The New Encyclopædia Britannica

Volume 7

MICROPÆDIA

Ready Reference

FOUNDED 1768
15TH EDITION

Encyclopædia Britannica, Inc.
Jacob E. Safra, Chairman of the Board
Jorge Aguilar-Cauz, President

Chicago
London/New Delhi/Paris/Seoul
Sydney/Taipei/Tokyo

First Edition	1768–1771
Second Edition	1777–1784
Third Edition	1788–1797
Supplement	1801
Fourth Edition	1801–1809
Fifth Edition	1815
Sixth Edition	1820–1823
Supplement	1815–1824
Seventh Edition	1830–1842
Eighth Edition	1852–1860
Ninth Edition	1875–1889
Tenth Edition	1902–1903

Printed in U.S.A.

Library of Congress Control Number: 2004110413
International Standard Book Number: 1-59339-236-2

Britannica may be accessed at http://www.britannica.com on the Internet.

How to use the MICROPAEDIA

The 12 volumes of the MICROPAEDIA contain tens of thousands of shorter articles on specific persons, places, things, and ideas, arranged in alphabetical order. The MICROPAEDIA can be used as an information resource on its own; and it can function as support for the longer articles in the MACROPAEDIA (to which it refers whenever appropriate). The MICROPAEDIA in turn is supported by references in the INDEX and by the lists of suggested readings in the PROPAEDIA. Finally, the MICROPAEDIA is the portion of the *Encyclopædia Britannica* best suited for the reader who wishes to browse among the countless subjects in all fields of human learning and history in all times and places.

Alphabetization

Entry titles are alphabetized according to the English alphabet, A to Z. All diacritical marks (such as in ö, ł, or ñ) and foreign letters without parallels in English (such as ayin [ʿ] and hamza [ʾ]) are ignored in the alphabetization. Apostrophes likewise are ignored. Titles beginning with numbers, such as **1812, War of**, are alphabetized as if the numbers were written out (**Eighteen-twelve, War of**).

Alphabetization proceeds according to the "word-by-word" principle. Thus, **Mount Vernon** precedes **mountain**; any **John** entry precedes **John Henry**, which in turn precedes **Johne's disease**. Any character or string of characters preceding a space, hyphen, or dash is treated as a word and alphabetized accordingly. Thus, **De Broglie** precedes **debenture**, and **jack-o'-lantern** precedes **jackal**. Titles with identical spellings are arranged in the following order: (1) persons, (2) places, (3) things.

For many rulers and titled nobility, chronological order, as well as alphabetical order, governs placement. Rulers of the same given name (*e.g.,* William) may be grouped together, separate from other entries, and indicated by the symbol •. They may be subgrouped alphabetically by country and, within each country, arranged chronologically (**William I, William II**, etc.). Nobility or peers of the same titled name (*e.g.,* **Essex, EARLS OF**) are similarly grouped together, separate from other entries; they are indicated by the symbol • and arranged chronologically.

Places with identical names are arranged in the alphabetical order of the countries where they are located. Identical place-names in the same country are alphabetized according to the alphabetical order of the state, province, or other political subdivision where they are found.

Entry arrangement

The titles of entries are arranged according to the forms commonly found in indexes and dictionaries, with some special conventions.

Entry titles for certain physical features, institutions, structures, events, and concepts are ordinarily inverted to place the substantive word first. Thus, the Bay of Bengal is entered as **Bengal, Bay of**; the Bank of England as **England, Bank of**; the Tower of London as **London, Tower of**; the Siege of Vienna as **Vienna, Siege of**; and the balance of power as **power, balance of**. If the name of a physical feature, institution, structure, event, or concept has two or more descriptors, it is entered under the descriptor appearing first. Thus, the Episcopal Church in Scotland is entered as **Episcopal Church in Scotland** (not **Scotland, Episcopal Church in**); the Leaning Tower of Pisa as **Leaning Tower of Pisa**; and the kinetic theory of gases as **kinetic theory of gases**.

The entries for most Western persons are arranged so that one can read a name in correct order by beginning after the first comma, proceeding to the end of the boldface type, returning to the beginning word or words, and proceeding forward to the first comma. Thus, the entry **March, Patrick Dunbar, 2nd Earl of**, is read "Patrick Dunbar, 2nd Earl of March"; the entry **Orléans, Louis, duc d'**, is read "Louis, duc d'Orléans." Names of Far Eastern origin are given in Oriental order, with the surname preceding the personal name (*e.g.,* **Tōjō Hideki**, **Deng Xiaoping**, **Nguyen Cao Ky**).

Cross-references

Some cross-reference entries appear in the MICROPAEDIA for the purpose of leading a reader from names that are familiar to alternate names that may not be. Cross-references also appear frequently within or at the ends of standard entries, where they are identified by *see, see also, see under, q.v.* (*quod vide,* "which see"), or *qq.v.* (*quae vide,* "which see," plural).

Certain entries serve both as relatively brief essays on general subjects and as cross-references to the same subjects treated at greater length and in greater depth in the MACROPAEDIA. Such an entry (*e.g.,* **igneous rock**) begins with a definition of the subject and then provides the following cross-reference: "A brief treatment of igneous rocks follows. For full treatment, *see* MACROPAEDIA: Minerals and Rocks.

Entries on certain broad subjects (*e.g.,* **music**) direct the reader to several relevant articles in the MACROPAEDIA and also to the PROPAEDIA for listings of related articles in the MICROPAEDIA.

Abbreviations

Abbreviations used in the MICROPAEDIA are given in a list that appears at the end of every MICROPAEDIA volume.

Territorial boundaries

In articles and maps indicating disputed geopolitical boundaries and territories, the attribution of sovereignty or administrative subordination to any specific area does not imply recognition of the status claimed by an administering power.

Krasnokamsk, city, Perm *oblast* (province), western Russia. Krasnokamsk lies along the Kama River. Founded in 1929 as a settlement in connection with the development of a pulp and paper mill, it became a town in 1938 and is now a satellite of Perm city. Oil was discovered nearby in 1934, and a small refinery opened in Krasnokamsk in 1943.

Oil refining and metalworking are the city's main industries. A technical college is devoted to studies for the paper industry. Pop. (1993 est.) 57,300.

Krasnoturinsk, also spelled KRASNOTURJINSK, town, Sverdlovsk *oblast* (province), western Russia. The town lies along the Turya River in the eastern foothills of the Northern Ural Mountains. Founded in 1758, it was called Turinskiye Rudniki ("Turinsky Mines") until 1944, when it became the town of Krasnoturinsk.

Now a centre of the aluminum industry based on local bauxite deposits, Krasnoturinsk has industrial and medical colleges located within its limits. The town also has a geologic and mineralogical museum. Pop. (1993 est.) 66,500.

Krasnov, Pyotr Nikolayevich (b. Sept. 10 [Sept. 22, New Style], 1869, St. Petersburg, Russia—d. Jan. 17, 1947, U.S.S.R.), imperial Russian army officer and a commander of anti-Bolshevik forces during the Russian Civil War. During World War II he helped organize anti-Soviet Cossack units for the Germans and urged the creation of a Cossack state under German protection.

The son of a Cossack general, Krasnov rose to divisional commander during World War I and was appointed head of a cavalry corps in August 1917 under the Provisional Government. At the time of the October Revolution, he was ordered to lead loyal troops from the front to Petrograd in what proved to be a failed attempt to defeat the Bolsheviks. Taken prisoner, he was released after promising not to oppose the new Soviet government.

Krasnov was nevertheless soon active in anti-Soviet efforts in the Don River region. Selected as commander of the so-called White forces, he organized a Cossack army and enjoyed initial military successes against the Soviets with the aid of German arms. After the Armistice (Nov. 11, 1918), however, the situation deteriorated, and in January 1919 Krasnov's forces suffered a major defeat. Resigning his command, Krasnov left Russia, later working with anti-Bolshevik Cossack groups in Europe and eventually becoming allied with the Nazis.

In 1944 the Germans established a Cossack puppet state in the Italian Alps, which Krasnov joined in 1945. Surrendering to the British in May, he was returned to the Soviet Union in accord with an agreement made at the Yalta Conference. In 1947 he was hanged by order of a Soviet military court.

Krasnovodsk (city, Turkmenistan): *see* Turkmenbashi.

Krasnoyarsk, also spelled KRASNOJARSK, or KRASNOIARSK, *kray* (region), east-central Russia. It occupies an area of Central Siberia and extends from the Severnaya Zemlya archipelago in the Arctic Ocean to the Sayan Mountains in the south. It includes the Evenky and Taymyr autonomous *okruga* (districts). The *kray,* which has its headquarters at Krasnoyarsk city, occupies almost all the Yenisey River basin; tributaries of the Yenisey River include the Angara, Podkamen Tunguska, Kureyka, and Turukhan rivers. The *kray* is also drained by the Chulym and Ket rivers of the Ob River basin. Much of Krasnoyarsk *kray* covers the Central Siberian Plateau, which reaches its highest point in the Putoran Plateau of the northwest. In the far south the Vostochny (East) and Zapadny (West) Sayan Mountains enclose the Minusinsk Basin. In the north the North Siberian Lowland separates the Byrranga Mountains of the Taymyr Peninsula from the plateau.

The *kray*'s vast area embraces a wide range of soils and vegetation, from the barren tundra of Taymyr to the steppe and rich soils of the Minusinsk Basin. The greater part of the *kray* consists of swampy forest, or taiga, of larch, pine, and birch that becomes sparser and more stunted in the north. The climate is continental, with very cold winters, especially in the north. Permafrost is common in much of the *kray*.

The population, which consists of Russians, Ukrainians, Tatars, and indigenous peoples, is concentrated in the south, along the Trans-Siberian Railroad and in the Minusinsk Basin; the remaining area is nearly uninhabited. The economic importance of the *kray* is threefold: its vast timber resources, which are exploited chiefly along the Trans-Siberian Railroad; its mineral wealth; and its hydroelectric potential. Its extensive drainage system makes possible the Krasnoyarsk and Sayan hydroelectric stations, among the largest in the world. Much lignite (brown coal) is mined at Kansk and Achinsk; nickel, cobalt, platinum, and copper at Norilsk; and gold in the southwestern plateau. Heavy industries of the region include machine building, metalworking, and smelting. Textiles, footwear, and leather are also produced. Meat and dairy cattle are raised, as are reindeer, sheep, horses, goats, and pigs. Hunting and fishing are important in the far north. Agriculture, chiefly wheat growing, is confined to the south. The *kray* is also a popular tourist area of Siberia. Area 903,400 square miles (2,339,700 square km). Pop. (1993 est.) 3,048,200.

Krasnoyarsk, also spelled KRASNOJARSK, or KRASNOIARSK, city and administrative centre of Krasnoyarsk *kray* (region), east-central Russia. The city stands on both banks of the Yenisey River where the river is crossed by the Trans-Siberian Railroad. One of the earliest Russian settlements in Siberia, it was founded as the fort of Krasny Yar in 1628 on the left bank of the Yenisey. The extension of the Great Siberian Post Road to this point in 1735 spurred Krasnoyarsk's development as the chief town of central Siberia. The discovery of gold in the area in the 19th century further accelerated its growth. After the arrival of the Trans-Siberian Railroad in the 1890s, Krasnoyarsk developed rapidly and spread onto the right bank, where it now extends for more than 18 miles (29 km) along the river. Krasnoyarsk's industrial growth was further stimulated by the evacuation to the town of many factories from the west in World War II. In the 1960s one of the largest hydroelectric stations in the world was constructed there on the Yenisey. During the 1980s a missile-tracking radar station was built near Krasnoyarsk. The Soviet government admitted in 1989 that the station was built in violation of the Treaty on Anti-Ballistic Missile Systems and in 1990 agreed to dismantle it.

Krasnoyarsk is a major industrial complex and one of the largest producers of aluminum in Russia. Its chemical industries make rayon and tire cord, synthetic rubber, and tires. Engineering plants manufacture cranes, harvesters, bulldozers, lumbering equipment, television sets, and refrigerators; there are shipbuilding and repair yards. Large-scale timber processing produces sawtimber, furniture, pulp, and paper. Krasnoyarsk has a forestry institute, polytechnic and medical institutes, and a number of research establishments, particularly associated with timber exploitation. Pop. (1993 est.) 919,300.

Krasnoye Selo, *rayon* (sector), St. Petersburg, northwestern Russia. The name Krasnoye Selo, meaning "beautiful village," has been in use since 1730, when it described three settlements located southwest of St. Petersburg. Krasnoye Selo was the site of one of the summer residences for the tsars and the summer camp for Russian soldiers stationed in St. Petersburg. A paper mill dating from 1764 is located there, as well as plastics, metalworking, and food-processing industries. The Troitskaya Church (1735) was rebuilt in 1854.

Krasnoye Selo became a city in 1925 and was incorporated into St. Petersburg (then Leningrad) in 1973.

Krasnyy Luch, Russian KRASNY LUCH, KRASNYI LUCH, or KRASNYJ LUČ, formerly (until 1929) KRINDACHYOVKA, or KRINDACHEVKA, city, Luhansk *oblast* (province), Ukraine, on the southern slopes of the Donets Hills. Originally established at the beginning of the 20th century as Krindachevka, it became the city of Krasnyy Luch in 1929.

Krasnyy Luch is an important anthracite-mining centre of the Donets Basin coalfield. There are coal-enriching plants, a machine-tools factory, and light industries. The city is linked by rail to Ivanivka. Pop. (1993 est.) 115,000.

Kraszewski, Józef Ignacy, pseudonym BOGDAN BOLESŁAWITA (b. July 28, 1812, Warsaw, Duchy of Warsaw [now in Poland]—d. March 19, 1887, Geneva, Switz.), Polish novelist, poet, literary critic, dramatist, historian, and journalist who was the dominant prose writer of Poland's Romantic period.

Kraszewski, detail of an oil painting by X.J. Kaniewski; in the National Museum, Warsaw

By courtesy of the Muzeum Narodowe, Warsaw

Kraszewski attended the University of Vilna, was imprisoned in 1830 on a charge of conspiracy against the Russian government, and was released in 1832. He lived in Volhynia (now in Ukraine) from 1834 to 1859, dividing his time between writing, farming, and social work. From 1841 he edited, and from 1849 to 1852 edited and published, the *Ateneum* review. Between 1859 and 1862 he edited the daily *Gazeta Codzienna* (later *Gazeta Polska*). Forced to leave Warsaw in January 1863 by Count Aleksander Wielopolski, head of the civil government, whom he had offended in an editorial, Kraszewski settled in Dresden, Germany. In 1883 the German government arrested him on a charge of espionage on behalf of France and in 1884 sentenced him to three and one-half years' imprisonment in the fortress at Magdeburg. Released in 1885, he went to Geneva, where he died.

Kraszewski's uneven but enduring works influenced other writers to support Polish nationalism. They fill more than 600 volumes and include 9 novels dealing with serfdom, 7 novels set against the background of Poland under the Saxon kings, and a cycle of 29 novels covering Polish history.

krater, also spelled CRATER, ancient Greek vessel used for diluting wine with water. It usually stood on a tripod in the dining room, where wine was mixed. Kraters were made of metal or pottery and were often painted or elaborately ornamented. In Homer's *Iliad* the prize offered by Achilles for the footrace at Patroclus' funeral games was a silver krater of Sidonian workmanship. The Greek historian Herodotus describes many enormous and costly kraters dedicated at temples or used in religious ceremonies to hold libations.

Attic red-figure volute krater attributed to the Painter of the Wooly Satyrs, *c.* 450 BC; in the Metropolitan Museum of Art, New York City

By courtesy of the Metropolitan Museum of Art, New York City, Rogers Fund, 1907

Kraters are large, with a broad body and base and usually a wide mouth. They may have horizontal handles placed near the base, or vertical handles rising from the shoulder. Among the many variations are the bell krater, confined to red-figure pottery, shaped like an inverted bell, with loop handles and a disk foot; the volute krater, with an egg-shaped body and handles that rise from the shoulder and curl in a volute (scroll-shaped form) well above the rim; the calyx krater, the shape of which spreads out like the cup or calyx of a flower; and the column krater, with columnar handles rising from the shoulder to a flat, projecting lip rim.

Kratie (Cambodia): *see* Krâchéh.

Kraus, Karl (b. April 28, 1874, Gitschin, Bohemia [now Jičín, Czech Republic]—d. June 12, 1936, Vienna, Austria), Austrian journalist, critic, playwright, and poet who has been compared with Juvenal and Jonathan Swift for his satiric vision and command of language. In German literature he ranks as an outstanding writer of the World War I era, but, because his work is almost untranslatably idiomatic, his talents have not been widely recognized.

Of Jewish parentage, Kraus attended the University of Vienna but abandoned his studies to earn his living as a writer. In 1899 he founded the literary and political review *Die Fackel* ("The Torch"), which ceased publication in 1936 with the rise of Nazism in Austria. Kraus never became associated with a particular literary movement or political persuasion.

Language, to Kraus, was of great moral as well as aesthetic importance, and he relentlessly criticized its dishonest, pretentious, or inexact use as symptomatic of the moral corruption of the age. He himself wrote with masterly precision, notably in such collections of aphorisms as *Sprüche und Widersprüche* (1909; "Proverbs and Contradictions") and *Nachts* (1919; "Nights") and in such essay collections as *Sittlichkeit und Kriminalität* (1908; "Morality and Criminality"), *Literatur und Lüge* (1929; "Literature and Lie"), and *Die Sprache* (1937; "Language"). His writing occasionally rises to apocalyptic heights, as in the lengthy satirical drama *Die letzten Tage der Menschheit* (1918; published 1922; "The Last Days of Mankind"), a visionary condemnation of the futility of World War I.

Kraus, 1908

By courtesy of the Bild-Archiv, Osterreichische Nationalbibliothek, Vienna

Kraus was the founder, editor, and from 1911 the sole author of *Die Fackel*, through which he achieved fame as a scathing critic of Austrian society. He gradually widened the range of his attacks from the Austrian middle classes and the Viennese liberal press to encompass all that he held responsible for what he viewed as the disintegration of the Austrian, and European, cultural traditions. His satire and mode of expression are idiosyncratic and essentially Austrian (even Viennese), but his influence has been far-reaching. He also wrote poetry (*Worte in Versen*, 9 vol., 1916–30), epigrams (1927), and dramatic parodies. He translated works of William Shakespeare and rediscovered the works of his compatriot Johann Nestroy.

Kraus's *Werke* were published in 14 volumes (1952–66).

BIBLIOGRAPHY. Frank Field, *The Last Days of Mankind: Karl Kraus and His Vienna* (1967); Harry Zohn, *Karl Kraus* (1971); Edward Timms, *Karl Kraus, Apocalyptic Satirist* (1986).

Krause, Karl Christian Friedrich (b. May 6, 1781, Eisenberg, Rhenish Palatinate [Germany]—d. Sept. 27, 1832, Munich, Bavaria), German philosopher who attracted a considerable following, especially in Spain, where his disciples, known as *krausistas*, greatly influenced the direction of Spanish education in the late 19th and early 20th centuries.

Krause's system of philosophy, which he called "panentheism" (essentially an attempt to reconcile pantheism and theism), asserts that God is an essence that contains the entire universe within itself but is not exhausted by it. He put particular emphasis on the development of the individual as an integral part of the life of the whole.

Among his major works are *Entwurf des Systems der Philosophie* (1804; "Sketch of the System of Philosophy"), *Vorlesungen über das System der Philosophie* (1828; "Lectures on the System of Philosophy"), and *Vorlesungen über die Grundwahrheiten der Wissenschaft* (1829; "Lectures on the Fundamentals of Knowledge").

Krâvanh Mountains, Khmer CHUŎR PHNUM KRÂVANH, formerly CARDAMOM MOUNTAINS, French CHAÎNE DES CARDAMOMES, range of high hills in southwestern Cambodia that is situated on a southeast-northwest axis and continues westward into the highland area around Chanthaburi, Thailand. The Krâvanh Mountains extend (some discontinuously) for about 100 miles (160 km) southeast and east to the Dâmrei Mountains, reaching their highest point (5,949 feet [1,813 m]) near Poŭthĭsăt in Cambodia. Farther west, they reach 5,128 feet (1,563 m) in Tumbol Hill, just east of the Thailand border.

Dense tropical rain forest prevails on their western slopes, which annually receive from 150 to 200 inches (3,800–5,000 mm) of rainfall; only 40 to 60 inches (1,000 to 1,500 mm) fall on the wooded eastern slopes in the rain shadow facing the interior Cambodian plain. On their slopes cardamoms and pepper have been commercially grown. The mountains were inhabited until 1975 by Dravidian peoples who may have emigrated from the Coromandel Coast of India; they were related to similar tribes in the Dângrêk, Dâmrei, and Annamitique mountains.

Kravchuk, Leonid Makarovich (b. Jan. 10, 1934, Velyky Zhityn, Ukraine, U.S.S.R.), president of Ukraine from 1991 to 1994. For 30 years a Communist Party functionary, he converted to nationalist politics after the collapse of the Soviet regime. He was the first democratically elected president of Ukraine.

In 1958 Kravchuk graduated from Kiev T.G. Shevchenko State University and joined the Communist Party. He taught political economics in Chernivtsi and began a political career, rising in the 1980s to top posts in the propaganda and ideology departments for Ukraine. He became chairman of the Ukrainian Supreme Soviet in July 1990, and as such he soon became the effective leader of the republic. As the central government in Moscow grew weaker, Kravchuk began to warm to the Ukrainian independence movement. After the failure of the coup attempt by Soviet Communist hardliners in August 1991, he expressed unqualified support for independence. He was elected president in December 1991 but lost reelection to Leonid D. Kuchma in July 1994.

Krebs, Edwin Gerhard (b. June 6, 1918, Lansing, Iowa, U.S.), American biochemist, winner with Edmond H. Fischer of the 1992 Nobel Prize for Physiology or Medicine for the discovery of reversible protein phosphorylation, a biochemical process that regulates the activities of proteins in cells and thus governs countless processes that are necessary for life.

Krebs received a medical degree from Washington University (St. Louis, Mo.) in 1943. From 1946 to 1948 he did research there under the biochemists Carl and Gerty Cori. In 1948 he joined the faculty of biochemistry at the University of Washington, Seattle, becoming full professor in 1957. In 1968 he moved to the University of California at Davis, returning to Washington University in 1977.

During the 1950s Krebs and Edmond Fischer began investigating the process by which muscle cells obtain energy from glycogen (the form in which the body stores sugar). The Coris had previously demonstrated that cells use an enzyme called phosphorylase to release glucose (the source of energy in cell function) from glycogen. Krebs and Fischer showed that phosphorylase could be converted from an inactive to an active form by the addition of a phosphate group taken from the compound adenosine triphosphate (ATP). The enzymes that catalyze this process are called protein kinases. Krebs and Fischer also showed that phosphorylase is inactivated by the removal of a phosphate group; this process is catalyzed by enzymes called phosphatases. Malfunctions in protein phosphorylation have been implicated in the causation of diseases such as diabetes, cancer, and Alzheimer's disease.

Krebs, Sir Hans Adolf (b. Aug. 25, 1900, Hildesheim, Ger.—d. Nov. 22, 1981, Oxford, Eng.), German-born British biochemist who received (with Fritz Lipmann) the 1953 Nobel Prize for Physiology or Medicine for the discovery in living organisms of the series of chemical reactions known as the tricarboxylic acid cycle (also called the citric acid cycle, or Krebs cycle). These reactions involve the conversion—in the presence of oxygen—of substances that are formed by the breakdown of sugars, fats, and protein components to

Sir Hans Adolf Krebs
By courtesy of the World Health Organization

carbon dioxide, water, and energy-rich compounds. The discovery of the citric acid cycle, which is central to nearly all metabolic reactions and the source of two-thirds of the food-derived energy in higher organisms, was of vital importance to a basic understanding of cell metabolism and molecular biology.

At the University of Freiburg (1932), he discovered (with the German biochemist Kurt Henseleit) a series of chemical reactions (now known as the urea cycle) by which ammonia is converted to urea in mammalian tissue; the urea, far less toxic than ammonia, is subsequently excreted in the urine of most mammals. This cycle also serves as a major source of the amino acid arginine.

The son of a Jewish physician, Krebs was forced in 1933 to leave Nazi Germany for England, where he continued his research at the University of Cambridge (1933–35). At Sheffield University, Yorkshire (1935–54), Krebs measured the amounts of certain four-carbon and six-carbon acids generated in pigeon liver and breast muscle when sugars are oxidized completely to yield carbon dioxide, water, and energy.

In 1937 he demonstrated the existence of a cycle of chemical reactions that combines the end-product of sugar breakdown, later shown to be an "activated" form of the two-carbon acetic acid, with the four-carbon oxaloacetic acid to form citric acid. The cycle regenerates oxaloacetic acid through a series of intermediate compounds while liberating carbon dioxide and electrons that are immediately utilized to form high-energy phosphate bonds in the form of adenosine triphosphate (ATP; the chemical-energy reservoir of the cell).

Krebs served on the faculty of the University of Oxford from 1954 to 1967. He wrote (with the British biochemist Hans Kornberg) *Energy Transformations in Living Matter* (1957). He was knighted in 1958, and the Royal Society awarded him its Copley Medal in 1961.

Krebs, Johann Ludwig (b. Oct. 10, 1713, Buttelstedt, Saxony [Germany]—d. January 1780, Altenburg), German organist and composer noted for his organ music.

Krebs studied under his father and was later a favourite pupil of the composer Johann Sebastian Bach at Leipzig. He was organist at Zwickau, Zeitz, and Altenburg. His organ music is composed in the forms used by Bach and leans heavily on Bach's style. It is technically very accomplished. Krebs also wrote trio sonatas, sonatas for flute and harpsichord, and some sacred vocal music.

Krebs cycle (biochemistry): *see* tricarboxylic acid cycle.

Krefeld, also spelled CREFELD, city and port, North Rhine–Westphalia *Land* (state), western Germany. The medieval city centre of Krefeld is situated 6 miles (10 km) west of the Rhine River. The city stretches in an east-west direction, with Uerdingen, a second city centre, lying along the Rhine itself and containing a harbour. Chartered in 1373, Krefeld belonged to the counts of Moers (Mörs) until it passed to the house of Orange in 1600; it passed to Prussia in 1702. In 1758 Ferdinand, duke of Brunswick, defeated the French near Krefeld in a major battle of the Seven Years' War. The city was long known for the manufacture of silks and velvets, which was begun in the 17th and 18th centuries by Protestant and Mennonite refugees. Krefeld absorbed several neighbouring towns between 1901 and 1929, including Uerdingen and its harbour. It was occupied by the Allies after World War I, from 1918 to 1926, and was severely bombed in World War II.

Krefeld is a rail hub. Steel, machinery, clothing (especially neckties), and chemicals are also manufactured. The city's cultural institutions include the Kaiser-Wilhelm-Museum, the Museum Burg Linn (a restored castle), a textile museum, and the Museum Haus Lange (modern art). Pop. (1998 est.) 245,606.

Kreis (German: "Circle"), any of the several imperial circles (administrative districts) of the Holy Roman Empire from the early 16th century until its dissolution in 1806, a period in which the empire became an increasingly looser federation of principalities. The *Kreise* were the Burgundian, Lower Rhine-Westphalian, Lower Saxon, Upper Saxon, Electoral Rhenish, Upper Rhenish, Franconian, Swabian, Bavarian, and Austrian. They were established by the emperor Maximilian I (1493–1519). The Diet of Augsburg in 1555 accorded them law-enforcement powers, including the right to carry out the decisions of the *Reichskammergericht,* or imperial chamber. Especially in western and southern Germany, the circles provided a measure of needed regional political cohesion during the great religious and political upheaval of the Reformation.

The *Kreis* (an abbreviation of *Landkreis,* "county") is an administrative unit in modern Germany. *Kreise* usually constitute the highest level of local government.

Kreisky, Bruno (b. Jan. 22, 1911, Vienna, Austria—d. July 29, 1990, Vienna), leader of the Social Democratic Party of Austria and chancellor of Austria (1970–83).

Kreisky joined the Social Democratic Party in 1926; he was active in the party until it was outlawed in 1934. In 1935 he was arrested for political reasons and imprisoned for 18 months. He was imprisoned again in 1938, shortly after graduating as doctor of law from the University of Vienna. Persecuted by the Gestapo because of his political beliefs and Jewish birth, he fled to Sweden, where he engaged in journalism and business during World War II. From 1946 to 1950 he served at the Austrian legation in Stockholm and then returned to Vienna to serve at the foreign ministry.

From 1956 he was a member of the Austrian Parliament, and in 1959 he was elected deputy chairman of the Social Democrats and became foreign minister. After the party's decisive defeat in the 1966 general election, he took the lead in an intraparty reform movement. He was narrowly elected chairman of the Social Democrats in 1967, and he became chancellor of Austria when the Social Democrats emerged from the 1970 elections as the strongest party; in 1971 they acquired an absolute majority. Kreisky was credited with successfully pursuing a policy of "active neutrality," smoothing relations with neighbouring Czechoslovakia and Yugoslavia and seeking cooperation with other nonaligned nations. Under his leadership, the Social Democrats preserved their parliamentary majority in elections in 1975 and 1979. He resigned in 1983.

Kreisler, Fritz (b. Feb. 2, 1875, Vienna, Austria—d. Jan. 29, 1962, New York, N.Y., U.S.), Austrian-born violinist who was a "secret" composer of short violin pieces.

At age seven Kreisler entered the Vienna Conservatory, and from 1885 to 1887 he studied composition and violin at the Paris Conservatory. After a successful concert tour of the United States (1888–89), he returned to Vienna to study medicine. He subsequently studied art in Paris and Rome and served as an officer in the Austrian army. In 1899 he returned to the stage as a concert violinist and became one of the most successful virtuosos of his time.

Kreisler's technique was characterized by an intensive vibrato and an economy in bowing. In 1910 he gave the first performance of Sir Edward Elgar's *Violin Concerto,* dedicated to him. After 1915 he lived mainly in the

Kreisler
By courtesy of RCA Records

United States but continued to tour widely in Europe. His concert programs frequently included many short pieces by him, among them "Caprice Viennois" ("Viennese Caprice") and "Schön Rosmarin" ("Pretty Rosemary"). His *Classical Manuscripts,* published as his arrangements of works by Antonio Vivaldi, François Couperin, Johann Stamitz, Padre Martini, and others, were admitted in 1935 to be works of his own.

To make the best use of the Britannica, consult the INDEX *first*

Kremenchuk, Russian KREMENCHUG, also spelled KREMENČUG, city, Poltava *oblast* (province), Ukraine. The city lies along the Dnieper River where it is crossed by the Kharkiv-Kirovohrad railway. Founded in 1571 as a fortress, Kremenchuk acquired city status in 1765. The modern city and the Kryukiv district across the river have developed important metallurgical and engineering industries that produce steel castings, rolling stock, heavy trucks, and harvesters. Iron ore is mined in the vicinity, and oil from the river's west-bank area is refined in Kremenchuk. In 1959 a large hydroelectric station was completed just north of the city. Pop. (1998 est.) 240,700.

kremlin, Russian KREML, formerly KREMNIK, central fortress in medieval Russian cities, usually located at a strategic point along a river and separated from the surrounding parts of the city by a wooden—later a stone or brick—wall with ramparts, a moat, towers, and battlements. Several capitals of principalities (*e.g.,* Moscow, Pskov, Novgorod, Smolensk, Rostov, Suzdal, Yaroslavl, Vladimir, and Nizhny Novgorod) were built around old kremlins, which generally contained cathedrals, palaces for princes and bishops, governmental offices, and munitions stores.

The Moscow Kremlin (1156) lost its importance as a fortress in the 1620s but was used as the centre of Russian government until 1712 and again after 1918. Originally constructed of wood, it was rebuilt in brick in the 14th century by Italian architects and later repaired and altered on numerous occasions. Its architecture thus reflects its long history and encompasses a variety of styles, including Byzantine, Russian Baroque, and classical. The structure is triangular in shape; its east side faces Red Square, and it has four gateways and a postern (back gate), concealing a secret passage to the Moscow River. Following the Bolshevik seizure of power in October 1917, the Moscow Kremlin became the headquarters of Lenin's Soviet government and the symbol of the communist dictatorship. After the collapse of the Soviet Union in 1991, it became the executive heaquarters of the Russian federation. *See also* Moscow.

The Moscow Kremlin, originally built 1156, frequent enlargements and reconstructions with present enclosure dating from the 16th century
Tass—Sovfoto

Krems, also called KREMS AN DER DONAU, city, Niederösterreich *Bundesland* ("federal state"), northeastern Austria, at the confluence of the Danube (Donau) and Krems rivers, northwest of Vienna. Mentioned in 995 as an imperial fortress, it was chartered in the 12th century, when it had a mint. Of its medieval fortifications, the Steiner Gate, the Pulverturm ("Powder Tower"), and the Gozzoburg remain. The adjacent towns of Stein an der Donau and Mautern (on the site of a Roman camp) were absorbed by Krems in 1938. Landmarks include the old Stadtburg (fortress; originally 13th century); the St. Veit parish church (restored 1616–30), one of Austria's oldest Baroque churches; and two Gothic churches in Stein. An old wine-producing town, Krems also has metal, textile, and chemical industries. Pop. (1991) 22,829.

Kremsier (Czech Republic): *see* Kroměříž.

Krenek, Ernst (b. Aug. 23, 1900, Vienna, Austria—d. Dec. 23, 1991, Palm Springs, Calif., U.S.), Austrian-American composer, one of the prominent exponents of the serial technique of musical composition.

Krenek studied in Vienna and Berlin and was musical assistant at the German opera houses of Kassel (1925–27) and Wiesbaden (1927–28). In 1938 he immigrated to the United States. He taught composition at Vassar College, Poughkeepsie, N.Y. (1939–42), and Hamline University, St. Paul, Minn. (1942–47).

Krenek's earliest compositions were influenced by Gustav Mahler (his father-in-law from 1923 to 1925). In his first operas, however, he turned to a dissonant, Expressionist style, as in *Zwingburg* (1924; *Dungeon Castle*). He gained international success with the opera *Jonny Spielt Auf!* (1927; *Johnny Strikes up the Band!*), written in an idiom that mixed Expressionist dissonance with jazz influences. After a period in which he espoused the Romanticism of Franz Schubert, he began in the 1930s to use the 12-tone method of Arnold Schoenberg. His first significant 12-tone work was the opera *Karl V* (1933; produced 1938). Other important 12-tone works were the *Second Piano Concerto* (1938) and the *Fourth Symphony* (1947).

Krenek experimented widely with styles and techniques of composition. In *Sestina* (1957) he used total serialization, in which not only pitch but all musical elements are arranged in basic series. In his *Third Piano Concerto* he temporarily abandoned the 12-tone method for traditional tonality; his *Fifth Symphony* is atonal but avoids serial technique. In his oratorio *Spiritus Intelligentiae* (1958) he utilized electronically produced sound. In *Pentagram,* for wind quintet (1952; revised 1958), and in *Fibonaci Mobile* (1965), mathematical ideas influence the musical content. Krenek's other compositions include sonatas for harp and for organ; *Twelve Short Piano Pieces,* an introduction to 12-tone technique; *Eleven Transparencies* for orchestra; and operas.

Krenek's books include *Über neue Musik* (1937; *Music Here and Now*); *Studies in Counterpoint* (1940); and *Selbstdarstellung* (1948; *Self-Analysis*), an autobiography.

krennerite, a gold mineral that usually occurs in veins formed at low temperatures, as at Kalgoorlie, Australia, and Cripple Creek, Colo., U.S. A gold telluride ($AuTe_2$), it forms orthorhombic crystals. Two chemically similar minerals, calaverite and sylvanite, form monoclinic crystals; they are more common than krennerite, are important primary ores of gold, and are sources of tellurium. All three substances have similar chemical and physical properties. For detailed physical properties, *see* sulfide mineral (table).

Kresge, S.S., in full SEBASTIAN SPERING KRESGE (b. July 31, 1867, Bald Mount, Pa., U.S.—d. Oct. 18, 1966, East Stroudsburg, Pa.), American merchant who established a chain of nearly 1,000 variety and discount stores throughout the United States.

Kresge worked as a traveling salesman before going into business with one of his customers, John G. McCrory, the owner of several department and five-and-ten-cent stores. They became partners in 1897 in two new five-and-dime stores in Memphis, Tenn., and Detroit, Mich. Two years later they traded interests, and Kresge became sole owner of the Detroit operation. He managed the store and opened seven others in major Midwest cities with his brother-in-law Charles Wilson under the firm name of Kresge & Wilson. By 1907 Kresge bought out Wilson and established the S.S. Kresge Company. When the firm was incorporated only five years later, it was capitalized at $7,000,000 and included 85 stores in the North and Midwest.

Kresge's original stores sold a wide selection of goods for 10 cents or less. His later stores included items for a price up to one dollar, and after World War II the company expanded into large discount stores in the United States, Puerto Rico, and Canada.

Kresge also established the Kresge Foundation in 1924 to benefit educational and charitable activities. By the time of Kresge's death in 1966, the foundation had distributed $70,000,000 in grants with a remaining net worth of $175,000,000.

Kresge Co., in full S.S. KRESGE CO.: *see* K mart Corporation.

Kress, S.H., in full SAMUEL HENRY KRESS (b. July 23, 1863, Cherryville, Pa., U.S.—d. Sept. 22, 1955, New York, N.Y.), American merchant and art collector who used the wealth from his chain of five-and-ten-cent stores to donate artwork to more than 40 U.S. museums.

With money saved from his teaching salary, Kress purchased a stationery store in Nanticoke, Pa., in 1887. With the profits, he bought a second store three years later in Wilkes-Barre, Pa., and, in 1896, opened a store in Memphis, Tenn. By consistently putting the stores' income into expansion, he had acquired 12 stores by 1900. His chain of stores offered fewer items than most variety stores, at lower prices, and he bought goods directly from manufacturers and relied on sales volume to make up for his low profit margin. By 1907 Kress had moved his headquarters to New York City and operated 51 stores. During his lifetime, his chain grew to include 264 stores selling $169,000,000 annually.

In 1921 Kress traveled to Europe, collecting medieval and Renaissance paintings, sculptures, and textiles. In 1929 he established the Kress Foundation, endowing it with 40 percent of the company's voting stock. The foundation donated works from his collection to art galleries in states in which he owned stores. In 1939 Kress gave the newly established National Gallery of Art in Washington, D.C., 375 paintings and 18 sculptures, valued at $25,000,000. Later gifts to the National Gallery included works of Watteau, Raphael, Titian, Fra Angelico, and Van Dyck. Fourteen city art museums also received works from his foundation. He also contributed to medical research and education, giving New York University-Bellevue Medical Center $8,000,000 for education in 1949 and in 1952 giving the Memorial Center for Cancer and Allied Diseases in New York City a betatron unit, along with funds for a research program.

Kretschmer, Ernst (b. Oct. 8, 1888, Wüstenrot, Ger.—d. Feb. 8, 1964, Tübingen, W.Ger.), German psychiatrist who attempted to correlate body build and physical constitution with personality characteristics and mental illness.

Kretschmer studied both philosophy and medicine at the University of Tübingen, remaining there as an assistant in the neurologic clinic after completing his studies in 1913. The next year, he published his dissertation on manic-depressive delusions, anticipating his later work in mental illness. He studied hysteria while a military physician during World War I, developing a treatment in which victims of battle hysteria were quieted in dark chambers and treated with electrical impulses. After the war, he returned to Tübingen as a lecturer and began writing books containing his psychological theories. His best-known work, *Körperbau und Charakter* (1921; *Physique and Character*), advanced the theory that certain mental disorders were more common among people of specific physical types. Kretschmer posited three chief constitutional groups: the tall, thin asthenic type, the more muscular athletic type, and the rotund pyknic type. He suggested that the lanky asthenics, and to a lesser degree the athletic types, were more prone to schizophrenia, while the pyknic types were more likely to develop manic-depressive disorders. His work was criticized because his thinner, schizophrenic patients were younger than his pyknic, manic-depressive subjects, so the differences in body type could be explained by differences in age. Nevertheless, Kretschmer's ideas to some extent entered into popular culture and generated further psychological research.

Kretschmer left Tübingen in 1926, when he became professor of psychiatry and neurology at the University of Marburg. During this period, he produced *Hysterie, Reflex und Instinkt* (1923; *Hysteria, Reflex, and Instinct,* 1960), in which he suggested that the formation of symptoms in hysteria is initially conscious but is then taken over by automatic mechanisms and becomes unconscious, and *Geniale Menschen* (1929; *The Psychology of Men of Genius,* 1931). In 1933 Kretschmer resigned as president of the German Society of Psychotherapy in protest against the Nazi takeover of the government, but unlike other prominent German psychologists he remained in Germany during World War II.

After the war, Kretschmer returned to Tübingen and remained there as professor of psychiatry and director of the neurologic clinic until 1959. He concerned himself with studies of physical constitution and mental illness in children and adolescents, developed new methods of psychotherapy and hypnosis, and studied compulsive criminality, recommending adequate provisions be made for the psychiatric treatment of prisoners.

Kretschmer, Paul (b. May 2, 1866, Berlin—d. March 9, 1956, Vienna), linguist who studied the earliest history and interrelations of the Indo-European languages and showed how they were influenced by non-Indo-European languages, such as Etruscan. A work on Greek vase inscriptions (1894) revealed how nonlinguistic materials could be exploited for their linguistic worth.

Paul Kretschmer, 1936
By courtesy of the Bild-Archiv, Osterreichische Nationalbibliothek, Vienna

Kretschmer's epochal study of pre-Greek elements in ancient Greek was his *Einleitung in die Geschichte der griechischen Sprache* (1896; "Introduction to the History of the Greek Language"). Comparing Greek place-names with their foreign counterparts in ancient Anatolia, he concluded that a non-Greek, Mediterranean culture had preceded the Greeks there, leaving extensive linguistic traces. The discoveries of the archaeologist Sir Arthur Evans at Knossos, Crete, around 1900 tended to confirm Kretschmer's views.

Following a professorship at the University of Marburg in Germany (1897–99), Kretschmer occupied the chair in comparative linguistics at the University of Vienna, where he remained until 1936. An adherent of the Neogrammarian school of linguistics, which stressed rigorous comparative methodology, he also contributed to Modern Greek dialectology and furthered the study of German linguistic geography.

In 1907 with Frans Skutsch he founded *Glotta*, a periodical devoted to classical linguistics.

Kretzer, Max (b. June 7, 1854, Posen, East Prussia—d. July 15, 1941, Berlin), German Expressionist writer who excelled in describing working conditions of the Berlin industrial proletariat in the 1880s and 1890s.

The son of a prosperous innkeeper whose business failed, Kretzer went to work in a factory at the age of 13, educated himself, and began to write when he was 25. Some of his minutely detailed sociological novels are based upon his working experience: *Der Fassadenraphael* (1911; "The Raphael of the Façades") describes his experience as a sign writer and *Der alte Andreas* (1911; "Old Andrew") records his work in a lamp factory. In other novels he treats pressing social problems of the day: prostitution in *Die Betrogenen* (1882; "The Deceived"); the fate of the urban workers in *Die Verkommenen* (1883; "The Depraved"); and the destruction of the small independent artisan by rapid industrialization in *Meister Timpe* (1888; "Master Timpe"), considered his best novel.

Kretzer was influenced by Émile Zola in his application of the Naturalistic view of literature and life to the Berlin environment with which he was familiar, and he was also an admirer of Charles Dickens.

Kreuger, Ivar (b. March 2, 1880, Kalmar, Swed.—d. March 12, 1932, Paris), Swedish financier, known as "the match king," who attempted to gain a worldwide monopoly over the production of matches.

After practicing as a civil engineer in the U.S. and in South Africa, Kreuger returned to Sweden in 1907 and founded a match company. During World War I the entire Swedish match industry was concentrated under Kreuger's initiative into a single firm, Svenska Tändsticks AB (the Swedish Match Company), with Kreuger as managing director. After the war, backed largely by U.S. capital, Kreuger launched a series of highly speculative financial operations, the aim of which was to secure a monopoly of the production and marketing of matches outside Sweden. The majority of Kreuger's transactions after 1925 took the form of long-term dollar loans to countries short of foreign currency in return for agreements granting him monopoly rights. By 1928 Kreuger's concern probably controlled more than half the match production of the world. But as the world depression developed, his position became increasingly strained. In 1932 Kreuger shot himself; it was discovered afterward that the assets and profits recorded for the business were largely fictitious. The concern disintegrated and many of its component companies went bankrupt.

Kreussen stoneware, German salt-glazed stoneware produced at Kreussen, in Bavaria, from the late 16th century until *c.* 1730–32. Squat tankards with pewter lids, four- or six-sided flasks (*Schraubflaschen*), and pear- or globular-shaped jugs were primarily produced; the best of these date from the 17th century. The stoneware is grayish-red, covered with a brown salt glaze. Decoration consists of plain applied reliefs, applied reliefs painted in bright opaque overglaze colours of blue, red, green, yellow, white, and occasionally gold, or plain surfaces with figures painted in the same overglaze colours. The earliest known example decorated with overglaze colours is dated 1622. Until this time painting pottery in overglaze colours had never been done in Europe; and, in all likelihood, the technique was learned from contemporary German and Bohemian glass enamelers. Decorative themes include the Apostles, the imperial electors, hunting scenes, the planets, and commemorations of families and marriages.

Kreutzberg, Harald (b. Dec. 11, 1902, Reichenberg, Bohemia—d. April 24, 1968, Gümligen, near Bern, Switz.), German modern dancer and choreographer best known for solos that combined dance with mime.

Trained at the Dresden Ballet School, Kreutzberg also studied modern dance with Mary Wigman and Rudolf Laban. Beginning in 1927 he appeared in plays directed by Max Reinhardt and in 1929 went with Reinhardt to New York City. Kreutzberg then toured the U.S., Canada, and Europe with the dancer Yvonne Georgi, and in 1932 he joined Ruth Page for tours of the U.S. and the Far East.

Kreutzberg in *Drei Irre Gestalten*
By courtesy of the Dance Collection, the New York Public Library at Lincoln Center, Astor, Lenox and Tilden Foundations

For the remainder of his concert career, he performed primarily as a soloist; his inventive choreographic style combined free dance movements with such elements of the theatre as mime and pictorial costuming. His works range from the tragic allegory of *Der Engel Luzifer* ("The Angel Lucifer") to the comic grotesque of *Der Hochzeitsstrauss* ("The Wedding Bouquet"). After retiring from the stage in 1959 he choreographed for others and taught at his own school, established in 1955 in Bern, Switz.

Kreutzer, Rodolphe (b. Nov. 16, 1766, Versailles, Fr.—d. Jan. 6, 1831, Geneva), composer and violinist, one of the founders of the French school of violin playing, and one of the foremost improvisers and conductors of his day.

Kreutzer was a pupil of the influential composer and conductor Anton Stamitz and in 1795 became professor of the violin at the Paris Conservatoire. In 1798 in Vienna he met Beethoven, who dedicated to him his *Sonata in A Major for Piano and Violin,* Opus 47, now known as the *Kreutzer Sonata.* Kreutzer did not appreciate the work and apparently never played it. He held solo violin positions at the Théâtre-Italien and the Paris Opéra and later was chamber musician to Napoleon and to Louis XVIII. He wrote about 40 operas—of which *Lodoïska* (1791) was particularly popular—several ballets, 19 violin concerti, and many chamber works. His *Méthode du violon,* written with the violinists Pierre Baillot and Pierre Rode, and his 40 *Études ou caprices* remain standard exercises for the violin.

Kreutzwald, F(riedrich) Reinhold (b. Dec. 26, 1803, Kadrina, Russian Estonia—d. Aug. 25, 1882, Tartu), physician, folklorist, and poet who compiled the Estonian national epic poem *Kalevipoeg* (1857–61, "The Son of Kalevi").

A graduate of Tartu University, Kreutzwald was municipal health officer in Voru for more than 40 years. In 1838, F.R. Faehlmann organized the Estonian Learned Society, which collected narrative folk songs for an epic in the tradition of Finland's *Kalevala.* Kreutzwald, a student and translator of German Romantic literature, wrote the epic, combining the collected material with original poetry.

In the epic, the *Kalevid* ("National Champion") is the symbol of ancient Estonian independence; the plot revolves around his romantic adventures. The *Kalevipoeg* was the central work of the Estonian national awakening of the 19th century and exercised considerable influence on the country's later literature, art, and music.

Kreuznach (Germany): *see* Bad Kreuznach.

Krėvė-Mickievičius, Vincas, also called VINCAS KRĖVĖ (b. Oct. 19, 1882, Subartonys, Russian Lithuania—d. July 7, 1954, Broomall, Pa., U.S.), Lithuanian poet, philologist, and playwright whose mastery of style gave him a foremost place in Lithuanian literature.

After serving as Lithuanian consul in Azerbaijan, Krėvė became professor of Slavonic languages and literature in Kaunas (1922–39) and later in Vilnius. He went into exile in 1944, shortened his name to Vincas Krėvė, and from 1947 was professor at the University of Pennsylvania.

Krėvė became internationally known by his collection of Lithuanian folk songs (*Dainos*). National feeling suppressed by foreign rule found expression in his plays and won him great popularity among Lithuanians. *Šarūnas, Dainavos kunigaikštis* (1912; "Sharunas, Prince of Dainava"), *Skirgaila* (1925; "Prince Skirgaila"), *Likimo keliais* (1926–29; "Along the Paths of Destiny"), and *Karaliaus Mindaugo mirtis* (1935; "The Death of King Mindaugas") have a romantic view of the past; but he was also a realistic observer with a deep understanding of human nature, as is shown in his village drama *Žentas* (1921; "The Son-in-Law") and in his short stories—particularly those contained in *Sutemose* (1921; "Twilight") or *Po šiaudine pastoge* (1922–23; "Under a Thatched Roof"). He also adapted Lithuanian legends in *Dainavos šalies senu žmoniu padavimai* (1912; "Legends of the Old People of Dainava") and themes from Oriental legends in *Rytu pasakos* (1930; "Tales of the Orient"). Among his last works, *Dangaus ir žemes sūnus* (1949; "The Sons of Heaven and Earth") shows great power of expression in portraying Hebrew life in Herod's time.

Kribi, port, southwestern Cameroon, west-central Africa. It lies at the edge of the tropical rain forest zone, on the Gulf of Guinea of the Atlantic Ocean. Ivory, cocoa, timber, and coffee are exported from the port, which is also a trade centre for local agricultural products and fish. Beautiful beaches and the Campo game reserve to the south attract tourists. Kribi is served by an airfield and has road connections with Edéa and Douala (north) and Ebolowa (east). Pop. (1984 est.) 18,000.

Krieger, Johann Philipp (b. Feb. 25, 1649, Nürnberg—d. Feb. 7, 1725, Weissenfels, Saxony), German composer known especially for his church cantatas, fugues, and keyboard suites.

Krieger studied at Nürnberg and Copenhagen and became court organist at Bayreuth in 1670. Later he studied and toured in Italy, working with Johann Rosenmüller in Venice and Bernardo Pasquini in Rome. After a brief return to Bayreuth, he became chapelmaster to the court of Halle and Weissenfels in 1680.

Only about 80 of Krieger's 2,000 cantatas are extant. Like his fugues, they represent an important stage in the development of their genre from the earlier Baroque style to that of J.S. Bach. Krieger was one of the principal composers of keyboard suites of his day. He also composed a number of suites for wind instruments and about 200 secular strophic airs, or songs.

Kriemhild, in Germanic heroic legend, sister of the Burgundian kings Gunther, Gernot, and Giselher. In Norse legend she is called Gudrun, and the lays in which she appears are variant tales of revenge. In the *Nibelungenlied,* she is the central character, introduced as a gentle princess courted by Siegfried. He wins Kriemhild's hand by performing feats for Gunther in the wooing of Brunhild. When Siegfried is later killed on Gunther's order because of Brunhild's spite at his role in wooing her, Kriemhild's grief transforms her into a "she-devil" in the second part of the epic. She marries Etzel (Attila the Hun) for revenge on her brothers, which she achieves by inviting them to Etzel's court, where she has them killed. She herself is killed by Hildebrand, the weapons master of Dietrich von Bern.

The origin of Kriemhild's legend may be traced to two historical events. In 437 a Burgundian king, Gundahar, and his followers were wiped out by Huns; and in 453 the Hunnish king Attila died in his sleep at the side of his new bride, a German girl named Hildico, or Ildico. These two events became fused in popular legend. In Old Norse legend, Hildico became Gudrun, who murdered Attila in revenge for his treacherous murder of her brothers. As the legend was reshaped in other Germanic regions where Attila was too much esteemed to be credited with atrocity, Etzel was pushed to the background, and Kriemhild became the murderess of her own brothers. *See* Atli, Lay of; Nibelungenlied.

Krige, (Mattheus) Uys (b. Feb. 4, 1910, Bontebokskloof, near Swellendam, Cape Province, S.Af.—d. Aug. 10, 1987, near Hermanus, Cape Province), South African dramatist, poet, translator, and short-story writer.

Krige was educated at the University of Stellenbosch and lived from 1931 to 1935 in France and Spain, where he learned Romance languages. He began his writing career as a reporter on the *Rand Daily Mail.* He began to make his reputation as a creative writer with a book of verse, *Kentering* (1935; "Turnings"); a play *Magdelena Retief* (1938); and a volume of poetic tales, *Die palmboom* (1940; "The Palm Tree"). He served as a war correspondent with the South African forces in North Africa (1940–41) and was captured at Tobruk. He was sent to Italy as a prisoner of war. His escape from the prisoner-of-war camp two years later became the basis for his first English-language book, *The Way Out* (1946). His earlier short stories were collected as *The Dream and the Desert* (1953), and his later short stories were published as *Orphan of the Desert* (1967). His plays *The Wall of Death* (1960), *The Sniper* (1962), and *The Two Lamps* (1964) solidified his international reputation as a dramatist.

Part of Krige's importance as a writer rests with his pivotal position in South African literature as one who bridges the gulf, both political and linguistic, between Afrikaans and English. He wrote equally effectively in both languages. His critical studies reveal his awareness of the underlying South African literary tradition of which he was a part. In 1968 he coedited *The Penguin Book of South African Verse,* which included translations of African-language poetry as well as Afrikaans poetry. Krige also translated a number of works in English, Spanish, and Italian literature into Afrikaans.

krill, any member of the crustacean suborder Euphausiacea or of the genus *Euphausia* within that suborder. The name is sometimes also used to refer to *Euphausia superba,* a single species. The Euphausiacea are shrimplike marine animals that are pelagic in habit

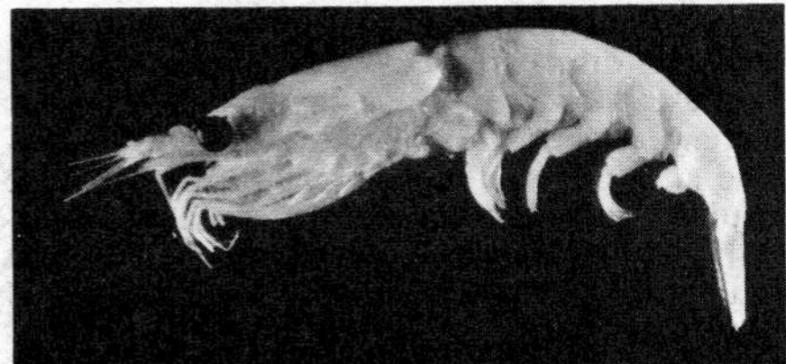

Krill (*Euphausia*)
G.A. Llane

(*i.e.,* they live in the open sea). They range in size from 8 to 60 mm (about ¼ to 2 inches). Eighty-two species have been described. Most have bioluminescent organs (photophores) on the lower side, making them visible at night. They are of great importance in certain regions of the sea as food for various fishes, birds, and whales, particularly blue whales and finback whales. Krill occur in vast swarms that may gather near the ocean surface or at depths greater than 2,000 m (about 6,600 feet).

The body of *E. superba* is about five centimetres long and translucent, with reddish brown blotches. The larvae pass through nine stages of development. Males mature in about 22 months, females in about 25 months. During a spawning period of about five and a half months the eggs are shed at a depth of about 225 m (740 feet). The krill larvae gradually move toward the surface as they develop, feeding on microscopic organisms.

From January to April swarms of *E. superba* in the Antarctic Ocean may contain as much as 20 kg of these animals per cubic metre (about 35 pounds per cubic yard). Because of their vast numbers and nutritive qualities, krill have been regarded by ecologists as a potential food source for man. They are an especially rich source of vitamin A.

Krimmitschau (Germany): *see* Crimmitschau.

Krimmler Waterfall, German KRIMMLER WASSERFÄLLE, waterfall on the Krimmler River, a tributary of the upper Salzach, in *Bundesland* (federal state) Salzburg, west-central Austria. The highest cataract in the Austrian

Krimmler Waterfall in the Austrian Alps
C. Ropke—Bavaria-Verlag

Alps, with a fall of 1,247 feet (380 m), it drops in three stages—upper, middle, and lower. Its upper fall is the most impressive, with a 460-foot (140-metre) drop. The falls can be reached by foot trail or bridle path from the nearby village of Krimml.

Krimpen, Jan van (b. Jan. 12, 1892, Gouda, Neth.—d. Oct. 20, 1958, Haarlem), outstanding modern designer of typefaces for books and postage stamps.

Van Krimpen received an art education at the academy of art at The Hague. An early interest in poetry led him in 1917 to publish the poetic works of his friends in a series for which he designed the format. He received a commission from the Dutch post office to draw the lettering for a special commemorative stamp to be printed by the prominent firm of Enschedé in 1923. The success of the design led Enschedé to invite him to design a new typeface for the firm. The typeface he produced, Lutetia (the Roman name for Paris), was the official lettering for an exhibition of Dutch art in Paris in 1927, and its reception led to his lifelong association with the firm. In addition to Lutetia, van Krimpen's well-known faces include Antigone Greek (1927), Romanée (1928), Romulus (1931), Cancelleresca Bastarda (1935), and Spectrum (1943). His types became well known in the United States through the Limited Editions Club and in England through the Nonesuch Press.

Krimskii Poluostrov (Ukraine): *see* Crimean Peninsula.

Krindachyovka, also spelled KRINDACHEVKA (Ukraine): *see* Krasny Luch.

Krishna, Sanskrit KṚṢṆA, one of the most widely revered and most popular of all Indian divinities, worshipped as the eighth incarnation (avatar, or *avatāra*) of the Hindu god Vishnu and also as a supreme god in his own right. Krishna became the focus of numerous bhakti (devotional) cults, which over the

Krishna and Rādhā in the rain with a musical maidservant, manuscript illumination from the Mewār period, 18th century; in the National Museum of India, New Delhi

Federico Borromeo—SCALA from Art Resource

centuries have produced a wealth of religious poetry, music, and painting. The basic sources of Krishna's mythology are the epic *Mahābhārata* and its 5th-century-AD appendix, the *Harivaṃśa,* and the *Purāṇa*s, particularly Books 10 and 11 of the *Bhāgavata-Purāṇa*. They relate how Krishna (literally "black," or "dark as a cloud") was born into the Yādava clan, the son of Vasudeva and Devakī, sister of Kaṃsa, the wicked king of Mathura (in modern Uttar Pradesh). Kaṃsa, hearing a prophecy that he should be destroyed by Devakī's child, tried to slay her children; but Krishna was smuggled across the Yamuna River to Gokula (or Vraja, modern Gokul), where he was raised by the leader of the cowherds, Nanda, and his wife Yaśodā.

The child Krishna was adored for his mischievous pranks; he also performed many miracles and slew demons. As a youth, the cowherd Krishna became renowned as a lover, the sound of his flute prompting the *gopīs* (wives and daughters of the cowherds) to leave their homes to dance ecstatically with him in the forests. His favourite among them was the beautiful Rādhā. At length Krishna and his brother Balarāma returned to Mathura to slay

Krishna River at Wai, Mahārāshtra state, India

David Channer—Nancy Palmer Agency

the wicked Kaṃsa. Afterward, finding the kingdom unsafe, he led the Yādavas to the western coast of Kāthiāwār and established his court at Dvāraka (modern Dwārkā, Gujarāt). He married the princess Rukmiṇī and took other wives as well.

Krishna refused to bear arms in the great war between the Kauravas and the Pāṇḍavas but offered a choice of his personal attendance to one side and the loan of his army to the other. The Pāṇḍavas chose the former, and Krishna thus served as charioteer for Arjuna. On his return to Dvāraka, a brawl broke out one day among the Yādava chiefs in which Krishna's brother and son were slain. As the god sat in the forest lamenting, a huntsman, mistaking him for a deer, shot him in his one vulnerable spot, the heel, killing him.

Krishna's personality is clearly a syncretic one, though the different elements are not easily separated. Vāsudeva-Kṛṣṇa, a Vṛṣṇi prince who was presumably also a religious leader, was elevated to the godhead by the 5th century BC; the cowherd Krishna is obviously the god of a pastoral community that turned away from the Indra-dominated Vedic religion. The Krishna who emerged from the blending of these ideologies was ultimately identified with the supreme god Viṣṇu-Nārāyaṇa and, hence, considered his avatar. His cult preserved distinctive traits, chief among them an exploration of the analogies between divine love and human love. Thus, Krishna's youthful dalliances with the *gopīs* are interpreted as symbolic of the loving interplay between God and the human soul.

The rich variety of legends associated with Krishna's life led to an abundance of representation in painting and sculpture. The child Krishna (Bālakṛṣṇa) is depicted crawling on his hands and knees or dancing with joy, a ball of butter held in his hands. The divine lover (the most common representation) is shown playing the flute, surrounded by adoring *gopīs*. In 17th- and 18th-century Rajasthani and Pahari painting, Krishna is characteristically depicted with blue-black skin, wearing a yellow dhoti (loincloth) and a crown of peacock feathers.

Krishna River, formerly KISTNA, river in southern India, rising in Mahārāshtra state in the Western Ghāts range near the old town of Mahābaleshwar, not far from India's west coast. It flows east to Wai and then in a generally southeasterly direction past Sāngli to the border of Karnātaka state. There the river turns east and flows in an irregular course across Karnātaka and into Andhra Pradesh state. It veers southeast and then northeast, flows east to its delta head at Vijayawāda, and from there flows into the Bay of Bengal after a course of about 800 mi (1,290 km).

The Krishna has a large and very fertile delta continuous with that of the Godāvari River, to the northeast. Although it is not navigable, the Krishna provides water for irrigation; a weir at Vijayawāda controls the flow of water into a system of canals in the delta. Because it is fed by seasonal monsoon rains, the river's flow undergoes great fluctuation during the year, limiting its usefulness for irrigation. The two largest tributaries are the Bhīma (north) and the Tungabhadra (south). The latter has a dam, completed in 1957, at Hospet, forming a reservoir and supplying electric power.

Krishnanagar, also called KRISHNAGAR, city, eastern West Bengal state, northeastern India, just south of the Jalangi River. A road and rail junction, it is the major agricultural distribution centre for the district. Sugar milling is the major industry, and Ghurnī, a suburb, is famous for the manufacture of coloured clay figures. The city, constituted a municipality in 1864, contains the residence of the maharaja of Nadia and is a Christian evangelistic centre. It is also the site of a hospital, a horticultural research station and jute nursery, and an agricultural training centre. A large fair is held annually. Pop. (2001 prelim.) 139,070.

Kristallnacht (German: "Crystal Night"), also called NIGHT OF BROKEN GLASS or NOVEMBER POGROMS, the night of Nov. 9–10, 1938, when German Nazis attacked Jewish persons and property. The name *Kristallnacht* refers to the litter of broken glass left in the streets after these pogroms. The violence continued during the day of November 10, and in some places acts of violence continued for several more days.

The pretext for the pogroms was the shooting in Paris on November 7 of the German diplomat Ernst vom Rath by a Polish-Jewish student, Herschel Grynszpan. News of Rath's death on November 9 reached Adolf Hitler in Munich, Ger., where he was celebrating the anniversary of the abortive 1923 Beer Hall Putsch. There, minister of propaganda Joseph Goebbels, after conferring with Hitler, harangued a gathering of veteran Storm Troopers, urging violent reprisals staged to appear as "spontaneous demonstrations." Telephone orders from Munich triggered pogroms throughout Germany, which then included Austria.

Just before midnight on November 9, Gestapo chief Heinrich Müller sent a telegram to all police units informing them that "in shortest order, actions against Jews and especially their synagogues will take place in all of Germany. These are not to be interfered with." Rather, the police were to arrest the victims. Fire companies stood by synagogues in flames with explicit instructions to let the buildings burn. They were to intervene only if a fire threatened adjacent "Aryan" properties.

In two days and nights, more than 1,000 synagogues were burned or otherwise damaged. Rioters ransacked and looted about 7,500 Jewish businesses, killed at least 91 Jews, and vandalized Jewish hospitals, homes, schools, and cemeteries. The attackers were often neighbours. Some 30,000 Jewish males age 16 to 60 were arrested. To accommodate so many new prisoners, the concentration camps at Dachau, Buchenwald, and Sachsenhausen were expanded.

After the pogrom ended, it was given an oddly poetic name: Kristallnacht—meaning "crystal night" or "night of broken glass." This name symbolized the final shattering of Jewish existence in Germany. After Kristallnacht, the Nazi regime made Jewish survival in Germany impossible.

The cost of the broken window glass came to millions of Reichsmarks. The Reich confiscated any compensation claims that insurance companies paid to Jews. The rubble of ruined synagogues had to be cleared by the Jewish community. The Nazi government imposed a collective fine of one billion Reichsmarks on the Jewish community. After assessing the fine, Hermann Göring remarked: "The swine won't commit another murder. Incidentally . . . I would not like to be a Jew in Germany."

The Nazi government barred Jews from schools on November 15 and authorized local authorities to impose curfews in late November. By December 1938, Jews were banned from most public places in Germany.

(Mi.Be.)

Kristensen, Knud (b. Oct. 26, 1880, Ringkøbing, Den.—d. Sept. 29, 1962, Hillerød), politician who, as leader of the first elected post-World War II Danish government, rekindled national hopes for the reacquisition of the historical territory of Schleswig from Germany. He also founded the Independent Party.

Entering Parliament in 1920, Kristensen became a leader of the Venstre (Left) Party. In 1940 he became minister of the interior in Thorvald Stauning's coalition government under the German occupation but resigned after Stauning's death in 1942, when Erik Scavenius, who sought accommodation with the Germans, became prime minister.

As prime minister of the postwar Venstre government (1945–47), Kristensen articulated a significant Danish sentiment for the incorporation of South Schleswig, retained by Germany after World War I, into Denmark. To a British inquiry, however, Kristensen replied that Denmark wished only to see a referendum by the German Schleswigers. His private stand in favour of an imposed border revision left no party to the territorial dispute satisfied, and his government fell in 1947. In 1953 he formed the small Independent Party, which advocated a return of southern Schleswig to Denmark and a repeal of most social welfare legislation.

Kristensen, Tom, in full AAGE TOM KRISTENSEN (b. Aug. 4, 1893, London, Eng.—d. June 4, 1974, Thurø, near Svendborg, Den.), Danish poet, novelist, and critic who was one of the central literary figures of the disillusioned generation after World War I.

Educated at the University of Copenhagen, Kristensen taught before he turned to writing. He was influential as a literary critic for the left-wing Copenhagen daily *Politiken* (1924–63). He also translated much literature into Danish, including works by Friedrich von Schiller, Theodore Dreiser, D.H. Lawrence, and Erich Maria Remarque. His art was considered radical both politically and artistically.

Kristensen's first volume of poetry, expressionistic in style, was *Fribytterdrømme* (1920; "Pirate Dreams"), which speaks of the beauty of the city and of technological achievements; the second, *Påfuglefjeren* (1922; "The Peacock Feather"), expresses his love of exotic-sounding names and brilliant colours and was inspired by a journey to China and Japan in 1922. A later volume of poetry, *Den sidste lygte* (1954; "The Last Lantern"), is meditative and philosophical. *Hærværk* (1930; *Havoc*, 1968), his best-known novel, is a bitter examination of conscience and an account of the interwar years of his generation. His autobiography *En bogorms barndom* ("A Bookworm's Boyhood") appeared in 1955.

Kristian (Swedish personal name): *see under* Christian.

Kristiania (city, Norway): *see* Oslo.

Kristiansand, town, seaport, and seat of Vest-Agder *fylke* (county), southern Norway. Located on the Skagerrak (strait between Norway and Denmark) at the mouth of the Otra River, it has a spacious, ice-free harbour, protected by offshore islands, and is the largest community of Sørlandet region. It was founded and fortified in 1641 by King Christian IV of Denmark and Norway, after whom it is named; in 1660 the Christiansholm fortress, now a tourist site, was built. Christian intended the town to be a leading commercial metropolis, but it remained relatively unimportant until the late 19th century. It is now a busy transportation centre and probably the most important town on the Oslo-Stavanger rail line (opened 1938). It provides ocean freight service to numerous European and American ports and a car ferry across the Skagerrak to Hirtshals, Den. Kjevik Airport, northeast of the town, has direct flights to the principal cities of Norway and to Copenhagen. An important industrial centre, Kristiansand has shipyards, textile mills, and metal- and wood-processing plants. Food processing (flour and fish) is also significant.

Notable buildings include the Lutheran cathedral (originating 1685–87 and rebuilt 1882–85), seat of the Church of Norway's bishopric of Agder, and the municipal theatre. Nearby is the ancient Oddernes Church (dating possibly to the 11th century) and the 18th-century Gimle Manor; Kongsgaard to the northeast houses the regional folklore museum. Pop. (2003 est.) 74,590.

Kristianstad, former *län* (county) of southern Sweden, merged with Malmöhus in 1997 to form the new county of Skåne.

Kristianstad, city, Skåne *län* (county), southern Sweden. It lies on Hammar Lake and the Helge River. It was founded in 1614 by King Christian IV of Denmark and Norway as a border defense against Sweden. It was ceded to Sweden in 1658, retaken by Christian V in 1676, and finally acquired by Sweden in 1678.

Tyggården, which was built in 1615 as a royal palace, was subsequently used as a royal stable and now houses a museum. The Technical College and Museum, with industrial, social history, and art exhibits, was occupied by King Stanisław I of Poland and his court from 1711 to 1714.

Kristianstad is a rail, commercial, and industrial centre, with engineering works, flour and textile mills, slaughterhouses, and food-processing plants. Its seaport, Åhus, is situated on the Baltic Sea, about 11 miles (18 km) southeast. There are air connections with Malmö and Stockholm. Pop. (2002 est.) 74,951.

Kristiansund, town and port, Møre og Romsdal *fylke* (county), western Norway. The town is situated on three tiny coastal islets facing the Norwegian Sea; its harbour is protected by an inlet in the adjacent island of Frei and by the island of Averøy (west). In the area around the town, ruins of habitations have been found that may date back to the Fosna culture (about 8000 BC). Long an important fishing port, it was incorporated as a city in 1742. Many of its residents are descendants of Scotsmen who came to supervise a fishing enterprise in the 18th century. During World War II, Kristiansund sustained heavy damage, especially by a German bombardment in April 1940. Completely rebuilt, it is now the home port for a large Norwegian trawler fleet. The town's principal export is fish (principally cod), fresh, salted, and frozen; local industry centres on fish processing. The town is postally known as Kristiansund N. (for Nord, "North"), to distinguish it from the similarly spelled town of Kristiansand, in southern Norway, which is postally written Kristiansand S. (for Sør, "South"). Pop. (2002 est.) 16,789.

Kristina (Swedish personal name): *see under* Christina.

Kristinehamn, town and port, in the *län* (county) of Värmland, west-central Sweden, on Vänern (lake). As early as the 14th century it was a trading centre known as Bro. It received a charter in 1582, when royal ironworks were established there, but lost both ironworks and charter within two years. In the 17th century, it became a regional iron centre as the place where iron prices were fixed. It was granted another charter in 1642 and adopted its present name in honour of Queen Christina. Destructive fires occurred in 1777 and 1893. Its leading industries are based on wood and iron; the products are shipped from its busy harbour. Pop. (2000 est.) 17,934.

Kristofer (Swedish personal name): *see under* Christopher.

Kritikón Pélagos: *see* Crete, Sea of.

Krivoy Rog (city, Ukraine): *see* Kryvyy Rih.

Križanić, Juraj (Croatian), Russian YURY KRIZHANICH (b. 1618, Obrh, near Podgorica, Croatia, Ottoman Empire [now in Montenegro, Yugos.]—d. Sept. 12, 1683, Vienna, Austria, Holy Roman Empire), Roman Catholic priest and scholar who became an early advocate of Pan-Slavism and of a program of cultural and social reform in Russia that foreshadowed the reforms made by Peter I the Great, who ruled from 1682 to 1725.

Križanić studied at various theological seminaries in Europe before going to Rome. He was trained to be a missionary to convert the Orthodox Slavs to Roman Catholicism and made a short expedition to Moscow to promote the unification of the two churches (1647).

After he returned from Russia, Križanić developed the idea of uniting all the Slav peoples in a single political entity centred at Moscow, a scheme that prompted his second trip to Moscow in 1659. Concealing his priestly profession, he offered his services to Tsar Alexis and was hired to undertake a study of Slavic grammar. But in January 1661, for unknown reasons, he was banished to Tobolsk in Siberia. He was provided with a substantial state stipend, however, and for the next 15 years he remained there, writing nine books on political, economic, religious, linguistic, and philosophical topics. Among them are the valuable philological work *Grammatichno izkazanye ob russkom yaziku* ("Grammatical Instruction on the Russian Language"), which advocates political unity among the Slavs through linguistic unity, and *Politika ili razgovor ob vladatelystvu* ("Politics; or, a Discourse on Government"), which criticizes the Muscovite government, outlines reforms based on education and on certain elements of Western culture, and advocates the union of all Slavs under the improved Russian state.

After Tsar Fyodor III succeeded Alexis in 1676, Križanić was allowed to return to Moscow and to go to western Europe (March 1677). He died during the Turkish siege of Vienna while on a journey to Rome. His works, which remained in the possession of the Russian tsars, influenced the ruling circles of Russia and helped prepare for the widespread reforms, patterned on western European examples, that Peter I later introduced.

Krk, Italian VEGLIA, Latin CURICUM, island, the largest and most northern of Croatia's Adriatic islands. With an area of 158 square miles (410 square km), it reaches maximum elevation at Obzova, 1,824 feet (556 m). Archaeological findings suggest that Krk has been continuously inhabited since the Neolithic Period. Roman influence, beginning in the 1st century BC, was followed by the arrival of the Slavs in the 7th century. The Romans retreated into the town of Krk on the island's west coast, which was renamed Vecla under the Byzantine Empire. A Greco-Roman dialect survived locally until the 19th century. From the year 1000, Venice competed for the island against the kingdom of Croatia, which won it in 1059; from 1133 to 1480, Krk was ruled by the counts of the Frankopan family, who recognized the sovereignty of the crown of Hungary and, at the same time, held a seat in the Great Council of Venice.

From about 1100, during the period of Croatian influence, comes the Baščanska Ploča ("Baška Inscription"), which was found on the island. It is a document written in the Glagolitic alphabet, one of the old Slav alphabets and a cornerstone of Croatian literary development. Ruled by Venice until 1797, Krk then passed to Austria, which held it until 1918. During World War II, in 1945, Yugoslav Partisans expelled the Germans there.

The stony, bare eastern part of the island contrasts with the western and central parts, in which Mediterranean fruits, viticulture, animal husbandry, and beekeeping support the population. The geologic structure of the island (karstic limestone and flysch zones) has allowed for the development of fast-flowing surface streams, such as the Ričina, and a number of springs. Two small lakes also provide water. The town of Krk lies on a hill above the sheltered Bay of Krk. It has a 12th-century cathedral and the castle of the Frankopan family.

In 1980 a bridge opened connecting the island of Krk to the mainland with the world's longest concrete arch (1,280 feet [390 m]). This arch forms the main span of the 4,296-foot (1,039-metre) bridge, carrying a 34-foot roadway and numerous pipelines, some carrying oil from the port of Omisalj on Krk to mainland refineries and some carrying fresh water to Krk, where there is little natural water. Pop. (1971) town, 1,531; (1991) island, 16,402.

Krkonoše (mountains, Czech Republic): *see* Giant Mountains.

Krleža, Miroslav (b. July 7, 1893, Zagreb, Croatia-Slavonia, Austria-Hungary [now in Croatia]—d. Dec. 29, 1981, Zagreb, Yugos.), novelist and playwright who was a dominant figure in modern Croatian literature.

Krleža trained for a military career but after World War I devoted himself to writing and founded a left-wing review in 1919. After World War II he was elected vice president of the Yugoslav Academy of Science and Art and later became director of the Croatian Institute of Lexicography and president of the Yugoslav Writers' Union. A man of vigorous and powerful intellect and wide learning, Krleža wrote with great intensity, fearlessly criticizing political and social injustices. Typical works are the dramatic trilogy *Glembajevi* (1932; "The Glembaj Family"), which is an indictment of the decadence of the Croatian bourgeoisie under the Austrian Empire; the novel *Povratak Filipa Latinovića* (1932; *The Return of Philip Latinovicz,* 1960); and works concerned with the past exploitation and sufferings of the Croatian peasants—*e.g.,* the stories in the collection *Hrvatski bog Mars* (1922; "The Croatian God Mars") and the *Balade Petrice Kerempuha* (1936; "Ballads of Petrica Kerempuh").

Kroc, Ray, byname of RAYMOND ALBERT KROC (b. Oct. 5, 1902, Chicago, Ill., U.S.—d. Jan. 14, 1984, San Diego, Calif.), American restaurateur and a pioneer of the fast-food industry with his worldwide McDonald's enterprise.

Ray Kroc
Sygma

After serving as an ambulance driver in World War I at the age of 15, Kroc returned to Chicago and held various jobs, including jazz pianist, real-estate salesman, and paper-cup salesman for Lily-Tulip Cup Co. In the early 1940s he became the exclusive distributor for the "multimixer," a blender that could simultaneously mix five milk shakes. In 1954 he visited a restaurant in San Bernardino, Calif., that used eight of his mixers. The restaurant was owned by two brothers, Maurice and Richard McDonald, who used an assembly-line format to prepare and sell a large volume of hamburgers, french fries, and milk shakes. Kroc decided to set up a chain of drive-in restaurants based on the McDonald brothers' format, and he agreed to pay the brothers 0.5 percent of gross receipts. The first of Kroc's McDonald's restaurants was opened April 15, 1955, in Des Plaines, Ill. Two more stores were opened that same year, and gross sales amounted to $235,000. Kroc continued to expand McDonald's, selling franchises on the condition that owners manage their restaurants. He instituted a training program for owner-managers and continually emphasized the automation and standardization of McDonald's operations.

Kroc bought out the McDonald brothers in 1961 for $2,700,000. By that time he had established 228 restaurants and sales had reached $37,000,000. At the time of his death there were some 7,500 McDonald's outlets worldwide, and three-fourths were run by franchise holders. Kroc served as president of McDonald's from 1955 to 1968, as chairman of the board from 1968 to 1977, and as senior chairman from 1977 until his death.

During his lifetime Kroc was an active supporter of numerous charitable organizations. From 1974 he was the owner of the San Diego Padres professional baseball team.

Krochmal, Nachman, also called (by acronym) RANAK (b. Feb. 17, 1785, Brody, Austrian Poland [now in Ukraine]—d. July 31, 1840, Tarnopol, Galicia, Austrian Empire [now Ternopil, Ukraine]), Jewish scholar and philosopher; his major, seminal work, *Moreh nevukhe ha-zeman* (1851; "Guide for the Perplexed of Our Time"), made pioneering contributions in the areas of Jewish religion, literature, and especially history.

Krochmal was married at the age of 14 (according to a contemporary custom) and went to live with his wealthy father-in-law. For the next 10 years, he read voraciously in the works of such authors as Moses Maimonides, the celebrated medieval Jewish philosopher (whose *Moreh nevukhim,* or *The Guide for the Perplexed,* later inspired Krochmal's own *Guide*); in Hebrew literature; in German philosophy, particularly the works of G.W.F. Hegel and Immanuel Kant; and in secular history.

During his lifetime Krochmal published only a few essays; his unfinished *Moreh nevukhe ha-zeman* was edited and published posthumously by the eminent Jewish scholar Leopold Zunz (1794–1886). Krochmal's aim, like that of Maimonides before him, was to reconcile the traditions of Judaism with modern secular knowledge. In order to accomplish this goal, Krochmal believed that it was necessary to trace the Jewish spirit through its manifestations in history, literature, and religious philosophy. A major achievement of Krochmal's book is that it shifted attention from Judaism as an abstract religion to Judaism as a process expressed through the activities of a people.

Krock, Arthur B., in full ARTHUR BERNARD KROCK (b. Nov. 16, 1886, Glasgow, Ky., U.S.—d. April 12, 1974, Washington, D.C.), principal political writer and analyst for *The New York Times* for a generation (1932–66). Krock became famous for his calm analysis of U.S. political and economic affairs and foreign relations. His column, "In the Nation," ran in the *Times* from 1933 until 1966. He was the first journalist ever to win four Pulitzer awards—two prizes (1935 and 1937) and two special awards (1950 and 1955).

Krock matriculated with the class of 1908 at Princeton University, but family financial reverses made it impossible for him to continue, and he went to Louisville, Ky., to find a newspaper job. The apprenticeship system then prevailing gave "cub" reporters no earnings, but he persuaded the *Louisville Herald* that he was an experienced reporter and was signed on to cover politics. He moved on to *The Courier-Journal,* where for a time he came under the influence of editor Henry Watterson. In 1910 he went to Washington, D.C., to be capital correspondent for the *Louisville Times,* and in 1911 took on duties for *The Courier-Journal* as well. He moved between Louisville and Washington in various newspapers and other assignments until 1923, when he was hired as assistant to the president and publisher of the *New York World.*

The New York Times engaged Krock in 1932 for its Washington bureau, and there he stayed for the rest of his career. He became a confidant of presidents. His columns identified him as a political conservative. The *Times* published a selection of his columns, *In the Nation: 1932–1966,* after his retirement. Krock wrote three books, *Memoirs: 60 Years on the Firing Line* (1968), *The Consent of the Governed and Other Deceits* (1971), and *Myself When Young: Growing Up in the 1890s* (1973).

Kroeber, A.L., in full ALFRED LOUIS KROEBER (b. June 11, 1876, Hoboken, N.J., U.S.—d. Oct. 5, 1960, Paris, France), influential American anthropologist of the first half of the 20th century, whose primary concern was to understand the nature of culture and its processes. His interest and competence ranged over the whole of anthropology, and he made valuable contributions to American Indian ethnology; to the archaeology of New Mexico, Mexico, and Peru; and to the study of linguistics, folklore, kinship, and social structure. His career nearly coincided with the emergence of academic, professionalized anthropology in the United States and contributed significantly to its development.

While a graduate student at Columbia University, Kroeber came under the influence of Franz Boas. He received a Ph.D. in 1901 for a study of decorative symbolism of the Arapaho Indians of Montana and that year founded the anthropology department at the University of California at Berkeley. Kroeber produced more than 500 articles, monographs, and books, and his most influential work is considered to be *Anthropology* (1923; rev. ed. 1948), one of the first general teaching texts on the subject.

Kroeber's first important contributions to archaeology were his studies of sites near Zuni, N.M. (1915–20), but his work centred mainly on expeditions to Mexico (1924 and 1930) and Peru (1925, 1926, and 1942). He introduced controlled excavational methods and used meticulous stylistic analyses to determine chronological sequences. An important resulting work was *Peruvian Archaeology in 1942* (1944). He also pioneered in dialect surveys of American Indians. His final work on California Indian languages was *Yokuts Dialect Survey* (1963).

Kroeber was concerned with culture as a universal human characteristic and believed that a complete understanding of culture must contain explanations not only of specific cultures but also of cultural elements and patternings that transcend specific cultures. One of his most ambitious efforts, *Configurations of Culture Growth* (1945), sought to trace the growth and decline of all of civilized man's thought and art. *The Nature of Culture* (1952) is a collection of Kroeber's essays.

Kroemer, Herbert (b. Aug. 25, 1928, Weimar, Ger.), German physicist who, with Zhores Alferov and Jack S. Kilby, was awarded the 2000 Nobel Prize for Physics for their work that laid the foundation for the modern era of microchips, computers, and information technology.

After receiving a Ph.D. from Georg August University, Göttingen, Ger. (1952), Kroemer worked at RCA Laboratories (1954–57) in Princeton, N.J., and Varian Associates (1959–66) in Palo Alto, Calif. In 1968 he became professor of electrical engineering at the University of Colorado at Boulder, and in 1976 he joined the faculty of the University of California, Santa Barbara.

In 1957 Kroemer carried out theoretical calculations showing that a heterostructure transistor would be superior to a conventional transistor, especially for certain high-frequency uses and other applications. (Most computer chips and other semiconductor components are made from one kind of material, whereas heterostructures are made of different materials.) Scientists later showed that he was correct—heterostructure transistors can operate at frequencies 100 times higher than conventional transistors, and they also work better as amplifiers. Alferov's research team in the Soviet Union applied Kroemer's theory, developing the first practical heterostructure electronic device in 1966. Alferov then pioneered electronic components from heterostructures, including the first heterostructure laser, which both men had proposed independently in 1963. Heterostructure devices made fibre-optic communications possible and are used in numerous everyday products, including computers and video players.

Krogh, August, in full SCHACK AUGUST STEENBERG KROGH (b. Nov. 15, 1874, Grenå, Den.—d. Sept. 13, 1949, Copenhagen), Danish physiologist who received the Nobel Prize for Physiology or Medicine in 1920 for his discovery of the motor-regulating mechanism of capillaries (small blood vessels).

Krogh studied zoology at the University of Copenhagen, becoming professor of animal physiology there in 1916. In 1906 he was awarded a prize by the Vienna Academy of

Krogh
By courtesy of Det Kongelige Bibliotek, Copenhagen

Science for investigations described in his treatise *Mechanism of Gas Exchange in Lungs.* He found that the capillaries contract or dilate in proportion to the tissue's requirement for blood—that active muscles, for example, have a greater number of open capillaries than do the less active. His study of the circulatory mechanisms that control the supply of oxygen to the tissues grew out of his primary interest, respiration, a subject in which he collaborated with his wife, Marie. He wrote *The Respiratory Exchange of Animals and Man* (1916) and *The Anatomy and Physiology of Capillaries* (1922).

Krokodil (Russian: "Crocodile"), humour magazine published in Moscow, noted for its satire and cartoons.

From 1922 to 1932 the periodical was published as a weekly illustrated supplement to the Soviet newspaper *Rabochaya gazeta* ("The Workers' Paper"). From 1932 until 1992 the magazine was published thrice-monthly but thereafter was forced by economic hardship to cut back to monthly publication.

The modern *Krokodil* is a 14- to 18-page magazine that features coloured type and cartoons. During the Soviet period its humour was chiefly directed against what it termed Western imperialism and bourgeois ideology, but it also assailed "undesirable elements" in Russian society. Vitaly Goryayev, one of its best-known cartoonists, became known for his comic portrayal of the "capitalist warmongers."

Kröller-Müller State Museum, Dutch RIJKSMUSEUM KRÖLLER-MÜLLER, collection in Otterlo, The Netherlands, primarily of late 19th- and 20th-century art, especially paintings by Vincent Van Gogh. The museum is named for Mrs. H.E.L.J. Kröller-Müller, the institution's principal benefactor.

The collection is housed in a building designed by the Belgian architect Henry van de Velde that was constructed between 1937 and 1954. It also contains collections of 16th–18th-century Dutch, Italian, and German paintings, European drawings and prints, furniture, Chinese objets d'art, and Chinese, Delft, Egyptian, French, and Greek ceramics.

Kromdraai, South African paleoanthropological site best known for its hominid fossils, which are associated with animals thought to be about 2 million years old. Kromdraai is a limestone cave that has occasionally had openings to the surface. The remains are of animals that were adapted to relatively dry and open habitats. The site also contains stone tools similar to those found at Olduvai Gorge. Kromdraai is one of three neighbouring South African sites where important evidence of human evolution has been found. Kromdraai, Sterkfontein, and Swartkrans (*qq.v.*) are parts of the Cradle of Humankind, a region designated a UNESCO World Heritage site in 1999.

Kroměříž, German KREMSIER, city, Jihomoravský *kraj* (region), Czech Republic, on the Morava River, northeast of Brno. The town dates from 1110, after which it was acquired by the bishops of Olomouc. It is best known historically because the Austrian constituent assembly used it as a refuge during the Vienna revolt (1848–49). In Kroměříž the assembly prepared the short-lived Kremsier constitution, designed to provide for the autonomy of national cultures under a liberal dynasty in Vienna. The town's historic buildings include the former summer residence of the archbishop of Olomouc, the Gothic Church of St. Maurice (1260), and the 18th-century Piarist Church of St. John.

Kroměříž lies at the southern edge of the Haná, a fertile agricultural region of barley, wheat, and sugar beets. In the town, generators, gasoline engines, and footwear are manufactured. Pop. (2003 est.) 29,180.

Krone, Julie, in full JULIEANNE LOUISE KRONE (b. July 24, 1963, Benton Harbor, Mich., U.S.), American jockey, the first woman to win a Triple Crown race.

Krone grew up on a horse farm in Eau Claire, Mich. In 1980 she won 20 races on Michigan's fair circuit. By 1987 she had become the first female leading rider at major racetracks, winning at Monmouth Park and the Meadowlands, both in New Jersey. She retained the leading riding title at Monmouth through 1989 and at the Meadowlands through 1990. On June 5, 1993, Krone made horse-racing history aboard 13-to-1 long shot Colonial Affair as the first woman to win the Belmont Stakes, one of the U.S. Triple Crown races. In 1995 she published an autobiography, *Riding for My Life.*

Kronecker, Leopold (b. Dec. 7, 1823, Liegnitz, Prussia [now Legnica, Pol.]—d. Dec. 29, 1891, Berlin, Ger.), German mathematician whose primary contributions were in the theory of equations and higher algebra.

Kronecker acquired a passion for number theory from Ernst Kummer, his instructor in mathematics at the Liegnitz Gymnasium, and earned a doctor's degree at the University of Berlin with a dissertation (1845) on those special complex units that appear in certain algebraic number fields. From 1861 to 1883 Kronecker lectured at the University of Berlin and in 1883 succeeded Kummer as professor there.

Kronecker was primarily an arithmetician and algebraist. His major contributions were in elliptic functions, the theory of algebraic equations, and the theory of algebraic numbers. In the last field he created an alternative

Kronecker, 1865
By courtesy of Bildarchiv Preussischer Kulturbesitz BPK, Berlin

to the theory of his fellow countryman Julius Dedekind. Kronecker's theory of algebraic magnitudes (1882) presents a part of this theory; his philosophy of mathematics, however, seems destined to outlast his more technical contributions. He was the first to doubt the significance of nonconstructive existence proofs (proofs that show something must exist, often by using a proof through contradiction, but that give no method of producing them), and for many years carried on a polemic against the analytic school of the German mathematician Karl Weierstrass concerning these proofs and other points of classical analysis. Kronecker joined Weierstrass in approving the universal arithmetization of analysis, but he insisted that all mathematics should be reduced to the positive whole numbers.

Kronoberg, *län* (county) of southern Sweden, part of the traditional *landskap* (province) of Småland. Kronoberg consists of a rolling plateau of woods and marshland. Of its numerous lakes, Åsnen and Möckeln are the largest; it is drained by the Mörrums, Helga, Lagan, and many smaller rivers. Industries are based largely on forest products, and Kosta is a well-known glass-manufacturing centre. Växjö is the capital. The *län* is crossed by the trunk railway from Malmö to Stockholm. Area 3,266 square miles (8,458 square km). Pop. (2002 est.) 176,978.

Kronotsky Nature Reserve, natural area set aside for research in the natural sciences, on the eastern coast of the Kamchatka Peninsula, eastern Russia. The reserve, established in 1934, has current boundaries that date from 1967 and an area of 4,243 square miles (10,990 square km). It contains the only geyser basin in Russia. The coastal mountain ranges have numerous extinct and active volcanoes, basalt rock flows, and thermal lakes and springs. The mountain and coastal tundra are composed of thickets of grasses, Russian rock birch forest, and dwarf birch scrub. Wildlife includes marmot, pika, Arctic ground squirrel, Steller's sea lion, ringed seal, brown bear, reindeer, sable, bighorn sheep, and geese, ducks, and swans.

Kronshtadt, also spelled KRONŠTADT, naval port, Leningrad *oblast* (province), northwestern Russia. It lies on Kotlin Island near the head of the Gulf of Finland. Peter I (Peter the Great) captured the island from the Swedes in 1703 and constructed a fort and docks—then called Kronslot—to protect the approaches to St. Petersburg. Until a channel to St. Petersburg was dredged in 1875–85, Kronshtadt was also a commercial port in which cargoes were transshipped to smaller craft.

Its fortifications, which were frequently reconstructed and strengthened, played a notable role in the defense of the old Russian capital, especially during the 1941–44 Siege of Leningrad (as St. Petersburg was then called). The sailors and garrison of Kronshtadt played major roles in several Russian revolutionary movements: a Kronshtadt officer led the mutiny of the Decembrists in St. Petersburg in 1825, and a Kronshtadt sailor was the leader of the military organization of the revolutionary Narodnaya Volya group and was shot in 1882. Mutinies broke out among the troops in 1905–06 but were suppressed. After the February Revolution (1917), the Kronshtadt Soviet opposed the provisional government, declared a "Kronshtadt Republic," and took part in the July 1917 mutiny. During the October Revolution (1917), the Baltic Fleet cruiser *Aurora* bombarded the Winter Palace in the capital as a preliminary to the Bolshevik seizure of power. In March 1921, in the so-called Kronshtadt Rebellion, Kronshtadt sailors mutinied against the Soviet government. Points of interest in the modern city include a Byzantine-style cathedral. Pop. (2002) 43,385.

Kronshtadt Rebellion, Kronshtadt also spelled KRONŠTADT (March 1921), one of several major internal uprisings against Soviet rule in Russia after the Civil War (1918–20). Conducted by sailors from the Kronshtadt naval base, it greatly influenced the Communist Party's decision to undertake a program of economic liberalization to relieve the hardships suffered by the Russian population.

The sailors, located at the Kronshtadt fortress in the Gulf of Finland overlooking Petrograd (now St. Petersburg), had supported the Bolsheviks in 1917; their cooperation had been crucial to the success of the October Revolution. During the Civil War, however, they had become disenchanted with the Bolshevik government, which had been unable to provide an adequate food supply to urban populations and had restricted their political freedoms and imposed harsh labour regulations.

When the urban workers responded (early 1921) with strikes and demonstrations, the Kronshtadt sailors, sympathizing with them, formed a Provisional Revolutionary Committee. In addition to economic reform, they demanded "soviets without Bolsheviks," the release of non-Bolshevik socialists from prison, the end of the Communist Party's dictatorship, and the establishment of political freedoms and civil rights.

Leon Trotsky and Mikhail N. Tukhachevsky led a force that crushed the rebels, shooting or imprisoning the survivors. Nevertheless, by dramatically demonstrating popular dissatisfaction with the Communists' policies, the rebellion forced the party to adopt the New Economic Policy (March 1921), which brought economic relief to Soviet Russia.

Kronstadt (Romania): *see* Brașov.

Kronstam, Henning (b. June 29, 1934, Copenhagen, Den.—d. May 28, 1995, Copenhagen), Danish dancer and associate director of the Royal Danish Ballet.

Kronstam was trained as a dancer at the Royal Danish Ballet School and joined the Royal Danish Ballet in 1952. He was one of the first Danish male dancers to be trained by the Russian teacher Vera Volkova after she emigrated to Denmark. In one of Kronstam's early performances he created the role of Romeo in Frederick Ashton's successful *Romeo and Juliet* (1955). This was a particular honour for the young dancer because it was the first full-length *Romeo and Juliet* to be produced outside of the Soviet Union. He danced all the great parts in the ballets of the 19th-century Danish choreographer August Bournonville. Kronstam specialized in demi-caractère roles (particularly known in Roland Petit's *Carmen* and *Cyrano de Bergerac*). He was the first to star in the leading roles of Flemming Flindt's *The Three Musketeers* (1966) and *Dreamland* (1974) and was considered an outstanding dancer in the classical repertory.

Kronstam was artistic director of the world famous Royal Danish Ballet from 1978 to 1985, succeeding the retiring director Flemming Flindt. He was also director of the Royal Danish Ballet School.

Kropotkin, Peter Alekseyevich (b. Dec. 21 [Dec. 9, Old Style], 1842, Moscow, Russia—d. Feb. 8, 1921, Dmitrov, near Moscow), Russian revolutionary and geographer, the foremost theorist of the anarchist movement. Although he achieved renown in a number of different fields, ranging from geography and zoology to sociology and history, he shunned material success for the life of a revolutionist.

Early life and conversion to anarchism. Kropotkin was the son of Prince Aleksey Petrovich Kropotkin and was educated in the exclusive Corps of Pages in St. Petersburg. For a year he served as an aide to Tsar Alexander II and, from 1862 to 1867, as an army officer in Siberia, where, apart from his military duties, he studied animal life and engaged in geographic exploration. On the basis of his observations, he elaborated a theory of the structural lines of mountain ranges that revised the cartography of eastern Asia. He also contributed to knowledge of the glaciation of Asia and Europe during the Ice Age.

Kropotkin's findings won him immediate recognition and opened the way to a distinguished scientific career. But in 1871 he refused the secretaryship of the Russian Geographical Society and, renouncing his aristocratic heritage, dedicated his life to the cause of social justice. During his Siberian service he already had begun his conversion to anarchism—the doctrine that all forms of government should be abolished—and in 1872 a visit to the Swiss watchmakers of the Jura Mountains, whose voluntary associations of mutual support won his admiration, reinforced his beliefs. On his return to Russia he joined a revolutionary group, the Chaiykovsky Circle, which disseminated propaganda among the workers and peasants of St. Petersburg and Moscow. At this time he wrote "Must We Occupy Ourselves with an Examination of the Ideal of a Future System?," an anarchist analysis of a postrevolutionary order in which decentralized cooperative organizations would take over the functions normally performed by governments.

Kropotkin
Brown Brothers

Caught in a police dragnet, he was imprisoned in 1874 but made a sensational escape two years later, fleeing to western Europe, where his name soon became revered in radical circles. The next few years were spent mostly in Switzerland until he was expelled at the demand of the Russian government after the assassination of Tsar Alexander II by revolutionaries in 1881. He moved to France but was arrested and imprisoned for three years on trumped-up charges of sedition. Released in 1886, he settled in England, where he remained, until the Russian Revolution of 1917 allowed him to return to his native country.

Philosopher of revolution. During his long exile, Kropotkin wrote a series of influential works, the most important being *Paroles d'un révolté* (1885; "Words of a Rebel"), *In Russian and French Prisons* (1887), *The Conquest of Bread* (1892), *Fields, Factories and Workshops* (1899), *Memoirs of a Revolutionist* (1899), *Mutual Aid* (1902), *Russian Literature* (1905), and *The Great French Revolution 1789–1793* (1909). In recognition of his scholarship, Kropotkin was invited to write an article on anarchism for the 11th edition of the *Encyclopædia Britannica*.

Kropotkin's aim, as he often remarked, was to provide anarchism with a scientific basis. In *Mutual Aid*, which is widely regarded as his masterpiece, he argued that, despite the Darwinian concept of the survival of the fittest, cooperation rather than conflict is the chief factor in the evolution of species. Providing abundant examples, he showed that sociability is a dominant feature at every level of the animal world. Among humans, too, he found that mutual aid has been the rule rather than the exception. He traced the evolution of voluntary cooperation from the primitive tribe, peasant village, and medieval commune to a variety of modern associations—trade unions, learned societies, the Red Cross—that have continued to practice mutual support despite the rise of the coercive bureaucratic state. The trend of modern history, he believed, was pointing back toward decentralized, nonpolitical, cooperative societies in which people could develop their creative faculties without interference from rulers, clerics, or soldiers.

In his theory of "anarchist communism," according to which private property and unequal incomes would be replaced by the free distribution of goods and services, Kropotkin took a major step in the development of anarchist economic thought. For the principle of wages he substituted the principle of needs. Each person would be the judge of his own requirements, taking from the common storehouse whatever he deemed necessary, whether or not he contributed a share of the labour. Kropotkin envisioned a society in which people would do both manual and mental work, both in industry and in agriculture. Members of each cooperative community would work from their 20s to their 40s, four or five hours a day sufficing for a comfortable life, and the division of labour would yield to a variety of pleasant jobs, resulting in the sort of integrated, organic existence that had prevailed in the medieval city.

To prepare people for this happier life, Kropotkin pinned his hopes on the education of the young. To achieve an integrated society, he called for an education that would cultivate both mental and manual skills. Due emphasis was to be placed on the humanities and on mathematics and science, but, instead of being taught from books alone, children were to receive an active outdoor education to learn by doing and observing firsthand, a recommendation that has been widely endorsed by modern educational theorists. Drawing on his own experience of prison life, Kropotkin also advocated a thorough modification of the penal system. In the future anarchist world, antisocial behaviour would be dealt with not by laws and prisons but by human understanding and the moral pressure of the community.

Kropotkin combined the qualities of a scientist and moralist with those of a revolutionary organizer and propagandist. For all his mild benevolence, he condoned the use of violence in the struggle for freedom and equality, and, during his early years as an anarchist militant, he was among the most vigorous exponents of "propaganda by the deed"—acts of insurrection that would supplement oral and written propaganda and help to awaken the rebellious instincts of the people. He was the principal founder of both the English and Russian anarchist movements and exerted a strong influence on the movements in France, Belgium, and Switzerland. But he alienated many of his comrades by supporting the Allied powers during World War I. His action, though prompted by the fear that German authoritarianism might prove fatal to social progress, violated the strong antimilitarist tradition among anarchists and touched off bitter polemics that nearly destroyed the movement for which he had laboured nearly half a century.

Return to Russia. Events, however, took an unexpected turn with the outbreak of the Russian Revolution in 1917. Kropotkin, by this time age 74, hastened to return to his homeland. When he arrived in Petrograd (now St. Petersburg) in June 1917, after 40 years in exile, he was greeted warmly and was offered the post of minister of education in the provisional government, a post he brusquely declined. Yet his hopes for a libertarian future were never brighter, for 1917 saw the spontaneous appearance of communes and soviets—soldiers' and workers' councils—that he felt might form the basis of a stateless society.

With the Bolshevik seizure of power in October 1917, however, his enthusiasm turned to bitter disappointment. "This buries the revolution," he remarked to a friend. The Bolsheviks, he said, have shown how the revolution was *not* to be made—that is, by authoritarian rather than libertarian methods. Kropotkin's last years were devoted to a history of ethics, which he was never to finish. He died at the village of Dmitrov near Moscow in 1921. His funeral, attended by tens of thousands of admirers, was the last occasion in the Soviet era when the black flag of anarchism was paraded through the Russian capital.

Kropotkin's life exemplified the high ethical standard and the combination of thought and action that he preached throughout his writings. He displayed none of the egotism, duplicity, or lust for power that marred the image of so many other revolutionaries. Because of this he was admired not only by his own comrades but by many for whom the label of anarchist meant little more than the dagger and the bomb. The French writer Romain Rolland said that Kropotkin lived what Leo Tolstoy only advocated, and Oscar Wilde called him one of the two really happy men he had known. (P.A.)

BIBLIOGRAPHY. George Woodcock and Ivan Avakumović, *The Anarchist Prince* (1950, reissued as *Peter Kropotkin,* 1990); Martin A. Miller, *Kropotkin* (1976); Caroline Cahm, *Kropotkin and the Rise of Revolutionary Anarchism, 1872–1886* (1989).

Krosno, former (1975–98) *województwo* (province), extreme southeastern Poland, now part of Podkarpackie and Małopolskie (*qq.v.*) provinces.

Krosno, city, Podkarpackie *województwo,* (province), extreme southeastern Poland. Set on the sloping plains of the Lower Beskid mountain range amid forests of beech and white fir, the city dates from the 14th century and is one of the oldest in the area. Krosno is the centre of Poland's mineral-oil industry and has food-processing plants and factories for the production of glass, textiles, and electrical machinery. A 14th-century Gothic church (rebuilt in the 17th century), buildings with connecting arcades from the 15th and 16th centuries, the Burgomaster House (Kamienica Wójtowa) built in 1525, and a regional museum are points of interest. Pop. (2002) 48,372.

Kroto, Sir Harold W., in full SIR HAROLD WALTER KROTO (b. Oct. 7, 1939, Wisbech, Cambridgeshire, Eng.), English chemist who, with Richard E. Smalley and Robert F. Curl, Jr., was awarded the 1996 Nobel Prize for Chemistry for their joint discovery of the carbon compounds called fullerenes.

Kroto received a Ph.D. from the University of Sheffield in 1964. He joined the faculty of the University of Sussex in 1967 and became a professor of chemistry there in 1985. In the course of his research, Kroto used microwave spectroscopy to discover long, chainlike carbon molecules in the atmospheres of stars and gas clouds. In order to study the vaporization of carbon to find out how these carbon chains formed, he went to Rice University (Houston, Texas), where Smalley had designed the laser-supersonic cluster beam apparatus, which could vaporize almost any known material and then be used to study the resulting clusters of atoms or molecules.

In a series of experiments carried out in September 1985, the two men, along with Smalley's associate at Rice, Robert Curl, generated clusters of carbon atoms by vaporizing graphite in an atmosphere of helium. Some of the spectra they obtained from the vaporization corresponded to previously unknown forms of carbon containing even numbers of carbon atoms ranging from 40 to more than 100 atoms. Most of the new carbon molecules had a structure of C_{60}. The researchers recognized that this molecule's atoms are bonded together into a highly symmetrical, hollow structure that resembles a sphere or ball. C_{60} is a polygon with 60 vertices and 32 faces, 12 of which are pentagons and 20 hexagons—the same geometry as a football (soccer ball).

In the 1985 paper describing their work, the discoverers chose the whimsical name buckminsterfullerene for C_{60}, after the American architect R. Buckminster Fuller, whose geodesic dome designs have a structure similar to that of C_{60}. The discovery of the unique structure of fullerenes, or buckyballs, as this class of carbon compounds came to be known, opened up an entirely new branch of chemistry.

Kru, any of a group of peoples inhabiting southern Liberia and southwestern Côte d'Ivoire. The Kru languages constitute a branch of the Niger-Congo family.

The Kru are known as stevedores and fishermen throughout the west coast of Africa and have established colonies in most ports from Dakar, Senegal, to Douala, Cameroon. With related tribes—the Basa and Grebo on the coast and the Sikon, Sapo, and Padebu in the interior—they occupy nearly one-third of Liberia. The Kru are thought to have entered the country from the northeast in the 15th to 17th century. There are about 24 subtribes with dialectal and cultural differences. Their political organization was traditionally uncentralized, each subtribe inhabiting a number of autonomous towns. Within each town social organization is based on exogamous patrilineal clans. Clan heads and titled officials make up the council of the town chief. Kru economy is based on fishing and the production of rice and cassava. The coastlands are cut by a series of unbridged rivers that have restricted economic progress, so that there has been a continuing exodus of young people to Monrovia, Liberia. By the late 20th century there were probably more Kru outside tribal territory than within, with the largest single Kru community in Monrovia.

Kruczkowski, Leon (b. June 28, 1900, Kraków, Poland, Austria-Hungary—d. Aug. 1, 1962, Warsaw, Pol.), Polish novelist and playwright.

Politically a socialist, Kruczkowski became famous upon the publication of his first novel, *Kordian i cham* (1932; "Kordian and the Churl"), which—as the author himself put it—was "an attempt to show the peasant question in Poland from the broad perspectives of historical development." Using the Marxist view of the historical process, he saw the causes of the November 1830 Polish insurrection in the light of class struggle. He continued his social and historical analysis in the novels *Pawie pióra* (1935; "Peacock's Feathers") and *Sidła* (1937; "The Trap").

Captured as a soldier in 1939, Kruczkowski spent World War II in a prison camp. After the war he joined the Polish Communist Party and was a prominent activist in state and party affairs. His finest play, *Niemcy* (1949; "The Germans"), analyzed the process of the rapid spread of Nazi ideology among the German people. In his last play, *Śmierć gubernatora* (1961; "Death of a Governor"), Kruczkowski examined the ethics of the capitalist world, to which he opposed the humanitarian principles of the socialist camp.

Krüdener, Barbara Juliane, Freifrau (Baroness) **von,** *née* VON VIETINGHOFF (b. Nov. 22, 1764, Riga, Livonia (now in Latvia)—d. Dec. 25, 1824, Karasubazar, Crimea, Russian Empire), mystic visionary who renounced a life of pleasure amid the

Russian nobility and won as a convert Tsar Alexander I, through whom she influenced the making of the Holy Alliance of 1815.

She was married to a Russian diplomat in 1782, but her life of amorous pleasure-seeking involved an affair that culminated in separation from her husband. After his death in 1802, she wrote the largely autobiographical novel *Valérie,* published anonymously in Paris in 1804. The same year she underwent a religious conversion at Riga; subsequently, she maintained a nervous and pietistic mysticism, at the same time manifesting unwavering tendencies toward romantic intimacies. Coming under the influence of apocalyptic visionaries, she held Bible classes and confessions in southwestern Germany and in Switzerland from 1808 to 1818. Despite her numerous and often wealthy admirers and protégés, however, her activities usually ended in banishment.

Among her successful efforts was her conversion of Alexander I, whom she met in 1815. Despondent since the military campaign of 1812 against France, he was revitalized through the mystical teachings of the Freifrau. She also claimed as her own achievement the Holy Alliance of Russia, Austria, and Prussia. For several months the tsar attended her Bible classes, but his revulsion at the character of some of her associates led to his withdrawal. In 1821 he expelled her from St. Petersburg because she had envisioned him as a new conqueror of Greece and had sought his support for the War of Greek Independence, a prospect Alexander did not welcome.

Krueger, Walter (b. Jan. 26, 1881, Flatow, West Prussia [now Złotów, Pol.]—d. Aug. 20, 1967, Valley Forge, Pa., U.S.), U.S. Army officer whose 6th Army helped free Japanese-held islands in the Pacific Ocean during World War II. He was regarded as one of the foremost strategists and tacticians in the U.S. armed forces.

Brought to the United States as a child in 1889, Krueger volunteered as an enlisted man during the Spanish-American War (1898) and was soon promoted to second lieutenant of infantry in the regular army (1901). In World War I he served in Europe as chief of the tank corps, American Expeditionary Force; he then attended several service schools and served with the War Department general staff. As U.S. participation in World War II evolved, he was placed in charge of the Southern Defense Command (May 1941–January 1943).

Early in 1943 General Krueger was given command of the newly activated U.S. 6th Army in Australia and New Guinea. In December his forces invaded New Britain and in April 1944 occupied Hollandia, capital of Dutch New Guinea. By land-hopping and leapfrog techniques that proved so suitable for island reconquest, Krueger's advance over six months measured more than 2,000 miles (3,200 km) to the Philippine Islands; he then led his troops in that campaign successfully, followed by the occupation of Japan (1945).

Krueger retired with the rank of general in July 1946. His memoirs, *From Down Under to Nippon,* appeared in 1953.

Kruger, Barbara (b. Jan. 26, 1945, Newark, N.J., U.S.), American artist who challenged cultural assumptions by manipulating images and text in her photographic compositions.

Kruger attended Syracuse University and continued her training in 1966 at New York City's Parsons School of Design. For a time she pursued a career as a graphic designer, eventually becoming chief designer at *Mademoiselle* magazine in New York. In the 1960s and '70s she also explored an interest in poetry.

By the late 1970s Kruger had developed her trademark style: large-scale photographic works that appropriate anonymous cultural images and text and juxtapose them in unexpected ways. In an untitled 1989 work, for example, she employed an oversized image of a model's face and divided it into sections.

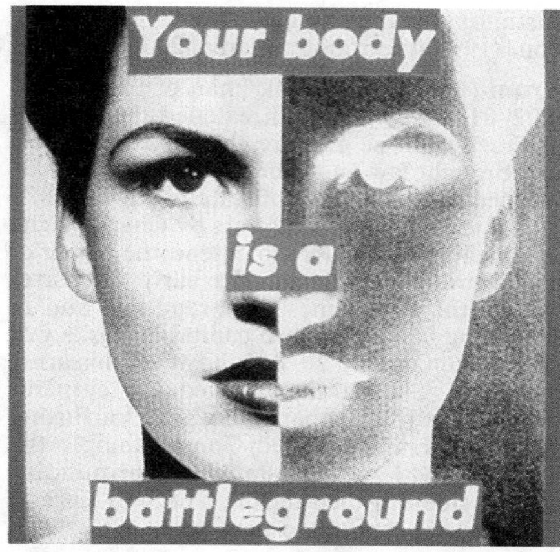

"Untitled" ("Your body is a battleground"), photographic silkscreen on vinyl by Barbara Kruger, 1989; in the Broad Art Foundation, Santa Monica, Calif.
Courtesy Mary Boone Gallery, New York, N.Y.

Placed across the image is the phrase "Your body is a battleground," by which she called into question the objectification of women and also raised the issue of women's reproductive rights. Such work embodied the deconstructivist concerns of much feminist art from the 1980s and '90s. By manipulating and recontextualizing imagery, Kruger sought to question the way accepted sources of power, in this case the mass media, present female identity. Her grounding in the theoretical connects her with contemporary developments in conceptual art.

Kruger, Paul, original name STEPHANUS JOHANNES PAULUS KRUGER, byname OOM ("Uncle") PAUL (b. Oct. 10, 1825, Cradock district, Cape Colony—d. July 14, 1904, Clarens, Switz.), farmer, soldier, and statesman, noted in South African history as the builder of the Afrikaner nation. He was president of the Transvaal, or South African Republic, from 1883 until his flight to Europe in 1900, after the outbreak of the South African (Boer) War.

Youth and early career. Kruger's parents were respectable farmers of Dutch descent on the northern outskirts of the British Cape Colony. He had little formal education but was able to express himself clearly in writing. Of more importance was the religious instruction he received from his parents according to the strict tenets of Dutch Calvinism. When he was 10, his family took part in the general emigration of frontier farmers who sought to found an independent political existence in the northern interior.

While still in his teens, Kruger played a part in public life as a local field-cornet, a post in which civil and military duties were combined. In January 1852 he was present when the Transvaal leader, Andries Pretorius, concluded the Sand River Convention with representatives of Great Britain, by which the independence of the Afrikaners (Boers) north of the Vaal River was recognized. He took part in 1855–56 as member of a commission that drew up the constitution of the new republic. During the civil disturbances of 1861–64, he played a prominent part as commandant general in unifying and pacifying the country in support of constitutional authority.

Leader of the Boers. Upon the British annexation of the Transvaal in 1877, Kruger became the recognized champion of his people in the struggle to regain independence. To that end, he visited England in 1877 and 1878, and, when he failed to persuade the government of Benjamin Disraeli to undo the annexation, he helped organize a movement of passive resistance to British administration in the Transvaal. Disappointed when the new Liberal government led by William Gladstone failed to live up to his expectations, Kruger succeeded in gaining the sympathy and political support of the Cape Colony against the British attempt to force South Africa, including the Transvaal, into a general federation. In December he led his people into active opposition, and, after a series of military victories that culminated in the Battle of Majuba Hill (Feb. 27, 1881), with great diplomatic skill he succeeded in negotiating peace based on a limited independence. In 1883 he was elected president of the restored republic.

Meanwhile, in 1883 Kruger again visited England and, after protracted negotiations, concluded a new convention in London on Feb. 27, 1884, which rectified the western border and removed any reference to British suzerainty over the Transvaal. On his return he found his republic embroiled with the Cape colonial authorities over control of the area along the western border, which was considered by Cecil Rhodes, the Cape statesman, to be the "Suez Canal" to the territory north of the Limpopo River. In 1885 Kruger was forced to accede to British demands to withdraw from the area in question and to agree to a British protectorate over Bechuanaland.

Gold rush in the Transvaal. Kruger's greatest problem began in 1886 with the discovery of gold in the Witwatersrand area, where a new metropolis, Johannesburg, arose, some 40 miles (64 km) south of the tiny republican capital, Pretoria. Large numbers of "outlanders" flocked to the Transvaal and established a cosmopolitan, mainly English community in the midst of a rural Boer society. Kruger saw this as a threat to the separate national identity of his people, "God's people," as he called them, and in 1890 he restricted the franchise to men resident at least 14 years. At the same time, he called into being a separate Volksraad (legislative body), in order to represent mining interests, but the mining magnates of Johannesburg criticized Kruger's economic and railway policy, which resulted in raising the cost of production of gold, and they complained of high railway tariffs.

Rhodes, the Cape premier, who had extensive gold interests and much political influence, hoped to achieve a united British South Africa. He supported the Rand capitalists and the outlander movement against Kruger's regime. When he failed to persuade Kruger to join a South African customs union, he decided to bring matters to a head. By 1895 Kruger was aware that trouble was brewing in Johannesburg and that, behind the scenes of the internal conflict within the Transvaal, a larger issue was at stake, that of British supremacy as against republican independence.

The South African (Boer) War. Ever since 1890 he also had had to contend with growing opposition from some of his own people; but when Rhodes, with the full knowledge of Joseph Chamberlain, the British colonial secretary, sponsored the ill-fated Jameson Raid against the republic at the end of 1895, Kruger handled the affair so successfully that his prestige soared again. In the presidential election in May 1898, he received almost unanimous support. While Rhodes was forced into the background, British imperial interests now came to the front. The colonial secretary took up the cudgels on behalf of the outlanders and, in 1897, sent Sir Alfred Milner to South Africa as governor of the Cape Colony and high commissioner, who began to force the issue and demanded that the residential qualification for voters in the Transvaal should be lowered to five years. In May 1899 a conference took place between Kruger and Milner. Although no agreement was reached, Kruger decided on a seven-year residential qualification. Milner refused the offer, tension increased, and Britain prepared an ultimatum. Both sides prepared for war, which was precipitated by Kruger when, on Oct. 9, 1899, he presented his own ultimatum, demanding the withdrawal of British troops from the border.

War broke out two days later, and, notwithstanding initial Boer successes, British invading armies occupied the two Boer capitals. Kruger was forced to retreat with the last Boer army along the Delagoa Bay railway. Being too old to keep up with the ensuing guerrilla struggle, he was delegated to Europe, where he lived in Holland to the end of the war in May 1902. He died in Switzerland in July 1904, and his body found a temporary resting place at The Hague. He was finally buried at Pretoria on Dec. 16, 1904. (D.W.K.)

BIBLIOGRAPHY. C.T. Gordon, *The Growth of Boer Opposition to Kruger, 1890–95* (1970), is based on original research, stressing important aspects of Kruger's policy. Johannes Stephanus Marais, *The Fall of Kruger's Republic* (1961), deals with British policy vis-à-vis Kruger and his republic up to the eve of the South African War, 1899–1902.

Kruger National Park, formerly the largest national park in South Africa. It was located in Northern and Mpumalanga provinces, west of the Lebombo Mountains on the Mozambique border. Established in part in 1898, the park in 1926 was named for Paul Kruger, former president of the South African Republic (the Transvaal). Headquartered at Skukuza, the park, with an area of 7,523 square miles (19,485 square km), was about 200 miles (320 km) long and 25 to 50 miles (40 to 80 km) wide. In 2002 Kruger National Park was combined with Mozambique's Limpopo Park and Zimbabwe's Gonarezhou National Park to form the Great Limpopo Transfrontier Park, the largest game park in Africa. The new park opened to visitors in early 2003.

The area has a generally flat terrain with low ranges of hills traversed by nearly 5,000 miles (8,000 km) of paved and gravel roads. Vegetation varies from open veld to dense bush that includes mopane, acacia, and baobab trees. Wildlife includes elephants, lions, leopards, cheetahs, buffalo, rhinoceroses, zebras, wildebeests, impalas, and numerous birds. Although six perennial rivers cross the park, droughts often make artificial watering necessary.

Kruger telegram (Jan. 3, 1896), a message sent by Emperor William II of Germany to President Paul Kruger of the South African Republic (the Transvaal), congratulating him on repelling the Jameson Raid, an attack on the Transvaal from the British-controlled Cape Colony. The telegram was interpreted in the Transvaal as a sign of possible German support in the future. William's intention was to demonstrate to the British that they were diplomatically isolated and should become friendly with Germany. Instead, it aroused the first wave of popular hostility against Germany in Britain in the pre-World War I period.

Krugersdorp, town, Gauteng province, South Africa. It lies on the Witwatersrand (ridge), at an elevation of 5,709 feet (1,740 m), northwest of Johannesburg. A mining and industrial centre, it was founded after the discovery of gold in 1887 and named for Paul Kruger, then president of the South African Republic (the Transvaal). Gold continues to be mined locally even though payable ore deposits have declined significantly. The world's first plant built to obtain uranium as a byproduct of gold recovery opened there in 1952 but ceased operations by the mid-1980s. Deposits of manganese, asbestos, and limestone are also worked. The Paardekraal Monument in Krugersdorp marks the site of the proclamation for an independent Transvaal pledged on Dec. 16, 1880. Nearby are paleontological sites (including Sterkfontein) that have yielded australopithecine and other hominid remains. Pop. (1996) metropolitan area, 203,168.

Krum (d. April 13, 814), khan of the Bulgars (802–814) who briefly threatened the security of the Byzantine Empire. His able, energetic rule brought law and order to Bulgaria and developed the rudiments of state organization.

With the defeat of the Avars by Charlemagne in 805, Krum was able to extend the power of the Pannonian Bulgars. His early offensives against the Byzantines were repulsed, and in the spring of 811 his own capital at Pliska was destroyed. On July 26, 811, however, his army crushed the Byzantines, killed the emperor Nicephorus I, and opened the way for further victories. Krum besieged Constantinople (Istanbul) in 813 and devastated the surrounding countryside but died during a second siege of the imperial capital the next year.

Krumbacher, Karl (b. Sept. 23, 1856, Kempten, Bavaria [Germany]—d. Dec. 12, 1909, Munich, Ger.), German scholar who developed the modern study of Byzantine culture. His writings and seminars were the basis for the specialized training of Byzantine scholars from all parts of the world.

Educated in the classics at the universities of Leipzig and Munich, Krumbacher turned to medieval Greek literature. His *Geschichte der byzantinischen Literatur* (1891; "History of Byzantine Literature") went through several revisions. In 1892 he founded the periodical *Byzantinische Zeitschrift* ("Byzantine Journal"), which became the central international organ for Byzantine studies.

In 1897 Krumbacher was appointed to the newly created professorial chair in medieval and modern Greek studies at the University of Munich. His other works include "Die griechischen Literatur des Mittelalters" (1905; "Greek Literature of the Middle Ages," a part of P. Hinneberg's *Die Kultur der Gegenwart* ["The Culture of the Present"]) and *Das Problem der neugriechischen Schriftsprache* (1902; "The Problem of the Modern Greek Literary Language").

Krupa, Gene (b. Jan. 15, 1909, Chicago, Ill., U.S.—d. Oct. 16, 1973, Yonkers, N.Y.), American jazz drummer who won widespread fame during the swing era.

Krupa was a respected professional drummer with the early Chicago jazz bands long before he studied drums academically. After working with such pioneers as Eddie Condon and Red Nichols, he joined the Benny Goodman orchestra in 1935, and by brilliant playing—represented by the recording "Sing Sing Sing"—he became internationally known. From 1938 to 1951 he led a successful band of his own and remained active as a touring soloist, retaining his technically accomplished style and gift for showmanship. He conducted serious studies of the percussion music of African and other cultures. Krupa appeared in numerous films, and he recorded the sound track for his highly fictionalized motion-picture biography, *The Gene Krupa Story* (1959).

Krupp, Alfred, byname THE CANNON KING, German DER KANONENKÖNIG (b. April 26, 1812, Essen, grand duchy of Berg [now in Germany]—d. July 14, 1887, Essen, Ger.), German industrialist noted for his development and worldwide sale of cast-steel cannon and other armaments. Under his direction the Krupp Works began the manufacture of ordnance (*c.* 1847).

His father, Friedrich Krupp, who had founded the dynasty's firm in 1811, died in 1826, leaving to his son the secret of making high-quality cast steel, together with a small workshop in which production had come almost to a standstill. Taking full charge of the firm at age 14, Alfred soon extended production to include the manufacture of steel rolls. He designed and developed new machines, invented the spoon roll for making spoons and forks, and manufactured rolling mills for use in government mints. He won new customers, extended his firm's purchases of raw materials, and secured funds to finance the expansion of his works. At the first world exhibition, the Great Exhibition, in London in 1851, he exhibited the largest steel ingot ever cast up to that time (4,300 pounds).

Alfred Krupp, portrait by Julius Grün, *c.* 1880
Archiv fur Kunst und Geschichte, Berlin

It was with the advent of railways that the rise of the firm really began. At first, railway axles and springs of cast steel were the only products made in this field, but in 1852 Krupp manufactured the first seamless steel railway tire. Later he adopted three superimposed railway tires, the "three rings," as the trademark of the firm. He was also the first to introduce the Bessemer and open-hearth steelmaking processes to Europe (1862 and 1869).

To prove the quality of his steel, Krupp turned to making cannons. Initially he could not sell his guns in Prussia, and the first orders came from Egypt (1856), Belgium (1861), and Russia (1863). As a result, however, of the performance of Krupp guns in the Franco-German War of 1870–71, the firm came to be called "the arsenal of the Reich." Krupp was in many ways the founder of modern warfare. At the time of his death he had armed 46 nations.

Recognizing early the human problems of industrialization, Krupp created a comprehensive welfare scheme for his workers. As early as 1836 he instituted a sickness and burial fund, and in 1855 he established a pension fund for retired and incapacitated workers. In 1861 he began to build housing settlements, hospitals, schools, and churches for his employees. His workers became fanatically loyal to him. He had started his steel plant with seven workers; at his death the enterprise was employing 21,000 persons.

Krupp AG, in full FRIED. KRUPP AG HOESCH-KRUPP, former German corporation that was one of the world's principal steelmakers and arms manufacturers until the end of World War II. An important manufacturer of building materials and industrial machinery, it became a limited-liability company in 1968 when its assets were transferred from the private ownership of the Krupp family to the Alfred Krupp von Bohlen und Halbach Foundation (*Stiftung*). In 1999 the corporation formally merged with Thyssen to form ThyssenKrupp AG.

The history of the Krupp industrial empire is essentially the history of the Krupp family. In 1811 Friedrich Krupp founded in Essen a plant to produce English cast steel and related products, called Gussstahlfabrik (cast-steel factory); and, in the course of the 19th century under his son, Alfred Krupp (*q.v.*), the company gained a worldwide reputation. It was the first to introduce the Bessemer and open-hearth steelmaking processes on the European continent. Alfred was best known, however, as the "Cannon King," producing in 1851 a cast-steel cannon that was the sensation of London's Great Exhibition, and, in the course of his career, he manufactured field guns and other armaments for nations around the world.

Under the direction of his son Friedrich Alfred Krupp (1854–1902), the business experienced enormous expansion resulting from the rise of the German navy and the demand for armour plates. Krupp acquired the Germania shipbuilding yards at Kiel in 1902. By that time the firm employed more than 40,000 people. Friedrich Alfred was succeeded by his elder daughter, Bertha Krupp (1886–1957); in 1906 she married Gustav von Bohlen und Halbach, and he was authorized by the emperor William II to add the name Krupp to his own (*see* Krupp von Bohlen und Halbach, Gustav). Meanwhile (in 1903), the family concerns were incorporated under the umbrella name Fried. Krupp Grusonwerk AG.

During World War I the firm secured special international significance by the manufacture of heavy guns such as the 42-cm howitzer "Big Bertha" and the long-range gun that in the spring of 1918 bombarded Paris at a distance of about 75 miles (120 km). After the war, the manufacture of arms was forbidden; parts of the works had to be dismantled, and the labour force reduced.

Adolf Hitler's policy of military conquest switched the Krupp combine back to armament products. During World War II the elderly Gustav was succeeded by his son Alfried, who, by the Lex Krupp (Krupp Law) of 1943, assumed the name Krupp and became the sole owner of his mother's vast holdings. Even before 1939, the extent of these holdings had become staggering. Within Germany, the Krupp concern had wholly owned 87 industrial complexes, held a controlling interest in 110 firms, and possessed substantial investments in 142 other German corporations. Abroad, Krupp works existed in almost every continental country; the family owned more than 50 percent of the stock in 41 foreign plants and large blocks of shares in another 25. There had been thousands of Krupp ore pits and coal mines, a chain of Krupp hotels, a group of Krupp banks, a Krupp cement works, and a score of private estates.

After the war, Alfried Krupp was convicted of war crimes at Nürnberg, specifically for employment of slave labour; but the company had also been guilty of plundering property and plants in all the occupied countries. Under the terms of an Allied decree of March 4, 1953, Krupp was ordered to sell about 75 percent of the value of the concern. There were ultimately no buyers, however, and by the early 1960s, Alfried had restored the prosperity of the firm, its value exceeding $1,000,000,000.

Krupp stock had never been traded on the stock exchanges until credit problems emerged in 1966–67. At the same time, Alfried's only son, Arndt, decided that he did not wish to take over the family business. In exchange for renouncing his succession rights, Arndt was granted $500,000 a year until his death (on May 12, 1986). On July 31, 1967, Alfried was found dead in Essen, and in the following January the firm became a corporation wholly owned by a foundation called Alfried Krupp von Bohlen und Halbach-Stiftung.

Krupp von Bohlen und Halbach, Alfried, original name (until 1943) ALFRIED VON BOHLEN UND HALBACH (b. Aug. 13, 1907, Essen, Ger.—d. July 30, 1967, Essen, W.Ger.), German industrialist, last member of the Krupp dynasty of munitions manufacturers.

Alfried Krupp was the son of Bertha Krupp, the heiress of the Krupp industrial empire, and Gustav Krupp von Bohlen und Halbach. Shortly after the outbreak of World War II it became evident that his father was drifting into senility. Alfried assumed his duties, and in 1943 Adolf Hitler issued an unprecedented decree, the Lex Krupp ("Krupp Law"), which, abolishing in this one case the laws of inheritance, preserved the firm as a family property. Alfried now assumed the name of Krupp and became the sole owner of his mother's vast holdings.

Alfried augmented this empire by seizing property in every country conquered by Germany. Already, in 1943, his salesmen were exporting finished machine products from his new Ukrainian plants and selling them in Bulgaria, Turkey, and Romania. When financier Robert Rothschild refused to sign over his French holdings to Alfried, Rothschild was shipped to the Auschwitz concentration camp and gassed. It was incidents of this kind, together with his exploitation of slave labour, that put Alfried in the prisoners' dock at the Nürnberg war-crimes trials after the war.

At first the victorious Allies, under the impression that Gustav had been in charge throughout the war, had indicted him. In fact, it was Alfried who had been the head of the family and the firm during the years when the inmates of 138 concentration camps worked for Krupp; Alfried who had built a fuse factory inside Auschwitz to take full advantage of prison labour; and Alfried who had Jewish prisoners at Auschwitz build a howitzer factory in Silesia.

The Nürnberg tribunal sentenced Alfried to 12 years in prison and ordered "forfeiture of all [his] property both real and personal." Seven months after the outbreak of the Korean War (1950–53), however, John J. McCloy, U.S. high commissioner in American-occupied Germany, granted Alfried amnesty and restored all his holdings. Operating with tremendous skill and zeal, Alfried quickly restored the family firm to its former supremacy. By the early 1960s he was worth more than a billion dollars.

Alfried Krupp's only son, Arndt, renounced his succession rights and his Krupp name. Thus, when Alfried died in 1967, the company went public, and the Krupp industrial family came to an end.

Krupp von Bohlen und Halbach, Gustav, original name GUSTAV VON BOHLEN UND HALBACH (b. Aug. 7, 1870, The Hague, Neth.—d. Jan. 16, 1950, Blühnbach, near Salzburg, Austria), German diplomat who married the heiress of the Krupp family of industrialists, Bertha Krupp, and took over operation of the family firm. At the time of their wedding, the Krupp name was added to his own.

Bertha's father, Friedrich Krupp, committed suicide in scandal in 1902, having been exposed in the newspapers as a homosexual. Because it was deemed unthinkable for the Krupp armament empire to be run by a woman, the emperor William II personally sought an acceptable husband for the young Bertha (1886–1957), eventually choosing Gustav von Bohlen und Halbach, a Prussian diplomat. They were married on Oct. 15, 1906, and Gustav was authorized by the emperor to add the name Krupp to his own.

In World War I, Gustav Krupp made many contributions to Germany's arsenal. One was the 98-ton howitzer that shelled Liège and Verdun. Others included the great cannon that bombarded Paris from a range of about 75 miles (120 km) and Germany's submarines, which were built at the family's Kiel shipyards. Because Germany was defeated, the war was, on the whole, bad business for Krupp but not a total loss. Before the war, in 1902, Vickers, Ltd., a British manufacturer of artillery shells, had leased a Krupp fuse patent. After the war, Vickers paid off in a settlement based on German artillery casualties, which placed Krupp in the awkward position of having profited from Germany's war dead.

With this money, and with subsidies from the government of the Weimar Republic, Gustav began the secret rearming of Germany within a year of the Armistice. In his words, he was determined that Krupp should be ready "again to work for the German armed forces at the appointed hour without loss of time or experience." Submarine pens were furtively built in Holland; new cannon were covertly perfected in Sweden. Krupp helped finance the Nazi "terror election" of 1933, tightening Adolf Hitler's grip on the reins of government, and, as president of the Reichsverband der Deutschen Industrie—Germany's equivalent of the U.S. Chamber of Commerce—expelled all Jewish industrialists and became one of the country's most ardent Nazis.

Growing senile, Gustav was succeeded by his son Alfried in 1943. After the war the Allies proposed to indict Gustav as a war criminal for his part in Germany's armament, but in view of his ill health he was never brought to trial.

Krupskaya, Nadezhda Konstantinovna (b. Feb. 14 [Feb. 26, New Style], 1869, St. Petersburg, Russia—d. Feb. 27, 1939, Moscow, Russia, U.S.S.R.), revolutionary who became the wife of Vladimir I. Lenin, played a central role in the Bolshevik (later Communist) Party, and was a prominent member of the Soviet educational bureaucracy.

A Marxist activist in St. Petersburg in the early 1890s, Krupskaya met Lenin about 1894. She was arrested in August 1896, and, when sentenced in 1898 to three years of exile, she obtained permission to spend her term with Lenin, who was then in exile in Shushenskoye, Siberia. On July 10 (July 22, New Style), 1898, Krupskaya and Lenin were married.

In 1901, after serving her term, Krupskaya joined Lenin (who had finished his sentence in 1900) in Munich. She subsequently settled with him in several European cities, returning briefly to Russia in 1905. Despite her ill health she served as Lenin's personal secretary as well as editorial secretary for his party newspapers and journals. She supported him in his factional feuds within the Russian Social-Democratic Workers' Party, helped found the Bolsheviks, and assumed a large degree of responsibility for organizing its members inside Russia.

Returning to Russia after the February Revolution of 1917, Krupskaya spread Bolshevik propaganda, carried messages from Lenin to his colleagues while he was hiding in Finland (July–October), and, after the Bolsheviks seized power (October 1917), became a member of the collegium of the People's Commissariat of Education.

After Lenin's death (1924), Krupskaya joined Joseph Stalin's opponents but later dissociated herself from the opposition and remained formally aloof from the intraparty struggles. She continued to serve the party, although her influence was never restored, and her memoirs, *Vospominaniya o Lenine* (1957; "Recollections of Lenin"), were criticized for erroneously depicting Lenin; her publications on education, *Pedagogicheskive sochineniya,* 11 vol. (1957–63; "Pedagogical Works"), were also condemned for conveying mistaken concepts of education and political training.

Krusenstern, Adam Johann (b. Nov. 19, 1770, Hagudi, [now Rapla], Estonia—d. Aug. 24, 1846, Revel [now Tallinn]), naval officer who commanded the first Russian expedition to explore the Pacific Ocean and circumnavigate the Earth (1803–06). Transporting a diplomatic mission bound for Japan and goods for delivery to the Kamchatka Peninsula of eastern Siberia, Krusenstern left Russia, rounded Cape Horn, and, crossing the Pacific, visited the Marquesas Islands. After stopping at Kamchatka, he visited Sakhalin, where he encountered the Mongols, but not

Krusenstern, detail of a portrait by an unknown artist
Novosti Press Agency

the native Ainu people. After a stop at Canton, Krusenstern made his way through Sunda Strait, circled the Cape of Good Hope, and returned to Russia. His writings include *Voyage Round the World . . .*, 2 vol. (1813).

Krušné hory (Europe): *see* Erzgebirge.

Krutch, Joseph Wood (b. Nov. 25, 1893, Knoxville, Tenn., U.S.—d. May 22, 1970, Tucson, Ariz.), American naturalist, conservationist, writer, and critic.

Krutch attended the University of Tennessee (B.A., 1915) and Columbia University, N.Y. (M.A., 1916; Ph.D., 1923). He served in the army (1918) and spent a year (1919–20) in Europe with his fellow student Mark Van Doren. Upon his return to the United States, he taught at Brooklyn Polytechnic and began to contribute book reviews and essays to periodicals. From 1924 through 1952, during which time he was drama critic for *The Nation,* he taught and lectured at various schools in the area and wrote a number of books, including *The Modern Temper* (1929). In the 1940s he wrote two critical biographies, *Samuel Johnson* (1944) and *Henry David Thoreau* (1948), which reflected his growing interest in common-sense philosophy and natural history. In 1952 Krutch moved to Arizona and wrote several nature books in addition to the essays he continued to publish. His later work included *The Measure of Man* (1954), *The Great Chain of Life* (1956), and his autobiography, *More Lives Than One* (1962).

Krylov, Ivan Andreyevich (b. Feb. 2 [Feb. 13, New Style], 1768/69, Moscow, Russia—d. Nov. 9 [Nov. 21], 1844, St. Petersburg), Russian writer of innocent-sounding fables that satirized contemporary social types in the guise of beasts. His command of colloquial idiom brought a note of realism to Russian classical literature. Many of his aphorisms have become part of everyday Russian speech.

Born to an impoverished family, Krylov had little formal education and began to work as a clerk at the age of nine. While still in his teens he wrote operas, comedies, and tragedies. After 1789 he enjoyed some success as a satirical journalist until government censorship intervened. In 1805 he began translating the fables of Jean de La Fontaine but found that his true medium was writing fables of his own. The publication of his first book of fables in 1809 gained him the patronage of the imperial family and virtually an official sinecure—a post in the St. Petersburg public library—which Krylov maintained for 30 years. He produced eight additional books of fables, all written in verse, and received many honours.

Although some of his themes were borrowed from Aesop and La Fontaine, they altered in Krylov's hands. His foxes and crows, wolves and sheep, whether wise or foolish, were always recognizable Russian types. His salty, down-to-earth parables emphasized common sense, hard work, and love of justice and made him one of the first Russian writers to reach a broad audience.

krypton (Kr), chemical element, rare gas of Group 0 (noble gases) of the periodic table, forming very few chemical compounds. About three times heavier than air, krypton gas is colourless, odourless, and tasteless. Although traces are present in meteorites and minerals, krypton is more plentiful in the Earth's atmosphere, which contains 1 part krypton in about 900,000. The element was discovered (1898) by the British chemists Sir William Ramsay and Morris W. Travers in the residue left after a sample of liquid air had boiled almost entirely away. Krypton is produced on a small commercial scale by fractional distillation of liquid air.

Krypton is used in certain fluorescent lamps and in a flash lamp employed in high-speed photography. Radioactive krypton-85 is useful for detecting leaks in sealed containers, with the escaping atoms detected by means of their radiation.

Krypton gas liquefies at −152.30° C (−242° F) and freezes 4° C lower. When a current of electricity is passed through a glass tube containing krypton at low pressure, a bluish white light is emitted. The wavelength of an orange-red component of light emitted by stable krypton-86, because of its extreme sharpness, served as the international standard for the metre from 1960 to 1983. (One metre equals 1,650,763.73 times the wavelength of this line.)

Krypton was considered for many years to be totally unreactive. In the early 1960s, however, krypton was found to react with the element fluorine when both are combined in an electrical-discharge tube; the compound formed is krypton difluoride, KrF_2. Few other krypton compounds have been reported. Clathrate "compounds," in which the element is trapped in cagelike structures of water or other molecules, are known. Molecules of krypton consist of single atoms.

Natural krypton is a mixture of six stable isotopes: krypton-84 (57 percent); krypton-86 (17.3 percent); krypton-82 (11.6 percent); krypton-83 (11.5 percent); krypton-80 (2.25 percent); and krypton-78 (0.35 percent). About 20 radioactive isotopes, produced by fission of uranium and by other nuclear reactions, also are known. Krypton-85 has a half-life of 10.73 years.

atomic number	36
atomic weight	83.80
melting point	−156.6° C (−249.9° F)
boiling point	−152.3° C (−242.1° F)
density (1 atm, 0° C)	3.733 g/litre
valence	0, 2
electronic configuration	2-8-18-8 or $(Ar)3d^{10}4s^24p^6$

Kryvyy Rih, Russian KRIVOY ROG, also spelled KRIVOI ROG, or KRIVOJ ROG, city, Dnipropetrovsk *oblast* (province), Ukraine, situated at the confluence of the Inhulets and Saksahan rivers. Founded as a village by Zaporozhian Cossacks in the 17th century, it had only 2,184 inhabitants in 1781. In 1881 a French company began to work the local iron-ore deposits, and a railway was constructed to the Donets Basin coalfield in 1884. After that date Kryvyy Rih became a significant iron-mining city.

Kryvyy Rih, with its suburbs, stretches for more than 18 miles (29 km) in a long, narrow belt along the iron-ore deposits. The local high-grade hematite ores are for the most part worked out except at great depth, but there are vast reserves that have a lower iron content. In and around the city are several ore-enriching and pelletizing plants to support the still-expanding ironworks and steelworks. Terny, which was annexed to Kryvyy Rih in 1969, has a major uranium mine. Other industry includes coking and machine building (especially for the mining industry); the production of diamond drills, cement, and foodstuffs; and timberworking. A canal brings additional water supplies from the Kakhovske Reservoir, on the Dnieper River. Kryvyy Rih has institutes for teacher training and for study in mining. Pop. (1993 est.) 737,000.

Ksar el-Boukhari, also called BOGHARI, town, north-central Algeria. Lying along the Wadi Chelif at the junction of the High Plateau and the Atlas Mountains, the town is almost totally surrounded by wooded mountain ridges. The old walled quarter (*ksar*) is on a hill, overlooking the modern town. Ksar el-Boukhari is a commercial centre for pastoral peoples of the interior, who trade in wool, livestock, and cereals. It also supports a local carpet industry. Immediately northwest is the village and fort of Boghar (Balcon du Sud), a strategic command post. Pop. (1987 prelim.) 39,003.

Ksar el-Kebir, also spelled AL-QAṢR AL-KABĪR, Spanish ALCAZARQUIVIR, city, northern Morocco. It lies along the Loukkos, or Lucus, River.

Originally a Greek and Carthaginian colony, the site was occupied by the Romans, whose ruins remain, and by the Byzantines. The Arab town, which was founded in the 8th century, has one of the oldest mosques of western Morocco, built with inscribed stones from an earlier Christian church. Ksar el-Kebir, which translates as "The Great Fortress," was plagued by war (it was the site in 1578 of the Battle of the Three Kings) until it was destroyed during the 19th-century civil wars. It was rebuilt after the Spanish occupation of 1912 and was incorporated into the Kingdom of Morocco in 1956. Ksar el-Kebir is near the crossroads between Fès, Rabat, and Tangier and is the main market for the irrigated Loukkos River valley. Pop. (1982) 73,541.

Ksar es-Souk (Morocco): *see* Rachidia, Er-.

Kschessinska, Mathilde, Kschessinska also spelled KSHESSINSKA, Russian in full MATHILDA-MARIA FELIKSOVNA KSHESINSKAYA (b. Aug. 19 [Aug. 31, New Style], 1872, Ligovo, near Peterhof [now Petrodvorets], Russia—d. Dec. 7, 1971, Paris, France), *prima ballerina assoluta* of the Imperial Russian Ballet and the first Russian dancer to master 32 consecutive *fouettés en tournant* ("whipped turns" done in place and on one leg), a feat previously performed only by Italian dancers and considered in that era the supreme achievement in dance technique.

Kschessinska studied under Christian Johansson and Enrico Cecchetti at the Imperial Ballet School in St. Petersburg, graduated in 1890, and joined the Mariinsky Theatre. In 1895 she became *prima ballerina assoluta,* a title awarded by the Imperial Ballet to only one other dancer, the Italian Pierina Legnani. Kschessinska interpreted major roles in *Cinderella, La Sylphide, Esmeralda, The Nutcracker*, and *The Sleeping Beauty*. In 1911 she danced in London with Vaslav Nijinsky in *Swan Lake* for Sergey Diaghilev's Ballets Russes.

Kschessinska was a close friend of both Nicholas II, who was executed in 1918, and his cousin the grand duke André, whom she married in 1921. She left Russia in 1920 and, for 30 years, taught in Paris; her pupils included Tatiana Riabouchinska and Margot Fonteyn. Her autobiography is *Souvenirs de la Kschessinska* (1960; *Dancing in Petersburg: The Memoirs of Kschessinska*).

Kshatrapa (Indian dynasty): *see* Śaka satrap.

Kshatriya, also spelled KSHATTRIYA, or KSATRIYA, Sanskrit KṢATRIYA, second highest in ritual status of the four varnas, or social classes, of Hindu India, traditionally the military or ruling class.

The earliest Vedic literature listed the Kshatriya (holders of *kṣatra,* or authority) as first in rank, then the Brahmans (priests and teachers of law), next the Vaisya (merchant-traders), and finally the Sudra (artisans and labourers). Movements of individuals and groups from one class to another, both upward and downward, were not uncommon; a rise in status even to the rank of Kshatriya was a recognized reward for outstanding services to the rulers of the day. The legend that the Kshatriya were destroyed by Paraśurāma, the sixth reincarnation of Vishnu, as a punishment for their tyranny is thought by some scholars to reflect a long struggle for supremacy between priests and rulers that ended in victory for the former. By the end of the Vedic era, the Brahmans were supreme, and the Kshatriya had fallen to second place. In modern times, the Kshatriya varna is held to include a broad class of caste groups, differing considerably in status and headed by the aristocratic Rājput lineages. *See also* varna.

Kṣitigarbha (Sanskrit: "Womb of the Earth"), bodhisattva ("buddha-to-be") who, though known in India as early as the 4th century AD, became immensely popular in China as Ti-ts'ang and in Japan as Jizō. He is the saviour

Kṣitigarbha, 13th-century Japanese painting on silk; in the Museum of East Asian Art, State Museums, Berlin

By courtesy of the Museum fur Ostasiatische Kunst, Staatliche Museen, Preussischer Kulturbesitz, Berlin—Art Resource

of the oppressed, the dying, and the dreamer of evil dreams, for he has vowed not to stop his labours until he has saved the souls of all the dead condemned to hell. In China he is considered the overlord of hell and is invoked when someone is about to die. In Japan, as Jizō, he does not reign over hell (the job of Emma-ō) but is venerated for the mercy he shows the departed and in particular for his kindness to dead children. His widespread worship in Central Asia is attested to by his frequent appearances on temple banners from Chinese Turkistan.

Kṣitigarbha is most commonly represented as a monk with shaved head but with a nimbus and with the *ūrṇā* (tuft of hair) between his eyebrows. He is depicted carrying the clerical staff (*khakkara*) with which he forces open the gates of hell, together with the flaming pearl (*cintāmaṇi*) with which he lights up the darkness. Because Kṣitigarbha has the ability to manifest himself according to the needs of the suffering, he is frequently shown, especially in Japan, in six aspects, each relating to one of the six worlds of desires.

K.T., knight of the Thistle, member of a Scottish order of knighthood. *See* Thistle, The Most Ancient and Most Noble Order of the.

ku, Pinyin GU, type of Chinese bronze vessel produced during the Shang dynasty (18th–12th century BC). It is a tall wine beaker

Bronze *ku* from An-yang, Shang dynasty (18th–12th century BC); in the William Rockhill Nelson Gallery and Mary Atkins Museum of Fine Arts, Kansas City, Mo.

The Nelson-Atkins Museum of Art, Kansas City, Missouri

with a trumpet-shaped top, a restricted centre section, and a slightly flared base—the whole silhouette being unusually taut and graceful. Decoration, which appears on the three sections of the vessel, includes snakes; cicadas; the *t'ao-t'ieh* (*q.v.*), or monster mask; and the *k'uei,* or dragonlike monster with curled tail and gaping jaw.

K'u-ch'e (city, China): *see* Kucha.

Ku K'ai-chih, Pinyin GU KAIZHI (b. *c.* AD 344, Wu-hsi, Kiangsu Province, China—d. *c.* AD 406), one of the earliest many-faceted artists in China, who probably set new standards for figure painting. Ku K'ai-chih was a courtier who protected himself from the hazards of public life in a turbulent age by playing the part of a harmless eccentric; but he is most famous as a painter of portraits and figure subjects and as a poet.

Ku K'ai-chih's art is known today from both written records and paintings that are associated with him. He is recorded as having been among the first to paint a representation of Vimalakīrti, the Buddhist saint who became popular in China. Ku is also represented by two versions of a painting recorded as having been painted by him, the hand scroll known as the "Nymph of the Lo River," illustrating a Taoist poem. His essay "Hua Yün-t'ai Shan Chi" ("On Painting the Cloud Terrace Mountain"), is also Taoist in content. The famous hand scroll entitled "The Admonitions of the Court Instructress" (in the British Museum) bears a signature of Ku K'ai-chih, though it is not originally recorded as having been painted by him. Nonetheless, it accurately maintains a pre-T'ang dynasty (618–906) style. The scroll illustrates, through a series of individual scenes separated by the text of a didactic Confucian poem, proper behaviour for court ladies. The line is carefully controlled, and the composition and highly selected details both illustrate and expand effectively upon the nature of the text.

"Nymph of the Lo River," detail from a scroll, 12th century, after a 4th–5th century design attributed to Ku K'ai-chih; in the Smithsonian Institution, Freer Gallery of Art, Washington, D.C.

By courtesy of the Smithsonian Institution, Freer Gallery of Art, Washington, D.C.

Ku Klux Klan, either of two distinct secret terrorist organizations in the United States, one founded immediately after the Civil War and lasting until the 1870s, the other beginning in 1915 and continuing to the present.

The 19th-century Klan was originally organized as a social club by Confederate veterans in Pulaski, Tenn., in 1866. They apparently derived the name from the Greek word *kyklos,* from which comes the English "circle"; "Klan" was added for the sake of alliteration and Ku Klux Klan emerged. The organization quickly became a vehicle for Southern white underground resistance to Radical Reconstruction. Klan members sought the restoration of white supremacy through intimidation and violence aimed at the newly enfranchised black freedmen. A similar organization, the Knights of the White Camelia, began in Louisiana in 1867.

In the summer of 1867, the Klan was structured into the "Invisible Empire of the South" at a convention in Nashville, Tenn., attended by delegates from former Confederate states. The group was presided over by a grand wizard (Confederate cavalry general Nathan Bedford Forrest is believed to have been the first grand wizard) and a descending hierarchy of grand dragons, grand titans, and grand cyclopes. Dressed in robes and sheets designed to frighten superstitious blacks and to prevent identification by the occupying federal troops, Klansmen whipped and killed freedmen and their white supporters in nighttime raids.

The 19th-century Klan reached its peak between 1868 and 1870. A potent force, it was largely responsible for the restoration of white rule in North Carolina, Tennessee, and Georgia. But Forrest ordered it disbanded in 1869, largely as a result of the group's excessive violence. Local branches remained active for a time, however, prompting Congress to pass the Force Act in 1870 and the Ku Klux Act in 1871.

These bills authorized the president to suspend the writ of habeas corpus, suppress disturbances by force, and impose heavy penalties upon terrorist organizations. President Grant was lax in utilizing this authority, although he did send federal troops to some areas, suspend habeas corpus in nine South Carolina counties, and appoint commissioners who arrested hundreds of Southerners for conspiracy. In *United States* v. *Harris* in 1882, the Supreme Court declared the Ku Klux Act unconstitutional, but by that time the Klan had practically disappeared.

It disappeared because its original objective—the restoration of white supremacy throughout the South—had been largely achieved during the 1870s. The need for a secret antiblack organization diminished accordingly.

The 20th-century Klan had its roots more directly in the American nativist tradition. It was organized in 1915 near Atlanta, Ga., by Colonel William J. Simmons, a preacher and promoter of fraternal orders who had been inspired by Thomas Dixon's book *The Clansman* (1905) and D.W. Griffith's film *The Birth of a Nation* (1915). The new organization remained small until Edward Y. Clarke and Mrs. Elizabeth Tyler brought to it their talents as publicity agents and fund raisers. The revived Klan was fueled partly by patriotism and partly by a romantic nostalgia for the old South, but, more importantly, it expressed the defensive reaction of white Protestants in small-town America who felt threatened by the Bolshevik revolution in Russia and by the large-scale immigration of the previous decades that had changed the ethnic character of American society.

This second Klan peaked in the 1920s, when its membership exceeded 4,000,000 nationally, and profits rolled in from the sale of its memberships, regalia, costumes, publications, and rituals. A burning cross became the symbol of the new organization, and white-robed Klansmen participated in marches, parades, and nighttime cross burnings all over the country. To the old Klan's hostility toward blacks the new Klan—which was strong in the Midwest as well as in the South—added bias against Roman Catholics, Jews, foreigners, and organized labour. The Klan enjoyed a last spurt of growth in 1928, when Alfred E. Smith, a Catholic, received the Democratic presidential nomination.

During the Great Depression of the 1930s the Klan's membership dropped drastically, and the last remnants of the organization temporarily disbanded in 1944. For the next 20 years the Klan was quiescent, but it had a resurgence in some Southern states during the 1960s as civil-rights workers attempted to force Southern communities' compliance with the Civil Rights Act of 1964. There were numerous instances of bombings, whippings, and shootings in Southern communities, carried out in secret but apparently the work of Klansmen. President Lyndon B. Johnson publicly denounced the organization in a nationwide television address announcing the arrest of four Klansmen in connection with the slaying of a civil-rights worker, a white woman, in Alabama.

The Klan was unable to stem the growth of a new racial tolerance in the South in the years that followed. Though the organization continued some of its surreptitious activities into the late 20th century, cases of Klan violence became more isolated, and its membership had declined to a few thousand. The Klan became a chronically fragmented mélange made up of several separate and competing groups, some of which occasionally entered into alliances with neo-Nazi and other right-wing extremist groups.

Ku-kung po-wu yüan (Peking): *see* Palace Museum.

ku-wen, Pinyin GUWEN (Chinese: "ancient script"), early form of Chinese writing, examples of which are found on bronze vessels and objects of the Shang (18th–12th century BC) and Chou (1111–255) dynasties. The term *chin-wen* ("metal script"), a reference to those metal objects, has also been used to designate *ku-wen* characters. *Ku-wen* is close in appearance to *chia-ku-wen* (*q.v.*), the ancient pictographic script found on oracle bones and turtle shells. Although no standardization of form had yet taken place and the arrangement and interrelationship of lines were different in every example, *ku-wen* showed a gradual development over *chia-ku-wen.* The number of strokes increased, and characters became more complex structurally and acquired additional meanings. They showed a transition from the pictographic to a more ideographic and abstract symbolization.

Ku-wen from a bronze *kuei*, 11th century BC; in the National Palace Museum, Taipei

By courtesy of the National Palace Museum, Taipei, Taiwan, Republic of China

Ku Yen-wu, Pinyin GU YANWU (b. July 15, 1613, K'un-shan, Kiangsu province, China—d. Feb. 15, 1682, Hua-yin, Shensi province), one of the most famous of the Ming dynasty loyalists, whose rationalist critiques of the useless book learning and metaphysical speculations of the neo-Confucian philosophy (that had been the underpinning of the Chinese empire for almost 1,000 years) started a new trend in scholarship during the Ch'ing dynasty. His works eventually provided the philosophical basis for the 19th-century movement that attempted to amalgamate Western learning and Chinese tradition by searching for empirical roots within Confucianism.

Having fought against the establishment of the Manchu Ch'ing dynasty as a young man, Ku spent the rest of his life traveling throughout China, studying the reasons for the Ming collapse. He viewed the decline of Chinese civilization as the result of the excessive orthodoxy of Chinese thought, which had confined Confucian thinking to certain set formulas and made it incapable of dealing with political and economic realities. As a remedy, Ku advocated knowledge "of practical use to society" (*ching-shih chih-yung*). Moreover, he proposed that scholars abandon the neo-Confucian commentaries that interpreted Confucius and return to the original classic as well as the commentaries of the Han scholars who had been close to the sages. The school of Han learning, which Ku thus founded, advocated the use of a broad inductive method and philological research to determine the original meanings of the classics.

Ku's travels and researches also resulted in the compilation of several valuable works on practical knowledge, including *T'ien-hsia chün-kuo li-ping shu* ("The Strategic and Economic Advantages of the Districts and States of the Empire") and *Jih-chih lu* ("Notes on Knowledge Accumulated from Day to Day"). Because of his continued emphasis on the classics as the ultimate source of knowledge, however, his movement eventually deteriorated into a dry concern with philological research and textual criticism.

Kuala Belait, town, western Brunei. It lies along the Belait River near the South China Sea, west of Seria, and is at the centre of an oil field that includes offshore wells. Kuala Belait is a river port on the coastal road that runs eastward to Seria and Bandar Seri Begawan, the national capital. Pop. (1991) 21,163.

Kuala Lumpur, capital of Malaysia. The city is located in west-central West (Peninsular) Malaysia, midway along the west coast tin and rubber belt and about 25 miles (40 km) east of its ocean port, Port Kelang, on the Strait of Malacca. It is the federation's largest urban area and its cultural, commercial, and transportation centre. In 1972 Kuala Lumpur was designated a municipality, and in 1974 this entity and adjacent portions of surrounding Selangor state became a federal territory.

Kuala Lumpur lies in hilly country astride the confluence of the Kelang and Gombak rivers; its name in Malay means "Muddy Confluence." Malaysia's Main Range rises nearby to the north, east, and southeast. The climate is equatorial, with high temperatures and humidity that vary little throughout the year. The area receives about 95 inches (2,400 mm) of rain annually; June and July are the driest months. Area federal territory, 94 square miles (243 square km). Pop. (2000 prelim.) city, 1,297,526; (2000) federal territory, 1,379,310.

History. The origin of Kuala Lumpur dates to 1857, when a group of 87 Chinese tin miners founded a settlement at what is now the suburb of Ampang. Strategically commanding both river valleys, the community flourished as a tin-collecting centre despite its malaria-infested jungle location. In 1880 Kuala Lumpur superseded Klang (now Kelang) as the state capital, and its rapid growth thereafter has been attributed to Sir Frank Swettenham, British resident after 1882. He initiated construction on the Klang–Kuala Lumpur Railway and encouraged the use of brick and tile in buildings as a precaution against fire and as an aid to better health. The city's central position led to its choice as capital of the Federated Malay States (1895).

The city was occupied by the Japanese

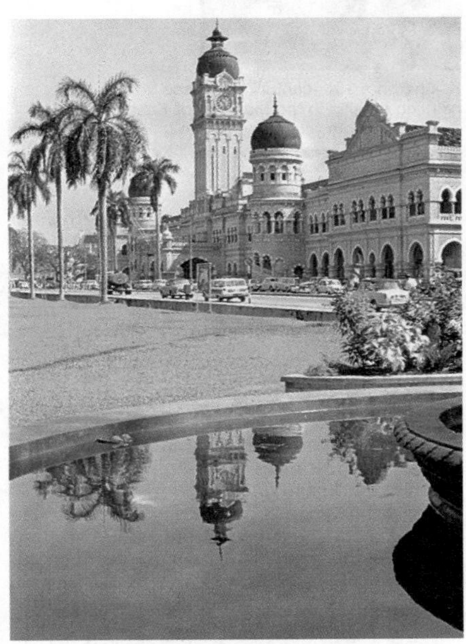

The Sultan Abdul Samad Building, Kuala Lumpur, Malaysia

Bernard Pierre Wolff—Photo Researchers

(1942–45) in World War II. Its population greatly increased in the postwar years during a long (1948–60) communist-led guerrilla insurgency, and under a resettlement program new villages were established on the city's outskirts. Kuala Lumpur became the capital of the independent Federation of Malaya in 1957 and of Malaysia in 1963. Growth continued, spurred by industrial development, the population reaching a half million in the mid-1960s and passing one million in the early 1980s.

The contemporary city. The city comprises a mixture of modern and Moorish-style architecture, traditional Chinese shop houses, squatters' huts, and Malay stilt *kampongs* ("villages"). While its centre along the embanked Kelang is heavily congested, its municipal area and suburbs are well planned. The commercial quarter, called the Golden Triangle, is concentrated on the river's east side. Among its sleek high-rise buildings are two of the world's tallest buildings, the 1,483-foot (452-m) Petronas Twin Towers, and one of the tallest broadcasting and telecommunications masts, the 1,381-foot (421-m) Kuala Lumpur Tower. Government buildings and the notable railway station (all influenced by Moorish design) are on the river's hilly west bank. This nucleus is surrounded by a zone of Chinese two-story wooden shop houses and mixed residential areas of Malay *kampongs*, modern bungalows, and middle-income brick flats. The exclusive Kenney Hill sector is a showcase for domestic architecture.

Malays, who are overwhelmingly Muslim, are the city's largest ethnic group. Despite the prevalence of Islāmic domes and minarets, however, the non-Muslim Chinese dominate the city and its economy. The Indian minority, connected with nearby rubber estates, is substantial. Kampong Baharu is one of the city's few concentrated Malay residential sections.

The industrial suburb of Sungai Besi ("Iron River") has iron foundries and engineering works and factories that process food and soap. The Sentul and Ipoh Road area is the site of railway (assembly and construction) and engineering workshops and sawmills, and cement is manufactured at Rawang to the north. While Kuala Lumpur has diversified manufacturing, the focus of industrial planning is in the adjacent suburbs of Petaling Jaya and Batu Tiga, notably in the high-technology sector. Kuala Lumpur is the country's centre of banking and finance; activities related to these and other services, including tourism, have become increasingly important. The local Batu Arang coalfield and the Connaught Bridge thermal-electric power station near Kelang are the main sources, respectively, of the city's fuel supply and power.

Kuala Lumpur is the hub of the peninsula's transportation system. Air service is largely through Kuala Lumpur International Airport, located about 30 miles (50 km) south at Sepang. The city itself has an extensive network of multilane roads and express highways, although these are inadequate for the growing number of cars and trucks. A light-rail public transit system, inaugurated in 1996, has eased traffic congestion somewhat.

There are several hospitals and state clinics, including the well-equipped Institute of Medical Research (1900). The Rubber Research Institute (1925) and Radio and Television Malaysia are headquartered there. The University of Malaya was founded at Kuala Lumpur in 1962, and the International Islāmic University Malaysia was established there in 1983. In addition, the Malay-language National University of Malaysia opened in Kuala Lumpur in 1970; the main campus is now in nearby Bangi, but there is still a branch in the city.

Lake Gardens, extending westward from the Kelang River opposite the central city, is an extensive greenbelt containing orchid and other gardens, wildlife areas, the government's Parliament House, and the National Museum of Malaysia (1963), the Islāmic Arts Museum Malaysia (1999), and the National Planetarium (1993). A smaller natural area, Bukit Nanas ("Pineapple Hill") Forest Reserve, is just northwest of the Golden Triangle. Nearby are the National Art Gallery (1958), the National Library of Malaysia (1966), and the National Theatre. Notable civic buildings include the Moorish-style Sultan Abdul Samad Building (formerly the Secretariat Building), the more contemporary National Mosque (Masjid Negara), and the old Sultan's Mosque (Masjid Jame). South of the city is the National Sports Complex, constructed for the 1998 Commonwealth Games, which includes the 100,000-seat National Stadium. To the east is the National Zoo and Aquarium. At the northern edge of the federal territory is Batu ("Rock") Caves, a complex of limestone grottoes including a 400-foot- (122-m-) high outcropping reached by hundreds of steps that contains a Hindu temple and is the scene of elaborate Dīpāvali (Thaipusam in Malay) New Year celebrations for local Hindus. North of the caves is Templer Park, a jungle preserve.

Kuala Terengganu, town, northeastern West (Peninsular) Malaysia, at the mouth of the Terengganu River, on the South China Sea. A sprawling town with wooden houses set on stilts amid trees, it is a collecting centre for the agricultural products of the river's delta. It is also a port engaged in coastal trade, with extensive road facilities and an airport at Seberang; and it is the residence of the sultan of Terengganu. Its cottage weaving industry (silk sarongs, mats made of screw-pine, and batiks) is well known. Petroleum and natural gas reserves have been developed offshore. Pop. (2000 prelim.) 250,528.

Kuan Han-ch'ing, Pinyin GUAN HANQING (b. 1241?, Ta-tu, now Peking—d. 1320?, China), dramatist who was considered by many critics to be the greatest playwright of the Chinese classical theatre.

Kuan Han-ch'ing, probably a scholar, belonged to a writers' guild that specialized in writing plays for performing groups. Fourteen of his plays (from more than 60 with known titles) have been preserved. Several of them are unquestionably masterpieces, and there is little doubt that Kuan played an important role in raising the early Chinese drama to a new level of excellence. His close association with performers may have contributed to his understanding of the common people displayed in his works. Many of his characters are women of low social standing, invariably portrayed with great sympathy and painstaking detail. His heroines always act with intelligence, integrity, and courage. Though Kuan's plots, following the fashion of his time, are unrealistic, his understanding of his characters and sympathy toward them always shine through. His style is simple and straightforward, probably closer to the spirit of early popular theatre than to the style of plays by his contemporaries. The action, often simple everyday happenings, is depicted with humour and poignancy. Some of his better known dramas include *Tou-o yüan* ("Injustice Suffered by Tou-o"), *Tan tou huei* ("Meeting Enemies Alone"), and *Chiu feng chen* ("Saving a Prostitute").

Kuan-hsiu, Pinyin GUANXIU (b. 832, Chin-hua, Chekiang Province, China—d. 912), T'ang dynasty Ch'an (in Japanese, Zen) painter known for his paintings of lohans (Buddhist holy men who have attained spiritual perfection). The best known of the lohan paintings that are attributed to him are a series of 16 in the Tokyo National Museum.

Kuan-hsiu eventually settled in the Shu-Han capital of Ch'eng-tu. His family name of Chiang was changed to Kuan-hsiu when he entered a Ch'an monastery as a youth. He was renowned not only as a painter but also as a poet and Buddhist savant.

kuan-hua: *see* Mandarin language.

Kuan Ti, Pinyin GUAN DI, historical name (Wade-Giles romanization) KUAN YÜ, also called KUAN KUNG, or WU TI, Chinese god of war.

Kuan Ti's immense popularity with the common people rests on the firm belief that his control over evil spirits is so great that even actors who play his part in dramas share his power over demons. Kuan Ti is not only a

Kuan Ti with (left) his son Kuan-p'ing and (right) his squire Ch'ou-ts'ang, painting on paper; in the Religionskundliche Sammlung der Philipps-Universität, Marburg, Ger.
Foto Marburg—Art Resource/EB Inc.

natural favourite of soldiers but has been chosen patron of numerous trades and professions. Peddlers of bean curd, for example, take him as their own, for Kuan Yü is said to have supported himself in like manner early in life.

Kuan Yü lived during the chivalrous era of the Three Kingdoms (3rd century AD) and has been romanticized in popular lore, in drama, and especially in the Ming dynasty novel *San Kuo yen-i*, as a sort of Chinese Robin Hood. When a magistrate was about to carry off a young girl, Kuan Yü came to her rescue and killed the man. Kuan Yü, fleeing for his life, came upon a guarded barrier. Suddenly his face changed to a reddish hue, and Kuan was able to pass unrecognized.

One of China's best known stories tells how he became one of the Three Brothers of the Peach Orchard. Liu Pei, a maker of straw sandals, intervened in a fight that was brewing between Kuan Yü and a prosperous butcher named Chang Fei. The three became friends and swore oaths of undying loyalty that they faithfully observed until death.

Kuan Yü was captured and executed in AD 219, but his fame continued to grow as rulers conferred successively greater titles upon him. Finally, in 1594, a Ming dynasty emperor canonized him as god of war—protector of China and of all its citizens. Thousands upon thousands of temples were constructed, each bearing the title Wu Miao (Warrior Temple) or Wu Sheng Miao (Sacred Warrior Temple). Many were built at government expense so that prescribed sacrifices could be offered on the 15th day of the second moon and on the 13th day of the fifth moon.

For a time the sword of the public executioner was housed in Kuan Ti's temple. After a criminal was put to death, the magistrate in charge of executions worshiped in the temple, certain that the spirit of the dead man would not dare to enter the temple or even follow the magistrate home.

In art Kuan Ti usually wears a green robe and has a reddish face. Almost always he is accompanied by his squire and his son. Other representations show Kuan Ti holding one of the Confucian classics, the *Tso Chuan,* which he reputedly memorized. This feat of memory led the literati to adopt him as the god of literature, a post he now shares with another deity, Wen Ti.

In the 17th century Kuan Ti's cult spread to Korea, where it was popularly believed that he saved the country from invasion by the Japanese.

Kuan ware, Pinyin GUAN, an imperial variety of stoneware of the Sung dynasty (AD 960–1279) of China. Kuan ware is characterized by a wash of brown slip and by glazes varying from pale green to lavender blue. A wide-meshed crackle is emphasized by the application of brown pigment. Made first in North China, Kuan ware was produced from about 1127 at Hang-chou, Chekiang province, in the south.

Kuan-yin, in Chinese Buddhism, the bodhisattva of infinite compassion and mercy. *See* Avalokiteśvara.

Kuan Yü (Chinese god): *see* Kuan Ti.

kuang, Pinyin GUANG, type of Chinese bronze vessel produced during the Shang (18th–12th century BC) and early Chou (1111–*c.* 900 BC) periods. It is a serving vessel for wine, with an unusually fine harmony between shape and decoration.

The *kuang* looks much like a sauce server, with a large spout extending from one end of

Ceremonial bronze *kuang,* Shang dynasty (18th–12th century BC); in the Freer Gallery of Art, Washington, D.C.

By courtesy of the Smithsonian Institution, Freer Gallery of Art, Washington, D.C.

the oval-section body and a vertical handle at the other end. All vessels classified as *kuang* properly have a lid that covers the entire top of the vessel, including the spout. The spout end of the lid typically has a bovine or feline head, the opposite end, an owl or birdlike mask. These elements harmonize with the decoration of the body, which may suggest the organic completion of the animals or provide complementary, zoomorphic motifs—such as the monster mask, or *t'ao-t'ieh*—characteristic of the bronze art of the Shang and early Chou.

Kuang-hsü, Pinyin GUANGXU (reign name), personal name (*hsing-ming*) TSAI-T'IEN, posthumous name (*shih*) CHING-TI, temple name (*miao-hao*) (CH'ING) TE-TSUNG (b. Aug. 14, 1871, Peking, China—d. Nov. 14, 1908, Peking), ninth emperor (reigned 1875–1908) of the Ch'ing dynasty, during whose reign the empress dowager Tz'u-hsi (1835–1908) totally dominated the government and thereby prevented the young emperor from modernizing and reforming the deteriorating imperial system.

When the previous emperor died, his mother, the empress dowager Tz'u-hsi, chose her four-year-old nephew as emperor. She adopted the boy as her son so that she could act as regent and dominate the government as she had since 1861. Although this action broke the sacred dynastic law of succession, opposition to the move was squelched, and on Feb. 25, 1875, the young prince ascended the throne, taking the reign name of Kuang-hsü.

Although the emperor came of age in 1887, he had to wait two more years before taking over the government from Tz'u-hsi, who continued to influence policy. In 1898, at the age of 27, he finally tried to assert himself. During what has come to be known as the "Hundred Days of Reform," he collected a group of progressively oriented officials around him and issued a broad series of reform edicts. Conservative officials were outraged. With the aid of the top imperial military commander, Jung-lu, Tz'u-hsi returned to the capital, confined the emperor to his palace, and spread rumours that he was deathly ill. Foreign powers, who let it be known that they would not take kindly to the emperor's death or dethronement, saved his life, but thereafter he had no power over the government.

On Nov. 15, 1908, Tz'u-hsi died, and, under highly suspicious circumstances, the theretofore healthy Kuang-hsü emperor was announced as having died the previous day. Tz'u-hsi's final decree passed the throne to the emperor's three-year-old nephew, who reigned as the Hsüan-t'ung emperor.

Kuang-hua (China): *see* Lao-ho-k'ou.

Kuang-wu ti, Pinyin GUANG WU DI (posthumous name, or *shih*), personal name (*hsing-ming*) LIU HSIU, temple name (*miao-hao*) (TUNG-HAN) SHIH-TSU (b. *c.* 5 BC—d. AD 57, Lo-yang, China), Chinese emperor (reigned AD 25–57) who restored the Han dynasty after the usurpation of Wang Mang, a former Han minister who established the Hsin dynasty (AD 9–25). Kuang-wu's restored Han dynasty is sometimes referred to as the Later Han, or the Eastern Han (AD 25–220).

Kuang-wu ti ("Shining Martial Emperor") was a member of the imperial Liu family and a supposed descendant of Kao-tsu (reigned 206–195 BC), the founder of the Han dynasty. In AD 22, when the radical reform measures of Wang Mang made his Hsin dynasty unpopular, Kuang-wu raised an army. Supported by the powerful Liu clan and other rich landowner families, he defeated Wang Mang in 23. Two years later he moved the capital to Lo-yang, in eastern China—hence the name Eastern Han—and proclaimed himself emperor.

The subsequent 10 years of Kuang-wu's reign were spent in consolidating his rule and subduing the numerous domestic rebellions that had arisen, including the Red Eyebrows revolt. He also suppressed the nomadic tribesmen of China's northern borders and returned imperial rule to the outlying areas of South China. Having restored peace to the empire, Kuang-wu became so weary of fighting that he forbade the mention of the word war in his presence.

The Later Han was never as powerful as the Former Han. In the wars that led to the founding of the Later Han dynasty, many of the vast, tax-exempt landed estates had been destroyed, thus eliminating one of the major problems that had plagued the last years of the Former Han. Nevertheless, Kuang-wu had risen to power with the support of a few aristocratic families, and he continued to depend on their military assistance. As a result, those families gradually increased their own holdings at the expense of the central government, and the dynasty grew to resemble a federation of great clans.

Kuangchou (China): *see* Canton.

Kuantan, city situated on the eastern coast of the Malay Peninsula, West Malaysia. It lies at the mouth of the Kuantan River, on the South China Sea. Situated on a wide alluvial plain north of the fertile Pahang River delta, Kuantan is Malaysia's most important east-coast port, shipping tin, rubber, and copra south to Singapore for export. Tin is extracted from the deep lode mine at Sungai Lembing to the northwest. As the only east-coast settlement that has a direct road link to Kuala Lumpur, Kuantan serves as a transfer point for westbound travelers.

Fishing villages dot the region's coastline, and local cottage industries produce textiles, dolls, screw-pine mats, and silver jewelry. A plywood factory and a tapioca-processing plant are in the city. Commercially valuable stone crabs inhabit Ular (Snake) Island, a small offshore isle that attracts skin-diving enthusiasts. Pop. (1991 prelim.) 198,356.

Kuanza River: *see* Kwanza River.

Kuba, also called BAKUBA, a cluster of about 16 Bantu-speaking groups in southeastern Zaire, living between the Kasai and Sankuru rivers east of their confluence.

Kuba cultivate corn (maize), cassava, millet, peanuts (groundnuts), and beans as staples. They grow raffia and oil palms, raise corn as a cash crop, and hunt and fish. They have kept aloof from modern life, and few have emigrated or engage in European-style occupations. The groups are divided into lineages related through matrilineal descent; the lineages are segments of numerous dispersed clans. The Kuba are united in a kingdom, ruled by the central Bushongo group, which emerged about 1600. The kingdom is a federation of chiefdoms, each ruled by a chief and two or three councils that represent the general population and noble clans. The ruling Bushongo chief is king by divine right. Uniting factors include bonds of common culture and group feeling, a royal army, and a common administration.

Nature spirits, the spirits of dead kings, and witchcraft dominate Kuba religion. Nearly all objects of daily use are decorated, and carved wooden figurines, initiation masks, cups, and beautifully embroidered handwoven raffia cloth are especially prized for export.

Kuba, former African kingdom in the interior of Zaire. It was bounded to the southwest by the Kasai and Lulua rivers and to the north by the Sankuru River, a tributary of the Kasai. Founded about 1600 by migrants from the area of the lower Kasai River, it was actually a federation of smaller, nearly autonomous subkingdoms such as the Bushongo and the Ngongo.

In the 19th century, rebellions in the east and Lulua invasions in the south weakened Kuba to the point of civil war. About 1910 the colonial regime of the Belgian Congo extended its control over the area and quelled the disorders, strengthening the Kuba kings by suppressing their subkings and rivals.

Kuba (Azerbaijan): *see* Quba.

Kuba carpet, any of several types of antique floor coverings of the Caucasus, many of which are of considerable length, but narrow. Rather than the town of Kuba (now Quba, Azerbaijan), which was founded about 1750 in Dagestan, the original source was probably the districts of Karabakh and Shirvan in Southern Caucasia, where rug workshops were operated under the sponsorship of the Iranian shāh ʿAbbās I in the early 17th century.

The most numerous group of Kuba carpets

are the Dragon rugs produced from the 17th into the 19th century. Sunburst carpets accent a motif that has persisted in the recent Eagle Kazaks, together with crude, hooked lancet leaves and egg-shaped palmettes. Other schemes offer variants of Kerman and East

Detail of the ground pattern of a Kuba carpet, 18th century; in the Textile Museum, Washington, D.C.
Textile Museum Collection, Washington, D.C.; photograph, Otto E. Nelson

Persian designs, each shape having become geometric, with bold draftsmanship and colouring. A later series has a modified Turkish silk pattern, with stylized palmettes in rows, placed between lancet leaves deformed into tree shapes. Kuba carpets normally were made entirely of wool until the 19th century, when cotton was sometimes used for warps or weft, or silk blended into the wool foundation yarns.

Kubaba, goddess of the ancient Syrian city of Carchemish. In religious texts of the Hittite empire (*c.* 1400–*c.* 1190 BC), she played a minor part and appeared mainly in a context of Hurrian deities and rituals. After the downfall of the empire her cult spread westward and northward, and she became the chief goddess of the successor kingdoms (the neo-Hittite states) from Cilicia to the Halys River.

Kubaba was represented as a dignified figure draped in a long robe, either standing or seated, and holding a mirror. Although her name was adopted by the Phrygians for their great mother goddess in the form of Cybebe (Cybele), the Phrygian goddess bore little resemblance to Kubaba in other respects.

Kuban River, river in southwestern Russia, 563 miles (906 km) in length and draining 23,600 square miles (61,000 square km). It rises from glaciers on Mount Elbrus in the Greater Caucasus and flows north through narrow gorges, with many rapids, to the Stavropol Upland, where it turns westward in a broad, marshy floodplain to enter the Sea of Azov. Much of its water is diverted for irrigation. The river is navigable to Krasnodar. The Kuban River gave its name to a Cossack group who settled along its northern bank in the late 18th and early 19th centuries.

Kubango River (Africa): *see* Okavango River.

Kubelík, Rafael, in full JERONYM RAFAEL KUBELÍK (b. June 29, 1914, Býchory, Bohemia, Austria-Hungary [now in Czech Republic]—d. Aug. 11, 1996, Lucerne, Switz.), Bohemian-born Swiss conductor, musical director, and composer, who was noted for his frequent guest appearances with major orchestras throughout the world.

He was a son of the violinist Jan Kubelík and studied composition and conducting at the Prague Conservatory. He conducted the Czech Philharmonic Orchestra from 1936 to 1939 and from 1942 to 1948. He left Czechoslovakia in 1948 after the Communist takeover, settling first in England and later in Switzerland, where he became a citizen in 1973. He became principal conductor of the Chicago Symphony Orchestra in 1950 but was forced to resign in 1953 amid controversy over his plans for staff changes and a concert program emphasizing modern compositions. As music director of the Covent Garden Opera from 1955 to 1958, he championed opera in English. From 1961 to 1979 he was principal conductor of the Bavarian Radio Symphony Orchestra. From 1973 to 1974 he was also musical director of the Metropolitan Opera in New York City. Kubelík's own compositions include two operas, three symphonies, choral works, and concertos.

Kubera, in Hindu mythology, the king of the *yakṣas* (nature spirits) and the god of wealth. He is associated with the earth, mountains, all treasures such as minerals and jewels that lie underground, and riches in general. According to most accounts he first lived in Laṅkā (Sri Lanka), but his palace was taken away from him by his half brother, Rāvaṇa, and he now resides in a beautiful mountain residence near Śiva's home on Mount Kailāsa, where he is attended by all manner of genies.

Kubera is the guardian of the north and is usually depicted as a dwarfish figure with a large paunch, holding a money bag or a pomegranate, sometimes riding on a man.

Kubera, stone figure from Orissa, *c.* 8th century AD; in the Indian Museum, Calcutta
Pramod Chandra

Also known as Vaiśrāvaṇa and Jambhala, he is a popular figure in Buddhist and Jaina mythology as well. In Buddhist sculptures he is often shown accompanied by a mongoose.

Kubin, Alfred (b. April 10, 1877, Leitmeritz, Bohemia, Austria-Hungary [now Litoměřice, Czech Republic]—d. Aug. 24, 1959, Zwickledt, Austria), Austrian graphic artist known for his drawings and paintings of dreamlike, often morbid, subjects.

In 1898 Kubin went to Munich to study art, and in 1902 he had his first exhibition at the Cassirer Gallery in Berlin. He traveled in France and Italy in 1905 and following years, and during this period he met the French painter Odilon Redon, whose work, along with that of the Belgian painter James Ensor, was a major influence on Kubin. In 1906 Kubin settled at Zwickledt, Austria, where he was to remain for most of his life. He exhibited with the Blaue Reiter group in Munich in 1911 and at the Der Sturm Autumn Salon in 1913. The nightmarish world created by Kubin in his illustrations reflects his own neurotic personality. Images of death and of various bizarre animals are depicted in dim light against shadowy backgrounds, evoking a haunting expectation of some sinister turn of events.

The books Kubin illustrated by such writers as Edgar Allan Poe, Oscar Wilde, and Fyodor Dostoyevsky seem to have been chosen on account of their macabre qualities. He also wrote a novel, *Die andere Seite* (1909; "The Other Side").

Kubitschek, Juscelino, in full JUSCELINO KUBITSCHEK DE OLIVEIRA (b. Sept. 12, 1902, Diamantina, Brazil—d. Aug. 22, 1976, near Resende), president of Brazil (1956–61) noted for his ambitious public works, especially the construction of the new capital, Brasília.

Kubitschek attended the Diamantina Seminary, worked his way through medical school at the University of Minas Gerais (graduated 1927), and did internships in surgery in Paris, Vienna, and Berlin. He became head of the surgical division of the military Medical Corps of the state of Minas Gerais in 1932 and represented Minas Gerais in the Federal Chamber of Deputies from 1934 to 1937 and 1946 to 1950. As mayor of Belo Horizonte (1940–45) he distinguished himself in city planning and the establishment of medical clinics and other public service facilties. As governor of Minas Gerais (1951–55) he concentrated on highway construction, power plants, and agricultural and industrial development.

Kubitschek campaigned for president on a platform of "power, transportation, and food" and won in a three-man race as the perceived political heir of the deceased Brazilian president Getúlio Vargas. While in office Kubitschek pushed forward the rapid development of Brazil's machinery, hydroelectric, steel, and other heavy industries, and he built 11,000 miles (18,000 km) of new roads and highways. Most important, perhaps, he moved the national capital from Rio de Janeiro to a new city called Brasília lying 600 miles (1,000 km) inland from the coast. Kubitschek intended the new inland capital to accelerate the settlement and development of Brazil's vast interior. The price of his ambitious development efforts was persistent and rapid inflation, however, a problem exacerbated by the need to spend vast sums for the rehabilitation of the drought-afflicted northeast region. Elected to the Senate in 1962, Kubitschek was nominated for president by the Social Democratic Party in 1964. The military junta that took power that same year forced him into exile. He returned to Brazil in 1967 to become a banker. He died in an automobile crash.

Kublai Khan, Kublai also spelled KHUBILAI, OR KUBLA (b. 1215—d. 1294), Mongolian general and statesman, grandson of Genghis Khan. He conquered China and became the first emperor of its Yüan, or Mongol, dynasty. He was thus at one and the same time the overlord of all the Mongol dominions—which included areas as diverse as that of the Golden Horde in southern Russia, the Il-Khanate of Persia, and the steppe heartlands where Mongol princes were still living the traditional nomadic life—and the ruler of his own realm of China. To govern China, with its long and individual political and cultural history, demanded statecraft of a special order.

Historical background. The Mongols were a parvenu nomadic power. Before the time of Genghis Khan they had been no more than a group of semibarbaric tribes, more or less unknown to history. They had only primitive cultural traditions, and, except for some organized hunting and the management of their herds, they had little experience of economic activity. Until a few years before Kublai's birth, they had been illiterate. They had only the most elementary ideas of statecraft.

This political incompetence contributed much to the rapid collapse of their empire.

Kublai Khan; in the National Palace Museum, Taipei

By courtesy of the National Palace Museum, Taipei, Taiwan, Republic of China

With a few outstanding exceptions, such as Kublai himself (whom the Mongols always called Setsen Khan, the Wise Khan), the rulers of the Mongols seem to have looked upon power as a personal, at most a family, possession, to be exploited for immediate gain. Hence, except in areas where, like China, there was a firm native political tradition, they never succeeded in organizing a durable state. In China, too, everything depended ultimately upon the willpower and ability of the ruler.

The Mongols had come to power in China, as elsewhere, by sheer force of arms; and with this prestige to back him, relying on his dominant personality, and building on the foundations of the brilliant civilization developed by the preceding Sung dynasty, Kublai for a while could maintain the illusion that Mongol supremacy was firmly based. Indeed, his reign must have appeared to be a period of solid expansion and lasting achievement to his contemporaries, including Marco Polo, the Venetian traveller who became Kublai's agent and whose book is the chief Renaissance source of information on the East.

Yet Kublai Khan was faced at the outset of his reign by an insoluble dilemma, which was given vivid expression in a memorial presented to him by one of his Chinese advisers: "I have heard that one can conquer the empire on horseback, but one cannot govern it on horseback." In other words, to administer China the inexperienced Mongols would have to adopt Chinese methods, even live according to a Chinese pattern; and, to the extent that they did so, they would be bound to become more and more assimilated and perhaps lose their identity altogether. If, on the other hand, they worked through Chinese and other agents they would become alienated from the mass of the population, which would reject them. In either case, the Mongols, culturally and numerically inferior and used to a different pattern of life, could not continue for long to rule China as a distinct and privileged caste; and only the brilliance of Kublai's personal achievement obscured this truth.

Rise to power. Kublai Khan was the fourth son of Tolui, the youngest of Genghis' four sons by his favourite wife. He began to play an important part in the extension and consolidation of the Mongol empire only in 1251, when he was in his middle 30s. His brother, the emperor Möngke, resolved to complete the conquest of Sung China, which had been planned by Genghis' third son, Ögödei, and also to subdue Persia—a task allotted to Kublai's brother Hülegü. Kublai was invested with full civil and military responsibility for the affairs of China. He appears never to have learned to read or write Chinese, but already he had recognized the superiority of Chinese thought and had gathered around himself a group of trustworthy Confucian advisers.

His attitude toward government was formed under the influence of these learned Chinese, who convinced him of the necessary interdependence of ruler and ruled and reinforced his innate tendency toward humanity and magnanimity. At home, in the fief allotted to him in the Wei River Valley (in modern Shensi Province), he established a competent administration and a supply base. In the field, he stressed to his generals the precepts of his mentors—the importance and effectiveness of clemency toward the conquered. This was a great advance in civilized behaviour compared to the methods of Genghis Khan and those of Kublai's contemporaries in Central Asia, where the massacre of the population was still the expected sequel to the capture of a city.

Kublai took Sung China in the flank, subjugating the Tai kingdom of Nanchao in present-day Yunnan before handing over command to his general Uriyangqadai. In 1257 Möngke assumed personal charge of the war, but he died in 1259. When Kublai, who with another army was besieging a city, heard that his brother, Arigböge, who had been left in charge of the homeland because he was the youngest, was planning to have himself elected khan, he patched up a truce with Sung. In April 1260 he arrived at his residence of K'ai-p'ing, or Shang-tu (the Xanadu of Samuel Taylor Coleridge's famous poem), in southeastern Mongolia. Here his associates held a *kuriltai,* or "great assembly," and on May 5 Kublai was unanimously elected khan in succession to Möngke.

Ten days later he announced his succession in a proclamation drawn up in Classical Chinese. Because primogeniture was not a recognized principle at the time, Arigböge, with some very powerful supporters, held a *kuriltai* at Karakorum and had himself declared khan, ignoring Kublai's action. In spite of Marco Polo's insistence that Kublai was the lineal and legitimate descendant of Genghis Khan and the rightful sovereign, there have always been doubts about this legitimacy. A legend recorded in Mongol chronicles to the effect that the dying Genghis designated the child Kublai as a future khan seems to have been contrived so as to provide retrospective justification of an act of usurpation.

In 1264 Kublai defeated Arigböge in battle and forced him to submit. He died two years later. But the family feud, of which this was one manifestation, continued throughout Kublai's reign. Against him were ranged those who resented the abandonment of the old ways of the steppe and the adoption of an alien, China-centred culture. The split was all the deeper because the leader of the opposition was Kaidu, who, as a grandson of Ögödei, who had been designated personally by Genghis as his successor, represented the cause of legitimacy. The throne had passed from the line of Ögödei to that of his brother Tolui in 1250 as a result of a coup d'etat. Kaidu never relaxed his hostility toward Kublai and remained master of Mongolia proper and Turkistan until his death in 1301.

The war with Kaidu showed how decisively Kublai had identified himself with the Chinese world and turned against the world of the nomads. Genghis had been strong and ruthless enough to compel the Mongols, always inclined to family feuds, to serve his cause; but Kublai, powerful though he was, could no longer control the steppe aristocracy effectively.

Unification of China. Kublai's achievement was to reestablish the unity of China, which had been divided since the end of the T'ang dynasty. This achievement was that much greater because he was a barbarian, nomadic conqueror. Even in Chinese official historiography the Mongol Kublai is treated with respect. As early as 1260 he instituted a reign period, in the Chinese manner, to date his reign; and in 1271, eight years before the disintegration of the Sung, he proclaimed his own dynasty under the title of Ta Yüan, or Great Origin. He never resided at Karakorum, Ögödei's short-lived capital in northern Mongolia, but set up his own capital at what is now Peking, a city known in his time as Ta-tu, the Great Capital.

The final conquest of Sung China took several years. Kublai might well have been content to rule the North and to leave the Sung dynasty nominally in control of South China, but the detention and ill treatment of envoys he had sent convinced him that the declining regime in the south must be dealt with decisively. Military operations opened once again in 1267. The Sung emperor was apparently badly served by his last ministers, who are said to have kept him misinformed of the true situation, whereas many Sung commanders went over voluntarily to the Mongols. In 1276 Kublai's general Bayan captured the child emperor of the day, but loyalists in the south delayed the inevitable end until 1279.

With all China in Mongol hands, the Mongol conquests in the south and east had reached their effective limit; but Kublai, seeking to restore China's prestige, engaged in a series of costly and troublesome wars that brought little return. At various times tribute was demanded of the peripheral kingdoms: from Burma, from Annam and Champa in Indochina, from Java, and from Japan. The Mongol armies suffered some disastrous defeats in these campaigns. In particular, invasion fleets sent to Japan in 1274 and 1281 were virtually annihilated, though their loss was due as much to storms as to Japanese resistance.

Kublai was never entirely discouraged by the indifferent results of these colonial wars nor by their expense, and they were brought to an end only under his successor. Marco Polo suggests that Kublai wished to annex Japan simply because he was excited by reports of its great wealth. It seems, however, that his colonial wars were fought mainly with a political objective—to establish China once more as the centre of the world.

Social and administrative policy. By themselves the Mongols were incapable of ruling China, and, though at the lower levels they made use of Chinese civil servants, posts of importance were allotted to foreigners. Of these Marco Polo is a familiar example. Kublai instituted a "nationalities policy" under which the population of China was divided into four categories. At the top were the Mongols, forming a privileged, military caste of a few hundred thousand, exempt from taxation, and living at the expense of the Chinese peasantry who worked the great estates allocated for their upkeep.

The foreign auxiliaries of the Mongols, natives for the most part of Central Asia, formed the second group, the se-mu jen, or persons with special status. This class furnished the higher officialdom, and its members, with their worldwide contacts and their privileged status, also formed a new breed of merchants and speculators. Like the Mongols, they were exempt from taxation and enjoyed preferential use of the official postroads and services.

The bulk of the population belonged to the

third and fourth classes, the *han-jen,* or northern Chinese, and the *man-tzu,* or southern barbarians, who lived in what had been Sung China. The expenses of state and the support of the privileged bore heavily on these two classes, with Kublai's continuing wars and his extravagant building operations at Ta-tu. Peasants were brought in as labourers, to the neglect of their farms. Food supplies in the north were inadequate for the new labour force and the unproductive Mongols, and large quantities had to be brought by sea and, when the sea routes proved insecure, along the Grand Canal. The repair and extension of this canal also demanded much labour.

Kublai, in common with other Mongol rulers, was much preoccupied with religion. His reign was a time of toleration for rival religions and of economic privilege for the favoured religions. Clerics and their communities were exempted from taxation, and Buddhist temples especially were granted generous donations of land and of peasants for their upkeep. The arrogance of the many Tibetan lamas who enjoyed a special status in China was particularly detested.

Such a discriminatory social policy was eventually bound to arouse strong resentment. Moreover, it was only on the surface that Kublai's China, with its intense commercial activity, was economically strong and wealthy. Trade was mainly carried on in the interests of a privileged, foreign merchant class, not those of the community at large. The common people of China were becoming progressively poorer. The old examination system, which admitted to the civil service only men with a proper knowledge of Confucian philosophy, had lapsed, and customary restraints upon absolutism and arbitrary rule, such as would have been imposed by the censorate (a body that scrutinized the conduct of officials) and a professional public service, were lacking.

The Chinese literati were excluded from public office and responsibility. As a result, adventurers could attain high positions, and even an emperor of Kublai's unique ability remained for years on end in ignorance of, and unable to check, the depredations of his dishonest foreign financial advisers. The extravagant policies that Kublai had countenanced and the financial ineptitude of later Mongol emperors, provoked, in the 14th century, the economically motivated uprisings that brought the dynasty down.

Kublai is celebrated, mainly because of Marco Polo's account, for his use of paper money. Paper money had, however, been in use in China under the Sung, and Kublai's innovation was merely to make it the sole medium of exchange. Toward the end of the dynasty, an incapable financial administration stimulated inflation by the overissue of paper money, but in Kublai's time the use of banknotes was essential. The supply of copper was too small to form a metal currency in a period of expanding trade, and in any case large quantities were diverted to the temples to be made into statues and other cult objects.

Assessment. Though celebrated above all as a Chinese emperor, Kublai also helped to form the political traditions of his own Mongol people. To him and to his adviser, the Tibetan grand lama 'Phags-pa, is attributed the development of the political theory known as the "dual principle"—that is, the parity of power and dignity of church and state in political affairs. This theory was turned to practical account on more than one occasion in the subsequent history of Mongolia and, for example, underlay the constitution of the theocratic monarchy proclaimed in 1911, when Mongolia recovered its independence from China.

Kublai's character is difficult to assess. The only personal account of him is by Marco Polo, and this is more of a panegyric than a sober appraisal. Marco presents Kublai as the ideal of a universal sovereign. Yet he does not overlook his human weaknesses, above all, an indulgence in feasting and hunting, a complicated and expensive sexual life, a failure to exercise proper supervision over his subordinates, and occasional outbursts of cruelty.

Kublai's career is interesting above all because of the way in which he interpreted—and finally failed to reconcile—his dual roles. As it turned out, he became a Chinese emperor of traditional type. China absorbed his interests and energies to the exclusion of the Mongol homeland, and for years he was actually engaged in civil war with rival Mongol princes of the steppes. Under him, China, and of course the privileged Mongols, enjoyed a brilliant spell of prosperity, but his politics, pursued with less skill by his successors, isolated the Mongols in China from their environment. With the collapse of the dynasty, the Mongols withdrew to the steppes and never again played any role of more than local importance. (C.R.B.)

BIBLIOGRAPHY. Morris Rossabi, *Khubilai Khan* (1987), discusses his life and times. Accounts of his life may also be found in histories of China and of the Mongols, especially in Wolfram Eberhard, *A History of China,* 4th ed. (1977); René Grousset, *The Empire of the Steppes: A History of Central Asia* (1970); and Robert Marshall, *Storm from the East: From Genghis Khan to Khubilai Khan* (1993).

Kubovy, Aryeh Leon, original name ARYEH LEON KUBOWITZKI (b. Nov. 2, 1896, Kuršėna, Lithuania—d. May 16, 1966, Jerusalem), Israeli lawyer, diplomat, and Zionist. He was a founder (1936) and general secretary (1945–48) of the World Jewish Congress.

After settling in Israel (1948), Kubovy served that country in diplomatic posts in Czechoslovakia, Poland, and several South American countries. He was chairman of Yad va-Shem (Martyrs' and Heroes' Remembrance Authority) from 1959 until his death.

Kubrick, Stanley (b. July 26, 1928, New York, N.Y., U.S.—d. March 7, 1999, Childwickbury Manor, near St. Albans, Eng.), American motion-picture director and writer whose films are characterized by a cool, formal visual style, meticulous attention to detail, and a detached, often ironic pessimism.

Having become interested in photography in high school, Kubrick became a staff photographer for *Look* magazine at age 17. His first film, *The Day of the Fight* (1951), is a short documentary about the boxing world. Two years later, his first feature-length film, *Fear and Desire* (1953), dealing with World War II, was released.

Paths of Glory (1957), a story of military injustice in the French army during World War I, brought Kubrick into prominence as a director. It was followed by films, mostly shot in England, that explored the incongruities and violence underlying modern life and reached imaginatively into the world of the future. After *Spartacus* (1960), a historical epic, Kubrick made *Lolita* (1962), based on the novel by Vladimir Nabokov; *Dr. Strangelove* (1964), which turned the possibility of a nuclear war into a grim joke; *2001: A Space Odyssey* (1968), which earned an Academy Award for special visual effects; *A Clockwork Orange* (1971), based on the dystopian novel by Anthony Burgess; *Barry Lyndon* (1975), based on William Makepeace Thackeray's novel of manners; *The Shining* (1980), a horror film based on the novel by Stephen King; *Full Metal Jacket* (1987), about the Vietnam War; and *Eyes Wide Shut* (1999), which was released posthumously.

Kubrick

Kubu, seminomadic forest dwellers found primarily in swampy areas near watercourses in southeastern Sumatra, Indonesia. The people appear to be a mixture of an early Veddoid stock and Negrito.

Contact of the Kubu with their neighbours had traditionally been primarily through "silent trade"; *i.e.,* goods for barter were put where traders could look them over. They, in turn, placed nearby what they were willing to give in exchange and retired to a distance. If the deal was satisfactory, the Kubu took what was offered and vanished into the bush. Shortly before World War II the Dutch forced some of these people into villages near the Malays and started them in agriculture, but these settlements were frequently deserted. Nevertheless, the contacts thus made, as well as those brought about by oil exploration in their territory, have broken down their isolation.

Traditional settlements normally consist of 20 to 30 persons living in frail houses made of bamboo and leaves. An older person serves as headman, but he has little authority. Jungle produce and small game provide most of the food, for in such a group there are no domestic animals other than an occasional dog or chicken. Dress consists of a bark loincloth and a headband to hold back the tangled hair. Little is known about their beliefs beyond the fact that they have mediums, or shamans, and that they make offerings to the spirits.

Kuch Bihār (India): *see* Cooch Behār.

Kucha, Chinese (Wade-Giles) K'U-CH'E, (Pinyin) KUQA, oasis city in the Sinkiang Uighur autonomous *ch'ü* (region), China. The oasis of Kucha lies at the foot of the southern slope of the Tien Shan (mountains) on the northern rim of the Tarim Basin. It is watered by the Kucha and Mu-cha-t'i rivers, which flow in rainy spells into the Tarim River but which for most of the year lose themselves in the salt marshes on the northern edge of the Takla Makan Desert.

Kucha was known to the Chinese from a very early date as a small independent kingdom under the name K'uei-tzu (spelled in a variety of ways). Its ancient population consisted of Aryan people speaking Tocharian B, or Kuchean, a form of Tocharian, an Indo-European language. The oasis, which is between A-k'o-su and Karashahr, was an important centre on the northern branch of the Silk Road through the Tarim Basin. Under the rule of the Min-chia (Po) peoples, Kucha became an important Buddhist centre; remains of this period are in the renowned Kizil caves. Many of the monks who introduced Buddhist teachings into China from the 3rd to the 7th century AD were from Kucha. The city was also famous in China for its musicians.

The T'ang government established a Chinese protectorate over Kucha in 658, but its power was challenged by the Tibetans in the south and the Turks in the north. After the middle of the 8th century, Chinese authority was nominal, and it ended by 790. In the 9th century, following the collapse of the Uighur empire, the Uighurs set up a regime in the Turfan region, which eventually came to control Kucha. In medieval times it was part of Uighuristan, and Chinese control was not reestablished there until the 18th century.

During the period of Uighur rule, most of the inhabitants were Muslims of Turkic origin. In modern times Kucha was divided into Muslim and Chinese sectors. The intensively irrigated oasis produces various grains and cotton and is known for its fruit, notably pears, grapes, and melons. The city is also renowned for its handicraft cutlery industry. Pop. (1990) 51,700.

Kuchan (Iran): *see* Qūchān.

Kuching, town, East Malaysia, on northwestern Borneo. The town was founded in 1839 by James (later Sir James) Brooke, who became ruler of Sarawak with the title of raja. He built the town's first European-style house on the jungled southern bank of the muddy, crocodile-infested Sarawak River, 15 miles (24 km) from the South China Sea. Now a busy administrative centre, Kuching is populated mainly by Chinese, although Malays, Land Dayaks, and Ibans live on its outskirts. Kuching exports rubber, pepper, and sago flour and has a seaport and an airport.

Its Sarawak Museum (1878), set in scenic gardens, has exhibits of ancient Bornean culture. The main government buildings include the Astana ("Palace"; 1870) and Supreme Court (1874). The region's heterogeneous quality is reflected in Anglican and Roman Catholic cathedrals and numerous mosques and Buddhist temples. Kuching contains a teacher-training college and an engineering college. Tourists frequent the nearby Land Dayak Longhouse, the seaside resort of Santubong, and Bako National Park. Pop. (1991) 147,729.

The Municipal Council building in Kuching, Malaysia

Victor Englebert—De Wys

kuchipudi, one of six classical dance styles of India. *Kuchipudi* is indigenous to the state of Andhra Pradesh and differs from the other five classical styles by the inclusion of singing. *Kuchipudi* originated in the 17th century with the creation by Sidhyendra Yogi of the dance-drama *Bhama Kalapam,* a story of Satyabhāma, the charming but jealous wife of the god Krishna. The dance performance begins with the sprinkling of holy water and the burning of incense. Other rituals are performed, the goddesses of learning, wealth, and energy are invoked, and the characters are introduced, together with songs concerning their function in the performance. All roles were traditionally played by men. As an offering to Krishna, every Brahman, or priest, of the village of Kuchipudi is expected to perform the role of Satyabhāma at least once in his life.

Kuchma, Leonid Danylovych (b. Aug. 9, 1938, Chaykyne, Ukraine, U.S.S.R.), Ukrainian engineer and politician who became prime minister (1992–93) and second president of Ukraine (from 1994). His administration supported increased privatization, free trade, and closer ties with Russia.

After graduating from Dnipropetrovsk State University (1960), Kuchma embarked on a career as an engineer, serving as Communist Party secretary (1972–82) for his company in Dnipropetrovsk. During those years he also retained a top-secret post as a technical manager in Baikonur, Kazakhstan, the centre of the Soviet space program. From 1986 to 1992, he served as the general director of Yuzhmash, the world's largest rocket construction firm, in Dnipropetrovsk.

In October 1992 Kuchma was appointed prime minister by Leonid M. Kravchuk, Ukraine's first democratically elected president. Kuchma clashed with Kravchuk over economic policies and resigned from the post after one year. In the 1994 presidential elections, Kuchma defeated the incumbent Kravchuk, a nationalist, by reaching out to former Communists.

Kuchumba language: *see* Amharic language.

Küçük Kaynarca, Treaty of, Küçük Kaynarca also spelled KUCHUK KAINARJI (July 10 [July 21, New Style], 1774), pact signed at the conclusion of the Russo-Turkish War of 1768–74 at Küçük Kaynarca, in Bulgaria, ending undisputed Ottoman control of the Black Sea and providing a diplomatic basis for future Russian intervention in internal affairs of the Ottoman Empire.

The territorial provisions of the treaty extended the Russian frontier to the southern Bug River, thus ceding to Russia the port of Azov, the fortresses of Kerch and Yenikale on the eastern end of the Crimean Peninsula, a part of the province of Kuban, and the estuary formed by the Dnieper and Bug rivers, including the Kinburn fortress. The territory of the Crimean khanate was to form an independent state, subject to the Ottoman sultan-caliph only in religious matters.

The treaty's commercial provisions gave Russia the right to establish consulates anywhere in the Ottoman Empire, to navigate freely in Ottoman waters through the Straits of the Bosporus and the Dardanelles, and to enjoy commercial privileges in Ottoman lands.

Most far-reaching, however, was a religious stipulation that accorded to Russia the privilege of representing, within the Ottoman Empire, the Greek Orthodox Christians in Moldavia and Walachia (which were to be returned to Turkey) and in the Aegean Islands. Later, Russia freely interpreted and employed this provision to support its claims to a protectorate over the Greek Orthodox Christians anywhere in the Ottoman Empire.

Kudamatsu, city, Yamaguchi *ken* (prefecture), western Honshu, Japan. Located on a deep cove of the Inland Sea, the original fishing village first started to grow through salt manufacturing and trade. When Kudamatsu was bypassed by a trunk line of the National Railway, its commercial activity declined.

Kudamatsu revived during World War I as an industrial city, assisted by its natural port and by factories built on reclaimed land previously used for salt manufacturing. Kudamatsu was designated a city in 1939, and its industrial complex includes heavy machinery and petrochemical factories, with power plants and shipyards. Pop. (1995) 53,472.

Kudirka, Vincas (b. Dec. 31, 1858, Paezeriai, Lithuania, Russian Empire—d. Nov. 6, 1899, Naumiestis [now Kudirkos-Naumiestis]), Lithuanian physician, writer, and patriot who, through an underground literary-political journal, *Varpas* (1889–1905; "The Bell"), articulated a broadly representative protest against Russian attempts to submerge the awakening national culture of its Lithuanian provinces.

Educated in medicine, as well as in history and philosophy, Kudirka was working as a physician when, in 1889, he founded *Varpas,* to which he soon devoted his full energies. *Varpas,* published in Tilsit, Prussia, and smuggled into the Russian Empire, offered poems and satires by Kudirka and others, as well as vociferous attacks on tsarist Russification policies. The journal also stirred social reform and was influential in liberal and socialist circles.

Kudirka translated the works of the 19th-century Romantic poets Lord Byron (English), Friedrich Schiller (German), and Adam Mickiewicz (Polish) into Lithuanian. His satires were influenced by the Russian writers Nikolay Gogol, Nikolay Nekrasov, and Count Mikhail Yevgrafovich Saltykov (N. Shchedrin). The first harmonizer of Lithuanian folk songs, Kudirka was also the author of the Lithuanian national anthem. The city of his death, Naumiestis, was later renamed for him.

kudu, any of certain handsome, slender antelopes of the genus *Tragelaphus,* family Bovidae (order Artiodactyla). The greater kudu (*T. strepsiceros*) lives in small groups in hilly bush country or open woods of eastern and southern Africa. It stands about 1.3 m (51 inches) at the shoulder. It has a fringe on the throat and a crest of hair on the neck and back, and it is reddish brown to blue-gray, with a white mark between the eyes and narrow, vertical white stripes on the body. The male has long, divergent, corkscrewlike horns.

Greater kudu (*Tragelaphus strepsiceros*)

Jeanne White—The National Audubon Society Collection

The lesser kudu (*T. imberbis*) lives in pairs or small groups in the hot, open bush country of eastern Africa. It stands about 1 m (39 inches) at the shoulder and is gray-brown to blue-gray, with markings like those of the greater kudu, but with two white patches on the throat and no throat fringe. It has smaller, more tightly spiraled horns.

Both species browse on shrubs and tree leaves. Apart from mating periods, mature kudu live in segregated groups of males and females.

kudurru (Akkadian: "frontier," or "boundary"), type of boundary stone used by the Kassites of ancient Mesopotamia. A stone block or slab, it served as a record of a grant of land made by the king to a favoured person.

The original *kudurrus* were kept in temples, while clay copies were given to the landowners. On the stone were engraved the clauses of the contract, the images or symbols of the gods under whose protection the gift was placed,

Kudurru of Melishipak II, carved black limestone, *c.* 1200 BC, found at Susa; in the Louvre

Cliche Musees Nationaux, Paris

and the curse on those who violated the rights conferred. The *kudurrus* are important not only for economic and religious reasons but also as almost the only works of art surviving from the period of Kassite rule in Babylonia (*c.* 16th–*c.* 12th century BC).

Kudymkar, city and administrative centre of Komi-Permyak autonomous *okrug* (district), Perm *oblast* (province), western Russia. It lies along the Inva River at the latter's confluence with the Kuva River in the Northern Ural Mountains. Founded in the 16th century, Kudymkar grew rapidly after 1925, and it became a town in 1938. Industrial enterprises include timber milling and food processing. Institutes for forestry, agriculture, and teacher training are located in the city. Pop. (1993 est.) 33,400.

kudzu vine (*Pueraria lobata,* or *P. thunbergiana*), twining perennial vine that is a member of a genus belonging to the family Leguminosae. The kudzu is a fast-growing, woody, somewhat hairy vine that may grow to a length of 18 m (60 feet) in one season. It has large leaves, long racemes with late-blooming reddish purple flowers, and flat, hairy seed pods. The plant is native to China and Japan, where it was long grown for its edible, starchy roots and for a fibre made from its stems. The kudzu was transplanted to North America with the intention of using it to anchor steep banks of soil and thereby prevent erosion. The plant has become a rampant weed in parts of the southeastern United States, however, since it readily spreads over trees and shrubs as well as exposed soil. The kudzu vine is a useful fodder crop for livestock, however, as well as an attractive ornamental. Northern winters tend to kill the plant's stems but allow the roots to survive.

kuei, Pinyin GUI (Chinese: "ghost," or "demon"), in indigenous Chinese religion, a troublesome spirit that roams the world causing misfortune, illness, and death.

Kuei are spirits of individuals who were not properly buried or whose families neglected the proper memorial offerings; they lack the means to ascend to the spirit world, hence their malevolent disposition. In traditional China, numerous protective rituals and talismans were devised to ward *kuei* away from the family abode, and the main entrance was usually screened by a protective "shadow wall." *See also* shen.

kuei, Pinyin GUI, type of Chinese bronze vessel produced during the Shang (18th–12th century BC) and Chou (1111–255 BC) dynasties. There are many varieties of the *kuei,* which is a wide-mouthed container for food, but the typical form consists of a ring base and an ample, bowl-shaped body with slightly rounded sides. The vessel probably often had a lid. The *kuei* shape is known in pottery of the Neolithic Period (*c.* 3000–1500 BC).

In the bronze art of the Shang dynasty, the *kuei* commonly has four lugs (ear-shaped protuberances) equally spaced on a decorative band just below the rim. As the shape developed in the Chou dynasty, the lugs were replaced by two and sometimes four sturdy

Ceremonial bronze *kuei,* late 11th–early 10th century BC, Chou dynasty; in the Freer Gallery of Art, Washington, D.C.

By courtesy of the Smithsonian Institution, Freer Gallery of Art, Washington, D.C.

handles, often modeled with fanciful animal motifs. A substantial, boxlike stand often anchored the vessel in the Chou period.

Kuei, Prince of: *see* Chu Yu-lang.

K'uei Hsing, Pinyin KUI XING, in Chinese mythology, a brilliant but ugly dwarf who as the god of examinations became the deity of scholars who took imperial examinations.

K'uei Hsing, whose name before deification was Chung K'uei, is said to have passed his own examination with remarkable success but was denied the usual honours when the emperor beheld his ugly features. Brokenhearted, K'uei attempted suicide. He would have died, according to one account, had not an *ao* fish (or an *ao* turtle) borne him to safety. Another account says that K'uei actually died.

As depicted in art, K'uei bends forward like a runner, his left leg raised behind, the other sometimes balanced on the head of a fish (or giant sea turtle). Sometimes he sits astride the animal. In his right hand K'uei holds a writing brush to check off the most outstanding scholar candidates whose names are listed on a paper belonging to Yü Ti, the great Jade Emperor. In his left hand K'uei holds an official seal (some say a bushel basket to measure the talents of examinees).

Before the imperial examinations were discontinued early in the 1900s, virtually every Chinese scholar gave K'uei a place of honour in his home, with images and name tablets.

K'uei Hsing, the god of examinations, a calligraphic depiction by Ma Te-chao, 19th century; in a private collection

Some delightful representations of the god merely stylized the Chinese character of his name (*k'uei*) in such a way that a man in motion was clearly visible. The arms are extended, the left leg is raised behind, and the right foot is sometimes balanced on the Chinese character for *ao* (sea turtle).

K'uei Hsing resides among the stars as the deity in charge of the Ursa Major constellation. He is also one of two assistants assigned to help Wen Ti, the god of literature.

Kuei-lin, also spelled KWEILIN, formerly LIN-KUEI, Pinyin GUILIN, or LINGUI, large city in northeastern Kwangsi Chuang autonomous *ch'ü* (region), China. It stands on the west bank of the Kuei River, which is a tributary of the Hsi. The natural route centre of the Kuei River basin, Kuei-lin lies along the easiest of all the routes leading from central China to Kwangtung province—that between the headwaters of the Hsiang River in Hunan province and the upper waters of the Kuei River. The two streams were linked in early times by the remarkable Ling Canal (*q.v.*), which thereby made it possible for small craft to pass between the Yangtze (north) and Hsi (south) river systems.

When the first emperor of the Ch'in dynasty (221–206 BC) undertook his great campaign against the state of Nan-yüeh in Kwangtung, his forces came by this route and are said to have set up the first administration in the area. In the 1st century BC, the Han dynasty (206 BC–AD 220) established a county seat there, called Shih-an. The modern county name, Lin-kuei, was first given during the T'ang dynasty (618–907). Under the Ming (1368–1644) and Ch'ing (1644–1911) dynasties, it became Kuei-lin superior prefecture; under the Ch'ing it was also the provincial capital of Kwangsi. In 1912 it reverted to county status, as Kuei-lin, and the provincial capital was moved to Nan-ning. It again became provincial capital in 1936 but was replaced for a second time by Nan-ning in 1949.

Kuei-lin has long been an important centre of trade and administration because of its location on an agriculturally rich valley floor that is also the easiest route south from Hunan. In 1939 the Hunan-Kwangsi railway was extended through Kuei-lin to Liu-chou via this corridor.

Kuei-lin has always been a handicraft centre, but until 1949 the only signs of modern industry were a power plant, a cement works, and some small textile mills. Since the 1950s Kuei-lin has developed industries engaged in the manufacture of chemicals, engineering and agricultural equipment, and paper, and it also has textile and cotton yarn factories. Food processing and the processing of local agricultural produce (especially sugar and oils) remain the most important industry. Kuei-lin is also a cultural centre.

As a major centre of Buddhism in the 7th century, it had many famous monasteries. Today the city has a university and a medical college. Kuei-lin (its name means "forest of sweet osmanthus") is set in a landscape of outstanding natural beauty and is renowned for its karst formations. Deep erosion of the limestone plateau has left a multitude of tall needle-shaped pinnacles out of whose steep sides trees sprout improbably. These fantastical mountains have long been memorialized in Chinese painting and poetry. The city also has many caves, the largest and most spectacular of which is Lu Ti Yen (Reed Flute Cave). Pop. (1999 est.) 458,333.

Kuei River, Wade-Giles romanization KUEI CHIANG, Pinyin GUI JIANG, conventional KWEI KIANG, northern tributary of the Hsi River, southern China. The Kuei River rises in the Mao-erh Mountains to the north of Kuei-lin in the northern part of the Kwangsi Chuang Autonomous Region and flows southward to join the Hsi River at Wu-chou on the border of Kwangsi Chuang and Kwangtung province. The level of the river varies from season to season, and its course has many dangerous rapids. Shallow-draft junks can reach P'ing-lo and, during the high-water season, get as far as Kuei-lin.

Above Kuei-lin the ancient Ling Canal, constructed in the 2nd century BC, leads over the watershed to connect the Kuei River with the upper waters of the Hsiang River in Hunan province. The Kuei River is also followed by a main highway from Hunan into Kwangsi Chuang and Kwangtung; the river itself serves as an important means of transporting the timber that is felled in the forests of northeastern Kwangsi Chuang to the Hsi River and thence to Canton.

Kuei-yang, also spelled KWEIYANG, Pinyin GUIYANG, city in central Kweichow *sheng* (province), China. Kuei-yang is the provincial capital. The city is situated on the Nan-ming River, a headstream of the Wu River, which eventually joins the Yangtze River at Fou-ling in Szechwan province. Kuei-yang is a natural route centre, with comparatively easy access northward to Szechwan and northeast to Hunan province.

Originally the area was populated by non-Chinese. The Sui dynasty (AD 581–618) had a commandery there, and the T'ang dynasty (618–907) a prefecture. They were, however, no more than military outposts, and it was not until the Yüan (Mongol) invasion of southwest China in 1279 that the area was made the seat of an army and a "pacification office." Chinese settlement in the area also began at that time, and, under the Ming (1368–1644) and Ch'ing (1644–1911) dynasties, the town became the seat of a superior prefecture named Kuei-yang.

Locally Kuei-yang was an important administrative and commercial centre with two distinct merchant communities, consisting of the Szechwanese, who lived in the "new" northern part of the city, and those from Hunan, Canton, and Kwangsi province, who lived in the "old" southern part. Nevertheless, until the Sino-Japanese War (1937–45), Kuei-yang was no more than the capital of one of China's least-developed provinces. As elsewhere in the southwest, considerable economic progress was made under the special circumstances of wartime. Highway communications with K'un-ming in Yunnan province and with Chungking in Szechwan (China's wartime provisional capital) and into Hunan were established. Work was begun on a railway from Liu-chou in Kwangsi, and after 1949 this development was accelerated. Kuei-yang has subsequently become a major provincial city and industrial base. In 1959 the rail link to Kwangsi was completed, and other lines also lead north to Chungking, west to K'un-ming, and east to Ch'ang-sha.

Coal is mined in the locality of Kuei-yang and An-shun, and there are large thermal generating plants at Kuei-yang and Tu-yün, supplying electricity for the city's industry. A large iron and steel plant came into production in Kuei-yang in 1960, supplying the local machinery-manufacturing industry. Large deposits of bauxite have been discovered to the north, and by the 1970s Kuei-yang had become a major producer of aluminum. Kuei-yang also manufactures industrial and mining equipment, as well as railway vehicles and equipment. It has a large chemical industry, producing fertilizers, and a rubber industry, manufacturing automobile tires. Kuei-yang also has textile plants and makes glass, paper, and other consumer goods.

The city is the cultural centre of Kweichow province and has a university, a teacher-training college, and a medical school. Pop. (1999 est.) 1,320,566.

Kūfah, also spelled KUFA, medieval city of Iraq that was a centre of Arab culture and learning from the 8th to the 10th century. It was founded in 638 as a garrison town by ʿUmar I, the second caliph. The city lay on the Hindīyah branch of the Euphrates River, about 7 miles (11 km) northeast of an-Najaf. It was populated largely by South Arabians and Iranians and served as the seat of the governor of Iraq, sometimes sharing this position with its sister city, Basra. In 655 the Muslims of Kūfah became the first to support the claims of ʿAlī, son-in-law of the prophet Muḥammad, against the caliph ʿUthmān; Kūfah subsequently served as ʿAlī's capital (656–661). Throughout Umayyad rule Kūfah remained a constant source of unrest. In 683, in the civil war following the death of the caliph Yazīd I, it recognized as caliph ʿAbd Allāh ibn az-Zubayr; then in 685 it violently resisted the Shīʿite doctrine forced on it by al-Mukhtār ibn Abū ʿUbayd at-Thaqafī.

Occupied by the ʿAbbāsids in 749, the city was maintained as an administrative capital for some years, until the founding of Baghdad. After being sacked by the Qarmaṭians in 924–925, 927, and 937, Kūfah declined steadily and was almost deserted in the 14th century when it was visited by the geographer Ibn Baṭṭūṭah. In its prime in the 2nd and 3rd Muslim centuries, Kūfah, along with Basra, was a centre for the study of Arabic grammar, philology, literary criticism, and belles lettres.

Kūfic script, in calligraphy, earliest extant Islāmic style of handwritten alphabet that was used by early Muslims to record the Qurʾān. This angular, slow-moving, dignified script was also used on tombstones and coins as well as for inscriptions on buildings. Some experts distinguish Kūfi proper from Meccan and Medinese scripts, which were also used to copy the Qurʾān.

The script was called Kūfi because it was thought to have been developed at Kūfah in Iraq—an early Islāmic centre of culture. Simple Kūfi was developed early in the Islāmic era; the earliest surviving copies of the Qurʾān—from the 8th to the 10th century—were copied in it. Later a floral Kūfi flourished, and several other varieties of the script developed, including foliated Kūfi, plaited or interlaced Kūfi, bordered Kūfi, and squared Kūfi. It went out of general use about the 12th century, although it continued to be used as a decorative element to contrast with the scripts that superseded it.

Kufrah, Al-, also spelled CUFRA, oasis group (about 30 miles [48 km] long and 12 miles [19 km] wide), southeastern Libya, in an elliptical trough near the centre of the Libyan Desert. Astride ancient caravan routes, the oasis was a thieves' stronghold until 1895, when it became the headquarters of the Sanūsī, a militant Muslim religious fraternity. The Italians began an aerial offensive against the oasis, the last haven of the Sanūsī, in 1930 and occupied it from 1931.

The main towns are Al-Jawf, Aṭ-Ṭulaylīb, and Aṭ-Ṭallāb; Aṭ-Ṭāj, on a sandstone plateau, has a Sanūsī religious school. There are extensive date groves, and an underground reservoir provides irrigation. Livestock raising is important. Pop. (latest est.) 12,606.

Kufstein, town, Tirol *Bundesland* (federal state), western Austria. It lies along the Inn River, between two ranges, the Kaiser Mountains and the Bavarian Alps, near the Bavarian (German) border. First mentioned in 788, it was held by the bishops of Regensburg under the dukes of Bavaria in the 13th and 14th centuries and was chartered in 1393. It was taken by the Holy Roman emperor Maximilian I in 1504 and thereafter belonged to Austria, except during a Bavarian occupation (1703–04) and a period of Bavarian rule from 1805 to 1814.

Geroldseck Fortress in Kufstein, Austria
S. Bohnacker—Bavaria-Verlag

The Geroldseck Fortress in the town, built in the early 13th century, was converted into a strong bastion by Maximilian. It now houses a local museum and the great "Heroes' Organ" (*Heldenorgel;* 1931), named for the daily recitals played to honour the war dead. A popular summer resort and winter-sports centre, Kufstein manufactures skis, glass, armatures, and metalware. Pop. (1998 est.) 14,931.

Kuft (Egypt): *see* Qifṭ.

Kuga Sorta (Mari: "Big Candle"), pacifist and theocratic movement among the Mari (or Cheremis), a Finno-Ugric tribal people living chiefly in Mari republic, Russia. The emergence of the cult around 1870 was an attempt by the Mari—who were nominally Christianized during the 16th–19th centuries—to resist Russian acculturation by a synthesis of their own religion with Christian elements.

The movement takes its name from the large candle central to its worship. The ritual is conducted in houses or forest groves, without priests or images. An ascetic ethic includes taboos on certain foods and stimulants and enjoins love, tolerance, respect for nature, and rejection of modern goods and medicine. Adherents believe that Christ was the greatest of prophets. Ancient marriage ceremonies, the cult of the dead, and mythology of the spirit world represent the Mari element in the religion, which has resisted the disapproval of both tsarist and Soviet governments.

Kühlmann, Richard von (b. May 17, 1873, Constantinople, Ottoman Empire [now Istanbul, Turkey]—d. Feb. 16, 1948, Ohlstadt, W.Ger.), German foreign minister for 10 months during World War I, who led the German delegation that concluded the Treaty of Brest-Litovsk with Russia (March 1918) and the Treaty of Bucharest with Romania (May 1918).

Kühlmann, 1948
Suddeutscher Verlag

Kühlmann, son of the director general of the Anatolian Railways, entered the German foreign service in 1899 and was posted to St. Petersburg, Tehrān, Tangier, Washington, The Hague, and then (1908–14) London. After the outbreak of World War I he served as German minister at The Hague and, later, as ambassador at Constantinople. On Aug. 6, 1917, he was appointed secretary of state for foreign affairs. The following June he told the Reichstag that the war could not be decided by military measures alone. As a result, the supreme army command forced his dismissal.

Kuhn, Richard (b. Dec. 3, 1900, Vienna, Austria-Hungary—d. Aug. 1, 1967, Heidelberg, W.Ger.), German biochemist awarded the 1938 Nobel Prize for Chemistry for work on carotenoids and vitamins. Forbidden by the Nazis to accept the award, he finally received his diploma and gold medal after World War II.

Kuhn took his doctorate from the University of Munich in 1922 for work on enzymes under Richard Willstätter. He spent 1926–29 at the technical school in Zürich and then became professor at the University of Heidelberg and director of the Kaiser Wilhelm Institute for Medical Research (later renamed for Max Planck) at Heidelberg.

Kuhn investigated the structure of compounds related to the carotenoids, the fat-soluble yellow colouring agents widely distributed in nature. He discovered at least eight carotenoids, prepared them in pure form, and determined their constitution. He discovered that one was necessary for the fertilization of certain algae. Simultaneously with Paul Karrer he announced the constitution of vitamin B_2 and was the first to isolate a gram of it. With coworkers he also isolated vitamin B_6. From 1948 he was an editor of *Justus Liebigs Annalen der Chemie* ("Justus Liebig's Annals of Chemistry").

Kuhn, Thomas S., in full THOMAS SAMUEL KUHN (b. July 18, 1922, Cincinnati, Ohio, U.S.—d. June 17, 1996, Cambridge, Mass.), American historian of science noted for *The Structure of Scientific Revolutions* (1962), one of the most influential works of history and philosophy written in the 20th century.

Kuhn earned bachelor's (1943) and master's (1946) degrees in physics at Harvard University but obtained his Ph.D. (1949) there in the history of science. He taught the history or philosophy of science at Harvard (1951–56), the University of California at Berkeley (1956–64), Princeton University (1964–79), and the Massachusetts Institute of Technology (1979–91).

In his first book, *The Copernican Revolution* (1957), Kuhn studied the development of the heliocentric theory of the solar system during the Renaissance. In his landmark second book, *The Structure of Scientific Revolutions,* he argued that scientific research and thought are defined by "paradigms," or conceptual world-views, that consist of formal theories, classic experiments, and trusted methods. Scientists typically accept a prevailing paradigm and try to extend its scope by refining theories, explaining puzzling data, and establishing more precise measures of standards and phenomena. Eventually, however, their efforts may generate insoluble theoretical problems or experimental anomalies that expose a paradigm's inadequacies or contradict it altogether. This accumulation of difficulties triggers a crisis that can only be resolved by an intellectual revolution that replaces an old paradigm with a new one. The overthrow of Ptolemaic cosmology by Copernican heliocentrism, and the displacement of Newtonian mechanics by quantum physics and general relativity, are both examples of major paradigm shifts.

Kuhn questioned the traditional conception of scientific progress as a gradual, cumulative acquisition of knowledge based on rationally chosen experimental frameworks. Instead, he argued that the paradigm determines the kinds of experiments scientists perform, the types of questions they ask, and the problems they consider important. A shift in the paradigm alters the fundamental concepts underlying research and inspires new standards of evidence, new research techniques, and new pathways of theory and experiment that are radically incommensurate with the old ones.

Kuhn's book revolutionized the history and philosophy of science, and his concept of paradigm shifts was extended to such disciplines as political science, economics, sociology, and even to business management. Kuhn's later works were a collection of essays, *The Essential Tension* (1977), and the technical study *Black-Body Theory and the Quantum Discontinuity* (1978).

Kuhn, Walt (b. Oct. 27, 1880, New York, N.Y., U.S.—d. July 13, 1949, White Plains, N.Y.), American painter instrumental in staging the Armory Show (New York City, 1913), the first exhibition of modern art in the United States.

"The Blue Clown," oil on canvas by Walt Kuhn, 1931; in the Whitney Museum of American Art, New York City
By courtesy of the Whitney Museum of American Art, New York City

Kuhn, a professional bicycle racer in the 1890s, moved in 1899 to San Francisco, where he worked as a cartoonist. He later studied art informally in Paris, then contributed cartoons to *Life, Puck, Judge,* and newspapers in New York City. Kuhn was also a consulting architect, set designer, and art promoter. As secretary of the Association of American Painters and Sculptors, he helped organize the Armory Show. After 1925 Kuhn devoted himself to painting, translating an early love of the circus and the theatre into simple and austere paintings of clowns, showgirls, and acrobats. They are bold and unpolished, with a slightly Spanish flavour; the figures are especially remarkable for dark penetrating eyes that are sometimes heavily outlined.

Kuhnau, Johann (b. April 6, 1660, Geising, Saxony [Germany]—d. June 5, 1722, Leipzig), German composer of church cantatas and early keyboard sonatas.

Kuhnau studied music from boyhood and became cantor at Zittau. From 1684 he was organist at the Church of St. Thomas in Leipzig and was cantor from 1701 until his death. He was succeeded at St. Thomas by J.S. Bach. In 1700, while also studying law, Kuhnau became musical director of the University of Leipzig and of two churches. He wrote 14 annual cycles of church cantatas, of which only a few remain, but he is best known for his clavier compositions. He introduced into many of his dance suites a prelude in free style. His sonatas are characterized by a feeling for the keyboard as an instrument of romantic expression. The biblical sonatas are program music illustrating such stories as that of David and Goliath. Kuhnau also wrote a satiric novel, *Der musickalische Quacksalber* (1700; "The Musical Charlatan"), deriding Italian musical affectation.

Kui Xing (Chinese god): *see* K'uei Hsing.

Kuibyshev (Russia): *see* Samara.

Kuiper, Gerard Peter, original name GERRIT PIETER KUIPER (b. Dec. 7, 1905, Harenkarspel, Neth.—d. Dec. 23, 1973, Mexico City, Mexico), Dutch-American astronomer known especially for his discoveries and theories concerning the solar system.

Kuiper graduated from the University of Leiden in 1927 and received his Ph.D. from that school in 1933. That same year he moved to the United States, where he became a naturalized citizen (1937). He joined the staff of Yerkes Observatory of the University of Chicago in 1936, twice serving as director (1947–49 and 1957–60) of both Yerkes and McDonald observatories. Kuiper founded the Lunar and Planetary Laboratory at the University of Arizona in 1960 and served as its director until his death.

After conducting research in stellar astronomy, Kuiper shifted his focus to planetary research in the 1940s. In 1944 he was able to confirm the presence of a methane atmosphere around Saturn's moon Titan. In 1948 he predicted (correctly) that carbon dioxide is a major component of the atmosphere of Mars, and he also correctly predicted that the rings of Saturn are composed of particles of ice. That same year he discovered the fifth moon of Uranus (Miranda), and in 1949 he discovered the second moon of Neptune (Nereid). In 1950 he obtained the first reliable measurement of the visual diameter of Pluto. In 1956 he proved that Mars's polar icecaps are composed of frozen water, not of carbon dioxide as had been previously assumed. Kuiper's 1964 prediction of what the surface of the Moon would be like to walk on ("it would be like crunchy snow") was verified by the astronaut Neil Armstrong in 1969.

In 1949 Kuiper proposed an influential theory of the origin of the solar system, suggesting that the planets had formed by the condensation of a large cloud of gas around the Sun. He also suggested the possible existence of a disk-shaped belt of comets orbiting the Sun at a distance of 500 to 1,000 astronomical units. The existence of this belt of millions of comets was verified in the 1990s, and it was named the Kuiper belt.

Kuiper Airborne Observatory, a C-141 jet transport aircraft, which made astronomical observations (1971–95) at high altitudes that, due to atmospheric absorption, could not be achieved with telescopes on Earth's surface. The observatory, equipped with a 0.9-m (36-inch) Cassegrain reflecting telescope, was typically flown at an altitude of 12,500 m (41,000 feet) to measure infrared radiation emitted by planets, stars, galaxies, and other cosmic objects. Its major discoveries included the rings of the planet Uranus, as well as new stars and molecules in interstellar space and in planetary atmospheres. Named for American astronomer Gerard P. Kuiper, it was operated by the National Aeronautics and Space Administration. It was superseded by a more sophisticated airborne observatory called SOFIA, built in the early 21st century.

Kujavia, also spelled KUJAWY, Latin CUJAVIA, lowland region of north-central Poland, bounded by the Vistula and Noteć rivers.

When King Bolesław III the Wry-Mouthed (ruled Poland 1102–38) divided his kingdom among his sons in 1138, Kujavia became part of the Mazovian-Kujavian duchy; later it was separated from Mazovia (1233) and subdivided into several duchies. In the beginning of the 14th century, however, one of its dukes, Władysław I the Short, undertook the reunification of Poland, and by 1363 all the Kujavian duchies had been reincorporated into two provinces (*województwa*)—Brześć Kujawski (the southeastern portion) and Inowrocław (the northwestern portion).

Prussia gained control of Inowrocław by the First Partition of Poland (1772) and acquired Brześć Kujawski by the Second Partition (1793). The two provinces were subsequently reunited as the province of Bydgoszcz and incorporated into the Grand Duchy of Warsaw, which was created by Napoleon in 1807. But in 1815, when the duchy was dismembered, only the eastern section of Kujavia was included in the newly formed Congress Kingdom of Poland; the remainder was returned to Prussia. In 1918 newly independent Poland reabsorbed all of Kujavia, dividing that region between the provinces of Pomerania (Polish: Pomorze) and Warsaw. In 1945 the entire area was included in the province of Bydgoszcz and now occupies a part of Kujawsko-Pomorskie.

Kujavia, *c.* 1320

Kujawsko-Pomorskie, *województwo* (province), north-central Poland. It comprises the former provinces (1975–98) of Bydgoszcz and Toruń, as well as a portion of Włocławek. It is predominantly a low-lying lakeland, drained by the Vistula, Drwęca, Brda, and Noteć rivers. The provincial capitals are Bydgoszcz and Toruń, both centres for the chemical and machine-building industries. The land is very fertile and primarily devoted to agriculture, notably the production of sugar beets, wheat, and milk. Northern recreational areas, such as Tuchola National Park and the resorts in Ciechocinek, are popular with tourists, as is the historic centre of Toruń. Area 6,938 square miles (17,970 square km). Pop. (2003 est.) 2,068,400.

Kūkā (religious sect): *see* Nāmdhārī.

Kūkai, original name SAEKI MAO, posthumous name KŌBŌ DAISHI (b. July 27, 774, Byōbugaura [modern Zentsūji], Japan—d. April 22, 835, Mount Kōya, near modern Wakayama), one of the best known and most beloved Buddhist saints in Japan, founder of the Shingon ("True Word") school of Buddhism that emphasizes spells, magic formulas, ceremonials, and masses for the dead. He contributed greatly to the development of Japanese art and literature and pioneered in public education.

Kūkai was born into an aristocratic family and as a youth was trained in the Confucian Classics. In 791, at the age of 17, he is said to have completed his first major work, the *Sangō shiiki* ("Essentials of the Three Teachings"), in which he proclaimed the superiority of Buddhism over Confucianism and Taoism. Desiring to learn more about Buddhism, Kūkai went to China in 804. In the T'ang-dynasty capital of Ch'ang-an, he met the great master of esoteric Buddhism, Hui-kuo (746–805; Japanese: Keika), and became the master's favourite disciple, receiving his secret teachings when he lay dying. Returning to Japan in 806, Kūkai was given imperial sanction to promulgate his new doctrines. In 816 he began building a monastery on Mount Kōya, in west-central Japan. This grew into one of the largest and most vigorous monastic complexes in the country, and the Shingon sect became one of the most popular forms of Japanese Buddhism.

Besides his role as philosopher and religious leader, Kūkai was also a poet, an artist, and a calligrapher. He exerted a great influence on the development of Japanese religious art over the next two centuries. In fact, much of the art that survives from this period depicts Shingon Buddhist deities. His major work, the *Jūjū shinron* ("The Ten Stages of Consciousness"), written in Chinese in a poetic style, classified Confucianism, Taoism, and all the existing Buddhist literature into 10 stages, the last and highest stage being that of Shingon philosophy. This work assured Kūkai a leading rank among the intellectual figures of Japanese Buddhism.

BIBLIOGRAPHY. Yoshito S. Hakeda (trans.), *Kūkai: Major Works* (1972), includes essays on Kūkai's life and thought.

Kukenaam Falls, Spanish SALTO CUQUENÁN, high waterfalls on the Guyana-Venezuelan border. They spring from a table mountain, Kukenaam (8,620 feet [2,627 m]), to the northwest of Mount Roraima (9,094 feet) and are the beginning of the Cuquenán River, a tributary of the Caroni River. The falls have a 2,000-foot (600-metre) drop, one of the highest drops in South America.

Kukhak (ancient Korean university): *see* Sŏnggyun'guan.

kukri snake, any of 50 to 60 species of snakes constituting the genus *Oligodon* of the family Colubridae. The snakes are named for their enlarged hind teeth, which are broad and curved like the Gurkha sword of this name. They occur in East and South Asia.

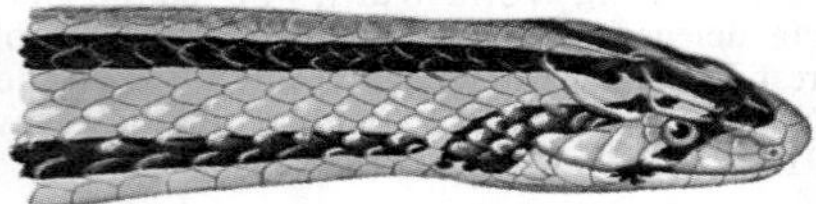
Kukri snake (*Oligodon*)
Painting by David M. Dennis

All kukri snakes are egg layers, and most are less than 90 cm (35 inches) long. They feed largely on bird and reptile eggs.

kul, also spelled KULA (Sanskrit: "assembly," or "family"), throughout India, except in the south, a family unit or, in some instances, an extended family. Most commonly *kul* refers to one contemporarily existing family, though sometimes this sense is extended—for example, when "family" implies a sense of lineage. As such, *kul* describes, in the Indian context, the patrilocal family unit, often made up of three generations who live together in a compound headed by the grandfather or his eldest son, into which the brides of the various generations are absorbed. The family holds its property in common, as division of possessions is traditionally frowned upon.

The splitting up of the joint family and the reforming into new units normally takes place on the death of the grandfather. The joint family system had a beneficial effect on the consolidation of landholdings and the sharing of resources but is steadily disappearing under modern pressures of economic mobility, improved communications, and widening job opportunities.

Special usages of *kul,* or *kula,* are found in such appellations as Agnikula ("Family of the Fire God"), a putative ancient dynasty from which the Rājputs of Rājasthān derive their claim to be Kshatriyas (nobles). Another is the *gurukula* ("guru's family") system of education, in which a pupil, after his initiation, lives in the house of his guru, or teacher, and studies the Veda and other subjects under his guru's guidance.

kula, exchange system among the people of the Trobriand Islands of southeast Melanesia, in which permanent contractual partners trade traditional valuables following an established ceremonial pattern and trade route. In this system, described by the Polish-born British anthropologist Bronisław Malinowski, only two kinds of articles, traveling in opposite directions around a rough geographic ring several hundred miles in circumference, were exchanged. These were red shell necklaces and white shell bracelets, which were not exchanged outside the ceremonial system. *Kula* objects, which sometimes had names and histories attached, were not owned in order to be used but rather to acquire prestige and rank.

Every detail of the transaction was regulated by traditional rules and conventions, and some acts were accompanied by rituals and ceremonies. A limited number of men could take part in the *kula,* each man keeping an article for a relatively short period before passing it on to one of his partners from whom he received the opposite item in exchange. The partnerships between men, involving mutual duties and obligations, were permanent and lifelong. Thus the network of relationships around the *kula* served to link many tribes by providing allies and communication of material and nonmaterial cultural elements to distant areas.

Kula carpet, Kula also spelled KOULA, or KULAH, floor covering handwoven in Kula, a town east of İzmir, in western Turkey. Kula prayer rugs were produced throughout the 19th century and into the 20th and have been favourites among collectors. Usually the arch (to indicate the direction of Mecca, the Holy City) is low and straight-sided; the columnar sides of the prayer niche may appear as broad, ribbonlike pendant forms. Central motifs are sometimes highly elaborate.

Kula prayer rug from Western Anatolia, 19th century; in the Metropolitan Museum of Art, New York City

By courtesy of the Metropolitan Museum of Art, New York City, gift of J.F. Ballard; photograph, Otto E. Nelson

Early Kula prayer rugs have strong reds and good blues; but the dyeing practices rapidly became slack, so that in most later examples the red has been exchanged for an assortment of muddy brown and yellow shades, often combined with a good surviving blue. Early carpets are not as finely woven as Ghiordes carpets, and late ones are quite loosely made. Additional types were produced, such as the Kumurju Kulas, dark carpets that often reproduce the designs of Transylvanian rugs, with prominent vases and yellow borders. Like other great carpet-weaving centres in Turkey, Kula produced many crudely woven carpets for the European market in the late 19th century.

kulak (Russian: "fist"), in Russian and Soviet history, a wealthy or prosperous peasant, generally characterized as one who owned a relatively large farm and several head of cattle and horses and who was financially capable of employing hired labour and leasing land. Before the Russian Revolution of 1917, the kulaks were major figures in the peasant villages. They often lent money, provided mortgages, and played central roles in the villages' social and administrative affairs.

During the War Communism period (1918–21), the Soviet government undermined the kulaks' position by organizing committees of poor peasants to administer the villages and to supervise the requisitioning of grain from the richer peasants. But the introduction in 1921 of the New Economic Policy favoured the kulaks. Although the Soviet government considered the kulaks to be capitalists and, therefore, enemies of socialism, it adopted various incentives to encourage peasants to increase agricultural production and enrich themselves. The most successful peasants (less than 4 percent) became kulaks and assumed traditional roles in the village social structure, often rivaling the authority of the new Soviet officials in village affairs.

In 1927 the Soviet government began to shift its peasant policy by increasing the kulaks' taxes and restricting their right to lease land; in 1929 it began a drive for rapid collectivization of agriculture. The kulaks vigorously opposed the efforts to force the peasants to give up their small privately owned farms and join large cooperative agricultural establishments. At the end of 1929 a campaign to "liquidate the kulaks as a class" ("dekulakization") was launched by the government. By 1934, when approximately 75 percent of the farms in the Soviet Union had been collectivized, most kulaks—as well as millions of other peasants who had opposed collectivization—had been deported to remote regions of the Soviet Union or arrested and their land and property confiscated.

Kuldja, also spelled KULJA, Chinese (Wade-Giles) I-NING, or (Pinyin) GULJA, or YINING, city in western Uighur Autonomous Region of Sinkiang, China. It is the chief city, agricultural market, and commercial centre of the I-li River valley, which is a principal route from the Sinkiang region into Central Asia. The valley is far wetter than any other part of Sinkiang and has rich grazing land. Kuldja has been a strategic centre since early times, being known to the T'ang dynasty (618–907) by the name K'ung-yüeh and to the Mongols as Almarikh, under which name it became the capital of the 13th-century Mongol conqueror Chagatai Khan. It first came under direct Chinese control in 1755–57, during the wars with the Dzungars. The Chinese subsequently established several forts near the I-li River. In the 1870s the area figured in a prolonged border dispute between China and Russia. Kuldja is a centre for textile manufacturing, food processing, and leather production. The valley is largely under cultivation, though the uplands still support the herding of sheep, cattle, and horses. The population is mostly Kazak, but around Kuldja there are a large settlement of Sibo (Tungusic) people and some Mongols. Pop. (1990 est.) 177,193.

Kuldja, Treaty of, Kuldja also spelled KULJA (1851), treaty between China and Russia regulating trade between the two countries. The treaty was preceded by a gradual Russian advance throughout the 18th century into Kazakstan.

Encouraged by the success of Britain, France, and other Western powers in extracting concessions from China in the wake of the trading conflict known as the first Opium War (1839–42), Russia began to send merchants into Chinese Central Asia in the mid-19th century. The resulting Treaty of Kuldja gave the Russians their first major foothold in the area.

Similar to other previous agreements between Russia and China, the treaty was negotiated on general terms of equality and reciprocity. It granted the Russians trading rights in the area, specifying the trade routes, the times of year trade was allowed, warehousing facilities, and place and number of official residences. It also established that the Russians were not subject to Chinese law while in the territory but could be under the control of their own consul at Chuguchak (modern T'a-ch'eng) and Kuldja, the city where the treaty was signed and the major city of the territory. The treaty was followed by an accelerated Russian expansion into Central Asia.

Kulebaki, city, Nizhegorod *oblast* (province), western Russia. It lies in the valley of the Tesha River, which is a tributary of the Oka River. The economic base of the city is metallurgy, including steel mills and the production of transportation equipment. Flour and timber milling are also important. A technical college in the city concentrates on metallurgical studies. Pop. (1991 est.) 45,700.

Kuleshov, Lev Vladimirovich (b. Jan. 1 [Jan. 13, New Style], 1899, Tambov, Russia—d. March 29, 1970, Moscow), Soviet film theorist and director who taught that structuring a film by montage (the cutting and editing of film and the juxtaposing of the images) was the most important aspect of filmmaking.

In 1910, after his father's death, Kuleshov and his mother moved to Moscow, where four years later he began to study painting. The next year he began designing sets for the Khanzhonkov Film Studio in Moscow and in 1917 directed his first film, *Proyekt inzhinera Prayta* (*The Project of Engineer Prite*), in which he experimented with montage and the effective use of close-ups. In the next 10 years he perfected his style in films such as *Na krasnom fronte* (1920; *On the Red Front*), the first Soviet film to combine documentary shots with acted sequences, and *Po zakonu* (1926; *According to the Law*), based on a Jack London story of three people snowbound in a cabin for an entire winter.

Kuleshov also trained actors and directors at the Kuleshov Workshop, which had been formed in 1920. After being officially censured in 1935 for emphasizing the technical composition of films rather than their social content, he produced no major films. His major theoretical works are *Art of the Cinema* (1929), *Practice of Film Direction* (1935), and *Fundamentals of Film Direction* (1941).

Kulhwch and Olwen, Welsh CULHWCH AC OLWEN (*c.* 1100), Welsh prose work that is one of the earliest-known Arthurian romances. It is a lighthearted tale that skillfully incorporates themes from mythology, folk literature, and history. The earliest form of the story survives in an early 14th-century manuscript called *The White Book of Rhydderch,* and the first translation of the story into modern English was made by Lady Charlotte Guest from *The Red Book of Hergest* (*c.* 1375–1425) and was included in her translation of *Mabinogion*.

The story uses the folk formula of a stepmother's attempt to thwart her stepson. Kulhwch, after refusing to marry the daughter of his stepmother, is told by her that he shall never wed until he wins Olwen, the daughter of the malevolent giant Yspadadden Penkawr. Because of a prophecy that if she marries, he will die, Olwen's father first tries to kill Kulhwch but then agrees to the marriage if Kulhwch performs several perilous feats and brings him the 13 treasures he desires. Kulhwch is aided in several of his adventures by his cousin Arthur and some of Arthur's men, including Kei (Sir Kay) and Gwalchmei (Sir Gawain). Kulhwch returns to Yspadadden with only part of his goal accomplished, kills him, and marries Olwen.

Kuliab (Tajikistan): *see* Kulyab.

Kulikovo, Battle of (Sept. 8, 1380), military engagement in which the Russians defeated the forces of the Golden Horde, thereby demonstrating the developing independence of the Russian lands from Mongol rule (which had been imposed in 1240). The battle occurred when Mamai, a Mongol general who effectively ruled the western portion of the Golden Horde, invaded the Russian lands. The Russians, whose respect for Mongol authority had been declining—particularly since a series of dynastic quarrels following the death of the khan Janibeg (1357) had weakened the Horde—resisted Mamai.

Led by Dmitry Ivanovich, prince of Moscow

and grand prince of Vladimir, the Russians met Mamai's forces at Kulikovo Pole ("Snipes' Field") on the upper Don River before Mamai's Lithuanian allies could join him. Although the Mongol armies gained an early advantage, they fled when the Russians sent in a reserve force. The battle was extremely bloody and casualties on both sides were heavy. In honour of the victory on the Don, Dmitry assumed the surname Donskoy ("of the Don").

But the great victory of the Russians was of little political consequence. Two years later (1382) Tokhtamysh, the khan who had overthrown Mamai in 1381 and extended his control over the entire Golden Horde, invaded Russia. He devastated the lands, looted and burned Moscow, and forced the Russians to recognize once again the suzerainty of the Golden Horde.

Kulin (d. 1204 or after), ruler of Bosnia from about 1180 as ban, or viceroy, of the king of Hungary.

During Kulin's rule, Hungarian influence dwindled and Bosnia functioned as a largely independent state. The country also enjoyed a period of peace and relative prosperity through increased trade. From the 1190s a number of regional rulers and Roman Catholic church leaders, most of whom had ulterior political motives, accused Kulin of sheltering Bogomil heretics in his domain. Some even claimed that the Bosnians had adopted Bogomilism on a large scale. In response, Kulin called a special church council at Bolino Polje in 1203, at which Bosnian church leaders affirmed the authority of the pope and committed themselves to a series of reforms correcting lax religious practices.

Kulja, Treaty of (1851): *see* Kuldja, Treaty of.

Kuljab (Tajikistan): *see* Kulyab.

Külpe, Oswald (b. Aug. 3, 1862, Kandau, Courland, Russian Empire [now Kandava, Latvia]—d. Dec. 30, 1915, Munich, Ger.), German psychologist and philosopher regarded as the guiding force behind the experimental study of thought processes identified with the Würzburg school of psychology.

After completing a dissertation on sensual feeling for Wilhelm Wundt, the founder of experimental psychology, at the University of Leipzig (1887), Külpe spent eight years at the Leipzig laboratory. During most of that time he acted as Wundt's assistant. In 1888 Külpe became *Privatdozent* (lecturer) at the university. He wrote *Grundriss der Psychologie* (1893; *Outlines of Psychology*), in which he defined psychology as a science concerned with experiences dependent on the experiencing individual and outlined the findings of experimental psychology.

In 1894 Külpe was appointed professor at the University of Würzburg, and under his inspiration and direction the institute published some 50 experimental studies before his departure for the University of Bonn in 1909. Best known is his research on the effects of attitudes and tasks on perception and the course of recall and thought.

In 1913 Külpe took a post at the University of Munich. At the time of his death he was writing another systematic treatment of experimental psychology. *Die Realisierung,* 3 vol. (1912–23; "Realization"), considered to be a valuable contribution to the theory of knowledge, was his last published work.

Kültepe (Turkish: "Ash Hill"), ancient mound covering the Bronze Age city of Kanesh, in central Turkey. Kültepe was known to archaeologists during the 19th century, but it began to attract particular attention as the reputed source of so-called Cappadocian tablets in Old Assyrian cuneiform writing and language. Finally, in 1925, Bedřich Hrozný found the source of the tablets in a fortified crescent-shaped area to the south and southeast of the mound proper. That area, called Karum Kanesh by archaeologists, had been inhabited by a mixture of Assyrian merchants and native population.

Lion-shaped vessel by Kültepe potters, "colony period" (1950–1750 BC); Archaeological Museum, Ankara, Tur.

By courtesy of the Archaeological Museum, Ankara; photograph, Josephine Powell, Rome

The excavations, resumed in 1948, were continued annually by the Turkish Historical Society under the direction of Tahsin and Nimet Özgüç. Their excavations added thousands of new tablet finds, dating from early in the 2nd millennium BC, and included the first such discoveries in the city mound itself.

The texts—the earliest historical documents found in Anatolia—are of Old Assyrian type; similar texts have been discovered at Alişar Hüyük and at Boğazköy, the site of the Hittite capital. All the texts belong to what is called the "colony period" in central Anatolia. At that time, Indo-European Hittites had already settled in Anatolia and assimilated into the indigenous population. From about the 20th to the 18th century BC there existed a number of Assyrian *karums* (trade outposts, of which Kanesh was probably the most important), which served as end stations for the caravan shipments from and to Assyria and as distribution centres. Assyrian textiles and items transshipped from Babylonia were traded for Anatolian copper and silver.

Kulturkampf (German: "culture struggle"), the bitter struggle (*c.* 1871–87) on the part of the German chancellor Otto von Bismarck to subject the Roman Catholic church to state controls. The term came into use in 1873, when the scientist and Prussian liberal statesman Rudolf Virchow declared that the battle with the Roman Catholics was assuming "the character of a great struggle in the interest of humanity."

Bismarck, a staunch Protestant, never fully trusted the loyalty of the Roman Catholics within his newly created German Empire and became concerned by the Vatican Council's proclamation of 1870 concerning papal infallibility. The Roman Catholics, who were represented politically by the Centre Party, distrusted the predominance of Protestant Prussia within the empire and often opposed Bismarck's policies.

The conflict began in July 1871, when Bismarck, supported by the liberals, abolished the Roman Catholic bureau in the Prussian Ministry of Culture (*i.e.,* ministry of education and ecclesiastical affairs) and in November forbade priests from voicing political opinions from the pulpit. In March 1872 all religious schools became subject to state inspection; in June all religious teachers were excluded from state schools, and the Jesuit order was dissolved in Germany; and in December diplomatic relations with the Vatican were severed. In 1873 the May Laws, promulgated by the Prussian minister of culture, Adalbert Falk, placed strict state controls over religious training and even over ecclesiastical appointments within the church. The climax of the struggle came in 1875, when civil marriage was made obligatory throughout Germany. Dioceses that failed to comply with state regulations were cut off from state aid, and noncompliant clergy were exiled.

Roman Catholics, however, strongly resisted Bismarck's measures and opposed him effectively in the German parliament, where they doubled their representation in the 1874 elections. Bismarck, a pragmatist, decided to retreat. He conceded that many of the measures were excessive and served only to strengthen the resistance of the Centre Party, whose support he needed for his new thrust against the Social Democrats. The advent of a new pope in 1878 eased compromise. By 1887, when Leo XIII declared the conflict over, most of the anti-Catholic legislation had been repealed or reduced in severity. The struggle had the consequence of assuring state control over education and public records, but it also alienated a generation of Roman Catholics from German national life.

Kulturkreis (German: "culture circle," or "cultural field"), plural KULTURKREISE, concept of a culture complex as an entity that develops from a centre of origin and becomes diffused over large areas of the world. It was the central concept of an early 20th-century German school of anthropology.

The theory developed under the ethnologists Fritz Graebner and Wilhelm Schmidt, who believed that a limited number of Kulturkreise developed at different times and in different places and that all cultures, ancient and modern, resulted from the diffusion of cultural complexes—functionally related groups of culture traits—from these cultural centres. Proponents of this school believed that the history of any culture could be reconstructed through the analysis of its culture complexes and the tracing of their origins to one or more of the Kulturkreise.

Later anthropologists questioned the accuracy of the concept for establishing culture histories and pointed out its many weaknesses. The basic complexes must be taken as axioms, arbitrary clusters of traits assumed to originate in a particular place. The proponents of the Kulturkreis theory often mistook analogous features for homologous ones and compared phenomena that were not really comparable. Contacts over unlikely distances were postulated, and allowances were not made for independent invention. Finally, most anthropologists considered the real complexity of cultural phenomena much too great to be explained by the interaction of a small number of Kulturkreise.

Kulu (India): *see* Kullu.

Kulunda Steppe, Russian KULUNDINSKAYA RAVNINA, Kazak QULYNDY ZHAZYGHY, lowland constituting the extreme southern extension of the West Siberian Plain. Most of the steppe lies in Russia, but its western part extends into Kazakstan. Roughly triangular in shape, with its point to the south, it covers an area of approximately 39,000 square miles (100,000 square km). With a poor drainage pattern because of low relative relief and meagre rainfall, the steppe has numerous lakes, mostly salt; Lake Kulunda is the largest. Glauber's salt (a sodium sulfate compound used in dyes and medicines) and soda are extracted from the lakes. The city of Pavlodar (*q.v.*) lies at its western margin.

Kulyab, also spelled KULIAB, or KULJAB, city, southwestern Tajikistan. It lies in the valley of the Iakhsu River and at the foot of the Khazratishokh Range, 125 miles (200 km) southeast of Dushanbe. The city was a trading point on the route from the Gissar (Hissar) valley to Afghanistan. Cotton and grain are cultivated throughout the surrounding region, and sheep are grazed in the mountain areas.

Kulyab was a main supply point for Afghan militias during the closing years of that country's civil war (*c.* 2000). The city and surrounding region were the political base of the ruling party following independence (1991). Pop. (2002 est.) 79,500.

Kŭm River, Korean KŬM-GANG, river, southwestern South Korea. It rises east of Chŏnju in North Chŏlla *do* (province) and flows north-northwest through North Ch'ungch'ŏng *do,* where it turns southwest and empties into the Yellow Sea at Kunsan. The Kŭm River is 249 miles (401 km) long and is navigable for 81 miles (130 km). It is located in an area of fertile plains and gold deposits. The 1,624-foot- (495-m-) long Taechong multipurpose dam, on a branch of the Kŭm River, was completed in 1980. It supplies the cities around its middle course (Ch'ŏngju, Nonsan, and Kanggyŏng) with water and electricity.

Kuma-Manych Depression, also called MANYCH, or MANYČ, Russian KUMO-MANYCHSKAYA VPADINA, geologic depression in western Russia that divides the Russian Plain (north) from the North Caucasus foreland (south). It is often regarded as the true frontier between Europe and Asia.

The depression runs northwest-southeast from the Don River valley to the Caspian lowlands. It is generally 12–19 miles (20–30 km) wide, though in the centre it is in places reduced to a mile or less. Its course is characterized by numerous salt lakes, such as the Manych-Gudilo, which is joined by canal to the Zapadny (Western) Manych River, a tributary of the Don. The Zapadny Manych drains the western part of the depression; the east is drained by the Vostochny Manych and lower Kuma rivers. The vegetation is typically feather grass and other semiarid types.

Kumagaya, city, Saitama *ken* (prefecture), Honshu, Japan, on the Ara River. It was named for the 12th-century warrior Kumagai Naozane. The city was a post town and silk market during the Tokugawa period (1603–1867) and marked the terminus of transport on the Ara River. The central part of Kumagaya was destroyed during World War II, but the city has since grown to be the commercial, administrative, and transport centre of northern Saitama *ken.* The silk-reeling industry is supplemented by heavy industry, introduced since 1961. Pop. (2000) 156,216.

Kumamoto, *ken* (prefecture), located in central Kyushu, Japan, facing the Amakusa Sea and including the Amakusa Archipelago. The city of Kumamoto (*q.v.*) is the capital.

The prefecture, once predominantly agricultural, now has a strong manufacturing and service-oriented economy. Rice, fruits and vegetables, and livestock all contribute to agricultural production. Forestry is important in the interior mountains, as is fishing along the coasts and islands. Manufactures include electronics (notably semiconductors), automobiles, and processed foods. Tourism, of growing importance, centres on the enormous crater of Mount Aso in Aso-Kujo National Park in the northeast. Yatsushiro, on the coast, was linked by Shinkansen (bullet train) to Kagoshima (south) in 2004. Area 2,859 square miles (7,404 square km). Pop. (2002 est.) 1,858,000.

Kumamoto, city and prefectural capital, Kumamoto *ken* (prefecture), central Kyushu, Japan. Kumamoto has long been the largest

Suizenji Park, Kumamoto, Japan
FPG

and most influential city of central Kyushu. It is known for its castle and for Suizenji Park, which is one of the three most famous gardens in Japan. The original castle, partly destroyed in 1877, was restored in 1960. The castle contains a museum of city history, with ancient Japanese armour and other relics. Suizenji Park was completed in 1632 by the priest Gentaku, under the auspices of the Hosokawa family, who ruled the region. A university was founded in Kumamoto in 1949. The Japanophile Lafcadio Hearn lived for three years in Kumamoto. The city's main industries are electrical equipment, machinery, and foodstuffs. Pop. (2000) 662,012.

Kuman (Turkic people): *see* Kipchak.

Kumanovo, city in northern Macedonia. It lies east-northeast of Skopje, on the rail and road link between Niš, Serbia and Montenegro, and Skopje. Agriculture and metal and tobacco processing contribute to the local economy. In 1912 the Serbians heavily defeated a Turkish army on the Kumanovo plain. About 8 miles (13 km) to the east of the city is the Staro Nagoričane Monastery, built by the Serbian king Milutin in 1318. It contains valuable frescoes. Also nearby is the 16th-century Matejić Monastery, an example of the "five cupola" style, and a spa resort with hot mineral waters. Pop. (2002) 103,205.

Kumāra (Hindu god): *see* Skanda.

Kumārajīva (b. 343/344—d. 413), Buddhist scholar and seer, famed for his encyclopaedic knowledge of Indian and Vedantic learning. He is recognized as one of the greatest translators of Buddhist scriptures from Sanskrit into Chinese, and it was largely owing to his efforts and influence that Buddhist religious and philosophical ideas were disseminated in China. Kumārajīva was raised in the tradition of Hīnayāna Buddhism and studied its teachings at Kashgar, China. He was later converted to the Mādhyāmika school of Buddhism and ordained at age 20. Captured by Chinese raiders, he was taken as prisoner to China and arrived at Ch'ang-an in 401. There he gained the approval of the imperial family and headed a famous school of translators that produced Chinese versions of the central Mādhyāmika texts.

Kumarhata (India): *see* Hālisahar.

Kumasi, also spelled COOMASSIE, city, south-central Ghana. Carved out of a dense forest belt among hills rising to 1,000 feet (300 m), Kumasi has a humid, wet climate. Osei Tutu, a 17th-century Ashanti king, chose the site for his capital and conducted land negotiations under a *kum* tree, whence the town's name. Located on north-south trade routes, Kumasi became a major commercial centre.

After defeating the Ashanti kingdom (1874), the British opened new trade routes in the region, thereby greatly reducing Kumasi's influence as a clearinghouse. The city did not revive until the early 1900s, when the British took over control; cacao cultivation was introduced, and the railroad from Sekondi was built. A rapid population increase led to the city's expansion and to the drainage of swamps, the installation of a sewage system, and modern city planning.

Kumasi remains the seat of Ashanti kings (the Asantehene) and of the golden stool, symbol of royal authority and unity of the people. The "Garden City of West Africa," Kumasi is zoned into commercial, industrial, and residential areas. Population is dense in the oldest part of town within a 2-mile (3-km) radius of the British fort (1897), which now houses the Ghana Regiment Museum. Nearby was the Ashanti palace, destroyed by the British in 1874.

The old town has been modernized with paved streets, parks, and gardens and is dominated by the Kumasi Central Hospital. Besides

Kumasi Central Hospital, Ghana
Stephanie Dinkins—Photo Researchers

schools and teacher-training colleges, there are the Kwame Nkrumah University of Science and Technology (founded 1951, university 1961) and research institutes for crops and soil. The Ashanti Cultural Centre supports a museum, a zoo, and a regional library.

The wealth of Kumasi is derived from its location at the junction of Ghana's main roads and from cacao farming in the hinterland. Trade and mining contribute to the local economy. Handicrafts, such as traditional *kente* cloth, are significant sources of income. Pop. (2001 est.) 601,600.

Kumayri (Armenia): *see* Gyumri.

Kumazawa Banzan (b. 1619, Kyōto, Japan—d. Sept. 9, 1691, Shimofusa), political philosopher who was a Japanese disciple of the Chinese Neo-Confucian philosopher Wang Yang-ming (d. 1529) and who was one of the first in Japan to attempt to put Wang's ideas into practice in his own daily life.

Born a *rōnin* (masterless samurai), Kumazawa showed such great promise that he was taken into the service of the great feudal lord of Okayama, Ikeda Mitsumasa, at the age of 15. Largely self-taught, Kumazawa was attracted to the ideas of Wang because of their antischolastic bent and emphasis on direct action. His commonsensical solutions to problems were held in great esteem, and in 1647 he was appointed chief minister of Okayama, an unprecedented honour for a man of his background. Among his many measures to foster agriculture, his attempts to return to the barter economy of Japan's simpler past provoked opposition, which was seized upon by his enemies. In 1656 Kumazawa was forced to resign, and he spent the rest of his years in study and writing.

Demonstrating his independent spirit by writing in colloquial Japanese rather than the classical Chinese usually used for philosophical works, Kumazawa criticized the prevailing government of his day. He advocated advancement based on individual merit rather than on hereditary status, an increased government responsibility for economic life, and a relaxation of central control over the great feudal lords. His ideas caused such a fury in the government that Kumazawa was kept in custody or under surveillance for the rest of his life.

Kumba, also spelled KOUMBA, town, southwestern Cameroon. It is an important regional transportation centre, connected by railway to Douala and by roads to Buea (south), Mamfe (north), Bafang (northeast), and Douala (southeast). Kumba is also a trade centre for locally grown oil palms, rubber, tea, bananas, plantains, and cocoa (the major export crop). Its food-processing, construction, and lumber industries use agricultural and forest products of the area. The town has a hospital and a medical-research centre. The surrounding region is noted for its many waterfalls and Lake Barombi Mbo, a crater lake several miles to the west. Pop. (1987 est.) 70,280.

Kumbakonam, city, east-central Tamil Nādu state, southeastern India, in the Cauvery River delta. It was a Cōḻa (Chola) capital in the 7th century AD and has numerous Vaishnava and Śaiva temples and a rare Brahmā temple. Also an ancient commercial centre, it is renowned for its trade in foods, particularly rice and betel leaves, and for its hand-spun silks and bell-metal pots. The city is situated on road and rail routes from Tranquebar (east) to Tiruchchirāppalli (west). Long a Brahman seat of learning, it has several colleges affiliated with Bharathidasan University. Pop. (1991 prelim.) city, 139,449; metropolitan area, 150,502.

The Vaishnava temple of Sarangapani, Kumbakonam, Tamil Nādu, India

Kumbh Mela, also called KUMBHA MELA, Hindi KUMBH MELĀ, greatest of the Hindu pilgrimage festivals. It is a riverside religious fair held four times every 12 years, rotating between Hardwār on the Ganges River, Ujjain on the Siprā, Nāsik on the Godāvari, and Allahābād, which lies at the confluence of the Ganges, the Yamuna, and the mythical Saraswati. Bathing in these rivers during the Kumbh Mela is seen as an act of great merit, cleansing body and soul, and it attracts millions.

The Chinese Buddhist traveler Hsüan-tsang recorded a visit to the Allahābād Kumbh Mela in the 7th century in the company of the emperor Harṣa, who distributed alms on the occasion. In the 8th century the philosopher Śaṅkara established four monasteries, in the north, south, east, and west of India, and exhorted the sadhus (holy men) to meet at the Kumbh Mela for an exchange of views. The informal assembly of ascetics and yogis that took place at the melas (festivals) served as a kind of "parliament of Hinduism" for the discussion of religious doctrine and possible reform and has remained a major attraction for the pilgrim. Sadhus who stay naked the year round, ascetics who practice the most severe physical disciplines, hermits who leave their isolation for these pilgrimages only, teachers who use modern microphones and public-address systems to talk to the crowds, frauds, and true saints—of all sects and from all parts of India—gather in camps along the riverbank and are visited by the pilgrims.

Pilgrimages have always been undertaken in India with a sense of possible danger, and though the cholera epidemics, widespread murder, and kidnappings of former Kumbha Melas have now been successfully controlled by the government, tragedies still occur. In 1954, at the Kumbha Mela at Allahābād, more than 500 people were killed in a sudden onrush of crowds toward the bathing area.

The explanation given in the *Purāṇa*s for the Kumbh Mela is that the gods and the demons fought over the pot (*kumbha*) of amrit (*amṛta*), the elixir that rose up from their joint churning of the milky ocean. During the battle, drops of the elixir fell on four earthly sites, these being the four sites of the mela. The fair's aspect as a fertility festival is evident in a tradition, said to have been carried out in former days, of dipping pots of grain in the river during this highly auspicious period. The consecrated grain was later sowed with other grain to ensure a good harvest.

Kumbi, also called KOUMBI SALEH, last of the capitals of ancient Ghana, a great trading empire that flourished in western Africa from the 9th through the 13th century. Situated about 200 miles (322 km) north of modern Bamako, Mali, Kumbi at the height of its prosperity, before 1240, was the greatest city of western Africa with a population of more than 15,000. Within its boundaries there were—as was the custom of the early kingdoms of the western Sudan—two cities, one of which was occupied by the king, the other by Muslim traders.

Kume Masao (b. Nov. 23, 1891, Ueda, Japan—d. March 1, 1952, Kamakura), novelist and playwright, one of Japan's most popular writers of the 1920s and '30s.

As a student, Kume was associated with the writers Akutagawa Ryūnosuke and Kikuchi Kan on the famous school literary journal *Shinshichō* ("New Currents of Thought"). He had started writing haiku in high school and published a book of poetry in 1914, but before graduating from Tokyo Imperial University in 1916, he had turned to theatre. A notable success during this time was the play *Gyūnyūya no kyōdai* (1914; "The Milkman's Younger Brother"). With Akutagawa, he became a disciple of the novelist Natsume Sōseki. *Jūkensei no shūki* (1916; "Notes of a Student Examinee"), *Tora* (1918; "The Tiger"), and *Hasen* (1922; "Shipwreck") are among his best works.

Kumi, city, Kyŏngsang-puk *do* (province), south-central South Korea. It lies near the junction of the Kumi River and the Naktong River. Developed after the Korean War (1950–53) as an industrial city, Kumi is the site of South Korea's largest inland planned industrial complex, covering an area of nearly 4 square miles (10 square km). Electronics is the principal manufacture. Mount Kumo (3,205 feet [977 m]) is 3 miles (5 km) southwest of the city. On the summit of the mountain is an old castle and Point Hanksa temple. Pop. (1990) 206,121.

Kumillā (Bangladesh): *see* Comilla.

Kummer, Ernst Eduard (b. Jan. 29, 1810, Sorau, Brandenburg, Prussia [Germany]—d. May 14, 1893, Berlin, Ger.), German mathematician whose introduction of ideal numbers, which are defined as a special subgroup of a ring, extended the fundamental theorem of arithmetic to complex number fields.

After teaching in gymnasiums one year at Sorau and 10 years at Liegnitz (now Legnica, Pol.), Kummer became professor of mathematics at the university at Breslau (now Wrocław, Pol.) in 1842. In 1855 he succeeded Peter Gustav Lejeune Dirichlet as professor of mathematics at the University of Berlin, at the same time also becoming professor at the Berlin War College.

In 1843 Kummer showed to Dirichlet an attempted proof of Fermat's last theorem ($x^n + y^n = z^n$, where n is an integer greater than 2, has no solution for positive integral values of x, y, and z); Dirichlet found an error. Kummer continued his search and developed the concept of ideal numbers. Using this concept he proved the insolubility of the Fermat relation for all but a small group of primes, and he thus laid the foundation for an eventual complete proof of Fermat's last theorem. For his great advance the Paris Academy of Sciences awarded him the Grand Prize in 1857. The ideal numbers have made possible new developments in the arithmetic of algebraic numbers.

Inspired by the work of William Hamilton on systems of optical rays, Kummer developed the surface named in his honour, based on the quartic (fourth-power) equation that is the singular surface of the quadratic line complex. This surface is the wave surface in space of four dimensions.

Kummer also extended the work of Carl Gauss on the hypergeometric series, adding developments that are useful in the theory of differential equations.

Articles are alphabetized word by word, not letter by letter

Kumo, town, Bauchi state, northeastern Nigeria. One of the largest towns of the traditional Gombe emirate, Kumo serves as a collecting point for peanuts (groundnuts), cotton, and corn (maize) and as a local trade centre for the sorghum, millet, cowpeas, cassava, peanuts, goats, cattle, sheep, fowl, horses, donkeys, and cotton raised by the Tangale, Fulani, and Hausa peoples of the surrounding area. The secondary highway between Gombe and Biliri serves the town. Pop. (1993 est.) 137,400.

kumquat, any of several evergreen shrubs or trees of the genus *Fortunella* (family Rutaceae). Native to eastern Asia, these small trees are cultivated throughout the subtropics, including southern California and Florida. They reach about 2.4 to 3.6 m (8 to 12 feet) high. The branches are mainly thornless and have

Fruit and flower of kumquat (*Fortunella*)
Encyclopædia Britannica, Inc.

dark green, glossy leaves and white, orangelike flowers, occurring singly or clustered in the leaf axils. The bright, orange-yellow fruit is round or oval, about 2.5 cm (1 inch) in diameter, with mildly acid, juicy pulp and a sweet, edible, pulpy skin.

Kumquats may be eaten fresh, preserved, or made into jams and jellies; in China they are frequently candied. Branches of the kumquat tree are used for Christmas decoration in parts of the United States and elsewhere.

The oval, or Nagami, kumquat (*F. margarita*) is the most common species. It is native to southern China and bears yellow fruits that are about 3 cm in diameter. The round, or Marumi, kumquat is *F. japonica;* it is indigenous to Japan and has orangelike fruits that are about 2.5 cm in diameter. The egg-shaped Meiwa kumquat (*F. crassifolia*), in which both the pulp and the rind of the fruit are sweet, is considered an intrageneric hybrid and is widely grown in China. In the United States, hybrids have been produced with limes, mandarin oranges, and other citrus fruits.

Kumran (Essene site): *see* Qumrān.

Kun (people): *see* Cuman.

kun (Japanese: "instruction"), one of two alternate readings (the other is *on*) for a kanji (Japanese: "character"). The ambiguity of a kanji arises from its having two values: the meaning of the original Chinese character from which the kanji is derived and a Chinese pronunciation of the character. In the *kun* reading the pronunciation given the kanji is a Japanese word or word element, often equivalent to a Chinese understanding of the meaning of the character.

Kun, Béla (b. Feb. 20, 1886, Szilágycseh, Transylvania, Austria-Hungary [now in Hungary]—d. Nov. 30, 1939?, U.S.S.R.), communist leader and head of the Hungarian Soviet Republic of 1919.

The son of a Jewish village clerk, Kun became active in Social Democratic politics early in life, working at first in Transylvania and later in Budapest. He was mobilized in the Austro-Hungarian army at the outbreak of World War I, became a prisoner of war in Russia in 1916, and joined the Bolsheviks. Attracting the attention of V.I. Lenin, Kun received training in revolutionary tactics and returned to Hungary after the collapse of the Central Powers in November 1918. He started a communist newspaper and founded the Hungarian Communist Party on Dec. 20, 1918. Though imprisoned in February 1919 by the government of Mihály Károlyi, Kun was allowed to continue directing Hungary's Communist Party from his cell. His extensive propaganda combined social agitation with promises that, if given power, he would secure Soviet aid against the Romanian forces then occupying parts of Hungary.

On March 20, 1919, Kun was released by Károlyi, and the following day, as commissar for foreign affairs, he assumed the dominant position in a new Communist–Social Democratic coalition government. His regime took advantage of an upsurge of popular nationalism and created a Red Army that rapidly reconquered a considerable portion of the territory lost to Czechoslovaks and Romanians. Kun also quickly eliminated the moderate elements in the government through terroristic measures. Soviet help, however, failed to arrive, and Kun alienated the peasantry by nationalizing Hungary's estates rather than dividing them among the peasants. As a consequence, food distribution broke down, and the army refused to fight. The regime collapsed on Aug. 1, 1919, and Kun fled to Vienna. As a leader of the Third International, he attempted to initiate revolutionary outbreaks several times in Germany and Austria during the 1920s. He was eventually accused of "Trotskyism" and fell victim to one of Joseph Stalin's purges in the late 1930s.

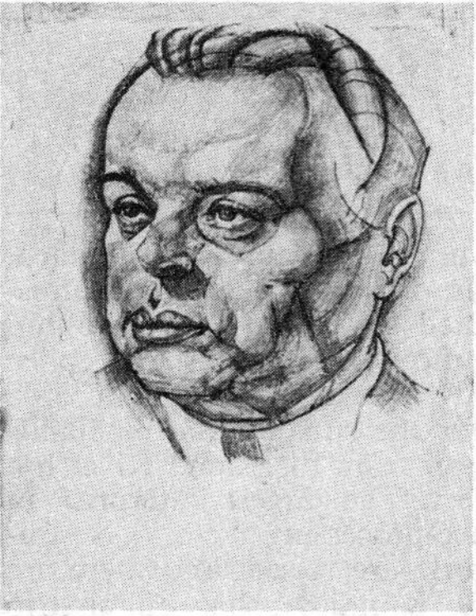

Béla Kun, drawing by Béla Uitz, 1930; in the Legújabbkori Történeti Múzeum, Budapest
By courtesy of the Legujabbkori Torteneti Muzeum, Budapest

Though possessing great energy and shrewdness, Kun was rigid in his communist views and was oblivious to the unpopularity of his policies during his brief rule in Hungary. Despite his organizational talents, he was unable to master the complexities of actual government or the tactics of power struggles within the international communist movement.

K'un-ming, Pinyin KUNMING, city in east-central Yunnan *sheng* (province), China. K'un-ming is the provincial capital of Yunnan. Situated in a fertile lake basin on the northern shore of the Tien Lake and surrounded by mountains to the north, west, and east, K'un-ming has always played a part in the communications of southwestern China.

In the 8th and 9th centuries it was known to the Chinese as T'o-tung city in the independent state of Nan-chao. It first came under the control of the Chinese central government with the Yüan (Mongol) invasion of the southwest in 1253. In 1276 it was founded as K'un-ming county and became the provincial capital of Yunnan. It is considered by scholars to have been the city of Yachi, described by the 13th-century Venetian traveler Marco Polo. During the Ming (1368–1644) and Ch'ing (1644–1911) dynasties, it was the seat of the superior prefecture of Yunnan. It reverted to county status in 1912, under the name K'un-ming, and became a municipality in 1935.

K'un-ming, Yunnan province, China
Roger Duzer

K'un-ming was a communications centre in early times and a junction of two major trading routes, one westward via Ta-li and T'eng-yüeh (modern T'eng-ch'ung) into Myanmar (Burma), the other southward through Meng-tzu to the Red River in Indochina. Eastward, a difficult mountain route led to Kuei-yang in Kweichow province and thence to Hunan province. To the northeast was a well-established trade trail to I-pin in Szechwan province on the Yangtze River. But these trails were all extremely difficult, passable only by mule trains or pack-carrying porters.

The opening of the K'un-ming area began in earnest with the completion in 1906–10 of the railway to Haiphong in Indochina. K'un-ming became a treaty port open to foreign trade in 1908 and soon became a commercial centre. In the 1930s its importance grew still further when the first highways were built, linking K'un-ming with Chungking in Szechwan and Kuei-yang in Kweichow to the east.

K'un-ming's transformation into a modern city resulted from the outbreak of the Sino-Japanese War in 1937. In the face of the advancing Japanese forces, great numbers of Chinese flooded into southwestern China and brought with them dismantled industrial plants, which were then reerected beyond the range of Japanese bombers. In addition, a number of universities and institutes of higher education were evacuated there. When the Japanese occupied French Indochina in 1940, the links of K'un-ming with the west, both via the newly constructed Burma Road and by air, grew increasingly vital. Industry became important in K'un-ming during World War II. The large state-owned Central Machine Works was transferred there from Hunan, while the manufacture of electrical products, copper, cement, steel, paper, and textiles expanded.

After 1949 K'un-ming developed rapidly into an industrial metropolis, second only to Chungking in the southwest. Its chief industries are the production of copper, lead, and zinc; its iron and steel industry has been greatly expanded. K'un-ming is also a centre of the engineering industry, manufacturing machine tools, electrical machinery and equipment, and automobiles. It has a major chemical industry, as well as cement works and textile factories. Its many processing plants, which include tanneries and woodworking and papermaking factories, use local agricultural products. K'un-ming remains a major cultural centre, with universities, medical and teacher-training colleges, technical schools, and scientific research institutes. About 60 miles (96 km) southeast of the city is the Stone Forest, a karst formation consisting of rock caves, arches, and pavilions. K'un-ming has daily air connections with Peking. Pop. (1999 est.) 1,350,640.

K'un-ming Ch'ih (China): *see* Tien Lake.

Kuncewicz(owa), Maria, *née* SZCZEPAŃSKA (b. Oct. 30 [Nov. 11, New Style], 1899, Samara, Russia—d. July 15, 1989, Kazimierz Dolny, Pol.), Polish writer of novels, essays, plays, and short stories.

A daughter of Polish parents who had been exiled to Russia after the Polish insurrection of January 1863, she was two years old when her family returned to Warsaw. She studied at the universities of Kraków, Warsaw, and Nancy. Her first novel, *Twarz mężczyzny* (1928; "The Face of the Male"), established her gift as a writer who excelled in penetrating psychological portraits, using subtle irony and poetical lyricism. Her *Cudzoziemka* (1936; *The Stranger*) is a masterpiece for which she was awarded the 1937 Warsaw Literary Prize. Episodes from her novel *Dni powszednie państwa Kowalskich* (1937; "The Daily Life of the Kowalskis") were broadcast by radio in Poland before World War II.

In 1939 she escaped from Warsaw to Paris, and in 1940 she went to England, where she wrote *Klucze* (1943; *The Keys*), a literary diary subtitled in the English version as *A Journey Through Europe at War*. In 1956 she moved to the United States, where she published an anthology of stories and essays entitled *The Modern Polish Mind* (1962) and taught Polish language and literature at the University of Chicago (1961–64). She continued to write novels, including *Gaj oliwny* (1961; *The Olive Grove*) and *Don Kichot i niańki* (1965; "Don Quixote and the Nannies").

Kunchev, Vasil Ivanov: *see* Levski, Vasil.

kuṇḍalinī, in some Tantric (esoteric) forms of Yoga, the cosmic energy that is believed to lie within everyone, pictured as a coiled serpent lying at the base of the spine. In the practice of Laya Yoga ("Union of Mergence"), the adept is instructed to awaken the *kuṇḍalinī*, also identified with the deity Shakti. Through a series of techniques that combine prescribed postures, gestures, and breathing exercises, the practitioner brings the *kuṇḍalinī* up along the spine to his head. On the way the *kuṇḍalinī* passes through six imagined centres, or *cakras*. When the *kuṇḍalinī* arrives at the seventh *cakra*, at the top of the head, the practitioner experiences an overwhelming and indescribable feeling of bliss that mystically represents the practitioner's reintegration with atman, or the eternal essence of the self.

The exercises used by the adept to achieve this union involve the purificatory practices, bodily postures, breathing, and meditation exercises that are common to other forms of Yoga.

Kundera, Milan (b. April 1, 1929, Brno, Czech.), Czech novelist, short-story writer, playwright, and poet who wrote various works combining erotic comedy with political criticism.

The son of a noted concert pianist and musicologist, Ludvik Kundera, the young Kundera studied music but gradually turned to writing, publishing his first volume of poetry, *Člověk zahrada širá* ("Man: A Broad Garden") in 1953. This and two other collections, *Poslední máj* (1955; "The Last May") and *Monology* (1957; "Monologues"), because of their ironic tone and eroticism, were condemned by the Czech political authorities. Meanwhile, he was in and out of the Communist Party (1948–50, 1956–70) and studied and taught in the Film Faculty of Prague's Academy of Music and Dramatic Arts.

Several volumes of short stories and a highly successful one-act play, *Majitelé Klíčů* (1962; "The Owners of the Keys"), were followed by his first novel and one of his greatest works, *Žert* (1967; *The Joke*), a comic, ironic view of the private lives and destinies of various Czechs during the years of Stalinism; translated into several languages, it achieved great international acclaim. His second novel, *Život je jinde* (1969; *Life Is Elsewhere*), about a hapless, romantic-minded hero who thoroughly embraces the Communist takeover of 1948, was forbidden Czech publication. Kundera had participated in the brief but heady liberalization of Czechoslovakia in 1967–68, and after the Soviet occupation of the country he refused to admit his political errors and consequently was attacked by the authorities, who banned all his works, fired him from his teaching positions, and ousted him from the Communist Party.

In 1975 Kundera was allowed to emigrate (with his wife, Vera Hrabankova) from his Czechoslovakian homeland to teach at the University of Rennes (1975–78) in France; in 1979 the Czech government stripped him of his citizenship. His subsequent novels, such as *Valčík na rozloučenou* (1976; "Farewell Waltz"; Eng. trans. *The Farewell Party*), *Kniha smíchu a zapomnění* (1979; *The Book of Laughter and Forgetting*), and *Nes nesitelná lehkost byti* (1984; *The Unbearable Lightness of Being*), were published in France and elsewhere abroad but until 1989 were banned in his homeland. *The Book of Laughter and Forgetting*, one of his most successful works, is a series of wittily ironic meditations on the modern state's tendency to deny and obliterate human memory and historical truth. A translation of Kundera's reflections on the art of the novel was published in 1988.

Consult
the
INDEX
first

Kundiawa, town, central Papua New Guinea. The town, built on an old Lutheran mission site, is located on a pine-covered hilltop surrounded by mountains, waterfalls, coffee plantations, and vegetable gardens. It is a trading centre for the surrounding highlands and receives power from the Ramu River hydroelectric project. The largest enterprise in the area, a coffee-processing factory, is situated nearby. Cattle are raised, and there are sawmills nearby. Kundiawa has an airstrip and lies on the Highlands Highway, which extends southeast to Lae on Huon Gulf. Pop. (1990) 4,800.

Kundt, August (Adolph Eduard Eberhard) (b. Nov. 18, 1839, Schwerin, duchy of Mecklenburg-Schwerin [Germany]—d. May 21, 1894, Israelsdorf, near Lübeck, Ger.), German physicist who developed a method for determining the velocity of sound in gases and solids.

Kundt studied at the University of Leipzig but afterward went to the University of Berlin. In 1867 he became an instructor at Berlin, and in the following year he became professor of physics at the Zürich Polytechnic. In 1872 he was called to Strasbourg, where he was one of the founders of that city's Physical Institute. In 1888 he succeeded to the chair of experimental physics and the directorship of the Berlin Physical Institute. In his experiments on sound, Kundt dusted the interior of a tube with a finely divided powder to show the position of the nodes of the sound waves, thereby determining their wavelength. He also studied the anomalous dispersion of light in liquids, vapours, and metals. In his work with magneto-optics, he showed the rotation, under magnetic influence, of the plane of polarization in certain gases and vapours.

Kundulun Khan (ruler of China): *see* Nurhachi.

Kuneitra, el- (Syria): *see* Qunayṭirah, al-.

Kunene, Mazisi (Raymond) (b. May 12, 1930, Durban, S.Af.), South African-born poet whose work reflects the influences of traditional Zulu poets.

Kunene began writing in the Zulu language when he was still a child and by age 11 had published a number of his poems in newspapers and magazines. In his University of Natal (M.A., 1959) master's thesis, "An Analytical Survey of Zulu Poetry, Both Traditional and Modern," Kunene criticized several tendencies in modern Zulu literature: its reliance on European stylistic techniques rather than adaptation of traditional ones; its unanalytical documentary writing; and a slide toward sentimentality and escapism that he saw as an influence of the Christian and the Romantic traditions.

In 1959 Kunene went to the University of London to complete his doctorate, but he soon found himself involved in politics and never completed his studies. He was an official representative of the African National Congress. He taught at the University of Iowa, Stanford University, and the University of California, Los Angeles.

His *Zulu Poems* (1979), a collection of his poetry translated from Zulu into English, was praised by critics for the freshness of the English translations, with patterns and imagery successfully carried over from Zulu vernacular traditions. Again translating his work from the original Zulu into English, Kunene published two epic poems—*Emperor Shaka the Great* (1979), a history of the Zulu king, and *Anthem of the Decades* (1981), a work dealing with Zulu religion and cosmology.

Kunene River, also spelled CUNENE, river rising in west-central Angola, southwestern Africa, about 20 miles (32 km) northeast of Huambo. Its total length is 587 miles (945 km).

At Chiamelu to the south the Kunene flows in a steep granite bed but leaves the granite uplands at Matala, falling about 42 feet (13 m) before entering the northern portion of the Kalahari Desert, where in the wet season it floods the sands. The Matala Dam raises the river 26 feet (8 m), giving a head of about 68 feet (21 m) for hydroelectric generation. At Olushandja the river turns sharply westward, flowing over a series of rapids, then falling 230 feet (70 m) at Ruacana Falls, where it is dammed for hydropower and irrigation. From that point it forms the boundary between Angola and Namibia. About 50 miles (80 km) west, the river enters its gorge tract through the Zebra and Baynes mountains, which rise to a height of about 7,200 feet (2,200 m), the riverbed being about 4,000 feet (1,200 m) below. In this gorge tract are the Epupa (or Montenegro) Falls, over 100 feet (30 m) high. The Kunene issues from the Baynes Gorge into the Namib Desert, where it generally has a small volume, before emptying into the Atlantic Ocean. The river's mouth is lagoonlike and closed in the dry season by a sand bar.

Küng, Hans (b. March 19, 1928, Sursee, Switz.), Swiss Roman Catholic theologian whose controversial liberal views led to his censorship by the Vatican in 1979.

Küng studied at Gregorian University in Rome and obtained a doctorate in theology from the Catholic Institute at the Sorbonne in 1957. He was ordained a Roman Catholic priest in 1954, and he taught at the University of Münster in West Germany (1959–60) and from 1960 at the University of Tübingen, where he also directed the Institute for Ecumenical Research from 1963. In 1962 he was named by Pope John XXIII a *peritus* (theological consultant) for the second Vatican Council.

Küng's prolific writings questioned such traditional church doctrine as papal infallibility, the divinity of Christ, and the dogma of the Virgin Mary. In 1979 a Vatican censure that banned his teaching as a Catholic theologian provoked international controversy, and in 1980 a settlement was reached at Tübingen that allowed him to teach under secular rather than Catholic auspices. His publications include *Rechtfertigung: Die Lehre Karl Barths und eine Katholische Besinnung* (1957; *Justification: The Doctrine of Karl Barth and a Catholic Reflection*), *Konzil und Wieder-*

vereinigung (1960; *The Council, Reform, and Reunion*), *Die Kirche* (1967; *The Church*), *Unfehlbar?* (1970; *Infallible?*), *Christ sein* (1974; *On Being a Christian*), *Existiert Gott?* (1978; *Does God Exist?*), and *Ewiges Leben?* (1982; *Eternal Life?*).

K'ung, H.H., in full K'UNG HSIANG-HSI (b. 1881, T'aiku, Shansi Province, China—d. Aug. 15, 1967, Locust Valley, N.Y., U.S.), banker and businessman who was a major figure in the Chinese Nationalist government between 1928 and 1945.

The son of an old merchant family, K'ung was educated in missionary schools in China and completed his education in the United States, where he received an M.A. in economics at Yale (1907). After returning to China, he became a friend of the Nationalist revolutionary leader Sun Yat-sen, who was married to a sister of K'ung's wife, Soong Ai-ling. When Sun Yat-sen died in 1925, K'ung helped promote Chiang Kai-shek to be leader of Sun's Kuomintang (Nationalist Party), even arranging Chiang's marriage to Mei-ling, another of Soong Ai-ling's sisters.

In 1928 K'ung became minister of industry and commerce in the new Nationalist government. Five years later he succeeded his brother-in-law T.V. Soong as minister of finance and soon took China's money off the silver standard and thus tied the Chinese economy to the international monetary system. That reform enabled China to survive the initial phase of the Sino-Japanese War without serious economic consequences.

K'ung succeeded Chiang Kai-shek briefly as president of the government in 1938, when Chiang resigned to devote all his time to prosecuting the war with Japan. Chiang resumed the presidency the following year, but K'ung continued to hold office throughout the war. In 1948, with Communist victory on the Chinese mainland imminent, he moved to the United States.

K'ung Chi (Chinese philosopher): *see* Tzu Ssu.

Kung Ch'in-wang (Prince), also called KUNG KUNG (Prince), Pinyin GONG QINWANG, or GONG GONG, original name (Wade–Giles romanization) I-HSIN, (b. Jan. 11, 1833, Peking—d. May 1898, Peking), leading official in the closing years of the Ch'ing dynasty (1644–1911), who tried to repair a weakened government and to effect a rapprochement with the West.

A brother of the Hsien-feng emperor (reigned 1851–61), Prince Kung was assigned to make peace with the British and French forces who had occupied the capital at Peking in 1860, during the "Arrow" War. After successfully concluding treaty negotiations, he urged that China try to understand and adopt some Western military techniques. As a result the Emperor created the Tsungli Yamen (Office for General Management), which assumed the function of a foreign affairs office and played an important role in the modernization of China over the next 40 years.

When the Hsien-feng emperor died, in August 1861, Prince Kung became a co-regent for the young T'ung-chih emperor (1861–75). Under Prince Kung's direction, the great Taiping Rebellion, which had occupied most of South China for more than a decade, was finally suppressed in 1864, and a restoration of the government was attempted. Arsenals were constructed to manufacture Western arms, and other foreign methods were studied. Corruption was stemmed, and good men were recruited for the bureaucracy and army. The empress dowager Tz'u-hsi (1835–1908), however, soon became the real power at the court. Prince Kung's authority was gradually undermined until, in 1884, he was dismissed to die in obscurity.

K'ung Ch'iu: *see* Confucius.

kung fu (Chinese: "skill"), Pinyin GONGFU, a martial art, both a form of exercise with a spiritual dimension stemming from concentration and self-discipline and a primarily unarmed mode of personal combat often equated with karate or tae kwon do. The term kung fu can also signify careful preparation for the performance of any skillful endeavour without interference from the intellect or emotions.

As martial art, kung fu can be traced to the Chou dynasty (1111–255 BC) and even earlier. As exercise it was practiced by the Taoists in the 5th century BC. Its prescribed stances and actions are based on keen observations of human skeletal and muscular anatomy and physiology, and it employs great muscular coordination. The various movements in kung fu, most of which are imitations of the fighting styles of animals, are initiated from one of five basic foot positions: normal upright posture and the four stances called dragon, frog, horse riding, and snake. There are hundreds of styles of kung fu, and armed as well as unarmed techniques have been developed. Kung fu performed as exercise resembles T'ai Chi ch'uan (*see also* martial art).

K'ung-fu-tzu: *see* Confucius.

Kung Hsien, Pinyin GONG XIAN (b. *c.* 1618, K'un-shan, Kiangsu Province, China—d. 1689), most important artist of the group known as the Eight Masters of Nanking. He spent most of his life in Nanking and was regarded by his contemporaries as aloof and eccentric. He died in poverty.

Short, broad vertical strokes characterize Kung's paintings, which, like those of Ni Tsan in the Yüan dynasty (1206–1368), typically contain no human figures; yet in contrast to that earlier artist, his paintings are rich with ink to produce unusually dense and even forbidding landscapes. While he knew well traditional Chinese painting and revealed such knowledge in his art, it has been suggested that his darkly contrasting surfaces owe something to Western illusionistic techniques, which were then to be seen in Nanking in engravings brought by Western missionaries.

kung-hung (Chinese guild): *see* cohong.

kung-pi, Pinyin GONGBI, in Chinese painting, meticulous brush technique that delimits details very precisely and without independent or expressive variation. It is often highly coloured and usually depicts figural or narrative subjects. The term *kung-pi* is also used to refer to paintings that are generally more descriptive than interpretive. *Kung-pi* paintings are considered to be the opposite of more freely and quickly sketched paintings called *hsieh-i*, or "sketching [one's] thoughts."

A term related to *kung-pi, chieh-hua,* or "boundary painting," refers to the accurate depiction of architectural forms with the aid of a ruler. One of the masters of *kung-pi* is the 16th-century painter Ch'iu Ying (*q.v.*).

Kung-sun Hung, Pinyin GONGSUN HONG (d. 121 BC, China), scholar who helped establish Confucianism as the official doctrine of the Chinese state.

According to tradition, Kung-sun Hung was a poor swineherd who did not begin the study of the Confucian Classics until he was 40 years old. In 140 BC he placed first among scholars examined by the Han emperor Wu and became one of his most important advisers. Primarily known for his ability to interpret portents and omens, Kung-sun Hung made an understanding of omens part of the officially accepted Confucian doctrine; future generations of administrative officials used his interpretations of natural phenomena in their attempt to check Imperial policies with which they disagreed.

In 124 BC Kung-sun Hung, together with the scholar Tung Chung-shu, established the first Imperial university. This school, which trained and tested future officials in the Confucian doctrines, became the predecessor of the later Confucian civil service examination system.

Kung-sun Lung, Pinyin GONGSUN LONG (b. 320? BC, Chao, now Shansi, China—d. 250?, China), one of the best known representatives of the Dialecticians, a Chinese philosophical school of the 3rd and 4th centuries BC whose adherents were concerned with analyzing the true meaning of words. The school had no influence after its own time.

Kung-sun Lung is famous for the discourse in which he discusses why "a white horse is not a horse." He explains that since the horse is white, it is a special kind of horse whose "form" is white; it is not the universal concept horse and hence is not a horse.

His *Kung-sun Lung-tzŭ* ("Master Kung-sun Lung") is the only independent work of ancient Chinese literature dealing with logic that has been even partially preserved. Only 6 of its original 14 chapters survive.

Kung-sun Lung, portrait by an unknown artist; in the National Palace Museum, Taipei, Republic of China

By courtesy of the Collection of the National Palace Museum, Taipei, Taiwan, Republic of China

Kung-sun Yang (Chinese emperor): *see* Shang Yang.

K'ung-tzu: *see* Confucius.

Kung Tzu-chen, also called KUNG TING-AN, Pinyin GONG ZIZHEN, or GONG DINGAN, courtesy name (Wade–Giles romanization) SE-JEN, or ERH-YÜ (b. Aug. 22, 1792, Hang-chou, Chekiang Province, China—d. Sept. 26, 1841, Nanking), a reform-minded Chinese writer and poet whose works both foreshadowed and influenced the modernization movements of the late Ch'ing dynasty.

Born into an eminent family of scholars and officials, Kung passed the state examinations and succeeded to a series of metropolitan posts in the Ch'ing administration. Concern over the Ch'ing failure to deal adequately with Western pressures and internal problems led Kung in 1830 to join other progressives like Lin Tse-hsü, later a key official in the Opium War with Britain, in founding a literary club to agitate for reform. Although his many essays on reform issues had great impact on later reform intellectuals like K'ang Yu-wei and Liang Ch'i-ch'ao, they were ill-received in the conservative Ch'ing councils of the time. Thus, Kung retired in disillusionment to a life of private letters in 1839. Famed chiefly as a prose stylist, Kung was also a master of lyrical *tz'u* poetry and published several verse collections, most notably his *Chi-hai tsa-shih* (1839; "Miscellaneous Verse").

Kungaku (Japanese painter): *see* Shiba Kōkan.

Kungur, city, Perm *oblast* (province), western Russia. It lies at the confluence of the Sylva, Iren, and Shakva rivers, 45 miles (72 km) south of Perm city. Founded in 1648 as a fortress, Kungur became an important post on routes to Siberia. It also became a noted centre for handicraft industries, especially in alabaster and crystal. Kungur now has machine-building and light industries. In the vicinity are alabaster-walled caves, notably the Kungur stalactite cave along the Sylva River. Pop. (2000 est.) 80,000.

Kungurian Stage, lowest stage of rock strata of the Late Permian Period (258 to 245 million years ago) in Russia and Kazakhstan, with well-developed exposures in the Ural region. The Kungurian exhibits complex facies relationships. In the Mugodzhar Hills (Kazakhstan) and southern Ural regions, Kungurian deposits are primarily terrigenous (formed by erosion), consisting of red beds and lagoonal sediment types; elsewhere, conglomerates, sandstones, and other red beds occur. To the east, thick evaporite sequences of gypsum, halite, and potash form the salt basin of the upper Kama River, the largest in the world. Marine limestones occur in the province of Perm, and reef carbonates occur in the western portions of the Mugodzhar Hills.

Kunie Island (New Caledonia): *see* Pins, Île des.

Kunikida Doppo, also called KUNIKIDA KAMEKICHI (b. Aug. 30, 1871, Chōshi, Chiba prefecture, Japan—d. June 23, 1908, Chigasaki, Kanagawa prefecture), writer whose short stories, deeply imbued with a Wordsworthian awareness of nature, brought to Japanese literature a new attitude toward the individual.

Kunikida grew up in southern Japan but went to Tokyo to enter Tokyo Senmon Gakkō (later Waseda University), where he adopted Christianity in 1889. He had already started to read the works of Ivan Turgenev, Thomas Carlyle, and Ralph Waldo Emerson when he went in 1893 to teach school in Saeki, on the southern Japanese island of Kyushu. That year, reinforced by his reading of William Wordsworth's poetry, was crucial in the development of his passionate devotion to nature. He returned to Tokyo, where he became a war correspondent during the Sino-Japanese War (1894–95).

Kunikida is identified by the Japanese with their naturalist movement in literature, but his poetic stories of tragedies in the lives of downtrodden common people are more romantic than harshly realistic. His love of nature can be seen in *Musashino* (1898; "The Musashi Plain"), his search for idealism in *Gyūniku to bareisho* (1901; *Meat and Potatoes*), and his poignant feeling for the fate of wretched men in *Gen oji* (1897; *Old Gen*) and *Haru no tori* (1904; *Spring Birds*).

Kunitz, Stanley, in full STANLEY JASSPON KUNITZ (b. July 29, 1905, Worcester, Mass., U.S.), American Pulitzer Prize-winning poet noted for his subtle craftsmanship and his treatment of complex themes.

Kunitz attended Harvard University, where he earned a B.A. in 1926 and an M.A. degree in 1927. While working as an editor, he contributed poems to magazines, eventually compiling them in his first book, *Intellectual Things* (1930). He served for two years in the army during World War II, after which he began working as a professor and visiting lecturer at several universities. His collection *Passport to the War* (1944), like his first book, contains meticulously crafted, intellectual verse. Most of the poems from these first two works were reprinted with some 30 new poems in *Selected Poems 1928–1958* (1958), which won the Pulitzer Prize in 1959. From 1974 to 1976 Kunitz was consultant in poetry to the Library of Congress (now poet laureate consultant in poetry); he was reappointed to the position in 2000.

With *The Testing-Tree* (1971), Kunitz departed from the formal structure and rational approach of his earlier verse and wrote shorter, looser, and more emotional poetry. Included in the book are "The Illumination," a compact poem about life's regrets, and "King of the River," which contemplates the nature of mystery. His later books of poetry include *The Terrible Threshold* (1974), *The Lincoln Relics* (1978), *The Poems of Stanley Kunitz* (1979), *The Wellfleet Whale and Companion Poems* (1983), and *Next-to-Last Things* (1985), which contains essays as well as verse. The poetry collection *Passing Through* (1995) won a National Book Award. The *Collected Poems* (2000) presents his work up to that year. Kunitz also edited numerous literary anthologies and cotranslated Russian writers Andrey Voznesensky and Anna Akhmatova (*qq.v.*) and Ukrainian Ivan Drach.

Kuniyoshi, Yasuo (b. Sept. 1, 1893, Okayama, Japan—d. May 14, 1953, Woodstock, N.Y., U.S.), Japanese-born American painter who was an influential teacher and a leader of artists' organizations.

Kuniyoshi, *c.* 1915
Peter A. Juley & Son

Kuniyoshi came to the United States in 1906 and in 1907 began to study painting at the Los Angeles School of Art and Design. In 1910 he moved to New York City to attend the National Academy of Design and the Art Students League. His early drawings and paintings are imbued with naive fantasy and delightful humour, using plants and animals as subjects. In his mature work—which shows his indebtedness to Jules Pascin—moody, sensuous women figure predominantly, as in "I'm Tired" (1938; Whitney Museum of American Art, New York City). With the beginning of World War II the artist developed a deep social and political consciousness for which he created his own pictorial symbols, which he believed were rooted in Japanese pictorial tradition. His colouring developed from earthen tones to luminous pastel hues.

In 1948 Kuniyoshi was the first living artist in the United States to be awarded a major retrospective at the Whitney Museum of American Art. He was the first president of the Artists Equity Association, and he taught at the Art Students League from 1933; at the New School for Social Research, New York City; and at the artists' colony in Woodstock, N.Y.

Kunjae (Korean painter): *see* Ch'oe Kyong.

Kunlun Mountains, Wade-Giles romanization K'UN-LUN SHAN, Pinyin KUNLUN SHAN, mountain system of Asia, extending for about 1,250 miles (2,000 km) through the western regions of China.

A brief treatment of the Kunlun Mountains follows. For full treatment, *see* MACROPAEDIA: Asia.

From the Pamir mountain area of Tajikistan, the Kunlun system runs due east along the border between the Chinese autonomous regions of Sinkiang Uighur and Tibet to the Sino-Tibetan ranges in the province of Tsinghai. The system unites dozens of High Asian mountain ranges and divides the northern limit of the high Plateau of Tibet from the interior plains of Central Asia. The full length of the Kunlun system is subdivided into two unequal sections—the smaller western and principal eastern parts. The western Kunluns, composed of three parallel chains of ranges separated only by narrow intermontane depressions, have a width of 60 miles (95 km). The eastern Kunluns are characterized by a complex branching of mountain chains that pass around broad intermontane valleys; their width reaches as much as 375 miles (605 km) in places. The A-erh-ko Mountains in the eastern section contain the highest peak, the 25,338-foot (7,723-metre) Mount Mu-tzu-t'a-ko (Muztagh).

Kunsan, city, Chŏlla-puk *do* (province), western South Korea. Kunsan is situated 25 miles (40 km) west-northwest of the provincial capital, Chŏnju, and 7.5 miles (12 km) from the mouth of the Kŭm River. From the time of the Yi dynasty (1392–1910), it was noted as a rice-shipping port, and much of its commercial activities centred on processing, storing, and transporting rice grown on the rich Kŭm River plain. A thermoelectric plant was constructed after independence was achieved in 1945, and paper, lumber, rubber, and plastic industries began to develop. Pop. (1995) 266,569.

Kunst, Jaap (b. Aug. 12, 1891, Groningen, Neth.—d. Dec. 7, 1960, Amsterdam), Dutch ethnomusicologist who was one of the founders of modern ethnomusicology.

Kunst began to study the violin at an early age and became seriously interested in the folk culture of The Netherlands, learning its songs, dances, and style of violin playing. After earning a law degree in 1917 from the University of Groningen, he worked in banking and law for two years before joining a string trio that toured the Dutch East Indies. Kunst remained in Java until the mid-1930s, both working for the government and collecting and studying the native music, especially that of the Javanese gamelan. In 1930 his growing reputation as an authority on Indonesian music brought him a position as musicologist for the Dutch government, and he began to make extensive field trips, assembling many musical instruments, recordings, books, and photographs.

Returning to The Netherlands in 1934, Kunst began a European lecture tour, and in 1936 he became curator of the Royal Tropical Institute of Amsterdam, beginning what was to become one of the greatest musicological collections in Europe. He later lectured in Europe and in the United States, joining the faculty of the University of Amsterdam in 1942. Kunst's written output was extensive; his studies of Indonesia remain standard reference works.

Kunsthaus Zürich (German: "Zurich Art House"), museum of art in Zürich, established in 1787 and, since 1910, occupying a building designed by Karl Moser. It houses a varied collection of European painting from the Renaissance to modern periods, along with sculpture, drawings, and prints. The museum specializes in German medieval paintings and wood and stone sculpture, as well as later paintings by Zürich-area artists. It features the works of the noted Swiss artists Henry Fuseli and Alberto Giacometti.

Kunsthistorisches Museum (German: "Museum of Art History"), art museum in

Vienna. In addition to its many famous paintings, the museum contains important collections of sculpture, Oriental art, and decorative arts.

The museum's acquisitions are in the main a result of the rich accumulation of treasures by successive Habsburg rulers from the 16th century onward, notably by Archduke Leopold William in the mid-17th century. The painting collection is especially noted for its Renaissance and Baroque pictures of the Italian, German, Flemish, and Spanish schools.

Künstlerroman (German: "artist's novel"), class of *Bildungsroman*, or apprenticeship novel, that deals with the youth and development of an individual who becomes—or is on the threshold of becoming—a painter, musician, or poet. The classic example is James Joyce's *Portrait of the Artist as a Young Man* (1916). The type originated in the period of German Romanticism with Ludwig Tieck's *Franz Sternbalds Wanderungen* (1798; "Franz Sternbald's Wanderings"). Later examples are Knut Hamsun's *Hunger* (1890) and Thomas Wolfe's *Look Homeward, Angel* (1929). Unlike many *Bildungsroman*, where the hero often dreams of becoming a great artist but settles for being a mere useful citizen, the *Künstlerroman* usually ends on a note of arrogant rejection of the commonplace life.

Kunstmuseum-Öffentliche Kunstsammlung Basel (German: "Basel Art Museum-Public Art Collection"), museum of art in Basel, Switz., established in 1662 by the city and its university. The founding collection, the first publicly owned art collection in Europe, was purchased from extensive holdings of the Amerbach family. Later acquisitions have usually been the gifts of Basel citizens. The museum is noted for its collections of European painting (especially from the Renaissance and modern periods) and of modern sculpture.

Kuntaur, town, port on the Gambia River, MacCarthy Island division, central Gambia. Oceangoing vessels of 17-ft (5-km) draft navigate 150 mi (240 km) upstream to Kuntaur to load peanuts (groundnuts) for export. The Gambia Produce Marketing Board, which has operated a peanut decorticating plant since 1956, is the town's chief employer. The town is a secondary administrative centre and a traditional market for peanuts and rice. Pop. (1983 prelim.) 2,052.

Harvesting rice for the market at Kuntaur, The Gambia

Photo Research International

Kuo Hsi, Pinyin GUO XI (fl. *c.* 1060–80; b. Wen-hsien, Lo-yang Province, China), one of the most famous artists of the Northern Sung period in China.

Kuo Hsi's collected notes on landscape painting, *Lin-ch'uan kao-chih* ("Lofty Record of Forests and Streams"), describes with much detail the purposes and techniques of painting and is a valuable aid to the understanding of the landscape painting of the Northern Sung Dynasty. Few of his paintings have survived; among the works that may be considered authentic are the famous "Early Spring of 1072" (in the National Palace Museum, Taiwan), which is dated 1072, and a handscroll entitled "The Coming of Autumn" (in the Freer Gallery of Art, Washington, D.C.). Both effectively capture the quality of their seasonal interests and are paramount examples of the Sung accomplishment, which balanced pictorial description with the expressive brush to provide, as Kuo Hsi himself wrote, landscapes in which one may physically and mentally ramble.

"Autumn in a River Valley," silk scroll in ink and colour by Kuo Hsi; in the Freer Gallery of Art, Washington, D.C.

By courtesy of the Smithsonian Institution, Freer Gallery of Art, Washington, D.C.

Kuo Hsiang, Pinyin GUO XIANG (d. AD 312, China), Chinese philosopher, a Neo-Taoist thinker to whom is attributed a celebrated commentary on the *Chuang-tzu*, one of the basic Taoist writings.

Kuo was a high government official. His *Chuang-tzu chu* ("Chuang-tzu Commentary") is thought to have been begun by another Neo-Taoist philosopher, Hsiang Hsiu. When Hsiang died, Kuo is said to have incorporated Hsiang's commentary into his own. For this reason the work is sometimes called the Kuo–Hsiang commentary.

Kuo deviated from Lao-tzu in interpreting Tao ("the Way") as nothingness. As nonbeing, Tao does not produce being—that is, it cannot be regarded as a first cause.

> We may claim that we know the causes of certain things. But if we push our investigation of these causes to the furthest limit, (we reach) something which is self-produced without any cause. Being self-produced, we can no longer ask what is the cause of this something. We can only accept it as it is. (Quoted in Fung Yu-lan, *A History of Chinese Philosophy*, vol. ii, pp. 209–210; Princeton, Princeton University Press, 1953.)

Kuo thus maintained that everything produces itself spontaneously. The "self-transformation" of a thing as well as its existence is conditioned by other things and in its turn conditions them. Applying this general principle to human affairs, Kuo argued that social institutions and moral ideas must be changed when situations change. Kuo also gave a more positive meaning to the Taoist term "nonaction" by interpreting it to mean spontaneous action, not sitting still. In these points Kuo deviated from original Taoism, but the result which he inferred from his conception of nonaction agreed with Chuang-tzu's thought. For Kuo meant also that everything has a definite nature; if it follows its own way, it finds satisfaction and enjoyment; if it is not content with what is, and craves to be what it is not, then there is dissatisfaction and regret. The Perfect Man ignores all such distinctions as right and wrong, life and death; his happiness is unlimited.

Kuo Mo-jo (Chinese writer): *see* Guo Moruo.

Kuo Sung-tao, Pinyin GUO SONGDAO (b. April 11, 1818, Hsiangyin, Hunan Province, China—d. July 18, 1891, Hsiangyin), Chinese diplomat and liberal statesman who was his country's first resident minister of modern times to be stationed in a Western nation.

Kuo served in various Chinese bureaucratic and administrative posts during the 1850s and '60s. He was notable for his advocacy of a peaceful response on China's part toward the growing Western presence in the area, a stance which prompted his fellow officials to accuse him of trying to gain favour with Westerners. In 1876 Britain and China signed the Chefoo Agreement stipulating that China must send a minister to England. Kuo was appointed and took up residence at the Court of St. James's in 1877. He was concurrently appointed minister to France in 1878 and briefly resided in Paris at that time. Kuo, in his dispatches, urged his government to discard superstitions and to introduce railways, telegraph facilities, and modern mining methods into China. His advocacy of Westernization provoked such a tremendous outcry against Kuo from officials at home that publication of the diary of Kuo's journey from Shanghai to London was halted and the printing blocks burned. The following year he was ordered to return to China. Fearing that his life would be in jeopardy if he appeared in the capital, he pleaded ill health and retired to his native village. He spent his later years teaching, writing, and advocating the modernization of China in order to regain an equal footing in relations with the West.

Kuo T'ai-ch'i, also spelled QUO TAI-CHI (b. 1888, Kwang-tsi, Hupeh Province, China—d. Feb. 29, 1952, Santa Barbara, Calif., U.S.), Chinese official and diplomat who played a major role in determining his country's foreign policy during the 1930s and '40s.

The son of a scholar, Kuo was sent by the Chinese government to study in the United States in 1904. The Chinese Revolution of 1911 broke out while he was studying political science at the University of Pennsylvania (B.S., 1911), and he returned to China in 1912. He promptly joined the Nationalist Party (Kuomintang) and served as a secretary and councillor first to Li Yuan-hung and later to Sun Yat-sen. After Sun's death in 1925, Kuo served under the Nationalists' new head, Chiang Kai-shek, in various posts concerned with foreign affairs. As a vice-minister of foreign affairs in 1932, Kuo was the chief Chinese delegate at the armistice negotiations in Shanghai which achieved a truce between the Chinese and Japanese forces fighting for control of that city.

Kuo served as China's minister and then ambassador to Great Britain from 1932 to 1941 and was concurrently a Chinese delegate to the League of Nations from 1932 to 1938; in both posts he sought international support for China over the issue of Japanese aggression in his country. He briefly served as China's minister of foreign affairs from July to December 1941, after which he played a major role in determining China's foreign policy as chairman of the foreign affairs committee of the Supreme National Defense Council. Kuo coordinated policy-making during the frequent absences of the foreign minister, T.V. Soong, who spent much of his time in the United States rallying American support for China.

As China's delegate to the United Nations from February 1946 to December 1947, Kuo served as chairman of the UN Security Council's first meeting in New York City in 1946. After the Communist takeover of China in 1949 he lived in retirement in California.

Kuo Tzu-i, Pinyin GUO ZIYI (b. 697, Shensi Province, China—d. 781, China), one of the greatest of Chinese generals, later deified in popular religion.

Kuo served three emperors of the T'ang dynasty and is most noted for his successful fight against the rebellion of the Chinese general An Lu-shan in 755–757. From 760 to 765 he was occupied in defending China's western provinces from incursions of the Tanguts and other nomadic peoples, and in 763 he recovered the T'ang capital city, Ch'ang-an, from the invading Turfans using only some 4,000 demoralized troops. In gratitude, the Emperor T'ai-Tsung ennobled Kuo and gave his daughter in marriage to Kuo's youngest son. Popular depictions of Kuo sometimes show him leading or carrying his son to the imperial court.

In Chinese popular religion, Kuo Tzu-i is identified, like many local and national heroes, with one or more deities. He is generally equated with Fu-hsing, the stellar god of happiness, though this honour is also given to the 6th-century mandarin Yang Ch'eng. In Szechwan, Kuo Tzu-i is known as T'sai-shen, the god of riches.

Kuo's deification is popularly explained by the legend of his encounter with Chih Nü, the heavenly weaving maiden. She appeared to Kuo on the night of her feast day and Kuo, recognizing her, begged for happiness and riches. Chih Nü called him the god of happiness and riches and promised that honours and riches would be his. This scene is a favourite subject of Chinese popular art.

Kuomintang, Wade-Giles romanization KUO-MIN TANG (Chinese political party): *see* Nationalist Party.

Kuopio, city, Itä-Suomen *lääni* (Eastern Finland province), south central Finland, on the Kallavesi (lake). Originally founded in 1653, Kuopio existed as little more than a village until 1776, when King Gustav III ordered new city plans drawn up. It received its municipal charter in 1782. Kuopio is the centre of the Finnish Orthodox Church and has a bishopric and a seminary. Accessible by major water and rail routes as well as air service, the city serves as the cultural and economic centre of the *lääni.* Industry is centred on wood products, flour processing, and liqueur distillation. It is a tourist centre for the Savo lake and forest country, and nearby Puijo hill is one of Finland's best known skiing centres. Kuopio hosts the annual Finland Ice Marathon.

Until Finland's administrative reorganization

Kuopio, Fin.
Shostal—EB Inc.

in the 1990s, Kuopio was the capital of Kuopio province. Kuopio now serves administratively as a subregion of Eastern Finland. Pop. (1999 est.) 86,575.

Consult the INDEX *first*

Kuosa-Aleksandriškis, Jonas (Lithuanian poet): *see* Aistis, Jonas.

Kupang, also spelled KOEPANG, city, *kabupaten* (regency), and capital of Nusa Tenggara Timur *propinsi* (East Nusa Tenggara province), Timor island, Indonesia, located near the southwestern tip of the island on Teluk (bay) Kupang of the Savu Sea. Roads link it with Soe and Dili on Timor; Kupang also has an airport and lies on the Java–Australia air route. It is a trade and transshipment centre; copra, hides, sandalwood, pearls, and fish are exported to Java, Irian Jaya, and Australia. The majority of the population is Papuan, with an admixture of Malayan and Polynesian peoples. Fishing and handicrafts, including wood carving, basket making, and leather tanning, are economically important. Coastal vessels are built in the port. The Universitas Nusa Cendana, founded in 1962, is located in Kupang. The Portuguese occupied the city in the 1530s but were expelled by the Dutch in 1613. The city was under Japanese occupation during World War II. Pop. (1990) city, 141,694; regency, 522,780.

Kupffer cell, any of the stellate (star-shaped) cells in the linings of the liver sinusoids. The sinusoids are microscopic blood channels. The Kupffer cells are phagocytic, *i.e.,* capable of ingestion of other cells and of foreign particles. They also store hemosiderin so that it is available for the production of hemoglobin, the oxygen-transporting component of the red blood cell. Hemosiderin is an iron-containing pigment that is formed from the hemoglobin of red blood cells that have disintegrated.

Kupka, František, also called FRANK KUPKA, or FRANÇOIS KUPKA (b. Sept. 23, 1871, Opočno, Bohemia—d. June 24, 1957,

"Portrait of the Artist with His Wife," oil on canvas by František Kupka, 1908; in the Národní Galerie, Prague
By courtesy of the National Gallery, Prague

Puteaux, Fr.), Czech-born French pioneer of abstract painting and one of the first completely nonrepresentational artists. His mature works contributed much to the foundations of pure abstract painting in the 20th century.

Kupka studied at the Prague and Vienna academies and at the École des Beaux-Arts in Paris, where he settled in 1895. In 1908–11 he experimented with Fauvism and with Pointillism, the latter a technique originating with the French painter Seurat, whose colour-contrast theories led Kupka to study the aesthetic properties of colours.

Kupka, in his painting "Disks of Newton" (1912; Philadelphia Museum of Art), and Robert Delaunay, in his similar "Disks" (1912), were the earliest exponents of curvilinear pure abstraction. This art was dubbed Orphism—an art of "musical" colour lyricism—by the poet and art critic Guillaume Apollinaire in 1912. Kupka painted abstractions with such titles as "Fugue in Red and Blue" (1912; Národní Galerie, Prague), making explicit his belief that abstract colour, like music, is capable of evoking profound feeling.

Küpper, Christian Emil Marie (Dutch painter): *see* Doesburg, Theo van.

Kuprin, Aleksandr Ivanovich (b. Sept. 7 [Aug. 26, old style], 1870, Narovchat, Russia—d. Aug. 25, 1938, Leningrad [now St. Petersburg]), Russian novelist and short-story writer, one of the last exponents of the great tradition of Russian critical realism.

Educated in military schools, he served as an officer in the army, a career he soon aban-

Kuprin
Novosti Press Agency

doned for a more lively and diversified life as a journalist, hunter, fisherman, actor, and circus worker. Literary fame came with *Poyedinok* (1905; *The Duel*), a realistically sordid picture of the emptiness of life in a remote military garrison. Its appearance during the Russo-Japanese War coincided with and confirmed a national wave of antimilitary sentiment. Kuprin wrote prolifically; his subjects might be best described by the title of one of his best known stories, *Reka zhizni* (1906; "The River of Life"). He is a fascinated and an undiscriminating observer of the stream of life and especially of any milieu that constitutes a world of its own—a cheap hotel, a factory, a house of prostitution, a tavern, a circus, or a race track. His best known novel, *Yama* (1909–15; *Yama: The Pit*), deals with the red-light district of a southern port city. It dwells with enthusiasm on the minutiae of the everyday life of the prostitutes, their housekeeping, economics, and social stratification. As Kuprin's spokesman in the novel puts it, "all the horror is just this—that there is no horror! Bourgeois work days—and that is all. . . ."

Kuprin's style is extremely natural. He picks up the slang and argot that is peculiar to his subject and describes everything with zest and colour and with a goodness of heart that compensates for any shortcomings he may have in originality or intellectual depth. After the Revolution, Kuprin became one of the many Russian émigrés in Paris, where he continued to write, although exile was not fruitful for his essentially extroverted, reportorial talent. In

1937 he was allowed to return to the Soviet Union.

Kura River, Turkish KURUÇAY, Georgian MTKVARI, river in Turkey, Georgia, and Azerbaijan. The Kura is the largest river in Transcaucasia. It rises on the slopes of Mount Kısırındağı in extreme eastern Turkey and cuts northward through the Little Caucasus range in a series of gorges with many rapids. Some distance after entering Georgia, the river swings eastward across the Kartli plain and takes a southeasterly course for the remainder of its length. Just above the Georgian capital of Tbilisi, a dam has been built along the Mtskheta narrows, and the river valley subsequently broadens out into an extensive lowland. Farther downstream, the narrows near Mingäçevir in Azerbaijan are the site of another dam and hydroelectric station that have created a large reservoir called Lake Mingäçevir. There is much flooding along the Kura's lower course. The river finally enters the Caspian Sea by a delta.

The Kura is 848 miles (1,364 km) long and drains an area of 72,500 square miles (188,000 sq km). Several of its tributaries also provide hydroelectric power, and the Kura itself is extensively used for irrigation purposes. The river is navigable upstream for 300 miles (480 km) as far as Yevlax, just south of Mingäçevir.

Kurakin, Boris Ivanovich, Prince (Knyaz) (b. July 20 [July 30, New Style], 1676, Moscow, Russia—d. Oct. 17 [Oct. 28], 1727, Paris, France), one of the first professional diplomats of Russia, who represented Peter I the Great in western Europe.

In 1691 Kurakin became Peter's brother-in-law by marrying the sister of the tsar's first wife, Eudoxia. Although he was a member of the old Muscovite aristocracy and often disapproved of Peter's nontraditional methods, Kurakin served the tsar faithfully.

After Russia entered the Great Northern War against Sweden, Kurakin fought in it as a soldier from 1700 to 1705. Shifted then to the diplomatic front, he persuaded Pope Clement XI to withhold his recognition of the pro-Swedish Stanisław I Leszczyński as king of Poland. After returning to Russia, Kurakin became head of the Semyonovsky Guards and took part in Russia's victory over the Swedes at Poltava (1709). Then for the remainder of the war he devoted himself to diplomatic activities, arranging in 1709 the marriage of Peter's son Alexis to Sophia Charlotte of Brunswick-Wolfenbüttel and serving as ambassador to London (*c.* 1710) and to The Hague (1716). He also negotiated (1710) a defensive treaty of friendship for Peter with George I, elector of Hanover and future king of Great Britain; concluded the Treaty of Greifswald (1715) between Peter and George (as elector of Hanover), in which they exchanged territorial guarantees; and participated with Peter in the Paris negotiations resulting in a French agreement not to provide Sweden with assistance.

After the Great Northern War was concluded (1721), Peter launched a campaign against Iran (1722–23), and Kurakin became coordinator of the work of all Russian diplomatic envoys. The following year he was appointed ambassador to Paris.

Ten volumes of Kurakin's papers, which include detailed descriptions of the main characters and events of his day, were published in *Arkhiv knyazya F.A. Kurakina* (1890–1902; "Archive of Prince F.A. Kurakin").

Kurashiki, city, Okayama *ken* (prefecture), western Honshu, Japan. It is situated on the eastern bank of the lower Takahashi River. During the Tokugawa period (1603–1867), it was an important trading centre for rice, cotton, and oil; many of its storage houses, built in traditional style, remain. The city has been known for its textile manufacturing since the

Ōhara Art Museum, Kurashiki, Japan
Bob Glaze—Artstreet

late 19th century. During World War II, a large aircraft-production plant was established there, which has since converted to automobile production. After 1964 the industrial centre moved south, where petrochemical and heavy chemical plants face the Inland Sea. Kurashiki is also a cultural centre that houses the Ōhara Art Museum. Pop. (1994 est.) 419,528.

Kurath, Hans (b. Dec. 13, 1891, Villach, Austria—d. Jan. 2, 1992, Ann Arbor, Mich., U.S.), American linguist, best known as the chief editor of the *Linguistic Atlas of New England,* the first comprehensive linguistic atlas of a large region.

Kurath emigrated from Austria to the United States in 1907 and became a citizen in 1912. He studied at the University of Texas (A.B., 1914) and the University of Chicago (Ph.D., 1920). He taught German at Northwestern University (Evanston, Ill.; 1920–27), German and linguistics at Ohio State University (Columbus; 1927–31) and at Brown University (Providence, R.I.; 1931–46), and English and linguistics at the University of Michigan, Ann Arbor (1946–62). His wife was the noted ethnomusicologist Gertrude Prokosch Kurath.

Kurath's career centred mainly on American English dialects. In addition to having edited the *Linguistic Atlas of New England,* 3 vol. (1939–43), he wrote the *Handbook of the Linguistic Geography of New England* (1939, rev. ed. 1973), *A Word Geography of the Eastern United States* (1949), and *The Pronunciation of English in the Atlantic States* (1961). From 1946 to 1962 he was also editor in chief of the *Middle English Dictionary.*

Kuratsukuri Tori (fl. early 7th century, Japan), the first great Japanese sculptor of the Asuka period (552–645).

Tori belonged to the hereditary *kuratsukuribe* ("saddlemakers' guild"), and, as an ardent Buddhist, he applied his technique of making gilt bronze ornaments for saddle trappings to the making of bronze Buddhas. Empress Suiko and Crown Prince Shōtoku, the great patron of Japanese Buddhism, commissioned Tori to do numerous works, including a statue of Shaka Nyorai (the Buddha) completed in 606 for the Asuka Temple, near modern Nara; and "Shakasanzonzō," or "Shaka Triad" (completed in 623), at the Golden Pavilion of the Hōryū Temple, also near modern Nara. Though made of bronze, the sculptures by Tori and his school clearly indicate the strong influence of the art of stonecutting, which had been developed in China when cave sculptures were popular during the Northern Wei dynasty (386–534).

Kurayoshi, city, Tottori *ken* (prefecture), Honshu, Japan. It lies along a tributary of the Tenjin River and occupies a strategic position on a plain bounded (south) by the Chūgoku Range. The city was the capital of Hōki province (now in Tottori prefecture) from

early historical times. A commercial centre, it developed its textile industry late in the Tokugawa period (1603–1867); the city is identified with a distinctive cotton cloth known as Kurayoshi-*kasuri* ("Kurayoshi splashed pattern"). Its modern industrial products include silk, agricultural machinery, beverages, and wood articles. Pop. (1990) 51,835.

Kurbsky, Andrey Mikhaylovich, Prince (Knyaz) (b. 1528, Russia—d. 1583, Poland-Lithuania), Russian military commander who was a close associate and adviser to Tsar Ivan IV the Terrible of Russia during the 1540s and '50s.

A member of the princely house of Smolensk-Yaroslavl, Kurbsky became attached to the special advisory council (Izbrannaya Rada, or "Chosen Council"), which Ivan formed in 1547 to assist him in the preparation of internal reforms and the formulation of foreign policy. At the age of 21, Kurbsky was appointed groom-in-waiting to the tsar and also began his military career, participating in the 1549 campaign against the khanate of Kazan. Although he was wounded while storming the city in 1552, he later took part in consolidating Russian power over the newly conquered Kazan (1553–56). During that period Kurbsky also became one of the tsar's intimate associates and in 1553 demonstrated his loyalty to Ivan, who was then seriously ill, by pledging to support Ivan's infant son Fyodor as heir, although many nobles refused to do so.

In 1556 Kurbsky was promoted to the rank of boyar, the aristocratic order just below the rank of ruling princes. After fighting the Crimean Tatars in the south (1556), he was named by Ivan to be one of the Russian commanders in the campaign to conquer Livonia and was sent to the western frontier (1557). Although militarily successful, after 1563 Kurbsky lost Ivan's favour and was effectively confined to Dorpat (now Tartu). When Ivan failed to renew his appointment, Kurbsky fled (April 30, 1564) to the camp of King Sigismund II Augustus of Poland-Lithuania, who granted him large estates and gave him a commission in his army to fight Ivan (September 1564).

Later Kurbsky defended the interests of the Orthodox population of Lithuania against encroachments from Catholics and Protestants. He also wrote religious works and an account of Ivan's reign (*Istoriya o velikom knyaze moskovskom;* "History of the Grand Duke of Muscovy"), in which he attacked Ivan's reign of terror. Kurbsky's letters are also interesting—the most famous being those he wrote to Ivan after his flight. From his correspondence it is evident that the Russian nobles—who until recently had been independent rulers of their principalities—found a spokesman in Kurbsky to voice their disapproval of Ivan's absolutist tendencies.

Kurchatov, Igor Vasilyevich (b. Jan. 12, 1903, Sim, Russia—d. Feb. 7, 1960, Moscow), Soviet nuclear physicist who guided the development of his country's first atomic bomb, the world's first practical thermonuclear bomb, and the first atomic electric-power station in the Soviet Union.

After graduation (1923) from the Crimean University in Simferopol, Kurchatov joined (1927) the staff of the Physico-Technical Institute of the Academy of Sciences in Leningrad. His initial studies concerned ferroelectricity, but by 1933 he was concentrating on nuclear physics. As director of the nuclear physics laboratory at the Physico-Technical Institute, he supervised the construction of the first Soviet cyclotrons. In 1939 he and his associates published studies of nuclear chain reactions, and in 1940 he reported the spontaneous fission of uranium, previously reported only a year earlier by Otto Hahn and Fritz Strassmann in Germany. During World War II, Kurchatov's nuclear research was suspended in favour of defense research concerning methods of protecting ships from magnetic mines.

Kurchatov directed the construction of the first Soviet cyclotron (1944) and, after the war, the first atomic reactor in Europe (1946). His team produced the first Soviet atomic bomb in 1949, four years after the United States. In 1953 the team detonated a thermonuclear (hydrogen) bomb, six months before the first U.S. thermonuclear bomb. The nonmilitary applications of atomic power explored and developed under Kurchatov's leadership included, besides electric-power stations (the first of which began operation in 1954), the nuclear-powered icebreaker *Lenin.* Kurchatov also directed research on the "ultimate power source," fusion energy, centring on a means of containment of the extremely high temperatures that are needed to initiate the fusion process.

In 1956 Kurchatov was publicly identified as director of the Institute of Atomic Energy of the Soviet Academy of Sciences (from 1960 called the I.V. Kurchatov Institute of Atomic Energy). The Kurchatov Medal was established by the Academy of Sciences for outstanding work in nuclear physics. Scientists in the Soviet Union proposed that the radioactive element with the atomic number 104 (which American scientists have called rutherfordium) be named kurchatovium, but neither group has been able to verify the results of the other, and both the name and priority of the discovery are still controversial.

kurchatovium (physics): *see* unnilquadium.

Kurd, member of an ethnic and linguistic group living in the Taurus Mountains of eastern Anatolia, the Zagros Mountains of western Iran, northern Iraq, and adjacent areas. Most of the Kurds live in contiguous areas of Iran, Iraq, and Turkey, a region generally referred to as Kurdistan ("Land of the Kurds"). A sizable, noncontiguous Kurdish population also exists in the Khorāsān region of northeastern Iran.

The Kurdish language is a West Iranian language related to Farsi and Pashto. The Kurds are thought to number more than 15 million, including communities in Armenia, Georgia, Kazakstan, Lebanon, and Syria, but sources for this information differ widely because of differing criteria of ethnicity, religion, and language; statistics may also be manipulated for political purposes.

The traditional Kurdish way of life was nomadic, revolving around sheep and goat herding throughout the Mesopotamian plains and the highlands of Turkey and Iran. Most Kurds practiced only marginal agriculture. The enforcement of national boundaries beginning after World War I impeded the seasonal migrations of the flocks, forcing most of the Kurds to abandon their traditional ways for village life and settled farming; others entered nontraditional employment.

The prehistory of the Kurds is poorly known, but their ancestors seem to have inhabited the same upland region for millennia. The records of the early empires of Mesopotamia contain frequent references to mountain tribes with names resembling "Kurd." The Kardouchoi who attacked Xenophon and the Ten Thousand in 401 BC (near modern Zākhū, Iraq, just south of the Turkish border) may have been Kurds, but some scholars dispute this claim. The name Kurd can be dated with certainty to the time of the tribes' conversion to Islām in the 7th century AD. Most Kurds are Sunnite Muslims, but among them there are also many Sufis and other mystical and heretical sects.

Despite their long-standing occupation of a particular region of the world, the Kurds never achieved nation-state status. Their reputation for military prowess has made them much in demand as mercenaries in many armies. Saladin, the Kurd best known to the Western world, epitomizes the Kurdish military reputation.

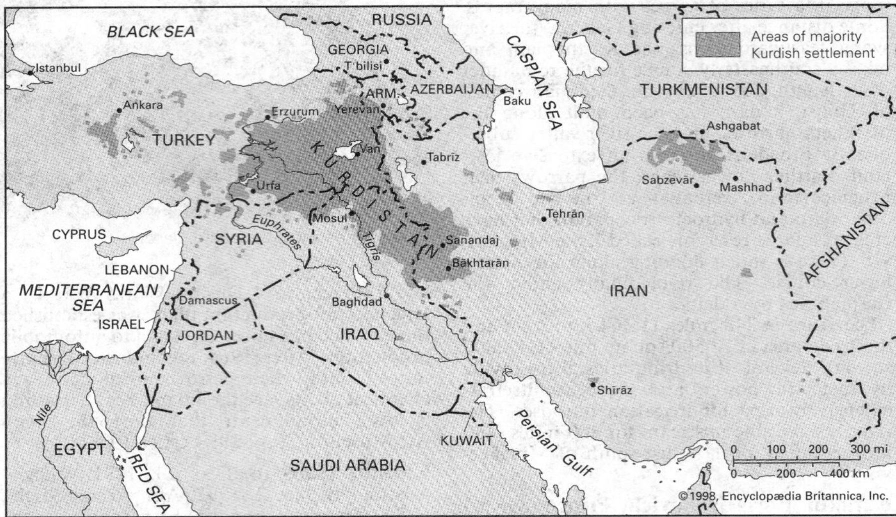

Areas of Kurdish settlement in Southwest Asia

The principal unit in traditional Kurdish society was the tribe, typically led by a sheikh, or an aga, whose rule was firm. Tribal identification and the sheikh's authority are still felt, though to a lesser degree, in the villages. Detribalization proceeded rapidly as Kurdish culture became urbanized and was nominally assimilated into several nations.

In traditional Kurdish society, marriage was generally endogamous. In nonurban areas, males usually marry at age 20 and females at age 12. Households typically consist of father, mother, and children. Polygamy, permitted by Islāmic law, is sometimes practiced, although it is forbidden by civil law in Turkey. The strength of the extended family's ties to the tribe varies with the way of life. Kurdish women—who traditionally have been more active in public life than Turkish and Iranian women—as well as Kurdish men, have taken advantage of urban educational and employment opportunities, especially in prerevolutionary Iran.

Kurdish nationalism, a recent phenomenon, came about through the conjunction of a variety of factors, including British introduction of the concept of private property, the partition of traditional Kurdistan by modern neighbouring states, and the influence of British, U.S., and Soviet interests in the Persian Gulf region. These factors and others combined with the flowering of a nationalist movement among a very small minority of urban, intellectual Kurds.

The first Kurdish newspaper appeared in 1897 and was published at intervals until 1902. It was revived at Istanbul in 1908 (when the first Kurdish political club, with an affiliated cultural society, was also founded) and again in Cairo during World War I. The Treaty of Sèvres, drawn up in 1920, provided for an autonomous Kurdistan but was never ratified; the Treaty of Lausanne (1923), which replaced the Treaty of Sèvres, made no mention of Kurdistan or of the Kurds. Thus the opportunity to unify the Kurds in a nation of their own was lost. Indeed, Kurdistan after the war was more fragmented than before, and various separatist movements arose among Kurdish groups. Short-lived armed rebellions occurred, and in 1931–32 and 1944–45 there were serious conflicts in Iraqi Kurdistan.

The Kurds of Turkey received particularly unsympathetic treatment at the hands of the government, which tried to deprive them of their Kurdish identity by designating them "Mountain Turks," by outlawing the Kurdish language (or representing it as a dialect of Turkish), and by forbidding them to wear distinctive Kurdish costume in or near the important administrative cities. The Turkish government suppressed Kurdish political agitation in the eastern provinces and encouraged the migration of Kurds to the urbanized western portion of Turkey, thus diluting the concentration of Kurdish population in the uplands. Kurds also felt strong assimilationist pressure from the national government in Iran and endured religious persecution by that country's Shīʿite Muslim majority.

Iraqi Kurds suffered relatively less cultural suppression. In 1958 the Iraqi monarchy was overthrown, but Kurdish hopes of a measure of administrative devolution, enhanced status for their language, and a fairer share of social services and development projects under the new government were not fulfilled. In 1970 a new Baʿthist government granted the Kurds of Iraq a limited autonomy that was nonetheless declared inadequate by Kurdish leaders. Unsuccessful, short-lived Kurdish rebellions continued into the late 20th century; slaughter, dislocation, and starvation were the usual consequences. *See also* Kurdistan.

Kurdish language, West Iranian language spoken in Kurdistan; it ranks as the third largest Iranian language group, after Persian and Pashto, and has numerous dialects. There are two main dialect groups. The northern group—spoken from Mosul, Iraq, into the Caucasus—is called Kurmānjī; in Turkey, Hawar (Turkized Latin) characters are used in the written form. The central group, called Kurdī, or Sōrānī, emerged as the major literary form of Kurdish. It is spoken within a broad region that stretches roughly from Orūmīyeh, Iran, to the lower reaches of traditional Kurdistan in Iraq. In Iraq, Kurdī is the official form of Kurdish. Subdialects of Kurdish include Kermanshahī, Lekī, Guranī, and Zaza.

Where the same name may denote a person, place, or thing, the articles will be found in that order

---

Kurdish rug, floor covering that is handcrafted by people of Kurdish stock in Iran, eastern Anatolia, or perhaps to a limited extent in Iraq and in the southernmost Caucasus. These rugs are stout and solid in structure, usually made in Ghiordes knotting upon a woolen foundation. Among older examples, created in the late 18th and early 19th centuries, the Garden carpets and those in the *harshang* design, with its repeat of "flaming" palmettes, are outstanding for their range of exuberant colours.

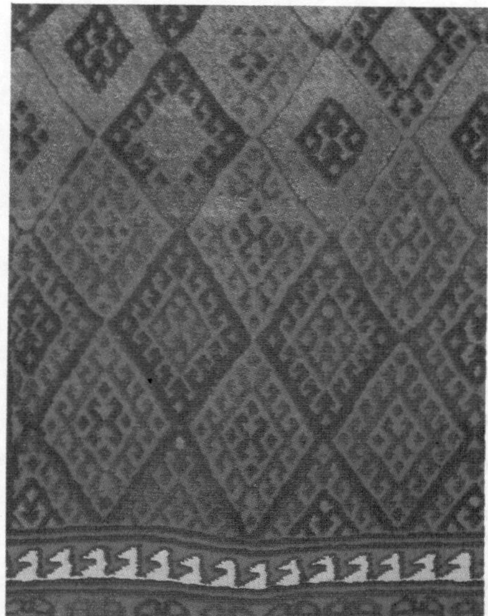

Diamond grid motif, detail of a Jaffi Kurdish rug from the Turko-Iranian borderland, 19th century; in the Textile Museum, Washington, D.C.
Textile Museum Collection, Washington, D.C.; photograph, Otto E. Nelson

Jaffi Kurdish rugs and saddlebag faces, from the Turko-Iranian borderland, show diamond grids, each lozenge containing a latch-hooked figure. Bījār carpets are Kurdish products, as are the surprisingly delicate rugs of Sanandaj.

Kurdistan, Arabic KURDESTĀN, Persian KORDESTĀN, traditional region, an extensive plateau and mountain area inhabited mainly by Kurds, including large parts of what are now eastern Turkey, northern Iraq, and northwestern Iran and smaller parts of northern Syria and Armenia. Of these, only Iran recognizes an area with the name Kordestān.

The name Kurdistan ("Land of the Kurds") refers to an area that roughly includes the mountain systems of the Zagros and the eastern extension of the Taurus. Since very early times the area has been the home of the Kurds, a people whose ethnic origins are uncertain. For 600 years after the Arab conquest and their conversion to Islām, the Kurds played a recognizable and considerable part in the troubled history of western Asia, but as tribes, individuals, or turbulent groups rather than as a nation.

Among the petty Kurdish dynasties that arose during this period the most important were the Shaddadids, ruling a predominantly Armenian population in the Ani and Ganja districts of Transcaucasia (951–1174); the Marwānids of Diyarbakir (990–1096); and the Hasanwaihids of Dīnavar in the Kermānshāh region (959–1015). Less is written of the Kurds under the Mongols and Turkmens, but they again became prominent in the wars between the Ottomans and the Ṣafavids. Several Kurdish principalities developed and survived into the first half of the 19th century, notably those of Bohtan, Hakari, Bahdinan, Soran, and Baban in Turkey and of Mukri and Ardelan in Persia. But Kurdistan, though it played a considerable part in the history of western Asia, never enjoyed political unity.

With the dissolution of the Ottoman Empire after World War I, and particularly with the encouragement of U.S. President Woodrow Wilson—one of whose Fourteen Points stipulated that the non-Turkish nationalities of the Ottoman Empire should be "assured of an absolute unmolested opportunity of autonomous development"—Kurdish nationalists looked to the eventual establishment of a Kurdistani state.

The Treaty of Sèvres, signed in 1920 by representatives of the Allies and of the sultan, provided for the recognition of the three Arab states of Hejaz, Syria, and Iraq and of Armenia and, to the south of it, Kurdistan, which the Kurds of the Mosul *vilāyet* (province), then under British occupation, would have the right to join. Owing to the military revival of Turkey under Kemal Atatürk, this treaty was never ratified. It was superseded in 1923 by the Treaty of Lausanne, which confirmed the provision for the Arab states but omitted mention of Armenia and Kurdistan. Mosul was excluded from the settlement, and the question of its future was referred to the League of Nations, which in 1925 awarded it to Iraq. This decision was made effective by the Treaty of Ankara, signed in 1926 by Turkey, Iraq, and Great Britain. *See also* Kurd.

Mountainous area of Kurdistan in northern Iraq
Tom Weir—Camera Press from Pictorial Parade

Kurdufān (Sudan): *see* Kordofan.

Kŭrdzhali, also spelled KŬRDŽALI, or KĂRDZHALI, town, south-central Bulgaria, in a broad valley on the Arda River between the Kŭrdzhali and Studen Kladenets dams, both important hydroelectric power and irrigation stations. The town became part of Bulgaria after the 1912–13 Balkan Wars. Its strong traditional Oriental character has been balanced by development as a modern industrial town. Formerly known chiefly as a tobacco-growing centre, it is now more diversified, with lead and zinc refining and asbestos production. Noteworthy are the "mushrooms" of Kŭrdzhali, pyramidal rock formations tinted green, rose-white, or yellow by minerals near the villages of Dobrovolets, Povet, and Zimzelen. Pop. (1989 est.) 58,995.

Kure, city, Hiroshima *ken* (prefecture), southwestern Honshu, Japan, on the Inland Sea. Its excellent natural harbour is surrounded by mountains and screened from the sea by mountainous islands. Because of its seclusion, Kure was chosen as the site of a major naval base in 1886. During World War II its shipyards and foundries produced the *Yamato,* one of the largest battleships ever built. The city now builds merchant ships and oil tankers for export. Kure's industries experienced serious economic depression after the 1973 oil-price increases. Pop. (1990) 216,717.

A shipyard in Kure, Japan
William C. Gagnon—Shostal

Kürenberger, Der also called DER VON KÜRENBERG (fl. 1160), the earliest of the German poet-musicians called minnesingers known by name.

All that is known of him is that he was an Austrian nobleman from near Linz. In his proud and imperious love songs there is as yet no evidence of the homage to women expressed by the later minnesingers and their French or Provençal models. His poems are written in stanzas of four lines, rhymed in pairs and divided into half lines by a caesura (pause). Because this is the form of the German heroic epic the *Nibelungenlied* ("the Nibelungenlied strophe") and because Kürenberger's style has an epic-dramatic quality, it has been conjectured that he may have written a lost German epic on which the unknown author of the *Nibelungenlied* based his poem.

Kurgan, *oblast* (province), west-central Russia, on the southern edge of the West Siberian Plain, in the Tobol Basin. It is a level plain with innumerable small lakes, often saline, in shallow depressions. The steppe-grass vegetation has been largely ploughed up, and many shelter belts of trees have been planted; in the north are extensive birch groves. Agriculture, greatly extended in the Virgin and Idle Lands campaign of the 1950s, dominates the economy. Spring wheat is the main crop, with rye, oats, and corn (maize), as well as vegetables, of some significance. Dairy farming is common in the north and sheep farming in the drier south. The towns, except Kurgan, the *oblast* headquarters, are small and concerned chiefly with processing agricultural produce. Area 27,400 square miles (71,000 square km). Pop. (1991 est.) 1,110,500.

Kurgan, city and administrative centre of Kurgan *oblast* (province), west-central Russia, on the Tobol River. In 1553 the fortified settlement of Tsaryovo Gorodishche was founded on a large ancient tumulus or artificial mound (Russian *kurgan*); it became a town in 1782, and by the late 19th century it was the focus of the surrounding farming area, especially after the building of the railways to Omsk, Chelyabinsk, and Yekaterinburg. The Tobol River, which is frozen from November until May, is navigable the rest of the year and links Kurgan to the Ob-Irtysh system. Agricultural and other machinery, medical preparations, and a wide range of foodstuffs are produced by local industries. The city has agricultural, teacher-training, and machine-building institutes. Pop. (1992 est.) 365,000.

Kurgan culture, seminomadic pastoralist culture that spread from the Russian steppes to Danubian Europe about 3500 BC. By about 2300 BC the Kurgans arrived in the Aegean and Adriatic regions. The Kurgans buried their dead in deep shafts within artificial burial mounds, or barrows. The word *kurgan* means "barrow," or "artificial mound," in Turkic and Russian.

Kurgan-Tyube, also spelled KURGAN-TIUBE, city, southwestern Tajikistan. It lies in the Vakhsh River valley, 62 miles (100 km) south of Dushanbe. Kurgan-Tyube has existed since the 17th century. It is on the railway line between Dushanbe and Kulyab.

Kurgan-Tyube has food-processing plants, clothing manufacturers, an electrical-transformer plant, and a cotton-ginning plant. The city also has a medical school and a power-engineering *tekhnikum* (technical college). In the surrounding area, cotton is the main crop and sheep are the main livestock. Pop. (1991 est.) 58,400.

Kuria Muria (Oman): *see* Khurīyā Murīyā.

Kuril Current (Pacific Ocean): *see* Oya Current.

Kuril Islands, Russian KURILSKIYE OSTROVA, Japanese CHISHIMA-RETTŌ, archipelago in Sakhalin *oblast* (province), far-eastern Russia. The archipelago extends for 750 miles (1,200 km) from the southern tip of the Kamchatka Peninsula (Russia) to the northeastern corner of Hokkaido island (Japan) and separates the Sea of Okhotsk from the Pacific Ocean. The 56 islands cover 6,000 square miles (15,600 square km).

The chain is part of the belt of geologic instability circling the Pacific and contains at least 100 volcanoes, of which 35 are still active, and many hot springs. Earthquakes and tidal waves are common; the tidal wave of 1737 attained a height of 210 feet (64 m), one of the highest on record. Parallel to the chain, in the Pacific floor, is the Kuril Trench, which reaches a depth of more than 6.5 miles (10.5 km). The climate in the islands is severe, with long, cold, snowy winters and cool, wet, foggy summers. The average annual precipitation is 30–40 inches (760–1,000 mm), most of which falls as snow, which may occur in any month from the end of September to the beginning of June. Vegetation ranges from tundra on the northern islands to dense forest on the larger southern islands. The only significant occupation is fishing, especially for crab. The principal centres are the towns of Kurilsk on Iturup, the largest island, and Severo-Kurilsk on Paramushir. Some vegetables are grown on the southern islands.

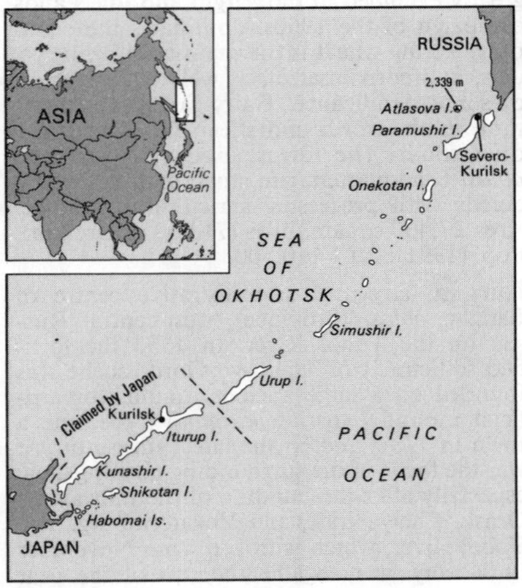

The Kurils were originally settled by the Russians, following their exploration in the 17th and 18th centuries. In 1855, however, Japan seized a group of the southern islands and in 1875 took possession of the entire chain. In 1945, as part of the Yalta agreements, the islands were ceded to the Soviet Union, and the Japanese population was repatriated and replaced by Soviets. Japan still claims historical rights to the southernmost islands and has tried repeatedly to persuade the Soviet Union and, from 1991, Russia to return the islands to Japanese sovereignty.

Kuril Islands

Kuril Trench, deep submarine depression in the western Pacific Ocean, situated on the east side of the Kamchatka Peninsula, the Kuril Islands, and Hokkaido island, Japan. Extending for about 1,800 miles (2,900 km) north-south, it has a maximum depth of 34,587 feet (10,542 m) and covers a total area of 102,000 square miles (264,000 square km). The steep slopes of the trench are characterized in places by an intermediate bench, or series of steps or terraces, which are sometimes interpreted as the scarps of giant, gravitationally slumped sheets of rock. The Kuril Trench marks the beginning of a chain of oceanic trenches extending from the southwestern edge of the Bering Sea to the southern tip of the Philippine Trench.

Kurland (region, Baltic seacoast): *see* Courland.

Kūrma (Sanskrit: "Tortoise"), second of the 10 avatars (incarnations) of the Hindu god Vishnu. In this incarnation Vishnu is associated with the myth of the churning of the cosmic ocean. The gods and the *asuras* cooperated in the churning to obtain the *amṛta,* the elixir of immortality. The great serpent Vāsuki offered himself as a rope, and Mount Mandara was torn out for use as a churning stick. A firm foundation was required to steady the mountain, so Vishnu took the form of a tortoise and supported the churning stick on his back. An earlier reference to a divine incarnation as a tortoise identifies the animal with Prajāpati (the god Brahmā), who took that shape in order to create offspring.

Kūrma, detail of sandstone sculpture from Garhwāl, Uttar Pradesh, India, 11th century

Pramod Chandra

The Kūrma avatar of Vishnu is usually represented in painting and sculpture in a mixed human-animal form. The human half, which is the upper half, is depicted wearing the same ornaments and holding the same weapons as in the usual images of Vishnu. Kūrma is also represented zoomorphically, as a tortoise.

A list of the abbreviations used in the MICROPAEDIA *will be found at the end of this volume*

Kürnberger, Ferdinand (b. July 3, 1821, Vienna, Austria—d. Oct. 14, 1879, Munich, Ger.), Austrian writer known for his participation in the Austrian revolution of 1848 and the Dresden rebellion of 1849.

Kürnberger was forced to leave Austria after his participation in the first rebellion and was jailed for his involvement in the second. He lived in Germany until 1864, when he became secretary for the Schiller Foundation, a position that he held for three years. He wrote many plays, the best known being *Catilina* (1855), as well as novels and critical essays. Among these works are *Der Amerika-Müde* (1855; "The One Who Is Tired of America"), a roman à clef about Nikolaus Lenau, a popular figure of the time; *Der Haustyrann* (1876; "The House Tyrant"); *Das Schloss der Frevel* (1904; "Frevel's Castle"); and two books of essays, *Siegelringe* (1874; "Signet Rings") and *Literarische Herzenssachen* (1877; "Literary Matters of the Heart"). His *Gesammelte Werke* ("Collected Works") was published in 1911.

Kurnell, historic site on the southern side of the entrance to Botany Bay, New South Wales, Australia. Kurnell was the first landing place in Australia of Captain James Cook on April 29, 1770. The First Fleet, the first group of British settlers in Australia, also landed there, in 1788, before moving on to Port Jackson. The area is now a public reserve, with several monuments and a museum.

Kurnool, city, west-central Andhra Pradesh state, southern India. It lies at the confluence of the Tungabhadra and Hindri rivers, about 240 miles (385 km) northwest of the city of Madras. Kurnool was made a municipality in 1866 and was the capital of Andhra Pradesh until 1956, when the capital was moved to Hyderābād.

Kurnool is a trade centre. In the city there are colleges of arts, sciences, and medicine, all of which are affiliated with Andhra University in Waltair. Of historical interest are the ruins of a royal fort dating back to the medieval kingdom of Vijayanagar, which flourished from the 14th to the 16th century. Pop. (1991 prelim.) 236,313.

Kuroda Kiyotaka, COUNT (Hakushaku) (b. Nov. 21, 1840, Satsuma province, Japan—d. Aug. 25, 1900, Tokyo), Japanese statesman who played a leading role in the Meiji Restoration, the 1868 overthrow of the Tokugawa shogunate and reestablishment of imperial rule in Japan. He served as prime minister from April 1888 to October 1889. Kuroda was one of the original genro, the handful of statesmen from Satsuma and Chōshū, who officially and unofficially dominated the Japanese government from 1868 until the end of World War I.

Having commanded the imperial forces that captured the northern Japanese island of Hokkaido for the Meiji government, Kuroda in 1870 was put in charge of colonizing and developing that relatively primitive area. He hired American agricultural experts, subsidized immigrants, and encouraged new industry. Within a decade the population of the island quadrupled, and the productivity markedly increased. As a result, Hokkaido became a secure part of the Japanese islands, safe from the threat of Russian penetration.

Kuroda rose rapidly within the government.

Although he was the only man in the Cabinet who in 1879 discouraged the establishment of a popular legislature, he was appointed prime minister in 1888. He resigned 18 months later in a dispute over revision of the "unequal treaties" the European nations had forced on Japan in the 1850s; but he continued to hold various other Cabinet positions and, as a member of the genro, to influence government policy until his death 11 years later.

Kuroda Nagamasa (b. 1568, Himeji, Japan—d. Aug. 29, 1623, Kyōto), noted Japanese warrior who rendered important service to two leaders, Toyotomi Hideyoshi and Tokugawa Ieyasu, in their campaigns to dominate Japan.

Upon his father's death, Kuroda succeeded him as one of Hideyoshi's generals in his battles to dominate Japan. When Hideyoshi invaded Korea in 1592, Kuroda served as one of the leading generals in the campaign, which continued for seven years. After Hideyoshi's death in 1598, however, Kuroda sided with Tokugawa, one of Hideyoshi's former subjects. At the Battle of Sekigahara in 1600, from which Tokugawa emerged as the dominant power in Japan, Kuroda rendered crucial support. As a result of this service, after the establishment of the Tokugawa regime in 1603, Kuroda was granted the large feudal fief of Fukuoka in northern Japan. His family continued to rule this fief until the late 19th century, when it was taken over by the newly established central government of the emperor Meiji (1868) and made into a province.

Kurosawa Akira (b. March 23, 1910, Tokyo, Japan—d. Sept. 6, 1998, Tokyo), first Japanese film director to win international acclaim, with such films as *Rashomon* (1950), *Ikiru* (1952), *Seven Samurai* (1954), *The Throne of Blood* (1957), *Kagemusha* (1980), and *Ran* (1985).

Kurosawa's father, who had once been an army officer, was a teacher who contributed to the development of gymnastic education in Japan. After leaving secondary school, Kurosawa attended an art school and began painting in the Western style. Although he was awarded important art prizes, he gave up his ambition to become a painter and in 1936 became an assistant director in the PCL cinema studio. Until 1943 he worked there mainly as assistant to Yamamoto Kajirō, one of Japan's major directors of World War II films. During this period Kurosawa became known as an excellent scenarist. Some of his best scenarios were never filmed but only published in journals; yet they were noticed by specialists for their freshness of representation and were awarded prizes.

In 1943 Kurosawa was promoted to director and made his first feature film, *Sanshiro Sugata,* from his own scenario; this story of Japanese judo masters of the 1880s scored a great popular success. In 1944 he made his second film, *The Most Beautiful,* describing an episode of girls at work in an arsenal. Immediately thereafter, he married the actress who had played the leading part in the picture, Yaguchi Yoko; they had two children, a son and a daughter. In August 1945, when Japan offered to surrender in World War II, he was shooting his picture *They Who Step on the Tiger's Tail,* a parody of a well-known Kabuki drama. The occupation forces, however, prohibited the release of most films dealing with Japan's feudal past, and this outstanding comedy was not distributed until 1952.

Kurosawa, 1961

Kurosawa's *No Regrets for Our Youth* (1946) portrays the history of Japanese militarism during the period from 1933 through the end of the war in terms of a person executed on suspicion of espionage during the war. Of the many postwar films criticizing Japanese militarism, this was the most successful, both artistically and commercially. It was *Drunken Angel* (1948), however, that made Kurosawa's name famous. This story of a consumptive gangster and a drunken doctor living in the postwar desolation of downtown Tokyo is a melodrama in which desperation and hope, as well as violent action and melancholic atmosphere, are intermingled. The gangster was portrayed by a new actor, Mifune Toshirō, who became a star through this film and who subsequently appeared in most of Kurosawa's films.

Rashomon was shown at the Venice Film Festival in 1951 and was awarded the Grand Prix. This was the first time a Japanese film had won such high international acclaim, and Japanese films now attracted serious attention all over the world. An adaptation of two short stories written by Akutagawa Ryūnosuke, the film deals with a samurai, his wife, a bandit, and a woodcutter in the 10th century; a rape and a murder are recollected by the four persons in distinctly different ways. This presentation of the same event as seen by different persons stimulated the imagination of the audience and advanced the idea of cinema as a means of probing a metaphysical problem.

Ikiru is regarded by many critics as one of the finest works in the history of the cinema. It concerns a petty governmental official who learns he has only half a year until he will die from cancer. He searches for solace in the affection of his family but is betrayed, then seeks enjoyment but becomes disillusioned and, in the end, is redeemed by using his position to work for the poor. In this film, which abounds in strong moral messages, Kurosawa depicted in an extremely realistic manner the collapse of the family system, as well as the hypocritical aspects of officials in postwar Japanese society. The film is an outstanding document of the life and spiritual situation of the Japanese people, who were beginning to recover from the desperation caused by defeat in the war.

Seven Samurai is considered the most entertaining of Kurosawa's films and also his greatest commercial success. It depicts a village of peasants and a few leaderless samurai who fight for the village against a band of marauding bandits; although it was inspired by his admiration of Hollywood western films, it was executed in an entirely Japanese style.

Record of a Living Being (1955) was a deeply honest film portraying a Japanese dentist's terror of the atomic tests conducted by the United States and the Soviet Union; its pessimistic conclusion, however, made it a commercial failure.

Kurosawa was also noted for his adaptations of European literary classics into films with Japanese settings. *The Idiot* (1951) is based upon the Fyodor Dostoyevsky novel of the same title, *The Throne of Blood* was adapted from Shakespeare's *Macbeth,* and *The Lower Depths* (1957) was from Gorky's drama; each of these films is skillfully Japanized. *The Throne of Blood,* which reflects the style of the sets and acting of the Japanese nō play and uses not a word of the original, has been called the best film of all the countless cinematized Shakespearean dramas.

Kurosawa's pictures contributed a strong sense of style to the artistic Japanese film, which had been pursuing a naturalistic trend. The violent action of his more commercial works also exerted a powerful influence.

In 1960 he set up Kurosawa Productions, of which he became president, and began to produce his own works. As producer, however, he was continually embarrassed by economic difficulties. Throughout the 1960s, Kurosawa made a number of entertainment films, mainly with samurai as leading characters; *Yojimbo* (1961) is a representative work. *Red Beard* (1965) combines the element of entertainment with a sentimental humanism. In the 1960s, however, Japanese cinema fell into an extreme depression, and Kurosawa's plans, in most cases, were found by film companies to be too expensive. As a result, Kurosawa attempted to work with Hollywood producers, but each of the projects ended in failure. At the Kyōto studio in 1968, for 20th Century-Fox, he started shooting *Tora, Tora, Tora!,* a war spectacle film dealing with the air attack on Pearl Harbor. The work progressed slowly, however, and the producer, fearing an excess in estimated cost, dismissed Kurosawa and replaced him with another director. After a six-year interval, Kurosawa at last managed to present another of his films, *Dodes'-ka-den* (1970); his first work in colour, a comedy of the poor people living in slums, it recaptured much of the poignancy of his best works but failed financially. The period of personal despondency and artistic silence that followed ended in the mid-1970s when Kurosawa filmed *Dersu Uzala* (1975) in Siberia at the invitation of the Soviet government. This story of a Siberian hermit won wide acclaim.

Kagemusha ("Shadow Warrior"), released in 1980, was the director's first samurai film in 14 years. It concerns a petty thief who is chosen to impersonate a powerful feudal lord killed in battle. This film was notable for its powerful battle scenes. Kurosawa's next film, *Ran* (1985; "Chaos"), was an even more successful samurai epic. An adaptation of Shakespeare's *King Lear* set in 16th-century Japan, the film uses sons instead of daughters as the aging monarch's ungrateful children. *Ran* was acclaimed as one of Kurosawa's greatest films in the grandeur of its imagery, the intellectual depth of its screen adaptation, and the intensity of its dramatic performances.

Although other Japanese filmmakers acquired substantial international followings after the pioneering success of *Rashomon,* Kurosawa's films continue to command the greatest interest in the West. They represent a unique combination of elements of Japanese art—in the subtlety of their feeling and philosophy, the brilliance of their visual composition, and their treatment of samurai and other historic Japanese themes—with a distinctly Western feeling for action and drama and a frequent use of stories from Western sources, both literary classics and popular thrillers. (T.S.)

BIBLIOGRAPHY. Kurosawa Akira, *Something Like an Autobiography* (1982), is an informal book of reminiscences. An informative list of sources about early works of Kurosawa is compiled in Patricia Erens, *Akira Kurosawa: A Guide to References and Resources* (1979). Donald Richie and Joan Mellen, *The Films of Akira Kurosawa,* rev. ed. (1984), is an excellent study written by authors familiar with the language and people of Japan; David Desser, *The Samurai Films of Akira Kurosawa* (1983), is a brief interpretive critical study of the genre that Kurosawa introduced to the West.

Kuroshio (Japanese: "Black Current"), also called JAPAN CURRENT, strong surface oceanic current of the Pacific Ocean, the northeasterly flowing continuation of the Pacific North Equatorial Current between Luzon of the Philippines and the east coast of Japan. The temperature and salinity of Kuroshio water are relatively high for the region, about 68° F (20° C) and 34.5 parts per thousand, respectively. Only about 1,300 feet (400 m) deep, the Kuroshio travels at rates ranging between 20 and 120 inches (50 and 300 cm) per second.

Flowing past Taiwan (Formosa) and the Ryukyu Islands, the current skirts the east coast of Kyushu, where, during the summer, it branches west and then northeast through the Korea Strait to parallel the west coast of Honshu in the Sea of Japan as the Tsushima Current. In the vicinity of latitude 35° N (about central Honshu), the bulk of the Kuroshio turns east to receive the southward-flowing Oya Current. This flow, known as the Kuroshio Extension, eventually becomes the North Pacific Current (also known as the North Pacific West Wind Drift). Much of this current's force is lost west of the Hawaiian Islands as a great south-flowing eddy, the Kuroshio countercurrent, joins the Pacific North Equatorial Current and directs the warm water back to the Philippine Sea. The remainder of the original flow continues east to split off the coast of Canada and form the Alaska and California currents. The Kuroshio exhibits distinct seasonal fluctuations. It is strongest from May to August. Receding some in late summer and autumn, it begins to increase from January to February only to weaken in early spring. Similar to the Gulf Stream (Atlantic) in its creation and flow patterns, the Kuroshio has an important warming effect upon the south and southeast coastal regions of Japan as far north as Tokyo.

The existence of the Kuroshio was known to European geographers as early as 1650, as shown by a map drawn by Bernhardus Varenius. It was also noted by Captain J. King, a member of the British expedition under Captain James Cook (1776–80). It is called Kuroshio ("Black Current") because it appears a deeper blue than does the sea through which it flows.

Kurozumi-kyō, prototype of the contemporary "new religions" of Japan, named for its founder, Kurozumi Munetada (1780–1850), a Shintō priest of the area that is now Okayama prefecture. The believers venerate the Shintō sun goddess Amaterasu as the supreme god and creator of the universe and consider the other traditional 8,000,000 Shintō kami (gods, or sacred powers) to be her manifestations. Devotional activities include daily morning worship of the sun, with breathing exercises, described as "swallowing the sun," intended to bring about spiritual union with the sun and consequent physical well-being. The cult was officially recognized as a Shintō sect in 1846 and reorganized under its present name in 1876. It is still recognized as a denomination of Sect Shintō and in the late 20th century claimed over 200,000 followers.

Kurri Kurri, town, now part of Greater Cessnock, eastern New South Wales, Australia. It was laid out in 1902 as a centre for the surrounding coalfields, its name coming from an Aboriginal term meaning either "man" or "the first." Nearby is the town of Weston, another coal-mining town, established in 1903. The principal industry in Kurri Kurri is an aluminum smelter, which began operating in 1969, but coal mining remains important, as does the manufacture of clothing. The surrounding area is given to poultry raising, orcharding, dairying, and sawmilling. Sydney lies 106 miles (170 km) to the south. Kurri Kurri was linked with Cessnock, Weston, and Bellbird in 1966 to form the local government area of Greater Cessnock. Pop. (1991) including Weston, 13,268.

Kursk, *oblast* (province), western Russia. The *oblast* is centred on Kursk city. It extends across the southern end of the Central Russian Upland. The surface is a rolling plateau, broken by broad, shallow valleys. Almost everywhere the natural forest-steppe vegetation has been replaced by farming, which in some parts has caused severe gully erosion. About three-fourths of the *oblast*'s land is arable, and grains, sugar beets, hemp, potatoes, and other vegetables are grown; pig keeping also is important. Most local industry is concerned with processing farm produce, but there are also large machine-building and chemical industries in Kursk city. In the 1950s exploitation of the extensive iron-ore deposits, known as the Kursk Magnetic Anomaly, was begun near Zhelezogorsk and developed very rapidly; much is mined by open-pit methods. Area 11,500 square miles (29,800 square km). Pop. (1995 est.) 1,349,000.

Kursk, city and administrative centre of Kursk *oblast* (province), western Russia. It lies along the upper Seym River, about 280 miles (450 km) south of Moscow. Kursk is one of the oldest cities in Russia. It was first mentioned in documents from 1032. Completely destroyed by the Tatars in 1240, it was not rebuilt until 1586, when it became a military outpost to protect the advancing Russian colonization from Tatar attack. The town, however, lost much of its importance at the beginning of the 18th century when the Russian border was moved farther south. In World War II fierce fighting took place around Kursk and the city was severely damaged; the Battle of Kursk in July–August 1943, the largest tank battle in World War II, ended in the defeat of the Germans. Kursk's industries include machine building, food processing, and the manufacture of electronic equipment and synthetic fibres. A large nuclear power station was completed in 1979. The city has medical, agricultural, and teacher-training institutes. Pop. (1994 est.) 438,900.

Monument to World War II dead in Kursk city, Russia
Vance Henry—Alpha Photos

Kursk, Battle of (July 5–August 23, 1943), unsuccessful German assault on the Soviet salient around the city of Kursk, in western Russia, during World War II. The salient was a bulge in the Soviet lines that stretched 150 miles (240 km) from north to south and protruded 100 miles (160 km) westward into the German lines. In an attempt to recover the offensive on the Eastern Front, the Germans planned a surprise attack on the salient from both north and south, hoping to surround and destroy the Soviet forces within the bulge. The German assault forces consisted of almost 50 divisions containing 900,000 troops, including 17 motorized or armoured divisions having 2,700 tanks and mobile assault guns. But the Soviets had surmised the German attack beforehand and had withdrawn their main forces from the obviously threatened positions within the salient. The Germans launched their attack on July 5, but they soon encountered deep antitank defenses and minefields, which the Soviets had emplaced in anticipation of the attack. The Germans advanced only 10 miles (16 km) into the salient in the north and 30 miles (48 km) in the south, losing many of their tanks in the process. At the height of the battle on July 12, the Soviets began to counterattack, having built up by then a marked preponderance of both troops and tanks. Their subsequent successes encouraged them to develop a broad offensive that recovered the nearby city of Orel (now Oryol) on August 5 and that of Kharkov (now Kharkiv, Ukraine) on August 23. The Battle of Kursk was the largest tank battle in history, involving some 6,000 tanks, 2,000,000 troops, and 4,000 aircraft. It marked the decisive end of the German offensive capability on the Eastern Front and cleared the way for the great Soviet offensives of 1944–45.

kuru, fatal degenerative disorder of the central nervous system. Kuru has been found only among the Fore people and related ethnolinguistic groups in Papua New Guinea (*kuru* is a Fore word for "trembling," or "shivering").

The first symptoms of the disease include joint pain and headaches, which typically are followed by loss of coordination, tremor, and dementia. After the onset of symptoms the disease progresses steadily, and death occurs within two years of the onset of symptoms. For many years medical investigators suspected that the disease was hereditary rather than infectious, although its pattern of incidence—it struck adult females and children of both sexes but rarely adult males—was unusual for a hereditary condition. The American physician D. Carleton Gajdusek established the infectious nature of the disease by injecting samples of brain tissue from subjects who had died from kuru into the brains of chimpanzees; the primates eventually developed and succumbed to the disease. The transmission of kuru is attributed to the Fore's cannibalistic rituals of mourning in which the brain of the dead was handled and eaten, especially by women and children. Since this practice was discontinued, the disease has virtually disappeared.

The exact nature of the infectious agent was difficult to discern. Originally a virus was believed to be the culprit, but research has revealed that an unusual infectious agent called a prion is responsible. A prion is a deviant form of a harmless protein normally found in the brain. The prion is thought to convert the conformation of the normal protein molecule to its own modified form. Unlike the normal protein, the aberrant prion protein is much more resistant to enzymatic breakdown. As a result, prions accumulate within nerve cells, damaging them and causing the characteristic neurodegeneration of the disease. Kuru is one of a group of prion diseases sometimes referred to as spongiform encephalopathies because the brains of those with the disease become riddled with holes.

Kurukh (people): *see* Oraon.

Kurukh language, a member of the North Dravidian subfamily of Dravidian languages, spoken by some 1.8 million people of the Oraon tribes of the Chota Nāgpur plateau of east-central India. It is also spoken in parts of Bangladesh. Lacking a written tradition, Kurukh is documented only since the European colonization of India, and in many areas it is being displaced by the Hindi language.

Kurukshetra, also spelled KURUKṢETRA, city, northeastern Haryāna state, northwestern India. It is connected by road and rail with Delhi (south) and Ambāla (north). Now united with Thānesar, it is an important Hindu pilgrimage centre. The city's large water reservoir is said to have been built by Raja Kuru, the ancestor of the Kauravas and Pāṇḍavas of the Hindu epic poem *Mahābhārata*. The name Kurukshetra means "field of Kuru." The bathing fair is attended by as many as half a million pilgrims on the occasion of a solar eclipse, when it is believed that the waters of all other tanks visit this one. Also of historical interest are many temples, a Muslim fort, and the tomb of Shaykh Chillī Jalāl (d. 1582), an octagonal building done in off-white marble. Kurukshetra University was established in 1956.

The area in which Kurukshetra is situated was the site of an early Aryan settlement in India (*c.* 1500 BC) and is associated with *Mahābhārata* legends and mentioned in the first verse of the *Bhagavadgītā*. The region contains more than 350 pilgrimage sites. The town of Thānesar was King Harṣa's capital (606–647); it was sacked by Maḥmūd of Ghazna in 1011. Pop. (1991 prelim.) city, 81,275.

Kuruman, town, Northern Cape province, South Africa. It is located in the northeastern corner of the province and is distantly southwest of Johannesburg. Originally a missionary station (1821), it later became an area of white settlement (town founded, 1885; incorporated, 1916). The town is chiefly known for a local spring—the Eye of Kuruman—which rises in a cave in this otherwise semidesert thornveld area and supplies at least 4,500,000 gallons (17,000,000 l) daily. Kuruman is also known for its dairy cattle and trade in butter. Pop. (1985) 6,931.

Kurumba, Negroid tribe living in the Cardamom and Nīlgiri hills, west-central Tamil Nadu state, southern India. Originally a pastoral people, the Kurumba were probably identical with or closely related to the Pallavas. With the decline of the Pallava dynasty in the 8th century, Kurumba forefathers dispersed over a wide area of southern India, becoming geographically separated from each other and culturally distinct. The members of these subdivisions survived by hunting and gathering, by petty agriculture, or as slaves. Today some Kurumba are field labourers or hunters who market jungle produce. Kurumba groups, which are commonly isolated from each other, are governed by a headman with two assistants, who handle disputes. Partially Hinduized, they have abandoned many traditional customs. The Kuruba, an ethnologically similar people who live on the plains as small landowners and herders of sheep, are now considered distinct from the hill Kurumba. In the late 20th century the Kuruba and Kurumba together numbered about 10,000.

Kurume, city, Fukuoka *ken* (prefecture), Kyushu, Japan. It lies at the centre of the Tsukushi Plain, on the Chikugo River. It was a castle town during the 17th century and a military centre from the late 19th century until World War II. Kurume is known for its patterned cotton textiles, which have been produced as a cottage industry since the 1700s. The city's economy is now based on the rubber industry, which produces tires, rubber shoes, and tubing. Kurume is also a market for agricultural produce and a railway hub. The nearby Suiten Shrine dedicated to the Shintō god of the sea was established in the late 12th century. Pop. (1993 est.) 232,-846.

Kurunegala, town, west-central Sri Lanka (Ceylon). It is situated 25 miles (40 km) northwest of Kandy amid steep hills that were used as citadels during its early history.

Kurunegala was the Sinhalese capital in the early 14th century, and later the town served as a way station between Kandy, the new capital, and its port, Puttalam. The contemporary town is the commercial centre of a populous agricultural area that produces rice, rubber latex, spices, cocoa, and, especially, coconuts. Kurunegala has good road and rail connections with the rest of Sri Lanka. Some 12 miles (20 km) northeast of the town lies Ridi Vihara, the "silver monastery," which was founded (100 BC) on the site of a vein of silver. Pop. (1990 est.) 28,000.

Kuryłowicz, Jerzy (b. Aug. 26, 1895, Stanislav, Galicia, Austria-Hungary—d. Jan. 28, 1978, Kraków, Poland), Polish historical linguist who was one of the greatest 20th-century students of Indo-European languages. His identification of the Hittite medial *ḫ* in 1927 substantiated the existence of the laryngeals, Indo-European speech sounds postulated by the Swiss linguist Ferdinand de Saussure in 1879. This discovery then stimulated much research in Indo-European phonology, the comparative study of changes in speech sounds.

Kuryłowicz
By courtesy of the Muzeum Historyczne Uniwersytetu Jagiellonskiego, Krakow, Poland

Kuryłowicz' contributions to Indo-European linguistics, particularly Romance and Germanic studies, began in 1924. In 1928 he became a professor at the university in Lwów (now Lviv, Ukraine) and wrote *Études indo-européennes I* (1935; "Indo-European Studies I"). After World War II he held professorships at the universities of Wrocław and Kraków, Poland. Two of his major works are *L'Apophonie en indo-européen* (1956; "Apophony in Indo-European") and *The Inflectional Categories of Indo-European* (1964).

Kurz, Hermann (b. Nov. 30, 1813, Reutlingen, kingdom of Württemberg [Germany]—d. Oct. 10, 1873, Tübingen, Ger.), German writer chiefly known for two powerful historical novels, *Schillers Heimatjahre* (1843; "Schiller's Homeland Years") and *Der Sonnenwirt* (1855; "The Proprietor of the Sun Inn"), both critical of the existing social order, and for his satirically humorous tales of Swabian life in *Erzählungen* (1858–63; "Tales").

Kurz, etching by Johann Lindner, *c.* 1870
Archiv fur Kunst und Geschichte, Berlin

Because the quality of his work went unrecognized, Kurz was forced to make his living by translating. He produced excellent translations of Ludovico Ariosto's epic *Orlando furioso* (1840–41) and, from the Middle High German, of Gottfried von Strassburg's *Tristan und Isolde* (1844). Kurz was also active between 1843 and 1854 as a political and literary journalist and as editor of the democratic newspaper *Der Beobachter* in Stuttgart. Later he became the university librarian at Tübingen.

Kurzeme, moraine region of western Latvia, roughly corresponding to the historic state of Courland (*q.v.*). Kurzeme is elevated slightly above the coastal plains of the Baltic Sea and the Gulf of Riga, which bound the moraine, and it rises to 604 feet (184 m) in the south. It is the source of many short rivers flowing northeast and northwest. Kurzeme is a region of farms that traditionally produce grain, potatoes, sugar beets, and flax and of woodland, mainly pine and spruce. It was a traditional province of Latvia, with its historic capital at Jelgava at the eastern edge of the region.

Kusaie (Caroline Islands): *see* Kosrae.

Kusanagi (Japanese: "Grass-Mower"), in Japanese mythology, the miraculous sword that the sun goddess Amaterasu gave to her grandson Ninigi when he descended to earth to become ruler of Japan, thus establishing the divine link between the imperial house and the sun. The sword, along with the mirror and jeweled necklace, still forms one of the three Imperial Treasures of Japan. The sword was discovered by the storm god Susanoo in the body of the eight-headed dragon (which he killed) and presented by him to his sister Amaterasu. It derives its name from an incident when the hero Yamato Takeru was attacked by Ainu warriors. They started a grass fire around him, from which he escaped by cutting down the burning brush with the sword.

Kusapura (India): *see* Sultānpur.

Kusch, Polykarp (b. Jan. 26, 1911, Blankenburg, Ger.—d. March 20, 1993, Dallas, Texas, U.S.), German-American physicist who, with Willis E. Lamb, Jr., was awarded the Nobel Prize for Physics in 1955 for his accurate determination that the magnetic moment of the electron is greater than its theoretical value, thus leading to reconsideration of and innovations in quantum electrodynamics.

Kusch was brought to the United States in 1912 and became a citizen in 1922. In 1937, at Columbia University, he worked with physicist Isidor I. Rabi on studies of the effects of magnetic fields on beams of atoms. He spent the wartime years in research on radar and returned to Columbia in 1946 as professor of physics, a position he held until 1972. Among other posts held by Kusch at Columbia were department chairman (1949–52, 1960–63), director of the radiation laboratory (1952–60), and academic vice president and provost (1969–72). In 1972 he took a position as professor at the University of Texas, Dallas; he remained there until his retirement in 1982.

In 1947, through precise atomic beam studies, Kusch demonstrated that the magnetic properties of the electron were not in agreement with existing theories. Subsequently, he made accurate measurements of the magnetic moment of the electron and its behaviour in hydrogen. In work characterized by great accuracy and reliability, he measured numerous atomic, molecular, and nuclear properties by radio-frequency beam techniques.

Kusevitsky, Sergey Aleksandrovich: *see* Koussevitzky, Serge.

Kusha, Chinese CHÜ-SHE, Buddhist school of philosophy introduced into Japan from China during the Nara period (710–784). The school takes its name from its authoritative text, the *Abidatsuma-kusha-ron* (Sanskrit: *Abhidharmakośa; q.v.*), by the 4th- or 5th-century Indian philosopher Vasubandhu. This text sets forth the doctrine of the Sarvāstivāda, an ancient Indian school that held that all things (dharmas), future, past, and present, actually exist; the self alone is illusory.

The text's translation into Chinese (651–654) by Hsüan-tsang led to the formulation of the Chü-she school in China. By the 9th century the school had died out as an active, separate faith in both China and Japan; in Japan it was appended to the Hossō school.

Kushān DYNASTY, also spelled KUṢĀṆA, ruling line descended from the Yüeh-chih (*q.v.*), a people that ruled over most of the northern Indian subcontinent, Afghanistan, and parts of Central Asia during the first three centuries of the Christian era. The Yüeh-chih conquered Bactria in the 2nd century BC and divided the country into five chiefdoms, one of which was that of the Kushāns (Kuei-shuang). A hundred years later, the Kushān chief Kujūla Kadphises (Chiu-Chiu-Chueh) secured the political unification of the Yüeh-chih kingdom under himself.

Under Kaniṣka I (fl. 1st century AD) and his successors, the Kushān kingdom reached its height. It was acknowledged as one of

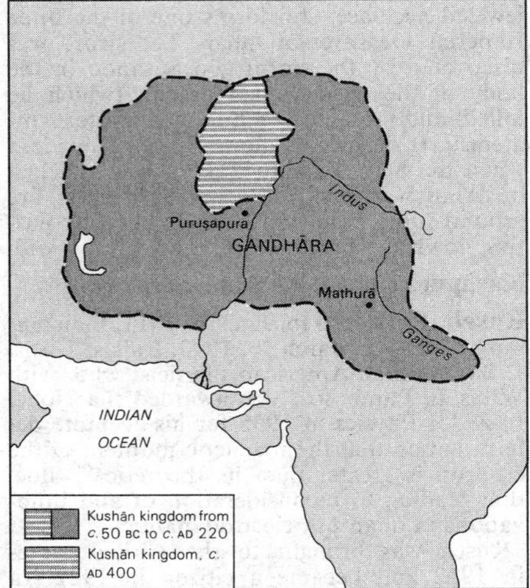

The Kushān empire
Adapted from *Westermann Grosser Atlas zur Weltgeschichte;* Georg Westermann Verlag, Braunschweig

the four great Eurasian powers of its time (the others being China, Rome, and Parthia). The Kushāns were instrumental in spreading Buddhism in Central Asia and China and in developing Mahāyāna Buddhism and the Gandhāra and Mathurā schools of art.

The Kushāns became affluent through trade, particularly with Rome, as their large issues of gold coins show. These coins, which exhibit the figures of Greek, Roman, Iranian, Hindu, and Buddhist deities and bear inscriptions in adapted Greek letters, are witness to the toleration and to the syncretism in religion and art that prevailed in the Kushān empire. After the rise of the Sāsānian dynasty in Iran and of local powers in northern India, Kushān rule declined.

Kushān art, also spelled KUṢĀṆA, art produced during the Kushān dynasty from about the late 1st to the 3rd century AD in an area that now includes parts of Central Asia, northern India, Pakistan, and Afghanistan.

The Kushāns fostered a mixed culture that is best illustrated by the variety of deities—Greco-Roman, Iranian, and Indian—invoked on their coins. At least two major stylistic divisions can be made among artifacts of the period: imperial art of Iranian derivation and Buddhist art of mixed Greco-Roman and In-

Kushān ivory carving of princesses, 2nd century; in the Kābul Museum, Kābul, Afghanistan
By courtesy of Smeets Lithographers, Weert, The Netherlands

dian sources. The best examples of the former are gold coins issued by the seven Kushān kings, the Kushān royal portraits (*e.g.,* the Kaniṣka statue), and princely portraits found at Surkh Kotal in Afghanistan. The style of Kushān artworks is stiff, hieratic, and frontal, emphasizing the power and wealth of the individual. There is little or no interest in the realistic rendering of anatomy or drapery, in contrast to the second style, which is typified by the Gandhāra and Mathurā (*qq.v.*) schools of Kushān art.

Kushbhawanpur (India): *see* Sultānpur.

Kushiro, city, Hokkaido *ken* (prefecture), eastern Hokkaido, Japan. It is situated along both banks of the Kushiro River where that river empties into the Pacific Ocean. The city was first settled by 537 Japanese immigrants in 1870. The natural harbour of the river mouth has since been developed into the largest commercial and fishing port of eastern Hokkaido.

Downtown Kushiro across the Kushiro River in Japan
Tokyo Photo—FPG

The Kushiro coalfield is worked near the city. Kushiro serves as the southern entrance to Akan National Park. Pop. (1990) 205,640.

Kushk River, Pashto DARYĀ-YE KOSHK, Russian KUSHKA, river in Afghanistan and Turkmenistan, formed by the confluence of two headstreams, the Āq Robāṭ and the Galleh Chaghar, which rise in northwestern Afghanistan. The river flows northwestward, passing the town of Koshk-e Kohneh (Kushk), where it turns north and receives the waters of the Moqor (Jōye Ḏarāb); for 10 miles (16 km) it forms the Turkmenistan-Afghanistan border. The river then turns northeast into Turkmenistan, where it receives the Egriyok River and eventually empties into the Murgab River near Tashkepri after a course of 172 miles (277 km). It drains a basin of about 4,100 square miles (10,700 square km). The river is completely dry in portions of its course during the summer months, but its waters irrigate farmlands along its middle and lower courses. The region through which the river flows is semiarid.

Kushtia, city, west-central Bangladesh, lying just south of the Padma (Ganges) River. The city is connected by rail with Saidpur and Calcutta and is a trade centre containing cotton-textile and sugar mills and a pottery cottage industry. Kushtia houses several government colleges that are affiliated with the University of Rājshāhi.

The surrounding area is a wide, fertile alluvial plain situated at the head of the Gangetic delta. Heavy trade is carried out on its network of waterways, including the Bhagirathi and Mātabhānga rivers. The region's chief crops are rice, jute, oilseeds, and pulses. Pop. (1981) city, 74,892.

Kushukh, also spelled KUSHUH, the Hurrian moon god. In the Hurrian pantheon, Kushukh was regularly placed above the sun god, Shimegi; his consort was Niggal (the Sumero-Akkadian Ningal). His home was said to be the city of Kuzina (location unknown), and his cult was later adopted by the Hittites. As Lord of the Oath he had as his special function the punishment of perjury. He was represented as a winged man with a crescent on his helmet and sometimes standing on a lion; in this form he appears among the images of Hittite gods at the rock sanctuary of Yazılıkaya (near modern Boğazköy in Turkey).

Kushva, also spelled KUŠVA, city, Yekaterinburg *oblast* (province), western Russia, at the foot of Mount Blagodat. Founded in 1735 after the discovery of iron-ore deposits on the mountain, it became a town in 1926, and until the 1950s open-pit mines were still in operation. Ore extraction is now conducted underground, and the deposits are the basis for a local metallurgical industry. Pop. (1991 est.) 43,300.

Kuskova, Yekaterina Dmitriyevna (b. 1869, Russia—d. Dec. 22, 1958, Geneva, Switz.), Russian political figure and publicist who opposed the Bolshevik government.

Becoming involved in radical activities in the mid-1890s, Kuskova wrote the *Credo,* a manifesto for the revisionist Marxist school called economism, earning the condemnation of Vladimir Lenin and other revolutionaries in the process. In 1906 she and her husband published a journal for the liberal Union of Emancipation, and later she contributed to other socialist newspapers. After the October Revolution in 1917, she opposed the Bolsheviks and Lenin's authoritarian policies. Appointed in 1921 to the All-Russian Committee to Aid the Starving, she was later arrested and charged with using the committee to conspire against the government. In 1922 she was expelled from the U.S.S.R. and spent the remainder of her life writing for émigré journals and agitating against the Soviets.

She was a longtime friend of the writer Maksim Gorky, having introduced him to various intellectuals in the 1890s; but, when Gorky decided to return to the Soviet Union in 1929, she cut all ties with him.

Kustanay, also spelled KUSTANAI, or KUSTANAJ, *oblast* (province), northern Kazakhstan, having an area of 44,200 square miles (114,500 square km). It contains a portion of the Turgay Lowland, which lies between the foothills of the Urals and the Kazakh Uplands and connects the West Siberian Plain in the north with the Turgay Tableland in the south. A wide, fertile black-earth belt in the northern part of the *oblast* changes into dry steppe toward the south. The climate is continental and dry. The main river is the Tobol, flowing north. There are a number of lakes, the largest of which is Kushmurun.

Mining, developed particularly since the 1950s, and agriculture dominate the *oblast*'s economy. Iron ore is mined in large quantities at Rudny and Lisakovsk, and there are also significant iron-ore deposits at Kachar, asbestos at Dzhetygara, and low-grade bauxite at Krasno-oktyabrsky. The *oblast* is a major producer of grain, particularly wheat, the sown area having quadrupled as a result of the Virgin and Idle Lands Campaign in the mid-1950s. Cattle and sheep are also raised. The *oblast*'s chief cities are Kustanay (the capital), Dzhetygara, Rudny, and Lisakovsk. The population is composed of Russians, Kazakhs, Ukrainians, Germans, Belarusians, and Tatars. Pop. (2001 est.) 972,300.

Kustanay, also spelled KUSTANAI, or KUSTANAJ, city and administrative centre, Kustanay *oblast* (province), Kazakhstan, on the Tobol River. Founded by Russian settlers from the Volga region in 1879, it became a centre of trade in the steppe, particularly in grain, a role that was enhanced by the construction of a branch railway in 1913. Kustanay was made an *oblast* centre in 1933, but its greatest expansion dates from the mid-1950s with the Virgin and Idle Lands Campaign, which extended agriculture and hastened the exploitation of mineral wealth, and the construction of rail lines in the region. The city's most economically important industries are food processing and other light enterprises, though there are vehicle and agricultural-equipment repair shops, and spare parts are produced for excavators and mining equipment. Kustanay has a teacher-training institute. Pop. (1999) 221,400.

Küstendil (Bulgaria): *see* Kyustendil.

Kūstī, also spelled KOSTI, town, central Sudan. It lies on the western bank of the White Nile, about 65 miles (104 km) south of Ad-Duwaym. Its basic agricultural economy is augmented by light manufacturing. The Kosti bridge, 4 miles (6 km) upstream from Kūstī, provides a railway connection with Al-Ubayyiḍ and accommodates motor-vehicular traffic. A domestic airport is located at Kūstī. Pop. (1993) 173,559.

Consult the INDEX *first*

Kusumi Morikage (b. 1610?, Edo [now Tokyo], Japan—d. 1700), Japanese painter of the early Tokugawa period (1603–1867) who excelled in painting farmers and common people.

Little is known of Kusumi's life, but a number of his paintings are extant, of which "Enjoying the Evening Cool Under a Gourd Trellis" and "Landscape Screen Depicting the Uji Bridge" are the most famous. He was one of the four best pupils of Kanō Tanyū (1602–74) of the Kanō school, which was founded in the 15th century and became the official school of painting in Japan under the strong influence of classical Chinese paintings, in particular of the Sung dynasty. Kusumi is said, however, to have been expelled by his teacher. He did not confine himself to the frequently formal and rigid style of the Kanō school but developed a more fluid and vivid way of painting. Kusumi also departed from the traditional way of rendering Chinese farming scenes and painted the actual life and customs of Japanese farmers.

"A Flock of Rooks," by Kusumi Morikage, *c.* 1690–1700, ink on paper; hanging scroll in the Richard P. Gale Collection, Mound, Minn.
By courtesy of Richard P. Gale

Kusunoki Masashige (b. 1294?, Japan—d. July 4, 1336, Minato-gawa, Settsu province, Japan), one of the greatest military strategists in Japanese history. Kusunoki's unselfish devotion and loyalty to the emperor have made him a legendary figure; after the imperial restoration of 1868, a splendid shrine was erected to him on the site of his death.

The head of a small fief, in 1331 Kusunoki joined the emperor Go-Daigo in a revolt to wrest the power of government from the shogunate, the hereditary military dictatorship that had dominated Japan since 1192. Although the numerically stronger shogunate troops captured the emperor, Kusunoki escaped into the hilly countryside, where he continued the war using guerrilla tactics.

Kusunoki's capture of the fortress of Chihaya near Nara in central Japan (in 1332) proved a major threat to the central government. The worried shogun then concentrated all his forces against Kusunoki, to the detriment of other parts of the country, where some warriors joined the rebel forces. In one of the most famous battles in Japanese history, Kusunoki successfully defended the fortress of Chihaya against the vastly superior shogunal forces.

Finally, early in 1333 the emperor, encouraged by reports of victory, bribed his guards and escaped from captivity. Ashikaga Takauji, the man who had been sent to capture the emperor, changed sides, and Nitta Yoshisada, another loyalist leader, captured the shogun's capital at Kamakura, thus ending the rule of the Hōjō family, who controlled the shogunate.

During the ensuing brief period of imperial rule, Kusunoki served as governor of the central Japanese provinces of Settsu, Kawachi, and Izumi and was a major figure in the central government. The real power in the countryside, however, continued to be held by the great hereditary lords, chiefly Ashikaga Takauji and Nitta Yoshisada, who openly vied to gain the loyalty of the minor feudal chieftains.

In 1335 Go-Daigo sided with Nitta Yoshisada against Ashikaga Takauji. As head of the imperial forces, Kusunoki defeated Takauji's troops in January 1336 and forced him to flee the capital. A few months later, however, Takauji returned at the head of a large combined army and navy. Kusunoki suggested that they temporarily retreat so that they could fight Takauji's forces at a point where the terrain was more favourable. The emperor insisted that Kusunoki advance and meet the much larger enemy forces before they occupied the capital. In the final battle at the Minato River, near modern Kōbe, Kusunoki fought bravely for many hours, but his troops were finally overwhelmed, and he committed suicide rather than face capture.

Kušva (Russia): *see* Kushva.

kut, trance ritual in Korean religion. *See* mudang.

Kūt, Al-, also called KŪT AL-ʿAMĀRAH, city, eastern Iraq. It lies along the Tigris River about 100 miles (160 km) southeast of Baghdad.

A relatively new town, Al-Kūt serves as a river port and agricultural centre for nearby farms. It is most noteworthy as the site of a famous British defeat in the Iraqi theatre of operations during World War I. Following a rapid advance from the south in 1915, British forces under General Charles Townsend occupied Al-Kūt, then continued their march toward Baghdad. Military reversals led the British to retreat to Al-Kūt, however, where they were enveloped by an Ottoman army on December 8. British forces surrendered on April 29, 1916, and about 10,000 British and Indian soldiers were taken prisoner. Other British forces retook Al-Kūt in February 1917. In the 1990s troops of an anti-Iranian militia, the Mojāhedīn-e Khalq, were stationed near the city. Al-Kūt saw little fighting during the Second Persian Gulf War (2003) but was the scene of political violence afterward.

Al-Kūt is a trade centre for agricultural produce grown in the surrounding area, where the Kūt Barrage diverts river water into irrigation canals. Al-Kūt's prosperity has always depended upon the Tigris River's course changes. Following a period of decline, the town revived when the present river system became established, making Al-Kūt a river port. Pop. (2002 est.) 380,000.

Kütahya, city, western Turkey. It lies along the Porsuk River, at the foot of a hill crowned by a ruined medieval castle. Kütahya, known as Cotyaeum in antiquity, lay on the great road from the Marmara region to the Mesopotamian plains; the town flourished and declined according to the changing importance of the trade routes. As a medieval Byzantine town, it was taken by the Seljuq Turks toward the end of the 11th century. It functioned as the capital of the Germiyan Turkmen principality from 1302 to 1429 before its absorption into the Ottoman Empire. During the 16th century, Kütahya emerged as a centre of the Ottoman ceramic industry, supplying tiles and faience for mosques, churches, and other buildings in Turkey and parts of the Middle East. Its importance was eclipsed by the growth of neighbouring Eskişehir at the end of the 19th century, but the development of industries at Kütahya in the mid-20th century restored some of the town's former importance. Its industries now include sugar refining, tanning, nitrate processing, pottery and carpet making, and the manufacture of smoking pipes and other articles from meerschaum (silicate of magnesium), which is extracted in the vicinity. Kütahya is linked by road and railway with Eskişehir (40 miles [65 km] northeast) and Afyon Karahisar (56 miles [90 km] southeast).

The city's old neighbourhoods have traditional Ottoman houses made of wood and stucco.

The area in which Kütahya is situated contains extensive areas of level or gently sloping agricultural land culminating in high mountain ridges to the north and west. Its products include cereals, fruits, and sugar beets. Large deposits of lignite are extensively worked at Tunçbilek and Değirmisaz, and stock raising is important. Pop. (1990) city, 130,944.

Ottoman houses in one of the older neighbourhoods of Kütahya, Turkey

© Ara Guler—Istanbul

Kutai (Indonesia): *see* Mahakam River.

Kutaisi, city, west-central Georgia. It lies along the Rioni River where the latter emerges from the Caucasian foothills into a lowland. One of the oldest cities of Transcaucasia, it served at various periods as the capital of successive kingdoms in Georgia: Colchis, Iberia (Kartli), Abkhazia, and Imeretia. After the Russian conquest, Kutaisi was made a provincial seat. It was sacked often in its stormy history, notably by the Turks in 1691; the ruins of the 11th-century Cathedral of Kutaisi, built by the Bogratids, stand on a hill above the city centre, which has narrow, winding streets. Just outside the city is the 12th-century Gelati cathedral and monastery; also on the outskirts is the Sataplia Nature Reserve, with limestone caverns and dinosaur fossils. Modern Kutaisi is an important industrial centre, producing trucks, pumps, mining machinery, textiles (especially silk), foodstuffs, and other consumer goods. There is a hydroelectric plant on the Rioni. Kutaisi has a teacher-training institute. Pop. (1991 est.) 238,200.

Kutang I (mountain, Nepal): *see* Manāslu.

Kutani ware, Japanese porcelain made in Kaga province (now in Ishikawa prefecture). The name "Old Kutani" refers to porcelain decorated with heavily applied overglaze enamels and produced in the Kaga mountain village of Kutani. The powerful Maeda family had established a kiln there by 1656. The clay bodies used were gray and coarse-grained. On most pieces—dishes and bowls were especially common—a white or blue-white matte glaze was decorated in dark, restrained colours, initially greens, yellows, and some reds, and later purples and dark blues. Some items had cobalt blue decoration under a white glaze. The most noted Old Kutani pieces are "Green Kutani," in which most of the surface is covered in a green or blue-green glaze to which one or two colours have been added (or the glaze is applied evenly over a design executed in black). The bold designs of Kutani ware drew freely from Chinese ceramics, paintings, and textiles. They are renowned for their rich pictorial ornament executed in lively, intense lines.

Owing to local financial problems and difficulties in obtaining the necessary pigments, the Kutani kiln was abandoned some time in the Genroku period (1688–1704). Ceramics production in Kaga enjoyed a renaissance early in the 19th century, however, including the establishment of another kiln at Kutani in the 1820s. In addition to a revival of the styles of Old Kutani ware, there arose a style using gold on a coral-red ground, which was perfected during another spate of activity that began in the 1860s. Technical advances were made and Western-style pigments were adopted, and by the 1890s modern Kutani ware had become a major item among Japan's exports.

The name "Kutani" is now losely applied to a great variety of 19th-century Japanese ceramics, many of which have no connection with Ishikawa prefecture. To further confuse matters, some authorities now assert that most Old Kutani ware was actually made at Arita, in present-day Saga prefecture.

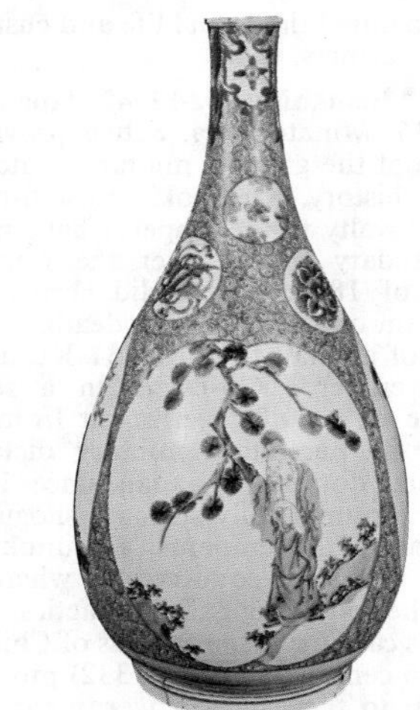

Kutani porcelain bottle, *c.* 1685, Tokugawa period; in the collection of Gerald Reitlinger

By courtesy of Gerald Reitlinger; photograph, Wilfred Walter

Kutch, Gulf of (India): *see* Kachchh, Gulf of.

Kutch, Rann of (mudflats, India-Pakistan): *see* Kachchh, Rann of.

Kutchin, a group of Athabascan-speaking North American Indian tribes inhabiting the basins of the Yukon and Peel rivers in eastern Alaska and the Yukon Territory—a land of coniferous forests interspersed by open barren ground. The name Kutchin, meaning "People," is given collectively to an indefinite number of distinct tribes, there being no precise agreement among authorities on whom to include under this cover name, which is as much linguistic as cultural.

The Kutchin had an unusual social organization, which divided each band or tribe into three exogamous castes or subgroups but recognized no ranks or heritable statuses. Men became chiefs through demonstration of leadership or prowess. The Kutchin were also noted for being warlike and merciless in the killing of enemy men, women, and children; slaves were never taken. Men were warriors, fishers, and hunters of caribou, moose, and other game; women were obliged to do all the day-to-day chores and portage and were excluded from most decision making. The aged and others unable to help themselves were customarily put to death.

The Kutchin's most influential neighbours were the Eskimo, with whom they traded and fought and from whom they borrowed such cultural traits as tailored caribou-skin clothing (most conspicuously, the Eskimo hood and mittens), various hunting weapons, and the sled. They also shared many customs, however, with Indians south and east—painting their faces and hair, wearing feathers as headdress, and decorating their clothing with fringes and beads. Their houses were domed huts of poles and fir boughs, banked with snow in winter and ventilated by a smoke hole at the top.

Little is known of Kutchin religion or beliefs, but they were well known for their feasts, games (especially wrestling), singing, and dancing. Only some 2,000 Kutchin remained in the late 20th century. They have been strongly influenced by the European way of life.

Kutenai, also spelled KOOTENAY, North American Indian tribe distributed over southeastern British Columbia, northern Idaho, and northwestern Montana. Their language is of uncertain classification, some authorities placing it in the Wakashan family and some classifying it independently. The tribe is probably descended from an ancient Blackfoot group that migrated westward from the Great Plains to the drainage of the Kootenai River, a tributary of the upper Columbia. Plentiful streams and lakes, adequate rainfall, and abundant game and fish made their range the most favourable part of the plateau between the Rockies and the Pacific coast ranges.

The Kutenai exhibit traits of both the Plains and the Plateau culture areas. After acquiring horses, they engaged in annual bison hunts through enemy country in the plains beyond the Rockies. War became more important, with formalized war honours becoming a means of social advancement and with slavery becoming more pervasive with the increase in war captives (women and children, mostly Blackfoot). The Kutenai dressed in skin clothing (breechclouts [breechcloths] for men, tunics for women), lived in conical skin tepees, and painted their garments, tents, and bodies much in the manner of the Plains Indians. Like other Plateau Indians, however, they engaged in communal fishing, built great bark and dugout canoes, and acknowledged a supreme chief only temporarily for special expeditions.

Among the Kutenai there were no clans, classes, or secret societies; they were divided loosely into bands, each with a nominal leader and an informal council of elders. They worshiped the Sun and believed in a multitude of spirits pervading all things in nature. Medicine men, or shamans, were persons of considerable influence.

Kutenai in modern times have become ranchers, sportsmen's guides, and labourers; they numbered fewer than 1,000 in the late 20th century.

Kutlah al-ʿAmal al-Waṭanī (Morocco): *see* National Action Bloc.

Kutná Hora, German KUTTENBERG, city, Středočeský *kraj* (region), Czech Republic. It lies on the high tableland above the Vrchlice River, 44 miles (71 km) east of Prague.

It began in the early 13th century as a silver-mining town, and from the 14th century Bohemian coins (*groš*) were minted there. The royal mint, which was transferred from Jihlava by King Wenceslas II, was in part of a royal residence called the Vlašský dvůr (Italian Court). Quarreling between the mainly German mining community and the surrounding Czechs, the Hussite Wars of the 15th century, and the Thirty Years' War (1618–48) ruined the city's prosperity, and the mines were virtually abandoned by the end of the 18th century.

Cathedral of St. Barbara, Kutná Hora, Czech Republic
Czechoslovak News Agency

The magnificent Gothic Cathedral of St. Barbara, built in the town's most flourishing period in the 13th century, resembles an imperial crown made of stone. Other historic buildings include the aforementioned Vlašský dvůr (now housing a coin museum) and the 14th-century St. James's Church. The Vocel Museum contains the Kutná Hora Bible (1489) and a collection of locally minted coins.

Under the Czech National Trust for the Preservation of Ancient Monuments, Kutná Hora is primarily a tourist attraction and a market centre for the surrounding countryside. Pop. (1991 prelim.) 21,541.

kutnohorite, a carbonate mineral, calcium manganese carbonate [$CaMn(CO_3)_2$]. Confirmed as a naturally occurring species in 1955, it was originally found at Kutná Hora, Bohemia; it also occurs in Franklin, N.J., U.S., and Chvaletice, Czech Republic. The manganese analogue of dolomite, it forms a chemical substitution (solid-solution) series with that mineral, in which magnesium replaces manganese in the crystal structure. It is probably intermediate in the discontinuous (at normal temperatures) solid-solution series between calcite ($CaCO_3$) and rhodochrosite ($MnCO_3$). For detailed physical properties, *see* carbonate mineral (table).

Kuts, Vladimir (b. Feb. 7, 1927, Aleksino, Ukraine, U.S.S.R.—d. Aug. 16, 1975, Moscow, Russia), Soviet distance runner who held the world record in the 5,000-metre race (1954–55, 1957–65), the 10,000-metre race (1956–60), and the three-mile race (1954).

An officer in the Soviet army and a member of the Communist Party from 1955, Kuts won gold medals for both the 5,000- and 10,000-metre races in the 1956 Olympic Games at Melbourne. He was the European champion in the 5,000-metre race in 1954 and was also Soviet champion at that distance and in the 10,000-metre race (1953–57). After 1957, illness forced him to retire from running, but he continued as a coach.

kuttāb (Muslim school): *see* maktab.

Kutuzov, Mikhail Illarionovich, Prince (Knyaz), original name MIKHAIL ILLARIONOVICH GOLENISHCHEV-KUTUZOV (b. Sept. 5 [Sept. 16, New Style], 1745, St. Petersburg, Russia—d. April 16 [April 28], 1813, Bunzlau, Silesia [now Bolesławiec, Pol.]), Russian army commander who repelled Napoleon's invasion of Russia (1812).

The son of a lieutenant general who had served in Peter the Great's army, Kutuzov attended the military engineering school at age 12 and entered the Russian army as a corporal when he was only 14. He gained combat experience fighting in Poland (1764–69) and against the Turks (1770–74), and he learned strategic and tactical techniques from General Aleksandr Suvorov, whom he served for six years in the Crimea. He was promoted to colonel in 1777 and by 1784 had become a major general.

Although he had received a severe head wound and lost an eye in 1774, he actively participated in the Russo-Turkish War of 1787–91, in which he was again severely wounded. After the war he held a variety of high diplomatic and administrative posts, but he fell into disgrace in 1802 and retired to his country estate. When Russia joined the third coalition against Napoleon three years later, however, Emperor Alexander I recalled Kutuzov and gave him command of the joint Russian-Austrian army that opposed the French advance on Vienna. Before Kutuzov's force could link up with the Austrians, however, Napoleon defeated the latter at the Battle of Ulm. Kutuzov skillfully retreated, after defeating the French at Dürrenstein on Nov. 11, 1805, and preserved his army intact. He proposed to fall back to the Russian frontier and await reinforcements, but Alexander overruled him and engaged the French army in battle at Austerlitz (December 2), suffering a disastrous defeat. Kutuzov was partly blamed for the disaster and was removed from his command. Subsequently Alexander returned Kutuzov to active duty as commander of an army in Moldavia after war had again broken out with Turkey. Kutuzov inflicted several defeats on the Turks and on May 28, 1812, concluded a Russo-Turkish peace settlement favourable to Russia (Treaty of Bucharest).

In June 1812 Napoleon's army entered Russia, and the Russians fell back before him. Under pressure of public opinion, Alexander

Kutuzov, detail of a portrait by G. Dawe, 1829; in the Hermitage, St. Petersburg
By courtesy of the State Hermitage Museum, St. Petersburg

on August 9 appointed Kutuzov commander in chief of all the Russian forces and, on the following day, made him a prince. Napoleon sought a general engagement, but Kutuzov's strategy was to wear down the French by incessant minor engagements while retreating and preserving his army. Under public pressure and against his better judgment, however, he fought a major battle at Borodino on September 7. Although the battle itself was inconclusive, Kutuzov lost almost half his troops and afterward withdrew to the southeast, allowing the French forces to enter Moscow.

Napoleon, having failed to make peace with the Russians and being unwilling to spend the winter in Moscow, left the city in October. He tried to move southwestward, but Kutuzov blocked his attempt to proceed along the fertile, southern route by giving battle at Maloyaroslavets (October 19). By forcing the disintegrating French army to leave Russia by the path it had devastated when it entered the country, Kutuzov destroyed his opponent without fighting another major battle. Kutuzov's troops harried the retreating French, engaging them at Vyazma and Krasnoye, and the remnants of Napoleon's army narrowly escaped annihilation at the crossing of the Berezina River in late November. In January 1813 Kutuzov pursued the French into Poland and Prussia, where he died of disease.

Kutuzov was the finest Russian commander of his day next to Suvorov himself. He typically relied on quick maneuvers and sought to avoid unnecessary battles, husbanding his forces to strike at the proper moment.

Kuujjuaq, formerly FORT-CHIMO, Eskimo (Inuit) community in Nouveau-Québec region, northeastern Quebec province, Canada. It lies along on the Koksoak River, about 20 miles (30 km) above the latter's mouth on Ungava Bay. Kuujjuaq is located in a region rich in iron ore. The Hudson's Bay Company established a trading post there in 1830. The post was closed from 1842 to 1866. A cooperative now operates a handicraft program for producing stuffed sealskin animals and birds, with emphasis on the *ookpik* (Arctic owl). Kuujjuaq has a Royal Canadian Mounted Police post, a health centre, a weather station, an airfield, and Roman Catholic and Anglican missions. An experimental farm is operated, and sheep farming is practiced. Pop. (1991) 1,405.

Kuusankoski, town, Kymen *lääni* (province), southeastern Finland. It lies along the Kymi River, just northwest of Kouvola. Part of a major industrial district that contains the Kymi Company factories, one of the largest paper and cellulose producers in Scandinavia, the town also has a hydroelectric-power station. Kuusankoski and neighbouring Voikka are linked by special rail service to Kouvola, and thence to Helsinki (the national capital) and Kotka. Pop. (1992 est.) mun., 21,774.

Kuusinen, Otto V., in full OTTO VILHELM KUUSINEN (b. Oct. 4, 1881, Laukaa, Fin.—d. May 17, 1964, Moscow, Russia, U.S.S.R.), a founder of the Finnish Communist Party and secretary of the Communist International (Comintern) who was prominent in the Communist Party of the Soviet Union.

Kuusinen joined the Social Democratic Party in Finland in 1905. Subsequently he held various important posts in the party, serving as minister of education in the short-lived Finnish socialist regime in early 1918. He fled to Russia in the same year, after the Finnish War of Independence had brought the socialist regime to an end, and became a key organizer of the Finnish Communist Party. Remaining in exile during the interwar years, he occupied the powerful position of secretary of the Comintern.

With the start, in 1939, of the "Winter War" between the U.S.S.R. and Finland, which had been assigned to the Russian sphere of influence in the German-Soviet Nonaggression Pact of 1939, Kuusinen was named head of a puppet Finnish socialist government. When the Soviet Union came to terms with Finland early in 1940, however, his government was quietly dissolved. From 1940 to 1956 he served as president of the supreme soviet (assembly) of the Karelo-Finnish Soviet Socialist Republic, which resulted from the union of Soviet eastern Karelia and Finnish western Karelia at the conclusion of the war in 1940. From 1946 to 1953 and from 1957 until his death, he was secretary and a presidium member of the Central Committee of the Communist Party of the Soviet Union.

kuvasz, plural KUVASZOK, Hungarian breed of guard and shepherd dog that earned a reputation as a watchdog unexcelled during the European Middle Ages, when it was kept by kings and nobles. The breed originated many centuries ago in Hungary, whence it spread to Turkey, India, Tibet, and China. The kuvasz of modern times stands about 66 cm (26 inches) and weighs about 36 kg (80 pounds). It is a large, sturdily built dog with a slightly wavy, pure-white coat and a handsomely shaped head. The kuvasz makes a loyal and stalwart companion, though it is not overly demonstrative. It is a fast and graceful runner and has a marked air of dignity. As a guard dog it is very protective, and it can act on its own initiative without instruction.

Kuvasz

Kuwait, officially STATE OF KUWAIT, Arabic AL-KUWAYT, or DAWLAT AL-KUWAYT, country lying at the upper northwestern corner of the Persian (Arabian) Gulf. The country spans a distance of about 100 miles (160 km) from north to south and about 90 miles (140 km) from east to west and is bordered by Iraq on the west and north and by Saudi Arabia on the south; it fronts the Persian Gulf to the east. The capital is Kuwait city. Area 6,880 square miles (17,818 square km). Pop. (2003 est.) 2,439,000.

A brief treatment of Kuwait follows. For full treatment, *see* MACROPAEDIA: Arabia.

For current history and for statistics on society and economy, *see* BRITANNICA BOOK OF THE YEAR.

The land. Kuwait lies on a gently sloping plain rising westward from the Persian Gulf and reaching an elevation of 951 feet (290 m) at Ash-Shaqāyā, the country's highest point, located near the extreme western border between Iraq and Saudi Arabia. Kuwait Bay extends 30 miles (48 km) inland from the Persian Gulf. Az-Zawr Escarpment, rising to 475 feet (145 m), extends along the northwestern shore of Kuwait Bay; a natural harbour and Kuwait, the capital city, occupy its southern shore. Except for Al-Jahrah Oasis, at the western end of Kuwait Bay, and a few fertile patches in the southeastern and coastal areas, the country is largely desert.

The climate is semitropical. The contrast between summer (April through October) and winter (November through March) is great. Summer precipitation is nearly nonexistent, and between April and September temperatures average 111° F (44° C) and occasionally go as high as 130° F (54° C). The country's 1 to 7 inches (25 to 180 mm) of annual precipitation fall almost exclusively in winter, filling the desert basins, or playas, in the north, west, and centre of the country with fresh water vital to the area's nomadic herdsmen. Winter temperatures average about 61° F (16° C) in the coolest months. Winds are frequent in Kuwait, and fierce dust storms occur, mostly in June and July.

Kuwait has almost no agricultural soil; its only resources are extensive petroleum and natural-gas fields. In the late 20th century its estimated reserves of petroleum represented almost 10 percent of global reserves and ranked Kuwait, in this respect, third only to Iraq and Saudi Arabia. Its natural-gas reserves are relatively small.

The people. Kuwait's population is overwhelmingly Arab and Muslim. Foreigners living in the country include non-Kuwaiti Arabs, South Asians, Westerners, and others.

Arabic, the official language, is spoken by the majority of Kuwait's population; Persian and English also are spoken. Nearly all the nation's population is urban. The annual rate of growth traditionally has been high and is mainly due to immigration. Citizenship, however, is reserved by the government for native Kuwaitis and for those who can prove Kuwaiti ancestry from before 1920.

The economy. Kuwait has a developing mixed government-owned and private-enterprise economy. The gross national product (GNP) is not growing as rapidly as the population, but the GNP per capita is nevertheless one of the highest in the non-Western world. The gross domestic product (GDP) originates primarily from crude petroleum and natural-gas production and refining.

Agriculture in Kuwait is a marginal economic activity and contributes little to the GDP. The little arable land is irrigated from recycled wastewater or brackish groundwater to grow garden produce and livestock feed. Pastures cover less than one-twelfth of the total land area; principal livestock are sheep, goats, and cattle.

Commercial fishing in the Persian Gulf yields silver pomfret for the local market and prawn and shrimp, which are frozen for export.

Manufacturing contributes about 7 percent of the GDP and employs about the same percentage of the labour force. Apart from various petroleum products, principal manufactures include plastics, cement, and ceramic and asbestos products; metal pipes; electric cables and dry-cell batteries; furniture; and woolen blankets. Industries are concentrated in Ash-Shuʿaybah and Mīnāʾ Abdullah industrial parks. All the country's electrical energy is produced by thermal-power plants.

Since the 1970s Kuwait's economic development has included the vertical integration of its oil industry by expanding its refining, shipping, and marketing capabilities. The Kuwaiti government owned all petroleum, natural-gas, and derivative industries; electrical-generation plants; and desalination plants. The private sector owns building-materials, construction, trade, and finance companies. Since the late 1970s the government has favoured the development of petroleum- and natural-gas-related industries and other low-pollution industries that require minimum labour, in an effort to decrease the country's large expatriate workforce. Kuwait also has invested much of its oil wealth overseas. Large petroleum revenues enable Kuwait to develop industries and a comprehensive social program for its citizens without budgetary deficits. More than one-half of all jobs in Kuwait are in the public-administration, defense, and services sectors. Kuwait's budgetary revenues derive overwhelmingly from petroleum and natural gas.

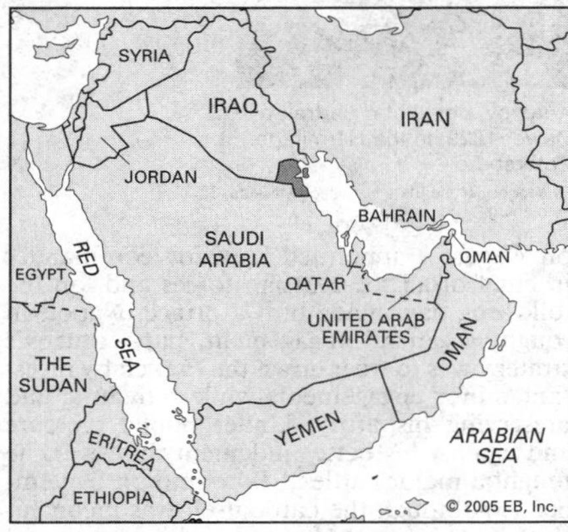

Kuwait

Virtually all of Kuwait's roads are paved. The principal ports are Ash-Shuʿwaykh and Ash-Shuʿaybah; Mīnāʾ al-Aḥmadi, the principal oil port, is located offshore. The international airport is located at Kuwait city. Most of the country's pipelines convey crude petroleum.

Kuwait's exports in the late 1970s and early 1980s had more than three times the value of imports; but, because of lower prices for oil on the international market, by the late 1980s the balance of trade had become more nearly equal. Exports consist primarily of crude petroleum, natural gas, and refined-petroleum products. Principal importers of Kuwaiti products are Japan, South Korea, and the United States. Imports consist mainly of machinery and transport equipment, basic manufactures, and food and live animals. Major import sources are the United States, Japan, and Germany.

Government and social conditions. Kuwait is a constitutional monarchy, governed by the Ṣabāḥ family (Āl Ṣabāḥ). The constitution, adopted in 1962, authorizes the ruling family to choose an emir, who serves as the country's head of state and who exercises his power through an appointed prime minister and Council of Ministers. In 1976 the emir dissolved the National Assembly, the country's unicameral legislature, and effectively suspended the constitution. The National Assembly met from 1981 until it was again suspended in 1986, under pressure from the Iran-Iraq War and falling oil prices. A new 50-seat National Assembly was elected in 1992. Kuwaiti law vests the highest judicial authority in the High Court of Appeal. Matters of civil and personal-status law are governed by Islāmic religious law.

Kuwait has a comprehensive social-welfare system. It provides financial assistance and housing to needy Kuwaitis and offers benefits to all employed citizens for work injury, old age, and disability. The government makes medical care available to all residents, regardless of nationality, at a low cost.

Health conditions are generally good; Kuwait has a fairly high ratio of doctors per capita. It also ranks high regionally in life expectancy, with rates of 76 years for men and 77 years for women. Relatively high infant mortality, however, remains a serious problem.

The government provides free education to native Kuwaitis at all school levels. Education is compulsory for native Kuwaitis between the ages of 6 and 14 years. Over three-fourths of the country's adult population is literate. The only major institution of higher learning is Kuwait University (founded 1962).

The Kuwaiti press is privately owned and generally free from censorship. The Council of Ministers, however, retains the authority to suspend newspapers that criticize the emir or the Kuwaiti economy. The Ministry of Information runs the government press and the radio and television broadcasting stations.

Cultural life. Kuwait has a Muslim cultural heritage. The country still serves as a transit point for some of those participating in the hajj, the pilgrimage to Mecca, Islām's holy city. Kuwait's Pilgrim's City offers these travelers board, lodging, and essential services.

History. Archaeological evidence, particularly on Faylakah island in Kuwait Bay, suggests that Kuwait was part of an early civilization contemporary with Sumer and the Indus valley (3rd millennium BC). Having close connections with the cities of Mesopotamia and the trading centre of Dilmun (widely identified with modern Bahrain), a Faylakah island settlement flourished until approximately 1200 BC, when it disappeared from the historical record. Greek colonists arrived on the island during the time of Alexander III the Great (*c.* 323 BC) and built a temple dedicated to Artemis. The island passed to the Seleucids but declined during Roman times.

At the beginning of the 18th century AD, the ʿAnizah tribe of central Arabia began an eastward search for better pasture and water and founded Kuwait city. (The traditional date of founding is 1710.) The foundation of the autonomous sheikhdom dates from 1756, when ʿAbd al-Raḥīm of the Āl Ṣabāḥ became sheikh. The Ṣabāḥ family continues to rule Kuwait.

Kuwait first came to the attention of European powers in the late 19th century, when Germany sought to extend the Berlin-Baghdad railway to the port of Kuwait. To thwart both German and Ottoman influences, Great Britain and Kuwait concluded an agreement (1899) whereby Britain assumed control of Kuwait's foreign affairs. Following the outbreak of war with the Ottomans in 1914, Britain established a protectorate over Kuwait.

Relations with Najd (later Saudi Arabia) were settled by the Treaty of al-Uqayr (1922), which involved the creation of the compromise Neutral Zone. The northern frontier with Iraq was agreed upon in 1923.

In June 1961 the British government announced its recognition of the full independence of Kuwait. This was followed by an Iraqi claim that all of Kuwait belonged to Iraq. The British sent troops to defend Kuwait, and, when the Arab League recognized Kuwait's independence on July 20, 1961, the Iraqi claim was dropped.

Kuwait typically followed a neutral policy among Arab states. The Iran-Iraq War (*q.v.*), however, seriously threatened Kuwait's security as well as the shipment of oil in the Persian Gulf. Kuwait sided tacitly with Iraq, making large loans to the latter throughout the 1980s. But after talks on the repayment of war debts and other issues broke down, Iraqi forces invaded and occupied Kuwait on Aug. 2, 1990. (*See* First Persian Gulf War.) The Kuwaiti government escaped and took refuge in Saudi Arabia, while Iraq systematically looted Kuwait of its economic assets. The United Nations approved a U.S.-led trade embargo against Iraq in an effort to force it out of Kuwait, and on November 29 the UN approved the use of force against Iraq for the same purpose. Early in 1991, after undertaking a month-long aerial bombardment of Iraq, a U.S.-led military coalition operating from Saudi Arabia drove Iraqi forces out of Kuwait on February 23–27. Kuwait's exiled rulers returned to their capital city several weeks later. Kuwait's initial reconstruction efforts were complicated by the fact that the retreating Iraqis had destroyed nearly half of the country's 1,300 oil wells, many of which continued to burn uncontrollably long after war's end, and that oil prices were low for much of the decade.

In the 1990s limited political reform was enacted, allowing select male citizens to vote in legislative elections, though the royal family still retained most political power. After years of political turmoil, in the 1999 elections nearly two-thirds of the winning candidates adopted antigovernment platforms. Kuwait supported the overthrow of the Iraqi government in the Second Persian Gulf War (2003).

Kuwait, Arabic AL-KUWAYT, city and national capital, eastern Kuwait. The city lies on the southern shore of Kuwait Bay of the Persian Gulf; its name is derived from the Arabic *kūt* ("fort").

Kuwait city was founded at the beginning of the 18th century by a group of families who migrated to the coast from the interior of the Arabian Peninsula. The old mud-walled city, only about 5 square miles (13 square km) in area, made its livelihood by fishing, pearling, and trading with the Indian subcontinent and eastern Africa. It was long the only populated place of consequence in the country.

ʿAbd Allāh al-Mubarraq aṣ-Ṣabāḥ Mosque in the city of Kuwait
Tor Eigeland—Black Star/EB Inc.

With the development of Kuwait's petroleum industry after World War II, the city and the surrounding area, including the residential suburb of Ḥawallī, began to grow rapidly. The mud wall was torn down in 1957, and only three gates remain. The city rapidly became an administrative, commercial, and financial centre; its banking facilities were among the largest in the Middle East. Kuwait city has many luxurious residences, as well as a number of parks and gardens; tree-lined avenues carry heavy automobile traffic. Kuwait University opened in 1966; the city's historical museum exhibits artifacts from Faylakah island.

When Iraq invaded and occupied Kuwait from August 1990 to February 1991, Iraqi forces systematically stripped Kuwait city of its food supplies, consumer goods, equipment, and other movable assets, and many of the city's inhabitants fled the country. Kuwait city suffered considerable damage to buildings and infrastructure, but after the war much of it was rebuilt. Pop. (1999) urban agglomeration, 1,165,000.

Kuwana, city, Mie *ken* (prefecture), Honshu, Japan. It is situated on the delta of the Ibi, Nagara, and Kiso rivers. Mentioned as a hamlet as early as the 10th century, it became a commercial port on Ise Bay during the Muromachi period (1338–1573). From the 16th to the 19th century, the city was controlled by several powerful families; it was one of the major post towns on the Tōkaidō ("Eastern Sea Highway"). The Kansai railway line running through the city was completed in 1899 and brought a decline in the port's activities.

Kuwana is now the centre of the Northern Ise Industrial Zone. The city produces metal castings, textiles, machinery, and processed foods and trades seaweed and clams. It is also the tourist base for Suigo Prefectural Park. Pop. (2000) 108,378.

Kuwatli, Shukri al- (b. 1891, Damascus [Syria]—d. June 30, 1967, Beirut, Leb.), statesman who led the anticolonialist movement in Syria and became that country's first president.

Kuwatli entered Syrian politics in the 1930s as a member of the National Bloc, an Arab group that led the opposition to French rule. Kuwatli assumed leadership of the movement in 1940. His tolerance for the corruption of his associates helped keep him in power. The National Bloc remained the dominant expression of Syrian nationalism, and, when Syria became independent in 1943, the bloc helped elect Kuwatli president. His major concern was to conclude a treaty with France, which had exercised control over Syria for more than 20 years. This was accomplished with British help, and by 1946 all foreign troops had left. In 1947 Kuwatli enacted an amendment that removed a one-term limit from the constitution, and he was reelected in 1948.

Because of the Israeli victory over Arab forces (1948), as well as dissatisfaction with Kuwatli's rule, he was overthrown by a military coup in March 1949. After a short imprisonment, he went into exile in Egypt, after which a series of coups paralyzed Syrian political life.

Shukri al-Kuwatli
Camera Press

Free elections once again took place in 1955, and Kuwatli, at the head of the National Party (the successor to the National Bloc), was elected president, a largely ceremonial post.

Kuyper, Abraham (b. Oct. 29, 1837, Maassluis, Neth.—d. Nov. 8, 1920, The Hague), Dutch theologian, statesman, and journalist who led the Anti-Revolutionary Party, an orthodox Calvinist group, to a position of political power and served as prime minister of The Netherlands from 1901 to 1905.

After serving as a pastor in Beesd, Utrecht, and Amsterdam (1863–74), Kuyper adopted the orthodox Calvinist views of Guillaume Groen van Prinsterer. *De Standaard,* the newspaper Kuyper founded in 1872, became an organ for Groen's ideas. Elected to the States General (national assembly) in 1874, he became the leader of Groen's political group, expanding it to form the Anti-Revolutionary Party (1878), the first properly organized Dutch political party. A far more practical politician than Groen, he built up a large lower-middle-class following with a program

Kuyper, portrait by H.J. Haverman; in the Haags Gemeentemuseum, The Hague

By courtesy of the Collection Haags Gemeentemuseum, The Hague

combining orthodox religious views and a progressive social program.

To provide a more thorough training in Calvinist doctrine for pastors, Kuyper founded the Free University at Amsterdam in 1880. After seceding from the Reformed Church (Hervormde Kerk) of The Netherlands (1886), which he viewed as overly aristocratic, he founded the Reformed Churches (Gereformeerde Kerken) in The Netherlands in 1892.

In 1888 Kuyper formed a coalition of the Anti-Revolutionary Party and the Roman Catholic group led by Hermanus Schaepman, which gained power and ended the era of Liberal rule. An education act passed by the coalition in 1889 introduced the first state subsidies for parochial schools. Having returned to the States General in 1894, Kuyper formed a coalition in 1897 of the three "church" groups: Catholic, Anti-Revolutionary, and Christian Historical parties, the last-named an aristocratic splinter group from the Anti-Revolutionaries. Becoming prime minister and home affairs minister in 1901, he mediated between England and the Boers during the South African War (1899–1902).

Although Kuyper repressed the railway and harbour workers' strike of 1903, he also advocated a wider franchise and social benefits. "Private" (denominational) universities first received official recognition in his administration. After the victory of a Liberal coalition in the 1905 elections, Kuyper's political influence declined. He was a representative in the Second Chamber (1908–12) and then in the First Chamber until his death.

Kuyuk (Mongol ruler): *see* Güyük.

Kuznets, Simon (Smith) (b. April 30 [April 17, Old Style], 1901, Kharkov, Ukraine, Russian Empire—d. July 8, 1985, Cambridge, Mass., U.S.), Russian-born American economist and statistician, winner of the 1971 Nobel Prize for Economics.

Kuznets emigrated to the United States in 1922, 15 years after his father had emigrated. (His father changed the family name to Smith, but the young Kuznets preferred his original name.) He was educated at Columbia University, receiving his Ph.D. in 1926. In 1927 he joined the National Bureau of Economic Research, working with its founder, Wesley Mitchell. It was there that Kuznets developed his pioneering studies of U.S. national income and his more general work on economic time series, resulting in comprehensive studies of the economic growth of nations. He later taught at a number of universities (University of Pennsylvania, 1930–54; Johns Hopkins, 1954–60; Harvard, 1960–71).

His work emphasized the complexity of underlying economic data, stressing the importance of large numbers of observations and the limitations of simple models based on one phase of historical experience. According to Kuznets, economic data must include information on population structure, technology, the quality of labour, government structure, trade, and markets in order to provide an accurate model. In particular, he emphasized, on the basis of the statistical series that he accumulated, how little of economic growth can be attributed in the conventional manner to the accumulation of labour and capital. He also described the existence of cyclical variations in growth rates (now called "Kuznets cycles") and their links with underlying factors such as population.

Kuznetsk (Russia): *see* Novokuznetsk.

Kuznetsk Coal Basin, byname KUZBASS, Russian KUZNETSKY UGOLNY BASSEYN, one of the largest producing coalfields of Russia, in Kemerovo *oblast* (province), south-central Russia. It lies in the basin of the Tom River between the Kuznetsk Alatau and Salair mountain ranges. The coalfield was first discovered in 1721. It covers about 10,000 square miles (26,000 square km) and contains proved, minable reserves of 725,000,000 tons, distinguished by thickness of seam and concentration. There are three main coal-bearing series; the Balakhonka Series, the oldest, contains 30–35 workable seams, some up to 50 feet (15 m) thick and in places reaching 130 feet (40 m). These seams contain anthracite and the richest coking and steam coals of the Kuznetsk Basin. Kuznetsk Basin coal is generally of high quality, with less than 1 percent sulfur but sometimes with a rather high ash content, necessitating pithead enrichment. About one-quarter of it is mined by opencast methods, chiefly in the north; as a result, production costs are low, especially in comparison with the Donets Basin coalfield, another of the major coal producers.

The first small diggings for coal, along the Kondoma River, date from 1721. Production long remained insignificant, but in the First Soviet Five-Year Plan (1928–32) large-scale exploitation was begun, and development since then has been rapid and continuous. The development of the coalfield was accompanied by the growth of a heavy-industrial area. Before World War II the Urals-Kuznetsk Basin *kombinat* (iron and steel complex) was established, with the Kuznetsk Basin supplying coking coal to the Urals and receiving iron ore in return. Giant iron- and steelworks were set up at Magnitogorsk in the Urals and at Stalinsk (now Novokuznetsk) in the Kuznetsk Basin. A second huge iron- and steelworks was built in Novokuznetsk in the 1960s. Nonferrous metallurgy is also important in the Kuznetsk Basin, especially at Novokuznetsk, and is based on bauxite from the Salair Ridge and on lead, zinc, tin, copper, and mercury from the adjoining Altay *kray* (region). Engineering and metalworking are widespread in all the major towns, with the emphasis on the production of heavy machinery. The coke-chemical industry is well developed in Novokuznetsk, Kemerovo, and Anzhero-Sudzhensk and forms the basis for the manufacture of plastics, fertilizers, and pharmaceutical goods. The main coal-mining centres are Anzhero-Sudzhensk, Kemerovo, Leninsk-Kuznetsky, Prokopyevsk, Osinniki, and Kiselyovsk.

Kuznetsov, Anatoly Vasilyevich, pseudonym A. ANATOLI (b. Aug. 18, 1929, Kiev, Ukraine, U.S.S.R.—d. June 13, 1979, London, Eng.), Soviet writer noted for the autobiographical novel *Baby Yar,* one of the most important literary works to come out of World War II.

Kuznetsov was 12 years old in 1941 when the invading German army occupied his home city of Kiev in the Ukraine. After World War II ended, he worked as a labourer at several construction sites and graduated from the Gorky Institute of Literature in 1960. His first literary success, *Prodolzheniye legendy* (1957; *Sequel to a Legend*), was based on his experiences as a labourer in Siberia; the book helped start the genre of "youth stories" that subsequently became popular in the Soviet Union. In 1966 Kuznetsov's controversial novel *Baby Yar* was published in the Soviet Union in a heavily censored and expurgated form. The book is an account of the horrors and injustices that the author witnessed during the brutal German occupation of Kiev from 1941 to 1944. (The title of the novel is taken from Baby Yar, a ravine in Kiev where the Germans killed and buried the bodies of more than 100,000 local inhabitants.)

Kuznetsov defected to the West during a trip to London in 1969. In 1970 he published the full and uncensored version of *Baby Yar* (or *Babi Yar*) and was promptly denounced as a traitor in the U.S.S.R. The complete *Baby Yar* is a scathing condemnation of both German and Soviet policies toward the Ukraine in the 1930s and '40s. The book is notable for its detached humour and ironical overtones and is enlivened by the author's remarkably vivid and penetrating descriptions of his efforts to survive the German occupation of Kiev.

Kuznetsov, Vasily Vasilyevich (b. Feb. 13 [Jan. 31, Old Style], 1901, Sofilovka, Russia—d. June 5, 1990, Moscow), Soviet official and diplomat.

Kuznetsov studied metallurgical engineering at the Leningrad Polytechnical Institute and joined the Communist Party in 1927; his career as an engineer (1927–44) was interrupted for further study in the United States (1931–33). Kuznetsov became chairman of the All-Union Central Council of Trade Unions in 1944. He became a member of the Central Committee of the Communist Party in 1952 and was a member of its Presidium (now the Politburo) in 1952–53. In 1953 he began a two-year term as Soviet ambassador to China. From 1955 to 1977 he was first deputy minister of foreign affairs. From 1977 to 1986 he was a candidate member of the Politburo and served as first deputy chairman (first vice president) of the Presidium of the Soviet Union. Upon the death of Leonid Brezhnev on Nov. 10, 1982, Kuznetsov served as acting president of the Soviet Union until Yury Andropov assumed the position of president on June 16, 1983.

Articles are alphabetized word by word, not letter by letter

Kvaran, Einar Hjörleifsson (b. Dec. 6, 1859, Vallanes, Ice.—d. May 21, 1938, Reykjavík), Icelandic journalist, novelist, short-story writer, playwright, and poet.

A clergyman's son, Kvaran studied at the University of Copenhagen and there joined a group of young Icelandic radicals. He went to Winnipeg, Man., in 1885 and for 10 years was a leading journalist and editor in the Icelandic immigrant community there. He spent the rest of his life as a journalist and writer in Reykjavík.

Kvaran had popular success. He expressed the contemporary longing for political independence, a better social structure, and better education. In Canada he had been converted to spiritualism, and he spent the rest of his life espousing it. Kvaran was a journalist until 1906 and from 1910 was subsidized as a writer by a government grant. His novels were often written to a thesis and were peopled with characters who were little more than vehicles for various ideas. His masterly short stories show him at his best.

Kvasir, in Norse mythology, a poet and the wisest of all men. Kvasir was born of the saliva of two rival groups of gods, the Aesir and the Vanir, when they performed the ancient peace ritual of spitting into a common vessel. He wandered around teaching and instructing, never failing to give the right answer to a question. Two dwarfs, Fjalar and Galar, who were weary of academics and learning, killed Kvasir and distilled his blood in Odhrǫrir, the magic caldron. When mixed with honey by the giant Suttung, his blood formed mead that gave wisdom and poetic inspiration to those who drank it. The story of Kvasir's murder is told in the *Braga Raedur* ("Conversations of Bragi"), one of the *Edda*s.

Kwa languages, branch of the Niger-Congo language family spoken by the inhabitants of an area extending along the Atlantic coast of Africa from Côte d'Ivoire to the Nigerian border and including the southern parts of Côte d'Ivoire, Ghana, Togo, and Benin. The Kwa languages include the Akan cluster, with 7 million speakers. The principal members of the Akan cluster are Asante Twi, Akuapem (Akuapim), and Fante in Ghana; Anyi and Baule (2 million) in Côte d'Ivoire; and Ewe (2 million) in southeast Ghana and southern Togo. The Kwa languages are tonal (*i.e.,* they use pitch levels to differentiate words that are otherwise pronounced identically), with a down-step system in which high tones are lowered after low tones. *See also* Niger-Congo languages.

Kwahu Plateau, plateau, southern Ghana. It comprises the uplifted southern edge of the Volta River basin and extends for 160 miles (260 km) northwest-southeast from Wenchi to Koforidua. It forms the main watershed of Ghana, separating rivers in the western half of Ghana that flow due south to the Atlantic Ocean (Birim, Pra, Ankobra) from those of the Volta system (Afram, Pru, Sene) in the eastern half of the country.

With an average elevation of 1,500 feet (460 m) and bordered north and south by bold erosional scarps, the plateau is deeply dissected by valleys and marked by prominent peaks (Mount Akwawa, 2,586 feet [788 m]). To the south it borders dense forest country, which it shields from the harmattan winds of the interior. Cacao cultivation has been introduced in the west, through which traditional trade routes lead to the Atlantic; vegetable cultivation is stressed in the eastern sector. Wenchi, Mampong, Mpraeso, and Abetifi are the principal towns.

Kwai River (Thailand): *see* Khwae Noi River.

Kwajalein Atoll, also called KWAJALONG, coral formation in the Ralik (western) chain of the Republic of the Marshall Islands, in the western Pacific Ocean. The string of some 90 islets has a total land area of 6 square miles (16 square km) and surrounds the world's largest lagoon (655 square miles [1,722 square km]). The islets of Kwajalein, Roi, and Namur were the first of the Marshall Islands captured by U.S. troops in World War II. The atoll serves as a seaport, an air stop, and a U.S. military missile testing site. Pop. (1988) 9,311.

Kwakiutl, Indians of the northwest Pacific coast of North America. The Kwakiutl live in British Columbia, Canada, along the shores of the waterways between Vancouver Island and the mainland opposite. They speak one of three major dialects: Haisla, spoken on the Gardner Canal and Douglas Channel; Heiltsuq, spoken from Gardner Canal to Rivers Inlet; and southern Kwakiutl, spoken from Rivers Inlet to Cape Mudge on the mainland and on the northern end of Vancouver Island. Kwakiutl is a Wakashan language. The Kwakiutl Indians are culturally related to the Nootka. The southern Kwakiutl are the best known.

The great importance of the Kwakiutl to anthropology stems from the ethnographic studies of the German-American anthropologist Franz Boas, who published more than 5,000 pages on their culture over a period of almost half a century. Boas' works describe almost every aspect of Kwakiutl culture, as well as analyzing their relationships to other Northwest Coast cultures, with whom they shared general features of technology and economy, art style, myths, and ceremonies.

The Kwakiutl subsisted mainly by fishing and had a technology based on woodworking. Their society was stratified by rank, which was determined primarily by the inheritance of names and privileges, such as the right to sing certain songs, use certain crests, and wear certain ceremonial masks.

The potlatch, a ceremonial distribution of property and gifts unique to Pacific Northwest Coast Indians, was elaborately developed by the southern Kwakiutl. Potlatches were held to celebrate major life events (*e.g.,* birth, marriage), as penalties for breaches of ceremonial taboo, for face-saving purposes, and in competition for a position or privilege. Potlatches were often combined with the performances of dancing societies, each having a series of ranked dances that dramatized ancestral experiences with supernatural beings. These beings were portrayed as giving gifts of ceremonial prerogatives such as songs, dances, and names, which became hereditary property.

Potlatch dish of the Kwakiutl Indians carved in human form from a single cedar log with the face representing the cannibal woman, Tsonoqua

The Portland Art Museum, Portland, Ore., The Rasmussen Collection of Northwest Coast Indian Art

KwaNdebele, former nonindependent black state and enclave in central Transvaal province, South Africa, that was a self-governing "national state" for Transvaal Ndebele people from 1981 to 1994. KwaNdebele was located in a 3,500-foot- (1,060-metre-) high dry savanna area about 100 miles (160 km) northeast of Johannesburg. It was established in 1979, when many Transvaal Ndebele were expelled from the nearby Bophuthatswana homeland. A massive resettlement program led to the creation of 12 camps in KwaNdebele, housing about 40 percent of the Transvaal Ndebele population in South Africa by the end of 1982. The capital was KwaMhlangu. The new constitution of South Africa abolished apartheid, and in 1994 KwaNdebele became part of the new province of Eastern Transvaal, which was subsequently renamed Mpumalanga province.

Kwando River, Portuguese RIO CUANDO, river in southern Africa, rising in central Angola and flowing southeast, forming for nearly 140 miles (225 km) the boundary between Angola and Zambia. Near the end of its course the Kwando reaches the northern boundary of the Caprivi Strip, which juts out from Namibia, and thereafter the river spreads into the Linyanti Marshes, covering about 550 square miles (1,425 square km) and including Lake Liambezi. The marshes drain eastward toward the Zambezi, both rivers sharing the same floodplain. The confluence of the rivers is about 6 miles (10 km) below an exposure of basalt that the Zambezi clears at the Mambova Rapids and the Kwando (known in this region as the Chobe, or the Linyanti) clears at the Kasane Rapids. In May the Chobe's water level rises at the northern Caprivi boundary, reaching high flood level in June. The total length of the river is 457 miles (731 km), and its drainage basin covers 37,366 square miles (96,778 square km).

Kwangju, also spelled GWANGJU, city and provincial capital, South Chŏlla *do* (province), southwestern South Korea. It has the status of a special city (area 193 square miles [501 square km]) under the direct control of the home minister, with administrative status equal to that of a province. An old city on the edge of the mountainous area of South Chŏlla province, it has been a centre of trade and of local administration since the time of the Three Kingdoms (about 57 BC). Modern industries, including cotton textiles, breweries, and rice mills, began with the building of a railway from Seoul in 1914. During the Korean War (1950–53) Kwangju's suburbs became a major military-training centre. From 1967, with the construction of an industrial zone centring on an automobile factory, the city developed rapidly. Developments included storage and processing facilities for agricultural products. Kwangju was the site of an armed uprising against the newly installed military government of Chun Doo Hwan in May 1980 that was suppressed with more than 140 civilian deaths.

Kwangju is a transportation junction of southwestern Korea, and it connects with Seoul in the north and Pusan to the east by air, rail, and road. Chosŏn University (1946) and several other colleges are there. The city has many historical remains, and there are old temples and tombs in the surrounding hills. Pop. (2000) 1,350,948.

Kwangsi, in full CHUANG AUTONOMOUS REGION OF KWANGSI, Chinese (Wade-Giles) KUANG-HSI CHUANG-TSU TZU-CHIH-CH'Ü, or (Pinyin) GUANGXI ZHUANGZU ZIZHIQU, autonomous region located in southern China and bounded by the Chinese provinces of Yunnan on the west, Kweichow on the north, Hunan on the northeast, and Kwangtung on the southeast and also by northern Vietnam and the Gulf of Tonkin on the southwest. The capital is Nan-ning.

A brief treatment of Kwangsi follows. For full treatment, *see* MACROPAEDIA: China.

The region's history began in 45 BC, during the late Chou dynasty. Various dynasties ruled it up to AD 1279, when the Yüan dynasty gave the province its present name. The Ming dynasty ruled there from 1368 to 1644, the Ch'ing dynasty until 1911, when the Chinese republic was established. Together with neighbouring Kwangtung, Kwangsi in the early 20th century became the base of the Nationalist revolution led by Sun Yat-sen. Following the rise of Chiang Kai-shek to power in 1927, Kwangsi leaders formed the Kwangsi Clique, in opposition to Chiang. This group did much to modernize Kwangsi, but their revolt was crushed by Chiang in 1929. During World War II, Kwangsi was a major target of Japanese attack. It was declared a province of the People's Republic of China in 1949. In 1958 the province was transformed into the Chuang Autonomous Region of Kwangsi.

The population is composed of Chinese, Chuang, Yao, Miao, and Tung. The Chuang, a Tai people, are found largely in the western two-thirds of the region, the Chinese in the eastern third. These two largest ethnic groups in Kwangsi have coexisted for centuries. The Yao, Miao, and Tung settlements are widely scattered.

Fishermen and their trained cormorants on the Li River in Chuang Autonomous Region of Kwangsi, China
Peter Carmichael—Aspect Picture Library, London

The greater part of the Kwangsi region is composed of hilly country lying at a height of between 1,500 and 3,000 feet (450 and 900 m). The predominance of limestone gives many parts of Kwangsi a spectacular type of landscape in which rocky hills, pinnacles and spires, strangely shaped caves and caverns, sinkholes, and subterranean streams abound.

The climate of Kwangsi is warm enough to assure agricultural production throughout the year. Because of the influence of the rain-bearing monsoon wind, precipitation is abundant. Agriculture is concentrated in the river valleys and on the limestone plain. Hillsides are terraced wherever possible. Major crops include rice, corn (maize), wheat, and sweet potatoes. The leading commercial crop is sugarcane; others are peanuts (groundnuts), sesame, ramie (China grass), tobacco, tea, cotton, and indigo. The province also produces citrus and other fruits.

The raising of livestock in Kwangsi is ancillary to farming. Water buffalo are used as draft animals in the paddies. Pigs, chickens, and ducks are raised on farms, and goats are raised in the hills. In many areas, silkworms are raised on mulberry leaves. Fishing is extensive, and complementary to it are aquaculture and the production of silkworms (the waste cocoons of silkworms are fed to the fish).

Kwangsi is also an important producer of timber and forest products. Several of the latter, including cardamom husks, cassia twigs, plantain seed, the seed of the wax tree, castor-oil seed, mugwort powder, dried lizard, mangosteen, and quinine, are vital to traditional Chinese medicine. Kwangsi has sufficient coal and iron deposits to support moderate industrial development. Its light industries produce textiles, paper, flour, silk, leather, matches, chemicals, and pharmaceuticals. Its heavy industries include the iron- and steelworks at Liu-chou and Lu-chai, machinery production at Nan-ning and Wu-chou, and the cement works at Liu-chou. Numerous traditional handicrafts are also produced.

Railways and highways criss-cross the region. The elaborate system of waterways provides transportation throughout the region. Area 85,100 square miles (220,400 square km). Pop. (1993 est.) 43,800,000.

Kwangtung, Wade-Giles romanization KUANG-TUNG, Pinyin GUANGDONG, *sheng* (province), the southernmost mainland province of China. Kwangtung constitutes the region through which South China's trade is primarily channeled. It is bounded by the Chuang Autonomous Region of Kwangsi to the west, the provinces of Hunan and Kiangsi to the north and Fukien to the northeast, and the South China Sea to the south. Kwangtung has one of the longest coastlines of any Chinese province. Along the coast of the province are two foreign holdings—the British crown colony of Hong Kong and the Portuguese territory of Macau. The provincial capital is Canton.

A brief treatment of Kwangtung follows. For full treatment, *see* MACROPAEDIA: China.

Historically, Kwangtung and Kwangsi often were governed jointly. Kwangtung was first incorporated into the Chinese empire in 222 BC. During the five centuries of the Sui, T'ang, and Northern Sung dynasties, from AD 581 to 1126, the military and agricultural colonization of the region gradually took place. This, combined with increasing overseas trade through Canton, led to an increase of Chinese migration into Kwangtung and to the rise of Canton as a metropolis with a population of hundreds of thousands. Further major migrations spurred the rapid development of Kwangtung. Its population growth was so fast that by the late 17th century the province had become an area from which emigration took place.

Kwangtung's topography separates it somewhat from the rest of China, and this factor, together with its long coastline, its contact with other countries through its overseas emigrants, and its early exposure to Western influence through the port of Canton, has resulted historically in the emergence of a degree of self-sufficiency, with which a tendency to separatism has also been associated. Canton dominates the economic, cultural, and political life of Kwangtung to an unusual extent.

The surface configuration of Kwangtung is diverse, being composed primarily of rounded hills cut by streams and rivers, and ribbonlike alluvial valleys. The greater part of eastern Kwangtung consists of the southerly extension of the Southern Uplands, which stretch down from Fukien and Chekiang provinces. Since much of Kwangtung lies south of the Tropic of Cancer, it is the only Chinese province with tropical and subtropical climates. Almost the entire province lies within an area in which two crops of rice can be grown per year. There is no true winter, but the hot summer varies in length in different regions.

Kwangtung is largely populated by Han Chinese. The most important dialect, which itself exhibits a variety of forms, is Cantonese. Most of the province's population lives in the villages, the greatest number of which are in the fertile river deltas and along the waterways. Other major cities in addition to Canton are Swatow, Sh'ao-kuan, Chiang-men, Chan-chiang, Fo-shan, Hai-k'ou, and Ch'ao-an.

In addition to its two rice crops, Kwangtung also produces nearly half of China's annual output of sugarcane and has a significant fruit production, particularly bananas and citrus fruits. Kwangtung, with its long coastline, produces about one-fifth of China's fish catch. More than 400 species of saltwater fish are caught from numerous fishing ports.

Kwangtung's light industry, which has long been important to its economy and which is located mostly in the Canton Delta, includes food processing, textile manufacturing, sugar refining, silk filature (the reeling of silk from cocoons), weaving, and rice milling; the latter is the largest and most widespread industry and takes place in nearly every county and municipality. The province's heavy industries include metal processing, the manufacture of machinery, shipbuilding and ship repairing, the production of hydroelectricity, and mining. Significant mineral deposits found in Kwangtung are hematite, coal, manganese, tungsten, and oil shale. Oil refineries have been established at Mao-ming.

Water transport accounts for much of Kwangtung's total traffic tonnage. The waterways are maintained by continual dredging, widening, and clearing of canals and other channels. Connections with other provinces depend principally on land transportation, however, and Kwangtung has developed the best highway network in China. The province also provides a crucial link in China's domestic and international air service, and its telecommunications and mail delivery are among the most advanced in the country. Area 76,100 square miles (197,100 square km). Pop. (1993 est.) 65,250,000.

Kwanto Plain (Japan): *see* Kantō Plain.

Kwanto Range (Japan): *see* Kantō Range.

Kwanza River, also spelled COANZA, CUANZA, QUANZA, or KUANZA, river in central Angola, rising about 50 miles (80 km) southeast of Chitembo in the Bié Plateau at 5,000 feet (1,500 m). It flows northward for about 320 miles (510 km) and then curves westward to enter the Atlantic Ocean 30 miles (48 km) south of Luanda, after a course of 600 miles (960 km). The Kwanza drains much of central Angola and is the only Angolan river of economic significance. At intervals during much of its upper and middle course, the Kwanza is broken by rapids and flows in a well-defined valley. The lowest fall is that at Cambambe (about 70 feet [20 m]), below which the river is navigable by small steamers to the sea, about 160 miles (255 km) distant. But the Kwanza is little used for transportation because of its shallowness in the dry season and because of a shifting sandbar at its mouth; moreover, much of the river's basin is served by the Luanda-Malanje railway. A right-bank tributary of the Kwanza, the Lucala, is also navigable and is noted for a 330-foot (100-metre) falls along its course. Cambambe Dam (1963) supplies electricity to the Angolan capital of Luanda and provides irrigation water for the valley of the Kwanza in its lower course.

Kwanzaa, also spelled KWANZA (Swahili: "First Fruits"), African-American holiday, celebrated each year from December 26 to January 1; it is patterned after various African harvest festivals.

Kwanzaa was created in 1966 by Maulana Karenga, a black-studies professor at California State University at Long Beach, as a nonreligious celebration of family and social values. By the early 1990s it was estimated to have more than 5 million celebrants. Each day of Kwanzaa is dedicated to one of seven principles: unity (*umoja*), self-determination (*kujichagulia*), collective responsibility (*ujima*), cooperative economics (*ujamaa*), purpose (*nia*), creativity (*kuumba*), and faith (*imani*). Each evening family members gather to light one of the candles in the *kinara*, a seven-branched candelabra, and discuss the principle for that day; often gifts are exchanged. On December 31 the family joins other members of the community for a feast, called the *karamu.*

Kwara, state, west-central Nigeria. It is bounded by Benin to the west and by the Nigerian states of Niger to the north, Kogi to the east, and Ekiti, Dsun, and Oyo to the south.

Kwara state consists mostly of wooded savanna, but there are forested regions in the south. Almost all of its savanna area was conquered by the Fulani in the early 19th century, and the region remained part of the greater Fulani empire until the forces of Sir George Goldie's Royal Niger Company defeated the emirs of Nupe and Ilorin in 1897. It was incorporated into the Protectorate of Northern Nigeria in 1900, in the amalgamated Colony and Protectorate of Nigeria in 1914, and in the Northern region in 1954; Kwara state was created in 1967, when the federal military government divided Nigeria into 12 new states. In 1976, when 19 states were formed, it lost to Benue state the three Igala divisions east of the Niger River. In 1991 it lost some of its territory in the northwest to Niger state and some of its territory in the southeast to the newly created Kogi state.

Kwara is one of the least densely populated regions in the country. Most of its inhabitants, chiefly Yoruba, Nupe, Busa, and Baatonun peoples, are Muslims engaged in farming. Yams, corn (maize), sorghum, millet, onions, and beans are the most important staple crops; rice and sugarcane are significant cash crops in the Niger floodplains. Cotton and tobacco are grown, and cotton weaving, pottery making, and the making of raffia mats are the traditional crafts.

Ilorin, the state capital and largest town, is an industrial and education centre. It has food-processing and iron-working industries and is the site of a university (1975) and a state polytechnic college. Jebba is another industrial town, with a pulp and paper mill and sugar refinery. A hydroelectric dam (completed in 1984) that forms part of the Niger Dams Project is situated at Jebba.

Kwara state's transportation facilities include river-borne transport on the Niger, now made navigable by locks at the Kainji Dam (in Niger state), up to Yelwa in Kebbi state. The main highway from Lagos passes through Ilorin and Jebba; it is paralleled through the state by the trunk railway from Lagos. The state also has a good network of local roads. Area 14,218 square miles (36,825 square km). Pop. (1995 est.) 1,751,464.

kwashiorkor, also called PROTEIN MALNUTRITION, condition caused by severe protein deficiency. Protein malnutrition is most often encountered in tropical and subtropical regions in which the diet is high in starch and low in proteins. Kwashiorkor is common in young children weaned to a diet consisting chiefly of cereal grains, cassava, plantain, and sweet potato or similar starchy foods.

The condition in children was first described in 1932 and was termed kwashiorkor, meaning "deposed child" (deposed from the mother's breast by a newborn sibling) in one African dialect and "red boy" in another dialect. The latter term comes from the reddish orange discoloration of the hair that is characteristic of the disease. Other symptoms include dry skin and skin rash, potbelly and edema, weakness and nervous irritability, and digestive disturbances with diarrhea, anemia, and fatty infiltration of the liver.

The consumption of dried skim milk has proved effective in treating kwashiorkor. Reports have suggested that protein malnutrition in early life may lead to an adult predisposition to certain diseases such as cirrhosis of the liver and may cause stunted mental development. There is strong evidence that an adequate level of dietary protein is a protection against the disease.

In addition to protein-deficient diet, other causes of kwashiorkor include intestinal malabsorption, chronic alcoholism, kidney disease, and infection, burns, or other trauma resulting in the abnormal loss of body protein. Protein malnutrition is often associated with deficiencies of one or more other nutrients and of calories. When the caloric intake is inadequate and the level of dietary protein is barely adequate, protein malnutrition may still develop, for some of the protein is metabolized to supply the body's energy needs.

The term protein-calorie malnutrition, or marasmus, covers the whole spectrum of deficiencies caused by lack of protein or calories or both. When both calories and protein are lacking, young children (usually one to four years old) may suffer from a general wasting of body tissues and become acutely emaciated and fail to grow; additions to the diet that provide both calories and good-quality protein can effect cures in a relatively short time.

Kwaśniewski, Aleksander (b. Nov. 15, 1954, Białogard, Pol.), Polish politician who served as president of Poland from 1995.

Kwaśniewski studied economics at the University of Gdańsk and became a leader in the student activist movement, serving as chair of the University Council of the Socialist Union of Polish Students (1976–77). In 1977 he joined the governing communist Polish United Workers' Party (PUWP) and moved to Warsaw to edit two of the party's youth newspapers. Kwaśniewski steadily rose through the party's ranks, serving as Minister of Youth Affairs (1985–87) and as chair of the Committee for Youth and Physical Culture (1987–90). The PUWP, however, faced growing unrest, particularly from the Solidarity labour movement, led by Lech Wałęsa (*q.v.*). As a cabinet minister, Kwaśniewski participated in the round-table negotiations in the late 1980s that ended communist rule. After the fall of communism, Kwaśniewski became a founding member (1991) of the Democratic Left Alliance, which in 1993 won a plurality of seats in the Sejm, the lower house of the legislature. Kwaśniewski then formed a ruling coalition with the Polish Peasant Party, which was similarly composed of former communists.

In 1995 Kwaśniewski won the presidency, narrowly defeating Wałęsa, the country's first post-communist president. He was easily reelected to a second term in 2000. As president, he continued market reforms and oversaw the approval of a new constitution in 1997. He also guided Poland into the North Atlantic Treaty Organization in 1999 and to the European Union in 2004. An agnostic, Kwaśniewski nevertheless sought to develop better relations with both the Vatican and Jewish groups.

Kwatah (Pakistan): *see* Quetta.

KwaZulu, former nonindependent black state, Natal, South Africa, that was the legal home of all of the nation's Zulus. Its area was scattered among 11 exclaves (detached sections) throughout Natal, occupying more than one-third of its territory. The capital, initially at Nongoma, was moved in 1980 to Ulundi, the last historic capital of the Zulu empire (founded in 1816 by Shaka), where the Zulu were defeated by the British in 1879 in the final battle of an extended period of British-Zulu warfare. The new constitution of South Africa abolished apartheid, and in 1994 KwaZulu was reincorporated into Natal province, which was renamed KwaZulu/Natal.

KwaZulu/Natal, formerly NATAL, province of the Republic of South Africa, occupying the southeastern portion of the country. It is bounded on the east by the Indian Ocean, on the south by Eastern province, on the west by Lesotho and Free State province, on the northwest by Mpumalanga province, and on the north by Swaziland and Mozambique. Within KwaZulu/Natal is an enclave of Eastern province consisting of the eastern portion of the former Griqualand East (around Umzimkulu). The joint provincial capitals are Pietermaritzburg and Ulundi.

Under the former system of apartheid, or racial separation, Natal province contained the nonindependent black state of KwaZulu, which served as the legal homeland of the country's Zulus. Following the repeal of apartheid and the resorption of KwaZulu in 1994, Natal was renamed KwaZulu/Natal. For the history of the province, *see* Natal.

KwaZulu/Natal is generally hilly or mountainous, especially along its western border, with land rising from the coast to more than 11,000 feet (3,300 m) along the Drakensberg Escarpment on the province's western border. The slope is not gradual, however, and various rocky outcrops render the terrain into steps of undulating land ascending from an elevation of 500 feet (150 m) along the coastal plain to areas of 2,000 and then 4,000 feet, respectively, in the centre of the province (and known as the Midlands). Beyond the province, to the west, lies the Highveld, or high plateau.

KwaZulu/Natal's climate varies from subtropical to temperate. Rainfall decreases from more than 50 inches (1,270 mm) annually along the coast to 30–40 inches (760–1,020 mm) inland. Temperatures decrease from the frost-free coastal area but still remain warm. In general, summers are hot with occasional rain, while the warm, dry, and sunny winters have made the coast the principal holiday playground of southern Africa.

KwaZulu/Natal's people belong to various ethnic groups. Peoples of black African descent, mostly Zulus, make up more than 82 percent of the population, while Asians of mostly Indian descent account for about 9 percent and whites account for 7 percent. Most of the people live along and behind the coast or in the centre of the province; the extreme west and northeast are lightly populated. Many blacks are concentrated in rural areas consisting of broken, rugged country. Most whites live in or near the port city of Durban or elsewhere along the coast.

The province's blacks have retained much of their cultural identity through their use of the Zulu language and through a rich heritage of folklore, ceremony, and customs that reflect a diversity of tribal allegiances. The rest of the Africans speak related Bantu languages. Most of South Africa's Asians live in KwaZulu/Natal province. About two-thirds of the province's Asians are Hindus, and one-fifth are Muslims. The province's whites are mostly of British descent.

A subsistence economy prevails in the areas that were formerly set aside for blacks. The economy in these areas rests mainly on cattle raising and corn (maize) cultivation and is supplemented by remitted earnings of blacks who work elsewhere in South Africa. The whites, by contrast, tend to operate in an advanced commercial economy, through which most of the province's resources have been exploited.

The mineral wealth of KwaZulu/Natal province consists mostly of coal, which is mined in the north around Newcastle and Dundee and provides South Africa with much of its coking and semi-anthracite coal. The most important agricultural area is along the coast, where sugarcane is the major crop. Sugar refining is mainly carried out in Durban. The province produces such subtropical fruits as pineapples and bananas, and the dairy industry is also important. Plantations of pine and eucalyptus in the Midlands provide raw materials for sawmills and for paper and rayon pulp mills.

Durban, together with neighbouring Pinetown, is the province's economic and industrial centre. It has most of KwaZulu/Natal's factories and is one of South Africa's most important industrial regions. Its factories are primarily concerned with textiles and clothing, food processing, chemicals, sugar refining, and oil refining. Pietermaritzburg, capital of the former Natal province, also has a number of industries, including an aluminum plant, several footwear factories, and food-processing plants. The province's road and rail networks are well developed. KwaZulu/Natal's chief port, Durban, is South Africa's main cargo port and serves much of the interior of southern Africa.

Pietermaritzburg and Durban both have campuses of the University of Natal. There is also the University of Durban-Westville at Durban and the University of Zululand at Kwa-Dlangezwa, near Empangeni. Area 35,560 square miles (92,100 square km). Pop. (2001) 9,426,017.

Kwei Kiang (China): *see* Kuei River.

Kweichow, Wade-Giles romanization KUEI-CHOU, Pinyin GUIZHOU, *sheng* (province) in southwestern China. It is bounded by the provinces of Yunnan on the west, Szechwan on the north, and Hunan on the east and by the Chuang Autonomous Region of Kwangsi on the south. Kweichow has rough topography, poor communications, and consequent isolation. The capital is centrally located Kuei-yang. Area 67,200 square miles (174,000 square km). Pop. (2000 est.) 35,250,000.

A brief treatment of Kweichow follows. For full treatment, *see* MACROPAEDIA: China.

Kweichow came under large-scale Chinese influence only in the modern era, particularly during the Ming dynasty (1368–1644), when it was made a province. During the Ch'ing dynasty (1644–1911), struggles broke out between the minorities, especially the Miao and the Chinese. Rebellions and suppressions became common. Serious revolts occurred in 1854 and 1871 and again between 1941 and 1944 as a result of exploitation and suppression by the warlord Wu T'ing-chang. Bitter struggles between the Miao and Wu armies went on until 1944.

Kweichow province is part of an old eroded plateau that is situated between the mighty Plateau of Tibet and the hilly regions of Hunan and Kwangsi and that forms part of a continuously ascending profile of the southwest. Incised valleys, steep gorges, and cliffs are common in the province. The entire terrain slopes at a steep angle from the centre toward the north, east, and south. Kweichow enjoys a mild climate with warm summers and mild winters. It is protected by mountain ranges from severe Siberian cold. Rainfall is fairly uniform and plentiful; typically, the province has high humidity, lengthy cloudy and rainy periods, and little sunshine. The province is said to be without three consecutive rainless days.

About three-fourths of the population is Han Chinese. Kweichow also has a large number of minority peoples, who intermingle with the Han people. At least 30 different groups have been identified. The most important of these are the Miao, the Puyi, the Shui, the Tung, and the Yi. Most of the population is rural. There are few cities in Kweichow. Kuei-yang is the largest and Tsun-i is a distant second.

The main crops produced are rice, corn (maize), wheat, barley, potatoes, and oats. Industrial crops include rapeseed, cured tobacco, peanuts (groundnuts), cotton, sugarcane, and sesame. Timber and other forestry products are plentiful. Among all the Chinese provinces, Kweichow ranks high in the production of raw lacquer and tung oil. It is also known for its production of *mao-tai* liquor—made from wheat and *kaoliang* (sorghum)—which has won a number of international prizes.

Mineral resources are rich in Kweichow. Metallic minerals include mercury, manganese, zinc, lead, antimony, aluminum, copper, iron, and gold. Nonmetallics are coal, petroleum, oil-shale, phosphate, gypsum, arsenic, limestone, and fluorite. Consequently, mining industries are important in the province. Other industries include iron and steel, machinery manufacture, cement, food processing, leather, production of silk and cotton textiles, and chemical fertilizers, soda acid, and other chemicals.

Kweichow has well-developed highway transportation and a growing railroad network. River transportation is of little importance owing to ubiquitous reefs and rapids. Area 67,200 square miles (174,000 square km). Pop. (2000 est.) 35,250,000.

Kweilin (China): *see* Kuei-lin.

Kwekwe, formerly QUE QUE, city, central Zimbabwe. Ancient gold-mine workings were discovered in the area in 1894. A settlement was established in 1902 and named for the Kwekwe River (meaning the sound of frogs, or "a crowd"). Kwekwe was created a village in 1904, a town in 1928, and a municipality in 1934. The city is now a busy industrial-commercial centre situated halfway between Harare (formerly Salisbury) and Bulawayo on the main road and rail lines. Located near the iron- and steelworks at Redcliff, Kwekwe processes rails, steel, and chrome. It also distributes tobacco, livestock, and general farm produce. Pop. (2002 prelim.) 88,000.

kwela (South African music): *see* kivela.

Kweni (people): *see* Guro.

Kwinana, town, southwestern Western Australia. It lies along Cockburn Sound, just south of Perth. The name was taken from a freighter wrecked offshore in 1922; it is an Aboriginal word meaning "young woman." The place was a small resort until the mid-1950s, when a large oil refinery with associated port facilities was completed to receive oil shipments from the Middle East. Since then, blast furnaces and rolling mills have been built to process iron ore shipped to Kwinana by rail from Koolyanobbing, which lies 250 miles (400 km) to the east. An alumina works processes bauxite from the nearby Darling Ranges, and there is a titanium-oxide treatment plant. A refinery processes nickel concentrates from the Kambalda nickel field. The area is rapidly becoming industrialized, with a power station and port development along the 14-mile (22-km) shoreline. Medina is among the growing residential areas. Pop. (2001) 20,812.

Oil refinery and port in Kwinana, Western Australia
G.R. Roberts

Ky, Nguyen Cao: *see* Nguyen Cao Ky.

kyanite, also spelled CYANITE, also called DISTHENE, silicate mineral that is formed during the regional metamorphism of clay-rich sediments. It is an indicator of deep burial of a terrain rather than high stress, as formerly thought. Kyanite occurs as elongated blades principally in gneisses and schists, and it is often accompanied by garnet, quartz, and mica. Its colour ranges from gray-green to black or blue, with blue and blue-gray being the most common colours. Kyanite varies in hardness according to the cleavage of its crystals. Occurrences include Switzerland; Trentino, Italy; the Urals, Russia; and New England, U.S. For detailed physical properties, *see* silicate mineral (table).

Kyanite is one of the many phases in the aluminum silicate (Al_2OSiO_4) system and can only form stably over a limited range of pressures and temperatures. At lower pressures, the minerals sillimanite, mullite, and andalusite exist as stable phases. Kyanite is a major raw material for the mullite used in spark plugs and other refractory porcelains. A clear, deep-blue variety is sometimes cut as a gemstone.

Kyaukse, town, central Myanmar (Burma). Lying on the Zawgyi River, 25 miles (40 km) south of Mandalay, it is served by the Mandalay-Yangôn (Rangoon) railway. The first Myanmar (Burmese) probably settled in the area about 800, and local 12th- and 13th-century inscriptions refer to Kyaukse as "the first home." Remains of pagodas and old cities are found throughout the area. The Shwethalyaung pagoda, built by King Anawrahta (reigned 1044–77), is located in Kyaukse.

The surrounding area consists of a level strip running south from Mandalay along the foothills of the Shan Plateau. The area is located in the heart of Myanmar's dry zone but is drained by the Panlaung and Zawgyi rivers, which were used for an ancient irrigation-canal system that predates Myanmar settlement in the area. The main lines of the canal system were supposedly dug by order of King Anawrahta in the 11th century. They are the largest of the historic irrigation works in Myanmar. The canalized area, traditionally the main Myanmar granary, was repaired and expanded under the British; it produces high yields of rice. Pop. (latest est.) 37,200.

Kyburg, also spelled KIBURG, countship prominent in medieval Swiss history. The first line of counts of Kyburg, with their seat in the castle of Kyburg just southeast of Winterthur (in the modern canton of Zürich), were influential in German politics from the 1020s; but their male line became extinct in 1078, and their possessions passed to a branch of the Swabian counts of Dillingen. This new line of counts of Kyburg in 1218 inherited a large part of the extensive lands of the deceased dukes of Zähringen in the present German state of Baden-Württemberg, but in 1264 the new line, too, became extinct. Its accumulated possessions were later divided between two branches of the house of Habsburg: those east of Switzerland's Aar River went to the future German king Rudolf I and, through him, to the successive dukes of Austria; those west of the Aar went to Rudolf's cousins of the house of Habsburg-Laufenburg.

Kyd, Thomas (baptized Nov. 6, 1558, London, Eng.—d. *c.* December 1594, London), English dramatist who, with his *The Spanish Tragedie* (sometimes called *Hieronimo,* or *Jeronimo,* after its protagonist), initiated the revenge tragedy (*q.v.*) of his day. Kyd anticipated the structure of many later plays, including the development of middle and final climaxes. Kyd in addition revealed an instinctive sense of tragic situation, while his characterization of Hieronimo in *The Spanish Tragedie* prepared the way for William Shakespeare's psychological study of Hamlet.

The son of a scrivener, Kyd was educated at the Merchant Taylors School in London. There is no evidence that he attended the university before turning to literature. He seems to have been in service for some years with a lord (possibly Ferdinando, Lord Strange, the patron of a theatrical troupe). *The Spanish Tragedie* was entered in the Stationers' Register in October 1592, and the undated first quarto edition almost certainly appeared in that year. It is not known which company first played it, nor when; but Strange's company played *Hieronimo* 16 times in 1592, and the Admiral's Men revived it in 1597, as apparently did the Chamberlain's Men. It remained one of the most popular plays of the age and was often reprinted.

The only other play certainly by Kyd is *Cornelia* (1594), an essay in Senecan tragedy, translated from the French of Robert Garnier's academic *Cornélie.* He may also have written an earlier version of *Hamlet,* known to scholars as the *Ur-Hamlet,* and his hand has sometimes been detected in the anonymous *Arden of Feversham,* one of the first domestic tragedies, and in a number of other plays.

About 1591 Kyd was sharing lodgings with Christopher Marlowe, and on May 13, 1593, he was arrested and then tortured, being suspected of treasonable activity. His room had been searched and certain "atheistical" disputations denying the deity of Jesus Christ found there. He probably averred then and certainly confirmed later, in a letter, that these papers had belonged to Marlowe. That letter is the source for almost everything that is known about Kyd's life. He was dead by Dec. 30, 1594, when his mother made a formal repudiation of her son's debt-ridden estate.

Articles are alphabetized word by word, not letter by letter

Kydones, Demetrios (theologian): *see* Cydones, Demetrius.

Kydones, Prochoros: *see* Cydones, Prochorus.

Kyffhäuser Mountains, German KYFFHÄUSER GEBIRGE, double line of hills on the northern edge of the Thüringer Basin in central Germany that extend for 13 miles (21 km) and reach a maximum height in the Kulpen-Berg (1,565 feet [477 m]). Lying in the lowland of Thuringia on the south side of the Harz Mountains, the range cuts off steeply to the north and slopes gently to the south. The northern hills look down upon the valley of the Goldene Aue and are crowned by two ruined castles, the 7th-century Rothenburg on the west and the 10th-century Kyffhäuser on the east. The hill of Kyffhäuser is surmounted by an imposing equestrian statue (erected 1896) of the German emperor William I. According to legend, the 12th-century Holy Roman emperor Frederick I Barbarossa is asleep within the mountain and one day will awaken to lead the united peoples of Germany to victory against their enemies.

Kyi language: *see* Khasi language.

Kyiv (Ukraine): *see* Kiev.

Kyle and Carrick, district, Strathclyde region, southwestern Scotland; created by the reorganization of 1975, it is part of the former county of Ayr. The district, area 498 sq mi (1,290 sq km), stretches along the shores of the Firth of Clyde and includes the steep rock of Ailsa Craig at its mouth. Cattle are raised on the Kyle plain and cattle and sheep on the Carrick uplands in the south, which are also extensively forested. The mild climate favours market gardening. Ayr, Prestwick, and Troon are seaside resorts, with some industry, and are known for their golf courses. Prestwick is Scotland's international airport, and Ayr has its best racecourse. Robert Burns, Scotland's national poet, was born at Alloway, just south of Ayr, the seat of the district authority. Pop. (1991 prelim.) 113,572.

kylix, also spelled CYLIX, in ancient Greek pottery, wide-bowled drinking cup with horizontal handles, one of the most popular pottery forms from Mycenaean times through the classical Athenian period. There was usually a painted frieze around the outer surface, depicting a subject from mythology or everyday life, and on the bottom of the inside a painting often depicting a dancing or drinking scene.

Attic red-figure kylix by Epictetus showing Heracles slaying Busiris, *c.* 520 BC; in the British Museum

By courtesy of the trustees of the British Museum

Kylver Stone, limestone slab that bears a 5th-century runic inscription, providing the oldest extant record of the Germanic runic series; it was found in a tomb in the province of Gotland in Sweden.

The runes faced the inside of a coffin and probably were intended either to protect the grave or to bind the dead person to it. In addition to the runic alphabet, the rune carver also carved a reinforced ṭ-rune that looked like a fir tree and the uninterpreted palindrome (a word that reads the same backward or forward) *sueus* in order to achieve the magical protection desired.

Kymi, in full KYMEN LÄÄNI, Swedish KYMMENE LÄN, *lääni* (province), southeastern Finland, bounded by the Gulf of Finland (south) and by Russia (east). The province has a land area of 4,145 square miles (10,736 square km) and includes the southern section of the Saimaa lake system, which is drained by the Kymijoki and Vuoksi rivers. Kymijoki valley industries include timber processing and wood products, iron and steel, textile milling, and granite and limestone quarrying. Kouvola, the administrative capital, has paper and pulp mills and is a major rail junction. Kotka and Hamina are two of the most important ports on the Gulf of Finland. The *lääni* was created in 1944 and encompasses the part of former Viipuri (present Vyborg) county that was not ceded to the U.S.S.R. Pop. (1991 est.) 334,905.

Kynaston, Edward, byname NED KYNASTON (b. *c.* 1640, London—d. January 1706), probably the last and the best of English boy actors playing female roles.

His last female role was in Beaumont and Fletcher's *Maid's Tragedy* with Killigrew's Company (1661). Earlier in that year the English diarist Samuel Pepys reports—having seen Kynaston play several parts in Ben Jonson's comedy *The Silent Woman,* one as a woman gallant in fine clothes—"And in them was clearly the prettiest woman in the whole house; and lastly, as a man; and then likewise did appear the handsomest man in the house."

Active by 1660, by 1665 he was one of the leading actors of male roles in the company at Covent Garden Theatre, London. He joined Thomas Betterton at Lincoln's Inn Fields in London in 1695, but his memory began to fail and he retired in 1699.

Kyneton, town, central Victoria, Australia, on the Campaspe River, about 50 mi (85 km) northwest of Melbourne. Squatters settled in the region in 1836–41; the town was surveyed in 1849 and named after Kineton (now known as Kington) in Hertfordshire, England. Kyneton is the service centre for an area producing wool, beef, dairy products, oats, wheat, and potatoes. There are abattoirs, knitting and timber mills, engineering works, and dairy factories in the town. Kyneton is a summer tourist resort, offering fishing and other sports, and is noted for its bluestone buildings, which have been classified by Australia's National Trust. Pop. (1989 est.) 4,010.

Kynewulf (Old English poet): *see* Cynewulf.

Kyō-yaki, decorated Japanese ceramics produced in Kyōto from about the middle of the 17th century. The development of this ware was stimulated by the appearance of enamelled porcelains in Kyushu, and it was not long after Sakaida Kakiemon successfully perfected overglaze enamels in Arita that Nonomura Ninsei also began production in Kyōto. *Kyō-yaki* contrasted with the enamelled wares of Arita that had been heavily influenced by Chinese models and produced with an eye to foreign export; instead, the Kyōto wares are in the classical Japanese style, retaining much of the traditional taste of the court.

A wide variety of tableware, tea utensils, and ornamental objects were produced. Many of these were formed on the wheel and have fine, classically proportioned walls. Pictorial motifs are painted in the style of both the Kanō school and *Yamato-e* traditions. A wide range of colors (red, blue, yellow, green, purple, black, silver, and gold) is used to create complex tonal harmonies.

Kyōdō tsūshinsha (Japanese: Cooperative News Agency) national news agency founded in November 1945 to replace the pre-World War II Dōmei tsūshinsha (Federated News Agency), which had served as the official news service of the Japanese government since 1936. Despite competition from the beginning with the Jiji news agency, formed by Dōmei employees who did not join Kyōdō, the latter gradually gained prestige among Japan's newspapers, in part by introducing technological innovations such as a teletype system for transmission of *kanji* (Japanese characters). By the 1980s the agency had representatives in major world cities, with some 110 subscribers in Japan, including radio and television stations as well as newspapers.

Kyoga Lake, also spelled KIOGA LAKE, lake in central Uganda, East Africa, north of Lake Victoria, formed by the Victoria Nile in its middle course. The many-armed lake is shallow, with swampy, papyrus-reeded shores; masses of papyrus are broken loose by strong winds and sometimes have completely blocked the river. Navigation for shallow-draft vessels is possible between Namasagali and Masindi Port. The lake is about 80 mi (129 km) long and is 3,390 ft (1,033 m) above sea level.

kyōgen, brief farce or comic interlude played during a Japanese Nō (lyric drama) cycle, expressed in the vernacular of the second half of the 16th century. Its effect is to relieve the tension of the drama. It is performed in ordinary dress and without masks (unless these are used in parody). There are normally four *kyōgen* interspersed among the usual five Nō pieces.

Kyōha Shintō, English SECT SHINTŌ, group of folk religious sects in Japan that were separated by a government decree in 1882 from the suprareligious national cult, State Shintō. They were denied public support, and their denominations were called *kyōkai* ("church"), or *kyōha* ("sect"), to distinguish them from the established shrines, called *jinja,* which were considered state institutions.

By 1908, 13 sects had been recognized by the government. Scholars have classified them into a number of groups according to characteristics of their religious faith. The main groups are:

(1) Revival Shintō: Shintō Taikyō ("Great Teaching of Shintō"); Shinrikyō ("Divine Truth Religion"); Izumo-ōyashirokyō, also called Taishakyō ("Religion of the Grand Shrine of Izumo").

(2) Confucian sects: Shintō Shūsei-ha ("Improving and Consolidating School of Shintō"); Shintō Taisei-ha ("Great Accomplishment School of Shintō").

(3) Mountain-worship sects: Jikkōkyō ("Practical Conduct Religion"); Fusōkyō ("Religion of Mount Fuji"); Mitakekyō, or Ontakekyō ("Religion of Mount Ontake").

(4) Purification sects: Shinshūkyō ("Divine Learning Religion"); Misogikyō ("Purification Religion").

(5) Utopian or faith-healing cults: Kurozumikyō ("Religion of Kurozumi," named after its founder); Konkōkyō ("Religion of Konkō," the name of the *kami,* or sacred power); Tenrikyō ("Religion of Divine Wisdom").

The sects developed many splinter sects and devotional associations, so that by the end of World War II, when they were allowed to separate themselves, they had multiplied from the original 13 to 75.

In their emphasis on elaborate doctrines, proselytization, and missionary activity, some were prototypes of the "new religions" that have sprung up in modern Japan. Most influential of the Kyōha Shintō is Tenrikyō.

Kyokujitsu-shō (Japan): *see* Rising Sun, Order of the.

Kyŏmja (Korean painter): *see* Chŏng Sŏn.

Kyŏnggi, *do* (province), northwestern South Korea. It is bounded by the truce line with North Korea (north), by the *do* of Kangwŏn (east) and Kyŏngsang-puk and Ch'ungch'ŏng-nam (south), and by the Yellow Sea (west). The nation's capital, Seoul, is in the middle of the province but was separated from it administratively in 1946 as a special city. Formerly Kyŏnggi *do* was the granary of Seoul; the Kyŏnggi plain, with the Han River and its tributaries flowing through it, produced rice, barley, and wheat. Dairying and truck farming and other types of horticulture are still carried on. As Seoul's industrial district has spread into the province's area, and with the construction of highways beginning in the late 1960s, a large part of the province has become the outer industrial region of Seoul. The cities of Anyang, Buchŏn, Sŏngnam, and Ŭijŏngbu have developed as satellites of Seoul, each carrying on various types of industries, such as shipbuilding, iron and steel manufacturing, and plate-glass production. The city of Inch'ŏn serves as Seoul's seaport; the city of Suwŏn is the provincial capital. The sea around Paengnyŏng *do* and Yŏnp'yŏng (islands) in the Kyŏnggi Gulf offer good fishing grounds for yellow corbinas and croakers. Area 4,196 square miles (10,867 square km). Pop. (2000) 8,937,752.

Kyŏngju, city, Kyŏngsang-puk *do* (province), southeastern South Korea. It is 17 miles (28 km) inland from the coast of the Sea of Japan (East Sea) and 34 miles (55 km) east of the provincial capital, Taegu. The capital of the Silla kingdom (57 BC–AD 935), its ancient name was Sŏrabŏl, which means "capital." Kyŏngju plain, surrounded by a double range of hills and mountains, formed a natural fortress for the city. Kyŏngju has hundreds of ancient historical remains such as temples, stone pagodas, imperial mausoleums, mounds, and castle sites. Sŏkkuram, a grotto shrine located on the summit of the mountain T'oham-san (2,444 feet [745 m]) near Pulguksa, was built in the 8th century and is known as one of the world's most excellent shrines for Buddhist art. Kyŏngju is one of the most important Korean tourist attractions, and more than a million people visit the city annually. It is connected with Seoul and Pusan by rail and highway. Pop. (1995) 273,968.

Consult the INDEX *first*

Kyŏngsang-nam, *do* (province), southeastern South Korea. It is bordered east by the Sea of Japan, south by the Korea Strait, west by Chŏlla-nam and Chŏlla-puk *do,* and north by Kyŏngsang-puk *do.* Pusan, capital of the province, was separated administratively in 1963, when it was elevated to the status of a special city. The Naktong River and its tributaries irrigate most of the province. The Kimhae delta plain, situated 9.5 miles (15 km) north to south and 4 miles (6.5 km) east to west, is one of the country's best granaries. In addition to rice, barley, beans, and potatoes, special agricultural products include cotton, flax, sesame, and fruits such as pears, oranges from the southern seaside, and sweet persimmons.

The length of the irregular coastline, including more than 400 islands, is about 1,400 miles (2,250 km). The interaction of warm and cold currents produces abundant sea life, and more than 40 kinds of marine products are caught annually, making the province one of the country's leading fisheries. Various light industries are carried on in the cities of Chinju, Ch'ungmo, and Samch'ŏnp'o, and there are

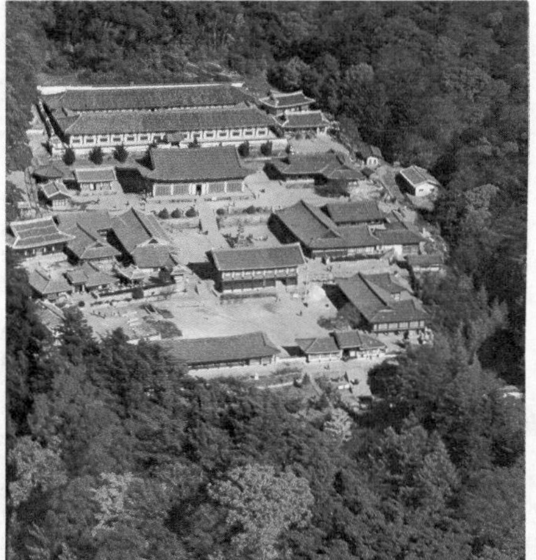

Haein Temple in Kyŏngsang-nam *do,* South Korea
Kim—Bavaria Verlag

heavy industries and chemical production in the large port cities of Ulsan, Masan, and Chinhae. The mountain Chiri-san (6,283 feet [1,915 m]), on the boundary with Chŏlla-puk *do,* is the centre of a national park in which Haein Temple, constructed in 802, is located. Area 4,579 square miles (11,859 square km). Pop. (2000) 2,970,929.

Kyŏngsang-puk, *do* (province), eastern South Korea. It is bounded on the east by the Sea of Japan (East Sea), on the south by Kyŏngsang-nam *do,* on the west by the *do* of Chŏlla-puk and Ch'ungch'ŏng-puk, and on the north by Kangwŏn *do.* It is South Korea's largest *do* in both size and population. The homeland of the Silla kingdom (57 BC–AD 935), of which there are historical remains, mainly in the Kyŏngju area, Kyŏngsang-puk has retained its cultural tradition. A number of scholars, artists, and political leaders have come from the province. Surrounded by the T'aebaek and Sobaek mountains and their spurs, it is the hottest province in South Korea during the summer and suffers from lack of rainfall; the amount per year at Taegu is about 37 inches (940 mm). The Naktong River, the second longest in Korea, and its tributaries flow toward the south, but the plains beside them are not broad. In addition to rice, barley, beans, and potatoes, its special agricultural product is apples from the vicinity of Taegu. Dairy farming and cattle breeding exist in several districts. Marine products from the seacoast and Ullŭng Island include seaweed, cuttlefish, and shellfish. Transportation has been well developed, and industries such as the manufacture of textiles, machinery, and chemicals are carried on in the cities of P'ohang and Kumi. Area 7,507 square miles (19,442 square km). Pop. (2000) 2,716,218.

Kyōto, *fu* (urban prefecture), Honshu, Japan, bounded by the *ken* (prefectures) of Fukui and Shiga (east), Nara (south), and Hyōgo (northwest), the *fu* of Ōsaka (southwest), and the Sea of Japan (north). Much of it is composed of the Tamba Mountains, which are sometimes considered to be the eastern extension of

Miyazu, port on Wakasa-wan near Maizuru, Kyōto *fu,* Japan
By courtesy of Fishery Aviation Manufacturing Co., Japan

the Chūgoku Range. From 1874 until World War II, Kyōto was the prefecture with the largest industrial production (especially of textiles) in Japan. Tokyo was ninth. Kyōto later became a part of the Kinki Industrial Zone. The prefectural headquarters are located in the former national capital of Kyōto. Other important cities include Uji, Fukuchiyama, and Maizuru. Area 1,781 square miles (4,613 square km). Pop. (2000 prelim.) 2,644,000.

Kyōto, city, seat of Kyōto *fu* (urban prefecture), west-central Honshu Island, Japan. The city, located about 29 miles (47 km) to the northeast of Ōsaka, is the principal centre of Japanese culture and of Buddhism in Japan. For more than 1,000 years—from 794 to 1868—Kyōto ("Capital City") was the capital of Japan and the place of residence of the imperial family.

A brief treatment of Kyōto follows. For full treatment, *see* MACROPAEDIA: Kyōto.

Kyōto is situated in the northern part of the great Kyōto (Yamashiro) fault basin and is surrounded on three sides by low mountains. Several streams, such as the Kamo and the Katsura, flow down from the mountains through the city to join the Yodo River to the south. Kyōto's climate is typical of inland Japan; it is hot in summer and cold in winter, with the annual rainfall of approximately 62 inches (1,575 mm) occurring mainly in summer.

The centre of the present city has moved northeastward since its earliest days. Most of the old city consists of small stores, workshops, and residences, all standing side by side. Buddhist temples (such as Higashi Hongan Temple and Tō Temple, with its famed five-story pagoda) and Shintō shrines (such as Heian Shrine and Yasaka Shrine) are found everywhere in the city and its surrounding hills. Although the city is divided into 11 wards (*ku*), Kyōto in popular usage consists of five districts: central Rakuchū, eastern Rakutō, northern Rakuhoku, western Rakusei, and southern Rakunan.

Kyōto is one of Japan's traditional centres for education and for training in the arts and sciences. Of the many national and private institutions of higher learning, some, such as Kyōto University (1897; formerly Kyōto Imperial University), are preeminent. The city is also the site of Dōshisha University (1875), a centre of Christian higher education, and several Buddhist universities.

Kyōto abounds with historical and cultural treasures, including architecture, paintings, carvings, fine examples of calligraphy, and gardens. Important cultural institutions include the Kyōto Municipal Museum of Art and the Kyōto National Museum (1889). Virtually every Buddhist temple has its own museum of Buddhist antiquities. Kyōto also has nō and kabuki theatres, and it is a centre for the tea ceremony and for flower arrangement. The old Kyōto Imperial Palace is one of the most representative examples of traditional Japanese architecture, and Nijō Castle (1603) is the most famous castle of the Tokugawa period (1603–1867). Kyōto's treasures and seasonal events draw millions of tourists to the city each year.

Most factories in Kyōto are small workshops, and the manufacture of traditional products overshadows machine and chemical industries. Most important are the manufacture of textiles (mainly silk), foods and drinks, porcelain ware, and traditional Japanese objects. Kyōto is the national centre for wholesale trade in textiles and is a banking and corporate headquarters. Railways and expressways link Kyōto with other cities. Area city, 236 square miles (610 square km). Pop. (1995 prelim.) city, 1,463,601.

Kyōto-Ōsaka-Kōbe Region: *see* Keihanshin Industrial Zone.

Kyōto University, Japanese KYŌTO DAIGAKU, coeducational state institution of higher education in Kyōto, Japan. It was founded in 1897 under the provisions of an 1872 Japanese law that established a system of imperial universities admitting small numbers of carefully selected students to be trained as scholars and imperial officials. Kyōto Imperial University (Kyōto Teikoku Daigaku), popularly called Kyōdai, soon became one of the most important imperial universities, surpassed in prestige only by Tokyo Imperial University (now the University of Tokyo).

After World War II the American forces of occupation encouraged the Japanese to establish a system of mass higher education. Although Kyōto was integrated into this system and the appellation "imperial" was dropped from the university's name, it maintained its prestige. Because admission to Kyōto or Tokyo is said to be essential for students who desire good jobs in Japanese industry or civil service, admission to these universities is highly competitive. The university has faculties of engineering, science, agriculture, and medicine, among others, and a college of liberal arts and sciences. It also has a large number of specialized research institutes dealing with various branches of the pure and applied sciences and technology.

Kyrenia, Greek KIRÍNIA, Turkish GIRNE, city, situated along the northern coast of Cyprus, in the Turkish Cypriot-administered area. Founded by the Achaeans, ancient Greek colonists, and fortified by the Byzantines, Franks, and Venetians, the city was the administrative headquarters of the Kyrenia district of the Republic of Cyprus until the Turkish intervention in 1974. Kyrenia city is a market centre and seaside resort. Its horseshoe-shaped harbour is flanked by a 12th-century castle fortress. The castle houses the remains of a ship dating to about 300 BC that was recovered in 1969 approximately 0.5 mile (0.8 km) offshore. Nearby in the Kyrenia Mountains are the 13th-century Abbey of Bellapais and the fortress of St. Hilarion. After the Turkish intervention, the city became the headquarters of the Turkish occupation forces. Mainland Turks subsequently settled in Kyrenia, and hotels were reopened for the tourist trade. Ferry service between Kyrenia and Mersin in Turkey began in 1977. Pop. (1987 est.) 7,107.

Kyrenia Mountains, mountain range in northern Cyprus extending east to west for about 100 miles (160 km) from Cape Andreas, on the Karpas Peninsula, to Cape Kormakiti. Rising from the coast a short distance inland, the range flanks a narrow coastal plain and reaches a maximum height of 3,360 feet (1,024 m) at Mount Kyparissovouno, in the western region, ending in low hills at the tip of Cape Andreas in the east. West of Melounda, the range is known as the Pentadaktylos ("Five Fingers"), from the fingered peak that is one of its main features. The first area extensively settled by mainland Turks after the Turkish intervention in Cyprus in 1974 stretches from the eastern part of Ayios Amvrosios to the Karpass Peninsula and across the Pentadaktylos mountains. The mountains are composed of a narrow fold of limestone with occasional deposits of marble.

Kyrgyz, also spelled KIRGIZ, or KIRGHIZ, Turkic-speaking people of Central Asia, most of whom live in Kyrgyzstan. Small numbers reside in Afghanistan, in western China, and in Kazakstan, Uzbekistan, Tajikistan, and Turkey. The Kyrgyz language belongs to the northwestern, or Kipchak, group of the Turkic languages. The people are Muslim in religion.

Like other Central Asian peoples, the Kyrgyz were traditionally nomadic and pastoral. During the second half of the 19th century, Kirgiziya (the country's Russian name) became a major area of Russian colonization, and much of the best land was given to Russian settlers. This was a major cause of the revolt of 1916, in the suppression of which the Kyrgyz suffered very heavily; whole villages were put to the torch, and nearly a third of the Kyrgyz fled to China. After the Russian Revolution of 1917, Kirgiziya was the scene of much guerrilla opposition to the Soviet regime. From 1926 to 1959 there was a heavy influx of Russians and Ukrainians into the area, and the proportion of Kyrgyz in the total population fell from about 66 percent to 40 percent. The development of agriculture and heavy industry, along with the growth of cities, did much to change the traditional Kyrgyz way of life.

Kyrgyz language, also spelled KIRGIZ, or KIRGHIZ, member of the Turkic subfamily of Altaic languages. It is spoken in Kyrgyzstan and in the Pamir Mountains on the border between Tajikistan, Afghanistan, and China. The language belongs to the northwestern, or Kipchak, division of the Turkic languages and is closely related to Kazak, Karakalpak, and Nogay.

Kyrgyz is also the name of the Old Turkic language found in inscriptions of the Yenisey River valley in Russia. The relationship between the speakers of Old Kyrgyz and the speakers of Central Asian Kyrgyz is unclear. *See also* Turkic languages.

Kyrgyzstan, officially KYRGYZ REPUBLIC, Kyrgyz KYRGYZ RESPUBLIKASY, formerly (1936–91) KIRGIZIYA, or KIRGHIZIA, or KIRGIZ SOVIET SOCIALIST REPUBLIC, historical region and country of Central Asia. Kyrgyzstan is bounded by Kazakstan on the north and northwest, Uzbekistan on the southwest, and Tajikistan on the south. On the southeast, the Kok Shaal-Tau Range, part of the Tien Shan (mountains), forms the border with China. The capital is Bishkek (formerly Frunze). Area 76,600 square miles (198,500 square km). Pop. (1996 est.) 4,521,000.

A brief treatment of Kyrgyzstan follows. For full treatment, *see* MACROPAEDIA: Central Asia.

For current history and for statistics on society and economy, *see* BRITANNICA BOOK OF THE YEAR.

Physical and human geography. Kyrgyzstan is, above all, a mountainous country. On the Chinese border is Victory (Pobedy) Peak, and Mount Khan-Tengri is nearby on the border with Kazakstan; these are among the highest peaks in the massive Tien Shan system. The crests of the ranges are mantled in perpetual ice and snow. Many short rivers with rapids cascade down the mountains. The Fergana and Chu valleys (in the southwest and north, respectively) are home to much of the country's population.

The remoteness of Kyrgyzstan from the oceans and the sharp change of elevation from neighbouring plains are two important influences on the climate. The country's lower reaches lie in belts of hot desert winds. At the higher elevations there is a cold desert. Between them is a transitional zone where westward and northward slopes receive more moisture. Except at the highest elevations, alpine and subalpine meadows abound. The lower valleys and the north-facing slopes are forested and support a mixture of European and Asian animal life. This includes the brown bear, wild pig, lynx, gray wolf, ermine, mountain sheep and goat, deer, and snow leopard.

The first Kyrgyz clans settled in the Tien Shan region in ancient times and were one of the great nomadic groups of Central Asia. After the advent of Soviet power and the development of the country, the nomadic life was almost completely abandoned. The Kyrgyz were moved into agricultural settlements, but only a small number adopted industrial employment, and two-thirds of the population still lives in rural areas. Kyrgyzstan's population is made up principally of Kyrgyz (about half the total population) and Russians (about one-fifth of the total), with minorities of Uzbeks, Ukrainians, and Germans deported from western Russia in 1941. Kyrgyz and Russian are the official languages. The Kyrgyz are predominantly Sunnite Muslims.

Kyrgyzstan

Kyrgyzstan was at one time wholly agricultural, but by the late 20th century the republic had become a source of nonferrous metals such as antimony and mercury ores. Coal mining continues to be important, and gold, tin, lead, zinc, and other metals have been discovered in the mountains. The republic is also a producer of machinery, hydroelectric power, and food products, and light industries produce textiles, clothing, and footwear. Industrialization has stimulated the mechanization of agriculture, which is dominated by livestock raising (especially sheep) and the cultivation of cereal grains, potatoes, cotton, sugar beets, tobacco, and opium poppies. The breeding of racehorses, the raising of pigs and rabbits, and beekeeping are pursued in the mountain regions.

Under the constitution adopted in 1993, Kyrgyzstan is a unitary federal republic founded on secular principles. There are a number of political parties. The president, who is head of state and has extensive executive powers, appoints the prime minister. There is a bicameral parliament. Judges of the three high courts are appointed by the president.

Medical care is free, but substandard. Kyrgyzstan's standard of living and educational and economic levels are among the lowest of the former Soviet republics.

Education is compulsory, at least officially, for nine years. Institutions of higher education include Kyrgyz State University (1951) in Bishkek and the Kyrgyz Academy of Sciences, which has about a dozen research institutes.

Kyrgyz cultural life has been influenced by a rich tradition of oral literature. Folk legacies have been handed on by the bards, who recite such poems as the long verse epic *Manas,* expressing the fiercely independent outlook of the Kyrgyz. Newspapers, magazines, and broadcast media are offered in both Kyrgyz and Russian; news media are not censored. A leading literary figure is the Kyrgyz writer Chingiz Aytmatov.

In music, earlier traditions are represented in ensembles of the three-stringed *komuz,* which is plucked like a lute; there is also a Kyrgyz symphony orchestra. There are vigorous folk-dance groups, and theatres perform plays in Kyrgyz and Russian. The Kyrgyz motion-picture studio, established since 1942, produces feature films as well as newsreels and popular-science films.

History. The origins of the Kyrgyz people are uncertain. Ethnographers tend to believe that they arrived in the region with the Khara-Khitais of Mongolia in the 12th century. Like Kazakstan and other Central Asian regions, Kirgiziya was largely nomadic before Russian invasion; it, too, was heavily settled by Russians in an attempt to suppress the nationalist movement. Kirgiziya became an autonomous *oblast* (province) within the Soviet Union in 1924, and it was made the Kirgiz Soviet Socialist Republic in 1936. It declared its independence in 1991, assuming the name Kyrgyzstan.

Kyrie, the vocative case of the Greek word *kyrios* ("lord"). The word *Kyrie* is used in the Septuagint, the earliest Greek translation of the Old Testament, to translate the Hebrew word Yahweh. In the New Testament, *Kyrie* is the title given to Christ, as in Philippians 2:11. As part of the Greek formula *Kyrie eleison* ("Lord, have mercy"), the word is used as a preliminary petition before a formal prayer and as a congregational response in the liturgies of many Christian churches.

Kyriotes, John: *see* Geometres, John.

kyūdō (Japanese: "way of the bow"), formerly KYŪJUTSU ("the technique of the bow"), traditional Japanese form of archery, closely associated with Zen Buddhism. When firearms supplanted the bow and arrow in warfare, the art of archery was retained by Zen monks and some members of the Japanese upper class as a mental and physical discipline. In *kyūdō* the primary aim is not to hit the target, as in Western archery, but to achieve through spiritual and physical training an intense concentration on the act of shooting and a style expressing perfect serenity.

Kyūdō bow drawn to its full extent
Haruo Satake

In *kyūdō* the *kyūjūtsushi* (archer) uses a traditional asymmetrical bow about 7.5 feet (2.3 m) long with a grip about one-third of the distance from the bottom. The bow is composite, made of strips of bamboo and mulberry and strung with hemp. The archer employs an Oriental, or Mongolian, grip, holding the string with the thumb supported by the fingers, and wears a special glove with a thumb reinforced by bone or wood. In the apparently continuous movements leading to the release of the arrow, there are eight recognized stages, each of which must be learned and practiced until the archer can move through them smoothly. There are many *kyūdō* schools in Japan, and tournaments are held annually in Kyōto and Tokyo.

Kyushu, Japanese KYŪSHŪ ("Nine Provinces"), southernmost and third largest of the four main islands of Japan. It is bordered by the East China Sea on the west and the Pacific Ocean on the east. Its name refers to the nine ancient provinces (*kuni*) into which the island was divided. It is separated from the island of Honshu to the north by the Shimonoseki Strait and from Korea to the northwest by the Tsushima Strait, or Eastern Channel. The island, with an area of 14,177 square miles (36,719 square km), is composed of a complex system of volcanic ranges. The climate in the south is subtropical, and Kyushu is known for its subtropical vegetation and heavy rainfall. It is the site of Mount Aso, the world's largest active volcanic crater, and of Aso-Kuju, Kirishima-Yaku, and Unzen-Amakusa national parks. Beppu is a well-known hot-springs resort.

The main crops raised on the island include rice, tea, tobacco, sweet potatoes, and citrus fruit. Industries, concentrated in northern Kyushu, include iron and steel and chemicals. Saga *ken* (prefecture) is famous for porcelain and pottery.

Kyushu is divided into the seven prefectures of Fukuoka, Kagoshima, Kumamoto, Miyazaki, Nagasaki, Ōita, and Saga. The chief cities are the northern industrial complex of Kita-Kyūshū, the commercial centre of Fukuoka, and Nagasaki. Pop. (1995 prelim.) 13,423,791.

Kyustendil, also spelled KÜSTENDIL, or KJUSTENDIL, town, southwestern Bulgaria. It lies on the margin of a small alluvial basin in the Struma River valley at the foot of the Osogov Mountains. It was known in Roman times as Pautalia, or Ulpia Pautalia. Located on the site of a Thracian fortified settlement, it became an important town during the Roman emperor Trajan's rule but was later badly damaged by barbarian invasions. During the first Bulgarian empire—from 1018 to the 14th century, when a local feudal lord, Constantine Dragash, established a short-lived independent principality—the town was known as Velbuzhd.

Kyustendil has developed from an Ottoman market town into an industrial centre that specializes in carpets and has factories for woolens, fruit canning, vegetable oils, and packaging. Hothouses produce early vegetables. The waters of local mineral springs heat the hothouses and serve the sanatoriums, which are popular as resorts. The town is the centre of what is called "Bulgaria's orchard"—extensive orchards and vineyards surround it—and a fruit-growing-research institute is located there. Pop. (1993 est.) 54,447.

Kyzyl, formerly (1914–18) BELOTSARSK, or (1918–26) KHEM-BELDYR, city and capital of Tuva republic, central Russia. It lies at the confluence of the Great Yenisey and Little Yenisey rivers where they form the upper Yenisey. Kyzyl's industries include tanning, timber working, brickworking, and food processing. The city has an agricultural college and a regional museum. Pop. (1995 est.) 93,-100.

Kyzyl-Kyya, also spelled KYZYL-KIYA, KYZYL-KIIA, or KYZYL-KIJA, city, southwestern Kyrgyzstan. It lies on the southern fringe of the Fergana Valley. Coal mining began there at the end of the 19th century, and the city is now one of the oldest mining centres in Kyrgyzstan. It became a city in 1938. The food industry and the production of firebricks and other refractory goods are important. Pop. (1991 est.) 49,400.

Kyzylkum, Uzbek QIZILQUM, Kazak QYZYLQUM ("Red Sand"), desert in Kazakstan and Uzbekistan. It has an area of about 115,000 square miles (about 300,000 square km) and lies between the Syr Darya and the Amu Darya (rivers), southeast of the Aral Sea. It consists of a plain sloping down toward the northwest, with a number of isolated bare mountains rising to 3,025 feet (922 m) and several large enclosed basins. Precipitation, 4–8 inches (100–200 mm) annually, occurs mainly in winter and spring. Mostly covered with sand ridges on which desert plants grow, the desert serves as pasture for Karakul sheep, horses, and camels, and there are several small oasis settlements. Important natural-gas deposits are exploited at Gazli in the southeast, and gold is mined at Muruntow in the centre.

Kzyl-Orda, Kazak QYZYLORDA, city, south-central Kazakstan, on the Syr Darya (river). Originally founded in the early 19th century as the Kokand fort of Ak-Mechet, it was renamed Perovsk after its capture by the Russians in 1853. After the Russian Revolution of 1917 the name of Ak-Mechet was restored, but in 1925 the city was renamed Kzyl-Orda, when it became the capital of the Kazakh A.S.S.R., a status that it lost to Alma-Ata (now Almaty) in 1929. There are some food and other light industries, as well as a Kazak theatre and a teacher-training institute. Pop. (1993 est.) 164,000.

L-D process: *see* basic oxygen process.

la (in proper names): *see* below and *see also* names spelled with no space after "la" (*e.g.,* LaFontaine, Sir Louis Hippolyte; Lagrange, Marie-Joseph) and continental European names alphabetized under the substantive word (*e.g.,* Vega, Garcilaso de la).

La Baule-Escoublac, also called LA BAULE, fashionable resort, Loire-Atlantique *département,* Bretagne *région,* France. It lies along the Atlantic coast near the mouth of the Loire River, west of Saint-Nazaire. Facing south and protected from the north wind by 1,000 acres (400 hectares) of dune-stabilizing maritime pines, it is on a crescent-shaped bay in the centre of a fine sand beach 5 miles (8 km) long. Headlands at each end of the bay shelter the town from east and west winds. Created in 1879, it and Biarritz are the best-known Atlantic resorts. Behind the line of the seafront hotels, luxurious villas are dotted among the pines. The town has a park, an open-air school, a casino, golf and tennis clubs, and a yacht harbour. Nearby are salt marshes. Pop. (1990) 14,845.

La Bourdonnais, Bertrand-François Mahé, Count (comte) **de** (b. Feb. 11, 1699, Saint-Malo, France—d. Nov. 10, 1753, Paris), French naval commander who played an important part in the struggle between the French and the British for control of India.

La Bourdonnais entered the service of the French East India Company as a lieutenant at 19, was promoted to captain in 1724, and took part in the capture of Mahé on the Malabar Coast (southwestern India) in 1726. From 1735 to 1740, he was governor of Île de France (Mauritius) and Île de Bourbon (Réunion) in the Indian Ocean, but with the outbreak of war between France and Great Britain, he was put in command of a fleet in Indian waters.

La Bourdonnais distinguished himself in the defense of the French outpost of Mahé and the relief of the governor-general of French East India, Joseph-François Dupleix, at Pondicherry; he defeated British forces in two naval actions. His blockade of Madras by sea enabled the French to capture this important port in September 1746. Bad relations with Dupleix, however, exacerbated by Dupleix's removal of him as governor of Île de France, obliged him to return to France. Although his ship was captured by the British, he was allowed to return home on parole. Arrested in 1748 on charges of corruption, he was imprisoned in the Bastille for more than two years. He was tried in 1751 and acquitted.

La Brea Tar Pits, tar pits, in Hancock Park (Rancho La Brea), Los Angeles, Calif., U.S. It is the site of "pitch springs" oozing crude oil, discovered by Gaspar de Portolá's expedition in 1769. The tar pits contain the fossilized skulls and bones of prehistoric animals that became entrapped in the sticky seepage of the pits. The remains of such Pleistocene mammals as imperial mammoth, mastodon, sabre-toothed cat, giant ground sloth, and camel have been recovered. Park exhibits include giant life-size figures of many such long-extinct creatures and an observation pit. The George C. Page Museum contains more than a million prehistoric specimens exhumed from the pits. Fossil remains from La Brea (Spanish: "The Tar") are also exhibited at the Natural History Museum of Los Angeles County.

La Bruyère, Jean de (b. August 1645, Paris, France—d. May 10/11, 1696, Versailles), French satiric moralist who is best known for one work, *Les Caractères de Théophraste traduits du grec avec les caractères ou les moeurs de ce siècle* (1688; *The Characters, or Manners of the Age, with the Characters of Theophrastus*), which is considered to be one of the masterpieces of French literature.

La Bruyère studied law at Orléans. Through the intervention of Jacques-Bénigne Bossuet, the eminent humanist and theologian, he became one of the tutors to the Duke de Bourbon, grandson of the Prince de Condé, and remained in the Condé household as librarian at Chantilly. His years there were probably unhappy because, although he was proud of his middle-class origin, he was a constant butt of ridicule because of his ungainly figure, morose manner, and biting tongue; the bitterness of his book reflects the inferiority of his social position. His situation, however, afforded him the opportunity to make penetrating observations on the power of money in a demoralized society, the tyranny of social custom, and the perils of aristocratic idleness, fads, and fashions.

La Bruyère, detail of an engraving by Pierre Drevet from Saint-Jean's frontispiece of *Les Caractères,* 1697

By courtesy of the Bibliotheque Nationale, Paris

La Bruyère's masterpiece appeared as an appendage to his translation of the 4th-century-BC character writer Theophrastus in 1688. His method was that of Theophrastus: to define qualities such as dissimulation, flattery, or rusticity and then to give instances of them in actual people, making reflections on the "characteristics" of the time, for the purpose of reforming manners. La Bruyère had an immense and richly varied vocabulary and a sure grasp of technique. His satire is constantly sharpened by variety of presentation, and he achieves vivid stylistic effects, which were admired by such eminent writers as the 19th-century novelists Gustave Flaubert and the Goncourt brothers.

Eight editions of the *Caractères* appeared during La Bruyère's life. The portrait sketches were expanded because of their great popularity. Readers began putting real names to the personages and compiling "keys" to them, but La Bruyère denied that any was a portrait of a single person.

Topical allusions in his book made his election to the French Academy difficult, but he was eventually elected in 1693. The Duke de Saint-Simon, the diplomat and memoirist, described him as honourable, lovable, and unpretentious.

La Calprenède, Gaultier de Coste, Seigneur de (b. *c.* 1610, château of Toulgon, near Sarlat, France—d. 1663, Grand-Andely), author of sentimental, adventurous, pseudo-historical romances that were immensely popular in 17th-century France. To this rambling and diffuse genre he imparted virility through swift-moving plots.

After studying at Toulouse, La Calprenède entered the regiment of the guards and campaigned in Germany. Pursuing military and literary careers simultaneously from 1635 to 1641, he wrote tragedies and tragicomedies, some based on episodes in English history, including *Jeanne Reyne d'Angleterre* (1636; "Jane, Queen of England") and *Le Comte d'Essex* (1638; "The Earl of Essex"). In 1642 he began a series of novels glorifying love and war: *Cassandre,* 10 vol. (1642–45), a history of the decline of the Persian empire; *Cléopâtre,* 12 vol. (1647–58), a story of Cleopatra's alleged daughter by Mark Antony; and *Faramond,* 12 vol. (1661–70), a Merovingian history, the last five volumes of which were completed after his death by Pierre d'Ortigue de Vaumorière. These well-plotted romances found immediate favour, and they continued to be popular to the end of the 18th century.

La Ceiba, city, northern Honduras. It lies along the Gulf of Honduras, in a lush, hot valley at the foot of 7,989-foot (2,435-metre) Mount Bonito.

Developed in the late 19th century as a banana port, La Ceiba is one of the nation's major Caribbean ports. Besides bananas, the port handles pineapples, citrus fruits, coconuts, abacá fibre, fish, meat, coffee, and lumber. The Standard Fruit and Steamship Company, which operates large banana, citrus-fruit, and coconut plantations in the hinterland, is centred in the city. La Ceiba is also an industrial centre; shoes, soap, jams, dairy products, furniture, cement, metalware, paper, plastics, and pharmaceuticals are manufactured in the city, which also contains the world's largest banana chip and puree plant, a major vegetable-oil plant, palm-oil processing factories, rice mills, sawmills, breweries, tanneries, and a winery. Fishing has become an important industry, and refrigeration and packing plants have been built.

In the 1970s La Ceiba became a major transit point for tourists to the Bay Islands. It has also developed banking and finance facilities. The city is linked to the other Caribbean ports and the Aguán River valley by railroad and highway, and it has an international airport. Pop. (1989 est.) 71,600.

La Chalotais, Louis-René de Caradeuc de (b. March 6, 1701, Rennes, France—d. July 12, 1785, Rennes), French magistrate who led the Breton Parlement (high court of justice) in a protracted legal battle against the authority of the government of King Louis XV. The struggle resulted in the purging and suspensions (1771–74) of the Parlements.

La Chalotais became advocate general in the Breton Parlement at Rennes in 1730 and attorney general in 1752. In 1761 he emerged as a leader of a growing anti-Jesuit campaign by issuing an attack on Jesuit control of France's secondary schools. The following year the Parlement of Paris, against the wishes of Louis XV, ordered the suppression of the Jesuits. La Chalotais's *Essai d'éducation nationale* (1763; "Essay on National Education") advanced proposals that helped the government overcome the ensuing educational crisis. Although his anti-Jesuit activities had made him a hero to the Philosophes (French writers of the Enlightenment), he had earned the hatred of the governor of Brittany, the Duke d'Aiguillon. In 1763 La Chalotais led his Parlement in challenging the government's right to impose a corvée (statute of forced labour for public works) on Brittany. Aiguillon retaliated by depriving La Chalotais's son of his right to inherit his father's office; the conflict reached its climax when, in 1765, the Breton Parlementaires staged a judicial strike. La Chalotais was arrested and imprisoned (November 1765), and upon his release he was exiled to Saintes (1767). In 1771 the king's chief minister, René-Nicolas de Maupeou, deprived the Parlements of their political powers, but, shortly after the accession of King Louis XVI in 1774, the authority of the Parlements was restored, and La Chalotais was reinstated in his judicial office.

La Chaussée, Pierre-Claude Nivelle de (b. 1692, Paris, France—d. March 14, 1754, Paris), French playwright who created the *comédie larmoyante* ("tearful comedy"), a verse-drama form merging tearful, sentimental scenes with an invariably happy ending. These sentimental comedies, which were precursors of Denis Diderot's *drames bourgeois,* were psychologically superficial and rhetorically exaggerated and were intended to contribute to the public's moral education. La Chaussée was the author of nine such plays—among them *L'École des Mères* (1744; "Mothers' School"), *Mélanide* (1741), and *Le Préjugé à la mode* (1735; "Stylish Prejudice").

La Chaussée was the scion of a prosperous bourgeois family and did not embark on a literary career until his middle age; his first play, *La Fausse Antipathie* ("False Antipathy"), was written when he was 41 years old. From that time, however, he wrote steadily. In addition to the *comédies larmoyantes,* he produced other comedies and several tragedies. He was elected to the French Academy in 1736.

"De," "la," and similar components of a name, when followed by a space, are alphabetized as separate words (e.g., *De Forest, Lee*). *When they are joined to the following part of a name, the combination is treated as a single word* (e.g., *DeForest, John William*).

La Chétardie, Jacques-Joachim Trotti, Marquis de (b. Oct. 3, 1705—d. Jan. 1, 1759, Hanau, Hesse-Kassel [Germany]), French officer and diplomat who helped raise the princess Elizabeth to the throne of Russia.

La Chétardie entered French military service at an early age and rose through the ranks, becoming lieutenant (1721), major (1730), and colonel (1734). He performed well and received assignments to Holland and Prussia and in 1739 became ambassador to Russia. In order to secure a government more favourable to French interests, La Chétardie joined with the supporters of the youngest daughter of Peter the Great, Elizabeth, and, with the help of her French physician Jean-Hermann, Count de Lestocq, directed the maneuvering that placed her on the throne on Dec. 6, 1741. After Elizabeth's ascension La Chétardie received the imperial orders of St. Andrew and St. Anne and soon became an intimate of the new empress.

He departed from St. Petersburg in 1742 but returned there as ambassador in 1743. La Chétardie seems to have annoyed Elizabeth with his excessive attentions, however, and he was expelled from Russia in 1744. Returning to France in disgrace, he was briefly imprisoned in the citadel of Montpellier before reentering the French army in 1745. He then served in Italy until 1748, becoming a lieutenant-general in that year. In 1749 he became ambassador to the court of Turin, and he reentered military service when the Seven Years' War broke out in 1756.

la ch'in (musical instrument): *see* yüeh-ch'in.

la chin (musical instrument): *see* ch'in.

La Condamine, Charles-Marie de (b. Jan. 28, 1701, Paris, France—d. Feb. 4, 1774, Paris), French naturalist and mathematician who accomplished the first scientific exploration of the Amazon River.

In 1735 La Condamine joined an expedition sent to Peru to determine the length near the Equator of a degree of the meridian. In 1743 he left the party, traveled from Quito (now in Ecuador), and began a four-month raft journey down to the mouth of the Amazon. During the trip he made ethnographic observations of the regions through which he passed. In addition to a scientific account of his journey, he published *Journal du voyage fait par ordre du roi a l'équateur* (1751; "Jour-

La Condamine, bust by d'Huez, 18th century

J.E. Bulloz

nal of a Voyage to the Equator Made by Order of the King").

La Crosse, city, seat (1851) of La Crosse county, western Wisconsin, U.S. It lies along the Mississippi River at the influx of the Black and La Crosse rivers, 129 miles (208 km) northwest of Madison. The settlement developed around a trading post (1841) on a site that French explorers named Prairie la Crosse, after the game of lacrosse played by the Indians there. A natural river port, it became an important transportation and sawmilling centre and was reached by rail in 1858. With the decline of lumbering around 1900, La Crosse developed diversified industries; products include air-conditioning systems, rubber footwear, and beer. The city is the seat of the University of Wisconsin at La Crosse (1909), Western Wisconsin Technical College (1911), and Viterbo College (1890). Its annual Oktoberfest attracts numerous visitors. Inc. 1856. Pop. (1991 est.) city, 51,662; La Crosse MSA, 99,167.

La Farge, John (b. March 31, 1835, New York, N.Y., U.S.—d. Nov. 14, 1910, Providence, R.I.), American painter, muralist, and stained-glass designer.

"Red and White Peonies," stained-glass window by John La Farge, 1886; in the Museum of Fine Arts, Boston

By courtesy of the Museum of Fine Arts, Boston

After graduating from college La Farge studied law, but in 1856 he went to Europe to study art. He worked independently, studying in Paris and coming under the influence of the Pre-Raphaelites in England. Returning to the United States, La Farge went in 1859 to Newport, R.I., where he came under the influence of the artist William Morris Hunt.

La Farge produced landscapes and figure compositions in the 1860s and was among the earliest American painters to incorporate into his own works stylistic elements derived from progressive French landscape painting of the mid-19th century. He took up mural painting in 1876 with his decorations of the interior of Trinity Church in Boston. His finest mural is the "Ascension" (1887), in the Church of the Ascension, New York City. About the same time, he became interested in stained glass. Through his invention of opalescent glass and his imaginative designing, as seen in the window "Red and White Peonies" (1886; Museum of Fine Arts, Boston), he brought about a revival of the art in America and won for himself an international reputation.

In later life La Farge undertook a series of travels to exotic places, and a notable series of watercolour scenes date from his trips to Japan and the South Pacific in the late 1880s and early '90s. His writings include *Considerations on Painting* (1895) and *An Artist's Letters from Japan* (1897).

La Farge, Oliver (Hazard Perry) (b. Dec. 19, 1901, New York, N.Y., U.S.—d. Aug. 2, 1963, Albuquerque, N.M.), American anthropologist, short-story writer, and novelist who acted as a spokesman for the American Indian through his political actions and his fiction.

At Harvard University La Farge pursued his interest in American Indian culture, specializing in anthropology and archaeological research. Although highly respected in this field, he abandoned his studies to publicize the Indians' dilemma, serving as president of the National Association on Indian Affairs (1933–37) and as president of the Association on American Indian Affairs (1937–42, 1946–63). La Farge rejected the popular sentimental image of the Indian in contemporary literature and countered it in his own writing. His first novel, *Laughing Boy* (1929; film version 1934), is a poetic but realistic story of the clash of two cultures; it was awarded the Pulitzer Prize for fiction in 1929. La Farge's novels have been called lyrical, yet they are always based on social awareness. *Sparks Fly Upward* (1931) is set in Central America, while *The Enemy Gods* (1937) centres on the inability of the Navajo to adapt to white civilization. *Long Pennant* (1933) and *The Copper Pot* (1942) have New Englanders as their main characters. La Farge's short stories were collected in *All the Young Men* (1935) and *A Pause in the Desert* (1957). La Farge's autobiography, *Raw Material,* was published in 1945.

La Farina, Giuseppe (b. July 20, 1815, Messina, Sicily, kingdom of Naples [now in Italy]—d. Sept. 5, 1863, Turin, Italy), Italian revolutionary, writer, and leader and historian of the Risorgimento.

The son of a Sicilian magistrate and scholar, La Farina received a law degree in 1835 and soon became involved with a secret committee for Italian unity; he was forced into exile after it attempted an insurrection in 1837. Receiving amnesty in 1838, he returned to Messina and took up literary work, while also engaging in revolutionary work in Naples and Palermo.

In Florence after 1841, La Farina lived by his pen; in 1847 he founded the political journal *L'Alba.* At the outbreak of revolution in 1848, he returned to Messina, served successively as deputy and secretary to the chamber of communes at Palermo, minister of public instruction and public works, and minister of war and the navy. But he was exiled again in April, when the revolution failed, and he remained in Paris until 1853, when he returned to Turin. In 1857 he helped found the Italian National Society, a nationalist organization.

After 1857 he was in frequent secret contact with the unification leader Count Cavour, planning annexation demands and policy and organizing military moves. Although he helped to furnish Sicilian funds for Giuseppe Garibaldi's conquest of Sicily and Naples in 1860, La Farina lost favour with Garibaldi when he began circulating an annexationist paper in Palermo called *L'Annessione,* and he was arrested and deported to Genoa in July 1860. Earlier that year, he had been elected to the Chamber of Deputies, and he later became a councillor of state.

La Farina's greatest literary work was the *Storia d'Italia dal 1815 al 1850* (1851–52), which included a discussion of Italy's future as a nation. His letters have been collected and edited by Ausonio Franchi in the two-volume *Epistolario di Giuseppe La Farina* (1869). La Farina's other works include the two-volume *Studi sul secolo XIII* (1841; "Study of the 13th Century"), the 10-volume *Storia d'Italia* (1846; "History of Italy"), and *Rivoluzione siciliana nel 1848 e 49* (1851; "Sicilian Revolution in 1848–49").

La Fayette, Gilbert Motier de (b. *c.* 1380, Auvergne, Fr.—d. Feb. 23, 1462, Auvergne), marshal of France during the Hundred Years' War and noted adviser to King Charles VII.

After serving in Italy under Marshal Jean le Meingre Boucicaut in 1409, he became steward of the Bourbonnais. In the wars with England, Jean I, duc de Bourbon, made him lieutenant general in Languedoc and Guyenne. After victories over the English and the Burgundians on the Loire, he was made governor of Dauphiné in 1420 and a marshal of France. Taken prisoner by the English in 1424, he was soon released and served with Joan of Arc at Orléans and Patay in 1429. A member of Charles VII's great council, he took part in the conferences of Nevers and Arras (1435), which prepared the King's reconciliation with Burgundy. La Fayette worked to reform the army from 1445 to 1448 and was recalled to military service in 1449 for a campaign against the English in Normandy. He remained a friend and adviser to the King all his life.

La Fayette, Marie-Joseph-Paul-Yves-Roch-Gilbert du Motier, marquis de: *see* Lafayette, Marie-Joseph-Paul-Yves-Roch-Gilbert du Motier, marquis de.

La Fayette, Marie-Madeleine (Pioche de la Vergne), comtesse de (countess of), byname MADAME DE LA FAYETTE (baptized March 18, 1634, Paris—d. May 25, 1693, Paris), French writer whose *La Princesse de Clèves* is a landmark of French fiction.

In Paris during the civil wars of the Fronde, young Mlle de la Vergne was brought into contact with Madame de Sévigné, now famous for her letters. She also met a leading political agitator, the future Cardinal de Retz. Married in 1655 to François Motier, comte de La Fayette (1616–83), she lived for some time with him on his estates in the province of Auvergne. In 1659, however, they separated, and she returned to Paris.

Marie-Madeleine de La Fayette; detail of an engraving by E.-J. Desroches

By courtesy of the Bibliotheque Nationale, Paris

Throughout the 1660s Madame de La Fayette was a favourite of Henrietta Anne of England, duchesse d'Orléans. During this time she also began what was to be a lasting and intimate friendship with the Duc de La Rochefoucauld, author of the famous *Maximes.* With him she formed a distinguished literary circle. After producing two conventional romances, she wrote her masterpiece, *La Princesse de Clèves,* published anonymously in 1678. Set in the middle of the 16th century, though its manners are those of the author's own time, it is notable as France's first serious "historical" novel, as distinct from "heroic" romances. It is the story of a virtuous young wife who suppresses her passion for a young nobleman. Its outstanding literary merits are the dignified pathos of the dialogue and the author's psychological insight into the theme of tragically but deliberately unconsummated love.

La Flesche, Francis (b. Dec. 25, 1857, Omaha Reservation, Nebraska—d. Sept. 5, 1932, near Macy, Neb., U.S.), U.S. ethnologist and champion of the rights of American Indians who wrote a book of general literary interest about his experiences as a student in a mission school in the 1860s. This memoir, *The Middle Five* (1900, new edition 1963), is rare in providing an account from an American Indian's viewpoint of his education by members of the majority culture.

His father—the son of a French trader and a woman of the Omaha tribe—chose the culture of his mother and became a chief. Believing that the Indians would have to come to terms with the white world, he sent his children to an English language school operated for Indians by the Presbyterians in Thurston County, Nebraska. Two of Francis La Flesche's sisters achieved prominence: Susette as a writer and activist for Indian causes, and Susan as a physician to the Omaha.

From 1881 to 1910 La Flesche was a clerk in the Bureau of Indian Affairs in Washington, D.C., meanwhile obtaining a law degree. He served as an ethnologist with the Bureau of American Ethnology from 1910 until his retirement in 1929. With Alice Cunningham Fletcher he wrote a study, *The Omaha Tribe* (1911). He also wrote two works, posthumously published, on the Osage: *A Dictionary of the Osage Language* (1932) and *War Ceremony and Peace Ceremony of the Osage Indian* (1938).

La Flesche, Susette, Indian name BRIGHT EYES (b. 1854, Omaha Reservation, Nebraska—d. May 26, 1903, near Bancroft, Neb., U.S.), American Indian writer, lecturer, and activist in the cause of Indian rights.

She was the daughter of an Omaha chief who was the son of a French trader and an Omaha woman. The father was familiar with both cultures, and though he lived as an Indian he sent his children to a Presbyterian mission school to provide them with an English language education. Her sister, Susan, became a physician, and her brother, Francis, an ethnologist. Susette was sent to Elizabeth, N.J., to continue her education, and she returned to the Omaha Reservation to teach at a government school.

Using her Indian name, Bright Eyes, she became involved in her people's struggle for justice. She and her father took up the cause of the Ponca Indians, a tribe related to the Omaha who had been uprooted from their lands by the U.S. government and moved to Oklahoma, where sickness and starvation beset them. When the Ponca chief and several of his followers returned to Nebraska in 1879 after a long and arduous journey, they were arrested. An editor of the *Omaha Herald,* Thomas H. Tibbles, whom Miss La Flesche was to marry in 1881, also assisted the Ponca's cause, and the Indian prisoners were eventually released. She continued to work against the arbitrary removal of Indians from their traditional lands, lecturing throughout the United States and in Scotland.

She and her husband settled on the Omaha Reservation, where she wrote and illustrated Indian stories and helped her husband with his editorial work. She edited and wrote the introduction for *Ploughed Under: The Story of an Indian Chief* (1881), an anonymous work.

La Follette, Robert M(arion) (b. June 14, 1855, Primrose, Wis., U.S.—d. June 18, 1925, Washington, D.C.), U.S. leader of the Progressive Movement, who as governor of Wisconsin (1901–06) and U.S. senator (1906–25) was noted for his support of reform legislation. He was the unsuccessful presidential candidate of the League for Progressive Political Action (*i.e.,* the Progressive party) in 1924, winning almost 5,000,000 votes, or about one-sixth of the total cast.

La Follette, 1906

By courtesy of the Library of Congress, Washington, D.C.

Early life and career. As a boy growing up in moderately prosperous rural areas, as a student at the University of Wisconsin (1875–79), as a county district attorney (1880–84) and congressman from southwestern Wisconsin, La Follette developed the personality and style that made him a popular leader. He combined an unusually outgoing personality, which made it natural for him to absorb the ideas and prejudices of his constituents, with an extraordinary flair for zealous oratory. As an eloquent spokesman for popular causes, La Follette exalted his constituents' wishes—even when those wishes ran counter to the desires of party leaders. His principal concerns in his three terms as congressman were economical government and protection for his district's farmers. He married his college sweetheart, Belle Case, on Dec. 31, 1881, after his first year as district attorney.

Defeated for reelection to Congress in a Democratic landslide of 1890, La Follette returned to Madison to practice law and develop the political organization that within 10 years would elect him governor and allow him to dominate Wisconsin politics until his death. His reputation as an enemy of political bosses began in 1891 when he announced that the state Republican boss, Sen. Philetus Sawyer, had offered him a bribe. For the next six years La Follette built a competing Republican faction on the support of other party members (Scandinavians, dairy farmers, young men, disgruntled politicians) with grievances against the dominant "stalwart" faction. His oratorical talents, combined with his natural charm, organizational skill, and driving ambition to become governor, made him the leader of his new group of Republicans.

Campaign for governor. In 1897 La Follette began to advocate programs that local-level progressives had popularized during the legislative session a few months earlier. Following their lead, he demanded tax reform, corporation regulation, and political democracy. In particular, he promoted steeper railroad taxes and a direct primary. Elected governor on this platform in 1900, he was reelected in 1902 and 1904.

As Wisconsin's governor La Follette developed new political techniques, which he later took to the U.S. Senate. The first, which received national attention as the "Wisconsin Idea," was the use of professors from the University of Wisconsin—57 at one point—to draft bills and administer the state regulatory apparatus created by the new laws. The second innovation was his public reading of the "roll call" in districts in which legislators had opposed his reform proposals.

With these new methods he secured the passage of several progressive laws. Believing that the railroads were the principal subverters of the political process, he persuaded the legislature to tax them on the basis of their property (1903) and to regulate them by commission (1905). The legislature enacted the direct primary in 1903 and state civil-service reform in 1905. His appointees to the Tax Commission, given new power by the legislature, equalized tax assessments. Wisconsin's leadership in these areas gave La Follette his reputation as a pioneering progressive.

United States senator. Resigning as governor in 1906, he was elected to the Senate at a time when that institution was widely believed to be a refuge for millionaires. La Follette acquired instant fame as a new type of senator, one who was not controlled by "the interests," and in his first three years there La Follette achieved the passage of laws aimed against the freight rates, labour policies, and financing practices of the railroads.

These laws reflected an emerging ideology that dominated La Follette's Senate activities thereafter. Politics, he believed, was a never-ending struggle between "the people," all men and women in their common roles as consumers and taxpayers, and the "selfish interests" for control of government; law-given privileges allowed "selfish interests" to dominate all facets of American life. He supported labour legislation because unions were battling the same enemies that menaced consumers and because consumers benefited directly from improvements in working conditions. He believed, for example, that his most famous achievement, the La Follette Seaman's Act of 1915, would increase the safety of passengers while it also improved working conditions for sailors. Beginning in 1908, with elaborate documentation during debate on the Aldrich-Vreeland Currency Act, La Follette argued that the nation's entire economy was dominated by fewer than 100 men who were, in turn, controlled by the J.P. Morgan and Standard Oil investment banking groups. Thereafter, he shifted his concern from the power of railroads to the power of their "owners," namely the large banks.

In 1909 La Follette founded *La Follette's Weekly,* later a monthly, and much later called *The Progressive.* The high point of his national popularity came in 1909–11 when he emerged as the leader of newly elected and newly converted progressives in Congress. Having led Republican opposition to the tariff, conservation, and railroad policies of President William Howard Taft, La Follette was widely promoted for the presidency in 1912. Most progressives backed La Follette because their first choice, Theodore Roosevelt, had refused to run; later, when Roosevelt entered the race early in 1912, they deserted La Follette. The bitterness of La Follette's attacks on Roosevelt cost him his reputation as a leader and left him an independent figure in the Senate. Although he had backed Woodrow Wilson in 1912 for the presidency, he was disgusted that the new president ignored the ideas of progressive Republicans and shaped most legislation in the Democratic caucus. While applauding the social justice laws, he believed that most of Wilson's regulatory acts—particularly the Federal Reserve Board—constituted government sponsorship of big business.

Anti-war position. Foreign affairs catapulted La Follette back into a leadership position in 1917, this time of the anti-war movement. Since 1910 he had argued that U.S. interventions in the problems of foreign governments were intended to protect the investments of U.S. corporations and to smash revolutions. Now he believed that the United States entered World War I in 1917 because U.S. businessmen needed protection for their investments and because Wilson had become isolated from public opinion. Confident that the majority opposed U.S. involvement, La Follette led the campaign for a popular referendum on war in 1916–17. He led the 1917 Senate filibuster against arming U.S. merchant ships and voted against the war declaration. Once war was declared, he opposed the draft, defended the civil liberties of the war's opponents, and insisted that wealthy individuals and corporations pay the costs of a war that mainly benefited them. Pro-war groups demanded his expulsion from the Senate for treason, but a Senate investigating committee exonerated him. As a martyr to the war hysteria, La Follette once again became a popular hero to millions of Americans.

Believing that the war had given large corporations nearly complete control over the federal government, La Follette concentrated on exposing the most flagrant corruption of the postwar years. His most significant contribution was his major role in publicizing the oil scandals of President Warren Harding's administration.

As labour and farm groups despaired of the conservatism of Democrats and Republicans alike in the 1920s, La Follette was frequently mentioned as a presidential candidate for a third party. Declining the pleas of the Farmer-Labor convention that he run in 1920, La Follette accepted the Progressive Party's nomination in 1924. His 1924 candidacy was supported by several farm groups, by organized labour (particularly the railroad brotherhoods, La Follette's oldest friends in the labour movement), by many old progressives, by the Socialist Party, and by the Scripps-Howard newspaper chain. In the end La Follette carried only the state of Wisconsin, although he placed second in 11 states and polled about one-sixth of the national total. He died in office.

Both of La Follette's sons carried on his work after his death. Robert M. La Follette, Jr. (1895–1953), was elected in 1925 to fill his father's unexpired term in the Senate and was reelected three times thereafter, serving until 1947. He generally supported President Franklin D. Roosevelt's New Deal, and he drafted the congressional reorganization bill of 1946 that streamlined the legislative process in Congress. That same year, though, he was defeated in the Republican senatorial primary by Joseph McCarthy.

Philip Fox La Follette (1897–1965) served as governor of Wisconsin in 1931–33 and 1935–39. In his first term he secured enactment of the first comprehensive unemployment compensation act in any U.S. state. He and his brother Robert organized a separate Progressive Party in Wisconsin in 1934, but it proved short-lived and returned to the Republican ranks in 1946. (D.P.T./Ed.)

BIBLIOGRAPHY. Biographies and analyses of La Follette and the Progressive movement include Belle Case La Follette and Fola La Follette, *Robert M. La Follette, June 14, 1855–June 18, 1925,* 2 vol. (1953, reissued 1971); David P. Thelen, *The Early Life of Robert M. La Follette, 1855–1884* (1966), and *Robert M. La Follette and the Insurgent Spirit* (1976, reissued 1985); Robert S. Maxwell, *La Follette and the Rise of the Progressives in Wisconsin* (1956, reprinted 1973); Fred Greenbaum, *Robert Marion La Follette* (1975); and Patrick J. Maney, *"Young Bob" La Follette* (1978).

Consult the INDEX *first*

La Fontaine, also called MLLE DE LAFONTAINE (b. 1655—d. 1738), French ballerina and the first woman professional ballet dancer.

Before La Fontaine's debut in 1681 at the Paris Opéra as première danseuse in Jean-Baptiste Lully's ballet *Le Triomphe de l'amour,* girls' roles on the public stage had been taken by young men. Although hampered by the long, confining costumes and limited ballet technique of the time, La Fontaine's grace and charm were such that she was called queen of the dance. After dancing at the Opéra for about a decade, in such works as *Persée, Amadis, Didon,* and *Le Temple de la paix,* she retired to a convent.

La Fontaine, Jean de (b. July 8?, 1621, Château-Thierry, Fr.—d. April 13, 1695, Paris), poet whose *Fables* rank among the greatest masterpieces of French literature.

Jean de La Fontaine, oil painting by François De Troy; in the Bibliothèque Publique et Universitaire, Geneva

By courtesy of the Bibliotheque Publique et Universitaire, Geneva; photograph, Jean Arlaud

Life. La Fontaine was born in the Champagne region into a bourgeois family. There, in 1647, he married an heiress, Marie Héricart, but they separated in 1658. From 1652 to 1671 he held office as an inspector of forests and waterways, an office inherited from his father. It was in Paris, however, that he made his most important contacts and spent his most productive years as a writer. An outstanding feature of his existence was his ability to attract the goodwill of patrons prepared to relieve him of the responsibility of providing for his livelihood. In 1657 he became one of the protégés of Nicolas Fouquet, the wealthy superintendent of finance. From 1664 to 1672 he served as gentleman-in-waiting to the dowager duchess of Orléans in Luxembourg. For 20 years, from 1673, he was a member of the household of Mme de La Sabliere, whose salon was a celebrated meeting place of scholars, philosophers, and writers. In 1683 he was elected to the French Academy after some opposition by the king to his unconventional and irreligious character.

The Fables. The *Fables* unquestionably represent the peak of La Fontaine's achievement. The first six books, known as the *premier recueil* ("first collection"), were published in 1668 and were followed by five more books (the *second recueil*) in 1678–79 and a twelfth book in 1693. The *Fables* in the second collection show even greater technical skill than those in the first and are longer, more reflective, and more personal. Some decline of talent is commonly detected in the twelfth book.

La Fontaine did not invent the basic material of his *Fables;* he took it chiefly from the Aesopic tradition and, in the case of the second collection, from the East Asian. He enriched immeasurably the simple stories that earlier fabulists had in general been content to tell perfunctorily, subordinating them to their narrowly didactic intention. He contrived delightful miniature comedies and dramas, excelling in the rapid characterization of his actors, sometimes by deft sketches of their appearance or indications of their gestures and always by the expressive discourse he invented for them. In settings usually rustic, he evoked the perennial charm of the countryside. Within the compass of about 240 poems, the range and the diversity of subject and of treatment are astonishing. Often he held up the mirror to the social hierarchy of his day. Intermittently he seems inspired to satire, but, sharp though his thrusts are, he had not enough of the true satirist's indignation to press them home. The *Fables* occasionally reflect contemporary political issues and intellectual preoccupations. Some of them, fables only in name, are really elegies, idylls, epistles, or poetic meditations. But his chief and most comprehensive theme remains that of the traditional fable: the fundamental, everyday moral experience of mankind throughout the ages, exhibited in a profusion of typical characters, emotions, attitudes, and situations.

Countless critics have listed and classified the morals of La Fontaine's *Fables* and have correctly concluded that they amount simply to an epitome of more or less proverbial wisdom, generally prudential but tinged in the second collection with a more genial epicureanism. Simple countryfolk and heroes of Greek mythology and legend, as well as familiar animals of the fable, all play their parts in this comedy, and the poetic resonance of the *Fables* owes much to these actors who, belonging to no century and to every century, speak with timeless voices.

What disconcerts many non-French readers and critics is that in the *Fables* profundity is expressed lightly. La Fontaine's animal characters illustrate the point. They are serious representations of human types, so presented as to hint that human nature and animal nature have much in common. But they are also creatures of fantasy, bearing only a distant resemblance to the animals the naturalist observes, and they are amusing because the poet skillfully exploits the incongruities between the animal and the human elements they embody. Moreover—as in his *Contes,* but with far more delicate and lyrical modulations—the voice of La Fontaine himself can constantly be heard, always controlled and discreet, even when most charged with emotion. Its tones change swiftly, almost imperceptibly: they are in turn ironical, impertinent, brusque, laconic, eloquent, compassionate, melancholy, or reflective. But the predominant note is that of *la gaieté,* which, as he says in the preface to the first collection, he deliberately sought to introduce into his *Fables.* "Gaiety," he explains, is not that which provokes laughter but is "a certain charm . . . that can be given to any kind of subject, even the most serious." No one reads the *Fables* rightly who does not read them with a smile—not only of amusement but also of complicity with the poet in the understanding of the human comedy and in the enjoyment of his art.

To the grace, ease, and delicate perfection of the best of the *Fables,* even close textual commentary cannot hope to do full justice. They represent the quintessence of a century of experiments in prosody and poetic diction in France. The great majority of the *Fables* are composed of lines of varying metre and, from the unpredictable interplay of their rhymes and of their changing rhythms, La Fontaine derived the most exquisite and diverse effects of tone and movement. His vocabulary harmonizes widely different elements: the archaic, the precious and the burlesque, the refined, the familiar and the rustic, the language of professions and trades and the language of philosophy and mythology. But for all this richness, economy and understatement are the chief characteristics of his style, and its full appreciation calls for keener sensitivity to the overtones of 17th-century French than most foreign readers can hope to possess.

Miscellaneous writings and the Contes. La Fontaine's many miscellaneous writings include much occasional verse in a great variety of poetic forms and dramatic or pseudodramatic pieces such as his first published work, *L'Eunuque* (1654), and *Climène* (1671), as well as poems on subjects as different as *Adonis* (1658, revised 1669), *La Captivité de saint Malc* (1673), and *Le Quinquina* (1682). All these are, at best, works of uneven quality. In relation to the perfection of the *Fables,* they are no more than poetic exercises or experiments. The exception is the leisurely narrative of *Les Amours de Psiché et de Cupidon* (1669; *The Loves of Cupid and Psyche*), notable for the lucid elegance of its prose, its skillful blend of delicate feeling and witty banter, and some sly studies of feminine psychology.

Like his miscellaneous works, La Fontaine's *Contes et nouvelles en vers* (*Tales and Novels in Verse*) considerably exceed the *Fables* in bulk. The first of them was published in 1664, the last posthumously. He borrowed them mostly from Italian sources, in particular Giovanni Boccaccio, but he preserved none of the 14th-century poet's rich sense of reality. The essence of nearly all his *Contes* lies in their licentiousness, which is not presented with frank Rabelaisian verve but is transparently and flippantly disguised. Characters and situations are not meant to be taken seriously; they are meant to amuse and are too monotonous to amuse for long. The *Contes* are the work far less of a poet than of an ingenious stylist and versifier. The accent of La Fontaine the narrator enlivens the story with playfully capricious comments, explanations, and digressions.

Personality and reputation. Though he never secured the favour of Louis XIV, La Fontaine had many well-wishers close to the throne and among the nobility. He moved among churchmen, doctors, artists, musicians, and actors. But it was literary circles that he especially frequented. Legend has exaggerated the closeness of his ties with Molière, Nicholas Boileau, and Jean Racine, but he certainly numbered them among his friends and acquaintances, as well as La Rochefoucauld, Mme de Sévigné, Mme de La Fayette, and many less well-remembered writers.

The true nature of the man remains enigmatic. He was intensely and naively selfish, unconventional in behaviour, and impatient of all constraint; yet he charmed countless friends—perhaps by a naturalness of manner and a sincerity in social relationships that were rare in his age—and made apparently only one enemy (a fellow academician, Antoine Furetière). He was a parasite without servility, a sycophant without baseness, a shrewd schemer who was also a blunderer, and a sinner whose errors were, as one close to him observed, "full of wisdom." He was accommodating, sometimes to the detriment of proper self-respect, but he was certainly not the lazy, absent-minded simpleton that superficial observers took him for. The quantity and the quality of his work show that this legendary description of him cannot be accurate: for at least 40 years La Fontaine, in spite of his apparent aimlessness, was an ambitious and diligent literary craftsman of subtle intelligence and meticulous conscientiousness.

He was an assiduous and discriminating reader whose works abound in judicious imitations of both the matter and the manner of his favourite authors. He was influenced by so many 16th- and 17th-century French writers that it is almost invidious to mention only François Rabelais, Clément Marot, François de Malherbe, Honoré d'Urfé, and Vincent Voiture. The authors of classical antiquity that he knew best were Homer, Plato, Plutarch—these he almost certainly read in translation—Terence, Virgil, Horace, and Ovid. Boccaccio, Niccolò Machiavelli, Ludovico Ariosto, and Torquato Tasso were his favourites among the Italians. La Fontaine was no romantic; his work derives its substance and its savour less from his experience of life than from this rich and complex literary heritage, affectionately received and patiently exploited.

Too wise to suppose that moral truths can ever be simple, he wrote stories that offer no rudimentary illustration of a certain moral but a subtle commentary on it, sometimes amending it and hinting that only the naive would take it at face value. Thus, what the *Fables* teach is trivial in comparison with what they suggest: a view of life that, although incomplete (for it takes little account of man's metaphysical anguish or his highest aspirations), is mature, profound, and wise. Enjoyed at many different levels, the *Fables* continue to form part of the culture of every Frenchman, from schoolchildren to such men of letters as André Gide, Paul Valéry, and Jean Giraudoux, who have given fresh lustre to La Fontaine's reputation in the 20th century.

(L.C.Sy./Ed.)

BIBLIOGRAPHY. Biographical and critical studies include Marie-Odile Sweetser, *La Fontaine* (1987); Agnes Ethel Mackay, *La Fontaine and His Friends: A Biography* (1972); John C. Lapp, *The Esthetics of Negligence: La Fontaine's Contes* (1971); and Richard Danner, *Patterns of Irony in the Fables of La Fontaine* (1985).

La Fosse, Charles de, de La Fosse also spelled DELAFOSSE (b. June 15, 1636, Paris, Fr.—d. Dec. 13, 1716, Paris), painter whose decorative historical and allegorical murals, while continuing a variant of the stately French Baroque manner of the 17th century, began to develop a lighter, more brightly coloured style that presaged the Rococo painting of the 18th century.

The greatest influence on La Fosse's painting was the work of his teacher, Charles Le Brun, the dictator of artistic matters in France during the reign of King Louis XIV. La Fosse was also impressed with the works of the 16th-century Italians Francesco Primaticcio (whose visible work was all in France), Titian, and Paolo Veronese, which he studied during his five-year stay in Rome and Venice (from 1658). In 1689–91 La Fosse decorated Montagu House in London. His greatest work was the decoration of the cupola of the Church of Les Invalides in Paris (1705), while the "Sacrifice of Iphigenia" in the Salon de Diane of Versailles and the "Sunrise" in the Salon d'Apollon are his most important works in the style of Charles Le Brun. More significant to later artists, however, are his smaller works, such as "The Finding of Moses" (1675–80; Louvre, Paris), remarkable for their use of light and their fresh colour sense. He became a member of the Royal Academy in 1673 and was named chancellor in 1715.

La Fresnaye, Roger de (b. July 11, 1885, Le Mans, Fr.—d. Nov. 27, 1925, Grasse), French painter who attempted to synthesize lyrical colour with the rigorous formalism of Cubism.

Although his paintings did much to popularize Cubism and to broaden its influence just prior to World War I, he later abandoned avant-garde art and became one of France's most influential advocates of traditional realism.

"Portrait of the Artist," oil on canvas by Roger de La Fresnaye, 1907; in the National Museum of Modern Art, Paris
Cliche Musees Nationaux, Paris

La Fresnaye studied at the École des Beaux-Arts and at the Ranson Academy in Paris. His work up to 1909 betrays the influence of the Symbolist paintings of Maurice Denis. During the next few years (1910–13) he developed an interest in Cubism. He became a member of the Cubist association known as the Section d'Or that met regularly at the studio of the painter Jacques Villon. Even at this early point, La Fresnaye's native sensitivity to colour gave his Cubism an unorthodox sensuousness. After being invalided out of the French army in 1917, he went to the south of France for his health. There he produced a number of Cubist watercolours and drawings that stress joyous colour and even romantic feeling. During the last years of his life, he began to paint such realistic works as "Portrait of Guynemer" (1921–23).

La Galissonnière, Roland-Michel Barrin, marquis de, also spelled ROLAND-MICHEL BARIN, MARQUIS DE LA GALISSONIÈRE (b. Nov. 10, 1693, Rochefort, France—d. Oct. 26, 1756, Montereau), mariner and commandant general of New France.

La Galissonnière was the son of a naval lieutenant-general and studied at the College of Beauvais in Paris. He became a midshipman in the French navy in 1710 and, in the following year, made the first of a number of voyages on the *Heros* carrying supplies to Canada. Some 26 years later he commanded the same vessel in the same trade, having earlier (1734–35) served as lieutenant commander in a West Indies campaign.

Through family influence, La Galissonnière was made captain and a knight of the Order of St. Louis in 1738. Subsequently he held a variety of commands in the Atlantic and in 1747 was named commandant general of New France—in effect, governor-general of Canada. War with the British over North American holdings had been under way for three years, and La Galissonnière, like his predecessors, sought to build and keep goodwill among the Indians. It was his hope to fortify a link along the Ohio River between French Canada and the Louisiana settlements, but the British presence in much of the projected link was too great. La Galissonnière also tried to establish French settlements in Detroit and the Illinois country, but the Canadian population was too sparse to enable sending colonists in any substantial numbers.

Upon his return to France in 1749, La Galissonnière served in Paris as a commissioner to the conference seeking to resolve the French disputes with the English over colonizing North America. He became a rear admiral in 1750, and in 1754 he was given command of a naval squadron operating to protect French shipping from the Barbary pirates. The following year he was elevated to lieutenant general of naval forces.

La Goulette (Tunisia): *see* Ḥalq al-Wādī.

La Grange, also spelled LAGRANGE, city, seat (1828) of Troup county, western Georgia, U.S. It lies just east of West Point Lake (impounded on the Chattahoochee River), about 50 miles (80 km) north of Columbus. Settled in 1826 and named for the French estate of the Marquis de Lafayette, the town developed as a trading centre in a cotton-growing area. During the American Civil War a women's militia confronted Union forces there, persuading them to spare the town (April 1865). In 2000 it became the first U.S. city to offer Internet access as a municipal utility.

Light manufacturing (rubber and plastic products, medical supplies), granite and quartz processing, high-technology industries, and tourism have diversified a textile-based economy since the 1960s. The Lamar Dodd Art Center and the Bellevue mansion are popular attractions. Warm Springs, Franklin D. Roosevelt State Park, and the Callaway Gardens are nearby recreational facilities. LaGrange College, the state's oldest independent liberal arts school, was founded in 1831. Inc. town, 1828; city, 1856. Pop. (2000) 25,998.

La Gruyère, German GREYERZ, region and southernmost district of Fribourg *canton,* western Switzerland. La Gruyère lies along the middle reach of La Sarine (Saane) River, on the edge of the Vaudois uplands and the Bernese Oberland (highland), south of Fribourg. The name is derived either from *gruyer,* a forestry officer, or from the crane (*grue*), the bird crest of the powerful counts of La Gruyère (923–1555). The principal towns of the district are Bulle, the capital, and Gruyères, the historic capital, site of the medieval castle of the counts. La Gruyère is famous for its dairy cattle and its cheese. Wood products and Gruyère cheese are produced at Bulle, and chocolate is made at Broc. The population of the district is French-speaking and Roman Catholic. Pop. (1990) 33,080.

La Guaira, city, northern *distrito federal* ("federal district"), northern Venezuela. One of the nation's leading seaports, La Guaira lies in the narrow, arid coastal zone along the Caribbean at the foot of the central highlands. Although the city dates to 1577, extremely high temperatures and the lack of room for expansion long hindered its growth. With the modernization of port facilities, development of several beach resorts, and construction of the international jet airport at nearby Maiquetía, La Guaira has prospered. It handles a major portion of Venezuela's foreign trade, including agricultural exports and imports of manufactured goods. The city is 20 miles (32 km) from Caracas. Pop. (1990 est.) 26,669.

La Guardia, Fiorello H., in full FIORELLO HENRY LA GUARDIA (b. Dec. 11, 1882, New York, N.Y., U.S.—d. Sept. 20, 1947, New York), American politician who served three terms (1933–45) as mayor of New York City.

La Guardia was reared in Arizona and at the age of 16 moved to Budapest with his mother. He was employed at the U.S. consulate there, and he later served in the American consulates at Trieste and Fiume, returning to the United States in 1906. While working at Ellis Island as an interpreter for the U.S. Immigration Service, he studied law at New York University and was admitted to the bar in 1910.

La Guardia was elected to the House of Representatives as a progressive Republican in 1916, but his term was interrupted by service as a pilot in World War I. He was returned to Congress in 1918 and, after serving as president of the New York City board of aldermen in 1920–21, was reelected to the House in 1922. He was reelected four more times, and in the House he opposed Prohibition and supported woman suffrage and child-labour laws. He cosponsored the Norris-LaGuardia Act (1932), which restricted the courts' power to ban or restrain strikes, boycotts, or picketing by organized labour.

In 1933 La Guardia ran successfully for mayor of New York on a "Fusion" (a Liberal and Republican party coalition) reform ticket dedicated to unseating Tammany Hall (the Democratic organization in New York) and ending its corrupt practices. As mayor, La Guardia earned a national reputation as an honest and nonpartisan reformer dedicated to civic improvement. He was an able and indefatigable administrator who obtained a new city charter, fought corrupt politicians and organized crime, improved the operations of the police and fire departments, expanded the city's social-welfare services, and began slum-clearance and low-cost-housing programs. Among his building projects were the La Guardia Airport and numerous roads and bridges. A colourful figure with a flair for the dramatic, La Guardia became known as "The Little Flower" in token of his first name.

After being reelected twice, La Guardia in 1945 refused to run for a fourth term as mayor. He was appointed director of the U.S. Office of Civilian Defense (1941) and director general (1946) of the United Nations Relief and Rehabilitation Administration.

La Guardia, 1941
UPI

La Guma, Alex (b. Feb. 20, 1925, Cape Town, S.Af.—d. Oct. 11, 1985, Havana, Cuba), black novelist of South Africa in the 1960s whose characteristically brief works (*e.g., A Walk in the Night* [1962], *The Stone-Country* [1965], and *In the Fog of the Season's End* [1972]) gain power through his superb eye for detail, allowing the humour, pathos, or horror of a situation to speak for itself.

La Guma was reared in a family active in the black liberation movement. In 1960 he joined the staff of the progressive newspaper *New Age.* During the next few years he was detained and imprisoned several times for his antiapartheid activities. The South African government banned his writing and speaking, and in 1966 he and his family moved to London, where he lived in exile until 1979.

His first novel, *A Walk in the Night,* presents the struggle against oppression by a group of characters in Cape Town's toughest district and, in particular, the moral dissolution of a young man who is unjustly fired from his job. Its general theme of protest is reiterated in *And a Threefold Cord* (1964), which depicts the degrading effect of apartheid upon a ghetto family, and in *The Stone-Country,* which grew out of La Guma's experiences in prison. His short stories appeared in many anthologies and magazines. The novel *Time of the Butcherbird* appeared in 1979. La Guma's high reputation is based on his vivid style, his colourful dialogue, and his ability to present sympathetically and realistically people living under sordid and oppressive circumstances.

La Habana, *provincia,* west-central Cuba, bounded on the north by the Straits of Florida and by Ciudad de la Habana *provincia;* on the south by the Gulf of Batabanó, an inlet of the Caribbean Sea; and on the east and west, respectively, by Matanzas and Pinar del Río *provincias.* It has an area of 2,213 square miles (5,731 square km) and is densely populated, being near the national and provincial capital city, Havana. The hills of northern and central La Habana province become a gently sloping plain in the south. The northern coast is characterized by terraces, sandy beaches, and the beautiful La Habana Bay; the swampy southern coast is covered with mangrove forests. The province yields considerable quantities of sugarcane, tobacco, fruits, vegetables, and milk for the Havana market. Many industrial plants are located in and around the capital. A thermal-power plant is located at Mariel, a port and a major centre of shrimp trawling southwest of Havana. The province has excellent communications, including a good network of modern highways, railways, and airways. Pop. (1989 est.) 636,889.

La Habra, city, Orange county, southern California, U.S., just north of Fullerton and southeast of Los Angeles. Its name apparently derives from the Spanish *abra* ("pass"), with reference to an opening in the nearby hills. The town was founded by a land grant in 1839, and it soon developed as a commercial centre for an extensive agricultural area (citrus fruit, avocados). A packinghouse was built after the arrival of the Pacific Electric Railroad in 1908. The nearby Coyote Hills oilfields were established in 1912. Since 1950 there has been zoned industrial development. Inc. 1925. Pop. (1990) 51,266.

La Halle, Adam de (poet): *see* Adam de la Halle.

La Harpe, Frédéric-César de (b. April 6, 1754, Rolle, Vaud, Switz.—d. March 30, 1838, Lausanne), Swiss political leader and Vaudois patriot, tutor and confidant to Tsar Alexander I of Russia and a central figure in the creation of the Helvetic Republic (1798).

Resentment of Bernese administration in his native Vaud caused La Harpe to go abroad, and at the Russian imperial court he found employment as tutor to the future tsar Alexander and his brother Constantine (1784). Following the outbreak of the French Revolution, he began to plot a Vaudois uprising from St. Petersburg. In 1794 he returned to Switzerland and thence to Paris, where he sought French assistance for releasing the Vaud from Bern's domination. In 1797 La Harpe published his *Essai sur la constitution du pays de Vaud* ("Essay on the Constitution of the Vaud"), an anti-Bernese tract, and on Dec. 9, 1797, on behalf of a group of refugees from the Vaud and Fribourg, he addressed a petition to the French Directory urging military intervention in Switzerland to secure Vaudois independence, thus providing the official pretext for the subsequent French invasion (March 1798). With Peter Ochs he succeeded in creating a unitary government for Switzerland, and on June 29, 1798, he entered the Directory (chief executive organ) of the new Helvetic Republic. After securing the deposition of Ochs (June 1799), La Harpe sought dictatorial power but was himself deposed in the coup of Jan. 7, 1800. Later, accused of conspiracy against the state and anti-French intrigue, he was forced to flee the country. With the fall of Napoleon, he secured from his protector and erstwhile pupil, Tsar Alexander I, a formal promise of Vaudois independence (1814) and made representations on behalf of Switzerland and his native canton at the Congress of Vienna (1815). Returning to the Vaud the following year, he served on its legislative council until 1828.

La Harpe, Jean-François de (b. Nov. 20, 1739, Paris, Fr.—d. Feb. 11, 1803, Paris), critic and unsuccessful playwright who wrote severe and provocative criticisms and histories of French literature.

Orphaned at 9 and imprisoned at 19 for allegedly writing a satire against his protectors at college, La Harpe became a bitter and caustic man. Of many uninspired plays he wrote, the best are perhaps his first tragedy, *Warwick* (1763), and *Mélanie* (1778), a pathetic drama never performed. He wrote criticism for and was editor of the *Mercure de France,* becoming respected, though often disliked, for his unsympathetic views. In 1786, after being coldly admitted to the French Academy, he began to lecture at the newly established Lycée. His lectures, published as the *Cours de littérature,* 16 vol. (1799–1805), show La Harpe at his best; he brought a clear and intelligent understanding to his treatment of 17th-century literature, as is also shown in his *Commentaire sur Racine* (1807). Although an extreme revolutionary, he became suspect and was imprisoned in April 1794. Shocked by the horrors around him, he became an ardent Roman Catholic and reactionary, attacking his former friends when he returned to the Lycée. His *Oeuvres* were published in 1821.

La Hire, Laurent de, La Hire also spelled LA HYRE (b. Feb. 27, 1606, Paris, Fr.—d. Dec. 28, 1656, Paris), French Baroque classical painter whose best work is marked by gravity, simplicity, and dignity.

He was the son of the painter Étienne de La Hire (*c.* 1583–1643) but was most influenced by the work of Georges Lallemont and Orazio Gentileschi. His picture of "Pope Nicolas V at the Tomb of Saint Francis" was done in 1630 for the Capuchins, for whom he executed several other works. For the goldsmiths' company he produced in 1635 "St. Peter Healing the Sick" and the "Conversion of St. Paul" in 1637. In 1648, with 11 other artists, he helped found the French Royal Academy. Cardinal Richelieu called him to the Palais-Royal about 1640 to paint decorative mythological scenes, and he later designed a series of tapestries for the Gobelins.

La Hontan, Louis-Armand de Lom d'Arce, baron de, La Hontan also spelled LAHONTAN (b. June 9, 1666, Mont-de-Marsan, Fr.—d. 1715, Hannover, Hanover [Germany]), French soldier and writer who explored parts of what are now Canada and the United States and who prepared valuable accounts of his travels in the New World.

La Hontan went to Canada in 1683 as a marine lieutenant. He participated in an unsuccessful campaign against the Iroquois Indians on Lake Ontario in 1684 and commanded Fort-Saint-Joseph (now Niles, Mich.) in 1687. In 1688–89 he explored territory along the Wisconsin and the Mississippi rivers.

On a return trip to France in 1692 with a plan for a fleet on the Great Lakes, La Hontan, now a captain, stopped at Newfoundland and defended the French colonists at Plaisance against the English. For this action he was made king's lieutenant at Plaisance but when the governor there accused him of insubordination, he fled to Portugal in 1693 and thereafter remained in Europe.

In 1703 La Hontan published *Nouveaux Voyages de Mr. le Baron de Lahontan dans l'Amérique septentrionale,* 2 vol. (*New Voyages to North-America*), considered the best 17th-century work on New France. The *New Voyages* also contained a series of dialogues describing the philosophy of the primitive way of life that influenced a subsequent growth of primitivism in France and England, as reflected in the works of Montesquieu, Voltaire, Jonathan Swift, and others.

La Junta, city, seat of Otero county, southeastern Colorado, U.S. It lies along the Arkansas River at the northern edge of the Comanche National Grassland, at an elevation of 4,052 feet (1,235 m). Founded in 1875, it was first called Otero, after a Spanish settler, and its present name is Spanish for "the junction," referring to its location at the convergence of the old Santa Fe and Navajo trails. La Junta developed as a shipping point to New Mexico and is now a railroad junction with large railroad shops. It lies in an irrigated-farming area devoted to sugar beets and vegetables; cattle auctions are important. Otero Junior College opened there in 1941. Inc. town, 1881; city, 1901. Pop. (1990) 7,637.

La Libertad, also called LIBERTAD, *departamento* (formed 1821) of northern Peru, stretching from the Pacific Ocean in the west to the Cordillera Central of the Andes in the east. The *departamento* occupies an area of 8,973 square miles (23,241 square km). The northward-flowing Marañón River has cut a narrow canyon between the cordilleras Occidental and Central.

Once the home of the Mochica and Chimú cultures—renowned for their ceramics, irrigation works, and vast urban centres such as Chan Chan—the area was eventually incorporated into the Inca empire. During the colonial era (1533–1821) it was of political, commercial, and ecclesiastical importance. It was the first *departamento* to proclaim independence from Spain.

Economic activity and population are concentrated in the irrigated coastal river valleys, especially around the capital, Trujillo (*q.v.*), and its port, Salaverry. Cotton, rice, and coffee are principal crops, but La Libertad is best known for its sugarcane production. In the mountains, cereals, corn (maize), and potatoes are cultivated, and cattle and sheep are grazed. The *departamento* has good transportation facilities; agricultural areas are linked by rail and highway to refineries and seaports. Roads penetrate the interior, and the Pan-American Highway runs the length of the coast. Pop. (1990 est.) 1,244,000.

La Libertad, city, southwestern El Salvador. Its open roadstead port as well as its location south of San Salvador encouraged La Libertad's development in the 19th century as a shipping outlet for balsam produced in Peru—a variety of balsam yielded from El Salvador's coastal forests. During the early 20th century La Libertad was one of the nation's largest ports, but in 1976 it was closed to international commercial traffic. It remains an important fishing port. Agriculture (livestock raising, sugarcane, and cotton) and beach-resort facilities augment fishing as important economic activities. Pop. (1985 est.) 12,675.

La Línea, in full LA LÍNEA DE LA CONCEPCIÓN, town, Cádiz *provincia,* in the *comunidad autónoma* ("autonomous community") of Andalusia, southwestern Spain. It lies along the Bay of Gibraltar, between San Roque and the British colony of Gibraltar. The name is derived from the *línea,* or boundary, dividing Spanish territory from the district of Gibraltar. The town processes fruit and vegetables for sale in Gibraltar, and manufactures include cork, liquor, and fish paste. La Línea is the site of a national military garrison and headquarters of the Spanish commandant of the línea of Gibraltar. Pop. (1981) 55,590.

La Louvière, town, Hainaut province, southwestern Belgium, on the Central Canal, about 11 mi (17 km) east of Mons. It has been a centre of coal mining since the 14th century. La Louvière is also a major centre of steel manufacturing and produces sheet metal, furniture, and ceramics. Nearby is the park of Mariemont, named for Mary of Hungary, sister of Charles V and queen of the Netherlands, who first built a palace there in 1554. A museum (built 1962–67) in the park contains Gallo-Roman and Merovingian antiquities, porcelain from Tournai, Far Eastern art, and has a library of 70,000 volumes. The town is connected by railway and road with Mons, Charleroi, and Brussels. Pop. (2000 est.) mun., 76,568.

La Ma'dukelleng: *see* Arung Singkang.

La Mancha, barren, elevated plateau (2,000 ft [610 m]) of central Spain, stretching between the Montes (mountains) de Toledo and the western spurs of the Cerros (hills) de Cuenca, and bounded on the south by the Sierra Morena and on the north by La Alcarria region. It includes portions of the modern provinces of Cuenca, Toledo, and Albacete, and most of Ciudad Real province. It constitutes the southern portion of the Castile-La Mancha autonomous community (region) and makes up most of the region. Known to the Arabs as al-Manshah (Dry Land or Wilderness), the region was an intermediate zone between Christian and Moorish forces during the Middle Ages. Down to the 16th century, the eastern portion was known as La Mancha de Montearagón or La Mancha de Aragon, and the western simply as La Mancha; afterward, the northeastern and southwestern sections, respectively, were distinguished by the epithets Alta and Baja (upper and lower). La Mancha remains almost exactly as Miguel de Cervantes (Saavedra) described it in his 17th-century novel *Don Quixote.* Many villages, such as El Toboso and Argamasilla de Alba, both near Alcázar de San Juan, are connected by tradition with Quixotic episodes.

Agriculture (wheat, barley, oats, wine grapes) is the primary economic activity, but it is severely restricted by unfavourable environmental conditions. In the north, hunting and fishing reserves draw increasing numbers of tourists.

La Marche, Olivier de (b. *c.* 1425, Villegaudin, Burgundy—d. Feb. 1, 1502, Brussels), Burgundian chronicler and poet who, as historian of the ducal court, was an eloquent spokesman of the chivalrous tradition.

La Marche, detail of an engraving

By courtesy of the trustees of the British Museum; photograph, J.R. Freeman & Co. Ltd.

After serving as a page to Philip the Good, duke of Burgundy, La Marche entered the service of the Duke's son, the count of Charolais (later called Charles the Bold). He became Charles's secretary and remained in Burgundian service all his life, representing Charles on many diplomatic missions throughout Europe. After Charles was killed at Nancy in 1477, La Marche continued to serve the Duke's heiress, Mary, and her husband, the Austrian archduke Maximilian.

La Marche's writings, the most important of which was *L'État de la maison du duc Charles de Bourgogne* (1474; "The State of the House of Charles, Duke of Burgundy"), for the most part glorify the House of Burgundy. His *Mémoires,* two books covering the periods 1435–67 and 1467–88, were completed about 1490. Though written with charm and liveliness, they are unreliable as history because La Marche makes mistakes in chronology and was too resolutely devoted to the House of Burgundy to be objective, especially in his judgments on French policy.

La Marmora, Alfonso Ferrero (b. Nov. 18, 1804, Turin, Piedmont—d. Jan. 5, 1878, Florence), Italian general and statesman who, while in the service of Sardinia–Piedmont, played an important role in the Risorgimento.

A graduate of the Turin Military Academy, La Marmora entered the army in 1823 and

La Marmora, detail of a lithograph by Masutti

By courtesy of the Museo Centrale del Risorgimento, Rome

first distinguished himself in the Italian wars of independence against Austria, especially at Borghetto and Pischiera (May 1848). He also commanded the Sardinian forces in the Crimea (1855). On Aug. 5, 1848, he rescued the Sardinian king Charles Albert from Milanese revolutionaries, who had resented the King's armistice with the Austrians. He was promoted to general in October and served as minister of war until November; he later suppressed an insurrection at Genoa (April 4–5, 1849). As minister of war again until 1860, he reorganized the Italian Army.

La Marmora served as premier of Piedmont from July 1859 to January 1860, as well as governor of Milan and the king's lieutenant in Naples. In September 1864 he again became premier, and as minister of foreign affairs in April 1866 he concluded Italy's alliance with Prussia against Austria. As chief of staff in the ensuing war, however, he was held responsible for the overwhelming defeat of the Italians by Austria at Custoza (June 24, 1866). La Marmora retired to private life shortly afterward, although, after Rome was annexed to the Kingdom of Italy in 1870, he was appointed the king's lieutenant there. Among his several works, *Un po' più di luce sugli eventi politici e militari dell'anno 1866* (1873; "A Little More Light on the Political and Military Events of the Year 1866") seeks to justify his actions at Custoza.

La Matanza, *partido* (political subdivision) of Gran (Greater) Buenos Aires, Arg., directly southwest of the city of Buenos Aires, in Buenos Aires province. The present-day *partido* was part of the Pago (country district) de las Conchas during the 17th and early 18th centuries. In 1730 the Pago de las Conchas was divided into four rural settlement areas, one of which was the Pago de la Matanza. The *partido* of La Matanza was established in 1784, and a justice of the peace was appointed to the region. Towns were established many years later. The present *cabecera* (administrative seat), San Justo, was founded in 1856.

The *partido* covers 125 sq mi (323 sq km) and is bordered by the *partidos* of Lomas de Zamora and Esteban Echeverría (southeast), as well as Marcos Paz (southwest), Merlo, Morón, and Tres de Febrero (northwest), and Cañuelas (south). The Río de la Matanza (Riachuelo) forms the southeastern border. Besides the *cabecera,* the major localities within the *partido* are Ciudad General Belgrano, Villa Madero, Villa Luzuriaga, Laferrere, Ramos Mejía, and Tablada.

The industries of La Matanza manufacture plows, automobile accessories, paper, and rubber goods. Agricultural lands, outside the built-up areas, grow wheat, corn (maize), barley, and alfalfa and support livestock.

With the growth of the national capital, La Matanza has been absorbed into the southwestern suburban fringe of Gran Buenos Aires. About half of the *partido* lies within the Gran Buenos Aires urban area, and its numerical population increase in both the 1960s and 1970s was greater than any other *partido* in Gran Buenos Aires. Pop. (1999 est.) 1,241,264.

La Mettrie, Julien Offroy de (b. Dec. 25, 1709, Saint-Malo, Fr.—d. Nov. 11, 1751, Berlin), French physician and philosopher whose Materialistic interpretation of psychic phenomena laid the groundwork for future developments of behaviourism and played an important part in the history of modern Materialism.

La Mettrie obtained a medical degree at Reims, studied medicine in Leiden under Herman Boerhaave (some of whose works he translated into French), and served as surgeon to the French military. A personal illness convinced him that psychic phenomena were directly related to organic changes in the brain and nervous system. The outcry following publication of these views in *Histoire naturelle de l'âme* (1745; "Natural History of the Soul") forced his departure from Paris. The book was burned by the public hangman. In Holland La Mettrie published *L'Homme-machine* (1747; *L'Homme Machine: A Study in the Origins of an Idea,* 1960), developing more boldly and completely, and with great originality, his Materialistic and atheistic views. The ethics of these principles were worked out in *Discours sur le bonheur ou l'anti-Sénèque* ("Discourse on Happiness, or the Anti-Seneca"). He was then forced to leave Holland but was welcomed in Berlin (1748) by Frederick the Great, made court reader, and appointed to the academy of science. In accord with his belief that atheism was the sole road to happiness and the pleasure of the senses the purpose of life (*Le Petit Homme à longue queue,* 1751; "The Small Man in a Long Queue"), he was a carefree hedonist to the end, finally dying of ptomaine poisoning. His collected works, *Oeuvres philosophiques,* were published in 1751, and selections were edited by Marcelle Tisserand in 1954.

La Mothe Le Vayer, François de, pseudonym OROSIUS TUBERO (b. 1588, Paris—d. 1672, Paris), independent French thinker and writer who developed a philosophy of Skepticism more radical than that of Michel de Montaigne but less absolute than that of Pierre Bayle.

La Mothe Le Vayer became an *avocat* in the Parlement of Paris, taking over his father's seat, but soon resigned when the attraction of belles lettres became stronger. His work *La Contrariété d'humeur entre la nation française et l'espagnole* (1636; "Conflicts of Interest Between the French and Spanish Nations") and *Considérations sur l'eloquence française* (1638) earned him admission to the Académie Française in 1639. He was admired by the powerful Cardinal de Richelieu and was tutor to several noble youths, including from 1652 to 1657 Louis XIV, for whom he wrote a complete series of texts. The king rewarded him by appointing him historiographer of France and councillor of state.

La Mothe Le Vayer, engraving by Jacques Lubin
Giraudon—Art Resource

His many philosophical works include *De la vertu des païens* (1642; "On the Goodness of the Pagans"); a treatise entitled *Du peu de certitude qu'il y a dans l'histoire* (1668; "On the Lack of Certitude in History"), which marked a beginning of historical criticism in France; and five skeptical *Dialogues,* published posthumously under the pseudonym Orosius Tubero, which are concerned, respectively, with diversity in opinions, variety in customs of life and sex roles, the value of solitude, the virtue of the fools of his time, and differences in religion.

La Noue, François de (b. 1531, Nantes, Fr.—d. Aug. 4, 1591, Moncontour), Huguenot captain in the French Wars of Religion (1562–98), known for his exploits as a soldier and for his military and historical writings.

La Noue became a Protestant in 1558 and soon began fighting for the Huguenot cause. Wounded at Fontenay (1570), he had one arm replaced by an iron device and was thereafter nicknamed Bras-de-Fer ("Arm of Iron"). After the Peace of Saint-Germain (1570), which provided a temporary break in the hostilities, he fought against the Spanish in the Netherlands. Commissioned by Charles IX to reconcile the inhabitants of La Rochelle to the king after the massacre of Protestants on St. Bartholomew's Day, 1572, he soon resigned his commission and from 1574 to 1578 acted as Huguenot general of La Rochelle. In 1580 he again fought in the Netherlands. Captured and imprisoned for five years by the Spanish, he wrote his *Discours politiques et militaires* (published 1587), a series of moral and military reflections together with a commentary on the state of France and an account of the early years of the Wars of Religion. After his release he eventually returned to France and served King Henry IV, dying of a wound received at the siege of Lamballe.

La Noue's other writings include *Observations sur Guicciardini,* 2 vol. (1592) and notes on Plutarch's *Lives.*

La Orotava, town, northern Tenerife island, Santa Cruz de Tenerife *provincia,* Canary Islands *comunidad autónoma* ("autonomous community"), Spain, just southwest of Santa Cruz de Tenerife city. The town is a health resort with its port, Puerto de la Cruz, on the coast immediately to the northwest. It lies in the Orotava Valley, known for its luxuriant vegetation and called the most beautiful in the world by the German traveler Alexander von Humboldt, who visited there in 1799. Its chief agricultural products are bananas, tobacco, and cochineal, a red dyestuff. Pop. (1999 est.) 35,775.

La Oroya, also called OROYA, city, Junín *departamento,* central Peru, at the junction of the Mantaro and Yauli rivers on a central plateau of the Andes, at an elevation of 12,195 feet (3,717 m). The city, located in a rich mining region based on the Cerro de Pasco, Morococha, and Casapalca mines, is a smelting and refining centre for copper, zinc, silver, and lead ores; it is also the site of a hydroelectric station fed by Pomacocha Reservoir, 20 miles (32 km) southwest. The first railroad in the area was completed in 1893 to spur silver production, and the first highway in 1943. La Oroya has become a communications link between Lima and the interior. Pop. (2002) 32,600.

La Palma, in full SAN MIGUEL DE LA PALMA, island, Santa Cruz de Tenerife *provincia* in the *comunidad autónoma* ("autonomous community") of Canary Islands, Spain. Located in the North Atlantic off the northwestern coast of Africa, it has an area of 281 square miles (728 square km). Its central geographic feature is La Caldera de Taburiente, a national park and a large volcanic caldera (6 miles [10 km] in diameter). The rim is breached on the west by a canyon but elsewhere forms a mountain ridge up to 7,950 feet (2,423 m) in elevation. Its well-watered slopes are densely wooded and deeply dissected by ravines. The more recent lava streams, including those formed in 1949, are naked. Santa Cruz de la Palma, the capital and port of the island, handles most of the exports of bananas, tomatoes, tobacco, and embroidery. The island has some motor roads and an airstrip. Pop. (1999 est.) 82,419.

La Pampa, *provincia,* central Argentina, immediately west of Buenos Aires *provincia* and geographically straddling drier sections of the Pampa (northeast) and semiarid sections of the Patagonian Desert (southwest). Its western and southern parts are comprised of low-lying tablelands (with a broad depression in the central west) occasionally broken by hillocks, saline marshes and lakes, and intermittent streambeds. The western part of La Pampa, in particular, is sparsely inhabited, while the plains of the northeast are more fertile and suited for the grazing of cattle and sheep and the cultivation of wheat and corn (maize). Occasional severe droughts make agriculture uncertain, however.

Not until after it was made a national territory in 1884 were there renewed efforts to extend the frontier and encourage European immigration. La Pampa attained provincial status in 1952, and from that time until the overthrow of President Juan Perón (1955), the area was known by his wife's name, Eva Perón.

Millet, sorghum, and sunflowers are also cultivated. The port of Bahía Blanca, in Buenos Aires *provincia,* serves as an outlet for the area's produce. Santa Rosa (*q.v.*), the provincial capital, and General Pico are the only important towns in La Pampa. Petroleum is extracted in the extreme southwest. Area 55,382 square miles (143,440 square km). Pop. (2000 est.) 306,113.

La Paz, city, capital of Bolivia, west-central Bolivia, situated some 42 miles (68 km) southeast of Lake Titicaca. La Paz is Bolivia's largest city and, at between 10,650 and 13,250 feet (3,250 and 4,100 m) above sea level, the world's highest capital. Visitors, upon arrival, find exertion difficult because of the rarefied atmosphere found at these elevations. The centre of the city lies in a deep, broad canyon formed by the La Paz, or Choqueyapu, River. The city's location, about 1,400 feet (430 m) below the surface of the Altiplano, or high intermontane plateau, affords some protection from the cold highland winds. Recent population growth has spread up the canyon walls to the edge of the Altiplano.

Founded in 1548 by the conquistador Captain Alonso de Mendoza as Nuestra Señora de La Paz ("Our Lady of the Peace") on the site of an Inca village, the city was renamed La Paz de Ayacucho in 1825, in commemoration of the last decisive battle in the wars of independence. The seat of national government was established there in 1898, but Sucre (*q.v.*) remains Bolivia's legal capital. The Plaza Murillo, on the northeastern side of the river, is the heart of the city and site of the huge modern cathedral and government and legislative palaces. Although few colonial buildings survive, the narrow, steep older streets, red-tile roofs, many skyscrapers, and highland Indians in colourful dress, with Nevado Illimani (20,741 feet [6,322 m]) and other snow-capped peaks of the Cordillera Real in the background, give La Paz a distinctive atmosphere. Its industries are chiefly food processing and the manufacture of consumer goods.

Government palace, La Paz, Bolivia
Art Resource

The University of San Andrés (1830), Bolivian Catholic University (1966), the National Museum of Art, and the National Museum of Archaeology are among the city's cultural assets.

La Paz is connected by railways and highways with Peruvian (via steamer across Lake Titicaca) and Chilean seaports and with Argentina and Brazil. Its international airport is located above the city on the plateau. Pop. (2000 est.) 1,000,899.

La Paz, town, southwestern Honduras, at an elevation of 2,461 feet (750 m) above sea level in the Comayagua River valley, on the eastern flanks of the Cordillera de Montecillos. It was founded in 1792 and has been called La Paz since 1861. The city serves as a commercial centre for the surrounding agricultural and pastoral lands, which yield primarily henequen, coffee, and cattle. The town has a sawmill, a tannery, and a liquor distillery. There is also some mining in the vicinity. La Paz is accessible by highway from Tegucigalpa, the national capital, and other centres. Pop. (2000) 16,900.

La Paz, city, capital of the *estado* ("state") of Baja California Sur, northwestern Mexico. Only 33 feet (10 m) above sea level on the La Paz Bay of the Gulf of California, the city has a hot, dry climate. The bay was discovered by the Spanish in 1596, and early in the 18th century it was temporarily the site of a Jesuit mission. The town was established in the early 1800s and was the capital of Baja California from 1828 until 1887, when the peninsula was divided between the United States and Mexico; La Paz then became the capital of the Mexican region. Fishing (shark and shrimp), agriculture (corn [maize], cotton, and dates), cattle raising, and tourism are the city's principal sources of income. The largest urban centre in the new state and a popular resort, it offers deep-sea fishing, boating, waterskiing and other water sports, and hunting in the nearby mountains. La Paz may be reached by road from Tijuana and Mexicali, to the north, by air, or by ferry from Mazatlán, on the Mexican mainland. Pop. (2000 prelim.) 162,795.

La Pérouse, Jean-François de Galaup, Count (comte) **de** (b. Aug. 22, 1741, near Albi, Fr.—d. *c.* 1788), French navigator who conducted wide-ranging explorations in the Pacific Ocean.

La Pérouse, detail from a mezzotint
H. Roger-Viollet

Commanding the ship *La Boussole,* which was accompanied by the *Astrolabe,* La Pérouse sailed from France on Aug. 1, 1785. After rounding Cape Horn, one of his stops in the South Pacific was Easter Island (April 9, 1786). Investigating tropical Pacific waters, he visited the Sandwich Islands (now Hawaii) and, with the object of locating the Northwest Passage from the Pacific, he made his way to North America. He reached the southern shore of Alaska, near Mount St. Elias, in June 1786 and explored the coast southward beyond San Francisco to Monterey. He then crossed the Pacific and reached the South China coast at Macau on Jan. 3, 1787. Leaving Manila on April 9, he began to explore the Asian coast. He sailed through the Sea of Japan up to the Tatar Strait, which separates the mainland from the island of Sakhalin, and also visited the strait, named for him, that separates Sakhalin from Hokkaido, Japan. At Petropavlovsk on the Siberian peninsula of Kamchatka, he dispatched his expedition journal and maps overland to France. The ships then made for the Navigators' (now Samoa) Islands, where the commander of the *Astrolabe* and 11 of his men were murdered. La Pérouse then went to the Friendly (now Tonga) and Norfolk islands on his way to Botany Bay in eastern Australia, from which he departed on March 10, 1788.

Nothing more was known of him until 1826–27, when the English captain-adventurer Peter Dillon found evidence that *La Boussole* and the *Astrolabe* had been near Vanikoro, one of the Santa Cruz Islands (now in Solomon Islands). In 1828 the French explorer Dumont d'Urville sighted wreckage and learned from islanders that about 30 men from the ships had been massacred on shore, though others who were well armed managed to escape. La Pérouse's records, *Voyage de La Pérouse autour du monde,* 4 vol. (1797; *A Voyage Round the World*), were edited by L.A. Milet-Mureau and published posthumously.

La Perouse Strait, Russian PROLIV LAPERUZA, Japanese SŌYA-KAIKYŌ, international waterway between the islands of Sakhalin (Russia) and Hokkaido (Japan). The strait, named after the French explorer Jean-François de Galaup, Count de La Pérouse, separates the Sea of Okhotsk from the Sea of Japan. It is 27 miles (43 km) wide at its narrowest part, between Cape Krilon (Sakhalin) and Cape Sōya (Hokkaido) and varies in depth from 167 to 387 feet (51 to 118 m). The strait is characterized by extremely strong marine currents. It is closed by ice in the winter.

La Piedad Cavadas, city, northwestern Michoacán *estado* ("state"), west-central Mexico. On the Lerma River, which forms the Michoacán-Guanajuato border, it is 314 miles (505 km) west-northwest of Mexico City and 119 miles (192 km) northwest of Morelia, the state capital. During the colonial era it was known as Zula la Vieja but was elevated to city rank and given its present name in 1871. Much of La Piedad's economy is based on the raising of livestock (cattle, pigs) and on dairying. The city is known for its cheeses and butter. Corn (maize), beans, wheat, and chick-peas also raised in the environs provide additional income. Several highways converge on La Piedad, and the Mexico City–Guadalajara railroad passes north-northeast of the city. Pop. (1995) 72,041.

La Plata, city, capital of Buenos Aires *provincia,* Argentina, 6 miles (9 km) inland from the southern shore of the Río de la Plata estuary. The site was selected in 1882 by the provincial governor of Buenos Aires, Dardo Rocha, as the new provincial seat, a move made necessary when Buenos Aires was federalized as the national capital (1880). The city plan was modeled on that of Washington, D.C.; and a municipal library, astronomical observatory, Gothic-style cathedral, and museum were included with the government buildings in the original construction. The museum, connected with the National University of La Plata (1897), houses one of the most important paleontological and anthropological collections in South America. Many advanced research institutes and other academies have been established there, furthering the city's reputation as a centre of culture.

The cathedral at La Plata, Arg.
Art Resource

The development of a heavy industrial zone (now including meat-packing houses, a petrochemical complex, and steel mill) between La Plata and the Río de la Plata led to the creation in 1957 of the separate localities of Ensenada and Berisso. La Plata's deepwater port facilities are located at Ensenada along with the national naval academy. In 1952 La Plata was renamed Eva Perón in memory of the wife of President Juan Perón; but following his overthrow in 1955, it resumed its original name. Pop. (1999 est.) city, 556,308; (1991) Greater La Plata (including Ensenada and Berisso), 642,979.

la Plata, Río de (Argentina): *see* Plata, Río de la.

La Plata River, Spanish RÍO DE LA PLATA, river in east-central Puerto Rico, rising on the western slope of Mount Santa (2,963 feet [903 m]), a peak of the Sierra de Cayey. Part of the stream is impounded by Lake Carite; the reservoir's outlet diverts waters for a series of hydroelectric stations on the Guamaní River in the coastal Guayama area to the south. The La Plata itself flows about 45 miles (70 km) northwest and north, dropping from 1,300 feet (400 m) to less than 500 feet (150 m), past Comerío and onto the northern coastal plain. The river then flows past the villages of Toa Alta and Toa Baja and empties into the Atlantic Ocean just north of Dorado, a small industrial town west of San Juan, the capital. Along its narrow alluvial plain and terraces, tobacco, cotton, grapefruit, and vegetables are grown.

La Révellière-Lépeaux, Louis-Marie de (b. Aug. 25, 1753, Montaigu, Fr.—d. March 27, 1824, Paris), member of the French Revolutionary regime known as the Directory.

La Révellière-Lépeaux, lithograph by F.-S. Delpech
By courtesy of the Bibliotheque Nationale, Paris

In 1789 La Révellière-Lépeaux was elected as a representative of the Third Estate (the unprivileged order) to the States General, which converted itself into the revolutionary National Assembly. In 1792 he became a member of the Convention, the new national assembly that governed France from 1792 to 1795. During the Terror of 1793–94, La Révellière-Lépeaux went into hiding, but after the fall of Robespierre he returned to the Convention and was appointed to the commission that drew up the Constitution of 1795. He served as president of the Convention and then as a member of the five-man Directory (1795–99). His policy was marked by a bitter hostility to the Christian religion, which he proposed to supplant with a deistic system. He was forced off the Directory on June 18, 1799, and thenceforth stayed out of politics, refusing to swear allegiance to Napoleon in 1804. After Napoleon's fall in 1814 La Révellière-Lépeaux was not banished by the royalist regime, even though as a member of the Convention he had voted for the execution of Louis XVI in 1793. His memoirs were published in 1873.

La Rioja, *provincia,* northwestern Argentina, extending southeastward from Chile. The *provincia*'s southeastern half is an arid to semiarid plain, while the northwestern section is crossed north to south by alternating mountain ranges and semiarid valleys associated with the Andean cordillera. Saline marshes and lakes of the southeast are formed by intermittent streams flowing out of the mountains.

Like the rest of northwestern Argentina, the region was conquered by Inca armies in the late 15th century and was settled by Spaniards exploring for gold and silver in the late 16th century. The capital, La Rioja, was founded in 1591 by the governor of Tucumán, and the area remained part of Tucumán *provincia* and under the control of the viceroyalty of Peru until 1782, when it came under the jurisdiction of the viceroyalty of Río de la Plata as part of the *intendencia* ("intendency") of Córdoba. After separating from Córdoba in 1816 and achieving the rank of *provincia* in 1820, La Rioja experienced 50 years of civil war and unrest. The establishment of an effective national government in Buenos Aires in the 1860s contributed to the *provincia*'s stability.

Water supply is the major problem of La Rioja. The small streams do not provide adequate volume, and both agriculture and mining have been seriously restricted for this reason. Dams erected on the Anzulón and La Rioja watercourses provide irrigation and electric power for the immediate area. The small-scale irrigated cultivation includes grapes, olives, and alfalfa. Cattle and sheep are generally grazed at lower elevations. There are significant copper and molybdenum reserves in the Famatina Mountains. A game reserve protecting diminishing herds of vicuña was created in 1980 near Laguna Brava in the high Andes. Area 34,626 square miles (89,680 square km). Pop. (1999 est.) 273,471.

La Rioja, city, capital of La Rioja *provincia,* northwestern Argentina, on La Rioja River at the foot of the Velasco Mountains. Founded in 1591 by explorers for gold and silver, it long remained a small commercial and administrative centre close to intermittently worked deposits of copper, silver, and lead ores in the high Andes to the west. Its destruction by earthquake in 1894 led to its reconstruction along modern lines. Contemporary commercial activities are based on agriculture (including cultivation of grapes, olives, apples, and pears), wine making, and elementary industries. The nearby dam on La Rioja (completed in 1930) is a source of power and irrigation. Notable landmarks include the ruins of a 16th-century Jesuit church and regional museums of archaeology and folklore. Pop. (1999 est.) 138,074.

"De," "la," and similar components of a name, when followed by a space, are alphabetized as separate words (e.g., *De Forest, Lee*). *When they are joined to the following part of a name, the combination is treated as a single word* (e.g., *DeForest, John William*).

La Rioja, *comunidad autónoma* ("autonomous community") and historical region of Spain coextensive with the north-central Spanish province of La Rioja (until 1980 called Logroño). As Logroño, the province was first organized in 1833. The autonomous community was established by the statute of autonomy of 1982. The region historically belongs to Old Castile.

The folds of the Obarenes Mountains rise in the northwest corner of La Rioja, marking the border with the province of Burgos. The Ebro River flows northwest to southeast, skirting the provinces of Álava and Navarre to the north. La Rioja is also bordered by the province of Zaragoza to the east. The Ebro basin rises southward into the hills of the upper Rioja. The Iberian range, dominated by the Demanda and Urbión mountain ranges, rises in the south and extends into the province of Soria. The southern sector, Cameros, also mountainous, is crossed by the Glera (Oja), Najerilla, Iregua, Leza, Cidacos, and Alhama rivers. A continental climate, modified by Atlantic influences, prevails. Temperatures are highest near the Ebro River; precipitation increases from east to west and south to north. Annual precipitation is moderate, ranging from 16 to 28 inches (400 to 700 mm).

The population is concentrated in the irrigated farmland (grapes, cereals, horticultural produce) along the Ebro River and its affluents. The latter were easily channeled and were tapped for traditional irrigation. The Canal of Lodosa, initiated in 1930, has channeled the Ebro River itself and greatly expanded the land under irrigation. The population of the lower Rioja tends to cluster in towns with 2,000 or more inhabitants, while the settlements of the Iberian range, where dry farming and animal husbandry predominate, have been steadily losing population. Emigration has centred on the city of Logroño (*q.v.*), the provincial capital, and on the provinces of Vizcaya, Guipúzcoa, Zaragoza, Barcelona, and Madrid.

The Iberian range has traditionally been a transhumant zone, but the number of livestock has declined sharply since the dissolution of royal grazing privileges in 1836.

The upper Rioja produces some of Spain's finest red wines. Basque capital financed the specialization of vineyards in the late 19th century; 12 were established between 1867 and 1900. The vineyards of the lower Rioja are noted for their slightly sweet red table wine. The introduction of quality control has favoured large vintners over small ones, though small producers in the lower Rioja have survived by forming cooperatives. The proximity of the Basque market has led to the diversification of agricultural production; new crops include gherkins, carrots, leeks, and asparagus.

Before the Industrial Revolution a modest textile industry centred on the towns of Cameros, Ortigosa, Munilla, Enciso, and Cervera del Río Alhama. Food processing has been the leading industry since the mid-19th century, but factories (mostly family-owned) suffer from low capital investment and offer only seasonal employment. The food-processing industry has been stagnant since the Spanish Civil War (1936–39), while the proximity of the industrialized zones of Navarre, Álava, Zaragoza, and Burgos has discouraged the industrial diversification of La Rioja. Oil was discovered at Nájera in 1980. The leading commercial centres are Logroño, Haro, Santo Domingo de la Calzada, Arnedo, and Calahorra.

Various popular festivals held throughout the region celebrate viticulture. The Vendimia Riojana is held during the third week of September in the city of Logroño to celebrate the grape harvest; festivities include a parade of carts and bullfights. Area 1,944 square miles (5,034 square km). Pop. (1998 est.) 2,724,544.

La Rive, Auguste-Arthur de (b. Oct. 9, 1801, Geneva, Switz.—d. Nov. 27, 1873, Marseille, Fr.), Swiss physicist who was one of the founders of the electrochemical theory of batteries.

La Rive was elected to the chair of natural philosophy at the Academy of Geneva in 1823, and for the next seven years he conducted studies on the specific heat of various gases and the temperature of the Earth's crust. His experiments in 1836 on the voltaic cell, an early type of battery, furthered the development of electrical theory. He shared the view of the English physicist Michael Faraday that voltaic electricity was caused by chemical

La Rive, lithograph by François Artus
By courtesy of the Bibliotheque Nationale Suisse, Bern

action. In 1840 he invented the process for electroplating gold onto silver and brass, and in 1841 he received a prize of 3,000 francs from the French Academy of Sciences for this process. His *Traité d'électricité théorique et appliquée* (1854–58; *Treatise on Theoretical and Applied Electricity*), was translated into several languages. Later, while carrying out research on the discharge of electricity through gases, he discovered that ozone is created when electrical sparks pass through oxygen.

La Roche, Sophie von, *née* GUTERMANN (b. Dec. 6, 1731, Kaufbeuern, Bavaria [Germany]—d. Feb. 18, 1807, Offenbach, Hesse), German writer whose first and most important work, *Geschichte des Fräuleins von Sternheim* (1771; *History of Lady Sophia Sternheim*), was the first German novel written by a woman and is considered to be among the best works from the period in which English novels, particularly those of Samuel Richardson, had great influence on many German writers.

Sophie von La Roche, oil painting by G.M. Kraus, 1799
Archiv fur Kunst und Geschichte, Berlin

She was engaged to her close friend and cousin, the well-known writer Christoph Martin Wieland, but the betrothal was dissolved, and in 1754 she married G.M. Franck von La Roche. She was to become the grandmother of Bettina von Arnim and Clemens Brentano, both associated with the Romantic movement. From 1771 she maintained a literary salon in Ehrenbreitstein to which the young J.W. von Goethe belonged. In that year Wieland edited and published her first novel. Both its insistent didacticism and its partially epistolary form follow English models, but it also is related to the new phase of fiction introduced by Jean-Jacques Rousseau's novel *La Nouvelle Héloïse;* in La Roche's novel, passion begins to take a place beside rational morality and virtue. Fräulein von Sternheim's melancholy moods and the "confessional" aspect lent to the novel by its letter form won it fame. This, like all La Roche's works, is imbued with the rational spirit of the Enlightenment and shows her interest in economic and social problems, including women's education.

La Roche-sur-Yon, town, capital of Vendée *département,* Pays de la Loire *région,* western France, south of Nantes. The Vendée region had been pacified at the time of the French Revolution but still remained disaffected after the counterrevolutionary insurrection of 1793; Napoleon in 1804 established a military and administrative town in the centre of the *département.* It was built on the site of the decayed township of La Roche-sur-Yon, which had been burned down by the Republican troops. The new town was built according to plan, with wide rectangular streets, barracks, stables, and a vast parade ground. The town is an agricultural centre. Traditional local industries include tanning and the manufacture of nails and needles; more recent industry includes household appliances. Pop. (1990) 48,-518.

La Rochefoucauld FAMILY, one of France's noblest families, traceable in Angoumois to the year 1019. Ducal titles belonging to it are: duke (duc) de La Rochefoucauld (1622); duke de La Roche-Guyon (1679); duke d'Anville (1732); duke d'Estissac; duke de Liancourt (1747); duke de Doudeauville (1780); duke (duca) di Bisaccia (Neapolitan title; 1851); and duke (duque) de Estrées (Spanish title; 1892). Its two best-known members, François VI, Duke de La Rochefoucauld, and François-Alexandre-Frédéric, Duke de La Rochefoucauld-Liancourt, are the subjects of separate articles. The family's claim to princely privileges in France was urged without success in the mid-17th century, but the bearers of the Bisaccia title were granted princely rank in Bavaria in 1855.

La Rochefoucauld, François VI, Duke (duc) **de,** also called (until 1650) PRINCE DE MARCILLAC (b. Sept. 15, 1613, Paris, Fr.—d. March 16/17, 1680, Paris), French classical author who had been one of the most active rebels of the Fronde before he became the leading exponent of the *maxime,* a French literary form of epigram that expresses a harsh or paradoxical truth with brevity.

Heritage and political activities. La Rochefoucauld was the son of François, Count (comte) de La Rochefoucauld, and his wife, Gabrielle du Plessis-Liancourt. In 1628 he was married to Andrée de Vivonne, with whom he had four sons and three daughters. He served in the army against the Spaniards in Italy in 1629, in the Netherlands and Picardy in 1635–36, and again in Flanders in 1639. The public lives of both father and son were conditioned by the policies of Louis XIV's government, which by turns threatened and flattered the nobility. Though his father was created duke and made governor of Poitou, he was later deprived of that post when the loyalty of the family was called into question. The younger La Rochefoucauld was allowed by Cardinal Mazarin, the infant king's chief minister, to resume the governorship in 1646. The fact that his château at Verteuil was demolished by the crown, apparently without notice, in 1650 throws light on a main cause of the series of revolts between 1648 and 1653 known as the Fronde: the distrust and fear felt by the monarchy for the local independence of the nobility.

La Rochefoucauld was more vulnerable than most of his contemporaries, because throughout his life he seems to have been susceptible to feminine charm. In 1635 the Duchess (duchesse) de Chevreuse had lured him into intrigues against Cardinal de Richelieu, the chief minister of Louis XIII, an adventure that only procured for La Rochefoucauld a humiliating interview with Richelieu, eight days of imprisonment in the Bastille, and two years of exile at Verteuil. Later, his hatred for Mazarin and his devotion to Anne de Bourbon, Duchess de Longueville, sister of the Great Condé, who was the leader of the Fronde, led to an even more disastrous outcome. His own account of the weary alternation of plots and campaigns of the mutinous nobles throughout the revolts (1648–53) may be read in his *Mémoires.* His loyalty to the House of Condé did not increase his popularity with the crown and prevented him from pursuing any single policy for reform of royal or ministerial government. How far toward treason he allowed himself to be led, when the intentions of the reforming princes and nobility were superseded by personal ambitions, is shown by the draft of the so-called Treaty of Madrid of 1651, which laid down conditions of Spanish help to the French nobility. La Rochefoucauld not only

La Rochefoucauld, detail of a 17th-century portrait in the palace of Versailles
Lauros—Giraudon from Art Resource

signed the treaty but is thought by one scholar to have drafted it.

Two other features of his public career deserve mention, since they explain much of his writing—courage and litigation. The man who was to pen the aphorisms on courage and cowardice had certainly been in the forefront of battle. Within six years he was wounded in no fewer than three engagements. The injuries to his face and throat were such that he retired from the struggle, his health ruined and his peace of mind lost.

His financial difficulties were no doubt intensified by war, his lands were heavily mortgaged, and but for the astute help of his agent he might not have been able to keep his establishment in central Paris, as he did from 1660 onward. He was forced to pay not only for fine living but for endless litigation. There is evidence of no fewer than five lawsuits in the space of three years, chiefly against other noble families, over questions of precedence and court ceremonial.

Yet in 1655 his literary endeavours were still before him. Thanks to the lasting and intellectually stimulating friendships with Mme de Sablé, one of the most remarkable women of her age, and Mme de Lafayette, he seems to have avoided politics for a while and gradually won his way back into royal favour, a feat sealed by his promotion to the knightly order of the Saint-Esprit at the end of 1661. Reading and intellectual conversation occupied his time as well as that of other men and women of a circle who listened to private readings of Pierre Corneille's classical tragedies and Nicolas Boileau's didactic poem on the principles of poetic composition, *L'Art poétique.* The circle was enlivened by a new game that consisted of discussing epigrams on manners and behaviour, expressed in the briefest, most pungent manner possible. The care with which La Rochefoucauld kept notes and versions of his thoughts on the moral and intellectual subjects of the game is clear from the surviving manuscripts. When the clandestine publication of one of them in Holland forced him to publish under his own name, it was clear that he had satisfied public taste: five editions of the *Maximes,* each of them revised and enlarged, were to appear within his lifetime.

The Maximes. The first edition of the *Maximes,* published in 1665, was called *Réflexions ou sentences et maximes morales* and did not contain epigrams exclusively; the most eloquent single item, which appeared only in the first edition and was thereafter removed by the author, is a three-page poetic description of self-interest, a quality he found in all forms of life and in all actions. The manuscripts also contain epigrams embedded in longer reflections; in some cases the various versions show the steps by which a series of connected sentences was filed down to the point of ultimate brevity. Beneath the general single statement, however, can be found a personal reaction to the Fronde, or to politics, often violent in its expression. For example:

> *Les crimes deviennent innocents, même glorieux, par leur nombre et par leurs qualités; de là vient que les voleries publiques sont des habiletés, et que prendre des provinces injustement s'appelle faire des conquêtes. Le crime a ses héros, ainsi que la vertu.* (Crimes are made innocent, even virtuous, by their number and nature; hence public robbery becomes a skillful achievement and wrongful seizure of a province is called conquest. Crime has its heroes no less than virtue has.)

It may have been hostile reception or the fear of revealing a political attitude that made him abandon this kind of epigram except for the almost unrecognizable No. 185: "*Il y a des héros en mal comme en bien*" ("Evil as well as good has its heroes"). Modern readers forget that La Rochefoucauld's contemporaries would read recent history into statements that appear cryptic and opaque to posterity.

The Fronde was to La Rochefoucauld one of those moments of history that seemed to reveal men's motives at their worst. His exposure of the self-seeking that lay beneath conventional homage to morality has earned for him the reputation of a cynic, but his keener contemporaries are no less severe. The pungency and absence of explanation make his epigrams seem more scornful than similar statements embedded in memoirs. But La Rochefoucauld was concerned with conveying something more than scorn, and beneath his professions of idealism he pinpointed a restless and unquenchable thirst for self-preservation. Virtue in the pure state was something he did not find:

> *Les vertus se perdent dans l'intérêt comme les fleuves se perdent dans la mer.* (Virtues are lost in self-interest as rivers are lost in the sea.)

This image of the sea recurred:

> *Voilà la peinture de l'amour-propre, dont toute la vie n'est qu'une grande et longue agitation; la mer en est une image sensible; et l'amour-propre trouve dans le flux et reflux de ses vagues continuelles une fidèle expression de la succession turbulente de ses pensées et de ses éternels mouvements.* (Such is the picture of self-love, of which all life is one continuous and immense ferment. The sea is its visible counterpart and self-love finds in the ebb and flow of the sea's endless waves a true likeness of the chaotic sequence of its thoughts and of its everlasting motion.)

La Rochefoucauld has been called an Epicurean but his imaginative insights attached him to no doctrine. Like Michel de Montaigne and Blaise Pascal, he was aware of the mystery around man that dwarfs his efforts and mocks his knowledge, of the many things about man of which he knows nothing, of the gap between thinking and being, between what man is and what man does: "*La nature fait le mérite et la fortune le met en oeuvre*" ("Nature gives us our good qualities and chance sets them to work"). Some epigrams show a respect for the power of indolence, and others reveal an almost Nietzschean respect for strength. All these insights seem common to the French classical school of which he is so brilliant a member—though as an aristocrat he disdained being called a writer. These insights also accounted for his fame and influence on his disciples: in England Lord Chesterfield, the orator and man of letters, and the novelist and poet Thomas Hardy; in Germany the philosophers Friedrich Nietzsche and Georg Christoph Lichtenberg; in France the writers and critics Stendhal, Charles-Augustin Sainte-Beuve, and André Gide.

Yet his chief glory perhaps is not as thinker but as artist. In the variety and subtlety of his arrangement of words he made the *maxime* into a jewel. It is not always the truth of the maxim that is so striking, but its exaggeration which can surprise one into a new aspect of the truth. He describes and defines—he has no time for more—but of the single metallic image he makes amazing use. He handles paradox to such effect that a final word can reverse the rest:

On ne donne rien si libéralement que ses conseils (We give nothing so generously as . . . advice). *C'est une grande folie de vouloir être sage tout seul* (It is great folly to seek to be wise . . . on one's own).

La Rochefoucauld authorized five editions of the *Maximes* from 1665 to 1678. Two years after the last publication, he died in Paris.

Though he did a considerable amount of writing over the years La Rochefoucauld actually published only two works, the *Mémoires* and the *Maximes.* In addition, about 150 letters have been collected and 19 shorter pieces now known as *Réflexions diverses.* These, with the treaties and conventions that he may have drawn up personally, constitute his entire work and of these only the *Maximes* stand out as a work of genius. Like his younger contemporary, Jean de La Bruyère, La Rochefoucauld was a man of one book. (W.G.Mo.)

BIBLIOGRAPHY. W.G. Moore, *La Rochefoucauld: His Mind and Art* (1969); Philip E. Lewis, *La Rochefoucauld: The Art of Abstraction* (1977); and Vivien Thweatt, *La Rochefoucauld and the Seventeenth-Century Concept of the Self* (1980).

La Rochefoucauld-Liancourt, François-Alexandre-Frédéric, Duke (duc) **de** (b. Jan. 11, 1747, La Roche-Guyon, Fr.—d. March 27, 1827, Paris), educator and social reformer who founded the École Nationale Supérieure des Arts et Métiers at Châlons and whose model farm at Liancourt contributed to the development of French agriculture.

La Rochefoucauld-Liancourt, lithograph by François-Séraphin Delpech, after a portrait by Jean-Baptiste Belliard

By courtesy of the Bibliotheque Nationale, Paris

La Rochefoucauld-Liancourt, the son of François-Armand de La Rochefoucauld, Duke d'Estissac, served in the army and, after going to England in 1769 to study farming methods, established his model farm, where he raised English and Swiss breeds of cattle and experimented with soils and grasses. He also founded an arts and crafts school for the children of poor soldiers, which in 1788 became the École des Enfants de la Patrie under the patronage of King Louis XVI. A representative of the nobility of Clermont and Beauvais, he went to the States General of 1789, became president of the Assembly on July 18, and defended the interests of the royal party. When the Bastille prison fell on July 14 and the king exclaimed, "Why, this is a revolt!" he replied, "No, sire, it is a revolution." He served as president of the medical committee of the National Assembly and established cotton mills at Liancourt in 1790.

Appointed to the command of a military division in Normandy, La Rochefoucauld-Liancourt offered Louis XVI a refuge in Rouen and, failing in that effort, donated a large sum of money for his support. After the capture of the king's palace in Paris in August 1792, he fled to England and then to the United States, not returning to France until 1799. During the Napoleonic era, he served on state commissions dealing with health, manufacturing, and prisons; he continued to sponsor progressive reforms, including the introduction of smallpox vaccination. He was a member of the Société de la Morale Chrétienne and a leader in the movement to abolish slavery. From 1800 to 1823 he served as government inspector of his school of arts and crafts, which had been moved to Châlons. In 1814 he was made a peer of France by Louis XVIII, and, on his return to Liancourt in 1825, he established one of the first savings banks.

La Rochefoucauld-Liancourt's writings, primarily on economic questions, include books on the English system of taxation, relief of the poor, and education, as well as on his experiences in the United States.

La Rochelle, town, Atlantic seaport and capital of Charente-Maritime *département,* Poitou-Charentes *région,* western France, situated on an inlet opposite Ré Island. The town, which has straight, regular streets, a large park, and shady promenades on the sites of its old fortifications, grew considerably after 1946, especially to the west. The old commercial harbour, too shallow for large ships, has been modernized and is now one of the foremost French fishing ports. It is directly connected to a renovated fish market. In 1890 a commercial port, accessible to larger vessels, was opened at La Pallice, 3.5 miles (5.5 km) west of the town; it has since been enlarged several times. Imports include fuel oil, nitrates, and phosphates. The two ports have attracted both industry and trade to the town, which has shipbuilding yards, aircraft works, railroad yards, automobile-assembly plants, and petroleum refineries. Other industries include food processing (fish canneries), sawmills, light metalworking, and chemical products.

The entrance to the old port is defended by two massive 14th-century towers. The pentagonal Saint-Nicolas Tower, the larger of the two, is an imposing fortress with crenellated walls and a keep. Opposite it stands the Tower de la Chaîne, so named because at night a big chain was strung between it and Saint-Nicolas

Harbour with Saint-Nicolas (left) and La Chaîne (right) towers, La Rochelle, Fr.

Art Resource

Tower to close the port. In the 15th century a third tower, the Tower de la Lanterne, a round base surmounted by an octagonal spire, was built as a lighthouse. Other buildings of interest are the Gothic Porte de la Grosse-Horloge, the Renaissance Hôtel de Ville, and the 18th-century Hôtel de la Bourse. The rue des Merciers is typical of the old streets. Many of the 16th- and 17th-century houses, built over arcades, are decorated with gargoyles and strange allegorical figures.

La Rochelle developed in the 12th century after the neighbouring town of Châtelaillon was destroyed by the dukes of Aquitaine. During the Hundred Years' War (1337–1453) it changed hands a number of times but was finally captured by the French in 1372. It became largely Protestant at the time of the Reformation and after the Massacre of St. Bartholomew's Day (1572), in which many French Protestants (Huguenots) were killed; many of the survivors took refuge there. Under Louis XIII (reigned 1610–43), La Rochelle sided with the English, who had invaded Ré Island. Richelieu, the king's minister, besieged the town and built a vast sea wall to prevent English ships from relieving their allies. After 15 months' siege, the town capitulated, three-fourths of its citizens having starved to death. It slowly recovered its former prosperity but declined once more after 1685, when the revocation of the Edict of Nantes, depriving French Protestants of religious and civil liberty, led to massive emigration. In the 18th century the loss of Canada by the French further reduced La Rochelle's trade. In World War II, it was the location of a German submarine base and suffered from Allied bombing. Pop. (1990) 73,744.

La Rocque, Jean-François de: *see* Roberval, Jean-François de La Rocque.

La Romana, city and port, southeastern Dominican Republic, on the Caribbean Sea opposite Catalina Island. Founded near the end of the 19th century, La Romana grew rapidly after the establishment of a large sugar mill in 1911. In addition to sugarcane, the surrounding region produces coffee, tobacco, beeswax, cattle, and hides. The city has food-processing and soap, shoe, and furniture plants. The port handles mainly sugar, and there is considerable fishing. New residential luxury resorts also have been built. La Romana is accessible by secondary highway from San Pedro de Macorís and El Seibo. Pop. (1986 est.) 101,350.

La Rue, Pierre de, German PETER VAN STRATEN, also called PIERCHON, PERCHON, or PIERSON DE LA RUE (b. *c.* 1460, Tournai, Flanders [now in Belgium]—d. Nov. 20, 1518, Courtrai [now Kortrijk, Belg.]), composer in the Flemish, or Netherlandish, style that dominated Renaissance music, known for his religious music.

La Rue worked in Brussels from 1492, where he served Philip the Handsome and from 1508, Margaret of Austria, regent of the Netherlands; with them he visited France and Spain. In 1516 he became canon at Courtrai. La Rue left more than 30 masses and about 45 motets, distinguished by their densely compressed style and skillful structure. His 32 surviving secular pieces include vocal part-songs and instrumentally accompanied solos.

La Sale, Antoine de, La Sale also spelled LA SALLE (b. *c.* 1386, near Arles, Provence [France]—d. *c.* 1460), French writer chiefly remembered for his *Petit Jehan de Saintré,* a romance marked by a great gift for the observation of court manners and a keen sense of comic situation and dialogue.

From 1400 to 1448 La Sale served the dukes of Anjou, Louis II, Louis III, and René, as squire, soldier, administrator and, ultimately, governor of René's son and heir, Jean (John of Calabria). The Angevin claims to the kingdom of Sicily brought him repeatedly into Italy, and his didactic works contain several accounts of his unusual and picturesque experiences there. He was in Italy for Louis II's 1409–11 campaign against Ladislas of Durazzo. In 1415 he took part in a Portuguese expedition against the Moors of Ceuta. La Sale visited the Sibyl's mountain near Norcia, seat of the legend later transported to Germany and attached to the name of Tannhäuser; he relates the legend in great detail in his *Paradis de la reine Sibylle.*

He became governor of the sons of Louis of Luxembourg, count of St. Pol in 1448. There he wrote *La Salle* (1451), a collection of moral anecdotes; *Le Petit Jehan de Saintré* (1456; *Little John of Saintré,* 1931); *Du Réconfort à Madame de Fresne* (1457; "For the Consolation of Madame de Fresne," on the death of her young son); and a *Lettre sur les tournois* (1459; "A Letter on the Tournaments").

Jehan de Saintré is a pseudobiographical romance of a knight at the court of Anjou who, in real life, achieved great fame in the mid-14th century. Modern criticism ascribes an important place to *Saintré* in the development of French prose fiction and also extols the grace, wit, sensibility, and realism of the writer.

La Salle, city, Montréal region, southern Quebec province, Canada, on the south shore of Île de Montréal (Montreal Island), at the head of the Lachine Rapids of the St. Lawrence River. Settlement of the site began in 1668, when Robert Cavelier, Sieur de La Salle, established a fortified townsite first known as Saint-Sulpice and later as La Petite Chine, or Lachine. Surviving an Iroquois Indian massacre in 1689, the community grew as a trade junction and western terminus of the Lachine Canal, 8 miles (13 km) long, bypassing the Lachine Rapids, built in the 1820s. In the 1850s the Montreal Aqueduct was built through the town from Lac Saint-Louis to serve the growing metropolis to the north. The origin of the name La Salle dates to 1912, when a group of townspeople moved to the modern site of Lachine, taking that name with them and allowing the old town of Lachine to become incorporated as a city under the name of its founder, La Salle. Following World War II, La Salle was engulfed by the spread of Montreal (in 1959 it joined the Montreal Metropolitan Corporation) and became primarily a residential suburb. Among the products manufactured there are alcoholic beverages, food products, roofing materials, plastics, chemicals, fabricated steel, pharmaceuticals, boxes, and heating and cooling equipment. Fleming Mill, a four-story conical windmill built in 1816, is a city landmark. La Salle is linked to Caughnawaga, on the south bank of the St. Lawrence, by the Honoré-Mercier Bridge. Inc. 1912. Pop. (1991) 73,804.

La Salle, city, La Salle county, north-central Illinois, U.S., on the Illinois River. With Peru (west) and Oglesby (south), it forms a tricity unit. Settled in 1830 and named for the explorer Robert Cavelier, Sieur de La Salle, its growth was stimulated by the Illinois and Michigan Canal (1848) and the arrival in the 1850s of the Illinois Central and Rock Island railroads. Its economy, based mainly on coal mining until the 1940s, now depends on agriculture, light manufacturing, and chemical, zinc, and metal works. Illinois Valley Community College (formerly La Salle–Peru–Oglesby Junior College; 1924) is in Oglesby. Starved Rock and Matthiessen state parks are nearby. Inc. 1852. Pop. (1990) 9,717.

La Salle, Antoine de: *see* La Sale, Antoine de.

La Salle, Saint Jean-Baptiste de (b. April 30, 1651, Reims, France—d. April 7, 1719, Rouen; canonized 1900; feast day April 7), French philanthropist, educator, and founder of the Brothers of the Christian Schools, the first Roman Catholic congregation of male nonclerics devoted solely to schools, learning, and teaching.

Of noble birth, La Salle was ordained priest in 1678 and devoted himself to education of the poor. He helped to establish charity schools in Reims and subsequently formed his teachers into a religious order (1680). He also set up boarding schools for middle-class boys, reformatories, and—for the first time—training colleges for secular teachers. In 1725 Pope Benedict XIII raised La Salle's congregation to the status of a papal institute. Among his writings are *Les Devoirs d'un chrétien* (1703; "The Duties of a Christian"), two series of *Méditations* (1730–31); and *La Conduite des écoles chrétiennes* (1720; "The Conduct of Christian Schools").

La Salle, René-Robert Cavelier, Sieur (Lord) de (b. Nov. 22, 1643, Rouen, France—d. March 19, 1687, near Brazos River [now in Texas, U.S.]), French explorer in North America, who led an expedition down the Illinois and Mississippi rivers and claimed all the region watered by the Mississippi and its tributaries for Louis XIV of France, naming the region "Louisiana." A few years later, in a luckless expedition seeking the mouth of the Mississippi, he was murdered by his men.

René-Robert Cavelier, Sieur de La Salle, engraving
By courtesy of the Bibliotheque Municipale, Rouen, France; photograph, Ellebe

Early life. La Salle was educated at a Jesuit college. He first studied for the priesthood, but at the age of 22 he found himself more attracted to adventure and exploration and in 1666 set out for Canada to seek his fortune. With a grant of land at the western end of Île de Montréal, La Salle acquired at one stroke the status of a seigneur (*i.e.,* landholder) and the opportunities of a frontiersman.

The young landlord farmed his land near the Lachine Rapids and, at the same time, set up a fur-trading outpost. Through contact with the Indians who came to sell their pelts, he learned various Indian dialects and heard stories of the lands beyond the settlements. He soon became obsessed with the idea of finding a way to the Orient through the rivers and lakes of the Western frontier.

If experience modified the visions of the dreamer, it enhanced the knowledge and skill of the pathfinder and trader. Having sold his land, La Salle set out in 1669 to explore the Ohio region. His discovery of the Ohio River, however, is not accepted by modern historians.

La Salle found a kindred spirit in the Count de Frontenac, the "Fighting Governor" of New France (the French possessions in Canada) from 1672 to 1682. Together, they pursued a policy of extending French military power by establishing a fort on Lake Ontario (Fort-Frontenac), holding the Iroquois in check, and intercepting the fur trade between the Upper Lakes and the Dutch and English coastal settlements.

Their plans were strongly opposed by the Montreal merchants, who feared the loss of their trade, and by the missionaries (especially the Jesuits), who were afraid of losing their influence over the Indians of the interior. Nevertheless, Fort-Frontenac was built where Kingston now stands, and La Salle was installed there as seigneur in 1675 after a visit to the French court, as Frontenac's representative. The governor had recommended him as "a man of intelligence and ability, more capable than anybody else I know here to accomplish every kind of enterprise and discovery . . . ." Louis XIV was sufficiently impressed by him to grant him a title of nobility.

Attempts to expand New France. At Fort-Frontenac, La Salle had control of a large share of the fur trade, and his affairs prospered. But his restless ambition drove him to seek greater ends. On another visit to France in 1677 he obtained from the king authority to explore "the western parts of New France" and permission to build as many forts as he wished, as well as to hold a valuable monopoly of the trade in buffalo hides.

Since the project had to be carried out at his own expense, however, he borrowed large sums in both Paris and Montreal, and he began to be enmeshed in a tangle of debts that was to blight all of his later enterprises. La Salle's proposals also roused still further the enmity of the Jesuits, who resolutely opposed all his schemes.

When he returned to Canada in 1678, La Salle was accompanied by an Italian soldier of fortune, Henri de Tonty, who became his most loyal friend and ally. Early in the following year, he built the "Griffon," the first commercial sailing vessel on Lake Erie, which he hoped would pay for an expedition into the interior as far as the Mississippi. From the Seneca Indians above the Niagara Falls he learned how to make long journeys overland, on foot in any season, subsisting on game and a small bag of corn. His trek from Niagara to Fort-Frontenac in the dead of winter won the admiration of a normally critical member of his expeditions, the friar Louis Hennepin.

La Salle's great scheme of carrying cargo in sailing vessels like the "Griffon" on the lakes and down the Mississippi was frustrated by the wreck of that ship and by the destruction and desertion of Fort-Crèvecoeur on the Illinois River, where a second ship was being built in 1680. Proud and unyielding by nature, La Salle tried to bend others to his will and often demanded too much of them, though he was no less hard on himself. After several disappointments, he at last reached the junction of the Illinois with the Mississippi and saw for the first time the river he had dreamed of for so long. But he had to deny himself the chance to explore it. Hearing that Tonty and his party were in danger, he turned back to aid them.

After many vicissitudes, La Salle and Tonty succeeded in canoeing down the Mississippi and reached the Gulf of Mexico. There, on April 9, 1682, the explorer proclaimed the whole Mississippi Basin for France and named it Louisiana. In name, at least, he acquired for France the most fertile half of the North American continent.

The following year La Salle built Fort-Saint-Louis at Starved Rock on the Illinois River (now a state park), and here he organized a colony of several thousand Indians. To maintain the new colony he sought help from Quebec; but Frontenac had been replaced by a governor hostile to La Salle's interests, and La Salle received orders to surrender Fort-Saint-Louis. He refused and left North America to appeal directly to the king. Welcomed in Paris, La Salle was given an audience with Louis XIV, who favoured him by commanding the governor to make full restitution of La Salle's property.

Last expedition. The last phase of his extraordinary career centred on his proposal to fortify the mouth of the Mississippi and to invade and conquer part of the Spanish province of Mexico. He planned to accomplish all this with some 200 Frenchmen, aided by buccaneers and an army of 15,000 Indians—a venture that caused his detractors to question his sanity. But the king saw a chance to harass the Spaniards, with whom he was at war, and approved the project, giving La Salle men, ships, and money.

The expedition was doomed from the start. It had hardly left France when quarrels arose between La Salle and the naval commander. Vessels were lost by piracy and shipwreck, while sickness took a heavy toll of the colonists. Finally, a gross miscalculation brought the ships to Matagorda Bay in Texas, 500 miles west of their intended landfall. After several fruitless journeys in search of his lost Mississippi, La Salle met his death at the hands of mutineers near the Brazos River. His vision of a French empire died with him.

La Salle provoked much controversy both in his own lifetime and later. Those who knew him best praised his ability unsparingly. He was considered "one of the greatest men of the age" by Tonty, who, like Frontenac, was among the very few who were able to understand the proud spirit of the dour Norman. Henri Joutel, who served under La Salle through the tragic days of the Texas colony until his death, wrote both of his fine qualities and of his insufferable arrogance toward his subordinates. In Joutel's view, this arrogance was the true cause of La Salle's death.

Undoubtedly, La Salle was hampered by faults of character and lacked the qualities of leadership. On the other hand, he possessed prodigious vision, tenacity, and courage. His claim of Louisiana for France, though but a vain boast at the time, pointed the way to the French colonial empire that was eventually built by other men. (D.C.G.S.)

BIBLIOGRAPHY. Louise P. Kellogg, *Early Narratives of the North-West, 1634–1699* (1917), contains translations of original narratives of La Salle's companions; Francis Parkman, *The Discovery of the Great West,* 5th ed. (1871, reissued 1956), embodies material from La Salle's own letters and other contemporary documents; John B. Brebner, *The Explorers of North America, 1492–1806* (1964), summarizes impartially various estimates of La Salle's character and achievements.

La Scala, in full TEATRO ALLA SCALA (Italian: Theatre at the Stairway), Milan, one of the principal opera houses of the world and the leading Italian house. Built in 1776 by the Empress Maria Theresa of Austria (which country then ruled Milan), it replaced an earlier theatre that had burned. In 1872 it became the property of the city of Milan. The house was closed during World War I. In 1920 the conductor Arturo Toscanini led a council that raised money to reopen it, organizing it as an autonomous corporation. The theatre, bombed during World War II, reopened in 1946, partly through funds raised by benefit concerts given by Toscanini.

La Scala's repertory is more varied than that of the other four or five leading opera houses. It tends to include a large number of unfamiliar works balanced by a limited number of popular favourites. Conductors are given control of casting and rehearsals. The composer Giuseppe Verdi was closely associated with the house during the 19th century. Toscanini's tenure as artistic director marked one of the finest periods in the theatre's existence.

Associated with the main theatre are a smaller theatre, La Piccola Scala; a ballet company and ballet school; and a singing school. The expenses of La Scala are met by a combination of ticket sales, a municipal tax, and an Italian governmental subsidy.

La Serena, capital of Coquimbo region, northern Chile, lying on a marine terrace overlooking Bahía (bay) de Coquimbo, just south of the Río Elqui and east of Coquimbo city. Founded *c.* 1543 on the river's northern bank, it was named after the Spanish birthplace of the conquistador Pedro de Valdivia. Razed by Diaguita Indians in 1549 and rebuilt on the present site the following year, La Serena received city status in 1552. It has survived pirate raids and earthquake damage. The seat of an archbishopric, the city has a cathedral, many churches, and several convents. It is the centre of an agricultural and dairy region and is also a popular tourist resort. Direct rail, bus, and air connections exist to Santiago. The nearby town of Vicuña, 30 mi (50 km) east, was the birthplace of the Chilean poet Gabriela Mistral, winner of the Nobel Prize for Literature in 1945. Pop. (1982 prelim.) 87,456.

La Seyne-sur-Mer (France): *see* Seyne-sur-Mer, La.

La Skhira (Tunisia): *see* Sukhayrah, as-.

La Soufriere: *see* Soufriere.

La Spezia, formerly SPEZIA, capital of La Spezia province, Liguria region, northern Italy. The city, a major naval base, is located at the head of the Golfo della Spezia, southeast of Genoa. The site was inhabited in Roman times, but little is known of its history before 1276, when it was sold to Genoa by the Fieschi family. It became a maritime prefecture in the French Empire and then part of the Duchy of Genoa in the Kingdom of Sardinia. After the transfer of the military fleet from Genoa in 1857, it became a naval headquarters, and in 1923 it became the provincial capital. It was severely damaged by bombing in World War II. Notable landmarks include the medieval Castel S. Giorgio, the 15th-century cathedral (rebuilt since 1945), and the naval arsenal (1861–69, rebuilt since 1945), with the adjacent naval museum. The archaeological museum has a collection of menhirs (prehistoric monoliths) cut in the form of human figures and of Roman artifacts from the nearby ancient city of Luni.

La Spezia's industries include shipbuilding, iron foundries, oil refineries, and mechanical engineering. Coal and oil are imported, and it is also a terminus for natural gas shipments from Libya. There is some tourism. Pop. (1983 est.) mun., 113,486.

La Taille, Jean de (b. *c.* 1540, Bondaroy, Fr.—d. *c.* 1607, Bondaroy), poet and dramatist who, through his plays and his influential treatise on the art of tragedy, helped to effect the transition from native French drama to classical tragedy.

While studying in Paris La Taille came under the influence, shown in his minor poems, of Pierre de Ronsard and Joachim du Bellay. His chief poems, prosaic but forceful, are a satire, *Le Courtisan retiré* ("The Retired Courtier"), and *Le Prince nécessaire*, a portrait of an ideal monarch.

A collection of his works appeared in 1572, including his tragedy *Saül le Furieux* (1562) and *De l'art de la tragédie*, the most important piece of French dramatic criticism of its time. La Taille wrote for the limited audience of a lettered aristocracy, depreciated the native drama, and insisted on the Senecan model. In his preface to the collecton of works he enunciates the unities of place, time, and action; he maintains that each act should have a unity of its own and that the scenes composing it should be continuous, and he objects to death on the stage as unconvincing and requires as a tragic subject an incident that is moving and developed by skillful intrigue. Although in *Saül* he did not completely carry out his program, the action is exciting and the principal character ably developed.

A second collection (1573) included a lesser tragedy, *La Famine, ou les Gabéonites*, neatly plagiarizing Seneca's *Troades*, and two comedies, *Le Négromant*, translated freely from Ariosto, and *Les Corrivaux* ("The Rivals"), remarkable for its colloquial prose dialogue. La Taille continued to write minor prose works, but the attribution to him of the political pamphlet *Histoire abrégée des singeries de la Ligue* ("A Short History of the Antics of the League"), often published with the *Satire Ménippée,* is questionable.

La Tène (French: The Shallows), archaeological site at the eastern end of Lake Neuchâtel, Switz., the name of which has been extended to distinguish the Late Iron Age culture of European Celts. La Tène culture originated in the mid-5th century BC, when the Celts came into contact with Greek and Etruscan influences from south of the Alps. This culture passed through several phases and regional variations during the next four centuries as the Celts expanded throughout most of northern Europe and the British Isles, but it came to an end in the mid-1st century BC, when most

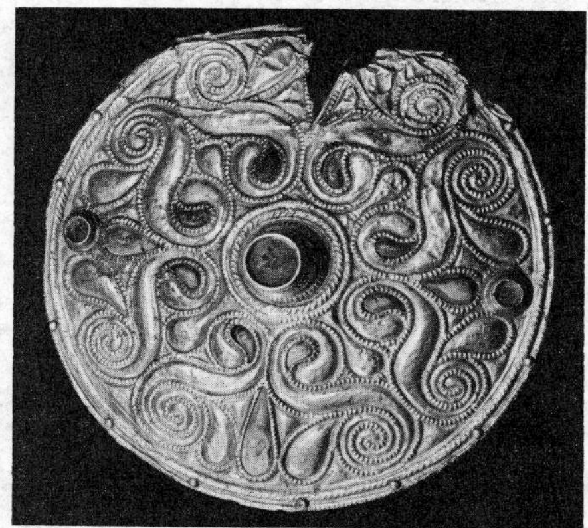

Gold disk found at Auvers, La Tène culture, 5th century BC

By courtesy of the Bibliotheque Nationale, Paris

of the Celts lost their independence to Rome.

During the first period, La Tène A (450–400/390 BC), Celtic tradition first encountered Greco-Etruscan imports and ideas. Though a short period, it seems to have been long enough to create the typical La Tène style, characterized by S-shapes, spirals, and round patterns symmetrically applied to every ornament.

In the La Tène B period (400/390–*c.* 300 BC), the unity of La Tène A was dissolved by the Celtic migrations. Throughout the region, however, certain features remained popular, such as long iron swords, lanceheads, heavy knives, and burial by flat inhumations in coffins or by covering the body with stone heaps.

In La Tène C (*c.* 300–*c.* 100 BC), the different branches of phase B continued, but there was a cultural intermixing between the aboriginals and the Celtic newcomers. Among the chief metal types were iron swords with decorated scabbards and heart shapes, warriors' iron chains as sword belts, broad-bladed heavy spearheads, wooden shields with iron bosses and supporters, and iron scissors and torques.

During the La Tène D period (*c.* 100–50/15 BC), Celtic power was ended by the perpetual pressure of German invaders from the north and by the Roman Empire from the south. Settlements of this period have revealed typical peasant's implements: iron sickles, scythes, axes, saws, ploughshares, and hammers, the majority resulting from contact with Roman civilization. Silver coinage, based on Greek and Roman prototypes, is more abundant than in La Tène C, when it began, and has been a valuable source for the knowledge of Celtic personal names.

La Tour, Charles (Turgis de Saint-Étienne de) (b. 1596, probably in Paris—d. 1666, Ft. St. John, Nova Scotia), French colonist and fur trader who served as governor of Acadia (Nova Scotia) under the French and the English.

La Tour went to Acadia with his father *c.* 1600. When the English destroyed the French settlements there in 1613–14, he went with Charles de Biencourt, commander of the devastated Port Royal (now Annapolis Royal, Nova Scotia), to live with the Indians. In 1623

Biencourt gave up his rights and possessions to La Tour.

Meanwhile La Tour's father had made an alliance with Sir William Alexander (later Earl of Stirling), the Scottish colonizer of Nova Scotia (the English name for Acadia), and La Tour was made an English baronet of the region, even though he refused to transfer his allegiance from France. He built Fort La Tour at the mouth of the St. John River and was made lieutenant governor of most of Acadia in 1631. La Tour disagreed violently with the governor, Charles de Menou, sieur d'Aulnay Charnisay, who represented the king of France, and violence resulted. La Tour escaped to Quebec, where he remained until d'Aulnay's death in 1650; he married d'Aulnay's widow in 1653. He returned to France and persuaded the king to make him governor of Acadia. When the English took over the territory in 1654, La Tour kept his post and, after visiting England, received a land grant.

La Tour, Georges de (b. March 19, 1593, Vic-sur-Seille, Lorraine, Fr.—d. Jan. 30, 1652, Lunéville), painter, mostly of candlelit subjects, who was well known in his own time but then forgotten until well into the 20th century, when the identification of many formerly misattributed works established his modern reputation as a giant of French painting.

La Tour became a master painter and eventually settled in Lunéville. King Louis XIII, Henry II of Lorraine, and the Duke de La Ferté were among the collectors of his work. Although the chronology of La Tour's output is uncertain, it is clear that he initially painted in a realistic manner and was influenced by the dramatic chiaroscuro of Caravaggio or his followers.

The paintings of La Tour's maturity, however, are marked by a startling geometric simplification of the human form and by the depiction of interior scenes lit only by the glare of candles or torches. His religious paintings done in this manner have a monumental simplicity and a stillness that expresses both contemplative quiet and wonder.

"St. Joseph the Carpenter," oil on canvas by Georges de La Tour, *c.* 1645; in the Louvre, Paris
Giraudon—Art Resource/EB Inc.

The body of his work was conclusively identified by the German art historian Hermann Voss and by other scholars after 1915. La Tour's work also exhibits a high degree of originality in colour and composition; the characteristic simplification of forms gives many of his pictures a deceptively modern appearance. Among La Tour's most impressive candlelit scenes are "The Newborn," "St. Joseph the Carpenter," and "The Lamentation over St. Sebastian." "The Hurdy-gurdy Player" and "The Sharper" are among his less numerous daylight compositions.

La Tour, Maurice-Quentin de, also spelled MAURICE QUENTIN DE LATOUR (b. Sept. 5, 1704, Saint-Quentin, Fr.—d. Feb. 17, 1788, Saint-Quentin), pastelist whose animated and sharply characterized portraits made him one of the most successful and imitated portraitists of 18th-century France.

Early in his youth La Tour went to Paris, where he entered the studio of the Flemish painter Jacques Spoede. He then went to Reims, Cambrai (1724), and England (*c.* 1725), returning to Paris to resume his studies in about 1727.

Maurice-Quentin de La Tour, self-portrait, pastel, *c.* 1760; in the Musée de Picardie, Amiens, Fr.
Telarci—Giraudon from Art Resource/EB Inc.

In 1737 La Tour exhibited the first of a splendid series of 150 portraits that formed one of the glories of the Salon for the next 37 years. He was able to endow his sitters with a distinctive air of charm and intelligence, and he excelled at capturing the delicate play of facial features. Among his subjects were the writers Jean-Jacques Rousseau and Voltaire, as well as Louis XV and his mistress, Mme. de Pompadour, of whom he did a life-size portrait (1756). In 1746 he was received into the Academy and in 1751 was promoted to councillor. La Tour was made portraitist to the king in 1750, a position he held until 1773, when he suffered a nervous breakdown. La Tour retired at the age of 80 to Saint-Quentin.

La Trémoille FAMILY, noble family that contributed numerous generals to France. The family's name was taken from a village in Poitou (modern La Trimouille). A Pierre de La Trémoille is recorded as early as the 11th century, but the family's ascendance dates from the 15th century. Early family members fought in several crusades. Gui (d. 1397) went with John the Fearless, duke of Burgundy, on the crusade to Hungary, was taken prisoner by the Turks at the battle of Nicopolis, and died in Rhodes on his way back to France. His son Georges (*c.* 1382–1446) first brought the family to prominence, serving as an adviser to Charles VII. He obstructed Joan of Arc's efforts to defeat the English and their Burgundian allies in the campaigns of 1429–30.

Georges de La Trémoille's son Louis I (*c.* 1431–83) brought the so-called principality of Talmont and the viscounty of Thouars into the family by marriage. His son Louis II (1460–1525) won a reputation for outstanding chivalry. Nicknamed *le chevalier sans reproche* ("the blameless knight"), he defeated rebellious French princes during Charles VIII's minority at Saint-Aubin-du-Cormier (1488) and served gloriously in the Italian campaigns until his death in the Battle of Pavia.

Because Louis's son had been killed in the Italian campaign at Marignan in 1515, his grandson François (1502–41) succeeded to the family estates. Through his marriage to Anne de Laval, granddaughter of Frederick of Aragon, deposed king of Naples, the family derived its pretension to the kingdom of Naples and the claim to recognition at the French court as foreign princes. François's children were the founders of three branches of the house. Louis III (1522–77), founder of the house of Thouars, was made Duke de Thouars in 1563; his descendants were Dukes de Thouars and de La Trémoille as well as Princes de Talmont and de Tarentes. Another son, Georges, established the house of the Marquis de Rohan and the Counts d'Olonne, while Claude (d. 1566) founded the branch of Noirmoutier.

Louis III's son Claude (1566–1604) at first fought in the campaigns against the Huguenots under Henry III but then changed sides, joining the Protestant king of Navarre, Henry III, in 1586. After Henry de Navarre became King Henry IV, of France, Claude was made a peer (1595).

Descendants of this line continued to distinguish themselves at war. Claude's grandson Henri-Charles (1620–72) fought against the crown in the Fronde (1648–53), a revolt that began in the Parlement of Paris against royal absolutism. Charles-Bretagne-Marie-Joseph (1764–1839) and his brother Antoine-Philippe (1765–94) were staunch royalists during the French Revolution. Both fought in the counter-revolutionary insurrection in the Vendée (1793–96).

La Trémoille, Georges de (b. *c.* 1382—d. May 6, 1446), powerful lord who exercised considerable influence over Charles VII of France.

At first allied with the duke of Burgundy in the power struggle that continued for many years during Charles VI's madness, La Trémoille switched his loyalty when the rival faction, the Armagnacs, came into power in 1413. He was a member of the pleasure-loving group that surrounded the dauphin, Louis (d. 1415), and then the queen, Isabella of Bavaria. In 1416 he married Jeanne, the widow of Jean de France, Duke de Berry, who died about 1423.

In 1427, with the help of the Constable de Richemont, La Trémoille had King Charles VII's favourite, Pierre de Giac, kidnapped and drowned; he then married Giac's widow, Catherine (who was probably an accessory), and took Giac's place on the king's council. Named grand chamberlain of France, he soon forced the Constable de Richemont to leave court.

France, at war with the English, was itself divided. The duke of Burgundy had allied himself with the English in 1419; Charles VII, although nominally king since 1422, was not consecrated until 1429, after Joan of Arc's advent. La Trémoille seems to have played a pernicious role during Joan of Arc's campaigns, obstructing her influence with the king and attempting to obtain a treaty with the duke of Burgundy for his personal advantage. His influence was undoubtedly a factor in the king's failure to obtain Joan's release after her capture at Compiègne in 1430.

La Trémoille's actions eventually caused his downfall; in 1433 he was wounded and kidnapped by de Richemont, who released him for ransom only after he had agreed to absent himself from court. Retired to his estates, he made Poitou a centre of discontent. In 1440 he joined the Praguerie, a revolt protesting the king's reforms (so called by analogy with an earlier uprising in Prague). Pardoned with the rest of the nobles, La Trémoille eventually returned to court shortly before his death.

La Trobe Valley (Australia): *see* Latrobe Valley.

La Tuque, town, Mauricie–Bois-Francs region, southern Quebec province, Canada, situated on the Saint-Maurice River. During the French regime, the site was occupied by a trading post of the Company of New France. The original lumbering settlement of 1908 was named for a rock on the river's edge that was shaped like a *tuque,* the woolen headgear that was worn by early French trappers. The town's economy depends chiefly on forestry and allied industries (pulp and paper) and a large hydroelectric installation on the river. The area is noted for its hunting, fishing, and skiing. A three-day lumberjacks' canoe race from La Tuque to Trois-Rivières city (103 miles [165 km] south) is held annually in late summer. Inc. town, 1911. Pop. (1991) 10,003.

La Unión, city, eastern El Salvador. It is located at the northern foot of Conchagua Volcano (about 4,100 feet [1,250 m]), on La Unión Bay, an inlet of the Gulf of Fonseca. The city's economic activity centres on a tortoiseshell industry, beach-resort facilities, and the nearby port of Cutuco, one of the country's largest ports. Situated along a spur of the Inter-American Highway, a section of the Pan-American Highway, La Unión is also the terminus of the International Railways of Central America, which link it with the Guatemalan Caribbean port of Puerto Barrios. Pop. (1987 est.) mun., 58,829.

La Vallière, Louise-Françoise de La Baume le Blanc, Duchess (duchesse) **de** (b. Aug. 6, 1644, Tours, France—d. June 6, 1710, Paris), mistress of King Louis XIV (reigned 1643–1715) from 1661 to 1667.

Mlle de La Vallière, detail of a portrait by Pierre Mignard; in the Palais de Longchamp, Marseille
Giraudon—Art Resource

La Vallière, the daughter of a military governor, was appointed maid of honour in 1661 to Louis XIV's sister-in-law Henrietta Anne of England, Duchess d'Orléans. Although Louis had been married to the Spanish infanta Marie-Thérèse for only about a year, he took La Vallière as his mistress in July 1661. In order to avoid offending his mother, Anne of Austria, the king did not publicly acknowledge the liaison, and La Vallière was too dependent and lacking in self-confidence to assert her rights as official mistress. Anne died in 1666, and in the following year La Vallière was supplanted in Louis's affections by the more worldly and ambitious Marquise de Montespan. He compensated La Vallière by making her a duchess. The marquise's husband, however, attempted to create a scandal by publicly calling attention to his wife's infidelity. To save himself embarrassment, Louis made La Vallière endure the humiliation of remaining at court as official mistress alongside his actual mistress. When La Vallière attempted to escape to a convent in 1671, the king forced her to return. Finally in 1674 the Marquis and Marquise de Montespan were legally separated; Louis then allowed La Vallière to enter a Carmelite convent in Paris, where she lived as a nun, imposing rigorous penances on herself until her death 36 years later. Two of her four children by Louis—a son and a daughter—survived infancy and were legitimized.

La Vega, in full CONCEPCIÓN DE LA VEGA, city, west-central Dominican Republic. It was founded in 1495 by Bartolomeo Colombo at the foot of Concepción fortress, which had been built by Christopher Columbus in 1494. La Vega was moved to the bank of the Camú River after an earthquake in 1564. La Vega is a prosperous commercial, manufacturing, and transportation centre in the fertile La Vega Real region, which yields cacao, coffee, tobacco, rice, fruits, and cattle. The railroad running westward from Sánchez, on Samaná Bay, ends in La Vega, which is also situated on the paved highway linking Santo Domingo, the national capital, with Montecristi. La Vega also has an airfield. Pop. (1986 est.) 60,250.

La Venta, ancient Olmec settlement, located near the border of modern Tabasco and Veracruz states, on the gulf coast of Mexico. La Venta was originally built on an island in the Tonalá River; now it is part of a large swamp. After petroleum was found there, many of the artifacts were moved to an archaeological park on the outskirts of the city of Villahermosa, some 80 miles (129 km) to the west.

Between about 800 and 400 BC La Venta was the most important settlement in Mesoamerica. All its major structures are set on an axis 8° west of north; they were probably originally aligned with some star or constellation. The site is dominated by a 100-foot- (30-metre-) high clay mound shaped like a fluted cone, which some archaeologists believe represents a volcano. North of this is a plaza and a ceremonial enclosure containing a number of tombs. There were three mosaic pavements representing jaguar masks, each measuring about 15 by 20 feet (4.5 by 6 m); these were deliberately buried soon after completion. In addition, there were numerous carved basalt monuments, notably colossal heads weighing some 18 tons. The basalt was quarried about 80 miles west of La Venta. Smaller artifacts include jade ornaments and polished iron-ore mirrors.

La Vérendrye, Pierre Gaultier de Varennes, et de (b. Nov. 17, 1685, Trois-Rivières, New France [now in Canada]—d. Dec. 5, 1749, Montreal), French-Canadian soldier, fur trader, and explorer whose exploits, little honoured during his lifetime, rank him as one of the greatest explorers of the Canadian West. Moreover, the string of trading posts he and his sons built in the course of their search for an overland route to the "western sea" broke the monopoly of the London-based Hudson's Bay Company and strengthened, for a while, French claims in North America.

La Vérendrye joined the army at the age of 12, took part in the French-Indian raid on Deerfield, Mass. (1704), and fought for France in Europe during the War of the Spanish Succession. Taken prisoner at the Battle of Malplaquet (1709), he was freed and returned to New France (Canada), where in 1726 he became a fur trader at Lake Nipigon, 35 miles (56 km) north of Lake Superior. From the Indians he heard of a great river that might lead to the Pacific and thence to the riches of the Orient. To discover the secrets of the West, he and his sons built a string of trading posts between 1731 and 1738 reaching from Rainy Lake in Ontario (Fort-Saint-Pierre) to Winnipeg (Fort-Rouge) in present Manitoba. To these convenient posts the Indians brought their furs and gave La Vérendrye crude maps of waterways they said would lead him to the "western sea."

In the fall of 1738 La Vérendrye reached the Mandan Indian villages on the Missouri River in present North Dakota, and in 1742 he sent two of his sons to push beyond the Missouri. It is possible that they penetrated Nebraska, Montana, and Wyoming and perhaps saw, but did not cross, the Rocky Mountains. On the return journey, they paused near present Pierre, S.D., where on March 30, 1743, they placed a lead tablet, claiming the country for France.

Despite having sent some 30,000 beaver pelts to Quebec annually (most of which would normally have gone to the rival Hudson's Bay Company) and having pushed farther west than any other white man, entirely at his own expense, La Vérendrye was severely criticized by French authorities for failing to find the western sea and was blamed for the deaths of one of his sons, a nephew, and a Roman Catholic priest at the hands of hostile Indians. Old and ill, he still pressed for another chance to explore the West. Permission was finally granted, but he died before he could leave Montreal.

La Victoria, quarter and district of the Lima-Callao metropolitan area of Peru, south of downtown Lima. It is mainly residential, with slums in the north, *pueblos jóvenes* ("young towns"), or squatter settlements, in the east, and middle-income housing in the south. The district is the site of Peru's largest wholesale and retail market area, near which are many light industries. La Victoria houses thousands of highland migrants who pour into Lima each year. Pop. (1990 est.) district, 325,319.

Laatste Nieuws, Het (Flemish: "The Latest News"), daily newspaper published in Brussels, the largest daily in Belgium. It was founded in 1888 to serve Flemish-speaking citizens.

A liberal paper with a serious approach to national and international news, it also publishes such features as comic strips, crossword puzzles, and cartoons. In the 1960s a large and attractive sports section of several pages was included. It is a morning paper using a seven-column page and having a dignified makeup style, with column and cutoff rules separating stories rather than columns.

Laâyoune (Western Sahara): *see* El Aaiún.

Labadie, Jean de (b. Feb. 13, 1610, Bourg, near Bordeaux, France—d. Feb. 13, 1674, Altona, near Hamburg), French theologian, a Protestant convert from Roman Catholicism who founded the Labadists, a Pietist community.

While a novice in the Jesuit religious order at Bordeaux, France, Labadie claimed a vision to reform the church. In 1639, however, seriously ill and increasingly dissatisfied with the Jesuits, he obtained their permission to leave

Labadie, engraving by Johannes Tangena
J.P. Ziolo

the order. In 1644 Labadie founded several small societies dedicated to frequent communion and holy life. Called pietistic for their stress on the practice of godliness, these communities influenced similar ones begun later by the founder of the German Pietist movement, P.J. Spener (1635–1705). Growing opposition from both civil authorities and the Jesuits caused Labadie to change residence several times. After reading John Calvin's *Institutes of the Christian Religion* (1536), he declared formal allegiance to the Reformed Church at Montauban in October 1650 and became professor of theology there the same year. Expelled for unorthodoxy in 1657, he sought refuge in Orange and then in 1659 in Geneva, where Spener heard him preach. In 1666, after being suspended from his ministry in the French church at Middleburg, Labadie fled to Amsterdam, where he founded a separatist group of Pietists. Excommunicated from the Reformed Church in 1670, he went with his group to Herford and then two years later to Altona, the Mennonite sanctuary.

By that time the basic Labadist principles centred upon an existence in which goods and meals were held in common. Labadie taught that the church consisted only of those regenerated by the Holy Spirit and asserted that the sacraments could be administered to them alone. He became increasingly separatist in his views during his later years, and his community never grew beyond a few hundred members. Although Labadist colonies were established by emigrants to the Western Hemisphere, they did not survive past 1730. The remaining community in Europe, at Wiewert, in West Friesland (now in The Netherlands), was dissolved in 1732. Among Labadie's more than 70 writings is *La Réforme de l'église par le pastorat* (1667; "The Reform of the Church Through the Clergy").

Laban, Rudolf, also called RUDOLF VON LABAN (b. Dec. 15, 1879, Bratislava, Austria-Hungary [now in Slovakia]—d. July 1, 1958, Weybridge, Surrey, Eng.), dance theorist and teacher whose studies of human motion provided the intellectual foundations for the development of central European modern dance. Laban also developed Labanotation, a widely used movement-notation system.

Originally interested in painting and architecture, Laban began to study dance in Paris. After choreographing ballets and directing several art festivals, he established his Choreographic Institute in Zürich in 1915 and later founded branches in Italy, France, and central Europe. In 1928 he published *Kinetographie Laban,* a practical method for recording all forms of human motion, now commonly known as Labanotation. In 1930 he became director of the Allied State Theatres of Berlin, where he choreographed many works for large "movement choirs."

Laban pointing to examples of Labanotation
By courtesy of the Laban Art of Movement Centre, Woburn Hill, Addlestone, Surrey, England

Laban's theories and teaching had great impact in central Europe. His analysis of forms in movement, known as choreutics, was a nonpersonal, scientific system designed, like Labanotation, to apply to all human motion. Based on the individual's relation to surrounding space, choreutics specified 12 primary directions of movement derived from complex geometric figures. Another of his theoretical systems, called eukinetics, was designed to increase the dancer's control of dynamic and expressional movement. Mary Wigman, one of his pupils and one of the originators of the modern dance in central Europe, based much of her dramatic choreography on a relationship between individual and space similar to the one Laban postulated in choreutics. Sigurd Leeder and Kurt Jooss, also pupils, further developed and made extensive use of eukinetics in their teaching and choreography.

In 1938 Laban joined Jooss and Leeder at their school at Dartington Hall in Devon, Eng. During World War II, Laban made a number of studies of industrial efficiency, devised a series of corrective exercises for factory employees, and published *Effort* (1947). In 1953 he moved to Addlestone, Surrey, where he continued his teaching and research; with Lisa Ullmann, he also conducted the Art of Movement Studio.

Labanotation, system of recording human movement, originated by Hungarian Rudolf Laban and first published in 1928 as *Kinetographie Laban.* The basic symbol used in writing Labanotation is the rectangle, which is

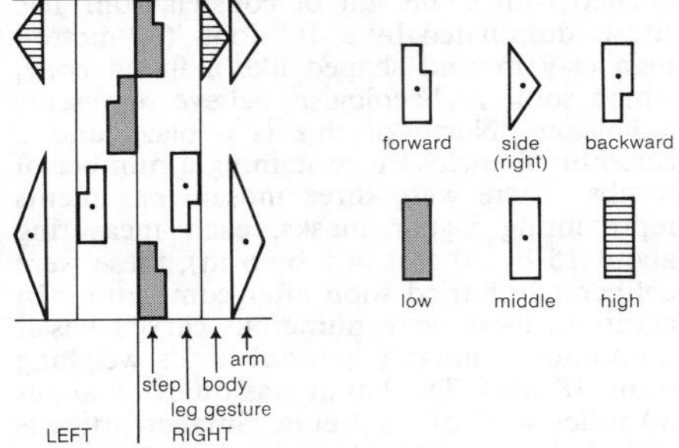

Labanotation

modified in shape to show direction of movement; in length to show duration of movement (rhythm); and in shade to show level. Labanotation is written on a vertical, three-line staff, with the centre line representing division of the body into left and right halves and the two columns used for symbols indicating means of support and left and right leg gestures. Additional columns of symbols show position for body, arms, hands, and head. The staff is read from bottom to top and is written from the performer's point of view rather than from the observer's.

Labanotation is the most widely used of all movement-notation systems, for it incorporates all necessary directives in one set of symbols and clearly indicates the relation of one movement to those that precede and follow. It has been used in anthropology, physical therapy, drama, and industrial production studies and in recording movement in such sports as diving and ice skating. It is most frequently utilized, however, in recording dance choreographies.

Unlike earlier dance-notation systems, Labanotation is not derived from or confined to a particular dance form and so has been employed to record a wide variety of dance styles, including ballet and modern, Spanish, African, and Hindu dance. Several major choreographers have made extensive use of Labanotation, because—unlike motion pictures or videotapes, which record only one particular performance—Labanotation is able to record with exactness all the original specifications of the choreographer. The increasingly widespread use of Labanotation has resulted in the establishment of several dance-notation centres, notably in the United States and Great Britain. Labanotation scripts are accepted for copyright purposes. *See also* dance notation.

Labarnas I, also spelled LABERNASH (fl. 17th century BC), early king of the Hittite Old Kingdom in Anatolia (reigned *c.* 1680–*c.* 1650 BC). Though perhaps not the first of his line, he was traditionally regarded as the founder of the Old Kingdom (*c.* 1700–*c.* 1500)—a tradition reinforced by the use in later times of his name and that of his wife, Tawannannas, as dynastic titles or throne names of subsequent rulers. Labarnas is known chiefly from a later Hittite text called the Edict of Telipinus, which states that from his capital, Kussara, in central Anatolia, Labarnas extended his territory south to the Mediterranean coast and installed his sons as governors in a number of conquered cities, such as Tuwanuwa, Hupisna, Landa, and Lusna (perhaps the classical Tyana, Cybistra, Laranda, and Lystra). According to later sources, he also conquered Arzawa, a country southwest of the Hittite heartland. Thus, a nucleus of empire was established and bequeathed to Labarnas' son Hattusilis I.

Labarnas II: *see* Hattusilis I.

labarum, sacred military standard of the Christian Roman emperors, first used by Constantine I in the early part of the 4th century AD. The labarum—a Christian version of the vexillum, the military standard used earlier in the empire—incorporated the Chi-Rho, the monogram of Christ.

The 4th-century historian Eusebius, in his *Life of Constantine,* describes the labarum as a long gilded pike, from whose crossbar hung a jeweled square of purple cloth; atop the spear a golden wreath enclosed the sacred monogram. According to Eusebius, before the victory over Maxentius (312), Constantine saw a sign of the cross in the sky and the words "in this sign thou shalt conquer" and used it as a talisman in battle. Dating of the labarum is documented by coins issued at Constantinople (now Istanbul) after Constantine's victory over Licinius in 324.

Labé, town, west-central Guinea. Located on the Fouta Djallon plateau (at 3,445 feet [1,050 m]) near the source of the Gambia River, it lies at the intersection of roads from Mamou to the Senegal border and from the Guinean towns of Mali, Tougué, and Télimélé. Founded in the 1720s by the Dialonke people and named for their chief, Manga Labé, the town became an important political and commercial centre of the 18th- and 19th-century Fulani state of Fouta Djallon.

It is now the chief trading centre (cattle, rice, millet, citrus fruits) for a densely populated region mainly inhabited by the Muslim Fulani people. Labé is a major collecting point for oranges, which are trucked to Dakar, Senegal, and to the fruit-juice canning plant at Mamou; it also processes orange, lemon, and jasmine oil, used in making soap and perfumes, for export. The town has a hospital, several secondary schools, a central mosque, and a Roman Catholic mission. Pop. (1983 prelim.) 65,439.

Labé, Louise, original name LOUISE CHARLY, byname LA BELLE CORDIÈRE (French: "The Beautiful Rope Maker") (b. *c.* 1524, Lyon, France—d. 1566, Parcieux-en-Dombes), French poet, the daughter of a rope maker (*cordier*).

Labé was a member of the 16th-century

Lyon school of humanist poets dominated by Maurice Scève. Her wit, charm, accomplishments, and the freedom she enjoyed provoked

Louise Labé, detail of an engraving, 1555
Giraudon—Art Resource

unverifiable legends, such as those claiming she rode to war and was a cultured courtesan. In 1555 she published a book of love sonnets, which are remarkable for their emotional intensity and their stylistic simplicity and which probably relate to her passion for the poet Olivier de Magny. The same volume also contained a prose dialogue, *Débat de Folie et d'Amour* ("Debate of Love and Folly").

label (architecture): *see* hoodmold.

labeo, any of numerous species of African and Asian river fishes belonging to the genus *Labeo* in the carp family, Cyprinidae. Labeos have a thick-lipped, sucking mouth on the underside of the head and two to four small mouth barbels. They are bottom feeders and eat algae and small animals. The rohu (*L. rohita*) of India is esteemed for food and sport and is cultured in ponds. Several African labeos are also valued game fishes, among them *L. altivelis,* a central and southern African species weighing up to 3 kg (6.5 pounds).

Two Asian species of *Labeo* are familiar to home aquarists: the red-tailed black "shark" (*L. bicolor*) and the black "shark" (*L.,* or *Morulius, chrysophekadion*). The former, about 12 cm (5 inches) long, is black with a bright red tail; the latter is totally black

Red-tailed black "shark" (*Labeo bicolor*)
Painting by Karen Allan

and grows to about 30 cm in aquariums. The fishes are called "shark" for their appearance.

Labeo, Marcus Antistius (d. AD 10/11), Roman jurist who was the greatest figure in imperial jurisprudence before the time of Hadrian.

Labeo came of a plebeian family of Samnite origin. His father, the jurist Pacuvius Labeo, had supported the republican revolutionary Marcus Junius Brutus, one of Julius Caesar's assassins. Although the younger Labeo likewise espoused an obsolescent Roman republicanism against the imperial form of government, he attained the praetorship under Augustus and declined that emperor's offer of the consulate.

Labeo is reputed to have written 400 books, including commentaries on the Law of the Twelve Tables, the praetorian edicts and pontifical law, collections of law cases (*Epistulae* and *Responsa*), and the *Pithana,* a collection of definitions and axiomatic legal propositions. He had a wide general culture and a special interest in dialectics and language as aids in legal exposition. His progressive outlook and bold innovations are confirmed in surviving fragments of his works and in the abundant citations and annotations of them by subsequent Roman jurists. Labeo's *Libri posteriores,* a systematic exposition of Roman law, was so called because it was published after his death. The esteem in which he was held is indicated by this posthumous publication, the only known instance in Roman legal history. Labeo was also a teacher and is regarded as the founder of the Proculian school of jurists, named for his follower Sempronius Proculus.

Laberius, Decimus (b. *c.* 105 BC—d. 43 BC), Roman knight with a caustic wit who was one of the two leading writers of mimes. In 46 or 45 BC he was compelled by Julius Caesar to accept the challenge of his rival, Publilius Syrus, and appear in one of his own mimes; the dignified prologue that he pronounced on this degradation has survived. Caesar awarded the prize to Publilius but restored Laberius to his equestrian rank, which he had forfeited by appearing as a mime. The titles of about 42 of his mimes have been preserved, with fragments.

Labernash I: *see* Labarnas I.

labialization (phonetics): *see* rounding.

Labiatae (plant family): *see* Lamiaceae.

Labiche, Eugène-Marin (b. May 5, 1815, Paris, France—d. Jan. 23, 1888, Paris), comic playwright who wrote many of the most popular and amusing light comedies of the 19th-century French stage.

Born into the bourgeois class that was to provide him with the social setting for most of his works, Labiche read for the bar and then briefly worked as a journalist before turning to

Labiche
J.P. Ziolo

writing fiction. In 1838 he published a novel, *La Clef des champs* ("The Key to the Fields"). Of his early plays, *Monsieur de Coislin,* written in collaboration with Marc Michel, was his first great success. A long series of hilarious full-length and one-act plays followed. Written together with other authors, these works were presented mostly at the Palais-Royal, the home of light comedy. Typically, the plays are based on an improbable incident evolving into an imbroglio that brings out the folly and frailty of the characters. The best of his works include *Le Chapeau de paille d'Italie* (1851; *The Italian Straw Hat*), which inspired René Clair's classic film of the same name (1927); *Le Misanthrope et l'Auvergnat* (1852); *Le Voyage de M. Perrichon* (1860); and *La Poudre aux yeux* (1861; "The Bluff").

Though full of dramatic devices, Labiche's plays nonetheless show real insight into human nature. When his plays were first presented, the exaggerated and slapstick style of his favourite actors—such as Jean Geoffroy, for whom many of the parts were written—somewhat obscured the delightfully precise delineations of character. With the publication of his *Théâtre complet,* 10 vol. (1878–83) while he was in retirement, Labiche was engulfed by renewed acclaim and success, including election to the French Academy. Sound and entertaining, his works raised the lowly farce to a much higher level of literary accomplishment.

Labinsk, city and administrative centre of Labinsk *rayon* (sector), Krasnodar *kray* (region), western Russia. Labinsk lies along the Laba River where it flows into a plain. Founded in 1840 as a fortress, it was known as Labinskaya Stanitsa (*stanitsa* meaning "Cossack village") until 1947, when it became a town. An agricultural centre, it has canning factories and timber milling, as well as a technical college. Pop. (1994 est.) 62,700.

Lablache, Luigi (b. Dec. 6, 1794, Naples [Italy]—d. Jan. 23, 1858, Naples), Italian operatic bass admired for his musicianship and acting.

Lablache studied at Naples and at the age of 18 appeared at the opera there as a basso buffo (*i.e.,* in comedy roles), later singing at Palermo, Milan, and Vienna. He had great success in London and Paris as Geronimo in Domenico Cimarosa's *Il matrimonio segreto* (*The Secret Marriage*). In 1836 he lived in London, where with Giulia Grisi, Giovanni Mario, and Antonio Tamburini he was part of the celebrated quartet of singers for whom Gaetano Donizetti wrote his *Don Pasquale*. He was admired by contemporary composers, among them Franz Schubert, who wrote songs for him.

labor: *see under* labour, except as below.

Labor Day, annual holiday devoted to the recognition of working people's contribution to society. Labor Day is observed on the first Monday in September in the United States and Canada and on May 1 or other dates in other countries.

The idea for such a holiday in the United States is attributed to Peter J. McGuire, a carpenter and labor union leader who later cofounded the precursor of the AFL-CIO. In 1882 he suggested to the Central Labor Union of New York that a celebration be held to honour the American worker. Acting on this idea, about 10,000 workers paraded in New York City on Sept. 5, 1882, under the sponsorship of the Knights of Labor. The date of the celebration was chosen simply because it filled up the long gap between Independence Day and Thanksgiving. In 1884 the Knights of Labor adopted a resolution that the first Monday in September should be considered Labor Day. The idea spread rapidly, and by 1885 Labor Day events were taking place in many states. Oregon in 1887 was the first state to grant legal status to Labor Day (though the state initially celebrated it on the first Saturday in June). That same year Colorado, New York, New Jersey, and Massachusetts established the holiday on the first Monday in September, and other states soon followed. In 1894 Congress passed a bill making Labor Day a national holiday.

Labor Day's associations with trade unions have gradually declined. The holiday marks the end of summer vacation for many American schoolchildren and is often celebrated at family picnics and sporting events. In most other countries, including former communist ones, May Day (*q.v.;* May 1) is the day generally chosen by labour unions and left-wing political parties to honour workers.

Labor-Management Relations Act (1947) (U.S. law): *see* Taft-Hartley Act.

Labor Party (Australia): *see* Australian Labor Party.

Labori, Fernand-Gustave-Gaston (b. April 18, 1860, Reims, France—d. March 14, 1917,

Paris), French lawyer who served as defense counsel in the prosecution of Alfred Dreyfus for treason.

Educated at Reims and Paris, Labori spent several years in England and Germany. He was called to the bar in 1884 and rapidly made a reputation as a brilliant lawyer and advocate, being counsel for the defense in most of the important political trials of the day during a period of nearly 30 years. His conduct of the Dreyfus case placed him at

Labori
H. Roger-Viollet

the top of his profession. He fought with unremitting energy for his client during both the first and second revisions of the trial, in 1898 and 1899. Labori was shot at and wounded at Rennes on the eve of his cross-examination of the witnesses for the prosecution. Dreyfus was not finally declared innocent until 1906, and Labori never once relaxed his efforts on behalf of the unfortunate officer.

Other notable trials in which Labori was concerned were the prosecution of Émile Zola for libel (1898), which arose out of the Dreyfus case, and the Humbert affair (1902). In another notorious case, Labori secured the acquittal of Mme Joseph Caillaux for the murder (March 16, 1914) of Gaston Calmette, editor of the journal *Le Figaro*. She shot Calmette to death for charging her husband, the minister of finance, with partiality in office and for publishing her private correspondence with Caillaux.

Laboulbeniomycetes, group of fungi (division Mycota) in the class Ascomycetes. It includes more than 1,500 species, which live off the chitin (exoskeleton) of arachnids (*e.g.,* spiders) and insects. The minute species are highly specialized, some attacking only specific areas on one sex of the host species. Asexual reproduction does not occur.

labour, also spelled LABOR, in economics, the general body of wage earners. It is in this sense, for example, that one speaks of "organized labour." In a more special and technical sense, however, labour means any valuable service rendered by a human agent in the production of wealth, other than accumulating and providing capital or assuming the risks that are a normal part of business undertakings. It includes the services of manual labourers, but it covers many other kinds of services as well. It is not synonymous with toil or exertion, and it has only a remote relation to "work done" in the physical or physiological senses. The application of the physical energies of people to the work of production is, of course, an element in labour, but skill and self-direction, within a larger or smaller sphere, are also elements. A characteristic of all labour is that it uses time, in the specific sense that it consumes some part of the short days and years of human life. Another common characteristic is that, unlike play, it is not generally a sufficient end in itself but is performed for the sake of its product or, in modern economic life, for the sake of a claim to a share of the aggregate product of the community's industry. Even the labourer who finds his chief pleasure in his work commonly tries to sell services or products for the best price that he can get.

If labour could be measured adequately in simple homogeneous units of time, such as labour-hours, the problems of economics would be considerably simplified. But labourers differ in the amount and character of their training, in their degree of skill, intelligence, and capacity to direct their own work or the work of others, and in the other special aptitudes that they require. Tasks differ in their irksomeness, in the prospects that they offer for permanent employment and advancement, in the social status associated with them, and in other characteristics that make one task more attractive than another. Apart from the circumstances that the mobility of labour is imperfect and that it cannot be transferred readily to the employments in which its products have the highest value, the wages of different kinds of labour cannot be taken to be payments for larger or smaller "quantities of labour." The price per unit of time that a particular kind of labour commands in the market depends not only upon the technical efficiency of the labourer but also upon the demand for the particular services that he is able to furnish, upon their relative scarcity, and upon the supply of other productive agents. Thus, the attempts of the earlier economists and of some socialists to find a simple and direct relation between the value of a product and the quantity of labour that it embodies proved fruitless.

Different uses of the available supply of labour, whatever its composition, can be compared with reference to the quantity and the value of the product that they yield. Such comparisons are made continuously in the planning and management of competitive business undertakings. By means of economic analysis, it is often possible to know whether a proposed change in the organization of the community's labour or in the uses to which it is put (as, for example, by encouraging certain types of industries at the expense of others) would be more likely to increase or to decrease the annual production of wealth. For the individual worker, as well as for the community as a whole, the practicable way of measuring the "labour costs" of production is by reference to the other products that might have been secured by means of the same labour or by reference to alternative uses of the time given to labour.

For international statistics on size and distribution of labour force, *see* the *Britannica World Data* section in the BRITANNICA BOOK OF THE YEAR.

labour, in human physiology, the physical activity experienced by the mother during parturition (*q.v.*), or childbirth.

labour, contract: *see* contract labour.

labour, division of, the separation of a work process into a number of tasks, with each task performed by a separate person or group of persons. It is most often applied to mass-production systems, where it is one of the basic organizing principles of the assembly line. Breaking down work into simple, repetitive tasks eliminates unnecessary motion and limits the handling of tools and parts. The consequent reduction in production time and the ability to replace craftsmen with lower-paid, unskilled workers result in lower production costs and a less expensive final product. The Scottish economist Adam Smith saw in this splitting of tasks a key to economic progress by providing a cheaper and more efficient means of producing economic goods.

The French scholar Émile Durkheim first used the phrase in a sociological sense in his discussion of social evolution. Rather than viewing division of labour as a consequence of a desire for material abundance, Durkheim stated that specialization arose from changes in social structure caused by an assumed natural increase in the size and density of population and a corresponding increase in competition for survival. Division of labour functioned to keep societies from breaking apart under these conditions.

The intensive specialization in industrial societies—the refinement and simplification of tasks (especially associated with a machine technology) so that a worker often produces only a small part of a particular commodity—is not usually found in nonindustrialized societies. There is rarely a division of labour within an industry in nonliterate communities, except perhaps for the production of larger goods (such as houses or canoes); in these cases the division is often a temporary one, and each worker is competent to perform other phases of the task. There may be some specialization in types of product (*e.g.,* one worker may produce pottery for religious uses; another, pottery for ordinary uses), but each worker usually performs all steps of the process.

A division of labour based on sex appears to be universal, but the form that this takes varies widely across cultures. Divisions on the basis of age, clan affiliation, hereditary position, or guild membership, as well as regional and craft specialization, are also found.

labour, hours of, the proportion of a person's time spent at work. Hours of labour have declined greatly since the middle of the 19th century. Workers in advanced industrial countries spend far fewer hours per year in a given place of work than they did formerly. Moreover, they spend a smaller portion of their lives in the labour force because of prolonged school enrollment and earlier retirement.

The movement for shorter hours began almost with the formation of unions but met with great employer resistance. In Great Britain it was not until 1847 that an effective limit of 10 hours per day was placed upon the factory employment of women and children. In the United States, state laws were enacted in the 1840s and '50s, but it was not until the 1870s that any such law contained enforcement provisions. The primary economic basis for employer resistance was that, during the 19th century, capital equipment was scarce and expensive relative to labour. In Australia, where the general shortage of labour made unions successful, the eight-hour day was established in the skilled trades by the 1850s.

A shorter working day was a major demand of trade unions in most countries during the latter part of the 19th century and throughout the first half of the 20th. Nevertheless, the length of the workweek declined only slowly prior to 1920. As technical progress made an hour of labour more productive, employers' resistance to shorter hours was reduced. During World War I, the eight-hour day and six-day week became standard in American factories. Most European countries also made substantial gains toward achieving the 48-hour week during the 1920s, many of them signing the international convention, sponsored by the newly formed International Labour Organisation, that declared the 8-hour day or 48-hour week to be a standard.

A principal argument for shorter hours, which gained prominence during the 1930s, was that scarce opportunities for gainful employment ought to be shared among the largest possible number of workers. A standard 40-hour week resulted in the United States when the Fair Labor Standards Act of 1938 imposed a financial penalty upon employers who hired workers for more than 40 hours. The 40-hour week was also established in France by its Popular Front government in 1936.

Australia had achieved a 40-hour week by 1948, and Canada had done so by the early 1960s. Most countries of Europe were approaching that figure by the late 1970s, while in Latin America the workweek averaged 45 hours. In most countries, provision is made for permitting work in excess of the prescribed number of hours. Such overtime work must usually be compensated at premium hourly rates.

Labour, Liberation of, also called EMANCIPATION OF LABOUR, Russian OSVOBOZHDENYE TRUDA, first Russian Marxist organization, founded in September 1883 in Geneva, by Georgy Valentinovich Plekhanov and Pavel Axelrod. Convinced that social revolution could be accomplished only by class-conscious industrial workers, the group's founders broke with the Narodnaya Volya and devoted themselves to translating works by Marx and Engels and to writing their own works emphasizing the need for economic and industrial development as a precondition for Socialism. They opposed terrorist tactics and revolution by violent means. In 1888 the group organized a Russian Social Democratic Union abroad (which became the Union of Russian Social Democrats in 1894). Finding that the union was losing its radicalism, they left it in 1900. Then, with Lenin, who had recently arrived in western Europe, the group published the newspaper *Iskra* and organized the Brussels–London congress (1903) of the Russian Social-Democratic Workers' Party. After the congress, Liberation of Labour joined that party and dissolved itself.

labour, statute: *see* statute labour.

Labour and Socialist International (LSI), organization in existence from 1923 until the advent of World War II that defined itself in its constitution as "a union of such parties as accept the principles of the economic emancipation of the workers from capitalist domination and the establishment of the Socialist Commonwealth as their object."

In 1921 delegates from the "centre" and "left" Socialist parties that had refused to join either the Second or the Third International met in a congress at Vienna and formed the International Working Union of Socialist Parties, also known as the Vienna Union, with the object of preparing the ground for an all-embracing International. In 1922 delegates from the Second and Third Internationals and the Vienna Union met in Berlin to explore the conditions of common action. No substantive agreements resulted. After the failure of the Berlin conference, the Second International and the Vienna Union drew closer together and ultimately united at a congress held in Hamburg in 1923, attended by 620 delegates representing 41 parties in 30 countries with an aggregate membership of 6,700,000 and a voting strength of 25,000,000. It adopted the name Labour and Socialist International and was closely associated with the International Federation of Trade Unions.

The LSI believed fascism to be the gravest menace to freedom and peace and considered the restoration of working-class unity as the most effective means to combat it. The LSI recognized in the economic conditions of the Versailles peace treaty one of the main sources from which both the Communist and Nazi movements in Germany derived their strength, and strove for a fair settlement of the reparations imposed upon the Weimar Republic. The LSI called on the Western powers to assist Germany when the German economy collapsed in the early 1930s. With Hitler's rise to power the LSI became mainly preoccupied with the danger of war. It supported the principle of collective security, pressed for the adoption of a general convention of the League of Nations to strengthen the means of preventing war, and opposed the rearmament of Nazi Germany. It helped to organize financial assistance on a large scale for political refugees from fascist countries, especially for the victims of Franco's war against the Spanish republic.

Hitler's conquests in western Europe destroyed the basis of the International in Europe. Only the British, Swedish, and Swiss Socialist parties survived, and the International ceased to function.

labour economics, the study of how workers are allocated among jobs, how their rates of pay are determined, and how their efficiency is affected by various factors. It is, in other words, the study of one of the traditional "factors of production," the others being land and capital and, sometimes, entrepreneurship. The aggregate claim of labour, among the factors, to a share of the national income is studied in distribution theory (*q.v.*).

A brief treatment of labour economics follows. For full treatment, *see* MACROPAEDIA: Work and Employment.

The labour force of a country is taken to include all who work for gain, in whatever capacity, as well as those who are unemployed but seeking work. In industrialized nations the labour force is typically about two-thirds of the portion of the population that is of working age, which is, in turn, typically two-thirds of the total population. The deployment and pay of labour depends upon a multitude of factors. The general health of the labour force, the general level of education, the distribution of special training and skills, and the degree of mobility are qualities of the labour force itself that play a large role in determining where workers are employed and how they are paid. The structural characteristics of the economy are of great significance—for example, the proportions of primary or extractive industries, heavy manufacturing, high-technology manufacturing, and service industries. Another set of factors are institutional, including the extent and power of trade unions and employers' associations and active interventions by government in such areas as hours and wages controls, minimum-wage laws, and arbitration of collective-bargaining problems. Various miscellaneous factors, such as custom and transient economic conditions, must also be considered.

Wage levels tend to be higher in industries that require higher levels of education or training and in economies that have high proportions of such industries. Wage levels tend to be higher in industries that are heavily unionized, although in the long run higher wage levels may be negated by higher price levels. Industries or regions whose wage rates are higher naturally tend to attract mobile labour, which under some circumstances may have a positive long-term effect on wage levels in other industries or regions.

Differences in wage rates among industries and among types of jobs within any industry may be accounted for in various ways. Classical economics held that different kinds of labour contained different quantities of a postulated "homogeneous labour time" and were rewarded accordingly. Other theories emphasize the status relations of different forms of labour and the relative power over the production process of different levels of skill.

labour law, body of law applied to such matters as employment, remuneration, conditions of work, trade unions, and labour–management relations. In its most comprehensive sense, it also includes old age and disability insurance.

A brief treatment of labour law follows. For full treatment, *see* MACROPAEDIA: Business Law.

Although labour-related laws have been traced as far back as the Code of Hammurabi, labour law as it is known today has its origin in the 18th century. It evolved from the influences and impact of the Industrial Revolution, the 18th-century Enlightenment, the French Revolution, and the political forces that fomented and were shaped by those historical movements.

Initially, labour laws were intended to provide protection to the working class, which, as a result of increasing mechanization, was being exposed to new abuses in the workplace. The first laws to protect children from abusive employment practices were enacted in England in 1802; but the bulk of labour laws in Europe were not passed until the late 19th century, and in the United States many laws were not enacted until the 1930s.

Legal recognition of the right of workers to associate for the purpose of trade-union activity has been most decisively influenced by political changes and still remains an area within labour law which is very sensitive to political fluctuations. In the United Kingdom in 1824 and in France in 1884, restrictions prohibiting trade-union association were repealed, but many subsequent changes in these laws have occurred. In the United States, the right of workers to associate in trade unions was not firmly granted until the 1930s. In Asia and Africa labour issues did not arise until the 1940s and '50s.

Employment laws. Legislation concerning long-term employment policy as a means of fostering economic stability and growth is a relatively new concept in labour law. This approach developed after the Great Depression of the 1930s and World War II. Its purpose was to enhance employment opportunities by assuring employers of sufficient manpower while guaranteeing employees their rights. Such legislation includes provisions for recruitment, vocational training, and apprenticeship. Also included under the category of employment laws are the rights to freedom from forced labour, equality of treatment, and unemployment compensation.

Employment laws that concern the individual's relation to the employer involve the contractual obligations of each party and the creation and termination of those obligations. However, with the development of labour laws, individual contracts have become limited by legal statutes, which fix many of the terms concerning the employment relationship.

Wage laws. Laws regarding wages concern the form and methods of payment, such as whether there has been proper notification of wage conditions and whether payment is to be made by legal tender or check. These laws allow workers the freedom to dispose of their wages, protect workers from unlawful deductions, and restrict the cases in which attachment of wages can be made.

The most important aspect of wage regulations has been movement away from their use as a means of controlling "social evils" and replacement of this system with one whose primary concern is overall economic stability. Many countries have administrative bodies such as the British Trade Board, which can set wages for various jobs for which collective agreements do not exist. These organizations also fix standards (such as minimum-wage laws) and other determinations for wages that in many cases are the basis for collective agreements. The primary concern here is again to regulate an economy and to keep control over inflationary practices.

Working conditions and social security laws. Legislation for working conditions includes provisions regulating hours, rest periods, vacations, child labour, and health and safety. This legislation was originally developed to protect women and children but now, for the most part, concerns all workers equally.

Health and safety regulations were once limited to high-risk occupations such as mining.

However, with the increased use of machines and chemicals, these regulations were applied to a broad range of fields. Provisions include accident-prevention services and health and safety standards concerning the risks of poisoning, dust, noise, and radiation.

Labour legislation in the area of social security has increased the amount of and opportunity for compensation for job-related injury and illness. Comprehensive social-security legislation began in Otto von Bismarck's Germany of the late 19th century, with the introduction of old-age benefits. Later, the Great Depression of the 1930s gave impetus to social-security legislation in the United States that now encompasses payment for sick leave, maternity leave, survivor's benefits, and medical care.

Trade-union relations and administrative bodies. Laws regarding trade unions and labour-management relations include the legal status of trade unions, the rights and obligations of workers' and employers' organizations, collective bargaining agreements, and rules for settling disputes, strikes, and lockouts. The laws in this category of labour law are complex and often have an impact that may affect the functioning of vital services to a community or a society at large. The general trend, therefore, is toward increasing legal involvement in these matters because of the potential for widespread disruption that may be caused by labour-management disputes.

Labour Party, British political party whose historic links with trade unions have led it to promote an active role for the state in the economy and in the provision of social services. In opposition to the Conservative Party, it has been the major democratic socialist party in Britain since the early 20th century.

History. The Labour Party was born at the turn of the 20th century out of frustration at the inability of working-class people to field parliamentary candidates through the Liberal Party, which at that time was the dominant social-reform party in Britain. In 1900 the Trades Union Congress (the national federation of British trade unions) cooperated with the Independent Labour Party (founded in 1893) to establish a Labour Representation Committee, which took the name Labour Party in 1906. The early Labour Party lacked a nationwide mass membership or organization; up to 1914 it made progress chiefly through an informal agreement with the Liberals not to run candidates against each other wherever possible. After World War I, however, the party made great strides, owing to a number of factors: first, the Liberal Party tore itself apart in a series of factional disputes; second, the 1918 Representation of the People Act extended the electoral franchise to all males aged 21 or over and to women aged 30 or over; and third, in 1918 Labour reconstituted itself as a formally socialist party with a democratic constitution and a national structure. The party committed itself to the pursuit of full employment with a minimum wage and a maximum workweek, democratic control and public ownership of industry, progressive taxation, and the expansion of educational and social services. By 1922 Labour had supplanted the Liberal Party as the official opposition to the ruling Conservative Party. In 1924–25 and again in 1929–31, with Liberal support, James Ramsay MacDonald was able to form the first Labour governments. In 1931, in a dispute over economic policy, MacDonald defied the objections of most Labour officials and formed a coalition National Government with Conservatives and Liberals. In the ensuing election, Labour's parliamentary representation was reduced from 288 to 52. The party remained out of power until 1940, when Labour ministers joined Winston Churchill's World War II coalition government.

Labour achieved a spectacular recovery in the general election of 1945, when it won a huge overall majority in Parliament. Under the leadership of Prime Minister Clement Attlee, the Labour governments of the following six years set about building on the state's recent experience of wartime intervention to construct a new postwar political consensus, based on a mixed economy, a much more extensive system of social welfare (including a National Health Service), and a commitment to the pursuit of full employment. Postwar economic recovery proved slow in the meantime, however, and in 1951 Labour lost power to the Conservatives.

Throughout the 1950s the question of whether, and how, to adapt the party's traditional socialist approach to an affluent society—especially the question of the nationalization of industry—divided Labour's ranks. "Bevanites" (followers of former health minister Aneurin Bevan) wanted a more socialist economic policy and less dependence on the United States; the "revisionists," led by Hugh Gaitskell, Attlee's successor as party leader, wished to drop the commitment to nationalization of industry. Labour did not regain power until 1964 under Harold Wilson, who was prime minister until 1970. The party held power again from 1974 to 1979, first under Wilson and then under James Callaghan. Ultimately, the moderate social-democratic approach exemplified by the Wilson-Callaghan years foundered on the twin rocks of Britain's chronic economic problems and Labour's worsening relations with its trade union allies.

After Labour's defeat by the Conservatives in the elections of 1979, the party's left wing succeeded in forcing through a number of internal organizational reforms that enhanced the power of grassroots activists and trade unions in the selection of parliamentary candidates and party leaders. In the 1983 general election Callaghan's successor, Michael Foot, presented a radical manifesto that proposed extensive nationalization of industry, unilateral nuclear disarmament, and the withdrawal of the United Kingdom from the European Economic Community. The result was Labour's worst national electoral defeat in more than 50 years. Foot was replaced by Neil Kinnock, who began a "modernization" process that contributed to Labour's electoral revival. The process was continued by Kinnock's successors as party leader, John Smith (1992–94) and Tony Blair (1994–). In a series of programmatic and organizational changes, the party reviewed its policies so as to re-embrace the mixed economy in the tradition of the revisionists of the 1950s, support Britain's continuing role within the European Union, drop the pretensions to a unilateralist defense policy, and jettison the party's commitment to public ownership of industry. Labour regained power after a landslide victory in the 1997 general election and again won by a wide margin in 2001.

Labour Party, Irish PÁIRTÍ LUCHT OIBRE, Irish political party founded in 1912 by James Larkin as an ancillary to the Trades Union Congress and formed as a separate party in 1930. James Connolly was its most important leader until 1916, when he was executed by the British for his part in the Easter Rising.

The Labour Party was the first opposition party in the Dáil Éireann (Irish Assembly) of the Irish Free State from 1922 to 1926. Never governing in its own right, it nevertheless supported the Eamon de Valera government of 1937–38 and participated in coalition governments (mostly with Fine Gael) in 1948–51, 1954–57, 1973–77, and 1981–82 and, except for a brief period, from 1982 to 1987.

The Labour Party is a member of the Socialist International and seeks wider social security and welfare services, public ownership of basic industries, and union with Northern Ireland. Its main base of power is in the Dublin area and among unionized workers.

Labour Party (Israel): *see* Israel Labour Party.

Labour Party (New Zealand): *see* New Zealand Labour Party.

labour union: *see* trade union.

Labrador, northeastern portion of the Canadian mainland. It embraces the great peninsula of northern Quebec and of Newfoundland and Labrador, an area of approximately 625,000 square miles (1,620,000 square km) that is bounded by the Hudson Strait (north), Atlantic Ocean (east), Gulf of St. Lawrence and Eastmain River (south), and Hudson Bay (west).

As a geographic entity, Labrador comprises the easternmost portion of the Canadian Shield, the rocky, glaciated plateau of eastern Canada. This plateau is characterized by numerous lakes draining into the Atlantic via the Churchill, Naskaupi, Eagle, and other rivers; by thin, poorly drained soils; and by a bleak, deeply indented coastline that is swept by the cold Labrador Current.

Labrador as a political entity refers to the Atlantic coast of Labrador, the Newfoundland and Labrador portion of the peninsula, whereas the Quebec portion is known as Ungava. The origin of the term Labrador is obscure, but it is believed to have been first applied to Greenland, called "Land of Labrador" by early Portuguese navigators, and later transferred to the northeastern North American mainland by cartographers. Political control of the peninsula passed between Newfoundland and Quebec, thus confusing the name's geographic significance until the Quebec-Newfoundland border was established in 1927.

Economic activity is centred along the southwestern part of the boundary between the two provinces, an area known as the Labrador Trough, which has immense iron-ore deposits. The region's largest towns—Schefferville, Que., and Labrador City and Wabush, Nfd. and Lab.—have sprung up since iron-ore exploitation began in the 1950s, powered by hydroelectric plants at Menihek and Churchill Falls. Fishing and lumbering are of local importance. Pop. (2001) Labrador section of Newfoundland and Labrador province, 27,864.

Labrador City, town, southwestern Labrador, Newfoundland and Labrador, Canada, near the Quebec border. It was developed in the 1950s as a planned community to serve the surrounding mining region (Carol Lake), one of Canada's largest producers of iron-ore concentrates and pellets. The community has an airport and rail connections with Schefferville, Que., to the north, and with Sept-Îles, Que., the ore transshipment port to the south at the mouth of the St. Lawrence River. Inc. 1961 as a local improvement district and in 1980 as a town. Pop. (2001) 7,774.

Labrador Current, surface oceanic current flowing southward along the west side of the Labrador Sea. Originating at the Davis Strait, the Labrador Current is a combination of the West Greenland Current, the Baffin Island Current, and inflow from Hudson Bay. The current is cold and has a low salinity; it maintains temperatures of less than 32° F (0° C) and salinities in the range of 30 to 34 parts per 1,000. The Labrador Current is limited to the continental shelf and reaches depths only slightly greater than 2,000 feet (600 m). Its volume of water transport varies between about 125,000,000 and 190,000,000 cubic feet (3,500,000 and 5,400,000 cubic m) per second and annually carries several thousand icebergs southward.

Labrador Sea, northwestern arm of the North Atlantic Ocean, between Labrador, Canada (southwest), and Greenland (northeast). It is connected with Baffin Bay (north) through Davis Strait and with Hudson Bay

Labrador Sea from the rocky coast of Labrador
Malak—Shostal

(west) through Hudson Strait. The cold, low-salinity Labrador Current flows southward along the Canadian coast, while the warmer and more saline West Greenland Current moves northward along the Greenland coast. Because the Labrador Current carries numerous icebergs, the main shipping routes are in the eastern part of the sea, where the navigation season extends from midsummer to late fall. Cod fishing is a major industry of the Greenland ports. Many early explorers passed through the Labrador Sea in search of the Northwest Passage, a presumed sea route between the Atlantic and Pacific oceans.

Labrador tea (*Ledum groenlandicum*), low-growing, perennial evergreen shrub of the heath family (Ericaceae), native to eastern North America. The name is also sometimes applied to *L. glandulosum,* a closely related shrub of the Rocky Mountains region.

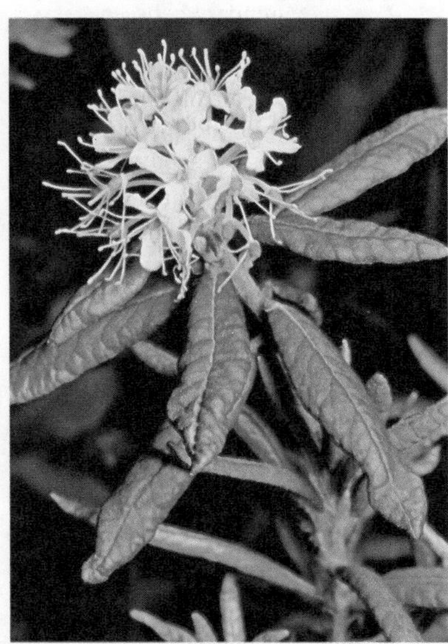

Labrador tea (*Ledum groenlandicum*)
Kenneth Fink—Root Resources

L. groenlandicum is found in cold boggy areas and grows to about 1 m (3 feet) high. The twigs are reddish. The fragrant leaves, which are sometimes used for making tea, are smooth-edged and elliptical and have a rusty "wool" on the underside. The leaf margins are curled under. The white or creamy flowers, 2 cm (0.8 inch) wide, are borne in a terminal cluster. There are five sepals and five petals.

labradorite, a feldspar mineral in the plagioclase (*q.v.*) series that is often valued as a gemstone and as ornamental material for its red, blue, or green iridescence. The mineral is usually gray or brown to black and need not be iridescent; when used as a gem it is usually cut en cabochon (with a rounded convex surface). Labradorite is one of the more common plagioclase varieties and occurs in many gabbros, dolerites, norites, and basalts. Anorthosite, a rock composed mainly of iridescent labradorite crystals up to about 2 m (6 to 7 feet) long, occurs in many of the world's mountain regions. Labradorite is named for its occurrence near Nain, on the coast of Labrador, Can.

Labriola, Antonio (b. July 2, 1843, Cassino, Kingdom of the Two Sicilies [Italy]—d. Feb. 12, 1904, Rome, Italy), philosopher who systematized the study of Marxist socialism in Italy. The first in his nation to expound orthodox Marxism, he profoundly influenced contemporaries of diverse political persuasions.

A student of the Hegelian philosopher Bertrando Spaventa, Labriola became a philosophy professor at the University of Rome in 1874. His independent and critical mind, together with his gift for oral expression, made him an exceptional teacher as well as a brilliant scholar. First favouring the political right, he became increasingly disturbed by the corruption in Italian politics and by 1885 adopted a radical socialist philosophy. It was in 1889, in presenting a course on the philosophy of history, that he began his lectures on Marxism, the first in Italy.

Labriola began a correspondence with Friedrich Engels in 1890 and undertook the systematic study of the texts of Karl Marx and Engels, approaching historical materialism from a critical, analytical point of view. Shortly thereafter, his Italian translation of *The Communist Manifesto* appeared. Labriola's writings include *In memoria del Manifesto dei Communisti* (1895; "In Memory of the Communist Manifesto"), *La concezione materialistica della storia* (1896; "The Materialist Conception of History"), and *Discorrendo di socialismo e di filosofia* (1897; "Speaking on Socialism and Philosophy").

Labrouste, Henri (b. May 11, 1801, Paris, France—d. June 24, 1875, Fontainebleau), French architect important for his early use of iron frame construction.

Labrouste entered the École des Beaux-Arts in Paris in 1819, won the Prix de Rome for architecture in 1824, and spent the period from 1825 to 1830 in Italy, after which he opened a studio in Paris.

Labrouste is primarily remembered for the two Parisian libraries he designed. The Bibliothèque Sainte-Geneviève, built between 1843 and 1850, is still admired for the attractiveness and restraint of its decoration and for the sensitive use of exposed iron structural elements (columns and arches). Labrouste's second library project, the reading room of the Bibliothèque Nationale, was constructed between 1862 and 1868. Its roof consists of nine decorated metal domes supported by slender cast-iron columns.

Labuan, island, East Malaysia, 6 miles (10 km) off northwestern Borneo in the South China Sea. Commanding the entrance to Brunei Bay, it is roughly triangular, with an area of 38 square miles (98 square km). Its chief town, Victoria, on the southeastern coast, is a free port whose deep, well-sheltered harbour is the principal transshipment point for the state of Brunei, northern Sarawak, and much of western Sabah. Low-lying and well-cultivated, the island has an extensive road network and a large airfield. Its chief products are rubber, copra, and sago. In 1990 the island was declared a tax haven by the Malaysian government as the first step toward developing it into an offshore financial centre.

Ceded to the British (1846) by the sultan of Brunei as a base to suppress piracy, Labuan became a crown colony in 1848. After a period of administration by North Borneo (1890–1906), it was incorporated into the Straits Settlements. In 1946 the island became part of the colony of North Borneo (now Sabah), and Victoria, which was demolished during World War II, was rebuilt. During the period of Indonesian armed opposition to Malaysia (1963–66), Labuan was the headquarters for the Commonwealth defense forces.

The island has broad, white beaches, and skin divers are attracted to the surrounding coral reefs. Historic landmarks include the war memorial cemetery and Surrender Point, where the Japanese surrendered to the Australians in 1945. Pop. (1997 est.) 70,400.

laburnum, any member of the genus (*Laburnum*) of trees and shrubs having butterfly-like flowers, and belonging to the subfamily Papilionoideae of the pea family (Leguminosae). The leaves are composed of three leaflets, and the flowers are disposed in hanging clusters. The pods are slender and compressed. *Laburnum anagyroides,* often called golden chain (*q.v.*), is native to southern Europe and is cultivated as an ornamental. The leaves have elongate stalks, and the bright yellow flowers hang in pendulous racemes up to a foot in length.

All parts of laburnums are poisonous, especially the seeds. The roots taste like licorice, which is a member of the same family. Occasionally, laburnum has proved fatal to cattle, though hares and rabbits are unharmed. The wood of laburnums has a striking greenish brown or reddish brown hue and takes a good polish. It is ideal for cabinetmaking and inlay and was at one time the most prized timber in Scotland.

labyrinth, also called MAZE, system of intricate passageways and blind alleys. "Labyrinth" was the name given by the ancient Greeks and Romans to buildings, entirely or partly subterranean, containing a number of chambers and passages that rendered egress difficult. Later, especially from the European Renaissance onward, the labyrinth or maze occurred in formal gardens, consisting of intricate paths separated by high hedges.

Pliny the Elder mentions the following as the four famous labyrinths of antiquity:

1. The Egyptian, of which a description is given by Herodotus and Strabo, was situated to the east of the Lake of Moeris, opposite the ancient site of Arsinoë, or Crocodilopolis. According to Egyptologists, the word means "the temple at the entrance of the lake." According to Herodotus, the entire building, surrounded by a single wall, contained 12 courts and 3,000 chambers, 1,500 above and 1,500 below ground. The roofs were wholly of stone, and the walls were covered with sculpture. On one side stood a pyramid about 243 feet (74 m) high. Herodotus himself went through

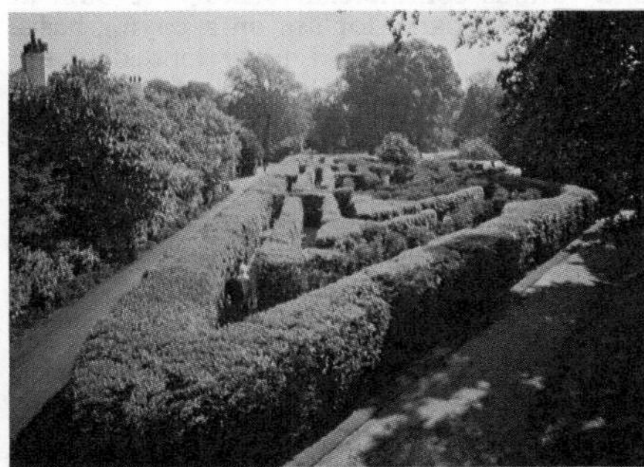

Maze in the gardens at Hampton Court Palace, Greater London
British Crown Copyright by permission of the Controller of Her Britannic Majesty's Stationery Office

the upper chambers but was not permitted to visit those underground, which he was told contained the tombs of the kings who had built the labyrinth and the tombs of the sacred crocodiles. Other ancient authorities considered that it was built as a place of meeting for the Egyptian nomes, or political divisions; but it is more likely that it was intended for sepulchral purposes. It was the work of Amenemhet III, of the 12th dynasty, who reigned from 1818 to 1770 BC. It was first located by the Egyptologist Karl R. Lepsius to the north of Hawara in the Fayum, and in 1888 Flinders Petrie discovered its foundation, the extent of which is about 1,000 feet long by 800 feet wide (300 by 250 m).

2. The Cretan, said to have been built by Daedalus on the plan of the Egyptian, is famous for its connection with the legend of the Minotaur. It is doubtful whether it ever had any real existence. By the older writers it was placed near Knossos, and it is represented on coins, but nothing corresponding to it has been found during modern excavations, unless the royal palace was intended. Later writers, such as Claudian, place it near Gortyna, but some winding passages and chambers close to that place are, in reality, ancient quarries.

3. The Lemnian was similar in construction to the Egyptian, with 150 columns.

4. The Italian was a highly intricate series of chambers in the lower part of the tomb of Porsena at Clusium. This tomb is said to be recognizable in the mound named Poggio Gajella, near Chiusi.

In gardening, a labyrinth or maze means an intricate network of pathways enclosed by hedges of which it is difficult to find the centre or exit. It is a descendant of the old geometrical style of gardening. The more common kind consists of walks, formerly called alleys, kept to an equal width by parallel hedges, which should be too close and thick for the eye readily to penetrate them. The task is to get to the centre, marked in some conspicuous way, then to return; but even those who know the key are apt to be perplexed. Sometimes the design consists of alleys only, with no centre. A design published in 1742 showed "six different entrances, whereof there is but one that leads to the centre, and that is attended with some difficulties and a great many stops."

The maze in the gardens at Hampton Court Palace, one of the finest examples in England, was planted in the reign of William III. It is constructed on the hedge-and-alley system and was, it is believed, planted with hornbeam, which was replaced by hollies, yews, and so on. The key to the centre is to go left on entering, then, on the first two occasions when there is an option, go right, but thereafter go left.

Navigating through an intricate maze had become a popular form of recreation in parts of Europe and in Japan by the late 20th century, and various commercial mazes were built at amusements parks for use on a paying basis. Commercial mazes in Europe tended to use hedges, while those in Japan were more complex and were constructed of movable wooden plank walls whose configuration could be periodically changed.

labyrinth fish, any of the small tropical fish of the suborder Anabantoidei (order Perciformes). Labyrinth fishes, like most other fishes, breathe with their gills, but they also possess a supplemental breathing structure, the labyrinth, for which they are named. This apparatus, located in a chamber above the gills, is liberally supplied with blood vessels. It enables the fishes to use oxygen from air gulped in through the mouth and thus to survive out of, or in oxygen-poor, water.

The labyrinth fishes are found in the freshwaters of Asia and Africa. They are often called bubble-nest builders because the males of most species build, guard, and maintain a foamy nest of soaplike bubbles that floats at the surface.

There are about 70 species of labyrinth fishes; some are commonly kept in home aquariums. The various species, once grouped together in the family Anabantidae, may be placed in five families: Badidae, Anabantidae, Belontiidae, Helostomatidae, and Osphronemidae.

For more information on labyrinth fish species and groups, *see* climbing perch; gourami; Siamese fighting fish.

labyrinth of the ear: *see* inner ear.

labyrinthitis, inflammation, either acute or chronic, of the inner ear (the labyrinth). It is often a complication of a respiratory-tract infection, of syphilis, or of inflammation of the middle ear. Symptoms include vertigo and vomiting. There is also a loss of hearing and equilibrium in the affected ear. If there is no suppuration (pus formation), recovery usually occurs after a number of days. If there is pus formation, the inner-ear structures on the affected side are usually totally destroyed, with permanent loss of hearing in that ear.

labyrinthodont, any member of an extinct order (Labyrinthodontia) or subclass of amphibians that constituted the dominant animals of Late Paleozoic and Triassic time (about 350 to 210 million years ago). Labyrinthodonts first appeared in the Late Devonian (374 to 360 million years ago) and may well have included the ancestors of all land vertebrates; some of them closely approached the reptiles in structure. Many were as large as alligators, some as small as salamanders. By the Permian Period (286 to 245 million years ago) certain genera had become terrestrial, but both the early members of the group and the late degenerate forms were aquatic. The body was stout and lizardlike, with short limbs. The large skull was solidly roofed (hence the term Stegocephalia, often applied to these and other early amphibians). The vertebrae, in contrast to those of most land vertebrates, had two parts.

lac, also spelled LACK, sticky, resinous secretion of the tiny lac insect, *Laccifer lacca,* which is a species of scale insect. This insect deposits lac on the twigs and young branches of several varieties of soapberry and acacia trees and particularly on the sacred fig, *Ficus religiosa,* in India, Thailand, Myanmar (Burma), and elsewhere in Southeast Asia. The lac is harvested predominantly for the production of shellac (*q.v.*) and lac dye, a red dye widely used in India and other Asian countries. Forms of lac, including shellac, are the only commercial resins of animal origin.

As early as about 1200 BC, lac products were being used in India as plastic and decorative materials. During the 17th century, after traders had introduced lac dye and, later, shellac to Europe, lac became commercially important there. Eventually, lac products came to be used in most of the industrialized countries of the world.

The word lac is the English version of Persian and Hindi words that mean "hundred thousand," indicating the large number of the minute insects required to produce lac. In fact, about 17,000 to 90,000 insects are needed to produce one pound of shellac.

The maximum yield of resin and dye is obtained by gathering stick lac (*i.e.,* the twigs with their living inhabitants) in June and November. Lac dye is obtained from ground stick lac by extraction with hot water or hot sodium carbonate solution.

Seed lac is the resin, freed from the lac dye. After the seed lac is melted, strained through canvas, spread, cooled, and flaked, it becomes the shellac of commerce. The palest orange lac is the most valuable. *See also* cochineal.

Lac Giao (Vietnam): *see* Buon Me Thuot.

Lacaille, Nicolas Louis de (b. May 15, 1713, Rumigny, France—d. March 21, 1762, Paris), French astronomer who mapped the constellations visible from the Southern Hemisphere and named many of them.

In 1739 Lacaille was appointed professor of mathematics in the Mazarin College, Paris, and in 1741 was admitted to the Academy of Sciences. He led an expedition (1750–54)

Lacaille, detail from an engraving
Boyer—H. Roger-Viollet

to the Cape of Good Hope, where he determined in only two years' time the positions of nearly 10,000 stars—many still referred to by his catalog numbers. His observations from South Africa of the Moon, Venus, and Mars, in conjunction with similar observations already made in the Northern Hemisphere, led to the calculation of more accurate values for the distances of these bodies.

Before leaving the Cape, Lacaille measured the first arc of a meridian in South Africa. After his return to France in 1754, he laboured alone in compiling his data, and overwork apparently hastened his death. His *Coelum Australe Stelliferum* ("Star Catalog of the Southern Sky") was published in 1763.

Lacan, Jacques, in full JACQUES MARIE ÉMILE LACAN (b. April 13, 1901, Paris, France—d. Sept. 9, 1981, Paris), French psychoanalyst who gained an international reputation as an original interpreter of Sigmund Freud's work.

Lacan earned a medical degree in 1932 and was a practicing psychiatrist and psychoanalyst in Paris for much of his career. He helped introduce Freudian theory into France in the 1930s, but he reached prominence only after he began conducting regular seminars at the University of Paris in 1953. He acquired celebrity status in France after the publication of his essays and lectures in *Écrits* (1966; Eng. trans. *The Language of the Self: The Function of Language in Psychoanalysis*). He founded and headed an organization called the Freudian School of Paris from 1964 until he disbanded it in 1980 for what he claimed was its failure to adhere with sufficient strictness to Freudian principles.

Lacan emphasized the primacy of language as the mirror of the unconscious mind, and he tried to introduce the study of language (as practiced in modern linguistics, philosophy, and poetics) into psychoanalytic theory. His major achievement was his reinterpretation of Freud's work in terms of the structural linguistics developed by French writers in the second half of the 20th century. The influence he gained extended well beyond the field of psychoanalysis to make him one of the dominant figures in French cultural life during the 1970s. In his own psychoanalytic practice, Lacan was known for his unorthodox, and even eccentric, therapeutic methods.

Lacandón, Mayan Indians living in a territory on the Mexico-Guatemala border. Some Lacandón probably live in Belize, across the

Lacandón men participating in a ceremony

J. Berrier—Atlas Photo

eastern border of Guatemala. Currently divisible into two major groups, the total number of Lacandón is less than 600 and decreasing. They inhabit a rich tropical rain forest, well supplied with water, fish, game, and fertile soil. The Lacandón have preserved until recently a quite isolated and primitive way of life. They are farmers, growing corn, beans, squash, and tomatoes together in mixed plots. Other vegetables and fruits may also be grown in separate gardens. They also gather wild fruit, hunt game, and fish.

Lacandón settlements may consist of single households or clusters of several households, known as *caribales.* The houses are thatched huts that may or may not have walls, supported on pole frameworks. Possessions are stored in the thatch, and food is hung from the roof in baskets. Crafts include the construction of dugout canoes, the spinning and weaving of cloth, leather tanning, and the making of bark cloth, nets, hammocks, pottery, flutes, bows, and stone-tipped arrows. Clothing usually consists of a long, loose tunic reaching almost to the ground, worn by both sexes. The hair is customarily worn long and loose by both sexes. There is still little trade or contact with the outside world.

The Lacandón are among the few Middle American Indian groups that successfully resisted the introduction of Roman Catholicism, and most have preserved their traditional beliefs. Unfortunately, disease and waning population have resulted in the loss of some elements of their traditional culture and religion, but prayer and several rituals are commonly practiced.

Laccadive, Minicoy, and Amīndīvi Islands (India): *see* Lakshadweep.

laccolith, in geology, any of a type of igneous intrusion that has split apart two strata, resulting in a domelike structure; the floor of the structure is usually horizontal. A laccolith is often smaller than a stock, which is another type of igneous intrusion, and usually is less than 16 km (10 miles) in diameter; the thickness of laccoliths ranges from hundreds of metres to a few thousand metres. They can be contrasted with sills, which are sheetlike intrusions oriented parallel to the bedding of the enclosing rock: a laccolith's ratio of diameter to thickness should be less than 10; a larger ratio would make the body a sill. Acidic rocks are more common than basic rocks in laccoliths. Although the lower portions of laccoliths are seldom visible, they usually are interpreted as having a relatively small feeder from a magma source below. A well-known example of a laccolith is found in the Henry Mountains, Utah.

lace, ornamental, openwork fabric formed by looping, interlacing, braiding (plaiting), or twisting threads. The dividing line between lace and embroidery, which is an ornamentation added to an already completed fabric, is not easy to draw; a number of laces, such as Limerick and filet lace, can be called forms of embroidery upon a more or less open fabric. On the other hand, fancy knitting, however much an ornamental openwork fabric, is not usually thought of as lace, though in some museums it is so classified. Openwork fabrics made on a loom (for example, brocaded gauze) are not considered lace.

Before 1800 the threads of lace were usually linen; after 1800 cotton was more common. Silk and metal thread and occasionally such other materials as wool, aloe fiber, and hair of various kinds were also used.

Almost all laces that have some claim to be called works of art are made in one of two techniques, needle lace and bobbin lace (*qq.v.*). Needle lace involves a very difficult technique and has seldom been used in folk art or, except at the beginning of its history, by amateurs. Bobbin lace in its simpler forms is a widespread craft and amateur pastime, but the more elaborate laces require the highest degree of skill. There are a number of minor techniques of lace making, including the following: drawn-thread work, or *punto tirato;* cutwork, or *punto tagliato;* filet, or network, lace; macrame, or knotted lace; *punto a groppo; punto avorio;* crochet; and tape lace.

Though ornamented openwork fabrics have been found in ancient Egyptian burial grounds, fully developed lace did not appear before the Renaissance; and, although some of the simple techniques may have originated in the Middle East, the art of lace is a European achievement. Some late 15th-century Italian and Flemish paintings show elaborate hemstitching and narrow lacelike insertions at the seams of linen garments and cushions, which represent the beginning of needle lace. The first bobbin lace is not well documented, but it probably originated early in the 16th century. Whether these lace techniques were developed first in Italy or in Flanders is a question that has remained unresolved. Most authorities, however, agree that needle lace originated in Italy, bobbin lace in Flanders.

By 1550 both of the main kinds of lace and a great deal of cutwork, drawn-thread work, and filet were being made. By 1600 lace, which had begun as a modest ornament for underlinen, was a fabric of the utmost luxury and an important article of commerce. Great quantities of lace were worn by both men and women. The chief centres of production in the 17th and 18th centuries were Italy, Flanders, and France, though lace was also made in Spain, Germany, and England.

In the 19th century the French Revolution and the Industrial Revolution led to great changes in the character of lace. The use of machine net for free-bobbin lace became general soon after 1800, making it considerably less expensive. Lace was no longer worn by men, and during the early part of the century women's fashions did not call for much of it; when the mode changed about 1840, enormous quantities of lace were readily made. Cotton, a cheaper but less satisfactory material, replaced linen. The design also deteriorated. The chief lace-making centres were Italy, Belgium, France, England, and Ireland. But lace was also made in Spain, Russia, Denmark, Turkey and elsewhere in the Levant, and in South American countries such as Paraguay and Brazil. The introduction of lace making into East Asia, especially China, took place late in the century.

Much handmade lace continued to be produced until World War I, despite increasing competition from machine-made types. A great deal of bobbin, needle, and filet lace was made in China for export to Europe and the United States. But by 1920 the industry was dying everywhere. In the second half of the 20th century, lace was still being made at such centres as Burano and Bruges, but chiefly as souvenirs.

lace bug, any insect of the easily recognized cosmopolitan family Tingidae (order Heteroptera), which numbers about 2,000 species. The adult, usually less than 5 mm (0.2 inch) long, has a lacelike pattern of ridges and membranous areas on its wings and upper body surface. It sucks the juices from foliage, causing a yellow spotting, then browning; the leaves eventually drop off. Nicotine sprays are used to control these insects.

The lace bug deposits its eggs on the underside of a leaf and covers them with a mucous secretion that hardens into a conelike form. The small, black, spiny nymphs do not resemble the adult. The life cycle takes between seven and nine weeks, and there are usually two generations each season. The lace bug, depending on the species, may pass the winter either in the adult or the egg stage.

Lace bug (*Corythucha juglandis*)

By courtesy of the U.S. Department of Agriculture

lace pattern book, collection of decorative lace patterns produced in the 16th and 17th centuries. The earliest known printed pattern books, beginning with those published in 1527 by Matio Pagano in Venice and Pierre de Quinty in Cologne, were dedicated to and intended for royal and noble ladies. The earliest booklets rarely provided technical instruction.

Books geared to a wider public were published eventually, and by the 17th century the lace and embroidery designs of Federico de Vinciolo of Paris (1587), Cesare Vecellio of Venice (1592), Isabetta Catanea Parasole of Venice (1595), and William Hoffman of Frankfurt (1604, expanded 1607) were popular. Also well known in England were Geoffrey Whitney's *A Choice of Emblemes* (1586), John Taylor's *The Needle's Excellency* (1621), and Richard Shorleyker's *A Schole House for the Needle* (1624).

Lacedaemon (Greece): *see* Sparta.

Lacépède, (Bernard-Germain-) Étienne de La Ville-sur-Illon, comte de (count of) (b. Dec. 26, 1756, Agen, Fr.—d. Oct. 6, 1825, Épinay-sur-Seine), French naturalist

Lacépède, detail of a portrait by an unknown artist

H. Roger-Viollet

and politician who made original contributions to the knowledge of fishes and reptiles.

Lacépède's *Essai sur l'électricité naturelle et artificielle* (1781; "Essay on Natural and Artificial Electricity") and *Physique générale et particulière* (1782–84; "General and Particular Physics") so impressed the naturalist G.-L.L. Buffon that he arranged the appointment (1785) of Lacépède as keeper and subdemonstrator at the Cabinet du Roi, associated with the Paris Botanical Garden. Buffon also invited him to make contributions to Buffon's own *Histoire naturelle* ("Natural History") series. Accepting, Lacépède published first the *Histoire naturelle des quadrupèdes ovipares* (1788; "Natural History of Oviparous Quadrupeds") and then *Histoire naturelle des serpents* (1789; "Natural History of Snakes"). During the Revolution he was appointed natural history professor in the study of fishes and reptiles at the relocated Paris Botanical Garden, where he completed the *Histoire naturelle des poissons,* 5 vol. (1798–1803; "Natural History of Fishes"). Although the work contained a number of errors because of insufficient research materials, it was recognized as the most original text on the subject at that time. The *Histoire naturelle des cétacés* (1804; "Natural History of Cetaceans") followed.

After the rise of Napoleon, Lacépède was elected to the French Senate in 1799. He became president of that body (1801) and grand chancellor of the Légion d'Honneur (1803). He was appointed minister of Bourbon state in 1809. After the restoration he returned to government, taking a seat in the Chamber of Peers (1819).

Lacerta, genus of lizards of the family Lacertidae that includes among its more than 50 species most European lizards and some Asian and African species. *Lacerta* species have well-developed limbs and deeply notched tongues. They have small back scales and large throat shields that form a well-defined collar.

lacewing, any of many species of neuropteran insects, especially those in the green lacewing family Chrysopidae and in the brown lacewing family Hemerobiidae, of the order Neuroptera.

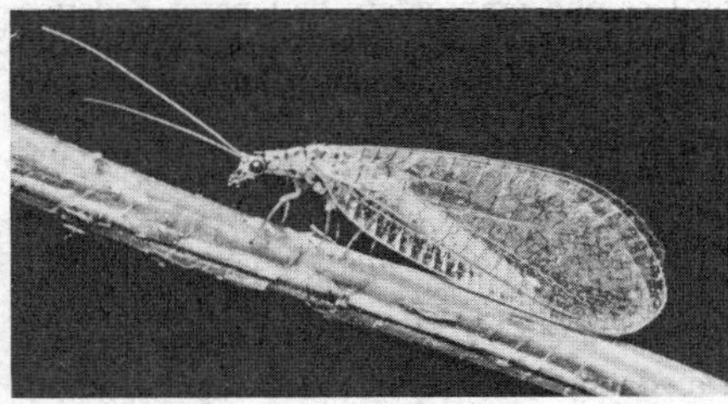

Lacewing (*Chrysopa*)
A.E.Mc.R. Pearce—Bruce Coleman Ltd.

The green lacewing, sometimes known as the golden-eyed lacewing, has long delicate antennae, a slender greenish body, golden- or copper-coloured eyes, and two pairs of similar veined wings. It is worldwide in distribution and flies near grasses and shrubs. The lacewing is also known as a stinkfly because it emits a disagreeable odour as a protective device. The female green lacewing secretes slender stalks and deposits one egg on top of each stalk; this prevents the larvae from devouring unhatched eggs. The larva has prominent sucking mouthparts and well-developed legs. The larva, often called an aphidlion, captures and drains body fluids from aphids and other soft-bodied insects. After about two weeks of continuous feeding, the larva spins a silken, pearl-sized cocoon on the underside of a leaf and remains in the pupal case approximately two weeks.

The brown lacewing resembles the green lacewing but is smaller in size, brown in colour, may have dark spots on the wings, and does not secrete stalks for its eggs. Some lacewing larvae hold debris (including the bodies of their victims) on their backs with hooks or bristles; this camouflage allows the lacewing larva to surprise its victims and also protects it from enemies.

Lachaise, Gaston (b. March 19, 1882, Paris—d. Oct. 18, 1935, New York City), French-born American sculptor known for his massively proportioned female nudes.

The son of a cabinetmaker, Lachaise at age 13 entered a craft school, where he was trained

"Standing Woman," bronze sculpture by Gaston Lachaise, 1932; in the Museum of Modern Art, New York City
By courtesy of the Museum of Modern Art, New York, Mrs. Simon Guggenheim Fund

in the decorative arts. He studied sculpture at the École des Beaux-Arts from 1898 to 1904. He began his artistic career as a designer of Art Nouveau decorative objects for René Lalique. His wife being an American, he emigrated to the United States in 1906 and worked in Boston for H.H. Kitson, an academic sculptor of military monuments. In 1912 he went to New York and worked as an assistant to the sculptor Paul Manship.

His most famous work, "Standing Woman" (1912–27), typifies the image that Lachaise worked and reworked—a female nude with enormous breasts and thighs and sinuous, tapered limbs. Bronze casts of this work are in many American museums. Lachaise is also known as a brilliant portraitist. He executed busts of such celebrities as John Marin, Marianne Moore, and e.e. cummings.

Laches (b. *c.* 475 BC—d. 418), a rich Athenian aristocrat who played a leading part in the first phase of the Peloponnesian War.

Laches was an associate of Socrates and was a conservative. Elected general in 427 BC, he was replaced in 425 after he undertook an unsuccessful mission to support Athenian interests in Sicily and was prosecuted by Cleon (Aristophanes satirized the trial in his comedy *The Wasps*). Temporarily eclipsed, he gained politically by the Athenian defeats of 424 at Megara and at Delium and proposed the decree that brought the year's armistice in 423. When the death of Cleon (422) made peace with Sparta possible, Laches served on the commission that negotiated terms. Then he supported Nicias' attempts to preserve the peace but could not prevent the dangerous alliance of Athens with Argos and Mantineia. He died in command of the Athenian force when this alliance was destroyed at the Battle of Mantineia (418). A dialogue of Plato's, on bravery, is known by his name.

Lachine, city, Montréal region, southern Quebec province, Canada. It is a western suburb of Montreal city in the Montreal Metropolitan Corporation. Lachine lies on the south shore of Montreal Island facing Lake Saint-Louis, which is a widening of the St. Lawrence River. First established in 1667 by the French explorer Robert Cavelier, sieur de La Salle, while he was searching for a route to China, it was named after a contraction of *la petite Chine* ("little China"). Settlement of the site began in 1675. In 1689 it was the site of a massacre of about 250 French settlers and soldiers by the Iroquois. Historically, Lachine was an important departure point for fur traders on their way to the West. The production of components used in bridge construction is the major industry, together with electrical appliance manufacture. Inc. 1848. Pop. (1991) 35,266.

Lachlan River, chief tributary of the Murrumbidgee River, in New South Wales, Australia. Rising in the Great Dividing Range (Eastern Highlands), 8 miles (13 km) east of Gunning, it flows northwest, and, 30 miles (48 km) upstream from Cowra, it is dammed to form Wyangala Reservoir. Continuing past Forbes and Condobolin, it turns southwest past Lake Cargelligo and Hillston and joins the Murrumbidgee, 130 miles (210 km) from that river's confluence with the Murray. The main stream, which is about 930 miles (1,500 km) long, and its principal tributaries, including the Abercrombie, Willandra Billabong, Eagle, and Goobang, drain a basin of 32,700 square miles (84,690 square km). Though usually perennial, the river may run dry in severe drought years. Explored in 1815 by George William Evans, it was named after Lachlan Macquarie, governor of New South Wales (1810–21). The Lachlan River valley supports wheat and sheep.

Lachman Dās, also called LACHMAN DEV (military leader): *see* Bandā Singh Bahādur.

Lachmann, Karl (Konrad Friedrich Wilhelm) (b. March 14, 1793, Braunschweig, duchy of Braunschweig [Germany]—d. March 13, 1851, Berlin, Prussia), German founder of modern textual criticism, or the methodology of determining the definitive text of a written work. His commentary (1850) on Lucretius' *De rerum natura* ("On the Nature of Things") was perhaps his greatest achievement and has been regarded as a major accomplishment of Latin scholarship.

Professor at the Friedrich Wilhelm University, Berlin (1825–51), Lachmann devoted his life to the research of language—especially of Old and Middle High German—and literature. He laid down the rules of textual criticism and delineated the phonetic and metrical principles of Middle High German in early works of 1816–17. His clarification of his rigorous method in a number of works published be-

Lachmann, detail of an engraving by A. Teichel, *c.* 1850
Archiv fur Kunst und Geschichte, Berlin

tween 1820 and 1836 led to the establishment of a school of textual criticism that gained many adherents.

In the area of classical studies he published editions of the poetry of Catullus and Tibullus (1829) and a number of other works. His views on Homer's *Iliad,* though no longer accepted, had considerable influence on Homeric criticism.

lachrymal duct and gland: *see* tear duct and gland.

Lachs, Manfred (b. April 21, 1914, Stanisławów, Austria-Hungary [now Ivano-Frankovsk, Ukraine]—d. Jan. 14, 1993, The Hague, Neth.), Polish writer, educator, diplomat, and jurist who profoundly influenced the postwar development of international law.

Lachs was educated at Jagiellonian University of Kraków, where he earned his law degrees, and did graduate work at the Consular Academy of Vienna and the London School of Economics before the outbreak of World War II.

His first public notice in the West came in 1945 with the publication of his first book, *War Crimes: An Attempt to Define the Issues.* Lachs was made a delegate to both the Paris Peace Conference and the first United Nations General Assembly (1946). The following year he was appointed director of the Legal and Treaties Department of the Foreign Ministry, a post he held until 1960. In that year he became legal adviser to Foreign Minister Adam Rapacki and played a central role in the development of the "Rapacki Plan" for making central Europe a nuclear-free zone. Lachs was a delegate to most General Assembly sessions through 1966. In that year he was elected a judge of the World Court, formally the International Court of Justice, at The Hague. He was president of the court in 1973–76 and was chairman of its committee on revising court procedures.

Throughout his political and legal careers Lachs continued to teach and lecture around the world; from 1952 he taught at the University of Warsaw. He published several books, including *The Teacher in International Law: Teachings and Teaching* (1982), and many articles.

Lachung, village, northeastern Sikkim state, northeastern India, on the Lachung River, a tributary of the Tista. A small trading centre (corn [maize] and pulses), it is equipped with a dispensary, rest house, and monastery and is linked to Gangtok, Sikkim's capital, 27 miles (43 km) south, by the North Sikkim Highway. It is the site of a government agricultural sta-

Dwellings on the Himalayan slopes at Lachung, Sikkim, India
Alice Kandell from Rapho/Photo Researchers

tion. To the north of its bazaar are seasonal grazing settlements, while to the south many hamlets are perched along the riverbanks. A trail from Lachung leads east to the Tibetan border pass of Thang Kar.

lack (resinous substance): *see* lac.

Lack, David Lambert (b. July 16, 1910, London, Eng.—d. March 12, 1973, Oxford, Oxfordshire), British ornithologist, best known as the author of *The Life of the Robin* (1943) and other works that popularized natural science.

Lack was educated at Magdalene College, Cambridge (M.A., 1936), and taught zoology in Devon from 1933 to 1938, when he joined an expedition to the Galápagos Islands. He served in the British army during World War II and in 1945 was appointed director of the Edward Grey Institute of Field Ornithology in Oxford. He was also a Fellow of Trinity College, Oxford, from 1963.

Lack is particularly noted for his argument that density of animal populations is more important than other factors (such as weather) in determining animal distribution and number (*The Natural Regulation of Animal Numbers,* 1954). His other works include *Darwin's Finches: An Essay on the General Biological Theory of Evolution* (1947, rev. ed. 1983), *Ecological Isolation in Birds* (1971), and *Island Biology* (1976), on the land birds of Jamaica.

Lackawanna, city, Erie county, western New York, U.S., on Lake Erie, adjoining Buffalo (north). Originally part of an Indian reservation, it was settled in the 1850s as part of West Seneca and was known as Limestone Hill. It was primarily a nursery and truck-farm area until 1899 when it was chosen as the site of the Lackawanna Steel Company, now the Bethlehem Steel Corporation. The steel-production facilities there, once among the largest in the United States, were extensively reduced in 1977. Inc. city, 1909. Pop. (1992 est.) 20,731.

Laclos, Pierre Choderlos de, in full PIERRE-AMBROISE-FRANÇOIS CHODERLOS DE LACLOS (b. Oct. 18, 1741, Amiens, France—d. Nov. 5, 1803, Taranto, Parthenopean Republic [now in Italy]), French soldier and writer, author of the classic *Les Liaisons dangereuses,* one of the earliest examples of the psychological novel.

Laclos chose a career in the army but soon left it to become a writer. His first novel, *Les Liaisons dangereuses* (1782), caused an immediate sensation. Written in epistolary form, the

Laclos, oil painting by an unknown artist; in a private collection
Giraudon—Art Resource

story deals with the seducer Valmont and his accomplice, Mme de Merteuil, who take unscrupulous delight in their victims' misery. Laclos' second novel, *De l'éducation des femmes* (1785; "On the Education of Women"), is of little importance except for the light it throws on the psychology of the earlier novel. His *Lettre à MM. de l'Académie Française sur l'éloge de M. le Maréchal de Vauban* (1786) mocked the French army and its hopelessly outdated methods of defense and, as a result, lost him his army commission. He then entered politics, working for a while as secretary to the duc d'Orléans. He again joined the army in 1792, however, and ultimately rose to the rank of general under Napoleon, serving in the Rhine and Italian campaigns.

Laconia, Modern Greek LAKONÍA, *nomós* (department) and historic region in the southeastern part of the Peloponnese, southern Greece. The present department of Laconia corresponds closely to the ancient province, which was bounded by Arcadia and Argolis on the north and Messenia in the west. Sparta, capital of the modern department, was once the capital of the ancient province.

Laconia has three distinctive topographic zones, running north-south and incorporating two of the three peninsulas of the southern Peloponnese: (1) the Taíyetos (ancient Taygetus) Mountains in the west, including Mount Ilías (7,887 feet [2,404 m]), the highest mountain of the Peloponnese, running south to the promontory of Cape Taínaron at the tip of the isolated Máni peninsula; (2) the central valley of the Evrótas River; and (3) the dissected eastern hills, which rise in the north to 6,348 feet (1,935 m) in Mount Párnon, terminate at the end of the Maléa peninsula, and reappear in the hills of the offshore islands of Elafónisos and Cythera (Kíthira). Laconia's only large rivers are the Evrótas River and its tributary, the Oinoús River. The coast, especially in the east, is rugged, with few good harbours.

Neolithic sites (before 2500 BC) are found in the Evrótas valley, the Maléa peninsula, and elsewhere; Yeráki, a quiet village southeast of Sparta, has been occupied continuously since Neolithic times and has remains from several periods of its history. In the Late Mycenaean period (1400–1100 BC) numerous settlements were founded; Laconia was a strong kingdom ruled by Menelaus, according to Homer. The Dorian Invasion (about 1100 BC) brought widespread destruction to the Peloponnese, and several centuries passed before Laconia began to reemerge. Throughout the classical period, the history of Laconia is that of its capital, Sparta, which at that time was called Lacedaemon.

In 195 BC towns on the coast were freed by Rome and became members of the Achaean League, which eventually included all of Laconia. In AD 267 and again in 395, Visigoths devastated Laconia, and in about 587 Slavic incursions brought on two centuries of barbarism. In 805 Laconia became part of the Byzantine Empire, and throughout the Middle Ages it was the scene of struggles between Slavs, Byzantines, Franks, Turks, and Venetians. Tradition holds that the last Byzantine emperor, Constantine Palaeologus, was crowned in the church of Hagios Demetrios, which still stands at Mistrás, just southwest of Sparta. In the Greek War of Independence (1821–29), inhabitants of the Máni peninsula played a prominent part.

The most important archaeological work—apart from that in Sparta, Gythium, and Vapheio—has been the systematic survey of Laconia begun in 1904 by the British School of Athens and continued intermittently. In antiquity the Taygetus range yielded iron and marble, while green porphyry (*lapis lacedaemonius*) was quarried at Croceae (modern Krokeaí). Laconia remains more hospitable to grazing than agriculture. Area 1,404 square miles (3,636 square km). Pop. (1991 prelim.) *nomós,* 94,916.

Laconia, Gulf of, Modern Greek LAKONIKÓS KÓLPOS, large, deep gulf on the southern Ionian Sea embraced by the two southernmost peninsulas of the Peloponnese, Greece, 35 miles (56 km) north-south and 30 miles (48 km) wide. Cape Maléa, which divides the Gulf of Laconia from the Aegean Sea, was once feared by sailors for its treacherous winds and harbourless coast. The surrounding region lies entirely within Laconia *nomós* (department). The major stream entering is the non-navigable Evrótas River, which rises in the Taíyetos range. Two promontories on the western shore form the Skoútari and Kolokithiás inlets, the latter fronting the port of Kótronas. The small island of Elafónisos is separated on the south by a channel from Cythera (Kíthira), an Ionian island.

Lacordaire, Henri, in full JEAN-BAPTISTE-HENRI LACORDAIRE (b. May 12, 1802, Recey-sur-Ource, France—d. Nov. 21, 1861, Sorèze), leading ecclesiastic in the Roman Catholic revival in France following the Napoleonic period.

Raised in a troubled time, Lacordaire renounced religion and studied jurisprudence at Dijon, France, following which he practiced law in Paris. After experiencing a religious awakening, however, he studied for the priesthood and was ordained in 1827. In 1830 he joined a small group of Roman Catholic writers under the direction of one of the most controversial and influential figures then in the French church, Hugues-Félicité-Robert de Lamennais. They founded *L'Avenir* ("The Future"), a journal advocating the separation of church and state. When Lamennais's doctrines were condemned in 1832 by Pope Gregory XVI, the journal was suppressed. Lacordaire and his colleagues submitted, but Lamennais was later excommunicated.

A period of disappointment followed, during which Lacordaire focused his energies on preaching. His sermons of 1834 appealed to Parisian intellectuals, and in 1835 the archbishop of Paris invited him to preach at Notre Dame, where his lectures became known as the Lenten Conferences. He gradually came to believe that the best means of strengthening the French church, the condition of which had been impaired by the Revolution, was to restore the religious orders destroyed by the Revolution. Favouring the Dominicans because they were especially devoted to preaching and education, he joined that order at Rome in 1838. He returned to Paris in 1840 and resumed his preaching at Notre Dame, using his pulpit as a means to express his support of liberty in church and state.

His major contribution to the religious reorientation in France was his reestablishment of the Dominicans, which began when he influenced the restoration of a novitiate at Nancy in 1843. He was head of the French Dominicans from 1850 to 1854 and helped to make the order a religious and educational power in France.

In favour of a republican France, Lacordaire openly attacked Napoleon III in a sermon at Paris (1853); his opposition to the emperor led him to retire to Sorèze in 1854. He was elected to the French Academy in 1860.

Lacoste, Rene, in full JEAN-RENE LACOSTE (b. July 2, 1904, Paris, France—d. Oct. 12, 1996, Saint-Jean-de-Luz), French tennis player who was a leading competitor in the late 1920s. As one of the powerful Four Musketeers (the others were Jean Borotra, Henri Cochet, and Jacques Brugnon), he helped France win its first Davis Cup in 1927, starting its six-year domination of the cup. Later on he was better known for his successful sportswear company.

Lacoste, who was nicknamed "the crocodile," won the Wimbledon singles in 1925 and 1928, the French singles in 1925, 1927, and 1929, and became the first foreigner to win the U.S. championship twice (1926–27). With Borotra, he won the British doubles in 1925 and the French doubles in 1924, 1925, and 1929.

A methodical player, Lacoste would study every aspect of tennis before a match, and he would wait for an opponent to weaken. His best-known game was perhaps the 1927 U.S. championship, in which he drove Bill Tilden to exhaustion in the two-hour final. After winning the 1929 French championship, Lacoste retired. Decades later, sportshirts and other items of apparel with his "crocodile" emblem (although somehow changed to an alligator) became popular throughout the world. He and his fellow "musketeers" were elected to the International Tennis Hall of Fame in 1976.

Lacq, village, centre of an industrial complex in the Béarn region, Pyrénées-Atlantiques *département,* southwestern France, northwest of Pau. The industrial complex was built after the discovery at Lacq of petroleum and, in 1951, of one of the greatest natural-gas fields in the world. Treatment of hydrogen sulfide in the gas yields about 700,000 tons of sulfur annually, making Lacq one of the world's largest sulfur producers and exporters. Other by-products include gasoline and propane, butane, and ethylene gas, used in chemical plants southeast of Lacq. A nearby gas-fired power station generates electricity for an aluminum plant. A new town has been constructed at Moureux to house employees of the Lacq complex. Pop. (1990) 657.

lacquer tree: *see* varnish tree.

lacquerwork, any of a variety of decorative objects and surfaces to which a coloured, highly polished, and opaque type of varnish called lacquer has been applied. Most true lacquerwork is Chinese or Japanese in origin, although the technique was copied by European craftsmen in the 18th and 19th centuries.

A brief treatment of lacquerwork follows. For full treatment, *see* MACROPAEDIA: Decorative Arts and Furnishings.

Lacquer takes its name from the substance known as lac, which is the basis of some lacquers. True lacquer, as used in East Asia, is the purified and dehydrated sap of a tree, the *Rhus vernicifera,* native to China and cultivated for centuries in Japan. The characteristic constituent of lacquer is called urushiol, from the Japanese word for lacquer, *urushi*. In Europe, where true lacquer was not available, various imitation substances were developed according to different formulas, though none of these had the hardness and brilliance of real Oriental lacquer.

The base to which lacquer is applied is usually wood, though porcelain and metal have sometimes been used. The wooden base, frequently of pine, must be specially prepared so that its surface is smooth and even. Any knots, cracks, knobs, or imperfections must be smoothed away or filled in. The lacquer itself in its natural state is a thick, syrupy whitish- or grayish-coloured sap that turns dark brown or black when exposed to the air. It must undergo special preparation before it is ready to be used. First it is purified, then it is stirred to liquefy it, and afterward it is heated and stored in an airtight container until required. Lacquer is characterized by its quality of becoming extremely hard, but not brittle, when exposed to air. Its other unique quality is that it can take a high polish, or shine, so that a lacquerware piece may be as brilliant as fine glazed porcelain.

In order to become as hard as possible, lacquer must "dry" in a damp atmosphere with plenty of moisture. This requirement led to the development of special techniques for hardening lacquerware. Lacquer is applied to the wooden base surface in many thin layers, and after each coat (20 to 30 is not an unusual amount) the surface must be allowed to harden and then be smoothed and rubbed. Various different qualities and types of lacquer are used in succession, and many different colours and decorative finishes are possible. Many days must elapse before the surface of the lacquerwork item is ready for decoration.

The different colours of lacquer are created by the addition of different substances, such as cinnabar for red. Greens, buff, brown, black, and purple are other possible colours. A wide variety of surface decorative techniques exist, some such as carving being peculiar to Chinese lacquerwork, and others, such as the use of gold, more characteristic of Japanese pieces. A design might be drawn on a piece of paper and then transferred to the lacquered surface, or it might be drawn directly onto the piece. Gold, silver, engraving, carving, and inlay have all been used to create decorative effects of extreme richness. Both Chinese and Japanese craftsmen favour shell inlays such as mother-of-pearl. Jade, ivory, porcelain, and coral inlays also are used in China.

The history of lacquerwork in China goes back to as far as the earliest legends of Chinese history. Lacquerwork of fine quality continued to be made until the 19th century, when it declined both in quality and in importance. The art was taken to Japan from China via Korea in the middle of the 6th century, when the lacquer tree, as well as Buddhism, was also introduced. By the 8th century a distinctive Japanese tradition had begun to develop, which was to continue until the 19th century. The finest work dates from the Genroku period between 1688 and 1703. The greatest Japanese lacquer artist of the 17th and 18th centuries was Ogata Kōrin. Other important artists include the families of Yamamoto Shunshō and Kajikawa.

After 1600 lacquerwork began to be imported quite widely from Asia to Europe, and imitation lacquerwork began to be made by European craftsmen, especially in England, France, and Venice. Many exquisite pieces, particularly lacquered furniture, were made, decorated often with motifs characteristic of the Rococo. The taste for Oriental-style lacquerwork in Europe was part of the general taste for things Chinese known as "chinoiserie." Lacquerwork in Europe was frequently known as "japanning," or "japan work."

"De," "la," and similar components of a name, when followed by a space, are alphabetized as separate words (e.g., *De Forest, Lee*). *When they are joined to the following part of a name, the combination is treated as a single word* (e.g., *DeForest, John William*).

Lacretelle, Jacques de (b. July 14, 1888, Cormatin, France—d. Jan. 2, 1985, Paris), French novelist, the third member of his family to be elected to the French Academy (1936).

Lacretelle wrote his first novel, *La Vie inquiète de Jean Hermelin* ("The Troubled Life of Jean Hermelin"), an autobiographical novel of adolescence, in 1914, and it was published in 1920. Lacretelle's next novel, *Silbermann* (1922), recounts the story of a Jewish boy's persecution during the time of the Dreyfus affair. Following the publication of *La Bonifas* (1925; *Marie Bonifas*), a minutely detailed study of provincial life, Lacretelle turned to shorter fiction and nonfiction, writing theatre reviews for *Nouvelle Revue Française,* fictional essays, and short stories. His return to novel writing was marked by the publication, in 1929, of *Amour Nuptiale* (Eng. trans. *A Man's Life*); this psychological study of a marriage won for Lacretelle the Prix du Roman of the French Academy.

From 1930 to 1935 Lacretelle wrote *Les Hauts-Ponts* ("High Bridges"), a long family saga set in the province of Vendée during the 19th century. *Sabine* (1932), the first of the four volumes in the series, was hailed as a masterpiece, though the other three were somewhat less well received. Lacretelle worked through the war years as a journalist for *Le Figaro,* of which he was a director. His postwar works include an autobiographical novel, *Le Pour et le contre* (1946; "For and Against"); a memoir, *Le Tiroir Secret* (1959; "The Secret Drawer"); and the antinovel *Les Vivants et leur ombre* (1977; "The Living and Their Shadows").

Lacretelle, Jean-Charles-Dominique de, THE YOUNGER (b. Sept. 3, 1766, Metz, France—d. March 26, 1855, Mâcon), French historian and journalist, a pioneer in the historical study of the French Revolution.

Jean-Charles-Dominique de Lacretelle, lithograph by H.-A. Valentin
Giraudon—Art Resource

Summoned in 1787 to Paris by his older brother Pierre, a lawyer and political activist, he became a member of the Feuillants, a party advocating a constitutional monarchy. He wrote for the *Journal des Débats* and the *Journal de Paris,* and, when he made no attempt to hide his monarchist sympathies in reporting the trial and death of Louis XVI (1792–93), his life was imperiled. He enlisted in the army for refuge but soon returned to Paris. There he became involved in the Royalist movement of 13 Vendémiaire (Oct. 5, 1795) and was condemned to deportation after the coup against the constitutional monarchists on 18 Fructidor (Sept. 4, 1797). Powerful sympathizers arranged for him to stay conveniently forgotten in prison until after the consulate under Napoleon came to power on Nov. 9, 1799, when he was set free. Under the empire, he began his historical writings and taught at the Faculté des Lettres in Paris. As *censeur royal,* he opposed proposed restrictions on the press (1827), causing both the defeat of the measure and his own removal from office.

Lacretelle's chief works, written with accurate information but lacking the insight and style of a great historian, are a series of histories, including *Précis historique de la Révolution française,* 5 vol. (1801–06; "A Short History of the French Revolution"); *Histoire de France pendant le XVIII*[e] *siècle,* 6 vol. (1808; "French History During the 18th Century"); and *Histoire de France depuis la restauration* (1829–35; "History of France Since the Restoration").

lacrimal duct and gland: *see* tear duct and gland.

Lacroix, Alfred, in full FRANÇOIS-ANTOINE-ALFRED LACROIX (b. Feb. 4, 1863, Mâcon, France—d. March 12, 1948, Paris), French mineralogist whose *Minéraux des roches* (1888; "The Minerals of Rocks"), written with the geologist Albert Michel-Lévy, was a pioneer study of the optical properties of rock-forming minerals.

Lacroix
Harlingue—H. Roger-Viollet

From 1893 to 1936 Lacroix was professor of mineralogy at the National Museum of Natural History in Paris. Lacroix's *Minéralogie de la France et de ses colonies* (1893–1913) and later his *Minéralogie de Madagascar* (1922–23), noted for their wide scope and comprehensive treatment, stand as unique in regional mineralogy. He contributed greatly to volcanology by his study of Mount Pelée in Martinique, *La Montagne Pelée et ses éruptions* (1904), and by his investigations of the 1906 eruption of Vesuvius in Italy. He became perpetual secretary of the Académie des Sciences, Paris, in 1920 and later wrote many biographies of great value to the history of science.

lacrosse (French: "the crosier"), competitive sport, modern version of the North American Indian game of baggataway, in which two teams of players use long-handled, racketlike implements (crosses) to catch, carry, or throw a ball down the field or into the opponents' goal. The goal is defined by uprights and a crossbar framing a loose net.

The distinctive feature of the game is the crosse, the implement used by the players to carry, catch, and pass the ball. The crosse is a staff of wood, usually hickory, the top being sharply bent to form a hook from the end of which a thong is drawn and fastened to the shaft about 2 or 3 feet (0.6 or 0.9 m) from the end of the handle, forming an oval triangle that is woven with a loose network of leather, nylon, or gut to form the pocket with which the ball is handled.

History. Lacrosse was played by the Six Nations of the Iroquois in what became upper New York state and lower Ontario long before Christopher Columbus landed in the New World. The sport was then much rougher than it is today. Among some tribes as many as a thousand players took part on each side, goals were miles apart, and a game could last as long as three days. Each player tried to disable as many opponents as possible with the stick he carried and afterward concentrate on scoring a goal. The Cherokee called their version of the game "little brother of war." Because of the endurance required and the injuries that had to be borne with fortitude it was considered excellent training for combat. Among many tribes the game was as much a mystic ceremony as a sport and was preceded by complex rituals and a solemn dance. In some areas men and women played together, and in other areas women had their own version of the game. Indians on government reservations in the United States and Canada still field strong teams.

To the first French settlers in Canada who saw the game, called baggataway, or *tewaraathon,* by the Indians, the shape of the implement used to catch, carry, and throw the ball suggested a bishop's crozier (*la crosse*), giving the sport its name.

Europeans in Canada started playing the game about 1840, and the first lacrosse organization, the Olympic Club, was founded in Montreal in 1842. In playing Indian teams, white players lost so frequently they were allowed to field extra men. Members of the Montreal Lacrosse Club (founded 1856) modified the rules somewhat, and in 1867 George Beers of Montreal, called "the father of lacrosse," made further changes that included replacing the Indian ball of deerskin stuffed with hair by a hard rubber ball, limiting the number of players on a team to 12, and improving the stick for easier catching and throwing of the ball. The 12 players were designated at that time as goal, point, cover point, first defense, second defense, third defense, centre, third attack, second attack, first attack, out home, and in home. In 1867 the National Lacrosse Association was formed, and the game was introduced to England. Captain W.B. Johnson of Montreal toured with a team of Caughnawaga Indians, appearing at Windsor Castle before Queen Victoria, who found the game "very pretty to watch." The English took to the sport and the game achieved popularity, notably in Lancashire, Cheshire, Yorkshire, Manchester, Bristol, and London. The English Lacrosse Union was founded in 1892, and the All-England Women's Lacrosse Association was formed in 1912. English teams exchanged visits with teams from the United States and Canada from time to time, and combined Oxford-Cambridge teams frequently exchanged visits with college or all-star teams from the United States. The game was also introduced in Ireland, Australia, and South Africa.

In the United States, a team of Indians introduced lacrosse at Troy, N.Y., about 1868, and a few years later teams were started in that city, New York City, and Brooklyn. In the 1880s Eastern schools including New York University, Princeton, Yale, and Harvard took up the sport. In 1884 a successful tour of Europe was made by a team of U.S. collegians, and in 1906 the U.S. Intercollegiate Lacrosse League was formed. The game received its greatest impetus, however, when it was introduced to Baltimore by some track-and-field athletes, who had seen the game played by Canadians on Long Island. The Baltimoreans actively promoted the sport, aiming at all age levels, so that Baltimore became the main U.S. centre of lacrosse. During the 1920s women field hockey players discovered lacrosse, and in 1931 the U.S. Women's Lacrosse Association was formed.

The Intercollegiate Lacrosse League was reorganized in 1926 as the U.S. Intercollegiate Lacrosse Association, which had about 120 member colleges. In 1970 the National Collegiate Athletic Association (NCAA), with more than 500 member colleges, undertook sponsorship of intercollegiate lacrosse competition, reflecting the growth of the sport in the country outside its traditional Eastern Seaboard stronghold. NCAA national championship tournaments for men began in 1971; women's tournaments began in 1982. The college team considered the best in the country is awarded the Wingate Trophy.

Lacrosse was included in the Olympic Games in 1904 and 1908 with teams representing Canada, the United States, and Great Britain. Teams from those countries also demonstrated the sport in exhibitions at the Games in 1928, 1932, and 1948, but it did not attract enough international interest to remain an Olympic sport. World Championships for men have been held since 1967. Women's World Championships were held from 1969 to 1982, when they were replaced by the World Cup. A variant of lacrosse, called box lacrosse (*q.v.*), was introduced in Canada in 1930.

The field and equipment. The field is 110 yards (about 100 m) long and 60 yards wide. The goals are 80 yards apart, the goal posts being 6 feet (1.8 m) high and the same distance apart, surmounted by a crossbar. The posts are fitted with a netting fastened to the ground behind the goal to stop passage of the ball after a successful shot. The goal-area lines, wing lines, and centre line act as restraints on the movements of certain players during play. Passing over a line into a prohibited area results in a penalty.

The ball is of sponge rubber, not less than 7.75 to 8 inches (19.7 to 20.3 cm) in circumference, and is from 5 to 5.25 ounces (142 to 149 g) in weight.

The width of the crosse at the top, or head, may not be more than 12 inches nor is it to be less than 7 inches. The length of the stick may not be more than 6 feet nor less than 3 feet, with the exception being the goalkeeper's stick, which may be of any length. Shoes have rubber, plastic, or metal cleats. Each player wears a helmet with a face mask or guard. Leather gloves protect the hands and wrists. Light pads are worn under the jersey to protect the shoulders and arms. The goalkeeper wears, in addition, a chest protector.

The game. Lacrosse is a very fast game, the object of which is to send the ball through the opponents' goal as many times as possible and to prevent one's opponents from scoring. A goal counts one point. Men's teams usually have 10 players: the goalkeeper, three defensemen, three midfielders (one of whom is the centre), and three attackmen. During play each team must have at least four players in its defensive half of the field and no fewer than three in its offensive half of the field. This rule prevents excessive crowding around a goal when it is under attack. Conventionally, the goalkeeper and the three defensemen stay in the defensive half, while the three attackmen stay in the offensive half. The midfielders are permitted to roam the field, reinforcing the attack or defense as needed. There are two officials, a referee and a judge.

The game is divided into four periods of 15 minutes each, with intervals of one minute between the first and second quarters and between the third and fourth quarters and a 10-minute rest at halftime. If the score is tied at the end of regulation time, play is resumed after an intermission of five minutes for two four-minute periods, with a one-minute rest in between. Free substitution is allowed.

A player may run with the ball, pass it in any direction, and catch it, but—with the exception of the goalkeeper—he may not touch it with his hand. A player may kick the ball or bat it, but not into the opponents' goal. A unique feature of the game is "cradling," in which the player rapidly rotates the stick in half-turns while holding it nearly upright as he runs. The centrifugal force developed keeps the ball in the pocket of the crosse and also puts it in position for accurate throwing. Defensive players are allowed to poke the ball-carrier in the body with their sticks or slap at his stick to dislodge the ball. Blocking the ball-carrier—*i.e.,* hitting him with the shoulder in an attempt to throw him off-balance or knock him down—is legal. For minor infractions of the rules the penalty is either suspension from the game for 30 seconds or an exchange of the ball. In the case of personal fouls of a more serious nature—for example, an illegal block—the offender is suspended from the game for one, two, or three minutes, and his team plays a man short for that period of time. Other serious fouls include tripping, slashing, and unnecessary roughness.

Play is started at the beginning of each quarter and after the scoring of a goal with a face-off at midfield, as in hockey. The two centres face each other, the heads of their sticks touching the ground. The referee places the ball between the two crosses and at his signal each player tries to gain control of the ball. He may keep it himself or bat it to a teammate. The player with the ball tries to advance it toward the opposing goal by running or passing to a teammate in the open. The defenders try to harry him into making a poor pass, intercept the ball when it is thrown, knock the ball from his stick, or occasionally knock it loose with a block. Players are in constant movement: dodging, hurling, or flipping the ball to a teammate; scooping up the ball while running at full speed; or making quick, deceptive shots at the goal. A unique ceremony at the beginning of the game consists of the teams lining up in the centre of the field opposite each other. Each player introduces himself to his particular opponent, shakes hands, and wishes him luck.

Women's lacrosse. Popular in the British Isles, Australia, Canada, New Zealand, South Africa, Switzerland, and the United States, women's lacrosse was first played in Scottish and English private schools in the early 1900s and was introduced to schools and colleges in the eastern United States by English women teachers. Frequent exchange visits by American and English women's teams followed, the latter showing themselves to be the best in the world. Britain-Ireland touring teams have excellent records against American teams.

The women's game allows no body contact or rough play with the stick. The goalkeeper wears a chest pad and leg guards. There are 12 players on a side. The goals are 90 to 110 yards apart, and there are no sidelines or end lines, the goal creases and centre circle being the only ground markings. A game consists of 25-minute halves, with a 10-minute intermission. There is no overtime in the case of a tie. The rules established by the All-England Ladies' Lacrosse Association are universally accepted by other nations. In the United States, the Philadelphia, Baltimore, and Boston areas furnish strong teams, while the main English centres of women's lacrosse are Hertfordshire, Kent, Norfolk, Essex, and Suffolk.

Lactantius, in full LUCIUS CAECILIUS FIRMIANUS LACTANTIUS, Caecilius also spelled CAELIUS (b. *c.* AD 240, North Africa—d. *c.* 320, Augusta Treverorum, Belgica [now Trier, Ger.]), Christian apologist and one of the most reprinted of the Latin Church Fathers, whose *Divinae institutiones* ("Divine Precepts"), a classically styled philosophical refutation of early-4th-century anti-Christian tracts, was the first systematic Latin account of the Christian attitude toward life. Lactantius was referred to as the "Christian Cicero" by Renaissance humanists.

Lactantius was appointed a teacher of rhetoric at Nicomedia (later İzmit, Tur.) by the Roman emperor Diocletian. When the emperor began persecuting Christians, however, Lactantius resigned his post about 305 and returned to the West. Later, in about 317, he came out of retirement to tutor the emperor Constantine's son Crispus, at Trier.

Only Lactantius' writings dealing with Christianity have survived. His principal work, the *Divinae institutiones,* depended more on the testimony of classical authors than on that of sacred Scripture. It repudiated what he termed the deluding superstitions of pagan cults, proposing in their place the Christian religion as a theism, or rationalized belief in a single Supreme Being who is the source creating all else. In a companion work, "On the Death of Persecutors," Lactantius held that the Christian God—in contradistinction to the remote, unconcerned God of Stoic deism—could intervene to right human injustice. Moreover, he maintained that Roman justice could be better perfected by rooting it in the Christian doctrine of divine fatherhood uniting the human race in universal fraternity through the mediation of Christ than by basing it on the Latin concept of *aequitas* ("equity").

Limited by an unprofound view of religion as popular morality, Lactantius was more adept in showing the incongruity of heathen polytheism than in establishing Christian teaching.

lactase, any of a group of enzymes found in the small intestine, liver, and kidney of mammals that catalyze the breakdown of lactose (milk sugar) into the simple sugars glucose and galactose. Lactase is particularly abundant during infancy. The enzyme is thought to be produced by the mucous membrane cells that line the intestinal walls; granules localize in the brush border (a chemical barrier through which food must pass to be absorbed) that coats the intestinal villi.

lactation, the secretion and yielding of milk by females after giving birth. The milk is produced by the mammary glands, which are contained within the breasts. (*See also* mammary gland.)

A brief treatment of human lactation follows. For full treatment, *see* MACROPAEDIA: Reproduction and Reproductive Systems.

Lactation is induced by a change in hormonal balance. Although the mammary glands enlarge during pregnancy, and some milk is formed, copious milk secretion begins about 3 days after the placenta is delivered or removed; this precipitates an increase in the secretion of prolactin, a hormone that stimulates the production of milk from the alveolar cells of the breast. The infant's action of nursing, or suckling, also stimulates the secretion of prolactin and of oxytocin, a pituitary hormone that causes the contraction of the muscle cells around the alveoli in the breast, resulting in the expulsion of milk.

Milk released during the first few days of lactation is called colostrum; it is richer in proteins, minerals, and immunoglobulins and is lower in calories and fat than the mature milk that develops over the following few weeks. The level of fats, lactose, and B vitamins gradually increases in breast milk during the first month of lactation. Mature breast milk is rich in the mother's white blood cells and hormones and substances such as immunoglobulins, which protect the infant against bacteria and other infectious agents.

The infant begins to outgrow the mother's milk supply around 4 to 6 months of age. Supplemental foods are generally introduced at this time to supply more calories and to acquaint the infant with the mechanisms of eating and drinking. As the child is weaned from nursing, lactation slowly declines and then stops. There is no typical age at which an infant must be weaned. The number of children who are breast-fed and the age at which they are weaned vary from country to country and among socioeconomic classes and regions within a country.

Lactation may be interrupted by insufficient oxytocin secretion, by an inadequate suckling pattern, or by maternal or infant physical difficulties. In addition, emotional factors such as stress can interfere with lactation and may be overcome by relaxation methods or by treatment with oxytocin and the reassurance gained as nursing becomes successful.

lactic acid, also called *α*-HYDROXYPROPIONIC ACID, or 2-HYDROXYPROPANOIC ACID, an organic compound belonging to the family of carboxylic acids, present in certain plant juices, in the blood and muscles of animals, and in the soil. It is the commonest acidic constituent of fermented milk products such as sour milk, cheese, and buttermilk.

First isolated in 1780 by a Swedish chemist, Carl Wilhelm Scheele, lactic acid is manufactured by the fermentation of molasses, starch, or whey in the presence of alkaline substances such as lime or calcium carbonate; it is available as aqueous solutions of various concentrations, usually 22–85 percent, and degrees of purity. Lactic acid is used in tanning leather and dyeing wool; as a flavouring agent and preservative in processed cheese, salad dressings, pickles, and carbonated beverages; and as a raw material or a catalyst in numerous chemical processes. Pure lactic acid, rarely prepared, is a colourless, crystalline substance that melts at 18° C (64° F); it rapidly absorbs moisture from the atmosphere.

Lactic acid occurs in the blood (in the form of its salts, called lactates) when glycogen is broken down in muscle and can be converted back to glycogen in the liver. Lactates are also the products of fermentation (*q.v.*) in certain bacteria.

lactic-acid bacterium, plural LACTIC-ACID BACTERIA, any member of several genera of gram-positive, rod- or sphere-shaped bacteria that produce lactic acid as the principal or sole end product of carbohydrate fermentation. Lactic-acid bacteria are aerotolerant anaerobes that are chiefly responsible for the pickling conditions necessary for the manufacture of pickles, sauerkraut, green olives, some varieties of sausage, and certain milk products, such as buttermilk. Under certain conditions, lactic-acid bacteria may contribute to dental caries. Important members include *Streptococcus, Lactobacillus,* and *Pediococcus.*

Lactobacillus, a genus of rod-shaped, gram-positive, non-spore-forming bacteria of the family Lactobacillaceae, widely distributed in animal feeds, silage, manure, and milk and milk products. *Lactobacillus delbrueckii,* a typical species, is 0.5 to 0.8 micrometre (μm; 1 μm = 10^{-6} metre) across by 2 to 9 μm long and occurs singly or in small chains. Various species of *Lactobacillus* are used commercially during the production of sour milks, cheeses, and yogurt. Lactobacilli have an important role in the manufacture of fermented vegetables (pickles and sauerkraut), beverages (beer, wine, and juices), sourdough breads, and some sausages. Lactobacilli are commensal inhabitants of animal and human intestinal tracts. Commercial preparations of lactobacilli are used to restore normal intestinal flora after the imbalance created by antibiotic therapy.

lactone, any of a class of cyclic organic esters, usually formed by reaction of a carboxylic acid group with a hydroxyl group or halogen atom present in the same molecule. Commercially important lactones include diketene and β-propiolactone used in the synthesis of acetoacetic acid derivatives and β-substituted propionic acids, respectively; the perfume ingredients pentadecanolide and ambrettolide; vitamin C; and the antibiotics methymycin, erythromycin, and carbomycin.

The γ- and δ-lactones, containing five- and six-membered rings, respectively, are the most common. They are formed by loss of water from the corresponding hydroxy acids, a process that often occurs spontaneously even in aqueous solution. Diketene and β-propiolactone are made by the reaction of ketene with itself or with formaldehyde, respectively. Lactones with 7 to 24 atoms in the ring are prepared by slow distillation of the appropriate hydroxy acids under greatly reduced pressure.

lactose, carbohydrate containing one molecule of glucose and one of galactose linked together. Composing about 2 to 8 percent of the milk of all mammals, lactose is sometimes called milk sugar. It is the only common sugar of animal origin. Lactose can be prepared from whey, a by-product of the cheese-making process. Fermentation of lactose by microorganisms such as *Lactobacillus acidophilus* is part of the industrial production of lactic acid. Human lactose intolerance is indicated by diarrhea and abdominal bloating and discomfort; lactose intolerance also may be a cause of diarrhea in newborns.

lacustrine ecosystem, any pond or lake viewed as an ecological unit of the biotic community and the physiochemical environment, within which mass and energy are cyclically exchanged. The factors affecting the lives and evolution of the organisms in still-water, or lentic, habitats vary according to the size of the body of water.

Ponds are relatively shallow, with considerable light penetration. They support a variety of rooted aquatic plants. Water is mixed well top to bottom, but there are great seasonal changes in wind, temperature, precipitation, and evaporation. It is a precarious habitat subject to much imbalance. The animal inhabitants must possess considerable physiological adaptability to survive.

Lakes are larger and deeper, often stratified in terms of light penetration, temperature range, and oxygen concentration. Such gradations from top to bottom profoundly affect the life of lakes in terms of distribution and adaptation. Seasonal changes are gradual and include spring and fall overturns of water and summer and winter stratification.

Three major zones of habitat are usually present: (1) littoral, the shallow-water zone, with light penetrating to the bottom and supporting rooted plants and bottom-dwelling animals; (2) limnetic, the water open to effective light penetration, supporting plant and animal plankton; and (3) profundal, the bottom and deepwater area beyond light penetration, supporting dark-adapted organisms.

Lacy, Franz Moritz, Count (Graf) **von** (b. Oct. 21, 1725, St. Petersburg, Russia—d. Nov. 24, 1801, Vienna, Austria), field marshal who served under the empress Maria Theresa and her successors and who reorganized the Austrian army.

Lacy's Irish father had served as a Russian officer. Lacy was educated in Germany and entered the Austrian service in 1743. During the War of the Austrian Succession (1740–48) he served in Italy, Bohemia, Silesia, and the Low Countries and during the Seven Years' War (1756–63) rose rapidly in rank. He was a field marshal by 1765 and then president of the supreme army council (1766–73). In the War of the Bavarian Succession (1778–79), Lacy and Gideon Ernst von Laudon were the chief Austrian commanders against Prussia, and, when Joseph II came to the throne (1765), Lacy became his most trusted associate. He was an excellent military administrator. Prematurely aged (perhaps because of numerous wounds), he was unsuccessful in the Turkish War of 1787–92 and had to hand over the command to his rival Laudon.

Ladākh, region of eastern Kashmir, part of Jammu and Kashmir state, in the northern part of the Indian subcontinent. It contains the western Himalayan Ladākh Range. Ladākh covers about 45,000 square miles (117,000 square km) and includes the Karakoram Range and the upper Indus River Valley.

Ladākh is one of the most elevated regions of the world. Its natural features consist mainly of high plains and deep valleys. The high plain predominates in the east, diminishing gradually westward. In the southeast of Ladākh lies Rupshu, an area of large, brackish lakes which has a uniform height of about 13,500 feet (4,100 m). To the northwest of Rupshu lies Zaskar, a bleak, inaccessible region where the people and the cattle remain indoors for much of the year because of the cold. Zaskar is drained by the Zaskar River, which, flowing northward, joins the Indus River below Leh. In Ladākh proper, farther to the north, cultivation by means of manuring and irrigation ranges from 9,000 to 15,000 feet (2,750 to 4,550 m). The people are divided into shepherds, who populate the upland valleys too high for cultivation, and the Ladākhis, who till the land around the valley villages. Leh, the most accessible town of Ladākh proper, is an important trade centre and lies 160 miles (260 km) east of Srinagar.

The climate of Ladākh is cold and dry. Average annual precipitation is $3\frac{1}{3}$ inches (84 mm); fine, dry, flaked snow is frequent, and sometimes the fall is heavy. Vegetation is confined to valleys and sheltered spots, where a stunted growth of tamarisk, furze, and other plants supply much-needed firewood. The principal products are wheat, barley, millet, buckwheat, peas, beans, and turnips. The only manufacture is woolen cloth.

Ladākh was contested by both India and Pakistan; after the cease-fire agreement of 1949, its southern portion went to India and the remainder to Pakistan. In the early 1960s Chinese forces gained control of the northeastern part of the Indian-held portion of Ladākh.

Ladākh Range, segment of the Karakoram Range, extending southeastward for 230 miles (370 km) from the mouth of the Shyok River in northern Pakistan across northern India to the Tibetan (China) border. With a crest line of about 20,000 feet (6,100 m), the range parallels the northeast bank of the Indus River. The Deosai Mountains, located southeast of the Indus River in northern Pakistan, are sometimes considered part of the range.

Ladd, George Trumbull (b. Jan. 19, 1842, Painesville, Ohio, U.S.—d. Aug. 8, 1921, New Haven, Conn.), philosopher and psychologist whose textbooks were influential in establishing experimental psychology in the United States. Though he called for a scientific psychology, he nonetheless viewed the role of psychology as ancillary to philosophy.

Ladd

By courtesy of the Archives of the History of American Psychology, the University of Akron, Ohio

Educated for the ministry, Ladd was pastor of a Congregational church in Milwaukee, Wis., for eight years before becoming professor of philosophy at Bowdoin College, Brunswick, Maine (1879–81). During those years, he began investigating the relationship between the nervous system and mental phenomena and introduced the first study of experimental psychology in the United States. From 1881 to 1905 he was a professor at Yale University, establishing the first American laboratory in experimental psychology. His main interest, however, was in writing *Elements of Physiological Psychology* (1887), the first such handbook in English. Because of its emphasis on neurophysiology, it long remained a standard work. His large-scale *Psychology, Descriptive and Explanatory* (1894) is important as a theoretical system of functional psychology, considering the human being as an organism with a mind purposefully solving problems and adapting the self to its environment.

Ladd-Franklin, Christine, *née* LADD (b. Dec. 1, 1847, Windsor, Conn., U.S.—d. March 5, 1930, New York, N.Y.), American scientist and logician known for contributions to the theory of colour vision.

She earned an A.B. at Vassar College, Poughkeepsie, N.Y., in 1869 and then studied mathematics at Johns Hopkins University, Baltimore. Although she held a fellowship, 1879–82, and fulfilled all the requirements for the Ph.D., she was not awarded the degree until 1926 because at the time of her graduate work the university did not officially recognize women candidates. She taught logic and philosophy at Johns Hopkins from 1904 to 1909 and lectured at Columbia University in New York City from 1910 to 1930.

She is probably best-known for her work on colour vision. While studying in Germany in 1891–92, she developed the Ladd-Franklin theory, which emphasized the evolutionary development of increased differentiation in colour vision and assumed a photochemical model for the visual system. Her theory, which criticized the views of Hermann von Helmholtz and Ewald Hering, was widely accepted for a number of years.

Earlier in her career, while investigating the problems of symbolic logic, she reduced syllogistic reasoning to an "inconsistent triad" with the introduction of the "antilogism," a form which made the testing of deductions easier. Ladd-Franklin also published numerous papers on mathematics and binocular vision. Her principal works are "The Algebra of Logic" (1883), "The Nature of Color Sensation" (1925), and *Colour and Colour Theories* (1929).

ladder-back chair, chair with a tall back constructed of horizontal slats or spindles between two uprights. The type is usually rustic, and the seat is often of cane or rush.

Appearing in the Middle Ages, ladder-back chairs had become widespread in England by the 17th century and were in common use in colonial America as well. By the middle of that century, they were also copied by fashionable furniture makers who used walnut instead of sycamore and tended to add elaborate refinements. The top slat, which even in simple types was usually larger than the others and was sometimes pierced for ease of handling, became more richly and heavily ornamented. As piercing of the back slats progressed, they began to resemble the sound holes of a violin, and this type of chair came to be known as a fiddle back (a term also applied, until the second half of the 18th century, to another type of shaped chair, the appearance of which was thought to resemble that of a violin).

Ladder-back armchair, Fairfield, Conn., 1700–35; in the Mary Allis Collection, Fairfield, Conn.

By courtesy of Mary Allis, Fairfield, Conn.

ladder shell (snail): *see* wentletrap.

Lādhiqīyah, al- (Syria): *see* Latakia.

ladies' fingers (herb): *see* kidney vetch.

Ladies' Home Journal, American monthly magazine, one of the longest-running in the country and long the trendsetter among women's magazines. It was founded in 1883 as a women's supplement to the *Tribune and Farmer* (1879–85) of Cyrus H.K. Curtis and was edited by his wife, Louisa Knapp. The *Journal* began independent publication in 1884 with a pious and demure editorial posture and a sentimental literary diet and had a circulation of 20,000. Curtis boosted circulation to more than 400,000 with an innovative multiple subscription "club" and a large advertising campaign.

Edward W. Bok became editor in 1889, and under him the *Journal* attracted great writers from Europe and the United States, offering quality fiction and nonfiction articles to women. By the turn of the century, its circulation surpassed all other American publications. As editor, Bok gave the magazine a sense of intimacy and established service departments to answer letters from readers. All of these contributed to the *Journal* 's outstanding success and revolutionized the women's magazine field.

The *Journal* instituted an advertising code to eliminate fraud and extravagant claims by advertisers and was noted for its attention to social causes. It refused, for example, to advertise patent medicine, and its subsequent muckraking campaign against those products helped bring about the passage of the U.S. Federal Food and Drugs Act in 1906. Its features on residential architecture, fine arts, and domestic life won renown. The *Journal* was often imitated, and it was long the leader of all American women's magazines in circulation, but after the mid-20th century it was overtaken by its older rival, *McCall's* (1873).

ladies' tresses, any plant of the genus *Spiranthes,* family Orchidaceae, numbering as many as 300 species of orchids found in woods and grasslands throughout most of the world. *Goodyera repens,* an unrelated British species, is known as creeping ladies' tresses.

Autumn ladies' tresses (*Spiranthes spiralis*)

Joan E. Rahn

Species of *Spiranthes* vary greatly in size and flower colour, but all have a spiral cluster of small whitish flowers borne at the top of a spike. Some species bloom in autumn, such as nodding ladies' tresses, or autumn tresses (*S. cernua*), in North America and autumn ladies' tresses (*S. spiralis*) in Europe. Slender ladies' tresses (*S. gracilis*) of North America has a single spiral of small, white flowers.

Lâdik carpet, handwoven floor covering usually in a prayer design and made in or near Lâdik, a town in the Konya Plain of south-central Turkey. Lâdik prayer rugs have either a high, stepped arch design or a triple arch with a dominating central portion. In a separate panel above or below the prayer-niche motif, a group of five or more flower stalks project upward from a band of crenellation.

Although a few date to the late 18th-century, most Lâdik carpets were made in the 19th century. The term column Lâdik has been applied to prayer rugs that, regardless of their actual places of origin, share a motif derived from a 16th-century Ottoman court design, consisting of three arches of unequal height supported upon slender columns and surmounted by a panel as described earlier. Most column Lâdiks have been found in Europe and presumably were made in the Balkans in the 17th and 18th centuries. A less sophisticated, more recent type, with bolder colouring, comes from the nearby city of Konya.

Lâdik prayer rug from Anatolia, early 19th century; in the Metropolitan Museum of Art, New York City

By courtesy of the Metropolitan Museum of Art, New York City, gift of J.F. Ballard; photograph, Otto E. Nelson

lading, bill of, document executed by a carrier, such as a railroad or shipping line, acknowledging receipt of goods and embodying an agreement to transport the goods to a stated destination. Bills of lading are closely related to warehouse receipts, which contain an agreement for storage rather than carriage. Both may be negotiable when they provide that the goods are to be delivered not to a fixed individual but, typically, to the order of a stated person; this person may endorse the document and give it to another, who will then be entitled to receive the goods. Such a negotiable document of title, which calls for the delivery of goods, must be distinguished from negotiable commercial paper such as notes and bills of exchange, which call for the payment of money. *See also* charter party.

Ladinian Stage, upper of two subdivisions in the Middle Triassic Series, representing all rocks deposited worldwide during the Ladinian Age (235 to 230 million years ago). No global stratotype section and point (GSSP) for the base of the stage has been approved by the International Commission on Stratigraphy. The stage's name is derived from the Ladin people, who inhabit the region of the Dolomites in northern Italy. The Duchenstein and Wengen beds comprise the Ladinian Stage in its type district. Five ammonite biozones, beginning with *Eoprotrachyceras subasperum* and ending with *Frankites sutherlandi,* are widely used to correlate this interval. The Ladinian Stage overlies the Anisian Stage and is itself overlain by the Carnian Stage in the Upper Triassic Series.

Ladino, Europeanized Central American person of predominantly Spanish origin. Despite regional variations, there is a cultural similarity among Ladinos stemming from their common Spanish origins and speech. Ladinos include urban classes, rural labourers, and peasantry. Although not always physically distinguishable from Indians, Ladinos may be recognized by their exclusive use of the Spanish language and by their Western dress.

Many Ladinos practice a subsistence agriculture much like that of their Indian neighbours, although with more stress on cash crops and participation in a regional market economy. They also differ from the Indians in their greater use of advanced cultivation equipment and methods, such as steel plows, irrigation, and fertilization. Many employ Indians or landless peasants as seasonal labour. In small towns, Ladinos very commonly engage in small-scale commerce, in addition to agricultural activities.

Ladino language, also called JUDEO-SPANISH, SEFARDIC, or SEPHARDIC, Romance language spoken by Sefardic Jews in the Balkans, the Middle East, North Africa, Greece, and Turkey; it is very nearly extinct in many of these areas. A very archaic form of Castilian Spanish, mixed somewhat with Hebrew elements, Ladino originated in Spain and was carried to its present speech areas by the descendants of the Spanish Jews who were exiled from Spain after 1492.

Ladino preserves many words and grammatical usages that have been lost in modern Spanish. It also has a more conservative sound system—for example, *f* and *g* sounds still occur where modern Spanish has an *h* (not pronounced): Ladino *fijo, fablar* versus Spanish *hijo, hablar,* and Ladino *agora* versus Spanish *ahora.* Ladino is usually written in Hebrew characters and has a literature of its own, including many works in translation.

Ladipo, Duro (b. Dec. 18, 1931, Oshogbo, Nigeria—d. Mar. 11, 1978, Oshogbo), Nigerian dramatist whose innovative folk operas incorporating ritual poetry and traditional rhythms performed on indigenous instruments were based on Yoruba history.

As a teacher in a church school at Oshogbo in 1960, Ladipo scandalized church members by including *bata* drums in the Easter cantata that he had composed for the church and was thereafter obliged to seek a secular outlet for his musical interests. In 1962 he founded the Mbari Mbayo Club, and for its inauguration his new theatre company performed his first opera, *Oba Moro* ("Ghost-Catcher King"). He premiered *Oba Koso* ("The King Did Not Hang") at the club's first anniversary in 1963 and a year later introduced *Oba Waja* ("The King is Dead"). All three operas are based on the history of the Oyo kingdom and are available in English in *Three Yoruba Plays* (1964).

Yoruba operas prior to Ladipo's were mostly moral exemplars based on Bible stories or folktales. Ladipo, by contrast, wished his operas to be reliable cultural and historical records, and he was painstaking in his pursuit of authenticity. In order to achieve greater dignity and dramatic impact, he dispensed with the traditional dances and the opening and closing "glees" usually employed for bracketing performances in Yoruba operas. For *Oba Koso,* his most successful work, he received a Nigerian government citation for cultural achievement in 1963. The work also proved to be popular throughout Europe and the United States.

Ladislas, also spelled LADISLAUS, or LADISLAW, name of rulers grouped below by country and indicated by the symbol •.

Foreign-language equivalents:

Czech	Ladislav
Hungarian	László
Italian	Ladislao

BOHEMIA

• **Ladislas:** *see* Ladislas V *under* Ladislas (Hungary).

HUNGARY

• **Ladislas I,** also called SAINT LADISLAS, Hungarian SZENT LÁSZLÓ (b. June 27, 1040, Poland—d. July 29, 1095, Nitra, Slovakia; canonized 1192; feast day June 27), king of Hungary who greatly expanded the boundaries of the kingdom and consolidated it internally; no other Hungarian king was so generally beloved by the people.

The son of Béla I of Hungary and the Polish princess Rycheza (Ryksa), Ladislas was born in exile. Returning to Hungary, he and his brother Géza refused to contest the throne against their cousin Salomon; however, they quarreled with him and drove him from the country (1073). Géza took the throne, and, on his death, in 1077, Ladislas succeeded him as king of Hungary.

Ladislas I, coin, 11th century; in the British Museum

By courtesy of the trustees of the British Museum; photograph, J.R. Freeman & Co. Ltd.

Ladislas extended Hungary's frontier in Transylvania and occupied Croatia (1091) to protect the rights of his sister, the widow of Zvonimir, prince of Croatia. In the investiture struggle over the nomination and installation of bishops, Ladislas sided with the pope, though he also initiated a policy of reconciliation with the Holy Roman emperor Henry IV. Ladislas rooted out heathens in his dominions with severity and introduced Roman Catholicism to Croatia, founding the bishopric of Zagreb (1091). He introduced an elaborate legal code that brought order and prosperity to his dominions.

Ladislas died suddenly while preparing for the First Crusade. The ideal Hungarian knight, he was regarded by the nation as a saint long before his canonization.

• **Ladislas IV,** byname LADISLAS THE CUMAN, or KUMAN, Hungarian KUN LÁSZLÓ (b. 1262—d. July 10, 1290, Körösszeg, Hung.), king of Hungary who, by his support of the German king Rudolf I at the Battle of Dürnkrut, helped to establish the future power of the Habsburg dynasty in Austria.

The son of Stephen V, Ladislas IV became king of Hungary on his father's death in 1272. His minority (until 1277) was troubled by palace revolutions and civil wars. His mother was a princess of the Cumans, a Turkic people from the Black Sea area that had settled in Hungary. She was engaged in a continuous struggle with rebellious vassals who had the support of the expansion-minded Otakar II of Bohemia: Otakar had designs on Slovakia, then part of Hungary. Thus, common interests impelled Ladislas to join forces with Rudolf, who was of the house of Habsburg, in his struggle with Otakar, and 56,000 Hungarians and Cumans helped Rudolf defeat Otakar at the Battle of Dürnkrut (Marchfeld; Aug. 26, 1278).

The Bohemian danger over, Ladislas, a talented but wild and reckless man, came into conflict with his own magnates. He had married Isabella of Anjou, a daughter of Charles I of Naples and Sicily, but had neglected her for Cuman mistresses. His enemies accused him of undermining Christianity by preferring the nomadic Cumans to the Magyars. After an inquiry by a papal legate, he was forced to war against the Cumans, whom he defeated at Hódmezö (May 1282).

Ladislas soon relapsed, however. He adopted Cuman dress, passed his time exclusively with Cumans, and abused his legitimate wife. At last, Pope Nicholas IV decided that the crown of Hungary should pass to the Angevin Charles Martel, son of Ladislas' sister Maria by her marriage to Isabella's brother Charles II of Naples and Sicily. On Aug. 8, 1288, the pope proclaimed a crusade against Ladislas.

For the next two years, civil war convulsed Hungary. Ladislas, who fought with desperate valour, was driven from one end of the kingdom to the other. On Dec. 25, 1289, he issued a manifesto to the lesser gentry, many of whom sided with him, urging them to fight on against the magnates and their foreign supporters. In the next year, however, he was murdered in his camp by the Cumans, who never forgave him for attacking them in 1282.

• **Ladislas V,** byname LADISLAS POSTHUMUS, Hungarian LÁSZLÓ POSTUMUS, Czech LADISLAV POHROBEK (b. Feb. 22, 1440, Komárom, Hung. [now Komarno, Slovakia]—d. Nov. 23, 1457, Prague, Bohemia [now in Czech Republic]), boy king of Hungary and of Bohemia (from 1453), who was caught up in the feud between his guardian Ulrich, count of Cilli, and the Hunyadi family of Hungary.

Ladislas was the posthumous only son of the Habsburg German king Albert II, who had also been king of Hungary and Bohemia. The estates of Hungary had already selected Władysław III of Poland to be their king as Ulászló I, but Ladislas' mother Elizabeth compelled the primate to crown Ladislas king at Székesfehérvár on May 15, 1440. She then placed him under the guardianship of his cousin, who was later to become Holy Roman emperor Frederick III. The estates, however, issued a charter declaring Ladislas' coronation null and void.

After Władysław died (1444), Ladislas was elected king of Hungary, but Frederick continued to act as guardian of both Ladislas and the crown until 1452. The child was later transferred to the guardianship of Ulrich, an enemy of János Hunyadi, who earlier had been elected governor of Hungary with full regal and administrative authority. Ulrich succeeded in instilling a hatred of the Hunyadi family in the young king.

Ladislas, still a minor, was crowned king of Bohemia as Ladislav I (Oct. 28, 1453). Thereafter, he spent most of his time in Prague and Vienna. Regents ruled both his realms: George of Poděbrady in Bohemia and Hunyadi in Hungary. After Hunyadi died (August 1456), his son Ladislas Hunyadi had Ulrich assassinated later that year. The subsequent execution of Ladislas Hunyadi (March 1457), after Ladislas V had sworn not to harm him, raised such a storm in Hungary that the king fled to Prague, where he died later that year. For centuries it was conjectured that Ladislas had died of poisoning by his political opponents or by his successor as king of Bohemia, George of Poděbrady. The scientific analysis of Ladislas' skeleton in 1987–88 established that he died of juvenile leukemia, however.

NAPLES

• **Ladislas** (b. Feb. 11, 1377, Naples [Italy]—d. Aug. 6, 1414, Naples), king of Naples (from 1386), claimant to the throne of Hungary (from 1390), and prince of Taranto (from 1406). He became a skilled political and military leader, taking advantage of power struggles on the Italian peninsula to greatly expand his kingdom and his power.

Succeeding his father, Charles III, in 1386, Ladislas was king at age nine under the regency of his mother, Margaret of Durazzo. Expelled from Naples in 1387 by the rival claimant Louis II of Anjou, he first subdued the recalcitrant Neapolitan barons and finally, in 1399, drove out Louis, who no longer was supported by France. In pursuance of his father's Hungarian ambitions, he led an expedition into Dalmatia and declared himself king of Hungary at Zara in August 1404, though he actually controlled very little territory. Thereupon, he returned to Naples to suppress once again the rebel barons.

When Boniface IX died in 1404, Ladislas supported the new pope, Innocent VII, against the antipope Benedict XIII, who was an ally of Louis. After Ladislas occupied Rome, Innocent proclaimed him protector of the church as well as governor of the Campagna and the Marittima. After the death of his powerful adversary Raimondo del Balzo-Orsini, prince of Taranto, he married the widowed Marie d'Enghien, thereby gaining the principality of Taranto.

When Gregory XII, who succeeded Innocent (1406), seemed ready to reach an accord to end the papal schism, Ladislas in the spring of 1408 occupied Rome, Lazio (Latium), and Umbria and tried to impede the Council of Pisa. Nevertheless, the council elected Alexander V pope in 1409, deposing both Gregory and Benedict. While Ladislas supported Gregory, Alexander's successor, the Pisan antipope John XXIII crowned Louis king of Naples (1411). Defeated by Louis at Roccasecca, Ladislas reorganized his forces, made peace with Florence, and won the aid of the skilled condottiere Muzio Attendolo Sforza. Ladislas' position was so much strengthened that Pope John agreed to give him money and land in return for Ladislas' disavowal of Gregory (1412).

An impending accord between Pope John and Sigismund, newly elected German king and claimant to the Hungarian throne, however, led Ladislas to occupy and sack Rome (June 1413). He advanced to Bologna to prevent John from joining Sigismund. After having made peace with Florence and Siena, Ladislas fell ill and was taken back to Naples, where he died.

Ladislaus (personal name): *see under* Ladislas.

Ladislav (Czech personal name): *see under* Ladislas.

Lado Enclave, region in central Africa bordering on Lake Albert Nyanza (now Lake Albert), on the west bank of the Upper Nile, that was administered by the Congo Free State in 1894–1909 and was incorporated thereafter into the Anglo-Egyptian Sudan.

Europeans first visited the northern part of the region in 1841–42, when an expedition was dispatched there by Muḥammad ʿAlī Pasha, the Ottoman sultan of Egypt. The neighbouring posts of Gondokoro, on the east bank, and Lado soon became stations for ivory and slave traders from Khartoum. After the discovery of Lake Albert Nyanza in 1864 by the British explorer Sir Samuel Baker, the whole region was overrun by slave raiders of diverse nationalities. Although Lado was claimed as part of the Egyptian Sudan, it was not until Baker arrived at Gondoroko in 1870 as governor of the equatorial provinces that any attempt to control the slave trade was made. Baker's successor, General C.G. Gordon, established a separate administration for the Baḥr al-Ghazāl (a southern province of the present-day republic of The Sudan). In 1877 Emin Paşa (a German administrator) became governor of the equatorial provinces and made his headquarters at Lado, whence he was driven in 1885 by Mahdists from the Sudan. He then removed southward to Wadelai, but in 1889 he was forced to withdraw to the east coast. The British claimed the Upper Nile region in February 1894, and that May they leased to Leopold II of Belgium, as sovereign of the Congo State, a large area west of the Upper Nile, which included the Baḥr al-Ghazāl and Fashoda. Pressed by France, however, Leopold agreed to occupy only that part of the area east of 30° E and south of 05°30′ N; thus, the actual limits of what was later called the Lado Enclave (the region occupied by Leopold) were defined.

After the French withdrew from Fashoda (1898), Leopold II revived his claim to the whole area leased to him by the British. Although he was unsuccessful, and the lease was annulled as a result of a new agreement with Great Britain, Leopold retained the enclave, with the stipulation that it should revert to the Anglo-Egyptian Sudan six months after the end of his reign. After Leopold's death in 1909, the Lado Enclave was incorporated into the Anglo-Egyptian Sudan in 1910.

Ladoga, Lake, Russian LADOZHSKOYE OZERO, or LADOZHSKOE OZERO, largest lake in Europe, located in northwestern Russia about 25 miles (40 km) east of St. Petersburg. It is 6,700 square miles (17,600 square km) in area—exclusive of islands—and 136 miles (219 km) long, with an average width of 51 miles (82 km) and an average depth of 167 feet (51 m). Its greatest depth, at a point west of Valaam Island, is 754 feet (230 m).

Lake Ladoga's basin has a total area of about 100,000 square miles (259,000 square km). The depression of the lake was produced by the action of glaciers. The northern shores are mostly high and craggy and are broken by deep, ice-covered, fjordlike inlets. There are numerous, mostly wooded islands there, with cliffs. The southern shores, which have many sandy or rocky beaches, are primarily low, slightly indented, and overgrown with willows and alders. In some places there are ancient coastal embankments overgrown with pines. There are approximately 50,000 lakes and 3,500 rivers more than 6 miles (10 km) long in the Lake Ladoga basin. The largest tributaries are the Volkhov, the Svir, and the Vuoksa.

The lake also contains approximately 660 islands of more than 2.5 acres (1 hectare) in area, occupying a total of 176 square miles (456 square km). The largest islands are Riyekkalan-Sari, Mantsinsari, Kilpola, Tulolansari, and Valaam.

The climate in the Lake Ladoga region is moderately cold. Mean annual precipitation is 24 inches (610) mm). The lake is highest in June and July and lowest in December and January; its average annual range of elevation is about 2.6 feet (0.8 m), and the absolute maximum annual variation was about 9.8 feet (3 m). Seiches, or temporary, sometimes drastic changes in the water level, can be observed.

Thermal conditions differ from the deep central to the shallow coastal regions of the lake. The coastal regions and inlets usually freeze at the beginning of December, and the open central area freezes in January or February; the average ice thickness is 20–23 inches (50–60 cm). The central part of the lake opens in late March or early April, the northern part not until the beginning of May.

Lake Ladoga's water, yellow-brown in colour, is fresh, with an average mineralization of about 56 parts per million of calcium hydrocarbonate. The lake abounds in fish of commercial importance. Water transportation and fishing are the principal commercial uses of Lake Ladoga. The lake is part of the Volga–Baltic water route and of the White Sea–Baltic Waterway system, through which freight is carried, without the need for transshipment, to points within Russia and to Finland, Germany, and other countries.

During World War II, when Leningrad (St. Petersburg) was under siege by the Germans from September 1941 to March 1943, Lake Ladoga was the lifeline connecting it with the rest of the Soviet Union. Supplies and military equipment were brought to the city across the water and ice, and the sick and wounded were evacuated over the same route.

The cities of Priozyorsk, Petrokrepost, and Sortavala are located on its shores.

lady, in Great Britain, a general title for any peeress below the rank of duchess and also for the wife of a baronet or knight. It is ordinarily used as a less formal alternative to the full title of a marchioness, countess, or viscountess; where the name is territorial, the "of" is dropped—thus, "the marchioness of A.," but "Lady A." The daughters of dukes, marquesses, and earls also have, by courtesy, the title of lady prefixed to their Christian name and surname, *e.g.,* Lady Jane Grey.

The style of address is used to refer to the wives of baronets and knights; but, whereas "The Lady A." is the style reserved for the wives of peers, the definite article is not used in referring to the wives of baronets and knights. *See also* lord.

Lady chapel, chapel attached to a church and dedicated to the Blessed Virgin. As the development of the chevet, or radiating system of apse chapels, progressed during the 12th and 13th centuries, custom began to dictate

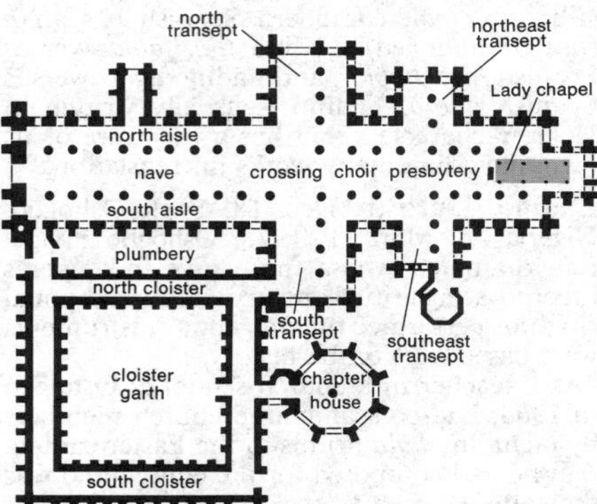

Plan of Salisbury cathedral, Wiltshire, England, showing the location of the Lady chapel

From M.S. Briggs, *Everyman's Concise Encyclopaedia of Architecture;* E.P. Dutton & Co., Inc., and J.M. Dent & Sons Ltd.

that the chapel dedicated to the Blessed Virgin be given the most important position, directly behind the high altar. The Lady chapel was frequently made larger than other chapels in the church.

No standard usage in building Lady chapels ever developed, however. In some French cathedrals they were emphasized (Reims; Le Mans; Amiens), whereas in others no distinction was made between them and other chapels (Notre-Dame, Paris; Bourges). In England, where the common plan of a square east end lent itself to the elaboration of the Lady chapel, it was more consistently emphasized, but there was considerable variation in location. In Spain and Italy the finest examples are late Gothic and Renaissance.

lady fern (species *Athyrium filix-femina*), a large, feathery fern classified in the family As-

Lady fern (*Athyrium filix-femina*)

A to Z Botanical Collection

pleniaceae (Aspidiaceae in some classification systems), widely cultivated for ornamentation. Leaves are about 75 cm (30 inches) long and 25 cm (10 inches) wide and grow in circular clusters. Characteristic of the genus are curved or horseshoe-shaped spore-producing clusters (sori) that are covered by a fringed, membranous protective structure. Lady ferns occur in moist, semi-shaded areas in the temperate zones of the world.

Lady Lever Art Gallery: *see* Lever Art Gallery.

Lady of Mercy, Order of Our: *see* Mercedarian.

ladybird beetle, also called LADYBUG, any of the approximately 5,000 widely distributed beetles of the family Coccinellidae (order Coleoptera). The name originated in the Middle Ages, when the beetle was dedicated to the Virgin Mary and called "beetle of Our Lady."

Ladybird beetles are hemispheric in shape and are usually 8 to 10 mm (0.3 to 0.4 inch) long. They have short legs and are usually brightly coloured with black, yellow, or reddish markings. The nine-spotted ladybird beetle (*Coccinella novemnotata*) has four black spots on each wing cover (elytron) and one shared spot.

The life cycle requires about four weeks, so that several generations are produced each

(Top) Larva and (bottom) adult of seven-spotted ladybird beetle (*Coccinella 7-punctata*)
(Top) N.A. Callow, (bottom) Stephen Dalton

summer. The long, slender, soft-bodied larvae—usually gray with blue, green, red, or black spots—feed on other insects and insect eggs. The larvae pass through four growth stages and then attach to some object and pupate in their last larval skin. Different groups of ladybird beetles usually hibernate each winter at the same location.

Clusters of ladybird beetles are often gathered and sold to farmers to control such insect pests as aphids, scales, and mites. The Australian ladybird beetle, or vedalia beetle (*Rodolia cardinalis*), was brought to western North America to help combat an outbreak of cottony-cushion scale (*Icerya purchasi*), which threatened to ruin orchards. Both the larvae and adults of the convergent ladybug (*Hippodamia convergens*) are important aphid predators.

Although most ladybird beetles and larvae are carnivorous, several feed on plants and are quite destructive—*e.g.,* the squash beetle (*Epilachna borealis*) and the Mexican bean beetle (*E. varivestis*).

The familiar children's rhyme "Ladybug ladybug, fly away home/ Your house is on fire, your children do roam" was a reference to the burning of the hop vines in England that took place following the harvest and cleared the fields but also killed numerous ladybird beetles. In folk medicine ladybird beetles have been prescribed as remedies for colic, measles, and toothaches.

ladyfish, also called TEN-POUNDER (*Elops saurus*), primarily tropical coastal marine fish of the family Elopidae (order Elopiformes), related to the tarpon and bonefish. The ladyfish is slender and pikelike in form and covered with fine silver scales; there are grooves into which the dorsal and anal fins can be depressed. A predatory fish, the ladyfish has small, sharp teeth and a bony throat plate between its mandibles. It ranges in length up to 90 cm (35 inches) and may weigh up to 13.6 kg (30 pounds). The young are transparent and eellike.

Ladyfish (*Elops saurus*)
Painting by Richard Ellis

The name ladyfish is also sometimes applied to other marine fishes, including the bonefish (*q.v.*). The Spanish ladyfish, or pudiano (*Bodianus rufus*), is a red and gold wrasse of the family Labridae.

lady's mantle, any of several herbaceous perennials of the genus *Alchemilla,* particularly *A. vulgaris,* within the rose family (Rosaceae). *A. vulgaris* is widely distributed in Eurasia and has been introduced into North America. It grows up to 60 cm (2 feet) tall on grasslands and rocky soils. The broad leaves are borne on long stalks, have shallow, rounded lobes and

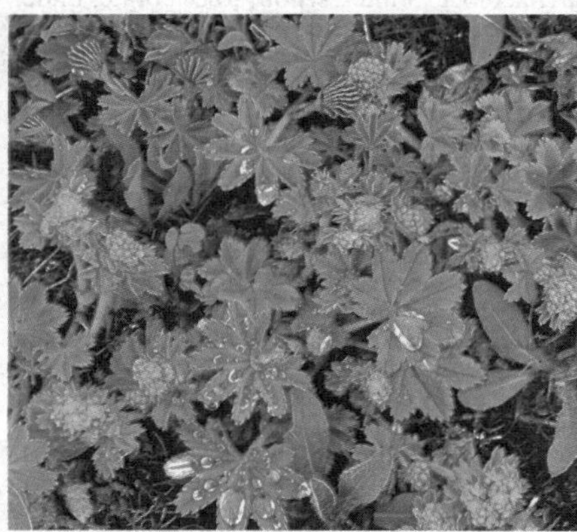

Lady's mantle (*Alchemilla vulgaris*)
Ingmar Holmasen

toothed edges, and are about 10 cm (4 inches) across. The tiny greenish yellow flowers grow in a terminal cluster.

lady's slipper, any member of several genera of orchids, family Orchidaceae, in which the lip of the flower is slipper-shaped. The genus *Cypripedium* has about 50 temperate and subtropical species. One well-known species is the yellow lady's slipper (*Cypripedium calceolus*); another is the pink lady's slipper (*C. acaule*), also known as the moccasin flower. Most species have one or two flowers on a stem about 30 to 60 cm (12 to 24 inches) tall.

About 12 species of lady's slippers constitute the genus *Phragmipedium.* They are narrow-leaved plants native to tropical America. One to six flowers with ribbonlike petals are borne on a stalk nearly 90 cm tall. The three species in the genus *Selenipedium,* also native to tropical America, may be 5 m (16 feet) tall. The leaves are folded, and the flowers are borne on a spike at the tip of the plant. Species of

Lady's slipper (*Cypripedium*)
Grant Heilman

Paphiopedilum, a genus of about 50 tropical Asian lady's slippers, have mottled or greenish leaves with a leathery texture and large, waxy flowers of various colours. Many hybrids have been developed.

Ladysmith, town, northwestern KwaZulu/Natal province, South Africa, on the Klip River. Founded in 1850 after the British annexed the area, it was named for the wife of Sir Harry Smith (then governor of Cape Colony). It was besieged by the Boers during the South African War from Nov. 1, 1899, until relieved by Sir Redvers Buller on Feb. 28, 1900. The 3,200 men who died in the defense and rescue of the town are commemorated in the stained-glass windows and marble tablets of the All Saints Anglican Church. An important rail junction and marshaling yard, Ladysmith markets and distributes agricultural produce over a wide area. Industry is based on food processing and the nearby KwaZulu/Natal coalfields. Pop. (1985) 25,102.

Lae, port city, northeastern Papua New Guinea. It is located near the mouth of the Markham River on Huon Gulf. Commercial activities centre on the export of timber, plywood, and coffee (transported by road from Bulolo and Wau) and the produce from the Central Range, which is airfreighted. Lae is also the marketing centre for the agricultural produce of the surrounding region.

The city originated as Lehe mission settlement and developed around an airport that was built in 1928 by Guinea Airways, Ltd. Although it was selected in 1938–39 to replace Rabaul as territorial capital, the transfer never took place because Lae was completely destroyed during World War II. It was later reconstructed with new wharves at Milfordhaven, sawmills and veneer mills, an abattoir, and modern amenities. It contains a war cemetery and botanical gardens. The Papua New Guinea University of Technology, founded in 1965, is located 6 miles (10 km) outside the city. Pop. (1990) 80,655.

Laelia, genus of orchids, family Orchidaceae, containing as many as 75 species of plants with attractively coloured flowers. Many species have been crossed with *Cattleya* and other genera to produce hybrid orchids for the commercial flower trade.

All *Laelia* species are epiphytic; that is, they are supported by other plants and have aerial roots exposed to the humid atmosphere. The

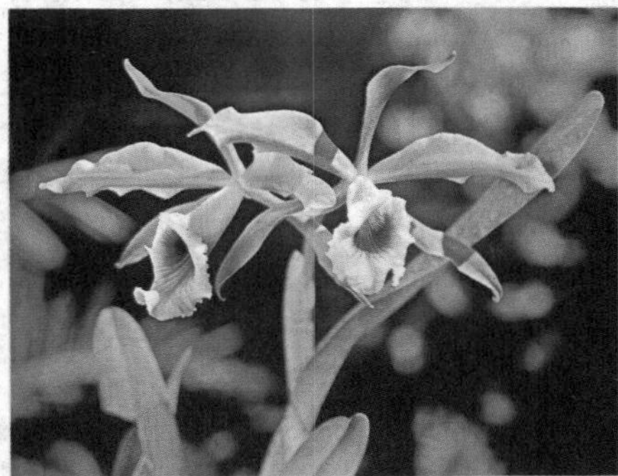

Laelia
Joyce R. Wilson

pseudobulbs (swollen stems) of various *Laelia* species may be long, oval, or rounded.

Laelius, Gaius (d. after 160 BC), Roman general and politician who contributed to Roman victory during the Second Punic War (218–201) between Rome and Carthage.

Owing his political advancement to his friend, the renowned commander Scipio Africanus, Laelius accompanied Scipio on his Spanish campaign (210–206). While in Africa with Scipio from 204 to 202, Laelius defeated the Numidian prince Syphax, an ally of the Carthaginians, and commanded the cavalry in Scipio's decisive victory over Hannibal at Zama (now in Tunisia; 202). After the war Laelius advanced from aedile (197) to praetor (196) to consul (190). In 160 he met Polybius and supplied the historian with a great deal of information about the life of Scipio Africanus.

Laelius Sapiens, Gaius, THE YOUNGER (fl. 2nd century BC), Roman soldier and politician known chiefly as an orator and a friend of Scipio Aemilianus. Laelius appears as one of the speakers in Cicero's *De senectute* ("On Old Age"), *De amicitia* ("On Friendship"; also called *Laelius*), and *De republica* ("On the Republic").

In 147 Laelius accompanied Scipio Aemilianus during the siege of Carthage and distinguished himself in the capture of the city's military harbour. Two years later he was praetor in Spain, and in 140 he became consul. Laelius helped prosecute the supporters of the agrarian reformer Tiberius Sempronius Gracchus (tribune in 133), and in 131 he opposed Gaius Papirius Carbo's bill to legalize the reelection of tribunes. In Cicero's works he appears as a member of the highly cultured Scipionic circle, a poet and a student of philosophy who sought to blend the better elements of Greek and Roman life.

Laënnec, René-Théophile-Hyacinthe (b. Feb. 17, 1781, Quimper, Fr.—d. Aug. 13, 1826, Kerlouanec), French physician who invented the stethoscope and is generally considered the father of chest medicine. Using a foot-long wooden cylinder that he placed on the chests of his patients, he was able to hear the various sounds made by the lungs and heart. For three years he studied patients' chest sounds and correlated them with the diseases found in autopsy. He described his methods and findings in the classic *De l'auscultation médiate* (1819; "On Mediate Auscultation"). Laënnec made numerous other contributions to the literature of respiratory and heart disease. A pupil of Jean-Nicolas Corvisart des Marets, whom he succeeded (1823) as physician at the Hôpital de la Charité in Paris, he also was appointed professor at the Collège de France (1822).

Laërtius, Diogenes: *see* Diogenes Laërtius.

Laetare Sunday, fourth Sunday in Lent in the Western Christian Church, so called from the first word ("Rejoice") of the introit of the liturgy. It is also known as mid-Lent Sunday, for it occurs just over halfway through Lent, and as Refreshment Sunday because it may be observed with some relaxation of Lenten strictness. In medieval England simnel cakes (special rich fruitcakes) were consumed on this day. In the Anglican churches it is sometimes called Mothering Sunday, with reference to a verse in Galatians (4:27).

Laetolil remains, hominid fossils found in the southern Serengeti Plains, about 25 miles (40 kilometres) from the Olduvai Gorge in northern Tanzania by Mary Leakey and coworkers in 1974–75, not far from where in 1938 L. Kohl-Larsen had unearthed a group of fossils. The 13 fragments of jaws found at the site by the Leakey party date from about 3,590,000 years ago and are among the oldest fossil hominids found in Africa.

The Laetolil remains belong to a species called *Australopithecus afarensis*, which had been discovered a few years earlier by D.C. Johanson in Ethiopia. Footprints of a family of these creatures were also recovered, indicating that *afarensis* was basically arboreal.

Laetus, Julius Pomponius (Latin), Italian GIULIO POMPONIO LETO (b. 1428, Diano, Kingdom of Naples—d. 1497, Rome), Italian Humanist and founder of the Academia Romana, a semisecret society devoted to archaeological and antiquarian interests and the celebration of ancient Roman rites.

As a youth, Laetus decided to dedicate his life to the study of the ancient world. He went to Rome *c.* 1450 and, in 1457, succeeded Lorenzo Valla, his former teacher, as professor of eloquence in the Gymnasium Romanum. From the outset he gathered round him a number of Humanists in a semisecret society, the Academia Romana. The members, who changed their Christian names to pagan ones, met not only to discuss their antiquarian and archaeological interests but to celebrate, under the direction of Laetus as pontifex maximus, rites and mysteries of pagan Rome, such as the birth of Romulus and the festival of the Palilia. Their admiration for the ancient world thus developed into a materialistic vision of life, in conscious opposition to Christian ideals, with the possible object of achieving revolutionary political reforms. Hence the Academia Romana fell under the suspicion of Pope Paul II, who in February 1468 dissolved it and arrested its members. Laetus, who for about a year had been living in Venice, was brought to Rome and imprisoned, but by May 1469 he and many of his associates were set free by an act of clemency. They did not regain full liberty until Sixtus IV, who succeeded Paul II in 1471, not only restored Laetus' professorship but also allowed the reconstitution of the Academia Romana.

Between his release and his death Laetus pursued his scholastic studies with extraordinary zeal, interrupted only by two visits to northern Europe (1472–73, 1479–83). His works of this period include treatises concerning Roman antiquities, commentaries on Latin authors, and, most important, some *editiones principes* among which are those of Curtius and Varro, Pliny's *Letters,* and Sallust. Laetus is not regarded highly as a Humanist: despite his erudition, the lack of rigour and absence of critical spirit in his method cause his philological achievements to be treated with reserve by modern scholars.

Lafayette, city, seat (1826) of Tippecanoe county, west central Indiana, U.S., on the Wabash River, 63 mi (101 km) northwest of Indianapolis. Laid out by William Digby on May 24, 1825, it was named for the Marquis de Lafayette, who was making his last visit to America. It is 4 mi northeast of the first white settlement in Indiana (Ft. Ouiatanon), built by the French in 1719 to exploit fur trade with the Indians. Lost to the English in 1763 and then to the Americans in 1779, it was a centre of Indian agitation. The fort, destroyed by the Scott and Wilkinson expeditions in 1791, has been restored as a memorial-museum. Tippecanoe County was named for the battle fought Nov. 7, 1811, when Gov. William Henry Harrison and his small army defeated an Indian confederacy under the leadership of the (Shawnee) Prophet, brother of Tecumseh. The battleground site, now a state park, is 7 mi north of the city. Lafayette is well industrialized (manufactures include aluminum, electrical and rubber products, prefabricated houses, and pharmaceuticals), and has a busy grain market. West Lafayette, across the river, is the seat of Purdue University (1869), a state institution and land-grant college named for a local businessman, John Purdue, whose gift secured its establishment there. Inc. 1853. Pop. (1990) city, 43,764; Lafayette–West Lafayette MSA, 130,598.

Lafayette, city, seat (1824) of Lafayette parish, south central Louisiana, U.S., on Vermilion River. The area was first settled by exiled Acadians from Nova Scotia in the late 18th century. The earliest village, Vermilionville, was established in 1824 but was renamed for the Marquis de Lafayette in 1884. Until World War II the economy was dependent upon intensive sugarcane, cotton, and corn production. After the war the city became a supply centre for much of the booming oil and gas industry of south Louisiana. Heymann Oil Center, headquarters for many companies, has its own post office and shopping facilities. Before the oil boom Lafayette was primarily a Cajun town, and the older culture is evident in the prevalence of French and the local Cajun dialect. A growing population attracted by the oil industry has created a more cosmopolitan community. Although many of the older customs have disappeared, the Live Oak Society still functions for the preservation of these noble trees, and the Camellia Show and Mardi Gras are still celebrated. The University of Southwestern Louisiana (1898) is there, as is the seat of a Roman Catholic diocese. Inc. 1836. Pop. (1990) city, 94,440; Lafayette MSA, 208,740.

Bald cypresses on the campus of the University of Southwestern Louisiana, Lafayette
Charles May—Shostal/EB Inc.

Lafayette, Marie-Joseph-Paul-Yves-Roch-Gilbert du Motier, marquis de, Lafayette also spelled LA FAYETTE (b. Sept. 6, 1757, Chavaniac, Fr.—d. May 20, 1834, Paris), French aristocrat who fought with the American colonists against the British in the American Revolution. Later, by allying himself with the revolutionary bourgeoisie, he became one of the most powerful men in France during the first few years of the French Revolution.

Born into an ancient noble family, Lafayette

Lafayette, lithograph by François-Séraphin Delpech after a portrait by Maurin
By courtesy of the trustees of the British Museum; photograph, J.R. Freeman & Co. Ltd.

had already inherited an immense fortune by the time he married the daughter of the influential duc d'Ayen in 1774. He joined the circle of young courtiers at the court of King Louis XVI but soon aspired to win glory as a soldier. Hence, in July 1777, 27 months after the outbreak of the American Revolution, he arrived in Philadelphia. Appointed a major general by the colonists, he quickly struck up a lasting friendship with the American commander in chief, George Washington. Lafayette fought with distinction at the Battle of Brandywine, Pennsylvania, on Sept. 11, 1777, and, as a division commander, he conducted a masterly retreat from Barren Hill on May 28, 1778. Returning to France early in 1779, he helped persuade the government of Louis XVI to send a 6,000-man expeditionary army to aid the colonists. Lafayette arrived back in America in April 1780 and was immediately given command of an army in Virginia. After forcing the British commander Lord Charles Cornwallis to retreat across Virginia, Lafayette entrapped him at Yorktown in late July. A French fleet and several additional American armies joined the siege, and on October 19 Cornwallis surrendered. The British cause was lost. Lafayette was hailed as "the Hero of Two Worlds," and on returning to France in 1782 he was promoted *maréchal de camp* (brigadier general). He became a citizen of several states on a visit to the United States in 1784.

During the next five years, Lafayette became a leader of the liberal aristocrats and an outspoken advocate of religious toleration and the abolition of the slave trade. Elected as a representative of the nobility to the States General that convened in May 1789, Lafayette supported the manoeuvres by which the bourgeois deputies of the Third Estate gained control of the States General and converted it into a revolutionary National Assembly. On July 11 he presented to the Assembly his draft of a Declaration of the Rights of Man and of the Citizen. After extensive revisions the document was adopted on August 27. Meanwhile on July 15, the day after a crowd stormed the Bastille, Lafayette had been elected commander of the newly formed national guard of Paris. His troops saved Louis XVI and Queen Marie-Antoinette from the fury of a crowd that invaded Versailles on October 6, and he then carried the royal family to Paris, where they became hostages of the Revolution.

For the next year, Lafayette's popularity and influence were at their height. He supported measures that transferred power from the aristocracy to the bourgeoisie, but he feared that further democratization would encourage the lower classes to attack property rights. Hence, he became alarmed as republicans began to assail the new system of constitutional monarchy. When a crowd of petitioners gathered on the Champ de Mars in Paris (July 17, 1791) to demand the abdication of the King, Lafayette's guards opened fire, killing or wounding about 50 demonstrators. The incident destroyed his popularity, and in October he resigned from the guard.

Appointed commander of the army at Metz in December 1791, Lafayette hoped to suppress the radical democrats (and perhaps rule in the King's name) after France went to war with Austria in April 1792. His plans failed, and on Aug. 10, 1792, the monarchy was overthrown in a popular insurrection. Lafayette would have been tried for treason had he not defected (August 19) to the Austrians, who held him captive until 1797. When Napoleon Bonaparte came to power in 1799, Lafayette returned to France and settled down as a gentleman farmer. He sat in the Chamber of Deputies during most of the reign of King Louis XVIII (1814–24), and in 1824–25 he visited the United States, where he was received with wild adulation. In July 1830 he commanded the national guard that helped overthrow King Charles X and install Louis-Philippe on the throne. Lafayette retired six months later.

BIBLIOGRAPHY. W. Woodward, *Lafayette* (1939); A. Maurois, *Adrienne: The Life of the Marquise de La Fayette* (Eng. trans., 1961); *see also* the series (1935–57) of biographical works on Lafayette by Louis Gottschalk.

Laffite, Jean, Laffite also spelled LAFITTE (b. 1780?, France—d. 1825?), privateer and smuggler who interrupted his illicit adventures to fight heroically for the United States in defense of New Orleans in the War of 1812.

Little is known of Laffite's early life, but by 1809 he and his brother Pierre apparently had established in New Orleans a blacksmith shop that reportedly served as a depot for smuggled goods and slaves brought ashore by a band of privateers. From 1810 to 1814 this group probably formed the nucleus for Laffite's illicit colony on the secluded islands of Barataria Bay south of the city. Holding privateer commissions from the republic of Cartagena (in modern Colombia), Laffite's group preyed on Spanish commerce, illegally disposing of its plunder through merchant connections on the mainland.

Because the Baratarian Bay was an important approach to New Orleans, the British during the War of 1812 offered Laffite $30,000 and a captaincy in the Royal Navy for his allegiance. Laffite pretended to cooperate, then warned Louisiana officials of New Orleans' peril. Instead of believing him, Gov. W.C.C. Claiborne summoned the U.S. Army and Navy to wipe out the colony. Some of Laffite's ships were captured, but his business was not destroyed. Still protesting his loyalty to the U.S., Laffite next offered aid to the hard-pressed forces of Gen. Andrew Jackson in defense of New Orleans if he and his men could be granted a full pardon. Jackson accepted, and in the Battle of New Orleans (December 1814–January 1815) the Baratarians fought with distinction. Jackson personally commended Laffite as "one of the ablest men" of the battle, and Pres. James Madison issued a public proclamation of pardon for the group.

Jean Laffite
The Bettmann Archive

Nevertheless, after the war the pirate chief returned to his old ways, and in 1817, with nearly 1,000 followers, he organized a commune called Campeche on the island site of the future city of Galveston, Texas, where he served briefly as governor in 1819. From this depot he continued his privateering against the Spanish, and his men were commonly acknowledged as pirates. When several of his lieutenants attacked U.S. ships in 1820, official pressure was brought to bear on the operation. As a consequence, the following year Laffite suddenly picked a crew to man his favourite vessel, "The Pride," burned the town, and sailed away—apparently continuing his depredations along the coast of Spanish America (the Spanish Main) for several more years.

Laffitte, Jacques (b. Oct. 24, 1767, Bayonne, Fr.—d. May 26, 1844, Maisons-sur-Seine), French banker and politician prominent in public affairs from the end of the Napoleonic period to the first years of the July Monarchy (1830–31).

The son of a carpenter, Laffitte became clerk in the banking house of Perregaux in Paris,

Jacques Laffitte, drawing by A. Devéria; in the Bibliothèque Nationale, Paris
By courtesy of the Bibliotheque Nationale, Paris

was made a partner in the business in 1800, and in 1804 succeeded Perregaux as head of the firm. The House of Perregaux, Laffitte et Cie, became one of the greatest in Europe, and Laffitte became regent (1809), then governor (1814) of the Bank of France and president of the Chamber of Commerce (1814). He raised large sums of money for the provisional government in 1814 and for Louis XVIII during the Hundred Days. Elected to the Chamber of Deputies in 1816, he took his seat on the Left and spoke chiefly on financial questions. In 1818 he saved Paris from a financial crisis by buying a large amount of stock, but the next year, in consequence of his heated defense of the liberty of the press and the electoral law of 1819, the governorship of the bank was taken from him. One of the earliest and most determined of the partisans of a constitutional monarchy under Louis-Philippe, duc d'Orléans, he was deputy for Bayonne in July 1830, when his house in Paris became the headquarters of the revolutionary party. When Charles X, after retracting the hated ordinances, tried to negotiate a change of ministry, the banker replied, "It is too late. There is no longer a Charles X."

Eager to avoid a republic, Laffitte, who was elected president of the Chamber of Deputies, did much to secure Louis-Philippe's accession to the throne. The new king made him a minister of state and finally, in November 1830, premier. He tried to help revolutionary movements abroad (particularly in Italy) but would not let France intervene, except in Belgium, thus provoking criticism from right and left alike. Laffitte resigned on March 13, 1831.

Laffitte, Pierre (b. Feb. 21, 1823, Béguey, France—d. Jan. 4, 1903, Paris), French philosopher, the closest disciple of the philosopher Auguste Comte, who taught in his doctrine of Positivism that only knowledge verifiable by the methods of the empirical sciences is valid.

On Comte's death in 1857, Laffitte, who was one of his executors, became head of the Comité Positiviste. He was appointed professor of the general history of science at the Collège de France in 1892. His works include *Leçons de cosmographie* (1853; "Lectures on Cosmography"), *Cours philosophique sur l'histoire générale de l'humanité* (1859; "Philosophic Course on the General History of Man"), *Considérations générales sur l'ensemble de la civilisation chinoise* (1861), *Les Grands Types de l'humanité* (1874; "The Great Symbols of Man"), *De la morale positive* (1880; "On the Positivist Ethic"), and *Le "Faust" de Goethe* (1899; "The 'Faust' of Goethe").

Lafia, formerly LAFIA BERI-BERI, town, Plateau State, central Nigeria. Originally the site of Anane, a small town of the Arago people, Lafia became the capital of a prominent local chiefdom in the early 19th century. During the rule of Mohamman Agwe (1881–1903), the Lafia market became important in the Benue Valley, and a trade route was opened to Loko (56 mi [90 km] southwest), a Benue River port. In 1903 the British, who controlled Northern Nigeria, recognized Chief Musa as Lafia's first emir. In 1967 the town became part of Benne-Plateau State, and in 1976 it was allocated to Plateau State.

Modern Lafia is a collecting point for sesame seeds and soybeans and is a trading centre for yams, sorghum, millet, and cotton. Besides farming, cotton weaving and dyeing are traditionally important activities of the town's permanent inhabitants—members of the Arago, Tiv, and Kanuri peoples—while Fulani herdsmen bring their cattle to graze in the vicinity during the dry season. Tin and columbite are mined nearby, and there is a deposit of coal southeast of the town.

In addition to the emir's palace, Lafia has a central mosque, a Roman Catholic secondary school, and a government health office. It is situated on the trunk railway from Port Harcourt and on the main highway between Makurdi and Jos. Pop. (1991) 79,387.

"De," "la," and similar components of a name when followed by a space, are alphabetized as separate words (e.g., *De Forest, Lee*). *When they are joined to the following part of a name, the combination is treated as a single word* (e.g., *DeForest, John William*).

Lafiagi, town, Kwara State, west-central Nigeria, on the south bank of the Niger River. It was founded in 1810 by Malam Maliki and his brother Manzuma, two Fulani leaders from Gwandu, 250 mi (400 km) north-northwest, as a fortified town in Nupe territory. Following Maliki's death in 1824, the emir of Gwandu named Manzuma as Lafiagi's first emir. The Lafiagi emirate survived serious Nupe revolts in the late 1820s and again in the late 1890s, with the aid of the forces of the Royal Niger Company. The Lafiagi ruler, whose title was changed from emir to chief in 1949, has served since 1954 as the chairman of the Federated Council of Lafiagi, Sharagi, and Shonga (20 mi northwest), founded by Maliki's son, Aliyu. Lafiagi is now the headquarters of the Edun Local Government Council. Most of the traditional emirate's inhabitants are Muslim Nupe people.

A market centre for rice, yams, sorghum, millet, corn (maize), sugarcane, kola nuts, peanuts (groundnuts), palm produce, fish, cattle, and cotton, the town is also a collecting point for the rice grown on the *fadamas* ("floodplains") of the Niger and for dried fish. Cotton and tobacco are local cash crops, and cotton weaving is traditionally important. Lafiagi has a government maternity clinic and dispensary. Pop. (latest est.) 53,500.

Lafitte, Jean: *see* Laffite, Jean.

Lafontaine, Henri-Marie (b. April 22, 1854, Brussels, Belg.—d. May 14, 1943, Brussels), Belgian international lawyer and president of the International Peace Bureau (1907–43) who received the Nobel Peace Prize in 1913.

Henri-Marie Lafontaine, 1924
H. Roger-Viollet

Lafontaine studied law at Brussels University. He was admitted to the bar in 1877 and established a reputation as an authority on international law. In 1893 he became professor of international law at the Université Nouvelle in Brussels and two years later was elected to the Belgian Senate as a member of the Socialist Party. He served as vice chairman of the Senate from 1919 to 1932.

Lafontaine took an early interest in the International Peace Bureau, founded in 1882, and was influential in the Bureau's efforts to bring about the Hague Peace Conferences of 1899 and 1907. He was a member of the Belgian delegation to the Paris Peace Conference in 1919 and to the League of Nations Assembly (1920–21). In other efforts to foster world peace, he founded the Centre Intellectuel Mondial (later merged into the League of Nations Institute for Intellectual Co-operation) and proposed such organizations as a world school and university, a world parliament, and an international court of justice.

Lafontaine was the author of a number of legal handbooks and a documentary history of international arbitration. He was also founder of the review *La Vie Internationale*.

LaFontaine, Sir Louis Hippolyte, BARONET (b. Oct. 4, 1807, Boucherville, Lower Canada—d. Feb. 26, 1864, Montreal), Canadian statesman, joint prime minister with Robert Baldwin of the United Province of Canada in 1842–43 and again during the "great ministry" of 1848–51, when responsible, or cabinet, government was finally achieved.

LaFontaine was called to the bar in Lower Canada in 1829, and a year later he began his political career when elected to the provin-

Sir Louis Hippolyte LaFontaine
By courtesy of the Public Archives of Canada

cial assembly for Terrebonne. He supported the French-Canadian grievances against the British governor in chief, but he did not condone the Rebellion of 1837. With a second outbreak of rebellion in 1838, LaFontaine was imprisoned but released without trial.

After the union of Upper and Lower Canada (1840) as Canada West and Canada East, LaFontaine took over the leadership of the French-Canadians. He declined the post of solicitor general offered by the first governor, Lord Sydenham, but responded to the request of the succeeding governor, Sir Charles Bagot, that LaFontaine form a ministry with Robert Baldwin, leader of the reformers in Canada West (now in Ontario). The ministry, formed in 1842, resigned within a year as a protest against Bagot's successor, Lord Metcalfe. After four years in opposition, LaFontaine formed a new administration with Baldwin under Lord Elgin, and they successfully established responsible government in Canada. LaFontaine's Rebellion Losses Bill (1848), compensating those who suffered damages during the rebellion, precipitated riots in Montreal.

He retired from office in 1851 and was appointed chief justice of Canada East and president of the seigneurial court in 1853. He was made a baronet in 1854. (His two sons died in infancy, and the baronetcy became extinct upon his death.)

Laforet (Díaz), Carmen (b. Sept. 6, 1921, Barcelona, Spain—d. Feb. 28, 2004, Madrid), Spanish novelist and short-story writer who received international recognition when her novel *Nada* (1944; "Nothingness"; Eng. trans., *Nada*) won the first Nadal Prize.

Educated in Las Palmas, Canary Islands, Laforet returned to Barcelona immediately after the Spanish Civil War (1936–39). The lives of the heroines in her novels strongly reflect the author's personal experiences. *Nada,* Laforet's first and most successful novel, is spontaneous and passionate. It is written in the postwar narrative style known as *tremendismo,* which is characterized by a tendency to emphasize misery and grotesque imagery. *Nada* presents a young girl who returns to Barcelona from abroad after the war and discovers a sordid, chaotic atmosphere and intellectual emptiness. A novel read for its narrative, political, and existential elements, *Nada* is direct and unaffected.

In contrast to her first novel, Laforet's later works, though better-constructed, are sentimental and less intense. In 1952 she published *La isla y los demonios* ("The Island and the Demons"), also autobiographical in nature. Laforet's conversion to Catholicism in 1951 is strongly reflected in *La mujer nueva* (1955; "The New Woman"), in which a worldly woman rediscovers her faith. Although this novel received the Menorca Prize in 1955 and the Premio Miguel de Cervantes the following year, many critics consider its main character unrealistic and its statement almost absurd to those who are not familiar with Laforet's own faith. In 1961 she wrote *Gran Canaria* ("Grand Canary"), a guide to the island on which she grew up.

Laforgue, Jules (b. Aug. 16, 1860, Montevideo, Uruguay—d. Aug. 20, 1887, Paris), French Symbolist poet, a master of lyrical irony and one of the inventors of vers libre ("free verse"). The impact of his work was felt by several 20th-century American poets, including T.S. Eliot, and he also influenced the work of the Surrealists. His critical essays, though somewhat neglected, are also notable.

Laforgue was brought up by relatives at Tarbes, Fr., from 1866 to 1876, when he joined his family in Paris. After finishing his schooling at the Lycée Fontanes, he attended the lectures of the literary critic and historian Hippolyte Taine at the École des Beaux-Arts. Through the writer Paul Bourget he became secretary to Charles Ephrussi, an art collector and editor of the *Gazette des Beaux-Arts,* who introduced him to Impressionist painting. In November 1881 he was appointed reader to the Empress Augusta in Berlin and remained in Germany for almost five years, during which time he wrote most of his works. He married an English woman, Leah Lee, in London on Dec. 31, 1886, and they returned to Paris, where, poverty-stricken, Laforgue died of tuberculosis the following year.

In the verse of *Les Complaintes* (1885), *L'Imitation de Notre-Dame la Lune* (1886; "The Imitation of Our Lady the Moon"), and *Le Concile féerique* (1886; "The Fairy Council"), Laforgue gave ironical expression to his obsession with death, his loneliness, and his boredom with daily routine. He was attracted by Buddhism and by German philosophy, especially by Arthur Schopenhauer's pessimism and Edward von Hartmann's theory of the unconscious. Inspired by the example of Tristan Corbière and Arthur Rimbaud, he forged new words, experimented with common speech, and combined popular songs and music-hall tags with philosophic and scientific terms to create an imagery that appears surprisingly modern. His search for new rhythms culminated in the vers libre that he and his friend Gustave Kahn invented almost simultaneously. He reinterpreted William Shakespeare, Richard Wagner, Gustave Flaubert, and Stéphane Mallarmé in a collection of short stories, *Moralités légendaires* (1887; *Six Moral Tales From Jules Laforgue*). His art criticism, published in the Symbolist reviews and subsequently in *Mélanges posthumes* (1923), testifies to his remarkable understanding of the Impressionist vision.

Lag ba-'Omer, also spelled LAG B'OMER, or LAG BE-OMER, a minor Jewish observance falling on the 33rd day in the period of the counting of the *'omer* ("barley sheaves"); on this day semimourning ceases and weddings are allowed. The origin of the festival is obscure. Among many traditions, one has it that manna first fell from heaven on this day; another tradition claims that a plague that raged among the followers of Rabbi Akiba ben Joseph during *'omer* ceased on this day. In Meron in Upper Galilee, Israel, Orthodox Jews by the thousands make a joyous pilgrimage to the burial site of the great rabbi Simeon ben Yoḥai, and young children receive their first haircuts as part of a popular celebration that includes playing with bows and arrows (symbols of the rainbow) and dancing around a bonfire at night.

Lagash, modern TELLOH, one of the most important capital cities in ancient Sumer, located midway between the Tigris and Euphrates rivers in southeastern Iraq. The ancient name of the mound of Telloh was actually Girsu, while Lagash originally denoted a site southeast of Girsu, later becoming the name of the whole district and also of Girsu itself. The French excavated at Telloh between 1877 and 1933 and uncovered at least 50,000 cuneiform texts that have proved one of the major sources for knowledge of Sumer in the 3rd millennium BC. Dedicatory inscriptions

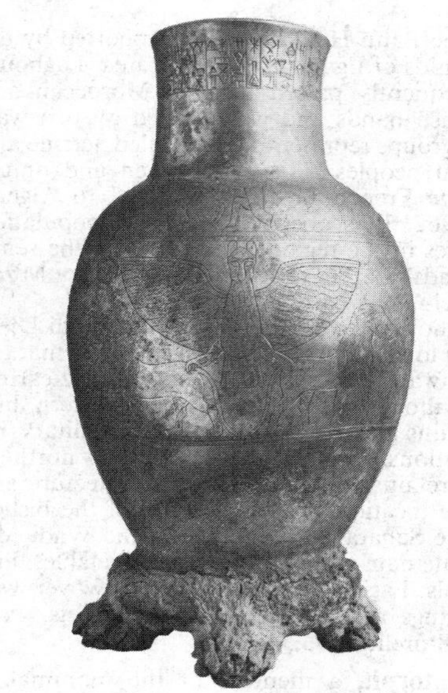

Engraved silver vase of King Entemena, from Lagash, Early Dynastic Period; in the Louvre, Paris
Archives Photographiques

on stone and on bricks also have provided invaluable evidence for assessing the chronological development of Sumerian art.

The city was founded in the prehistoric Ubaid Period (*c.* 5200–*c.* 3500 BC) and was still occupied as late as the Parthian era (247 BC–AD 224). In the Early Dynastic Period the rulers of Lagash called themselves "king" (*lugal*), though the city itself never was included within the official Sumerian canon of kingship. Among the most famous Lagash monuments of that period is the Stele of the Vultures, erected to celebrate the victory of King Eannatum over the neighbouring state of Umma. Another is the engraved silver vase of King Entemena, a successor of Eannatum. Control of Lagash finally fell to Sargon of Akkad (reigned *c.* 2334–2279 BC), but about 150 years later Lagash enjoyed a revival. It prospered most brilliantly under Gudea, who was probably a governor rather than an independent king and was nominally subject to the Guti, a warlike people who controlled much of Babylonia from about 2230 to about 2130.

Lagash was endowed with many temples, including the Eninnu, "House of the Fifty," a seat of the high god Enlil. Architecturally the most remarkable structure was a weir and regulator, once doubtless possessing sluice gates, which conserved the area's water supply in reservoirs.

Lågen, also called NUMEDALSLÅGEN, river, southeastern Norway. Rising in the Hardanger Plateau, the Lågen flows generally east and north, then southeast through Numedalen, a valley in Buskerud *fylke* (county), past Rødberg and Kongsberg, through Vestfold *fylke* and into the Skagerrak (an arm of the North Sea) at Larvik. With a total length of 209 miles (337 km), it is the third longest river in the country. Near Kongsberg, silver was mined from the early 17th century until the mid-20th century, and the oldest school of mines in the world (founded 1757) is in the town. Above Kongsberg, lumbering and hydroelectric power generation are the main economic resources; below Kongsberg, agriculture becomes important. Larvik is an important lumber-products centre on the southern coast. Small towns in the river valley have many interesting medieval stave churches.

Lågen, also called GUDBRANDSDALSLÅGEN, river, south-central Norway. The name Lågen is applied to the portion of the river in Oppland *fylke* (county); it rises in small lakes and streams in the Dovre Plateau at the northern end of Gudbrands Valley and flows southeast for 122 miles (199 km) through Gudbrands Valley to Mjøsa Lake at Lillehammer. It flows out from Mjøsa as the Vorma River (in Akershus *fylke*) southeast to its confluence with the Glåma River at Årnes, more than 100 miles (160 km) from its source. It drains an area of about 4,600 square miles (11,900 square km) through its main tributaries—the Otta, Sjoa, Vinstra, and Gausa rivers. Many large hydroelectric power generating stations have been built along the Lågen. The main road and rail routes between Trondheim and Oslo follow the river for most of its length.

lager beer, light-coloured, highly carbonated type of beer (*q.v.*).

Lagerkvist, Pär (Fabian) (b. May 23, 1891, Växjö, Swed.—d. July 11, 1974, Stockholm), novelist, poet, dramatist, and one of the major Swedish literary figures of the first half of the 20th century. He was awarded the Nobel Prize for Literature in 1951.

Lagerkvist was reared in a traditional religious manner in a small town. The influence of his early years remained strong despite his introduction to modern scientific ideas and his eventual break with the religion of his forefathers. He became involved with socialism and soon began to support artistic and literary radicalism, as demonstrated in his manifesto entitled *Ordkonst och bildkonst* (1913; "Literary and Pictorial Art"). In *Teater* (1918; "Theatre"), the three one-act plays *Den Svåre Stunden* ("The Difficult Hour") illustrate a similar modernist viewpoint.

Lagerkvist, 1951
By courtesy of the Nobel Foundation, Stockholm

The extreme pessimism that pervaded Lagerkvist's works during World War I, such as *Ångest* (1916; "Anguish"), slowly subsided, starting with *Det eviga leendet* (1920; *The Eternal Smile*) and his autobiographical novel *Gäst hos verkligheten* (1925; *Guest of Reality*), until finally he declared his faith in man in the great prose monologue *Det besegrade livet* (1927; "The Triumph over Life"), which became a positive point of departure for much of his later work.

When the new creeds of violence were being proclaimed in the early 1930s, he quickly recognized their danger. His prose work *Bödeln* (1933; *The Hangman*), later dramatized, is a protest against the everlasting brutality in the world. The play *Mannen utan själ* (1936; *The Man Without a Soul*) is also an expression of Lagerkvist's indignation with Fascism. During the 1940s he wrote his most unusual play, sometimes called a "stage oratorio," *Låt människan leva* (1949; *Let Man Live*), which deals with man's readiness throughout history to judge his fellows and condemn them even to death.

It was not until his novel *Dvärgen* (1944; *The Dwarf*) appeared that he had unqualified success with Swedish critics; it became his first best-seller. With *Barabbas* (1950) he achieved world recognition.

Evening Land=Aftonland (1975) is a literal

translation into English by Leif Sjöberg and verse rendering by W.H. Auden of 66 of Lagerkvist's poems. *The Marriage Feast* (1973) contains English translations of 19 Lagerkvist short stories.

Lagerlöf, Selma (Ottiliana Lovisa) (b. Nov. 20, 1858, Mårbacka, Swed.—d. March 16, 1940, Mårbacka), novelist whose work is rooted in legend and saga, and who in 1909 became the first woman and also the first Swedish writer to win the Nobel Prize for Literature.

An illness left her lame for a time, but otherwise her childhood was happy. She was taught at home, then trained in Stockholm as a teacher, and in 1885 went to Landskrona as schoolmistress. There she wrote her first novel, *Gösta Berlings saga,* 2 vol. (1891). A chronicle of life in the heyday of her native Värmland's history, the age of prosperous iron founders and small manors, the book recounts the story of the 12 Cavaliers, led by Gösta Berling, a renegade priest of weak character but irresistible charm. Written in a lyrical style, full of pathos, it showed the influence of Thomas Carlyle and played a part in the Swedish Romantic revival of the 1890s. In 1894 she published a collection of stories, *Osynliga länkar* (*Invisible Links*), and in 1895 she won a traveling scholarship, gave up teaching, and devoted herself to writing. After visiting Italy she published *Antikrists mirakler* (1897; *The Miracles of Antichrist*), a socialist novel about Sicily. Another collection, *En herrgårdssägen* (*Tales of a Manor*), is one of her finest works. A winter in Egypt and Palestine (1899–1900) inspired *Jerusalem,* 2 vol. (1901–02), which established her as the foremost Swedish novelist. Other notable works were *Herr Arnes Penningar* (1904), a tersely but powerfully told historical tale; and *Nils Holgerssons underbara resa genom Sverige,* 2 vol. (1906–07; *The Wonderful Adventures of Nils* and *Further Adventures of Nils*), a geography reader for children.

Selma Lagerlöf, 1909
By courtesy of the Nobel Foundation, Stockholm

World War I disturbed her deeply, and for some years she wrote little. Then, in *Mårbacka* (1922), *Ett barns memoarer* (1930; *Memories of My Childhood*), and *Dagbok för Selma Lagerlöf* (1932; *The Diary of Selma Lagerlöf*), she recalled her childhood with subtle artistry and also produced a Värmland trilogy: *Löwensköldska ringen* (1925; *The Ring of the Löwenskölds*), set in the 18th century; *Charlotte Löwensköld* (1925); and *Anna Svärd* (1928). She was deeply attached to the family manor house at Mårbacka, which had been sold after her father's death but which she bought back with her Nobel Prize money. Selma Lagerlöf ranks among the most naturally gifted of modern storytellers.

Lages (Brazil): *see* Lajes.

Laghouat, town and oasis north-central Algeria, at the southern edge of the Saharan Atlas, on the route linking Algiers with central Africa. The oasis (625 acres [253 hectares]) was probably settled in the 11th century after the Banū Hilāl invaders, supported by the Fāṭimids of Egypt, crossed the area. Laghouat subsequently passed through Moroccan and Turkish hands and was divided by two warring groups representing the Ouled Serrine and Hallaf peoples. The oasis, taken and united by the French in 1852, reverted to Algeria in 1962. It is one of four major population centres in the region; the others are the seminomads' market town of Aflou and the M'zab and el-Golea oases groups.

Laghouat lies on the Wadi Mzi (Wadi Djedi in its lower course), built on two hills that are northward extensions of Mount Tizigarine. The modern quarter, on the southern hill, contains the administrative and military installations. The old section, on the northern hill, retains its Saharan-style architecture and is the location of the cathedral of the bishop of the Sahara. Three dams on the Wadi Mzi irrigate date palms, fruit trees, vegetables, and cereals. Laghouat is known for its woven wall hangings and knotted woolen carpets. Pop. (1998 prelim.) 96,342.

lagomorph, a member of the mammalian order Lagomorpha, which includes the rabbits and hares and the rarer pikas, or mouse hares. Long ears, a short tail, and powerful hind limbs that give them an ability to bound from place to place characterize hares and rabbits, while pikas have shorter ears, no exterior tail, and less-developed hind limbs.

A brief treatment of lagomorphs follows. For full treatment, *see* MACROPAEDIA: Mammals.

Living lagomorphs belong to two families: Leporidae (rabbits and hares) and Ochotonidae (pikas). Ranging in size from the smallest pikas at 15 cm (about 6 inches) in length and 100 g (3½ ounces) in weight to the largest hares at 70 cm (27½ inches) and 4.5 kg (10 pounds), lagomorphs are found nearly worldwide. Wild lagomorphs have long been sought by hunters for sport as well as for food and fur. Domestic rabbits, descended from the Old World, or European, rabbit (*Oryctolagus cuniculus*), are raised for meat and skins and are used in biological and medical research. Wild rabbits and hares can become pests, especially in areas where man has eliminated their natural predators and they are free to deplete vegetation and damage young trees and orchards. Pikas, usually inhabiting regions far from human activity, are of little importance economically to man.

Most rabbits and hares have a coat that is brownish or reddish brown above and lighter to white below, but there are wide differences according to species, location, and season. Their habitats include grassland, desert, forest, marsh, brushland, and tundra. Rabbits burrow or inhabit the abandoned burrows of other animals. Hares shelter in natural depressions. Pikas are found in northern steppes, semideserts, some forests and scrub thickets of Asia, and rocky terrain. They may burrow or find natural shelter, depending on habitat.

Rabbits and hares usually vocalize only when frightened or injured; pikas have a whistle or bark and a chattering call used in giving alarm signals and in maintaining territorial boundaries. Unlike rabbits and hares, whose major activity takes place from dusk to after dawn, pikas are active during the day.

All lagomorphs are herbivorous. Their well-developed incisors are suited to severing plant stems and gnawing on bark, and they continue to grow throughout life, offsetting the abrasive effects of a herbivorous diet. Rabbits and hares are not known to store food, but pikas not only store but dry or cure vegetation for winter. Some lagomorphs are capable of reingesting moist and nutritionally rich fecal pellets, a practice considered comparable to cud-chewing in ruminants. Lagomorphs themselves are the dietary staple of many carnivorous mammals and birds, among them wolves, foxes, bobcats, weasels, predatory hawks, and owls.

The long-eared hares rely on keen hearing and strong hind limbs to escape danger by bounding through their open-country habitat as fast as 80 km (50 miles) per hour. The shorter-eared rabbits, with their weaker hind limbs, lack the endurance of hares and seldom venture far from cover. The pikas' still-shorter ears and weaker hind limbs keep them in areas where secure cover can be reached in a quick scamper.

The proverbial fecundity of rabbits and hares yields several litters during each breeding season, with two or three litters common among hares and three to six among rabbits. Rabbits gestate for approximately 28 days and hares for 47; litter size is usually between two and eight. Young rabbits, naked and blind at birth, are cared for in a nest; hares, born in the open, have open eyes, are furred, and can run soon after birth. The pikas, whose reproduction cycle is less well-known, gestate for about 30 days and produce a litter of two to six, with two or three litters born each year. In some pikas the young are born lightly furred and with closed eyes and ears, but they gain the ability to move about after approximately eight days.

Northern Asia was apparently the place of origin of the order Lagomorpha, most likely by the end of the Paleocene Epoch (about 55,000,000 years ago). The family of rabbits and hares was in North America by the end of the Eocene, and by the Pliocene (about 7,000,000 years ago) it was present in Europe and had become reestablished in Asia. Leporids now are to be found throughout those ranges and down to South Africa and as far south as northern Argentina. The pika family spread from Asia to Europe and eastern North America in the Pleistocene (about 1,000,000 years ago).

lagoon, area of relatively shallow, quiet water with access to the sea but separated from it by sandbars, barrier islands, or coral reefs. The term lagoon is used to describe two classes of phenomena that share the physical characteristics described but are otherwise quite distinct. These are coastal lagoons, found on most land margins, and coral-reef lagoons, which occur only in areas of the ocean where warm-water corals thrive.

A brief treatment of lagoons follows. For full treatment, *see* MACROPAEDIA: Oceans.

Coastal lagoons are found most commonly on coasts with low to moderate tidal ranges and have been estimated to constitute 13 percent of the total world coastline. They are usually elongated parallel to the general trend of the coastline and are separated from the open sea by barrier islands or by barriers of sand or shingle. One or more narrow openings permit the passage of water between the lagoon and sea.

Lagoon barriers are formed initially by the action of waves or longshore currents working on coarse sediments derived from the coast or the seabed. The protected water behind them, often fed by rivers, acts as a trap for transported mud and eventually silts up to form an extension of the coastal plain.

The water circulation in coastal lagoons is dominated by tides that alternately empty and fill them through gaps in the lagoons' barriers. Because of the large volume of water that has to pass through a narrow opening with each rising and falling tide, currents may be strong near inlets, although they are weak enough over most of the lagoon area to permit sediment deposition and the formation of tidal flats.

Because the ratio of surface area to depth is larger than for the open sea, lagoons are subject to extreme variations in properties that depend on interaction with the atmosphere. Their water is, for example, colder than the sea in winter and warmer in summer. In warm regions, evaporation may more than balance any freshwater input, and if inlets are restricted, it results in hypersaline water and even the accumulation of crystalline salt. When accompanied by geologic subsidence, this accumulation may be instrumental in the formation of thick salt deposits.

Coral-reef lagoon surrounding Raiatea and Tahaa in the Society Islands, Pacific Ocean

Coral-reef lagoons occur on marginal reefs such as the Great Barrier Reef of Australia, but the most spectacular examples are the atolls of the Pacific Ocean, some of which are more than 50 km (30 miles) across. Some atolls consist only of a lagoon, often with a fairly uniform depth, surrounded by a low-lying coral reef; some include one or more high, rocky volcanic islands, and others are complex, with small reefs surrounded by lagoons within a larger reef. All are thought to have been built by the upward growth of coral during a relative rise in sea level due to subsidence and eustatic change.

Lagoon Nebula (catalog numbers NGC 6523 and M8), ionized-hydrogen region located in the constellation Sagittarius at 1,200 parsecs (3,900 light-years) from the solar system. The nebula is a cloud of interstellar gas and dust approximately 10 parsecs (33 light-years) in diameter. A group of young, hot stars in the cloud ionize the nearby gas. As the atoms in the gas recombine, they produce the light emitted by the nebula. Interstellar dust within the nebula absorbs some of this light and appears almost to divide the nebula, thus producing a lagoonlike shape.

Lagos, state, southwestern Nigeria, on the coast of the Bight of Benin. It is bounded by the state of Ogun on the north and east, by the Bight of Benin on the south, and by the Republic of Benin on the west. From 1914 to 1954 the area included in the state was administered by the British as part of the colony of Nigeria. The provisions of the 1954 constitution led to the creation of the Federal Territory of Lagos (the 27-square-mile [70-square-kilometre] area of Lagos Island, including the city of Lagos) and to the transfer of the city's hinterland to the administrative region of Western Nigeria. This arrangement restricted the expansion of Lagos city onto the mainland, however, and in 1967 the creation of Lagos state by the national government restored to the city sovereignty over its hinterland.

The state's mainly Yoruba population has grown more heterogeneous with the migration of other Nigerians and West Africans to Lagos city. Lagos state's agricultural and fishing output includes cassava, palm oil and kernels, coconuts, corn (maize), vegetables, fruits, and fish. These products are collected in the lagoon ports of Badagry, Epe, and Ikorodu and shipped to markets in Lagos city.

Because of the limited space available on the three islands that constitute central Lagos city, industry has been concentrated at estates both inside (Apapa, Ijora, and Yaba) and outside (Ikeja and Mushin) the city, while the central city has increasingly become a commercial, financial, transportation, and service centre. In response to the overcrowding and congestion of Lagos, the federal government selected a new capital site, Abuja, which replaced Lagos as the national capital in December 1991. The state government centred in Lagos city was shifted to Ikeja in 1975. Additional bridges and feeder roads have also been constructed from the central city to the mainland, and the ports at Apapa and Tin Can Island have been incorporated into the metropolitan area to reduce harbour congestion.

Lagos state is served by a main line of the Nigerian Railways (which has its central yards in Lagos city) and the trunk highway system; Ikorodu, Mushin, and Ikeja are thereby linked to Lagos city. Epe, the state's other major town, is served by secondary highways and is also a seaport. Lagos city has an international airport located in the suburb of Ikeja. Area 1,292 square miles (3,345 square km). Pop. (1995 est.) 6,357,253.

Lagos, city and chief port, Lagos state, Nigeria. Until 1975 it was the capital of Lagos state, and until December 1991 it was the federal capital of Nigeria. Ikeja replaced Lagos as the state capital, and Abuja replaced Lagos as the federal capital. Lagos, however, remained the unofficial seat of many government agencies. The city's population is centred on Lagos Island, in Lagos Lagoon, on the Bight of Benin in the Gulf of Guinea. Lagos is Nigeria's largest city and one of the largest in sub-Saharan Africa.

By the late 15th century Lagos Island had been settled by Yoruba fishermen and hunters, who called it Oko. The area was dominated by the kingdom of Benin, which called it Eko, from the late 16th century to the mid-19th century. The Portuguese first landed on Lagos Island in 1472; trade developed slowly, however, until the Portuguese were granted a slaving monopoly a century later. The local obas (kings) enjoyed good relations with the Portuguese, who called the island Onim (and, later, Lagos) and who established a flourishing slave trade. British attempts to suppress the slave trade culminated in 1851 in a naval attack on Lagos and the deposition of the oba. The slave trade continued to grow, however, until Lagos came under British control in 1861.

Apapa Quay, Lagos, Nigeria

Originally governed as a British crown colony, Lagos was part of the United Kingdom's West African Settlements from 1866 to 1874, when it became part of the Gold Coast Colony (modern Ghana). In 1886 it again achieved separate status under a British governor, and in 1906 it was amalgamated with the Protectorate of Southern Nigeria. When Southern and Northern Nigeria were amalgamated in 1914, Lagos was made the capital of the Colony and Protectorate of Nigeria. In 1954 most of the hinterland was incorporated into the region of Western Nigeria, while the city itself was designated as federal territory. In 1960 Lagos became the capital of independent Nigeria. Control of its hinterland was returned to the city in 1967 with the creation of Lagos state. After 1975 a new national capital, centrally situated near Abuja, was developed to replace Lagos, which by then suffered from slums, industrial pollution, and traffic congestion.

The topography of Lagos is dominated by its system of islands, sandbars, and lagoons. The city itself sprawls over four main islands: Lagos, Iddo, Ikoyi, and Victoria, which are connected to each other and to the mainland by a system of bridges. All the territory is low-lying, the highest point on Lagos Island being only 22 feet (7 m) above sea level. The original settlement on the northwestern tip of Lagos Island is now a slum area characterized by narrow streets, poor housing, and overcrowding. The main business district occupies Lagos Island's southwestern shore and contains an increasing number of multistory buildings. This is the heart of the city, the centre of commerce, finance, administration, and education. The principal manufacturing industries in Lagos include automobile and radio assembly, food and beverage processing, metalworks, and the production of paints and soap. Textile, cosmetic, and pharmaceutical manufacturing are also economically important. There is also a fishing industry.

The port of Lagos consists of Customs Quay, on Lagos Island, and the more important Apapa Quay, on the mainland, which serves as the principal outlet for Nigeria's exports. The creeks and lagoons are plied by small coastal craft. The city is the western terminus of the nation's road and railway networks, and the airport at Ikeja provides local and international services.

The Lagos metropolitan area is also a major educational and cultural centre. The University of Lagos (1962), the National Library, the Lagos City Libraries, and the National Museum (1957), with excellent historical examples of Nigerian arts and crafts, are all located in the city or its suburbs. The city is also the headquarters of the Federal Radio Corporation of Nigeria and the Nigerian Television Authority. Pop. (1996 est.) 1,518,000.

Lagrange, Joseph-Louis, COUNT (comte) DE L'EMPIRE, original Italian GIUSEPPE LUIGI LAGRANGIA (b. Jan. 25, 1736, Turin, Sardinia-Piedmont [Italy]—d. April 10, 1813, Paris, Fr.), Italian-French mathematician who made great contributions to the theory of numbers and to analytic and celestial mechanics. His most important book is *Mécanique analytique* (1788; "Analytic Mechanics"), the textbook on which all later work in this field is based.

Lagrange was from a well-to-do family of French origin on his father's side. His father was treasurer to the king of Sardinia and lost his fortune in speculation. Lagrange later said, "If I had been rich, I probably would not have devoted myself to mathematics." His interest in mathematics was aroused by the chance reading of a memoir by the English astronomer Edmond Halley. At 19 (some say 16) he was teaching mathematics at the artillery school of Turin. He was to be instrumental in founding the Turin Academy of Sciences. His early publications, on the propagation of sound and on the concept of maxima and minima, were well received; Leonhard Euler, in Berlin, praised Lagrange's version of his theory of variations. The young mathematician continued to surprise his contemporaries with his discoveries.

Joseph-Louis Lagrange, engraving by Robert Hart

By courtesy of the trustees of the British Museum; photograph, J.R. Freeman & Co. Ltd.

By 1761 he was already recognized as one of the greatest living mathematicians. In 1764 he was awarded a prize offered by the Paris Academy of Sciences for an essay on the libration of the Moon, *i.e.,* the apparent oscillation that causes the slight changes in position of lunar features on the face that the Moon presents to the Earth. In this essay he used the equations that now bear his name. His success encouraged the academy in 1766 to propose, as a problem, the theory of the motions of the satellites of Jupiter. The prize was again awarded to Lagrange, and he won the same distinction in 1772, 1774, and 1778. In 1766, on the recommendation of Euler and the French mathematician Jean d'Alembert, Lagrange went to Berlin to fill a post at the academy vacated by Euler, at the invitation of Frederick the Great, who expressed the wish of "the greatest king in Europe" to have "the greatest mathematician in Europe" at his court.

Lagrange stayed in Berlin until 1787. His productivity in those years was prodigious: he published papers on the three-body problem, which concerns the evolution of three particles mutually attracted according to Sir Isaac Newton's law of gravity; differential equations; prime-number theory; the fundamentally important number-theoretic equation that has been identified (incorrectly by Euler) with John Pell's name; probability; mechanics; and the stability of the solar system. In his long paper "Réflexions sur la résolution algébrique des équations" (1770; "Reflections on the Algebraic Resolution of Equations"), he inaugurated a new period in algebra and inspired Évariste Galois to his group theory.

A kind and quiet man, living only for science, Lagrange had little to do with the factions and intrigues around the king. When Frederick died, Lagrange preferred to accept Louis XVI's invitation to Paris. He was given apartments in the Louvre, was continually honoured, and was treated with respect throughout the French Revolution. From the Louvre he published his classic *Mécanique analytique,* a lucid synthesis of the hundred years of research in mechanics since Newton, based on his own calculus of variations, in which certain properties of a mechanistic system are inferred by considering the changes in a sum (or integral) that are due to conceptually possible (or virtual) displacements from the path that describes the actual history of the system. This led to independent coordinates that are necessary for the specifications of a system of a finite number of particles, or "generalized coordinates." It also led to the so-called Lagrangian equations for a classical mechanical system in which the kinetic energy of the system is related to the generalized coordinates, the corresponding generalized forces, and the time. The book was typically analytic; he stated in his preface that "one cannot find any figures in this work."

The revolution that began in 1789 pressed Lagrange into work on the committee to reform the metric system and then into teaching. When the great chemist Antoine-Laurent Lavoisier was guillotined, Lagrange commented: "It required only a moment to sever that head, and perhaps a century will not be sufficient to produce another like it." When the École Polytechnique was opened in 1795, he became, with Gaspard Monge, its leading professor of mathematics. His lectures were published as *Théorie des fonctions analytiques* (1797; "Theory of Analytic Functions") and *Leçons sur le calcul des fonctions* (1804; "Lessons on the Calculus of Functions") and were the first textbooks on real analytic functions. In them Lagrange, worried about the weak foundation of the calculus having to do with the ratios of small quantities and the limits of such ratios, namely, the derivatives, tried to base it on algebra and thus eliminate the infinitesimal—a gallant but unsuccessful attempt. He also continued to work on his *Mécanique analytique,* but the new edition appeared only after his death.

Napoleon honoured the aging mathematician, making him a senator and a count of the empire, but he remained the quiet, unobtrusive academician, a venerable figure wrapped in his thoughts. He married twice. His second wife, the daughter of the astronomer Pierre-Charles Le Monnier, was much younger than he. (D.J.S.)

Lagrange, Marie-Joseph (b. March 7, 1855, Bourg-en-Bresse, Fr.—d. March 10, 1938, Marseille), French theologian and outstanding Roman Catholic biblical scholar.

Lagrange became a Dominican in 1879 and was ordained in 1883. After teaching church history at Toulouse (1884–88), he studied Oriental languages at the University of Vienna before his order sent him to Jerusalem in 1890 to establish the School of Biblical Studies. There he also founded (1892) a journal, the *Revue Biblique* ("Biblical Review"), and in 1903 began a series of scholarly commentaries on the Bible, the *Études bibliques* ("Biblical Studies"), to which he contributed three volumes: on the historical method of Old Testament criticism, on the Book of Judges, and on the Semitic religions.

Europe was at that time experiencing the effects of papally censured modernism, an intellectual movement that sought to reinterpret traditional Roman Catholic teaching. Although Lagrange welcomed the papal anti-modernist pronouncements, his commentary on Genesis (1906) so clearly represented the modernist viewpoint that he was subjected to strong criticism. In 1912 opposition to some of his methods caused his superiors to recall him to France. He was later sent back to Jerusalem, where he taught, except during World War I, until his death.

Lagrange wrote important commentaries for the *Études* on Mark (1911), Romans (1916), Galatians (1918), Luke (1921), Matthew (1923), and John (1925). His chief books include *Le Judaïsme avant Jésus-Christ* (1931; "Judaism Before Jesus Christ"), *Histoire ancienne du canon du Nouveau Testament* (1933; "Ancient History of the Canon of the New Testament"), and *Critique textuelle—La Critique rationelle* (1935; "Textual Criticism—The Rational Criticism"), considered to be his masterpiece.

BIBLIOGRAPHY. F.-M. Braun, *The Work of Père Lagrange* (1963).

Lagrangian function, also called LAGRANGIAN, quantity that characterizes the state of a physical system. In mechanics, the Lagrangian function is just the kinetic energy (energy of motion) minus the potential energy (energy of position).

One may think of a physical system, changing as time goes on from one state or configuration to another, as progressing along a particular evolutionary path, and ask, from this point of view, why it selects that particular path out of all the paths imaginable. The answer is that the physical system sums the values of its Lagrangian function for all the points along each imaginable path and then selects that path with the smallest result. This answer suggests that the Lagrangian function measures something analogous to increments of distance, in which case one may say, in an abstract way, that physical systems always take the shortest paths.

In the special case of a ray of light, the path of system configurations is just the ordinary path of the light through space, and the Lagrangian function reduces simply to a measure of the passage of time. The particular curved path that a light ray takes through a refracting lens is therefore just the one that takes the least time.

The principle is, however, much more general than that, and it is a remarkable discovery that it seems to describe all phenomena equally well, including, for example, the travel of a rocket to the moon, and the likelihood that colliding subatomic particles will scatter each other in selected directions.

Lagrangian point, in astronomy, a point in space at which a small body, under the gravitational influence of two large ones, will remain approximately at rest relative to them. The existence of such points was deduced by the French mathematician and astronomer Joseph-Louis Lagrange in 1772. In 1906 the first examples were discovered: these were minor planets moving in Jupiter's orbit, under the influence of Jupiter and the Sun. (*See also* Trojan planets.)

In each system of two heavy bodies (*e.g.,* Sun-Jupiter, or Earth-Moon) there exist five theoretical Lagrangian points, but only two are stable—*i.e.,* will tend to retain small bodies despite slight perturbations by outside gravitational influences. Each stable point forms one tip of an equilateral triangle having the two massive bodies at the other vertices.

Consult the INDEX *first*

Laguna Beach, city, Orange county, southwestern California, U.S., on the Pacific Ocean. Originally called Lagonas (for the two lagoons at the head of Laguna Canyon), it was founded in 1887 as Lagona. Renamed Laguna Beach (1904), it developed as a coastal resort and art colony. Since 1932 the Festival of Arts and Pageant of the Masters have been held at Irvine Bowl, a natural amphitheatre just east of the city. Laguna has schools of painting, photography, ballet, sculpturing, and ceramics. Mission San Juan Capistrano is a

Laguna Beach, Calif.
Edward Garey—Shostal

few miles southeast. Inc. 1927. Pop. (2000) 23,727.

Laguna District, agricultural area comprising adjoining portions of western Coahuila and eastern Durango *estados* ("states"), northern Mexico. The district, which contains approximately 312,000 acres (126,000 hectares) of irrigable land, occupies the western portion of the Mayrán Basin; it was named for the shallow lakes (*lagunas*) formed on the plain.

The land, once used only for grazing, belonged to a large hacienda until the 1850s. In 1936, under the agrarian reform program of President Lázaro Cárdenas, it was divided among Indian communities under the Mexican cooperative system of *ejidos* (with ownership retained by the government), and water from the Rivers Nazas and Aguanaval was used for irrigation. Cotton production in the district increased dramatically for a number of years but declined sharply after severe drought in the early 1950s. Many farm families were relocated, and the government initiated new irrigation projects. The major cities of the district are Torreón and Gómez Palacio.

Lahaina, city, Maui county, on the northwest coast of Maui Island, Hawaii, U.S. Extending for 2 miles (3 km) along the leeward (southern) shore, the city is backed by volcanic peaks culminating in Puu Kukui (5,788 feet [1,764 m]) and sheltered by thick groves of coconut palms.

A section of Lahaina, Maui, Hawaii
Ray Atkeson

Lahaina was actively associated during the 19th century with the Hawaiian royal family, European whalers, and American missionaries. In 1820 King Kamehameha II transferred his capital to Lahaina (meaning "cruel sun"), where it remained until replaced by Honolulu in 1845. The Wainee Church Cemetery is sacred to islanders as a burial place of Hawaiian monarchs. Lahaina Roadstead, on Auau Channel, was a favourite anchorage of Pacific whaling fleets. The stone prison of Hale Paahao, built by missionaries in 1851, was built for drunken and disorderly sailors. Lahainaluna High School (1831) is also a relic of missionary days, and on its campus Hawaii's first newspaper, *Ka Lama Hawaii* ("The Torch of Hawaii"), was published in 1834.

At the centre of the city is a historic banyan tree planted in 1873 and claimed to be the largest in the islands. The Olowalu Petroglyphs, 5 miles east, are rock carvings up to 300 years old depicting occupations of the early Hawaiians. Tourism, pineapple canning, and sugar refining are Lahaina's chief sources of income. Pop. (2000) 9,118.

lahar, mudflow of volcanic material. Lahars may carry all sizes of material from ash to large boulders and produce deposits of volcanic conglomerate. Lahars may be the result of heavy rain on loose ash material such as deposits of nuées ardentes (dense clouds of gases charged with incandescent dust, discharging volcanic sand in avalanche fashion); or they may result from the mixing of debris with river water, the flooding of ash by snow or ice melted by an eruption, or the emptying of crater lakes onto loose material. A variation is the hot lahar ordinarily produced by the heating of the crater lake water by the quiet upwelling of lava or an explosion. Lahars move downslope at very high speeds and may extend for tens of miles. A lahar deposit usually has a hummocky or hilly surface. They often cause much death and destruction, as at Herculaneum during the eruption of Vesuvius in AD 79.

Lahbabi, Mohammed Aziz (b. Dec. 25, 1922, Fès, Mor.—d. Aug. 23, 1993, Rabat?), Moroccan novelist, poet, and philosopher whose works are marked by a humanist perspective that stresses the importance of dialogue and of the universal.

Lahbabi taught philosophy at the University of Rabat, where he was dean of the faculty of letters as well as professor, and at the University of Algiers. He also founded the Union of Arab Writers of the Maghrib, over which he presided, and he directed the review *Afaq* ("Horizons").

Lahbabi's training in philosophy in Paris led to a doctorate, and his dissertation was published in two parts as *De l'être à la personne* (1954; "From Being to Person") and *Liberté ou libération* (1956). Lahbabi attempted to forge a philosophy based on Muslim humanism, using a personalist methodology influenced by the writings of Henri Bergson and Emmanuel Mounier. With the Qur'ān and traditional Islāmic writings as his guides, Lahbabi analyzed the autonomy of the person, personal awareness, responsibility, the sense of self, and the conscience. From this work came *Le Personnalisme musulman* (1964), an overview of Muslim thought, and *Du Clos à l'ouvert* (1961; "From the Closed to the Open"), a study in culture and civilization.

In addition to numerous essays on literary and philosophical subjects, Lahbabi published a number of volumes of poetry and a novel, *Espoir vagabond* (1972), which appeared in both Arabic and French. His works also include *L'Économie marocaine: notion essentielles* (1977; "The Moroccan Economy: Essential Elements"), the first volume being *Les Fondements de l'économie marocaine* (1977; "The Foundations of the Moroccan Economy"), and *Le Monde de demain: le Tiers-Monde accuse* (1980; "The World of Tomorrow: the Third World Challenges").

Laḥij, also spelled LAHEJ, town, southwestern Yemen. Situated on the Wadi Tibban in the coastal plain, some 30 miles (45 km) north of Aden, it is the centre of an agricultural area. Its sparse rainfall occurs chiefly in the winter season.

Under the former Aden Protectorate, a British-ruled area, it was capital of the ʿAbdali Sultanate, abolished when Yemen (Aden) became independent in 1967. The sultan's palace is now a school of agriculture. For a brief period in the 1960s, the town was renamed Al-Hawtah or Al-Houta. Laḥij is on the main road from Aden city to the northern parts of western Yemen and is a regional trade centre. Pop. (latest est.) 11,000.

Lahina (Sikh Gurū): *see* Aṅgad.

Lahmu and Lahamu, in Mesopotamian mythology, twin deities, the first gods to be born from the chaos that was created by the merging of Apsu (the watery deep beneath the earth) and Tiamat (the personification of the salt waters); this is described in the Babylonian mythological text *Enuma elish* (*c.* 12th century BC).

Usually, Lahmu and Lahamu represent silt, but in some texts they seem to take the form of serpents, and, because the wavy line of a gliding snake is similar to the ripple of water, some scholars believe that Lahmu and Lahamu may have been only synonyms of Tiamat. Lahmu and Lahamu were rather vague deities who do not seem to have played any significant part in subsequent myths, although they may have been the progenitors of Anshar and Kishar (*q.v.*).

Lahn River, river, a right-bank tributary of the Rhine River, rising on the Jagd Berg (2,218 feet [676 m]), a summit of the Rothaar Hills in western Germany. The river, which is 152 miles (245 km) long, first flows eastward and then southward to Giessen, before turning southwestward and, with a winding course, reaching the Rhine at Lahnstein. Small barges are able to navigate to Giessen on the partly canalized river. Its valley, the lower part of which divides the Taunus (mountains) from the Westerwald (mountains), is often very narrow.

The cathedral (centre) at Limburg on the bank of the Lahn River, Germany
EB Inc.

Among the towns and sites of interest on the Lahn's banks are Marburg and Giessen, each with a university; Wetzlar, with a cathedral; Runkel, with a castle; Limburg, with a cathedral; the castles and medieval ruins of Schaumburg, Balduinstein, Laurenburg, Langenau, Burg Stein, and Nassau; and the health resort of Bad Ems.

Lahnda language, also called JATKI, or WESTERN PANJABI, language belonging to the western group of Indo-Aryan languages and spoken mainly in the western Punjab, Pakistan. One of the most important of its numerous dialects is Multani. Lahnda has a large number of Persian and Arabic loanwords and shares features with Kashmiri and Sindhi. There is little recorded literature in the language. The Muslims use the Persian form of the Arabic script to write Lahnda; the Hindus use the Lahnda script.

Lahore, second largest city of Pakistan and the capital of Punjab province. It lies in the upper Indus plain on the Rāvi River, a tributary of the Indus.

Little is known of the history of the settlement prior to the Muslim period. Hindu legend attributes the founding of Lahore to Lava, or Loh, son of Rāma, after whom it is said to have been named Lohawar. It was the capital of the Ghaznavid dynasty from 1152 to 1186. During the 14th century the city was repeatedly attacked by the Mongols, and in 1524 the city was captured by the Mughal Bābur's troops. Lahore's golden age began under the Mughals, and the city occasionally became the place of royal residence. It was greatly expanded during the reign of Shāh Jahān (1628–57) but declined in importance during the reign of Aurangzeb.

From the death of Aurangzeb (1707), Lahore was subjected to a power struggle between Mughal rulers and Sikh insurrectionists. With the invasion of Nādir Shāh in the mid-18th century, Lahore became an outpost of his empire. However, it soon was associated with the rise of the Sikhs, becoming once more the seat of a powerful government during the rule of Ranjit Singh (1799–1839). After Singh's death, the city rapidly declined, and it passed under British rule in 1849. When the Indian subcontinent received independence in 1947, Lahore became the capital of West Punjab province; in 1955 it was made the capital of the newly created West Pakistan province, which was reconstituted as Punjab province in 1970.

Lahore consists of an old city area flanked on the southeast by newer commercial, industrial, and residential areas ringed by suburbs. The old city was at one time surrounded by a wall and a moat, but these structures have been replaced, except in the north, by parklands. A circular road around the rampart provides access to the old city by 13 gates. Notable structures within the old city include the mosque of Wazīr Khān (1634) and Lahore Fort. A walled complex that covers some 36 acres (14.5 hectares), the fort is a splendid example of Mughal architecture; it was partially built by Akbar (reigned 1556–1605) and extended by the next three emperors. The mosque and the fort are decorated in marble and kashi, or encaustic tile work. Other historic landmarks include the Bādshāhī (Imperial) Mosque, built by Aurangzeb and still one of the largest mosques in the world; the 14-foot- (4.3-metre-) long Zamzama, or Zam-Zammah, a cannon immortalized (along with other details of the city) in Rudyard Kipling's novel *Kim* (1901); Ranjit Singh's buildings and mausoleum; the Shāhdara gardens, containing the tomb of the Mughal emperor Jahāngīr; and the magnificent Shālīmār Garden, laid out east of the city in 1642 by Shāh Jahān as a refuge for the royal family. Jahān's refuge consists of about 80 acres (32 hectares) of terraced, walled gardens, with about 450 fountains. The fort and Shālīmār Garden were added to UNESCO's World Heritage List in 1981.

The fort at Lahore, Pak.
Frederic Ohringer—Nancy Palmer Agency

An important educational centre, Lahore is the seat of the University of the Punjab (1882), which is the oldest university in Pakistan. Near the university is the Lahore Museum (1864), which houses eclectic collections of art and historical items. The University of Engineering and Technology, Lahore (1961), and numerous other colleges and institutes also are located in the city.

Lahore is a leading commercial, banking, and industrial centre. Textiles are the single most important industry, but there are many rubber factories, as well as iron, steel, and other mills. Railways and air services link Lahore with other major cities of Pakistan. Pop. (1998) including cantonments, 5,063,499.

Lahore Museum, also called CENTRAL MUSEUM, in Lahore, Pak., archaeological museum opened in 1894 and containing examples of the arts and crafts of the province of Punjab, including sculpture, coins, and Kangra (Pahari) and Mughal paintings and fabrics. Greco-Buddhist sculptures excavated from sites in the Peshāwar district are on display, as is a stūpa drum of Sikri carved with scenes from the Buddha's life. The museum's collection of jewelry is especially notable, with objects from the Trans-Indus territory. There are also a comprehensive collection of musical instruments and a good collection of elaborately ornamented arms and armour.

Lahti, city, Hämeen (Häme) *lääni* (province), southern Finland. It lies at the southern end of Vesi Lake northeast of Helsinki. Founded in 1878, it was incorporated in 1905. A developing industrial centre linked to the rest of Finland by major rail, road, and lake routes, it produces most of the nation's furniture, as well as numerous other wood products, and has a glassworks, breweries, and clothing and machine-tool factories. Lahti is the home of Finland's primary radio and television stations. It is also internationally known for winter sports, with annual championship ski races and other games on the glacially formed Salpaus Ridge. The town hall (1912) was designed by Eliel Saarinen. The city has an arts museum and a historical museum. Pop. (1999 est.) mun., 96,666.

Lahti, Fin.
Ernst A. Jahn

Lāhūn, al-, also spelled EL LAHUN, or IL-LAHUN, ancient Egyptian site situated just north of the turn of the Baḥr Yūsuf canal into the Fayum in al-Fayyūm *muḥāfaẓah* (governorate); it was the location of a Middle Kingdom (1938–*c.* 1600? BC) pyramid and of a workmen's village of approximately the same date. The pyramid, built by King Sesostris II (reigned 1844–37 BC), fourth of the eight kings of the 12th dynasty, was unusual in that the entrance to the burial chamber was not in the north side of the pyramid but was found instead to the south of the structure. Although the pyramid itself was robbed in antiquity, a treasure of jewelry was discovered in the tombs of the princesses, located within the pyramid-enclosure wall. In technical and artistic mastery this collection easily rivals all other Middle Kingdom objects of its type.

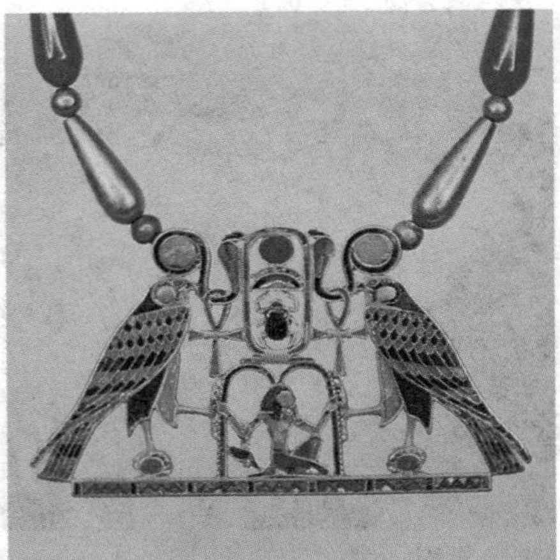
Jeweled pectoral of Sesostris II from al-Lāhūn
By courtesy of the Metropolitan Museum of Art, New York, contribution from Henry Walters and the Rogers Fund, 1916

Excavation of the village, which was also inhabited during the Second Intermediate Period (*c.* 1630–1540 BC), revealed a remarkable degree of town planning. Innumerable pieces of furniture and other household items and a mass of papyri dealing with various topics were uncovered, picturing clearly everyday life during the Middle Kingdom.

lai, medieval poetic and musical form, cultivated especially among the trouvères, or poet-musicians, of northern France in the 12th and 13th centuries but also among their slightly earlier, Provençal-language counterparts, the troubadours, and, called *Leich,* by the German minnesingers. The lai was a long poem having nonuniform stanzas of about 6 to 16 or more lines of 4 to 8 syllables. One or two rhymes were maintained throughout each stanza. The text might address the Virgin Mary or a lady, or in some cases might be didactic. The lais of the poet Marie de France (late 12th century) are short stories in verse on romantic and magical themes and are not lais in the musical sense.

In musical form, the lai was influenced by the sequence, a long liturgical hymn having the general musical pattern *x aa bb cc . . . y;* the repeated pairs are termed double versicles. In lais, however, triple and quadruple repetitions and unrepeated lines might occur, and the first and last lines of music were not always unrepeated. Each stanza had its own music.

This basic form could be varied in a number of ways. A set of several double versicles could be repeated, giving musical unity in the setting of a long poem; the last few notes of a melody might be altered on the repetition, the first ending being called *ouvert* (open), the second, *clos* (closed); and the melody might be varied on the repetition. Shorter variants and offshoots of the lai included patterns such as *aabb,* set to short poems; and strophic songs (*i.e.,* the same music for every stanza) using short double-versicle patterns such as *abbc.*

The lai was monophonic music, having one unharmonized melody line. But in the 14th century the poet and composer Guillaume de Machaut set 2 of his 18 lais polyphonically, using a form called the chace, a three-part canon at the unison (all voices in strict melodic imitation at the same pitch level). Machaut typically wrote lais of 12 stanzas, the last of which shared the melody and poetic form of the first; each stanza used double or quadruple versicles.

Laibach, Congress of (Jan. 26–May 12, 1821), meeting of the Holy Alliance powers (all European rulers except those of Britain, the Ottoman Empire, and the papacy) at Laibach (now Ljubljana, Slovenia) that set the conditions for Austrian intervention in and occupation of the Two Sicilies in action against the Neapolitan revolution (July 1820). As such, it was a triumph for antiliberal Austrian policy, and also, because of British and French dissension, it was a demonstration of the decline of the congress system.

Attended by the monarchs of Russia, Austria, and Prussia and their chief ministers, the kings of the Two Sicilies and Sardinia-Piedmont, the dukes of Modena and Tuscany, and British and French observers, the congress proclaimed its hostility to revolutionary regimes, agreed to abolish the Neapolitan constitution, and authorized the Austrian army to restore the absolutist monarchy. The British and French protested the decision, thereby encouraging unsuccessful resistance among the Neapolitans. A similar revolt in Piedmont was put down by the Austrians at Novara on April 8, 1821.

Laidoner, Johan (b. Feb. 12, 1884, Viiratsi, near Viljandi, Estonia, Russian Empire—d. March 13, 1953, Penza, Russian S.F.S.R.), Estonian soldier and patriot who led the Estonian liberation army in 1918 and supported the authoritarian regime of Konstantin Päts in the 1930s.

Educated in Russia for a military career, Laidoner earned the rank of lieutenant colonel in Russian service. He served in World War I (1914–18) as an intelligence officer and then as a divisional chief of staff. In 1918 Laidoner became commander in chief of the new Estonian army, which drove the German and Russian occupiers out of Estonia in 1918–19. He left the army in 1920 but returned to it in 1924 to put down an attempted communist coup d'état. In 1925 he headed a League of Nations commission that dealt with a British–Turkish Mosul frontier dispute.

In 1934 Laidoner again led the Estonian army in putting down an attempted government takeover by the right-wing "Vap" movement, and thereafter he headed the military support of President Päts's authoritarian regime. Laidoner was deported to the Soviet Union when the Soviets occupied Estonia in June 1940, and he died there.

Laie, town, Honolulu county, on Laie Bay, northeastern Oahu Island, Hawaii, U.S. The land was acquired by Mormon missionaries in 1864 and settled by a colony of Hawaiian Mormons. The impressive white Laie Temple, where the highest rites of the Mormon church can be performed, was built (1919) on the site of an ancient Hawaiian "city of refuge" (a sanctuary for the pursued). The Polynesian Cultural Center, a project of the Mormon church, is Laie's main tourist attraction. Brigham Young University-Hawaii campus (formerly the Church College of Hawaii [1955]) is also there. The nearby Waiapuka Pool is known in Hawaiian literature as the refuge of the beautiful Princess Laieikawai ("Leaf in the Water"), dedicated to the Sun God and guarded from her father, who had vowed to kill her. Pop. (1990) 5,577.

Laigin (Ireland): *see* Leinster.

Laima, also called LAIMA-DALIA (from Lithuanian *laimė,* "happiness," "luck"), in Baltic religion, the goddess of fate, generally associated with the linden tree. Together with Dievs, the sky, and Saule, the sun, Laima determines the length and fortune of human life. In the course of each life she helps arrange marriages, oversees weddings, protects pregnant women, and appears at childbirth to pronounce each infant's destiny.

Revered as patroness of cows and horses, Laima decides the life span of plants and animals and determines the length of the day.

Three other demigoddesses with analogous functions are preserved in Latvian mythology—Dēkla, protector of babies, Kārta, spinner of the thread of life, and Māra, goddess of fertility.

Laing, Alexander Gordon (b. Dec. 27, 1793, Edinburgh, Scot.—d. Sept. 26, 1826, near Tombouctou, Fulani Empire [now Timbuktu, Mali]), Scottish explorer of western Africa and the first European known to have reached the ancient city of Tombouctou.

Serving with the British army in Sierra Leone (1822), Laing was sent among the Mande people of the region by the governor, Charles (later Sir Charles) M'Carthy, to attempt to develop trade in goods and to abolish that in slaves. He also visited the capital of the Susu people, Falaba, now in Sierra Leone. In 1823–24 Laing fought in the war between the British and the Ashanti kingdom and returned to England with the news of M'Carthy's death in action.

Alexander Gordon Laing, engraving
BBC Hulton Picture Library

His next mission was to visit Tombouctou and to explore the Niger River basin. In July 1825 he left the North African coast at Tripoli, Libya, on his journey across the Sahara. He reached Ghudāmis (Ghadames) in northern Fezzan, now in Libya, by September and then entered the vast country of the Tuareg people. Before reaching Tombouctou on Aug. 18, 1826, he had to fight for his life and was severely wounded. He left Tombouctou on September 24 and was murdered two days later. The journal of his earlier explorations, *Travels in the Timannee, Kooranko, and Soolima Countries in Western Africa,* was published in 1825.

Laing, R(onald) D(avid) (b. Oct. 7, 1927, Glasgow, Scot.—d. Aug. 23, 1989, St. Tropez, Fr.), British psychiatrist noted for his alternative approach to the treatment of schizophrenia.

Laing was born into a working-class family and grew up in Glasgow. He studied medicine and psychiatry and earned a doctoral degree in medicine at the University of Glasgow in 1951. After serving as a conscript psychiatrist in the British army (1951–52) and teaching at the University of Glasgow (1953–56), he conducted research at the Tavistock Clinic (1956–60) and at the Tavistock Institute of Human Relations (1960–89). He had a private practice in London.

Throughout much of his career Laing has been interested in the underlying causes of schizophrenia. In his first book, *The Divided Self* (1960), he theorized that ontological insecurity (insecurity about one's existence) prompts a defensive reaction in which the self splits into separate components, thus generating the psychotic symptoms characteristic of schizophrenia. He was opposed to the standard treatments for schizophrenics, such as hospitalization and electroshock. He further analyzed the inner dynamics of schizophrenia in *The Self and Others* (1961) and published, with Aaron Esterson, *Sanity, Madness, and the Family* (1965), a group of studies of people whose mental illnesses he viewed as being induced by their relationships with other family members. Among his other works are *The Politics of Experience* (1967), in which madness is viewed as a form of transcendence of the normal state of alienation, and *The Politics of the Family* (1971). Laing's early approach to schizophrenia was quite controversial, and he modified some of his positions in later years. His book *Wisdom, Madness and Folly: The Making of a Psychiatrist, 1927–1957* (1985) was autobiographical.

Laird, Macgregor (b. 1808, Greenock, Renfrewshire, Scot.—d. Jan. 9, 1861, London, Eng.), Scottish explorer, shipbuilder, and merchant who contributed to the knowledge of the Niger River.

In 1832 Laird accompanied his Liverpool firm's expedition, commanded by the Cornish explorer Richard Lander, to the delta of the Niger River. Among the three ships was the *Alburkah,* a 55-ton paddle-wheeler designed by Laird and the first iron vessel to make an ocean voyage. The expedition proved that the lower Niger could be navigated by oceangoing ships. Laird ascended the Niger to a place about 550 miles (880 km) from the sea and its principal eastern tributary, the Benue, about 80 miles (130 km) above the confluence and formed an accurate idea of its course and source. Of the expedition's 48 European members, all but 9 died from fever or wounds, and Laird never fully recovered from the many hardships of the expedition.

After returning to Liverpool in 1834, he published, with R.A.K. Oldfield, *Narrative of an Expedition into the Interior of Africa by the River Niger . . . in 1832, 1833, 1834* (1837). He subsequently devoted himself to developing trade in the Niger territory and in 1854 promoted a second expedition, led by the Scottish explorer William Balfour Baikie, which penetrated the Benue about 250 miles (400 km) farther than any earlier European exploration. As a result of good organization and the use of quinine to control malaria, not a life was lost, and the venture, a landmark in the development of western Africa, led to expeditions by other traders. Laird also developed transatlantic steamship routes, and his company's ship *Sirius* was the first to cross the Atlantic from Europe to the United States (1838) entirely under steam power.

laissez-faire (French: "allow to do"), policy based on a minimum of governmental interference in the economic affairs of individuals and society. The origin of the term is uncertain, but it is usually associated with the economists known as Physiocrats, who flourished in France from about 1756 to 1778. The policy of laissez-faire received strong support in classical economics as it developed in Great Britain under the influence of Adam Smith.

Belief in laissez-faire was a popular view during the 19th century; its proponents cited the assumption in classical economics of a natural economic order as support for their faith in unregulated individual activity. The British economist John Stuart Mill was responsible for bringing this philosophy into popular economic usage in his *Principles of Political Economy* (1848), in which he set forth the arguments for and against government activity in economic affairs.

Laissez-faire was a political as well as an economic doctrine. The pervading theory of the 19th century was that the individual, pursuing his own desired ends, would thereby achieve the best results for the society of which he was a part. The function of the state was to maintain order and security and to avoid interference with the initiative of the individual in pursuit of his own desired goals.

The philosophy's popularity reached its peak around 1870. In the late 19th century the acute changes caused by industrial growth and the adoption of mass-production techniques proved the laissez-faire doctrine insufficient as a guiding philosophy. Although the original concept had to yield to new theories in attracting wide support, the general philosophy still retains some supporters.

Laja River, Spanish in full RÍO DE LA LAJA, river in Guanajuato *estado* ("state"), north-central Mexico. After rising in the Sierra Madre Occidental near San Felipe (Doctor Hernandez Alvarez), the Laja arches eastward and then southeastward through the central plateau, past the cities of Dolores Hidalgo, San Miguel de Allende, Comonfort, and San Miguel Octopan. It joins the Apaseo River, a tributary of the Lerma River, 3 miles (5 km) southeast of Celaya. A portion of the Mexico City–Piedras Negras railroad parallels the river's lower course. The Laja is approximately 85 miles (135 km) long.

Lajes, also spelled LAGES, city, east-central Santa Catarina *estado* ("state"), southern Brazil, lying north of the Caveiras River in the Paraná Mountains, at 3,000 feet (900 m) above sea level. Formed as a municipality in 1800, it was settled chiefly by Germans and

Lumber stacked around a tall araucaria (Paraná pine) tree, near Lajes, Brazil
Ernst Jahn

in 1866 was elevated to city status. Livestock raising and industry are now the main economic activities. Principal products include lumber, corn (maize), *feijão* (beans), wheat, potatoes, and oats. Lajes is on the main highway linking São Paulo and Pôrto Alegre. Pop. (1991 prelim.) 137,169.

Lajes, town, northeast Terceira Island, Portuguese Azores. In 1941 the Portuguese government selected the town's site, 10 miles (16 km) northeast of the city of Angra do Heroísmo, as an air base. It became a major Allied air installation during World War II and later a joint U.S. and Portuguese base within the North Atlantic Treaty Organization (NATO). The airfield is also an important weather-forecasting point for the North Atlantic. Pop. (1981) 2,863.

Lajos (Hungarian personal name): *see under* Louis.

Lajpat Rai, Lala (b. 1865, Jagraon, India—d. Nov. 17, 1928, Lahore [now in Pakistan]), Indian writer and politician, outspoken in his advocacy of a militant anti-British nationalism in the Congress Party and as a leader of the Hindu supremacy movement.

After studying law at the Government College, Lahore, Lajpat Rai practiced at Hissār and Lahore, where he helped to establish the nationalistic Dayananda Anglo-Vedic School and became a follower of Dayananda Sarasvati, the founder of the conservative Hindu society Arya Samaj ("Society of Aryans"). After joining the Congress Party and taking part in political agitation in the Punjab, Lajpat Rai was deported to Mandalay, Burma (Myanmar), without trial in May 1907. In November, however, he was allowed to return when the viceroy, Lord Minto, decided that there was insufficient evidence to hold him for subversion. Lajpat Rai's supporters attempted to secure his election to the presidency of the party session at Surāt in December 1907, but elements favouring cooperation with the British refused to accept him, and the party split over the issues.

During World War I, Lajpat Rai lived in the United States, but he returned to India in 1919 and in the following year led the special session of the Congress Party that launched the noncooperation movement. Imprisoned from 1921 to 1923, he was elected to the legislative assembly on his release. In 1928 he introduced the legislative assembly resolution for the boycott of the British Simon Commission on constitutional reform. Shortly thereafter he died after being attacked by police during a demonstration.

Lajpat Rai's most important writings include *The Story of My Deportation* (1908), *Arya Samaj* (1915), *The United States of America: A Hindu's Impression* (1916), and *Unhappy India* (1928).

Lak-Dargin languages, also called LAK-DARGWA, two related languages spoken in central Dagestan in the Caucasus—Lak and Dargin. Both are written languages. The dialects of Dargin differ considerably from one another and are considered by some scholars to be separate languages. The Lak-Dargin languages are often placed in the Dagestanian group of the Nakho-Dagestanian (Northeast Caucasian) languages, together with the Avar-Andi-Dido and Lezgian languages. *See also* Dagestanian languages.

lakabi ware, lakabi also spelled LAQABI, also called KĀSHĀN WARE, in Islāmic ceramics, a style of pottery associated with Kāshān, Persia (Iran), from about the middle of the 11th century until the end of the 14th century. The name (*lakabi,* "painted") is a misnomer, actually referring to an incised design decorated with different coloured glazes separated by clay threads. Colours used were blue, yellow, purple, and green. Some *lakabi* wares were also made at Ar-Raqqah, on the Euphrates.

Lakanal, Joseph (b. July 14, 1762, Serres, France—d. Feb. 14, 1845, Paris), educator who reformed the French educational system during the French Revolution.

At the outbreak of the French Revolution in 1789, Lakanal was working as a teacher. In 1792 he was elected to the revolutionary legislature known as the National Convention. He voted for the execution of King Louis XVI (January 1793).

Lakanal, portrait after a medallion by Pierre-Jean David
By courtesy of the Bibliotheque Nationale, Paris

As a member of the Convention's Committee of Public Instruction, Lakanal in June 1793 presented a bill (*Projet d'éducation nationale*) proposing that the state provide free elementary education for boys and girls. The plan was rejected, but, after the fall of Robespierre's Jacobin regime (1794), Lakanal became president of the education committee. In October he presented a version of his plan for elementary schools that was enforced for about a year. He also presented a plan for *écoles centrales* (secondary schools), which was followed until the lycées were set up in 1802. In 1795 he started the *école normale* for training teachers. Proscribed as a regicide, he went to the United States in 1815 after the second Restoration of the monarchy; Lakanal returned to France in 1834.

Consult the INDEX *first*

lake, any relatively large body of slow-moving or standing water that occupies an inland basin.

A brief treatment of lakes follows. For full treatment, *see* MACROPAEDIA: Lakes.

Lakes occur throughout much of the world, but they are most abundant in high northern latitudes and in mountain regions, particularly those that have been glaciated in recent geologic times. They commonly occur along rivers with low gradients and wide flats and are associated with variations in the river channel. Many lakes are found in lowlands near the sea, especially in wet climates.

A lake may contain either fresh water or salt water. Freshwater lakes constitute about 0.009 percent of the Earth's free surface water, while saline lakes account for a somewhat smaller percentage. In general, salt lakes occur in arid regions where the lakes occupy landlocked basins and the surrounding lands are rich in saline and alkaline compounds; the salts brought into the lakes in solution remain and are concentrated as the lake waters evaporate. Extremely salty lakes, such as the Great Salt Lake in northern Utah, occur in areas where the climate has changed from humid to arid.

Lakes vary significantly in size. Most have a surface area of about 260 square km (100 square miles) or less, but a few exceed 3,900 square km (1,506 square miles). Lake Superior, located in North America and covering roughly 82,100 square km (31,700 square miles), is the largest freshwater lake in terms of surface area. The freshwater lake with the largest volume, however, is Lake Baikal in Siberia. Its total volume is approximately 23,000 cubic km (5,500 cubic miles).

Lakes may form in any large undrained depression or in any sizable depression that has an outlet somewhat above the lowest parts of the depression where there is an adequate supply of water to keep the depression filled. The primary sources of lake water are melting ice and snow, springs, rivers, immediate runoff from the land surface, and direct precipitation.

Unquestionably, more of the world's existing lakes have been produced by glacial action than by any other single agent. The extensive ice sheets that covered Canada, the northern United States, Finland, and portions of Sweden during the Pleistocene Epoch (1,600,000 to 10,000 years ago) gouged out undrained depressions in the bedrock of these areas, thereby producing tens of thousands of rock-shored lakes. Such continental glaciers also created lakes by depositing rock debris across preexisting drainage patterns. The sedimentary material dammed up streams and creeks, causing lakes to form. In some cases, glacial debris spread indiscriminately over the landscape left scattered shallow swales, or depressions, and these formations now hold lakes. When glacial ice melts, it sometimes leaves deep pits called kettle holes, which fill with water and become lakes. Most lakes in

Largest natural lakes of the world

name and *location*	area*	
	sq mi	sq km
Africa		
Victoria, *Kenya–Tanzania–Uganda*	26,828	69,485
Tanganyika, *Burundi–Tanzania–Zaire–Zambia*	12,700	32,900
Nyasa (Malaŵi), *Malaŵi–Mozambique–Tanzania*	11,430	29,604
Chad, *Cameroon–Chad–Niger–Nigeria*	6,875†‡	17,800†‡
Bangweulu, *Zambia*	3,800	9,800
Rudolf (Turkana), *Ethiopia–Kenya*	2,473	6,405
Albert (Mobutu Sese Seko), *Uganda–Zaire*	2,160	5,600
Mweru, *Zaire–Zambia*	1,900	4,920
Kyoga, *Uganda*	1,710	4,430
Tana, *Ethiopia*	1,418	3,673
Kivu, *Rwanda–Zaire*	1,040	2,700
Rukwa, *Tanzania*§	1,000	2,600
Chilwa, *Malaŵi–Mozambique*§	1,000	2,600
Mai-Ndombe (Leopold II), *Zaire*	890	2,300
Edward, *Uganda–Zaire*	830	2,150
Abaya, *Ethiopia*	448	1,160
Stefanie, *Ethiopia*§	425	1,100
Eyasi, *Tanzania*§	400	1,050
Natron, *Tanzania*§	350	900
Abe, *Djibouti–Ethiopia*§	300	780
America, North		
Superior, *Canada–United States*	31,700	82,100
Huron, *Canada–United States*	23,000	59,600
Michigan, *United States*	22,300	57,800
Great Bear, *Northwest Territories, Can.*	12,028	31,153
Great Slave, *Northwest Territories, Can.*	11,031	28,570
Erie, *Canada–United States*	9,910	25,667
Winnipeg, *Manitoba, Can.*	9,417	24,390
Ontario, *Canada–United States*	7,340	19,010
Nicaragua, *Nicaragua*	3,156	8,157
Athabasca, *Saskatchewan–Alberta, Can.*	3,064	7,936
Reindeer, *Saskatchewan–Manitoba, Can.*	2,568	6,651
Nettilling, *Northwest Territories, Can.*	2,140	5,543
Winnipegosis, *Manitoba, Can.*	2,075	5,374
Nipigon, *Ontario, Can.*	1,872	4,848
Manitoba, *Manitoba, Can.*	1,799	4,659
Great Salt, *Utah, U.S.*§	1,700†	4,400†
Lake of the Woods, *Canada–United States*	1,679	4,349
Dubawnt, *Northwest Territories, Can.*	1,480	3,833
Amadjuak, *Northwest Territories, Can.*	1,203	3,116
Wollaston, *Saskatchewan, Can.*	1,035	2,681
Iliamna, *Alaska, U.S.*	1,000	2,590
Mistassini, *Quebec, Can.*	902	2,336
Nueltin, *Northwest Territories–Manitoba, Can.*	880	2,279
Southern Indian, *Manitoba, Can.*	868	2,248
Michikamau, *Newfoundland, Can.*	784	2,031
Baker, *Northwest Territories, Can.*	729	1,888
Okeechobee, *Florida, U.S.*	700	1,813
Martre, *Northwest Territories, Can.*	686	1,777
Williston, *British Columbia, Can.*	641	1,660
Seul, *Ontario, Can.*	640	1,658
Yathkyed, *Northwest Territories, Can.*	559	1,448
Claire, *Alberta, Can.*	555	1,437
Cree, *Saskatchewan, Can.*	554	1,435
Ronge, *Saskatchewan, Can.*	546	1,414
Eau Claire, *Quebec, Can.*	534	1,383
Moose, *Manitoba, Can.*	528	1,368
Cedar, *Manitoba, Can.*	522	1,352
Kasba, *Northwest Territories, Can.*	518	1,342
Bienville, *Quebec, Can.*	482	1,248
Island, *Manitoba, Can.*	472	1,222
St. Clair, *Canada–United States*	460	1,191
Becharof, *Alaska, U.S.*	458	1,186
Lesser Slave, *Alberta, Can.*	451	1,168
Red, *Minnesota, U.S.*	451	1,168
Gods, *Manitoba, Can.*	444	1,150
Champlain, *Canada–United States*	435	1,127
Aberdeen, *Northwest Territories, Can.*	425	1,101
Chapala, *Mexico*	417	1,080
Napaktulik, *Northwest Territories, Can.*	417	1,080
Mackay, *Northwest Territories, Can.*	410	1,062
Managua, *Nicaragua*	400	1,035
Saint-Jean, *Quebec, Can.*	387	1,002
Pipmuacan, *Quebec, Can.*	378	979
Garry, *Northwest Territories, Can.*	377	976
Contwoyto, *Northwest Territories, Can.*	370	958
Abitibi, *Ontario, Can.*	360	932
Rainy, *Canada–United States*	360	932
Hottah, *Northwest Territories, Can.*	354	917
Salton (Sea), *California, U.S.*§	344	890
Aylmer, *Northwest Territories, Can.*	327	847
Eskimo North, *Northwest Territories, Can.*	324	839
Nipissing, *Ontario, Can.*	321	831
Teshekpuk, *Alaska, U.S.*	315	816
Nonacho, *Northwest Territories, Can.*	303	785
Peter Pond, *Saskatchewan, Can.*	300	777
Atlin, *British Columbia–Yukon, Can.*	299	774
Minto, *Quebec, Can.*	294	761
Cross, *Manitoba, Can.*	292	756
Simcoe, *Ontario, Can.*	287	743
Clinton Colden, *Northwest Territories, Can.*	284	736
Selwyn, *Northwest Territories, Can.*	277	717
Point, *Northwest Territories, Can.*	271	702
Ennadai, *Northwest Territories, Can.*	263	681
Wholdaia, *Northwest Territories, Can.*	262	679
Tulemaiu, *Northwest Territories, Can.*	258	668
Big Trout, *Ontario, Can.*	255	660
Playgreen, *Manitoba, Can.*	254	658
America, South		
Maracaibo, *Venezuela*	5,150	13,300
Titicaca, *Peru–Bolivia*	3,200	8,300
Poopó, *Bolivia*§	1,000	2,600
Buenos Aires, *Chile–Argentina*	865	2,240
Chiquita, *Argentina*§	714	1,850
Argentino, *Argentina*	546	1,415
Viedma, *Argentina*	420	1,088
San Martin (O'Higgins), *Argentina–Chile*	391	1,013
Llanquihue, *Chile*	330	860
Colhué Huapi, *Argentina*	310	803
Asia		
Caspian Sea, *Turkmenistan–Kazakhstan–Russia–Azerbaijan–Iran*	149,200	386,400
Aral (Sea), *Kazakhstan–Uzbekistan*§	13,000	33,800
Baikal, *Russia*	12,200	31,500
Balkhash, *Kazakhstan*§	6,650†	17,250†
Tonle Sap, *Cambodia*	2,525†	6,350†
Ysyk-Köl (Issyk-Kul), *Kyrgyzstan*§	2,408	6,236
Urmia, *Iran*§	2,150†	5,600†
Koko Nor, *Tsinghai, China*§	1,770†	4,583†
Taymyr, *Russia*	1,760	4,560
Khanka (Hsing-k'ai), *Russia–China*	1,690†	4,380†
Van, *Turkey*§	1,434	3,713
P'o-yang, *Kiangsi, China*	1,383†	3,583†
Uvs, *Mongolia*§	1,300	3,350
Tung-t'ing, *Hunan, China*	1,089†	2,820†
Alaköl, *Kazakhstan*§	1,025	2,650
Hövsgöl, *Mongolia*	1,012	2,620
Chany, *Russia*§	960	2,500
T'ang-ku-la-yu-mu (Tangra), *Tibet, China*§	950	2,460
T'ai, *Chekiang–Kiangsu, China*	936	2,425
Hu-lun, *Inner Mongolia, China*	894†	2,315†
Lama, *Russia*	772	2,000
Lop Nor (Lo-pu), *Sinkiang, China*§	770 ‖	2,000 ‖
Hung-tse, *Anhwei–Kiangsu, China*	757	1,960
Hammar, *Iraq*	750	1,950
Na-mu (Nam), *Tibet, China*§	741	1,920
Ch'i-lin (Zilling), *Tibet, China*§	720	1,864
Har Us, *Mongolia*	680	1,760
Tengiz, *Kazakhstan*§	614	1,590
Tuz, *Turkey*§	580	1,500
Po-ssu-t'eng (Baghrash), *Sinkiang, China*	580	1,500
Hyargas, *Mongolia*§	543	1,407
Toba, *Sumatra, Indonesia*	440	1,140
Dead (Sea), *Israel–Jordan*	394	1,020
Wei-shan, *Kiangsu–Shantung, China*	386	1,000
Ebi, *Sinkiang, China*§	386	1,000
Bay, *Luzon, Philippines*§	356	922
P'u-mo (Pomo), *Tibet, China*	340	881
Cha-jih-nan-mu (Terinam), *Tibet, China*	313	810
Yang-cho-yung (Yamdrok), *Tibet, China*	309	800
Ch'ao, *Anhwei, China*	309	800
Seletytengiz (Siletiteniz), *Kazakhstan*	300	777
Namak, *Iran*	290	750
Sasyk, *Kazakhstan*	284	736
Pyasino, *Russia*	284	735
Kulundin, *Russia*§	281	728
Wu-lun-ku (Ulyungur), *Sinkiang, China*	270	700
Mapam (Ma-fa-mu; Mānasarowar), *Tibet, China*	270	700
Kao-yu, *Anhwei–Kiangsu, China*	270	700
To-ko-ts'o-jen (Montcalm), *Tibet, China*§	270	700
Huang-kai, *Hunan–Hupeh, China*	270	700
Biwa, *Honshu, Japan*	259	672
Beysehir, *Turkey*	253	656
Ngoring, *Tsinghai, China*	250	650
Europe		
Ladoga, *Russia*	6,826	17,678
Onega, *Russia*	3,753	9,720
Vänern, *Sweden*	2,156	5,585
Iso Saimaa, *Finland*	1,690	4,377
Peipsi, *Estonia–Russia*	1,373	3,555
Vättern, *Sweden*	738	1,912
Sevan, *Armenia*	525	1,360
Mälaren, *Sweden*	440	1,140
Inari, *Finland*	425	1,102
Päijänne, *Finland*	407	1,054
Ilmen, *Russia*	379†	982†
Oulu, *Finland*	345	893
Pielinen, *Finland*	335	868
Imandra, *Russia*	314	812
Oceania		
Eyre, *South Australia*§	3,600 ‖	9,300 ‖
Torrens, *South Australia*§	2,230 ‖	5,776 ‖
Gairdner, *South Australia*§	1,845 ‖	4,780 ‖
Frome, *South Australia*§	900 ‖	2,400 ‖
Amadeus, *Northern Territory, Australia*§	340 ‖	880 ‖
Taupo, *North Island, New Zealand*	234	606

*Conversions for rounded figures have been rounded, thousands to the nearest hundred and hundreds to the nearest ten. †Area of lake varies according to season; figure given represents mean area. ‡In the 1990s the area was reported as 1,000 square miles (2,600 square km). §Salt lake. ‖ Usually dry.

mountain valleys are glacial in origin, having been formed by mountain, or valley, glaciers by the same process of erosion and deposition. A few mountain lakes were formed as a result of landslides or mudflows blocking streams. Ordinarily, such a lake is relatively short lived because the outlet at the lower end is quickly cut down through the fairly unresistant material in the natural dam. Lakes so formed by lava flows, however, are likely to be permanently established.

Other barriers to preexisting drainage that result in lake formation are sand dunes deposited across a small stream, beach deposits across the mouth of a river, or the alluvium laid down by a large river across the course of a smaller tributary. Deltaic deposits that are laid down in a sluggish stream by a silt-laden, more swiftly flowing stream may dam the former and produce a lake upstream. The floodplains of rivers contain bodies of water called oxbow lakes that were formed in what were once river channels.

The craters of extinct or dormant volcanoes commonly contain lakes. Crater Lake in Oregon is one of the best known examples. At various places, the Earth's crust has been warped or broken into depressed blocks filled with water. Several large African lakes (*e.g.,* Nyasa and Tanganyika) lie in the Great Rift Valley, an enormous down-dropped block of the terrestrial crust.

Regions underlain by highly soluble limestone develop depressions known as sinkholes, which may fill with water under certain conditions to become lakes. The lake region of north-central Florida is of this type.

Viewed on the geological time scale, lakes are short-lived. Almost as soon as they are formed, three processes begin their eventual destruction. All inflowing streams carry sediment into a lake, thereby starting the process of filling the basin. If the basin is filled enough for the lake to overflow, the outflowing stream tends to erode a notch through the lip of the basin and thereby drains the depression. Lastly, the accumulation of organic deposits from vegetation may cause shallow lakes to become bogs or swamps and, ultimately, dry land.

In the upper part of lakes there is a good supply of light, heat, oxygen, and nutrients, well distributed by currents and turbulence. As a result, a large number of diverse aquatic organisms can be found there. The most abundant forms are plankton (chiefly diatoms), algae, and flagellates. In the lower levels and in the sediments, the main forms of life are bacteria.

Although organic wastes are efficiently digested through the symbiotic relationship between algae and bacteria, the presence of toxic matter in some industrial and domestic wastes may seriously disrupt a lake's normal biological activity. Anaerobic conditions (the absence of free oxygen) may prevail, and the diversity of life may also be harmed by agricultural pesticides and herbicides carried by streamflow, and by air pollutants carried by rain.

In modern industrial societies, requirements for water—a large percentage of which is derived from lakes—include its use for dilution and removal of municipal and industrial wastes, for cooling purposes, for irrigation, for transportation, for power generation, and for recreation. With each of these uses is associated a variety of abuses of the very characteristics of lakes that make them desirable for any of these purposes. Municipalities and industries have polluted lakes chemically and thermally, the shipping that plies large inland water bodies leaves oil and other refuse in its wake, water used for irrigation often contains chemical residues from fertilizers and biocides when it is returned to lakes, and the populace that demands clean bodies of water for its recreation often ignores basic sanitary and antipollution practices, to the ultimate detriment of the waters enjoyed. These abuses of lake waters, however, are being ameliorated by better resource management.

lake, any of a class of pigments composed of organic dyes that have been rendered insoluble by interaction with a compound of a metal. The interaction may involve the precipitation of a salt in which the proportions of dye to metal are fixed, or it may be a less well defined attraction between the dye and the surfaces of particles of the inorganic compound. Some lakes are prepared by a combination of both processes. Lakes considerably extend the range of colours available in the production of paints, cosmetics, and inks for printing and lithography.

Dyes of several chemical classes are made into lakes by techniques that vary according to the nature of the salt-forming groups in the dye molecule. Mordant dyes and acid dyes form insoluble salts with metal ions, such as those of calcium and aluminum. Basic dyes contain amino groups and form insoluble salts with inorganic metal-containing acids such as phosphotungstic or phosphomolybdic acids.

Lake (of Delhi and of Aston Clinton), Gerard Lake, 1st Viscount (b. July 27, 1744, Harrow, Middlesex, Eng.—d. Feb. 20, 1808, London), British general, most prominent for his role in suppressing the Irish Rebellion of 1798 and for his campaigns in India from 1801 to 1806 against Daulat Rāo Sindhia of Gwalior and Jaswant Rāo Holkar, leaders of the Marāthā confederacy.

1st Viscount Lake, detail of an engraving by P. Lightfoot
BBC Hulton Picture Library

Lake served in the Seven Years' War, in the American Revolutionary War, and in the wars of the French Revolution. He took command of the British Army in Ireland in April 1798, and when rebellion broke out, defeated the insurgents at Vinegar Hill on June 21. He also stopped a landing of French troops at Killala Bay in September.

In 1800 Lake was made commander in chief in India, and after arriving in Calcutta in July 1801 strove to modernize the Indian Army. He became a full general the following year and in 1803 won victories over the disunited Marāthās, capturing Delhi and defeating Sindhia's French-trained army at Laswari on November 1; rewarded with a peerage, he went on to rout Holkar at Farrukhābād, in November 1804, but was repulsed at Bharatpur early in 1805 and was forced to make peace in April. He was then removed from his command, but was made a viscount on his return to England.

Lake, Simon (b. Sept. 4, 1866, Pleasantville, N.J., U.S.—d. June 23, 1945, Bridgeport, Conn.), U.S. inventor who built the "Argonaut," the first submarine to operate extensively in the open sea.

Lake's first experimental submarine, the "Argonaut, Jr.," built in 1894, had a wooden hull and was about 14 feet (4 metres) long. It travelled the sea bottom on wheels turned by hand. The "Argonaut," built in 1897, was 36 feet (11 metres) long and was powered by a 30-horsepower gasoline engine. Air for the engine and crew was drawn down from the surface through a floating hose, later through rigid tubes. The "Argonaut" also had wheels for movement along the bottom. In 1898 it voyaged about 300 miles (500 kilometres) from Norfolk, Va., to New York City.

Lake's "Protector" (1906), about 60 feet (18 metres) long, was rejected by the Congress for purchase for the U.S. Navy. Lake sold it to Russia, and it was shipped to Vladivostok. Lake went there for several years to supervise its reassembly and the training of crews. He built more submarines for the Russian government and, during World War I, more than 100 for other nations, including 55 for the U.S. He also helped develop the submarine periscope and invented other underwater gear.

Lake Charles, city, seat (1852) of Calcasieu parish, southwestern Louisiana, U.S., on the Calcasieu River. Adjacent to the town of Sulphur, it is a port of entry on a 32-mi (51-km) deepwater channel (completed 1926) and linked to the Gulf of Mexico via the 20-mi-long Calcasieu Lake. The site was first settled *c.* 1781 and was named for Charles Sallier, an early lakeside settler. In the 1880s it was promoted as a base for the exploitation of heavily timbered pinelands to the north and west. The advent of railroads stimulated the timber industry and brought grain farmers from the Midwest, who developed nearby what is now the principal rice-growing area of the United States. Exploitation of local mineral deposits—sulfur, oil, and gas—has made Lake Charles one of the nation's leading petrochemical production centres. Fur-bearing animals are trapped nearby in coastal marshes, and there is offshore oil drilling. McNeese State University was established (1939) in the city. The Sam Houston State Park is nearby. Inc. town, 1867; city, 1904. Pop. (1990) city, 70,580; Lake Charles MSA, 168,134.

Lake City, city, seat (1832) of Columbia county, northern Florida, U.S., near Osceola National Forest, 60 mi (97 km) west of Jacksonville. It occupies the site of a Seminole village once ruled by a chief called Halpatter-Tustennuggee (meaning "alligator warrior"). The Indians left under the terms of an 1824 treaty, and white settlers moved in. An important settlement in early Florida, it was called Alligator until 1859, when it was incorporated and renamed Lake City for the myriad lakes that surround it. The only significant Civil War battle (Feb. 20, 1864) fought in Florida took place at Olustee, 15 mi west; it resulted in a Confederate victory, and the battlefield is now a state historic site. The city developed as a centre for mixed farming and has a tobacco auction. Other economic factors include tourism, phosphate mining, forest products, and some manufacturing, including aircraft repair facilities. Pop. (1990) 10,005.

Lake Clark National Park and Preserve, formerly LAKE CLARK NATIONAL MONUMENT, national park and preserve in southern Alaska, U.S., on the western shore of Cook Inlet, southwest of Anchorage. It was proclaimed a national monument in 1978 and the boundaries and name were altered in 1980. Lake Clark, more than 40 mi (65 km) long and the largest of more than a score of glacial lakes on the rim of the Chigmit Mountains, is the headwaters for the most important spawning ground for red salmon in North America. With great geologic diversity, the park includes jagged peaks, granite spires, dozens of glaciers, hundreds of waterfalls, tundra plains, and active volcanoes. Wildlife includes caribou, Dall sheep, brown and grizzly bears, bald eagles, and peregrine falcons. The total area is 3,653,000 ac (1,478,900 ha).

Lake District, famous scenic region and national park in the county of Cumbria, England. The national park covers an area of 866 sq mi (2,243 sq km). It contains the principal English lakes, including Windermere (10½ mi [17 km] long), and the highest English mountains (Scafell Pike, 3,210 ft [978 m]). The famous lake-strewn valleys of the region radiate from a core of central mountains, thus making through routes difficult to establish but also contributing to the distinctive character that makes the entire Lake District attractive to tourists.

The geological structure is basically a dome, with hard, pre-Carboniferous rocks forming most of the principal summits, such as Scafell Pike, Scafell (3,162 ft), and Helvellyn (3,118 ft). To the north softer Ordovician rocks give more rounded hills (Skiddaw [3,054 ft] and Saddleback [2,847 ft]). In the south, lower hills of Silurian slates and grits surround the lakes of Windermere, Esthwaite Water, and Coniston Water.

This structure has been influenced by glacial action that deepened existing valleys, both scooping out the rock basins that now contain the lakes and also creating (by truncating former tributary valleys) a number of "hanging valleys" with attractive waterfalls.

The area was long isolated from the south and east by moorlands, peat bogs, lakes, and forests. Two Roman roads were built across the region, and later Norse invasions resulted in a period of forest clearance. The Cistercian abbeys of Furness and Byland, exploiting the area for wool production, continued the process of deforestation, which was accelerated by iron-ore smelting and, later, by the extraction of lead and copper. These activities became uneconomic after the 1870s, and labour was diverted into slate and building stone quarries. The state Forestry Commission has covered large areas with conifers but has agreed to leave the central fell (upland) area in its deforested state with fragmentary deciduous woodland.

The Lake District became a national park in 1951, and the increased social mobility of the population of the industrial regions of northern England has stimulated the tourist industry. Traditional forms of extensive agriculture (cattle and sheep rearing) have been intensified and include the production of milk and eggs.

The increased demand for water by industrial northwest England has resulted in the use of Thirlmere Lake as a reservoir, precluding its use for recreation.

The Lake District was the home of William Wordsworth, who was born at Cockermouth and is buried beside his sister and his wife in Grasmere churchyard. Since the early 19th century, the region has had many other well-known literary visitors and residents.

Lake Dwellings, German *Pfahlbauten*: "pile structures," remains of prehistoric settlements within what are today the margins of lakes in southern Germany, Switzerland, France, and Italy. According to the theory advanced by the Swiss archaeologist Ferdinand Keller in the mid-19th century, the dwellings were built on platforms supported by piles above the surface of the water, and all appear very similar in construction. First, the wooden piles, the ends burned to a point, were driven deep into the mud and surrounded with heavy stones. A lacework of tree trunks and smaller branches was built across the piles, forming a platform; on the platform were built one- or two-roomed rectangular huts with beaten clay floors. Although the clay floors were used especially as a precaution against fire, the vast majority of pile dwellings appear to have ended in conflagration—either accidental or the result of enemy attack. Cattle and sheep were also raised on the platforms.

Because the Lake Dwellers usually rebuilt the new village on top of the remains of the old one, archaeologists were able to work out a culture sequence for central Europe and in the process confirmed what the Danish archaeologist Christian Thomsen had postulated for Scandinavia—that the Stone Age was immediately followed by the Bronze Age. Pile dwellings continued to be built during the Bronze Age and the Iron Age.

Anthropologists now believe that the pile dwellings may have been built above swampy land on the lake shore rather than above the waters of the lakes themselves. Similar houses and storage buildings on platforms supported by wooden piles or stone foundations are in use today in humid subtropical and tropical areas (*e.g.,* Malaysia).

Lake Erie, Battle of (Sept. 10, 1813), major U.S. naval victory in the War of 1812, ensuring U.S. control over Lake Erie and precluding any territorial cession in the Northwest to Great Britain in the peace settlement. On Sept. 10, 1813, Master Commandant Oliver Hazard Perry's fleet of nine ships engaged six British

"Battle of Lake Erie," detail of a painting by Thomas Birch, 1814; in Pennsylvania Academy of the Fine Arts, Philadelphia

By courtesy of Pennsylvania Academy of the Fine Arts, Philadelphia

warships under Capt. Robert Heriot Barclay in Lake Erie. After Perry's flagship, "Lawrence," had suffered heavy casualties and had been reduced to a defenseless wreck, he transferred to a sister ship, the "Niagara," and sailed directly into the British line, firing broadsides and forcing its surrender. The British lost 40 men, with 94 wounded; the Americans, 27 killed and 96 wounded. The destruction of the British squadron on Lake Erie reversed the course of the northwest campaign and forced the British to abandon Detroit.

Lake Forest, city, Lake county, extreme northeastern Illinois, U.S., on Lake Michigan, a northern suburb of Chicago. Settled in 1835, it was laid out in 1856, and its wooded lakeshore became the setting for numerous estates. Special areas were reserved for the establishment of three educational institutions: Lake Forest College, opened in 1857; Lake Forest Academy, in 1861; and Ferry Hall (now a part of the academy), in 1869. Also in the city are Barat College of the Sacred Heart (1904) and Woodlands Academy (preparatory), operated by the Society of the Sacred Heart. Inc. 1861. Pop. (1990) 17,836.

Lake Geneva, city, Walworth county, southeastern Wisconsin, U.S., on the northeastern shore of Lake Geneva at its outlet (the White River), 52 mi (84 km) southwest of Milwaukee. Named for Geneva, N.Y., it developed after 1840 and has been a popular year-round resort for more than a century, with many summer homes and estates (most of which are now permanent residences) on the lake and the wooded hills. The Northwestern Military and Naval Academy moved there in 1911 from Highland Park, Ill. Lake Geneva is the site of the University of Chicago's Yerkes Astronomical Observatory (at Williams Bay). There are some light manufactures. The lake, covering 5,230 ac (2,120 ha) is 7.7 mi long and 2 mi across at its widest point; it is partly spring-fed, has a shoreline of 26 mi and a maximum depth of 140 ft (45 m), and is angled for several types of fish. At its western end is Fontana, the site in the 1830s of the Potawatomi village of Chief Big Toe (or Big Foot). Big Foot Beach State Park is at the lake's eastern edge, and the smaller lakes Como and Delavan are nearby. Inc. village, 1844; city, 1883. Pop. (1990) 5,979.

Lake Havasu City, year-round resort, Mohave county, western Arizona, U.S., in the Chemhuevi Valley along the Colorado River, west of the Mohave Mountains. The city, founded in 1963, was promoted by industrialist Robert P. McCulloch as the focal point of a recreational and retirement development. Although unincorporated it has become the county's largest community. It centres on the 45-mi (72-km) long Lake Havasu (impounded by Parker Dam and 3 mi across at its widest point) and London Bridge. The latter, designed by John Rennie with multiple masonry arches and completed in 1831 over the Thames River in London, was transplanted stone by stone and reerected to span a man-made inlet on the Colorado; dedicated in 1971 it has generated unusual tourist interest. Havasu Lake National Wildlife Refuge is to the north, and Lake Havasu State Park is across the lake in San Bernardino County, Calif. Cattle ranching is a basic local economic activity but light manufacturing (notably chain saw production) has developed in Lake Havasu City. Pop. (1990) 24,363.

lake herring, also called CISCO, any of several whitefish (*q.v.*) species.

Lake IJssel (The Netherlands): *see* IJsselmeer.

Lake Louise, unincorporated place, southwestern Alberta, Canada, on the Bow River, in Banff National Park, immediately northeast of the icy, blue-green lake of the same name, which is a renowned beauty spot. Originally settled in 1884 as a Canadian Pacific Railway construction camp, it was known as Holt City and later Laggan, until renamed in 1914 for the lake, which had been discovered in 1882 by railroad workers and named to honour Princess Louise, the daughter of Queen Victoria and wife of the Marquess of Lorne

Lake Louise, with Victoria Mountain and Glacier in the background, near the village of Lake Louise, Alta.

Josef Muench

(governor-general of Canada, 1878–83). Since 1892, when the locality became part of the national park, the locality has been administered by the Canadian Department of Indian Affairs and Northern Development. It is a noted tourist resort and excursion centre on the Trans-Canada and Banff-Jasper highways. The lake, at an elevation of 5,680 feet (1,731 m), springs from Victoria Glacier; it is about 1.5 miles (2.4 km) long and 0.75 mile (1.2 km) wide and reaches a depth of more than 220 feet (70 m). Pop. (1991) 500.

Lake Nicaragua shark, species of shark in the family Carcharhinidae. *See* carcharhinid.

Lake of ———: *see under* substantive word (*e.g.,* Ozarks, Lake of the; Woods, Lake of the).

Lake Placid, village in North Elba Town (township), Essex county, northeastern New York, U.S., on Mirror Lake and Lake Placid, at the foot of Whiteface Mountain (4,868 feet [1,484 m]), in the Adirondacks. The site was settled in 1800 but was abandoned after crop failures. Resettled during the 1840s, it was promoted in 1850 as a summer resort, and Melvil Dewey (deviser of the Dewey Decimal Classification system for libraries) founded the exclusive Lake Placid Club there in 1895. Numerous hotels, golf courses, ski resorts, a bobsled run (on Mount Van Hoevenberg), and the surrounding forest and mountain scenery (including Mount Marcy [5,344 feet], the state's highest peak) form the basis of a year-round tourist economy. The village's Olympic Arena and Convention Hall was built for the 1932 Olympic Games and adjoins the Fieldhouse built for use during the 1980 Winter games. The farm and grave of Abolitionist John Brown is 3 miles (5 km) south. Inc. 1900. Pop. (1990) 2,485.

Lake poet, any of the English poets William Wordsworth, Samuel Taylor Coleridge, and Robert Southey, who lived in the English Lake District of Cumberland and Westmorland (now Cumbria) at the beginning of the 19th century. They were first described derogatorily as the "Lake school" by Francis (afterward Lord) Jeffrey in *The Edinburgh Review* in August 1817, and the description "Lakers" was also used in a similar spirit by the poet Lord Byron. These names confusingly group Wordsworth and Coleridge together with Southey, who did not subscribe in his views or work to their theories of poetry.

Lake Ridge (North America): *see* Niagara Escarpment.

Lake Superior Provincial Park, park, central Ontario, Canada, on the eastern shore of Lake Superior. Established in 1944 to preserve the rugged shoreline and surrounding region of pink granitic hills, it has an area of 595 square miles (1,540 square km). Among the park's attractions are the Agawa pictographs, rock paintings created over many millennia by Indians. Moose, bear, white-tailed deer, and red squirrel inhabit the forests of maple, poplar, and spruce. The park has many recreational facilities, including trails throughout its hilly, wooded areas and fishing in its lakes and rivers.

lake trout, also called MACKINAW TROUT, GREAT LAKES TROUT, or SALMON TROUT (*Salvelinus namaycush*), large, voracious char, family Salmonidae, widely distributed from northern Canada and Alaska, U.S., south to New England and the Great Lakes basin. It is usually found in deep, cool lakes. The fish are greenish gray and covered with pale spots. In spring, lake trout of about 2.3 kg (5 pounds) are caught in shallow water; in summer, larger fish, up to about 45 kg (100 pounds), are caught by trolling in deep water. Lake trout spawn among reefs in fall, the heavy eggs

Lake trout (*Salvelinus namaycush*)

Painted especially for *Encyclopaedia Britannica* by Tom Dolan, under the supervision of Loren P. Woods, Chicago Natural History Museum

sinking to the bottom. They were of commercial value in the Great Lakes until sea lampreys, entering through the Welland Canal in the 1930s, reduced them almost to extinction. Lake trout have been introduced in parts of the western United States, South America, and Europe, as well as in New Zealand.

The term lake trout is also frequently applied to any of various other trout and salmon found in lakes.

Lake Wales, city, Polk county, central Florida, U.S., 55 miles (89 km) east of Tampa. The site was surveyed in 1879 by Sidney Wailes, and the lake (originally called Watts) was renamed for him. The town was laid out in 1911, and in 1915 its name was changed to Wales by the post office. It developed as a centre for lumber milling and fruit processing, and later its setting amid myriad lakes made it a popular tourist spot. Mountain Lake Sanctuary was established on the slopes of nearby Iron Mountain (324 feet [99 m], the highest point in peninsular Florida) by Edward W. Bok, Pulitzer prizewinner (1920) and editor of the *Ladies' Home Journal*. The sanctuary, famed for its bird life, forms a peaceful setting for the Bok Singing Tower, 205 feet (62 m) high, with a carillon of 57 bells. Pop. (1992 est.) 10,080.

Lake Washington Ship Canal, waterway, Washington state, U.S., 8 miles (13 km) long, with a minimum depth of 28.5 feet (8.7 m), connecting Shilshole Bay (Puget Sound) in the state of Washington with Lake Washington, passing through Lake Union, Portage Bay, and Union Bay. The locks near the west end of the canal, which overcome the difference of 26 feet (8 m) between water levels, accommodate ships up to 760 feet (230 m) long.

Lakehead (city, Ontario, Canada): *see* Thunder Bay.

Lakehurst, borough, Ocean county, eastern New Jersey, U.S., 8 miles (13 km) northwest of the community of Toms River. It is surrounded by fish and wildlife management areas, and small Lake Horican lies within its boundaries. Originally a part of Manchester, it became a separate municipality in 1925. At Lakehurst's eastern edge is the naval air station associated in the history of flight with rigid, lighter-than-air craft. There in 1923 the *Shenandoah,* the first American airship, made her maiden flight, and in 1929 the *Graf Zeppelin* began and ended a 21-day round-the-world trip. The Lakehurst station continued to serve as a terminal for transatlantic airships until 1937, when the huge German zeppelin *Hindenburg* burned in the air while landing, with a loss of 36 lives. Hangar One (807 feet [245 m] long, 268 feet [82 m] wide, and 172 feet [52 m] high), built in 1921 and a relic of the airship era, was designated a registered historic landmark in 1968. The U.S. Navy continued to use the air station for blimps through World War II until 1962, when the program was abandoned. Several naval air commands, including a school for parachute riggers, now occupy the site and form the borough's primary economic interest. Pop. (1990) 3,078.

Lakeland, city, Polk county, central Florida, U.S., 32 miles (51 km) northeast of Tampa. Founded in 1883, it was named for the many lakes in the area, several of them within city limits. Pebble phosphate mining and the citrus industry are important, and the city is the seat of the regulatory Florida Citrus Commission. Lakeland is also a popular winter resort, and its Civic Center houses a large sports-recreation-convention complex. It is the seat of Southeastern College of the Assemblies of God (1935) and Florida Southern College (1885), whose campus has a large concentration of buildings designed by the architect Frank Lloyd Wright. Inc. 1885. Pop. (1992 est.) city, 73,575; Lakeland–Winter Haven MSA, 422,603.

Lakeland terrier, breed of dog originally used to hunt and kill foxes in the Lake District of England. Formerly known as the Patterdale terrier, the Lakeland terrier was bred for gameness when in pursuit of foxes and otters. Somewhat like a small Airedale terrier in appearance, it stands about 33 to 38 cm (13 to 15 inches), weighs about 7 to 8 kg (15 to 18 pounds), and is characteristically a bold, friendly, sturdily built dog. Its dense, wiry, weather-resistant coat is commonly black and tan in colour.

Lakes Entrance, port city, at the entrance of a channel cut in 1889 to the Gippsland Lakes in southeastern Victoria, Australia. It is a resort centre for the lakes region embracing the Lakes National Park and the Ninety Mile Beach and is linked to Melbourne, 165 miles (266 km) to the west, by both rail and the Prince's Highway. The beach is a curving sand-dune coast extending southward to near Yarram and paralleled by the lakes, a group of interconnected shallow lagoons of fresh water occupying an area of 150 square miles (390 square km) and including Lakes Wellington, Reeve, King, and Victoria.

Lakes Entrance, Victoria

Ted Spiegel from Rapho/Photo Researchers

Natural gas and oil are extracted in nearby Bass Strait, the source of about half of Australia's domestic crude oil. The port's trawler fleet catches lake and ocean fish for the Melbourne market. Local forests yield timber. Buchan Caves (36 miles [58 km] north) are notable limestone formations. Pop. (1986) 4,104.

Lakeview, city, seat of Lake county, southern Oregon, U.S., north of Goose Lake. It was founded in 1876 on a former cattle ranch. Earlier settlement had been discouraged by Indian attacks that subsided in 1871 with the establishment of Indian reservations. Lakeview was destroyed by fire in 1900 but was rebuilt soon after. It is the headquarters of Fremont National Forest and the trading centre for a vast conservation and livestock area. Several recreation areas, with activities ranging from water sports to snow skiing, are close by. Abert Rim, one of North America's largest exposed fault scarps, is 25 miles (40 km) north; "Old Perpetual," a 40-foot (12-metre) geyser, is 2 miles north; and Hart Mountain National Antelope Refuge is about 40 miles northeast. Inc. 1889. Pop. (1994 est.) 2,557.

Lakewood, township, Ocean county, eastern New Jersey, U.S., on South Branch Metedeconk River, in a pine forest and lake region. It is the site of Georgian Court College (1908) for women, located on the former Gould estate, and of Ocean County Park 1 (the former Rockefeller estate and a noted arboretum). Settled by the Dutch and English in 1800, the township was known successively as Three Partners' Mill, Washington's Furnace, Bergen Iron Works, Bricksburg, and, finally, Lakewood. In the 1890s wealthy New Yorkers built country mansions around Lake Carasaljo; Lakewood is now a popular health and winter resort. Inc. 1892. Pop. (1994 est.) 46,909.

Lakewood, city, Cuyahoga county, northeastern Ohio, U.S., on Lake Erie, just west of Cleveland. Surveyed in 1806, it was known as Rockport (1819) and East Rockport (1871) until renamed in 1889 for its wooded lakeshore. It is mainly residential with some light industry. The Great Lakes Shakespeare Festival is an annual summer event; the Lakewood Little Theater is also in the city. Inc. village, 1903; city, 1911. Pop. (1994 est.) 57,063.

Lakhīmpur, city, north-central Uttar Pradesh state, northern India, on the North-Eastern Railway. It is just northwest of Kheri town, with which it is almost contiguous. The surrounding region is known for its extensive tea gardens; rice, jute, and other crops are also grown, and silkworms are raised. Lakhīmpur has several colleges affiliated with Dibrugarh University. Pop. (1991 prelim.) 79,549.

Lakhmid DYNASTY, pre-Islāmic Bedouin tribal dynasty that aided Sāsānian Iran in its struggle with the Byzantine Empire and fostered early Arabic poetry.

Centred at the Christian city of Al-Ḥīrah, near present-day Al-Kūfah in southern Iraq, the Lakhmid kingdom originated in the late 3rd century AD and developed essentially as an Iranian vassal state. Gaining a voice in Iranian affairs under King al-Mundhir I (*c.* 418–462), who raised Bahrām V to the throne of the Sāsānian empire, the Lakhmids reached the height of their power in the 6th century, when al-Mundhir III (503–554) raided Byzantine Syria and challenged the pro-Byzantine Arab kingdom of Ghassān. His son ʿAmr ibn Hind (554–569) was patron of the pre-Islāmic Arabic poetry of Ṭarafah and others associated with *Al-Muʿallaqāt* ("The Suspended Odes"). The dynasty became extinct with the death, in 602, of an-Nuʿmān III, who was a Nestorian Christian.

Laki, volcanic fissure and mountain in southern Iceland, just southwest of Vatna Glacier (Vatnajokull), the island's largest ice field. Mount Laki was the only conspicuous topographic feature in the path of the developing fissure eruption that is now known as Lakagígar (English: "Laki Craters").

The fissure, which extends northeast-southwest, is divided into two nearly equal halves by the 2,684-foot (818-metre) mountain, which rises some 650 feet (200 m) above its immediate surroundings. Mount Laki was not completely breached by the fissure; between the fissure cuts on the slopes of the mountain, there are only a few very small craters that extruded small amounts of lava. The eruption began on June 8, 1783. Until July 29 activity was confined to the fissure southwest of Mount Laki. On July 29 the fissure northeast of the mountain became active, and from that time almost all activity was confined to that half of the fissure. The eruption lasted until early February 1784, and it is considered to be the greatest lava eruption on Earth in historical times. The commonly accepted figure for the volume of lava extruded is about 2.95 cubic miles (12.3 cubic km); that for the area covered, about 220 square miles (565 square km). The enormous quantity of volcanic gases that was released caused a conspicuous haze over most of continental Europe; haze was even reported in Syria, in the Altai Mountains in western Siberia, and in North Africa. The vast quantities of sulfurous gases stunted crops and grasses and killed most of the domestic animals in Iceland; the resulting Haze Famine eventually killed about one-fifth of Iceland's population.

Lakshadweep, formerly (1956–73) LACCADIVE, MINICOY, AND AMĪNDĪVI ISLANDS, union territory of India, comprising a group of islands in the Arabian Sea, about 185 miles (300 km) off the southwestern coast of the Indian mainland. The territory includes 27 islands (only 10 of which are inhabited), with a total land area of 12 square miles (32 square km). The capital is Kavaratti.

A brief treatment of Lakshadweep follows. For full treatment, *see* MACROPAEDIA: India.

Most of the islands came under the control of the mainland Hindu Kulaśekhara dynasty and passed subsequently to the Coḷa (Kolathiri). When a Kolathiri princess married a Muslim convert in the 12th century, the islands became a part of the only Islāmic dominion in the Kerala region. The Portuguese first visited the islands in May 1498 and built forts there, but about 1545 the inhabitants rose against them. The British obtained sovereignty over the islands about the end of the 18th century and assumed direct administration in 1908. Having passed to India upon its independence in 1947, the island groups were consolidated in 1956 into the nation's smallest union territory.

Of the territorial group, Minicoy Island in the south is separated from the Amīndīvi (northernmost) and the Laccadives by the Nine Degree Channel. The islands are small, none exceeding about a mile in breadth, and the soil is light coral sand, beneath which, a few feet down, lies a stratum of coral stretching over the whole of the islands.

The people are Moplahs (of mixed Indian and Arab descent), and the great majority are Muslim. Malayālam is by far the most commonly spoken language. Coconut fibre, copra, and fish are notable economic products. Pop. (1991) 51,707.

Lakṣmī, also spelled LAKSHMI, also called ŚRĪ, Hindu goddess of wealth and good fortune. The wife of Vishnu, she is said to have taken different forms in order to be with him in each of his incarnations. Thus when he was the dwarf Vāmana, she appeared from a lotus and was known as Padmā, or Kamalā; when he was the ax-wielding Paraśurāma, the destroyer of the warrior caste, she was his wife Dharaṇī; when he was King Rāma, she was his queen Sītā. In the most widely received account of Lakṣmī's birth, she rose from the churning of the milky ocean, seated on a lotus and holding another blossom in her hand. (*See also* churning of the milky ocean.) Controversy arose between the gods and demons over possession of her.

Lakṣmī, from the north gateway of stupa No. 1 at Sānchi, Madhya Pradesh, 1st century BC
P. Chandra

Lakṣmī is often represented in sculpture seated on a lotus, full-breasted, broad-hipped, beneficently smiling, and sometimes being anointed by a pair of elephants. Her vehicle is the white owl. She continues to be worshiped by modern Hindus, particularly in the home (every Friday) and on regular festival days throughout the year. She is greatly revered by members of the Jainist faith.

Lala, a people of eastern Nigeria. The Lala belong to a small cluster of linguistically related peoples in geographic proximity, the Ga-Anda, Yungur, Handa, and Mboi living north of the Benue River.

The Lala and other small indigenous groups of the mountainous Nigeria-Cameroon borderlands have had somewhat complicated relations with migrant peoples, particularly Hausa peddlers and Fulani pastoralists. For some time the Lala defended themselves from Fulani raids by means of a habitat characterized by hills, plateaus, and fields hedged with milkbush. At other times, Fulani herdsmen paid fees to the Lala for cattle-grazing rights. The Ga-Anda have even employed Fulani to tend the larger herds, paying the herdsmen with milk. By the 20th century, however, the Lala were politically subordinate to the Yola emirate of the Muslim Fulani.

Crops such as cassava, corn (maize), and millet are cultivated by Lala women, and goats, sheep, and chickens are raised. The smelting of iron ore from local riverbeds died out during British colonial administration.

Lalande, Jérôme, in full JOSEPH-JÉRÔME LEFRANÇAIS DE LALANDE, Lefrançais also spelled LE FRANÇAIS, LEFRANÇOIS, or LE FRANÇOIS (b. July 11, 1732, Bourg-en-Bresse, France—d. April 4, 1807, Paris), French astronomer whose tables of the planetary positions were considered the best available until the end of the 18th century.

A law student in Paris, Lalande became interested in astronomy while he was lodging at the Hôtel de Cluny, where the noted astronomer Joseph-Nicolas Delisle had his observatory. In 1751 Lalande went to Berlin to make lunar observations in concert with the work of Nicolas-Louis de Lacaille at the Cape of Good Hope. The success of this task and the subsequent calculation of the Moon's distance secured for Lalande, before he reached the age of 21, admission to the Academy of Berlin and the post of adjunct astronomer to the Academy of Paris.

Lalande then devoted himself to the improvement of planetary theory, publishing in 1759 a corrected edition of the tables of Halley's Comet. He helped organize international collaboration in observing the transits of Venus in 1761 and 1769; the data obtained made possible the accurate calculation of the distance between the Sun and the Earth. In 1762 Lalande was appointed to the chair of astronomy in the Collège de France, Paris, a position that he held for 46 years. A popularizer of astronomy, he in 1802 instituted the Lalande Prize for the chief astronomical contribution of each year.

Among his voluminous works are *Traité d'astronomie* (1764; "Treatise on Astronomy"), *Histoire céleste française* (1801; "French Celestial History"), and *Bibliographie astronomique* (1803; "Astronomical Bibliography").

Lalande, Michel-Richard de (French composer): *see* Delalande, Michel-Richard.

Lalībela, historically ROHA, religious and pilgrimage centre, north-central Ethiopia. Roha, capital of the Zague dynasty for about 300 years, was renamed for its most distinguished monarch, Lalībela (late 12th–early 13th century), who according to tradition built the 11 monolithic churches for which the place is famous. The churches were hewn out of solid rock (entirely below ground level) in a variety of styles. Generally, trenches were excavated in a rectangle, isolating a solid granite block.

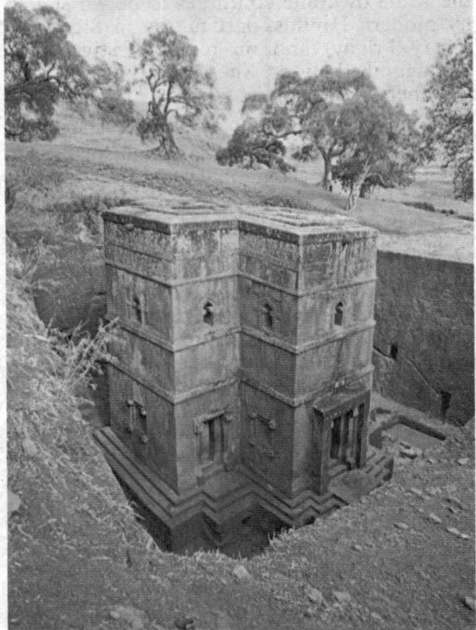

House of Giorgis rock church in Lalībela, Eth.
Richard Abeles

The block was then carved both externally and internally, the work proceeding from the top downward.

The churches are arranged in two main groups, connected by subterranean passageways. One group, surrounded by a trench 36 feet (11 m) deep, includes House of Emmanuel, House of Mercurios, Abba Libanos, and House of Gabriel, all carved from a single rock hill. House of Medhane Alem ("Saviour of the World") is the largest church, 109 feet (33 m) long, 77 feet (23 m) wide, and 35 feet (10 m) deep. House of Giorgis, cruciform in shape, is carved from a sloping rock terrace. House of Golgotha contains Lalībela's tomb, and House of Mariam is noted for its frescoes. The interiors were hollowed out into naves and given vaulted ceilings.

The expert craftsmanship of the Lalībela churches has been linked with the earlier church of Debre Damo near Aksum and tends to support the assumption of a well-developed Ethiopian tradition of architecture. Emperor Lalībela had most of the churches constructed in his capital, Roha, in the hope of replacing ancient Aksum as a city of Ethiopian preeminence. Recent restoration indicates that some of them may have been used originally as fortifications and royal residences.

The popularity of the churches eventually caused Roha to be renamed Lalībela. They attract thousands of pilgrims during the major holy day celebrations and are tended by more than 1,000 Coptic priests. The town also serves as a market centre for the Amhara people. Pop. (1986 est.) 5,604.

Lalique, René (b. April 6, 1860, Ay, Fr.—d. May 5, 1945, Paris), French jeweler during the early 20th century, whose designs in

Enamel, glass, and topaz hair ornament and brooch by Lalique, 1900; in the Victoria and Albert Museum, London
By courtesy of the Victoria and Albert Museum, London

jewelry and glass contributed significantly to the Art Nouveau movement at the turn of the century.

Trained at the School of Decorative Arts, Paris, and in London (1878–80), Lalique founded his own firm at Paris in 1885. His Art Nouveau brooches and combs attracted great attention at the Paris international exhibition in 1900, after which he became a celebrated jeweler. Among his patrons was the renowned French actress Sarah Bernhardt, for whom he designed some of his finest creations. He was also a technical innovator, successfully introducing new materials, such as horn, by emphasizing their hitherto neglected visual and tactile qualities. His favourite motifs were women—represented with sensuous hair and diaphanous drapery—and animals, especially snakes or insects. Reacting against machine production of more manneristic jewelry featuring precious gems, he created jewelry of elegant and fantastic designs with relatively few precious stones.

Lalique's interest in rock crystal and architectural glass led him to artistic experiments in those media. By 1910 he had established a glass factory at Combs-la-Ville, Fr., and in 1918 he acquired a larger factory at Wingen-sur-Moder, Fr. An order for perfume bottles led him to develop that style of molded glass with which he is generally associated: it is characterized by iced surfaces, elaborate or partially realistic patterns in relief, and occasionally applied or inlaid colour. His relief decoration was produced by blowing into molds or by pressing. His new designs shown at the Paris Exhibition, 1925, greatly enhanced his reputation. Used for luxury articles, Lalique glass was the height of fashion during the 1920s. He was a leading advocate of the use of glass in architecture, and much of his work was in the form of lighting equipment and other details of interior decoration. Under the direction of his son Marc, Lalique's factory continued to produce glass in his own personal style after his death.

Lalitavistara (Sanskrit: "Detailed Narration of the Sport [of the Buddha]"), legendary life

A relief inspired by the *Lalitavistara* of the Buddha as Siddhārtha competing at archery; from the temple at Borobuḍur, Indon., AD 750–850
J. Powell, Rome

of the Gautama Buddha, written in a combination of Sanskrit and a vernacular. The text apparently is a recasting, in the Mahāyāna ("Greater Vehicle") tradition, of a work from the Sarvāstivāda school. Like the *Mahāvastu* ("Great Story"), the subject matter of which is the same, the *Lalitavistara* contains late material but also preserves some very ancient passages. It shares with the Hindu *Purāṇas* (encyclopaedic collections of legends and other lore) similarities of style as well as the concept of a divine being's earthly activities as "sport," or "play." In characteristic Mahāyāna fashion, an introductory chapter describes the Buddha, deep in meditation and surrounded by a divine effulgence, about to reveal the contents of the text to an assemblage of 12,000 monks and some 32,000 bodhisattvas ("those destined to become enlightened"). In the ensuing narrative it is especially with regard to the Buddha's conception and birth that this work adds to the miraculous and mythological elements of earlier accounts.

The *Lalitavistara* is regarded as especially sacred in Mahāyāna circles, and it has inspired a considerable amount of Buddhist art. A version of it appears to have been translated into Chinese in AD 308.

A list of the abbreviations used in the MICROPAEDIA *will be found at the end of this volume*

Lalitpur, town, southwestern Uttar Pradesh state, northern India, situated 56 miles (90 km) south of Jhānsi town. According to legend it was founded by a southern Indian king who named it after his wife, Lalita. It is built on raised river frontage along the Shahjad River on the east and Biana stream on the north. Its cottage industries include tanning, sawmilling, shoemaking, ironsmithing, and soapmaking. Nehru College, affiliated with Bundelkhand University at Jhānsi, is in the town. About 0.5 mile (0.8 km) south is the Govind Sāgar Dam; nearby is a Muslim tax-collecting post, called *bansa,* dating from about 1360. An airfield for civil and military aircraft is 5 miles (8 km) outside the town. Lalitpur has major road and railway connections. Pop. (1981) 55,756.

Lalitpur, also called PĀTAN, town, central Nepal, in the Kāthmāndu Valley near the Bāghmati River, about 3 miles (5 km) southeast of Kāthmāndu. According to Nepalese chronicles, Lalitpur was founded by King Varadeva in AD 299. Some scholars believe that it was the capital of the Licchavi, Thakuri, and Malla dynasties; this theory, however, is now disputed. When Prithvi Narayan Shah conquered the valley in 1769, Lalitpur was plundered and the people treated with great brutality.

The town, which is the headquarters for the Banra sect of the Newār people, has an agricultural economy (barley, rice, wheat, millet, vegetables, and fruit). Lalitpur is known for its craftsmen, particularly metalworkers and wood-carvers. There are a number of fine Buddhist temples, including the Temple of Machendranāth in Durbar Square. A feature of the town is the number of viharas, originally Buddhist monasteries but now inhabited by descendants of the priests who once occupied them. According to legend, the Indian emperor Aśoka visited the town about 250 BC and built the four large stupas (Buddhist temples and burial mounds) that still exist on the four sides of the town. Pop. (1981) 79,875.

Lally, Thomas-Arthur, comte de (count of) (b. Jan. 13, 1702, Romans, Fr.—d. May 9, 1766, Paris), French general who was executed for capitulating to the British in India during the Seven Years' War (1756–63).

The son of an Irish Jacobite exile, Lally served in the Irish Brigade of the French army under Maurice, comte de Saxe, and accompanied Charles Edward, the Stuart Pretender, on his invasion of Scotland and England in 1745. In 1758 he was sent to India, where his lack of tact alienated the native princes allied with France. Defeated by the British under Sir Eyre Coote at Wandiwash (January 1760) and besieged at Pondicherry, he surrendered in January 1761. He voluntarily returned to France to stand trial on charges of treason and was convicted and beheaded after a long imprisonment.

Lalo, Édouard (-Victor-Antoine) (b. Jan. 27, 1823, Lille, Fr.—d. April 22, 1892, Paris), French composer, best known for his *Symphonie espagnole* and notable for the clarity of his orchestration.

Born into a military family of Spanish descent, Lalo pursued music studies against his

Lalo

J.P. Ziolo

father's will and went to Paris, without funds, in 1839 toward that end. There he studied violin at the Paris Conservatory and composition privately. He supported himself by working as a violinist and teacher. In 1848 he published his first songs and in 1855 joined the Armingaud quartet as viola player. Though he wrote little in the early 1860s, he won success with his *Symphonie espagnole* for violin and orchestra, first performed by Pablo Sarasate in 1875; for his cello concerto (1876); and for his ballet *Namouna* (1882). *Namouna* foreshadowed the ballets of Diaghilev in that it merited attention more for its musical score than for its choreography. There followed the *Symphony in G Minor* (1887) and the final version of his opera *Le Roi d'Ys* (1888; libretto by Edouard Blau). Perhaps better known for his orchestral works, Lalo was also a master of chamber pieces. His chamber works, which were influential, include a string quartet, three piano trios, and cello and violin sonatas. He also wrote concerti for violin and for piano and many lyrical songs and song collections (written for performance by his wife, a contralto). His music, although it shows some affinity with Robert Schumann and Carl Weber, is the product of a highly original talent.

Lalor, Peter (b. Feb. 5, 1827, Tinakill, Queen's County, Ire.—d. Feb. 9, 1889, Melbourne, Australia), Irish-born Australian

Lalor, detail of a lithograph by L. Becker, 1856

By courtesy of the National Library of Australia, the Rex Nan Kivell Collection

leader of the 1854 gold miners' uprising at the Eureka Stockade in Ballarat, Victoria, the most celebrated rebellion in Australian history; subsequently he became a politician.

Lalor was the son of a Home Rule supporter and landowner, and he was trained as a civil engineer in Ireland. In the mass migration that followed the great Irish famine in the mid-19th century, Lalor and one of his brothers immigrated to Australia in 1852 (three other brothers went to America). Lalor found work on the Melbourne-Geelong railway and then at the Eureka goldfield in 1853. He joined the Ballarat Reform League, formed by miners on Nov. 11, 1854, to protest high license fees, police mistreatment, lack of representation, and shortage of land. When the league's petition for reform went unanswered by the government, the miners organized to fight on November 30 and chose Lalor as their leader. He and other rebellious miners were driven out of the Eureka Stockade on December 3, and Lalor was wounded in the assault and lost an arm. He went into hiding for several weeks. Soon after he emerged, charges against the rebels' leaders were dropped. After the Eureka uprising, most of the miners' grievances were redressed.

Lalor was one of the first goldfield representatives, elected to the Victoria Legislative Council in 1855 and then to the Legislative Assembly (lower house) in 1856–71 and 1875–87. He served as postmaster general (1875), commissioner of trade and customs (1875, 1877–80), and speaker of the Assembly from 1880 to 1887.

Lama (people): *see* Lamba.

lama, Tibetan BLA-MA ("superior one"), in Tibetan Buddhism, a spiritual leader. Originally used to translate "guru" (Sanskrit: "venerable one") and thus applicable only to heads of monasteries or great teachers, the term is now extended out of courtesy to any respected monk or priest. The common Western usage of "lamaism" and "lamasery" are, in fact, incorrect terms of reference for Tibetan Buddhism and a Tibetan monastery.

Some lamas are considered reincarnations of their predecessors. These are termed *sprul-sku* lamas, as distinguished from "developed" lamas, who have won respect because of the high level of spiritual development they have achieved. The highest lineage of reincarnate lamas is that of Dalai Lama (*q.v.*), who was, until 1959, when he went into exile, the temporal ruler of Tibet. The title is given to the head of the dominant order of Tibetan Buddhists, the Dge-lugs-pa (Yellow Hat sect). He is considered the physical manifestation of the compassionate bodhisattva ("buddha-to-be") Avalokitesvara. The second highest line of succession is that of the Paṇchen Lama (*q.v.*), head abbot of the Tashilhunpo monastery, believed to be the manifestation of the self-born buddha Amitābha. Other, lesser *sprul-sku* lamas are revered as reincarnations of great saints or teachers, ranked by the Dalai Lama as great, middle, or lesser incarnations. The idea probably originated from the tradition of the 84 *mahāsiddhas,* or master yogins (spiritual adepts, or ascetics), many of whom were identified as manifestations of earlier sages, coupled with the accepted Buddhist belief in rebirth.

The process of discovering the rebirth of a reincarnated lama can be elaborate and exacting, particularly in the selection of a Dalai Lama, which has many political implications. The rebirth may take place at any time, from days to years, following the death of the previous lama. The state oracle at Nechung is consulted for the whereabouts of the newly born Dalai Lama. Remarks made by the Dalai Lama before his death are frequently accepted as indications of a favoured place for rebirth, as are any unusual signs that are observed during his death or during a birth thereafter.

Often two or more candidates are subjected to a critical physical and mental examination, which includes recognition of personal belongings handled by the previous lama. In case of doubt, lots may be drawn. After selection, the young child is given extensive monastic training from an early age. During the years of search for and education of a newly incarnated lama, a regent is appointed to rule in his stead.

Lamaism: *see* Tibetan Buddhism.

Lamar, city, seat of Barton county, southwest Missouri, U.S., on a branch of the Spring River, 100 miles (160 km) south of Independence. Founded in 1856 and named for Mirabeau B. Lamar, president of the Texas Republic (1838–41), it developed as the centre of a farming community. Lamar is the birthplace of Harry S. Truman, 33rd president of the United States, and the house has been restored as a state historic site. Pop. (1990) 4,168.

Consult the INDEX *first*

Lamar, Joseph R(ucker) (b. Oct. 14, 1857, Elbert county, Ga., U.S.—d. Jan. 2, 1916, Washington, D.C.), associate justice of the United States Supreme Court (1911–16).

Admitted to the bar in 1878, Lamar taught Latin for a year at Bethany College in Georgia and married the daughter of the college president. In 1880 he started his practice in the capital city of Augusta. He rose rapidly at the bar, while also serving two terms in the state legislature and writing on the history of Georgia jurisprudence. In 1893 he was appointed one of three commissioners to recodify the laws of Georgia. The compilation, *The Code of the State of Georgia* (1896), was well received and contributed to his later appointment to the state Supreme Court in 1904. He served briefly, stepping down owing to ill health, but in 1911 he was appointed to the U.S. Supreme Court by President William Howard Taft.

Joseph R. Lamar

By courtesy of the Library of Congress, Washington, D.C.

He gave the court's opinion on two important cases: *Gompers* v. *Bucks Stove and Range Company* (1911), which upheld the power of the courts to punish violations of injunctions but set aside the convictions of Samuel Gompers and other labour leaders on procedural grounds, and *United States* v. *Midwest Oil Company* (1914), which upheld the president's right to withhold public oil lands from private entry.

Lamar represented President Woodrow Wilson at a conference called in 1914 to settle differences between Mexico and the United States arising out of Wilson's refusal to recognize President Victoriano Huerta of Mexico.

Lamar, Lucius Q.C., in full LUCIUS QUINTUS CINCINNATUS LAMAR (b. Sept. 17, 1825, Putnam county, Ga., U.S.—d. Jan. 23, 1893, Vineland, Ga.), American lawyer, politician, and jurist who served the Confederacy during the American Civil War (1861–65) and later became an associate justice of the U.S. Supreme Court.

Lamar was admitted to the bar in Georgia in 1847 and was a member of the Georgia House of Representatives (1853). He moved to Mississippi in 1855 and was elected to the U.S. House of Representatives the following year, serving until December 1860, when he resigned to participate in the Mississippi secession convention. He was the author of the Mississippi ordinance of secession (Jan. 9, 1861) and served in the Confederate army.

After the war Lamar taught law at the University of Mississippi (1866–73). He then served in the U.S. Congress, both in the House (1873–77) and in the Senate (1877–85), where his moderating influence during Reconstruction won him the sobriquet "the Great Pacificator." President Grover Cleveland appointed Lamar secretary of the interior (1885) and later associate justice of the U.S. Supreme Court (1888). His most important opinion while a justice of the Court was a dissent in *In re Neagle* (1890), which expressed his conviction that the authority of the federal executive is limited to the powers specifically granted by the Constitution and statutes.

"De," "la," and similar components of a name, when followed by a space, are alphabetized as separate words (e.g., *De Forest, Lee*). *When they are joined to the following part of a name, the combination is treated as a single word* (e.g., *DeForest, John William*).

Lamar, Mirabeau Buonaparte (b. Aug. 16, 1798, Louisville, Ga., U.S.—d. Dec. 19, 1859, Richmond, Texas), second president of the Republic of Texas.

After an unsuccessful career as a merchant in Alabama, Lamar took a position as secretary to the governor of Georgia. He later became editor of a distinctly states-rights newspaper, the *Columbus* (Georgia) *Enquirer*. Following the death of his wife in 1833 and the failure of his bid for a congressional seat, Lamar moved to Texas, where he quickly became involved in the independence struggle against Mexico.

Lamar won distinction as cavalry commander at the Battle of San Jacinto in April 1836 and soon after assumed the position of secretary of war in the provisional government of Texas. Later that year he was elected vice president of Texas under President Sam Houston; in 1838 Lamar himself won a three-year term as president of the republic.

During his presidency, Lamar sought to strengthen the independence of Texas in order to avoid U.S. annexation. He planned a national bank and comprehensive school system, and he initiated diplomatic contacts with France, England, and Holland. An expansionist, Lamar founded the new capital at Austin at the farthest reach of settlement, and he tried to win for Texas the allegiance of parts of New Mexico.

Lamar's constant military campaigning against the Indians and his costly exploits into New Mexico nearly bankrupted Texas. When he left office in 1841, the republic's debt stood at more than $7,000,000.

By 1844 Lamar was advocating U.S. annexation of Texas on the basis that it would assure the continuation and safety of slavery. During the Mexican War (1846–48) he again distinguished himself in battle, joining Zachary Taylor's forces and fighting gallantly at Monterrey, Mexico. He then retired to his plantation at Richmond, Texas, where he remained for most of his life, except for a brief tenure (1857–59) as U.S. minister to Nicaragua and Costa Rica.

Lamarck, Jean-Baptiste de Monet, Chevalier (Knight) **de**, in full JEAN-BAPTISTE-PIERRE-ANTOINE DE MONET, CHEVALIER DE LAMARCK (b. Aug. 1, 1744, Bazentin-le-Petit, Picardy, France—d. Dec. 18, 1829, Paris), pioneer French biologist who is best known for his idea that acquired traits are inheritable, an idea known as Lamarckism, which is controverted by Darwinian theory.

Lamarck, detail of an engraving by W.H. Lizars

By courtesy of the Museum National D'Histoire Naturelle, Paris

Life. Lamarck was the youngest of 11 children of a baron and lieutenant of infantry. Intended for the priesthood, he was sent to a Jesuit school at Amiens, but after his father died he took the opportunity to enlist in an infantry regiment, serving several years (1761–68). He became interested in plants while stationed on the Riviera and, following his resignation from the army, embarked upon the study first of medicine and then of botany. He soon devoted himself entirely to botany under the French botanist Bernard de Jussieu at the Jardin du Roi (the royal botanical gardens) in Paris.

Drawing on nine years of field study and collecting, Lamarck published a three-volume flora of France in 1778. Botany had become universally popular, and a wide public greeted his *Flore française* ("French Flora") as a useful manual of identification. It did not adhere slavishly to the methods of the Swedish botanist Carolus Linnaeus and won for Lamarck appointment to the Academy of Sciences, which at that time was restricted to 42 members. Count Georges de Buffon, the leading naturalist of the day, engaged him as tutor to his son during two years of travel in central Europe visiting botanical gardens and other learned institutions. He devoted the years following to voluminous botanical writings for the *Encyclopédie méthodique* ("Methodic Encyclopaedia"), successor of the famous *Encyclopédie* founded by Denis Diderot, and to working as curator of the royal herbarium.

Modernizing of museum collections. The revolution of 1789 was devoted to remaking institutions of intellect as well as of politics, and so the royal collection of natural history was discontinued. Lamarck addressed a memoir to the National Assembly condemning the random cabinets for display of curiosities built up by well-meaning amateurs and urged instead that collections be applied to the progress of science through the establishment of a great museum of natural history. Within such a collection objects "ought to be arranged in methodical or properly systematic order," not for display at random: each division of nature (animal, vegetable, and mineral) should be subdivided by classes, and those in turn by orders, and so to genera, with a written catalogue that would be the basis for systematic knowledge. Lamarck was one of the originators of the modern concept of the museum collection, an array of objects whose arrangement constitutes a classification under institutional sponsorship, maintained and kept up to date by knowledgeable specialists. When the Jardin des Plantes (National Museum of Natural History) was founded in 1793, Lamarck was placed in charge of the invertebrates, of which he had already made an important collection. He seems to have been the first to relate fossils to the living organisms to which they corresponded most closely.

By the end of the 18th century, enough had been learned in the sciences of chemistry and physiology to persuade the most acute inquirers that new understandings might be attained through patient search for clues to fundamental relationships. To Lamarck it seemed that the new chemistry of Antoine Lavoisier led away from grand facts into a labyrinth of details. Lamarck feared that science would cease to be a coherent system whereby all men might understand the world and their place in it, becoming instead the confined domain of a few specialists. So he conceived a plan for a series of treatises, elaborating a unified view of physical processes, chemistry, geology, climate, and life.

The first of these was a two-volume speculative treatment of matter and energy, *Recherches sur les causes des principaux faits physiques, et particulièrement sur celles de la combustion* (1794; "Research on the Causes of Principal Physical Facts, and Particularly on Those of Combustion"), followed in 1796 by *Réfutation de la théorie pneumatique, ou de la nouvelle doctrine des chimistes modernes* ("Refutation of the Pneumatic Theory, or of the New Doctrine of Modern Chemists"), in which he opposed his own theory of combustion to the views of Lavoisier and Count Antoine de Fourcroy. Neither of Lamarck's works was calculated to appeal to the mood of caution then coming to govern most serious scientific work, and Lamarck did not know how to dramatize his views for a wider public.

His *Hydrogéologie* (1802; *Hydrogeology*) offered a history of the earth interpreted as a series of inundations by a global sea, each accompanied by organic deposits building up the continents. Among the insights that were highly advanced for his day was Lamarck's recognition that the type of fossil occurring in a deposit would permit inferences as to whether the deposit had been built up as deep-marine sediments or as coastal deposits. The book also revealed an extraordinary perception of the vastness of geologic time. "Time is insignificant and never a difficulty for Nature. It is always at her disposal and represents an unlimited power with which she accomplishes her greatest and smallest tasks." This treatise was also neglected, to Lamarck's deepening sorrow. Increasingly, science was being conducted through networks of mutual criticism in which evidence and data were employed to secure wide acceptance of essential facts before general theories were attempted. Scorning these procedures, Lamarck was transformed into a scientific outcast and gradually became an embittered solitary.

Systematic biology of the invertebrates. In 1800 he announced a revision of the classification of lower animals that had been left in a confused state by Linnaeus. He was able to penetrate superficial resemblances in form, as between certain worms and mollusks, through discriminating analysis of the functions and complexity of essential organs. This work he placed on an empirical foundation, "having at my disposal the magnificent collections of the Museum and another fairly rich, which I have myself made in the course of nearly thirty years' work." Published as *Système des animaux sans vertèbres, ou table général des classes* ("System of Invertebrate Animals, or General Table of Classes") in 1801, Lamarck's first major work on the invertebrates reflected current research, most notably the anatomical studies of Cuvier, and established the basic arrangement for these animals that served as a guide to inquiry throughout the 19th century and is still largely accepted. These systematic studies of invertebrates were climaxed by the publication of his life's work, *Histoire naturelle des animaux sans vertèbres* ("Natural History of Invertebrate Animals"), from 1815 to 1822, a complete vindication of his proposal to establish museum collections as the basis for revisionary work in systematic biology.

Lamarck imagined a vast sequence of life forms extending like a series of staircases from the simplest to the most complex. Impelled by "excitations" and "subtle and ever-moving fluids," the organs of animals became more complex and took their place on successively higher levels. This was the summary view of the relationship between physical energy and the overall organization of life set forth in *Recherches sur l'organisation des corps vivans* (1802; "Research on the Organization of Living Bodies") and the *Philosophie zoologique* (1809; *Zoological Philosophy*). In the latter work he stated two "laws" that he held to govern the ascent of life to higher stages: first, that organs are improved with repeated use and weakened by disuse; second, that such environmentally determined acquisitions or losses of organs "are preserved by reproduction to the new individuals which arise." Thus, in a celebrated example, the forelegs and neck of giraffes have become lengthened through their habit of browsing. With the publication of Charles Darwin's *Origin of Species* 50 years later, these views of Lamarck became the centre of interest and controversy. Lamarckism was discredited by most geneticists after the 1930s, except in the Soviet Union, where, as Lysenkoism, it dominated Soviet genetics until the 1960s. As originally formulated, however, Lamarckism was part of an elaborate surmise about processes for whose operation Lamarck had no direct evidence. To apply excerpts from so general a course of speculation to questions made much more precise through the application of Darwinian theory a century or more later—especially within the field of genetics, of which Lamarck had no conception—necessarily entails radical alterations of his meaning. From a lifelong, direct exposure to plants and animals Lamarck gained an intuitive sense of the dynamic quality of life, the close interdependence of physical and vital processes upon which the modern science of biology rests. Indeed Lamarck was the first to use the word biology, in 1802. But in the history of that science he may best be considered a forerunner rather than a founder, except in the systematic biology of the invertebrates, for which he established not only the best procedures of inquiry but also the kind of institution within which these inquiries have since been most successfully pursued.

Lamarck died blind and in poverty. (P.C.R.)

BIBLIOGRAPHY. There is no modern biography of Lamarck. Information on his work may be found in H. Bentley Glass, O. Temkin, and W.L. Straus (eds.), *Forerunners of Darwin: 1745–1859* (1959), an appraisal of Lamarck's contribution to evolutionary thought; and Philip C. Ritterbush, *Overtures to Biology: The Speculations of Eighteenth-Century Naturalists* (1964), a general account of speculative themes in 18th-century natural history. Two important translations of Lamarck's writings are by Hugh Elliott, *Zoological Philosophy* (1914, reprinted 1963), his major speculative work; and by Albert V. Carozzi, *Hydrogeology* (1964), an excellent modern edition of his work on the physical globe.

Lamartine, Alphonse de (b. Oct. 21, 1790, Mâcon, Fr.—d. Feb. 28, 1869, Paris), French poet and statesman whose lyrics in *Méditations poétiques* (1820) established him as one of the key figures in the Romantic movement in French literature.

Lamartine, oil painting by François Gérard; in the Musée National de Versailles et des Trianons
Giraudon—Art Resource/EB Inc.

Alphonse's father, an aristocrat, was imprisoned during the culminating phase of the French Revolution known as the Reign of Terror but was fortunate enough to escape the guillotine. Alphonse was educated at the college at Belley, which was maintained by the Jesuits though they were suppressed in France at this time.

Lamartine had wanted to enter the army or the diplomatic corps, but because France was ruled by Napoleon, whom his faithful royalist parents regarded as the usurper, they would not allow him to serve. Thus he remained idle until the Bourbon monarchy was restored in 1814, when he served in Louis XVIII's bodyguard. The following year, however, Napoleon returned from exile and attempted to rebuild his empire during the Hundred Days. Lamartine emigrated to Switzerland. After Napoleon's defeat at Waterloo and the Second Bourbon Restoration, he abandoned the military profession.

Attracted to literature, he wrote some tragedies in verse and a few elegies. By this time his health was not good, and he left for the spa of Aix-les-Bains, where, in October of 1816, on the shore of Lake Bourget, he met the brilliant but desperately ill Julie Charles. Early in 1812 Lamartine had fallen deeply in love with a young working girl named Antoniella. In 1815 he had learned of her death, and later he was to recast her as Graziella in his prose "anecdote" of that name. He now became passionately attached to Charles, who, because of her vast connections in Paris, was able to help him find a position. After her death in December 1817, Lamartine, who had already dedicated many strophes to her (notably "Le Lac"), devoted new verses to her memory (particularly "Le Crucifix").

In 1820 Lamartine married Maria Ann Birch, a young Englishwoman connected by marriage to the Churchills. The same year he published his first collection of poetry, *Méditations poétiques,* and finally joined the diplomatic corps, as secretary to the French embassy at Naples. *Méditations* was immensely successful because of its new romantic tone and sincerity of feeling. It brought to French poetry a new music; the themes were at the same time intimate and religious. If the vocabulary remained that of the somewhat faded rhetoric of the preceding century, the resonance of the sentences, the power of the rhythm, and the passion for life sharply contrasted with the often-withered poetry of the 18th century. The book was so successful that Lamartine attempted to extend it two years later with his *Nouvelles méditations poétiques* and his *Mort de Socrates,* in which his preoccupation with metaphysics first became evident. *Le Dernier Chant du pèlerinage d'Harold,* published in 1825, revealed the charm that the English poet Lord Byron exerted over him. Lamartine was elected to the French Academy in 1829, and the following year he published the two volumes of *Harmonies poétiques et religieuses,* a sort of alleluia, filled with deist—and even occasionally Christian ("L'Hymne au Christ")—enthusiasm.

That same year (1830), when Louis-Philippe acceded to the throne as constitutional monarch after the July Revolution, Lamartine abandoned his diplomatic career to enter politics. He refused to commit himself to the July Monarchy, however, and, preserving his independence, he set out to draw attention to social problems. After two unsuccessful attempts he was elected deputy in 1833. Yet he still wanted to write a poem, *Les Visions,* that he had been thinking about since 1821 and that he had conceived of as an "epic of the soul." The symbolic theme was that of a fallen angel cast out of heaven for having chosen the love of a woman and condemned to successive reincarnations until the day on which he realized that he "preferred God." Lamartine wrote the last fragment of this immense adventure first, and it appeared in 1836 as *Jocelyn.* It is the story of a young man who intended to take up the religious life but, instead, when cast out of the seminary by the Revolution, falls in love with a young girl; recalled to the order by his dying bishop, he renounces his love and becomes a "man of God," a parish priest, consecrating his life to the service of his fellow men. In 1838 Lamartine published the first fragment of this vast metaphysical poem under the appropriate title *La Chute d'un ange* ("The Fall of an Angel"). In 1832–33 he travelled to Lebanon, Syria, and the Holy Land. He had by then definitively lost the Catholic faith he had tried to recover in 1820; a further blow was the death in Beirut, on Dec. 7, 1832, of his only remaining child, Julia. A son born in Rome in 1821 had not survived infancy.

After a collection published in 1839 under the title *Recueillements poétiques* ("Poetic Meditations"), Lamartine interrupted his literary endeavours to become more active as a politician. He was convinced that the social question, which he himself called "the question of the proletariat," was the principal issue of his time; he deplored the inhumanity of the worker's plight; he denounced the trusts and their dominant influence on governmental politics, directing against them two discourses, one in 1838, another in 1846; he held that a working-class revolution was inevitable and did not hesitate to hasten the hour, promising the authorities, in July 1847, a "revolution of scorn." In the same year he published his *Histoire des Girondins,* a history of the right, or moderate, Girondin Party during and after the French Revolution, which earned him immense popularity with the left-wing parties.

After the revolution of Feb. 24, 1848, the Second Republic was proclaimed in Paris, and Lamartine became, in effect, head of the provisional government. The propertied classes, who were at first startled, pretended to accept the new circumstances, but they were unable to tolerate the fact that the working class possessed arms with which to defend themselves. In April 1848 Lamartine was elected to the National Assembly by 10 *départements.* The bourgeoisie, represented by the right-wing parties, thought they had elected in Lamartine a clever manipulator who could placate the proletariat, while military forces capable of establishing order, such as they conceived of it, were being reconstituted. The bourgeoisie was enraged to discover, however, that Lamartine was, indeed, as he had proclaimed himself to be, the spokesman of the working class. On June 24, 1848, he was thrown out of office and the revolt crushed.

A broken man, Lamartine entered the "twilight" of his life. He was 60 years old in 1850, and his debts were enormous, not because he had been personally extravagant but because of the allowances he gave his sisters to compensate for the total property inheritance he had received as the only male in the Lamartine family. For 20 years he struggled desperately, though in vain, against bankruptcy, publishing book after book: *Raphaël,* a transposed account of his love for Julie Charles; *Les Confidences* and *Nouvelles Confidences,* wherein he intermingled real and imaginary elements (*Graziella* is a fragment of it); novels: *Geneviève* (1851), *Antoniella, Mémoires politiques* (1863), the last work being of great historical interest; a periodical titled *Cours familiers de littérature* (1856–1868/69), in which he published such poems as "La Vigne et la maison" and "Le Désert"; some historical works that remained unequaled, including *Histoire des Constituants* (1854), *Histoire de la Restauration* (1851–52), *Histoire de la Russie, Histoire de la Turquie.* He died nearly forgotten by his contemporaries.

(He.Gu./Ed.)

BIBLIOGRAPHY. William Fortescue, *Alphonse de Lamartine: A Political Biography* (1983), provides a well-researched account of his political career; while H. Remson Whitehouse, *The Life of Lamartine,* 2 vol. (1918, reprinted 1969), is a comprehensive work. Mary Ellen Birkett, *Lamartine and the Poetics of Landscape* (1982), offers a brief but detailed study of the major poems; and Charles M. Lombard, *Lamartine* (1973), contains brief summaries and commentary on all of Lamartine's writings.

Lamas, Carlos Saavedra: *see* Saavedra Lamas, Carlos.

Lamashtu (Akkadian), Sumerian DIMME, in Mesopotamian religion, the most terrible of all female demons, daughter of the sky god Anu (Sumerian: An). A wicked female who slew children, drank the blood of men, and ate their flesh, she had seven names and was often described in incantations as the "seven witches." Lamashtu accomplished a variety of evil deeds: she disturbed sleep and brought nightmares; she killed foliage and infested rivers and streams; she bound the muscles of men, caused pregnant women to miscarry, and brought disease and sickness. Lamashtu was often portrayed on amulets as a lion- or bird-headed female figure kneeling on an ass; she held a double-headed serpent in each hand and suckled a dog at her right breast and a pig or another dog at her left breast.

Lamaze, method of childbirth that involves psychological and physical preparation by the mother for the purpose of suppressing pain and facilitating delivery without drugs.

The Lamaze method, one of the more popular methods of childbirth preparation, was introduced by Fernand Lamaze in the 1950s as an attempt to lessen pain-increasing tension and anxiety of childbirth. Lamaze emphasized education about the stages of labour and delivery (to reduce tension generated by fear based on ignorance of the process) and taught physical and psychological methods for relaxing the voluntary muscles during labour. Applying Pavlov's theory of conditioned reflexes, Lamaze taught the use of distraction techniques to decrease women's perceptions of discomfort during labour contractions. These techniques include deep and shallow breathing, rhythmic light abdominal massage (effleurage), and concentration on external focal points or on internal visualization of pleasant experiences; all are designed to draw attention away from the pain of the childbirth process.

Lamaze and other methods of prepared, or "natural," childbirth rely on supervised training and practice in relaxation techniques during the weeks before the birth. Both the mother-to-be and a supportive partner, who helps to distract the mother, are fully trained in Lamaze techniques. Expectant mothers perform exercises to strengthen the abdomen and relax the muscles around the birth canal; this preparation helps to reduce the strain of pushing during delivery. Another exercise is the rehearsal of deep chest breathing and rapid, shallow breathing during periods of maximum strain; this technique helps to reduce uterine tension. By frequent repetition, proper breathing techniques become semiautomatic. Lamaze training also includes instruction in the processes of labour and delivery.

lamb, live sheep before the age of one year, and the flesh of such animals. Mutton refers to the flesh of the mature ram or ewe at least one year old; the meat of sheep between 12 and 20 months old may be called yearling mutton. The meat of sheep 6 to 10 weeks old is usually sold as baby lamb, and spring lamb is from sheep of five to six months.

The mild flavour of lamb is preferred in most Western countries; the stronger flavour of mutton is considered desirable in many Middle and Far Eastern countries. Milk-fed lamb is especially delicate in flavour. The colour of the lean deepens as the animal grows older. In the lamb it ranges from light to dark pink; in yearling mutton it is medium pink to light red; in mutton it is light to dark red in colour. The fat, soft and creamy white to pale pink in the lamb, hardens and whitens in older sheep. Bones also harden and whiten, becoming porous in the yearling and extremely hard in the mature animal.

In the United States the carcass may be separated into sides and then divided into wholesale cuts; it may be cut straight across into saddles; or it may be cut into leg, loin, shoulder, breast, and shank. The outer fat covering, or fell, may be removed from the cuts. U.S. quality grades for lamb include prime, choice, good, utility, and cull; mature mutton grades are choice, good, utility, and cull.

The primary lamb- and mutton-consuming countries (on a per capita basis) are New Zealand, Australia, Greece, Uruguay, and Ireland. The leg, saddle (upper back portion of the carcass from last rib to legs), and shoulder, although they contain higher proportions of bone to meat, are considered the finest cuts by some cooks. In the United States popular cuts include individual chops from the ribs or loin, the leg, and the so-called crown roast, made by forming the rib section, or rack, into a circle. A regional specialty, virtually unknown outside of the state of Kentucky, is barbecued mutton. Curried mutton, served with rice, is a favourite dish of Jamaicans.

The traditional British lamb roast is distinguished by a fresh mint sauce. Lamb also plays an important part in classic French cuisine; unlike American- or English-style preparation, however, French recipes often call for shorter cooking times, yielding rare or pinkish meat.

Lamb predominates in the cuisines of Greece, Turkey, and the Middle East, commonly marinated and roasted on a skewer (shish kebab) or cooked with local vegetables. A classic Middle Eastern dish is *kibbe,* a mixture of ground lamb and cracked wheat.

Lamb, Charles (b. Feb. 10, 1775, London, Eng.—d. Dec. 27, 1834, Edmonton, Middlesex), English essayist and critic, best-known for his series of miscellaneous "Essays of Elia," but also among the greatest of English letter writers, and a perceptive literary critic.

Lamb's father, a scrivener, acted as confidential clerk to Samuel Salt, a bencher of London's Inner Temple. The boy read avidly among Salt's books, and at the age of seven he went to school at Christ's Hospital, where he studied until 1789. He was a near contemporary there of Samuel Taylor Coleridge, with whom he began what was to be a lifelong friendship, and of Leigh Hunt. He was a good scholar and, but for a stutter, would probably have proceeded to holy orders. Instead, he left school just before the age of 15 and in 1792 found employment as a clerk at India House, remaining there until retirement in 1825. In 1796 Lamb's sister, Mary, in a fit of madness (which was to prove recurrent) killed their mother. Lamb reacted with courage and loyalty, taking on himself the burden of looking after Mary, and being rewarded by her affectionate devotion.

Charles Lamb, detail of an oil painting after Henry Meyer; in the National Portrait Gallery, London

Lamb's first appearances in print were as a poet, with contributions to collections by Coleridge (1796) and by Charles Lloyd (1798). *A Tale of Rosamund Gray,* a prose romance, appeared in 1798, and in 1802 he published *John Woodvil,* a poetic tragedy. None of these publications brought him much fame or fortune. "The Old Familiar Faces" (1789) remains his best-known poem, although "On an Infant Dying As Soon As It Was Born" (1828) is his finest poetic achievement.

In 1807 Lamb and his sister published, at the invitation of William Godwin, *Tales from Shakespear,* a retelling of the plays for children, and in 1809 they published *Mrs. Leicester's School,* a collection of stories supposedly told by pupils of a school in Hertfordshire. In 1808 Charles published a children's version of the *Odyssey,* called *The Adventures of Ulysses.*

Concurrently with these works, Lamb published *Specimens of English Dramatic Poets Who Lived About the Time of Shakespear,* a selection of scenes, much-edited, from Elizabethan dramas. The book included some passages of implicit criticism. Lamb also contributed critical papers on Shakespeare and on Hogarth to Leigh Hunt's *Reflector.* The only lengthy piece of criticism that he undertook, on William Wordsworth's *Excursion,* was characteristically "gelded" by William Gifford, editor of the *Quarterly Review,* in which publication it appeared. Lamb's letters, however, contain much of his most perceptive criticism and reveal his personal tastes. The criticism often appears in the form of marginalia, reactions, and responses: brief comments, delicately phrased, but hardly ever argued through.

Lamb's greatest achievements in prose were the essays that he wrote under the pseudonym Elia for *London Magazine,* which was founded in 1820. The essays are almost wholly autobiographical (though often he appropriated to himself the experiences of others). Many of the best deal with things half a century past: vistas revealed by an imagination looking back down the experiences of a lifetime. The subject of his first essay was the South Sea house, where his elder brother, John, was a clerk. In order to spare his brother's feelings, Lamb called himself Elia (the name of another clerk at the South Sea house). The persona of

Elia predominates in nearly all of the essays. Lamb's style, therefore, is highly personal and mannered, its function being to "create" and delineate this persona, and the writing, though sometimes simple, is never plain. The essays conjure up, with humour and sometimes with pathos, old acquaintances such as Samuel Salt; they recall scenes from childhood and from later life, indulge the author's sense of playfulness and fancy, and avoid only whatever is urgent or disturbing—politics, suffering, sex, religion. The first essays were published separately in 1823; a second series appeared, as *The Last Essays of Elia,* in 1833.

After Lamb's retirement from the India House, a worsening of his sister's condition obliged the pair to move to Edmonton. This separation from the friends who gave him life and courage did not help his spirits. His tendency to drink too heavily became more pronounced. He died at Edmonton from complications to a wound suffered in a fall.

The standard edition of the works of Charles and Mary Lamb, edited by E.V. Lucas, appeared in seven volumes in 1903–05. An edition of the letters, edited by Lucas, appeared in three volumes in 1935. A projected six-volume edition by Edwin W. Marrs, Jr., includes vol. 1, 1796–1801 (1975); vol. 2, 1801–09 (1976); vol. 3, 1809–17 (1978).

BIBLIOGRAPHY. The standard biography is E.V. Lucas, *The Life of Charles Lamb,* 5th ed. rev., 2 vol. (1921, reprinted 1968). George L. Barnett, *Charles Lamb* (1976), is a shorter modern treatment. Roy Park (ed.), *Lamb as Critic* (1980), is an anthology of Lamb's critical writings and a reassessment of him as a critic.

Lamb, Sir Horace (b. Nov. 27, 1849, Stockport, near Manchester, Eng.—d. Dec. 4, 1934, Cambridge, Cambridgeshire), English mathematician who contributed to the field of mathematical physics.

Sir Horace Lamb
Walter Stoneman

In 1872 Lamb was made a fellow and assistant tutor of Trinity College, Cambridge, and three years later he became professor of mathematics at Adelaide University, Australia. He returned to England in 1885 to become professor of mathematics at Victoria University, Lancashire. Lamb wrote the *Mathematical Theory of the Motion of Fluids* (1878) and *Hydrodynamics* (1895); the latter was, for many years, the standard work on hydrodynamics. His many papers, principally on applied mathematics, detailed his researches on wave propagation, electrical induction, earthquake tremors, and the theory of tides and waves.

Lamb made valuable studies of airflow over aircraft surfaces for the Aeronautical Research Committee from 1921 to 1927. He was made a fellow of the Royal Society of London in 1884 and was knighted in 1931. His other publications include *Infinitesimal Calculus* (1897), *Dynamical Theory of Sound* (1910), and *Higher Mechanics* (1920).

Lamb, Mary Ann (b. Dec. 3, 1764, London, Eng.—d. May 20, 1847, London), English writer, known for *Tales from Shakespear,* written with her brother Charles.

Born into a poor family, Mary Lamb received little formal education. From an early age she helped support the family by doing needlework. Her mother was an invalid, and for many years she was entirely dependent on

Mary Ann Lamb, detail of an oil painting by Francis S. Cary, 1834; in the National Portrait Gallery, London
By courtesy of the National Portrait Gallery, London

Mary's care. On Sept. 22, 1796, in a fit of madness, Mary stabbed and killed her mother. It is believed that there was a hereditary strain of mental illness in the family and that Mary's illness was precipitated by overwork. She was declared temporarily insane and placed under the guardianship of her brother Charles. For the rest of her life Mary was subject to recurrent bouts of mental illness.

In 1807 Mary and Charles published *Tales from Shakespear,* a collection of prose adaptations of William Shakespeare's plays, intended for children. Mary wrote the preface and the 14 comedies and histories, and Charles contributed the 6 tragedies; only Charles's name, however, appeared on the title page. The book was successful, and it established Charles Lamb's literary reputation. In 1809 Charles and Mary published two collaborative works, *Mrs. Leicester's School,* a book of children's stories, and *Poetry for Children.*

After Charles's death, Mary's mental health deteriorated. She survived him by 13 years.

Lamb, Sydney M(acDonald) (b. May 4, 1929, Denver, Colo., U.S.), American linguist and originator of stratificational grammar, an outgrowth of glossematics theory. (Glossematics theory is based on glossemes, the smallest meaningful units of a language.)

Lamb obtained his Ph.D. in 1958 from the University of California, Berkeley. He taught at the same institution from 1956 to 1964, directing the Machine Translation Project from 1958 to 1964. He began teaching at Yale University in 1964. In 1977 he joined the staff of Semionics Associates in Berkeley, Calif.

Lamb's seminal work, *Outline of Stratificational Grammar* (1966), describes his theory of the four levels necessary for sentence analysis: the sememic, the lexemic, the morphemic, and the phonemic. These levels are hierarchically related, each "realized" by the elements in the level structurally beneath it.

Lamb, Willis Eugene, Jr. (b. July 12, 1913, Los Angeles, Calif., U.S.), American physicist and joint winner, with Polykarp Kusch, of the Nobel Prize for Physics in 1955 for experimental work that spurred refinements in the quantum theories of electromagnetic phenomena.

Lamb joined the faculty of Columbia University in 1938 and worked in the radiation laboratory there during World War II. Though the quantum mechanics of Paul A.M. Dirac had predicted the hyperfine structure of the lines that appear in the spectrum (dispersed light, as by a prism), Lamb applied new methods to measure the lines and in 1947 found their positions to be slightly different from what had been predicted. While a professor of physics at Stanford University, California, (1951–56), Lamb devised microwave techniques for examining the hyperfine structure of the spectral lines of helium. He was professor of theoretical physics at the University of Oxford until 1962, when he was appointed professor of physics at Yale University. In 1974 he became professor of physics and optical sciences at the University of Arizona.

Lamb of God: *see* Agnus Dei.

Lamba, also called LAMA, or NAMBA, a Bantu-speaking people living in the Kéran River valley and Togo Mountains of northeastern Togo and adjacent areas of Benin. The Lamba, like the neighbouring and related Kabre, claim descent from autochthonous Lama; megaliths and ancient pottery attest to the "paleonegritic" status assigned to the Lamba by some authors.

Although by their name the Lamba are "people of the forest," they have cleared their lands of all but an occasional baobab, mango, shea tree, or oil palm. Fields are not allowed to lie fallow but are maintained by the use of ash and manure and by the alternation of corn (maize), sorghum, millet, and taro with legumes for nitrogen replenishment.

Lamba attend their own small markets or larger ones in towns in or adjacent to their lands (such as Niamtougou, or Lama-Kara). Weaving, basketry, pottery, and blacksmithing are well developed, and some crafts are exported. Many Lamba have participated in the rapid urbanization of Lama-Kara, Togo, in recent decades; others migrate southward toward Lomé or westward into Benin seeking land or work.

The Lamba live in homesteads separated from others by fields; descent is patrilineal. Before colonial rule there were no authorities other than ritual headmen in each family group, although loose neighbourhood groups (*tegu*) might join for defense or attack. Age-sets reinforce the egalitarian nature of Lamba society. Lamba (and the neighbouring Kabre) are known in Togo for wrestling matches held among boys of the first age-set. A hierarchy of chiefs that was introduced by German and developed by French colonizers integrates Lamba communities into the Togolese national government.

Lamballe, Marie-Thérèse-Louise de Savoie-Carignan, Princess (princesse) **de** (b. Sept. 8, 1749, Turin, Piedmont [Italy]—d. Sept. 3, 1792, Paris, Fr.), the intimate compan-

The Princess de Lamballe; detail from a portrait by an unknown artist, 18th century; in the Palace of Versailles
Giraudon—Art Resource

ion of Queen Marie-Antoinette of France; she was murdered by a crowd during the French Revolution for her alleged participation in the queen's counterrevolutionary intrigues.

The daughter of Prince Louis-Victor de Savoie-Carignan, she was married in 1767 to Louis-Alexandre-Stanislas de Bourbon, Prince de Lamballe, who died the following year. She went to live at the royal court at Versailles upon the marriage (1770) of the dauphin Louis to Marie-Antoinette, and, by the time Louis ascended the throne as King Louis XVI in 1774, Marie-Antoinette had singled her out as a confidante. The following year she became superintendent of the queen's household.

In October 1789, several months after the outbreak of the Revolution, Lamballe accompanied the royal family to Paris, where her salon became the meeting place for Marie-Antoinette's secret intrigues with royalist sympathizers in the revolutionary National Assembly. Lamballe was also suspected of abetting the queen's private dealings with France's Austrian enemies. After the overthrow of the monarchy on Aug. 10, 1792, she was imprisoned with the queen in the Temple prison but was transferred to La Force prison on August 19. Having refused to take an oath against the monarchy, Lamballe was on September 3 delivered over to the fury of the populace, who cut off her head and carried it on a pike before the windows of the queen.

Lambaréné, city, west-central Gabon, located on an island in the Ogooué River at a point where the river is over half a mile wide. It is a trading and lumbering centre with a steamboat landing, an airport, and road connections

Lambaréné on the Ogooué River, Gabon
Agence HOA-QUI

to Kango, Ndjolé, and Mouila. Lambaréné is best known for its hospital founded in 1913 by Albert Schweitzer (*q.v.*), the theologian and mission doctor. There is a small museum devoted to Schweitzer's life and work. The Paris Mission Society first established a mission there in 1876, and Lambaréné became the headquarters of Protestant missions in the former French Equatorial Africa. The town has a Protestant church and teacher-training school, a Roman Catholic church, a mosque, and a government medical centre and secondary school.

Plantation rubber has been introduced in the area, and petroleum is drilled to the northwest. Lambaréné has a large palm oil factory, and lumber and palm products are sent down the Ogooué to Port-Gentil, 100 miles (160 km) west, for export. Pop. (1993) 15,033.

Lambayeque, *departamento* (formed 1874) of northern Peru. It consists of an arid desert coastal plain that climbs gently eastward from the Pacific Ocean to the Andes Mountains. Vast irrigation projects have made Lambayeque one of Peru's major agricultural regions and a leading department in rice and sugarcane production. Cotton, fruit, and corn (maize) are also cultivated. Railways connect agricultural areas with the departmental capital of Chiclayo (*q.v.*) and the seaports of Pimentel and Eten, which are on the Pan-American Highway. Area 5,495 square miles (14,231 square km). Pop. (1998 est.) 1,050,280.

Lambeau, Curly, byname of EARL LOUIS LAMBEAU (b. April 9, 1898, Green Bay, Wis., U.S.—d. June 1, 1965, Sturgeon Bay, Wis.), American football coach who had one of the longest and most distinguished careers in the history of the game. A founder of the Green Bay Packers in 1919, he served through 1949 as head coach of the only major team in U.S. professional sports to survive in a small city.

After playing briefly for the University of Notre Dame, Lambeau collaborated with George Calhoun, a Green Bay newspaperman, in organizing a professional football team, called the Packers because it received a subsidy from a local meat-packing firm. In 1921 the Packers entered the American Professional Football Association (in 1922 the National Football League [NFL]). Lambeau led the team to six NFL championships (1929, 1930, 1931, 1936, 1939, 1944). In addition to coaching and serving as general manager, he played halfback (1919–29) and was noted as a forward passer.

Lambeau was dismissed after the 1949 season in a dispute with the Packers' business management. Subsequently he coached the Chicago Cardinals (1950–51) and the Washington Redskins (1952–54).

Lambeosaurus, genus of duck-billed dinosaurs (hadrosaurs) found as fossils in Late Cretaceous rocks (66.4 to 97.5 million years old) of North America. *Lambeosaurus* was first discovered in the Oldman Formation, Alberta, Canada; more recently, larger specimens, up to 16.5 m (54 feet) in length, have been found in Baja California, Mexico.

Lambeosaurus is notable for the hatchet-shaped hollow bony crest on top of its skull. This crest contained complex chamber extensions of the breathing passage between the nostrils and the trachea. The function of these chambers is not known, but it has been suggested that they served as resonating chambers (for honking) or as expanded olfactory membranes to increase the sense of smell. Other researchers believe that the crest served in species recognition. As in all duck-billed dinosaurs, the dentition was expanded and adapted for chewing large quantities of harsh plant tissues.

Lambermont, August, Baron (b. March 25, 1819, Dion-le-Val, Neth.—d. March 7, 1905, Brussels), Belgian statesman who in 1863 helped free Belgium's maritime commerce by

Lambermont, detail of an oil painting by Emile Wauters, 1903; in the Musées Royaux des Beaux Arts de Belgique, Brussels

By courtesy of the Musees Royaux des Beaux Arts de Belgique; photograph, © A.C.L., Brussels

negotiating a settlement of the Schelde Question—the dispute over Dutch control of the maritime commerce of Antwerp, Belgium's main port.

After distinguished service in Spain for the army of Queen Isabella II during the First Carlist War (1833–39), Lambermont returned to Belgium in 1842 and entered the foreign-affairs ministry, where he remained for 63 years. Seeing the importance of developing Belgium's trade, he transferred to the commercial branch of the foreign office; in 1856 he began to work on freeing Belgian commerce on the Schelde River, Antwerp's only outlet to the sea. His efforts made possible the signing of an international convention at Brussels in July 1863 that ended the remaining Dutch tolls on Antwerp's maritime trade. For that achievement he was made a baron. He was also prominent between 1874 and 1890 at several international conferences dealing with the laws and customs of war and with Central African affairs.

lambert, unit of luminance (brightness) in the centimetre-gram-second system of physical measurement. It is defined as the brightness of a perfectly diffusing surface that radiates or reflects one lumen per square centimetre. The unit was named for the 18th-century German physicist Johann Heinrich Lambert. It is used by astronomers as well as by physicists, engineers, and photographers.

Lambert OF **HERSFELD** (b. 1025—d. *c.* 1088), chronicler who assembled a valuable source for the history of 11th-century Germany.

Educated in Bamberg, Lambert joined the Benedictine convent of Hersfeld in March 1058 and was ordained the following fall, traveling to the Holy Land the same year. He moved to the Abbey of Hasungen in 1077, helping to initiate its acceptance of the reforms of the Benedictines' Cluniac order in 1081.

His *Annales Hersveldenses* (first published in 1525) were written about 1077–79, covering the period from the Creation to 1077. An erudite scholar, he used as historical and rhetorical models the works of the Roman historians Livy, Sallust, and Suetonius. His coverage of the period from Genesis to 1040 is brief and primarily a compilation of other sources, but the description of events from 1040 to 1077 is highly detailed and based on the annals of the Hersfeld abbey as well as information from other sources and personal experience. Thus, the *Annales* are valuable as documentation of ecclesiastical and political developments in 11th-century Germany, particularly on the relations between the state and the papacy (though criticized for their pro-papal bias). They are also valued for their literary elegance and as a primary source on the relations between Emperor Henry IV and Pope Gregory VII.

Lambert OF **SPOLETO**, Italian LAMBERTO DI SPOLETO (d. Oct. 15, 898, Marengo, Lombardy [Italy]), duke of Spoleto, king of Italy, and Holy Roman emperor (892–898) during the turbulent late Carolingian Age. He was one of many claimants to the imperial title.

Crowned coemperor with his father, Guy of Spoleto, at a ceremony in Ravenna in 892, Lambert ruled alone after his father's death in 894. The following year Arnulf of Carinthia, king of Germany, invaded Italy and besieged Rome, taking the city in February 896. He was crowned emperor by Pope Formosus, who declared Lambert deposed. Marching on Spoleto, Arnulf was suddenly taken ill and had to return to Germany, leaving Lambert once more in possession of the empire.

Almost a year after Formosus' death in 896, Lambert avenged the pope's crowning of Arnulf by having Formosus' body exhumed by the new pope, Stephen VI (VII), dressed in his pontifical robes, and tried and convicted in St. Peter's for a variety of crimes. Then, naked and mutilated, the body was flung into a potter's field and eventually thrown into the Tiber. Lambert died the following year in a hunting accident.

In 898 Berengar, marquis of Friuli, Guy of Spoleto's former rival, marched on Pavia. Lambert, who had been hunting near Marengo, south of Milan, counterattacked and defeated Berengar. On his return to Marengo, he was killed, either by assassination or by a fall from his horse.

Lambert, Constant (b. Aug. 23, 1905, London—d. Aug. 21, 1951, London), English composer, conductor, and critic who played a leading part in establishing the ballet as an art form in England.

Lambert was commissioned in 1926 by Diaghilev to compose the ballet *Romeo and Juliet*. In 1929 he became conductor of the Camargo Society that led to the creation of the Sadler's Wells Ballet, which he then directed until 1947. His works include the ballet *Horoscope* (first produced 1938) and the song cycle *Eight Chinese Songs* (composed 1926). A perspicacious critic, his *Music Ho! A Study of Music in Decline* (1934) is an illuminating study of 20th-century music.

Lambert, Franz, also called FRANÇOIS LAMBERT D'AVIGNON (b. 1486, Avignon, Fr.—d. April 18, 1530, Frankenberg-Eder, Hesse), Protestant convert from Roman Catholicism and leading Reformer in the German province of Hesse.

At age 15 Lambert entered the Franciscan monastery at Avignon, where the city father was a papal official. After 1517 he became an itinerant friar, travelling through France, Italy, and Switzerland. He left his cloister permanently in 1522 after reading some of Martin Luther's writings, although he withheld commitment from both Luther and the Swiss Reformer Huldrych Zwingli (1484–1531).

After a meeting with Luther in Wittenberg, where he had gone to lecture, he returned to Strassburg in 1524 to preach Reformation doctrines to the French-speaking population. There he encountered the Reformer Jakob Sturm, who recommended him to the landgrave Philip of Hesse, the German prince most favourably inclined toward the Reformation. Encouraged by Philip, Lambert drafted *Reformatio ecclesiarum Hassiae* ("The Reformation of the Churches of Hesse"), submitted by Philip to the synod at Homberg (1526). Lambert's document called for democratic principles of congregational representation in church government, by which pastors were to be elected by their congregations. He believed he was expressing Luther's views, including the abolition of bishoprics, but Luther and his adherents pronounced the plan too democratic, and Philip abandoned it. Nevertheless, Lambert's influence persisted in Hesse, where with Philip's assent the Anabaptists, firm advocates of congregationalism, were permitted to flourish. In 1527 Philip founded the University of Marburg and recognized Lambert's service by appointing him head of the theological faculty.

Lambert, Gerard Barnes (b. May 15, 1886, St. Louis, Mo., U.S.—d. Feb. 25, 1967, Princeton, N.J.), U.S. merchandiser and advertiser who marketed his father's invention of Listerine mouthwash by making bad breath a social disgrace.

After graduating from Princeton and studying architecture at Columbia University, Lambert fought in World War I and then joined his father's firm, Lambert Pharmacal Co. The firm later became Warner-Lambert Pharmaceutical Co. As president of the firm in 1923, Lambert focussed on the advertising efforts for Listerine, an antiseptic that his father had invented. To carry out his advertising ideas, Lambert formed the advertising agency of Lambert & Feasley. With Lambert in charge, the pharmaceutical firm saw profits increase 60 times.

He sold his share of the business in 1928 and, after a three-year retirement, joined the Gillette Safety Razor Co., which was in need of a reorganization. In three years he turned the company around by helping to develop the Gillette Blue Blade.

Relying on his architectural training, Lambert developed plans for the first low-cost subsidized housing for New Brunswick and Princeton, N.J., in 1938. Lambert was also a proficient yachtsman, an amateur archaeologist, an art collector, and a writer. His works include a mystery, *Murder in Newport* (1938), a yachting memoir, *Yankee in England* (1937), and his autobiography, *All out of Step: A Personal Chronicle* (1956).

Lambert, Johann Heinrich (b. Aug. 26, 1728, Mülhausen, Alsace,—d. Sept. 25, 1777, Berlin), Swiss-German mathematician, astronomer, physicist, and philosopher who provided the first rigorous proof that π (the ratio of a circle's circumference to its diameter) is irrational, meaning it cannot be expressed as the quotient of two integers.

Johann Lambert, detail of a lithograph by Gottfried Englemann, after a portrait by Pierre-Roch Vigneron
Archiv fur Kunst und Geschichte, West Berlin

The son of a tailor, Lambert was largely self-educated and early began geometric and astronomical investigations by means of instruments he designed and built himself. He worked for a time as a bookkeeper, secretary, and editor. As a private tutor in 1748, he gained access to a good library, which he used for self-improvement until 1759, when he resigned his post to settle in Augsburg. In 1764 he went to Berlin, where he received the patronage of Frederick the Great. His memoir containing the proof that π is irrational was published in 1768. In 1774 at Berlin, he became editor of *Astronomisches Jahrbuch oder Ephemeriden*, an astronomical almanac.

Lambert made the first systematic development of hyperbolic functions. He is also responsible for many innovations in the study of heat and light. The lambert, a measurement of light intensity, was named in his honour. Among his most important works are *Photometria* (1760), *Die Theorie der Parallellinien* (1766; "The Theory of Parallel Lines"), and *Pyrometrie* (1779). The *Neues Organon* (1764; "New Organon"), his principal philosophical work, contains an analysis of a great variety of questions, among them formal logic, probability, and the principles of science.

Lambert, John (b. autumn 1619, Calton, West Riding, Yorkshire, Eng.—d. March 1684, St. Nicholas Isle, off Plymouth, Devon), a leading Parliamentary general during the English Civil Wars and the principal architect of the Protectorate, the form of republican government existing in England from 1653 to 1660.

Coming from a well-to-do family of gentry, Lambert joined the Parliamentary army as a captain at the outbreak of the Civil War between King Charles I and Parliament. He first distinguished himself in encounters with the Royalists at Bradford, Yorkshire, in March 1644, and he fought bravely in the major Parliamentary victory at Marston Moor, Yorkshire, in July 1644. A major general at the age of 28, he helped Henry Ireton draw up the "Heads of the Proposals," a draft constitution aimed at reconciling the conflicting interests of the army, Parliament, and the king.

At the beginning of the second phase of the Civil War in 1648, Lambert was commander of the troops of northern England. He and Oliver Cromwell routed the Scottish Royalist invaders at Preston, Lancashire, in August 1648, and on March 22, 1649, Lambert captured Pontefract, Yorkshire, the last Royalist stronghold in England.

Second in command under Cromwell during the campaigns against the Royalists in Scotland in 1650 and 1651, Lambert was also with Cromwell on Sept. 3, 1651 when he decisively defeated Charles I's son, Charles II, at Worcester in the final battle of the Civil War.

In succeeding years Lambert played a key role in Cromwell's experimental governments. He persuaded Cromwell to dissolve the Rump Parliament in 1653, but was unhappy with Cromwell's plan for a nominated Parliament. When it failed, Lambert was responsible for drawing up the Instrument of Government under which Cromwell assumed power as Lord Protector of the Commonwealth in 1653. Lambert served on the Council of State and was Cromwell's right-hand man until, in 1657, he outspokenly opposed the proposal that Cromwell be made king. When he refused to swear allegiance to the Protector after a new constitution had been established, Cromwell deprived him of his offices but granted him a substantial annual pension.

John Lambert, portrait after Robert Walker; in the National Portrait Gallery, London
By courtesy of the National Portrait Gallery, London

After Cromwell's death (September 1658), Lambert gradually returned to politics. He did not openly cooperate with the army officers who deposed Cromwell's son and successor, Richard, in May 1659, but he was one of the most powerful figures in the ensuing power struggle. Although he helped restore the Rump Parliament in May 1659, he soon broke with it and dissolved it by force. Shortly thereafter, his army was defeated by the forces of Gen. George Monck, who marched from Scotland to reinstate the Rump. Monck proceeded to restore King Charles II to power (1660), and in June 1662 Lambert was sentenced to death for his part in the Civil War. He was granted a reprieve and spent the rest of his life in prison. See W.H. Dawson, *Cromwell's Understudy* (1938).

Lambert, Piggy, byname of WARD L. LAMBERT (b. May 28, 1888, Deadwood, S.D.,

U.S.—d. Jan. 20, 1958, Lafayette, Ind.), U.S. collegiate basketball coach who pioneered the fast break, an offensive drive down the court at all-out speed. Lambert got his nickname from the pigtails he wore as a child.

As a basketball player at Crawfordsville (Ind.) High School and at Wabash College (Crawfordsville; B.S. in chemistry, 1911), Lambert was considered by many to be the greatest small-college player. He was obsessed with motion and speed. After graduate study in chemistry at the University of Minnesota (Minneapolis), he taught physics and chemistry and coached at Lebanon (Ind.) High School (1912–16) before becoming coach at Purdue University (West Lafayette, Ind.), where his teams won or shared in 11 Big Ten (Western Conference) championship titles. As a coach Lambert stressed self-confidence, aggressiveness, speed, and positive attitude. Among his All-American players was John Wooden, who became a foremost collegiate coach. Lambert retired from coaching in 1946, served until 1949 as commissioner of the professional National Basketball League, and then returned to Purdue as head freshman basketball and baseball coach, giving up the former in 1955 but retaining the latter. He also worked as a chemist. Lambert was elected to the Basketball Hall of Fame in 1960.

Lambert conformal projection, conic projection for making maps and charts in which a cone is, in effect, placed over the Earth with its apex aligned with one of the geographic North Pole. The cone is so positioned that it cuts into the Earth at one parallel and comes out again at a parallel farther south; both parallels are chosen as standards, or bounds, of the area to be charted. Points on the Earth are then projected onto the cone along lines radiating from the centre of the Earth; the map or chart results when the cone is slit along one side and laid out flat.

Lambessa, also spelled LAMBÈSE, formerly LAMBAESIS (modern Tazoult-Lambese), an Algerian village notable for its Roman ruins; it is located in the Batna *département,* 80 mi (128 km) south-southwest of Constantine by road.

The remains of the Roman town (Lambaesis) and camp include two triumphal arches, temples, an aqueduct, an amphitheatre, baths, and many private houses. The camp of the third legion, charged with defending North Africa, was moved to Lambessa between AD 123 and 129. Its remains, located north of the modern village, are dominated by a praetorium (commandant's house) dating from AD 268. Lambaesis became a town during the reign of Marcus Aurelius (AD 161–180) and the capital of the Roman province of Numidia under the emperor Septimius Severus (AD 193–211). With the departure of the legion in 392 the ancient town soon declined.

Praetorium at Lambessa, Algeria, AD 268

J. Powell, Rome

The modern settlement was founded in 1848 by French agriculturalists attracted by the fertile soil. A large convict prison for French political deportees was established there in 1852. Pop. (1987 prelim.) 16,057.

Lambeth, inner borough of London, part of the historic county of Surrey, extending southward from the River Thames. It includes the districts of (roughly north to south) Lambeth, Vauxhall, Kennington, South Lambeth, Stock Well, and Brixton, along with large parts of Clapham, Balham, Streatham, and Norwood. It was established in 1965 by the amalgamation of the former metropolitan boroughs of Lambeth and Wandsworth (in part).

Settlement of the area dates to Roman times or earlier, and many of its place-names may be of ancient derivation. The borough was sparsely populated until the 18th century, and the majority of its inhabitants lived and worked along the Thames. Direct access to the left bank was by ford, horse ferry, or boat until 1750, when Westminster Bridge was opened. Because of its proximity to central London and the use of the river for bulk transportation, Lambeth's northern section became an important manufacturing centre by the 18th century.

The riverfront is graced by one of Europe's major cultural centres, the South Bank arts complex, which includes the Royal Festival Hall, Queen Elizabeth Hall, the Purcell Room, the Royal National Theatre, the National Film Theatre, the Museum of the Moving Image, and the Hayward Gallery. In Archbishop's Park the parish church, St. Mary's, lies alongside Lambeth Palace, the London residence of the archbishop of Canterbury. The Oval cricket ground is in Kennington, and the borough's parklands include large parts of Clapham, Tooting Bec, and Streatham commons. Area 11 square miles (27 square km). Pop. (1998 est.) 269,500.

Lambeth Conference, any of the gatherings of bishops of the Anglican Communion held periodically at Lambeth Palace, the London house of the archbishop of Canterbury, who convenes and presides over them. They are important as a means of expressing united Anglican opinion, but the Anglican Communion has no central, authoritative government. The bishops meet and deliberate as equals, with the archbishop of Canterbury as host and chairman. The time between conferences has varied, but the normal interval is 10 years.

The first conference was held in 1867 as a result of a request from the Anglican Church of Canada. Many English bishops questioned the status and wisdom of the international gathering, although the archbishop of Canterbury, Charles Thomas Longley, carefully explained the limited scope of the deliberations: "We merely purpose to discuss matters of practical interest, and pronounce what we deem expedient in resolutions which may serve as safe guides to future action." He later stated that it was not proposed "that questions of doctrine should be submitted for interpretation in any future Lambeth Conference. . . ." Despite this cautious approach, only 76 of the 144 Anglican bishops attended the first conference. Attitudes changed, however, and, in 1978, 440 bishops attended. The first conference lasted only four days, but later conferences each lasted several weeks.

In 1897 a permanent continuation committee, the Consultative Body of the Lambeth Conference, was established to help prepare the agenda for the conferences. An Advisory Council on Missionary Strategy was established in 1948. At the Lambeth Conference of 1958 it was decided to appoint a bishop to serve as executive officer of the Anglican Communion and to work with these two inter-Anglican organizations. Action taken at the 1968 conference merged the two organizations into the Anglican Consultative Council, with headquarters in London, which carries on the cooperative work of the Anglican Communion between meetings of the Lambeth Conference.

Lambeth Conferences are the primary means of joint consultation for Anglican leaders on relations with other churches, internal Anglican matters, and theological, social, and international questions. The conferences normally issue an encyclical letter, a series of resolutions, and the reports prepared by committees. The decisions of the conferences have no power over Anglican churches, which must adopt them by synodical or other constitutional means to make them legally binding.

Lambeth Quadrilateral, four points that constitute the basis for union discussions of the Anglican Communion with other Christian groups: acceptance of Holy Scripture as the rule of faith; the Apostles' and the Nicene creeds; the sacraments of Baptism and the Lord's Supper; and the historic episcopate. Declared by the General Convention of the Protestant Episcopal Church in Chicago in 1886, they were amended and adopted by the Anglican Communion's Lambeth Conference of 1888. The first three points are widely accepted. The fourth point, episcopacy (church government based on bishops), has been the principal block to union of Anglican and Protestant churches.

Lambeth walk, ballroom dance of the late 1930s, supposedly representing the strut of the Cockney residents of the Lambeth section of London. Adapted from the choreography of the 1937 British musical *Me and My Girl,* the dance was performed with walking steps in march time. Each dancer held his hands free at shoulder level, thumbs out. Couples walked side by side or face to face, linked arms to turn, or slapped their knees and shouted "hoy." The dance was especially popular as a respite from the exhausting jitterbug.

Lambeth walk

Culver Pictures

Lambing Flat Riots (1860–61), wave of anti-Chinese disturbances in the goldfields of New South Wales, Australia, which led to restriction of Chinese immigration. Many white and Chinese miners had flocked to the settlement of Lambing Flat (now called Young) when gold was discovered in the area in the summer of 1860. The first disturbance grew out of a demonstration organized by a white miners' vigilance committee against gambling dens and other alleged vice on Dec. 12, 1860. After venting their rage on these establishments, the miners attacked the Chinese quarter of the settlement, killed several people, and wounded many others. Other attacks followed the December incident; eventually the Chinese miners had to abandon the fields. While the white miners justified their brutality by claiming that the Orientals were squandering the water supply so vital to alluvial prospecting, racism was probably an equally significant factor.

A military detachment restored order at the flat from March until June 1861, and most of the Chinese returned to the settlement. Soon after the departure of the troops, however, a final, devastating riot occurred on June 30. Several thousand miners descended on the Orientals, plundering their dwellings; mounted pursuers overtook the fleeing Chinese and degraded, beat, and robbed them. The authorities returned quickly and restored order. The Lambing Flat Riots led the New South Wales government to pass the Chinese Immigration Act in November 1861, severely limiting the flow of Chinese into the colony.

lambkill, also called DWARF LAUREL, SHEEP LAUREL, or WICKY (species *Kalmia angustifolia*), an open upright woody shrub of the heath family (Ericaceae). Lambkill is 0.3–1.2 m (1–4 feet) tall and has glossy, leathery, evergreen leaves and showy pink to rose flowers. It contains andromedotoxin, a poison also common to other *Kalmia* species (including mountain laurel and bog laurel) and other members of the heath family. In northwestern North America, where these plants occur, livestock (especially sheep) that graze on nonfertile soils of abandoned pastures and meadows may ingest sufficient lambkill to become poisoned. Symptoms include excessive salivation and nasal discharge, paralysis, and coma and may ultimately lead to death.

lamb's lettuce (plant): *see* corn salad.

lamb's quarters, also called PIGWEED (species *Chenopodium album*), an annual weed of the goosefoot family (Chenopodiaceae) of wide distribution in Asia, Europe, and North America. It can grow up to 3 m (about 10 feet) but is usually seen as a smaller plant. The blue-green leaves are variable in size and shape but are often white and mealy beneath. The tender young shoots in spring are sometimes gathered for potherbs.

Lambton, John George: *see* Durham, John George Lambton, 1st Earl of.

lamellaphone, also called MBIRA, LIKEMBE, KALIMBA, or THUMB PIANO, African musical instrument consisting of a set of tuned metal or bamboo tongues (lamellae) of varying length attached at one end to a soundboard that often has a box or calabash resonator. Board-mounted lamellaphones are often played inside gourds or bowls for increased resonance, and the timbre may be modified by attaching rattling devices to the board or resonator or by attaching metal cuffs at the base of the tongues.

Mbira (a lamellaphone) with bamboo tongues, central Africa; in the James Blades Collection
James Blades

The lamellaphone is often classified as a plucked idiophone, *i.e.,* an instrument whose sounding parts are resonant solids. This term, however, is not strictly accurate, because the tongues are not plucked but rather depressed and released with the thumbs and fingers. The lamellaphone is commonly played as an accompaniment to song, but in some areas it is used for purely instrumental music.

The lamellaphone was described by European travelers as early as 1586. It is widely distributed throughout sub-Saharan Africa in the same regions as the xylophone, to which its tuning is similar and with which it shares several local names. It was taken to Latin America by African slaves during the 19th century, where it gave rise to the Afro-Cuban marimba.

Lamennais, (Hugues-) Félicité (-Robert de) (b. June 19, 1782, Saint-Malo, Fr.—d. Feb. 27, 1854, Paris), French priest and philosophical and political writer who attempted to combine political liberalism with Roman Catholicism after the French Revolution. A brilliant writer, he was an influential but controversial figure in the history of the church in France.

Lamennais was born to a bourgeois family whose liberal sympathies had been chastened by the French Revolution. He and his elder brother, Jean, early conceived the idea of a revival of Roman Catholicism as the key to social regeneration. After Napoleon's restoration of the Roman Catholic church in France, the brothers sketched a program of reform in *Réflexions sur l'état de l'église. . .* (1808; "Reflections on the State of the Church. . ."). Five years later, at the height of Napoleon's conflict with the papacy, they produced a defense of ultramontanism (a movement supporting papal authority and centralization of the church, in contrast to Gallicanism, which advocated the restriction of papal power). This book brought Lamennais into conflict with the emperor, and he had to flee to England briefly during the Hundred Days in 1815.

Lamennais, detail from a portrait by Paulin Guerin, 1826; in the National Museum of the Chateau of Versailles
Cliche Musees Nationaux, Paris

Having returned to Paris, Lamennais was ordained a priest in 1816, and in the following year he published the first volume of his *Essai sur l'indifférence en matière de religion* ("Essay on Indifference Toward Religion"), which won him immediate fame. In this book he argued for the necessity of religion, basing his appeals on the authority of tradition and the general reason of mankind rather than on the individualism of private judgment. Though an advocate of ultramontanism in the religious sphere, Lamennais in his political beliefs was a liberal who advocated the separation of church and state and the freedoms of conscience, education, and the press. Though he attacked the Gallicanism of the French bishops and the French monarchy in his book *Des progrès de la révolution et de la guerre contre l'Église* (1829; "On the Progress of the Revolution and the War Against the Church"), this work showed his readiness to combine Roman Catholicism with political liberalism.

After the July Revolution in 1830, Lamennais founded *L'Avenir* with Henri Lacordaire, Charles de Montalembert, and a group of enthusiastic liberal Roman Catholic writers. This daily newspaper, which advocated democratic principles and church-state separation, antagonized both the French ecclesiastical hierarchy and King Louis-Philippe's government. And despite its ultramontanism, the paper also found little favour in Rome, for Pope Gregory XVI had no wish to assume the revolutionary role it advocated for him. Publication of the paper was suspended in November 1831, and after a vain appeal to the pope its principles were condemned in the encyclical *Mirari Vos* (August 1832). Lamennais then attacked the papacy and the European monarchs in *Paroles d'un croyant* (1834; "The Words of a Believer"); this famous apocalyptic poem provoked the papal encyclical *Singulari Nos* (July 1834), which led to Lamennais' severance from the church.

Thenceforth Lamennais devoted himself to the cause of the people and put his pen at the service of republicanism and socialism. He wrote such works as *Le Livre du peuple* (1838; "The Book of the People"), and he served in the Constituent Assembly after the Revolution of 1848. He retired after Louis-Napoleon's coup d'état in 1851. Because he refused to be reconciled to the church, upon his death Lamennais was buried in a pauper's grave.

BIBLIOGRAPHY. Alexander R. Vidler, *Prophecy and Papacy: A Study of Lamennais, the Church, and the Revolution* (1954); Peter N. Stearns, *Priest and Revolutionary: Lamennais and the Dilemma of French Catholicism* (1967).

Lament for the Destruction of Ur, ancient Sumerian composition bewailing the collapse of the 3rd Dynasty of Ur (*c.* 2112–*c.* 2004 BC) in southern Mesopotamia. The lament, primarily composed of 11 "songs" or stanzas of unequal length, begins by enumerating some of the prominent cities and temples of Sumer and the deities who had deserted them. In the second "song," the people of Ur and of other cities of Sumer are urged to set up a bitter lament. The third "song" relates that the goddess Ningal hears the pleas of the people of Ur, but she is not able to dissuade the gods Anu and Enlil from their decision to destroy the city, and the remaining "songs" relate the devastating results of Ur's defeat in battle. The last stanza ends with a plea to Nanna, the husband of Ningal, that the city may once more rise up and that the people of Ur may again present their offerings to him.

Lamentations of Jeremiah, The, also called THE LAMENTATIONS OF JEREMIAS, Old Testament book belonging to the third section of the biblical canon, known as the Ketuvim, or Writings. In the Hebrew Bible, Lamentations stands with Ruth, the Song of Solomon, Ecclesiastes, and Esther and with them makes up the Megillot, five scrolls that are read on various festivals of the Jewish religious year. In the Jewish liturgical calendar, Lamentations is the festal scroll of the Ninth of Av, a day commemorating the destruction of the First and Second Temples of Jerusalem.

Most of the Christian English translations of the Bible, following the lead of the later Greek versions and the Latin versions, call the book The Lamentations of Jeremiah, though its title in the Talmud and the Septuagint is simply Lamentations. The content and style, however, argue against Jeremiah's authorship. Each of the first four chapters consists of an acrostic poem. Although the 5th chapter consists of 22 verses, it is not, strictly speaking, an alphabetic acrostic. The poems are independent units, but their mood and content provide a unity to the book as a whole. Because the poems are laments over the destruction of Judah, Jerusalem, and the Temple by the Babylonians in 586 BC, they must be dated during the exile that followed.

Lamerie, Paul de (b. April 9, 1688, 's Hertogenbosch, Neth.—d. Aug. 1, 1751, London, Eng.), well-known Dutch-born English silversmith.

His parents were Huguenots who probably left France for religious reasons in the early 1680s; they had settled in Westminster by 1691. After serving as an apprentice to a London goldsmith, Pierre Platel, de Lamerie registered his mark and established his own shop in 1712. Early in his career he made simple vessels, such as tankards and teapots, in an unornamented Queen Anne style, and more pretentious works, such as a large wine cistern for the first Earl of Gower (1719), in an ornamented style associated with the work of French Huguenot craftsmen.

Silver Newdegate centrepiece by Paul de Lamerie, 1743; in the Victoria and Albert Museum, London

By courtesy of the Victoria and Albert Museum, London

In the 1730s de Lamerie produced works, particularly covered cups, in his version of the Rococo style. A notable example of 1737 is a cup whose handles are in the form of realistic snakes. A further example of his rich Rococo decoration is a ewer (1741) with a handle in the form of the figure of a triton. Unlike the silversmiths on the Continent, de Lamerie made many uncommissioned works that were intended to be stocked for later sale.

Lameth, Alexandre (-Theodore-Victor), comte de (count of) (b. Oct. 28, 1760, Paris, Fr.—d. March 18, 1829, Paris), French nobleman who was a leading advocate of constitutional monarchy in the early stages of the French Revolution of 1789.

Lameth and his brothers, Charles and Théodore, fought for the colonists in the American Revolution. On returning to France, Lameth was appointed colonel of a cavalry regiment (1785). He was elected a representative for the nobility to the Estates General that convened on May 5, 1789, but on June 25 he joined the unprivileged Third Estate, which had declared itself a revolutionary National Assembly. He helped draft the Assembly's Declaration of the Rights of Man and of the Citizen (August 1789), and he supported measures abolishing feudalism and restricting the hitherto absolute powers of King Louis XVI. In September, Lameth and his two close associates, Antoine Barnave and Adrien Duport—the "triumvirate"—blocked legislation that would have created a separate legislative chamber for the nobility.

Lameth, engraving by Jean-Baptiste Vérité, late 18th century

By courtesy of the Bibliotheque Nationale, Paris

Nevertheless, by the spring of 1791 Lameth and his friends felt that continuation of the Revolution might endanger the monarchy and private property. They then became secret advisers to the royal family, which subsidized their newspaper, the *Logographe.* Louis XVI's abortive attempt to flee from France in June 1791, however, discredited the new system of constitutional monarchy. In an attempt to consolidate their forces, Lameth and his associates withdrew from the Jacobin Club and formed the Club of the Feuillants. The triumvirs were ineligible to sit in the Legislative Assembly, which convened on Oct. 1, 1791, but they directed the Feuillants of the Assembly in their unsuccessful struggle against the Jacobins.

When France went to war with Austria in April 1792, Lameth became an officer in the Army of the North. He emigrated with the Marquis de Lafayette after the fall of the monarchy on Aug. 10, 1792. Interned for more than three years in Austria, Lameth settled in Hamburg in 1796. After Napoleon came to power in France, Lameth returned to his homeland (1800) and served as a prefect from 1802 until 1815. He was a member of the liberal parliamentary opposition during the reigns of kings Louis XVIII and Charles X.

Lamia, in classical mythology, a female daemon who devoured children. According to late myths she was a queen of Libya who was beloved by Zeus. When Hera robbed her of her children from this union, Lamia killed every child she could get into her power. She was also known as a fiend who, in the form of a beautiful woman, seduced young men in order to devour them.

Lamía, city of central Greece in the Sperkhiós River valley at the foot of the Óthris Mountains, near the Gulf of Euboea. It is the capital of the Fthiótis *nomós* (department) and the seat of a bishop of the Greek Orthodox church. Lamía commands the strategic Foúrka Pass leading northwestward into Thessaly (Thessalía).

The original Lamía was founded in the 5th century BC as the centre of the tribes of Malis, a semi-indigenous Dorian people who contributed to the construction of a temple at Delphi. Upon the decline of Sparta and Thebes in the second half of the 4th century BC, Lamía passed under the influence of Macedonia and Thessaly. It was besieged by the Second Athenian Confederation during the Lamian War (323–322) in that confederation's futile attempt to throw off Macedonian hegemony. In the 3rd century Lamía came under the influence of the expanded Aetolian League, which invited the Seleucid king Antiochus III to Lamía (192); this imprudent gesture provoked the Romans, who destroyed Lamía. In the Middle Ages Lamía was renamed Gipton and turned into a stronghold of the Frankish dukes of Athens. The succeeding Catalans named it El Cito, and to the Turks it was known as Zituni or Zeytun. The acropolis dominating the modern city has ruins that range from classical wall foundations to Roman, Catalan, and Turkish battlements.

Lamía's industries include soap, cotton textiles, and tobacco processing, and there is trade in wheat, olives, and citrus from the Sperkhiós valley. It is linked to Vólos and Larissa by the Athens-Thessaloníki (Salonika) superhighway, and a spur from the Athens-Thessaloníki railway runs to Lamía and its port, Stilís. The area has both iron and manganese deposits. Pop. (1981) 41,846.

Lamiaceae, also called LABIATAE, the mint family of flowering plants, with about 160 genera and 3,500 species, the largest family of the order Lamiales. It is important to humans for herb plants useful for flavour, fragrance, or medicinal properties. Most members of the family have square stems; paired, opposite, simple leaves; and two-lipped, open-mouthed, tubular corollas (united petals), with five-lobed, bell-like calyxes (united sepals).

The 40 to 50 species of the genus *Lamium* are known as dead nettles; they are low weedy plants that are sometimes cultivated. There are about 300 to 400 species in the genus *Thymus,* all Eurasian. Wild thyme (*T. serpyllum*), with scented leaves, is a creeping plant that is native in Europe but naturalized in eastern North America. Its foliage and flower heads resemble those of garden thyme (*T. vulgaris*), the source of the kitchen herb (*see* thyme).

(Top) Betony (*Betonica officinalis*), (bottom) self-heal (*Prunella vulgaris*)

(Top) A to Z Botanical Collection—EB Inc., (bottom) Thomas W. Martin from Rapho/Photo Researchers—EB Inc.

Among the approximately 100 species of the genus *Phlomis* is Jerusalem sage (*P. tuberosa*), which rises to almost 2 m (6.5 feet) and has clusters of purple flowers. It is native to Eurasia and is naturalized in North America.

Of the 150 tropical species of *Ocimum,* one sacred to Hindus is basil, or *tulsī* (*Ocimum basilicum*); this plant is native in Africa and Asia but is cultivated as a culinary herb in other regions (*see* basil). The genus *Origanum,* native in Europe, includes 15 to 20 species, chief among them being marjoram (*Origanum *majorana,* or *Majorana hortensis; see* marjoram).

Best known for its sharp fragrance is rosemary (*q.v.; Rosmarinus officinalis*), a Mediterranean species. Also Mediterranean is lavender (*Lavandula officinalis*), with fragrant blue to lavender flowers in leafless spikes (*see* lavender).

One of the 40 species of the African genus *Leonotis, L. nepetaefolia,* is naturalized throughout the tropics; it has red-orange globe clusters of profuse flowers at the top of the one- to two-metre plants. Hyssop (*Hyssopus officinalis*) was once used as a curative herb (*see* hyssop).

Catnip, or catmint (*Nepeta cataria*), a Eurasian perennial, grows to about 1 m and has downy, heart-shaped leaves with an aroma that is stimulating to cats. Betony (*Betonica,* or *Stachys, officinalis*) was once regarded as a cure-all, and other plants of the genus *Stachys,* or the woundworts generally, had supposed value as folk remedies. Self-heal, or heal all (*Prunella vulgaris*), provided another important herbal medicine. *See also* Coleus; Mentha; Monarda.

Consult the INDEX *first*

Lamiales, the mint order of the flowering plants, belonging to the class called dicotyledon (Magnoliopsida; characterized by two seed leaves). It comprises some 7,800 species in four families. The mint (Lamiaceae) and the verbena (Verbenaceae) families account for some three-quarters of the species. Members of these two families are represented on all habitable continents. All four families in the order have low-growing, herbaceous members; only the verbena group is noted for large trees.

With some exceptions, plants of the Lamiales possess simple, opposite leaves; flowers with both stamens (male) and pistils (female); and two-lipped flowers in which one half (as viewed longitudinally) is the mirror image of the other (bilateral symmetry, or irregular flowers). Many genera of the Lamiaceae and the Verbeniaceae have distinctive, four-angled stems.

Most of the roughly 3,200 species of the mint family are annual or perennial herbs. Their primary centre of distribution is the Old World, from the Canary Islands to the Himalayas, with lesser centres in Ethiopia, Madagascar, southern areas of Africa and India, Sri Lanka, and oceanic regions eastward. Centres of distribution in the New World range from the mountains in central Mexico into Argentina and Chile, with secondary centres radiating northward and eastward.

Essential oils, which are used medicinally, for flavouring foods and beverages, and in perfumery, are derived from many genera of the mint family. The oils from horehound (*Marrubium vulgare*) and clary (*Salvia sclarea*) have medicinal value. *Mentha* cultivars (horticultural varieties) grown commercially for their oils are *M. arvensis* for menthol; *M.* × *gentilis* and *M. spicata* for spearmint; and *M.* × *piperita* for peppermint. Spice plants include marjoram (*Origanum majorana*), European marjoram (*O. vulgare*), sweet basil (*Ocimum basilicum*), sage (*Salvia officinalis*), savory (*Satureja hortensis*), lemon balm (*Melissa officinalis*), and thyme (*Thymus vulgaris*). Perfumes are derived from lavender (*Lavandula angustifolia*) and rosemary (*Rosmarinus officinalis*).

Border, bedding, and ground cover plants of the mint family include *Levendula, Mentha,* and the so-called dead-nettle (*Lamium maculatum*), a semievergreen.

Among the ornamental plants of Lamiaceae are species of *Salvia* that range in colour from blue to the orange-red Brazilian scarlet-sage (*S. splendens*). Bells-of-Ireland (*Molucella laevis*) develops an unusual, green, open-faced calyx much used in floral arrangements. Hundreds of named cultivars of *Coleus,* notable for their colourful leaves, are prized as houseplants and for protected outdoor plantings. Wildflowers and cultivated varieties of *Monarda,* the bergamots, are also appreciated for their colour in summer.

The verbena, or vervain, family (Verbenaceae), composed of some 2,600 species, is distributed largely in tropical and subtropical South America and Africa. Other places of origin include central Asia, Japan, and islands near India; few members are native to Europe, Asia Minor, and North America.

The most important commercial plant of Verbenaceae is *Tectona grandis,* the teak native to India, Myanmar (Burma), and Malaysia; it is also grown in other warm areas for its valuable wood. Another Asian tree, *Vitex altissima,* produces commercial timber; wood of the related *V. divaricata* is used for shingles and the bark for tanning. A related smaller tree, the aromatic *V. agnus-castus* (chaste tree) is a hardy ornamental in warm temperate regions. Fiddlewood (*Citharexylum fruticosum*) of the West Indies, with the general appearance of a cherry tree, produces valuable timber and blossoms in all seasons.

Species of *Avicennia,* the black mangrove, inhabit the coastal mud flats of Florida and many tropical lands. Their large seeds germinate while still attached to the parent plant. When released from the parent, the root of this seedling gets stuck in the mud and quickly grows into a new plant. In addition, numerous stilt roots and special roots growing upward from the watery soil permit the mangroves to literally invade the sea.

Other notable plants of the Lamiales include the evergreen beautyberry (*Callicarpa americana*), lemon verbena (*Aloysia triphylla*), yellow sage (*Lantana camara*), and *Verbena* × *hybrida,* a desirable ground cover.

The carpet bugleweed (*Ajuga reptans* of the Lamiaceae), native to Europe, spreads by stolons (above-ground runners), and *A. pyramidalis* produces rhizomes to form enlarged colonies vegetatively. Reproduction in the mint order is, however, accomplished most efficiently by seeds.

The predominant inflorescence (flower cluster) is a raceme in which the lowest flowers of the branched system open first. Most genera produce bisexual flowers bearing both stamens and pistils. A representative flower is four- or five-parted, sepals are partially fused to form a bell-shaped calyx, and petals form a tubular corolla that is two-lipped. Typically two united carpels form the pistil, which consists of a basal ovary, a slender style, and the pollen-receptive stigma.

After pollination and fertilization, the ovule becomes the seed and the ovary the fruit. The ovary in the Lamiales is deeply four-lobed with the style arising from the central depression. When mature, the fruit separates into four nutlets, a characteristic that distinguishes the mint family from most members of the Verbenaceae. Fruits in the verbena family may also split apart, but many are berries or drupes (outer layer fleshy, but inner one stony).

Lamian War, also called GREEK WAR (323–322 BC), conflict in which Athenian independence was lost despite efforts by Athens and its Aetolian allies to free themselves from Macedonian domination after the death of Alexander the Great. Athenian democratic leaders, in conjunction with the Aetolian League, fielded an army of 30,000 men in October 323. They seized Thermopylae and kept a Macedonian army under Antipater blockaded in the city of Lamía until the spring of 322, when the arrival of enemy reinforcements from Asia forced them to raise the siege. Outnumbered and deserted by their allies, the Athenians were defeated at the Battle of Crannon (September 322) and surrendered unconditionally. Abandoning Alexander's liberal policy, Antipater forced Athens to accept an oligarchical government subservient to him and had Hyperides and Demosthenes, leaders of the anti-Macedonian party, sentenced to death.

laminar flow, type of fluid (gas or liquid) flow in which the fluid travels smoothly or in regular paths, in contrast to turbulent flow, in which the fluid undergoes irregular fluctuations and mixing. In laminar flow, sometimes called streamline flow, the velocity, pressure, and other flow properties at each point in the fluid remain constant. Laminar flow over a horizontal surface may be thought of as consisting of thin layers, or laminae, all parallel to each other. The fluid in contact with the horizontal surface is stationary, but all the other layers slide over each other. A deck of new cards, as a rough analogy, may be made to "flow" laminarly.

Laminar flow in a straight pipe may be considered as the relative motion of a set of concentric cylinders of fluid, the outside one fixed at the pipe wall and the others moving at increasing speeds as the centre of the pipe is approached. Smoke rising in a straight path from a cigarette is undergoing laminar flow. After rising a small distance, the smoke usually changes to turbulent flow, as it eddies and swirls from its regular path.

Laminar flow is common only in cases in which the flow channel is relatively small, the fluid is moving slowly, and its viscosity is relatively high. Oil flow through a thin tube or blood flow through capillaries is laminar. Most other kinds of fluid flow are turbulent except near solid boundaries, where the flow is often laminar, especially in a thin layer just adjacent to the surface.

Laminaria, genus of brown algae commonly known as kelp (*q.v.*).

lamination, in technology, the process of building up successive layers of a substance, such as wood or textiles, and bonding them with resin to form a finished product. Laminated board, for example, consists of thin layers of wood bonded together; similarly, laminated fabric consists of two or more layers of cloth joined together with an adhesive, or a layer of fabric bonded to a plastic sheet. *See also* plywood; veneer.

Lamington Plateau, section of the McPherson Range, southeastern Queensland, Australia, near the New South Wales border. With an average elevation of 2,000 feet (600 m), it occupies an area of about 75 square miles (195 square km). The headwaters of the Nerang, Coomera, Albert, and Logan rivers rise there. The plateau, named after Baron Lamington (Charles W. Baillie), a former state governor, is the site of Lamington National Park, which contains scenic wooded peaks, including Mount Wanugara (3,925 feet), more than 500 waterfalls, ancient stands of Antarctic beech trees, and rare birds and plants. The area is accessible via the Mount Lindesay Highway from Brisbane (70 miles [110 km] north).

lammergeier, also spelled LAMMERGEYER, or LAMMERGEIR (German: "lamb vulture"), also called BEARDED VULTURE (species *Gypaetus barbatus*), big eaglelike vulture of the Old World (family Accipitridae), frequently over 1 m (40 inches) long, with a wingspread of nearly 3 m (10 feet). Brown above and tawny below, the lammergeier has spots on the breast, black and white stripes on the head, and long bristles on the "chin." Eaglelike features are the feathered face and legs, curved beak, strongly prehensile feet, and long curved claws. The lammergeier inhabits mountainous regions from Central Asia and eastern Africa to Spain. It usually nests on ledges of cliffs, laying one or two whitish eggs about 10 cm (4 inches) in length. It feeds on carrion, especially bones, which it drops from heights as

Lammergeier (*Gypaetus barbatus*)
Paul Johnsgard from Root Resources—EB Inc.

great as 260 feet (80 m) onto flat rocks below. The bird thereby obtains access to the marrow of the bones that have broken.

Lamont, Johann von (b. Dec. 13, 1805, Braemar, Aberdeenshire, Scot.—d. Aug. 6, 1879, Munich, Ger.), Scottish-born German astronomer noted for discovering that the magnetic field of the Earth fluctuates with a period somewhat in excess of 10 years.

In 1827 Lamont began working at the Royal Observatory, Bogenhausen, near Munich. He adopted German nationality and worked at Bogenhausen for the rest of his life, as director of the observatory from 1835 and also as professor of astronomy at the University of Munich from 1852. In addition to his other work, he determined the orbits of Saturn's satellites Enceladus and Tethys, the periods of Uranus' satellites Ariel and Titan, and the mass of Uranus. He also cataloged more than 34,000 stars. He established a magnetic observatory at Bogenhausen in 1840 and 10 years later discovered the variation in the Earth's magnetic field. In 1862 he discovered the existence of large-scale surges of electrical charge within the Earth's crust that are associated with ionospheric disturbances. Lamont's most noteworthy work is *Handbuch des Erdmagnetismus* (1849; "Handbook of Terrestrial Magnetism"). He was elected a foreign member of the Royal Society of London in 1852.

Lamont, Thomas William (b. Sept. 30, 1870, Claverack, N.Y., U.S.—d. Feb. 2, 1948, Boca Grande, Fla.), American banker and financier who began his career by reorganizing corporations and went on to help establish financial stability in countries around the world.

Lamont graduated from Harvard University in 1892 and, after a brief stint on the financial desk of the *New York Tribune,* began working for Cushman Brothers Co., a New York food importer and exporter. The firm suffered financial problems, and Lamont came to its rescue with a reorganization plan and new capital, thus creating in 1898 the firm of Lamont, Corlis & Co. with his brother-in-law. Lamont's success earned him a reputation as a financial problem solver.

In 1903, when the Bankers Trust Co. was formed, Lamont was asked to be its secretary and treasurer by Henry P. Davison, who had been impressed with Lamont's handling of the Cushman reorganization. Within two years he was vice president of the new bank. Before leaving the bank in 1909, Lamont went to Europe for the American Bankers Association to establish an internationally accepted system of drafts known as travelers' checks. Two years later he became the youngest partner in the bank of J.P. Morgan, a relationship that he maintained until his death, serving for the last five years of his life as chairman of the board. In 1918 Lamont satisfied his lifelong fascination with journalism by purchasing the *New York Evening Post,* only to sell it four years later at a significant loss.

During World War I Lamont, with his friend Davison, arranged the financing and purchasing of supplies in the United States to be sent to France and England. After the war he negotiated reconstruction financing and the conditions for German reparations payments as a member of the American delegation to the Paris Peace Conference (1919) and as one of the participants in the drafting of the Dawes (1924) and Young (1929) plans. In the mid-1920s Lamont helped stabilize the French franc and the Italian lira by arranging $100 million lines of credit. After a devastating earthquake in Japan in 1923, he helped arrange a loan for that country for $250 million. He traveled annually to Europe, South America, and East Asia to help solve international monetary problems and consult with world and financial leaders.

A list of the abbreviations used in the MICROPAEDIA *will be found at the end of this volume*

Lamontagne-Beauregard, Blanche (b. 1889, Les Escoumains, Que., Can.—d. 1958, Canada), French-Canadian poet who is recognized as the first important female poet of French Canada.

Lamontagne studied literature at the University of Montreal. Her early writing explored historical themes, but she later shifted to regionalism, extolling her homeland, the Gaspé Peninsula, in a robust, emotional style. Her collections of lyric poetry include *Visions Gaspésiennes* (1913; "Views of the Gaspé"), *Par nos champs et nos rives* (1917; "Through Our Fields and Shores"), *Ma Gaspésie* (1928; "My Gaspé"), and *Moisson nouvelle* (1926; "New Harvest").

Lamoricière, Christophe-Louis-Leon Juchault de (b. Feb. 5, 1806, Nantes, Fr.—d. Sept. 11, 1865, Prouzel), French general and administrator noted for his part in the conquest of Algeria.

After entering the engineers in 1829, Lamoricière was sent to Algiers (1830) as a captain in the Zouaves. In 1833 he played a prominent role in the creation of the Arab Bureau, which was to coordinate information on French Arab colonies. Military success at Constantine led to his promotion to colonel (1837) and thereafter he rose rapidly to marshal (1840) and to governor of a division (1843). An efficient and distinguished general, he served as governor general of Algeria during the incumbent's absence in 1845.

Lamoricière, lithograph, *c.* 1848
By courtesy of the Bibliotheque Nationale, Paris

In France in 1846, Lamoricière was elected deputy for Sarthe and submitted a plan for free, rather than military, colonization of Algeria. He was concerned that a war of extermination against the Arabs would leave Algeria a barren wasteland instead of a rich and useful colony. He served as minister of war (1848) and was sent to Russia on a diplomatic mission (1850–51) dealing with political, military, and colonial affairs. As an opponent of the rising power of Louis-Napoléon, he was arrested (1851) and exiled, but was allowed to return in 1857. In 1860 he led the papal troops against Piedmont but was defeated at Castelfidardo and returned to France.

lamp, a device for producing illumination, consisting originally of a vessel containing a wick soaked in combustible material, and subsequently such other light-producing instruments as gas and electric lamps.

The lamp was invented at least as early as 70,000 BC. Originally it consisted of a hollowed-out rock filled with moss or some other

Roman bronze oil lamp with lions and dolphins, from the Baths of Julian, Paris, 1st century AD; in the British Museum
By courtesy of the trustees of the British Museum

absorbent material that was soaked with animal fat and ignited. In the Mediterranean area and the Middle East, the earliest lamp had a shell shape. Originally, actual shells were used, with sections cut out to provide space for the lighting area; later these were replaced by pottery, alabaster, or metal lamps shaped to resemble their natural prototypes. Another basic type of primitive lamp, found in ancient Egypt and China, was the saucer lamp. Made of pottery or bronze, it was sometimes provided with a spike in the centre of the declivity to support the wick, which was used to control the rate of burning. Another version had a wick channel, which allowed the burning surface of the wick to hang over the edge. The latter type became common in Africa and spread into East Asia as well.

In ancient Greece lamps did not begin to appear until the 7th century BC, when they replaced torches and braziers. Indeed, the very word lamp is derived from the Greek *lampas,* meaning a torch. The pottery version of a Greek lamp was shaped like a shallow cup, with one or more spouts or nozzles in which the wick burned; it had a circular hole in the top for filling and a carrying handle. Such lamps usually were covered with a heat-resisting red or black glaze. A more expensive type was produced in bronze. The standard form had a handle with a ring for the finger and a crescent above for the thumb. Hanging lamps made of bronze also became popular.

The Romans introduced a new system of manufacturing terra-cotta lamps, using two molds and then joining the parts together. In metal, shapes became more complex, sometimes assuming animal or vegetable forms; very large versions for use in circuses and other public places appeared during the 1st century AD.

Very little information is available about medieval lamps, but it would appear that such as existed were of the open, saucer type, and considerably inferior in performance to the closed lamps of the Romans. The great step forward in the evolution of the lamp occurred in Europe in the 18th century with the introduction of a central burner, emerging from a closed container through a metal tube and controllable by means of a ratchet. This advance coincided with the discovery that the flame produced could be intensified by aeration and a glass chimney. Until the late 18th century, the primary fuels burned in lamps included vegetable oils such as olive oil and tallow, beeswax, fish oil, and whale oil. With the drilling of the first well for petroleum oil in 1859, the kerosene lamp (paraffin in British usage) grew popular. In the meantime, however, coal gas and then natural gas for illumination were coming into wide use. Coal gas had been used as a lamp fuel as early as 1784, and a "thermolampe" using gas distilled from wood was patented in 1799. Although coal gas was denounced as unsafe, it won increasing favour for street lighting, and by early in the 19th century most cities in the United States and Europe had gaslighted streets and increasing numbers of homes converted to the new fuel.

The early gas lamps made use of a simple burner in which the yellow light of the flame itself was the source of the illumination. But during the 1820s a new form of burner was introduced in which a controlled amount of air was admitted to the gas current, producing a high-temperature but nonluminous flame that heated a refractive, noncombustible material to a very high temperature. This became the source of light; the higher the temperature of the material, the whiter the colour of the light and the greater the output. By the 1880s, a woven network of cotton threads impregnated with thorium and cerium salts was the standard light-emitting material used in gas lamps.

The development of the electric lamp at the turn of the 19th century stemmed the trend toward gas lamps, and by 1911 the conversion of gas fixtures for use with electricity had begun. Soon electricity was rapidly replacing gas for general illuminating purposes. In England and Europe, however, gas enjoyed wide use for a number of years longer.

Electric lamps. Modern lamps and lighting began with the invention of the incandescent electric lamp about 1870. An incandescent lamp (*q.v.*) is one in which a filament gives off light when heated to incandescence by an electric current. The incandescent lamp was not the first lamp to use electricity, however; lighting devices employing an electric arc struck between electrodes of carbon had been developed early in the 19th century. These arc lamps, as they were called, were reliable but cumbersome devices that were best used for street lighting. In 1876 Pavel Yablochkov, a Russian electrical engineer, introduced the Yablochkov candle. This was an arc lamp having parallel carbon rods separated by porcelain clay, which vaporized during burning of the arc. Alternating current was used to ensure equal rates of consumption of the two points of the rods. This lamp was widely used in street lighting for a time.

In the decades before the Edison incandescent carbon-filament lamp was patented in 1880, numerous scientists had directed their efforts toward producing a satisfactory incandescent lighting system. Outstanding among them was Sir Joseph Wilson Swan of England. In 1850 Swan had devised carbon filaments of paper; later he used cotton thread treated with sulfuric acid and mounted in glass vacuum bulbs (only possible after 1875).

The final development of the incandescent lamp was the result of concurrent work by Swan and Thomas A. Edison of the United States, using the vacuum pump of Hermann Sprengel and Sir William Crookes. These lamps by Swan and Edison consisted of a filament of carbon wire in an evacuated glass bulb, two ends of the wire being brought out through a sealed cap and thence to the electric supply. When the supply was connected, the filament glowed and, by virtue of the vacuum, did not oxidize away quickly as it would have done in air. The invention of a completely practical lamp ordinarily is credited to Edison, who began studying the problem in 1877 and within a year and a half had made more than 1,200 experiments. On Oct. 21, 1879, Edison lighted a lamp containing a carbonized thread for the filament. The lamp burned steadily for two days. Later he learned that filaments of carbonized visiting card paper (bristol board) would give several hundred hours' life. Soon carbonized bamboo was found acceptable and was used as the filament material. Extruded cellulose filaments were introduced by Swan in 1883.

Concurrently, recognizing that the series wiring systems then used for arc lights would not be satisfactory for incandescent lamps, Edison directed much effort toward the development of dynamos and other necessary equipment for multiple circuits.

The first commercial installation of Edison's lamp was made in May 1880 on the steamship *Columbia.* In 1881 a New York City factory was lighted with Edison's system, and the commercial success of the incandescent lamp was quickly established.

The most important subsequent improvement in the incandescent lamp was the development of metallic filaments, particularly of tungsten. Tungsten filaments quickly replaced ones made of carbon, tantalum, and metalized carbon in the early 1900s, and they are still used in most filament lamps today. Tungsten is highly suitable for such lamps because of all the materials suitable for drawing into filament wires, it has the highest melting point. This means that lamps can operate at higher temperatures and therefore emit both whiter light and more light for the same electrical input than was possible with less durable and less refractory carbon filaments. The first tungsten-filament lamps, introduced in the United States in 1907, made use of pressed tungsten. By 1910 a process (patented in 1913) for producing drawn tungsten filaments had been discovered.

The early tungsten lamps, like carbon lamps, suffered from the migration of filament molecules to the glass bulb, causing a blackening of the bulb, a loss in light output, and progressive thinning of the filament until it broke. About 1913 it was found that the introduction of a small amount of inert gas (argon or nitrogen) reduced migration and enabled the filament to be run at a higher temperature, giving a whiter light, higher efficiency, and longer life. Further improvements followed, including the development of the coiled filament.

Electric discharge lamps. During the late 19th century, Sir William Crookes and other physicists experimented with methods of generating radiation by striking an arc between electrodes in an evacuated tube to which small amounts of an elemental gas had been admitted. In about 1910 the French physicist Georges Claude developed such a tube with neon gas as the filling; when a high voltage was applied to the two electrodes at either end of the tube, it emitted a deep red light. Neon signs soon decorated the exteriors of commercial buildings in the world's cities, and experiments with other vapour fillings—such as mercury, argon, helium, krypton, and xenon—enabled a variety of colours to be produced.

Using the same basic principle, Peter Cooper Hewitt marketed the mercury-arc lamp in 1901, the energy efficiency of which proved to be two or three times that of the contemporary incandescent lamp. Creating a nearly shadow-free light and less glare, the lamp immediately found wide use for industrial and street lighting in the United States.

A promising electric discharge lamp developed in Europe by 1931 was the high-intensity sodium-vapour lamp (*q.v.*), and although it was not satisfactory for commercial or domestic use because of its characteristic yellow colour, by the mid-20th century sodium-vapour lamps were being used for street and highway lighting and for the illumination of bridges and vehicular tunnels all over the world.

Despite these inventions, electric discharge lamps were little used in interior lighting until the development in the 1930s of the fluorescent tube. This is a long tube with a mercury-vapour filling, and inner walls coated with a material which fluoresces white or near white when subjected to the radiation of the mercury discharge. This fluorescence multiplies the lamp's light emission by a hundredfold. Fluorescent lamps gradually became a mainstay of interior lighting, particularly in offices, factories, and other work environments.

Modern electrical light sources. By the mid-20th century the atmospheric arc lamp was used chiefly in large-wattage units for searchlights, for projectors calling for a high intensity and concentrated source, and for other special applications requiring small but powerful sources of blue and ultraviolet energy.

Incandescent electric lamps remain the most common source of home illumination and are used for most portable lamps. They are inexpensive, reliable, and readily available, but they are inefficient in their use of energy.

Luminescent lamps, which produce less heat than incandescent lamps, include electric discharge lamps, semiconductor lamps, and chemical lamps. Of the electric discharge lamps, the fluorescent lamp (*q.v.*) gives off a neutral white light, the sodium-vapour lamp emits a yellow-orange light, and the mercury-vapour lamp gives off a whitish blue-green light.

Glow lamps are very low-power electric discharge lamps, with large metal electrodes in an atmosphere of neon. The neon glows orange near the negative electrode, producing a dim light suitable for pilot or indicator lamps. Neon lamps for signs are also electric discharge lamps. The light-emitting diode (LED) is a form of luminescent lamp. The device is a crystalline semiconductor diode; when current flows through the diode, electrons combine with "holes" (localized positive charges) and drop to a state of lower energy. Part of the released energy is emitted as a photon. The colour of light given off depends on the crystal material used. Green LED's, for example, are made of gallium phosphide treated with nitrogen. LED's do not produce enough light for illumination, but are used for indicators. Segmented LED's provide the digital displays on many electronic devices.

The electroluminescent lamp, another semiconductor lamp, consists of a flat-plate capacitor with a phosphor (similar to those used with fluorescent lamps) in the dielectric; it is used with alternating current. These lamps are used for night-lights and engineering applications such as luminous instrument panels.

Lamp of Diogenes (monument): *see* Choragic Monument of Lysicrates.

lamp shell, also called BRACHIOPOD, any member of the phylum Brachiopoda, a group of bottom-dwelling marine invertebrates that superficially resemble bivalve mollusks.

Although no longer numerous, they were once one of the most abundant forms of life. Great diversity existed among brachiopods in the past; modern brachiopods, however, exhibit little variety. They are commonly tongue-shaped, with a surface that may be smooth, spiny, covered with platelike structures, or ridged. Most modern brachiopods are yellowish or white, but some have red stripes or spots; others are pink, brown, or dark gray. The tongue-shaped shells of *Lingula* are brown with dark-green splotches; rarely, they are cream yellow and green.

The shells of brachiopods are fundamentally dissimilar from those of the mollusks, as the valves of the shell enclose the body dorsally and ventrally, rather than laterally as in mollusks. The lower valve is often larger than the upper one, with an upturned 'beak' and rounded aperture near the hinge—a shape reminiscent of a Roman lamp, from which the name lamp shell is derived. Internally brachiopods differ from bivalve mollusks even more markedly. The body of the brachiopod is surprisingly small, measuring only about 5 to 100 millimetres (0.2 to 4 inches). A few brachiopods occur in deep water, but most are confined to shallow continental-shelf habitats. They are typically attached to solid surfaces either by a stalk or by direct cementation of the ventral valve.

Other than their usefulness in dating geological periods, members of this phylum have no economic value, except as curios and museum pieces.

Lampang, town and *changwat* (province) in the Northern region of Thailand, located in the forested Khun Tan Range. The provincial capital of Lampang (or Lakhon) is a commercial centre located on the Mae Nam Wang (Wang River). One of Thailand's largest provincial towns, it was once the seat of an independent principality and retains the old walled city as its nucleus. There is a large sugar plant nearby at Ko Kha. The town is on the Bangkok–Chiengmai railway and at the junction of highways to Chiengmai and Chiang Rai. There is an airport with scheduled flights to other Thai cities.

The province occupies an area of 4,839 sq mi (12,534 sq km). The forests are a source of teak; and mineral products include lignite, antimony, lead, and tungsten. Tobacco, rice, beans, cotton, and sugarcane are grown. Pop. (2000 prelim.) town, 69,600; province, 779,215.

Lampedusa, Giuseppe Tomasi di (Italian author): *see* Tomasi di Lampedusa, Giuseppe.

Lampedusa Island, Italian ISOLA DI LAMPEDUSA, Latin LOPADUSSA, largest island (area 8 sq mi [21 sq km]) of the Isole (islands) Pelagie (which include Linosa and Lampione islets), in the Mediterranean Sea between Malta and Tunis, 105 mi southwest of Licata, Sicily. Administratively the group is part of Agrigento province, Sicily, Italy. Lampedusa's greatest length is about 7 mi (11 km), its greatest width about 2 mi; it rises to 436 ft (133 m) above sea level. The Lopadusa of the Greek geographer Strabo and the Lipadosa of the poet Ludovico Ariosto's *Orlando furioso,* the island has remains of prehistoric hut foundations, Punic tombs, and Roman buildings. In 1436 it was given by Alfonso of Aragon to Don Giovanni de Caro, baron of Montechiaro. A thousand slaves were taken from its population in 1553 by the Turks. In 1661 its then owner, Ferdinand Tommasi, received the title of prince from Charles II of Spain. In 1737 the English earl of Sandwich visited the island and found only one inhabitant. Some French settlers established themselves there in 1760, and in 1843 Ferdinand II of Naples founded a colony. After the Allied victory in North Africa in World War II, British and U.S. planes bombed Lampedusa. It surrendered on June 12, 1943, and Linosa and Lampione submitted on June 13.

Lampedusa's soil is calcareous; it was covered with scrub until comparatively recent times, but this has been cut, and the rock is now bare. The poor soil and lack of irrigation have limited the cultivation of figs and olives. The valleys, however, are fertile, and grapes and wheat are grown. Fishing is the economic mainstay of the island, and sardines and anchovies are packed for export. Coral and sponges are also collected. The village of Lampedusa, on the southern part of the island, is the centre of the commune of the same name, which includes Linosa and Lampione. The village has a harbour dredged to a depth of 13 ft. Linosa, about 30 mi north-northeast, has an area of 2 sq mi and is entirely volcanic. It has landing places on the south and west and is more fertile than Lampedusa, but suffers water shortages from lack of springs. Pop. (2000 est.) Lampedusa and Linosa mun., 5,937.

Lamphun, also spelled LAMPOON, town and *changwat* (province) in the Northern region of Thailand. Lamphun, the provincial capital, is an old walled city on the Nam Mae (river) Kuang, 16 mi (26 km) south of Chiengmai. Although located on the Bangkok–Chiengmai railway, it lost its commercial importance to Chiengmai after 1921. Wat Phra That Haripunjaya is Lamphun's most famous temple; the intricate doors of its sanctuary are covered in gold leaf. Neighbouring Pa Sang produces colourful cotton cloth as a major cottage industry.

The province, occupying an area of 1,740 sq mi (4,506 sq km), was the site of an early Mon kingdom, founded in the 6th century. The kingdom fell to Thai forces in the 13th century with the rise of Chiengmai and remained a province of the Lanno Thai kingdom until the late 19th century. Fluorite is mined and teak is forested in the western mountains. Rice and tobacco are the main crops. Pop. (2000 prelim.) town, 15,000; province, 411,231.

Lampman, Archibald (b. Nov. 17, 1861, Morpeth, Ont.—d. Feb. 10, 1899, Ottawa), important Canadian poet of the Confederation group, whose most characteristic work sensitively records the feelings evoked by scenes and incidents of the outdoors.

Educated at Trinity College in the University of Toronto, he lived in Ottawa, employed in the post office department of the Canadian civil service, from 1883 until his death. He collaborated with two other Ottawa poets in the writing of a weekly column, "At the Mermaid Inn," in the Toronto *Globe* (1892–93).

Lampman, 1891
By courtesy of the Public Archives of Canada

Lampman was repelled by the mechanization of urban life and escaped to the countryside whenever possible. After being influenced by the craftsmanship and perfection of form of classical poetry and by the lyrical verse of such English Romantic poets as Wordsworth, Shelley, Tennyson, and Keats, he wrote nature poems celebrating the beauties of Ottawa and its environs and the Gatineau countryside of Quebec. Although Lampman was a Socialist and a critic of party politics and organized religion, only a few short poems reflect his radical ideas on politics and economics.

During his lifetime Lampman published two volumes of verse, *Among the Millet and Other Poems* (1888) and *Lyrics of Earth* (1893). After his death, his friend and literary executor, Duncan Campbell Scott, edited *The Poems of Archibald Lampman* (1900) and *Lyrics of Earth: Poems and Ballads* (1925). Several uncollected poems were published in 1943.

Lampong, also called ABUNG, people indigenous to Lampung province on the Sunda Strait in southern Sumatra, Indonesia. They speak Lampong, a Malayo-Polynesian language that has been written in a script related to the Hindu alphabet. A dependency of the Sultan of Bantam (western Java) after 1550, southern Sumatra contains many Lampong whose ancestors were granted noble titles. Great value continues to be placed on such distinctions; titles are commonly bought from tribal chiefs. Former foreign rule has strengthened the internal clan organization of Lampong villages, which in turn comprise the larger tribal unit, the *marga,* headed by a chief. The Lampong are organized patrilineally; inheritance passes only to the eldest son, who must support the family if the father dies. A few noble or wealthy Lampong preserve a matriarchal arrangement in which only women can own property. Marriage is clan exogamic. The Lampong practice swidden agriculture, growing dry rice, coffee, and pepper, the last as a cash crop for trade in nearby towns. Although mostly converted to Islām, the Lampong also still observe their traditional religious animism and customary law, even when these contradict Islāmic practices.

Lampoon (Thailand): *see* Lamphun.

lampoon, virulent satire in prose or verse that is a gratuitous and sometimes unjust and malicious attack on an individual. Although the term came into use in the 17th century from the French, examples of the lampoon are found as early as the 3rd century BC in the plays of Aristophanes, who lampooned Euripides in *The Frogs* and Socrates in *The Clouds.* In English literature the form was particularly popular during the Restoration and the 18th century, as exemplified in the lampoons of John Dryden, Thomas Brown, and John Wilkes and in dozens of anonymous satires.

Lamprecht, Karl Gottfried (b. Feb. 25, 1856, Jessen, Saxony—d. May 10, 1915, Leipzig), German historian who was one of the first scholars to develop a systematic theory of psychological factors in history.

He studied history, political science, economics, and art at the universities of Göttingen, Leipzig, and Munich (1874–79). In 1878 he completed his doctoral dissertation at Leipzig on the 11th-century French economy. The influence upon him of Jacob Burckhardt's *Civilization of the Renaissance in Italy,* with its emphasis on psychological characteristics of certain historical epochs, was evident in one of Lamprecht's earliest essays, also published in 1878, "Individuality and Its Comprehension in the German Middle Ages," which first stated his critique of exterior factual data as the focus of scientific history. In 1879 he tutored in Cologne and taught at the Friedrich Wilhelm Gymnasium. His *Initialornamentik. . .* (1882) dealt with the psychological implications of 8th- to 13th-century artistic ornamentation and symbolism and provided the core for his later and more elaborated theory.

Lamprecht moved to Bonn (1881), where he jointly established a society for the study of Rhenish history (1883) and a journal on West German history and art (1882) and was appointed professor at the University of Bonn (1885). While he was at Bonn one of his best works, *Deutsches Wirtschaftsleben im Mittel-*

alter, 3 vol., (1885–86; "German Economic Life in the Middle Ages"), appeared. In 1890 he taught at the University of Marburg and a year later was made professor of history at the University of Leipzig.

Lamprecht's master work was the massive *Deutsche Geschichte,* 12 vol. (1891–1901; "German History"). It was a major contribution to the development of the Kulturgeschichte (History of Civilization) school in Germany and the centre of a heated controversy over the meaning of "scientific history." While he put special emphasis on economic groups and mass movements in social history, his principal thesis was that history achieves scientific status not through exactitude of detail in particular instances but rather through the achievement of a general and philosophical synthesis arising from the comparative study of collective psychologies in given periods of time.

Lamprecht's approach to history provoked great controversy, and he was highly criticized for his reductionist analysis, a priori system, and inadequately documented generalizations. It led, however, to a reexamination of historical methods and to the acceptance of social and cultural history as a legitimate sphere of scholarly research.

lamprey, any of about 22 species of primitive, fishlike, jawless vertebrates placed with hagfishes in the class Agnatha. Lampreys belong to the family Petromyzonidae. They live in coastal and freshwaters and are found in temperate regions around the world, except in Africa. Eel-like, scaleless animals, they range

Lamprey (*Lampetra*) on rainbow trout
Oxford Scientific Films—Bruce Coleman Ltd.

from about 15 to 100 centimetres (6 to 40 inches) long. They have well-developed eyes, one or two dorsal fins, a tail fin, a single nostril on top of the head, and seven gill openings on each side of the body. Like the hagfishes, they lack bones, jaws, and paired fins. The skeleton of a lamprey consists of cartilage; the mouth is a round, sucking aperture provided with horny teeth.

Lampreys begin life as burrowing, freshwater larvae (ammocoetes). At this stage, they are toothless, have rudimentary eyes, and feed on microorganisms. After several years, they transform into adults and typically move into the sea to begin a parasitic life, attaching to a fish by their mouths and feeding on the blood and tissues of the host. To reproduce, lampreys return to freshwater, build a nest, then spawn (lay their eggs) and die.

Not all lampreys spend time in the sea. Some are landlocked and remain in freshwater. A notable example is the landlocked race *Petromyzon marinus dorsatus* of the sea lamprey. This form entered the Great Lakes of North America and, because of its parasitic habits, had a disastrous killing influence on lake trout and other commercially valuable fishes before control measures were devised. Other lampreys, such as the brook lamprey (*Lampetra planeri*), also spend their entire lives in freshwater. They are nonparasitic, however, and do not feed after becoming adults; instead they reproduce and die.

Lampreys have long been used to some extent as food. They are, however, of no great positive value to man.

lamprophyre, any of a group of dark gray to black intrusive igneous rocks that generally occur as dikes (tabular bodies inserted in fissures). Such rocks are characterized by a porphyritic texture in which large crystals (phenocrysts) of dark, iron-magnesium (mafic) minerals are enclosed in a fine-grained to dense matrix (groundmass). The abundance, large size, well-formed crystal outline, and brilliantly reflecting cleavage faces of the mafic phenocrysts give the rock a striking appearance. Mafic minerals, including biotite, hornblende, augite, or olivine, not only constitute virtually all of the phenocrysts but occur in the groundmass as well, together with much potash feldspar, plagioclase, or feldspathoid.

Petrographically, lamprophyres are set apart from most other igneous rocks by the presence of mafics, by the lack of feldspar phenocrysts, and by the abundance of mafics combined with alkali-rich feldspar. Chemically, the lamprophyres are unique because of their low silica content and a high iron, magnesium, and alkali content. The commonest lamprophyres are associated with large masses of granite and diorite. Classic examples occur in the Highlands and southern uplands of Scotland, the Lake District of Ireland, the Vosges, the Black Forest, and the Harz Mountains.

Lamprophyres show a strong tendency to weather and decompose. Many have been altered, undoubtedly while the rocks lay some distance beneath the surface. The common alteration products include carbonatite, chlorite, serpentine, and limonite.

Lampsacus, ancient Greek city on the Asiatic shore of the Hellespont, best known for its wines, and the chief seat of the worship of Priapus, a god of procreation and fertility. Colonized in 654 BC by Ionian Phocaea, the city had a fine harbour. It took part in the Ionian revolt against Persia (499) and later joined the Delian League. Upon the fall of Athens in 405, Lampsacus came under Persian control until Alexander freed it with the rest of Greece during his invasion in 334.

The city, which became the site of one of Alexander's mints, seems to have been prosperous, as indicated by the high tribute it paid to the Delian League.

Lampung, *propinsi* (province), southern Sumatra, Indonesia, bounded by the Java Sea on the east, the Sunda Strait on the south, the Indian Ocean on the west, and Sumatera Selatan (South Sumatra) province on the north and northwest. It covers an area of 12,860 sq mi (33,307 sq km) and includes the islands of Sebuku, Sebesi, Sertung, and Rakata in Sunda Strait. The area formed part of the kingdom of Kantoli in southern Sumatra in the beginning of the 6th century and in the 14th century was included in the Hindu Majapahit Empire of eastern Java. Hindu and Buddhist archaeological remains have been found at Palas, Talangpadang, Liwa, and Gunung (mount) Besar. In the 16th century, Lampung was part of the Muslim state of Bantam (now Banten) under Hasanuddin (ruled 1552–70). The Dutch incorporated Lampung into their colonial empire in 1860. It became part of the Republic of Indonesia in 1950.

The Banjaran (mountains) Bengkulen, a portion of the Pegunungan (mountains) Barisan, run the length of the province from the northwest to southeast and are surmounted by volcanic cones including Gunung Batai 5,518 ft (1,682 m) and Tangkit (mount) Tebak, 6,939 ft. The mountains are flanked by narrow coastland on the southwest and by rapidly descending highlands on the northeast. The eastern lowland area of Lampung stretches from the foothills of the Banjaran Bengkulen to the belt of swamps along the eastern coast. The Sungai (river) Sekampung, Sungai Seputih, and Wai (stream) Tulangbewang descend the eastern slopes of the Bengkulen and drain eastward into the Java Sea. Mangrove and freshwater swamp forests are found along the coast; tropical lowland evergreen rain forests extend from the coastal swamps into the mountains.

Most of the population is engaged in agriculture; rubber, tea, coffee, soybeans, sweet potatoes, corn (maize), peanuts (groundnuts), copra, and palm oil are produced. Deep-sea fishing is also important. Industries include wood carving, food processing, cloth weaving, mat and basket making, and the production of handmade paper. Road and railway transport is confined to the foothills of the Banjaran Bengkulen and link Tanjung Kurang, the provincial capital, with Kotabumi, Panjang, and Telukbatung. The eastern half of the province relies mainly on riverine transport. The population is a mixture of Malay, Javanese, and Minangkabau. The Javanese are the most numerous because of a large influx of rural Javanese into Lampung in the early 20th century. Pop. (1995 est.) 6,680,000.

Lamu, town, port, and island in the Indian Ocean off the East African coast, 150 mi (241 km) north-northeast of Mombasa. It is administered as part of the Coast Province, Kenya. The port lies on the southeastern shore of the island. A former Persian, then Zanzibari, colony, Lamu Island rivalled Mombasa until the late 19th century as an entrepôt for gold, spices, and slaves. Pop. (1989) town, 8,800.

A list of the abbreviations used in the MICROPAEDIA *will be found at the end of this volume*

Lamut (people): *see* Even.

län, administrative subdivision (county) of Sweden; *see* landskap.

Lan Caihe (in Chinese mythology): *see* Lan Ts'ai-ho.

Lan Chang: *see* Lan Xang.

Lan-chou, Pinyin LANZHOU, conventional LANCHOW, capital of Kansu Province (*sheng*), China. A prefecture-level municipality (*shih*), it is also the command headquarters of the Lan-chou Military Region, incorporating Tsinghai, Kansu, and Shensi provinces, and Ningsia Hui Autonomous Region. It is situated on the upper course of the Huang Ho (river), where the river emerges from the mountains. Lan-chou has been a centre since early times, being at the southern end of the route leading via the Kansu Corridor across Central Asia; it also commands the approaches to the ancient capital area of Sian (Ch'ang-an) in Shensi Province from both the west and the northwest, as well as from the area of Koko Nor (lake) via the upper waters of the Huang Ho and its tributaries.

Petroleum refinery at Lan-chou, Kansu Province, China
Marc Riboud—Magnum

Originally in the territory of the Western

Ch'iang peoples, Lan-chou became part of the territory of Ch'in in the 6th century BC. In 81 BC, under the Han dynasty (206 BC–AD 220), it became the seat of Chin-ch'eng *hsien* (county) and later of Chin-ch'eng *chün* (commandery), the county being renamed Yün-wu. In the 4th century it was briefly the capital of the independent state of Earlier Liang. The Northern Wei dynasty (386–534) reestablished Chin-ch'eng commandery, renaming the county Tzu-ch'eng. Under the Sui dynasty (581–618) the city became the seat of Lan-chou prefecture for the first time, retaining this name under the T'ang dynasty (618–907). In 763 the area was overrun by the Tibetans and was then recovered by the T'ang in 843. Later it fell into the hands of the Hsi-Hsia (Tangut) dynasty (which flourished in Tsinghai from the 11th to 13th century) and was subsequently recovered by the Sung dynasty (960–1126) in 1041. The name Lan-chou was reestablished, and the county renamed Lan-chuan. After 1127 it fell into the hands of the Juchen dynasty, and after 1235 it came into the possession of the Mongols. Under the Ming dynasty (1368–1644) the prefecture was demoted to a county and placed under the administration of Lin-t'ao superior prefecture, but in 1477 Lan-chou was reestablished as a political unit. In 1739 the seat of Lin-t'ao was transferred to Lan-chou, which was later made a superior prefecture called Lan-chou. When Kansu became a separate province in 1666, Lan-chou became its capital.

The city was badly damaged during the rising of Kansu Muslims in 1864–75; in the 1920s and '30s it became a centre of Soviet influence in northwest China. During the Sino-Japanese War (1937–45) Lan-chou, linked with Hsi-an (Ch'ang-an) by highway in 1935, became the terminus of the 2,000-mile (3,200-kilometre) Chinese-Soviet highway, used as a route for Soviet supplies destined for the Hsi-an area. This highway remained the chief traffic artery of northwest China until the completion of the railway from Lan-chou to Wu-lu-mu-ch'i (Urumchi) in the Sinkiang Uighur autonomous region. During the war Lan-chou was heavily bombed by the Japanese.

Since 1949 Lan-chou has been transformed from the capital of a poverty-stricken province into the centre of a major industrial area. The Lung-hai Railway line was extended westward to Lan-chou from T'ien-shui by 1953. Later Lan-chou was linked with Peking via Pao-t'ou in Inner Mongolia, and lines were also constructed northwest to Wu-lu-mu-ch'i and westward via Hai-yen on the Koko Nor to Golmud (in Tsinghai). A thermal generating plant is supplied with coal from fields in Tsinghai. In addition, there is a hydroelectric station at Chu-la-ma Gorge in Kansu, and a large multipurpose dam has been built in the Liu-chia Gorge on the Huang Ho above Lan-chou.

The city is a centre of the petrochemical industry and has a large refinery linked to the fields at Yü-men by pipeline; it also manufactures equipment for the oil industry. In addition, Lan-chou produces locomotives and rolling stock for the northwestern railways, as well as machine tools and mining equipment. Aluminum products, industrial chemicals, and fertilizers are produced on a large scale, and there is a large rubber industry. Copper is mined in nearby Kao-lan. Lan-chou remains the collecting centre and market for agricultural produce and livestock from a wide area. Its textile industry is noted for the production of woolens. Leather goods are also produced. Since the 1960s Lan-chou has become the centre of China's atomic energy industry.

The city is the cultural centre of Kansu and the seat of Lan-chou University (founded 1909). The National Minorities Institute at Lan-chou and a number of scientific institutes are also located there. Pop. (1999 est.) 1,429,-673.

Lan Ts'ai-ho, Pinyin LAN CAIHE, in Chinese mythology, one of the Pa Hsien, the Eight Immortals of Taoism, whose true identity is much disputed. Artists depict Lan as a young man—or girl—carrying a flute or a pair of clappers and occasionally wearing only one shoe. Sometimes a basket of fruit is added.

Lan Ts'ai-ho, wood sculpture, 18th century; in the Musée Guimet, Paris

By courtesy of the Musee Guimet, Paris

In Chinese theatre, Lan is dressed in female clothes but speaks with a male voice. Lan traveled the streets singing ballads, some of which are still preserved, before being carried off to heaven in an intoxicated state by a stork, one of several Chinese symbols for immortality. *See also* Pa Hsien.

Lan-ts'ang Chiang (Asia): *see* Mekong River.

Lan Xang, also spelled LAN CHANG, Laotian kingdom that flourished from the 14th century until it was split into two separate kingdoms, Vien Chang and Luang Prabang, in the 18th century. Conflict with its Myanmar (Burmese) and Thai (Siamese) neighbours forced the kingdom's rulers to transfer the capital from Luang Prabang to Vientiane (1563), but the kingdom maintained its power and was at the height of its glory when the Dutch merchant Gerrit van Wusthof visited Vientiane in 1641.

Lanai, island, Maui county, Hawaii, U.S., across the Auau channel from Maui Island. Formed by the extinct volcano Palawai (3,370 feet [1,027 m]), it has an area of 140 square miles (363 square km). In 1854 a group of Mormon elders formed a colony there that failed 10 years later. Lanai was used primarily for cattle grazing until 1922, when it was purchased by the Dole Corporation for use as a pineapple plantation. In 1961, Castle & Cook, Inc., after merging with Dole, took over the management of the island. It is the largest privately owned isle in the Hawaiian chain. The principal company settlements are Lanai City and the port of Kaumalapau on the west coast. At the ruined village of Kaunolu, once the resort place of King Kamehameha I, can be seen the remains of houses and a *heiau* (temple). Lanai (meaning "conquest day") is the only one of the inhabited Hawaiian islands to have a known etymology. Most of the important place-names in the islands are so ancient that no translation is possible. Pop. (2000) 3,193.

Lanao, Lake, lake, west-central Mindanao, Philippines. It is situated just south of Marawi, northwest of the Butig Mountains. Lake Lanao is the second largest lake in the Philippines and has an area of 131 square miles (340 square km). Its outlet is the Agus River, which flows north, over Maria Cristina Falls, where there is a hydroelectric power plant, to Iligan Bay. There are numerous Muslim villages around the lake.

Lanark, royal burgh (town), South Lanarkshire council area, historic county of Lanarkshire, south-central Scotland, situated by the right bank of the River Clyde, southeast of the Glasgow metropolitan area. The town developed around a castle built by David I of Scotland (reigned 1124–53), who made the town a royal burgh.

Lanark is now primarily a residential town and an agricultural market centre, with regular livestock sales. New Lanark, 1 mile (1.6 km) south, was founded in 1785 as a cotton-spinning centre by David Dale with the support of Sir Richard Arkwright, inventor of the spinning frame. New Lanark became well known for its humane working and living conditions, brought about by the experiments of the socialist Robert Owen, Dale's son-in-law. New Lanark now houses a historic village and visitor centre with interpretive tours and exhibits. Pop. (1991) Lanark, 8,877.

Lanark, William Hamilton, Earl of: *see* Hamilton, William Hamilton, 2nd Duke of.

Lanarkshire, also called LANARK, historic county of south-central Scotland, roughly coinciding with the basin of the River Clyde. It is bounded to the south by the historic county of Dumfriesshire, to the east by Peeblesshire, Midlothian, and West Lothian, to the north by Stirlingshire and Dunbartonshire, and to the west by Renfrewshire and Ayrshire. It encompasses all of the council areas of South Lanarkshire and the City of Glasgow, most of the council area of North Lanarkshire, and part of the council area of East Dunbartonshire.

Lanarkshire probably became an administrative region during the reign of David I (1124–53). The county was the scene of several notable episodes in Scottish history. The Scottish nationalist William Wallace attacked the garrison at Lanark in 1297. In 1568 Mary, Queen of Scots, and her supporters were defeated in the Battle of Langside (located in Lanarkshire); this defeat led to her flight to England and imprisonment. The battles of Drumclog and Bothwell Bridge (both in 1679), between the Covenanters and government forces, also took place in the county. During the 17th and 18th centuries, Glasgow prospered as a port by tapping the growing trade with the American colonies. It subsequently became a major shipbuilding centre. Rapid industrial development, based mainly on textile manufacture, began in Lanarkshire in the middle of the 18th century. With the discovery of large iron deposits in the 19th century, an iron and steel industry developed. The county was in the forefront of the struggle to improve the lot of the working classes. In the early 19th century Robert Owen conducted his influential social welfare programs at his cotton mills in New Lanark. The decline of Lanarkshire's textile manufacture and traditional heavy industries during the late 20th century brought a period of difficult economic adjustment.

Lancashire, administrative, geographic, and historic county in northwestern England, bounded on the north by Cumberland and Westmorland (in the present administrative county of Cumbria), on the east by Yorkshire, on the south by Cheshire, and on the west by the Irish Sea. The administrative, geographic, and historic counties occupy somewhat different areas. The administrative county comprises 12 districts: West Lancashire; the boroughs of Burnley, Chorley, Fylde, Hyndburn, Pendle, Preston, Ribble Valley, Rossendale, South Ribble, and Wyre; and the city of Lancaster. The geographic county comprises the entire administrative county and the unitary authorities of Blackburn with Darwen and Black-

The village of Downham, Lancashire
Authenticated News International

pool. The administrative and geographic counties include a large area in the eastern boroughs of Pendle and Ribble Valley that belongs to the historic county of Yorkshire.

Apart from this area, the historic county of Lancashire encompasses the entire geographic county and the following areas: the Furness region, comprising the borough of Barrow-in-Furness and part of the district of South Lakeland in the administrative county of Cumbria; a small area west of Todmorden in the metropolitan borough of Calderdale; the parts of the unitary authorities of Halton and Warrington that lie north of the River Mersey; the city of Liverpool and all other metropolitan boroughs in the metropolitan county of Merseyside except Wirral; and most of the metropolitan county of Greater Manchester, including the historic core of Manchester and all or part of every metropolitan borough.

The geographic county comprises two principal physical regions. In the east the gritstones and shales of the Pennines form level, elevated plateaus. The highest summits are Wards Stone at 1,836 feet (560 m), Pendle at 1,831 feet (558 m), and Fair Snape at 1,701 feet (518 m). Coal-bearing rocks in the south form lower plateaus and benches that surround the heather moorlands of Rossendale. In the north are the scenic ridges of the Forest of Bowland. The western lowlands, formerly covered by extensive peat bogs, have largely been reclaimed. The flat coastline encouraged the growth of ports and resorts.

Neolithic artifacts have been found on the moorlands around Rochdale, and bronze implements at Winmarleigh, Colne, and Pilling. Several stone circles stand in Furness. Ribchester, Lancaster, Kirkham, Wigan, and Manchester (Mamucium) were occupied by the Romans. During the 7th and 8th centuries the Anglians, an Anglo-Saxon people, penetrated the area, and it became a province of the Danish in the 9th century. Lancashire was not a rich area in the Middle Ages. The Scottish border wars, the Black Death, and the drawn-out Wars of the Roses drained resources.

The key to the region's economic development was the textile industry. During the 16th and 17th centuries the towns of Lancashire began to prosper with the manufacture of linen and woolen cloth. The Industrial Revolution originated in Lancashire during the 18th century with the introduction of cotton manufacture. Industrial development led to the rapid growth of manufacturing towns such as Manchester, Bolton, and Blackburn; and Liverpool thrived as the main port.

Textiles and coal mining, the historic staple industries of the area, declined during the 20th century. After an economic downturn during the late 20th century, the economy began to stablilize around a mix of light industry, engineering, and service activities. The rich lowlands remain important agricultural regions. In the Fylde region, intensive dairy farming and other forms of livestock husbandry predominate. Market gardening flourishes north and south of the Ribble estuary. Lancaster and Preston are market and industrial centres, while the many coastal towns are tourist centres. Area administrative county, 1,119 square miles (2,898 square km); geographic county, 1,188 square miles (3,078 square km). Pop. (1998 est.) administrative county, 1,136,300; geographic county, 1,426,800.

Lancaster, urban area and city (district), administrative and historic county of Lancashire, England, at the head of the estuary of the River Lune, 7 miles (11 km) from the Irish Sea. Lancaster grew on the site of a Roman station, and traces of the Roman fortification walls remain. In the 11th century a feudal landowner, Roger of Poitou, founded or enlarged a castle on an eminence there and also founded the Priory of St. Mary as a cell of his Benedictine priory. The town grew around these institutions and was granted its first charter in 1193. Although twice destroyed by the Scots (in 1322 and 1389), Lancaster became a market centre, and in 1688 six trade companies were incorporated. It flourished briefly as a port in the late 18th century, but silting of the estuary caused its decline. In the English Civil Wars of the mid-17th century, the castle, held by the Parliamentarians, was three times besieged by Royalist forces.

The city has a range of industries, including furniture and linoleum manufacture. Because of its distance from the great urban centres of Manchester and Liverpool, attempts to found a cotton textile industry proved abortive, but synthetic fibres have become established, and the city is the headquarters of shoe manufacturer Reebok. The town remains a major market centre, having one of the largest livestock markets in northwestern England. A high proportion of professional, distributive, and retail employment reflects its traditional status as a regional centre for northern Lancashire. Lancaster lies on the railway line between southern Lancashire and the city of Carlisle and on the major British motorway between the city of Birmingham and Scotland.

Lancaster's buildings include a castle on the site of the Roman castrum, St. Mary's Church (mainly 15th-century), and the Roman Catholic Cathedral of St. Peter (built in 1859). The University of Lancaster (founded in 1964) is located in the city. The Storey Institute has technical and art schools, an art gallery, and a museum. Market Square contains a civic and regimental museum. In addition to the town of Lancaster, the city (district) includes a substantial rural and agricultural area and the seaside resort of Morecambe. Area 223 square miles (577 square km). Pop. (1991) urban area, 44,497; (1998 est.) city, 136,700.

Lancaster, city, Los Angeles county, southwestern California, U.S., in the Antelope Valley at the western edge of the Mojave Desert. It began as a Scottish settlement organized by M.L. Wicks (1882), who perhaps named it for his hometown in Pennsylvania. The valley largely supported cattle ranching until the early 1900s, when water, pumped by gasoline engines, transformed it into an agricultural area. Lancaster shares with Palmdale (south) development of aircraft, aerospace, and electronics industries. Edwards Air Force Base is immediately northeast. Borax, mined locally, is economically significant. Antelope Valley (junior) College (1929) is in Lancaster. Pop. (2000) 118,718.

Lancaster, city, seat (1800) of Fairfield county, south-central Ohio, U.S., on the Hocking River, 30 miles (48 km) southeast of Columbus. It was founded (1800) by Ebenezer Zane on land granted to him in payment for blazing Zane's Trace, a 266-mile (428-kilometre) wilderness road from Wheeling, W.Va. (then a part of Virginia) to Limestone (now Maysville), Ky. The first settlers came over this road in 1798; many of them were from Lancaster, Pa., for which the new town was named. Completion (1808) of the Lancaster Lateral Canal, connecting with the Ohio and Erie Canal, and the arrival (1851) of the Muskingum Valley Railroad spurred economic progress, which was further enhanced by the discovery (1887) of natural gas in the vicinity. Lancaster's economy is well diversified; it is a trading centre for an agricultural region chiefly supporting dairying, beef cattle, pigs, corn, wheat, and soybeans, while varied manufactures include glassware, cereal, paper products, industrial lighting, auto parts, boiler equipment, and electronics. A branch campus (1956) of Ohio University is in the city.

The birthplace of the American Civil War general William Tecumseh Sherman and his brother John Sherman, sponsor of the Sherman Antitrust Act, is preserved as a state memorial. Mount Pleasant, a 250-foot (75-metre) rock overlooking the city, was a favourite Indian lookout, while the nearby Tarlton Cross Mound State Memorial is the only known Indian earthwork shaped in the form of a cross. Several covered bridges are in the vicinity. Inc. 1831. Pop. (2000) 35,335.

Lancaster, city, seat of Lancaster county, southeastern Pennsylvania, U.S., and the centre of a metropolitan area comprising a number of small towns and boroughs, 71 miles (114 km) west of Philadelphia. The original site on Conestoga Creek, known as Gibson's Pasture, or Hickory Town, was made the county seat in 1729, the year after Lancaster county (named for the English city and shire) was created. During the American Revolution, the Continental Congress, fleeing from Philadelphia, held a one-day session there (Sept. 27, 1777), and the Supreme Executive Council of Pennsylvania took refuge in the city for nine months in 1777–78. Lancaster was considered for the new national capital in 1790. From 1799 to 1812 it was the capital of Pennsylvania.

The stone-surfaced turnpike from Lancaster to Philadelphia was completed in 1794. President James Buchanan lived in Lancaster, and his home, Wheatland (1828), has been restored; he is buried in Woodward Hill Cemetery. Thaddeus Stevens, Abolitionist congressman, also lived in the city; he is buried in a small cemetery amid the graves of blacks. The

Wheatland, home of President James Buchanan, Lancaster, Pa.
Bond

18th-century Conestoga wagon (symbol of the pioneers' trek westward) and the Pennsylvania (Kentucky) rifle were produced in Lancaster, which after the Revolution became an iron-founding centre. It was in Lancaster that F.W. Woolworth opened (1879–80) his first successful "5-and-10 cent" store. The city's modern economy is balanced between agriculture (cattle, dairy products, grain, and tobacco), services, and industry. Manufactures include linoleum, electrical products, and farm machinery; printing is also important.

In the heart of the Pennsylvania Dutch country, Lancaster's residents include members of the Amish, Mennonite, and Dunkard churches, distinguished by their black, buttonless attire and nonuse of modern devices. The restored Hans Herr House (1719) is an early example of medieval Germanic architecture; it was used as a Mennonite meetinghouse. The state's agricultural history is depicted at the nearby Amish Farm and House and the Pennsylvania Farm Museum of Landis Valley. Franklin and Marshall College was formed in 1853, and Lancaster Bible College was founded in 1933. Also nearby is the Ephrata Cloister, site of a German monastic community, which flourished in the mid-18th century. Inc. borough, 1742; city, 1818. Pop. (1992 est.) city, 57,171; Lancaster MSA, 427,316.

Lancaster, city, seat of Lancaster county, northern South Carolina, U.S., near the Catawba River. It was founded in the 1750s by settlers from Lancaster, Pa. The architect Robert Mills designed the jail (1823) and the courthouse (1828). In the early 19th century the community was identified with the Waxhaw Revival, part of the Great Revival (a nationwide movement of religious vagaries), and witchcraft was once legally recognized. A textile-based economy prevails, supplemented by light industries. The University of South Carolina at Lancaster was opened in 1959. A state historical park 8 miles (13 km) north marks the site of President Andrew Jackson's birthplace. Inc. village, 1802; town, 1830; city, 1898. Pop. (1992 est.) 9,060.

Lancaster, EARLS AND DUKES OF, titled English nobility of several creations, grouped below chronologically and indicated by the symbol •.

•Lancaster, Edmund, 1st Earl of, byname CROUCHBACK (b. Jan. 16, 1245, London, Eng.—d. *c.* June 5, 1296, Bayonne, France), fourth (but second surviving) son of King Henry III of England and Eleanor of Provence, who founded the house of Lancaster.

At the age of 10, Edmund was invested by Pope Innocent IV with the kingdom of Sicily (April 1255), as an expression of his conflict with the Holy Roman Emperor, who held Sicily; but Edmund was never more than an absentee titular king, and Pope Alexander IV canceled the grant (December 1258).

In 1265 Edmund received the earldom of Leicester, and two years later was created Earl of Lancaster. He joined the crusade of his elder brother, the Lord Edward (1271–1272); and Edward, on his accession as King Edward I, found in Edmund a loyal supporter. In 1275, two years after the death of his first wife, Edmund married Blanche of Artois, the widow of Henry III of Navarre and Champagne, and assumed the title Count Palatine of Champagne and Brie. When the court of King Philip IV of France pronounced that the king of England had forfeited Gascony, Edmund renounced his homage to Philip and withdrew with his wife to England. He was appointed lieutenant of Gascony in 1296 but died in the same year, leaving his son Thomas to succeed him in his English possessions.

Edmund's nickname "Crouchback" (meaning "Crossback," or crusader) was misinterpreted, probably intentionally, by his direct descendant, King Henry IV, who, in claiming the throne (1399), asserted that Edmund had really been Henry III's eldest son but had been disinherited as a hunchback.

•Lancaster, Thomas, 2nd Earl of, EARL OF LEICESTER, EARL OF DERBY (b. *c.* 1278—d. March 22, 1322, Pontefract, Yorkshire, Eng.), a grandson of King Henry III of England and the main figure in the baronial opposition to King Edward II. His opposition to royal power derived more from personal ambition than from a desire for reform.

The son of Edmund ("Crouchback"), 1st Earl of Lancaster, he became involved in politics during the controversy over Edward II's favourite, Piers Gaveston, and was among the earls who demanded Gaveston's banishment in 1308 and who compelled Edward in 1310 to surrender his power to a committee of "Ordainers," among whom he himself was numbered. After Gaveston returned to England in December 1311, Lancaster and other barons formed a confederacy to defend the Ordinances, and in the ensuing conflict it was on Lancaster's territory that Gaveston was executed in 1312.

Pardoned by Edward II in 1313, Lancaster forced changes in the royal household in 1314 and by 1315 virtually controlled England. But his ambition became apparent, and a failure of statesmanship led to a fresh baronial grouping that by the compromise Treaty of Leake (1318) effected a formal reconciliation between him and the king. The rise of Hugh Le Despenser the Elder and Hugh Le Despenser the Younger as royal favourites by 1318 renewed Lancaster's quarrel with Edward, who, after their banishment in 1321, took up arms on their behalf. Lancaster was defeated by the king's forces at Boroughbridge and was executed near his castle of Pontefract, where his tomb became a centre of pilgrimage.

•Lancaster, Henry, 3rd Earl of, EARL OF LEICESTER, LORD LANCASTER (b. *c.* 1281—d. Sept. 22, 1345), second son of Edmund ("Crouchback"), 1st Earl of Lancaster, and the brother of Thomas, 2nd Earl of Lancaster.

After his brother's execution in 1322, Henry was so little suspected of opposing King Edward II that he was allowed possession of another of the family titles, the earldom of Leicester (1324). He held lands adjacent to the increasing possessions in South Wales of Edward II's favourites, Hugh Le Despenser and his son and namesake, and in September 1326 he joined Queen Isabella and Roger Mortimer after their return from France to depose the king. Henry captured Edward II at Neath Abbey and detained him at Kenilworth. He was a member of the deputation that informed the king of his deposition. In 1327 he was made chief of the Council of Regency, and after entering a petition in Parliament he was reinstated to much of the Lancastrian inheritance and allowed the title of Earl of Lancaster.

He soon quarreled with Mortimer. Lancaster complained that the Council of Regency was ignored and refused to attend the Salisbury Parliament of October 1328. He gathered troops at Winchester but was compelled to make peace. In 1330 he was one author of the plot that, with King Edward III's approval, overthrew Mortimer. About this time his eyesight failed, and after Mortimer's fall he retired from public life.

•Lancaster, Henry, 1st Duke and 4th Earl of, EARL OF LEICESTER, EARL OF DERBY, EARL OF LINCOLN, EARL OF MORAY, LORD LANCASTER (b. *c.* 1300, perhaps at Grosmont Castle, Monmouthshire, Wales—d. March 24, 1361, Leicester, Leicestershire, Eng.), soldier and diplomatist, the most trusted adviser of King Edward III of England (reigned 1327–77). He was unquestionably the most powerful feudal lord in England at that time.

The son of Henry, 3rd Earl of Lancaster, he was the great-grandson of King Henry III and grandfather of King Henry IV. Created Earl of Derby in 1337, he succeeded to his father's earldoms of Lancaster and Leicester in 1345. In 1349 he was made Earl of Lincoln and in 1351 Duke of Lancaster, with sovereign (or palatine) powers within his domains. King David II of Scotland created him Earl of Moray in 1359.

During the Hundred Years' War between France and England (1337–1453), Henry served in the naval battles off Sluis (now in The Netherlands) in 1340 and off Winchelsea, Sussex, in 1350. From 1345 to 1347 he was Edward III's lieutenant and captain in southwestern France; he won a notable victory over a superior French force at Auberoche in Périgord, October 1345, and sacked Poitiers in October 1346. In 1349 he was appointed captain and vice-regent of Gascony and Poitou. As Edward's commissioner in France, he was largely responsible for negotiating in May 1360 the provisional Treaty of Brétigny, ending the first phase of the war. At various times he was sent on embassies to most of the courts of Europe. He died of the plague.

Upon the death of Lancaster's older daughter, Maud, in 1362, the Lancastrian titles and estates passed to his younger daughter, Blanche, and her husband, John of Gaunt. Their son became King Henry IV, the first Lancastrian ruler of England.

•Lancaster, John of Gaunt, Duke of: *see* John of Gaunt, Duke of Lancaster.

Lancaster, HOUSE OF, a cadet branch of the house of Plantagenet (*q.v.*). In the 15th century, it provided three kings of England—Henry IV, Henry V, and Henry VI—and, defeated by the house of York (*q.v.*), passed on its claims to the Tudor dynasty.

The family name first appeared in 1267, when the title earl of Lancaster was granted to Edmund "Crouchback" (1245–96), the youngest son of Henry III. Two of Edmund's sons by his second wife, Blanche of Artois, succeeded to the title: Thomas, Earl of Lancaster (d. 1322), and Henry, Earl of Lancaster (d. 1345). Henry's son, Henry, 1st Duke of Lancaster (d. 1361), was survived only by two coheiresses. The elder daughter, Maud, married to William, duke of Bavaria, died without issue a year after her father. The Lancastrian inheritance thus fell to the younger daughter, Blanche, and to her husband, John of Gaunt (d. 1399), third surviving son of Edward III. After Gaunt's death his son Henry of Lancaster deposed Richard II and became king himself, as Henry IV. On his accession the duchy of Lancaster was merged in the crown, and the house of Lancaster, in the persons of Henry IV, Henry V, and Henry VI, ruled England for more than 60 years.

Henry V alone had the strength to rule; and his marriage to the daughter of the mad King Charles VI of France did not improve his son's chances. Henry IV had founded his title to the throne on the descent of Lancaster from Henry III in order to avoid the greater claim of the heirs of Gaunt's elder brother Lionel, Duke of Clarence; in the end his grandson was defeated by Edward IV of the house of York—the heir both of Clarence and of Gaunt's younger brother Edmund, Duke of York.

The last remaining fragment of Lancastrian title was that which Henry VII derived through Gaunt's legitimized bastard line, the Beaufort family. By the time Henry VII had inaugurated the Tudor monarchy, the Lancaster lands were firmly in the hands of the crown.

Lancaster, Burt, original name BURTON STEPHEN LANCASTER (b. Nov. 2, 1913, New York, N.Y., U.S.—d. Oct. 20, 1994, Century City, Calif.), American film actor known for his portrayal of physically tough, emotionally sensitive characters.

After two years at New York University in the mid-1930s, Lancaster became part of a two-man acrobatic team that toured with various circuses, providing him with the experience to later perform his own stunt work in films. After World War II service in Italy, he was discovered by a stage producer who gave him a part in a short-lived play, *A Sound of Hunting* (1945). A talent scout took him to Hollywood, where he made a successful entry into motion pictures with *The Killers* (1946).

Despite Lancaster's obvious ability to give

exciting performances in adventure films such as *The Crimson Pirate* (1952), he soon showed a sincere, sensitive side in such powerful films as *Come Back, Little Sheba* (1952), *From Here to Eternity* (1953), *The Rose Tattoo* (1955), and *Separate Tables* (1958). His title role in *Elmer Gantry* brought him an Oscar from the Academy of Motion Picture Arts and Sciences in 1960, and in 1962 he won the Venice Festival Award for *The Birdman of Alcatraz.* The following year he appeared as the title character in the Italian film *Il Gattopardo* (*The Leopard*), adapted by Luchino Visconti from the Giuseppe de Lampedusa novel about an aging nobleman during the period of Italian unification. His later films included *The Swimmer* (1968), *1900* (1976), *Atlantic City* (1981), and *Local Hero* (1983).

Lancaster, Sir James (b. *c.* 1554, Basingstoke, Hampshire, Eng.—d. June 6, 1618, London), merchant who commanded the first English vessel to reach the East Indies and who established the first English trading post in Southeast Asia.

In 1588 Lancaster served under Sir Francis Drake as commander of the *Edward Bonaventure* against the Spanish Armada. On April 10, 1591, commanding the same ship, he sailed from Plymouth for the East Indies. He reached the island of Penang, west of the Malay Peninsula, in June 1592, remaining there until September and plundering every vessel he encountered. He returned to England in May 1594.

In April 1601, in command of the *Red Dragon,* Lancaster went on the first trading expedition of the East India Company. At Bantam, Java, he established the first of the company's trading posts. He was knighted after his return to England in 1603. Lancaster remained a director of the company, and he sponsored several voyages in search of the Northwest Passage, the American Arctic waterway linking the Atlantic and Pacific oceans.

Lancaster, Joseph (b. Nov. 25, 1778, London, Eng.—d. Oct. 24, 1838, New York, N.Y., U.S.), British-born educator who developed the system of mass education known as the Lancasterian method, a monitorial, or "mutual," approach in which brighter or more proficient children were used to teach other children under the direction of an adult. In the early 19th century the system, as developed by Lancaster, Andrew Bell, and Jean-Baptiste Girard, was widely used to provide the rudiments of education for numbers of poor children in Europe and North America.

Lancaster's teaching career began in 1789 when he asked his father's permission to bring some poor children home in order to teach them to read. Crowds of children came to him; since he couldn't afford to hire extra teachers or assistants, he had the idea of making those pupils who knew a little more teach the others, and he devised a workable system to this effect. His school, his lectures, and his pamphlet *Improvements in Education as It Respects the Industrious Classes of the Community* (1803) attracted the attention of philanthropically minded people, and he felt encouraged to expand the school and to found others. But he proved to be vain, rash, and extravagant and soon fell heavily into debt. Friends of the school paid his creditors, became trustees of the school, and organized the Royal Lancasterian Institution, later known as the British and Foreign School Society (1810). Lancaster's techniques for mass teaching spread rapidly, and there were soon about 30,000 pupils being taught in 95 Lancasterian schools.

Meanwhile, Lancaster severed his connections with his original school and opened a new secondary-level boarding school, which soon ended in bankruptcy. In 1818 he emigrated to the United States, where his work was well known. Nothing, however, came of Lancaster's own projects in the United States, and so he welcomed an invitation from Simón Bolívar to move to Venezuela in 1825. He quarreled with the Latin-American leader and returned north in 1827, spending the last decade of his life in Canada and the United States making various experiments with his system.

In Lancaster's monitorial system (*q.v.*), from 200 to 1,000 pupils were gathered in one room and seated in rows, usually of 10 pupils each. The adult schoolmaster taught the monitors, or prefects, each of whom relayed the lesson to his own row. Besides monitors who taught, there were monitors who took attendance, who examined and promoted pupils, and who prepared or distributed writing slates and books. Schoolroom activity proceeded with military precision, according to directions

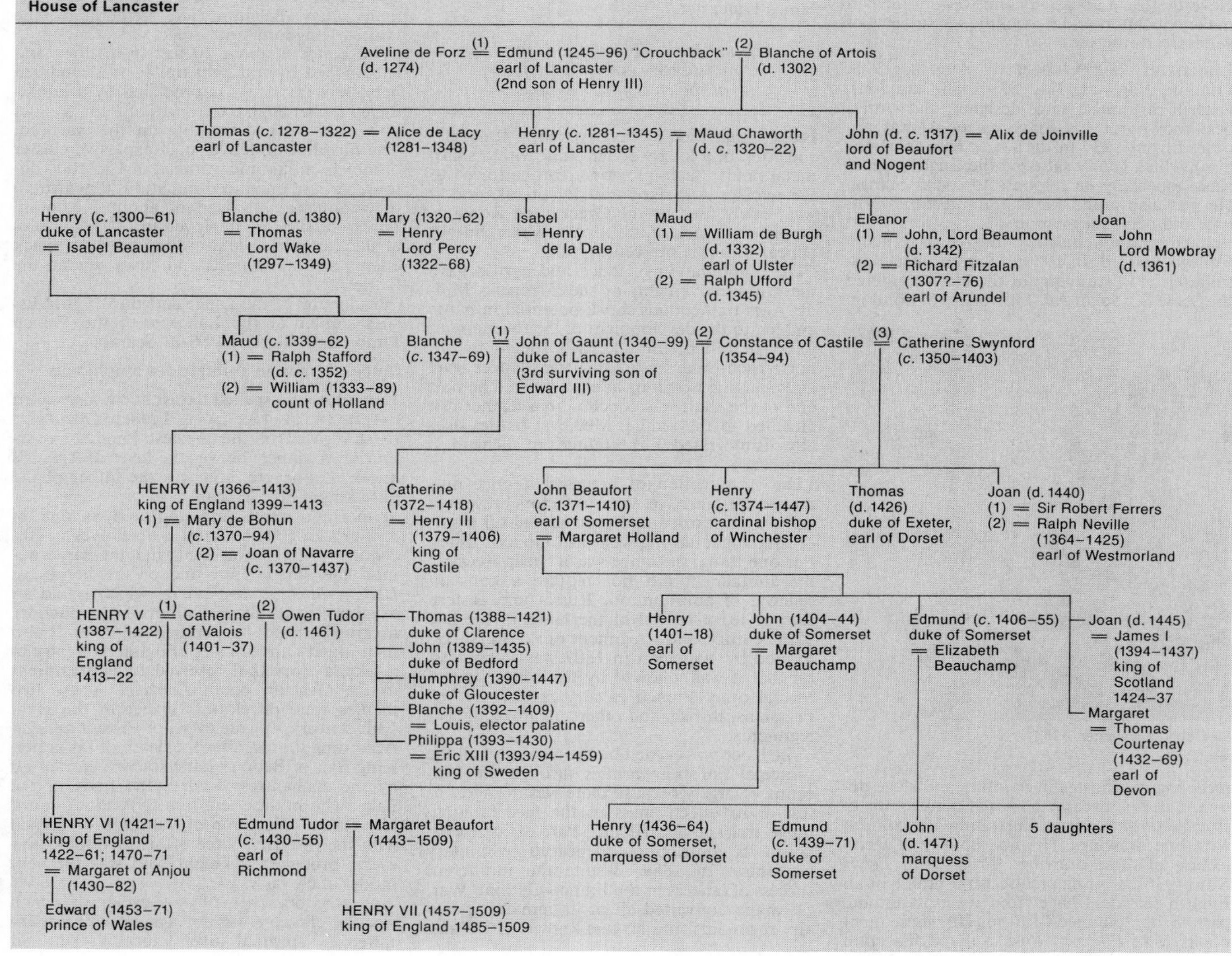

laid down by Lancaster and from which even the slightest deviations were not permitted. The defect of this system was that in order to achieve mass results and mass economies the schoolmaster was relegated to the position of a bystander, learning was reduced to drill and memorization, and the curriculum was reduced to particles of information and rote sequences. The whole process of teaching and learning was thus routinized and formalized to a point at which opportunities for creative thinking and initiative scarcely existed. Nevertheless, Lancaster's innovations helped make education and its techniques subjects of widespread interest.

Joseph Lancaster, portrait by J. Hazlitt; in the National Portrait Gallery, London

By courtesy of the National Portrait Gallery, London

Lancaster, Sir Osbert (b. Aug. 4, 1908, London, Eng.—d. July 27, 1986, London), English cartoonist, stage designer, and writer, best-known for his suave cartoons that appeared from 1939 in the *Daily Express* (London), which gently satirized the English upper class, especially its response to social change. He was also noted for his architectural writings and personal memoirs.

Lancaster took his B.A. degree at Lincoln College, Oxford, in 1930. After an unsuccessful attempt at studying for the bar, he entered the Slade School of Art, University of London, receiving certificates in painting and stage design. Later he became a regular contributor to *Architectural Review,* illustrating his column with line drawings. His first book was a collection of these drawings: *Progress at Pelvis Bay* (1936), a biting architectural profile of an English seaside village from its most remote past to its "planned" future. His subsequent books were *Pillar to Post,* a witty dissection of English architectural history (1938), and *Homes, Sweet Homes* (1939), in a similar vein and concerned with English interior decoration. These works were later combined, with additional material on American architecture and design, in *Here, of All Places* (1958).

Sir Osbert Lancaster, 1960

Jane Bown

In 1951 Lancaster entered the field of stage design and for the next 20 years successfully designed sets and costumes for numerous theatrical, ballet, and opera productions. He published two volumes of memoirs: *All Done from Memory* (1953) and *With an Eye to the Future* (1967). Lancaster's subsequent publications included *Sailing to Byzantium: An Architectural Companion* (1969); *Noblesse Oblige: An Enquiry into the Identifiable Characteristics of the English Aristocracy* (1973); *The Pleasure Garden: An Illustrated History of British Gardening* (1977); and *Scene Changes* (1978). In 1982 he published *The Life and Times of Maudie Littlehampton,* an assortment of vintage cartoons tracing the development of his classic character Maudie Littlehampton. He was knighted in 1975.

Lancaster Sound, western arm of Baffin Bay (an inlet of the North Atlantic), in north-central Baffin region, Northwest Territories, Canada. The Sound is 200 miles (320 km) long and 40 miles (64 km) wide. It extends between Devon Island (north) and Baffin Island (south) and joins the Barrow Strait northeast of Somerset Island. All feasible routes of the Northwest Passage, a seaway through the Canadian Arctic Archipelago connecting the Atlantic and Pacific oceans, pass through the sound. It was discovered in 1616 by William Baffin, the English navigator, who named the sound for the promoter of his expedition, Sir James Lancaster.

A list of the abbreviations used in the MICROPAEDIA *will be found at the end of this volume*

---

lance, spear used by cavalry troops. It usually consisted of a long wooden shaft with a sharp metal point. Its employment can be traced to the ancient Assyrians and Egyptians, and it was widely used by the Greeks and Romans, despite their lack of the stirrup, which did not appear until the 6th century AD.

The combination of lance and stirrup gave the armoured knights of the European Middle Ages tremendous shock potential in battle and led to the development of the tournament joust, in which single knights sought to unhorse each other by holding their lances level and charging headlong at each other. The butt end of the shaft was couched in a leather rest attached to the saddle. Medieval battles usually disintegrated into hundreds of such single combats.

The introduction of firearms at once outmoded the lance, yet various factors prevented its being discarded and even brought it a surprising vogue lasting well into modern times. For one thing, the lance was a cheap weapon; for another, it did not require a constant renewal of ammunition. Russia and eastern Europe led a revival of the lance in the late 18th century, and a regiment of Polish lancers formed by Napoleon in 1807 was so successful that it was followed by the conversion of several other French cavalry regiments. The Prussians, British, and others organized lancer regiments.

The lance was carried by the cavalry of all the principal European armies through the 19th century, largely because there was no rigorous test of its effectiveness in the face of long-range musket or rifle fire. Part of its appeal lay in its contribution to peacetime military pageantry. In 1889, despite the indifferent success of lancers in the Franco-German War, Germany converted all of its remaining cavalry regiments into lancers known as Uhlans. In 1914 they briefly carried their antique weapons into a machine-gun war, as did the British and French—men were run through with lances at the first Battle of the Marne. Through hard experience, the general staffs of Europe eventually (and reluctantly) conceded that a charge of lancers or any other cavalry contingent could easily be mowed down by machine-gun fire before reaching the defenders' lines. And so by the 1920s the lance had quietly faded out of the Western armory. The lance made an anachronistic battlefield appearance in the hands of Polish cavalrymen who futilely charged German tank columns in September 1939, at the beginning of World War II.

Lance Formation, division of Late Cretaceous rocks in the western United States (the Cretaceous period began about 144 million years ago and ended 66.4 million years ago). Where it occurs, the Lance Formation is the uppermost rock unit of the Cretaceous. It was named for exposures studied near Lance Creek, Niobrara county, Wyoming. The Lance Formation varies in thickness from about 90 m (300 feet) in North Dakota to almost 600 m (2,000 feet) in parts of Wyoming and consists of grayish sandy shales, light-coloured sandstones, and thin lignite beds. It is well-known for its Late Cretaceous fossils, which include plants, dinosaurs, and mammals. The duckbilled dinosaur *Trachodon,* the great carnivore *Tyrannosaurus,* the herbivores *Triceratops* and *Ankylosaurus,* and mammals and marsupials have been found in the Lance.

Lance missile, U.S.-made short-range ballistic missile, adopted by the U.S. Army in 1972 and subsequently by the armies of West Germany, Italy, Belgium, The Netherlands, the United Kingdom, and Israel.

The Lance is about 20 feet (6 m) long and is launched from a light trailer or a modified personnel carrier. It is propelled by a liquid-fueled rocket engine to ranges of 5 to 75 miles (8 to 120 km), depending on the warhead. The missile can deliver high-explosive cluster bomblets, an atomic warhead of 1 to 100 kilotons, or an enhanced-radiation ("neutron") thermonuclear warhead of about 1 kiloton. Lance missiles are deployed in NATO armies at the corps level and are intended to attack enemy armoured units and bases beyond the battlefront.

Production of the Lance ended in 1980. Missiles similar to the Lance were the French Pluton and the Soviet SS-21 Scarab.

lancelet (marine animal): *see* amphioxus.

Lancelot, also spelled LAUNCELOT, also called LANCELOT OF THE LAKE, French LANCELOT DU LAC, one of the greatest knights in Arthurian romance; he was the lover of Arthur's queen, Guinevere, and was the father of the pure knight Sir Galahad.

Lancelot's name first appeared as one of Arthur's knights in Chrétien de Troyes's 12th-century romance of *Erec,* and the same author later made him one of the heroes in *Le Chevalier de la charette,* which retold an existing legend about Guinevere's abduction, making Lancelot her rescuer and lover. It also mentioned Lancelot's upbringing by a fairy in a lake, a story that received fuller treatment in the German poem *Lanzelet.* These two themes were developed further in the great 13th-century Vulgate cycle, or Prose *Lancelot.* According to this, after the death of his father, King Ban of Benoic, Lancelot was carried off by the enchantress Vivien, the Lady of the Lake, who in time sent him to Arthur's court. Her careful education of Lancelot, combined with the inspiring force of his love for Guinevere, produced a knight who was the very model of chivalry.

In later branches of the cycle, in which worldly chivalry was set against chivalry inspired by spiritual love, Lancelot's son, Sir

Galahad, whom he fathered by Elaine, daughter of the Grail keeper King Pelleas, displaced him as the perfect knight. Lancelot's adulterous love for the queen, moreover, caused him to fail in the quest for the Holy Grail and set in motion the fatal chain of events that brought about the destruction of the knightly fellowship of the Round Table.

In medieval English romance, Lancelot played a leading role in the late 14th-century *Le Morte Arthur,* which told of a fatal passion for Lancelot conceived by Elaine the Fair of Astolat and which described the tragic end of Lancelot's love for Guinevere. He also played a central role in Malory's 15th-century prose work *Le Morte Darthur,* in which it was essentially the conflict between Lancelot's love for Guinevere and his loyalty to his lord that led to Arthur's "dolorous death and departing out of this world."

Lancet, The, British medical journal established in 1823. The journal's founder and first editor was Thomas Wakley, considered at the time to be a radical reformer. Wakley stated the intent of the new journal was to report on the metropolitan hospital lectures and to describe the important cases of the day. *The Lancet* has since played an important role in medical and hospital reform movements in England and has become a highly prestigious medical journal around the world.

lancet fish, either of two species of widely distributed, deepwater marine fish of the genus *Alepisaurus* (the family Alepisauridae). Lancet fish are elongated and slender, with a long, very tall dorsal fin and a large mouth that is equipped with formidable fanglike teeth. The fish grow to a large size, attaining a maximum length of about 1.8 m (6 feet). Voracious and carnivorous, they feed on a variety of fish

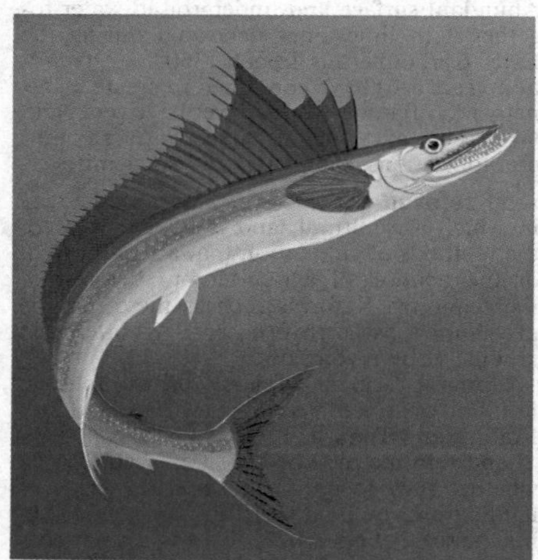

Longnose lancet fish (*Alepisaurus ferox*)

and invertebrates. The longnose lancet fish (*A. ferox*) is found in the Atlantic Ocean; the Pacific lancet fish (*A. richardsoni* or *A. borealis*), in the Pacific.

lancet window, narrow, high window capped by a lancet, or acute, arch. The lancet arch is a variety of pointed arch in which each of the arcs, or curves, of the arch have a radius longer than the width of the arch. It takes its name from being shaped like the tip of a lance. The lancet window is one of the typical features of the Early English (13th century) period in Gothic architecture.

lancewood, tough, heavy, elastic, straight-grained wood obtained from several different trees of the custard-apple family (Annonaceae). True lancewood, *Oxandra lanceolata,* of the West Indies and Guianas, furnishes most of the lancewood of commerce in the form of spars about 13 feet (4 m) in length and 5 inches (13 cm) in diameter at the small end. Lancewood was formerly used by carriage builders for shafts. The smaller wood is used for whip handles, for the tops of fishing rods, and for various minor purposes where even-grained elastic wood is desired. The black lancewood, or carisiri, of the Guianas, *Guatteria virgata,* grows to a height of about 50 feet (15 m) and has a remarkably slender trunk that is seldom more than 8 inches (20 cm) in diameter. The yellow lancewood tree (*Duguetia quitarensis*), or yari-yari, of the Guianas, is of similar dimensions and is used by the Indians for arrow points as well as for spars and beams. Trees of the genus *Rollinia* of the Guianas are also called lancewood. Australian lancewood is derived from several species of *Backhousia* (family Myrtaceae). Florida lancewood, of the genus *Nectandra* (family Lauraceae), is not used commercially.

Lanchester, Frederick William (b. Oct. 23, 1868, London, Eng.—d. March 8, 1946, Birmingham, Warwickshire), English automobile and aeronautics pioneer who built the first British automobile (1896).

In 1891, after attending Hartley University College (now the University of Southampton) and the National School of Science, Lanchester went to work for a gas-engine works in Birmingham. During his employment at the firm he improved its products by designing a pendulum governor and a starter. After five years he left to set up his own automobile-manufacturing firm, producing his first car, a one-cylinder, five-horsepower model, in 1896. A second model, with two cylinders, and a third led to financial backing for the Lanchester Engine Company, which produced several hundred cars over the next few years. Among notable design features of his cars were a relative freedom from vibration, a graceful appearance with fewer of the knobs and levers that bristled in most driver's compartments, and a luggage rack.

Lanchester's interest in aeronautics was first expressed in a paper he wrote in 1897, a work ahead of its time in appreciation of the principles of heavier-than-air flight. In 1907–08 he published a two-volume work embodying distinctly advanced aerodynamic ideas. As a member of the Advisory Committee on Aeronautics in 1909 and, later, as a consultant to the Daimler Motor Company, Ltd., he also contributed to the development of operations research.

Lanciani, Rodolfo Amadeo (b. Jan. 1, 1847, Rome, Papal States [Italy]—d. May 21, 1929, Rome), Italian archaeologist, topographer, and authority on ancient Rome who discovered many antiquities at Rome, Tivoli, and Ostia. He published a 1:1,000-scale map of classical, medieval, and modern Rome in *Forma Urbis Romae* (1893–1901).

At 20 Lanciani assisted in the excavation of Emperor Trajan's harbour at Porto, and his description (1868) of that site remains authoritative. He was appointed director of excavations and professor of ancient topography at the University of Rome in 1878, and he also lectured in the United States and England (1886–87). His major works include *Ancient Rome in the Light of Modern Discoveries* (1888) and *Storia degli scavi di Roma,* 4 vol. (1902–12; "History of the Excavation of Rome").

Lanciano, town, Chieti *provincia,* Abruzzi *regione,* south-central Italy. An archbishopric and agricultural centre, it has textile, machinery, and furniture manufactures. It originated as the Roman Anxanum. The town's Cistercian-Gothic church of Santa Maria Maggiore dates from 1227, and its cathedral has a late 13th-century campanile. Up to the 17th century Lanciano held fairs that attracted merchants from all over Italy, as well as from France and the Balkans. Pop. (1989 est.) mun., 34,541.

Lancisi, Giovanni Maria (b. Oct. 26, 1654, Rome, Papal States [Italy]—d. Jan. 20, 1720, Rome), Italian clinician and anatomist who is considered the first modern hygienist.

Lancisi graduated in medicine from the University of Rome at age 18. He was appointed physician to Pope Innocent XI in 1688 and subsequently was physician to Popes Innocent XII and Clement XI. Lancisi's monographs on influenza, cattle plague (rinderpest), and malaria revealed his gifts as an epidemiologist. In his book *De noxiis paludum effluvis* (1717; "On the Noxious Effluvia of Marshes") he related the prevalence of malaria in swampy

Lancisi, miniature by an unknown artist
Alinari—Art Resource/EB Inc.

districts to the presence of mosquitoes and recommended drainage of the swamps to prevent the disease. He wrote the classic monograph *De subitaneis mortibus* (1707; "On Sudden Death") at the request of Clement XI to explain an increase in the number of sudden deaths in Rome. Lancisi attributed sudden death to such causes as cerebral hemorrhage, cardiac hypertrophy and dilatation, and vegetations on the heart valves. This treatise and *De motu cordis et aneurysmatibus* (1728; "On the Motion of the Heart and on Aneurysms"), in which he discussed the various causes of heart enlargement and was the first to describe aneurysms of syphilitic origin, markedly contributed to knowledge of cardiac pathology.

Lanclos, Anne de: *see* Lenclos, Ninon de.

Lancret, Nicolas (b. Jan. 22, 1690, Paris, Fr.—d. Sept. 14, 1743, Paris), French genre painter whose brilliant depictions of fêtes galantes, or scenes of courtly amusements taking place in Arcadian settings, reflected the society of his time.

Lancret was influenced by both Antoine Watteau and Claude Gillot. Much admired as a decorator, he executed numerous commissions for the mansions of many great collectors. Among his favourite subjects were balls, fairs, and village weddings. In 1719 he was received into the Royal Academy, and in 1735 he was made councillor of the Academy. His best-known work is a series of illustrations for the *Contes* of Jean de La Fontaine.

Land, Edwin Herbert (b. May 7, 1909, Bridgeport, Conn., U.S.—d. March 1, 1991, Cambridge, Mass.), American inventor and physicist whose one-step process for developing and printing photographs culminated in a revolution in photography unparalleled since the advent of roll film.

While a student at Harvard University, Land became interested in polarized light, *i.e.,* light in which all rays are aligned in the same plane. He took a leave of absence, and, after intensive study and experimentation, succeeded (1932) in aligning submicroscopic crystals of iodoquinine sulfate and embedding them in a sheet of plastic. The resulting polarizer, for which he envisioned numerous uses and which he dubbed Polaroid J sheet, was a tremendous advance. It allowed the use of almost any size of polarizer and significantly reduced the cost.

With George Wheelwright III, a Harvard physics instructor, Land founded the Land-Wheelwright Laboratories, Boston, in 1932. He developed and, in 1936, began to use numerous types of Polaroid material in sunglasses and other optical devices. Polaroid was later used in camera filters and other optical equipment.

Land founded the Polaroid Corporation, Cambridge, Mass., in 1937. Four years later he developed a widely used, three-dimensional motion-picture process based on polarized light. During World War II he applied the polarizing principle to various types of military equipment.

Land began work on an instantaneous developing film after the war. In 1947 he demonstrated a camera (known as the Polaroid Land Camera) that produced a finished print in 60 seconds. The Land photographic process soon found numerous commercial, military, and scientific applications. Many innovations were made in the following years, including the development of a colour process. Land's Polaroid Land cameras, which were able to produce developed photographs within one minute after the exposure, became some of the most popular cameras in the world.

Land's interest in light and colour resulted in a new theory of colour perception. In a series of experiments he revealed certain conflicts in the classical theory of colour perception. He found that the colour perceived is not dependent on the relative amounts of blue, green, and red light entering the eye; he proposed that at least three independent image-forming mechanisms, which he called retinexes, are sensitive to different colours and work in conjunction to indicate the colour seen.

Land received more than 500 patents for his innovations in light and plastics. In 1980 he retired as chief executive officer of Polaroid but remained active in the field of light and colour research by working with the Rowland Institute of Science, a nonprofit centre supported by the Rowland Foundation, Inc., a corporation that Land founded in 1960. Under Land's direction, Rowland researchers discovered that perception of light and colour is regulated essentially by the brain, rather than through a spectrum system in the retina of the eye, as was previously believed.

Land and Freedom (Russian revolutionary party): *see* Zemlya i Volya.

land bridge, any of several isthmuses that have connected the Earth's major landmasses at various times, with the result that many species of plants and animals have extended their ranges to new areas. A land bridge that had a profound effect on the fauna of the New World extended from Siberia to Alaska during most of the Tertiary and Quaternary periods (beginning 66.4 million years ago), with some interruptions. Across this strip of land passed a number of organisms of Old World origin, including man.

Another important land bridge, the Isthmus of Panama, was submerged during most of the Tertiary, with the result that the faunas of North and South America evolved largely separately, except during the Pliocene Epoch (5.3 to 1.6 million years ago) for periods of several hundred thousand years, when the isthmus was elevated.

land crab, any crab of the family Gecarcinidae (order Decapoda of the class Crustacea), typically terrestrial, square-bodied crabs that only occasionally, as adults, return to the sea. They occur in tropical America, West Africa, and the Indo-Pacific region. All species feed on both animal and plant tissue. *Cardisoma guanhumi,* a land crab of Bermuda, the West Indies, and the southern United States, lives in fields, swamps, and mangrove thickets. Some penetrate inland as far as 8 km (about 5 miles). Adults weigh about 0.5 kg (18 ounces) and measure about 11 cm (4 inches) across the carapace, or back. *Gecarcinus lateralis,* occurring from Bermuda to Guyana, is 9 cm wide. Like *Cardisoma,* it may live a considerable distance from the ocean.

Land crab (*Gecarcinus*)
Walter Dawn

land-grant college, any of numerous American institutions of higher learning that were established under the first Morrill Act (1862). This act was passed by the U.S. Congress and was named for the act's sponsor, Vermont congressman Justin Smith Morrill.

Under the provisions of the act, each state was granted 30,000 acres of federal land for each member of Congress representing that state. The lands were sold and the resulting funds were used to finance the establishment of one or more schools to teach "agriculture and the mechanic arts." Though the act specifically stated that other scientific and classical studies need not be excluded, its intent was clearly to meet a rapidly industrializing nation's need for trained technicians. Military training was required to be included in the curriculum of all land-grant schools, and this provision led to the establishment of the Reserve Officers Training Corps, an educational program for future army, navy, and air force officers.

Some states established new schools with their land-grant funds; others turned the money over to existing state or private schools to be used for the establishment of schools of agriculture and mechanics (these came to be known as "A & M" colleges). Altogether, 69 land-grant schools were founded offering programs in agriculture, engineering, veterinary medicine, and other technical subjects. Cornell University in New York (in part), Purdue in Indiana, Massachusetts Institute of Technology, Ohio State University, the University of Illinois (Urbana), and the University of Wisconsin (Madison) are among the best-known land-grant schools.

With the second Morrill Act (1890), Congress began to make regular appropriations for the support of these institutions, and these appropriations were increased through subsequent legislation. Since the act withheld funds from states that refused to admit nonwhite students unless those states provided "separate but equal" facilities, it encouraged the foundation of black colleges. (This practice was ended by the 1954 Supreme Court decision that declared "separate but equal" schools to be unconstitutional.) Acts in 1847 and 1914 appropriated funds to the land-grant colleges to promote the development of scientific methods of agriculture.

The influence of the land-grant colleges on American higher education has been formidable. In recent years almost one-fifth of all students seeking degrees in the United States were enrolled in land-grant institutions. Pioneering research in physics, medicine, agricultural science, and other fields has been done at land-grant colleges. And, because their admissions policies were more open than most other institutions of the day, land-grant schools made it possible for women, working-class students, and students from remote areas to obtain undergraduate and professional education at low cost.

Land League, Irish agrarian organization that worked for the reform of the country's landlord system under British rule. The league was founded in October 1879 by Michael Davitt, the son of an evicted tenant farmer and a member of the Fenian (Irish Republican) Brotherhood. Davitt asked Charles Stewart Parnell, leader of the Irish Home Rule Party in the British Parliament, to preside over the league; this linking of the land reform movement with parliamentary activity constituted a new departure in the Irish national movement.

The league's program was based upon the "three F's": fair rent, fixity of tenure, and free sale of the right of occupancy. The passage in 1881 of Gladstone's Land Act, restricting the privileges of landlords, was a victory for the league. Parnell's increasingly violent speeches, however, led to his arrest on Oct. 13, 1881, and the league called on tenants to withhold all rents. The government used this "no-rent manifesto" as a pretext for its suppression of the league on October 20.

land mine, stationary explosive charge used against military troops or vehicles. *See* mine.

Land of Ten Thousand Sinks, in west-central Kentucky, U.S., area of numerous sinkholes and caves in the Pennyrile (or Pennyroyal) region. The area includes the interconnected caves of Mammoth Cave National Park and Flint Ridge Cave System (*qq.v.*). Abundant surface and underground water together with limestones deposited during the Early Carboniferous Epoch (360 to 320 million years ago) have combined to create a vast network of underworld caverns, rivers, and lakes. The caves include extensive sulfate mineral formations, stalactites, and stalagmites.

land reform, a purposive change in the way in which agricultural land is held or owned, the methods of cultivation that are employed, or the relation of agriculture to the rest of the economy. Reforms such as these may be proclaimed by a government, by interested groups, or by revolution.

A brief treatment of land reform follows. For full treatment, *see* MACROPAEDIA: Land Reform and Tenure.

Land reforms may be classified according to whether they focus on altering the terms of landholding; on land redistribution; on changing the scale of operations; on altering patterns of cultivation; or on supplementary measures such as marketing, credit, or education reforms.

The most common political objective of land reform is to abolish feudal or (if the landowners are foreign) colonial forms of landownership; in either case, exploitation of peasants is the target. The social status of peasants is often a concern of land reform as well. Economic objectives of land reform may include encouraging more intensive cultivation and coordinating agricultural production with the rest of the economy, particularly with an eye to supporting an industrialization program.

Evaluating the success of land reform programs is often complicated by vaguely stated objectives. Some are virtually impossible to put into measurable terms, and often there are inherent contradictions. Economic success is the easiest to measure; it may be indicated by a sustained increase in per capita real income, substantial capital investment in agriculture, a rise in productivity, a decrease in rural unemployment, or by the responsiveness of the agricultural sector to the specific demands of the rest of the economy. Social and political indicators are less reliable.

The inadequacies of these indicators are highlighted by several paradoxes of land reform: land redistribution implies the loss of the landlord's economic and managerial contributions; reform often means breaking up efficiently run farms; compensation to evicted landlords drains the economy; farmers tend to spend increased incomes on consumption rather than saving for investment; reforms often lead to increased participation in social and political institutions before an adequate educational system can be implemented; and measures to prevent future concentration of ownership may prevent the creation of efficient operations.

The earliest record of land reform is from 6th-century-BC Athens, where Solon abolished the debt system that forced peasants to mortgage their land and labour as tenants of their creditors. The reforms of the Gracchi in Rome in 133 BC redistributed public lands that had been usurped by the nobility and specified minimum and maximum individual landholdings. In 121 BC, however, the reform was reversed, and land concentration became the rule throughout Europe for many centuries.

The French Revolution largely realized the social and political aims of the reformers; feudalism and serfdom were abolished, along with any debt not based on real property, and the lands of the clergy and political emigrants were seized and sold at public auction. While little if any economic benefit occurred, the small family farm became the cornerstone of French democracy. In England reform was facilitated by the great movement of peasants into urban centres during the Industrial Revolution. Sweden and Denmark peacefully abolished serfdom in the late 1820s; Germany, Italy, and Spain did so after the revolutions of 1848. Reform in Ireland was not completed until the 1930s.

Tsar Alexander II emancipated Russia's serfs in 1861, but the reform was partial and economically unsuccessful. The Russian Revolution of 1917 introduced public ownership and collectivization of agricultural land. At first the Soviet reforms entailed much bloodshed and loss of capital, but the eventual mechanization of farms resulted in the release of many farm workers to the industrial sector.

After the revolution of 1915, Mexico moved to abolish conditions that had resulted in virtual serfdom for large numbers of peasants and the impoverishment of rural, especially Indian, populations. Only a relatively small amount of redistribution was attempted, but this resulted in lasting political stability for the country. Land reform in Latin America has typically reflected internal instability and international pressure and is complicated by a rapidly increasing population, extremely high land ownership concentrations, extensive foreign ownership, inadequate cultivation methods, and the dependence of the economy on a few staple export items. Cuba, under a Communist government, has made comprehensive reforms, with greater social than economic success.

Egypt instituted in 1952 the most drastic reforms outside of Communist countries, although probably because of the country's underdeveloped industrial sector, the economic effects have been minimal. Land reform was also instituted in many other countries of North Africa and the Middle East, usually following independence or revolution. Of the tropical African nations, Ethiopia and Mozambique have initiated the more radical land reforms, vesting the land title in the state and guaranteeing the right of use to those who till the land and to their descendants.

Another notable example of land reform was instituted after the Communists came to power in China; the Chinese commune system, with its more recent incentive and individual-responsibility programs, is generally held to be successful and quite effective.

land snail, any of the approximately 22,000 species of snails adapted to life away from water. Most are members of the subclass Pulmonata (class Gastropoda); a few are members of the subclass Prosobranchia. Typically, land snails live on or near the ground, feed

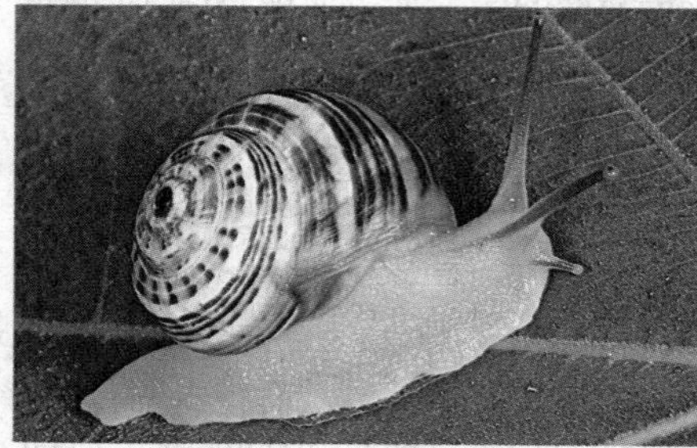

European land snail (*Helix*)
Jacques Six

on decaying plant matter, and lay their eggs in the soil. They are most common on tropical islands but occur also in cold regions, where they hibernate. Arboreal forms, such as *Liguus* of Florida and Cuba, tend to be brightly coloured; terrestrial forms usually are drab. Largest in size are those of the genus *Achatina,* of Africa, some 20 cm (8 inches) across. Several common land snails (*Helix* species) of Europe are table delicacies, especially in France. *See* gastropod.

land tenure, feudal: *see* feudal land tenure.

Landa, Diego de (b. 1524?, Cifuentes, Spain—d. 1579, Yucatán, Mexico), Spanish Franciscan priest and bishop of Yucatán who is best known for his classic account of Mayan culture.

Landa was born to a noble family and when quite young joined the Franciscans (1541). His religious fervour manifested itself early, and he asked to be sent as a missionary to the New World. Once in Mexico he tried to help the Indians, who were decimated by disease and starvation, through charitable works, and he protected them as much as possible from the Spanish authorities. He became the Franciscan provincial of Yucatán in 1561.

Landa was an acute and intelligent observer, and his opus on Mayan life and religion, *Relación de las cosas de Yucatán* (1566), remains the classical text on Mayan civilization. While Landa was sympathetic to the Mayan people, he abhorred certain of their practices, particularly human sacrifice. When traces of human sacrifice were found in a cave containing sacred statues of the Maya, Landa, in his religious zeal, ordered all their idols destroyed and all Mayan books to be burned; he was surprised at the distress this caused the Indians. It was reported that 157 Indians were killed in the process, but an investigation by crown authorities exonerated Landa, and he was appointed bishop of Yucatán in 1572.

Modern scholars regard Landa with a mixture of frustration and admiration. At the same time he wrote his comprehensive work on Mayan culture, his orders to destroy all icons and hieroglyphics obliterated the Mayan language forever, helping to undermine and destroy the civilization he so vividly described. Yet his book, which was not printed until 1864, provided a phonetic alphabet that made it possible to decipher about one-third of the Mayan hieroglyphs, and many of the remainder have since been deciphered.

Landau, in full LANDAU IN DER PFALZ, city, Rhineland-Palatinate *Land* (state), southwestern Germany. It is picturesquely situated along the Queich River, at the slope of the Haardt Mountains. The settlement was first mentioned in 1106, and an Augustinian monastery was founded there in 1276. Landau became an imperial free town in 1291. It was occupied by the French (1680–1815) and granted to Bavaria in 1816. The city's Gothic Protestant church dates from 1333, St. Catherine's Chapel from 1344, and the church of the former monastery from 1405. Of the early fortifications, the Deutsches Tor remains, as do the ruins of a fortress built (1688–91) by Sébastien de Le Prestre Vauban, the French military engineer. The town is known for its zoo and spacious gardens and parks. Landau gave its name to the famous four-wheel town carriage (17th–18th century) with a convertible top. The city's industries include iron founding and the manufacture of tobacco, shoes, furniture, and machinery. Cattle markets are held, and there is an important wine trade. Pop. (1989 est.) 36,297.

landau, four-wheeled carriage, invented in Germany, seating four people on two facing seats with an elevated front seat for the coachman. It was distinguished by two folding hoods, one at each end, which met at the top to form a boxlike enclosure with side windows. It was a heavy vehicle, often drawn by a team of four horses, and was widely used from the 18th century in England. Usually, landaus

Landau, 1890; in the Suffolk Museum and Carriage House, Stony Brook, Long Island, N.Y.
By courtesy of the Suffolk Museum and Carriage House at Stony Brook, Long Island, N.Y., Melville Collection

were severely cut away beneath at each end, so that the bottom of the door was the lowest point of the carriage body.

The landaulet, or landaulette, was a landau coupé, appearing as if the front were cut away, with a forward-facing seat for two people. It had an elevated coach seat for the coachman, and a folding, or falling, top.

Landau, Ezekiel (b. Oct. 8, 1713, Opatów, Pol.—d. April 29, 1793, Prague), Polish rabbi, the learned author of a much-reprinted book on Jewish law (Halakha).

In 1734 Landau's reputation for learning led to his appointment as head of the rabbinical court at Brody, and in 1745 he became rabbi of Jampol, Podolia (then part of Poland). There he gained fame by his diplomacy in arbitrating the Emden–Eybeschütz controversy (Rabbi Jacob Emden, a fiery opponent of religious unorthodoxy, had accused Rabbi Jonathan Eybeschütz of dispensing heretical amulets). In 1755 he went to Prague as rabbi and remained there until his death. His Halakhic decisions (responsa), collected under the title *Nodaʿ be-Yehuda* ("Known in Judah"), reveal Landau's fine analytical mind and careful scrutiny of sources.

He was an implacable opponent of the two major currents of Judaism that arose in his generation: Ḥasidism ("Pious Ones") and Haskala ("Enlightenment"). Ḥasidism, a mystical movement that valued joy and devotion in the service of God over learning, he opposed as sinfully ignorant; Haskala, a movement that encouraged assimilation as a means of ending prejudice and gaining civil rights for the Jews, he attacked as a threat to Jewish identity. Landau even went so far as to order the public burning of a famous Ḥasidic polemic, the *Toledot Ya'aqov Yosef* ("History of Jacob Joseph") of Jacob Joseph of Polonnoye (died about 1782).

Landau, Lev Davidovich (b. Jan. 22, 1908, Baku, Azerbaijan, Russian Empire—d. April 1, 1968, Moscow), Soviet physicist who worked in such fields as low-temperature physics, atomic and nuclear physics, and solid-state, stellar-energy, and plasma physics. Several physics terms bear his name. He was awarded the 1962 Nobel Prize for Physics.

Lev Davidovich Landau
USSR Magazine—Sovfoto

Landau had science-oriented parents. His father was an engineer who worked in the Baku oil industry and his mother a doctor who had at one time done physiological research. Landau was graduated at 13 from the Gymnasium and, because he was too young to go to the university, attended the Baku Economical Technical School. He matriculated in 1922 at Baku University, studying physics and chemistry, and transferred in 1924 to the Leningrad State University, which at that time was the centre of Soviet physics. Graduating in 1927, he continued research at the Leningrad Physico-Technical Institute.

At that time there were practically no outstanding senior theoretical physicists in the Soviet Union, and, since the younger men had to teach themselves and each other, it was important for them to go abroad and be in touch with the Western theoretical physics schools that were flourishing in such centres as Copenhagen and Munich. Landau got his first chance to go abroad in 1929, on a Soviet government travelling fellowship supplemented by a Rockefeller Fellowship. After brief stays in Göttingen and Leipzig, he went to Copenhagen to work in Niels Bohr's Institute for Theoretical Physics. It is probably no exaggeration to say that the development of present-day theoretical physics owes more to Bohr's Institute than to any other place in the world. Almost all of the leading theoretical physicists of the 1920s and 1930s spent some period at this institute. Landau always considered himself a pupil of Bohr's, and his attitude to physics was greatly influenced by Bohr's example. After his stay in Copenhagen he visited Cambridge and Zürich before returning to the Soviet Union. Apart from short visits to Copenhagen in 1933 and 1934, Landau spent the remainder of his life in his own country.

In 1932 Landau went to Kharkov to become the head of the Theoretical Division of the Ukrainian Physico-Technical Institute, a position he combined in 1935 with that of head of the Department of General Physics at the Kharkov A.M. Gorky State University. In Kharkov Landau began to build a Soviet school of theoretical physics, so that Kharkov soon became the centre of theoretical physics in the U.S.S.R. It was also in Kharkov that, with his friend and former student, E.M. Lifshits, he started to write the well-known *Course of Theoretical Physics,* a set of nine volumes that together span the whole of the subject. His great interest in the teaching of physics is also shown in his plans for a "Course of General Physics" and even a series "Physics for Everybody."

Landau required that his students master all necessary mathematical techniques before coming to him. After that he expected them to master the so-called theoretical minimum, which included a basic knowledge of all the domains of theoretical physics. Only the ablest of the students were able to pass this minimum. In this way his students became proper physicists, rather than narrow specialists.

In 1937 Pyotr Leonidovich Kapitsa, a low-temperature experimentalist, persuaded Landau to move to Moscow and to head the Theory Division of the S.I. Vavilov Institute of Physical Problems, which had been created by the U.S.S.R. Academy of Sciences. There, Landau's close interest in experimental physics led to his development of the theory of liquid helium, the last of the elements to be liquefied and the most remarkable of all liquids. Kapitsa had found that liquid helium was super-fluid—that is, that it had less resistance against moving through a tube than any other known liquid. Landau's theory to explain this peculiar behaviour was the work for which he was awarded the Nobel Prize for Physics.

Landau's attitude to physics and physicists was critical; he did not suffer fools gladly. While always willing to help anybody, he hated pomposity. People either adored him or were his bitter enemies, and he was imprisoned during the Stalin era, in 1938, and only a personal intervention by Kapitsa freed him.

In 1937 Landau married K.T. Drobanzeva, and in 1946 they had a son, Igor, who became an experimental physicist.

In Moscow Landau continued to make significant contributions to almost all parts of physics. The topics he covered range from low-temperature to nuclear physics, from the theory of metals to stellar energy, from cosmic rays to plasmas, from hydrodynamics to atomic physics. Landau's contributions are partly reflected in such terms as Landau diamagnetism and Landau levels in solid-state physics, Landau damping in plasma physics, the Landau energy spectrum in low-temperature physics, or Landau cuts in high-energy physics.

On Jan. 7, 1962, Landau was involved in a car accident. He was unconscious for six weeks and was several times declared clinically dead, but he somehow revived. Distinguished specialists from several countries helped to save his life. After Landau had regained consciousness his faculties slowly returned to him, but he was no longer able to perform creative work. His physical condition never returned to normal, and he died six years later.

Apart from the Nobel Prize, Landau received many other honours. In the U.S.S.R. he was directly elected a member of the Academy of Sciences, was given the title of Hero of Socialist Effort, and was awarded three State Prizes, as well as a Lenin Prize. He was a foreign member of the Royal Society of London and of the academies of The Netherlands, Denmark, and the United States, as well as a recipient of the Max Planck Medal and the Fritz London Prize. (D.t.H.)

BIBLIOGRAPHY. A popular account of Landau's life, and especially of his last six years after his accident, may be found in A. Dorozynski, *The Man They Wouldn't Let Die* (1966). His scientific papers were published in D. ter Haar (ed.), *Collected Papers of L.D. Landau* (1965). All his books have been published in English translation.

Landen, John (b. Jan. 23, 1719, Peakirk, Northamptonshire, Eng.—d. Jan. 15, 1790, Milton, Northamptonshire), British mathematician who made important contributions on elliptic integrals.

Landen became known as a mathematician by his essays in *The Ladies' Diary* for 1744, and he was elected a fellow of the Royal Society of London in 1766. His researches on elliptic integrals are remembered for Landen's point and Landen's transformations. The theorem known by his name appeared in his memoir of 1775 and later was included in the first volume of his *Mathematical Memoirs,* 2 vol. (1780–89). Landen's theorem expresses the arc of a hyperbola in terms of the arcs of two ellipses.

Landen also wrote on a variety of subjects, including astronomy and physics. He made early contributions to the study of rotary motion and explained a minor error Newton had made in calculating the effects of precession (the slow rotation of a rotating body's axis). In *A Discourse Concerning the Residual Analysis* (1758), Landen tried to rid calculus of the difficult concept of infinitesimals by basing it on the accepted principles of algebra and geometry.

Lander, city, seat (1884) of Fremont county, west central Wyoming, U.S., on the Popo Agie River, east of the Wind River Range, at an altitude of 5,360 ft (1,634 m). It was settled in the 1870s around Fts. Augur and Brown and named for Col. F.W. Lander. Ranching, lumber, oil wells, coal mines, iron ore, and uranium are its economic assets. To the north is the Wind River Indian Reservation (Shoshoni and Arapahoe tribes) with the grave of Sacajawea (Shoshone guide of the Lewis and Clark expedition). Sinks Canyon State Park and the Shoshoni National Forest are immediately southwest. The city sponsors the annual One-Shot Antelope Hunt. Inc. 1890. Pop. (1990) 7,023.

Lander, Harald (b. Feb. 25, 1905, Copenhagen—d. Sept. 14, 1971, Copenhagen), Danish dancer and choreographer who was primarily responsible for rebuilding the faltering Royal Danish Ballet into a superb performing organization.

Lander studied under the great ballet master and reformer Michel Fokine in 1926–27 and danced in leading roles until 1945. As ballet master of the Royal Danish Ballet (1932–51) he enriched its repertoire with productions of Fokine's masterpieces—*e.g., Les Sylphides, Petrushka,* and *Prince Igor*—and revivals of works by the great 19th-century Danish choreographer August Bournonville. His own compositions include the frequently performed *Études* (1948), a one-act ballet that begins with traditional ballet exercises at a dance studio's "barre" and ends with spectacular displays by advanced students.

After becoming ballet master of the Paris Opéra in 1953, he became a French citizen in 1956 and opened a studio in Paris in 1964. He was decorated by the governments of Denmark, Belgium, and France for his contributions to modern ballet. Lander returned to Copenhagen shortly before his death. He was married to the outstanding Danish ballerinas Margot Lander (1931; divorced 1950) and Toni Lander (1950; divorced 1965).

Lander, Richard Lemon (b. Feb. 8, 1804, Truro, Cornwall, Eng.—d. Feb. 6, 1834, Fernando Po), British explorer of West Africa who traced the course of the lower Niger River to its delta.

He accompanied the Scottish explorer Hugh Clapperton as a servant on his second expedition to the region now lying within northern Nigeria. After Clapperton's death near Sokoto (April 1827), Lander proceeded southeast to Kano and then returned to the coast through the country of the Yoruba people. He published *Journal of Richard Lander from Kano to the Sea Coast* (1829) and *Records of Captain Clapperton's Last Expedition to Africa, with the Subsequent Adventures of the Author* (1830), based on his leader's journal, which he had saved.

At the request of the British government, Lander went again to West Africa. Accompanied by his brother John, he landed at Badagri, now in Nigeria, on March 22, 1830, and traveled inland to Bussa. From there they explored the Niger upstream for about 100 miles (160 km) and then began a hazardous canoe trip downstream to the river's delta.

Richard Lander, detail from an oil painting by W. Brockedow, *c.* 1835; in the National Portrait Gallery, London
By courtesy of the National Portrait Gallery, London

Seized by inhabitants of the delta, the brothers were held captive until a large ransom was paid and passage was secured for them to the island of Fernando Po. Their exploration was recounted in *Journal of an Expedition to Explore the Course and Termination of the Niger* (1832). On a trading expedition up the Niger, Lander was wounded by tribesmen attacking his canoe, and he died soon thereafter.

Landes, also called LES LANDES, forest region bordering the Bay of Biscay in the Aquitaine Basin of southwestern France, extending northward to the Garonne Estuary and southward to the Adour River. With an area of 5,400 square miles (14,000 square km), Landes occupies three-quarters of the Landes *département,* half of Gironde, and about 175,000 acres (70,000 hectares) of Lot-et-Garonne. Formerly a vast tract of marshland and moors, it now consists chiefly of the most extensive forest in France. The monotonous, sandy plain was originally covered with lakes and ponds and was bordered by dunes of moving sands. In 1801 the sand dunes were stabilized with plantations of maritime pines. Early in the second half of the 19th century, the plain was drained by canals, and a vast pine forest was planted that provided timber and turpentine. Three-quarters of the forest was destroyed in disastrous fires in 1937 and 1950, but much of the burned area was replanted, and paper mills were established in the region to improve the economy. Great tracts of land were also made suitable for mixed farming. Several seaside resorts have been established, and the resort area was named the Côte d'Argent (Silver Coast).

Landes, *département,* Aquitaine region, southwestern France, created from parts of the historic provinces of Guyenne, Gascony, and Béarn (*qq.v.*). Its 3,569 square miles (9,243 square km) front the Bay of Biscay for nearly 70 miles (110 km) in a straight, harbourless coastline fringed with sand dunes and bounded on the south by the Adour River (*q.v.*). The area also embraces three-quarters of the flat, monotonous sandy plain known as Les Landes. Mont-de-Marsan (*q.v.*), the *département*'s capital, and the ancient city of Dax (*q.v.*) lie in the southwest, which is hilly and wooded and has good agricultural land. The oceanic climate is mild and pleasant.

Landes has a leading place in France's production of pâté de foie gras and asparagus. Saint-Vincent-de-Paul, formerly Pouy, was the birthplace of the saint after whom it was renamed. There is a missile base near Biscarrosse Lagoon and oil wells at Parentis-en-Born. The *département,* which has two *arrondissements*—Mont-de-Marsan and Dax—is in the educational division of Bordeaux. Pop. (1985 est.) 302,000.

landfill, sanitary: *see* sanitary landfill.

landform, any conspicuous topographic feature on the Earth or a similar planetary body or satellite. Familiar examples are mountains (including volcanic cones), plateaus, and valleys. Comparable structures have been detected on Mars, Venus, the Moon, and certain satellites of Jupiter and Saturn. The term landform also can be applied to related features that occur on the floor of the Earth's ocean basins, as, for example, seamounts, mid-oceanic ridges, and submarine canyons.

A brief treatment of landforms follows. For full treatment of those on the Earth, *see* MACROPAEDIA: Continental Landforms. For coverage of the topographic features of the so-called terrestrial planets and of various major satellites, *see* Solar System.

The distribution and structure of landforms reflect the geomorphic processes that created them. Most landforms occurring at the surface of the terrestrial land masses result from the interaction of two fundamental types of processes over geologic time. These are (1) vertical tectonic movements and extrusion of magma (molten rock material) and (2) denudational processes, which encompass the weathering and erosion of rocks and the accumulation of the resulting sedimentary debris.

Relief features produced chiefly by uplift and subsidence of the Earth's crust or by upward magmatic movements can be classified as tectonic landforms. They include rift valleys, plateaus, mountains, and volcanic cones. Other topographic features, such as pediments, sand dunes, subterranean caves, fjords, and beaches, are formed by denudational processes. These features, categorized as structural landforms, are attributable to the erosional and depositional action of rivers, wind, groundwater solution, glaciers, sea waves, and other external agents.

Although tectonic and denudational processes account for the origin of most landform types, a few have been produced by other means. Impact craters, for one, are formed by collisions with asteroids, comets, and meteorites. Biogenic landforms, for another, are produced—as the term implies—by living organisms. They range from giant termite mounds and coral reefs to open-pit mines and dams created by humans.

landgrave, feminine LANDGRAVINE, a title of nobility in Germany and Scandinavia, dating from the 12th century, when the kings of Germany attempted to strengthen their position in relation to that of the dukes (*Herzoge*). The kings set up "provincial counts" (*Landgrafen*) over whom the dukes would have no control and who would have rank and authority equivalent to those of dukes. Later—and more commonly—the title was given to counts in order to make them directly dependent on the king (or emperor).

The first landgraviate was Thuringia (conferred on the Ludowing family in 1130 by King Lothair II). The title survived into the 20th century in the House of Hesse and also in a branch of the House of Fürstenberg, which acquired the landgraviate of Stühlingen in 1639.

Landgrave, landgravine
foreign-language equivalents

	masculine	feminine
Danish	lensgreve	lensgrevinde
Dutch	landgraaf	landgravin
German	Landgraf	Landgräfin
Norwegian	landgreve	landgrevinne
Swedish	länsgreve	länsgrevina

Landini, Francesco, Landini also spelled LANDINO (b. *c.* 1335, Fiesole, near Florence—d. Sept. 2, 1397, Florence), leading composer of 14th-century Italy, famed during his lifetime for his musical memory, his skill in improvisation, and his virtuosity on the organetto, or portative organ, as well as for his compositions. He also played the flute and the rebec.

The son of Jacopo the Painter, Landini was blinded in childhood by smallpox. He attained in his youth a reputation for learning in philosophy, astrology, and music, and he was crowned with a laurel wreath as the winner of a poetical contest at Venice in 1364. In *Il Paradiso degli Alberti del 1389,* Giovanni da Prato described Landini as playing his songs so sweetly "that no one had ever heard such beautiful harmonies, and their hearts almost burst from their bosoms."

Landini's surviving works include numerous songs, of which his favourite form was the ballata, an Italian song form modeled on the French virelay or on the native Italian *lauda spirituale.* The melodies (top part predominating) are vocal in character and highly ornamental. As in other songs of the period, they are distinguished by elaborate patterning, syncopations, roulades, and an evident lack of emotional connection between the words and the music. The songs were performed by voices, instruments, or, typically, a mixture of both. Their stylized elegance, gay preciosity, and clear, limpid texture characterize all of Landini's songs.

In addition to his 140 settings of ballate (91 for two voices, 49 for three), his surviving compositions include 12 madrigals, a virelay, and a caccia.

One distinctive cadence formula that was common in 14th-century music, particularly that of Landini, is known as the Landini cadence, in which the leading tone drops to the sixth of the scale before approaching the final tonic note.

Landis, Kenesaw Mountain (b. Nov. 20, 1866, Millville, Ohio, U.S.—d. Nov. 25, 1944, Chicago), American federal judge who, as the first commissioner of organized professional baseball, was noted for his uncompromising measures against persons guilty of dishonesty or other conduct he regarded as damaging to the sport.

Landis, 1928
UPI—EB Inc.

He was named for a mountain near Atlanta, Ga., where his father, a Union soldier, was wounded during the Civil War. Landis attended the University of Cincinnati and in 1891 was graduated from the Union College of Law, Chicago. He practiced law in Chicago until March 1905, when President Theodore Roosevelt appointed him U.S. district judge for the northern district of Illinois. Two years later, Landis won nationwide fame by fining the Standard Oil Company more than $29,000,000 for granting unlawful freight rebates. (The decision was reversed on appeal.) During World War I he presided at sedition trials of Socialist and labour leaders.

In 1915 the Federal League, a "third major league" operating outside the structure of organized professional baseball, brought suit against the American and National leagues. The case came before Landis, who neither granted nor denied the injunction that was requested but withheld his decision until the Federal League had disbanded on terms satisfactory to all three leagues. Following the Black Sox baseball scandal (in which eight Chicago White Sox players were accused of accepting bribes to lose the 1919 World Series), Landis was proposed for the office of commissioner. Replacing the three-man National Baseball Commission, which had failed to deal adequately with the Black Sox problem, Landis took office in January 1920.

Although disliked and even feared for his autocratic methods and patriarchal sternness, the commissioner held office until his death, and none of his decisions ever was reversed. He was elected to the Baseball Hall of Fame in 1944.

ländler, traditional couple dance of Bavaria and Alpine Austria. To lively music in $\frac{3}{4}$ time, the dancers turn under each other's arms using complicated arm and hand holds, dance back to back, and grasp each other firmly to turn around and around. These figures and the

Ländler
Culver Pictures

triple rhythm have appeared in turning dances characteristic of German peasant dances from the Middle Ages. Ländler melodies became fashionable in 18th- and 19th-century Vienna, and the dance greatly influenced the evolution of the waltz.

The ländler has many variants, among them the *Steyrischer,* with improvised satiric verse and syncopated hand clapping, and the *Schuhplattler,* a courtship dance in which the men perform exuberant, acrobatic displays, stamp their feet, slap their hands and body, and end by lifting the women high off the ground. The *Schuhplattler* is one of several European courtship dances, such as the Basque *aurresku,* the Norwegian halling, and the Ukrainian *hopak,* in which the men show off for their partners.

landlord and tenant, also called LESSOR AND LESSEE, the parties to the leasing of real estate, whose relationship is bound by contract. The landlord, or lessor, as owner or possessor of a property—whether corporeal, such as lands or buildings, or incorporeal, such as rights of common or of way—agrees through a lease, an agreement for a lease, or other instrument to allow another person, the tenant, or lessee, to enjoy the exclusive possession and use of the property for a specified period, usually upon payment of a rent. Generally speaking, any person may grant or take a lease, though there are several common-law and statutory qualifications and exceptions (notably with regard to minors, aliens, felons, the legally insane, *et al.*). Also, generally speaking, any owner of an interest in property may grant a valid tenancy for any estate equal to or less than his own; thus, a person who has merely a tenancy himself may grant a subtenancy for any period equal to or shorter than his own tenancy.

The principal forms of tenancy are as follows: (1) A "lease for a fixed period" may be granted for any certain period, whether as short as a week or less or for as long as several hundred years. Tenancies for a fixed period end automatically with the expiration of the period. (2) A "periodic tenancy"—granted yearly, quarterly, monthly, weekly, or for some other period—continues indefinitely until ended by a notice to quit given by either landlord or tenant. A certain required period of prior notice is governed by law and mutual consent. (3) A "tenancy at will" endures at the will of both landlord and tenant. Such tenancies are comparatively rare but are sometimes used to meet temporary necessities. If no rent is agreed upon, the landlord is entitled to compensation for use and occupation. (4) A "tenancy in sufferance" is one in which a tenant came into possession by a lawful means but "holds over," or remains in occupation, after his estate is ended; the tenant is considered a "tenant at sufferance" and not a trespasser. A tenancy in sufferance, like a tenancy at will, is readily converted into a periodic tenancy; and the tenant is similarly liable to pay compensation for use and occupation. Under certain circumstances, he may be subject to penalties, such as double rent.

A lease or tenancy may come to an end by expiration of the fixed term for which it was granted, by expiration of notice to quit, or by forfeiture. It is usual to insert in a lease an express provision for forfeiture of the lease if the tenant fails to pay the rent or breaks any of his covenants. If a right of forfeiture arises, it lies with the landlord to decide whether or not to enforce it. In most cases, he is required to serve on the tenant a notice specifying the breach, requiring it to be remedied, if possible, and requiring compensation, if desired. The ancient remedy of distress whereby the landlord might enter, seize, and retain personal property in the possession of the tenant until arrears of rent were paid is still available in some jurisdictions, though in a considerable number it has been abolished, leaving only the ordinary legal processes for the collection of a debt and the summary procedure for ejection of the tenant.

Landnámabók (Icelandic: "Book of Settlements"), also called LANDNÁMA, unique Icelandic genealogical record, probably originally compiled in the early 12th century by Ari Thorgilsson the Learned, though it exists in several versions of a later date. It lists the names of 400 original settlers of Iceland, their Norwegian origins, and their descendants. Their landholdings also are described with minute topographical accuracy. Occasionally the lists of names are enlivened by anecdotes of marriages or feuds or by brief but vivid character sketches. The *Landnámabók* served as the source for many Icelandic sagas.

Lando, Latin LANDUS (b. Rome—d. February 914), pope from July/August 913 to early 914. He reigned during one of the most difficult periods in papal history—from *c.* 900 to 950. The Holy See was then dominated by the relatives and dependents of the senior Theophylact.

Lando DI **Sezze** (pope): *see* Innocent (III).

Landoma (people): *see* Landuma.

Landon, Alfred M(ossman), byname ALF LANDON (b. Sept. 9, 1887, West Middlesex, Pa., U.S.—d. Oct. 12, 1987, Topeka, Kan.), governor of Kansas (1933–37) and unsuccessful U.S. Republican presidential candidate in 1936.

Alfred M. Landon
By courtesy of the Kansas State Historical Society

Landon went with his parents to Independence, Kan., in 1904. He received a law degree from the University of Kansas in 1908 and entered the oil business in 1912. He attended the Bull Moose Convention of the Progressive Party in that same year and campaigned in Kansas for the Progressive Party presidential candidate, Theodore Roosevelt. Thereafter, Landon's political affiliation remained with Kansas progressivism. During World War I he served in the U.S. Army chemical warfare service.

After the war Landon returned to his oil business and Kansas politics. He was elected governor in 1932 and was reelected in 1934, the only Republican gubernatorial incumbent to win that year. This victory led to the "Landon Boom" and to his presidential candidacy of 1936. Although nearly 17,000,000 Americans voted the Republican ticket, Landon won the electoral votes of only Maine and Vermont. After losing the election he continued to participate in Kansas politics but did not again play an important role in national affairs. His daughter Nancy Landon Kassebaum was also a Republican senator from Kansas.

Landon, Letitia Elizabeth, also called L.E.L. (b. Aug. 14, 1802, London—d. Oct. 15, 1838,

Letitia Landon, detail of a drawing by D. Maclise; in the National Portrait Gallery, London
By courtesy of the National Portrait Gallery, London

Gold Coast Colony [now Ghana]), English poet and novelist who, at a time when women were conventionally restricted in their themes, wrote of passionate love. She is remembered for her high-spirited social life and mysterious death and for verse that reveals her lively intelligence and emotional intensity.

Landon's first volume of verse came out in 1821; it and the eight collections that followed were extremely popular, and she was in great demand as a contributor to magazines and giftbooks, annuals produced in the 1820s and '30s as gifts for ladies. Her four novels, published in 1831–42, were also successful.

Landon captivated London society by her wayward charm. Her engagement to John Forster, a journalist and man of letters, ended unhappily. In 1838 she married George Maclean, then chief administrator of the Cape Coast settlement (now in Ghana). She died of poisoning, presumably by accident, soon after her arrival in Africa.

Landor, Walter Savage (b. Jan. 30, 1775, Warwick, Warwickshire, Eng.—d. Sept. 17, 1864, Florence, Italy), English writer best remembered for *Imaginary Conversations,* prose dialogues between historical personages.

Educated at Rugby School and at the University of Oxford, both of which he left after disagreement with school officials, Landor spent a lifetime quarreling with his father, neighbours, wife, and any authorities at hand who offended him. Paradoxically, though, he won the friendship of literary men from Robert Southey, Samuel Taylor Coleridge, and Charles Lamb among the Romantics to Charles Dickens and Robert Browning. A proficient classicist from boyhood, he wrote many of his English works originally in Latin. He wrote lyrics, plays, and heroic poems, but *Imaginary Conversations,* 2 vol. (1824; vol. 3, 1828; and thereafter sporadically to 1853), was his great work.

Landowska, Wanda, in full WANDA LOUISE LANDOWSKA (b. July 5, 1879, Warsaw, Pol., Russian Empire—d. Aug. 16, 1959, Lakeville, Conn., U.S.), Polish-born harpsichordist who initiated the revival of the harpsichord in the 20th century.

Wanda Landowska, 1953
UPI

Landowska studied composition in Berlin in 1896, and in 1900 she went to Paris, where, influenced by her husband, Henry Lew, an authority on folklore, she researched old music and keyboard instruments. She taught at the Schola Cantorum, first played the harpsichord in public in 1903, and in 1909 published, with her husband, *Musique ancienne,* a study of 17th- and 18th-century music. She remained until the beginning of World War II the principal exponent of 17th- and 18th-century harpsichord music, particularly that of J.S. Bach and François Couperin, on whose works she wrote several studies. In 1925 she founded a school for the study of old music at Saint-Leu-La-Forêt, near Paris, and in 1941 settled in the United States. Among the modern works she inspired were the harpsichord concerti of Manuel de Falla and Francis Poulenc. Her theories of technique are the basis of contemporary harpsichord playing.

Landrum-Griffin Act, formally the LABOR-MANAGEMENT REPORTING AND DISCLOSURE ACT (1959), a legislative response to widespread publicity about corruption and autocratic methods in certain American labour unions during the 1950s. Even though the AFL-CIO (American Federation of Labor–Congress of Industrial Organizations) expelled three of the worst offenders (the Teamsters, the Bakery and Confectionery Workers, and the Laundry Workers Union), President Dwight D. Eisenhower and the McClellan committee, which had investigated ties between labour and organized crime, insisted on a law to put internal union affairs on a more honest and democratic basis.

Thus, the Landrum-Griffin Act instituted federal penalties for labour officials who misused union funds, who had been found guilty of specific crimes, or who had violently prevented union members from exercising their legal rights. The act contained other provisions that strengthened parts of the Taft-Hartley Act (*q.v.*), which was detested by nearly all elements of organized labour. These provisions included a strict ban on secondary boycotts (union efforts to stop one employer from dealing with another employer who is being struck or boycotted) and greater freedom for individual states to set the terms of labour relations within their borders. The latter provision hampered labour organizing in the South, the least unionized region in the United States.

Landry, Tom, byname of THOMAS WADE LANDRY (b. Sept. 11, 1924, Mission, Texas, U.S.—d. Feb. 12, 2000, Dallas, Texas), American professional football coach, notably with the National Football League (NFL) Dallas Cowboys from 1960 to 1989. He molded the Cowboys into a dominant team from the late 1960s to the early '80s.

Landry began his professional career as a player with the All America Football Conference New York Yankees (1949) and moved to the NFL New York Giants (1950–55) as a cornerback. He was a player-coach (1954–55) and an assistant coach in charge of defense through the 1959 season.

Landry became coach of the newly formed Cowboys team in 1960, and in his first season they won no games, lost 11, and tied 1. Losing seasons continued for the team through 1964. The Cowboys then went on to 20 consecutive winning seasons. They competed in two NFL championship games, in 10 National Football Conference championship games, and in five Super Bowls, losing three games (1971, 1976, and 1979) and winning two (1972 and 1978).

After several consecutive losing seasons, Landry was dismissed as coach of the Cowboys in 1989, when the team was sold to a new owner. In 1990 he was elected to the National Professional Football Hall of Fame.

Land's End, Cornish PEDN-AN-LAAZ, westernmost peninsula of the county of Cornwall,

Natural arch and sea stacks off the coast of the peninsula at Land's End, Cornwall
G.F. Allen—Bruce Coleman

England. Composed of a granite mass, its tip is the southwesternmost point of England and lies about 870 miles (1,400 km) by road from John o' Groats, traditionally considered the northernmost point of Great Britain. The popular expression "from Land's End to John o' Groats" means "from end to end of Britain." Land's End is a major British tourist attraction. Off its rocky but scenic coast lie dangerous reefs, one group of which, a mile from the mainland, is marked by the Longships lighthouse.

Consult the INDEX *first*

Landsat, byname of EARTH RESOURCES TECHNOLOGY SATELLITE (ERTS), any of a series of unmanned U.S. scientific satellites. The first three Landsat satellites were launched in 1972, 1975, and 1978. These satellites were primarily designed to collect information about the Earth's natural resources, including the location of mineral deposits and the condition of forests and farming regions. They were also equipped to monitor atmospheric and oceanic conditions and to detect variations in pollution level and other ecological changes. All three satellites carried various types of cameras, including those with infrared sensors. Landsat cameras provided images of surface areas 115 miles (184 km) square; each such area could be photographed at 18-day intervals. These pictures were the basis of a far more comprehensive survey than could be made from airplanes.

A fourth Landsat satellite was launched in 1982 and a fifth in 1984. In 1985 Landsat was transferred to a private commercial operator, the Earth Observation Satellite Company (EOSAT). In 1992 the U.S. government again assumed control of the program. The newer models contained two sensors, a multispectral scanner and a thematic mapper (which provides 100-foot [30-metre] spatial resolution in seven spectral bands). Landsat 6 failed to achieve orbit after its launch in 1993. Landsat 7 was launched successfully in 1999.

Landsberg an der Warthe (city, Poland): *see* Gorzów Wielkopolski.

landscape architecture, the development and decorative planting of gardens, yards, grounds, parks, and other planned green outdoor spaces. Landscape gardening is used to enhance nature and to create a natural setting for buildings, towns, and cities. It is one of the decorative arts and is allied to architecture, city planning, and horticulture.

A brief treatment of landscape architecture follows. For full treatment, *see* MACROPAEDIA: Garden and Landscape Design.

Landscape architects begin with the natural terrain and enhance, re-create, or alter existing landforms. "Garden" generally connotes a smaller, more intensively cultivated area, frequently created around a domestic building or other small structure. "Landscape" denotes a larger area such as a park, urban area, campus, or roadside.

Trees, bushes, shrubs, hedges, flowers, grasses, water (lakes, streams, ponds, and cascades), and rocks are used to alter or create a pleasing natural setting. Such artificial devices as decks, terraces, plazas, pavement, fences, gazebos, and fountains are also used. The importance of man-made components relative to natural components varies according to the designer, the purpose of the particular site, and the prevailing culture and fashion.

A garden or landscape's aesthetic aspects include form, plants, colour, scent, size, climate, and function. Gardens need continual maintenance in order to keep weeds and other unwanted natural phenomena from asserting themselves. Gardens change with the seasons and climate and with their plants' cycle of growth and decay.

Historically, gardens have been designed more for private than for public pleasure. The ancient Egyptians, Greeks, and Romans each evolved their own characteristic garden designs. Hadrian's Villa, near Tivoli, Italy, contains a vast pleasure garden that had great influence on subsequent designs. The Italian Renaissance developed formal gardens in which the outdoor landscape was considered an extension of a building. The 16th-century Villa d'Este at Tivoli is a remarkable example.

In the 17th century André le Nôtre, influenced by the Italian Renaissance, created for Louis XIV of France gardens at Versailles in which symmetry, vistas, and grandiose fountains predominated. Such a design was much copied and perhaps matched human dominance over natural landscape. These classical gardens are beautiful but immaculate, formal, hard, elaborate, and logical, with straight lines, circles, trees, and hedges tamed into geometric shapes and with compartmentalized beds for flowers. They are extensions of contemporary architecture.

In 18th-century England the Earl of Burlington and the landscape gardeners William Kent, Lancelot "Capability" Brown, and Humphrey Repton brought about a change whereby a "natural" philosophy of garden design began to recommend the irregular and informal. Late in the century artificial ruins and grottoes were cultivated as picturesque accessories. Famous examples include the gardens at Rousham, Stowe, and Stourhead. In the United States the leading figure in garden and landscape design was Frederick Law Olmstead.

In the East a completely separate tradition of landscape gardening evolved, starting in China and spreading via Korea to Japan. The Oriental attitude to the garden was closely linked to religious traditions. The garden was designed to induce a certain state of mind and enhance a distinctive perception. Nature predominated over man-made symmetry. Rocks were especially important and in Japanese gardens were religious symbols. The scale tended to be smaller than in Western gardens, with emphasis on tiny details. Water, trees, and bridges were vital elements. The Japanese tea garden was supposed to induce a suitable mood in the person approaching a teahouse to participate in the tea ceremony. Oriental landscape gardening, particularly Japanese, has exerted considerable influence on modern Western designs.

Landseer, Sir Edwin (Henry) (b. March 7, 1802, London, Eng.—d. Oct. 1, 1873, London), British painter and sculptor best known for his paintings of animals.

Landseer learned drawing from his father, an engraver and writer, and also studied at the Royal Academy. His paintings of animals were based on sound anatomical knowledge and, at first, were marked by healthy animation. His later works were marred, however, by anthropomorphism that lapsed into sentimentality. His "Shoeing" (1844) and "Rout of Comus" (1843) exhibit his best style. The four bronze lions at the base of Nelson's Column in Trafalgar Square, London (unveiled 1867), are his. He was elected to the Royal Academy (1831) and knighted (1850).

Landshut, city, Bavaria *Land* (state), southeastern Germany, on the Isar River. Named for its early position as the protector (*Hut*) of the neighbouring district, it was founded in 1204, when the duke of Bavaria built a fortress there, and was chartered in 1279. It remained a ducal seat until 1503 and was the site of the university of the Bavarian state from 1802 to 1826. Although surrounded by modern suburbs, the city retains its medieval character. It is dominated by the ducal castle of Trausnitz (13th–16th century) and by the Gothic St. Martin's Church (1389–1450), with one of the world's highest brick steeples (436 feet [133 m]). Other landmarks include the Renaissance ducal palace (1536–43); the Cistercian nunnery of Seligenthal (founded 1232), with a Rococo church; and the former Dominican monastery, which was the seat of the university. There are other medieval, Renaissance, and Baroque buildings, as well as many gabled houses. Landshut has several museums with collections of art.

Floodlit spire of St. Martin's Church and Trausnitz Castle, Landshut, Ger.
Malak—Shostal/EB Inc.

An important rail junction, Landshut received more than 12,000 refugees after World War II, stimulating new industries such as electrotechnics and machinery. Older industries include brewing, milling, chocolate making, and tobacco processing and the manufacture of textiles, furniture, and chemicals. Pop. (1989 est.) 57,194.

landskap, traditional subdivision (province) of Sweden. The 25 *landskaper* (provinces) developed during the pre-Viking and Viking eras and were governed by councils that met outdoors. Although they no longer have any political or administrative significance, their names remain in common use and appear in official tabulations of data. The *landskaper* overlap and occasionally coincide with the 26 *län* (counties) that came into being during the later European Middle Ages. The *län*, established in their present form in the 17th century, still serve as Sweden's main administrative subdivisions.

Landskrona, town and port, in the *län* (county) of Malmöhus, southern Sweden, on The Sound (Öresund), north-northwest of the city of Malmö. It has the only natural harbour on The Sound. It was founded by Eric of Pomerania, king of Sweden, Denmark, and Norway, and chartered in 1413. Although it was fortified after being burned in 1428 by the Hanseatic League, it was again sacked during wars of the 16th and 17th centuries.

Earthen walls, among the largest and best preserved in Europe, still surround the 16th-century castle and fortress. The island of Ven, now a part of the town, contains the ruins of astronomer Tycho Brahe's observatory. Principal industries include shipbuilding, metalworking, tanning, food processing, and the manufacture of machinery and artificial fertilizers. The town is also a popular summer resort and has regular ferry connections with Copenhagen. Pop. (1989 est.) mun., 35,393.

landslide, also called LANDSLIP, downward mass movement of earth or rock on unstable slopes, including a number of forms that result from differences in rock structure, coherence of material involved, degree of slope, amount of included water, extent of natural or artificial undercutting at the base of the slope, relative rate of movement, and relative quantity of material involved. Many terms cover these variations; creep, earthflow, mudflow, solifluction, and debris avalanche are related forms in which mass movement is achieved by flowage.

If shearing movement occurs on a surface on consolidated rock, the dislocated mass is a debris slide. Cliffs may become so steepened through undercutting by rivers, glaciers, or waves that masses of rock will fall freely and constitute a rockfall type of landslide.

Landstad, Magnus Brostrup (b. Oct. 7, 1802, Måsøy, Nor.—d. Oct. 8, 1880, Kristiania [now Oslo]), pastor and poet who published the first collection of authentic Norwegian traditional ballads (1853).

After ordination, Landstad served in several parishes before going to Christiania (later Kristiania), where he remained the rest of his life. His *Norske folkeviser* ("Norwegian Folk Ballad") dates back for its material to the European Middle Ages and revolves around the adventures of trolls, heroes, knights, and gods; a supplement contains folk melodies collected by L.M. Lindeman. Though a later, more authoritative collection was published, Landstad's book continued to be the most influential; Henrik Ibsen drew many of the themes for his early dramas from the Landstad collection.

Landstad was later given responsibility for the preparation of a national hymnal. He included about 50 of his own hymns and completed the editing in 1861.

Landsteiner, Karl (b. June 14, 1868, Vienna, Austrian Empire [Austria]—d. June 26, 1943, New York, N.Y., U.S.), immunologist and pathologist, who received the 1930 Nobel Prize for Physiology or Medicine for his discovery of the major blood groups and development of the ABO system of blood typing that has made blood transfusion a routine medical practice.

Landsteiner
By courtesy of the World Health Organization

A research assistant at the Vienna Pathological Institute (1898–1908), Landsteiner found basic differences in human blood that explained the danger involved in indiscriminate transfusions of whole blood. He was able to show (1901) that there were at least three major types of human blood that vary according to the kinds of sugar-containing substances, known as antigens, attached to the plasma membrane (outer envelope) of the red blood cells. Landsteiner labeled the types A, B, and O. A fourth group, possessing both antigens A and B (type AB) and no AB antibodies, was found in the following year. He later discovered the additional blood groups M and N (1927) and the Rhesus, or Rh, factor (1940), named for the species of monkey in which it was discovered. The Rh factor is the basis of a series of events that can occur in the blood of a mother and fetus, causing abortion, miscarriage, or a dangerous illness in the newborn.

Landsteiner's work added an important chapter to the development of legal medicine, providing admissible evidence in paternity suits and murder trials. Proof that blood types are inherited through specific genes has provided an effective tool for the study of human genetics and anthropology.

Landsteiner was appointed professor of pathology at the University of Vienna (1909–19); and at the Rockefeller Institute for Medical Research, New York City (1922–43). He wrote *The Specificity of Serological Reactions* (1936), a classic text that helped to establish the science of immunochemistry.

Landuma, also spelled LANDOMA , people located principally in Guinea, 30 to 60 miles inland along the border of Guinea-Bissau. Their language belongs to the West Atlantic branch of the Niger-Congo family and is related to Baga. The Landuma are agriculturalists—maize, millet, groundnuts (peanuts), and rice being the major crops. Social organization centres in a paramount chief, with villages governed by subordinate chiefs. Marriage is frequently polygamous, and inheritance goes to members of the mother's family. Religious beliefs centre on the activities of departed spirits.

Landus (pope): *see* Lando.

Landwirte, Bund der (Germany): *see* Agrarian League.

Lane, Alfred Church (b. Jan. 29, 1863, Boston—d. April 15, 1948, New York City), U.S. geologist and educator who originated, promoted, and directed research on the determination of the age of the Earth. He was petrographer, assistant state geologist, and state geologist for the Michigan State Geological Survey from 1889 to 1909. He served as professor of geology and mineralogy at Tufts University, Medford, Mass., from 1909, resigning in 1936 in protest against a state teachers' oath.

Lane was chairman of the committee on the measurement of geologic time of the National Research Council (1922–46) and advanced worldwide research on this subject. He was among the first of the world's scientists to undertake the study of neutrons, and in 1926, with German physicist Otto Hahn, he instituted an international plan for exchanging scientific information on nuclear fission. He was the first American to receive information of Hahn's splitting the uranium atom in 1938.

Lane, Sir Allen, original name ALLEN LANE WILLIAMS (b. Sept. 21, 1902, Bristol, Gloucestershire, Eng.—d. July 7, 1970, Northwood, Middlesex), 20th-century pioneer of paperback publishing in England, whose belief in a market for high-quality books at low prices helped to create a new reading public and also led to improved printing and binding techniques.

In 1919 Lane was apprenticed to his uncle, publisher John Lane of The Bodley Head, London, of which he became managing editor on his uncle's death six years later. Lane left Bodley in 1935 and founded Penguin Books, Ltd., which published Penguin paperback reprints priced at 6 pence (12 cents, U.S.). Encouraged by the success of the Penguin venture, he extended his efforts to include other series, such as Pelicans (serious nonfiction) and topical Penguin Specials. The Penguin Shakespeare was published in 1937, and the Puffin Story Books, published from 1941, revolutionized children's literature. Penguin's best-selling reprint, D.H. Lawrence's *Lady Chatterley's Lover* (1960), sold more than 3,500,000 copies after a much-publicized court case held that the novel was neither obscene nor corrupting.

Lane, who had been knighted in 1952, retired as managing director of Penguin in 1969 after publication of the 3,000th Penguin title—James Joyce's *Ulysses*.

Lane, Franklin K(night) (b. July 15, 1864, near Charlottetown, Prince Edward Island, Can.—d. May 18, 1921, Rochester, Minn., U.S.), U.S. lawyer and politician who, as secretary of the interior (1913–20) made important contributions to conservation.

The Lane family moved from Canada to California in 1871. Lane worked as a journalist to finance his college education and later (1891) became a part owner and the editor of the *Tacoma Daily News*. He attended Hastings College of Law (San Francisco) and was admitted to the bar in 1888. Lane practiced in San Francisco, he entered politics in 1898 when he was elected city attorney, a post to which he was twice reelected. After running unsuccessfully for governor of California (1902) and for mayor of San Francisco (1903), he was appointed to the Interstate Commerce Commission in 1905 and served briefly as its chairman in 1913. In that year he was named secretary of the interior by Pres. Woodrow Wilson. During his seven years in that post Lane promoted greater autonomy for American Indians, and encouraged development in the West and Alaska. At Lane's urging, Congress in 1916 created the National Park Service; Lane appointed as its first director the noted conservationist Stephen Tyng Mather.

Lane, Sir Hugh Percy (b. Nov. 9, 1875, Ballybrack, County Cork, Ire.—d. May 7, 1915, at sea), Irish art dealer known for his collection of Impressionist paintings.

Lane travelled extensively in Europe as a boy. He began to work in art galleries in London in 1893, and in 1898 set up his own. He established a gallery of modern art in Dublin to advance Irish painting, acted as adviser to galleries at Johannesburg and Cape Town in South Africa, and was appointed director of the National Gallery of Ireland, Dublin, in 1914. His death in the sinking of the "Lusitania" stirred a controversy over his collection, the bequest of which was unclear; ultimately it was divided between museums in London and Dublin. He had been knighted in 1909.

Lane, Jonathan Homer (b. Aug. 9, 1819, Geneseo, N.Y., U.S.—d. May 3, 1880, Washington, D.C.), U.S. astrophysicist who was the first to investigate mathematically the Sun as a gaseous body. His work demonstrated the interrelationships of pressure, temperature, and density inside the Sun and was fundamental to the emergence of modern theories of stellar evolution.

Lane became an assistant examiner in the U.S. Patent Office in 1848 and three years later became principal examiner. From 1857 he worked as an expert counsellor in patent cases. His solar studies culminated in Lane's law, which states that as a gaseous body contracts (under the influence of gravity, for example), the contraction generates heat. He used this law to explain how the Sun built up its intense heat over the eons. His most important publication is *On the Theoretical Temperature of the Sun* (1870).

Lane also studied electricity and worked on a machine for calculating mathematical roots. In addition, he devised an electromechanical governor, a "visual telegraph," and an air pump; he also experimented with mechanical refrigeration.

Lanfranc (b. *c.* 1005, Pavia, Lombardy—d. May 28, 1089, Canterbury, Kent, Eng.), Italian Benedictine who, as archbishop of Canterbury (1070–89) and trusted counsellor of William the Conqueror, was largely responsible for the excellent church–state relations of William's reign after the Norman Conquest of England.

Originally a lawyer, Lanfranc won a reputation as a teacher at a school he established at Avranches, Normandy (1039–42). He then entered the Benedictine monastery at Bec, where, after three years of seclusion, he became prior and resumed teaching. He was at first an opponent of the marriage of William of Normandy to Matilda of Flanders (1053), but he and William were later reconciled and thereafter maintained a relationship of mutual respect. William made Lanfranc first abbot of St. Stephen's at Caen (*c.* 1063) and after the Conquest nominated him to the see of Canterbury as soon as the incumbent, Stigand, was deposed.

Lanfranc embarked upon a successful reform and reorganization of the English Church. Although a firm supporter of papal sovereignty, he assisted William in maintaining the fullest possible independence for the English Church. At the same time he protected the church from royal and other secular influence. His concern for the separate responsibilities and prerogatives of state and church shaped a memorable ordinance that divided the ecclesiastical from the secular courts (*c.* 1076). His policy, in accord with that of the King, was to replace native English bishops with Normans, but he remained on friendly terms with Wulfstan of Worcester, the last of the Anglo-Saxon prelates. Perhaps his greatest service to the King was his detection in 1075 of the conspiracy formed against him by the earls of Norfolk and Hereford. On the death of the Conqueror in 1087, Lanfranc secured the succession for William II Rufus, inducing the English militia to support him against the partisans of his elder brother, Robert II Curthose, Duke of Normandy.

Lanfranco, Giovanni, also called GIOVANNI DI STEFFANO, or IL CAVALIERE GIOVANNI LANFRANCHI (b. Jan. 26, 1582, Parma—d. Nov. 30, 1647, Rome), Italian painter, one of the early exponents of High Baroque illusionism. He was a pupil of Agostino Carracci in Parma (1600–02) and later studied with Annibale Carracci in Rome. The decisive influence on his work, however, was not the Baroque classicism of the Carracci but the dynamic illusionism of the dome paintings in Parma by Correggio. Lanfranco's painting in the dome of S. Andrea della Valle in Rome (1621–25) derives directly from Correggio in its virtuoso use of vigorously posed figures floating in the clouds over the spectator's head. Lanfranco worked in Naples from 1633/34 to 1646, his best known work there being the dome of the chapel of S. Gennaro in the cathedral (1641–46). He was a bitter rival of Domenichino, both in Rome and later in Naples.

Lang, Andrew (b. March 31, 1844, Selkirk, Selkirkshire, Scot.—d. July 20, 1912, Banchory, Aberdeenshire), Scottish scholar and man of letters noted for his collections of fairy tales and translations of Homer.

Educated at St. Andrews University and at Balliol College, Oxford, he held an open fellowship at Merton College until 1875, when he moved to London. He quickly became famous for his critical articles in *The Daily News* and other papers. He displayed talent as a poet in *Ballads and Lyrics of Old France* (1872), *Helen of Troy* (1882), and *Grass of Parnassus* (1888) and as a novelist with *The Mark of Cain* (1886) and *The Disentanglers* (1902). He earned special praise for his 12-volume collection of fairy tales, the first volume of which was *The Blue Fairy Book* (1889) and the last *The Lilac Fairy Book* (1910). His own fairy tales, *The Gold of Fairnilee* (1888), *Prince Prigio* (1889), and *Prince Ricardo of Pantouflia* (1893) became children's classics.

Lang also did important pioneer work in such volumes as *Custom and Myth* (1884) and *Myth, Ritual and Religion* (1887). Later he turned to history and historical mysteries, notably *Pickle the Spy* (1897), *A History of Scotland from the Roman Occupation*, 4 vol. (1900–07), *Historical Mysteries* (1904), and *The Maid of France* (1908). His lifelong devotion to Homer produced well-known prose translations of the *Odyssey* (1879), in collaboration with S.H. Butcher, and of the *Iliad* (1883), with Walter Leaf and Ernest Myers. He defended the theory of the unity of Homeric literature, and his *World of Homer* (1910) is an important study.

Lang (of Lambeth), (William) Cosmo Gordon Lang, Baron (b. Oct. 31, 1864, Fyvie Manse, Aberdeen, Aberdeenshire, Scot.—d. Dec. 5, 1945, Kew Gardens, Surrey, Eng.), influential and versatile Anglican priest who, as archbishop of Canterbury, was a close friend and adviser to King George VI. He was also briefly suspected of having conspired to bring about the abdication in 1936 of King Edward VIII, who married the U.S. divorcee Wallis Simpson.

Baron Lang of Lambeth, 1929
BBC Hulton Picture Library

Abruptly abandoning a legal career on the eve of his appointment to the bar, Lang enrolled at Cuddesdon Theological College. After an assistant curacy in a Leeds slum, he became dean of divinity at Magdalen College, Oxford (1893–96), and vicar of the university church (1894–96). He then served successively as vicar of Portsea, Hampshire; suffragan bishop of Stepney, London; and archbishop of York. He was archbishop of Canterbury from 1928 until his retirement in 1942, when George VI created him Baron Lang of Lambeth and granted him a home at Kew.

Also a prominent member of the House of Lords, Lang was an ardent ecumenicist and was active in the ministry to slum and industrial areas. Public opinion later acquitted him of wrongdoing during the intrigue of 1936, when various officials of the British government sought the abdication of Edward VIII to prevent his romance with Wallis Simpson from dividing the country. Lang's life and work is outlined in J.G. Lockhart's *Cosmo Gordon Lang* (1949).

Lang, Fritz (b. Dec. 5, 1890, Vienna—d. Aug. 2, 1976, Los Angeles), Austrian-born U.S. motion-picture director whose films, dealing with fate and man's inevitable working out of his destiny, are considered masterpieces of visual composition.

The son of an architect, Lang briefly studied architecture at Vienna's Technical University, then travelled widely before settling for a time in Paris as a painter. While recovering from wounds suffered in the service of Austria during World War I, he started to write screenplays; after the war he went to Berlin to work with Erich Pommer, a German film producer.

His first successful picture as a director was *Der müde Tod* (1921; *Between Worlds*). *Dr. Mabuse, der Spieler* (1922; *Dr. Mabuse*) studied a criminal mastermind; *Die Nibelungen* (1924; released in two parts in the United States, *Siegfried* and *Kriemhild's Revenge*) was based on the early 13th-century German poem; *Metropolis* (1926) was an Expressionist vision of the future; and *M* (1931), his most famous German film, explored the compulsion to murder. *Das Testament des Dr. Mabuse* (1932; *The Last Will of Dr. Mabuse*), in which a madman speaks Nazi philosophy, attracted the attention of Joseph Goebbels, the Nazis' chief propagandist, who invited Lang to supervise German films. Lang left for Paris the same evening and later moved to the United States.

Fritz Lang checking model street for *Hangmen Also Die*, 1943
By courtesy of Fritz Lang

Fury (1936), a study of a lynch mob, is his most praised American film. Others include *You Only Live Once* (1937), *Western Union* (1941), *Hangmen Also Die* (1943), *Scarlet Street* (1945), *Clash by Night* (1952), *Rancho Notorious* (1952), *Moonfleet* (1955), and *Beyond a Reasonable Doubt* (1956). Paul M. Jensen's *The Cinema of Fritz Lang* was published in 1969.

Lang, Jack, in full JOHN THOMAS LANG (b. Dec. 21, 1876, Sydney—d. Sept. 27, 1975, Sydney), Australian statesman and Labor premier of New South Wales (1925–27, 1930–32) whose defiance of Australia's Labor prime minister James Henry Scullin's economic policies contributed to Scullin's defeat in 1931 and to the decline of the Labor Party from national power.

After entering the New South Wales Parliament in 1913, Lang rose to party secretary and state treasurer (1920–22), becoming premier and treasurer in 1925. During his first ministry he developed Australia's first child endowment plan and sponsored a widows' pension bill. He led the Labor parliamentary opposition (1927–30) and was elected premier in 1930 on a platform opposing the deflationary policies of the federal Labor government.

Jack Lang
Camera Press

Refusing to pay New South Wales's interest payments on overseas loans in April 1931, Lang modified his position three months later. Lang's actions deepened the split in the national Labor Party, leading to Scullin's defeat in 1931, and encouraged the development of the right-wing New Guard movement in opposition to Lang's policies. In February 1932, he rejected the new federal statute requiring payment of state revenues to the commonwealth and was dismissed by Gov. Philip Game. He served in the New South Wales Parliament in 1943–49 (although expelled from the Labor Party in 1943), and then briefly in the federal Parliament, before settling into a very long and active retirement. In 1972 the party reinstated his membership.

Consult the INDEX *first*

Lang, John Dunmore (b. Aug. 25, 1799, Greenock, Scot.—d. Aug. 8, 1878, Sydney), Australian churchman and writer, founder of the Australian Presbyterian Church, and an influence in shaping colonization of that continent.

Lang studied at the University of Glasgow, was ordained in September 1822, and was sent to Australia in 1823 on behalf of the established Church of Scotland to be its first regular minister there. In 1836 he persuaded the English government to subsidize those who wished to emigrate to Australia, which had hitherto been settled largely by convicts. He also recruited ministers and teachers for the Australian church. He served in the legislature for a number of years as the representative of Port Philip, Moreton Bay, and Sydney. He visited England six times, mainly to encourage the emigration of upper-working-class Protestants to Australia.

Lang, (Alexander) Matheson (b. May 15, 1879, Montreal—d. April 11, 1948, Bridgetown, Barbados), English romantic actor and dramatist whose imposing presence, commanding features, and fine voice were as well suited to Othello as to such popular and picturesque characters as Mr. Wu and the Wandering Jew.

Matheson Lang, 1936
By courtesy of the National Film Archive, London

Lang began his career as a Shakespearean actor in 1897, first played in London in 1900, and acted Benedick to the Beatrice of Ellen Terry in 1903. His sonorous and passionate Othello was first seen in 1907 at Manchester, and his highly romantic Romeo was a feature of the 1908 London season. For the next 30 years he toured the English-speaking world, acting also in grandiose plays by Temple Thurston, Rafael Sabatini, and many others. His career also included several films, and he produced and dramatized many works. In 1914 he and his actress-wife, Hutin Britton (1876–1965), inaugurated the Shakespeare seasons at the Old Vic Theatre, London.

Lang, Matthäus (b. 1468, Augsburg, Ger.—d. March 30, 1540, Salzburg, Austria), German statesman and cardinal, counsellor of the emperor Maximilian I.

Matthäus Lang, detail from an engraving by Daniel Hopfer
By courtesy of the Bildarchiv, Osterreichische Nationalbibliothek, Vienna

Of bourgeois origin, Lang studied law, entered Maximilian's service about 1494, and became indispensable as the emperor's secretary. He received numerous benefices and ecclesiastical offices prior to his ordination as a priest in 1519. In many ways, he typified the worldly absentee bishops against whom the reformer Martin Luther protested.

Lang negotiated the League of Cambrai with France, Spain, the Netherlands, and later Pope Julius II, against Venice (1508). In 1511, however, when Julius, at peace with Venice, wanted Maximilian's help in driving the French from Italy, Lang was sent to Bologna to reconcile the pope with France and to isolate Venice. They failed to reach agreement then, partly because Lang's arrogant conduct scandalized the papal officials, but Lang returned to Italy in 1512 and persuaded Julius to unite with Maximilian against Venice. The pope in turn obtained the emperor's agreement to the convening of the fifth Lateran Council and a promise of armed support. Lang's elevation as cardinal was announced on Nov. 24, 1512, the papal-imperial alliance on the 25th.

After Lang negotiated the settlement in Vienna (1515) that ultimately gave the Habsburgs the thrones of Bohemia and Hungary, he became prince-archbishop of Salzburg (1519) and ceased to be a Habsburg official. In the 1520s he overcame rebellions of his nobles and of the citizens of Salzburg and, supported by the Swabian League, suppressed a fierce peasant uprising. He maintained authoritarian conservatism in religion and government until his death.

Langbaurgh-on-Tees, formerly LANGBAURGH, district and borough, county of Cleveland, England. It extends on the south side of the River Tees between Middlesbrough and the rocky coastline and then southward along the coastline past the highest cliffs of England at Boulby, which rise more than 600 feet (180 m) from the North Sea.

Langbaurgh-on-Tees takes its name from a division dating to the Danish colonization 2,000 years ago. The district includes modern steelworks (at Lackenby and Redcar) and petrochemical plants (Wilton), as well as older iron-making towns such as Grangetown and South Bank along the bay shoreline that was followed by the Redcar railway of 1846. The estuary mudflats of the River Tees below Middlesbrough have been extensively reclaimed to provide spacious sites for industrial and port installations, which include an oil refinery and the new international port of Teesport. Since 1977 oil has been received from the North Sea by direct pipeline.

The district is scenic. The coastal resort of Saltburn-by-the-Sea and the inland market town of Guisborough are favoured residential towns. In the south Langbaurgh-on-Tees extends into the North York Moors National Park. Area district, 93 square miles (242 square km). Pop. (1991 prelim.) 141,700.

Langdell, Christopher Columbus (b. May 22, 1826, New Boston, N.H., U.S.—d. July 6, 1906, Cambridge, Mass.), American educator, dean of the Harvard Law School (1870–95), who originated the case method of teaching law.

Langdell studied law at Harvard (1851–54) and practiced in New York City until 1870, when he accepted a professorship and then the deanship of the Harvard Law School. American legal education at that time was a leisurely process, with no examinations or fixed requirements for the bachelor of laws (LL.B.) degree. Langdell raised the law program to university standards by instituting a regular progression of mandatory courses and tests. Later he devised the case method, so that students might read and discuss original authorities and derive for themselves the principles of the law.

A book by Langdell, *Selection of Cases on the Law of Contracts* (1871), was the first case-method text. Most of the early casebooks, however, were edited by James Barr Ames (1846–1910), a law professor at Harvard from 1873 and Langdell's successor as dean. Eventually the method became universal in American law schools.

Lange, Antoni (b. *c.* 1861, Warsaw, Pol.—d. March 17, 1929, Warsaw), Polish poet, literary critic, and translator.

Lange studied linguistics, philosophy, and literature in Paris (1886–90), and shortly after his return to Warsaw he became one of the leading personalities in literary circles. His intellectual curiosity was unlimited, and he was one of the first to popularize Indian philosophy and literature in Poland. In his *Studia z literatury francuskiej* (1897; "Studies on French Literature") he not only wrote about the French Parnassians and Symbolists but also made their works available to Polish readers in excellent translations. Lange's own poems did not win him recognition, and the last phase of his life was poisoned by feelings of bitterness.

Lange, Christian Lous (b. Sept. 17, 1869, Stavanger, Nor.—d. Dec. 11, 1938, Oslo), Norwegian peace advocate, secretary-general of the Inter-Parliamentary Union (1909–33), and cowinner (with Karl Branting) of the Nobel Prize for Peace in 1921.

Christian Lous Lange
Norsk Telegrambyra, Oslo

Lange graduated in languages from the University of Oslo in 1893 and in 1919 received a doctorate for a thesis on the history of internationalism. He served as secretary (1900–09) to the Nobel Committee in Oslo and was instrumental in organizing the library of the Nobel Institute, which was founded in 1904. In 1907 he was a delegate to the second peace conference at The Hague. In 1909 he became secretary-general of the Inter-Parliamentary Union, the conference of delegates from the legislative bodies of the world's nations. Under his leadership it grew and prospered despite great difficulties during World War I. Lange was also active in the League of Nations as a Norwegian delegate, interesting himself particularly in disarmament. In 1932 he received the Grotius Medal of The Netherlands.

Lange, David (Russell) (b. Aug. 4, 1942, Otahuhu, N.Z.), New Zealand lawyer and politician who in 1984 became the youngest prime minister of that country in the 20th century.

The son of a left-wing physician, Lange grew up in a working-class suburb of Auckland. After receiving a law degree from the University of Auckland, he chose to provide low-cost legal aid to the poor rather than pursue a more lucrative practice. At age 25 he moved to London for a year, during which time he was greatly influenced by the preaching of a Methodist minister in a mission for the poor.

Lange was elected to the New Zealand Parliament in 1977 after having lost his first bid to win a seat in 1976. He quickly earned a reputation as an outstanding orator, was chosen leader of the opposition Labour Party in 1983, and, as such, was elected prime minister in his party's sweeping victory in 1984.

As prime minister Lange took various measures to deal with the economic problems he had inherited from the previous government. His administration fulfilled its campaign promise to deny New Zealand's port facilities to nuclear-armed and nuclear-powered vessels in the hope of securing a "nuclear-free" Pacific. The ban primarily affected U.S. warships, and Lange was chided by the U.S. government for his unwillingness to cooperate with the Western global nuclear strategy. His policy effectively terminated the ANZUS (Australia–New Zealand–U.S.) defense alliance. Lange was also forthright in confronting France after that nation's agents blew up a ship belonging to the environmentalist group Greenpeace in Auckland Harbour shortly before the ship was to set off to protest a planned French nuclear test in the South Pacific. He pressed for an apology and reparations from France for the sinking of the vessel. The Labour Party won the national election of August 1987, and so Lange continued as prime minister until 1989, when he resigned from office owing to health reasons.

Lange, Dorothea (b. May 26, 1895, Hoboken, N.J., U.S.—d. Oct. 11, 1965, San Francisco, Calif.), American documentary photographer whose studies of the victims of the Great Depression of the 1930s greatly influenced later documentary and journalistic photographers.

Lange studied photography under Clarence White, a member of the group of photographers called the Photo-Secession, and then, at the age of 20, decided to travel around the world, earning money as she went by selling her photographs. She got as far as San Francisco before her money ran out, settled there, and opened a portrait studio in 1916.

During the Depression, Lange sought to broaden the dimensions of her work by photographing the homeless men who wandered the streets. Such pictures as "White An-

Dorothea Lange, 1964
Wayne Miller—Magnum

gel Breadline" (1932), showing the hopeless condition of these men, received immediate recognition from the photographers of Group *f*.64 and led to Lange's being hired by the federal Resettlement Administration (later called the Farm Security Administration) to bring the conditions of the poor to public attention. Her photographs of migrant workers were captioned with the words of the workers themselves and were so effective that the state established camps for the migrants.

In 1939 Lange published a collection of her photographs in the book *An American Exodus: A Record of Human Erosion.* Two years later she received a Guggenheim Fellowship, which she gave up, however, after the attack on Pearl Harbor so that she could record the mass evacuation of Japanese-Americans to detention camps. After World War II, she did a number of photo-essays, including "Mormon Villages" and "The Irish Countryman," for *Life* magazine. Even during long periods of inactivity because of illness, her reputation continued to rise.

Lange, Friedrich Albert (b. Sept. 28, 1828, Wald, near Solingen, Prussia—d. Nov. 21, 1875, Marburg, Ger.), German philosopher and Socialist, important for his refutation of materialism and for establishing a lasting tradition of Neo-Kantianism at the University of Marburg.

Lange was the son of theologian Johann Peter Lange and was educated at Cologne, Bonn, and Duisburg. In 1861 he became involved in politics. Among his best known works are *Die Leibesübungen* (1863; "On Physical Exercise"); *Die Arbeiterfrage* (1865; "The Worker Question"); *Die Grundlagen der mathematischen Psychologie* (1865; "The Foundation of Mathematical Psychology"); *Geschichte des Materialismus und Kritik seiner Bedeutung in der Gegenwart* (1866; *History of Materialism*); *J. St. Mill's Ansichten über die soziale Frage* (1866; "John Stuart Mill's Theories About the Social Question"). Lange left Germany in 1866 and moved to Winterthur, near Zürich, to write for a democratic newspaper. He also wrote the *Neue Beiträge zur Geschichte des Materialismus* (1867; "A New Contribution on the History of Materialism") and in 1870 became professor of philosophy at the University of Zürich, resigning his post in 1872 because of the pro-French sympathies of the Swiss in the Franco-German War. He then accepted the chair of philosophy at the University of Marburg and was largely responsible for a Kantian revival there. His *Logische Studien* ("Studies in Logic") was published in 1877, after his death.

Langeland, island (area 110 sq mi [284 sq km]), Fyns *amtskommune* (county), Denmark, in the Baltic Sea between Fyn (Funen) and Lolland islands. Langeland's castle of Tranekær has been a royal residence since 1231 (rebuilt 1550), and its principal town, Rudkøbing, was chartered in 1287. The undulating, well-wooded land has fertile clay loams that support grain and sugar beets. There is a well-preserved Stone Age barrow in the southern part of the island, and Rudkøbing has several medieval churches and houses. Pop. (1981 est.) 16,092.

Langen, Eugen (b. Oct. 9, 1833, Cologne—d. Oct. 2, 1895, Cologne), German engineer who pioneered in building internal-combustion engines.

In 1864 Langen formed a partnership with Nikolaus A. Otto, with whom he collaborated for the rest of his life. In 1867 they designed their first internal-combustion engine. Later, recognizing the theoretical advantages of a four-stroke cycle, they incorporated it in their "silent engine" (patented 1877), the first operating example of the modern automobile engine. Langen also conceived the idea of an overhead suspension monorail, as put into operation in 1901 at Wuppertal, Ger.

Langer, František (b. March 3, 1888, Prague—d. Aug. 2, 1965, Prague), physician and writer, one of the outstanding Czech dramatists of the interwar period.

Langer studied medicine in Prague and wrote a collection of short stories and two unsuccessful plays before joining the Austrian army as a surgeon. Sent to the Galician front during World War I, he was taken prisoner by the Russians (1916) and subsequently joined the Czechoslovak Legion, which fought the Communists in the Russian Civil War. After the war, he served in the medical corps of the Czech army and continued his literary career.

Langer achieved his greatest success with *Velbloud uchem jehly* (1923; *The Camel Through the Needle's Eye*), a comedy about lower-class life. *Periferie* (1925; "The Outskirts"), a psychological drama, deals with a murderer who is frustrated in his attempts to be legally condemned. Of his later writing, only *Jízdní hlídka* (1935; "The Cavalry Watch") compared with his earlier successes; it was based upon his experiences with the legion.

Langer went to England in 1939 and did not return to his home until after World War II; he retired from the army with the rank of general. The postwar Communist government did not allow him to publish new work until the late 1950s.

Langer, Susanne K(nauth) (b. Dec. 20, 1895, New York City—d. July 17, 1985, Old Lyme, Conn.), American philosopher and educator who wrote extensively on linguistic analysis and aesthetics.

Langer studied with Alfred North Whitehead at Radcliffe College, Cambridge, Mass., and she received her Ph.D. in philosophy from Harvard University, Cambridge, Mass. in 1926. From 1927 to 1942 she was a philosophy tutor at Radcliffe. She lectured in philosophy at Columbia University, New York City, from 1945 to 1950, and from 1954 to 1961 (after 1961, emeritus) she was a professor of philosophy at Connecticut College in New London.

In her best known book, *Philosophy in a New Key: A Study in the Symbolism of Reason, Rite and Art* (1942), she attempted to give art the claim to meaning that science was given through Whitehead's analysis of symbolic modes. Distinguishing nondiscursive symbols of art from discursive symbols of scientific language in *Feeling and Form* (1953), she submitted that art, especially music, is a highly articulated form of expression symbolizing direct or intuitive knowledge of life patterns; *e.g.,* feeling, motion, and emotion, which ordinary language is unable to convey. In the three-volume work *Mind: An Essay on Human Feeling* (1967, 1972, and 1982), Langer attempted to trace the origin and development of the mind.

Langerhans, islets of, also called ISLANDS OF LANGERHANS, irregularly shaped patches of endocrine tissue located within the pancreas of most vertebrates. They are named for the German physician Paul Langerhans, who first described them in 1869. The normal human pancreas contains about 1,000,000 islets. The islets consist of four distinct cell types, of which three (alpha, beta, and delta cells) produce important hormones; the fourth component (C cells) has no known function.

The most common islet cell, the beta cell, produces insulin, the major hormone in the regulation of carbohydrate, fat, and protein metabolism. Insulin is crucial in several metabolic processes: it promotes the uptake and metabolism of glucose by the body's cells; it prevents production and release of glucose by the liver; it causes muscle cells to take up amino acids, the basic components of protein; and it inhibits the breakdown and release of fats. The release of insulin from the beta cells can be triggered by growth hormone (somatotropin) or by glucagon, but the most important stimulator of insulin release is glucose; when the blood glucose level increases—as it does following a meal—insulin is released to counter it. The inability of the islet cells to make insulin or the failure to produce amounts sufficient to control blood glucose level are the causes of diabetes mellitus.

The alpha cells of the islets of Langerhans produce an opposing hormone, glucagon, which releases glucose from the liver and fatty acids from fat tissue. In turn, glucose and free fatty acids favour insulin release and inhibit glucagon secretion. The delta cells produce somatostatin, a strong inhibitor of somatotropin, insulin, and glucagon; its role in metabolic regulation is not yet clear. Somatostatin is also produced by the hypothalamus and functions there as a counterbalance to somatotropin, one of the major pituitary hormones.

Langey, Guillaume du Bellay, seigneur de (lord of): *see* Bellay, Guillaume du.

Langfjellet, English LONG MOUNTAINS, mountainous area lying south and west of the Dovrefjell (plateau) in west central Norway. Langfjellet includes the Jotunheimen (mountains), the Jostedalsbreen and Hardangerjøkulen (ice fields), the Hardangervidda (plateau), the Bykleheiane (upland), and many lesser features. The highest mountains in Scandinavia are found in the group, with Galdhøpiggen (8,100 ft [2,469 m]) and Glittertinden (8,110 ft; including glacier at summit) being the two loftiest peaks. Several major fjords penetrate the region, including Boknafjorden, Hardangerfjorden, and Sognafjorden, the longest fjord in Norway. Jostedalsbreen, in the northwestern part of Langfjellet region, is the largest ice field in continental Europe. Most of the principal rivers of southern Norway originate in Langfjellet. The region, generally sparsely populated, is a centre for both winter and summer tourism.

Langhorne, John (b. March 1735, Winton, Somerset, Eng.—d. April 1, 1779, Blagdon, Somerset), poet and English translator of the 1st-century Greek biographer Plutarch; his work anticipates that of George Crabbe in its description of the problems facing the poor. He was a country rector after 1766. His best work is perhaps *The Country Justice* (3 parts, 1774–77). His translation—jointly with his brother William—of Plutarch appeared in 1770. He also contributed reviews to *The Monthly Review* (1761–79) and edited the poems of William Collins (1765).

Langhorne, Nancy Witcher: *see* Astor (of Hever Castle), Nancy Witcher Astor, Viscountess.

Langiewicz, Marian (Melchior) (b. Aug. 5, 1827, Krotoszyn, near Poznań, Pol., Prussia—d. May 11, 1887, Constantinople), Polish soldier and patriot who played a key role in the Polish Insurrection of 1863.

After a year in the Prussian Army as a lieutenant of artillery, Langiewicz took a teaching position at the Polish military school in Paris (1860), but in the same year he joined Garibaldi's Neapolitan campaign. In 1861 he taught at a short-lived Polish military school in Cuneo, in the Piedmont.

Langiewicz joined in plans for a Polish insurrection against Russia in 1862; and when it began in 1863, he headed a ragtag army in the Sandomierz (Sandomir) region of southern Poland. Because of Langiewicz' early successes against Russian forces, conservative elements in the insurrection offered him dictatorship of the revolutionary regime in March, bypassing and hoping to check the more radical leadership in Warsaw. Langiewicz accepted the

Langiewicz, portrait by an unknown artist

By courtesy of Panstwowe Wydawnictwo Naukowe, Warsaw

post and won partial recognition from the outmaneuvered Warsaw leaders. Within a few days, however, his forces suffered serious defeats against the Russians, which, along with factionalism among his troops, caused him to flee to Austria on March 21; his dictatorship thus ended after 10 days.

Langiewicz was imprisoned by the Austrians until 1865 and then lived in Switzerland for a while. Later he entered the service of the Ottoman Empire as Langie Bey. He wrote *Relacya o kampanii własney 1863 r.* (1905; "Report on My Campaign of 1863") and *Pisma wojskowe* (1920; "Military Writings").

Langjökull (Icelandic: "Long Glacier"), large ice field, west-central Iceland. Langjökull is 40 miles (64 km) long and 15 miles (24 km) wide and covers an area of 395 square miles (1,025 square km). It rises to 4,757 feet (1,450 m) above sea level in the centre and feeds several rivers, including the Hvítá and Ölfusá. Haga Lake (Hagavatn) is at the foot of the glacier.

Langkawi Island, Malaysian PULAU LANGKAWI, main island of the Langkawi group, in the Strait of Malacca, West Malaysia (Malaya). It lies just south of the Thai island of Tarutao. Langkawi, 18 miles (29 km) long and 10 miles (16 km) wide, with an area of 203 square miles (526 square km), rises to 2,887 feet (880 m) at Raya Mountain.

While most of its inhabitants are fishermen, the island is well cultivated (coconuts and rubber). Kauh, the main village on the southern shore, is linked by road to the coastal settlements of Air Hangat and Padang Masirat. Langkawi Island has ferry connections with Kuala Kedah on the mainland and is frequented for its beaches, waterfalls, hot springs, coloured cliffs, historic caves, and fishing grounds. Its steep-sided limestone hills are favoured by climbers. Pop. (1991) 42,755.

Langland, William (b. *c.* 1330—d. *c.* 1400), presumed author of one of the greatest examples of Middle English alliterative poetry, generally known as *Piers Plowman,* an allegorical work with a complex variety of religious themes. One of the major achievements of *Piers Plowman* is that it translates the language and conceptions of the cloister into symbols and images that could be understood by the layman. In general, the language of the poem is simple and colloquial, but some of the author's imagery is powerful and direct.

There are three versions of *Piers Plowman:* the A version of the text is the earliest, the B and C versions consist of revisions and further amplifications of the major themes of A, and C is thought by some scholars to be not entirely attributable to Langland. The version described here is from the B text, which consists of (1) a prologue and seven passus (divisions) concerned primarily with the life of man in society, the dangers of Meed (love of gain), and manifestations of the seven capital sins; and (2) 13 passus ostensibly dealing with the lives of Do-wel, Do-bet, and Do-best; in effect, with the growth of the individual Christian in self-knowledge, grace, and charity.

In its general structure the poem mirrors the complexity of the themes with which it deals, particularly in the recurring concepts of Do-wel, Do-bet, and Do-best, all in the end seen as embodied in Christ. They are usually identified with the active, contemplative, and "mixed" religious life, but the allegory of the poem is often susceptible to more than one interpretation, and some critics have related it to the traditional exegetical way of interpreting the Scriptures historically, allegorically, anagogically, and topologically.

Little is known of Langland's life: he is thought to have been born somewhere in the region of the Malvern Hills, in Worcestershire, and if he is to be identified with the "dreamer" of the poem, he may have been educated at the Benedictine school in Great Malvern. References in the poem suggest that he knew London and Westminster as well as Shropshire, and he may have been a cleric in minor orders in London.

Langland clearly had a deep knowledge of medieval theology and was fully committed to all the implications of Christian doctrine. He was interested in the asceticism of St. Bernard of Clairvaux, and his comments on the defects of churchmen and the religious in his day are nonetheless concomitant with his orthodoxy.

Langley, city ("district municipality"), southwestern British Columbia, Canada, just east-southeast of Vancouver, near the U.S. (Washington) border. The historic Hudson's Bay Company post, Fort Langley (named for Thomas Langley, a company director), was established nearby on the south bank of the Lower Fraser River in 1827; it was moved 2 miles (3 km) upstream in 1839 and played an important role in securing British influence in the coastal region before its closure in 1885. In 1858 the fort became the provisional capital of the Crown Colony of British Columbia when the colony was proclaimed there and Sir James Douglas sworn in as governor. Some of the fort's structures have been restored within a national historic park. The city, established in 1873 and incorporated in 1955, is now a suburb in the metropolitan area of Vancouver with some light industry and agricultural interests (dairying, vegetables, fruits). Pop. (1996) 22,523.

Langley, Edmund of: *see* York, Edmund of Langley, 1st Duke of.

Langley, Samuel Pierpont (b. Aug. 22, 1834, Roxbury, Mass., U.S.—d. Feb. 27, 1906, Aiken, S.C.), American astronomer, physicist, and aeronautics pioneer who contributed to the knowledge of solar phenomena as related to meteorology and built the first heavier-than-air flying machine to achieve sustained flight.

Langley

By courtesy of the Smithsonian Institution, Washington, D.C.

After practicing civil engineering and architecture in Chicago, Ill., and St. Louis, Mo., Langley returned to Boston, received an assistantship at the Harvard Observatory, and later taught mathematics at the U.S. Naval Academy, Annapolis, Md. In 1867 he accepted the directorship of the Allegheny Observatory and became professor of physics and astronomy at the University of Pittsburgh.

His chief interest was solar activity and its effect on the weather. In 1878 he invented the bolometer, a radiant-heat detector that is sensitive to differences in temperature of one hundred-thousandth of a degree. This device enabled him to study the solar spectrum (light rays from the Sun) far into its infrared (heat-ray) region and to measure the intensity of solar radiation at various wavelengths.

While at Allegheny, Langley made important experiments on the lift and drag of an aircraft moving through the air at a measured speed. Backed by these experiments, he was the first to offer a clear explanation of the way birds soar and glide without appreciable wing movement.

In 1896 he became the first to build heavier-than-air machines capable of sustained (although uncontrolled) flight. Both of his unmanned crafts had two sets of 14-foot (4.3-metre) wings, weighed 26 pounds (11.8 kg), and were powered by steam engines. His first manned aircraft, powered by a five-cylinder air-cooled gasoline engine designed by Langley's assistant Charles M. Manly and piloted by Manly, snagged upon launching from a catapult, and it crashed into the Potomac River for the second and last time on Dec. 8, 1903, just nine days before the successful flights of the Wright brothers near Kitty Hawk, N.C. It had a wingspan of 48 feet (14.6 m) and a total weight (with pilot) of 850 pounds (386 kg). Some authorities believe that if his catapult had not failed, Langley would have been the first to achieve sustained flight in a manned heavier-than-air machine.

Langlois, Charles-Victor (b. May 26, 1863, Rouen, France—d. June 25, 1929, Paris), one of the leading French scholars of the late 19th century, who is best known for his bibliographic and historical studies of medieval France.

Langlois received his doctorate in 1887 and was named lecturer at the faculty of letters of Douai. In 1909 he became a professor at the University of Paris, where he taught paleography, bibliography, and the history of the Middle Ages.

Langlois's work *Le Règne de Philippe III le Hardi* (1887; "The Reign of Philip III the Bold"), emphasizing the political and institutional conditions of 13th-century France, remains one of the best histories of a single reign. In 1904 he published *Manuel de bibliographie historique,* 2 vol. (1896–1904; "Manual of Historical Bibliography"), a fundamental work in historical scholarship that provides valuable discussions of bibliographic method.

Among his other treatises are *La Vie en France au moyen âge, de la fin du XIIe au milieu du XIVe siècle,* 3 vol. (1925–27; "Life in France in the Middle Ages from the End of the 12th to the Middle of the 14th Century"), a description of French life illustrated by edited selections from medieval texts, and *Les Archives de l'histoire de France* (1891–93), a bibliographic description of archives in all parts of France. Langlois became director of the Archives Nationales in 1913 and was later appointed to the Académie des Inscriptions et Belles-Lettres (1917).

Langmuir, Irving (b. Jan. 31, 1881, Brooklyn, N.Y., U.S.—d. Aug. 16, 1957, Falmouth, Mass.), American physical chemist whose studies of molecular films on solid and liquid surfaces opened new fields in colloid research and biochemistry and won him the Nobel Prize in Chemistry for 1932.

After studying metallurgical engineering at Columbia University, Langmuir worked under Walther H. Nernst, a pioneer physical chemist, at the University of Göttingen, Germany, where he took his Ph.D. in 1906. In the United States he conducted research for the General Electric Company, Schenectady, N.Y. (1909–50).

Investigating electrical discharges in gases, electron emission, and the high-temperature surface chemistry of tungsten, Langmuir greatly extended the life of the tungsten-filament light bulb. He also developed a vacuum pump, high-vacuum tubes used in radio broadcasting, and an atomic hydrogen blowtorch capable of producing temperatures greater than 3,000° C (6,000° F).

Working independently of the U.S. atomic chemist Gilbert N. Lewis, Langmuir formulated theories of atomic structure and chemical bond formation and introduced the term covalence. In 1946 he and his associates began to explore the possibility of inducing rainfall by seeding clouds with silver iodide and solidified carbon dioxide.

Lango, people inhabiting the marshy lowlands northeast of Lakes Kwania and Kyoga in northern Uganda and speaking an Eastern Sudanic language of the Chari-Nile branch of the Nilo-Saharan family.

The Lango cultivate millet for food and for making beer and also grow numerous vegetables. Men and women share the agricultural work, but men have sole custody of cattle.

The population was traditionally divided into a number of patrilineal clans, each having its own territory and inhabiting a compact and usually stockaded village. Marriage involved a substantial bride-price in livestock. Hereditary chiefs had authority over all inhabitants of their clan areas, regardless of kinship. There was, however, no hereditary aristocracy. Above these chiefs were senior chiefs (*rwot*) who won their positions by personal merit, each controlling from three to six hereditary chiefs. Men also were divided into a series of age grades.

Lango traditionally believed that every human had a guardian spirit (*winyo*, or "bird") that attended him during life and that must be ritually liberated from the corpse. There was also a belief in a shadow self, or immaterial soul (*tipo*), that after death eventually was merged into a vague entity called Jok, their god or supreme force. Ancestors, of whom Jok was held the universal sublimation, were worshiped along with Jok at shrines and sacred trees by prayer and sacrifice.

Milton Obote, the first president of the Republic of Uganda (1966–71; 1980–85), was a member of the Lango people.

Langport, town ("parish"), South Somerset district, county of Somerset, England, at the head of the Somerset marshes and for centuries the main crossing point of the River Parrett. Founded as a royal borough in Saxon times, by 1086 the town had 34 burgesses. It remained in direct communication with the Bristol Channel until the establishment of the port of Bridgwater in 1200. In 1563 the first charter of the town granted it fairs and a market. The river trade, which had made Langport such an important market, declined with the advent of railways; borough status was lost in 1886. Pop. (1991) 2,882.

Langres, town, eastern France, Haute-Marne *département,* Champagne-Ardenne *région,* north-northeast of Dijon. A medieval fortified city, it is situated 1,529 feet (466 m) above sea level on a promontory at the northern end of the Langres Plateau. The walls encompassing the town contain a 2nd-century Roman gate, 15th- to 16th-century towers, and other 16th- to 18th-century gates. The severe 12th-century Saint-Mammès Cathedral, marking the transition between Burgundy Romanesque and Gothic architecture, has an 18th-century facade. A statue of the encyclopaedist Denis Diderot, who was born in Langres, stands in the centre of the town. A stronghold of the Lingones, a Gallic tribe, Langres later became an important Gallo-Roman town called Andematunum. At the end of the 2nd century St. Bénigne introduced Christianity to the town, and, at the beginning of the 3rd century, St. Sénateur was the first bishop of Langres. From the 12th to the 18th century the bishops of Langres, who had the title of duke, were ecclesiastical peers of the realm of France. Today the town is a centre of local agricultural industry; manufactures include electrical and nonelectrical machinery, as well as plastics. Pop. (1999) 9,586.

Langston, John Mercer (b. Dec. 14, 1829, Louisa county, Va., U.S.—d. Nov. 15, 1897, Washington, D.C.), black leader, educator, and diplomat, who is believed to have been the first black ever elected to public office in the United States.

The son of a Virginia planter and a slave mother, Langston was emancipated at the age of five, attended school in Ohio, and graduated from Oberlin College in 1849. He quickly became a leader among free blacks and was elected to local offices in Brownhelm Township, Ohio (1855), and Oberlin (1865–67). In 1864 he helped organize the National Equal Rights League, of which he was the first president.

After the American Civil War Langston moved to Washington, D.C., practiced law, and was professor of law and dean of the law department (1869–77) and vice president (1872–76) of Howard University. He was U.S. minister to Haiti and chargé d'affaires to Santo Domingo (1877–85) and was elected president of the Virginia Normal and Collegiate Institute (1885). In 1888 he was a Republican candidate from Virginia for the U.S. House of Representatives, and, after a challenge of the election returns that took almost two years, he succeeded in unseating his Democratic opponent and served in Congress from Sept. 23, 1890, to March 3, 1891.

Langtoft, Peter (d. *c.* 1307), author of an Anglo-Norman chronicle in alexandrines, canon of the Augustinian priory at Bridlington. He took his name from the village of Langtoft in East Yorkshire. It is known that he acted as procurator for the prior or chapter (1271–86), but he later seems to have been in disgrace.

His *Chronicle* deals with the history of England from the earliest times to the death of Edward I and seems to have as its aim the glorification of that king. The early part relies ultimately upon Geoffrey of Monmouth and other writers, but for the reign of Edward I it is an original and valuable authority, with a strong anti-Scottish bias. The latter part of the *Chronicle* was translated into English verse by Robert Mannyng of Brunne (completed 1328). The complete *Chronicle* was edited by Thomas Wright (1866–68).

Langton, Stephen (d. July 9, 1228, Slindon, Sussex, Eng.), English cardinal whose appointment as archbishop of Canterbury precipitated King John's quarrel with Pope Innocent III and played an important part in the Magna Carta crisis.

Langton, son of a lord of a manor in Lincolnshire, became early in his career a prebendary of York. He then (*c.* 1181) went to Paris and, having graduated from that university, became one of its most celebrated theologians, serving 25 years there. Pope Innocent III then summoned him to Rome and in 1206 created him cardinal-priest of St. Chrysogonus. Immediately afterward Langton was drawn into the vortex of English politics.

After the death of Hubert Walter (1205), a dispute immediately arose as to who should be the new archbishop of Canterbury; but after two years of political turmoil involving king and clergy, the Pope suggested that the suffragans of Canterbury elect Langton, who was consecrated at Viterbo on June 17, 1207. King John, however, refused to allow the new archbishop access to his province, seized the revenues of Canterbury, and banished the monks; Innocent replied by laying England under an interdict (March 1208). Langton crossed to Dover (October 1209) in an attempt to achieve negotiation with the king, but John would go no nearer than Chilham, Kent, and after a week the archbishop left the country, and John's excommunication was published (November 1209).

By 1212 John was seriously planning the recovery of the French territories lost to Philip II in 1204. The need to embark on this enterprise unhampered by ecclesiastical censure, Innocent's threat of deposing him, and the news that Philip was planning (April 1213) an invasion of England finally caused John to submit. He at once agreed to receive the archbishop, and Langton, who had been residing mainly at the Cistercian abbey of Pontigny, crossed to England (July 1213) and absolved the king.

Langton was not only associated with the baronial opposition against King John; he advised and supported it, suggesting that the barons take their stand on the coronation oath and the charter of Henry I. Later he withdrew, disapproving violent means, and at Runnymede (June 1215) appeared as one of the king's commissioners. He therefore probably influenced such "non baronial" clauses of Magna Carta as the one confirming ecclesiastical liberties. During 1218–28 he supported Henry III's party, being responsible for the 1225 reissue of Magna Carta, and that year convened a clerics' council to determine a grant to the king. He was responsible for the recall of the papal legate, and during his life no other one resided in England, thus strengthening the archbishop of Canterbury's claim to be *legatus natus* (a legate in his own right). In 1222 he also promulgated some important constitutions.

Langton, Walter (b. probably West Langton, Leicestershire, Eng.—d. Nov. 9/16, 1321, London), a leading adviser of King Edward I of England; he was treasurer of the exchequer from 1295 to 1307 and bishop of Lichfield from 1296 until his death. In both capacities he was greedy and unpopular.

From June 1296 to November 1297, Langton was in France and Flanders on diplomatic missions for Edward I. After Edward's death (July 7, 1307), Langton, whose enemies included Robert Winchelsey, archbishop of Canterbury, was dismissed by Edward II, with whom he had quarreled. His ecclesiastical holdings and revenues were seized, and he was imprisoned until January 1312.

He was released because Edward II wished to use him to undermine the strength of the lords ordainers, the committee of barons that attempted to reduce the power of the king and to rid the country of his favourite, Piers Gaveston. The barons, however, would not countenance Langton's reappointment as treasurer, and the king was forced to dismiss him from the privy council in 1315.

Langtry, Lillie, byname of EMILIE CHARLOTTE, LADY DE BATHE, née LE BRETON, also called (1874–97) EMILIE CHARLOTTE LANGTRY (b. Oct. 13, 1853, Isle of Jersey, Channel Islands—d. Feb. 12, 1929, Monte-Carlo, Monaco), British beauty and actress, known as the Jersey Lily.

She was the daughter of the dean of Jersey. In 1874 she married Edward Langtry, who died in 1897, and in 1899 she married Hugo

Lillie Langtry
Mansell Collection

de Bathe, who became a baronet in 1907. In 1881 Langtry caused a sensation by being the first society woman to go on the stage, making her first notable appearance at the Haymarket Theatre, London, as Kate Hardcastle in *She Stoops to Conquer*. For some time the critics did not take her seriously, but she became a competent actress, her most successful part being Rosalind in *As You Like It*. She also toured the provinces and the United States. She turned the old Aquarium Theatre in London into the Imperial Theatre, modeled on a Greek temple, and opened it under her own management in 1901. Her last appearance on the stage was in 1917. Lillie Langtry also maintained a successful racing stable at Newmarket. One of the most beautiful women of her time, she had many distinguished admirers, including the Prince of Wales, subsequently King Edward VII.

language, a system of conventional spoken or written symbols by means of which human beings, as members of a social group and participants in its culture, communicate. Language so defined is the peculiar possession of humans. Other animals interact by means of sounds and body movements, and some can learn to interpret human speech to an extremely limited extent. But no other species of being has conventionalized its cries and utterances so that they constitute a systematic symbolism in the way that language does. In these terms, then, humans may be described as the talking animals.

A brief treatment of language follows. The subject is treated in a number of articles in the MACROPAEDIA. For a general treatment, encompassing physiological, structural, semantic, cultural, and historical aspects, *see* Language. For full treatment of particular languages and language groups, *see* Languages of the World. For a treatment of the scientific study of the evolution, components, forms, and uses of language, *see* Linguistics. For a treatment of the phonetic and physiological aspects of spoken language, *see* Speech. For a treatment of written language and writing systems, *see* Writing. For a treatment of the particular linguistic function of naming, *see* Names.

For a description of the place of language in the circle of learning, and for a list of both MACROPAEDIA and MICROPAEDIA articles on the subject, *see* PROPAEDIA: Part Five, Section 514. For statistical data on major languages by country, *see* BRITANNICA BOOK OF THE YEAR.

Language has a structure or a series of structures, and this structuring can be analyzed and systematically presented. When language is spoken, a complex series of events takes place. These events are on many planes of experience: physical (the sound waves); chemical (the body chemistry); physiological (the movements of nerve impulses and of muscles); psychological (the reaction to stimuli); general cultural (the situation of the speaker in respect to the cultural system of his society); linguistic (the language being spoken); and semantic (its meaning).

Languages are classified genetically if they are descendants of a common ancestral language. The conservative genetic classification of languages into a language family is based on an abundance of cognates (related words) in the member languages. Using these terms, one may treat the languages of the world according to the following geographic divisions: Europe, South Asia, North Asia, Southwest Asia, East Asia, Southeast Asia, Africa, and the Americas.

The languages of Europe and of regions inhabited by descendants of Europeans (*e.g.,* the English- and Spanish-speaking peoples of the Americas) are primarily of the Indo-European and Uralic, or, more specifically, Finno-Ugric, language families. In the Indo-European family, Portuguese, Spanish, Catalan, French, Romansh, Ladin, Friulian, Italian, and Romanian constitute the Romance subgroup of the Italic branch. The extant Germanic language groups spoken are English, Frisian, Netherlandic-German, Insular Scandinavian, and Continental Scandinavian, with these groups dividing further on national criteria (*e.g.,* Continental Scandinavian divides into Norwegian, Danish, and Swedish). The Celtic branch of Indo-European is composed of Welsh, Breton, Irish Gaelic, and Scottish Gaelic. The literary languages within the Slavic branch of Indo-European may be divided into three geographic zones: East Slavic, West Slavic, and South Slavic, of which zones Russian, Polish, and Serbo-Croatian are respective examples. The three remaining branches of Indo-European are Baltic, Greek, and Albanian. Languages of the Finno-Ugric family, such as languages of the Sami (Lapp) and Baltic-Finno groups (*e.g.,* Sami, Finnish, and Livonian), are spoken in parts of Norway, Sweden, Finland, and Russia. Hungarian is also a member of the Finno-Ugric family.

In South Asia, the languages of India, Bangladesh, Pakistan, and the border states are genetically classified into the Indo-Aryan and Iranian subgroups of the Indo-Aryan branch of Indo-European. There are more than 20 members of the Indo-Aryan subgroup and many more dialects, but the most widely spoken are Bengali-Assamese, West Hindi, Bihārī, and East Hindi. The languages of the Iranian subgroup have fewer speakers in South Asia than the Indo-Aryan languages: Kashmiri and Shina, the most widely spoken Iranian languages in South Asia, are spoken only in Jammu and Kashmir. A few indigenous languages, such as the Dravidian languages of Telugu and Tamil, are spoken in South Asia, as are a few Sino-Tibetan languages. In many parts of postcolonial South Asia, English is still spoken as an interstate and international language.

The languages of North Asia are those spoken from the Arctic Ocean on the north to South Asia and China on the south and from the Caspian Sea and Ural Mountains in the west to the Pacific Ocean in the east. These languages are genetically classified into either the Uralic family, the Altaic group, the Indo-European family, or the Paleo-Siberian group. Although speakers of the Uralic languages are few in number, many speakers of Altaic languages are found in Iran, Afghanistan, and the Kansu province of China. Most Indo-European languages, such as Iranian, have been introduced into North Asia only recently. The Paleo-Siberian languages are not genetically linked to each other or to the other languages of North Asia and are spoken largely in northeasternmost Siberia.

In Southwest Asia—*i.e.,* in Iran, Iraq, Saudi Arabia, Jordan, Syria, Lebanon, and Israel—the languages spoken are either Indo-European, Turkic, Caucasian, or Semitic. Of the Indo-European languages, almost all the Iranian languages, including Persian, Pashto, Kurdish, and Balochi, are spoken in Iran; and Armenian is spoken in Armenia and Georgia. The Turkic language Turkish is spoken in Turkey, and other Turkic languages are spoken in the Caucasus, where more than 30 Caucasian languages are spoken. Of the Semitic languages spoken in Southwest Asia, Arabic is spoken in North Africa, the Arabian Peninsula, and much of the rest of the Middle East. Hebrew is spoken in Israel, and West Aramaic dialects are spoken in Lebanon and Syria.

In East Asia the languages spoken are largely Chinese languages (or dialects) in China, Japanese in Japan, and Korean in Korea, though the Altaic group is represented in China by Uighur, a Turkic language, and Manchu, a Manchu-Tungus language. Of the Chinese languages, Mandarin, Wu, and Cantonese are the most widely spoken. Mandarin, the native language of 70 percent of the Chinese, has more native speakers than any other language in the world. Tai and Miao-Yao languages are spoken in south-central China, Vietnam, Laos, and Thailand.

Southeast Asia is composed of a mainland subregion south of China and east of India, insular Malaysia, Indonesia, and the Philippines, and the name of the language generally corresponds to the name of the country. The languages on the mainland belong to the Austroasiatic, Tai, and Sino-Tibetan language groups, while the insular languages are all members of the Austronesian family. More than 50 Austroasiatic languages, such as Khmer in Cambodia, Mon in Thailand, and Vietnamese in Vietnam, are spoken on the mainland of Southeast Asia. The Tai and Sino-Tibetan families are represented by Thai in Thailand, Lao in Laos and Cambodia, and Burmese in Myanmar (Burma). In insular Southeast Asia, more than 500 Austronesian languages are spoken, the largest group of which is the Western Indonesian subgroup, which includes Tagalog, the basis for Pilipino, and 100 other languages spoken in the Philippines. While New Guinea and Australia may be said to belong to insular Southeast Asia, they contain only non-Austronesian languages, predominantly the Papuan languages of New Guinea and the more than 200 Australian Aboriginal languages.

Although, in many parts of Africa, European languages imported with 19th-century colonialism are still spoken as functional national languages, the native African language families are the Afro-Asiatic (formerly Hamito-Semitic), Nilo-Saharan, Niger-Congo, and Khoisan families. The Afro-Asiatic languages are spoken across North Africa from Mauritania to Somalia and beyond into southern Asia. The Nilo-Saharan languages are spoken in central interior Africa. The Niger-Congo languages, of which there are almost 900, are spoken from Mauritania to Kenya and south into South Africa. The Khoisan languages consist of about 50 languages spoken in southern Africa and Tanzania.

In the Americas, European languages such as Spanish, English, Portuguese, and French predominate. English is the language of most of North America, while Spanish and Portuguese are the dominant languages in South and Central America. The Western Hemisphere's indigenous languages, which came from Asia with the ancestors of the American Indians, are classified into the North and Central American Indian language families and the South American Indian language families. The North and Central American Indian language family is in part composed of the 20

Athabascan languages, the 13 Algonkian languages, the Macro-Siouan languages, and the Penutian languages, the only North American Indian language group successfully traced into South America. The South American Indian languages are much more numerous: the Andean-Equatorial group, for example, includes 14 families and almost 200 languages spoken from French Guiana to Colombia and south to Paraguay, as well as along the Amazon.

language, ideal (philosophy): *see* ideal language.

Languedoc, historical and cultural region encompassing the southern French *départements* of Hérault, Gard, and Ardèche and parts of Haute-Loire, Lozère, Tarn, Tarn-et-Garonne, Haute-Garonne, and Ariège and coextensive with the former province of Languedoc.

Languedoc is a centre of the distinctive civilization of the south of France. Its name is derived from the traditional language of southern France, in which the word *oc* means "yes," in contrast to *oïl,* or *oui,* in northern French. From the 13th century the name applied to

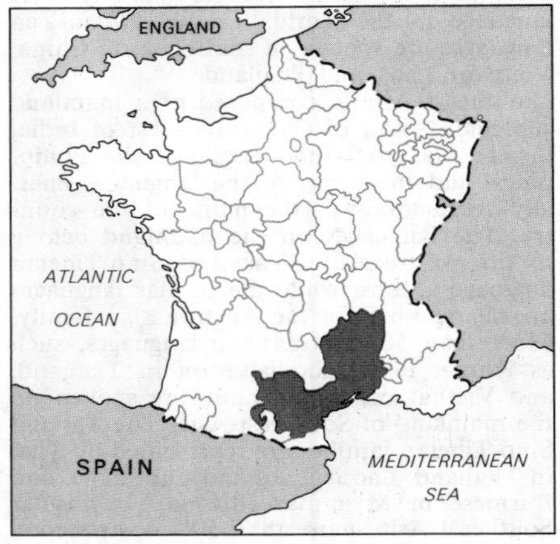

The *gouvernement* of Languedoc in 1789

the entire area in which the Languedoc, or Occitan, language was spoken and came to apply specifically to the territory of the feudal county of Toulouse.

From 121 BC the territory that constituted Languedoc was part of the Roman province of Gallia Narbonensis, which connected Italy to Spain, and was strongly influenced by Roman culture. With the breakdown of the Roman Empire, the region was controlled by the Visigoths in the 5th century and was partially conquered by the Franks in the 6th century. Septimania, the coastal strip, came under Arab rule in the early 8th century and was not conquered by the Franks until 759; under the Carolingians it was formed into a march for the protection of Aquitaine. The Toulousain (area around Toulouse) was reunited with the march in 924, the date marking the origin of the county of Toulouse. By 1050 the counts of Toulouse were suzerains not only of Toulousain and Septimania but also of Quercy, Rouergue, and Albi to the north, making the county one of the great fiefs of France. The power of the counts over much of this territory was largely nominal, being limited by the independence of their vassals, by the large ecclesiastical estates, and by the self-government of the towns.

From the mid-12th century, the Cathari, a Manichaean sect, won wide support from the people and the nobles of Languedoc; the Cathari were sometimes called Albigenses because of their strength around the town of Albi. They were branded as heretics by the Roman Catholic church, and Pope Innocent III preached a crusade against them, precipitating an invasion of Languedoc by a northern French army in 1209. The ensuing wars, which lasted until the mid-13th century, ended the political independence of Languedoc. The eastern part of the county of Toulouse was annexed by the French crown in 1229 and organized into the *sénéchaussées* ("seneschalships") of Carcassonne and Beaucaire. The rest remained with Raymond VII (count of Toulouse from 1222 to 1249), who agreed to the marriage of his daughter and heiress Jeanne to Alphonse of Poitiers, brother of King Louis IX. On the death of the couple without heirs in 1271, the rest of Languedoc was added to the holdings of the French crown. The Hundred Years' War exposed Languedoc not only to invasion from the west but also to the rapacity of the French king's own representatives, whose extortions provoked riots in the towns and finally the peasant rebellion of the Tuchins (1382–83).

By the 15th century Languedoc was organized into a *gouvernement* and from the 16th century was divided into the *généralités* ("generalities") of Montpellier and Toulouse. The province had institutions that insured its local privileges; the estates (assembly) of Languedoc gained prominence during the Hundred Years' War (1337–1453) for their taxing power over the south of France and continued to function until the French Revolution, and the Parlement of Toulouse, created in 1443, was second only to that of Paris as a high court.

In the 16th century Languedoc became a centre of French Protestantism. The government's attempt to impose Catholicism there gave rise to the peasant insurrection of the Protestant Carmisards in the early 18th century. With the Revolution, Languedoc lost its distinctive institutions and was divided into *départements.*

The physiography of Languedoc consists of Mediterranean lowlands of France extending from the Pyrenees in the southwest eastward some 125 miles (200 km) to the right bank of the Rhône River as far north as its junction with the Isère. The prevalence of malaria in the extensive coastal marshes of the Rhône delta (the Camargue) and westward discouraged the development of the coast well into the 19th century, and older villages tend to be inland. Traditional farmsteads around Toulouse have one story and are built of rough brick.

Roman Catholicism predominates outside the mountains of the Cévennes above the Plain of Languedoc. There are large Protestant enclaves around Florac in Lozère and Vigan, Nîmes, and Alès in Gard. Catholicism is particularly strong in the Massif Central and less so in the plains. Freemasons are numerous in Gard. Repatriated émigrés from Algeria and immigrants from Spain and Italy have settled in Haute-Garonne, Hérault, Gard, and Tarn. The Communist Party has numerous adherents throughout Languedoc.

The vineyards of the plains in Languedoc produce fine muscatels. *Blistelle* is a sweet wine whose fermentation is artificially stopped; new cultures are then added and the wine is allowed to age. Regional cuisine relies heavily on olive oil and garlic; pork fat is widely used in the Cévennes. Soups include *aigo bouillido,* which is made with garlic, and *oulade,* which is made with potatoes and seasoned with pickled pork and various herbs. *Aligot* is a puree of potatoes and cheese and is seasoned with garlic. The Occitan language continues to be widely spoken around Nîmes and Uzès and in Haute-Loire and Ardèche.

Languedoc Canal (France): *see* Midi Canal.

Languedoc language: *see* Occitan language.

Languedoc-Roussillon, *région,* encompassing the southern French *départements* of Lozère, Gard, Hérault, Aude, and Pyrénées-Orientales and roughly coextensive with the former province of Languedoc (*q.v.*). The capital is Montpellier. The region has an area of 10,570 square miles (27,376 square km) and is bounded by the *départements* of Ariège to the west, Haute-Garonne, Tarn, Aveyron, and Cantal to the northwest, Haute-Loire to the north, Ardèche to the northeast, and Vaucluse and Bouches-du-Rhône to the east. Gard, Hérault, Aude, and Pyrénées-Orientales face the Mediterranean to the southeast; Spain borders Pyrénées-Orientales to the south. The Massif Central extends into Lozère and marks the northwestern borders of Gard, Hérault, and Aude. The plain of Languedoc faces the Mediterranean and is separated from the plain of Roussillon to the southwest by the mountains of Corbières. The Pyrenees rise to the south. A Mediterranean climate prevails along the coast and a mountain climate in Lozère and the Pyrenees.

The population of Languedoc declined by nearly 10 percent between 1900 and 1954, in common with most predominantly rural areas of France during this period, but has subsequently increased. Immigrants from Spain, Italy, and North Africa have accounted for much of the increase. Demographic recovery has favoured Hérault, Gard, and Pyrénées-Orientales over Lozère and Aude. The proportion of urban population approaches the national average.

Viticulture is concentrated in the plains of Aude, Hérault, and Gard, which produce about one-half of France's grapes. Animal husbandry predominates in the Causses region. The Compagnie Nationale d'Aménagement de la Région du Bas-Rhône et du Languedoc ("National Company for the Development of the Region of the Lower Rhône and Languedoc") has brought approximately 500,000 acres (200,000 hectares) under irrigation in an effort to diversify agricultural output. Manufacturing is underdeveloped outside the lower Rhône. Plutonium is processed at Marcoule in Gard, while Ardoise in Gard is the site of the electrometallurgical centre of Ugine-Kuhlmann. Tourism is being developed along the Mediterranean. Pop. (1990) 2,114,985.

langur, any of several oriental monkeys belonging to the family Cercopithecidae and including the genera *Presbytis, Pygathrix, Rhinopithecus,* and *Simias.* Like the related guerezas of Africa, langurs have large, complex stomachs adapted to a diet of leaves, fruit, and other vegetation.

The langurs, or leaf monkeys, of the genus *Presbytis* (sometimes placed in *Pygathrix*) comprise about 14 species including the sacred

Sacred monkey, or Hanuman langur (*Presbytis entellus*)
Phyllis Dolhinow

monkey, or Hanuman langur (*P. entellus*), of India. Members of this genus are gregarious, diurnal, basically arboreal monkeys with long tails, slender bodies, and long, slender limbs, hands, and feet. Depending on species, the head and body are about 40 to 80 cm (16 to 31 inches) long and the tail is about 50 to 110 cm long. These monkeys have long fur, and many species have characteristic caps or crests of long hair. Adults usually have black faces; colour varies among the species but is commonly gray, brown, or black. The colour of the young, born singly after about 168 days gestation, differs from that of adults and possibly serves to arouse maternal protectiveness.

The Hanuman langur, typical of this genus, is almost black when newborn and gray, tan, or brown when adult. Regarded as sacred in India, it roams at will in villages and temples, raiding crops or the stores of merchants. The Hanuman langur lives in bands of about 20 to 30. Males have clearly marked dominance positions, but females have no fixed status. Mothers are protective but allow other females to help care for the young. The douc langur (*Pygathrix nemaeus*) is a large, forest-dwelling monkey of Southeast Asia. It has short, gray fur marked with red and white. Snub-nosed langurs (*Pygathrix roxellanae* and *P. avunculus*) live in the forests of China and northern Vietnam and are stocky with upturned noses and long fur of gray, black, or brownish overlaid with yellow. The pig-tailed langur (*Nasalis concolor*) is a snub-nosed, brownish, macaque-like monkey of wet Indonesian forests. Apart from *Presbytis entellus,* all species mentioned are classified as either endangered or rare.

languriid beetle: *see* lizard beetle.

Lanier, Nicholas, Lanier also spelled LANIERE (baptized Sept. 10, 1588, London, Eng.—d. February 1666, London), English composer, singer, and painter, who probably introduced Italian monody into England. In 1617 he painted the scenery, composed the music for, and sang in Ben Jonson's masque *Lovers Made Men,* using the new monodic recitative style. In 1626 he became music master to Charles I and after the Restoration (1660) to Charles II.

Lanier's use of the Italian recitative style, or *stylo recitativo,* brought a significant Italian influence to English music. His skillful experimentation with speech rhythms, characteristic of Italian recitative, contributed to the development of the Baroque style, later brought to maturity by John Blow and Henry Purcell.

Lanier, Sidney (b. Feb. 3, 1842, Macon, Ga., U.S.—d. Sept. 7, 1881, Lynn, N.C.), American musician and poet whose verse often suggests the rhythms and thematic development of music.

Lanier was reared by devoutly religious parents in the traditions of the Old South. As a child he wrote verses and was especially fond of music. After graduation in 1860 from Oglethorpe College (now University), Atlanta, Ga., he served in the Civil War until his capture and subsequent imprisonment at Point Lookout, Md., where he contracted tuberculosis. In 1867 he married Mary Day, also of Macon; and in the same year he published his first book, the novel *Tiger-Lilies,* a mixture of German philosophy, Southern traditional romance, and his own war experiences. After working in his father's law office at Macon, teaching school at Prattville, Ala., and traveling for his health in Texas, he accepted in 1873 a position as first flutist in the Peabody Orchestra, Baltimore. With numerous poems already published in magazines, he wrote several potboilers and played private concerts and delivered lectures to small groups.

Sidney Lanier, *c.* 1870–80
By courtesy of the Library of Congress, Washington, D.C.

"Corn" (1875), a poem treating agricultural conditions in the South, and "The Symphony" (1875), treating industrial conditions in the North, brought Lanier national recognition. Adverse criticism of his "Centennial Meditation" in 1876 launched him on an investigation of verse technique that he continued until his death. *The Song of the Chattahoochee,* a volume of poems, was published in 1877. Appointed to Johns Hopkins University in 1879, he delivered a series of lectures on verse technique, the early English poets, and the English novel, later published as *The Science of English Verse* (1880), *Shakspere and his Forerunners* (1902), and *The English Novel* (1883; rev. ed. 1897). In the spring of 1881, when advanced tuberculosis made further work impossible, he established camp quarters at Lynn, N.C., where he died. Three years later his wife published an enlarged edition of his poems. The complete edition of his works (10 volumes) appeared in 1945.

BIBLIOGRAPHY. Aubrey Harrison Starke, *Sidney Lanier: A Biographical and Critical Study* (1933, reissued 1964); Jack De Bellis, *Sidney Lanier* (1972); and Jane S. Gabin, *A Living Minstrelsy: The Poetry and Music of Sidney Lanier* (1985).

Laniidae (bird family): *see* shrike.

Lanikai (Hawaii, U.S.): *see* Kailua-Lanikai.

Länkäran, Russian LENKORAN, city, Azerbaijan. It lies on the shore of the Caspian Sea, south-southwest of Baku. First mentioned in the 17th century, it was capital of the Talysh khanate of Iran in the 18th century. It was held by Russia from 1728 to 1735 but only fell definitively to Russia in 1813. It is now the centre of a rich agricultural region, where subtropical crops, such as tea and citrus, are grown. There is a brickyard, furniture factory, and timber combine. Pop. (1991 est.) 45,400.

Laṅkāvatāra-sūtra, in full SADDHARMA-LAṄKĀVATĀRA-SŪTRA (Sanskrit: "Sūtra of the Appearance of the Good Doctrine in Laṅkā"), distinctive and influential philosophical discourse in the Mahāyāna Buddhist tradition that is said to have been preached by the Buddha in the mythical city Laṅkā. Dating from perhaps the 4th century, although parts of it may be earlier, it is the chief canonical exposition of Vijñānavāda ("Doctrine of Consciousness"), or subjective idealism. It teaches, in other words, that the world is an illusory reflection of ultimate, undifferentiated mind and that this truth suddenly becomes an inner realization in concentrated meditation.

The thought of the *Laṅkāvatāra* is reflected in the Yogācāra school and provides some of the philosophical background of Zen. It is distinct from two other main thrusts in Mahāyāna, the *Prajñāpāramitā* ("Perfection of Wisdom") emphasis and the worship of Amitābha, the Buddha of Infinite Light. The sutra was first translated into Chinese in the 5th century and has been the subject of many treatises and commentaries.

Lankester, Sir Edwin Ray (b. May 15, 1847, London, Eng.—d. Aug. 15, 1929, London), British authority on general zoology at the turn of the 19th century, who made important contributions to comparative anatomy, embryology, parasitology, and anthropology.

In 1871, while a student at the University of Oxford, Lankester became one of the first persons to describe protozoan parasites in the blood of vertebrates, an important development in the diagnosis and treatment of such parasitic diseases as malaria. While professor of zoology and comparative anatomy at the University of London (1874–90), his research in invertebrate morphology and embryology provided evidence in support of the theories of evolution and natural selection. He further supported these theories through his pioneering research in anthropology, which he pursued during his terms as professor at Oxford (1890–98) and at the Royal Institution, London (1898–1900), and as director of the British Museum of Natural History (1898–1907). He was knighted in 1907.

In "The Significance of the Increased Size of the Cerebrum in Recent as Compared with Extinct Animals" (1899), Lankester emphasized that an inherited ability to learn, allowing cultural advances to be transmitted between generations socially, was an important factor in human evolution. His discovery of flint implements in Suffolk demonstrated the presence of skilled workers during the Pliocene Epoch (5.3 to 1.6 million years ago).

He wrote some 200 scientific papers and edited the *Quarterly Journal of Microscopical Science* (1869–1920), founded by his father in 1860. Among his larger works are *Comparative Longevity in Man and the Lower Animals* (1870), *Degeneration* (1880), and *Great and Small Things* (1923).

Lanman, Charles Rockwell (b. July 8, 1850, Norwich, Conn., U.S.—d. Feb. 20, 1941, Boston, Mass.), American scholar of Sanskrit who wrote the widely used *Sanskrit Reader* (1884) and helped edit the "Harvard Oriental Series," which offered scholarly English translations of the ancient Hindu Vedic texts.

He received his doctorate from Yale University, where he studied Sanskrit under William Dwight Whitney. After further study in Germany, Lanman was appointed to Johns Hopkins University (1876) and later to Harvard University (1880), where he became Wales professor of Sanskrit (1903–26). In 1891 Lanman became editor of the Harvard Oriental Series, founded and financed by his friend and pupil Henry Clark Warren. During Lanman's editorship 31 volumes were issued; and many of them, such as Whitney's *Atharva Veda* and Arthur B. Keith's *Yajur Veda* and *Rig Veda Brahmanas,* furnished for the first time scholarly translations into English of ancient Sanskrit texts. In 1884 Lanman published the first edition of his *Sanskrit Reader,* which formed a standard introduction to that language for English-speaking students, remaining in print into the second half of the 20th century.

Lannes, Jean, DUKE (duc) DE MONTEBELLO (b. April 11, 1769, Lectoure, France—d. May 31, 1809, Vienna, Austrian Empire), French general who, despite his humble origins, rose to the rank of marshal of the First Empire; Napoleon said of him, "I found him a pygmy and left a giant."

Lannes, the son of a stable boy, learned to read and write from a village priest and was apprenticed to a dyer. In 1792 he joined the national volunteers of Gers and, as sergeant major, served in the Army of the Pyrénées-Orientales against the Spanish. His great courage in the Battle of Dego (1796), in the Italian campaign, brought him to the attention of Napoleon, who made him a general in 1796. In 1798–99 he took part in the capture of Cairo and went on the Syrian campaign as commander of an army division, playing a leading role in the siege of Gaza and

Saint-Jean d'Acre, though he was seriously wounded at the Battle of Aboukir. Returning to France, he took command of the 9th and

Lannes, portrait by François Gérard; in a private collection
Lauros—Giraudon from Art Resource/EB Inc.

10th divisions. He took part in the coup d'etat of 18 Brumaire (Nov. 9, 1799), which brought Napoleon to power. Entrusted with the vanguard that crossed the Alps into Italy in May 1800, he defeated the Austrians at Montebello on June 9, thus contributing greatly to Napoleon's victory at Marengo five days later.

In May 1804 Lannes was made one of the 18 marshals of the empire and fought in the battles of Ulm (October 1805), Austerlitz (December 1805), and Jena (October 1806). At the Battle of Pultusk in Poland on Dec. 26, 1806, he defeated a much larger Russian force and contributed to a second victory over the Russians at Friedland in June 1807.

In 1808 Lannes was created duc de Montebello in honour of his greatest victory. Sent to Spain, he directed the bloody siege of Saragossa, which was captured on Feb. 20, 1809. At the Battle of Aspern-Esseling, however, he was struck in the legs by a cannon ball, and nine days later, after having undergone a double amputation, he died. A tough, impetuous, hot-tempered fighter, he was one of Napoleon's ablest generals.

lanolin, purified form of wool grease or wool wax (sometimes erroneously called wool fat), used either alone or with soft paraffin or lard or other fat as a base for ointments, emollients, skin foods, salves, superfatted soaps, and fur dressing. Lanolin, a translucent, yellowish-white, soft, unctuous, tenacious substance, is readily absorbed by the skin and thus makes an ideal base for medicinal products intended to be absorbed.

Lanolin is obtained from raw wool by kneading it in water, or by scouring with soap solution, and then centrifuging. The wool grease so obtained is refined, bleached, deodorized, and dried.

Chemically, lanolin consists of a mixture of several sterols, fatty acids, and their esters.

Lanrezac, Charles (-Louis-Marie) (b. July 31, 1852, Pointe-à-Pitre, Guadeloupe—d. Jan. 18, 1925, Neuilly-sur-Seine, Fr.), French army commander during the first part of World War I who, though a capable tactician, proved unable to stop the German advance in northern France and was consequently replaced.

Rising steadily in the French army, Lanrezac had by 1914 become a member of the Conseil Supérieur de la Guerre (Supreme War Council) and commander of the 5th Army. Poised on the left flank of the French force that was expected to sweep eastward into Germany through Alsace and Lorraine at the outbreak of World War I, he was compelled to swing his army northward to face the German armies advancing through Belgium. Forced to retreat south under pressure from Gen. Karl von Bülow's German 2nd Army, he became increasingly pessimistic about the outcome of the campaign. On orders of the French commander in chief, Gen. Joseph Joffre, he nevertheless supported the British expeditionary force east of Paris, winning a brilliant tactical victory at Guise (Aug. 29, 1914). His continued retreat, however, led Joffre to replace him on September 3.

Lansbury, George (b. Feb. 21, 1859, near Halesworth, Suffolk, Eng.—d. May 7, 1940, London), leader of the British Labour Party (1931–35), a Socialist and poor-law reformer who was forced to resign the party leadership because of his extreme pacifism.

A railway worker at the age of 14 and later a timber merchant, he became a propagandist for Henry Mayers Hyndman's Social Democratic Federation in 1892 but eventually repudiated its strict Marxism. He helped to found (1912) and for a time edited, the *Daily Herald,* the first British newspaper devoted to labour subjects. In World War I he defended the rights of conscientious objectors.

A Labour member of the House of Commons (1910–12, 1922–40), he served as first commissioner of works in the Labour government of 1929–31 and then became leader

Lansbury, oil painting by Sylvia Gosse; in the National Portrait Gallery, London
By courtesy of the National Portrait Gallery, London

of the parliamentary opposition. Unwilling to join his associates in calling for economic sanctions that might have led to war against Italy for its aggression in Ethiopia, Lansbury resigned in 1935 and was succeeded as party leader by his deputy, Clement Attlee (prime minister, 1945–51). In 1937 Lansbury visited Adolf Hitler and Benito Mussolini in the belief that his personal influence could stop the movement toward war.

Lansdowne, Henry Charles Keith Petty-Fitzmaurice, 5th marquess of, also called (until 1866) VISCOUNT CLANMAURICE (b. Jan. 14, 1845, London—d. June 3, 1927, Clonmel, County Tipperary, Ire.), Irish nobleman and British diplomat who served as viceroy of Canada and of India, secretary for war, and foreign secretary.

The eldest son of the 4th Marquess, he attended Eton and on the death of his father succeeded, at age 21, to the marquessate and great lands and wealth. Joining the Liberal Party he was a lord of the Treasury (1868) and under secretary for war (1872–74) and for India (1880). As governor general of Canada (1883–88) he effected an agreement with rebelling Indians and used his French language ability to facilitate acceptance.

Conservative Prime Minister Salisbury ap-

5th Marquess of Lansdowne, detail of a portrait by P.A. de László, 1920; in the National Portrait Gallery, London
By courtesy of the National Portrait Gallery, London

pointed him viceroy of India, and his administration (1888–94) was marked by peace except for a short rising in the independent state of Manipur, for which the leader Tikendrajit was executed. Lansdowne founded an imperial library and record office, abolished the presidential army system, closed Indian mints to the free coinage of silver, reorganized the police, reconstituted legislative councils, gave council members rights of financial discussion and interpolation, and extended railway and irrigation works. The independent kingdom of Sikkim was brought under British protection in 1888 and its boundary with Tibet demarcated; Hunza and Nagar on the Afghan frontier were annexed in 1892.

Lansdowne became secretary of state for war in 1895, and charges of unpreparedness for the South African War brought demands for his impeachment in 1899. After the 1900 elections the Conservative government remodelling brought him in as foreign secretary (1900–06) amid protests. In 1906–10 he was leader of the minority Conservative opposition in the House of Lords and deplored the disparity of parties there. He was minister without portfolio (1915–16) in Asquith's government. His controversial published "Lansdowne Letter" (1917), calling for a statement of intentions from World War I Allies, was criticized as contrary to public policy.

Lansdowne, William Petty-Fitzmaurice, 1st marquess of, also called (1761–84) 2ND EARL OF SHELBURNE (b. May 13, 1737, Dublin—d. May 7, 1805, London), British statesman and prime minister (July 1782 to April 1783) during the reign of George III.

The son of John Fitzmaurice, who took the additional name of Petty on succeeding to the Irish estates of his uncle and who was created earl of Shelburne (1753), William was educated privately and at Christ Church, Oxford (1755–57), and, entering the army, served in the Seven Years' War. While abroad he was elected to Parliament for the family borough of Chipping Wycombe (1760). In 1761 he was reelected and was also returned to the Irish Parliament for County Kerry, but his father's death in May of that year made him ineligible to sit in either House of Commons and removed him to the English House of Lords.

He declined office under Lord Bute but became first lord of trade in the Grenville ministry (1763). He resigned, however, a few months later and attached himself to William Pitt, under whom, in 1766, he served as secretary of state for the southern department. Differences with his colleagues on colonial questions caused him to resign in 1768. In 1782 he took office under Lord Rockingham as home secretary and was appointed prime minister on Rockingham's death in July, but the Foxite Whigs refused to serve under him and combined with Lord North to defeat him in 1783. When the younger Pitt formed his ministry in December 1783 following the dismissal of the coalition, Shelburne was left out.

His arrogance and aloofness, as well as his popularity with the King, had alienated those with whom he had acted, and he was accused of being the King's tool as much as North had been. Pitt never even consulted him but Shelburne, realizing his own unpopularity, made no effort to embarrass Pitt and the breach was not permanent, for in December 1784 he was created marquess of Lansdowne. He no longer took an active part in politics.

Lansel, Peider (b. Aug. 15, 1863, Pisa—d. Dec. 9, 1943, Geneva), Romansh leader of the revival of Rhaeto-Romance language and culture and one of its most accomplished lyric poets.

Spending every summer at his family's native village of Sent in the Engadine, Lansel devoted himself to the collection and critical examination of Rhaeto-Romance texts of the previous four centuries, work that was crowned by publication of the lyric anthology *La musa ladina* (1910, 2nd ed., 1918) and amplified in *Musa rumantscha* (1950) and by his study *Ils retoromans* (1935), translated into English, German, Italian, French and Esperanto. In his nostalgic and exquisitely controlled verse (definitive ed., *Il vegl chalamer*, 1920), he was able to sublimate a tragic love affair of his youth in the celebration of the beauty of his Alpine valley, with its age-old culture rooted in the soil. His poems and stories (*Grusaidas albas*, 1931) signalled the rebirth of Rhaeto-Romance literature, purging it of impurities and turning it back to its beginnings in the 16th century.

Lansing, capital of Michigan, U.S., in Ingham county, on the Grand River at its junction with the Red Cedar River. The site was a wilderness when the state capital was moved there from Detroit (85 mi [137 km] southeast) in 1847. Called Michigan, in 1848 it assumed

State Capitol, Lansing, Mich.
Milt and Joan Mann from CameraMann

the name of Lansing for the township (named for Lansing, N.Y.), in which it was located. The State Capitol (erected 1873–78) stands in a 10-ac (4-ha) park in the centre of the city. Connected by road to Detroit in 1852, and to out-of-state areas by railroad in the 1870s, the city grew industrially after 1887 with the establishment of the Olds Motor Works and the Reo Motor Car Company by Ransom Eli Olds; it is now a major automobile production centre with a wide range of manufactures. Lansing Community College (1957) and the Michigan School for the Blind (1879) are located there. Adjacent East Lansing is the home of Michigan State University (1855). Inc. city, 1859. Pop. (1990) city, 127,321; Lansing–East Lansing MSA, 432,674.

Lansing, Robert (b. Oct. 17, 1864, Watertown, N.Y., U.S.—d. Oct. 30, 1928, Washington, D.C.), international lawyer and U.S. secretary of state (1915–20), who negotiated the Lansing–Ishii Agreement (1917) attempting to harmonize U.S.–Japanese relations toward China; he eventually broke with Pres. Woodrow Wilson over differences in approach to the League of Nations.

Lansing, 1915
By courtesy of the Library of Congress, Washington, D.C.

Appointed associate counsel in the Bering Sea arbitration (1892–93), he served frequently thereafter as federal counsel or agent before international tribunals, including the Alaskan Boundary Tribunal (1903) and the North Atlantic Coast Fisheries Tribunal of Arbitration (1910). In 1914 President Wilson appointed him counsellor to the state department, and the following year, after the resignation of William Jennings Bryan, Lansing became secretary of state. Wilson made all major foreign policy decisions, however, and relied upon his friend, Col. Edward M. House, to handle delicate negotiations abroad. Lansing did draft important notes upholding the rights at sea of the United States as a neutral power during World War I, including a challenge to the British blockade of western Europe. He persuaded the government of Denmark to sell to the United States its islands in the West Indies (now the U.S. Virgin Islands) to prevent possible German occupation of them; and after the entry of the United States into World War I, he negotiated the Lansing–Ishii agreement (1917), in which the United States recognized the special interests of Japan in China in return for Japan's commitment to the Open Door Policy of equal trading rights for all countries there.

Following the Armistice (November 1918) a rift developed when Wilson ignored Lansing's advice that the President should not attend the peace conference. In Paris Wilson delegated little responsibility to him and seldom consulted him. Their views diverged fundamentally: to Wilson the League of Nations was essential and needed to be created immediately; to Lansing the conclusion of the peace treaty was more urgent, and he felt the matter of the League might better be postponed. Lansing also opposed certain provisions that Wilson inserted in the League Covenant. In Washington, however, Lansing exerted himself to gain Senate approval of the peace treaty, despite his known reservations. During nearly five months following Wilson's illness (September 1919), he directed foreign policy and conducted Cabinet meetings. Wilson resented this show of independence and requested Lansing's resignation, which became effective Feb. 13, 1920.

Lansing returned to his law practice in Washington and wrote *The Peace Negotiations* (1921) and *The Big Four and Others of the Peace Conference* (1921).

Lansing–Ishii Agreement (Nov. 2, 1917), attempt to reconcile conflicting U.S. and Japanese policies in China during World War I by a public exchange of notes between the U.S. secretary of state, Robert Lansing, and Viscount Ishii Kikujirō of Japan, a special envoy to Washington. Japan promised respect for China's independence and territorial integrity and for the U.S.-sponsored Open Door Policy (equal trading rights for all foreign nations in China); the U.S. recognized Japan's right to protect its special interests in areas of China bordering on its own territory. Ishii later asserted that the U.S. had thus recognized the "paramount" interest of Japan in Manchuria, a claim that embarrassed the U.S. Ambiguously worded and designed to patch over differences between two wartime allies, the agreement was terminated by a further exchange of notes on March 30, 1923.

Lansky, Meyer, original name MAIER SUCHOWLJANSKY (b. July 4, 1902, Grodno, Russia—d. Jan. 15, 1983, Miami Beach, Fla., U.S.), one of the most powerful and richest of U.S. crime syndicate chiefs and bankers, who had major interests in gambling, especially in Florida, pre-Castro Cuba, Las Vegas, and the Bahamas.

A Polish Jew born in Russia's Pale of Settlement, Lansky immigrated with his parents to New York's Lower East Side in 1911. By 1918 he and Bugsy Siegel were running a floating crap game and then graduated into highly lucrative auto theft and resale. In the course of the 1920s Lansky's gang branched into burglaries, liquor smuggling, and other rackets and came under the aegis of crime boss Giuseppe Masseria. Lansky and Siegel had also developed a squad of professional murderers for hire, the prototype for the later Murder, Inc., headed by Louis Buchalter and Albert Anastasia. Lansky became a naturalized citizen in 1928.

It was allegedly Lansky who persuaded Lucky Luciano to have Masseria assassinated in 1931 and loaned Bugsy Siegel for the purpose, making the four-man hit team representative of the major New York factions. Between 1932 and 1934 Lansky joined Luciano in forming the national crime syndicate and became one of its major overseers and bankers, often laundering funds through foreign accounts.

By 1936 Lansky had begun to develop gambling operations in Florida and New Orleans and also in Cuba, where he arranged payoffs to Cuban dictator Fulgencio Batista. He also financed Bugsy Siegel's casino developments in Las Vegas (and ordered Siegel's execution in 1947, when Siegel welshed on the syndicate). When Fidel Castro came to power in Cuba in 1959, Lansky turned to the Bahamas, building casinos on Grand Bahama and Paradise islands in the 1960s after nurturing government cooperation. He also extended his gambling empire to other areas of the Caribbean and even across the Atlantic to London. He was also into narcotics smuggling, pornography, prostitution, labour racketeering, and extortion and had control of such legitimate enterprises as hotels, golf courses, and a meat-packing plant. Monies were secreted in Swiss banks. By 1970 his total holdings were estimated at $300,000,000.

In 1970, fearing both a call to a grand jury and indictment for income-tax evasion, he fled to Israel, seeking to remain under the Law of Return; however, Israel eventually expelled him, and he ended up back in the United States facing several indictments. In 1973 he was convicted of both grand jury contempt and income-tax evasion. He remained out of prison on appeals, and indictments on other charges lay dormant, partly because of his chronic ill health. In 1979 the House of Representatives Assassinations Committee, ending its two-year investigation of the Warren Commission report, linked Lansky with Jack Ruby, the nightclub owner who killed presidential assassin Lee Harvey Oswald.

Lansky died of lung cancer and was buried in Miami in an Orthodox Jewish ceremony.

Lantana, genus of more than 150 shrubs native to tropical America and Africa and belonging to the verbena family (Verbenaceae), order Lamiales. Common lantana (*L. camara*), growing to 3 metres (10 feet) tall, is a weed in tropical America, but elsewhere it is much used as a garden plant. It blooms almost continuously with yellow, orange, pink, and white flower heads in various colour combinations. The aromatic leaves are rough and oval. Clusters of poisonous black berries follow the flowers.

Trailing lantana (*L. montevidensis*), from South America, is a small-leaved, drooping, thinly branched species that bears rose-lavender flowers. Other species are variously known as yellow sage, weeping (or trailing) lantana, and polecat geranium.

Common lantana (*Lantana camara*)
D.W. Woodruff—EB Inc.

Lantao Island, also spelled LAN TAU, island located about 6 miles (10 km) west of Hong Kong Island, part of the New Territories of the British Crown Colony of Hong Kong. About 17 miles (27 km) long and 6 miles (9.5 km) wide, it has an area of 58 square miles (150 square km). Consisting of mountains rising to 3,064 feet (934 m) at Lantao Peak, the island is covered by grass and scrub with pockets of arable land along its coasts. Rice and vegetables are grown. Shek Pik Reservoir in the southwest is a catchment facility; the island has a road system and is linked by ferry with Tuen Mun and Victoria.

Lanterloo (card game): *see* Loo.

lantern, a case, ordinarily metal, with transparent or translucent sides, used to contain and protect a lamp.

Lamp-containing lanterns have been found at Pompeii, Herculaneum, and other classical sites. They have been made of iron, silver, gold, and tin and their sides of horn, talc, leather, oiled paper, and glass. Designs have ranged from crude boxes pierced with nail holes to Oriental openwork bronze and exquisitely delicate examples of Renaissance and Baroque craftsmanship.

The bull's-eye lantern, with one or more sides of bulging glass, was in popular use from the early 18th century, similar devices having been made at least as early as the 13th century. Dark until it was suddenly switched on by opening its door, it focused its light to some extent and served the purpose of the modern flashlight.

The hurricane lantern, or hurricane lamp, still in use as a warning flare, has a shield of glass and perforated metal surrounding its flame to protect it from strong winds.

Consult the INDEX *first*

lantern, in architecture, originally an openwork timber construction placed on top of a building to admit light and allow smoke to escape. Something of this idea persists in medieval examples such as the lantern above the central octagon of Ely Cathedral (14th century). The term lantern soon came to refer to the open top story of a tower, because such a construction resembled a lamp container and because beacons were occasionally placed there.

In Renaissance and Baroque architecture, lantern came to mean the small cupola-like structure, usually with decorative arcades, mounted on top of a dome. Although at times its function is to admit light to the interior, it is essentially a proportional element in the visual design. Typical are the lanterns capping the domes of the Cathedral of Florence (1436–71), St. Peter's in Rome (1506), St. Paul's Cathedral in London (1689), and the Capitol in Washington, D.C.

Lantern on top of the dome of the Cathedral of Florence, Italy, designed by Filippo Brunelleschi, 1436; completed *c.* 1436–71
Robert Harding Picture Library

lantern-eye fish, also spelled LANTERNEYE FISH, any of three species of fishes in the family Anomalopidae (order Beryciformes), characterized by the presence of luminescent organs just below the eye. They are among the few species of non-deep-sea fishes to possess such organs. Phosphorescent bacteria create the light continuously, but each species has its own mechanism for decreasing the luminescence; when swimming, some fishes create a blinking effect by alternately covering and uncovering the light.

Each of the three species of lantern-eye fishes is in a separate genus. Two are found in tropical marine habitats of the Indo-Pacific region; the third lives in the Caribbean. All are small, the maximum length being 30 cm (1 foot). The name lantern-eye fish refers most specifically to *Anomalops kaptoptron* and *Photoblepharon palpebratus,* both found in the East Indies.

lantern fish, any of the numerous species of small, abundant, deep-sea fish of the family Myctophidae. Lantern fish live in the depths by day, but at night they may approach the surface and can sometimes be attracted to lights. They are somewhat elongated fish with large mouths and eyes and numerous light organs on the head, underside, and tail base. The arrangement of these lights may aid species or sex recognition. The pattern also provides an important means of identifying the 150 or more species. Fully grown lantern fish range from about 2.5 to 15 cm (1 to 6 inches) long.

Lantern fish (*Symbolophorus veranys*)

lantern tree (*Crinodendron hookeranum*), tree of the family Elaeocarpaceae native to western South America and cultivated in other regions for its handsome flowers. It grows to 4.5 to 7.5 m (15 to 25 feet) in height. The urn-shaped, dark red flowers are about 2 cm (0.8 inch) long.

Flower of the lantern tree (*Crinodendron hookeranum*)
A to Z Botanical Collection—EB Inc.

lanternfly (*Lanternaria phosphorea*), a large, brightly coloured South American plant hopper (order Homoptera) that lives on trees and is relatively uncommon. Its most remarkable feature is the inflated anterior prolongation of the head, which contains a pouchlike extension from the digestive tract. This structure appears to be luminous at times, a phenomenon that may be related to mating behaviour.

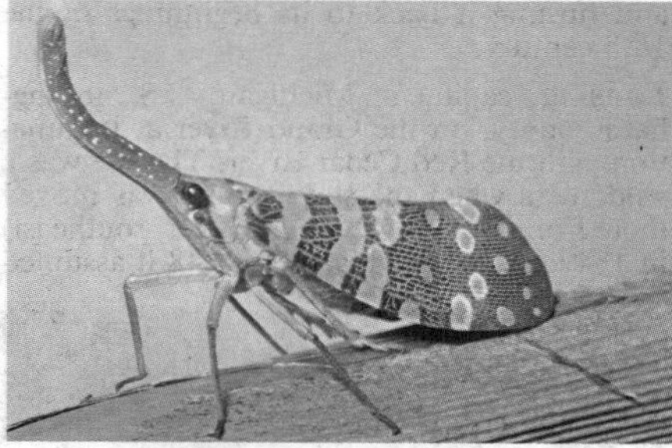

Lanternfly (*Lanternaria phosphorea*)
E.S. Ross

Some lanternflies secrete a white wax in the form of long filaments or a powder. The Amazonian Indians believed that the lanternfly bite caused death.

lanthanide contraction, in chemistry, the steady decrease in the size of the atoms and ions of the rare-earth elements with increasing atomic number from lanthanum (atomic number 57) through lutetium (atomic number 71). For each consecutive atom the nuclear charge is more positive by one unit, accompanied by a corresponding increase in the number of electrons present in the $4f$ orbitals surrounding the nucleus. The $4f$ electrons very imperfectly shield each other from the increased positive charge of the nucleus, so that the effective nuclear charge attracting each electron steadily increases through the lanthanide elements, resulting in successive reductions of the atomic and ionic radii. The lanthanum ion, La^{3+}, has a radius of 1.061 angstroms, whereas the heavier lutetium ion, Lu^{3+}, has a radius of 0.850 angstrom. Because the lanthanide contraction keeps these rare-earth ions about the same size and because they are all generally trivalent, their chemical properties are very similar, with the result that at least small amounts of each one are usually present in every rare-earth mineral. The lanthanide contraction also is a very significant factor in the extremely close chemical similarity of zirconium (atomic number 40) and hafnium (atomic number 72) of the IVb group of the periodic table. Because of the lanthanide contraction, heavier hafnium, which immediately follows the lanthanides, possesses a radius nearly identical to the lighter zirconium.

lanthanide series, in chemistry, the elements with atomic numbers from 58 to 71—*i.e.,* from cerium through lutetium. Lanthanum is sometimes included in this group, owing to its similar chemical and physical properties. *See* rare-earth metal.

lanthanum (La), chemical element, rare-earth metal of transition Group IIIb of the periodic table, prototype of the lanthanide series of elements. Lanthanum is a ductile and malleable, silvery-white metal, soft enough to be cut with a knife. The element was discovered as the oxide (lanthana) in 1839 by Carl Gustaf Mosander, who distinguished it from cerium oxide (ceria). Its name is derived from the Greek *lanthanein,* meaning "to be concealed," indicating that it is difficult to isolate.

Lanthanum occurs in the rare-earth minerals monazite and bastnaesite. It is concentrated commercially by crystallization of ammonium lanthanum nitrate. Ion-exchange and solvent extraction methods are used when high purity is desired. The metal itself is prepared by electrolysis of fused anhydrous halides or by reduction of its halides by alkali or alkaline-earth metals (*e.g.,* reduction of the fluoride with calcium). Misch metal—used as cigarette-lighter flints, as a getter that removes traces of oxygen in electron tubes, and in metallurgy—is one-fourth lanthanum.

Lanthanum exhibits three allotropic (structural) forms. Two isotopes occur in nature: stable lanthanum-139 (99.911 percent) and very long-lived radioactive lanthanum-138 (0.089 percent). The isotope lanthanum-140 has been detected as a fission product in snow after nuclear-test explosions.

Lanthanum is the second most reactive of the rare-earth metals (europium is first); it rapidly tarnishes in dry air, ignites in air at 440° C (824° F), and reacts vigorously with hot water. It is exclusively trivalent in its compounds. The ionic radius is the largest of the rare-earth trivalent ions, and as a consequence the white oxide La_2O_3 is the most alkaline rare-earth oxide.

Highly purified lanthanum oxide is an ingredient in the manufacture of low-dispersion, high-refraction glasses for lens components. The technical grade fluoride is used as core material for arc-light carbons.

atomic number	57
atomic weight	138.91
melting point	920° C (1,688° F)
boiling point	3,454° C (6,249° F)
specific gravity	6.166 (25° C)
valence	3
electronic config.	2-8-18-18-9-2 or (Xe)$5d^16s^2$

Lantian man, Lantian also spelled LAN-T'IEN, hominid species identified on the basis of fossils found in 1963 and 1964 by Chinese archaeologists at two sites in Lan-t'ien district, Shensi province, China. One specimen was found at each site: a cranium (skullcap) at Kung-wang-ling (Gongwangling) and a mandible (lower jaw) at Ch'en-chia-wo (Chenjiawo). Both fossils have been classified as female. The remains are believed to be about 600,000 years old, or as old as Java man, an early form of *Homo erectus,* and older than Peking man, another form. The cranial capacity of 780 cubic cm (48 cubic inches) also indicates its resemblance to the small-brained Java man. Named by its discoverers *Sinanthropus lantianensis,* Lantian man is classified by most scholars as *Homo erectus.* Stone implements from a third site in Lan-t'ien may be contemporary with the fossils.

Lantz, Walter (b. April 27, 1900, New Rochelle, N.Y., U.S.—d. March 22, 1994, Burbank, Calif.), American motion-picture animator, cartoon producer, and creator of the cartoon character Woody Woodpecker. In 1930 Lantz produced the opening scenes of *King of Jazz,* the first Technicolor cartoon sequence ever screened.

Lantz began his career as a newspaper cartoonist but in 1916 experimented with animation. In 1922 he went to work for Bray Studios in New York City, where he collaborated on several series, among them *The Katzenjammer Kids, Happy Hooligan, Mutt and Jeff,* and *Colonel Heeza Liar.*

Lantz went to California in 1927, where he found work as a gagman for Mack Sennett and Hal Roach. In the late '20s he began working for Universal Studios; he continued their *Oswald the Rabbit* series and developed *Andy Panda, Li'l Eight Ball,* and *Winchester the Tortoise.* He did a brief stint with Walt Disney in the 1930s but returned to Universal, where he remained until the early '70s. At Universal he created Woody Woodpecker, giving him a bit part in the 1940 cartoon short *Knock, Knock.* In 1941 the animated bird got star billing. Lantz's wife, Gracie Lantz (Grace Stafford), became the voice of Woody Woodpecker.

During World War II, Lantz produced cartoons that were used as training films by the army and navy. After that he produced educational films, commercial pictures, and the *Woody Woodpecker Show* for television. In 1979 the Academy of Motion Picture Arts and Sciences presented him with an honorary award "in recognition of his unique animated motion pictures."

Lanza, Giovanni (b. Feb. 15, 1810, Casale Monferrato, Piedmont, French empire [now in Italy]—d. March 9, 1882, Rome, Italy), Italian statesman and political activist of the Risorgimento who was premier in 1870 when Rome became the capital of a united Italy and who helped organize the political forces of the centre-left.

After graduating from the University of Turin as a doctor of medicine, Lanza concentrated on agricultural improvement in Piedmont. In 1848 he enlisted as a volunteer in a Piedmontese force sent to help the Lombards against the Austrians. Elected a deputy of the Piedmontese Chamber, he opposed the peace treaty (Aug. 9, 1849) with Austria and became one of the most effective leaders of the centre-left. He became vice president of the Chamber in 1853, and, as minister of education from May 1855, he instituted many important reforms. Later (January 1858) he was named Piedmontese minister of the interior. In March 1861 he presided over the parliament that proclaimed Victor Emmanuel II king of all Italy. After further service as minister of the interior (1864–65) and again as president of the Italian Chamber, he formed his own cabinet on Dec. 14, 1869, and achieved the final step in the unification of Italy by taking possession of Rome (Sept. 20, 1870). His fairness and impartiality won him the deep respect of the Italian people.

Lanzarote, island, Las Palmas *provincia,* in Canarias *comunidad autónoma* ("autonomous community"), Spain. It is the easternmost of the Canary Islands in the North Atlantic. It has an area of 307 square miles (795 square km), and, although it rises to only 2,198 feet (670 m), it is mountainous, with numerous small craters and extensive lava flows.

About 1730 the appearance of half the island was altered by volcanic eruptions. The last violent activity was in 1824, but crevices in the Montañas del Fuego (Fire Mountains) still emit sufficient heat to fry eggs. Timanfaya National Park (20 square miles [51 square km]) was established in 1974. By remarkable dry-farming methods, cereals, vegetables, wine grapes, and other crops are produced on terraces on the steep sides of the volcanoes. Tourists are drawn to the island because of its fine black-sand beaches and sport fishing.

Raking salt evaporated from seawater for use in the fish-preserving industry on Lanzarote

Robert Davis—Photo Researchers

Arrecife, the chief port, has a fishing and fish-preserving industry. Regular sea and air services connect Lanzarote with Las Palmas de Gran Canaria. Pop. (1981) 53,452.

Lanzhou (China): *see* Lan-chou.

Lao Cai, town, northwestern Vietnam, on the China-Vietnam border. It lies at the junction of the Red River (Song Hong) and the Nam Ti River about 160 miles (260 km) northwest of Hanoi. It is a market town for timber from the surrounding mountains and is strategically important because of its location on the Haiphong railway to Yunnan province, China. It has a carbide factory.

Lao-chün (Chinese philosopher): *see* Lao-tzu.

Lao-ho-k'ou, formerly KUANG-HUA, Pinyin LAOHEKOU, or GUANGHUA, town in northern Hupeh *sheng* (province), China. It is situated on the Han River at its confluence with the Lao River, some 30 miles (50 km) northwest of Hsiang-fan.

Lao-ho-k'ou is a communications centre of some importance, being situated on the major southeast-to-northwest highway, via the Han River valley, where the highway joins the route to Nan-yang and the province of Honan. Lao-ho-k'ou is also the head of navigation for junks up to 50 tons on the Han River and is on a spur of the rail line, completed in 1978, extending up the Han River valley from Hsiang-fan via An-k'ang in Shensi province to Ch'ung-ch'ing (Chungking) in Szechwan province.

Lao-ho-k'ou was the seat of a county called Yin-ch'eng from the late 5th century AD. In the 18th and 19th centuries, although Lao-ho-k'ou remained administratively subordinate to Hsiang-fan, it grew into a commercial centre with a sphere of influence extending into the newly colonized area of the Upper Han River in southern Shensi province and into northeastern Szechwan. Bankers and merchant firms from Han-k'ou (Wu-han) and Shanghai and from Shansi and Kiangsi provinces had flourishing branches in the city, and it was nicknamed "Little Hankow." In the 1930s Lao-ho-k'ou was estimated to have a population of 120,000 people. Since then, however, much of the trade of Lao-ho-k'ou has been transferred to Hsiang-fan, and the importance of the city has declined. Pop. (1990) 123,366.

Lao Issara, English FREE LAOS, Laotian political movement against French colonial control, founded in 1945. The departure of the Japanese from Laos in 1945 left the Laotian ruling elite divided over the issue of the restoration of French control. The king welcomed the French return, but Prince Phetsarath, the viceroy, and his brothers, Souvanna Phouma and Souphanouvong, were prominent in the noncommunist Lao Issara, which demanded full independence. The granting of limited independence within the French union in 1949 split the Lao Issara, one faction becoming the left-oriented Pathet Lao.

Lao language, also called LAOTIAN, one of the Tai languages of Southeast Asia, and the official language of Laos. Lao occurs in various dialects, which differ among themselves at least as much as Lao as a group differs from the Tai dialects of northeastern Thailand. The latter are usually called Northeastern Thai, but the difference between Lao and Northeastern Thai is more political than linguistic. Like the other Tai languages, Lao is generally monosyllabic in word form and uses tones (pitch differences) to distinguish between words that are otherwise pronounced alike. Some polysyllabic Lao words do occur; for the most part, they are borrowed from Pāli (the language of the Buddhist scriptures, related to Sanskrit) and from Cambodian. Lao has also received influence from the neighbouring, and closely related, Standard Thai, the national language of Thailand. The language is written in a script of Indic origin, similar to that of Thai. *See also* Tai languages.

Lao She, Pinyin LAO SHE, pseudonym of (Wade–Giles romanization) SHU SHE-YÜ, original name SHU CH'ING-CH'UN (b. Feb. 3, 1899, Peking, China—d. Aug. 24?, 1966, Peking), Chinese author of humorous, satiric novels and short stories and, after the onset of the Sino-Japanese War (1937), of patriotic and propagandistic plays and novels.

Lao She served as principal of an elementary school at age 17 and soon worked his way up to district supervisor. In 1924 he went to England, teaching Mandarin Chinese to support himself and collaborating for five years on a translation of the great Ming-dynasty novel *Chin p'ing mei.* By reading the novels of Charles Dickens to improve his English, Lao She was inspired to write his first novel, which was published in China in the *Hsiao-shuo yüeh-pao* ("Short-Story Magazine") and enjoyed some success. He also completed two more novels, in which he developed the theme that the strong, hardworking individual could reverse the tide of stagnation and corruption plaguing China.

When Lao She returned to China in 1931, he found that he had achieved some fame as a comic novelist, and so he continued to create his humorous, action-packed works.

In *Niu T'ien-tz'u chuan* (1934; "The Life of Niu T'ien-tz'u"), Lao She changed his individualist theme to one stressing the importance of the total social environment and the futility of the individual's struggle against such an environment. His new theme found its clearest expression in his masterpiece, *Lo-t'o Hsiang-tzu* (1936; "Hsiang-tzu the Camel"), the tragic story of the trials of a ricksha puller in Peking. An unauthorized and bowdlerized English translation, titled *Rickshaw Boy* (1945), with a happy ending quite foreign to the original story, became a best seller in the United States.

During the Sino-Japanese War and World War II, Lao She headed the All-China Anti-Japanese Writers Federation, encouraging writers to produce patriotic and propagandistic literature. His own works were inferior and overly infused with propaganda.

In 1946–47 Lao She traveled to the United States on a cultural grant, lecturing and overseeing the translation of several of his novels, including *The Yellow Storm* (1951) and his last novel, *The Drum Singers* (1952), which never appeared in Chinese. Upon his return to China he was active in various cultural movements and literary committees and continued to write his propagandistic plays, among them the popular *Lung-hsü kou* (1951; "Dragon Beard Ditch") and *Ch'a-kuan* (1957; "The Teahouse"), which displayed his fine linguistic talents in its reproduction of the Peking dialect.

Lao She fell victim to persecution at the outset of the Cultural Revolution in 1966, and it is widely believed that he died as a result of a beating by Red Guards.

Lao-tzu, Pinyin LAOZI (Chinese: "Master Lao," or "Old Master"), original name (Wade-Giles romanization) LI ERH, deified as LAO-CHÜN, T'AI-SHANG LAO-CHÜN, or T'AI-SHANG HSÜAN-YÜAN HUANG-TI, also called LAO TUN, or LAO TAN (fl. *c.* 6th century BC, China), the first philosopher of Chinese Taoism and alleged author of the *Tao-te Ching* (*q.v.*), a primary Taoist writing. Modern scholars discount the possibility that the *Tao-te Ching* was written by only one person but readily acknowledge the influence of Taoism on the development of Buddhism. Lao-tzu is venerated as a philosopher by Confucianists and as a saint or god by some of the common people and was worshiped as an imperial ancestor during the T'ang dynasty (618–907). (*See also* Taoism.)

Lao-tzu (centre), detail from a Taoist temple fresco, southern Shansi, China, Yüan dynasty (1206–1368); in the Royal Ontario Museum, Toronto

By courtesy of the Royal Ontario Museum, Toronto

The life of Lao-tzu. Despite his historical importance, Lao-tzu remains an obscure figure. The principal source of information about his life is a biography in the *Shih-chi* ("Historical Records") by Ssu-ma Ch'ien. This historian, who wrote in about 100 BC, had little solid information concerning the philosopher. He says that Lao-tzu was a native of Ch'ü-jen, a village in the district of Hu in the state of Ch'u, which corresponds to the modern Lu-yi in the eastern part of Honan province. His family name was Li, his proper name Erh, his appellation Tan. He was appointed to the office of *shih* at the royal court of the Chou dynasty (*c.* 1111–255 BC). *Shih* today means "historian," but in ancient China the *shih* were scholars specializing in matters such as astrology and divination and were in charge of sacred books.

After noting the civil status of Lao-tzu, the historian proceeds to relate a celebrated but questionable meeting of the old Taoist with the younger Confucius (551–479 BC). The story has been much discussed by the scholars; it is mentioned elsewhere, but the sources are so inconsistent and contradictory that the meeting seems a mere legend. During the supposed interview, Lao-tzu blamed Confucius for his pride and ambition, and Confucius was so impressed with Lao-tzu that he compared him to a dragon that rises to the sky, riding on the winds and clouds.

No less legendary is a voyage of Lao-tzu to the west. Realizing that the Chou dynasty was on the decline, the philosopher departed and came to the Hsien-ku pass, which was the entrance to the state of Ch'in. Yin Hsi, the legendary guardian of the pass (*kuan-ling*), begged him to write a book for him. Thereupon, Lao-tzu wrote a book in two sections of 5,000 characters, in which he set down his ideas about the Tao (literally "Way," the Supreme Principle) and the *te* (its "virtue"): the *Tao-te Ching.* Then he left, and "nobody knows what has become of him," says Ssu-ma Ch'ien.

After the account of the voyage of Lao-tzu and of the redaction of the book, Ssu-ma Ch'ien alludes to other men with whom Lao-tzu was sometimes identified. One was Lao-Lai-tzu, a Taoist contemporary of Confucius; another was a great astrologer named Tan. Ssu-ma Ch'ien adds, "Maybe Lao-tzu has lived one hundred and fifty years, some say more than two hundred years."

To explain why the life of Lao-tzu is so shrouded in obscurity, Ssu-ma Ch'ien says that he was a gentleman recluse whose doctrine consisted in nonaction, the cultivation of a state of inner calm, and purity of mind. Indeed, throughout the whole history of China, there have always been recluses who shunned worldly life. The author (or authors) of the *Tao-te Ching* was probably a person of this kind who left no trace of his life.

The question of whether there was a historical Lao-tzu has been raised by many scholars, but it is rather an idle one. The *Tao-te Ching,* as we have it, cannot be the work of a single man; some of its sayings may date from the time of Confucius; others are certainly later; and the book as a whole dates from about 300 BC. Owing to these facts, some scholars have assigned the authorship of the *Tao-te Ching* to the astrologer Tan; while others, giving credit to a genealogy of the descendants of the philosopher, which is related in the biography by Ssu-ma Ch'ien, try to place the life of Lao Tan at the end of the 4th century BC. But this genealogy can hardly be considered as historical. The name Lao-tzu seems to represent a certain type of sage rather than an individual.

Hagiographical legends. Beyond the biography in the *Shih-chi* and sporadic mentions in other old books, several hagiographies were written from the 2nd century AD onward. These are interesting for the history of the formation of religious Taoism (Tao-chiao). During the Eastern, or Later, Han dynasty (AD 25–220), Lao-tzu had already become a mythical figure who was worshiped by the people and occasionally by an emperor. Later, in religious circles, he became the Lord Lao (Lao-chün), revealer of sacred texts and saviour of mankind. There were several stories about his birth, one of which was influenced by the legend of the miraculous birth of Buddha. Lao-tzu's mother is said to have borne him 72 years in her womb and he to have entered the world through her left flank. One legend gives an explanation of his family name, Li: the baby came to light at the foot of a plum tree (*li*) and decided that *li* ("plum") should be his surname. Two legends were particularly important in the creed of the Taoists. According to the first, the Lao-chün was believed to have adopted different personalities throughout history and to have come down to the earth several times to instruct the rulers in the Taoist doctrine. The second legend developed from the story of Lao-tzu's voyage to the west. In this account the Buddha was thought to be none other than Lao-tzu himself. During the 3rd century AD an apocryphal book was fabricated on this theme with a view to combating Buddhist propaganda. This book, the *Lao-tzu Hua-hu ching* ("Lao-tzu's Conversion of the Barbarians"), in which Buddhism was presented as an inferior kind of Taoism, was often condemned by the Chinese imperial authorities.

Lao-tzu has never ceased to be generally respected in all circles in China. To the Confucianists he was a venerated philosopher; to the people he was a saint or a god; and to the Taoists he was an emanation of the Tao and one of their greatest divinities. (Ma.K.)

BIBLIOGRAPHY. Holmes Welch, *Taoism: The Parting of the Way,* rev. ed. (1966); Max Kaltenmark, *Lao Tzu and Taoism* (1969).

Laoag, city, northwestern Luzon, Philippines. It lies on the north bank of the nonnavigable Laoag River, a few miles above the latter's mouth. Laoag was first occupied by the Spaniards in 1572 and is now the largest city in northern Luzon.

A trade centre for an agricultural region producing corn (maize), rice, and tobacco, the city has warehouses, wholesale outlets, and several cigarette factories. It is also the base of a sizable fishing industry. Laoag is served by good roads and national ports at nearby Gaang and Salomaque bays. The city is also located on the Pan-Philippine Highway, and it has an airport. Pop. (2000) 94,466.

Consult the INDEX *first*

Laocoön, in Greek legend, a seer and a priest of the god Apollo; he was the son of Agenor of Troy or, according to some, the brother of Anchises (the father of the hero Aeneas). Laocoön offended Apollo by breaking his oath of celibacy and begetting children. Thus, while preparing to sacrifice a bull on the altar of the god Poseidon (a task that had fallen to him by lot), Laocoön and his twin sons, Antiphas and Thymbraeus (also called Melanthus), were crushed to death by two great sea serpents, Porces and Chariboea (or Curissia or Periboea), sent by Apollo. An additional reason for his punishment was that he had warned the Trojans against accepting the wooden horse left by the Greeks. The legend found its most famous expressions in Virgil's *Aeneid* (ii, 109 *et seq.*) and in the Laocoön statue (now in the Vatican Museum) by three Rhodian sculptors, Agesander, Polydorus, and Athenodorus, dating probably from the 2nd century BC.

Laodicea, the ancient name of several cities of western Asia, mostly founded or rebuilt in the 3rd century BC by rulers of the Seleucid dynasty, and named after Laodice, the mother of Seleucus I Nicator, or after Laodice, daughter (or possibly niece) of Antiochus I Soter and wife of Antiochus II Theos. Established as commercial centres on newly opened or reconditioned trade routes, or as strongholds for the pacification of parts of the Seleucid empire, the cities aided in the Hellenization of western Asia and subsequently in the spread of Christianity in the region.

The most important of the cities was Laodicea ad Lycum (near modern Denizli, Turkey); its church was one of the seven to which Saint John addressed the Revelation. Laodicea ad Mare (modern Latakia, Syria) was a major seaport.

Laoet (Indonesia): *see* Laut Island.

Laoighis, also spelled LAOIS, or LEIX, county in the province of Leinster, Ireland, formerly called Queen's county. It is bounded by County Offaly (north and west), by Kildare (east), by Carlow and Kilkenny (south), and by Tipperary (southwest). The county consists mainly of the valleys of the upper Nore and upper Barrow rivers. Within the county are the greater part of the Slieve Bloom, a range of mountains reaching 1,732 feet (528 m) in Arderin, and the northern part of the Castlecomer Plateau. The county seat is Portlaoighise (Portlaoise). Most of the county is lowland between the Slieve Bloom and the Castlecomer Plateau. More than four-fifths of the county is improved land.

More than one-third of the county's population lives in towns and villages. A county council meets at Portlaoighise. Most of the farms in Laoighis are from about 70 to 80 acres (28 to 32 hectares) in size, and about three-fifths of the county's land area is permanent pasture, one-fifth bog, and one-fifth crops. Wheat, barley, and sugar beets for the factory at Carlow are the most important crops. Farming is mixed, with cattle fattening as a source of income. There is sheep rearing in the Slieve Bloom, where there are also forestry plantations. The country's industries include woodworking in Portarlington, a bacon factory in Mountmellick, a woolen mill in Portlaoighise, and pharmaceuticals at Abbeyleix. A branch of the Grand Canal was built through Portarlington to Mountmellick in the early 19th century. The main railway line to Cork from Dublin passes through Portarlington (which has a branch to Portlaoighise). Area 664 square miles (1,719 square km). Pop. (2002 prelim.) 58,732.

Laomedon, legendary king of Troy and father of Podarces (later famous as King Priam of Troy). Laomedon refused to give the gods Apollo and Poseidon their wages after they had built the walls of Troy for him. The gods therefore sent a pestilence and a sea monster to ravage the land, which could be delivered only by the sacrifice of the king's daughter Hesione. But the Greek hero Heracles, who happened to be at Troy at the time, killed the monster and rescued the maiden on the understanding that Laomedon should give him his divine horses. When Laomedon later refused, Heracles returned with a band of warriors, captured Troy, and slew Laomedon and all his sons except Priam. Laomedon was buried near the Scaean Gate, and, according to legend, as long as his grave remained undisturbed the walls of Troy would remain impregnable.

Laon, town, capital of Aisne *département,* Picardie *région,* northern France. It lies northwest of Reims and northeast of Paris. The

The Chapel of the Templars in the garden of the Museum of Laon, France
Bernard Cardon—Shostal

picturesque old town, situated on the summit of a scarped hill, stands high above the new town, which spreads out over the surrounding plain about 330 feet (100 m) below the old town. The railway station and the main industries are located in the lower town.

The Laon Cathedral in the old town was begun in the second half of the 12th century and completed in 1235. Adjoining the cathedral is a 13th-century cloister. The nearby Episcopal Palace (partly 13th century) now houses law courts and has a 12th-century chapel. On the cathedral's other side lies a 13th-century abbey with a large underground Gothic hall, now a hospital. The Museum of Laon has a collection of Roman and medieval jewelry. It also contains paintings by the three brothers Le Nain, 17th-century painters who were born in Laon. A 12th-century octagonal Chapel of the Templars stands in the museum gardens. The old town has a monument to the explorer Jacques Marquette, also born in Laon.

The hilly district of Laon (Latin: Laudunum) has always been of some strategic importance and was fortified by the Romans. At the end of the 5th century, Saint-Rémi, archbishop of Reims, instituted a bishopric in the town, and it remained a religious and intellectual centre until the Renaissance. Laon was the medieval capital of the Carolingian kings. Hugh Capet, however, who became king in 987, seized the town with the connivance of the local bishop and then moved the capital to Paris. In the 12th century Laon revolted against the authority of the bishops, but Louis VI quashed the rebellion. During the Hundred Years' War (1337–1453) Laon changed hands a number of times but was finally retaken by the French king. The bishopric was abolished in 1790 during the French Revolution. In 1870, when the Germans invaded, an engineer blew up the powder magazine, killing 500 people and damaging the cathedral. Laon was occupied during World Wars I and II, and the new town was severely damaged in 1944.

Laon is a minor industrial centre that has benefited from the decentralization of Paris. The main industries include metal founding, printing, and the production of heating equipment and plastics. Pop. (1999) 27,050.

Laos, officially LAO PEOPLE'S DEMOCRATIC REPUBLIC, Lao SATHALANALAT PAXATHIPATAI PAXAXÔN LAO, French RÉPUBLIQUE DÉMOCRATIQUE POPULAIRE LAO, landlocked country situated in the centre of the Indochinese peninsula of Southeast Asia. The country's maximum length from northeast to southwest is about 650 miles (1,050 km), and its maximum width from east to west is 290 miles (470 km). Laos is bordered on the north by China, on the northeast and east by Vietnam, on the south by Cambodia, on the west by Thailand, and on the northwest by Myanmar (Burma). The Mekong River forms the boundary with Myanmar and the greater part of the boundary with Thailand also. The capital is Vientiane (Lao: Viangchan). Area 91,400 square miles (236,800 square km). Pop. (2002 est.) 5,777,000.

A brief treatment of Laos follows. For full treatment, *see* MACROPAEDIA: Southeast Asia.

For current history and for statistics on society and economy, *see* BRITANNICA BOOK OF THE YEAR.

The land. Laos is mountainous with more than 90 percent of its land more than 600 feet (180 m) above sea level. Of its two physiographic zones, northern Laos is the

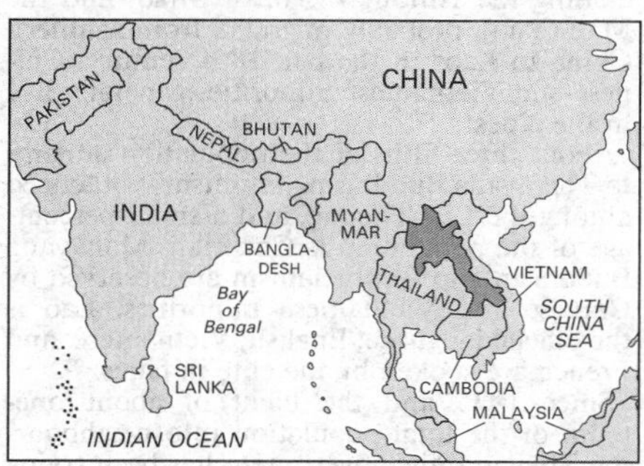

Laos

more mountainous and is deeply dissected by narrow, deep river valleys running generally northwest to southeast. Several mountain ranges rise to about 5,000 feet (1,500 m) in elevation, and the country's highest point is Mount Bia (9,245 feet [2,818 m]). The Plain of Jars, situated on the Xiangkhoang Plateau, is politically and strategically important. Apart from the mountains of the Annamese Cordillera (elevation 5,000 to 8,000 feet [1,500 to 2,400 m]), which form a barrier between Laos and Vietnam to the east, southern Laos is a region of lower elevations. The Annamese Cordillera extend along the country's eastern margin. The western border of Laos is largely formed by the Mekong River, which is the centre of the country's economic life. The Bolovens Plateau, at an elevation of about 3,600 feet (1,100 m), is in the far south. The only lowlands are along the eastern bank of the Mekong River, where fertile floodplains provide the major wet-rice fields of the country.

The climate is subequatorial and monsoonal, with a wet season from May to October and a dry season from November to April. Temperatures average between 60° and 70° F (16° and 21° C) in the cool months of December and February and more than 90° F (32° C) in March and April. Annual precipitation ranges from 60 to 67 inches (1,500 to 1,700 mm) in the lowlands to 160 inches (4,100 mm) on the Bolovens Plateau.

Only about 4 percent of the total area of Laos is suitable for agriculture. Rice is the principal crop, and about one-third of the rice fields are irrigated. Tropical forests cover more than half of the country's total land area and consist chiefly of broadleaf evergreen forests (containing oak, pine, magnolia, and laurel) in the north and deciduous monsoon forests (teak, rosewood, ebony, sandalwood, and bamboo) in the south. The country's animal life includes tiger, elephant, leopard, gibbon, and water buffalo.

A variety of minerals are found in Laos, but only tin, gypsum, and rock salt are mined in commercial quantities; the tin reserves are limited. Other minerals include coal, iron ore, copper, gold, potash, lead, zinc, and gemstones. Although the rivers represent an enormous potential for water storage and hydroelectric power, their potential has not yet been widely tapped.

The people. Laos has four major ethnolinguistic groups. The Lao-Lum, or valley Lao, speak Laotian Tai and live in the lowlands and cities and along the Mekong River. The Lao-Lum comprise about two-thirds of the country's total population. The Lao-Tai, or tribal Tai, include the Black Tai and Red Tai (so-called in reference to the colour of their women's dress), who live throughout the country, especially at higher elevations. The Lao-Theung (Mon-Khmer) are thought to be descendants of the earliest populations of the region; they live throughout Laos and in neighbouring countries. The Lao-Soung group, including the Hmong (Meo, or Miao) and the Man (Yao), probably migrated from southern China to Laos in the late 18th century. Chinese and Vietnamese minorities generally live in the cities.

About three-fifths of the population adheres to Theravāda Buddhism. Animism is practiced among the Lao-Theung, and a small percentage of the population is Christian. Mahāyāna Buddhism and Confucianism are observed by Chinese and Vietnamese minorities. Lao is the official language; English, Vietnamese, and French are spoken by the elite in cities.

Since 1975 and the flight of about one-tenth of the total population into neighbouring Thailand, the government has been trying to expand Laos's population. The birth rate has remained substantial; more than two-fifths of the total population is less than 15 years of age. The formerly high death rate decreased significantly in the 1980s.

About half the population lives in the lowlands and is engaged in rice cultivation. Only one-fifth of the population live in urban areas. The country's four largest cities, including Louangphrabang (formerly the royal capital, Luang Prabang) and Vientiane (the nation's largest city and chief commercial centre), are located on the Mekong River.

The economy. Laos is one of the world's poorest countries. It has a slowly developing, largely centrally planned economy based mainly on agriculture and international aid. The gross national product (GNP) per capita is one of the world's lowest.

Agriculture employs about three-fourths of the workforce and is dominated by the production of rice. After the (communist) Pathet Lao took control of the country in 1975, all land was nationalized and the government encouraged the spread of agricultural cooperatives. By the early 1990s, however, the government had begun taking steps to liberalize the economy, such as permitting the return to family-based farms and allowing foreign investment. Farmers are allowed to sell rice on the open market; the quantity of rice sold to the state has increased sharply as a result of higher prices and a lowering of the agricultural tax. Production of rice, however, frequently falls short of domestic demand and is supplemented by imports from Thailand. Significant quantities of sweet potatoes, sugarcane, cassava, potatoes, pineapples, corn (maize), spices, coffee, medicinal oils, tobacco, and cotton are also produced. Opium is an important cash crop in northern Laos, the Laotian portion of the "Golden Triangle." Pigs, water buffalo, and cattle are reared. Forestry and fishing are also elements of the economy. Fish from ponds and the Mekong River are the major source of protein in the Laotian diet.

The country's manufacturing industries are of negligible importance outside Vientiane and centre on the processing of agricultural products and domestic raw materials, of which timber is the most important. Electricity is generated almost entirely from hydroelectric power. Most electricity generated by the Nam Ngum Dam is exported to Thailand and serves as a major source of foreign exchange. Wood, coffee, tin, and gypsum are other important exports. Much of Laos's external trade, including the import of food, fuels, and manufactured goods, is ordinarily channeled through Thailand. Thailand, Japan, China, and Hong Kong are the country's main trading partners.

Government and social conditions. Laos is a republic governed by the only legal political party, the Lao People's Revolutionary Party (LPRP). In the late 1980s and '90s this party followed the lead of Vietnam in sponsoring economic reforms while retaining its tight hold on political power. The constitution of 1991 provides for a National Assembly. Executive power is exercised by the president, who is head of state, and the Council of Ministers, under the leadership of the prime minister, who also is the party chairman. The LPRP selects candidates for public office. The LPRP's structure is similar to that of other communist parties, with the Central Committee's Politburo the highest policy-making body. The army is the largest branch of the armed forces. Laos continues to receive some military support from Vietnam.

Health conditions are poor, as reflected in the average life expectancy of about 50 years. Extension of medical and public-health services to more remote areas has been a high priority of the government. Malaria, influenza, dysentery, and pneumonia are the major health problems, and malnutrition is widespread. The literacy rate, although increasing, remains relatively low at 84 percent. The educational system includes five-year primary, six-year secondary, and technical schools. The government controls the communications media.

Cultural life. Laotian literature is predominantly religious and linked to the Buddhist tradition. There is also a secular literary tradition based on themes of the Hindu epic poems, which have been transmuted into popular language.

Laotians have a variety of folk arts, including weaving, basketmaking, wood and ivory carving, and silverwork and goldwork. Professional dance troupes draw upon themes from the Indian epics.

History. The Lao people, a branch of the Tai peoples, migrated into Laos from southern China after the 8th century AD, gradually displacing various indigenous tribes who are now known as the Kha. During the 12th and 13th centuries the principality of Muong Swa (later Luang Prabang, now Louangphrabang) was established. In the 14th century Fa Ngum founded the first Laotian state, Lan Xang, with the help of the Khmer sovereign at Angkor. Except for a period of rule by Myanmar (1574–1637), the Lan Xang kingdom ruled Laos until 1713, when it split into three separate kingdoms—Vien Chan (now Vientiane), Champassak, and Luang Prabang.

During the 18th century the rulers of the three Laotian kingdoms became vassals of Siam, paying tribute to Siamese rulers. In the 19th century Chao Anou, king of Vien Chan, tried unsuccessfully to break the Siamese yoke by uniting his kingdom with Vietnam. Anou was defeated, and Vien Chan became a Siamese province. During the late 19th century France gained control of all Siamese territory east of the Mekong River. In the early 20th century Laos became a French protectorate.

In March 1945 the Japanese drove the French from Indochina and declared the independence of Laos. After World War II French rule was restored, but in 1946 France recognized a united Laos under the king of Luang Prabang. In 1949 a constitution was promulgated, and Laos was granted limited autonomy within the French Union. The leftist Pathet Lao ("Land of the Lao") movement joined the Viet Minh of Vietnam in the First Indochina War against the French in the early 1950s. By the end of the war the Pathet Lao controlled two provinces of the country.

At the Geneva Conference (1954), a unified and independent Laos was established as a buffer state between communist-aligned North Vietnam and Western-oriented Thailand (formerly Siam). During the 1950s the Pathet Lao struggled with rightist and neutralist factions for control of Laos. A second Geneva Conference (1962) formed a neutral coalition government that included the Pathet Lao. For the rest of the decade Laos became increasingly involved in the war in Vietnam. Pathet Lao forces aligned themselves with North Vietnam and fought Laotian government forces for control of the country.

In 1973 a cease-fire was signed, and the next year a Provisional Government of National Unity, composed of the Pathet Lao and rightists, was formed. In 1975, coinciding with the fall of the anticommunist regimes of Saigon and Phnom Penh, the Pathet Lao took control of the country, revealed the existence of a secret Laotian communist party, and established the Lao People's Democratic Republic. Laos maintained a close relationship with Vietnam during the 1980s, but Vietnamese influence had diminished by the early 1990s. The country held its first election in 1989 and promulgated a new constitution in 1991.

Laotian language: *see* Lao language.

Laozi (Chinese philosopher): *see* Lao-tzu.

Lapai, town and traditional emirate, southeastern Niger state, west-central Nigeria. It lies near the Gurara River, which is a tributary to the Niger River. It was originally inhabited by the Gbari (Gwari) people, who were subject to the Hausa kingdom of Zazzau and, after 1804, to the Fulani emirate of Zaria (to the north). In 1825 the Fulani requested the emir of Gwandu (Gando), the overlord of the western Fulani emirates, to create a new emirate independent of the emirates of Zaria and Agaie (to the west). Thus the Lapai emirate was founded that same year.

Lapai town was burned after the emirate had given military aid to Bida (50 miles [80 km] west) in its campaign against the British Royal Niger Company in 1897. The emirate was incorporated into Niger province in 1908; and, in 1938, its traditional seat was moved to Badeggi-Lapai (now Badeggi) 9 miles (14 km) west.

Lapai serves as a market centre for the sorghum, yams, rice, millet, shea nuts, peanuts (groundnuts), and cotton grown by the area's Gbari and Nupe peoples. Swamp rice is cultivated in the Gurara and Niger floodplains. The site of a government dispensary, Lapai is on the road to Abuja. Pop. (1972 est.) town, 6,039; (1991) local government area, 88,172.

"De," "la," and similar components of a name, when followed by a space, are alphabetized as separate words (e.g., *De Forest, Lee*). *When they are joined to the following part of a name, the combination is treated as a single word* (e.g., *DeForest, John William*).

---

laparoscopy, also called PERITONEOSCOPY, procedure that permits visual examination of the abdominal cavity with an optical instrument called a laparoscope, which is inserted through a small incision made in the abdominal wall. The term comes from the Greek word *laparo,* meaning "flank," and *skopein,* meaning "to examine."

The laparoscope is a type of endoscope—*i.e.,* a device similar to a small telescope that is equipped with a light source. Laparoscopy came into use early in the 20th century. It was first used as a means of diagnosing abdominal pain. By the 1960s gynecologists were using the laparoscope in operations such as tubal ligations. Modern laparoscopes have been fitted with fibre-optic lights and small video cameras that allow a surgical team to view the abdominal tissues and organs on a monitor in the operating room. These improvements have expanded the applications of laparoscopy. The technique is now not only used to obtain diagnostic information but employed in a variety of surgeries, including removal of the gall bladder (cholecystectomy), appendectomy, hysterectomy, repair of hernias, and removal of cancerous tumours.

Laparoscopy is a minimally invasive surgical procedure because it requires a much smaller incision than traditional surgery does, causing less damage to nerves, muscles, and skin. It can be performed using only local anesthesia and a mild sedative. To begin the procedure, carbon dioxide is pumped into the abdomen, thereby expanding the abdominal cavity to provide the physician with space to maneuver instruments. Next a small incision is made for the laparoscope. Additional tiny cuts can be made if surgical instruments such as forceps and scissors are needed in the procedure. The benefits of laparoscopic surgery include a reduction in postoperative pain, brief recovery times, and shortened hospital stays.

lapidary style, in calligraphy, style of lettering characteristically used for inscription in marble or other stone by chisel strokes, as, for example, on Trajan's Column in the Forum at Rome. The words of the inscription may be painted upon the stone slab first as a guide for the stonecutter, and the effect of his cut letters may be heightened by later painting or

Replica of the lapidary style inscription on Trajan's Column in Rome, *c.* AD 106–113; in the Victoria and Albert Museum, London

By courtesy of the Victoria and Albert Museum, London

gilding them. The play of light and shade on the planes of the incised strokes enhances the precision of the technique. The lapidary style reached its zenith of elegance and restraint in the square roman capital alphabet.

lapiés, also spelled LAPIAZ, weathered limestone surface found in karst regions and consisting of etched, fluted, and pitted rock pinnacles separated by deep grooves. This rugged surface is formed by the solution of rock along joints and areas of greater solubility by water containing carbonic and humic acids. It is not clearly understood whether lapies forms on bare rock or forms under soil mantle and is exposed later. The grooves of the lapies may vary in depth from a few millimetres to several metres. Lapies commonly forms on tilted rocks, and the limestone base becomes extremely hard.

lapillus, plural LAPILLI, unconsolidated volcanic fragment with a diameter between 4 and 32 mm (0.16 and 1.26 inches) that was ejected during a volcanic explosion. Lapilli may consist of fresh magma, solid magma from a prior eruption, or basement rocks through which the eruption passed. Accretionary lapilli are pellets formed by the accretion of volcanic ash or dust around moisture droplets; as in hailstones formed of water, these volcanic "hailstones" may show concentric rings—some as much as 10 cm (four inches) across—when they are carried through the eruption cloud several times by turbulent updrafts.

Lapin lääni (Finland): *see* Lappi.

lapis lazuli, semiprecious stone valued for its deep blue colour. The source of the pigment ultramarine (*q.v.*), it is not a mineral but a rock coloured by lazurite (*see* sodalite). In addition to the sodalite minerals in lapis lazuli, small amounts of white calcite and of pyrite crystals are usually present. Diopside, amphibole, feldspar, mica, apatite, titanite (sphene), and zircon may also occur.

Because lapis is a rock of varying composition, its physical properties are variable. It usually occurs in crystalline limestones and is a product of contact metamorphism. The most important sources are the mines in Badakhshan, northeastern Afghanistan, and those near Ovalle, Chile, where it is usually pale rather than deep blue. Much of the material that is sold as lapis is an artificially coloured jasper from Germany that shows colourless specks of clear, crystallized quartz and never the goldlike flecks of pyrite that are characteristic of lapis lazuli and have been compared with stars in the sky.

Lapita culture, cultural complex of what were presumably the original human settlers of Melanesia, much of Polynesia, and parts of Micronesia, and dating from between 1600 and 500 BC. It is named for a type of fired pottery that was first extensively investigated at the site of Lapita in New Caledonia.

The Lapita people were originally from New Guinea or some other region of Austronesia. They were highly mobile, seaborne explorers and colonists who had established themselves on the Bismarck Archipelago (northeast of New Guinea) by 2000 BC. Beginning about 1600 BC they spread to the Solomon Islands; they had reached Fiji, Tonga, and the rest of western Polynesia by 1000 BC; and they had dispersed to Micronesia by 500 BC.

The Lapita people are known principally on the basis of the remains of their fired pottery, which consists of beakers, cooking pots, and bowls. Many of the pottery shards that have been found are decorated with geometric designs made by stamping the unfired clay with a toothlike implement. A few shards with figurative designs have also been found. Lapita pottery has been found from New Guinea eastward to Samoa. Fishhooks, pieces of obsidian and chert flakes, and beads and rings made of shells are the other principal artifacts of the Lapita culture.

The Lapita appear to have been skilled sailors and navigators who subsisted largely, but not entirely, by fishing along the coasts of the islands on which they lived. They may also have practiced domestic agriculture and animal husbandy to a limited extent, although the evidence for this remains fragmentary.

Laplace, Pierre-Simon, marquis de, also called (1806–17) COMTE DE LAPLACE (b. March 23, 1749, Beaumount-en-Auge, Normandy, France—d. March 5, 1827, Paris), French mathematician, astronomer, and physicist who is best known for his investigations into the stability of the solar system.

Laplace successfully applied the Newtonian theory of gravitation to the solar system by accounting for all the observed deviations of the planets from their theoretical orbits and developed a conceptual view of evolutionary change in the physical universe. He also demonstrated the usefulness of the probabilistic interpretation of scientific data.

Laplace was the son of a peasant farmer. Little is known of his early life except that he quickly showed his mathematical ability at the military academy at Beaumont. At age 18 he left his humble surroundings for Paris, determined to make his way in mathematics. He then composed a letter on principles of mechanics for the mathematician Jean d'Alembert, who recommended him to a professorship at the École Militaire.

In 1773 he began his major lifework—applying Newtonian gravitation to the entire solar system—by taking up a particularly troublesome problem: why Jupiter's orbit appeared to be continuously shrinking while Saturn's continually expanded. The mutual gravitational interactions within the solar system were so complex that mathematical solution seemed impossible; indeed, Newton had concluded that divine intervention was periodically required to preserve the system in equilibrium. Laplace announced the invariability of planetary mean motions, carrying his proof to the cubes of the eccentricities and inclinations. This discovery in 1773, the first and most important step in establishing the stability of the solar system, was the most important advance in physical astronomy since Newton. It won him associate membership in the Academy of Sciences the same year.

Applying quantitative methods to a comparison of living and nonliving systems, Laplace and the chemist Antoine Lavoisier in 1780, with the aid of an ice calorimeter that they had invented, showed respiration to be a form of combustion. Returning to his astronomical investigations with an examination of the entire subject of planetary perturbations—mutual gravitational effects—Laplace in 1786 proved that the eccentricities and inclinations of planetary orbits to each other will always remain small, constant, and self-correcting. The effects of perturbations were therefore conservative and periodic, not cumulative and disruptive. The opposite and secular inequalities of Jupiter and Saturn (acceleration and deceleration, respectively), for example, were due to a changing effect with a period of 929 years. Their inequalities were therefore not cumulative but periodic.

Turning to the subject of the attraction between spheroids, Laplace in 1784–85 proved that his theorem concerning spheroids of revolution is true for any spheroids with common focuses, and he explored the problem of the attraction of any spheroid upon a particle situated outside or upon its surface. Through his discovery that the attractive force of a mass upon a particle, regardless of direction, could be obtained directly by differentiating a single function, Laplace laid the mathematical foundation for the scientific study of heat, magnetism, and electricity.

Laplace removed the last apparent anomaly from the theoretical description of the solar system in 1787 with the announcement that lunar acceleration depends on the eccentricity of the Earth's orbit. Although the mean motion (average angular velocity) of the Moon around the Earth depends mainly on the gravitational attraction between them, it is slightly diminished by the pull of the Sun on the Moon. This solar action depends, however, on changes in the eccentricity of the Earth's orbit resulting from perturbations by the other planets. As a result, the Moon's mean motion is accelerated as long as the Earth's orbit tends to become more circular; but, when the reverse occurs, this motion is retarded. The inequality is therefore not truly cumulative, Laplace concluded, but is of a period running into millions of years. The last threat of instability thus disappeared from the theoretical description of the solar system.

In 1796 Laplace published *Exposition du système du monde* (*The System of the World*), a semipopular treatment of his work in celestial mechanics and a model of French prose. The book included his "nebular hypothesis"—attributing the origin of the solar system to cooling and contracting of a gaseous nebula—which strongly influenced future thought on planetary origin. His *Traité de mécanique céleste* (*Celestial Mechanics*), appearing in five volumes between 1798 and 1827, summarized the results obtained by his mathematical development and application of the law of gravitation. He offered a complete mechanical interpretation of the solar system by devising methods for calculating the motions of the planets and their satellites and their perturbations, including the resolution of tidal problems. The book made him a celebrity.

In 1814 Laplace published a popular work for the general reader, *Essai philosophique sur les probabilités* (*A Philosophical Essay on Probability*). This work was the introduction to the second edition of his comprehensive and important *Théorie analytique des probabilités* ("Analytic Theory of Probability"), first published in 1812, in which he described many of the tools he invented for mathematically predicting the probabilities that particular events will occur in nature. He applied his theory not only to the ordinary problems of chance but also to the inquiry into the causes of phenomena, vital statistics, and future events, while emphasizing its importance for physics and astronomy.

Probably because he did not hold strong political views, he escaped imprisonment and execution during the Revolution. Laplace was president of the Bureau des Longitudes (Board of Longitude), aided in the organization of the metric system, helped found the Society of Arcueil, a scientific society, and was created a marquis. He served for six weeks as minister of the interior under Napoleon, who thought his record as an administrator was undistinguished. (G.J.W.)

BIBLIOGRAPHY. Laplace's collected works were published as *Œuvres complètes de Laplace,* 14 vol. in 15 (1878–1912). Translations of Laplace's works include *Mécanique céleste,* trans. by Nathaniel Bowditch, 4 vol. (1829–39, reprinted as *Celestial mechanics,* 1966–69), with a wealth of commentary; *The System of the World,* 2 vol. (1830), a classic, semipopular treatment of his work on celestial mechanics; and *A Philosophical Essay of Probabilities* (1902, reprinted 1951), also a classic. An excellent account of Laplace's work is by Edmund T. Whittaker in *The Mathematical Gazette,* 33:1–12 (1949). E.T. Bell, *Men of Mathematics* (1937, reissued 1986), chapter 11, also contains a lively biographical essay. An important source of information is M.P. Crosland, *The Society of Arcueil: A View of French Science at the Time of Napoleon I* (1967).

Laplace transform, in mathematics, a particular integral transform. The Laplace transform $f(p)$, also denoted by $L\{F(t)\}$ or Lap $F(t)$, is defined by the integral

$$f(p) = \int_0^\infty e^{-pt} F(t)\,dt,$$

involving the exponential parameter p in the kernel $K = e^{-pt}$. The linear Laplace operator L thus transforms each function $F(t)$ of a certain set of functions into some function $f(p)$. The inverse transform $F(t)$ is written $L^{-1}\{f(p)\}$ or $\mathrm{Lap}^{-1} f(p)$. The Laplace transform has many applications, such as in solution of linear differential equations with constant coefficients or the study of boundary value problems. These problems often arise in connection with calculations relating to physical systems. Notable early success in solving this type of problem was achieved by the 19th–20th-century British physicist-engineer Oliver Heaviside, who developed a procedure called operational calculus. *See also* Fourier transform; integral transform.

Laplace's equation, second-order partial differential equation widely useful in physics, because its solutions R (known as harmonic functions) occur in problems of electrical, magnetic, and gravitational potentials, of steady-state temperatures, and of hydrodynamics. The equation is named for the 18th–19th-century French mathematician and astronomer Pierre-Simon Laplace.

Laplace's equation states that the sum of the second-order partial derivatives of R, the unknown function, with respect to the Cartesian coordinates, equals zero:

$$\frac{\partial^2 R}{\partial x^2} + \frac{\partial^2 R}{\partial y^2} + \frac{\partial^2 R}{\partial z^2} = 0.$$

The sum on the left often is represented by the expression $\nabla^2 R$, in which the symbol ∇^2 is called the Laplacian, or the Laplace operator.

Many physical systems are more conveniently described by the use of spherical or cylindrical coordinate systems. Laplace's equation can be recast in these coordinates; for example, in cylindrical coordinates, Laplace's equation is

$$\nabla^2 R = \frac{\partial^2 R}{\partial r^2} + \frac{1}{r}\frac{\partial R}{\partial r} + \frac{1}{r^2}\frac{\partial^2 R}{\partial \theta^2} + \frac{\partial^2 R}{\partial z^2} = 0.$$

Lapland, Finnish LAPI, or LAPPI, Swedish LAPPLAND, region of northern Europe largely within the Arctic Circle, stretching across northern Norway, Sweden, and Finland and into the Kola Peninsula of Russia. It is bounded by the Norwegian Sea on the west, the Barents Sea on the north, and the White Sea on the east. Lapland is named for the Sami, or Lapp, people, who have sparsely inhabited the region for several thousand years. (*See* Sami.) Lapland straddles several national borders and does not exist as any unified administrative entity.

Lapland is a region of great topographical variety. To the west it embraces the northern part of the Kolen Mountains, which reach elevations of more than 6,500 feet (2,000 m). On its Norwegian (western) side this range slopes abruptly and is deeply eroded into fjords and headlands and fractured into archipelagoes. The eastern flank of the range, which is situated in Swedish Lapland (*see* Lappland), slopes more gradually into a broad piedmont studded with large, fingerlike lakes that feed the rivers flowing into the Gulf of Bothnia. Farther to the east, Finnish Lapland (*see* Lappi) is a relatively low-lying region with many bogs and small lakes.

Sami (Lapps) outside their reindeer-skin tent in Finnish Lapland

Norwegian Lapland is largely open and windswept, with timber growth only in sheltered tracts and the more protected interior. Southern and central Lapland occupies the zone of the taiga, or swampy coniferous forest, with its saturated land and many bogs and swamps. Forests of pine and spruce give way to the dwarf birch, heath, and lichens of the tundra farther north and at higher elevations.

Many of the Sami have adopted a sedentary life and intermarried with Scandinavians and Finns. The region is still home to several hundred thousand reindeer, but the traditional reindeer country has been intruded upon by permanent farming, forestry, mining, and hydroelectric and even industrial enterprises. Those who practice reindeer herding have liberty of movement across the open boundaries of Finland, Norway, and Sweden.

Lapland (province, Finland): *see* Lappi.

Lapland Nature Reserve, Russian LAPLANDSKY ZAPOVEDNIK, natural area set aside for research in the natural sciences, in the western part of the Kola Peninsula, northwestern Russia. It lies west of Lake Imandra and has an area of 1,036 square miles (2,684 square km). The reserve was established (1930) mainly to protect the natural habitat of the reindeer. It is in a region of plains and low mountains; glaciated landforms, bogs and lakes, and exposed crystalline rocks of the Baltic Shield are common. Most of the reserve's vegetation is pine, with some reindeer moss and fir; there are also areas of mountain lichen tundra (with willow, rhododendron, and mountain aven) and open forest of downy and silver birch. Wildlife includes beaver, elk, brown bear, pine marten, otter, and wolverine, and birds such as ptarmigan, golden eagle, osprey, grouse, and the Siberian tit and jay. The muskrat was introduced in 1931 and the American mink, by accident, in 1958. The reserve is used for scientific research on reindeer, fur-bearing animals, and fish.

Lapp (people): *see* Sami.

Lapp language: *see* Sami language.

Lappeenranta, Swedish VILLMANSTRAND, city, Kymi *lääni* (province), southeastern Finland. Lappeenranta lies at the southern end of Lake Saimaa, northeast of Kotka. It was a major trade centre during the Middle Ages, with a municipal charter granted by Per Brahe, the Swedish governor-general of Finland, in 1649.

Lake Saimaa harbour, Lappeenranta, Fin.
By courtesy of the Embassy of Finland, Washington, D.C.

A border fortress and the headquarters of the administrative district of Kyminkartano after the Treaty of Uusikaupunki (1721), Lappeenranta was destroyed by the Russians in 1741. After the Treaty of Åbo (Turku) in 1743, the city became a Russian possession until 1812. Lappeenranta's notable sites include the mineral baths (established in 1824), the wooden Lappee Church (1791; restored 1929), and a Greek Orthodox church (1785); the remains of the old town and its ramparts and fortifications are on a promontory overlooking the harbour.

Lappeenranta is the rail junction point between many eastern Finnish cities and Vyborg and St. Petersburg in Russia and is a major harbour for several of Lake Saimaa's shipping routes. The National Sulphuric-Acid Works is located there, as well as lumber mills, lime and cement factories, and machine shops. Because of its fine lakeside location and its mineral baths, Lappeenranta is known as a health resort. Pop. (1994 est.) 55,843.

Lappenberg, Johann Martin (b. July 30, 1794, Hamburg [Germany]—d. Nov. 28, 1865, Hamburg), German archivist who was also a prolific scholar of German and English history.

Lappenberg was intended for his father's profession, medicine, and studied in Edinburgh and London, where he conceived the ambition of entering British politics or serving in that country's diplomatic service. He therefore studied law at the universities of Berlin and Göttingen but became convinced after visiting Britain again that his ambition must remain unfulfilled. Returning to Hamburg, Lappenberg was appointed keeper (curator) of the city's historical archives in 1823. He published copiously, contributing editions of early documents to the series *Monumenta Germaniae Historica* and to the archives of the Society for Early German History. He meanwhile conducted assiduous research on the Hamburg archives and on the history of the Hanseatic League. His *Geschichte von England*, 2 vol. (1834–37; *A History of England*), proved a useful work to historians until the end of the 19th century.

Lappenberg became government secretary to the Hamburg Senate, and in 1850 he represented his native city at the Frankfurt parliament.

To make the best use of the Britannica, consult the INDEX *first*

lappet, any member of the insect genus *Tolype* of the Lasiocampidae family of moths (order Lepidoptera). The genus includes the eggars, named for their egg-shaped cocoons, and the tent caterpillars, which spin huge, tent-shaped communal webs in trees. Lappets in the larval stage have lateral lobes, or lappets, on each segment of their body.

Adults are stoutbodied and usually bluish gray, with a typical wingspan of 25 to 75 mm (1 to 3 inches). Many species have feathery antennae and hairy bodies, legs, and eyes. The larvae are often brightly coloured and can defoliate forest, fruit, and ornamental trees. *T. laricis* larvae feed on larch, while *T. vellida* prefers apple, poplar, and syringa.

Lappi, in full LAPIN LÄÄNI, Swedish LAPPLANDS LÄN, also called LAPLAND, *lääni* (province), northern Finland. It is bounded on the north by Norway, on the east by Russia, and on the west by Sweden. Its land area, extending mainly north of the Arctic Circle, comprises more than one-fourth of Finland's total area. The province is drained southwestward to the Gulf of Bothnia by the Kemi River and northward to the Barents Sea by the Paats River. Lappi is sparsely populated and is the most underdeveloped area in Finland. Forestry, waterpower, reindeer husbandry, and summer tourism provide the principal occupations. Finland's two largest national parks, Pallas-Ounastunturi and Lemmenjoki, are located in the province. Important towns include Tornio and Kemi, both seaports on the Gulf of Bothnia, and Rovaniemi, the administrative capital. Lappi was created in 1938 when the *lääni* of Oulu was divided in two parts. Area 35,930 square miles (93,057 square km). Pop. (1995 est.) 202,325.

Lappland (region, Europe): *see* Lapland.

Lappland, *landskap* (province) of northern Sweden. Lappland is bounded on the west by Norway, on the north by Finland, on the east by the *landskaper* (provinces) of Norrbotten and Västerbotten, and on the south by those of Ångermanland and Jämtland. Administratively it lies within the *län* (counties) of Västerbotten and Norrbotten. The *landskap* covers about one-fourth of the total area of Sweden, but it is sparsely settled. Its landscape is characterized by the highest mountains in Sweden, notably Mounts Kebne (Kebnekaise) and Sarek (Sarektjåkkå), as well as rolling hills, plains, forests of spruce, pine, and birch, long chains of lakes, rushing rivers, waterfalls, and glaciers. The climate is typically Arctic, with a short growing season.

A hiker in Stora Sjöfallet National Park, Swedish Lappland
© Hans Nelsater/Bildarkivet

Archaeological finds indicate habitation of Lappland as early as the Stone Age. By early medieval times the area was occupied by reindeer-herding Sami (Lapps). Swedes from farther south were attracted by its valuable furs and brought the area under their domination. Territorial subdivisions called *lappmark* were established for the regulation and taxation of the fur trade. As Swedish cultivators settled the coastal provinces (Västerbotten and Norrbotten) and began to move up the rivers into the interior, conflicts arose with the indigenous Sami. Twice, "limits of cultivation" were established by decree, setting bounds on the Swedish migration inland; these limits became the boundary of Lappland with Västerbotten and Norrbotten.

The development of mining, beginning in the 1630s, increased settlement, and by the 1860s northern Lappland had a population of almost 6,000 people. The coming of railroads, together with large-scale mining operations, resulted in further growth. There are still a few thousand Sami in the *landskap,* but the majority of the people are descendants of the settlers from other parts of Sweden who moved there to work in the mines or in the forest industries.

Lappland has some of the richest iron-ore mines in the world, at Kiruna, Gällivare, and Malmberget. The *landskap*'s rushing torrents have been harnessed for hydroelectric power, notably at Porjus and Harsprånget. Because of the short growing season, agriculture is limited; chief crops are potatoes, barley, and rye. Tourism has become increasingly important, receiving impetus from such attractions as Sarek and Stora Sjöfallet national parks. Abisko, Björkliden, and Riksgränsen are well-known winter-sports resorts. Lappland is accessible by road, rail, or air. Area 42,356 square miles (109,702 square km). Pop. (1994 est.) 112,717.

lapse, doctrine of, in Indian history, formula devised by Lord Dalhousie, governor-general of India (1848–56), to deal with questions of succession to Hindu Indian states. It was a corollary to the doctrine of paramountcy, by which Great Britain, as the ruling power of the Indian subcontinent, claimed the superintendence of the subordinate Indian states and so also the regulation of their succession.

According to Hindu law an individual or a ruler without natural heirs could adopt a person who would then have all the personal and political rights of a son.

Dalhousie asserted the paramount power's right of approving such adoptions and of acting at discretion in their absence in the case of dependent states. In practice this meant the rejection of last-minute adoptions and British annexation of states without a direct natural or adopted heir, because Dalhousie considered that Western rule was preferable to Eastern and to be enforced where possible. Annexation in the absence of a natural or adopted heir was enforced in the cases of Sātāra (1848), Jaitpur and Sambalpur (1849), Baghat (1850), Chota Udaipur (1852), Jhānsi (1853), and Nāgpur (1854). Though the scope of the doctrine was limited to dependent Hindu states, these annexations aroused much alarm and resentment among the Indian princes and the old aristocracy who served them. They have generally been regarded as having contributed to the discontent that was a factor in the outbreak of the Indian Mutiny (1857) and the widespread revolt that followed.

lapse rate, rate of temperature change observed in passing upward through the Earth's atmosphere. The lapse rate is considered positive when the temperature decreases with elevation, zero when the temperature is constant with elevation, and negative when the temperature increases with elevation (temperature inversion [*q.v.*]). The lapse rate of nonrising air—commonly referred to as normal temperature, or actual, lapse rate—is highly variable, being affected by radiation, convection, and condensation processes; it averages about 6.5° C per km (18.8° F per mile). It differs from adiabatic lapse rate, which involves temperature change due to the rising or sinking of an air parcel. Adiabatic lapse rate is usually differentiated as dry or moist.

The dry rate for air depends only on the specific heat of air at constant pressure and the acceleration caused by gravity. The dry adiabatic lapse rate for the Earth's atmosphere equals 9.8° C per kilometre (28.3° F per mile); thus, the temperature of an air parcel that ascends or descends 5 km (3 miles) would fall or rise 49° C (85° F), respectively.

When an air parcel that is saturated with water vapour rises, some of its moisture will condense, releasing heat and causing the parcel to cool more slowly than it would if it were not saturated. This moist adiabatic lapse rate varies considerably. The greater the amount of moisture contained in the air, the smaller the adiabatic lapse rate; as the air parcel rises, cools, and loses its moisture through condensation, its lapse rate increases and approaches the dry adiabatic.

The comparison between the normal lapse rate in the atmosphere and the dry and moist adiabatic lapse rates determines the vertical stability of the atmosphere—*i.e.,* the tendency of an air particle to return to its original position or to accelerate away from its original position after being given a slight vertical displacement. For this reason, the lapse rate is of prime importance to meteorologists in forecasting certain types of cloud formations, the incidence of thunderstorms, and the intensity of atmospheric turbulence.

Laptev Sea, Russian MORE LAPTEVYKH, marginal sea of the Arctic Ocean off the coast of Northern Siberia (Russia), bounded by the Taymyr Peninsula (Poluostrov) and the islands of Severnaya Zemlya on the west and by the New Siberian Islands and Kotelny Island on the east. It is connected in the west with the Kara Sea and in the east with the East Siberian Sea. Formerly called the Siberian Sea, it was renamed in 1935 after Khariton and Dmitry Laptev, the brothers who first mapped its shores (1735–40). Its area is about 276,000 square miles (714,000 square km), the average depth 1,896 feet (578 m), and the greatest depth 9,774 feet (2,980 m).

Large bays cut into the shore, and numerous rivers, the largest being the Lena, flow into the sea. Several rivers form extensive deltas. Dozens of islands, primarily in the west, vary in landscape and origin.

Ancient rivers and glaciers were important in forming the bottom relief and shoreline. The floor of the sea is a gently sloping plain, breaking off abruptly toward the Arctic Ocean. The bottom of the deepwater part is covered with silt, the shallower areas with sand and silt. In the east, under a thin layer of deposits, occurs a layer of very old "relic" ice. As regards salinity, the thawing of ice and the inflow of fresh river water might have resulted in a layer of fresh water 53 inches (135 cm) thick. In winter the salinity in the southeastern part of the sea is 20–25 parts per thousand, in the northern part up to 34, and in summer the salinity falls to 5–10 parts per thousand in the southeast and 30–32 in the north.

Air temperature below 32° F (0° C) occurs in the north during about 11 months and in the south 9 months. The average temperature in January is −24° to −29° F (−31° to −34° C), the minimum about −58° F (−50° C). In July the average temperature in the north is just above the freezing point, in the south about 43° F (6° C), with a maximum of 50° F (10° C). On the shores the maximum can reach 75° F (24° C). In winter there are frequent gales, blizzards, and snowstorms; in the summer, snow squalls and fogs.

For most of the year the sea is covered with ice. In the winter the temperature of the water under the ice is 30.6° F (−0.8° C) in the southeast and 28.8° F (−1.8° C) in the north; in the deep regions it is from 29.1° to 28.9° F (−1.6° to −1.7° C). In the summer, in ice-free regions, a thin layer of water warms to above the freezing point.

At the mouths of the rivers people live by catching salmon and other fish. Mammals include various seals, walrus, and polar bear. The Laptev Sea is on the Northern Sea Route, with Tiksi the main port. Timber, building materials, and furs are the primary cargoes.

"De," "la," and similar components of a name, when followed by a space, are alphabetized as separate words (e.g., *De Forest, Lee*). *When they are joined to the following part of a name, the combination is treated as a single word* (e.g., *DeForest, John William*).

Lapu-Lapu, city, northwestern Mactan Island, Philippines, on a narrow channel of the Bohol Strait opposite Cebu City. Formerly called Opon, the city was renamed in honour of Chief Lapulapu, who, on April 27, 1521, killed the navigator Ferdinand Magellan. The chief is considered a national hero. A coconut-growing and fishing centre, it has an international airport nearby and excellent port facilities, including petroleum installations. Inc. city, 1961. Pop. (1990 prelim.) 146,000.

Lapua Movement (1929–32), fascist movement in Finland that threatened the young state's democratic institutions and for a time dictated the policies of the government. It was named for the parish of Lapua, where a fascist group disrupted a meeting of communists late in 1929. The movement, engendered by the Great Depression and influenced by Italian fascism, espoused anticommunism and hatred of Russia. Through 1930 the movement gained wide popular support, and in 1930–31 it unofficially dominated the government, forcing it to outlaw the Finnish Communist Party, to curb radical trade unions, and to intimidate the press. The tactics of the movement included mass demonstrations and kidnapping, raids on newspaper offices, and other forms of terror. Military units of the Lapua under General K.M. Wallenius assembled in February 1932 in preparation for a coup d'état. The government took up the challenge, however, and ordered the units to disarm. The rebels complied, Wallenius and others received mild prison sentences, and early in 1932 Parliament banned the Lapua Movement. Financial and popular support soon evaporated, and the movement collapsed.

lapwing, any of numerous species of birds of the plover family, Charadriidae (order Charadriiformes), especially the Eurasian lapwing, *Vanellus vanellus,* of farmlands and grassy plains. The name lapwing, which refers to the birds' slow wingbeat, is sometimes applied broadly to members of the subfamily Vanellinae. Lapwings are about 30 cm (12 inches) long, with broad, rounded wings. Several species have crests, and some have wing spurs (sharp projections at the bend of the wing for use in fighting).

The Eurasian lapwing is green-glossed black above with white cheeks. The throat and breast are black, the belly is white, and the tail is white with a black band. This species has a notable crest. It breeds in Britain, in much of Europe, and across temperate Asia to eastern China. Some northern birds go south in winter, particularly to northern Africa. The brownish, black-marked eggs of this species are the plover eggs of commerce.

Eurasian lapwing (*Vanellus vanellus*)
Ingmar Holmasen

There are about 24 other species of lapwings in South America, Africa, southern Asia, Malaya, and Australia. The crowned lapwing (*Stephanibyx coronatus*), of Africa, has a black cap with a white ring around it. The red-wattled lapwing, *Vanellus* (sometimes *Lobivanellus*) *indicus,* and the yellow-wattled lapwing (*V. malabaricus*), of southern Asia, have wattles on the face. Others are the gray-headed lapwing (*Microsarcops cinereus*), of eastern Asia, and the long-toed lapwing (*Hemiparra crassirostris*), of Africa.

Lapworth, Charles (b. Sept. 30, 1842, Faringdon, Berkshire, Eng.—d. March 13, 1920, Birmingham), English geologist who proposed what came to be called the Ordovician period (505 to 438 million years old) of geologic strata.

In 1864 Lapworth became a schoolmaster at Galashiels and began his studies of the early Paleozoic (570 to 245 million years old) strata of the Southern Uplands. He used the occurrence of graptolite fossils to establish the order of these strata and in 1873 published a paper that detailed his findings and opened the way for similar stratigraphic research over the world. In 1879 Lapworth proposed that a complex series of strata (considered to be Lower Silurian by Sir Roderick I. Murchison and to be Upper Cambrian by Adam Sedgwick) was in fact a separate system. He proposed that the series of rocks be called the Ordovician System.

From 1881 to 1913 he held the newly established chair of geology and physiography at Mason College, Birmingham University. In 1882 he began excursions into the Durness–Eireboll region of the northwest Highlands, where he conducted a detailed study of the main geologic features. He was elected a fellow of the Royal Society in 1888.

laque burgauté, also spelled LAC BURGAUTÉ, in the decorative arts, East Asian technique of decorating lacquer ware with inlaid designs employing shaped pieces of the iridescent blue-green shell of the sea-ear (Haliotis). This shell inlay is sometimes engraved and occasionally combined with gold and silver. Workmanship is exquisite; therefore, *laque burgauté* is principally used to decorate such small-scale objects as tiny boxes, miniature table screens, vases, and especially little silver-lined wine cups, usually made in sets of five.

Laque burgauté seems to have originated in China, with examples occurring as early as the Ming dynasty (1368–1644), and was especially popular in the Ch'ing dynasty (1644–1911/12), when it was also used to cover unglazed

Bottom of a circular flat-topped box, *laque burgauté* on black ground, Chinese, *c.* 1700; in the collection of Kurt Herberts, Germany

By courtesy of Kurt Herberts

porcelain. It was widely used by Japan craftsmen in the Tokugawa (Edo) period (1603–1867). In China this technique is referred to as *lo tien*, and in Japan it is called *aogai*. Like many of the artistic techniques and objects imported into 17th- and 18th-century Europe from eastern Asia, the Western name is derived from the French—sea-ear (*burgau*) lacquer (*laque,* or *lac*).

L'Aquila, city, capital of L'Aquila province and of Abruzzi region, central Italy, on a hill above the Aterno River, northeast of Rome. The district was settled by the Sabini, an ancient Italic tribe, after their town Amiternum was destroyed by the Romans and later by the barbarians. The city was founded *c.* 1240 by Holy Roman emperor Frederick II and became an episcopal see in 1257. An important centre in the Middle Ages, it was contended for by the Angevin dynasty (House of Anjou) and Aragonese and later passed to the Kingdom of Naples. It took part in the resistance to the French invasion of 1798–99 and in the rebellions of the 19th century against the reactionary Neapolitan kingdom; it became part of the Kingdom of Italy in 1860.

Notable buildings include the majestic castle (1535) housing the archaeological and artistic National Museum of the Abruzzi; the churches of S. Bernardino (1454–72; 1527 facade), containing the mausoleum (1505) of St. Bernardine of Siena, and Sta. Maria di Collemaggio (1283–88); and the 14th-century cathedral, rebuilt after earthquakes in 1703. The medieval city walls are still largely extant. There are many palaces, a large provincial library, and a municipal hospital of ancient foundation.

The chief point of departure for the nearby Gran Sasso d'Italia mountain group, L'Aquila is a skiing centre and summer resort. Woollen cloth, radio equipment, bricks, and furniture are manufactured, and agriculture, lacework, and other crafts are practiced. A motorway connects L'Aquila to Rome and is being extended to the Adriatic coast. Pop. (2000 est.) mun., 69,839; province, 303,839.

Lar, plural LARES, in Roman religion, any of numerous tutelary deities. They were originally gods of the cultivated fields, worshipped by each household at the crossroads where its allotment joined those of others. Later the Lares were worshipped in the houses in association with the Penates, the gods of the storeroom (*penus*) and thus of the family's prosperity; the household Lar (Familiaris) was conceived as the centre of the family and of the family cult.

Originally each household had only one Lar. It was usually represented as a youthful figure, dressed in a short tunic, holding in one hand a drinking horn, in the other a cup. Under the empire, two of these images were commonly to be found, one on each side of the central figure of the *genius*, of Vesta, or of some other deity. The whole group came to be called indifferently Lares or Penates. A prayer was said to the Lar every morning, and special offerings were made at family festivals.

The public Lares belonged to the state religion. Among these were included the *Lares compitales*, who presided over the crossroads (*compita*) and the whole neighbouring district. They had a special annual festival, called the Compitalia.

The state itself had its own Lares, called *praestites*, the protecting patrons and guardians of the city. They had a temple and altar on the Via Sacra and were represented as men wearing the chlamys (military cloak), carrying lances, seated, with a dog (the emblem of watchfulness) at their feet.

Lara, state, northwestern Venezuela. Bordered on the north by Falcón, east by Yaracuy, south by Portuguesa and Trujillo, and west by Zulia, the territory comprises 7,645 sq mi (19,800 sq km) and lies in the Segovia Highlands, a hilly region plagued by recurring droughts. Subsistence agriculture, the traditional way of life, persists, although the growing of sisal and coffee supplements the cultivation of cacao, corn (maize), potatoes, and tobacco. Goats are important in the north; cattle raising is widespread, especially around Carora. There is a small amount of mining in the state, but the copper mines of Aroa, once owned by Simón Bolívar, have been abandoned. Lara accounts for almost all of Venezuela's sisal; its manufacture into bags, sacks, and cordage is an important industry. The state is traversed by highways that link Barquisimeto (*q.v.*), the state capital, with the major urban centres to the northeast. Pop. (1997 est.) 1,491,940.

Larache, Arabic EL-ARAISH, Atlantic port city, northern Morocco, at the mouth of the Oued Loukkos (Lucus River). The ruins of ancient Lixus, successively a Phoenician, Carthaginian, and Roman settlement, are 2 mi (3 km) northeast on the river's north bank. Larache was under Spanish rule from 1610 to 1689 and from 1912 to 1956. The old walled city rises in terraces to two forts that dominate it on the north and south. The ancient

The fort of La Cigogne in Larache, Mor.

Salmer—Plessner International

Kebibat fortress (now a hospital) rises out of the sea; the fort of La Cigogne (*c.* 1700) was built by the Spaniards. The modern quarter stretches from the port across the coastal plateau, with gardens and orchards bordering the river. Larache is a busy agricultural and fishing centre, exporting produce, timber, and wool. Pop. (1971) 45,710.

Laramide orogeny, a series of mountain-building events that affected much of western North America in Late Cretaceous and Early Tertiary time (the Cretaceous period ended 66.4 million years ago and was followed by the Tertiary period). Evidence of the Laramide orogeny is present from Mexico to Alaska, but the main effects appear centred in the eastern portion of the Cordilleran Geosyncline from southern Nevada to the Northern Rockies and Northern Cordillera in western Canada, in the Central Rockies of Montana and Wyoming, in the Southern Rockies of Colorado and New Mexico, and in southern Arizona, southwestern New Mexico, and northern Mexico.

The evidence consists of great eastward-directed thrust faults and folds with only slight basement involvement in the eastern portion of the Cordilleran Geosyncline from Nevada northward to British Columbia; initial vertical uplift accompanied by the development of flanking, coarse clastic basin sediments and unconformities in the Central and Southern Rockies; and acidic plutonic intrusions ranging from 50,000,000 to 70,000,000 years in age that are much smaller in bulk than those that accompanied the Nevadan orogeny, with the exception of the portion in southern Arizona.

Clastic wedges that were derived from Laramide uplifts in the Cordilleran Geosyncline were shed eastward into parts of Wyoming and Utah.

The Laramide orogeny originally was believed to mark the Cretaceous–Tertiary boundary. It is now considered to have been a polyphase orogeny consisting of many disparate pulses of deformation that varied in intensity and age from place to place in western North America. Events ascribed to the Laramide range in date from Late Cretaceous to as late as Oligocene time (the Oligocene epoch occurred from 36.6 to 23.7 million years ago). Laramide igneous intrusions, however, are generally centred around the Cretaceous-Tertiary time boundary.

Laramie, city, seat of Albany county, southeastern Wyoming, U.S., on the Laramie River, 49 mi (79 km) west of Cheyenne, surrounded by divisions of the Medicine Bow National Forest (headquartered at Laramie). It was founded in 1868 when several thousand persons made a settlement—a jumble of tents and shanties on the treeless plain—during construction of the Union Pacific Railroad. Most of the builders moved on, leaving a handful to build a permanent city from a heretofore lawless settlement.

Laramie's growth was slow but steady. It attracted attention in 1870 as the site of the first "mixed" jury trial in the United States, when six women served on a grand jury. Humorist Edgar Wilson (Bill) Nye lived in Laramie; the *Laramie Boomerang,* a newspaper which he helped found in 1881, is still published.

For years the search for precious metals in the Medicine Bow Mountains, 30 mi to the west, provided employment. The railroad, cattle and sheep ranches, forest products, and the University of Wyoming (founded there in 1886) are important factors in the economy, as are tourism and cement making. The University Stock Farm is in the city, and the Geological Museum on the main campus exhibits a dinosaur skeleton discovered in the area.

Laramie city, river, plains, and mountains take their name from Jacques La Ramie, a French-Canadian fur trapper killed by Indians on the river *c.* 1819. Inc. 1874. Pop. (2000) 27,204.

Laramie Mountains, range of the central Rocky Mountains, in southeastern Wyoming, U.S. A northern section of Colorado's Front Range, it stretches north-northwestward for 125 mi (200 km) from the Wyoming–Colorado border, between Laramie and Cheyenne, to the North Platte River, around Casper. The range (roughly 25–50 mi wide) rises about 3,000 ft (900 m) from the Great Plains on the east and 1,500 ft from the Laramie Basin on the west. It exceeds 9,000 ft in many places, with Laramie Peak (10,274 ft) being the high point. Its low southern portion provides a relatively easy path into the Rockies for the Union Pacific Railroad, as well as for a cross-country highway. Two divisions of the Medicine Bow National Forest encircle the mountains, which were named for Jacques La Ramie (*see* Laramie).

Laramie River, river in Colorado and Wyoming, U.S., rising in the Front Range in Roosevelt National Forest, northern Colorado. It flows north across the Wyoming border and then turns northwest past the city of Laramie, through the Laramie Plains and Wheatland reservoirs, to enter the North Platte River at Fort Laramie after a course of 216 mi (348 km). The Laramie supplies irrigation projects in northern Wyoming.

Consult the INDEX *first*

Larbaud, Valery-Nicolas (b. Aug. 29, 1881, Vichy, Fr.—d. Feb. 2, 1957, Vichy), French novelist and critic, an erudite cosmopolitan who became a literary intermediary between France and Europe, especially England and Spanish-speaking countries.

Larbaud's personal fortune permitted him a life of travel and leisure. His novels and stories are largely based on personal experiences: *Fermina Marquez* (1911), a novel of adolescence, deals with the effects of the visit of a beautiful South American girl to a boys' school; *A.O. Barnabooth* (1913; Eng. trans., 1924) is the journal and verse of a South

Larbaud
H. Roger-Viollet

American millionaire—Larbaud's alter ego—a cultivated, sensuous adventurer, whose haunts are international sleeping cars and luxury hotels. *Enfantines* (1918) is a collection of nostalgic childhood reminiscences, and *Amants, heureux amants* (1923), dealing with men and women in love, uses the interior-monologue technique developed by the Irish novelist James Joyce. Larbaud's other works comprise essays and reflections inspired by his travels, such as *Jaune, bleu, blanc* (1927; "Yellow, Blue, White") and *Aux couleurs de Rome* (1938). His translations include works of the 17th-century English miscellaneous prose writer Sir Thomas Browne, the 19th-century English novelist Samuel Butler, the U.S. poet Walt Whitman, and James Joyce. He also wrote two volumes of criticism of English and French literature, *Ce Vice impuni, la lecture* (1925) and *Ce Vice impuni, domaine français* (1941). In 1952 Larbaud received the Grand Prix National des Lettres.

larceny, in criminal law, the trespassory taking and carrying away of personal goods from the possession of another with intent to steal. Larceny is one of the specific crimes included in the general category of theft (*q.v.*).

larch, any of about 10 to 12 species of coniferous trees constituting the genus *Larix* of the family Pinaceae, native to cool temperate and sub-Arctic parts of the Northern Hemisphere. One species, *Larix griffithii,* is found only in the Himalayas. A larch has the pyramidal growth habit typical of conifers; but the leaves are shed in autumn, like deciduous trees. The short, needlelike leaves are arranged spirally

Tamarack (*Larix laricina*)
Joy Spurr—Bruce Coleman Inc.

on new growth and in whorls at the tips of short spurs on older twigs. There are 10 to 30 soft, light-green needles on each spur. The related golden larch (*q.v.*) has cones that disintegrate at maturity; those of *Larix* species often remain on the trees several years, then fall intact.

The most widely distributed North American larch is tamarack, hackmatack, or eastern larch (*L. laricina*). The bracts on its small cones are hidden by the scales. Eastern larch trees mature in 100 to 200 years. They may grow 12 to 30 metres (about 40 to 100 feet) tall and have gray to reddish-brown bark. A taller species, the western larch (*L. occidentalis*) of the Pacific Northwest, has bracts that protrude beyond the cone scales.

The European larch (*L. decidua* or *L. europaea*), native to mountainous areas of northern and central Europe and Siberia, usually is 24 to 42 m (about 80 to 140 ft) tall. It has reddish-gray bark and produces a clear oleoresin known as Venetian turpentine.

Several species of *Larix* are grown as ornamentals, especially the Japanese larch (*L. leptolepis*) and *L. decidua* variety *pendula,* a variety of the European larch. Larch wood is coarse-grained, strong, hard, and heavy; it is used in ship construction and for telephone poles, mine timbers, and railroad ties.

Larche, Col de (French), English LARCHE PASS (France–Italy): *see* Maddalena Pass.

lard, soft, creamy, white solid or semisolid fat with butter-like consistency, obtained by rendering or melting the fatty tissue of hogs. A highly valued cooking and baking fat, lard is blended, frequently after modification by molecular rearrangement or hydrogenation, with other fats and oils to make shortening. Antioxidants are usually added to lard and shortenings to protect against rancidity. Lard is also used in pharmacy and perfumery to make ointments and pomades.

Lard varies with the production method and the fat-bearing animal parts used. Steam- or wet-rendered lard is made by injecting steam under pressure into a closed vessel containing hog fats. Open-kettle-rendered or dry-rendered (enclosed-system) lards, which are darker in colour, are made by melting hog fats in steam-jacketed vessels; the residue is called cracklings. Neutral lard is prepared by melting leaf fat (from around the kidneys) and back fat at about 49° C (120° F). Continuous rendering involves grinding, rapid heating, and separation of fat from the cells by centrifuging. Lard composition varies with the diet of the hogs. The predominant fatty acids are oleic, palmitic, stearic, and linoleic.

Lard oil is the clear, colourless oil pressed from pure lard after it has been crystallized, or grained, at 7° C (45° F). It is used as a lubricant, in cutting oils, and in soap manufacture. The solid residue, lard stearin, is used in shortenings and as a source of saturated fatty acids.

Lardner, Ring, original name RINGGOLD WILMER LARDNER (b. March 6, 1885, Niles, Mich., U.S.—d. Sept. 25, 1933, East Hampton, N.Y.), U.S. writer, one of the most gifted, as well as the most bitter, American satirists and a fine storyteller with a true ear for the vernacular.

Lardner came of a well-to-do family, although his father lost most of his fortune during Lardner's last year in high school. He attended Armour Institute of Technology in Chicago for one term and then worked at a series of jobs before beginning his writing career in 1905 as a reporter for the *South Bend* (Ind.) *Times.* He went on to papers in Chicago, where he established a reputation as a sportswriter specializing in baseball stories. From 1913 to 1919 he wrote a daily column, "In the Wake of the News," for the *Chicago Tribune* and from 1919 to 1927 a humorous weekly column for the Bell syndicate. Meanwhile, in 1914, he had begun publishing fiction and had won success with his stories about a comic baseball player, Jack Keefe, some of which were collected in *You Know Me Al* (1916).

Lardner moved to New York in 1919, and the scope of his stories spread beyond the baseball diamond. He first attracted critical interest with his collection *How to Write Short Stories* (1924). Some of Lardner's best stories—"My Roomy," "Champion," "The Golden Honeymoon," and "Some Like Them Cold"—appeared in the 1924 collection. Equally good was his next: *The Love Nest and Other Stories* (1926), with its notable title story (dramatized by Robert E. Sherwood in 1927), "A Day with Conrad Green," and "Haircut."

He contracted tuberculosis and was in and out of hospitals during his last seven years, turning his hand to all manner of writing to support his family. He collaborated on two plays that had Broadway runs: *Elmer the Great* (1928) with George M. Cohan and *June Moon* (1929) with George S. Kaufman. His spoof autobiography, *The Story of a Wonder Man,* appeared in 1927.

Among the works on Lardner's life are Jonathan Yardley, *Ring: A Biography of Ring Lardner* (1977), and Ring Lardner, Jr., *The Lardners: My Family Remembered* (1977).

Laredo, city, seat (1848) of Webb County, southern Texas, U.S., on the Rio Grande (there bridged to Nuevo Laredo, Mex.), 153 mi (246 km) southwest of San Antonio. It was established in 1755 by Tomás Sánchez as a ferry crossing and was named for Laredo, Spain. For more than 200 years it was the scene of violence: Indian wars, border banditry, and the rowdyism of adventurers on their way to the California goldfields. After the

Texas revolt against Mexico (1836), Laredo was in a no-man's-land and became the seat of the short-lived (1839–41) Republic of the Rio Grande; the building that served as the capitol, over which seven flags have flown, is now a museum. With its adobe houses, church buildings, mission bells, and plazas, Laredo has retained much of the feeling of the frontier, and the influence and language of Spain and Mexico are apparent. The city has a diversified economic base, which includes tourism and a considerable export-import trade; it is the commercial centre for an area of irrigated farms and ranches and of gas and oil industries and has a range of manufactures, including bricks, clothing, and electronic components. Laredo Junior College was founded in 1947, and Laredo State University in 1970. Inc. 1852. Pop. (1990) city, 122,899; Laredo MSA, 133,239.

Lares (in Roman religion): *see* Lar.

large intestine, posterior section of the vertebrate intestine, consisting typically of four regions: the cecum, colon, rectum, and anal canal (*qq.v.*). The term colon is sometimes used to refer to the entire large intestine.

For a depiction of the large intestine in the human anatomy, shown in relation to other parts of the body, *see* the colour Trans-Vision in the PROPAEDIA: Part Four, Section 421.

The large intestine is wider and shorter than the small (in humans, approximately 5 feet, or 1.5 metres, in length as compared with 22 to 25 feet, or 6.7 to 7.6 metres, for the small intestine) and has a smooth inner wall. In the proximal, or upper, half of the large intestine, enzymes from the small intestine complete the digestive process, and bacteria produce the B vitamins (B_{12}, thiamin, and riboflavin) as well as vitamin K. The large intestine's primary function, however, is absorption of water and electrolytes from digestive residues (which in humans usually takes about 24 to 30 hours) and storage of fecal matter until it can be expelled. Churning movements of the intestine gradually expose digestive residue to the absorbing walls. A progressive and more vigorous type of movement known as mass movement (gastrocolic reflex), which occurs only two or three times daily, propels the material toward the anus.

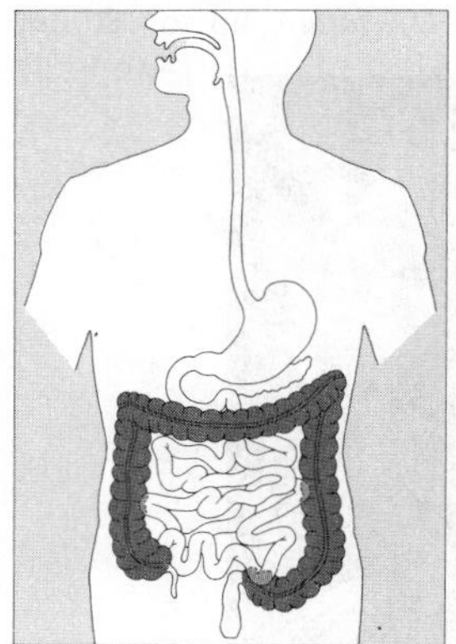

Large intestine

In primarily vegetarian animals the large intestine is usually longer. The immature frog (or tadpole), for example, eats mainly plant matter and has a long, highly coiled large intestine. As the frog matures and begins to eat mostly insects, its intestine becomes considerably shorter. High-protein food, such as meat, can readily be digested by the small intestine; much more chemical action and agitation are required, however, to reduce the tough cellulose fibres of plant cells. The large intestine performs this function with its slow digestive process.

In newborn humans, the large intestine does not contain the bacteria essential for production of vitamin K, lack of which may cause excessive bleeding. Infant diets should be supplemented with this vitamin for a few weeks until the infant is capable of producing its own supply. Common afflictions of the large intestine include inflammation, such as colitis; diverticulosis; and abnormal growths, such as benign or malignant tumours.

large mouse-eared bat, species of brown bat (*q.v.*).

Large White (breed of pig): *see* Yorkshire.

Largeau (Chad): *see* Faya.

Largillière, Nicolas de (baptized Oct. 10, 1656, Paris—d. March 20, 1746, Paris), French historical and portrait painter who excelled in painting likenesses of the wealthy middle classes. Most artists of his time took as their standard of excellence the adherence to classical models and emphasis on drawing, while some broke away in favour of the style of Rubens and an emphasis on colour. Trained in Antwerp and showing great admiration for the Flemish masters, Largillière came to be looked upon as a pioneer by those 18th-century artists who followed the later, more modern course. Highly honoured in his lifetime, he was made chancellor of the Academy in 1743.

"Self-portrait," oil painting by Largillière; in the Musée National de Versailles et des Trianons, France

Cliche Musees Nationaux

Largo Caballero, Francisco (b. Oct. 15, 1869, Madrid—d. March 23, 1946, Paris), Spanish Socialist leader, prominent during the Second Republic, of which he became prime minister soon after the outbreak of the civil war of 1936–39.

Largo Caballero worked in Madrid as a plasterer before joining the Socialist Party in 1894. He soon became an official in the party's trade union federation, the Unión General de Trabajadores (UGT), and rose to become chief lieutenant of the union's head, Pablo Iglesias. Sentenced to life imprisonment for his part in the general strike of August 1917, he was released on his election to Parliament in 1918. In 1925 he succeeded Iglesias as head of the UGT. He cooperated with the government of dictator Primo de Rivera (1923–30) in hopes of increasing Socialist strength and standing. Minister of labour from 1931 to 1933 in the second Spanish Republic (1931–39), he introduced progressive labour legislation.

After the general elections of 1933, which inaugurated a period of centre-right government, Largo Caballero moved further to the left, spoke increasingly of Socialist revolution, and supported the abortive uprising of October 1934.

In September 1936, following the electoral victory of the Popular Front, Largo Caballero became prime minister and minister of defense. He attempted to tighten army discipline and endeavoured to secure respect for governmental authority in the Republican war zone. But an extreme left uprising in Barcelona (May 3–10, 1937) was used by the Communists to provoke a cabinet crisis, and he was forced to resign.

After his fall, Largo Caballero was politically isolated by the new government of Juan Negrín. In 1939 he went into exile in France. During World War II he was interned by the Germans in Dachau concentration camp, but he survived the war and died in exile.

Laridae, family of birds (of the order Charadriiformes) that comprises the gulls (subfamily Larinae) and the terns (subfamily Sterninae). *See* gull; tern.

Lario (lake, Italy): *see* Como, Lake.

Larionov, Mikhail Fyodorovich (b. June 3 [May 22, old style], 1881, Tiraspol, near Odessa, Russia—d. May 11, 1964, Paris), Russian-born French painter and stage designer, a pioneer of pure abstraction in painting, most notably through his founding, with Natalya Goncharova, whom he later married, of the Rayonist movement (*c.* 1910).

Larionov's early work was influenced by Impressionism and Symbolism, but with the painting "Glass" (1909) he introduced a nonrepresentational style conceived as a synthesis of Cubism, Futurism, and Orphism. In the Rayonist manifesto of 1913, he asserted the principle of the reduction of form in figure and landscape compositions into rays of reflected light.

"Glass," oil painting by Mikhail Larionov, 1909; in the Solomon R. Guggenheim Museum

Collection, The Solomon R. Guggenheim Museum, New York City

Both Larionov and Goncharova participated in the first Jack of Diamonds exhibition of avant-garde Russian art in Moscow in 1910. In 1914 they moved to Paris, where both achieved renown as designers for Sergey Diaghilev's Ballets Russes.

"De," "la," and similar components of a name, when followed by a space, are alphabetized as separate words (e.g., *De Forest, Lee*). *When they are joined to the following part of a name, the combination is treated as a single word* (e.g., *DeForest, John William*).

Larissa, Modern Greek LÁRISA, town, capital of the *nomós* (department) of Lárisa and the chief town of Thessaly (Thessalía), Greece, on the Piniós Potamós (river). Since the 9th century it has been the seat of a bishop.

In antiquity Larissa was the seat of the Aleuad clan, founded by Aleuas, who claimed descent from Heracles. The poet Pindar and the physician Hippocrates, attracted by the Aleuad court, died there. In 480 BC the Aleuads supported the Persians. During the Peloponnesian War (431–404 BC), they supported Athens; thereafter the city was weakened by civil strife. In 357 BC the last Aleuads called in Philip II of Macedonia against the tyrants of Pherae, and from 344 to 196 Larissa remained under Macedonia. Rome then made it capital of the reorganized Thessalian League.

The emperor Justinian fortified the city, whose name means Citadel, but in AD 985 it fell to the Bulgars, and in 1204 it was occupied by the Franks of the Fourth Crusade. It was conquered by the Serbs in 1348 and in 1393 by the Turks, who held it until 1881, when Thessaly was annexed to the kingdom of Greece, beginning an exodus of Turkish residents, all of whom had left by the 1920s. In 1941 Larissa was devastated by an earthquake, and it also suffered considerably during the German occupation (1941–44).

The centre of Thessaly's thriving agricultural economy, Larissa is in the midst of the Thessaly plain. The city produces high-quality ouzo (anise liqueur) and silk cloth; it has direct rail links to Vólos and Athens and airport facilities. In the 1960s there was some industrial development, and there are large factories to manufacture sugar from locally grown sugar beet, as well as a paper-pulp plant. Pop. (1981) city, 102,426; *nomós,* 254,295.

Laristan, also spelled LĀRESTĀN, or LURISTAN, extensive region in southeastern Fārs *ostān* (province), Iran. Situated between the Persian Gulf coast and the main water divide, it is characterized by ridges, dissected uplands, and depressions. The area, sparsely settled, contains nomadic Khamseh peoples of Turkish, Arab, and Iranian origin.

The first mention of the region is in a chronicle written by Mostowfi, a Persian traveler, in the 14th century AD, when it was ruled by the Muẓaffarid dynasty of Kermān. The Muẓaffarids were conquered by Timur (Tamerlane) in the late 1300s. After the death of Timur in 1405, Laristan was ruled by a series of local chiefs (*khān*) who continued to be quasi-independent under the Ṣafavid dynasty (1501–1736). The last *khān* was deposed and put to death by ʿAbbās I the Great (ruled 1587–1629).

The region is one of the more economically undeveloped areas of Iran; many of its inhabitants have migrated as far as Mashhad, Tehrān, and Khorramshahr in search of livelihood. The land reforms of the mid-20th century resettled the nomadic population and made agriculture more productive. Crops grown include cereals and fruits; industry includes brick and tile making and carpet weaving.

Lār, the chief town, lies at 3,000 ft (900 m) above sea level on a plain bordered by mountains separating the town from the Persian Gulf and on the road from Shīrāz to Bandar ʿAbbās. Lār contains the Qaisarieh, a travelers' lodge, and the Masjid-e Jomeh (Friday Mosque), both built during the Ṣafavid period. Pop. (1985 est.) Lār, 32,600.

Larius, Lacus (Italy): *see* Como, Lake.

Larivey, Pierre de (b. *c.* 1540, Champagne, Fr.—d. Feb. 12, 1619, Troyes), chief French comic dramatist of the 16th century, whose free translations of Italian comedy provided material for Molière and others.

Larivey's surname was gallicized from his original Italian family name, Giunti (The Arrived), to a variation of the translation of it, L'Arrivé. He lived in Paris, then returned to his native Troyes to become canon and there compiled almanacs and books of predictions.

Larivey's most successful *Comédies facétieuses* (1579, 1611) were free adaptations from Italian playwrights, with French settings and idioms added. These comedies of intrigue were popular for their sudden twists in plot, swift reversals of fortune, and realistic, racy language. Molière used situations from Larivey's *Les Esprits* and *Le Fidèle* for his *L'Avare* and *Les Femmes savantes.*

lark, family name ALAUDIDAE, any of about 75 species of a songbird family (order Passeriformes). Larks occur throughout the continental Old World; only the horned, or shore, lark (*Eremophila alpestris*) is native to the New World. The bill is quite variable: it may be small and narrowly conical or long and downward-curving; and the hind claw is long and sometimes straight. Plumage is plain or streaked (sexes usually alike) in a colour closely matching the soil. Body length is 13 to 23 centimetres (5 to 9 inches).

Horned lark (*Eremophila alpestris*)
Herbert Clarke

Flocks of larks forage for insects and seeds on the ground. All species have high, thin, melodious voices; in courtship the male may sing in the sky or audibly clap his wings aloft. The male Old World skylark (*Alauda arvensis*) is particularly noted for his rich, sustained song. The species breeds across Europe and has been introduced into Australia, New Zealand, Hawaii, and Vancouver Island, B.C.

The name lark is also given, chiefly because of habitat, to several birds belonging to other families. *See* meadowlark; songlark. For fieldlark, or titlark, *see* pipit. For mudlark, *see* Grallinidae.

Larka Kol (people): *see* Ho.

Lārkāna, town and district, Sukkur division, Sind Province, Pakistan. The town, the district headquarters, lies on the Ghar Canal just west of the Indus River; it derives its name from the neighbouring Lārak tribe. A railway junction, it is divided into two parts by the rail lines: the old city to the east, and Lahori village and the Civil Lines (mostly official residences) to the west. It was incorporated as a municipality in 1855. It is an important grain marketing and trade centre and is noted for its brass and metal wares. Once the capital of Sind under the Kalhōṛās, it contains many historic buildings. Several colleges are affiliated with the University of Sind.

Lārkāna district (area 2,866 sq mi [7,423 sq km]), formed in 1901, occupies a fertile plain known as the "Garden of Sind," except for its mountainous western portion (Kīrthar Range). Irrigated by canals, the plain yields sugarcane, wheat, rice, gram, rape, and fruit (mango, date, guava). Camel breeding is widespread, and there are numerous rice-husking, flour, and dyeing mills. Coarse salt and saltpetre are easily obtainable. Mohenjo-daro (Mound of the Dead), a key archaeological site of the Indus Valley civilization (*c.* 2500 BC), lies 15 mi (24 km) south of Lārkāna. Pop. (1981) town, 123,890; district, 1,138,580.

Larkin, Philip (Arthur) (b. Aug. 9, 1922, Coventry, Warwickshire, Eng.—d. Dec. 2, 1985, Kingston upon Hull, Humberside), most representative and highly regarded of the poets who gave expression to a clipped, antiromantic sensibility prevalent in English verse in the 1950s.

Larkin was educated at Oxford University on a scholarship, an experience that provided material for his first novel, *Jill* (1946; rev. ed. 1964). (His first book of poetry, *The North Ship,* was published at his own expense in 1945.) Another novel, *A Girl in Winter,* followed in 1947. He became well known with *The Less Deceived* (1955), a volume of verse the title of which suggests Larkin's reaction and that of other British writers who then came into notice (*e.g.,* Kingsley Amis and John Wain) against the political enthusiasms of the 1930s and what they saw as the emotional excesses of the poetry of the 1940s. His own verse is not without emotion, but it tends to be understated.

Larkin became librarian at the University of Hull, Yorkshire, in 1955 and was jazz critic for *The Daily Telegraph* (1961–71), from which occupation were gleaned the essays in *All What Jazz: A Record Diary 1961–68* (1970). *The Whitsun Weddings* (1964) and *High Windows* (1974) are his later volumes of poetry. He edited the *Oxford Book of Twentieth-Century English Verse* (1973). *Required Writing* (1982) is a collection of miscellaneous essays.

larkspur, any of about 300 species of herbaceous plants constituting the genus *Delphinium* of the buttercup family (Ranunculaceae), many of which are grown for their showy flower stalks.

Annual larkspurs (sometimes separated as the genus *Consolida*) include the common rocket larkspur (*D. ajacis* or *C. ambigua*) and its varieties, up to 60 centimetres (2 feet) tall, with bright blue, pink, or white flowers on branching stalks. Perennial larkspurs, which tend toward blue flowers but vary to pink, white, red, and yellow, include a puzzling assemblage of species, among them *D. cashmerianum* and *D. grandiflorum,* from 30 to 100 cm tall, and *D. elatum,* up to 180 cm tall. Many hybrids have arisen, notably the Belladonna and Bellamosa types, which bear large blue to violet flowers on tall branched spires.

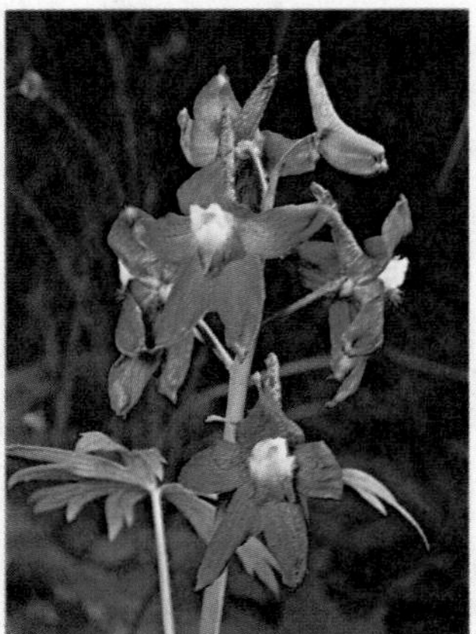

Dwarf larkspur (*Delphinium tricorne*)
Louise K. Broman from Root Resources—EB Inc.

Larmor, Sir Joseph (b. July 11, 1857, Magheragall, County Antrim, Ire.—d. May 19, 1942, Holywood, County Down), Irish physicist, the first to calculate the rate at which energy is radiated by an accelerated electron, and the first to explain the splitting of spectrum lines by a magnetic field. His theories were based on the belief that matter consists entirely of electric particles moving in the ether.

Educated in Belfast and at Cambridge, Larmor taught at Queen's College, Galway (1880–85), and at Cambridge (1885–1932). Knighted in 1909, he represented his university in the British Parliament from 1911 to 1922.

Larnaca, Greek LÁRNAX, Turkish LÂRNAKA, or ISKELE, port town and district, southeastern Republic of Cyprus. The modern town, on the bay between Capes Kiti and Pyla, overlays much of ancient Citium, founded by the Mycenaeans in the 13th century BC; it was rebuilt by the Byzantines. Citium was the birthplace of the Greek philosopher Zeno, the founder of Stoicism. Its modern name (Greek: Funerary Urn) recalls the many tombs under its soil. The modern port, developed during Turkish occupation (1571–1878), was enlarged after the Turkish intervention (1974) in northern Cyprus closed the island's main port at Famagusta. Larnaca's port accommodates small craft at dockside; larger ships anchor in the roadstead and are served by lighters (barges) or use two floating pontoons completed in 1977. Potatoes and cement are exported through Larnaca. A developing industrial base includes a tannery, an oil refinery, a cooperative cheese factory, and the production of commercial salt, brooms, processed food, and chemicals. Larnaca International Airport has expanded since opening as a temporary facility in 1974 after the closing of the international airport at Nicosia.

Larnaca is known for its schools, which include the American Academy (1908). According to tradition, Lazarus of Bethany settled there after his resurrection and became its first bishop; the chief church bears his name. Artifacts from archaeological excavations in the area are displayed in the regional museum housed in a Turkish fortress erected in 1625.

Larnaca district is bounded by the districts of Nicosia and Famagusta on the north, Limassol on the west, by the Dhekelia British Sovereign Base Area on the east, and the Mediterranean Sea on the south. It covers an area of 436 sq mi (1,229 sq km). The northern tip of the district is in the Turkish Cypriot administered area. The Troödos Mountains cover much of the western part of the district; the highest elevation is 4,606 ft (1,404 m), on the border with Nicosia district. The northern tip of the district lies in the Mesaoria Plain and has patches of woodland in which eucalyptus, acacia, cypress, and lowland pine predominate. The eastward-flowing Vasilikos, Syrkatis, Xerapotamos, Pouzi, and Tremithios rivers drain southeastward across the coastal plain into the Mediterranean Sea. Under the Turks (1570–1914) the region probably formed part of the Mesaoria district. In 1914 British forces occupied the district as part of the British annexation of Cyprus. The northeastern portion of the district has been under Turkish Cypriot administration since 1974, when Turkish troops invaded northern Cyprus.

Crops include wheat, barley, potatoes, fruits, vegetables, and nuts. Industry produces milled flour, canned fruit and vegetables, beverages, wood and furniture, paper products, textiles, and margarine. Salt is extracted, and copper and gypsum are mined at Kalavasos in the west. Larnaca town, the district headquarters, is linked by roads with Dhekelia, Pano Kophinou, and Mazotos. A short railway line in the southwestern corner of the district connects Vasilikos and Kalavasas. Pop. (1998 est.) urban area, 68,000; (1999 est.) district, 111,400.

Larne, Irish LATHARNA, town, seat, and district (established 1973), formerly in County Antrim, Northern Ireland, bordering the Irish Sea north of Belfast. The Scot Edward Bruce landed near the present town site in 1315 when he attempted to free Ireland from English rule. His death three years later ended all hopes of an independent Scots-Irish kingdom. Larne town developed as a holiday resort after 1900. In 1914 Ulster Unionists opposed to a Roman Catholic-dominated independent Ireland unloaded large numbers of German-made rifles in Larne harbour. Contemporary Larne town is an important port equipped with modern loading facilities. Passenger and commercial services operate regularly between Larne and Stranraer and Cairnryan in Scotland, and commercial ships also transit to ports in England. Local manufactures include electrical equipment and textiles.

Larne district, extending from the village of Ballynure in the south to the headland of Garron Point in the north and from the peninsula of Island Magee in the east to the peaks of the Antrim Mountains in the west, covers an area of 131 sq mi (340 sq km). Northern Larne is composed of high rolling moorlands, dissected near the coast by scenic wooded glens, while in the southern part of the district the high moors descend more gradually into hills and lowlands and then to the flat shores of Larne Lough (inlet of the sea). Tourism and harbour services at Larne town are the main industries. The Antrim Coast Road, one of the greatest tourist attractions in Northern Ireland with its many miles of bays, headlands, and cliffs, begins at Larne town. Sheep, dairy cattle, and pigs are raised where possible in the pastoral countryside. Limestone is quarried for cement at Magheramorne. Pop. (1991) town, 17,575; (1996 est.) district, 30,200.

Larne River, river, in County Antrim, Northern Ireland, rising in the low watershed (400 ft [122 m]) between its own valley and that of the Six-Mile-Water and flowing northeastward to the important Irish Sea port of Larne, where it swings east and enters Larne Lough (inlet of the sea) after a course of about 9 mi (14.5 km). The valleys of the Larne and Six-Mile-Water cut across the Antrim plateau to form a through-route to the Irish Sea coast from the lowlands east of Lough (lake) Neagh.

Consult the INDEX *first*

Laromiguière, Pierre (b. Nov. 3, 1756, Livignac, Fr.—d. Aug. 12, 1837, Paris), French philosopher who became famous for his thesis on the rights of property in connection with taxation, which he held to be arbitrary and therefore illegal. For the thesis he was censured by the French Parlement.

After the French Revolution he was appointed professor of logic at the École Normale and spent the rest of his life in various teaching posts. He became a member of the Académie des Sciences Morales et Politiques in 1833.

Although he was essentially a follower of Étienne Bonnot de Condillac, who held that the source of all knowledge is sense perception, he took issue with several points of Condillac's doctrine, maintaining that some functions of the mind originate from within the mind itself. His major works include *Projet d'éléments de métaphysique* (1793; "Elements of Metaphysics"), *Les Paradoxes de Condillac* (1805; "The Paradoxes of Condillac"), and *Leçons de philosophie* (1815–18; "Lessons on Philosophy"), an extremely popular work in his day. He also edited the works of Condillac (1795).

Larousse, in full LIBRAIRIE LAROUSSE, Parisian publishing house specializing in encyclopaedias and dictionaries, founded in 1852 by Augustin Boyer and Pierre Larousse, editor of the *Grand Dictionnaire universel du XIXe siècle* (15 vol., 1866–76; 2 supplements, 1878 and 1890). The many reference works later published by descendants of the founders derived from Larousse's *Grand Dictionnaire.*

The *Grand Dictionnaire universel du XIXe siècle,* in the compilation of which Larousse was guided by the motto *vulgariser sans abaisser* ("popularize without debasing"), combined features of the dictionary and of the general short-entry encyclopaedia in offering concise, alphabetically arranged entries that included etymologies and examples of usage of the title words.

At the turn of the century, under the direction of Larousse's nephew, Claude Augé, the *Nouveau Larousse illustré* (7 vol., 1897–1904; supplement, 1907), which was a modernized form of the *Grand Dictionnaire,* further exploited the Larousse short-entry style. It was especially noted for its articles on individual works of art. In 1907 Augé inaugurated a serial supplement to the Larousse publications, the monthly *Larousse mensuel illustré: revue encyclopédique universelle* (1907–40 and 1947–57), in which the articles are relatively long.

The *Larousse du XXe siècle* (6 vol., 1927–33; revised 1948–50; supplement, 1954), edited by Paul Augé, devoted special attention to World War I. In adopting a more popular approach and in using shorter entries than Pierre Larousse's *Grand Dictionnaire,* it resembled the *Nouveau Larousse illustré,* of which it approximated a new edition.

The *Grand Larousse encyclopédique* (10 vol., 1960–64), also edited by Paul Augé, succeeded the three previous major Larousse encyclopaedias but was the first to be profusely illustrated and to offer comprehensive biographies.

Other Larousse publications include shorter general encyclopaedias, such as the *Larousse pour tous: dictionnaire encyclopédique* (2 vol., 1908), superseded in 1922 by the two-volume *Larousse universel: dictionnaire encyclopédique;* dictionaries, notably Pierre Larousse's *Dictionnaire de la langue française* (1856) and its successor, *Petit Larousse illustré* (1906), edited by Claude Augé; children's encyclopaedias, including the topically arranged *Encyclopédie pour la jeunesse* (5 vol., 1958–62); and the topically arranged encyclopaedia *Grand Mémento encyclopédique* (2 vol., 1936–37), re-edited as the *Encyclopédie Larousse méthodique* (1955).

The *Pequeño Larousse ilustrado* (1912), in later printings entitled *Nuevo Pequeño Larousse ilustrado,* is an adaptation in Spanish of the *Petit Larousse illustré.*

Larousse, Pierre(-Athanase) (b. Oct. 23, 1817, Toucy, Fr.—d. Jan. 3, 1875, Paris), grammarian, lexicographer, and encyclopaedist who published many of the outstanding educational and reference works of 19th-century France, including the *Grand Dictionnaire universel du XIXe siècle* (15 vol., 1866–76; supplements 1878 and 1890), a comprehensive encyclopaedia of lasting value.

The son of a blacksmith, Larousse obtained a bursary to study at Versailles and then returned to Toucy as a schoolmaster. In 1840 he went to Paris, supporting himself meagrely while beginning his researches. His first work, a basic vocabulary textbook, was published in 1849, followed soon after by a steady stream of grammars, dictionaries, and other textbooks he had written, brought out by his own publishing house after 1852. Success was immediate and provided a financial base for the *Grand Dictionnaire,* which was issued in fortnightly parts over 11 years. The work was imbued with Larousse's attitude of scientific progressivism: he attempted to disseminate all of the newly developed scientific attitudes, even when these were not conventionally acceptable. "My first ambition was to teach children," he wrote; "I wanted to continue by trying to teach everyone about everything."

Larra (y Sánchez de Castro), Mariano José de (b. March 24, 1809, Madrid—d. Feb.

13, 1837, Madrid), Spanish journalist and satirist who attacked contemporary society for its social habits, literary tastes, and political ineptitude.

Larra, drawing by F. de Madrazo, 1834; in the Museo Español de Arte Contemporáneo, Madrid
Archivo Mas, Barcelona

Larra's family was forced to move to France in 1814 owing to public resentment against his father for having collaborated with the French during the Napoleonic occupation of Spain. They returned in 1818, and Larra's father became the personal physician to the brother of Fernando VII. In 1828 Larra published his own newspaper, *El duende satírico del día,* for which he wrote his first journalistic essays. He later published another paper, *El pobrecito hablador* (1832–33), and then became drama critic for the nation's finest newspaper, *La revista española,* under the pen name Fígaro. In 1834 his play *Macías* was produced and he published his only novel, *El doncel de Don Enrique el doliente.*

Larra's personal life was filled with unhappiness, and his work became increasingly bitter and pessimistic. When he was 16 he fell in love with a woman who, he later discovered, was his father's mistress. He married early and unhappily in 1829, and his wife's third child—a daughter who later became the mistress of King Amadeus—was reputedly not Larra's. He committed suicide after being rejected by a woman with whom he had had a long affair.

Unlike most other writers of prose sketches of the customs of society (*costumbristas*), who took a nostalgic approach, Larra exposed in his mordant and vitriolic sketches the pretentiousness and absurdity of contemporary Spanish society. In journalistic essays and articles he directed his trenchant wit and sarcasm against almost every aspect of Spain's political, social, and intellectual life, describing the corruption, conservatism, bigotry, laziness, apathy, intellectual vacuity, and hypocrisy that he saw. What distinguishes Larra is the analytical depth and penetration of his criticism, along with a certain reforming zeal and a morally constructive emphasis; these qualities prompted the Generation of '98 to hail him as a prophetic forerunner.

Larreta, Enrique Rodríguez (b. March 4, 1875, Buenos Aires—d. July 7, 1961, Buenos Aires), Argentine novelist famous for *La gloria de Don Ramiro* (1908; *The Glory of Don Ramiro*), one of the finest historical novels in Spanish American literature.

After taking a degree in law at the University of Buenos Aires, Larreta went to Madrid, where he met the French novelist Maurice Bárrès, who influenced him to write his famous novel. Larreta spent five years in Spain researching his book and prided himself on its historical accuracy. He was appointed minister to France in 1910, and he spent a large part of his later years in Madrid. His major works include *Zogoibi* (1926; "The Unfortunate One"); *Gerardo o la torre de las damas* (1953; "Gerardo, or the Tower of the Ladies"); its sequel, *En la pampa* (1955; "On the Pampa"—issued with *Gerardo* in one volume as *El gerardo* in 1956); and *La naranja* (1948; "The Orange"), a volume of memoirs and essays.

Larsa, modern TALL SANKARAH, one of the ancient capital cities of Babylonia, located about 20 miles (32 km) southeast of Uruk (Erech; Arabic Tall al-Warkā'), in southern Iraq. Larsa was probably founded in prehistoric times, but the most prosperous period of the city coincided with an independent dynasty inaugurated by a king named Naplanum (*c.* 2025–*c.* 2005 BC); he was a contemporary of Ishbi-Erra, who founded a dynasty at the rival city of Isin. Naplanum was succeeded by a line of 13 kings, many of whom exercised great authority in Babylonia and represented the new hegemony of Semitic Akkadian elements that superseded the Sumerians.

Isin and Larsa seem to have existed in a state of armed neutrality for more than a century, but by the time of the fifth and sixth kings of Larsa, Gungunum (*c.* 1932–*c.* 1906 BC) and Abisare (1905–1895), Larsa was already on the road to dominance. The 12th king of the dynasty, Silli-Adad (*c.* 1835), reigned for only a year and was then deposed by a powerful Elamite, Kutur-Mabuk, who installed his son Warad-Sin (1834–23) as king. This act apparently caused little disruption in the economic life of Larsa, and this was in fact a most prosperous period, as many thousands of business documents attest. Agriculture and stock breeding flourished; much attention was given to irrigation; and long-distance trade connected the Euphrates with the Indus valley through a commerce in hides, wool, vegetable oil, and ivory. Under Warad-Sin's son Rim-Sin (1822–1763), the arts, especially the old Sumerian scribal schools, received great encouragement. The days of Larsa were numbered, however, for Hammurabi of Babylon, who had long been determined to destroy his most dangerous enemy, defeated Rim-Sin in 1763 BC and substituted his own authority for that of Larsa over southern Mesopotamia.

Larsen Ice Shelf, ice shelf in the northwestern Weddell Sea, adjoining the east coast of the Antarctic Peninsula and named for Captain Carl A. Larsen, who sailed along the ice front in 1893. It originally covered an area of 33,000 square miles (86,000 square km), excluding numerous small islands within the ice shelf. The shelf was narrow in its southern half but gradually widened toward the Antarctic Circle to the north before narrowing again. As air temperatures over the Antarctic Peninsula warmed slightly in the second half of the 20th century, the Larsen shelf shrank dramatically. In January 1995 the northern portion (known as Larsen A) disintegrated, and a giant iceberg calved from the middle section (Larsen B). Larsen B steadily retreated until February–March 2002, when it too collapsed and disintegrated. These events left the Larsen Ice Shelf covering only 40 percent of its former area.

Lartet, Édouard Armand Isidore Hippolyte (b. April 1801, Saint Guiraud, near Castelnau-Barbarens, Fr.—d. January 1871, Seissan), French geologist, archaeologist, and a principal founder of paleontology, who is chiefly credited with establishing a date for the Upper Paleolithic Period of the Stone Age.

A magistrate in the *département* of Gers, Lartet made his first discovery of fossil remains in 1834 near Auch in southwestern France. From 1863, with the support of the English banker-ethnologist Henry Christy, he excavated a number of sites in the Dordogne district that are now well known, including Les Eyzies and La Madeleine, where a mammoth bone bearing the engraved figure of an extinct animal was found in an undisturbed Ice Age deposit. From 1869 to his death Lartet was professor of paleontology at the museum of the Jardin des Plantes, Paris.

Lartigue, Jacques-Henri (-Charles-Auguste) (b. June 13, 1894, Courbevoie, near Paris—d. Sept. 12, 1986, Nice, Fr.), French painter and photographer particularly noted for photographs dating from his boyhood that have a beguiling spontaneity, freshness, and joyful humour.

Born into a prosperous French family Lartigue was given his first camera at the age of seven, a large plate camera that he operated by standing on a stool. His distress at not being able to capture motion with the cumbersome machine resulted in his being given a hand camera, a Brownie No. 2, for the following Christmas. Lartigue's boyhood photographs were almost always candids taken of his family and friends. His upbringing in an upper-middle-class situation allowed him varied and interesting scenes for his pictures.

For the next decade Lartigue enthusiastically photographed such subjects as automobile races, fashionable ladies at the seashore and the park, and kite flying. These photographs, with their informal approach to everyday subjects, reveal his free spirit and love of life, rather than a concern for photographic technique and craft. After they were finally discovered and published in the early 1960s, his photographs were acclaimed in part precisely because of his departure from the formal, posed portraits that had been typical of ear-

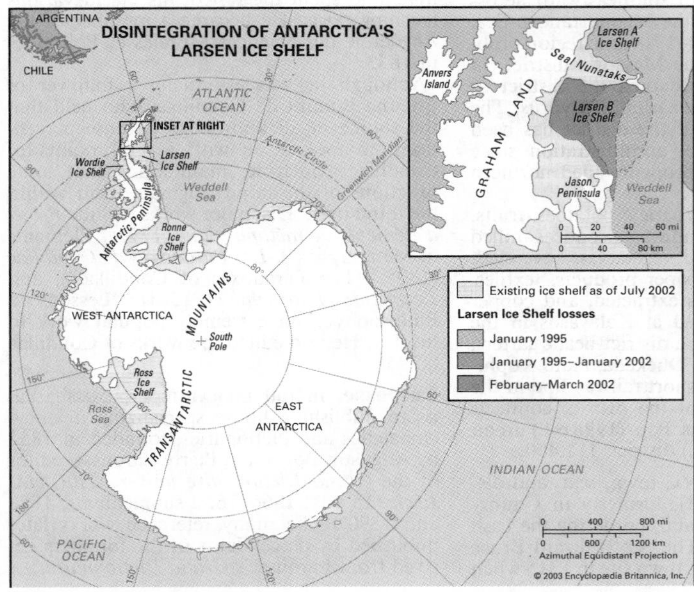

Lartigue with his mother and grandmother in the Bois de Boulogne, Paris, 1905
Henri Lartigue—Rapho/Photo Researchers

lier photographers. Lartigue's boyhood diary of photos, notes, and drawings, as well as his documentation of World War I, display an ingenuous charm.

Lartigue's interest in photography waned after the war in favour of painting, although he continued to make photographs for the rest of his life. He was made Chevalier de la Légion d'honneur. A collection of his work, *Diary of a Century,* was published in 1970. Later collections of Lartigue's work include *Les femmes aux cigarettes* (1980; "Women Holding Cigarettes") and *Les autochromes de J.-H. Lartigue, 1912–1927* (1980; *The Autochromes of J.H. Lartigue*).

"De," "la," and similar components of a name, when followed by a space, are alphabetized as separate words (e.g., *De Forest, Lee*). *When they are joined to the following part of a name, the combination is treated as a single word* (e.g., *DeForest, John William*).

---

larva, plural LARVAE, or LARVAS, stage in the development of many animals, occurring after birth or hatching and before the adult form is reached. These immature, active forms are structurally different from the adults and are adapted to a different environment.

In some species the larva is free-living and the adult is an attached or nonmobile form; in others the larva is aquatic and the adult lives on land. In forms with nonmobile adults, the mobile larva increases the geographic distribution of the species. Such larvae have well-developed locomotor structures. A larva sometimes functions as a food gatherer—in many species the larval stage occurs at a time when food is abundant—and has a well-developed alimentary system. It stores food so that the transformation to the adult stage can occur. Some larvae function in both dispersion and nutrition.

The amount of time in the life cycle spent in the larval stage varies among species. Some have long larval periods, either hatching early, metamorphosing into adults late, or both. Some organisms have a short-lived larval phase or no larvae at all.

Larvae appear in a variety of forms. Many invertebrates (*e.g.,* cnidarians) have a simple ciliated larva called a planula. Flukes have several larval stages, and annelids, mollusks, and crustaceans have various larval forms. The larval forms of the various insects are called caterpillars, grubs, maggots, and nymphs (*q.v.*). Echinoderms (*e.g.,* starfish) also have larval forms. The larva of the frog is called a tadpole.

larvacean, also called APPENDICULARIAN, any member of the class Larvacea, of the subphylum Urochordata, or Tunicata, belonging to the phylum Chordata. Reaching lengths of 5 mm (0.2 inches), larvaceans are transparent, larva-like organisms that live in the open sea. The U-shaped body consists of a trunk and tail. The body secretes a structure larger than itself, within which the animal moves freely.

Larvae (in Roman religion): *see* Lemures.

laryngeal cancer, malignant tumour of the larynx. There are two types of tumours found on the larynx that can be malignant. One is called a carcinoma; the other, called a papilloma, often is benign but occasionally becomes malignant.

The papilloma is the most common tumour of the larynx. It is a small warty growth that attaches to the vocal cords or at the joints between the cartilage plates. It is most frequent in singers, announcers, and people who use their voices strenously and often. In adults it may form many polyps (lumps of tissue) that can plug the larynx; after removal it may reappear. A similar condition may occur in children, except that when they reach puberty the growths usually disappear spontaneously.

Carcinoma of the larynx occurs more often in males. It frequently arises from chronic irritation, overuse of the voice, or alcohol and tobacco abuse. There are two types, called, respectively, intrinsic and extrinsic. The intrinsic form attacks the vocal cords. The tumour originates from the lining of the larynx. It often remains confined to the larynx, and the patient has a good chance of recovery when the tumour is removed. The extrinsic form grows in the area above the vocal cords and folds and may extend to the epiglottis (a flap of cartilage above the larynx) or the pharynx, the upper throat. It usually invades the surrounding tissue and can spread by way of the lymphatic vessels.

Carcinoma begins as a small hard patch or papillary tumour. There may be extensive destruction, ulcers, and abscesses. Laryngeal cancer is a relatively common disease that can be treated in the early stages. Unfortunately, 8 to 10 months may elapse before the first symptoms of hoarseness appear and a diagnosis is made.

laryngitis, inflammation of the larynx or voice box, caused by chemical or mechanical irritation or bacterial infection. Laryngitis is classified as simple, diphtheritic, tuberculous, or syphilitic laryngitis.

Simple laryngitis is usually associated with the common cold or similar infections. Nonbacterial agents such as chlorine gas, steam, or sulfur dioxide can also cause severe inflammation. Usually the mucous membrane lining the larynx is the site of prime infection; it becomes swollen and filled with blood, secretes a thick mucous substance, and contains many inflammatory cells. When the epiglottis, which closes the larynx during swallowing, becomes swollen and infected by influenza viruses, the larynx can become obstructed, and suffocation may result. Chronic laryngitis is produced by excessive smoking, alcoholism, or overuse of the vocal cords. The mucous membrane becomes dry and covered with polyps, small lumps of tissue that project from the surface. The wall of the larynx may thicken and become inflamed.

Diphtheritic laryngitis is caused by the spread of diphtheria from the region of the upper throat down to the larynx. It may cause a membrane of white blood cells, fibrin (blood clotting protein), and diseased skin cells to attach to and infiltrate the surface mucous membrane. When looser portions of this false membrane become dislodged from part of the larynx, they may consolidate at the vocal

cords and cause an obstruction there. A similar type of membrane covering can occur in streptococcal infections.

Tuberculous laryngitis is a secondary infection spread from the initial site in the lungs. Tubercular nodule-like growths are formed in the larynx tissue. The bacteria die after infecting the tissue, leaving ulcers on the surface. There may be eventual destruction of the epiglottis and laryngeal cartilage.

Syphilitic laryngitis is one of the many complications of syphilis. In the second stage of syphilis, sores or mucous patches can form; as the disease advances to the third stage, there is tissue destruction followed by healing and scar formation. The scars can distort the larynx, shorten the vocal cords, and produce a permanent hoarseness of the voice.

laryngology, a branch of medicine dealing with the larynx, nose, and pharynx. *See* otolaryngology.

larynx, also called VOICE BOX, a hollow, tubular structure connected to the top of the windpipe (trachea); air passes through the larynx on its way to the lungs. The larynx also produces vocal sounds and prevents the passage of food and other foreign particles into the lower respiratory tracts.

For a depiction of the larynx in human anatomy, shown in relation to other parts of the body, *see* the colour Trans-Vision in the PROPAEDIA: Part Four, Section 421.

The larynx is composed of an external skeleton of cartilage plates that prevents collapse of the structure. The plates are fastened together by membranes and muscle fibres. The front set of plates, called thyroid cartilage, has a central ridge and elevation commonly known as the Adam's apple. The plates tend to be replaced by bone cells beginning from about 20 years of age onward.

The epiglottis, at the upper part of the larynx, is a flaplike projection into the throat. As food is swallowed, the whole larynx structure rises to the epiglottis so that the passageway to the respiratory tract is blocked. After the food passes into the esophagus (food tube), the larynx relaxes and resumes its natural position.

The centre portion of the larynx is reduced to slitlike openings in two sites. Both sites represent large folds in the mucous membrane lining the larynx. The first pair is known as the false vocal cords, while the second is the true vocal cords (glottis). Muscles attached directly and indirectly to the vocal cords permit the opening and closing of the folds. Speech is normally produced when air expelled from the lungs moves up the trachea and strikes the underside of the vocal cords, setting up vibrations as it passes through them; raw sound emerges from the larynx and passes to the upper cavities, which act as resonating chambers (or in some languages, such as Arabic, as shapers of sound), and then passes through the mouth for articulation by the tongue, teeth, hard and soft palates, and lips. If the larynx is removed, the esophagus can function as the source for sound, but the control of pitch and volume is lacking.

In other forms of animal life, sounds can be produced by the glottis, but in most, the ability to form words is lacking. Reptiles can produce a hissing sound by rushing air through the glottis, which is at the back of the mouth. Frogs produce their croaking sounds by passing air back and forth over the vocal folds; a pair of vocal sacs near the mouth serve as resonating chambers. In birds the larynx is a small structure in front of the trachea; it serves only to guard the air passage.

Las Alpujarras, mountainous district, Granada and Almería provinces, southern Spain, stretching northward from the towns of Motril and Almería to the foothills of the Sierra Nevada and forming a trough between the latter and the coastal mountains. Deep fertile and secluded valleys have been cut by the Guadalfeo (west) and Andarax (east) rivers and by smaller streams. Frequently, villages are located on ledges overhanging gorges, and it is to these villages that the name Alpujarras is sometimes more exclusively applied.

Given to the vanquished Moorish leader Muhammad XI (Boabdil) and his followers after the Catholic conquest of Granada in 1492, the district became a hotbed of Moorish rebellions. The inhabitants of Moorish descent (Moriscos) were finally evacuated in 1570 (and expelled from Spain) and were replaced by colonists from Extremadura and Galicia.

The district has a range of vegetation unparalleled in Europe: from sugarcane and palm on the coast, it extends through belts of citrus, vine, olive, chestnut, and oak to alpine flora on the heights. Wild and poverty-stricken, the region was first cultivated for fruit and vegetables. Construction of modern roads is stimulating development, and the exploitation of iron, lead, and mercury is increasing. Chief cities include Órjiva and Ugíjar; Lanjarón is a notable mineral spa.

Las Bela, also spelled LASBELA, district of Kalāt division, Baluchistan Province, Pakistan. A former princely state, it has an area of 7,048 sq mi (18,254 sq km) and is bounded north by Khuzdār district, east by the Kīrthar Range (separating it from Sind), south by the Arabian Sea, and west by the Hāla Range. An agriculturally underdeveloped zone with untapped water resources, it is mountainous in the east and has a central alluvial lowland drained by the Porāli and Kūd rivers; in the west is a narrow coastal strip dotted with mangrove swamps.

Cultivation depends upon flood irrigation, with *jowār* (sorghum) and oilseeds being the chief crops. Sheep, camels, and goats are bred extensively, and fishing is important along the coast. Sonmiāni is the principal seaport.

Bela (ancient Armabel, Armel), the district headquarters until it was replaced by Uthal, and site of the *jām's* (chief's) residence, lies just east of the Porāli at the apex of the Las Bela Plain; it is linked by roads with Karāchi and with Quetta via Kalāt and Mastung. Rugs, embroidery, and crochet work are local handicrafts. The caves at Gondrāni (north of Bela), hewn out of solid rock, are probably of Buddhist origin.

Las Bela is strategically located on the Makrān coastal trade route between Sind and Iran (Persia). The army of Alexander the Great retreated to Persia through the southern part in 325 BC, and the Arab general Muḥammad ibn al-Qāsim followed the same path *c.* AD 711. Stone ruins at Gondakeha on the Kūd, 10 mi (16 km) northwest of Bela, indicate ancient Arab (possibly Ḥimyaritic) occupation.

Las Bela princely state acceded to Pakistan in 1948. In 1955 it became a district of Kalāt division and in 1961 of Karāchi division; it was returned to Kalāt after 1972. Its population is Muslim. The Lumris or Lasis, whence the prefix Las, are the dominant tribal groups; other tribes include the Baluchi and Brahui. Pop. (1981 prelim.) town, 11,000; district, 187,000.

Las Casas, Bartolomé de (b. August 1474, Seville?—d. July 17, 1566, Madrid), early Spanish historian and Dominican missionary in the Americas, who was the first to expose the oppression of the Indian by the European and to call for the abolition of Indian slavery. His several works include *Historia de las Indias* (first printed in 1875). A prolific writer and in his later years an influential figure of the Spanish court, Las Casas nonetheless failed to stay the progressive enslavement of the indigenous races of Latin America.

Las Casas, engraving
By courtesy of the Organization of American States

The son of a small merchant, Las Casas is believed to have gone to Granada as a soldier in 1497 and to have enrolled to study Latin in the academy at the cathedral in Seville. In 1502 he left for Hispaniola, in the West Indies, with the governor, Nicolás de Ovando. As a reward for his participation in various expeditions, he was given an *encomienda* (a royal land grant including Indian inhabitants), and he soon began to evangelize the Indians, serving as *doctrinero,* or lay teacher of catechism. Perhaps the first person in America to receive holy orders, he was ordained priest in either 1512 or 1513. In 1513 he took part in the bloody conquest of Cuba and, as priest-*encomendero* (land grantee), received an allotment of Indian serfs.

Although during his first 12 years in America Las Casas was a willing participant in the conquest of the Caribbean, he did not indefinitely remain indifferent to the fate of the natives. In a famous sermon on Aug. 15, 1514, he announced that he was returning his Indian serfs to the Governor. Realizing that it was useless to attempt to defend the Indians at long distance in America, he returned to Spain in 1515 to plead for their better treatment. The most influential person to take up his cause was Francisco Jiménez de Cisneros, the archbishop of Toledo and future co-regent of Spain. With the help of the Archbishop, the *Plan para la reformación de las Indias* was conceived, and Las Casas, named priest-procurator of the Indies, was appointed to a commission to investigate the status of the Indians. He sailed for America in November 1516.

Las Casas returned to Spain the next year. In addition to studying the juridical problems of the Indies, he began to work out a plan for their peaceful colonization by recruiting farmers as colonists. His stirring defense of the Indians before the Spanish Parliament in Barcelona in December 1519 persuaded King Charles I (the emperor Charles V), who was in attendance, to accept Las Casas' project of founding "towns of free Indians"—*i.e.,* communities of both Spaniards and Indians who would jointly create a new civilization in America. The location selected for the new colony was on the Gulf of Paria in the northern part of present-day Venezuela. Las Casas and a group of farm labourers departed for America in December 1520. The failure to recruit a sufficient number of farmers, the opposition of the *encomenderos* of Santo Domingo, and, finally, an attack by the Indians themselves all were factors that brought disaster to the experiment in January 1522.

Upon his return to Santo Domingo, the unsuccessful priest and political reformer abandoned his reforming activities to take refuge in religious life; he joined the Dominican order in 1523. Four years later, while serving as prior of the convent of Puerto de Plata, a town in northern Santo Domingo, he began to write the *Historia apologética.* One of his major works, the *Apologética* was to serve as the introduction to his masterpiece, the *Historia de las Indias.* The *Historia,* which by his request was not published until after his death, is an account of all that had happened in the Indies just as he had seen or heard of it. But, rather than a chronicle, it is a prophetic interpretation of events. The purpose of all the facts he sets forth is the exposure of the "sin" of domination, oppression, and injustice that the European was inflicting upon the newly discovered colonial peoples. It was Las Casas' intention to reveal to Spain the reason for the misfortune that would inevitably befall her when she became the object of God's punishment.

He interrupted work on the book only to send to the Council of the Indies in Madrid three long letters (in 1531, 1534, and 1535), in which he accused persons and institutions of the sin of oppressing the Indian, particularly through the *encomienda* system. After various adventures in Central America, where his ideas on the treatment of the natives invariably brought him into conflict with the Spanish authorities, Las Casas wrote *De único modo* (1537; "Concerning the Only Way of Drawing All Peoples to the True Religion"), in which he set forth the doctrine of peaceful evangelization of the Indian. Together with the Dominicans, he then employed this new type of evangelization in a "land of war" (a territory of still-unconquered Indians)—Tuzutlan, near the Golfo Dulce (Sweet Gulf) in present-day Costa Rica. Encouraged by the favourable outcome of this experiment, Las Casas set out for Spain late in 1539, arriving there in 1540.

While awaiting an audience with Charles V, Las Casas conceived the idea of still another work, the *Brevísima relación de la destrucción de las Indias* ("A Brief Report on the Destruction of the Indians"), which he wrote in 1542 and in which the historical events described are in themselves of less importance than their theological interpretation: "The reason why the Christians have killed and destroyed such an infinite number of souls is that they have been moved by their wish for gold and their desire to enrich themselves in a very short time." (*Destrucción,* page 36).

Las Casas' work finally seemed to be crowned with success when King Charles signed the so-called New Laws (Leyes Nuevas). According to these laws, the *encomienda* was not to be considered a hereditary grant; instead, the owners had to set free their Indians after the span of a single generation. To ensure enforcement of the laws, Las Casas was named bishop of Chiapas in Guatemala, and in July 1544 he set sail for America, together with 44 Dominicans. Upon his arrival in January 1545, he immediately issued *Avisos y reglas para confesores de españoles* ("Admonitions and Regulations for the Confessors of Spaniards"), the famous *Confesionario,* in which he forbade absolution to be given to those who held Indians in *encomienda.* The rigorous enforcement of his regulations led to vehement opposition on the part of the Spanish faithful during Lent of 1545 and forced Las Casas to establish a council of bishops to assist him in his task. But soon his uncompromisingly pro-Indian position alienated his colleagues, and in 1547 he returned to Spain.

Las Casas then entered upon the most fruitful period of his life. He became an influential figure at court and at the Council of the Indies. In addition to writing numerous *memoriales* (petitions), he came into direct confrontation with the learned Juan Ginés de Sepúlveda, an increasingly important figure at court by reason of his *Democrates II* ("Concerning the Just Cause of the War Against the Indians"), in which he maintained, theoretically in accordance with Aristotelian principles, that the Indians "are inferior to the Spaniards just as children are to adults, women to men, and, indeed, one might even say, as apes are to men." Las Casas finally confronted him in 1550 at the Council of Valladolid, which was presided over by famous theologians. The argument was continued in 1551, and its repercussions were enormous.

The servitude of the Indians was already irreversibly established, and, despite the fact that Sepúlveda's teachings had not been officially approved, they were, in effect, those that were followed in the Indies. But Las Casas continued to write books, tracts, and petitions, testimony to his unwavering determination to leave in written form his principal arguments in defense of the American Indian.

During his final years Las Casas came to be the indispensable adviser both to the Council of the Indies and to the king on many of the problems relating to the Indies. In 1562 he had the final form of the *Prólogo* to the *Historia de las Indias* published, although in 1559 he had left written instructions that the work itself should be published only "after forty years have passed, so that, if God determines to destroy Spain, it may be seen that it is because of the destruction that we have wrought in the Indies and His just reason for it may be clearly evident." At the age of 90 Las Casas completed two more works on the Spanish conquest in the Americas. Two years later he died in the Dominican convent of Nuestra Señora de Atocha de Madrid, having continued to the end his defense of his beloved Indians, oppressed by the colonial system that Europe was organizing.

At the suggestion of Francisco de Toledo, the viceroy of Peru, the king ordered all the works, both published and unpublished, of Las Casas to be collected. Although his influence with Spain and the Indies declined sharply, his name became well known in other parts of Europe, thanks to the translations of the *Destrucción* that soon appeared in various countries. In the early 19th century the Latin-American revolutionary Simón Bolívar himself was inspired by some of the letters of Las Casas in his struggle against Spain, as were some of the heroes of Mexican independence. His name came into prominence again in the latter half of the 20th century, in connection with the so-called Indigenistas movements in Peru and Mexico. The modern significance of Las Casas lies in the fact that he was the first European to perceive the economic, political, and cultural injustice of the colonial or neocolonial system maintained by the North Atlantic powers since the 16th century for the control of Latin America, Africa, and Asia.

The most complete edition of Las Casas' works is Juan Antonio Llorente (ed.), *Colección de las obras del venerable obispo de Chiapas don Bartolomé de Las Casas* (1822, reprinted 1981). (E.Du.)

BIBLIOGRAPHY. Lewis Hanke, *Bartolomé de Las Casas: An Interpretation of His Life and Writings* (1951), *Bartolomé de Las Casas: Bookman, Scholar and Propagandist* (1952), *Bartolomé de Las Casas: Historian* (1952), and *Aristotle and the American Indians* (1959), provide a comprehensive survey of his life and work. Other studies include Arthur Helps, *The Life of Las Casas: The Apostle of the Indies* (1868, reissued 1980); Henry Raup Wagner, *The Life and Writings of Bartolomé de Las Casas* (1967); and Helen Rand Parish, *Las Casas as a Bishop* (1980).

Las Cases, Emmanuel, Count (comte) **de,** in full EMMANUEL-AUGUSTIN-DIEUDONNÉ-JOSEPH, COUNT DE LAS CASES (b. June 21, 1766, Languedoc, France—d. May 15, 1842, Passy), French historian best known as the recorder of Napoleon's last conversations on St. Helena, the publication of which contributed greatly to the Napoleonic legend in Europe.

An officer of the royal navy, Las Cases in 1790 emigrated from France to England, where he wrote and published his *Atlas Historique . . .* (1802), a work that attracted Napoleon's attention. Consequently, on his return to France (1809) with other Royalists rallying to Napoleon, Las Cases was given a minor position on the council of state and created count in 1810. After Napoleon's defeat (1814), he returned to England but joined Napoleon during the Hundred Days (1815), following him into exile at St. Helena. For 18 months he recorded his conversations with Napoleon on his principles of warfare, his identification of the French Revolution with the Empire, his political philosophy, and his sentiments on religion and philosophy. A letter of complaint about Napoleon's treatment led to Las Cases' deportation and to the seizure of his manuscript by the British government. Forbidden to enter England, he traveled in Germany and Belgium until he was allowed to return to France after the death of Napoleon in 1822. Recovering his manuscript, he published his *Mémorial de Sainte-Hélène* (1823), which at once became extremely popular. A deputy for Saint-Denis (1831–34; 1835–39), he sat with the extreme left, opposing the rule of Louis-Philippe.

Las Cases' *Mémorial de Sainte-Hélène* was the first defense of Napoleon after his defeat. Although prejudiced in Napoleon's favour, the identification of the idea of the Revolution with Napoleon furthered a union of liberals with Bonapartists, thus contributing to the rise of Napoleon III.

Las Cruces, city, seat (1852) of Doña Ana county, southern New Mexico, U.S. It lies along the Rio Grande 38 miles (61 km) northwest of El Paso, Texas. It was founded in 1848. Old accounts tell how a Spanish caravan of oxcarts was ambushed by Apaches and the bodies left at the spot where the town now stands. Another caravan, following along, buried the dead and placed crosses over the graves, whence the name Las Cruces (Spanish: "the crosses"). Cotton and pecans are grown in the area, which is irrigated by Elephant Butte Dam. New Mexico State University (1888) is in nearby University Park. White Sands Missile Range and White Sands National Monument are to the northeast. Historic Mesilla (briefly the Confederate capital of Arizona Territory) and the Indian community of Tohtugas are nearby. Inc. 1907. Pop. (1992 est.) city, 66,466; Las Cruces MSA, 141,405.

Las Hurdes, region of western Spain in Cáceres *provincia,* in the Extremadura *comunidad autónoma* ("autonomous community"), northwest of Plasencia. The high plateau of Salamanca in the central Cordillera Ridge rises almost imperceptibly to the western ranges of the Sierra de Peña de Francia, which on their southern flank have been fractured and plunge precipitously more than 1,000 feet (300 m) to the Alagón Basin. These step mountains (which were early deforested and are mostly barren) comprise Las Hurdes, a very poor region that is remote from the rest of the country. It consists of a land area of about 180 square miles (470 square km). Until the 16th century, the three parallel valleys of Las Hurdes were legendary as the home of evil spirits and savage peoples.

The Hurdanos who inhabit the region are thought originally to have been political or religious refugees. They remain distinct and inhabit hamlets on the hard slates of the Sierra de Gata to the southwest. Their meagre economy is based upon stock raising, which does not adequately support the region's population of about 6,000. Before the Spanish Civil War (1936–39), a new road was built from La Alberca (a national monument and site of a ruined Carmelite monastery built in 1599 to exorcise the region's evil spirits) to Las Batuecas Valley.

Las Marismas, coastal marshes along the Guadalquivir estuary in Andalusia, southern Spain. For centuries the region, noted for its birdlife, served as a hunting ground for the dukes of Medina-Sidonia. In 1963, at the suggestion of the World Wildlife Fund, it was established as a nature reserve, and in 1969 it became part of the Doñana National Park. It is the winter home of ducks and geese and a sanctuary for hundreds of other bird species, although only about 20 are year-round residents. The park is virtually the only remaining habitat of the southern European lynx; fallow and red deer, mongoose, wild boar, and wild cat are also found there.

Las Navas, El de (Spanish: "He of Las Navas"): *see* Alfonso VIII *under* Alfonso (Spain: Castile and Leon).

Las Palmas, *provincia,* in the *comunidad autónoma* ("autonomous community") of the eastern Canary Islands, Spain. It consists of Gran Canaria, Fuerteventura, Lanzarote (*qq.v.*), and a few smaller islands. The city of Las Palmas on the island of Gran Canaria is the capital of the province. Area 1,572 square miles (4,072 square km). Pop. (1991) 767,969.

Las Palmas, in full LAS PALMAS DE GRAN CANARIA, city, capital of Las Palmas *provincia,* Canary Islands *comunidad autónoma* ("autonomous community") of Spain. Located on the northeastern coast of Gran Canaria Island, it is the largest city of the island. Founded in 1478 at the mouth of a ravine, it was named for the abundant palms there. The city was the headquarters for the Spanish conquest of Tenerife and La Palma islands and was later a major supply port for ships bound for Spanish America. The oldest houses, dating from the late 15th century, are found in the colonial quarter (Vegueta), along with the cathedral of Santa Ana (begun 1497) and the house of Christopher Columbus. Other notable landmarks include the Canario Museum, which contains relics of the extinct island inhabitants known as the Guanches (*see* Guanche and Canario), and the Pueblo Canario, a group of buildings in the old Canary style of architecture.

Growth of Las Palmas was slow until 1883, the year in which construction of the port was begun. The modern section lies mostly below 100 feet (30 m) in elevation and within 0.5 mile (0.8 km) of the sea, which it fronts for 5 miles (8 km). Development of the modern

The modern seafront section of Las Palmas on Gran Canaria Island

Charles Bear—Shostal

city is largely attributable to foreign (especially British) merchants. The port of La Luz, located 4 miles (6 km) north of the colonial quarter, has a well-equipped harbour. It is sheltered westward by a rocky promontory, La Isleta, which is joined to the island by a narrow sandy isthmus (now built over) and eastward by long breakwaters. The port, with oil-bunkering facilities, is on the main shipping routes between Europe and South America and is entered annually by thousands of ships. Chief exports include bananas, tomatoes, and other agricultural produce. Tourism, based on the mild winter climate, excellent beaches, and resort facilities, is important economically. Pop. (1998 est.) 352,641.

Las Peñas (Mexico): *see* Puerto Vallarta.

Las Piedras, city, southern Uruguay. It is situated in a wine-growing district just north of Montevideo. It was the site of a decisive battle (1811) in Uruguay's struggle for independence, in which the revolutionaries defeated Spanish forces. Las Piedras is among the largest cities in Uruguay. It is known for its ostrich farming and horse racing. Las Piedras is on the main highway and railroad linking Montevideo with Tacuarembó and Rivera. Pop. (1985) 58,288.

Las Tunas, *provincia,* south-central Cuba. It is bounded on the north by the Atlantic Ocean and on the southwest by the Caribbean Sea. Part of former Oriente *provincia* until 1976, Las Tunas consists of rolling plains; swamps exist in the southwest along the Gulf of Guacanayabo. The principal economic activities traditionally have been cattle raising and sugarcane growing. In addition, tobacco, corn (maize), beans, rice, peanuts (groundnuts), cassava, and fruits (bananas and oranges) are grown. Cedars are raised on plantations near Victoria de las Tunas, the *provincia*'s capital, and sugar is refined near Puerto Padre, on Puerto Padre Bay. The central highway and main railway of Cuba run through the *provincia.* Area 2,544 square miles (6,589 square km). Pop. (1998 est.) 523,810.

Las Vacas (Mexico): *see* Ciudad Acuña.

Las Vegas, city, seat (1909) of Clark county, southeastern Nevada, U.S. It is the principal city of Nevada and the hub of a large commercial, recreational, and mining area. It is one of the fastest growing metropolitan areas in the country.

Anasazi and Paiute peoples were early inhabitants of the region, which was first visited by European explorers in 1829. Mormons from Utah were the first settlers (1855), attracted by the artesian springs in the arid valley of the Mojave Desert along the Old Spanish Trail, hence the name Las Vegas ("The Meadows"). The Mormons abandoned the site in 1857, and the U.S. Army built Fort Baker there in 1864. With the coming of the railroad in 1905, Las Vegas was officially founded and became a railroad town. Its growth was stimulated by legalized gambling (1931) and by construction in the 1930s of the Hoover Dam (29 miles [47 km] east) on the Colorado River. Lake Mead (impounded by the dam), along with nearby Red Rock Canyon National Conservation Area, Lake Mead National Recreation Area, Valley of Fire State Park, and Death Valley National Park, have become popular tourist attractions.

Las Vegas is famous as a unique year-round desert resort. The city's commercial core is a four-mile section of Las Vegas Boulevard known as "the Strip," an array of luxury hotels, casinos, and nightclubs featuring gambling and exotic entertainment. The buildings along the Strip are notable for their bright neon signage, colourful electronic billboards, and extravagant facades and interiors.

In the city's early years, its economy was based on agriculture. By the 1980s, only outlying areas remained dependent on agriculture; and, as delivering water to fields became more difficult, farming diminished in importance. Tourism and related services, particularly casino gambling, are the basis of the modern economy. The city is a leading vacation destination in the country, with some 30 million visitors annually. Nellis Air Force Base, adjacent to North Las Vegas, is also a primary economic factor, and the city has some mining and manufacturing. McCarren International Airport has been expanding rapidly to accommodate the growing crowds of tourists, and construction of the Las Vegas Beltway, a 53-mile loop around much of the Las Vegas Valley, was begun in 1993 to help ease traffic flow as the city's population increased.

Las Vegas first began to grow rapidly after 1940 with the arrival of defense industries. The city's connections to the national crime syndicate began in 1946, when gangster Benjamin ("Bugsy") Siegel opened the Flamingo Hotel with financing by his associate Meyer Lansky and others. With its legalized gambling, and with the growth of American travel after World War II, Las Vegas began to earn a reputation as a popular tourist destination and to attract notoriety as a "sin city"—though the city's connection with organized crime had essentially been severed by the 1960s.

The city's growth surged in the mid-1950s as more casinos were built and again in the mid-1960s when the industrialist Howard Hughes bought many local businesses and properties. Another economic boom began in the mid-1980s with a new spate of extravagant hotel-casino complexes, this time emphasizing family entertainment. The Mirage (1989) was the first of the new style of hotel-casino complexes featuring a theme-park atmosphere; other complexes replicate the New York City skyline, a medieval castle, and an Egyptian pyramid. The last of the city's 1950s-era hotels was demolished in 1993. Las Vegas is also known as a wedding destination; the city has dozens of wedding chapels providing everything from formal events to drive-through services.

In addition to the air base, Nellis Air Force Range (the site of nuclear weapons testing in the 1950s and '60s) lies 60 miles (100 km) northwest. The city has a branch of the University of Nevada (1957). Inc. 1911. Pop. (1999 est.) city, 418,658; Las Vegas MSA 1,381,086.

Lasa (Tibet, China): *see* Lhasa.

Lascaris, Constantine (b. 1434, Constantinople, Byzantine Empire [now Istanbul, Turkey]—d. 1501, Messina, Sicily [Italy]), Byzantine exile, primarily a grammarian and copyist, who taught Greek in Italy.

After the fall of Constantinople (1453), Lascaris went to Milan, where he became tutor to the Duke of Milan's daughter, Ippolita Sforza, and wrote for her his *Erotemata* (1476). Published in Milan, this was the first book printed entirely in Greek and enjoyed long popularity as an elementary grammar. He held university chairs at Naples in 1465 and at Messina from 1467 to his death; he tutored the writer Pietro Bembo in 1491–93. A scholarly copyist, Lascaris produced many valuable manuscripts, including collections of the Greek rhetoricians and epistolographers.

Lascaris, John, also called JANUS LASCARIS (b. *c.* 1445, Constantinople, Byzantine Empire [now Istanbul, Turkey]—d. *c.* 1535, Rome, Papal States [Italy]), Greek scholar and diplomat whose career shows the close connections that linked political interests and humanist effort before the Protestant Reformation.

A librarian to Lorenzo de' Medici, Lascaris toured the Levant (1489–92), and his records of the manuscripts he sought, examined, or purchased are of great value for the history of learning. Simultaneously, he collected information about the Ottoman Empire, producing some useful first printed editions, including ones of the *Greek Anthology,* Callimachus, Musaeus, and Lucian. His knowledge, connections, and devotion to Greek freedom were appreciated by rulers contemplating an active eastern policy. After the temporary decline of the Medici family he served the French court in various diplomatic posts, helped Pope Leo X to establish in Rome the short-lived Quirinal college for training young Greeks, and was chosen in 1525 to present Pope Clement VII's appeal for a crusade to the emperor Charles V. Appointed French ambassador in Venice in 1503, he helped Aldus Manutius with his edition of the *Rhetores Graeci,* and through his friendships with Jacques Lefèvre d'Étaples and Guillaume Budé he presided over the beginnings of the French Renaissance.

Lascaux Grotto, French GROTTE DE LASCAUX, cave containing one of the most outstanding displays of prehistoric art yet discovered, located above the Vézère valley near Montignac, in Dordogne, France. First investigated by four young men in September 1940, the cave consists of a main cavern and several steep galleries, all magnificently decorated with engraved, drawn, and painted animals. The paintings were done on a light background in various shades of yellow, red, brown, and black. Some of the most remarkable pictures include three huge aurochs, their horns portrayed in a "twisted perspective"; a curious unicorn-type animal, perhaps intended as a mythical creature; several red deer; oxen; horses; the heads and necks of several stags, which appear to be swimming across a river; and a rare narrative composition.

"Frieze of Little Horses," cave painting in Lascaux Grotto, near Montignac, France
Jean Vertut

The cave is believed to have served over a long period of time as a centre for the performance of hunting and magical rites—a belief supported by the number of arrows and traps portrayed on or near the animals. From the style of the paintings, the animal species portrayed, and carbon-14 dating tests, the Lascaux paintings have been dated to the late Aurignacian (Perigordian) period (*c.* 15,000–13,000 BC). The cave, though in perfect condition when first discovered, was almost immediately opened to the public, and the ensuing traffic caused the once vivid colours to fade and algae and bacteria to grow over some of the paintings. In 1963 the cave was again closed and in 1983 a partial replica was opened nearby to the public.

laser, any of a class of devices that produces an intense beam of light of a very pure single colour. This light beam may be intense enough to vaporize the hardest and most heat-resistant materials. The word laser is an acronym derived from "light amplification by stimulated emission of radiation."

Fundamental principles. Atoms and molecules exist at low and high energy levels. Those at low levels can be excited to higher levels, usually by heat, and after reaching the higher levels they give off light when they return to a lower level. In ordinary light sources the many excited atoms or molecules emit light independently and in many different colours (wavelengths). If, however, during the brief instant that an atom is excited, light of a certain wavelength impinges on it, the atom can be stimulated to emit radiation that is in phase (in step) with the wave that stimulated it. The new emission thus augments or amplifies the passing wave; if the phenomenon can be multiplied sufficiently, the resulting beam, made up of wholly coherent light (*i.e.,* light of a single frequency or colour in which all the components are in step with each other), will be tremendously powerful.

Albert Einstein recognized the existence of stimulated emission in 1917, but not until the 1950s were ways found to use it in devices. The American physicists Charles H. Townes and A.L. Schawlow showed that it was possible to construct such a device using optical light. Two Soviet physicists proposed related ideas independently. The first laser, constructed in 1960 by Theodore H. Maiman of the United States, used a rod of ruby. Since then many types of lasers have been built.

Of the several different types of lasers produced by different means and used for different purposes, the following are most important.

Optically pumped solid-state lasers. One way to achieve the excitation of atoms to the higher energy level for laser action to take place is by illuminating the laser material with light of a frequency higher than that which the laser is to emit. This process is called optical pumping; the light pump must be of high intensity, as the process is usually rather inefficient.

An optically pumped solid-state laser consists of a rod of the material chosen, with its ends polished flat and parallel and coated with mirrors to reflect the laser light. The sides are left clear to admit the light from the pumping lamp, which may be a pulsed gas discharge, flashing on and off like a photographer's electronic flash bulb. It may be wound around the laser rod, positioned alongside, or focused on it by a mirror. The first operating laser employed a rod of pink ruby, an artificial crystal of sapphire (aluminum oxide). Many other rare-earth elements have since been employed, the most widely used being neodymium. Power outputs in the form of brilliant flashes of light of thousands of watts can be obtained.

Liquid lasers. Solid-state lasers have the disadvantage of occasional breakdown and damage at higher power levels because of the intense heat generated within the material and by the pumping lamp. The liquid laser is not susceptible to such damage; the crystalline or glassy rod is replaced by a transparent cell containing a suitable liquid, such as a solution of neodymium oxide or chloride in selenium oxychloride. Such cells can be made as large as desired to increase power output. Only a small number of inorganic liquids, however, will function as lasers.

Dye lasers. Certain organic dyes are capable of fluorescing—*i.e.,* re-radiating light of a different colour. Though the excited state of their atoms lasts only a small fraction of a second and the light emitted is not concentrated in a narrow band, many such dyes have been made to exhibit laser action, with the advantage that they can be tuned to a wide range of frequencies.

Dyes such as rhodamine 6G, which emits orange-yellow light, can be made to lase (provide laser action) by excitation by another laser. Rhodamine 6G was the first dye for which continuous, rather than pulsed, operation was achieved, making possible the production of a continuous beam of tunable laser light. Another dye, methylumbelliferone, with the addition of hydrochloric acid, can be made to lase at wavelengths varying across the light spectrum from ultraviolet to yellow, producing laser light of almost any desired frequency within this range.

Gas-discharge lasers. Atoms in a gas discharge can be excited to radiate and produce light, as in a neon sign. Occasionally, a particular energy level will cause an exceptionally high number of atoms to accumulate within it. If mirrors are positioned at the ends of the discharge tube, laser action results. Though the conditions are unusual and occur for only a few of the many wavelengths at which the discharge emits, most gases can be made to exhibit laser action at some wavelength under certain discharge conditions. Gas-discharge lasers commonly use a helium–neon mixture, though those designed to produce laser action at infrared wavelengths employ such gases as carbon monoxide and hydrogen cyanide.

Gas dynamic lasers. If a hot gas is allowed to cool rapidly, the number of molecules in a low-energy state may decrease more rapidly and fall below the number in a higher energy state, thus permitting laser action. This condition can be achieved by expanding burning carbon monoxide mixed with nitrogen through jet nozzles. High power outputs of more than 30,000 watts can be obtained.

Chemical lasers. Certain chemical reactions produce enough high-energy atoms to permit laser action to take place. Laser action can occur in carbon dioxide, for example, if it is present when the elements hydrogen and fluorine are reacting to produce hydrogen fluoride. Large amounts of energy can be released when only moderate amounts of the appropriate materials react.

Semiconductor lasers. A semiconductor laser consists of a flat junction of two pieces of semiconductor material, each of which has been treated with a different type of impurity. Aluminum gallium arsenide and gallium arsenide typically are used in lasers of this type, though pairs of other so-called III-V compound semiconductors may be employed (*see* semiconductor device). When a large electrical current is passed through such a device, laser light emerges from the junction region. Power output is limited, but the low cost, small size, and comparatively high efficiency make these devices suitable for use as light sources in optical fibre communications systems (see below) and in compact digital audio disc players.

Free-electron lasers. Lasers of this type are more efficient than any other variety in producing beams of very high power radiation. Furthermore, these devices are tunable, so that they can be made to operate at microwave to ultraviolet wavelengths. (Theoretically they have the potential of generating laser radiation of X-ray wavelength, though present technology is still incapable of such short wavelengths.) In a free-electron laser, free electrons (*i.e.,* those not bound to nuclei) from a particle accelerator or some other source are passed through an undulator (commonly called a "wiggler"), a device consisting of a linear array of electromagnets. An alternating magnetic field in the undulator bends the electrons into a spiral path around the lines of force, whereby they are accelerated to velocities approaching the speed of light and emit energy in the form of synchrotron radiation (*q.v.*). The intensity and wavelength of this radiation can be adjusted by modifying certain parameters of the magnetic field. Because of this ability to produce laser light tunable over a broad range of wavelengths and high efficiency, researchers believe that the free-electron laser, with further development, will prove especially suitable in such applications as isotope separation, semiconductor research, and ballistic missile defense (namely, as a laser beam weapon).

Lasers producing short, intense pulses. A shutter placed between the amplifying column and the end mirrors of a laser can prevent laser action as long as it is closed. If conditions are otherwise correct for laser action and the shutter is suddenly opened, the stored energy is released as a giant pulse of light lasting only a tiny fraction of a second and having a peak power capacity that may be as high as several hundred thousand kilowatts. This is known as Q-switching. The Q-switch may be a mechanical shutter or, more usually, a liquid or solid optical shutter that is normally opaque but can be made transparent by the application of an electrical pulse. The shutter may also be an opaque dye which becomes transparent when exposed to laser light.

Normally a laser oscillates in several modes—*i.e.,* at several different frequencies. By synchronizing these modes, a process called mode-locking, even shorter, more powerful pulses can be obtained. Such pulses are useful in scientific investigations and in puncturing holes so rapidly that the surrounding material is not affected.

Laser applications. The light produced by lasers is in general far more monochromatic, directional, powerful, and coherent than that from any other light sources. Nevertheless, the individual kinds of lasers differ greatly in these properties as well as in wavelength, size, and efficiency. There is no single laser suitable for all purposes, but some of the combinations of properties can do things that were difficult or impossible before lasers were developed.

A continuous visible beam from a laser using a gas, such as the helium–neon combination, provides a nearly ideal straight line for all kinds of alignment applications. The beam from such a laser typically diverges by less than one part in a thousand, approaching the theoretical limit. The beam's divergence can be reduced by passing it backward through a telescope, although fluctuations in the atmosphere then limit the sharpness of a beam over a long path. Lasers have come to be widely used for alignment in large construction—*e.g.,* to guide machines for drilling tunnels and for laying pipelines.

A pulsed laser can be used in a light radar, sometimes called LIDAR, and the narrowness of its beam permits sharp definition of targets. As with radar, the distance to an object is measured by the time taken for the light to reach and return from it, since the speed of light is known. LIDAR echoes have been returned from the Moon, facilitated by a multiprism reflector that was placed there by the first astronauts to land there. Distances can be measured from an observatory on Earth to the lunar mirror with an accuracy of several centimetres. Simultaneous measurements of the mirror's distance and direction from two observatories on different parts of the Earth could give an accurate value for the distance between the two observatories. A series of such measurements can tell the rate at which continents are drifting relative to each other.

A vertically directed laser radar in an airplane can serve as a fast, high-resolution device for mapping fine details, such as the contours of steps in a stadium or the shape of the roof of a house. With a pulsed laser radar, returns can be obtained from dust particles and even from air molecules at higher altitudes. Thus air densities can be measured and air currents can sometimes be traced.

The high coherence of a laser's output is very helpful in measurement and other applications involving interference of light beams. If a light beam is divided into two parts that travel different paths, when the beams come together again they may be either in step so that they reinforce each other or out of step so that they cancel one another. Thus the brightness of the recombined wave changes from light to dark, producing interference fringes, when the difference in path lengths is changed by one-half of a wavelength. Such devices are called laser interferometers. Very small displacements can be detected, and larger distances can be measured with precision. With lasers, these measurements can be carried out over extremely long distances. Laser interferometers are used to monitor small displacements in the Earth's crust across geological faults. In manufacturing, such devices are employed to gauge fine wires, to monitor the products of automated machine tools, and to test optical components.

Lasers can be so monochromatic that a small shift in the light frequency can be detected. Light reflected from an object that is moving toward the laser is raised in frequency by an amount depending on the velocity of the object (Doppler effect). For a receding object, the frequency is lowered. In either case, if some of the original and the shifted light are recombined at a photodetector, a signal at the difference frequency (the difference in frequency between the original and the shifted light) is observed, and even small velocities can be measured.

The brightness and coherence of laser light make it especially suitable for visual effects and photography that simulate third dimensional depth—*e.g.,* holography (*q.v.*).

The light from many lasers is relatively powerful and can be focused by a conventional lens system to a small spot of great intensity. Thus even a moderately small pulsed laser can vaporize a small amount of any substance and drill narrow holes in the hardest materials. Ruby lasers, for example, are used to drill holes in diamonds for wire drawing dies and in sapphires for watch bearings. For biological research, a finely focused laser can vaporize parts of a single cell, thus permitting microsurgery of chromosomes.

Strong heating can be produced by a laser at a place where no mechanical contact is possible. Thus one of the earliest applications of lasers was for surgery on the retina of the eye.

Lasers are also used for small-scale cutting and welding. They can trim resistors to exact values by removing material and can alter connections within integrated arrays of microcircuit elements. A pulse of light from a laser can vaporize a sample of a substance for analysis by suitable instruments. By this method an extremely small sample can be analyzed without introducing contaminants.

The high brightness, pure colour, and directionality of laser light make it ideally suited for experiments on light scattering. Even a small amount of light that is scattered with a change of wavelength or direction can be detected. Notably, a type of scattering known as the Raman effect produces characteristic wavelength shifts by which molecular species can be identified. With laser sources and sensitive spectrography, small samples of transparent liquids, gases, or solids can be analyzed. It is even possible to measure contaminants in the atmosphere at a considerable distance by the Raman scattering of light from a laser beam.

Laser beams can be used for communications. Because the light frequency is so high (around 5×10^{14} hertz for visible light), the intensity can be rapidly altered to encode very complex signals. In principle, one laser beam could carry as much information as all existing radio channels. Laser light can, however, be blocked by rain, fog, or snow so that, for reliable communications on Earth, the laser beam would need to be enclosed in a protective medium. Optical fibres made of glass and covered with a cladding material are employed for this purpose. Waveguides of this kind are being used increasingly in long-distance telephone systems (*see* fibre optics).

Laser technology is integral to optical disc recording and storage systems. In such a system, digital data are recorded by burning a series of microscopic holes, commonly referred to as pits, with a laser beam into thin metallic film on the surface of a small-diameter disc. In this manner, information from magnetic tape is encoded on a master disc, which is replicated by a process known as stamping. In the read mode, laser light of low intensity is reflected off the disc surface and is "read" by light-sensitive diodes. The amount of light received by the diodes varies according to the presence or the absence of the pits, and this input is digitized by the diode circuits. The digital signals are subsequently converted to analog information on a video screen. Compact audio disc players work in much the same way except that the digital signals are transformed into sound impulses.

Lasers also are used in a major type of computer printer. Laser printers employ a laser beam and a system of optical devices to etch images on a photoconductor drum. The images are carried from the drum to paper by means of electrostatic photocopying.

Lases (Roman deities): *see* Lar.

Lashley, Karl S(pencer) (b. June 7, 1890, Davis, W.Va., U.S.—d. Aug. 7, 1958, Paris), American psychologist who conducted quantitative investigations of the relation between brain mass and learning ability.

Lashley
By courtesy of Harvard University Archives; photograph, Fabian Bachrach

While working toward his Ph.D. in genetics at Johns Hopkins University, Baltimore, Md. (1914), Lashley became associated with the influential psychologist John B. Watson. During three years of postdoctoral work on vertebrate behaviour (1914–17), he began formulating the research program that was to occupy the remainder of his life. He cooperated with Watson on studies of animal behaviour and also gained the skills in surgery and microscopic tissue study needed for studying the neural basis of learning. In 1920 he became an assistant professor of psychology at the University of Minnesota, Minneapolis, where his prolific research on brain function gained him a professorship in 1924. His monograph *Brain Mechanisms and Intelligence* (1929) contained two significant principles: mass action and equipotentiality. Mass action postulates that certain types of learning are mediated by the cerebral cortex (the convoluted outer layer of the cerebrum) as a whole, contrary to the view that every psychological function is localized at a specific place on the cortex. Equipotentiality, associated chiefly with sensory systems such as the visual, relates to the finding that some parts of a system take over the functions of other parts.

Lashley was a professor at the University of Chicago (1929–35) and Harvard University (1935–55) and also served as director of the Yerkes Laboratories of Primate Biology, Orange Park, Fla., from 1942. His work included research on brain mechanisms related to sense receptors and on the cortical basis of motor activities. He studied many animals, including primates, but his major work was done on the measurement of behaviour before and after specific, carefully quantified, induced brain damage in rats.

Lasker, Albert (Davis) (b. May 1, 1880, Freiburg, Ger. [now in West Germany]—d. May 30, 1952, New York, N.Y., U.S.), American advertising executive and philanthropist credited as the founder of modern advertising because he insisted that advertising copy actively sell rather than simply inform.

Lasker was brought to the United States from Germany in his infancy and graduated from high school in Galveston, Texas. In 1898 he went to Chicago to work for the Lord & Thomas advertising agency as an office boy. When Lasker started in advertising, agencies were chiefly responsible for taking copy that clients had already prepared and placing it in various publications. Lasker seized on the newer ideal of advertising that was emerging—that it should seek not merely to passively inform the public about a particular product but rather to actively sell that product by changing people's attitudes through the use of images, slogans, endorsements, and other sales techniques. By putting to work his definition of advertising as "salesmanship in print," Lasker quickly rose through the company ranks, becoming head copywriter in 1905 and sole owner of the agency in 1912. His agency's campaigns revolutionized the industry while making Lord & Thomas the biggest advertising agency in the world. Among their successes were the "Oranges for health, California for wealth" campaign, which popularized both orange juice and the state of California, and "The grains that are shot from guns" campaign for Quaker puffed cereals.

Lasker introduced such products as sanitary napkins (Kotex in 1921) and facial tissues (Kleenex in 1924) to the public. He broke down the taboo against women's smoking with his advertisement of "Reach for a Lucky instead of a sweet," showing actresses and female opera stars smoking Lucky Strike cigarettes. The slogan made Lucky Strike one of America's best-selling cigarette brands.

The high-pressure world of advertising took a heavy toll on Lasker, however. During his career he suffered three nervous breakdowns, and in 1942 he finally decided to dissolve the agency in order to devote himself fully to his philanthropies. Lord & Thomas was then reorganized as Foote, Cone, and Belding.

In 1942 Lasker and his third wife, Mary Lasker (*née* Woodard), set up a foundation, the Albert and Mary Lasker Foundation, to distribute medical research grants and awards. Mary Lasker, an art dealer, carried on his philanthropies in medicine and public health after her husband's death.

Lasker, Eduard (b. Oct. 14, 1829, Jarotschin, Posen, Prussia [now Poznań, Pol.]—d. Jan. 5, 1884, New York City), Prussian Liberal conspicuous for his opposition to Bismarck; he was one of the most important parliamentarians of the German Empire.

Eduard Lasker, engraving, 1861
By courtesy of the Staatsbibliothek, Berlin

After legal training he joined the Prussian government service and became a judge. Lasker was a deputy in the Prussian diet from 1865 to 1879 and in the *Reichstag* of the

North German Confederation and then of the German Empire from 1867 to 1883. He took the lead in the formation of the National Liberal Party in 1866 and supported Bismarck's unification of Germany. He was most active in working out the unification of the legal administration and procedure of the empire (1877) and of its economic structure.

An opponent of Bismarck's exploitation of parliamentarianism and a convinced adherent of the tenets of free trade, Lasker broke with the National Liberal Party after quarrels over constitutional reform and the introduction of a protective tariff in 1878. This "secession" was followed in 1884 by the fusion of Lasker's followers with the German Progressive Party to form the German Radical Party. He died while on a visit to the United States.

Lasker, Emanuel (b. Dec. 24, 1868, Berlinchen, Prussia [Ger.]—d. Jan. 11, 1941, New York, N.Y., U.S.), German chess master, the world champion from 1894 to 1920, who is often regarded as one of the greatest players of all time.

The son of a Jewish cantor, Lasker first left Prussia in 1889 and only five years later won the world chess championship from Wilhelm Steinitz. He went on to a series of stunning wins in St. Petersburg, Nürnberg, London, and Paris before concentrating on his education. In 1902 he received his doctorate for research on abstract algebraic systems.

In 1904 Lasker resumed his chess career, publishing a magazine, *Lasker's Chess Magazine,* for four years and winning against the top masters. Though the championship title was finally taken from him in 1921 by José Raúl Capablanca, he continued to play successfully until he was 67, considered a unique achievement.

Lasker changed the nature of chess, not in its strategy but in its economic base. After he was financially ruined by the Great Depression, he became the first chess master to demand high fees, thus paving the way to strengthening the financial status of professional chess players. He invented new endgame theories and then retired for some years to study philosophy and to teach and write. At 66, however, he returned to tournament playing and was again successful at several international matches. His book *Common Sense in Chess* (1896) is considered a classic.

Lasker-Schüler, Else, *née* SCHÜLER (b. Feb. 11, 1869, Elberfeld, Ger.—d. Jan. 22, 1945, Jerusalem, Palestine), German poet, short-story writer, playwright, and novelist of the early 20th century.

Of Jewish parentage, Schüler settled in Berlin after her marriage to the physician Berthold Lasker in 1894 (divorced 1903). In Berlin she frequented avant-garde literary circles, and her lyric poems and short stories began appearing in periodicals. Her second marriage (1901–11) was to Herwarth Walden, the editor of a leading Expressionist journal. Her first book, a poetry collection entitled *Styx* (1902), was followed by *Meine Wunder* (1911; "My Miracles"), *Hebräische Balladen* (1913; "Hebrew Ballads"), and several other volumes of lyric poetry. Her other important works are the play *Die Wupper* (1909), the autobiographical novel *Mein Herz* (1912; "My Heart"), and the short stories collected in *Der Prinz von Theben* (1914; "The Prince of Thebes") and *Der Wunderrabbiner von Barcelona* (1921; "The Wonder Rabbi of Barcelona"). She emigrated to Switzerland in 1933 after the Nazis came to power in Germany, and in 1940 she resettled in Jerusalem in Palestine. She had always led an eccentric and unpredictable life, and she spent her last years in poverty.

Lasker-Schüler's poems exploit a rich vein of fantasy and symbolism and alternate between pathos and ecstasy in their intensely personal evocation of her childhood and parents, romantic passion, art, religion, and other themes. Many of her short stories reinterpret Arabian nights tales in a mode of modern fantasy that is rich with visual images. Though rich in atmosphere and symbolism, her stories tend to have a weak narrative focus and little or no plot. Lasker-Schüler's reputation as an important German lyric poet of the early 20th century is assured, however.

Laski, Harold J(oseph) (b. June 30, 1893, Manchester, Eng.—d. March 24, 1950, London), British political scientist, educator, and prominent member of the British Labour Party who turned to Marxism in his effort to interpret the "crisis in democracy" in Britain in the 1930s.

Laski, 1946
The Press Association Ltd.

Laski was educated at New College, Oxford, and left England to teach at McGill University, Montreal, from 1914 to 1916. He then obtained a post at Harvard University, where he taught from 1916 to 1920, and during this period he wrote *Authority in the Modern State* (1919) and *The Foundations of Sovereignty, and Other Essays* (1921). In these works he attacked the notion of an all-powerful sovereign state, arguing instead for political pluralism. In his *Grammar of Politics* (1925), however, he defended the opposite position and came to see the state as "the fundamental instrument of society."

After his return to England in 1920, Laski became an active worker for the Labour Party in the election campaign of 1923. In 1926 he accepted a position at the London School of Economics and Political Science, where he taught political science until his death. His doubts about the eventual implementation of reform by the ruling class led him to embrace Marxism during the Great Depression of the 1930s. In *The State in Theory and Practice* (1935), *The Rise of European Liberalism: An Essay in Interpretation* (1936), and *Parliamentary Government in England: A Commentary* (1938), Laski argued that economic difficulties of the capitalist system might lead to the destruction of political democracy. He came to view socialism as the only available and possible alternative to the rising menace of fascism. During World War II, Laski lectured throughout England and served as assistant to Clement Attlee, deputy prime minister to Winston Churchill. In *Reflections on the Revolution of Our Time* (1943) and *Faith, Reason, and Civilization: An Essay in Historical Analysis* (1944) he again called for broad economic reforms. In 1945 he was chosen chairman of his party and felt that his cause was at least partially vindicated by Labour's electoral triumph that year. Among his many other works are *The American Presidency: An Interpretation* (1940) and the lengthy and controversial *The American Democracy: A Commentary and Interpretation* (1948).

BIBLIOGRAPHY. Kingsley Martin, *Harold Laski, 1893–1950: A Biographical Memoir* (1953, reissued 1969); Herbert A. Deane, *The Political Ideas of Harold J. Laski* (1955, reissued 1972).

Laspeyres index, index proposed by the German economist Étienne Laspeyres (1834–1913) for measuring current prices or quantities in relation to those of a selected base period. A Laspeyres price index is computed by taking the ratio of the total cost of purchasing a specified group of commodities at current prices to the cost of that same group at base-period prices, and multiplying by 100. The base-period index number is thus 100, and periods with higher price levels will have index numbers greater than 100. The distinctive feature of the Laspeyres index is that it uses a group of commodities purchased in the base period as the basis for comparison. In other words, in computing the index, a commodity's relative price (the ratio of the current price to the base-period price) is weighted by the commodity's relative importance to all purchases during the base period. *Compare* Paasche index.

Some observers believe that the Laspeyres price index tends to overstate price increases because, as prices change, consumers normally alter their patterns of consumption to include smaller amounts of products with large price increases and larger amounts of products with little or no price increases. If they can do this without reducing their total satisfaction, the use of base-period commodity selections tends to overstate declines in the standard of living. The Laspeyres quantity index operates in a similar way, using base-period prices to compare aggregate production levels in two periods.

Lassalle, Ferdinand (b. April 11, 1825, Breslau, Prussia [now Wrocław, Pol.]—d. Aug. 31, 1864, near Geneva, Switz.), leading spokesman for German socialism, a disciple of Karl Marx (from 1848), and one of the founders of the German labour movement.

Early years. Lassalle was born of Jewish parents; his father, Heymann Lasal, or Loslauer, was a wholesale silk merchant and town councillor.

Lassalle, *c.* 1860
Archiv fur Kunst und Geschichte, Berlin

Ferdinand Lassalle—the spelling of the name dates from a stay in Paris in 1846—attended the Breslau classical high school but was expelled when he forged a signature on a school report. He attended a trade school in Leipzig in 1840, returned to Breslau in 1841, and passed his school-leaving examination in 1843. In 1843–44 he began to study philosophy, history, philology, and archaeology at the University of Breslau. In 1844–45 he continued his studies in Berlin, where he first encountered the ideas of the German philosophers G.W.F. Hegel and Ludwig Feuerbach and of the French Utopian thinkers. Intending to take his degree and to qualify as a university lecturer with a thesis on the philosophy of Heracleitus, he made repeated studies of the subject in Paris between 1845 and 1847. Here he met the French social theorist Pierre-Joseph Proudhon and Heinrich Heine, the German poet.

Champion of Countess Hatzfeld. In 1846, in Düsseldorf, he met the unhappily married countess Sophie Hatzfeld, who was trying to divorce her husband. Although not a lawyer, Lassalle conducted 35 lawsuits in her behalf and in 1854 finally obtained a divorce for her. Henceforth, he received an annual pension of 4,000 thalers from the countess, thus becoming financially independent. His lifelong relationship with the countess, though it was nothing more than that of son and mother, "stimulated gossip about Lassalle and immensely impeded his political career." Lassalle lived in Düsseldorf from 1848 to 1857 and took part in the revolution of 1848–49, by which the liberal middle class tried to attain a constitutional monarchy that would grant such civil rights as freedom of assembly and freedom of the press. During those days he established contact with Karl Marx and Friedrich Engels, the socialist leaders. When Lassalle urged the militia to open revolt in November 1848, he was arrested and held in prison until his trial in July 1849. Although he was repeatedly arrested, indicted, and sentenced to prison, Lassalle counted his years in Düsseldorf, where he was able to be active both as a writer and as a labour organizer, among the happiest of his life. In the period of reaction following the abortive revolution, he traveled to Switzerland, to the World's Fair in Paris in 1855, and to the Orient in 1856. He completed the Heracleitus manuscript and the tragedy *Franz von Sickingen* (1859), which assigns to personality a role in determining the course of history.

Lassalle and Bismarck. In 1857 Lassalle went back to Berlin, and in 1859 he settled permanently in the capital, where he became active as a political journalist. He met Marx in 1861, but, although they continued to correspond, they gradually became estranged. In contrast to Marx, Lassalle believed that the revolutionary phase had come to an end and that only a legal and evolutionary approach could hold hopes of success. With this goal in mind he held discussions with the Prussian prime minister Otto von Bismarck in 1863–64. Fourteen years after Lassalle's death Bismarck said of him, "He was one of the most intelligent and amiable men I have ever associated with, a man of great ambition and by no means a republican." Finding himself in a difficult political situation, Bismarck was, in the early 1860s, seeking allies in his struggle against the majority liberal opposition, while Lassalle was considering the concept of a monarchical welfare state. This was to be based on a universal suffrage for the three classes rather than on the existing suffrage that favoured the upper classes. He thus hoped, by integrating the working class into political and social life, to achieve a transition from a bourgeois state based on private property to a democratic constitutional state. Lassalle and Bismarck were attracted to each other by their many common characteristics. Lassalle in particular was distinguished by his charismatic personality and his paternalist notions of democracy, which were understandable in the context of Germany's largely politically apathetic population.

The year 1862 produced a crisis in Lassalle's thinking when the uprising in Italy led by Giuseppe Garibaldi did not, contrary to Lassalle's expectations, spread to other countries. The Prussian government meanwhile remained utterly unreceptive to his ideas. Realizing that lecturing and distributing pamphlets to artisans' clubs and citizens' associations were not producing sufficient results, Lassalle began agitating in workingmen's associations in order to make his political aims known to the masses.

Organization of the "Suffrage Army." In December 1862, Lassalle was asked by the executive committee of the "Central Committee to Convoke a General Congress of German Workers" to write a program for the congress. Lassalle at once recognized in the congress an opportunity to organize a "Suffrage Army." "Organize yourselves as a general German workingmen's association to agitate legally and peacefully, but untiringly and ceaselessly, for the introduction of universal and direct suffrage in all German provinces! This is the banner you must raise! This is the sign under which you will be victorious!"

In 1863–64 Lassalle hurled himself into the struggle for workers' rights, especially in the Rhineland. "Only the working class matters to me," he declared. When the ADAV (Allgemeiner Deutscher Arbeiterverein, or General German Workers' Association) was founded on May 23, 1863, in Leipzig, Lassalle was elected president for a five-year term. In Cologne he collaborated with a socialist writer, Moses Hess, but other associates rebelled against Lassalle's authoritarian leadership and the cult of his personality he did nothing to discourage. His generally incendiary speeches were often followed by lawsuits.

Exhausted and disappointed over the insignificant results of his propaganda activity, Lassalle went to Switzerland for a rest in July 1864. There he met Helene von Dönniges. He courted her passionately, but, encountering opposition from the young girl's family, he challenged her father and her former fiancé, Yanko von Racowitza, to a duel. Racowitza accepted, and on August 28, in a little forest near Geneva, the senseless duel was fought. Lassalle was struck in the abdomen and died three days later. He was buried in the Jewish cemetery in Breslau.

Assessment. Lassalle was for many decades considered a reformist heretic by the worker's movement, which then adhered to the deterministic notions of popular Marxism according to which the dictatorship of the proletariat was foreordained by history. By others Lassalle continued to be romantically glorified as a pioneer of socialism.

Only since the time of Eduard Bernstein and the era of revisionism, when the German Social Democratic Party, aiming at becoming a mass political party, adopted the aims of parliamentary democracy and participation in government, has the modern significance of Lassalle been acknowledged. It is not the theorist or the organizer of a workers' party who is remembered, but, in the words of the German Social Democratic leader Carlo Schmid, a Lassalle "who in place of scientific analysis constantly fixed his sights on the true aim on history's horizon: the liberation of man from the position of object and the elimination of man's alienation from himself through the power of his own will." (Wi.M.)

BIBLIOGRAPHY. Eduard Bernstein, *Ferdinand Lassalle As a Social Reformer* (1893, reissued 1970); Georg Brandes, *Ferdinand Lassalle* (1911, reprinted 1970); David Footman, *The Primrose Path: A Life of Ferdinand Lassalle* (1946; also published as *Ferdinand Lassalle, Romantic Revolutionary,* 1947, reprinted 1969).

Lassell, William (b. June 18, 1799, Bolton, Lancashire, Eng.—d. Oct. 5, 1880, Maidenhead, Berkshire), amateur English astronomer who discovered Ariel and Umbriel, satellites of Uranus; and Triton, a satellite of Neptune. He also discovered a satellite of Saturn, Hyperion (also discovered independently by William Bond and George Bond).

Lassell started a brewery business about 1825, after a seven-year apprenticeship. He became interested in astronomy and, in 1844, began construction of a 24-inch reflecting telescope, using a machine of his own design for polishing the mirror. With this telescope, the first of its size to be set in an equatorial mounting, he discovered Triton on Oct. 10, 1846, only 17 days after Neptune itself had been discovered. In 1848 he discovered Hyperion (on the night that the Bonds made the same discovery). Two years later Lassell made his first sighting of the dark inner ring of Saturn (called the crepe ring); he spent the entire night verifying the discovery only to find in his morning newspaper an article announcing Bond's discovery of the same phenomenon.

Lassell discovered Ariel and Umbriel in 1851–52 while at Malta, and there in 1861 he erected a 48-inch reflector, which he used to observe and catalog hundreds of new nebulae. He was elected a fellow of the Royal Society of London in 1849 and was president of the Royal Astronomical Society from 1870 to 1872.

To make the best use of the Britannica, consult the INDEX *first*

Lassen Peak, also called MOUNT LASSEN, peak standing at the southern end of the Cascade Range in northern California, U.S., 50 miles (80 km) east of Redding. Lassen Peak is 10,457 feet (3,187 m) high. It erupted without warning on May 30, 1914, and larger explosions occurred on May 19, 1915, when hot lava spilled 1,000 feet (300 m) down the

Lassen Peak in Lassen Volcanic National Park, California
Ray Atkeson—EB Inc.

mountain, melting snow and causing mudflows. Three days later a blast of hot gases felled many trees. The eruptions ceased in 1921, but evidence has suggested the possibility of a 65-year cycle for volcanic activity in the area. Lassen Peak is the principal attraction of Lassen Volcanic National Park, which was created in 1916.

Luis Argüello, a Spanish officer, was the first European to sight the peak, in 1821. It is named for Peter Lassen, an explorer who guided settlers through the surrounding area.

Lasseran-Massencôme, Blaise de: *see* Monluc, Blaise de Lasseran-Massencôme, seigneur de.

Lasso, Orlando di, Latin ORLANDUS LASSUS, also called ROLAND DE LASSUS (b. 1530/32, Mons, Spanish Hainaut—d. June 14, 1594, Munich), Flemish composer whose music stands at the apex of the Franco-Nether-

Lasso, engraving by James Caldwall
By courtesy of the Royal College of Music, London

landish style that dominated European music of the Renaissance.

As a child he was a choirboy at St. Nicholas in Mons and because of his beautiful voice was kidnapped three times for other choirs. He was taken into the service of Ferdinand of Gonzaga, general to Charles V, and travelled with the imperial army in its French campaign in 1544. He accompanied Gonzaga to Italy in 1544, where he remained for 10 years. From 1553 to 1554 he was chapelmaster of the papal church of St. John Lateran at Rome, a post later held by Palestrina. Following a sojourn in Antwerp (1555–56), he joined the court chapel of Duke Albrecht V of Bavaria in Munich, where, except for some incidental journeys, he remained for the rest of his life. In 1570 the Emperor Maximilian raised him to the nobility; and, when Lasso dedicated a collection of his masses (1574) to Pope Gregory XIII, he received the knighthood of the Golden Spur.

Of Lasso's more than 2,000 compositions, many appeared in print between 1555, when his first book of Italian madrigals was published in Venice, and 1604, when a posthumous collection of 516 Latin motets (religious choral works), *Magnum Opus Musicum*, was published by his sons. Certain volumes stand out as landmarks in his career: his first collection of motets (1556) established his mastery in a field to which he contributed all his life; a comprehensive anthology of his chansons, or French part-songs (1570), helped to consolidate his position as the leading composer in this genre. In addition to his madrigals (Italian choral pieces) and chansons, he published seven collections of lieder (German part-songs). Probably his best known work is his sombre, impressive collection of penitential psalms, *Psalmi Davidis Poenitentiales* (1584). Its rediscovery and edition in 1838 by S.W. Dehn initiated a revival of interest in Lasso's works.

Lasso was a master in the field of sacred music and was equally at home in secular composition. In the latter field his internationalism is striking, encompassing Italian, French, and German genres. His religious works have a particular emotional intensity. He took great care to mirror the meaning of his texts in his music, a trait that looked forward to the Baroque style of the early 17th century.

Lassois, Mont, site of great Celtic fortifications near Châtillon-sur-Seine in the Côte-d'Or *département*, France. The hill-fort of Vix, on Mt. Lassois, seems to have been the centre of widespread political authority and extensive trade relations, especially during the 6th century BC. The rich Celtic and Greek artifacts found there, as well as those from the nearby tumulus burials near the villages of Vix and Sainte-Colombe-sur-Seine, indicate a frequent interchange of trade and gifts not only among the Celts themselves but also between the Celts and the Greeks.

Lasswell, Harold D(wight) (b. Feb. 13, 1902, Donnellson, Ill., U.S.—d. Dec. 18, 1978, New York City), influential U.S. political scientist known for seminal studies of power relations and of personality and politics, and for other major contributions to contemporary behavioral political science.

Lasswell received his Ph.B. in 1922 and his Ph.D. in 1926 from the University of Chicago and studied at the universities of London, Geneva, Paris, and Berlin in the summers of 1923, 1924, and 1925. He taught political science at the University of Chicago (1922–38) and then went to Yale University, where he was a visiting lecturer at the Law School (1938), professor of law (1946–70), professor of political science (1952–70), and Ford Foundation professor of law and social sciences and emeritus fellow of Bramford College (1970–76). He served at the Washington School of Psychiatry (1938–39) and was director of war communications research at the U.S. Library of Congress (1939–45). He was also professor of law at John Jay College of the City University of New York (1970–73) at Temple University (1973–76). He was a visiting lecturer at campuses throughout the world and was a consultant to numerous U.S. government agencies.

For Lasswell, political science was the study of changes in the distribution of the value patterns in society, and, since influence is crucial to distribution, power served as the focal point of his discussion. For him, values were defined as desired goals and power was participation in decisions; political power was conceived of only as producing intended effects over other people. In *Politics: Who Gets What, When, How* (1936) he concentrated on the elite as the primary holders of power, but in *Power and Society: A Framework for Political Inquiry* (1950), written with Abraham Kaplan, the discussion was broadened to include a general framework for political inquiry, examining key analytic categories such as person, personality, group, and culture.

Psycho-political works by Lasswell include *Psycho-pathology and Politics* (1930), which seeks the means of channelling the desire for domination to healthy ends, *World Politics and Personal Insecurity* (1935), and *Power and Personality* (1948), which deals with the problem of the power-seekers who sublimate personal frustrations in power. Lasswell moved toward a moralistic posture as he called for the social and biological sciences in particular to reorient themselves toward policy science that would serve the democratic will for justice. Other contemporary features of political science that can be traced to Lasswell include systems theory and functional and role analysis, as well as content analysis.

Other works by Lasswell include: *Propaganda Technique in the World War* (1927); *World Revolutionary Propaganda* (with D. Blumenstock, 1939), *Politics Faces Economics* (1946); *The Policy Sciences: Recent Developments in Scope and Method* (with D. Lerner, 1951); and *The Future of Political Science* (1963).

Last Judgment, a general, or sometimes individual, judging of the thoughts, words, and deeds of persons by God, the gods, or by the laws of cause and effect. In some religions (*e.g.,* Christianity) the judgment is of both the living and the dead; in others (*e.g.,* certain primitive religions in Africa) the judgment in which God rewards or punishes men according to their actions occurs only after death.

The Western prophetic religions (*i.e.,* Zoroastrianism, Judaism, Christianity, and Islām) developed concepts of the Last Judgment that are rich in imagery. Zoroastrianism, founded by the 6th-century-BC Iranian prophet Zoroaster, teaches that after death the soul waits for three nights by the grave and on the fourth day goes to the Bridge of the Requiter, where his deeds are weighed. If the good outweigh the bad, the soul is able to cross the bridge to heaven; if the bad outweigh the good deeds, the bridge becomes too narrow for the soul to cross, and it plunges into the cold and dark abyss of hell. This is not the end, however, for there will be a final overthrow of Ahriman, the prince of demons, by Ahura Mazdā, the Wise Lord, who will resurrect all men, preside over a Last Judgment, and restore the world to goodness.

Early Judaic writers emphasized a day of Yahweh, the God of Israel, which is also called the day of the Lord. This day, which will be a day of judgment of Israel and all nations, will inaugurate the Kingdom of God.

Christianity, further developing the concept of the Last Judgment, teaches that it will occur at the Parousia (the Second Coming, or Second Advent, of Christ in glory), when all men will stand before a judging God. In early Christian art the scene is one of Christ the judge, the resurrection of the dead, the weighing of souls, the separation of the saved and the damned, and representations of paradise and hell. Romanesque artists produced a more terrible vision of the Last Judgment: Christ is shown as a stern judge, sometimes carrying a sword and surrounded by the four mystical beasts—eagle, lion, ox, and winged man—of the apocalypse; the contrast between paradise and hell is between the awesome and the ferocious. In the gentler, more humanistic art of the Gothic period, a beautiful Christ is shown as the Redeemer, his right side undraped to reveal the wound of the lance, and both wounded hands raised high in a gesture that emphasizes his sacrifice. He is surrounded by the instruments of his Passion—cross, nails, lance, and crown of thorns. The intercessors are restored, and the scene of the Judgment is treated with optimism. In the 16th century, Michelangelo produced a radically different version of the Last Judgment in his fresco in the Sistine Chapel in Rome (1533–41): a vengeful Christ, nude like a pagan god, gestures menacingly toward the damned.

Islām likewise is rich in its imagery and conceptual expansion of the doctrine of the Last Judgment. The Day of Judgment is one of the five cardinal beliefs of Muslims. After death, persons are questioned about their faith by two angels: Munkar and Nakīr. If a person has been a martyr, his soul immediately goes to paradise; others go through a type of purgatory (*q.v.*). At doomsday all persons will die and then be resurrected to be judged according to the records kept in two books, one containing a person's good deeds, and the other his evil deeds. According to the weight of the book that is tied around a person's neck, he will be consigned to paradise or hell.

In addition to the Western religions and some primitive religions, ancient Near Eastern religions had developed beliefs in a Last

Tympanum of The Last Judgment, church facade at Conques, Fr., 1130–1135
Lauros—Giraudon from Art Resource/EB Inc.

Judgment. In ancient Egyptian religion, for example, a dead person's heart was judged by being placed on a balance held by the god Anubis. If the heart was light, thus indicating a person's comparative goodness, the soul was allowed to go to the blessed region ruled by Osiris, god of the dead. If the heart was heavy, the soul might be destroyed by a hybrid creature called the Devouress.

In the Asian religions (*e.g.*, Hinduism, Jainism, and Buddhism) that believe in reincarnation (*q.v.*), the concept of a Last Judgment is not uncommon.

Last Mountain Lake, also called LONG LAKE, lake in south central Saskatchewan, Canada, which drains southward to the Qu'Appelle River. Named after a hill 12 mi (19 km) to the east, the lake averages only 2 mi in width but extends northward for nearly 60 mi. It has an area of 89 sq mi (231 sq km). Since the establishment (*c.* 1865) by Isaac Cowie, the trader-author, of a Hudson's Bay Company post near Silton at its southern tip, the lake has been noted for fishing; most lucrative commercially are its buffalo fish, which were mistaken for black bass when imported from the U.S. for stocking. The lake is known as a bird sanctuary and as a stopping place on a flyway, notably for whooping and sandhill cranes during spring and fall migrations. It is also a popular vacation area, with several beach resorts and Buffalo Pound (2,340 ac [947 ha]) and Rowan's Ravine (652 ac) provincial parks along its shores, serving the nearby cities of Regina (20 mi southeast) and Moose Jaw. The Company trading post has been reconstructed within Last Mountain House Historic Park.

Last Supper, also called LORD'S SUPPER, in the New Testament (Matt. 26:17–29; Mark 14:12–25; Luke 22:7–38; I Cor. 11:23–25), the final meal shared by Jesus and his disciples in an upper room in Jerusalem, the occasion of the institution of the Eucharist. According to the biblical account, Jesus sent two of his disciples to prepare for the meal and met with all the disciples in the upper room. He told them that one of them would betray him. After blessing bread and wine and giving it to them to eat and drink, Jesus told them that it was his body and his blood of the Covenant.

The Synoptic Gospels and the traditions of the church affirm that the Last Supper occurred on the Passover. Although the account of the Crucifixion in the Gospel According to John indicates that the Last Supper could not have been a Passover meal, many interpreters accept the account given in the Synoptic Gospels. Two aspects of the Last Supper have been traditionally depicted in Christian art: Christ's revelation to his Apostles that one of them will betray him and their reaction to this announcement, and the institution of the sacrament of the Eucharist with the communion of the Apostles. Early Christian art (*c.* 2nd–*c.* 6th century) stressed neither aspect of the Last Supper to the exclusion of the other, but thereafter the East generally favoured compositions emphasizing the symbolic aspects of the event, and the West favoured those emphasizing the narrative.

In early Christian art the presence of a fish on the table symbolizes the institution of the Eucharist. This symbol appeared in Western depictions of the communion of the Apostles until the 15th century, when a chalice and wafer were substituted for it.

"Odysseus and Nausicaa," painting by Pieter Lastman; in the Alte Pinakothek, Munich

By courtesy of the Alte Pinakothek, Munich

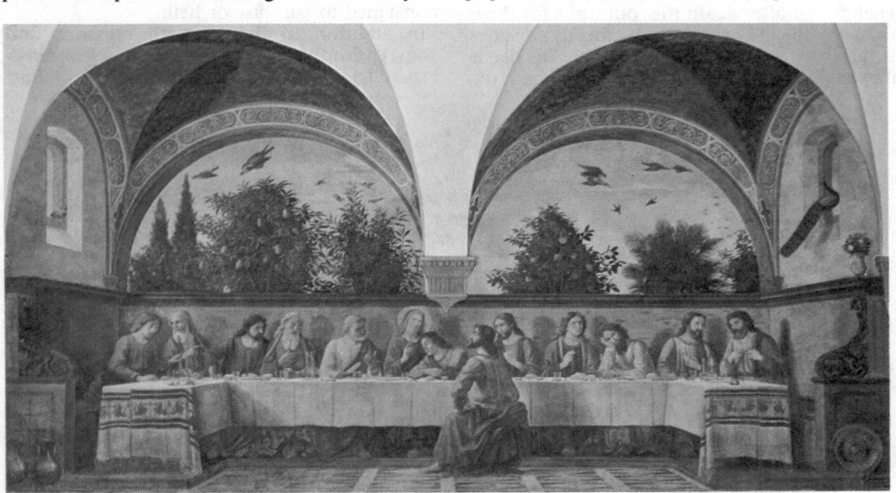

"Last Supper," fresco by Domenico Ghirlandajo, 1480; in the Church of Ognissanti, Florence

SCALA—Art Resource/EB Inc.

Consult the INDEX *first*

Lastman, Pieter (b. 1583, Amsterdam—d. 1633, Amsterdam), Dutch painter of biblical and mythological scenes in antique landscapes who had a strong influence on the young Rembrandt, who worked in his Amsterdam studio in 1624.

Lastman received his earliest training from a pupil of Cornelis van Haarlem, a painter of the post-Renaissance Mannerist school. He also shared stylistic affinities with Hendrik Goltzius, another prominent painter in Haarlem. He worked in Rome about 1603–07, where he was profoundly influenced by an important German landscape painter, Adam Elsheimer. By the time he returned to Amsterdam in 1607, he had assimilated Elsheimer's sensitive feeling for light and atmosphere in landscape. Rembrandt's "Angel and the Prophet Balaam" (1626; Musée Cognacq-Jay, Paris) is based on Lastman's earlier painting of the same subject (1622; Palmer Collection, England). Lastman's "Coriolanus and the Roman Woman" (Trinity College, Dublin) and "The Baptism of the Chamberlain" (Alte Pinakothek, Munich) also influenced the early narrative style of Rembrandt.

László (Hungarian personal name): *see under* Ladislas.

Lāt, al-, North Arabian goddess of pre-Islāmic times to whom a stone cube at aṭ-Ṭā'if (near Mecca) was held sacred as part of her cult. Two other North Arabian goddesses, Manāt (Fate) and al-ʿUzzā (Strong), were associated with al-Lāt in the Qur'ān (Islāmic sacred scriptures). The Prophet Muḥammad once recognized these three as goddesses, but a new revelation led him to abrogate the approving verses he had earlier recited and to abandon his attempt to placate Meccan pagans. Members of the tribe of Quraysh circumambulated the Kaʿbah in Mecca (now a central shrine of Islām in Mecca's al-Ḥaram mosque) chanting the praises of al-Lāt, al-ʿUzzā, and Manāt. Each of the three had main sanctuaries near Mecca that were sites of pious visits and offerings until Muḥammad ordered them destroyed. The goddesses were also worshipped by various Arab tribes located as far away as Palmyra, Syria.

Latacunga, capital of Cotopaxi province, north central Ecuador, in an Andean basin on the upper Río Patate, at an elevation of 9,055 ft (2,760 m). The city dates from precolonial times, when it was frequented by Incan royalty because of its thermal springs. Latacunga lies 20 mi (32 km) southwest of the active volcano Cotopaxi and has been seriously damaged by eruptions and by attendant earthquakes. Although completely destroyed in 1797, it was subsequently rebuilt.

The city serves as a commercial centre for the surrounding cattle-raising and farming region. Industrial activities include flour milling and the manufacture of building stone (from local lava rock), furniture, pottery, and gunpowder. Latacunga has been a Roman Catholic episcopal see since 1963. Pop. (1981 prelim.) 55,979.

Latakia, Arabic AL-LĀDHIQĪYAH, city and *muḥāfaẓah* (governorate), northwestern Syria. The city, capital of the governorate, is situated on the low-lying Raʾs Ziyārah promontory that projects into the Mediterranean Sea. It was known to the Phoenicians as Ramitha and to the Greeks as Leuke Akte. Its present name is a corruption of Laodicea, for the mother of Seleucus II (3rd century BC).

Ancient Ramitha replaced the earlier settlement of Ugarit (Ras Shamra) to the north,

Triumphal arch of Septimus Severus, Latakia, Syria
Sam Abboud—FPG/EB Inc.

which was destroyed in the 12th century BC. During the Seleucid period (3rd and 2nd centuries BC), it flourished as a port and one of north Syria's principal cities, but in the following centuries earthquakes twice destroyed the city. Latakia was taken in AD 638 by the Arabs, in 1103 by the crusaders, and in 1188 by Saladin. Subsequently the town was administered by Christians from Tripoli, Muslims from Ḥamāh, and the Ottoman Turks; it came within the French mandate of Syria and Lebanon in 1920.

Latakia is now the principal port of Syria; it is located on a good harbour, with an extensive agricultural hinterland. Exports include bitumen and asphalt, cereals, cotton, fruit, eggs, vegetable oil, pottery, and tobacco. Cotton ginning, vegetable-oil processing, tanning, and sponge fishing are local industries. The University of Latakia (renamed Tishrīn University in 1977) was founded in 1971. The city is linked by road to Aleppo, Tripoli, and Beirut. All but a few classical buildings have been destroyed, often by earthquakes; those remaining include a Roman triumphal arch and Corinthian columns known as the colonnade of Bacchus.

Latakia governorate has an area of 887 sq mi (2,297 sq km) and embraces Syria's fertile Mediterranean coastal area. It is an important agricultural region, producing abundant crops of tobacco, cotton, cereal grains, and fruits. Pop. (1981 prelim.) city, 196,791; governorate, 554,783.

late blight, disease of potato and tomato plants that is caused by the fungus *Phytophthora infestans.* The disease occurs in humid regions with temperature ranges of between 40° and 80° F (4° and 29° C); hot, dry weather checks its spread. Potato or tomato vines that are infected may rot within two weeks. The Irish potato famines of 1845–60 were caused by late blight. The disease destroyed more than half of the tomato crop in the eastern United States in 1946, leading to the establishment of a blight-forecasting service in 1947.

When plants have become infected, lesions (round or irregularly shaped areas that range in colour from dark green to purplish black and resemble frost injury) appear on the leaves, petioles, and stems. A whitish growth of spore-producing structures may appear at the margin of the lesions on the underleaf surfaces. Potato tubers develop rot up to 15 millimetres (0.6 inch) deep. Secondary fungi and bacteria (*Erwinia* species) often invade potato tubers and produce rotting that results in great losses during storage, transit, and marketing.

The *Phytophthora* fungus survives in stored tubers, dump piles, field plants, and greenhouse tomatoes. Sporangia are airborne to nearby plants, in which infection may occur within a few hours. At temperatures below 59° F (15° C) sporangia germinate by producing zoospores that encyst and later form a germ tube. Above that temperature most sporangia produce a germ tube directly. Foliage blighting and a new crop of sporangia are produced within four to six days after infection. The cycle is repeated as long as cool, moist weather prevails.

Latécoère, Pierre (b. 1883, Bagnères-de-Bigorre, Fr.—d. Aug. 11, 1943, Paris), French aircraft manufacturer who aided the development of international airline service.

The Compagnie Latécoère began commercial air flights between Toulouse, Fr., and Barcelona on Dec. 25, 1918, and extended its route to Morocco in 1919 and to Dakar, Senegal, in 1925. In 1927 the line was renamed Compagnie Générale Aéropostale, and, at the end of the decade, it temporarily operated a transatlantic route to Buenos Aires. After financial failure in 1932, the company was taken over by Air France.

Founded in 1917, Latécoère's aircraft-building company had factories at Toulouse and Bayonne and a seaplane base at Biscarrosse, Landes. At various times the author-aviator Antoine de Saint-Exupéry was employed by both the airline and the manufacturing concern.

lateen sail, triangular sail that was of decisive importance to medieval navigation. The ancient square sail permitted sailing only before the wind; the lateen was the earliest fore-and-aft sail. The triangular sail was affixed to a long yard or crossbar, mounted at its middle to the top of the mast and angled to extend aft far above the mast and forward down nearly to the deck. The sail, its free corner secured near the stern, was capable of taking the wind on either side, and, by en-

Lateen-rigged ship, first used about the 2nd century AD in the eastern Mediterranean
From Bjorn Landstrom, *The Ship,* illustration copyright 1961 by Bjorn Landstrom; reproduced by permission of Doubleday & Company, Inc.

abling the vessel to tack into the wind, the lateen immensely increased the potential of the sailing ship.

The lateen is believed to have been used in the eastern Mediterranean as early as the 2nd century AD, possibly imported from Egypt or the Persian Gulf. Its effective use by the Arabs caused its rapid spread throughout the Mediterranean, contributing significantly to the resurgence of medieval commerce. Combined with the square sail, it produced the ocean-conquering full-rigged ship. The Sunfish class of one-design sailboats is lateen-rigged.

latent heat, characteristic amount of energy absorbed or released by a substance during a change in its physical state that occurs without changing its temperature. The latent heat associated with melting a solid or freezing a liquid is called the heat of fusion; that associated with vaporizing a liquid or a solid or condensing a vapour is called the heat of vaporization.

For example, when a pot of water is kept boiling, the temperature remains at 100° C (212° F) until the last drop evaporates, because all the heat being added to the liquid is absorbed as latent heat of vaporization and carried away by the escaping vapour molecules. Similarly, while ice melts it remains at 0° C (32° F), and the liquid water that is formed with the latent heat of fusion is also at 0° C.

The structure of a crystalline solid is maintained by forces of attraction between the individual molecules or ions, which oscillate slightly about their mean positions in the array. When heat is absorbed, these motions increase until at the melting point the attractive forces can no longer preserve the orderly arrangement, and the solid changes into a liquid, in which the individual particles move about independently, attracted to each other only by forces much weaker and less specifically directed in space. When a substance is heated sufficiently, even the weak forces that hold the particles together in the liquid state are overcome, and at the boiling point the liquid transforms into vapour.

Latent heat is associated with processes other than changes between solid, liquid, and vapour phases of a single substance. Many solids exist in different crystalline modifications, and the transitions between these are generally attended by absorption or evolution of latent heat. The process of dissolving one substance in another often involves heat; if the solution process is a strictly physical change, the heat is a latent heat. Sometimes, however, the process is accompanied by a chemical change, and part of the heat is that associated with the chemical reaction. *See also* thermal fusion.

latent image, in photography, the invisible configuration of silver halide crystals on a piece of film after exposure to image-bearing focussed light; it is distinguishable from unexposed silver halide only by its ability to be reduced to metallic silver by a developing agent.

According to current theories of latent image formation, small specks of silver atoms (one ten-millionth the size of the halide) are formed on exposure by condensation and act as points of attack for the developer, which can then reduce the whole silver halide crystal to silver.

latent infection: *see* infection.

Later Le DYNASTY, Vietnamese NHA HAU LE (1428–1788), the greatest and longest lasting dynasty of traditional Vietnam. Its predecessor, the Earlier Le, was founded by Le Hoan and lasted from 980 to 1009.

The Later Le was established when its founder, Le Loi, began a resistance movement against the Chinese armies then occupying Vietnam; by 1428 he had liberated the country and was free to begin the process of recovering the southern portion of the Indochinese Peninsula from the Indianized kingdom of Champa. In 1471 Le Thanh Tong, the greatest of the Le rulers, permanently subjugated Champa. Le Thanh Tong divided Vietnam into 13 provinces or circuits, based on the Chinese model, and established a triennial Confucian civil service examination. He also promulgated a new legal code, the Hong Duc code. This administrative system showed some Chinese influence but also contained distinctly Vietnamese elements.

The rulers following Le Thanh Tong came under the control of a series of ambitious feudal magnates. In 1527 the throne was even usurped by a member of the powerful Mac family. Although a Le emperor was restored in 1533 with the help of the Nguyen family, the Le rulers were thereafter only theoretically supreme. Real power was shared between two families, the Trinh in the north and the Nguyen, with their capital at Hue, in the south. By about 1630 the cleavage between the two had become so acute that the southerners built two walls across the plain of Dong Hai (at latitude 18° north) to the jungle, sealing off the north until the late 18th century.

In 1771 a peasant uprising led by the Tay Son brothers spread throughout the country and seven years later overthrew the dynasty. Members of the Nguyen family, however, were able to obtain French aid and reunite the nation under the Nguyen dynasty.

Later Ly DYNASTY, Vietnamese NHA HAU LY (1009–1225), first of the three great dynasties of Vietnam. The kingdom, known later as Dai Viet, was established by Ly Thai To in the Red River Delta area of present northern Vietnam. Its capital was Thang Long (Hanoi). (It is "later" with respect to the Earlier Ly dynasty, founded by Ly Bon and lasting from 544 to 602/603.) The Later Ly was the first stable Vietnamese dynasty and helped establish many of the characteristics of the modern Vietnamese state.

A Chinese style of administration was one of the more significant changes wrought by the Later Ly. Through this system the local lords were replaced by a nine-tiered hierarchy of civil servants and state officials. An institution for the training of civil administrators was established, as was an academy of learning. This centralized form of government enabled the Ly to establish universal military service, which kept the invading Chinese and Champa at bay for two centuries. More importantly, the administrative system enabled the Ly to develop the great Red River Delta system of dikes and canals that prevented summer flooding and winter drought and made the region one of the most fertile rice-growing areas in the world. The Ly promoted literature and art, and during their reign, knowledge of classical Chinese literature was widespread. Under the Ly, Vietnamese influence spread southward into the area controlled by the Indianized kingdom of Champa.

lateral, in phonetics, a consonant sound produced by raising the tip of the tongue against the roof of the mouth so that the airstream flows past one or both sides of the tongue. The *l* sounds of English, Welsh, and other languages are laterals.

lateral line system, network of sensory receptors located along the head and sides of fishes and amphibians. The system serves to detect movements and pressure changes in the surrounding water. The individual receptor, called a lateral line organ, or neuromast, consists of a cluster of innervated hairs surrounded by a jellylike projection (cupula) that bends in response to water movements. The neuromasts of most bony fishes are set in a series of interconnected depressions, forming a canal, with openings at intervals to the environment.

lateral secretion, geological process by which ore minerals dissolved from wall rocks by percolating waters are redeposited in nearby openings. Put forth in 1847, the theory was vigorously attacked in the late 1800s by geologists who contended that the deposits were formed by hot water ascending from deep-seated sources; it was generally dismissed about the beginning of the 20th century, but modern studies have attributed some deposits to lateral secretion.

laterality, in physiological psychology, the development of specialized functioning in each hemisphere of the brain or in the side of the body which each controls.

The most obvious example of laterality is handedness, the tendency to use one hand or the other to perform activities. It is the usual practice to classify persons as right-handed, left-handed, or ambidextrous (two-handed). People differ considerably in the range of activities for which they prefer a given hand as well as in the degree of disparity in skill between their two hands. Probably no one favours his right or left hand exclusively.

Origin and development. There is no extensive agreement on the origin of manual preferences. Some authors believe such laterality is inherited; others, that the child is trained to it; and still others, that biases are initiated in an infant during pregnancy by some organization of intrauterine forces, such as those producing twinning, or some extrauterine environmental influences. It is possible all three hypotheses are, in some measure, correct. It does seem clear that left-handed parents more frequently have left-handed offspring than do right-handed parents; that even at birth most babies tend to move one arm—usually the right—more than the other; and that, if a systematic effort is made to keep infants from developing a preference, they still come to favour one hand. It is equally apparent that most babies shift their preference once or twice during their first year. The consistency with which children use one hand in preference to the other increases with age, at least through the preschool years and probably longer. By far, most children are right-handed.

There is some data suggesting that humans are genetically biased toward right-handedness. During the third and fourth months of gestation, for example, a fetus' fingerprints are larger on the right hand than the left. Recent research, however, suggests that right-handedness and left-handedness are not genetically encoded within the body's genes but rather are coded in the spatial structure of ovarian cells. Other scientists believe handedness is not biologically determined at all, but is a factor of the environment. Most children can be trained to use and to prefer the right hand for any activity, and many have been so trained without obvious harmful effects. The wisdom of interfering with a child's spontaneous preference, however, has been questioned.

Laterality in the body. One of the first to suggest the relationship between the brain's hemispheres and specialized functions was the French pathologist and anthropologist Paul Broca (1824–80). He localized the brain centre for articulate speech in the third convolution of the left frontal lobe. He referred to this area as the "convolution of Broca" (mainly known as Broca's area). Broca also realized that damage to the brain's left hemisphere could lead to the loss of certain abilities such as the comprehension of spoken language and such functions as speech, reading, and writing. Loss of these functions is referred to as aphasia, alexia, and agraphia, respectively. Broca's work seems supported by evidence that the brain speech centre tends to be located in the hemisphere (usually left) opposite to the side of the dominant hand (usually right) and that brain waves from corresponding parts of the two cerebral hemispheres are more conspicuous on the nondominant side. Neither of these bits of evidence shows conclusively, however, that the cortical organization a person inherits is responsible for his hand preference. There is little support for the view, as the theory of a dominant cerebral hemisphere might lead one to expect, that the body structures under the control of one hemisphere are uniformly more efficient than those under control of the other. Indeed, the dominant hand is not always on the side of the dominant foot, and about three-fourths of right-handed and one-third of left-handed persons are right-eyed in sighting.

Lateran Council, any of the five ecumenical councils of the Roman Catholic Church held in the Lateran Palace in Rome.

The first Lateran Council, the ninth ecumenical council (1123), was held during the reign of Pope Calixtus II; no acts or contemporary accounts survive. The council promulgated a number of canons (probably 22), many of which merely reiterated decrees of earlier councils. Much of the discussion was occupied with disciplinary or quasi-political decisions relating to the Investiture Controversy settled the previous year by the Concordat of Worms; simony was condemned, laymen were prohibited from disposing of church property, clerics in major orders were forbidden to marry, and uncanonical consecration of bishops was forbidden. There were no specific dogmatic decrees.

The second Lateran Council, the 10th ecumenical council (1139), was convoked by Pope Innocent II to condemn as schismatics the followers of Arnold of Brescia, a vigorous reformer and opponent of the temporal power of the pope, and to end the schism created by the election of Anacletus II, a rival pope. Supported by St. Bernard of Clairvaux and later by Emperor Lothair II, Innocent was eventually acknowledged as the legitimate pope. Besides reaffirming previous conciliar decrees, the second Lateran Council declared invalid all marriages of those in major orders and of professed monks, canons, lay brothers, and nuns. The council repudiated the heresies of the 12th century concerning holy orders, matrimony, infant Baptism, and the Eucharist.

The third Lateran Council, the 11th ecumenical council, was convoked in 1179 by Pope Alexander III and attended by 291 bishops who studied the Peace of Venice (1177), by which the Holy Roman emperor, Frederick I Barbarossa, agreed to withdraw support from his antipope and to restore the church property he had seized. This council also established a two-thirds majority of the College of Cardinals as a requirement for papal election and stipulated that candidates for bishop must be 30 years old and of legitimate birth. The heretical Cathari (or Albigenses) were condemned, and Christians were authorized to take up arms against vagabond robbers. The council marked an important stage in the development of papal legislative authority.

The fourth Lateran Council, the 12th ecumenical council (1215), generally considered the greatest council before Trent, was years in preparation. Pope Innocent III desired the widest possible representation, and more than 400 bishops, 800 abbots and priors, envoys of many European kings, and personal representatives of Frederick II (confirmed by the council as emperor of the West) took part. The purpose of the council was twofold: reform of the church and the recovery of the Holy Land. Many of the conciliar decrees touching on church reform and organization remained in effect for centuries. The council ruled on such vexing problems as the use of church property, tithes, judicial procedures, and patriarchal precedence. It ordered Jews and Saracens to wear distinctive dress and obliged Catholics to make a yearly confession and to receive Communion during the Easter season. The council sanctioned the word transubstantiation as a correct expression of eucharistic doctrine. The teachings of the Cathari and Waldenses were condemned. Innocent also ordered a four-year truce among Christian rulers so that a new crusade could be launched.

The fifth Lateran Council, the 18th ecumenical council (1512–17), was convoked by Pope Julius II in response to a council summoned at Pisa by a group of cardinals who were hostile to the Pope. The Pope's council had reform as its chief concern. It restored peace among warring Christian rulers and sanctioned a new concordat with France to supersede the Pragmatic Sanction of Bourges of 1438. In dogmatic decrees the council affirmed the immortality of the soul and repudiated declarations of the councils of Constance and Basel that made church councils superior to the pope.

Lateran Treaty, also called LATERAN PACT OF 1929, treaty (effective 1929 to 1985) between Italy and the Vatican. It was signed by Benito Mussolini for the Italian government and by cardinal secretary of state Pietro Gasparri for the papacy and confirmed by the Italian constitution of 1948.

Upon ratification of the Lateran Treaty, the papacy recognized the state of Italy, with Rome as its capital. Italy in return recognized papal sovereignty over the Vatican City, a minute territory of 44 hectares (109 acres), and secured full independence for the pope. A number of additional measures were agreed upon. Article 1, for example, gave the city of Rome a special character as the "centre of the Catholic world and place of pilgrimage." Article 20 stated that all bishops were to take an oath of loyalty to the state and had to be Italian subjects speaking the Italian language.

By article 34 the state recognized the validity of Catholic marriage and its subjection to the provisions of canon law; nullity cases were therefore reserved to the ecclesiastical courts, and there could be no divorce.

The state agreed by article 36 of the concordat to permit religious instruction in the public primary and secondary schools and conceded to the bishops the right to appoint or dismiss those who imparted such instruction and to approve the textbooks that they used.

With the signing of the concordat of 1985, Roman Catholicism was no longer the state religion of Italy. This change in status brought about a number of alterations in Italian society. Perhaps the most significant of these was the end to compulsory religious education in public schools. The new concordat also affected such diverse areas as tax exemptions for religious institutions and ownership of the Jewish catacombs.

laterite, soil layer that is rich in iron oxide and derived from a wide variety of rocks weathering under strongly oxidizing and leaching conditions. It forms in tropical and subtropical regions where the climate is humid. Lateritic soils may contain clay minerals; but they tend to be silica-poor, for silica is leached out by waters passing through the soil. Typical laterite is porous and claylike. It contains the iron oxide minerals goethite, $HFeO_2$; lepidocrocite, FeO(OH); and hematite, Fe_2O_3. It also contains titanium oxides and hydrated oxides of aluminum, the most common and abundant of which is gibbsite, $Al_2O_3 \cdot 3H_2O$. The aluminum-rich representative of laterite is bauxite.

Laterite is frequently pisolitic (pealike). Exposed surfaces are blackish-brown to reddish and commonly have a slaggy, or scoriaceous, lavalike appearance. Commonly lighter in colour (red, yellow, and brown) where freshly broken, it is generally soft when freshly quarried but hardens on exposure.

Laterite is not uniquely identified with any particular parent rock, geologic age, single method of formation, climate per se, or geographic location. It is a rock product that is a response to a set of physiochemical conditions, which include an iron-containing parent rock, a well-drained terrain, abundant moisture for hydrolysis during weathering, relatively high oxidation potential, and persistence of these conditions over thousands of years.

Laterite has been used as an iron ore and, in Cuba, as a source of nickel.

Lateur, Frank: *see* Streuvels, Stijn.

latex, colloidal suspension, either the milky white liquid emulsion found in the cells of flowering plants such as the Para rubber tree (*Hevea brasiliensis*) or any of various manufactured water emulsions consisting of synthetic rubber or plastic.

The plant product is a complex mixture of substances, including various gum resins, fats, or waxes and, in some instances, poisonous compounds, suspended in a watery medium in which salts, sugars, tannins, alkaloids, enzymes, and other substances are dissolved. It is produced especially by the cells of plants of the family Asclepiadaceae but also by those in the families Apocynaceae, Sapotaceae, Euphorbiaceae, Papaveraceae, Moraceae, and Asteraceae (Compositae). The latex circulates in branched tubes that penetrate the tissues of the plant in a longitudinal direction, conducting substances and acting as an excretory reservoir. The chief commercial products of latex are rubber, gutta-percha, chicle, and balata (*qq.v.*). The latex of the opium poppy (*Papaver somniferum*) is the source of opium and the alkaloid morphine.

In the paint and coatings industry, aqueous dispersion polymers, or polymer emulsions called latexes, have come into widespread use since the late 1940s. These synthetic latexes include a binder dispersed in the water and form films by fusion of the plastic particles as the water evaporates. The properties of the films—such as hardness, flexibility, toughness, adhesion, colour retention, and resistance to chemicals—depend on the composition of the plastic. Polymers based on butadiene, styrene, vinyl acetate, and acrylic monomers have been used commercially.

latex foam: *see* foam rubber.

lath, any material fastened to the structural members of a building to provide a base for plaster. Lath can be of wood, metal, gypsum, or insulated board. In older residential buildings, narrow wood strips were generally used.

One of the most common laths is gypsum lath. It is manufactured with an air-entrained gypsum core sandwiched between two layers of fibrous absorbent paper. Sheets with reflective foil backing provide insulation and act as a vapour barrier.

Metal lath, a mesh formed by expanding a perforated metal sheet, is made in a variety of forms (diamond-mesh, flat-ribbed, and wire lath). The sheets of metal are slit and drawn out to form numerous openings, creating an irregular surface for the keying of the plaster. It is often used in bathrooms and kitchens, where ceramic tile is applied over a plaster base.

Latharna (Northern Ireland): *see* Larne.

lathe, machine tool that performs turning operations in which unwanted material is removed from a workpiece rotated against a cutting tool.

The lathe is one of the oldest and most important machine tools. Wood lathes were in use in France as early as 1569. During the Industrial Revolution in England the machine was adapted for metal cutting. The rotating horizontal spindle to which the workholding device is attached is usually power driven at speeds that can be varied. On a speed lathe the cutting tool is supported on a tool rest and manipulated by hand. On an engine lathe the tool is clamped onto a cross slide that is power driven on straight paths parallel or perpendicular to the work axis. On a screwcutting lathe the motion of the cutting tool is accurately related to the rotation of the spindle by means of a lead screw that drives the carriage on which the cutting tool is mounted.

Internal turning is known as boring and results in the enlargement of an already existing hole. For internal turning on solid workpieces, holes are drilled first; engine lathes are equipped for drilling coaxial holes. *See also* boring machine; drilling machines.

Lathrop, Mother Alphonsa, original name ROSE HAWTHORNE (b. May 20, 1851, Lenox, Mass., U.S.—d. July 9, 1926, Hawthorne, N.Y.), U.S. author, nun, and founder of the Servants of Relief for Incurable Cancer, a Roman Catholic congregation of nuns affiliated with the Third Order of St. Dominic and dedicated to serving victims of terminal cancer.

The daughter of the author Nathaniel Hawthorne, Rose was an infant when her family moved to Liverpool, where her father served as consul. After two years in Italy, the family went to Concord, Mass., in 1860. Eleven years later Rose married George Parsons Lathrop, who later was assistant editor of *The Atlantic Monthly,* Boston. Their son, Francis, born in 1876, died five years later. During that period Rose wrote short stories and verse, including a book of poems, *Along the Shore* (1888). Although a Unitarian of Puritan heritage, she converted to Roman Catholicism in 1891.

Legally separated from her husband, Rose trained at Memorial Hospital, New York City, so that she could help cancer patients. In the midst of a campaign to procure funds for her cause, she wrote *Memories of Hawthorne* (1897). She acquired a house on the city's Lower East Side, opening it to victims of cancer. In the spring of 1899, a year after her husband's death, she moved to larger quarters, which she named St. Rose's Free Home for Incurable Cancer. Having joined the Dominicans, she made her vows on Dec. 8, 1900, taking the religious name Alphonsa. With the aid of her first companion, Sister M. Rose, she founded the Dominican Congregation of St. Rose of Lima, later called the Servants of Relief for Incurable Cancer. She became her order's first superior general.

In 1901 Mother Alphonsa opened Rosary Hill Home, Hawthorne (now the motherhouse), where she directed the growth of the Servants, founding the magazine *Christ's Poor.* Subsequent homes were established in New York, Pennsylvania, Massachusetts, Georgia, and Minnesota. Biographies of Mother Alphonsa include K. Burton's *Sorrow Built a Bridge: A Daughter of Hawthorne* (1937) and M. Joseph's *Out of Many Hearts* (1961).

Lathrop, Julia Clifford (b. June 29, 1858, Rockford, Ill., U.S.—d. April 15, 1932, Rockford), American social welfare worker who was the first director of the federal Children's Bureau.

Lathrop graduated from Vassar College in Poughkeepsie, N.Y., in 1880. In 1890 she joined the staff of Hull House, Jane Addams' settlement in Chicago, with which Lathrop remained associated for 20 years. In 1893 she was appointed the first woman member of the Illinois State Board of Charities; her work there contributed to such reforms as the appointment of female doctors and nurses in state hospitals, the removal of the insane from poorhouses, and the establishment of the first juvenile court in the United States (1900).

In 1912 President William Howard Taft named Lathrop chief of the newly created Children's Bureau. Lathrop directed pioneering studies of infant mortality, child labour, juvenile delinquency, and illegitimacy. She also promoted legislation that resulted in the Sheppard-Towner Act of 1921, which laid the groundwork for the maternal and child health provisions of the Social Security Act. Lathrop resigned from the Children's Bureau in 1921. In 1925 she was appointed to the Child Welfare Committee of the League of Nations.

latifundium, plural LATIFUNDIA, any large ancient Roman agricultural estate that used a large number of peasant or slave labourers.

The ancient Roman latifundia originated from the allocation of land confiscated by Rome from certain conquered communities, beginning in the early 2nd century BC. Earlier, in classical Greece of the 5th century BC, sizable estates were cultivated for high profit, based on what was known of scientific agriculture. Later, in the Hellenistic Age (from 323 BC), large estates were held by rulers, ministers, and other wealthy people and by some great temples. On such estates there were a number of economic activities and, consequently, a wide division of labour, some slave, some free.

Upper-class Romans who owned latifundia had enough capital to improve their crops and livestock with new strains, putting peasant smallholders at a competitive disadvantage. Thus latifundia virtually supplanted the small farm as the regular agricultural unit in Italy and in the provinces by the 3rd century AD. On the latifundium stood the villa, or manor house; slaves were counted with the cattle, farm tools, and other movable property. In the later days of the empire, slave labour grew more expensive, and more *coloni,* or tenant farmers, who cultivated small plots, replaced them. As the empire declined and disappeared in the West (5th century AD), the latifundia assumed great importance not only as economic but also as local political and cultural centres.

Latimer, Hugh (b. *c.* 1485, Thurcaston, Leicestershire, Eng.—d. Oct. 16, 1555, Oxford), English Protestant who advanced the cause of the Reformation in England through his vigorous preaching and through the inspiration of his martyrdom.

Latimer was the son of a prosperous yeoman farmer. Educated at the University of Cambridge, he was ordained a priest about 1510. At first he subscribed to orthodox Roman Catholicism, but in 1525 he came into contact with a group of young Cambridge divines who were influenced by Martin Luther's new doctrines. He attributed his conversion to Protestantism to the ministrations of the group's spiritual leader, Thomas Bilney. After gaining royal favour by speaking out in support of the efforts of King Henry VIII to obtain an annulment of his marriage to Catherine of Aragon, Latimer received the benefice of West Kington, Wiltshire, in 1531. He soon befriended two rising Reformers: Thomas Cromwell, who was to become the king's chief minister, and the future archbishop of Canterbury Thomas Cranmer. Such powerful backers, however, could not protect him from accusations of heretical preachings. Before investigators Latimer refused in January 1532 to subscribe to certain articles of faith such as the existence of purgatory and the need to venerate saints. Consequently, he was excommunicated and imprisoned until he made a complete submission (April 1532).

Nevertheless, thanks to Cromwell's influence, Latimer was elevated in 1535 to the bishopric of Worcester. By 1536 he was generally regarded as one of the Reform leaders. As a

Latimer, detail of a panel painting by an unknown artist, 1555; in the National Portrait Gallery, London

result of a temporary reaction in England in favour of orthodox Catholicism, Latimer was forced to resign his see in 1539, and, upon the sudden fall of Cromwell in July 1540, he lost his main support at court.

For the remainder of Henry's reign Latimer existed in the shadows. Apparently he incurred suspicion of heresy at intervals and spent some time in the Tower of London, where he was incarcerated during the last few months before the accession of the boy king Edward VI in January 1547. The new regime, with its rapid advance toward Protestantism, gave Latimer a chance to exercise his talents. He refused to resume his bishopric, because he wanted to be free to preach without fear or favour. His sermons attracted large crowds and were often patronized by the court. But because of his success in popularizing the idea of the Reformation, Latimer was immediately marked for proscription when the Catholic Mary Tudor ascended the throne. In September 1553 he was arrested on charges of treason; taken to Oxford for trial, he was burned there with the Reformer Nicholas Ridley on Oct. 16, 1555. At the stake Latimer immortalized himself by exhorting his fellow victim Ridley with the words "we shall this day light such a candle, by God's grace, in England as I trust shall never be put out."

BIBLIOGRAPHY. Harold S. Darby, *Hugh Latimer* (1953); Allan G. Chester, *Hugh Latimer, Apostle to the English* (1954, reprinted 1978).

Latin, the ancient people of Latium (*q.v.*).

Latin alphabet, also called ROMAN ALPHABET, most widely used alphabetic writing system in the world, the standard script of the English language and the languages of most of Europe and those areas settled by Europeans. Developed from the Etruscan alphabet at some time before 600 BC, it can be traced through Etruscan, Greek, and Phoenician scripts to the North Semitic alphabet used in Syria and Palestine about 1100 BC. The earliest inscription in the Latin alphabet appears on the Praeneste Fibula, a cloak pin dating from about the 7th century BC, which reads, "MANIOS MED FHEFHAKED NUMASIOI" (in Classical Latin: "*Manius me fecit Numerio,*" meaning "Manius made me for Numerius"). Dated not much later than this is a vertical inscription on a small pillar in the Roman Forum, and the Duenos inscription on a vase found near the Quirinal (a hill in Rome) probably dates to the 6th century BC. Although experts disagree on the dating of these objects, the inscriptions are generally considered to be the oldest extant examples of the Latin alphabet.

The classical Latin alphabet consisted of 23 letters, 21 of which were derived from the Etruscan alphabet. In medieval times the letter *I* was differentiated into *I* and *J* and *V* into *U, V,* and *W,* producing an alphabet equivalent to that of modern English with 26 letters. Some European languages currently using the Latin alphabet do not use the letters *K* and *W,* and some add extra letters (usually standard Latin letters with diacritical marks added or sometimes pairs of letters read as one sound).

In ancient Roman times there were two main types of Latin script, capital letters and cursive. There were also varieties of writing that mixed capitals and cursive or semicursive letters; Latin uncial script developed from such a mixed form in the 3rd century AD. In the Middle Ages many different Latin scripts developed from capital, cursive, and uncial forms. The round "humanistic" handwriting, used for copying books, and a more angular cursive script, used for legal and commercial purposes in 15th-century Italy, gave rise, respectively, to the roman and italic typefaces currently used in printing.

Latin America, the countries of South America and North America (including Central America and the islands of the Caribbean) whose inhabitants speak a Romance language. Most frequently the term Latin America is restricted to countries whose inhabitants speak either Spanish or Portuguese, but the French-speaking areas of Haiti, French Guiana, and the French West Indies may also be included.

A brief treatment of the history of Latin America follows. For full treatment, *see* MACROPAEDIA: Latin America, The History of. *See also* the following MACROPAEDIA articles: Pre-Columbian Civilizations; South America; Central America; West Indies; North America; as well as individual Latin American countries.

Human beings first entered the Western Hemisphere at least 20,000 years ago, probably from Siberia by way of Alaska. They spread over North and Central America, reached South America by way of the Isthmus of Panama, and eventually reached the tip of South America. Their cultures ranged from simple hunting and gathering societies to sophisticated civilizations such as those of the Aztec of central Mexico and the Inca of the central Andes. For all the indigenous peoples, however, contact with Europeans brought conquest and devastating epidemics.

Colonial period. The colonial era in Latin America and the Caribbean began in the late 15th century with the first voyages of discovery to the New World and ended in the 19th century with successful movements for independence from the European powers.

In search of a westward route to the spice-rich lands of Asia that was shorter than rounding the continent of Africa, the Genoese seafarer Christopher Columbus set out for the Indies in 1492 under Spanish royal patronage. The Caribbean islands of Cuba and Hispaniola, which he reached that year, became the proving grounds for methods of Spanish conquest and exploitation. About 1500 the explorer Amerigo Vespucci concluded that the so-called Indies were not part of eastern Asia but were in fact a new continent. A derivative of Vespucci's name, "America," was later applied to the entire New World, whose natives retained the (inaccurate) name "Indians."

The Spaniards soon conquered and settled the major islands of the Caribbean. In 1519 the Spanish conquistador Hernán Cortés led an expedition to the Mexican mainland. After brief struggles, many of the area's Indian peoples allied themselves with the Spaniards, who seized the Aztec leader Montezuma II and captured the island-capital of Tenochtitlán. Using tactics similar to those employed in the Caribbean and Mexico, conquistadores pushed to the north and south, and in 1532 Francisco Pizarro captured the emperor Atahuallpa and took over the Inca empire based in Peru. That same year the first Portuguese settlement was made in Brazil.

Spanish and Portuguese colonists sailed to the New World in increasing numbers to exploit its rich deposits of gold and silver. The basic economic unit in the new colonies was the encomienda, which was the Spanish crown's grant to a colonist of a group of Indians in a particular area. The Indians served the colonist with either labour or gold tribute, and in return he protected them. In actuality, the encomienda became a form of slavery that enriched the colonists while their Indian subjects were decimated through overwork and mistreatment. The main factor in the Indians' catastrophic population decline in the 16th century, however, was the spread of diseases of European origin to which the Indians had no immunity or resistance. Gradually a mestizo (mixed European and Indian) population emerged, and African slaves were imported—especially to Brazil, the Caribbean, and coastal regions—to replace the Indians. The decline of the Indian population left land vacant and reduced the flow of foodstuffs to the cities and mines, thereby stimulating the rapid growth of Spanish agricultural estates (haciendas) to produce grain and meat.

The political organization of Latin America reflected the centralized absolutist rule of Spain. The highest officials—*i.e.,* the members of the Council of the Indies, the viceroys, and the captains general—were all appointed by the crown. Latin America was organized into viceroyalties—those of New Spain, New Granada, Peru, Río de La Plata, and the (Portuguese) Viceroyalty of Brazil. Though formal power lay in the hands of royal officials, on the local level actual power was often exercised by large landowners. The Roman Catholic church established a widespread presence in Latin America, and some clergy led in the drive against the enslavement and mistreatment of the Indians.

Spain's technically backward economy could not supply its Latin American colonies with adequate manufactured goods, so they obtained such goods by exporting silver, sugar, coffee, cacao, tobacco, hides, and other commodities to the more advanced northern European nations. As the European demand for colonial products grew, economic activity was spurred by Spain's Bourbon kings, who widened trade connections and decentralized the governance of the colonies in the second half of the 18th century. These reforms brought material prosperity to the upper-class Creoles (*i.e.,* persons of Spanish descent who had been born in the Americas), who were nevertheless excluded from high church and state offices by native-born Spaniards.

The decentralizing reforms, the new commercial prosperity of the Creoles and their dissatisfaction with crown policies, the ideals of the Enlightenment, and most importantly, Napoleon's invasion of Spain and Portugal in 1807–08, catalyzed Latin Americans' desire for national independence. Following an unsuccessful rebellion in 1810–15, Mexico won its independence in 1820–21. In South America, Buenos Aires revolted in 1810 yet proved unable to win the support of outlying provinces. In 1817 forces under José de San Martín and Bernardo O'Higgins won independence for Chile, but San Martín's thrust into Peru stalled on the coast. In the north Simón Bolívar's early struggles (1812–16) met with defeat, but he won the crucial Battle of Boyacá in 1819 and the Battle of Carabobo in 1821, and with Antonio José de Sucre, he freed Ecuador the following year. San Martín resigned his command after a meeting with Bolivar, who then proceeded with the liberation of Peru and Upper Peru (Bolivia). In 1824 Sucre won the Battle of Ayacucho, and within two years the last of the Spanish loyalists in South America had been defeated. Brazil's independence was marked by far less violence. Fleeing Napoleon's army in 1808, Prince Regent John (later King John VI) transferred the royal court from Lisbon to Rio de Janeiro. When, at the end of the Napoleonic Wars, the king was obliged to return, he left Brazil in the hands of his son Dom Pedro, who oversaw the break with Portugal in 1822.

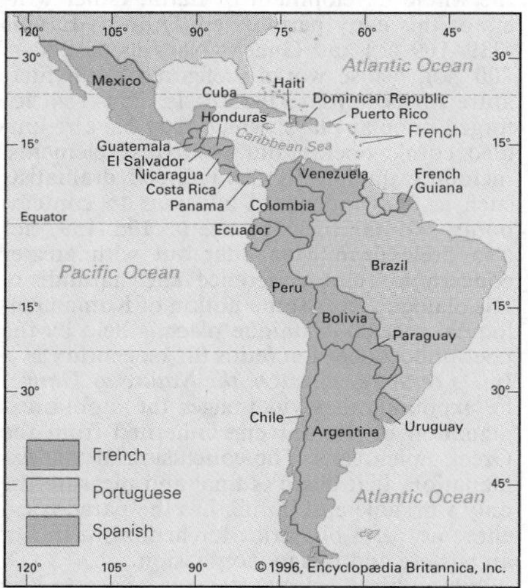

Romance languages of Latin America

Post-Independence. With the removal of the Spanish crown from the political arena, much of Latin America descended into political chaos. Federal republics were soon promulgated across the region, but few of their leaders evinced consistent respect for the often idealistic provisions of constitutions. Violent political bosses or military dictators (caudillos) rose to power across Latin America.

Creole elites were the greatest beneficiaries of independence. Despite the official abolition of caste systems, Indians and many mestizos saw only limited improvements. Slavery was outlawed in most areas by about 1850 but continued into the late 19th century in Cuba and Brazil.

After about 1850 the countries of Latin America began to pursue economic development even as they veered politically between oligarchic rule, dictatorship, and liberal republicanism. European investment capital financed the building of railroads that in turn greatly aided Latin America's export of its commodities. As development proceeded, the large landowners and other elites who depended on the thriving export economy increasingly tended to dominate politics. Regions of Brazil, Argentina, and Chile were transformed by the influx of large numbers of new immigrants from Europe.

In the first half of the 20th century, some Latin American nations, notably Argentina, Brazil, Chile, Mexico, Uruguay, and Costa Rica, achieved a measure of political stability as well as significant industrial growth; while others, such as Colombia, Bolivia, Peru, Ecuador, and the nations of Central America and the Caribbean, remained politically unstable and economically underdeveloped. The poorer countries' reliance on single-product exports, often managed by state-run companies, brought boom and bust periods depending on world markets. The United States became the dominant foreign influence on Latin America's political and economic affairs.

The decades after World War II were marked by a renewed tilt towards right-wing dictatorship in some Latin American countries, but with the end of the Cold War in the 1990s, a trend toward democratic rule reemerged. High rates of population growth were a major impediment to raising general standards of living and drove increasing numbers of landless labourers to burgeoning cities in search of work. In the 1990s many state-run industries were privatized, and efforts toward regional economic integration were accelerated.

Latin American Central of Workers, Spanish CENTRAL LATINOAMERICANA DE TRABAJADORES (CLAT), regional Christian Democrat trade union federation linked to the World Confederation of Labour. Its affiliated trade unions represent some 10,500,000 workers in more than 30 countries. From its founding in 1954 until 1971 it was known as the Latin American Christian Trade Union Federation (Confederación Latinoamericana Sindical Cristiana). Its origins can be traced to the efforts of the Roman Catholic church in Latin America to combat the rise of socialist ideas with its own ideology of Christian corporatism.

In 1978 the federation began to move away from its founding tenets to stress commitment to workers' control, participatory socialism, and human rights. However, rhetoric was often divorced from action, as with the affiliated Venezuelan Confederation of Autonomous Trade Unions, which collaborated with the Christian Democrats.

Latin American Integration Association, Spanish ASOCIACIÓN LATINOAMERICANA DE INTEGRACIÓN (ALADI), organization that was established by the Treaty of Montevideo (August 1980) and became operational in March 1981. It seeks economic cooperation among its 11 members—Argentina, Bolivia, Brazil, Chile, Colombia, Ecuador, Mexico, Paraguay, Peru, Uruguay, and Venezuela.

ALADI replaced the Latin American Free Trade Association (LAFTA; Asociación Latinoamericana de Libre Comercio), which had been established in 1960 with the aim of developing a common market in Latin America. The scheme made little progress, and ALADI was created with a more flexible and more limited role of encouraging free trade but with no timetable for the institution of a common market. Members approved the Regional Tariff Preference scheme in 1984 and expanded upon it in 1987 and 1990.

Latin-American literature, the body of writings produced in the Spanish-speaking countries of the Western Hemisphere and in Portuguese-speaking Brazil. It also includes the literary expression—the poetry, theatre, and mythicohistorical writing—of the advanced American Indian civilizations encountered by the Spanish conquistadores.

A brief treatment of Latin-American literature follows. For full treatment, *see* MACROPAEDIA: Latin-American Literature.

Among the earliest works of Latin-American literature are the soldierly reports and historiographical writings of the men who participated in the discovery, conquest, and settlement of the New World. Notable examples of such first-hand accounts include the vividly written dispatches of Hernán Cortés and Bernal Díaz del Castillo's unpolished yet colourful chronicle of the conquest of Mexico. Reflecting the Renaissance predilection for narrative literature of a heroic mold, many of the later, more cultivated Spanish soldiers of fortune chronicled their adventures and deeds in epic poems. The finest work of this type was Alonso de Ercilla y Zúñiga's *La Araucana* (1569–89; *The Araucaniad*), a historical poem depicting the struggle between the Spaniards and Araucanian Indians of Chile. The Portuguese colonization of Brazil yielded quite a different kind of literature; much of the writings of the Portuguese explorers and missionaries were devoted to describing and extolling the beauty and virtues of the new land.

As Latin-American colonial society stabilized during the 16th and 17th centuries, close ties with the European homeland promoted the development of parallel literary trends. The epic was supplanted by satire and lyric poetry. The latter consisted largely of uninspired imitations of the Spanish Baroque poet Luis de Góngora y Argote, but a few works, such as the simple poems of religious and profane love by the Mexican nun Sor Juana Inés de la Cruz, displayed genuine literary merit. French customs and letters and the ideas of the French Revolution became highly influential in the 1700s. The fervent spirit of the Latin-American revolutionary wars (1808–24) found expression in patriotic odes and heroic verse, such as those of José Joaquín Olmedo and José Mariá Heredia.

By the mid-1800s, the Romantic movement had spread to all the new Latin-American republics. For their subject matter, the Romantics turned to native scenes and local types, as for example the Indian, the gaucho of the Pampas (horseman of the southern plains), and the *sertanejo* (man of the backlands) of northeastern Brazil. These motifs continued to hold sway in subsequent literature, giving rise to such distinctively Latin-American literary genres as the gaucho literature of the River Plate region and the *Indianista* novel of Brazil. Another indigenous literary form that developed around midcentury was *costumbrismo,* poetically realistic sketches of manners and customs depicting varied aspects of contemporary life in provincial regions. *Costumbrismo* later evolved into the realistic novel of manners, which focused on social problems rather than on the picturesque.

In the late 1870s, there emerged throughout much of Latin America a literary movement known as Modernismo, or Modernism. This movement, which reached its apex under the leadership of the Nicaraguan poet Rubén Darío, promoted the doctrine of "art for art's sake" and embraced as its ideals the beautiful, the exotic, and the refined, amalgamating many diverse trends both native and European (*e.g.,* Symbolism, Parnassianism, and Decadentism).

The horrors of the Mexican Revolution (1910–20) awakened among Latin-American writers an intense social consciousness. Rejecting the modernist literature of artistic escape, they produced prose fiction that focused on the mistreatment and plight of the masses—the Indian, the black man, the mestizo peasant, and the poor city worker. Examples of this form of writing include Mariano Azuela's *Los de abajo* (1915; *The Under Dogs*) and Jorge Icaza's *Huasipungo* (1934; *The Villagers*). In poetry César Vallejo, Pablo Neruda, and others created pieces that combined sociopolitical concerns with daring innovations in verse forms and imagery. In drama, significant attempts at experimentation and renovation were undertaken, particularly in Mexico and Brazil, during the late 1920s and '30s under the influence of movements ranging from Expressionism to the Theatre of the Absurd.

Latin-American literature in the last half of the 20th century has become more universal in its themes and symbols and has fully entered the mainstream of Western literature. It has exhibited an increased preoccupation with philosophical questioning—with the problem of modern man as the victim of alienating forces, solitude, existential despair, and evil. Also evident is an enduring fascination with psychological analysis and magic realism—the interplay of reality and fantasy or dream. Such are particularly characteristic of the prose fiction of a host of contemporary authors, including Jorge Luis Borges, Eduardo Mallea, Julio Cortázar, Gabriel García Márquez, and Isabel Allende.

Latin Averroism, the teachings of a number of Western Christian philosophers who, in the later Middle Ages and during the Renaissance, drew inspiration from the interpretation of Aristotle put forward by Averroës, a Muslim philosopher. The basic tenet of Latin Averroism was the assertion that reason and philosophy are superior to faith and knowledge founded on faith. The Latin Averroists, represented in Paris by John of Jandun and in Italy by Taddeo of Parma and Angelo of Arezzo, also held that the creation of matter and of spirits was necessary and eternal and that there is but one "intellective soul" for all of humanity (thereby denying individual personality and immortality). They espoused also psychological determinism, which precluded moral responsibility.

Latin-Faliscan languages, language group proposed by some scholars to be included in the Italic branch of Indo-European languages. The group includes Latin, which emanated from Rome, and Faliscan, spoken in the Falerii district in southeastern Etruria. Closely related to Latin, Faliscan is known from a few short inscriptions written in the Etruscan alphabet. The other subdivision of Italic is the Osco-Umbrian languages.

Latin language, Latin LINGUA LATINA, Indo-European language belonging to the Italic group; it is the language ancestral to the modern Romance languages.

A brief treatment of the Latin language follows. For full treatment, *see* MACROPAEDIA: Languages of the World: *Romance languages*.

Originally spoken by small groups of people living along the lower Tiber River, Latin spread with the increase of Roman political power, first throughout Italy and then throughout most of western and southern Europe and the central and western Mediterranean coastal regions of Africa. The modern Romance languages developed from the spoken Latin of various parts of the Roman Empire. During the Middle Ages and until comparatively recent times, Latin was the language most widely used in the West for scholarly and literary purposes. Until the latter part of the 20th century its use was required in the liturgy of the Roman Catholic church.

The oldest example of Latin extant, perhaps dating to the 7th century BC, consists of a four-word inscription in Greek characters on a cloak pin; this text shows the preservation of full vowels in unstressed syllables in contrast to the language in later times, which has reduced vowels. Early Latin had a stress accent on the first syllable of a word, in contrast to the Latin of the republican and imperial periods, in which the accent fell on either the next or second to the last syllable of a word.

Latin of the Classical period had six regularly used cases in the declension of nouns and adjectives (nominative, vocative, genitive, dative, accusative, ablative), with traces of a locative case in some declensional classes of nouns. Except for the *i*-stem and consonant stem declensional classes, which it combines into one group (listed in grammar books as the third declension), Latin kept distinct most of the declensional classes inherited from Indo-European.

During the Classical period there were at least three types of Latin in use: Classical written Latin, Classical oratorical Latin, and the ordinary colloquial Latin used by the average speaker of the language. Spoken Latin continued to change, and it diverged more and more from the Classical norms in grammar, pronunciation, and vocabulary. During the Classical and immediate post-Classical periods, numerous inscriptions provide the major source for spoken Latin, but, after the 3rd century AD, many texts in a popular style, usually called Vulgar Latin, were written. Such writers as St. Jerome and St. Augustine, however, in the late 4th and early 5th centuries, wrote good literary Late Latin.

Subsequent development of Latin continued in two ways. First, the language developed on the basis of local spoken forms and evolved into the modern Romance languages and dialects. Second, the language continued in a more or less standardized form throughout the Middle Ages as the language of religion and scholarship; in this form it had great influence on the development of the West European languages. *See also* Vulgar Latin.

Latin League, originally a confederation of about 30 villages and tribes in the neighbourhood of ancient Rome that joined for mutual protection and defense against hostile adjoining communities. The city of Alba Longa, the leader of this federation, was the site of religious ceremonies, which included worship of Jupiter on the Alban Mount. It was also the place where league members assembled to dispense justice.

Rome first entered into an alliance with the league about 493 BC for mutual defense. As Rome gained territory the political power of the league diminished. Their treaty was renewed in 358 BC with changes that secured Rome's leadership. This led to an outbreak of war from which Rome emerged victorious in 338 BC, when the Latin League was dissolved.

Latin literature, the body of writings in Latin, primarily produced during the Roman republic and empire, when Latin was a spoken language, and also during the medieval and Renaissance periods, when it was used as a language of ritual, scholarship, and officialdom.

It has been said that the development of ancient, or classic, Latin literature was determined by its dependence on Greek originals, but this is only partly true. From an early stage a quality of "Latinity" asserted itself, and part of the beauty and vigour of Latin literature arises from the fusion of Greek elements with that robust native element. When the 1st-century BC poet Virgil forged out of the Latin language an instrument as subtle and polished as the poetry used in the *Aeneid,* he did not discard its pristine qualities such as the percussive alliteration that is met, in cruder form, in 3rd-century BC poets.

It was the Greeks, however, who bequeathed most of the genres of literature produced by the Romans: epic, drama, lyric and other personal types of poetry, history, oratory, and philosophy. To these the Romans added satire (literally "a medley") and a forerunner of the novel.

A brief treatment of Latin literature follows. For full treatment, *see* MACROPAEDIA: Latin Literature.

Ancient. Given the pattern of Roman dependence on Greek culture, it is not surprising that the first significant Latin writer, Lucius Livius Andronicus (*c.* 284–*c.* 204 BC), was a Greek, a freed slave from the Greek colony of Tarentum. Among other things, he translated Homer's *Odyssey* into Latin. From the fragments that survive it appears that he drew imaginatively on the latent resources of the Latin language to coin equivalents for Homer's immense vocabulary. This influenced the whole development of Latin. Other writers of this early period were Quintus Ennius (239–169 BC) and Gnaeus Naevius (*c.* 270–*c.* 200 BC), whose works prefigured Latin literature in its heyday. Plautus (*c.* 254–184 BC) forged popular plays, which may have resembled comic operas, out of diverse elements, including quotations from Greek dramatists such as Menander and allusions to contemporary Roman life. Terence (*c.* 195–159? BC) also drew from Menander but with greater concern for plot coherence and naturalism. His dialogue gives some notion of Roman colloquial speech. A unique place is held by the poet-philosopher Lucretius (fl. 1st century BC). In *De rerum natura* (*On the Nature of Things*) he expounds in vivid images the atomic explanation of the universe inherited from the Greek Epicureans. The conclusion of that explanation, that death is final and pleasure the only workable end in life, has the paradoxical effect not of a blueprint for hedonism but of an austere and melancholy vision.

Philosophical eclecticism was characteristic of Cicero (106–43 BC), a politician, advocate, orator, voluminous letter writer, theorist on an encyclopaedic scale, and skilled versifier (though hardly a poet). He left works that form the largest single source for the history and culture of republican Rome. In the *Commentaries* of Julius Caesar (100–44 BC), a propagandistic treatment of his conquest of Gaul is veiled in a clear, low-key style.

From the time of the effective acquisition of power in the Roman world in 31 BC by Octavian (later the emperor Augustus), Latin literature was conditioned by the necessity for a writer, if he was to remain active (or even alive and in possession of his property), somehow to adapt to the regime. For a number of writers this meant entering powerful coteries, such as that of the wealthy and adroitly diplomatic Gaius Maecenas (*c.* 70–8 BC). During the republic it had been possible for writers to criticize public figures with impunity, and Gaius Valerius Catullus (*c.* 84–*c.* 54 BC) had attacked both Caesar and Pompey in his poems. He was an emotional and outspoken writer, ranging from exquisite sensibility to scabrous comment. No later writer surpassed his sheer technical brilliance.

It is, however, Virgil (70–19 BC) who is preeminent in Latin poetry. He enjoyed the patronage of Augustus, but before writing his epic, the *Aeneid,* in which discreet lip service to emperor worship is discernible, he wrote other works such as the Eclogues, consisting of ten pastorals modeled on the Greek *Idylls* of Theocritus, and the highly wrought *Georgics*. Virgil also introduced to Maecenas' circle Horace (65–8 BC)—the refinement, humour, and inventiveness of whose *Odes, Epodes,* and *Satires* made him one of the most important poets of his day. Perhaps from policy, his poetry conceals as much as it reveals: his invectives are not addressed to real persons, nor are his love poems. A quality of humanity pervades them, however, and Horace is often taken to exemplify Roman *humanitas* (the civilized virtues). The urbane Ovid (43 BC–AD 17) was less discreet than Horace and was banished by Augustus to a cultural backwater on the Black Sea. Of his many works the one that most influenced posterity was the epic *Metamorphoses,* a long series of transformation stories.

An equally vivid storyteller, in a different genre, was the historian Livy (59 BC–AD 17), whose compendious history of Rome reflected an admiration for the traditional values of early Rome and the hope that Augustus might restore some of them. Livy's reconstruction of past events was masterly, but his stylistic vagaries were criticized by some contemporaries as provincial. The real horrors of the dynastic succession initiated by Augustus were eventually described by the historian Tacitus (*c.* AD 56–*c.* 120) in a vigorous and ironical style. Suetonius (*c.* AD 69–after 122) made undiscriminating use of gossip but did have some good sources (such as Augustus' letters) for his biographies of the emperors. The genre of natural history was represented by Pliny the Elder (AD 23–79), who died in the pursuit of science, going too near the fumes of the erupting Vesuvius.

The gloom of the historian Tacitus had reflected a moral viewpoint—namely, that virtue was possible but had failed because of inertia and corruption. Another moralist, the poet Juvenal (50/65–after 127), reacted to Rome's moral decay by bitterly attacking it in his *Satires* with clinical accuracy. His poetry is frequently indecent, as are the epigrams of his friend Martial (38/41–*c.* 103).

Although the Romans did not consciously invent the novel, the foundations were laid in the long, rambling, and mesmerizing narrative called the *Satyricon,* written in the 1st century AD by Petronius Arbiter, about the adventures of a couple of disreputable young men. What survives is only a portion of what must have been a work of immense length. It is interlaced with quotations, sometimes in Greek, and gives some notion of ordinary colloquial Latin speech (though possibly not that of polite society). Though quickly lost sight of in antiquity, the *Satyricon* reemerged in comparatively modern times.

Medieval. The rise to dominion of Christianity in the 4th century and the conquest of Rome by barbarian tribes in the late 5th century produced a basic shift in the institutional foundations of Latin literature. Whereas previously the governing classes of the Roman Empire, based in the cultural metropolis of Rome, had ensured the continued use of Latin, now it was the Christian church that insured its survival, if only as a language of liturgy and theological and historical scholarship. Latin henceforth came to be preserved as a literature in the monasteries and cathedral schools of western Europe, which during the Middle Ages formed the major and at times the only means for the transmission of classical texts and the culture they described. Christian Latin literature began in the growing Christian communities in the West, particularly the Roman province of Africa. The literary language was enriched by a new vocabulary conditioned by Christian needs. The Old Latin versions of the Bible as well as the idioms of everyday speech were influential. A group of 3rd- and 4th-century African writers—Tertullian, Minucius Felix, Cyprian, Arnobius, and Lactantius—were the creators of Christian Latin literature.

In *De doctrina christiana* Augustine discussed the Christian acceptance of the secular methods of the schools, while pointing out that the "lowly style" of the Scriptures contained a rhetoric of its own. The same problem had tormented Jerome, but in the Vulgate (his translation of the Bible), which was to be influential throughout the Middle Ages, he produced a model of Christian Latin. The devices of rhetoric were employed in religious themes by a host of poets; such were Juvencus, Sedulius, Avitus of Vienne, Arator, Blossius Aemilius Dracontius, Prudentius, and Paulinus of Nola. Christian history in the West was represented by Tyrannius Rufinus, Sulpicius Severus, and Paulus Orosius. Two pagan writers of the 5th century, Ambrosius Theodosius Macrobius and Martianus Minneus Felix Capella, exercised for centuries a great influence in the schools. The most original literary creation of the 4th century was the Latin Christian hymn. Hilary of Poitiers composed hymns, and St. Ambrose's compositions formed the core of later hymnals.

To the 6th century and to the period of Ostrogothic rule in Italy belong Boethius and Cassiodorus. The former had a profound influence on the literature and philosophy of the Middle Ages, and the latter laid down a program of study that was followed for centuries. Ennodius and Maximian display in their verse the still persistent secularism of the Italian schools. The Lombard invasions had disastrous results for Italian culture, but Gregory the Great, whose writings reflect at once his genius and the decay of learning, by sending Augustine to convert the English brought a new people into the orbit of Latin culture.

Latin literature in England began in the 7th century with Aldhelm, bishop of Sherborne, whose prose and verse show the mingled influences of the Irish tradition and of the new learning from Rome. The Venerable Bede, whose ecclesiastical history is a source of the first order, is the most conspicuous representative of this revival. His scheme of studies, based on the seven arts, was carried over to the school of York from which Alcuin went to be master of the palace school at Aachen and the most prominent figure in the Carolingian revival of learning.

The Carolingian period (8th–9th century) saw a revival of Latin letters under the enlightened leadership of Charlemagne. The scholar Alcuin and the poet Theodulf of Orléans were the most prominent literary figures at this time, writing historical and biographical works and composing both sacred and profane verse in a variety of metres.

The age of monasteries was followed in the 12th century by that of the cathedral schools, the precursors of the universities. Under Gerbert at Reims and Fulbert at Chartres a wider range of studies was established, with a more intelligent devotion to the authors. Bernard Silvestris and Alain of Lille were influential Platonists.

The *Historia regum Britanniae* by Geoffrey of Monmouth (d. 1155) had an unprecedented success in a century that took a great interest in romantic tales. At the same time, there was an immense growth of historical writing by such authors as Sigebert of Gembloux, Guibert of Nogent, Orderic Vitalis, William of Malmesbury, Suger of St. Denis, Otto of Freising, William of Tyre, Saxo Grammaticus, and, later, Matthew Paris.

The most original poetical creation of the Latin Middle Ages was the sequence, sung between the epistle and the gospel at the Mass. Beginning as poetical prose, it had as its most famous exponent the 9th-century Notker Balbulus of St. Gall. By the 12th century, it had developed into an elaborate rhymed and rhythmical composition, reaching its perfection in the sequences of Adam of St. Victor.

From the late 11th century onward there was a growing stream of devotional and religious writing. Anselm of Canterbury put his *Monologion, Proslogion,* and *Cur deus homo* into literary form, and his prayers gave a great impulse to the movement of personal devotion, to which belong Bernard of Clairvaux, William of St. Thierry, and Aelred of Rievaulx. The meditations of Guigo are unparalleled in medieval Latin literature, while Hugh of St. Victor and Richard of St. Victor represent a conservative theology. Devotional literature culminates in England in Richard Rolle of Hampole and, on the continent of Europe, in Thomas à Kempis.

Renaissance. The term Renaissance Latin is associated with Dante, Petrarch, Giovanni Boccaccio, Albertino Mussato, Coluccio Salutati, Leonardo Bruni, and Aeneas Silvius Piccolomini (Pope Pius II). In verse there was a return to classical models. In prose, Latin was still a necessary medium for the abundant literature—humanistic, historical, scientific, philosophical, and religious—of the age.

In Italy the three major centres of learning in the 15th and 16th centuries were Florence, Rome, and Naples. Poggio Bracciolini, Marsilio Ficino, Giovanni Pico della Mirandola, Politian, and Francesco Landini belonged to the Florentine circle. In Rome were Pietro Bembo, Giovanni Cotta, Marco Vida, and many others. At the court of Naples Giovanni Pontano was preeminent. Battista Spagnoli (Mantovano), general of the Carmelite order, was a prodigious composer of verse whose eclogues were widely read. In the Renaissance centuries the pastoral was a favourite genre.

Succeeding centuries after the Renaissance saw the continued use of Latin in scholarship, but its purely literary use gradually declined. Until the early 18th century, Latin was still the international language for historical and scientific studies. But by that time it had completely ceased to be used for literary or artistic purposes, having been utterly supplanted by the vernacular languages of western Europe.

Latin rights (Roman law): *see* jus Latii.

Latina, city, capital of Latina *provincia,* Lazio (Latium) *regione,* south-central Italy, 40 miles (64 km) southeast of Rome. Built in 1932 as the first centre of the newly reclaimed Agro Pontino (*see* Pontine Marshes), it became the provincial capital when Latina province was formed from Roma province in 1934. Both the town and the province were known as Littoria until 1947. Latina has a beet-sugar refinery, a fruit and vegetable cannery, and glass factories. There is a nuclear-power station nearby. Pop. (1989 est.) mun., 100,663; province, 470,784.

Latini, Brunetto (b. *c.* 1220, Florence? [Italy]—d. 1294, Florence), Florentine scholar who helped disseminate ideas that were fundamental to the development of early Italian poetry. He was a member of the Guelph party

Latini (left), detail of the fresco "Il Paradiso" attributed to Giotto; in the Museo Nazionale, Florence

Alinari—Art Resource/EB Inc.

and a leading figure in the political life of Florence.

After the defeat of the Guelphs at Montaperti (1260), Latini went into exile in France but returned to Tuscany in 1266, holding public office for about 20 years from 1267 and becoming famous as a master of rhetoric. Between 1262 and 1266 he wrote a prose encyclopaedia in French, *Li Livres dou Trésor,* and an abridged version in Italian verse called the *Tesoretto.* His works profoundly influenced the young Dante, and, although he is depicted in the *Inferno* (XV, 30–124) as condemned for sodomy, the poet addresses him with great respect.

Latino sine Flexione (language): *see* Interlingua.

Latinus, in Roman legend, king of the aborigines in Latium and eponymous hero of the Latin race. He was believed to be either the son of the Greek hero Odysseus and the enchantress Circe or the son of the Roman god Faunus and the nymph Marica. Latinus was a shadowy personality who was perhaps invented to explain the origin of Rome and its relations with Latium.

According to the *Aeneid,* the hero Aeneas landed at the mouth of the Tiber River and was welcomed by Latinus, the peaceful ruler whose daughter Lavinia he ultimately married.

latissimus dorsi, widest and most powerful muscle of the back. It is a large, flat, triangular muscle covering the lower back. It arises from the lower half of the vertebral column and iliac crest (hipbone) and tapers to a rounded tendon inserted at (attached to) the front of the upper part of the humerus (upper-arm bone).

The action of the latissimus dorsi draws the upper arm downward and backward and rotates it inward, as exemplified in the downstroke in swimming the crawl. In climbing it joins with the abdominal and pectoral muscles to pull the trunk upward. The two latissimus dorsi muscles also assist in forced respiration by raising the lower ribs.

latite, also called TRACHYANDESITE, extrusive igneous rock very abundant in western North America. Usually coloured white, yellowish, pinkish, or gray, it is the volcanic equivalent of monzonite (*q.v.*). Latites contain plagioclase feldspar (andesine or oligoclase) as large, single crystals (phenocrysts) in a fine-grained matrix of orthoclase feldspar and augite. They also contain phenocrysts of diopside, and sometimes biotite and hornblende; accessory minerals include apatite, zircon, leucite, and magnetite. Latites are chemically intermediate to trachytes and andesites; when the matrix contains considerable quartz, the rock is transitional to dacite.

latitude and longitude, coordinate system by means of which the position or location of any place on the Earth's surface can be determined and described.

Latitude is a measurement on a globe or map of location north or south of the Equator. Technically there are different kinds of latitude—geographic, astronomical, and geocentric—but there are only minor differences between them. In most common references, geographic latitude (the kind used in mapping) is implied. Given in degrees, minutes, and seconds, geographic latitude is the arc subtended by an angle at the centre of the Earth and measured in a north-south plane poleward from the Equator. Thus, a point at 30°15′20″ N subtends an angle of 30°15′20″ at the centre of the globe; similarly, the arc between the Equator and either geographic pole is 90° (one-fourth the circumference of the Earth, or $\frac{1}{4} \times 360°$), and thus the greatest possible latitudes are 90° N and 90° S. As aids to indicate different latitudinal positions on maps or globes, equidistant circles are plotted and drawn parallel to the Equator and each other; they are known as parallels, or parallels of latitude.

Different methods are used to determine geographic latitude, as by taking angle-sights on certain polar stars or by measuring with a sextant the angle of the noon Sun above the horizon. The length of a degree of arc of latitude is approximately 111 km (69 miles), varying, because of the nonuniformity of the Earth's curvature, from 110.567 km (68.706 miles) at the Equator to 111.699 km (69.41 miles) at the poles.

Perspective of the globe with grid formed by parallels of latitude and meridians of longitude

Longitude is a measurement of location east or west of the prime meridian at Greenwich, the specially designated imaginary north-south line that passes through both geographic poles and Greenwich, London. Measured also in degrees, minutes, and seconds, longitude is the amount of arc created by drawing first a line from the centre of the Earth to the intersection of the Equator and the prime meridian and then another line from the centre of the Earth to any point elsewhere on the Equator. Longitude is measured 180° both east and west of the prime meridian. As aids to locate longitudinal positions on a globe or map, meridians are plotted and drawn from pole to pole where they meet. The distance per degree of longitude at the Equator is about 111.32 km (69.18 miles) and at the poles, 0.

The combination of meridians of longitude and parallels of latitude establishes a framework or grid by means of which exact positions can be determined in reference to the prime meridian and the Equator: a point described as 40° N, 30° W, for example, is located 40° of arc north of the Equator and 30° of arc west of the Greenwich meridian.

latitudinarian, any of the 17th-century Anglican clerics whose beliefs and practices were viewed by conservatives as unorthodox or, at best, heterodox. After first being applied to the Cambridge Platonists, the term was later used to categorize churchmen who depended upon reason to establish the moral certainty of Christian doctrines rather than argument from tradition. Limiting that doctrine to what had to be accepted, they allowed for latitude on other teachings. The Latitudinarians thus became the precursors of the similar Broad Church (*q.v.*) movement in the 19th-century Church of England.

Latium, ancient area in west-central Italy, originally limited to the territory around the Alban Hills, but extending by about 500 BC south of the Tiber River as far as the promontory of Mount Circeo. It was bounded on the northwest by Etruria, on the southeast by Campania, on the east by Samnium, and on the northeast by the territory of the Sabini, Aequi, and Marsi. The modern region of Lazio extends farther to include the entire coastal plain between the Fiora River in the north and Garigliano River in the south and is bounded by the Apennines on the east. The history of Latium is inseparable from the destiny of ancient Rome.

The Latins (or Latini) were sprung from those Indo-European tribes that, during the 2nd millennium BC, came to settle in the Italian peninsula. By the first centuries of the 1st millennium BC, the Latins had developed as a separate people, originally established on the mass of the Alban Hills, which was isolated and easy to defend. The Latin tribes that settled there were influenced both by the civilization of the Iron Age of southern Italy and by the Villanovan civilization of southern Etruria. The Latins cremated their dead and deposited their ashes in urns of Villanovan type as well as in hut-shaped urns that were faithful imitations of the huts of the living. The decoration of these funerary containers is of a simple geometric type, similar to that engraved on bronze objects found in these tombs, such as razors, spindles, weapons, and brooches. The material used for the tombs in the Alban Hills resembles the material found in contemporary tombs in Rome but is occasionally rougher and coarser in appearance.

In approximately 600 BC, when the Etruscans occupied Latium and settled in Rome, the influence of Etruscan civilization and art made itself felt as much in the other Latin towns as in Rome itself. But Rome soon became a large city, similar to the powerful cities of southern Etruria, and it took precedence over its neighbours. According to the annalistic tradition, it was a specifically Roman uprising that drove the Etruscans from Rome in 509. In fact it was a coalition of Latins and Greeks that led to the Etruscans' withdrawal from Latium in 475 BC.

After the departure of the Etruscans the fortunes of Latium changed; it became impoverished. Rome lost its preeminence over the neighbouring cities and took a long time to recover it. Throughout the 5th century BC the Latin League imposed its policy on Rome. Every year the delegates of the Latin cities elected a dictator who commanded a federal army, which included Roman troops. In this league Tusculum seemed to exercise the leadership that Rome had held in the Etruscan period. The territory of Rome did not extend beyond the sixth mile from the city.

The Latin people were threatened by the proximity of turbulent peoples: the Volsci, who dwelt in Antium, and the Aequi, who ruled Praeneste and Tibur. The legendary story of Coriolanus shows how, in the early 5th century BC, Rome began to extend its territory toward the south by fighting on the side of Ardea and Aricia against the Volsci. At the end of the 5th century Roman colonies were established in the Monti Lepini. In the 4th century BC Rome began to take precedence among the sister cities of Latium, weakened by their dissensions. In 358 BC, however, Rome and the Latin confederacy concluded a treaty of alliance on a basis of equality. They nominated in turn the dictator of the league. But the strength of Rome grew, and it established two tribes in Volscian territory. In 340 war broke out between Rome and the Latins. It ended in 338 in the defeat of the Latins and the dissolution of their league. The Latin cities were given political statutes that limited or abolished their autonomy. Thereafter Roman hegemony in Latium was an accomplished fact, and the life of the Latin country was soon modeled on that of the city.

Latium (Italy): *see* Lazio.

Latona (Greek mythology): *see* Leto.

Latour, Maurice Quentin de (French painter): *see* La Tour, Maurice-Quentin de.

Latreille, Pierre-André (b. Nov. 29, 1762, Brive-la-Gaillarde, France—d. Feb. 6, 1833, Paris), French zoologist and Roman Catholic priest, father of modern entomology, who achieved the first detailed classification of crustaceans and insects.

Although he was a devoted student of natural history, Latreille was educated for the priesthood and was ordained in Paris in 1786. Publication of his *Précis des caractères génériques des insectes disposés dans un ordre naturel* (1796; "Summary of the Generic Characteristics of Insects, Arranged in a Natural Order") marked the beginnings of modern entomology, the scientific study of insects. It also brought him the position of head of the entomology department at the National Museum of Natural History, Paris (1799). In this capacity Latreille published many works, among them *Histoire naturelle générale et particulière des crustacés et insectes*, 14 vol. (1802–05; "Comprehensive Natural History of Crustaceans and Insects"). In 1829 he succeeded Jean Lamarck as professor of zoology in crustaceans, arachnids, and insects at the National Museum of Natural History.

Latreille, detail of an engraving after a portrait, 1823
H. Roger-Viollet

Latrobe, Benjamin (Henry) (b. May 1, 1764, Fulneck, near Leeds, Yorkshire, Eng.—d. Sept. 3, 1820, New Orleans, La., U.S.), British-born architect and civil engineer who established architecture as a profession in the United States. Latrobe was the most original proponent of the Greek Revival style in American building.

Latrobe attended the Moravian college at Niesky, Saxony, and traveled in France and Italy, acquiring a knowledge of advanced French architecture. After returning to England in 1784, he studied with the Neoclassical architect Samuel Pepys Cockerell. Latrobe may also have studied engineering under John Smeaton, a well-known civil engineer. Having begun his own practice about 1790, Latrobe designed Hammerwood Lodge, Sussex, which shows his subsequent combinations of bold geometric forms with classical details.

Latrobe emigrated in 1795 to the United States, where his first important work was the State Penitentiary in Richmond, Va. (1797–98; demolished 1927). Latrobe then moved to Philadelphia and in 1798 received the commission for his Bank of Pennsylvania, whose Ionic porticoes inspired countless imitations; the building is now considered the first monument of the Greek Revival in America. It is clear, however, that Latrobe did not feel himself confined by styles, as his Sedgeley House, Philadelphia, built about the same time, is thought of as the first Gothic Revival structure in the United States.

The Basilica of the Assumption of the Blessed Virgin Mary, Baltimore, by Benjamin Latrobe, begun 1805
Sandak, Inc.

In Richmond, Latrobe had met Thomas Jefferson, who, in 1803, made him surveyor of the public buildings of the United States. In this post Latrobe inherited the task of completing the U.S. Capitol in Washington, D.C. In the House of Representatives and the Senate chambers, he incorporated American floral motifs—corn cobs, tobacco leaves—into the classical scheme. His Supreme Court Chamber (designed 1806–07) in the Capitol is a notably original American classical interior.

Latrobe's most famous work is the Basilica of the Assumption of the Blessed Virgin Mary, the Roman Catholic cathedral of Baltimore (begun 1805), a severe, beautifully proportioned structure slightly marred by the onion-shaped domes added, after Latrobe's death, to the towers above the portico.

Latrobe was also active as an engineer, especially in the design of waterworks. His more inventive schemes, involving engines, steamboats, and similar projects, brought him to financial ruin. While supervising his waterworks project for New Orleans, Latrobe contracted yellow fever and died. Latrobe set high standards of design and technical competence that were adopted by his foremost pupils, Robert Mills and William Strickland.

Latrobe Valley, Latrobe also spelled LA TROBE, river valley in southeastern Victoria, Australia. It is one of the most important economic areas in the state.

The Latrobe River rises in the Eastern Highlands near Mount Baw Baw in the Gippsland district. Flowing in a southeasterly direction, it passes the cities of Moe and Yallourn, where it turns to flow almost directly east, past Traralgon. The Latrobe is joined by its main tributaries, the Thomson and Macalister rivers, near Sale, 6 miles (10 km) from where it enters Lake Wellington, one of the Gippsland lakes. Originally called the Glengarry, the 70-mile- (112-kilometre-) long river was renamed to honour Charles La Trobe, first lieutenant governor of Victoria. The seasonal variations in its flow are marked.

Near the river's mouth, agriculture—primarily dairying—is the main economic activity. Farther west, the middle Latrobe Valley has one of the world's largest deposits of brown coal; it has been exploited since 1919. There are large thermal power stations at Yallourn, Morwell, and Hazelwood, all fueled by coal, and briquettes are produced. The valley also has some forestry, which supplies its wood pulp and paper mills, and there is a plant that processes natural gas.

Latter-day Saints, Church of Jesus Christ of, the largest denomination of the Mormon religion. *See* Mormon.

Latter Day Saints, Reorganized Church of Jesus Christ of: *see* Reorganized Church of Jesus Christ of Latter Day Saints.

Latter Rain revival, early name for the Pentecostal movement within U.S. Protestantism; it began in the late 19th and early 20th centuries in Tennessee and North Carolina and took its name from the "latter rain" referred to in Joel 2:23. The Bible passage states that the former (fall) rain and latter (spring) rain were poured down from God. These rains marked the beginning and end of the Jewish harvest. According to Pentecostal interpretation, the "former rain" referred to speaking in tongues during the first Christian Pentecost, when the Holy Spirit was poured down on the followers of Christ, and the "latter rain" referred to a second period, when people would again receive the Holy Spirit and speak in tongues as a sign that the Second Coming of Christ would soon occur.

Lattes, C.M.G., in full CÉSARE MANSUETO GIULIO LATTES (b. July 11, 1924, Curitiba, Brazil), Brazilian physicist who, with American physicist Eugene Gardner, in 1948 confirmed the existence of heavy and light mesons formed during the bombardment of carbon nuclei with alpha particles.

Lattes studied at the University of São Paulo with Giuseppe Occhialini in the 1940s and accompanied him in 1946 to the University of Bristol, where with Cecil Frank Powell they demonstrated that the two types of mesons could be identified by tracks left on photographic plates exposed to cosmic rays atop a mountain in the Bolivian Andes. Lattes became a full professor at the University of São Paulo in 1948 and also taught at the University of Brazil after 1948 and, in the 1950s, as a research associate in the United States.

Lattimore, Owen (b. July 29, 1900, Washington, D.C., U.S.—d. May 31, 1989, Providence, R.I.), American sinologist, a victim of McCarthyism in the 1950s.

The brother of poet Richmond Lattimore, Owen Lattimore spent much of his childhood in China, where his father was a teacher. From 1926 he was engaged in research and writing, traveling throughout Mongolia, Sinkiang, and Manchuria. He was director of the Page School of International Relations at Johns Hopkins University in Baltimore, Md., from 1939 to 1953 and was a lecturer at Johns Hopkins from 1938 to 1963. In 1963–70 he was director of the Department of Chinese Studies at the University of Leeds, Eng.

In 1950 Senator Joseph McCarthy accused Lattimore of being a Soviet espionage agent. A Senate committee exonerated him later that year, but the investigation was revived by the Senate Internal Security subcommittee, and in 1952 he was indicted for perjury in connection with testimony that he had given before the subcommittee. In 1955 the Justice Department dropped all charges against him.

Fluent in Chinese, Russian, and Mongol, Lattimore was regarded as a leading expert on the China-Russia frontier. He published many books on Asia and an account of the McCarthy episode, *Ordeal by Slander* (1950).

Lattimore, Richmond, in full RICHMOND ALEXANDER LATTIMORE (b. May 6, 1906, Paotingfu, China—d. Feb. 26, 1984, Rosemont, Pa., U.S.), American poet and translator renowned for his disciplined yet poetic translations of Greek classics.

Lattimore graduated from Dartmouth in 1926 and from the University of Oxford in 1932. He received his Ph.D. from the University of Illinois (1935). While in college, Lattimore wrote poetry that touched on Greek, Anglo-Saxon, and Norse tradition. He later focused on composing lyric poetry: as a classical scholar, he would equate the process of writing lyrics with that of interpreting texts. His translations include Homer's *Iliad* (1951) and *Odyssey* (1967), and *The Four Gospels and the Revelation* (1979); he coedited, with David Grene, *Complete Greek Tragedies* (1959). His translations of the works of Aeschylus, Euripides, Aristophanes, and Pindar were particularly highly praised. Lattimore's version of the *Iliad* is widely regarded as the authoritative contemporary translation.

Lattimore was a professor of Greek at Bryn Mawr College from 1935 to 1971. A collection of his poetry, *Poems from Three Decades,* appeared in 1972. He also wrote criticism, such as *Story Patterns in Greek Tragedy* (1964).

Lattre de Tassigny, Jean de, in full JEAN-MARIE-GABRIEL DE LATTRE DE TASSIGNY (b. Feb. 2, 1889, Mouilleron-en-Pareds, France—d. Jan. 11, 1952, Paris), French army officer and posthumous marshal of France who became one of the leading military figures in the French forces under General Charles de Gaulle during World War II. He was also the most successful French commander of the First Indochina War (1946–54).

After service in World War I and Morocco (1921–26), de Lattre held a staff commission early in World War II, becoming commander of an infantry division in May 1940. After France collapsed in June 1940, he was imprisoned by the Germans but escaped to North Africa in October 1943. He then commanded the French 1st Army in the Allied landing operations in southern France (Aug. 16, 1944) and the subsequent drive across France and into southern Germany and Austria. On May 8, 1945, he represented France at the signature of the German capitulation.

De Lattre
By courtesy of the Bibliotheque Nationale, Paris

After serving as commander of the Western European Union ground forces, he went in December 1950 to French Indochina, where he mobilized French civilians for the war effort against the nationalist revolutionary Viet Minh movement. He halted General Vo Nguyen Giap's Red River delta offensive of 1951, but illness forced his return to France.

Latuka (people): *see* Lotuko.

Latvia, officially REPUBLIC OF LATVIA, Latvian LATVIJA, or LATVIJAS REPUBLIKA, country of northeastern Europe. The capital and chief city is Riga. Latvia lies along the shores of the Baltic Sea and the Gulf of Riga. It borders on Estonia in the north, Russia in the east, and Lithuania in the south. Area 24,938 square miles (64,589 square km). Pop. (2003 est.) 2,348,800.

Latvia

A brief treatment of Latvia follows. For full treatment, *see* MACROPAEDIA: Baltic States.

For current history and for statistics on society and economy, *see* BRITANNICA BOOK OF THE YEAR.

Physical and human geography. Latvia is essentially an undulating plain, with fairly flat lowlands alternating with hills. The shores of the Baltic and the Gulf of Riga are very regular. The climate is influenced by the prevailing air masses coming from the Atlantic Ocean. Summers are cool and rainy. Winter sets in slowly and lasts from mid-December to mid-March. Some two-thirds of Latvia is covered with forests, meadows, pastures, swamps, and wasteland. Latvia's forests are mixed, and its fauna include squirrel, fox, hare, lynx, badger, and ermine.

Only about three-fifths of the population are ethnic Latvians. The Latvians, or Letts, speak Latvian, one of two surviving Baltic languages, the other being Lithuanian. Ethnic Russians make up almost one-third of the population.

Latvia is a fully industrialized nation. During the Soviet era, labour-intensive goods, such as radios and scientific instruments, were produced in quantity, as were durable consumer goods. Heavy industry (principally the production of ships, railcars, streetcars, and vehicle parts) once was a stronger sector of activity than it is today. Now leading manufactures tend toward lighter industry, including alcoholic beverages, wood products, foodstuffs, and clothing.

All types of transport—rail, road, air, and internal waterways—are available in Latvia, and much foreign trade is conducted via the Latvian seaports of Riga and Ventspils. In addition to Russia and the Baltic states, Latvia's main trading partners are Germany, Finland, and Sweden. Riga has air links with Moscow and other large European cities.

With the collapse of the Soviet Union, Latvia won its independence in 1991. It formed a unitary multiparty republic, holding the first elections for its legislative body, the Saeima (Parliament), in 1993. It also introduced a new domestic currency, the lats, to replace the Russian ruble. Privatization grew, as did foreign investment from outside Russia.

Primary and secondary education are free and compulsory in Latvia. Teaching is in Latvian or Russian or both, but education reforms in 2003 called for greater instruction in Latvian. There are numerous higher-education institutions as well as scientific institutes. Health conditions in Latvia are quite good. Still, in the early 21st century, the natural increase rate was decreasing and was well below the world average. Life expectancy was about 65 years for men and 77 years for women.

History. Latvia was originally settled by the ancient people known as Balts. In the 9th century the Balts came under the overlordship of the Varangians, or Vikings, but a more lasting dominance was established over them by their German-speaking neighbours to the west, who Christianized Latvia in the 12th and 13th centuries. The Knights of the Sword, who merged with the German Knights of the Teutonic Order in 1237, conquered all of Latvia by 1230, and German overlordship of the area continued for three centuries, with a German landowning class ruling over an enserfed Latvian peasantry. From the mid-16th to the early 18th century, Latvia was partitioned between Poland and Sweden, but by the end of the 18th century the whole of Latvia had been annexed by expansionist Russia. German landowners managed to retain their influence in Latvia, but indigenous Latvian nationalism grew rapidly in the early 20th century. Following the Russian Revolution of 1917, Latvia declared its independence, and, after a confused period of fighting, the new nation was recognized by Soviet Russia and Germany in 1920.

Independent Latvia was governed by democratic coalitions until 1934, when dictatorial rule was established. In 1939 Latvia was forced to grant military bases on its soil to the Soviet Union, and in 1940 the Soviet Red Army moved into Latvia, which was soon incorporated into the Soviet Union. Nazi Germany held Latvia from 1941 to 1944, when it was retaken by the Red Army. Latvia's farms were forcibly collectivized in 1949, and its flourishing economy was integrated into that of the Soviet Union. Latvia remained one of the most prosperous and highly industrialized parts of the Soviet Union, however, and its people retained strong memories of their brief 20-year period of independence. With the liberalization of the Soviet regime undertaken by Mikhail Gorbachev in the late 1980s, Latvian nationalist sentiments resurfaced.

In 1991 Latvia attained its independence and, with the free elections of 1993—the first since 1940—the constitution of 1922 was restored. In 2004 Latvia became a member of both the North Atlantic Treaty Organization (NATO) and the European Union (EU).

Latvian language, also called LETTISH, Latvian LATVIESU VALODA, East Baltic language spoken primarily in Latvia, where it has been the official language since 1918. It belongs to the Baltic branch of the Indo-European family of languages. (*See* Baltic languages.) In the late 20th century Latvian was spoken by about 1.5 million people.

The earliest texts in Latvian, a Roman Catholic catechism and a Lutheran catechism, both written in Gothic script, date from the 16th century. The first grammar of the language appeared in the 18th century, and by the end of the 19th century the literary language was well developed. A modified Latin alphabet was adopted in 1922.

Latvian has three dialect groups: East, or High, Latvian; West Latvian; and Central Latvian. The last is more conservative and was the basis for the modern literary language.

Although closely related to Lithuanian, Latvian is more innovating than Lithuanian in many respects; for example, the reduction of vowels in final syllables has progressed much further in Latvian. Furthermore, because of the influence of Finnish, word accent has been fixed on the first syllable.

Articles are alphabetized word by word, not letter by letter

Latvian literature, body of writings in the Latvian language. Latvia's loss of political independence in the 13th century prevented a natural evolution of its literature out of folk poetry. Much of Latvian literature is an attempt to reestablish this connection. Written literature came late, fostered by German clergymen. Latvian secular literature began in the 18th century with G.F. Stender who, in the spirit of the Enlightenment, produced didactic tales or idyllic portrayals of country life and vainly attempted to supplant the folk songs by ditties of his own—thus, in his own way, verifying that the great wealth of folk songs (some 400,000 published, and about a million recorded but unpublished) has been in all ages a pervasive presence in Latvian literature. Already in the 17th century, C. Fuereccerus, a sensitive poet who introduced new metrical conventions and rhymes, at times also made use of stylistic elements from Latvian folk songs, and G. Mancelius, founder of Latvian prose, battled against folklore more in a spirit of affection than hostility.

During the "national awakening" of the mid-19th century, the Latvians established their literary independence. Juris Alunāns' book of verse *Dziesmiņas* (1856; "Little Songs") founded the modern Latvian lyric. Folk poetry became a source of literary inspiration, as in the lyrics of Auseklis (M. Krogzems) and in Andrejs Pumpurs' epic poem *Lāčplēsis* (1888; "Bearslayer"). The first major Latvian novel, *Mērnieku laiki* (1879; "The Times of the Land-Surveyors"), by Reinis and Matīss Kaudzītes, portrayed Latvian peasant life realistically. Modern Latvian plays and short stories began with Rūdolfs Blaumanis.

In the 1890s the "new movement" demanded realism, but the major poet of that time, Jānis Rainis (pseudonym of Jānis Pliekšāns), wrote in a Symbolic manner, using the imagery of folk poetry in his depictions of contemporary problems. His wife, Aspazija (pseudonym of Elza Pliekšāna, *née* Rozenberga), took up the struggle for women's rights but displayed rather Romantic tendencies in her later work. Jānis Poruks introduced New Romanticism, whereas in the following decade "Decadents" or "Symbolists" propounded art for art's sake.

A great emotional experience was the Revolution of 1905, when the Latvians tried to break away from imperialistic Russian and local German tutelage. Lyricism then began to predominate. In the verse and fairy tales of the great poet Kārlis Skalbe, the ethical world of folk poetry was reborn. A new generation of authors arose when Latvia became independent in 1918. Jānis Akurāters portrayed himself or romantic heroes with aesthetic ideals in the spirit of Friedrich Nietzsche, and his lyrics were powerful but improvised. A. Upītis, inspired by French and Russian naturalism, idealized working-class heroes. Edvarts Virza (pseudonym of Edvarts Lieknis) created lyrics in strict classical forms; his prose poem *Straumēni* (1933) praised the patriarchal farmstead. Lyrical emotionalism was disciplined in Jānis Jaunsudrabiņš, whose best novel was a trilogy, *Aija, Atbalss,* and *Ziema.* World War I provided many themes for works such as K. Štrāls' *Kaŗš* (1922–27), Anna Brigadere's *Kvēlošā lokā* (1922), and Aleksandrs Grīns's *Dvēseļu putenis* (1932–34); the postwar atmosphere found expression in well-composed short stories by Jānis Ezeriņš and Kārlis Zariņš. Jānis Veselis tried to harmonize the spirit of the age with that of Latvian folk poetry; this is successfully realized in the poetry of Zinaīda Lazda and Andrejs Eglītis and also in that of Veronika Strēlerte.

Latvians found it difficult to achieve a unified view of the world in the 20th century, however, and so turned to psychological detail. The stories of Mirdza Bendrupe show Freudian influence, and Ēriks Ādamsons depicted the neuroses of modern man. Anšlavs Eglītis delighted in caricaturing and intensifying one particular human quality at a time. Mārtiņš Zīverts, the best modern Latvian dramatist, evolved a long, one-act play culminating in a great monologue, as in his historical tragedy *Vara* (1944).

Several poets were still influenced or inspired by folk songs, but Aleksandrs Čaks (pseudonym of Aleksandrs Čadarainis) created a new tradition, describing in free verse, with exaggerated images, the atmosphere of the suburbs. His outstanding work was a ballad cycle, *Mūžības skartie* (1937–39; "Marked by Eternity"), about the Latvian riflemen of World War I. His influence was felt in a new generation of poets who migrated to the West after World War II.

The poetry of Velta Sniķere contains certain elements of Surrealism in verse reminiscent of ancient Latvian magic formulas. A fusion of Čaks's Imaginist poetry and the experience of big American cities led to the poetry of Linards Tauns and Gunars Saliņš. Čaks's verse may have appeared too avant-garde to find an echo in the work of poets in present-day Latvia; but three gifted poets there, Vizma Belševica, Ojārs Vācietis, and Imants Ziedonis, gave individual expression to their inner worlds of experience constrained by external pressures. In the West, new vistas were opening up in the poetry of Astrīde Ivaska, Aina Kraujiete, and Baiba Bičole. In the field of prose, Alberts Bels, a noteworthy writer in Latvia, portrayed a many-faceted reality; in the West, Ilze Šķipsna moved from existentialism to profound Symbolism working at various levels, as in her novel *Neapsolītās zemes* (1971). (J.A.A.)

BIBLIOGRAPHY. Jānis Andrups and Vitauts Kalve, *Latvian Literature* (1954); Aleksis Rubulis, *Baltic Literature* (1970); Rolfs Ekmanis, *Latvian Literature Under the Soviets, 1940–1975* (1978).

Latynina, Larisa Semyonovna (b. Dec. 27, 1934, Kherson, Ukraine, U.S.S.R.), Soviet gymnast, first woman athlete to win nine gold medals in the Olympic Games.

In the 1956 Games in Melbourne, Latynina, who was educated at the Kiev State Institute of Physical Culture, won the women's competition in all-around individual exercises, the horse vault, and floor exercises (in which she tied for first place). In Rome in 1960 she again placed first in the all-around and floor exercises, and in Tokyo in 1964 she captured her third consecutive gold medal in floor exercises. Latynina won three additional first-place medals as a member of the Soviet Union's six-member women's gymnastics team in 1956, 1960, and 1964. She also was awarded five silver (second-place) and four bronze (third-place) medals in those three Olympics. After retirement from competition Latynina was a teacher and national senior coach and was active in the planning of the 1980 Olympics at Moscow.

Lau Group, also called EASTERN GROUP, island cluster of Fiji in the South Pacific Ocean, east of the Koro Sea. Mainly composed of limestone, the 57 islands and islets cover a land area of 188 square miles (487 square km) and are scattered over 44,000 square miles (114,000 square km) of the South Pacific. The chief island is Vanua Balavu, site of Lomaloma, now a copra port. The second most important island is Lakeba, site of the first Wesleyan missionary venture in Fiji (1835). The town of Tubou is on Lakeba. The Lau Group's islanders exhibit a greater admixture of Polynesian and Melanesian characteristics than is found in Fiji's more westerly groups. Pop. (1986) 14,203.

Lauchen, Georg Joachim von: *see* Rheticus, Georg Joachim.

Laud, William (b. Oct. 7, 1573, Reading, Berkshire, Eng.—d. Jan. 10, 1645, London), archbishop of Canterbury (1633–45) and religious adviser to King Charles I of Great Britain. His persecution of Puritans and other religious dissidents resulted in his trial and execution by the House of Commons.

Laud, detail of a painting by Sir Anthony Van Dyck, 1633; in Lambeth Palace, London

Early life and career. Laud was the son of a prominent clothier. From Reading Grammar School he went on to St. John's College, Oxford, and until he was nearly 50 combined the successful but unspectacular careers of academic and churchman. He was soon associated with the small clerical group, followers of the patristic scholar Lancelot Andrewes, who, in opposition to Puritanism, stressed the continuity of the visible church and the necessity, for true inward worship, of outward uniformity, order, and ceremony. In 1608 Laud entered the service of Richard Neile, bishop of Rochester, with whose help he secured a succession of ecclesiastical appointments. From 1611 he was a royal chaplain and came gradually to the notice of King James I. His lifelong conflict with John Williams, later bishop of Lincoln and archbishop of York, began when both sought advancement through the patronage of Charles's favourite, the Duke of Buckingham. During Buckingham's years of power, Laud was his chaplain and confidant, and he established a dominant voice in church policies and appointments. He became a privy councillor in 1627 and, a year later, bishop of London.

In his London diocese, Laud devoted himself to combating the Puritans and to enforcing a form of service in strict accordance with the Book of Common Prayer. The wearing of surplices, the placing of the communion table—railed off from the congregation—at the east end of the chancel, and such ceremonies as bowing at the mention of the name of Jesus were imposed, though cautiously enough to avoid unmanageable opposition. Churches, from St. Paul's Cathedral down to neglected village chapels, were repaired, beautified, and consecrated. To religious radicals, all such reforms seemed moves toward popery.

At Oxford, where Laud was chosen president of St. John's in 1611 and chancellor in 1629, new statutes, new endowments, and new buildings improved the university, both as a centre of learning and as a training ground for Laudian religion. On the death of George

Abbott in 1633, Laud became archbishop of Canterbury, but he had already, by instructions issued in the King's name and by his ruthless energy in the royal prerogative courts of Star Chamber and High Commission, extended his authority—with varying success—over the whole country.

Persecution of Puritans. From 1634 to 1637 visitations of every diocese (including, after strong resistance by Williams, that of Lincoln) showed the extent of deficiencies within the Anglican Church and the strength of Puritan practices. A succession of detailed orders from the Archbishop laid down the remedies. Preaching, to Puritans the essential task of the ministry, was to Laud a most dangerous source of "differences" in religion to be curtailed and controlled. In London his attack on Puritan "lectureships" culminated in the overthrow of the "feoffees for impropriations," the City organization for buying up tithes and church patronage for the benefit of Puritan clergy. The printed word was dangerous, too: celebrated Puritan propagandists such as Alexander Leighton and William Prynne were mutilated and imprisoned. Occasionally, Laud was less harsh than his enemies admitted, especially to the clergy. But he rejected all conciliation of the Puritan movement, whose strength and qualities he never understood. He had, in fact, much in common with some forms of it: the unrelenting quest for the godly life, the intolerant certainty of his own rectitude, the hatred of corruption and extravagance. He could do much to diminish inefficiency, pluralism, absenteeism, and sheer idleness. But his wider efforts to overcome the poverty of clergy and parishes and restore something of the church's position as a great and powerful landowner had extremely limited success.

To Laud, the strength of the church was inseparable from that of the state. Conflict between royal and ecclesiastical power was a possibility he never faced: under Charles I both could be exalted simultaneously. Holding no state office, he used his position on the privy council and his influence over the King to attack "the Lady Mora" (delay) in what he considered her first personification, the treasurer Richard Weston, and afterward in other ministers. His most effective direct impact on government was in the social policy he applied through the council and the courts. Exacting landlords and unscrupulous officials were attacked, and the poor were protected against everyone except the state itself.

In all this his one constant ally was Thomas Wentworth (later the earl of Strafford), from 1633 lord deputy in Ireland. Laud and Wentworth corresponded regularly and frankly on their joint struggle to establish "thorough," as their rigorous policy came to be called. But by 1637 both began to see, dimly, the storm that was about to break upon them. The further trial of Prynne, together with other radical Puritans such as Bastwick and Burton, demonstrated not success for Laudian suppression but rather huge popular support for the opposition. The resistance of the gentry was consolidated by the extended demand for "ship money," the most hated of Charles's non-parliamentary levies. Attempts by Charles and Laud to impose Anglican forms of worship in Scotland provoked fierce resistance there. English forces were sent northward, and in 1639 the "Bishops' Wars" began.

Trial and execution. In the spring of 1640 Parliament met for the first time in 11 years and with it the clerical assembly, the Convocation, which laid down in a new set of canons the principles of the Laudian church. They explained the prescribed ceremonies as "fit and convenient" rather than essential. But they added to the popular hatred of Laud shown in mass demonstrations, petitions, and leaflets. In December, formally accused of high treason, he was taken to the Tower. His trial, managed enthusiastically by Prynne, began only in 1644, in the midst of the Civil War. As with Strafford, the Commons had to abandon legal proof and resort to an ordinance of attainder, accepted hesitantly by the lords. On Jan. 10, 1645, the Archbishop was beheaded.

Laud was never much liked, even by his allies. A humourless, dwarflike figure, uninterested in court pleasures, unmarried, tactlessly impartial in his condemnations, he could never establish a party of influential supporters. During the war and interregnum, royalists and peacemakers generally preferred to forget him. At the Restoration, in 1660, outward Laudian forms were accepted but by a church less significant than ever to the community and the individual. Few in the 18th century saw Laud as a martyr. In the 19th century the historian Thomas Babington Macaulay's fierce contempt for the "ridiculous old bigot" inspired the schoolbooks of many generations. The Oxford Movement, a movement of High Anglican reform in the 1840s, tried unconvincingly to reestablish him as a religious leader, and High Anglican clergy have remained his principal supporters. But at the turn of the 19th century, the Civil War historian Samuel Rawson Gardiner stressed Laud's abilities and integrity and regarded the links with authoritarian politics as his "misfortune."

In the 20th century, the eminent English historian H.R. Trevor-Roper has set against his narrow-minded methods the comprehensive idealism of his social policy, "coloured over by the accepted varnish of an appropriate religious doctrine." Laud, as he himself was well aware, failed; but his devotion to a coherent purpose and his repudiation of hypocrisy, compromise, and corruption in allies and enemies of whatever class were rare and admirable qualities. (D.H.P.)

BIBLIOGRAPHY. H.R. Trevor-Roper, *Archbishop Laud, 1573–1645,* 2nd ed. (1962); W.M. Lamont, *Godly Rule,* ch. 3 (1969), stressing Laud's idea of the "Elect Church"; Christopher Hill, *Economic Problems of the Church, from Archbishop Whitgift to the Long Parliament,* pt. 3 (1956), on Laud's large but unsuccessful schemes for restoring the church's economy; J.W. Allen, *English Political Thought, 1603–1644,* vol. 1, pt. 2 (1938, reprinted 1967), showing the vagueness of his political ideas; E.C.E. Bourne, *The Anglicanism of William Laud* (1947), an uncompromisingly favourable clerical view.

lauda, also spelled LAUDE (Italian: "canticle, hymn of praise"), plural LAUDE, or LAUDI, a type of Italian poetry or a nonliturgical devotional song in praise of the Virgin Mary, Christ, or the saints.

The poetic *lauda* was of liturgical origin, and it was popular from about the mid-13th to the 16th century in Italy, where it was used particularly in confraternal groups and for religious celebrations. The first *lauda* in Italian was St. Francis' moving canticle in praise of "Sir Brother Sun," "Sister Moon," "Brother Wind," "Sister Water," "Brother Fire," and "Mother Earth"—a work that has been called *Laudes creaturarum o Cantico del Sole* ("Praises of God's Creatures or the Canticle of the Sun"). Another outstanding early master of the *lauda* was the gifted 13th-century Franciscan poet Jacopone da Todi, who wrote many highly emotional and mystical *laudi spirituali* ("spiritual canticles") in the vernacular. Jacopone is also the reputed author of a famous Latin *lauda,* the *Stabat mater dolorosa,* which, with another 13th-century *lauda* in Latin, the *Dies irae,* has been part of Roman Catholic liturgy for centuries.

Laude were frequently written in ballata form for recitation by religious confraternities, their content usually consisting of exhortations to a moral life or of events in the lives of Christ and the saints. These recitations evolved into dialogues and eventually became part of the Italian version of the miracle play, the *sacra rappresentazione,* a form of religiously inspired drama, which became secularized during the Renaissance. Later in the Renaissance some *laude* were written for musical settings.

Laude songs were first associated with the early Franciscan friars (early 13th century); later, confraternities, or Laudisti, to encourage devotional singing were founded in Florence and the rest of northern Italy.

Although there were many writers of *lauda* poetry, the composers were often unknown. *Laude* were simple and popular in style. Their musical form depended on that of the period, and at times folk melodies were used to set *lauda* texts. The earliest *laude,* from the 13th century, were monophonic (single-line) compositions. By the 16th century the *laude* appear in polyphonic (several-voice) settings, usually in chordal style. Collections of *laude* from the secular Congregazione dell'Oratorio, founded by St. Philip Neri (d. 1595), are extant, because the singing of *laude* formed an essential part of their meetings. The 16th-century *lauda* was important as a step in the development of the oratorio. The *lauda* remained important in Italian devotional life until the 19th century.

Laudenbach, Pierre-Jules-Louis: *see* Fresnay, Pierre.

Lauder, Estée (b. 1910?, New York City), U.S. co-founder of a large fragrance and cosmetics company.

In 1946 Estée Lauder and her husband, Joseph Lauder, founded Estée Lauder, Inc., and offered their first six products to the public in Saks Fifth Avenue, New York City. The products, including skin treatments, a rouge, and a make-up base, had been developed with the help of Lauder's uncle, a cosmetic chemist.

When no agency would handle their small $50,000 advertising budget, the Lauders spent the money on samples, which they gave away at fashion shows and in mailings. Their strategy succeeded. From a company employing five persons and grossing $850,000 in sales in 1958, Estée Lauder, Inc., grew to employ 1,000 and earn $100,000,000 in sales by 1973.

The company maintained a policy of emphasizing skin care and protection while distributing their products only through department and specialty stores rather than less prestigious outlets. Their best known products included Youth Dew fragrance and bath oils, added in 1953; Clinique allergy-tested cosmetics, first developed in 1968; and Aramis men's products, begun in 1965.

The company's products are sold in more than 70 countries. All stock in the company is owned by the family.

The Lauders built three adventure playgrounds in New York City's Central Park. In 1978 Estée Lauder was honoured by the French government for her contributions to restoring the Palace of Versailles.

Lauder, Sir Harry (MacLennan) (b. Aug. 4, 1870, Portobello, Edinburgh—d. Feb. 26, 1950, near Strathaven, Lanarkshire, Scot.), Scottish music-hall comedian who excited enthusiasm throughout the English-speaking world as singer and composer of simplehearted Scottish songs.

While a child labourer in a flax mill he won singing competitions but worked in a coal mine for 10 years before joining a concert party that took him to Belfast, Birkenhead, and other places that claim to have seen his professional debut. The first songs that he wrote and sang were Irish or English, but when he came to London, to Gatti's music hall in May 1900, he was wearing the kilt. Later he wore trousers for his character studies only, such as "Saftest of the Family" and "It's Nice To Get Up in the Morning." During his week's engagement at Gatti's a gap occurred

Sir Harry Lauder
BBC Hulton Picture Library

in the program at the Tivoli, and Lauder stepped into it with "Lass o' Killiekrankie," an immediate success. Until then his songs had all been comic. With "I Love a Lassie" he struck the homely poetic note that gave charm to "When I Get Back Again to Bonnie Scotland" and "Roamin' in the Gloamin'." His range extended from the bibulous "A Wee Deoch an' Doris" to the hortatory "End of the Road." With a large repertory of his own songs (some verses partly by other persons) he toured America, South Africa, and Australia, and during World War I he sang to troops in France. He gave many concerts for war charities and was knighted in 1919. He wrote four books of reminiscences and acted in several films. He made 22 American tours and entertained troops again in World War II.

Articles are alphabetized word by word, not letter by letter

Lauder, William (d. 1771, Barbados, West Indies), Scottish literary forger, known for his fraudulent attempt to prove Milton a plagiarist.

Educated at the University of Edinburgh, Lauder was a competent classical scholar. He was, however, embittered by a series of failures, and seeking public recognition, he published in 1747 a series of essays in the *Gentleman's Magazine,* subsequently collected as *An Essay on Milton's Use and Imitation of the Moderns in his Paradise Lost* (1750). In preparation for his essays, Lauder interpolated lines from a Latin translation of *Paradise Lost* into the Latin verse of several 17th-century poets, notably Hugo Grotius, Jacobus Masenius, and Andrew Ramsay. By citing these lines and garbling others, he "proved" that *Paradise Lost* was merely a patchwork of stolen quotations. As most of the allegedly plagiarized passages were absent from the extant editions of their Latin sources, Lauder's forgery was soon detected by several scholars and exposed definitively by the scholar John Douglas in 1750. When this occurred, Dr. Samuel Johnson, who had unwittingly supported Lauder's early inquiries, extracted from him a public confession and apology.

Although Lauder later attempted to recoup his reputation, vacillating between an arrogant defense of his position (in 1753 he charged that Milton had robbed a total of 97 authors) and a weak insinuation that the whole affair was a joke, he was regarded with great contempt and ended his days in the West Indies as a poor storekeeper.

Lauderdale (Scotland): *see* Ettrick and Lauderdale.

Lauderdale, James Maitland, 8th earl of, BARON LAUDERDALE OF THIRLESTANE (b. Jan. 26, 1759, Ratho, Midlothian, Scot.—d. Sept. 13, 1839, Thirlestane, Berwickshire, Eng.), Scottish politician and economic writer who pursued what was initially a radical career in Parliament and openly displayed sympathies with the French Revolutionaries, although he ultimately moved to the opposite end of the political spectrum and opposed the Reform Bill of 1832.

Lauderdale was educated at the universities of Edinburgh and Glasgow. He was elected to the House of Commons (1780, 1784) where, in spite of his abilities, he ran into difficulties due to his volatile temper. After his succession to his father's title, Lauderdale served sporadically in the House of Lords, where he became known for his unremitting hostility to various cabinets. In 1806 he was created Baron Lauderdale of Thirlestane, thus becoming a peer of Great Britain. At this time, as a member of the Privy Council he tried unsuccessfully to negotiate a peace treaty with France. Lauderdale was elected to the Order of the Thistle (1821), and from this time on, a marked conservatism pervaded his previously liberal politics. Lauderdale was the great-grandfather of Arthur Balfour, prime minister of Great Britain.

His chief work in economics was his *Inquiry into the Nature and Origin of Public Wealth* (1804). He stands well outside the mainstream of classical economists on a number of issues. In particular, he was a forerunner of Malthus in his belief in the possibility of oversaving and in concern about the level of aggregate demand. He followed Jean-Baptiste Say's subjective value theory and, like him, rejected the distinction between productive and unproductive labour on the grounds that any labour which created utility was productive. The main reason for his position on this issue was his belief that emphasis on the need for parsimony to secure a sufficiently high level of investment was mistaken; indeed, he looked to government expenditure and the creation of the national debt to offset excess private saving. Consistent with this view is his mercantilist view that the national debt did not harm society but was merely a debt owed by one part to another.

Lauderdale, John Maitland, duke of (b. May 24, 1616, Lethington, East Lothian, Scot.—d. Aug. 20/24, 1682, Tunbridge Wells, Kent, Eng.), one of the chief ministers of King Charles II of England (ruled 1660–85); he earned notoriety for his repressive rule in Scotland during Charles II's reign.

The son of a Scottish lord, Maitland signed the Solemn League and Covenant (1638), pledging to protect Scottish Presbyterianism against encroachments by England's king Charles I. During the first phase (1642–47) of the English Civil War between Charles I and Parliament, he helped ally Scotland with the Parliamentarians. Nevertheless, after Charles I was taken captive by Parliament in 1647, Maitland secured from the King a secret agreement, known as the Engagement, by which Charles promised to impose Presbyterianism on England in exchange for aid against the rebels. Maitland helped the Scottish Engagers mount their ill-fated invasion of England in 1648, and in 1651 he was captured while fighting with Charles II (the late Charles I's son and successor) against Oliver Cromwell's forces at the Battle of Worcester.

Lauderdale, detail of an oil painting by J. Huysmans, 1665–70; in the National Portrait Gallery, London
By courtesy of the National Portrait Gallery, London

Imprisoned in England, Maitland was released upon the Restoration of Charles II in 1660. Over the course of the next few years he became Charles's principal administrator in Scotland and a member of the King's ministry known as the Cabal. He was not privy to the secret Treaty of Dover (1670), in which Charles promised to convert to Catholicism in return for French funds.

Although Maitland was created duke of Lauderdale in the Scottish peerage in 1672, he was widely hated for the ruthlessness with which he suppressed Covenanters who resisted the restoration of episcopacy in Scotland. Fears were sparked in the English Parliament that his policies would lay the foundation for arbitrary government enforced by a standing army. Ill health caused him to resign in 1680.

Laudon, Gideon Ernest, Freiherr von (baron of), Laudon also spelled LOUDON (b. Feb. 2, 1717, Tootzen, Swedish Livonia—d. July 14, 1790, Neutitschein), Austrian field marshal who was one of the most successful Habsburg commanders during the Seven Years' War (1756–63) and the Austro-Turkish War of 1787–91.

The son of a Swedish officer of Scottish descent, Laudon entered the Russian Army as a cadet in 1732. After an unsuccessful bid to serve Prussia, he joined the Austrian forces in 1741. He distinguished himself during the War of the Austrian Succession (1740–48), but his rapid rise began with the Seven Years' War, a worldwide conflict that in Europe involved the struggle between Austria and Prussia for supremacy in Germany. Laudon defeated Frederick II the Great of Prussia at Kunersdorf (1759) and Landshut (1760) and became Austrian commander in chief for Bohemia, Moravia, and Silesia. Although he was crushed by Frederick at Liegnitz (1760), he captured Schweidnitz in a surprise attack in 1761 in the last Austrian success of the war. After retiring in 1763, he served without distinction during the War of the Bavarian Succession (1778–79). Recalled in 1788, he crowned his career by capturing Belgrade from the Turks in 1789 and was made commander in chief of the Austrian armed forces.

Laue, Max (Theodor Felix) von (b. Oct. 9, 1879, Pfaffendorf, near Koblenz, Ger.—d. April 23, 1960, Berlin), German recipient of the Nobel Prize for Physics in 1914 for his work on the diffraction of X-rays in crystals. This enabled scientists to study the structure of crystals and hence marked the origin of solid-state physics, an important field in the development of modern electronics.

Laue became professor of physics at the University of Zürich in 1912. In that year he was the first to use a crystal to diffract X-rays and thus demonstrated that X-rays are electromagnetic radiations similar to light. His success also provided experimental proof that the atomic structure of crystals is a regularly repeating arrangement. He championed Albert Einstein's theory of relativity, did research on the quantum theory, the Compton effect (change of wavelength in light under certain conditions), and the disintegration of atoms. He became director of the Institute for Theoretical Physics at the University of Berlin in 1919 and director of the Max Planck Institute for Research in Physical Chemistry, Berlin, in 1951.

Laue diffraction pattern, in X-rays, a regular array of spots on a photographic emulsion resulting from X-rays scattered by certain groups of parallel atomic planes within a crystal. When a thin, pencil-like beam of X rays is allowed to impinge on a crystal, those of certain wavelengths will be oriented at just the proper angle to a group of atomic planes so that they will combine in phase to produce intense, regularly spaced spots on a film or plate centred around the central image from the beam, which passes through undeviated. Laue patterns, first detected by Max von Laue (*q.v.*) are invaluable for crystal analysis.

Lauenburg, former duchy of northern Germany, stretching from south of Lübeck to the Elbe and bounded on the west and east, respectively, by the former duchies of Holstein and Mecklenburg, an area that since 1946 has been part of the federal *Land* (state) of Schleswig-Holstein.

A duchy under the Ascanian dynasty from the 13th century, Lauenburg was acquired by George William, the Welf duke of Brunswick-Lüneburg-Celle, in 1702. In 1728 his nephew George Louis, elector of Hanover and, as George I, king of Great Britain and Ireland, was recognized as heir by Emperor Charles VI; thus, Lauenburg became attached to Hanover. The Congress of Vienna (1814–15) awarded it to Prussia, which granted it to Denmark in exchange for the previously Swedish part of Pomerania. After the Danish–Prussian War of 1864, it passed to Prussia; Prussia's king, William I, became duke of Lauenburg. Lauenburg was integrated into Prussia's Schleswig-Holstein in 1876. Otto von Bismarck, Prussian prime minister and chancellor of the Reich, was granted large estates in Lauenburg and in 1890 was also granted the ducal title, which he never used. The duchy was abolished in 1918.

Laufer, Berthold (b. Oct. 11, 1874, Cologne, Ger.—d. Sept. 13, 1934, Chicago, Ill., U.S.), American scholar who, for 35 years, was virtually the only sinologist working in the United States.

Laufer took his doctorate at the University of Leipzig, then in the forefront of Far Eastern studies. He made four major expeditions to the Himalayas and was curator of Asiatic Ethnology and Anthropology at the Field Museum of Natural History, Chicago.

His more than 150 monographs on a wide variety of attributes of Chinese and Tibetan culture are indispensable reference works, many of them on highly specialized aspects of primitive technology. His extensive knowledge of Tibetan, Chinese, and Japanese antiquities resulted in his being commissioned to collect books, manuscripts, and artifacts, and he made major contributions to the collections of the Field Museum and the Newberry Library in Chicago.

Laugerud García, Kjell Eugenio (b. Jan. 24, 1930, Guatemala City, Guat.), president of Guatemala (1974–78), minister of defense and chief of the armed forces (1970–74).

Laugerud attended the Politécnica, Guatemala's military academy. He was elected president of Guatemala in March 1974 in an election accompanied by violence, political assassinations, and accusations of fraud. Inaugurated on July 1, he announced an economic austerity program. Throughout his administration he conducted a vigorous campaign to reestablish Guatemalan sovereignty over neighbouring Belize but was hindered by international opposition. In 1977 he broke diplomatic relations with Panama over this issue. He was successful in obtaining loans from the Interamerican Development Bank for the construction of roads, hospitals, and electric lines and the promotion of the fishing and construction industries. Following the disastrous earthquake of 1976 he managed the distribution of relief supplies and maintained order. The political unrest which accompanied his election continued to grow, however. Amnesty International repeatedly condemned the actions of the White Hand, a right-wing civilian death squad, and charged that Laugerud tacitly condoned the terrorism.

laughing dove, also called SENEGAL DOVE (*Streptopelia senegalensis*), bird of the pigeon family, Columbidae (order Columbiformes), a native of African and southwest Asian scrublands that has been successfully introduced into Australia. The reddish brown bird has blue markings on its wings, a white edge on its long tail, purplish legs, and a black bill. The copper-tipped feathers on the neck are prominent during the "bowing display" of courtship. The monogamous pair care for a clutch of two white eggs. Its call has a musical, bubbly quality.

laughing owl (*Sceloglaux albifacies*), an extinct bird of the family Strigidae (order Strigiformes) that was native to New Zealand. It was last seen in the early 1900s. Laughing owls nested on the ground, where they fell prey to cats, rats, goats, and weasels. About 40 centimetres (about 1.3 feet) long and brownish in colour, they ate rodents, lizards, and insects.

laughing thrush, also called JAY-THRUSH, any of the 45 species of the Asian genus *Garrulax,* large, strong-billed, sometimes strikingly patterned song-babblers, family Timaliidae. The name laughing thrush is sometimes used for the song-babbler (*q.v.*) group generally. These shy birds of forests form sizable flocks and reveal their presence by cackling and screaming loudly. A widespread example, from the Himalayas to Sumatra (and frequently seen in captivity), is the white-crested laughing thrush (*G. leucolophus*), 30 centimetres (12 inches) long and reddish-brown, except for white foreparts, puffy white crest, and black mask. The hua-mei (*G. canorus*), also called Chinese thrush, is a slightly smaller and plainer species, widespread in eastern Asia and introduced in Hawaii.

White-crested laughing thrush (*Garrulax leucolophus*)
Painting by H. Jon Janosik

Laughlin, Robert B. (b. Nov. 1, 1950, Visalia, Calif., U.S.), American physicist who, with Daniel C. Tsui and Horst Störmer, received the Nobel Prize for Physics in 1998 for the discovery that electrons in a semiconductor placed in a powerful magnetic field at very low temperatures can act as if they have only a fraction of a whole electron charge. This effect is known as the fractional quantum Hall effect.

After receiving a Ph.D. from the Massachusetts Institute of Technology in 1979, Laughlin conducted research at Bell Laboratories (1979–81) in Murray Hill, N.J., and at the Lawrence Livermore National Laboratory (1981–82) in Livermore, Calif. In 1985 he joined the faculty at Stanford University.

Laughlin received his share of the Nobel Prize for explaining the puzzling experimental results obtained by Tsui and Störmer in 1982. The two men extended the work of Klaus von Klitzing, who in 1980 had shown that, in a current-carrying material in a strong magnetic field at temperatures near absolute zero, the Hall resistance (the ratio of the Hall voltage to the current in the material [*see* Hall effect]) changes in a series of discrete integer steps. They found that, in a material subjected to even lower temperatures and stronger fields, the Hall resistance changes in fractional increments of the steps observed by Klitzing, suggesting that the charge carriers involved carry a fraction of an electron's charge. Laughlin provided the theoretical explanation for these results in 1983, positing that the electrons condense into a quantum fluid, where they behave as fractionally charged "quasiparticles."

Laughton, Charles (b. July 1, 1899, Scarborough, Yorkshire [now North Yorkshire], Eng.—d. Dec. 15, 1962, Hollywood, Calif., U.S.), English-born American actor who defied the Hollywood typecasting system to emerge as one of the most versatile performers of his generation.

Laughton, who attended the Royal Academy of Dramatic Art, was able to avoid the usual typecasting brought on by a homely face and bulky frame, playing a wide variety of characters both villainous and virtuous. He made his film debut in the British comedy *Bluebottles* in 1928, the same year that he met his future wife, actress Elsa Lanchester. In 1931 he went to New York City, where he repeated his London stage success in *Payment Deferred* (1932); he became a U.S. citizen in 1950. Cast as a lunatic in his first American picture, *The Devil and the Deep* (1932), he immediately counteracted this image with his portrayal of a good-natured industrialist in *The Old Dark House* (1932). Shortly afterward he switched gears again to play the depraved Nero in *The Sign of the Cross* (1932). In 1933 he returned to England to play the title role in *The Private Life of Henry VIII,* for which he won an Academy Award.

Continuing to play such unpleasant film characters as Javert in *Les Misérables* (1935) and Captain Bligh in *Mutiny on the Bounty* (1935), Laughton balanced these assignments with such sympathetic roles as the mild-mannered British valet in *Ruggles of Red Gap* (1935) and Quasimodo in *The Hunchback of Notre Dame* (1939). He even dabbled in broad comedy, most memorably in *Abbott and Costello Meet Captain Kidd* (1952). Laughton's inclination toward hammy self-indulgence was not universally appreciated by his coworkers, but audiences adored him. Near the end of his career his acting style mellowed considerably, and many regard his performances in *Spartacus* (1960) and *Advise and Consent* (1962) as his finest work. Laughton also produced and directed the long-running Broadway drama *The Caine Mutiny Court Martial* (1953).

lauma (Latvian), Lithuanian LAUMĖ, or DEIVĖ, in Baltic folklore, a fairy who appears as a beautiful naked maiden with long fair hair. *Laumas* dwell in the forest near water or stones. They yearn for children, but being unable to give birth, they often kidnap babies to raise as their own. Sometimes they marry young men and become excellent wives, perfectly skilled in all domestic work. They are noted as swift spinners and weavers, and when they spin on Thursday evenings and launder after sunset on the other days, no mortal woman is allowed to do the same.

Laumas are very temperamental. They are benevolent, motherly beings, helpful to orphans and poor girls, but they are extremely vindictive when angered, particularly by disrespectful men.

Among the Lithuanians, a *laumė* was sometimes called *laumė-ragana,* indicating that she may have been a prophetess (*ragana*) at one time. By the 18th century *laumė* was totally confused with *ragana* and came to denote a witch or hag capable of changing into a snake or toad. Not only could a *laumė* fly, she could also transform people into birds, dogs, and horses and dry up a cow's milk. Similarly, in modern Latvian *lauma* is a hag and *lauminet* means "to practice witchcraft."

laumontite, common hydrated calcium and sodium aluminosilicate mineral in the zeolite family, formulated $(Ca,Na_2)Al_2Si_4O_{12} \cdot 4H_2O$. Its white to yellow or gray prismatic crystals typically occur filling veins and vesicles in igneous rocks. It is one of the more abundant zeolites present in sedimentary rocks and is found, among other places, in Transylvania (Romania); in the Tirol, Austria; and in California, Oregon, and New Jersey, U.S. Its crystals have a framework structure of linked silicate and aluminate tetrahedra, water molecules, and large cations located within cavities. Cations such as calcium, sodium, and potassium readily replace one another in the structure, making laumontite useful in water softeners. For detailed physical properties, *see* zeolite (table).

Laumontite on chabazite from Little Pines, Ore., U.S.
Floyd R. Getsinger

Launcelot (Arthurian knight): *see* Lancelot.

Launceston, chief city and port of northern Tasmania, Australia, lying where the North and South Esk rivers meet to form the River Tamar, a navigable tidal estuary that winds 40 miles (65 km) to Bass Strait. In 1804 Lieutenant Colonel William Paterson established George Town at the mouth of the Tamar, from which a settlement was established upstream on the present site of Launceston (at first called Patersonia). Surveyed in 1826, it was named for the Cornish birthplace of Philip Gidley King, third governor of New South Wales (1800–07). During the 1830s Launceston developed as a whaling port and market centre for an agricultural district. It was proclaimed a municipality in 1852, a town in 1858, and a city in 1888.

The city is now the largest population and commercial centre in northern Tasmania. Located at the junction of the West and East Tamar, Tasman, and Midland highways, it is the headquarters of the state railway system, has direct air connections to Hobart and Melbourne, and is close to the mainland ferry at Devonport. The fertile coastal plain around Launceston yields fruits, livestock, wool, and grains, which are shipped from local wharves or from larger docks at Beauty Point farther north on the estuary. Other exports are textiles and lumber and aluminum from the Bell Bay refinery. Industries include heavy-engineering works; motor-body, textile, and machine-making plants; and flour mills and breweries. Launceston has a maritime college, the Queen Victoria Museum and Art Gallery, St. John's Church (1824–30), and Entally House (1820). One of the world's first hydroelectric stations (1895) lies within the city on Cataract Gorge of the South Esk. Pop. (1991) 62,504.

Launceston, town ("parish"), North Cornwall district, county of Cornwall, England. Situated on the Devon county border, Launceston has sometimes been described as "the gateway to Cornwall." The keep of the Norman castle of Dunheved still dominates the town, which has grown up around it. A parish church, built in 1524, stands in the market square. Pop. (1981) 6,092.

launch, also called LONGBOAT, largest of a ship's boats, at one time sloop-rigged and often armed, such as those used in the Mediterranean Sea during the 18th and 19th centuries. Although present-day launches can travel under sail or by oar, most are power-driven. Because of their weight, they are seldom used by merchant ships but are often deployed as armed craft from warships. Launches are capable of carrying large numbers of men and are also useful for transporting anchors, cannons, and other heavy objects.

launch vehicle, rocket system that boosts a spacecraft into Earth orbit or beyond the gravitational dominance of the Earth. A wide variety of launch vehicles have been used to lift payloads ranging from a few pounds to the giant Skylab and Soyuz space stations.

Many of the early launch vehicles were originally developed as intercontinental ballistic missiles, including the Atlas rocket that served as a booster for the U.S. Mercury (*q.v.*) series and the Titan rocket modified for the U.S. Gemini (*q.v.*) program. Most launch vehicles used to lift heavier spacecraft consist of two or three rocket propulsion systems mounted one on top of the other. The Saturn V, which carried Apollo spacecraft to the Moon, was made up of three stages, the first two of which were equipped with a single engine. In such a system, the propellant tank and the vehicle structure in each stage are cast off as soon as the fuel is depleted, in order to lighten the load. The U.S. space shuttle (*q.v.*) system that became operational in 1981 represents a significant technical advance over traditional launch vehicles. Unlike the Saturn V, it can make more than one flight, since most of its principal components are designed to be recovered and refurbished for repeated use.

Laura, the beloved of the Italian poet Petrarch and the subject of his love lyrics, written over a period of about 20 years, most of which were included in his *Canzoniere,* or *Rime* (1360). Laura has traditionally been identified as a Laura de Noves of Avignon (now in France), a married woman and a mother; but since Petrarch gives no clues as to who she was, several other Lauras have also been suggested and some critics believe there was no actual Laura at all. Petrarch was supposed to have seen Laura for the first time in St. Claire Church in Avignon on April 6, 1327. In his poetry she appears to give him little encouragement, but his love for her became a lifelong obsession, even after her death on April 6, 1348.

Petrarch wrote more than 300 Italian sonnets to Laura, as well as other short lyrics and one long poem. Those included in his *Canzoniere* are divided into *Rime in vita Laura* (263 poems) and *Rime in morte Laura* (103 poems). The poems treat a variety of moods and subjects, but particularly his intense psychological reactions to his beloved. Many of his similes, such as burning like fire and freezing like ice, beautifully stated in the sonnet beginning "I find no peace, and all my war is done," were to be frequently repeated by the sonneteers of Elizabethan England and later became poetic clichés. Some of the poems express the very simple, human wish to be with her and to be treated kindly. After Laura's death, his poems continued on the same themes, expressing his sorrow and describing her return to him in dreams.

Earlier Italian poets had written splendid sonnets expressing their love for a particular woman, but it was Petrarch's poems that spawned a whole generation of translators and imitators in Europe and particularly in England, where his example inspired the great love-sonnet cycles of Sir Philip Sidney, Edmund Spenser, Michael Drayton, and William Shakespeare. *See also* sonnet.

Laurales, order of flowering plants, characterized by woodiness, aromatic plant parts, and a single strand of conducting tissues continuing from the stem into the leaf. Laurales belongs to the class called dicotyledon (*q.v.;* characterized by two seed leaves) and contains 8 families, between 72 and 97 genera, and some 2,600 species of trees, shrubs, or vines, distributed mostly in the tropics and warmer regions of the world. Lumber, medicinal extracts, essential oils used in perfumery, and camphor are all derived from the Laurales, and several genera in different families are ornamentally important.

A brief treatment of Laurales follows. For full treatment, *see* MACROPAEDIA: Angiosperms.

The laurel family, Lauraceae, consists of about 2,200 species in 45 genera, many of which are aromatic and evergreen. The avocado, or alligator pear (*Persea americana*), is an economically important berry appreciated for its buttery green or bright yellow meat. Several cultivars (horticultural varieties) now are grown in many nations and the southern United States.

Cinnamomum, another genus of Lauraceae, is remarkable for the utility of several of its species. *C. camphora,* a handsome tree 100 feet (30 m) in height, yields camphor, which is used medicinally and in the manufacture of explosives. The most favoured cinnamon spice is derived from the bark of *C. zeylanicum.* One of the oldest spices, Chinese cinnamon (cassia), is produced in the bark of *C. cassia.* Korintje cinnamon is the product of *C. burmanii* of Southeast Asia.

The bay laurel (*Laurus nobilis*), also of the Lauraceae and native to the Mediterranean region, provides essential oils for perfumery and medicine, and its leaves (known as bay leaves) are used in cooking. In ancient Greece a chaplet of leaves and branches from this tree was a symbol of honour presented to victorious athletes and other heroes.

Some Laurales reproduce vegetatively. Near the base of the stems in laurel and Carolina allspice (*Calycanthus floridus*), buds may arise to form suckers, which can be transplanted for propagation. Reproduction by seeds, however, is the universal manner of propagation in this order.

The Laurales order demonstrates great diversity in vegetative and floral structure. Inflorescences (flower clusters) are classed as spikes, racemes, panicles, and umbels, depending upon the degree of branching and the ultimate shape of the assemblage. A representative flower of this order is small. The outermost two series may resemble petals, but units likely to be designated sepals and petals appear to be similar or to intergrade. As many as 12 stamens in four whorls are common; some may not produce pollen. The pistil is differentiated into a pollen-receptive stigma, a style, and a basal ovary; it consists of one carpel. In some genera, stamens and the pistil develop in separate flowers, but generally both kinds are borne on the same plant.

Pollen grains of all the Laurales have no more than two grooves. In the Calycanthaceae, pollination is accomplished by beetles; in the Lauraceae and Monimiaceae, nectar derived from stamen glands attracts pollinating bees.

Following pollination and fertilization, the ovule becomes the seed and the ovary the fruit. In several families the floral tube becomes a part of the fruit or surrounds it partially or even wholly. Depending upon the genus, fruits are berries or drupes (having an inner stony layer); a few families produce winged fruits.

Most of the Laurales are more advanced in several respects than members of the order Magnoliales. The two orders are so closely related, however, that several families have been shifted from one order to the other by various authorities.

Laurana, Francesco (b. *c.* 1430, Vrana, Dalmatia, republic of Venice [now in Italy]—d. before March 12, 1502, Avignon, France), early Italian Renaissance sculptor and medallist, especially distinguished for his severely elegant portrait busts of women and as an early disseminator of the Renaissance style in France.

Laurana's early career is obscure, the first notice of him, in 1453, being when he was

"Eleonora of Aragon," portrait bust by Francesco Laurana; in the National Archaeological Museum, Palermo, Sicily
Alinari—Art Resource

paid by Alfonso II of Aragon for work on the Castel Nuovo in Naples. He probably designed and sculptured the triumphal gate of the Castel. Between 1461 and 1466 he was at the court of René, duke d' Anjou, rival claimant to the throne of Naples. By 1468, however, he was in Sicily, and he seems to have spent the remainder of his life there, at Naples, and in the south of France.

Laurana's documented works include a series of medals executed for René, statues of the Madonna and bas-reliefs in Italy and Sicily, and tombs and architectural sculpture in the south of France. His portrait busts include those of Baptista Sforza (Bargello, Florence), Beatrice of Aragon (Kunsthistorisches Museum, Vienna), and Ippolita Maria Sforza (National Gallery of Art, Washington, D.C.). They are characterized by serene, detached dignity and reserve. Laurana created an ideal image of aristocratic elegance by reducing details to a minimum and concentrating on the essential geometry of forms harmoniously balanced, clearly and precisely carved. In its seriousness and gravity of impression, as well as in its simplification of forms, Laurana's work may be compared to that of Piero della Francesca, whom he may have known in Urbino, since his relative Luciano Laurana, the architect, was active there.

Laurana, Luciano (b. *c.* 1420, Zadar, Dalmatia [now in Croatia]—d. 1479, Pesaro, Papal States [Italy]), principal designer of the Palazzo Ducale at Urbino and one of the main figures in 15th-century Italian architecture.

Nothing is known of Laurana's training. Because the triumphal arch of Alfonso of Aragon in Naples has much in common with Laurana's later works at Urbino, some speculate that he may have begun his career in Naples.

The courtyard of the Palazzo Ducale, Urbino, Italy, by Luciano Laurana
SCALA—Art Resource

He is known to have been at Mantua in 1465, when Leon Battista Alberti was directing the construction of the Church of San Sebastiano.

In Urbino from about 1466, he may have immediately begun making designs for the renovation of the ducal palace of Federico da Montefeltro. In 1468 he was named chief architect of the court, considered during the last half of the 15th century to be the most celebrated intellectual centre in Italy. The palace Laurana designed was part of a comprehensive town plan, one of the most ambitious and successful attempted up to that time. Although there are problems of attribution associated with the palace—the original structure dated from medieval times—Laurana is thought to have been responsible for the courtyard and entrance facade, both noted for their perfect proportions.

In the courtyard, Laurana borrowed elements of the Florentine palace but handled them with a sophistication and elegance that surpassed any contemporaneous examples in Florence. The ground floor of the courtyard, a delicate arcaded portico, supports an enclosed second story where narrow windows and Corinthian pilasters alternate. This work strongly influenced the foremost architect of the following generation, Donato Bramante. Laurana also probably designed the floor plan of the palace and contributed to the fine interior detail work, the best of the period that has survived. He left Urbino in 1472 for Naples, where he was employed as a "master of artillery," and in his last years he worked on the fortress at Pesaro.

Laurasia, hypothetical continental mass in the Northern Hemisphere that included North America, Europe, and Asia (except peninsular India). Its existence was proposed by Alexander Du Toit, a South African geologist, in "Our Wandering Continents" (1937), a reformulation of the continental drift (*q.v.*) theory advanced by the German meteorologist Alfred Wegener. Whereas Wegener had postulated a single supercontinent, Pangaea (*q.v.*), Du Toit theorized that there were two such great landmasses: Laurasia in the north and Gondwanaland (*q.v.*) in the south, separated by an oceanic area called Tethys. Laurasia is thought to have fragmented into the present continents largely during the Mesozoic Era (from approximately 245 million to 66.4 million years ago).

Laurel, city, Prince Georges county, Maryland, U.S., on the Patuxent River, midway between Washington, D.C., and Baltimore. The land was patented to the Snowden family, who arrived about 1669 and founded the community. Montpelier Manor (1740; Georgian), built by Thomas Snowden, is now owned by the Maryland-National Park and Planning Commission. Named for the local laurel trees, the community experienced steady growth as a residential and industrial centre after World War II. The Washington D.C. International horse race is run each November at Laurel Race Course, and there is harness racing at Laurel Raceway. Patuxent Wildlife Research Center (southeast) is between Fort Meade (an army training centre) and the National Research Agricultural Center. T. Howard Duckett Reservoir and Dam are immediately northwest. Inc. town, 1870. Pop. (1991 est.) 19,757.

Laurel, city, seat (1906) of Jones county, southeastern Mississippi, U.S., on Tallahala Creek, 84 miles (135 km) southeast of Jackson. Founded in 1882 as a lumber camp, it was named for laurel shrubs, native to the surrounding forests. By 1920 it was the world's largest shipping centre for yellow-pine lumber, but as the forests were depleted the city faced economic collapse. Soon after, William Mason, an associate of Thomas Edison, moved to Laurel and developed a type of hardboard (Masonite) made from sawmill waste. The Masonite Corporation remains a major industrial concern. The petroleum industry and light manufacturing have boosted economic development. The Chickasawhay District of the De Soto National Forest extends southeastward from Laurel. The Lauren Rogers Library and Museum of Art has a notable collection of North American Indian baskets. The Southeastern Baptist College (1949) is in the city. James Street, a native of Laurel, in his novel *Tap Roots* (1942) popularized the legend that Jones County had seceded from the Confederacy during the American Civil War period. Inc. village, 1888; town, 1896; city, 1901. Pop. (1991 est.) 18,964.

laurel, any of several evergreen shrubs and small trees of the genus *Laurus* within the family Lauraceae; the name is chiefly applied to *L. nobilis* (also called bay, sweet bay, bay laurel, and bay tree), native to the Mediterranean region but now widely cultivated in other regions of the world. The plant is the source of bay leaf (*q.v.*), a cooking herb. In ancient Greece the wreath of honour placed upon the heads of heroes was made from the leaves and branches of laurel.

Laurel (*Laurus nobilis*)
W.H. Hodge

Laurus nobilis grows 6–18 m (20–60 feet) tall. The stiff, alternate, oval leaves are dull and leathery and about 7.5–10 cm (3–4 inches) long; the leaf edges are smooth and often wavy. The small and inconspicuous flowers are yellowish or greenish white. The fruit, a green, purple, or blackish berry, contains one seed.

Laurel, José Paciano (b. March 9, 1891, Tanauan, Luzon, Phil.—d. Nov. 6, 1959, Manila), president of the Philippines (1943–45), during the Japanese occupation of World War II.

After receiving law degrees from the University of the Philippines (1915) and from Yale University (1920), he was elected to the Philippine Senate in 1925 and appointed associate justice of the Supreme Court in 1936.

After the Pearl Harbor attack, Laurel stayed in Manila after President Manuel Quezon escaped first to Bataan and then to the United States. He offered his services to the Japanese; and because of his criticism of U.S. rule of the Philippines he held a series of high posts

José Laurel
Popperfoto

in 1942–43, climaxing in his selection as president in 1943. Twice in that year he was shot by Philippine guerrillas but recovered. In July 1946 he was charged with 132 counts of treason but was never brought to trial; he shared in the general amnesty in April 1948.

As the Nationalist Party's nominee for the presidency of the Republic of the Philippines in 1949, he was narrowly defeated by the incumbent president, Elpidio Quirino, nominee of the Liberal Party. Elected to the Senate in 1951, Laurel helped to persuade Ramón Magsaysay, then secretary of defense, to desert the Liberals and join the Nationalists. When Magsaysay became president, Laurel headed an economic mission that in 1955 negotiated an agreement to improve economic relations with the United States. He retired from public life in 1957.

Laurel, Stan; and Hardy, Oliver, original names respectively ARTHUR STANLEY JEFFERSON and OLIVER NORVELL HARDY, JR. (respectively b. June 16, 1890, Ulverston, Lancashire, Eng.—d. Feb. 23, 1965, Santa Monica, Calif., U.S.; b. Jan. 18, 1892, Harlem, Ga., U.S.—d. Aug. 7, 1957, North Hollywood, Calif.), the first great Hollywood motion-picture comedy team.

Laurel and Hardy in *Way Out West,* 1937
Culver Pictures

Stan Laurel, the skinny member of the team, performed in circuses, musicals, dramas, and vaudeville before acting in silent films. In 1926 he joined Oliver Hardy, the fat member of the partnership, who had traveled in the United States in singing and vaudeville acts and had been in silent comedies since 1913. The two men joined Hal Roach's studio separately in 1926, and Roach persuaded them to team up. Their first successful film comedy together was *Putting Pants on Philip* (1927). They made the transition to sound motion pictures fairly easily, using dialogue scantily for plot development.

Laurel and Hardy made nearly 90 comedies from 1927 to 1951. Laurel, the bumbling and easily distressed innocent, acted as foil to the pompous and overbearing Hardy, whose confident mien was as unwarranted as his partner's fearful timidity. The pair frequently managed to convert simple, everyday situations into disastrous tangles by acts of incredible naïveté and stupidity. Laurel worked out most of the two men's comic routines.

Many of Laurel and Hardy's best films were shorts made under the direction of Leo McCarey of the Hal Roach studios in the late 1920s and '30s. Among them are *The Battle of the Century* (1927), *Leave 'em Laughing* (1927), *The Music Box* (1932), *Sons of the Desert* (1933), and *Way Out West* (1937).

laurel leaf: *see* bay leaf.

Lauren, Ralph, original name RALPH LIPSCHITZ (b. Oct. 14, 1939, New York, N.Y., U.S.), American fashion designer who, by developing his brand around the image of an elite, American lifestyle, built one of the world's most successful fashion empires.

Lauren grew up in the Bronx, in New York City. After high school, he took business classes at night school and worked in sales by day. While working for a tie company, he was inspired to begin designing his own neckwear, and in 1967 he went into business for himself, changing his last name to Lauren and marketing his unique line of ties under the name Polo.

From the inception of his brand, Lauren's creations were characterized by a monied style that evoked the look of English aristocracy, as adapted by the sporty, East-Coast American elite. His first menswear line in 1968 featured classic, preppy tweed suits, and his first womenswear line in 1971 continued his explorations of classic tailoring and good taste, but with a feminine twist. In 1972 Lauren debuted what would become his signature piece: the mesh sport shirt, available in a variety of colours and featuring his trademark emblem of the most aristocratic of athletes, the polo player. The Ralph Lauren style became a nationwide phenomenon after he dressed the male actors in the 1974 film adaptation of *The Great Gatsby* in clothing from his current line. The film's evocation of the lost, elegant era of F. Scott Fitzgerald provided a perfect vehicle for Lauren's classic, sometimes nostalgic, vision. The designer received further attention when he created the clothing for *Annie Hall* (1977), in which Woody Allen sported traditional oxford button-down shirts, chinos, and tweeds, and Diane Keaton wore a quirky, modern blend of Lauren's signature pieces for both men and women. Lauren once said of his style, "I'm interested in longevity, timelessness, style—not fashion." His work throughout the following decades reflected this motto, as his exploration of new ideas—including Southwestern themes and safari looks—was always grounded in his central focus on classic American clothing.

Lauren's vision appealed to a wide spectrum of people, and his label quickly turned into an empire. Seeing how his clothing was associated with a certain lifestyle, starting in 1983 he expanded his business to include a range of home accessories that would eventually include pillows, throws, bed and bath products, furniture, and household paint. Lauren also diversified the appeal of his label by creating lines of clothing and accessories targeted at a wide range of price points and demographics, including a jeans line and a children's line. By the 1990s, the presence of both his shops and his brand name had become global. Among his numerous awards, Lauren has won the Council of Fashion Designers. of America (CFDA) awards for Lifetime Achievement (1992), Womenswear Designer of the Year (1995), and Menswear Designer of the Year (1996).

Laurence: *see under* Lawrence, except as below.

Laurence, (Jean) Margaret, *née* WEMYS (b. July 18, 1926, Neepawa, Man., Can.—d. Jan. 5, 1987, Lakefield, Ont.), Canadian writer whose novels portray strong women striving for self-realization while immersed in the daily struggle to make a living in a male-dominated world.

Her first publications reflect her life with her engineer husband (later divorced) in Somaliland (1950–52) and Ghana (1952–57). Her first novel, *This Side Jordan* (1960), dealt with how old colonials and native Africans suffered through the exchange of power as Ghana became a nation. *The Prophet's Camel Bell* (1963; also published as *New Wind in a Dry Land*) is an account of her life in Africa. *The Tomorrow-Tamer* (1963) is a collection of African stories.

Laurence's next three novels were set in Canada and were woman-centred. In *The Stone Angel* (1964), an ancient prairie woman tells her life struggles. *A Jest of God* (1966; made into the motion picture *Rachel, Rachel* in 1968) and *The Fire Dwellers* (1969) are about two sisters, a Manitoba schoolteacher and a Vancouver housewife, each trying to achieve personal fulfillment. After her fifth and sixth novels, *The Diviners* (1974) and *Heart of a Stranger* (1977), Laurence turned to writing children's stories.

Laurencin, Marie (b. Oct. 31, 1883, Paris, Fr.—d. June 8, 1956, Paris), French painter and printmaker, known particularly for her delicate watercolours of elegant, vaguely melancholic women.

At the Académie Humbart, where she studied art, Georges Braque was among her classmates. Gertrude Stein was one of the first buyers of her work. Although she flourished in the Montmartre milieu of the Cubists, Laurencin did not herself exploit the movement's idiom. The distinct femininity of her subject matter, colourism, and technique earned her the nickname "La Fauvette."

As companion to the poet Guillaume Apollinaire, she produced several portraits of him and of their friends. Her stage designs include scenery for the Ballets Russes (1924) and the Comédie Française (1928).

Laurens, Henri (b. Feb. 18, 1885, Paris, Fr.—d. May 8, 1954, Paris), principal French sculptor of the Cubist movement in art.

Laurens worked as a stonemason and decorator before he became a sculptor. He was influenced by Auguste Rodin and became a friend of Georges Braque in 1911. His early sculptures were painted in colours that emphasized their various planes in a Cubist manner.

In the 1920s he began producing numerous works on marine themes, particularly nudes and sirens, in marble and bronze. Laurens had an intense interest in the human form but interpreted it from a Cubist and somewhat Expressionist perspective, as in "The Farewell" (1940). His work shows a consistent sensual and poetic concern, and the influence of his contemporary Aristide Maillol is evident in many pieces.

Laurens, Henry (b. March 6, 1724, Charleston, S.C. [U.S.]—d. Dec. 8, 1792, near Charleston, S.C., U.S.), early American statesman who served as president of the Continental Congress (1777–78).

After pursuing a profitable career as a merchant and planter, Laurens espoused the patriot cause in the disputes with Great Britain preceding the American Revolution. He was made president of the South Carolina Council of Safety and vice president of the state in 1776. Sent as a delegate to the Continental Congress meeting at Philadelphia, he was soon elected chief officer of that body.

In August 1780 Laurens embarked on a mission to Holland to negotiate on behalf of Congress a $10,000,000 loan, but he was captured off Newfoundland and imprisoned in the

Tower of London. When his papers were found to contain a draft of a proposed treaty between the Americans and the Dutch, war broke out between Great Britain and Holland. On Dec. 31, 1781, he was released on parole and finally exchanged for the British general Charles Cornwallis. The following June he was appointed one of the U.S. commissioners for negotiating peace with the British, but, because of failing health, he was absent from the signing of the final peace treaty and retired to his plantation.

Laurent, Auguste (b. Nov. 14, 1807, La Folie, Fr.—d. April 23, 1853, Paris), French chemist who advanced knowledge of the structure of organic compounds.

He held various industrial posts before becoming professor of chemistry at Bordeaux (1838) and was an assayer at the Paris mint from 1848.

Laurent discovered several important organic compounds and, with Charles Gerhardt, developed a systematic classification of them. They attempted to rationalize the composition and reactions of organic compounds in terms of a "unitary" theory of their atomic structure, which was opposed by Justus von Liebig and Jöns Berzelius, who adhered to the dualistic view that every chemical compound represents a combination of an electropositive and an electronegative component. Laurent advanced the accurate determination of atomic weights by helping to win acceptance of Avogadro's law. His *Méthode de chimie* (1854; "Chemical Method") brought him posthumous respect.

Laurent, François (b. July 8, 1810, Luxembourg—d. Feb. 11, 1887, Ghent, Belg.), Belgian administrator, legal scholar, and historian noted as the author of a monumental universal history and a series of comprehensive works on civil law.

After gaining his degree in law in 1832, he served as the head of a division at the Belgian Ministry of Justice and in 1836 was appointed professor of civil law at the University of Ghent. His liberal views were attacked by the Roman Catholic church, but his position with the Belgian government permitted him to retain his chair at the university.

His greatest work was *Études sur l'histoire de l'humanité,* 18 vol. (1861–70), a political and cultural history of man that was extremely popular in France, Germany, and England. It was praised for its great erudition but criticized for its theistic scheme and contention that man's progress is the result of a providential plan. His other works include *Principes de droit civil français,* 33 vol. (1869–78; "Principles of French Civil Law"), which placed him in the top ranks of juridical scholars; and *Droit civil international,* 8 vol. (1880–82; "International Civil Law"). After 1879 he worked on problems of legal reform, producing *Avant-Project de revision du code civil,* 6 vol. (1882–84; "Rough Draft of a Revision of the Civil Code"), and participated in philanthropic activities, including the establishment of a workers' society at Ghent.

Laurentian Library: *see* Medicean-Laurentian Library.

Laurentian Mountains, French LES LAURENTIDES, mountains forming the Quebec portion of the Canadian Shield, particularly the area partially bounded by the Ottawa, St. Lawrence, and Saguenay rivers. One of the world's oldest mountain regions, it consists of Precambrian rocks (those more than 540 million years old). The range was gradually scoured and worn down and now forms a rocky peneplain (a vast erosional plain) with relatively uniform crests of 3,000 feet (900 m) and a maximum elevation of 3,905 feet (1,190 m).

The heavily forested area, with its innumerable lakes and swift rivers, supports large-scale lumbering, pulp and paper-milling, and mining operations, hydroelectric installations, and an important tourist industry. Two provincial parks, Laurentides and Mont Tremblant, are popular vacation areas easily accessible from Montreal and Quebec.

Laurentian Trough, submarine glacial trough in the eastern continental shelf of North America, the most impressive such feature on Earth. It extends from the mouth of the St. Lawrence River eastward through the Gulf of St. Lawrence to the edge of the continental shelf, about 190 miles (306 km) south of Newfoundland. It has a mean width of 50 miles (80 km) and a depth as great as 1,700 feet (518 m) below sea level.

The topography of the Laurentian Trough is believed to have been greatly modified by glacial activity during the Pleistocene Epoch (1,600,000 to 10,000 years ago). The depression of the Earth's crust owing to the forward movement of glaciers caused silt blankets and submerged shorelines along the trough. The floor of the trough forms a basin, and the trough has both tributaries and distributaries.

Laurentide Ice Sheet, principal glacial cover of North America during the Pleistocene Epoch (1,600,000 to 10,000 years ago). At its maximum extent it spread as far south as latitude 37° N and covered an area of more than 13,000,000 square km (5,000,000 square miles). In some areas its thickness reached 2,400–3,000 m (8,000–10,000 feet) or more. The Laurentide Ice Sheet probably originated on the Labrador-Ungava plateau and on the mountains of the Arctic islands of Canada, and centred over Hudson Bay. As it spread, the glacial ice mass appears to have combined with other ice caps that had formed on local highlands in eastern Canada and in the northeastern United States.

Laurentius, English LAWRENCE (fl. early 6th century, Italy), antipope in 498 and from 501 to about 505/507, whose disputed papal election gave his name to the Laurentian schism, a split in the Roman Catholic church.

Late in the 5th century, the Roman church's relations with the Eastern church in Constantinople became badly strained. Pope Anastasius II attempted conciliation, which alarmed some of the Roman clergy, and factions arose. Upon Anastasius' death (Nov. 19, 498), two parties confronted each other—one led by Laurentius, an archpriest who favoured Anastasius' policy, and the other under the Sardinian deacon St. Symmachus. Three days later a minority of clergy elected Laurentius pope, while a majority chose Symmachus. The Ostrogothic king Theodoric the Great, then master of Italy, was considered to be impartial, and thus both parties appealed to him to decide the legal claimant. Theodoric finally favoured Symmachus, based on the majority vote.

Laurentius submitted to the decision and was then appointed bishop of Nocera in Campania. After his partisans continued in active opposition, however, Theodoric summoned Symmachus to Ravenna. When the pope fled, Theodoric convoked a Roman synod (501) to judge Symmachus, whose party was mauled en route to the synod by the Laurentians. The synod's final decrees dissatisfied Theodoric, and he allowed Laurentius to return to Rome, where he was proclaimed pope by the Laurentians. A period of civil chaos and factional wars ensued. In 505(?) the Alexandrian deacon Dioscorus induced Theodoric to declare Symmachus the legal pontiff. Laurentius was forced out of Rome and retired under the protection of the patrician Festus.

Laurentius OF CANTERBURY, SAINT, also called LAWRENCE, or LAURENCE (d. Feb. 2, 619, Canterbury, Kent, Eng.; feast day February 3), second archbishop of Canterbury, missionary who played a large part in establishing the Anglo-Saxon church.

In 597 Pope Gregory I the Great assigned Laurentius, who was then probably a Benedictine friar, to the first Anglo-Saxon mission aimed at converting England to Roman Catholicism. The mission was led by St. Augustine, later first archbishop of Canterbury. Laurentius reported to Rome on the mission's progress and returned with more missionaries in 601. He succeeded Augustine as archbishop about 604.

Like Augustine, Laurentius endured persecution and hostilities by the Britons while fruitlessly trying to convince the Celtic Christians to adopt Roman practices. Anti-Christian attitudes increased upon the death (616) of King Aethelberht I of Kent and the succession of his son, Edbald.

Gregory's plan was to have two archbishoprics (London and York); Laurentius attempted to establish his see at London but was ejected by antagonists and retired to Canterbury, where the provincial see remained. About 617 opposition encouraged by Edbald caused Laurentius to consider departing for France, but a dream of St. Peter reminded him of his mission. Before he died he succeeded in converting Edbald.

Lauricocha, Lake, Spanish LAGO LAURICOCHA, northernmost of a chain of glacier-fed lakes in the Andes Mountains, central Peru, about 100 miles (160 km) north-northeast of Lima. It lies at an elevation of 12,615 feet (3,845 m). The Marañón River, the main stream of the Amazon River, issues from the lake; hence, it was once regarded as the source of the Amazon. The lake lies in one of Peru's most sparsely populated areas.

Laurier, Sir Wilfrid (b. Nov. 20, 1841, Saint-Lin, Canada East [now Quebec, Can.]—d. Feb. 17, 1919, Ottawa, Ont., Can.), the first French-Canadian prime minister of the Dominion of Canada (1896–1911), noted especially for his attempts to define the role of French Canada in the federal state and to define Canada's relations to Great Britain. He was knighted in 1897.

Early life and education. Laurier was born of French-Canadian parents and studied at the college at l'Assomption, where he received literary training under Catholic priests. He then studied law at McGill University in Montreal

Laurier
National Film Board of Canada Phototheque

and was called to the bar in 1864. His bicultural education, most unusual at the time, may have played a part in his lifelong dedication to Canadian unity. While at McGill, he became a leading member of the Institut Canadien, a political club of advanced liberals (Les Rouges) with anticlerical and republican views. Later he joined the law offices of one of the leading Rouge politicians and contributed a number of articles to radical newspapers, one of which he edited for a few months in the mid-1860s.

In 1866, for reasons of health, Laurier moved to Athabaska, where he opened his own law practice. In 1868 he married Zoë Lafontaine of Montreal, and, despite a long relationship with Emilie Lavergne, his law partner's wife, his childless marriage seems to have been a happy one. In 1871 he was elected to the opposition benches of the provincial legislature of Quebec, where his first speech, an eloquent plea for educational reform, attracted much attention. In 1874 he was elected to the Canadian House of Commons, of which he was to be a member until his death.

Rise to leadership. As Laurier gradually rose to become minister of internal revenue (1877–78) and eventually to leadership of the opposition Liberal Party in 1887, he persistently sought to bring together his countrymen on the issues that have since been recognized as the dominant themes of modern Canadian politics: the relations of church and state, the bicultural entente between French- and English-speaking Canadians, and the country's association with the British Empire and relations with the United States. One of the political highlights of these years for Laurier was his famous speech on Liberalism delivered in 1877 in the city of Quebec. In that speech he set himself against both the Quebec politicians who attempted to form a Catholic party and the extremist elements in his own group who sought to exclude the clergy from all political activity. Because of his skillful statesmanship, the cold antagonism between conservative churchmen and liberal politicians gradually began to thaw; after 1896 no anticlerical ever attained important public office and no cleric officially interfered in politics.

In 1885 Laurier became a national figure when he delivered a moving plea of clemency for Louis Riel, who had led a rebellion of the Métis (people of mixed French and Indian extraction) in Manitoba and whose death sentence provoked violent outbursts between the French Catholic nationalists in Quebec and the Britannic groups in Ontario. Showing great courage, Laurier, though not condoning Riel's actions, charged the government with mishandling the rebellion. Although he did not succeed in saving Riel, he established his reputation as a man of principle and high ideals. Throughout his political life, he emphasized moderation and compromise and gradually became recognized as the only leader able to effect a national reconciliation.

At the same time he was turning his personal magnetism into a valuable political weapon. Between 1887 and 1896 he perfected his party's organization, refined Liberal strategy, made political alliances, assessed local partisans, and judiciously applied his personal charm to winning over Conservative adversaries and dissident Liberals. He infused new life into his party, for instance, by campaigning vigorously for unrestricted reciprocity, the grant of mutual commercial privileges, with the United States. After the policy had served its purpose, however, he dropped it from his platform in 1893. Between 1895 and 1896 he spoke at between 200 and 300 meetings, thus personally reaching some 200,000 voters. In mid-1896, with the Conservative government divided and disorganized, he easily carried the Liberal Party to victory in the general election.

Laurier's "national policy." Intent on heading an administration of national unity, Laurier attracted to his first Cabinet men who had won distinction in their own provinces. His "national policy" consisted of protection for Canadian industries, the settlement of the west, and the building of an effective transportation system. The years between 1896 and 1911 became a boom period for which the Prime Minister himself provided the slogan: "The Twentieth Century belongs to Canada." The budget of 1897 lowered tariffs but established a protection policy that lasted until 1911. Laurier's land and emigration policy remains as perhaps the basic achievement of his government. During 15 years more than 1,000,000 people moved into Manitoba and into the western territories, which in 1905 became the provinces of Saskatchewan and Alberta. Wheat became the major product of the new Prairie Provinces; towns and ports sprang up; railroads flourished; and in 1903 Laurier announced that a second transcontinental rail system would be built: the Canadian west had become the granary of the world.

Meanwhile, the Prime Minister's attention had been diverted to external affairs. In 1897, 1902, 1907, and 1911 he attended Imperial Conferences at which he steadily resisted British proposals for closer ties that might commit Canada to defense responsibilities. He sincerely admired the institutions and liberal policies of Great Britain—he accepted a knighthood (1897) and once declared that he would be proud to see a Canadian of French descent affirming the principles of freedom in the British Parliament—yet he would never agree to any dilution of Canadian autonomy. Thus, from his policies there began to emerge the modern concept of a British Commonwealth of independent states.

Britain's South African War of 1899 marked the start of Laurier's decline. Quebec nationalists denounced his decision to send a force of 1,000 men, while English Canadians thought the number insufficient. Then, a series of invidious disputes—over denominational schools in the Northwest, Sunday observance laws, the restrictions of French linguistic rights in Manitoba and Ontario—kept widening the rift between the nationalities in the east and new Canadians in the west and between Laurier and his Cabinet. As the election of 1911 approached, the Prime Minister attempted to reunite his factious party by negotiating a treaty of reciprocity with the United States, but he failed. Reciprocity did not distract Quebec from the convincing argument that each one of Laurier's compromises was a surrender of French Canada's fundamental rights. Among the Britannic Canadians, reciprocity seemed an opportunistic capitulation to the United States, the first step toward annexation. In a month of bitter campaigning in 1911, the 70-year-old prime minister delivered more than 50 speeches yet could not overcome the powerful combination of imperialist business interests and bigoted nationalism. He retired with the dignity Canadians had learned to expect of him and spent his remaining years as leader of the opposition.

Assessment. To his faithful followers, especially in Quebec, where his surname is used as a first name by many other Canadians, Laurier is a charismatic hero whose term of office was a happy time in Canadian history. He worked all his life for cooperation between French- and English-speaking Canadians while he strove to keep Canada as independent as possible from Britain. His personal charm and dignity, his great skill as an orator, and his great gifts of intellect won the admiration of all Canadians and non-Canadians alike.

(J.Mo.)

BIBLIOGRAPHY. Authoritative and sympathetic biographies of Laurier are L.O. David, *Laurier: sa vie—ses oeuvres* (1919); and O.D. Skelton, *The Life and Letters of Sir Wilfrid Laurier,* 2 vol. (1921, reprinted 1965). Also laudatory is Sir John Willison, *Sir Wilfrid Laurier and the Liberal Party: A Political History,* 2 vol. (1903). More recent reappraisals of Laurier's life and work include Paul Stevens, "Wilfrid Laurier: Politician," in M. Hamelin (ed.), *The Political Ideas of the Prime Ministers of Canada* (1969).

Laurium, Modern Greek LÁVRION, industrial town of the *nomós* (department) of Attica, on the Aegean Sea, famous in antiquity for its silver mines. Its port, sheltered by Makrónisos island, imports coal, loads ore, and handles coastal and insular shipping.

The mines may have been worked as early as 1000 BC, but in 483 BC Athenians exploited the veins to finance construction of a large fleet, which then defeated the Persians at Salamis in 480. Sparta forced the closing of the mines after their occupation of Decelea in 413. Production remained low until after 350, when, as Demosthenes' speeches show, large fortunes were being made by the proprietors. The Laureot Owls, Athenian silver coinage attributed to the mines, were circulated throughout the classical world, but by Roman times the mines lay neglected because of competition from the gold and silver mines of Pangaeum in Macedonia and piratical raids on the Laurium mines. About the beginning of the Christian Era, the silver was exhausted, and not until after 1860, when franchises were granted to Greek, French, and U.S. companies for reworking the ancient slag heaps—for lead and the extraction of cadmium and manganese—were the mines again active.

The best preserved of the ancient shafts and tunnels are found in the Verzeko Valley just west of Laurium, running south from the village of Áyios Konstandínos. Poisonous fumes have killed all vegetation around Laurium, but workshop chimneys are located on hillsides to render the fumes less noxious. The port is linked by railway to Athens. Pop. (1981) 10,124.

"De," "la," and similar components of a name, when followed by a space, are alphabetized as separate words (e.g., *De Forest, Lee*). *When they are joined to the following part of a name, the combination is treated as a single word* (e.g., *DeForest, John William*).

Lausanne, capital of Vaud canton, western Switzerland, on the northern shore of Lake Geneva (Lac Léman); built on the southern slopes of the Jorat heights, its altitude ranges from 1,240 ft (378 m) at Ouchy, its lake port, to 2,122 ft at Le Signal, its highest point. Two short streams, the Flon and the Louve, which formerly flowed through the centre of the city, have been filled in, leaving numerous

The Cathédrale de Notre-Dame in Lausanne, Switz.
Sven Samelius

depressions; as a result, Lausanne has a hilly appearance, built on many connecting levels.

The ancient Celtic Lausonium, or Lausonna, was originally on the shore of the lake southwest of the present city. During the invasion of the Alemanni (*c.* 379), the inhabitants took refuge in the hills above, building a settlement on the site of the present Cité district. In 590 Bishop Marius of Aventicum (now Avenches) established his diocese there. The settlement eventually joined with the Burgundian settlement of Bourg across the Flon and with a colony around the church of Saint-Laurent to the west. The bishops, princes of the Holy Roman Empire from the 12th century, retained their great temporal powers until 1536, when Lausanne, with the rest of the Pays de Vaud, was conquered by the Bernese, who introduced the Protestant Reformation. The Bernese occupation lasted until 1798, and Lausanne became the capital of the new Vaud canton of Napoleon's Helvetic Republic in 1803.

Two major international treaties were signed at Lausanne: between Italy and Turkey in 1912 and between Turkey and the Allies of World War I in 1923. In 1932 a conference was held there to liquidate reparations payments by Germany to the Allies. In 1964 it was the site of the Swiss National Exhibition, held every 25 years in a different Swiss city.

Historic buildings include the early Gothic Cathedral of Notre-Dame, consecrated in 1275 by Pope Gregory X in the presence of the Holy Roman emperor Rudolf I; the Saint-François Church, erected during the same period but partly rebuilt in the late 14th century; and the city hall (rebuilt 1674). The castle, now housing the Historical Museum of the Ancient Bishopric, is the only vestige of the 13th-century residences of the bishops. The Château Saint-Maire (1397–1431), the former bishop's castle, is now the seat of the cantonal government. More recent landmarks are the Palais de Rumine (1903), the principal building of the university, which also houses the cantonal museums, and the federal court of justice (1927), seat of the Swiss Supreme Court.

Lausanne rivals Geneva as the intellectual and cultural centre of French Switzerland. Its university (1891) originated as a theological academy in 1537. The city was the birthplace of the noted literary figures Benjamin Constant de Rebecque, Alexandre Vinet, Juste Olivier, and Charles-Ferdinand Ramuz and of the philosopher Charles Secrétan. Many famous men of letters, including Voltaire, Jean-Jacques Rousseau, Victor Hugo, Charles Dickens, and Edward Gibbon, resided there.

The headquarters of the International Olympic Committee are at Lausanne, and an Olympic Museum, surrounded by a public park, opened in 1993. Lausanne is also the site of the Federal Institute of Technology (founded 1853, present status 1969) and of the annual national fair Comptoir Suisse.

A junction for railway lines from Geneva, Fribourg, Bern, and Vallorbe (for Paris), Lausanne gained greatly in commercial importance when the opening of the Simplon Tunnel in 1906 placed it on the great international route from Paris to Milan. Principal industries include the manufacture of precision instruments and clothing, metal and leather work, printing, and food processing. The city is also an important tourist and convention centre. Pop. (2002 est.) 116,332.

Lausanne, Treaty of (1923), final treaty concluding World War I. It was signed by representatives of Turkey (successor to the Ottoman Empire) on one side and by Britain, France, Italy, Japan, Greece, Romania, and the Kingdom of Serbs, Croats, and Slovenes (the future Yugoslavia) on the other. The treaty was signed at Lausanne, Switz., on July 24, 1923, after a seven-month conference.

The treaty recognized the boundaries of the modern state of Turkey. Turkey made no claim to its former Arab provinces and recognized British possession of Cyprus and Italian possession of the Dodecanese. The Allies dropped demands of autonomy for Turkish Kurdistan and Turkish cession of territory to Armenia, abandoned claims to spheres of influence in Turkey, and imposed no controls over Turkey's finances or armed forces. The Turkish straits between the Aegean Sea and the Black Sea were opened to all shipping.

Lausanne Conference (June–July 1932), conference that was held to liquidate the payment of reparations by Germany to the former Allied and Associated powers of World War I. Attended by representatives of the creditor powers (Great Britain, France, Belgium, and Italy) and of Germany, it resulted in agreement on July 9, 1932, that the world economic crisis made the continued reparation payments impossible. Germany, however, was to deliver to the Bank for International Settlements 5 percent redeemable bonds to the value of three billion Reichsmarks. The creditor governments canceled war debts as between themselves but made a "gentleman's agreement" that the Lausanne Protocol would not be ratified until they had reached a satisfactory agreement with respect to their own war debts to the United States. Although the agreement was never ratified, the protocol in effect put an end to attempts to exact reparations from Germany.

Laut Island, Indonesian PULAU LAUT, Laut also spelled LAOET, island off the southeastern coast of Borneo, Kalimantan Selatan *provinsi* ("province"), Indonesia. Laut Island lies in the Makassar Strait, 105 miles (169 km) east of Banjarmasin city. It is 60 miles (100 km) long north to south and 20 miles (30 km) wide east to west, and it covers an area of about 796 square miles (2,062 square km). The island is low-lying and flat except in the northeast, where hills rise to about 2,600 feet (800 m). Much of the island is covered with sago and coconut palms and mangrove trees. The coastal climate is hot and humid.

Most of the population is engaged in the production of spices (especially pepper) and rubber, both grown in extensive plantations. The main industry is coal mining. Copra, pepper, and coal are the major exports. Transportation is by boat across the narrow Laut Strait. The chief town and port is Kotabaru on the northern tip of the island; it is connected by road with Karambu on the western coast.

Lautaro (b. before 1535—d. April 29, 1557, Mataquito, Chile), Araucanian (Mapuche) Indian who led the native uprising against the Spanish conquerors in south-central Chile from 1553 to 1557.

Lautaro was probably born in northern Chile; according to tradition, during his boyhood he was captured by the Spanish and forced to serve as a groom in the stables of the conquistador Pedro de Valdivia. Escaping southward into Araucanian Indian country soon after Valdivia began conquering it in 1550, Lautaro joined the Araucanians, unified their tribal organization, and with their chief, Caupolicán, led them in battle, further improving on the shrewd tactics and stratagems by which they had often defeated the Spaniards.

In a battle in December 1553, near Tucapel, Lautaro captured Valdivia; he executed him the next month. Lautaro himself was killed in a battle at the Mataquito River in 1557. The Araucanians continued their resistance, and the region was not finally pacified until the 1880s. Now regarded by Chileans as a national hero, Lautaro is the hero of the epic poem *La Araucana* (1569–89), written by Alonso de Ercilla y Zúñiga, one of Valdivia's soldiers.

Lauterbur, Paul, in full PAUL CHRISTIAN LAUTERBUR (b. May 6, 1929, Sidney, Ohio, U.S.), American chemist who, with Sir Peter Mansfield, won the 2003 Nobel Prize for Physiology or Medicine for the development of magnetic resonance imaging (MRI), a computerized scanning technology that produces images of internal body structures.

After receiving a Ph.D. (1962) from the University of Pittsburgh, Lauterbur was a professor at the University of New York at Stony Brook from 1969 to 1985, when he accepted the post of professor at the University of Illinois at Urbana-Champaign and director of its Biomedical Magnetic Resonance Laboratory.

In the early 1970s Lauterbur began work using nuclear magnetic resonance (NMR), a key tool in chemical analysis that uses absorption measurements of very high-frequency radio waves to provide information about the nuclear structure of various solids and liquids. He realized that if the magnetic field was made nonuniform, information in the signal distortions could be used to create two-dimensional images of a sample's internal structure. This led to the development of MRI as Mansfield turned Lauterbur's work into a practical medical tool. Noninvasive and lacking the harmful side effects of X-ray and other examinations, MRI became widely used in medicine.

Lautoka, city on the northwest coast of Viti Levu (island), Fiji, in the South Pacific. Situated on the dry side of the island, Lautoka (originally called Namoli) serves an important sugarcane-growing district and is Fiji's leading sugar export port. Large mills in the city are supplied with cane by a private railroad. Roads link Lautoka to Suva (about 140 miles [225 km] southeast). Lautoka is 17 miles (27 km) north of the international airport at Nandi (Nadi). Pop. (1996) 36,083.

Lautréamont, Count (comte) **de,** pseudonym of ISIDORE-LUCIEN DUCASSE (b. April 4, 1846, Montevideo, Uruguay—d. Nov. 4, 1870, Paris, France), poet, a strange and enigmatic figure in French literature, who is recognized as a major influence on the Surrealists.

The son of a chancellor in the French consulate, Lautréamont was sent to France for schooling; he studied at the imperial lycées in Tarbes (1859–62) and Pau (1863–65). He set out for Paris in 1867, ostensibly to attend the École Polytechnique, and disappeared into obscurity. Little more is known of his life. He took the name of Lautréamont and his title from the arrogant hero of Eugène Sue's historical novel *Latréaumont* (1837).

The first stanza of his prose poem *Les Chants de Maldoror* was published anonymously in 1868. A complete edition was printed in 1869, but the Belgian publisher, alarmed by its violence and fearing prosecution, refused to distribute it to booksellers. The *Poésies,* a shorter work, was printed in June 1870. Lautréamont died in Paris later that same year, possibly a victim of the police during the siege of Paris.

Maldoror was republished in 1890. The work received little notice until the Surrealists, struck by its disquieting juxtaposition of strange and unrelated images, adopted Lautréamont as one of their exemplars. Above all it was the savagery of protest in *Maldoror,* as if revolt against the human condition had achieved definitive blasphemy, that created a ferment among the poets and painters of the early 20th century.

Lauzun, Antonin-Nompar de Caumont, Count and Duke (comte et duc) **de,** also called MARQUIS DE PUYGUILHEM (b. May 1633, Lauzun, Fr.—d. Nov. 19, 1723, Paris),

Lauzun, detail of a portrait by Sir Peter Lely

Giraudon—Art Resource, New York City

French military officer who was imprisoned by King Louis XIV to prevent him from marrying the Duchesse de Montpensier (known as La Grande Mademoiselle), the wealthiest heiress in Europe.

The son of Gabriel de Caumont, comte de Lauzun, he was at first known as the marquis de Puyguilhem. In 1658 he was appointed colonel of Louis XIV's foreign dragoons. When Louis became infatuated with Puyguilhem's lover, Mme de Monaco, the Marquis displayed such brazen jealousy that the King sent him to the Bastille for six months (1665). He became colonel general of the dragoons in 1688, but the following year he was again sent to the Bastille for venting his rage against Louis's mistress, Mme de Montespan, who had dissuaded the King from appointing him grand master of the artillery. Quickly released, he was made a captain of the King's bodyguard.

In 1670 the Duchesse de Montpensier astonished the court by proposing marriage to the Comte de Lauzun (as Puyguilhem was now known). Louis at first consented to the match but withdrew his consent after objections from the princes and from Mme de Montespan, who desired the vast Montpensier inheritance for her children. Showered with compensatory honours, Lauzun indulged in more outbursts against Mme de Montespan. He was arrested in November 1671 and imprisoned in the fortress of Pignerol, Italy, until April 1681, when he consented to renounce the lands granted to him by the Duchesse. Soon after returning to Paris in 1682 he seems to have secretly married the Duchesse, but in 1684 they separated. Lauzun, having commanded French troops in Ireland in 1690, was created duc in 1692.

Lauzun, Armand-Louis de Gontaut, duc de (duke of): *see* Biron, Armand-Louis de Gontaut, duc de.

lava, magma (molten rock) poured out onto the Earth's surface at temperatures from about 700° to 1,200° C (1,300° to 2,200° F). The viscosity ranges from about 100,000 times that of water to the point that the lava can scarcely flow at all.

Mafic (ferromagnesian, dark-coloured) lavas, such as basalt, characteristically form flows known by the Hawaiian names pahoehoe and aa. Pahoehoe lava flows are characterized by smooth, gently undulating, or broadly hummocky surfaces. The liquid lava flowing beneath a thin, still-plastic crust drags and wrinkles it into tapestry-like folds and rolls resembling twisted rope. Pahoehoe lava flows are fed almost wholly internally by streams of liquid lava flowing through natural pipes known as lava tubes. Typically, the margin of a pahoehoe flow advances by protruding one small toe after another.

In contrast to pahoehoe, the surface of aa lava is exceedingly rough, covered with a layer of partly loose, very irregular fragments commonly called clinker. Aa lava flows are fed principally by rivers of liquid lava flowing in open channels. Typically, such a feeding river forms a narrow band, 8–15 metres (25–50 feet) wide, along the centre line of the flow, with broad fields of less actively moving clinker on each side of it. At the front of the flow, clinker from the top rolls down and is overridden by the pasty layer.

Thin basaltic lava flows generally contain many holes, or vesicles, left by bubbles of gas frozen into the congealing liquid. Thick flows, which remain hot for long periods, may lose most of their gas before the lava congeals, and the resulting rock may be dense with few vesicles.

Pahoehoe and aa flows may be identical in chemical composition. In fact, it is common for a flow that leaves the vent as pahoehoe to change to aa as it progresses downslope. The greater the viscosity, and the greater the stirring of the liquid (as by rapid flow down a steep slope), the greater the tendency for the material to change from pahoehoe to aa. The reverse change does not occur.

Lavas of andesitic or intermediate composition commonly form a somewhat different type of flow, known as a block lava flow. These resemble aa in having tops consisting largely of loose rubble, but the fragments are more regular in shape, most of them polygons with fairly smooth sides. Flows of more siliceous lava tend to be even more fragmental than block flows. Apparently the escape of gas from the cooling and crystallizing magma causes a series of minute explosions all through the flow, thoroughly shattering the lava into a mass of blocks that are little separated from each other.

Lava Beds National Monument, region of recent lava flows and related volcanic formations, including deep chasms, cinder cones that rise to 300 ft (90 m) from the lava, and chimneys, in northern California, U.S., south of the city of Tule Lake.The main battle sites of the Modoc Indian War (1872–73) are located within the monument, which occupies 72 sq mi (186 sq km).

lava cave, cave or cavity formed as a result of surface solidification of a lava flow during the last stages of its activity. A frozen crust may form over still mobile and actively flowing liquid rock as a result of surface cooling. A dwindling supply of lava may then cause the molten material to drain out from under this crust and leave long cylindrical tunnels. Volcanic gases from bubbles in the lava collect under the tunnel roof and support it. As this gas mixes with air from vents in the roof, more intense heating from oxidation may raise the temperature sufficiently to re-fuse the ceiling rock, which then drips with the remelted lava. Such lava may congeal in place to form rude stalactites. Caves of this type commonly have solidified lava streams along their floors; in places, the roofs may collapse to form pits or depressions on the ground surface.

Consult the INDEX *first*

Laval, city, seat of Montréal region, southern Quebec province, Canada. It occupies the whole of Île Jésus (Jesus Island), just north of Île de Montréal from which it is separated to the south by the Rivière des Prairies and from the mainland to the north by the Rivière des Mille Îles; both rivers are extensions of the Ottawa, which flows into the St. Lawrence below Montreal city. Île Jésus, 20 mi (32 km) long by 8 mi wide, with an area of 95 sq mi (246 sq km), was first settled in 1681. In 1699 it was granted to the Society of Jesus, and named for François de Montmorency Laval, the first Roman Catholic bishop of Canada. By 1702 a parish known as Saint-François de Sales was established.

Development of Montreal suburban communities on the island was relatively slow until the post-World War II years. In 1959, because of industrialization and urban growth, the Interurban Corporation of Île Jésus was formed. In 1965 the city of Laval was created by merging the island's cities of Chomedey, Duvernay, Laval-des-Rapides, Laval Ouest, Pont-Viau, Sainte-Rose, and the towns of Auteuil, Fabreville, Îles-Laval, Laval-sur-le-Lac, Sainte-Dorothée, Saint-François, Saint-Vincent-de-Paul, and Vimont.

Since the opening of industrial parks in the 1960s, planned industrial development has been rapid. Manufactures include television and radio sets, lithographic printed materials, paper, aluminum, iron and steel products, pharmaceuticals, and dairy foods. Inc. city, 1965. Pop. (2001) 343,005.

Laval, town, capital of Mayenne *département,* Pays de la Loire region, northwestern France, east of Rennes. The old quarters of the town, which have fine 16th- and 18th-century houses and two châteaus, are located on the west bank slopes of the Mayenne River and are surrounded by the modern town on both sides of the river. The old castle of the counts of Laval, a medieval stronghold, has

Château of the count of Laval overlooking the Pont Vieux (Old Bridge) on the Mayenne River, Laval, Fr.
Ralph Luce—Shostal/EB Inc.

been restored and houses a museum. The Château Neuf (New Chateau), a Renaissance building also called the Gallery of the Counts of Laval, was restored and enlarged in the 19th century to become the Palais de Justice. The cathedral, dating partly from the 11th century, has been considerably reconstructed and enlarged. The old castle, around which the town of Laval grew, was built early in the 10th century by Guy II, one of the first lords of Laval. The lords, and later the counts, of Laval among whom were the Montmorencys and the Montforts, played a prominent role in French history. After the French Revolution the counterrevolutionary Vendéen army, during the Wars of the Vendée at the end of the 18th and beginning of the 19th centuries, twice captured the castle from the Republicans. When the Republicans crushed the insurgents they executed the Prince de Talmont, lord of Laval and general of the Vendéen cavalry, in front of the castle gates. Today Laval is a centre for a textile industry (linen and cotton) and manufactures shoes and leather goods. Industrial growth has occurred in manufactures such as electronics and printing. Pop. (1999) 54,379.

Laval, Carl Gustaf Patrik de (b. May 9, 1845, Blasenborg, Swed.—d. Feb. 2, 1913, Stockholm), Swedish scientist, engineer, and inventor who pioneered in the development of high-speed turbines.

After 1872 he was an engineer with the Klosters-Bruck Steel Works. In 1878 he invented the centrifugal cream separator, and later he applied the principle of rotation to the manufacture of glass bottles.

Laval built his first impulse steam turbine in 1882. Further advances followed, and in 1893 he built and operated a reversible turbine for marine use. A Laval reaction turbine (patented in 1883) attained a speed of 42,000 revolutions per minute. He continued improving his turbine until by 1896 he was operating a complete power plant using an initial steam pressure of 3,400 pounds per square inch. He invented and developed the divergent nozzle used to deliver steam to the turbine blades. His flexible shaft, used to eliminate wobbling, which can be dangerous at high speeds, and his special double-helical gear formed the foundation for most steam-turbine development that followed.

Laval, François de Montmorency (b. April 30, 1623, Montigny-sur-Avre, Fr.—d. May

6, 1708, Quebec), the first Roman Catholic bishop in Canada, who laid the foundations of church organization in France's North American possessions.

Born into one of the greatest families of France, Laval was ordained priest in 1647. After taking a degree in canon law at the Sorbonne, he was named archdeacon of the diocese of Évreux. He later resigned that post, however, and lived (1654–58) at the Ermitage of Caen, a spiritual school under the direction of Jean de Bernières.

In June 1658 Laval was made a bishop and vicar apostolic of New France, and a year later he took up residence in Quebec. A man of great vision and strong character, Laval was quarrelsome by nature and became involved in frequent conflicts with the civil authorities of the colony. His staunch opposition to

François de Montmorency Laval, portrait by Frère Luc

liquor sales to the Indians brought him into conflict with the governor, Baron d'Avaugour, in 1662. Laval departed for France in August and succeeded in bringing about d'Avaugour's recall the following year.

Laval returned to Quebec in 1663 and in that year founded the Seminary of Quebec, which was intended to be both a training school for priests and a home for retired priests. It was not long, however, before he quarrelled also with the new governor, who, in 1664, removed from the Sovereign Council four men who were protégés of Laval.

Laval's political power declined somewhat with the arrival of the new intendant (royal agent) Jean-Baptiste Talon, who had instructions to make certain that the authority of the clergy be subordinated to that of the civil government. Yet, in spiritual matters, Laval's authority remained preeminent. In 1674 he was made bishop of Quebec. The newly created diocese of Quebec, which included all French territory in North America, was placed under the direct supervision of Rome.

In 1684 Laval, suffering from ill health, left Quebec and presented his resignation to the court, which reluctantly accepted it. Although he technically continued in office for several more years, his destined successor, Monsignor de Saint-Vallier, took office in Quebec in 1685 with the title of vicar general. Upon Laval's official resignation in 1688, Saint-Vallier succeeded him. Laval resided at the Seminary of Quebec until his death.

In 1852 the Seminary was named after its founder, becoming Laval University. His cause of canonization was introduced in 1878; the decree stating that Laval was a man of saintly virtues was promulgated by Pope John XXIII in 1960.

Laval, Pierre (b. June 28, 1883, Châteldon, Fr.—d. Oct. 15, 1945, Paris), French politician and statesman who led the Vichy government in policies of collaboration with Germany during World War II, for which he was ultimately executed as a traitor to France.

Pierre Laval, 1931
Harris & Ewing

A member of the Socialist Party from 1903, Laval became a lawyer in Paris in 1909 and promptly made a name for himself by his defense of trade unionists and leftists. Elected deputy for Aubervilliers in 1914, he urged a negotiated peace to end World War I. Defeated in the 1919 election, he left the Socialist Party in 1920, became mayor of Aubervilliers (1923–44), and was reelected deputy in 1924, leaving the Chamber to become a senator in 1927. After gaining experience as minister of public works (1925), undersecretary of state (1925), minister of justice (1926), and minister of labour (1930), when he was responsible for steering the Social Insurance Act through both of the National Assembly chambers, he became premier for the first time in 1931. He early displayed a tendency to act over the heads of his ministers, especially in regard to foreign affairs. Defeated in 1932, he became minister of colonies and then minister of foreign affairs in 1934 under Gaston Doumergue and then under Pierre Flandin. Becoming premier again in 1935, Laval also took the portfolio for foreign affairs. Concerned to create a stable Europe, he made the cornerstone of his policy a strong Franco-Italian rapprochement, which eventually collapsed over the Ethiopian crisis in 1936. Domestically, Laval met financial crises by refusing to devalue the franc, cutting expenditures instead.

Laval's Cabinet fell in 1936, shortly before the Popular Front victory. In 1940 he entered Marshal Pétain's government as minister of state and was largely responsible for persuading the government to remain in France and accept an armistice so that there would be a legal government in Paris that could negotiate advantageous terms and, perhaps, eventually a peace treaty. He was also responsible for persuading the Assembly to dissolve itself, thus ending the Third Republic on July 10, 1940, and for the revision of the constitution. Certain of an ultimate German victory, he became convinced that France's best course lay in collaboration with Germany in order to assure France a strong role in the future. He began negotiations on his own initiative, arousing the mistrust of his fellow ministers; Pétain dismissed him in December 1940.

When he returned as head of the government in 1942, France could no longer expect to be Germany's collaborator, but instead was fighting for survival as an independent state. To assure Germany of France's goodwill, Laval agreed to provide French labourers for German industries. In a famous speech (June 1942) asking for volunteers, he announced that he desired a German victory. In general, however, he tried to protect France by hard-fought compromises in negotiations with Hitler. Laval's control of France deteriorated with the growth of the resistance movement and the attacks of extremist collaborators such as Marcel Déat, with whom the Germans forced him to work.

When Germany collapsed, Laval fled to Spain, where he prepared his defense, returning to France in July 1945. On trial for treason he found himself in a hostile court, faced by a heckling jury, his defense constantly cut off. He was executed, after attempting to poison himself, on Oct. 15, 1945.

Laval University, French UNIVERSITÉ LAVAL, a French-language, Roman Catholic university located on the outskirts of the city of Quebec. Laval's predecessor institution, the Seminary of Quebec, considered the first Canadian institution of higher learning, was founded by François de Montmorency Laval, first bishop of Quebec, in 1663. Queen Victoria granted the seminary a university charter in 1852, and it was recognized by a papal bull in 1872. In 1970 the university was reorganized and given a new charter by the national assembly of Quebec. Laval currently carries on an active educational exchange with French-language universities in Africa, Europe, and the Caribbean. Several scientific research institutes are affiliated with the university.

lavaliere, ornament hung from a chain worn around the neck. The lavaliere, which came into fashion in the 17th century, was usually a small, jewelled gold locket, though it could also be an enamelled locket or pendant.

The lavaliere was named for the Duchesse de La Vallière, the mistress of Louis XIV in the 1660s. The term was sometimes also used during the Third Republic in France to describe a man's silk scarf that was worn loosely knotted with long hanging ends.

Lavalleja, department, southeastern Uruguay, named for Juan Antonio Lavalleja, a hero of Uruguay's struggle for independence. The department has an area of 3,867 sq mi (10,016 sq km) and contains some of the most mountainous areas of Uruguay, including the Cuchilla Grande (Great Ridge). Much of northern Lavalleja is used for livestock raising, the department's principal economic activity. Lands in the south are devoted primarily to production of milk, vegetables, and industrial crops for the Montevideo market. Slate and limestone are quarried, and galena marble, iron ore, emery, and dolomite are mined in the Cuchilla Grande. The Pan-American Highway traverses Lavalleja southwest–northeast, passing through Minas (*q.v.*), the capital. Lavalleja is also linked to Montevideo by rail. Pop. (1996) 60,618.

Lavater, Johann Kaspar (b. Nov. 11, 1741, Zürich—d. Jan. 2, 1801, Zürich), Swiss writer, Protestant pastor, and founder of physiognomics, an anti-rational, religious, and literary movement.

Lavater served as pastor of St. Peter's Church in Zürich. He was deported to Basel for a time because of his protest against the violence of the French Directory. His studies in physiognomy and his interest in "magnetic" trance conditions had their source in his religious beliefs, which drove him to search for demonstrable traces of the divine in human life. His belief in the interaction of mind and

Lavater, oil painting by an unknown artist, 18th century; in the Schweizerisches Landesmuseum, Zürich
By courtesy of the Swiss National Museum, Zurich

body led him to seek influences of the spirit upon the features.

His *Physiognomische Fragmente zur Beförderung der Menschenkenntnis und Menschenliebe*, 4 vol. (1775–78; *Essays on Physiognomy*, 1789–98) established his reputation throughout Europe. Goethe worked with Lavater on the book, and the two enjoyed a warm friendship that was later severed by Lavater's zeal for conversion.

Lavater's most important books are *Aussichten in die Ewigkeit* (1768–78), *Geheimes Tagebuch von einem Beobachter seiner selbst* (1772–73; *Secret Journal of a Self Observer*, 1795), *Pontius Pilatus* (1782–85), and *Nathanael* (1786). His lyrical and epic poems are imitations of Klopstock.

"De," "la," and similar components of a name, when followed by a space, are alphabetized as separate words (e.g., *De Forest, Lee*). *When they are joined to the following part of a name, the combination is treated as a single word* (e.g., *DeForest, John William*).

lavatoe (dance): *see* volta, la.

Lavelle, Louis (b. July 15, 1883, Saint-Martin-de-Villeréal, Fr.—d. Sept. 1, 1951, Saint-Martin-de-Villeréal), French philosopher recognized as a forerunner of the psychometaphysic movement, which teaches that self-actualization and ultimate freedom develop from seeking one's "inward" being and relating it to the Absolute. Much of his thought drew upon the writings of Nicolas Malebranche and St. Augustine.

Lavelle received a doctorate from the Lycée Fustel de Coulanges, Strasbourg (1921), before becoming professor of philosophy at the Sorbonne (1932–34) and the Collège de France (1941–51). He was appointed inspector general of national education (1941) and elected to the Académie des Sciences Morales et Politiques in 1947. His major works include *La Dialectique du monde sensible* (1921; "The Dialectic of the World of the Senses"), *La Conscience de soi* (1933; "Self-Awareness"), *La Présence totale* (1934; "The Total Presence"), *Le Mal et la souffrance* (1940; "Evil and Suffering"), and *Introduction à l'ontologie* (1947; "Introduction to Ontology").

lavender, any plant of the genus *Lavandula*, comprising about 20 species of the mint family Labiatae, native to countries bordering on the Mediterranean. English lavender (*L. officinalis, L. spica, or L. vera*) is cultivated widely for its essential oil and for its narrow fragrant leaves and spikes of purple flowers that are dried and used in sachets. French lavender (*L. stoechas*) and *L. lanata,* native to

French lavender (*Lavandula stoechas*)
W.H. Hodge

Spain, are also widely cultivated. The ancient Romans used lavender in their baths, and the dried flowers have long been used to scent chests and closets.

Lavender is a small evergreen shrub with gray-green, hoary, linear leaves, and light-purple flowers sparsely arranged on spikes at the tips of long, bare stalks. The fragrance of the plant is caused by shining oil glands imbedded among tiny star-shaped hairs with which the flowers, leaves, and stems are covered. The plants in cultivation do not produce seed, and propagation is by slips or by dividing the roots. In Britain and the United States, lavender is cultivated for its essential oil, while in the south of Europe the flowers are an object of trade.

Lavender oil is obtained by distillation of the flowers and is used chiefly in fine perfumes and cosmetics. It is a colourless or yellow liquid, the fragrant constituents of which are linalyl acetate, linalool, pinene, limonene, geraniol, and cineole. Lavender water, a solution of the essential oil in alcohol with other added scents, is used in a variety of toilet preparations.

Spike oil, or spike lavender oil, is distilled from a somewhat inferior grade of lavender having grayer leaves. Oil of spike is used in painting on porcelain, in soap manufacture, and to scent other products.

laver, Japanese NORI, any member of the genus *Porphyra,* a group of marine red algae.

Laver (*Porphyra*)
J.R. Waaland

The thallus, a sheet of cells embedded in a thin gelatinous mass, varies in colour from deep brown or red to pink; sexual reproductive structures are at the margin. Laver grows at the high-water mark of the intertidal zone in both Northern and Southern hemispheres. It grows best in nitrogen-rich water, such as is found near sewage outlets. Laver is harvested, dried, and used as food in greater amounts than any other seaweed. Cultivated as a major food crop in artificial seawater factories in the Orient, it is used as a soup base, a flavouring for other food, and a salt for meat. In the British Isles laver is grilled on toast (sloke) and has an oyster-like taste.

Laver, Rod(ney George) (b. Aug. 9, 1938, Rockhampton, Queensland, Australia), outstanding Australian tennis player, the second male player in the history of the game (after Don Budge in 1938) to win the four major singles championships—Australia, France, Great Britain (Wimbledon), and the United States—in one year (1962) and the first to repeat this grand slam (1969).

The son of two tournament lawn tennis players, Laver was introduced early to the game. Considered too small to become a good player, he began vigorous practice as a youth in the Australian outback. Later he came to the attention of the Australian Davis Cup captain, Harry Hopman, and became a member of the Australian Davis Cup squad at the age of 18. He first toured overseas in 1956, and his first outstanding success was winning the Australian doubles championship with Robert Mark and the Wimbledon mixed doubles with Darlene Hard in 1959. He won the Australian singles in 1960. In Wimbledon play, Laver won the men's singles four times (1961–62, 1968-69), the mixed doubles twice (1959–60), and the men's doubles once (1971). In 1962 he added the Italian and German singles titles to his four grand slam victories. From 1959 through 1962 he played for the Australian team in Davis Cup competition; in 1962 he won all three of his matches—two singles and one doubles—in the challenge (final) round.

Laver turned professional in 1963 and dominated the professional game until the introduction of open tournaments in 1968, when he won the first open Wimbledon championship. His championship play continued into the 1970s. In 1971 he became the first professional tennis player to surpass the $1,000,000 mark in career prize money, and he held on to his position as tennis' all-time leading money-winner until 1978. In 1976 the 38-year-old Laver joined the San Diego team in World Team Tennis competition and was named the league's Rookie of the Year.

Laveran, (Charles-Louis-)Alphonse (b. June 18, 1845, Paris—d. May 18, 1922, Paris), French physician, pathologist, and parasitologist who in 1880 in Algeria discovered the parasite that causes human malaria. For this and later work on protozoal diseases he received the Nobel Prize for Physiology or Medicine in 1907.

Educated at the Strasbourg faculty of medicine, he served as an army surgeon in the Franco-German War (1870–71) and practiced and taught military medicine until 1897, when he joined the Pasteur Institute, Paris.

Laveran was a powerful influence in developing research in tropical medicine, carrying on fruitful work in trypanosomiasis, leishmaniasis, and other protozoal diseases, as well as his epochal work in malaria. He established the Laboratory of Tropical Diseases at the Pasteur Institute (1907) and founded the Société de Pathologie Exotique (1908).

Laveran's extensive writings include *Trypanosomes et trypanosomiasis* (with Félix Masnil; 1904); *Traité des fièvres palustres avec la description des microbes du paludisme*

Laveran
BBC Hulton Picture Library

(1884); and *Traité des maladies et épidémies des armées* (1875).

Lavigerie, Charles (-Martial-Allemand) (b. Oct. 31, 1825, near Bayonne, Fr.—d. Nov. 25?, 1892, Algiers), cardinal and archbishop of Algiers and Carthage (now Tunis, Tunisia) whose dream to convert Africa to Christianity prompted him to found the Society of Missionaries of Africa, or White Fathers.

He was ordained priest in 1849 after studies at Saint-Sulpice, Paris. He taught at the Sorbonne but resigned his professorship to become director of the Society for the Promotion of Education in the Near East (Oeuvre des Écoles d'Orient), through which he raised aid for those Maronites (Lebanese Christians) who had survived the massacre of 1860 led by the Druzes, a Middle Eastern people whose religion is derived from Islām. His tour of Lebanon at that time inspired his missionary plans.

Consecrated bishop of Nancy, Fr., in 1863, he was appointed archbishop of Algiers in 1867. With the support of Emperor Napoleon III of France, Lavigerie overrode the local government's disapproval of missionary work among Algerian Muslims and established vil-

Lavigerie, detail of a painting by Léon Bonnat, 1888; in the Palais du Luxembourg, Paris

H. Roger-Viollet

lages for orphans. He founded the White Fathers in 1868 for work in northern Algeria, and by 1878 he had encouraged the society to extend its missions to equatorial Africa. Expanding his activities into Tunisia, he was named cardinal in 1882 by Pope Leo XIII, who in 1884 made him primate of Africa and archbishop of the restored see of Carthage.

He had always opposed slavery, and he spent his last years organizing antislavery societies to protect the people of central Africa. Three years after his death, the White Fathers were working in West Africa, and the society was finally approved by Pope St. Pius X in 1908.

Lavinium, modern PRATICA DI MARE, Italy, an ancient town of Latium, 19 miles (30 kilometres) south of Rome, regarded as the religious centre of the early Latin peoples. Roman tradition maintained that it had been founded by Aeneas and his followers from Troy and named after his wife, Lavinia. Here he is supposed to have built a temple establishing the worship of the household gods, the Penates. Certain classes of Roman officials sacrificed regularly at Lavinium to the Penates and Vesta. Lavinium remained loyal to Rome in the wars of the 5th and 4th centuries BC. Thereafter it fell into decay, although archaeological evidence reveals that settlements on the site, beginning in early Villanovan times, lasted as late as *c.* AD 400. The later town was known as Laurolavinium.

Lavoisier, Antoine-Laurent (b. Aug. 26, 1743, Paris—d. May 8, 1794, Paris), French scientist usually regarded as the founder of modern chemistry. He made quantitative discoveries leading to the discovery of oxygen and the composition of water and various organic compounds. During the reign of Louis XVI (including the early Revolutionary period) he was an important public official and was later guillotined.

A brief account of the life and works of Antoine-Laurent Lavoisier follows; for a full biography, *see* MACROPAEDIA: Lavoisier.

Lavoisier had simultaneous careers in public service and in science. He was a member of the Ferme générale, the main tax-collecting agency; he instituted improvements in the manufacture of gunpowder, demonstrated the advantages of scientific agriculture, planned improvements in the social and economic condition of the province of Orléans, and was a member of the commission appointed to secure uniformity of weights and measures throughout France. The report of that commission led to the adoption of the metric system.

Lavoisier's initial scientific achievements (1772) were concerned with the gain or loss of weight that occurs when substances are burned or reduced with charcoal; he ascribed the changes in weight to absorption or loss of "air," a substance he identified with the "dephlogisticated air" prepared by Joseph Priestley in 1774. In a memoir presented in 1777, Lavoisier proposed the name oxygen ("acid producer") for dephlogisticated air, believing that all acids result from its union with other substances. Adoption of Lavoisier's chemical doctrines, as presented in *Traité élémentaire de chimie* (1789), marked the end of the phlogiston theory of combustion.

lavolta (dance): *see* volta, la.

Lávrion (Greece): *see* Laurium.

Lavrov, Pyotr (Lavrovich), original name PYOTR LAVROVICH MIRTOV (b. June 14 [June 2, old style], 1823, Melekhovo, Russia—d. Feb. 6 [Jan. 25, old style], 1900, Paris), Russian Socialist philosopher whose sociological thought provided a theoretical foundation for the activities of various Russian revolutionary organizations during the second half of the 19th century.

A member of a landed family, he graduated from an artillery school in St. Petersburg in 1842 and taught mathematics at military schools in St. Petersburg from 1844 to 1866. Becoming involved in antigovernment activities in 1857, Lavrov joined a secret revolutionary society and edited an underground newspaper. Arrested and sentenced to internal banishment in 1867, he escaped to Paris, arriving in time to participate in the Paris Commune of 1871. Later he went to London, where he became friends with Karl Marx and Friedrich Engels.

Lavrov was a prolific writer. He edited a number of the various publications of the Narodnaya Volya ("People's Will") revolutionary organization and organized Socialist discussion circles in Paris and elsewhere. His philosophical works include *Historical Letters* (1868–69) and *The State Element in the Future Society* (1876).

law, the discipline and profession concerned with the customs, practices, and rules of conduct of a community that are recognized as binding by the community. Enforcement of the body of rules is through a controlling authority.

The law is treated in a number of articles in the MACROPAEDIA. For a description of legal training and a general background, *see* Law, The Practice and Profession of. Articles that delineate the relationship of law to political structures are Constitution and Constitutional Government; Ideology; Political Parties and Interest Groups; Political Systems. For articles that discuss the importance of law regarding social justice and other social issues, *see* Human Rights; Land Reform and Tenure; Social Welfare. For an examination of comparative legal systems and the relationship of the law to the social sciences, *see* Social Sciences, The. For a description of canon law, *see* Christianity. For a description of Islāmic law, *see* Islām, Muḥammad and the Religion of. For a description of Jewish law, *see* Judaism. For an analysis of the role of law in the administration of government, *see* Cities; Public Administration. For an exposition of social restrictions and their enforcement, *see* Censorship; Crime and Punishment; Police. For a description of the legal aspects of war and the military, *see* War, The Theory and Conduct of. For a discussion of legal philosophy, *see* Philosophies of the Branches of Knowledge. For an exposition of various types of legal systems, *see* Judicial and Arbitrational Systems; Legal Systems, The Evolution of Modern Western. For international aspects of law, *see* International Law; United Nations. For an examination of the laws covering specific fields, *see* Business Law; Constitutional Law; Criminal Law; Family Law; Inheritance and Succession; Medicine; Procedural Law; Property Law; Taxation; Torts; Transportation Law.

For a description of the place of law in the circle of learning and for a list of both MACROPAEDIA and MICROPAEDIA articles on the subject, *see* PROPAEDIA: Part Five, Division V.

Law, (Andrew) Bonar (b. Sept. 16, 1858, Kingston, N.B., Can.—d. Oct. 30, 1923, London), prime minister of Great Britain from Oct. 23, 1922, to May 20, 1923, the first holder of that office to come from a British overseas possession. He was the leader of the Conservative Party during the periods 1911–21 and 1922–23.

The son of a Presbyterian minister of Ulster ancestry, Law from the age of 12 was reared by wealthy cousins in Scotland. Leaving school at age 16, he eventually became a

Bonar Law, 1919

BBC Hulton Picture Library

partner in a Glasgow firm of iron merchants. Elected to the House of Commons as a Conservative in 1900, he adhered to the party's imperialist faction led by Joseph Chamberlain, whose illness (from 1906) left Law and Chamberlain's son Austen as the leading advocates of a protective tariff. Late in 1911 the former prime minister Arthur James Balfour resigned as Conservative Party leader; the deadlock between the leading candidates for the succession, Austen Chamberlain and Walter Long, was broken by their withdrawal in favour of Law, a compromise candidate, who was elected unanimously on November 13. On that occasion and afterward, his chief adviser was his friend William Maxwell Aitken (Lord Beaverbrook from 1917), who later became a powerful newspaper publisher.

Until the outbreak of World War I, Law was concerned primarily with the tariff question and with Irish Home Rule, which, as an Ulsterman, he furiously opposed. On May 25, 1915, he became secretary for the colonies in the wartime coalition government that he had virtually forced H.H. Asquith to lead. He took part in the intrigues resulting in Asquith's resignation on Dec. 5, 1916; asked by King George V to form a government, he recommended instead David Lloyd George, who assumed office the next day. In the new coalition, Law was leader of the House of Commons, a member of the war cabinet, and chancellor of the Exchequer, in which capacity he astutely managed war-loan and war-bond programs. Exchanging the chancellorship for the office of lord privy seal on Jan. 10, 1919, he remained leader of the Commons until

March 1921, when ill health forced him to resign his offices.

In 1922 the Conservatives were angered successively by a scandal over the sale of honours, the Çanak incident (when a wholly unnecessary war with Turkey seemed imminent), and a proposal that an election be called to approve a new coalition to be headed by Lloyd George. On October 19, at a party meeting in the Carlton Club, London, Law spoke against another coalition. Lloyd George at once resigned, taking with him most of the leading Tories in the government. Law then formed a Conservative government ("of the second eleven," as Winston Churchill described it), which in November 1922 was approved by a comfortable majority of voters. The principal events of his premiership occurred in January 1923, when he almost resigned in dissatisfaction with Chancellor of the Exchequer Stanley Baldwin's settlement of the British war debt to the United States and when he broke off diplomatic relations with France because of her occupation of the Ruhr. Aware of an inoperable malignancy in his throat, he resigned in May and was succeeded by Baldwin. A biography, *The Unknown Prime Minister* (1955), was written by Robert N.W. Blake.

Consult the INDEX *first*

Law, Edward: *see* Ellenborough, Edward Law, earl of.

Law, John (baptized April 21, 1671, Edinburgh—d. March 21, 1729, Venice), Scottish monetary reformer and originator of the "Mississippi scheme" for the development of French territories in America.

Law studied mathematics, commerce, and political economy in London. After killing an adversary in a duel, he fled to Amsterdam, where he studied banking operations. A decade later he returned to Scotland and wrote his best-known work, *Money and Trade Considered, with a Proposal for Supplying the Nation with Money* (1st ed., 1705; 2nd ed., 1720). He submitted his banking reform plan to the Scottish parliament, but it was rejected.

After several other rejections, Law received permission in 1716 to try his plan in France. The French government was heavily in debt as a result of the extensive wars of Louis XIV, who died in 1715; and Law's program, which promised to reduce the public debt, held obvious appeal. With Law, however, lowering the public debt was somewhat incidental. He shared with his mercantilist contemporaries a belief that money is a creative force in economic development and that an increase in its quantity would stimulate a larger national product and would increase national power. He differed from other mercantilists in looking upon a central bank as an agency for manufacturing money in the form of bank notes that would circulate in place of gold and silver, which were scarce.

In Paris, Law founded a bank with authority to issue notes. Later he combined with his bank the Louisiana Company, which had exclusive privileges to develop the vast French territories in the Mississippi Valley of North America. Law's plan worked well for a few years but ran afoul of speculative complications and political intrigue, neither of which were directly attributable to Law. As the author of the program, popularly known as the "Mississippi Bubble," Law was responsible and was forced to flee France in 1720. He died in Venice a poor man.

law, wager of (early English law): *see* compurgation.

Law, William (b. 1686, King's Cliffe, Northamptonshire, Eng.—d. April 9, 1761, King's Cliffe), English author of influential works on Christian ethics and mysticism.

He entered Emmanuel College, Cambridge, in 1705 and in 1711 was elected a fellow there and was ordained. Upon the accession of George I in 1714, however, he was dismissed from Cambridge as a nonjuror (refusing to take an oath of allegiance). By 1727 he was serving as tutor to Edward Gibbon, father of the historian. From 1740 Law lived in retirement at his birthplace.

His chief contribution lies in his delineation of the Christian ethical ideal for human life and its actualization through the disciplined practices of private mysticism. His *Practical Treatise Upon Christian Perfection* (1726) and his *Serious Call to a Devout and Holy Life* (1728), considered his best work, both espouse a mild mysticism within the bounds of the normative Christian tradition. His stress upon the union between the Creator and the creature, however, as expressed in *The Way to Divine Knowledge* (1752), *The Spirit of Prayer* (1749), and *The Spirit of Love* (1752), has seldom found acceptance among Christian moral theologians. Each of these works was strongly criticized by such contemporaries as John Wesley. Nevertheless John and Charles Wesley both expressed an indebtedness to Law's work.

law code, also called LEGAL CODE, a more or less systematic and comprehensive written statement of laws. Law codes were compiled by the most ancient peoples. The oldest extant evidence for a code are tablets from the ancient archives of the city of Ebla (now at Tell Mardikh, Syria), which date to around 2400 BC. The best known ancient code is that of the Babylonian king Hammurabi of the 18th century BC (*see* Hammurabi, Code of). Roman legal records began in the 5th century BC, but there was no major codification of Roman law until that of the emperor Justinian in the 6th century AD, long after the dissolution of the Western Empire. The peoples who overran the Roman Empire, such as the Burgundians, the Visigoths, and the Salian Franks, also made codes of law (*see* Salic Law). During the later Middle Ages in Europe, various collections of maritime customs were drawn up for the use of merchants and lawyers and acquired great authority throughout Europe.

From the 15th through the 18th century, movements in various European countries to organize and compile the numerous laws and customs resulted in local and provincial compilations rather than national ones. The 19th century brought movements for national codifications, the first of which were the five Napoleonic codes of 1804–10: the civil code, the code of civil procedure, the commercial code, the code of criminal procedure, and the penal code (*see* Napoleonic Code). Since then, similar codes have been enacted by other civil-law countries (*see* German Civil Code; Swiss Civil Code; Japanese Civil Code).

In common-law countries, such as England and the United States, general law codes are the exception rather than the rule, largely because much of the law is based on previous judicial decisions. In the United States these codifications tend to be narrower, covering different types of procedure or penal and probate law. States adopt their own codes, although there have been attempts to establish uniform codes in various areas of law; the most comprehensive of these is the Uniform Commercial Code adopted by numerous jurisdictions. In Great Britain some codes have been adopted in narrow areas such as sale and partnership, but there has been considerable work done in revising and consolidating existing statutes.

In international law there have been few concrete results, despite considerable effort at codification of international public and private law. Drafts have been prepared on such matters as arbitration and sale of goods, but so far the difficulty of achieving acceptance by nations with various legal systems has not been overcome.

law merchant, during the Middle Ages, the body of customary rules and principles relating to merchants and mercantile transactions and adopted by traders themselves for the purpose of regulating their dealings. Initially, it was administered for the most part in special quasi-judicial courts, such as those of the guilds in Italy and, later, regularly constituted piepoudre courts in England (*see* piepoudre court).

The law merchant was developed in the early 11th century in order to protect foreign merchants not under the jurisdiction and protection of the local law. Foreign traders often were subject to confiscations and other types of harassment if one of their countrymen had defaulted in a business transaction. A kind of law was also needed by which the traders themselves could negotiate contracts, partnerships, trademarks, and various aspects of buying and selling. The law merchant gradually spread as the traders went from place to place. Their courts, set up by the merchants themselves at trade fairs or in cities, administered a law that was uniform throughout Europe, regardless of differences in national laws and languages. It was based primarily on Roman law, although there were some Germanic influences; it formed the basis for modern commercial law.

Law of ———: *see under* substantive word (*e.g.*, Guarantees, Law of; Sea, Law of the; Twelve Tables, Law of the), except as below.

law report, in common law, published record of a judicial decision that is cited by lawyers and judges for their use as precedent in subsequent cases. The report of a decision contains the title of the case, a statement of the facts giving rise to the litigation, and its history in the courts. It then reproduces the opinion of the court and concludes with the judgment of the court; *e.g.*, affirming or reversing the judgment of the court below. The report of a modern decision is usually preceded by a headnote—*i.e.*, an analytical summary of the opinion, stating the points decided.

The earliest English court reports were the *Year Books* produced from the late 13th century until the 16th. From 1537 until 1865 hundreds of series of English reports were published under the names of the reporters themselves. During both periods reporting was a disorganized private enterprise, the reporters being volunteers who made and circulated notes of court proceedings and decisions. Their work was very uneven, and reports were often overlapping and irreconcilable. The modern report form was standardized in the second half of the 18th century, and in 1865 the *Law Reports,* though still privately published, were established as semiofficial. In England today a law reporter must be a barrister-at-law, who signifies that he has followed the hearing and can vouch for the accuracy of the report. Although all decisions of the highest English appellate court, the House of Lords, are reported, other court of appeals decisions are reported only if they reveal a new principle of law or a new application. Comparatively few decisions of lower courts are reported.

The first state and federal reports in the United States were also privately published under the reporter's name, although the appointment of an official reporter was an early development. Today reported opinions are almost invariably written by the court and are officially published. Late in the 19th century a private publishing concern began unofficial publication of all state and federal reports in the National Reporter System, which continues today.

The decisions of most U.S. appellate courts are reported and published unless they deal with settled propositions of law. Since trial courts do not ordinarily write opinions, their findings are not ordinarily reported. In jurisdictions such as New York, Pennsylvania, and the federal district courts, where trial courts prepare opinions in a substantial number of cases, these opinions are reported and published. By the 1970s published U.S. decisions numbered nearly 4,500,000, with about 40,000 new cases being added each year—a volume of legal precedent that has created considerable burdens for both scholarship and libraries.

Lawa (people): *see* Wa.

Lawes, Henry (baptized Jan. 5, 1596, Dinton, Wiltshire, Eng.—d. Oct. 21, 1662, London), English composer noted for his continuo songs.

Lawes studied under one of the foremost English musicians of the time, John Coperario, and became a gentleman of the Chapel Royal in 1626 and a royal musician for lutes and voices in 1631. In 1634 he wrote the music for Thomas Carew's masque *Coelum Britannicum* and for John Milton's *Comus,* and in 1636, for Sir William Davenant's *The Triumph of the Prince d'Amour* (with his brother William Lawes). His *Choice Psalmes* (1648) also contained music by his brother and a commendatory sonnet by Milton. He lost his court appointments during the English Civil Wars (1642–51) but regained them at the Restoration (1660). In 1656 he contributed music to Davenant's *The Siege of Rhodes.*

Henry Lawes, portrait by an unknown artist; in the collection of the Faculty of Music, Oxford

By courtesy of the Faculty of Music, Oxford

Lawes's songs, influenced by the Italian recitative style, are characterized by rhyme emphasis, word repetition, many cadences, and deliberate rhythmic discontinuity.

Lawes, Sir John Bennet, 1ST BARONET (b. Dec. 28, 1814, Rothamsted, Harpenden, Hertfordshire, Eng.—d. Aug. 31, 1900, Rothamsted), English agronomist who founded the artificial fertilizer industry and Rothamsted Experimental Station, the oldest agricultural research station in the world.

Lawes inherited his father's estate, Rothamsted, in 1822. In 1842, after long experimentation with the effects of manures on potted plants and field crops on his estate, he patented a process for treating phosphate rock with sulfuric acid to produce superphosphate. That year he opened the first fertilizer factory, thus initiating the artificial fertilizer industry. The following year, the chemist J.H. (later Sir Henry) Gilbert joined him, and they began a collaboration lasting more than a half century; Lawes considered 1843 the year of the station's foundation. Together, the pair studied the effects of different fertilizers on crops. They also researched animal nutrition, including the value of different fodders and the sources of animal fat.

In 1867 the Royal Society awarded Lawes and Gilbert jointly a Royal Medal. In 1882 Lawes was created a baronet. Seven years later he ensured the continuation of the Rothamsted experiments by setting up the Lawes Agricultural trust.

Lawes, William (baptized May 1, 1602, Salisbury, Wiltshire, Eng.—d. 1645, Chester, Cheshire), English composer, prominent during the early Baroque period, noted for his highly original instrumental music.

The brother of the composer Henry Lawes, he entered the household of the Earl of Hertford about 1612 and in 1635 became a musician to Charles I. Lawes fought with the Royalists during the English Civil Wars (1642–51) and was killed at the siege of Chester. His instrumental music includes *Great Consort* for violin, bass viol, theorbo, and harp; *The Royal Consort* (a set of dance suites); and some fine fantasias, anthems, and psalms. His daring harmonies employ unusual dissonances. He was a skilled contrapuntalist who after some difficulty mastered the idiom of the Baroque. He was also one of the principal masque composers, composing the music for James Shirley's *The Triumph of Peace* (1634) and *The Triumph of Beauty* (*c.* 1644) and Sir William Davenant's *The Triumph of the Prince d'Amour* (1636; with Henry Lawes) and *Britannia Triumphans* (1638).

Lawler, Ray, in full RAYMOND EVENOR LAWLER (b. 1921?, Footscray, Melbourne, Vic., Australia), actor, producer, and playwright whose *Summer of the Seventeenth Doll* is credited with changing the direction of modern Australian drama.

Lawler left school at 13 and worked in a variety of jobs before joining the National Theatre Company in Melbourne as an actor, writer, and producer. In 1955 the newly formed Elizabethan Theatre Trust chose his *Summer of the Seventeenth Doll* for its first staging of an original Australian play. Lawler played the lead in Melbourne (1956); the play's success led to productions in London (1957; with Lawler again in the lead) and New York City (1958), and a film version was made in 1959. Its criticism of Australian cultural stereotypes—combined with a natural style and a language free of cliché—represented a major break with tradition and inspired a new phase of dramatic realism in Australia.

Lawler's other plays include *Cradle of Thunder* (1949), *The Piccadilly Bushman* (1959), *The Unshaven Cheek* (1963), *A Breach in the Wall* (1967), *The Man Who Shot the Albatross* (1972), and two additional plays in "The Doll Trilogy": *Kid Stakes* (1975) and *Other Times* (1976). His play *Godsend* was produced in 1982.

lawn, fine-textured turf (*q.v.*) of grass that is kept mowed.

lawn bowls (game): *see* bowls.

lawn croquet (game): *see* croquet.

lawn-leaf (plant): *see* Dichondra.

lawn tennis: *see* tennis.

Lawrance, Charles Lanier (b. Sept. 30, 1882, Lenox, Mass., U.S.—d. June 24, 1950, East Islip, N.Y.), American aeronautical engineer who designed the first successful air-cooled aircraft engine, used on many historic early flights.

After attending Yale University Lawrance joined a new automobile firm that was later ruined by the financial panic of 1907. He then went to Paris, where he studied architecture at the Beaux-Arts School and experimented with aeronautics at the Eiffel Laboratory, designing and building an 8-cylinder, 200-horsepower engine. He also designed a new type of wing section with an exceptionally good lift-to-drag ratio; the wing design was used widely in World War I.

Returning home in 1914, Lawrance continued his research, which culminated in the development of the engine later named the Wright Whirlwind by the Curtiss-Wright Company, of which he was chief of engineering. The Whirlwind, air-cooled with the aid of cooling fins on the cylinder heads, was improved in a succession of models for the U.S. Army and Navy and general aviation. By the mid-1920s its power and reliability had been demonstrated so effectively that a remarkable series of long-distance flights became possible: those of Admiral Byrd in the Arctic, that of Charles Lindbergh from New York City to Paris, and those of Amelia Earhart, Byrd, and Clarence Chamberlin across the Atlantic.

In 1930 Lawrance left Curtiss-Wright to form his own engineering firm, the Lawrance Engineering & Research Corporation, which, among other projects, built thousands of auxiliary electric-generating plants for World War II bombers.

Although the recipient of many honorary degrees and other distinctions, Lawrance remained relatively obscure despite the sensational publicity of the Lindbergh flight, an irony on which he commented, "Who remembers Paul Revere's horse?"

Lawrence: *see under* Laurence, except as below.

Lawrence (antipope): *see* Laurentius.

Lawrence, city, seat (1855) of Douglas county, eastern Kansas, U.S., on the Kansas (Kaw) River. It was founded in 1854 by antislavery radicals who had come to Kansas under the auspices of the New England Emigrant Aid Company to outvote proslavery settlers and thus make Kansas a nonslave state. The town was named for Amos A. Lawrence, a New England textile manufacturer. It was a noted station on the Underground Railroad by which slaves escaped into free territory. As a Jayhawker (Abolitionist) headquarters, the town was sacked in 1856 by proslavery militia under a former Democratic senator from Missouri, David Rice Atchison, and in 1863 by the Confederate guerrilla William Clarke Quantrill, who massacred more than 150 citizens. In 1866 the University of Kansas was opened there, and in 1884 Haskell Institute (now Haskell Indian Junior College) was established for American Indians. Baker University (1858) is in Baldwin City, 13 miles (21 km) south. Lawrence has some small factories, but it is essentially a college town. Inc. 1858. Pop. (1992 est.) city, 66,810; Lawrence MSA, 83,293.

Lawrence, city, seat (with Newburyport and Salem) of Essex county, northeastern Massachusetts, U.S. It lies along the Merrimack River, 27 miles (43 km) north-northwest of Boston. The site at Bodwell's Falls (the source of abundant waterpower) was promoted for industry in 1845 by the Essex Company, formed by a group of Boston financiers including Abbott Lawrence, for whom the town was named. In 1847 it was set off from Andover and Methuen and incorporated as a town, and it developed as one of the largest woolen-textile centres in the United States after completion of the Boston and Maine Railroad (now closed). In 1912 Lawrence was the scene of a great strike involving out-of-town militia and the Industrial Workers of the World; the strike was settled with the workers winning a one-cent hourly increase. The city's industry has diversified since 1950, and its manufactures now include leather, paper, clothing, chemicals, machinery, plastic, rubber, and fabricated metal products. Inc. city, 1853. Pop. (1992 est.) city, 69,991; (1990) Lawrence-Haverhill PMSA, 393,516.

Lawrence, SAINT, Lawrence also spelled LAURENCE (d. 258, Rome [Italy]; feast day August 10), one of the most venerated Roman martyrs, celebrated for his Christian valour.

Lawrence was among the seven deacons of the Roman church serving Pope St. Sixtus II, whose martyrdom preceded Lawrence's by a few days: they were executed during the persecution under the Roman emperor Valerian. It is said that Lawrence gave the church's treasures to the poor and the sick before his arrest. Although Lawrence was probably beheaded, Bishop St. Ambrose of Milan and the Latin poet Prudentius, among others, recorded that he was roasted to death on a gridiron, remarking to his torturers at one point, "I am cooked on that side; turn me over, and eat." Many conversions to Christianity throughout Rome reportedly followed Lawrence's death, including those of several senators witnessing his execution. The Basilica of San Lorenzo, Rome, was built over his burial place. He is named in the canon of the Roman mass.

Lawrence OF ARABIA: *see* Lawrence, T(homas) E(dward).

Lawrence OF BRINDISI, SAINT, Lawrence also spelled LAURENCE, Italian SAN LORENZO DA BRINDISI, original name CESARE DE ROSSI (b. July 22, 1559, Brindisi, Kingdom of Naples [Italy]—d. July 22, 1619, Belem, Port.; canonized 1881; feast day July 21), doctor of the church and one of the leading polemicists of the Counter-Reformation in Germany.

He joined the Capuchin Friars Minor, a strict offshoot of the Franciscans, at Verona, Italy, in 1575, taking the name Lorenzo (Lawrence). A gifted linguist, he mastered several languages including Greek, Hebrew, Aramaic, and Syriac. Under Popes Gregory XIII and Clement VIII he was appointed apostolic preacher to the Roman Jews. During the Battle of Stuhlweissenburg, Hung. (Oct. 9–14, 1601), Lawrence accompanied Emperor Rudolf II's forces to victory against the Turkish army of Sultan Mehmed III; this victory was attributed in great part to the indomitable spirit of the saint, who had communicated his ardour and confidence to the Christian troops. He fought against the rise of German Protestantism and founded Capuchin houses at Madrid and at Munich, where he took part in the political discussions preceding the Thirty Years' War. Lawrence died near Lisbon while on a mission to King Philip III of Spain for the Neapolitans, who were being oppressed by the Duke of Osuna, Italy. He was beatified by Pope Pius VI in 1783 and declared a doctor of the church by John XXIII in 1959. Lawrence's works were published in nine volumes (1928–45).

BIBLIOGRAPHY. A. Brennan, *Life of St. Laurence of Brindisi* (1911); A. da Carmignano, *St. Lawrence of Brindisi* (1963).

Lawrence OF CANTERBURY, SAINT: *see* Laurentius of Canterbury, Saint.

Lawrence, Abbott (b. Dec. 16, 1792, Groton, Mass., U.S.—d. Aug. 18, 1855, Boston, Mass.), American merchant and philanthropist who was a major developer of the New England textile industry. He led in founding the town of Lawrence, Mass., named in his honour, and built several mills there, making it a textile centre.

Lawrence joined his brother, Amos Lawrence (1786–1852), in business in Boston in 1808, and together they founded in 1814 the firm of A. and A. Lawrence, which became one of the largest American mercantile houses of the time. Starting as a retailer of English and then exclusively American textiles, he began manufacturing in 1830, building large cotton and wool cloth mills in Lawrence in 1845. He also promoted New England railways, chiefly the line between Boston and Albany, N.Y.

A popular advocate of New England business interests, Lawrence was elected to the U.S. House of Representatives (1835–37, 1839–40) and was U.S. minister to Great Britain (1849–52). His donations established the Lawrence Scientific School at Harvard University. Amos Lawrence's son, Amos Adams Lawrence (1814–86), founded Lawrence University in Appleton, Wis., and a college in Lawrence, Kan., named in his honour, which became the University of Kansas in 1866.

Lawrence, D.H., in full DAVID HERBERT LAWRENCE (b. Sept. 11, 1885, Eastwood, Nottinghamshire, Eng.—d. March 2, 1930, Vence, France), English author of novels, short stories, poems, plays, essays, travel books, and letters. His novels *Sons and Lovers* (1913), *The Rainbow* (1915), and *Women in Love* (1920) made him one of the most influential English writers of the 20th century.

Youth and early career. Lawrence was the fourth child of a north Midlands coal miner who was a dialect speaker, a drinker, and virtually illiterate. Lawrence's mother, who came from the south of England, was educated, refined, and pious. Lawrence won a scholarship to Nottingham High School (1898–1901) and left at 16 to earn a living as clerk in a factory, but he had to give up work after a first attack of pneumonia. Convalescing, he began visiting the Haggs Farm nearby and began an intense friendship (1902–10) with Jessie Chambers. He became a pupil-teacher in Eastwood in 1902 and, encouraged by Jessie, began to write in 1905; his first story was published in a local newspaper in 1907. He studied at University College, Nottingham, from 1906 to 1908, earning a teachers' certificate, and went on writing poems and stories and drafting his first novel, *The White Peacock.*

The Eastwood setting, especially the contrast between mining town and unspoiled countryside, the life and culture of the miners, the strife between his parents, and its effect on his tortured relationship with Jessie all became themes of Lawrence's early short stories and novels. He kept on returning to Eastwood in imagination long after he had left it in fact.

In 1908 Lawrence went to teach in Croydon, a London suburb. Jessie Chambers sent some of his poems to Ford Madox Hueffer (Ford Madox Ford), editor of the influential *English Review.* Hueffer recognized his genius, the *Review* began to publish his work, and Lawrence was able to meet such rising young writers as Ezra Pound. Hueffer recommended *The White Peacock* to the publisher William Heinemann, who published it in 1911, just after the death of Lawrence's mother and his break with Jessie. His second novel, *The Trespasser* (1912), gained the interest of the influential editor Edward Garnett, who secured the third novel, *Sons and Lovers,* for his own firm, Duckworth. In the crucial year of 1911–12 Lawrence had another attack of pneumonia and decided to give up teaching and live by writing. Most importantly, he fell in love and eloped with Frieda Weekley (*née* von Richthofen), the aristocratic German wife of a professor at Nottingham. The couple went first to Germany and then to Italy, where Lawrence completed his third novel, *Sons and Lovers.* They were married in England in 1914 after Frieda's divorce.

Sons and Lovers. Lawrence's first two novels, first play, and most of his early short stories, including such masterpieces as "Odour of Chrysanthemums" and "Daughters of the Vicar" (collected in *The Prussian Officer, and Other Stories,* 1914), use early experience as a departure point. *Sons and Lovers* carries this process to the point of quasi-autobiography. The book depicts Eastwood and the Haggs Farm, the twin poles of Lawrence's early life, with vivid realism. The central character, Paul Morel, is naturally identified as Lawrence; the miner-father who drinks and the powerful mother who resists him are clearly modeled on his parents; and the painful devotion of Miriam Leivers resembles that of Jessie Chambers. An older brother, William, who dies young, parallels Lawrence's brother Ernest, who met an early death. In the novel, the mother turns to her elder son William for

D.H. Lawrence
Elliott and Fry

emotional fulfillment in place of his father, and when William dies, his younger brother Paul becomes the mother's mission and, ultimately, her victim. Paul's adolescent love for Miriam is undermined by his mother's dominance; though fatally attracted to Miriam, Paul cannot be sexually involved with anyone so like his mother, and the sexual relationship he forces on her proves a disaster. He then, in reaction, has a passionate affair with a married woman, Clara Dawes, in what is the only purely imaginary part of the novel. Clara's husband is a drunken workingman whom she has undermined by her social and intellectual superiority, so their situation mirrors that of the Morels. But Paul can manage sexual passion only when it is split off from commitment; their affair ends after Paul and Dawes have a murderous fight, and Clara returns to her husband. Paul, for all his intelligence, cannot fully grasp his own unconscious motivations, but Lawrence silently conveys them in the pattern of the plot. Paul can only be released by his mother's death, and at the end of the book, he is at last free to take up his own life, though it remains uncertain whether he can finally overcome her influence. The whole narrative turns Lawrence's own life history into a powerful psychoanalytic study of a young man's Oedipal attraction toward his mother and its consequences on his relations with other women.

The Rainbow and Women in Love. During World War I Lawrence and his wife were trapped in England and living in poverty. At this time he was engaged in two related projects. The first was a vein of philosophical writing that he had initiated in the "Foreword" to *Sons and Lovers* and continued in "Study of Thomas Hardy" (1914) and later works. The other, more important project was an ambitious novel of provincial life that Lawrence rewrote and revised until it split into two major novels: *The Rainbow,* which was immediately suppressed in Britain as obscene; and *Women in Love,* which was not published until 1920. In the meantime the Lawrences, living in a cottage in remote Cornwall, had to endure growing suspicion and hostility from their rural neighbours on account of Lawrence's pacifism and Frieda's German origins. They were expelled from the county in 1917 on suspicion of signaling to German submarines and spent the rest of the war in London and Derbyshire. Though threatened with military conscription, Lawrence wrote some of his finest work during the war.

The Rainbow extends the scope of *Sons*

and Lovers by following the Brangwen family (who live near Eastwood) over three generations, so that social and spiritual change are woven into the chronicle. The Brangwens begin as farmers so attached to the land and the seasons as to represent a premodern unconsciousness, and succeeding generations in the novel evolve toward modern consciousness, self-consciousness, and even alienation. The book's early part, which is poetic and mythical, records the love and marriage of Tom Brangwen with the widowed Polish exile Lydia in the 1860s. Lydia's child Anna marries a Brangwen cousin, Will, in the 1880s. These two initially have a stormy relationship but subside into conventional domesticity anchored by work, home, and children. Expanding consciousness is transmitted to the next generation, Lawrence's own, in the person of their daughter Ursula. The last third of the novel describes Ursula's childhood relationship with her father and her passionate but unsuccessful romantic involvement with the soldier Anton Skrebensky. Ursula's attraction toward Skrebensky is negated by his social conventionality, and her rejection of him is symbolized by a sexual relationship in which she becomes dominant. Ursula miscarries their child, and at the novel's end she is left on her own in a convalescence like Paul Morel's, facing a difficult future before World War I.

Women in Love takes up the story, but across the gap of changed consciousness created by World War I. The women of the title are Ursula, picking up her life, still at home, and doubtful of her role as teacher and her social and intellectual status; and her sister Gudrun, who is also a teacher but an artist and a free spirit as well. They are modern women, educated, free from stereotyped assumptions about their role, and sexually autonomous. Though unsure of what to do with their lives, they are unwilling to settle for an ordinary marriage as a solution to the problem. The sisters' aspirations crystallize in their romantic relationships: Ursula's with Rupert Birkin, a university graduate and school inspector (and also a Lawrence-figure), Gudrun's with Gerald Crich, the handsome, ruthless, seemingly dominant industrialist who runs his family's mines. Birkin and Gerald themselves are deeply if inarticulately attached to each other. The novel follows the growth of the two relationships: one (Ursula and Birkin) is productive and hopeful, if difficult to maintain as an equilibrium of free partners. The other (Gudrun and Gerald) tips over into dominance and dependence, violence and death. The account is characterized by the extreme consciousness of the protagonists: the inarticulate struggles of earlier generations are now succeeded at the verbal level by earnest or bitter debate. Birkin's intellectual force is met by Ursula's mixture of warmth and skepticism and her emotional stability. The Gerald-Gudrun relationship shows his male dominance to be a shell overlying a crippling inner emptiness and lack of self-awareness, which eventually inspire revulsion in Gudrun. The final conflict between them is played out in the high bareness of an Alpine ski resort; after a brutal assault on Gudrun, Gerald wanders off into the snow and dies. Birkin, grieving, leaves with Ursula for a new life in the warm symbolic south, in Italy.

The search for a fulfilling sexual love and for a form of marriage that will satisfy a modern consciousness is the goal of Lawrence's early novels and yet becomes increasingly problematic. None of his novels ends happily: at best, they conclude with an open question.

Later life and works. After World War I Lawrence and his wife went to Italy (1919), and he never again lived in England. He soon embarked on a group of novels consisting of *The Lost Girl* (1920), *Aaron's Rod* (1922), and the uncompleted *Mr. Noon* (published in its entirety only in 1984). In 1921 the Lawrences decided to leave Europe and go to the United States, but eastward, via Ceylon (now Sri Lanka) and Australia. Since 1917 Lawrence had been working on *Studies in Classic American Literature* (1923), which grew out of his sense that the American West was an uncorrupted natural home. His other nonfiction works at this time include *Movements in European History* (1921) and two treatises on his psychological theories, *Psychoanalysis and the Unconscious* (1921) and *Fantasia of the Unconscious* (1922).

Lawrence wrote *Kangaroo* in six weeks while visiting Australia in 1922. This novel is a serious summary of his own position at the time. The main character and his wife move to Australia after World War I and face in the new country a range of political action: his literary talents are courted alike by socialists and by a nationalist quasi-fascist party. He cannot embrace either political movement, however, and an autobiographical chapter on his experiences in England during World War I reveals that the persecution he endured for his antiwar sentiments killed his desire to participate actively in society. In the end he leaves Australia for America.

Finally reaching Taos, N.M., from where he visited Mexico in 1923 and 1924, Lawrence embarked on the ambitious *The Plumed Serpent* (1926). In this novel Lawrence maintains that the regeneration of Europe's crumbling postwar society must come from a religious root, and if Christianity is dead, each region must return to its own indigenous religious tradition. *The Plumed Serpent*'s prophet-hero, a Mexican general, revives Aztec rites as the basis of a new theocratic state in Mexico whose authoritarian leaders are worshiped as gods. The Lawrence-representative in the story, a European woman, in the end marries one of the leader-gods but remains half-repelled by his violence and irrationality. In his disillusionment and bitterness after World War I, Lawrence dreamed of replacing Christianity and Western democratic political values with primitive mysticism and political authoritarianism. After pursuing this theme to its logical conclusion in *The Plumed Serpent,* however, he abandoned it, and he was reduced to his old ideal of a community where he could begin a new life with a few like-minded people. Taos was the most suitable place he had found, but he was now beginning to die; a bout of illness in 1925 produced bronchial hemorrhage, and tuberculosis was diagnosed.

Lawrence returned to Italy in 1925, and in 1926 he embarked on the first versions of *Lady Chatterley's Lover.* Privately published in 1928, *Lady Chatterley's Lover* led an underground life until legal decisions in New York (1959) and London (1960) made it freely available—and a model for countless literary descriptions of sexual acts. The London verdict allowing publication capped a trial at which the book was defended by many eminent English writers. In the novel Lawrence returns for the last time to Eastwood and portrays the tender sexual love, across barriers of class and marriage, of two damaged moderns. Lawrence had always seen the need to relate sexuality to feeling, and his fiction had always extended the borders of the permissible—and had been censored in detail. In *Lady Chatterley's Lover* he now fully described sexual acts as expressing aspects or moods of love, and he also used the colloquial four-letter words that naturally occur in free speech.

The dying Lawrence moved to the south of France, where in 1929 he wrote *Apocalypse* (published 1931), a commentary on the biblical Book of Revelation that is his final religious statement. He was buried in Vence, and his ashes were removed to Taos in 1935.

Poetry and nonfiction. The fascination of Lawrence's personality is attested by all who knew him, and it abundantly survives in his fiction, his poetry, his numerous prose writings, and his letters. Lawrence's poetry deserves special mention. In his early poems his touch is often unsure, he is too "literary," and he is often constrained by rhyme. But by a remarkable triumph of development, he evolved a highly spontaneous mode of free verse that allowed him to express an unrivaled mixture of observation and symbolism. His poetry can be of great biographical interest, as in *Look! We Have Come Through!* (1917), and some of the verse in *Pansies* (1929) and *Nettles* (1930) is brilliantly sardonic. But his most original contribution is *Birds, Beasts and Flowers* (1923), in which he creates an unprecedented poetry of nature, based on his experiences of the Mediterranean scene and the American Southwest. In his *Last Poems* (1932) he contemplates death.

No account of Lawrence's work can omit his unsurpassable letters. In their variety of tone, vivacity, and range of interest, they convey a full and splendid picture of himself, his relation to his correspondents, and the exhilarations, depressions, and prophetic broodings of his wandering life. Lawrence's short stories were collected in *The Prussian Officer, England My England, and Other Stories* (1922), *The Woman Who Rode Away, and Other Stories* (1928), and *Love Among the Haystacks and Other Pieces* (1930), among other volumes. His early plays, *The Widowing of Mrs. Holroyd* (1914) and *The Daughter-in-Law* (performed 1936), have proved effective on stage and television. Of his travel books, *Sea and Sardinia* (1921) is the most spontaneous; the others involve parallel journeys to Lawrence's interior.

Assessment. D.H. Lawrence was first recognized as a working-class novelist showing the reality of English provincial family life, and—in the first days of psychoanalysis—as the author-subject of a classic case-history of the Oedipus complex. In subsequent works, Lawrence's frank handling of sexuality cast him as a pioneer of a "liberation" he would not himself have approved. From the beginning readers have been won over by the poetic vividness of his writing and his efforts to describe subjective states of emotion, sensation, and intuition. This spontaneity and immediacy of feeling coexists with a continual, slightly modified repetition of themes, characters, and symbols that express Lawrence's own evolving artistic vision and thought. His great novels remain difficult because their realism is underlain by obsessive personal metaphors, by elements of mythology, and above all by his attempt to express in words what is normally wordless because it exists below consciousness. Lawrence tried to go beyond the "old, stable ego" of the characters familiar to readers of more conventional fiction. His characters are continually experiencing transformations driven by unconscious processes rather than by conscious intent, thought, or ideas.

Lawrence was ultimately a religious writer who did not so much reject Christianity as try to create a new religious and moral basis for modern life by continual resurrections and transformations of the self. These changes are never limited to the social self, nor are they ever fully under the eye of consciousness. Lawrence called for a new openness to what he called the "dark gods" of nature, feeling, instinct, and sexuality; a renewed contact with these forces was, for him, the beginning of wisdom. (M.H.Bl.)

BIBLIOGRAPHY. A critical edition of Lawrence's works is being published by Cambridge University Press (1980–); these texts use manuscripts and typescripts to restore censored or deleted passages, notably in *Sons and Lovers* (1992), and add hitherto unpublished material and much draft material. A standard biography of Lawrence is

John Worthen, *D.H. Lawrence* (1991–). Edward Nehls (ed. and compiler), *D.H. Lawrence: A Composite Biography,* 3 vol. (1957–59), assembles the testimony of contemporaries. E.T. (Jessie Chambers), *D.H. Lawrence: A Personal Record* (1935, reprinted 1980), is also worth consulting. Two biographical studies by John Middleton Murry, *Son of Woman* (1931, reissued 1980), and *Reminiscences of D.H. Lawrence* (1933, reprinted 1971), provoked a third: Catherine Carswell, *The Savage Pilgrimage* (1932, reprinted 1981). Paul Delany, *D.H. Lawrence's Nightmare* (1978), deals with the years 1914–18. F.R. Leavis, *D.H. Lawrence, Novelist* (1955, reissued 1979), is the starting-point for modern criticism; the literature is enormous. Convenient one-volume introductions are Graham Hough, *The Dark Sun* (1956, reissued 1973); H.M. Daleski, *The Forked Flame* (1965, reissued 1987); Keith Sagar, *The Art of D.H. Lawrence* (1966, reissued 1981); and Frank Kermode, *D.H. Lawrence* (also published as *Lawrence,* 1973).

Lawrence, Ernest Orlando (b. Aug. 8, 1901, Canton, S.D., U.S.—d. Aug. 27, 1958, Palo Alto, Calif.), American physicist, winner of the 1939 Nobel Prize for Physics for his invention of the cyclotron, the first particle accelerator to achieve high energies.

Lawrence earned his Ph.D. at Yale University in 1925. An assistant professor of physics at Yale (1927–28), he went to the University of California, Berkeley, as an associate professor and became full professor in 1930.

Lawrence first conceived the idea for the cyclotron in 1929. One of his students, M. Stanley Livingston, undertook the project and succeeded in building a device that accelerated hydrogen ions (protons) to an energy of 13,000 electron volts (eV). Lawrence then set out to build a second cyclotron; when completed, it accelerated protons to 1,200,000 eV, enough energy to cause nuclear disintegration. To continue the program, Lawrence built the Radiation Laboratory at Berkeley in 1936 and was made its director.

One of Lawrence's cyclotrons produced technetium, the first element that does not occur in nature to be made artificially. His basic design was utilized in developing other particle accelerators, which have been largely responsible for the great advances made in the field of particle physics. With the cyclotron, he produced radioactive phosphorus and other isotopes for medical use, including radioactive iodine for the first therapeutic treatment of hyperthyroidism. In addition, he instituted the use of neutron beams in treating cancer.

During World War II he worked with the Manhattan Project as a program chief in charge of the development of the electromagnetic process of separating uranium-235 for the atomic bomb. In 1957 he received the Fermi Award from the U.S. Atomic Energy Commission. Besides his work in nuclear physics, Lawrence invented and patented a colour-television picture tube. In his honour were named Lawrence Berkeley Laboratory at Berkeley; Lawrence Livermore National Laboratory at Livermore, Calif.; and element 103, lawrencium.

Lawrence, Frederick William: *see* Pethick-Lawrence, Frederick William Pethick-Lawrence, 1st Baron.

Lawrence, Gertrude, original name GERTRUD ALEXANDRA DAGMA LAWRENCE KLASEN (b. July 4, 1898, London, Eng.—d. Sept. 6, 1952, New York, N.Y., U.S.), English actress noted for her performances in Noel Coward's sophisticated comedies and in musicals, especially *Lady in the Dark.*

Lawrence's father was a singer in variety shows and musicals. She made her first stage appearance in December 1910 in *Babes in the Wood* and toured in musicals until 1916, when she was engaged for a London revue. Two years later she took over the lead in another revue when Beatrice Lillie was injured and, costarring with Lillie and Jack Buchanan, came with a revue to New York (1924). She starred there in the Gershwin musical *Oh, Kay!* in 1926. Her first dramatic role was in *Icebound* (London, 1928). Later she played in *Candle Light, Private Lives* (written for her by Coward), *Tonight at 8:30,* and *Susan and God,* among others. Perhaps her greatest triumph was as Liza Elliot in Moss Hart's musical play *Lady in the Dark* (1941). An early marriage to the English director Francis Gordon-Howley ended in divorce. In 1940 she married Richard Aldrich, an American producer, and she spent her later years in the United States. Her last appearance was as Anna in the Rodgers and Hammerstein musical *The King and I* (1951). Her autobiographical *A Star Danced* was published in 1945.

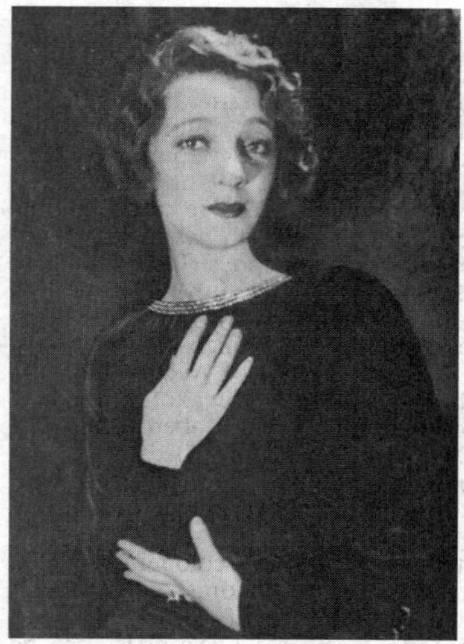
Gertrude Lawrence
Cecil Beaton

Lawrence, Sir Henry Montgomery (b. June 28, 1806, Matura, Ceylon [now Sri Lanka]—d. July 4, 1857, Lucknow, India), English soldier and administrator who applied a keen sense of Indian politics in helping to consolidate British rule in the Punjab.

After joining the Bengal artillery in 1823, Lawrence served at the capture of Arakan in the First Anglo-Burmese War (1824–26). He studied Urdu, Hindi, and Persian languages and in 1833 joined the survey department of the North-Western Provinces. Placed in charge of Ferozepur, in the Punjab (1839), he acquired a substantial knowledge of Sikh politics. After holding several other posts, he in 1846 was appointed agent, and later resident, at Lahore. He reduced the Sikh army, suppressed mutinies in the Kāngra district and in Kashmir, and deposed the *wazīr* (Muslim executive officer) Lal Singh.

After the Treaty of Bhairowal (1846), the British part in Sikh rule was apparent when Lawrence prepared a Sikh legal code that gave him the power to forbid suttee (self-immolation by widows on their husbands' funeral pyres), infanticide, and forced labour. Knighted in 1848 while on home leave, he returned to India when the Second Sikh War (1848–49) broke out. He was made president of the board of administration of the newly annexed Punjab. He was in charge of political affairs while his younger brother, John, supervised finance. Henry favoured treating the Sikh aristocracy with generosity by granting them life pensions and large estates, while John wished to improve the status of the common people by reducing taxes and limiting landlords' rights.

Policy conflicts with his brother led Henry to seek a transfer, and in 1852 he was assigned to Rājputāna. In 1857 he was summoned to Oudh, where annexation, precipitate land reforms, and a mutinous army had created a grave situation. He effectively delayed the mutiny at Lucknow and prepared the residency for its famous six-month siege during the Indian Mutiny. He was mortally wounded on July 2, and at his death he did not know that the British government had nominated him provisional governor-general.

Lawrence, Jacob (b. Sept. 7, 1917, Atlantic City, N.J., U.S.—d. June 9, 2000, Seattle, Wash.), black American painter whose works portray scenes of black life and history with vivid, stylized realism.

At the age of 13 Lawrence moved with his family to the Harlem section of New York City. At free art classes he showed a talent for creating lively, decorative masks, a motif that would later figure strongly in his narrative painting. At the Harlem Art Workshop (sponsored by the Works Progress Administration) in 1932 he studied under Charles H. Alston.

Gouache and tempera were Lawrence's characteristic mediums. His use of sombre browns and black for shadows and outlines in an otherwise vibrant palette lent his work a distinctive overtone. His best-known works are his series on historical or social themes, including ". . . And the Migrants Kept Coming" (1940), "Life in Harlem" (1942), and "War" (1947). In 1964 he visited Nigeria, where he painted scenes of local life. His later works include a powerful series on the struggles of desegregation. Lawrence taught at various schools and colleges and became a professor of art at the University of Washington in Seattle in 1971.

Lawrence, James (b. Oct. 1, 1781, Burlington, N.J., U.S.—d. June 1, 1813, in a sea battle off Boston, Mass.), U.S. naval officer of the War of 1812 whose dying words, "Don't give up the ship," became one of the U.S. Navy's most cherished traditions.

Lawrence entered the navy as a midshipman (1798) and fought against the Barbary pirates. He was first lieutenant to Lieutenant Stephen Decatur when the USS *Philadelphia,* which had been captured by the Tripolitans, was destroyed in Tripoli harbour by Decatur-led forces (1804). During the War of 1812 Lawrence commanded the USS *Hornet* in the capture of HMS *Peacock.* Shortly thereafter he was promoted to captain of the frigate *Chesapeake.* On June 1, 1813, the *Chesapeake* accepted HMS *Shannon*'s challenge to a sea fight off Boston. The *Chesapeake* was decisively defeated in less than an hour and Lawrence was mortally wounded.

James Lawrence, detail of an engraving by W. Rollinson after a portrait by Gilbert Stuart
By courtesy of the Library of Congress, Washington, D.C.

Lawrence (of the Punjab and of Grately), John Laird Mair Lawrence, 1st Baron (b. March 4, 1811, Richmond, Yorkshire, Eng.—d. June 27, 1879, London), British viceroy and governor-general of India whose institution in the Punjab of extensive economic, social, and political reforms earned him the sobriquet "Saviour of the Punjab."

In 1830 Lawrence travelled to Calcutta with his brother Henry and then to Delhi, where he served for 19 years as an assistant judge, magistrate, and tax collector and where he came to oppose the oppression of the peasantry by the *talukdars* (tax collectors). After home leave (1840–42), he successfully organized the transport of supplies from Delhi to the Indo-British army fighting in the Punjab in the First Sikh War (1845–46). He was rewarded at age 35 with promotion to the commissionership of the newly annexed district of Jullundur. In this capacity he subdued the hill chiefs, prepared a revenue settlement, established courts and police posts, curbed female infanticide and suttee (self-destruction by widows on their husbands' funeral pyres), and trained a group of officials. He twice deputized for his brother as resident at Lahore.

Impatient with the Sikh council, Lawrence was eager to place financial reform under British control. As a member of the Punjab board of administration under Henry, after the Second Sikh War (1848–49), he made a first summary revenue settlement, abolished internal duties, introduced a uniform currency and postal system, and encouraged road and canal construction. To finance this work, he economized, curtailing the privileges of chiefs' estates and thus coming into conflict with his brother Henry. James Ramsay, Lord Dalhousie, governor general, dissolved the Punjab board in 1853, appointing John Lawrence chief commissioner in the executive branch.

On the outbreak of the mutiny in 1857, Lawrence restricted the sepoy (Indians employed as soldiers) battalions to the Punjab and negotiated a successful treaty with the Afghan ruler Dōst Moḥammad Khān, for which he was made a baronet and Knight Grand Cross of the Bath. After a brief visit to England, he returned to India in 1864 as a member of the civil service and was appointed viceroy and governor general.

Lawrence sought British security in a sepoy army of divided loyalty and in the weakening of princely forces; he resisted the appointment of Indians to high civil service posts but promoted increased educational opportunities. He wisely refrained from intervening in the succession dispute in Afghanistan after the death of Amīr Dōst Moḥammad in 1863, rejected entanglements in the affairs of Arabia and the Persian Gulf, and recognized any chief who secured power. He was created Baron Lawrence of the Punjab and of Grately, Hampshire, after his return to England in 1869.

Lawrence, Stringer (b. March 6, 1697, Hereford, Herefordshire, Eng.—d. Jan. 10, 1775, London), British army captain whose transformation of irregular troops into an effective fighting force earned him credit as the real founder of the Indian army under British rule.

Stringer Lawrence, oil painting by Thomas Gainsborough; in the National Portrait Gallery, London

By courtesy of the National Portrait Gallery, London

During 20 years of army service, Lawrence rose from ensign to captain and served at Gibraltar, in Flanders (Belg.), and at the Battle of Culloden Moor (Inverness). Joining the East India Company early in 1748, he commanded company troops at Madras. He so trained his mixed force of Europeans, *topasses* (Christian Indo-Portuguese), and sepoys (Indian soldiers in British employ) that by June 1748 he was able to foil a French attack on Cuddalore; he was captured by the French, however, and released after the Treaty of Aix-la-Chappelle (1748). In the capture of Devakottai in 1749, his subordinate officer was Robert (afterward Lord) Clive, who eventually became a lifelong friend. In 1750 Lawrence resigned from service to the British government over a pay dispute.

Promoted to lieutenant colonel in 1752, Lawrence returned to Madras and immediately relieved the town of Tiruchchirāppalli (Trichinopoly). With Clive's assistance he then destroyed the French force under Jacques Law, won another victory at Bahur, and for 17 months in 1753–54 successfully defended Tiruchchirāppalli in campaigns that frustrated French plans; in Madras in 1758 he again repulsed the French. In 1761 he was made commander in chief of all East India Company forces, with a seat on the council and a royal commission as major general. In 1766 he left India for retirement. Robert Clive, when presented a gift sword by the East India Company, refused to accept it unless a similar honour was presented to his veteran commander, Lawrence, who had been ignored. Later, Clive helped relieve Lawrence's financial straits by arranging an early pension of £500 for him.

"De," "la," and similar components of a name, when followed by a space, are alphabetized as separate words (e.g., *De Forest, Lee*). *When they are joined to the following part of a name, the combination is treated as a single word* (e.g., *DeForest, John William*).

Lawrence, T(homas) E(dward), byname LAWRENCE OF ARABIA, also called (from 1927) T.E. SHAW (b. Aug. 15, 1888, Tremadoc, Caernarvonshire, Wales—d. May 19, 1935, Clouds Hill, Dorset, Eng.), British archaeological scholar, military strategist, and author best known for his legendary war activities in the Middle East during World War I and for his account of those activities in *The Seven Pillars of Wisdom* (1926).

T.E. Lawrence

By courtesy of Lowell Thomas and Harry A. Chase

Early life. Lawrence was the son of Sir Thomas Chapman and Sara Maden, the governess of Sir Thomas' daughters at Westmeath, with whom he had escaped from both marriage and Ireland. As "Mr. and Mrs. Lawrence," the couple had five sons (Thomas Edward was the second) during what was outwardly a marriage with all the benefits of clergy. In 1896 the family settled in Oxford, where T.E. (he preferred the initials to the names) attended the High School and Jesus College. Medieval military architecture was his first interest, and he pursued it in its historical settings, studying crusader castles in France and (in 1909) in Syria and Palestine and submitting a thesis on the subject that won him first-class honours in history in 1910. (It was posthumously published, as *Crusader Castles,* in 1936.) As a protégé of the Oxford archaeologist D.G. Hogarth, he acquired a demyship (travelling fellowship) from Magdalen College and joined an expedition excavating the Hittite settlement of Carchemish on the Euphrates, working there from 1911 to 1914, first under Hogarth and then under Sir Leonard Woolley, and using his free time to travel on his own and get to know the language and the people. Early in 1914 he and Woolley, and Capt. S.F. Newcombe, explored northern Sinai, on the Turkish frontier east of Suez. Supposedly a scientific expedition, and in fact sponsored by the Palestine Exploration Fund, it was more a map-making reconnaissance from Gaza to Aqaba, destined to be of almost immediate strategic value. The cover study was nevertheless of authentic scholarly significance; written by Lawrence and Woolley together, it was published as *The Wilderness of Zin* in 1915.

The month the war began, Lawrence became a civilian employee of the Map Department of the War Office in London, charged with preparing a militarily useful map of Sinai. By December 1914 he was a lieutenant in Cairo. Experts on Arab affairs—especially those who had travelled in the Turkish-held Arab lands—were rare, and he was assigned to intelligence, where he spent more than a year, mostly interviewing prisoners, drawing maps, receiving and processing data from agents behind enemy lines, and producing a handbook on the Turkish Army. When, in mid-1915, his brothers Will and Frank were killed in action in France, T.E. was reminded cruelly of the more active front in the West. Egypt at the time was the staging area for Middle Eastern military operations of prodigious inefficiency; a trip to Arabia convinced Lawrence of an alternative method of undermining Germany's Turkish ally. In October 1916 he had accompanied the diplomat Sir Ronald Storrs on a mission to Arabia, where Ḥusayn ibn ʿAlī, *amīr* of Mecca, had the previous June proclaimed a revolt against the Turks. Storrs and Lawrence consulted with Ḥusayn's son Abdullah, and Lawrence received permission to go on to consult further with another son, Fayṣal, then commanding an Arab force southwest of Medina. Back in Cairo in November, Lawrence urged his superiors to abet the efforts at rebellion with arms and gold and to make use of the dissident shaykhs by meshing their aspirations for independence with general military strategy. He rejoined Fayṣal's army as political and liaison officer.

Guerrilla leader. Lawrence was not the only officer to become involved in the incipient Arab rising, but from his own small corner of the Arabian Peninsula he quickly became—especially from his own accounts—its brains, its organizing force, its liaison with Cairo, and its military technician. His small but irritating second front behind the Turkish lines was a hit-and-run guerrilla operation, focussing upon the mining of bridges and supply trains and the appearance of Arab units first in one place and then another, tying down enemy forces that otherwise would have been deployed elsewhere, and keeping the Damascus-to-Medina railway largely inoperable, with potential Turkish reinforcements thus helpless to crush the uprising. In such fashion Lawrence—"Amīr Dynamite" to the admiring Bedouins—committed the cynical, self-serving shaykhs for the moment to his king-maker's vision of an Arab nation, goaded them with examples of his own self-punishing personal valour when their spirits flagged, bribed them with promises of enemy booty and English gold sovereigns.

Aqaba—at the northernmost tip of the Red Sea—was the first major victory for the Arab guerrilla forces; they seized it after a two-month march on July 6, 1917. Thenceforth, Lawrence attempted to coordinate Arab movements with the campaign of General Sir Edmund Allenby, who was advancing toward Jerusalem, a tactic only partly successful. In November Lawrence was captured at Darʿā by the Turks while reconnoitring the area in Arab dress and was apparently recognized and homosexually brutalized before he was able to escape. The experience, variously reported or disguised by him afterward, left real scars as well as wounds upon his psyche from which he never recovered. The next month, nevertheless, he took part in the victory parade in Jerusalem and then returned to increasingly successful actions in which Fayṣal's forces nibbled their way north, and Lawrence rose to the rank of lieutenant colonel with the Distinguished Service Order (DSO).

By the time the motley Arab army reached Damascus in October 1918, Lawrence was physically and emotionally exhausted, having forced body and spirit to the breaking point too often. He had been wounded numerous times, captured, and tortured; had endured extremities of hunger, weather, and disease; had been driven by military necessity to commit atrocities upon the enemy; and had witnessed in the chaos of Damascus the defeat of his aspirations for the Arabs in the very moment of their triumph, their seemingly incurable factionalism rendering them incapable of becoming a nation. (Anglo-French duplicity, made official in the Sykes-Picot Agreement, Lawrence knew, had already betrayed them in a cynical wartime division of expected spoils.) Distinguished and disillusioned, Lawrence left for home just before the Armistice and politely refused, at a royal audience on Oct. 30, 1918, the Order of the Bath and the DSO, leaving the shocked king George V (in his words) "holding the box in my hand." He was demobilized as a lieutenant colonel on July 31, 1919.

Postwar activities. A colonel at 30, Lawrence was a private at 34. In between he lobbied vainly for Arab independence at the Paris Peace Conference in 1919 (even appearing in Arab robes) and lobbied vainly against the detachment of Syria and Lebanon from the rest of the Arab countries as a French mandate. Meanwhile he worked on his war memoir, acquiring for the purpose a research fellowship at All Souls College, Oxford, effective (for a seven-year term) in November 1919. By that time his exploits were becoming belatedly known to a wide public, for in London in August 1919 an American war correspondent, Lowell Thomas, had begun an immensely popular series of illustrated lectures, "With Allenby in Palestine and Lawrence in Arabia." The latter segment soon dominated the program, and Lawrence, curious about it, went to see it himself.

Adviser on Arab affairs. Lawrence was already on a third draft of his narrative when, in March 1921, he was wooed back to the Middle East as adviser on Arab affairs to the colonial minister, then Winston Churchill. After the Cairo political settlements, which redeemed a few of the idealistic wartime promises Lawrence had made, he rejected all offers of further positions in government; and, with the covert help of his wartime colleague, Air Marshal Sir Hugh Trenchard, enlisted under an assumed name (John Hume Ross) in the Royal Air Force on Aug. 28, 1922. He had just finished arranging to have eight copies of the revised and rhetorically inflated 330,000-word text of *The Seven Pillars of Wisdom* run off by the press of the *Oxford Times* and was emotionally drained by the drafting of his memoir. Now he was willing to give up his £1,200 Colonial Office salary for the daily two shillings ninepence of an aircraftman, not only to lose himself in the ranks but to acquire material for another book. He was successful only in the latter. The London press found him at the Farnborough base, the *Daily Express* breaking the story on December 27. Embarrassed, the RAF released him early the next month.

Finding reinstatement impossible, Lawrence looked around for another service and through the intervention of a War Office friend, Sir Philip Chetwode, was able to enlist on March 12, 1923, as a private in the Royal Tank Corps, this time as T.E. Shaw, a name he claimed to have chosen at random, although one of the crucial events of his postwar life was his meeting in 1922, and later friendship with, George Bernard Shaw. (In 1927 he assumed the new name legally.) Posted to Bovington Camp in Dorset, he acquired a cottage nearby, Clouds Hill, which remained his home thereafter. From Dorset he set about arranging for publication of yet another version of *Seven Pillars;* on the editorial advice of his friends, notably George Bernard Shaw, a sizable portion of the Oxford text was pruned for the famous 128-copy subscription edition of 1926, sumptuously printed and bound and illustrated by notable British artists commissioned by the author.

Major literary works. Lawrence's *The Seven Pillars of Wisdom* (posthumous trade edition 1935, with subsequent editions since) remains one of the few 20th-century works in English to make epical figures out of contemporaries. Though overpopulated with adjectives and often straining for effects and "art," it is, nevertheless, an action-packed narrative of Lawrence's campaigns in the desert with the Arabs. The book is replete with incident and spectacle, filled with rich character portrayals and a tense introspection that bares the author's own complex mental and spiritual transformation. Though admittedly inexact and subjective, it combines the scope of heroic epic with the closeness of autobiography.

To recover the costs of printing *Seven Pillars,* Lawrence agreed to a trade edition of a 130,000-word abridgment, *Revolt in the Desert.* By the time it was released in March 1927, he was at a base in India, remote from the publicity both editions generated; yet the limelight sought him out. Unfounded rumours of his involvement as a spy in Central Asia and in a plot against the Soviet Union caused the RAF (to which he had been transferred in 1925 on the intervention of George Bernard Shaw and John Buchan with the prime minister, Stanley Baldwin) to return him to England in 1929. In the meantime he had completed a draft of a semifictionalized memoir of Royal Air Force recruit training, *The Mint* (published 1955), which in its explicitness horrified Whitehall officialdom and which in his lifetime never went beyond circulation in typescript to his friends. In it he balanced scenes of contentment with air force life with scenes of splenetic rage at the desecration of the recruit's essential inviolate humanity. He had also begun, on commission from the book designer Bruce Rogers, a translation of Homer's *Odyssey* into English prose, a task he continued at various RAF bases from Karāchi in 1928 through Plymouth in 1931. It was published in 1932 as the work of T.E. Shaw, but posthumous printings have used both his former and adopted names.

Little else by Lawrence was published in his lifetime. His first postwar writings, including a famous essay on guerrilla war and a magazine serial version of an early draft of *Seven Pillars,* have been published as *Evolution of a Revolt* (edited by S. and R. Weintraub, 1968). *Minorities* (1971) reproduced an anthology of more than 100 poems Lawrence had collected in a notebook over many years, each possessing a crucial and revealing association with something in his life.

Last years. Lawrence's last years were spent among RAF seaplanes and seagoing tenders, although officialdom refused him permission to fly. In the process, moving from bases on the English Channel to those on the North Sea and leading charismatically from the lowest ranks as Aircraftman Shaw, he worked on improved designs for high-speed seaplane-tender watercraft, testing them in rigorous trials and developing a technical manual for their use.

Discharged from the Royal Air Force on Feb. 26, 1935, Lawrence returned to Clouds Hill to face a retirement, at 46, filled alternately with optimism about future publishing projects and a sense of emptiness. To Lady Astor, an old friend, he described himself as puttering about as if "there is something broken in the works . . . my will, I think." A motorcycling accident on May 13 solved the problem of his future. He died six days later without regaining consciousness.

Assessment. Lawrence became a mythic figure in his own lifetime even before he published his own version of his legend in *The Seven Pillars of Wisdom.* His accomplishments themselves were solid enough for several lives. More than a military leader and inspirational force behind the Arab revolt against the Turks, he was a superb tactician and a highly influential theoretician of guerrilla warfare. Besides *The Seven Pillars of Wisdom,* his sharply etched service chronicle, *The Mint,* and his mannered prose translation of the *Odyssey* added to a literary reputation further substantiated by an immense correspondence that establishes him as one of the major letter writers of his generation.

Lawrence found despair as necessary as ambition. He lived on the masochistic side of asceticism, and part of his self-punishment involved creating within himself a deep frustration to immediately follow, and cancel out, high achievement by denying to himself the recognition he had earned. At its most extreme, this impulse involved a symbolic killing of the self, a taking up of a new life and a new name. Under whatever guise, he was a many-sided genius whose accomplishments precluded the privacy he constantly sought. By the manufacture of his myth, however solidly based, he created in his own person a characterization rivaling any in contemporary fiction. (S.We./Ed.)

BIBLIOGRAPHY. Biographies include Robert Graves, *Lawrence and the Arabs* (1927, reissued 1991), a book vetted by Lawrence; A.W. Lawrence (ed.), *T.E. Lawrence, by His Friends* (1937, reprinted 1980), a mostly adulatory but biographically important collection; Jean Béraud-Villars, *T.E. Lawrence; or, The Search for the Absolute* (1959), one of the best studies of Lawrence, with sound scholarship where it does not exaggerate Lawrence's Francophobia; John E. Mack, *A Prince of Our Disorder: The Life of T.E. Lawrence* (1976), a comprehensive study of the personal side of Lawrence's life; H. Montgomery Hyde, *Solitary in the Ranks* (1977), a chronicle of Lawrence's life after he left the Middle East; Michael Yardley, *T.E. Lawrence* (1987); Malcolm Brown and Julia Cave, *A Touch of Genius: The Life of T.E. Lawrence* (1988); and Jeremy Wilson, *Lawrence of Arabia: The Authorised Biography of T.E. Lawrence* (1989). Other studies include Jeffrey Meyers, *The Wounded Spirit: T.E. Lawrence's Seven Pillars of Wisdom* (1973, reissued 1989), a critique of the narrative's literary merits, with substantial background information and a lengthy bibliography; Stanley Weintraub and Rodelle Weintraub, *Lawrence of Arabia: The Literary Impulse* (1975), a study of Lawrence as a writer; and Jeffrey Meyers (ed.), *T.E. Lawrence: Soldier, Writer, Legend: New Essays* (1989).

Lawrence, Sir Thomas (b. April 13, 1769, Bristol, Gloucestershire, Eng.—d. Jan. 7, 1830, London), painter and draftsman who was the most fashionable English portrait painter of the late 18th and early 19th centuries.

He was the son of an innkeeper who owned the "Black Bear" at Devizes, where the young

"Queen Charlotte," oil on canvas by Sir Thomas Lawrence, *c.* 1789; in the National Gallery, London

By courtesy of the trustees of the National Gallery, London; photograph, J.R. Freeman & Co. Ltd.

Lawrence won a reputation as a prodigy for his profile portraits in pencil of guests. Later he began to work in pastel, and in 1780, when his family moved to Bath, he set up professionally. He had little regular education or artistic training, but was working in oils by the time he moved to London in 1787. There he studied at the Royal Academy schools for a short time and was given encouragement by Sir Joshua Reynolds. He was handsome, charming, and exceptionally gifted. His early success was phenomenal, and when he was 20 years of age he was summoned to Windsor to paint the portrait, later widely acclaimed, of Queen Charlotte. He was elected associate of the Royal Academy in 1791 and academician in 1794.

Lawrence was a highly skilled draftsman. He soon abandoned pastels but continued to make portraits in pencil and chalks. These were separate commissions and were rarely studies for paintings, as it was his usual practice to make a careful drawing of the head and sometimes the whole composition on the canvas itself and to paint over it. There are highly interesting references to his working methods in Joseph Farington's *Diary.*

After the death of Reynolds, Lawrence was the leading English portrait painter. His works exhibit a fluid touch, rich colour, and an ability to realize textures. He presented his sitters in a dramatic, sometimes theatrical, manner that produced Romantic portraiture of a high order. After the death of John Hoppner in 1810 he was patronized by the Prince Regent, who knighted him in 1815 and sent him in 1818 to the political congresses of Aix-la-Chapelle and Vienna, where he painted 24 large full-length portraits of the military leaders and heads of state of the Holy Alliance. Executed with sovereign verve and elegance, these works now hang together in the Waterloo Chamber at Windsor Castle—a unique historical document of the period. By these works Lawrence was recognized as the foremost portrait painter of Europe. On his return to England in 1820 he was elected president of the Royal Academy.

Lawrence was also a distinguished connoisseur. His collection of old-master drawings was one of the finest ever assembled, and he was instrumental in securing the collection of Greek sculptures known as the Elgin Marbles for the nation and in the founding of the National Gallery.

lawrencium (Lr), synthetic chemical element, the 14th member of the actinide series in Group IIIb of the periodic table, atomic number 103. Not occurring in nature, lawrencium (as the isotopes lawrencium-257, lawrencium-258, and lawrencium-259) was produced (1961) by Albert Ghiorso, T. Sikkeland, A.E. Larsh, and R.M. Latimer at the University of California, Berkeley, by bombarding a mixture of the longest lived isotopes of californium (atomic number 98) with boron ions (atomic number 5) accelerated in a heavy-ion linear accelerator. A team of Soviet scientists at the Joint Institute for Nuclear Research in Dubna discovered (1965) lawrencium-256 (35-second half-life), which the Berkeley group used to show that lawrencium behaves more like the tripositive elements in the actinide series than like the predominantly dipositive nobelium (atomic number 102).

atomic number	103
stablest isotope	256
valence	3
electronic config.	2-8-18-32-32-9-2 or (Rn)$5f^{14}7s^2$

laws, conflict of, the existence worldwide of a multiplicity of different sets of courts and different sets of private law (*i.e.*, the law governing relations between private individuals or between an individual and the state considered as an individual without special position or privilege). The "law of the conflict of laws"—also called private international law—has to do with the resolution of the problems resulting from such diversity of courts and law.

A brief treatment of conflict of laws follows. For full treatment, *see* MACROPAEDIA: Procedural Law.

Conflict of laws refers to an area of law concerned with the principles by which the governing laws of different states, provinces, and nations are to be applied, recognized, or enforced by others. When a country encompasses a number of smaller powers (states or provinces, for example), each of which is governed by a set of laws in addition to those applicable to the country as a whole, this situation is referred to as a diversity of laws. This can also arise when a country is newly formed, divided, or brought into the dominion of another country; and it often exists between a national power and its colonies. Even within a nation there may be a diversity of laws among different religious or ethnic groups, as the Muslims, Jews, and Christians who are governed by separate legal codes in Lebanon and in Israel.

The rules of conflict of laws are designed to determine which set of laws is applicable to a given case, which judicial system is most appropriate for trial of the case (jurisdiction), and the extent to which foreign powers will honour or enforce the outcome of the trial. Despite 19th-century attempts to establish a consistent international code for the determination of these questions, in current practice every nation establishes its own set of laws and determines its relations with the laws of other states, often through treaties and other forms of mutual agreement. Each power also defines the extent of its jurisdiction, generally limiting the cases accepted for trial to (1) those cases whose proceedings do not severely inconvenience the court schedule or require drastic relocation of one or both parties in the dispute and (2) those cases whose results are enforceable within national boundaries. In some countries that consist of a number of states or provinces, jurisdiction among the states is determined by a uniform national law, as in Germany, while in other countries such as the United States and the British domain, each state is empowered to define the range of its own jurisdiction within certain limits; in the United States, states authority is limited by the Constitution. In common practice, countries generally extend jurisdiction to all cases in which both parties accept it. Under the continental European civil-law system, suit is usually brought against a defendant in the locality where he resides, while in the Anglo-American common-law system the trial may proceed in any area in which notice of trial can be personally served on the defendant. Both systems allow their courts to govern questions of land within their jurisdiction, regardless of where the owner resides.

Generally, each country determines for itself the extent to which it will enforce or recognize decisions rendered by a foreign power, unless the two countries follow a practice established by mutual agreement. Policies vary widely among different countries concerning the acceptance of *in rem* judgments, the enforcements of penalties, and the application of *res judicata*, which prevents a case from being brought to trial a second time on the same grounds. When a foreign decision is accepted, it is generally converted into a form consistent with the practice of the accepting power, through a special procedure called *exequatur* that establishes the validity of the original trial but does not require a reopening of the case; in some Scandinavian countries, however, court proceedings must be newly initiated. Decisions not to accept a foreign judgment may be the result of a lack of jurisdiction in the first court, improper conduct of the trial, or severe disruption or inconvenience for the accepting power. In the United States, each state is bound by the Full Faith and Credit clause of the Constitution to recognize and enforce judgments rendered by the court of any other state acting within its proper jurisdiction.

In order to try parties under the law where the action was taken, states and countries may occasionally elect to conduct a trial according to the laws of the foreign power rather than that of their own. Though efforts have been made to simplify the principles governing this practice, known as "choice of law" provisions, they remain complex and highly diversified among different nations. Generally, the determination of a person's legal status is conducted on the basis of his nationality, which is considered by common-law countries to be his country of residence. Disputes over the ownership of land are settled according to the laws of the locality where the land is situated, and wills are commonly validated in compliance with the laws of the area where they are signed. Contract disputes between businesses are also usually conducted under the laws of the state of execution or according to the laws by which both parties explicitly agree to be bound as a provision of the contract.

Laws of ——— : *see under* substantive word (*e.g.*, Indies, Laws of the).

Lawson, Andrew Cowper (b. July 25, 1861, Anstruther, Fife, Scot.—d. June 16, 1952, San Leandro, Calif., U.S.), Canadian-U.S. geologist who made important discoveries of Precambrian rock structures (more than 570,000,000 years old) and headed the commission appointed to investigate the disastrous California earthquake of 1906.

In 1882 Lawson joined the Canadian Geological Survey and began his epic studies of the Precambrian rocks of southwestern Ontario. His revolutionary interpretation of these strata was published in 1881, and, although considered heretical at first, his conclusions soon gained general acceptance. In 1890 he left the Survey to become professor of mineralogy and geology at the University of California at Berkeley, where he remained until he retired in 1928. He organized the university's instruction in mineralogy and petrography, developed a geology field course, and became a powerful influence throughout academic and professional circles. He founded and for 35 years edited the *Bulletin of the Department of Geology.* The report of his commission's investigation of the 1906 California earthquake marked an epoch of study in that field. A milestone in the understanding of earthquakes, the report was the most complete ever made of a major earthquake and initiated the theory of elastic rebound of shock waves as the cause of certain earthquakes.

Lawson, Edward Levy- (English newspaperman): *see* Burnham, Edward Levy-Lawson, 1st Baron.

Lawson, (Victor) Fremont, Fremont also spelled FREEMONT (b. Sept. 9, 1850, Chicago—d. Aug. 19, 1925, Chicago), newspaper editor and publisher, probably the first in the United States to assign correspondents to live and gather news in major cities outside the country. Before this innovation (1898) U.S. newspapers relied on dispatches from British or other foreign sources. He also led the successful effort of Western publishers to rescue the Associated Press (AP) from a combine that leaked its news to the rival United Press (UP).

Fremont Lawson

Reprinted with permission from the Chicago *Daily News*

Already the owner of a Norwegian-language paper in Chicago, Lawson in 1876 bought an interest in the Chicago *Daily News,* which had been founded in 1875 by Melville Elijah Stone (1848–1929) as the first one-cent newspaper in the Middle West. Under Lawson's business management the circulation of the *Daily News* increased markedly within a year. In 1881 Lawson and Stone started a morning edition that later (1883) was called the Chicago *Record.* After numerous mergers and variations in name, it was known as the *Record-Herald* when Lawson sold his interest (1914) and as the *Chicago's American* when it ceased publication (1969). Lawson retained proprietorship of the *Daily News* until his death.

Lawson's active interest in the AP began with concern over delayed and inconsistent New York financial reports reaching Chicago newspapers. Investigation led him to discover that the majority owners of the profit-making UP were in de facto control of AP, a nonprofit cooperative. He rallied Western newspapers against collusive Eastern publishers in a successful and sweeping reorganization of the AP that began the agency's climb to dominance. Lawson was a director of AP (1893–1925) and its president (1894–1900) while Stone was its manager. His advocacy of a U.S. postal savings bank caused him to be called the father of the law that established it (1910). Lawson was also a leading benefactor of the Congregational Church and the Young Men's Christian Association.

Lawson, Henry (Archibald) (b. June 17, 1867, near Grenfell, N.S.W., Australia—d. Sept. 22, 1922, Abbotsford, N.S.W.), Australian writer of short stories and balladlike verse noted for his realistic portrayals of bush life.

He was the son of a former Norwegian sailor and an active feminist. Hampered by deafness from the time he was nine and by the poverty and unhappiness in his family, he left school at 14 to help his father as a builder. About 1884 he moved to Sydney, where the *Bulletin* published his first stories and verses (1887–88). During those years he worked for several newspapers but also spent much time wandering. Out of these experiences came material for his vivid, realistic writing, which, by its often pessimistic blend of pathos and irony, captured some of the spirit of Australian working life. His later years were increasingly unhappy, and the quality of his writing deteriorated.

Lawson's principal works are collections of poems or stories and include: *In the Days When the World Was Wide and Other Verses* (1896); *While the Billy Boils* (1896); *On the Track and over the Sliprails* (1900); *Joe Wilson and His Mates* (1901); *Children of the Bush* (1902); and *Triangles of Life and Other Stories* (1913).

Lawson, John Howard (b. Sept. 25, 1894, New York City—d. Aug. 11, 1977, San Francisco), U.S. playwright, screenwriter, and member of the "Hollywood Ten," who was jailed (1948–49) and blacklisted for his refusal to tell the House Committee on Un-American Activities about his political allegiances.

Lawson's early works, such as *Roger Bloomer* (1923) and *Processional* (1925), are notable examples of Expressionism. He later portrayed problems of the working class: *The International* (1928) depicts a world revolution of the proletariat; *Marching Song* (1937) concerns a sit-down strike. Lawson's plays emphasize ideology and innovation and are powerful and effective.

During the 1930s and 1940s Lawson devoted his time to the movies. He wrote such scripts as *Action in the North Atlantic* (1943) and *Sahara* (1943) and was the co-founder and first president of the Screen Writers Guild. This new employment led to *Theory and Technique of Playwriting and Screenwriting* (1949), a revised edition of his earlier *Theory and Technique of Playwriting* (1936).

In the late 1940s the uproar over alleged Communist influence in the motion picture industry led to his jail sentence and the blacklisting of Lawson in Hollywood. These events reaffirmed Lawson's interest in American cultural tradition, explored in *The Hidden Heritage: A Rediscovery of the Ideas and Forces That Link the Thought of Our Time with the Culture of the Past* (1950).

Consult the INDEX *first*

Lawton, city, seat (1907) of Comanche county, southwestern Oklahoma, U.S., on the Cache Creek. Originally part of the Choctaw-Chickasaw lands in the Indian Territory, the area was settled in 1869 by the Kiowa and Comanche Indians; Ft. Sill was established to control the Indians. A settlement near the fort was organized as a city in 1901 and was named for Gen. Henry W. Lawton, sent to capture the Apache leader Geronimo. Indian lands were then opened to auction, and more than 25,000 white settlers came to participate. Lawton is in an area of farms, grazing lands, limestone and granite quarries, and oil wells. It is the site of Cameron University (1901). Wichita Mountains Wildlife Refuge is in the vicinity. The huge Ft. Sill Military Reservation is 4 mi (6 km) north. Pop. (1990) city, 80,561; Lawton MSA, 111,486.

lawyer, one trained and licensed to prepare, manage, and either prosecute or defend a court action as an agent for another and who also gives advice on legal matters that may or may not require court action.

The lawyer applies the law to specific cases. He investigates the facts and the evidence by conferring with his client and reviewing documents, and he prepares and files the pleadings in court. At the trial he introduces evidence, interrogates witnesses, and argues questions of law and fact. If he does not win the case, he may seek a new trial or relief in an appellate court.

In many instances, the lawyer can bring about the settlement of a case without trial through negotiation, reconciliation, and compromise. In addition, the law gives individuals the power to arrange and determine their legal rights in many matters and in various ways, as through wills, contracts, or corporate bylaws, and the lawyer aids in many of these arrangements. During the 20th century a rapidly developing field of work for lawyers has been the representation of clients before administrative committees and courts and before legislative committees.

A lawyer has several loyalties in his work. They include that to his client, to the administration of justice, to the community, to his associates in practice, and to himself. When these loyalties conflict, the standards of the profession are intended to effect a reconciliation.

Legal practice varies from country to country. In England lawyers are divided into barristers, who plead in the higher courts, and solicitors, who do office work and plead in the lower courts. In the United States attorneys often specialize in limited areas of law such as criminal, divorce, corporate, probate, or personal injury, though many are involved in general practice.

In France numerous types of professionals and even nonprofessionals handle various aspects of legal work. The most prestigious is the *avocat,* who is equal in rank to a magistrate or law professor. Roughly comparable to the English barrister, the *avocat*'s main function is to plead in court. In France, as in most civil-law countries, the examination of witnesses is conducted by the magistrate rather than the attorney as in common-law countries. In the *avocat*'s pleading, he develops his argument and points out discrepancies in the testimony of witnesses; this is the primary means open to the *avocat* to persuade the court on legal and factual points. Formerly, in addition to the *avocats,* there were also *avoués* and *agréés;* the former represented litigants in all procedural matters except the oral presentation, prepared briefs, and negotiated settlements, while the latter, few in number, were responsible for pleading in certain commercial courts. Today the distinction between *avoués* and *avocats* has been abolished in all but the appellate courts, where *avoués* continue to practice as before.

In addition to these professional groups there are nonprofessional legal counsellors who give advice on various legal problems and are often employed by business firms. In almost all civil-law countries there are notaries (*see* notary), who have exclusive rights to deal with such office work as marriage settlements and wills.

In Germany the chief distinction is between lawyers and notaries. The German attorney, however, plays an even smaller courtroom role than the French *avocat,* largely because presentations on points of law are limited and litigation is often left to junior partners. Attorneys are often restricted to practice before courts in specific territories. There are further restrictions in that certain attorneys practice only before appeals courts, often necessitating a new attorney for each level of litigation. In Germany lawyers are employed in the administration of government to a greater extent than in common-law countries.

In communist countries lawyers are widely used as advisers to government bureaus but have far less scope in representing individuals. *See also* advocate; barrister; solicitor.

laxative, any drug that stimulates the bowel's smooth muscles or affects the stool's consistency to promote the evacuation of feces.

Laxative, cathartic, purgative, and drastic denote increasing intensity of effect in promoting defecation, a gradation sometimes achieved simply by increasing the dosage of a single drug. Laxatives produce their effect by several mechanisms. Irritant, or stimulant, laxatives act directly on the muscles of the intestine, stimulating the wavelike muscular contractions (peristalsis) that result in defecation. The stimulants include cascara sagrada, senna, castor oil, bisacodyl, and phenolphthalein. Bulk-forming laxatives promote evacuation by increasing the stool's water content and bulk volume. The bulk laxatives include the hydrophilic (water-attracting) colloids, which consist of such indigestible fibrous matter as dietary bran, agar, psyllium seeds, methylcellulose, and polycarbophil. The action of saline laxatives is not completely understood, but it is certain that they draw water into the intestine from adjacent tissues. The increased water content and bulk of the stool are believed to stimulate evacuation. Saline laxatives include magnesium sulfate (Epsom salts), magnesium hydroxide (milk of magnesia), magnesium citrate, and such phosphate salts as disodium phosphate. Glycerin is another substance that attracts water into the stool. Lubricant laxatives make the bowel walls and stool moist and slippery, thus facilitating defecation. The principal lubricant laxatives are mineral oil and certain vegetable oils. Stool-softening laxatives such as dioctyl sulfosuccinate help liquids mix into the stool and thus prevent dry, hard stools from forming.

Laxatives are secondary in importance to a high fibre diet in correcting simple intestinal constipation. Other valid uses include prevention of strain when anorectal disorders or diseases of arterial vessels exist. They also alleviate constipation caused by various illnesses or drug treatment. A secondary use is the elimination of bowel contents prior to surgery.

Laxdaela saga (Icelandic: "Saga of [the Men of] Laxárdal"), one of the Icelanders', or family, group of sagas. The tale, written about 1245 by an anonymous author (possibly a woman), is the tragic story of several generations of an Iceland warrior-family descended from Ketill Flatnose. One of the best English translations is by Magnus Magnusson and Hermann Pálsson in 1969. This is included with other sagas in the five-volume *Complete Sagas of Icelanders* (1997).

Laxness, Halldór, pseudonym of HALLDÓR KILJAN GUDJÓNSSON (b. April 23, 1902, Reykjavík, Ice.—d. Feb. 8, 1998, near Reykjavík), Icelandic novelist who was awarded the Nobel Prize for Literature in 1955. He is considered the most creative Icelandic writer of the 20th century.

Laxness spent most of his youth on the family farm. At age 17 he traveled to Europe, where he spent several years and, in the early 1920s, became a Roman Catholic. His first major novel, *Vefarinn mikli frá Kasmír* (1927; "The Great Weaver from Kashmir"), is about a young man who is torn between his religious faith and the pleasures of the world. Rebellious in its attitude and experimental in style, this modernistic novel marked the beginning of his dissociation from Christianity. While living in the United States (1927–29), Laxness turned to socialism, an ideology that is reflected in his novels written in the 1930s and '40s.

After his return to Iceland, he published a series of novels with subjects drawn from the social life of Iceland: *Salka Valka* (1931–32; Eng. trans. *Salka Valka*), which deals with the plight of working people in an Icelandic fishing village; *Sjálfstætt fólk* (1934–35; *Independent People*), the story of an impoverished farmer and his struggle to retain his economic independence; and *Heimsljós* (1937–40; *World Light*), a four-volume novel about the struggles of a peasant poet. These novels criticized Icelandic society from a socialist viewpoint, and they attracted a great deal of controversy. Although he had initially rejected the literary tradition of his native country, Laxness later embraced the medieval Icelandic saga and was credited by the Swedish Academy, which awards the Nobel Prize, with having "renewed the great narrative art of Iceland." The nationalistic trilogy *Íslandsklukkan* (1943–46; "Iceland's Bell") established him as the country's leading writer. Beginning in the late 1950s, Laxness increasingly turned from social issues to philosophical questions and problems of the individual. The novels from this period, including *Brekkukotsannáll* (1957; *The Fish Can Sing*) and *Paradísarheimt* (1960; *Paradise Reclaimed*), are more lyrical and introspective. In *Kristnihald undir Jökli* (1968; *Christianity at Glacier*) and *Innansveiterkronika* (1970; "Domestic Chronicle") he even engaged in modernist experimentation as he had in his early works.

Laxness also published plays, poetry, short stories, critical essays, and translations, and he edited several Icelandic sagas. In the 1970s and '80s he published several volumes of memoirs, including *Sagan af brauddinu dýra* (1987; *The Bread of Life*) and *Dagar hjá múnkum* (1987; "Days with Monks").

BIBLIOGRAPHY. Peter Hallberg, *Halldór Laxness* (1971).

Lay, Elzy, byname of WILLIAM ELLSWORTH LAY (b. Nov. 25, 1868, McArthur, Ohio, U.S.—d. Nov. 10, 1934, Los Angeles, Calif.), western American outlaw, a member of the Wild Bunch (*q.v.*) and the favourite friend and ally of Butch Cassidy in train and bank robberies. Following a train robbery near Folsom, N.M., in which two sheriffs were killed, Elzy Lay was captured and on Oct. 10, 1899, sentenced to life imprisonment—under his alias William McGinnis. While in the New Mexico Territorial Prison he helped to quell a riot and in 1906 was granted a governor's pardon. He then drifted north to Wyoming (still retaining his alias), married one Mary Calvert, and operated a ranch. From 1916 he guided geologists in the area and became an amateur geologist and prospector.

Lay, Horatio Nelson (b. 1832—d. May 4, 1898, Forest Hill, Kent, Eng.), British diplomat who organized the Maritime Customs Bureau for the Chinese government in 1855.

In 1854 a rebellion had cut off the North China trading city of Shanghai from the capital, Peking (Bejing); and, because the Western powers in Shanghai were required by treaty to pay a tariff on all goods that they brought into the country, they set up a bureau to collect the tariff for the Chinese government. Lay, as head of the bureau, made plans to extend its services to other Chinese cities and, in 1861, was appointed inspector general of customs for all 14 ports through which Western goods entered China.

Two years later, at the request of the Chinese, he procured a fleet of eight gunboats with crews from the British, assuming the Chinese would transmit orders through him. They refused to allow such control to a foreigner, however, and the fleet was sold.

Lay-Osborn flotilla, fleet of ships bought for China in the mid-19th century by a British consular official, Horatio Nelson Lay, which created a tremendous controversy when Lay falsely assumed that the Chinese government would transmit all orders to the fleet through him. This controversy prompted a decision by the Chinese government to discontinue leasing or purchasing vessels from abroad and instead to manufacture vessels in China.

In 1863 the Chinese government decided to buy a fleet of gunboats to aid in suppressing the great Taiping Rebellion (1850–64), which was sweeping the southern provinces. Lay, who had undertaken to contract the vessels for the Chinese government, procured the gunboats and hired Captain Sherard Osborn and a British crew to run them. After the flotilla arrived in Chinese waters in 1863, Lay and Osborn refused to comply with the wishes of the Chinese that they surrender command of the ships and continue to serve only as technical advisers. Lay revealed much about Western attitudes toward the Chinese when he stated that "the notion of a gentleman acting under an Asiatic barbarian is preposterous." The Chinese government revoked the purchase and dismissed Lay from its service.

Layamon, more properly spelled LAWAMON (fl. 12th century), early Middle English poet, author of the romance-chronicle the *Brut* (*c.* 1200), one of the most notable English poems of the 12th century, when English was nearly eclipsed by French and Latin as a literary language. It is the first work in English to treat of the "matter of Britain"—*i.e.,* the legends surrounding Arthur and the knights of the Round Table.

Layamon describes himself as a priest living at Arley in Worcestershire. His source was the *Roman de Brut* by Wace, an Anglo-Norman verse adaptation of Geoffrey of Monmouth's *History of the Kings of Britain.* In about 16,000 long alliterative lines (often broken into short couplets by rhyme), the *Brut* relates the legendary history of Britain from the landing of Brutus, great-grandson of the Trojan Aeneas, to the final Saxon victory over the Britons in 689. One-third of the poem deals with Arthurian matter, but Layamon's is not a high chivalric treatment: mass war is the staple, with Arthur the splendid war leader of Germanic tradition.

Layard, Sir Austen Henry (b. March 5, 1817, Paris, France—d. July 5, 1894, London, Eng.), English archaeologist whose excavations greatly increased knowledge of the ancient civilizations of Mesopotamia.

Layard, drawing by G.F. Watts; in the National Portrait Gallery, London

In 1839 he left his position in a London law office and began an adventuresome journey on horseback through Anatolia and Syria. In 1842 the British ambassador at Istanbul, Sir Stratford Canning, employed him for unofficial diplomatic missions. Spending much time in the vicinity of Mosul, Ottoman Mesopotamia (now in Iraq), Layard became increasingly interested in locating and unearthing the great cities of biblical renown. Mistaking Nimrūd, site of the Assyrian capital of Calah, for Nineveh, he excavated there (1845–51) and discovered the remains of palaces of 9th- and

7th-century-BC kings and a large number of important artworks. These included sculptures from the reign of King Ashurnasirpal II and a huge winged bull that remain among the most valued treasures of the British Museum.

After his celebrated and unprecedented success, he turned his attention in 1849 to the mound opposite Mosul on the eastern bank of the Tigris River, where he found Nineveh. His new effort uncovered the palace of Sennacherib and many extraordinary artworks. Perhaps most important, however, was his discovery of large numbers of cuneiform tablets from the state archives, from which much about Assyrian and Babylonian culture and history was eventually learned. He also made soundings at Ashur, Babylon, Nippur, and other sites in Babylonia and Assyria. His *Discoveries in the Ruins of Nineveh and Babylon* (1853), an account of this expedition, was extremely popular.

During his later career in government and diplomacy, Layard served in Parliament (1852–57 and 1860–69), became under secretary of foreign affairs (1861–66), and was appointed chief commissioner of works and privy councillor (1868) and ambassador at Istanbul (1877–80). He was knighted in 1878.

"De," "la," and similar components of a name, when followed by a space, are alphabetized as separate words (e.g., *De Forest, Lee*). *When they are joined to the following part of a name, the combination is treated as a single word* (e.g., *DeForest, John William*).

Laye, Camara (b. Jan. 1, 1928, Kouroussa, French Guinea [now in Guinea]—d. Feb. 4, 1980, Senegal), one of the first African writers from south of the Sahara to achieve an international reputation.

Laye grew up in the ancient city of Kouroussa, where he attended local Qur'ānic and government schools before leaving for Conakry to study at the Poiret School, a technical college. Scholarship aid then enabled him to pursue an engineering course at Argenteuil, Fr.

His autobiographical novel *L'Enfant noir* (1953; *The Dark Child*) recreates nostalgically his childhood days in Guinea in a flowing, poetic prose. The life he depicts in a traditional African town is an idyllic one in which human values are paramount and the inevitable alienation from the land that accompanies Western technology has not yet taken its toll.

Upon his return to Guinea in 1956, he worked as an engineer for two years and then as director of a research centre for the Ministry of Information. During the next 10 years he wrote numerous short stories for such periodicals as *Black Orpheus* and *Présence Africaine.*

In 1954, *Le Regard du roi* (*The Radiance of the King*), the novel considered by some critics to be Laye's best work, appeared. It describes a white man's journey through the jungle in quest of an audience with an African king, and interpretations of its meaning vary from the human search for God to a journey into the unconscious, or a seeking after identity. Its nightmarish intensity is reminiscent of the works of Franz Kafka and of Amos Tutuola, the Nigerian writer.

The sequel to *L'Enfant noir,* entitled *Dramouss* (1966; *A Dream of Africa*), is less nostalgic than its predecessor and much more heavily weighted with social commentary, because the chief character, returning to his native land after six years in Paris, finds that political violence has replaced the values and way of life he had so longed for when abroad.

From 1964 Laye lived in exile in Senegal and worked as a research fellow in Islāmic studies at the University of Dakar.

laying on of hands (Christian ritual): *see* hands, imposition of.

Layton, Irving (Peter) (b. March 12, 1912, Neamţ, Rom.), poet who treated the Jewish-Canadian experience with rebellious vigour.

Layton's family immigrated to Canada in 1913. He earned a degree in agriculture (1939) and served in the Canadian Air Force during World War II. His poems, lyrical and romantic in tone and classical in form, developed from the early descriptive poetry collected in *Here and Now* (1945) and *Now Is the Place* (1948) into the tough and denunciatory expressions of his hatred of the bourgeoisie and all other enemies of spontaneity contained in *In the Midst of My Fever* (1954) and *The Cold Green Element* (1955). He later turned from social satire to concern for the universal human condition—*e.g., A Red Carpet for the Sun* (1959), *The Swinging Flesh* (1961), *Balls for a One-Armed Juggler* (1963), *For My Brother Jesus* (1976), *For My Neighbours in Hell* (1980), and *Europe and Other Bad News* (1981). *Collected Poems* (1965) was revised in 1971. He also published volumes of prose containing assortments of essays, stories, and letters, including *Engagements* (1972) and *Taking Sides* (1978).

Layton was a teacher and lecturer in Montreal from 1945 to 1960, and from 1970 to 1978 he was professor of literature at York University, Toronto.

Laz language, Laz LAZURI NENA, Georgian ČANURI ENA, also called CHAN LANGUAGE, unwritten language spoken along the coast of the Black Sea in Georgia and in the adjacent areas of Turkey. Some scholars believe Laz and the closely related Mingrelian language to be dialects of the Svan language rather than independent languages.

Both Laz and Mingrelian have made a number of linguistic changes in comparison to Georgian and Svan, which are relatively conservative in both their grammatical and phonological characteristics. The Laz, Mingrelian, Georgian, and Svan languages constitute the Kartvelian, or South Caucasian, language family. *See also* Kartvelian languages.

Lazarev, Pyotr Petrovich (b. April 13 [April 1, Old Style], 1878, Moscow—d. April 23, 1942, Alma-Ata, Kazakh S.S.R.), Soviet physicist and biophysicist known for his physicochemical theory of the movement of ions and the consequent theory of excitation in living matter, which attempts to explain sensation, muscular contraction, and the functions of the central nervous system.

Educated in medicine at the University of Moscow (1903), he did scientific research at Strasbourg and in 1907 was appointed privatdocent (unsalaried lecturer) in physics and assistant to Pyotr N. Lebedev at the University of Moscow. In 1912 he became professor at the Higher Institute of Technology in Moscow and from 1920 to 1931 was director of the Biophysics Institute there. From 1938 to his death he directed the Biophysical Laboratories of the Soviet Academy of Sciences.

Lazarist (religious society): *see* Vincentian.

Lazarsfeld, Paul Felix (b. Feb. 13, 1901, Vienna, Austria—d. Aug. 30, 1976, New York, N.Y., U.S.), Austrian-born American sociologist whose studies of the mass media's influence on society became classics in his field.

Lazarsfeld was educated at the University of Vienna and took his Ph.D. there (1925) in applied mathematics. His interest having turned to applied psychology, he founded a research institute for applied social psychology (1929) in Vienna. He was appointed lecturer in applied psychology at the University of Vienna (1929–33).

A Rockefeller Foundation grant for psychological research enabled Lazarsfeld to come to the United States in 1933, where he eventually obtained U.S. citizenship. He served as director of the Office of Radio Research, a Rockefeller project at Princeton University (1937–40), and, when the project was transferred to Columbia University in 1940 (it was later renamed the Bureau of Applied Social Research), he continued as its director and was appointed to the sociology department of that university. Under his leadership (1940–50) the bureau became a well-known laboratory for empirical social research. He remained a professor at Columbia until 1970.

Lazarsfeld addressed a great variety of topics in his research. Chief among them was his use of statistical means to determine the impact of radio and the print media on Americans' voting habits and preferences. He conducted large-scale studies on the effect of newspapers, magazines, radio, and motion pictures on society, and he carried out particularly detailed investigations of the radio-listening habits of the American public with his associates, the psychologist Hadley Cantril and Frank Stanton, the then-head of research for the CBS broadcasting company. Among Lazarsfeld's more important works are *Radio and the Printed Page* (1940; coauthored with Cantril and Stanton), *The People's Choice* (1944), *Voting* (1954), and the textbook *An Introduction to Applied Sociology* (1975).

Lazarus, from Hebrew ELEAZAR ("God Has Helped"), either of two figures mentioned in the New Testament.

The story of Lazarus is known from the Gospel narrative of John (11:18, 30, 32, 38). Lazarus of Bethany was the brother of Martha and Mary and lived at Bethany, near Jerusalem. When Lazarus died, he was raised by Jesus from the dead after he had been entombed for four days. This miraculous raising of Lazarus from the dead inspired many Jews to believe in Jesus as the Christ.

Lazarus is also the name given by Luke (ch. 16) to the beggar in the parable of the rich man and Lazarus. It is the only proper name attached to a character in the parables of Jesus.

Lazarus, Emma (b. July 22, 1849, New York, N.Y., U.S.—d. Nov. 19, 1887, New York City), American writer best known for her sonnet "The New Colossus," written to the Statue of Liberty.

Born into a cultured family of Sefardic (Spanish Jewish) stock, Lazarus learned languages and the classics at an early age. Her first book (1867) included poems and translations and caught the attention of Ralph Waldo Emerson, with whom she corresponded thereafter. At 21 she published *Admetus and Other Poems* (1871). She also wrote a prose romance (*Alide*) based on J.W. von Goethe's autobiography; a tragedy (*The Spagnoletto*); and a translation, *Poems and Ballads of Heinrich Heine* (1881). About 1881 she took up the defense of persecuted Jews and began working for the relief of new immigrants in the United States. "The New Colossus" (1883), written to express her faith in America as a refuge for the oppressed, closes with the lines:

> Give me your tired, your poor,
> Your huddled masses, yearning to breathe free,
> The wretched refuse of your teeming shore.
> Send these, the homeless, tempest-tost to me,
> I lift my lamp beside the golden door!

This sonnet was chosen to be inscribed on a bronze plaque inside the base of the statue, which was dedicated in 1886. *By the Waters of Babylon,* a series of prose poems, was published in the *Century* in 1887.

Lazarus, Fred, Jr. (b. Oct. 29, 1884, Columbus, Ohio, U.S.—d. May 27, 1973, Cincinnati, Ohio), American merchandiser who parlayed his family's small but successful department store into a $1.3 billion holding company known as Federated Department Stores.

At age 10 Lazarus began selling in his family's department store, F. & R. Lazarus, in Columbus, Ohio. At 18 he left Ohio State University to work full time. The store operated on the belief that the customer had to be happy, and, as a result, business prospered.

Lazarus in 1921 suggested to a merchants group, the Retail Research Association, that all its members keep their books the same way in order to share profit and sales information. The idea was accepted. The group formed the Associated Merchandising Corp.

In 1930 Lazarus joined forces with the owners of William Filene's Sons in Boston and of Abraham & Straus in Brooklyn and finally with the owners of Bloomingdale's in Manhattan and formed Federated Department Stores. Lazarus took the leadership of Federated in 1945 at the age of 61 and developed it into a huge corporation before turning control over to his son Ralph in 1966. By that time the company had some 200 stores nationwide.

Lazarus, Moritz (b. Sept. 15, 1824, Filehne, Prussia [now Wieleń, Pol.]—d. April 13, 1903, Meran, Austria [now Merano, Italy]), Jewish philosopher and psychologist, a leading opponent of anti-Semitism in his time and a founder of comparative psychology.

The son of a rabbinical scholar, Lazarus studied Hebrew literature and history, law, and philosophy at Berlin. He served as professor at Bern (1860–66), at the Kriegs Akademie in Berlin (1867–73), and at the Friedrich Wilhelm University (now Humboldt University of Berlin) in Berlin (1873).

The fundamental principle of Lazarus' philosophy stated that truth must be sought not in metaphysical or a priori abstractions but in psychological investigation; further, this investigation cannot confine itself successfully to the individual consciousness but must be devoted primarily to society as a whole. The psychologist must study humanity from the historical or comparative standpoint, analyzing the elements that constitute the fabric of society, with its customs, its conventions, and the main tendencies of its evolution. To further this *Völkerpsychologie* (German: "folk," or comparative, psychology), he founded, with the philologist H. Steinthal, the journal *Zeitschrift für Völkerpsychologie und Sprachwissenschaft* (1859). His chief philosophical work is *Das Leben der Seele,* 3 vol. (1855–57; "The Life of the Soul").

In both 1869 and 1871 Lazarus was president of the Liberal Jewish synods at Leipzig and Augsburg. As a leading defender of Judaism against the anti-Semitism of his day, he was an outstanding spokesman. His works on Jewish subjects include *Treu und frei: Reden und Vorträge über Juden und Judenthum* (1887; "Faithful and Free: Speeches and Lectures About Jews and Judaism"); a monograph on the prophet Jeremiah (1894); and *Die Ethik des Judentums,* 2 vol. (vol. 1, 1898; vol. 2, 1911; *The Ethics of Judaism*), which soon achieved the rank of a standard work.

Moritz Lazarus, 1892

By courtesy of the Staatsbibliothek Preussischer Kulturbesitz, Berlin

Lazear, Jesse William (b. May 2, 1866, Baltimore county, Md., U.S.—d. Sept. 26, 1900, Quemados, Cuba), American physician and member of the commission that proved that the infectious agent of yellow fever is transmitted by a mosquito, later known as *Aëdes aegypti.*

Lazear received his medical degree (1892) from the College of Physicians and Surgeons of Columbia University. After a period of study in Europe, he joined the staff of Johns Hopkins Hospital, Baltimore, where he was among the first to investigate the structure of the malarial parasite. In 1900 he went to Cuba as a surgeon with the U.S. Army. There he was asked to join the yellow-fever commission, which included Walter Reed, James Carroll, and Aristides Agramonte. In the course of his research he was bitten by a mosquito, contracted yellow fever, and died.

Lazio, Latin LATIUM, *regione,* west-central Italy, fronting the Tyrrhenian Sea and comprising the provinces of Roma, Frosinone, Latina, Rieti, and Viterbo. In the east Lazio is dominated by the Reatini, Sabini, Simbruini, and Ernici ranges of the central Apennines, rising to 7,270 feet (2,216 m) at Mount Terminillo. Although the mountains are mainly limestone, the valleys and lower foothills of the pre-Apennines are fertile. The western part of the region is a coastal plain centring on the Roman Campagna (Campagna di Roma) and extending northwestward into the Maremma and southeastward through the Pontine Marshes (Agro Pontino) to the plains of Fondi and Formia. Northwest and southeast of Rome are four groups of ancient volcanoes, the Volsini, Cimini, Sabatini, and Albani mountains, each containing one or more crater lakes, those of Bolsena, Vico, Bracciano, Albano, and Nemi. Southeast of the volcanic Alban Hills (Colli Albani), the stark, denuded Lepini, Ausoni, and Aurunci mountains extend to the Garigliano River, the southern limit of Lazio. Until the late 19th century, much of the lowland area of Lazio was marshy and malarial. Major reclamation works in the Maremma, the Campagna di Roma, and the Pontine Marshes (*qq.v.*) in the early 20th century resulted in drainage and repopulation of the plain and transformed the region's agriculture. Migratory grazing was greatly reduced; wheat, corn (maize), vegetables, fruit, meat, and dairy products now dominate in the lowlands, while olive groves and vineyards cover the slopes. Vineyards abound near Montefiascone, on the Alban Hills, and around Terracina and Formia. Civitavecchia and Gaeta are the main fishing ports.

Light industry has developed with the help of a regional development program, the Cassa per il Mezzogiorno (Fund for the South), particularly in and around the new satellite towns of Aprilia, Pomezia, and Latina, south of Rome. Rome is the region's commercial and banking centre, but it has little industry apart from artisan and specialist industries, such as fashions. Large numbers of persons are employed by the government. In the rest of the region only chemical and pharmaceutical plants, food industries, papermaking, and a few small machine industries are of significance. Rome, including the Vatican, is Italy's largest tourist centre, and tourism is also important at resorts in the Alban Hills, the Apennines, and along the coast.

Lazio's transportation is also dominated by Rome, which is the rail and road hub of central Italy and has one of Europe's busiest international airports. Civitavecchia, the only port of importance, is noted chiefly for its trade with Sardinia. For history of the region, *see* Latium. Area 6,642 square miles (17,203 square km). Pop. (1991) 5,145,763.

lazulite, phosphate mineral, a basic magnesium and aluminum phosphate [$MgAl_2(PO_4)_2(OH)_2$], that often occurs as blue, glassy crystals, grains, or masses in granite pegmatites, aluminous metamorphic rocks and quartzites, and quartz veins. It is found in Werfen, Austria; Västarå, Sweden; Mocalno, Calif., U.S.; and Minas Gerais, Brazil.

Lazulite (from German *Lazurstein,* "blue stone") may be distinguished from lapis lazuli by the presence of cleavage planes. Although lazulite is most often opaque or subtranslucent, transparent granular material has been cut en cabochon (with rounded, convex, polished surface) for gems. Iron commonly substitutes for some of the magnesium in the crystal structure; in nature there is a complete chemical variation, called a solid-solution series, between pure lazulite, which contains no iron, and pure scorzalite, which contains no magnesium but is similar to lazulite in physical properties. For detailed physical properties, *see* phosphate mineral (table).

lazurite, blue variety of the mineral sodalite (*q.v.*) that is responsible for the colour of lapis lazuli.

lazzo (Italian: "joke"), plural LAZZI, improvised comic dialogue or action in the commedia dell'arte. The word may have derived from *lacci* (Italian: "connecting link"), comic interludes performed by the character Arlecchino (Harlequin) between scenes, but is more likely a derivation of *le azioni* ("actions"). Lazzi were one of the prime resources of the commedia actors, consisting of verbal asides on current political and literary topics, manifestations of terror, pratfalls and other acrobatics, and similar actions. Arlecchino, a character particularly congenial to lazzi, might throw cherry stones in another servant's face or mime the catching and eating of a fly. The ability to improvise ingenious and engaging lazzi contributed to the reputations of many actors; many lazzi were frequently performed with slight variations and became part of the commedia repertoire. Lazzi were implicit in many of the comedies of Molière and those of William Shakespeare, in which they came to be called jigs.

LBK culture, formerly DANUBIAN CULTURE, Neolithic culture that expanded over large areas of Europe north and west of the Danube River (from Slovakia to the Netherlands) about the 5th millennium BC. Farmers probably practiced a form of shifting cultivation on the loess soil. Emmer wheat and barley were grown, and domestic animals, usually cattle, were kept. The name LBK derives from an abbreviation of the German Linienbandkeramik, or Linearbandkeramik, a reference to the culture's characteristic pottery, which was ornamented with pairs of parallel lines arranged in spiral or meander patterns. The most common stone tool was a polished stone adze. The people occupied large rectangular houses grouped in medium-sized village communities or as small, dispersed clusters.

LC Classification: *see* Library of Congress Classification.

LCA: *see* Lutheran Church in America.

LCUSA: *see* Lutheran Council in the United States of America.

le (in proper names): *see* below and *see also* names spelled with no space after "le" (*e.g.,* LeRoy, Mervyn).

Le DYNASTY (Vietnamese history): *see* Later Le dynasty.

Le Bel, Joseph-Achille (b. Jan. 21, 1847, Péchelbronn, France—d. Aug. 6, 1930, Paris), French chemist whose explanation of why some organic compounds rotate the plane of polarized light helped to advance stereochemistry.

Le Bel
Harlingue—H. Roger-Viollet

Le Bel studied at the École Polytechnique in Paris and was an assistant to A.-J. Balard and C.-A. Wurtz. He perceived that a molecule in which four different atoms or groups were linked to a carbon atom would exist in two forms, mirror images that could not be superimposed. Either of the pair would be dissymmetric and thus optically active. He published his ideas independently of, but almost simultaneously with, those of Jacobus van't Hoff (1874). He also predicted correctly that other elements also would give rise to optically active compounds.

Le Bon, Gustave (b. May 7, 1841, Nogent-le-Rotrou, France—d. Dec. 13, 1931, Marnes-la-Coquette), French social psychologist best known for his study of the psychological characteristics of crowds.

After receiving a doctorate of medicine, Le Bon traveled in Europe, North Africa, and Asia and wrote several books on anthropology and archaeology. His interests later shifted to natural science and social psychology. In *Les Lois psychologiques de l'évolution des peuples* (1894; *The Psychology of Peoples*) he developed a view that history is the product of racial or national character, with emotion, not intelligence, the dominant force in social evolution. He attributed true progress to the work of an intellectual elite.

Le Bon believed that modern life was increasingly characterized by crowd assemblages. In *La psychologie des foules* (1895; *The Crowd*), his most popular work, he argued that the conscious personality of the individual in a crowd is submerged and that the collective crowd mind dominates; crowd behaviour is unanimous, emotional, and intellectually weak.

Le Brun, Charles, Le Brun also spelled LEBRUN (b. Feb. 24, 1619, Paris, France—d. Feb. 12, 1690, Paris), painter and designer who became the arbiter of artistic production in France during the last half of the 17th century. Possessing both technical facility and the capacity to organize and carry out many vast projects, Le Brun personally created or supervised the production of most of the paintings, sculptures, and decorative objects commissioned by the French government for three decades during the reign of Louis XIV. Under his direction French artists created a homogeneous style that came to be accepted throughout Europe as the paragon of academic and propagandistic art.

"The Chancellor Séguier," painting on canvas by Charles Le Brun, 1661; in the Louvre, Paris
Giraudon—Art Resource

A protégé of the chancellor Pierre Séguier, Le Brun studied first with the painter Guillaume Perrier and then with Simon Vouet. In 1642 he went to Rome, and during the four years he spent there he learned much from Nicolas Poussin, Pietro da Cortona, and other contemporary Baroque painters. On his return to Paris he was given large decorative and religious commissions; his work for the Hôtel Lambert and for Nicolas Fouquet, the influential minister of finance, at Vaux-le-Vicomte in the 1650s made his reputation. His first commission from Louis XIV dates from 1661, when he painted the first of a series of subjects from the life of Alexander the Great. "The Tent of Darius" delighted Louis, who liked to think of himself as a latter-day Alexander. Le Brun was made first painter to the king, given an enormous salary, and until his death occupied a position of paramount importance in the artistic life of France not equaled until the advent of the painter Jacques-Louis David at the end of the 18th century.

Fouquet's successor as minister of finance, Jean-Baptiste Colbert, was quick to recognize and to use Le Brun's organizing capacities to the greatest advantage. In 1663 Le Brun was appointed director of the Gobelins, which, from being a small tapestry manufacture, expanded into a sort of universal factory supplying all the royal houses. From the 1660s, commissions for decoration of the royal palaces, notably Versailles, were given automatically to Le Brun and his assistants, and in 1663 the Academy of Painting and Sculpture was reorganized with Le Brun as director. In 1666 he organized its satellite, the French Academy at Rome, which played an influential role in the artistic affairs of France for more than a century. These institutions gave French art its characteristic homogeneity.

Le Brun's own painting style was a more dramatic and sensuous version of Poussin's static and monumental manner—seen in "Horatius Cocles Defending Rome" (1644)—which became dulled and generalized when applied to large surfaces. As a portrait painter, however, he was consistently distinguished, as in "The Banker Jabach and His Family" (1647). His position declined after Colbert's death in 1683, although he continued to receive the king's support.

Le Carré, John, pseudonym of DAVID JOHN MOORE CORNWELL (b. Oct. 19, 1931, Poole, Dorset, Eng.), English writer of suspenseful, realistic spy novels based on a wide knowledge of international espionage.

Educated abroad and at the University of Oxford, Le Carré was an instructor in French and Latin at Eton College before becoming a member of the British foreign service in West Germany in 1959. He began to devote his full time to writing as a result of the success of his third novel, *The Spy Who Came in from the Cold* (1963). Its protagonist is an aging British intelligence agent entrusted with the destruction of an East German official. Unlike the usual glamorous spies of fiction, the agent is a lonely and alienated man, without a respectable career or a place in society; the book was adapted into a highly successful film in 1965. This novel was followed by *The Looking Glass War* (1965) and *A Small Town in Germany* (1968).

Tinker, Tailor, Soldier, Spy (1974) was the first in a trilogy of novels centred on the shrewd but self-effacing British intelligence agent George Smiley, Le Carré's best-known character. Smiley's nemesis was the Soviet master spy Karla, and their struggle was continued in *The Honourable Schoolboy* (1977) and culminated in *Smiley's People* (1980) with a successful attempt by Smiley to force Karla's defection to the West. *The Little Drummer Girl* (1983) describes a struggle between the Israeli secret service and a Palestinian terrorist.

Le Carré
Horst Tappe from Camera Press—Publix

Le Carré's later novels include *A Perfect Spy* (1986), the story of a double agent; *The Russia House* (1989); *The Secret Pilgrim* (1991); and *The Night Manager* (1993).

Le Chapelier, Jean, also called ISAAC LE CHAPELIER (b. June 12, 1754, Rennes, France—d. April 22, 1794, Paris), French Revolutionary leader who in 1791 introduced in the National Assembly the Loi ("Law") Le Chapelier, which made any association of workers or of employers illegal. In force until 1884, the law actually affected only workers, who found it much more difficult to conceal their activities than employers did.

Beginning his career as a barrister, Le Chapelier in 1789 was elected to the Estates-General as a deputy of the Third Estate (the bourgeoisie, or middle class) for Rennes. He founded the Club Breton at Versailles, which was the precursor of the Jacobin Club, and was president of the National Assembly (August 1789). But after Louis XVI's flight to Varennes in 1791, Le Chapelier allied himself with the moderate reformers. He left the Jacobins and joined the Feuillants, a group that advocated limiting the vote to property owners. Le Chapelier was arrested and executed (1794) during the Reign of Terror after his return from a visit to England.

Le Chatelier, Henry-Louis (b. Oct. 8, 1850, Paris, France—d. Sept. 17, 1936, Miribel-les-Échelles), French chemist who is best known for the principle of Le Chatelier, which makes it possible to predict the effect a change of conditions (temperature, pressure, and concentration of reaction components) will have on a chemical reaction. This principle proved invaluable in the chemical industry for developing the most efficient chemical processes.

Le Chatelier was educated at the Collège Rollin, École Polytechnique, and École des Mines, Paris. After working two years as a mining engineer, he was named professor of chemistry at the École des Mines in 1877. He became an authority on metallurgy, cements, glasses, fuels, and explosives, and his interests turned to the study of heat. He developed a platinum and rhodium thermocouple for measuring high temperatures and an optical pyrometer, which measures intense heat by analyzing the light from the heat source. Le Chatelier first enunciated his principle in 1884 and dealt with the effect of changing pressures and other conditions in his *Loi de stabilité de l'equilibre chimique* (1888; "Law of Stability of Chemical Equilibrium"). He was unaware for some time that his conclusions had been anticipated in part by the American physicist J. Willard Gibbs, whose works Le Chatelier later translated into French.

At Le Chatelier's suggestion (1895) the oxyacetylene torch was developed for use in welding and cutting metal. In 1908 he became professor of chemistry at the University of Paris, and from 1914 to 1918 he worked for the Ministry of Armaments.

The Le Chatelier principle states that if a system (a substance or a collection of substances) in a balanced, or equilibrium, state is disturbed, the system will readjust in such a way as to neutralize the disturbance and restore equilibrium. The principle may be illustrated by the behaviour of a reversible chemical reaction such as that of hydrogen and nitrogen to form ammonia. The reaction is represented by the equation: $3H_2 + N_2 \rightleftharpoons 2NH_3$. The double arrows indicate that while ammonia is being formed it is also being decomposed. The formation reaction is accompanied by evolution of heat while the decomposition reaction requires absorption of heat. At equilibrium, *i.e.,* when the velocity by which ammonia is being formed is just balanced by the velocity by which it is being decomposed, a definite amount of ammonia as well as hydrogen and nitrogen will be present. According to the Le Chatelier principle, if the mixture is heated, the equilibrium condition will be displaced in such a way that the resultant increase in temperature will be minimized, that is, in a direction that consumes heat energy. Thus, the addition of heat energy will favour the decomposition of ammonia, this being the reaction that absorbs heat, until finally a new equilibrium condition point is reached. In this new equilibrium state there will be less ammonia present and more hydrogen and nitrogen. The principle therefore predicts that at a higher temperature the reaction will yield less ammonia than at a lower temperature. This conclusion is the basis for the use of low temperature in view of the high pressure employed in the industrial manufacture of ammonia.

The Le Chatelier principle applies not only to reversible chemical reactions but equally to reversible physical processes, such as evaporation or crystallization.

Le Creusot, industrial town, Saône-et-Loire *département,* Bourgogne *région,* east-central France. It is located about 40 miles (65 km) southwest of Dijon. In 1782 a foundry and blast furnaces, using coal instead of wood for the first time in France, were built at Le Creusot. Shortly afterward, John Wilkinson, an English ironmaster, built coke-burning blast furnaces and began producing arms with machinery brought from England. The town's metallurgical industry subsequently declined until 1836, when the brothers Adolphe and Eugène Schneider founded the Société des Forges et Ateliers du Creusot ("Creusot Forge and Workshop Company"), which produced the first French locomotives as well as armour plate. Iron is no longer manufactured in Le Creusot, but the working of steel into fabricated products for rail transportation, agriculture, and the military is still of importance. The Schneider company, which merged in 1970 with the Ateliers et Forges de la Loire (Workshop and Forge Company of the Loire), is an important French firm producing heavy mechanical equipment and specialized steel. Le Creusot has been one of the chief armaments-producing centres of Europe, and cast-iron cookware bearing the city's name is sold worldwide. Pop. (1990) 28,909.

Le Duan, also called LE DUNG (b. April 7, 1908, Quang Tri province [now Binh Tri Thien province], Vietnam—d. July 10, 1986, Hanoi), Vietnamese Communist politician.

Le Duan was a founding member of the Indochina Communist Party in 1930. Twice imprisoned by the French, he joined the Viet Minh, Ho Chi Minh's anti-French Communist-led front, and attained an influential position on the Central Committee of Ho's new Republic of Vietnam in Hanoi in 1945. After Vietnam's division in 1954, Le Duan was put in charge of establishing an underground Communist Party organization in South Vietnam. He thus oversaw the creation in 1962 of the People's Revolutionary Party, a crucial component of the National Liberation Front.

Upon Ho's death in 1969, Le Duan, as first secretary to the Vietnam Worker's Party, assumed party leadership—a position that he retained after the party's reorganization as the Vietnamese Communist Party in 1976. At that time, his official title became secretary-general. After the end of the Vietnam War in 1975, Le Duan led the party through a difficult period that witnessed the formal reunification of Vietnam, the Vietnamese invasion of Cambodia, and the country's break with China and the expulsion of much of its ethnic Chinese community. Vietnam under Le Duan entered into a close alliance with the Soviet Union and became a member of the Council for Mutual Economic Assistance.

Though adept at party organizing and at mobilizing human resources in pursuit of victory during the Vietnam War, Le Duan proved less pragmatic afterward as a maker of peacetime economic and foreign policy.

Le Duc Tho, original name PHAN DINH KHAI (b. Oct. 14, 1911, Nam Ha province, Vietnam—d. Oct. 13, 1990, Hanoi), Vietnamese politician and corecipient in 1973 (with Henry Kissinger) of the Nobel Prize for Peace, which he declined.

Le Duc Tho was one of the founders of the Indochinese Communist Party in 1930. For his political activities he was imprisoned by the French in 1930–36 and 1939–44. After his second release he returned to Hanoi in 1945 and helped lead the Viet Minh, the Vietnamese independence organization, as well as a revived communist party called the Vietnam Workers' Party. He was the senior Viet Minh official in southern Vietnam until the Geneva Accords of 1954. From 1955 he was a member of the Politburo of the Vietnam Workers' Party, or the Communist Party of Vietnam, as it was renamed in 1976. During the Vietnam War (1955–75) Tho oversaw the Viet Cong insurgency that began against the South Vietnamese government in the late 1950s. He carried out most of his duties during the war while in hiding in South Vietnam.

Tho is best known for his part in the cease-fire of 1973, when he served as special adviser to the North Vietnamese delegation to the Paris Peace Conferences, 1968–73. He eventually became his delegation's principal spokesman, in which capacity he negotiated the cease-fire agreement that led to the withdrawal of the last American troops from South Vietnam. It was for this accomplishment that he was awarded the Nobel Peace Prize. Tho oversaw the North Vietnamese offensive that overthrew the South Vietnamese government in 1975, and he played a similar role in the first stages of Vietnam's invasion of Cambodia in 1978. He remained a member of the Politburo until 1986.

Le Fanu, Sheridan, in full JOSEPH SHERIDAN LE FANU (b. Aug. 28, 1814, Dublin, Ire.—d. Feb. 7, 1873, Dublin), Irish writer of ghost stories and mystery novels, celebrated for his ability to evoke the ominous atmosphere of a haunted house.

Le Fanu belonged to an old Dublin Huguenot family and was related on his mother's side to Richard Brinsley Sheridan. Educated at Trinity College, Dublin, he became a lawyer in 1839 but soon abandoned law for journalism. *The Purcell Papers,* written while he was a student, show his mastery of the supernatural and were collected in three volumes in 1880. Between 1845 and 1873 he published 14 novels, of which *Uncle Silas* (1864) and *The House by the Churchyard* (1863) are the best known. He contributed numerous short stories, mostly of ghosts and the supernatural, to the *Dublin University Magazine,* which he owned and edited from 1861 to 1869. *In a Glass Darkly* (1872), a book of five long stories, is generally regarded as his best work. Le Fanu also owned the *Dublin Evening Mail* and other newspapers.

Le Fanu, oil painting by Brindsley Le Fanu, 1916; in the National Gallery of Ireland, Dublin

By courtesy of the National Gallery of Ireland, Dublin

"De," "la," and similar components of a name, when followed by a space, are alphabetized as separate words (e.g., *De Forest, Lee*). *When they are joined to the following part of a name, the combination is treated as a single word* (e.g., *DeForest, John William*).

Le Gallienne, Eva (b. Jan. 11, 1899, London, Eng.—d. June 3, 1991, Weston, Conn., U.S.), actress, director, and producer, one of the outstanding figures of the 20th-century American stage.

The daughter of the British poet Richard Le Gallienne, Eva Le Gallienne felt a vocation for the theatre from the age of seven, when she saw Sarah Bernhardt perform. She made her London debut in 1914 as a walk-on in *Monna Vanna.* In 1915 she traveled to the United States, where she appeared in various minor and supporting roles before achieving a major success as the star of *Liliom* (1921).

In 1926 she founded the Civic Repertory Theatre in New York City to present classics and important foreign plays at low admission prices. Through her productions and translations, she introduced American audiences to the works of Anton Chekhov, Henrik Ibsen, and others; she directed and acted in most of the theatre's productions. The Civic Rep was hard hit by the Depression, and it closed in 1933. In 1946 she cofounded the American Repertory Theatre in New York City with Cheryl Crawford and Margaret Webster; it closed after a year. She continued in later years to act, produce, and direct; her last performance was as the White Queen in a 1982 revival of *Alice in Wonderland,* a role in which she had had a great success 50 years earlier.

Le Gallienne won many awards, including the National Medal of Arts (1986). In addition to translations, she published two volumes of memoirs, *At 33* (1934) and *With a Quiet Heart* (1953), a children's book, and a biography of the actress Eleonora Duse.

Le Havre, seaport and town, Seine-Maritime *département,* Haute-Normandie *région,* northern France. It is on the English Channel coast and on the right bank of the Seine estuary, 134 miles (216 km) west-northwest of Paris and 53 miles (85 km) west of Rouen by road.

Le Havre was only a fishing village until 1517, when Francis I had a harbour built there named Havre-de-Grâce ("Haven of Grace"). Enlarged and fortified under the Cardinal de Richelieu and Louis XIV in the 17th century, it was adapted to accommodate bigger vessels under Louis XVI in the late 18th century and was further improved under Napoleon III in the mid-19th century. During World War II the Belgian government was transferred there for a short time after the fall of Antwerp and Ostend to the Germans.

Almost three quarters of Le Havre's buildings were destroyed during World War II but were subsequently rebuilt. The Place de l'Hôtel de Ville in the centre is one of the most spacious public squares in Europe. The 16th–17th-century Church of Notre-Dame is one of the few surviving old buildings; although damaged during World War II, it was restored in the 1970s. The Church of Saint-Joseph is an unusual reinforced-concrete edifice. The new museum, built in 1961, houses a collection saved from the old museum, which was destroyed in 1944. Paintings by the 19th-century painter Eugène Boudin and the 20th-century artist Raoul Dufy are housed there.

The harbour, rebuilt after World War II, was expanded in the early 1970s. Le Havre is the second port of France after Marseille and acts as an outport (seaward terminal for deep-draft vessels) of Paris. Before World War II it was one of the principal centres of passenger traffic with North America. This role has virtually ceased, however, because of air travel. Regular car-ferry services run to England and Ireland. Le Havre's main imports are fuel oil and tropical goods (cotton, coffee). Pipelines connect the port to refineries east of the town and carry the refined product to the Paris region. Petroleum-storage facilities exist at nearby Antifer. Elsewhere, major industrialization efforts have been made. Le Havre's industries now include the manufacture of machinery and automobiles, as well as the older, traditional manufacture of rope and the handling of timber. Pop. (1990 prelim.) 196,000.

Le Jeune, Claude (b. *c.* 1527, Valenciennes, Burgundian Hainaut [now in France]—d. *c.* 1600, Paris), French composer known for his psalm settings and for his *musique mesurée,* a style reflecting the long and short syllables of classical prosody.

Le Jeune was choirmaster to François d'Anjou, brother of Henry III, and later was music master to Henry IV. He died a Huguenot. Le Jeune was associated with the poet Antoine de Baïf who, following the theories of *vers mesurés* of Pierre Ronsard, sought to revive the poetry of classical antiquity. Compositions in *musique mesurée* were settings of poetry in *vers mesurés* with long and short syllables matched by long- and short-note values. Le Jeune also composed a famous series of metrical psalm settings from the Genevan Psalter, published posthumously in 1606. His other works include madrigals, chansons, and motets.

Le Loi, also called BINH DINH VUONG, or THUAN THIEN, reign title LE THAI TO (b. Lam Son, Thanh Hoa province, Vietnam; fl. 1428–43), Vietnamese general and emperor who won back independence for Vietnam from China in 1428, founded the Later Le dynasty (*q.v.*), and became the most honoured Vietnamese hero of the medieval period.

A wealthy upper-class landowner, Le Loi despised the Vietnamese aristocrats who collaborated with the Chinese governors of Vietnam (then known as Dai Viet). Though his country had basically been independent from China since the rebellion of 939, the Ming occupation, which began in 1407, irritated Le Loi, who was greatly affected by the social conditions of the common people, who suffered while the Chinese and the aristocracy thrived at their expense. He declared himself the "Prince of Pacification" and in 1418 led a series of revolts aimed at removing the Chinese overlords from the country. The revolts began in Thanh Hoa province, south of the Red River valley in northern Vietnam. There he secured the lowlands and gradually forced the Chinese to retreat to Tay-do. Le Loi took that centre in 1424–25, then captured Hanoi the following year.

After defeating the Chinese army by clever military strategy, Le Loi assisted their beleaguered forces in returning to China. Thereafter he was diplomatic in his relations with the Chinese, sending tribute to the Ming emperors, who grudgingly acknowledged his kingdom in 1428. Ascending the throne as the emperor Le Thai To, he established the third great Vietnamese dynasty, the Later Le, which maintained itself in Vietnam for nearly 360 years. From the time of his accession, China retained only nominal control over Vietnam, which was launched as an independent state.

Among the achievements of Le Loi's reign were land reforms to help the peasant class. He announced that all people, including women and children, were entitled to a fair share of the land. The land was not divided on an equal basis, however; he repaid his faithful soldiers and generals, and members of the royal family and their kin also received more than did the landless peasants.

Le Maçon, Robert, Le Maçon also spelled LE MASSON (b. 1365?, Anjou, Fr.—d. Jan. 28, 1443, Anjou), chancellor of France, a leading adviser of Charles VII of France, and a supporter of Joan of Arc.

After being ennobled in 1401, Le Maçon was a counselor to Louis II, duke of Anjou and titular king of Naples, from 1407. Appointed chancellor (1414) to Queen Isabella, wife of Charles VI of France, he later became chancellor to the Duke of Touraine, the future Charles VII, whom he helped to escape from Paris when the Burgundians attacked in May 1418. He gave up his position as chancellor in 1422 but remained a member of the French council until 1436.

Le Maistre, Antoine, important figure in the Jansenist religious movement in France, a member of the Arnauld family (*q.v.*).

Le Maistre de Sacy, Isaac-Louis, important figure in the Jansenist religious movement in France, a member of the Arnauld family (*q.v.*).

Le Mans, town, capital of Sarthe *département,* Pays de la Loire *région,* northwestern France. Situated in the former province of Maine, the town lies southwest of Chartres at the confluence of the Sarthe and Huisne rivers.

Le Mans derives its name from the ancient Gallic tribe of the Cenomani, whose capital it was. In the late 3rd century AD the Gallo-Romans surrounded the town with walls, parts of which still survive. Also in the 3rd century, St. Julien evangelized the city and established a bishopric there. After the 6th century Le Mans became the seat of the counts of Maine. In the early 12th century the countship passed to the Plantagenets, counts of Anjou. Henry II, the first Plantagenet king of England, was born in Le Mans in 1133. Le Mans reverted to the French crown in the 13th century. The English invaded it during the Hundred Years' War between England and France (1337–1453). Royalists and republicans successively took over the town during the French Revolution.

The old city, which is mainly cramped within the old Gallo-Roman walls on the left bank of the Sarthe, contrasts strikingly with the new town, which surrounds it.

Saint-Julien Cathedral (11th–15th century), which towers over the old city, combines Romanesque and Gothic styles. On the right side there is a beautifully sculptured 12th-century portal and, at the end of the transept, a 12th–15th-century tower 210 feet (64 m) high. The choir (13th century), which is one of the tallest and handsomest in France, is exteriorly supported by buttresses of an exceptionally light and elegant design. The cathedral features magnificent 13th-century stained-glass windows and two fine Renaissance tombs.

Saint-Julien Cathedral, Le Mans, Fr.
Shostal—EB Inc.

The Church of Notre-Dame-de-la-Couture (10th–13th century) possesses a Gothic facade with remarkable 13th-century sculptures. The Church of Sainte-Jeanne-d'Arc, which was founded by Henry II of England (reigned 1154–89), is also of interest. The picturesque old town has a number of Renaissance and 17th-century houses.

Le Mans was mainly a market town for the agricultural products of the region until the mid-19th century, when new industries developed and later expanded, principally producing railway, motorcar, and agricultural machinery; textiles; and tobacco. More recently, the plastics and electrical-machinery industries have been added, as well as a growing service sector, especially the insurance industry.

Every year the Le Mans Grand Prix d'Endurance, probably the world's best-known automobile race, is held at the Sarthe road-racing circuit just outside the town. Nearby there is a museum of early motorcars. Pop. (1990 prelim.) 146,000.

Le Mans Grand Prix d'Endurance, byname LE MANS 24-HOUR RACE, probably the world's best-known automobile race, run annually with few exceptions since 1923 at the Sarthe road-racing circuit, near Le Mans, Fr. Since 1928 the winner has been the car that travels the greatest distance in a 24-hour time period. The racing circuit is 8.3 miles (13.4 km) long, and the race is open only to sports cars (modified cars that are built for highway driving). The race is run in June, on one of the shortest nights of the year. The Le Mans Grand Prix is sanctioned by the International Automobile Federation (FIA) and is included in the FIA's annual series of races to determine a world manufacturer's championship. For winners, *see* Sporting Record: *Automobile Racing.*

Le Moyne de Bienville, Jean-Baptiste: *see* Bienville, Jean-Baptiste Le Moyne de.

Le Moyne d'Iberville, Pierre: *see* Iberville, Pierre Le Moyne d'.

Le Nain, Antoine, Louis, and Mathieu (respectively b. *c.* 1588, Laon, Fr.—d. May 25, 1648, Paris; b. *c.* 1593, Laon—d. May 23, 1648, Paris; b. 1607, Laon—d. April 20, 1677, Paris), three brothers whose paintings of peasant life have a realism unique in 17th-century French art.

By 1630 they had established a common workshop in Paris. They remained unmarried and are traditionally said to have worked in harmony, often collaborating on the same picture. In 1648 all were received into the newly founded French Academy. The "Le Nain problem" of determining which of them painted what is complicated because no signed work bears a first initial and no work completed after 1648 is dated. Evaluation of the three personalities early in the 20th century was therefore based on what was traditionally known of each brother and on the dubious establishment of three stylistic groups. Art scholars today no longer try to attribute individual works, and the three brothers are treated as a single artist. Their portraits of peasants and beggars remain their most important works, although "A Blacksmith in His Forge" was one of the most admired and copied paintings in the Louvre in the 19th century. Their domestic scenes of peasant life depict humble people with human dignity, with a classical composure that is characteristically French.

Mathieu became an official painter to the city of Paris (1633) and was made a chevalier. He excelled in large compositions and in portraiture. His career was prosperous, and, from the large number of portraits and religious works produced in his studio, he must have had several assistants.

Le Nôtre, André (b. March 12, 1613, Paris, Fr.—d. Sept. 15, 1700, Paris), one of the greatest French landscape architects, his masterpiece being the gardens of Versailles.

Le Nôtre grew up in an atmosphere of technical expertise; his father, Jean Le Nôtre, was the master gardener of King Louis XIII at the Tuileries. At the studio of painter François Vouet he studied the laws of perspective and optics, which he meticulously followed in his plans, and from François Mansart, uncle of Jules Hardouin-Mansart, the principal architect of Versailles, he learned the principles of architecture. Succeeding his father (1637), Le Nôtre redesigned the Tuileries gardens, revealing his genius for expansive vistas. He continued the main avenue, later called the Champs-Élysées, as far as the eye could see.

Le Nôtre, detail of a painting by Carlo Maratti; in the Musée National de Versailles et des Trianons

Cliche Musees Nationaux, Paris

Le Nôtre was subsequently named to a succession of official posts. For finance minister Nicolas Fouquet he designed the château grounds of Vaux-le-Vicomte, near Melun (1656–61), suiting his layout to the relief of the ground. He extended from the parterres great blocks of trees, contracting progressively to accentuate the perspective, and related them to fountains, waterworks, and statuary, obtaining the maximum reflection by attention to water levels. So delighted with the result was Louis that he charged Le Nôtre with planning the gardens at Versailles, where the grounds covered more than 15,000 acres (6,000 hectares). Transforming a muddy swamp into a park of magnificent vistas, he extended and enhanced the architecture of the palace, and his monumental style reflected and heightened the splendour of Louis XIV's court.

Le Nôtre's other designs include the gardens of the Trianon, Saint-Cloud, and Chantilly and the parks of Saint-Germain-en-Laye and Fontainebleau. His genius was in demand throughout the capitals of Europe. He visited London (1662), where he is believed to have been responsible for St. James's Park, and Italy (1679). His students and collaborators, working in Germany, Austria, and Spain, spread his style of landscape planning and garden design across the European continent. A century later Pierre-Charles L'Enfant's plan for the U.S. capital at Washington, D.C., was influenced by Le Nôtre's design for the grounds of Versailles.

Le Pautre, Antoine, Le Pautre also spelled LEPAUTRE (b. Jan. 15, 1621, Paris, Fr.—d. 1691, Paris), French Baroque architect.

Born into a family of architects and decorators, Le Pautre was appointed architect to the king's buildings in 1644. He then designed the Chapelle de Port-Royal (begun 1646), an austere building that suited Jansenist sobriety. He was commissioned in 1654 to design the Hôtel de Beauvais on the rue François Miron in Paris. This is considered his masterwork because of his ingenious treatment of the irregular building site, in which no side of the building is parallel to any other.

Le Pautre published *Desseins de plusieurs palais* ("Designs for Several Palaces") in 1652, a volume of engravings that includes a famous project for an immense château. Among its features are semicircular concave bays connecting the end pavilions to the building's centre. The bays are contrasted to the convex periphery of the "drum-without-dome" that crowns the structure. In 1659 Le Pautre was appointed controller of building works to the Duke d'Orléans, the king's brother. In the 1660s and '70s he designed several country mansions. Le Pautre spent his final years restoring the theatre and other rooms at the Palais Royal. His building style veered throughout his career between dramatic and imaginative Baroque designs influenced by Italian models and simpler, more restrained structures.

Le Pen, Jean-Marie (b. June 20, 1928, La Trinité, Fr.), French nationalist politician whose National Front political party constituted the main right-wing opposition to the country's mainstream conservative parties from the 1970s through the turn of the 21st century. He was widely regarded as the leader of French neofascism.

Le Pen was born in a coastal village in Brittany and attended a Jesuit boarding school in Vannes. In the 1940s he studied law at the University of Paris and in 1954 joined the French Foreign Legion, serving as a paratrooper in Algeria and in French Indochina. Upon his return to France, Le Pen became a follower of the publisher Pierre Poujade, who was then leading an anti-tax movement. In 1956 he was elected to the National Assembly (parliament) as its youngest deputy. After being defeated for reelection in 1962, he founded a society that sold recordings of Nazi speeches and German military songs.

In 1972 Le Pen helped to found the National Front political party, becoming its leader later that year. From the outset, the National Front stressed the threat to France posed by immigration—particularly of Arab immigration from France's former colonies in North Africa. The party also opposed European integration, favoured the reintroduction of capital punishment, and sought prohibitions on the building of additional mosques in France. Le Pen himself was constantly embroiled in political controversy. In 1990, for example, he was found guilty of violating a law against denying the Holocaust for his 1987 remark that the Holocaust was a mere "detail" in the history of World War II; and in 1998 he was convicted of assaulting a political opponent and was banned from holding or seeking office for two years.

Nevertheless, Le Pen's policies captured significant public support, particularly from the working class, which suffered from rising crime and high unemployment during the 1980s and '90s. He ran several times for the presidency; though he captured less than 1 percent in 1974, in 1988 and 1995 he won some 15 percent. In 2002 Le Pen defeated Prime Minister Lionel Jospin in the first round of the presidential election, winning 18 percent of the vote. Alarmed at his success, nearly the entire French political establishment—including the Socialist Party and the Communist Party—endorsed his opponent, conservative President Jacques Chirac, who defeated Le Pen by a wide margin in the second round. In the 1980s and '90s, Le Pen was elected to the European Parliament.

Le Puy, town, capital of Haute-Loire *département,* Auvergne *région,* southern France. Le Puy is situated in the Massif Central, at 2,251 feet (686 m) above sea level, 2 miles (3 km) from the left bank of the Loire River. It lies in the middle of a basin that is surrounded by basalt plateaus bristling with strange volcanic peaks. The town was already a Christian centre in the 4th century. After Muslim invasions forced the neighbouring bishop to seek refuge there in the 6th century, Le Puy became one of the main pilgrimage centres in France. During the Wars of Religion, in the latter part of the 16th century, it sided with the Catholic League.

On the highest hill in the town, called Corneille Peak, a statue (53 feet high) of Our Lady of France was erected in 1860. At the foot of the hill, on a platform surrounded by the steep narrow streets of the Old Town, stands the mainly 13th-century Romanesque Cathedral of Notre-Dame, which shows Byzantine influence in its octagonal cupolas and decoration. The adjacent cloister is mainly Romanesque but has Carolingian capitals. On the outskirts of the town a volcanic needle 260 feet (80 m) high is crowned by an 11th-century church, Saint-Michel-d'Aiguilhe, that was ingeniously designed to cover the irregular surface of the rock. About 3 miles (5 km) away, the ruined castle of Polignac stands on a basalt plateau rising sheer from the plain.

Le Puy is primarily a market town but has also been a centre for lace making since the 17th century; a fine collection of lace is kept in the Crozatier Museum. The traditional workshops of the town's lace, leather, and brewing industries are in decline, however. Pop. (1999) 20,490.

Le Sueur, Eustache, Le Sueur also spelled LESUEUR (baptized Nov. 19, 1617, Paris, Fr.—d. April 30, 1655, Paris), painter known for his religious pictures in the style of the French classical Baroque. Le Sueur was one of the founders and first professors of the Royal Academy of Painting and Sculpture.

Le Sueur studied under the painter Simon Vouet and was admitted at an early age into the guild of master painters. Some paintings reproduced in tapestry brought him notice, and his reputation was further enhanced by a series of decorations for the Hôtel Lambert that he left uncompleted. He painted many pictures for churches and convents, among the most important being "St. Paul Preaching at Ephesus" (Louvre), and his famous series of 22 paintings of the "Life of St. Bruno" (Louvre), executed in the cloister of the Chartreux. Stylistically dominated by the art of Nicolas Poussin, Raphael, and Vouet, Le Sueur had a graceful facility in drawing and was always restrained in composition by a fastidious taste.

Le Tellier, François-Michel: *see* Louvois, François-Michel Le Tellier, marquis de.

Le Tellier, Michel (b. April 19, 1603, Paris, Fr.—d. Oct. 30, 1685, Paris), secretary of state for war (1643–77) and then chancellor who created the royal army that enabled King Louis XIV to impose his absolute rule on France and establish French hegemony in Europe.

The son of a Parisian magistrate, Le Tellier became a *procureur* (attorney) for King Louis XIII in 1631 and intendant (royal agent) to the French army in Italy in 1640. In April 1643, a month before the four-year-old Louis XIV succeeded to the throne, Le Tellier was made secretary of state for war by the chief minister, Cardinal Jules Mazarin. During the aristocratic uprising known as the Fronde (1648–53), he remained loyal to Mazarin, serving as principal adviser to the queen regent, Anne of Austria, while the cardinal was in exile.

Le Tellier, detail from a marble portrait bust by A. Coysevox; in the Bibliothèque Sainte-Geneviève, Paris

Giraudon—Art Resource/EB Inc.

The experience of the Fronde taught Le Tellier and Louis that the army must be removed from the control of the nobles and made totally dependent on the king. Le Tellier began to reorganize it in the mid-1650s, and, when Louis assumed personal control of the government upon the death of Mazarin in 1661, Le Tellier was admitted to the king's three-member inner council (Conseil d'en Haut). His major army reforms were instituted over the next 16 years. Aided by his son François-Michel Le Tellier, Marquis de Louvois, he drastically increased the size of the army, creating a 100,000-man standing peacetime force that was quadrupled in times of war. Officers loyal to the king were promoted to newly created general commands, and the discipline of the troops was greatly improved. In addition, Le Tellier perfected a centralized military transport system that enabled the king to deprive disobedient officers of supplies. The new army organization survived, with minor changes, to the outbreak of the French Revolution in 1789.

Although he was appointed to the chancellorship in 1677, Le Tellier continued to help his son direct the war ministry. In his new post he reformed law studies and improved recruitment to the magistracy. His hatred of Protestantism caused him to encourage the persecution of Huguenots, and shortly before his death he helped to draft the revocation of the Edict of Nantes (1598), which had secured for the Huguenots some measure of religious liberty.

Le Thai To (Vietnamese emperor): *see* Le Loi.

Le Thanh Tong, also called LE THANH TON, or THUAN HOANG DE (d. 1497, Dong Kinh [now Hanoi, Vietnam]), the greatest ruler of the Later Le dynasty (*q.v.;* 1428–1788) in Vietnam. Though the early years of Le Thanh Tong's reign were marked by a struggle for power, he eventually developed a governmental power base. He established a Chinese-style centralized administration and expanded dynastic control southward, at the expense of the once great kingdom of Champa, located on the southern coast of modern Vietnam.

Ascending the throne in 1460, Le Thanh Tong divided the empire into 13 circuits (similar to Chinese provinces), each of which was subdivided into prefectures (*phu*), districts (*huyen*), and departments (*chau*). These were ruled by centrally appointed officials, who were selected on the basis of their performance in the Confucian civil service examinations given every three years. The population was registered; a land tax (based on the nature of the crops and the amount of arable land) was instituted and revised triennially; new penal and civil codes were drawn up utilizing Confucian moral precepts; and, following the practices of the Chinese Ming dynasty (1368–1644), hortatory works of Confucian moral precepts were periodically read in every village in the country.

Continuing the southward push of his dynasty down the Vietnamese peninsula, Le Thanh Tong established a series of military colonies in the south. In 1471 he finally defeated Champa, ending the attacks on Vietnam by the Cham people. Champa was reduced to a narrow remnant along the southern edge of the peninsula.

Le Touquet-Paris-Plage, town, Pas-de-Calais *département,* Nord-Pas-de-Calais *région,* northern France, at the mouth of the Canche River. Situated on the English Channel 20 miles (32 km) south of Boulogne, it is a fashionable seaside resort with casinos, sports facilities, fine sands, and a forested background. Its airport is one of the main car cross-channel air-ferry points with Britain. Pop. (1982) 5,204.

Le Van Duyet (b. 1763, Quang Ngai province, Vietnam—d. July 30, 1832, Saigon [now Ho Chi Minh City, Vietnam]), Vietnamese military strategist and government official who served as a diplomatic liaison between Vietnam and France and defended Christian missionaries against the early Nguyen emperors.

From early youth, Duyet, who grew up in the Mekong River delta near My Tho, was attached to the Vietnamese court, first as a counselor to Prince Nguyen Anh, who became Emperor Gia Long, and later as an adviser to Emperor Minh Mang. Duyet accompanied Anh on military campaigns, and in 1801 he engineered a naval defeat of other contenders for the throne of Vietnam. Duyet's military strategy, combined with Western armaments and techniques supplied by the French, enabled Anh to conquer all Vietnam and to ascend the throne in 1802. In 1813 Duyet was named viceroy of the southernmost portion of the kingdom of Vietnam and was given the title grand eunuch of the court of Hue. (Duyet had been a eunuch from birth.)

As Gia Long's trusted adviser, Duyet often acted as intermediary between the emperor and the Europeans who visited Vietnam. He often interceded on behalf of European missionaries, because Gia Long was not sympathetic to their cause. Gia Long's successor, Minh Mang, who made Duyet governor of Gia Dinh province (1820–32), was more outspoken in his dislike of all Westerners. When Minh Mang ordered the persecution of Roman Catholic missionaries, Duyet refused to apply the orders in the provinces he governed. In defense of the Christians, he wrote to the emperor, "We still have between our teeth the rice which the missionaries gave us when we were starving." For a time, Minh Mang allowed the missionaries to continue their preaching.

When Duyet died, Minh Mang began his persecution in earnest, killing, imprisoning, or banishing missionaries from the kingdom and indicting Duyet posthumously. The emperor ordered Duyet's grave desecrated and had a plaque placed over the ruins with the inscription "Here lies the eunuch who resisted the law." During the reign of Thieu Tri (1841–47) the grave was restored and declared a national monument.

Le Van Trung (Vietnamese religious leader): *see* Ngo Van Chieu.

Le Verrier, Urbain-Jean-Joseph (b. March 11, 1811, Saint-Lô, Fr.—d. Sept. 23, 1877, Paris), French astronomer who predicted by mathematical means the existence of the planet Neptune.

Appointed a teacher of astronomy at the École Polytechnique ("Polytechnic School"), Paris, in 1837, Le Verrier first undertook an extensive study of the theory of the planet Mercury's orbit and compiled greatly improved tables of the motion of that planet.

In 1845 he turned his attention to the irregular orbit of Uranus, which he explained by assuming the presence of a previously unknown planet. Independently of the English astronomer John C. Adams, he calculated the size and position of the unknown body and asked the German astronomer Johann G. Galle to look for it. On Sept. 23, 1846, after only an hour of searching, Galle found Neptune within one degree of the position that had been computed by Le Verrier. As a result of this achievement Le Verrier received, among other awards, the Copley Medal from the Royal Society of London and was named an officer in the Legion of Honour. A chair of astronomy was created for him at the University of Paris.

In 1854 Le Verrier became director of the Observatory of Paris. He reestablished the efficiency of this institution, but some of the uncompromising measures taken raised a storm of protest that was appeased only by his removal in 1870. On the death of his successor in 1873 he was reinstated, but with his authority restricted by the supervision of an observatory council.

During his difficulties as director of the observatory, he carried out a complete revision of the planetary theories and compared them with the best observations then available. In particular, in 1855 he took up the problem of explaining an unusual characteristic of the motion of Mercury. He postulated a second asteroid belt inside Mercury's orbit, and, when an amateur astronomer reported finding an inner planet, Le Verrier assumed it was one of the larger of his asteroids and named it Vulcan. Further observations failed to confirm the find, however. The unusual orbital motion of Mercury, which includes an advance of its perihelion, was completely explained in 1915 by Albert Einstein's general theory of relativity.

Lea, River, river rising in the county of Hertfordshire, England, and flowing for 46 miles (74 km) east and then south to enter the River Thames at Bromley-by-Bow, in the London borough of Tower Hamlets. In the 17th century an important aqueduct known as the New River was constructed in the Lea River valley. Much of the valley has seen considerable industrial development, gravel is dug there, and many large reservoirs supplying water for London are located in the area. In 1967 the Lea Valley Regional Park Authority was formally constituted, and the regional park is now an important British recreational centre.

leaching, in geology, loss of soluble substances and colloids from the top layer of soil by percolating precipitation. The materials lost are carried downward (eluviated) and are generally redeposited (illuviated) in a lower layer. This transport results in a porous and open top layer and a dense, compact lower layer. The rate of leaching increases with the amount of rainfall, high temperatures, and the removal of protective vegetation. In areas of extensive leaching, many plant nutrients are lost, leaving quartz and hydroxides of iron, manganese, and aluminum. This remainder forms a distinctive type of soil, called laterite, or latosol, and may result in deposits of bauxite. In such areas rapid bacterial action results in the absence of humus in the soil, because fallen plant material is completely oxidized and the products are leached away. Accumulations of residual minerals and of those redeposited in lower layers may coalesce to form continuous, tough, impermeable layers called duricrusts.

Leacock, Stephen (Butler) (b. Dec. 30, 1869, Swanmore, Hampshire, Eng.—d. March 28, 1944, Toronto, Ont., Can.), internationally popular Canadian humorist, educator, lecturer, and author of more than 30 books of lighthearted sketches and essays.

Leacock immigrated to Canada with his parents at the age of six. He attended Upper Canada College (1882–87) and later received a B.A. degree from the University of Toronto (1891). After teaching for eight years at Upper Canada College, he entered the University of Chicago and was awarded a Ph.D. in 1903. Appointed that same year to the staff

Leacock, photograph by Yousuf Karsh

© Karsh from Rapho/Photo Researchers—EB Inc.

of McGill University in Montreal, he became head of the department of economics and political science in 1908 and served in that capacity until his retirement in 1936. Although Leacock was the author of nearly 20 works on history and political economy, his true calling was humour, both as a lecturer and as an author.

His fame now rests securely on work begun with the beguiling fantasies of *Literary Lapses* (1910) and *Nonsense Novels* (1911). Leacock's humour is typically based on a comic perception of social foibles and the incongruity between appearance and reality in human conduct. Sarcasm is foreign to his work; it is, rather, characterized by youthful zest and the invention of lively comic situations.

He also wrote *Humour: Its Theory and Technique* (1935), a discussion of his humour, and *The Boy I Left Behind Me* (1946), an uncompleted autobiography.

Lead, city, Lawrence county, western South Dakota, U.S. It lies in the northern Black Hills, 30 miles (48 km) northwest of Rapid City. Situated just southwest of Deadwood at the head of Gold Gulch Run, it spreads out over the tops of the nearby hills. Established in 1876 following the discovery of gold, its name was inspired by the lode mines in the area, a ledge or outcrop of ore being termed a "lead." It is the site of the Homestake Mine, one of the largest gold mines in the Western Hemisphere. The basic economy, which depends on mining and allied industries, is supplemented by tourism, ranching, and lumbering. Inc. 1890. Pop. (1990) 3,632.

lead (Pb), a soft, silvery-white or grayish metal in Group IVa of the periodic table. Lead is very malleable, ductile, and dense and is a poor conductor of electricity. Known in antiquity and believed by the alchemists to be the oldest of metals, lead is highly durable and resistant to corrosion, as is indicated by the continuing use of lead water pipes installed by the ancient Romans.

A brief treatment of lead follows. For full treatment of lead and lead mining and refining, *see* MACROPAEDIA: Industries, Extraction and Processing. For comparative statistical data on lead production and reserves, *see* mining (table).

Occurrence, properties, and uses. Rarely found free in nature, lead is present in several minerals; but all are of minor significance except the sulfide, PbS (galena, or lead glance), which is the major source of lead production throughout the world. Lead may be extracted by roasting the ore and then smelting it in a blast furnace or by direct smelting without roasting. Additional refining removes impurities present in the lead bullion produced by either process. Almost half of all refined lead is recovered from recycled scrap.

When freshly cut, lead oxidizes quickly, forming a dull gray coating, formerly thought to be lead suboxide, Pb_2O, but now recognized as a mixture of lead and lead monoxide, PbO, which protects the metal from further corrosion. Similarly, although lead is soluble in dilute nitric acid, it is only superficially attacked by hydrochloric or sulfuric acids because the insoluble chloride or sulfate coatings that are formed prevent continued reaction. Because of this general chemical resistance, considerable amounts of lead are used in roofing, as coverings for electric cables placed in the ground or underwater, and as linings for water pipes and conduits and structures for the transportation and processing of corrosive substances.

Lead has many other applications; the largest is in the manufacture of storage batteries. It is used in ammunition (shot and bullets) and as a constituent of various low-melting alloys, such as solder, type metal, and pewter. In the construction of large buildings, lead sheets are used in the walls to block the transmission of sound; and pads of lead and asbestos are used in the foundations to absorb the vibrations caused by street traffic and other sources. Because lead effectively absorbs electromagnetic radiation of short wavelengths, it is used as a protective shielding around nuclear reactors, particle accelerators, X-ray equipment, and containers used for transporting and storing radioactive materials.

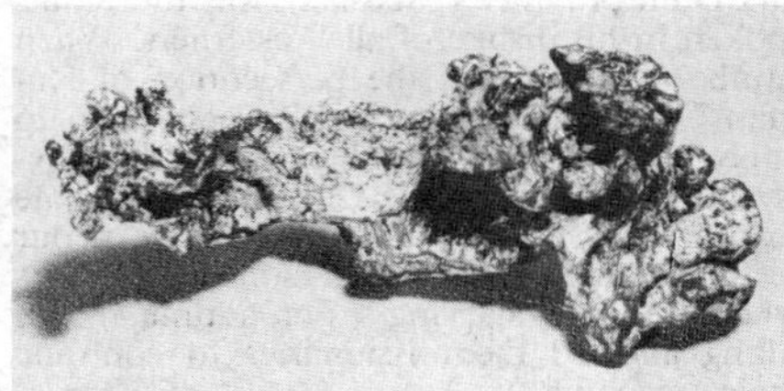

Lead with pyrochroite from Långban, Swed.

By courtesy of the Illinois State Museum; photograph, John H. Gerard—EB Inc.

Lead and its compounds are toxic and are retained by the body, accumulating over a long period of time—a phenomenon known as cumulative poisoning—until a lethal quantity is reached. In children the accumulation of lead may result in cognitive deficits; in adults it may produce progressive renal disease. *See also* lead poisoning.

Lead has four stable isotopes, all of which are the end products of the radioactive decay of other elements; their relative abundances are: lead-204, 1.48 percent; lead-206, 23.6 percent; lead-207, 22.6 percent; and lead-208, 52.3 percent. More than 20 radioactive isotopes have been reported.

Compounds. Lead shows valences of +2 and +4 in its compounds. Among the many important lead compounds are the oxides: lead monoxide, or lead(II) oxide, PbO; lead dioxide, or lead(IV) oxide, PbO_2; and trilead tetroxide, Pb_3O_4. Lead monoxide exists in two modifications, litharge and massicot. Litharge, or alpha lead(II) oxide, is a red or reddish yellow solid, has a tetragonal crystal structure, and is the stable form at temperatures below 488° C (910° F). Massicot, or beta lead(II) oxide, is a yellow solid and has an orthorhombic crystal structure; it is the stable form above 488° C. Both forms are insoluble in water but dissolve in acids to form salts containing the Pb^{2+} ion or in alkalies to form plumbites, which have the PbO_2^{2-} ion. Litharge is produced by air oxidation of lead. Except for tetraethyllead $[Pb(C_2H_5)_4]$, an organic compound that has been used as a gasoline antiknock additive, litharge is the most important commercial compound of lead; it is used in large amounts directly and as the starting material for the preparation of other lead compounds. Considerable quantities of lead(II) oxide are consumed in manufacturing the plates of lead-acid storage batteries. High-quality glassware contains as much as 30 percent litharge, which increases the refractive index of the glass and makes it brilliant, strong, and resonant. Litharge is also employed as a drier in varnishes and in making sodium plumbite, which is used for removing malodorous thiols (a family of organic compounds containing sulfur) from gasoline.

Lead(IV) oxide, found in nature as the brown-to-black mineral plattnerite, is commercially produced from trilead tetroxide by oxidation with chlorine. It decomposes upon heating and yields oxygen and lower oxides of lead. Lead(IV) oxide is used as an oxidizing agent in the production of dyestuffs, chemicals, pyrotechnics, and matches and as a curing agent for polysulfide rubbers. Trilead tetroxide (known as red lead, or minium) is produced by further oxidation of lead(II) oxide. It is the orange-red to brick-red pigment commonly used in corrosion-resistant paints for exposed iron and steel. It also reacts with iron(III) oxide to form a ferrite used in making permanent magnets.

Another economically significant compound is lead(II) acetate, $Pb(C_2H_3O_2)_2$, a water-soluble salt made by dissolving litharge in strong acetic acid. The common form, the trihydrate $[Pb(C_2H_3O_2)_2 \cdot 3H_2O]$, called sugar of lead, is used as a mordant in dyeing and as a drier in certain paints. In addition, it is utilized in the production of other lead compounds and in gold cyanidation plants, where it primarily serves to precipitate soluble sulfides from solution.

Various other salts, most notably basic lead carbonate, basic lead sulfate, and basic lead silicate, were once widely employed as pigments for white exterior paints. Since the mid-20th century, however, the use of such so-called white lead pigments has decreased substantially because of a concern over their toxicity and attendant hazard to human health. The use of lead arsenate in insecticides has virtually been eliminated for the same reason.

atomic number	82
atomic weight	207.19
melting point	327.5° C (621.5° F)
boiling point	1,744° C (3,171.2° F)
density (20° C)	11.29 g/ml
oxidation states	+2, +4
electron config.	2-8-18-32-18-4 or $6s^2 6p^2$ or $1s^2 2s^2 2p^6 3s^2 3p^6 3d^{10} 4s^2 4p^6 4d^{10} 4f^{14} 5s^2 5p^6 5d^{10} 6s^2 6p^2$

lead-210 dating, method of age determination that makes use of the ratio of the radioactive lead isotope lead-210 to the stable isotope lead-206. The method has been applied to the ores of uranium. In the series of unstable products from the radioactive decay of uranium-238, lead-210 results from the decay of radon-222 and is a precursor of the stable isotope lead-206. Lead-210 dating is particularly useful for determining the ages of relatively recent lacustrine and coastal marine sediments and so has been applied increasingly to studies concerned with the impact of human activity on the aquatic environment (*e.g.,* measuring the accumulation rates of pollutants in sediments).

lead crystal: *see* flint glass.

lead glance (mineral): *see* galena.

lead poisoning, also called PLUMBISM, deleterious effect of a gradual accumulation of lead in body tissues, as a result of repeated exposure to lead-containing substances.

In the home, the main sources of lead are usually lead-based paint and drinking water carried through lead pipes; lead-based paints are especially harmful to children who chew on painted toys and furnishings and eat paint peelings from the walls. Industries in which workers encounter lead-containing solids, dusts, or fumes are the petroleum industry, mining and smelting, printing, cutlery and storage-battery manufacture, plumbing and gas fitting, paint and pigment manufacture, and manufacture of ceramics, glass, and ammunition. Other possible sources of lead poisoning include the agricultural use of insecticides containing lead compounds; the spraying of fruits and vegetables may affect the workers and, eventually, the consumers. Constant exposure to the exhaust fumes of motor vehicles powered by fuel containing tetraethyl lead is also suspected of causing lead poisoning, especially in children.

Individual susceptibility to lead poisoning varies widely. Symptoms also vary; they may develop gradually or appear suddenly after chronic exposure. The poison affects the entire body—especially the nervous system, the gastrointestinal tract, and the blood-forming tissues. The victim usually becomes pallid, moody, and irritable and may complain of a metallic taste. Digestion is deranged, the appetite fails, and there may be severe abdominal pain, with spasms of the abdominal muscles ("lead colic") and constipation. A black line ("lead line") may appear at the base of the gums. There is often anemia. In later stages, headache, dizziness, confusion, and visual disturbances may be noted. Peripheral nerve involvement results in a paralysis ("lead palsy") that generally first affects the fingers, hands, and wrists ("wrist drop"). Among children, the brain itself may be affected, resulting in some cases in permanent damage, such as blindness and deafness, or in convulsions and coma ending in death. Brain injury may also occur in adults after massive exposure.

The lead in the tissues may be removed gradually with substances such as the calcium salts of ethylene diamine, tetraacetic acid, and penicillamine. A lengthy treatment may be necessary, but recovery is usually complete, except when there is major involvement of the brain structures. Until the last half of the 20th century, damage to the brain caused by lead poisoning ended in death in about 25 percent of the cases; about half of those who survived showed some degree of permanent mental deterioration.

Leadbelly, byname of HUDDIE WILLIAM LEDBETTER (b. *c.* Jan. 21, 1885?, Mooringsport, La., U.S.—d. Dec. 6, 1949, New York, N.Y.), American folk-blues singer, songwriter, and guitarist whose ability to perform a vast repertoire of songs, in conjunction with his notoriously violent life, made him a legend.

Musical from childhood, Leadbelly played accordion, 6- and 12-string guitar, bass, and harmonica. He led a wandering life, learning songs by absorbing oral tradition. For a time he worked as an itinerant musician with Blind Lemon Jefferson. In 1918 he was imprisoned for murder; after serving six years, he was pardoned by the governor of Texas, who had visited the prison and heard him sing.

Resuming a life of drifting, Leadbelly was imprisoned for attempted murder in 1930 in the Angola, La., prison farm. There he was discovered by the folklorists John and Alan Lomax, who were collecting songs for the Library of Congress. A campaign spearheaded by the Lomaxes secured his release in 1934, and he embarked on a concert tour of eastern colleges. Subsequently, he published 48 songs and commentary (1936) about Depression-era conditions of blacks, recorded extensively, and from 1937, when he settled in New York City, performed for political causes. He worked with Woody Guthrie, Sonny Terry, Brownie McGhee, and others as the Headline Singers, performed on radio, and appeared in a short film in 1945. In 1949, shortly before his death, he gave a concert in Paris.

Leadbelly died penniless, but within six months his song "Goodnight, Irene" had become a million-record hit for the singing group The Weavers; along with other pieces from his repertoire, among them "The Midnight Special" and "Rock Island Line," it became a standard.

leader, in meteorology, a luminous lightning discharge from a cloud to the ground that precedes a much brighter return stroke to the cloud. The first leader in a lightning flash is called the stepped leader because it descends in a series of very rapid steps. It forms an electrically conductive path along which the return stroke travels. Subsequent leaders are called dart leaders and may or may not be stepped. As many as 40 leaders have been observed in a single flash.

Leadville, city, seat (1878) of Lake county, central Colorado, U.S., in the upper Arkansas River valley in a Rocky Mountain area of national forests, at an elevation of 10,200 feet (3,109 m). It is the centre of one of the nation's most celebrated mining districts, which has yielded gold, silver, lead, zinc, manganese, and molybdenum. Gold was discovered in nearby California Gulch in 1859, and Oro City, south of present Leadville, had a population of 5,000 in 1860. Gold mining declined in 1866, but the discovery that the carbonates of lead ores were laden with silver resulted in the founding of Leadville in 1878. When the Denver and Rio Grande Western Railroad reached the city in 1880, the population exceeded 30,000. More than 30 silver mines on Fryer's Hill continued to yield heavily until the silver market collapsed in 1893, after which the population declined.

Much of the world's molybdenum is produced at nearby Climax. The National Mining Hall of Fame and Museum, the Matchless Mine, and the Tabor Opera House are among the features of the city that recall life during the mining boom. The Colorado Mountain College (Timberline Campus) was opened during the 1960s in Leadville. Inc. 1878. Pop. (1990) 2,629.

leadwork, sculpture, ornamental objects, and architectural coverings and fittings made of lead. Although the ease with which lead is smelted from lead ores ensured its early discovery, the softness of the metal restricted its use until Roman times. The earliest known use of lead dates from about 3000 BC in Egypt and Asia Minor, when it was used in making small statuettes and votive figures. Lead was used infrequently, however, until about 500 BC, when the Greeks began using it for small sculptures, toys, and market weights. The Romans used lead extensively for ornamental purposes in decorative boxes, wine cups, and other household items. Roman engineers developed architectural uses—for roof coverings, masonry, gutters, water pipes, and cisterns—that were continued for centuries.

During the European Middle Ages, lead was put to wide use as a covering for roofs, domes, and cathedral spires. It was also used in fashioning stained-glass windows, coffins, coins, tokens, and inscribed plaques for buildings. Lead was sometimes decorated by tinning, painting, lacquering, or gilding. Lead trappings were often added to statues carved from stone. Lead casts well, preserving fine detail from the mold. Although often rejected in favour of other materials (particularly bronze), lead has found continual use in sculpture. Its ability to withstand corrosion has proven a major asset, although large lead sculptures need internal reinforcement to prevent the weight of the work from causing it to collapse.

leaf, in botany, any usually flattened, green outgrowth from the stem of a vascular plant. Leaves manufacture food for plants, which in turn ultimately nourish and sustain all land animals. Botanically, leaves are an integral part of the stem system, and they are initiated in the apical bud along with the tissues of the stem itself. Certain organs that are superficially very different from the usual green leaf are formed in the same manner and are actually modified leaves; among these are the sharp spines of the Japanese barberry and the scales of an asparagus stalk or a lily bulb.

Typically a leaf consists of a broad, expanded blade (the lamina), attached to the plant stem by a stalklike petiole; leaves are, however, quite diverse in size, shape, and various other characteristics, including the nature of the blade margin and the type of venation (arrangement of veins). Veins, which support the lamina and transport materials to and from the leaf tissues, radiate through the lamina from the petiole. The venation is characteristic for different kinds of plants: for example, dicotyledons have netlike venation and usually free vein endings; monocotyledons have parallel venation and rarely free vein endings. The leaf may be simple—with a single blade—or compound—with separate leaflets; it may also be reduced to a spine or scale.

The main function of a leaf is to produce food for the plant by photosynthesis. Chlorophyll, the substance that gives plants their characteristic green colour, absorbs light energy. The internal structure of the leaf is protected by the leaf epidermis, which is continuous with the stem epidermis. The central leaf, or mesophyll, consists of soft-walled, unspecialized cells of the type known as parenchyma. As much as one-fifth of the mesophyll is composed of chlorophyll-containing chloroplasts, which absorb sunlight and, in conjunction with certain enzymes, use the radiant energy in decomposing water into its elements, hydrogen and oxygen. The oxygen liberated from green leaves replaces the oxygen removed from the atmosphere by plant and animal respiration and by combustion. The hydrogen obtained from water is combined with carbon dioxide in the enzymatic processes of photosynthesis to form the sugars that are the basis of both plant and animal life. Oxygen is passed into the atmosphere through stomates—pores in the leaf surface.

Chlorophylls, green pigments, are usually present in much greater quantities than other pigments. In autumn the chlorophylls break down and bleach away, and the colours of other pigments are revealed. These include carotene (yellow), xanthophyll (pale yellow), anthocyanin (red if the sap is slightly acidic, bluish if it is slightly alkaline, with intermediate shades between), and betacyanin (red).

Leaves are essentially short-lived structures. Even when they persist for two or three years, as in coniferous and broad-leaved evergreens, they make little contribution to the plant after the first year. The fall of leaves, whether in the first autumn in deciduous trees or after several years in evergreens, results from the formation of a weak zone, the abscission layer, at the base of the petiole. Abscission layers may form when leaves are seriously damaged by insects, disease, or drought. Their normal formation in autumn appears to be due, in part at least, to the shortening of the day. Perhaps the shorter days accentuate the senile changes normal in older leaves. As a result, a zone of cells across the petiole becomes softened until the leaf falls. A healing layer then forms on the stem and closes the wound, leaving the leaf scar, a prominent feature in many winter twigs and an aid in identification.

leaf beetle, any member of the 25,000 species of leaf-feeding insects of the family Chrysomelidae (order Coleoptera). Leaf beetles occur throughout the world but are concentrated in the tropics. They are oval and short-legged and tend to be less than 12 mm (0.5 inch) long; the antennae are about half the body length. Many are important pests. The family is divided into numerous subfamilies.

leaf blister, also called LEAF CURL, worldwide disease of many woody plants and ferns caused by fungi of the genus *Taphrina.* Following cold, wet weather at budbreak, leaves become swollen, crinkled, and distorted with

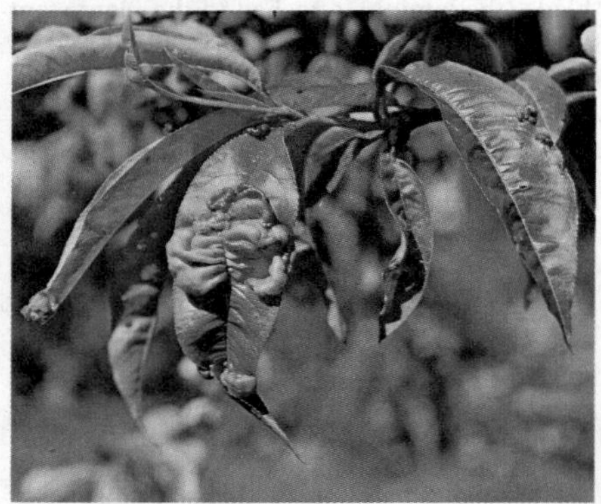
Leaf blister on a peach tree
G.R. Roberts

yellow, red, purple, brown, whitish, or gray blisters. Such leaves usually die and drop early, weakening the plant. A second growth of healthy leaves often appears later. Young peach and nectarine fruits may drop early or are knobby with discoloured warty spots; plum fruits become greatly swollen, distorted, and hollow (plum pockets); witches'-brooms may form on alder, *Amelanchier,* apricot, birch, cherry, cherry laurel, California buckeye, and plum stems; alder and poplar catkins are enlarged and deformed.

leaf cactus, also called ORCHID CACTUS, the genus *Epiphyllum,* of about 15 species, family Cactaceae, native to tropical and subtropical America, including the West Indies. The plants are mostly epiphytes (perched on other plants) but sometimes grow from the ground.

Common names are leaf cactus—for the mostly flattened, nonspiny stems that function as leaves—or orchid cactus—for the spectacular large flowers of many colours. These names also refer to hybrids often grown in cultivation. Flowers are red, white, or yellow, on tubes up to 38 cm (about 15 inches) long, usually nocturnal, and often fragrant; they are among the largest in the cactus family. Many species have edible fruit.

leaf-cutter bee, also called LEAF-CUTTING BEE, any of the insects in the family Megachilidae (order Hymenoptera), particularly certain species in the genus *Megachile.* Leaf-cutter bees differ from related species in that they collect pollen on their abdomens rather than on their hind legs. The solitary female, having mated with the male, makes a nest in soil, a hollow plant stalk, or a cavity in wood, lining it with pieces of green leaf to envelop the brood. She obtains these pieces by standing on a leaf and cutting carefully around herself, leaving an almost circular hole at the growing leaf's edge. The foliage of rose bushes is favoured by some leaf-cutter species.

leaf fibre, hard, coarse fibre obtained from leaves of monocotyledonous plants (flowering plants that usually have parallel-veined leaves, such as grasses, lilies, orchids, and palms), used mainly for cordage. Such fibres, usually long and stiff, are also called "hard" fibres, distinguishing them from the generally softer and more flexible fibres of the bast, or "soft," fibre group. Commercially useful leaf fibres include abaca, cantala, henequen, Mauritius hemp, phormium, and sisal.

Leaf fibre is mainly obtained from sword-shaped leaves that are thick, fleshy, and often hard-surfaced, such as those of plants of the agave family (Agavaceae), a major source. The leaves are strengthened and supported by fibre bundles, often several feet long, composed of many overlapping cells, or true plant fibres, held together by gummy substances. The fibre generally traverses the length of the leaf and is often densest near the leaf undersurface. Leaves of the abaca plant, with fibre bundles concentrated in the stalks, are an exception.

The leaves are hand-harvested, and their fibre is separated from the surrounding leaf tissue by decortication, a hand or machine scraping or peeling process, then cleaned and dried. The released fibre bundles, or strands, are not separated into individual fibre cells and are called fibres in the trade.

Leaf fibres are chiefly employed for such cordage as rope and twine. They may also be used for woven fabrics, usually requiring no spinning for this purpose. Sisal, abaca, and henequen lead in world production. Many potentially useful leaf fibres remain unexploited

Leaf fibres of sisal drying on poles, near Tanga, Tanzania
Lynn McLaren from Rapho/Photo Researchers

because of the limitations of existing cultivation and processing methods and the increased use of synthetic fibres for cordage.

leaf fish, any of about 10 species of fishes in the family Nandidae (order Perciformes). All live in fresh water, although some species may enter brackish water. Their geographic distribution is circumtropical, including the Amazon River basin, western Africa, India, southeastern Asia, and the Malay Archipelago.

The name leaf fish is applied specifically to *Monocirrhus polyacanthus,* a South American species that is known for its close resemblance in both appearance and swimming behaviour to a dead, drifting leaf. This species is about 7.5 cm (3 inches) long and is coloured a mottled brown; it has serrated dorsal and anal fins that resemble the saw edges of leaves and a chin barbel that looks like a broken leaf stem. It lives in quiet waters, drifting about, often head down, and propelling itself with a transparent tail and pectoral fins. When feeding, it awaits an unsuspecting small fish or moves toward it slowly, taking it with a sudden gape of the huge mouth. Many members of the Nandidae family are popular aquarium fishes.

leaf-footed bug: *see* coreid bug.

leaf insect, also called WALKING LEAF, flat green insect with a leaflike appearance, belonging to the family Phylliidae (order Phasmatodea) of about 25 species. The female has large leathery forewings (tegmina) that lie edge to edge on the abdomen and resemble, in their vein pattern, the midrib and veins in a leaf;

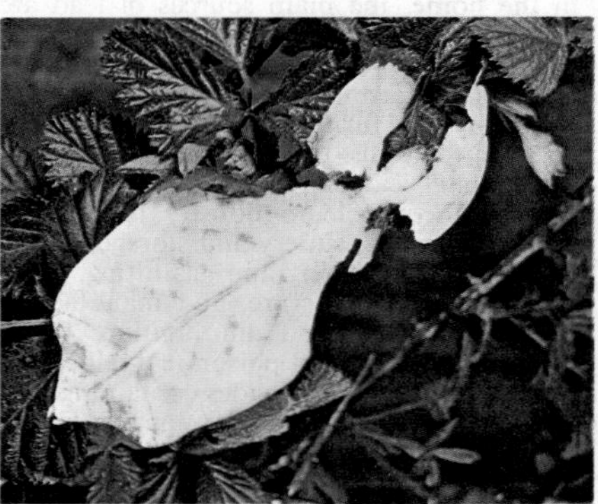
Leaf insect (*Phyllium*)
S.C. Bisserot

the hindwings have no function. The male has small tegmina and ample, non-leaflike, functional hindwings. Newly hatched young are reddish in colour; they become green after feeding on leaves. Colour and form provide protection for the insect, as does the similarity between its eggs and various types of seeds.

The leaf insect, about 60 mm (2.3 inches) long, ranges from India to the Fiji Islands. It is related to the stick insect (family Phasmatidae; *compare* walkingstick).

leaf miner, any of a number of insect larvae that live and feed within a leaf. Leaf miners include caterpillars (order Lepidoptera), sawfly larvae (order Hymenoptera), beetle and weevil grubs or larvae (order Coleoptera), and maggots (larvae) of two-winged flies (order Diptera).

Most leaf-miner burrows or tunnels are either thin, winding, whitish trails or broad, whitish or brownish blotches. Although leaf miners do not usually cause injury, they do mar the appearance of ornamental trees and shrubs. One method of control on garden plants is to remove and burn infested leaves. Spraying with nicotine solutions or dusting with various insecticides is effective only when the adults are emerging; the larval mining stage is unaffected by spray or dust.

leaf monkey, species of langur (*q.v.*).

leaf-nosed bat, any of the bats belonging to the families Phyllostomatidae and Hipposideridae (*qq.v.*).

leaf-nosed snake, any of four species of small burrowing snakes of the family Colubridae that have the nose shield enlarged and flattened, with free edges. Several subspecies of each also exist. The two members of the genus *Phyllorhynchus* are found in creosote-bush deserts of the southwestern United States and Mexico, where they hunt at night for lizards and insects. The two species of the

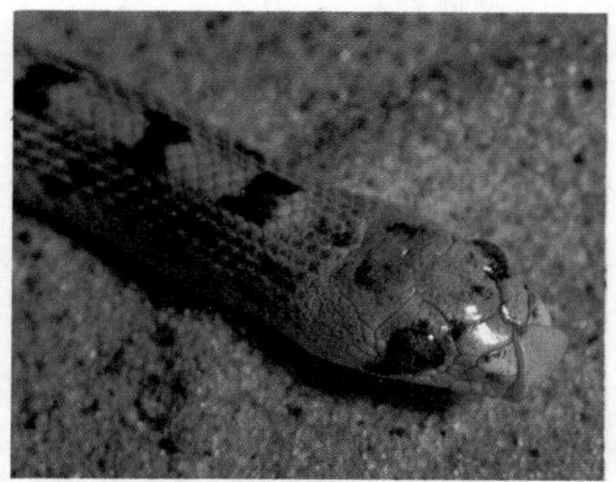

Spotted leaf-nosed snake (*Phyllorhynchus decurtatus*)

Bucky Reeves

genus *Lytorhynchus* are abundant in the dry country of northern Africa and southwestern Asia.

leaf roller moth, also called BELL MOTH, any member of the worldwide insect family Tortricidae (order Lepidoptera), named for the characteristic leaf rolling habit of the larvae. The name bell moth arises from the shape of the adult's folded, squarish forewings. These moths are characterized by their stout bodies, small antennae, reduced mouthparts, and broad, slightly fringed wings that can expand to 25 mm (1 inch).

The larvae usually feed from nests made of rolled leaves. Many species (*e.g.,* those of *Archips, Cacoecia*) are gregarious, congregating and constructing large communal nests of silk, twigs, and leaves. The destructive larval tortricids include the spruce budworm (*Choristoneura fumiferana*), one of the most destructive North American pests. It attacks evergreens, feeding on needles and pollen, and can completely defoliate spruce and related trees, causing much loss for the lumber industry. Other species are pests of evergreen and deciduous trees: the European oak roller, or pea-green, moth (*Tortrix viridana*) and the North American ugly-nest caterpillar (*Archips cerasivoranus*).

Leaf roller moth

Ken Brate—Photo Researchers/EB Inc.

leaf-rolling weevil, any of the beetles of the subfamily Attelabidae of the family Curculionidae (order Coleoptera), so named because of the way in which females protect their newly laid eggs by rolling them up inside a growing leaf. After hatching, the larvae eat the leaf from within. Adults are free-living but associated with certain tree species. *Attelabus nitens,* for example, is associated with oak, and *Rhynchites populi* with poplar. Two species of leaf-rolling weevils lay their eggs in hazel trees: *R. betuleti,* which rolls the whole leaf, and *Apoderus coryli,* which rolls only one side of the leaf.

leafbird (genus *Chloropsis*), any of about eight species of short-legged, grass-green birds (family Irenidae, order Passeriformes), from Southeast Asia and the Philippines. Some authorities place the leafbird in the bulbul family (Pycnonotidae).

Leafbirds are about 17 to 20 cm (6.5 to 8 inches) long. They live high up in the jungle canopy, feeding mainly on nectar, plus some insects and berries. They are excellent mimics, although often aggressive towards other birds. The loosely made cuplike nest may contain two to three cream-coloured eggs. The golden-fronted leafbird (*C. aurifrons*) is a popular cage bird.

leafhopper, any of the small, slender, often beautifully coloured and marked sap-sucking insects of the large family Cicadellidae (Jassidae) of the order Homoptera. They are found on almost all types of plants; however, individual species are host specific. Although a single leafhopper does no damage to a plant, collectively they can be serious economic pests. Their feeding may injure the plant in any of several ways: by removing sap, destroying chlorophyll, transmitting diseases, or curling leaves. The host plant is also punctured during egg laying.

Most leafhoppers are several millimetres long; some may grow to 15 mm (0.6 inch). They excrete honeydew, a sweet by-product of digestion, and are responsible for hopperburn, a diseased condition caused by the insects' injection of a toxin into the plant as they feed. Control is by contact insecticides. Common types of leafhoppers include the following:

The apple leafhopper (*Empoasca maligna*) causes apple foliage to pale and become specked with white spots. The adult insects are greenish white, and they are host specific for either apple or rose. There is one generation per year.

The beet leafhopper (*Circulifer tenellus*) is the carrier of a viral disease known as "curly top" that curls sugar beet leaves and stunts plant growth. The adults are pale green or yellow and are about 3 mm (0.1 inch) long. There are three or more generations per year. In addition, beet leafhoppers infect tomato, cantaloupe, cucumber, spinach, and other garden plants.

The grape leafhopper (*Erythroneura*) is a slender yellow-coloured insect with red markings and is about 3 mm long. It feeds on developing leaves and overwinters among fallen grape leaves. It is found on the grapevine, Virginia creeper, and apple tree and is controlled by spraying or dusting.

The potato leafhopper (*Empoasca fabae*) is a destructive potato pest that causes that plant's leaves to turn brown and curl; the insect plugs the plant's xylem and phloem vessels, thus interfering with the transportation of food products. Adult potato leafhoppers are green with white spots on the head and thorax and are about 3 mm long. Instead of hibernating in the north, they overwinter on legumes in warm climates. This insect carries viral diseases and infects beans and apples as well as potatoes.

The rose leafhopper (*Edwardsiana rosae*) is a serious rose and apple pest. It is creamy white to light yellow in colour and is about 3 mm long. It overwinters in the egg stage and produces two generations per year. It does not cause hopperburn.

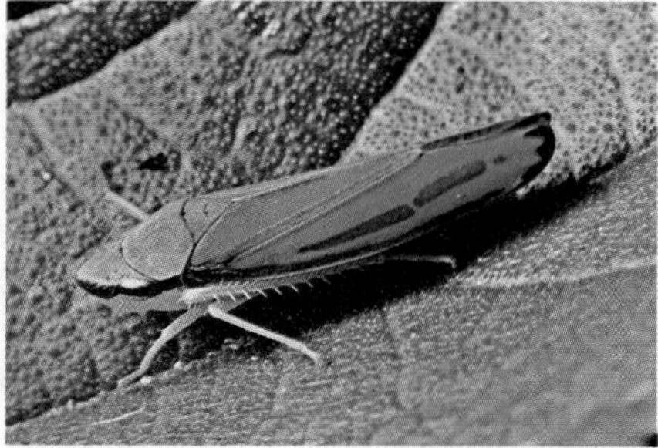

Red-banded leafhopper (*Graphocephala*)

Stephen Collins—Photo Researchers/EB Inc.

The six-spotted leafhopper (*Macrosteles fascifrons*) is greenish yellow with six black spots. It produces several generations per year. It infects asters and other garden plants and transmits aster yellow virus, which causes excessive branching, stunted growth, and foliage to turn yellow.

leafy liverwort, also called SCALE MOSS, any of numerous species of liverworts (class Hepaticae), generally of the order Jungermanniales, in which the plant body is prostrate and extends horizontally in leaflike form with an upper and lower surface. About three-quarters of all liverworts species belong to this order.

Most leafy liverworts are found in moist habitats—in swamps and bogs and in damp forests, where they grow on rotted logs or in damp soil. Others are found in colder environments, and still others are aquatic. The plant's leaves are spirally arranged around the stem, most often in rows of three. The leaves are usually lobed, and those of some species may have toothed or fringed edges and may curve upward. New growth covers the old, which then dies for lack of light.

The mature gametophyte of the leafy liverwort can be either dioecious (each individual bears either male or female reproductive structures) or monoecious (each individual bears both male and female reproductive structures). The fertilized egg eventually develops into the sporophyte, which remains dependent on the gametophyte for water and nutrients. The sporophyte's spore-containing capsule (sporangium) is usually attached to the gametophyte by an elongate setae. The sporangium ruptures and releases spores, which germinate, ultimately into the gametophyte. The gametophyte remains attached to the substratum by way of filamentous rhizoids.

The greatest number and variety of leafy liverworts are found in tropical Central and South America and in the Malay Archipelago. *Plagiochila,* a very species-rich genus, is found throughout the world. The large family Lejeuneaceae, which is extremely diverse in the tropics, shows an extraordinary variety of form and ecology. Many species of *Frullania* are able to tolerate drying and can revive after drought, thus allowing them to grow in areas where rains are seasonal.

league, any of several units of measure ranging from 2.4 to 4.6 statute miles (3.9 to 7.4 km). In English-speaking countries the land league is generally accepted as 3 statute miles (4.8 km). An ancient unit derived from the Gauls and introduced into England by the Normans, the league was estimated by the Romans to be equal to 1,500 paces—a pace, or *passus,* in Roman measure being nearly 5 feet (1.5 m).

Land leagues of about 2.63 miles (4.23 km) were used by the Spanish in early surveys of parts of the American Southwest. At one time the term was also used as a unit of area measurement. Old California surveys show square leagues equal to 4,439 acres (1,796 hectares). In the late 18th century the league also came to be the distance a cannon shot could be fired at menacing ships offshore. This resulted in the 3-mile offshore territorial limit.

League for the Independence of Vietnam: *see* Viet Minh.

League of ———: *see under* substantive word or words (*e.g.,* Nations, League of), except as below.

League of Augsburg, War of the: *see* Grand Alliance, War of the.

Leah, also spelled LIA, in the Old Testament (primarily in Genesis), first wife of Jacob (later Israel) and the traditional ancestor of five of the 12 tribes of Israel. Leah was the mother of six of Jacob's sons: Reuben, Simeon, Levi, Issachar, Zebulun, and Judah; Judah was the ancestor of King David and, according to the New Testament, of Jesus.

After Jacob had deprived his brother Esau of his birthright and blessing, he fled from the wrath of Esau and took refuge in the household of his uncle Laban. There he fell in love with Laban's younger daughter, Rachel, working for Laban seven years to win her hand. On the night of the nuptial feast, however, Laban deceived him by sending in the "tender-eyed" Leah ("tender-eyed" is an uncertain phrase, possibly denoting poor vision); thus, Laban compelled Jacob to work another seven years for Rachel. Because of this trickery, even after he married Rachel, Jacob did not love Leah, but God consoled her with children before allowing Rachel to become pregnant. Leah lived on after Rachel (though no details of this portion of her life are recorded), and, according to some traditions, she was buried in Hebron on the west bank of the Jordan River.

Leahy, Frank, byname of FRANCIS WILLIAM LEAHY (b. Aug. 27, 1908, O'Neill, Neb., U.S.—d. June 21, 1973, Portland, Ore.), American collegiate-football coach, whose teams at the University of Notre Dame, South Bend, Ind., won 87 games, lost 11, and tied 9, a record second only to that of Knute Rockne.

Leahy played at Notre Dame under Rockne in 1929, but a knee injury in 1930 ended his playing career. While he was recuperating from a knee operation, he shared a hospital room with Rockne, who was struck with his football acumen and made him informally a coach of the tackles until his graduation in 1931. Leahy began his coaching career in earnest as line coach at Georgetown University, Washington, D.C. (1931), and at Michigan State University, East Lansing (1932). He became line coach under Jim Crowley at Fordham University, Bronx, New York City (1933–38), creating the formidable line called the Seven Blocks of Granite. Leahy became a head coach at Boston College in 1939 and went to Notre Dame in 1941. During his career at Notre Dame (he retired in 1953), his teams won four national championships and Notre Dame remained unbeaten in 39 consecutive games (1946–50).

After his retirement from football, he was a business executive, a sports columnist, and a television commentator.

Leahy, William D., in full WILLIAM DANIEL LEAHY (b. May 6, 1875, Hampton, Iowa, U.S.—d. July 20, 1959, Bethesda, Md.), American naval officer who served as personal chief of staff to President Franklin D. Roosevelt during World War II.

A graduate of the U.S. Naval Academy, Annapolis, Md. (1897), Leahy saw service in the Spanish-American War (1898), the Philippine insurrection (1899–1901), and the Boxer Rebellion in China (1900). In command of a navy transport during World War I, he formed a lasting friendship with Roosevelt, then assistant secretary of the navy. He reached the

William D. Leahy
By courtesy of the National Archives, Washington, D.C.

rank of admiral in 1936 and was chief of naval operations from 1937 to 1939.

Leahy's first career ended with retirement because of age in August 1939, and his second career began a few months later, when President Roosevelt named him governor of Puerto Rico. He held that post until December 1940, when he was appointed ambassador to the Vichy government of unoccupied France. After the United States entered World War II (December 1941), he was given the newly created position of chief of staff to the president. He was made a fleet admiral in December 1944 and accompanied Roosevelt to the Yalta Conference the following year.

After Roosevelt's death (April 1945), Leahy retained his post under President Harry S. Truman. He retired in 1949 and wrote his war memoirs, *I Was There* (1950).

Leakey, Louis S.B., in full LOUIS SEYMOUR BAZETT LEAKEY (b. Aug. 7, 1903, Kabete, Kenya—d. Oct. 1, 1972, London, Eng.), Kenyan archaeologist and anthropologist whose fossil discoveries in East Africa proved that man was far older than had previously been believed and that human evolution was centred in Africa, rather than in Asia, as earlier discoveries had suggested. Leakey was also noted for his controversial interpretations of these archaeological finds.

Born of British missionary parents, Leakey spent his youth with the Kikuyu people of Kenya, about whom he later wrote. He was educated at the University of Cambridge and began his archaeological research in East Africa

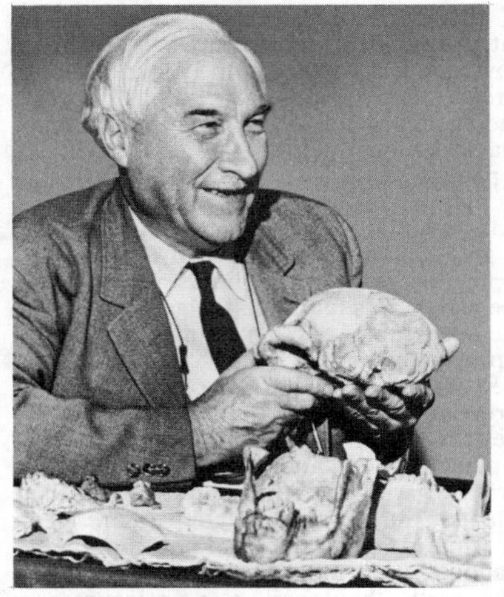

Louis S.B. Leakey
AP/Wide World Photos

in 1924; he was later aided by his second wife, the archaeologist Mary Douglas Leakey (*née* Nicol), and their sons. He held various appointments at major British and American universities and was curator of the Coryndon Memorial Museum in Nairobi from 1945 to 1961.

In 1931 Leakey began his research at Olduvai Gorge in Tanzania, which became the site of his most famous discoveries. The first finds were of animal fossils and crude stone tools, but in 1959 Mary Leakey uncovered a fossil hominid that was given the name *Zinjanthropus* (now generally regarded as a form of *Australopithecus*) and believed to be about 1.7 million years old. Leakey later theorized that *Zinjanthropus,* or *Australopithecus,* was not a direct ancestor of modern man; he claimed this distinction for other hominid fossil remains that his team had discovered at Olduvai Gorge in 1960–63 and which Leakey named *Homo habilis.* Leakey held that *H. habilis* lived contemporaneously with *Australopithecus* in East Africa and represented a more advanced hominid on the direct evolutionary line to *Homo sapiens.* Initially many scientists disputed Leakey's interpretations and classifications of the fossils he had found, although they accepted the significance of the finds themselves. They contended that *H. habilis* was not sufficiently different from *Australopithecus* to justify a separate classification. Subsequent finds by the Leakey family and others, however, established that *H. habilis* does indeed represent the evolutionary link between the australopithecines (who eventually became extinct) and *Homo erectus,* who was the direct ancestor of modern man.

Among the other important finds made by Leakey's team was the discovery in 1948 at Rusinga, an island in Lake Victoria, of the remains of *Proconsul africanus,* a common ancestor of both humans and apes that lived about 25 million years ago. At Fort Ternan, east of Lake Victoria, in 1962, Leakey's team discovered the remains of *Kenyapithecus,* another link between apes and early man that lived about 14 million years ago.

Leakey's discoveries formed the basis for the most important subsequent research into the earliest origins of human life. He was also instrumental in persuading Jane Goodall and Dian Fossey to undertake their pioneering long-term studies of chimpanzees and gorillas in those animals' natural habitats.

Leakey wrote *Adam's Ancestors* (1934; rev. ed., 1953), *Stone-Age Africa* (1936), *White African* (1937), *Olduvai Gorge* (1952), *Mau Mau and the Kikuyu* (1952), *Olduvai Gorge, 1951–61* (1965), *Unveiling Man's Origins* (1969; with Jane Goodall), and *Animals of East Africa* (1969).

Leakey, Mary Douglas, *née* NICOL (b. Feb. 6, 1913, London, Eng.—d. Dec. 9, 1996, Nairobi, Kenya), English-born archaeologist and paleoanthropologist who made several of the most important fossil finds subsequently interpreted and publicized by her husband, the noted anthropologist Louis Leakey.

After undergoing sporadic schooling, she participated in excavations of a Neolithic site at Hembury, Devon, Eng., by which time she had become skilled at making reproduction-quality drawings of stone tools. She met Louis Leakey in 1933, they were married in 1936, and she bore three surviving children.

Working alongside her husband for the next 30 years, Mary Leakey oversaw the excavation of various prehistoric sites in Kenya. In 1948 she discovered the skull of *Proconsul africanus,* an apelike ancestor of both apes and early humans that lived about 25 million years ago. In 1959 she discovered at Olduvai Gorge the skull of an early hominid named *Zinjanthropus* by Louis Leakey, though it is now regarded as a type of australopithecine. In 1978 she discovered at Laetoli, a site south of Olduvai Gorge, several sets of footprints made in volcanic ash by early hominids who lived about 3.5 million years ago. The footprints indicated that their makers walked upright; this discovery pushed back the advent of human bipedalism to a date earlier than had previously been suspected by the scientific community. Among Mary Leakey's books were *Olduvai Gorge: My Search for Early Man* (1979) and the autobiographical *Disclosing the Past* (1984).

Leakey, Richard, in full RICHARD ERSKINE FRERE LEAKEY (b. Dec. 19, 1944, Nairobi, Kenya), Kenyan physical anthropologist and paleontologist responsible for extensive fossil finds of human ancestral forms in East Africa. His investigations suggested that relatively intelligent, tool-using ancestors of true man lived in eastern Africa as early as 3 million years ago, or almost twice the time span of previous estimates.

The son of noted anthropologists Louis Leakey and Mary Leakey, he was originally reluctant to follow his parents' career and became a safari guide. When, in 1963, he found an australopithecine jaw while exploring the

Lake Natron region in northeast Tanzania, he decided that he would, after all, become an anthropologist. In London, Leakey completed a two-year secondary-education program in six months but, running out of funds and out of interest in classrooms, returned to Kenya without a university education.

In 1967 he joined an expedition to the Omo River valley in Ethiopia. It was during this trip that he first noticed the site of Koobi Fora, along the shores of Lake Rudolf (now Lake Turkana) in Kenya, where he led a preliminary search that uncovered several stone tools. From this site alone in the subsequent decade, Leakey and his fellow workers uncovered some 400 hominid fossils, representing perhaps 230 individuals, making Koobi Fora the site of the richest and most varied assemblage of early human remains found to date anywhere in the world.

Leakey proposed controversial interpretations of his fossil finds. In two books written with science writer Roger Lewin, *Origins* (1977) and *People of the Lake* (1978), Leakey presented his view that, some 3 million years ago, three hominid forms coexisted with each other: *Homo habilis, Australopithecus africanus,* and *Australopithecus boisei.* He argued that the two australopithecine forms eventually died out and that *H. habilis* evolved into *Homo erectus,* the direct ancestor of *Homo sapiens,* modern human beings. At Koobi Fora he claimed to have found evidence to support this theory. Of particular importance is an almost completely reconstructed fossil skull found in more than 300 fragments in 1972 (coded as Skull 1470), which Leakey believed to represent *H. habilis* and to date from more than 2 million years ago. The skull created quite a stir in the scientific community because it lacked the pronounced brow of other hominid skulls and had a cranial capacity nearly twice that of *Australopithecus* and more than half that of modern humans. Leakey's team went on to make further finds supporting his contention that a relatively large-brained, upright, bipedal form of the species *Homo* lived in eastern Africa as early as 2.5 million or even 3.5 million years ago. Further elaboration of Leakey's views was given in his work *The Making of Mankind* (1981).

In 1968 Leakey became administrative director of the National Museums of Kenya. He also founded the Louis Leakey Memorial Institute for African Prehistory, a fossil repository and postgraduate study centre and laboratory.

Leal, Juan de Nisa Valdés: *see* Valdés Leal, Juan de Nisa.

Leamington Spa (England): *see* Royal Leamington Spa.

Lean, Sir David (b. March 25, 1908, Croydon, Surrey, Eng.—d. April 16, 1991, London), leading motion-picture director in the post-World War II renaissance of the British movie industry. His films evidence a strong cinematic sense and a mastery of the technical aspects of filmmaking.

Lean began his film career in 1928 with a job at Gaumont Studios. Though starting at the bottom, he advanced rapidly to cameraman and assistant director. In 1930 he became the head film editor for Gaumont Sound News and, later, for British Movietone News. He soon achieved a reputation as one of the most accomplished editors in the British film industry.

Lean codirected the award-winning war film *In Which We Serve* (1942) with the playwright Noël Coward and then directed the films *This Happy Breed* (1944), *Blithe Spirit* (1945), and *Brief Encounter* (1945), all closely based on plays by Coward. Lean then directed highly successful film adaptations of Charles Dickens' *Great Expectations* (1946) and *Oliver Twist* (1948), followed by *Breaking the Sound Barrier* (1952).

Lean
AP/Wide World Photos

After the huge popular and critical success of *The Bridge on the River Kwai* (1957), a story of British prisoners of war in the jungles of Burma (now Myanmar) during World War II, Lean became identified with long, beautifully shot epics that often took years to produce. His next film, *Lawrence of Arabia* (1962), a chronicle of T.E. Lawrence's guerrilla exploits in Arabia during World War I, matched its predecessor's critical and commercial appeal and made actor Peter O'Toole a star. These two films garnered a total of 14 Academy Awards. Lean's two subsequent epics, *Dr. Zhivago* (1965) and *Ryan's Daughter* (1970), received mixed reviews but were admired for their pictorial beauty. His last film, *A Passage to India* (1984), based on the novel by E.M. Forster, was on the level of his finest work. Lean was knighted in 1984.

Leander (Greek mythology): *see* Hero and Leander.

Leaning Tower of Pisa, Italian TORRE PENDENTE DI PISA, medieval structure in Pisa, Italy, that is famous for the settling of its foundation, causing it to lean 17 feet (5.2 m) from the perpendicular. The bell tower, begun in 1174 as the third and final structure of the city's cathedral complex, was designed to stand 185 feet (56 m) high and was constructed of white marble. Three of its eight stories were completed when the uneven settling of the building's foundation in the soft ground became noticeable.

Bonnano Pisano, the engineer in charge, sought to compensate for the lean by making the new stories slightly taller on the short side, but the extra masonry caused the structure to sink still further. Work was suspended several times as engineers sought solutions, but the tower was ultimately topped out in the 14th century, still leaning.

Leaning Tower of Pisa
Edwin Smith

In modern times the foundations have been strengthened by the injection of cement grouting, but in the late 20th century the structure was still in danger of collapse, and various schemes were being considered to save it.

leap of faith, metaphor used by the 19th-century Danish philosopher Søren Kierkegaard in his *Afsluttende uvidenskabelig Efterskrift* (1846; *Concluding Unscientific Postscript*) to describe commitment to an objective uncertainty, specifically to the Christian God. For Kierkegaard, God is totally other than man; between God and man there exists a gulf that faith alone can bridge. Kierkegaard was equally opposed to the German philosopher G.W.F. Hegel's rationalized Christianity and to orthodox attempts to demonstrate the truth of the Christian faith by rational argument, and he insisted that religious truth is incapable of objective proof and can be appropriated only by an act of will. Kierkegaard praised aesthetic and ethical responses to life but maintained that they do not free man from dread and despair. Man requires a relationship with God founded on a commitment that has no conclusive evidence to recommend it; faith is a risk or, as the 17th-century French writer Blaise Pascal put it, a "wager."

Kierkegaard's emphasis on the God-man dichotomy influenced 20th-century religious existentialism and neo-orthodox theology, especially as embodied in the work of the Swiss theologian Karl Barth.

leap year, year containing some intercalary period, especially a Gregorian year having a 29th day of February instead of the standard 28 days. The astronomical year, the time taken for the Earth to complete its orbit around the Sun, is about 365.242 days, or, to a first approximation, 365.25 days. To account for the odd quarter day, an extra calendar day is added every four years, as was first done in 46 BC, with the establishment of the Julian calendar. Over many centuries, the difference between the approximate value 0.25 day and the more accurate 0.242 day accumulates significantly. In the Gregorian calendar now in general use, the discrepancy is adjusted by adding the extra day to only those century years exactly divisible by 400 (*e.g.,* 1600, 2000). For still more precise reckoning, every year evenly divisible by 4,000 (*i.e.,* 16,000, 24,000, etc.) is made a common (not leap) year.

Lear, legendary British king and central character of William Shakespeare's play *The Tragedy of King Lear.* The name derives from that of a sea god of the ancient Britons called Llyr. The story of Lear's kingdom—his division of it among his daughters and the consequences of his action—was told in Geoffrey of Monmouth's early 12th-century *Historia regum Britanniae* (*History of the Kings of Britain*), an inventive work from which Raphael Holinshed borrowed material when compiling the early part of his *Chronicles* (1577). This latter was, in turn, a major source for Shakespeare's historical plays and for his *Macbeth* and *Cymbeline.* Shakespeare may, therefore, have used Holinshed's work when writing *King Lear,* performed in 1605 or 1606, though he was perhaps more directly influenced by an anonymous play, *The True Chronicle History of King Leir,* performed and printed in 1605.

The story of Lear was handled by Edmund Spenser in his heroic poem, *The Faerie Queene,* and it was one of the "tragedies" told in the mid-16th-century compilation *A Myrrour for Magistrates.*

Shakespeare's play, centred upon the old king

who cannot distinguish truth from falsehood, is considered by many his most pessimistic work. A subplot, dealing with the sufferings of the Earl of Gloucester and his son Edgar through the malice of Gloucester's bastard son Edmund, echoes the theme of family tragedy.

Lear, Edward (b. May 12, 1812, Highgate, near London—d. Jan. 29, 1888, San Remo, Italy), English landscape painter who is more widely known as the writer of an original kind of nonsense verse and as the popularizer of the limerick. His true genius is apparent in his nonsense poems, which portray a world of fantastic creatures in nonsense words and show a Tennysonian feeling for word colour, variety of rhythm, and often a deep underlying sense of melancholy. Their quality is matched, especially in the limericks, by that of his engaging pen-and-ink drawings.

Edward Lear, drawing by William Holman Hunt, 1857; in the Walker Art Gallery, Liverpool

By courtesy of the Walker Art Gallery, Liverpool

The youngest of 21 children, he was brought up by his eldest sister, Ann, and from the age of 15 earned his living by drawing. He subsequently worked for the British Museum, made drawings of birds for John Gould, a zoologist, and, during 1832–37, made illustrations of the Earl of Derby's private menagerie at Knowsley, Lancashire. Lear had a natural affinity for children, and it was for the earl's grandchildren that he produced his first *Book of Nonsense* (1846, enlarged 1861, 1863). In 1835 he decided to become a topographical landscape painter.

Lear, a homosexual, suffered all his life from epilepsy and melancholia. After 1837 he lived mainly abroad. Though naturally timid, he was a constant and intrepid traveler, exploring Italy, Greece, Albania, Palestine, Syria, Egypt, and, later, India and Ceylon. An indefatigable worker, he produced innumerable pen and watercolour sketches of great topographical accuracy. He worked these up into the carefully finished watercolours and large oil paintings, showing Pre-Raphaelite influence, that were his financial mainstay. During his nomadic life he lived, among other places, at Rome, Corfu, and, finally, with his celebrated cat "Foss," at San Remo.

Lear published three volumes of bird and animal drawings; seven illustrated travel books (notably *Journal of a Landscape Painter in Greece and Albania,* 1851); and four books of nonsense—*The Book of Nonsense* mentioned earlier, *Nonsense Songs, Stories, Botany and Alphabets* (1871), *More Nonsense, Pictures, Rhymes, Botany, etc.* (1872), and *Laughable Lyrics* (1877). A posthumous collection, *Queery Leary Nonsense* (1911), was compiled by Lady Strachey.

BIBLIOGRAPHY. The definitive biography is Vivien Noakes, *Edward Lear: The Life of a Wanderer,* new ed. (1985). A study of his art is found in Philip Hofer, *Edward Lear as a Landscape Draughtsman* (1967).

Lear, William P(owell) (b. June 26, 1902, Hannibal, Mo., U.S.—d. May 14, 1978, Reno, Nev.), self-taught American electrical engineer and industrialist whose Lear Jet Corporation was the first mass-manufacturer of business jet aircraft in the world. Lear also developed the automobile radio, the eight-track stereo tape player for automobiles, and the miniature automatic pilot for aircraft.

The child of immigrant parents and a broken home, Lear said that at the age of 12 he had worked out a blueprint of his life, based upon profiting by inventing what people wanted. He held some 150 patents at his death.

After completing eighth grade, Lear quit school to become a mechanic and at the age of 16 joined the navy, lying about his age. During World War I, Lear studied radio and after his discharge designed the first practicable auto radio. Failing to secure the financial backing to produce the radio himself, Lear sold the radio to the Motorola Company in 1924.

In 1934 he designed a universal radio amplifier (*i.e.,* one that would work with any radio.) The Radio Corporation of America purchased the plans, giving Lear the capital he needed to expand his operations. He founded the Lear Avia Corporation in 1934 to make radio and navigational devices for aircraft. In 1939 he founded Lear, Inc. By 1939 more than half the private airplanes in the United States were using Lear radio and navigational equipment. In World War II, the company manufactured cowl-flap motors and other precision devices for Allied aircraft. After World War II, Lear, Inc. introduced a new, miniaturized autopilot that could be used on small fighter aircraft.

Between 1950 and 1962 the sales of Lear, Inc., rose to $90,000,000. New plants were added in the Midwest and on both coasts, and the company embarked on the manufacture of stereophonic sound systems and miniature communications satellites. Lear himself wanted to expand into low-priced, small jet aircraft for businessmen. When his board of directors would not approve the expenditure, Lear sold his share of the company and formed Lear Jet, Inc., Wichita, Kan., which produced its first compact jet in 1963. The new company's jets became among the world's most popular private jet aircraft. Lear sold his interest in the corporation in 1967 and formed Lear Motors Corporation (1967–69) to produce a steam car.

Learmont, Thomas: *see* Thomas the Rhymer.

learning, the alteration of behaviour as a result of individual experience. When an organism can perceive and change its behaviour, it is said to learn.

A brief treatment of learning and learning theories follows. For full treatment, *see* MACROPAEDIA: Learning, Animal; Learning and Cognition, Human.

Types of learning. The array of learned behaviour includes associative, or conditioned, learning (both classical and operant; *see* conditioning); discrimination learning, where a subject learns to respond to a limited range of sensory characteristics, such as a particular shade of coloration; habituation, the cessation of responses to repeated stimulation; concept formation (*q.v.*), the process of sorting experiences according to related features; problem solving; perceptual learning (*q.v.*), the effects of past experience on sensory perceptions; and psychomotor learning (*q.v.*), the development of neuromuscular patterns in response to sensory signals. Imitation, insight learning, and imprinting are other types of learning.

Learning theorists from the 17th through the mid-20th century had in common a desire to demonstrate scientifically that certain universal principles governed all learning processes and could explain how and why they worked. Rigorous, "objective" methodology was attempted so that the behaviour of all organisms could be comprehended under a unified system of laws modeled on those posited in the physical sciences. By the 1970s, however, the leaks in comprehensive theories had led psychologists to hold out the possibility that no single theory of learning may be appropriate.

The last attempts to integrate all knowledge of psychology into a single, grand theory occurred in the 1930s. Three seminal thinkers were E.R. Guthrie (1886–1959), Clark L. Hull (1884–1952), and E.C. Tolman (1886–1959). Guthrie reasoned that responses (not perceptions or mental states) were the ultimate and most important building blocks of learning. Hull argued that "habit strength," a result of practiced, stimulus–response (S–R) activities promoted by reward, was the essential aspect of learning, which he viewed as a gradual process. Tolman contributed the insight that learning is a process that is inferred from behaviour. Several themes these men sounded remain vital to researchers.

Association is one such theme. Its essence lies in the observation that a subject perceives something in the environment (sensations) and the result is an awareness of what is out there (ideas). Associations leading to ideas were said to include closeness of objects or events in space or time, similarity, frequency, salience, and attractiveness. Associative learning, the ability of an animal to connect a previously irrelevant stimulus with a particular response, occurs mainly through the process of conditioning, where reinforcement crystallizes new behaviour patterns. The earliest well-known conditioning experiment was performed by the 19th-century Russian physiologist Ivan Petrovich Pavlov (*q.v.*), who conditioned dogs to salivate to the sound of bells.

S–R theories failed to account satisfactorily for many learned phenomena, however, and seemed overly reductive, ignoring a subject's inner activities. Tolman headed another, less "objective" camp that held that associations involved a stimulus and a subjective sensory impression (S–S).

Another current theme is reinforcement, a concept developed to account for the finding that a subject's performance is facilitated when his practiced activities are rewarded. A heated dispute has continued over the theoretical mechanisms of reinforcement.

Many psychologists discount any universal applicability of association theory, saying that other considerations are crucial to learning. Gestalt psychologists, for instance, believe that important learning processes involve a restructuring of relationships in the environment, not simply associating them. Psycholinguists (those who study the psychological aspects of language ability) argue that language learning involves too many words and combinations to be satisfactorily explained by association theory. Instead, these researchers argue that some basic organizing structure underlies language learning, perhaps a native "grammar" inherited genetically.

Other major issues of contemporary theories of learning include the role of motivation in performance; the transfer of training (*q.v.*) between a task already learned and one yet to be learned; learning stages; and the processes and nature of recall, forgetting, and information retrieval (*see* memory). Behaviour genetics (*q.v.*) has contributed to such major issues as the distinction between learned and inherited behaviour. Other scientists are exploring nonquantifiable concepts such as image, cognition (*q.v.*), awareness, and volition.

Physiological basis of learning. The mechanisms of learning and remembering seem to depend on relatively enduring changes in the nervous system. Apparently the effects of learning are first retained in the brain by some reversible process, after which a more permanent neural change takes place. Two types of neurological processes have therefore been suggested. The short-term function of memory, temporary and reversible, may be achieved through a physiological mechanism (*e.g.,* synaptic electrical or chemical change) that keeps the memory trace alive over a limited period of time. The ensuing, more permanent (long-term) storage may depend on changes in the physical or chemical structure of neurons; synaptic changes seem to be particularly important.

Akin to the problem of learning are the relatively complex activities of reasoning, problem solving, and intelligent and linguistic behaviour. *See also* attention; developmental psychology; intelligence; motivation; sensorimotor skill; thought.

lease, a contract for the exclusive possession of property (usually but not necessarily land or buildings) for a determinate period or at will. The person making the grant is called the lessor, and the person receiving the grant is called the lessee. Two important requirements for a lease are that the lessee have exclusive possession (nonexclusive possession would call for a license) and that the lessor's term of interest in the property be longer than the term of the lease (a grant involving an equal term or period would comprise a conveyance or assignment, not a lease).

leather, animal skins and hides that have been treated to preserve them and make them suitable for use.

The term hide is used to designate the skin of larger animals (*e.g.,* cowhide or horsehide), whereas "skin" refers to that of smaller animals (*e.g.,* calfskin or kidskin). The preservation process employed is a chemical treatment called tanning, which converts the otherwise perishable skin to a stable and nondecaying material. Although the skins of such diverse animals as ostrich, lizard, eel, and kangaroo have been used, the more common leathers come from seven main groups: cattle, including calf and ox; sheep and lamb; goat and kid; equine animals, including horse, mule, and zebra; buffalo; pig and hog; and such aquatic animals as seal, walrus, whale, and alligator.

The hides of mammals are composed of three layers: epidermis, a thin outer layer; corium, or dermis, the thick central layer; and a subcutaneous fatty layer. The corium is used to make leather after the two sandwiching layers have been removed. Fresh hides contain between 60 and 70 percent water by weight and 30 to 35 percent protein. About 85 percent of the protein is collagen, a fibrous protein held together by chemical bonds. Basically, leather making is the science of using acids, bases, salts, enzymes, and tannins to dissolve fats and nonfibrous proteins and strengthen the bonds between the collagen fibres.

Leather making is an ancient art that has been practiced for more than 7,000 years. Primitive man dried fresh skins in the sun, softened them by pounding in animal fats and brains, and preserved them by salting and smoking. Beginning with simple drying and curing techniques, the process of vegetable tanning was developed by the Egyptians and Hebrews about 400 BC. During the Middle Ages the Arabs preserved the art of leather making and so improved it that morocco and cordovan (from Córdoba, Spain) became highly prized leathers. By the 15th century, leather tanning was once more widespread in Europe, and, by the mid-19th century, power-driven machines that performed such operations as splitting, fleshing, and dehairing were introduced. Toward the end of the 19th century, chemical tannage—in particular, the use of chrome salts—was introduced.

The modern commercial leather-making process involves three basic phases: preparation for tanning, tanning, and processing tanned leather. As a preliminary step, a hide must be carefully skinned and protected both in storage and transportation before reaching the tannery. A hide will begin to decompose within hours of an animal's death; to prevent this from happening, the hide is cured by a dehydrating process that involves either air-drying, wet or dry salting, or pickling with acids and salts before being shipped to a tannery.

At the tannery the hide is soaked to remove all water-soluble materials and restore it to its original shape and softness. Hair is loosened usually by a process called liming, accomplished by immersing the hides in a mixture of lime and water; the hair and extraneous flesh and tissue are removed by machine. The hide is then washed, delimed, bated (the enzymatic removal of nonfibrous protein to enhance colour and suppleness), and pickled (to provide a final cleansing and softening).

The tanning process derives its name from tannin (tannic acid), the agent that displaces water from the interstices of the hide's protein fibres and cements these fibres together. Vegetable tanning, which is the oldest of tanning methods, is still important. Extracts are taken from the parts of plants (such as the roots, bark, leaves, and seed husks) that are rich in tannin. The extracted material is processed into tanning liquors, and the hides are soaked in vats or drums of increasingly strong liquor until they are sufficiently tanned. The various vegetable-tanning procedures can take weeks or months to complete. The end result is a firm, water-resistant leather.

Mineral tanning, which uses mineral salts, produces a soft, pliable leather and is the preferred method for producing most light leathers. Use of this method can shorten the tanning period to days or even hours. Chromium salt is the most widely used mineral agent, but salts from aluminum and zirconium are also used. In mineral tanning the hides are soaked in saline baths of increasing strength or in acidic baths in which chemical reactions deposit salts in the skin fibres.

Oil tanning is an old method in which fish oil or other oil and fatty substances are stocked, or pounded, into dried hide until they have replaced the natural moisture of the original skin. Oil tanning is used principally to make chamois leather, a soft, porous leather that can be repeatedly wetted and dried without damage. A wide variety of synthetic tanning agents (or syntans), derived from phenols and hydrocarbons, are also used.

After the basic tanning process is completed, the pelts are ready for processing, the final phase in leather production. The tanned pelt is first thoroughly dried and then dyed to give it the appropriate colour; common methods include drum dyeing, spraying, brush dyeing, and staining. Blended oils and greases are then incorporated into the leather to lubricate it and to enhance its softness, strength, and ability to shed water.

The leather is then dried to about 14 percent moisture, either in the air or in a drying tunnel or by first stretching the leather and then air or tunnel drying it. Other less frequently used methods include paste and vacuum drying. The dried leather is finished by reconditioning with damp sawdust to a uniform moisture content of 20 percent. It is then stretched and softened, and the grain surface is coated to give it additional resistance to abrasion, cracking, peeling, water, heat, and cold.

The leather is then ready to be fashioned into any of a multitude of products. These include shoes and boots, outer apparel, belts, upholstery materials, suede products, saddles, gloves, luggage and purses, and recreational equipment as well as such industrial items as buffing wheels and machine belts.

leatherleaf, also called CASSANDRA (*Chamaedaphne calyculata*), evergreen shrub of the heath family (Ericaceae). The name is also sometimes applied to a stiff-leaved fern.

Chamaedaphne calyculata occurs in Arctic regions and in North America as far south as Georgia. It forms large beds at the edges of swamps and boggy meadows. The plant grows to about 1.2 m (4 feet) in height. The brownish, alternate leaves, 1–5 cm (about 0.5–2 inches) long, are oblong or lance-shaped. The flowers, which often appear while snow is still on the ground, are small, white, and bell-shaped. They are borne in a leafy, terminal cluster. The fruit is a small, dry pod.

Leatherleaf (*Chamaedaphne calyculata*)
L. West

Léaud, Jean-Pierre (b. May 5, 1944, Paris), French screen actor who played leading roles in some of the most important French New Wave films of the 1960s and '70s, particularly ones by François Truffaut.

The son of a scriptwriter and an actress, Léaud, at age 14, was chosen to play the misunderstood adolescent Antoine Doinel in François Truffaut's first feature-length film, *Les Quatre Cents Coups* (1959; *The 400 Blows*). Léaud appeared in four more Truffaut films which traced Doinel's progress through physical maturity, courtship, marriage, fatherhood, and finally divorce: these films are *L'Amour à vingt ans* (1962; *Love at Twenty*), *Baisers volés* (1968; *Stolen Kisses*), *Domicile conjugale* (1970; *Bed and Board*), and *L'Amour en fuite* (1979; *Love on the Run*). Léaud was perfectly suited to play the part of Doinel, an engaging young man who is not well-equipped to meet the responsibilities of adult life. Léaud appeared in several other films by Truffaut, including *Les Deux Anglaises et le continent* (1971; *Two English Girls; Anne and Muriel*), and *La Nuit américaine* (1973; *Day for Night*).

Léaud played roles in several of Jean-Luc Godard's most important films: *Masculin-Féminin* (1966), *La Chinoise* (1967), and *Le Week-End* (1967). He also played parts in films by Jerzy Skolimowski and Bernardo Bertolucci, appearing in the latter's *Last Tango in Paris* (1972). He later appeared in *36 Fillette* (1988), *I Hired a Contract Killer* (1990), and *Irma Vep* (1996). An actor of limited range, Léaud nevertheless endowed the role of a scatter-brained young man with both emotional intensity and a wry humour.

leavening agent, substance causing expansion of doughs and batters by the release of gases, producing baked products with porous structure. Such agents include air, steam, yeast, baking powder, and baking soda.

Leavening of baked foods with air is achieved by vigorous mixing that incorporates air bubbles, producing foam. Egg white is well suited to this purpose because it produces voluminous and strong foams that retain their expanded structure when dried by the baking process. Egg white is used in such baked products as angel food and chiffon cakes and sponge cakes. Gluten, the elastic protein of flour, may also be whipped to produce a foam, as in beaten biscuits.

Puff pastes, which are used for light, flaky pastries, are expanded by water-vapour (steam) pressure. During baking, as the interior of the product nears the boiling point, the vapour exerts pressure within bubbles that have been incorporated earlier by other means, producing swelling.

Leavening may be achieved by the process of fermentation, which releases carbon dioxide gas. Bakers' yeast, composed of living cells of the yeast strain *Saccharomyces cerevisiae,* is available as a pressed cake and in a powdered form. When added to doughs, yeast initiates fermentation by acting upon certain sugars contributed by other dough ingredients, releasing both carbon dioxide and substances that affect the flavour and aroma of the baked product. Yeast-leavened products include most types of breads and rolls and such sweet-dough products as coffee cakes, raised doughnuts, and Danish pastries. The sourdough method, used for rye breads, employs a small portion of dough, or sponge, in which sugar-fermenting bacteria have been allowed to develop. When added to a fresh dough mixture, the sponge produces fermentation. Commercial sour cultures are sometimes used as substitutes for naturally fermented sourdoughs.

Chemical leavening agents also produce expansion by the release of carbon dioxide. Modern baking powders are combinations of baking soda (sodium bicarbonate) and dry acids or acid salts, usually with starch added for stability in storage. Single-acting baking powders, containing tartaric acid or cream of tartar, release carbon dioxide at room temperature, and mixtures in which they are used must be baked immediately to avoid loss of most of the gas. Slow-acting baking powders, containing phosphates, release part of their gas at room temperature and part when heated. Double-acting baking powder, the most widely used type, contains sodium aluminum sulfate and calcium acid phosphate and releases a small amount of gas when mixed and the balance when heated.

Baking soda is added to doughs and batters in which acid is provided by other ingredients, such as honey, sour cream, molasses, or cocoa. If used without acid ingredients, baking soda may produce yellowing and undesirable odours and flavours in the finished product. Mixtures leavened with baking soda require quick handling to avoid release of most of the gas before baking.

Leavenworth, city, seat (1855) of Leavenworth county, northeastern Kansas, U.S., on the Missouri River. First settled in 1827 by Colonel Henry H. Leavenworth to protect travelers on the Santa Fe Trail, the town was organized and laid out in 1854. The following year Leavenworth became the first incorporated community in the Kansas Territory. By 1857 it was a prosperous supply base for the settlement of the West. During the American Civil War the city supported the Union, though earlier it had been strongly proslavery. The city is now a trading centre for a diversified farming area; industries include steel and iron plants and the manufacture of wood and food products. It is the seat of St. Mary College (1923). Fort Leavenworth, 3 miles (5 km) north, includes the U.S. Army Command and General Staff College, a federal penitentiary, a national cemetery, and a museum. Pop. (1991 est.) 38,765.

Leavis, F.R., in full FRANK RAYMOND LEAVIS (b. July 14, 1895, Cambridge, Cambridgeshire, Eng.—d. April 14, 1978, Cambridge), English literary critic who introduced a new seriousness into a field still influenced by the informal narrative approach taken by George Saintsbury and other English critics.

Born in Cambridge, Leavis attended the university and then served throughout World War I as an ambulance bearer on the Western Front. He lectured at Emmanuel College, Cambridge, from 1925 but moved in the early 1930s to Downing College, where he was elected into a fellowship in 1936. He retired in 1962 and thereafter served as visiting professor at a number of English universities. In 1967 he delivered the Clark Lectures at Trinity College, Cambridge (published in 1969 as *English Literature in Our Time and the University*). He was made a Companion of Honour in 1978.

In 1932 with his wife, the former Queenie Dorothy Roth, he founded *Scrutiny,* a quarterly journal of criticism that was published until 1953 and is regarded by many as his greatest contribution to English letters. Always expressing his opinions with severity, Leavis believed that literature should be closely related to criticism of life and that it is therefore a literary critic's duty to assess works according to the author's moral position.

Leavis' criticism falls into two phases. In the first, influenced by T.S. Eliot, he devoted his attention to English verse. In *New Bearings in English Poetry* (1932) he attacked English late Victorian poetry and proclaimed the importance of the work of T.S. Eliot, Ezra Pound, and Gerard Manley Hopkins. In *Revaluation: Tradition and Development in English Poetry* (1936), he extended his survey of English poetry back to the 17th century. In the 1940s his interest moved toward the novel. In *The Great Tradition* (1948) he reassessed English fiction, proclaiming Jane Austen, George Eliot, Henry James, and Joseph Conrad as the great novelists of the past and D.H. Lawrence as their only successor (*D.H. Lawrence: Novelist,* 1955). After 1955 other novelists, notably Dickens and Tolstoy, engaged his attention in *Anna Karenina and Other Essays* (1967) and *Dickens the Novelist* (1970), written with his wife. His range is perhaps best shown in the collection *The Common Pursuit* (1952).

BIBLIOGRAPHY. William Walsh, *F.R. Leavis* (1980), combines criticism and biography. Analyses of his writing include R.P. Bilan, *The Literary Criticism of F.R. Leavis* (1979); and Francis Mulhern, *The Moment of "Scrutiny"* (1979).

Leavitt, Henrietta Swan (b. July 4, 1868, Lancaster, Mass., U.S.—d. Dec. 12, 1921, Cambridge, Mass.), American astronomer known for her discovery of the relationship between period and luminosity in Cepheid variables, pulsating stars that vary regularly in brightness in periods ranging from a few days to several months.

Leavitt graduated from the women's college that was affiliated with Harvard College, Cambridge, Mass., in 1892. In 1902, after working as a volunteer research assistant, Leavitt became a permanent staff member of the Harvard College Observatory. She conducted studies of stellar magnitudes (star brightness) and became head of the department of photographic stellar photometry. In 1912, after about five years of single-minded study, she found that the periods of the Cepheids were proportional to their luminosity, a relationship that became important to the measurement of interstellar and intergalactic distances. She also discovered four novae (stars that become suddenly brighter and within a few months gradually fade away) and more than 2,400 variable stars.

Lebachia, a genus of extinct cone-bearing plants known from fossils of the Late Carboniferous and Early Permian epochs (from about 320 to 258 million years ago). *Lebachia* and related genera in the family Lebachiaceae, order Coniferales (sometimes family Voltziaceae, order Voltziales), appear to be among the immediate ancestors of all extant conifers except the yews. A tree of uncertain size with pinnately arranged side branches (like the barbs of a feather), *Lebachia* apparently had a growth habit similar to that of the present-day Norfolk Island pine. It bore both pollen-bearing and seed-bearing cones (the latter, as detached fossils, are called *Gomphostrobus*) at the ends of the side branches.

Lebanon, officially REPUBLIC OF LEBANON, Arabic LUBNĀN, or AL-JUMHŪRĪYAH AL-LUBNĀNĪYAH, predominantly mountainous country located on the Levant (eastern littoral of the Mediterranean Sea). Lebanon extends about 135 miles (215 km) from north to south and is about 55 miles (90 km) at its widest from east to west. It is bounded by Syria (north and east), Israel (south), and the Mediterranean Sea (west). The capital is Beirut. Area 3,950 square miles (10,230 square km). Pop. (1993 est.) 2,872,000.

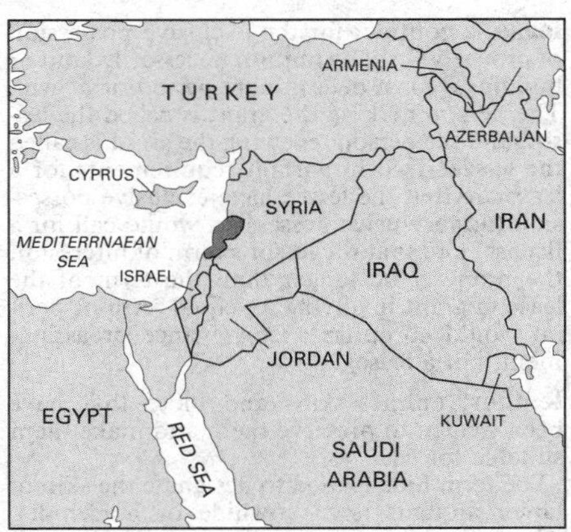

Lebanon

A brief treatment of Lebanon follows. For full treatment, *see* MACROPAEDIA: Lebanon.

For current history and for statistics on society and economy, *see* BRITANNICA BOOK OF THE YEAR.

The land. Lebanon can be divided into four distinct physiographic regions from west to east: the narrow and flat coastal strip along the Mediterranean Sea; the Lebanon Mountains (Jabal Lubnān), extending north to south at elevations of 6,600 to 9,800 feet (2,000 to 3,000 m); the 110-mile- (175-kilometre-) long fertile Al-Biqāʿ (Beqaa) valley, running parallel to the Lebanon Mountains; and, forming the eastern border, the approximately 6,500-foot- (2,000-metre-) high Anti-Lebanon (Al-Jabal ash-Sharqī) and more elevated Mount Hermon ranges. The Līṭānī, Lebanon's only year-round river, flows southward through most of Al-Biqāʿ valley before discharging into the Mediterranean near the historic city of Tyre (modern Ṣūr).

A variety of climatic conditions exists in Lebanon because of the differences in relief and the extensions of the main ranges across the path of the prevailing westerly winds. Precipitation is high by Middle Eastern standards with about 30 to 40 inches (750 to 1,000 mm) of rain falling annually (mostly in winter) along the coast. High elevations in the Lebanon Mountains receive up to 60 inches (1,500 mm) and Al-Biqāʿ 15 to 25 inches (380 to 630 mm).

Originally much of the country was heavily forested, but forests now cover only about 8 percent of the terrain. After centuries of exploitation, the few remaining of the famed cedars of Lebanon are now concentrated on mountainside groves. The country has few mineral resources.

The people. Between 1974 and 1979 Lebanon's total population is estimated to have declined by one-eighth or more because of internal and external migration resulting from the 1975–76 civil war and subsequent ongoing civil strife. By the early 1990s and because of the return of many Lebanese from abroad, the population was approximately the same size as it had been in 1974.

The Lebanese are ethnically a mixture of

Phoenician, Greek, Armenian, and Arab elements. Arabic is the official language. French and English are widely understood, and many Lebanese are trilingual. Arabic speakers compose most of the population, and speakers of Turkish and Armenian account for a small percentage. Religious affiliation of the population is unevenly divided between Muslims (Sunnite and Shīʿite), estimated at slightly more than 50 percent, and Christians (Maronite, Greek Orthodox, and others), between 24 and 40 percent. The Druze form about 7 percent of the population.

Lebanon is one of the most densely populated countries among the major Arab states. Because of the civil war, a substantial influx and recurrent relocation of Palestinian refugees and the relocation of Lebanese Christians and Muslims have occurred. More than four-fifths of the total population is urban. More than one-third of the population is less than 15 years of age.

The economy. Lebanon has a market economy. The country's traditional role as the commercial and financial centre of the Middle East, however, has been undermined by recurrent civil strife and the intervention of foreign troops. The gross national product (GNP) per capita, which was one of the highest among the world's developing countries in the early 1970s, has declined substantially.

Agriculture, which ordinarily accounts for almost one-tenth of the gross domestic product (GDP), has been severely disrupted. Agriculture is concentrated along the Mediterranean coast and in Al-Biqāʿ valley, and farms tend to be small and highly fragmented. Lebanon is not agriculturally self-sufficient, and it traditionally has imported large quantities of vegetable products and meat. Wheat is the leading cereal. Apples, citrus fruits, and grapes are leading cash crops; hashish and opium poppies have also become major cash crops. Goats and sheep are the principal livestock.

Manufacturing, which normally accounts for about one-seventh of the GDP, is small-scale but more developed than that of most other countries in the Middle East. Textiles and processed foods traditionally have accounted for nearly one-half of the industrial output. War casualties and emigration have depleted the skilled workforce, however, and in the 1980s cement, textiles, wheat flour, leather goods, and paper were among the few industrial products still being produced.

The financial sector of Lebanon's economy, including banking and insurance, has remained relatively stable, and monetary reserves (mostly in foreign currency) have risen despite the civil war and postwar fighting.

Government and social conditions. Lebanon's parliamentary democracy has been rendered largely ineffective by continuing civil strife. The national constitution, promulgated in 1926, concentrates executive power in a president and legislative power in a unicameral parliament, the National Assembly. The fighting of the 1970s and '80s made elections to the National Assembly (which was only sporadically active from 1974) impossible. A general election, the first since 1972, was held in 1992, and a new National Assembly of 128 members was elected. One-half of the assembly's membership is Christian and one-half Muslim/Druze. The judiciary is modeled after the French system.

Lebanon's traditionally high standard of living was wrecked by the civil war. Beirut, southern Lebanon, and the Palestinian refugee camps have been particularly affected by armed strife and the accompanying destruction of housing. The displacement of settled populations and occupation of homes and villages by militias, foreign military troops, and others created chaos in property rights.

Education is not compulsory and consists of five primary years, followed by a seven-year secondary or four-year vocational program. Lebanon's literacy rate is one of the highest in the Arab world. Higher education is primarily private.

History. Much of present-day Lebanon corresponds to the ancient land of the Phoenicians, who probably arrived in the region in about 3000 BC. Commercial and religious connections were established with Egypt after about 2613 BC and continued until the end of the Egyptian Old Kingdom and the invasion of Phoenicia by the Amorites (*c.* 2200 BC).

Other groups invading and periodically controlling Phoenicia included the Hyksos (18th century BC), the Egyptians of the New Kingdom (16th century BC), and the Hittites (14th century BC). Seti I (1290–79 BC) of the New Kingdom reconquered most of Phoenicia, but Ramses III (1187–56 BC) lost it to invaders from Asia Minor and Europe.

Between the withdrawal of Egyptian rule and the western advance of Assyria (10th century BC), the history of Phoenicia is primarily the history of Tyre. This city-state rose to hegemony among Phoenician states and founded colonies throughout the Mediterranean region.

The Achaemends, an Iranian dynasty under the leadership of Cyrus II, conquered the area in 538 BC. Sidon, 20 miles (32 km) north of Tyre, became a principal coastal city of this empire. In 332 BC Tyre capitulated to the army of Alexander the Great after resisting for eight months. This event marked the demise of Tyre as a great commercial city, as its inhabitants were sold into slavery. In 64 BC Phoenicia was incorporated into the Roman province of Syria.

Emperors embracing Christianity protected the area during the later Roman and Byzantine periods (*c.* AD 300–634). A 6th-century Christian group fleeing persecution in Syria settled in what is now northern Lebanon, absorbed the native population, and founded the Maronite Church. In the following century, Arab tribesmen settled in southern Lebanon after the Muslim conquest of Syria. Four hundred years later, many of this Arab group coalesced their beliefs into the Druze faith. In the coastal towns the population became mainly Sunnite Muslim.

By the end of the 11th century Lebanon had become part of the crusader states, and it later became part of the Mamlūk state of Syria and Egypt. Lebanon was able to evolve a social and political system of its own between the 15th and the 18th century. Throughout this period European, particularly French, influence was growing. In 1516 the Ottoman Turks replaced the Mamlūks.

The social system came under severe strain as the Christian population grew. The Ottoman Turks ended the local rule of the Druze Shihāb princes in 1842, exacerbating already poor relations between the Maronites and the Druze. The French intervened in behalf of the Christians, forcing the Ottoman sultan to form an autonomous province within the Ottoman Empire for the mountainous Christian area, known as Mount Lebanon.

Following World War I, Lebanon was initially administered by the French military; in 1923 the League of Nations formally granted a mandate to France for the administration of Syria and Lebanon.

In 1945 the French withdrew, and by the end of 1946 Lebanon was fully independent. Thereafter the government of independent Lebanon functioned under an unwritten agreement, called the National Pact (1943), which upheld the principle of equal representation of the country's disparate religious communities in the government and administration. Thus the president of Lebanon was traditionally a Maronite Christian, the prime minister was a Sunnite Muslim, and the speaker of the National Assembly was a Shīʿite Muslim. This power-sharing compromise (in which the Christians held a subtle primacy) worked reasonably well during the first two decades of Lebanon's independence. Lebanon became a viable, functioning democracy and blossomed economically as a major banking and commercial centre of the Middle East.

In 1958 Lebanon's Muslims, inspired by pan-Arab ideals and aware that their population was growing faster than that of the Christians', launched an insurrection that was put down by the central government with the aid of U.S. troops. Tranquillity subsequently returned to Lebanon, but the Muslim community remained dissatisfied over what it saw as the disproportionately large Christian share in Lebanon's government and administration.

Following the Arab-Israeli War of 1948–49, several hundred thousand Palestinian refugees resettled in camps in southern Lebanon. In 1970 the Palestine Liberation Organization (PLO) transferred its military activities and headquarters to Lebanon after it had been driven out of Jordan. In the early 1970s the PLO launched raids across the border into northern Israel, and in response the Christian-dominated Lebanese government tried to curb the PLO's military activities on Lebanese soil. The PLO in its turn shifted its support to Lebanon's Muslims in the intensifying conflict between Christians and Muslims in the country. By 1975 this conflict had degenerated into open warfare between Muslims and Palestinians on one side and Christians on the other.

In 1975 and 1976 hardly a day passed without a battle taking place, as Muslims and Palestinians fought against the Christians. As the Christians began to lose the civil war, Syria, prompted by fears of Israeli intervention, sent some 20,000 troops into Lebanon to prevent destruction of the Christian community. From 1976 to 1982 several thousand Syrian troops and a multinational United Nations force attempted to maintain a tenuous cease-fire between Christians, Muslims, Palestinians, and Israelis.

In June 1982 Israeli forces invaded Lebanon with the stated intent of driving the Palestinian forces out of southern Lebanon. Israel's armed forces withdrew from all but a small strip of southern Lebanon in 1985, leaving the conflict between the country's religious groups unresolved. By this time the intermittent civil war had reduced sections of the country to ruins, and thousands had been killed in the internecine fighting.

An accord signed by all parties in al-Ṭāʾif, Saudi Arabia, in 1989 put an effective end to the civil war, though violence continued in small pockets throughout the country during the 1990s. The Ṭāʾif agreement placed limits on the authority of factions by reinstituting an adjusted version of the power sharing formula worked out after the French withdrawal of 1945. Disputes over power within the government remained, however, and despite a full Israeli withdrawal from the country in 2000, the continued presence of Syrian troops in Lebanon guaranteed that country's influence in Lebanese politics.

Lebanon, town (township), New London county, east-central Connecticut, U.S. Settled in 1695 and incorporated in 1700, its name was inspired by a nearby cedar forest that suggested the biblical cedars of Lebanon. In colonial times the town was on the most direct road between New York City and Boston. The home of Jonathan Trumbull (1740), American Revolutionary governor of Connecticut, is preserved in Lebanon, and the Revolutionary War office (1727), which served as the governor's headquarters from which Connecticut's war effort was directed, is now a museum. Poultry and dairy farming are the mainstays of the town's economy. Pop. (1999 est.) 6,261.

Lebanon, city, seat (1849) of Laclede county, south-central Missouri, U.S., in the Ozark

Mountains. Founded *c.* 1849, it was named for Lebanon, Tenn. During the Civil War the town was occupied alternately by Federal and Confederate troops because of its strategic location on the military road (later U.S. Route 66, now Interstate 44) between Springfield and St. Louis. Agriculture, dairying, manufacturing (aluminum boats, clothing, barrels), and tourism are the economic mainstays. Harold Bell Wright was pastor (1905–07) of the Lebanon Christian Church, which was the setting of his novel *The Calling of Dan Matthews* (1909). Nearby are Bennett Springs State Park (west), Mark Twain National Forest (east), and Lake of the Ozarks (north). Inc. 1877. Pop. (1990) 9,983.

Lebanon, city, seat (1813) of Lebanon county, southeastern Pennsylvania, U.S., in the Lebanon Valley, 23 mi (37 km) east of Harrisburg. Settled by Germans in the 1720s, it was laid out (1756) by George Steitz and was first called Steitztown. Later it was renamed for the biblical Lebanon. Its location near the famous Cornwall ore mines and other mineral deposits led to its development before the American Revolution as an iron centre. Its growth was spurred by construction of the Union Canal (1827) and the Lebanon Valley Railroad (1857). Principal manufactures include iron and steel products, pharmaceuticals, shoes, and textiles. Lebanon Valley College (1866) is at Annville, 5 mi west. Inc. borough, 1821; city, 1885. Pop. (1990) city, 24,800; Harrisburg-Lebanon-Carlisle MSA, 587,986.

Lebanon, city, seat of Wilson county, north central Tennessee, U.S., 30 mi (48 km) east of Nashville and 6 mi south of the Cumberland River. Established in 1802 on an overland stagecoach route, it was named for the biblical Lebanon (because of a profusion of cedar trees) and developed as a trading centre for livestock and farm products. The most important cash crop is tobacco. Industrial activities include flour milling and the manufacture of bedding, clothing, leather and rubber goods, auto parts, furniture, and clocks. Cedarwood is a significant economic factor, and the nearby Cedars of Lebanon State Park and Forest has one of the largest stands of virgin cedar in the U.S. The city is the seat of Cumberland (junior) College of Tennessee (1842) and Castle Heights Military Academy (1902). The Hermitage, home of Pres. Andrew Jackson, is 18 mi west. Lebanon is where Sam Houston, who became president of the Republic of Texas, began his legal practice (1818). Inc. town, 1805; city, 1819. Pop. (1990) 15,208.

Lebanon Mountains, Arabic JABAL LUBNĀN, French MONT LIBAN, also called JABAL AL-GHARBĪ, or MT. LEBANON, mountain range, extending almost the entire length of Lebanon, paralleling the Mediterranean coast for about 150 mi (240 km), with northern outliers extending into Syria.

The northern section, north of the saddle, or pass, of Ḍahr al-Baydar (through which the Beirut-Damascus railroad and highway run), is the widest and loftiest part of the mountains, which average 7,000 ft (2,100 m) above sea level, with a few snowcapped peaks, including Qurnat as-Sawdā', at 10,131 ft. On the western flanks, east of Bsharrī, are the remaining groves of the renowned Cedars of Lebanon. South of the pass the mountains average 5,000–6,000 ft in altitude. In southern Lebanon they are broken by the 900-ft-deep gorge of the Nahr (river) al-Līṭānī. Although the porous limestone of the mountains forms poor, thin soil, it has helped create numerous underground springs that make irrigated cultivation of the lower and middle slopes possible. A variety of tree crops (including olives, apricots, and apples) are grown on the coastal side. The view presented by the snow-clad peaks may have given Lebanon its name in antiquity; *laban* is Aramaic for "white."

Lebbaeus, SAINT: *see* Judas, Saint.

Lebedev, Pyotr Nikolayevich (b. March 8 [Feb. 24, old style], 1866, Moscow—d. March 14 [March 1, O.S.], 1912, Moscow), Russian physicist who demonstrated experimentally the minute pressure that light exerts on bodies (1910).

Lebedev studied physics under August Kundt at Strasbourg, where he took his doctorate (1891). He became professor at the University of Moscow (1900). He published *Experimental Research on Light Pressure* (1901) and also worked on the origin of the Earth's magnetism. The P.N. Lebedev Physical Institute, Moscow, was named in his honour.

Pyotr Nikolayevich Lebedev
Novosti Press Agency

Lebedev, Sergey Vasilyevich (b. July 25 [July 13, old style], 1874, Lublin, Pol.—d. May 2, 1934, Leningrad), Russian chemist who developed a method for industrial production of synthetic rubber.

Lebedev joined the faculty of St. Petersburg University in 1902 and in 1910, while researching processes by which small molecules combine to form large ones, Lebedev produced an elastic rubber from butadiene. He founded the Laboratory for Petroleum Refining in 1925 and served as director of the Laboratory of Synthetic Rubber in Leningrad (1928–30). He was made a fellow of the Soviet Academy of Sciences in 1932. During World War II his process of obtaining butadiene from ethyl alcohol was used not only by the Soviet, but also the German, rubber industry.

Lebenswelt (philosophy): *see* life-world.

Lebesgue, Henri-Léon (b. June 28, 1875, Beauvais, Fr.—d. July 26, 1941, Paris), French mathematician whose generalization of the Riemann integral revolutionized the field of integration. He was *maître de conférences* (lecture master) at the University of Rennes until 1906, when he went to Poitiers, first as *chargé de cours* (assistant lecturer) of the faculty of sciences and later as professor. About six years later he went to Paris as *maître de conférences,* and afterward he became professor at the Collège de France. In 1917 he was awarded the Prix Saintour, and in 1922 he was elected to the Paris Academy of Sciences. He was made an honorary member of the London Mathematical Society in 1924 and a foreign member of the Royal Society of London in 1930.

Lebesgue, portrait by an unknown artist, 1929
By courtesy of the Bibliotheque Nationale, Paris

One of the greatest mathematicians of his day, Lebesgue's pavement theorem is an important contribution to topology, and he did some work on Fourier series and potential theory (the theory of functions describing a conservative energy field). However, his main work was in integration.

Toward the close of the 19th century, mathematical analysis was limited effectually to continuous functions, and artificial restrictions were necessary to cope with discontinuities that cropped up with greater frequency as more exotic functions were encountered. The Riemann method of integration was applicable only to continuous and a few discontinuous functions. Influenced by the work of Émile Borel, Camille Jordan, and others on theories of measure and content, Lebesgue formulated his theory of measure in 1901. In 1902 he framed a new definition of the definite integral. This Lebesgue integral is one of the great achievements of modern real analysis. With Lebesgue integration, any bounded, summable function is the derivative of its indefinite integral, except perhaps for an ensemble of points with zero measure. Lebesgue integration was also instrumental in greatly expanding the scope of Fourier analysis.

In addition to about 50 papers, Lebesgue wrote two major books, *Leçons sur l'intégration et la recherche des fonctions primitives* (1904; "Lessons on Integration and Analysis of Primitive Functions") and *Leçons sur les séries trigonométriques* (1906; "Lessons on the Trigonometric Series").

Lebesgue integral, way of extending the concept of area inside a curve to include functions that do not have graphs representable pictorially. The graph of a function is defined as the set of all pairs of *x*- and *y*-values of the function. A graph can be represented pictorially if the function is piecewise continuous, which means that the interval over which it is defined can be divided into subintervals on which the function has no sudden jumps. Because the Riemann integral is based on the Riemann sums, which involve subintervals, a function not defined in this way will not be Riemann integrable.

For example, the function that equals 1 when x is rational and equals 0 when x is irrational has no interval in which it does not jump back and forth. Consequently, the Riemann sum $f(c_1)\Delta x_1 + f(c_2)\Delta x_2 + \ldots + f(c_n)\Delta x_n$ has no limit but can have different values depending upon where the points c are chosen from the subintervals Δx.

Lebesgue sums are used to define the Lebesgue integral of a bounded function by partitioning the y-values instead of the x-values as is done with Riemann sums. Associated with the partition $\{y_i\}$ $(= y_0, y_1, y_2, \ldots y_n)$ are the sets E_i composed of all x-values for which the corresponding y-values of the function lie between the two successive y-values y_{i-1} and y_i. A number is associated with these sets E_i, written as $m(E_i)$ and called the measure of the set, which is simply its length when the set is composed of intervals. The following sums, resembling the upper and lower Darboux sums (*see* Riemann sum), are then formed: $S = m(E_0)y_1 + m(E_1)y_2 + \ldots + m(E_{n-1})y_n$ and $s = m(E_0)y_0 + m(E_1)y_1 + \ldots + m(E_{n-1})y_{n-1}$. As the subintervals in the y-partition approach 0, these two sums approach a common value that is defined as the Lebesgue integral of the function.

The Lebesgue integral is the concept of the measure (*q.v.*) of the sets E_i in the cases in which these sets are not composed of intervals, as in the rational/irrational function above, which allows the Lebesgue integral to be more general than the Riemann integral.

Leblanc, Maurice, in full MAURICE-MARIE-ÉMILE LEBLANC (b. Dec. 11, 1864, Rouen, France—d. Nov. 6, 1941, Paris), French author and journalist, known as the creator of Arsène Lupin, French gentleman-thief turned detective, who is featured in more than 60 of Leblanc's crime novels and short stories.

Leblanc abandoned his law studies to become a pulp crime writer. Commissioned in 1905 to write a crime story for the French periodical *Je sais tout,* he created "L'Arrestation d'Arsène Lupin" ("The Arrest of Arsène Lupin") and achieved immediate and long-lasting popular success. His first collection of short stories appeared in 1907. Leblanc used as a recurrent element the suspicion that Lupin may not have reformed completely. Many of LeBlanc's stories were adapted into successful films in the 1930s; in some, Lupin was portrayed by John Barrymore.

LeBlanc was awarded the French Legion of Honour.

Leblanc, Nicolas (b. 1742?, Issoudun, France—d. Jan. 16, 1806, Saint-Denis), French surgeon and chemist who in 1790 developed the process for making soda ash (sodium carbonate) from common salt (sodium chloride). This process, which bears his name, became one of the most important industrial-chemical processes of the 19th century.

Leblanc was the son of the director of an ironworks. He received a medical education, and about 1780 he became a private surgeon to the Duke d'Orléans. Five years earlier the Academy of Sciences had offered a prize for a process to convert salt to soda ash. Extracted at that time by crude methods from wood or seaweed ashes, soda ash was used in making paper, glass, soap, and porcelain; if these industries were to expand, a cheaper process was needed. Because salt and soda ash are simple compounds of sodium, scientists correctly reasoned that transformation was possible.

In the Leblanc process, salt was treated with sulfuric acid to obtain salt cake (sodium sulfate). This was then roasted with limestone or chalk and coal to produce black ash, which consisted primarily of sodium carbonate and calcium sulfide. The sodium carbonate was dissolved in water and then crystallized.

The Leblanc process was simple, cheap, and direct, but because the French Revolution had begun by the time Leblanc completed his experiments in 1790, he never received his prize. The National Assembly awarded him a 15-year patent in September 1791 but confiscated his patent and factory three years later with only token compensation. Though Napoleon returned the factory about 1800, Leblanc was never able to raise enough capital to reopen it and died a suicide in 1806.

Leboeuf, Edmond (b. Dec. 5, 1809, Paris, France—d. June 7, 1888, Moncel-en-Trun), French general who was marshal of the Second Empire and minister of war in the crucial period at the opening of the Franco-German War.

Leboeuf studied at the École Polytechnique and participated in the Revolution of July 1830 that led to the accession of Louis-Philippe; subsequently, he served as an artillery officer in Algeria and distinguished himself in the siege of Constantine. Becoming a colonel in 1852 and a brigade general in 1854, he took part in the siege of Sevastopol during the Crimean War and was promoted to divisional general in December 1857. As commander in chief of the artillery detachments, he contributed greatly to the victory at Solferino during the Italian campaign against Austria in 1859.

After serving as aide-de-camp to Emperor Napoleon III, Leboeuf commanded the military camp at Châlons in 1868 and the VI Army Corps the following year. Appointed minister of war on Aug. 21, 1869, and marshal of France on March 24, 1870, he was confident of the abilities of French arms against the Prussians, but after the disastrous battles of Reichshoffen and Forbach in the Franco-German War, he resigned as minister of war and took to the field as commander of the III Army Corps. He fought well at Mars-la-Tour but was captured with the Metz garrison in October 1870. When the Germans released him, he went to The Hague but returned to France in 1873 to testify forcefully against Marshal Achille-François Bazaine, the commander of the main French armies in the war, in Bazaine's court-martial for treason.

Lebombo Mountains, also called LUBOMBO MOUNTAINS, long, narrow mountain range in South Africa, Swaziland, and Mozambique, southeastern Africa, about 500 miles (800 km) long and consisting of volcanic rocks. The mountains' name is derived from a Zulu word, Ubombo, that means "big nose." The mountains extend from south of the Mkuze River (KwaZulu/Natal province) north into Kruger National Park (Northern province). The Lebombo Mountains form the boundary between the province of KwaZulu/Natal, S.Af., and Swaziland, between Swaziland and Mozambique, and between Eastern Transvaal and Northern provinces, S.Af., and Mozambique, extending north of the Olifants River. The average elevation of the range is about 1,970 feet (600 m) above sea level; Mount Mananga, on the border between Eastern Transvaal province, S.Af., and Swaziland, rises to about 2,500 feet (760 m). A number of rivers, including the eastward-flowing Mkuze, Olifants, Pongola, Ingwavuma (Ngwavuma), and Usutu, cut their way through the range, and the latter two have formed especially spectacular gorges. An immense storage dam has been built in the Pongola gorge. The vegetation on the range is mostly tropical forest and savanna, with ironwood and ebony on the better-drained slopes. In the narrow ravines, tree growth is dense and includes the large khoya tree, which resembles mahogany.

Lebon, Philippe (b. May 29, 1767, Brachay, France—d. Dec. 2, 1804, Paris), French engineer and chemist, inventor of illuminating gas.

While employed as an engineer at Angoulême, Lebon was called to be professor of mechanics at the School of Bridges and Highways in Paris. In 1797 he began work that led to his invention of gas lighting and heating. His "thermolampe," which he patented and exhibited in 1799, burned gas distilled from wood. Invited to aid in preparations for the coronation of Napoleon I in 1804, he was murdered by prowlers on the day of the ceremony, according to the most common account of his mysterious death.

Lebon is also credited with having planned a gas motor that was provided with an electric fuel pump and spark ignition. He may also have been the first to suggest (1801) the value of compression of the charge in an internal-combustion engine.

Lebowa, former nonindependent black state that was in northern Transvaal, South Africa. The state was made up of two major and several minor exclaves (detached portions). It was designated by the South African government as the national territory for the northern Sotho people (Pedi, Lovedu, Kanga-Kone, and others).

A territorial assembly, established in 1962, was replaced by a legislative assembly in 1971. The following year Lebowa was granted self-government. Political parties became defined soon after the first election, held in 1973. The Lebowa People's Party, under Chief Minister C.N. Phatudi, controlled the legislative assembly, while the Lebowa National Party, led by M.M. Matlala, constituted the opposition. By 1978, Lebowa was the actual residence of more than half of South Africa's northern Sotho people, all of whom were legally Lebowa citizens. The new constitution of South Africa abolished apartheid, and in 1994 Lebowa became part of the new South African province of Northern.

Lebowakgomo, new town, Northern province, South Africa. It was the capital of the former nonindependent black state of Lebowa. Lebowakgomo lies southeast of Pietersburg. The town, established in 1974 with a population of only 115 inhabitants, was enlarged and developed in the early 1980s. The commercial establishments included bakeries, bottle stores, wood and coal yards, and butchering establishments. Industries at nearby Pietersburg, Potgietersrus, Tzaneen, and Phalaborwa employ a number of workers from Lebowakgomo. The lake called Chuniespoortdam supplies water to the town, which is linked by road to Pietersburg. Pop. (1985) 8,369.

Lebrija, city, Seville *provincia,* Andalusia *comunidad autónoma* ("autonomous community"), southwestern Spain. It is located south of the city of Seville in the lower basin of the Guadalquivir River. Founded as Nebritza by the Phoenicians, it was called Nebrixa by the Romans, Nebrisa by the Arabs, and Nebrija, or Lebrija, by the Spaniards, who reconquered it in 1249. Lebrija was the birthplace of the humanist scholar Elio Antonio de Nebrija, author of the first Castilian grammar, and of Juan Díaz de Solís, the first European to explore the Río de la Plata in South America.

The city's architecture reflects the Moorish influence in various Mozarabic temples, in the Church of Santa María de la Oliva (12th–16th century) with its early sculptures of Alonso Cano, and in the ruins of a Moorish castle. Lebrija markets local agricultural products (cereals, foodstuffs, meats) and exports aluminum silicate from nearby mines. Pop. (1991 prelim.) 28,597.

Lebrun, Albert (b. Aug. 29, 1871, Mercy-le-Haut, France—d. March 6, 1950, Paris), 14th and last president (1932–40) of France's Third Republic. During the first year of World War II, he sought to preserve French unity in the face of internal political dissension and the German military threat, but he failed to provide effective leadership.

Lebrun, a mining engineer, was educated at the Nancy Lycée, the École Polytechnique,

Albert Lebrun

By courtesy of the Bibliotheque Nationale, Paris

and the École Nationale Supérieure des Mines. He was elected deputy for Lorraine in 1900, senator in 1920, and president of the Senate in 1931. Other posts he held during that period included: minister of colonies (1911–13; 1913–14), of war (1913), and of blockade and of liberated regions (1917–19).

Lebrun, himself a moderate conservative, was elected president of the republic on May

10, 1932, largely as a compromise candidate acceptable to all factions. In his role as mediator and as a symbol of unity, Lebrun easily adapted to governments of both the right and the left, rarely exerting political influence on cabinet appointments or policy. On April 15, 1939, Lebrun was reelected president, only the second among the presidents of the Third Republic to be so honoured.

When Germany successfully invaded France early in World War II, Lebrun complied with the cabinet's decisions of June 1940 that led to the armistice with Germany, although he personally would have preferred heading a government-in-exile. In July, Lebrun acquiesced in the constitutional revisions at Vichy through which Marshal Philippe Pétain took over as head of state. Lebrun retired to Vizille near Grenoble and was later interned by the Germans at Itter in Tirol (1943–44). By acknowledging General Charles de Gaulle as head of the provisional government as the Allies liberated France, Lebrun ended his own political career. In his autobiography, *Témoignage* (1945; "Testimony"), he attempted to clarify the confusing events in which he had participated.

Lebrun, Charles (French painter): *see* Le Brun, Charles.

Lebrun, Charles-François, DUKE (duc) DE PLAISANCE, PRINCE DE L'EMPIRE (b. March 19, 1739, Saint-Sauveur-Lendelin, France—d. June 16, 1824, Saint-Mesmes), French politician who served as third consul from 1799 to 1804, as treasurer of Napoleon's empire from 1804 to 1814, and as governor-general of Holland from 1811 to 1813.

While he was a lawyer in Paris, Lebrun served as royal censor in 1766, and two years later he became inspector general of the crown lands. As secretary and protégé of the chancellor René-Nicolas de Maupeou, he assisted him in the judicial reforms of 1771, but after Maupeou fell out of favour, Lebrun occupied himself translating *Gerusalemme liberata* ("Jerusalem Delivered"), by the 16th-century Italian poet Torquato Tasso, and parts of the *Iliad.*

During the sessions of the Estates-General of 1789, Lebrun was deputy for the Third Estate of Dourdan, and after the Revolution he continued to represent Dourdan in the National Assembly. A moderate liberal, he was imprisoned by the left-wing Jacobins; but after the coup d'état of 9 Thermidor (July 27, 1794), which brought the Terror to an end, he represented the *département* of Seine-et-Oise in the Conseil des Anciens, one of the legislative chambers of the Directory. After Napoleon's coup d'état of 18 Brumaire (Nov. 9, 1799), Lebrun served as third consul, selected by Napoleon because his royalist sympathies would satisfy the conservatives. At the proclamation of the empire in May 1804, he was named *prince et archetrésorier* and instituted the Cours de Comptes, which became an important institution in French financial administration. From 1805 to 1806 he supervised the integration of Liguria into the French empire; although he disapproved of Napoleon's aristocracy, he reluctantly accepted the title Duke de Plaisance (Piacenza) in 1808. As governor-general of Holland, Lebrun ruled wisely and moderately, earning the title "le bon Stadhouder."

After Napoleon's abdication, Louis XVIII made him a peer of France. During the Hundred Days, however, after Napoleon returned from exile in Elba, Lebrun accepted the post of grand master of the University of Paris and was therefore excluded from the peerage after the return of the Bourbons in 1815. He was not reinstated until 1819. His *Memoires* were published posthumously in 1829.

Lebu, capital of Arauco *provincia,* Bío-Bío *región,* south-central Chile. It lies on the Pacific coast at the mouth of the Lebu River. Founded in 1739 but destroyed several times by Araucanian Indians, it became the provincial capital in 1875 and now serves an agricultural and mining hinterland.

The principal products of the locality are grains, legumes, livestock, and coal. A minor transportation hub, Lebu is a coal port and is linked by road and railroad to provincial towns and to Concepción, 65 miles (105 km) north. Tourism, based on nearby beaches, is an added source of income. The picturesque Lake Lanalhue is 39 miles (63 km) southeast. Pop. (1992) mun., 24,671.

Lecce, city, capital of Lecce *provincia,* Puglia (Apulia) *regione,* southeastern Italy. It lies on the Salentina peninsula, or "heel" of Italy, east of Taranto. Possibly built on the site of the ancient Roman town of Lupiae, Lecce was contested by the Byzantines, Lombards, and Saracens after the fall of the Roman Empire. It became a diocese in the 6th century and was captured and elevated to a countship by the Normans in the mid-11th century. The city passed in 1463 to the Aragonese kings of Naples, who fortified it.

The city's classical remains include an underground burial chamber of the 4th century BC and a Roman amphitheatre. Lecce flourished in the 16th and 17th centuries and has many examples of Apulian Baroque architecture; many of its buildings are built of the characteristic *pietra leccese,* a light yellow, easily worked limestone. The cathedral, the Basilica of Santa Croce, and the Church of SS. Niccolo e Cataldo are notable, all rebuilt in the Baroque style. Other fine Baroque buildings include the bishop's palace, the seminary, and the Palazzo della Prefettura, housing the provincial museum.

Lecce's industries include flour milling, wine and olive-oil processing, food canning, and the manufacture of pottery, glass, and papier-mâché religious objects and toys. Pop. (1993 est.) mun., 100,508.

Lecco, town, capital of Lecco *provincia,* Lombardia (Lombardy) *regione,* northern Italy. It lies at the southern end of the eastern arm of Lake Como, at the outflow of the Adda River. Earlier the seat of a marquessate, Lecco was granted to the bishops of Como in the 11th century and passed to Milan in the 12th century. It was fortified by the Visconti family in the 14th century and was an object of continuous contention until it became a countship in 1647. Little remains of its past except for the Ponte Grande, a bridge (1336–38; modernized) over the Adda; a tower from the former Castello Visconteo, housing the historical museum; and a 17th-century palace, housing the civic museum. There is a monument to Alessandro Manzoni, who took Lecco and its environs as the setting for his novel *I promessi sposi* (1825–27; *The Betrothed*).

Lecco is a tourist centre and has metallurgical, mechanical, textile, and food-canning industries. The local cheese market is noted for its Gorgonzola. Pop. (1993 est.) mun., 46,109.

lechatelierite, a natural silica glass (silicon dioxide, SiO_2) that has the same chemical composition as coesite, cristobalite, keatite, quartz, and tridymite but has a different crystal structure. Two varieties are included: meteoritic silica glass, produced when terrestrial silica is fused in the intense heat and pressure created by the impact of large meteorites; and fulgurite (*q.v.*), glass produced when silica is fused in the heat generated by a lightning strike. Tektites, tear-shaped meteoritic glass, the silica content of which is usually between 68 and 82 percent, often contain strings or grains of lechatelierite. Meteoritic silica glass has been found in and near large meteorite craters, as at Winslow, Ariz., in the United States, and not associated with particular craters but still with meteoritic impact, as in the Libyan Desert.

Lechitic languages: *see* Lekhitic languages.

Lechoń, Jan, pseudonym of LESZEK SERAFINOWICZ (b. March 13, 1899, Warsaw, Pol., Russian Empire—d. June 8, 1956, New York, N.Y., U.S.), poet, editor, diplomat, and political propagandist, considered one of the foremost Polish poets of his generation.

Lechoń's first volume, *Karmazynowy poemat* (1920; "The Scarlet Poem"), dealt with patriotic themes, followed by *Rzeczpospolita Babińska* (1921; "The Republic of Babin"). In 1924 he collected his lyric poems in *Srebrne i czarne* ("Silver and Black"). In 1926 he became editor of a satirical weekly, *Cyrulik Warszawski* ("The Barber of Warsaw"), and in 1932 was appointed cultural attaché to the Polish embassy in Paris, where he remained until France capitulated to the Nazis, when he escaped to Lisbon and finally to Rio de Janeiro.

In 1941 Lechoń went to New York City, where for four years he edited a Polish weekly. His *Lutnia po Bekwarku* ("Bekwark's Lute") appeared in 1942 in London; it was followed in 1945 by another volume of verses. Lechoń worked for Radio Free Europe from 1952 until his death by his own hand.

lechwe, antelope species of the genus *Kobus* (*q.v.*).

lecithin, also called PHOSPHATIDYL CHOLINE, any of a group of phospholipids (phosphoglycerides) that are important in cell structure and metabolism. Lecithins are composed of phosphoric acid, cholines, esters of glycerol, and two fatty acids; the chain length, position, and degree of unsaturation of these fatty acids vary, and this variation results in different lecithins with different biological functions. Pure lecithin is white and waxy and darkens when exposed to air. Commercial lecithin is brown to light yellow, and its consistency varies from plastic to liquid.

The term lecithin is also used for a mixture of phosphoglycerides containing principally lecithin, cephalin (specifically phosphatidyl ethanolamine), and phosphatidyl inositol. Commercial lecithin, most of which comes from soybean oil, contains this mixture and, commonly, about 35 percent neutral oil. It is widely used as a wetting and emulsifying agent and for other purposes. Among the products in which it is used are animal feeds, baking products and mixes, chocolate, cosmetics and soaps, dyes, insecticides, paints, and plastics.

Lecky, William Edward Hartpole (b. March 26, 1838, Newtown Park, near Dublin, Ire.—d. Oct. 22, 1903, London, Eng.), Irish historian of rationalism and European morals whose study of Georgian England became a classic.

Lecky was educated at Kingstown, Armagh, at Cheltenham, and at Trinity College, Dublin. His early works, *Religious Tendencies of the Age* (1860) and *Leaders of Public Opinion in Ireland* (1861), published anonymously, were the products of his eclectic reading while a student and had small success. He had been influenced by the theologian Richard Whately and the historian Henry Thomas Buckle; and his next book, the *History of Rationalism* (1865), while owing something to them, was welcomed by readers made familiar with evolutionary theory by Charles Darwin and the geologist Sir Charles Lyell. Lecky offered a broadly ranging narrative, showing the emergence of modern scientific thought and rational inquiry since the Middle Ages. The impression made by the considerable learning of this work was deepened by the appearance of its companion study, the two-volume *History of European Morals* (1869), which explored themes initiated in the former work—the declining sense of the miraculous, the aesthetic expressions of religious belief, and the complex relationship of society and morality. Pervading it was a desire to show the "natural causes" underlying the prevalence of certain theological and moral beliefs.

In 1871 he married Elizabeth van Dedem, lady-in-waiting to Queen Sophia of The Netherlands; but, while this involved him in social duties, it did not interrupt research upon his *History of England in the Eighteenth Century,* which appeared in 8 volumes (12 in the 1892 edition) from 1878 to 1890 to considerable praise. Lecky's claim to impartiality was not inconsistent with a desire to refute the very different views expressed by James Anthony Froude, particularly evident in the sections dealing with Ireland.

In 1892 Lecky declined the chair of modern history at the University of Oxford and entered politics, being elected in 1895 as a Liberal Unionist to represent Dublin University. His political philosophy is best represented by *Democracy and Liberty* (1896). He feared the advent of socialism as retrogressive and prophesied a new despotism of the state founded on nationalism and a mass franchise. In Parliament he supported ameliorative measures for Ireland but opposed Home Rule. He was made a privy councillor in 1897 and in 1902 received the Order of Merit.

"De," "la," and similar components of a name, when followed by a space, are alphabetized as separate words (e.g., *De Forest, Lee*). *When they are joined to the following part of a name, the combination is treated as a single word* (e.g., *DeForest, John William*).

Leclair, Jean-Marie, THE ELDER (b. May 10, 1697, Lyon—d. Oct. 22, 1764, Paris), French violinist and composer who established the classical French violin school that supplanted the earlier Italian school.

In 1722 Leclair was principal dancer and ballet master at Turin. After finishing his violin studies with G.B. Somis, he went to Paris

Leclair, engraving by Jean-Charles François, 1741
The Andre Meyer Collection—J.P. Ziolo

and began in 1728 a brilliant career as a violinist-composer. By 1732 he was the subject of an article in J.G. Walther's *Musicalisches Lexicon.*

He later became a musician of the royal chamber and visited several princely courts. Leclair, whose last years were clouded by despair and distrust, was murdered, possibly by his estranged wife.

He published four books of sonatas for violin and continuo, two books of sonatas for two unaccompanied violins, five sets of *Récréations* for two violins and continuo, and two sets of string concerti. He also wrote an opera, *Scylla et Glaucus.*

His brothers Jean-Marie Leclair the Younger (1703–77) and Pierre Leclair (1709–84) were also composers.

Leclanché, Georges (b. 1839, Paris—d. Sept. 14, 1882, Paris), French engineer who in about 1866 invented the battery that bears his name. In slightly modified form, the Leclanché battery, now called a dry cell, is produced in great quantities and is widely used in devices such as flashlights and portable radios.

After completing a technical education in 1860, Leclanché began work as an engineer. Six years later he developed his battery, which contained a conducting solution (electrolyte) of ammonium chloride, a negative terminal of zinc, and a positive terminal of manganese dioxide.

In 1867 he gave up his job to devote full time to his invention; a year later it was adopted by the telegraph service of Belgium. He subsequently opened a factory to produce the battery and other electric devices; the business was taken over by his brother Maurice upon Georges's death in 1882.

Leclerc, Charles (-Victor-Emmanuel) (b. March 17, 1772, Pontoise, Fr.—d. Nov. 2, 1802, Cap-Français, Saint-Domingue), French general, brother-in-law of Napoleon, who suppressed the Haitian revolt led by the former slave Toussaint-Louverture.

Leclerc joined the army in 1791 and distinguished himself at the siege of Toulon. It was in this campaign that he met Napoleon Bonaparte, who developed a great affection for him; Leclerc would serve Napoleon faithfully for the rest of his life. Leclerc was promoted to general after duty in Napoleon's Italian campaign. The relationship was further strengthened by Leclerc's marriage (1797) to Napoleon's sister, Pauline. In 1799 Leclerc played a decisive role in the coup that brought Napoleon to power.

After proving his abilities as a general both in the Egyptian campaign and in Germany (1800), Leclerc was sent by Napoleon to subdue the rebellion in Haiti, at that time known as Saint-Domingue. Leclerc, accompanied by 45,000 of the best French troops, landed in Haiti in 1802 and soon took possession of most of the island and made peace with the rebel leaders Henri Christophe, Toussaint-Louverture, and Jean-Jacques Dessalines. By treachery, Leclerc captured Toussaint-Louverture and sent him to France. This and Napoleon's restoration of slavery on Guadeloupe touched off renewed fighting with the black rebels and at a time when Leclerc's army was decimated by a yellow fever epidemic. Leclerc himself succumbed in November and the blacks then resumed the offensive under Christophe and Dessalines. Within a year the French were driven from the island.

Leclerc, Georges-Louis (French naturalist): *see* Buffon, Georges-Louis Leclerc, comte de.

Leclerc, Jacques-Philippe, byname of PHILIPPE-MARIE, VISCOMTE (viscount) DE HAUTECLOCQUE, also called (from 1945) JACQUES-PHILIPPE LECLERC DE HAUTECLOCQUE (b. Nov. 22, 1902, Belloy-Saint-Leonard, Fr.—d. Nov. 28, 1947, Colomb-Bechar, Alg.), French general and war hero who achieved fame as the liberator of Paris.

Born into a patrician family, he graduated from the prestigious military schools Saint-Cyr (1924) and Saumur. In 1939, as a captain of infantry, he was wounded and captured by the Germans, but he managed to escape to England. Upon hearing that Gen. Charles de Gaulle was rallying Free French forces from London, he took the pseudonym Leclerc (so as to spare his family in France any reprisals) and joined de Gaulle. Promoted to colonel by de Gaulle, he achieved a number of military victories in French Equatorial Africa. After being promoted to general, he staged a spectacular 1,000-mile march from Chad to Tripoli in Libya to join the forces of the British Eighth Army, capturing Italian garrisons along the way.

He took part in the Normandy invasion of 1944 as commander of a French armoured division. On August 25, the commander of the German garrison in Paris surrendered to Leclerc and on Aug. 26, 1944, Leclerc and de Gaulle entered Paris in triumph. Leclerc liberated Strasbourg (Nov. 23, 1944) and then led his men on into Germany, capturing Berchtesgaden. In July 1945, Leclerc was named commander of the French Expeditionary Force to the Far East. That same year, he legally changed his name from Philippe-Marie, vicomte de Hautecloque, to Jacques-Philippe Leclerc de Hautecloque, using his wartime pseudonym.

In March 1946 Leclerc was sent to French-occupied Indochina. Perceiving that the nature of the problems there was more political than military and arousing controversy with that message in France, he resigned his post and took over in July 1946 as inspector-general of the French forces stationed in North Africa. He was killed in an airplane accident. The nation named him posthumously marshal of France.

Leclerc, Jean, Latin JOHANNES CLERICUS (b. March 19, 1657, Geneva—d. Jan. 8, 1736, Amsterdam), encyclopaedist and biblical scholar who espoused advanced principles of exegesis (interpretation) and theological method.

Educated at Geneva and also in France at Grenoble and Saumur (all noted for a radical approach to biblical and patristic documents), Leclerc broke with scholastic Calvinism. In 1684 he was appointed to the Remonstrant Seminary faculty at Amsterdam. He made a lasting contribution to biblical studies as editor of three encyclopaedias: *Bibliothèque universelle et historique* (26 vol., 1686–93), *Bibliothèque choisie* (28 vol., 1703–13), and *Bibliothèque ancienne et moderne* (29 vol., 1714–30). His views on the Scriptures included the denial of Mosaic authorship of the Pentateuch as well as of the divine inspiration of Ecclesiastes, Job, Proverbs, and the Song of Solomon.

In addition to *Harmonia Evangelica* (1699), Leclerc also wrote commentaries on the Pentateuch (1699), a translation of the New Testament (1703), and commentaries on other Old Testament books.

Lecocq, (Alexandre) Charles (b. June 3, 1832, Paris—d. October 24, 1918, Paris), one of the principal French composers of operettas after Offenbach, especially known for his *La Fille de Madame Angot.*

Lecocq studied at the Paris Conservatoire under François Bazin, Fromental Halévy, and François Benoist. His first operetta, *Le Docteur Miracle* (1857), written for a competition organized by Offenbach, shared the prize with a setting of the same libretto by Bizet. He produced six one-act operettas, but his first real success was the three-act *Fleur de thé* (1868). Eleven operettas followed, including *Les Cent*

Lecocq
H. Roger-Viollet

Vierges (1872) and *La Fille de Madame Angot* (1872). The last was performed in Europe and the U.S., and in 1947 some of the music was arranged by Gordon Jacob as a ballet, *Mam'zelle Angot*. Lecocq also wrote polkas, mazurkas, schottisches, and other dances and five volumes of songs. He kept alive the spirit of Offenbach in the French operetta, adapting it to the more sober style of light opera prevalent after the Franco-German war.

Lecompton Constitution (1857), instrument framed in Lecompton, Kan., by Southern pro-slavery advocates of Kansas statehood. It contained clauses protecting slaveholding and a bill of rights excluding free blacks, and it added to the frictions leading up to the U.S. Civil War. Though it was rejected in a territorial election (January 1858), Pres. James Buchanan subsequently recommended statehood for Kansas under its provisions. Congress balked, and a compromise was offered calling for resubmission of the constitution to the territory's voters. Kansas again rejected it the following August and was admitted to the Union as a free state on Jan. 29, 1861.

Leconte de Lisle, Charles-Marie-René (b. Oct. 22, 1818, Saint-Paul, Réunion—d. July 17, 1894, Louveciennes, near Paris), poet, leader of the Parnassians, who from 1865 to 1895 was acknowledged as the foremost French poet apart from the aging Victor Hugo.

Leconte de Lisle's theories, reacting against Romanticism and stressing the need for impersonality and discipline in poetry, were expressed with deliberate provocativeness and exaggeration. His epic poetry is often overweighted by erudition and ornamentation, but his shorter poems convey a compelling and individual vision, and "Qaïn" (1869; "Cain") is one of the most impressive short epics of the 19th century.

Leconte de Lisle was sent to the Université de Rennes in 1837 but gave up law for literature. Recalled to Réunion by his family, he remained unwillingly on the island from 1843 to 1846, when he returned to France to work on *La Démocratie pacifique*, a daily journal that propagated the utopian social theories of Charles Fourier. In the poems of the next few years he drew on Greek mythology for symbols of his Revolutionary views; he wrote political articles and unsuccessfully attempted practical work for the February Revolution of 1848. Later, while remaining a republican, he became convinced that the poet should not engage in direct political action.

His first volume of poetry was published in 1852. He eventually arranged the poems, which had appeared in different collections during his lifetime, to form *Poèmes antiques*, *Poèmes barbares*, and *Poèmes tragiques*. *Derniers poèmes* was published in 1895.

He spent most of his life in financial need, attempting to support his mother, sisters, and wife by his writings. He published a series of translations from Greek and Latin; three anticlerical and republican booklets (1871–72); and, under the pseudonym Pierre Gosset, *Histoire du Moyen Âge* (1876). In 1873 he obtained a sinecure as librarian of the Senate and in 1886 was elected to succeed Hugo as a member of the Académie Française.

At the centre of Leconte de Lisle's poetry is a sense of the impermanence of a vast and pitiless universe. Influenced by the new study of comparative religion and by contemporary scientific discoveries, his epics show the death of religions and civilizations—Greek, Indian, Celtic, Scandinavian, Polynesian, Jewish, and Christian. Some of Leconte de Lisle's finest poems describe scenes of cosmic destruction with exultation rather than terror. They assert that, in the face of the cruel forces that create and destroy an ephemeral world, the poet must savour the more sharply its rich physical beauty.

Lecoq de Boisbaudran, Paul-Émile (b. April 18, 1838, Cognac, Fr.—d. May 28, 1912, Paris), French chemist who developed improved spectroscopic techniques for chemical analysis and discovered the elements gallium (1875), samarium (1880), and dysprosium (1886).

In 1858 Lecoq de Boisbaudran began working in the family wine business, though he pursued scientific studies in his spare time. He took up the study of spectroscopic analysis and began a search for new elements in 1859. In 1869 Mendeleyev published his periodic table, from which he predicted the existence and properties of several unknown elements, including one he called eka-aluminum. When Lecoq de Boisbaudran discovered gallium, he found it had the predicted properties of eka-aluminum, and thus it was the first of Mendeleyev's elements to be uncovered. His discovery paved the way for the general acceptance of the periodic table.

Lecouvreur, Adrienne (b. April 5, 1692, Damery, Fr.—d. March 20, 1730, Paris), leading French actress whose life inspired a tragic drama a century after her death.

At the age of 14 she participated in an amateur performance of Pierre Corneille's *Polyeucte*. She then received instruction in acting from the actor-manager Paul Legrand and as a professional actress was first seen on the stage at Lille. On May 14, 1717, she made

Adrienne Lecouvreur, lithograph by C. Motte after a drawing by P. Vigneron

By courtesy of the Bibliotheque de l'Arsenal, Paris; photograph, J.E. Bulloz

her debut at the Comédie-Française in Prosper Jolyot Crébillon's *Électre*. To this role, to the Monime in Jean Racine's *Mithridate*, and to the Angélique in Molière's *George Dandin*, she brought a naturalness and simplicity not characteristic of the style of acting then current; this factor, combined with her beauty and charm, made her extraordinarily popular.

Lecouvreur found a friend and teacher in the celebrated actor Michel Baron, who in 1720 returned to the stage at the age of 67, and she was admired by Voltaire. After 1721 she was the mistress of Maurice Saxe, who abandoned her some time before her death. She died in her prime and, not having renounced acting as a profession, was refused Christian burial. Though Lecouvreur enacted comedy parts with spirit and intelligence, her real domain was tragic acting. The more sensational aspects of her life were exploited by Eugène Scribe and Ernest Legouvé in their play *Adrienne Lecouvreur* (1849), which is unsatisfactory as biography but provided a leading role played by Rachel and later by Sarah Bernhardt. Jack Richtman's *Adrienne Lecouvreur: The Actress and the Age* (1971) throws new light on her death.

lectionary, in Christianity, a book containing portions of the Bible appointed to be read on particular days of the year. The word is also used for the list of such Scripture lessons. The early Christians adopted the Jewish custom of reading extracts from the Old Testament on the sabbath. They soon added extracts from the writings of the Apostles and Evangelists. During the 3rd and 4th centuries, several systems of lessons were devised for churches of various localities. One of the first attempts for a diocese to fix definite readings for special seasons during the year was made by Musaeus of Marseille in the mid-5th century.

At first, the lessons were marked off in the margins of manuscripts of the Scriptures. Later, special lectionary manuscripts were prepared, containing in proper sequence the appointed passages. The Greek Church developed two forms of lectionaries, one (*Synaxarion*) arranged in accord with the ecclesiastical year and beginning with Easter, the other (*Mēnologion*) arranged according to the civil year (beginning September 1) and commemorating the festivals of various saints and churches. Other national churches produced similar volumes. Among the Western churches during the medieval period the ancient usage at Rome prevailed, with its emphasis on Advent.

During the 16th-century Reformation the Lutherans and Anglicans made changes in the Roman Catholic lectionaries. Luther was dissatisfied with the choice of many of the lessons from the letters in the Roman system, and he included a greater proportion of doctrinal passages. In the Anglican Church, the first edition of *The Book of Common Prayer* assigned for each day a passage of the Old Testament and the New Testament to be read at both the morning and evening services. Nearly all the saints' days were dropped, and the new system assigned chapters of the Bible to be read consecutively. Present-day liturgists in many denominations have been active in revising traditional lectionary systems.

Consult the INDEX *first*

lectisternium (from Latin *lectum sternere*, "to spread a couch"), ancient Greek and Roman rite in which a meal was offered to gods and goddesses whose representations were laid upon a couch positioned in the open street. On the first occasion of the rite, which originated in Greece, couches were prepared for three pairs of gods: Apollo and Latona, Hercules and Diana, Mercury and Neptune. The feast, lasting for seven or eight days, was also celebrated by private individuals; the citizens kept open house, debtors and prisoners were released, and everything was done to banish sorrow. In later times, similar honours were paid to other divinities. The rite largely replaced the old Roman *epulum* and *daps*, in which the god was not visibly represented. In Christian times, the word was used for a feast in memory of the dead.

lector, also called READER, in Christianity, a person chosen or set apart to read Holy Scripture in the church services. In the Eastern Orthodox churches lector is one of the minor orders in preparation for the priesthood. Although formerly a minor order in the Roman Catholic Church, the office was named a ministry by Pope Paul VI in a *motu proprio* (initiated by the Pope without advice, effective Jan. 1, 1973) and was opened to laymen. Officially this ministry is reserved to men, although in practice women may serve as lectors without being formally installed in the ministry.

In Protestant churches the person who functions as a reader, either lay or clergy, is generally called a lector.

Leda, in Greek legend, usually believed to be the daughter of Thestius, king of Aetolia, and wife of Tyndareus, king of Lacedaemon. Some ancient writers thought she was the mother by Tyndareus of Clytemnestra, wife of King Agamemnon, and of Castor, one of the Heavenly Twins. She was also believed to have been the mother (by Zeus, who had approached her in the form of a swan) of the other twin, Pollux, and of the Trojan Helen, both of whom hatched from eggs. Variant legends gave divine parentage to both the twins and possibly also to Clytemnestra, with all three of them having hatched from the eggs of Leda, while yet other legends say that Leda bore the twins to her mortal husband, Tyndareus. Still other variants say that Leda may have hatched out Helen from an egg laid by the goddess Nemesis, who was similarly approached by Zeus in the form of a swan. In any case, the divine swan's encounter with Leda was a subject depicted by both ancient Greek and Italian Renaissance artists; Leonardo da Vinci undertook a painting (now lost) of the theme, and Correggio's "Leda" (*c.* 1530s) is a well-known treatment of the subject.

Ledbetter, Huddie (musician): *see* Leadbelly.

Ledebour, Georg (b. March 7, 1850, Hannover, Hanover [Germany]—d. March 31, 1947, Bern, Switz.), German socialist politician who was radicalized by the outbreak of war in 1918 and became a leader of the Berlin communist uprising of January 1919.

A Social Democrat member of the Reichstag (national parliament) from 1900, Ledebour initially stood among the left centrists of his party. With the outbreak of World War I, however, he formed, with his fellow socialist Hugo Haase, a solitary opposition to the voting of German war credits (August 1914) and later, again with Haase, led other party dissidents in the formation of the Independent Social Democratic Party (1917). A leading proponent of political and social revolution during the closing weeks of the war, he headed, with Karl Liebknecht, the revolutionary committee that in January 1919 directed the abortive communist uprising in Berlin. Subsequently, as a member of the Weimar Reichstag (1920–24), he was the head of a small independent faction. In 1931 Ledebour joined the Socialist Workers' Party, but he emigrated from Germany when the National Socialists came to power in 1933.

Lederberg, Joshua (b. May 23, 1925, Montclair, N.J., U.S.), American geneticist, pioneer in the field of bacterial genetics, who shared the 1958 Nobel Prize for Physiology or Medicine (with George W. Beadle and Edward L. Tatum) for discovering the mechanisms of genetic recombination in bacteria.

Lederberg
By courtesy of Stanford University, Stanford, Calif.

Lederberg studied under Tatum at Yale (Ph.D., 1948) and taught at the University of Wisconsin (1947–59), where he established a department of medical genetics. In 1959 he joined the faculty of the Stanford Medical School, serving as director of the Kennedy Laboratories of Molecular Medicine there from 1962 to 1978, when he moved to New York City to become president of Rockefeller University.

With Tatum he published "Gene Recombination in *Escherichia coli*" (1946), in which he reported that the mixing of two different strains of a bacterium resulted in genetic recombination between them and thus to a new, crossbred strain of the bacterium. While biologists who had not previously believed that "sex" existed in bacteria such as *E. coli* were still confirming Lederberg's discovery, he and his student Norton D. Zinder reported another and equally surprising finding. In the paper "Genetic Exchange in *Salmonella*" (1952), they revealed that certain viruses were capable of carrying a bacterial gene from one bacterium to another, a phenomenon they termed transduction. Lederberg's discoveries made bacteria as important a tool of genetic research as the fruit fly *Drosophila* and the bread mold *Neurospora*. He also developed ingenious breeding techniques in bacterial genetics.

Lederman, Leon Max (b. July 15, 1922, New York City), American physicist who, along with Melvin Schwartz and Jack Steinberger, received the Nobel Prize for Physics in 1988 for their joint research on neutrinos.

Lederman was educated at the City College of New York (B.S., 1943) and received his Ph.D. in physics from Columbia University, New York City, in 1951. He joined the faculty at Columbia that same year and became a full professor there in 1958. He was director of the Fermi National Accelerator Laboratory in Batavia, Ill., from 1979 to 1989.

From 1960 to 1962, Lederman, together with his fellow Columbia University researchers Schwartz and Steinberger, collaborated in an important experiment at the Brookhaven National Laboratory on Long Island, N.Y. There they used a particle accelerator to produce the first laboratory-made beam of neutrinos—elusive subatomic particles that have no detectable mass and no electric charge and that travel at the speed of light. It was already known that when neutrinos interact with matter, either electrons or electron-like particles known as muons (mu mesons) are created. It was not known, however, whether this indicated the existence of two distinct types of neutrinos. The three scientists' work at Brookhaven established that the neutrinos that produced muons were indeed a distinct (and previously unknown) type of neutrino, one which the scientists named muon neutrinos. The discovery of muon neutrinos subsequently led to the recognition of a number of different "families" of subatomic particles, and this eventually resulted in the standard model, a scheme that has been used to classify all known elementary particles.

Ledo Road (Burma): *see* Stilwell Road.

Ledoux, Claude-Nicolas (b. March 21, 1736, Dormans-sur-Marne, Fr.—d. Nov. 19, 1806, Paris), French architect who developed an eclectic and visionary architecture linked with nascent pre-Revolutionary social ideals.

Ledoux studied under J.-F. Blondel and L.-F. Trouard. His imaginative woodwork at a café brought him to the notice of society, and he soon became a fashionable architect. In the 1760s and early '70s he designed many private houses in an innovative Neoclassical style for the higher social circles in France. Among such few surviving works are the Pavilion Hocquart (1764–70), the Château de Bénouville, Normandy (1770), and the famous chateau for Madame du Barry at Louveciennes (1771–73).

In the mid-1770s Ledoux took on the planning for a new saltworks and its surrounding town at the Salines de Chaux, at Arc-et-Senans. He devised a radial concentric plan for the settlement, with rings of workers' dwellings enclosing a central salt-extraction factory. Less than half of the project was completed, but the remaining structures show Ledoux's striking simplifications of cubes and cylinders to create squat, massive, boldly rusticated (roughhewn) versions of classical building types. His layout of the town to both facilitate economic production and ensure healthy and happy conditions for the workers anticipated similar planning efforts by Robert Owen and other 19th-century Utopian socialists.

The Director's Pavillion, salt mines at Arc-et-Senans, near Besançon, Fr., by Ledoux, 1773–75
By courtesy of the Caisse Nationale des Monuments Historiques, Paris

Ledoux's Theatre of Besançon (1771–73) was a revolutionary design in its provision of seats for the ordinary public as well as for the upper classes. The private houses he designed in the 1780s had brilliantly eccentric features, including odd layouts, discontinuous elevations, and a striking use of Doric architectural elements. Ledoux's most important public project in the last phase of his career was to design 60 tollhouses situated at the city gates of Paris. He turned what might have been modest customs offices into a series of monumental gates and other structures called the Portes de Paris. Of the 50 such tollhouses, or *barrières,* actually built (1785–89) in the four years preceding the French Revolution, only four, including the famous Barrière de la Villette, still survive. In the *barrières* Ledoux took his interest in squat, colossal geometric forms to its furthest extent, fashioning rotundas, Greek temples, porticoes, and vaulted apses with rusticated masonry and Doric columns. The cost of these buildings proved ruinous to the public treasury, however, and he was dismissed from his project in 1789. Many of the *barrières* were subsequently torn down by mobs of resentful taxpayers during the Revolution. Ledoux himself was arrested during the Terror, and this event and the deaths of several members of his family ended his active career as an architect. After his release he spent his last years writing and compiling *L'architecture considérée sous le rapport de l'art, des moeurs et de la législation* (1804; "Architecture Considered with Respect to Art, Customs, and Legislation"), which contains his own engravings of his works.

Ledoux was the most prolific, productive, and original architect of late 18th-century France. The powerful and brilliantly simplified geometry of his buildings held little appeal for the following generations, however, and wholesale demolitions and vandalism during the 19th century have left only a handful of his works still standing.

Ledru-Rollin, Alexandre-Auguste (b. Feb. 2, 1807, Paris—d. Dec. 31, 1874, Fontenay-aux-Roses, Fr.), French lawyer whose radical political activity earned him a prominent position in the French Second Republic; he helped bring about universal male suffrage in France.

Called to the bar in 1829, Ledru-Rollin established his reputation by his defense of republicans charged with political offenses. He also began a notable contribution to French jurisprudence with his edition of the *Journal du Palais,* 27 vol. (1791–1837; "Journal of the Palace of Justice"), later (1837–47) to be supplemented by 17 volumes and by the *Répertoire général de la jurisprudence française,* 8 vol. (1843–48; "General Repertoire of French Law").

Alexandre-Auguste Ledru-Rollin, detail of a portrait by Angélique Mongez, 1853; in the collection of the Bibliothèque Nationale, Paris
By courtesy of the Bibliotheque Nationale, Paris

He was elected to the Chamber of Deputies in 1839 on a platform calling for universal suffrage and popular sovereignty. In the legislature his continued insistence on the need for a republican form of government left him isolated from other leftists.

Upon the outbreak of the Revolution of 1848, Ledru-Rollin proclaimed his support for a republic and joined the provisional government set up after the abdication of Louis-Philippe. He became minister of the interior, and through his influence the elections for a new legislature were held under universal manhood suffrage. In May 1848 Ledru-Rollin opposed the revolutionary extremists who were attempting to set up a new government. This lost him a great deal of working-class support.

In June 1849 Ledru-Rollin attacked the new president, Louis-Napoléon, whose impeachment he demanded on June 11. Two days later Ledru-Rollin headed a demonstration that ended as an attempted insurrection. After heading a provisional government for two hours, he fled to England, where he wrote a great many revolutionary pamphlets. Under the full general amnesty of 1870, Ledru-Rollin returned to France. An edition of his speeches and political writings appeared in 1879.

Ledyard, John (b. 1751, Groton, Conn. [U.S.]—d. Jan. 10, 1789, Cairo, Egypt), American adventurer and explorer who accompanied Captain James Cook on his voyage to find a Northwest Passage to the Orient (1776–79).

After trying the life of a missionary among the North American Indians, Ledyard shipped out as a common seaman (1774). In the course of his voyage with Cook, Ledyard developed what was to become a lifelong interest in establishing a lucrative fur trade with China. After numerous efforts to secure financial support for his proposals proved futile, Ledyard conceived the daring scheme of attracting interest in the commercial possibilities of the Pacific Northwest by walking eastward across Russia (including Siberia), crossing the Bering Strait, and then continuing on foot across the North American continent. He set out from St. Petersburg in September 1787 and by the following February had gotten as far as Irkutsk, where he was arrested and ordered out of the country. Ledyard's last adventure was an expedition into Africa in search of the source of the Niger River, but he got no farther than Cairo before he died.

Lee, Ann, byname MOTHER ANN (b. Feb. 29, 1736, Manchester, Eng.—d. Sept. 8, 1784, Watervliet, N.Y., U.S.), religious leader who brought the Shaker sect from England to the American Colonies.

The daughter of a blacksmith, she was a factory worker who in 1758 joined the Shaking Quakers, a radical offshoot of the Quakers. She married in 1762, an unhappy union that probably influenced her later doctrinal insistence on celibacy.

In 1770, during a period of religious persecution by the English authorities, she was imprisoned and while in jail became convinced of the truth of certain religious ideas perceived in a vision. She came to believe that only through celibacy could men and women further Christ's kingdom on Earth. Four years later, commanded as the result of another vision, Lee persuaded her husband, brother, and six other followers to emigrate to America. There, her followers founded a settlement near Albany (in present-day New York state). The Shaker movement began to spread throughout New England to embrace thousands. Mother Ann, as she came to be known, was believed to have ushered in the millennium, for the Shakers asserted that as Christ had embodied the masculine half of God's dual nature, so she embodied the female half.

In 1780 Mother Ann was imprisoned for treason because of her pacifist doctrines and her refusal to sign an oath of allegiance. She was soon released and in 1781–83 toured New England. According to witnesses, she performed a number of miracles, including healing the sick by touch. *See also* Shaker.

Lee, Arthur (b. Dec. 21, 1740, Westmoreland county, Va. [U.S.]—d. Dec. 12, 1792, Middlesex county, Va., U.S.), diplomat who sought recognition and aid in Europe for the Continental Congress during the American Revolution.

Lee gave up a medical practice for the study of law and then became interested in colonial politics. He wrote political tracts, among them a series of 10 essays called "The Monitor's Letters" in the *Virginia Gazette* in 1768. In 1770 he became an agent for the colony of Massachusetts, and in 1776 he, Benjamin Franklin, and Silas Deane were appointed commissioners to negotiate an alliance with France and to solicit aid from other European governments. Important treaties of commerce were signed with France in 1778; however, Lee's quarrels with his associates led to the recall of Lee and Deane to the United States. He was elected to the Virginia House of Delegates in 1781 and served as a delegate to the Continental Congress (1782–84). He was on the U.S. Treasury Board (1785–89). After the adoption (1789) of the federal Constitution, which he opposed, he retired to Landsdowne, his Virginia estate.

Lee, David M., in full DAVID MORRIS LEE (b. Jan. 20, 1931, Rye, N.Y., U.S.), American physicist who, with Robert C. Richardson and Douglas D. Osheroff, was awarded the Nobel Prize for Physics in 1996 for their joint discovery of superfluidity in the isotope helium-3.

Lee received a bachelor's degree from Harvard University in 1952 and a Ph.D. in physics from Yale University in 1959. He joined the faculty of Cornell University (Ithaca, N.Y.) in 1959, becoming a full professor there in 1968. Lee and Richardson built a special cooling apparatus for their research in the low-temperature laboratory at Cornell. They discovered superfluidity in helium-3 by accident in 1972. They had cooled that compound to within a few thousandths of a degree above absolute zero (−273° C) when Osheroff, a graduate student working with them, noticed odd changes in the sample's internal pressure. The team eventually determined that these deviations marked helium-3's phase transition to superfluidity. Because the atoms in superfluid helium-3 move in a coordinated manner, that substance lacks all internal friction and flows without resistance. Helium-3 in this state behaves according to quantum mechanical laws. The discovery of superfluidity in helium-3 enabled scientists to study directly in macroscopic (visible) systems the strange quantum mechanical effects that previously could only be studied indirectly in molecules, atoms, and subatomic particles.

Lee, Gypsy Rose, original name ROSE LOUISE HOVICK (b. Jan. 9, 1914, Seattle, Wash., U.S.—d. April 26, 1970, Los Angeles, Calif.), American striptease artist, a witty and sophisticated entertainer who was one of the first burlesque artists to imbue a striptease with grace and style.

Lee's stage-mother manager, Madam Rose, put her daughters Rose (Gypsy) and June on stage at lodge benefits. Later, without June, Gypsy became the star of Madam Rose's Dancing Daughters. She made her debut in burlesque in Kansas City in 1929. Within two years she was the headliner at Billy Minsky's Republic Theatre on Broadway. In 1936 Lee appeared in the *Ziegfeld Follies.* When New York's burlesque houses were closed the following year, she went to Hollywood to appear in a series of motion pictures. She starred in *The Streets of Paris* at the New York World's Fair (1940), was featured in the musical play *Star and Garter* (1942), and appeared in nightclubs and on television. She published an autobiography, *Gypsy* (1957), which was the basis for the musical play (1959) and motion picture (1962) of that name.

Gypsy Rose Lee, 1944
By courtesy of United Artists Corporation; photograph, from the Museum of Modern Art Film Stills Achive, New York

Lee, Harper, in full NELLE HARPER LEE (b. April 28, 1926, Monroeville, Ala., U.S.), American writer nationally acclaimed for her one novel, *To Kill a Mockingbird* (1960).

Related to Robert E. Lee's family, Harper Lee was the daughter of a lawyer apparently rather like the hero-father of her novel in his sound citizenship and warmheartedness. Lee attended the University of Alabama (spending a year as exchange student at Oxford University) but left for New York City before obtaining her own law degree. In New York she worked as an airlines reservationist but soon received financial aid from friends that allowed her to write full-time. With the help of an editor, she transformed a series of short stories into *To Kill a Mockingbird.*

The narrator of the novel is lawyer Atticus Finch's six-year-old daughter "Scout." Scout and her brother Jem learn the principles of racial justice and social tolerance from their father, whose just and compassionate acts include an unpopular defense of a black man falsely accused of raping a white girl. They also develop tolerance and the strength to follow their convictions in their acquaintance and eventual friendship with a recluse who has been demonized by the community. *To Kill a Mockingbird* received a Pulitzer Prize in 1961. Criticism of its tendency to sermonize has been matched by praise of its insight and stylistic effectiveness. It became a memorable film in 1962 and was filmed again in 1997.

Lee remained in her hometown of Monroeville. In addition to her novel she wrote a few short essays, including the 1983 "Romance and High Adventure," devoted to Alabama history.

Lee, Henry, byname LIGHT-HORSE HARRY LEE (b. Jan. 29, 1756, Prince William county, Va. [U.S.]—d. March 25, 1818, Cumberland Island, Ga., U.S.), American cavalry officer during the American Revolution. He was the father of Robert E. Lee and the author of the resolution passed by Congress upon the death of George Washington containing the celebrated apothegm "first in war, first in peace, and first in the hearts of his countrymen."

Henry Lee, portrait by Gilbert Stuart; in a private collection

By courtesy of Carter Lee Refo, Richmond, Va.

A graduate of the College of New Jersey (now Princeton University), Lee joined Washington's army immediately upon the outbreak of the American Revolution (1775–83). In 1778 he advanced to the rank of major and commanded three troops of cavalry and three companies of infantry with which he won notable engagements and gained his nickname. His storming of Paulus Hook, N.J. (Aug. 19, 1779), won praise from Washington, and as a lieutenant colonel of dragoons in the Southern theatre (1780–81) he added further lustre to his name.

After the war Lee served in the Virginia legislature (1785–88; 1789–91), in the Congress under the Articles of Confederation (1785–88), in the Virginia Convention of 1788 that ratified the federal Constitution, and as governor of the state (1791–94). In 1794 his political career was interrupted while he commanded the army assembled to put down the Whiskey Rebellion, an uprising of farmers resisting the federal whiskey tax, in western Pennsylvania. From 1799 to 1801 he served in the U.S. House of Representatives.

After 1800 he became involved in unfortunate land speculation and was twice imprisoned for debt. In 1812 he was badly crippled in a Baltimore riot while defending the editor of an antiwar newspaper. The next year he went to the West Indies for his health, although some said he had gone to escape his creditors. He died while returning home.

Lee was the author of *Memoirs of the War in the Southern Department of the United States,* published in 1812 and reprinted in 1869 with a biographical sketch by Robert E. Lee.

Lee, Ivy Ledbetter (b. July 16, 1877, Cedartown, Ga., U.S.—d. Nov. 9, 1934, New York, N.Y.), American pioneer of 20th-century public-relations methods, who persuaded various business clients to woo public opinion.

A graduate of Princeton University, Lee worked as a newspaper reporter in New York City from 1899 to 1903. In 1906 he became press representative for a group of coal miners, and in 1912 he began representing the Pennsylvania Railroad Company. By 1917 he had acquired a string of powerful clients, including the Rockefeller interests. Lee's greatest innovation was his frank, open policy toward the press.

Lee's clients included the American Red Cross during World War I, the German dye trust in the early Nazi era, and the American-Russian Chamber of Commerce in the era when the Soviet Union was striving for U.S. recognition.

Lee, Mary Ann (b. 1823, Philadelphia, Pa., U.S.—d. 1899), one of the first American ballet dancers. Her 10-year career included the first American performance of the classic ballet *Giselle* (Boston, 1846).

Lee made her debut in 1837 in *The Maid of Cashmere* (an English version of Auber's opera-ballet *Le Dieu et la Bayadère*). After several tours of the United States, Lee studied at the Paris Opéra with Jean Coralli, the principal choreographer of *Giselle,* and returned to tour the United States with the dancer George Washington Smith. Together they presented authentic productions of *Giselle, La Fille du Danube,* and other ballets. Lee's health began to fail in 1846, and she retired the following year at the age of 24.

Lee, Nathaniel (b. 1649?—buried May 6, 1692, London, Eng.), English playwright whose heroic plays were popular but marred by extravagance. Lee's earliest play, *Nero,* was performed in 1674. A blank-verse tragedy, *The Rival Queens* (1677), made his reputation; it remained popular until the 19th century. *Lucius Junius Brutus* (1680) was prohibited for antimonarchical sentiments. Lee collaborated with John Dryden in *Oedipus* (1678) and *The Duke of Guise* (1682).

Lee, Richard Henry (b. Jan. 20, 1732, Stratford, Va. [U.S.]—d. June 19, 1794, Chantilly, Va., U.S.), American statesman.

Richard Henry Lee, portrait by Charles Willson Peale, 1784; in the Independence National Historical Park, Philadelphia

By courtesy of the Independence National Historical Park Collection, Philadelphia

Educated in England, Lee served in the Virginia House of Burgesses (1758–75). He opposed arbitrary British policies at the time of the Stamp Act and the Townshend Acts, and, with Patrick Henry and Thomas Jefferson, he originated a plan for intercolonial committees of correspondence (March 1777).

Lee was an active member of the First Continental Congress, where admirers of his oratory compared him with Cicero. In the Second Continental Congress he introduced three resolutions: (1) for declaring independence; (2) for forming foreign alliances; and (3) for preparing a plan of confederation. His first resolution was adopted on July 2, and the Declaration of Independence followed two days later. He remained active in Congress until forced to resign in 1779 because of poor health. In 1777, 1780, and 1785 he served in the Virginia House of Delegates and in 1784 was back in Congress, where he remained until 1787, acting as its president in 1784. He opposed ratification of the federal Constitution because it created a "consolidated" government and lacked a bill of rights. He served, nonetheless, as senator from Virginia in the first Congress from 1789 to 1792, when he retired from public life.

Lee, Robert E., in full ROBERT EDWARD LEE (b. Jan. 19, 1807, Stratford, Westmoreland county, Va., U.S.—d. Oct. 12, 1870, Lexington, Va.), Confederate general, commander of the Army of Northern Virginia, the most successful of the Southern armies during the American Civil War (1861–65). In February 1865 he was given command of all the Southern armies. His surrender at Appomattox Courthouse April 9, 1865, is commonly viewed as signifying the end of the Civil War.

Robert E. Lee, 1865

By courtesy of the Library of Congress, Washington, D.C.

Heritage and youth. Robert Edward Lee was the fourth child of Colonel Henry Lee and Ann Hill Carter. On both sides, his family had produced many of the dominant figures in the ruling class of Virginia. Lee's father, known as "Light-Horse Harry," had been a cavalry leader during the Revolution, a post-Revolution governor of Virginia, and the author of the famous congressional memorial eulogy to his friend, George Washington. Intermarriage with most of Virginia's ruling families was a tradition, and Robert would eventually marry a distant cousin, Mary Anne Randolph Custis, the great-granddaughter of George Washington's wife and heiress of several plantation properties.

With all his aristocratic connections, Robert lacked the advantages of wealth. His father had no aptitude for finance and, dying when Robert was a child, left in straitened circumstances an ailing widow with seven children. Robert, the youngest boy, was the closest of the children to his mother and was deeply influenced by her strength of character and high moral principles. All reports of his childhood and youth stress that the pinched gentility of his formative years, in such marked contrast to the life on the great plantations of his kinspeople, was a strong influence goading him to excel at whatever task he was assigned.

Unable to afford a university education, Lee obtained an appointment to the United States Military Academy at West Point, where his high aspirations and native gifts produced what a fellow cadet, the Confederate general Joseph Johnston, called his natural superiority. Always near the top of his class, he won the appointment to corps adjutant, the highest rank a cadet could attain, and was graduated second in his class in 1829. With handsome features, a massive head, and superb build, he combined dignity with kindness and sympathy with good humour, to win, as Johnston said, "warm friendship and command high respect."

Early military career. Commissioned into the elite engineering corps, later transferring to the cavalry because of slow advancement in the engineers, he did the best he could at routine assignments and on relatively uninspiring engineering projects. Not until the Mexican War (1846–48), when he was a captain on the staff of Gen. Winfield Scott, did he have the opportunity to demonstrate the brilliance and heroism that prompted General Scott to write that Lee was "the very best soldier I ever saw in the field."

In October 1859, while on leave at Arlington to straighten out the entangled affairs of his late father-in-law, he was ordered to suppress the slave insurrection attempted by John Brown at Harpers Ferry, Va. Although Lee put down the insurgency in less than an hour, the very fact that it was led by a white man made him aware of the gathering crisis between the North and the South.

Lee was back at his command in Texas when on Feb. 1, 1861, Texas became the seventh Southern state to secede, and, with the rest of the U.S. Army forces, he was ordered out of the state. Without a command, he returned to Arlington to wait to see what Virginia would do. On April 18 he was called to Washington and offered command of a new army being formed to force the seceded states back into the Union. Lee, while he opposed secession, also opposed war, and "could take no part in an invasion of the Southern states." Meanwhile, President Lincoln called on Virginia to furnish troops for the invasion. A Virginia convention, which had previously voted 2 to 1 against secession, now voted 2 to 1 against furnishing troops for an invasion and to secede, and Lee resigned from the army in which he had served for 36 years to offer his services to the "defense of [his] native state."

Role in Civil War. As commander in chief of Virginia's forces, Lee saw it as his first task to concentrate troops, armaments, and equipment at major points where the invasion might be expected. During this period, Confederate troops joined the Virginia forces and subdued the Federal Army at the first Battle of Bull Run. The attempt at a quick suppression of the Southern states was over and, as Lee was one of the first to realize, a long, all-out war began. Between July 1861 and June 1862, Confederate president Jefferson Davis appointed Lee to several unrewarding positions, the last of which was the trying post of military adviser to the president. Here, however, Lee, working independently of Davis, was able to introduce a coherent strategy into the Confederacy's defense.

During May 1862, General Johnston was leading a heterogeneous collection of Confederate troops back toward Richmond from the east, before the methodical advance of Gen. George B. McClellan's superbly organized, heavily equipped Army of the Potomac. Lee collaborated with Thomas Jonathan (Stonewall) Jackson to concentrate scattered garrisons in Virginia into a striking force in the Shenandoah Valley, where he surprised the Federal forces into retreating and posed a threat to Washington. Jackson's threat from the valley caused Lincoln to withhold from McClellan the large corps of Gen. Irvin McDowell, with whom McClellan planned a pincer movement on Richmond from the east and north. On May 31, Johnston delivered an attack on McClellan's forces seven miles east of Richmond in the indecisive Battle of Fair Oaks (Seven Pines). The battle became a turning point for Lee: Johnston was seriously wounded, and Lee was at last given field command.

In three weeks he organized Confederate troops into what became the famed Army of Northern Virginia; he tightened command and discipline, improved morale, and convinced the soldiers that headquarters was in full command. McClellan, waiting vainly for McDowell to join the wing of his army on the north side of the Chickahominy River, was moving heavy siege artillery from the east for the subjugation of Richmond when Lee struck. Combining with Jackson, who moved in from the valley, Lee defeated Porter's right wing and was on McClellan's supply line to his base on the York River.

In a series of hard fights, the Seven Days' Battles (around Richmond), McClellan withdrew his army to the wharves of Berkeley Plantation, where he was aided by the U.S. Navy. Because it was the first major victory for the Confederacy since Bull Run, and because it halted a succession of military reversals, Lee emerged overnight as the people's hero, and his soldiers developed an almost mystical belief in him.

Lee never believed that the Confederate troops had the strength to win in the field; for the next two years his objectives were to keep the enemy as far away as possible from the armament-producing centre of Richmond as well as from the northern part of the state, where farmers were harvesting their crops, and, finally, to inflict defeats of such decisiveness as to weaken the enemy's will to continue the war. To nullify the Federals' superiority in manpower, armaments, and supply, Lee always sought to seize the initiative by destroying the enemy's prearranged plans.

Until the spring of 1864, he was successful in keeping the enemy away from Richmond and from the northern part of the state, twice expelling the enemy out of Virginia altogether. He inflicted several severe defeats on the enemy, most strikingly at the Second Battle of Bull Run (Second Manassas), Aug. 29–30, 1862. To shift the fighting out of Virginia, Lee crossed into Maryland, where he hoped for support from Southern sympathizers. But his plans fell into Northern hands, and his forces were nearly destroyed at Antietam (Sharpsburg) on Sept. 17, 1862. He was, however, able to withdraw the remnants across the Potomac, to reorganize his army, and to resume his series of victories at Fredericksburg in December of that year. At Chancellorsville (May 1–4, 1863) he achieved another notable victory, although outnumbered two to one, by splitting up his army and encircling the enemy in one of the most audacious moves in military history.

But he was producing no more than a stalemate on the Virginia front, while Federal forces won important victories in other parts of the Confederacy, and time was against him. While the Federals always replaced their losses, Lee's army was dwindling in size, suffering an irreplaceable drain in its command—particularly through the loss of Stonewall Jackson, who had been mortally wounded at Chancellorsville—and increasingly acute shortages of food and clothing, which undermined the physical condition of the soldiers.

Largely to resupply his troops and to draw the invading armies out of Virginia, Lee once more crossed the Potomac. The first invasion had ended with the Battle of Antietam, and the second ended in Lee's repulse at Gettysburg (July 1–3, 1863). There, operating for the first time without Jackson, Lee was failed by three of his top generals in using the discretionary orders that had worked so effectively with Jackson, his "right arm."

Then, in May 1864, Ulysses S. Grant, the newly appointed commanding general of all Union forces, drove at Lee with enormous superiority in numbers, armaments, and cavalry. The horses of the troopers of Confederate general Jeb Stuart were in poor condition, and Stuart was killed early in the campaign. Grant could neither defeat nor outmanoeuvre Lee, however, and the superb army Grant inherited sustained losses of 50,000 men in the May and early June battles of the Wilderness, Spotsylvania Court House, the North Anna, and Cold Harbor.

Grant, however, his losses replaced by fresh recruits, had advanced within seven miles of Richmond, while Lee, his soldiers too weakened physically and his officers too inexperienced to attempt countering manoeuvres, had lost the initiative. Lee himself was, moreover, physically declining and frequently incapacitated by illness. When Grant, abandoning his advance on Richmond, moved south of the James River to Petersburg—Richmond's rail connection with the South—Lee could only place his starving tatterdemalions in defensive lines in front of Petersburg and Richmond.

Beginning at Spotsylvania Court House, Lee had nullified Grant's numbers by using his engineering experience to erect fortifications that were in advance of any fieldworks previously seen in warfare. At Petersburg, Lee extended the field fortifications into permanent lines that presaged trench warfare. While Lee's lines enabled him to withstand Grant's siege of the two cities from late June 1864 to April 1, 1865, once his mobile army was reduced to siege conditions, Lee said the end would be "a mere question of time."

The time came on Sunday, April 2, when his defensive lines were stretched so thin that the far right broke under massive assaults, and Lee was forced to evacuate Petersburg and at last uncover Richmond. When the survivors of his army pulled out of the trenches, an agonizing week of a forlorn retreat began for him; his men fell out from hunger, animals dropped in the traces, and units dissolved under demoralized officers. At Appomattox Court House on April 9, 1865, his way west was blocked and there was nothing left except to bear with dignity the ordeal of surrender, which was made less painful for him by Grant's considerate behaviour.

Postwar years and position in history. Lee spent several months recuperating from the physical and mental strain of retreat and surrender, but he never regained his health. He was, moreover, deeply concerned about the future of his seven children, for his wife's Arlington plantation had been confiscated by the U.S. government, and he was without income at the age of 58. Both to earn subsistence for his family and to set an example for his unemployed fellow officers, he accepted the post of president of Washington College (later Washington and Lee University) in Lexington, Va.

Lee was a surprisingly progressive educator; by employing his lifelong practices in economy, he placed the institution on a sound basis and awakened in his students—many of whom were veterans of the recent war—the desire to rebuild their state with the goal of good citizenship in a nation that in time would become reunited.

He died in 1870 at his home at Washington College.

Although history knows him mostly as "the Rebel General," Lee was a disbeliever in slavery and secession and was devoutly attached to the republic that his father and kinsmen had helped bring into being. He was, moreover, very advanced in his rejection of war as a resolution of political conflicts—a fact that has been almost entirely ignored by posterity. As a U.S. Army colonel in Texas during the secession crises of late 1860, he wrote, "[If] strife and civil war are to take the place of brotherly love and kindness, I shall mourn for my country and for the welfare and progress of mankind."

As the idol of a defeated people, Lee served as an example of fortitude and magnanimity during the ruin and dislocations, the anguish and bitterness of the war's long aftermath. He became an enduring symbol to the Southern people of what was best in their heritage. (C.Do.)

BIBLIOGRAPHY. Douglas Southall Freeman, *R.E. Lee*, 4 vol. (1934–35, reissued 1962), is the definitive biography of Lee. There is also a one-volume abridgment by Richard Harwell, *Lee* (1961, reissued 1982). Later biographies reevaluate Freeman's interpretation of the second day of the Battle of Gettysburg; these include Clifford Dowdey, *Lee* (1965), and *Death of a Nation* (1958, reprinted 1988). Thomas L. Connelly, *The Marble Man: Robert E. Lee and His Image in American Society* (1977), emphasizes the complex nature of Lee's personality. Lee's years as president of Washington College are chronicled in Charles Bracelen Flood, *Lee—The Last Years* (1981). Combined biographies of Lee and Grant include Gene Smith, *Lee and Grant* (1984); and Nancy Scott Anderson and Dwight Anderson, *The Generals—Ulysses S. Grant and Robert E. Lee* (1988).

Lee, Spike, byname of SHELTON JACKSON LEE (b. March 20, 1957, Atlanta, Ga., U.S.), American filmmaker known for his uncompromising, provocative approach to controversial subject matter.

Lee majored in communications at Atlanta's Morehouse College and later attended New York University's graduate film school. There he gained national attention with his master's thesis, the short subject *Joe's Bed-Stuy Barbershop: We Cut Heads* (1983), which earned him a student award from the Academy of Motion Picture Arts and Sciences.

His feature film debut was *She's Gotta Have It* (1986), a prismatic character study about the love life of a contemporary black woman. The film, which was made on a $175,000 budget, was hailed as "Godardesque" at the Cannes Film Festival. Establishing a career-long pattern, Lee wrote, produced, directed, and edited the film, in addition to playing a key supporting role. His next film, based on his experiences at Morehouse, was *School Daze* (1988), a scatological satire of skin-tone prejudice, snobbery, and betrayal within the black academic community. The infamous Howard Beach incident, in which a black man was chased and killed by three rampaging white youths, was the inspiration for Lee's third feature, *Do the Right Thing* (1989), an impassioned but evenhanded work that neither blamed any specific group for racial violence nor absolved any from it. Virtually all of his subsequent films dealt head-on with issues of race and racism in the modern United States, sometimes with righteous and justifiable indignation (*Jungle Fever*, 1991), sometimes with charm and wry humour (*Get on the Bus*, 1996).

With the notable exception of his monumental biographical film *Malcolm X* (1992), many of Lee's later works—such as *Mo' Better Blues* (1990), *Summer of Sam* (1999), and *Bamboozled* (2000)—received mixed reviews. Some observers complained about the excessive length of his films, his perpetuation of ethnic stereotypes, and the way he presents his female characters. Nevertheless, Lee's skill as a filmmaker, characterized by his inventive use of the camera and striking visual metaphors, has never been in doubt.

Lee, Tsung-Dao (b. Nov. 25, 1926, Shanghai, China), Chinese-born American physicist who, with Chen Ning Yang, received the Nobel Prize for Physics in 1957 for discovering major refinements in particle-physics theory.

Lee immigrated to the United States in 1946, and, although he had no undergraduate degree, he entered the graduate school in physics at the University of Chicago, where he began his collaboration with Yang. He was appointed assistant professor of physics at Columbia University in 1953.

In 1956 Lee and Yang concluded that the theta-meson and tau-meson, previously thought to be different because they decay by modes of differing parity, are in fact the same particle (now called the K-meson). Because the law of parity conservation prohibits a single particle from having decay modes exhibiting opposite parity, the only possible conclusion was that for weak interactions, at least, parity is not conserved. They suggested experiments to test their hypothesis, and in 1957 Wu Chien-hsiung, working at Columbia University, experimentally confirmed their theoretical conclusions.

In 1960 Lee was appointed professor of physics at the Institute for Advanced Study, and three years later he returned to Columbia to assume the first Enrico Fermi professorship in physics. From 1964 he made important contributions to the explanation of the violations of time-reversal invariance, which occur during certain weak interactions.

Lee, William (b. 1550?, Calverton, Nottinghamshire, Eng.—d. 1610?, Paris, France), English inventor who devised the first knitting machine (1589), the only one in use for centuries. Its principle of operation remains in use.

Lee's first machine produced a coarse wool, for stockings. Refused a patent by Queen Elizabeth I, he built an improved machine that produced a silk of finer texture, but the queen again denied him a patent because of her concern for the security of the kingdom's many hand knitters. With support from Henry IV of France, Lee began stocking manufacture in Rouen, France, and prospered until Henry's assassination in 1610. After Lee's death his brother returned to England and slowly established the knitting industry there, against the opposition of the hand knitters.

Lee, Yuan T., in full YUAN TSEH LEE (b. Nov. 29, 1936, Hsin-chu, Taiwan), Taiwanese-American chemist who, with Dudley R. Herschbach and John C. Polanyi, received the Nobel Prize for Chemistry in 1986 for his role in the development of chemical-reaction dynamics.

Lee was educated in Taiwan and at the University of California at Berkeley (Ph.D., 1965). He did postdoctoral work at Harvard University and Berkeley and then taught at the University of Chicago from 1968 to 1974. He became a U.S. citizen in 1974 and moved from Chicago to Berkeley, where he continued his research.

As a postdoctoral researcher, Lee experimented with and further developed Herschbach's invention of the "crossed molecular beam technique"—a technique (derived from elementary particle physics) in which beams of molecules are brought together at supersonic speeds under controlled conditions to allow detailed observation of the events that occur during chemical reactions. Lee extended Herschbach's technique to enable the study of larger and more complex molecules.

Lee Commission, body appointed by the British government in 1923 to consider the racial composition of the superior Indian public services of the government of India. The chairman was Lord Lee of Fareham, and there were equal numbers of Indian and British members.

In 1924 the Lee Commission proposed that 40 percent of future entrants should be British, 40 percent Indians directly recruited, and 20 percent Indians promoted from the provincial service. By the date of independence in 1947, more than half the service of about 1,000 members were Indians, many with long experience and holding high positions.

Lee-Enfield rifle, rifle adopted by the British army as its basic infantry weapon in 1902. The short, magazine-loaded Lee-Enfield (Mark I, or SMLE) superseded the longer Lee-Enfield that was first produced in 1895. The short rifle had a length of 44.5 inches (111.6 cm) and combined the bolt action devised by the Scots-American James P. Lee and the rifling standard at the British arsenal at Enfield—*i.e.,* five grooves with a leftward twist. It fired .303-calibre ammunition with a rimmed cartridge carried in a 10-round box magazine. The magazine could also be loaded with five-round clips or single rounds. Though less accurate than the Springfield rifle at longer ranges, it could hold twice the number of cartridges and was capable of a faster rate of fire. Late in World War I it was modified to fire U.S. standard .30-06 ammunition and was widely used by U.S. troops unable to obtain the Springfield rifle. The various models of Lee-Enfield rifles were the standard weapons of British infantry troops in both World Wars I and II.

Lee Kuan Yew (b. Sept. 16, 1923, Singapore), politician and lawyer who was prime minister of Singapore from 1959 to 1990.

Lee was born into a wealthy Chinese family that had been established in Singapore since the 19th century. His first language was English; only upon entering politics did he acquire a command of Chinese as well as Malay and Tamil. After attending school in Singapore, Lee entered the University of Cambridge, England. There he headed the honours list; he also became a socialist. In 1950 he was admitted to the English bar. Instead of practicing as a barrister, however, Lee returned to Singapore. Appointed legal adviser to the Postal Union, he participated in negotiations to obtain higher wages for postal workers and subsequently did similar work for other trade unions.

A British crown colony and the site of Britain's principal naval base in the Far East, Singapore was ruled by a governor assisted by a legislative council. The council's members consisted primarily of wealthy Chinese businessmen, most of whom were appointed rather than elected. When, in the early 1950s, constitutional reform was in the air in Singapore, Lee formed an alliance with two other political newcomers—David Saul Marshall, a lawyer, and Lim Yew Hock, a trade unionist—to challenge the hold of the businessmen on the council. Lee, however, soon broke with his two colleagues to take a more radical stand, becoming secretary-general of his own party, the People's Action Party (PAP), which included some communists, Lee having accepted communist support for some years.

In 1955 a new constitution was introduced increasing the number of elected seats on the council to 25 out of a total of 32. In the elections, the Labour Front, founded by Lee's for-

Lee Kuan Yew
Keystone

mer colleagues, won 13 seats, while the PAP won 3—one of which, for a district inhabited by many of the poorest Chinese in Singapore, was won by Lee.

The following year Lee returned to London as a member of a Singaporean delegation that unsuccessfully sought self-rule for the colony. Unrest in Singapore followed, during which a number of PAP leaders were imprisoned. In 1957 the London negotiations were resumed, again with Lee on the delegation. After agreement was reached on a measure of self-government, Lee won a by-election in Singapore by an overwhelming majority. A brief power struggle within the PAP then ensued: in August Lee was ousted from the secretary-generalship by the party's left wing, but he regained his post in October.

The next year (1958) in London, Lee helped negotiate the status of a self-governing state within the Commonwealth for Singapore. Elections were held under Singapore's new constitution in May 1959, and Lee campaigned on an anticolonialist, anticommunist platform calling for social reforms and eventual union with Malaya. Lee's party won a decisive victory, gaining 43 of the 51 seats, but Lee refused to form a government until the British freed the left-wing members of his party who had been imprisoned in 1956. After their release, Lee was sworn in as prime minister on June 5, 1959. He introduced a five-year plan calling for slum clearance and the building of new public housing, the emancipation of women, the expansion of educational services, and industrialization. In 1961 the PAP's left-wing members broke away from the party to form the Barisan Sosialis ("Socialist Front"), and Lee subsequently broke his remaining ties with the communists.

In 1963 Lee took Singapore into the newly created Federation of Malaysia. In elections held soon afterward, the PAP retained its control of Singapore's Parliament, and Lee thus continued as prime minister. In 1964, however, he made the mistake of entering his party, 75 percent of whose members were Chinese, in the Malaysian national elections. The growing tension between Chinese and Malays resulted in communal rioting in Singapore itself. In August 1965 Lee was told by his Malaysian colleagues in the federal government that Singapore must leave the federation. Although Lee passionately believed in the multiracialism that the federation represented, Singapore had to secede. It then became a sovereign state with Lee as its first prime minister.

Lee's principal aims were to ensure the physical survival of the new state and to retain Singapore's national identity. Surrounded by more powerful neighbours (including China and Indonesia), Lee did not press for the immediate withdrawal of Commonwealth forces from Singapore. Instead, he sought to phase them out slowly and to replace them with a Singaporean force locally trained and patterned on the Israeli model.

Recognizing that Singapore needed a strong economy to survive as an independent country, Lee launched an industrialization program to transform the country into a major exporter of finished goods. He encouraged foreign investment and secured agreements between labour unions and businesses that ensured both labour peace and a rising standard of living for workers. While improving health and social-welfare services, Lee emphasized the need for cooperation, discipline, and austerity on the part of the average Singaporean.

Lee's dominance of the nation's political life was made easier when the main opposition party, the Barisan Sosialis, decided to boycott Parliament from 1966. As a result, the PAP won every seat in Parliament in the elections of 1968, 1972, 1976, and 1980, after which opposition parties managed to claim one or two seats. Lee sometimes resorted to press censorship to stifle left-wing dissent over his government's fundamental policies.

Lee brought his country an efficient administration and spectacular prosperity at the cost of a mildly authoritarian style of government that sometimes infringed on civil liberties. By the 1980s Singapore under Lee's guidance had a per capita income second in East Asia only to Japan's, and the country had become a chief financial centre of Southeast Asia.

The PAP won the general elections of 1984 and 1988, and Lee continued as prime minister, though the question of the succession of leadership became an issue during that decade. After satisfactorily arranging the succession, Lee resigned the office of prime minister in November 1990, though he remained the leader of the PAP until 1992.

Lee Teng-hui (b. Jan. 15, 1923, near Tanshui, Taiwan), first Taiwan-born president of the Republic of China (Taiwan; 1988–2000).

Lee attended Kyōto University in Japan and National Taiwan University (B.A., 1948) and studied agricultural economics in the United States at Iowa State University (M.A., 1953) and Cornell University (Ph.D., 1968). From 1958 to 1978 he was professor of economics at National Taiwan University, Taipei; during this period he also served as a member of Taiwan's Joint Commission on Rural Reconstruction. He was mayor of Taipei from 1978 to 1981 and governor of Taiwan province from 1981 to 1984. In 1984 he became vice president of Taiwan, becoming president in 1988 after the death of President Chiang Ching-kuo. In 1990 he was reelected by an overwhelming majority of members of the National Assembly, and in 1996 he won Taiwan's first direct popular presidential election.

President Lee worked to democratize Taiwan's political system. He favoured a policy of "flexible diplomacy" in dealing with the People's Republic of China, and he eased restrictions on travel to that country and on trade. China, however, was wary of Lee, believing that he supported an independent Taiwan. Tensions flared in 1999 when Lee's announcement that contacts between China and Taiwan should be on the basis of "special state-to-state relations" effectively moved Taiwan closer to independence. Lee retired when his term ended in 2000, and the KMT lost power for the first time in Taiwan's history.

lee wave, vertical undulation of airstreams on the lee side of a mountain. (The lee side is the side that is sheltered from the wind.) Airstreams are often deep enough to flow directly over a mountain range; they sometimes form strong vertical currents, the speed of which commonly reaches 5 m (16 feet) per second. The first wave occurs above the mountain that causes it, but in most deep airstreams a series extends downstream; over 100 have been reported where they are not interfered with by other mountains, as over the sea. These waves may produce clouds, called wave clouds, and have an important effect on the weather.

Lee waves occur most often when a deep airstream with stronger winds in the higher levels and stably stratified air in the lower levels flows across a long ridge having a steep lee slope. The strongest up current then occurs not over the wind-facing slope but at the front of the first lee wave. If the lee slope is very steep and high, the waves may be of sufficient amplitude for a rotor, a vortex with a horizontal axis of rotation perpendicular to the direction of flow, to occur. In a rotor, the wind at the ground blows toward the mountain.

The regular spacing between the waves is usually 2 to 8 km (1 to 5 miles). If this spacing coincides approximately with the spacing of the hills, the waves become large; if not, the lee waves of one mountain may be annulled as the air passes over a second. In hilly country with a complicated topography, intense waves may be temporarily set up in one or two places; such strong winds may occur under the wave troughs that large stretches of forest are blown down.

By day, the winds up a lee slope inhibit the formation of lee waves by inducing the flow to break away from the hilltops. At night, the shallow downslope (katabatic) wind induces the airflow to adhere to the slope so that waves are formed; a deep, strong wind then blows down the lee slope.

One of the most fully explored and spectacular lee waves is the Sierra wave, which occurs in a westerly wind to the lee of the Sierra Nevada Range in California. It is best developed when a jet stream associated with a front blows across the range. In it, gliders have soared to elevations of more than 14,000 m.

leech, any worm of the class Hirudinea (phylum Annelida). About 300 species are known. A small sucker, which contains the mouth, is at the anterior end; a large sucker is at the posterior end. All leeches have 34 body segments. The length of the body ranges from minute to about 20 cm (8 inches) or even longer when the animal stretches. Leeches occur primarily in freshwater and on land. Members of the order Rhynchobdellida occur in the sea as well as in freshwater. Some species of leeches are predators on other animals; some eat organic debris; others are parasitic.

Leeches breathe through the skin. The digestive system contains a crop, or pouch, in which food can be stored for several months. One to four pairs of eyes are located at the anterior end. Individuals are hermaphroditic—*i.e.,* functional reproductive organs of both sexes occur in the same individual. Leeches are not self-fertilizing, however, for the sperm of one individual fertilizes only the eggs of other individuals. The eggs are laid in a cocoon, which may be deposited on land or in water. Development and growth are direct, without a larval stage.

Aquatic leeches may feed on the blood of fishes, amphibians, birds, and mammals, or they may eat snails, insect larvae, and worms. True land leeches feed only on the blood of mammals. Three jaws set with sharp teeth make a Y-shaped incision in the flesh. The leech's saliva contains substances that anesthetize the wound area, dilate the blood vessels to increase blood flow, and prevent the blood from clotting. The anticoagulant hirudin, which is extracted from the body tissues of the European medicinal leech (*Hirudo medicinalis*), is used medically.

Land leeches await their victim in damp vegetation, poising one end in the air. The victim is often unaware that he has been bitten until blood is discovered running from the wound; blood flow may continue because of the anticoagulant still present.

Leeches that attack humans belong to the family Gnathobdellidae. Some species have been used medically for centuries; in Europe the use of leeches to drain off blood reached its height of popularity in the 19th cen-

European medicinal leech (*Hirudo medicinalis*)
Jacques Six

tury. Diseases commonly treated with leeches included mental illness, tumours, skin disease, gout, and whooping cough. A common treatment for headache was to apply several leeches to each temple. In addition to *H. medicinalis* of Europe, the Algerian dragon (*H. troctina*) was used. *Gnathobdella ferox* was commonly used in Asia. After *H. medicinalis* was introduced into North America, it established itself there as a wild species. It grows to 10 cm (4 inches) in length and is green, with four to six brown stripes.

Other land leeches that attack humans are primarily of the genus *Haemadipsa* in Asia, the Philippines, the East Indies, and Madagascar. Leeches of the genus *Philaemon* are parasitic on humans in Australia.

Aquatic leeches, particularly *Limnatis nilotica,* may enter the body in drinking water. Some may enter the excretory openings of persons who bathe in infested waters. *L. nilotica,* which inhabits lakes and streams of southern Europe, North Africa, and the Middle East, attains lengths of up to 12 cm (4.75 inches). The younger, smaller specimens are most likely to enter the body. When ingested with drinking water they may first attach themselves to the linings of the nose or throat and then be inhaled into the lungs. A person infected with many such leeches may suffer from anemia resulting from loss of blood. In external wounds secondary infection is more likely to occur than anemia. Leeches can cause suffocation and death of the host by blockage of the breathing passages; in Asia, in particular, domestic animals commonly die in this way.

Leech, John (b. Aug. 29, 1817, London, Eng.—d. Oct. 29, 1864, London), English caricaturist notable for his contributions to *Punch* magazine.

Leech was educated at Charterhouse, where he met William Makepeace Thackeray, who was to be his lifelong friend. He then began to study medicine but soon drifted into the artistic profession and in 1835 published *Etchings and Sketchings by A. Pen, Esq.,* comic character studies from the London streets. In 1840 Leech began contributing to magazines with a series of etchings in *Bentley's Miscellany;* he also collaborated with George Cruikshank, whose work his own resembled in both style and subject. Later, however, he excluded the horrific and satirical elements present in the tradition of English caricature established in the late 18th and early 19th centuries by James Gillray and Thomas Rowlandson. Leech developed in his caricatures a comfortable, warmly humorous middle-class urbanity, in which character is underlined by emphatic contrasts of stock types. These qualities emerge from the four etchings illustrating Charles Dickens' *Christmas Carol* (1844), the *Comic History of England* (1847–48), and the woodcuts for the *Comic History of Rome* (1852). These were followed by numerous etchings and woodcuts of sporting scenes in the novels of his friend R.S. Surtees.

"Mr. Briggs, anxious to become a 'complete angler,' studies the 'gentle art' of fly-fishing," cartoon from *Mr. Briggs and His Doings* by John Leech, 1860

By courtesy of the trustees of the British Museum; photograph, J.R. Freeman & Co. Ltd.

Leech's first contribution to *Punch* appeared in the issue of Aug. 7, 1841. This was the beginning of a fruitful connection that resulted in about 3,000 caricatures and other illustrations for the magazine. Leech concentrated on social caricature, as in *Pictures of Life and Character from the Collection of Mr. Punch* (1854, 1860, and 1863). Leech and the English illustrator Sir John Tenniel were the creators of the conventional image of John Bull—a jovial and honest Englishman, solid and foursquare, sometimes in a Union Jack waistcoat and with a bulldog at heel. He also contributed to *Punch* almanacs and pocketbooks, to *Once a Week,* and to *The Illustrated London News,* as well as to numerous novels and miscellaneous volumes.

leechee (fruit): *see* litchi.

Leeds, urban area, city, and metropolitan borough, metropolitan county of West Yorkshire, historic county of Yorkshire, England. It lies along the River Aire about 30 miles (48 km) northeast of Manchester. The coal and iron ore deposits in the locality, a plentiful supply of water from the Aire's tributaries, and the city's excellent transportation links helped make it the industrial capital of Yorkshire. It is the largest city in Yorkshire and one of Britain's major cultural centres.

Leeds originated as an Anglo-Saxon township on the north bank of the Aire. It grew as a local market centre and was incorporated in 1626. By then the town was a cloth-finishing centre for a wide area where domestic weaving, introduced by 14th-century Flemish weavers, was pursued. By the 16th century Leeds challenged the supremacy of York and Beverley in the woolen-manufacturing trade. With the Industrial Revolution and development of the local coalfield, the woolen industry was surpassed in importance by engineering. The completion in 1816 of the Leeds and Liverpool Canal also stimulated Leeds's growth, and after 1848 the railway made the city a major centre of locomotive engineering. The late 19th century saw a great expansion of the factory production of ready-made clothing, drawing labour from an influx of Jewish immigrants.

In the modern city, factories are largely concentrated in the south and east, where engineering and electronics, printing and publishing, food processing, chemicals, and furniture are especially noteworthy among a great diversity of industries. Leeds is also an important regional centre for insurance and financial services and is the major shopping and commercial centre for West Yorkshire.

Retail shopping markets, grain and stock exchanges, and some fine Victorian arcades occupy the old town site. Nearby is the Town Hall (1858), an imposing Victorian building that contains law courts and a large concert hall; triennial musical festivals are held in the Town Hall. Leeds has two universities, many specialized colleges, and a boys' grammar school that was founded in 1552. Other amenities include a nationally famous cricket ground at Headingley, a football (soccer) ground at Elland Road, a championship golf course at Moortown, and more than 200 parks and open spaces, chief among which is Roundhay Park.

Besides the historic town and urban area of Leeds, the city and metropolitan borough include the towns of Morley, Pudsey, Horsforth, Garforth, Kippax, and Rothwell and an area of open countryside, woodlands, and rural villages. The M1 motorway from London to Leeds crosses the M62 motorway connecting Liverpool and Manchester with Kingston upon Hull. Northwest of Leeds is an airport at Yeadon. Area metropolitan borough, 215 square miles (557 square km). Pop. (1991) Leeds urban area, 424,194; (1998 est.) metropolitan borough, 727,400.

Leeds, Thomas Osborne, 1st Duke of, MARQUESS OF CARMARTHEN, EARL OF DANBY, VISCOUNT LATIMER OF DANBY, VISCOUNT OSBORNE OF DUNBLANE, BARON OSBORNE OF KIVETON, also called (1647–73) SIR THOMAS OSBORNE, 2ND BARONET (b. Feb. 20, 1632—d. July 26, 1712, Easton Neston, Northamptonshire, Eng.), English statesman who, while chief minister to King Charles II, organized the Tories in Parliament. In addition he played a key role in bringing William and Mary to the English throne in 1689.

Leeds, detail of a painting from the studio of Sir Peter Lely, 1689; in the National Portrait Gallery, London

By courtesy of the National Portrait Gallery, London

The son of a Royalist Yorkshire landowner, Osborne did not become active in politics until Charles II was restored to the throne in 1660. He then held local posts in Yorkshire, and in 1665 he won a seat in Parliament. Advancing in office through the patronage of the influential George Villiers, 2nd Duke of Buckingham, Osborne became joint treasurer of the Royal Navy in 1668 and lord treasurer of England in 1673. His success in stabilizing the government's financial position soon made him Charles's chief minister and earned him the title Earl of Danby (June 1674).

Danby set about using crown patronage and bribery to build in Parliament a court party based on royal (as opposed to parliamentary) supremacy, strict Anglicanism (especially through enforcement of the Test Act), and hostility to France. As part of his anti-French and pro-Protestant policy, he engineered a marriage (1677) between Princess Mary, Charles's niece, and William of Orange, stadholder of Holland, the foremost opponent of France on the European continent. At the same time, Charles made him secretly obtain a yearly subsidy from the French king Louis XIV. When this was made public in 1678, against the background of a nation alarmed by the Popish Plot, Danby was immediately impeached by Parliament and committed (1679) to the Tower of London.

Released in 1684, he returned to politics in June 1688, when he and six other conspirators invited William of Orange to invade England and seize power from the Roman Catholic king James II. Danby raised northern England in support of William's cause, and he helped persuade the Convention Parliament of 1689 to make William and Mary joint sovereigns of England (though he initially favoured making Mary alone the reigning sovereign). By the spring of 1690 he had virtually reestablished himself as chief minister in the new regime. For the next four years Danby managed to maintain an uneasy balance among the feuding factions at William's court.

He was created Duke of Leeds in 1694, but in 1695 he was impeached by Parliament for taking a bribe from the East India Company. Danby's influence thereafter declined. In 1699 he was deprived of all his offices.

BIBLIOGRAPHY. Andrew Browning, *Thomas Osborne, Earl of Danby and Duke of Leeds, 1632–1712,* 3 vol. (1944–51).

leek (species *Allium porrum*), hardy, vigorous, biennial plant of the lily family (Liliaceae). Related to the onion, it has a mild, sweet, onionlike flavour. The leek is widely used in European soups and stews, especially as a complement to potatoes, and it is cooked whole as a vegetable.

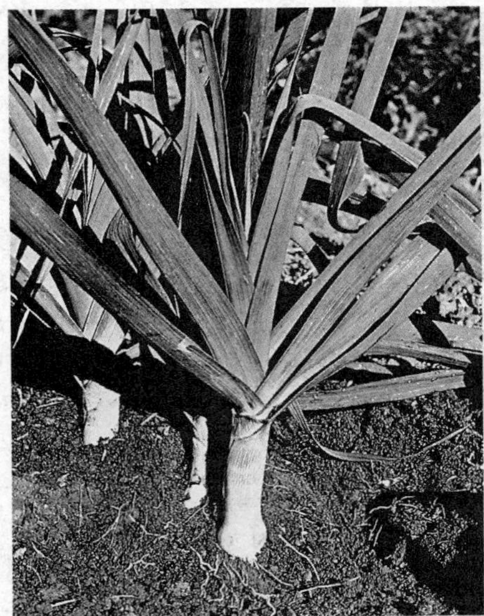

Leek (*Allium porrum*)
G.R. Roberts

The leek is native to eastern Mediterranean lands and the Middle East, where it was cultivated in ancient times. The Romans probably brought it to Europe and the British Isles. The vegetable became the national emblem of Wales following an ancient victory by an army of Welshmen who wore leeks as a distinguishing sign.

In the plant's first season of growth, long linear leaves arise from a compressed stem or stem plate; the thick leaf bases overlap and are arranged concentrically in a nearly cylindrical bulb. The bulb is little if any larger at the base than at the neck. A tuft of fibrous, shallow roots grows from the base of the stem plate. In the second season, a tall solid stalk arises bearing leaves and a large globular umbel with many perfect flowers. The seeds are small, black, irregular, and angular.

Leet, Court: *see* Court Leet.

Leeuwarden, Frisian LJOUWERT, *gemeente* (commune) and capital, Friesland *provincie,* northern Netherlands. Leeuwarden lies at the junction of the Harlinger-Trek Canal and the Dokkumer Ee Canal. Originally a port on the Middelzee (reclaimed since the 13th century), it was chartered in 1435, became the capital of Friesland in 1504, and was from 1582 to 1747 the residence of the Frisian stadtholders of the house of Orange-Nassau, ancestors of the present Dutch royal family. A noted centre of goldwork and silverwork in the 16th–18th century, it is now the economic centre of Friesland. Leeuwarden is a rail junction, has an important cattle market (Friesland Hall), and processes dairy foods; it manufactures tin, wood, and paper packings.

The city's Frisian Museum is the most extensive provincial museum in The Netherlands, with comprehensive cultural exhibits. The Princessehof Museum has Oriental displays, and the Pier Pander Museum features works of that sculptor. Historic buildings include the Kanselarij, a Renaissance building and originally the seat of the Frisian government and law courts; the former Weighhouse (1598); the town hall (1724); the Oldehove (1529), an unfinished tower (130 feet [40 m]) that leans slightly; and the Sint Bonifatius Church. Pop. (1989 est.) 85,296.

Leeuwen, Denys van, also spelled DE LEEUWIS: *see* Dionysius the Carthusian.

Leeuwenhoek, Antonie van (b. Oct. 24, 1632, Delft, Neth.—d. Aug. 26, 1723, Delft), Dutch microscopist who was the first to observe bacteria and protozoa. His researches on lower animals refuted the doctrine of spontaneous generation, and his observations helped lay the foundations for the sciences of bacteriology and protozoology.

Little is known of Leeuwenhoek's early life. When his stepfather died in 1648, he was sent to Amsterdam to become an apprentice to a linendraper. Returning to Delft when he was 20, he established himself as a draper and haberdasher. In 1660 he obtained a position as chamberlain to the sheriffs of Delft. His income was thus secure and sufficient enough to enable him to devote much of his time to his all-absorbing hobby, that of grinding lenses and using them to study tiny objects.

Leeuwenhoek made microscopes consisting of a single, high-quality lens of very short focal length; at the time, such simple microscopes were preferable to the compound microscope, which increased the problem of chromatic aberration. Although Leeuwenhoek's studies lacked the organization of formal scientific research, his powers of careful observation enabled him to make discoveries of fundamental importance. In 1674 he began to observe bacteria and protozoa, his "very little animalcules," which he was able to isolate from different sources, such as rainwater, pond and well water, and the human mouth and intestine, and he calculated their sizes.

Leeuwenhoek, detail of a portrait by Jan Verkolje; in the Rijksmuseum, Amsterdam
By courtesy of the Rijksmuseum, Amsterdam

In 1677 he described for the first time the spermatozoa from insects, dogs, and man, though Stephen Hamm probably was a codiscoverer. Leeuwenhoek studied the structure of the optic lens, striations in muscles, the mouthparts of insects, and the fine structure of plants and discovered parthenogenesis in aphids. In 1680 he noticed that yeasts consist of minute globular particles. He extended Marcello Malpighi's demonstration in 1660 of the blood capillaries by giving (in 1684) the first accurate description of red blood cells. In his observations on rotifers in 1702, Leeuwenhoek remarked that "in all falling rain, carried from gutters into water-butts, animalcules are to be found; and that in all kinds of water, standing in the open air, animalcules can turn up. For these animalcules can be carried over by the wind, along with the bits of dust floating in the air."

A friend of Leeuwenhoek put him in touch with the Royal Society of England, to which, from 1673 until 1723, he communicated by means of informal letters most of his discoveries and to which he was elected a fellow in 1680. His discoveries were for the most part made public in the society's *Philosophical Transactions.* The first representation of bacteria is to be found in a drawing by Leeuwenhoek in that publication in 1683.

His researches on the life histories of various low forms of animal life were in opposition to the doctrine that they could be produced spontaneously or bred from corruption. Thus, he showed that the weevils of granaries (in his time commonly supposed to be bred from wheat as well as in it) are really grubs hatched from eggs deposited by winged insects. His letter on the flea, in which he not only described its structure but traced out the whole history of its metamorphosis, is of great interest, not so much for the exactness of his observations as for an illustration of his opposition to the spontaneous generation of many lower organisms, such as "this minute and despised creature." Some theorists asserted that the flea was produced from sand, others from dust or the like, but Leeuwenhoek proved that it bred in the regular way of winged insects.

Leeuwenhoek also carefully studied the history of the ant and was the first to show that what had been commonly reputed to be ants' eggs were really their pupae, containing the perfect insect nearly ready for emergence, and that the true eggs were much smaller and gave origin to maggots, or larvae. He argued that the sea mussel and other shellfish were not generated out of sand found at the seashore or mud in the beds of rivers at low water but from spawn, by the regular course of generation. He maintained the same to be true of the freshwater mussel, whose embryos he examined so carefully that he was able to observe how they were consumed by "animalcules," many of which, according to his description, must have included ciliates in conjugation, flagellates, and the *Vorticella.* Similarly, he investigated the generation of eels, which were at that time supposed to be produced from dew without the ordinary process of generation.

The dramatic nature of his discoveries made him world famous, and he was visited by many notables—including Peter I the Great of Russia, James II of England, and Frederick II the Great of Prussia.

Leeuwenhoek's methods of microscopy, which he kept secret, remain something of a mystery. During his lifetime he ground more than 400 lenses, most of which were very small—some no larger than a pinhead—and usually mounted them between two thin brass plates, riveted together. A large sample of these lenses, bequeathed to the Royal Society, were found to have magnifying powers of between 50 and, at the most, 300 times. In order to observe phenomena as small as bacteria, Leeuwenhoek must have employed some form of oblique illumination, or other technique, for enhancing the effectiveness of the lens, but this method he would not reveal. Leeuwenhoek continued his work almost to the end of his long life of 90 years.

Leeuwenhoek's contributions to the *Philosophical Transactions* amounted to 375 and those to the *Memoirs of the Paris Academy of Sciences* to 27. Two collections of his works appeared during his life, one in Dutch (1685–1718) and the other in Latin (1715–22); a selection was translated by S. Hoole, *The Select Works of A. van Leeuwenhoek* (1798–1807).

BIBLIOGRAPHY. Clifford Dobell, *Antony van Leeuwenhoek and His "Little Animals"* (1932, reissued 1960); and Brian J. Ford, *Single Lens: The Story of the Simple Microscope* (1985).

Leeward Islands, French ÎLES SOUS LE VENT, Spanish ISLAS DE SOTOVENTO, an arc of West Indian islands that constitute the most westerly and northerly of the Lesser Antilles, at the northeastern end of the Caribbean Sea, between latitudes 16° and 19° N and longitudes 61° and 65° W. The major islands are, from north to south, the Virgin Islands of the United States and the United Kingdom (geologically a part of the Greater Antilles); Anguilla, a British dependency; Saint-Martin (Sint Martin), an island half French (a dependency of Guadeloupe) and half Dutch (a part of the Netherlands Antilles and, with nearby Saba and Sint Eustacius, the group called administratively by the Dutch the "Windward Islands," though geographically they are part of the Leewards); Saint Kitts and Nevis, an independent English-speaking nation; Antigua and Barbuda, an independent English-speaking nation; Montserrat, a British dependency; and Guadeloupe, a *département* of France. Just south of this chain is Dominica, sometimes classified as part of the Leewards but usually designated as part of the Windward Islands (*q.v.*).

The Virgin Islands are part of a submerged mountain chain, like the other islands of the Greater Antilles. Areas of Antigua, Anguilla, Barbuda, and eastern Guadeloupe consist of formations of coral limestone, whereas the small chain from Saint Kitts to Montserrat and including western Guadeloupe form a volcanic ridge; the volcano Soufrière on Guadeloupe is the highest mountain in the Lesser Antilles (at 4,813 feet [1,467 m]). The climate of the Leeward Islands is drier than that farther south but does vary from region to region and in different parts of a single island; rainfall increases with elevation and in more southerly latitudes. Tradewinds ameliorate the tropical heat. Hurricanes occur occasionally from June to October.

The population of the Leewards is predominantly black, though tourism, as a leading source of income, seasonally brings in a large mixture of nationalities from mainland North America and from Europe.

"De," "la," and similar components of a name, when followed by a space, are alphabetized as separate words (e.g., *De Forest, Lee*). *When they are joined to the following part of a name, the combination is treated as a single word* (e.g., *DeForest, John William*).

Leeward Islands, Portuguese ILHAS DE SOTAVENTO, island group in the Atlantic Ocean off the coast of western Africa, constituting one of two *distritos* ("districts") of Cape Verde and consisting of the following islands: Brava, Fogo, Maio, and São Tiago (*qq.v.*). The islands are of volcanic origin and have a tropical climate. Rainfall is scarce, and drought is a constant problem.

Lefèbvre, Anne: *see* Dacier, Anne.

Lefebvre, (Pierre-) François-Joseph, DUC (duke) DE DANTZIG (b. Oct. 20, 1755, Rouffach, Fr.—d. Sept. 14, 1820, Paris), French general who was one of the 18 marshals of the empire appointed by Napoleon in May 1804.

Lefebvre, the son of an Alsatian miller, worked for a time as a clerk before entering a military career in the French Guards in 1773. A sergeant at the outbreak of the French Revolution in 1789, he was, between September 1792 and January 1793, promoted rapidly from captain to divisional general. Between 1793 and 1796 he commanded the vanguard of the Army of the Rhine, serving with distinction at the battles of Fleurus (June 1794), which repulsed the Austrians, and Duisburg (September 1795). In 1798 he served briefly as commander of the Army of the Sambre and Meuse and was appointed governor of Paris the following year. His position as governor proved extremely useful to Napoleon, who persuaded him to support the coup d'état of 18 Brumaire (Nov. 9, 1799), which resulted in Napoleon's being proclaimed first consul.

Created a senator in 1800 and a marshal in 1804, Lefebvre carried the sword of Charlemagne at Napoleon's imperial coronation. He with his German accent and his illiterate wife, née Catherine Hubscher and nicknamed Madam Sans-Gêne ("Overfamiliar," or "Cheeky") for her uninhibited behaviour, made themselves fine figures at court, but he wanted active service. Lefebvre commanded the imperial infantry guard at Jena (Oct. 14, 1806) and captured the city of Danzig on April 27, 1807, an exploit that earned him the title Duke de Dantzig in 1808. He served in Spain in 1808 and the following year, as commander of Bavarian troops, fought at Eckmühl and Wagram. In 1812 he fought in Russia. Although he opposed the invasion of France by the Allied armies attempting to depose Napoleon in 1814, he voted for Napoleon's abdication in the Senate; for this action Louis XVIII made him a peer of France. But he rejoined Napoleon in his attempt during the Hundred Days to recapture his empire and was deprived of his title when the Bourbons were restored for the second time in July 1815.

Lefebvre, Georges (b. Aug. 6, 1874, Lille, Fr.—d. Aug. 28, 1959, Boulogne-Billancourt), French historian noted for his studies of various aspects of the French Revolution.

Lefebvre's major work, *Les Paysans du Nord pendant la Révolution française* (1924; "The Peasants of the North During the French Revolution"), was the result of 20 years of research into the role of the peasantry during the Revolution, during which time he supported himself as a secondary school teacher. This four-volume study deals with what might be called the rural sociology of a single *département,* that of Nord, before and during the Revolution. Obtaining a doctoral degree, Lefebvre began university teaching, and in 1935 he was made a professor at the Sorbonne. Among his other books are *Napoléon* (1935) and *Quatre-vingt-neuf* (1939; *The Coming of the French Revolution*), which was written for the nonspecialist and is perhaps the best general picture of the ancien régime available in English. Lefebvre's exhaustive knowledge of the French peasantry of the 18th century was his sure guide in analyzing the society of the time, since four-fifths of the people were peasants and the social positions of the aristocracy, the bourgeoisie, and the town labouring classes were defined largely by their relation to the rural population.

Lefebvre, Marcel (-François) (b. Nov. 29, 1905, Tourcoing, Fr.—d. March 25, 1991, Martigny, Switz.), ultraconservative Roman Catholic archbishop who opposed the liberalizing changes begun by the Second Vatican Council (1962–65) and who was excommunicated in 1988 for consecrating new traditionalist bishops without the approval of the Holy See in Rome. He created the bishops in order to perpetuate his crusade after his death.

Lefebvre studied at the Sacred Heart College in Tourcoing and at the French Seminary in Rome and was ordained a priest in 1929. After a brief assignment in Lille, Fr., he served in missionary posts in Gabon (1932–46) and Senegal (1947–62), becoming archbishop of Dakar, Senegal, in 1948. As a member of the preparatory commission (1960–62) for the Second Vatican Council, he helped frame traditionalist proposals that the convening bishops in the subsequent council sessions strongly rejected. The bishops substituted more liberal reforms, such as saying mass in the vernacular rather than in Latin, reconciling Roman Catholicism with other religions, and promoting the collegiality of the pope and the bishops in leading the church. Lefebvre came to denigrate such reforms as "heretical," "anti-Christ," and "satanic."

From 1962 to 1968 Lefebvre was superior general of the Holy Ghost Fathers. In 1969 he founded the Priestly Confraternity of Saint Pius X in Fribourg, Switz. (the namesake, Pope Pius X, had been a staunch conservative), and in 1970 he established the society's seminary at Ecône, a villa near Riddes in Valais canton, Switz., to train priests according to his traditionalist model. Soon the Vatican and Lefebvre were to exchange vigorous criticisms, and in 1975 the Vatican withdrew approval of the order. In 1976 Pope Paul VI suspended Lefebvre, forbidding him to carry out priestly and episcopal functions. Lefebvre not only defied Rome in continuing his priesthood but set about establishing regional headquarters in various countries for his variety of Roman Catholicism. Several negotiating efforts to avoid a schism failed; and on June 30, 1988, upon consecrating four traditionalist bishops at Ecône in defiance of Pope John Paul II's orders, Lefebvre was excommunicated. His group, then numbering more than 60,000 followers, was deemed schismatic.

Lefevre, Pierre: *see* Faber, Peter.

Lefèvre d'Étaples, Jacques, Latin JOHANNES FABER STAPULENSIS (b. *c.* 1455, Étaples, Picardy [France]—d. March 1536, Nérac, Fr.), outstanding French humanist, theologian, and translator whose scholarship stimulated scriptural studies during the Protestant Reformation.

Ordained a priest, Lefèvre taught philosophy in Paris from about 1490 to 1507. During visits to Italy in 1492 and 1500, he studied Greek classics and Neoplatonist mysticism. In Paris he influenced the church reformers Guillaume Farel and François Vatable. From 1507 he worked for the Saint-Germain-des-Prés Abbey, Paris, where his former pupil Guillaume Briçonnet was abbot. Appointed bishop of Meaux in 1516, Briçonnet began reforms in his diocese and made Lefèvre his vicar general in 1523. When the clergy of the diocese were suspected of Protestantism in 1525, Lefèvre moved to Strasbourg, later returning to Blois, under the protection of King Francis I. In 1531 he fled to Nérac, where he was supported by Margaret of Angoulême, queen of Navarre.

Lefèvre's work shows an effort to divorce religious studies from the older Scholasticism. Between 1492 and 1506 he wrote student manuals on physics and mathematics and published new, annotated translations or paraphrases of Aristotle's works on ethics, metaphysics, and politics. He seems to have undergone a religious crisis in 1505, and, influenced by the ideals of the Brethren of the Common Life (communal Dutch clergymen who sponsored scholarship), he turned to mysticism. That year he published a volume of contemplations by the Catalan author and philosopher Ramon Llull and later published works by the celebrated mystic Jan van Ruysbroeck and by Nicholas of Cusa. In 1509 he issued his *Psalterium quintuplex* (five Latin versions of the Psalms). That work—along with his commentary on the letters of St. Paul (1512), which has sometimes been interpreted as embodying the cardinal doctrine of the Reformation—had some influence on Martin Luther.

In 1521 his book rejecting the view of the three Marys of the Gospels as being one person was condemned by the Sorbonne. He wrote Latin commentaries on the Gospels (1522) and on the Catholic Letters (1527). Understanding the importance of using the vernacular for religious and other prose works, he translated the whole Bible into French from the Vulgate (1530). Lefèvre had considerable influence on younger scholars, who improved on his methods. By reason of his biblical studies, his edition of the Psalms, and his commentaries on St. Paul, he is often hailed as a reformer on the eve of the Reformation. J. Barnaud's *Lefèvre d'Étaples* appeared in 1936.

Lefkoşa (Cyprus): *see* Nicosia.

Left Communist, in Soviet history, one of a group within the Communist Party which in the first half of 1918 opposed Lenin's practical policies for preserving Communist rule in Russia. The group was led by Nikolay I. Bukharin.

Rather than make peace, the Left Communists favoured waging a revolutionary war. They contended that it was impossible for Soviet Russia, an economically underdeveloped country, to build Socialism until other Socialist revolutions succeeded in western Europe.

On the industrial issue, the Left Communists insisted that the proletariat should run the economy and that the workers' control of industrial enterprises that had developed during 1917 was a step toward this goal and should not be sacrificed for short-range, opportunistic purposes.

The Left Communists initially had substantial support within the party. They dominated the Supreme Council of National Economy, an institution created in December 1917 to supervise the economy; in January 1918 there were more votes in the Central Committee favouring a revolutionary war than a peace treaty. But in March 1918 they were defeated at the seventh Party Congress, which approved the Brest-Litovsk peace treaty; they also lost their positions on the Supreme Council of National Economy and shortly afterward lost their control of the Moscow and Urals regional organizations. When the Soviet government nationalized all large industrial enterprises in late June, many Left Communists considered this to be a correct economic policy and shifted their support back to Lenin. By the end of the summer the Left Communists no longer existed as a distinct opposition group.

Lefuel, Hector-Martin (b. Nov. 14, 1810, Versailles, Fr.—d. Jan. 1, 1881, Paris), French architect who completed the new Louvre in Paris, a structure that was seen as a primary symbol of cosmopolitan architecture in the late 19th century.

Lefuel was the son of a building contractor. He studied with Jean-Nicolas Huyot and received the grand prix of the Academy in 1839. His design for the theatre at Fontainebleau, in an 18th-century style, led to his appointment as successor to L.-T.-J. Visconti in the project to build a connecting structure between the old Louvre and the Tuileries. He retained much of Visconti's original plan but introduced some modifications of his own, especially on the side of the rue de Rivoli, where he added rich ornamentation and made extensive use of iron. Lefuel relied on structural motifs already present in the older buildings, but the resulting effects were almost entirely original. Most striking are the corner and central pavilions. Projecting from the corners of the steep mansard roof are stone dormers ornamented in a nearly Baroque manner. The central pavilions, at either end of the Cour du Carrousel, have convex mansard roofs forming, as it were, "square" domes. Such features were imitated all over the world for the next 30 years and came to be symbolic of Second Empire architectural style. Ironically, the new Louvre is not typical of Parisian architecture during this time.

Lefuel's other works include the Hôtel Fould and Hôtel Nieuwerkerke, both at Paris, and a *palais provisoire* of wood for the Exposition of 1855.

leg, limb or appendage of an animal, used to support the body, provide locomotion, and, in modified form, assist in capturing and eating prey (as in certain shellfish, spiders, and insects). In four-limbed vertebrates all four appendages are commonly called legs, but in bipedal animals, including humans, only the posterior or lower two are so called.

The bones of the human leg, like those of other mammals, consist of a basal segment, the femur (thighbone); an intermediate segment, the tibia (shinbone) and the smaller fibula; and a distal segment, the pes (foot), consisting of tarsals, metatarsals, and phalanges (toes).

For the actions of the major muscles of the mammalian leg, *see* adductor muscles; biceps muscle; gastrocnemius muscle; gluteus muscles; quadriceps femoris muscle; sartorius muscle; and soleus muscle.

In birds and bats the foreleg has evolved into the wing (*q.v.*). Various other adaptations of the leg include modifications for swimming, digging, leaping, and running, as seen in the porpoise, mole, kangaroo, and horse, respectively. The appendages of many invertebrates are also known as legs.

leg triceps (anatomy): *see* gastrocnemius muscle.

legacy, also called BEQUEST, in law, generally a gift of property by will or testament. The term is used to denote the disposition of either personal or real property in the event of death.

In Anglo-American law, a legacy of an identified object, such as a particular piece of real estate, or a described object of personal property, is called a specific legacy. A general legacy, on the other hand, would involve such things as a sum of money or a number of objects identified generically, such as any 100 shares of common stock. If the total value of the estate is insufficient to satisfy all legacies, the specific legacies are satisfied first.

A legacy is termed residuary if the beneficiary is to receive only what is left of the estate after the satisfaction of all specific and general legacies.

In civil-law countries (*e.g.,* Germany, Japan) legacy and legatee have somewhat different meanings than in Anglo-American law. In Roman law, upon the death of a person, the totality of his legal rights and duties passed to a universal successor, the heir. If there was no valid testament, the heir was determined by the rules of intestate succession. An heir, however, could also be instituted by testament, and in his testament the testator could charge his heir with legacies—that is, duties to a third party, called a legatee, to whom the heir had to pay certain sums of money or give certain assets of the estate. This terminology is still used in the law of Germany and those countries with similar systems, such as Switzerland and Japan. In the French civil code and those countries that follow its pattern, however, the term heir is limited to the universal intestate successor. A person to whom a testator leaves his entire estate is called a *légataire universel;* when the estate is divided, the beneficiaries are called *légataires à titre universel.* A person who is to receive a fixed sum of money or a particular asset of the estate—*i.e.,* a legacy—is called a *légataire particulier.*

legal aid, the professional legal assistance given, either at no charge or for a nominal sum, to indigent persons in need of such help. In criminal cases most countries—especially those in which a person accused of a crime enjoys a presumption of innocence—provide the services of a lawyer for those who have insufficient means of their own. In some countries defender offices with salaried personnel, either publicly or privately supported, have been found to be the most economical solution. In other countries where there is no shortage of lawyers skilled in criminal law and trial practice, private lawyers undertake this duty, being assigned by the court or being chosen by the accused person himself. In many countries these private lawyers receive no remuneration or only a nominal fee paid either by the state or from charitable funds. In an increasing number of countries, the provision by the state of a fund sufficient to pay an adequate fee and to cover all allied expenses is considered to be necessary to ensure that the person receiving this aid gets proper service.

Traditionally, in many countries, as one of the public-service responsibilities attached to the practice of law, lawyers also undertake to give legal aid in civil cases.

In 1958 the International Bar Association sponsored the organization of the International Legal Aid Association, the purpose of which is to (1) compile and maintain a directory of legal aid agencies, (2) collect and distribute information concerning both the services provided by such organizations and laws and other provisions regulating legal aid in the various nations, (3) develop facilities for the referral of cases on a basis of reciprocal service among the cooperating agencies, and (4) encourage the establishment of legal aid services in all countries where they may be needed and to cooperate with bar associations, the judiciary, social welfare agencies, and other international organizations interested in extending and improving legal aid and defender services. The need for such an international organization was recognized by the League of Nations in 1924 and later by the International Red Cross and other international agencies concerned with social welfare, especially those dealing with migration.

legal association: *see* bar association.

legal code: *see* law code.

legal fiction, a rule assuming as true something that is clearly false. A fiction is often used to get around the provisions of constitutions and legal codes that legislators are hesitant to change or to encumber with specific limitations. Thus, when a legislature has no legal power to sit beyond a certain midnight but has five hours more of work still to do, it is easier to turn back the official clock from time to time than it is to change the law or constitution.

In ancient Rome, where every family needed a male heir, the lack of one was overcome through the legal fiction of adoption. In England, when courts handling civil cases were full, the Court of Queen's (or King's) Bench, a criminal court, could take some of the load by pretending that the defendant in a simple civil suit had been arrested and was in custody.

Almost any legal fiction can be stated in terms of fact. Thus, the fiction that a corporation is, for many purposes, a person separate from its members is equivalent to saying that, for those purposes, the law deals with the group as a unit, disregarding for the moment the group's individual members as such.

legal glossator, in the Middle Ages, any of the scholars who applied methods of interlinear or marginal annotations (*glossae*) and the explanation of words to the interpretation of Roman legal texts. The age of the legal glossators began with the revival of the study of Roman law at Bologna at the end of the 11th century. One of their first tasks was to reconstruct Justinian's *Digest*, the 6th-century compilation of Roman law, by comparing the existing manuscripts.

In the middle of the 13th century Franciscus Accursius, a professor at Bologna and the last of the glossators, undertook the task of collecting and arranging the vast number of annotations made by his predecessors in one complete work. This compilation, the *Glossa ordinaria,* supplemented by the annotations of Accursius himself, was known as the *Glossa magna* (Great Gloss). For nearly a century its authority was no less than that of the original Roman texts.

The glossators laid the foundation for the study of Roman law in Europe at a time when increasing commercial relations among individuals and among states were soon to necessitate an advanced legal system. Whether they were concerned with these trends or even with the current legal needs of their day is open to doubt. Their discussions tended to be academic rather than practical. It was the task of their successors of the 14th century, the commentators or postglossators, to effect a closer liaison between the revived Roman law and the law of the Italian cities and to find a way to apply Roman law to the practical legal needs of the day.

The influence of the glossators and commentators spread beyond Italy. Many students were attracted to the Bologna school, from which lawyers went out into governments and courts of Europe. Their work affected both the processes and the substance of legal thinking for many centuries.

legal maxim, in Anglo-American law, a broad proposition (usually stated in a fixed Latin form), a number of which have been used by lawyers since the 17th century or earlier. Some of them can be traced to early Roman law. Much more general in scope than ordinary rules of law, legal maxims commonly formulate a legal policy or ideal that judges are supposed to consider in deciding cases. Maxims do not normally have the dogmatic authority of statutes; but in California some have been incorporated into the civil code, such as: "Anyone may waive the advantage of a law intended solely for his benefit. But a law established for a public reason cannot be contravened by a private agreement." (Thus, an agreement not to invoke the statute of limitations is binding, but an agreement not to plead that a certain contract constitutes an illegal restraint of trade is not.) "The law never requires impossibilities": *Lex non cogit ad impossibilia.* (Thus, an actress who becomes ill is excused from performing although her contract does not so state.)

With the expansion of commerce and industry in the 16th and 17th centuries English courts were called upon to decide many novel cases for which the rules of medieval common law provided little or no guidance, and the judges felt the need for broad, authoritative principles to support their decisions. In the 17th century Francis Bacon composed a collection of maxims of the common law in Latin with an elaborate English commentary on each; and Sir Edward Coke's writings were replete with similar Latin aphorisms, some borrowed from Roman law, others invented. Collections of maxims, usually followed by explanatory comments and references to illustrative cases, continued to appear during the next three centuries in England and the United States. With the accumulation of statutes, precedents, and voluminous textbooks, however, the maxims steadily declined in importance. Eventually, they were criticized by judges for what had once been considered their most valuable characteristic: their generality and vagueness. Although some of the ideas embodied in them retain considerable influence, the maxims themselves are now less often referred to.

legal medicine: *see* medical jurisprudence.

legal procedure, Roman: *see* Roman legal procedure.

Legal Tender Cases (1870, 1871), two cases decided by the U.S. Supreme Court regarding the power of Congress to authorize government notes not backed by specie as money that creditors had to accept in payment of debts.

To finance the Civil War, the federal government in 1862 passed the Legal Tender Act, authorizing the creation of paper money not redeemable in gold or silver. About $430 million worth of "greenbacks" were put in circulation, and this money by law had to be accepted for all taxes, debts, and other obligations—even those contracted prior to the passage of the act.

In *Hepburn* v. *Griswold* (Feb. 7, 1870), the Court ruled by a four-to-three majority that Congress lacked the power to make the notes legal tender. Chief Justice Salmon P. Chase, who as secretary of the Treasury during the Civil War had been involved in enacting the Legal Tender Act, wrote the majority opinion, declaring that the congressional authorization of greenbacks as legal tender violated Fifth Amendment guarantees against deprivation of property without due process of law.

On the day the decision was announced, a disapproving President Grant sent the nominations of two new justices to the Senate for confirmation. Justices Bradley and Strong were confirmed, and at the next session the court agreed to reconsider the greenback issue. In *Knox* v. *Lee* and *Parker* v. *Davis* (May 1, 1871), the Court reversed its *Hepburn* v. *Griswold* decision by a five-to-four majority, asserting that the Legal Tender Act of 1862 represented a justifiable use of federal power at a time of national emergency.

Consult the INDEX *first*

Legalism, school of Chinese philosophy that attained prominence during the turbulent Warring States era (475–221 BC) and, through the influence of the philosopher Han Fei-tzu, formed the ideological basis of China's first Imperial dynasty, the Ch'in (221–206 BC).

The Legalists believed that political institutions should be modelled in response to the realities of human behaviour and that men were inherently selfish and short-sighted. Thus social harmony could not be assured through the recognition by the people of the virtue of their ruler, but only through strong state control and absolute obedience to authority. The Legalists advocated government by a system of laws that rigidly prescribed punishments and rewards for specific behaviours. The Legalists stressed the direction of all human activity toward the goal of increasing the power of the ruler and the state. The brutal implementation of this policy by the authoritarian Ch'in dynasty led to that dynasty's overthrow and the permanent discrediting of Legalist philosophy in China.

Legaré, Hugh Swinton (b. Jan. 2, 1797, Charleston, S.C., U.S.—d. June 20, 1843, Boston), U.S. lawyer, a conservative Southern intellectual who opposed the attempts of South Carolina's radicals to nullify the Tariff of 1832.

Legaré studied for a year under Moses Waddel before going on to become the valedictorian of his class at South Carolina College (now the University of South Carolina, Columbia). Following three years of studying law in the United States, Legaré went to Europe to advance his education. In 1820 he returned to South Carolina, where he served in the state legislature for most of the decade.

In 1828 he helped found the *Southern Review*, one of the best literary journals of the era. He became attorney general of South Carolina in 1830 and two years later accepted appointment as U.S. chargé d'affaires in Belgium. Before he left the country, however, he led the Unionist forces in South Carolina during the nullification controversy, opposing John C. Calhoun's theory of state sovereignty and right to secession (*see* nullification).

When he returned from Belgium in 1836, Legaré served one term in the U.S. House of Representatives. Then, when his good friend and fellow Southern aristocrat John Tyler succeeded to the presidency in 1841, Legaré became U.S. attorney general. When Daniel Webster resigned as secretary of state (1843), Legaré—a month before his death—was appointed to replace him.

Legaspi, also spelled LEGAZPI, chartered city, capital of Albay province, southeastern Luzon, Philippines, near an inlet on Albay Gulf. Founded *c.* 1639, it was named for Miguel López de Legazpi, conquistador and first Spanish governor general of the Philippines. The city lies at the southern base of the active volcanic Mt. Mayon, the 1815 eruption of which killed more than 1,000 people and levelled nearby Cagsawa. The mountain is the site of a national park.

Legaspi is the primary port for a region that exports copra and abaca. The city has facilities for storing petroleum, and it is the centre of a large abaca-fibre handicraft industry. Its harbour, although well protected, has poor wharfage facilities because of deep water inshore and the frequency of typhoons. Legaspi is the southernmost point on the Manila-South Railroad; it also has an airport. It is the seat of Bicol University (1969). Inc. city, 1959. Pop. (2000) 157,010.

legate, Latin LEGATUS ("deputy"), plural LEGATI, official who acted as a deputy general to governors of provinces conquered by ancient Rome in the 2nd and 1st centuries BC, during the period of the republic. In the latter part of the 1st century BC, Julius Caesar initiated the practice of appointing legates to command legions in the army. This practice became customary under the emperor Augustus (27 BC–AD 14). Under the early empire, in the 1st and 2nd centuries AD, a province containing one or more legions was governed by a military commander with the title *legatus Augusti pro praetore* (propraetorian legate of the emperor).

legate, also called PAPAL LEGATE, in the Roman Catholic Church, a cleric sent on a mission, ecclesiastical or diplomatic, by the pope as his personal representative. Three types of legates are recognized by canon law. A *legatus a latere* (a legate sent from the pope's side, as it were) is a cardinal who represents the pope on some special assignment with such powers as are delegated to him. Nuncios and internuncios are sent to countries that have diplomatic relations with the Holy See; they promote friendly relations and observe and report to the pope on the state of the church in that region. Apostolic delegates are sent to countries that do not have diplomatic relations with the Holy See; they channel information between the local ecclesiastical hierarchy and the Holy See.

legation, Italian LEGAZIONE, major administrative division of the Papal States ruled by a cardinal legate during the 18th and 19th centuries. In the mid-19th century, on the eve of Italian unification, there were four such legations: Bologna (including Ferrara and Romagna), Urbino (covering the Marche), Perugia (covering Umbria), and Velletri (covering southern Lazio).

Legazpi, Miguel López de (b. *c.* 1510, Zumárraga, Spain—d. Aug. 20, 1572, Manila), Spanish explorer who established Spain's dominion over the Philippines that lasted until the Spanish–American War of 1898.

Legazpi went to New Spain (Mexico) in 1545, serving for a time as clerk in the local government. Although Ferdinand Magellan had discovered the Philippine archipelago in 1521, no European settlements had been made there, so Luis de Velasco, the viceroy of New Spain, sent Legazpi to claim it in 1564. He left Acapulco with five ships and reached Cebu, one of the southern islands of the archipelago, in April 1565, founding the first Spanish settlement on the site of modern Cebu City.

Legazpi served as the first governor of the Philippines, from 1565 until his death. In 1570 he sent an expedition to the northern island of Luzon, arriving there himself the next year. After deposing a local Muslim ruler, in 1571 he established the city of Manila, which became the capital of the new Spanish colony and Spain's major trading port in East Asia.

Legazpi repulsed two attacks by the Portuguese, in 1568 and 1571, and easily overcame the poorly organized Filipinos' resistance. The Muslims in the southern islands resisted Spanish rule up to the 19th century, but Islām was weak in Luzon and the northern islands, and Legazpi and his chaplain, Andrés de Urdaneta, were able to lay the foundations for the conversion of the people to Christianity, which proved their most durable legacy.

Legdan (Mongol chief): *see* Ligdan.

legend, traditional story or group of stories told about a particular person or place. Formerly the term legend meant a tale about a saint. Legends resemble folktales in content; they may include supernatural beings, elements of mythology, or explanations of natural phenomena, but they are associated with a particular locality or person and are told as a matter of history.

Some legends are the unique property of the place or person that they depict, such as the story of young George Washington, the future first president of the United States, who confesses to chopping down the cherry tree. But many local legends are actually well-known folktales that have become attached to some particular person or place. For example, a widely distributed folktale of an excellent marksman who is forced to shoot an apple, hazelnut, or some other object from his son's head has become associated with the Swiss hero William Tell. Another popular tale, of a younger son whose only inheritance is a cat, which he sells for a fortune in a land overrun with mice, has become associated with Richard Whittington, thrice lord mayor of London in the early 15th century. The story told about King Lear is essentially the folktale "Love Like Salt."

Local legends sometimes travel. Though the Pied Piper of Hamelin is famous through literary treatment, many other European towns have a similar legend of a piper who lured their children away. *See also* folktale.

Legendre, Adrien-Marie (b. Sept. 18, 1752, Paris, France—d. Jan. 10, 1833, Paris), French mathematician whose distinguished work on elliptic integrals provided basic analytic tools for mathematical physics.

Legendre was professor of mathematics at the École Militaire, Paris, from 1775 to 1780 and in 1795 became a professor at the École Normale. Although he was appointed to several minor government positions, he was never offered offices commensurate with his ability because of the jealousy of his colleague Pierre-Simon Laplace, who appropriated some of Legendre's work with scant acknowledgment.

One of the problems Legendre studied at an early age was the attraction of spheroids. In the first of his four great memoirs on this subject, published in 1783, he introduced the celebrated function that has been named after him. Legendre's *Nouvelles méthodes pour la détermination des orbites des comètes* (1806; "New Methods for the Determination of Comet Orbits") contains the first comprehensive treatment of the method of least squares. He also made important contributions to geodesy and was widely known for his *Éléments de géométrie* (1794).

Legendre, detail of a lithograph by F.-S. Delpech after a portrait by Z. Belliard

In his *Éléments* Legendre greatly rearranged and simplified many of the propositions from Euclid's *Elements* to create a more effective textbook. Legendre's work replaced Euclid's *Elements* as a textbook in most of Europe and, in succeeding translations, in the United States and became the prototype of later geometry texts. In *Éléments* Legendre gave a simple proof that π (pi) is irrational, as well as the first proof that π^2 is irrational, and conjectured that π is not the root of any algebraic equation of finite degree with rational coefficients.

In 1786 Legendre took up research on elliptic integrals at the point that Leonhard Euler of Germany, John Landen of England, and Joseph-Louis Lagrange of France had left off. In his most important work, *Traité des fonctions elliptiques* (1825–37; "Treatise on Elliptic Functions"), he reduced elliptic integrals to three standard forms now known by his name. Shortly after his work appeared, the independent discoveries of Niels Henrik Abel and Karl Jacobi revolutionized the subject of elliptic integrals completely.

Legendre published his own researches in number theory and those of his predecessors in a systematic form under the title *Théorie des nombres,* 2 vol. (1830). This work included his proof of the law of quadratic reciprocity. Regarded by the greatest mathematician of his day, Carl Friedrich Gauss, as the "gem of arithmetic," this law was the most important general result in number theory since the work of Pierre de Fermat in the 17th century.

Léger, Fernand (b. Feb. 4, 1881, Argentan, France—d. Aug. 17, 1955, Gif-sur-Yvette), French painter, deeply influenced by modern industrial technology, who developed "machine art," or a style characterized by monumental mechanistic forms in bold colours arranged in highly disciplined compositions.

Léger was born into a peasant family in a small town in Normandy. He served a two-year apprenticeship in an architect's office at Caen and then, in 1900, went to work in Paris, first as an architectural draftsman and later as a retoucher of photographs. In 1903 he enrolled in the Paris École des Arts Décoratifs and, although failing to get into the École des Beaux-Arts, began to study under two of its professors as an unofficial pupil. A large retrospective of the work of Paul Cézanne at the Paris Salon d'Automne of 1907 influenced him profoundly.

In 1908, the year Cubism began, Léger rented a studio at La Ruche ("The Beehive"), an artists' settlement on the edge of Montparnasse, and there he soon found himself in the centre of several avant-garde tendencies. Eventually, he got to know the painters Robert Delaunay, Marc Chagall, and Chaim Soutine; the sculptors Jacques Lipchitz, Henri Laurens, and Alexander Archipenko; and the poets Guillaume Apollinaire, Max Jacob, Blaise Cendrars, and Pierre Reverdy. Through the poets, in particular, there was a connection with the Cubist movement, the early centre of which was in Montmartre, where Pablo Picasso and Georges Braque had their studios.

Léger had been painting in a style that mixed Impressionism with Fauvism; now, under the pressure of his new environment, he evolved rapidly. In 1909 he produced "La Couseuse" ("The Seamstress"), in which he reduced his colours to a combination of blue-gray and buff and the human body to a construction of slabs and cylinders that resembled a robot. That same year he began "Nus dans la forêt" ("Nudes in the Forest"), completed the following year, in which the geometric volumes composing the figures are broken into large fragments.

By 1913 Léger was painting, in brighter colours, the series of dynamic, sometimes completely abstract studies he called "Contrast of Forms"; here his style, aptly nicknamed "tubism," was intended to illustrate his theory that the way to achieve a maximum of pictorial effect was to multiply contrasts of colour, contrasts of curved and straight lines, and contrasts of solids with each other or with flat planes. In 1914, in a lecture entitled "Les Révélations picturales actuelles" ("Contemporary Achievements in Painting"), he added to this aesthetic basis of his art an affirmation of his faith in modern life and popular culture.

Léger, photograph by Arnold Newman, 1941

During World War I, in which he fought as a sapper in the front lines, Léger acquired a strengthened sense of reality and a renewed interest in cylindrical shapes, as found in weaponry. "Without transition," he remembered, "I found myself at the level of the entire French people. . . . At the same time I was dazzled by the breech of a 75 [artillery piece] in full sunlight, by the magic of the light on the bare metal. . . . Total revolution, as man and as painter." Gassed at the Battle of Verdun, he was hospitalized for a long period and was finally released from the army in 1917. That year he completed "La Partie de Cartes" ("The Card Party"), which he regarded as "the first picture in which I deliberately took my subject from our own epoch." By 1919 he was in what has been called his mechanical period, which was marked by a fascination for motors, gears, bearings, furnaces, railway crossings, and factory interiors.

In the mid-1920s, Léger was associated with the French formalist movement called Purism, which had been launched by the painter Amédée Ozenfant and the painter-architect Charles-Édouard Jeanneret (Le Corbusier). But from then on, Léger's art was essentially figurative, and the only significant change in his style was a tendency, begun during World

War II, to separate his bands of colour from his drawing and to leave them abstract.

Léger was concerned all his life about the relationship of colour to public buildings, and he was able to realize some of his ideas in the mosaic facade of Notre-Dame de Toute-Grâce at Plateau d'Assy, in southeastern France (1949); in a mosaic for the crypt of the American memorial at Bastogne (1950); in a mural for the United Nations building in New York City; and in several projects for stained-glass windows, such as those for Sacré-Coeur of Audincourt, France (1951).

His desire to bring his art closer to the life of ordinary people may have been one of his reasons for joining the French Communist Party in 1945—although in fact he never practiced the Social Realism that was then favoured by Communist leaders. During the last years of his life, Léger's major paintings were "Les Constructeurs" (1950) and "La Grande Parade" (1954). A large number of studies and variations can be linked to both pictures.

Few 20th-century artists accepted the Industrial Revolution with as much enthusiasm as Léger displayed during his long and, although qualitatively uneven, remarkably consistent career. Since his death his reputation, although somewhat that of a period figure, has grown. At Biot, in southern France, there is a museum devoted to his work. (R.McMu./Ed.)

BIBLIOGRAPHY. Biographical and critical studies include Robert Delevoy, *Léger* (1962); Jean Cassou and Jean Leymarie, *Fernand Léger: Drawings and Gouaches* (1973); Christopher Green, *Leger and the Avant-Garde* (1976); Werner Schmalenbach, *Fernand Léger* (1976); *Fernand Leger* (1982), with essays by Robert T. Buck, Edward F. Fry, and Charlotta Kotik; and Peter De Francia, *Fernand Léger* (1983).

Legg–Calvé–Perthes syndrome, also called COXA PLANA, bone disease, a form of osteochondrosis (*q.v.*).

Leggett, Anthony J. (b. March 26, 1938, London, Eng.), British physicist who won the Nobel Prize for Physics in 2003 for his seminal work on superfluidity. He shared the award with the Russian physicists Alexey A. Abrikosov and Vitaly L. Ginzburg.

After receiving a Ph.D. (1964) from the University of Oxford, Leggett joined the faculty of the University of Sussex in 1967. He taught there until 1983, when he moved to the University of Illinois at Urbana-Champaign.

Scientists have known since the 1930s that the common form of helium, the isotope helium-4, becomes a superfluid when chilled. Although a theoretical explanation was produced for the phenomenon, researchers in the 1970s discovered it did not work for the much rarer helium isotope helium-3, which was also a superfluid. Leggett filled the gap in theoretical research by showing that electrons in helium-3 form pairs in a situation similar to, but more complicated than, the electron pairs that form in superconducting metals. His work in identifying and describing the phase transitions that occur during these pairing interactions found wide application in science.

legion, a military organization, originally the largest permanent organization in the armies of ancient Rome. The term legion also denotes the military system by which imperial Rome conquered and ruled the ancient world.

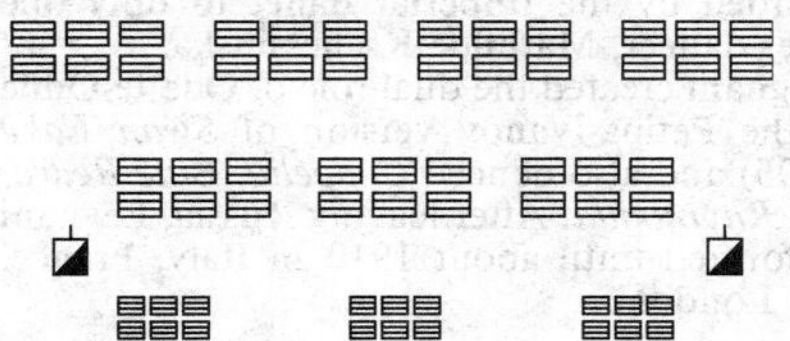

Legion in battle order
Four cohorts in the first line and three each in the second and third lines with cavalry
Encyclopædia Britannica, Inc.

The expanding early Roman Republic found the Greek phalanx formation too unwieldy for fragmented fighting in the hills and valleys of central Italy. Accordingly, the Romans evolved a new tactical system based on small and supple infantry units called maniples. Each maniple numbered 120 men in 12 files and 10 ranks. Maniples drew up for battle in three lines, each line made up of 10 maniples and the whole arranged in a checkerboard pattern. (*See* the Figure.) Separating each unit was an interval equivalent to a maniple's front of 18 m (60 feet), so that the maniples of the first line could fall back in defense into the intervals of the second line. Conversely, the second line could merge with the first to form a solid front 10 ranks deep and 360 m (1,200 feet) wide. In the third line, 10 maniples of light infantry were supplemented by smaller units of reserves. The three lines were 75 m (250 feet) apart, and from front to rear one maniple of each line formed a cohort of 420 men; this was the Roman equivalent of a battalion. Ten cohorts made up the heavy-infantry strength of a legion, but 20 cohorts were usually combined with a small cavalry force and other supporting units into a little self-supporting army of about 10,000 men.

Two infantry weapons gave the legion its famous flexibility and force; the *pilum,* a 2-m (7-foot) javelin used for both throwing and thrusting; and the *gladius,* a 50-cm (20-inch) cut-and-thrust sword with a broad, heavy blade. For protecton each legionary had a metal helmet, cuirass, and convex shield. In battle, the first line of maniples attacked on the double, hurling javelins and then diving in with swords before the enemy had time to recover. Then came the maniples of the second line, and only a resolute foe could rally from the two successive shocks.

As Roman armies of the late Republic and Empire became larger and more professional, the cohort, with an average field strength of 360 men, replaced the maniple as the chief tactical unit within legions. In the military operations of Lucius Cornelius Sulla and Julius Caesar, a legion was composed of 10 cohorts, with 4 cohorts in the first line and 3 each in the second and third lines. The 3,600 heavy infantry were supported by enough cavalry and light infantry to bring the legion's strength up to 6,000 men. Seven legions in three lines, comprising about 25,000 heavy infantry, occupied a mile and a half of front.

As Rome evolved into a defending power, the cohort was increased to a field strength of 500–600 men. These still depended on the shock tactics of *pilum* and *gladius,* but the 5,000–6,000 heavy infantry in a legion were now combined with an equal number of supporting cavalry troops and light infantry made up of archers, slingers, and javelin men. In order to deal with mounted barbarian raiders, the proportion of cavalry rose from one-seventh to one-fourth. By the 4th century AD, with the empire defending its many fortified border outposts, as many as 10 catapults and 60 ballistae were assigned to each legion.

In modern times the term legion has been applied to a corps of foreign volunteers or mercenaries, such as the French provincial legions of Francis I and the second-line formations of Napoleon. "Foreign legion" often signifies the irregular corps of foreign volunteers raised by states at war. The most famous of these is France's Foreign Legion (Légion Étrangère).

Legion of Honour, officially ROYAL ORDER OF THE LEGION OF HONOUR, French ORDRE ROYALE DE LA LÉGION D'HONNEUR, premier order of the French republic, created by Napoleon Bonaparte, then first consul, on May 19, 1802, as a general military and civil order of merit conferred without regard to birth or religion provided that anyone admitted swears to uphold liberty and equality.

Napoleon's ideas for this order, which finally prevailed, aroused some opposition, particularly from those who felt the Legion should have purely military qualifications. After becoming emperor, Napoleon presided over the first investiture into the Legion, which took place in 1804 at the Hôtel des Invalides, Paris. During the Restoration, the Legion became a royal order, ranked below the restored military and religious orders of the ancien régime. Upon the downfall of the monarchy, the Legion once again became the highest-ranking order and decoration in France.

True to the stated ideals of Napoleon, the membership of the Legion is remarkably egalitarian; both men and women, French citizens and foreigners, civilians and military personnel, irrespective of rank, birth, or religion, can be admitted to any of the classes of the Legion. Admission into this order, which can be conferred posthumously, requires 20 years of civil achievement in peacetime or extraordinary military bravery and service in times of war. Admission for war services automatically carries with it the award of the Croix de Guerre, the highest French military medal.

During the Consulate and the First Empire, Napoleon served as the grand master of the order, while a grand council of seven grand officers administered the 15 territorial units, or "cohorts," into which the order was divided. Currently, the president of France serves as grand master, and the order is administered by a civil chancellor with the help of a council nominated by the grand master. The Legion has five classes, listed in descending rank: grand cross (limited to 80 members), grand officer (200), commander (1,000), officer (4,000), and knight, or chevalier (unlimited). Foreign recipients in the classes higher than chevalier are supernumerary. Promotion from a lower grade to a higher grade is done according to the service performed in the lower. However, extraordinary services may admit candidates at once to any rank.

The changes in design of the insignia reflect the vicissitudes of French history. Originally, the star of the order depicted a crown surrounded by oak and laurel wreaths with the head of Napoleon, while the reverse displayed an eagle holding a thunderbolt with the motto emblazoned "Honneur et Patrie" ("Honour and Country"). During the first Restoration, Louis XVIII, in 1814, replaced the head of Napoleon with that of King Henry IV of France, and on the other side introduced the royal fleur-de-lis emblem. Napoleon III, in 1870, restored the original design, although he replaced the head of Napoleon with the female head of the Republic. The badge of the Legion depicts this head with the inscription "République Française"; the reverse side has a set of crossed tricolours with the motto "Honneur et Patrie."

Legionnaire's disease, form of pneumonia first identified in 1976 as caused by a previously unknown bacillus subsequently named *Legionella pneumophila*. The name of the disease (and of the bacterium) derives from a 1976 state convention of the American Legion, a U.S. military veterans' organization, at a Philadelphia hotel where 182 Legionnaires contracted the disease, 29 of them fatally. The largest known outbreak of Legionnaire's disease, confirmed in more than 300 people, occurred in Murcia, Spain, in 2001.

Medical detective work by the U.S. Centers for Disease Control in Atlanta, Ga., pieced together clues and laboratory work, discovering that the organism had many unique properties and was unlike any bacterium previously encountered in medical bacteriology. Investigators found that *L. pneumophila* would grow slowly and only in a greatly enriched, moist culture medium within a narrow range of acidity (optimally pH 6.9 to 7.0) and that the bacterium could survive for a year in tap water. Later studies of stored tissue and serum samples revealed that a number of mysterious outbreaks of unknown pneumonia-like diseases throughout the world actually were episodes of Legionnaire's disease.

Typically, but not uniformly, the first symptoms of Legionnaire's disease are general malaise and headache, followed by high fever, often accompanied by chills. Coughing (often without sputum production), shortness of breath, pleurisy-like pain, and abdominal distress are common, and occasionally some mental confusion is present. Although healthy individuals can contract Legionnaire's disease, the most common patients are elderly or debilitated individuals or persons whose immunity is suppressed by drugs or disease. Measurement of *Legionella* protein in the urine is a rapid and specific test for the majority of *L. pneumophila* subtypes.

Although it is fairly well documented that the disease is rarely spread like pneumococcal pneumonia through person-to-person contact, the exact source of the outbreaks has yet to be determined. It is suspected that contaminated water in central air-conditioning units can serve to disseminate *L. pneumophila* in droplets into the surrounding atmosphere. Potable water and drainage systems are suspect, as is water at construction sites. Treatment for Legionnaire's disease is with the antibiotic azithromycin, augmented in unusually severe cases by rifampin.

Pontiac fever, an influenza-like illness characterized by fever, headache, and muscle pain, represents a milder form of *Legionella* infection.

legislative apportionment, also called LEGISLATIVE DELIMITATION, process by which representation is distributed among the constituencies of a representative assembly. The use of the term apportionment is limited almost exclusively to the United States. In most other countries, particularly the United Kingdom and the countries of the Commonwealth, the term used is delimitation.

Apportionment can take relatively simple forms: in the assembly of ancient Athens, for example, each citizen represented himself. During later centuries, in the East as well as the West, the courts and councils of kings and emperors were formed of representatives of several classes, such as the nobility, clergy, and delegates of such bodies as guilds and centres of learning. With the growth of democracy, the extension of suffrage, and the rise of political parties, however, legislative apportionment became a complex problem. Apportionment had to be methodically and mathematically arranged to ensure that the distribution of legislative seats would reflect most accurately the will of the electorate.

Although practice varies widely, it is possible to distinguish five general types of legislative apportionment, each giving rise to a particular form of constituency:

1. Territorial apportionment: constituencies have specified boundaries, and ideally the number of voters in each of the constituencies is about equal; this is the most common form of apportionment.

2. Apportionment among self-contained governing units (such as towns, counties, cities, states, etc.): the unit of local government acts as the constituency and is represented in higher legislative bodies.

3. Apportionment among official bodies that act as constituencies: local or provincial bodies choose representatives (*e.g.,* the state legislatures chose U.S. senators before the 17th Amendment established popular election).

4. Apportionment among functional groupings of the population: the electorate is grouped according to social or economic characteristics, resulting in such divisions as the nobility, clergy, and commoners of early English Parliaments or the occupational, industrial, professional, national, and other groupings used as the basis for apportionment in guild socialism.

5. Apportionment among party interests: systems of proportional representation are designed to reflect as many facets of voter opinion as possible (*see* proportional representation). Under the latter two systems, the group or party is regarded as the constituency.

Disparity of constituency sizes has been a recurring problem in legislative apportionment everywhere. Electoral reforms have often been instituted to eliminate such malapportionments as the system of rotten boroughs (*see* rotten borough) in Britain and the practice of gerrymandering (*q.v.*) in the United States. Periodic reapportionments by constituency boundary commissions have been adopted by legislatures in order to adjust apportionment to changes in population.

The authority to adjust apportionment can be an important tool in maintaining the power of the incumbent party. Constituencies can be defined, for example, in a way that concentrates the power of the opposition into relatively few districts, while giving the ruling party narrow majorities in a large number of districts, thus giving the incumbent party a disproportionately large share of seats. Or, by a different strategy, individual incumbents may influence the apportionment to give themselves districts with no substantial opposition. While such politically motivated apportionment is generally regarded as an abuse, various minority groups in the United States have recently begun to call for what amounts to gerrymandering to preserve the integrity and power of special-interest blocs of voters in large cities.

Legislative Assembly, French ASSEMBLÉE LÉGISLATIVE, national parliament of France during part of the Revolutionary period and again during the Second Republic. The first was created in September 1791 and was in session from Oct. 1, 1791, to Sept. 20, 1792, when it was replaced by the National Convention, marking the formal beginning of the (First) Republic. During the Second Republic it lasted from May 28, 1849, to Dec. 2, 1851, when Napoleon III dissolved it; the republic itself ended less than one year later.

Legislative Corps (France): *see* Corps Législatif.

legislative investigative powers, powers of a lawmaking body to conduct investigations. In most countries this power is exercised primarily to provide a check on the executive branch of government. The U.S. Congress, however, has exercised broad investigative powers, beginning in 1792 with an investigation of a military disaster.

In the 1820s Congressional committees regularly began to summon witnesses to testify about proposed legislation. In 1857 it provided criminal penalties for witnesses who refuse to answer questions, although in *Kilbourn* v. *Thompson* (1881), the Supreme Court held that Congress may not inquire "into the private affairs of the citizen." Nearly four decades later, in *Sinclair* v. *United States* (1929), the court, less hostile to congressional inquiries, ruled that a witness could not refuse to answer questions on the grounds that questions related to his private affairs.

In the 1950s, investigations conducted by the House Un-American Activities Committee into alleged Communist activities prompted claims that congressional investigations were violating First Amendment rights by "engaging in exposure for exposure's sake." Because these cases invariably included allegations of Fifth Amendment violations, the court disposed of the cases on Fifth Amendment grounds, thus avoiding the First Amendment issue. Several contempt-of-Congress convictions were sustained, however, before the judicial climate changed in the 1960s.

In *Gibson* v. *Florida Legislative Commission* (1963) the Supreme Court held that a state legislative investigation of the Miami National Association for the Advancement of Colored People (NAACP) was a violation of First Amendment rights. Writing for the majority, Justice Arthur Goldberg stated that "groups which themselves are neither engaged in subversive or other illegal or improper activities . . . are to be protected in their rights of free and private association." Later, in *DeGregory* v. *New Hampshire Attorney General* (1966), the court held that the First Amendment prevents the government from "using the power to investigate enforced by the contempt power," in the absence of any showing of "overriding and compelling state interest that would warrant intrusion into the realm of political and associational privacy protected by the First Amendment."

"De," "la," and similar components of a name, when followed by a space, are alphabetized as separate words (e.g., *De Forest, Lee*). *When they are joined to the following part of a name, the combination is treated as a single word* (e.g., *DeForest, John William*).

Legitimist, French LÉGITIMISTE, in 19th-century France, any of the royalists who from 1830 onward supported the claims of the representative of the senior line of the house of Bourbon to be the legitimate king of France. They were opposed not only to republicans but also to the other monarchist factions: to the Orleanists, royalist adherents of the house of Bourbon-Orléans, who at the July Revolution of 1830 recognized Louis-Philippe as king of France; and to the Bonapartists, who favoured a restoration of the French Empire. The Legitimist position was theoretically unassailable as long as the Count de Chambord, whom they recognized as Henry V of France, was alive. The Count de Chambord's intransigence, however, precluded a coalition between the Legitimists and Orleanists even when the collapse of the Second Empire (1852–70) seemed to make a restoration of the monarchy possible. After the Count de Chambord's death without heirs in 1883, most Legitimists switched their support to the Orleanist pretender, Louis-Philippe-Albert, Count de Paris.

Legnani, Pierina (b. 1863, Italy—d. 1923, Italy), Italian ballerina whose virtuoso technique inspired Russian dancers to develop their now-characteristic technical brilliance.

After appearing in Milan, Paris, London, and Madrid, Legnani went in 1893 to the Mariinsky Theatre in St. Petersburg, where she danced *Cinderella* and astonished audiences with 32 consecutive *fouettés en tournant* ("whipped turns" done in place and on one leg), a tour de force that she originated and first performed in London. Though initially engaged for one season only, Legnani performed in Russia until 1901 and received the title *prima ballerina assoluta,* an honour awarded by the Imperial Ballet to only one other dancer, Mathilde Kschessinska.

Legnani created the dual role of Odette-Odile in the Petipa-Ivanov version of *Swan Lake* (1895) and also danced *Coppélia, Blue Beard,* and *Raymonda*. After leaving Russia, Legnani performed until about 1910 in Italy, France, and London.

Legnano, Latin LEUNIANUM, city, Milano *provincia,* Lombardia (Lombardy) *regione,* northern Italy, on the Olona River. An unimportant Roman settlement called Leunianum, it became the site of a fortified castle of the bishops of Milan in the 11th century and in 1176 was the scene of a decisive defeat of the Holy Roman emperor Frederick I Barbarossa by the forces of the Lombard League. A monument built in 1876 by Enrico Butti commemorates the victory.

Notable landmarks in the city include the Church of San Magno (1529), with an altarpiece by Bernardino Luini, and the remains of a castle of the Visconti family, who controlled the region in the 14th and 15th centuries.

A northwestern industrial satellite of Milan, Legnano has important metallurgical and cotton-textile plants and machinery, soap, and candle works. Pop. (2001) 53,797.

Legnica, German LIEGNITZ, former (1975–98) *województwo* (province), southwestern Poland, now part of Dolnośląskie (*q.v.*) province.

Legnica, German LIEGNITZ, city, Dolnośląskie *województwo* (province), southwestern Poland. It lies along the Kaczawa River in the western lowlands of Silesia (Śląsk). A 12th-century Silesian stronghold, Legnica became the capital of an autonomous principality in 1248. At the Battle of Liegnitz, or Legnica, on April 15, 1241, the Mongols defeated a Polish army under Henry II, prince of Lower Silesia. Legnica received municipal rights in 1252 and soon became an important trade centre, with an economy based on its extensive weaving industry. Long ruled by the Piast dynasty, the town passed to the Habsburgs (1675) and to the Prussians (1741). It suffered extensive damage in World War II. Traditional industries include metalworking (principally brass), textiles, and food production and, more recently, metallurgy and copper processing. Legnica is the capital of the local Roman Catholic diocese, established in 1992. The city operates a copper museum, art gallery, theatre, cultural centre, and public library. Pop. (2002) 107,100.

Legrenzi, Giovanni (b. 1626, Clusone, near Bergamo, Republic of Venice [Italy]—d. May 27, 1690, Venice), Italian composer, one of the greatest of the Venetian Baroque. His trio sonatas are among the best chamber music of the period before Arcangelo Corelli.

Little is known about Legrenzi's early years. He studied with his father, a violinist and minor composer, and he was ordained as a priest in 1651. After serving as organist and

Legrenzi

© Lebrecht Music and Arts Photo Library

chaplain at the Santa Maria Maggiore Church in Bergamo, he was maestro di cappella at the Academy of the Holy Spirit in Ferrara from 1656 to 1665. His first opera, *Nino il giusto* (1662; "Nino the Just"), dates from this period. In 1681 he obtained the post of second maestro di cappella at the San Marco Basilica in Venice, succeeding to maestro di cappella in 1685. He enlarged the orchestra at San Marco's and completely reorganized the music.

During his lifetime Legrenzi composed some 19 operas, in addition to sonatas, masses, motets, oratorios, and other pieces. At the time of his death, he had attained an international reputation. Legrenzi's music is characteristic of the final stage of the late Baroque style. He was equally adept at the composition of sacred music, opera, and chamber music. His compositions for the church attest to the advances he made in polyphonic writing. His instrumental sonatas are his most forward-looking works, particularly in the handling of structure; they exerted a strong influence on the works of Domenico Scarlatti, Antonio Vivaldi, and J.S. Bach. Themes from Legrenzi's compositions were used by Bach in his *Fugue in C Minor* for organ and by G.F. Handel in a chorus from his oratorio *Samson*.

Legros, Alphonse (b. May 8, 1837, Dijon, France—d. Dec. 8, 1911, Watford, Hertfordshire, Eng.), French-born British painter, etcher, and sculptor, now remembered chiefly for his graphics on macabre and fantastic themes. An excellent draftsman, he taught in London, revitalizing British drawing and printmaking during a period of low ebb.

Legros first attracted attention at the Paris Salon of 1857 with a profile portrait of his father. Other well-received early works are the "Angelus" (1859) and the "Ex Voto" (1861). He became closely associated with Gustave Courbet, James McNeill Whistler,

"Women at Prayer," oil painting by Alphonse Legros; in the Tate Gallery, London

By courtesy of the trustees of the Tate Gallery, London; photograph, John Webb

and Édouard Manet and was hailed by Charles Baudelaire and other champions of a "new realism" as an important figure. His paintings exhibit his characteristic fine draftsmanship, in the tradition of Jean-Auguste-Dominique Ingres, but have come to be regarded as perhaps too obviously sentimental.

Encouraged by Whistler, Legros settled in London (1863) and taught etching until his appointment as Slade professor of Fine Art, University College, London (1876–92), where he insisted on sound constructional drawing.

Leguía y Salcedo, Augusto Bernardino (b. Feb. 19, 1863, Lambayeque, Peru—d. Feb. 7, 1932, Lima), businessman and politician who, during his first of two terms as president of Peru (1908–12; 1919–30), settled the country's age-old boundary disputes with Bolivia and Brazil.

Leguía was a member of one of the more distinguished families of the Peruvian oligarchy. Before entering politics, he acquired a great deal of experience in business, founding his own insurance company in 1896 and serving on the board of a large British sugar company during the 1890s.

He served Peru as minister of finance and premier from 1903 to 1908. After his election as president in 1908, Leguía encouraged economic development by introducing fiscal and administrative reforms, and he improved the health-care system by founding hospitals and building drainage systems in the cities. After complicated negotiations, he also resolved the controversies with Bolivia and Brazil over disputed territories. For the most part he remained the tool of the Peruvian oligarchy during this term. He spent the interval between his two presidential terms in London.

When in 1919 Leguía was recalled to the presidency, elements of the oligarchy revolted, but his followers staged a coup d'état on July 4, 1919, to install him in office. As a result, during his second term Leguía broke with the

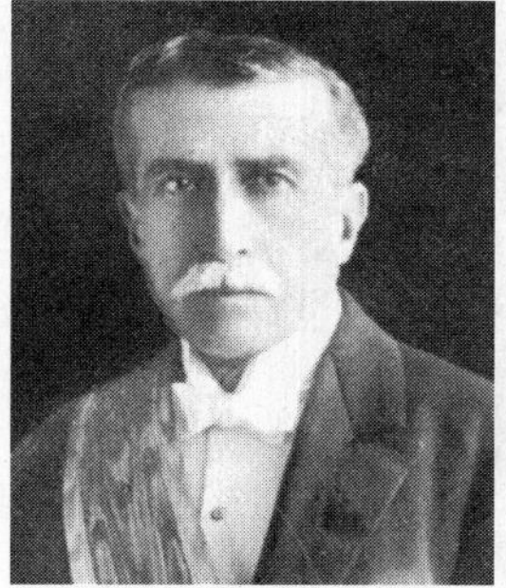

Leguía y Salcedo, 1925

By courtesy of the Organization of American States

old oligarchy that had dominated Peruvian politics for the previous two decades, and he forced many prominent politicians into exile. Although he presided over the creation of a new constitution, he disregarded constitutional norms and ruled as a dictator. In 1930 Leguía was removed from office by a coup.

legume, also called POD, fruit of plants of the order Fabales (*q.v.*), consisting of the single family Leguminosae, or Fabaceae (peas, beans, vetch, and so on). The dry fruit releases its seeds by splitting open along two seams. Legumes furnish food for humans and animals and provide edible oils, fibres, and raw material for plastics. Nutritionally, they are high in protein and contain many of the essential amino acids. For important legumes, *see* alfalfa; bean; broom; clover; cowpea; pea; peanut; soybean; vetch.

Leguminosae, plant family comprising the order Fabales (*q.v.*).

Leh, town, eastern Jammu and Kashmir state, India, in the Kashmir region of the northern part of the Indian subcontinent. The town is located in the remote valley of the upper Indus River at an elevation of 11,550 feet (3,520 m), surrounded by the towering peaks of the Ladākh Range (the southeastern extension of the Karakoram Range). Leh is one of the highest permanently inhabited towns in the world. Built as a terminus for caravans from Central Asia, it is reached only by one main highway, the Treaty Road, which connects it with Srīnagar to the west and to Dêmqog (Tien-chiao), Tibet, to the southeast. The economy relies mainly on trade, but agriculture, including fruit growing, is also important. An old palace of the Ladākhī kings, as well as the Sankar monastery, overlook the town. Pop. (2001 prelim.) 27,513.

Lehár, Franz (b. April 30, 1870, Komárom, Hung., Austria-Hungary—d. Oct. 24, 1948, Bad Ischl, Austria), Hungarian composer of operettas who achieved worldwide success with *Die lustige Witwe* (*The Merry Widow*).

He studied at the Prague Conservatory. Encouraged by Antonín Dvořák to follow a musical career, Lehár traveled in Austria as a bandmaster from 1890. In 1896 he produced his operetta *Kukuschka.* In *The Merry Widow* (1905), with libretto by Viktor Léon and Leo Stein, Lehár created a new style of Viennese operetta, introducing waltz tunes and imitations of the Parisian cancan dances as well as a certain satirical element. Its success was such that two years later it was played at Buenos

Aires at five theatres simultaneously. Many other operettas by Lehár followed and became well known in England and the United States under their English titles. Among them were *The Man with Three Wives* (1908), *The Count of Luxembourg* (1909), *Gypsy Love* (1910), and *The Land of Smiles* (1923). Several of his works were filmed, including *The Merry Widow* and *The Land of Smiles.* He wrote a single grand opera, *Giuditta* (1934), which was less successful.

Lehár
By courtesy of the Osterreichische Nationalbibliothek, Vienna

Lehigh Valley Railroad Company, American railroad whose growth was based on hauling coal from the anthracite mines of northeastern Pennsylvania. Originally founded in 1846 as the Delaware, Lehigh, Schuylkill, and Susquehanna Railroad Company, it changed its name to Lehigh Valley in 1853. It acquired other small lines in Pennsylvania and New Jersey until it reached New York City in the east and Buffalo in the west, for a total length of about 1,400 miles (2,250 km).

With the decline of anthracite as a heating fuel, the Lehigh entered upon bad years until by the end of the 1950s it was near bankruptcy. In 1962 the Pennsylvania Railroad Company purchased most of the Lehigh stock, but the line continued to decline and entered bankruptcy in 1970. Most of its assets were absorbed by the federally chartered Consolidated Rail Corporation (*q.v.*) in 1976.

Lehman Caves, numerous caverns at Great Basin National Park in east-central Nevada, U.S. The caves lie 5 miles (8 km) west of Baker on the eastern slope of Wheeler Peak (13,063 feet [3,982 m]) in the Snake Range. They are made of light gray and white limestone that is honeycombed by tunnels and galleries containing a spectacular array of stalactites and stalagmites. Established in 1922 as a national monument, the Lehman Caves became part of the Great Basin National Park in 1986. Some of the caves were used as burial places by prehistoric Indians.

Lehmann, Johann Gottlob (b. Aug. 4, 1719, Langenhennersdorf, near Pirna, Saxony [Germany]—d. Jan. 22, 1767, St. Petersburg, Russia), German geologist who contributed to the development of stratigraphy, the scientific study of order and sequence in bedded sedimentary rocks.

Lehmann received his M.D. from the University of Wittenberg in 1741 and established a medical practice in Dresden. In Saxony he discovered his real field of interest, mines and mining. His publications on ore deposits and their chemical composition won for him, in 1750, an official commission by the Royal Prussian Academy of Sciences in Berlin to study mining procedures in the Prussian provinces. His explanation of the origin of mineral deposits in specific strata was summarized in the first geologic profile, published in 1756. He recognized that rocks do not fall in haphazard position but rather form in historical sequence; this principle serves as the foundation of modern stratigraphy. The Freiberg Bergakademie, a technical research institute, was founded in 1765 at Lehmann's urging.

Lehmann was invited to St. Petersburg by the Imperial Academy of Sciences; in 1761 he became professor of chemistry at the university there and director of the academy's natural-history collection. His investigations in Russia became the model for geologic explorations carried out after his early death.

Lehmann, John, in full JOHN FREDERICK LEHMANN (b. June 2, 1907, Bourne End, Buckinghamshire, Eng.—d. April 7, 1987, London), English poet, editor, publisher, and man of letters whose book-periodical *New Writing* and its successors were an important influence on English literature from the mid-1930s through the 1940s.

Educated at Eton and at Trinity College, Cambridge, Lehmann worked as a journalist and poet in Vienna from 1932 to 1936 and returned to England to found *New Writing,* which was issued under various titles until 1950. *New Writing* published the work of W.H. Auden, Christopher Isherwood, V.S. Pritchett, and others. Lehmann was general manager of the Hogarth Press (1938–46), founded by Leonard and Virginia Woolf, and advisory editor of *The Geographical Magazine* (1940–45). He and his sister, the novelist Rosamond Lehmann, directed the publishing firm of John Lehmann Ltd. (1946 to 1953). In 1954 he founded *The London Magazine,* a literary review that he edited until 1961.

His first volume of poems, *A Garden Revisited,* appeared in 1931, and several other volumes preceded his *Collected Poems* (1963). His autobiography, which throws much light on the literary life of his time, appeared in three volumes—*The Whispering Gallery* (1955), *I Am My Brother* (1960), and *The Ample Proposition* (1966)—and in a condensed one-volume version in the United States—*In My Own Time* (1969). *Thrown to the Woolfs* (1978) details his difficulties with Leonard Woolf at the Hogarth Press. Lehmann also published a biography of the poet Rupert Brooke in 1980.

Lehmann, Lilli (b. Nov. 24, 1848, Würzburg, Bavaria [Germany]—d. May 17, 1929, Berlin), German operatic soprano and lieder singer, known especially for her performances as Isolde in Richard Wagner's opera *Tristan und Isolde.*

Lehmann made her debut in Prague in 1865 as the First Boy in W.A. Mozart's *Die Zauberflöte* (*The Magic Flute*). In 1870 she joined the Berlin Opera and was a coloratura singer in such roles as the Queen of the Night in *Die Zauberflöte*. She was coached by Wagner in the parts of one of the Rhinemaidens and the Forest Bird for the first Bayreuth performances of his cycle *Der Ring des Nibelungen*. She later undertook dramatic soprano roles and became the greatest Isolde of her day. She was equally outstanding in Ludwig van Beethoven's *Fidelio*. In 1885–89 and 1891–92 she sang at the Metropolitan Opera in New York City.

Lehmann was admired for her dramatic presence and fine voice and for her versatility: her repertory encompassed 170 operatic roles, from Wagner to Vincenzo Bellini to Jacques Offenbach, and 600 lieder. She gave memorable lieder recitals and was active from 1905 in the organization of the Salzburg Festivals. She wrote an autobiography, *Mein Weg* (1913; *My Path Through Life*), and *Meine Gesangskunst* (1902; *How to Sing*).

Lehmann, Lotte (b. Feb. 27, 1888, Perleberg, Ger.—d. Aug. 26, 1976, Santa Barbara, Calif., U.S.), German lyric-dramatic soprano, particularly renowned for her performances of the songs of Robert Schumann and in the roles of Leonore in Ludwig van Beethoven's opera *Fidelio* and of the Marschallin in Richard Strauss's *Der Rosenkavalier* (*The Knight of the Rose*).

Lotte Lehmann as the Marschallin in *Der Rosenkavalier*
The Granger Collection, New York City

Lehmann received her early training in Berlin and made her first major operatic appearance in Hamburg as Freia in Richard Wagner's *Das Rheingold* in 1910. She went to the Vienna State Opera in 1914 and became closely associated with pre-World War II Viennese culture; there Richard Strauss, who later composed for her the title role in *Arabella* (1933), chose her for roles in several of his operas. Lehmann also appeared successfully on English stages from 1913 and in the United States from 1930. At the Metropolitan Opera in New York City she sang chiefly Wagnerian roles. From 1938 she lived in the United States, becoming a citizen and continuing an active career as both a leading performer (until her retirement in 1961) and a teacher.

Lehmann was the author of a novel, *Orplid, mein Land* (1937; *Eternal Flight*), and three volumes of memoirs. She was not related to the celebrated earlier German soprano Lilli Lehmann.

"De," "la," and similar components of a name, when followed by a space, are alphabetized as separate words (e.g., *De Forest, Lee*). *When they are joined to the following part of a name, the combination is treated as a single word* (e.g., *DeForest, John William*).

Lehmann, Orla, in full PETER MARTIN ORLA LEHMANN (b. May 19, 1810, Copenhagen, Den.—d. Sept. 13, 1870, Copenhagen), political reformer who successfully advocated parliamentary government in 19th-century Denmark.

As a student leader in the 1830s, Lehmann was an outspoken critic of Denmark's absolute monarchy. In the 1840s he was a leader of the National Liberal Party, which called for parliamentary government, a liberal economic system, and incorporation of the affiliated duchy of Schleswig into the Danish state.

Lehmann was a leader of the nationalistic demonstrations of March 1848, which resulted in a liberal constitution, a popular ministry, and war against the separatists of Schleswig. He also became a minister without portfolio in the March (provisional) cabinet. Although a liberal until 1848, Lehmann turned to the political right after that year, especially over the issue of increased peasant representation. In 1851 he was elected to the lower house of the new Parliament, and from 1854 to 1870 he sat in the conservative upper house. He also served as a member of the Council of State (1855–66). In 1861–63 he served as minister of the interior in the National Liberal government, which precipitated the disastrous Danish war against Prussia and Austria (1864).

Lehmann, Rosamond Nina (b. Feb. 3, 1901, Bourne End, Buckinghamshire, Eng.—d. March 12, 1990, London), English novelist noted for her sensitive portrayals of girls on the threshold of adult life. An accomplished stylist, she was adept at capturing nuances of moods. She was the sister of the editor and publisher John Lehmann.

She was educated privately and at Girton College, Cambridge, scene of a portion of her first novel, *Dusty Answer* (1927), a finely told story of a girl moving through childhood and adolescence to the complexity of mature emotions. *Invitation to the Waltz* (1932) is a slight, but wholly realized, work about a girl's timid confrontation with social demands. The girl appears again, this time in an affair with a married man, in *The Weather in the Streets* (1936).

Lehmann's style grew more complex, and her subject matter took in more of the world, in her later books: *The Ballad and the Source* (1944), in which a dominating old woman is seen through the eyes of a 14-year-old girl, and *The Echoing Grove* (1953), elaborating on a girl's growing awareness of a love triangle. Her autobiography is entitled *The Swan in the Evening* (1967). Her novel *A Sea-Grape Tree* was published in 1976. She was made a Commander of the Order of the British Empire in 1982.

Lehmbruck, Wilhelm (b. Jan. 4, 1881, Meiderich, near Duisburg, Ger.—d. March 25, 1919, Berlin), printmaker, painter, poet, and one of the most important sculptors of the Expressionist movement in Germany. He is best known for the pathos of his sculptures of elongated nudes.

Lehmbruck's youthful work was in the tradition of academic realism. But by 1905 he was greatly impressed with the monumental works of the famed French sculptor Auguste Rodin, as can be seen in Lehmbruck's "The Bather" (1905) and his life-sized "Mankind" (1909).

In 1910 Lehmbruck moved to Paris, where he executed not only sculpture but also a number of paintings, etchings, and lithographs. The full, boldly modeled forms of his "Standing Woman" (1910) reveal his new enthusiasm for the classicism of the French sculptor Aristide Maillol. The idealized face is softly modeled and evokes a sensitive, introspective mood that anticipates works of Lehmbruck's mature style, such as the "Kneeling Woman" (1911). The harmonious repose of this figure's angular, yet feminine, limbs and her melancholy

"Seated Youth," statue by Wilhelm Lehmbruck, 1918; in the Wilhelm-Lehmbruck Museum, Duisburg, Ger.

By courtesy of Erben Lehmbruck and the Wilhelm-Lehmbruck Museum, Duisburg, Ger.

facial expression suggest a resigned pessimism that characterizes Lehmbruck's mature works. His bronze "Standing Youth" (1913) is similarly elongated. But, in contrast to the "Kneeling Woman," it exhibits a masculine hardness and brooding power.

At the outbreak of World War I, Lehmbruck returned to Germany, where he worked in a hospital. His experiences with wounded and dying soldiers led him to create such poignant works as "The Fallen" (1915–16) and "Seated Youth" (1918), revealing the artist's state of utter depression. He committed suicide one year later.

Lehn, Jean-Marie (b. Sept. 30, 1939, Rosheim, Fr.), French chemist who, together with Charles J. Pedersen and Donald J. Cram, was awarded the Nobel Prize for Chemistry in 1987 for his contribution to the laboratory synthesis of molecules that mimic the vital chemical functions of molecules in living organisms.

Lehn earned a Ph.D. in chemistry from the University of Strasbourg in 1963, and in 1970 he became a professor of chemistry at Louis Pasteur University in Strasbourg. From 1979 he was also a professor at the Collège de France in Paris.

Lehn expanded on Pedersen's achievement in creating crown ethers, a class of two-dimensional, ring-shaped organic compounds that are capable of selectively recognizing and combining with other molecules. In the course of his efforts to synthesize three-dimensional molecules that would possess similar reactive characteristics, Lehn created a molecule that combines with the chemical acetylcholine, which is an important neurotransmitter in the brain. His work raised the possibility of creating totally artificial enzymes that would have characteristics superior to their natural counterparts in the human body.

Lehna (Sikh Gurū): *see* Aṅgad.

Lehtonen, Joel (b. Nov. 27, 1881, Sääminki, Fin.—d. 1934, Helsinki), Finnish novelist in the naturalistic tradition of Émile Zola and Maksim Gorky.

The first stage of Lehtonen's career was characterized by the Neoromanticism of the turn of the century, and his first novel, *Paholaisen viula* (1904; "The Fiddle of the Devil"), is highly indebted to Selma Lagerlöf's *Gösta Berlings saga* (1891). In *Rakastunut rampa* (1922; "The Amorous Cripple"), however, Lehtonen bitterly rejects the tributes to individualism and genius worship that marked his youthful phase. The main character has deluded himself into believing that he is a superman, but as circumstances assail him he becomes overwhelmed with shame and finally commits suicide. Lehtonen returns in the short-story collection *Kuolleet omenapuut* (1918; "The Dead Apple Trees") to the subject of the Finnish civil war and views it with doubt and disgust. Nihilism dominates his view of man in *Putkinotko* (1919–20). In it, Lehtonen despairs of the future and views the growth of industrial society as a disease. The same cultural pessimism appears in *Henkien taistelu* (1933; "The Struggle of Spirits") and in his poems, *Hyvästijättö Lintukodolle* (1934; "Farewell to the Bird's Nest"), which were written shortly before his suicide. Lehtonen's influence on Finnish literature has increased over the years.

lei, a garland or necklace of flowers given in Hawaii as a token of welcome or farewell. Leis are most commonly made of carnations, kika blossoms, ginger blossoms, jasmine blossoms, or orchids and are usually about 18 inches (46 cm) long. They are bestowed with a kiss as a sign of hospitality. The traveler customarily tosses the farewell lei onto the harbour waters as his ship leaves; the drift of the lei back to the shore indicates that he will someday return to the islands. The custom of wearing leis originated with the indigenous Hawaiians, who wove necklaces of leaves or ferns or sometimes strung dried shells, fruits, beads, or bright feathers for personal adornment. Hawaiians celebrate Lei Day on May 1, symbolizing their tradition of friendliness.

Lei-chou Pan-tao (China): *see* Luichow Peninsula.

Lei Kung, Pinyin LEI GONG (Chinese: "Duke of Thunder"), also called LEI SHEN ("Thunder God"), Chinese Taoist deity who, when so ordered by heaven, punishes both earthly mortals guilty of secret crimes and evil spirits who have used their knowledge of Taoism to harm human beings. Lei Kung carries a drum and mallet to produce thunder and a chisel to punish evildoers.

Lei Kung is depicted as a fearsome creature with claws, bat wings, and a blue body and wears only a loincloth. Temples dedicated to him are rare, but some persons do him special honour in the hope that he will take revenge on their personal enemies.

Since Lei Kung's specialty is thunder, he has assistants capable of producing other types of heavenly phenomena. Tien Mu ("Mother of Lightning"), for example, uses flashing mirrors to send bolts of lightning across the sky. Yün T'ung ("Cloud Youth") whips up clouds, and Yü-tzu ("Rain Master") causes downpours by dipping his sword into a pot. Roaring winds rush forth from a type of goatskin bag manipulated by Feng Po ("Earl of Wind"), who was later transformed into Feng P'o P'o ("Madame Wind"). She rides a tiger among the clouds.

Lei Shui (China): *see* Luan River.

Leibl, Wilhelm (b. Oct. 23, 1844, Cologne [Germany]—d. Dec. 4, 1900, Würzburg), painter of portraits and genre scenes who was one of the most important German realists of the late 19th century.

"Three Women in Church," oil on wood by Wilhelm Leibl, 1878–82; in the Kunsthalle, Hamburg

By courtesy of the Kunsthalle, Hamburg

Leibl entered the Munich Academy in 1864. From 1866 to 1868 he worked with the artist Avon Ramberg and in 1869 with Karl von Piloty. In 1870 he went to Paris to work with the painter Gustave Courbet but returned to Munich after only nine months because of the outbreak of the Franco-German War. He resided in Munich for three years and then settled in a number of small country places in Bavaria (Berbling, 1878–81; Aibling 1881–92; and Kutterling 1892–1900), drawing on the peasant life he witnessed there for subject matter.

Leibl's painting was in opposition to the prevailing aesthetic in Germany of romantic idealism. Leibl's objective style, like that of Gustave Courbet in France, was based on a direct, careful recording of nature, objects, figures, and situations. His most characteristic and popular works are from his "Holbein period," *c.* 1870–80 (*e.g.,* "Three Women in Church," 1878–82). Later he abandoned the hard brilliance of his former works and drew softer outlines. He followed his own strong instinct for colour, reproducing what he saw with a bold, sure touch (*e.g.*, "In the Kitchen," 1898; Staatsgalerie, Stuttgart). His superb technique enabled him to paint liquidly and broadly and yet to render detail with the utmost delicacy.

Consult the INDEX *first*

Leibniz, Gottfried Wilhelm (b. July 1 [June 21, old style], 1646, Leipzig—d. Nov. 14, 1716, Hannover, Hanover), German philosopher, mathematician, and political adviser,

Leibniz, detail of an oil painting by A. Scheits, 1695; in the Herzog Anton Ulrich-Museum, Braunschweig

By courtesy of the Herzog Anton Ulrich-Museum, Braunschweig

important both as a metaphysician and as a logician and distinguished also for his independent invention of the differential and integral calculus.

Early life and education. Leibniz was born into a pious Lutheran family near the end of the Thirty Years' War, which had laid Germany in ruins. As a child, he was educated in the Nicolai School but was largely self-taught in the library of his father, who had died in 1652. At Easter time in 1661, he entered the University of Leipzig as a law student; there he came into contact with the thought of men who had revolutionized science and philosophy—men such as Galileo, Francis Bacon, Thomas Hobbes, and René Descartes. Leibniz dreamed of reconciling—a verb that he did not hesitate to use time and again throughout his career—these modern thinkers with the Aristotle of the Scholastics. His baccalaureate thesis, *De Principio Individui* ("On the Principle of the Individual"), which appeared in May 1663, was inspired partly by Lutheran nominalism (the theory that universals have no reality but are mere names) and emphasized the existential value of the individual, who is not to be explained either by matter alone or by form alone but rather by his whole being (*entitate tota*). This notion was the first germ of the future "monad." In 1666 he wrote *De Arte Combinatoria* ("On the Art of Combination"), in which he formulated a model that is the theoretical ancestor of some modern computers: all reasoning, all discovery, verbal or not, is reducible to an ordered combination of elements, such as numbers, words, sounds, or colours.

After completing his legal studies in 1666, Leibniz applied for the degree of doctor of law. He was refused because of his age and consequently left his native city forever. At Altdorf—the university town of the free city of Nürnberg—his dissertation *De Casibus Perplexis* ("On Perplexing Cases") procured him the doctor's degree at once, as well as the immediate offer of a professor's chair, which, however, he declined. During his stay in Nürnberg, he met Johann Christian, Freiherr von Boyneburg, one of the most distinguished German statesmen of the day. Boyneburg took him into his service and introduced him to the court of the prince elector, the archbishop of Mainz, Johann Philipp von Schönborn, where he was concerned with questions of law and politics.

King Louis XIV of France was a growing threat to the German Holy Roman Empire. To ward off this danger and divert the King's interests elsewhere, the Archbishop hoped to propose to Louis a project for an expedition into Egypt; because he was using religion as a pretext, he expressed the hope that the project would promote the reunion of the church. Leibniz, with a view toward this reunion, worked on the *Demonstrationes Catholicae.* His research led him to situate the soul in a point—this was new progress toward the monad—and to develop the principle of sufficient reason (nothing occurs without a reason). His meditations on the difficult theory of the point were related to problems encountered in optics, space, and movement; they were published in 1671 under the general title *Hypothesis Physica Nova* ("New Physical Hypothesis"). He asserted that movement depends, as in the theory of the German astronomer Johannes Kepler, on the action of a spirit (God).

In 1672 the Elector sent the young jurist on a mission to Paris, where he arrived at the end of March. In September, Leibniz met with Antoine Arnauld, a Jansenist theologian (Jansenism was a nonorthodox Roman Catholic movement that spawned a rigoristic form of morality) known for his writings against the Jesuits. Leibniz sought Arnauld's help for the reunion of the church. He was soon left without protectors by the deaths of Freiherr von Boyneburg in December 1672 and of the Elector of Mainz in February 1673; he was now, however, free to pursue his scientific studies. In search of financial support, he constructed a calculating machine and presented it to the Royal Society during his first journey to London, in 1673.

Late in 1675 Leibniz laid the foundations of both integral and differential calculus. With this discovery, he ceased to consider time and space as substances—another step closer to monadology. He began to develop the notion that the concepts of extension and motion contained an element of the imaginary, so that the basic laws of motion could not be discovered merely from a study of their nature. Nevertheless, he continued to hold that extension and motion could provide a means for explaining and predicting the course of phenomena. Thus, contrary to Descartes, Leibniz held that it would not be contradictory to posit that this world is a well-related dream. If visible movement depends on the imaginary element found in the concept of extension, it can no longer be defined by simple local movement; it must be the result of a force. In criticizing the Cartesian formulation of the laws of motion, known as mechanics, Leibniz became, in 1676, the founder of a new formulation, known as dynamics, which substituted kinetic energy for the conservation of movement. At the same time, beginning with the principle that light follows the path of least resistance, he believed that he could demonstrate the ordering of nature toward a final goal or cause.

The Hanoverian period. Leibniz continued his work but was still without an income-producing position. By October 1676, however, he had accepted a position in the employment of John Frederick, the duke of Braunschweig-Lüneburg. John Frederick, a convert to Catholicism from Lutheranism in 1651, had become duke of Hanover in 1665. He appointed Leibniz librarian, but, beginning in February 1677, Leibniz solicited the post of councillor, which he was finally granted in 1678. It should be noted that, among the great philosophers of his time, he was the only one who had to earn a living. As a result, he was always a jack-of-all-trades to royalty.

Trying to make himself useful in all ways, Leibniz proposed that education be made more practical, that academies be founded; he worked on hydraulic presses, windmills, lamps, submarines, clocks, and a wide variety of mechanical devices; he devised a means of perfecting carriages and experimented with phosphorus. He also developed a water pump run by windmills, which ameliorated the exploitation of the mines of the Harz Mountains, and he worked in these mines as an engineer frequently from 1680 to 1685. Leibniz is considered to be among the creators of geology because of the observations he compiled there, including the hypothesis that the Earth was at first molten. These many occupations did not stop his work in mathematics: In March 1679 he perfected the binary system of numeration (*i.e.,* using two as a base), and at the end of the same year he proposed the basis for analysis situs, now known as general topology, a branch of mathematics that deals with selected properties of collections of related physical or abstract elements. He was also working on his dynamics and his philosophy, which was becoming increasingly anti-Cartesian. At this point, Duke John Frederick died on Jan. 7, 1680, and his brother, Ernest Augustus I, succeeded him.

France was growing more intolerant at home—from 1680 to 1682 there were harsh persecutions of the Protestants that paved the way for the revocation of the Edict of Nantes on Oct. 18, 1685—and increasingly menacing on its frontiers, for as early as 1681, despite the reigning peace, Louis XIV took Strasbourg and laid claim to 10 cities in Alsace. France was thus becoming a real danger to the empire, which had already been shaken on the east by a Hungarian revolt and by the advance of the Turks, who had been stopped only by the victory of John III Sobieski, king of Poland, at the siege of Vienna in 1683. Leibniz served both his prince and the empire as a patriot. He suggested to his prince a means of increasing the production of linen and proposed a process for the desalinization of water; he recommended classifying the archives and wrote, in both French and Latin, a violent pamphlet against Louis XIV.

During this same period Leibniz continued to perfect his metaphysical system through research into the notion of a universal cause of all being, attempting to arrive at a starting point that would reduce reasoning to an algebra of thought. He also continued his developments in mathematics; in 1681 he was concerned with the proportion between a circle and a circumscribed square and, in 1684, with the resistance of solids. In the latter year he published *Nova Methodus pro Maximis et Minimis* ("New Method for the Greatest and the Least"), which was an exposition of his differential calculus.

Leibniz' noted *Meditationes de Cognitione, Veritate et Ideis (Reflections on Knowledge, Truth, and Ideas)* appeared at this time and defined his theory of knowledge: things are not seen in God—as Nicolas Malebranche suggested—but rather there is an analogy, a strict relation, between God's ideas and man's, an identity between God's logic and man's. In February 1686, Leibniz wrote his *Discours de métaphysique (Discourse on Metaphysics).* In the March publication of *Acta,* he disclosed his dynamics in a piece entitled *Brevis Demonstratio Erroris Memorabilis Cartesii et Aliorum Circa Legem Naturae* ("Brief Demonstration of the Memorable Error of Descartes and Others About the Law of Nature"). A further development of Leibniz' views, revealed in a text written in 1686 but long unpublished, was his generalization concerning propositions that in every true affirmative proposition, whether necessary or contingent, the predicate is contained in the notion of the subject. At this time, with the exception of the word monad (which did not appear until 1695), his philosophy of monadology was defined.

In 1685 Leibniz was named historian for the House of Brunswick and, on this occasion, *Hofrat* ("court adviser"). His job was to prove, by means of genealogy, that the princely house had its origins in the House of Este, an Italian princely family, which would allow Hanover to lay claim to a ninth electorate. In search of these documents, Leibniz began travelling in November 1687. Going by way of southern Germany, he arrived in Austria, where he learned that Louis XIV had once again declared a state of war; in Vienna, he was well received by the Emperor; he then went to Italy. Everywhere he went, he met scientists and continued his scholarly work, publishing essays on the movement of celestial bodies and on the duration of things. He returned to Hanover in mid-July 1690. His efforts had not been in vain. In October 1692 Ernest Augustus obtained the electoral investiture.

Until the end of his life, Leibniz continued his duties as historian. He did not, however, restrict himself to a genealogy of the House of Brunswick; he enlarged his goal to a history of the Earth, which included such matters as geological events and descriptions of fossils. He searched by way of monuments and linguistics for the origins and migrations of peoples; then for the birth and progress of the sciences, ethics, and politics; and, finally, for the elements of a *historia sacra.* In this project of a universal history, Leibniz never lost sight of the fact that everything interlocks. Even though he did not succeed in writing this history, his effort was influential because he devised new combinations of old ideas and invented totally new ones.

In 1691 Leibniz was named librarian at Wolfenbüttel and propagated his discoveries by means of articles in scientific journals. In 1695 he explained a portion of his dynamic theory of motion in the *Système nouveau* ("New System"), which treated the relationship of substances and the preestablished harmony between the soul and the body: God does not need to bring about man's action by means of his thoughts, as Malebranche asserted, or to wind some sort of watch in order to reconcile the two; rather, the Supreme Watchmaker has so exactly matched body and soul that they correspond—they give meaning to each other—from the beginning. In 1697, *De Rerum Originatione (On the Ultimate Origin of Things)* tried to prove that the ultimate origin of things can be none other than God. In 1698, *De Ipsa Natura* ("On Nature Itself") explained the internal activity of nature in terms of Leibniz' theory of dynamics.

All of these writings opposed Cartesianism, which was judged to be damaging to faith. Plans for the creation of German academies followed in rapid succession. With the help of the electress Sophia Charlotte, daughter of Ernest Augustus and soon to become the first queen of Prussia (January 1701), the German Academy of Sciences in Berlin was founded on July 11, 1700.

On Jan. 23, 1698, Ernest Augustus died, and his son, George Louis, succeeded him. Leibniz found himself confronted with an uneducated, boorish prince, a reveller who kept him in the background. Leibniz took advantage of every pretext to leave Hanover; he was constantly on the move; his only comfort lay in his friendship with Sophia Charlotte and her mother, Princess Sophia. Once again, he set to work on the reunion of the church: in Berlin, it was a question of uniting the Lutherans and the Calvinists; in Paris, he had to subdue Bishop Bénigne Bossuet's opposition; in Vienna (to which Leibniz returned in 1700) he enlisted the support of the Emperor, which carried great weight; in England, it was the Anglicans who needed convincing.

The death in England of William, duke of Gloucester, in 1700 made George Louis, great-grandson of James I, a possible heir to the throne. It fell to Leibniz, jurist and historian, to develop his arguments concerning the rights of the House of Braunschweig-Lüneburg with respect to this succession.

The War of the Spanish Succession began in March 1701 and did not come to a close until September 1714, with the Treaty of Baden. Leibniz followed its episodes as a patriot hostile to Louis XIV. His fame as a philosopher and scientist had by this time spread all over Europe; he was named a foreign member by the Academy of Sciences of Paris in 1700 and was in correspondence with most of the important European scholars of the day. If he was publishing little at this point, it was because he was writing *Théodicée,* which was published in 1710. In this work he set down his ideas on divine justice.

Leibniz was impressed with the qualities of the Russian tsar Peter the Great, and in October 1711 the ruler received him for the first time. Following this, he stayed in Vienna until September 1714, and during this time the Emperor promoted him to the post of *Reichhofrat* ("adviser to the empire") and gave him the title of *Freiherr* ("baron"). About this time he wrote the *Principes de la nature et de la Grâce fondés en raison,* which inaugurated a kind of preestablished harmony between these two orders. Further, in 1714 he wrote the *Monadologia,* which synthesized the philosophy of the *Théodicée.* In August 1714, the death of Queen Anne brought George Louis to the English throne under the name of George I. Returning to Hanover, where he was virtually placed under house arrest, Leibniz set to work once again on the *Annales Imperii Occidentis Brunsvicenses* (1843–46; "Braunschweig Annals of the Western Empire"). At Bad-Pyrmont, he met with Peter the Great for the last time in June 1716. From that point on, he suffered greatly from gout and was confined to his bed until his death.

Leibniz was a man of medium height with a stoop, broad-shouldered but bandy-legged, as capable of thinking for several days sitting in the same chair as of travelling the roads of Europe summer and winter. He was an indefatigable worker, a universal letter writer (he had more than 600 correspondents), a patriot and cosmopolitan, a great scientist, and one of the most powerful spirits of Western civilization.

(Y.B./Ed.)

BIBLIOGRAPHY. Nicholas Rescher, *Leibniz: An Introduction to His Philosophy* (1979); and Charlie D. Broad and C. Lewy, *Leibniz: An Introduction* (1975), are excellent overviews of his philosophy; Gottschalk E. Guhrauer, *Gottfried Wilhelm, Freiherr von Leibniz: eine Biographie,* 2 vol. and suppl. (1842–46, reissued 1966; with partial Eng. trans. by J. Milton Mackie, *Life of Godfrey William von Leibniz,* 1845), a fundamental work; Wilhelm Totok and Carl Haase, *Leibniz: sein Leben, sein Wirken, seine Welt* (1966), completes and corrects Guhrauer in several respects; Yvon Belaval, *Leibniz: Initiation à sa philosophie,* 4th ed. (1975), places the philosophical development of Leibniz in the context of the history of his time; Bertrand Russell, *A Critical Exposition of the Philosophy of Leibniz,* 2nd ed. (1937, reissued 1975), still of great value; Leroy E. Loemker, *Struggle for Synthesis: The Seventeenth Century Background of Leibniz's Synthesis of Order and Freedom* (1972), discusses the intellectual background.

Leibovitz, Annie, original name ANNA-LOU LEIBOVITZ (b. Oct. 2, 1949, Westbury, Conn., U.S.), American photographer who is renowned for her revealing, eye-catching portraits of celebrities.

Leibovitz enrolled in the San Francisco Art Institute in 1967, intending to become a painter. After being introduced to photography in a night class, she quickly switched her focus to that medium. In 1970, while still a student, she was given her first commercial assignment for *Rolling Stone* magazine. Leibovitz became the publication's chief photographer in 1973, creating images of the major personalities of contemporary rock music. In 1975 she documented the Rolling Stones' six-month concert tour, during which she produced several widely reproduced photographs of lead singer Mick Jagger. Perhaps her most famous work from this period is a nude portrait of John Lennon wrapped fetus-like around his wife, Yoko Ono.

In 1983 Leibovitz produced a 60-print show that toured Europe and the United States. The accompanying book, *Annie Leibovitz: Photographs*, was a best-seller. That same year she moved to *Vanity Fair* magazine, which broadened her pool of subjects to include film stars, athletes, and political figures, and in 1986 she moved into advertising photography, working for such clients as Honda, American Express, and the Gap. (The American Express ad campaign that used her photos won a Clio Award, recognizing advertising excellence worldwide, in 1987.) Her style throughout these projects is characterized by carefully staged settings and her trademark use of vivid primary colours. Leibovitz typically spends two days observing her subjects' daily lives and views her photographic sessions as a collaboration.

In 1991 Leibovitz had her first museum exhibit at the National Portrait Gallery in Washington, D.C., one of only two such exhibits that the institution had devoted to a living photographer. A companion book, *Photographs: Annie Leibovitz 1970–1990*, was published in 1991. She also earned much praise for her portraits of American Olympians taken for an exhibit at the 1996 Summer Games in Atlanta, Ga., which were later published in the book *Olympic Portraits* (1996). In 1999 she published a collection of photographs entitled *Women*, with an essay by Susan Sontag.

Leicester, unitary authority, England, lying on the River Soar and the Grand Union Canal.

Remains of a Roman settlement mark the point where the Fosse Way crossed the River Soar, and Leicester had a considerable burgess community by Norman times. The medieval castle was dismantled in 1645, but a few ruins remain. The abbey was founded in 1143. A royal charter of incorporation was granted in 1589. In 1832 the railway joined the town with the small Leicestershire coalfield to the northwest, and rapid industrial development followed. The oldest industry is hosiery and knitwear, but in the 19th century Leicester became famous for footwear manufacture. Light engineering followed.

The focal centre of the town is the Clock Tower, from which shopping streets radiate. The central area has been redeveloped since World War II, and modern housing estates have replaced the deteriorating dwellings of the Industrial Revolution.

A modern concert hall is named after Simon de Montfort, earl of Leicester. Nearby is the University of Leicester (chartered 1957; formerly a university college, founded 1918). There are also technical and arts schools. The Guildhall, Newarke Gateway to the castle, and Trinity Hospital all date from the 14th century and Wyggeston School from the 16th. St. Martin's Church became a cathedral in 1926 when the diocese of Leicester was constituted. The district has an area of 28 sq mi (73 sq km). Pop. (1998 est.) 294,300.

Leicester, Robert Dudley, earl of, BARON DENBIGH, also called (1550–64) SIR ROBERT DUDLEY (b. June 24, 1532/33—d. Sept. 4, 1588, Cornbury, Oxfordshire, Eng.), favourite

Robert Dudley, earl of Leicester, miniature by Nicholas Hilliard, 1576; in the National Portrait Gallery, London

By courtesy of the National Portrait Gallery, London

and possible lover of Queen Elizabeth I of England. Handsome and immensely ambitious, he failed to win the Queen's hand in marriage but remained her close friend to the end of his life. His arrogance, however, undermined his effectiveness as a political and military leader.

He was the fifth son of John Dudley, duke of Northumberland, virtual ruler of England during the later part of the reign of Edward VI. After the failure of his father's conspiracy to put Lady Jane Grey on the throne in 1553, Robert was imprisoned in the Tower of London, but he was released the following year and served with the English forces in France in 1557.

With the accession of Elizabeth in 1558, Dudley's fortunes soared rapidly. She at once made him master of the horse, and in April 1559 he became a privy councillor and Knight of the Garter. He soon won the Queen's affection and favour, but his pretensions aroused bitter jealousy at court. When his wife, Amy, *née* Robsart, died in September 1560, it was widely rumoured that Dudley had murdered her in order to marry Elizabeth. Although there is no evidence to support this suspicion, Dudley did become an active suitor of the Queen. She rejected him, however, and even proposed that he wed Mary, Queen of Scots. Probably to further this design, Elizabeth made him earl of Leicester and Baron Denbigh in September 1564.

In 1571 Leicester began an affair with the dowager Lady Sheffield. They were almost certainly never married, and he cast her off in 1578, when he secretly wed Lettice Knollys, widow of Walter Devereux, earl of Essex. A Puritan, Leicester became the leader of those Protestants who favoured vigorous action against Spain abroad and against the Roman Catholics at home. His zeal caused him to be attacked, presumably by a Catholic writer, in a famous but highly distorted exposé of his character known as *Leicester's Commonwealth* (1584).

In 1585 Elizabeth sent Leicester in command of a force of 6,000 troops to the United Provinces (the Netherlands) to assist their revolt against Spain. He proved to be not only an incompetent commander but also a failure in his political role. His policies, in violation of Elizabeth's instructions, and his arrogant manner alienated the Dutch and resulted in his recall to England in 1587. Despite his shortcomings, the Queen appointed him in 1588 lieutenant general of the army mustered at Tilbury against the Spanish Armada. Later that year he died suddenly at his home.

Leicester, Simon de Montfort, earl of: *see* Montfort, Simon de.

Leicestershire, administrative county, within the East Midlands region of England, bordered by Nottinghamshire, Lincolnshire, Northamptonshire, Warwickshire, and Derbyshire. Its central axis, containing most of its population and industry, is the valley of the River Soar, which crosses the county from south to north on its way to join the River Trent. East of the Soar Valley lies an upland reaching 300–500 ft (100–150 m), which forms a deeply rural and scenically attractive area. This sparsely populated upland is the territory of some of England's most famous fox hunts (*e.g.*, the Cottesmore and the Fernie).

West of the Soar Valley lie the wooded hills of Charnwood Forest, an area where some of Britain's oldest bedrock is exposed at the surface in the form of Precambrian gritstone. North and west of the forest lies the Leicestershire coalfield, where some of the earliest developments of the Industrial Revolution in canal and rail transport took place. Only a few mines are still open around Coalville, but plans have been made to develop a large new coalfield in the northeastern corner of the county in the Vale of Belvoir.

Leicestershire's agriculture has traditionally been pastoral and livestock-based, the county being famous for its sheep, Stilton cheese, and pork pies. Its industry is varied, but hosiery has been of special importance; framework knitting began in the 16th century in adjoining Nottinghamshire and was first introduced into the county at Hinckley in 1640. Both hosiery and footwear are still manufactured, although the industries have been seriously reduced in scale by foreign competition. Along the Soar Valley, much of which is occupied by the cities of Leicester and Loughborough and their industrial plants, engineering and the manufacture of machinery are important and sufficiently varied to maintain a high level of employment.

Leicestershire is a county of country houses rather than of great buildings. It is the site of Oakham Castle, a Norman structure, and there are fine medieval churches at Leicester, Lutterworth (where the reformer John Wycliffe was parish priest in the 1380s), Melton Mowbray, Ashby-de-la-Zouch, and elsewhere. There is a cathedral at Leicester, and modern universities are located at both Leicester and Loughborough. The area of the county is 805 sq mi (2,084 sq km). It has seven districts: Blaby, Charnwood, Harborough, Hinckley and Bosworth, Melton, North West Leicestershire, and Oadby and Wigston. Pop. (1998 est.) 598,700.

Leichhardt, (Friedrich Wilhelm) Ludwig (b. Oct. 23, 1813, Trebatsch, Prussia—d. after April 4, 1848, Australia), explorer and naturalist who became one of Australia's earliest national heroes and whose mysterious disappearance aroused efforts to find him for nearly a century.

While Leichhardt was a student at the universities of Berlin (1831, 1834–36) and Göttingen (1833), he turned from philosophy to natural science. He also met a fellow student from England, William Nicholson, with whom he returned to England in 1837. The two pursued their own course of study: medicine and natural science at the Royal College of Surgeons and the British Museum in London and at the Jardin des Plantes in Paris. They also did field work in England, France, Italy, and Switzerland. In 1841 Nicholson provided Leichhardt with funds and paid his way to Australia.

Leichhardt landed at Sydney in 1842 intent on exploring the interior of Australia. From 1842 to 1844 he did field work in the Hunter River Valley, arranged plant and rock collections, and worked on geological notes, lecturing the while. An official overland expedition had been proposed to the Colonial Office, but Leichhardt impatiently arranged his own with a public subscription. He sailed from Sydney with six companions in August 1844, picked up four more members of the party, and departed from the farthest outpost on Darling Downs in October to cross to Port Essington. Two members turned back and one was killed by Aboriginals, but the rest reached Port Essington in December 1845. The party had been given up for dead, and their return to Sydney was greeted with the greatest astonishment and joy. They received a government grant of £1,000 and private subscriptions of more than £1,500. Leichhardt's journal of the expedition was published in 1847.

The second expedition, a party of eight, set out in December 1846 to cross from Darling Downs to the west coast and south to the Swan River settlement. Forced back by loss of animals taken for food and by fever, the party set out again in June 1847 but had to return. Leichhardt organized a party of six others and set out in March 1848, but the party was never heard of after leaving a point near the present town of Roma, from which he wrote his last letter, on April 4. Leichhardt had expected the expedition to take two years. Search for the party began in 1852 and continued into the 1930s, spurred on in its latest stages by rumours of white men living among the Aboriginals. Many of the searching parties brought back valuable information for later settlement.

Leichhardt's expeditions discovered extensive areas suitable for settlement and many important streams and provided an early map. His early success was rewarded by a share of the 1847 prize of the Geographical Society of Paris and by the Patron's medal of the Royal Geographical Society of London. Prussia forgave him his failure to perform his military service. Records of his scientific work and his lectures were published worldwide.

His legend provided the basis for the hero of Patrick White's novel *Vass* (1957). A biography by A.H. Chisholm was published in 1941, revised in 1955, and published under the title *Strange Journey* (1973). Leichhardt's letters (3 vol.) were published in 1968.

Leiden, English LEYDEN, *gemeente* (municipality), Zuidholland *provincie* (province), western Netherlands, at the confluence of the Oude Rijn and Nieuwe Rijn (Old Rhine and New Rhine) rivers, northeast of The Hague. The name of Lugdunum Batavorum sometimes applied to it is not of Roman origin but was given to it by Janus Dousa (Johan van der Does), statesman and defender of Leiden against the Spaniards, in his *Nova Poemata* (1575; "New Poems"). First mentioned in 922 as a holding of Utrecht diocese, Leiden grew around the 12th-century castle (Burcht); its charter was confirmed and extended in 1266. Until 1420 it was governed by a representative of the court of Holland. In the 14th century, an influx of weavers from Ypres laid the basis for textile prosperity. Leiden became a noted printing centre after the Elzevir family (from Louvain) established their press there *c.* 1581. During the Dutch revolt against Spain, the city endured a Spanish siege (May–October 1574) that was relieved only when the dikes were cut, flooding the countryside and enabling Dutch ships to carry provisions to the townspeople. In reward for the citizens' bravery during the siege, the University of Leiden was founded in 1575 by William I the Silent, prince of Orange, and became a centre of Dutch Reformed theology and of science and medicine in the 17th and 18th centuries, with such scholars as

Joseph Justus Scaliger, Hugo Grotius, Jacobus Arminius, Daniël Heinsius, Franciscus (Frans) Hemsterhuis, and Hermann Boerhaave. Institutions affiliated with the university include the Royal Institute of Linguistics and Anthropology, the National Museum of Antiquities, the National Museum of Ethnology of Asia, the Museum of the History of Science, the botanical gardens (1587), and the observatory. The city was the birthplace of many famous painters including Rembrandt, Jan van Goyen, Jan Steen, Gabriel Metsu, and Gerard Dou; in the 17th century it became a centre of the Dutch artistic Renaissance.

Historic buildings include the Gemeenlandshuis van Rijn (1596; partly restored 1878), the Weighhouse (1658; restored 1957–58), and the Municipal Museum (1869) in the old Lakenhal, or Cloth Hall (1640). The 17th-century town hall burned in 1929 and has been rebuilt. The Pilgrim Fathers house (dedicated 1957) contains documents concerning the stay of the Pilgrims in Leiden (1609–20) prior to their settling in Plymouth, Mass.; the medieval St. Peter's Church contains a memorial to their pastor, John Robinson. Gothic Hooglandse Kerk (St. Pancras Church) dates from the 15th century.

The decline of the textile industry in the 18th century caused a period of economic stagnation until the industrialization of the late 19th century. Economic activities now include metallurgy, the graphic arts, the manufacture of building materials, and food processing. Leiden's cheese and cattle markets are among the nation's largest, and there are bulb-growing farms to the west. Nearby are the seaside resorts of Noordwijk and Katwijk. There has been considerable development of the outlying residential areas since World War II, but the old town remains the centre of the city's activities. Pop. (1983 est.) 103,819; metropolitan area, 175,457.

"De," "la," and similar components of a name, when followed by a space, are alphabetized as separate words (e.g., *De Forest, Lee*). *When they are joined to the following part of a name, the combination is treated as a single word* (e.g., *DeForest, John William*).

Leiden, State University of, Dutch RIJKSUNIVERSITEIT TE LEIDEN, university in Leiden, Neth., founded in 1575 by William of Orange. It was originally modelled on the Academy of Geneva, an important centre of Calvinistic teaching. By the early 17th century Leiden had an international reputation as a centre of theology, science, and medicine. Hermann Boerhaave (*q.v.*), who was largely responsible for Leiden's reputation in the study of medicine, spent his professional life there.

Institutes connected with the university include the Royal Institute of Linguistics and Anthropology, the Rijksmuseum van Oudheden (prehistory of The Netherlands and antiquities), the botanical gardens, Leiden Observatory, and the National Museum of Ethnology of Asia.

Leidy, Joseph (b. Sept. 9, 1823, Philadelphia—d. April 30, 1891, Philadelphia), zoologist, one of the most distinguished and versatile scientists in the United States, who made important contributions to the fields of comparative anatomy, parasitology, and paleontology.

Soon after his appointment as librarian and curator at the Philadelphia Academy of Natural Sciences (1846), he became chairman of the Board of Curators (1847–91). The founder of paleontology in the United States, he made extensive studies of fossil deposits in the western states. The first of his many works on the subject, "On the Fossil Horse of America" (1847), showed that the horse had lived and

Leidy

By courtesy of the University of Pennsylvania, Philadelphia

become extinct on the North American continent long before the arrival of Columbus. He subsequently proved the prehistoric presence in the western United States of the lion, tiger, camel, and rhinoceros.

In 1848 he published *Researches into the Comparative Anatomy of the Liver*, the first thorough study made of that organ. Upon his appointment as professor of anatomy at the University of Pennsylvania (1853–91), he established himself as a leader in parasitology with the publication of *A Flora and Fauna Within Living Animals* (1853), the first important study of the parasites of the alimentary canal. His discovery of *Trichina spiralis* in pork led to Rudolf Leuckart's discovery of the cause of trichinosis in man.

The chief U.S. authority of his time on protozoa, Leidy published several works on the lower animal orders. One, *Fresh Water Rhizopods of North America* (1879), became a standard work. In all, he published more than 600 works, among which are the *Elementary Treatise on Human Anatomy* (1861), recognized as a classic American text on the subject, and "On the Extinct Mammalia of Dakota and Nebraska" (1869), described by the prominent U.S. paleontologist Henry Osborn as possibly the most important paleontological work produced in the United States.

Leif Eriksson THE LUCKY, Eriksson also spelled ERICSON, or ERIKSON, Norwegian LEIV ERIKSSON DEN HEPNE (fl. 11th century), Norse explorer widely held to have been the first European to reach the shores of North America. The 13th- and 14th-century Icelandic accounts of his life and additional later evidence show that he was certainly a member of an early Norse Viking voyage to North America; but it remains doubtful whether he led the initial expedition.

The second of three sons of Erik the Red, the first European colonizer of Greenland, Leif sailed from Greenland to Norway in 1000, according to the Icelandic *Eiríks saga* ("Saga of Erik"), and was there converted to Christianity by the Norwegian king Olaf I Tryggvason. The following year Leif was commissioned by Olaf to urge Christianity upon the Greenland settlers. He sailed off course on the return voyage and landed on the North American continent at a region he called Vinland (possibly Nova Scotia), perhaps because of the wild grapes and fertile land he found there. On returning to Greenland he proselytized for Christianity and converted his mother, who built the first Christian church in Greenland, at Brattahild.

According to the *Groenlendinga saga* ("Tale of the Greenlanders") in the *Flateyjarbók* ("Songbook"), considered more reliable than the *Eiríks saga* by many modern scholars, Leif learned of Vinland from the Icelander Bjarni Herjulfsson, who had been there 14 years earlier. The *Saga* pictures Leif as reaching North America several years after 1000 and visiting Helluland (possibly Labrador) and Markland (possibly Newfoundland) as well as Vinland. Further expeditions to Vinland were then made by Thorvald, Leif's brother, and by the Icelander Thorfinn Karlsefni.

Leigh, Vivien, original name VIVIAN MARY HARTLEY (b. Nov. 5, 1913, Darjeeling, India—d. July 8, 1967, London), English motion-picture star and stage actress noted for her delicate beauty.

She made her first film in 1934, *Things Are Looking Up*, and her stage debut a year later in *The Mask of Virtue*. Following a well-publicized talent hunt for the role of Scarlett O'Hara in *Gone with the Wind* (1939), Leigh not only got the part but received an Oscar from the Academy of Motion Picture Arts and Sciences. She was honoured with a second Oscar in 1951 for her portrayal of Blanche du Bois in *A Streetcar Named Desire*, a role she originally created on stage. Leigh toured extensively with the Old Vic and Stratford companies in productions of Shakespeare. Among her notable stage vehicles were *The Skin of Our Teeth, Antigone, Caesar and Cleopatra, The Sleeping Prince,* and *Duel of Angels*.

Leigh's later film and stage appearances were limited because of poor health. She made her last film, *Ship of Fools*, in 1965.

Leigh Creek, town and coalfield, east central South Australia, 350 mi (563 km) by rail north of Adelaide. Lignite coal, discovered there in 1888, was mined underground from 1892 to 1908 and then abandoned until 1941, when wartime shortages forced the government to explore the possibilities of reopening the field. By 1944 commercial quantities of coal were being extracted again. The opencut mines were taken over by the Electricity Trust of South Australia in 1948, which has since developed them as the fuel source for large power generators in Port Augusta. The town, named for a stockman who settled in the vicinity in 1856, was established in 1941 and in 1981 was moved 8 mi south to enable the mining of coal beneath the old town. It lies on the Central Australian Railway. In addition to large coal reserves, magnesite, gypsum, ochre, and pigment clays are worked locally. Fossil deposits of soft-bodied marine animals at Ediacara Reserve and Lake Callabonna are of worldwide interest. Pop. (1981) 1,635.

Leighton (of Stretton), Frederic Leighton, Baron, also called (1886–96) SIR FREDERIC LEIGHTON, BARONET (b. Dec. 3, 1830, Scarborough, Yorkshire, Eng.—d. Jan. 25, 1896, London), academic painter of immense prestige in his own time. After an education in many European cities, he went to Rome in 1852, where his social talents won him the friendship of (among others) the English novelist William Makepeace Thackeray, the French novelist George Sand, and the English poet Robert Browning.

Leighton's painting "Cimabue's Madonna," shown at the Royal Academy's exhibition in 1855, was bought by Queen Victoria. It marked the entry into England of a new cosmopolitan academic manner in which grandeur of scale and forms of classical Greek and High Renaissance extraction were used to embody subject matter of an anecdotal and superficial nature. Leighton came to London in 1858 to enjoy this triumph but did not settle there until 1860.

In 1869 he was made a member of the Royal Academy and in 1878 its president. In 1878 he was knighted, in 1886 he was made a baronet, and, on the day before he died, he became a baron, being the first English painter to be so honoured. (He did not marry, and the titles became extinct upon his death).

Leighton, Margaret (b. Feb. 26, 1922, Barnt Green, near Birmingham, Worcestershire, Eng.—d. Jan. 13, 1976, Chichester, West Sussex), English actress of stage and screen noted for her versatility in classic and contemporary roles.

Leighton made her stage debut as Dorothy in *Laugh With Me* (1938) at the Birmingham Repertory Theatre and then studied at Sir Barry Jackson's theatre school in Birmingham. She earned critical acclaim during her years as a member of England's prestigious Old Vic company, making her London debut as the troll king's daughter in *Peer Gynt* (1944) and her first New York City appearance as Lady Percy in *Henry IV, Part I* (1946). Leighton worked steadily both in London and on Broadway for several years. At home her notable roles included Celia Coplestone in *The Cocktail Party* (1950) and Orinthia in a revival of *The Applecart* (1953); in New York City she received a Tony (Antoinette Perry) Award for *Separate Tables* (1956), and another for *The Night of the Iguana* (1962).

Leighton is also remembered for several fine screen performances; among the best of her more than 20 films were *The Astonished Heart* (1949), *The Winslow Boy* (1948), *The Sound and the Fury* (1959), *The Madwoman of Chaillot* (1969), and *The Go-Between* (1970). For the last she was honoured as best supporting actress by the British Society of Film and Television Arts. Exceptional television performances included her roles as Miss Havisham in a 1974 production of *Great Expectations* and as Queen Gertrude in a production of *Hamlet* (1970), for which she won an Emmy award. Leighton appeared at both Stratford-upon-Avon and the Chichester Festivals; her last appearance was with Alec Guinness in *A Fame and a Fortune* in London (1975).

Leighton, Robert (b. 1611, England, probably in London—d. June 25, 1684, London), Scottish Presbyterian minister and devotional writer who accepted two Anglican bishoprics in Scotland in an attempt to reconcile proponents of the presbyterian form of church government with their episcopal opponents.

The son of Alexander Leighton, a Presbyterian who had been persecuted by the Anglican bishop William Laud, Leighton was attracted to the piety and antipapal attitudes of the Jansenist movement during the several years he spent in France after his education at Edinburgh. He was also influenced by the devotional work *Imitatio Christi,* often attributed to Thomas à Kempis.

On his return to Scotland in 1641, Leighton was ordained a Presbyterian minister and installed at Newbattle, Midlothian. Two years later he signed the Solemn League and Covenant of 1643, a concord between the Scots and the English Parliament that was used by Scottish Presbyterians to swear mutual loyalty when their system of church government and worship came under attack. In 1653 Leighton was appointed principal of the University of Edinburgh and professor of divinity.

In 1661, a year after Charles II was restored to the British throne and episcopacy once more was established in Scotland, Leighton was consecrated as Anglican bishop of Dunblane. He accepted the bishopric because he believed its traditional functions could be modified. His hopes proved futile, however, under the unconciliatory attitude adopted by Charles and the government. He had persisted in trying to persuade the Presbyterian clergy to come to an "accommodation" with the Anglicans but finally gave up his struggle for a comprehensive church in Scotland, comparing it to one in which he seemed to be "fighting against God." When he failed to induce Charles's government to cease persecution of the Covenanters, he went to London in 1665 to resign his bishopric. Charles persuaded him to continue, but four years later he was back in London on behalf of the Covenanters. With reluctance he accepted the bishopric of Glasgow in 1670, where he renewed his unsuccessful efforts at conciliation. He resigned in 1674 to spend his last decade in retirement. Among his works are *Sermons* (1692) and *Rules and Instructions for a Holy Life* (1708).

Leilan, Tell (ancient Syrian site): *see* Shubat Enlil.

Léim an Mhadaidh (Northern Ireland): *see* Limavady.

Leiner, Benjamin (boxer): *see* Leonard, Benny.

Leino, Eino, pseudonym of ARMAS EINO LEOPOLD LÖNNBOHM (b. July 6, 1878, Paltamo, Russian Finland—d. Jan. 10, 1926, Tuusula, Fin.), prolific and versatile poet, the scope of whose talent ranges from the visionary and mystical to topical novels, pamphlets, and critical journalism.

Leino
By courtesy of the Federation of Finnish Writers, Helsinki

Leino studied at the University of Helsinki and worked as a journalist, principally as literary and dramatic critic on the liberal newspapers *Päivälehti* and *Helsingin Sanomat.* The last part of his life he spent in bohemian excess. He translated into Finnish a number of world classics, including Dante's *Divina Commedia.*

In his first collection of poems, *Maaliskuun lauluja* (1896, "Songs of March"), Leino's mood was gay and his style free and melodic; he was influenced by his compatriot J.L. Runeberg, the German poet Heinrich Heine, and Finnish folk songs. But gradually his mood darkened, and he turned to poems of confession and solitude, patriotic poems about the period of Russian oppression, desolate ballad themes, and mythical motifs. The last dominate *Helkavirsiä* (1903–16; *Whitsongs,* 1978), Leino's main work, in which he revives the metre and spirit of folklore.

Other poetry includes *Talviyö* (1905, "Winter Night"), *Halla* (1908, "Frost"), and a historical poem *Simo Hurtta* (1904–19; "Simo the Bloodhound"). He also wrote plays, collected in *Naamioita* (1905–11, "Masks"), contemporary novels, animal fables, and essays. His work is uneven, but his best poems are among the finest Finnish lyrics.

Leinsdorf, Erich (b. Feb. 4, 1912, Vienna, Austria-Hungary—d. Sept. 11, 1993, Zürich, Switz.), Austrian-born American pianist and conductor.

Following musical studies at the University of Vienna and the State Academy, Leinsdorf served as rehearsal, and then solo, pianist for Anton von Webern's Singverein der Sozialdemokratischen Kunststelle (Choral Society of the Social Democratic Arts Council). Bruno Walter took him as his assistant at Salzburg in 1934, and that same year Arturo Toscanini engaged him as pianist for a special performance in Vienna. In 1937, having already established a name in Italy as a conductor of opera, Leinsdorf was invited to join the New York Metropolitan Opera as assistant conductor. He was later promoted to full conductor and in 1939 was put in charge of the German repertory.

Leinsdorf succeeded Artur Rodzinsky at the Cleveland Orchestra in 1943 but sacrificed the post when he was inducted into the U.S. Army. He returned from overseas in 1947 to a position with the Rochester Philharmonic. In 1956 he was musical director of the New York City Opera and then in 1957 resumed work with the Metropolitan as conductor and musical consultant. He succeeded Charles Munch at the Boston Symphony Orchestra in 1962, remaining there until 1969. In 1978 he was named chief conductor of the Radio Symphony of West Berlin, a post he retained until 1980.

He made guest appearances with virtually every major orchestra in Europe and the United States, and he recorded extensively. The autobiographical *Cadenza: A Musical Career* was published in 1976, and a book on conducting, *The Composer's Advocate,* in 1981.

Leinster, Old Irish LAIGIN, the southeastern province of Ireland, comprising the counties of Carlow, Dublin, Kildare, Kilkenny, Offaly, Longford, Louth, Meath, Leix, Westmeath, Wexford, and Wicklow. In its present form it incorporates the ancient kingdom of Meath (Midhe) as well as that of Leinster, which was bounded by the peninsula of Howth and the River Liffey on the north and by the Slieve Bloom Mountains on the west. In the early Middle Ages, kings of Leinster fought constantly against the Uí Néill, the line of high kings whose capital was at Tara in Meath. In the late 15th and early 16th centuries, Leinster was virtually independent, under the earls of Kildare.

Leinster, The Book of, compilation of Irish Gaelic verse and prose from older manuscripts and oral tradition and from 12th- and 13th-century religious and secular sources. It was tentatively identified in 1907 and finally in 1954 as the *Lebar na Núachongbála* ("The Book of Noughval"), thought lost; thus it is not the book formerly known as *The Book of Leinster* or *The Book of Glendalough* and by various Irish titles. Ascribed to Áed Hún Crimthaind, the abbot of Tír-dhá-ghlas (Terryglass, Tipperary), the work is notable for its calligraphy.

The Book of Leinster was written about 1160, completed sometime between 1201 and 1224, and is one of the most important extant Middle Irish collections, especially for the period before the Normans came to Ireland in the second half of the 12th century. It contains historical and genealogical poems, mainly on Leinster kings and heroes; mythological and historical accounts of invasions and battles; descriptive prose and verse topographical lists giving the history and etymology of nearly 200 place-names; treatises on bardic and Greek metres; Latin hymns; a version of the hero tale *The Cattle Raid of Cooley;* and the oldest version of *The Fate of the Sons of Usnech* (the legend of Deirdre).

Leiothrix, genus of birds of the babbler family Timaliidae (order Passeriformes), with two species: the silver-eared mesia, or silver-ear (*L. argentauris*), and the red-billed leiothrix (*L. lutea*), which is known to cage-bird fanciers as the Pekin, or Chinese, robin (or nightingale). Both range from the Himalayas to Indochina; *L. lutea* has been introduced into Hawaii, where it is commonly called hill robin. The silver-ear has yellow, gray, red, and black markings; the "robin" has a golden throat, orange or red breast, yellow wings marked with blue (and red, in the male), and a blue-tipped tail that is forked and outcurved. Both species are 15 cm (6 inches) long and have brief, sweet songs.

Leipoldt, C. Louis, in full CHRISTIAAN FREDERIK LOUIS LEIPOLDT (b. Dec. 28, 1880, Worcester, Cape Colony [now in South Africa]—d. April 12, 1947, Cape Town, S.Af.), South African doctor, journalist, and a leading poet of the Second Afrikaans Language Movement.

Though trained as a doctor, Leipoldt was more attracted to a literary career. He began as a journalist writing for *De kolonist, Het dagblad,* and the *South African News,* and during the South African War he was a war correspondent for several pro-Boer papers. He was a versatile writer: poetry, drama, travel books, detective stories, books on cookery—all flowed with equal felicity from his pen.

Leipoldt's poetry gave searing expression to the Afrikaner's feelings of humiliation and protest after the war and extolled the beauties of the South African landscape. He specialized in a cryptic, very personal poem with metaphysical overtones for which he coined the untranslatable name *Slampamperliedjie.* Leipoldt's best poetry is to be found in *Oom Gert vertel en ander gedigte* (1911; "Uncle Gert's Story and Other Poems"), *Uit drie wêrelddele* (1923; "From Three Continents"), and *Skoonheidstroos* (1932; "The Consolation of Beauty"). In *Die heks* (1923; "The Witch") and *Die laaste aand* (1930; "The Last Evening"), Leipoldt wrote the first notable dramatic works in Afrikaans.

Leipzig, city, east-central Germany, situated in the western part of Saxony *Land* (state). It lies just above the junction of the Pleisse, Parthe, and Weisse Elster rivers, 113 miles (182 km) southwest of Berlin. Leipzig is situated in the fertile, low-lying Leipzig Basin, which has extensive deposits of lignite (brown coal). Although encircled by a belt of parks and gardens, the city is a major industrial centre and transport junction, and it lies at the core of the Halle-Leipzig metropolitan agglomeration. The countryside around the city consists of a plain that is intensively farmed.

Leipzig entered recorded history in AD 1015 as the fortified town of Urbs Libzi and was granted municipal status by 1170. Its favourable position in the middle of a plain intersected by the principal trade routes of central Europe stimulated the town's commercial development. Its two annual markets, at Easter and at Michaelmas, were raised in 1497 to the rank of imperial fairs. Additional economic privileges enabled Leipzig to become the foremost German commercial centre by about 1700, a development that in turn promoted the growth of a network of roads converging on the town. Leipzig's focal geographic situation had another, less fortunate consequence: several important battles were fought in or near the town. These included two at Breitenfeld (now a suburb) in 1631 and 1642 and one at Lützen in 1632, during the Thirty Years' War, and in particular the Battle of Leipzig (or Battle of the Nations) in October 1813, in the Napoleonic Wars.

The New Town Hall, Leipzig

Karl Droste—Bavaria Verlag

The town's enviable economic status stimulated a notable cultural life, based particularly on the early development of the printing industry but also including the musical efflorescence associated with Johann Sebastian Bach. Trade continued to be the most important economic activity in the town, the main commodities traded being books, furs, yarns, and textiles. In 1839 the first German railroad was opened between Leipzig and Dresden, and the accompanying growth of banks provided capital for the city's growing textile and metallurgical industries.

One-quarter of Leipzig was destroyed in the last years of World War II. After the devastation of the war, the restoration and reconstruction of the city were carried out under the communist policies of East Germany. With renewed attention being paid to the Leipzig Fair and other exhibitions held in the city, Leipzig continues to play an important role among European cities. Peaceful but massive demonstrations by citizens of Leipzig in late 1989 played a significant role in bringing an end to the communist regime of East Germany.

The traditional fur and book-publishing industries of Leipzig are still well known. Modern industries include heavy constructional engineering and the manufacture of electrical products, textiles, clothing, chemicals, and machine tools. The annual Leipzig Fair, held in the spring, is one of the most important forums for international trade between eastern and western Europe. Leipzig is the centre of many railway lines, and its main railway station is one of the most important passenger stations in central Europe. Leipzig is also the focus of several major roads, and two airports serve the city.

Leipzig is a major intellectual and cultural centre. The University of Leipzig (called Karl Marx University of Leipzig from 1953 to 1990) dates from 1409. Leipzig has many museums, and its academies of dramatic art, musical history, graphic arts, and bookmaking are internationally known.

Among the city's libraries are the German Library and the Comenius Library, which is Europe's largest library specializing in education. The university library, the Leipzig City Library, and the City Archives are also important. Musical traditions are carried on by the Thomaner Choir, the Gewandhaus Orchestra, and the Radio Symphony Orchestra. There is also a fine opera house (1963).

Historic landmarks that were restored after World War II include the Old Town Hall, the Old Commercial Exchange, the old residential and market squares, Auerbach's Cellar, and the 13th-century Church of St. Thomas. The skyline of the modern city now includes the university tower and new hotels and commercial and residential buildings. Within the city, former woodlands along the riverbanks have been partly converted to parks and fulfill an important recreational function. Pop. (1994 est.) 490,851.

Leipzig, Battle of, also called BATTLE OF THE NATIONS (Oct. 16–19, 1813), decisive defeat for Napoleon, resulting in the destruction of what was left of French power in Germany and Poland. The battle was fought at Leipzig, in Saxony, between approximately 185,000 French and other troops under Napoleon, and approximately 320,000 allied troops, including Austrian, Prussian, Russian, and Swedish forces, commanded respectively by Prince Karl Philipp Schwarzenberg, General Gebhard Leberecht Blücher, General Leonty Leontyevich Bennigsen, and the Swedish crown prince Jean Bernadotte. After his retreat from Russia in 1812, Napoleon mounted a new offensive in Germany in 1813. His armies failed to take Berlin, however, and were forced to withdraw west of the Elbe River. When the allied armies threatened Napoleon's line of communications through Leipzig, he was forced to concentrate his forces in that city. On October 16 he successfully thwarted the attacks of Schwarzenberg's 78,000 men from the south and Blücher's 54,000 men from the north, but he failed to defeat either decisively. The number of troops surrounding him increased during the lull on the 17th, when Bennigsen and Bernadotte arrived.

The allied attack on the 18th, with more than 300,000 men, converged on the Leipzig perimeter. After nine hours of assaults, the French were pushed back into the city's suburbs. At 2 AM on October 19, Napoleon began the retreat westward over the single bridge across the Elster River. All went well until a frightened corporal blew up the bridge at 1 PM, while it was still crowded with retreating French troops and in no danger of allied attack. The demolition left 30,000 rear guard and injured French troops trapped in Leipzig, to be taken prisoner the next day. The French also lost 38,000 men killed and wounded. Allied losses totaled 55,000 men. This battle, one of the most severe of the Napoleonic Wars (1800–15), marked the end of the French Empire east of the Rhine.

Leipzig, University of, German UNIVERSITÄT LEIPZIG, coeducational state-controlled institution of higher education in Leipzig, Ger. It was renamed Karl Marx University of Leipzig in 1953 by the communist leadership of East Germany; the original name was restored in 1990. The University of Leipzig was founded in 1409 by German students and professors who withdrew from the University of Prague when Wenceslas IV, king of Bohemia, turned that four-nation university over to the Czechs. The University of Leipzig was confirmed by papal bull in 1409. In 1539 Leipzig accepted the Reformation, which thoroughly penetrated the university. In the 18th and 19th centuries, the university became one of the leading literary and cultural centres of Europe because of its eminent scholars and professors. The literary theorist Johann Gottsched was perhaps its most famous professor, and the mathematician Gottfried Leibniz, the literary figure Johann Wolfgang von Goethe, the philosopher Johann Fichte, and the composer Richard Wagner were students there.

Leiria, town and capital of Leiria *distrito* ("district"), Portugal. The town is located 70 miles (115 km) north of Lisbon, a few miles inland from the Atlantic Ocean. It originated as the Roman town of Collippo and was captured by the Moors early in the 8th century. After its reconquest in 1135 by Afonso I, a Romanesque church was built that still remains, as does a well-preserved medieval castle (restored *c.* 1300). The first Portuguese printing press was established there in 1466. An episcopal see, Leiria has a Renaissance cathedral. The town is an agricultural trade centre for a fertile farming area (wine, olives, corn [maize], sheep) and has tanneries and cement works.

Leiria district contains Portugal's largest pine forest. Besides the capital, important towns in the district include Alcobaça, famous for its abbey; Marinha Grande, with a noted glass industry; and Peniche and Nazaré, picturesque fishing villages. Area district, 1,354 square miles (3,508 square km). Pop. (1991 prelim.) town, 27,531; (1993 est.) district, 426,200.

Leiris, Michel (b. April 20, 1901, Paris, France—d. Sept. 30, 1990, Saint-Hilaire), French writer who was a pioneer in modern confessional literature and was also a noted anthropologist, poet, and art critic.

Leiris studied at the Sorbonne (University of Paris) and at the School for Advanced Scientific and Religious Studies. While associated with the Surrealists, Leiris published a collection of poems, *Simulacre* (1925; "Simulacrum"), and, in the late 1920s, wrote a novel, *Aurora,* published in 1946. The novel and his numerous collections of poems all show his fascination with puns and wordplay and with the associative power of language. In precarious mental health, Leiris temporarily abandoned literary life in 1929 and drew on his university training as an ethnologist to join the Dakar-Djibouti expedition of 1931–33. Upon his return to France he was employed at the Museum of Man (Musée de L'Homme) in Paris and resumed writing.

In 1939 Leiris published the autobiographical *L'Âge d'homme* (*Manhood*), which attracted much attention and was reissued in 1946. Self-deprecating and punitive, the work catalogs Leiris' physical and moral flaws; he introduced the 1946 edition with an essay, "De la littérature considérée comme une tauromachie" (1946; *The Autobiographer as Torero*), comparing the courage required to write with that required of a matador. In 1948 he began another autobiography, *La Règle du jeu* ("The Rules of the Game"), which was published in four volumes as *Biffures* (1948; "Erasures"), *Fourbis* (1955; "Odds and Ends"), *Fibrilles* (1966; "Fibrils"), and *Frêle Bruit* (1976; "Frail Noise") and which was replete with memories of childhood humiliations, sexual fantasies, and contemplations of death.

Leiris served as director of research at the National Centre for Scientific Research from 1935 to 1970. His *Journal 1922–1989* was published in 1992.

Leisewitz, Johann Anton (b. May 9, 1752, Hannover, Hanover [Germany]—d. Sept. 10, 1806, Braunschweig, Brunswick), German dramatist whose most important work, *Julius von Tarent* (1776), was the forerunner of Friedrich Schiller's famous Sturm und Drang masterpiece *Die Räuber* (1781; *The Robbers*).

Leisewitz studied law and entered the Brunswick administrative service, in which he rose to high position. His impressive tragedy *Julius von Tarent* shows Gotthold Ephraim Lessing's, rather than J.W. von Goethe's, influence. The play, treating the favourite Sturm und Drang theme of fratricide, postulated a fundamental conflict between the political state and the individual heart. It exhibits calculated restraint and finely drawn characters. Leisewitz's short dramatic sketches *Die Pfändung* (1775; "The Distraint") and *Der Besuch um Mitternacht* (1775; "The Midnight Visit") pursue the Sturm und Drang trend toward the theme of social injustice, which he had divorced from the tragic conflict in *Julius von Tarent.*

Leisewitz, engraving by C.F.T. Uhlemann after a portrait by Kaurdorf

Bavaria-Verlag

leishmaniasis, human protozoal infection spread by the bite of a sandfly. Leishmaniasis occurs worldwide but is especially prevalent in tropical areas. Three major forms of the disease are recognized: visceral, cutaneous, and mucocutaneous.

Leishmaniasis is caused by various species of the flagellate protozoan *Leishmania,* of the order Kinetoplastida. These parasites infect a variety of vertebrate animals, such as rodents and canines. They are transmitted to humans by the bite of a bloodsucking sandfly, which belongs to the genus *Lutzomyia* in the Americas and to *Phlebotomus* in the Old World. Leishmanial parasites have two morphologic stages in their life cycle. One form, which inhabits the digestive tract of the sandfly, is an elongated, motile, flagellated form called a promastigote or leptimonad. The other, a round or oval, nonmotile form, called an amastigote, is found in certain cells (*i.e.,* macrophages) of vertebrates. If a sandfly dines on an infected vertebrate, it will ingest cells containing amastigotes, which develop into promastigotes in its gut. There the promastigotes multiply, eventually entering the fly's saliva. From here they can enter another vertebrate through the wound made during the sandfly's next blood meal, thus initiating a new infection.

Depending on the species of *Leishmania* that invades a host and on the host's immunologic response to the infection, one of three principal types of leishmaniasis can arise. Visceral leishmaniasis, also called kala-azar, is produced by several subspecies of *L. donovani.* It occurs throughout the world but is especially prevalent in the Mediterranean area, Africa, Asia, and Latin America. This form of the disease is systemic, primarily affecting the liver, spleen, bone marrow, and other viscera. Symptoms, which include fever, weight loss, reduction in the number of white blood cells, and enlargement of the spleen and liver, usually appear two months or more after infection. The disease is usually fatal if not treated. Cutaneous leishmaniasis is caused by several *Leishmania* species. It is characterized by lesions that range from pimples to large ulcers located on the skin of the legs, feet, hands, and face, most of which heal spontaneously after many months. A distinction is made between cutaneous leishmaniasis of the Old World and of the New World. That of the Old World, also called Oriental sore, is endemic in areas around the Mediterranean, in central and northeast Africa, and in south and west Asia. It is caused primarily by *L. major, L. tropica,* and *L. aethiopica*. Cutaneous leishmaniasis of the New World, which is found in Central and South America and parts of the southern United States, is caused mainly by *L. mexicana* and *L. viannia braziliensis.* This infection may spread to the oral and nasal mucous membranes, a complication referred to as mucocutaneous leishmaniasis, or espundia. Destruction of the lips, throat, palate, and larynx can ensue. Mucocutaneous leishmaniasis may not appear until years after an initial cutaneous lesion has healed.

All types of leishmaniasis are treated with compounds of antimony, such as sodium stibogluconate. Spread of the disease is prevented by controlling sandfly populations.

Leisler, Jacob (b. 1640, Frankfurt am Main [Germany]—d. May 16, 1691, New York, N.Y. [U.S.]), provincial militia captain who seized the reins of British colonial government in New York (Leisler's Rebellion) and exercised effective control over the area for more than 18 months in 1689–91.

Emigrating to New Netherland (New York) at the age of 20, Leisler quickly became one of the colony's wealthiest merchants. Remaining there after control of the colony passed from the Dutch to the English in 1664, he was one of many colonists who strongly resisted the unified administration (called the Dominion of New England) imposed by King James II (1685–89) on New York and New England.

When James was overthrown in 1689, Leisler took the opportunity to lead a revolt against the crown's agent in New York, Lieutenant Governor Francis Nicholson. Nicholson fled to England when his fort was seized by Leisler's rebellious force on May 31. Supported by small farmers and city workers, Leisler set himself up as head of a revolutionary government that subsequently appointed him commander in chief. In December he assumed the title of lieutenant governor and, appointing a council, took charge of the entire province. He also summoned the first intercolonial congress in North America, which met in New York (May 1, 1690) to plan concerted action against the French and Indians.

Although he proclaimed loyalty to the new king, William III, Leisler refused to recognize the authority of Major Richard Ingoldsby, who arrived with English soldiers in January 1691. Fighting broke out in March, shortly before the arrival of Colonel Henry Sloughter, who had been commissioned governor of the province. After reluctantly surrendering, Leisler was charged with treason and, with his son-in-law, Jacob Milborne, was convicted and hanged. Parliament reversed the attainder in 1695 and restored the confiscated estates to the family heirs.

Leith, port of Edinburgh, lying north of the city on the southern shore of the Firth of Forth, in the region of Lothian, southeastern Scotland. Leith was once an independent town and before the railway era was the chief port of entry for travelers to Scotland. Mary, Queen of Scots, landed and stayed there at Lamb's House on her return to Scotland (1561). Leith was incorporated into Edinburgh in 1920 and is now part of the Forth Ports Authority, which includes Burntisland, Grangemouth, Granton, Kircaldy, and Methil.

leitmotiv (German: "leading motive"), recurring musical theme appearing usually in operas but also in symphonic poems. It is used to reinforce the dramatic action, to provide psychological insight into the characters, and to recall or suggest to the listener extramusical ideas relevant to the dramatic event. In a purely musical sense the repetition or transformation of the theme also gives cohesion to large-scale works.

The term was first used by writers analyzing the music dramas of Richard Wagner, with whom the leitmotiv technique is particularly associated. They applied it to the "representative themes" that characterize his works. The close thematic musical structure of his dramas, from *Der Ring des Nibelungen* onward, including *Tristan und Isolde* and *Die Meistersinger,* demands skillful contrivance and keen intelligence in order to make the themes work satisfyingly in a symphonic way and at the same time enrich the dramatic events.

The leitmotiv has two distinct dramatic functions, which may operate separately or together: one is allusion (to dramatic events), the other transformation, or continual modification of the theme. Both were used long before Wagner. W.A. Mozart's four-measure phrase "Così fan tutte" ("Thus do they all"), in his opera of the same name, is allusive, but it appears as a recurrent motto rather than as a true leitmotiv. Another early example of such allusive use is in Carl Maria von Weber's opera *Der Freischütz* (*The Freeshooter*), when Max hesitates to descend into the wolves' glen and the orchestra echoes the mocking chorus that had teased him in the first act.

Weber also used the leitmotiv in a purely instrumental fashion, as in his opera *Euryanthe,* where at least 13 motifs are transformed or developed in the orchestra. Also, in Hector

Berlioz' *Symphonie fantastique,* the idée fixe ("fixed idea," or leitmotiv) appears in different forms, first as a poet's thought of his beloved as an ideal and last in a nightmarish vision of her taking part in the witches' sabbath. But Berlioz' idée fixe was not yet an organic part of the symphonic fabric.

In the works of Wagner, allusion and transformation are used in rich abundance. Purely allusive is the three-note death theme in *Tristan und Isolde.* In contrast, the horn call in the second act of *Siegfried* is changed in *The Twilight of the Gods* from $\frac{6}{8}$ to $\frac{4}{4}$ time, becoming the theme for the matured and heroic Siegfried. Further modified in rhythm and texture, it forms the basis for the great orchestral threnody after his death. Similarly, in *The Rhinegold,* the Rhine maidens' joyful song about their treasure becomes transformed when the theme represents the evil power of the gold in the hands of the dwarf Alberich.

Richard Strauss often used musical allusion with great subtlety, as in his opera *Der Rosenkavalier.* His thematic transformations, in contrast, are most often musical developments, rather than dramatic references. He used leitmotiv most dramatically in his symphonic poems, where there is no stage action to carry the plot. Other followers of Wagner have done little to extend his methods, partly because he left them little to do.

Wagner's original contribution to the use of the leitmotiv is that of allusion. Transformation was not his invention, for it was already well advanced in the works of Berlioz and the symphonic poems of Franz Liszt. Claude Debussy used the principle in its most purely musical form, *e.g.,* in his opera *Pelléas et Mélisande.*

Georges Bizet and Giacomo Puccini employed representative themes effectively as reminiscences, as did Giuseppe Verdi, who frequently recalled a past happiness during a final tragic situation by means of a melody associated with the earlier happiness. Charles Gounod used it most effectively in *Faust* when Marguerite in prison recalls her meeting with Faust.

Consult the INDEX *first*

Leitneriales, order of dicotyledonous flowering plants comprising the single rare species *Leitneria floridana,* the North American corkwood. It is a shrub or small tree found in swampy and riverside localities from southern Missouri to Texas and Florida. *Leitneria* is characterized by soft, lightweight, close-grained, pale-yellow wood with resin canals; simple, smooth-margined leaves arranged alternately on the stems and lacking stipules (basal appendages); and separate male and female flowers borne on different plants.

The flowers are in distinctive clusters called catkins. The male catkins are lax and dangling; those of the female are stiffly erect. The male flowers, which lack petals or sepals, consist of 3 to 12 stamens (male pollen-producing structures) set in the angle of a large, hairy, leaflike bract; 40 to 50 such overlapping bracts make up the male catkin. The female flowers have three to eight small petallike structures at the base of a one-chambered ovary, which encloses one ovule and is prolonged above into a stout elongated upper extension (style). The style is characteristically constricted at the point of union with the ovary and bears the pollen-receptive area (stigma) along one side of the curved upper end. Pollination is by wind.

As the corkwood tree is isolated taxonomically, its evolutionary relationships are largely unknown, but it is thought to have ancestors in the witch hazel order (Hamamelidales) or one of its precursors. *Leitneria* is of little economic importance except for occasional ornamental use.

Leitrim, Irish LIATROIM (Gray Ridge), county in the province of Connaught (Connacht), Ireland. With an area of 589 square miles (1,525 square km), it is bounded on the north by County Donegal, on the east by Northern Ireland and Cavan, on the south by Longford, and on the west by Roscommon and Sligo. The southern part of the county is a lowland covered by glacial drifts; most of it is used as farmland, though there are peat bogs and many small lakes. The western boundary follows the River Shannon, on which boats can ascend to Carrick-on-Shannon, the county town (seat). At Drumshanbo, close to Lough (lake) Allen, the terrain changes to a series of plateaus, mainly 1,400 feet to 1,800 feet (425 m to 550 m) high. There are relics of past ironworks in the south and some coal seams, with many traces of past mining. The plateaus are split up by a number of deep valleys, in one of which Lough Allen covers about 14 square miles (36 square km).

Leitrim formed part of the ancient kingdom of Bréifne, the country of the O'Rourkes. In 1588 Sir Brian O'Rourke sheltered 1,000 Spaniards after the Armada had been destroyed by the English fleet; for this he was driven from the country and executed in 1591. Since 1841 the population of Leitrim has declined consistently. Less than one-fifth of the people live in towns and villages, of which the largest is Carrick-on-Shannon. The county has a county council and is united with Sligo under a county manager.

In 1891 several parts of the county ranked as "congested districts" because of their poverty, but the reduction of population made possible the union of farms into larger holdings. Much of the land is poor, with pasture as the main use. In the uplands there are sheep as well as cattle, but in the south cattle are the main stock. Potatoes and oats are the principal crops. The towns are small market centres. Industries include textiles, electrical accessories, and automotive parts. Pop. (1986) 27,035.

Leix (Ireland): *see* Laoighis.

Leixões, Port of, Portuguese PORTO DE LEIXÕES, principal port serving the city of Porto and northern Portugal. It is an artificial harbour on the Atlantic Ocean, within the town of Matosinhos, 5.5 miles (9 km) northwest of central Porto. Porto is prevented by a sandbar from having a deepwater harbour of its own. The Leixões harbour is formed by two curved breakwaters that are 5,240 feet (1,597 m) and 3,756 feet (1,145 m) long. The port's original docking facilities were completed in 1890 and were subsequently expanded in the early 1930s and early 1970s. The principal export is port wine.

Leizhou Bandao (China): *see* Luichow Peninsula.

Lejeune, Louis-François, Baron (b. Feb. 3, 1775, probably at Strasbourg, Fr.—d. Feb. 29, 1848, Toulouse), general, painter, and lithographer who was chiefly responsible for the introduction into France of lithography as an artistic medium.

He took part in many of the Napoleonic campaigns, and his vigorous battle pictures, executed mainly from sketches and studies made in the field, enjoyed a great vogue. The campaign of 1806 brought him to Munich, where he visited the workshop of Aloys Senefelder, inventor of lithography. Fascinated, Lejeune drew on the stone his famous "Cosaque" and immediately pulled 100 proofs of it, one of which he later submitted to Napoleon.

Lejeune also painted many landscapes and portraits. In 1837 he became director of the École des Beaux-Arts and curator of the museum at Toulouse.

lek, in animal behaviour, communal area in which two or more males of a species perform courtship displays. Lek behaviour, also called arena behaviour, is found in a number of insects, birds, and mammals. Varying degrees of interaction occur between the males, from virtually none to closely cooperative dancing. Females visit the lek briefly to select mates and to copulate, but they do not form lasting pair bonds with the males.

Lekain, original name HENRI-LOUIS CAIN (b. March 31, 1729, Paris—d. Feb. 8, 1778, Paris), French actor whom Voltaire regarded as the greatest tragedian of his time.

The son of a goldsmith, he was trained to follow his father's trade but had a passion for the theatre. He frequented the Comédie-Française and in 1748 began organizing amateur productions in which he starred. Voltaire witnessed one of his performances and, though impressed, nonetheless tried to discourage his stage career. When Lekain could not be dissuaded, Voltaire decided to coach him and to help him financially; Lekain made his debut at the Comédie-Française in 1754 as Titus in Voltaire's tragedy *Brutus.*

Lekain, detail from an engraving, late 18th century
H. Roger-Viollet

Though contemporaries described Lekain as small, ugly, and harsh-voiced, he overcame these disadvantages on the stage and became enormously popular with the public. He scored his greatest successes in plays by Voltaire, notably as Genghis Khan in *L'Orphelin de la Chine* and in the title role of *Tancrède.* In 1759 he drew up plans for a royal school of dramatic art. He strove to reform theatrical costume, discarding, for instance, the traditional heroic paraphernalia when playing Oreste in Racine's *Andromaque* and adopting a pseudo-Grecian costume instead. As a disciple of Voltaire, he campaigned successfully for more realistic scenery and for abolishing the contemporary custom of allowing privileged spectators to sit on the stage. His *Mémoires* were published in 1801.

Lekhitic languages, also spelled LECHITIC, group of West Slavic languages composed of Polish, Kashubian and its archaic variant Slovincian, and the extinct Polabian language. All these languages except Polish are sometimes classified as a Pomeranian subgroup.

In the early Middle Ages, before their speakers had become Germanized, Pomeranian languages and dialects were spoken along the Baltic in an area extending from the lower Vistula River to the lower Oder River. Kashubian and Slovincian survived into the 20th century; there were still a considerable number of native speakers of Kashubian in Poland in the 1970s, but the Slovincian speech community was limited to only a few families. The extinct Polabian language, which bordered the Sorbian dialects in eastern Germany, was spoken by the Slavic population of the Elbe River region until the 17th or 18th century; a dictionary and some phrases written in the language exist. *See also* Polish language.

lekythos, in ancient Greek pottery, oil flask used at baths and gymnasiums and for funerary offerings. The flask has a long, cylindrical body gracefully tapered to the base, and a narrow neck with a loop-shaped handle. Its decoration was often superior to the sentimentality of most late Attic pottery.

Attic red-figure lekythos, 510 BC; in the Museum of Fine Arts, Boston

By courtesy of the Museum of Fine Arts, Boston, Francis Bartlett Fund

Leland, Charles Godfrey (b. Aug. 15, 1824, Philadelphia—d. March 20, 1903, Florence), American poet and writer of miscellany, best-known for the "Hans Breitmann Ballads," which reproduce the dialect and humour of the Philadelphia Germans (also called Pennsylvania Dutch).

Leland studied for two years in Germany, where he became fascinated with German culture. On his return to America he studied and then practiced law. In 1853 he turned to journalism and worked for a number of years on Barnum's *Illustrated News,* the Philadelphia *Evening Bulletin,* and *Vanity Fair.* He also edited *Graham's Magazine,* where he published the first of his German-English poems, "Hans Breitmann's Barty" (1857). Written in a mixture of German and broken English and first published in the 1860s and 1870s, the poems were later collected in *The Breitmann Ballads* (new ed., 1895).

After inheriting his father's estate in 1869, Leland abandoned journalism, preferring to pursue his interest in folklore, mysticism, and the occult. He lived mostly in Italy and Germany after 1884.

Leland, Henry Martyn (b. Feb. 16, 1843, Danville, Vt., U.S.—d. March 26, 1932, Detroit), American engineer and manufacturer whose rigorous standards contributed to the development of the automobile.

After an apprenticeship as a machinist in Worcester, Mass., he worked in the U.S. Armory at Springfield, Mass., during the American Civil War and for the next 18 years at a factory in Providence, R.I., where he supervised the sewing-machine division.

In 1890 Leland moved to Detroit, where he soon organized Leland & Faulconer Manufacturing Company to build engines for automobile makers. In 1903 he created his own motorcar, the Model A Cadillac, a machine that proved successful and remained in production for several years. In 1908 the British distributor of Cadillac dramatized Leland's meticulous production system at the Royal Automobile Club's test facility at Brooklands, near London, by having three Cadillacs disassembled, the parts scrambled, and all three cars reassembled; each performed flawlessly in 500-mile tests, winning Leland the Dewar Trophy. In 1917 Leland resigned from the Cadillac company, of which he was president, to start the Lincoln Motor Company, which passed into the hands of Henry Ford. Among Leland's automotive innovations were the V-8 engine and adoption of the electric starter.

Leland, John, Leland also spelled LEYLAND (b. *c.* 1506, London—d. April 18, 1552, London), chaplain and librarian to King Henry VIII. He was the earliest of a notable group of English antiquarians.

Leland was educated at St. Paul's School and Christ's College, Cambridge (B.A., 1522), later studying at All Souls' College, Oxford, and in Paris. He took holy orders and by 1530 was chaplain and librarian to Henry VIII; the special position of king's antiquary was created for him in 1533, and he was authorized to search cathedral and monastic libraries for manuscripts of historical interest. Probably from 1534 and certainly from 1536 to 1542 he was engaged on an antiquarian tour of England and Wales. He supported Henry VIII's church policy (though the havoc that resulted among the monastic manuscripts at the dissolution of the monasteries caused him great distress), and his loyalty was rewarded with his presentation to the rectory of Haseley in Oxfordshire, a canonry at King's College (afterward Christ Church), Oxford, and a prebend at Salisbury. But he resided mainly in London, where he was certified insane in March 1550. He did not regain his reason before he died.

At the conclusion of his tour of England and Wales, Leland presented to the king a plan of his proposed works, a volume later edited as *The Laboryouse Journey and Serche of J. Leylande for Englandes Antiquities, Given of Hym as a Newe Yeares Gyfte to Kinge Henry the VIII* (1549). He intended to write a book ("History and Antiquities of the Nation") that would provide a topographical account of the British Isles and the adjacent islands, and to add a description of the nobility and of the royal palaces. Illness and death intervened, however, before these works were prepared. After passing through various hands, the bulk of Leland's manuscripts—including his important five-volume *Collectanea,* with notes on antiquities, catalogs of manuscripts in monastic libraries, and Leland's account of British writers—was deposited (1632) in the Bodleian Library at Oxford. They had in the meantime been freely drawn upon by many other antiquarians, notably by John Bale (who edited the *Newe Yeares Gyfte*).

Lelantine War, conflict arising during the late 8th century BC from colonial disputes and trade rivalry between the Greek cities of Chalcis and Eretria.

The two cities (both on the island of Euboea) had jointly founded Cumae in Italy (*c.* 750). When they fell out, the war between them split the Greek world in two: Samos, Corinth, Thessaly, and perhaps Erythrae joined Chalcis, while Miletus, Megara, and perhaps Chios took the Eretrian side.

The war appears to have consisted of a series of loosely connected contests all over the Greek world, with no decisive overall result. It derives its name from the Chalcidic victory won by Thessalian cavalry at the Lelantine Plain separating Eretria and Chalcis. Otherwise, events were scattered. In the West, Corinthians displaced Eretrian colonists from Corcyra (Corfu), and Chalcidians expelled Megarians from Leontini in Sicily. Chalcis held both sides of the Strait of Messina and colonized the richest agricultural sites in Sicily. In the East, its ally Samos suffered eclipse. In the home island of Euboea, Eretria was to become the more prominent city, while its allies Miletus and Megara prospered and colonized the best sites of the Bosporus.

Lelewel, Joachim (b. March 22, 1786, Warsaw—d. May 29, 1861, Paris), prominent Polish historian, regarded as one of the founders of modern Polish historical thought.

Descendant of a Polonized German family, Lelewel completed his studies at the Polish University of Wilno, received an assistant professorship there (1815–24), and then a full professorship in European history (1822–24). Deprived of his chair by the Russian governor, he moved to Warsaw, where he engaged in political activity. After the defeat of the Polish insurrection of 1830–31, he set out on foot across Germany to Paris. Expelled from France upon the intervention of the Russian ambassador, he walked to Brussels, where he published his writings in French.

Lelewel produced more than 20 volumes of Polish and European history. His *Numismatique du moyen âge* (1835; "Numismatics of the Middle Ages") and *Géographie du moyen âge,* 5 vol. (1852–57; "Geography of the Middle Ages") are of fundamental importance, as is his *Poland of the Middle Ages,* 4 vol. (in Polish, 1846–51).

Leloir, Luis Federico (b. Sept. 6, 1906, Paris—d. Dec. 2, 1987, Buenos Aires, Arg.), Argentine biochemist who won the Nobel Prize for Chemistry in 1970 for his investigations of the processes by which complex carbohydrates are broken down into simple sugars.

After serving as an assistant at the Institute of Physiology, University of Buenos Aires, from 1934 to 1935, Leloir worked a year at the biochemical laboratory at the University of Cambridge and in 1937 returned to the Institute of Physiology, where he undertook investigations of the oxidation of fatty acids. In 1947 he obtained financial support to set up the Instituto de Investigaciones Bioquímicas, Buenos Aires, where he began research on the formation and breakdown of lactose, or milk sugar, in the body. That work ultimately led to the discovery of sugar nucleotides, key elements in the natural processes of carbohydrate metabolism. He also investigated the formation and utilization of glycogen and discovered certain liver enzymes that are involved in its synthesis from glucose.

Lelouch, Claude (b. Oct. 30, 1937, Paris), motion-picture director, noted chiefly for his lush visual style, who achieved prominence in 1966 with his film *Un Homme et une femme* (*A Man and a Woman*), which shared the Grand Prize at the Cannes Film Festival and won two Oscars from the Motion Picture Academy of Arts and Sciences as best foreign film and best original story and screenplay.

The son of a Jewish businessman, whose family had resided in Algeria for three generations, Lelouch won a prize at the Cannes Amateur Film Festival at the age of 13 with his film *Le Mal du siècle,* but he did not become a film professional until 1956. He made television commercials before serving in the military from 1957 to 1960. After his release from military service Lelouch made his first feature with financial backing from his family. *Le Propre de l'homme* (1960; "The Right of Man")—in which he produced, wrote the script, and acted—was not a success. Lelouch's mature films include *Vivre pour vivre* (1967; "Live for Life"), *Toute une vie* (1974; *And Now*

My Love), *Mariage* (1974; *Marriage*), *Robert et Robert* (1978; *Robert and Robert*), *A nous deux* (1979; *An Adventure for Two*), *Les uns et les autres* (1981; *The Ins and Outs*), and *Bolero* (1982).

"De," "la," and similar components of a name, when followed by a space, are alphabetized as separate words (e.g., *De Forest, Lee*). *When they are joined to the following part of a name, the combination is treated as a single word* (e.g., *DeForest, John William*).

Lely, Sir Peter, original name PIETER VAN DER FAES (b. Oct. 14, 1618, Soest, Westphalia [Germany]—d. Dec. 7, 1680, London, Eng.), Baroque portrait painter known for his Van Dyck-influenced likenesses of the mid-17th-century English aristocracy. The origin of the name Lely is uncertain.

He studied in Holland at Haarlem, where he became a guild member in 1637. He probably arrived in England in about 1643, and he soon gained the patronage of the court, painting portraits of Charles I and James, duke of York. He was a buyer at the sale of Charles I's picture collection (1649–53) and in about 1651 petitioned Parliament for the mural decoration of Whitehall. Lely was a connoisseur and was known for his own fine collection of art. He prospered during the Commonwealth and even more during the Restoration, when he produced his finest portraits. In 1661 he received a pension of £200 a year, "as formerly to Van Dyck." He was knighted in 1679.

"Duchess of Cleveland," oil painting by Sir Peter Lely; in the Courtauld Institute of Art, London

By courtesy of Earl Spencer; photograph, Courtauld Institute of Art, London

Lely was the most technically proficient painter in England after the death of Van Dyck. During the Commonwealth he adopted a severe, puritanical style, but his Restoration portraits of women are noted for their subtle colouring, skillful rendering of silk, and the air of sensuous languor with which they invest their subjects—*e.g.*, the portrait series of court ladies entitled "The Windsor Beauties" (1660s; Hampton Court, London). Simultaneously he painted the portrait series of the "Admirals" (1666–67) at Greenwich, the best of them rugged and severely masculine characterizations. Lely's late works are marred by stylistic mannerisms and decreasing vitality.

Lelystad, *gemeente* (municipality) and capital, Flevoland *provincie* (province), north-central Netherlands, on the IJsselmeer (Lake IJssel). After the East Flevoland Polder was drained in 1957, the town was built on a foundation of piles driven into the subsoil. It was named after Cornelis Lely (d. 1929), an engineer-statesman who designed the Zuiderzee reclamation project. It became the capital of the newly created Flevoland province in 1986. Located next to a land-reclamation dike, Lelystad has a small fishing harbour; boats have access to Amsterdam through the Oostvaarder Canal. Several inland canals on the polder supply water for the surrounding agricultural area, where flowers, apples, cereals, and dairy cattle are raised. The town has five residential areas that are separated from each other by parks, and industrial zones are located on its periphery. Construction of the dike and road between Lelystad and Enkhuizen across the IJsselmeer was completed in 1976 as the first step toward the reclamation of Markerwaard Polder to the east. The Informatiecentium Nieuw Land is an exhibition in Lelystad about the Zuiderzee project. The Oostvaarderplassen, a waterfowl reserve, is located southwest of the town. Pop. (1984 est.) 55,141.

Lemain Island (The Gambia): *see* MacCarthy Island.

Lemaire de Belges, Jean (b. *c.* 1473, Bavai, Hainaut [now in Belgium]—d. *c.* 1525), Walloon poet, historian, and pamphleteer, who, writing in French, was the last and one of the best of the school of poetic *rhetoriqueurs* ("rhetoricians") and the chief forerunner, both in style and in thought, of the Renaissance humanists in France and Flanders.

Lemaire led a wandering life in the service of various princes and was often at the court of Margaret of Austria (d. 1530), the regent of the Netherlands; he acted as her librarian at Malines. An innovator of wide intellectual curiosity, he had a sense of literary beauty that set his works apart from those of his contemporaries. Most of his poems are occasional pieces in memory of some prince. His two *Épitres de l'amant vert* (1505) are charming and witty letters in light verse describing the grief of Margaret of Austria's parrot during her mistress's absence. Lemaire traveled in Italy and was an admirer of Italian culture. His *Concorde des deux langages* (after 1510; modern ed. 1947) attempts to reconcile the influence of the Italian Renaissance with French tradition. His most extensive work is a legendary romance in prose, *Illustrations de Gaule et singularitez de Troye* (*c.* 1510), showing exuberant imagination and a modern appreciation of classical antiquity.

Lemaître, Georges (b. July 17, 1894, Charleroi, Belg.—d. June 20, 1966, Louvain), Belgian astronomer and cosmologist who formulated the modern big-bang theory, which holds that the universe began in a cataclysmic explosion of a small, primeval "super-atom."

A civil engineer, Lemaître served as an artillery officer in the Belgian Army during World War I. After the war he entered a seminary and in 1923 was ordained a priest. He studied at the University of Cambridge's solar physics laboratory (1923–24) and then at the Massachusetts Institute of Technology, Cambridge (1925–27), where he became acquainted with the findings of the American astronomers Edwin P. Hubble and Harlow Shapley on the expanding universe. In 1927, the year he became professor of astrophysics at the University of Louvain, he proposed his big-bang theory, which explained the recession of the galaxies within the framework of Albert Einstein's theory of general relativity. Although expanding models of the universe had been considered earlier, notably by the Dutch astronomer Willem de Sitter, Lemaître's theory, as modified by George Gamow, has become the leading theory of cosmology.

Lemaître also did research on cosmic rays and on the three-body problem, which concerns the mathematical description of the motion of three mutually attracting bodies in space. His works include *Discussion sur l'évolution de l'univers* (1933; "Discussion on the Evolution of the Universe") and *L'Hypothèse de l'atome primitif* (1946; "Hypothesis of the Primeval Atom").

Lemaître, (François-Élie-)Jules (b. April 27, 1853, Vennecy, Fr.—d. Aug. 4, 1914, Tavers), French critic, storyteller, and dramatist, now remembered for his uniquely personal and impressionistic style of literary criticism.

After leaving the École Normale, Lemaître was a schoolmaster and then professor at the University of Grenoble before resigning to devote himself to writing. His first essay (1894), on the French historian and dramatist Joseph Renan, showed his independence of mind and lively style and was the beginning of a long career as a theatrical and literary critic. His critical essays from the *Journal des Débats* were collected in *Les Contemporains* (vol. 1–7, 1885–99; vol. 8, 1918; selections translated into English as *Literary Impressions*) and *Impressions du théâtre* (vol. 1–10, 1888–98; vol. 11, 1920). Lemaître was an enemy of critical dogmatism and critical systems; like his contemporary Anatole France, he emphasized his individual, human perceptions of works, controlled only by knowledge and taste. His essays, although inevitably dated, remain readable, not only as valuable documents on the writing of his time but also because of their wit, wide knowledge, and lack of pedantry.

His other works include penetrating and authoritative collections of lectures: one published in 1907 on the philosopher Jean-Jacques Rousseau, a second published in 1908 on the French tragedian Jean Racine, another published in 1910 on the writer and political figure Fénelon, and still more on various subjects. Of his plays, *Revoltée* (1889; "Rebellious Woman"), *Les Rois* (1893; "The Kings"), and *La Massière* (1904; "The Treasurer") had moderate success. His best collections of stories include *Serenus* (1886) and *En marge des vieux livres* (1905–07; *On the Margins of Old Books*), a compilation of tales created around the characters from classic works of literature and history.

Jules Lemaître

H. Roger-Viollet

Léman, Lac (Europe): *see* Geneva, Lake.

Lemass, Sean F(rancis) (b. July 15, 1899, Dublin—d. May 11, 1971, Dublin), Irish patriot, politician, and prime minister from 1959 to 1966.

As early as the age of 16, Lemass became a freedom fighter in the streets of Dublin, engaging in the Easter Rising (April 1916) and other hostilities and landing in jail again and again; his brother Noel died as a revolutionary. After establishment of the Irish Free State, he joined Eamon De Valera and the other holdouts, becoming a member of the headquarters staff of the Irish Republican Army in 1922 and sharing in the founding of the new party, Fianna Fáil, in 1926. After De Valera rose to the premiership in 1932, Lemass held portfolios in all his cabinets for 21 of the next 27 years, notably as minister of industry and commerce and then as deputy prime minister.

When De Valera became president in 1959, Lemass inherited the office of prime minister. Under him the nation took a more outward-looking approach, and he especially pressed for Ireland's entry into the European Economic Community (Common Market). Ill health, however, forced him to relinquish the leadership of his party in 1966 and withdraw from politics in 1969. Ireland's membership in the Common Market was not secured until 1973, after his death.

LeMay, Curtis E(merson) (b. Nov. 15, 1906, Columbus, Ohio, U.S.—d. Oct. 1, 1990, March Air Force Base, Calif.), U.S. Air Force officer whose expertise in strategic bombardment techniques was important during World War II and afterward.

Entering the U.S. Army Air Corps in 1928, LeMay advanced to the position of bombardment group commander by 1942. Flying with the 8th Air Force from England (1942–44), he became known for his development of advanced bomber tactics, including pattern bombing and the combat box formation. After commanding B-29s in India and China (1944), LeMay took over the 21st Bomber Command in the Mariana Islands (January 1945); in that post he planned and originated the low-altitude incendiary-bombing tactics that burned out parts of Tokyo and a number of other Japanese cities in an effort to force a surrender before the Allied invasion of Japan, which was planned for the end of that year.

LeMay
By courtesy of the U.S. Air Force

After the war LeMay commanded the U.S. air forces in Europe, and in that capacity he directed the Berlin airlift in 1948. He headed the U.S. Strategic Air Command from 1948 to 1957 and built it into a global strike force. He was promoted to the rank of general in 1951. In 1957 he was named vice chief of staff and four years later chief of staff of the U.S. Air Force. He retired in 1965.

In 1968 he was the vice presidential candidate on the third-party (American Independent) ticket headed by George C. Wallace.

Lemberg (Ukraine): *see* Lviv.

Lemdiyya (Algeria): *see* Médéa.

Lemercier, Jacques, Lemercier also spelled LE MERCIER (b. 1585, Pontoise, Fr.—d. June 4, 1654, Paris), French architect who, along with François Mansart and Louis Le Vau, defined French classical architecture.

Lemercier belonged to a famous family of builders. For several years between 1607 and 1614 he was in Rome, where he probably studied with Rosato Rosati, whose Church of San Carlo ai Catinari was Lemercier's model for the Church of the Sorbonne, in Paris.

Following his completion of the Church of l'Oratoire (1616; begun by C. Métezeau), Lemercier became recognized as the new master of classicism in France. He was commissioned by Louis XIII to carry out the enlargement of the old Louvre courtyard (now the Cour Carrée), planned by Pierre Lescot, and to this purpose he built the Pavillon de l'Horloge and the adjoining wings to the north. The rich ornament and complex proportions of the Pavillon de l'Horloge make it one of his most successful buildings.

The Cardinal de Richelieu soon became his patron, and Lemercier built for him the Palais-Cardinal, subsequently renamed the Palais Royal, in Paris (1629). The theatre of the Palais was one of the first structures in France built exclusively for theatrical use. It was also for Richelieu that Lemercier built the Church of the Sorbonne (begun 1626), perhaps the earliest French building to have a dome set on a high drum. The most ambitious project carried out for his patron was the design of a château and surrounding town at Richelieu in Indre-et-Loire (begun 1631; now mostly destroyed).

In 1646 Lemercier took over the completion of François Mansart's Church of the Val-de-Grâce in Paris. The dramatic exterior of the Italianate dome that he added is regarded as a masterpiece of French classicism, as is the interior of his dome for the Sorbonne church. Lemercier died just after beginning Saint-Roch (1653), which became the principal Parisian church of the early 18th century.

Lemercier, (Louise-Jean) Népomucène (b. April 21, 1771, Paris, Fr.—d. June 7, 1840, Paris), poet and dramatist, a late proponent of classical tragedy over Romanticism, and the originator of French historical comedy.

An accident caused Lemercier lifelong partial paralysis, which he faced with considerable courage. He made a precocious literary debut, attempting a comedy at age 9 and having his first tragedy, *Méléagre,* produced at the Comédie-Française before he was 16. His *Tartuffe révolutionnaire* (1795) created a succès de scandale and was quickly suppressed because of its bold political allusions. The orthodox tragedy *Agamemnon* (1794) was probably Lemercier's most celebrated play. *Pinto* (1800), a historical comedy treating the Portuguese revolution of 1640, was original in attempting to divest historical events of poetic ornament and the high seriousness of tragedy, thus foreshadowing Eugène Scribe's unheroic approach. This more experimental attitude was also shown in *Christophe Colomb* (1809), a Shakespearean comedy, and *Richard III et Jeanne Shore* (1824), imitated from William Shakespeare and Nicholas Rowe. Despite these excursions outside the classical realm, Lemercier had no sympathy with the Romantics, and in the Académie Française, to which he was elected in 1810, he consistently opposed them, refusing his vote to Victor Hugo's admittance. The most successful of his later plays was *Frédégonde et Brunehaut* (1821), a "regular" tragedy in which he claimed to portray, from early French history, a modern equivalent of the classic house-of-Atreus theme. Most of his plays were helped by the acting of the great tragedian François-Joseph Talma. Lemercier also wrote a number of philosophical epic poems. His reputation as a writer declined long before his death.

Népomucène Lemercier, engraving by Boilly, 1820
H. Roger-Viollet

Lemesós (Cyprus): *see* Limassol.

lemming, any of several small rodents belonging to the family Cricetidae (order Rodentia) and found primarily in north temperate and polar regions of North America and Eurasia. Lemmings are placed in four genera: *Dicrostonyx* (collared, or Arctic, lemmings); *Lemmus* ("true" lemmings); *Myopus* (wood, or red-backed, lemmings); and *Synaptomys* (bog lemmings). Lemmings are short-legged, with small ears and long, soft fur. They are 10 to 18 cm (4 to 7 inches) long, including the stump of a tail, and are grayish or reddish brown above, paler below. The wood lemming (*Myopus schisticolor*) of the Old World has a reddish back. The collared lemmings of the Arctic regions of Russia and Canada have dark back and face stripes, except in winter, when their fur is completely white. Lemmings feed on roots, shoots, and grasses and live in burrows or rock crevices. They breed from spring to fall, the female producing up to nine young after a gestation period of 20 to 22 days.

Collared lemmings (*Dicrostonyx groenlandicus*) in summer coat
By courtesy of Walt Disney Productions

Lemmings are noted for the regular fluctuations of their populations and for their periodic migrations. Their population "explosions" occur about three or four years apart in the genus *Lemmus* and are not completely understood. Factors influencing their population explosions and migrations include the following: natural increase in numbers after the last migration and its subsequent population decline; reduction in predators resulting from the decline in lemmings, their prey, after a migration; and optimal breeding conditions for lemmings.

The migrations of lemmings tend to occur in spring and in fall. After several years of optimal breeding conditions and low rates of mortality from predation, the lemmings in an area may move in detectable waves away from centres of denser lemming population. The emigrating lemmings begin to move in greater numbers, at first erratically and under cover of darkness and later in bold groups that may travel in daylight. The movements of the Norway lemming (*Lemmus lemmus*) are the most dramatic, as many of the migrants may end by drowning in the sea. The animals tend to follow paths and roadways established by people or animals, and they apparently move outward in all directions from a central area. Lemmings hesitate to enter water and generally try to avoid swimming across rivers and other bodies of water, seeking land crossings whenever possible. They do not, as is popularly supposed, plunge into the sea in a deliberate, suicidal death march.

Lemmon, Jack, in full JOHN UHLER LEMMON III (b. Feb. 8, 1925, Boston—d. June 27, 2001, Los Angeles), American screen and stage actor noted for his character portrayals in American films from the 1950s onward.

Lemmon graduated from Harvard University in 1947 and then went to New York City to work as an actor. He worked as a piano player, acted in radio and television dramas, and began acting on Broadway in 1953. His first film appearance was in *It Should Happen to You* (1954), and his performance as Ensign Pulver in *Mister Roberts* (1955) established his career in Hollywood. His performances in leading roles in *Some Like It Hot* (1959) and *The Apartment* (1960) reinforced the character type he played, that of a tense, excitable, and baffled individual who painfully progresses to a deeper understanding of the world. His major films of the 1960s were *Days of Wine and Roses* (1962), *The Fortune Cookie* (1966), and *The Odd Couple* (1968). In the 1970s he starred in *The Out-of-Towners* (1970), *Save the Tiger* (1973), *The Front Page* (1974), and *The China Syndrome* (1979), and in the 1980s his most notable performance was in *Missing* (1982). He won Academy Awards as best supporting actor in *Mister Roberts* and for best actor in *Save the Tiger*.

Lemnos, Modern Greek LÍMNOS, isolated Greek island in the Aegean Sea, midway between Mount Áthos (in northeastern mainland Greece) and the Turkish coast, in the *nomós* (department) of Lesbos. Composed mainly of volcanic rock, its western region rises to 1,410 feet (430 m) at Múrtzeflos Cape and is more rugged than the eastern portions, which are separated from the west by two deep inlets, Pourniá in the north and Moúdhros in the south. The 184-square-mile (476-square-kilometre) island is treeless in the west, but the valleys and eastern plains are fertile. The chief town and port, Mírina, on the west coast, is the seat of the metropolitan bishop of Lemnos and the island of Áyios Evstrátios to the south. The second town is Moúdhros, on the bay of the same name, one of the best natural harbours in the Aegean. There is a major airfield on the island.

Excavations conducted by the Italian School in 1931–36 at Poliochni on the east coast revealed four ancient superimposed settlements: Early Bronze Age (*c.* 3000 BC); beneath it a Copper Age (*c.* 5000 BC) city; and beneath that the remains of two Neolithic cities, equipped with stone baths, representing the most advanced Neolithic civilization yet found in the Aegean. Near the ancient town of Hephaestia an extensive necropolis (cemetery) of the 8th to 6th century BC has been found. Located on Pourniás Bay, Hephaestia was the principal city of Lemnos in classical times; today it is occupied by the hamlet of Palaiópolis.

Toward the end of the 6th century BC, the island was conquered by Otanes, a general of the Persian king Darius. From 477 Lemnos was a member of the Delian League, and later, except for a Spartan interlude, it was controlled by Athens. In 197 BC Rome declared it free but gave it over in 166 BC to Athens, which retained nominal possession of the island until the time of the Roman emperor Septimius Severus (AD 193–211).

In the 4th century the island had a Byzantine bishop and became a metropolitan see in the reign of Leo VI (reigned 928). It was settled by Venetian merchants in the 11th and 12th centuries, and in 1204, after disruption of the Byzantine Empire, the Venetians established themselves on the island. During the following centuries, rule alternated among Venice, Genoa, and the Turks, who after 1670 used it as a place for banishment of exiles. Lemnos joined the Greek kingdom after the Balkan Wars (1912–13). From the Órmos Moúdhrou in 1915 the Allies launched their unsuccessful invasion of the Dardanelles; in the same bay, the Allied armistice with Turkey was concluded in 1918. In classical times Lemnian earth (*Lemnia sphragis*) was used as an astringent for snakebites and wounds and in the 16th century for the plague. This medicinal soil was dug ceremonially once a year from a mound near Hephaestia. Pop. (1981) 15,721.

lemon (*Citrus limon*), small tree or spreading bush of the rue family (Rutaceae) and its edible fruit. The lemon forms a spreading bush or a small tree, 3–6 m (10–20 feet) high if not pruned. Its young leaves have a decidedly reddish tint; later they turn green. In some varieties, the young branches of the lemon are angular; some have sharp thorns at the axils of the leaves. The flowers have a sweet odour and are rather large, solitary or in small clusters in the axils of the leaves. Reddish-tinted in the bud, the petals are white above and reddish purple below.

The fruit is oval with a broad, low, apical nipple and 8 to 10 segments. The outer rind, or peel, yellow when ripe and rather thick in some varieties, is prominently glandular-dotted. The white, spongy inner part of the peel, called the mesocarp, or albedo, is nearly tasteless and is the chief source of commercial grades of pectin. The seeds are small, ovoid, and pointed; occasionally, fruits are seedless. The pulp is decidedly acid. The predominant acid present is citric acid, which may amount

Lemon (*Citrus limon*)
J. Horace McFarland Co.

to 5 percent or more by weight of the lemon's juice. Lemon juice is rich in vitamin C and contains smaller amounts of the B vitamins, particularly B1, B2, and niacin.

The lemon was probably unknown to the ancient Greeks and Romans, but it was introduced into Spain and North Africa some time between the years AD 1000 and 1200. It was further distributed through Europe by the crusaders, who found the fruit growing in Palestine. In 1494 the fruit was being cultivated in the Azores and shipped largely to England. The lemon was thought by the 18th-century Swedish botanist Linnaeus to be a variety of the citron (*Citrus medica*), though it is now known to be a separate species.

The chief varieties of lemons were formerly the Lisbon, a variety introduced from Australia, and the Eureka, a variety that originated from a seedling tree grown in California. Since the mid-20th century, new, more vigorous varieties such as the Frost Lisbon and the Frost Eureka have been developed that have a higher resistance to infection from fungal and other plant diseases. As a cultivated tree, the lemon is now grown to a limited extent in most tropical and subtropical countries.

Lemon trees for commercial planting are usually propagated by budding the desired variety on seedlings of other citrus species, such as the sweet orange, grapefruit, mandarin orange, sour orange, or tangelo. Seedlings of these species are superior to lemon seedlings as rootstocks because they are more uniform and less susceptible to the various crown- and foot-rot diseases.

The relatively cool, equable climatic zones of coastal Italy and California are especially favourable for lemon cultivation. The trees are commonly grown in orchards, spaced 5–8 m (16–26 feet) apart. Lemon trees usually bloom throughout the year, and the fruit is picked 6 to 10 times a year. Full-sized fruit for commercial purposes is about 50 mm (2 inches) in diameter. The fruit is usually picked while still green and, after curing, may be kept three months or more in storage.

Young lemon trees reach bearing age as early as the third year after planting, and commercial crops may be expected during the fifth year. The average orchard yield per tree is 1,500 lemons a year. Because lemons bruise easily, the pickers must wear gloves and take great care when picking and handling the fruit. Careful handling is essential to prevent the loss of fruit in storage and transit due to fungal diseases. Picked lemons are graded in the packing house according to their maturity, which is indicated by their colour; yellow fruits are already fully ripe and must be sold immediately, while fruits that are still green are held in storage until they become a uniform yellow in colour.

The United States and Italy are major producers of lemons. Other producing countries include Spain, Greece, Turkey, Argentina, Lebanon, Chile, Brazil, Israel, Australia, Tunisia, South Africa, Algeria, Cyprus, and Portugal. About half of the lemon crop is usually shipped to the fresh-fruit market.

Juice of the lemon is a characteristic ingredient in many pastries and desserts, such as tarts and the traditional American lemon meringue pie. The astringent, distinctive flavour of the fruit is also used to enhance many poultry, fish, and vegetable dishes worldwide. Lemonade, made with lemon, sugar, and water, is a popular warm-weather beverage, and the juice itself is commonly added to tea.

Among the important by-products of lemons are citric acid, citrate of lime, lemon oil, and pectin. Preparation of the oil, used in perfumes, soap, and flavouring extract, is an important industry in Sicily. Citric acid is used in beverage manufacturing. Pectin has long been an important material for making fruit jellies; it has also been used in medicine in the treatment of intestinal disorders, as an antihemorrhagic, as a plasma extender, and for other purposes.

lemon shark, species of shark in the family Carcharhinidae. *See* carcharhinid.

lemon verbena (*Aloysia triphylla,* or *Lippia citriodora*), tropical perennial shrub belonging to the family Verbenaceae, originating in

Lemon verbena (*Aloysia triphylla*)
G.R. Roberts

Argentina and Chile. Growing more than 3 m (10 feet) high in warm climates, it is also grown as a potted plant reaching a height of about 25.4 cm (10 inches).

The leaves are long, narrow, and pointed,

with yellowish green colour. They are rich in aromatic oil and have a clear lemonlike flavour and scent. Lemon verbena is used in sweet drinks, salads, jellies, and puddings. Used alone or in combination with other herbs, the leaves make an excellent herbal tea. They are also used for their fragrance in colognes and sachets.

LeMond, Greg, in full GREGORY JAMES LEMOND (b. June 26, 1961, Lakewood, Calif., U.S.), bicycle racer and the first non-European to win the Tour de France (*q.v.*), cycling's most challenging event. In his career he won the Tour de France three times (1986, 1989, 1990) and twice won the World Professional Road Racing Championship (1983, 1989).

LeMond began cycling as a teenager in Nevada and turned professional in 1980. In 1983 LeMond won his first world championship, and the next year he entered his first Tour de France, finishing third. At the 1985 Tour de France, LeMond deferred to his teammate Bernard Hinault and finished second while aiding the Frenchman to his fifth Tour title. The next year LeMond defeated Hinault to win his first Tour de France.

In 1987 LeMond was shot and nearly killed in a hunting accident, but he regained top form for the 1989 Tour de France. On the last day of that three-week race, LeMond raced through a time trial (*q.v.*), making up 58 seconds on the leader, Laurent Fignon, and won the Tour by 8 seconds, the smallest victory margin in the history of the event.

LeMond retired from competitive cycling in 1994 when he was diagnosed with mitochondrial myopathy, a rare cellular disorder.

Lemonnier, (Antoine-Louis-) Camille (b. March 24, 1844, Ixelles, near Brussels, Belg.—d. June 13, 1913, Ixelles), novelist, writer of short stories, and art critic, one of the outstanding personalities of the 19th-century French literary renaissance in Belgium.

Lemonnier, pen-and-ink drawing by an unknown artist; in the Bibliothèque Royale, Brussels
By courtesy of the Bibliotheque Royale, Brussels

His first novel, *Un Mâle* (1881; "A Male"), shows the influence of the naturalism of Émile Zola. Like his other novels, it is a work of great violence, describing characters of unbridled instincts and passions. *Happe-chair* (1886) deals with the drudgery of mill workers' lives. Later, his work turned to psychological analysis, condemning the conservative tendencies of the bourgeoisie. Finally, he returned to naturalism with a subtler but no less forceful style. Many consider *Le Petit Homme de Dieu* (1902; "The Little Man of God"), a late naturalist novel, his masterpiece.

Lemonnier's works seem somewhat dated partly because his prose is pretentious and heavy. In spite of his frequent word coinages and laboured effects, many of his novels are still worth reading for their psychological insight, their feeling for nature, and their faithful descriptions of the Flemish countryside.

Lemoyne, Jean-Baptiste (b. Feb. 15, 1704, Paris, Fr.—d. May 25, 1778, Paris), French sculptor renowned for his portrait busts.

The pupil of his father, Jean-Louis Lemoyne, and of Robert Le Lorrain, he was appointed sculptor to Louis XV. Lemoyne executed many likenesses of the king, either as large sculptures—the statues in the royal squares at Bordeaux (1743) and at Rennes (1754)—or as busts. Most of these were destroyed in the French Revolution. He also produced many portraits of the leaders of French society of his day, including busts of Voltaire (1748), Montesquieu (1767), and Madame de Pompadour (1761). His works are essentially Baroque in style, with an elegance of decorative handling that is Rococo.

Lempa River, Spanish RÍO LEMPA, river in Central America. It rises in Guatemala near Esquipulas, crosses a corner of Honduras, and enters El Salvador at Citalá. After cutting across El Salvador's northern mountain range, it flows eastward for over 80 miles (130 km) and then southward for 65 miles (105 km) across the southern mountain range to enter the Pacific Ocean after a total course of about 200 miles (320 km). It is El Salvador's largest and only navigable river. Its northern valley has hydroelectric projects that supply power to much of El Salvador. Its southern basin has been developed agriculturally.

lemur, generally, any of the more primitive primates except the tree shrews. In this sense, the term covers not only the typical lemurs (family Lemuridae) but also the avahi, indri, sifaka, aye-aye, loris, potto, and galago (*qq.v.*). All these animals are characterized by a naked, moist tip to the muzzle; comblike, forward-directed lower front teeth; and a clawlike nail on the second toe of the foot.

Typical lemurs are slender primates that are found only on Madagascar and the Comoro Islands. They have large eyes, foxlike faces, monkeylike bodies, and long hind limbs. Lemurs range in length (excluding the tail) from about 13 cm (5 inches) in the dwarf lemur to about 60 cm in the true lemurs. The bushy tails of lemurs may be longer than their bodies. The animals' woolly fur is reddish, gray, brown, or black; some species are variously marked or striped.

Ring-tailed lemur (*Lemur catta*)
Tierbilder Okapia, Frankfurt am Main

Lemurs are lower on the evolutionary scale and are less intelligent than monkeys. Their sense of smell is more acute, but they lack binocular vision. Lemurs are docile, gregarious animals, and some species live in groups of 10 or more. Most are active at night and sleep during the day. Lemurs spend most of their time in the trees, eating fruits, leaves, buds, insects, and small birds and birds' eggs. Some species are more carnivorous than others. A single young is usually born after two to five months' gestation.

The family Lemuridae includes three genera and about nine species, with the typical genus being that of the true lemurs (*Lemur*). The best-known of these is the ring-tailed lemur (*L. catta*), which is unique in both its habitat (the dry, rocky areas of Madagascar) and in its striped tail, since all other lemurs have solid-coloured tails. Another species of true lemur is the black lemur (*L. macaco*), in which the male is black and the female is reddish brown. Another genus within the family Lemuridae is that of the nocturnal, bamboo-eating gentle lemurs (*Hapalemur*). The sportive lemurs make up a separate family (Lepilemuridae), as do the dwarf (*Cheirogaleus*) and mouse (*Microcebus*) lemurs, which together make up the family Cheirogaleidae. Mouse and dwarf lemurs are small types that store fat in their rumps and tails and estivate during dry periods.

A number of lemurs are listed in the *Red Data Book* as rare or endangered animals.

Lemurs first appeared in the Early Eocene Epoch (57.8 to 52 million years ago), though their origins may be traced to the preceding Paleocene Epoch. These early lemuroids were moderately abundant and are found as fossils in deposits in North America and Europe. One Eocene form, *Notharctus* (*q.v.*), is particularly well-known from complete fossil remains. At the close of the Eocene (36.6 million years ago), *Notharctus* and related forms disappeared from the Northern Hemisphere. The lemurs continued in tropical forests, however, and were particularly successful in Madagascar, where they were relatively free from competition with more advanced primates.

Lena River, major river of Russia and one of the longest rivers in the world. It flows 2,734 miles (4,400 km) from its source in a small Siberian mountain lake west of Lake Baikal in Central Asia, northward across Russia, to the mouth of its delta on the Arctic Laptev Sea.

A brief treatment of the Lena River follows. For full treatment, *see* MACROPAEDIA: Asia.

The Lena River basin covers an area of about 961,000 square miles (2,490,000 square km). Its major tributaries include the Vitim, Aldan, Great Patom, Olyokma, and Nyuya rivers. Three main sections form the Lena, each about 900 miles (1,450 km) long: the upper section flows from the source to the Vitim tributary; the middle course from the Vitim to the mouth of the Aldan; and the lower section from the Aldan to the Laptev Sea. The river's upper section flows through a deeply cut valley that gradually widens, becoming a large, deep riverbed in the upper half of the middle course. The surrounding slopes are gentle and green with forests, and there is a large water meadow in which many small lakes are scattered. The character of the valley changes sharply in the lower half of the middle course. There the Lena flows along the bottom of a narrow valley with sheer, broken slopes; the area is a popular site for tourists and rock climbers. In the lower section, as the Lena enters the Yakut Lowland, the riverbed widens and water meadow abounds once again.

The climatic conditions of the Lena basin are determined by its continental location. Air temperatures in the winter are severe, the average monthly figure in January being −22° to −40° F (−30° to −40° C). In July temperatures range between 50° and 68° F (10° and 20° C). Because of its remoteness from the sea, the amount of precipitation in the basin is slight, falling mainly in the summer; on the average no more than 2 inches (50 mm) of snow fall each year. Typical of the Lena basin are high floods, especially flash floods, in the summer, and very little flow in the winter. The average annual discharge is 579,000 cubic feet (16,400 cubic m) per second. In some locations the riverbed and floodlands are covered with permanent ice. A large part of the basin is covered with taiga (swampy northern coniferous forest); tundra is found along the lower course near the Arctic.

Farms produce cereal crops and raise livestock on the Yakut Lowland. The basin is rich in coal and natural gas, and gold occurs in exploitable quantities. Yakutsk is the chief city among many industrial centres on the Lena, and Osetrovo is the river's leading modern port.

Lenard, Philipp, in full PHILIPP EDUARD ANTON LENARD (b. June 7, 1862, Pressburg, Hung. [now Bratislava, Slovakia]—d. May 20, 1947, Messelhausen, Ger.), German physicist, winner of the Nobel Prize for Physics in 1905 for his research on cathode rays and the discovery of many of their properties. His results had important implications for the development of electronics and nuclear physics.

Lenard
Bavaria-Verlag

After serving as a lecturer and as an assistant to Heinrich Hertz at the University of Bonn in 1893, Lenard was professor of physics successively at the universities of Breslau (1894), Aachen (1895), Heidelberg (1896), and Kiel (1898). In 1907 he returned to the University of Heidelberg as professor of physics, where he stayed until his retirement in 1931.

Applying the discovery that cathode rays pass through thin leaves of metal, Lenard constructed (1898) a cathode-ray tube with an aluminum window through which the rays could pass into the open air. Using a phosphorescent screen, he showed that the rays decreased in number as the screen was drawn away from the tube and that they ceased at a distance. The experiments also demonstrated that the power of substances to absorb the rays depends on their density and not on their chemical nature and that absorption decreases with increasing velocity of the rays. In similar experiments in 1899 he proved that cathode rays are created when light strikes metal surfaces; this phenomenon later became known as the photoelectric effect.

Lenard's extensive research also included studies of ultraviolet light, the electrical conductivity of flames, and phosphorescence. He wrote a considerable number of books on cathode rays, relativity, and related subjects, including *Über Kathodenstrahlen* (1906; "On Cathode Rays") and *Deutsche Physik,* 4 vol. (1936–37; "German Physics").

An ardent supporter of Nazism, Lenard publicly denounced "Jewish" science, including Albert Einstein's theory of relativity.

Lenau, Nikolaus, pseudonym of NIKOLAUS FRANZ NIEMBSCH, LORD (edler) VON STREHLENAU (b. Aug. 13, 1802, Csatád, Hung.—d. Aug. 22, 1850, Oberdöbling, near Vienna, Austria), Austrian poet known for melancholy lyrical verse that mirrors the pessimism of his time as well as his personal despair.

Severe depression and dissatisfaction characterized Lenau's life. He began, but never completed, studies in law, medicine, and philosophy. A legacy in 1830 enabled him to devote himself to writing. Frequent moves, a number of unhappy love affairs, and a disastrous year-long emigration to the United States in 1832–33 further exemplified the general disappointment he felt at the failure of his life and acquaintances to measure up to his artistic ideals. He recognized that his inability to keep separate the spheres of poetic expression and real life was both the source of his depression and the root of his art.

Lenau's fame rests predominantly on his shorter lyrical poems. These early poems, which were published in *Gedichte* (1832; "Poems") and *Neuere Gedichte* (1838; "Newer Poems"), demonstrate close ties to the Weltschmerz ("World Pain") mood of the Romantic period and reveal a personal, almost religious relationship to nature. His later poems, *Gesammelte Gedichte,* 2 vol. (1844), and the religious epics *Savonarola* (1837) and *Die Albigenser* (1842; "The Albigensians"), deal with his relentless and unsuccessful search for order and constancy in love, nature, and faith. Following J.W. von Goethe's death in 1832, the appearance in 1833 of the second part of his *Faust* inspired many renditions of the legend. Lenau's *Faust: Ein Gedicht* (published 1836, revised 1840) is noticeably derivative of Goethe's, but Lenau's version has Faust confronting an absurd life that is devoid of any absolute values, the same position in which Lenau felt himself to be. Lenau's lifelong mental illness resulted in a complete breakdown in 1844 and later to near-total paralysis from which he never recovered. His epic *Don Juan* (1851) appeared posthumously. His letters to Baroness Sophie von Löwenthal, with whom he was in love from 1834 to his death, were published in 1968.

"De," "la," and similar components of a name, when followed by a space, are alphabetized as separate words (e.g., *De Forest, Lee*). *When they are joined to the following part of a name, the combination is treated as a single word* (e.g., *DeForest, John William*).

Lenbach, Franz von (b. Dec. 13, 1836, Schrobenhausen, Bavaria [Germany]—d. May 6, 1904, Munich, Ger.), painter whose powerful characterizations made him the favoured portraitist of late 19th-century Germany.

In 1857 Lenbach became a pupil of Karl von Piloty, with whom he traveled in Italy. The works of this first journey were painted from nature and were frequently attacked for their "trivial realism." Shortly after his return to Germany in 1862, Lenbach was appointed professor at the academy at Weimar. From 1863 to 1868 he copied old masters for private collectors, especially Count Schack, in the museums and private collections of Germany, Italy, and Spain.

After 1868 Lenbach devoted himself to portraiture. Among his sitters were the foremost men of his time: Emperor William I, Richard Wagner, Franz Liszt, Hermann von Helmholtz, and William Gladstone. His portraits of Otto von Bismarck, of whom he painted about 80 pictures, are particularly famous. Stylistically, Lenbach relied on the chiaroscuro, colour, and painterly qualities of Titian, Rembrandt, Diego Velázquez, and Joshua Reynolds. The later years of his life were spent between Munich, Vienna, and Berlin, with visits to Egypt and Rome.

Lenca, Indians of the northern highlands of Honduras and El Salvador who are somewhat intermediate culturally between the Maya to the north and circum-Caribbean peoples such as the Cuna to the south. The aboriginal culture of the Lenca has virtually disappeared and is not well known. It is thought that formerly each village was autonomous, controlled by a chief and a council who managed the village lands and officiated in all disputes.

Today the pattern of organization of Lenca villages varies greatly from town to town. The old class system has disappeared for the most part; although some chiefs, or caciques, still inherit their positions, others are elected. Land is owned by the village and distributed among individuals for farming, the method of distribution varying. The principal crop is corn (maize), although some European crops have been adopted. Crafts include pottery and basketry; the weaving of cloth seems to have been abandoned. In general, the Lenca have been much influenced by the modern cultures around them.

Although nominally Roman Catholic, the Lenca have retained many traditional beliefs and practices. The village shaman plays an important role in curing the sick.

Lenclos, Ninon de, byname of ANNE DE LENCLOS, Lenclos also spelled LANCLOS (b. 1620, Paris, Fr.—d. Oct. 17, 1705, Paris), celebrated French courtesan.

From her father, Henri de Lenclos, sieur de La Douardière, she acquired a lasting interest in Epicurean philosophy. Although her father fled from France after killing a man in 1632, she remained in Paris and established there a salon that attracted a number of the most prominent literary and political figures of the age. Her lovers included Gaspard de Coligny, Marquis d'Andelot; Louis de Bourbon, Duke d'Enghien (later known as the Great Condé); Pierre de Villars; both the Marquis de Sévigné and his son, Charles de Sévigné; and Louis de Mornay, Marquis de Villarceaux, by whom she had a son. Among her intellectual admirers were included the playwright Molière, the poet Paul Scarron, and the skeptic Saint-Évremond.

Ninon de Lenclos's irreligious attitudes caused King Louis XIV's mother, Anne of Austria, to have her confined to a convent in 1656, but her sympathizers quickly secured her release. She defended her philosophy and conduct in her book *La Coquette vengée* (1659; "The Coquette Avenged"). During the 1670s she was protected by Scarron's widow, who later became (as Madame de Maintenon) the wife of Louis XIV.

After she retired from her career as a courtesan in 1671, Mlle de Lenclos's receptions became not only fashionable but also highly respectable. François Arouet, father of Voltaire, managed her business dealings during the fi-

Ninon de Lenclos, portrait by an unknown French artist, 17th century; in the Versailles Museum, France
Giraudon—Art Resource

nal years of her life; in her will she left money for books for young Voltaire.

BIBLIOGRAPHY. Edgar H. Cohen, *Mademoiselle Libertine* (1970).

lend-lease, system by which the United States aided its World War II allies with war materials, such as ammunition, tanks, airplanes, and trucks, and with food and other raw materials. President Franklin D. Roosevelt had committed the United States in June 1940 to materially aiding the opponents of fascism, but, under existing U.S. law, Great Britain had to pay for its growing arms purchases from the United States with cash. By the summer of 1940, the new British prime minister, Winston Churchill, was warning that his country could not pay cash for war materials much longer.

In order to remedy this situation, Roosevelt on Dec. 8, 1940, proposed the concept of lend-lease, and the U.S. Congress passed his Lend-Lease Act in March 1941. This legislation gave the president the authority to aid any nation whose defense he believed vital to the United States and to accept repayment "in kind or property, or any other direct or indirect benefit which the President deems satisfactory." Though lend-lease had been authorized primarily in an effort to aid Great Britain, it was extended to China in April and to the Soviet Union in September. The principal recipients of aid were the British Commonwealth countries (about 63 percent) and the Soviet Union (about 22 percent), though by the end of the war more than 40 nations had received lend-lease help. Much of the aid, valued at $49,100,000,000, amounted to outright gifts. Some of the cost of the lend-lease program was offset by so-called reverse lend-lease, under which Allied nations gave U.S. troops stationed abroad about $8,000,000,000 worth of aid.

L'Enfant, Pierre-Charles (b. Aug. 2, 1754, Paris, France—d. June 14, 1825, Prince Georges county, Md., U.S.), French-born American engineer, architect, and urban designer who designed the basic plan for Washington, D.C., the capital city of the United States.

L'Enfant studied art under his father at the Royal Academy of Painting and Sculpture from 1771 until he enlisted in 1776 as a volunteer in the American Revolutionary Army. In recognition of his services, Congress made him major of engineers in 1783. The medal and diploma of the Society of the Cincinnati, an association of former Revolutionary officers, were designed by L'Enfant, and upon returning to Paris he helped organize the French branch of the society. L'Enfant came again to America in 1784 and settled in New York City. There, in addition to small architectural jobs, he renovated the old city hall for the U.S. Congress as Federal Hall (1787). For this, his first major architectural essay, he added star decorations to the Doric order in honour of his adopted country. He also designed the grandiose Morris House in Philadelphia, a mansard-styled structure that was begun in 1794 but was never completed.

When Congress decided to build a federal capital on the Potomac River, President George Washington hired L'Enfant in 1791 to prepare a plan for it. The plan he created was a gridiron of irregular rectangular blocks upon which broad diagonal avenues were superimposed. It was devised to focus on the Capitol and the presidential mansion and to form many squares, circles, and triangles at street intersections where monuments and fountains could be placed. The plan used to advantage the uneven ground and prepared for future transportation needs as well. Secretary of State Thomas Jefferson had provided L'Enfant with maps of various European cities to use as models, but instead of copying any one of them L'Enfant took ideas from several. The influence of Baroque planning at Versailles by André Le Nôtre appears in his plan, and it also bears resemblances to the London plans of Sir Christopher Wren and John Evelyn.

Washington was forced to dismiss L'Enfant in 1792 for his obstinacy in defying the commissioners of the city, and particularly for his high-handed procedure in removing the house of Daniel Carroll, an influential Washington resident, to make way for an avenue. Nevertheless, his plan of the city was generally followed. L'Enfant later attempted to obtain $95,500 as payment for his services. Congress gave him what it thought to be proper, the sum of about $3,800. In his old age L'Enfant lived with friends at "Green Hill," a Maryland estate, where he died penniless. In 1909 his body was removed to Arlington National Cemetery, where a suitable monument was erected to him by Congress.

Leng-hu, Pinyin LENGHU, new town, northwestern Tsinghai *sheng* (province), western China. Leng-hu is situated in the northwest of the Tsaidam Basin, to the southwest of Tang-chin Pass, which leads from the Tsaidam into western Kansu province and to the Sinkiang Uygur autonomous region. Leng-hu is one of the major centres of the oil fields developed in the Tsaidam Basin during the 1960s and has its own refinery. It is also linked by a highway with the western Tsaidam oil field around Mang-ya, and by pipeline with oil fields to the northwest of Yü-men. Another highway links it with Golmud in the south-central Tsaidam Basin and with Hsi-ning in the east. Pop. (1982 est.) 17,000.

Lenglen, Suzanne (b. May 24, 1899, Compiègne, France—d. July 4, 1938, Paris), French tennis player and six-time Wimbledon champion who dominated women's amateur lawn tennis from 1919 until 1926, when she turned professional. She was also one of the greatest women players of hard-court tennis in her time. Her game, temperamental vagaries, and daring court dress were remarkable even in the 1920s, an era rich in colourful sports personages.

Chief among Lenglen's lawn-tennis titles were the Wimbledon (properly All-England; considered the world championship) singles (1919–23, 1925), women's doubles (1919–23, 1925), and mixed doubles (1920, 1922, 1925); and the French singles (1920–23, 1925–26), women's doubles (1925–26), and mixed doubles (1925–26). In the 1920 Olympic Games (Antwerp, Belg.) she earned gold medals in singles and mixed doubles. In world hard-court championship play she won the singles four times (1914, 1921–23), the women's doubles three times (1914, 1921–22), and the mixed doubles three times (1921–23). Her career was interrupted twice, first by World War I and later (1924) by illness.

In amateur lawn tennis Lenglen lost only one match: to Molla Bjurstedt Mallory in the 1921 U.S. tournament (Forest Hills, N.Y.). At Cannes, Fr., in 1926, she defeated the great American player Helen Wills 6–3 and 8–6 in their only meeting, a widely publicized match. Later that year she traveled to the United States to join a professional tennis tour. She died of pernicious anemia.

Lenin, world's first nuclear-powered surface ship, a large icebreaker built by the Soviet Union in Leningrad (St. Petersburg) in 1957. The *Lenin* is 440 feet (134 m) long, displaces 16,000 tons, and cruises in normal waters at 18 knots (nautical miles per hour). It is powered by three nuclear reactors, two of which are normally used for operation and the third of which is kept in reserve. Despite high initial costs, nuclear propulsion proved to be highly advantageous because it allowed virtually unlimited cruising range under extremely severe conditions.

Nuclear-powered icebreaker *Lenin*
Tass—Sovfoto

Lenin, Order of, highest civilian award of the U.S.S.R. It was established in 1930 by the Central Executive Committee of the Soviet Union and awarded to individuals, collectives, institutions, or organizations for outstanding achievements in research, art, technology, or economics or for the solution of tasks vital to the state. The order had one class. It was awarded automatically to "Heroes of the Soviet Union" and "Heroes of Socialist Labour." It also was conferred on foreigners for services strengthening cooperation and friendship between the U.S.S.R. and other nations.

The badge consisted of a circular portrait of Lenin framed in a gold wreath of ears of rye and crowned by a red flag with Lenin's name. On the left side was a red star, and at the base were the hammer and sickle emblems.

Lenin, Vladimir Ilich, original name VLADIMIR ILICH ULYANOV (b. April 10 [April 22, New Style], 1870, Simbirsk, Russia—d. Jan. 21, 1924, Gorki [later Gorki Leninskiye], near Moscow), founder of the Russian Communist Party (Bolsheviks), inspirer and leader of the Bolshevik Revolution (1917), and the first head of the Soviet state (1917–24). As a thinker, he was the formulator of Marxism-Leninism, which until the late 1980s and early '90s was the official ideology of the Soviet Union and several other communist nations.

A brief treatment of Lenin follows. For full treatment, *see* MACROPAEDIA: Lenin.

Lenin was born into a middle-class family but became a revolutionary through the influence of his brother Aleksandr. He became an adherent of Marxism in 1889. He received a degree in law in 1891 from St. Petersburg University, as an external student. Between 1887 and the autumn of 1893 he lived in various places, all on or near his native Volga. By the time he moved to St. Petersburg in 1893 he had become an authority on Marxism. Arrested as a subversive in 1895, he served a term of exile in Siberia; after 1900, he lived mostly in western Europe, where he emerged as the leader of the Bolshevik faction among the Russian Social Democrats. He returned to Russia after the overthrow of the tsarist regime in March 1917, and under his leadership the Bolsheviks, the only group with strict discipline and definite purpose, emerged from the chaos of wartime Russia and channeled the leaderless discontent of the Russian masses into revolutionary action. Lenin thus led the Bolsheviks to power in the October Revolution (in November, New Style) of 1917. The new Bolshevik (or Soviet) government established a dictatorship, abolished the newly won political and civil liberties in Russia, and renamed its political party the Communist Party. Lenin became the head of the new government and guided the Soviet state through its earliest formative years. The Soviet state maintained itself in power during the Russian Civil War (1918–20) largely through the dynamic leadership of Lenin and Leon Trotsky.

In economics, Lenin initially tried to introduce a socialist system into the Soviet Union by the forced abolition of markets, exchange, and money, but in 1921 he retreated from this policy and allowed the Soviet Union's temporary reversion to a market economy.

From 1922 until his death Lenin was incapacitated by serious health problems. The body of political principles that Lenin formulated and attempted to put into practice is known as Leninism (*q.v.*).

Lenin Library: *see* Russian State Library.

Lenin Peak, Russian PIK LENINA, formerly MOUNT KAUFMAN, highest summit (23,406 feet [7,134 m]) of the Trans-Alay Range on the frontier of Kyrgyzstan and Tajikistan. Once thought to be the highest mountain in what was then the Soviet Union, Lenin Peak was relegated to third place by the discovery in 1932–33 that Stalin Peak (called Communism Peak after 1962) was higher and by the finding in 1943 that Victory Peak was also higher. The peak is named after the Soviet leader Vladimir I. Lenin.

Lenin Peak was discovered by the Russian explorer A.P. Fedchenko in 1871. Its steep flanks are covered with glaciers. The first ascent was made in 1928 from the south by German alpinists included in the First Pamirs Expedition of the Academy of Sciences of the U.S.S.R. The first ascent by Soviet climbers, from the north, followed in 1934.

Lenin Volga-Baltic Waterway: *see* Volga-Baltic Waterway.

Leninabad (city, Tajikistan): *see* Khudzhand.

Leninakan (city, Armenia): *see* Kumayri.

Leningrad, *oblast* (province), northwestern Russia. It comprises all the Karelian Isthmus and the southern shore of the Gulf of Finland as far west as Narva. It extends eastward along the southern shore of Lake Ladoga and the Svir River as far as Lake Onega. In the north the Karelian Isthmus consists of long, winding morainic hills, separated by hollows with lakes and swamps. In the west-central part of the *oblast* lies the city of Saint Petersburg (formerly [1924–91] Leningrad). In the centre of the *oblast* are extensive lowlands, rising in the east to a line of uplands. There are innumerable lakes. The *oblast* is named after the Soviet leader Vladimir I. Lenin.

The proximity of the Baltic Sea and the activity of Atlantic climatic depressions make the *oblast*'s climate less cold, but damper and more variable, than that of most of European Russia. Rainfall varies from about 18 to 19 inches (450 to 475 mm) a year in the lowlands to 24 inches (610 mm) on higher ground, with a marked summer maximum. In the *oblast*'s north, east, and centre is swampy forest, or taiga, largely of spruce, pine, and birch. The west has mixed forest; alder and aspen are widespread in the wetter areas. Swamps of peat bog and grass marsh are everywhere, though many have been drained.

Leningrad *oblast*'s economy is overshadowed by that of Saint Petersburg city and its suburbs, and much of the *oblast*'s industry serves that major metropolitan area. Timberworking, paper, and pulp making are highly developed industries. Along the shores of the Gulf of Finland and Lake Ladoga, fishing is important, with Vyborg and Primorsk the main centres. The *oblast*'s agriculture serves Saint Petersburg's large urban population. Widespread natural pastures form a basis for intensive dairying, many pigs are kept, and poultry farming is carried on throughout the *oblast*. The arable land is dominated by market gardening and fodder crops. In the north and east, less land is arable, and rye and oats are more widely grown than vegetables. More than 90 percent of the *oblast*'s population is urban. Area 33,200 square miles (85,900 square km). Pop. (1993 est.) 6,626,500.

Leningrad (city, Russia): *see* Saint Petersburg.

Leningrad, Siege of, also called 900-DAY SIEGE (Sept. 8, 1941–Jan. 27, 1944), prolonged siege of the city of Leningrad (St. Petersburg) in the Soviet Union by German and Finnish armed forces during World War II. The siege actually lasted 872 days.

After Nazi Germany invaded the Soviet Union in June 1941, German armies by early September had approached Leningrad from the west and south while their Finnish allies approached to the north down the Karelian Isthmus. Leningrad's entire able-bodied population was mobilized to build antitank fortifications along the city's perimeter in support of the city's 200,000 Red Army defenders. Leningrad's defenses soon stabilized, but by early November it had been almost completely encircled, with all its vital rail and other supply lines to the Soviet interior cut off.

The ensuing German blockade and siege claimed 650,000 Leningrader lives in 1942 alone, mostly from starvation, exposure, disease, and shelling from distant German artillery. Sparse food and fuel supplies reached the city by barge in the summer and by truck and ice-borne sled in winter across Lake Ladoga. These supplies kept the city's arms factories operating and its two million inhabitants barely alive in 1942, while one million more of its children, sick, and elderly were being evacuated. Starvation-level food rationing was eased by new vegetable gardens that covered most open ground in the city by 1943.

Soviet offensives in early 1943 ruptured the German encirclement and allowed more copious supplies to reach Leningrad along the shores of Lake Ladoga. In January 1944 a successful Soviet offensive drove the Germans westward from the city's outskirts, ending the siege. The Soviet government awarded the Order of Lenin to Leningrad in 1945 and bestowed the title Hero City of the Soviet Union on it in 1965, thus paying tribute to the city's successful endurance of one of the most grueling and memorable sieges in history.

Vyborg, on the Gulf of Finland in Leningrad *oblast*, Russia
Sovfoto/TASS

Leningrad Affair (1948–50), in the history of the Soviet Union, a sudden and sweeping purge of Communist Party and government officials in Leningrad and the surrounding region. The purge occurred several months after the sudden death of Andrey A. Zhdanov (Aug. 31, 1948), who had been the Leningrad party boss as well as one of Joseph Stalin's most powerful lieutenants in the postwar period. The purge, which also affected the leadership of the Russian Soviet Federated Socialist Republic, resulted in the execution and imprisonment in labour camps of thousands of party officials, managers, and technical personnel, most of whom were associates and followers of Zhdanov. Although the actual motivation for the purge is still unknown, it probably climaxed a struggle for power within the party between the Georgy M. Malenkov–Lavrenty P. Beria faction on the one hand and the by-then leaderless Zhdanov faction on the other.

Among those executed during the Leningrad Affair were Nikolay A. Voznesensky (Politburo member and head of the State Planning Commission), his brother Aleksandr A. Voznesensky (minister of education of the Russian S.F.S.R.), Aleksey A. Kuznetsov (Central Committee secretary responsible for state security organs), Pyotr S. Popkov (first secretary of the party organization in Leningrad), and Mikhail N. Rodionov (chairman of the Russian S.F.S.R. Council of Ministers).

Though never officially announced or acknowledged, the purge was mentioned by Nikita S. Khrushchev in his secret speech to the party's Central Committee in February 1956. At that time, Khrushchev noted that the charges of treason and conspiracy levied against the victims of the purge had been fabrications. He charged that Lavrenty P. Beria, the late chief of security police, and V.S. Abakumov, minister of state security (1947–51), had been responsible for making up the cases against Zhdanov and his followers and for convincing Stalin of the authenticity of the accusations. In July 1957, Khrushchev further identified Malenkov as "one of the chief organizers" of the purge. Abakumov was executed in December 1954 for his role in the affair, and Khrushchev effectively exploited Malenkov's involvement to consolidate his own hold on the party leadership. There is some creditable speculation that Stalin himself not only sanctioned the purge but actively participated in it because of his paranoid suspicion and jealousy of the rising young leaders of the Leningrad party faction.

Leninism, principles expounded by Vladimir I. Lenin, who was the preeminent figure in the Russian Revolution of 1917. Whether Leninist concepts represented a contribution to or a corruption of Marxist thought has been debated, but their influence on the subsequent development of communism in the Soviet Union and elsewhere has been of fundamental importance.

In the *Communist Manifesto* (1848), Karl Marx and Friedrich Engels defined communists as "the most advanced and resolute section of the working-class parties of every country, that section which pushes forward all others." This conception was fundamental to Leninist thought. Lenin saw the Communist Party as a highly committed intellectual elite who (1) had a scientific understanding of history and society in the light of Marxist principles, (2) were committed to ending capitalism and instituting socialism in its place, (3) were bent on forcing through this transition after having achieved political power, and (4) were committed to attaining this power by any means possible, including violence and revolution if necessary. Lenin's emphasis upon action by a small, deeply committed group stemmed both from the need for efficiency and discretion in the revolutionary movement and from an authoritarian bent that was present in all of his political thought. The authoritarian aspect of Leninism appeared also in its insistence upon the need for a "proletarian dictatorship" following the seizure of power, a dictatorship that in practice was exercised not by the workers but by the leaders of the Communist Party.

At the root of Leninist authoritarianism was a distrust of spontaneity, a conviction that historical events, if left to themselves, would not bring the desired outcome—*i.e.,* the coming into being of a socialist society. Lenin was not at all convinced, for instance, that the workers would inevitably acquire the proper revolutionary and class consciousness of the communist elite; he was instead afraid that they would be content with the gains in living and working conditions obtained through trade-union activity. In this, Leninism differed from traditional Marxism, which predicted that material conditions would suffice to make workers conscious of the need for revolution. For Lenin, then, the communist elite—the "workers' vanguard"—was more than a catalytic agent that precipitated events along their inevitable course; it was an indispensable element.

Just as Leninism was pragmatic in its choice of means to achieve political power, it was also opportunistic in the policies it adopted and the compromises it made to maintain its hold on power. A good example of this is Lenin's own New Economic Policy (1921–28), which temporarily restored the market economy and some private enterprise in the Soviet Union after the disastrous economic results of War Communism (1918–21).

In practice, Leninism's unrestrained pursuit of the socialist society resulted in the creation of a totalitarian state in the Soviet Union. If the conditions of Russia in its backward state of development did not lead to socialism naturally, then, after coming to power, the Bolsheviks would legislate socialism into existence and would exercise despotic control to break public resistance. Thus, every aspect of the Soviet Union's political, economic, cultural, and intellectual life came to be regulated by the Communist Party in a strict and regimented fashion that would tolerate no opposition. The building of the socialist society proceeded under a new autocracy of Communist Party officials and bureaucrats. Marxism and Leninism originally expected that, with the triumph of the proletariat, the state that Marx had defined as the organ of class rule would "wither away" because class conflicts would come to an end. Communist rule in the Soviet Union resulted instead in the vastly increased power of the state apparatus. Terror was applied without hesitation, humanitarian considerations and individual rights were disregarded, and the assumption of the class character of all intellectual and moral life led to a relativization of the standards of truth, ethics, and justice. Leninism thus created the first modern totalitarian state.

Leninist Communist League of Youth, All-Union: *see* Komsomol.

Leninogorsk, formerly (until 1941) RIDDER, city, northeastern Kazakhstan. The city is situated in the southwestern Altai Mountains along the Ulba River, at an elevation of more than 3,300 feet (1,000 m). An Englishman, Philip Ridder, discovered a small mine containing gold, silver, copper, and lead there in 1786, and systematic mining started in 1791. Present-day Leninogorsk is an important centre of the lead and zinc industry and is connected to the Turk-Sib Railway. Pop. (1991 est.) 69,500.

Lenin's Testament, formally LETTER TO THE CONGRESS, Russian PISMO K SYEZDU, two-part document dictated by Vladimir I. Lenin on Dec. 23–26, 1922, and Jan. 4, 1923, and addressed to a future Communist Party Congress. It contained guideline proposals for changes in the Soviet political system and concise portrait assessments of six party leaders (Joseph Stalin, Leon Trotsky, Grigory Y. Zinovyev, Lev B. Kamenev, Nikolay Bukharin, and Georgy Pyatakov). The testament, written while Lenin was recovering from a severe stroke, concluded with a recommendation that Stalin be removed from his position as secretary-general of the party. The document has been variously interpreted as an attempt by Lenin to guide the party's choice of his successor or as an attempt to undermine the efforts of his colleagues who, he thought, were trying to usurp his power. He may have intended the letter to provoke mutual distrust among the party leaders and thereby to preclude the possibility of any single one of them succeeding him.

The first part of the testament suggested that the Central Committee be enlarged; it also stated that the most serious threat to unity within the Central Committee was the strained relationship between Stalin and Trotsky. Lenin then asserted that Stalin was not cautious enough to be entrusted with the large amount of power he had personally accumulated and that, although Trotsky was the most capable individual on the Central Committee, he was too self-assured and overly inclined toward purely administrative functions. Bukharin was cited as the party's most eminent theoretician, although he had failed to master the dialectic. The testament also warned that the party should not condemn Kamenev and Zinovyev for their behaviour in October 1917 (they had opposed the Bolshevik coup d'état and published the plans for the insurrection).

The second part was a postscript, dictated after Lenin had become convinced that Stalin was not only mishandling the suppression of dissent in Georgia but was being abusive to Lenin's wife, Krupskaya. The addendum described Stalin as "too rude" and proposed that the Congress consider removing him from the post of secretary-general. Several copies of the testament were made and sealed with the instruction that they were to be opened by Lenin personally or, in case of his death, by Krupskaya.

In May 1924, four months after Lenin's death and a few days before the 13th Party Congress convened, Krupskaya transmitted the testament to the Central Committee, indicating that it was Lenin's wish that it be communicated to the Congress. The Central Committee, however, already largely dominated by Stalin, decided that it should only be read to the individual delegations rather than be presented to the entire assembled Congress and prohibited its publication or reproduction, including quotations. As a result of this partial suppression, the existence of the testament was not generally known within the Soviet Union; with Stalin's ascendancy it became a forbidden subject, and all overt reference to it disappeared for almost three decades.

The testament soon found its way out of the Soviet Union, however. Max Eastman obtained portions of it and published them in *Since Lenin Died* in 1925, and *The New York Times* printed the entire testament, obtained indirectly through Krupskaya, who had joined the opposition against Stalin, in October 1926. Within the Soviet Union, however, it was not generally known and thus did little to retard Stalin's rise to power. At the 20th Party Congress (1956), Nikita S. Khrushchev included portions of the testament in his famous secret speech to the Central Committee in order to support his indictment of Stalin and add Lenin's authority to his de-Stalinization campaign.

Leninsk-Kuznetsky, formerly (until 1925) KOLCHUGINO, city, in Kemerovo *oblast* (province), central Russia. It lies along the Inya River, a tributary of the Ob. In 1912 a French company started coal-mining operations there; from the 1930s the city developed rapidly to become a major coal-mining centre, with many pits located in the city itself. Other industries produce chemicals, mining machinery, electric lamps, and timber goods. Pop. (1993 est.) 131,700.

Lenkoran (city, Azerbaijan): *see* Länkäran.

Lennep, Jacob van (b. March 24, 1802, Amsterdam, Neth.—d. Aug. 25, 1868, Oosterbeek), Dutch novelist, poet, and leading man of letters in the mid-19th century.

Van Lennep, detail of an oil painting by Johan Georg Schwartze; in a private collection

By courtesy of the Iconographisch Bureau, The Hague

Early in his career van Lennep found his natural genre, the historical novel, and his first such work, *De pleegzoon* (1833; *The Adopted Son*), was set in the 17th century. Like many of his later works it contains a strong element of adventure and a complicated plot. *De lotgevallen van Ferdinand Huyck* (1840; *The Count of Talavera*) is a tale of great charm and ingenuity told with humour and realism. Although he was the most popular Dutch writer of his time, van Lennep was weak in characterization, and few of his works appeal to the modern reader. His five-volume *De lotgevallen van Klaasje Zevenster* (1865; "The Adventures of Klaasje Zevenster") was a failed attempt to write a modern novel on the French model.

Lenngren, Anna Maria, *née* MALMSTEDT (b. June 18, 1754, Uppsala, Sweden—d. March 8, 1817, Stockholm), Swedish poet whose Neoclassical satires and pastoral idylls show a balance and moderation characteristic of the Enlightenment period and are still read for their gaiety and elegance.

Educated by her father, a lecturer at the University of Uppsala, Lenngren began to publish poetry at age 18. In 1780 she married Carl Lenngren, founder (with J.H. Kellgren) and later editor of the influential *Stockholms-posten,* to which she thereafter contributed anonymously. Her best work was written in the 1790s. Her most famous idylls are "Den glada festen" (1796; "The Merry Festival") and "Pojkarne" (1797; "The Boys"). Of her satires, "Portraiterne" (1796) and "Grefvinnans besök" (1800; "The Countess's Visit") are especially fine. Although, as she says, she was "seldom far from home," she combined clear-sighted knowledge of the world with kindly tolerance of its foibles. Her poetry, collected in 1819, is classical in form and remarkable for its restraint and purity of style and diction.

Lenni Lenape (people): *see* Delaware.

Lennoaceae, the sand food family, composed of three genera and four to six species of curious, parasitic plants, which send out rootlike structures (haustoria) that penetrate the roots of other plants for food. Once the parasite's haustoria have entered the host roots, the parasite develops its aboveground portions, usually club-shaped, fleshy, yellowish or brownish stems on which a head of flowers appears. The scalelike leaves lack chlorophyll.

Two species of *Lennoa* in Mexico are typical. *Flor de tierra* ("flower of the earth"; *L. madreporoides*) is highly selective, growing usually on roots of the Mexican sunflower (*Tithonia*). The oval, mushroomlike stem is 5–15 cm (2–6 inches) tall, yellowish or brownish in colour, and covered with oval to lance-shaped scales. The plant's domelike head is covered at maturity with small, starlike flowers, violet with yellow throats. It is native in cornfields of south-central Mexico, at about 1,500 m (5,000 feet) altitude. A blue-flowered species, *L. caerulea,* grows on higher land, near Mexico City and Puebla. Two genera occur in southwestern North America: sand food (*Ammobroma*) and desert Christmas tree (*Pholisma*).

Lennox, Charles Lennox, 1st Duke of: *see* Richmond, Charles Lennox, 1st Duke of.

Lennox, Charlotte, *née* RAMSAY (b. 1720, New York, N.Y., U.S.—d. Jan. 4, 1804, London, Eng.), American-born English novelist whose work, especially *The Female Quixote* (1752), was much admired by leading literary figures of her time, including Samuel Johnson and the novelists Henry Fielding and Samuel Richardson.

Charlotte Lennox, detail of an engraving by Francesco Bartolozzi after a portrait by Sir Joshua Reynolds

By courtesy of the trustees of the British Museum; photograph, J.R. Freeman & Co. Ltd.

In 1735 Lennox left New York for London, there marrying Alexander Lennox in 1748. She made the first comparative study of William Shakespeare's source material, called *Shakespear Illustrated;* . . . (1753–54), a project in which she was probably assisted by Dr. Johnson. She died in poverty.

Lennox, Margaret Douglas, Countess of (b. Oct. 8, 1515, Harbottle Castle, Northumberland, Eng.—d. March 7, 1578), prominent intriguer in England during the early reign of Queen Elizabeth I.

Lady Margaret Douglas was the daughter of Archibald Douglas, 6th Earl of Angus, and Margaret Tudor (daughter of King Henry VII of England and widow of King James IV of Scotland), and in 1544 she married Matthew Stewart (1516–71), 4th Earl of Lennox. Because of her nearness to the English crown, Lady Margaret Douglas was brought up chiefly at the English court in close association with Princess Mary (afterward Queen Mary I), who remained her fast friend throughout life.

On Elizabeth I's accession in 1558 Lady Lennox retired to Yorkshire, where her home at Temple Newsom became a centre for Roman Catholic intrigue. She was determined to secure the succession to both thrones for her family, and by a series of successful maneuvers she married her son Henry Stewart, Lord Darnley, to Mary Stuart, Queen of Scots.

Lady Lennox was sent to the Tower of London in 1566, but after the murder of Darnley in 1567 she was released. She was at first loud in her denunciations of Mary, but was eventually reconciled with her daughter-in-law. Lennox was sent to the Tower again in 1574 because of the marriage of her son Charles, Earl of Lennox, to Elizabeth Cavendish, daughter of the Earl of Shrewsbury, and she was pardoned only after her son's death in 1577. Lady Lennox died the following year, in great poverty, but her life was successful in its main purpose, for her grandson James became King James VI of Scotland and afterward King James I of England.

Leno, Dan, original name GEORGE GALVIN (b. Dec. 20, 1860, London, Eng.—d. Oct. 31, 1904, London), popular English entertainer who is considered the foremost representative of the British music hall at its height in the 19th century. In 1901 Leno gave a command performance for King Edward VII, becoming the first music-hall performer to be so honoured.

Born into a family of traveling entertainers, Leno first appeared on stage at the age of four as a tumbler and contortionist. Within five years he achieved prominence as a clog dancer with an act that included singing and comic patter. From 1888 until his death, Leno was the star of the Drury Lane's annual Christmas pantomime and played to sell-out crowds in music halls throughout England the rest of the year. His wistful and comic caricatures endeared him to audiences. His autobiography appeared in 1901.

Lenoir, (Jean-Joseph-) Étienne (b. Jan. 12, 1822, Mussy-la-Ville, Belg.—d. Aug. 4, 1900, La Varenne-Saint-Hilaire, Fr.), Belgian inventor who devised the first commercially successful internal-combustion engine.

Lenoir's engine was a converted double-acting steam engine with slide valves to admit the air-fuel mixture and to discharge exhaust products. A two-stroke cycle engine, it used a mixture of coal gas and air. Though only about 4 percent efficient in fuel consumption, it was a smooth-running and durable machine (some machines were in perfect condition after 20 years of continuous operation), and by 1865 more than 400 were in use in France and 1,000 in Britain, used for such low-power jobs as pumping and printing.

In 1862 Lenoir built the first automobile with an internal-combustion engine. He had adapted his engine to run on liquid fuel and with his vehicle made a 6-mile (10-kilometre) trip that required two to three hours. His other inventions include an electric brake for trains (1855), a motorboat using his engine (1886), and a method of tanning leather with ozone.

Lenormand, Henri-René (b. May 3, 1882, Paris, Fr.—d. Feb. 16, 1951, Paris), French dramatist, the most important of those playwrights concerned with subconscious motivation who flourished between World Wars I and II.

The son of a composer, Lenormand was educated at the University of Paris and spent much of his adult life writing for the Parisian stage. He was the author of a number of somewhat gloomy plays that explore inner emotional conflicts and the tragedies of human destiny. His dissections of the human personality centre on subsconscious instincts and motivations, which are mostly of a negative character.

Lenormand's first play exploring the tragedy of human destiny was *Le Temps est un songe* (1919; "Time Is a Dream"). His best-known play, *Les Ratés* (1920; "The Failures"), traces the physical and moral disintegration of a playwright and his mistress, a mediocre actress, who, under the pressure of adversity, end their lives in murder and suicide. To elucidate the conflicts of the human psyche, Lenormand often chose abnormal or pathological types for his characters, and to portray their inner struggles, he made use of tableaux, *i.e.,* a succession of very short scenes occupying only part of the stage and serving to show the various facets of the characters' inner personalities. Stage settings and effects that convey such symbolism are an essential element in many of his plays.

Lenormand's play *Le Simoun* (1920; "The Simoom") depicts the demoralizing influence of the life and climate of the tropics on a European man who becomes obsessed with an incestuous passion for his adult daughter. *Le Lâche* (1925; "The Coward") is a psychological study of fear in a man about to go to war as a soldier. Two of Lenormand's plays, *Le Mangeur de rêves* (1922; "The Dream Eater") and *L'Homme et ses fantômes* (1924; "Man and His Phantoms"), earned him a reputation as a Freudian for their explorations of the Oedipal complex. His other plays include *Les Possédés* (1909; "The Possessed"), *À l'Ombre du mal* (1924; "The Shadow of Evil"), *Une Vie secrète* (1929; "A Secret Life"), and *Asie* (1931; "Asia"). Many of Lenormand's plays received excellent first productions in Paris by the director-stage designer Georges Pitoëff and the actor Firmin Gémier.

Lenormand, Louis-Sebastien (b. 1757, France—d. 1839, France), French aeronaut, generally recognized as the first person to make a parachute descent. He was not the inventor of the parachute; the ancient Chinese may have devised one, and it was known to medieval Europe in the form of a toy.

Information about Lenormand's life is scanty, but it is believed that he made his first jump from the top of a tree; in December 1783 he mounted the tower of the Montpellier Observatory in France and jumped with a 14-foot (4.3-metre) parachute, landing unharmed. Apparently he thought of the device as a kind of portable fire escape that would enable persons trapped in burning buildings to leap to safety.

Lenormant, François (b. Jan. 17, 1837, Paris, Fr.—d. Dec. 9, 1883, Paris), French Assyriologist and numismatist who recognized, from cuneiform inscriptions, a language now known as Akkadian that proved valuable to the understanding of Mesopotamian civilization 3,000 years before the Christian era. He published his first archaeological paper at 14 and went on to become a scholar of wide achievement. He published *La Monnaie dans l'antiquité,* 3 vol. (1873–79; "Coins in Antiquity"), *Les Sciences occultes en Asie* (1874–75; "The Occult Sciences in Asia"), and *Les Origines de l'histoire d'après la Bible et les traditions des peuples orientaux* (1880–82; "The Origins of History According to the Bible and the Traditions of the Oriental Peoples").

Lenox, town ("township"), Berkshire county, western Massachusetts, U.S. It lies in the Berkshire Hills, just south of Pittsfield. Settled around 1750 and originally called Yokuntown, it was set off from Richmond in 1767 and was probably named for Charles Lennox, Duke of Richmond and a defender of colonial rights. Early industries include an iron foundry, a marble works, and a glass factory. Lenox, now a noted summer resort, is the site of Tanglewood, summer home of the Boston Symphony Orchestra and of the annual Berkshire Music Festival. A writers' colony flourished there in the 19th century; authors who lived or visited there included Nathaniel Hawthorne, Fanny Kemble, Catharine Sedgwick, Henry Ward Beecher, and Edith Wharton. Hawthorne's cottage, where he wrote *Tanglewood Tales,* was burned in 1891 and rebuilt in 1948. Lenox is the seat of Berkshire Christian College (founded in 1897 as the Boston Bible School and relocated in 1958). October Mountain State Forest and Pleasant Valley Wildlife Sanctuary are nearby. Inc. 1775. Pop. (1990) 5,069.

Lenox, James (b. Aug. 19, 1800, New York, N.Y., U.S.—d. Feb. 17, 1880, New York City), American philanthropist and pioneer book collector.

Lenox' father was a wealthy Scottish merchant from whom Lenox inherited several million dollars as well as valuable properties in New York City. A graduate of Columbia College (1818) and a member of the bar, Lenox devoted the bulk of his life to collecting rare books, manuscripts, and art objects and to public and private philanthropy. His special interests in collecting were Bibles, books about North and South America, early Americana, first-person accounts of the great voyages of the age of discovery, and all editions of the works of John Bunyan, William Shakespeare, and John Milton. The collection was originally intended for the use of scholars but in 1870 was made available to the public. In 1895 the Lenox Library (containing about 85,000 volumes), the Astor Library, and the Tilden Foundation were consolidated to become the New York Public Library.

Lens, industrial town, Pas-de-Calais *département,* Nord-Pas-de-Calais *région,* northern France, south-southwest of Lille. It is the chief urban centre of the Pas-de-Calais coal basin (a portion of which was scheduled to be abandoned after 1983); the urban agglomeration includes the mining settlements of Liévin, Bruay-en-Artois, and Hénin-Liétard. The town is active in both service industries and trade and thus was well adapted for the transition from an industrial to a service economy. The town, which was completely destroyed in World War I, was damaged again in World War II. Pop. (1982) 38,006.

lens, in anatomy, a colourless, nearly transparent biconvex structure suspended behind the iris of the eye, the sole function of which is to focus light rays onto the retina. The lens is made up of unusual elongated cells that have no blood supply but obtain nutrients from the surrounding fluids, the aqueous humour in front and the vitreous behind. The shape of the lens—essentially that of a flattened globe—can be altered by the relaxation and contraction of the ciliary muscles surrounding it, thus enabling the eye to focus clearly on objects at widely varying distances. The ability of the lens to adjust from a distant to a near focus, called accommodation, gradually declines with age, often requiring correction. Clouding or opacity of the lens, called a cataract, may also occur with age and cannot be corrected except by surgical removal of the lens.

lens, in optics, piece of glass or other transparent substance that is used to form an image of an object by focusing rays of light from the object. A lens is a piece of transparent material, usually circular in shape, with two polished surfaces, either or both of which is curved and may be either convex (bulging) or concave (depressed). The curves are almost always spherical, *i.e.,* the radius of curvature is constant. A lens has the valuable property of forming images of objects situated in front of it. Single lenses are used in eyeglasses, contact lenses, pocket magnifiers, projection condensers, signal lights, viewfinders, and on simple box cameras. More often a number of lenses made of different materials are combined together as a compound lens in a tube to permit the correction of aberrations. Compound lenses are used in such instruments as cameras, microscopes, and telescopes.

A lens produces its focusing effect because light travels more slowly in the lens than in the surrounding air, so that refraction, an abrupt bending, of a light beam occurs both where the beam enters the lens and where it emerges from the lens into the air.

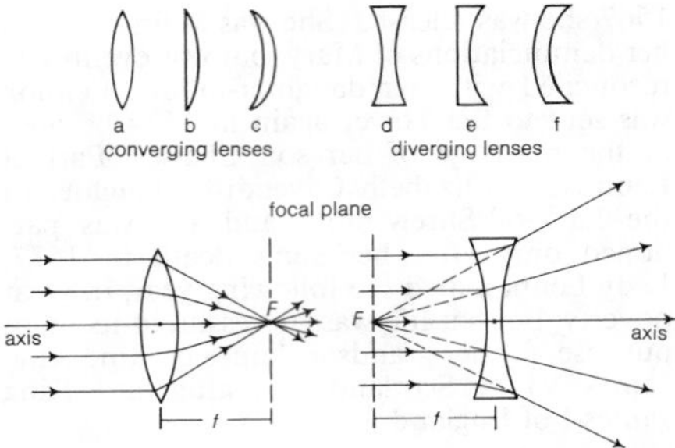

Figure 1: *Lenses*
(Top) Cross-sections of standard forms of common lenses; (bottom) the refraction of light by converging and diverging lenses showing the principal axis, principal focus (or focal point) *F*, focal length *f*, and focal plane

From *Classical and Modern Physics* by H. White © 1940 by Litton Educational Publishing, Inc. Reprinted by permission of Van Nostrand Reinhold Company

A single lens has two precisely regular opposite surfaces; either both surfaces are curved, or one is curved and one is plane. Lenses may be classified according to their two surfaces as biconvex (a in Figure 1), plano-convex (b), concavo-convex (c; converging meniscus), biconcave (d), plano-concave (e), and convexo-concave (f; diverging meniscus). Because of the curvature of the lens surfaces, different rays of an incident light beam are refracted through different angles, so that an entire beam of parallel rays can be caused to converge on, or to appear to diverge from, a single point. This point is called the focal point, or principal focus, of the lens, as shown in the lower part of Figure 1. Refraction of the rays of light reflected from or emitted by an object causes the rays to form a visual image of the object. This image may be either real—photographable or visible on a screen—or virtual—visible only upon looking into the lens, as in a microscope. The image may be much larger or smaller than the object, depending on the focal length (see Figure 1) of the lens and on the distance between the lens and the object. The focal length of a lens is the distance from the centre of the lens to the point at which the image of a distant object is formed. A long-focus lens forms a larger image of a distant object, while a short-focus lens forms a small image.

Usually the image formed by a single lens is not good enough for precise work in such fields as astronomy, microscopy, and photography; this is because the cone of rays emitted by a single point in a distant object is not united in a perfect point by the lens but instead forms a small patch of light. This and other innate imperfections in a lens's image of a single object point are known as aberrations. To correct such aberrations, it is often necessary to combine in one mount several lens elements (single lenses), some of which may be convex and some concave, some made of dense high-refractive or high-dispersive glass, and others made of low-refractive or low-dispersive glass. The lens elements may be cemented together or mounted at carefully calculated separations to correct the aberrations of the individual elements and obtain an image of acceptable sharpness (*see also* aberration). The precise mounting also ensures that all lenses are properly centred; that is, the centres of curvature of all the lens surfaces lie on a single straight line called the principal axis of the lens. A frequently used measure of the quality of any lens system is its ability to form an image that is sharp enough to separate, or resolve, two very close dots or lines in an object. Resolving power depends on how well the various aberrations in a lens system are corrected.

The simplest compound lens is a thin cemented combination of two single lenses, such as that used in the objective (the lens nearest the object) of a small refracting telescope. Microscope objectives may contain as many as eight or nine elements, some of which may be made of different materials in order to bring all colours of light to a common focus, and thus prevent chromatic aberration. The objective lenses used in cameras may contain from two to 10 elements, while a so-called zoom or variable-focal length lens may have as many as 18 or 20 elements in several groups, the different groups being movable along the axis by levers or cams in order to produce the desired change in focal length without a shift of the focal plane. Lenses also vary greatly in diameter, from as small as 0.16 cm (1/16 inch) for an element in a microscope objective to as large as 100 cm (40 inches) for an astronomical telescope objective. In reflectors and several other types of astronomical telescopes, concave mirrors are used for the objective instead of lenses.

In the manufacture of lenses, slabs of glass are cut with a glass saw or slitting disk; a piece of the desired type and shape is chipped to a rough, round blank, or the pieces may be heated to softness, rolled to a round shape, and pressed in a mold to the desired size and to approximately the desired curvature of the surfaces. The surfaces are then ground, or lapped, to the final form, using coarse emery, carborundum, or diamond as an abrasive. Lens surfaces are ground on an iron tool, either flat or suitably curved, using progressively finer grades of one of the abrasives mentioned above. In the grinding process, a rotating cup-shaped tool is mounted so that its axis of rotation intersects the axis of the lens at the centre of curvature, C, of the desired spherical surface. (See Figure 2.) The obliquity of the tool axis must be adjusted so that the rim of

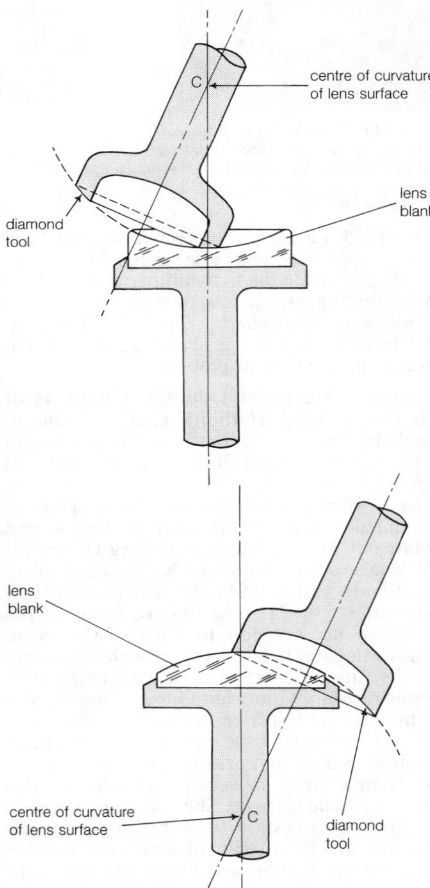

Figure 2: Cross section of a curve generator for (top) concave and (bottom) convex surfaces

the tool cuts across the centre of the (concave) lens being generated. For convex lenses, the centre of the rotating tool face cuts the rim of the lens blank. As both tool and lens rotate about their respective axes, a spherical surface of the desired radius of curvature is generated on the lens.

Fine grinding, or smoothing, is done using carefully graded emery flour as an abrasive. A number of fine-ground lens blanks are then mounted with pitch on a block so that they can be polished together. The polishing tool

A recessed block to hold several lenses during smoothing and polishing

is covered with a thin layer of pitch, wax, or even coarse cloth, and wet rouge or certain other mineral oxides are also used as polishing agents. The polishing of glass is a slow process, requiring lenses to be oscillated back and forth, sometimes for hours, against the rotating polisher. After both sides have been polished, the lens is ground around the edge to centre it and give it the correct diameter. If a compound objective is being made, several single lenses must be mounted together in a precise coaxial arrangement, and their thicknesses, separations, and centring must be kept very close to the prescribed values, or the aberration corrections laboriously determined by the lens designer will not be realized. The finished lens's resolving power is then tested by using the lens to form an image of a point source or other suitable test object. Sophisticated variants of this basic testing procedure have been developed using photoelectric cells or interferometers to obtain greater measuring accuracy.

lens dislocation, abnormal position of the crystalline lens of the eye. The dislocation, which may be congenital or acquired, has as its immediate cause weakness or loss of a portion of the ligaments that anchor the lens to the ciliary muscle.

Congenital dislocation of the lens. The defect is present in about 50 percent of the children who have Marfan's syndrome, also called arachnodactyly—"spider fingers"—because of the unusual length of the fingers and toes. Dislocation of the lenses may also be a feature of the Ehlers-Danlos syndrome, a condition marked by great elasticity of the skin and by double-jointedness. The usual management of the lens dislocation is improvement of vision by means of glasses.

Acquired dislocation of the lens. Dislocation of the lens that is not congenital is usually the result of a blow, as from the fist. If the dislocation is slight and there are no complications, there are usually no symptoms and treatment is not required. Severe dislocation may impair vision and cause double images or extreme farsightedness. In such instances extraction of the lens may be necessary.

Lent, in the Christian church, a period of penitential preparation for Easter. In Western churches it begins on Ash Wednesday, 6½ weeks before Easter, and provides for a 40-day fast (Sundays are excluded), in imitation of Jesus Christ's fasting in the wilderness. In Eastern churches it begins 8 weeks before Easter (both Saturdays and Sundays are excluded as fast days).

Since apostolic times a period of preparation and fasting has been observed before the Easter festival. It was a time of preparation of candidates for baptism and a time of penance for sinners. In the early centuries fasting rules were strict, as they still are in Eastern churches. One meal a day was allowed in the evening, and meat, fish, eggs, and butter were forbidden. In the West these fasting rules have gradually been relaxed. The strict law of fasting among Roman Catholics was dispensed during World War II, and only Ash Wednesday and Good Friday are now kept as Lenten fast days. But the emphasis on penitential practice remains.

In the Anglican churches *The Book of Common Prayer* prescribes that Lent be observed with fasting. In Lutheran and many other Protestant churches Lent is observed with various services and practices.

Lenthall, William (b. June 1591, Henley-on-Thames, Oxfordshire, Eng.—d. Sept. 3, 1662, Burford, Oxfordshire), English Parliamentarian who, as speaker of the House of Commons, was at the centre of repeated struggles between the Parliamentarians and Royalists during the English Civil Wars. His later cooperation with the Royalists earned him a reputation as a political opportunist.

Lenthall, portrait miniature by S. Cooper, 1652; in the National Portrait Gallery, London

By courtesy of the National Portrait Gallery, London

Trained in law, Lenthall was chosen speaker of the House at the beginning of the Long Parliament in November 1640. When on Jan. 4, 1642, King Charles I personally entered the Commons to arrest five opposition leaders, Lenthall refused to reveal their whereabouts, uttering the famous words "May it please your Majesty, I have neither eyes to see nor tongue to speak in this place but as the House is pleased to direct me, whose servant I am here." During the Civil Wars he sided with Parliament, and upon the outbreak (1647) of the power struggle between the Presbyterians and Independents he supported the Independents. At the same time he was probably secretly in sympathy with the Royalist cause.

Lenthall continued as speaker in the first Parliament (1654) held under Oliver Cromwell's Protectorate, and after the collapse of the Protectorate in 1659 he was speaker of the restored Long Parliament. Although he supported the Restoration of King Charles II in 1660, he was thereafter barred from public office. He soon gained royal favour by testifying against a man accused of participating in the trial and execution (1649) of Charles I.

lentil (species *Lens esculenta*), small annual legume of the pea family (Leguminosae) and its lens-shaped edible seed, which is rich in protein and one of the most ancient of cultivated foods. Of unknown origin, the lentil is widely cultivated throughout Europe, Asia, and North Africa but is little grown in the Western Hemisphere. The seeds are used chiefly in soups and the herbage as fodder. Lentils are a good source of protein, vitamin B, iron, and phosphorus.

The plant varies from 15 to 45 cm (6 to 18 inches) in height and has many long, ascending branches. The leaves are alternate, with six pairs of oblong-linear leaflets about 15 mm (0.5 inch) long and ending in a spine. Two to four pale blue flowers are borne in the axils of the leaves in June or early July. The pods are about 15–20 mm long, broadly oblong, and slightly inflated and contain two seeds the shape of a doubly convex lens and about 4–6 mm in diameter. There are many cultivated varieties of the plant, differing in size, hairiness, and colour of the leaves, flowers, and seeds. The seeds may be more or less compressed in shape, and the colour may vary from yellow or gray to dark brown; they are also sometimes mottled or speckled.

The lentil has been found in the lake dwellings of St. Peter's Island, Lake Biel, Switz., dating from the Bronze Age. The red pottage of lentils for which Esau sold his birthright (Genesis 25:30–34) probably was made from the red Egyptian lentil. This lentil is cultivated in one or another variety in the Middle East, North Africa, and Europe along the Mediterranean coast and as far north as Germany, The Netherlands, and France. In Egypt, Syria, and other Middle Eastern countries, the parched seeds are sold in shops and are esteemed the best food to carry on long journeys.

Lentini, Giacomo da (Italian poet): *see* Giacomo da Lentini.

Lentulus, Publius Cornelius, byname SURA (Latin: "Calf of the Leg") (d. Dec. 5, 63 BC, Rome), a leading figure in Catiline's conspiracy (63 BC) to seize control of the Roman government.

In 81 Lentulus was quaestor to Lucius Cornelius Sulla. When Sulla later accused him of having squandered public funds, Lentulus scornfully held out the calf of his leg, a gesture normally used by ball-playing boys inviting punishment for an error. He was praetor in 74 and consul in 71. Although expelled from the Senate for immorality in 70, he was elected to a second praetorship in 63. It was while serving in this office that he joined Catiline. When Catiline fled from Rome after Cicero's speech *In Catilinam,* Lentulus assumed leadership of the remaining conspirators. He planned to murder Cicero and set fire to Rome, but the plot failed because of his indiscretion in communicating it to the ambassadors of the Allobroges, then in Rome, in the hope of securing armed assistance from them. The ambassadors betrayed him, and Lentulus and his co-conspirators were arrested, forced to confess, and then executed.

Lentulus Crus, Lucius Cornelius (d. Sept. 29, 48 BC, Egypt), Roman politician, a leading member of the senatorial party that vigorously opposed Julius Caesar.

In 61 BC Lentulus was the chief accuser of Publius Clodius on a charge of sacrilege at a festival. Lentulus was a praetor in 58. As consul in 49 he advocated the rejection of all peace terms offered by Caesar in his conflict with the Senate. On the outbreak of the Civil War in 49, Lentulus joined Pompey's senatorial forces at Dyrrhachium. Pompey's army was crushed at Pharsalus in 48, and Lentulus then fled to Egypt, where he was murdered.

Lentulus Spinther, Publius Cornelius (d. *c.* 48 BC), a leading supporter of the Roman general Pompey the Great during the Civil War (49–45 BC) between Pompey and Julius Caesar.

As curule aedile, Lentulus in 63 helped Cicero suppress Catiline's conspiracy to overthrow the government. He was praetor in 60 and with Caesar's aid became governor of the province of Nearer Spain in 59. After serving as consul in 57, he governed Cilicia from 56 to 53. Despite his debt to Caesar, Lentulus joined the Pompeians in 49. Captured at the battle of Corfinium, Italy, he was granted clemency by Caesar, but he subsequently again went over to Pompey. After Pompey was decisively defeated at Pharsalus, Thessaly, in 48, Lentulus escaped to Rhodes; soon thereafter he fell into Caesar's hands and was executed.

Lenya, Lotte, original name KAROLINE BLAMAUER (b. Oct. 18, 1900, Penzing, Austria—d. Nov. 27, 1981, New York City), Austrian actress-singer who popularized much of the music of her first husband, the composer Kurt Weill, and appeared frequently in the musical dramas of Weill and his longtime collaborator Bertolt Brecht.

Lenya studied ballet and drama in Zurich from 1914 to 1920, was a member of the corps de ballet at the Zürich Stadttheater, and played in Shakespeare in Berlin in the 1920s. She married Weill in 1926 and appeared in the controversial Brecht–Weill work *Mahagonny* ("Little Mahagonny") at the Baden-Baden Festival in 1927. She alternated in the roles of Jenny and Lucy in *Die Dreigroschenoper* (1928; "The Threepenny Opera") and starred in other Weill vehicles, among them a full-length operatic version of *Mahagonny,* entitled *Aufsteig und Fall der Stadt Mahagonny* (1930; "The Rise and Fall of the City of Mahagonny").

Fleeing Nazi Germany, Lenya and Weill went to Paris in 1933, where she appeared in *Die sieben Todsünden* (1933; "The Seven Deadly Sins"), a ballet-drama written for her by Brecht and Weill. From Paris the Weills moved to New York City; Lenya made her U.S. debut as Miriam in *The Eternal Road* (1937). She appeared as Cissy in *Candle in the Wind* (1944) and Duchess in *The Firebrand of Florence* (1945), after which she retired for a few years to assist Weill with composing. After his death in 1950, she returned to the stage as Xantippe in *Barefoot in Athens* (1951) and, throughout the 1950s, played in revivals of previous plays, most notably the long-running, off-Broadway production of *The Threepenny Opera,* as well as in several Kurt Weill Memorial Concerts. Lenya also played in the revue *Brecht on Brecht* (New York City and London, 1962), *Mother Courage and Her Children* (at the Ruhr Festival, Recklinghausen, W.Ger., 1965), and *Cabaret* (1966). She appeared in several films, including *Die Dreigroschenoper* (1930), *The Roman Spring of Mrs. Stone* (1960), *From Russia with Love* (1964), and *The Appointment* (1969); for her portrayal in *Roman Spring* Lenya was nominated for an Academy Award in 1961. She also did extensive recording, made television appearances, and performed in concert in West Germany and the United States.

Lenz, Jakob Michael Reinhold (b. Jan. 12, 1751, Sesswegen, Livonia, Russia—d. May 24, 1792, Moscow), Russian-born German poet and dramatist of the Sturm und Drang (Storm and Stress) period, who is considered an important forerunner of 19th-century Naturalism and of 20th-century Expressionistic theatre.

Lenz studied theology at Königsberg University but gave up his studies in 1771 to travel to Strasbourg as a tutor and companion to two young barons von Kleist. In Strasbourg he became a member of Goethe's circle and was strongly influenced by the Sturm und Drang sentiments of that group of dramatists. Lenz made his reputation with plays from the Strasbourg years, an eccentric didactic comedy, *Der Hofmeister oder Vortheile der Privaterziehung* (published 1774, performed 1778, Berlin; "The Tutor, or the Advantages of Private Education"), and his best play, *Die Soldaten* (performed 1763, published 1776; "The Soldiers"). His plays have dramatic and comic effects arising from strong characters and the swift juxtaposition of contrasting situations. *Anmerkungen übers Theater* (1774; "Observations on the Theatre") contains a translation of Shakespeare's *Love's Labour's Lost* and outlines Lenz's theories of dramaturgy, summarizing conceptions of theatre that he shared with other members of the Sturm und Drang movement. These include contempt for classical conventions, particularly the unities of time and place, and a search for utterly realistic depiction of character.

Consumed by the ambition to become Goethe's equal, Lenz made himself ridiculous by imitating both Goethe's writing style and his personal life in Strasbourg and at court in Weimar, where Lenz followed Goethe in 1776. His eccentricities were thought to be harmless and amusing until a tactless parody angered the Duke, who therefore expelled Lenz from the court in disgrace. The remaining years of his life were spent in aimless drifting and poverty and, eventually, in insanity. Georg Büchner, a 19th-century dramatist whose technique owes much to Lenz's innovations, portrayed episodes of Lenz's insanity in his short novel *Lenz* (1839).

Lenz's law, in electromagnetism, statement that an induced electric current flows in a direction such that the current opposes the change that induced it. This law was deduced in 1834 by the Russian physicist Heinrich Friedrich Emil Lenz (1804–65).

Thrusting a pole of a permanent bar magnet through a coil of wire, for example, induces an electric current in the coil; the current in turn sets up a magnetic field around the coil, making it a magnet. Lenz's law indicates the direction of the induced current. Because like magnetic poles repel each other, Lenz's law states that when the north pole of the bar magnet is approaching the coil, the induced current flows in such a way as to make the side of the coil nearest the pole of the bar magnet itself a north pole to oppose the approaching bar magnet. Upon withdrawing the bar magnet from the coil, the induced current reverses itself, and the near side of the coil becomes a south pole to produce an attracting force on the receding bar magnet.

A small amount of work, therefore, is done in pushing the magnet into the coil and in pulling it out against the magnetic effect of the induced current. The small amount of energy represented by this work manifests itself as a slight heating effect, the result of the induced current encountering resistance in the material of the coil. Lenz's law upholds the general principle of the conservation of energy. If the current were induced in the opposite direction, its action would spontaneously draw the bar magnet into the coil in addition to the heating effect, which would violate conservation of energy.

Leo, name of rulers grouped below by country or papacy and indicated by the symbol •.

Foreign-language equivalents:

Armenian	Levon
Greek	Leon
Latin	Leo

ARMENIA

• **Leo I:** *see* Levon I.

BYZANTINE EMPIRE

• **Leo I** (d. Feb. 3, 474), Eastern Roman emperor from AD 457 to 474.

Leo was a Thracian who, beginning his career in the army, became a protégé of General Aspar. In proclaiming Leo Eastern emperor at Constantinople (Feb. 7, 457), Aspar expected to use him as a puppet ruler. Leo, who had recognized Majorian as emperor of the West in 457, withheld recognition from Majorian's successor, Libius Severus, in 461. Six years later he installed Anthemius as the Western emperor.

In 468 Leo opened a disastrous joint campaign with Anthemius against the Vandals under King Gaiseric in North Africa. Leo is said to have assembled a fleet of 1,113 ships and to have embarked an army of 100,000 men, but he made the mistake of entrusting the command to Basiliscus, his wife's brother. Gaiseric outwitted Basiliscus and destroyed the Roman fleet. As a result of this defeat the Roman treasury was left nearly bankrupt for a generation.

In matters of the church, Leo was firmly orthodox. Aspar's influence on internal policies persisted for the first few years of Leo's reign. To free himself from the general's control, Leo began to rely on a force of Isaurians from the mountains of southern Anatolia to counterbalance Aspar's German troops. With Aspar's overthrow and murder in 471, Leo's power was unchallenged. In October 473, the year before his death, Leo appointed his grandson, Leo II, as colleague and successor.

• **Leo II** (d. Nov. 10, 474), Roman emperor of the East, grandson of Leo I, and son of Zeno. His grandfather, growing ill, felt compelled to name a successor but, deciding that his son Zeno, an Isaurian, was unpopular, made his grandson co-emperor, as Caesar and then Augustus, at the young age of five (or six). After his grandfather's death (Feb. 3, 474), Leo II became emperor, and his father was made co-emperor (February 9), but he survived only several months, leaving the throne to Zeno.

• **Leo III,** byname LEO THE ISAURIAN (b. *c.* 675–680, Germanicia, Commagene, Syria—d. June 18, 741, Constantinople), Byzantine emperor (717–741), who founded the Isaurian, or Syrian, dynasty, successfully resisted Arab invasions, and engendered a century of conflict within the empire by banning the use of religious images (icons).

Military accomplishments. Born at Germanicia (Marʿash) in northern Syria (modern Maraş, Tur.), as a youth he was taken by his parents (who apparently were prosperous) to Mesembria, in Thrace. Emperor Justinian II appointed the young man to the prestigious rank of *spatharius* (attendant) as a reward for assisting him in the recovery of his throne in 705. But the Emperor soon developed a distrust of him and therefore sent him to perform a perilous mission among the Alani on

Leo III, gold solidus, 8th century; in the British Museum

Peter Clayton

the remote eastern frontier, anticipating that he would never return. Despite the danger, Leo accomplished his assignment, managed to preserve his life, and ultimately, at the hands of a subsequent emperor, Anastasius II (713–715), received appointment as commander of the Anatolikon, the largest theme, or military-district army, in Asia Minor. As the result of a military revolt in 715, Anastasius was deposed, exiled to a monastery, and replaced by Theodosius III. Leo, in alliance with Artavasdos, the commander of the Armeniakon theme (the second largest in Asia Minor), refused to recognize the new emperor and continued to champion the cause of Anastasius. Meanwhile, Arab armies had invaded Asia Minor. Leo deceived them into believing that he would subjugate the empire for them, and thus he won their goodwill and support for his own attempt to seize the throne. After persuading them to spare Byzantine territory, he marched on Constantinople. The feeble Theodosius III abdicated, realizing that opposition was futile. Leo became emperor on March 25, 717.

Leo's first task as emperor was the organization of the defense of Constantinople against the Arab troops under Maslamah ibn ʿAbd al-Malik, who angrily perceived the deception. They besieged the city by land and sea from Aug. 15, 717, to Aug. 15, 718. Leo's skillful defense, which was aided by Greek fire (an igneous petroleum mix), a severe winter, desertions from the Arab fleet, and a Bulgarian assault upon those Arabs who had encamped in Thrace, compelled Maslamah to abandon the siege, which was the second and supreme Arab effort to capture Constantinople. Leo's victory marked an important check to Arab expansionism, preventing their establishment of a bridgehead in southeastern Europe. His complicated negotiations with the Arabs, as well as those earlier with the Alani, brought him a contemporary reputation for cleverness.

Leo consolidated his authority by crushing a rebellion in Sicily and a plot of army officers and officials to restore former emperor Anastasius II to the throne. Leo then sealed an alliance with his associate Artavasdos by marrying his daughter Anna to him. Throughout the reign, Artavasdos remained the second most powerful man in the empire by virtue of his control of several important military posts. Leo's wife, Maria, bore him a son, Constantine, whom he crowned in 720. An able diplomat, Leo married Constantine in 733 to a daughter of the Khagan of the Khazars; the marriage brought Leo a valuable military alliance with the Khazars in the trans-Caucasus against the Arabs.

Leo maintained peaceful relations with the Bulgarians to the north, enabling him to concentrate his military abilities against the Arab menace to Asia Minor. In 740 he won a major victory over the Arabs at Akroïnos (Afyonkarahisar). This victory freed Asia Minor from any immediate serious threat of Arab conquest, and it made possible the forceful counteroffensive and reconquest of some lost territory in the subsequent reign of his son Constantine V (741–775). He also repaired the extensive walls of Constantinople.

An energetic soldier-emperor, who personally led his troops in battle, Leo displayed great concern for the efficiency of his army. His victories improved army morale. He subdivided some of the very large military-district armies, or themes, which had proved, as his own career demonstrated, so large and powerful that their commanders might attempt to seize the throne. Whether or not this administrative reorganization was itself responsible for subsequent stability, he did succeed in halting the vulnerability of the throne to military overthrow. He unquestionably left the army a more effective instrument at his death than he had found it on his accession. It no longer seems probable, however, that he planned or established a comprehensive system of social and institutional reforms.

Religious policies. Leo's military achievements earned him great popularity with his soldiers and the people and may have given him the confidence to pursue his religious policies forcefully. He not only held firm religious opinions but he also had a profound belief in his duty as emperor to implement them as he understood them. In 722 he ordered the forcible baptism of Jews and Montanists (a Christian heretical group). He personally investigated but did not prosecute adherents of the Paulician heresy. The origins and nature of his policy of Iconoclasm, the most singular religious development in his reign, are obscure and controversial. He was deeply religious and seems to have become genuinely convinced of the sacrilegious character of religious pictures and relics as objects of veneration in worship services. It is uncertain whether any boyhood experiences in northern Syria, including contact with Muslims, influenced his Iconoclastic views, as his critics often charged. The Iconoclastic opinions of certain bishops in western Asia Minor did, however, have some effect upon him. Thus, in 726 he began to speak out publicly against the use of sacred pictures. Opposition to his doctrines may have been the cause for an unsuccessful rebellion against him in the Cyclades Islands in 727.

In 730 he proclaimed Iconoclasm the official policy of the empire and ordered the removal and destruction of sacred pictures in churches. When Patriarch Germanus I of Constantinople refused his demand for approval of these policies, Leo removed him and appointed a patriarch of his own choice, Anastasius. Where necessary, Leo employed harsh penalties, such as beatings and imprisonment, against recalcitrant ecclesiastics. His policies met particularly strong opposition from monastic circles. Popes Gregory II and Gregory III also strongly rejected his efforts to impose Iconoclasm upon Byzantine-controlled areas of Italy. Leo retaliated by halting financial contributions to the papacy from southern Italy, and he may also have removed the churches of Sicily, Calabria, and Illyria from papal jurisdiction and placed them under the patriarch of Constantinople. At any rate, his actions severely strained relations with the papacy, causing the popes to turn increasingly to the Frankish kings as alternative protectors of the Holy See in Rome and weakening the Byzantine position in the Italian peninsula. Other harsh taxation and administrative measures added to his unpopularity in Sicily and southern Italy. Although an able commander, Leo neglected to maintain strong naval forces in the western Mediterranean and thus further weakened Byzantine power there.

Legal and other accomplishments. One of Leo's most important acts was the promulgation, in 726, of the Ecloga, a law code of modest length, which represented a revision of Roman legal practices as embodied in the 6th-century Corpus Juris Civilis (Body of Civil Law) of Emperor Justinian I. Consciously attempting to revise Roman law in accordance with Christian principles, Leo devoted much space in the Ecloga to the regulation of marriage and property rights. Amputation and mutilation often were substitutes in this new code for the former death penalties. Leo provided regular salaries for legal officials to discourage the corrupt custom of offering gifts or bribes to judges and bureaucrats. An important codification of military law, the so-called Soldiers' Law, is sometimes attributed to Leo, but its true ascription is uncertain.

Other than his sincere predilection for theological topics, Leo's intellectual interests are unknown. He possessed, doubtless from boyhood, a speaking knowledge of Arabic. Although there is little evidence of intellectual activity during his reign, the earlier charge that he halted higher education in Constantinople by closing an ecclesiastical academy (because of the faculty opposition to Iconoclasm) can no longer be credited with certainty. Similarly, there is little source material on economic or demographic developments during his reign, but the numerous earthquakes doubtless inflicted major damage on towns and the countryside.

Leo was buried in the Church of the Holy Apostles at Constantinople. There is inadequate information on internal history in the last eight years of his reign, but he certainly failed to silence opposition to his Iconoclastic policies; in fact, Iconoclasm divided the empire for another century. He had instilled his Iconoclastic opinions and his grasp for military tactics in his son Constantine V, who ably followed and even intensified the policies of his father. Although Leo's memory was reviled by those later Byzantines who deplored his Iconoclasm, he was admired, especially in certain military circles, for his forceful and generally successful efforts to strengthen the state. (W.E.K.)

BIBLIOGRAPHY. Karl Schenk, *Kaiser Leon III.* (1880), a biography of his early life; *A Manual of Roman Law: The Ecloga, Published by the Emperors Leo III and Constantine V . . . A.D. 726,* trans. by Edwin Hanson Freshfield (1926), contains a useful introduction; J.B. Bury, *A History of the Later Roman Empire from Arcadius to Irene, 395 A.D. to 800 A.D.,* 2 vol. (1889), an old but useful narrative; G. Ostrogorsky, *Geschichte des byzantinischen Staates* (1963; *History of the Byzantine State,* 2nd ed., 1968), including a useful bibliography; R. Jenkins, *Byzantium: The Imperial Centuries, A.D. 610–1071,* pp. 61–68, 74–89 (1966), a good narrative; E.J. Martin, *A History of the Iconoclastic Controversy* (1930).

"De," "la," and similar components of a name, when followed by a space, are alphabetized as separate words (e.g., *De Forest, Lee*). *When they are joined to the following part of a name, the combination is treated as a single word* (e.g., *DeForest, John William*).

• **Leo IV,** byname LEO THE KHAZAR (b. Jan. 25, 749—d. Sept. 8, 780), Byzantine emperor whose reign marked a transition between the period of Iconoclasm and the restoration of the icons.

Leo became Byzantine emperor in 775 at the death of his father, Constantine V. The following year, at the request of the army and with the support of the Senate and the citizens, Leo's young son Constantine was crowned co-emperor, passing over the caesar Nicephorus, a stepbrother of Leo. The resulting conspiracy in favour of the caesar Nicephorus was, however, suppressed, and the conspirators were exiled.

Leo profited from discord among the Bulgars by granting the Bulgar khan Telerig asylum in Constantinople (776–777) and marrying him to a cousin of his wife Irene. He also conducted three campaigns against the Arabs between 777 and 780.

At the beginning of his reign Leo made no attempt to continue his father's fierce Iconoclastic policy that forbade the use of icons (religious images). Instead he showed considerable moderation toward the proponents of icons, even appointing them to bishoprics. This action may have resulted from the influence of Irene, who was strongly orthodox. In 780, however, shortly before the close of his reign, he reversed his policy and initiated a persecution of those favouring the use of icons.

• **Leo V,** byname LEO THE ARMENIAN (b. Armenia—d. Dec. 25, 820, Constantinople), Byzantine emperor responsible for inaugurating the second Iconoclastic period in the Byzantine Empire.

When Bardanes Turcus and Nicephorus I were fighting over the Byzantine throne in 803, Leo at first joined Bardanes but later sided with Nicephorus. Leo distinguished himself as a general under Nicephorus I and Michael I and became *strategus* ("general") of the Anatolikon district of the empire. He took part in the campaign of 813 against the Bulgars, but, when Michael unwisely refused the peace terms they offered, the Asian troops under Leo deserted at the Battle of Versinikia, near Adrianople. Leo then deposed Michael I and in July 813 replaced him.

Meanwhile, Krum, the Bulgarian khan, had reached the walls of Constantinople. Leo succeeded in drawing him back and concluded a treaty with Krum's successor, Omortag, that determined the boundary between the two countries and provided a 30-year peace.

In March 815 Leo deposed the Orthodox patriarch Nicephorus and convoked a synod for the following month that reimposed the decrees of the Iconoclast synod of Hieria of 754, which had opposed the use of icons (religious images). Leo was assassinated during a Christmas service in the church of Hagia Sophia by friends of Michael the Amorian, whom Leo had condemned to death the day before on a charge of treason. After the assassination Michael ascended the throne as Michael II.

• **Leo VI,** byname LEO THE WISE, OR THE PHILOSOPHER (b. Sept. 19, 866—d. May 11, 912, Constantinople), Byzantine coemperor from 870 and emperor from 886 to 912, whose imperial laws, written in Greek, became the legal code of the Byzantine Empire.

Leo was the son of Basil I the Macedonian, who had begun the codification, and his second wife, Eudocia Ingerina. Made coemperor in 870, Leo succeeded to the throne on his father's death. His foreign policy was directed mainly against the Arabs and the Bulgars. The able commander Nicephorus Phocas the Elder was recalled from his successful campaigns against the Lombards in south Italy to assist in the Balkans. After this Byzantium met with reverses in the West: Sicily was lost to the Arabs in 902, Thessalonica was sacked by Leo of Tripoli, and the Aegean was open to constant attack from Arab pirates. Steps were taken to strengthen the Byzantine navy, which successfully attacked the Arab fleet in the Aegean in 908. But the naval expedition of 911–912 was defeated by Leo of Tripoli. Byzantium's enemy to the north was Simeon, the Bulgar ruler. Hostilities arose out of a trade dispute in 894, and the Byzantines, aided by the Magyars of the Danube-Dnieper region, forced Simeon to agree to a truce. With the help of the nomadic Pechenegs, however, Simeon in 896 took revenge on the Byzantines, forcing them to pay an annual tribute to the Bulgars.

During Leo's reign the Russian prince Oleg sailed to Constantinople and in 907 obtained a treaty regulating the position of Russian merchants in Byzantium, which was formally ratified in 911. Because of his anxiety for a male heir Leo married four times, thus incurring the censure of the church.

Educated by the patriarch Photius, Leo was more scholar than soldier. In addition to completing the canon of laws, he wrote several decrees (novels) on a wide range of ecclesiastical and secular problems. He also wrote a funeral panegyric on his father, liturgical poems, sermons and orations, secular poetry, and military treatises. Leo's image is in a mosaic over the central door of Hagia Sophia.

PAPACY

• **Leo I,** SAINT, byname LEO THE GREAT (b. late 4th century, Tuscany?—d. Nov. 10, 461, Rome; Western feast day November 10 ([formerly April 11], Eastern feast day February 18), pope from 440 to 461, master exponent of papal supremacy. His pontificate—which saw the disintegration of the Roman Empire in the West and the formation in the East of theological differences that were to split Christendom—was devoted to safeguarding orthodoxy and to securing the unity of the Western church under papal supremacy.

Leo I, detail of a miniature from the menologion of Basil II, 10th century; in the Vatican Library (Vat. Gr. 1613 folio 412)
Biblioteca Apostolica Vaticana

Consecrated on Sept. 29, 440, as successor to St. Sixtus III, Leo immediately worked to suppress heresy, which he regarded as the cause of corruption and disunity. Yet his most significant theological achievement was not his negative suppression of heresy but his positive formulation of orthodoxy.

His treatment of the monk Eutyches of Constantinople provides an example. The monk had founded Eutychianism, an extreme form of monophysitism holding that Christ had only one nature, his human nature being absorbed in his divine nature. Patriarch Flavian of Constantinople excommunicated Eutyches, who then appealed to Leo. After examining the case, Leo sent Flavian (449) his celebrated *Tome,* which rejected Eutyches' teaching and presented a precise, systematic doctrine of Christ's Incarnation and of the union of both his natures. The Council (451) of Chalcedon (modern Kadikoy, Turkey), summoned to condemn Eutychianism, declared that Leo's *Tome* was the ultimate truth. Furthermore, the council recognized Leo's doctrine as "the voice of Peter." Thus for the church Leo's *Tome* established the doctrine that Christ's natures coexist and his Incarnation reveals how human nature is restored to perfect unity with divine, or absolute, being.

Leo's 432 letters and 96 sermons expound his precept of papal primacy in church jurisdiction. He held that papal power was granted by Christ to St. Peter alone, and that that power was passed on by Peter to his successors. In one letter, for example, he cautioned the Bishop of Thessalonica that although he had been entrusted with office and shared Leo's solicitude, he was "not to possess the plenitude of power."

Leo further enhanced the prestige of the papacy and helped to place Western leadership in its hands by dealing with invading barbaric tribes. He persuaded the Huns, a nomadic people terrorizing northern Italy, not to attack Rome (452), and the Vandals, a Germanic people, not to sack Rome when they occupied it three years later. Leo was declared a doctor of the church by Pope Benedict XIV in 1754.

• **Leo II,** SAINT (b. Sicily—d. July 3, 683; feast day July 3, formerly June 28), pope from 681 to 683.

Leo was elected about December 681 to succeed St. Agatho but was not consecrated until Aug. 17, 682, because of a delay in confirmation by the Byzantine emperor Constantine IV. He ratified the decision of the sixth ecumenical Council of Constantinople (680) to condemn monothelitism, a heresy concerning the will of Christ, as well as the conciliatory policies of Pope Honorius I (d. 638). Because Honorius had not directly denounced monothelitism, Leo called him one who "by unholy betrayal tried to overthrow the immaculate faith." During Leo's pontificate, the see of Ravenna, having in 666 been freed from the pope's jurisdiction by the Byzantine emperor Constans II Pogonatus, was again made papally dependent, by order of Constantine.

• **Leo III,** SAINT (b. Rome—d. June 12, 816; canonized 1673; feast day June 12), pope from 795 to 816.

Leo was a cardinal when elected to succeed Pope Adrian I on Dec. 26, 795; he was consecrated the next day. Unlike Adrian, who had tried to maintain independence in the growing estrangement between East and West by balancing the Byzantine emperor against

Leo III, detail from a mosaic, 8th century; on the exterior of the church of S. Giovanni Laterano, Rome
Alinari—Art Resource

Charlemagne, Leo immediately yielded to Charlemagne by recognizing him as *patricius* of the Romans. On April 25, 799, during a Roman procession, Leo was physically attacked by assailants incited by Adrian's supporters, who accused him of misconduct and whose ultimate plan was to blind Leo and remove his tongue, thus disqualifying him for the papacy. He fled across the Alps to his protector, Charlemagne, at Paderborn. Exactly what was negotiated there is unknown, but Leo was safely escorted back to Rome in November by a commission that discredited the complaints against him and arrested and deported his accusers.

Confusion in Rome continued, however, and Charlemagne in the autumn of 800 went there "to restore the state of the church, which was greatly disturbed." In the presence of Charlemagne, on December 23, Leo solemnly purged himself of the charges against him. Two days later, at a large gathering in St. Peter's Basilica for the consecration of Charlemagne's son (Louis I the Pious) as king, Leo suddenly crowned Charlemagne as emperor. By this act, Leo obliterated his earlier humiliation and established the legal precedent that only the pope could confer the imperial crown. More important, however, Leo made his position secure by becoming the immediate beneficiary of the coronation, itself an illegal and revolutionary proceeding. His motive to create a new Western empire alongside the Eastern one proved ineffectual, for the Byzantines regarded Charlemagne as a usurper. Leo's act, which had clearly been prepared in advance, also carried wide connotations: it separated East and West, causing a rivalry persisting until the 13th century; by allying the papacy with the Western empire, it involved Charlemagne and his successors ever more deeply in the ecumenical pretensions of the papacy.

Although the relations between Pope and Emperor were relatively amiable, Charlemagne controlled imperial administration and ecclesiastical reform. Yet in 809, when approached by Charlemagne's theologians, Leo confirmed the dogmatic correctness of the *Filioque* clause (the doctrine that the Holy Spirit proceeds from both the Father and the Son) introduced into the Nicene Creed; but, because that clause had always been rejected by the Eastern churches, Leo, in the interest of peace with the Greeks, urged that the creed should not be chanted in the public liturgy.

Upon Charlemagne's death in 814, the hatred of the Roman nobility against Leo reasserted itself. He had some conspirators executed and submitted an account of his action to Louis, who had succeeded his father. Leo died soon afterward.

• **Leo IV,** Saint (b. Rome—d. July 17, 855, Rome; feast day July 17), pope from 847 to 855.

A Benedictine monk, Leo served in the Curia under Pope Gregory IV and was later made cardinal priest by Pope Sergius II, whom he was elected to succeed. Leo rebuilt Rome after it had been sacked by the Saracens (Arab enemies) in 846 and fortified the city to protect it against future attacks. In 849 he arranged an alliance among several Greek cities in Italy, and their combined forces defeated an invading Saracen fleet off Ostia, Italy. In 854 Leo fortified Civitavecchia, Italy, a popular Saracen target. Thereafter, the town was named Leopoli in his honour.

At a Roman synod in April 850, he crowned as co-emperor the Frankish emperor Lothair I's son Louis II. In church affairs, Leo took a firm hand against abuses by important ecclesiastics. He censured the powerful archbishop Hincmar of Reims for excommunicating an imperial vassal without papal approval, and he excommunicated Cardinal Anastasius of San Marcello (later the antipope Anastasius Bibliothecarius), in 853, to enforce ecclesiastical obedience to Rome.

A list of the abbreviations used in the MICROPAEDIA *will be found at the end of this volume*

• **Leo V** (b. Priapi?, Italy—d. September 903), pope from July to September 903. Elected while a priest to succeed Pope Benedict IV, Leo assumed the pontificate in a dark period of papal history. He was deposed and imprisoned by the antipope Christopher. Leo was perhaps murdered, either by Christopher or his successor, Pope Sergius III.

• **Leo VI** (b. Rome—d. probably December 928, Rome), pope from May to December 928. He was Pope John VIII's prime minister and later a cardinal priest when elected by the *senatrix* Marozia, then head of the powerful Roman Crescentii family, who deposed and imprisoned Leo's predecessor, Pope John X. His principal act was the regulation of the jurisdiction of the hierarchy in Dalmatia.

• **Leo VII** (b. Rome—d. July 13, 939, Rome), pope from 936 to 939. Leo was probably a Benedictine monk when he succeeded John XI, who had been imprisoned by Duke Alberic II of Spoleto. In 936 he invited Abbot St. Odo of Cluny (then one of the most influential abbeys in western Europe) to help him settle the struggle between Hugh of Provence, king of Italy, and Alberic over Hugh's siege of Rome. He encouraged reform of the German clergy and forbade Archbishop Frederick of Mainz to enforce the conversion of Jews to Christianity, yet at the same time allowed him to expel all Jews who would not embrace Christianity.

• **Leo VIII** (b. Rome—d. March 1?, 965), pope, or antipope, from 963 to 965.

A Roman synod in December 963 deposed and expelled Pope John XII for dishonourable conduct and for instigating an armed conspiracy against the Holy Roman emperor Otto I the Great. Otto, who had marched into Rome with his army and had called the synod, subsequently influenced the election of Leo, then only a layman.

When Otto departed, John and his partisans returned to Rome, where in February 964 John conducted a synod that deposed Leo, who then fled to Otto. John died suddenly in the following May. Ignoring Otto's candidate, Leo, the Romans elected Benedict V. The furious Otto again came to Rome, reinstated Leo by force in June 964, and deported Benedict. Some scholars regard Leo as an antipope until after Otto compelled his acceptance. Others consider either Leo or Benedict as antipopes.

• **Leo IX,** Saint, original name Bruno, Graf (count) von Egisheim und Dagsburg (b. June 21, 1002, Egisheim, Alsace, Upper Lorraine—d. April 19, 1054, Rome; feast day April 19), head of the medieval Latin Church (1049–54), during whose reign the papacy became the focal point of western Europe, and the great East–West Schism of 1054 became inevitable.

Early life. Bruno of Egisheim was born into an aristocratic family. He was educated at Toul, where he first became canon and then was consecrated bishop on Sept. 9, 1027, at the early age of 25. Dynamic, purposeful,

Leo IX (left) consecrating the rebuilt monastery church of St.-Arnould-de-Metz, which is being offered to him by Abbot Warinus of Metz, 11th-century codex; in the Burgerbibliothek, Bern, Switz. (Cod. 292, f. 72)

and zealous in the cause of reform, he began to raise the moral standards of important monasteries in his diocese, as well as those of the secular diocesan clergy, by holding frequent meetings and by constant exhortations. In accordance with prevailing practice, he was appointed pope at the age of 47 by the emperor Henry III. He insisted, however, upon being elected by the people and clergy of Rome, an action that implicitly indicated his opposition to the firmly entrenched lay intervention, especially by the emperors, in purely ecclesiastical matters. After having obtained approval by the Romans, he was enthroned as pope on Feb. 12, 1049.

Papal reforms. Leo IX's aim was the eradication of what he saw as the chief evils of the time—that is, concubinage (clerical marriage), simony (buying and selling of ecclesiastical offices), and lay investiture (conferment of an ecclesiastical office by a lay ruler). In order to achieve these ends it was necessary for the Roman Church itself to be made the centre of Christian society and life. Leo therefore called to Rome men whom he had known in his capacity as bishop of Toul. They not only were aware of the pressing need for reform but were also first-class scholars and administrators as well as men who realized the difficulties with which they were to be confronted. Among them were Humbert of Moyenmoutier, Frederick of Lorraine (later Pope Stephen IX), and Hugh of Remiremont, all of whom became cardinals. A notable monk at Cluny, Hildebrand, also obeyed the call to Rome, where he was destined to play a historic role as Pope Gregory VII, becoming the consummator of the reform initiated by Leo. These men and their assistants infused new blood into the Roman Church. Leo also entertained regular contact with other leading churchmen, such as Peter Damian and Abbot Hugh of Cluny, who by virtue of their reputations exercised great influence upon their immediate surroundings and thus prepared the way for the acceptance of measures to reform Christian society.

These men succeeded in transforming the papacy from a local Roman institution into an international power. This farsighted and able group was determined to make papal ideology a social reality. The pivotal point in this ideology was the primatial position of the pope as so-called successor of St. Peter—an ecclesiastical expression for papal monarchy. The organizational apparatus of the papacy experienced a great expansion at this time, notably the chancery, which became the nerve centre of the papacy in which the universally valid and applicable law and the instructions and mandates to distant ecclesiastical officers were drafted.

Although the effect of these legal measures was not immediately conspicuous, they nevertheless prepared the ground for their subsequent successful implementation. During Leo IX's pontificate the cardinals became more and more prominent as the most intimate counsellors of the pope, and within a few years they were to form the body known as the Sacred College of Cardinals.

The validity of priestly ordinations administered by simoniac bishops proved a serious problem, because most theologians held that simony prostituted the sacrament of ordination. Leo IX ordered a number of simoniacally ordained priests to be "reordained." This order called forth a great spate of controversial literature, but the problem was not solved until several decades later. A synod that was under Leo's presidency condemned as heretical in 1050 the views propounded by Berengar of Tours (died 1088) on the Eucharist (that the bread and wine only symbolically became the body and blood of Christ).

Leo IX was intent on making the primatial position of the pope real by his own physical presence outside Rome. To this end he held more than a dozen councils in Italy, France, Germany, and Sicily, which reenacted the decrees of earlier councils and popes and initiated practical measures to eliminate the worst excesses from which Christian society suffered. The personal attendance of St. Peter's successor and his chairmanship of these councils were factors that powerfully contributed to the accelerated ascendancy of the papacy. The frequent journeyings enabled the Pope to establish direct contact with the higher and lower clergy as well as with leading secular personages.

The Schism of 1054. The most significant event of Leo IX's pontificate—the actual break with the Eastern Church—resulted, at least partially, from an ill-fated military involvement.

After their settlement in Sicily in the second decade of the 11th century, the Normans presented considerable dangers to the existence of the papal state. In their marauding expeditions they plundered and devastated many churches and monasteries. In conjunction with Emperor Henry III, Leo resolved to undertake a military campaign against the Normans; but Henry withdrew and, with a weak and inexperienced army under his command, Leo had to face the Normans alone. They inflicted a crushing defeat upon the papal army, and on June 18, 1053, they took the Pope prisoner. He was, nevertheless, allowed to maintain contact with the outside world and to receive visitors. After nine months he was released.

The Norman venture, however, brought the papacy into conflict with the Eastern Church centred in Constantinople, which, since the 8th century, had exercised jurisdiction over large areas of southern Italy and Sicily. The forcefully enunciated papal theme of primacy in Leo's pontificate complicated the relations between Rome and Constantinople still further because the patriarch of Constantinople, Michael I Cerularius, considered this sheer provocation.

He closed the Latin (Western) churches in Constantinople and raised serious dogmatic charges against the Roman Church, notably in connection with the Eucharist. Cardinal Humbert attacked the Patriarch in a vitriolic and passionate manner by arguing the case for Roman primacy and also quoting extensively from the forged "Donation of Constantine" (allegedly bestowing sovereignty in the West on the papacy). A legation under Humbert's leadership left for Constantinople in April 1054, but, despite several meetings between Patriarch, Emperor, and legates, no concrete results emerged. On July 16, 1054, in the full view of the congregation, Humbert put the papal bull of excommunication—already prepared before the legation left Rome—on the altar of the church of Hagia Sophia in Constantinople. Thereupon the Patriarch excommunicated the legation and its supporters. This marked the final breach between Rome and Constantinople. This schism was to last, with short interruptions, until the modern age.

Whether the excommunication of Michael I Cerularius was valid, because Leo had been dead for three months, is merely a technical problem. The Roman legates were legates of the papacy, and the bull of excommunication had been a measure of the reigning pontiff. In any case, the excommunication merely formalized in a dramatic and spectacular manner a state of affairs that had long existed. Although this occurred after the death of Leo IX, the outbreak of the formal schism correctly belongs to his pontificate, which in several ways therefore marked a caesura in the history of the papacy in medieval times.

(W.U.)

BIBLIOGRAPHY. Lucien Sittler and Paul Stintzi (eds.), *Saint Léon IX, le pape alsacien* (1950), a competent and readable account; Horace K. Mann, *The Lives of the Popes in the Early Middle Ages*, vol. 6, *The Popes of the Gregorian Renaissance*, pp. 19–182 (1910), the fullest account in English, although in many respects outdated; *Pour le neuvième centénaire de la mort de saint Léon IX* (1954), a memorial volume commemorating the ninth centenary of Leo's death and concerning a number of aspects of his pontificate; Owen J. Blum in the *New Catholic Encyclopedia*, vol. 8, pp. 642–643 (1967); V. Grumel, "Les Préliminaires du schisme de Michel Cérulaire ou la question romaine avant 1054," *Revue des études byzantines*, 10:5–23 (1952), an examination of the historical background of the schism; Steven Runciman, *The Eastern Schism: A Study of the Papacy and the Eastern Churches During the XIth and XIIth Centuries* (1955); Donald M. Nicol, "Byzantium and the Papacy in the 11th century," *Journal of Ecclesiastical History*, 13:1–20 (1962), a very competent survey of the subject; F. Dvornik, *Byzance et la primauté romaine* (1964; *Byzantium and the Roman Primacy*, 1966), an original assessment based on the author's own research.

• **Leo X,** original name GIOVANNI DE' MEDICI (b. Dec. 11, 1475, Florence—d. Dec. 1, 1521, Rome), one of the most extravagant of the Renaissance popes (reigned 1513–21), who made Rome a centre of European culture and raised the papacy to significant political power in Europe. He depleted the papal treasury, and, by his response to the developing Reformation, he contributed to the dissolution of the unified Western church. Leo excommunicated Martin Luther in 1521.

Leo X, contemporary medallion; in the coin collection of the Vatican Library
Leonard von Matt—EB Inc.

Early life and ecclesiastical career. Born Giovanni de' Medici, he was the second son of Lorenzo the Magnificent, the ruler of the Florentine republic, and by custom thus destined for a religious life. At the early age of eight young Giovanni received the tonsure—a ceremony involving the cutting of hair from the head, thus indicating the change of status from lay to clerical—and five years later became the cardinal-deacon of Sta. Maria in Dominica. He received the finest education available in Europe at the court of his father under several tutors, including the philosopher Pico della Mirandola (1463–94). From 1489 to 1491 the youthful ecclesiastic studied theology and canon law at the University of Pisa. In 1492 he became a member of the Sacred College of Cardinals and attempted to take up residence in Rome. The death of his father later in the same year, however, brought him back to Florence where he lived with his older brother, Piero.

The election of Pope Alexander VI took him back to Rome for the conclave (assembly of cardinals to elect the pope); otherwise he lived in Florence until he was exiled in November 1494 with the other members of the Medici family on the charge of their betraying the republic. For the next six years Cardinal de' Medici travelled throughout northern Europe. In 1500 he returned to Italy and settled in Rome. Upon the death of his brother Piero, Giovanni became the head of the Medici family. During 1503 he took part in the conclaves that elected first Pius III (September) and then Julius II (October). Named papal legate to Bologna and Romagna in 1511, he supervised the reestablishment of Medici control of Florence the following year; and, although his younger brother Giuliano actually held the first place in the Florentine republic, it was the Cardinal who ruled.

Election to the papacy. With the death of Julius II on Feb. 21, 1513, the Sacred College of Cardinals was summoned to elect a successor. The conclave met on March 4, and with minimal deliberation the cardinals, who desired a peace-loving successor to the warlike Julius, elected Cardinal de' Medici on March 11. Taking the title of Leo X the pontiff-elect was ordained a priest on March 15 and consecrated bishop of Rome on the 17th. Two days later the papal coronation took place.

At 37 years of age the new pope was the personification of Renaissance ideals. Having spent his youth at the court of Lorenzo de' Medici, he had acquired the mannerisms and tastes of one of the most brilliant societies of Europe and posed a sharp contrast to the soldier-pope whom he succeeded. He fit extremely well into the atmosphere of calm and quiet of which Rome was desirous after 10 years under Julius II. Leo was lavish in his spending not only of the church's money but also of his own. Under his patronage Rome again became the cultural centre of the Western world. The construction of St. Peter's Basilica—initiated under Julius II—was accelerated, the holdings of the Vatican Library were greatly increased, and the arts flourished. Even the piety of the papacy was revised to some extent after the low reputation it had reached under the Borgia popes (Calixtus III and Alexander VI).

The fifth Lateran Council occupied the new pope during the first five years of his pontificate. Called by Julius II two years before his death, the council was designed to nullify the efforts of nine rebellious cardinals who had called for a council to meet at Pisa in order to revive the conciliar movement—intending to place ecclesiastical authority in councils, rather than the papacy—of the previous century. Although "Pisa II" collapsed when first the German emperor (Maximilian I, 1459–1519) and then the French king (Louis XII, 1462–1515) withdrew their support, the Lateran Council opened in 1512. Leo X, who inherited the council before it was a year old, was little inclined to preside over the sweeping reforms that the church so desperately needed on the eve of the Protestant Reformation. Poorly attended, and dominated by Italian bishops, the council debated the principal issues of the day; but there was neither direction nor encouragement from the pontiff, nor the urgency and necessity that would spur on the Council of Trent some 40 years later. Thus the council was dissolved (March 16, 1517), without significant action, on the very eve of Martin Luther's posting of his Ninety-five Theses.

Struggle for political power. Leo X was not only the head of the Christian Church, he was also the temporal ruler of the Papal States and head of the Medici family that ruled the Florentine republic. To exert his influence in Italy he resorted to the common practice of nepotism (granting offices or benefits to relatives, regardless of merit). To the influential archbishopric of Florence he appointed his cousin, and future pope (Clement VII), Giulio de' Medici. He also named his younger brother Giuliano and his nephew Lorenzo to be Roman patricians. Giuliano's premature death in 1516 brought an end to the Pope's plan to create a central Italian kingdom for him. On July 1, 1517, following and as a result of an attempt upon his life earlier in the same year, Leo named 31 new cardinals, thus prejudicing the College of Cardinals with papal supporters. One cardinal (Alfonso Petrucci) was strangled in prison, and others were imprisoned and executed when they were implicated in the attempted assassination.

In his struggle to dominate Italy, Leo X was confronted by the awesome power of Spain and the determination of the French kings. Louis XII of France marched into Italy in

1513 to make good his claims to Milan and Naples. Reluctantly Leo formed the League of Mechlin, in which Spain provided the major military strength. The French were defeated at Novara, and Louis renounced his claims and withdrew his army. The peace was short-lived. The ascent of Francis I (1494–1547) in 1515 to the throne of France led to the renewal of the war. Although Leo renewed the coalition of Spain, the Empire, and England, Francis won the Battle of Marignano (Sept. 14, 1515). The Pope made peace with the French king and then followed it up with the Concordat of Bologna. Promulgated in the form of a papal bull (*Primitiva*) on Aug. 18, 1516, the concordat regulated church–state relations in France for the next 275 years. The French kings were given the power to nominate bishops, abbots, and priors, though the popes did retain the right to nominate candidates to fill vacant benefices *in curia* and certain other benefices. Though the pope always had the power to veto a nomination of the king's, in practice the lay monarch's choice was tantamount to an appointment. This control over the church in France on the part of the kings explains, in part, why the monarchy showed little interest in Protestantism during the 16th century.

The death of the Holy Roman emperor, Maximilian I, in 1519 brought Leo further into the political arena. The Habsburg candidate, Charles (1500–58) of Spain, had succeeded his maternal grandparents Ferdinand II of Aragon (1452–1516) and Isabella I of Castile (1451–1504) in 1516 and now sought to follow his paternal grandfather, Maximilian, to the powerful German throne. Both Francis I and Frederick the Wise (1463–1525) of Saxony, however, immediately put forward their candidacy. Leo—fearing that if the empire were joined to either France or Spain, Italy would come under the power of the victor—threw his support in favour of Frederick. The election of Charles I of Spain as Charles V of the Holy Roman Empire led to war between France and Spain, and although Leo would have preferred to remain neutral he cast his lot with the new emperor when Francis again invaded Italy.

Conflict with Luther. The ever-pressing financial undertakings of the papacy kept Leo X in constant need of new means of raising revenue. The wars with France, his lavish support of the arts, the construction of St. Peter's, and a projected crusade against the Turks all contributed to the financial needs of the papacy. One important source of revenue had long been the dispensing of indulgences (remission of the temporal penalty for sins) for money. During the reign of Julius II, indulgences had been authorized for financial contributions for the construction of St. Peter's. Leo, who was very much interested in continuing this work, reaffirmed the indulgence shortly after his ascent. Nevertheless, because of its unpopularity in northern Europe, based primarily on economic reasons, it was not until early in 1517 that a Dominican friar actually began to preach the indulgence in the archdioceses of Mainz and Magdeburg (Germany). In response to this preaching, Martin Luther posted his Ninety-five Theses on the door of the Wittenberg Castle Church.

By the following year (1518) Luther's ideas had reached Rome, and Leo ordered the head of the Augustinian order, of which Luther was a member, to discipline the troublesome monk. When this failed the Pope tried to work through Frederick of Saxony, but again to no avail. During the course of the Leipzig debates in the summer of 1519, the Catholic theologian Johann Eck (1486–1543) manoeuvred Luther into publicly professing heresy on three accounts. On June 15, 1520, Leo issued a document condemning Luther of heresy on 41 accounts and ordered him to submit to the authority of Rome within 60 days or suffer excommunication. Luther, who by this time had gained the support of influential figures in Germany, openly defied the Pope. Thus, Leo was left no alternative but to issue a papal bull (*Decet Romanum Pontificem*) of excommunication on Jan. 3, 1521.

Leo X had not taken the Lutheran movement with the seriousness that history later indicated was warranted. But the church, after all, had withstood the teachings of an English reformer, John Wycliffe (*c.* 1330–84), and a Bohemian reformer, Jan Hus (*c.* 1372/73–1415), and was at the time weathering those of the Renaissance humanist Erasmus (*c.* 1466–1536). Leo viewed Luther as merely another heretic whose teachings would lead some of the faithful astray but that, as had happened in the past, the true religion would triumph in time. Furthermore, the political climate of Germany was not favourable for strong action against Luther and his supporters. Thus, the new movement spread rapidly in the north with relatively little interference from the papacy. In December 1521 Leo X died suddenly, leaving behind him political turmoil in Italy and religious turmoil spreading across northern Europe. (J.G.G.)

BIBLIOGRAPHY. William Roscoe, *The Life and Pontificate of Leo the Tenth,* 2 vol. (1853, new ed. 1973), the standard biography of Leo X (well documented and containing a good index); Ludwig von Pastor, *The History of the Popes, from the Close of the Middle Ages,* 3rd ed., vol. 7–8 (1950), the best source on the life and times of Leo X (well documented and well indexed); E.P. Rodocanachi, *Le Pontificat de Léon X, 1513–1521* (1930), contains an excellent bibliography; G.K. Brown, *Italy and the Reformation to 1550* (1933), a study of Pope Leo as a principal figure of the Reformation.

Consult the INDEX *first*

• **Leo XI,** original name ALESSANDRO OTTAVIANO DE' MEDICI (b. June 2, 1535, Florence—d. April 27, 1605, Rome), pope from April 1–27, 1605. Pope Gregory XIII made him bishop of Pistoia, Italy, in 1573, archbishop of Florence in 1574, and cardinal in 1583. Elected to succeed Clement VIII on April 1, 1605, he died within the month.

Leo XI, detail from a tomb monument by Alessandro Algardi, 1634–44; in St. Peter's Basilica, Rome
Alinari—Art Resource/EB Inc.

• **Leo XII,** original name ANNIBALE SERMATTEI DELLA GENGA (b. Aug. 22, 1760, near Spoleto, Papal States—d. Feb. 10, 1829, Rome), pope from 1823 to 1829.

Ordained in 1783, Della Genga became private secretary to Pope Pius VI, who in 1793 sent him as ambassador to Luzern, Switz. In 1794 he was appointed ambassador to Cologne, subsequently being entrusted with missions to several German courts. Pope Pius VII created him cardinal bishop of Senigallia in 1816 (which office he resigned in 1818) and vicar general of Rome in 1820.

Against Austria's opposition, Della Genga was elected pope on Sept. 28, 1823, by the influential *zelanti* (*i.e.,* conservatives who objected to Pius VI's conciliatory policies and to Cardinal Ercole Consalvi's reforming liberalism). Under Leo, authoritarianism was reinstated in the Papal States, a reaction that caused the bourgeoisie to resent a "government by priests." Although he reduced expenditure, thus reducing taxation, the precarious economic situation remained unchanged. In doctrinal matters, Leo strove to prevent the infiltration of liberal ideas and to strengthen the efficiency of the Inquisition. Thus, as was expected, he reversed Pius VI's policies.

In the Papal States, Leo pursued a repressive policy while endeavouring to reorganize financial administration, but other governments opposed his foreign policies, thus effecting a political change. After some clumsy moves inspired by the *zelanti,* he recognized the need for moderation in view of the new outbreak of liberal propaganda and the revival of Gallicanism, an essentially French ecclesiastical doctrine advocating restriction of papal power. Following Consalvi's moderate lines, he negotiated concordats advantageous to the papacy with Hanover (1824) and with The Netherlands (1827). He condemned (May 1825) indifferentism, a doctrine advocating the equality of all religions, and Freemasonry, because of its secret practices that he considered pagan. That year he also revived the practice of holding jubilees, periodic observances in which all the faithful are invited to prayer and works of charity and penance for the sanctification of themselves and the world. After some hesitation he formally recognized (1827) the reorganized Hispanic dioceses; he had resisted because Spain demanded royal patronage in the Latin-American colonies.

• **Leo XIII,** original name VINCENZO GIOACCHINO PECCI (b. March 2, 1810, Carpineto Romano, Papal States—d. July 20, 1903, Rome), head of the Roman Catholic Church (1878–1903) who brought a new spirit to the papacy, manifested in more conciliatory positions toward civil governments, by care taken that the church not be opposed to scientific progress and by an awareness of the pastoral and social needs of the times.

Early career. Vincenzo Gioacchino Pecci was the sixth child of a family of the lower nobility. After his early education in Viterbo and Rome, he completed his studies at the Accademia dei Nobili Ecclesiastici (Academy of Noble Ecclesiastics) in Rome. In 1837 he was ordained a priest and entered the diplomatic service of the Papal States. His superiors immediately appreciated his qualities: flexibility and lucidity and great energy, despite

Leo XIII, 1878
The Bettmann Archive

his delicate health. Thus promotions came quickly; he was made delegate (the equivalent of provincial governor) of Benevento in 1838 and was transferred in 1841 to the more important delegation of Perugia. In January 1843 he was appointed nuncio (a papal legate of the highest rank, permanently attached to a civil government) to Brussels and shortly after was consecrated an archbishop.

Pecci's stay in Belgium, lasting only three years, was an important stage in the life of the future pope. He discovered how Catholics in a modern constitutional government could profit from the parliamentary system and from freedom of the press. But the Belgian nunciature halted the young prelate's career, which had begun so auspiciously. Pecci showed initiative and independence in several delicate situations, but he was severely criticized at the time, and King Leopold I, considering him less docile than his predecessor, soon demanded his recall.

He was then named, early in 1846, bishop of Perugia, a small diocese to which he was confined for 32 years, despite his having been made a cardinal in 1853. He suffered from this obscurity and made many attempts to win Rome's favour, but in vain: his harsh judgment of the opposition in the Papal States to the Roman Revolution of 1848 and his concern to avoid useless conflicts with the Italian authorities after the annexation of Umbria in 1860 made Rome suspect him—quite wrongly—of liberal sympathies and of tepidity with respect to temporal powers.

A weaker personality would undoubtedly have been dulled and embittered by this prolonged period of disfavour, but for Pecci these years of retreat were extremely fertile. He zealously applied himself to the systematic reorganization of his diocese and to the spiritual and intellectual improvement of his clergy. He also had available a great deal of leisure time in which to read and meditate. He occupied himself with the renewal of Christian philosophy and studied particularly the writings of St. Thomas Aquinas, the 13th-century Scholastic philosopher, to whom he had been introduced by his brother Giuseppe, a Jesuit seminary professor. He was also led to reconsider the problem of the relations between the church and modern society and became increasingly convinced of the mistake committed by ecclesiastical authorities in taking a fearful, negative attitude toward the aspirations of the times. The fruits of this silent maturation were revealed to his surprised contemporaries in his pastoral letters of 1877 and 1878, which attracted attention even beyond Italy's borders. He also received notice when, in 1877, he was named camerlengo, the office of chief administrator of the church in the event that the pope dies.

Pontificate. At the death of Pius IX in February 1878, Pecci's name was mentioned frequently among those of the principal *papabili,* those considered possible successors to the papacy. His candidacy was strongly supported by most of the non-Italian cardinals, who were impressed by the self-control and energy with which he acquitted his duties as camerlengo and who noted that one who had been away for so long from Rome would be less compromised by the decisions of the preceding pope. Cardinal Pecci was elected on Feb. 20, 1878, on the third ballot. He announced that he would take the name Leo in memory of Leo XII, whom he had always admired for his interest in education, for his conciliatory attitude toward temporal governments, and for his desire to create links with Christians who had separated from the Roman Catholic Church. The age of the new pope and his delicate health caused speculation that his pontificate would be brief. But, in fact, he directed the church for a quarter of a century.

The pontificate of Leo XIII's predecessor, Pius IX, had been long and controversial. From shortly after the beginning of his reign, Pius IX had been a strong, conservative authoritarian, both in his governing of the church and in his opposition to the new Italian government that annexed the Papal States. Although the pontificate of Leo XIII had a new spirit, the new pope was as intractable as his predecessor on the principle of the temporal sovereignty of the pope and continued to consider the traditional doctrine of the Christian state as an ideal. He reacted as strongly as had Pius IX against Freemasonry (a secret society that both popes viewed as opposed to Christianity) and secular liberalism. In church administration he continued to accentuate the centralization of authority in the papacy rather than in the national churches and reinforced the power of the nuncios. In addition, Leo XIII followed Pius IX in encouraging the devotion to the Sacred Heart of Jesus and to Mary. He renewed the condemnations of Rationalism—the theory that reason is the primary source of knowledge and of spiritual truth—and pursued with fresh vigour the reestablishment of the philosophy of St. Thomas Aquinas.

In other respects, however, there is no doubt that Leo XIII's pontificate was characterized by a new spirit. In his relations with civil governments, Leo XIII showed his preference for diplomacy. He achieved many incontestable successes through diplomacy, although his ability in this area was definitely less than is customarily asserted. The true greatness of Leo XIII was precisely that, in spite of his taste for politics, he was not exclusively a political pope. He was also an intellectual sympathetic to scientific progress and to the need for the Roman Catholic Church to demonstrate itself open to such progress, and he always remained a pastor who was concerned for the church's internal life and for the spreading of its message throughout the world.

This concern toward renewing the dialogue between the church and the world was manifested especially in his many encyclical letters giving instructions to Catholics throughout the world. In 1893 the encyclical *Providentissimus Deus* ("The Most Provident God"), now outdated but originally a pioneering work, defined in fairly broad-minded manner the principles on which Catholics should interpret the Bible. In several instructions he recommended that church and state live together in peace within the framework of modern society. The encyclical *Rerum Novarum* ("Of New Things") in 1891, though rather cautious in its approach, showed that the papacy had taken cognizance of the problems of the working class. He attempted to support the organization of the Catholic laity and was concerned about renewed dialogue with non-Catholics, as is demonstrated in the interest he showed in the attempt to create a link between the Anglican Church and Rome and in his respect for the traditions of the Eastern churches.

During the last years of Leo XIII's pontificate, until his death in 1903, there was a hardening of church policy and a more reserved attitude toward Christian democracy. Nevertheless, Leo XIII succeeded in gaining great prestige for the papacy, as was shown by the increase in countries having diplomatic relations with the Vatican, even non-Christian countries. He was a man gifted with a superior intelligence, an energetic temperament, a keen awareness of his personal worth, and a discriminating sense for public relations. Although his pontificate did not bring about many immediate changes in the relationship of the Roman Catholic Church to society, it did initiate many new attitudes that began to mature in succeeding decades. (R.-F.-M.A.)

BIBLIOGRAPHY. C. de T'Serclaes, *Le pape Léon XIII,* 3 vol. (1894–1906), gives the official Vatican viewpoint (the first two volumes were reviewed by the Pope himself); M. Spahn, *Leo XIII* (1905), offers critical evaluations (in German) from the point of view of German "Reformkatholizismus" ("Critical Catholicism"); a French point of view is found in F. Hayward, *Léon XIII* (1937). The essay by R. Aubert, "Léon XIII," in *I cattolici italiani dall'800 ad oggi,* pp. 189–220 (1964), utilizes the most recent works. On the various aspects of the work of Leo XIII as pope, see E.T. Gargan (ed.), *Leo XIII and the Modern World* (1961); and E. Soderini, *Il pontificato di Leone XIII,* 3 vol. (1932–33).

Leo (Latin: Lion), in astronomy, zodiacal constellation lying between Cancer and Virgo, at about 10 hours 30 minutes right ascension (the coordinate of the celestial sphere analogous to longitude on the Earth) and 15° north declination (angular distance north of the celestial equator). Regulus (Alpha Leonis), the brightest star, is of the first magnitude. The November meteor shower called the Leonid has its radiant, or point of apparent origin, in Leo.

Leo, illumination from a Book of Hours, Italian, *c.* 1475; in the Pierpont Morgan Library, New York City (MS. G.14)

By courtesy of the Pierpont Morgan Library, New York, the Glazier Collection

In astrology, Leo is the fifth sign of the zodiac, considered as governing the period *c.* July 23–*c.* August 22. Its representation as a lion is usually linked with the Nemean lion slain by Heracles (Hercules).

Leo AFRICANUS, Italian GIOVANNI LEONE, original Arabic AL-ḤASAN IBN MUḤAMMAD AL-WAZZĀN AZ-ZAYYĀTĪ, or AL-FĀSĪ (b. *c.* 1485, Granada, Kingdom of Granada—d. *c.* 1554, Tunis), traveller whose writings remained, for some 400 years, one of Europe's principal sources of information about Islām.

Educated at Fès, in Morocco, Leo Africanus travelled widely as a young man on commercial and diplomatic missions through North Africa and may also have visited the city of Timbuktu, now in Mali, as well as the valley of the Niger River. While in Egypt (1516–17), he ascended the Nile to Aswan. On his voyage homeward through the Mediterranean he was captured by Christian pirates and, because he revealed extraordinary intelligence, was presented as a gift to Pope Leo X. Impressed with his slave's learning, the pontiff freed him after a year and, having persuaded him to profess Christianity, stood sponsor at his baptism in 1520. As Giovanni Leone (John Leo), the new convert enjoyed favour in scholarly Roman society, learned Latin and Italian, and taught Arabic. Around 1526 he completed his greatest work, *Descrittione dell'Africa* (1550; *A Geographical Historie of Africa,* 1600). He eventually returned to North Africa, where he is believed to have died a Muslim.

Leo DE BAGNOLS, also called LEO HEBRAEUS: *see* Levi ben Gershom.

Leo THE ARMENIAN: *see* Leo V *under* Leo (Byzantine Empire).

Leo THE GREAT: *see* Leo I *under* Leo (Papacy).

Leo THE ISAURIAN: *see* Leo III *under* Leo (Byzantine Empire).

Leo THE KHAZAR: *see* Leo IV *under* Leo (Byzantine Empire).

Leo THE WISE, also called LEO THE PHILOSOPHER: *see* Leo VI *under* Leo (Byzantine Empire).

Leo, Heinrich (b. March 17, 1799, Rudolstadt, Thuringia—d. April 24, 1878, Halle, Ger.), Prussian conservative historian.

As a student at the universities of Breslau, Jena, and Göttingen, Leo joined the extreme revolutionary wing of the students' association. But, after reading Edmund Burke and Albrecht Haller and after a friend of his murdered the reactionary dramatist August von Kotzebue, Leo rejected radicalism and grew increasingly conservative. He taught at the universities of Berlin and Halle (1826–78).

As a historian Leo was a pioneer in acknowledging the importance of social and geographical factors in the development of a state. His first major work was *Geschichte der italienischen Staaten* (1829–32; "History of the Italian States"). His most ambitious work, *Lehrbuch der Universalgeschichte* (1839–44; "Textbook of Universal History"), was published in six volumes. Leo was a philologist as well as a historian, and he published several books on ancient Germanic languages. Leo was a leading opponent of the Prussian historian Leopold von Ranke.

Leo, Leonardo (Ortensio Salvatore de) (b. Aug. 5, 1694, S. Vito degli Schiavi, near Brindisi, Kingdom of Naples [Italy]—d. Oct. 31, 1744, Naples), composer who was noted for his comic operas and who was instrumental in forming the Neapolitan style of opera composition.

Leo entered the Conservatorio della Pietà dei Turchini at Naples in 1709, where his earliest-known work, a sacred drama, *L'infedeltà Abbattuta,* was performed by his fellow students in 1712. In 1714 he produced an opera, *Pisistrato,* for the court theatre. He later held various posts at the royal chapel and taught at the conservatory. His operas include *La 'mpeca scoperta* (1723), a comic opera in Neapolitan dialect; *Demofoonte* (1735) and *L'Olimpiade* (1737), both serious operas. Leo is probably best remembered for the comic opera *Amor Vuol Sofferenze* (1739). His sacred works include six or seven oratorios, of which *S. Elena al Calvario* (1732) was particularly esteemed; five or six masses; and a *Miserere* for double choir. He also wrote instrumental works, among them six concerti for cello and strings, organ fugues, and harpsichord toccatas. Leo's serious operas suffer from a coldness and severity of style, but in his comic operas he shows a keen sense of humour.

Consult the INDEX *first*

Leoben, town, *Bundesland* ("federal state") Steiermark, southeast-central Austria, on the Mur River, northwest of Graz. An ancient settlement, it was reestablished as a town by Ottokar II of Bohemia in about 1263. Medieval buildings include the Maria am Waasen Church (12th century, rebuilt 15th century) with magnificent Gothic stained-glass windows, the parish church (1660–65), and the bell tower that has become a symbol of the city. Leoben is the home of the University of Mining and Metallurgy, established 1840, as well as other technical schools. A centre of upper Styrian lignite mining, the town manufactures iron, textiles, and beer; it is also a tourist centre. The industrial suburbs of Donawitz and Göss were incorporated into Leoben in 1939. Pop. (1998 est.) 27,138.

Leochares (fl. mid-4th century BC), Greek sculptor to whom the "Apollo Belvedere" (Roman copy, Vatican Museum) is often attributed. About 353–*c.* 350 BC Leochares worked with Scopas on the Mausoleum at Halicarnassus, one of the Seven Wonders of the World. Most of his attributions are from ancient records. The base of a statue inscribed with his name, however, has been found in Athens. This work, a bronze lion hunt of Alexander, was executed by Leochares and Lysippus at Delphi. He was commissioned by King Philip of Macedon to produce gold and ivory statues of the king's family, which were installed in the Philippeum at Olympia about 338 BC. The Vatican statuette of "Ganymede and the Eagle" is thought to be a copy of a work by Leochares.

Leofric (d. Aug. 31, 1057, Bromley, Eng.), Anglo-Saxon earl of Mercia (from some date prior to 1032), one of the three great earls of 11th-century England, who took a leading part in public affairs. On the death of King Canute in 1035, Leofric supported the claim of Canute's son Harold to the throne against that of Hardecanute; and, during the quarrel between Edward the Confessor and Earl Godwine in 1051, he played the part of a mediator. Through his efforts civil war was averted, and in accordance with his advice the settlement of the dispute was referred to the Witan.

Because Chester was his principal residence and the seat of his government, he is sometimes called Earl of Chester. His wife was Godgifu, famous in legend as Lady Godiva (*q.v.*). Both husband and wife were noted as liberal benefactors to the church, among their foundations being the famous Benedictine monastery at Coventry.

Leominster, town ("parish"), unitary authority and historic county of Herefordshire, England, situated on the River Lugg, a tributary of the Wye. A religious house was founded on the site in 660, and the parish church of Saints Peter and Paul was the former priory church. The town was incorporated in 1554 and was a centre for the wool trade from the 13th to the 18th century. The contemporary economy is based on agricultural produce and livestock, and there are cattle and sheep markets. Agricultural implements also are manufactured. Half-timbered houses include the reconstructed 17th-century town hall. Pop. (1991) 9,543.

Leominster, city, Worcester county, north-central Massachusetts, U.S., on the Nashua River, just southeast of Fitchburg. The site, purchased from the Nashua Indians in 1701, was originally part of Lancaster. It was separately incorporated as a town in 1740 and named for Leominster, Eng. Combs, first made there in 1775 by Obadia Hills from animal horns, subsequently became the leading economic activity. After the introduction of celluloid as a material for comb making in the 20th century, a more diversified economy developed to include the manufacture of plastic articles, paper products, clothing, furniture, machinery, and chemicals. Leominster was the birthplace of the traveling orchardist John Chapman (Johnny Appleseed), and the Johnny Appleseed Civic Day is celebrated in June. Benjamin Hill and Pheasant Run ski areas are nearby. Inc. city, 1915. Pop. (2000) city, 41,303; Fitchburg-Leominster PMSA, 142,284.

Leon (personal name): *see under* Leo.

Leon, Spanish LEÓN, medieval Spanish kingdom. Leon proper included the cities of León, Salamanca, and Zamora—the adjacent areas of Vallodolid and Palencia being disputed with Castile, originally its eastern frontier. The kings of Leon ruled Galicia, Asturias, and much of the county of Portugal before Portugal gained independence about 1139.

The rise of the medieval Leonese kingdom began with García I (909–914), who set up his court on the site of the former Roman permanent camp of the Legio VII Gemina, abandoning the former Asturian capital at Oviedo (*see* Asturias). The period of Leonese hegemony in Christian Spain nominally lasted until the death of Alfonso VII (1157), but it had, long before, been seriously undermined by the conquests of Sancho III Garcés the Great (1000–35) of Navarre and by the elevation, on his death, of Castile from county to kingdom. During the 10th century, when the caliphate of Córdoba was at its most powerful, Leon lost ground in the struggle with the Moors, and its kings often had to accept a de facto submission to the caliphs. Leon, however, had inherited from the Asturian monarchy a strong attachment to Visigothic tradition, and its rulers, sometimes taking the title of emperor or king of all Spain, furthered the Reconquest wherever possible.

The second period in Leonese history runs from 1157 to 1230, when the kingdom was ruled, in separation from Castile, by its own kings, Ferdinand II (1157–88) and Alfonso IX (1188–1230). Relations with Castile were rarely friendly, but Leon was a stable political entity during this time and won notable victories over the Moors in Leonese Extremadura. After the final union with Castile (1230), Leonese political and administrative institutions were, for a time, maintained, and the records of the Cortes show that some sense of the separate identity of Leon survived into the first half of the 14th century.

During the first century of its existence, there was a large influx of Mozarabic immigrants into Leon. These introduced strong Arabic linguistical and cultural influences into the kingdom. Modern Spanish historiography—concerned often to justify medieval Castilian separatism—has tended to portray medieval Leon as an archaizing, Byzantine type of state overready to compromise with the Moors. The evidence for this is not wholly convincing. Leon successfully bore the brunt of the caliphate's attacks and seems to have been the first Peninsular kingdom to evolve popular parliamentary institutions.

The modern provinces of León, Salamanca, and Zamora, roughly coterminous with the medieval kingdom, were incorporated after 1979 into the *comunidad autónoma* ("autonomous community") of Castile-León (*q.v.*).

León, in full LEÓN DE LOS ALDAMAS, city, northwestern Guanajuato *estado* ("state"), central Mexico. It stands in a fertile plain on the Turbio River, 6,182 feet (1,884 m) above sea level. Although Léon was first settled in 1552, it was not formally founded until 1576 and was given city status in 1830. At that time the words "*de los Aldamas*" were added to its name, in honour of Juan Aldama, a leader in the struggle for Mexican independence.

Once subject to disastrous floods, the city is now protected by a large dam and has developed into an important industrial and commercial centre for the surrounding hinterland, considered one of the richest cereal-producing districts of Mexico. Leather goods, gold and silver embroideries, steel products, textiles, and soap are manufactured in the city, which also contains tanneries and flour mills. León, northwest of Mexico City and northeast of Guanajuato, can be reached by rail, highway, or air. Pop. (2000 prelim.) 1,133,576.

León, city situated in western Nicaragua. The city of León was founded on the edge of Lake Managua in 1524, but after an earthquake it was moved in 1610 to the site of the old Indian capital and shrine of Sutiaba. León was the capital of the Spanish province and of the Republic of Nicaragua until 1855, although its great political and commercial rival, Granada, long disputed the honour. The rivalry brought on civil wars that resulted in the coming of William Walker, the American filibuster, who was expelled in 1857. León was a scene of heavy fighting between Sandinista guerrillas and government troops in 1978–79, leaving much of the centre of the city in ruins.

León long has been noted as a liberal political and intellectual centre of Nicaragua. In 1952 the University of León (founded in 1812) became part of the National University of Nicaragua. Rubén Darío, one of the greatest Spanish-American poets, lived and was educated there. Nicaragua's second largest city, León is the centre of an important agricultural and commercial region: cotton, sugarcane, and rice are the principal crops; cattle are raised for export; and manufactures include processed cotton, cigars, shoes, and saddlery. León is linked to Managua, the national capital, and other cities by the Pacific Railway and a paved road. Pop. (1985 est.) 100,982.

León, *provincia,* in the Castile-León *comunidad autónoma* ("autonomous community"), northwestern Spain, consisting of the northern part of the former Kingdom of Leon. It has an area of 5,972 square miles (15,468 square km). In the north are the lofty Cantabrian Mountains, the highest peak of which is the Torre de Cerredo (8,668 feet [2,642 m]). The natural regions are El Bierzo, a lowland in the northwest drained by the Sil River, where mining has replaced agriculture; La Montaña; and the Meseta Central (plateau), a dry desert with fertile strips, as along the Orbigo River. The main catchment is the basin of the Esla River, a tributary of the Duero (Portuguese: Douro) River and site of a large dam at Ricobayo.

León is the leading producer of hops in Spain; other main crops include cereals and flax. The *provincia* also has timber resources (oak, beech, and chestnut), and cattle, donkeys, and sheep are bred. Mineral resources are considerable and include deposits of anthracite, iron, bituminous coal, and mica; Ponferrada is a major coal- and iron-mining area. Chemical factories in León (*q.v.*) city, the provincial capital, manufacture antibiotics. Pop. (1986 est.) 527,493.

León, city, capital of León *provincia,* in the Castile-León *comunidad autónoma* ("autonomous community"), northwestern Spain, lying on the northwestern part of the Meseta Central (plateau), at the confluence of the Bernesga and Torío rivers. The city developed from the camp of the Roman 7th Gemina Legion; its modern name is a corruption of the Latin *legio.* It was held by the Goths during the 6th and 7th centuries, falling to the Moors, who held it until 850. In the 10th century León became the capital of the kingdom of Asturias and Leon when García I transferred his court there from Oviedo. On the pilgrimage route to Santiago de Compostela, León exercised considerable political, cultural, and economic influence during the Middle Ages. It was an important commercial centre, with many craft guilds and well-known fairs and markets. The street names of the old part of the city recall the offices and structure of the medieval town. A monumental city with a wealth of artistic interest, it attracts large numbers of tourists. Especially notable are the fine Gothic cathedral of Santa María de Regla (founded 1199) with its fine stained-glass windows known as the Pulchra Leonina; the Romanesque collegiate church of San Isidoro (11th century); and the Renaissance-style church and monastery of San Marcos, converted into a state-run inn.

The economic life of the city declined in the 16th century and did not revive until the 19th with the development of mining. By the mid-20th century, León was resurgent, with a new city and industrialization. Pop. (1986 est.) 133,537.

Leon OF MODENA: *see* Modena, Leone.

León, Juan Ponce de: *see* Ponce de León, Juan.

León, Luis de (b. 1527, Belmonte, Cuenca Province, Spain—d. Aug. 23, 1591, Madrigal de las Altas), mystic and poet who contributed greatly to Spanish Renaissance literature.

Luis de León, engraving by Pacheco del Río
Archivo Mas, Barcelona

León was a monk educated chiefly at Salamanca, where he obtained his first chair in 1561. Academic rivalry between the Dominicans and the Augustinians, whom he had joined in 1544, led to his denunciation to the Inquisition for criticizing the text of the Vulgate, imprudent at that period in Spain, particularly because one of his great-grandmothers had been Jewish. After almost five years' imprisonment (1572–76), he was exonerated and restored to his chair, which, however, he resigned in favour of the man who had replaced him. But he subsequently gained a new one, also at Salamanca; a second denunciation, in 1582, did not succeed. His prose masterpiece, *De los nombres de Cristo* (1583–85), a treatise in the dialogue form popularized by the followers of Erasmus on the various names given to Christ in Scripture, is the supreme exemplar of Spanish classical prose style: clear, lofty, and, though studied, entirely devoid of affectation. His translations from Greek, Latin, Hebrew, and Italian include the Song of Solomon (modern edition by J. Guillén, 1936) and the Book of Job, both with commentary. León's poems, containing many of the motifs of *De los nombres de Cristo,* were posthumously published by Francisco Gómez de Quevedo y Villegas in 1631 because their sincerity of expression and emphasis on content rather than form were useful in the struggle against the attempts of the Gongorists to re-Latinize the language. The Spanish classicists of the 18th century used his lyrics as models. Among his more familiar poems are "Vida retirada" (1557; "Withdrawn Life") and "Noche Serena" (1571; "Serene Night"). His poetic works reflect the tension between his Horatian ideals of moderation and the turbulent life of a man of an honest and naturally pugnacious temperament inhabiting a world of ecclesiastical intrigue and rancorous academic politics. His other works include theological treatises and commentaries in Latin on various psalms and books of the Bible and *La perfecta casada* (1583; "The Perfect Married Woman"), a commentary in Spanish on Proverbs 31, incorporating elements of the medieval ascetic tradition of misogyny interspersed with picturesque glimpses of feminine customs of the day.

Leonard, Benny, byname of BENJAMIN LEINER (b. April 7, 1896, New York City—d. April 18, 1947, New York City), American world lightweight (135-pound) boxing champion from May 28, 1917, when he knocked out Freddy Welsh in nine rounds in New York City, until Jan. 15, 1925, when he retired. He is regarded as one of the cleverest defensive boxers in the history of professional boxing.

A professional fighter from 1911 to 1942, he had 210 bouts, winning 89 (45 by knockouts), with 115 no-decision bouts. He was noted for distracting his opponents by talking to them. Leonard retired after successfully defending the lightweight title seven times and losing on a foul in an attempt to win the welterweight (147-pound) championship from Jack Britton (June 26, 1922). In 1931–32, after several years of inactivity, he had numerous fights in the welterweight division, but he retired once more after being knocked out by Jimmy McLarnin on Oct. 7, 1932. He died while refereeing a bout in the St. Nicholas Arena, New York City.

Leonardi, Piero (b. Jan. 29, 1908, Valdobbiadene, Italy), Italian geologist and prehistorian, known for his research on the stratigraphy and paleontology of the Triassic invertebrates (from 190,000,000 to 225,000,000 years ago) and the Permian vertebrates (from 225,000,000 to 280,000,000 years ago).

Leonardi was a fellow at the University of Ferrara, Italy (1935–49), where he later served as professor of geology and director of the geology institute. His works include studies of the tectonics (the movement and deformation of the Earth's surface) and stratigraphy (the description and interpretation of rock successions) of the Dolomite Alps and development of a new theory on their evolution. He also discovered a new Mousterian prehistoric culture, the Bernardinian. He wrote *L'evoluzione dei viventi* (1950; "The Evolution of Living Things"), *Carlo Darwin* (1966), *Le Dolomiti* (1967), and *Trattato di geologia* (1963; "Treatise of Geology").

Leonardian Stage, post-Wolfcampian time of deposition of the Lower Permian Series of rock strata in the United States, especially well-developed in the Southwest (the Permian Period began about 280,000,000 years ago and lasted about 55,000,000 years). The Leonardian is defined on the basis of exposures seen in the Lenox hills in the Glass Mountains, Texas, where it consists of more than 600 m (2,000 feet) of gray, silty shales interbedded with light-gray limestones. In central Texas, Leonardian strata are seen as red beds, channel sandstones, gray shales, and thin, widespread limestones. These strata contain a well-developed reptile and amphibian faunal assemblage. In the Guadalupe Mountains and the Diablo Mountains, wholly marine Leonardian strata exhibit two strikingly distinct facies: a white limestone, the Victorio Peak Limestone, and a black, thin-bedded limestone formation, the Bone Spring Limestone. The Victorio Peak Limestone was deposited on a broad platform with shallow lagoons; the black Bone Spring Limestone accumulated in deep, poorly oxygenated, fetid basins where conditions were inimical to life and organically rich sediments accumulated slowly.

Leonardo DA VINCI (b. 1452, Vinci, Republic of Florence [now in Italy]—d. May 2, 1519, Cloux, Fr.), Italian painter, draftsman, sculptor, architect, and engineer whose genius, perhaps more than that of any other figure, epitomized the Renaissance humanist ideal. His "Last Supper" (1495–97) and "Mona Lisa" (1503–06) are among the most widely popular and influential paintings of the Renaissance. His notebooks reveal a spirit of scientific inquiry and a mechanical inventiveness that were centuries ahead of his time.

A brief account of the life and works of Leonardo da Vinci follows; for a full biography, *see* MACROPAEDIA: Leonardo da Vinci.

Leonardo was probably apprenticed to the sculptor Andrea del Verrocchio, receiving a diversified training, and painted in Florence until 1481. He worked (1482–99) in Milan as artist and technical adviser on architecture and engineering, already displaying his amazing versatility. After short visits to Mantua and Venice (1499/1500), he returned, honoured, to Florence, remaining there until 1506, though he visited Rome in 1502 and 1503. Again in Milan (1506–13), he later went, by way of Rome (1513–16), to France at the invitation of King Francis I. His prestige remained high at the French court and later contributed to Vasari's fable, now discredited, of Leonardo's having died in the arms of the king.

Leonardo's surviving works consist primarily of a few paintings together with many drawings, scientific diagrams, and notes on diverse subjects. Even though relatively little of his oeuvre has survived, Leonardo's genius has maintained its power to fire the imagination.

Leonardo PISANO, English LEONARDO OF PISA, original name LEONARDO FIBONACCI (b. *c.* 1170, Pisa?—d. after 1240), medieval Italian mathematician who wrote *Liber abaci* (1202; "Book of the Abacus"), the first European work on Indian and Arabian mathematics.

Life. Little is known about Leonardo's life beyond the few facts given in his mathematical writings. During Leonardo's boyhood his father, Guglielmo, a Pisan merchant, was appointed consul over the community of Pisan merchants in the North African port of Bugia (now Bejaïa, Alg.). Leonardo was sent to study calculation with an Arab master. He later went to Egypt, Syria, Greece, Sicily, and Provence, where he studied different numerical systems and methods of calculation.

When Leonardo's *Liber abaci* first appeared, Hindu-Arabic numerals were known to only a few European intellectuals through translations of the writings of the 9th-century Arab mathematician al-Khwārizmī. The first seven chapters dealt with the notation, explaining the principle of place value, by which the position of a figure determines whether it is a unit, 10, 100, and so forth, and demonstrating the use of the numerals in arithmetical operations. The techniques were then applied to such practical problems as profit margin, barter, money changing, conversion of weights and measures, partnerships, and interest. Most of the work was devoted to speculative mathematics—proportion (represented by such popular medieval techniques as the Rule of Three and the Rule of Five, which are rule-of-thumb methods of finding proportions), the Rule of False Position (a method by which a problem is worked out by a false assumption, then corrected by proportion), extraction of roots, and the properties of numbers, concluding with some geometry and algebra. In 1220 Leonardo produced a brief work, the *Practica geometriae* ("Practice of Geometry"), which included eight chapters of theorems based on Euclid's *Elements* and *On Divisions*.

The *Liber abaci,* which was widely copied and imitated, drew the attention of the Holy Roman emperor Frederick II. In the 1220s Leonardo was invited to appear before the emperor at Pisa, and there John of Palermo, a member of Frederick's scientific entourage, propounded a series of problems, three of which Leonardo presented in his books. The first two belonged to a favourite Arabic type, the indeterminate, which had been developed by the 3rd-century Greek mathematician Diophantus. This was an equation with two or more unknowns for which the solution must be in rational numbers (whole numbers or common fractions). The third problem was a third-degree equation (*i.e.,* containing a cube), $x^3 + 2x^2 + 10x = 20$ (expressed in modern algebraic notation), which Leonardo solved by a trial-and-error method known as approximation; he arrived at the answer

$$1^{0}\ 22^{\mathrm{I}}\ 7^{\mathrm{II}}\ 42^{\mathrm{III}}\ 33^{\mathrm{IV}}\ 4^{\mathrm{V}}\ 40^{\mathrm{VI}} \quad \left(1 + \tfrac{22}{60} + \tfrac{7}{3{,}600} + \tfrac{42}{216{,}000} + \cdots\right)$$

in sexagesimal fractions (a fraction using the Babylonian number system that had a base of 60), which, when translated into modern decimals (1.3688081075), is correct to nine decimal places.

Contributions to number theory. For several years Leonardo corresponded with Frederick II and his scholars, exchanging problems with them. He dedicated his *Liber quadratorum* (1225; "Book of Square Numbers") to Frederick. Devoted entirely to Diophantine equations of the second degree (*i.e.,* containing squares), the *Liber quadratorum* is considered Leonardo's masterpiece. It is a systematically arranged collection of theorems, many invented by the author, who used his own proofs to work out general solutions. Probably his most creative work was in congruent numbers—numbers that give the same remainder when divided by a given number. He worked out an original solution for finding a number that, when added to or subtracted from a square number, leaves a square number. His statement that $x^2 + y^2$ and $x^2 - y^2$ could not both be squares was of great importance to the determination of the area of rational right triangles. Although the *Liber abaci* was more influential and broader in scope, the *Liber quadratorum* alone ranks Leonardo as the major contributor to number theory between Diophantus and the 17th-century French mathematician Pierre de Fermat.

Except for his role in spreading the use of the Hindu-Arabic numerals, Leonardo's contribution to mathematics has been largely overlooked. His name is known to modern mathematicians mainly because of the Fibonacci sequence (see below) derived from a problem in the *Liber abaci:*

> A certain man put a pair of rabbits in a place surrounded on all sides by a wall. How many pairs of rabbits can be produced from that pair in a year if it is supposed that every month each pair begets a new pair which from the second month on becomes productive?

The resulting number sequence, 1, 1, 2, 3, 5, 8, 13, 21, 34, 55 (Leonardo himself omitted the first term), in which each number is the sum of the two preceding numbers, is the first recursive number sequence (in which the relation between two or more successive terms can be expressed by a formula) known in Europe. Terms in the sequence were stated in a formula by the French-born mathematician Albert Girard in 1634: $u_{n+2} = u_{n+1} + u_n$, in which u represents the term and the subscript its rank in the sequence. The mathematician Robert Simson at the University of Glasgow in 1753 noted that, as the numbers increased in magnitude, the ratio between succeeding numbers approached the number a, the golden ratio, whose value is 1.6180 . . . , or $(1 + \sqrt{5})/2$. In the 19th century the term Fibonacci sequence was coined by the French mathematician Edouard Lucas, and scientists began to discover such sequences in nature; for example, in the spirals of sunflower heads, in pine cones, in the regular descent (genealogy) of the male bee, in the related logarithmic (equiangular) spiral in snail shells, in the arrangement of leaf buds on a stem, and in animal horns. (F.C.Gi./Ed.)

BIBLIOGRAPHY. Joseph Gies and Frances Gies, *Leonard of Pisa and the New Mathematics of the Middle Ages* (1969), summarizes Leonardo's life and surveys his works, and contains a brief overview of the history of numerical notation and of medieval Pisa. Specialized treatments include Verner E. Hoggatt, Jr., *Fibonacci and Lucas Numbers* (1969), an introduction to the Fibonacci numbers and sequence, with propositions and exercises for mathematics students; N.N. Vorobev, *The Fibonacci Numbers* (1961); and Andreas N. Philippou, Gerald E. Bergum, and Alwyn F. Horadam (eds.), *Fibonacci Numbers and Their Applications* (1986).

Leonardo da Vinci Museum of Science and Technology, Italian MUSEO NAZIONALE DELLA SCIENZA E DELLA TECNICA "LEONARDO DA VINCI," in Milan, museum devoted to the evolution of science since the 15th century, including transport, metallurgy, physics, and navigation. It is housed in the old Olivetan convent of San Vittore, which dates from the early 16th century. The building has fine frescoes by Bernardino Luini. The Leonardo Gallery contains models of machines and inventions by Leonardo. Other galleries illustrate aspects of physics, astronomy, radio communications, optics, and telecommunications. There is also a collection of early motor cars. In an outside pavilion are some steam locomotives and airplanes.

A separate section founded in 1922 displays ship models and navigational instruments.

Leoncavallo, Ruggero (b. March 8, 1858, Naples—d. Aug. 9, 1919, Montecatini Terme, near Florence), Neapolitan opera composer whose fame rests on the opera *Pagliacci,* which, with Pietro Mascagni's *Cavalleria rusticana* (1890), represented a reaction against Richard Wagner and against Romantic Italian opera; both works substituted for the quasi-historical plot a sensational story from everyday life.

Leoncavallo

C. Cauboue—J.P. Ziolo

Leoncavallo studied at the Naples Conservatory and subsequently supported himself by giving café concerts and piano and singing lessons. His first operas, *Chatterton* (after Alfred de Vigny) and *I Medici* (first part of a projected trilogy inspired by the Italian Renaissance), failed to attract attention. He followed them with *Pagliacci,* composed in the *verismo,* or realistic, style of Mascagni. Produced in Milan in 1892, it was an immediate success. His *La Bohème* (1897) suffered from comparison with Giacomo Puccini's *La Bohème. Zazà* (1900) was more successful, but *Der Roland* (1904), commissioned by Wilhelm II to glorify the Hohenzollerns, was a failure. A number of later works achieved passing success. For most of his operas Leoncavallo was his own librettist and showed a distinct literary ability and a flair for theatrical effect.

Leone, Giovanni: *see* Leo Africanus.

Leone, Sergio (b. Jan. 3, 1929, Rome, Italy—d. April 30, 1989, Rome), motion-picture director known primarily for his popularization of the Italian "spaghetti western."

As the son of a film-industry pioneer, Leone became involved in Italian filmmaking at an early age. He worked for years as an assistant to Italian directors as well as American directors—such as Fred Zinnemann, Robert Wise, William Wyler, and Raoul Walsh—who were working in Italy.

Leone was a second-unit director on a number of productions and collaborated as a screenwriter for *Nel segno di Roma* (1958; *Sign of the Gladiator*) and *Gli ultimi giorni di Pompei* (1959; *The Last Days of Pompeii*). He chose *Il Colosso di Rodi* (1961; *The Colossus of Rhodes*), a pseudo-historical epic, for his directing debut and then went on to direct a series of stylized, violent westerns, including *Per un pugno di dollari* (1964; *A Fistful of Dollars*), *Per qualche dollaro in più* (1965; *For a Few Dollars More*), *Il buono, il brutto, il cattivo* (1966; *The Good, The Bad, and the Ugly*), and *C'era una volta il West* (1968; *Once Upon a Time in the West*). These films were extremely successful financially, attracting large audiences throughout the world. At first they were poorly received by critics, but Leone was eventually recognized for his meticulous care for historical accuracy and his powerful sense of visual composition. The last film he completed was *Once Upon a Time in America* (1984).

Leoni, Leone (b. 1509, Arezzo, republic of Florence [Italy]—d. 1590, Milan), Florentine sculptor, goldsmith, and medalist who had significant influence on Spanish sculpture.

During much of his career, Leoni was master of the imperial mint in Milan. His portrait medals of the Spanish court and his work on the high altar of the palace-monastery of El Escorial, produced in collaboration with his son Pompeo, have a refined, classical quality. Leoni's "Bust of Emperor Charles V" (1553–55) shows his powers of observation and deep sensitivity.

Other well-known works include "Charles V Restraining Fury" (1549–55) and "Charles V Triumphant over Discord," which has removable armour. Leoni's palatial residence in Milan, Casa Degli Omenoni (1565–70), is a tribute to the Roman emperor Marcus Aurelius; six larger-than-life-size sculptures of barbarians (possibly representing Aurelius' conquests) project from the house's facade.

Leoni, Pompeo (b. 1533, Milan [Italy]—d. Oct. 13, 1608, Madrid, Spain), Italian late Renaissance sculptor and medalist who, like his father, Leone, was known for his expressive sculpture portraits.

In 1556 Pompeo went to Spain to help his father. He produced a large-scale sculpture for the wedding of King Philip II and Anna of Austria in 1570. Also in that year, under the patronage of Philip II, he produced his most famous work, the bronze effigy portraits of the Holy Roman emperors Charles V and Philip II and their families, which now stand on either side of the main altar of the church of the monastic palace of El Escorial.

Leoni was appointed to serve the regent, Joan of Austria, and made Madrid his home. From 1576 to 1587 he worked on the tomb of Fernando de Valdés, archbishop of Seville and inquisitor general, which has life-size marble figures. The Spanish influence on Leoni's work is evident in his use of jewels.

Leonidas (d. 480 BC, Thermopylae, Locris [Greece]), Spartan king whose stand against the invading Persian army at the pass of Thermopylae in central Greece is one of the enduring tales of Greek heroism, invoked throughout Western history as the epitome of bravery exhibited against overwhelming odds.

A member of the Agiad house, Leonidas succeeded his half brother, Cleomenes I, as king, probably in 490. He was married to Cleomenes' daughter, Gorgo, and may have supported Cleomenes' aggressions against other Greek cities.

In 480 Leonidas commanded the small Greek force that resisted the advance through Thermopylae of the vast army of the Persian king Xerxes. For two days Leonidas withstood Persian attacks; he then ordered most of his troops to retreat, and he and his 300-member royal guard fought to the last man. This episode made a deep impression on the Greek imagination and gave rise to the legend that Spartans never surrendered.

Leonidas OF TARENTUM (fl. first half of the 3rd century BC), Greek poet more important for his influence on the later Greek epigram than for his own poems.

Leonidas was among the earlier Hellenistic epigrammatists, and about 100 of his epigrams survive, all but two collected in the *Greek Anthology.* They contain little personal information; he speaks of himself as an impoverished wanderer who expected to die far from home.

Leonidas is a facile versifier but seldom more. Not many of his sepulchral or dedicatory epigrams can have been intended for inscriptions; the deaths often seem contrived, the dedications highly ornate. For generations after his death, epigrammatists lacking inspiration aped his manner and composed variations on his poems.

Leonidov, Leonid Mironovich, pseudonym of L.M. VOL'FENZON (b. May 22, 1873, Odessa, Ukraine, Russian Empire—d. Aug. 6, 1941, Moscow, Russia, U.S.S.R.), Russian actor, director, and teacher who represented in his work and teaching the precepts of Konstantin Stanislavsky.

Leonidov studied at the Moscow Imperial Theatrical School and worked as an actor in Kiev, Odessa, and at Moscow's Korsh Theatre before joining the Moscow Art Theatre in 1903 to work under Stanislavsky. He made his debut there playing Pepel in Maksim Gorky's *The Lower Depths,* and, although he received favourable notice in a few comedy roles (Borkin in Anton Chekhov's *Ivanov* and Skalozub in Aleksandr S. Griboyedov's *Woe from Wit*), he went on to receive greater acclaim for his dramatic performances. His most brilliant performance was as Dmitry Karamazov in *The Brothers Karamazov* (1910). Among his outstanding roles were Cassio in *Julius Caesar* (1903) and the title roles in *Peer Gynt* (1912) and *Othello* (1930).

Leonidov's motion-picture career, begun in 1919, also emphasized his dramatic talents; his Ivan the Terrible in *The Wings of a Serf* (1926) and his portrayal of the title role in *Gobsek* (1935) are especially noteworthy. Leonidov was particularly adroit in conveying the theories and practice of his director, Stanislavsky, to theatre neophytes. He began teaching at the State Institute of Theatre Arts in 1935 and was its dean and artistic director from 1939 until his death.

He was also active as a theatre director; among his credits were stagings of Nikolay Y. Virta's *Earth* in 1937 and Gorky's *Dostigaev and the Others* in 1938. He was honoured as a People's Artist of the U.S.S.R. in 1936 and was the recipient of an Order of Lenin and an Order of the Red Banner of Labour.

Léonin, Latin LEONINUS (fl. late 12th century), leading liturgical composer of his generation, associated with the Notre Dame, or Parisian, school of composition.

The details of Léonin's life are not known. To him is attributed the *Magnus liber organi* (*c.* 1170; "Great Book of Organum"), a collection of two-voiced organum settings, notably of Gradual, Alleluia, and Responsory chants, for the complete liturgical year. (Organum is the elaboration of a plainchant melody by a countermelody sung above it.) In the *Magnus liber,* melismatic, or florid, and note-against-note, or "discantus," styles were combined within compositions characterized by the use of rhythmic modes, or short repeated patterns in triple rhythm. His discantus style is not strictly note-against-note but is an early instance in which the chant melody is organized into small rhythmic units with the same pulse as the added voice. *See also* organum; mode; rhythmic mode.

Leonov, Aleksey Arkhipovich (b. May 30, 1934, near Kemerovo, Russia, U.S.S.R.), Soviet cosmonaut, the first man to climb out of a spacecraft in space.

After early schooling in Kaliningrad, Leonov joined the Soviet air force in 1953. He completed his flight training in 1957 and served as a fighter pilot until 1959, when he was selected for cosmonaut training.

On March 18, 1965, Voskhod 2 was launched into space with Leonov and Pavel Belyayev aboard. During the second orbit Leonov let himself out of the spacecraft by means of an air lock while about 110 miles (177 km) above

Aleksey Leonov, 1968
Tass—Sovfoto

the Crimea. Tethered to the ship, Leonov made observations, took motion pictures, and practiced maneuvering in free-fall for about 10 minutes before reentering Voskhod 2 over western Siberia. The ship landed after completing 17 orbits (26 hours) in space. A decade later, Leonov was commander of the Soviet Soyuz craft that linked in orbit with the U.S. Apollo craft on July 17, 1975. Later in his career, he worked at the cosmonaut training centre.

Leonov, Leonid Maksimovich (b. May 19 [May 31, New Style], 1899, Moscow, Russia—d. Aug. 8, 1994, Moscow), Russian novelist and playwright who was admired for the intricate structure of his best narratives and for his ability to convey the complex moral and spiritual dilemmas faced by his characters. His multilayered, psychological approach was strongly influenced by—and often compared to—that of Fyodor Dostoyevsky.

Leonov went to school in Moscow and published his first stories in a newspaper in Arkhangelsk, where his father, the poet Maksim L. Leonov, had been exiled. He served as a soldier and journalist in the Red Army during the Russian Civil War (1918–20). In 1924, after publishing several more short stories and novellas, Leonov established his literary reputation with his epic first novel, *Barsuki* (*The Badgers*), which he followed with *Vor* (1927; *The Thief*), a pessimistic tale set in the Moscow criminal underworld.

His other major novels include *Sot* (1930; *Soviet River*), *Skutarevsky* (1932), and *Doroga na okean* (1935; *Road to the Ocean*). In the 1930s and '40s Leonov's fiction conformed somewhat more closely to the prevalent style of Socialist Realism, as did his 12 plays, 11 of which were staged in Moscow. His last major novel, *Russky les* (1953; *The Russian Forest*), won the Lenin Prize in 1957. Leonov devoted the remainder of his life to revising his earlier works. He was elected to the U.S.S.R. Academy of Sciences in 1972.

Leonowens, Anna Harriette, *née* CRAWFORD (b. Nov. 5, 1834, Carnarvon, Carnarvonshire, Wales—d. Jan. 19, 1914, Montreal, Que., Can.), British writer and governess employed by King Mongkut (Rama IV) of Siam for the instruction of his children, including his son and successor, Prince Chulalongkorn.

At age 15 Anna went to Asia, where she married Maj. Thomas Lewis Leonowens of the Indian Army. After the major died in 1858, she lived in Singapore with her two children until she was invited (1862) by King Mongkut to serve as governess to the royal children. For five years she was part of the royal household in Bangkok. After leaving Siam she wrote two books, *The English Governess at the Siamese Court* (1870) and *The Romance of the Harem* (1872). According to King Mongkut's biographer, Abbot Low Moffat (*Mongkut, the King of Siam*), Mrs. Leonowens' accounts of Siamese court life were exaggerated, and her description of King Mongkut as a cruel tyrant was unfair.

Her adventures in Siam inspired a popular book by Margaret Landon, *Anna and the King of Siam* (1944), on which was based the musical by Richard Rodgers and Oscar Hammerstein II, *The King and I,* two motion pictures, and a television serial.

Leontes (Lebanon): *see* Līṭānī, Nahr al-.

Leontief, Wassily (b. Aug. 5, 1906, Leningrad—d. Feb. 5, 1999, New York, N.Y.), Russian-born U.S. economist who has been called the father of input-output analysis in econometrics and who won the Nobel Prize for Economics in 1973.

Leontief was a student at the University of Leningrad (1921–25) and the University of Berlin (1925–28) and came to the United States in 1931, teaching at Harvard University from 1931 to 1975. From 1948 to 1975 he was director of the Harvard Economic Research Project on the Structure of the American Economy. In 1975 he became professor of economics at New York University, a position that he retained after being appointed director of the school's Institute for Economic Analysis three years later.

The core of his complex input-output system is a gridlike table showing what individual industries buy from and sell to one another. With the addition of government, consumers, foreign countries, and other elements, there emerges a general outline of the goods and services circulating in a national economy. The input-output method of economic analysis is used in more than 50 industrialized countries for planning and forecasting.

Leontief is also distinguished for having developed linear programming, a mathematical technique for solving complex problems of economic operations. He also is known for the "Leontief Paradox," his finding that, in the United States, capital rather than labour is the relatively scarce factor of production.

Among his major publications are *The Structure of the American Economy 1919–1929: An Empirical Application of Equilibrium Analysis* (1941) and *Input-Output Economics,* 2nd ed. (1986).

Leontini, ancient Greek town of southeastern Sicily, 22 miles northwest of Syracuse. Originally held by the Sicels (Siculi), its command of the fertile plain on the north made it an attractive site to the Chalcidians from Naxos, who colonized it in 729 BC. Early in the 5th century Hippocrates of Gela subjugated the city, and in 476, Hieron of Syracuse, having destroyed the towns of Catana and Naxos, relocated their inhabitants in Leontini. Twice the appeals of Leontini for aid led to unsuccessful Athenian expeditions into Sicily: in 427, following a Syracusan attack on the city, and in 415, when its democrats had been expelled by Syracuse-supported oligarchs. Marcus Claudius Marcellus stormed Leontini in 214 BC, as did the Muslims in AD 846–847. It was almost totally ruined by the earthquake of 1693.

The historian Polybius describes it as lying in a valley between two hills, each topped by an acropolis. Excavations in 1950 unearthed a Sicel hut village and the remains of the Castellaccio, a strongly fortified medieval castle, on the eastern acropolis.

The modern town of Lentini, Sicily, a prosperous agricultural centre of over 20,000 inhabitants, lies somewhat to the northwest of the original site.

Leontius OF BYZANTIUM (b. *c.* 485, probably Constantinople—d. *c.* 543, Constantinople), Byzantine monk and theologian who provided a breakthrough of terminology in the 6th-century Christological controversy over the mode of union of Christ's human nature with his divinity. He did so through his introduction of Aristotelian logical categories and Neoplatonic psychology into Christian speculative theology. His work initiated the later intellectual development of Christian theology throughout medieval culture.

Leontius became a monk while young and took active part at Rome in the theological disputes of the time. Moving to a new monastery near Jerusalem *c.* 520, he returned to Constantinople in 531 to participate in a conciliar meeting on the Christological question and, *c.* 542, to seek judgment in a dispute over monastic theology.

In the controversy over Christ, Leontius at first tended to favour the Nestorians (*q.v.*). Exposing certain of the Monophysites' (*q.v.*) fraudulent uses of patristic authorities, Leontius criticized them and the followers of Eutyches (*q.v.*). Later, however, in his principal work, *Libri tres contra Nestorianos et Eutychianos* ("Three Books Against the Nestorians and the Eutychians"), he assumed a moderate, orthodox position, having been influenced by the leading Nestorian adversary, Cyril of Alexandria.

The "Three Books," a primary source for verbatim expressions of the various theological schools, develops the concept that eventually played the key role in reaching a mediatory orthodox formulation at the general council of Constantinople in 553, thus integrating the partial conclusions from the previous councils at Ephesus in 431 and at Chalcedon in 451.

Involved with promoting the monastic influence of Origen (*q.v.*), Leontius was the object of a negative judgment at Constantinople.

A list of the abbreviations used in the MICROPAEDIA *will be found at the end of this volume*

Leontyev, Konstantin Nikolayevich, Leontyev also spelled LEONTIEV (b. Jan. 25 [Jan. 13, old style], 1831, Kudinovo, near Kaluga, Russia—d. Nov. 24 [Nov. 12, O.S.], 1891, near Moscow), Russian essayist who questioned the benefits derived by Russia from following contemporary industrial and egalitarian developments in Europe.

A military surgeon in the Crimean War, Leontyev later entered the Russian consular service, where he held posts in Crete, Edirne, and Salonika. In 1879 he became assistant editor of the newspaper *Varshavsky dnevnik* ("Warsaw Diary"), and a year later he joined the staff of the Moscow censorship department. In 1887 he settled in a small house near the Optina monastery, where he secretly took monastic vows but never lived under strict monastic discipline.

Leontyev wrote with a clarity and a persistent personal conviction rare among Russian political thinkers. He tried to find in the Russian empire an alternative which could civilize an Eastern world that already recoiled from the commercial-minded, democratic West. He elaborated this analysis and his answer to it in a number of remarkable essays, many of which were collected in the volume *Vostok, Rossiya i slavyanstvo* (1885–86; "The East, Russia and Slavdom"). Leontyev also wrote novels and short stories and a revealing autobiography, *Moya literaturnaya sudba* (1875; "My Literary Destiny"). He has been called the Russian Nietzsche.

leopard, formerly PARD, or PARDUS, also called PANTHER (*Panthera pardus*), large cat closely related to the lion, tiger, and jaguar. The name leopard was originally given to the cat now called cheetah—the so-called hunting leopard—which was once thought to be a cross between the lion and the pard. The term pard was eventually replaced by the name leopard.

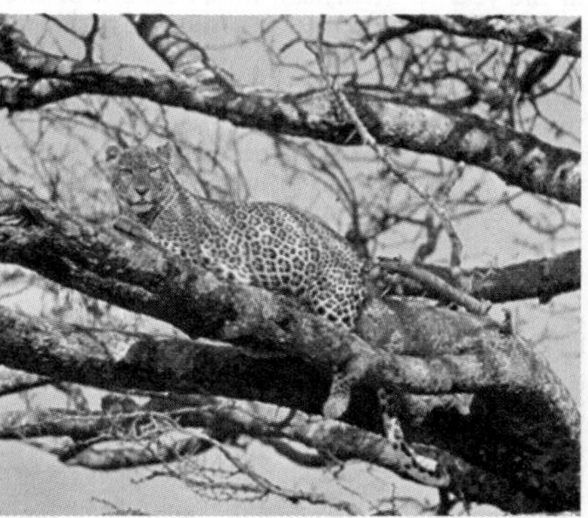

Leopard (*Panthera pardus*)
Leonard Lee Rue III

The leopard is found over nearly the whole of Africa south of the Sahara, in northeast Africa, and from Asia Minor through Central Asia and India to China and Manchuria. It varies greatly in size and markings. The average size is from 50 to 90 kilograms (110 to 200 pounds) in weight, 210 centimetres (84 inches), excluding the 90-cm tail, in length, and 60 to 70 cm in shoulder height. The leopard can, however, grow much larger. The ground colour is typically yellowish above and white below. Dark spots are generally arranged in rosettes over much of the body and are without the central spot characteristic of the coat of the jaguar (*q.v.*); the ground colour within the rosettes is sometimes a darker yellow, and the size and spacing of the spots vary greatly. As a result of these differences in pattern, several races of leopard have been named.

The leopard is a solitary animal of the bush and forest and is mainly nocturnal in habit, although it sometimes basks in the sun. It is an agile climber and frequently stores the remains of its kills in the branches of a tree. It feeds upon any animals it can overpower, from small rodents to waterbuck, but generally preys on the smaller and medium-sized antelopes and deer; it appears to have a special liking for dogs as food and, in Africa, for baboons. It sometimes takes livestock and may attack human beings.

There is no definite breeding season; the female produces from two to four, usually three, cubs after a gestation period of about three months. The calls of the leopard vary and include a series of harsh coughs, throaty growls, and deep, purring sounds. The animal takes to water readily and is a good swimmer.

A black form, in which the ground colour, as well as the spots, is black, is widely known as the black panther; it is more common in the Far East than in other parts of the range of the leopard. The races known as the Barbary, South Arabian, Anatolian, Amur, and Sinai leopards are listed as endangered in the *Red Data Book.*

The lion, tiger, leopard, and jaguar also belong to the genus *Panthera.* The ounce (snow leopard), leopard cat, and clouded leopard (*qq.v.*), although called leopards, are distinct genera.

leopard cat (*Felis bengalensis*), forest-dwelling cat, family Felidae, found in India and Southeast Asia and noted for its leopard-like colouring. The coat of the leopard cat is usually yellowish or reddish brown above, white below, and heavily marked with dark spots and streaks. Length of the animal ranges from 45 to 75 centimetres (18 to 30 inches) excluding the 23–35-cm tail. The leopard cat is a nocturnal hunter, preying on birds and small mammals (including domestic fowl in some areas). It breeds in spring (possibly again later in the year in Malaysia); litters consist of two to four young, and the gestation period is about 56 days.

leopard frog (*Rana pipiens*), North American frog (family Ranidae) often used in laboratories and, for teaching purposes, in schools. It is a common frog found in the United States and Canada, and it frequents a variety of habitats, including marshes, meadows, and ponds. It often strays far from water.

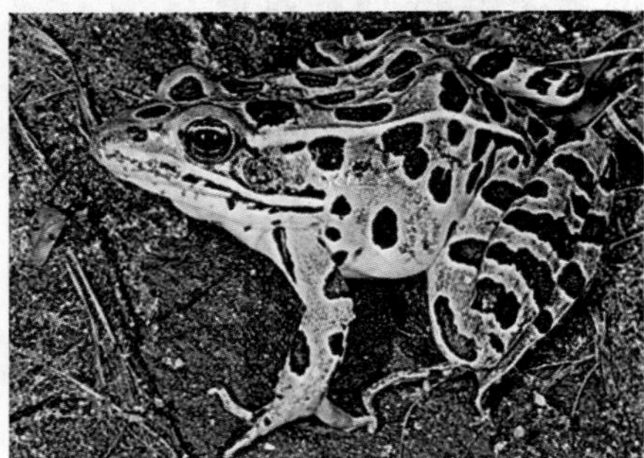

Leopard frog (*Rana pipiens*)
John Kohout—Root Resources

The leopard frog is about 5 to 13 centimetres (2 to 5 inches) long and is gray, green, or brown with paler lengthwise ridges on its back. Light-edged, dark spots are usually present on the upper surface of the body. Its call consists of throaty snoring and grunting sounds. Its close relatives—the southern leopard frog (*R. utricularia*), the plains leopard frog (*R. blairi*), the Rio Grande leopard frog (*R. berlandieri*), and the pickerel frog (*R. palustris*)—are similar and extend the family's range into Mexico.

leopard lily: *see* blackberry lily.

leopard lizard, any member of the species *Gambelia* (or *Crotaphytus*) *wislizeni* in the lizard family Iguanidae. These large, spotted lizards are inhabitants of arid and semi-arid areas in the southwestern United States and northern Mexico.

Leopard lizards feed upon a variety of insects, seeds, and flowers as well as on small mammals and other lizards. When disturbed they can run rapidly across open habitat using only the hind feet. Leopard lizards lay 2–10 white shelled eggs and exhibit no signs of parental care.

leopard moth (*Zeuzera pyrina*), widely distributed insect of the family Cossidae (order Lepidoptera), known particularly for its destructive larva.

The adult moth has a fluffy white body and pale wings (span about four to six centimetres) with numerous black or blue spots and blotches. They fly at night and are strongly attracted to bright lights. Larvae bore into stems of shrubs and trees, especially apples, pears and plums, where they do much damage by eating the heartwood. When fully grown the larva is about 5 cm long, white and fleshy with black spots and a dark head capsule. Development takes two or three years.

leopard seal, also called SEA LEOPARD (*Hydrurga leptonyx*), generally solitary, earless seal (family Phocidae) that inhabits Antarctic and sub-Antarctic regions. The only seal that feeds on penguins, young seals, and other warm-blooded prey, the leopard seal is a slender animal with a relatively long head and long, three-cusped cheek teeth. It is named for its black-spotted, gray coat, and it attains a maximum length and weight (greater in the female) of about 3.5 metres (12 feet) and 380 kilograms (840 pounds). The leopard seal has a reputation for ferocity but is not known to make unprovoked attacks on man; it is of no commercial importance.

Leopard seal (*Hydrurga leptonyx*)
John Warham

leopard shark (*Triakis semifasciata*), small shark of the family Triakidae found in shallow water along the Pacific coast of the United States. A slim, narrow-headed shark with small, three-cusped teeth, it grows about 90 to 150 centimetres (3 to 5 feet) long. It is gray, distinctively marked with transverse black bars on its back and black spots on its sides. It preys on fishes and crustaceans. Though often considered harmless to man, it may bite.

Leopard shark (*Triakis semifasciata*)
Painting by Richard Ellis

Leopardi, Giacomo (b. June 29, 1798, Recanati, Papal States—d. June 14, 1837, Naples), Italian poet, scholar, and philosopher whose outstanding scholarly and philosophical works and superb lyric poetry place him among the great writers of the 19th century.

A precocious, congenitally deformed child of noble but apparently insensitive parents, Giacomo quickly exhausted the resources of his tutors. At the age of 16 he independently had mastered Greek, Latin, and several modern languages, had translated many classical works, and had written two tragedies, many Italian poems, and several scholarly commentaries. Excessive study permanently damaged his health: after bouts of poor vision, he eventually became blind in one eye and developed a cerebrospinal condition that afflicted him all his life. Forced to suspend his studies for long periods, wounded by his parents' unconcern, and sustained only by happy relationships with his brother and sister, he poured out his hopes and his bitterness in poems such as *Appressamento della morte* (written 1816, published 1835; "Approach of Death"), a visionary work in terza rima, imitative of Petrarch and Dante but written with considerable poetic skill and inspired by a genuine feeling of despair.

Two experiences in 1817 and 1818 robbed Leopardi of whatever optimism he had left: his frustrated love for his married cousin, Gertrude Cassi (subject of his journal *Diario d'amore* and the elegy "Il primo amore"), and the death from consumption of Terese Fattorini, young daughter of his father's coachman, subject of one of his greatest lyrics, "A Silvia." The last lines of this poem express the anguish he felt all his life: "O nature, nature, / Why dost thou not fulfill / Thy first fair promise? / Why dost thou deceive / Thy children so?"

Leopardi's inner suffering was lightened in 1818 by a visit from the scholar and patriot Pietro Giordani, who urged him to escape from his painful situation at home. At last he went to Rome for a few unhappy months (1822–23), then returned home for another painful period, brightened only by the 1824 publication of his verse collection *Canzoni.* In 1825 he accepted an offer to edit Cicero's works in Milan. For the next few years he travelled between Bologna, Recanati, Pisa, and Florence and published *Versi* (1826), an enlarged collection of poems; and *Operette morali* (1827; "Minor Moral Works"), an influential philosophical exposition, mainly in dialogue form, of his doctrine of despair.

Lack of money forced him to live at Recanati (1828–30), but he escaped again to Florence through the financial help of friends and published a further collection of poems, *I canti* (1831). Frustrated love for a Florentine beauty, Fanny Targioni-Tozzetti, inspired some of his saddest lyrics. A young Neapolitan exile, Antonio Ranieri, became his friend and only comfort.

Leopardi moved to Rome, then to Florence, and finally settled in Naples in 1833, where, among other works, he wrote *Ginestra* (1836), a long poem included in Ranieri's posthumous collection of his works (1845). The death that he had long regarded as the only liberation came to him suddenly in a cholera epidemic in Naples.

Leopardi's genius, his frustrated hopes, and his pain found their best outlet in his poetry, which is admired for its brilliance, intensity, and effortless musicality. His finest poems are probably the lyrics called "Idillii" in early editions of his poetry, among which is "A Silvia." One English translation of his prose works is James Thomson's *Essays, Dialogues, and Thoughts* (1905). Among many translations of Leopardi's poetry are R.C. Trevelyan's *Translations From Leopardi* (1941) and J.-P. Barricelli's *Poems* (1963).

leopard's bane, any plant of the genus *Doronicum* of the family Asteraceae, consisting of about 20 to 30 species of perennial herbs native to Eurasia. They have large flower heads with yellow disk flowers and one row of yellow ray flowers.

Leopard's bane (*Doronicum grandiflorum*)
Anthony J. Huxley—EB Inc.

Some leaves are clustered at the base and others alternate along and sometimes clasp the stout, usually single stem. Several species, especially *D. cordatum* and *D. plantagineum,* are cultivated as garden ornamentals.

Leopold, name of rulers grouped below by country and indicated by the symbol •.

Foreign-language equivalents:

Dutch	Leopold
French	Leopold
German	Leopold
Hungarian	Lipot
Italian	Leopoldo

ANHALT-DESSAU

• Leopold I, byname THE OLD DESSAUER, German DER ALTE DESSAUER (b. July 3, 1676, Dessau, Prussia—d. April 7, 1747, Dessau), prince of Anhalt-Dessau, Prussian field marshal and reformer, inventor of the iron ramrod and responsible for the introduction of the modern bayonet; he founded the old Prussian military system that, generally unchanged until 1806, enabled Frederick II the Great to propel Prussia to the position of a European power.

Beginning his military career serving against the French in 1695, Leopold commanded the Prussian contingent in the allied forces during most of the War of the Spanish Succession (1701–14). A friend of the Austrian field marshal Prince Eugene of Savoy, he fought in Germany, Italy, the Netherlands, and France, distinguishing himself at the battles of Höchstädt an der Donau (Bavaria; 1703), Cassano d'Adda (Italy; 1705), Turin (1706), Tournai (Belgium), and Malplaquet (France; both 1709). In 1715 he commanded the Prussian Army against Charles XII of Sweden, defeating him at Stralsund and on the island of Rügen.

The long peace that followed gave Leopold the chance to use his considerable organizational talents. Introducing the iron ramrod (wooden ones tended to break in the heat of battle), the modern bayonet (replacing the plug bayonet that had to be removed from the barrel to fire the weapon), and the uniform marching step in his own regiment in the late 1690s, he extended these improvements to the entire Prussian Army after 1715. Under his strict, often brutal tutelage, the Prussian infantry achieved the discipline and rapidity of fire that made possible Frederick II's victories against vastly more numerous and powerful foes. In this endeavour, Leopold had the confidence and cooperation of his monarch, King Frederick William I (ruled 1713–40). As a result of his experience in the field, the Prince always favoured his own branch of the service, infantry, over cavalry and artillery.

After the succession of Frederick II in 1740, war again broke out. Leopold, by now an old man, once more took a field command. On Dec. 14, 1745, as Frederick was hurrying to his aid, the "Old Dessauer" defeated a superior Austrian and Saxon army at Kesselsdorf, Saxony, the final action of his long career.

AUSTRIA

• Leopold I–II: *see* Leopold I–II (Germany/Holy Roman Empire).

BELGIUM

• Leopold I, French in full LÉOPOLD-GEORGES-CHRÉTIEN-FRÉDÉRIC, Dutch in full LEOPOLD GEORGE CHRISTIAAN FREDERIK (b. Dec. 16, 1790, Coburg, Saxe-Coburg-Saalfeld—d. Dec. 10, 1865, Laeken, Belg.), first king of the Belgians (1831–65), who helped strengthen the nation's new parliamentary system and, as a leading figure in European diplomacy, scrupulously maintained Belgian neutrality.

The fourth son of Francis, duke of Saxe-Coburg-Saalfeld, Leopold served with the allies against Napoleon's forces during the Napoleonic Wars (1800–15); in 1816 he married Charlotte, the only child of the future king George IV of Great Britain. Although the Princess died in 1817, Leopold continued to

Leopold I, photograph by Nadar (Gaspard-Félix Tournachon)
Archives Photographiques, Paris

live in England until 1831, when he accepted his election as king of the Belgians, having declined the Greek crown the previous year. He immediately began to strengthen the Belgian Army and, with assistance from France and England, fought off the attacks of William I of The Netherlands, who refused until 1838 to recognize Belgium as an independent kingdom.

Until 1839 Leopold helped maintain a Liberal–Catholic coalition that expanded the educational system. In 1836 he granted greater political autonomy to large towns and rural areas. The coalition ended in 1839 with the removal of Dutch pressure through William I's recognition of the Belgian kingdom. Leopold signed commercial treaties with Prussia (1844) and France (1846) and maintained a neutral foreign policy, most notably during the Crimean War (1853–56). His throne was not seriously challenged during the revolutions of 1848. After the accession of a hostile regime under Napoleon III in France (1852), he sponsored a fortification of the Antwerp area, completed in 1868.

Often referred to as the "Nestor of Europe," Leopold was highly influential in European diplomacy and used marriages to strengthen his ties with France, England, and Austria. He married Marie-Louise of Orléans, daughter of the French king Louis-Philippe, in 1832; in 1840 he helped to arrange the marriage of his niece Victoria, queen of England, to his nephew Prince Albert of Saxe-Coburg-Gotha. He also helped negotiate the marriage of his daughter Carlota to Maximilian, archduke of Austria and later emperor of Mexico, in 1857. Leopold's influence declined with the growing power of Napoleon III and of Otto von Bismarck of Prussia.

• Leopold II, French in full LÉOPOLD-LOUIS-PHILIPPE-MARIE-VICTOR, Dutch in full LEOPOLD LODEWIJK FILIPS MARIA VICTOR (b. April 9, 1835, Brussels—d. Dec. 17, 1909, Laeken, Belg.), king of the Belgians from 1865 to 1909; he led the first European efforts to develop the Congo Basin, making possible the formation of the Congo Free State in 1885, annexed in 1908 as the Belgian Congo (now Zaire).

The eldest son of Leopold I, first king of the Belgians, and his second wife, Marie-Louise of Orléans, Leopold became duke of Brabant in 1846 and served in the Belgian Army. In 1853 he married Maria Henrietta, daughter of the Austrian archduke Joseph, palatine of Hungary, and became king of the Belgians on his father's death in December 1865. Although the domestic affairs of his reign were dominated by a growing conflict between the Liberal and Catholic parties over suffrage and education issues, Leopold II concentrated on developing the nation's defenses. Aware that Belgian neutrality, maintained during the Franco-German War (1870–71), was imperilled by the increasing strength of France and Germany, he persuaded Parliament in 1887 to finance the fortification of Liège and Namur. A military conscription bill, for which he had long argued, was passed shortly before his death.

Leopold had meanwhile become deeply involved in the Congo region, founding the Association Internationale du Congo (1876) to explore the area, with Sir Henry Morton Stanley as his main agent. In 1884–85 he defeated an Anglo-Portuguese attempt to conquer the Congo Basin and gained recognition by the U.S. and the leading European powers as the sovereign of the État Indépendant du Congo (Congo Free State), an area 80 times the size of Belgium. The chief industry, wild rubber

Leopold II, portrait by Louis-Joseph Ghemar
By courtesy of the Bibliotheque Royale Albert I, Brussels

production, became especially lucrative after 1891, but in 1904 exposure of mistreatment of natives in the rubber industry marked the onset of the decline of Leopold's personal rule in the region. Great Britain, with U.S. aid, pressured Belgium to annex the Congo state to redress the "rubber atrocities"; the area became part of Belgium in November 1908. Since Leopold's only son had predeceased him, a nephew, Albert I, succeeded to the throne.

• Leopold III, French in full LÉOPOLD-PHILIPPE-CHARLES-ALBERT-MEINR AD-HUBERTUS-MARIE-MIGUEL, Dutch in full LEOPOLD FILIPS KAREL ALBERT MEINRAD HUBERTUS MARIA MIGUEL (b. Nov. 3, 1901, Brussels—d. Sept. 25, 1983, Brussels), king of the Belgians whose actions as commander in chief of the Belgian Army during the German conquest of Belgium (1940) in World War II aroused opposition to his rule, eventually leading to his abdication in 1951.

The son of Albert I and his consort Elisabeth of Bavaria, Leopold served as a private soldier during the final campaign of World War I. On Nov. 10, 1926, he married Princess Astrid of Sweden (died August 1935); their children were Joséphine-Charlotte, Baudouin, and Albert. Leopold became king of the Belgians following his father's death on Feb. 17, 1934. Favouring an independent foreign policy, but not strict neutrality, he withdrew Belgium from its defensive alliance with France and from the Pact of Locarno—a peace agreement among Germany, France, Belgium, Italy, and Great Britain—after German occupation of the Rhineland (1936). Determined to resist aggression with help from Britain and France, he sponsored construction of a fortified defense line from Antwerp to Namur, facing Germany.

With the outbreak of World War II, Leopold assumed supreme command of the Belgian Army and surrendered his encircled forces on

May 28, 1940, 18 days after the German invasion began. The Belgian government's repudiation of his decision to surrender and to remain with his troops, rather than join the London government in exile, laid the foundation for the postwar conflict over his claim to the throne. He was held prisoner by the Germans at his royal château near Brussels until 1944 and then in Austria to the end of the war. His letter to Adolf Hitler in 1942 is credited with saving an estimated 500,000 Belgian women and children from deportation to munitions factories in Germany. He married Mary-Lilian Baels on Sept. 11, 1941, whom he made princesse de Réthy; their children were Alexandre, Marie-Christine, and Maria Esmeralda.

After his brother Charles had been appointed regent in 1944, Leopold remained in Switzerland (1945–50), awaiting resolution of the "royal question," the controversy over his pending return to the throne. In a plebiscite held March 12, 1950, nearly 58 percent of the voters favoured the King's return, largely reflecting Catholic Fleming support. But unrest fomented by Liberal, Socialist, and Walloon opposition led Leopold to renounce his sovereignty on Aug. 11, 1950, in favour of his son Baudouin, who became king the following year. Leopold and the princess de Réthy continued to live in Laeken, however, the traditional home of Belgian kings, until his son's marriage in 1969. Critics of Leopold had felt that his residence in Laeken gave him too much influence over King Baudouin.

GERMANY/HOLY ROMAN EMPIRE

•**Leopold I** (b. June 9, 1640, Vienna—d. May 5, 1705, Vienna), Holy Roman emperor during whose lengthy reign (1658–1705) Austria emerged from a series of struggles with the Turks and the French to become a great European power, in which monarchical absolutism and administrative centralism gained ascendancy.

Leopold I, detail of a portrait bust, *c.* 1700; in the Kunsthistorisches Museum, Vienna
By courtesy of the Kunsthistorisches Museum, Vienna

Early years. Leopold, the second son of Ferdinand III's first marriage, to his cousin Maria Anna, daughter of Philip III of Spain, was destined for the church. He received a careful education by excellent teachers, among whom the cultured count Johann Ferdinand Portia was the leading personality. Made lord high steward by his pupil, Portia retained his influence with Leopold until his death in 1665. From an early age Leopold showed an inclination toward learning. He learned easily and became fluent in Latin, Italian, and Spanish, but he did not like French and later would not have it spoken at court. Besides concerning himself with antiquarian studies, history, literature, natural science, and astronomy, his special interest was music, having inherited the musical talents of his father. The keynote of his personality was a deep devotion, which made him the personification of *pietas Austriaca,* the loyal Catholic attitude of his house. From his religiosity, however, also derived a fatalistic strain, which had its negative side for a ruling monarch. He rejected all political compromising on denominational questions.

Accession. When his elder brother, Ferdinand IV, died quite unexpectedly (July 9, 1654), Leopold suddenly found himself heir apparent to the Austrian Habsburg lands. In 1655 the Lower Austrian estates did homage, and he was elected and crowned king of Hungary, the Bohemian coronation following in 1656. Then, in 1657, his father died, and a new imperial election was due. After long and difficult struggles against the opposition of France, Leopold was elected and crowned in the summer of 1658.

Leopold acquired a claim to the Spanish throne by his first marriage, in 1666, to Margarita Teresa, daughter of Philip IV of Spain; she died in 1673. Leopold's health was bad, and, when he fell dangerously ill in 1670, everybody expected the Austrian line of the Habsburgs to become extinct. He recovered, however, and in 1673 married Claudia Felicitas from the Tirolian branch of the Austrian Habsburgs. In 1676 the Emperor solemnized his third marriage, with Eleonore of Palatinate–Neuburg; this proved a happy union and produced 10 children, among them the future emperors Joseph I and Charles VI.

With untiring energy and a deep sense of duty, Leopold undertook the unwonted task of government. From the beginning he had to fight wars, first of all against the Turks. In 1683 they appeared before Vienna, and for the second time in its history the city suffered a Turkish siege. Leopold had left the capital with his court to await the outcome at Passau. An imperial army was summoned, and from the time of their repulse at Vienna the Turks were gradually forced into the defensive, especially after the military genius of Prince Eugene of Savoy appeared on the scene in 1696. In the Treaty of Carlowitz (1699), almost the whole of Hungary was freed from Turkish rule.

The Hungarian nobles, however, who were mostly Calvinists, did not want to exchange Turkish rule for a centralized Habsburg government, which threatened to introduce the Counter-Reformation. Their opposition had been a serious problem all the time, and Leopold, who usually showed clemency, took a firm stand for once, refusing to recall the cruel sentences after the so-called Nobles' Plot. Three of the most prominent Hungarian noblemen were executed, and Hungarian resistance flared up again in the fierce Kuruc risings.

The struggle with France. Though Leopold's policy toward Catholic France was undecided at first, he finally had to agree to a coalition with the Protestant naval powers, Holland and England. In the course of the long struggle with France, the empire scored several military successes; but in the end French diplomacy remained victorious, always dividing the enemy at the decisive moment. The Emperor was accused of a wavering attitude and lack of initiative, and these character traits were indeed partly responsible for the failure of his policies. The war ended in the unfavourable Treaty of Rijswijk (1697), under the terms of which Strasbourg had to be ceded to France, a great discredit to Leopold.

Apart from some contributions from the empire and subsidies from its allies, the financial burden of all these wars had to be borne by Leopold's hereditary countries, the finances of which were badly organized. During his long reign Leopold found it impossible to arrive at a sound financial basis; indeed, he was careless in these matters and for years suffered the treasury to be mismanaged by Count Sinzendorf.

Emperor Leopold was not always fortunate in the choice of his ministers. There was, for example, Count Eusebius Pötting, with whom he had formed a warm friendship but who was not the right man for the post of ambassador to Madrid. On the other hand, councillors who had convinced the Emperor of their sincerity and honesty found excellent chances for a court career, even if they were middle class, like the Austrian court chancellor Johann Paul Hocher.

Leopold no longer regarded the empire as his primary responsibility; rather, in his view, concern for the power and prestige of the Habsburg dynasty and lands took the first place. From the outset the Spanish succession formed the central aim of his politics. What lay behind this was the idea of the unity of the House of Habsburg, the two lines being considered only as parts of the same entail. At the death (1700) of the childless Charles II of Spain, his throne and the vast Spanish holdings passed by bequest to Philippe, duc d'Anjou, a grandson of Louis XIV of France. There could be no question for Emperor Leopold that the Spanish heritage had to be defended by force of arms. In the middle of the War of the Spanish Succession (*q.v.*; 1701–14), Leopold died. He was buried in the Habsburg mausoleum of the Capuchins at Vienna.

Personal traits. The Emperor was of medium size, rather slender in his youth but stout in later life. His face was pale, and he had dark hair and the typical Habsburg traits of a strongly developed lower lip and a protruding chin. A Turkish traveller described him as a cultivated man of extreme ugliness.

If the Emperor, who had not been trained for the throne, rarely interfered with the course of events, he, nevertheless, impressed contemporaries with an imperturbability founded in personal piety, which did not fail him even during the worst crises to his long reign. His biographer, the Jesuit Hans Jacob Wagner von Wagenfels (died 1702), quite aptly praises his magnanimity as his most conspicuous character trait. The interest Leopold took in all matters of learning, his gift for music, and his preoccupation with historiography made him a patron of renown and, notwithstanding the military conflicts of the time and his precarious finances, gave enormous impetus to learning and the arts throughout the Austrian countries and especially made Vienna a famous cultural centre. His reign saw the first flourishing of Baroque culture in Austria.

In spite of the Emperor's great personal simplicity, the sums expended to maintain the imperial court were gigantic. At all occasions the Emperor was anxious to emphasize his imperial dignity; official journeys, such as his coronation journey to Frankfurt in 1658, as well as the numerous pilgrimages he undertook to assure divine assistance against his enemies, were used for ostentation. A special concern of the Emperor was to reshape Vienna into a worthy imperial residence. The Vienna court was famous for its costly theatricals, in which at times the Emperor and Empress also took part. Italian operas and ballets were lavishly staged, often with some additional music composed by Leopold himself. As the Emperor was very fond of hunting, courtly pleasures also included heron hawking and hunting wild boars and stags in the vicinity of the residence. Though Leopold undertook no more extensive journeys after 1693, he enjoyed these regular hunting expeditions until his death.

Leopold I was a devoted book collector and, in the director of the court library, Peter Lambeck, found a helper of great renown. He was known for the encouragement he extended to learning, whereby he tried to secure the services of famous scholars for his court.

(H.Di./Ed.)

BIBLIOGRAPHY. The best presentation of his reign is still to be found in Oswald Redlich, *Weltmacht des Barock: Österreich in der Zeit Kaiser Leopolds I.* (1927, reprinted 1961) and *Das Werden einer Grossmacht: Österreich von 1700 bis 1740,* 2nd ed. (1942, reprinted 1962), with references to source materials and a detailed bibliography. A good biography in English is John P. Spielman, *Leopold I of Austria* (1977). A modern summary of recent research may be found in Erich Zollner, *Geschichte Österreichs,* 4th ed. (1970), with bibliography.

• **Leopold II** (b. May 5, 1747, Vienna—d. March 1, 1792, Vienna), Holy Roman emperor from 1790 to 1792, one of the most capable of the 18th-century reformist rulers known as the "enlightened despots."

The third son of the Habsburg Maria Theresa and the emperor Francis I, Leopold succeeded his father as duke of Tuscany when his eldest brother became emperor as Joseph II in 1765. Like Joseph, Leopold was influenced by the ideas of the Enlightenment and was determined to construct an efficient state apparatus at the expense of feudal interests. During his 25-year reign over the Grand Duchy of Tuscany, he rationalized his states' taxation and tariff systems and encouraged the development of representative institutions.

After Joseph II died in February 1790, Leopold was elected emperor (and also became king of Hungary and archduke of Austria). Although he dismantled some of the centralized state machinery that Joseph had set up in the Habsburg domains, he kept in force Joseph's decrees that emancipated the peasantry and granted increased religious liberty to non-Catholics. At first Leopold reacted cautiously to the explosive situation created in Europe by the French Revolution. In August 1791, however, he joined with the Prussians in issuing the Declaration of Pillnitz, appealing to the European sovereigns to use force to assure the maintenance of monarchical government in France. Austria and Prussia concluded a defensive alliance in February 1792, but Leopold died less than two months before France declared war on Austria.

HUNGARY

• **Leopold I–II:** *see* Leopold I–II (Germany/Holy Roman Empire).

TUSCANY

• **Leopold II** (b. Oct. 3, 1797, Florence—d. Jan. 29, 1870, Rome), last reigning grand duke of Tuscany (ruled 1824–59).

Succeeding his father, Ferdinand III, on June 18, 1824, Leopold continued liberal administrative, judicial, and educational reforms and improved the transportation system. After the election (1846) of the popular and democratic Pope Pius IX, whose reforms and policies unloosed liberal enthusiasm throughout Italy, Leopold became one of the first Italian rulers to grant a constitution for representative government (Feb. 17, 1848). Popular pressure forced him to send Tuscan troops to fight against the Austrians in Lombardy. As radical agitation grew, however, he left Tuscany (Jan. 30, 1849), stating that he could not agree to the planned constituent assembly, and on February 21 joined the pope at the fortified port of Gaeta south of Rome; Pius IX had fled the radical extremists in Rome.

Leopold II, portrait bust by Ottavio Giovannozzi, 1846; in the Uffizi, Florence
Alinari—Art Resource/EB Inc.

After the Austrian victory over the Piedmontese at Novara (March 23), the Tuscan Assembly installed a dictator whose brief rule proved unsuccessful; the Assembly then invited Leopold to return (April 12). He accepted but secretly arranged for Austrian troops to march in first (May 25, 1849). Leopold himself did not return until July 28; the Austrians remained until 1855. Leopold prorogued the parliament in September 1850, finally revoked the constitution on May 5, 1852, and imprisoned the Tuscan revolutionaries.

Despite the end of Austrian occupation in 1855, Leopold's prestige remained low. He refused the popular demand to join the French and Sardinians in their war against Austria in 1859, and, in the face of mounting opposition, he quietly left Tuscany (April 27) to abdicate in favour of his son Ferdinand IV (July), who never reigned.

Leopold II, Lake (Africa): *see* Mai-Ndombe, Lake.

Leopold, Carl Gustaf af (b. March 26, 1756, Stockholm—d. Nov. 9, 1829, Stockholm), Swedish court poet in the service of the enlightened monarch Gustav III and of his successor, the reactionary Gustav IV.

After study at Uppsala and Greifswald, Leopold began his career in 1792 with skillful articles and polemical essays propagating the rational ideas of the Enlightenment and parrying the criticism of the younger generation of Romantics. A member of the Swedish Academy from its foundation in 1786, he became, on the death of the poet and critic J.H. Kellgren (1795), the dominant arbiter of classical taste in Sweden. His philosophical, didactic poetry is typified by his ode "Försynen" (1793; "Providence").

Carl Gustaf af Leopold, oil painting by J.G. Sandberg, 1832; in Gripsholm Castle, Sweden
By courtesy of the Svenska Portrattarkivet, Stockholm

Leopold was ennobled in 1809. His last years were saddened by his wife's insanity and by his own blindness.

Leopold, Jan Hendrik (b. May 11, 1865, 's Hertogenbosch, Neth.—d. June 21, 1925, Rotterdam), poet whose unique expression and masterly technique set him apart from other heirs to the Dutch literary renaissance of the 1880s. His poetry is often wistful and melancholy in mood, conveying a desolating solitude of spirit that was probably accentuated by his deafness; he himself describes his work as "one long plaint."

He was first influenced by Pieter Cornelis Boutens and Herman Gorter but soon developed along his own lines. He made his debut in the periodical *De nieuwe gids* ("The New Guide") in 1893 and later collaborated on Albert Verwey's *Tweemaandelijks tijdschrift* ("Bimonthly Periodical").

His most highly rated work is the epic poem "Cheops" (1915), which describes in rich, musical language the journey of a pharaoh's soul after death through the spiritual regions of the universe and its return, disillusioned, to its burial pyramid.

Consult the INDEX *first*

Leopold, Nathan F(reudenthal), Jr.; and Loeb, Richard A. (respectively b. Nov. 19, 1904, Chicago—d. Aug. 29, 1971, San Juan, P.R.; b. June 11, 1905, Chicago—d. Jan. 28, 1936, Stateville Penitentiary, Ill., U.S.), two celebrated Chicago murderers of 1924, who confessed to the kidnapping and murder of 14-year-old Robert ("Bobbie") Franks for an "intellectual" thrill. Pleading guilty, they were defended in a bench trial by famed lawyer Clarence Darrow, who secured them life imprisonment rather than execution.

Wealthy and intellectually brilliant (Leopold had graduated from the University of Chicago at 18, Loeb from the University of Michigan at 17), the two had committed several petty acts of theft and arson before attempting the "perfect murder"—in the kidnap of Bobbie Franks in a rented automobile on May 21, 1924, on Chicago's south side; Loeb, the more ruthless of the two, hit the boy on the head with a chisel and stuffed a gag in his mouth; the boy died within minutes. They half-buried the body in a railway culvert and, by phone and notes, demanded $10,000 in ransom from the boy's wealthy parents. The body, however, was unexpectedly found, and several clues, including the discovery of Leopold's eyeglasses at the culvert, led the police to Leopold and Loeb. They quickly confessed.

For 33 days in July–August 1924, Darrow, hired by Leopold's father, defended the two before Judge John R. Caverly, offering an eloquent appeal against capital punishment. The judge finally sentenced them each to life imprisonment for murder and 99 years for kidnapping. They were sent to Northern Illinois Penitentiary near Joliet.

In January 1936, Loeb was razor-slashed and killed by a fellow inmate, toward whom Loeb allegedly had made sadistic homosexual advances. Leopold was paroled in 1958 and worked as a hospital technician in Puerto Rico, where he married a widow in 1961. He died of a heart attack 10 years later. He wrote *Life Plus 99 Years* (1958).

Leopoldo (Italian personal name): *see under* Leopold.

Léopoldville (Zaire): *see* Kinshasa.

Leotychides, also spelled LEOTYCHIDAS (b. *c.* 545 BC—d. *c.* 469), Spartan king of the Eurypontid family and a successful military commander during the Greco-Persian wars.

In 491 he acceded to the throne held by his cousin, Demaratus, after the coruler (Sparta having a dual kingship), Cleomenes I, had bribed the Delphic oracle to declare Demaratus illegitimate. Shortly thereafter, Leotychides tried unsuccessfully to arrange a truce in the war between Athens and the island of Aegina. The island had earned the enmity of Athens by submitting to the Persians, who were expanding their sphere of influence to the west.

By 479, when most of the Persian invaders had been driven from mainland Greece, Leotychides was commander of the Greek fleet. In that year he crushed the Persian army and navy at Mycale on the coast of Lydia, a victory that prepared the way for the liberation of the Greeks of western Asia Minor from Persian rule. Leotychides led an army to Thessaly, around 476, to punish the aristocratic family of the Aleuads for having aided the Persians, but he withdrew after allegedly accepting a bribe. Convicted on this charge at Sparta, he fled to Tegea, in Arcadia. A sentence of exile was passed upon him; his house was razed, and his grandson, Archidamus II, ascended the throne.

Leotychides should not be confused with an earlier Spartan king of the same name who fought against the Messenians in the Second Messenian War (*c.* 650 BC).

Leovigild, also spelled LIUVIGILD, Spanish LEOVIGILDO (d. April/May 586, Toledo, Spain), the last Arian ruler in Visigothic Spain, who did much to restore the extent and power of the Visigothic kingdom.

Brother of King Athanagild (d. 567), Leovigild succeeded (568) to that part of the Visigothic kingdom that lay south of the Pyrenees. Another brother, Liuva, ruled in Septimania, but after his death (572) Leovigild became sole king. Throughout his reign he was constantly at war. He took (569) Leon and Zamora from the Suebi in the northwest and Córdoba (571–572) from the Greeks in the south. One of Leovigild's sons, Hermenegild, married Ingund, daughter of Brunhild and of the Frankish king Sigebert, and was converted by her to Catholicism. He received support from his father's enemies, and Leovigild had to fight on all fronts. Leovigild defeated the Suebi, ultimately annexing their kingdom, and after a two-year siege he wrested Seville from the Byzantines (581–583). Hermenegild was executed in 585, his wife fleeing to Africa. On a pretext of avenging her treatment, the Frankish kings Childebert II and Guntram attacked Septimania and sent a fleet to help the Suebi; they were repulsed by Leovigild. At his death he was succeeded by his remaining son Reccared.

Lepanto, Battle of (Oct. 7, 1571), naval engagement between allied Christian forces and the Ottoman Turks during an Ottoman campaign to acquire the Venetian island of Cyprus. Seeking to drive Venice from the eastern Mediterranean, the forces of Sultan Selim II invaded Cyprus in 1570. The Venetians formed an alliance with Pope Pius V and Philip II of Spain (May 25, 1571). Philip sent his half brother, Don John of Austria, to command the allied forces. By the time the allies assembled at Messina, Sicily (Aug. 24, 1571), the Turks had captured Nicosia (Sept. 9, 1570), besieged Famagusta, and entered the Adriatic. Their fleet lay in the Gulf of Patras, near Lepanto (Návpaktos), Greece. The allied fleet of more than 200 ships sailed for Corfu on September 15 and on October 7 advanced in four squadrons against the Ottoman fleet, commanded by Ali Paşa, Muḥammad Saulak (governor of Alexandria), and Uluj Ali (dey of Algiers). After about four hours of fighting, the allies were victorious, capturing 117 galleys and thousands of men. Of little practical value (Venice surrendered Cyprus to the Turks in 1573), the battle had a great impact on European morale and was the subject of paintings by Titian, Tintoretto, and Veronese.

Lepchā, also called RONG, people of eastern Nepal, western Bhutan, Sikkim state, and the Darjeeling district of West Bengal in India. They number about 46,000 (11,000 in India; 25,000 in Sikkim; and 10,000 in Bhutan). They are thought to be the earliest inhabitants of Sikkim, but have adopted many elements of the culture of the Bhutia people, who entered Sikkim from Tibet in the 14th century and afterward. The Bhutia are mainly pastoralists in the high mountains; the Lepchā usually live in the remotest valleys. While some intermarriage has occurred between the two groups, they tend to stay apart and to speak their own languages, which are dialects of Tibetan. Neither group has much to do with the Hindu Nepalese settlers, who have entered Sikkim since the 18th century and in the late 20th century comprised about two-thirds of the population.

The Lepchā are primarily monogamous, although a married man may invite a younger unmarried brother to live with him and share his fields and his wife. Occasionally, also, a man may have more than one wife. The Lepchā trace their descent through the paternal line and have large patrilineal clans.

They were converted to Tibetan Buddhism by the Bhutia, but still retain their earlier pantheon of spirits and their shamans, who cure illnesses, intercede with the gods, and preside over the rites accompanying birth, marriage, and death.

Traditionally hunters and gatherers, the Lepchā now also engage in farming and cattle breeding.

Lepidodendron, one of the most commonly encountered genera of extinct treelike club mosses, order Lepidodendrales, class (or subdivision) Lycopsida. Some of its species, prominent during the Upper Carboniferous Period (ending 280,000,000 years ago), exceeded 30 metres (100 feet) and 1 metre (40 inches) in diameter. It was named originally for twig and branch fragments. Other so-called form genera were subsequently constructed for other parts not known to belong definitely to *Lepidodendron:* cones (*Lepidostrobus*), leaves (*Lepidophylloides,* or *Lepidophyllum*), seeds (*Lepidocarpon*), and underground parts (*Stigmaria*). Later, as more complete specimens were discovered in each genus, many species were created to accommodate them.

Fossil fragment of *Lepidodendron*
Louise K. Broman from Root Resources—EB Inc.

lepidolite, also called LITHIA MICA, the most common lithium mineral, basic potassium and lithium aluminosilicate; a member of the common mica group. It is economically important as a major source of lithium. Because it is one of the few minerals containing appreciable amounts of rubidium, it is useful in determining geological age according to strontium–rubidium ratios. Lepidolite occurs almost exclusively in granite pegmatites. For chemical formula and detailed physical properties, *see* mica (table).

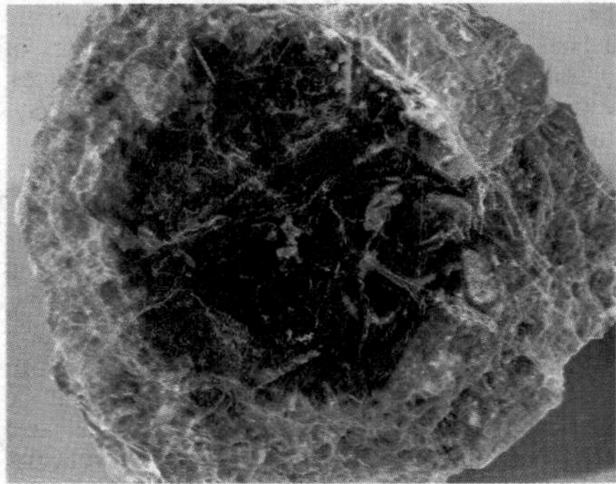
Lepidolite mica from Brazil
By courtesy of the Joseph and Helen Guetterman collection; photograph, John H. Gerard—EB Inc.

"De," "la," and similar components of a name, when followed by a space, are alphabetized as separate words (e.g., *De Forest, Lee*). *When they are joined to the following part of a name, the combination is treated as a single word* (e.g., *DeForest, John William*).

lepidopteran, a member of the insect order Lepidoptera, which includes the butterflies, the moths, and the skippers. They are among the most familiar and easily recognizable insects and have long been popular objects of study and collecting. The order contains over 100,000 species, making it the second largest of the insect orders. The name Lepidoptera, derived from Greek words meaning "scaly wing," in reference to the dusting of minute scales that covers the wings and body, was first applied by Linnaeus in 1735.

A brief treatment of lepidopterans follows. For full treatment, *see* MACROPAEDIA: Insects.

The order Lepidoptera is divided into three suborders: the Zeugloptera, which includes only a few scattered species; the Monotrysia, which includes the swifts and ghost moths (family Hepialidae), midget moths (Nepticulidae), and fairy moths (Incurvariidae); and the Ditrysia, which includes flannel moths (Megalopygidae), clothes moths (Tineidae), bagworms (Psychidae), ermine moths (Yponomeutidae), leaf roller moths (Tortricidae), silkworm moths (Bombycidae), tent caterpillar moths (Lasiocampidae), regal moths (Citheroniidae), measuring worm moths (Geometridae), hawk or sphinx moths (Sphingidae), tiger moths (Arctiidae), tussock moths (Liparidae), the skippers (superfamily Hesperioidea), and the true butterflies (superfamily Papilionoidea).

The moths, by far the most numerous of the Lepidoptera, are in general stoutly built, dull coloured, and nocturnal in habit. Butterflies are diurnal and are frequently brightly coloured. Skippers occupy a position intermediate between the moths and the butterflies; they are also diurnal.

Lepidopterans, being nearly all phytophagous (plant-eating), are present wherever plants are, and thus are found on every continent except Antarctica. Some families are cosmopolitan, while others are found only in certain restricted areas. In part this is due to the tendency of many species to feed upon only one type of plant, so that it is confined to those habitats suited to that plant.

Many types of lepidopteran, including hawk moths and a few types of butterflies, migrate from one region to another. Some have crossed thousands of miles of ocean to populate remote islands in the Atlantic, Pacific, and Indian oceans. The only species to make a true migration—a two-way flight by the same individuals—is the monarch butterfly (*Danaus plexippus*) of North America. Every fall the entire monarch population of North America migrates southward to a high mountain ridge in Mexico, whence they return in spring.

The body of a lepidopteran, like those of all insects, is composed of three basic regions; head, thorax, and abdomen. The head is small and features two well-developed compound eyes and often also a pair of simple eyes (ocelli). The antennae are prominent and segmented; in moths they are tapered and frequently branched or feathered, while in skippers and butterflies they end in clublike knobs. Smell, taste, and hearing are highly developed in various species. The mouth parts are equipped for sucking only, by means of a slender, tubular proboscis, which is coiled up when not in use. In some species the mouth parts are reduced, and some lepidopterans do not eat at all when they reach adulthood.

The thorax bears three pairs of legs and two pairs of wings. The forewings are longer and usually have a more pronounced apex, while the hindwings are smaller and rounder. The abdomen consists of 10 segments and contains the reproductive organs and other viscera. The females of nearly all species have two reproductive openings, one for copulation and the other for egglaying.

A female may lay from a few to as many as a thousand or more eggs at a time. The eggs may be merely dropped on foliage, or the female may lay them carefully on the undersides of leaves or in covered masses. After the eggs hatch, development occurs in three stages. The larvae are known as caterpillars. This is a stage of active feeding; for some caterpillars the first meal is the remains of the shell from which they hatched. Caterpillars have chewing mouth parts rather than the sucking mouth parts of the adult forms, and they consume great quantities of plant tissue. At the end of this stage, in most species, a cocoon is spun to protect the insect during the pupal stage. During pupation the insect undergoes a complete metamorphosis; the adult features are developed at this time.

Lepidopterans are an important element in many food chains. Both adult and larval forms of virtually every species serve as food for one or more predator—spiders, beetles, wasps, toads, lizards, bats, birds, and monkeys. Some adult forms are protected by repellent substances or toxins acquired when the larval forms fed on certain plants, such as the milkweeds favoured by monarch caterpillars.

Many types of lepidopterans are pests and can cause severe damage to grain, cotton, or beet crops, various fabrics, and timber.

Lepidus, Marcus Aemilius (d. 152 BC), Roman statesman who held the highest offices of the republic.

As ambassador to Greece, Syria, and Egypt in 200, he delivered to Philip V at Abydos the Senate's ultimatum warning Macedonia not to make war on any Greek state. Consul in 187 and 175, censor in 179, *pontifex maximus* from 180 onward, and *princeps senatus* from 179 to 152, Lepidus fought against the Ligurians, directed the construction of the Via Aemilia from Ariminum (modern Rimini) to Placentia (modern Piacenza), and founded colonies at Mutina (modern Modena) and Parma. The district of northern Italy called Emilia preserves his name.

Lepidus, Marcus Aemilius (d. *c.* 77 BC, Sardinia), Roman senator who attempted unsuccessfully to overthrow the constitution imposed by the dictator Sulla.

Although he had supported Sulla's rise to power and became wealthy in the Sullan proscriptions, Lepidus was elected consul for 78 with the help of Pompey, despite Sulla's opposition. When Sulla died in 78, Lepidus sought to rescind the dictator's measures. He called for the renewed distribution of cheap grain, recall of exiles, restoration of confiscated lands, and, ultimately, the reestablishment of the office of tribune. When his proposals were rejected by the Senate, he gathered forces in Etruria and Cisalpine Gaul and marched on Rome, demanding reelection to the consulship for 77. After being repelled by the other consul, Quintus Lutatius Catulus, at Rome's Milvian Bridge, Lepidus was driven by Pompey into the port of Cosa (modern Ansedonia) in Etruria. From there he escaped to Sardinia, where he died shortly thereafter, after suffering a series of defeats at the hands of the propraetor, Gaius Valerius Triarius. His son Marcus Aemilius Lepidus was one of the triumvirs who ruled Rome after 43.

Lepidus, Marcus Aemilius (d. 13/12 BC), Roman statesman, one of the triumvirs who ruled Rome after 43.

He was the son of a prominent politician (d. *c.* 77) of the same name. Lepidus joined the Caesarian side during the Civil War (49–45) between Caesar and the adherents of Pompey. He was praetor in 49, governor of Hither Spain in 48–47, and consul in 46. In 45 he became Caesar's *magister equitum* ("master of the cavalry"). After the murder of Caesar, Lepidus joined the Caesarian leader Mark Antony against the conspirators. Antony obtained for Lepidus the office of *pontifex maximus* ("high priest"). When Antony was defeated in the fighting near Mutina (modern Modena) and fled to Gaul, Lepidus sided with Antony and was declared a public enemy by the Senate. In October 43 Lepidus formed the triumvirate with Antony and Octavian (later the emperor Augustus) at Bononia (modern Bologna). Lepidus received both Hither and Further Spain, along with southern Gaul, as his portion. He was consul again in 42, but his two colleagues soon deprived him of most of his power. His provinces of Gaul and Spain were taken from him, and he was confined to the government of Roman Africa and only formally included in the renewed triumvirate of 37. In 36 he attempted to raise Sicily in revolt against Octavian, but his soldiers deserted his cause. He was removed from even nominal membership in the Triumvirate, and, although he was allowed to remain *pontifex maximus* until his death, he was forced to retire from public life.

Lepontine Alps, Italian ALPI LEPONTINE, French ALPES LÉPONTIENNES, German LEPONT(IN)ISCHE ALPEN, segment of the Central Alps along the Italian–Swiss border, bounded by the Simplon Pass and Pennine Alps (*q.v.*; west-southwest), the Upper Rhône and Vorderrhein river valleys (north), Splügen Pass (Italian Passo dello Spluga) and the Rhaetian Alps (east-northeast), and the Italian lake district (south). At the western end of the range lies Mt. Leone (11,657 ft [3,553 m]), the highest peak; and along the south slope are the deep Leventina and Mesolcina valleys. Important passes include Simplon, St. Gotthard (*qq.v.*), Lukmanier, and San Bernardino. The portion of the range east of St. Gotthard Pass is sometimes called the Adula Alps. The sources of the Rhône and Rhine rivers lie on the borders of this section of the Alps. Mountain climbing is popular in the region.

leprechaun, in Irish folklore, fairy in the form of a tiny old man often with a cocked hat and leather apron. Solitary by nature, he is said to live in remote places and to make shoes and brogues. The sound of his hammering betrays his presence. He possesses a hidden crock of gold; if captured and threatened with bodily violence, he might, if his captor keeps his eyes on him, reveal its hiding place. But usually the captor is tricked into glancing away, and the fairy vanishes.

The word derives ultimately from Old Irish *luchorpan,* "little body."

leprosy, also called HANSEN'S DISEASE, chronic infectious disease that affects the skin, peripheral nerves, and mucous membranes of the nose, throat, and eyes. It is caused by the leprosy bacillus, *Mycobacterium leprae.* Destruction of the peripheral nerves leads to a loss of sensation, which, together with progressive tissue degeneration, may result in the extremities becoming deformed and eroded.

In almost all cultures throughout history, leprosy has aroused dread and loathing. Lepers were ostracized as unclean and were isolated in leper colonies to control contagion. In reality the leprosy bacillus is not highly infectious, and today leprosy is entirely curable. Nevertheless, more than 500,000 people currently require treatment, and some 600,000 new cases arise every year. The disease is still common in Asia, Africa, Central and South America, and the Pacific Islands. More than 60 percent of infected persons are in India.

The leprosy bacillus was discovered by a Norwegian physician, G.H. Armauer Hansen, in 1873. It is passed from person to person only after prolonged close contact, as among family members. The bacillus probably enters the body through a break in the skin or through the mucous membranes of the nose. Even then, some 95 percent of humans are not susceptible to the bacillus and will never develop leprosy. Among the few who do contract the disease, in most cases it is self-limiting and disappears before symptoms become apparent.

Among the few who do contract leprosy, there are two principal types of disease. In the tuberculoid type, the bacilli are trapped in hard nodules, or tubercles, in the skin, underlying tissues, sweat glands, hair follicles, and nerve fibres. Loss of nervous transmission results in loss of sensation and circulation, frequently leading to claw hand and deformity of the foot. The face is frequently paralyzed, and open ulcers can form. In the lepromatous type, the bacilli multiply freely and spread widely through the body via the lymphatic system. The face is very often involved; the skin thickens, nodules and sometimes open sores appear, and the septum of the nose and palate can be destroyed. The disease seldom cuts life short.

Leprosy is treated through multidrug therapy. Patients with localized infection receive the antibacterial drugs dapsone and rifampicin for six months. Patients with more widespread disease receive dapsone, clofazimine, and rifampicin for two years. Relapses occur in fewer than 1 in 1,000 treated patients. Occasionally the infection persists despite continued therapy. Severe nerve and tissue damage cannot be repaired, so that many former patients require physical therapy, training, or surgery.

Lepsius, Richard, in full KARL RICHARD LEPSIUS (b. Dec. 23, 1810, Naumburg an der Saale, Saxony [now in Germany]—d. July 10, 1884, Berlin), German Egyptologist and a founder of modern, scientific archaeology who did much to catalog Egyptian archaeological remains and to establish a chronology for Egyptian history.

Following studies in archaeological philology and comparative languages, Lepsius became a lecturer at the University of Berlin. From 1843 to 1845, under the patronage of Frederick William IV of Prussia, he led a scientific expedition to Egypt and the Sudan. He found evidence of pyramids dating from about 3000 BC; studied 130 mastabas, the oblong burial structures peculiar to the Old Kingdom (*c.* 2686–*c.* 2160 BC); and, at Tell el Amarna (ancient Akhetaton), found the first evidence

Richard Lepsius

By courtesy of the Deutsche Staatsbibliothek, Berlin

to delineate the character of King Ikhnaton (Amenhotep IV), the controversial religious reformer. First to measure the Valley of the Tombs of the Kings, he also collected a great number of casts of temple reliefs and inscriptions, supervised the preparation of many drawings, and secured papyri and antiquities. Perhaps most important, he was the first to perceive the developing panorama of Egyptian history.

Hypostyle hall of the Temple of Amon at Karnak, illustration from Richard Lepsius' *Denkmäler aus Ägypten und Äthiopien* (1849–59)
Archivo Iconografico, S.A./Corbis

After returning to Prussia, he became professor at the University of Berlin (1846) and began publishing works that still attract interest, notably *Chronologie der Ägypter* (1849; "Egyptian Chronology"), *Königsbuch der Alten Ägypter* (1858; "Book of Egyptian Kings"), and the enormous *Denkmäler aus Ägypten und Äthiopien,* 12 vol. (1849–59; "Egyptian and Ethiopian Monuments"). In 1866 he returned to Egypt and discovered the Canopus Decree, an inscription similar to the Rosetta Stone, which further substantiated the position of Egyptologist Jean-François Champollion on the deciphering of hieroglyphs. Under Lepsius' direction, the Egyptian collection of the Berlin Museum became one of the world's finest. In 1873 he also became director of the Royal Library, Berlin.

Leptis Magna, also spelled LEPCIS MAGNA, Punic transliteration LABQI, or LPQI, modern LABDAH, largest city of the ancient region of Tripolitania. It is located 62 miles (100 km) southeast of Tripoli on the coast of Libya. Lying 2 miles (3 km) east of what is now Al-Khums (Homs), Leptis contains some of the world's finest remains of Roman architecture. It was designated a UNESCO World Heritage site in 1982.

Founded as early as the 7th century BC by Phoenicians of Tyre or Sidon, it was later settled by Carthaginians, probably at the end of the 6th century BC. Its natural harbour at the mouth of the Wadi Labdah facilitated the city's growth as a major Mediterranean and trans-Saharan trade centre, and it also became a market for agricultural production in the fertile coastland region. Near the conclusion of the Second Punic War, it passed in 202 BC to Masinissa's Numidian kingdom, from which it broke away in 111 BC to become an ally of Rome. Through the 1st century AD, however, it retained several of its Punic legal and cultural traditions, including its municipal constitution and the official use of the Punic language. The Roman emperor Trajan (reigned AD 98–117) designated Leptis a *colonia* (community with full rights of citizenship). The emperor Septimius Severus (AD 193–211), who was born at Leptis, conferred upon it the *jus Italicum* (legal freedom from property and land taxes) and became a great patron of the city. Under his direction a building program was initiated, and the harbour, which had been enlarged in the 1st century AD, was improved again. Over the following centuries, however, Leptis began to decline because of the increasing insecurity of the frontiers, culminating in a disastrous incursion in 363, and the growing economic difficulties of the Roman Empire. After the Arab conquest of 642, the status of Leptis as an urban centre effectively ceased, and it fell into ruin.

Buried by sand until the early 20th century, Leptis still preserves traces of early Punic structures near the excavated shell of its amphitheatre (AD 56) and its old forum. From this nucleus, the city spread westward along the coast and inland. Second-century buildings include well-preserved baths erected under the emperor Hadrian (117–138) and a circus (racecourse) some 1,500 feet (460 m) long. The largest surviving monuments were erected during the reign of Severus. Linking the city centre to the harbour was a colonnaded street roughly 1,350 feet (410 m) long that terminated in a circular piazza dominated by an intricately designed *nymphaeum* (ornamental fountain house). Among the other structures erected during that period were an aqueduct 12 miles (19 km) long, an elaborate complex of buildings on the left bank of the wadi, and the well-preserved Hunting Baths, with colourfully painted scenes of hunting exploits (including a 2nd- or 3rd-century painting of a leopard hunt) and the still-legible names of honoured hunters on the walls.

The basilica, which stood on the western side of the colonnaded street, was dedicated in 216 (five years after Severus' death). Measuring 525 feet (160 m) long and 225 feet (69 m) wide, it was a three-aisled, colonnaded hall with an apse at each end. Flanking the apses were ornately sculpted pilasters depicting the life of Dionysus and the twelve labours of Hercules (both favourites of the Severus family). Adjoining the basilica was the new forum.

The Severan Basilica at Leptis Magna, completed by Caracalla, son of Septimius Severus, in AD 216
By courtesy of the British School at Rome

From the early 20th century the Libyan Antiquities Service and groups of Italian archaeologists diligently laboured to preserve the site. During World War II the Royal Air Force sought to erect a radar station there, but the intervention of the British art historians and archaeologists Col. Mortimer Wheeler and Major John Ward-Perkins saved the site. Many of the works of art uncovered there are displayed at the nearby Leptis Magna Museum or at the Al-Saraya Al-Hamra (castle) museum in Tripoli.

Work in the late 20th century included the uncovering of Roman villas on the outskirts of Leptis. In the 1990s excavations within the city revealed a house with an intact water system, including a well and underground cisterns.

Leptis Minor, also called LEPTIMINUS, or LEPTI MINUS, modern LAMTAH, small Carthaginian city located 10 miles (16 km) from modern Al-Munastir (Ruspinum), Tunisia. In Roman times it was the centre of a prosperous olive-growing district, and its exports included olive oil and pottery. It was Julius Caesar's base before the Battle of Thapsus in 46 BC. Under Justinian it was with Capsa one of the two residences of the army commander of the province of Byzacenia, and it was later the seat of a bishopric.

leptochlorite, subgroup of chlorite minerals. *See* chlorite.

Leptodactylidae, family of frogs (order Anura), including more than 900 species, most of

South American bullfrog (*Leptodactylus pentadactylus*)
Cy LaTour at the Philadelphia Zoo

which are found in South and Central America. Leptodactylid frogs live in water, on land, or in trees. More than 300 species, most of them West Indian or Central American, are of the genus *Eleutherodactylus,* or robber frogs. The young of this genus hatch as small frogs, rather than as tadpoles. The greenhouse frog (*E. planirostis*), a small brown frog commonly found in gardens, is a Cuban frog introduced into the southern United States. Many species have a very restricted distribution, such as *E. jasperi,* which is restricted to the cloud forests of Puerto Rico.

The genus *Leptodactylus,* or nest-building frogs, includes frogs that have a wide variety of reproductive modes. Some species lay their eggs on land in a frothy mass, the young living in the foam until washed into a pool by rain. The South American bullfrogs are of this genus. These animals resemble true frogs (*Rana*) but lack webbing on the feet. The edible *L. pentadactylus* of Panama and South America is a large form with a maximum length of more than 15 centimetres (6 inches).

Horned frogs (*Ceratophrys*) are frog-eating South American forms that typically have a projecting flap, or "horn," of skin above each eye. They have wide heads and mouths and range in length from about 2.5 cm (one inch) in the small species to more than 15 cm (6 in.) in the Amazonian *C. cornuta*. Horned frogs may be aggressive when disturbed; some are capable of giving sharp bites.

The numerous Australian frogs of the families Limnodynastidae and Myobatrachidae (*q.v.*) are considered by some authorities to belong to the Leptodactylidae.

Leptodesma, extinct genus of pelecypods (clams) found as fossils in Silurian to Mississippian rocks (between 430,000,000 and 325,000,000 years old). Its distinct shell, roughly oval except for a sharp outgrowth that extends

Leptodesma
From H. Shimer and R. Shrock, *Index Fossils of North America,* by permission of the M.I.T. Press, Cambridge, Massachusetts, Copyright 1944 by the Massachusetts Institute of Technology, Copyright renewed 1972 by the Massachusetts Institute of Technology

posteriorly, makes *Leptodesma* easy to identify. A troughlike flange connects the spinous outgrowth to the main body of the shell. Concentric growth lines are also present.

Leptodus, extinct genus of articulate brachiopods, or lamp shells, of the Permian period (286 to 245 million years ago). *Leptodus,* a very specialized form characterized by an aberrant morphology, had an oysterlike pedicle valve, which anchored the shell to the

Leptodus

By courtesy of the trustees of the British Museum (Natural History); photograph, Imitor

substrate and was probably attached to other shells by cementation. The brachial (upper) valve was flat and very thin. It is likely that *Leptodus* inhabited the flanks of reefs developed in shallow Permian seas of North America.

Leptolepis, genus of marine fish thought to represent the ancestral form that gave rise to the teleosts, the dominant group of fishes in the world today. *Leptolepis* was abundant between 208 million and 144 million years ago in the world's Jurassic seas and was herringlike

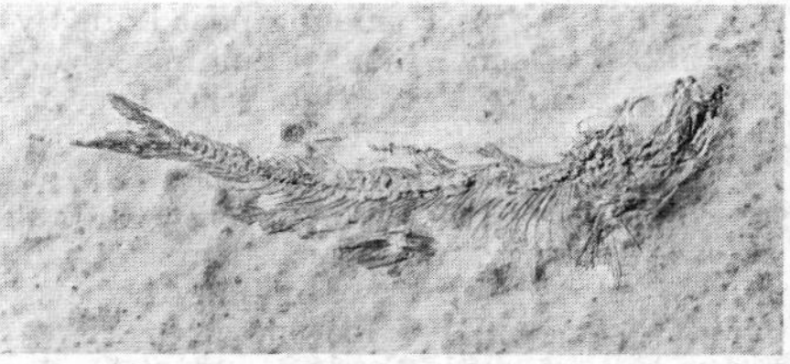

Leptolepis sprattiformis, collected from Solnhofen, Ger.

By courtesy of the Buffalo Museum of Science, Buffalo, N.Y.

in size and appearance. Fragmentary remains from earlier and later rocks may indicate an earlier origin and longer persistence for the genus than the Jurassic period dates indicate. In many anatomical details, *Leptolepis* is intermediate between the more primitive holosteans and the more advanced teleost fish.

lepton, in particle physics, any member of a class of fermions that respond only to electromagnetic, weak, and gravitational forces and do not take part in strong interactions. Like all fermions, leptons have a half-integral spin. (In quantum-mechanical terms, spin constitutes the property of intrinsic angular momentum.) Leptons obey the Pauli exclusion principle, which prohibits any two identical fermions in a given population from occupying the same quantum state. Leptons are said to be fundamental particles; that is, they do not appear to be made up of smaller units of matter.

Leptons can either carry one unit of electric charge or be neutral. The charged leptons are the electrons, muons, and taus. Each of these types has a negative charge and a distinct mass. Electrons, the lightest leptons, have a mass only 0.0005 that of a proton. Muons are heavier, having more than 200 times as much mass as electrons. Taus, in turn, are approximately 3,700 times more massive than electrons. Each charged lepton has an associated neutral partner, or neutrino (*i.e.,* electron-, muon-, and tau-neutrino), that has no electric charge and no significant mass. Moreover, all leptons, including the neutrinos, have antiparticles called antileptons. The mass of the antileptons is identical to that of the leptons, but all of the other properties are reversed.

The total number of leptons appears to remain the same in every particle reaction. Mathematically, total lepton number L (the number of leptons minus the number of antileptons) is constant. In addition, a conservation law for leptons of each type seems to hold. The number of electrons and electron neutrinos, for example, is conserved separately from the number of muons and mu-neutrinos. The current limit of violation of this conservation law is one part per million.

The electroweak theory of electromagnetic and weak interactions, proposed during the late 1960s, has enabled physicists to better understand the interactions of leptons. This apparent theoretical conquest, however, has also generated a host of new questions. Other, more recent theoretical schemes seeking to intertwine strong interactions with the weak and the electromagnetic have had a similar effect. A law akin to that of the conservation of lepton number exists for strongly interacting fermions, the baryons (*e.g.,* protons). The new "grand unified" theories suggest that a proton decays into leptons and other particles, thereby simultaneously violating lepton and baryon number conservation. In such theories the quantity $B-L$, the number of baryons minus the number of leptons, is conserved. *See also* fermion; gauge theory.

Leptospermum, genus of about 40 species of subtropical evergreen shrubs or small trees, in the myrtle family (Myrtaceae), native to Australasia. Several species have been introduced to temperate regions and grown in greenhouses for their showy roselike flowers and almost needlelike foliage.

Many species are called tea trees: the Australian tea tree (*Leptospermum laevigatum*), growing to a height of 6 m (20 feet), has shredding bark and white flowers. It is used for reclamation planting and erosion control on sandy soils. The woolly tea tree (*L. lanigerum*) differs in having fuzzy young shoots. The

New Zealand tea tree (*Leptospermum scoparium*)

A to Z Botanical Collection—EB Inc.

shrubby New Zealand tea tree, or manuka (*L. scoparium*), has several cultivated varieties with white to rose-red flowers and gray-green to brownish leaves.

leptospirosis, also called WEIL'S DISEASE, INFECTIOUS JAUNDICE, PEA PICKER'S DISEASE, or SWINEHERD'S DISEASE, contagious disease of animals, occasionally communicable to humans, caused by a pathogenic spirochete of the genus *Leptospira.*

The reservoir of leptospires includes rodents and certain domestic animals. These animals excrete live, fully virulent organisms in their urine and contaminate the environment. Outside the animal body, leptospires can live for several weeks in fresh water. Thus infection takes place by direct contact with urine of infected animals or by indirect contact with contaminated food or water. Leptospires can readily penetrate mucous membranes but probably cannot gain entrance to the body through intact skin. A scratch or abrasion, as well as the nasal mucosa and eye, are excellent portals of entry; thus the origin of many infections can be traced to wading, swimming, or other contact with water containing virulent leptospires. The incidence in humans depends upon the opportunity for exposure in swimming, the harvesting of rice, and contact with animals.

Clinical evidence of disease in humans varies depending upon the infecting type of leptospire. Usually after an incubation period of about a week, fever, weakness, and pains in the legs, back, and abdominal muscles are noted. Nausea, vomiting, and diarrhea are not uncommon. One characteristic symptom is congestion of the conjunctival blood vessels around the corneas of the eyes. Jaundice may occur after the first week of illness. The death rate is approximately 30 percent of the severely ill and jaundiced patients.

Lerdo de Tejada, Sebastián (b. April 25, 1827, Jalapa, Veracruz, Mexico—d. April 1889, New York, N.Y., U.S.), president of Mexico from 1872 to 1876.

Lerdo de Tejada

By courtesy of the Library of Congress, Washington, D.C.

Lerdo, orphaned and impoverished as a child, struggled to obtain an education and became professor of jurisprudence and rector of the College of San Ildefonso in Mexico City. A political liberal, he joined Benito Juárez during the period of French intervention in Mexico (1861–67), becoming president of the Tribunal Supremo (Supreme Court) and de facto vice president of the Mexican republic after its restoration in 1867.

After Juárez' death in 1872, Lerdo became president of Mexico, only to be immediately challenged by Porfirio Díaz, another of Juárez' lieutenants. Opposed by provincial chieftains who resented Lerdo's centralized government, by the church for his connection with the anticlerical reforms of Juárez, and by progressives who criticized his failure to undertake public works, Lerdo was driven into exile by an uprising led by Díaz in 1877.

Lérida, *provincia,* in the *comunidad autónoma* ("autonomous community") of Catalonia, northeastern Spain. It was bounded by France and Andorra to the north and by the *provincias* of Gerona and Barcelona (east), Tarragona (south), and Zaragoza and Huesca (west). It was formed in 1833 with an area of 4,644 square miles (12,028 square km). With Barcelona, Gerona, and Tarragona, Lérida became one of the four provinces of the newly created autonomous region of Catalonia in 1979.

The northern half lies within the Mediterranean sector of the Pyrenees Mountains and contains some of the finest scenery in the whole Pyrenean chain, including the valleys of Aran and Cerdaña and large tracts of forest. It is watered by many rivers, the largest of which is the Segre, a left-bank tributary of the Ebro, with important hydroelectric power developments.

The southern half, in contrast, is a rolling, well-irrigated plain stretching to the Ebro. Agriculture is well mechanized, and the province does a thriving trade in wine, wool, timber, and cattle, but the importance of the traditional mule and horse trade is diminishing.

The olive oil produced in the town of Borjas Blancas is known for its purity. Fruits, especially pears and lemons, are exported. Industrial development is slight, centred on the provincial capital, Lérida city. Seo de Urgel, near the headwaters of the Segre, is an episcopal see with a close historical connection with Andorra. Pop. (1988 est.) 354,026.

"De," "la," and similar components of a name, when followed by a space, are alphabetized as separate words (e.g., *De Forest, Lee*). *When they are joined to the following part of a name, the combination is treated as a single word* (e.g., *DeForest, John William*).

Lérida, capital of Lérida *provincia,* in the *comunidad autónoma* ("autonomous community") of Catalonia, northeastern Spain, on the Segre River near its confluence with the Ebro River. Of Iberian origin, the town then called Ilerda was taken in 49 BC from Pompey (Gnaeus Pompeius Magnus) by Julius Caesar during the Roman Civil War. The site of a Visigothic council (546), Lérida was captured in 713 by the Moors, who called it Lareda or Lerita. It was reconquered in 1149 by Ramón Berenguer IV of Aragon. A university, founded there in the 13th century, was transferred to Cervera (1717) after the War of the Spanish Succession, during which Lérida took the side of the Habsburg archduke Charles.

The old cathedral in Byzantine-Gothic style, with a Moorish admixture, was begun in 1203 and consecrated in 1278 but has not been used since 1707; it has been restored and declared a national monument. Other notable buildings include the new cathedral (1761–81); the Church of San Lorenzo (14th century); the La Pahería Palace with its 13th-century facade, the meeting place of the municipal council; and La Alcazaba (castle). This castle, built in 1149, dominates the older quarter, a maze of narrow streets on the right bank of the Segre. On the left bank are the modern suburbs.

The city's economy is based primarily on agriculture; Lérida is well known for its cattle, agricultural, and fruit shows. Industrial development is slight. Pop. (1988 est.) 109,795.

Lérins, Abbey of, Cistercian monastery, originally founded about 410 by St. Honoratus of Arles on a Mediterranean island opposite Cannes (now in France). It flourished in the 5th century, when it was a centre of intellectual activity. Many highly educated monks, trained elsewhere, were attracted by its spiritual discipline and became residents. Vincent of Lérins was its chief theologian, and St. Hilary and St. Caesarius of Arles were also from Lérins.

The abbey adopted the Benedictine Rule about 660. Monastic life ended for a time after the monks were massacred (*c.* 732) when Saracens occupied the island. Restored and reformed by Cluny in the late 10th century, the monastery prospered materially and spiritually during the next centuries. In the 15th century a decline began. The monastery was suppressed in 1786, and in 1791 its buildings were sold.

In 1871 a Cistercian congregation established a community on the island and rebuilt the monastery. Some of the earlier buildings remain, including some ancient chapels and a tower.

Lerma, Francisco Gómez de Sandoval y Rojas, duque de (duke of) (b. 1553, Seville, Spain—d. May 17, 1625, Valladolid), Spanish statesman who died a cardinal, having been the first of the *validos*—strong men or favourites—through whom the Habsburg kings were to govern Spain until the end of the 17th century.

The son of the 4th marqués de Denia, he was brought up at Seville, where his uncle, Cristóbal de Rojas, was archbishop. A grandee and one of the gentlemen of the king's chamber under Philip II, he won the confidence of the heir to the throne, who on becoming king as Philip III in 1598 entrusted him with the conduct of public affairs and, in 1599, created him Duke de Lerma.

Believing that Philip III might maintain Spanish supremacy in Europe to some extent by relying on dynastic hegemony, he worked to continue the series of marriages between members of the Spanish royal house and Viennese Habsburgs or French Bourbons. He achieved the peace of London between Spain and England (1604) and the 12-year truce with the United Provinces of the Netherlands (1609).

It was Lerma who sponsored the decrees (1609–14) for the expulsion of the Moriscos, or officially Christianized Moors, from Spain—a decision affecting about 350,000 people. Motivated by religious and political rather than economic considerations, he wanted to stop a controversy that could be solved only by drastic means in view of the failure to assimilate the Moriscos with the Spanish Christians.

Lerma accumulated an immense personal fortune—a fact that his enemies exploited when they launched their final attack on his position. His own son Cristóbal, Duke de Uceda, cleverly manipulated by the ambitious Count (later Duke) de Olivares, took part in the conspiracy against Lerma. Foreseeing his fall from favour, Lerma sought leave to retire into private life but first obtained a cardinal's hat from Pope Paul V (March 1618). He was dismissed from power a few months later (October 1618).

Lerma River, Spanish RÍO LERMA, river in west-central Mexico. It rises on the central plateau 15 miles (24 km) southeast of Toluca and flows northwestward through the state of México, forms the short border between the states of Querétaro and Michoacán, and then meanders generally west-northwestward through Guanajuato. After looping southward, the Lerma separates Guanajuato and Michoacán, and Michoacán and Jalisco before flowing, after a course of about 350 miles (560 km), into Lake Chapala, 15 miles (24 km) west-southwest of La Barca. The Río Grande de Santiago, which leads for 250 miles (400 km) from Lake Chapala northwestward to the Pacific Ocean, is sometimes considered an extension of the Lerma. Although the Lerma is not navigable, its waters are used extensively for hydroelectric plants and for irrigation. With its major tributaries, the Laja, Apaseo, and Turbio, and including the Santiago, the Lerma constitutes Mexico's largest river system. Many large cities, particularly in the basins of Toluca, Guanajuato, and Jalisco, lie on its banks.

Lermontov, Mikhail (Yuryevich) (b. Oct. 15 [Oct. 3, Old Style], 1814, Moscow, Russia—d. July 27 [July 15], 1841, Pyatigorsk), the leading Russian Romantic poet and author of the novel *Geroy nashego vremeni* (1840; *A Hero of Our Time*), which was to have a profound influence on later Russian writers.

Life. Lermontov was the son of Yury Petrovich Lermontov, a retired army captain, and Mariya Mikhaylovna, *née* Arsenyeva. At the age of three he lost his mother and was brought up by his grandmother, Yelizaveta Alekseyevna Arsenyeva, on her estate in Penzenskaya province. Russia's abundant natural beauty, its folk songs and tales, its customs and ceremonies, the hard forced labour of the serfs, and stories and legends of peasant mutinies all had a great influence in developing the future poet's character. Because the child was often ill, he was taken to spas in the Caucasus on three occasions, where the exotic landscapes created lasting impressions on him.

In 1827 he moved with his grandmother to Moscow, and, while attending a boarding school for children of the nobility (at Moscow University), he began to write poetry and also studied painting. In 1828 he wrote the poems *Cherkesy* ("Circassians") and *Kavkazsky plennik* ("Prisoner of the Caucasus") in the vein of the English Romantic poet Lord Byron, whose influence then predominated over young Russian writers. Two years later his first verse, *Vesna* ("Spring"), was published. The same year he entered Moscow University, then one of the liveliest centres of culture and ideology, where such democratically minded representatives of nobility as Aleksandr Herzen, Nikolay Platonovich Ogaryov, and others studied. Students ardently discussed political and philosophical problems, the hard fate of serf peasantry, and the recent Decembrist uprising. In this atmosphere he wrote many lyrical verses, longer, narrative poems, and dramas. His drama *Stranny chelovek* (1831; "A Strange Man") reflected the attitudes current among members of student societies: hatred of the despotic tsarist regime and of serfdom. In 1832, after clashing with a reactionary professor, Lermontov left the university and went to St. Petersburg, where he entered the cadet school. Upon his graduation in 1834 with the rank of subensign (or cornet), Lermontov was appointed to the Life-Guard Hussar Regiment stationed at Tsarskoye Selo, close to St. Petersburg. As a young officer, he spent a considerable portion of his time in the capital, and his critical observations of aristocratic life there formed the basis of his play *Maskarad* ("Masquerade"). During this period his deep—but unreciprocated—attachment to Varvara Lopukhina, a sentiment that never left him, was reflected in *Knyaginya Ligovskaya* ("Duchess Ligovskaya") and other works.

Lermontov, detail of an oil painting by Pyotr Yefimovich Zabolotsky, 1837; in the State Tretyakov Gallery, Moscow

By courtesy of the State Tretyakov Gallery, Moscow

Lermontov was greatly shaken in January 1837 by the death of the great poet Aleksandr Pushkin in a duel. He wrote an elegy that expressed the nation's love for the dead poet, denouncing not only his killer but also the court aristocracy, whom he saw as executioners of freedom and the true culprits of the tragedy. As soon as the verses became known to the court of Nicholas I, Lermontov was arrested and exiled to a regiment stationed in the Caucasus. Travel to new places, meetings with Decembrists (in exile in the Caucasus), and introduction to the Georgian intelligentsia—to the outstanding poet Ilia Chavchavadze, whose daughter had married a well-known Russian dramatist, poet, and diplomatist, Aleksandr Sergeyevich Griboyedov—as well as to other prominent Georgian poets in Tiflis (now Tbilisi) broadened his horizon. Attracted to the nature and poetry of the Caucasus and excited by its folklore, he studied the local languages and translated and polished the Azerbaijanian story "Ashik Kerib." Caucasian themes and images occupy a strong place in his poetry and in the novel *Geroy nashego vremeni,* as well as in his sketches and paintings.

As a result of zealous intercession by his grandmother and by the influential poet V.A. Zhukovsky, Lermontov was allowed to return to the capital in 1838. His verses began to appear in the press: the romantic poem *Pesnya pro tsarya Ivana Vasilyevicha, molodogo oprichnika i udalogo kuptsa Kalashnikova* (1837; "A Song About Tsar Ivan Vasilyevich, His Young Bodyguard, and the Valiant Merchant Kalashnikov"), the realistic satirical poems *Tambovskaya kaznacheysha* (1838; "The Tambov Paymaster's Wife") and *Sashka* (written 1839, published 1862), and the romantic poem *Demon.* Soon Lermontov became popular; he was called Pushkin's successor and was lauded for having suffered and been exiled because of his libertarian verses. Writers and journalists took an interest in him, and fashionable ladies were attracted to him. He made friends among the editorial staff of *Otechestvennye zapiski,* the leading magazine of the Western-oriented intellectuals, and in 1840 he met the prominent progressive critic V.G. Belinsky, who envisioned him as the great hope of Russian literature. Lermontov had arrived among the circle of St. Petersburg writers.

At the end of the 1830s, the principal directions of his creative work had been established. His freedom-loving sentiments and his bitterly skeptical evaluation of the times in which he lived are embodied in his philosophical lyric poetry ("Duma" ["Thought"], "Ne ver sebye . . . " ["Do Not Trust Yourself . . . "]) and are interpreted in an original fashion in the romantic and fantastic images of his Caucasian poems, *Mtsyri* (1840) and *Demon,* on which the poet worked for the remainder of his life. Finally, Lermontov's mature prose showed a critical picture of contemporary life in his novel *Geroy nashego vremeni,* containing the sum total of his reflections on contemporary society and the fortunes of his generation. The hero, Pechorin, is a cynical person of superior accomplishments who, having experienced everything else, devotes himself to experimenting with human situations. This realistic novel, full of social and psychological content and written in prose of superb quality, played an important role in the development of Russian prose.

In February 1840 Lermontov was brought to trial before a military tribunal for his duel with the son of the French ambassador at St. Petersburg—a duel used as a pretext for punishing the recalcitrant poet. On the instructions of Nicholas I, Lermontov was sentenced to a new exile in the Caucasus, this time to an infantry regiment that was preparing for dangerous military operations. Soon compelled to take part in cavalry sorties and hand-to-hand battles, he distinguished himself in the heavy fighting at Valerik River, which he describes in "Valerik" and in the verse "Ya k vam pishu . . . " ("I Am Writing to You . . . "). The military command made due note of the great courage and presence of mind displayed by the officer-poet.

As a result of persistent requests by his grandmother, Lermontov was given a short leave in February 1841. He spent several weeks in the capital, continuing work on compositions he had already begun and writing several poems noted for their maturity of thought and talent ("Rodina" ["Motherland"], "Lyubil i ya v bylye gody" ["And I Was in Love"]. Lermontov devised a plan for publishing his own magazine, planned new novels, and sought Belinsky's criticism. But he soon received an order to return to his regiment and left, full of gloomy forebodings. During this long journey he experienced a flood of creative energy: his last notebook contains such masterpieces of Russian lyric poetry as "Utes" ("The Cliff"), "Spor" ("Argument"), "Svidanye" ("Meeting"), "Listok" ("A Leaf"), "Net, ne tebya tak pylko ya lyublyu" ("No, It Was Not You I Loved So Fervently"), "Vykhozhu odin ya na dorogu . . . " ("I go to the Road Alone . . . "), and "Prorok" ("Prophet"), his last work.

On the way to his regiment, Lermontov lingered on in the health resort city of Pyatigorsk for treatment. There he met many fashionable young people from St. Petersburg, among whom were secret ill-wishers who knew his reputation in court circles. Some of the young people feared his tongue, while others envied his fame. An atmosphere of intrigue, scandal, and hatred grew up around him. Finally, a quarrel was provoked between Lermontov and another officer, N.S. Martynov; the two fought a duel that ended in the poet's death. He was buried two days later in the municipal cemetery, and the entire population of the city gathered at his funeral. Later, Lermontov's coffin was moved to the Tarkhana estate, and on April 23, 1842, he was buried in the Arsenyev family vault.

Assessment. Only 26 years old when he died, Lermontov had proved his worth as a brilliant and gifted poet-thinker, prose writer, and playwright, the successor of Pushkin, and an exponent of the best traditions of Russian literature. His youthful lyric poetry is filled with a passionate craving for freedom and contains calls to battle, agonizing reflections on how to apply his strengths to his life's work, and dreams of heroic deeds. He was deeply troubled by political events, and the peasant mutinies of 1830 had suggested to him a time "when the crown of the tsars will fall." Revolutionary ferment in western Europe met with an enthusiastic response from him (verses on the July 1830 revolution in France, on the fall of Charles X), and the theme of the French Revolution is found in his later works (the poem *Sashka*).

Civic and philosophical themes as well as subjective, deeply personal motifs were closely interwoven in Lermontov's poetry. He introduced into Russian poetry the intonations of "iron verse," noted for its heroic sound and its energy of intellectual expression. His enthusiasm for the future responded to the spiritual needs of Russian society. Lermontov's legacy has found varied interpretations in the works of Russian artists, composers, and theatrical and cinematic figures. His dramatic compositions have played a considerable role in the development of theatrical art, and his life has served as material for many novels, poems, plays, and films. (V.V.Z.)

BIBLIOGRAPHY. Laurence Kelly, *Lermontov: Tragedy in the Caucasus* (1977, reissued 1983), is a detailed biography. Shorter biographical sketches are found in the works of literary criticism, such as John Mersereau, *Mikhail Lermontov* (1962); Janko Lavrin, *Lermontov* (1959); B.M. Eikhenbaum, *Lermontov: A Study in Literary-Historical Evaluation* (1981); and John Garrard, *Mikhail Lermontov* (1982), which discuss both the romantic poetry and prose of the writer. Lermontov's largest and most important prose work is analyzed in C.J.B. Turner, *Pechorin: An Essay on Lermontov's "A Hero of Our Time"* (1978); and William Mills Todd III, *Fiction and Society in the Age of Pushkin: Ideology, Institutions, and Narrative* (1986). Good translations of Lermontov into English are found in Charles Johnston (trans.), *Narrative Poems by Alexander Pushkin and by Mikhail Lermontov* (1983); and Guy Daniels (trans.), *A Lermontov Reader* (1965).

Lerner, Alan Jay (b. Aug. 31, 1918, New York, N.Y., U.S.—d. June 14, 1986, New York, N.Y.), American librettist and lyricist who collaborated with composer Frederick Loewe on the hit Broadway musicals *Brigadoon* (1947), *Paint Your Wagon* (1951), *My Fair Lady* (1956), and *Camelot* (1960) and the film *Gigi* (1958).

Lerner, whose parents were prosperous retailers (Lerner Stores, Inc.), was educated at Bedales School, Hampshire, Eng.; Choate School, Wallingford, Conn.; the Juilliard School of Music, New York City; and Harvard University (B.S., 1940), where he contributed lyrics to Hasty Pudding shows. He wrote more than 500 radio scripts between 1940 and 1942, the year he met Loewe (who had been composing theatrical songs with little success) at The Lambs theatrical club in New York City. One Lerner and Loewe Broadway production failed, and a second had a five-month run before the 1947 success of *Brigadoon.*

My Fair Lady, their fifth musical, based on George Bernard Shaw's *Pygmalion,* was an unprecedented triumph in American musical theatre. Produced by Columbia Broadcasting System, it set a record at the time for the longest original run of any musical production in London or New York City, was mounted in more than 20 countries, translated into 11 languages, toured the United States for several years, and was revived several times. The film version (1964) won seven Academy Awards. *Brigadoon* (1954), *Paint Your Wagon* (1969), and *Camelot* (1967) were also made into popular motion pictures. *Gigi,* Lerner and Loewe's collaboration directly for film, received nine Academy Awards.

Without Loewe, Lerner wrote the book and lyrics for Kurt Weill's *Love Life* (1948), and he produced scripts for several films, including *An American in Paris* (1951), for which he won an Academy Award. He attempted to collaborate with Richard Rodgers in the 1960s, but the partnership did not work out; and Lerner joined the composer Burton Lane for *On a Clear Day You Can See Forever,* successfully produced on Broadway in 1965 and filmed in 1970. Lerner also collaborated with Lane on *Carmelina* (1979) and with the composers André Previn on *Coco* (1969), Leonard Bernstein on *1600 Pennsylvania Avenue* (1976), and Charles Strouse on *Dance a Little Closer* (1983).

In 1978 Lerner published an autobiography, *The Street Where I Live* (the title being an echo of one of the famous songs in *My Fair Lady*).

Lernet-Holenia, Alexander (b. Oct. 21, 1897, Vienna, Austria—d. July 3, 1976, Vienna), prolific and popular dramatist, poet, and novelist, many of whose works exhibit nostalgia for pre-World War I Austrian aristocracy. In particular, his novel *Die Standarte* (1934), by depicting military unrest in Serbia in 1918, illustrates the loss of authority in the disintegrating empire.

Lernet-Holenia served as an Austrian cavalry officer in World War I. He wrote several successful plays after the war, ranging from society comedies to farces and melodrama: *Österreichische Komödie* (performed 1926, published 1927; "Austrian Comedy"), *Ollapotrida* (performed and published 1926; "Mishmash"), *Erotik* (performed and published 1927), *Parforce* (performed and published 1928; "By

All Means"), *Die nächtliche Hochzeit* (performed 1928, published 1929, published as a novel 1930; "The Nightly Marriage"), and *Die Frau des Potiphar* (performed and published 1934; "Potiphar's Wife"). His poetry, including *Pastorale* (1921), *Das Geheimnis Sankt Michaels* (1927; "St. Michael's Secret"), and *Die goldene Horde* (1935; "The Golden Horde"), mingles the classical tradition and modern influences. During the 1930s Lernet-Holenia also wrote detective and adventure novels, included among which are *Ich war Jack Mortimer* (1933; "I Was Jack Mortimer") and *Die Auferstehung des Maltravers* (1936; "The Resurrection of Maltraver").

Lernet-Holenia spent part of World War II in an army film unit. Throughout his life, except during the war years, Lernet-Holenia traveled and spent time in South America.

His later works—including the novel *Prinz Eugen* (1960) and the collection of short stories *Mayerling* (1960)—reflect a nostalgia for the old Austria.

Léros, island, one of the Dodecanese islands of Greece, in the Aegean Sea, east of the Cyclades and off the southwest coast of Turkey. It is surrounded by numerous islets and is full of creeks, with many promontories and deep bays. Léros is mountainous (rising to 1,073 feet [327 m]) and consists of three peninsulas joined by two isthmuses, with a total area of 20 square miles (53 square km). Bathing beaches are found on the east and west coasts. It is believed that Léros and Kálymnos just to the southeast comprise the Kalydrian isles referred to by Homer; it was famous in ancient times for its honey and for a temple of Artemis. Léros was first inhabited by Carians, then, successively, by Cretans, Ionians, Byzantines, and Rhodians; the last two quarreled over it until Rhodes took possession of it in 1319. Most of the property on the island belongs to women as a result of an old custom of handing down estates to the daughters. An annual festival derived from ancient Dionysian competitions is celebrated in houses where a marriage has taken place during the previous year. Adults compose satirical verses and children dressed as monks recite them. The chief economic activities of the island are agriculture and fishing; the fertile valleys in the centre of the island yield olives, figs, carobs, tobacco, fruit, and grapes for wine. Léros is linked to Piraeus, Rhodes, and Samos by ferry.

lerot, small rodent, a species of dormouse (*q.v.*).

Leroux, Gaston (b. May 6, 1868, Paris, Fr.—d. April 15/16, 1927, Nice), French novelist, best known for his *Le Fantôme de l'opéra* (1910; *The Phantom of the Opera*), which became famous in film and stage renditions.

After leaving school, Leroux worked as a clerk in a law office and, in his free time, began writing essays and short stories. By 1890 he had become a full-time journalist, and from 1894 to 1906 he sailed the world as a correspondent, reporting back to Paris various adventures in which he took part, notably during the Russian Revolution of 1905. In the early 1900s he began writing novels, his first success being *Le Mystère de la chambre jaune* (1907; *The Mystery of the Yellow Room*), starring an amateur detective Joseph Rouletabille. A number of sequels followed, none quite so successful. In 1910 *The Phantom of the Opera* appeared serially (before publication as a novel) and received only moderate sales and somewhat poor reviews; the melodrama of the hideous recluse abducting a beautiful young woman in a Paris opera house did not achieve international celebrity until the American actor Lon Chaney created the title role in the silent-film version of 1925.

Leroux published several other novels and a few plays but, except among mystery aficionados, never achieved wide fame as a writer of horror and crime stories.

LeRoy, Mervyn (b. Oct. 15, 1900, San Francisco, Calif., U.S.—d. Sept. 13, 1987, Beverly Hills, Calif.), American motion-picture director whose wide variety of 75 films included dramas (*Little Caesar* [1930], *I Am a Fugitive from a Chain Gang* [1932], *Thirty Seconds over Tokyo* [1944]), romances (*Tugboat Annie* [1933], *Waterloo Bridge* [1940], *Random Harvest* [1942]), epics (*Anthony Adverse* [1936], *Quo Vadis* [1951]), comedies (*Three Men on a Horse* [1936], *Mister Roberts* [1955]), and musicals (*Gold Diggers of 1933* [1933], *Lovely to Look At* [1952], *Gypsy* [1962]). He also produced several films, including the classic *The Wizard of Oz* (1939).

LeRoy, an impoverished youth, worked as a newsboy and then appeared in vaudeville for nine years before getting work in films from a relative, film pioneer Jesse L. Lasky, as a wardrobe handler. He worked his way up to directing his first feature, *No Place to Go,* in 1927. After establishing his reputation with *Little Caesar,* he turned out scores of films during his 41-year career. He touched the public's conscience with motion pictures decrying such brutalities as lynch mobs and savage prison conditions, and in 1946 he received a special Academy Award for the documentary *The House I Live In,* an indictment of intolerance. In 1957 he successfully persuaded Motion Picture Academy officials to allow the academy rather than studios to choose whether a performer should be nominated in a leading or a supporting role. A memoir, *Mervyn LeRoy: Take One,* written with Dick Kleiner, appeared in 1974. At the Oscar ceremonies in 1976, LeRoy received the Irving G. Thalberg Memorial Award for outstanding work as a producer.

Lerroux, Alejandro (b. March 4, 1864, Córdoba, Spain—d. June 27, 1949, Madrid), leader of the Spanish Radical Party who headed four governments during the period of centre-right rule (1933–35) in the Second Republic (1931–39).

The son of a sergeant major, Lerroux practiced as a lawyer and worked as a journalist in Barcelona before becoming leader of the Radical Party. In 1901 he was elected to the Spanish Parliament, and in the 1903 elections his party defeated the Catalan nationalists. His republican views led to his exile in 1907, when he fled to Argentina. After his young followers were in 1909 accused of burning convents in Barcelona, he became less extreme, and the Radicals became representative of moderate middle-class liberalism.

Lerroux welcomed the inauguration of the Second Republic in 1931 and became its first foreign minister. The general elections of November 1933 inaugurated a period of centre-right government in which he, aided by the right, played a major part. His first government (November 1933–April 1934), though composed entirely of Radicals, depended upon rightist support. Lerroux believed the republic had moved too far to the left and sought to reconcile conservatives, but, in doing so, he angered leftist groups. In October 1934 a major left-wing uprising was suppressed with great severity. Throughout 1935 Lerroux cooperated with José Maria Gil Robles, the parliamentary leader of the right, and headed several coalition cabinets that were largely ineffective.

Lerroux failed to recover politically from the "Straperlo" scandal in late 1935, in which several of his relatives and Radical Party associates were charged with corruption involving gambling concessions. In the elections of February 1936 he lost his seat in parliament in the midst of a Radical electoral debacle. He went to Portugal during the civil war (1936–39) and did not return to Spain until 1947.

Lerwick, chief town of Scotland's Shetland Islands, an archipelago lying 130 miles (210 km) north of the Scottish mainland. Situated on a fine natural harbour on Bressay Sound, Lerwick is the most northerly town in Britain. It is the administrative centre of the Shetland Islands council area.

Lerwick originated as a fishing village and continued as such until the 19th century, when it became one of the major herring ports of Britain; the "old town," huddled along the shore, contains many 17th-century buildings—including Fort Charlotte, first built by Oliver Cromwell and later burned and restored by George III, whose queen it was named after. Today whitefish, crabs, and lobsters are the mainstay. The North Sea oil boom beginning in the 1970s resulted in increased port traffic and the emergence of Lerwick as an oil supply and service base.

The name Lerwick is of Norse derivation, and the strong Norse tradition of Shetland is dramatically represented in Lerwick's Up-Helly-Aa (Fire Festival) at the end of January, when a full-sized model of a Norse longship is dragged through the town in a torchlight procession and then burned.

Les Baux-en-Provence, also called LES BAUX, village, Bouches-du-Rhône *département,* Provence-Alpes-Côte d'Azur *région,* southeastern France, on a spur of the Alpilles Hills rising abruptly from the valley floor, northeast of Arles. On this rocky hill, about 1,000 yards (900 m) long and 220 yards (200 m) wide, are a ruined château and streets of abandoned houses, plus a church, a museum, and small modern tourist installations. In the European Middle Ages this was the seat of the mighty lords of Baux, who in the 11th century held 72 towns and domains in Provence and the Dauphiné including the principality of Orange. In the 13th century their *cours d'amour* drew highborn ladies and troubadours. Over the centuries their struggles against the pope, the rulers of Provence, and the kings of France reduced the power of the house. In 1632 Louis XIII destroyed the château and city walls. Although the city later became a marquisate under the Grimaldis, its prominence was ended. The windmill (now a museum) that inspired Alphonse Daudet's *Lettres de mon moulin* is at nearby Fontvieille. Bauxite, the mineral that is the raw material for the refining of aluminum, was named for Les Baux, near which it was discovered in 1821. Local deposits are still worked. Pop. (1982) 62.

Les Cayes, also called CAYES, or AUX CAYES, town, southwestern Haiti, on the southern Caribbean shore of the southern peninsula. Founded in 1786, it was plagued by disease and pirates during colonial times. In 1815 the South American liberator Simón Bolívar visited the port to accept Haitian arms and a contingent of troops to aid him in his fight against Spain. The town was badly damaged by fire in 1908 and by hurricane in 1954. Les Cayes is Haiti's leading southern port, exporting sugar, coffee, bananas, cotton, timber, dyewood, and hides. Historic landmarks include an arsenal and several forts dating from buccaneer times. Pop. (1997 est.) 48,838.

Les Combarelles, cave famous for its prehistoric engraved designs, located near Les Eyzies in Dordogne, Fr. Thousands of superimposed engravings dating from the late Aurignacian through the middle Magdalenian periods suggest that the cave long served as the centre of a hunting cult.

Bison and reindeer are the main subjects, but grotesque humans with parts of other animals are also portrayed, perhaps intended as decoys or hunting magicians. Some of the engraved animals are lively, others stiff. Most scholars rank Les Combarelles as one of the finest products of the Ice Age.

Les Landes (France): *see* Landes.

Lesage, Alain-René, Lesage also spelled LE SAGE (b. May 6, 1668, Sarzeau, Fr.—d. Nov. 17, 1747, Boulogne), prolific French satirical dramatist and author of the novel *Gil Blas,* which was influential in making the picaresque form a European literary fashion.

Although he was orphaned at 14 and was always quite poor, Lesage was well educated at a Jesuit college in Brittany and studied law in Paris. He abandoned his legal clerkship to dedicate himself to literature and received a pension from the Abbot of Lyonne, who also taught him Spanish and interested him in the Spanish theatre.

Lesage, engraving by J.-B. Guélard, 18th century

By courtesy of the trustees of the British Museum; photograph, J.R. Freeman & Co. Ltd.

Lesage's early plays were adaptations of Spanish models and included the highly successful adapted comedy *Crispin, rival de son maître* (*Crispin, Rival of His Master*), performed in 1707 by the Théâtre Français. His prose work *Le Diable boiteux* (1707; *The Devil upon Two Sticks*) is of Spanish inspiration, but its satire is aimed at Parisian society. The more popular Théâtre de la Foire gave Lesage greater freedom as an author, and he composed for that company more than 100 *comédies-vaudevilles,* for which he is considered successor to Molière.

Lesage's *Histoire de Gil Blas de Santillane* (1715–1735; *The Adventures of Gil Blas of Santillane*) is one of the earliest realistic novels. It concerns the education and adventures of an adaptable young valet as he progresses from one master to the next. In the service of the quack Dr. Sangrado, Gil Blas practices on the poorer patients and soon achieves a record equal to his master's, *i.e.,* 100 percent fatalities. In service to Don Mathias, a notorious seducer, he also learns to equal and surpass his master. The sunnier spirit of *Gil Blas* had a civilizing effect on the picaresque tradition. Unlike most novels of the genre, it ends happily, as Gil Blas retires to marriage and a quiet country life.

Lesage, Jean (b. June 10, 1912, Montreal, Que., Can.—d. Dec. 12, 1980, near Quebec, Que.), Canadian public official who was premier of Quebec during the period of reform in the early 1960s.

Lesage received a law degree in 1934 from Laval University, Quebec, and in 1939–44 served as a crown attorney. In 1945 he was elected to the national House of Commons—to serve as parliamentary assistant to leading members of the Cabinet and also as a delegate to the United Nations. In 1953 he was appointed minister of resources and development in the national government. In 1958 he was elected leader of the provincial Liberal Party, resigning his national portfolio and Commons seat. In the provincial elections of 1960 he led the Liberal Party's victory over the conservative Union Nationale, which had been in office since 1944.

With a platform calling for social and cultural reform as well as greater provincial autonomy, Lesage set out to lead Quebec's "Quiet Revolution." He formed a Cabinet of diverse personalities who were dubbed *l'équipe de tonnerre* ("the team of thunder"). They included the first woman elected to the Quebec legislature; the left-wing nationalist René Lévesque, later to lead the separatist Parti Québecois; and the conservative champion of law and order Claude Wagner.

Lesage fought and decisively won the 1962 provincial election on the issue of the nationalization of hydroelectric power. Under Lesage's administration, the provincial government became more active in the fields of social welfare, municipal reform, and culture. He appointed the first minister of education in Quebec; the school system and the civil service were modernized; and clerical influence was reduced. His administration was active in developing closer ties with France through cultural accords.

In 1966 the Liberals were defeated by the renovated Union Nationale. Lesage was thereafter leader of the opposition until 1970, when he was succeeded by his protégé Robert Bourassa.

lesbianism, also called SAPPHISM, or FEMALE HOMOSEXUALITY, the quality or state of intense emotional and usually erotic attraction of a woman to another woman.

As it was first used in the late 16th century, the word *lesbian* was the capitalized adjectival term referring to the Greek island of Lesbos. Its connotation of "female homosexuality" was added in the late 19th century, when an association was made with the tender and often passionate poetry written by Lesbian poet Sappho (*c.* 610–*c.* 580 BC) to and about other women in her female coterie. The history of lesbianism to the present has been largely reconstructed by late 20th-century European and American theorists; perceptions from other cultures are not readily available.

Just as heterosexual orientation produces a great variety of behaviours, so, too, lesbianism presents no unified face. Some lesbians hide or deny their orientation, marrying in order to be accepted by their families and communities. Others—often in the relative anonymity of an urban setting—prefer to live openly as lesbians, sometimes bearing and rearing children.

Broadly speaking, in Europe and North America, many of the issues faced by lesbians at the turn of the 21st century were not radically different from those that concerned either heterosexual women or many gay men. Like heterosexual women, lesbians are affected by such issues as equal pay or the historical exclusion of women from medical research studies, the latter of which has led to a lack of understanding about the effect of lesbian sexuality on women's health. Like many gay men, many lesbians in long-term relationships regret the lack of legal recognition for same-sex unions. Other issues of concern to lesbians include child rearing (ranging from the inability to adopt a partner's offspring to laws barring same-sex adoption), the sharing of medical health benefits with a partner, the right to make health decisions for a partner, taxes, inheritance, and so on.

Lesbos, Modern Greek LÉSVOS, also called MITILÍNI (after its capital), largest island after Crete and Euboea in the Aegean Sea, forming with Lemnos and Áyios Evstrátios islands the *nomós* (department) of Lesbos, Greece. The capital of the *nomós* is Mytilene (*q.v.*), chief town of the 629.5-square-mile (1,630.5-square-kilometre) island and seat of a Greek Orthodox bishop. Sometimes grouped with the Greek Southern Sporades, Lesbos (the name is pre-Hellenic) was among the earlier sites of Aegean settlement. Lesbos is separated from the Asia Minor coast by two shallow channels ranging from 6 to 14 miles (10 to 23 km) wide, the Muselim (north) and the Mitilini (east), which form the entrance to the Turkish Gulf of Edremit.

The irregular coast of Lesbos is penetrated by two narrow-mouthed bays, Géras (southeast) and the Gulf of Kallonís (southwest). The island is largely volcanic in the west, and numerous thermal springs indicate the unstable subterranean structure that has caused severe earthquakes throughout history. The principal peak, Mount Lepethymnus (Áyios Ilías), reaches 3,176 feet (968 m).

Mytilene, the port, was built on an island and later connected to Lesbos by causeway, forming the two harbours. Lesbos took its name "Pentapolis" from the five cities of Mytilene, Methymna, Antissa, Eresus, and Pyrrha. (Another important city was Arisba, northwest of Kalloní, which was destroyed by an earthquake in the 5th century BC.) Pyrrha, which lies in a small valley off the Gulf of Kallonís, suffered from an earthquake about 231 BC. Antissa, on the northwestern coast just north of the present Ándissa, was destroyed by the Romans in 168 BC. Eresus, on the southwest coast, is the birthplace of the 7th-century-BC poet Sappho and the 4th–3rd-century-BC philosopher Theophrastus, Aristotle's successor. Methymna, on the north coast, has given its pre-Greek name to a town and artists' colony (formerly Mólivos) and is the second largest city after Mytilene.

Lesbos, near the Hellespont trade routes (modern Dardanelles), long has had strategic and commercial importance. In 1929–33 the British School excavated Thérmi, north of Mytilene, and Antissa, both important early Bronze Age (*c.* 3000–2750 BC) towns. Thérmi apparently was settled by Troas, judging from its Troy I-like black pottery. Cycladic influences predominated in Lesbos until 2000 BC, when the island was depopulated.

About 1050 Aetolians migrating to Lesbos made it their chief settlement and Mytilene their capital. The island prospered after Pittacus (*c.* 650–570) ended civil strife as *aisymnētēs* ("dictator"). The lyric poetry of Greece owed much to the 7th-century Lesbos-born musician Terpander and the dithyrambist Arion as well as Alcaeus and Sappho.

After a protracted struggle with Athens for Sigeum on the Hellespont (Dardanelles) and a naval defeat, Lesbos in 527 submitted to Persia, being freed only in 479 with the defeat of Persian naval forces. Lesbos then joined the Delian League under Athenian leadership. Early in the Peloponnesian War (431–404 BC), the Mytilene oligarchy forced a revolt that ended (428–27) with Athenian reprisals. Thereafter, Lesbos was repeatedly attacked by the Peloponnesians, falling to Sparta in 405. In 389 Thrasybulus recovered most of the island for Athens; in 377 it joined the Second Athenian League but in 333 served as a base for the Persian admiral Memnon against Alexander the Great of Macedonia and subsequently for other invaders until the Roman Pompey made Mytilene a free city.

As a Byzantine dominion the island flourished; in AD 809 the empress Irene was exiled there. In 821, 881, and 1055, it swayed before Saracen attacks and fell in 1091 to the Seljuq Turks. In 1224 the Byzantine emperors recovered it and in 1354 gave it to a Genoese trading family. After a prosperous century, it came under Turkish domination (1462–1911) and then joined the Greek kingdom.

Lesbos' fertile plains and valleys produce grapes, cereals, and, the principal product and export, olives. Hides, soap, and tobacco are also produced; sardine fishery is important. Lesbos is handicapped by severe earthquakes such as that which destroyed Mytilene (1867), and this may partly account for the few ancient remains. Pop. (1981) 104,620.

Lescaze, William (b. March 27, 1896, Geneva, Switz.—d. Feb. 9, 1969, New York, N.Y., U.S.), Swiss-born American architect best known for conceiving, in conjunction with George Howe, the Philadelphia Savings Fund Society Building, or PSFS (1931–32), which effectively introduced the International style of architecture into the United States. It is considered one of the best-designed skyscrapers of the pre-World War II era of modern architecture.

Lescaze studied in Zürich under the modernist architect Karl Moser and worked in France until 1920, when he went to the United States. He practiced first in Cleveland and then moved to New York City. His first important commission was for the Oak Lane Country Day School, near Philadelphia, a structure notable for its scaling down to child size of many features, such as stairs, and for its use of cork floors to reduce knee injuries. In 1929 he entered into a five-year partnership with George Howe, after which he headed his own firm. His own house in Manhattan (1934) and the Longfellow Building (1941) were notable early examples of the International style in the United States.

After World War II, Lescaze was a successful designer of office buildings in New York City, two of which were under construction at the time of his death. Among his important late works were the Borg-Warner Building, Chicago (1955); the chancery building of the Swiss embassy, Washington, D.C. (1959); and the Church Peace Center Building, New York City (1962).

Lesch-Nyhan syndrome, hereditary metabolic disorder affecting the central nervous system and characterized by incoordination, mental retardation, aggressive behaviour, and compulsive biting. The cause of the syndrome is a defective organic catalyst or enzyme, hypoxanthine-guanine-phosphoribo-syltransferase, which normally is particularly active in brain cells and is involved in the metabolism of purines. The Lesch-Nyhan syndrome is transmitted by a recessive sex-linked gene, affecting chiefly males, and it is possible to detect it before birth in the offspring of women known to be carriers of the trait.

Leschetizky, Theodor, original name TEODOR LESZETYCKI (b. June 22, 1830, Łańcut, Pol., Austrian Empire [now in Poland]—d. Nov. 14, 1915, Dresden, Ger.), Polish pianist and teacher who, with Franz Liszt, was the most influential teacher of piano of his time.

Leschetizky studied under Carl Czerny in Vienna and thus was linked indirectly with the playing of Czerny's teacher, Ludwig van Beethoven. In 1852 he went to St. Petersburg as a pianist and teacher. From 1878 he taught in Vienna. As one of the great pianists of the Romantic era, he approached the printed note with a certain amount of freedom. As a teacher, he stressed thorough understanding of the music, absolutely sound technique, and, above all, beauty of tone. Although the celebrated "Leschetizky method" of teaching was much discussed, he himself claimed to have no fixed method, and his students affirmed that he developed the individual characteristics of each student. His pupils included many of the leading pianists of the 19th and early 20th centuries, among them Artur Schnabel, Ossip Gabrilowitsch, and Ignacy Paderewski.

Lescluse, Charles de: *see* Clusius, Carolus.

Lescot, Pierre (b. *c.* 1515, Paris, Fr.—d. 1578, Paris), one of the great French architects of the mid-16th century who contributed a decorative style that provided the foundation for the classical tradition of French architecture.

In his youth Lescot, who came from a wealthy family of lawyers, studied mathematics, architecture, and painting. There is no evidence that he visited Italy, although much of his design was classical; it appears that he acquired his knowledge of architecture from illustrated books and from Roman ruins in France.

Lescot, marble portrait bust by Julie Charpentier, 1814; in the Musée de Versailles, France
Archives Photographiques

Lescot's most important contribution to architecture was his rebuilding of the Louvre, which he began in 1546 as a commission from Francis I. The style and design of Lescot's work on the Louvre reflect a revolution in French architecture marked by the influence of classical elements. His work on the facade combined traditional French elements and classical features to create a unique style of French classicism. Lescot's other work includes the Hôtel Carnavalet (1545), which still survives in part; a screen at Saint-Germain-l'Auxerrois (1554); the Fontaine des Innocents (1547–49); and the château of Vallery. Unfortunately, none of these works has survived intact.

Lesdiguières, Charles I de Blanchefort, duc de (duke of): *see* Créquy, Charles I de Blanchefort, marquis de.

Lesdiguières, François de Bonne, duc de (duke of) (b. April 1, 1543, Saint-Bonnet-en-Champsaur, Fr.—d. Sept. 21, 1626, Valence), constable of France and Protestant leader who late in life abjured the faith.

Lesdiguières had begun to study law at Paris when he joined the Huguenot troops in Dauphiné and distinguished himself in mountain warfare. In 1575 he became the acknowledged leader of Huguenot resistance in the province and fought there for several years to secure better terms for the Protestants.

Lesdiguières took up arms for Henry of Navarre in 1585 and, after the truce of 1588–89, secured the submission of Dauphiné. For the next several years he fought to defend France against the Spanish and Savoyards, with the war against the latter proceeding on and off until 1601.

Lesdiguières was made marshal of France in 1609, duke and peer of France in 1611, and governor of Dauphiné in 1612. He moderated the political claims made by his coreligionists under the terms of the Edict of Nantes, which had acknowledged Protestant religious and political rights. In 1622 he formally abjured the Protestant faith and took up arms against Protestants in the south; he became constable of France and received the Order of the Saint Esprit. Much of his official correspondence was published in 1878–84.

leshy, in Slavic mythology, the forest spirit. The *leshy* is a sportive spirit who enjoys playing tricks on people, though when angered he can be treacherous. He is seldom seen, but his voice can be heard in the forest laughing, whistling, or singing. When the *leshy* is spotted, he can be easily recognized; for, though he often has the appearance of a man, his eyebrows, eyelashes, and right ear are missing, his head is somewhat pointed, and he lacks a hat and belt. In his native forest the *leshy* is as tall as the trees, but, the moment he steps beyond, he shrinks to the size of grass.

The *leshy* is a spirit of fairly homogeneous characteristics that are familiar to most Slavs living in heavily forested areas; the Ukrainians living in steppe country lack a fully articulated *leshy* and know about him from hearsay.

Lesina (Croatia): *see* Hvar.

lesion, in physiology, a structural or biochemical change in an organ or tissue produced by disease processes or a wound. The alteration may be associated with particular symptoms of a disease, as when a gastric ulcer produces stomach pain, or it may take place without producing symptoms, as in the early stages of cancer. Certain lesions, such as the genital chancre of syphilis, are diagnostic of a particular disease, and early recognition of the physical or biochemical injury can help to prevent later, more serious manifestations of a disease; thus, the recognition and classification of disease lesions is a major part of pathology.

Lesions may be classified as anatomic (evident to the unaided senses), histologic (evident only under a microscope), or biochemical (evident only by chemical analysis). A typical gross anatomic lesion might be the solid tumour of a carcinoma of the colon, while the corresponding histological lesion would be the atypical cells (dysplasia) that precede or surround the gross tumour; and a biochemical lesion associated with the same disease process would be the abnormal carcinoembryonic antigen found in the blood of some colon cancer patients.

Consult the INDEX *first*

Leskov, Nikolay Semyonovich, pseudonym STEBNITSKY (b. Feb. 16 [Feb. 4, Old Style], 1831, Gorokhovo, Russia—d. March 5 [Feb. 21], 1895, St. Petersburg), novelist and short-story writer who has been described as the greatest of Russian storytellers.

As a child Leskov was taken to different monasteries by his grandmother, and he used those early memories of Russian monastic life with good effect in his most famous novel, *Soboryane* (1872; *Cathedral Folk,* 1924). A junior clerk of a criminal court in Orel and Kiev, he later joined an English firm and traveled all over Russia; it was during these travels that he obtained the material for most of his novels and short stories. Leskov began his writing career as a journalist. In 1865 he

Leskov
Novosti Press Agency

published his best known story, *Ledi Makbet Mtsenskogo uezda* (*Lady Macbeth of the Mtsensk District,* 1961), the passionate heroine of which lives and dies by violence. His most popular tale, however, remains *Skaz o Tulskom kosom Levshe i o stalnoy Blokhe* (1881; "The Tale of Cross-eyed Lefty from Tula and the Steel Flea"), a masterpiece of Gogolesque comedy in which an illiterate smith from Tula outwits the skill of the most advanced British craftsman. Another story, the picaresque *Ocharovanny strannik* (1873; *Enchanted Wanderer,* 1961), was written after a visit to the monastic islands on Lake Ladoga in 1872. His early novels *Nekuda* (1864; "Nowhere to Go") and *Na nozhakh* (1870–71; "At Daggers Drawn") were violently attacked by the Russian radicals as revealing an attitude of uncompromising hostility toward the Russian revolutionary movement, an attitude Leskov later modified. In 1969 W.B. Edgerton translated into English, for the first time, 13 of Leskov's stories, with a new translation of "The Steel Flea."

Leslie, Alexander: *see* Leven, Alexander Leslie, 1st earl of.

Leslie, John, Leslie also spelled LESLEY (b. Sept. 29, 1527, Scotland—d. May 31, 1596, near Brussels), Scottish Roman Catholic bishop and historian and an adviser of Mary Stuart, queen of Scots. He was involved in plots to overthrow the Protestant government of Queen Elizabeth I and to place Mary on the throne of England.

John Leslie, detail of an engraving
BBC Hulton Picture Library

The illegitimate son of a parson at Kingussie, Inverness-shire, Leslie studied at the universities of Aberdeen, Paris, and Poitiers. From about 1554 he taught canon law at King's College, Aberdeen, and held a diocesan administrative post. When Mary Stuart, the recently widowed queen consort of France, returned to reign in Scotland in 1561, Leslie became her adviser, holding judicial office, a privy councillorship, and (from 1566) the bishopric of Ross. Unhappy with Mary's attachment to the Earl of Bothwell, he accused the Earl of seducing her with black magic. Leslie was loyal to Mary even after her forced abdication of the Scottish throne. He tried to defend her before the board of inquiry convened at York (Oct. 4, 1568) by Queen Elizabeth, and in 1569 he became Mary's accredited representative at Elizabeth's court.

Leslie was implicated in an unsuccessful revolt in the north of England in January 1569 but was acquitted. He then joined Roberto Ridolfi, a Florentine businessman living in London, in planning a more ambitious rebellion. Elizabeth was to be deposed (and murdered) in favour of Mary, with the aid of Spanish armed forces; Mary was to be married to Thomas Howard, 4th duke of Norfolk. Leslie's confessions (October–November 1571) and other evidence led to Norfolk's execution for treason (June 2, 1572) and to his own imprisonment. Released late in 1573, Leslie tried without success to obtain assistance for Mary from continental rulers. From 1579 he lived in France, where he was suffragan and vicar general of the diocese of Rouen. At Rome in 1578 Leslie published his history of Scotland, *De origine, moribus et rebus gestis Scotorum.* Partly derived from the works of Hector Boece and John Major, it presents a strongly Catholic viewpoint.

Leslie, Sir John (b. April 10, 1766, Largo, Fife, Scot.—d. Nov. 3, 1832, Coates), Scottish physicist and mathematician who first created artificial ice.

In 1802 Leslie's explanation of capillary action was the first that is consistent with present-day theory. Two years later he published *An Experimental Inquiry into the Nature and Propagation of Heat.* In 1810 he froze water by using an air pump. Elected to the chair of mathematics at the University of Edinburgh in 1805, he was transferred to the chair of natural philosophy in 1819 and was knighted in 1832.

Leśmian, Bolesław, original name BOLESŁAW LESMAN (b. Jan. 12, 1878, Warsaw—d. Nov. 5, 1937, Warsaw), lyric poet among the first to adapt Symbolism and Expressionism to Polish verse.

Of Jewish origin, Leśmian was educated in Kiev, wrote some of his early poems in Russian, and spent most of his life practicing law in a provincial town. In later years he was elected to the Polish Academy of Literature.

His small output includes *Sąd rozstajny* (1912; "Orchard"); *Łąka* (1920; "The Meadow"), the volume that established his reputation; *Napój cienisty* (1936; "The Shadowy Drink"); and *Dziejba leśna* (1938; "Woodland Tale"). Though the difficulty of his work, which is often symbolic in nature, tended to obscure its excellence, Leśmian has nevertheless achieved widespread recognition since his death.

Leśniewski, Stanisław (b. March 30, 1886, Serpukhov, Russia—d. May 13, 1939, Warsaw), Polish logician and mathematician who was a co-founder and leading representative of the Warsaw school of logic.

Life. Leśniewski was the son of one of the civil engineers chiefly responsible for the construction and supervision of the trans-Siberian railroad. After preliminary schooling in Russia and the Gymnasium in Siberia, he attended—as was the custom of the time—several universities in continental Europe, finally taking his doctoral degree in 1912 at the Polish University of Lwów (now Lviv, Ukraine), then a part of Austria. His dissertation was approved by Kazimierz Twardowski, who, for his wide-ranging influence on Polish intellectual life, is known as the father of contemporary Polish philosophy. Twardowski, like Edmund Husserl (the founder of Phenomenology), was a student in Vienna of Franz Brentano, an Aristotelian and Scholastic philosopher who, although not himself interested in formal logic, was noted for his precise and thorough analysis of philosophical problems. Under his influence, Leśniewski's first scholarly interests focussed upon problems of philosophical logic, such as those that had concerned John Stuart Mill in 19th-century England and Husserl and others of the Austrian school. Thus, his doctoral dissertation of 1911 dealt with the analysis of existential propositions.

The intellectual activity of Leśniewski divides into three distinct periods. The first extends from his dissertation to the appearance in 1916 of his first work on the theory of collective sets. Leśniewski attributed the discovery of his true intellectual vocation to the influence of Jan Łukasiewicz, also a pupil of Twardowski and then a *privat dozent* at the University of Lwów. Already learned in the history of logic, to which he was to make outstanding contributions, Łukasiewicz was at the time studying the work of the German logicians Gottlob Frege and Ernst Schröder, the importance of which he was mainly responsible for making known in Poland, and teaching his first course in mathematical logic. It was Łukasiewicz' book *O Zasadzie Sprzeczności u Arystotelesa* (1910; "On the Principle of Contradiction in Aristotle") that awakened Leśniewski from his dogmatic slumber. From it he became interested in the problem posed by the discovery of the antinomies, or paradoxes, in logic and mathematics that threatened to undermine the foundations of all deductive science. His efforts to overcome and solve these antinomies, with which Frege and Bertrand Russell were also wrestling, eventually led to the great discoveries for which he is known.

Although Leśniewski then definitely turned his back on philosophy in favour of logic—he later spoke of himself as a renegade from philosophy—his initial impression of mathematical logic was not at all favourable. He distrusted its technical formal notation, the scant attention given to its relation to ordinary language, and the resulting equivocations in the use of such terms as class, implies, and true. In attempting to clear away the equivocations in the work of Russell, however, he soon became convinced that the formal and artificial language of mathematical logic was essential for his work, that ordinary language was too clumsy and imprecise. The writings of this period were completed, however, before he had adopted the rigorous methods of mathematical logic and were all later repudiated by him.

The period from 1916 to 1927 was one of intensive and creative research in which he accumulated a mass of results but refrained from publishing them. In 1915, upon the reopening of the University of Warsaw, Łukasiewicz had been called from Lwów to become professor of philosophy. Leśniewski, after teaching for two years at a Warsaw Gymnasium and spending the war years in Moscow, followed his friend and colleague to Warsaw in 1919 as professor of the philosophy of mathematics. They soon established a thriving centre of research that attracted talented students from all sides.

Leśniewski finally felt constrained to start publishing some account of his findings, even though they were not yet in as perfect a form as he would have desired. Beginning with the publication, in 1927, of his first mature work on the foundations of mathematics and extending until his death, in 1939, he published a series of papers expounding the main lines of his theories of logic and mathematics. These publications gained a worldwide reputation for the Warsaw school. Yet, just as it was reaching its height, Leśniewski died suddenly and unexpectedly on the eve of the war that shortly engulfed the school in the common fate of Poland.

Many of Leśniewski's findings remained unpublished at his death. Although all of his manuscripts were destroyed by the war, many of the unpublished results of his researches have since been made known through the work of his students, particulary that of Bolesław Sobociński and Alfred Tarski.

Major work in logic. The distinctive and original contribution of Leśniewski consists in the construction of three interrelated logical systems, to which he gave the names, derived from the Greek, of protothetic, ontology, and mereology (*q.v.*). The logical basis of the whole theory, and hence its name (*prōtos,* "first"), is provided by protothetic, which is the most comprehensive theory yet developed of the relations between propositions. The other two systems are based on a distinction the lack of which, Leśniewski claimed, was the source of Russell's difficulties with the antinomies: that between a distributive and a collective class. In its distributive use, a class expression is identical with a general name; thus, to say that a person belongs to the class of Poles is to say that that person is a Pole. Hence, ontology (*on,* "being") is the logic of names; and, combined with protothetic, it yields all of the theorems of syllogistic (traditional Aristotelian logic) and of logical algebra, as well as of the logic of sets and relations. Mereology (*meros,* "part") is the logic of a whole conceived as though physically constituted by its parts—*i.e.,* of the collective class, as the class of all automobiles in Chicago consists of the entire collection of them. Hence, mereology is a general theory of the relation between part and whole.

In developing these theories, Leśniewski gave great care to the statement of their metalogic and, for this purpose, elaborated a general theory of semantic categories, which is analogous, on the one hand, to the traditional doctrine of the parts of speech and, on the other, to Husserl's "meaning categories."

Leśniewski developed his logical systems with a clarity and precision that established a new standard for mathematical rigour. In their powers of implication, they are strong enough to provide a logical foundation for all of classical mathematics. They also overcome the antinomies in a way that Leśniewski claimed is better and truer than any other solution. In his opinion, modern mathematicians and logicians are often too neglectful, if not contemptuous, of humanity's naive and basic intuitions of the way things are. For this very reason, Alfred Tarski, one of his students who later went to the United States, described his position as "an intuitive formalism." Leśniewski was openly critical of a pure formalism that would consider logic and mathematics as nothing more than a game of symbols. It is true that he advocated and employed formalist methods for their rigour and precision, but he maintained that a theory ultimately must be judged for its accord with reality. Nevertheless, Leśniewski maintained that his logical systems are neutral in that they make no metaphysical assumptions and are equally well adapted to diverse and even conflicting philosophical interpretations.

(O.A.B.)

BIBLIOGRAPHY. Eugene C. Luschei, *The Logical Systems of Lesniewski* (1962); Z.A. Jordan, *Philosophy and Ideology: The Development of Philosophy and Marxism-Leninism in Poland Since the Second World War* (1963); Tadeusz Kotarbiński, *Gnosiology: The Scientific Approach to the Theory of Knowledge* (1966); Zbigniew Stachniak, *Introduction to Model Theory for Leśniewski's Ontology* (1981); Jan T.J. Srzednicki, V.F. Rickey, and J. Czelakowski (eds.), *Leśniewski's Systems* (1984); Jan Woleński, *Logic and Philosophy in the Lvov-Warsaw School* (1989); Peter Simons, *Philosophy and Logic in Central Europe from Bolzano to Tarski: Selected Essays* (1992).

Lesotho, officially KINGDOM OF LESOTHO, formerly BASUTOLAND, independent kingdom in southern Africa, an enclave within the east-central part of the Republic of South Africa. Lesotho's maximum length from north to south is about 150 miles (240 km), and maximum width from east to west is also about 150 miles. The capital is Maseru. Area 11,720 square miles (30,355 square km). Pop. (2003 est.) 1,802,000.

A brief treatment of Lesotho follows. For full treatment, *see* MACROPAEDIA: Southern Africa.

For current history and for statistics on society and economy, *see* BRITANNICA BOOK OF THE YEAR.

The land. About two-thirds of Lesotho's total land area is mountainous (elevations more than 10,000 feet [3,000 m] above sea level), with higher elevations in the northeast and east in the Drakensberg Range. Mount Ntlenyana (11,424 feet [3,482 m]), on the

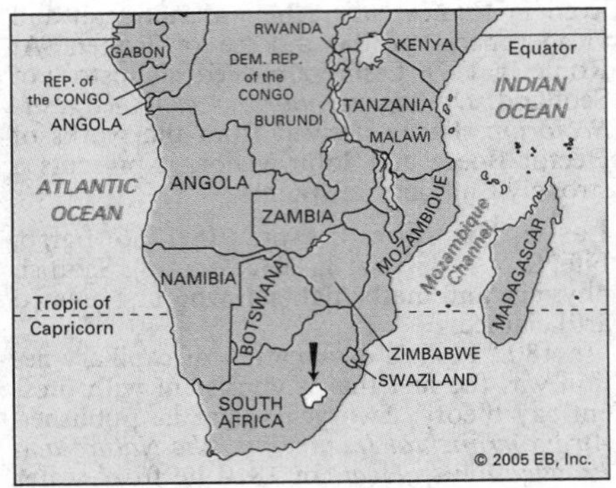

Lesotho

northeastern border with KwaZulu/Natal province, is the highest point in Lesotho and in southern Africa. The terrain gradually descends westward to a foothill region and farther west to a fertile and densely populated lowland region (elevations between 5,000 and 6,000 feet [1,500 and 1,800 m]), which forms a narrow (25-mile- [40-kilometre-] wide) corridor along the Caledon River. The Maloti Mountains in the central northwest are the source of two of South Africa's largest rivers—the eastward-flowing Tugela and the westward-flowing Orange River.

Lesotho has a temperate subtropical climate. The mean summer temperature is 68° F (20° C), and the mean winter temperature is 50° F (10° C). In the highlands of the northeast the temperature range is much wider, and frost occurs frequently. Precipitation, usually concentrated in torrential thunderstorms, averages about 28 inches (710 mm) annually and decreases from 40 inches (1,016 mm) in the east to 30 inches (762 mm) in the west. The Maloti Mountains are usually snowcapped in winter. Lesotho's climatic conditions are most favourable for grasslands; the subtropical meadows of the mountain slopes are excellent grazing grounds for cattle, sheep, and goats, the latter providing wool and mohair, the principal agricultural products of the country. Indigenous animal life is limited to small antelopes, hare, and hyrax. Lesotho is the last stronghold of the bearded vulture, or lammergeier.

Lesotho's most important natural mineral resource is diamonds; its diamond deposits are mostly located in the northeast. The Lesotho Highlands Water Project (a five-dam scheme under construction since the late 1980s), when completed, will harness the country's fast-flowing rivers for hydroelectric power. The project is expected to solve most of the country's energy problems and to bring in substantial revenue from the sale of water to South Africa.

The people. Four-fifths of Lesotho's population is Sotho, a Bantu-speaking people. Most of the rest are Zulu. The Kwena are the largest Sotho subgroup in the country; the Natal (North) Nguni, the Mahlape, and the Cape (South) Nguni (Thembu) are among the other subgroups. The official languages are Southern Sotho (Sesotho) and English. Afrikaans, Zulu, Xhosa, and French are also spoken. About 90 percent of the population is Christian, with Roman Catholics dominating. A small number practice traditional religions.

Lesotho's population is overwhelmingly rural. About half of the adult males leave to seek work in the mines of South Africa, and about one-third are unemployed. Lesotho's growth rate is lower than that of most African nations. More than one-third of the total population is under age 15.

The economy. Lesotho has a developing mixed economy in which both the public and private sectors participate. The economy is dependent on agriculture and remittances from citizens working in South Africa. The gross national product (GNP) is not growing as rapidly as the population, and the GNP per capita remains low.

Agriculture accounts for more than one-tenth of the gross domestic product (GDP) but employs almost two-fifths of the workforce. The king nominally owns all land in trust for the nation, and chiefs allocate arable land to individuals and families. Under the Land Tenure Act of 1979, the king awards leases for 99 years to farmers. Agricultural productivity in Lesotho is low, and production of corn (maize), potatoes, wheat, and sorghum, which are the chief staples, must be supplemented by imports from South Africa. Significant quantities of manufactured goods (mostly clothing), as well as machinery and transport equipment, beverages, and wool are exported.

The production of diamonds continues to be dominated by De Beers Consolidated Mines of South Africa, but large-scale exploitation ceased in 1982 because of the world recession in the diamond market and the low diamond recovery rates at the mine. The development of domestic manufacturing industries, which account for about one-eighth of the GDP, is promoted by the Lesotho National Development Corporation. Industries include food processing, textile and apparel making, and furniture making. Lesotho's external trade is dominated by South Africa.

Government and social conditions. Lesotho attained independence in 1966 as a constitutional monarchy, with a parliamentary system of government. But after the ruling Basotho National Party (BNP) staged a coup in 1970 to maintain itself in power, the constitution was suspended. One-party rule continued until 1986, when a coup sponsored by South Africa and carried out by Lesotho's paramilitary forces established a Military Council to rule the country in consultation with the king; political activity was banned. Following another coup in 1991 the reorganized Military Council promised a new constitution and announced that political activity could resume.

The constitution now in effect (following general elections held in 1993) makes the hereditary king the head of state. There is a bicameral legislature consisting of a nonelective Senate (mostly principal chiefs) and a National Assembly, whose members are elected by universal suffrage to five-year terms; the king appoints as prime minister the leader of the political party or coalition that commands the support of a majority of members. The judicial system consists of a High Court, a court of appeal, and subordinate courts.

Worsening health conditions were reflected in the average life expectancy of about 47 years (down from 59 years in the 1990s) and a high infant mortality rate. Health facilities are concentrated in urban areas, and there is a shortage of medical personnel. Public health facilities are also inadequate, with a major proportion of the population lacking a potable water supply. Lesotho has a high incidence of infectious and parasitic diseases. Malnutrition is also a serious problem, and nearly one-third of the population is HIV-positive.

Lesotho's literacy rate of about 80 percent for men and about 60 percent for women is among the highest in Africa. Education is free and compulsory in seven-year primary schools. A large majority of the school-aged children attend primary schools, but only half attend secondary schools.

Cultural life. Lesotho has a strong literary tradition, which has been stimulated by the extension of the educational system. Folklore, both oral and written, flourishes, as do village crafts such as woodwork, pottery, weaving, and basketwork.

History. The Lesotho region was probably first inhabited by San. About the 16th century Bantu-speaking farmers began to settle the area, and a number of chiefdoms arose. A series of violent upheavals throughout the region in the 1820s annihilated or dispersed many of these groups, but a few strong chiefs arose to form defensive kingdoms. The most powerful of these chiefs was Moshoeshoe of the Moketeli, a minor Kwena lineage. In 1824 he occupied Thaba Bosiu ("Mountain of the Night"), and from this defensive centre he organized the Basotho.

From that time until his death (1870), Moshoeshoe was the undisputed leader of the Basotho. In 1843 he negotiated British protection as tension between the Basotho and the South African Boers increased. In 1868 Lesotho became a British territory. After Moshoeshoe's death Lesotho was annexed by the Cape Colony (1871). Administration by the Cape Colony ignored many Basotho customs, and in 1880 open revolt erupted when the government attempted to disarm the people. In 1884 Lesotho ceased to be part of the Cape Colony and became a British High Commission Territory. Basotho chiefs were allowed to govern according to tradition and custom. The success of self-government under British control is attributed to the early resident commissioners and the paramount chief Lerotholi. In 1905 Lerotholi died, and the national council, with British concurrence, elected his son Letsie II as paramount chief.

In 1910, when the four South African colonies were united under the Union of South Africa, Lesotho remained under the control of the British. South Africa assumed that it would ultimately annex Lesotho, but in 1964 a constitution adopted in Lesotho provided for its independence as a constitutional monarchy, with the paramount chief serving as king. In 1965 general elections were held in which the Basutoland National Party, headed by Chief Leabua Jonathan, won. Chief Jonathan became the first prime minister of independent Lesotho under its king, Moshoeshoe II. Jonathan remained prime minister for the next 20 years. Moshoeshoe's demand in 1966 for powers wider than those of a constitutional monarch were denied, however. In 1970 Jonathan retained power by a coup after his party had apparently lost a general election to an opposition party.

Jonathan and his party had initially supported cooperation with South Africa, but he adopted a more independent foreign policy in the 1970s and '80s, criticizing his neighbour's apartheid policies and giving refuge to members of the outlawed African National Congress. In response South Africa mounted an economic blockade of Lesotho in early 1986, and Jonathan was soon overthrown in a military coup and replaced by Major General Justin Lekhanya. Relations between Lesotho and South Africa subsequently improved, with each country agreeing not to permit its territory to be used to mount attacks on or subvert the other.

Meanwhile, Lesotho's economy had continued to deteriorate owing to overpopulation and a shortage of agricultural land. These economic pressures and internal political discontent led to continuing government instability in the early 1990s. Elections held in 1993, however, resulted in a landslide victory for the antiapartheid Basotho Congress Party led by Ntsu Mokhehle, who became prime minister. King Moshoeshoe II, who had been dethroned in 1990 and had regained the throne in 1995, died in 1996 and was succeeded by his eldest son, who had reigned as Letsie III in 1990–95.

lespedeza, also called BUSH CLOVER, any member of a genus (*Lespedeza*) of herbaceous plants in the pea family (Fabaceae), some of which are useful as forage and green manure crops. The approximately 40 species in the genus are native to North America, tropical and East Asia, and Australia. The lespedezas may be roughly grouped as herbaceous perennials, small shrubs, and annuals. Lespedezas are either erect or trailing in habit, and some perennial species can reach heights of up to 3 m (10 feet). The best-known species have alternate, toothless leaves that are made up of three leaflets. All lespedezas are adapted to warm, humid climates.

Lespedezas are among the principal hay and pasture crops in the southeastern and south-central United States (along with alfalfa). Two of the most widely used annual species are the common lespedeza (*L. striata*) and the Korean lespedeza (*L. stipulacea*), both native to Asia. A perennial species, the sericea lespedeza (*L. cuneata*), is also used in American agriculture, both as a pasture crop and to combat soil erosion. Owing to its great root system, its dense growth canopy, and its ability to grow on badly eroded soils, the sericea lespedeza is extremely useful in American soil conservation. Some shrublike lespedeza species, such as the bicolour lespedeza (*L. bicolor*), are grown as ornamentals. Lespedezas are also valuable for birds and other wildlife, affording them food and cover.

"De," "la," and similar components of a name, when followed by a space, are alphabetized as separate words (e.g., *De Forest, Lee*). *When they are joined to the following part of a name, the combination is treated as a single word* (e.g., *DeForest, John William*).

Lespinasse, Julie de, in full JULIE-JEANNE-ÉLÉANORE DE LESPINASSE (b. 1732, Lyon, France—d. May 23, 1776, Paris), hostess of one of the most brilliant and emancipated of Parisian salons and the author of several volumes of passionate letters that reveal her romantic sensibility and genuine literary gifts.

The natural child of the comtesse d'Albon, she was sent to convent school and made governess to the marquise de Vichy, her mother's legitimate daughter. Madame du Deffand, one of the reigning aristocratic Parisian hostesses, recognized Mademoiselle de Lespinasse's intelligence and charm and persuaded her to come to Paris and assist at her literary salon from 1754 to 1764, when she became jealous of her younger companion's popularity and dismissed her.

Julie de Lespinasse, detail of a watercolour by L. Carmontelle; in the Condé Museum, Chantilly, Fr.
Giraudon/Art Resource, New York City

Mademoiselle de Lespinasse set up her own salon in the rue Saint-Dominique, and the philosopher and mathematician Jean Le Rond d'Alembert eventually joined her there; she nursed him through a serious illness but never returned his deep love for her. Instead, she was torn between her passions for unworthy men of fashion—the marquis de Mora and the comte de Guibert. Her *Lettres* (1809) show her intensely experienced emotions of love, remorse, and despair. She died brokenhearted as a result of her unrequited affection for Guibert, leaving d'Alembert the letters she had intended for Guibert.

Lesse River, river in southeastern Belgium. The Lesse River rises west of Libramont in the Ardennes and follows a short (52-mile [84-kilometre]), meandering northwesterly course to the Meuse River at Anseremme, a few miles south of Dinant. The river's early northward course lies in a shallow valley of the Ardennes, where it receives the Lomme tributary. Reaching the less-resistant rocks (limestone and shale) of the Famenne depression, it abruptly turns westward toward the Meuse. Disappearing underground for about a mile at Han-sur-Lesse, the river has created the celebrated Grottoes of Han, which are renowned for their stalactites and stalagmites. One of the grottoes measures 505 feet (154 m) long and 450 feet (137 m) wide. In its lowest section, from Houyet to Anseremme, the Lesse River flows in a deep, winding valley between steep limestone cliffs. In the cavern of Naulette, situated on the left bank, some prehistoric remains, which have been assigned to the Mousterian industry period, were discovered in 1866.

lessee: *see* landlord and tenant.

Lesseps, Ferdinand, vicomte de, in full FERDINAND-MARIE, VICOMTE DE LESSEPS (b. Nov. 19, 1805, Versailles, France—d. Dec. 7, 1894, La Chenaie, near Guilly), French diplomat famous for building the Suez Canal across the Isthmus of Suez (1859–69) in Egypt.

Lesseps was from a family long distinguished in government service. Appointed assistant vice-consul at Lisbon in 1825, he was sent in 1828 to Tunis and in 1832 to Alexandria, where he studied a proposal (by one of Napoleon's engineers) for a Suez Canal. At Alexandria the survey report of J.-M. Le Père, one of Napoleon's chief engineers, on the Isthmus of Suez, and his friendship with Muḥammad ʿAlī, the Turkish viceroy of Egypt, and his son, Saʿīd Pasha, led Lesseps to hope that he might one day finish the canal that Le Père had begun. For the time, however, he could not pursue his plans. From 1833 to 1837, Lesseps was consul at Cairo, where he gained distinction in combating an outbreak of plague. Two years later he was transferred to Rotterdam. Subsequently he served at Málaga and at Barcelona, where he was promoted to consul general. From 1848 to 1849, after the proclamation of the Second Republic, he was minister of France at Madrid. In May 1849 he sent a mission to Rome, from where Pope Pius IX had fled and where Giuseppe Mazzini had proclaimed the republic. This mission was ambiguous: it was a question of "placing a limit on the pretensions of Austria . . . of ending by arbitration . . . the differences which divided . . . the peninsula. . . ." Lesseps tried to reconcile the irreconcilables: the papacy and the republic. But at the end of May, when the French Legislative Assembly, conservative by nature, followed the Constituent Assembly, which held republican views, he was recalled,

Lesseps
Culver Pictures

handed over to the Council of State, and censured. French troops reestablished pontifical power in Rome. The diplomatic career of Lesseps was shattered. But in 1854, an invitation from Saʿīd Pasha, newly appointed viceroy, or khedive, of Egypt, revived his ambitions. On Nov. 30, 1854, Saʿīd Pasha signed the first act of concession authorizing Lesseps to pierce the isthmus of the Suez.

A first scheme, directed by Lesseps, was immediately drawn up by the surveyors Linant Bey and Mougel Bey (L.-M. Linant de Bellefonds and E. Mougel) providing for direct communication between the Mediterranean and Red Sea, and, after being slightly modified, it was adopted by an international commission of engineers in 1856. Encouraged by this approval, Lesseps allowed no obstacles to retard the work, and he succeeded in rousing the French people to subscribe more than half the capital needed to form the company, which was organized in 1858. The first blow of the pickax was given by Lesseps at Port Said on April 25, 1859; and 10 years later, on Nov. 17, 1869, the Suez Canal was officially inaugurated by the empress Eugénie, who had been invited by the host of the celebrations, the khedive (viceroy), Ismāʿīl Pasha. In 1875 the British government, on the initiative of the prime minister, Benjamin Disraeli, purchased the khedive Ismāʿīl's Suez Canal shares and became the largest shareholder. Lesseps cooperated loyally with the British (in spite of the fact that they had earlier tried to block the building of the canal because of their suspicions of the French) and facilitated the transfer of ownership. Though he usually tried to keep out of politics, Lesseps stood as a Bonapartist candidate for a seat in the Chamber of Deputies at Marseille in 1869 but was defeated by Léon Gambetta, later one of the founders of the Third Republic.

In 1879, when the International Congress of Geographical Sciences met in Paris and voted in favour of the construction of a Panama canal, the 74-year-old Lesseps undertook to carry out the project. His despotic temper and stubbornness, however, made him fail to appreciate the difficulties of the task: at first he thought that it would be possible to pierce a canal without locks, even though the route was barred by the Culebra cut and by the torrential Chagres River. The task proved to be beyond the capacities of a private company, so that eventually, in 1889, the company that Lesseps had formed had to liquidate. After an official inquiry in 1892, the French government instituted the prosecution of the company's administrators, and in February 1893 Lesseps and his son Charles (1849–1923) were sentenced to five years' imprisonment. Only Charles, however, was imprisoned, and in June an appeals court reversed the decision. On the other hand, the fact that members of the government and parliamentarians were accused of having accepted bribes from the company made the Panama scandal a political affair as well as a financial one, with important repercussions in the history of the Third French Republic.

Lesseps was a member of the French Academy, of the Academy of Sciences, and of numerous scientific societies. He was also decorated with the grand cross of the Legion of Honour and the Star of India and received the freedom of the City of London. His great gifts, unselfishness, and social charm made him everywhere respected, and the scandal that clouded his last years has done nothing to tarnish his reputation. (A.Da.)

BIBLIOGRAPHY. John Pudney, *Suez: De Lesseps' Canal* (1969), describes the construction of the canal and Lesseps' involvement and traces the canal's history to 1967. Maron J. Simon, *The Panama Affair* (1971), recounts the history of the French Panama Canal Company and the scandal of its financial collapse.

Lesser Antilles, formerly CARIBBEES, long arc of small islands in the Caribbean Sea extending in a north–south direction from the Virgin Islands to Trinidad and then in an east–west direction from Margarita to Aruba off the northern coast of Venezuela. They comprise 6 percent of the total land area of the West Indies. The term Caribbees derives from the Carib Indians, who inhabited many of the islands at the time of their European discovery.

Since the early times of Spanish colonization the Lesser Antilles have been divided into two groups; the division was adopted by the French, Dutch, and Germans. The Spanish names of the subgroups reflect the importance to the region of the prevailing easterly trade winds; they are Barlovento (Windward, or Upwind) and Sotavento (Leeward, or Downwind). The islands called windward are those ranging south from Dominica to Grenada; those that arc generally westerly from Guadeloupe to the Virgin Islands are the leeward group. The east–west chain of islands, close to the South American coast, are arid because the tradewinds drop their moisture on the Windward group. Three small islands (Margarita, Coche, and Cubagua) form the Venezuelan state of Nueva Esparta (*q.v.*), and some 70 others, mostly uninhabited, also belong to Venezuela. *See also* Leeward Islands; Windward Islands; Netherlands Antilles.

Lesser Armenia: *see* Little Armenia.

Lesser Atlas (mountains, North Africa): *see* Anti-Atlas.

Lesser Himalayas, also called INNER HIMALAYAS, LOWER HIMALAYAS, or MIDDLE HIMALAYAS, middle section of the Himalayan mountain ranges, extending southeastward across north Pakistan, north India, Nepal, Sikkim (India), and into Bhutan. The range lies between the Great (north) and Siwālik, or Outer (south), Himalayan ranges and has an average height of 12,000 to 15,000 feet (3,700 to 4,500 m). It includes portions of the Punjab, Kumaun, Nepal, and Assam Himalayas.

Lesser Khingan Range, Wade–Giles romanization HSIAO HSING-AN LING, Pinyin XIAO HINGGAN LING, mountain range in the northeastern section of Heilungkiang *sheng* (province), China. The range is connected to the Greater Khingan Range by the I-lo-hu-li Mountains, which run northwest–southeast for some 375 miles (600 km), extending southwest of the Amur River until, beyond the Sungari River, in the area of Chia-mu-ssu, they merge into the eastern Manchurian mountain system in the Wan-ta Range.

Although they share the same name, the Lesser Khingan Range is a completely different mountain system from the Greater Khingan Range. The Greater Khingan Range is largely composed of rocks that are igneous (formed from the molten state) and metamorphic (formed under conditions of heat and pressure) and was formed in the Jurassic Period, whereas the Lesser Khingan was until Quaternary times a part of the great intermontane trough formed by the Manchurian and Zeya-Bureya plains. The range was formed by the uplift of its comparatively young sedimentary rocks in comparatively recent geologic times. The relief is generally rounded and gentle, the main sharp fault line running along the Amur Valley, giving the northeastern face a somewhat sharper contour than the southwest, which merges gently into the Sungari plain. The range forms a watershed between the Amur River system and the Sungari and Nen River system. The Lesser Khingan is lower than the Greater Khingan and has elevations averaging between 1,650 and 3,300 feet (500 and 1,000 m), with most of the range being less than 2,000 feet (600 m). The Lesser Khingan's climate is slightly more temperate and much more humid. Winters, nevertheless, are still long and bitterly cold, and much of the area is under permafrost.

The whole area is covered with timber, mostly consisting of larch and birch in the north, and of mixed broad-leafed and coniferous forests (cedar, spruce, yew, birch, elm, and larch) in the south. Forestry is the main economic base, and in the southern part of the range a number of railways, centring on Nan-ch'a and I-ch'un, have been constructed to transport lumber. The southern end of the range is marked by the great fault line of the Sungari River valley. The name Lesser, or Outer, Khingan (Wai Hsing-an) is also given by the Chinese to ranges in Russia, to the north of the Amur, in the region of Birobidzhan.

Lesser Slave Lake, lake in central Alberta, Canada, 130 miles (209 km) northwest of Edmonton and 400 miles (640 km) south of Great Slave Lake (in the Northwest Territories). It is 60 miles (97 km) long by 12 miles (19 km) wide and has an area of 451 square miles (1,168 square km). Fed by many small streams, it drains eastward into the Athabasca River via the Lesser Slave River. The name, first used by the Cree Indians, refers to the Slave (Dogrib) Indians, who once inhabited its shores. The lake was an important transportation link to the Peace River district from 1910 until 1916, when its significance declined with the building of the Northern Alberta Railway along the southern shore. The lake and its periphery are now important for lumbering, farming, and commercial fishing. The Lesser Slave Lake Provincial Park (28 square miles [73 square km]) adjoins its northeastern shore, 4 miles (6 km) north of the town of Slave Lake.

Lessing, Doris (May) (b. Oct. 22, 1919, Kermanshah, Iran), British writer whose novels and short stories are largely concerned with people involved in the social and political upheavals of the 20th century.

Her father was serving in Iran as a captain in the British army at her birth. The family moved to a farm in Rhodesia, where she lived from 1924 until she settled in England in 1949. In her early adult years she was an active communist. *In Pursuit of the English* (1960) tells of her initial months in England, and *Going Home* (1957) describes her reaction to Rhodesia on a return visit.

Her first published book, *The Grass Is Singing* (1950), is about a white farmer and his wife and their African servant in Rhodesia. Her most substantial work is her series of novels about Martha Quest, who also grows up in southern Africa and settles in England. They were published in two volumes as *Children of Violence* (1964–65). *The Golden Notebook* (1962), in which a woman writer attempts to come to terms with the life of her times through her art, is one of the most complex and the most widely read of her novels. *The Memoirs of a Survivor* (1975) is a prophetic fantasy. A master of the short story, Lessing has published several collections, including *The Story of a Non-Marrying Man* (1972); her African stories, collected in *This Was the Old Chief's Country* and *The Sun Between Their Feet* (both 1973); and *Stories* (1978).

Lessing turned to science fiction in a five-novel sequence titled *Canopus in Argos: Archives* (1979–83). The novels *The Diary of a Good Neighbour* (1983) and *If the Old Could . . .* (1984) were published pseudonymously, under the name Jane Somers, to dramatize the problems of unknown writers. In 1985 Lessing published *The Good Terrorist,* a novel about a group of revolutionaries in London. *The Fifth Child,* a horror story about a family destroyed by the birth of a monstrous child, was published in 1988.

Lessing, Gotthold Ephraim (b. Jan. 22, 1729, Kamenz, Upper Lusatia, Saxony [Germany]—d. Feb. 15, 1781, Braunschweig, Brunswick [Germany]), German dramatist, critic, and writer on philosophy and aesthetics. He helped free German drama from the influence of classical and French models and wrote the first German plays of lasting importance. His critical essays greatly stimulated German letters and combated conservative dogmatism and cant while affirming religious and intellectual tolerance and the unbiased search for truth.

Gotthold Lessing, detail of an oil painting by Georg May, 1768; in the Gleimhaus, Halberstadt, Ger.
By courtesy of the Gleimhaus, Halberstadt, Ger.

Education and first dramatic works. Lessing's father, a highly respected theologian, was hard put to support his large family even though he occupied the position of *pastor primarius* (chief pastor). At the age of 12, Lessing, even then an avid reader, entered the famous *Fürstenschule* ("elector's school") of St. Afra, in Meissen. He was a gifted and eager student and acquired a good knowledge of Greek, Hebrew, and Latin, while his admiration for the plays of the Latin dramatists Plautus and Terence fired him with the ambition to write comedies himself.

In the autumn of 1746 Lessing entered the University of Leipzig as a student of theology. His real interests, however, lay toward literature, philosophy, and art. Lessing became fascinated by the theatre in Leipzig, which had recently been revitalized by the work of a talented and energetic actress, Caroline Neuber. Neuber took an interest in the young poet and in 1748 successfully produced his comedy *Der junge Gelehrte* ("The Young Scholar"). The play is a delightful satire on an arrogant, superficial, vain, and easily offended scholar, a figure through which Lessing mocked his own bookishness. The other comedies belonging to this Leipzig period of 1747–49 (*Damon, Die alte Jungfer* ["The Old Maid"], *Der Misogyn* ["The Misogynist"], *Die Juden* ["The Jews"], *Der Freigeist* ["The Free Thinker"]) are witty commentaries on human weaknesses—bigotry, prejudice, nagging, fortune hunting, matchmaking, intrigue, hypocrisy, corruption, and frivolity. Set against this background are virtuous men and women who are considerate and selfless, sensitive and helpful, forthright, and faithful in love. In *Die Juden* Lessing praised unappreciated nobility of mind and thus struck a blow for tolerance toward the Jews at a time when they were still confined to a ghetto life. Lessing had set himself the goal of becoming the German Molière: in these comedies he most interestingly begins to draw his characters as recognizable individuals, breaking away from the traditional dramatic "types."

Early in 1748 Lessing's parents, who disapproved of his association with the theatre in Leipzig, summoned him home. But he managed to win their consent to begin studying medicine and was soon allowed to return to Leipzig. He quickly found himself in difficulties because he had generously stood surety for some members of the Neuber company—although himself heavily in debt. When the company folded, he fled from Leipzig in order to avoid being arrested for debt. He eventually reached Berlin in 1748, where he hoped to find work as a journalist through his cousin Mylius, who was by this time an established editor. In the next four years he undertook a variety of jobs, mainly translating French and English historical and philosophical works into German. But he also began to make a name for himself through his brilliant and witty criticism for the *Berlinische privilegirte Zeitung,* on which he was book review editor. He also launched a periodical of his own, *Beiträge zur Historie und Aufnahme des Theaters* ("Contributions to the History and Improvement of the Theatre"), which was discontinued in 1750.

Rising reputation as dramatist and critic. From 1751 to 1752 Lessing was in Wittenberg, where he took his degree in medicine. He then returned to Berlin, where he started another periodical, *Theatralische Bibliothek* ("Theatrical Library"), but this too had to be closed down after only four volumes. The most significant event during this time was the publication in 1753–55 of a six-volume edition of his works. Apart from some witty epigrams, the edition contained the most important of his Leipzig comedies. It also contained *Miss Sara Sampson,* which is the first major *bürgerliches Trauerspiel,* or domestic tragedy, in German literature. Middle-class writers had long wanted to do away with the traditional class distinctions in literature, whereby heroic and tragic themes were played out by aristocratic figures, while middle-class characters appeared only in comedy. Lessing was, in fact, not the first German writer to challenge this tradition, but it is fair to say that his play marks the decisive break with the classical French drama that still dominated the German stage. *Miss Sara Sampson* was inspired by George Lillo's *London Merchant* (1731) and by the novels of Samuel Richardson—with their praise of middle-class feminine virtue—and, to a lesser degree, by the sentimental *comédie larmoyante* ("tearful comedy"), originated in France by the early 18th-century dramatist Pierre-Claude de La Chausée. It is the first German play in which *bürgerlich* characters bear the full burden of a tragic fate, and it had its successful premiere at Frankfurt an der Oder in 1755. Its reflective prose skillfully lays bare the psychology of the situation—a conflict between the demands of virtue and the heart, between conscience and passion—and its characters are finely drawn. The plot centres on an innocent, sensitive heroine of a bourgeois family; she becomes the victim of Lady Marwood, her vampirelike rival in love, who disregards all restraints and inhibitions, and of Mellefont, a weak man who vacillates between the two women but finally atones for his guilt by his death.

Characteristic of Lessing's writings at this period is his *Rettungen* ("Vindications"), which is outstanding for its incisive style and clarity of argument. In its four essays he aimed to defend independent thinkers such as the Reformation-period writers Johannes Cochlaeus and Gerolamo Cardano, who had been unjustly slandered and persecuted. His scintillating and biting polemic *Vade Mecum für den Herrn Samuel Gotthold Lange* (1754) was directed against the carelessly corrupt translations of the poetry of Horace by the arrogant scholar S.G. Lange, whose literary reputation was demolished by Lessing's attack. From this point on, Lessing was justly feared as a literary adversary who used his command of style as a finely honed weapon. The philosopher Moses Mendelssohn and the writer and publisher C.F. Nicolai stand out among Lessing's Berlin friends. With these men Lessing conducted a truly epoch-making correspondence (*Briefwechsel über das Trauerspiel,* 1756–57; "Correspondence About Tragedy") on the aesthetic of tragic drama. Tragedy, Lessing maintained, should not preach morality but rather should arouse admiration and pity in the audience as evidence of emotional involvement.

Between November 1755 and April 1758 Lessing lived again at Leipzig, but he moved back to Berlin in May 1758 and remained there until November 1760. There he contributed regularly to Nicolai's weekly, *Briefe, die neueste Literatur betreffend* ("Letters Concerning the Latest Literature"), writing a number of essays on contemporary literature. The central point of these was a vigorous attack on the influential theatre critic J.C. Gottsched for his advocacy of a theatre modeled on French drama, especially that of the 17th-century tragedian Pierre Corneille. Lessing maintained that the courtly, mannered drama of France was alien to the German mentality. Instead, he demanded a truly national drama, belonging to the people, based on faithfulness to nature and reality. He urged German playwrights to take Shakespeare as their model. In the 17th *Literaturbrief* he published a stirring scene from his own fragmentary Faust drama. In this scene, Lessing sketches out a "Faust without evil" whose relentless spirit of inquiry is justified before God, notwithstanding his pact with the devil. He thus paved the way for his young contemporary Johann Wolfgang von Goethe and his great dramatic version of the Faust story.

In 1759 Lessing published some masterly prose fables, largely social criticism, and with them an essay on the fable form itself, in which he formulated the particular laws of the genre by analyzing its didactic and allegorical structure. In 1760 Lessing went to Breslau as secretary to General Tauentzien, the military governor of Silesia. He studied philosophy and aesthetics in the Breslau libraries, the result being the great treatise *Laokoon: oder über die Grenzen der Malerei und Poesie* (1766; "Laocoon; or, On the Limits of Painting and Poetry"). Here he took issue with the contemporary art historian Johann Winckelmann, specifically over his interpretation of the "Laocoon," a famous sculpture of Hellenistic times (*c.* 1st century BC), which shows the priest Laocoon and his sons as they are about to be killed by the serpents that hold them entwined. In the *Laokoon* Lessing attempted to fundamentally define the separate functions of painting and of poetry. He pointed out that whereas painting is bound to observe spatial proximity—and must, therefore, select and render the seminal and most expressive moment in a chain of events—poetry has the task of depicting an event organically and in its temporal sequence. The essence of poetry thus lies not in description but in the representation of the transitory, of movement.

The poetic fruit of Lessing's stay in Breslau was the comic masterpiece *Minna von Barnhelm* (1767), which marks the birth of classical German comedy. Goethe was to praise it for its contemporary relevance and for its central theme (the struggle between Prussia and Saxony in the Seven Years' War), which was an event of national significance. The central characters are a Prussian officer, Major Tellheim, and a young gentlewoman from Thuringia, Minna. The upright officer's conscientiousness and rigid interpretation of the code of honour has endangered his relationship with Minna. She, charming and spirited, takes matters into her own hands and, prompted by her heart's perceptions, resolutely overcomes the obstacles that war and occupation have placed in the way of their union and resolves the conflict between the claims of conscience and those of happiness. Thus, in thinking and acting like true representatives of the Enlightenment, the two eventually behave like ordinary people and so bear witness to Lessing's concept of humanity. The two protagonists are supported by forcefully drawn secondary characters, and Lessing's dialogue enhances a lively dramatic action that can still hold an audience's attention.

On returning to Berlin in 1765 Lessing tried for the post of director of the royal library; but since he had quarreled with Voltaire, who lived as a favourite at Frederick the Great's court, the king (who in any case thought little of German authors) rejected his application. Lessing then accepted the offer of some Hamburg merchants to act as adviser and critic in their privately funded venture of a national theatre. The project collapsed within a year, however, and Lessing recognized with some bitterness that the time for a German national theatre was not yet ripe. Even so, his reviews of more than 50 performances were published, in the form of 104 brief essays on basic principles of the drama, under the title of *Hamburgische Dramaturgie* (1767–69). Here, too, Lessing argued against tragedy modeled on that of Corneille and Voltaire, although he praised the realism of the contemporary French writer Denis Diderot's descriptions of middle-class life. Lessing interpreted Aristotle's famous and much-discussed concept of tragic catharsis (purging) as meaning the emotional release that follows tension generated in spectators who witness tragic events; he concludes that the sensations evoked by pity and fear should afterward exert a moral influence on the audience by being transformed into virtuous action. In 1768–69 he published *Briefe antiquarischen Inhalts* ("Letters of Antiquarian Content"), an attack on the pretentious learning and elitist attitudes of the Halle professor C.A. Klotz. Another result of this dispute was the lucid and perceptive essay *Wie die Alten den Tod gebildet* ("How the Ancients Depicted Death").

Final years at Wolfenbüttel. Being extremely poor, in 1770 Lessing had no choice but to accept the badly paid post of librarian at Wolfenbüttel, which he had earlier visited in 1766. His years there were unhappy and tempestuous but rich in achievement. Lessing became involved in perhaps the most bitter controversy of his career when he also published extracts containing extremely radical ideas from the papers of the recently deceased biblical critic and scholar H.S. Reimarus under the title *Fragmente eines Ungenannten* (1774–77; "Fragments of an Unknown"). Theologians viewed these publications as a serious challenge to religious orthodoxy, even though Lessing himself had taken up a mediating position toward the radical theses of Reimarus, who had rejected the basic tenets of the Christian faith. Lessing went into battle against the orthodox clergy, involving himself in violent controversies with their leader, the chief pastor of Hamburg, J.M. Goeze. Against this rigid dogmatist, who was a man of almost pharisaical narrow-mindedness, Lessing launched some of his most cutting polemics, notably "Anti-Goeze" (1778), in which he expounded his belief that the search for truth is more valuable than the certainty gained by clinging to doctrinaire orthodoxy.

Lessing's tragedy *Emilia Galotti* was performed in 1772. Written in intense and incisive prose, this brilliantly constructed play deals with a conflict of conscience at the court of an Italian prince. In 1779 appeared the "dramatic poem" in iambic verse *Nathan der Weise.* This is a didactic play of a theological and philosophical nature, combining ethical profundity with many comic touches, and is a work of high poetic quality and dramatic tension. *Nathan der Weise* symbolizes the equality of three great religions in regard to their ethical basis, for the play celebrates man's true religion—love, acting without prejudice and devoted to the service of mankind. Among the representatives of the three religions—Islāmic (Saladin), Christian (the Templar), and Jewish (Nathan)—only the Jew, in whose character Lessing paid tribute to his old friend Moses Mendelssohn, lives up to the ideal of full humanity; he alone is capable of complete self-abnegation and has the courage to speak the truth even to the mighty. The fact that the main characters discover in the end that they are blood relatives serves to underscore their common membership in the larger family of mankind.

Lessing's last work, *Die Erziehung des Menschengeschlechts* (1780; *The Education of the Human Race*), is a treatise that closely reflects the working of his mind and expresses his belief in the perfectibility of the human race. In the history of the world's religions, Lessing saw a developing moral awareness that would, he believed, eventually attain the peak of universal brotherhood and moral freedom that would transcend all dogmas and doctrines.

Thus the last decade of his life spent at Wolfenbüttel produced a rich harvest of philosophical and literary works. But his life there was otherwise full of tribulations. His health had begun to give way, and it was a lonely existence, with only a few trips to break the monotony. In 1776 he had finally been able to marry Eva König, the widow of a Hamburg merchant and a friend of long standing. But she died in 1778 while giving birth to their only child. Lessing's last years were lonely and poor, and upon his death he was buried in a pauper's grave at public expense.

(J.Mu./Ed.)

BIBLIOGRAPHY. Siegfried Seifert, *Lessing-Bibliographie* (1973), a comprehensive bibliography; *Sämmtliche Schriften,* ed. by his brother C.G. Lessing, J.J. Eschenburg, and C.F. Nicolai, 31 vol. (1771–1825), the first volumes of which were published during Lessing's lifetime; *Gotthold Ephraim Lessings sämmtliche Schriften,* ed. by Karl Lachmann, 3rd ed. by Franz Muncker, 23 vol. (1886–1924, reissued 1968), a standard and complete historical-critical edition; *Lessings Werke,* ed. by Julius Peterson and Waldemar Von Olshausen, 25 vol. (1925), likewise a complete edition. Erich Schmidt, *Lessing: Geschichte seines Lebens und seiner Schriften,* 4th ed., 2 vol. (1923), a complete biography written in the positivistic method; Theodor W. Danzel and G.E. Guhrauer, *Gotthold Ephraim Lessing: sein Leben und seine Werke,* 2nd ed. rev. by W. Von Maltzahn and R. Boxberger, 2 vol. (1880–81), a basic work, complementary to Schmidt; Ilse Graham, *Goethe and Lessing* (1973), seeks the sources of their inspiration; Henry B. Garland, *Lessing: The Founder of Modern German Literature,* 2nd ed. (1962), compressed and to the point; Paul Rilla, *Lessing und sein Zeitalter* (1960; reissued 1977), the first total presentation from a Marxist viewpoint; Karl S. Guthke, *Gotthold Ephraim Lessing,* 3rd ed. (1979), an important study; Francis J. Lamport, *Lessing and the Drama* (1981), a study of the tension between the modern content and the classical form of his drama.

lessivé soil: *see* podsolic soil.

lessor and lessee: *see* landlord and tenant.

L'Estrange, Sir Roger (b. Dec. 17, 1616, Hunstanton, Norfolk, Eng.—d. Dec. 11, 1704, London), one of the earliest of English journalists and pamphleteers, an ardent supporter of the Royalist cause during the English Civil Wars and Commonwealth period (1649–60), who was eventually rewarded for his loyalty by being appointed surveyor of the imprimery. In this position he had the power to license and control the press, and he energetically weeded out unlicensed printers who issued antigovernment propaganda.

L'Estrange, detail of an oil painting attributed to John Michael Wright, *c.* 1680; in the National Portrait Gallery, London

By courtesy of the National Portrait Gallery, London

L'Estrange was deeply implicated in an unsuccessful attempt to recapture the town of Lynn, Norfolk, from anti-Royalist forces in 1644, and he was imprisoned for four years. He later withdrew to the Netherlands. Just before the restoration of the monarchy he attacked the poet John Milton, a leading apologist for the Commonwealth, in a pamphlet called *No Blinde Guides* (1660), a reference to Milton's blindness. Appointed surveyor in 1663, he also published three news sheets: the *Intelligencer* and the *News* (both 1663–66) and the *Observator* (1681–87), as well as numerous pamphlets in support of the government. He was knighted in 1685 after helping to discredit the Popish Plot, a fictitious story alleging that the Jesuits were planning to assassinate King Charles II.

The "bloodless revolution" of 1688, in which King James II lost the throne, cost L'Estrange his official post. Accomplished in languages, he afterward supported his wife and himself chiefly by translations of many standard authors, including the lively *Fables of Aesop, and other Eminent Mythologists: with Morals and Reflexions* (1692).

Lestres, Alonié de: *see* Groulx, Lionel-Adolphe.

Lesueur, Jean-François (b. Feb. 15, 1760, Drucet-Plessiel, near Abbeville, Fr.—d. Oct. 6, 1837, Paris), composer of religious and dramatic works who helped to transform French musical taste during the Revolution.

In 1781 Lesueur was appointed chapelmaster at the cathedral of Dijon and in 1786 at Notre-

Jean-François Lesueur, engraving

J.P. Ziolo

Dame in Paris. There he aroused controversy by introducing a large orchestra to accompany his masses, which, he maintained, should make a dramatic appeal. Though Lesueur's masses, admired by opera goers, caused Notre-Dame to be described as *L'Opéra des gueux* ("The Beggars' Opera"), he succeeded in blending the sacred and secular styles, thus anticipating the religious works of Hector Berlioz and Charles Gounod, and also the *Requiem* of Verdi. He knew Gregorian chant well and made a study of the Greek modes. In his Christmas oratorio he transformed themes in a manner suggesting Wagner's use of leitmotiv. After 1789 he wrote several odes and chants for performance at the open-air celebrations of the Revolution by vast numbers of choristers and instrumentalists. Between 1793 and

1796 he wrote his operas *La Caverne, Paul et Virginie,* and *Télémaque.* He was inspector of the Paris Conservatoire from 1795 to 1802 and in 1804 was made director of music to Napoleon I, to whom he dedicated his opera *Ossian ou les bardes.* He was later director of music to Louis XVIII and in 1818 professor of composition at the Conservatoire, where his pupils included Berlioz, Gounod, Ernest Guiraud, and Ambroise Thomas.

LeSueur, Lucille (American actress): *see* Crawford, Joan.

Lésvos (Greece): *see* Lesbos.

leśyā (Sanskrit: "light," "tint"), according to Jainism, a religion of India, the special aura of the soul that can be described in terms of colour, scent, touch, and taste and that indicates the stage of spiritual progress reached by the creature, whether human, animal, demon, or divine. The *leśyā* is determined by the adherence of karmic matter to the soul, resulting from both good and bad actions. This adherence is compared to the way in which particles of dust adhere to a body smeared with oil.

The *jīva,* or soul, is classified according to the good or bad emotions that hold sway. Thus the *saleśī* ("having *leśyā*") are all those who are swayed by any of the emotions, and the *aleśī* are those liberated beings (*siddhas*) who no longer experience any feelings, neither pain nor pleasure, not even humour. The three bad emotions (ill will, envy, and untruthfulness) give the *leśyā* a bitter taste, harsh or dull colour, a smell that can be likened to the odour of a dead cow, and a texture rougher than the blade of a saw. The three good emotions (good will, union with goodness, and nondistinction) lend the aura the fragrance of sweet flowers, the softness of butter, a taste sweeter than fruit or honey, and a pleasing hue ranging from bright red to pure white.

Leszczyński, Stanisław (king of Poland): *see* Stanisław I.

Leszetycki, Teodor: *see* Leschetizky, Theodor.

Leszno, German LISSA, former (1975–98) *województwo* (province), west-central Poland, now part of Wielkopolskie and Dolnośląskie (*qq.v.*) provinces.

Leszno, German LISSA, city, Wielkopolskie *województwo* (province), west-central Poland. The town is a rail junction and an agricultural and manufacturing centre. It was founded in the 15th century by the prominent Leszczyński family, whose tombs are in the parish church. In the 16th century a band of Protestant Moravian Brothers, expelled from Bohemia, made Leszno a centre of the Reformation. The educator John Amos Comenius lived and taught there. During the 17th and 18th centuries, the town prospered as a textile and academic centre. It passed to Prussian rule, returning to Poland after World War I. Pop. (2002) 63,660.

Letchworth, town ("parish"), North Hertfordshire district, administrative and historic county of Hertfordshire, England, north of London. Britain's first planned "garden city," much copied elsewhere, it was founded in 1903 by Sir Ebenezer Howard, who established the new town movement. The commercial centre and the residential and industrial areas are carefully separated. Industries include engineering, printing and publishing, and light manufactures. Pop. (2001) 42,798.

lethal injection, method of execution whereby a prisoner is administered chemicals that induce death. Now the most widely used method of execution in the United States, lethal injection was first adopted by Oklahoma in 1977 because injection was considered cheaper and more humane than electrocution and lethal gas. Used in a majority of the U.S. states, lethal injection can also be employed at the national level, in federal and military prisons. It is the sole method of execution in some states. Other countries that have adopted this form of captial punishment include Guatemala, China, Guam, and the Philippines.

Lethbridge, city, southern Alberta, Canada, on the Oldman River, near its junction with the St. Mary River, in the foothills of the Canadian Rockies, 135 miles (217 km) south-southeast of Calgary. Founded in the 1880s as a mining town called Coalbanks, it was renamed Lethbridge, after William Lethbridge, president of the Northwest Coal and Navigation Company, upon arrival of the Canadian Pacific Railway (1885). While coal is still important, the discovery of oil and natural gas in the vicinity and the growth of agricultural industries has brought about a diversification of the economy. Lethbridge is the centre of an irrigation network, begun in 1900, that has become the most extensive in Canada (more than 1,000,000 acres [400,000 hectares]), watering fields for ranching, grains, and vegetables (especially sugar beets).

A replica of Fort Whoop-Up (1860), once notorious for its whiskey trade with the Indians, stands in Indian Battle Park; on the banks of the Oldman River, the park marks the site of the last great encounter (1870) between the Cree and the Blackfoot Indians prior to a peace treaty of 1871. The Nikka Yuko centennial garden (created 1967) is one of the largest authentic Japanese gardens in North America. The city is the provincial headquarters of the Royal Canadian Mounted Police and holds the annual (July) Whoop-Up Days exhibition and rodeo. The University of Lethbridge was founded in 1967, and Lethbridge Community College in 1957. Inc. town, 1891; city, 1906. Pop. (2001) 67,374.

Lethe (Greek: "Oblivion"), in Greek mythology, daughter of Eris (Strife) and the personification of oblivion. Lethe is also the name of a river or plain in the infernal regions.

In Orphism, a Greek mystical religious movement, it was believed that the newly dead who drank from the River Lethe would lose all memory of their past existence. The initiated were taught to seek instead the river of memory, Mnemosyne, thus securing the end of the transmigration of the soul. At the oracle of Trophonius near Lebadeia (modern Levadhia, Greece), which was thought to be an entrance to the underworld, there were two springs called Lethe and Mnemosyne.

Aristophanes' *The Frogs* mentions a plain of Lethe. In Book X of Plato's *The Republic* the souls of the dead must drink from the "river of Unmindfulness" before rebirth. In the works of the Latin poets Lethe is one of the five rivers of the underworld.

Lethington, Sir Richard Maitland, Lord: *see* Maitland, Sir Richard.

Leticia, capital of Amazonas *departamento,* southeastern Colombia, on the Amazon River, at the point where the borders of Colombia, Brazil, and Peru meet. Founded as a military outpost and river port by Peruvians in 1867, the jungle village passed into Colombian hands in the 1930s. Despite recent growth and the introduction of tourism and regular air service, Leticia retains the atmosphere of an outpost. Indians, who subsist on hunting and gathering, live around the town; there is almost no industry, and rubber gathering is the principal economic activity. Leticia possesses a customs house and, though not accessible by road, has regular river connections with Iquitos (Peru), Manaus (Brazil), Florencia (Caquetá department), and other jungle towns. Pop. (2003) 27,782.

Leto, Latin LATONA, in classical mythology, a Titan, the daughter of Coeus and Phoebe, and mother of the god Apollo and the goddess Artemis. The chief places of her legend were Delos and Delphi. Leto, pregnant by Zeus, sought a place of refuge to be delivered. She finally reached the barren isle of Delos, which, according to some, was a wandering rock borne about by the waves until it was fixed to the bottom of the sea for the birth of Apollo and Artemis. In later versions the wanderings of Leto were ascribed to the jealousy of Zeus's wife, Hera, who was enraged at Leto's bearing Zeus's children. The foundation of Delphi followed immediately upon the birth of Apollo.

Leto has been plausibly identified with the Lycian goddess Lada; she was also known as a goddess of fertility and as Kourotrophos (Rearer of Youths).

Leto, Giulio Pomponio: *see* Laetus, Julius Pomponius.

letter of ——— : *see under* substantive word (*e.g.,* credit, letter of).

letterpress printing, also called RELIEF PRINTING, or TYPOGRAPHIC PRINTING, in commercial printing, process by which many copies of an image are produced by repeated direct impression of an inked, raised surface against sheets or a continuous roll of paper. Letterpress is the oldest of the traditional printing techniques and remained the only important one from the time of Gutenberg, about 1450, until the development of lithography late in the 18th century and, especially, offset lithography early in the 20th.

Originally the ink-bearing surface for printing a page of text was assembled from individual types by a typesetter or compositor, letter by letter and line by line. The first keyboard-actuated typesetting machines, the Linotype and the Monotype (*qq.v.*), were introduced in the 1890s. If only a small number of copies is to be made, printing can be done directly from the hand- or machine-set blocks of type assembled in forms, but for long press runs, duplicates—stereotypes or electrotypes (*qq.v.*)—are made to prevent wear and damage of the expensive types.

Letterpress was originally carried out on platen presses, in which the paper is pressed against the flat, inked form by a flat platen; later, the platen was replaced by a roller in the flat-bed cylinder press; still later, the printing form was wrapped around one cylinder and the paper was passed between this cylinder and a second, creating a rotary press (*see* printing).

Several procedures have been developed for the production of line drawings or reproduction of photographs in the form of halftone pictures by letterpress. The most widely used method of preparing a printing plate for such matter is photoengraving (*q.v.*).

Letterpress can produce work of high quality at high speed, but it requires much time to adjust the press for varying thicknesses of type, engravings, and plates. Because of the time needed to make letterpress plates and to prepare the press, many newspapers have changed to offset printing. To combat this trend, letterpress printers have developed printing plates made from a photosensitive plastic sheet that can be mounted on metal. *See also* flexography.

letterset (printing): *see* dry offset.

Lettish language: *see* Latvian language.

Lettow-Vorbeck, Paul von (b. March 20, 1870, Saarlouis, Rhine Province, Prussia [now in Germany]—d. March 9, 1964, Hamburg), lieutenant colonel commanding Germany's small African force during World War I, who became a determined and resourceful guerrilla leader hoping to influence the war in Europe by pinning down a disproportionately large number of Allied troops in his area.

A member of the South West Colonial Forces in 1914, Lettow-Vorbeck served on the expedition to put down the Herero and Hottentot rebellion, during which he gained experience in bush fighting. Appointed commander of the (German) East African Colonial Forces, he repelled a British landing at Tanga (Tanzania) in November of that year. For four years, with a force that never exceeded about 14,000 (3,000 Germans and 11,000 askaris, or native Africans), he held in check a much larger force (estimates range from 130,000 to more than 300,000) of British, Belgian, and Portuguese troops.

On his return to Germany in January 1919, Lettow-Vorbeck was welcomed as a hero. In July 1919 he led a corps of right-wing volunteers that occupied Hamburg to prevent its take-over by the left-wing Spartacists. He was a deputy to the Reichstag (parliament) from May 1929 to July 1930. Though a member of the right wing, he was not a Nazi and unsuccessfully tried to organize a conservative opposition to Hitler.

lettre de cachet: *see* cachet, lettre de.

"De," "la," and similar components of a name, when followed by a space, are alphabetized as separate words (e.g., *De Forest, Lee*). *When they are joined to the following part of a name, the combination is treated as a single word* (e.g., *DeForest, John William*).

lettuce (*Lactuca sativa*), cultivated annual salad plant, probably derived from the prickly lettuce (*L. scariola*) of the family Asteraceae. Four botanical varieties of lettuce are cultivated: (1) asparagus lettuce (variety *asparagina*), with narrow leaves and a thick, succulent, edible stem; (2) head, or cabbage, lettuce (variety *capitata*), with the leaves folded into a compact head; (3) leaf, or curled, lettuce (variety *crispa*), with a rosette of leaves that are curled, finely cut, smooth-edged or oakleaved in shape; and (4) cos, or romaine, lettuce (variety *longifolia*), with smooth leaves that form a tall, oblong, loose head. There are two classes of head lettuce: the butter-head types with soft heads of thick, oily leaves, and crisp-head types with brittle-textured leaves that form very hard heads under proper temperature conditions.

Lettuce (*Lactuca sativa*, variety *capitata*)
Derek Fell

For successful cultivation lettuce requires ample water, especially in warmer weather. During unseasonable weather, protection is furnished and growth stimulated with greenhouses, frames, cloches, or polyethylene covers. In many parts of the world the leaf and butter-head types are most popular. They are not suitable for shipping, so they are usually grown on truck farms or market gardens relatively close to markets. The crisp-head varieties, well adapted for long-distance shipment, are dominant in the U.S., where over five-sixths of the acreage is located in California and Arizona. In Great Britain cabbage and cos types dominate. Although most commonly consumed in salads, lettuce may also be served as a cooked vegetable.

Letzeburg (city, Luxembourg): *see* Luxembourg.

Leucas, Modern Greek LEVKÁS, also called LEVKÁDHIA, Greek island in the Ionian Sea, forming with the island of Meganísi the *nomós* (department) of Levkás. The 117-sq-mi (303-sq-km) island is a hilly mass of limestone and bituminous shales culminating in the centre in Mt. Eláti (3,799 ft [1,158 m]). The chief town, Levkás, lies at the northeastern corner, which in antiquity was separated by a marshy isthmus. It was formerly called Amaxíkhi or Santa Maura; the latter is also the Venetian name for the island. Most of the population inhabit the wooded east coast and its valleys.

Mycenaean remains at Nidhrí on the east coast testify to early occupation and convince some scholars that Leucas, not Ithaca, was the home of Odysseus. In the mid-7th century BC, Corinthian colonists established themselves just south of the present capital and dug a canal through the isthmus. Under Roman rule in the 2nd century BC, a stone bridge, of which there are some remains, was constructed to the main island. In 167 the Romans made Leucas a free city. During the 13th century AD the island was subject to the Despotate of Epirus, and in 1479 it was seized by the Turks. The island was alternately under Turkish and Venetian control until 1718, when it was formally ceded to Venice. After the 18th century it shared the political fortunes of the other Ionian islands under British rule. In 1864 it was restored to Greece.

The island has suffered for centuries from severe earthquakes; those of 1867 and 1948 severely damaged the capital. Cape Leucatas at the southwestern tip of the island has fragments of the ruined temple of Apollo Leucatas; nearby are the 200-ft white cliffs that give the island its Greek name. In antiquity they served as a trial by ordeal (the "Leucadian leap") for accused persons, survivors being picked up by boat. According to legend, Sappho, desperate with love, ended her life here. Economic activities include considerable olive-oil production but meagre cereal cultivation. The currant, introduced about 1859, has been one of the chief cash crops. Cotton, flax, tobacco, and valonia are produced, and much red wine is exported. In 1903 the isthmus was cut by a ship canal. Pop. (1981) 21,863.

leucine, an amino acid obtainable by the hydrolysis of most common proteins. Among the first of the amino acids to be discovered (1819), in muscle fibre and wool, it is present in large proportions (about 15 percent) in hemoglobin (the oxygen-carrying pigment of red blood cells) and is one of several so-called essential amino acids for rats, fowl, and man; *i.e.,* they cannot synthesize it and require dietary sources. In plants and microorganisms it is synthesized from pyruvic acid (a product of the breakdown of carbohydrates).

Leucippus (fl. 5th century BC, probably at Miletus, on the west coast of Asia Minor), Greek philosopher credited by Aristotle and by Theophrastus with having originated the theory of atomism. It has been difficult to distinguish his contribution from that of his most famous pupil, Democritus. Only fragments of Leucippus' writings remain, but two works believed to have been written by him are *The Great World System* and *On the Mind.* His theory stated that matter is homogeneous but consists of an infinity of small indivisible particles. These atoms are constantly in motion, and through their collisions and regroupings form various compounds. A cosmos is formed by the collision of atoms that gather together into a "whirl," and the drum-shaped Earth is located in the centre of man's cosmos.

leucite, one of the most important feldspathoid minerals, a potassium aluminosilicate ($KAlSi_2O_6$). It occurs only in igneous rocks, particularly potassium-rich, silica-poor, recent lavas. Some important localities include Rome; Uganda; and Leucite Hills, Wyo., U.S. Leucite is used as a fertilizer in Italy (because of its high potassium content) and as a source of commercial alum. For detailed physical properties, *see* feldspathoid (table).

leucitite, extrusive igneous rock, coloured ash gray to nearly black, that contains leucite and augite as large, single crystals (phenocrysts) in a fine-grained matrix (groundmass) of leucite, augite, sanidine, apatite, sphene, magnetite, and melilite; in this regard it is similar to nephelinite (*q.v.*), which contains nepheline in place of leucite.

Leucitites are rare rocks and are known mostly from Tertiary or Recent strata; hence, they are generally younger than 66,400,000 years. Perhaps the best known occurrence is near Rome, where leucite lavas are thinly spread from Mt. Vesuvius, 200 kilometres (125 miles) south of the city, to Lago (lake) di Bolsena, 80 kilometres (50 miles) north. Other occurrences include the Mufumbiro region, Uganda; the West Kimberley region, Australia; and the eastern slope of the Rocky Mountains, U.S.

Like the nephelinites, leucite-rich basalts are divided according to their mineralogical composition: leucitite contains no olivine or plagioclase; leucite-basalt contains olivine but no plagioclase; leucite-tephrite contains plagioclase but no olivine; and leucite-basanite contains both plagioclase and olivine. In all other respects these rocks are similar. With an increase in the nepheline content, leucite-rich basalts pass over into the nepheline-rich varieties, as at Hamberg, near Bühne, Ger.

Leuckart, (Karl Georg Friedrich) Rudolf (b. Oct. 7, 1822, Helmstedt, Ger.—d. Feb. 6, 1898, Leipzig), German zoologist and teacher who initiated the modern science of parasitology. He described the complicated life histories of various parasites, including tapeworms and the liver fluke, and demonstrated that some human diseases, such as trichinosis, are caused by multicellular animals of the various wormlike phyla. His textbook, *Die menschlichen Parasiten* (1863–76; Eng. trans., *The Parasites of Man*, 1886), was of fundamental importance; he also wrote many scientific papers.

Though remembered primarily for his work in parasitology, Leuckart did other innovative work in zoology; for example, in systematics he showed that the radial symmetry of the coelenterates (such as jellyfish) and echinoderms (starfish) did not indicate a close relationship between the two groups.

He taught successively at the universities of Göttingen (where he was educated), Giessen, and Leipzig.

leucocyte (blood): *see* leukocyte.

leucorrhoea (disease): *see* leukorrhea.

Leucosolenia, also called LEUCOSELENIA, genus of tubular branched sponges of the class Calcispongiae (phylum Porifera). Found in tide pools and on wharves and represented by numerous species, the widespread genus includes most of the asconoids, structurally the simplest sponges.

Most species of *Leucosolenia* are 2.5 centimetres (one inch) or less in length. They grow as a group of slender individuals connected by a common stolon—*i.e.,* a rootlike process—which also attaches the group to the bottom or to some other surface. Water—which enters the central cavity (spongocoel) of the animal through numerous tiny perforations—is expelled through one large opening, the osculum, at the tip. The water current is created by flagella attached to the choanocytes, the cells that line the spongocoel. The outer body wall consists of thin, flat cells called pinacocytes. Between the two cell layers is a jellylike matrix, the mesoglea, which usually contains freely moving cells (amoebocytes) and skeletal spicules often shaped like slender three- or four-pointed stars. The spicules, which provide support for the body tube, are produced by special amoebocytes.

New individuals usually develop as free-swimming flagellated larvae from eggs produced by amoebocytes. These larvae enter the spongocoel of the parent and then pass through the osculum, eventually attaching themselves permanently to a surface. Some leucosolenids—for example, *L. botryoides*—also may reproduce by budding, a process in which a fingerlike extension of the parent body breaks off. The tip of the extension becomes the lower end of the new individual when it attaches to a new site.

Leucothea (Greek: White Goddess [of the Foam]), in Greek mythology, a sea goddess first mentioned in Homer's *Odyssey,* in which she rescued the Greek hero Odysseus from drowning. She was customarily identified with

Leucothea giving Dionysus a drink from the Horn of Plenty, antique bas-relief; in the Lateran Museum, Rome

Alinari—Art Resource/EB Inc.

Ino, daughter of the Phoenician Cadmus; because she cared for the infant god Dionysus, the goddess Hera drove Ino (or her husband, Athamas) mad so that she and her son, Melicertes, leaped terrified into the sea. Both were changed into marine deities—Ino as Leucothea, Melicertes as Palaemon. The body of Melicertes was carried by a dolphin to the Isthmus of Corinth and deposited under a pine tree. There Melicertes' body was found by his uncle Sisyphus, who removed it to Corinth and instituted the Isthmian games and sacrifices in his honour. Leucothea's link with Cadmus suggests possible Semitic connections; Melicertes may be identical with the Phoenician god Melqart.

Leucothoë, genus of about 50 species of shrubs, of the heath family (Ericaceae), native to North and South America and eastern Asia. Many species are grown as ornamentals, chiefly for their large, usually evergreen leaves and the white (sometimes tinged with pink) flowers. Most species grow to about 1.8 metres (6 feet) in height. The leaves are alternate and have short petioles (leaf stalks) and toothed edges. The urn-shaped flowers have five small

Drooping leucothoe (*Leucothoë catesbaei*)

A to Z Botanical Collection—EB Inc.

teeth at the mouth and are borne in clusters along the branches or at the branch tips.

Leuctra, Battle of (371 BC), battle fought on the plain of Leuctra (near modern Levktra) in southern Boeotia, in which a Boeotian army under Epaminondas defeated a Spartan army under King Cleombrotus. This Spartan defeat in the Boeotian–Athenian war against Sparta of 379–371 destroyed the reputation of the Spartan hoplite phalanx and established Theban hegemony in Greece (371–362). Epaminondas' tactical innovations of oblique order and concentration of forces against the enemy's command brought about the Theban–Boeotian victory.

After the Theban refusal to sign the peace agreement of 371, Cleombrotus, who was in Phocis with about 10,000 Spartan and allied hoplites and 1,000 cavalry, was ordered to invade Boeotia and attack Thebes. He was met by Epaminondas' Theban force, consisting of about 6,000 hoplites (heavily armed infantrymen) and an unknown number of cavalry. Eschewing the usual battle formation of cavalry heading a continuous hoplite phalanx, with the commander on the right wing, Epaminondas massed hoplites to a depth of 50 on his left wing and advanced it ahead of the centre and right wings. When the superior Theban cavalry drove the Spartan cavalry back on the phalanx, the Theban left wing attacked and routed the Spartan right, killing Cleombrotus, the Spartan king. Xenophon, a contemporary historian, reports nearly 1,000 Spartan dead.

Leuenberger, Niklaus (b. *c.* 1611—d. Sept. 6, 1653, Schönholz bei Rüderswil, Bern), Swiss peasant hero, spokesman for rural discontent, and leader of the peasant revolt at Bern (1653), for which he earned the sobriquet King of the Peasants.

By the mid-17th century, Swiss peasants had come to bitterly resent the domination of the towns and to openly complain of oppressive taxation and the infringement of local rights. In 1653 the leadership of a movement expressing this unrest fell to Leuenberger. A rustic of origins as obscure as most of his fellows, he had as his primary claims to leadership a measure of literacy and native intelligence. Having acquired some local prominence in the district of Trachselwald (canton of Bern), he was appointed head of the movement at an intercantonal peasant assembly at Sumiswald (April 23, 1653). Although he was opposed to violent methods, Leuenberger led a peasant force of 16,000 against Bern (May 1653), where he secured a number of concessions to local grievances. Federal forces soon intervened, however, and, after the peasants' defeat at Herzogenbuchsee (June 8, 1653), the movement collapsed. Leuenberger was arrested June 12 and was executed at Bern.

leukemia, malignant disease of the blood-forming tissues characterized by large increases in the numbers of leukocytes (white blood cells) in the circulation. A number of different leukemias are classified according to the course of the disease and the predominant type of white blood cell involved, generally granulocytes, myelocytes, or lymphocytes. Some types of leukemia have been related to radiation exposure, especially noted in the Japanese population exposed to the first atomic bomb at Hiroshima; other evidence suggests hereditary susceptibility. Viruses are known to produce leukemia in animals but have never been clearly demonstrated to cause the human disease.

Acute leukemias develop rapidly, with symptoms including anemia, fever, bleeding, and swelling of the lymph nodes. The most common form in children, acute lymphocytic leukemia, once killed more than 90 percent of its victims within six months; drug therapies that were later developed allowed the disease to be controlled in many cases. The majority of patients achieve complete remissions, with no evidence of malignant cells in the blood; more than half remain free of disease for five years or longer on continued therapy and are presumed to be cured.

Treatment results in other leukemias have not been as positive. In acute myelogenous, or granulocytic, leukemia, which is more common in adults, more than half of the patients experience remissions; these remissions, however, are of short duration, and few patients survive for long periods without recurrences.

Chronic leukemias also occur more frequently in adults. They are characterized by more gradual onset and a more protracted course. Chronic myelogenous leukemia, which has a peak incidence in adults in their 40s, may remain quiescent for long periods before weight loss, low fever, weakness, and other symptoms develop. Chemotherapy relieves these symptoms somewhat but has questionable value in prolonging survival.

Chronic lymphocytic leukemia occurs primarily in old people and may also be inactive for months or years. Treatment is generally delayed until the appearance of anemia; survival rates are better than in myelogenous leukemia, with one-third of patients alive 10 years after diagnosis. Chronic lymphocytic leukemia is in itself rarely the cause of death but renders the patient more vulnerable to fatal infection or hemorrhage.

leukocyte, also spelled LEUCOCYTE, also called WHITE BLOOD CELL, or WHITE CORPUSCLE, a cellular component of blood, millions of which in the circulation and tissues help defend the body from infection by ingesting foreign materials and by providing antibodies. Five mature forms of white blood cells may be distinguished: (1) neutrophils (also called heterophils), (2) basophils, (3) eosinophils, (4) monocytes and macrophages, and (5) lymphocytes. Neutrophils, basophils, and eosinophils (named for the stains they take in the laboratory) are collectively called granulocytes, because they are characterized by having granules in their cytoplasm, and are also called polymorphonuclear leukocytes, because their nuclei have a wide variety of shapes. All five cell types are nucleated and are capable of movement, having characteristic modes and speeds of progression.

White blood cells function mostly in the body tissues; those in the bloodstream are being transported to a site of need. Neutrophils, which are eosinophils, and monocytes are attracted to sites of injury or infection by chemicals emanating from bacteria or foreign particles, a process called chemotaxis. Neutrophils, which are the most numerous type of leukocyte in vertebrates, are phagocytic; *i.e.,* they engulf and sometimes digest bacteria at the site of infection. Monocytes, which are the largest cells of the blood, ingest protozoa, particulate matter, and aging red blood cells. After circulating for several hours in the blood, monocytes settle in the lymphoid tissues and, having acquired more phagocytic capacity, become macrophages. Macrophages are large cells, capable of amoeboid movement, that ingest damaged and infected body cells and debris. Eosinophils, which are especially prominent during allergic reactions, engulf antigen–antibody complexes and apparently limit the effects of certain chemicals (*e.g.,* histamine) that appear during a foreign-body reaction. Basophils are most numerous at sites of healing or chronic inflammation. Lymphocytes are of two types—B cells and T cells—both of which can recognize and bind to foreign substances (antigens) in the body. B cells produce antibodies upon activation by antigens and release the antibodies into the bloodstream. Some T cells bind to and kill infected body cells; others activate or inhibit the action of other T cells and B cells. Both classes of lymphocytes are active in the lymphoid tissues and organs. (*See* lymphocyte.)

The normal adult human has between 5,000 and 10,000 leukocytes per cubic millimetre of blood. The blood leukocyte count rises after exercise, convulsions, and strong emotional reactions; during pain, pregnancy, and labour; and also during many disease states, such as infections and intoxications. Specific types of cells are associated with different illnesses and reflect the special function of that cell type in body defense. A fall in leukocyte count, which is called leukopenia, occurs in states such as debilitation, anaphylactic shock, and overwhelming infection. In general, newborns have a high white blood cell count that gradually falls to the adult level during childhood. An exception is the lymphocyte count, which is low at birth, reaches its highest levels in the first four years of life, and thereafter falls gradually to a stable adult level. *See also* blood; blood cell formation.

leukocytosis, abnormally high number of white blood cells (leukocytes) in the blood circulation, defined, for statistical purposes, as more than 10,000 leukocytes per cubic millimetre of blood. Leukocytosis commonly occurs after strenuous exercise, convulsions (*e.g.,* epilepsy), strong emotional reactions, ether anesthesia, the administration of epinephrine, pregnancy and labour, and oxygen lack (as in the early phases of adaptation to high altitude). Leukocytosis is also observed in many disease states, including infections, parasitic infestations, intoxications (metabolic or chemical), chronic diseases (*e.g.,* leukemia), and allergic reactions.

leukoderma (medicine): *see* vitiligo.

leukopenia, abnormally low number of white blood cells (leukocytes) in the blood circulation, defined, for statistical purposes, as less than 5,000 leukocytes per cubic millimetre of blood. Leukopenia often accompanies certain infections, especially those caused by viruses or protozoans, as well as any overwhelming infection. Other causes of the condition include debilitation, malnutrition, chronic anemias, some spleen disorders, agranulocytosis, lupus erythematosus, and anaphylactic shock.

leukoplakia, precancerous tumour of the mucous membranes, most common in older men and usually seen on the lips or tongue, but also known to occur in women on the vagina or vulva. Leukoplakia first appears as a small, smooth, white spot but develops into a larger area of thickening with a rough texture and colour varying from white to gray; red areas within the leukoplakia pose a particularly high risk of becoming malignant. Older lesions may have numerous fissures and sores and tend to bleed after slight injury.

Tertiary syphilis was a common cause of leukoplakia in the past. Most cases now result from external irritants, notably tobacco smoke. Other factors believed to contribute to this disease include exposure to sunlight, poor dental hygiene, and ill-fitting dentures. Leukoplakia may persist for many years without becoming malignant, but the high risk of squamous-cell carcinoma dictates complete removal of the tumour by surgery or freezing, as well as the elimination of all predisposing factors.

Hairy leukoplakia is a white lesion on the tongue or mouth floor, often having rough hairlike projections. It often occurs in persons with acquired immune deficiency syndrome (AIDS) or the AIDS-related complex (ARC). The Epstein-Barr virus has been isolated from the lesions.

leukorrhea, also spelled LEUCORRHOEA, abnormal flow of a whitish or yellowish discharge from the vagina of the female. Such discharges may originate from the vagina, ovaries, fallopian tubes, or, most commonly, the cervix. The discharge may be caused by gonorrhea or some other infection of these structures. Nongonorrheal infection of the cervix is a frequent cause of leukorrhea and is indeed one of the most common gynecological disorders. The infection has a tendency to irritate the mucus glands of the cervix and cause them to secrete an excess of mucus mixed with pus. The vagina and vulva of adult women are frequently infected by *Trichomonas vaginalis* (a protozoan parasite) and by various fungi, which may give rise to an irritating discharge that is often quite resistant to treatment. A tampon, diaphragm, or other foreign object left too long in the vagina can also cause the discharge. Douching may provide temporary relief from a discharge and its associated pain and itching, but a clinical examination to determine the cause of the discharge is the recommended course of action. *See also* cervicitis; vulvitis.

Leutze, Emanuel (b. May 24, 1816, Schwäbisch-Gmünd, Württemberg [Germany]—d. July 18, 1868, Washington, D.C., U.S.), German-born American historical painter whose picture "Washington Crossing the Delaware" (1851; Metropolitan Museum of Art, New York City) numbers among the most popular and widely reproduced images of an American historical event.

Leutze was brought to the United States as a child. In 1841 he returned to Germany to study at the Academy in Düsseldorf. He remained in Germany for almost 20 years and was primarily occupied with painting a series of canvases based on U.S. history. Sentimental and anecdotal in content, they are painstakingly executed in the highly finished style of the Düsseldorf school, characterized by firm drawing, careful rendering of detail, and filled-in colour.

Leutze returned to the United States in 1859 and in 1860 was commissioned by the U.S. Congress to decorate a stairway in the Capitol at Washington, D.C., for which he painted a large composition, "Westward the Course of Empire Takes Its Way" (often erroneously called "Westward Ho"), illustrating the settlement of the Far West.

Leuven (Belgium): *see* Louvain.

Levallois-Perret, city, Hauts-de-Seine *département,* Paris *région,* France. The city is a northwestern industrial and residential suburb of Paris and is located on the right bank of the Seine River, 4 miles (6.5 km) northwest of Notre Dame cathedral. With an area of less than 1 square mile (2.5 square km), it is connected to Paris by subway and has important automobile-manufacturing plants. Most of the garages of the taxi fleets of Paris are located in Levallois-Perret. The Hertford British Hospital is situated in a street bordering the western suburb of Neuilly. Pop. (1982) 53,485.

Levalloisian stone-flaking technique, toolmaking technique of prehistoric Europe and Africa, characterized by the production of large flakes from a tortoise core (prepared core shaped much like an inverted tortoise shell). Such flakes, seldom further trimmed, were flat on one side, had sharp cutting edges, and are believed to have been used as skinning knives. Sometimes the butts of Levalloisian flakes were trimmed in a way that suggests hafting onto a handle. The Levalloisian technique gradually replaced the Acheulian in much of Europe during the Third Interglacial period and continued into the Fourth Glacial period. In Africa the prepared core technique had a long history of development in association with the Acheulian industry. The Levalloisian technique was often and widely employed for flake production in Mousterian industries in Europe, western Asia, and northern Africa, as well as in other industries (*e.g.,* Stillbay) in sub-Saharan Africa during the late Pleistocene epoch.

levalto (dance): *see* volta, la.

Levant (from the French *lever,* "to rise," as in sunrise, meaning the east), historically the countries along the eastern Mediterranean shores. Common use of the term is associated with Venetian and other trading ventures and the establishment of commerce with cities such as Tyre and Sidon as a result of the Crusades. It was applied to the coastlands of Asia Minor and Syria, sometimes extending from Greece to Egypt. It was also used for Anatolia and as a synonym for the Middle or Near East. In the 16th and 17th centuries, the term High Levant referred to the Far East. The name Levant States was given to the French mandate of Syria and Lebanon after World War I, and the term is sometimes still used for those two countries, which became independent in 1946.

levanter, also spelled LEVANTE, strong wind of the western Mediterranean Sea and the southern coasts of France and Spain. It is mild, damp, and rainy and is most common in spring and fall. Its name is derived from Levant, the land at the eastern end of the Mediterranean, and refers to the wind's eastward direction. The levanter reaches its maximum intensities in the Strait of Gibraltar, where it sometimes brings eastward-flying airplanes almost to a standstill. It causes foggy weather on the Spanish coast for up to two days at a time. The levanter results from a merging of the clockwise winds of a high-pressure centre over central Europe with the counterclockwise winds of a low-pressure centre over the southwestern Mediterranean.

Levassor, Émile (b. 1844?—d. 1897, France), French businessman and inventor who developed the basic configuration of the automobile.

Levassor took over a firm that made woodworking machinery. When René Panhard joined the firm in 1886, the renamed firm of Panhard and Lavassor began to make metal-sawing machines as well. Around 1890 Levassor managed to gain control of the French licenses to the automobile engine patents of Gottlieb Daimler. By 1891 Levassor had designed a radically new motorcar to house Daimler's engine. He broke with tradition by placing the engine in front of the driver rather than under him, thereby obtaining better traction for the steering (front) wheels. He replaced the typical belt drive with a shaft-and-gear transmission that could be selectively engaged with a clutch to give different speed ratios. These and other innovations and existing designs were brilliantly combined by Levassor in the automobiles that his firm started selling in 1892. His vehicles were the first true, if embryonic, automobiles, rather than being simply carriages that had been modified for self-propulsion.

In June 1895 Levassor gave a sensational demonstration of the effectiveness of his design by finishing first in a field of 18 gasoline, steam, and electric motorcars in a race from Paris to Bordeaux and back, a distance of 730 miles (1,200 km). Levassor died of injuries sustained in a race in 1897.

levator muscle, any of the muscles that raise a body part. In humans these include the levator anguli oris, which raises the corner of the mouth; the levator ani, collective name for a thin sheet of muscle that stretches across the pelvic cavity and helps hold the pelvic viscera in position, forming a kind of sphincter around the vagina in the female and the anal canal in both sexes; the levatores costarum, which help raise the ribs during respiration; the levator labii superioris and levator labii superioris alaeque nasi, which raise the upper lip; the levator palpebrae superioris, which raises the upper eyelid; the levator prostatae, a part of the levator ani in the male that supports the prostate gland and is involved in control of urination; the levator scapulae, a straplike muscle of the shoulder that helps raise and rotate the shoulder blade; and the levator veli palatini, which raises the soft palate of the mouth.

levee, any low ridge or earthen embankment built along the edges of a stream or river channel to prevent flooding of the adjacent land. Artificial levees are typically needed to control the flow of rivers meandering through broad, flat floodplains. Levees are usually embankments of dirt built wide enough so that they will not collapse or be eroded when saturated with moisture from rivers running at unusually high levels. Grass or some other matlike vegetation is planted on the top of the levee's bank so that its erosion will be kept to a minimum.

Levees protecting inhabited river valley areas against inundations during floods were among the earliest engineering works. In ancient Egypt a series of levees was built along the left bank of the Nile River for more than 600 miles (966 km), from Aswan to the Mediterranean. The cooperative and coordinated enterprise involved in building such long, massive embankments must have been a strong incentive for the development of an organized society and a unified government in ancient Egypt, as well as in ancient Mesopotamia and China, which engaged in similar hydraulic engineering projects.

One of the largest modern systems of levees is that built along the Mississippi River and its tributaries and backwaters in the broad alluvial valley extending southward from Cape Girardeau, Mo., to the Mississippi delta, a distance of about 1,000 miles (1,600 km) by river channel. These levees, begun by French settlers in Louisiana in the early 18th century, were in 1735 about 3 feet (0.9 m) high and had been constructed along the river's banks from 30 miles (48 km) north of New Orleans to 12 miles (19 km) south of that city. The system was extended until by the mid-1980s it included more than 3,500 miles (5,600 km) of levees having an average height of about 24 feet (7 m), with some levees reaching 50 feet (15 m) in height.

Some silt-laden streams, as their flow slows, may deposit sediment in their bed between their enclosing levees and thus build their channels up higher than the surrounding floodplains. Such streams commonly breach the levees, flowing out onto lower ground and causing catastrophic floods. The lower portions of the Huang Ho in China are noted for this type of behaviour. The lower reaches of the Mississippi River also are poised on such "mid-valley ridges."

level, device for establishing a horizontal plane. It consists of a small glass tube containing alcohol or similar liquid and an air bubble; the tube is sealed and fixed horizontally in a wooden or metallic block or frame with a smooth lower surface. The glass tube is slightly bowed, and adjustment to the horizontal is indicated by movement of the bubble. The device is on a level surface when the bubble is in the middle of the glass tube. The level's sensitivity is proportional to the radius of the curvature of the glass.

Leveler, also spelled LEVELLER, member of a republican and democratic faction in England during the period of the Civil Wars and Commonwealth. The name Levelers was given by enemies of the movement to suggest that its supporters wished to "level men's estates."

The Leveler movement originated in 1645–46 among radical supporters of Parliament in and around London. The Civil War had been waged in the name of Parliament and people: the Levelers demanded that real sovereignty should be transferred to the House of Commons (to the exclusion of king and lords); that manhood suffrage, a redistribution of seats, and annual or biennial sessions of Parliament should make that legislative body truly representative; and that government should be decentralized to local communities. They put forward a program of economic reform in the interests of small property holders—complete equality before the law, the abolition of trading monopolies, the reopening of enclosed land, security of land tenure for copyholders, no conscription (impressment) or billeting, drastic law reform, the abolition of tithes (and so of a state church), and complete freedom of religious worship and organization. Disappointed by Parliament's attitude, the Levelers turned directly to the people—and to the New Model Army.

In April 1647 the army rank and file elected agitators who were largely influenced by Leveler ideas. The generals had to accept an army council that included these ordinary soldiers, as well as officers. At Putney, in October 1647, this representative body discussed the Agreement of the People, a document presented by the Levelers as a new social contract to refound the state that had been dissolved by Parliament's victory in the Civil War. The Putney debates on this document ended in deadlock, however, and the generals restored discipline in the army by force. In March 1649, John Lilburne and other Leveler leaders were imprisoned. A mutiny of Leveler troops in London was suppressed, and in May a more serious revolt was put down in Oxfordshire. That was the end of the Levelers as an organized political force.

The Levelers never won national support. Their sea-green colours held London's streets, and the troops listened to them eagerly, but propaganda was difficult among a population used to taking its ideas from the church and the landed aristocracy. The Leveler failure to capture the support of the army was decisive. But had they been allowed time to educate a democratic electorate, their program was well calculated to appeal to peasant farmers and artisans—the overwhelming majority of the people. Their ideas were more likely to command widespread support than had those of the communistic Diggers, for they also sought to appeal to men of small property and independence. Their appeal to reason against arguments drawn from precedent or biblical authority marks a milestone in political thought, and the pamphlets of some of their leaders are important in the evolution of popular English prose. Some of their social ideas were taken over by the Quakers.

Leven, Alexander Leslie, 1st Earl of, LORD BALGONIE (b. *c.* 1580—d. April 4, 1661, Balgonie, Fife, Scot.), commander of the Scottish army that from 1644 to 1646 fought on the side of Parliament in the English Civil Wars between Parliament and King Charles I.

Leslie joined the Swedish army in 1605 and served brilliantly in the Thirty Years' War

Leven, portrait by an unknown artist; in the Scottish National Portrait Gallery, Edinburgh

By courtesy of the Scottish National Portrait Gallery, Edinburgh

in central Europe. In 1628 he distinguished himself by successfully defending Stralsund against the imperial commander Wallenstein, and in 1636 he became a field marshal under the Swedish king Gustavus II Adolphus.

By the time he returned to Scotland in 1637, the country was in turmoil over King Charles I's attempts to impose Anglican forms of worship on the Presbyterian Church of Scotland. Leslie readily pledged to defend the Presbyterian religion and indeed had encouraged Scottish troops on the European continent to do so. During the nearly bloodless First and Second Bishops' Wars (1639–41) between England and Scotland, he commanded the Scottish army. He occupied northeastern England in August 1640, remaining there until the war's end. In a fruitless attempt to win his allegiance, Charles then made him Earl of Leven and Lord Balgonie (October 1641).

Leven led Scottish troops against Roman Catholic rebels in Ireland in 1642–43, but he returned to Scotland (January 1644) to take charge of the Scottish army that entered England to fight for Parliament. He played a leading role in the campaigns of 1644–45, and in May 1646 Charles I surrendered to him at Newark, Nottinghamshire. After handing the king over to Parliament (January 1647), Leven returned with his army to Scotland and retired from active service. He was powerless to prevent the Scottish Royalists from sending troops into England in 1648, but the execution of Charles I by the Independents (radical Puritans) brought him into the Royalist camp of King Charles II. In 1650–51 the aged general commanded the forces that defended Scotland from the invading army of Oliver Cromwell. Captured by English dragoons at Alyth in August 1651, Leven was confined until 1654, when he once more retired.

Leven, Loch, famous trout-fishing lake in Perth and Kinross district, Tayside region, Scotland. Roughly circular in shape and about 3 miles (5 km) in diameter, it is one of the shallowest of the Scottish lochs (mean depth 15 feet [4.5 m]) and has become important as a nature reserve. The loch is a roosting area for geese in winter and a resting area for ducks. Its trout, a subspecies of *Salmo trutta,* or brown trout, are known as Loch Leven trout and have been widely transplanted elsewhere in the world.

The largest of Loch Leven's seven islands, St. Serf's, contains the ruins of a priory that was made over in 1150 to the Augustinians of St. Andrews. On Castle Island are the ruins of a late 14th-century castle, which served as a place of detention for many important persons, including Mary, Queen of Scots; in 1567 she signed her abdication there. During her escape in 1568, the castle keys were thrown into the loch, where they were found 300 years later.

Pink-footed geese (*Anser fabalis brachyrhynchus*) in flight over Loch Leven

David and Katie Urry—Bruce Coleman Ltd.

Levene, Phoebus (Aaron Theodor), original name FISHEL AARONOVICH LEVIN (b. Feb. 25, 1869, Sagor, Russia—d. Sept. 6, 1940, New York, N.Y., U.S.), Russian-born American chemist and pioneer in the study of nucleic acids.

On receiving his M.D. degree from the St. Petersburg Imperial Medical Academy in 1891, Levene fled from Russian anti-Semitism and settled in New York City. While practicing medicine there, he studied chemistry at Columbia University and ultimately decided to devote his life to chemical research. From 1905 to 1939 he worked at the Rockefeller Institute for Medical Research.

Although Levene's studies encompassed nearly every major class of organic compounds, his most valuable work was on the nucleic acids. He isolated the nucleotides, the basic building blocks of the nucleic acid molecule; and in 1909 he isolated the five-carbon sugar d-ribose from the ribonucleic acid (RNA) molecule. Twenty years later he discovered 2-deoxyribose (a sugar derived from d-ribose by removing an oxygen atom), which is part of the deoxyribonucleic acid (DNA) molecule. He also determined how the nucleic acid components combine to form the nucleotides and how the nucleotides combine in chains. Although the importance of the nucleic acids was unrecognized when he began his research, later discoveries showed DNA and RNA to be key elements in the maintenance of life.

Leventon, Alla: *see* Nazimova, Alla.

lever, simple machine used to amplify physical force. All early people used the lever in some form, for moving heavy stones or as digging sticks for land cultivation. The principle of the lever was used in the swape, or shaduf, a long lever pivoted near one end with a platform or water container hanging from the short arm and counterweights attached to the long arm. A man could lift several times his own weight by pulling down on the long arm. This device is said to have been used in Egypt and India for raising water and lifting soldiers over battlements as early as 1500 BC.

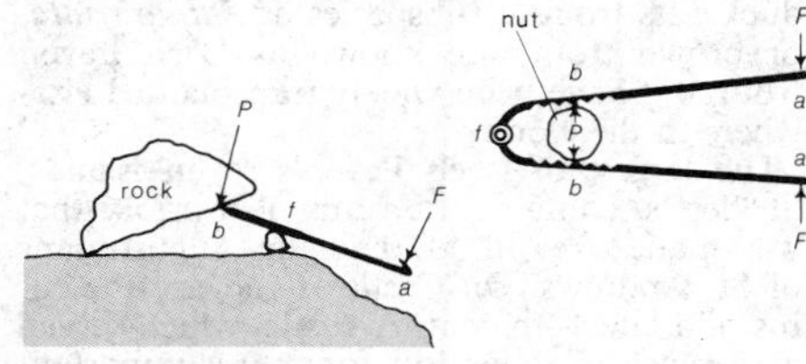

Two types of levers

Another interesting lever device, probably used in Egypt about 5000 BC, was a balance beam for weighing, consisting of a bar pivoted at its centre and weights that were hung on one end to balance the object being weighed on the other end.

The illustration (left) shows how a lever, for example, a crowbar that is supported and can turn freely on the fulcrum *f*, enables a man to create at *b* a force *P* that is greater than the force *F* that he exerts at *a*. If, for example, the length *af* is five times *bf*, the force *P* is five times *F*. In the nutcracker, shown at the right, the two bars are connected by a pin joint at the fulcrum *f*; if *af* is three times *bf*, the force *P* at *b* is three times the force *F* exerted by the hands at *a*.

Lever, Charles James (b. Aug. 31, 1806, Dublin, Ire.—d. June 1, 1872, Trieste, Austria-Hungary [now in Italy]), Irish editor and writer whose novels, set in post-Napoleonic Ireland and Europe, featured lively, picaresque heroes.

In 1831, after study at Trinity College, Cambridge, he qualified for the practice of medicine. His gambling and extravagance, however, left him short of money despite his income and his inheritance, and he began to utilize his gifts as a raconteur. In 1837 *The Confessions of Harry Lorrequer* appeared serially in the *Dublin University Magazine*, where it was a definite success. His novel *Charles O'Malley*, which ranges from the west of Ireland to the Peninsular War, appeared in 1841; *Jack Hinton* and *Tom Burke of "Ours,"* a vigorous story of an Irishman in the service of the French empire, in 1843.

In 1842 Lever assumed the editorship of the *Dublin University Magazine*. He traveled to the European continent in 1845, visited resorts, and served as British consul at La Spezia and Trieste. He continued to write novels, among them *The Knight of Gwynne* (1847), *Confessions of Con Cregan* (1849), and *Roland Cashel* (1850). These novels mark a transition from the loosely constructed picaresque works of his youth to the less ebullient, more analytic manner of his last books, among which are *The Fortunes of Glencore* (1857) and *Lord Kilgobbin* (1872). Rough and ready though they are, the vivacity of his early novels, the picture they present of the devil-may-care, hard-riding gentry and their ragged adherents, and a down-to-earth Irish realism make them perennially attractive.

Lever Art Gallery, in full LADY LEVER ART GALLERY, in Port Sunlight, a model village founded for workers in Bebington, Cheshire (now in Merseyside), Eng. The museum was a gift to the public of the 1st Viscount Leverhulme, as a memorial to his wife, who died in 1913. The building was begun in 1914 and opened in December 1922. The collection of works exhibited at the gallery was formed by Lord Leverhulme and records his personal taste, which was strongly biased in favour of British works, especially of the Victorian period. There is also a very fine collection of Chinese ceramics and a collection of Napoleonic relics, including a bronze death mask of Napoleon. The gallery also has a superb collection of English furniture and an unrivaled collection of Wedgwood ware. There are important paintings by members of the Pre-Raphaelite Brotherhood and their followers including John Everett Millais, William Holman Hunt, Frederic Leighton, and Ford Madox Brown. There is an important series of 18th-century portraits, including examples by Joshua Reynolds, George Romney, and John Hoppner.

Lever Brothers, predecessor company of Unilever (*q.v.*).

Leverhulme (of The Western Isles), William Hesketh Lever, 1st Viscount, BARON LEVERHULME OF BOLTON-LE-MOORS (b. Sept. 19, 1851, Bolton, Lancashire, Eng.—d. May 7, 1925, Hampstead, London), British soap and detergent entrepreneur who built the international firm of Lever Brothers.

Lever entered the soap business in 1885, when he leased a small, unprofitable soap-works. With his brother, James Darcy Lever, he began to make soap from vegetable oils instead of tallow and registered the name "Sunlight" for the product. At Port Sunlight in 1888 their company financed a model industrial village; and the brothers soon instituted other employee benefits, including pensions, medical care, unemployment compensation, profit sharing, and free insurance. By 1925 the firm served a world market through a system of 250 associated companies.

Leverhulme, detail of an oil painting by Augustus John, 1920; in Thornton Hough Manor, Cheshire

By courtesy of Unilever Ltd., London

William Lever, elected to Parliament in 1906, was raised to the peerage as a baron in 1917 and became a viscount in 1922. "Leverhulme" was a combination of his own name and his wife's maiden name, Hulme.

Leverkusen, city, North Rhine-Westphalia *Land* (state), west-central Germany, on the Rhine River at the mouth of the Wupper River, in the Dhünn valley just north of Cologne. Formed in 1930 by the union of the villages of Schlebusch, Rheindorf, and Steinbüchel with the town of Wiesdorf, it is well served by highway and rail and is the site of the Bayer Works (chemicals, pharmaceuticals, and photographic film). Iron products and textiles are also manufactured. The Morsbroich Castle houses a museum of modern art and is used for plays and concerts. There are numerous parks and open spaces. Pop. (1987 est.) 154,700.

Levertin, Oscar Ivar (b. July 17, 1862, near Stockholm, Swed.—d. Sept. 22, 1906, Stockholm), Swedish poet and scholar, a leader of the Swedish Romantic movement of the 1890s.

Levertin, oil painting by C.O. Larsson, 1906; in the Bonniers' Collection, Stockholm

By courtesy of the Svenska Portrattarkivet, Stockholm

Levertin was educated at Uppsala University and became in 1899 professor of literature at the University of Stockholm. After the death of his first wife and an attack of tuberculosis, which sent him to Davos, Switz., he abandoned his early Naturalism for Romanticism. In Davos he completed his first volume of poems, *Legender och visor* (1891; "Legends and Songs"), which placed him at the head of the new Romantic movement. In this poetry—which he describes as "black with purple-coloured threads"—he drew his material partly from medieval legend and art and partly from Jewish tradition and history. In *Nya dikter* (1894; "New Poems"), the atmosphere and colouring are less melancholy; the combined influence of Ernest Renan and Friedrich Nietzsche is prominent. *Dikter* (1901) has a simpler and more compressed style and has genuine Swedish themes. His last and perhaps finest poetical work was *Kung Salomo och Morolf* (1905; "King Solomon and Morolf"), based on material drawn from Oriental tales and medieval romances.

As a literary historian Levertin concentrated on the 18th century, the same period that was the background in his volume of short stories, *Rococonoveller* (1899; "Rococo Novels"). From 1897 until his death he was the leading literary critic of the *Svenska Dagbladet* and exerted great influence on contemporary readers and writers. Among his books on the history of art, *Jacques Callot* (1911) is the most important.

Levertov, Denise (b. Oct. 24, 1923, Ilford, Essex [now in Greater London], Eng.—d. Dec. 20, 1997, Seattle, Wash., U.S.), English-born American poet who wrote deceptively matter-of-fact verse.

Educated entirely at home, Levertov became a civilian nurse during World War II, serving in London throughout the bombings. Her first volume of verse, *The Double Image* (1946), was not very successful. She settled in New York the next year with her husband and was naturalized in 1955. She credited the spare, clear, objective work of the poet William Carlos Williams with being the greatest influence on the development of her style.

Here and Now (1957) was quickly followed by *Overland to the Islands* (1958), and five more volumes appeared in the 1960s. She translated the Buddhist work *In Praise of Krishna: Songs from the Bengali* (1967; with Edward Dimock, Jr.). *Relearning the Alphabet* (1970) discloses her concern with social issues. Opposed to the war in Vietnam, she was active in the War Resisters League and edited for it the collection *Out of the War Shadow* (1967).

In *Footprints* (1972) she reverted to the mystical tone of her earlier works. Levertov's later efforts included essays and prose, as in *The Poet in the World* (1973), and several collections of poetry, including *Candles in Babylon* (1982) and *Breathing the Water* (1987).

Lévesque, René (b. Aug. 24, 1922, New Carlisle, Que., Can.—d. Nov. 1, 1987, Montreal), premier of the French-speaking Canadian province of Quebec (1976–85) and a leading advocate of independence from English-speaking Canada.

Lévesque went to school in Gaspésie and afterward to Laval University, Quebec. Already a part-time journalist while still a student, he broke off his law studies to serve in Europe (1944–45) as a reporter and correspondent attached to the U.S. forces. Back in Quebec after the war, he joined the international service of the Canadian Broadcasting Corporation in 1946, became a war correspondent in Korea in 1952, and from 1956 to 1959 was commentator on a popular TV program.

Lévesque entered politics in 1960 and was elected to the Quebec National Assembly as a Liberal member for Gouin, joining Jean Lesage's government as minister of public works and hydraulic resources (1960–61). He then held the newly created portfolio of natural resources (1961–65), and in 1966, during the last months of the Lesage government, he was minister of family and social welfare. Meanwhile he had been reelected in the constituency of Laurier in the 1962 and 1966 legislative elections.

In October 1967 Lévesque, with others, founded the Mouvement Souveraineté-Association, which the following year combined with other separatist groups to form the Parti Québécois, with Lévesque as its first president. He was unsuccessful in the elections of 1970 and 1973 and returned to journalism, writing daily political articles in the *Journal de Montréal* and the *Journal de Québec*, until 1976, when his party won control of the provincial National Assembly and he became the premier of Quebec. He was reelected premier in April 1981.

The goal of Lévesque and his Parti Québécois government was the independence option termed "sovereignty-association." The concept envisaged Quebec enacting its own laws, collecting taxes from its people, and establishing relations with foreign countries. Simultaneously, it would form an economic union with the rest of Canada based on a common currency.

This plan was rejected by 59.6 percent of the Quebec electorate in a popular-referendum vote on May 20, 1980, amid one of the highest voter turnouts in Quebec's history. Despite this serious setback to his plan for "sovereignty-association," Lévesque (as his reelection demonstrates) retained his personal popularity.

In June 1985, largely because of failing health, Lévesque resigned from the leadership of the Parti Québécois and later gave up the premiership of Quebec, at a time when the power of his party was waning.

Levi (Apostle of Jesus): *see* Matthew (the Evangelist), Saint.

Levi, Carlo (b. Nov. 29, 1902, Turin, Italy—d. Jan. 4, 1975, Rome), Italian writer, painter, and political journalist whose first documentary novel became an international literary sensation and enhanced the trend toward social realism in postwar Italian literature.

Levi was a painter and a practicing physician when he was exiled (1935–36) to the southern district of Lucania for anti-Fascist activities. His *Cristo si è fermato a Eboli* (1945; *Christ Stopped at Eboli*) reflects the visual sensitivity of a painter and the compassionate objectivity of a doctor. Quickly acclaimed a literary masterpiece, it was widely translated.

Though Levi's first novel is unquestionably his masterpiece, he wrote other important nonfiction works. His *Paura della libertà* (1947; *Of Fear and Freedom*) proclaims the necessity of intellectual freedom despite an inherent human dread of it. *L'orologio* (1950; *The Watch*) deals with a postwar Cabinet crisis in Rome; *Le parole sono pietre* (1955; *Words Are Stones*) is a study of Sicily; and *La doppia notte dei tigli* (1959; *The Linden Trees*, or *The Two-Fold Night*) is a presentation of postwar Germany.

Levi directed a periodical in Florence for a time and contributed to several other magazines. Later he devoted himself to painting.

Levi, Primo (b. July 31, 1919, Turin, Italy—d. April 11, 1987, Turin), Italian-Jewish writer and chemist, noted for his restrained and moving autobiographical account of and reflections on survival in the Nazi concentration camps.

Levi was brought up in the small Jewish community in Turin, studied at the University of Turin, and graduated summa cum laude in chemistry in 1941. Two years later he joined friends in northern Italy in an attempt to connect with a resistance movement, but he was captured and sent to Auschwitz. While there, Levi worked as a slave labourer for an I.G. Farbenindustrie synthetic-rubber factory. Upon the liberation of Auschwitz by the Soviets in 1945, Levi returned to Turin, where in 1961 he became the general manager of a factory producing paints, enamels, and synthetic resins; the association was to last some 30 years.

Levi's first book, *Se questo è un uomo* (1947; *If This Is a Man*, or *Survival in Auschwitz*), demonstrated extraordinary qualities of humanity and detachment in its analysis of the atrocities he had witnessed. His later autobiographical works, *La tregua* (1963; *The Truce*, or *The Reawakening*) and *I sommersi e i salvati* (1986; *The Drowned and the Saved*), are further reflections on his wartime experiences. *Il sistema periodico* (1975; *The Periodic Table*) is a collection of 21 meditations, each named for a chemical element, on the analogies between the physical, chemical, and moral spheres; of all of Levi's works, it is probably his greatest critical and popular success. He also wrote poetry, novels, and short stories. His death was apparently a suicide.

Lévi, Sylvain (b. March 28, 1863, Paris—d. Oct. 30, 1935, Paris), French Orientalist who wrote on Eastern religion, literature, and history and is particularly noted for his dictionary of Buddhism.

Appointed a lecturer at the school of higher studies in Paris (1886), he taught Sanskrit at the Sorbonne (1889–94) and wrote his doctoral dissertation, *Le Théâtre indien* (1890; "The Indian Theatre"), which became a standard treatise on the subject. After his appointment as professor at the Collège de France (1894–1935), he toured India and Japan (1897 and 1898) and published *La Doctrine du sacrifice dans les Brâhmanas* (1898; "The Doctrine of Sacrifice in the Brāhmaṇas"). Another book resulting from these travels was *Le Népal: Étude historique d'un royaume hindou*, 3 vol. (1905–08; "Nepal: Historical Study of a Hindu Kingdom"). In *L'Inde et le monde* (1926; "India and the World"), he discussed India's role among nations.

Subsequent Far Eastern travels (1921–23) generated his major work, *Hôbôgirin. Dictionnaire du Bouddhisme d'après les sources chinoises et japonaises* (1929; "Hōbōgirin. Dictionary of Buddhism Based on Chinese and Japanese Sources"), produced in collaboration with the Japanese Buddhist scholar Takakusu Junjirō.

Lévi also worked with the French linguist Antoine Meillet on pioneer studies of the Tocharian language spoken in Chinese Turkistan in the 1st millennium AD. He determined the dates of texts in Tocharian B and published *Fragments de textes koutchéens . . .* (1933; "Fragments of Texts from Kucha").

Levi ben Gershom, also called GERSONIDES, LEO DE BAGNOLS, LEO HEBRAEUS, or (by acronym) RALBAG (b. 1288, Bagnols-sur-Cèze, Fr.—d. 1344), French Jewish mathematician, philosopher, astronomer, and Talmudic scholar.

In 1321 Levi wrote his first work, *Sefer ha-mispar* ("Book of the Number"), dealing with arithmetical operations, including extraction of roots. In *De sinibus, chordis et arcubus* (1342; "On Sines, Chords, and Arcs") he presented an original derivation of the sine theorem for plane triangles and tables of sines calculated to five decimal places. On the request of Philip of Vitry, bishop of Meaux, he composed a book on geometry, preserved only in Latin translation, *De numeris harmonicis* (1343; "The Harmony of Numbers"), containing commentaries on the first five books of Euclid and original axioms.

Influenced by the works of Aristotle and the 12th-century Islāmic philosopher Averroës,

Levi wrote *Sefer ha-hekkesh ha-yashar* (1319; Latin *Liber syllogismi recti;* "Book of Proper Analogy"), criticizing several arguments of Aristotle; he also wrote commentaries on the works of both philosophers.

Although Levi's biblical commentaries are complex, he presupposed an audience familiar with these commentaries, medieval astronomical literature, and the works of Averroës when he wrote (1317–29) his major work, *Sefer milḥamot Adonai* ("The Book of the Wars of the Lord"; partial trans. *Die Kämpfe Gottes,* 2 vol.). Divided into six parts, the work treats exhaustively of the immortality of the soul; dreams, divination, and prophecy; divine knowledge; providence; celestial spheres and separate intellects and their relationship with God; and the creation of the world, miracles, and the criteria by which one recognizes the true prophet. In the fifth part, he describes "Jacob's staff," an instrument that he used to measure the angular distance between celestial bodies.

Levi's work has often been criticized because of his bold expression and the unconventionality of his thought, which continued to exercise wide influence into the 19th century.

Levi-Civita, Tullio (b. March 29, 1873, Padua, Italy—d. Dec. 29, 1941, Rome), Italian mathematician known for his work in differential calculus and relativity. At the University of Padua (1891–95) he studied under Curbastro Gregorio Ricci, with whom he later collaborated in founding the absolute differential calculus (now known as tensor analysis). Levi-Civita became an instructor there in 1898 and a professor of rational mechanics in 1902. He taught at the University of Rome from 1918 until 1938, when he was removed because of his Jewish origins.

With Ricci, Levi-Civita wrote the pioneering work on the calculus of tensors, *Méthodes de calcul differéntiel absolu et leurs applications* (1900; "Methods of the Absolute Differential Calculus and Their Applications"). In 1917 Levi-Civita made his most important contribution to this branch of mathematics, the introduction of the concept of parallel displacement in general curved spaces. This concept immediately found many applications and in relativity is the basis of the unified representation of electromagnetic and gravitational fields. In pure mathematics as well, his concept was instrumental in the development of modern differential theory of generalized spaces in topology.

Levi-Civita concerned himself also with differential geometry, hydrodynamics, and engineering. He made great advances in the study of the three-body problem, which involves the motion of three bodies as they revolve around each other. His *Questioni di meccanica classica e relativistica* (1924; "Questions of Classical and Relativistic Mechanics") and *Lezioni di calcolo differentiale assoluto* (1925; *The Absolute Differential Calculus*) became standard works, and his *Lezioni di meccanica razionale,* 3 vol. (1923–27; "Lessons in Rational Mechanics"), is a classic.

Levi-Montalcini, Rita (b. April 22, 1909, Turin, Italy), neurologist who, with Stanley Cohen, shared the Nobel Prize for Physiology or Medicine in 1986 for her discovery of a bodily substance that stimulates and influences the growth of nerve cells. She held dual citizenship in Italy and the United States.

Levi-Montalcini studied medicine at the University of Turin and did research there on the effects that peripheral tissues have on nerve cell growth. She went into hiding in Florence during the German occupation of Italy (1943–45) because of her Jewish ancestry but was able to resume her research at Turin after the war. In 1947 she accepted a post at Washington University, St. Louis, Mo., with the zoologist Viktor Hamburger, who was studying the growth of nerve tissue in chick embryos.

In 1948 it was discovered in Hamburger's laboratory that a variety of mouse tumour spurred nerve growth when implanted into chick embryos. Levi-Montalcini and Hamburger traced the effect to a substance in the tumour that they named nerve-growth factor (NGF). Levi-Montalcini showed that the tumour caused similar cell growth in a nerve-tissue culture kept alive in the laboratory, and Cohen, who by then had joined her at Washington University, was able to isolate the nerve-growth factor from the tumour. NGF was the first of many cell-growth factors to be found in the bodies of animals. It plays an important role in the growth of nerve cells and fibres in the peripheral nervous system. Levi-Montalcini remained active in the field, working at Washington University until 1961 and afterward at the Institute of Cell Biology in Rome. An autobiographical work, *In Praise of Imperfection,* was published in 1988.

Lévi-Strauss, Claude (b. Nov. 28, 1908, Brussels, Belg.), French social anthropologist and leading exponent of structuralism, a name applied to the analysis of cultural systems (*e.g.,* kinship and mythical systems) in terms of the structural relations among their elements. Structuralism has influenced not only 20th-century social science but also the study of philosophy, comparative religion, literature, and film.

After studying philosophy and law at the University of Paris (1927–32), Lévi-Strauss taught in a secondary school and was associated with Jean-Paul Sartre's intellectual circle. He served as professor of sociology at the University of São Paulo, Brazil (1934–37), and did field research on the Indians of Brazil. He was visiting professor at the New School for Social Research in New York City (1941–45), where he was influenced by the work of linguist Roman Jakobson. From 1950 to 1974 he was director of studies at the École Pratique des Hautes Études at the University of Paris, and in 1959 he was appointed to the chair of social anthropology at the Collège de France.

Lévi-Strauss
AP/Wide World Photos

In 1949 Lévi-Strauss published his first major work, *Les Structures élémentaires de la parenté* (rev. ed., 1967; *The Elementary Structures of Kinship*). He attained popular recognition with *Tristes tropiques* (1955; *A World on the Wane*), a literary intellectual autobiography. Other publications include *Anthropologie structurale* (rev. ed., 1961; *Structural Anthropology*), *La Pensée Sauvage* (1962; *The Savage Mind*), and *Le Totémisme aujourd'hui* (1962; *Totemism*). His massive *Mythologiques* appeared in four volumes: *Le Cru et le cuit* (1964; *The Raw and the Cooked*), *Du miel aux cendres* (1966; *From Honey to Ashes*), *L'Origine des manières de table* (1968; *The Origin of Table Manners*), and *L'Homme nu* (1971; *The Naked Man*). In 1973 a second volume of *Anthropologie structurale* appeared. *La Voie des masques,* 2 vol. (1975; *The Way of the Masks*), analyzed the art, religion, and mythology of native American Northwest Coast Indians. In 1983 he published a collection of essays, *Le Regard éloigné* (*The View from Afar*).

Lévi-Strauss's structuralism was an effort to reduce the enormous amount of information about cultural systems to what he believed were the essentials, the formal relationships among their elements. He viewed cultures as systems of communication, and he constructed models based on structural linguistics, information theory, and cybernetics to interpret them.

Levi Strauss & Co., world's largest maker of pants, noted especially for its blue denim jeans called Levi's (registered trademark). It also manufactures tailored slacks, jackets, hats, shirts, skirts, and belts and licenses the manufacture of novelty items. The company is headquartered in San Francisco.

The company traces its origin to Levi Strauss (1829–1902), a Bavarian immigrant who arrived in San Francisco in 1850 during the Gold Rush, bringing dry goods for sale to miners. Hearing of the miners' need for durable pants, Strauss hired a tailor to make garments out of tent canvas. (Later, denim was substituted, and copper riveting was added to pocket seams.) A merchandising partnership of Strauss and his two brothers, Jonas and Louis, was formed in 1853.

After Strauss's death in 1902, leadership of the company passed to four nephews and, after 1918, to in-laws, the Haas family. The company's most spectacular growth occurred after 1946, when it decided to abandon wholesaling and concentrate on manufacturing clothing under its own label. By the 1960s Levi's and other jeans—once worn chiefly by Western cowboys—became popular worldwide. In 1985 the Haas family, along with other descendants of Levi Strauss, staged a leveraged buyout that returned the company to private ownership. In 1986 Levi Strauss & Co. introduced a new line of casual pants called "Dockers."

Levin, Meyer (b. Oct. 8, 1905, Chicago, Ill., U.S.—d. July 9, 1981, Jerusalem, Israel), American author of novels and nonfiction about the Jewish people and Israel.

Levin first became known with the novel *Yehuda* (1931). In 1945 he wrote and produced the first Palestinian feature film, *My Father's House* (book, 1947), which tells of Jews who are driven out of Poland and reunite in Palestine. Other major works are *Citizens* (1940)—about the 1937 steel strikes in Chicago, in which 10 strikers were killed—and *Compulsion* (1956)—about the Leopold–Loeb murder case.

From 1933 to 1939 Levin worked as an associate editor and film critic with *Esquire* and was a reporter of the Loyalist side in the Spanish Civil War. He was also a war correspondent during World War II. Other works include *The Settlers* (1972) and *The Illegals* (1977), a film telling the story of the journey of Jewish immigrants from Poland to Israel.

Levine, Jack (b. Jan. 3, 1915, Boston, Mass., U.S.), painter prominent in the American Social Realist school of the 1930s.

Trained first at the Jewish Welfare Center, Roxbury, Mass., and later at the Boston Museum of Fine Arts, from 1929 to 1931 he studied at Harvard University. In 1935 Levine joined the Works Progress Administration (WPA) Federal Art Project. He set up his studio in the slums of Boston, where he painted the poor and satirically portrayed corrupt politicians. Technically, he was influenced by the dramatic distortions of the European Expressionists. His "Brain Trust," exhibited in 1936, and "The Feast of Pure Reason," the following year, brought him to prominence. His first one-man show was held in 1939 in New

Jack Levine, 1970
Budd Studio

York City. "The Trial" (1953–54), "Gangster Funeral" (1952–53), "The Patriarch of Moscow on a Visit to Jerusalem" (1975), and the triptych "Panethnikon" (1978), depicting an imaginary meeting of the United Nations Security Council) continued his vein of biting social satire.

It was because of Levine's satirical tendency that he drew sharp criticism from President Dwight D. Eisenhower for some of his works in a State Department show in Moscow in 1959. Interestingly, the Vatican demonstrated a greater appreciation for Levine's work. In 1973, upon the purchase of his "Cain and Abel" canvas, Levine was told by Pope Paul VI that his work would always be welcome in the Vatican Museum—an unusual distinction for an American artist.

Levine, James (b. June 23, 1943, Cincinnati, Ohio, U.S.), American conductor and pianist, especially noted for his work with the Metropolitan Opera of New York City.

As a piano prodigy Levine made his debut in 1953 with the Cincinnati Orchestra. He studied piano with Rosina Lhévinne and conducting with Jean Morel at the Juilliard School in New York City. In 1965 George Szell invited him to become the assistant conductor of the Cleveland Orchestra, where he remained until 1970. He made his Metropolitan Opera debut in 1971 with *Tosca;* he became the company's principal conductor in 1973, musical director in 1975, and artistic director in 1986. In addition to making guest appearances in the U.S. and Europe, Levine was musical director of the Chicago Symphony Orchestra at its Ravinia (Ill.) summer festival from 1973 to 1993. Among his important recordings were operas by W.A. Mozart, Giuseppe Verdi, and Richard Wagner and the symphonies of Johannes Brahms and Gustav Mahler. Levine's straightforward interpretations were marked by vitality and architectural clarity. He remained active as a recitalist and recorded chamber music in collaboration with cellist Lynn Harrell.

Levinson, Salmon Oliver (b. Dec. 29, 1865, Noblesville, Ind., U.S.—d. Feb. 2, 1941, Chicago, Ill.), lawyer who originated and publicized the "outlawry of war" movement in the United States.

Levinson practiced law in Chicago from 1891 and became noted for his skill in reorganizing the finances of distressed corporations. In an article in the *New Republic,* March 9, 1918, he argued that violence by nation-states should be declared illegal. During the waning months of World War I he was able to win leaders in many fields to his cause. Levinson later assisted in drafting the Kellogg-Briand Pact (1928), which "outlawed" war in a legal sense.

levirate, custom or law decreeing a dead man's brother to be the preferred, and in rare cases the mandatory, marriage partner of the widow. The term comes from the Latin *levir,* meaning "husband's brother." In ancient Hebrew society, the levirate served to perpetuate the line of a man who died without offspring. In some nonliterate societies the rights and duties of the first husband continue; among the Nuer people of the Sudan, for example, the children of a remarried widow belong to the first husband's line, and they consider the deceased to be their father even if the new husband is their biological genitor. Often, the brother who marries his former sister-in-law is a proxy for the deceased, and no new marriage is contracted, since all progeny are socially acknowledged as the seed of the dead man. The "brother" may be an actual sibling of the deceased or a person so classified, and where he is required to be a younger man the custom is called the junior levirate.

Levi's (apparel): *see* jeans.

Lévis-Lauzon, city, Chaudière-Appalaches region, southern Quebec province, Canada, on the south shore of the St. Lawrence River, opposite the city of Quebec, with which it is linked by ferry. The settlement, founded in 1647, was formerly called Aubigny in honour of the Duke of Richmond (who had inherited the title of Duke d'Aubigny). From the heights above the town, the British general James Wolfe bombarded and destroyed part of Quebec city in 1759. In 1861 the community's name was changed to honour François Gaston, Duke de Lévis, who commanded the French forces in Canada after the death of the Marquis de Montcalm during Wolfe's siege.

Now an industrial centre, Lévis has dry docks equipped to accommodate the largest ships. Major manufactures are foundry and machine-shop products, lumber, tobacco, and furniture. The city's Lowtown, between high cliffs and the river, is occupied chiefly by railroad yards and wharves; its Hightown, atop a steep incline, is largely residential. Lauzon, a major industrial and shipbuilding centre just to the northeast of Lévis, was a separate community until the early 1990s. Inc. Lévis, 1916. Pop. (1991) 39,452.

"De," "la," and similar components of a name, when followed by a space, are alphabetized as separate words (e.g., *De Forest, Lee*). *When they are joined to the following part of a name, the combination is treated as a single word* (e.g., *DeForest, John William*).

Levita, Elijah, Hebrew in full ELIYAHU BEN ASHER HA-LEVI ASHKENAZI, byname BAḤUR ("Young Man," or "Student") (b. Feb. 13, 1469, Neustadt an der Aisch, Nürnberg [Germany]—d. Jan. 28, 1549, Venice [Italy]), German-born Jewish grammarian whose writings and teaching furthered the study of Hebrew in European Christendom at a time of widespread hostility toward the Jews.

Levita went to Italy early in life and in 1504 settled at Padua. There he wrote a manual of Hebrew (1508) that was appropriated by his transcriber, Benjamin Colbo, who made interpolations and published it under his own name. The work enjoyed wide popularity among both Jewish and Christian students, but Levita did not receive credit for writing it until 1546, when he published a corrected edition.

Forced to flee Padua when it was taken and sacked by the League of Cambrai in 1509, he settled in Venice and in 1513 went to Rome, where he enjoyed the patronage of Gilles of Viterbo, general of the Augustinian religious order and later a cardinal. Encouraged by Gilles to write a treatise on Hebrew grammar, Levita produced *Sefer ha-Baḥur* (1518; "Book of Baḥur"), which was widely used and went into many editions. About the same time, he published a table of paradigms and an annotated dictionary of irregular word forms found in the Bible. A work on phonetics and various aspects of Hebrew grammar, *Pirqe Eliyahu* ("Chapters of Elijah"), appeared in 1520.

In 1527 Levita again lost his property and many of his manuscripts and was forced to leave Rome when it was sacked by the imperial army. He again settled in Venice, correcting Hebrew works for a printer, teaching, and completing *Sefer ha-zakhronot* ("Book of Memoirs"), a Masoretic, or Hebrew biblical, concordance. Though never published, the manuscript brought offers of professorships from church prelates, princes, and the king of France, Francis I. He declined all of them, however. Another Masoretic work, *Massarot ha-massarot* (1538; "Tradition of Tradition") remained a subject of debate among Hebraists for nearly three centuries.

During the last years of his life Levita produced, among others, two major works. *Sefer meturgeman* (1541; "A Translator's Book") was the first dictionary of the Targums, or Aramaic books of the Old Testament. His lexicon *Tishbi* (1542) explained much of the late Hebrew language and was a supplement to two important earlier dictionaries.

levitation, rising of a human body off the ground, in apparent defiance of the law of gravity. The term designates such alleged occurrences in the lives of saints and of spiritualist mediums, generally during a séance; levitation of furniture and other objects during a séance has also been reported. Levitation of witches and other figures of folklore is called transvection and is said to involve the rubbing of "flying ointment" on their bodies before flying to the sabbath (*see* witches' sabbath). The levitation of saints is usually directly upward, whereas that of witches has the dynamic purpose of transportation. Theologians long debated whether transvection was illusion or fact; levitation, however, has been subject to less controversy, though its practice has often been discouraged.

Levite, member of a group of clans of religious functionaries in ancient Israel who apparently were given a special religious status, conjecturally for slaughtering idolaters of the golden calf during the time of Moses (Ex. 32:25–29). They thus replaced the firstborn sons of Israel who were "dedicated to the service of the Lord" for having been preserved from death at the time of the first Passover (Ex. 12).

Inconclusive evidence has been presented to show that the Levites originally constituted a secular tribe that was named (some say only symbolically) after Levi, the third son born to Jacob and his first wife, Leah. If the Levites were a secular tribe, scholars generally believe it no longer existed when the Israelites took possession of the Promised Land; for the Levites, unlike the 12 tribes of Israel, were not assigned a specific territory of their own but rather 48 cities scattered throughout the entire country (Numbers 35:1–8). Other scholars, however, argue that it would have been improper for the Levites to possess land, even if they were a secular tribe, for as priestly officials "the offerings by fire to the Lord God of Israel are their inheritance" (Joshua 13:14). The history of the Levites is further obscured by the possibility that their ranks may have included representatives of all the tribes.

Because the priestly functions of the Levites evidently changed during the course of centuries, historians are still unable to explain satisfactorily such problems as the relationship that existed between the Levites and the members of the priesthood, who were descendants of Aaron, himself a descendant of Levi. The priests of Aaron clearly acquired sole right to the Jewish priesthood. Those who performed subordinate services associated with public worship were known as Levites. In this capacity, the Levites were musicians, gate keepers, guardians, Temple officials, judges, and craftsmen.

In modern synagogue practice, a Levite is called upon to bless the reading of the second portion of the Law during a service.

Leviticus, Hebrew WAYIQRA' ("And He Called"), the third book of the Latin Vulgate Bible, the name of which designates its contents as a book (or manual) primarily concerned with the priests and their duties. Although Leviticus is basically a book of laws, it also contains some narrative (chapters 8–9, 10:1–7, 10:16–20, and 24:10–14). The book is usually divided into five parts: sacrificial laws (chapters 1–7); the inauguration of the priesthood and laws governing their office (chapters 8–10); laws for ceremonial purity (chapters 11–16); laws governing the people's holiness (chapters 17–26); and a supplement concerning offerings to the sanctuary and religious vows (chapter 27).

Scholars agree that Leviticus belongs to the Priestly (P) source of the Pentateuchal traditions. This material is dated according to one theory in the 7th century BC and is regarded as the law upon which Ezra and Nehemiah based their reform. Older material, however, is preserved in P, particularly the "Holiness Code" (chapters 17–26), dating from ancient times.

Because the closing chapters of the preceding book (Exodus) and the opening chapters of the following book (Numbers) are also P materials, the existence of Leviticus as a separate book is presumably a secondary development. This hypothesis suggests that Leviticus properly belongs to a larger literary unit that is variously understood to include the first four, five, or six books of the Old Testament.

Levitsky, Ivan, pseudonym of IVAN NECHUY-LEVITSKY, also spelled NECHÚI-LEVÝTSKY, or NEČUJ-LEVYC'KYJ (b. Nov. 25 [Nov. 13, old style], 1838, Steblev, Kiev province, Ukraine, Russian Empire—d. April 15 [April 2, O.S.], 1918, Kiev), Ukrainian Realist novelist of the postserfdom reform period. He drew upon his background as a seminary student and, later, a provincial teacher, to depict the educated and lower classes in some of the earliest social novels in Ukrainian literature. His works include *Prichepa* (1869; "The Intruder"), *Khmari* (1874; "Clouds"), *Kaydasheva semya* (1879; "The Kaydashev Family"), and *Burlachka* (1881; "A Factory Girl"). Use of objective narrative and details of folklore strengthen the realistic effect of his works.

Levitt, Helen (b. Aug. 31, 1913, New York, N.Y., U.S.), American photographer whose work captures the bustle, squalour, and beauty of everyday life in New York City.

Levitt began her career in photography at age 18 working in a portrait studio in the Bronx and taking photographs in her spare time. During this period Levitt often chose children, especially the underprivileged, as her subject matter. Her first show, "Photographs of Children," was held at the Museum of Modern Art in New York in 1943 and featured the humanity that infuses much of her work. Included in this show were photographs from her visit in 1941 to Mexico City, where she photographed the city's street life. Her friend the novelist James Agee wrote the introduction to Levitt's book of photographs entitled *A Way of Seeing: Photographs of New York,* which she compiled in the late 1940s. In it, he praised her photographs, finding them "as beautiful, perceptive, satisfying and enduring as any lyrical work that I know."

In the mid-1940s Levitt collaborated with Agee, filmmaker Sidney Meyers, and painter Janice Loeb on *The Quiet One,* a prizewinning documentary about a young African-American boy, and with Agee and Loeb on the film *In the Street,* which captures everyday life in East Harlem. For most of the 1960s she concentrated on film editing and directing. Levitt resumed photography in the 1970s, with a major Museum of Modern Art show in 1974.

Levittown, unincorporated residential community in Hempstead town (township), Nassau county, western Long Island, New York, U.S. Developed between 1946 and 1951 by the firm of Levitt & Sons, Inc., Levittown was an early example of a completely preplanned and mass-produced housing complex. More than 17,000 low-cost homes were built, with accompanying shopping centres, playgrounds, swimming pools, community halls, and schools. The name Levittown became a national symbol for suburbia during the post-World War II building boom. Many of the homes were subsequently remodeled or redesigned, and few of the original structures remain. Pop. (2000) 53,067.

Levittown, extensive, unincorporated suburban housing development in Bucks county, eastern Pennsylvania, U.S., near the big bend of the Delaware River, approximately midway between Philadelphia and Trenton, N.J. It was built in 1951–58 by Levitt & Sons, Inc., who repeated there the planned construction formula first used in Levittown, N.Y., in the late 1940s. The first occupants arrived in June 1952. The name Levittown is now equated with similar developments throughout the country. Pop. (2000) 53,966.

Lévka Mountains, Modern Greek LÉVKA ÓRI, also called MADHÁRES ÓRI, highest and most precipitous massif in western Crete, located a few miles south of the Cretan capital, Khaniá (Canea), in the *nomós* (department) of Khaniá, Greece. The limestone peaks have been hollowed out by erosion into high plains such as the Omalós (1,650–3,300 ft [500–1,000 m]), which gives access from the village of Lákkoi to the Samaria gorge, 11 mi (18 km) long and 1,000 ft deep.

Bearing a stream during the wet season, the Samaria provides the only route of transit to the south coast over the Lévka range. The massif is separated from Mt. Apopigádhi (4,367 ft) on the west by a depression carrying the road from Khaniá to Ayía Iríni; on the east it is defined by the depression carrying the road from Vrísai to Chóra Sfakíon. At least four of the Lévka peaks exceed 6,600 ft. The highest is Mt. Lévka at 8,045 ft (2,452 m). The major stream rising from the Lévka is the Plataniás, which flows past Lákkoi northwestward into the Kólpos (gulf) Khaníon. The region is believed to be the last habitat of the Cretan agrimi, a wild goat.

Levkádhia, also spelled LEVKÁS (Greece): *see* Leucas.

Levkosía (Cyprus): *see* Nicosia.

Levnî, Abdülcelil (b. late 17th century, probably Edirne, Rumelia—d. 1732, Constantinople), the most accomplished and famous Ottoman painter of the early 18th-century "Tulip Period."

He went as a young man to Constantinople, where he studied at the academy of painting at the Topkapı Palace. He later became chief court painter to the Ottoman sultan Mustafa II, and he probably held the same post under the successor to the throne, Ahmed III.

Levnî painted at a time when the maxim of Ottoman society was "enjoy today," and much of his work depicts entertainments. His masterpiece consists of more than 100 illustrations for the two-volume poem *Surname-i Vehbi,* by the Ottoman poet Vehbi. Levnî preferred to use softer colours and severely limited the amount of gold leaf illumination, two departures from the past. His paintings show a love of movement and action, strong powers of observation, and touches of humour.

"Dancers and Entertainments Before Sultan Ahmed III," miniature from the *Surname-i Vehbi,* illustrated by Levnî, *c.* 1720–25; in the Topkapı Saray Museum, Istanbul

By courtesy of the Topkapi Saray Museum, Istanbul

His works also include a series of 50 plates, mostly portraits, showing the sultan, his family, and his court as well as formal portraits of Sultan Mustafa II and Ahmed III.

Levon I, byname LEVON THE GREAT (fl. early 13th century), king of Armenia (reigned 1199–1219), who rallied the Armenians after their dispersion by the Seljuq Turks and consolidated the kingdom in Cilicia, southeastern Asia Minor. Through his friendly relations with the German emperors Frederick I Barbarossa and Henry VI, he was crowned by Pope Celestine III's legate, Cardinal Conrad von Wittelsbach, and allied Lesser Armenia to the West, despite overtures from the Byzantine emperor.

Levski, Vasil, byname of VASIL IVANOV KUNCHEV (b. July 6, 1837, Karlovo, Rumelia—d. Feb. 6, 1873, near Sofia), Bulgarian revolutionary leader in the struggle for liberation of Bulgaria from Ottoman rule.

Initially a monk (1858–64), Vasil Kunchev soon dedicated himself to the work of freeing Bulgaria and for his courage was nicknamed Levski (Lionlike). Levski united the two legions of Bulgarian volunteers organized in Serbia (1862, 1868) but, disappointed in the Serbian government, decided to return to Bulgaria in order to organize an uprising. He introduced a new phase in the Bulgarian national movement by transferring revolutionary activity from abroad into the country itself.

In 1869 in Bucharest, Levski, together with Lyuben Karavelov, organized the Bulgarian Central Revolutionary Committee, which established a network of agents (called apostles) in Bulgaria. In 1872, during one of his secret missions to Bulgaria, Levski was caught by the Turks and was later hanged.

Levuka, town on the east coast of Ovalau island, central Fiji, South Pacific, and capital of Lomaiviti Province at the western edge of the country's Eastern Division. Settled by a U.S. adventurer in 1822, the area was the centre of a cotton boom during the U.S. Civil War (1861–65), when world cotton supplies were disrupted. Levuka was chosen as the capital of Fiji in 1874, when the islands were annexed by Great Britain, but lost this distinction to Suva in 1882. It is now a tuna-fishing port for Japanese, South Korean, and Taiwanese fishermen. Pop. (1996 est.) 3,700.

Levy, Edward (English newspaperman): *see* Burnham, Edward Levy-Lawson, 1st Baron.

Levy, Joseph Moses (b. Dec. 15, 1812, London, Eng.—d. Oct 12, 1888, Ramsgate, Kent), English newspaperman, founder of the London newspaper *Daily Telegraph*.

Educated at Bruce Castle school and in Germany, Levy acquired a printing shop on Fleet Street in London and, in 1855, became proprietor of the *Sunday Times* (which he kept for a year) and the *Daily Telegraph and Courier*, which he acquired from a Colonel Sleigh in settlement of debts. The paper's name was abbreviated to *Daily Telegraph* and became the first London daily to sell for a penny.

With the assistance of his eldest son, Edward (*see* Burnham, Edward Levy-Lawson, 1st Baron), Levy created one of the most dynamic and creative newspapers of the day. He invested heavily in the enterprise, hired some of the leading writers and journalists of the day, and contributed many of the artistic and theatrical articles himself.

Lévy-Bruhl, Lucien (b. April 19, 1857, Paris, France—d. March 13, 1939, Paris), French philosopher whose study of the psychology of primitive peoples gave anthropology a new approach to understanding irrational factors in social thought and primitive religion and mythology.

Lévy-Bruhl was professor of philosophy at the Sorbonne from 1899 to 1927. His first major work, *La Morale et la science des moeurs* (1903; *Ethics and Moral Science*), reflected the positivism of Auguste Comte. Contending that theoretical moralities cannot prevail, this book laid the groundwork for a pluralistic, relativistic sociology. Much of his subsequent attention was devoted to the mentality of people in so-called primitive societies, which he first examined at length in *Les Fonctions mentales dans les sociétés primitives* (1910; *How Natives Think*). From the French sociologist Émile Durkheim he adopted the concept of *représentations collectives,* or group ideas, which account for differences in reasoning between people in primitive societies and those in modern Western ones. He suggested that primitive thought and perceptions are pervaded by mysticism and that the primitive mentality, though not opposed to the laws of logic, is not governed exclusively by them.

Lévy-Bruhl continued his examination of primitive mentality and transitional stages in several other works, including *La Mentalité primitive* (1922; *Primitive Mentality*), *L'Âme primitive* (1927; *The "Soul" of the Primitive*), and *Le Surnaturel et la nature dans la mentalité primitive* (1931; *Primitives and the Supernatural*).

Levy-Lawson, Edward (English newspaperman): *see* Burnham, Edward Levy-Lawson, 1st Baron.

Lévy-Roussy syndrome, also called ROUSSY-LÉVY SYNDROME, hereditary condition characterized by a loss of muscular coordination and progressive atrophy of the muscles, along with certain skeletal abnormalities. The atrophy and other muscular symptoms are apparently secondary to a neurologic defect. Symptoms first appear in early childhood and progress slowly through life. Affected persons have impaired equilibrium, making walking or standing difficult, and lose certain neuromuscular reflexes of the knees and ankles. There may be severe curvature of the spine (scoliosis) and clubfoot.

levyne, also called LEVYNITE, mineral in the zeolite family, similar in composition and structure to chabazite (*q.v.*).

Lewald, Fanny (b. March 24, 1811, Königsberg, Prussia [now Kaliningrad, Russia]—d. Aug. 5, 1889, Dresden, Ger.), popular German novelist and feminist who wrote mainly on family, marriage, and social problems.

She first began writing at the age of 30 with the encouragement of her cousin August Lewald, a journalist and editor. The novels *Clementine* (1842) and *Jenny* (1843) describe circumscribed lives built around family virtues. *Die Familie Darner,* 3 vol. (1888; "The Darner Family"), and *Von Geschlecht zu Geschlecht,* 8 vol. (1863–65; "From Generation to Generation"), are realistic novels about the lives of family members over several generations. *Diogena* (1847) is a parody of *Gräfin Faustine,* a sentimental novel by Lewald's rival, Ida, Countess von Hahn-Hahn. In the historical novel *Prinz Louis Ferdinand,* 3 vol. (1849), Rahel Varnhagen von Ense, an early 19th-century Berlin literary hostess, is the central figure.

Lewald also wrote travel books about Italy, Scotland, and England and an autobiography, *Meine Lebensgeschichte,* 3 vol. (1861–62; "My Life Story"). While traveling in Italy in 1845 she met Adolf Stahr, whom she married in 1854 after his marriage was dissolved. Although she began writing after their works were banned in 1835, Lewald was influenced by the Young Germany group, a largely political movement whose writers scorned the excesses of the late Romantics and sought to use literature for utilitarian and political ends. The emancipation of women was one of the issues the movement espoused. Lewald was also influenced by the French feminist writer George Sand.

Lewen, John, Lewen also spelled LOWEN, or LOWYN: *see* Lowin, John.

Lewes, district, county of East Sussex, England. The district is bordered on the northwest by the county of West Sussex and on the southwest by the borough of Brighton. On the south it stretches along the English Channel coast to include the port of Newhaven and the resort of Seaford. The chalk ridge of the South Downs runs across it from east to west, with the town of Lewes occupying the gap where the River Ouse cuts through the ridge to the sea. East of the gap lies Glyndebourne, known for its operatic productions. Area 113 square miles (292 square km). Pop. (1992 est.) 88,900.

Lewes, town (parish), Lewes district, county of East Sussex, England. Lewes lies at a gap in the South Downs and along the River Ouse where it is still tidal. A castle was built in the 11th century, and its ruins still dominate the town, which grew below as a market centre and river port of some importance, although the port later gave way to Newhaven on the coast. In 1264 Simon de Montfort vanquished Henry III at the Battle of Lewes.

The Barbican House, the house of Anne of Cleves (fourth queen of Henry VIII), and Shelley's Hotel all date from the 16th century. Southover Grange, also built in the 16th century, together with its walled gardens, is municipal property.

A historic assize town, Lewes in modern times has developed as the county town (seat) of East Sussex. It also has some light industries and is still an important market. Glyndebourne, the world-famous opera centre, is only 3 miles (5 km) from the town. Pop. (1981) 14,772.

Lewes, city, Sussex county, southeastern Delaware, U.S. It lies at the mouth of Delaware Bay just west of Cape Henlopen (state park), where it is protected by Delaware Breakwater (built 1825–35). Founded in 1631 by Dutch colonists, it was the first white settlement along the Delaware River. Originally called Zwaanendael, the town was renamed (*c.* 1685) for Lewes, Sussex, Eng., after William Penn was granted the rights to the area. A port of entry, the town has a seafaring tradition dating back more than 300 years. It was bombarded by the British during the War of 1812 and has been the site of many shipwrecks. Lewes is now a resort community known for saltwater fishing. Its industries include fish processing and canning and the manufacture of clothing. Zwaanendael House (1931), a replica of the town hall in Hoorn, Neth., is maintained as a memorial to the early settlers. Restored buildings, maintained by the Lewes Historical Society, depict the city's past. Regular ferry service links Lewes to Cape May, N.J. Inc. town, 1857; city, 1969. Pop. (1994 est.) 2,476.

Lewes, George Henry (b. April 18, 1817, London, Eng.—d. Nov. 28, 1878, London), English philosopher, literary critic, dramatist, actor, scientist, and editor, remembered chiefly for his decades-long liaison with the novelist Mary Ann Evans (better known by her pseudonym, George Eliot).

Lewes was the grandson of the actor Charles Lee Lewes and the son of the manager of Liverpool's Theatre Royal. After a desultory education, he spent two years in Germany and returned to London in 1840. During the next decade he wrote frequently for various journals and in the early 1840s corresponded with John Stuart Mill, through whom he became acquainted with the positivist philosophy of Auguste Comte, usually considered the founder of sociology. In 1850 Lewes and his friend Thornton Leigh Hunt founded a radical weekly called *The Leader,* for which he wrote the literary and theatrical features. His *Comte's Philosophy of the Sciences* (1853) originally appeared as a series of articles in *The Leader.*

Lewes, detail of a pencil drawing by Anne Gliddon, 1840; in the National Portrait Gallery, London

By courtesy of the National Portrait Gallery, London

Lewes married in 1841, and the couple lived communally with Hunt, Mrs. Hunt, and two other couples. Though initially a success, the arrangement failed after Mrs. Lewes had two children by Hunt. Lewes willingly registered the first child under his family name and remained friends with Hunt and his own wife. In 1851, however, after the birth of the second child, Lewes ceased to regard Mrs. Lewes as his wife. In the same year, after their estrangement, he met Mary Ann Evans. Legal divorce was impossible for Lewes because he had condoned the adultery, but from his separation in 1854 until his death, Lewes and Evans lived happily together.

All of Lewes' major writings were stimulated by his association with Evans, which included mutual consultation about articles and attendance at plays and operas that Lewes reviewed for *The Leader.* Before turning to scientific studies, he published *Life and Works of Goethe,* 2 vol. (1855), which is still considered the best introduction in English to the poet. Besides numerous papers on motor and sensory nerves, he published *Seaside Studies* (1858), *Physiology of Common Life,* 2 vol. (1859–60), and *Studies in Animal Life* (1862). These were followed by a study of Aristotle (1864) and his most ambitious work,

Problems of Life and Mind, 5 vol. (1873–79). He edited *The Fortnightly Review* (1865–66), contributing articles in science, politics, and literary criticism.

A versatile writer and thinker in many fields, Lewes contributed most significantly to the development of empirical metaphysics; his treatment of mental phenomena as related to social and historical conditions was a major advance in psychological thought.

BIBLIOGRAPHY. Rosemary Ashton, *G.H. Lewes: A Life* (1991).

Lewin, Kurt (b. Sept. 9, 1890, Mogilno, Ger. [now in Poland]—d. Feb. 12, 1947, Newtonville, Mass., U.S.), German-born American social psychologist known for his field theory of behaviour, which holds that human behaviour is a function of an individual's psychological environment.

Lewin received a doctorate from the University of Berlin in 1914. After World War I, he joined the faculty of the Berlin Psychoanalytic Institute. In 1933 he moved to the United States, settling at the State University of Iowa's Child Welfare Research Station (1935–45). In 1945 he founded and became director of the Research Center for Group Dynamics at the Massachusetts Institute of Technology, Cambridge. He retained that position until his death.

Lewin proposed that human behaviour should be seen as part of a continuum, with individual variations from the norm being a function of tensions between perceptions of the self and of the environment. He devoted the last years of his life to research on group dynamics, believing that groups alter the individual behaviour of their constituents. On the basis of research examining the effects of democratic, autocratic, and laissez-faire methods of leadership on groups of children, Lewin claimed that small groups operated most successfully when they were conducted in a democratic manner.

Lewis, Alun (b. July 1, 1915, Aberdare, Glamorganshire, Wales—d. March 5, 1944, Goppe Pass, Arakan, Burma [Myanmar]), at his early death one of the most promising Welsh poets, who described his experiences as an enlisted man and then an officer during World War II.

The son of a schoolmaster, Lewis grew up in a mining valley of South Wales, where he forged a bond of sympathy with the impoverished coal miners. Scholarships enabled him to attend the universities of Aberystwyth and Manchester. He worked as a schoolteacher before entering the army shortly after the outbreak of the war. Most of the poems in *Raiders' Dawn* (1942) are about army life in training camps in England, as are the short stories in *The Last Inspection* (1942). *Ha! Ha! Among the Trumpets* (1945) contains the verse he wrote after leaving England for military duty in the East, where he was killed. *Letters from India* (1946) and *Selected Poetry and Prose* (1966) were also published posthumously.

Consult the INDEX *first*

Lewis, Sir Arthur, in full SIR WILLIAM ARTHUR LEWIS (b. Jan. 23, 1915, Castries, St. Lucia, British West Indies—d. June 15, 1991, Bridgetown, Barbados), British economist who shared (with Theodore W. Schultz, an American) the 1979 Nobel Prize for Economic Science for his studies of economic development and his construction of an innovative model relating the terms of trade between less developed and more developed nations to their respective levels of labour productivity in agriculture.

Lewis attended the London School of Economics after winning a government scholarship. He graduated in 1937 and received a Ph.D. in economics there in 1940. He was a lecturer at the school from 1938 to 1947, professor of economics at the University of Manchester from 1947 to 1958, principal of University College of the West Indies in 1959–62, and professor at Princeton University from 1963 to 1983. He helped establish, and in 1970–73 headed, the Caribbean Development Bank. Lewis was knighted in 1963.

He also wrote several books, including *The Principles of Economic Planning* (1949), *The Theory of Economic Growth* (1955), *Development Planning* (1966), *Tropical Development 1880–1913* (1971), and *Growth and Fluctuations 1870–1913* (1978).

Lewis, C. Day: *see* Day-Lewis, C(ecil).

Lewis, C.I., in full CLARENCE IRVING LEWIS (b. April 12, 1883, Stoneham, Mass., U.S.—d. Feb. 3, 1964, Cambridge, Mass.), American logician, epistemologist, and moral philosopher.

Educated at Harvard University, Lewis taught there from 1920 until his retirement in 1953, serving as a full professor of philosophy from 1930. His principal works are *Symbolic Logic* (with Cooper Harold Langford; 1932), *An Analysis of Knowledge and Valuation* (1947), and *The Ground and Nature of the Right* (1955).

In epistemology and ethics Lewis was a conceptualistic pragmatist within a Kantian framework; *i.e.,* he sought to develop philosophical concepts in the manner of Kant as rooted in empirical reality. According to Lewis, epistemological problems are a matter of the subjective interpretations that individuals make about their sensory experiences. The only possible certainty is that provided by what Lewis calls terminating judgment, which involves a statement about reality that has been verified empirically. Terminating judgments must refer to appearances, while nonterminating judgments may refer to other objects or values. Certainty and meaning may, however, exist in nonterminating judgments if a terminating judgment stands behind them.

In logic, Lewis criticized contemporary formal systems using material implication and proposed an alternative system of logic based upon strict implication. That is, he rejected systems that do not limit themselves strictly to what is implicit in experience. Because concepts arise from experience, in his system no concept is fixed or indispensable, and the abstract categories of traditional logic are subject to change.

Lewis, C.S., in full CLIVE STAPLES LEWIS (b. Nov. 29, 1898, Belfast, Ire. [now in Northern Ireland]—d. Nov. 22, 1963, Oxford, Oxfordshire, Eng.), British scholar, novelist, and author of about 40 books, most of them on Christian apologetics, the most widely known being *The Screwtape Letters.* He also achieved fame with a trilogy of science-fiction novels and with the *Chronicles of Narnia,* a series of seven children's books that have become classics of fantasy literature.

During World War I, Lewis fought in France with the Somerset Light Infantry and was wounded in 1917. The following year he went to University College, Oxford, where he achieved an outstanding record as a classical scholar. From 1925 to 1954 he was a fellow and tutor of Magdalen College, Oxford, and from 1954 to 1963 he was professor of medieval and Renaissance English at the University of Cambridge.

Lewis lapsed into atheism in his teens but experienced a reconversion to Christianity in 1931. His first work to attract attention was *The Pilgrim's Regress: An Allegorical Apology for Christianity, Reason and Romanticism* (1933). In 1936 came the critical and characteristic *Allegory of Love: A Study in Medieval Tradition,* considered by many to be his finest scholarly work. The first of his science fiction novels (a genre then scarcely known), *Out of the Silent Planet* (1938), was followed by the equally remarkable fictions *Perelandra* (1943) and *That Hideous Strength* (1945). These three books, which form one of the best of all science fiction trilogies, centre on an English linguist named Ransom who voyages to Mars and Venus and becomes involved in a cosmic struggle betwen good and evil in the solar system.

Lewis's *The Problem of Pain* (1940) brought him wide recognition as a lay expositor of Christian apologetics, but it was far exceeded by the fictional best-selling *Screwtape Letters* (1942). This satire consists of 31 letters in which an elderly, experienced devil named Screwtape instructs his junior, Wormwood, in the subtle art of tempting a young Christian convert. Lewis's first story for children was *The Lion, the Witch and the Wardrobe* (1950), the first of seven tales about the kingdom of Narnia. The Narnia books are exciting, often humorous, inventive, and, in the final scenes of *The Last Battle* (1956), deeply moving. Notable among Lewis's other books are a volume of autobiography, *Surprised by Joy; The Shape of My Early Life* (1955), and a novel based on the story of Psyche and Cupid, *Till We Have Faces: A Myth Retold* (1956).

BIBLIOGRAPHY. W.H. Lewis (ed.), *Letters* (1966), compiled by C.S. Lewis's brother, includes a memoir. Dabney Adams Hart, *Through the Open Door* (1984); and A.N. Wilson, *C.S. Lewis* (1990), are biographies. Critical studies include Chad Walsh, *The Literary Legacy of C.S. Lewis* (1979); and Margaret Patterson Hannay, *C.S. Lewis* (1981).

Lewis, Carl, in full FREDERICK CARLTON LEWIS (b. July 1, 1961, Birmingham, Ala., U.S.), American track-and-field athlete who won nine Olympic gold medals during the 1980s and '90s.

Lewis qualified for the U.S. Olympic team in 1980 but did not compete because of the U.S. boycott of the Moscow Games. At the 1984 Games in Los Angeles, Lewis won gold medals in the 100-metre and 200-metre races, the long jump, and the 4 × 100-metre relay, where he anchored the U.S. team. Lewis became the third track-and-field athlete to win four gold medals in one Olympics, joining Americans Al Kraenzlein (1900) and Jesse Owens, the latter of whom won the same four events at the 1936 Olympics in Berlin.

Lewis added two more gold medals and a silver medal at the 1988 Games in Seoul, South Korea, becoming the first Olympic athlete to win consecutive long-jump gold medals. Lewis's other gold medal at the 1988 Games came in the 100 metres, after Canadian Ben Johnson, who had won in world record time (9.79 sec), was disqualified three days later after testing positive for anabolic steroids. Lewis settled for a silver in the 200 metres, in which Joe DeLoach took the gold.

At the 1992 Olympics in Barcelona, Spain, Lewis won two more gold medals, including his third consecutive long-jump title. Again anchoring the American 4 × 100-metre relay team, Lewis won his eighth gold medal as the U.S. team set a world and Olympic record of 37.40 sec. He won his fourth consecutive long-jump title and ninth gold medal at the 1996 Olympics in Atlanta, Ga. In 1997 he retired from competition.

Lewis, Edward B. (b. May 20, 1918, Wilkes-Barre, Pa., U.S.—d. July 21, 2004, Pasadena, Calif.), American developmental geneticist who, with geneticists Christiane Nüsslein-Volhard and Eric F. Wieschaus (*qq.v.*), was awarded the 1995 Nobel Prize for Physiology or Medicine for discovering the functions that control early embryonic development.

Lewis' interest in genetics was kindled in high school. He studied biostatistics at the

University of Minnesota (B.A., 1939) and genetics at the California Institute of Technology (Ph.D., 1942), where he spent his professional career. Working independently of Nüsslein-Volhard and Wieschaus, Lewis based his research on studies of the fruit fly, or vinegar fly (*Drosophila melanogaster*), a popular species for genetic experiments. By crossbreeding thousands of flies he was able to establish that genes are generally arranged on the chromosome in the same order as their corresponding body segments—*e.g.,* the first set of genes controls the head and thorax; the middle set, the abdomen; and the final set, posterior parts. This orderliness is known as the colinearity principle. Lewis also found that genetic regulatory functions may overlap. For example, a fly with an extra set of wings has a defective gene not in the abdominal region but in the thoracic region, which normally functions as a regulator of such mutations.

Lewis' work on the fruit fly helped to explain mechanisms of general biological development, such as the causes of congenital deformities, in humans and other higher organisms. The results of his longtime research were published in *Nature* magazine in 1978. He was elected to the National Academy of Sciences in 1968 and received the National Medal of Science in 1990.

Lewis, G.N., in full GILBERT NEWTON LEWIS (b. Oct. 23, 1875, Weymouth, Mass., U.S.—d. March 23, 1946, Berkeley, Calif.), American chemist whose theory of the electron pair fostered understanding of the covalent bond and extended the concept of acids and bases.

Lewis took his Ph.D. at Harvard University (1899), studied at the universities of Leipzig and Göttingen, and entered research in thermodynamics at the Massachusetts Institute of Technology, Cambridge (1905). He became professor of physical chemistry and dean of the College of Chemistry at the University of California, Berkeley in 1912.

About 1916 Lewis began to advance the idea that a chemical bond could be formed by the sharing of valence electrons as well as by the transfer of electrons. He published his views in *Valence and the Structure of Atoms and Molecules* (1923). He also published, with Merle Randall, *Thermodynamics and the Free Energy of Chemical Substances* (1923), a textbook that became a classic work.

The first to isolate deuterium, an isotope of hydrogen, he prepared a pure sample of heavy water (deuterium oxide) in 1933. His later researches contributed to the understanding of fluorescence, phosphorescence, and colour in organic substances.

A list of the abbreviations used in the MICROPAEDIA *will be found at the end of this volume*

Lewis, Isaac Newton (b. Oct. 12, 1858, New Salem, Pa., U.S.—d. Nov. 9, 1931, Hoboken, N.J.), U.S. Army officer and inventor best known for the Lewis machine gun, widely used in World War I and later.

Lewis graduated from the U.S. Military Academy, West Point, N.Y., in 1884. In 1891 he patented an artillery ranging device, the first of a succession of military inventions, including a ranging system for coastal artillery, an artillery fire-control system, a quick-firing field gun, and a gas-propelled torpedo. He also patented several devices with nonmilitary applications, including an electric car-lighting system. Lewis patented his machine gun in 1911, but it failed to win adoption by the U.S. Army. Retiring from active service in 1913 with the grade of colonel, Lewis went to Europe, where he found immediate interest in the weapon. He built a factory in Liège, Belg., and began manufacturing the gun. With the outbreak of World War I he moved his operation to England, where he merged it with the Birmingham Small Arms Company. Some 100,000 Lewis guns were used by the Allied armies; an adaptation of his gun was especially valuable on airplanes because of its minimal recoil. This advantage finally won it acceptance by the U.S. Army after new tests and considerable controversy.

Lewis, John, in full JOHN AARON LEWIS (b. May 3, 1920, La Grange, Ill., U.S.), American jazz pianist and composer-arranger.

Reared in New Mexico by academically oriented parents, Lewis studied piano from childhood and, until 1942, anthropology and music at the University of New Mexico. He served in the U.S. Army (1942–45) and subsequently worked as a pianist with Dizzy Gillespie, arranging "Two Bass Hit," "Emanon," "Minor Walk," and his own "Toccata for Trumpet and Orchestra" for Gillespie's big band. He also worked with Miles Davis (having arranged "Move," "Budo," and "Rouge" for Davis's album *Birth of the Cool*), Charlie Parker, Lester Young, and Illinois Jacquet.

In 1952 he became the leader of the Modern Jazz Quartet, which—with vibraphonist Milt Jackson, bassist Percy Heath, and drummer Connie Kay—was one of the longest-lived and best-received groups in jazz history. It was active throughout most of the 1950s and '60s, disbanded in 1974, and resumed performing on a part-time basis in 1981. Its music was subtle and polite, quite close to Baroque chamber music, and often classed with the "cool jazz" category. Lewis also composed for nonjazz settings and wrote musical scores for cinema, ballet, and theatre. "Django" is the Lewis composition most frequently played by others. In 1974 Lewis became an instructor at the Davis Center for the Performing Arts at City College of the City University of New York.

Lewis, John L., in full JOHN LLEWELLYN LEWIS (b. Feb. 12, 1880, near Lucas, Iowa, U.S.—d. June 11, 1969, Washington, D.C.), American labour leader who was president (1920–60) of the United Mine Workers of America (UMWA) and chief founder and first president (1936–40) of the Congress of Industrial Organizations (CIO).

The son of immigrants from Welsh mining towns, Lewis left public school in the seventh grade and went to work in the mines at age 15. In the coal-mining town of Panama, Ill., he became head of a UMWA local, and in 1911 he became an organizer for the American Federation of Labor (AFL), with which the miners' union was affiliated. He became a vice president of the UMWA in 1917, acting president in 1919, and president in 1920 of the largest trade union in the United States. He would remain the UMWA's leader for the next 40 years. Lewis led a successful national coal strike in 1919, but during the 1920s the UMWA's membership shrank from 500,000 to less than 100,000 as unemployment spread among UMWA members in northern states and nonunionized mines in the southern Appalachians increased their production.

Beginning in 1933, President Franklin D. Roosevelt's New Deal presented organized labour with opportunities that Lewis exploited with energy and imagination. The National Industrial Recovery Act (1933), which guaranteed labour the right to bargain collectively, enabled him to launch new organizing campaigns in the Appalachian and other coalfields and triple the UMWA's membership within a few years. In 1935 Lewis joined several other AFL union leaders and formed the Committee for Industrial Organization with the intention of organizing workers in mass-production industries. The more traditional leaders of the AFL favoured limiting its membership to craft unions and refused to support the new strategy, so Lewis and seven other dissident union heads left the AFL to organize what became the Congress of Industrial Organizations (CIO), with Lewis as its president. Beginning in 1935–36 Lewis presided over the often-violent struggle to introduce unionism into previously unorganized industries such as steel, automobiles, tire, rubber, and electrical products. The CIO proved so successful that by the end of 1937 it had more members than did the AFL.

John L. Lewis, 1963
AP/Wide World Photos

Lewis was a lifelong Republican, but he left his party and supported Franklin D. Roosevelt for the presidency in 1932 and 1936. He opposed a third term for Roosevelt, however, and threatened to resign as CIO president if Roosevelt won. Interpreting Roosevelt's victory as a repudiation of his own leadership, Lewis resigned as president of the CIO in 1940 and in 1942 pulled the UMWA out of the parent body. A series of miners' strikes called by Lewis in the 1940s won wage increases and new benefits for miners but alienated large segments of the public. The strikes spurred the passage of the Smith-Connally Act (1943) and the Taft-Hartley Act (1947), both of which placed new restrictions on labour unions.

In the 1950s Lewis reverted to his more conciliatory attitude of the '20s; he worked closely with mine operators to mechanize the industry, a strategy that increased productivity and ultimately enlarged the miners' union benefits. After retiring as UMWA president in 1960, he served as chairman of the board of trustees of the UMWA's welfare and retirement fund. A man of imposing appearance, with overhanging brows and a bulldog chin, Lewis studded his sonorous oratory with literary allusions and sometimes with harsh epithets.

BIBLIOGRAPHY. Melvyn Dubofsky and Warren Van Tine, *John L. Lewis* (1977); Robert H. Zieger, *John L. Lewis: Labor Leader* (1988).

Lewis, Matthew Gregory, byname MONK LEWIS (b. July 9, 1775, London, Eng.—d. May 14, 1818, at sea), English novelist and dramatist who became famous overnight after the sensational success of his Gothic novel *The Monk* (1796). Thereafter he was known as "Monk" Lewis.

Matthew Gregory Lewis, detail of an oil painting by H.W. Pickersgill; in the National Portrait Gallery, London
By courtesy of the National Portrait Gallery, London

Educated at Westminster School and Christ Church, Oxford, Lewis served as attaché to the British embassy at The Hague and was a member of Parliament from 1796 to 1802. In 1812 he inherited a fortune and large properties in Jamaica. Sincerely interested in the conditions of his 500 slaves, he made two West Indian voyages, contracted yellow fever on his return from the second, and died at sea.

The Monk, written when Lewis was 19, was influenced by the leading Gothic novelist, Ann Radcliffe, and also by stronger contemporary German Gothic literature. Its emphasis on horror rather than romance, its violence, and its eroticism made it avidly read, though universally condemned. Its success was followed by a popular musical drama in the same vein, *The Castle Spectre* (1798), which was produced by the dramatist Richard Brinsley Sheridan. Lewis' other lasting work was a triumph of a very different nature, the *Journal of a West India Proprietor* (published 1834), attesting to his humane and liberal attitudes.

Consult the INDEX *first*

Lewis, Meade, byname LUX (b. 1905, Louisville, Ky., U.S.—d. June 7, 1964, Minneapolis, Minn.), U.S. musician and one of the leading exponents of boogie-woogie piano.

A former violin student who moved to piano playing in Chicago nightclubs, he owed his belated fame to a single record made in 1929 and unearthed seven years later: his "Honky Tonk Train Blues." One of the most vibrant and exhilarating of all boogie-woogie expositions, it had a great deal to do with the feverish if transient craze for the idiom in the late 1930s. He re-recorded the theme on at least four occasions. He also appeared with Pete Johnson and Albert Ammons as part of a famous six-handed piano team. He spent the last 20 years of his career as he had begun it, playing piano in nightclubs. His style, with its hypnotically insistent right-hand figures and its powerful, mechanistic left-hand rhythms, had enormous impact on the idiom.

Lewis, Meriwether (b. Aug. 18, 1774, near Charlottesville, Va.—d. Oct. 11, 1809, near Nashville, Tenn., U.S.), U.S. explorer who with William Clark led the first overland expedition to the Pacific Northwest (1804–06).

Meriwether Lewis, portrait by Charles Willson Peale; in Independence National Historical Park, Philadelphia

By courtesy of the Independence National Historical Park Collection, Philadelphia

As a boy, Lewis developed a love of the wilderness and became an expert hunter. After serving in the militia during the Whiskey Rebellion (1794) in western Pennsylvania, he transferred into the regular army.

In 1801 Lewis became private secretary to Pres. Thomas Jefferson, who for the next two years unofficially prepared Lewis for leadership of a transcontinental exploring expedition. At Lewis' request, another Virginian, Lieut. William Clark, was appointed to share the command with him. Upon the U.S. purchase of the Louisiana Territory (1803), Congress appropriated $2500 for its exploration. To round out his background before leaving, Lewis went to Philadelphia to study botany, zoology, and celestial navigation.

The three-year expedition, from St. Louis to the Pacific Ocean and back, succeeded not only because of the party's skills but also because its two leaders worked together in such close harmony. Following Jefferson's instructions, Lewis and his colleagues kept a detailed journal of the trip, thus contributing a priceless narrative of North American exploration. These diaries helped dispel ignorance about the region and did much to open the way for westward expansion.

Along with Clark, Lewis received 1,600 acres of public land as a reward. On his resignation from the army, he was named governor of Louisiana Territory in 1808. He died under mysterious circumstances in an inn on the Natchez Trace while en route to Washington. Whether his death resulted from murder or suicide is still a subject of controversy. A reliable biography is Richard H. Dillon's *Meriwether Lewis: A Biography* (1965). *See also* Lewis and Clark Expedition.

Lewis, (Harry) Sinclair (b. Feb. 7, 1885, Sauk Centre, Minn., U.S.—d. Jan. 10, 1951, near Rome), U.S. novelist and social critic who punctured American complacency with his broadly drawn, widely popular satirical novels. He won the Nobel Prize for Literature (1930), the first given to an American.

Sinclair Lewis

The Granger Collection

Lewis graduated from Yale University (1907) and was for a time a reporter and also worked as an editor for several publishers. His first novel, *Our Mr. Wrenn* (1914), attracted favourable criticism but few readers. At the same time he was writing with ever-increasing success for such popular magazines as *The Saturday Evening Post* and *Cosmopolitan*, but he never lost sight of his ambition to become a serious novelist. He undertook the writing of *Main Street* as a major effort, assuming that it would not bring him the ready rewards of magazine fiction. Yet its publication in 1920 made his literary reputation. *Main Street* is seen through the eyes of Carol Kennicott, an Eastern girl married to a Middle Western doctor who settles in Gopher Prairie, Minn. (modelled on Lewis' hometown of Sauk Centre). The power of the book derives from Lewis' careful rendering of local speech, customs, and social amenities. The satire is double-edged—directed against both the townspeople and the superficial intellectualism that despises them. In the years following its publication, *Main Street* became not just a novel but the textbook on American provincialism.

In 1922 Lewis published *Babbitt,* a study of the complacent American whose individuality has been sucked out of him by Rotary clubs, business ideals, and general conformity. The name Babbitt passed into general usage to represent the optimistic, self-congratulatory, middle-aged businessman whose horizons were bounded by his village limits.

He followed this success with *Arrowsmith* (1925), a satiric study of the medical profession, with emphasis on the frustration of fine scientific ideals. His next important book, *Elmer Gantry* (1927), was an attack on the ignorant, gross, and predatory leaders who had crept into the Protestant Church. *Dodsworth* (1929), concerning the experiences of a retired big businessman and his wife on a European tour, offered Lewis a chance to contrast U.S. and European values and the very different temperaments of the man and his wife.

Lewis' later books were not up to the standards of his work in the 1920s. *It Can't Happen Here* (1935) dramatized the possibilities of a Fascist takeover of the U.S. It was produced as a play by the Federal Theatre with 21 companies in 1936. *Kingsblood Royal* (1947) is a novel of race relations.

In his final years Lewis lived much of the time abroad. His reputation declined steadily after 1930. His two marriages (the second was to the political columnist Dorothy Thompson) ended in divorce, and he drank excessively. His biography, *Sinclair Lewis: An American Life* (1961), was written by Mark Schorer.

Lewis, (Percy) Wyndham (b. Nov. 18, 1882, on a yacht near Amherst, Nova Scotia, Can.—d. March 7, 1957, London), English artist and writer who founded the abstract Vorticist movement, which, in painting and literature before World War I, sought to relate art to the industrial process.

About 1893 Lewis moved to London with his mother when his father separated from her. At the age of 16 he won a scholarship to London's Slade School of Art, but, leaving three years later without completing his course, he went to Paris, where he practiced painting and attended lectures at the Sorbonne. On his return to London in 1909 he began to write stories and to exhibit his paintings. In 1914 the first of two numbers of *Blast,* a Vorticist review, appeared. Lewis' writings in this journal show the influence of Imagist poetry, while the designs by Lewis and others, in their violent and theatrical handling of harsh shapes, have much in common with Futurism (*q.v.*), a movement that sought to glorify speed and the machine.

In World War I Lewis served at the front as an artillery officer and then, commissioned as a war artist, produced some memorable paintings and drawings of battle scenes. His first novel, *Tarr,* was published in 1918; he then worked in seclusion until 1926, when a remarkable series of books began to appear: *The Art of Being Ruled* (political theory); *Time and Western Man* (an attack on subjectivity and the cult of flux in modern art); *The Lion and the Fox* (a study of Shakespeare and Machiavelli); and *The Wild Body* (short stories and essays on satire). In 1930 he caused a furor in literary London with his huge satirical novel, *The Apes of God,* in which he scourged wealthy dilettantes.

The 1930s brought great accomplishments but few rewards. Though Lewis produced some of his most noted paintings, including "The Surrender of Barcelona" (1936) and a portrait of the poet T.S. Eliot (1938), and wrote some of his finest books, including *Men Without Art* (literary criticism; 1934), *Blasting and Bombardiering* (memoirs; 1937), and *The Revenge for Love* (a novel; 1937), he was deeply in debt by the end of the decade. Two successful libel actions brought against him in 1932 had made publishers wary of Lewis, while books and articles championing Fascism had lost him many friends. Though Lewis later admitted his errors of political judgment, his reputation never recovered.

In 1939 Lewis and his wife journeyed to the

Wyndham Lewis, 1904
BBC Hulton Picture Library

United States, where he hoped to recoup his finances with a lecture tour and portrait commissions. The outbreak of World War II made return impossible; after a brief, unsuccessful stay in New York City, they went to Canada, where they lived in poverty for three years in a dilapidated Toronto hotel. His 1954 novel, *Self-Condemned,* is a fictionalized account of those years.

At the war's end, Lewis and his wife returned home; he became art critic for *The Listener,* a publication of the British Broadcasting Corporation. Until his sight failed in 1951, he produced a memorable series of articles for that journal, praising several young British artists, such as Michael Ayrton and Francis Bacon, who later became famous. He also wrote a second volume of memoirs (*Rude Assignment,* 1950), satirical short stories (*Rotting Hill,* 1951), and the continuation of a multivolume allegorical fantasy begun in 1928 (*The Human Age,* 1955–56). A year before his death he was honoured with a retrospective exhibition at London's Tate Gallery.

BIBLIOGRAPHY. Jeffrey Meyers, *The Enemy* (1980), is a biography. Critical studies include William H. Pritchard, *Wyndham Lewis* (1968); Walter Michel, *Wyndham Lewis: Paintings and Drawings* (1971); Robert T. Chapman, *Wyndham Lewis: Fictions and Satires* (1973); Timothy Materer, *Wyndham Lewis, the Novelist* (1976); Jeffrey Meyers (ed.), *Wyndham Lewis: A Revaluation* (1980); and SueEllen Campbell, *The Enemy Opposite: The Outlaw Criticism of Wyndham Lewis* (1988).

Lewis and Clark Caverns, limestone cave in Jefferson county, southwestern Montana, U.S. It lies 47 miles (76 km) east of Butte, near the confluence of the Madison and Missouri rivers, and is the focus of a state park. The cave, largest in the Northwest, was discovered in 1902 by Don Morrison, a prospector, but was closed after 1912 for several years to prevent damage by vandals. There are guided tours through the cave's intricate chambers with their colourful stalactite and stalagmite formations.

Lewis and Clark Expedition (1804–06), first U.S. overland expedition to the Pacific coast and back. It was conducted under the leadership of Captain Meriwether Lewis and Lieutenant William Clark. Preparations for the expedition were initiated by President Thomas Jefferson before the Louisiana Purchase in 1803. All members of the expedition, numbering about 40 and ranging in age from 29 to 33 years, had had vigorous outdoor training and were variously skilled in botany, meteorology, zoology, celestial navigation, Indian sign language, carpentry, gun repair, and boat handling.

Engraving in Patrick Gass's *Voyage des capitaines Lewis et Clarke . . ., 1810*
By courtesy of the Library of Congress, Washington, D.C.

After a winter near St. Louis spent in military training and in gathering supplies and equipment, the group started up the Missouri River in three boats on May 14, 1804. En route, they supplemented their pork, flour, salt, and biscuits with wild game and fish. By November they had made the difficult ascent of the Missouri to what later became North Dakota. There they built a small fort and spent a comfortable winter among the friendly Mandan Sioux. Before leaving the next spring, Lewis and Clark employed a French-Canadian interpreter, Toussaint Charbonneau, who brought along his Indian wife, Sacajawea, and their infant son. Sacajawea also served as an interpreter and helped win the friendship of the Shoshoni Indians. The expedition pushed westward to what is now Montana. Obtaining horses, they traveled over the Continental Divide to arrive at the headwaters of the Clearwater River. There canoes were built to carry them down the Clearwater to the Snake River and then to the mouth of the Columbia, which they reached on November 15. After building Fort Clatsop, where they wintered, the explorers began their return trip the following March, traveling via the Marias and Yellowstone rivers, continuing downstream on the Missouri, and arriving amid much excitement at St. Louis on Sept. 23, 1806.

Following Jefferson's instructions, Lewis and Clark brought back diaries and maps that contained much information. They did much to dispel ignorance about the area, especially the myth of an easy water crossing of the continent (the long-sought Northwest Passage). The journals include accounts of many stirring adventures. Considering that the expedition encountered hostile Indians, accidents, sickness, grizzly bears and rattlesnakes, exposure, and near starvation, it is remarkable that only one member died en route.

The two leaders were each given 1,600 acres (650 hectares) of public land, and each of their men received 320 acres (130 hectares) and double pay. Lewis later became the governor of the Louisiana Territory and Clark of the Missouri Territory.

Lewis and Harris, largest and most northerly of the Outer Hebrides, island group off the western coast of Scotland, separated from the mainland by the North Minch, 24 miles (39 km) wide. Although the island forms one continuous unit, it is usually referred to as two separate islands. The larger and more northerly part is the island of Lewis; Harris is in the south. Local government in both islands is administered by the Western Isles Islands Council, established in 1975.

The terrains of the two areas contrast sharply. Lewis is covered by peat moor and has many small inland lakes, while Harris is hilly, with more than 30 summits over 1,000 feet (300 m). The coastline is deeply indented and the many rivers abound with salmon, trout, and wild fowl. There is little cultivable land, but sheep and cattle are raised. Most of the land is tenanted by crofters (tenants of divided farms) whose holdings average less than 7 acres (3 hectares). There are approximately 4,000 of these crofter holdings and 168 crofter townships, nearly all situated on the coast, for the crofters were formerly dependent on the inshore fishing to supplement their livelihood. Since the advent of the steam trawler, the importance of local fisheries, including the herring industry once located in Stornoway, in Lewis, has declined. In 1918, Lord Leverhulme, a British industrialist, bought estates on the island and planned, without success, to develop the fishing on more modern lines. About 3,000 people, mainly young men, left the island; but the later rise of the Harris tweed industry compensated, in part, for the decline in fishing. The tweed industry provides employment in the country areas as well as at Stornoway, for it is essentially a cottage industry. The development of the North Sea oil industry has had little effect on the Western Isles. An attempt at supplying barges and steel fabrications for that industry experienced difficulty obtaining orders. Stornoway, the only sizable town in the Outer Hebrides, functions as a port and commercial and administration centre for the islands and accommodates more than half of the island's population. Gaelic language and culture survive on Lewis and Harris, and tourism is an important part of the island's economy. Pop. (1981) 23,390.

Croft (farm) at Balallan on the peat moors of the Isle of Lewis, Scotland
Tourist Photo Library

Lewis Range, segment of the northern Rockies, extending south-southeastward for 160 miles (260 km) from the Alberta, Can., border, near Waterton Lake, to the Blackfoot River in northwestern Montana, U.S. Many peaks exceed 10,000 feet (3,000 m), with Mount Cleveland (10,479 feet [3,194 m]) being the highest point. The northern portion of the range is within the Waterton-Glacier International Peace Park, while most of the remainder is included in the Flathead and Lewis and Clark national forests and the Bob Marshall Wilderness Area. Marias Pass (5,216 feet [1,590 m]) is crossed by rail and highway. Tourism is promoted in the park area, but development in the southern portions of the range is restricted by their inaccessibility.

"De," "la," and similar components of a name, when followed by a space, are alphabetized as separate words (e.g., *De Forest, Lee*). *When they are joined to the following part of a name, the combination is treated as a single word* (e.g., *DeForest, John William*).

Lewis theory, generalization concerning acids and bases introduced in 1923 by the U.S. chemist Gilbert N. Lewis, in which an acid is regarded as any compound which, in a chemical reaction, is able to attach itself to an unshared pair of electrons in another molecule. The molecule with an available electron pair is called a base. The reaction between an acid and a base (neutralization) results in the formation of an addition compound, in which the electron pair that constitutes the chemical bond comes from only one reactant. Included in the Lewis definition of acids are the metal ions; the oxides of certain nonmetallic elements, such as sulfur, phosphorus, and nitrogen; substances able to donate hydrogen ions or protons; and certain solid compounds, such as aluminum chloride, boron trifluoride, silica, and alumina.

In practice, substances that are considered acids by the Lewis definition, other than those associated with hydrogen ions and protons, are specifically referred to as Lewis acids. Lewis bases include ammonia and its organic derivatives, the oxides of the alkali and alkaline earth metals, and most atoms and molecules with negative electrical charges (anions).

Lewisburg, city, seat (1778) of Greenbrier county, southeastern West Virginia, U.S. It is a mountain resort and farming centre (dairying, poultry, and fruit) near the Greenbrier River and the Greenbrier State and Jefferson National forests, just west of White Sulphur Springs. Strategically situated at the junction of the Seneca and Kanawha trails, settlement developed after 1769 around Camp Union, rendezvous of the Virginia militiamen of Gen. Andrew Lewis (for whom the town was named) prior to their successful campaign against the Indians under the Shawnee chief Cornstalk that culminated in the Battle of Point Pleasant (Oct. 10, 1774). The Old Stone Presbyterian Church (1796; replacing an earlier log structure) is a notable landmark. Lewisburg is the seat of West Virginia School of Osteopathic Medicine (1972) and Greenbrier Community Mental Health/Mental Retardation Centre (1973). The locality abounds in limestone caves, including the Lost World Caverns and Organ Cave (used by Gen. Robert E. Lee as a refuge during the Civil War). Fairlea, just south, is the site of West Virginia's annual State Fair (August). Inc. 1782. Pop. (1990) 3,598.

Lewisham, inner borough of Greater London, covering an area of 13 sq mi (35 sq km). Various light industries and electrical engineering firms are located in the borough, especially along the valley of the River Ravensbourne, and Lewisham has a major shopping centre. Goldsmith's College of the University of London was built at New Cross Road in 1843 and now specializes in teacher training and the social sciences. Open spaces include Horniman Gardens with the Horniman Museum and Library, Beckenham Place Park, part of Blackheath, Ladywell Fields, and Deptford Park. Pop. (1982 est.) 233,600.

Lewisian Complex, also called LEWISIAN GNEISS, major division of Precambrian rocks in northwestern Scotland (the Precambrian began with the formation of the Earth's crust about 3.8 billion years ago and ended 570 million years ago). In the region where they occur, Lewisian rocks form the basement, or lowermost, rocks; they form all of the Outer Hebrides, as well as the islands of Coll and Tiree, and are exposed along the northwestern coast of Scotland. The oldest rocks of the Lewisian have been dated by radiometric techniques at between 2.4 billion and 2.6 billion years old, whereas the youngest Lewisian rocks have been dated at 1.6 billion years. Lewisian rocks originally consisted of both igneous and sedimentary rocks that have been altered from their original composition and structure through time by heat, pressure, and the action of solutions of one sort or another. The dominant rock type is grayish gneiss that is rich in quartz, feldspar, and iron-rich minerals. Some sedimentary-derived Lewisian rocks, especially in the region of Loch Maree and South Harris, still retain some of their original sedimentary features and indicate that the sediments were originally shales, sandstones, and some limestones. Many igneous intrusions also occur, including granites, pegmatites, and dolerites. Three major subdivisions of the Lewisian Complex are recognized: the lowermost Scourian Complex, followed by the Inverian Complex and the Laxfordian Complex. Rocks of the Lewisian Complex are overlain by those of the Torridonian Series. Lewisian rocks have been profoundly affected by two major periods of deformation, the first of which occurred during the time represented by the Scourian Complex and the second during the Laxfordian. The radiometric dates obtained for the age of the Lewisian are essentially the dates of these periods of deformation.

lewisite, in chemical warfare, poison blister gas developed by the United States for use during World War I. Chemically, the substance is dichloro(2-chlorovinyl)arsine, a liquid whose vapour is highly toxic when inhaled or when in direct contact with the skin. It blisters the skin and irritates the lungs. Any part of the body that is contacted by the liquid or vapour suffers inflamation, burns, and tissue destruction. Lewisite was developed in retaliation for German gas attacks during World War I, but was never actually used. It was in the process of manufacture when the armistice was signed.

Lewiston, city, seat (1861) of Nez Perce county, northwestern Idaho, U.S., just south of Moscow and adjacent to Clarkston, Wash. (west), at the confluence of the Snake and Clearwater rivers. Established as a gold-mining town on a site where the explorers Meriwether Lewis (for whom it was named) and William Clark camped (1805, 1806), it is Idaho's oldest incorporated community (1861) and was the first territorial capital (1863–64). The economy is based on lumbering and agriculture, supplemented by small manufactures. The Port of Lewiston (1958) is the terminus of river barge traffic from Astoria-Portland, Ore. The city is the seat of Lewis-Clark State College (1893). Lapwai, 10 mi (16 km) east, is the headquarters of the Nez Perce Indian Reservation and a part of Nez Perce National Historical Park. Pop. (1990) 28,082.

Lewiston, city, Androscoggin county, southwestern Maine, U.S., on the Androscoggin River opposite Auburn, with which it forms a metropolitan area, 34 mi (55 km) north-northeast of Portland. Paul Hildreth of Dracut, Mass., in 1770, settled the site of Lewiston Falls (supposedly named for a drunken Indian called Lewis who drowned there). Textile operations began in 1819 and expanded with the formation of the Androscoggin Falls, Dam Locks and Canal Company in 1836 (reorganized in 1842 as the Lewiston Water-Power Company). Lewiston remains a leading textile centre, with two hydroelectric dams giving the community ample waterpower. There are several footwear and metallurgical plants, and one of the nations's first electronically automated poultry hatcheries is also there. The city is the seat of Bates College (1864). The Memorial Armoury (1927) houses one of the state's largest auditoriums, and a youth centre (1959) has an unusually large covered ice rink. Mt. David, 340 ft (104 m) high, offers a panoramic view of the city. The Thorncrag Sanctuary for wild birds is 1½ mi east. Inc. town, 1795; city, 1861. Pop. (1990) city, 39,-757; Lewiston-Auburn MSA, 88,141.

Lewistown, borough, seat (1789) of Mifflin county, south central Pennsylvania, U.S., on the Juniata River, 45 mi (72 km) northwest of Harrisburg. Opened for settlement (1754) by a treaty with the Iroquois, it was laid out in 1790 on the site of the Shawnee Indian village, Ohesson. It was one of the state's pioneering iron-manufacturing centres and was named for William Lewis, an early ironmaster. Nearby Ft. Granville was built by settlers in 1755 and destroyed the following year in the French and Indian Wars. Lewistown became an important shipping point with the opening of the Pennsylvania Canal in 1829. Minerals, diversified farming, and manufactures (rayon, electronic equipment, steel, and farm machinery) form its economic base. The Greenwood Furnace (restored early ironworks) and Reeds Gap State parks, and Lewistown Narrows, a scenic gorge on the river, are nearby. Inc. 1795. Pop. (1990) 9,341.

Lex XII Tabularum (ancient Roman law code): *see* Twelve Tables, Law of the.

Lex Salica: *see* Salic law.

lex talionis (early legal principle): *see* talion.

Lexington, urban town (township), Middlesex county, eastern Massachusetts, U.S., primarily a residential suburb, 10 mi (16 km) northwest of Boston. Settled in 1640 and organized as the parish of Cambridge Farms in 1691, it became an independent township in 1713 and was named for Lexington (now Laxton), Eng. The town is traditionally regarded as the site of the first military engagement (April 19, 1775) of the American Revolution. (*see* Lexington and Concord, Battles of). The event is commemorated by Lexington Green (sometimes called Battle Green), with the battleground marked by a boulder and plaque inscribed with Capt. John Parker's words to his men: "Stand your ground; don't fire unless fired upon, but if they mean to have war, let it begin here," and with its Revolutionary and Minuteman monuments. The Hancock–Clarke House (1698), Munroe Tavern (1695), and Buckman Tavern (1710) are among colonial buildings that have been preserved. In 1839, the first public normal (teachers' training) school in the U.S. (later moved to Framingham) was established in Lexington. Pop. (1990) 28,974.

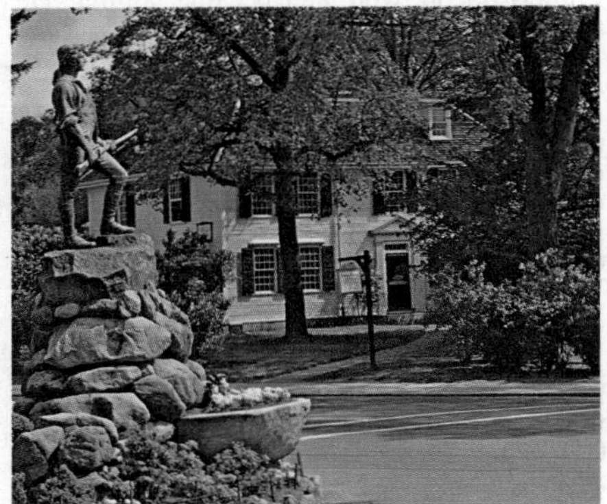

Minuteman Statue, Lexington, Mass.
Arthur Griffin—EB Inc.

Lexington, city, seat (1823) of Lafayette county, west central Missouri, U.S., on the Missouri River (there bridged to Henrietta), 35 mi (56 km) east of Kansas City. The site, around William Jack's Ferry, was settled after 1819. The town was laid out in 1822 and named for Lexington, Ky. At the beginning of the Civil War, Lexington was the most important river town between St. Louis and St. Joseph and commanded the river approach to Ft. Leavenworth, Kan. The Battle of Lexington (Sept. 18–21, 1861) resulted in a bloody victory for Confederate troops under Maj. Gen. Sterling Price over the Federal forces of Col. James A. Mulligan. The battlefield, overlooked by Anderson House (1853; restored) which was used as a field hospital by both sides, is a state historic site. The Lexington County Courthouse (1847) retains battle scars, and Linwood Lawn (*c.* 1850) is a notable antebellum mansion. The nation's first Masonic college functioned in Lexington from 1846 to 1859, and Wentworth Military Academy was founded there in 1880. The city's economy now depends on agriculture (corn [maize]), coal mines, rock quarries, tourism, and light manufactures (cables, dies, wood products, and shirts). Inc. 1845. Pop. (1990) 4,860.

Lexington, city, seat, but administratively independent, of Rockbridge county, western Virginia, U.S., in the Shenandoah Valley, on the Maury River, 30 miles (48 km) northwest of Lynchburg. Established by the Virginia Assembly in 1777 as the county seat, it was named for the Revolutionary Battle of Lexington and Concord (April 19, 1775). The town was almost completely destroyed by fire in 1796. During the American Civil War, it was bombarded (June 10, 1864) by the Federal troops of General David Hunter.

Lexington is the seat of Washington and Lee University (founded as Augusta Academy in 1749) and the Virginia Military Institute (VMI; founded 1839). The former was named for George Washington, its greatest benefactor, and for the Confederate general Robert E. Lee, who served as its president from 1865 to 1870; Lee Memorial Chapel, on the campus, contains the crypt of the Lee family and a museum. Former teachers of the VMI include the Confederate general "Stonewall" Jackson and Matthew Fontaine Maury, naval explorer and inventor. The Stonewall Jackson Memorial Hall contains Benjamin Clinedinst's mural depicting the cadets' heroic charge at New Market, and the George C. Marshall Research Library (1964) is named for the VMI's most famous graduate, the general and statesman George Marshall. The Stonewall Jackson Cemetery holds the graves of Stonewall Jackson and many other Confederate soldiers. Nearby are Natural Bridge and Goshen Pass. Lexington was the birthplace of Sam Houston, the Texas military hero, and Cyrus McCormick, inventor of the reaper.

Aside from its status as a "shrine of the South," it is also a shopping centre for an agricultural area (beef cattle, sheep, and dairying). Inc. town, 1841; city, 1966. Pop. (1990) 6,959.

Lexington and Concord, Battles of (April 19, 1775), initial skirmishes between British regulars and American provincials, marking the beginning of the U.S. War of Independence. Acting on orders from London to suppress the rebellious colonists, General Thomas Gage, recently appointed royal governor of Massachusetts, ordered his troops to seize the colonists' military stores at Concord. En route from Boston, the British force of 700 men was met on Lexington Green by 77 local minutemen and others who had been forewarned of the raid by the colonists' efficient lines of communication, including the ride of Paul Revere. It is unclear who fired the first shot. Resistance melted away at Lexington, and the

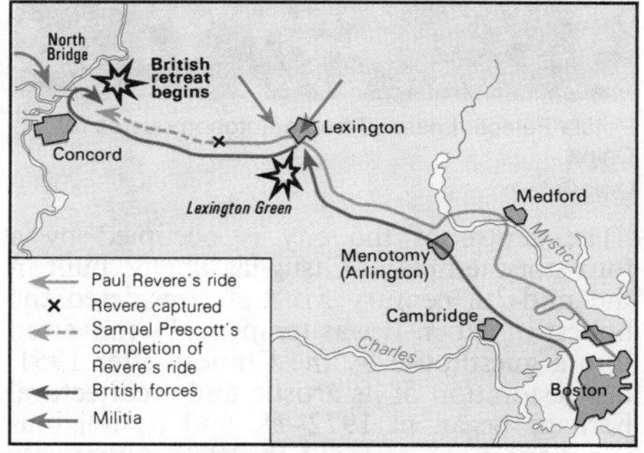

Operations around Lexington and Concord, April 18–19, 1775

Adapted from *The American Heritage Pictorial Atlas of United States History;* copyright © 1966 by American Heritage Publishing Co., Inc.

British moved on to Concord. Most of the American military supplies had been hidden or destroyed before the British troops arrived. A British covering party at Concord's North Bridge was finally confronted and forced to withdraw by 320 to 400 American patriots. The march back to Boston was a genuine ordeal for the British, with Americans continually firing on them from behind roadside houses, barns, trees, and stone walls. This experience established guerrilla warfare as the colonists' best defense strategy against the British. Total losses were British 273, American 95. The Battles of Lexington and Concord confirmed the alienation between the majority of colonists and the mother country, and it roused 16,000 New Englanders to join forces and begin the Siege of Boston, resulting in its evacuation by the British the following March.

Lexington-Fayette, city and urban county, coextensive with Fayette county, north-central Kentucky, U.S., the focus of the Bluegrass region and a major centre for horse breeding. Named in 1775 for the Battle of Lexington, Mass., it was chartered by the Virginia legislature in 1782 and was the meeting place (1792) for the first session of the Kentucky legislature. Lexington in the early 1880s, boasting Transylvania College (1780; now University), street lights, a public subscription library, a theatre, and a musical society, called itself the Athens of the West. In 1817 it presented the first Beethoven symphony heard in the United States.

Horse racing on the town common was prohibited in 1788, and the racecourse was rebuilt in another part of town. Devotion to fine

The Red Mile race course at Lexington, Ky.

Tony Leonard—Shostal/EB Inc.

horseflesh remains a local passion (flat racing at Keeneland; trotting at the "Red Mile"). The American Thoroughbred Breeders Association has its headquarters in Lexington. Surrounded by rich farmlands, the city is an important market for beef cattle, sheep, spring lambs, bluegrass seed, and loose-leaf tobacco. Its manufactures include bourbon whiskey, paper products, and electronic equipment. The University of Kentucky and Lexington Theological Seminary were founded there in 1865; there are also two business colleges. The U.S. Government Hospital for Narcotics Addicts and the Lexington-Blue Grass Army Depot Headquarters are in the city.

John C. Breckinridge, who was vice president of the United States from 1857 to 1861, as well as the Confederate general John Hunt Morgan, the Todd family, and U.S. Senator Henry Clay, are buried in Lexington Cemetery. The homes of Clay, Morgan, and Mary Todd Lincoln are public shrines. The Headley Museum on the Old Frankfurt Pike displays bibelots executed in precious jewels. Lexington was incorporated as a city in 1832. In 1974 Lexington city and Fayette county merged, thus creating an urban county government. Pop. (1990) city, 225,366; Lexington-Fayette MSA, 348,428.

Ley, Robert (b. Feb. 15, 1890, Niederbreidenbach, Ger.—d. Oct. 25, 1945, Nürnberg), Nazi politician and head of German labour, who helped supervise the recruitment of slave labour during World War II.

The son of a small landowner, Ley studied at the universities of Jena and Bonn, received a Ph.D. in chemistry, and worked for IG Farbenindustrie, before he was discharged in 1928 for "political activity." He was elected as Nazi member to the Prussian Diet in 1929 and to the Reichstag in 1932.

Ley was made head of the German workers' front after Hitler's accession to power. To weld German labour into a solid organization backing Hitler, Ley abolished the democratic trade unions and built up a powerful labour organization designed to facilitate German militarization and war preparations. He was also head of the Bund der Auslanddeutsche (Union of Germans Living Abroad).

During World War II, Ley supervised the mobilization of foreign as well as German labour for war work. Near the war's end he fled to the mountains near Berchtesgaden, where he was captured by U.S. troops on May 16, 1945. He attempted to take his life but failed and was arraigned as a war criminal. On October 25 he hanged himself with a towel in the lavatory in the Nürnberg prison, where he and 23 other Nazis were awaiting trial as war criminals.

Leyden (The Netherlands): *see* Leiden.

Leyden, Lucas van: *see* Lucas van Leyden.

Leyden jar, device for storing static electricity, discovered accidentally and investigated by the Dutch physicist Pieter van Musschenbroek of the University of Leiden in 1746, and independently by the German inventor Ewald Georg von Kleist in 1745. In its earliest form it was a glass vial, partly filled with water, the orifice of which was closed by a cork pierced with a wire or nail that dipped into the water. To charge the jar, the exposed end of the wire was brought into contact with a friction device that produced static electricity. When the contact was broken, a charge could be demonstrated by touching the wire with the hand and receiving a shock. In its present form, the inner and outer surfaces of an insulating jar are coated with sheets of metal foil. The outer coating is connected to earth, and a suitable connection is made with the inner coating through a central brass rod that projects through the mouth of the jar. In addition to its use for classroom demonstrations, the Leyden jar is of importance as a prototype of capacitors, which are widely used in radios, television sets, and other electrical and electronic equipment.

Leyster, Judith (b. July 28, 1609, Haarlem, Neth.—d. Feb. 10, 1660, Heemstede, near Amsterdam), Dutch painter, one of the few female artists of the era to have emerged from obscurity. Among her known works are portraits and genre and still-life paintings.

Leyster was the daughter of a brewer. She began to paint while still quite young, and by the age of 24 she had become a member of the Haarlem painters' guild. Her subject matter embraced a greater range than was typical of Dutch painters of the era, and she was one of the first to exploit the domestic genre scene. The influence of Frans Hals on her work is clear; she also, however, was interested in the tenebrist style of the Utrecht school. The majority of her dated works were painted between 1629 and 1635. In 1636 she married genre painter Jan Meinse Molenaer and moved with him to Amsterdam.

Many of Leyster's works were in the past attributed to her male contemporaries. Among her best-known paintings are "The Proposition" (1631) and "Boy Playing the Flute" (*c.* 1635).

Leyte, island, one of the Visayan group in the Philippines, lying east of Cebu and Bohol across the Camotes Sea. It lies southwest of the island of Samar, with which it is linked by a 7,093-foot (2,162-metre) bridge (completed in 1973) across the narrow San Juanico Strait.

The Samar and Bohol (Mindanao) seas lie to the north and south, and Leyte Gulf occupies a large basin between eastern Leyte and southern Samar Island.

The island is irregular in shape and has an area of 2,785 square miles (7,213 square km); it has a rugged mountain backbone, which reaches its maximum height at Mount Lobi (4,426 feet [1,349 m]) in the centre. A complex system of short streams drain northward to Carigara Bay or westward to Leyte Gulf. The mountains are broken by a low gap at the narrowest part of the island, there crossed by a highway. Rolling plains are found in the coastal areas, particularly in the north near Tacloban and Ormoc.

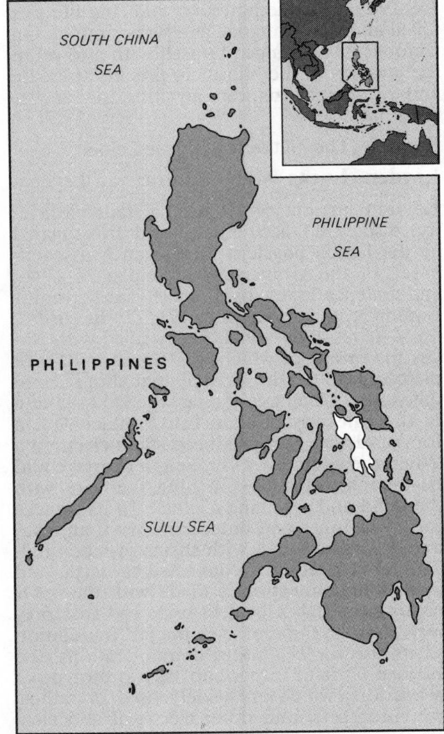

Leyte

The island was known to 16th-century Spanish explorers as Tandaya. Its population grew rapidly after 1900, especially in the Leyte and Ormoc valleys. In World War II, U.S. forces landed on Leyte (Oct. 20, 1944), and, after the Battle of Leyte Gulf, the Japanese were expelled. Because the availability of land has been exhausted, Leyte has supplied a large number of migrants to Mindanao.

Most inhabitants are farmers. Fishing is a supplementary activity. Rice and corn (maize) are the main food crops; cash crops include coconuts, abaca, tobacco, bananas, and sugarcane. There are some manganese deposits, and sandstone and limestone are quarried in the northwest.

The island has two major cities, Ormoc and the port of Tacloban. Other population centres include Barugo, Carigara, Baybay, Burauen, and Maasin. Pop. (1990 est.) including adjoining islands, 1,897,714.

Leyte Gulf, Battle of (Oct. 23–26, 1944), decisive air and sea battle of World War II, which crippled the Japanese Combined Fleet, permitted U.S. invasion of the Philippines, and gave the Allies control of the Pacific.

The battle was precipitated by a U.S. amphibious assault on the central Philippine island of Leyte on October 20. The Japanese responded with Sho-Go (Victory Operation), a plan to decoy the U.S. 3rd Fleet north, away from the San Bernardino Strait, while converging three forces on Leyte Gulf to attack the landing; the 1st Attack Force was to move from the north across the Sibuyen Sea through the San Bernardino Strait, with the 2nd Attack Force and C Force moving from the south across the Mindanao Sea through the Surigao Strait.

As the Japanese forces moved into position southwest of Leyte, submarines of the U.S. 7th Fleet discovered the 1st Attack Force and sank two heavy cruisers west of Palawan on October 23. A series of almost continuous surface and air clashes followed, especially in the Sibuyen Sea, while the U.S. 3rd Fleet chased the Japanese decoy. Finally, on October 25, the three major engagements of the battle were fought, almost simultaneously. At the Surigao Strait, battleships and cruisers from the 7th Fleet destroyed C Force and forced the 2nd Attack Force to withdraw. Meanwhile, the 1st Attack Force passed through the unguarded San Bernardino Strait and inflicted heavy damage on the 7th Fleet carriers off Samar but withdrew unexpectedly just as they seemed ready to attack the landing operations. In the north, off Cape Engaño, part of the 3rd Fleet sank the Japanese decoy carriers while another part moved south, attacking and pursuing the 1st Attack Force.

A list of the abbreviations used in the MICROPAEDIA *will be found at the end of this volume*

Lezama Lima, José (b. Dec. 19, 1910, Havana, Cuba—d. Aug. 9, 1976, Havana), poet, novelist, and essayist whose writing profoundly influenced other Cuban writers.

After studying law in Havana, Lezama became one of the founders and supporters of *Verbum* (1937) and other literary reviews, and he was leader of the literary group associated with *Orígenes* (1944–56). They published the work of a number of excellent young poets who revolutionized Cuban letters.

His solid foundation in the Spanish classics of the Golden Age and his knowledge of the French Symbolists greatly influenced his early work. *Muerte de Narciso* (1937; "Death of Narcissus"), Lezama's first book of poems, reveals his vast cultural background. *Enemigo rumor* (1941; "Enemy Rumor"), in addition to aesthetic preoccupations about the essence of poetry, reveals the poet's belief that the act of creation is laden with religious and metaphysical possibilities. In *Aventuras sigilosas* (1945; "Silent Adventures"), he recreates incidents of his youth and treats his mother's powerful influence on his artistic and cultural growth after his father's death in 1919. His novel *Paradiso* (1966) has a similar tone and content. It is considered to be his masterpiece and reaffirms faith in his art and in himself.

The poems in *La fijeza* (1949; "Stability") are an attempt to recapture his past experiences. *Analecta del reloj* (1953; "Selected Work of the Clock"), a collection of essays, is notable for "Las imágenes posibles" ("Possible Images"), which gives his poetic credo. *La expresión americana* (1957) includes essays that attempt to decipher the essence of Latin-American reality. His *Tratados en la Habana* ("Treatises on Havana") was published in 1958, and in 1959 Fidel Castro named him director of the Department of Literature and Publications of the National Council of Culture.

lezginka, also spelled LEZGHINKA, folk dance originating among the Lezgian people of the Caucasus. It is a male solo dance (often with a sword) and also a couple dance. The man, imitating the eagle, falls to his knees, leaps up, and dances with concise steps and strong, sharp arm and body movements. When the dance is performed in pairs, couples do not

Lezginka as performed by the song and dance ensemble of the Azerbaijan Soviet Socialist Republic

Sovfoto

touch; the woman dances quietly as she regards the man's display.

LH: *see* luteinizing hormone.

Lha-mo, in Tibetan Buddhism, the only goddess among the "Eight Terrible Ones," who are defenders of the faith. *See* dharmapāla.

Lhasa, Wade-Giles romanization LA-SA, Pinyin LHASA, capital of the Tibetan autonomous *ch'ü* (region) of the People's Republic of China. It is located at an elevation of 11,975 feet (3,650 m) in the Tibetan Himalayas near the Lhasa River, a tributary of the Brahmaputra.

Lhasa had been designated as the capital of Tibet by the 9th century AD. National power was decentralized following the assassination of the Tibetan king in 842, and Lhasa lost its position as the country's capital, though it gained in religious importance in succeeding centuries. It served as the national religious centre of Tibet, and much of its population was composed of Buddhist monks and laymen. In 1642 Lhasa was again the seat of the central government, a position it held into the 20th century. Although Lhasa and Tibet came under Chinese occupation in 1951, the city and the country remained under the Tibetan government until 1959, when direct Chinese administration was imposed.

Potala Palace, Lhasa, Tibetan autonomous *ch'ü*, China

Ewing Galloway

The centre of the city is occupied by a four-story temple of Gtsug-lag-khang, built in the mid-7th century AD and considered the holiest in Tibet. It was temporarily converted into a guesthouse by the Chinese after 1951, but restoration of its artistic and architectural heritage began in 1972–75, and its religious functions were restored in 1979. Other city landmarks include the temple of Klu-khang; the Potala Palace, once the winter residence of the Dalai Lama; and the former summer palace of the Dalai Lama, the Nor-bu-gling-ka (Jewel Palace), which is now the People's Pleasure Park. The monasteries of 'Bras-spungs (Drepung) and Se-ra, two of the largest in Tibet, have received renovation.

Before the Chinese occupation, the city's economy was based on the historic trade routes that converged on Lhasa from China, India, Nepal, and Bhutan. Except for handicrafts, the only industries were those of the ammunitions factory and mint. The Chinese administration reopened Lhasa to foreign trade in the 1980s and has established experimental farms outside the city and encouraged the scientific breeding of livestock. Small-scale industries include chemical production, electric-motor manufacturing, tanning, wool processing, pharmaceutical and fertilizer production, motor-vehicle maintenance and repair, tractor assembly, rug and carpet making, and cement production. The city has a teacher-training college and an airport. Roads connect Lhasa with the major cities in the Chinese provinces of Szechwan and Tsinghai and the autonomous region of Sinkiang. Pop. (1988 est.) 106,000.

Lhasa apso, breed of dog from Tibet, where it is called *abso seng kye* ("bark lion sentinel dog") and is used as an indoor guard dog. The Lhasa apso is characteristically hardy, intelligent, and watchful. Longer than it is tall, it stands 25.5 to 28 cm (10 to 11 inches) and weighs 6 to 7 kg (13 to 15 pounds). It has a heavily haired tail that curls over its back and a long, profuse coat that covers its eyes. The coat of the Lhasa apso may be of various colours, but golden-brown shades are preferred by most breeders.

Lhasa apso
Sally Anne Thompson—EB Inc.

L'Hermite, Tristan, pseudonym of FRANÇOIS L'HERMITE: *see* Tristan l'Hermite.

Lhevinne, Josef (b. Dec. 13, 1874, Oryol, Russia—d. Dec. 2, 1944, New York, N.Y., U.S.), piano virtuoso in the Romantic tradition, noted for his masterly technique, sonorous tone, and careful musicianship.

He studied at the Moscow Conservatory, made his debut in 1889 in Moscow, and won the coveted Rubinstein Prize in 1895. From 1902 to 1906 he was professor of piano at the Moscow Conservatory. His American debut in 1906 brought an offer of 150 concerts in the United States during the 1907–08 season. He taught in Berlin while continuing to give concerts in Europe and the United States. During World War I he was interned in Germany. In 1919 he settled in the United States, where he taught privately and at the Juilliard School in New York City.

His wife, Rosina Lhevinne, *née* Bessie (1880–1976), was an eminent pianist and teacher (her pupils included Van Cliburn) and frequently appeared in two-piano recitals with her husband.

L'Hospital, Michel de, L'Hospital also spelled L'HÔPITAL (b. 1507, Aigueperse, Fr.—d. March 13, 1573, Bellebat), statesman, lawyer, and humanist who, as chancellor of France from 1560 to 1568, was instrumental in the adoption by the French government of a policy of toleration toward the Huguenots.

L'Hospital studied law at Toulouse but was forced into exile because of his father's association with the traitor Charles de Bourbon; he subsequently continued his legal studies at Padua and Bologna. He was able to return to France about 1534, and in 1537 he became a councillor in the Parlement of Paris (supreme court). Henry II made him his envoy to the Council of Trent in 1547, and in 1553, on the recommendation of Charles, cardinal de Lorraine, he was made a master of requests, responsible for petitions to the king. In 1555 he became first president of the Chambre des Comptes. In 1560, during the brief reign of Francis II, he was made chancellor of France and was retained in that position by the regent, Catherine de Médicis.

L'Hospital played an important role in both the shaping and the implementation of government policy. As the Huguenots and Catholics prepared to fight each other, L'Hospital advocated a policy of religious toleration favoured by the regent, Catherine, and presented the government's policies in numerous speeches to the various provincial estates and other local assemblies. But he was not merely expressing Catherine's policies: a perusal of his works shows that much government policy was indeed his own policy. His *Traicté de la réformation de la justice* ("Treatise on the Reform of Justice") and his *Mémoire sur la nécessité de mettre un terme à la guerre civile* (*c.* 1570; "Memoir on the Necessity of Putting an End to the Civil War") are the most complete presentations of the case for toleration of his time. He argued that the ruler should not favour one religion over another but should safeguard the welfare of his subjects as a whole. While he favoured unity of religion, he believed that if force were used the opposite effect would be achieved.

His philosophies of toleration and moderation and his policies in office caused him to be considered a founder of the Politiques, the moderate Roman Catholic group that tried to bring peace to France during the later years of the Wars of Religion. L'Hospital disapproved of rebellion as a means of bringing about change, and he loathed tyrannicide; he regarded the monarchy as divinely instituted and the king as the supreme lawgiver, but he believed that the king should remain in close touch with his subjects by summoning the States General frequently.

L'Hospital, detail of a portrait by an unknown French artist, 1566; in the Musée Condé, Chantilly, Fr.
By courtesy of the Musee Conde, Chantilly, Fr.; photograph, Giraudon—Art Resource/EB Inc.

During his term of office he worked hard for judicial reform and in 1566 promoted the Ordonnance de Moulins, which went far to rectify many problems in judicial administration and also stipulated policies for the administration and centralization of the royal domain (crown lands). In September 1567 civil war broke out again, and Catherine lost confidence in L'Hospital's policy of toleration. Seeing that he had lost favour, he asked to be dismissed and then retired (1568) to his estate, where he spent his remaining years writing. His *Oeuvres complètes* were published in 1824–26.

Lhote, André (b. July 5, 1885, Bordeaux, Fr.—d. Jan. 24, 1962, Paris), French painter, sculptor, writer, and educator who was an outstanding critic and teacher of modern art.

Largely self-taught, Lhote was initially associated with Fauvism, but his mature painting style (*i.e.,* "Rugby," 1917; Musée d'Art Moderne, Paris) is Cubist in manner. In 1922 he founded his own influential art school. As a critic he worked for *La Nouvelle Revue Française* until 1940, and he also wrote *Traité du paysage* (1939; "Treatise on Landscape Painting") and *Traité de la figure* (1950; "Treatise on Figure Painting").

Lhote, 1962
© Etienne Hubert

Lhotse, also called E[1], one of the world's highest mountains (27,940 feet [8,516 m]), consisting of three Himalayan summits on the Nepalese-Tibetan (Chinese) border just south of Mount Everest, to which it is joined by a 25,000-foot (7,600-metre) ridge. On May 18, 1956, Fritz Luchsinger and Ernest Reiss, two Swiss climbers, made the first ascent of the mountain. It is sometimes considered part of the Mount Everest massif. Lhotse is Tibetan for "south peak"; E[1] was the original survey symbol (denoting Everest 1) given by the Survey of India (1931).

Li, aboriginal people of Hainan Island, off the southern coast of China. They live in the mountainous southern portion of the island and share with the Miao people the Hai-nan Li-Miao Autonomous Prefecture. Their many dialects are related to Tai and Malayo-Polynesian (or Austronesian). The Li number about 980,000. The majority of Li, who are settled in upland river valleys, grow paddy or wet rice and raise water buffalo and cattle. They worship local earth gods, as well as ancestral and other spirits.

li, Pinyin LI, type of Chinese bronze vessel originally produced in the Shang dynasty (18th–12th century BC). It is a wide-mouthed cooking vessel supported by three legs, shaped like pointed lobes, which are well articulated

Bronze *li* vessel, Western Chou dynasty (*c.* 1111–771 BC); in the Museum of Fine Arts, Boston
By courtesy of the Museum of Fine Arts, Boston, 1941 Purchase Fund and Grace M. Edwards Fund

with the body of the vessel and which form an extension of the interior volume.

A coarse pottery *li* was made in Neolithic times (*c.* 3000–1500 BC); the shape appeared in the bronze art of the Shang dynasty and was continued into the Chou and beyond. It also reappeared in the pottery of early historical periods. The vocabulary of animal motifs that so typically decorates ritual bronze vessels is generally limited on the li.

li, Confucian concept often rendered as "proper conduct," or "propriety." Originally li denoted magic rites performed to sustain social and cosmic order. Confucians, however, reinterpreted it to mean formal social patterns that, in their view, the ancients had abstracted from cosmic models to order communal life. From customary patterns, li came to mean conventional norms, yielding a new concept of an internalized code of civility that defined proper human conduct. It is this concept that is detailed in the Confucian Classic called the *Li chi* ("Record of Rites"). Yet even in this context, li transcends mere politeness or convention, for, as a derivative of natural order, it retains a cosmic role, harmonizing man with nature.

Li Ang (Chinese emperor): *see* Wen-tsung.

Li Ao, Pinyin LI AO (d. *c.* 844, China), Chinese scholar and official who helped reestablish Confucianism at a time when it was being severely challenged by Buddhism and Taoism. Li helped lay the groundwork for the later Neo-Confucianists of the Sung dynasty (960–1279), who systematically reformulated Confucian doctrine.

Although Li was a high official of the T'ang dynasty (618–907), little is known of his life. He was apparently friends with or a disciple of the great Confucian stylist and thinker Han Yü, with whom he is usually linked. Unlike Han, however, who was vehemently opposed to Buddhism, Li was much influenced by it, helping to integrate many Buddhist ideas into Confucianism and beginning the development of a metaphysical framework to justify Confucian ethical thinking. Li is especially known for his insistence that the questions of human nature and human destiny were central to Confucianism, ideas that became the core of later Neo-Confucianism. Moreover, his quotations from the *Ta hsüeh* ("Great Learning"), the *Chung yung* ("Doctrine of the Mean"), and the *I Ching* ("Classic of Changes") helped bring recognition to these previously obscure works and led to their eventual enshrinement as part of the great body of Confucian Classics. Finally, Li helped establish Mencius for later Neo-Confucians as almost the equal of Confucius.

Li Bi (Vietnamese leader): *see* Ly Bon.

Li Bo (Chinese poet): *see* Li Po.

Li Chi, Pinyin LI JI (b. 1896, Chung-hsiang, Hupeh province, China—d. Aug. 1, 1979, Taipei, Taiwan), archaeologist chiefly responsible for establishing the historical authenticity of the semilegendary Shang dynasty of China. The exact dates are in dispute, but, traditionally, the period of the Shang dynasty is considered to be from about 1766 to about 1122 BC.

One of many students sent to the West for an education under the Chinese Republic's attempt at modernizing China, Li studied anthropology and received a Ph.D. from Harvard University in 1923. After being associated briefly with the Freer Gallery of Art, Washington, D.C., he returned to China, taught for a short time, and then in 1928 became the director of archaeology for the Academia Sinica, the Chinese national research organization.

Near the end of 1928, he made a preliminary sounding of the ancient Shang capital at An-yang, Honan province, and, in 1929, under the patronage of the Academia Sinica and the Freer Gallery, he began the organized excavation that continued intermittently from 1929 to 1937. The harsh climate permitted only brief digging seasons; and traditional Chinese opposition to any disturbance of the earth, civil war (1930), large-scale grave looting, and threats by organized bandits all militated against his archaeological efforts. During the final seasons of work, with an armed guard and the official protection of Chiang Kai-shek, great progress was made. More than 300 tombs, including 4 important royal burial sites, were uncovered and carefully studied. Some 1,100 skeletons and animal bones inscribed with oracles in an early Chinese script, unquestionably linked with the Shang period, were recovered.

Following the Japanese invasion of China in 1937 and the expulsion of the Chinese Nationalists from the mainland in 1949, many of Li's An-yang remains and notes were lost. After escaping to Taiwan, he became the head of anthropology and archaeology at the National University in Taipei (1950) and began directing publication of his remaining An-yang materials. He published a number of books, including *The Beginnings of Chinese Civilization* (1957).

Li chi (Chinese: "Record of Rites"), one of the Five Classics (*Wu ching*) of Chinese Confucian literature, the original text of which is said to have been compiled by the ancient sage Confucius (551–479 BC). During the 1st century BC the text had apparently been so reworked by Elder Tai (Ta Tai) and his cousin Younger Tai (Hsiao Tai) that scholars presume the original title *Li ching* ("Classic of Rites") was dropped so that *ching* ("classic") would be reserved for works more directly connected with Confucius.

In general, *Li chi* underscores moral principles in its treatment of such subjects as royal regulations, development of rites, ritual objects and sacrifices, education, music, the behaviour of scholars, and the doctrine of the mean (*chung yung*).

In 1190 Chu Hsi, a Neo-Confucian philosopher, gave two chapters of *Li chi* separate titles and published them together with two other Confucian texts under the name *Ssu shu* ("Four Books"). This collection is generally used to introduce Chinese students to Confucian literature.

li-chia, Pinyin LIJIA, system of social organization in Ming China. *See* pao-chia.

Li Chih (Chinese emperor): *see* Kao-tsung (AD 628–683).

li-chin (Chinese tax): *see* likin.

Li Chin-chung (Chinese courtier): *see* Wei Chung-hsien.

Li Ch'ing-chao, Pinyin LI QINGZHAO (b. 1081, Tsinan, Shantung province, China—d. after 1141, Chin-hua, Chekiang province), China's greatest woman poet, whose work, though it survives only in fragments, continues to be as highly regarded as it was in her own day.

Li Ch'ing-chao was born into a literary family. In 1101 she married Chao Ming-ch'eng, a noted antiquarian, but their extremely happy marriage was cut short in 1129 by his death in their escape from the Juchen dynasty's takeover of K'ai-feng. Continuing alone, she arrived at Hangchow by 1132. Two years later she fled to Chin-hua, where she probably died about 1150.

Li Ch'ing-chao produced seven volumes of essays and six volumes of poetry, but unfortunately all her work is lost except for some poetry fragments. She was a writer of *tz'u* poetry; this was a form of lyric poetry written to music and is a type generally associated with the Sung dynasty. Li's poems are noted for their feminine sensibilities and striking diction.

Li Dazhao, Wade-Giles romanization LI TA-CHAO (b. Oct. 6, 1888, Hopeh province, China—d. April 28, 1927, Peking), cofounder of the Chinese Communist Party (CCP) and mentor of Mao Zedong.

After studying at Tientsin and at Waseda University in Tokyo, Li became an editor for *Hsin ch'ing-nien* ("New Youth"), the principal journal of the new Western-oriented literary and cultural movements. In 1918 he was appointed chief librarian of Peking University, and in 1920 he became, concurrently, professor of history. Inspired by the success of the Russian Revolution in 1917, Li began to study and lecture on Marxism, influencing many students who later became important communist leaders, including Mao Zedong (then an impoverished student whom Li had employed as a library clerk).

When the Marxist study groups that Li had created evolved into the formally organized Chinese Communist Party (CCP) in July 1921, he was instrumental in carrying out the policy dictated by the Communist International and in effecting cooperation between the minuscule CCP and the national leader Sun Yat-sen's Kuomintang (Nationalist Party). As a party leader, Li's role was limited to North China. In 1927 he was seized at the Soviet Embassy in Peking, where he had taken refuge, by the Manchurian warlord Chang Tso-lin, who had him hanged.

A seminal Chinese Marxist thinker, Li was more party theoretician than party leader. Like most of the Chinese communists of his day, he was intensely nationalistic before he embraced Marxism. Li was unwilling to wait for the international proletarian revolution to occur in the West and liberate China, and he was convinced that China's small urban working class was unable to carry out the revolution by itself. Because of these views he disregarded or played down the doctrine of proletarian class struggle presented in Marxism–Leninism. The communist revolution, in Li's conception, became a populist revolution against the exploitation and oppression of foreign imperialism, with an overwhelming emphasis on the central role of China's impoverished peasantry. In a country that was seething with national resentment against foreign aggression, chafing at its own backwardness, and composed chiefly of peasants, Li's ideas had decisive relevance and formed the core of the thinking of Mao Zedong, who later formulated the military strategy by which the peasantry could carry out its revolution. After his death Li became the most venerated of Chinese communist martyrs.

Li Erh (Chinese philosopher): *see* Lao-tzu.

Li-fan yüan, Pinyin LIFAN YUAN, governmental bureau established in the 17th century by China's Ch'ing (Manchu) dynasty to handle relations with the peoples of Inner Asia. The first bureau of its kind in the history of Chinese administration, it signified the growing interest of China in Inner Asia.

The office appointed governors to supervise Chinese territory in Inner Asia and Tibet, granted permits to merchants to trade in these areas, took charge of Russian students and traders who came to China, and supervised the Russian religious mission in Peking. In 1861 responsibility for Russian affairs was taken over by the newly created foreign office, the Tsungli Yamen. The Li-fan yüan continued in existence until 1906, when it was reorganized as the Ministry of Dependencies.

Li Fei-kan: *see* Ba Jin.

Li Gonglin: *see* Li Kung-lin.

Li Ho, Pinyin LI HE (b. 791, China—d. 817, Ch'ang-ku), brilliant Chinese poet whose untimely death at the age of 26 ended what might have become one of China's greatest poetic careers.

Literary legend describes Li Ho as a man of *kuei-ts'ai* ("devilish talent") who composed his haunting verses by jotting down single lines on small slips of paper while on horseback, dropping the slips into an embroidered black bag, and assembling a finished poem each evening. Composing verse from the early age of seven, Li Ho promised to do well on the literary examinations necessary for an official career. Unfortunately, the poet was excluded from the examinations by a minor technicality; his resulting disappointment was said to have triggered the poor health that led to his death a few years later. Li Ho's verse is characterized by its vivid imagery, odd diction, striking juxtapositions, and unrelieved pessimism.

Li Hou-chu (Chinese poet and ruler): *see* Li Yü.

Li-hsien Chiang (river, China–Vietnam): *see* Black River.

Li Hsiu-ch'eng, Pinyin LI XIUCHENG (d. Aug. 7, 1864, Nanking), Chinese general and leader of the Taiping Rebellion, the giant religious–political uprising that occupied most of South China between 1850 and 1864. After 1859, when the Taipings were beset by internal dissension, poor leadership, and corruption, Li's military and administrative genius kept the movement going. Between 1860 and 1862, Li tried to expand the Taiping conquests by taking the large North China trading city of Shanghai. As a result, Western forces based in the city began to aid the Imperial government. Repeatedly driven off by these Western mercenary armies, Li had to abandon his efforts and go to aid in the defense of the Taiping capital at Nanking. Having given his best horse to the young heir-apparent to the Taiping throne and taken a poor mount for himself when the capital fell to the enemy in 1864, he was captured by government troops, forced to confess, and then executed.

Li Hung-chang, Pinyin LI HONGZHANG (b. Feb. 15, 1823, Ho-fei, Anhwei Province, China—d. Nov. 7, 1901), leading Chinese statesman of the 19th century who made strenuous efforts to modernize his country. In 1870 he began a 25-year term as governor-general of the capital province, Chihli, during which time he initiated projects in commerce and industry and, for long periods, conducted China's relations with the Western powers.

Li Hung-chang
Charles Phelps Cushing

Early life and career. Both Li's father and Tseng Kuo-fan, who became his mentor, took terminal degrees in the Confucian examinations, earning the status of "advanced scholars." Li started on his official career in 1844 under Tseng's guidance in Peking, the capital; in 1847 he earned his terminal degree.

In 1850 the Taiping Rebellion, a great national religious–political upheaval, broke out and threatened to topple the dynasty. When their homeplace was threatened, Li and his father organized a local militia. Li became so involved that he stayed (unofficially) at his post even when his father died in 1855, in defiance of the traditional Confucian mourning retirement. He earned a judgeship in 1856.

Tseng Kuo-fan, who in 1860 was governor-general of the Liangkiang provinces (central China), was organizing irregular anti-Taiping forces, and Li later joined his staff. In 1862 Li was made acting governor of Kiangsu Province and traveled to Shanghai with his own troops in rented steamers. Hitherto, steamers had given the West a great advantage in two wars with China (1839–42 and 1856–60) from which came the so-called unequal treaties, whereby China unilaterally surrendered such things as tariff autonomy and extraterritorial jurisdiction.

At just under 40 years of age, Li enjoyed high civil provincial rank and independent military power, a combination that had been forced on the central government by the exigencies of the rebellion.

For the next few years, Li worked partly with foreigners and their weapons in the anti-Taiping effort around Shanghai. Best known of these Westerners was Charles ("Chinese") Gordon, then a 30-year-old English army officer who led the "Ever-Victorious Army," a force, later put at Li's disposal, made up of foreign mercenaries. Although Westerners tended to credit this alien force with putting down the rebellion, it was really Tseng Kuo-fan and subordinates such as Li who accomplished the task. The immediate director of the 1864 campaign against Nanking, the Taiping capital, was a brother of Tseng Kuo-fan, but Li disregarded his orders to assist in that terminal action because he felt that jealousies might arise—a delicacy that hinted at Li's own eminence.

Between 1865 and 1870, Li was heavily involved in various high official assignments in central, northern, and western China, mostly to suppress other rebellions. He kept his interest in the Western-style arsenals he had established in Nanking and Shanghai because he wanted to strengthen China against the West—or encroachment by Japan, whose modernization in the late 1860s was increasingly alarming to Li.

Appointment as governor-general of Chihli. In 1870 Li was appointed governor-general of the capital province, Chihli. Also at this time he served as a grand secretary (a central government post) and superintendent of trade for the north and thus was responsible for supervising trade with the West out of the so-called treaty ports north of the Yangtze River. Although there was a new Peking agency for China's Western diplomatic relations, the Tsungli Yamen, Li became the Chinese negotiator most familiar to foreigners. Thus, he had positions in both the central and the provincial structures, military forces at his disposal, growing prestige abroad, and, it developed, an unprecedented 25-year term of office in Chihli.

During this long tenure, Li interested himself in several major modernizing projects: another arsenal at Tientsin and improved fortifications there, the sending of young Chinese to the United States to learn new skills, a commercial steamship line, Western-built warships, a coal mine, a railroad, a telegraph line, a cotton mill, a military academy, a modern mint, and two modern naval bases. He even talked about change in the procrustean Confucian examinations. There were few other Chinese officials interested in such projects.

During these years, Li also engaged heavily in negotiations with the Japanese, the British, the French, and other treaty powers. If his efforts were not ultimately successful, this was largely a reflection of China's continuing relative military weakness, of which Li, throughout his "self-strengthening" efforts, was acutely aware. China sent a mission of apology to Great Britain in 1876 after the murder of a British official. In the same year, Japan made a treaty with Korea that ignored China's traditional suzerainty over the peninsula, and Li was not able, in a later treaty of commerce between the United States and Korea that he tried to manipulate, to get U.S. recognition of the old relationship. In 1879 China lost to Japan its suzerainty over the Liuchiu (Ryukyu) Islands. Li sought French acceptance of Chinese suzerainty over Annam, but the result of the Sino-French War (1883–85) was that French suzerainty was substituted for it. Li's efforts to recover China's prestige in Korea were undercut by Japan, and, in 1885, Li and the leading Japanese statesman, Itō Hirobumi, in effect agreed to a joint protectorate over the contested peninsula. In 1894 Japan went to war with China over Korea.

In this war, Li's northern fleet bore the brunt of the conflict with Japan; virtually no assistance came from China's two other modern fleets. Again China lost a modern naval war and had to cede Formosa (Taiwan) and the Liaotung Peninsula to Japan, to recognize Korean independence, to open new treaty ports, to pay a large indemnity to Japan, and to grant to the Japanese all of the advantages hitherto preempted by Westerners under the unequal treaties. Li had tried to avoid this war, but his influence, nonetheless, suffered because of it. He personally opened peace negotiations in Japan in March 1895 but was wounded by a Japanese fanatic—and, ironically, it was this attack, which excited Japanese sympathy, that somewhat ameliorated the harsh peace terms. (Certain Western powers, including Russia, forced the retrocession of the Liaotung Peninsula—which Russia in effect appropriated in 1898 anyway.)

State visits abroad. Nevertheless, to many Westerners, Li was the leading Chinese statesman. In 1896 he attended the tsar's coronation and while in Russia negotiated a secret alliance between the two countries that was modern China's first equal treaty. Although he journeyed in state through western Europe and was received in Washington, D.C., by President Grover Cleveland, his homecoming was chilly; probably the empress dowager had to use her influence to protect him (it was said that he bribed her for the favour). He kept his trade superintendency and in 1899 was made acting governor-general of the Liangkwang provinces. His prestige was still such that he was selected to negotiate with the aggrieved Western powers after the 1900 Boxer Rebellion fiasco. Again Li had to preside at a national humiliation. He died in 1901.

Li Hung-chang did not exemplify all of the Confucian virtues. He did not have the reputation for financial disinterest enjoyed by Tseng Kuo-fan, and much of his innovating enterprise was made with an eye to personal profit. But the terminal crisis of the dynastic Confucian system in China cannot be explained thus. Li and a few contemporaries modernized parts of China's forces to protect the old system, but within that system, with its peculiar values and organization, the modern devices could not give full service. Li saw something of this contradiction; he hoped that examination reform would give prestige to the scientific modes, but his proposals were truncated, and he was nearly alone in making them. He did support the education mission noted heretofore, but, when conservatives at court decried it as subversive to Confucian norms, Li did not stake his reputation on it, and in 1881 it was terminated. Li was adroit in manipulating the system and was unquestionably loyal to it. China's late 19th-century modernization, which was designed to save the dynasty and the traditional life, was disastrously hampered by institutional contradictions, which are nowhere better illustrated than in Li's unprecedented career.

(J.L.Ra.)

BIBLIOGRAPHY. Stanley Spector, *Li Hung-chang and the Huai Army: A Study in Nineteenth-century Chinese Regionalism* (1964); Mary C. Wright, *The Last Stand of Chinese Conservatism* (1957).

Li Ji (Chinese archaeologist): *see* Li Chi.

Li K'o-yung, Pinyin LI KEYONG (d. 908, Shansi province, China), T'ang general of Turkish origin who suppressed the great peasant rebellion of Huang Ch'ao (d. 884), which threatened the T'ang dynasty (618–907) in its last years. Afterward the empire was divided between powerful warlords, and Li became a leading contender for power in North China. Driven out of the central-northern area near the capital at Ch'ang-an, he established himself in the northwestern province of Shansi. When Chu Wen (854–914), Li's principal competitor, usurped the T'ang throne in 907, Li established the independent state of Chin in Shansi.

Consult the INDEX *first*

Li Kung-lin, Pinyin LI GONGLIN, also called LI LUNG-MIEN (b. 1049, Shu-ch'eng, Anhwei province, China—d. 1106), one of the most lavishly praised Chinese connoisseurs and painters in a circle of scholar-officials during the Northern Sung period.

Li Kung-lin was born into a scholarly home, received the *chin-shih* ("advanced scholar") degree in 1070, and followed the common career of going to the capital in K'ai-feng to serve as an official. There he became acquainted with many of the literary lights of the day. Li Kung-lin developed high standards of critical taste by collecting and copying old masters, and in his own painting he rejected pure description and obvious dexterity for a greater emphasis upon scholarly knowledge of the antique and self-expression within those modes—the ideal of "literati painting" (*wen-jen-hua*). No completely reliable paintings of Li Kung-lin are still in existence, and many styles and attitudes of painting are associated with him. Generally he is known as a painter of horses, Buddhist subjects, landscapes, and figures. In spite of a conventional association with a rather sketchy style appropriate to his literary tastes, he is also linked with a very refined, elegant, and skillful outline painting of figures and architecture without further colour added.

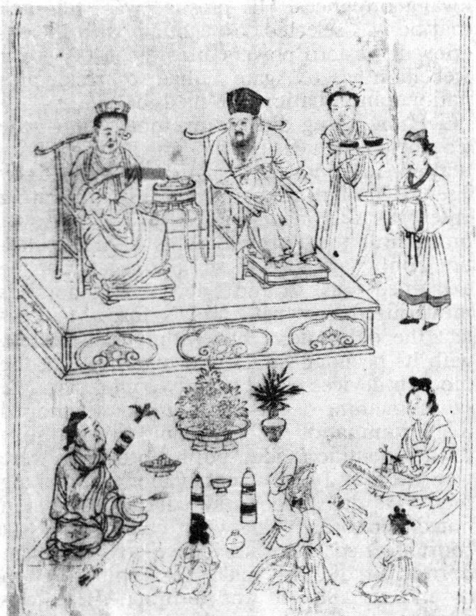

"The Classic of Filial Piety," detail of a handscroll attributed to Li Kung-lin, ink on silk; in The Art Museum, Princeton University, N.J.

The Art Museum, Princeton University, anonymous loan

Li Lisan, Wade-Giles romanization LI LI-SAN (b. 1896, Li-ling, Hunan province, China—d. 1967, China), Chinese revolutionary who was Mao Zedong's chief rival for power within the Chinese Communist Party (CCP) from 1928 to 1930.

Li joined the CCP in Paris in 1921 and then returned to China to become one of the party's principal labour organizers. After 1928 he became the effective head of the CCP. On orders from the Communist International (Comintern), he implemented what became known as the "Li Lisan line"; this strategy followed established Marxist-Leninist doctrine in its encouragement of large-scale worker uprisings in urban centres and was different in emphasis from the peasant-oriented rural strategy of the revolutionist Mao Zedong.

In July 1930 Li's small Communist army attacked and took over Ch'ang-sha, the capital of the central Chinese province of Hunan. The Communists suffered heavy losses, however, when the government's forces recaptured the city three days later. The major centre of CCP activity then shifted to Mao Zedong's guerrilla forces. Denounced by the Comintern as responsible for the debacle at Ch'ang-sha, Li was recalled to Moscow for corrective study.

He returned to China in 1945, and, after the establishment of the People's Republic of China in 1949, he was minister of labour. Owing to conflict with the party leadership, however, Li resigned this post by 1954. He subsequently held a series of modest posts in the party. Li reportedly committed suicide when he came under attack in the Cultural Revolution in 1967.

Li Lung-chi (Chinese emperor): *see* Hsüan Tsung (AD 685–762).

Li Nang-hsiao (Chinese emperor): *see* Li Yüan-hao.

Li Peng, Wade-Giles romanization LI P'ENG (b. October 1928, Ch'eng-tu, Szechwan province, China), prime minister of the People's Republic of China from 1988.

The son of writer Li Shuo-hsün (Li Shouxun), who was executed by the Nationalist Party (Kuomintang) in 1930, Li Peng from 1939 was cared for by Deng Yingchao, the wife of Zhou Enlai. In 1948 Li was sent to Moscow, where he studied at the Moscow Power Institute. He returned to China in 1955. From 1955 to 1979 he supervised a number of major power projects in China, and between 1979 and 1982 he served as vice minister and minister of power industry and first vice minister of water resources and electric power. He also rose through the ranks of the Chinese Communist Party (CCP), joining the Central Committee in 1982 and becoming an elected member of the Political Bureau (Politburo) and the Secretariat of the CCP 12th Central Committee in 1985. Earlier that year he had been named minister of the State Education Commission. In 1987 Li became a member of the powerful standing committee of the Politburo. In April 1988 he was chosen by Deng Xiaoping to succeed Zhao Ziyang as prime minister after the latter had assumed the post of general secretary of the CCP.

Li advocated a cautious approach to economic liberalization, and his chief concern was the maintenance of economic and political stability under the direction of the central government. When massive student protests calling for more democratic government broke out in Peking in April 1989, Li was foremost among those advocating the demonstrators' suppression by force if necessary. He won Deng Xiaoping's support for his stance, and on May 20 he declared martial law in Peking. In early June Li sent the armed forces into central Peking to crush the pro-democracy movement, with the consequent loss of hundreds of lives.

Li Po, Pinyin LI BO, Wade-Giles romanization LI T'AI-PO (b. 701, Szechwan province, China—d. 762, Tang-t'u, Anhwei province), Chinese poet who rivaled Tu Fu for the title of China's greatest poet.

Li Po liked to regard himself as belonging to the imperial family, but he actually belonged to a less-exalted family of the same surname. At 19 he left home and lived with a Taoist recluse. After a period of wandering, he married and lived with his wife's family, north of Han-chou. He had already begun to write

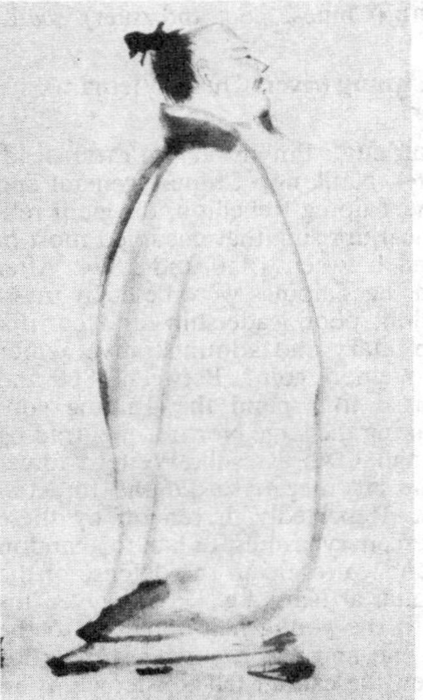

Li Po, pen-and-ink portrait by Liang K'ai, 13th century; in the Tokyo National Museum

By courtesy of the International Society for Educational Information, Tokyo

poetry and showed some of it to various officials, in the vain hope of becoming employed as a secretary. A visit to a friend in northeast China in 734 began another period of wandering, and in 742 he arrived at Ch'ang-an, the capital, no doubt hoping to be given a post at court. No official post was forthcoming, but he was accepted into a group of distinguished court poets. In the autumn of 744 he began his wanderings again.

At this point he met the other towering poet of the period, Tu Fu, then scarcely known, while Li Po's fame was already immense. Tu Fu, it is clear, was completely carried away by the dash and verve of the older man, who was becoming increasingly wrapped up in Taoism and alchemical studies and at about that time was definitely accepted as a Taoist initiate, receiving a diploma of spiritual progress from the hands of a high Taoist dignitary.

In 756 Li Po became unofficial poet laureate to the military expedition of Prince Lin, the emperor's 16th son. The prince was soon accused of intending to set up an independent kingdom and was executed; Li Po was arrested and imprisoned at Chiu-chiang. A high official, reviewing sentences passed in connection with the troubles, looked into Li Po's case, had him released, and made him a staff secretary. In the summer of 758 the charges against Li Po were revived, and he was banished to Yeh-lang. Before he arrived, he benefited by a general amnesty; he returned to eastern China, where he died in a relative's house, though popular legend says that he drowned when, sitting drunk in a boat, he tried to seize the moon's reflection in the water.

Li Po was a romantic in his view of life and

in his verse. One of the most famous wine drinkers in China's long tradition of imbibers, Li Po frequently celebrated the joy of drinking. He also wrote of friendship, solitude, the passage of time, and the joys of nature. Popularly referred to as a "banished Immortal," he wrote with brilliance and great freshness of imagination. Arthur Waley's biography, *The Poetry and Career of Li Po,* appeared in 1951.

Li Qingzhao (Chinese poet): *see* Li Ch'ing-chao.

Li Shang-yin, Pinyin LI SHANGYIN (b. 813, Ho-nei, Honan Province, China—d. 858, Cheng-chou, Honan Province), Chinese poet remembered for his elegance and obscurity.

A member of a family of minor officials, Li Shang-yin pursued a generally unsuccessful career as a government official, composing poetry during and between his various posts. He died a disillusioned but proud man whose genius few of his contemporaries recognized.

Until the second half of the 20th century little of Li Shang-yin's poetry had been studied seriously by Western critics, despite the fact that Chinese scholars since the Sung dynasty (960–1269) had paid close attention to his work. To Chinese critics he has been one of the most controversial, difficult, and complex of poets because of his use of exotic imagery, abstruse allusions, political allegory, and personal satire involving both historical and contemporary events and figures. These qualities also make his poetry difficult to translate, and little of it has appeared in European languages.

Li Shang-yin's works reflect the social and political conditions of his time, and they greatly influenced early Sung poets.

Li Shao-chün, Pinyin LI SHAOJUN (fl. 2nd century BC, China), noted Chinese Taoist who was responsible for much of the mystical content of popular Taoist thought. Li was not only the first known Taoist alchemist but also the first to make the practice of certain hygienic exercises a part of Taoist rites. He was also the first to claim that the ultimate goal of the Taoist was to achieve the status of *hsien,* or a kind of immortal sage.

Gaining the confidence of the great Han emperor Wu Ti in 133 BC, Li persuaded him that immortality could be achieved by eating from a cinnabar vessel that had been transmuted into gold. When that occurred, Li said, one would suddenly see the famous sages on P'eng-lai, the legendary isles of immortality. If one performed the proper rituals while gazing on these *hsien,* one would never die.

According to Li, the first step in the transmutation of cinnabar involved prayers to Tsao Chün, the Furnace Prince. These prayers became an established part of Taoist ritual, and shortly after Li's death Tsao Chün came to be considered the first of the great Taoist divinities; Li was thus responsible for making the worship of a specific divine figure a part of Taoist ritual.

So great was his influence that Li was able to persuade the usually realistic Wu Ti that Li was several centuries old, having discovered the secret of immortality long before Wu's time. Even after Li's death the emperor's faith in Li was unshaken; he declared that Li had merely transformed himself into another state, departing his old body.

Li Shih-chen (fl. 16th century, China), Chinese scholar of the Ming dynasty (1368–1644) who compiled a giant materia medica, the *Pen-ts'ao kang-mu* ("Great Pharmacopoeia"), which described more than 2,000 drugs and presented directions for preparing more than 8,000 prescriptions. Completed in 1578, the book was in part a compilation of other smaller works of the same kind. It contained 142 illustrations and descriptions of 1,074 vegetable, 443 animal, and 217 mineral substances. Li described such seemingly modern processes as distillation and the uses of mercury, ephedrine, chaulmoogra oil, iodine, and even smallpox inoculation.

Li Shih-min (Chinese emperor): *see* T'ai Tsung (AD 600–649).

li-shu, Pinyin LISHU (Chinese: "clerical script," or "chancery script"), in Chinese calligraphy, a style that may have originated in the brush writing of the Shang and Chou dynasties (*c.* 1600–221 BC); it represents a more informal tradition than the *chuan-shu* ("seal script"), which was more suitable for inscriptions cast in the ritual bronzes. While examples of *li-shu* from the 3rd century BC have been discovered, the style was most widely used in the Han dynasty (206 BC–AD 220). Though somewhat square and angular, with strong emphasis on the horizontal strokes, the *li-shu* is a truly calligraphic style, making full use of the flexible brush to modulate the thickness of the line. Many Han examples survive, written with a brush on bamboo slips or carved in stone. Characters were approximately uniform in size and evenly spaced within a composition, but the construction of characters and individual strokes varied greatly. At the end of the Han dynasty the *li-shu* developed into the more supple and fluent *k'ai-shu.*

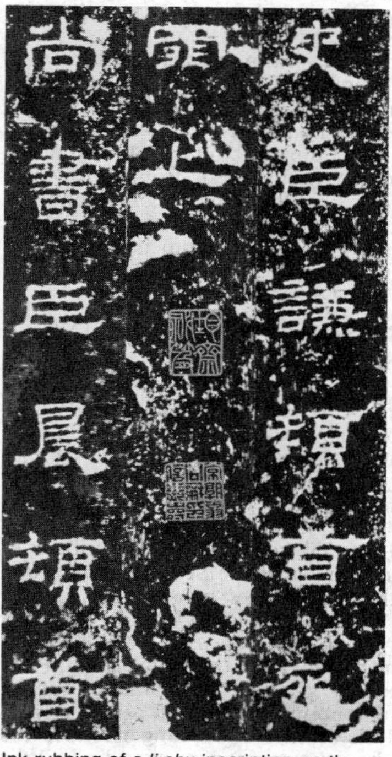

Ink rubbing of a *li-shu* inscription on the stele of Shih Ch'en, AD 169, Han dynasty; in the collection of Wan-go H.C. Weng, New York

By courtesy of Wan-go H.C. Weng, New York

Li Ssu, Pinyin LI SI (b. 280 BC?, Ch'u state, central China—d. 208 BC, Hsien-yang), Chinese statesman who utilized the ruthless but efficient ideas of the political philosophy of Legalism to weld the warring Chinese states of his time into the first centralized Chinese empire, the Ch'in dynasty (221–206).

In 247 he entered the state of Ch'in to begin almost 40 years of service under the ruler later known as Shih Huang-ti ("First Sovereign Emperor"). As minister to the emperor, Li was responsible for most of the radical political and cultural innovations made in Ch'in after 221.

Li caused the empire to be divided into 36 regions, each governed by a centrally appointed official. Under his guidance the emperor standardized coinage and weights and measures and began construction of the Great Wall to keep out barbarians from the north. Li Ssu also was influential in creating a unified writing system, which remained substantially the same until recent times. Finally, in an effort to prevent the growth of subversive thought, Li in 213 forbade the teaching of history and ordered the "burning of the books," for which he earned the opprobrium of all future generations of Confucian scholars. When the emperor died in 209, Li became involved in the eunuch Chao Kao's plot to void the proper succession. But the two conspirators quarreled, and Chao Kao had Li executed. *See also* Ch'in.

Li Ssu-hsün, Pinyin LI SIXUN (b. 651—d. 716), Chinese painter who was later seen as the chief exponent of a decoratively coloured landscape style of the T'ang dynasty and as the founder of the so-called Northern school of professional painters, in contrast to the scholar-painters of the Southern school, of which Wang Wei was the first.

Li Ssu-hsün was related to the T'ang Imperial family, led an active political life including exile and restoration, and was given the honorary rank of general. His son, Li Chao-tao, was also a famous painter, and thus the father is sometimes called Big General Li and the son Little General Li. While no genuine works survive, both Li Ssu-hsün and Li Chao-tao are known to have painted in a highly decorative and meticulous fashion, employing especially the colours blue and green (*ch'ing-lü*), often together with white and gold. While the later division (by Tung Ch'i-ch'ang) into the decorative tradition begun by Li Ssu-hsün and the scholar's tradition of Wang Wei certainly overstated the original situation, it undoubtedly reflected the expressive range of landscape art in the T'ang period.

Li Ta-chao (Chinese Communist): *see* Li Dazhao.

Li T'ai-po (Chinese poet): *see* Li Po.

Li T'ang, Pinyin LI TANG (b. Ho-yang, Honan Province, China; fl. *c.* 1080—*c.* 1130), major Chinese painter who lived during both the Northern and the Southern Sung dynasties and established a style of painting that became the base for the academy-style landscape of the Southern Sung.

He earned the highest rank in the academy of painting of Emperor Hui Tsung, and, after the North fell to the Mongols, went to the South and entered the academy of Emperor

"Whispering Pines in the Mountains," hanging scroll by Li T'ang, 1124; in the National Palace Museum, Taipei

By courtesy of the National Palace Museum, Taipei

Sung Kao Tsung. His landscapes—of which one dated 1124 (National Palace Museum, Taipei, Taiwan) is the most reliably ascribed—serve as a vital link between the earlier, and essentially Northern, variety of monumental landscape, and the more lyrical Southern style of the Ma-Hsia school. Li T'ang perfected the brush texture stroke known as the ax stroke, which gives a tactile sense to painted rocks and suggests the precise and comprehensive reality that Southern Sung artists sought to give their landscapes.

Li T'ieh-kuai, Pinyin LI TIEGUAI, in Chinese mythology, one of the Pa Hsien, the Eight Immortals. He was an ascetic for 40 years, often foregoing food and sleep, until Lao-tzu (also surnamed Li) agreed to return to earth and instruct his fellow clansman on worldly vanities. Returning one day from a celestial visit to his master, Li found his earthly body had been cremated by a disciple to whom it had been entrusted. He thereupon assumed a new identity by entering the deformed body of a beggar who had died of hunger. Li is thus depicted in art as an old man with an iron crutch (*t'ieh kuai*), a gourd often slung over his shoulder or held in his hand. The gourd served as a bedroom for the night and held medicine, which Li dispensed with great beneficence to the poor and needy. *See also* Pa Hsien.

Li T'ieh-kuai with his iron crutch, painting on paper; in the Religionskundliche Sammlung of the Philipps-Universität, Marburg, Ger.

Foto Marburg—Art Resource/EB Inc.

Li Tzu-ch'eng, Pinyin LI ZICHENG (b. Oct. 3, 1605?, Michih, Shensi Province, China—d. 1645, Hupeh Province), Chinese rebel leader who dethroned Ch'ung-chen, the last emperor of the Ming dynasty (1368–1644).

A local village leader, Li joined the rebel cause in 1631 following a great famine that had caused much unrest in the northern part of the country. Making his headquarters in the northwestern province of Shensi, Li called himself the Ch'uang Chiang (Dashing General). A superb military leader, he gradually increased his following and began to organize raids into neighbouring provinces.

After 1639 several scholars rallied to Li's cause. Relying on their advice, he prevented his troops from pillaging and began to distribute the food and land he had confiscated to the poor. Stories and legends of his heroic qualities were purposefully spread throughout the land, and he also began to set up an independent government over the territory he controlled, conferring titles and issuing his own coinage. Finally, in 1644 he proclaimed himself first emperor of the Ta Shun, or Great Shun, dynasty and advanced on the capital at Peking.

Li took the city easily because the last Ming emperor was betrayed by a group of his eunuch generals, but his stay in the capital was short-lived. Wu San-kuei (1612–78), a general loyal to the Emperor, induced the Manchu tribes on the northeastern frontier to enter China and restore the Ming. A combined force of Ming and Manchu troops drove Li from the capital. He fled into Hupeh Province in the north, where he is thought to have been killed by local villagers.

Li Xiucheng (Chinese general): *see* Li Hsiu-ch'eng.

Li Yü, Pinyin LI YU, Wade-Giles romanization LI HOU-CHU (Chinese: The Last Ruler) (b. 937, modern Nanking—d. Aug. 15 (?), 978, Pien, now K'ai-feng, Honan Province, China), Chinese poet and the last ruler of the Southern T'ang dynasty (937–975) who succeeded his poet father, Li Ching, in 961.

Though Li Yü had paid annual tribute to T'ai Tsu, founder of the Sung dynasty (960–1279), the Sung forces invaded his country in 974. When his capital, Chin-ling (modern Nanking), fell the next year, Li Yü surrendered and was taken to the Sung capital, Pien. There he was given a nominal title, but his life was one of misery. When T'ai Tsu died in 976 and his brother T'ai Tsung ascended the throne, the new emperor, angered by Li Yü's poems, had him poisoned.

Li Yü was a master of the *tz'u* (*q.v.*). More than 30 of his lyrics have survived. The earlier poems reflect the gay and luxurious life at his court, though some are tinged with romantic melancholy. Li Yü achieved his greatness, however, in his later poems in which he expressed his grief and despair at the loss of his kingdom. Their direct and powerful emotional appeal has won them lasting popularity. In addition to being a poet, Li Yü was also a painter, calligrapher, collector, and musician.

Li Yüan (Chinese emperor, T'ang dynasty): *see* Kao-tsu.

Li Yüan-hao, Pinyin LI YUANHAO, also called LI NANG- HSIAO, posthumous name, or *shih*, WU-LIEH TI, temple name (HSI HSIA) CHING TSUNG (fl. 11th century, China), leader of the Tangut tribes, a Tibetan people who inhabited the northwestern region of China in the area of modern Kansu Province. Li founded the Hsia dynasty (1038–1227), usually referred to as the Hsi Hsia, or Western Hsia.

The Tanguts were originally a vassal state of China, but in 1038 Li ended his people's tribute shipments to the Sung (960–1279) rulers and proclaimed himself emperor of the Hsia. He tried to create a Chinese-style system of government and even adopted a system of writing the Tangut language using Chinese-style ideographs. A warlike state, the Hsia preserved its independence until the coming of the Mongols (1209), who so decimated the country that little is now known of the Tangut people or culture.

Li Yüan-hung, Pinyin LI YUANHONG (b. 1864, Hupeh Province, China—d. June 5, 1928, Tientsin), the only president of the Republic of China at Peking who served for two terms.

In 1911 Li was a divisional commander in the army and was stationed in the city of Wu-han (Hupeh Province), where the anti-Imperial Revolution of 1911, which brought a republican government to China, erupted among army units. The uprising had been planned to occur at a later date; hence, no recognized leaders were on hand. As the only figure of stature who had not fled the area, Li was forced by his troops to become the head of the new government, despite the fact that he had no previous association with the revolutionaries. His enthusiasm for his new position increased as the success of the revolution became assured. Sun Yat-sen, a leader of national prominence, returned from abroad, where he had been raising funds, and he was elected president of the republic on Dec. 29, 1911. Li was elected vice president, a position he continued to hold when Sun resigned in favour of the former general Yüan Shih-k'ai.

On the death of Yüan in June 1916, Li succeeded him as president and held office until the brief restoration of the boy emperor in July 1917. In 1922 he was prevailed upon to resume the presidency, but in September of the following year he was compelled to resign. Li was unsuccessful in his efforts to reunify the country by negotiation rather than by military force.

Li Zicheng (Chinese rebel leader): *see* Li Tzu-ch'eng.

Lia (first wife of Jacob): *see* Leah.

liability, in law, a broad term including almost every type of duty, obligation, debt, responsibility, or hazard arising by way of contract, tort, or statute.

The extent of liability is often regulated by contract. For example, a limited partnership may often be formed so that certain partners designated as limited—as opposed to general—are liable for the firm's obligations only to the extent of their contribution to the firm's capital. Liability may also be governed by the customs of tort, as when children, insane persons, and other legally incompetent persons are not considered to be legally responsible for their actions.

The amount of liability may also be determined by reference to a statute. Thus, stockholders under certain statutes have a personal liability making them individually responsible for the debts of the corporation to the extent of the par value of their stock or some other specified limit.

liability, manufacturer's: *see* manufacturer's liability.

liability insurance, insurance against losses or damage a policyholder might incur. The largest component of the protection provided by liability insurance is against losses resulting from acts or omissions which are legally deemed to be negligent and which result in damage to the person, property, or legitimate interests of others.

In comparison with most other forms of insurance, liability insurance is a relatively recent phenomenon. A very modest amount was written before 1890, but it was principally the introduction of the automobile after that year that spurred the rapid growth of this form of insurance, which now extends to a great many activities in addition to the operation of an automobile.

Other types of liability insurance include professional liability for doctors and other professionals (malpractice insurance), marine liability for boatowners and operators, and products liability for manufacturers of consumer goods. Protection can also be provided against the possibility that one may be unable to fulfill the terms of a contract or against the risks involved in activities that are considered so dangerous to other people or property that the law requires persons engaged in them to assume responsibility for their consequences no matter how much care is taken to avoid damage. Examples of this last type, called absolute liability, vary from one legal jurisdiction to another but may include, for example, the ownership of dangerous wild animals.

Policyholders pay premiums to the insurance company and, in the event damage or injury does occur, the insurance company pays reparations up to the limit set forth in the particular policy.

Product liability and malpractice insurance present special problems because of the increasingly high cost of court awards of damages and because of the public's high expectations of product safety and physician performance. An additional problem for product liability insurance is that the courts have tended to award damages even in cases where the product was willfully misused. The worldwide nuclear power industry faces a special liability problem because of the immense amount of damage a major nuclear accident can cause. In the United States this problem was dealt with by legislation that enabled the government to provide liability insurance and stipulated the amount of private insurance a nuclear power facility must carry. Similar measures have been adopted in other countries.

Liadov, Anatoly Konstantinovich: *see* Lyadov, Anatoly.

liana, also spelled LIANE, any long-stemmed woody vine that is rooted in the soil and climbs or twines around other plants for support. Lianas are characteristic plants of rainforests in tropical areas and may grow up to 60 cm (about 2 feet) in diameter and 100 m (about 330 feet) in length. Flattened or twisted lianas often become tangled together to form a hanging network of vegetation.

Liana encircling a tree in a rainforest in Brazil

E. Aubert de la Rue

Liang Ch'en-yü, Pinyin LIANG CHENYU (b. 1520, K'un-shan, Kiangsu province, China—d. *c.* 1593, China), Chinese playwright and author of the first play of the K'un school (*k'un-ch'ü*) of dramatic singing. When his great actor-friend Wei Liang-fu developed a new, more subtle and quiet style of dramatic singing, he asked Liang Ch'en-yü to create a showcase for his new style, and Liang complied by writing the *Huan sha chi* ("Washing the Silken Gauze"), a *k'un-ch'ü* drama that initiated the type of theatre that was to dominate the Chinese stage until the end of the 18th century. The plot, concerning the feud between the states of Wu and Yüeh, is unimportant; rather, the drama is admired for its elegant lyrics and fine soft music.

Liang Ch'i-ch'ao, Pinyin LIANG QICHAO (b. Feb. 23, 1873, Hsinhui, Kwangtung province, China—d. Jan. 19, 1929, Peking), the foremost intellectual leader of China in the first two decades of the 20th century.

Liang was a disciple of the great scholar K'ang Yu-wei, who reinterpreted the Confucian Classics in an attempt to utilize tradition as a justification for the sweeping innovations he prescribed for Chinese culture. After China's humiliating defeat by Japan (1894–95), the writings of K'ang and Liang came to the attention of the emperor and helped usher in the Hundred Days of Reform. During this period (summer 1898) the emperor acted on the advice of these scholars in an attempt to renovate the imperial system. The suggested changes included setting up modern schools, remaking the 2,000-year-old civil service examination system, and reorganizing virtually every activity of the government. When the empress dowager Tz'u-hsi halted the reform movement because she felt it too inclusive, warrants were issued for the arrest of K'ang, Liang, and other reformers. Liang fled to Japan. During his exile his iconoclastic journalism affected a whole generation of young Chinese.

Liang returned to China in 1912 after the establishment of the Republic of China. As a founder of the Progressive Party (Chinputang) he sided with Yüan Shih-k'ai, the autocratic president of the republic, against the liberal nationalist leader Sun Yat-sen and his Nationalist Party (Kuomintang). Liang, however, organized a successful resistance to Yüan's attempt to overturn the republic and have himself declared emperor. English translations of Liang's works include *History of Chinese Political Thought During the Early Tsin Period* (1930) and *Intellectual Trends in the Ch'ing Period* (1959).

Liang K'ai, Pinyin LIANG KAI (b. *c.* 1140, Tung-p'ing, Shantung province, China—d. *c.* 1210), Chinese painter known primarily for paintings that reflect his interest in Ch'an (Japanese: Zen) Buddhism.

Liang was originally a painter in attendance at the imperial painting academy in Hang-chou during the Southern Sung period. For uncertain reasons, he left the academy to become a Ch'an Buddhist priest, and his later paintings, those that reflect his involvement with Buddhism, are of most interest. He became a priest in a temple near Hang-chou, the capital city of the Southern Sung dynasty. Because Ch'an painting generally and that of the Southern Sung in particular has not been popular with the Chinese collector of more restrained Confucian sensibility, all the extant works that can be accepted as by Liang K'ai are now in Japan. They have been much prized and imitated there. Though varied, the general effect of Liang K'ai's paintings is appropriate to Ch'an belief: explosive and intense, an immediate release of passion and sure knowledge with a matching mastery of brush technique.

Liang Shih-ch'iu (b. Dec. 8, 1902, Peking, China—d. Nov. 3, 1987, Taipei, Taiwan), writer, translator, and literary critic known for his devastating critique of romantic modern Chinese literature and for his insistence on the aesthetic, rather than the propagandistic, purpose of literary expression.

After completing his preparatory education in China, Liang Shih-ch'iu graduated from Colorado College (in Colorado Springs, Colo., U.S.) in 1924 and went on to Columbia and Harvard universities for graduate study. At Harvard, where he was greatly influenced by the conservative literary critic Irving Babbitt, he wrote a paper outlining the romantic excesses of modern Chinese literature and suggested the development of a new Chinese literature that would borrow from the forms of Western literature. He later expanded these ideas into a book, *Lang-man-ti ku-tien-ti* (1927; "The Romantic and the Classic"), which was published in China.

At the time of his return to China in 1926, Liang Shih-ch'iu also insisted upon the aesthetic and independent purposes of literary creation. He and others, including Hu Shih and Hsü Chih-mo, founded the Crescent Moon Society in 1927 and published their ideas in the journal *Hsin-yueh* ("Crescent Moon"). Liang Shih-ch'iu taught English literature at Peking University (1934–37) and worked on his translation into vernacular Chinese of the complete works of Shakespeare (completed 1967). When the Communists took control of China in 1949, he moved to Taiwan.

Besides his many critical works on Chinese and Western literature, Liang Shih-ch'iu was an able translator who made available to Chinese readers such varied works as the 12th-century love letters of the monk Abelard to Héloïse, Sir James Barrie's *Peter Pan,* and Emily Brontë's *Wuthering Heights.* He also wrote a history of English literature in Chinese and compiled a Chinese-English dictionary.

Liang Shu-ming, Pinyin LIANG SHUMING (b. Oct. 18, 1893, Kweilin, Kwangsi province, China—d. June 23, 1988, Peking), Neo-Confucian philosopher and writer who attempted to demonstrate the relevance of Confucianism to China's problems in the 20th century. A believer in the unity of thought and action, Liang became a leader in attempts at peasant organization. He also was active in the ill-fated Democratic League, a political organization that tried to steer a middle course between the Chinese Communists and the Nationalist Party of Chiang Kai-shek.

Originally a Buddhist, Liang in 1917 was appointed to the faculty of Peking University as the first professor of Buddhism ever to serve on the staff of a Chinese university. In 1918, however, his father's suicide prompted him to return to Confucianism. His influential *Tung-hsi wen-hua chi ch'i che-hsueh* (1921; "The Cultures of East and West and Their Philosophies") attempted to demonstrate to an increasingly iconoclastic and Westernized Chinese intelligentsia the modern relevance of Chinese, especially Confucian, culture. Characterizing the Western attitude as one of struggle, the Chinese attitude as one of harmonization through adjustment, and the Indian attitude as escapist, Liang theorized that after World War I, Western culture was dominant; this phase, he claimed, would soon be replaced by another era, in which the Chinese way would adapt the material successes of the West to man's moral and ethical needs. In an even more distant era, the Indian attitude would prevail.

By the 1930s, however, Liang had come to believe that Western methods and doctrines would never be suitable to China but that once the Chinese countryside was awakened by enlightened understanding, it would become a repository of traditional Confucian values; continued struggle or revolution on the part of the Chinese people would therefore cease. To this end, Liang helped found the Shantung Rural Reconstruction Research Institute.

In 1937, when the Sino-Japanese War forced his institute to close, Liang became an organizing member of the Democratic League. He remained in China after the Communists came to power in 1949, though he refused, despite frequent criticism, to acknowledge the validity of Marxism. In 1980 he served on the committee for the revision of the Chinese constitution, and he was also a member of the presidium of the Chinese People's Political Consultative Conference, a body of scholars who serve in an advisory capacity.

Lianyungang (China): *see* Lien-yün-kang.

Liao DYNASTY, Pinyin LIAO (907–1125), dynasty formed by the nomadic Khitan tribes in much of present-day Manchuria (Northeast Provinces) and Mongolia and the northeastern corner of China proper. Adopting the Chinese dynastic name of Liao, the Khitan created a dual government to rule their conquests. The southern government, which ruled the Chinese parts of the empire, was modeled after the administration of the T'ang dynasty (618–907), which the Khitan had helped destroy. The northern government, which was set up on a tribal basis, ruled over the nomads of the Inner Asian steppes.

Afraid that their use of Chinese advisers and administrative techniques would blur their own ethnic identity, the Khitan made a conscious effort to retain their own tribal rites, food, and clothing and refused to use the Chinese language, devising a writing system for their own language instead.

After the establishment of the Sung dynasty (960–1279) in China proper, the Liao carried on a border war with the Sung for control of North China. The war was eventually settled in 1004, when the Sung agreed to pay an annual tribute to the Liao. The Liao dynasty, which continued many of the cultural practices of the Sung, was destroyed in 1125 by the Juchen tribes, who had formerly been subjects of the Khitan and who rose in rebellion against them with the aid of the Sung. The Juchen went on to defeat the Sung and, as the Chin dynasty (1115–1234), establish rule over North China. The Chin adopted most of the Liao governmental system.

Liao River, Wade-Giles romanization LIAO HO, Pinyin LIAO HE, river in the southern Northeast (Manchuria) region in Liaoning province and Inner Mongolian autonomous region, China. The Liao River system drains the southern part of the Liao and Sungari plains of central Northeast China. Its drainage area is divided from the Sungari basin by a belt of land that has been subject to gentle uplift, while the plain area has in general been gently subsiding since the Mesozoic Era. The watershed area experienced intensified uplift in recent geological time, and this uplifting was accompanied by volcanic activity along the southern part of the divide. The plain as a whole is formed of thick sediments and is extremely flat and in parts swampy.

In its upper reaches the Liao River divides into two main systems. The eastern Liao drains the foothills of the eastern mountains of the Northeast, while the western Liao, with its upper tributaries—the Lao-ha, the Ying-chin, and the Hsin-k'ai rivers—drain the arid Jehol Uplands in southeastern Inner Mongolia. The volume of water varies greatly from season to season and has a marked summer maximum. The gradient in the plain is very low, and the lower Liao River valley has regularly suffered from summer flooding in spite of an extensive and long-established system of dikes. The river also carries a heavy load of silt. The area is icebound for about three months a year; extensive flooding often occurs during the spring thaw. The length of the Liao River is 836 miles (1,345 km), and its drainage basin is 83,000 square miles (215,000 square km).

The Liao is not very important as a waterway; though its mouth, near the port of Ying-k'ou, is constantly silting up, it is navigable for small steamboats as far as San-chiang-k'ou, where the eastern and western Liao rivers diverge. Its principal tributary is the Hun River, which flows into the Liao not far above its mouth and drains the foothills of the Liaotung Peninsula and Ch'ang-pai Mountains, passing through Shen-yang (Mukden) in Liaoning province.

Liao T'ai Tsu (Mongol ruler): *see* A-pao-chi.

Liao-yang, Pinyin LIAOYANG, city in central Liaoning *sheng* (province), China. Liao-yang is situated on the T'ai-tzu River, some 30 miles (50 km) southwest of Shen-yang (Mukden), and 12 miles (19 km) northeast of the great industrial city of An-shan.

Liao-yang is located in the most ancient area of Chinese settlement in Manchuria. The Han dynasty (206 BC–AD 220) set up Liao-yang commandery in the 2nd century BC, with its seat at P'ing-hsiang, northwest of the modern city. During the 4th and 5th centuries AD it formed part of the territories of the successive Yen kingdoms, and in the 640s was occupied by the T'ang dynasty (618–907) as a base area for their invasions of the Korean area. When the Chinese protectorate over southern Manchuria ended in 756, Liao-yang became a southern frontier district of the P'o-hai (Korean Parhae) state, which flourished in the 8th and 9th centuries. Early in the 10th century it was overrun by the Khitan people and incorporated in their state of Liao-tung. In 919 their king rebuilt the city and forcibly resettled Chinese and P'o-hai captives to populate it. In 928 it was designated the eastern capital of the Liao dynasty; it remained one of the capitals under both the Liao and their successors, the Juchen (Chin) dynasty (12th and early 13th centuries).

The area was the seat of a rebellion in the early 13th century, and the rebels submitted to the Mongols in 1215–16. From 1269 to 1367 Liao-yang served as the capital of the province of Liao-yang Lu, but the area seems to have been extensively depopulated by the Mongols. At the beginning of the Ming dynasty (1368–1644), the city became a crucial defensive base for the northeastern frontier. Walled in 1368–72, it was the centre of a network of guard posts and garrisons. With the rise of the Manchus at the end of the 16th century, however, its defenses proved inadequate, and it was overrun by the armies of Nurhachi, a Manchurian tribal chieftain, in 1621. Nurhachi made it his capital, and began the construction of a large new capital city some 3 miles (5 km) to the east. Laid out on a grand scale, this city was never finished. In 1625 Nurhachi moved his court to Mukden; the abandoned new capital fell into ruins. Subsequently, Liao-yang became a superior prefecture and remained an important administrative centre.

Owing to its strategic location, Liao-yang was the site of several fierce battles during the Russo-Japanese War (1904–05). With the foundation of the Chinese republic (1911) it was demoted to the status of a county seat but continued to flourish as the centre of a rich and densely peopled agricultural area producing rice, grain, soybeans, cotton, tussah silk (a tan silk), and a variety of vegetables and foodstuffs. Various industries associated with agriculture, such as brewing, textiles, and oil extraction, also grew up.

With the rapid growth from the 1930s onward of nearby An-shan, one of the principal industrial centres of China, Liao-yang's economy has been to a large extent subordinated to An-shan's needs. The city provides much of the foodstuffs consumed by An-shan. It has developed a large cotton mill and engineering and cement manufacturing plants. It is connected by railway to Shen-yang, An-shan, and Lü-ta. Pop. (1990) 492,559.

Liao-yüan, also called TUNG-LIAO, Pinyin LIAOYUAN, or DONGLIAO, city, southwestern Kirin *sheng* (province), China. Liao-yüan is on the north bank of the upper Tung-liao River, about 60 miles (100 km) south of Ch'ang-ch'un. Standing on the border between the plains and the hills, it was originally a Manchu hunting preserve, which was first opened to legal colonization by Chinese farmers in the late 19th century. Liao-yüan then became a rural market and collecting centre for soybeans, grain, and other agricultural products. In 1911 coal was discovered in the area, and Liao-yüan became the centre of a major coalfield, with pits located at such neighbouring centres as Hsi-an (Ch'ang-an) and P'ing-kang. The field has enormous reserves of good quality coal, mostly bituminous. The mines, badly damaged at the end of World War II, were extensively reequipped in the early 1950s, those at Hsi-an with Soviet aid. By 1960 Liao-yüan had become the chief coal-producing district in Kirin province. Besides providing fuel for industrial use in the province, Liao-yüan has a large thermal generating plant, which is connected with the power grid linking the major industrial centres of Northeast China. The city's other industries include engineering, chemical and fertilizer plants, paper mills, and factories for cotton weaving, silk reeling, and oil pressing. It is connected by rail via Ssu-p'ing to Ch'ang-ch'un and to T'ung-hua. Pop. (1990) 354,141.

Consult the INDEX *first*

Liaoning, Wade-Giles romanization LIAO-NING, Pinyin LIAONING, *sheng* (province) of northeastern China, southernmost of the three that form the region of Manchuria, bounded on the northeast by Kirin province, on the east by North Korea, on the south by the Yellow Sea, on the southwest by Hopeh province, and on the northwest by the Inner Mongolian autonomous region.

A brief treatment of Liaoning follows. For full treatment, *see* MACROPAEDIA: China.

The area was known as Sheng-ching in Manchu times (1644–1911). It was redefined in 1903 and named Feng-t'ien; in 1928 the boundaries were altered once again and it was renamed Liaoning. From 1932 to 1945, the province was part of the Japanese puppet state of Manchukuo. Shen-yang (then called Mukden), the capital, fell to the Chinese Communists in 1948. In 1954, Liaoning was established as a single province and was given its present form in 1956.

Liaoning consists of a central lowland, with Shen-yang at its centre and mountain masses to the east and west. A southward extension of the eastern highlands forms the Liaotung Peninsula. There are four main topographical regions: the central plains, the Liaotung Peninsula, the western highlands, and the eastern mountain zone. Summer rainfall is often torrential. Strong winds occur in spring and the scarcity of spring precipitation tends to leave growing crops short of water.

Most of the Liaoning population is Han Chinese. Significant minorities are Manchu, located mainly in the Liao River valley and around Shen-yang, and the Mongols, who live near the frontier of Inner Mongolia.

Liaoning is rich in mineral resources, especially iron ore and coal. Petroleum is produced from oil shale. There are rich reserves of manganese and magnesium ore and substantial deposits of copper, lead, zinc, bauxite, and gold. Sea salt is produced for use in food and in the chemical industry.

The province ranks first in China in heavy industrial production, producing steel, cement, crude oil, and approximately one-fifth of the nation's electrical power. Other Liaoning industries include nonferrous-metals processing; the manufacture of electrical, agricultural, mining, and transport machinery and machine tools; textiles, including both cotton and silk; foodstuffs; paper; and cement. Most of these manufactures are produced in five cities: Shen-yang, An-shan, Lü-ta, Fu-shun, and Pen-ch'i.

Although agricultural development has not matched industrial development in the growth of Liaoning, much of the climate, topography, and soils are favourable to agriculture. The degree of farm mechanization is very high by Chinese standards. Industrial and export crops are yielded from a small portion of the cultivated area; the majority is used for grain crops, vegetables, and soybeans.

The rail transportation facilities of Liaoning are the best in China, and the tonnage transported is also the highest for any province. Highways are extensive but of poor quality. There is little internal sea or river traffic, but sea navigation is of great importance for transport to other parts of China. Lü-ta is the largest port, followed by Ying-k'ou. Area 58,300 square miles (151,000 square km). Pop. (1995 est.) 40,670,000.

Liaotung Peninsula, Wade-Giles romanization LIAO-TUNG PAN-TAO, Pinyin LIAODONG BANDAO, large peninsula jutting out in a southwesterly direction from the southern coastline of Liaoning province, northeastern China. It partly separates the Po Hai (Gulf of Chihli) (west) from Korea Bay (east), and, with the Shantung Peninsula to the south, it delimits the Po Hai Strait.

The Liaotung Peninsula forms a part of a larger mountain belt, with a southwest-northeast axis, which is continued in the Ch'ang-pai Mountains of the Northeast (Manchuria)–North Korean border area. On the peninsula, the range is known as the Ch'ien Mountains. The backbone of the peninsula consists of a number of parallel ridges of mountains formed from very ancient granites and shales. They have been weathered into sharp peaks and ridges and are rarely more than 3,300 feet (1,000 m) in elevation, but the highest peak, Mount Pu-yün, reaches 3,712 feet (1,131 m). Most of the southern part of the peninsula is gentler in its relief, seldom exceeding 1,650 feet (500 m). The mountains are deeply dissected by a complex river system, which drains partly into the Yalu River to the east, partly into the Liao River to the west, and partly into the sea. The river valleys of the peninsula proper are narrow, with no large alluvial plains.

The climate of the Liaotung Peninsula is somewhat warmer in winter than is the surrounding area of northeastern China. It receives 20 to 30 inches (500 to 750 mm) of precipitation annually, about two-thirds of which falls in the very hot summer months (July to September). The area is extensively used for orchard and fruit farming, especially apples; and wheat, corn (maize), and rice are grown. Chestnut-leaved oaks are grown in the highlands for use in tussah silk production. Mineral resources include iron ore, gold, copper, and magnesite. Boron and salt are also mined. Near the southern tip of the peninsula lies the major city and port of Lü-ta, which is made up of the ports of Ta-lien and Lü-shun (Dairen and Port Arthur). A north-south railway connects Lü-ta to Ying-k'ou, at the western base of the peninsula, and continues beyond the peninsula to Shen-yang. Lü-ta and other cities in the area grew rapidly in the late 20th century.

Liapchev, Andrei (b. Nov. 30, 1866, Resen, Macedonia, Ottoman Empire—d. Nov. 6, 1933, Sofia, Bulg.), statesman, prime minister of Bulgaria through several years of continuing national tension (1926–31).

As a student Liapchev took a prominent part in the movement for the unification of Bulgaria and Eastern Rumelia (1885). In the following years he provided journalistic support for the Macedonian revolutionary cause and eventually became editor of the Democratic Party organ, *Priaporets.*

Almost continuously in Bulgaria's Parliament after 1908, Liapchev served successively as minister of agriculture and commerce and minister of finance from 1908 to 1911. In 1908 he signed the treaty establishing Bulgaria's independence from Ottoman Turkey. Again serving as finance minister in 1918, Liapchev signed the armistice (September 1918) that marked Bulgaria's military defeat in World War I, and in November 1918 he was appointed minister of war. Imprisoned in 1922 under the dictatorship of Aleksandŭr Stamboliyski, he was released after Stamboliyski's fall in June 1923.

Thereafter he was a leader of the political coalition, the "Democratic Entente," that had formed around Prime Minister Aleksandŭr Tsankov, and in January 1926 he succeeded Tsankov as prime minister. The tolerance of Liapchev's government for the violent Internal Macedonian Revolutionary Organization (IMRO) reinforced tensions with Greece and Yugoslavia and permitted IMRO's virtual control of certain areas of Bulgaria. During 1927–28 his government secured League of Nations stabilization loans to assist in repatriating Bulgarian refugees in Yugoslavia, but the Great Depression soon brought further national discontent that continued through the end of his ministry (1931).

Liaquat Ali Khan (b. Oct. 1, 1895, Karnāl, India—d. Oct. 16, 1951, Rāwalpindi, Pak.), first prime minister of Pakistan.

Born the son of a landowner, Liaquat was educated at Alīgarh, Allahābād, and Exeter College, Oxford. A barrister by profession, like his leader, Mohammed Ali Jinnah, he entered politics in 1923, being elected first to the provincial legislature of the United Provinces and then to the central legislative assembly. He joined the Muslim League and soon became closely associated with Jinnah. By degrees he won first the respect and then the admiration of the Muslim community for his share in the struggle for Pakistan; when victory was won, and Jinnah became the first governor-general, Liaquat was the obvious choice as prime minister. In this post his achievements were outstanding. If Jinnah founded Pakistan, Liaquat established it, laying down the main lines of policy, domestic and foreign, which afterward guided the country. After Jinnah's death, Liaquat was acclaimed as *qaid-i-millet* ("leader of the country"). His assassination at Rawalpindi in 1951 was the work of fanatics who resented his steady refusal to contemplate war with India.

liar paradox, also called EPIMENIDES' PARADOX, the paradox that if "This sentence is not true" is true, then it is not true, and if it is not true, then it is true. This example shows that certain formulations of words, though grammatically correct, are logically nonsensical. The English philosopher Bertrand Russell, in developing the theory of types, used the following illustration: the statement, "I am lying" is true only if it is false, and false if it is true. Epimenides, a 6th-century-BC Cretan prophet, first recorded such a paradox.

Liard River, river in northwestern Canada. It rises in the Saint Cyr Range of the Pelly Mountains, Yukon Territory, and flows southeast into British Columbia, then northeast to join the Mackenzie River at Fort Simpson in the Northwest Territories, after a course of 693 miles (1,115 km). Its upper course is characterized by rapids and canyons; its lower course is navigable for small boats from Fort Simpson to Fort Liard, 165 miles upstream. Part of the river's valley is followed by the Alaska Highway. Its tributaries include the Hyland, Kechika, Coal, Beaver, Petitot, Fort Nelson, and South Nahanni rivers. It is named for the liards (poplar trees) along its course.

Liatris, genus of perennial herbs of the family Asteraceae, containing approximately 30 species, native to North America. They have tall spikelike clusters of purple or pinkish purple flower heads that are surrounded by many scaly bracts (leaflike structures). Their long thin leaves alternate along the stem and frequently bear resinous dots. Some species of *Liatris* are cultivated as border plants or in wildflower gardens. Some are known variously as button snakeroot, gay feather, and blazing star.

Blazing star (*Liatris squarrosa*)
H.R. Hungerford

Libanius (b. AD 314, Antioch, Syria—d. 393), Greek Sophist and rhetorician whose orations and letters are a major source of information on the political, social, and economic life of Antioch and of the eastern part of the Roman Empire in the 4th century.

After beginning his teaching career in Constantinople and Nicomedia, Libanius went to Antioch (354), where his school soon became famous. Devoted to the classical authors in both teaching and writing, he tried to maintain the Greek tradition in the face of the rise of Rome, and as a friend of the emperor Julian, he attempted to live and write as though Christianity did not exist, though he knew and esteemed individual Christians. His works give valuable pictures of contemporary education.

Libau, also called LIBAVA (Latvia): *see* Liepāja.

Libavius, Andreas (Latin), German ANDREAS LIBAU (b. *c.* 1540, Halle [Germany]—d. July 25, 1616, Coburg), German chemist, physician, and alchemist who made important chemical discoveries but is most noted as the author of the first modern chemistry textbook.

Libavius was professor of history and poetry at the University of Jena from 1586 to 1591 and then became town physician and inspector of the *Gymnasium* at Rothenburg. In 1605 he established the Gymnasium Casimirianum at Coburg.

Of his numerous works, all of which were noted for clear, unambiguous writing, the most important was *Alchymia* (1606; "Alchemy"), a work that established the tradition for 17th-century French chemistry textbooks. Although he was a firm believer in the transmutation of base metals into gold, Libavius was renowned for his vitriolic attacks against the mysticism and secretiveness of his fellow alchemists. Libavius pioneered in the analytic approach to chemistry. Among his discoveries were methods for the preparation of ammonium sulfate, antimony sulfide, hydrochloric acid, and tin tetrachloride.

Libby, Willard Frank (b. Dec. 17, 1908, Grand Valley, Colo., U.S.—d. Sept. 8, 1980,

Los Angeles, Calif.), American chemist whose technique of carbon-14 (or radiocarbon) dating provided an extremely valuable tool for archaeologists, anthropologists, and earth scientists. For this development he was honoured with the Nobel Prize for Chemistry in 1960.

Libby received his Ph.D. from the University of California, Berkeley, where he was a member of the faculty from 1933 to 1945. He was with the Institute for Nuclear Studies at the University of Chicago (1945–59) and then was professor of chemistry at the University of California, Los Angeles, until his death.

While associated with the Manhattan Project (1941–45), Libby helped develop a method for separating uranium isotopes, an essential step in the creation of the atomic bomb. In 1946 he showed that tritium, the heaviest isotope of hydrogen, was produced by cosmic radiation. The following year he and his students developed the carbon-14 dating technique. This technique is used to date material derived from former living organisms as old as 50,000 years. It measures small amounts of radioactivity from the carbon-14 in organic or carbon-containing materials and is able to identify older objects as those having less radioactivity. Libby also served on the U.S. Atomic Energy Commission (1955–59) and wrote *Radiocarbon Dating* (1952).

Liber and Libera, in Roman religion, a pair of fertility and cultivation deities of uncertain origin. Liber, though an old and native Italian deity, came to be identified with Dionysus. The triad Ceres, Liber, and Libera (his female counterpart) represented in Rome, from early times and always under Greek influence, the Eleusinian Demeter, Iacchus-Dionysus, and Kore (Persephone). At the festival of the Liberalia, held at Rome on March 17, the *toga virilis* was commonly assumed for the first time by boys who were of age.

liberal arts, college or university curriculum aimed at imparting general knowledge and developing general intellectual capacities in contrast to a professional, vocational, or technical curriculum. In the medieval European university the seven liberal arts were grammar, rhetoric, and logic (the trivium) and geometry, arithmetic, music, and astronomy (the quadrivium). In modern colleges and universities the liberal arts include the study of literature, languages, philosophy, history, mathematics, and science as the basis of a general, or liberal, education.

Liberal-Democratic Party (LDP), Japanese JIYŪMINSHUTŌ, Japan's largest political party, which has held power almost continuously since its formation in November 1955. The party generally has worked closely with business interests and followed a pro-American foreign policy. During more than four decades of almost uninterrupted power, the LDP oversaw Japan's recovery from World War II and its development into an economic superpower.

The LDP is descended from parties that existed in the 19th century. In 1880 the Liberal Party (Jiyūtō), itself descended from an older protest group, campaigned for a Japanese constitutional government with a national assembly. A more moderate group, the Progressive Party (Kaishintō), advocated government along British lines. Under the Meiji Constitution of 1889, the parties became active in parliamentary government. From 1918 to 1931 they wielded substantial power under the respective names of Friends of Constitutional Government (Rikken Seiyūkai) and Democratic Party (Minseitō), but all political parties lost influence with the rise of militarism in Japan; in 1940 they disbanded.

The Japanese surrender at the end of World War II in 1945 was followed by four years of political confusion. New parties were formed from the remnants of the old ones: the Liberal Party built on the old Seiyūkai, whereas the Progressive Party drew on factions of both the Seiyūkai and the Minseitō. Alliances wavered. From 1945 to 1954, the Progressives changed their name four times, successively from Progressive Party to Democratic Party to National Democratic Party to Reform Party. In 1947 and 1948 the Progressives, who had received 19 percent of the vote in the 1946 elections, participated in a coalition government with left-wing parties. In the 1949 elections, however, they received only 16 percent of the vote and moved rightward. In November 1954 they joined with a faction of the Liberal Party to form the Japanese Democratic Party (Nippon Minshutō)—which in turn united with the remaining Liberals in 1955 to form the Liberal-Democratic Party.

In the 1950s and early '60s the LDP consistently won about 60 percent of the vote. After the mid-1960s the LDP's popularity wavered considerably, but it maintained control of the government. In the mid-1970s and again in the late '80s and early '90s, the party was shaken by a number of major financial and other scandals. The party weathered the 1970s scandal; but the second series forced the consecutive resignations of two LDP prime ministers, and in elections held in July 1993, the party lost its majority in parliament and, for the first time in its history, control of the government. The LDP returned to power the following year as the largest party in a three-party coalition, though Tomiichi Murayama of the Social Democratic Party held the office of prime minister. After Murayama's resignation in 1996, the LDP held the prime minister's office continuously through the rest of the 1990s and into the next decade. At the beginning of the 21st century, however, the party's popularity began to decline, though it was able to remain in power.

Liberal Democrats, also called LIBERAL DEMOCRATIC PARTY, a British political party founded in 1988 through a merger of the Liberal Party and the Social Democratic Party (*qq.v.*), or SDP. In the middle ground between the dominant Labour and Conservative parties, the Liberal Democrats occupy a centre-left, libertarian position.

Almost from the very founding of the SDP, the Liberals and Social Democrats were allied with each other, and on March 3, 1988, the two parties were formally merged as the Social and Liberal Democratic Party. The present name was adopted in 1989.

In the 1992 general election, the Liberal Democrats won 18 percent of the popular vote, establishing themselves as a significant force in British politics. They more than doubled their parliamentary representation in 1997 and also increased their seats in 2001.

Liberal Party, a British political party that emerged in the mid-19th century as the successor to the historic Whig Party. It was the major party in opposition to the Conservatives until 1918, after which it was supplanted by the Labour Party. The Liberals continued as a minor party until 1988, when they merged with the Social Democratic Party to form what is now the Liberal Democratic Party (*q.v.*).

After Britain's First (electoral) Reform Act of 1832, the mainly aristocratic Whigs were joined in the House of Commons by increasing numbers of middle-class members and by a smaller number of Radicals, who, from about 1850, tended to work together in cooperation with the Peelites (antiprotectionist Tories). By 1839 Lord John Russell was referring to "the Liberal party" in his letters to Queen Victoria. Russell's administration of 1846 is sometimes regarded as the first Liberal government; others reserve the distinction for Lord Palmerston's 1855 administration. The first unequivocally Liberal government was formed in 1868 by William E. Gladstone, under whose leadership the Liberals became a cohesive parliamentary party. After 1865 Gladstone dominated the party, which held power under him for a total of more than 12 years between 1868 and 1894. The main achievement of the Liberal Party under Gladstone was its reforms. These included the establishment of a national system of education, voting by secret ballot, the legalization of trade unions, the enfranchisement of the working class in rural areas, reconstruction of the army (involving the abolition of the purchase of commissions), and reform of the judicial system.

In 1886 the party was weakened by the defection of the Liberal Unionists, who disliked Gladstone's plan for Home Rule of Ireland and eventually joined the Conservatives. By the early 20th century the Liberal Party seemed moribund, but a Conservative split helped the Liberals to victory. The period 1906–15, during which the foundations of the British welfare state were laid, was the last during which the Liberals held power alone.

In 1915, during World War I, the Liberal H.H. Asquith formed a national coalition government with the Conservative and Labour parties. However, during the war the Liberals clustered into two distinctly different camps, centred on the rival personalities of Asquith and his successor, David Lloyd George. Aligned with Asquith were those who felt that cherished Liberal beliefs were being threatened by such wartime exactions as military conscription, introduced in 1916. Allied to Lloyd George were those who sided with the Conservatives in seeking a more rigorous prosecution of the war. The Liberals' divisions became more firmly drawn after the postwar election of December 1918, in which Lloyd George's Coalition Liberals ran unopposed by their Conservative partners while Asquith's Independent Liberals were routed. In the years that followed, the party's internal conflicts exacted a terrible toll on it at precisely the time when the Labour Party was emerging as a coherent and effective source of reform in the country. In 1924, the Liberals' parliamentary representation was reduced to 40. Their last experience of national government was provided by their participation in Winston Churchill's World War II coalition of 1940–45.

During the 1950s the Liberals polled as little as 2.5 percent of the popular vote. Under the successive leadership of Jo Grimond, Jeremy Thorpe, and David Steel, the Liberals eventually managed to regain almost 20 percent of the popular vote, but they continued to be severely hampered by the lack of proportional representation. The strategic importance of the party was enhanced by the emergence of the Social Democratic Party (SDP) in 1981. An Alliance was forged between the two parties in time for the 1983 general election, and a formal merger followed in 1988.

During its period as a major political party, the Liberal Party was characterized by certain attitudes rather than a precise ideology. Central to Liberal attitudes was a trust in rationality, faith in the idea of progress, attachment to individualism, emphasis on human rights, and an eagerness to emancipate underprivileged groups. But Liberals' distrust of the enlargement of the functions of the state eventually came into conflict with the egalitarian political aspirations of the party, leaving it unprepared to adopt the role subsequently taken up by the emergent Labour Party. On the one hand, the Liberal Party championed individualism, free trade, and private enterprise, opposing what it saw as the centralizing and stultifying power of the state; on the other, it pursued policies of active social reorganization to prevent abuses of private power, to promote social justice, and to extend the role of the state in fields such as education, social welfare, and industrial relations. The Liberal Party always sought reform of the system of government, and Liberal reforms molded most of Britain's political institutions. In overseas policy, Liberal attitudes were pacific and internationalist. The party was wary of imperial expansion in the 19th century and supported the independence of colonial peoples in the 20th century. It constantly promoted international cooperation.

Liberal Party (Italy): *see* Italian Liberal Party.

Liberal Party of Australia, major Australian political party, founded in 1944.

The original Liberals emerged in 1910 as an alliance of radical protectionists and laissez-faire free traders who were united mainly in opposition to the growing strength of what became the Australian Labor Party. Known in 1910 as the Fusion, they first fought an election under the Liberal label in 1913, losing to Labor, against whom, at this stage, they were able to offer no distinctive program.

The Liberals first came to power during World War I when, as a result of a Labor split over conscription, they merged with pro-conscription elements of that party to form the Nationalist Party. Following a general election of 1922, the Nationalists sought an alliance with the newly emerged Country Party (now the National Party). This permitted the Liberal contingent of the Nationalist Party to remove the Labor leadership of that party, which was renamed the Nationalist-Country alliance and which became more conservative. The alliance dominated federal politics until 1929, when it was defeated partly as a result of the increasingly hard line that was adopted toward the unions in the bitter labour disputes of the 1920s. At the end of 1931, however, following an alliance with elements of the Labor Party, the Nationalists came back into office as the United Australia Party. Their policy was to counter the effects of the Great Depression with a program of reduction in government expenditure. The United Australia Party, usually in coalition with the Country Party, was dominant until 1937, after which it was weakened by internal division and lack of a clear program; it eventually fell, in 1941.

Out of the remains of the United Australia Party a new Liberal Party was established in October 1944. In 1949, in cooperation with the Country Party, it was led back to power by Robert Gordon Menzies, who was prime minister of Australia from 1949 to 1966. This coalition dominated Australian politics and controlled the government until 1972, when Labor came to power, and again from 1975 to 1983. Led by John Howard, the Liberal Party regained power from Labor in 1996, forming a coalition government with the National Party. Under Howard's leadership, the Liberal Party and its coalition partner, the National Party, won reelection in 1998, 2001, and 2004. Important elements of the Liberal program have been strong ties with the business community and close cooperation with the United States.

Liberal Party of Canada, French PARTI LIBÉRAL DU CANADA, centrist Canadian political party, one of the major parties in the country since the establishment of the Dominion of Canada in 1867. The Liberal Party has been the governing party at the federal level for most of the period since the late 1890s.

The Liberal Party originated in the reformist opposition groups that emerged in the mid-19th century in what are now the provinces of Quebec and Ontario—"Rouges" (Reds) in the former and Clear Grits in the latter. The looseness and instability of all party formations at the time was especially persistent on what came to be called the Liberal side.

Both before and after the 1867 creation of the Canadian federation, the Conservatives were more successful than the Liberals in forging a durable coalition. In 1873 Alexander Mackenzie became the first Liberal prime minister, but his parliamentary group was undisciplined and lacked coherence. The party was swept from office in 1878, largely because of its support for unpopular free-trade policies. In 1887 Wilfrid Laurier assumed the Liberal leadership and was able to unify the party around a centrist platform and to bridge (for a time) the linguistic and regional divisions that had fragmented it. Laurier became the country's first French-Canadian prime minister in 1896, holding power until 1911.

In 1921 William Lyon Mackenzie King was elected prime minister, a position he retained for all but five years until his retirement in 1948. Under his leadership, the Liberals had some success in mediating French-English and regional differences. The party was able to attract broad support by fashioning pragmatic centrist policies that included some social reforms.

Louis St. Laurent replaced Mackenzie King as party leader in 1948 and served as prime minister until the Liberals' defeat in 1957. St. Laurent oversaw significant expansion of the welfare state in his early years, but the party also retained pro-business policies and a complacent attitude toward increased economic integration with the United States.

Led by Nobel Prize-winning diplomat Lester Pearson, the Liberals narrowly regained power in 1963. They once again expanded social insurance programs, introducing a comprehensive national health-care system. Pearson's government also sought to accommodate the growing nationalist movement in Quebec, allowing the province to opt out of some federal programs and extending official bilingualism in federal government operations.

Pierre Trudeau, who had been an elected legislator for only a few years, replaced Pearson as party leader in 1968 and was prime minister for all but a brief period in 1979–80 until his retirement from federal politics in 1984. Trudeau turned away from the party's previous attempts to recognize Quebec's special status and favoured policies reflecting a Canadian nationalist wariness of American domination. He also focused attention on the defense of individual rights, engineering the inclusion of a Charter of Rights and Freedoms in the new Canadian constitution of 1982. In 1984 the party was swept from office by the Progressive Conservatives, a defeat fueled in part by discontent in Quebec and in western Canada.

Jean Chrétien returned the party to office in 1993. He presided over a pragmatic mixture of policies characteristic of the party's history, but one in which the balance between welfare and business liberalism had shifted in favour of reduced social spending and a diminished governmental role in the economy. Chrétien focused on cutting the federal government's budget deficit, and this resulted in significant reductions in financial transfers to provincial governments for social services. His position on Quebec reflected that of Trudeau, in whose cabinet he had served. Aided by the fragmentation of conservative forces at the federal level, Chrétien led the party to successive election victories in 1997 and 2000.

Since its founding, the Liberal Party has lacked a clear ideology. Like the Conservatives (from 1942 the Progressive Conservatives), the party was composed of diverse regional, ethnic, religious, and class interests.

As with most Canadian political parties, policy making is dominated by the leader, who typically presides over a highly disciplined group of parliamentarians. The party has local constituency associations, along with representative bodies at the regional and national levels. These play important roles in elections and in choosing party leaders. At other times, they are relatively inactive.

There are Liberal parties in each of the provinces, and the federal party is formally distinct from them, in terms of both organization and policy. The federal Liberals traditionally have been strongest in Ontario (*e.g.*, in 2000 they secured 100 of the province's 103 seats in the House of Commons). The party also generally runs well in Quebec and the Atlantic region. (D.Ra.)

liberal socialism: *see* market socialism.

Liberale DA VERONA, also called LIBERALE DI JACOPO DALLA BRAVA (b. *c.* 1445, Verona, Republic of Venice [Italy]—d. 1526/29, Verona), early Renaissance artist, one of the finest Italian illuminators of his time.

"Jesus Before the Gates of Jerusalem," manuscript illumination by Liberale da Verona, 1470–74; in the Piccolomini Library, Siena, Italy

SCALA—Art Resource

Liberale's name derives from his native city of Verona, where he trained as a miniaturist and panel painter. He was influenced initially by Andrea Mantegna and by the Mantegnesque miniaturist Girolamo da Cremona, with whom he worked (1467–69) illuminating choir books. In 1470–74 he illuminated the choir books of Siena Cathedral, now preserved in the Piccolomini Library. These are some of the finest and most ornate Italian miniatures of their time. Their calligraphic style and imagery exercised a deep influence in Siena, above all on the paintings of Matteo di Giovanni and Francesco di Giorgio. About 1488 Liberale returned to Verona, where he executed (*c.* 1490) some frescoes in the Cappella Bonaveri in Sant'Anastasia. Though such frescoes as the "Lamentation over the Dead Christ" reveal Liberale as a forceful and expressive artist, his panel paintings seldom approach the quality of his illuminations.

liberalism, the creed of those who believe in individual liberty. More specifically, since "no government allows absolute liberty" (Locke), it is the belief that it is desirable to maximize the amount of liberty in the state.

A brief treatment of liberalism follows. For full treatment, *see* MACROPAEDIA: Socioeconomic Doctrines and Reform Movements, Modern.

Traditionally, a liberal believes that the primary function of the state is to protect the rights of the citizens. These rights are often ascribed to nature (natural rights) and frequently affirmed in proclamations, petitions, bills of rights, declarations of the rights of man, and so forth. Particularly at the beginning of liberal movements, liberals are reformers, enemies of entrenched institutions, traditions, and customs. Liberal programs, therefore, seek to place constraints on governmental power. Sometimes this may be achieved in the structure of the government itself, through a parliamentary system of government or a constitutional monarchy, or through the separation of governmental powers into functionally differentiated agencies such as executive, legislative, and judiciary, the classical example being the U.S. government. These constraints may also include barring the government so far as possible from the marketplace, as in the policies known as laissez-faire economics. Finally, these constraints may be introduced in the form of more specific limitations on governmental power, such as guarantees of habeas corpus, bail, rights of speech and assembly, and so on.

As the word liberty is ambiguous, however, so is the word liberal. A liberal may believe that freedom is a matter for the individual alone and that the role of the state should be minimal, or he may believe that freedom is a matter for the state and that the state can and should be used as an instrument to promote it. The former view in its extreme tends toward anarchism, while the latter in its extreme tends toward socialism, called social, or welfare, liberalism. In between are myriad gradations. Rarely has a liberal movement been unaffected by this ambiguity; some have even collapsed because of it.

Great Britain was the birthplace of both modern liberalism and modern conservatism. The term liberal first appeared in that country in the early 19th century. Originally, it carried a pejorative sense; the Tories began to refer to their Whig opponents as "liberales" after the Spanish political party by that name. The philosophical foundations of British liberalism were laid by John Locke, while Adam Smith developed the classical laissez-faire economic theory associated with liberalism. The British Liberal Party was formed upon the dissolution of the old Whigs and was forged into a strong parliamentary party by William E. Gladstone. The party ultimately split in 1918, however, between one faction tending toward classical laissez-faire liberalism and another tending more toward social liberalism.

In France the seeds of a similar split were already present in the writings of Jean-Jacques Rousseau, a precursor of French liberalism. The first sentence of his *Social Contract* reads: "Man is born free, but is everywhere in chains"—a classical individualistic liberal position. Yet a few pages later Rousseau writes that this situation can only be overcome if the individual submits himself, with all his rights, to the state; he continues in a vein familiar to later social liberals. Voltaire, François Guizot, and others took the individualist side of liberalism; various figures of the French Revolution and the young Napoleon I himself took the socialist side. In France and in other European countries, liberalism is also associated with anticlericalism.

The path of liberalism in the United States was much less difficult than that of European movements. American liberalism was not forced to struggle with the remnants of aristocratic traditions and institutions, and the U.S. Constitution took shape at a time when liberal ideals were in full bloom.

liberalism, theological: *see* theological liberalism.

Liberation, Union of, Russian SOYUZ OSVOBOZHDENIYA, first major liberal political group in Russia. The Union was founded in St. Petersburg in January 1904 to be a covert organization working to replace absolutism with a constitutional monarchy. Originally the creation of liberal nobility, it soon was dominated by middle-class, professional people, who gave the union a new militance.

liberation theology, in late 20th-century Roman Catholicism, a movement centred in Latin America that sought to apply religious faith by aiding the poor and oppressed through involvement in political and civic affairs. It stressed both heightened awareness of the socioeconomic structures that caused social inequities and active participation in changing those structures.

Liberation theologians believed that God speaks particularly through the poor and that the Bible can be understood only when seen from the perspective of the poor. They perceived that the Roman Catholic church in Latin America was fundamentally different from the church in Europe—*i.e.,* that the church in Latin America was a church for and of the poor. In order to build this church, they established *communidades de base,* or base communities, local Christian groups composed of 10 to 30 members each, that both studied the Bible and attempted to meet their parishioners' immediate needs for food, water, sewage disposal, and electricity. A great number of base communities, led mostly by laypersons, sprang into being throughout Latin America.

The birth of the liberation theology movement is usually dated to the second Latin American Bishops' Conference, which was held in Medellín, Colom., in 1968. At this conference the attending bishops issued a document affirming the rights of the poor and asserting that industrialized nations enriched themselves at the expense of Third World countries. The movement's seminal text, *Teología de la liberación* (1971; *A Theology of Liberation*), was written by Gustavo Gutiérrez, a Peruvian priest and theologian. Other leaders of the movement included Archbishop Oscar Arnulfo Romero of El Salvador (killed in 1980), Brazilian theologian Leonardo Boff, Jesuit scholar Jon Sobrino, and Archbishop Helder Câmara of Brazil.

The liberation theology movement gained strength in Latin America during the 1970s. Because of their insistence that ministry includes involvement in the political struggle of the poor against wealthy elites, liberation theologians were often criticized—both formally, from within the Roman Catholic church, and informally—as naive purveyors of Marxism and advocates of left-wing social activism. By the 1990s the Vatican, under Pope John Paul II, had begun trying to curb the movement's influence through the appointment of more conservative prelates in Brazil and elsewhere in Latin America.

Liberation Tigers of Tamil Eelam (LTTE), terrorist guerrilla organization seeking to establish an independent Tamil state in northern and eastern Sri Lanka. Formed in 1972, the LTTE has been considered one of the world's most sophisticated and tightly-organized insurgent groups. By 1985 it controlled the port of Jaffna and most of the Jaffna Peninsula in northern Sri Lanka. After losing control of Jaffna to an Indian peacekeeping force in 1987, the LTTE carried out several attacks, including a bombing that killed 10 senior Sri Lankan military commanders, the assassinations of the Sri Lankan president and the former Indian prime minister (though the LTTE denied involvement in the latter killing), and a suicide bombing in the capital of Colombo that killed 100 people. Negotiations between the LTTE and the government broke down in the mid-1990s. Fighting intensified in the late 1990s and continued despite efforts to revive peace talks.

Liberator (U.S. aircraft): *see* B-24.

Liberator, The, weekly newspaper of abolitionist crusader William Lloyd Garrison for 35 years (Jan. 1, 1831–Dec. 29, 1865). It was the most influential antislavery periodical in the pre-Civil War period of U.S. history. Although *The Liberator,* published in Boston, could claim a paid circulation of only 3,000, it reached a much wider audience with its uncompromising advocacy of immediate emancipation for the millions of black Americans held in bondage throughout the South. In the North, Garrison's message of moral suasion challenged moderate reformers to apply the principles of the Declaration of Independence to all people, regardless of colour. Fearful slaveholders in the South, erroneously assuming that *The Liberator* represented the majority opinion of Northerners, reacted militantly by defending slavery as a "positive good" and by legislating ever more stringent measures to suppress all possible opposition to its "peculiar institution." Garrison's publication further altered the course of the American antislavery movement by insisting that abolition, rather than African colonization, was the answer to the problem of slavery.

Liberec, German REICHENBERG, city, Severočeský *kraj* (region), northern Czech Republic. It lies in the valley of the Lužická Nisa (German: Lausitzer Neisse) River amid the Giant (Krkonoše) Mountains. Founded in the 13th century and chartered in 1577, Liberec was inhabited mainly by Germans until their expulsion after World War II. Called the "Bohemian Manchester," Liberec has been a textile centre since the 16th century, manufacturing chiefly broadcloth, rugs, tapestries, and cotton and silk fabrics. The city's North Bohemian Museum has an outstanding collection of medieval Flemish tapestries. After 1945 there was Czech resettlement of the city and a revival of industry, including traditional textile and glass production. Pop. (1999 est.) 99,794.

Liberia, city, northwestern Costa Rica. It lies along the Liberia River, a tributary of the Tempisque, at the foot of the Cordillera de Guanacaste. Liberia is a commercial centre for the surrounding agricultural lands on which livestock is raised and fruits, grains, and sugarcane are cultivated. No railroad serves the city, but it is on the Pan-American Highway; another highway leads southward to towns on the Nicoya Peninsula. Pop. (1993 est.) 31,366.

Liberia, officially REPUBLIC OF LIBERIA, republic of western Africa. It is bounded by Sierra Leone on the northwest, by Guinea on the north, by Côte d'Ivoire (Ivory Coast) on the east, and by the Atlantic Ocean along its southwestern coast. The capital is Monrovia. Area 37,743 square miles (97,754 square km). Pop. (2000 est.) 3,164,000.

A brief treatment of Liberia follows. For full treatment, *see* MACROPAEDIA: Western Africa. For current history and for statistics on society and economy, *see* BRITANNICA BOOK OF THE YEAR.

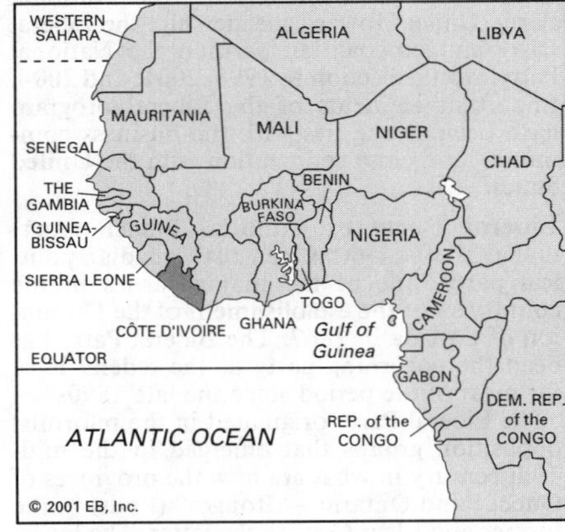

Liberia

The land. Liberia's coastal terrain, extending approximately 350 miles (560 km) along the Atlantic Ocean, is sandy, low, and interspersed with lagoons and mangrove swamps. Inland is a belt of low rolling hills running parallel to the coast for most of its length. Dense tropical rain forest blankets much of this belt. Farther inland is a dissected plateau with scattered low mountains, varying in elevation from 600 to 2,000 feet (180 to 600 m) above sea level, where the forest is less dense. Mount Nimba, near the Guinea frontier, is the nation's highest mountain, with a peak of 4,540 feet (1,380 m) at Guest House Hill. The country's major rivers flow southwestward into the Atlantic Ocean, and the Cavalla River, which separates Liberia from Côte d'Ivoire, is partly navigable.

The climate is warm year-round and has marked wet (May to October) and dry (November to April) seasons. The deforestation and drought conditions of the Sahel have lengthened the dry season in some areas. Mean annual temperatures range between 65° F (18° C) in the northern highlands to 80° F (27° C) along the coast. Yearly rainfall is as high as 200 inches (5,100 mm) on the coast, decreasing to about 70 inches (1,800 mm) in areas farthest inland. Roughly one-fifth of Liberia consists of tropical rainforest. Monkeys, chimpanzees, various antelopes, snakes, and crocodiles are common, but other animals, such as elephants and leopards, are gradually disappearing.

The people. The people most closely associated with the founding of the Liberian state were black freedmen (freed slaves) from the New World. Known historically as Americo-Liberians, they migrated to Liberia from the United States mostly between 1820 and 1865. Blacks from the Americas have continued to migrate intermittently, but Americo-Liberians have remained a minority of the country's population. The languages of Liberia's African indigenous peoples all are from the Mande, Kwa, Kru, or Atlantic branches of the Niger-Congo language family. The Mande, including the Kpelle, Loma, and Mano tribes, inhabit northern, northwestern, and central Liberia, as well as other nearby countries. The Kwa and Kru include the Bassa, De, Grebo, and Kru tribes of the coast and the Krahn (Kran), Sapo, and other tribes of the interior and southern half of the country. The Atlantic group comprises mostly the Gola and Kissi in the north. The country's official language is English. About two-thirds of the population practice traditional religious beliefs, about one-sixth are Muslim, and almost one-fifth are Christian.

More than two-fifths of Liberia's population is age 15 or younger. The birth and death rates are high by world standards, as is the annual population growth rate. More than half of the population is rural.

Economy. Liberia has a developing market economy that is largely based on agriculture and iron-ore exports. Economic growth, particularly in the iron-ore industry, was steadily undercut during the late 20th century by rising fuel costs, civil war, and other problems. The gross national product (GNP) is not growing as rapidly as the population.

Agriculture accounts for about one-third of the gross domestic product (GDP) and employs more than two-thirds of the workforce. The principal cash crops are rubber and logs and timber. The rubber industry is dominated by plantations owned by large foreign companies. Its exports generally have accounted for almost 10 percent of the GNP, but by the early 21st century they had risen to more than half, as other sectors were depressed. The staple crops are cassava and rice. Liberia's forest resources are extensive.

Manufacturing and mining account for somewhat less than one-fifth of the GDP but employ only a small portion of the workforce. Few secondary industries based on iron ore or rubber have been established, and import-substitution goods predominate in manufacturing. The infrastructure had been developing rapidly but was undermined by years of war.

The Liberian government officially encourages private foreign investment in order to stimulate development. Substantial foreign aid for development is provided as grants and loans from a variety of Western countries, particularly the United States, as well as the International Monetary Fund and the World Bank. Exports include mainly rubber and wood. Imports consist of machinery and transport equipment, fuels, basic manufactures, and foodstuffs. Chief trading partners include South Korea, Japan, Norway, and Germany.

Government and social conditions. Following a coup in 1980, Liberia came under military rule. Under the new constitution, approved by national referendum in 1984 and in effect since 1986, the elected president is the head of state, head of government, and commander in chief of the armed forces. The legislature consists of a 26-member Senate and a 64-member House of Representatives. Following the outbreak of civil war in 1990, an interim president took office; pending presidential and general elections, he has governed in association with a multiparty cabinet and an interim National Assembly. The highest judicial body is the People's Supreme Court; its justices are appointed by the president with the consent of the Senate.

Since 1939 education has been compulsory for children between ages 7 and 16. Six years of primary-school education are followed by three in middle school and three in high school. Less than half of the children of school age, however, attend school. The University of Liberia (dating to 1851) is in Monrovia.

Health and housing conditions have remained poor, although progress has been made in providing better health facilities. The standard of living in Liberia is also poor, and wages are extremely low by Western standards. Economic and social divisions are more keenly felt between the coastal and rural areas because a cash economy is relatively new inland.

History. Liberia is Africa's oldest republic. It was originally intended to be a home for freed American slaves under the auspices of the American Colonization Society (founded 1816). The society established a small colony at Cape Mesurado (Montserrado) in 1821–22. In late 1822 Jehudi Ashmun, a Methodist minister, became the director of the settlement and Liberia's real founder. In 1824 the colony was named Liberia, and its main settlement was named Monrovia. Joseph Jenkins Roberts, Liberia's first nonwhite governor, proclaimed Liberian independence in 1847, expanded its boundaries, and worked to end the illicit slave trade on Africa's western coast.

Border disputes with the French and British lasted until 1892, when the final treaty defining Liberia's boundaries was signed. French encroachment continued, however, and in 1919 an agreement was signed transferring to France 2,000 square miles (5,180 square km) of hinterland that Liberia could not control.

Liberia's economic situation deteriorated steadily into the 20th century. Unable to pay off its loans, Liberia granted a 1,000,000-acre (400,000-hectare) concession to the Firestone Tire and Rubber Company in 1926 and received a $5,000,000 loan to pay off foreign obligations. The loan further taxed the country, which later became embroiled in a League of Nations investigation (1931) into charges of complicity in forced labour and slavery activities. The government resigned, and new arrangements were negotiated with Firestone that put Liberia on the road to recovery.

The value of Liberia's rubber during World War II led the United States to sign a defense agreement that also resulted in the building of roads, an international airport, and a deepwater harbour at Monrovia.

President William V.S. Tubman was Liberia's president from 1944 until his death in 1971. His successor was overthrown in a 1980 coup that terminated more than a century of rule by the True Whig Party and also marked the end of the Americo-Liberians' long political dominance over the indigenous, inland-dwelling Africans. Presidential and legislative elections were held in 1985; General (formerly Master Sergeant) Samuel K. Doe, leader of the 1980 coup and subsequent military ruler of Liberia, was elected president and took office in 1986. In 1989 a rebellion broke out that developed into a countrywide civil war. Doe was assassinated; bitter ethnic and political rivalries racked the nation for several years despite the intervention of the Economic Community of West African States (ECOWAS) and the United Nations. A truce was finally achieved, and elections were held in 1997. Charles Taylor of the National Patriotic Front of Liberia Party, who had launched the civil war, was victorious with a large legislative majority. Government troops, however, were unable to keep peace after the withdrawal of peacekeeping troops two years later. In 2003 Taylor was forced into exile, and the UN took over peacekeeping operations.

Consult the INDEX *first*

Liberius (b. Rome [Italy]—d. Sept. 24, 366, Rome), pope from 352 to 366. He was elected on May 17, 352, to succeed Pope St. Julius I.

Liberius was pope during the turbulence caused by the rise of Arianism—a heresy teaching that Christ was not truly divine but was rather a created being. Liberius was pope under the Arian Roman emperor Constantius II, who opposed both the Council of Nicaea (which had condemned Arianism) and Bishop St. Athanasius of Alexandria (who was Arianism's most virulent opponent). Liberius' first act as pope was to write Constantius requesting a council at Aquileia, Italy, to discuss Athanasius, but the emperor independently effected Athanasius' condemnation. In 355 Liberius was one of the few bishops who refused to sign the condemnation, which had been imposed at Milan by imperial command upon all the Western bishops. Consequently, Constantius exiled Liberius to Beroea (modern Véroia, Greece), and the Arian archdeacon Felix (II) appropriated the papacy.

In late 357 Liberius went to Sirmium (modern Sremska Mitrovica, Serb.-Mont.). Supposedly dejected, he agreed to sign certain unorthodox formulas that served to emasculate the Nicene Creed (the creed had implicitly disavowed Arianism). Liberius also agreed to sever relations with Athanasius and submitted to the authority of the emperor. But Constantius recalled him to Rome, where he returned in 358, joyfully received by the Roman Christians. Felix fled to Porto, Italy, but Constantius decreed that Felix and Liberius should corule.

Although this imperial order was disregarded, Liberius' prestige was impaired. Neither he nor Felix was invited to the great council that met at Rimini, Italy, in 359 to terminate the Arian crisis. This temporary humiliation prevented the papacy's involvement in the council's capitulation to imperial despotism and in its compromise with heresy. After Constantius' death in 361, Liberius annulled the decrees of Rimini. In 362, with his authority renewed, he received some Eastern bishops and had them profess the Nicene faith and anathematize the formulary of Rimini. The curious phenomenon of the papacy's double occupation ended when Felix died in 365.

libertarianism, political philosophy that takes individual liberty to be the primary political value. It is properly understood as a form of liberalism.

Liberalism seeks to define and justify the legitimate powers of government in terms of certain natural rights, such as the rights to life, liberty, private property, freedom of speech and association, freedom of worship, government by consent, equality under the law, and moral autonomy. According to liberals, government exists solely to protect those rights, and government power should be limited to that which is necessary to accomplish that task. Libertarians are liberals who strongly emphasize the individual right to liberty. They believe that individuals should be free to behave and to dispose of their property as they see fit, provided that their actions do not infringe on the equal freedom of others.

Historical origins. Both liberalism and libertarianism trace their roots to ancient Israel and ancient Greece, whose religious and intellectual traditions accepted the idea of a higher moral law, and to Christian theologians such as Tertullian and St. Thomas Aquinas, who stressed the moral worth of the individual. In the late Middle Ages, libertarians opposed the growth of royal absolutism. During the English Civil Wars (1642–51) the radical Levelers produced the first coherent statement of libertarian principles, including "self-ownership" (the right of each individual to exclusive control of his choices, actions, and body), private property, legal equality, religious toleration, and limited, representative government. In the late 17th century, John Locke developed a theory of natural rights, including the right to private property and to government by consent, that served as a philosophical foundation of libertarianism. In the 18th century, Adam Smith's studies of free markets greatly advanced the liberal theory of "spontaneous order," according to which some aspects of society arise naturally and spontaneously, without central direction, from the independent activities of individuals.

In the United States Declaration of Independence (1776), Thomas Jefferson enunciated many liberal and libertarian ideas, including the belief in "unalienable Rights" to "Life, Liberty, and the pursuit of Happiness" and the belief in the "right" and "duty" of citizens to "throw off such Government" that violates those rights. In the late 19th and early 20th centuries, as liberal governments established themselves in the United States and Europe, many liberals worried that persistent inequalities of wealth were undermining democracy and threatening other liberal values. They advocated government regulation of markets, heavier taxation of the rich, and the introduction of various government-funded social services. Meanwhile, classical liberals insisted that the welfare of the poor would be best served by free markets and minimal government. As liberalism became increasingly associated with government intervention, some classical liberals abandoned the old term and began to call themselves "libertarians."

Libertarian philosophy. Libertarians have sought to define the proper extent of individual liberty in terms of the notion of self-ownership. Because no individual has the right to control the peaceful activities of other self-owning individuals—*e.g.*, their religious practices, their occupations, or their pastimes—no such power can be properly delegated to government. Legitimate governments are therefore severely limited in their authority. Because government power is inherently dangerous, it should be limited and divided through a written constitution and a system of checks and balances.

Libertarians believe that all acts of aggression against the rights of others are unjust and that the primary purpose of government is to protect citizens from the illegitimate use of force. They embrace individualism insofar as they attach supreme importance to the rights and freedoms of individuals. Another aspect of libertarian individualism is its insistence on understanding the legal order in terms of the individual rather than the group or the state.

In keeping with the theory of spontaneous order, libertarians hold that the most important institutions of human society—such as language, law, customs, money, and markets—develop by themselves, without central direction. Free markets, according to libertarians, are necessary for the production of wealth and indeed for individual survival and flourishing. Accordingly they believe that self-help, mutual aid, charity, and economic growth do more to alleviate poverty than government social-welfare programs.

Libertarians consider the rule of law to be a crucial underpinning of a free society. Laws should be generally applicable and publicly known and not subject to the arbitrary decisions of kings, presidents, or bureaucrats.

Contemporary libertarianism. In the early 21st century the political and economic systems of most Western countries—especially the United Kingdom and the United States—continued to be based largely on classical liberal principles. Accordingly, libertarians tended to focus on smaller deviations from liberal principles, creating the perception among many that their views were radical or extreme. Libertarian political parties have generally garnered little support, even among self-professed libertarians. Most politically active libertarians support classical liberal parties (such as the Free Democratic Party in Germany) or conservative parties (such as the Republican Party in the United States or the Conservative Party in Great Britain). (Da.D.B.)

Liberty, Sons of, organizations formed in the American colonies in the summer of 1765 to oppose the Stamp Act. They took their name from a speech given in the British Parliament by Isaac Barré (February 1765), in which he referred to the colonials who had opposed unjust British measures as the "sons of liberty." They rallied support for colonial resistance through the use of petitions, assemblies, and propaganda, and they sometimes resorted to violence against officials of the mother country. Instrumental in preventing the enforcement of the Stamp Act, they remained an active pre-Revolutionary force against the crown.

Liberty, Statue of: *see* Statue of Liberty.

Liberty Bell, large bell, a traditional symbol of U.S. freedom, commissioned in 1751 by the Pennsylvania Provincial Assembly to hang in the new State House (renamed Independence Hall) in Philadelphia. It was cast in London by the Whitechapel Bell Foundry, purchased for about £100, and delivered in August 1752. It was cracked by a stroke of the clapper while being tested and was twice recast in Philadelphia before being hung in the State House steeple in June 1753. It weighs about 2,080 pounds (943 kilograms), is 12 feet (3.7 metres) in circumference around the lip, and measures 3 feet from lip to crown. It bears the motto, "Proclaim liberty throughout all the land unto all the inhabitants thereof" (Leviticus 25:10).

The legend that on July 4, 1776, the bell was rung to signal the Continental Congress' adoption of the Declaration of Independence is untrue; it was rung four days later on July 8 to celebrate the first public reading of the document. In 1777, when British forces entered Philadelphia, it was hidden in an Allentown, Pa., church. Restored to Independence Hall, it cracked, according to tradition, while tolling for the funeral of Chief Justice John Marshall in 1835. The name "Liberty Bell" was first applied in 1839 in an abolitionist pamphlet. It was rung for the last time for George Washington's birthday in 1846, during which it cracked irreparably. On Jan. 1, 1976, the bell was moved to a new pavilion about 100 yards from Independence Hall.

Liberty Island, formerly (until 1956) BEDLOE'S ISLAND, island off the southern tip of Manhattan Island, New York City, U.S., in Upper New York Bay. It has an area of about 10 acres (4 hectares) and is the site of Bartholdi's "Liberty Enlightening the World" (*see* Statue of Liberty) and of the American Museum of Immigration. Known to the Mohegans as Minnissais and to early colonists as Great Oyster Bay, it was renamed for Isaack Bedloo, who bought it in the 1660s. The city of New York acquired it in 1758, and it was ceded to the federal government in 1796. It was the site of U.S. Ft. Wood (1841–1937) until the National Park Service gained jurisdiction.

Liberty Party, U.S. political party (1840–48) created by abolitionists who believed in political action to further antislavery goals. Organized in Warsaw, N.Y., the party nominated James G. Birney, a Kentuckian and former slaveholder, for president. The party's first national convention took place at Albany, N.Y., on April 1, 1840, when Birney's nomination was confirmed. Liberty Party supporters hoped to dramatize the antislavery issue, pressure legislators into taking firmer antislavery positions, prevent slavery from extending beyond the states where it existed into the federal territories, and eradicate both the interstate slave trade and the institution itself within the boundaries of the nation's capital.

Although the Liberty Party collected only 7,000 votes in 1840, it raised that total to 62,000 in 1844 (when Birney was again its candidate), probably denying the state of New York—and with it the presidency—to Henry Clay. In January 1848 the party nominated John P. Hale, who later withdrew from the race. The Liberty Party dissolved when many of its members joined "Barnburner" Democrats and "Conscience" Whigs in forming the Free-Soil Party (Aug. 9, 1848).

Libertyville, village, northern suburb of Chicago, Lake county, northeastern Illinois, U.S., on the Des Plaines River. It was founded in 1836 by settlers from New England and originally called Independence Grove. The patriotic theme was continued when it was renamed in 1837. Mainly residential, Libertyville has some industry, including telecommunications and plastics manufacture. Inc. 1882. Pop. (2003 est.) 21,113.

liberum veto, in Polish history, the legal right of each member of the Sejm (legislature) to defeat by his vote alone any measure under consideration or to dissolve the Sejm and nullify all acts passed during its session. Based on the assumption that all members of the Polish nobility were absolutely equal politically, the veto meant, in practice, that every bill introduced into the Sejm had to be passed unanimously. It was first used to dissolve a session of the Sejm in 1652. Subsequently, it was used extensively, often paralyzing the government, making a centralization of power (opposed by nobles jealous of their independence) impossible, and leaving Poland vulnerable to the influence of foreign powers, which habitually bribed delegates to the Sejm to force the adjournment of sessions that threatened to pass legislation contrary to their interests.

Although King Stanisław II August Poniatowski (ruled 1764–95) attempted to make constitutional reforms, among them a limitation upon the right of liberum veto, he succeeded only in provoking a civil war and Russian military intervention (1767), which culminated in the First Partition of Poland (1772). Only after Poland suffered these misfortunes did its political leaders adopt the Constitution of May 3, 1791, which abolished the liberum veto.

libido, concept originated by Sigmund Freud to signify the instinctual physiological or psychic energy associated with sexual urges and, in his later writings, with all constructive human activity. In the latter sense of eros, or life instinct, libido was opposed by thanatos, the death instinct and source of destructive urges; the interaction of the two produced all the variations of human activity. Freud considered psychiatric symptoms the result of misdirection or inadequate discharge of libido.

Carl Jung used the term in a more expansive sense, encompassing all life processes in all species. Later theories of motivation have substituted for libido such related terms as drive and tension.

Libitina, in Roman religion, goddess of funerals. At her sanctuary in a sacred grove (perhaps on the Esquiline Hill), a piece of money was deposited whenever a death occurred. There the undertakers (*libitinarii*) had their offices, and there all deaths were registered for statistical purposes. The word Libitina thus came to be used for the business of an undertaker, funeral requisites, and, by poets, for death itself.

Libitina was often mistakenly identified with Venus Lubentia (Lubentina), an Italian goddess of gardens. Libitina may have been originally an earth goddess connected with luxuriant nature and the enjoyments of life; because all such deities were connected with the underworld, she also became the goddess of death, that side of her character predominating in later conceptions.

Lībīyah, aṣ-Ṣaḥrā' al- (Africa): *see* Libyan Desert.

Libourne, town, Gironde *département,* Aquitaine *région,* southwestern France. Libourne lies northeast of Bordeaux, at the confluence of the Isle and Dordogne rivers. It is a port for ocean-going vessels and is the centre of a wine-producing district. Libourne (Leybornia) takes its name from Roger de Leyburn, English seneschal of Gascony, who founded it as a *bastide* (fortified town) in 1270. It was united to France in the 15th century. Its Clocktower Gate dates from the 14th century and its town hall from the 16th. Pop. (1990) 21,931.

Old tower gate, Libourne, Fr.
Richard Chatagneau

Libra (Latin: "Balance"), in astronomy, zodiacal constellation lying between Scorpius and Virgo, at about 15 hours 30 minutes right ascension (the coordinate on the celestial sphere analogous to longitude on the Earth) and 15° south declination (angular distance south of the celestial equator). Its stars are faint.

In astrology, Libra is the seventh sign of the zodiac, considered as governing the period from about September 22 to October 23. It is represented by a woman (sometimes identified with Astraea, the Roman goddess of justice), holding a balance scale or by the balance alone.

Libra, illumination from a Book of Hours, Italian, *c.* 1475; in the Pierpont Morgan Library, New York City (MS. G.14)
By courtesy of the Pierpont Morgan Library, New York, the Glazier Collection

libra, the basic Roman unit of weight, equal to 0.722 pounds avoirdupois (1.59 kg). The abbreviation "lb" for pound is derived from libra. One-twelfth of the libra, the Roman uncia, is the ancestor of the English ounce.

The libra also is one of the nonmetric units of weight still used today in Spain, Portugal, and several Spanish-speaking countries of the Americas. Most of the New World libras weigh about the same as the U.S. avoirdupois pound.

Librairie Larousse (French publishing house): *see* Larousse.

library, collection of books used for reading or study, or the building or room in which such a collection is kept. The word derives from the Latin *liber,* "a book," whereas a Latinized Greek word, *bibliotheca,* is the origin of the word for library in German, Russian, and the Romance languages. Today's libraries frequently contain periodicals, microfilms, tapes, videos, compact discs, online services, and other materials, as well as books.

A brief treatment of libraries follows. For full treatment, *see* MACROPAEDIA: Libraries.

History. The origin of libraries lies in the practice of keeping records; as early as the 3rd millennium BC, records on clay tablets were stored in a temple in the Babylonian town of Nippur. In the 7th century BC the Assyrian king Ashurbanipal assembled and organized a collection of records, of which some 20,000 tablets and fragments have survived. The first libraries as repositories of books were those of the Greek temples and those established in conjunction with the Greek schools of philosophy (4th century BC). Important libraries of the ancient world were those of Aristotle, the great Library of Alexandria with its thousands of papyrus and vellum scrolls, its rival at Pergamum that included many works on parchment, the Bibliotheca Ulpia of Rome, and the Imperial Library at Byzantium set up by Constantine the Great in the 4th century AD. China also has a long tradition of record keeping and book collecting, in private libraries as well as in centralized government libraries.

Extant Greek and Roman literary works were preserved alongside the early Christian literature in Constantine's library and (beginning in the 2nd century) in libraries of monasteries. These libraries were joined by those of the universities—founded in the 13th century in Europe—as learning centres in the late Middle Ages.

The Renaissance witnessed the beginning of changes in society that were to produce decisive effects on the size and function of libraries down to modern times: the growth of mercantilism and the beginnings of a middle class; an interest in the new humanist learning, owing in part to the rediscovered classical texts; the invention of printing; and widening literacy.

Religious wars and political and even intellectual revolutions intermittently interfered with the growth of libraries. For example, in England an edict from Henry VIII reflecting the humanist rejection of the old learning of the Middle Ages resulted in the dispersion of the collections of the monastic libraries and the destruction of countless manuscripts.

The 17th and 18th centuries saw the amassing of great private collections, many of which became the basis of modern national libraries such as France's Bibliothèque Nationale and the library of the British Museum (later part of the British Library). The U.S. Library of Congress in Washington, D.C., and the Lenin Library (now the Russian State Library) in Moscow were begun in 1800 and 1917, respectively. The National Library of Peking and the National Diet Library in Tokyo are among the world's largest libraries. In many cases, national libraries also began to serve as repositories of all copyrighted published materials. University libraries that rivaled the national collections were begun at Oxford in 1602 and Harvard in 1638. Free town and school libraries also proliferated, and in the late 18th century subscription libraries—which circulated books and provided reference services to paying members—became common.

Main reading room in the Russian State Library, Moscow; built 1930
Tass—Sovfoto

Library architecture. The principles of library architecture have changed in response to changes in the rarity (and preciousness) of books. Handwritten books and the earlier printed books were rare and valuable objects that had to be protected from theft, and so in the libraries of medieval monasteries and cathedrals, the large folios (books made of paper folded once) and quartos (with sheets folded into fourths) were chained to cupboards and could be used only at the attached desks. The long rooms of benches and stalls gradually gave way to wall shelving when printed books began to be produced in smaller sizes and became less expensive. Opening the stacks (bookstacks) to readers in the late 19th century meant that books had to be accessible on lower shelves and arranged according to a simple system. After World War II, modular systems were deemed most functional for libraries that were adapting to the needs of growing numbers of users.

Types. Libraries are usually classified in one of two ways: by ownership or purpose (*e.g.,* national, county or municipal, university, research, school, industrial, club, private) or by subject content (*e.g.,* general or special, the latter including medical, legal, theological, scientific, engineering, music). Many of these institutions are lending libraries, from which users may borrow books for a limited time. The 20th century has seen an increase in special libraries to keep up with the publication—frequently in periodicals—of information in the sciences, engineering, medicine, business, and law. These libraries act as information services (with access to references and bibliographies) as well as repositories for books and periodicals, and they are often sponsored by industry or professional associations. Some general libraries contain special collections or departments.

Large libraries such as the Russian State Library have complex systems of organization—with many catalogs, indexes, and a large staff—while small private libraries have a much simpler arrangement. Faced with the astounding growth of information as well as a multiplicity of tools for information processing, modern libraries have had to incorporate sophisticated mechanical and electronic systems for searching and retrieving. While providing greater efficiency than such methods as card catalog searches, these systems generally require some form of training. They have both increased user accessibility and changed the role of the librarian and the very perception of the library as an institution.

Library operations and use. All libraries follow some selection policy because facilities and budgets do not allow acquisition of all published materials. Public libraries must endure a continuing struggle between the need to provide recreational materials for the majority of users and the need to satisfy the specific demands of intellectually elite minorities. Many libraries can make available to their patrons the use of information not in their own collection by borrowing materials from other collections and libraries through a well-developed system of interlibrary loans. In the late 20th century, many of the larger libraries also enabled their patrons to electronically search remote databases and not only to capture a wide variety of enhanced information, such as abstracts, but also, on occasion, to obtain full-text documents.

Once the desired books have been obtained, librarians must initiate the cataloging process. Cataloging consists of listing the bibliographic descriptions of materials—usually by author, title, and subject or by some combination of these. Books and other library materials are usually cataloged by cataloging agencies in national libraries, such as the Library of Congress, and by other large libraries. The resulting information is made available to other libraries, which in turn can use computers to search the catalog records and display them to their users. Although card catalogs are still common, many libraries rely entirely on computerized catalogs that allow their users to search by author, title, subject, keyword, or some combination of these.

In addition to cataloging, the organization of materials involves the assignment of classification numbers, a function that groups similar materials together. By means of the classification system, the user can locate a particular book and can also find other books that treat the same subject. The most common classification systems in use in the United States are the Dewey Decimal Classification and the Library of Congress Classification (*qq.v.*). (*See also* Bliss Classification; Colon Classification.)

Another service of libraries is that of preservation. Most books, journals, and newspapers printed in the 19th and 20th centuries will soon become brittle and crumble into dust. A number of libraries are involved in the attempt to save these materials from disintegration, usually by reformatting them. Other, more evident services provided by libraries include the circulation of reading materials, instruction in library use, general information services offered by reference departments, and specialized information services such as Selective Dissemination of Information (SDI) or the use of computerized information-retrieval systems. These and a number of additional information services—depending on the type of library—provide users with ready access to a wide variety of information that can be used for education, recreation, and general interest. *See also* information science.

library classification, system of arrangement adopted by a library to enable patrons to find its materials quickly and easily. While cataloging provides information on the physical and topical nature of the book (or other item), classification, through assignment of a call number (consisting of class designation and author representation), locates the item in its library setting and, ideally, in the realm of knowledge. Arranging similar things in some order according to some principle unites and controls information from various sources.

Classification can be distinguished by type: (1) natural, or fundamental—*e.g.,* books by subject, (2) accidental—*e.g.,* chronological or geographic, and (3) artificial—*e.g.,* by alphabet, linguistic base, form, size, or numerical order. Degree of classification (*e.g.,* close, with the most minute subdivisions, or broad, with omission of detailed subdivisions) may also characterize a system. Several systems of classification have been developed to provide the type of access and control that a particular library and its clientele need. Generally, each system consists of a scheme that arranges knowledge in terms of stated principles into classes, then divisions and subdivisions.

Current predominating systems include the Dewey Decimal Classification, the Library of Congress Classification, the Bliss Classification, and the Colon Classification (*qq.v.*); many special and research libraries devise their own unique systems.

Library of Congress: *see* Congress, Library of.

Library of Congress Classification, byname LC CLASSIFICATION, system of library organization developed during the reorganization of the U.S. Library of Congress. It consists of separate, mutually exclusive, special classifications, often having no connection save the accidental one of alphabetical notation.

Unlike the Dewey Decimal Classification, this system was based on an actual collection of some million books and incorporated the best features of existing systems with individual subject schemes or schedules devised by subject specialists. The arrangement, based on the order devised by the American librarian Charles Cutter in *Expansive Classification* (1891–93), roughly follows groupings of social sciences, humanities, and natural and physical sciences. It divides the field of knowledge into 20 large classes and an additional class for general works. Each main class has a synopsis that also serves as a guide. The resulting order is from the general to the specific and from the theoretical to the practical.

Special features include differentiation between general and general specific (books treating general works in a special way); minute groupings of subjects and geographic places for individual titles; and association of subject by country rather than topic in certain classes (philosophy, social sciences, political sciences). The quarterly appearance of LC Classification schedules testifies to the constant revision.

The Library of Congress does not publish a general index to the classification schedules, but a *Combined Indexes to the Library of Congress Classification Schedules,* compiled by Nancy B. Olson, was published independently in 1975. In place of standard subdivisions, each class may incorporate divisions for literary form and geography. Terminology may be explicit, exact, scientific, or popular, depending on the situation. There is no attempt to give mnemonic (memory) aids, and the fullness of each class varies. Subdivisions in the Library of Congress system are arranged roughly on a historical basis, and the notation is mixed: capital letters (single and double sets) and Arabic numerals. More combinations and, hence, greater specificity is possible, yet excessively long notations do not occur. Hence, university, special, and government libraries favour its use.

library science, the principles and practices of library operation and administration, and their study. Libraries have existed since ancient times, but only in the second half of the 19th century did library science emerge as a separate field of study. With the knowledge explosion in the 20th century, it was gradually subsumed under the more general field of information science (*q.v.*).

By the second half of the 19th century, Western countries had experienced such a proliferation of books of all sorts that the nature of the librarian's work was radically altered; being well-read was no longer a sufficient characteristic for the post. The librarian needed some means of easy and rapid identification as well as strong organizational and administrative skills, and the necessity for specialized training soon became clear. One of the earliest pioneers in library training in the United States was Melvil Dewey (*q.v.*), who established the first training program for librarians in 1887. These training programs in the United States evolved into graduate programs in library education accredited by the American Library Association (ALA; founded 1876).

In the 20th century, advances in the means of collecting, organizing, and retrieving information changed the focus of libraries, enabling a great variety of institutions and organizations, as well as individuals, to conduct their own searches for information without the involvement of a library or library staff. As a result, universities began to offer combined graduate programs in library science and information science. These programs usually provide a master's degree and may provide more advanced degrees, including doctorates. Particulars of admission and course requirements vary from school to school. In the United States and Canada, the appropriateness of graduate programs in library and information science in preparing students to become professional librarians is still ensured by accreditation by the ALA. Increasingly, however, graduates of these programs are finding themselves qualified for a variety of professional positions in other parts of the information industry.

In many countries the furtherance of librarianship and library systems is promoted by national and regional library associations. The Chicago-based ALA, for example, in addition to its promotion of library service and librarianship, has an extensive publishing program and holds annual national conferences. Professional associations of a similar nature exist throughout the world.

libration, in astronomy, an oscillation, apparent or real, of a satellite, such as the Moon, the surface of which may as a consequence be seen from different angles at different times from one point on its primary body.

The latitudinal libration of the Moon occurs

because its axis is tilted slightly, relative to the plane of its orbit around the Earth; this makes the Moon's north and south poles apparently alternate in tipping slightly toward the Earth as the Moon moves through its orbit. The Moon's longitudinal libration (a back and forth turning, a "headshaking" motion) results from its moving at slightly different speeds at different points in its orbit (in accord with Kepler's second law).

These and other small librations allow about 59 percent of the Moon's surface to be seen from Earth, though it presents nearly the same face to the Earth at all times.

libretto (Italian: "booklet"), plural LIBRETTOS, or LIBRETTI, text of an opera, operetta, or other kind of musical theatre. It is also used, less commonly, of a musical work not intended for the stage. A libretto may be in verse or in prose; it may be specially designed for a particular composer, or it may provide raw material for several; it may be wholly original or an adaptation of an existing play or novel.

Writing a libretto demands techniques different from those for writing spoken drama. Music moves at a slower pace than speech, and an orchestra can suggest emotions that would need to be made explicit in a play. When sung, elaborate literary artifices and unnatural word orders would present audiences with unnecessary problems, but simple words and repetitions of phrases provide aids to understanding.

The earliest operas, beginning in 1597 with Ottavio Rinuccini's *Dafne,* set to music by Jacopo Peri, were court entertainments, and as a commemoration the words were printed in a small book, or "libretto." In the 1630s Venetian opera became a public spectacle, and audiences used printed librettos to follow the drama. The early French and Italian librettists regarded their works as poetic dramas, and the composer was expected to pay faithful regard to the accents of the words. A tendency to more lyrical treatment of the text developed in Venice, however, and purely musical demands began to outweigh strict subservience to the poetry. Despite the enhancement of the composer's role, full operatic scores were rarely printed. It was usually only the librettist who saw his name in print.

The early 17th-century librettists drew their subject matter from pastoral drama of the 16th century, which dealt with mythological subjects, as in Alessandro Striggio's *Orfeo* (1607), set to music by Claudio Monteverdi. Other trends soon developed. In 1642 Gian Francesco Busenello based his *L'incoronazione di Poppea* (*The Coronation of Poppea,* music by Monteverdi) on incidents in the life of Nero, and, from that point on, historical subjects became increasingly popular. While they appealed to the common people by the inclusion of love intrigues that were not required to reflect historical occurrence, historical librettos that portrayed magnanimous rulers flattered the aristocracy on whom many opera centres were financially dependent.

The style of 18th-century librettos was exemplified by Pietro Metastasio and by Apostolo Zeno, both of whom aimed at raising libretto standards by banishing comic characters from serious opera and creating a lofty poetic drama. Their elevated style eventually came under criticism as unnatural and occasionally absurd. The movement for reform was most noticeable in the works of Christoph Gluck. Ranieri Calzabigi, working closely with Gluck, wrote the libretto for *Orfeo ed Euridice;* the result, in marked contrast with contemporary librettos, supported Gluck's musical aims of simplicity and profundity.

In the late 18th century, librettists began to turn aside from mythology and antiquity. In contrast to serious opera, comic opera had always dealt with subjects from real life, and it now became the framework for works that were largely serious in intention. An example of this approach is Mozart's *Die Zauberflöte* (1791; *The Magic Flute*), to Emanuel Schikaneder's libretto. After the French Revolution (1789) the "rescue opera" with its theme of resistance to tyranny became popular, culminating in Beethoven's *Fidelio,* based on Jean-Nicolas Bouilly's play *Léonore.*

Nineteenth-century Romanticism encouraged texts dealing with medieval history and legends of the supernatural, such as Friedrich Kind's libretto for Carl Maria von Weber's *Der Freischütz* (1821; *The Freeshooter*) and the librettos written for Giacomo Meyerbeer by Eugène Scribe, *e.g., Les Huguenots* (1836). Exotic subjects and themes drawn from folklore and regional culture found their way into 19th- and 20th-century librettos, among them Karel Sabina's for Bedřich Smetana's *The Bartered Bride* (1866) and Giacomo Puccini's *Turandot* (1926), adapted from the Oriental fable of Carlo Gozzi. Demand for librettos of high literary quality also rose; Richard Wagner wrote his own, as did Hector Berlioz (*e.g., Les Troyens,* 1858; *The Trojans*) and such later composers as Alban Berg, Leoš Janáček, Arnold Schoenberg, and Gian Carlo Menotti.

Close collaboration between librettist and composer provided another solution to the question of textual quality. Perhaps the best example of successful partnership is that of Hugo von Hofmannsthal and Richard Strauss, who collaborated on *Elektra* (1909), *Der Rosenkavalier* (1911), two versions of *Ariadne auf Naxos* (1912 and 1916), *Die Frau ohne Schatten* (1919), *Die ägyptische Helena* (1928), and *Arabella* (produced—after von Hofmannsthal's death—in 1933).

Among the rare successful uses of spoken-drama texts are Claude Debussy's setting of Maurice Maeterlinck's *Pelléas et Mélisande* (1902) and Richard Strauss's setting of Oscar Wilde's *Salomé* (1905). The growth of realism in spoken drama also influenced opera, notably in Georges Bizet's *Carmen* (1875), based on Prosper Mérimée's novel.

Libreville, city and capital of Gabon, located on the north shore of the Gabon Estuary, which empties into the Gulf of Guinea. It is built on a succession of hills overlooking a well-sheltered port. The former European sector (modern in appearance and the site of the principal administrative and commercial buildings) climbs a plateau that rises from the sea; traditional African villages partially surround this community, ending at the estuary. The international airport is 7 miles (11 km) north, and a growing system of roads links the city with towns in the interior.

Libreville, Gabon, on the Gabon Estuary

Art Resource

Pongoue (Mpongwe) people first settled the estuary after the 16th century, followed by the Fang, who had migrated south from the Cameroon area, in the 19th century. Fort-d'Aumale was built by the French in 1843 on the estuary's north bank, and a Catholic mission was founded a year later. In 1849 a settlement of freed slaves from the ship "Elizia" and a group of Pongoue villages were given the name Libreville (meaning "free town"). In 1850 the French abandoned their fort and resettled on the plateau that is now the site of the administrative and commercial sector. Between 1860 and 1874, the British, Germans, and Americans established businesses in Libreville, which from 1888 to 1904 was the capital of French Equatorial Africa.

Although second to Port-Gentil as a port and economic centre, Libreville is well industrialized and is the educational centre for Gabon. It is the site of the Omar Bongo University (1970), a library (1960), and research institutes for tropical agriculture and livestock, geology and mining, and forestry. A modern hospital, Roman Catholic and Protestant churches, and a mosque also serve the community.

Industrial development caused the population to more than double in the 1960s. Both Libreville and the new deepwater port at Owendo, 9 miles (14.5 km) south-southeast, handle regional exports. Lumber has long been the major export (okoumé wood, ebony, walnut, mahogany), but cocoa, rubber, and palm products also are shipped overseas. Libreville's industries include sawmills, plywood and cloth-printing factories, and brewing, milling of flour, and shipbuilding. Oil was discovered offshore north of the city, and an experimental rice project began in the 1970s at Akok, 26 miles (42 km) east-northeast. The city saw widespread rioting and political unrest in 1990. Pop. (1993) 362,386.

Consult
the
INDEX
first

Libya, officially GREAT SOCIALIST PEOPLE'S LIBYAN ARAB JAMAHIRIYA, Arabic AL-JAMĀHĪRĪYAH AL-ʿARABĪYAH AL-LĪBĪYAH ASH-SHAʿBĪYAH AL-ISHTIRĀKĪYAH AL-ʿUẒMĀ, formerly SOCIALIST PEOPLE'S LIBYAN ARAB JAMAHIRIYA, country of North Africa along the Mediterranean coast, the fourth largest in Africa. The capital is Tripoli (though policy-making bodies often meet at Surt). Large parts of the country fall within the arid Sahara (desert), and it spans 820 miles (1,320 km) east to west. It is bordered to the west by Tunisia and Algeria, to the south by Niger and Chad, to the southeast by The Sudan, to the east by Egypt, and to the north by the Mediterranean Sea. Area 678,400 square miles (1,757,000 square km). Pop. (2002 est.) 5,365,000.

A brief treatment of Libya follows. For full treatment, *see* MACROPAEDIA: North Africa.

For current history and for statistics on society and economy, *see* BRITANNICA BOOK OF THE YEAR.

The land. Libya, with an average elevation of 600 to 2,000 feet (200 to 600 m) above sea

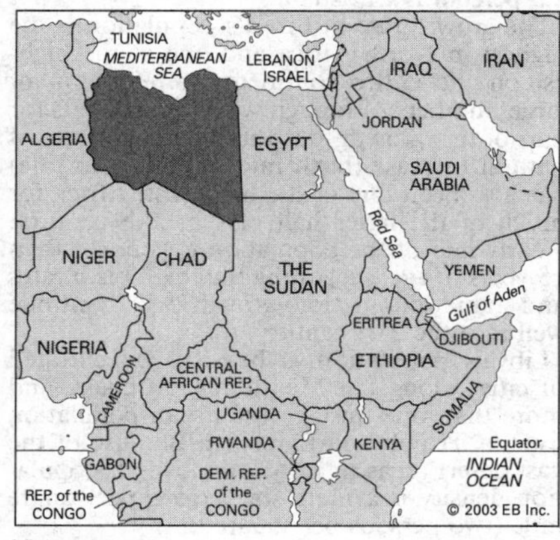

Libya

level, forms the northern slopes of the vast plateau of North Africa. It can be divided into three physiographic regions. All but two tiny fractions of Libya are covered by the Saharan plateau. The exceptions are the northwest corner, Tripolitania; and the northeast, Cyrenaica. Tripolitania (north to south) is a string of carefully cultivated coastal oases, the triangular Al-Jifārah plain (6,000 square miles [15,540 square km]), and the 200-mile- (320-kilometre-) long limestone Nafūsah Plateau (2,000 to 3,000 feet [600 to 915 m] in elevation). It is the most important agricultural area of Libya and its most populated. Cyrenaica's Al-Marj coastal plain gives way to the Akhḍar Mountains, which merge southward into semidesert grasslands. The vast Saharan plateau is largely composed of bare rock and wind-driven sand, with a few scattered oases. The sand dunes of the Fezzan region in the southwest rise several hundred feet in elevation and range to some 100 miles (160 km) in length. Beneath the Surt Basin in the north lie the country's major petroleum deposits. In the Tibesti Mountains of the south, Bette Peak, the highest point in the country, rises to 7,500 feet (2,286 m). There are no perennial rivers, but extensive underground aquifers support the artesian wells and springs that supply some 60 percent of the country's area.

Libya's arid desert climate is moderated along the coast by the Mediterranean Sea. Average January (winter) temperatures range from 52° F (11° C) in the north to 63° F (17° C) in the south; corresponding figures for July (summer) are 82° F (28° C) and 100° F (38° C). Precipitation ranges from 16 to 20 inches (400 to 500 mm) in the northern hills to less than 5 inches in most of the south, and 1 inch in the Libyan Desert. A drought of one or two years occurs every five or six years. Sabhā in the Fezzan region is one of the most arid places on Earth. Natural vegetation is minimal. Wildlife includes desert rodents, hyena, fox, jackal, gazelle, and wildcat. Eagles, hawks, and vultures are common.

Libya's principal mineral resource is its enormous reserves of petroleum, Africa's largest and among the world's largest. Apart from natural gas associated with the petroleum, other minerals include natron (hydrated sodium carbonate), manganese, gypsum, iron ore, and lignite (brown coal).

The people. The tribe, or *qabīlah,* remains the fundamental unit of Libya's social structure. Berbers, who were formerly the major ethnic group, have been largely assimilated into the Arab culture. Arabic is the principal language; a minority of Berbers speak their own Hamitic language, and many are bilingual. Italians, Greeks, Jews, and black Africans are among the other ethnic groups. Most of the population is Sunnite Muslim, and about 2.5 percent is Christian.

The growth rate of Libya's population is the highest in North Africa and one of the highest on the entire continent. Immigration of large numbers of foreign workers accounts for part of this growth, but Libya's annual rate of natural increase (birth rate minus death rate) has also been one of the highest in Africa for much of the latter half of the 20th century. Nearly half of the population is younger than 15 years of age, suggesting that high birth rates and rapid population growth will continue well into the 21st century.

Libya's population is heavily concentrated in cities along the Mediterranean coast, and more than one-third of the urban population lives in Tripoli and Banghāzī. Because of the vast desert areas in Libya, the overall population density is a mere six persons per square mile (two persons per square km).

The economy. Libya has a centrally planned economy based largely on the production and export of petroleum. The government controls almost all sectors of the economy. There is a shortage of skilled labour, and foreign technicians have been recruited to work in the oil fields and develop the country's infrastructure. The gross national product (GNP) declined with the drop in oil prices during the 1980s, but the GNP per capita has remained the highest in Africa.

Agriculture accounts for about 5 percent of the gross domestic product (GDP) but employs approximately one-fifth of the work force. Harvests of barley, the main staple, fluctuate from year to year, and Libya is not agriculturally self-sufficient. In addition to barley, wheat, tobacco, and olives are grown in the north; dates and figs are grown on the oases; and grapes are cultivated on the mountain slopes. The government sponsors land reclamation and hydroponic agriculture and has sold expropriated land to peasants at subsidized prices. It also provides credits for seed, fertilizers, and machinery and has greatly expanded the land under irrigation.

Pastures cover about 8 percent of the land, and sheep and goat rearing is an important activity in the north. Cattle have been imported from the United Kingdom. Offshore fisheries and sponge beds are exploited by Greek, Italian, and Maltese vessels.

The production and export of petroleum and natural gas account for almost one-third of the GDP, employ about 2 percent of the work force, and provide the central bank with large reserves of foreign exchange and gold. The assets of most international oil companies in Libya were nationalized in 1973; the government subsequently encouraged exploration by foreign firms while maintaining a controlling interest in production. Italian capital has helped to finance the construction of oil refineries, and tankers have been purchased from Japan and Sweden to transport Libyan petroleum. Cement production and the extraction of iron ore are also controlled by the government.

The government has encouraged investment by foreign firms in manufacturing industries, which account for less than 10 percent of the GDP and employ about the same share of the labour force. The development of industries has been hindered by the uneven distribution of the population and by a lack of natural resources other than petroleum. Manufactures include processed food, textiles, carpets, and footwear; the production of petrochemicals and construction materials is expanding.

Electricity is generated thermally from domestic fuels. Libya has purchased uranium from Niger and has sought to develop nuclear power. Per capita consumption of electricity is higher than that of any other African country.

The General Federation of Trade Unions coalesced in 1972 and is effectively a part of the ruling and only political party. Foreign workers account for about one-fifth of the work force and come primarily from other North African countries and Turkey.

The country's substantial trade surplus has been partially offset by expenditures on development and foreign aid. Food, raw materials, capital and consumer goods, and armaments dominate imports. Chief trading partners include Italy, Germany, Spain, France, and the United Kingdom.

Government and social conditions. Libya is a socialist republic governed by the Arab Socialist Union, the sole political party. A radical revision of the 1969 constitution espouses direct democracy and vests supreme power in the people through a General People's Congress (GPC), a body of 750 members formed from local elected and appointed bodies, which elects a five-member General Secretariat to make policy and serve as its permanent body. The GPC also elects the General People's Committee, a cabinet, and the "revolutionary leader," or head of state. This intricate system has perpetuated the rule of the man who overthrew the monarchy, Colonel Muammar al-Qaddafi. The judicial system is headed by the Supreme Court.

Greatly expanded and improved social services have resulted in significantly improved health conditions. The average life expectancy remains relatively low, however, at 61 years. Social security programs provide old-age, disability, and survivor pensions, as well as compensation for sickness, maternity, and work injury. Free medical care is available through a network of expanding and well-dispersed hospitals, clinics, and health centres, and additional medical personnel have been recruited from other Arab and European countries. While some diseases such as malaria and trachoma are now generally under control, typhoid, hepatitis, schistosomiasis (a parasitic infection of the liver), meningitis, and venereal diseases remain a serious threat.

Libya's literacy rate is the highest in North Africa, but the female literacy rate is only about three-fourths that of males. Education is free at all levels and compulsory between the ages of 6 and 15. The educational system consists of six-year primary, three-year intermediate and vocational, and three-year secondary and advanced vocational schools. Tripoli and Banghāzī each have a university.

The press is strictly controlled, and the broadcast media are owned by the government.

Cultural life. Libyan culture centres on folk arts and traditions, highly influenced by Islām's prohibitions of graphic representation of living beings.

History. The Greeks designated most of North Africa west of the Nile Libya, deriving the name from a tribe living in eastern Cyrenaica during the 2nd millennium BC. In the 7th century BC Phoenicians settled in Tripolitania, which later became the eastern province of the Carthaginian state (centred on modern Tunis). Greeks settled in Cyrenaica in the same century, establishing several cities. When the Romans conquered the region (1st century BC), Tripolitania became part of the Africa Nova province, and Cyrenaica became a province combined with Crete. The ancient Phazania (Fezzan) region was inhabited by the Garmantes people prior to Roman conquest (19 BC). The Byzantine Empire gained control of the territory after the decline of Rome, and in the 7th century Muslim Arabs began their long domination.

For about 350 years Tripolitania was ruled by the Berber Almohads from Morocco, while Cyrenaica was under Egyptian control. Early in the 16th century the Ottoman Turks subdued the three regions of Libya and combined Fezzan, Cyrenaica, and Tripolitania under one regency in Tripoli. In the early 18th century the Karamanli dynasty was established in Tripoli and ruled for about 120 years, during which the three regions were gradually consolidated. In 1835 the Ottomans reasserted their control.

The Sanūsīyah (Sennusiyah) Islāmic religious order was established in 1837 and was very influential in Libyan political life during the late 1800s and early 1900s. In 1911 Italy invaded Ottoman-controlled Libya, claiming control, which was hardly acknowledged by Turkey and tenaciously resisted in Libya. Nevertheless, by the outbreak of World War II some 150,000 Italians had settled there. Most of the Italian influence was destroyed during that war.

In 1951 Libya became an independent state with a Sanūsī monarch, and in 1953 it became a member of the Arab League. The discovery of oil in 1959 transformed Libya into an oil-rich monarchy, and a decade later a group of army officers led by Colonel Muammar al-Qaddafi deposed the king and made the country a Pan-Arab and puritanically Muslim republic. Qaddafi severed ties with the United Kingdom and the United States, while maintaining support for Palestinian Arabs and guerrilla and revolutionary movements in Africa and elsewhere. In 1977 hostilities erupted with Egypt. Libya changed its name to the Socialist People's Libyan Arab Jamāhīrīyah. Libya's alleged aid to international terrorist groups and its military adventurism in various parts of Africa brought a storm of international protest and mounting political isolation for the country.

Attempts by Qaddafi to project a more conciliatory attitude beginning in the 1980s met with some success among Libya's North African and Middle Eastern neighbours. However, these efforts failed to dissuade the United States and United Nations from imposing harsh economic sanctions on Libya in 1996 for its alleged involvement in international terrorist attacks. UN sanctions were ended in 2003, and many U.S. injunctions were ended the following year, after Libya forswore the use of terrorism as a means of political change.

Libyan Desert, Arabic AṢ-ṢAḤRĀʾ AL-LĪBĪYAH, northeastern portion of the Sahara, extending from eastern Libya through southwestern Egypt into the extreme northwest of The Sudan. The desert's bare rocky plateaus and stony or sandy plains are harsh, arid, and inhospitable. The highest point is Mount Al-ʿUwaynāt (6,345 feet [1,934m]), located where the three countries meet; the Qattara Depression (Munkhafaḍ al-Qaṭṭārah) of Egypt descends to 436 feet (133 m) below sea level. The very few inhabitants are mainly concentrated in the Egyptian oases of Siwa, Al-Baḥrīyah, Al-Farāfirah, Ad-Dākhilah, and Al-Khārijah and the Libyan oasis of Al-Kufrah. The Egyptian part, known as the Western Desert (Aṣ-Ṣaḥrāʾ al-Gharbīyah), was a critical area of operations in World War II.

Licata, town, Agrigento *provincia,* southern Sicily, Italy, and a Mediterranean port at the mouth of the Salso River (ancient Himera Meridionalis), northwest of Ragusa. It lies at the foot of the promontory of Sant'Angelo (ancient Ecnomus), the site of the town of Phintias, founded about 281 BC. During World War II Licata was an initial invasion point where Allied forces from North Africa landed on July 10, 1943. Vegetables and cereals are grown, and sulfur is mined and exported. Chemical fertilizers, pasta, and flour are produced. Pop. (2001) 37,976.

Licchavi, also spelled LICHCHHAVI, a people who settled (6th–5th century BC) on the north bank of the Ganges River in modern Bihār state, India, with their capital city at Vaiśālī. The Licchavi were renowned for their republican government, having a general assembly of the heads of the leading Kshatriya-caste families. They were, for a time, of considerable importance and rivaled the rising power of Magadha, forming a confederacy with other tribal groups (the so-called Vr̥jjian, or Vajjian, confederacy).

The Licchavi remained influential in northern India and Nepal until about the 4th century AD. In Nepal a Licchavi dynasty is commemorated in a dating system, the Licchavi era, that began in AD 110.

lice (insects): *see* louse.

lich-gate: *see* lych-gate.

lichen, any of about 15,000 species of thallophytic plants that consist of a symbiotic association of algae (usually green) and fungi (mostly Ascomycetes and Basidiomycetes).

Lichens were once classified as single organisms until the advent of microscopy, when the association of algae and fungi became evident. There is still some discussion about how to classify lichens.

Lichens have been used by humans as food and as sources of medicine and dye. They also provide two-thirds of the food supply for the caribou and reindeer that roam the far northern ranges.

The composite body of a lichen is called a thallus (plural thalli). The homoeomerous type of thallus consists of numerous algal cells (called the phycobionts) distributed among a lesser number of fungal cells (called the mycobionts). The heteromerous thallus differs in that it has a predominance of fungal cells. Hairlike growths that anchor the thallus to its substrate are called rhizines. Lichens that form a crustlike covering that is thin and tightly bound to the substrate are termed crustose. Squamulose lichens are small and leafy with loose attachments to the substrate. Foliose lichens are large and leafy, reaching diameters of several feet in some species, and are usually attached to the substrate by their large, platelike thalli at the centre.

It is not certain when fungi and algae came together to form lichens for the first time, but it was certainly after the mature development of the separate components. The basis of their relationship is the mutual benefit that they provide each other. Algae form simple carbohydrates that, when excreted, are absorbed by fungi cells and transformed into a different carbohydrate. In at least one case, *Peltigera polydactyla,* the exchange occurs within two minutes. Algae also produce vitamins that the fungi need. Fungi contribute to the symbiosis by absorbing water vapour from the air and by providing much-needed shade for the light-sensitive algae beneath.

Lichens grow relatively slowly, and there is still some question as to how they propagate. Most botanists agree that the most common means of reproduction is vegetative; that is, portions of an existing lichen break off and fall away to begin new growth nearby.

Lichfield, city and district, administrative and historic county of Staffordshire, England, on the northern margin of both the West Midlands plateau and the metropolitan complex centred on Birmingham. A nearby site is traditionally held to be the scene of the martyrdom in AD 286 of 1,000 Christians. The cathedral in Lichfield, one of the smallest in England, dates from the 13th and early 14th centuries. The town was incorporated in 1548, but its municipal history began much earlier. Lichfield is associated with Samuel Johnson, the celebrated lexicographer, who was born there in 1709; the house in which he was born is preserved as a museum. A variety of light industries provides employment. Area district, 129 square miles (333 square km). Pop. (2001) city, 27,900; district, 92,232.

lichi (fruit): *see* litchi.

Lichtenberg, a *Stadtbezirk* (urban district) of Berlin, Germany. A distinct town dating from before the 1280s, it underwent rapid industrial growth between the Franco-German War of 1870–71 and the beginning of World War I in 1914. In 1920 Lichtenberg, enlarged to include Friedrichsfelde and other rural parishes, was made a district of the city of Berlin. Its area of 10 square miles (26 square km) includes open areas on the outskirts of the city as well as industrial and densely residential areas near the centre. Manufacturing includes tools, clothing, and furniture. The district has one of Berlin's principal railway stations. Pop. (2000 est.) 155,050.

Lichtenberg, Georg Christoph (b. July 1, 1742, Ober-Ramstadt, near Darmstadt, Hesse [Germany]—d. Feb. 24, 1799, Göttingen, Hanover), German physicist and satirical writer, best known for his ridicule of metaphysical and romantic excesses.

Lichtenberg was the 17th child of a Protestant pastor, who taught him mathematics and natural sciences. In 1763 he entered Göttingen University, where in 1769 he became extraordinary professor of physics and in 1775 ordinary professor. This post he held until his death. Lichtenberg did research in a wide variety of fields—including geophysics, volcanology, meteorology, chemistry, astronomy, and mathematics—but most important were his investigations into physics. Notably, he constructed a huge electrophorus and, in the course of experimentations, discovered in 1777 the basic principle of modern xerographic copying; the images that he reproduced are still called "Lichtenberg figures."

As a satirist and humorist Lichtenberg takes high rank among the German writers of the 18th century. His biting wit involved him in many controversies with well-known contemporaries, such as Johann Kaspar Lavater, whose science of physiognomy he ridiculed, and Johann Heinrich Voss, whose views on Greek pronunciation called forth a powerful satire, *Über die Pronunciation der Schöpse des alten Griechenlandes* (1782; "On the Pronunciation of the Muttonheads of Old Greece"). In 1769 and again in 1774 he resided for some time in England, and his *Briefe aus England* (1776–78; "Letters from England") are the most attractive of his writings. He contributed to the *Göttinger Taschenkalender* ("Göttingen Pocket Almanac") from 1778 onward and to the *Göttingisches Magazin der Literatur und Wissenschaft* ("Göttingen Magazine of Literature and Science"), which he edited for three years (1780–82) with J.G.A. Forster. He also published in 1794–99 an *Ausführliche Erklärung der Hogarthschen Kupferstiche* ("Full Explanation of Hogarthian Copper Engravings").

Lichtenstein, Roy (b. Oct. 27, 1923, New York, N.Y., U.S.—d. Sept. 29, 1997, New York, N.Y., U.S.), American painter who was noted for his pioneering role in the Pop

Roy Lichtenstein with his work

art (*q.v.*) movement, which took its subject matter from the phenomena of mass culture.

Lichtenstein received his master of fine arts degree from Ohio State University in 1949. He taught at Ohio State (1946–51), at New York State University College, Oswego (1957–60), and at Douglass College of Rutgers University, New Brunswick, N.J. (1960–63).

At the beginning of his career, in 1951, he painted cowboys and Indians in modern art styles. In 1957 he tried Abstract Expressionism. His interest in the comic-strip cartoon as an art theme probably began with a painting he made of Mickey Mouse in 1960 for his children. In later paintings, comic-strip characters were vastly enlarged, the dots of the benday screen being simulated by means of a metal screen used as a stencil. The result was a combination of commercial art and abstraction. Brilliant colours outlined in deep black contributed to the intense visual impact. The first one-man show of his comic-strip painting (New York City, 1962) was a sensation, and by 1968 interest in his unusual work had spread so widely that he had the distinction of being the first American artist to have an exhibition at London's Tate Gallery.

Lichtenstein continued in this vein for a while, taking subjects from sentimental romance magazines. He enclosed speeches in balloons and made landscapes in the comic-book idiom. Quite different, though related, was his sculpture in 1967–68, in which he consciously evoked the glass and curved-chrome styles of the 1930s. Lichtenstein's works of the 1970s and '80s marked a significant departure from his earlier style in their use of brushstrokes and depiction of still lifes. These works stemmed from a more eclectic vision of art and were influenced by various periods of art history, especially by Pablo Picasso, Henri Matisse, and Salvador Dalí.

Licinius, in full VALERIUS LICINIANUS LICINIUS (d. 325), Roman emperor from 308 to 324.

Born of Illyrian peasant stock, Licinius advanced in the army and was suddenly elevated to the rank of augustus (November 308) by his friend Galerius, who had become emperor. Galerius hoped to have him rule the West, but since Italy, Africa, and Spain were held by the usurper Maxentius, while Constantine reigned in Gaul and Britain, Licinius had to content himself with ruling Pannonia. When Galerius died in 311, Licinius took over Galerius' European dominions. He married Constantine's half sister Constantia (313) and in the same year defeated the Eastern emperor Maximinus at Tzurulum, east of Adrianople, Thrace, pursuing him into Asia, where Maximinus died. Licinius thus added the entire eastern half of the empire to his dominion.

After a brief accord between the two augusti, Constantine forced Licinius to surrender the provinces of Pannonia and Moesia. There followed 10 years of uneasy peace in which Licinius built up his army and accumulated a huge reserve of treasure. In 324 Constantine defeated him at Adrianople and again at Chrysopolis (now Üsküdar, Tur.). Licinius surrendered, was exiled to Thessalonica, and was executed the next year on a charge of attempted rebellion.

During the campaign against Maximinus, Licinius had made his army use a monotheistic form of prayer closely resembling that later imposed by Constantine. On June 5, 313, he had issued an edict granting toleration to the Christians and restoring church property. Hence his contemporaries, the Latin writer Lactantius and Bishop Eusebius, hailed him as a convert. But he eventually became alienated from the Christians and about 320 initiated a mild form of persecution.

Licking River, river, rising in Magoffin County, east Kentucky, U.S., and flowing about 320 mi (515 km) generally northwest to enter the Ohio River at Covington, Ky., opposite Cincinnati, Ohio. It is joined by north and south forks near Falmouth in Pendleton County.

The Licking River, partly navigable and an early trade route, courses through an area of numerous saline springs, where animals went for salt licks. By the river, in the Bluegrass region of Kentucky 40 mi northeast of Lexington, stands the Blue Licks Battlefield State Park, commemorating a Revolutionary skirmish (Aug. 19, 1782) in which Kentucky pioneers were defeated by a British-Indian force.

licorice (species *Glycyrrhiza glabra*), also spelled LIQUORICE, perennial herb of the Fabaceae family, and the flavouring, confection, and medicine made from its roots, similar in their sweet, slightly bitter flavour to anise. The Greek name *glykyrrhiza,* of which the word licorice is a corruption, means "sweet root."

Native to southern Europe, licorice is cultivated around the Mediterranean and in parts of the United States. An effective mask for the taste of medicines, licorice is an ingredient in cough lozenges, syrups, and elixirs. It is a flavouring agent in candies and tobacco. In medicine, licorice has been used to treat peptic ulcers and Addison's disease.

The herb may grow up to 1 metre (3 feet) tall and has compound leaves with four to eight oval leaflets, axillary clusters of blue flowers, and flat pods from 7 to 10 centimetres (3 to 4 inches) long. The roots used are about 1 m long and about 1 cm (0.4 in.) in diameter. They are soft, fibrous, and flexible and are coloured bright yellow inside. The distinctive sweetness of licorice is imparted by a substance called glycyrrhizin.

The preparation of the juice by boiling crushed and ground roots is an industry along the Mediterranean coasts. The pliable, semivitreous stick form of licorice candy, also called licorice paste or black sugar, is processed from the thickened juice.

Spanish licorice (*Glycyrrhiza glabra*)
A-Z Botanical Collection

lictor, plural LICTORS, or LICTORES, member of an ancient Roman class of magisterial attendants, probably Etruscan in origin and dating in Rome from the regal period. Lictors carried the fasces (*q.v.*) for their magistrate and were constantly in his attendance in public; they cleared his way in crowds, and summoned and punished offenders for him. They also served as their magistrate's house guard.

Emperors originally had 12 lictors, but after Domitian (reigned AD 81–96) they had 24; dictators, 24; consuls, 12; praetors, 6; legates, 5; and priests, one.

Lictors were mostly freedmen, exempt from military duties. They held annual, regularly renewed appointments at fixed salaries. The Comitia Curiata (a popular assembly) was summoned by the lictors until the late republic, when the Comitia met less frequently and the 30 divisions of the people, or curiae, delegated 30 lictors as their representatives.

Lida, city and centre of Lida *rayon* (sector), Grodno *oblast* (province), Belarus. Lida emerged in the 13th century as a fortified point of the Lithuanian duke Gediminas on the border between the Principality of Grodno and Grand Duchy of Lithuania. The city eventually passed to Poland and then to Russia (1795). It reverted to Poland in 1919 but was ceded to the Soviet Union in 1945. It contains the ruins of the 14th-century Gediminas Castle. Lida was for long a trading centre but is now a centre for food processing, with agricultural machine building and electrical engineering industries. Pop. (1991 est.) 95,000.

Liddell, Henry George (b. Feb. 6, 1811, Bishop Auckland, County Durham, Eng.—d. Jan. 18, 1898, Ascot, Berkshire), British lexicographer and co-editor of the standard *Greek–English Lexicon* (1843; 8th ed., 1897; revised by H.S. Jones and others, 1940; abridged, 1957; intermediate, 1959). In 1834 he and a fellow student at Oxford, Robert Scott, began preparing the *Lexicon,* basing their work on the Greek–German lexicon of Francis Passow, professor at the University of Breslau.

Liddell, portrait bust by Henry Richard Hope-Pinker, 1888; in the National Portrait Gallery, London
By courtesy of the National Portrait Gallery, London

A tutor at Balliol College, Oxford (1836–45), Liddell was ordained in the Church of England (1838) and in 1846 was appointed domestic chaplain to Prince Albert. He was headmaster of Westminster School prior to serving as dean of Christ Church, Oxford (1856–91). He devoted much of his spare time to revising and enlarging the *Lexicon.* He also wrote a *History of Ancient Rome,* 2 vol. (1855), abridged in 1871 under the title *The Student's Rome: A History of Rome from the Earliest Times to the Establishment of the Empire.* It was for Liddell's daughter Alice that Lewis Carroll wrote *Alice in Wonderland.*

Liddell Hart, Sir Basil (Henry) (b. Oct. 31, 1895, Paris—d. Jan. 29, 1970, Marlow, Buckinghamshire, Eng.), British military historian and strategist known for his advocacy of mechanized warfare.

Liddell Hart left studies at Cambridge University when World War I broke out in 1914 and became an officer in the British Army. In 1920 he wrote the Army's official *Infantry Training* manual that included his "battle drill" system evolved in 1917 and his so-called "expanding torrent" method of attack, which grew out of infiltration tactics introduced in 1917–18. Liddell Hart became an early advocate of air power and mechanized tank warfare. Defining strategy as "the art of distributing military means to fulfil the ends of policy," he favoured an "indirect approach" that aimed at dislocating the enemy and reducing his means of resistance. Drawing on his wartime experiences, he emphasized the elements of mobility and surprise.

Invalided in 1924, Liddell Hart retired as a

captain in 1927. He was military correspondent of the *Daily Telegraph* in 1925–35 and military adviser to *The Times* in 1935–39. In 1937–38 he served as personal adviser to Leslie Hore-Belisha, secretary of state for war, and saw many of his advocated reforms implemented. His efforts to mechanize the Army with tank and antiaircraft forces were resisted by most professional officers.

Liddell Hart's writings were more influential in Germany than in France or England. His "expanding torrent" theory, along with the doctrines of General J.F.C. Fuller on employment of tanks, was adopted by German pioneers of armoured warfare, and became the basis for the blitzkrieg warfare through which German armies mastered the European continent in 1939–41. For the duration of the war, Liddell Hart wrote for the *Daily Mail*. Dubious of nuclear deterrence, he stressed conventional defense forces during the postwar years and also opposed the concept of total war. In 1966 he was knighted by Queen Elizabeth II.

Liddell Hart was the author of a number of military biographies, several works on military strategy, and a history of World War II.

Liddesdale, valley of the Liddel Water, district of Roxburgh, Borders region, Scotland, extending more than 20 miles (32 km) southwest from Peel Fell to the River Esk, which flows into the head of the Solway Firth. For 7 miles (11 km) the Liddel forms the Anglo-Scottish border, and its dale was long ravaged by border warfare and cattle raiders. The most important fortification is Hermitage Castle (1244), but the countryside is studded with minor fortified buildings (pele-towers). It is still very rural in character, with the sheep farms of the enclosed valley land set between steep hills of rough summer grazing.

Liddon, Henry Parry (b. Aug. 20, 1829, North Stoneham, Hampshire, Eng.—d. Sept. 9, 1890, Weston-super-Mare, Gloucestershire), Anglican priest, theologian, close friend and biographer of the Oxford Movement leader Edward Bouverie Pusey (1800–82), and a major advocate of the movement's principles, which included an elaborated liturgy, a recovery of 18th-century church discipline, and an emphasis on classical learning.

Liddon, chalk drawing by George Richmond, 1866; in the National Portrait Gallery, London

By courtesy of the National Portrait Gallery, London

Ordained in 1852, Liddon became vice principal at the new seminary at Cuddesdon, Oxfordshire, in 1854 and vice principal at St. Edmund Hall, Oxford, in 1859. He used his post at Oxford to maintain and advance the movement, which had suffered a setback after the conversion in 1845 of its chief figure, John Henry Newman, to Roman Catholicism. In 1864 Liddon became chaplain to W.K. Hamilton, bishop of Salisbury and one of the few bishops then favourable to the Oxford Movement's renewal of Roman Catholic principles within the Anglican church. His stature as a spokesman was enhanced by his Bampton Lectures of 1866, published the following year as *The Divinity of Our Lord and Saviour Jesus Christ*.

In 1870 Liddon became a canon of St. Paul's, London, and Ireland professor of exegesis at Oxford. His sermons at St. Paul's attracted vast congregations for the next 20 years. Like others in the movement, he consistently opposed preferment (the ecclesiastical system of promotions) and is known to have refused at least two bishoprics. His concern with Christian unity prompted him to participate in developing the Old Catholic movement after the Vatican Council of 1869–70, and he traveled in Russia and the Middle East, contacting Orthodox church leaders.

As an associate and admirer of Pusey at Oxford, he favoured Pusey's attitudes, in contrast to those of younger thinkers in the movement; after Pusey's death in 1882, Liddon began Pusey's authorized biography, published posthumously as *Life of Edward Bouverie Pusey,* 4 vol. (1893–97).

Lidice, village, Středočeský *kraj* (region), Czech Republic, just northwest of Prague. Before World War II it was a mining settlement of the Kladno coal basin and had a population of about 450. On June 10, 1942, it was "liquidated" by German armed forces as part of a massive reprisal for the assassination by Czech underground fighters of Reinhard Heydrich ("Heydrich the Hangman"), deputy leader of the SS. On June 9, five days after Heydrich died of bomb injuries, the SS rounded up Lidice's inhabitants. The 172 men were shot the next day. The women, except for 7 who were shot on the spot or who had been shot earlier trying to flee, were transported to the Ravensbrück concentration camp, where 49 died (7 by gas) and 3 "disappeared." The 90 children, after one had been shot running away, were screened and found "racially pure" and were dispersed through Germany to be renamed and raised as Germans. Local miners (19 men) who were missed on the first round were executed later in Prague. When the massacre and deportation were complete, the SS burned Lidice, dynamited what was left standing, and leveled the debris.

A similar devastation—albeit on a larger scale—occurred two years to the day after the Lidice massacre at the French village of Oradour-sur-Glane.

In 1947 a new village site was designated nearby. A museum, with a monument and an international rose garden, marks the site of the original village.

Lidköping, town, *län* (county) of Skaraborg, southwestern Sweden, at the mouth of the Lidån River on Kinneviken Bay, Lake Vänern. It is of medieval origin and was chartered in 1446. After devastation by several fires, it was rebuilt, beginning in 1672. The manufacture of porcelain is the principal industry. The old town hall (1676–1882) originally was a hunting lodge belonging to Count Magnus Gabriel De la Gardie (1622–86), head of King Charles XI's administration from 1660 to 1680. About 15 miles (24 km) north of the town is Läckö Castle, with more than 200 rooms; although its oldest parts date from 1298, when it was built as the residence of the bishop of Skara, it is essentially a 17th-century structure. Another attraction near Lidköping is Kinnekulle, a ridge underlain by igneous rock, once used by the Goths as a watch hill from which they could signal the approach of an enemy. Pop. (1998 est.) mun., 36,833.

Lidman, Sara (b. Dec. 30, 1923, Missenträsk, Swed.), novelist, one of the most acclaimed and widely read of the post-World War II generation of Swedish writers.

Lidman grew up in the remote West Bosnian region of northern Sweden. Her studies at the University of Uppsala were interrupted by tuberculosis, and she began to write. She had an immediate success with her first two novels, *Tjärdalen* (1953; "The Tar Still") and *Hjortronlandet* (1955; "Cloudberry Land"), both of which deal with the rural life of her

Sara Lidman

Lennart Nilsson

childhood and youth. Another well-known work is *Regnspiran* (1958; *The Rain Bird,* 1962). In the 1960s she visited Africa and produced two novels protesting the oppression of the blacks. *Samtal i Hanoi* (1966; "Conversations in Hanoi") is a record of her trip to Vietnam, and *Fåglarna i Nam Dinh* (1972; "Birds in Nam Dinh") covers the Vietnam war. Her regional novels blend realism with a fairy-tale-like atmosphere, and her works of social criticism express her commitment to the rights of the underprivileged. Lidman repudiated her earlier fiction in favour of reporting social conditions. *Gruva* (1968; "The Mine") is a study of Lapland iron miners. *Marta, Marta* (1970) is a folk saga. In the 1970s she began a series of novels, including *Din tjänare hör* (1977; "Your Servant is Listening"), *Nabots sten* (1981; *Naboth's Stone*), and *Järnkronan* (1985; "The Iron Crown"), set in the far north of Sweden; the books describe the introduction of the railroad in the late 19th century and its effect on the region and its inhabitants.

Lidner, Bengt (b. March 16, 1757, Göteborg, Swed.—d. Jan. 4, 1793, Stockholm), Swedish dramatic and epic poet of early Romanticism, noted for his choice of spectacular subjects.

A courtier in the favour of Gustav III, Lidner toured the continent at royal expense. His best works were written between 1783 and 1787. *Grefvinnan Spastaras Död* (1783), the text for a cantata, deals with a woman who attempts to rescue her son during an earthquake. Both are killed, and the poem follows the mother to heaven, where she meets Lidner's mother, who had died when Lidner was a boy. In

Lidner, detail of an oil painting by Carl-Fredrik von Breda; in Gripsholm Castle, Sweden

By courtesy of the Svenska Portrattarkivet, Stockholm

the operatic libretto *Medea* (1784), a deceived wife kills her sons on the stage. The heroine of the epic *Yttersta Domen* (1788; "The Last Judgment") is Eve: its opening, in which images of sound and light combine to evoke an intense atmosphere of death, is famous. Lidner's motto *In lacrimis voluptas* ("There is pleasure in tears") reflects the emotionally charged atmosphere of his works.

lidocaine, synthetic organic compound used in medicine, usually in the form of its hydrochloride salt, as a local anesthetic. Lidocaine produces prompter, more intense, and longer lasting anesthesia than does procaine (Novocaine). It is widely used for infiltration, nerve-block, and spinal anesthesia in a 0.5 to 2 percent aqueous or saline solution and is also applied to mucous membranes (2 to 4 percent) for mucosal anesthesia.

Lie, Jonas (Lauritz Idemil) (b. Nov. 6, 1833, Hokksund in Eiker, Nor.—d. July 5, 1908, Stavern), novelist whose goal was to reflect in his writings the nature, the folk life, and the social spirit of his native Norway. He is considered one of "the four great ones"

Jonas Lie, engraving
By courtesy of the Royal Norwegian Embassy

of 19th-century Norwegian literature, together with Henrik Ibsen, Bjørnstjerne Bjørnson, and Alexander Kielland.

He studied law in Kristiania (Oslo) and began to practice but went bankrupt in 1868. With much encouragement from his wife and with her collaboration, Lie wrote his first novel, *Den fremsynte eller billeder fra Nordland* (1870; *The Visionary or Pictures from Nordland,* 1894). The first Norwegian story of the sea and of business life, *Tremasteren "Fremtiden" eller liv nordpå* (1872; *The Barque "Future,"* 1879), followed. Two novels from his Naturalistic period are *Livsslaven* (1883; *One of Life's Slaves,* 1895), which tells of the social misfortunes of a boy born out of wedlock, and *Familien paa Gilje* (1883; *The Family at Gilje,* 1920), a novel that deals with the position of women, the most popular question of his day. The latter is a classic of Norwegian literature.

Toward the end of his life Lie wrote two volumes of fairy tales called *Trold* (1891–92; some translated as *Weird Tales from Northern Seas,* 1893).

Lie, (Marius) Sophus (b. Dec. 17, 1842, Nordfjordeid, Nor.—d. Feb. 18, 1899, Kristiania), Norwegian mathematician who made significant contributions to the theories of algebraic invariants and differential equations.

In 1869 Lie went to Berlin, where he met Felix Klein, with whom he later collaborated in publishing several papers. In Paris in 1870, Lie discovered contact transformations. Using these transformations, a one-to-one correspondence can be established between lines and spheres in such a way that tangent spheres correspond to intersecting lines. In 1871 he became an assistant tutor at the University of

Sophus Lie, detail of an engraving *c.* 1885
Archiv fur Kunst und Geschichte, West Berlin

Kristiania (Oslo). In the same year he submitted for his doctor's degree a memoir in which he advanced the theory of tangential transformations (a process of changing an expression to another expression of different form). Appointed extraordinary professor in 1872, he began his researches on continuous transformation groups in 1873.

After nine years' collaboration with Ernst Engel, Lie published *Theorie der Transformationsgruppen,* 3 vol. (1893; "Theory of Transformation Groups"). This work contains the results of his investigations of the general theory of finite continuous groups of substitutions. It was followed by *Geometrie der Berührungstransformationen* (1896; "Geometry of Contact Transformations"). In 1886 he succeeded Klein in the chair of mathematics at the University of Leipzig, with Engel as his assistant. In 1898 he returned to Kristiania to accept a special post created for him, but his health was already broken. Besides his development of transformations, he made contributions to differential geometry; his primary aim, however, was the advancement of the theory of differential equations.

An analysis of Lie's works is given in the *Bibliotheca Mathematica* (1900). His collected works are contained in *Gesammelte Abhandlungen,* 6 vol. (1922–37; "Collected Essays"). Two other standard works are his *Differentialgleichungen* (1891; "Differential Equations") and *Vorlesungen über continuierliche Gruppen* (1893; "Lectures on Continuous Groups").

Lie, Trygve (Halvdan) (b. July 16, 1896, Kristiania, Nor.—d. Dec. 30, 1968, Geilo), Norwegian politician and diplomat, the first secretary general of the United Nations (1946–52), who resigned largely because of the Soviet Union's resentment of his support of UN military intervention in the Korean War.

Trygve Lie
H. Roger-Viollet

Educated at the University of Kristiania (Oslo), Lie practiced law and became a leading member of the Norwegian Labour Party (Arbeiderpartiet). After the German invasion of Norway in April 1940, he was appointed foreign minister of the Norwegian government-in-exile in London.

On Feb. 1, 1946, Lie was elected UN secretary general for a term of five years. He first was nominated (by Andrey A. Gromyko of the Soviet Union) for president of the General Assembly, a less important office, but was defeated by Paul-Henri Spaak of Belgium. One of Lie's first tasks was helping to secure the evacuation of Soviet troops from northern Iran. From May 1947 he had to deal with the war in Palestine that followed the proclamation of the state of Israel and throughout 1948 with the Indian–Pakistani conflict over Kashmir. Only temporary solutions were found to these problems.

In 1950 Lie undertook a "peace mission" to the capitals of the great powers, promoting a "20-Year Peace Program" and trying to resist the Soviet attempt to expel Nationalist China from the UN. Also in 1950 he urged that the UN admit the People's Republic of China (Communist China).

After UN armed forces had been authorized to aid the Republic of Korea (South Korea; June 27, 1950), Lie was subjected to official hindrance and personal insult by the Soviet Union. When it became certain that the Soviet Union would veto his reelection in the Security Council, his term was extended for three years (without formal reelection) by the General Assembly. The Soviet Union thereupon ceased to recognize him as secretary general. He also encountered opposition in the United States as a result of the investigations led by Sen. Joseph R. McCarthy against suspected Communists in the UN. Lie's secretariat was accused of giving jobs to disloyal U.S. citizens, but no charge of subversion of the United States within the UN could be proved.

His mediatory work having become nearly impossible, Lie resigned his office on Nov. 10, 1952. His book *In the Cause of Peace* was published in 1954.

lie detector, also called POLYGRAPH, instrument for recording physiological phenomena such as blood pressure, pulse rate, and respiration of a human subject as he answers questions put to him by an operator; these data are then used as the basis for making a judgment as to whether or not the subject is lying. Used in police interrogation and investigation since 1924, the lie detector is still controversial among psychologists and not always judicially acceptable.

Physiological phenomena usually chosen for recording are those not greatly subject to voluntary control. A pneumograph tube is fastened around the subject's chest, and a blood pressure–pulse cuff is strapped around the arm. Pens record impulses on moving graph paper driven by a small electric motor.

Lieber, Francis, original name FRANZ LIEBER (b. March 18, 1798, Berlin—d. Oct. 2, 1872, New York City), German-born U.S. political philosopher and jurist, best known for formulating the "laws of war." His *Code for the Government of Armies in the Field* (1863) subsequently served as a basis for international conventions on the conduct of warfare.

Lieber was educated at the university at Jena. A liberal political activist, he was twice imprisoned under the Prussian government. He fled to England and, in 1827, immigrated to the United States. There he began to compile and edit the first edition of the *Encyclopedia Americana* (1829–33). He was appointed professor of history and political economics at South Carolina College (Columbia) in 1835 and joined the faculty of Columbia College, New York City, in 1857. During this period he produced two of his most important works, *Manual of Political Ethics,* 2 vol. (1838–39) and *On Civil Liberty and Self-Government,* 2 vol. (1853). In his *Code for the Government of Armies,* drafted for the Union Army during the U.S. Civil War, Lieber recognized the need for a systematic, institutionalized code of behaviour to mitigate the devastation of war, protect civilians, and regulate the treatment of prisoners of war.

Lieber, Thomas: *see* Erastus, Thomas.

Liebermann, Max (b. July 20, 1847, Berlin—d. Feb. 8, 1935, Berlin), painter and etcher known for his objective studies of the life and labour of the poor and as the leader of the German Impressionist school.

After studying under Steffeck (1866–68), Liebermann attended the Weimar Kunstschule (1868–72). The straightforward realism and direct simplicity of his first exhibited picture, "Women Plucking Geese" (1872; Nationalgalerie, Berlin), presented a striking contrast to the romantically idealized art then in vogue. This picture earned him the epithet "disciple of the ugly." A summer spent at Barbizon in 1873, where he became acquainted with Jean-François Millet and studied the works of Corot, Constant Troyon, and Charles-François Daubigny, resulted in the brightening of his palette.

Liebermann returned to Munich in 1878 and finally settled in Berlin in 1884. During this period he found his subjects in the orphanages and asylums for the old in Amsterdam and among the peasants and urban labourers of Germany and The Netherlands (*e.g.*, "The Flax Spinners," 1887). In these works Liebermann did for German art what Millet had done for French painting.

"The Flax Spinners," oil on canvas by Max Liebermann, 1887; in the National-Galerie, Berlin

By courtesy of the Staatliche Museen zu Berlin, National-Galerie, Berlin

After 1890 Liebermann's style was influenced by French Impressionism—initially by the works of Manet and later by Degas. He became a member (1898) and later president of the Berlin Academy, despite his role as the founder and leader of the Berliner Sezession (1899), a group of artists who supported the academically unpopular styles of Impressionism and Art Nouveau.

Liebig, Justus, Freiherr von (baron of) (b. May 12, 1803, Darmstadt, Hesse-Darmstadt—d. April 18, 1873, Munich), German chemist who made many important contributions to the early systematization of organic chemistry, to the application of chemistry to biology (biochemistry), to chemical education, and to the basic principles of agricultural chemistry.

Liebig, photograph by F. Hanfstaengl, 1868

By courtesy of the Gesellschaft Liebig-Museum, Giessen, Ger.

After studying pharmacy for a short time Liebig followed his ambition to become a chemist by entering the University of Bonn to study with a leading chemist of the day, Karl Wilhelm Gottlob Kastner. When Kastner moved to the University of Erlangen, Liebig accompanied him and received his doctorate there in 1822. He then received a grant from the Hessian government to study in Paris. Through the influence of Alexander von Humboldt he was able to work in the private laboratory of Joseph-Louis Gay-Lussac.

In 1824 he joined the faculty of the University of Giessen, where he became a full professor in 1826. At Giessen he established the first laboratory in which the methods of chemical research were taught systematically to young chemists. The laboratory soon became world famous, and students from all over Europe came to study with him. Among them were many of the notable chemists of the following generation, including August Wilhelm von Hofmann, Sir Edward Frankland, F.A. Kekule von Stradonitz, and Charles-Adolphe Wurtz. Liebig's laboratory set the pattern for chemical education that came to prevail in Germany and was in large part responsible for the great development of German chemistry later in the 19th century. In 1845 he was made a baron, and in 1852 he became professor of chemistry at the University of Munich, where he remained until his death.

Liebig was active in many fields of inorganic and organic chemistry, but some of his studies stand out because of their great significance in the later development of chemistry. His early studies on the isomerism of cyanic and fulminic acids made a great impression on his contemporaries and led him into organic chemistry. Through his work in organic chemistry, he became acquainted with another outstanding chemist, Friedrich Wöhler. His friendship with Wöhler lasted a lifetime, and the two men collaborated in several investigations. The most important of these was the study of bitter almond oil (benzaldehyde), in which the same chemical group was found to pass unchanged through a great variety of reactions. Such a group was called a radical, and the radical theory that Liebig did much to develop was the first major attempt at systematization in organic chemistry.

Liebig's studies in organic chemistry were greatly aided by the simple method he developed for the analytical determination of carbon and hydrogen. He also developed a method for the analytical determination of halogens, published important work on polybasic organic acids, and did much to support the hydrogen theory of acids. He popularized, but did not invent, the Liebig condenser, still used in many laboratory distillations.

After 1838 Liebig's interest shifted from pure organic chemistry to the chemistry of plants and animals. He made a large number of analyses of tissues and body fluids and carried out a study of the nitrogenous products of the animal organism. A by-product of this investigation was the Liebig extract of beef. He then became greatly interested in agricultural problems and in 1840 published *Organic Chemistry in Its Application to Agriculture and Physiology.* This book exerted very great influence on practical agriculturalists. He rejected the old theory that humus supplied plants with food and showed that plants took carbon dioxide, water, and ammonia from the air and soil. He advocated the use of mineral fertilizers to supply other elements that might become depleted in soils.

In his later years Liebig's reputation became so great that he was regarded as the final authority in chemical matters. He never hesitated to express his sometimes rather rigid views. As a result he was often involved in scientific controversies in which he was not always in the right. Much of his work was published in the journal that he founded in 1832, the *Annalen der Pharmacie,* which ultimately became the *Annalen der Chemie,* one of the major chemical journals.

After he accepted the professorship at Munich, Liebig gradually lost his enthusiasm for laboratory work. He soon refused to accept new students and devoted himself more and more to literary activities. In these, aside from his frequent polemics, he was occupied in stressing the broader applications of chemistry to human life. (H.M.L.)

BIBLIOGRAPHY. Most of the biographies of Liebig have been written in German. A good account is by F. Haber in E. Farber, *Great Chemists* (1961). The work of Liebig and its results are treated in *Liebig and After Liebig,* ed. by F.R. Moulton (1942). An excellent picture of Liebig's relations with his contemporaries is H. von Dechend (ed.), *Justus von Liebig in eigenen Zeugnissen und Solchen seiner Zeitgenossen,* 2nd ed. (1963).

Liebknecht, Karl (b. Aug. 13, 1871, Leipzig—d. Jan. 15, 1919, Berlin), German Social Democrat, who, with Rosa Luxemburg and other radicals, founded the Spartakusbund (Spartacus League), a Berlin underground group that became the Communist Party of Germany, dedicated to a socialist revolution. Liebknecht was killed in the Spartacus Revolt of January 1919.

Karl Liebknecht, 1913

Interfoto-Friedrich Rauch, Munich

The son of Wilhelm Liebknecht, Karl grew up during the years when the Anti-Socialist Law was in force against his father's Social-ist Labour Party (which became the Social Democratic Party in 1891). With financial help from the party, he studied law and political economy, first at Leipzig and then at Berlin, where he earned his doctor's degree. He planned to devote his career to the defense of Marxism.

After serving with the Imperial Pioneer Guards in Potsdam during 1893–94 and subsequently as a junior barrister in Westphalia, he returned to Berlin in 1898. In 1900, the year of his father's death, he married his first wife, Julie Paradies, by whom he had three children. She died 10 years later, and in 1912 he married Sophia Ryss, a woman of Russian birth who had graduated from the University of Heidelberg.

In 1904, at a trial at Königsberg, he defended propertyless peasants accused of infiltrating socialist propaganda from East Prussia into tsarist Russia. His defense of the accused was primarily an apology for social democracy and provided him with a platform for his attacks against militarism. In 1907 he played a principal role in the establishment of the International Union of Socialist Youth Organizations in Stuttgart. His publication of *Militarismus und Antimilitarismus* in the same year earned him a jail sentence of 18 months in Glatz, Silesia. While still in prison, he won a seat in the Prussian Landtag, and in 1912 he entered the Reichstag as the chief spokesman against the government and against the growing movement within the Social Democratic Party to revise its Marxist doctrine.

During World War I Liebknecht became a leading figure in the development of opposition movements to the wartime government. He was the first in the Reichstag to vote against war credits and spoke out publicly, as early as January 1915, for the transformation of the national war into a civil or class war. The government conscripted him as a noncombatant but furloughed him to fulfill his duties as a deputy in the Reichstag and the Prussian Assembly. He served on the Düna sector of the Russian front, felling trees, peeling potatoes, and burying the rotting corpses of the dead, until he suffered physical collapse in October 1915. In 1916 he was expelled from the Social Democratic Party for opposing its leadership. The ouster brought him into close alliance with another revolutionary personality, Rosa Luxemburg. Together, they provided the leadership for illegal opposition to the war through the subversive Spartakusbund, which disseminated through its network of confidential underground agents various kinds of revolutionary propaganda. Liebknecht edited the famous illegal "Spartacus Letters," the "official" organ of the Spartakusbund.

On May 1, 1916, Liebknecht participated in a May Day demonstration in Berlin and called for the overthrow of the government and an end to the war and was tried and imprisoned. In October 1918 the climate in Germany had become more revolutionary and Liebknecht was granted an amnesty by the government of Prince Max of Baden.

Liebknecht entered the maelstrom of the German revolutionary period with great expectations. The Russian Soviet government celebrated his release from prison by a dinner for him at its embassy in Berlin. He planned to develop, through the Spartakusbund, a German revolution after the Soviet pattern. While the Social Democratic Party, under the leadership of Friedrich Ebert, channeled the revolution along moderate lines, Liebknecht harangued the masses to win support for a "real" revolution. He played a leading role in the formation of the German Communist Party, which attempted without success to organize the radical elements. A series of bloody clashes between the provisional government formed by Ebert after the downfall of the monarchy and the extreme radicals culminated in the January 1919 putsch in which Liebknecht resorted to force, a tactic both he and his father had strongly opposed. His use of force stimulated the growth of the counterrevolution, and both he and Rosa Luxemburg were among its first victims. On Jan. 15, 1919, they were shot to death by counterrevolutionary volunteers on the pretext of attempted escape while under arrest.

BIBLIOGRAPHY. Karl W. Meyer, *Karl Liebknecht: Man Without a Country* (1957), stresses his political activities. Helmut Trotnow, *Karl Liebknecht (1871–1919): A Political Biography* (1984), also offers a new look at the history of the Social Democratic Party.

Liebknecht, Wilhelm (b. March 29, 1826, Giessen, Hesse [Germany]—d. Aug. 7, 1900, Berlin), German socialist, close associate of Karl Marx, and later cofounder of the German Social Democratic Party.

Liebknecht was still a child when his father died, but he was brought up comfortably.

Wilhelm Liebknecht, *c.* 1890
Archiv fur Kunst und Geschichte, Berlin

He attended the universities of Giessen, Marburg, and Berlin and developed an interest in French socialist thinking. He accepted an invitation to teach at a Swiss elementary school and then decided to study law and be called to the bar in Switzerland (1847).

On Feb. 23, 1848, revolution erupted in Paris. He arrived too late to become involved and returned to Germany, where he participated in several revolutionary insurrections that failed. During an attempt to fan the fading revolutionary embers in Baden, he was captured and held prisoner for eight months. In 1849, after his release, he returned to Switzerland.

Liebknecht's stay in Switzerland was short, for the Austrian and Prussian governments, fearful of his growing influence among the Swiss workers, succeeded in having him expelled from Geneva. In 1849 he went to England, where he remained for 13 years. In London he joined the Communist League, working closely with Karl Marx and Friedrich Engels and supporting himself as London correspondent for the *Augsburger allgemeine Zeitung* ("Augsburg Gazette"). In 1862 the Prussian government granted him amnesty; he returned to Berlin and became a writer for the *Norddeutsche allgemeine Zeitung* ("North German Gazette"), soon becoming an influential socialist. But Otto von Bismarck, who had become minister president (prime minister) in 1862, resented Liebknecht's influence among the working classes and, failing to gain his support, had him expelled from Prussia in 1865.

In Leipzig, where he moved, Liebknecht joined the floundering Allgemeiner Deutscher Arbeiterverein (General German Worker's Association), founded by the socialist leader Ferdinand Lassalle in 1863. He also formed a friendship with August Bebel, a woodturner, who on his travels as a journeyman had become familiar with the poverty of the masses throughout Germany. Liebknecht, the writer, and Bebel, the orator and practical politician, complemented one another and together they provided the leadership for German socialism for the remainder of the century. In Leipzig, Liebknecht worked hard to win new recruits for the cause and continued his efforts to educate the masses through the *Demokratisches Wochenblatt* ("Democratic Weekly"). In 1867 the workers elected Liebknecht to the North German Reichstag, where he opposed Lassalle's advocacy of a "paternalistic" state socialism. In 1869, at a congress at Eisenach, Liebknecht and Bebel organized the Sozialdemokratische Arbeiterpartei (Social Democratic Labour Party) and affiliated it with the First International (International Workingmen's Association), headquartered in London.

The outbreak of the Franco-German War in 1870 put Liebknecht's devotion to international socialism to a practical test. His failure to vote for war credits and his writings against the war and the government resulted in his conviction on charges of "treasonable intentions" in 1872. He was sentenced to two years' confinement in the fortress of Hubertusburg, along with Bebel, who was similarly charged.

The Prussian military victory in 1871 did nothing to abate the socialists' growing strength in the Reichstag, and Liebknecht continued to be a thorn in Bismarck's side. Bismarck's determination to repress the socialists brought about the merger of the Lassalleans and Liebknechtians as the Sozialistische Arbeiterpartei Deutschlands (Socialist Labour Party) at Gotha in 1875. The Gotha Program, a compromise between the positions of the two parties—although criticized by Marx for its call for government-aided productive organizations—remained the charter of German socialism until the adoption of the Erfurt Program in 1891, which discarded the state-aid provisions of the Gotha Congress and pledged the party to a Marxist program. Bismarck won his battle to repress the socialists in 1878 when the Reichstag adopted the Anti-Socialist Law that, among other things, forbade the publication of socialist literature.

Notwithstanding a dozen years of repression, the party continued to grow significantly. When the law expired in 1890, it was obvious that Liebknecht's tactic of education, not conspiracy, had been productive. When the liberated party met at Erfurt in 1891, it adopted a charter embodying the 19th century's fullest expression of social democratic ideas. Thereafter, the party was known as the German Social Democratic Party. During the final nine years of his life, Liebknecht was one of its leading spokesmen, primarily as a writer for *Vorwärts,* the party's most prominent newspaper.

BIBLIOGRAPHY. Raymond H. Dominick III, *Wilhelm Liebknecht and the Founding of the German Social Democratic Party* (1982), examines both his personal qualities and his political career.

Consult the INDEX *first*

Liebler, Thomas: *see* Erastus, Thomas.

Liechtenstein, officially PRINCIPALITY OF LIECHTENSTEIN, German FÜRSTENTUM LIECHTENSTEIN, tiny European principality located between Switzerland and Austria; it has an area of only 62 square miles (160 square km). The national capital is at Vaduz.

The eastern two-thirds of the country is composed of the rugged foothills of the Rhätikon Massif, part of the central Alps. The mountains rise to elevations between 5,900 and 8,600 feet (1,800 and 2,623 m). Their lower slopes are covered by evergreen forests and alpine flowers, while their bare peaks are blanketed by snow. The mountains contain three major valleys and are drained by the Samina River.

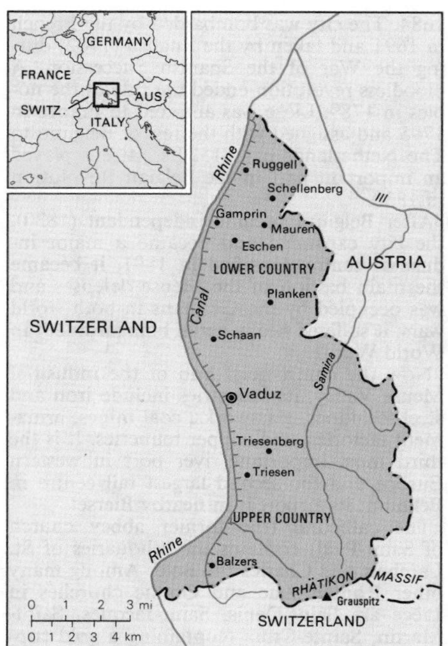

Liechtenstein

The western section of the country is occupied by the Rhine River floodplain. This, together with the valley of the Ill River, forms a triangular lowland widening northward. The river valley was once marshy, but a drainage channel built in the 1930s has made its rich soils highly suitable for agriculture.

The climate is mild and is greatly affected by the warm southerly wind known as the foehn. The annual totals of rainfall and snowfall range, according to location, from 36 to 45 inches (914 to 1,143 mm). In winter the temperature rarely falls below 5° F (−15° C), while in summer the average daily maximum temperature varies from 68° to 82° F (20° to 28° C). These conditions allow for the cultivation of grapes and corn (maize), unusual in a mountainous area.

Liechtenstein has a remarkable variety of vegetation. Water milfoil and mare's-tail as well as reeds, bulrush, bird's eye primrose, and orchids can be found. The forests comprise a mixed woodland with copper beeches, common and Norway maple, sycamore, lime, elm, and ash. As to the animal life, Liechtenstein is rich in red deer, roe deer, chamois, hare, marmot, blackcock, pheasant, hazel grouse, partridge, fox, badger, marten, polecat, stoat, weasel, and others.

The Rhine plain has always been the focus of settlement. For centuries, the valley was occupied by two independent lordships of the Holy Roman Empire, Vaduz and Schellenberg. The principality of Liechtenstein, consisting of these two lordships, was founded in 1719 and remained part of the Holy Roman Empire. It was included from 1806 to 1815 in the Rhine Confederation, and from 1815 to 1866 in the German Confederation. In 1866 Liechtenstein became independent. The traditional regions of Vaduz and Schellenberg are still recognized as unique regions—the Upper Country and the Lower Country, respectively—and they form separate electoral districts. Throughout most of its history, Liechtenstein was a quiet, rural corner of the world that was largely unaffected by its European neighbours. After World War II, however, the country underwent a remarkably rapid period of industrialization.

Liechtenstein is a constitutional monarchy in which governmental power derives from both the prince and the populace. Succession to the throne is hereditary through the male line and is determined by the regulations of the princely house. The constitution of 1921 provides for a unicameral Landtag, or parliament, composed of 15 members who are elected for four-year terms. The franchise extends to all male citizens over 20 years of age. In 1984 female citizens over 20 years of age were granted the right to vote on national, but not on local, issues.

The government consists of a head and deputy head of government and three councillors who are appointed by the prince, on proposition of the Landtag, for four-year terms. The 11 *Gemeinden* (communes) are governed autonomously—but under government supervision—by mayors and city councils, elected every three years. The government maintains a nominal police force, but the standing army was abolished in 1868.

Liechtenstein has no natural resources of commercial value, and virtually all raw materials, including wood, have to be imported. Industrialization, therefore, has as yet been free of the pollution problems suffered by other developed areas. All of the principality's forested areas are protected in order to maintain the ecology of the mountain slopes and to guard against erosion. There is no heavy industry, and the small manufacturing concerns are spread throughout the country. Production includes metalworking, pharmaceuticals, optical lenses, electronic equipment, food processing, and the manufacture of consumer goods. In 1921 Liechtenstein adopted Swiss currency, and in 1923 it joined the Swiss customs union.

Despite the small and declining percentage of the population engaged in agriculture, farming units have been increasing in size; the largest concerns concentrate on stock breeding and dairying. Corn and potatoes are traditional crops, but the production of cereals and vegetables is increasing. Vineyards are few and are split into small units. The Alpine slopes are used for grazing during the summer.

Tourism is sponsored by the government. Most visitors come from the surrounding European countries and centre their activities around Vaduz. The registration of foreign firms in Liechtenstein provides a source of tax income. The country has also become a centre of banking because of its stable political situation and its absolute bank secrecy.

There is a network of excellent roads connecting the country with its neighbours. The railway, part of the Paris–Vienna express route, passes through the northern sections of the country. There is no airport.

The Liechtensteiners are descended from the Alemanni tribe that came into the region after AD 500. Although the official language is German, the population still speaks an Alemanni dialect containing local variations in pronunciation and vocabulary. The Walsers, descendants of immigrants from the Swiss canton of Valais, settled in Triesenberg at the end of the 13th century and continue to speak a particularly distinctive form of the language. The majority of the population is Roman Catholic.

To the south, the more industrial Upper Country contains the communes of Vaduz, Balzers, Triesen, Triesenberg, Schaan, and Planken. The Lower Country, to the north, is divided into the communes of Eschen, Mauren, Gamprin, Ruggell, and Schellenberg. As a result of postwar industrialization, there has been a movement of people to the larger communes. The most populous communes are Vaduz, the administrative and commercial centre, and Schaan, the principal industrial community.

Matters of public health are in the hands of a committee of public health, which is headed by a state medical officer. Liechtenstein's small medical institutions are supplemented by the excellent neighbouring Swiss facilities, to which the principality contributes support. Social security is sustained by a variety of compulsory insurance schemes; the financing of these comprehensive plans is shared by employers, employees, and the government, the last also assuming any deficits.

Education is supervised by the National Board of Education. The school system consists of eight-year primary schools, three-year secondary schools, a vocational school, grammar school, commercial high school, music school, and a technical college. All citizens over the age of seven are literate.

The world-famous art collections of the princes of Liechtenstein, exhibited in the Engländerhaus in the centre of Vaduz, include outstanding works of many 17th-century Dutch and Flemish painters. There is also a State Art Collection (1969).

The Liechtenstein Postal Museum (founded in 1930) exhibits a large stock of stamps, including national issues since 1912. The Liechtenstein National Museum in Vaduz houses primarily early and Roman artifacts. The Liechtenstein National Library was established in 1961 as a public foundation. Pop. (1988 est.) 27,700.

lied, plural LIEDER, any of a number of particular types of German song, as they are referred to in English and French writings. The earliest so-called lieder date from the 12th and 13th centuries and are the works of minnesingers, poets and singers of courtly love (*Minne*). Many surviving *Minnelieder* reflect southern German origins and are written in a group of manuscripts of somewhat later date. These songs occur in a number of forms based on poetic models. The lied proper, like many other forms, commonly comprises two sections, the first phrase of music (*a*) repeated with different words, and the second phrase (*B*), again with different words *aaB*. This is the *Bar* form much favoured by German composers and often expanded in various ways.

The monophonic (single melodic line) *Minnelieder* are virile, abounding in small leaps; they are attractively contoured and make use of modal scales (melodic patterns characteristic of medieval and Renaissance music until the advent of the major–minor scale system). Because musical notation of this period is not precise regarding rhythmic values, the rhythmic interpretation of *Minnelieder* is controversial. Among important minnesingers (some of the lesser nobility) are Walther von der Vogelweide, Tannhäuser, Wolfram von Eschenbach, and Neidhart von Reuenthal, the first three known today through the operas of Richard Wagner.

The 14th century brought a decline of the monophonic lied and the introduction of polyphonic lieder for two or more voices or voice and instruments. One of the most popular polyphonic lieder is the two-voice "Wach auff myn Hort" ("Awake, my darling") by Oswald of Wolkenstein (1377–1455).

The 15th century saw a flowering of polyphonic lieder for as many as four voices singing together. These polyphonic settings, unlike the courtly *Minnelieder*, are addressed to educated scholars and clergy as well as nobles. *Bar* form and romantic texts predominate, and through-composed pieces (*i.e.*, devoid of sectional repetition) occur. The tunes are usually sung by the middle part (tenor); often the parts accompanying the tenor are played on instruments. The tenor melody is often a preexistent, familiar one, not a tune newly composed for the polyphonic lied. Franco-Flemish influences appear in the relations among the parts (usually three); sometimes the texture is chordal, otherwise one part may imitate the melody of another voice for part of a phrase. When three parts are present, whether sung or played and sung, the tenor and top part (descant) form a harmonic unity, while the third part (countertenor) skips between and below the other two.

Polyphonic lieder reached a climax in the mid-16th century with the songs of Ludwig Senfl and his contemporaries. The invention of printing helped disseminate the secular polyphonic lieder, and many of the most popular ones were turned into sacred pieces by simply substituting a new text. Thus lieder became important vehicles for spreading Protestantism. By the late Renaissance (*c.* 1580), lieder were composed deliberately in an Italian style: textures often chordal, phrases of regular length and well-articulated, melodies in the top part with the words carefully declaimed. Under the influence of the new madrigal (a polyphonic Italian secular form), the old lied tradition decayed.

The 19th century saw German composers again turning to lied production. Late 18th- and early 19th-century Romanticism gave great impetus to serious popular poetry, and many poems of such masters as Goethe were set by lied composers. Franz Schubert, who composed more than 600 lieder, Robert Schumann, Johannes Brahms, and Hugo Wolf are among the finest 19th-century lied composers. Although the verse in lieder often was mediocre, for the Romantics, poetry and music were of equal importance. Romantic lieder are generally for a solo voice with piano accompaniment, which often required a virtuoso technique. The songs were primarily salon music: individual lieder lack the scope of contemporary opera arias, but are more intimate and emotionally refined. Composers often wrote cycles of lieder, all related by a single topic but giving scope for considerable musical development. A lied may be either through-composed or strophic, *i.e.,* repeating the music for each new stanza of the poem. Occasionally lieder are arranged for accompaniment by full orchestra or, in the case of several lied cycles, for chamber ensemble of reduced strings and winds.

Liège (French), Flemish LUIK, province (area 1,491 sq mi [3,862 sq km]), eastern Belgium, bordering Germany on the east. It is divided into four administrative *arrondissements*—Huy, Liège, Verviers, and Waremme—with the capital at Liège. Primarily French-speaking, it includes the German-language territory of Eupen-et-Malmédy (*q.v.*), Sankt Vith, and the former neutral district of Moresnet, where German is still widely spoken.

For nearly 1,000 years Liège was the focus of the independent prince-bishops of Liège, dependencies of whom then extended from Upper Gelderland to the French frontier (Champagne), but the borders of the bishopric were deeply indented and enclosed dependencies of neighbouring states. Its position between the northwestern and southeastern areas of the Burgundian Netherlands lent the province particular importance in the 15th century. From the 16th century its prince-bishops generally collaborated with the Habsburg rulers of the Netherlands. The French encroached on the territory during the next century and annexed it (1795) during the French Revolutionary Wars. Assigned to The Netherlands in 1815, the lands became Belgian in 1830.

Drained by the Meuse, Amblève, Ourthe, and Vesdre rivers, its soils support varied agriculture. The Hesbaye, a chalk plateau in the northwest with its overlay of clay loams, produces cereals and sugar beets, and supports cattle. The humid clay loams of the Pays de Herve Plateau in the northeast support grazing lands, orchards, and syrup and cheese production. The Meuse Valley provides market garden and dairy produce. In the south and southeast are the Condroz and Hautes Fagnes areas of the Ardennes (*q.v.*), where agriculture is limited; pigs and dairy cattle are bred on the uplands, and dairy farming and the cultivation of oats, rye, wheat, clover, and potatoes are carried on in the valleys. Tourism at Spa (*q.v.*) and along the Ourthe and Amblève rivers contributes to the province's economy. Parts of the Ardennes are thickly wooded, particularly in the Eupen-et-Malmédy district; and parts of the wild Hautes Fagnes heathlands are set aside as natural reserves.

There are two major industrial regions: along the Meuse Valley centred on Liège and its satellite towns and in the Vesdre Valley around Verviers. The most easterly basin of the Sambre-Meuse coalfield occurs around Liège, and collieries, coke ovens, steelworks, and chemical and metallurgical factories extend along the Meuse Valley; coal exploitation has, however, been reduced. The Verviers region is the hub of the Belgian wool industry. Other population centres are Huy, in the Meuse Valley, and the market and resort towns of Eupen, Spa, Stavelot, and Sankt Vith in the Ardennes. The province is served by the canalized Meuse, the Albert Canal, six main roads, and several international railway routes. There are many old castles and monasteries, particularly in the Amblève and Ourthe valleys. Pop. (1983 est.) 995,576.

Liège (French), Flemish LUIK, German LÜTTICH, capital of Liège province, eastern Belgium, on the Meuse River at its confluence with the Ourthe. (The grave accent in Liège was officially approved over the acute in 1946.) The site was inhabited in prehistoric times and was known to the Romans as Leodium. A chapel was built there to honour St. Lambert, bishop of Maastricht, who was murdered there in 705. Liège became a town when St. Hubert transferred his see there in 721.

Under Notger, its first prince-bishop, it grew in importance as a centre of Liège principality and of the Mosan school of art and as a major European intellectual centre. After it was granted a communal magistracy (1185) and citizens' charter (1195), and the guilds were granted representation on the city council (1303), there was a struggle for power between the guilds and the nobles. The nobles failed in a sudden attack, and their armed party was burned to death by the populace in the church of Saint-Martin in 1312, an event known as Male Saint-Martin. Political equality was granted to the labourers and to most of the trade guilds in 1313.

During the 15th-century Burgundian domination of the Netherlands, Liège resisted and was sacked twice by Charles the Bold (1467, 1468). After Charles's death (1477) the city was rebuilt and experienced renewed prosperity in the 16th century under Prince-Bishop Evrard de La Marck. Renewed strife between the prince-bishops and the citizens resulted in the destruction of democratic institutions in 1684. The city was bombarded by the French in 1691 and taken by the English (1702) during the War of the Spanish Succession. A bloodless revolution ended the rule of the nobles in 1789; Liège was annexed to France in 1795 and assigned with the rest of Belgium to The Netherlands in 1815. Its citizens played an important part in the Belgian Revolution in 1830.

After Belgium became independent (1830), the city expanded and became a major industrial centre. Fortified in 1891, it became the main bastion of the Meuse defenses and was occupied by the Germans in both world wars; it suffered heavy aerial bombardment in World War II.

Now the commercial hub of the industrial Meuse Valley, its industries include iron and steel foundries, glassworks, coal mines, armament factories, and copper refineries. It is the third most important river port in western Europe and the second largest rail centre in Belgium; its airport is in nearby Bierset.

The cathedral (the former abbey church of Saint-Paul) contains the reliquaries of St. Lambert and Charles the Bold. Among many other Romanesque and Gothic churches in Liège are Saint-Denis, Saint-Jacques, Saint-Martin, Sainte-Croix (containing a gold triptych from 1150), and Saint-Barthélemy, with a baptismal font (1108). The palace of the prince-bishops (built in the 15th century and repaired in the 18th and 19th centuries) is now the Palais de Justice. Saint-Laurent, an old Benedictine abbey, has been a military hospital since 1796.

Central Liège, cut by the Meuse River, Belg.
Photo Research International

As the cultural centre of Wallonia (French-speaking Belgium), Liège has concert halls, theatres, an opera, and many fine museums—particularly those of fine arts and of Walloon life, the Ansembourg Museum of decorative art, the archaeological museum (in the Maison Curtius, *c.* 1600), the arms museum, and the house of the composer César Franck. The state university (1817) was entirely rebuilt in the 1960s on a new site to the south. The Royal Conservatory of Music (1887) is famous for the violin school established by Eugène Ysäye. There are also several national research laboratories and technical schools associated with the major industries of Liège. Pop. (1983 est.) mun., 207,496.

liege (probably from German *ledig,* "empty" or "free"), in European feudal society, an unconditional bond between a man and his overlord. Thus, if a tenant held estates of various overlords, his obligations to his liege lord (usually the lord of his largest estate or of that he had held the longest), to whom he had done "liege homage," were greater than, and in the event of conflict overrode, his obligations to the other lords, to whom he had done only "simple homage." This concept of liegeance is found in France as early as the 11th century and may have originated in Normandy. By the 13th century it was important because it determined not so much which lord a man should follow in a war or a dispute but which lord was entitled to the traditional pecuniary profits of overlordship from that particular tenant. In some places, such as Lotharingia (Lorraine), the distinction became virtually meaningless, men doing liege homage to several lords. In any case, the king was always considered a subject's liege lord, and clauses reserving the allegiance due to him came to be inserted in all feudal contracts. For this reason a ceremony of homage became part of the English coronation rite from the late 13th century.

Liège, State University of, French UNIVERSITÉ DE L'ÉTAT À LIÈGE, state-financed, partially autonomous coeducational French-language institution of higher learning in Liège, Belg., founded in 1816 under King William I of The Netherlands. Following Belgian independence (1831), the university was designated a state university in 1835. It has faculties of philosophy and letters, sciences, law (including economics and political and social sciences), medicine, veterinary medicine, and applied sciences (engineering and architecture). There are institutes of psychology and education and of physical education, and a school of business administration.

Liegnitz (Poland): *see* Legnica.

Lieh-tzu, Pinyin LIEZI, original name (Wade-Giles) LIEH YÜK'OU (fl. 4th century BC, China), one of the three primary philosophers who developed the basic suppositions of Taoist thought, and the presumed author of the Taoist work *Lieh-tzu*. Many of the writings traditionally attributed to Lieh-tzu and included in the book bearing his name have been identified as later forgeries. This fact and the omission of Lieh-tzu's name in the biographical notices of the historian Ssu-ma Ch'ien in 100 BC have led many to consider Lieh-tzu a fictitious person. Most modern scholars, however, think that such a man did exist.

Little is known of Lieh-tzu's life save the fact that, like his contemporaries, he had a large number of disciples and roamed through the different warring states into which China was then divided, advising kings and rulers. His work is distinguished stylistically by its wittiness and philosophically by its emphasis on determinism. Unlike the other two major Taoist philosophers, Lao-tzu and Chuang-tzu, Lieh-tzu taught that cause and effect, rather than fate, are primarily responsible for the condition of men.

Lieh-tzu, Pinyin LIEZI, also called CH'UNG HSÜ CHIH TE CHEN CHING, Pinyin CHONGXU ZHIDE ZHENJING (Chinese: "True Classic of the Perfect Virtue of Simplicity and Emptiness"), Chinese Taoist classic bearing the name of Lieh-tzu (*q.v.*). As in earlier Taoist classics (from which it borrowed heavily), emphasis in the *Lieh-tzu* centres on the mysterious Tao (Way) of Taoism, a great unknowable cosmic reality of incessant change to which human life should conform. In its present form, the *Lieh-tzu* possibly dates from the 3rd or 4th century AD.

The "Yang Chu" chapter of the classic gives the *Lieh-tzu* a particular interest, for this chapter—named after a legendary figure of the 5th–4th century BC, incorrectly identified as its author—acknowledges the futility of challenging the immutable and irresistible Tao; it concludes that all man can look forward to in this life is sex, music, physical beauty, and material abundance, and even these goals are not always satisfied. Such "fatalism" implies a life of radical "self-interest" (a new development in Taoism), according to which a person should not sacrifice so much as a single hair of his head for the benefit of others.

Lieh Yük'ou (Taoist philosopher): *see* Lieh-tzu.

lien, in property law, claim or charge upon property securing the payment of some debt or the satisfaction of some obligation or duty. Although the term is of French derivation, the lien as a legal principle was a recognized property right in early Roman law.

The English common law early recognized the creditor's possessory lien, a right of a creditor to retain possession of a debtor's goods until the satisfaction of the debt, generally the payment of the purchase price. In time, the common law developed two kinds of possessory liens: specific liens and general liens. The specific lien extended only to the indebtedness of the property owner for the value of services rendered to or in connection with his property—that is, the price for the repair or improvement of the property. The general lien extends not only to the value of services rendered in regard to the specific property but also to all indebtedness on general account by the property owner to the creditor. Whether a creditor had a general or specific possessory lien came to be determined by custom and trade usage. This classification of creditor's possessory liens was largely superseded in the eventual refinement of common-law contract remedies.

In addition to the common-law possessory liens, there are also equitable and statutory liens. Courts of equity will in certain situations recognize a creditor's interest in a debtor's property even though the property remains in the debtor's possession. An example of a statutory lien in general use in the United States is the mechanic's lien, most commonly of statutory creation, that confers upon builders, contractors, and others furnishing labour and materials for land improvement an interest in the land so improved as security for payment for their services.

Mortgages, pledges, and pawns are a generic species of the lien to the extent that they create creditor interests in property, although the law governing these differs substantially from that which applies to the lien.

Lien-yün-kang, formerly HSIN-HAI-LIEN, Pinyin LIANYUNGANG, or XINHAILIAN, city and seaport in northern Kiangsu *sheng* (province), China. The city is situated near the mouth of the Ch'ang-wei River and at the northern end of a network of canals centred on the Yün-yen River, associated with the innumerable salt pans of the coastal districts of northern Kiangsu.

Lien-yün-kang was founded as Hai-chou in AD 549 at a point somewhat farther east. It was already a centre of salt production in the 7th century. In Ming times (1368–1644) the *fu* (prefecture) was subordinated to Huai-an, but from 1726 onward it was independent. At the time of the foundation of the republic in 1911, it became a *hsien* (county) seat. Opened to foreign trade in 1905, it became a collecting centre not only for salt but also for agricultural produce from inland, which was shipped to Tsingtao, in Shantung province, and to Shanghai. Its modern growth began with the construction of the Lung-hai Railway, an east–west route running through Pao-chi, in Shensi province, in the Wei River valley. Hai-chou was the eastern terminus, and a harbour was constructed in the estuary at Ta-p'u. This, however, rapidly silted up; and in 1933 the railway was extended to the coast at a village called Lao-yao, where a new port called Lien-yün-kang was constructed in a location protected by Tung-hsi-lien Island. The port, however, which was built in 1933–36 by a Dutch company, encountered unexpected difficulties and rapidly silted up. Part of the port was used by the Lung-hai Railway, the management of which was inefficient, and part by the Chung-hsing Company to export coal from the Ts'ao-chuang mines. Although the port was linked with places as far west as Hsi-an (Ch'ang-an) in Shensi and was the centre of a network of canals, it did not grow rapidly, and it remained under the customs administration of Tsingtao. The real growth of the city began with the Japanese occupation in 1938. Although the Chinese, before withdrawing, had demolished much of the port, it was rebuilt and dredged. It handled large exports of coal, phosphates, iron ore, salt, and grain to Japan.

After 1949 Hai-chou and its older river ports of Hsin-p'u and Ta-p'u were merged. They became the municipality of Hsin-hai-lien. Subsequently its name was changed to Lien-yün-kang. The city has continued to grow as a port, and its facilities have been improved. It has also become a fishing port and a centre of the salt industry. There has been some industrial growth, and in 1984 Lien-yün-kang was designated one of China's "open" cities in the new open-door policy inviting foreign investment. Pop. (1988 est.) 317,000.

Lienz, town, *Bundesland* (federal state) Tirol, southern Austria, on the Drava (Drau) and Isel rivers at the northern end of the rugged Lienzer Dolomiten. The ruined Aguntum, which is situated immediately to the east, was the site of an Illyrian settlement (1100–500 BC) and subsequently of a Roman town. Lienz was chartered in 1252. Notable landmarks include the 16th-century Lieburg (castle); the nearby Bruck Castle, a seat of the counts of Görz-Tirol from 1271 to 1500; the parish church of St. Andreas (*c.* 1450); the church of the former Dominican monastery (*c.* 1250; rebuilt 1798); and the Franciscan church (*c.* 1439). Lienz is the principal town and market centre of the East Tirol district. It is a summer and winter tourist resort and has some manufacturing (textiles and leather goods). Pop. (1981) 11,699.

Liepāja, German LIBAU, Russian LIBAVA, city and port, Latvia, on the west (Baltic Sea) coast at the northern end of Lake Liepāja. First recorded in 1253, when it was a small Kurish settlement, Liepāja was the site of a fortress built by the Knights of the Teutonic Order in 1263. It was created a town in 1625, and in 1697–1703 a canal was cut to the sea and a port was built. In 1701, during the Great Northern War, Liepāja was captured by Charles XII of Sweden, but the end of the war saw the city in Polish possession. It was taken by Russia in the Third Partition of Poland, in 1795.

Liepāja's importance as a port, especially for grain export, was greatly stimulated in 1876 by the construction of the railway from Romny in the Ukraine. In 1893 a naval port was built, and its function as a naval base persisted through World Wars I and II, when the city suffered heavy damage, to the present. Modern Liepāja has important industries, producing steel, agricultural machinery, linoleum, sugar, canned fish, textiles, and footwear. It is a deep-sea fishing base and has several schools including a college of navigation and a branch of the Riga Polytechnic Institute. Pop. (1989 prelim.) 114,000.

Lier (Flemish), French LIERRE, *commune,* Antwerp *province,* northern Belgium, at the junction of the Great and Little Nete rivers, southeast of Antwerp. Probably settled in the 8th century, it developed around the Chapel of St. Peter (1225) on the site of an earlier wooden chapel. An important textile centre by the 14th century, it was granted many town privileges by Henry I and John I of Brabant.

It was besieged and captured by the Spanish in 1582, by the Dutch in 1595, and by the English in 1706 during the War of the Spanish Succession. Belgian nationalists repelled a Dutch attack there in 1830.

Although the town was partly destroyed during the bombardment of Antwerp in 1914, some medieval buildings survived, including the *béguinage* (a retreat for secular nuns; 13th century), the Gothic belfry (1369), and Saint Gommarus' Church (1425–1577). The church, a fine example of the Brabantine High Gothic style, is noted for its stained-glass windows, paintings, and sculptures, as well as its museum. The town hall (1740) replaced the old Cloth Hall. A conspicuous landmark is the 17th-century Zimmer Tower (named for a local astronomer and clockmaker) with its multifaced astrological clock. An art museum exhibits works by Dutch and Flemish masters. Educational institutions include a normal school (1817) and a state college (1843). The Flemish writer Felix Timmermans was born in Lier. Traditional industries include lace making, embroidery mills, and the manufacture of clothing, beaded bags, and musical instruments. Pop. (1990 est.) mun., 30,918.

Liesegang ring, in physical chemistry, any of a series of usually concentric bands of a precipitate (an insoluble substance formed from a solution) appearing in gels (coagulated colloid solutions). The bands strikingly resemble those occurring in many minerals, such as agate, and are believed to explain such mineral formations. The rings are named for their discoverer, the 20th-century German chemist Raphael Eduard Liesegang.

Liestal, capital (since 1833) of the half canton of Basel-Landschaft (Bâle-Campagne), northern Switzerland. It lies along the Ergolz River, southeast of Basel. First mentioned as a village in 1189, it passed to the bishop of Basel in 1305 and to the city of Basel in 1400. Notable landmarks are the 15th-century town hall, Saint Martin's church, and the Upper Gate. Liestal manufactures textiles, chemicals, ironware, machinery, and motors. The population is German speaking and mainly Protestant. Pop. (1987 est.) 12,161.

Lietz, Hermann (b. April 28, 1868, Dumgenewitz, Rügen, Prussia—d. June 12, 1919, Haubinda, Ger.), German educational reformer.

In 1898 he visited the progressive Abbotsholme school for boys, founded in Derbyshire, Eng., in 1889 by Cecil Reddie. Lietz was impressed by the Abbotsholme system of education, which combined comprehensive individual instruction with physical exercise and recreation. By 1904 he had founded three *Landerziehungsheime* (country boarding schools), based on Reddie's model, for boys of different ages, in Ilsenburg, Haubinda, and Bieberstein. Lietz eventually succeeded in establishing five more *Landerziehungsheime*.

Lietzmann, Hans (b. March 2, 1875, Düsseldorf, Ger.—d. June 25, 1942, Locarno, Switz.), German scholar and Lutheran church historian noted for his investigations of Christian origins.

While a professor of classical philology and church history at the University of Jena (1905–24) and the University of Berlin (1924–42), Lietzmann began and directed the *Handbuch zum Neuen Testament,* 23 vol. (1906–31; "Handbook to the New Testament"). Impressed by his linguistic expertise in biblical interpretation, his colleagues, in 1920, chose him to edit the *Zeitschrift für neutestamentliche Wissenschaft* ("Journal of New Testament Scholarship"). He gained respect for his precision and depth of judgment, even when he overturned long-held opinions. He shed new light on the evolution of the eucharistic communion service with his *Messe und Herrenmahl* (1926; *The Mass and the Lord's Supper*), which detected a possible fusion of two distinct types of 1st- and 2nd-century prayer services. His extensive research on St. Peter and St. Paul provided insights into the development of the church's organization in 1st-century Rome. *Geschichte der alten Kirche,* 4 vol. (1932–44; *A History of the Early Church*), indicates the breadth of his scholarship.

lieutenant, company grade officer, the lowest rank of commissioned officer in most armies of the world. The lieutenant normally commands a small tactical unit such as a platoon.

In the British Army and in the United States Army, Air Force, and Marine Corps, a second lieutenant is the lowest ranking commissioned officer. Above him in the U.S. services comes a first lieutenant (lieutenant in the British Army), then a captain. In the Russian Army there is still another rank, senior lieutenant. The term lieutenant has a somewhat different meaning in the U.S. and British navies, in which the lowest ranking commissioned officer is an ensign (U.S.) or sublieutenant (British). The next higher rank is lieutenant junior grade (U.S. and British), followed by lieutenant and lieutenant commander. A U.S. navy lieutenant is thus equal in rank to an army, air force, or Marine Corps captain; a U.S. navy ensign is equal in rank to a second lieutenant in the other services. In the Royal Air Force a flight lieutenant ranks below a squadron leader and above a flying officer.

The word also appears in combination with other military and civilian titles to denote a second-in-command or one of lower rank. A lieutenant colonel, for example, ranks below a colonel and above a major. A lieutenant general ranks below a general and above a major general. In the U.S. and British navies a lieutenant commander, as noted above, ranks between a lieutenant and a commander.

Lievens, Jan, also called LIEVENS DE OUDE, LIVIUS JOHANIS LE VIEUX, or JOHANNIS LIVENS, Lievens also spelled LIEVERSZ(OON), LYRINS, or LEYRENS (b. Oct. 24, 1607, Leiden, Neth.—buried June 4, 1674, Amsterdam), versatile painter and printmaker whose style derived from both the Dutch and Flemish schools of Baroque art.

A contemporary of Rembrandt, he was a pupil of Joris van Schooten (1616–18) and of Rembrandt's teacher Pieter Lastman in Amsterdam (1618–20). After residing in Leiden for a time, Lievens worked in England (1632–35) and then in Antwerp (1635–44). In 1644 he returned to Amsterdam, where he received important commissions and where his work was greatly admired. Yet his last years were troubled by debts, loneliness, and wandering.

Lievens is remembered primarily for the works of his Leiden period, which show the influence of, and the competition with, his friend Rembrandt, with whom he shared a studio there. He painted religious, allegorical, and mythological subjects; portraits; genre scenes; and landscapes. Some of his landscapes were long attributed to his friend Adriaen Brouwer. During his stay in Antwerp his art acquired a strong flavour of the style of Van Dyck. In his later years in Holland, Lievens' mastery of the Flemish grand manner recommended him to official circles, and he was commissioned to paint decorative canvases for the town hall in Amsterdam and other buildings. Some of his early etchings are of Rembrandt quality.

Liezi (Taoist philosopher): *see* Lieh-tzu.

Lifar, Serge (b. April 2, 1905, Kiev—d. Dec. 15, 1986, Lausanne, Switz.), Russian-born French dancer, choreographer, and ballet master (1929–45, 1947–58) of the Paris Opéra Ballet who enriched its repertoire, reestablished its reputation as a leading ballet company, and enhanced the position of male dancers in a company long dominated by ballerinas.

Lifar was introduced to dance in 1920 by Bronislava Nijinska, under whom he began to study. Brought to France to join Sergey Diaghilev's Ballets Russes, Lifar studied with the eminent teacher Enrico Cecchetti and became premier danseur of the company in 1925 and created the title roles in a number of George Balanchine's early ballets, including *The Prodigal Son* (1929). Lifar was a dramatic and athletic dancer who had a charismatic stage presence. The first ballet he himself choreographed was *Le Renard* (1929; "The Fox," music by Igor Stravinsky).

Lifar in *Night,* 1930
BBC Hulton Picture Library

After Diaghilev's death, in 1929, Lifar joined the Paris Opéra Ballet as premier danseur and ballet master and soon instituted weekly ballet performances, thus abolishing the Opéra's practice of producing ballet only in conjunction with opera. In 1932 he was awarded the title of *professeur de danse* and began reforms of the Opéra's school to enable its dancers to perform the more modern ballets, particularly his own.

Lifar believed that dance was more important than the music and decor in a ballet, and he held that since ballet technique has its own innate formal values, its choreography should not derive from music. Lifar first experimented with this controversial concept in *Icare* (1935; "Icarus"), in which he created the title role. The work was performed solely to a percussion accompaniment that was added after the choreography had been completed. In later ballets he utilized more conventional music but continued to dictate to his composers or musical arrangers the rhythms necessary to coincide with his choreography.

Apart from revivals of classical ballets, Lifar staged more than 50 works for the Opéra, including *Promethée* (1929), *David triomphant* (1936), *Le Chevalier et la damoiselle* (1941), *Joan de Zarissa* (1942), *Les Mirages* (1947), *Phèdre* (1950), and *Les Noces fantastiques* (1955). Most of his ballets were considered modern but classical in structure. Many were narrative works, with themes drawn from classical mythology and legend or from the Bible. His ballets often attempted to convey the drama through appropriate technique and choreography, rather than through mime-dance, and, in contrast to prevalent Opéra custom, frequently gave leading, rather than supporting, roles to men.

Dismissed from the Paris Opéra Ballet after World War II because of his social association with high German officers during the war, Lifar returned to the Opéra in 1947, retired as a dancer in 1956, and, after 1958, choreographed or staged ballets for various European companies. In 1960 he appeared in the film *Le Testament d'Orphée.* He wrote many books on the theory and history of dance.

life, the state of a material complex or individual characterized by the capacity to perform certain functional activities, including metabolism, growth, reproduction, and some form of responsiveness and adaptation. Life is further characterized by the presence of complex transformations of organic molecules, and by the organization of such molecules into the successively larger units of protoplasm, cells, organs, and organisms.

A brief treatment of life follows. For full treatment, see MACROPAEDIA: Life.

Metabolism involves a living system's continual exchange of some of its materials with its surroundings, principally in the process of building up or destroying its protoplasm. Growth involves an increase in the size of an organism, which in turn is usually due to its having a higher metabolic rate of synthesis of protoplasm than a rate of breakdown of that matter. Reproduction, perhaps the most striking hallmark of life, involves at its most basic level the division of one cell into two cells. This process is ultimately mediated by the hereditary information contained in large molecules, called genes, that are composed of nucleic acids. The reproduction of genes themselves passes the instructions for the various characteristics of an organism on to the next generation. Responsiveness and adaptation represent the ability of an organism to change in response to alterations in its environment. These two qualities are fundamental determinants of the process of natural selection, through which the hereditary characteristics of organisms evolve over long periods of time and many generations.

Opinion concerning the essential nature of life has been historically divided between vitalist and mechanistic concepts. Vitalism asserts the existence of some "vital force" that separates living from nonliving matter and forms life's underlying principle. Mechanism, on the other hand, asserts that the wondrous phenomena of life are merely processes and transformations obeying elementary chemical and physical laws, and that a living system is ultimately reducible to its constituent atoms and molecules, and nothing more.

Procaryotic bacteria and blue-green algae are the earliest known forms of life on Earth. Fossils of these organisms, discovered in the Fig Tree chert of the Transvaal, have been dated at 3.5 billion years old. This suggests that living systems appeared within a few hundred million years after the origin of their host planet, since the Earth itself is thought to be about 4.6 billion years old.

Hypotheses of the origin of life range from religious concepts of life's creation out of inanimate matter by a divine agency to the more scientifically acceptable theory that life began on the early Earth by a series of progressive chemical reactions. According to this hypothesis, which has been supported by recent laboratory experimentation, inorganic compounds such as methane, ammonia, and water vapour that were plentiful in early times on the Earth formed into simple organic molecules with the aid of atmospheric electric discharges and ultraviolet radiation as energy sources. The question of how the resulting simple amino acids eventually became the much more highly organized and self-replicating systems known as life is much more difficult to answer, however, and is still far from being resolved.

Life, weekly picture magazine (1936–72) published in New York City. *Life* was a pioneer in photojournalism and one of the major forces in that field's development. It was long one of the most popular and widely imitated of American magazines. It was founded by Henry Luce, publisher of *Time,* and quickly became a cornerstone of his Time–Life Publications.

From its start *Life* emphasized photography, with gripping, superbly chosen news photographs, amplified by photo features and photo essays on an international range of topics. Its photographers were the elite of their craft and enjoyed worldwide esteem. *Life*'s war coverage of World War II, Korea, Vietnam, and numerous regional wars was consistently vivid, authentic, and moving. Gradually, the magazine began to admit more writing to its pages, carefully choosing its writers and text editors. *Life* ceased publication largely because the costs of preparing, printing, and mailing each issue outstripped its revenues from advertising. After 1972 it reappeared in several special issues, and then, in 1978, on a reduced scale and on a regular basis as a monthly.

life cycle, in biology, the series of changes that the members of a species undergo as they pass from the beginning of a given developmental stage to the inception of that same developmental stage in a subsequent generation.

In many simple organisms, including bacteria and various protists, the life cycle is completed within a single generation: an organism begins with the fission of an existing individual; the new organism grows to maturity; and it then splits into two new individuals, thus completing the cycle. In higher animals, the life cycle also encompasses a single generation: the individual animal begins with the fusion of male and female sex cells (gametes); it grows to reproductive maturity; and it then produces gametes, at which point the cycle begins anew (assuming that fertilization takes place).

In most plants, by contrast, the life cycle is multigenerational. An individual plant begins with the germination of a spore, which grows into a gamete-producing organism (the gametophyte). The gametophyte reaches maturity and forms gametes, which, following fertilization, grow into a spore-producing organism (the sporophyte). Upon reaching reproductive maturity, the sporophyte produces spores, and the cycle starts again. This multigenerational life cycle is called alternation of generations; it occurs in some protists and fungi as well as in plants.

The life cycle characteristic of bacteria is termed haplontic. This term refers to the fact that it encompasses a single generation of organisms whose cells are haploid (*i.e.,* contain one set of chromosomes). The one-generational life cycle of the higher animals is diplontic; it involves only organisms whose body cells are diploid (*i.e.,* contain two sets of chromosomes). Organisms with diplontic cycles produce sex cells that are haploid, and each of these gametes must combine with another gamete in order to obtain the double set of chromosomes necessary to grow into a complete organism. The life cycle typified by plants is known as diplohaplontic, because it includes both a diploid generation (the sporophyte) and a haploid generation (the gametophyte).

life insurance, method by which large groups of individuals equalize the burden of financial loss from death by distributing funds to the beneficiaries of those who die. Life insurance is most developed in wealthy countries, where it has become a major channel of saving and investing. (*See* insurance.)

The three basic types of life insurance contracts are term, whole life, and endowment. Under term insurance contracts, issued for a specified number of years, protection expires at the end of the period and there is no cash value remaining. Whole life contracts run for the whole of the insured's life and also accumulate a cash value, which is paid when the contract matures or is surrendered; the cash value is less than the policy's face value. Endowment contracts run for a specified time period and pay their full face value at the end of the period.

Upon the death of the insured, the beneficiary may accept a lump sum settlement of the face amount, may choose to receive the proceeds over a given period, may leave the money with the insurer temporarily and draw interest on it, or may use it to purchase an annuity guaranteeing regular payments for life.

life span, the period of time between the birth and death of an organism, ranging from one day for the mayfly to thousands of years for the bristlecone pine. A maximum life span probably exists for each species.

A brief treatment of life spans follows. For full treatment, *see* MACROPAEDIA: Growth and Development, Biological.

The life span of each organism depends on different environmental pressures (availability of food, shelter, climate, predators), variation in physical condition (disease, accidents), and heredity (offspring from long-lived parents have a longer life expectancy than those from short-lived parents).

Among single-celled organisms, which reproduce by cell division, the concept of an individual life span loses some validity, as in a sense the individual continues to exist indefinitely. Thus arbitrary definitions of individual lives, such as the period between reproductive divisions, may be used to estimate life span, but such estimates are not comparable to those for sexually reproducing organisms.

In most species the maximum life span can be estimated from the longest observed survival of individual members of the species. The maximum human life span is reported to be between 115 and 150 years. In many animals, the maximum life span has been calculated from survival in captivity, where safety from predators allows many individuals to live to an advanced old age seldom reached in the wild. Typical vertebrate life spans range from about one year for some small rodents to 177 years for the giant tortoise; the longest-lived mammal appears to be the human. Invertebrate animals generally have shorter life spans, some surviving for only a few days, but some snails, crayfish, and beetles have been observed to live for up to 30 years. Although the maximum life span of humans is over 100 years, the average life span today is only about 70 years, compared with 30 years in the 1700s. More humans are thus likely to survive to the hypothetical maximum life span in the present generation. Nevertheless, there is no evidence that maximum life span has increased, and persons surviving the risks of infancy and childhood in historic times had life spans roughly similar to present-day averages.

The life span of plants is more difficult to determine than that of animals, but in general, plant species seem to have longer maximum survivals than animals. Bristlecone pine trees in California and Nevada have been confirmed to have lived for 4,900 years, and several other trees, including oaks, redwoods, and junipers, may live for more than 1,000 years. Some flowering plants, such as English ivy, also may have life spans in the hundreds of years, and the mycelia of fungi may survive 400 years, putting forth transient reproductive bodies such as mushroom caps whenever conditions are appropriate. Except for trees, which have annual growth rings that make possible an accurate assessment of age, it is almost impossible to state the age of a given plant unless there are clear records of its individual existence from planting onward. Some mosses have been estimated to have lived for as long as 2,800 years, but the proven survival of these species is considerably less.

Several herbaceous plant species survive for only a single growing season, producing flowers and seeds and then dying off; for such plants, called annuals, average and maximum life spans are more or less equivalent. Other herbaceous plants live for two growing seasons, storing food in the first and putting forth flowers and seeds in the second; again, average and maximum life spans are the same. Other plants, called perennials, survive for several years before reproducing.

Estimates of plant life spans are also made more difficult because the life span of plants is sometimes determined from the formation of seeds or spores rather than from their germination. Many seeds retain viability for years, producing normal plants when they are finally planted; in such cases, the period between germination and death of the plant may be considerably less than the total life span from the first formation of the seed.

life-span psychology: *see* developmental psychology.

life-support system, any mechanical device that enables a person to live and usually work in an environment such as outer space or underwater in which he could not otherwise function or survive for any appreciable amount of time. Life-support systems provide all or some of the elements essential for maintaining physical well being, as for example oxygen, nutrients, water, disposal of body wastes, and control of temperature and pressure. The danger of contaminants and psychological factors must also be considered. Life-support systems are designed not only to enable survival in inhospitable environments but also to obviate the extreme difficulty people sometimes have in working under such conditions; thus life-support systems promote comfort, efficiency, and safety as well.

The development of life-support systems can be traced to the work of Paul Bert, a 19th-century French physiologist, engineer, and physician. During the 1870s Bert conceptualized the basic principle of using supplementary oxygen to supply balloonists and mountain climbers who had ascended beyond the levels at which the oxygen in air is sufficient for breathing. Two of Bert's colleagues took a supply of about 150 litres of 70 percent oxygen on a balloon flight in 1875; but they failed to use it soon enough, and only one of the two survived. On this flight the oxygen was stored at ambient pressure in "goldbeater's bags" (made from cow's intestines) and was to be inhaled by mouth tube through a humidifier containing an aromatic liquid whose purpose was both to humidify the gas and to counteract the odour of the bags. Bert also designed a tank and regulator system with a capacity of 330 litres whereby mountain climbers could breathe oxygen near the peak on their ascent.

Since Bert's pioneering efforts, various kinds of sophisticated life-support systems have been developed. They include the pressurized cabins and auxiliary environmental control mechanisms of high-altitude aircraft, spacecraft, and submarines and other submersibles. Examples of personal life-support devices are the pressure suits and extravehicular activity (EVA) backpacks (*i.e.*, portable systems that contain cooling fluid, oxygen flow and recirculation equipment, waste containment unit, power source, and communications apparatus) worn by astronauts when working outside of their spacecraft; the self-contained underwater breathing equipment (scuba gear) used by divers; and the protective garments and breathing systems employed by firefighters. Another variety of devices that are sometimes classified as life-support systems include the anesthesia machine and the incubator unit (apparatus for housing premature or sick babies) utilized in hospitals.

life-world, German LEBENSWELT, in Phenomenology, the world as immediately or directly experienced in the subjectivity of everyday life, as sharply distinguished from the objective "worlds" of the sciences, which employ the methods of the mathematical sciences of nature; although these sciences originate in the life-world, they are not those of everyday life. The life-world includes individual, social, perceptual, and practical experiences. The objectivism of science obscures both its origin in the subjective perceptions of the life-world and the life-world itself. In analyzing and describing the life-world, Phenomenology attempts to show how the world of theory and science originates from the life-world, strives to discover the mundane phenomena of the life-world itself, and attempts to show how the experience of the life-world is possible by analyzing time, space, body, and the very givenness or presentation of experience.

lifeboat, watercraft especially built for rescue missions. There are two types, the relatively simple versions carried on board ships and the larger, more complex craft based on shore. Modern shore-based lifeboats are generally about 40–50 feet (12–15 metres) long and are designed to stay afloat under severe sea conditions. Sturdiness of construction, self-righting ability, reserve buoyancy, and manoeuvrability in surf, especially in reversing direction, are prime characteristics.

As early as the 18th century, attempts were made in France and England to build "unsinkable" lifeboats. After a tragic shipwreck in 1789 at the mouth of the Tyne, a lifeboat was designed and built at Newcastle that would right itself when capsized and would retain its buoyancy when nearly filled with water. Named the "Original," the double-ended, ten-oared craft remained in service for 40 years and became the prototype for other lifeboats. In 1807 the first practical line-throwing device was invented. In 1890 the first mechanically powered, land-based lifeboat was launched, equipped with a steam engine; in 1904 the gasoline engine was introduced, and a few years later the diesel.

A typical modern land-based lifeboat is either steel-hulled or of double-skin, heavy timber construction; diesel powered; and equipped with radio, radar, and other electronic gear. It is manned by a crew of about seven, most of whom are usually volunteers who can be summoned quickly in an emergency.

lifesaving, any activity related to the saving of life in cases of drowning, shipwreck, and other accidents on or in the water and to the prevention of drowning in general.

Drowning involves suffocation by immersion in a liquid, usually water. Water closing over the victim's mouth and nose cuts off the body's supply of oxygen. Deprived of oxygen, the victim stops struggling, loses consciousness, gives up the remaining tidal air in his lungs, and sinks to the bottom. There the heart may continue to beat feebly for a brief interval, but eventually it ceases and death ensues. Lifesaving consists of aiding or rescuing the drowning persons and reviving the apparently drowned.

The act of saving a drowning person is immensely complicated by the panicked struggles of the victim to stay afloat and breathing. The victim may convulsively grip his would-be rescuer, impeding his movements and quite possibly dragging them both down to the bottom in his efforts to stay alive. Contact with a drowning person poses no threat to the trained lifesaver, however, who is skilled in ways of avoiding or releasing the grip of the victim. For the person unskilled in lifesaving to come within the grasp of a drowning person can mean death for both of them. There are ways, however, in which anyone can give effective aid to a victim whether he is a skilled lifesaver or not, even if he cannot swim at all.

So many persons get into difficulty close to safety that the rescuer may often act without entering the water at all. For those very close to the rescuer, a hand reach while retaining a firm position or handhold on dry support is enough. To make contact with a victim just beyond hand reach, an oar, paddle or anything else to serve as an extension may be held by one end while the other end is thrust into the victim's grasp and he is drawn to safety. A drowning victim beyond reach of extensions may be aided by flinging within his grasp ring buoys, life vests, inflated tubes, or anything that has enough buoyancy to enable him to keep his head above water until he can be brought to safety.

A swimming rescue may be made as a last resort by a person who is a strong swimmer, provided he is willing to take the risk involved. The rescuer approaches the drowning person from the rear even though it involves circling the victim. Watching his chance, the rescuer swims to within arm's reach of the victim and assumes an upright position in the water with the legs in stroking position, a little forward of perpendicular. The rescuer then grasps the victim firmly by the hair, collar, or upper body and immediately turns on his side and starts swimming strongly with his legs and free arm. The holding arm is kept rigid. No attempt is made to lift the victim's head above water, because the act of swimming away not only brings the victim's face above the surface so that he may breathe but also planes the victim's body to the horizontal position and thus makes towing him easier.

Lifesaving in the 20th century has been augmented by new techniques involving the use of the life jacket, or vest, which largely replaced the doughnut-shaped life preserver except for use on bridges or waterfronts; and by the use of powered boats and helicopters to rescue the shipwrecked. As the recreation of swimming became popular in the 19th century, a variety of organizations sprang up in the United States and in western Europe that were dedicated to teaching lifesaving and water-safety techniques, as well as certifying persons trained to prevent drowning.

Among the bodies offering such services in the late 20th century were the Royal Life Saving Service, the American Red Cross, whose involvement with lifesaving dates from 1914, and the U.S. Coast Guard, as well as the beach personnel of local and municipal governments and those yacht clubs, marinas, and boating associations which provided training in lifesaving techniques. *See also* artificial respiration.

Liffey, River, Irish AN LIFE, river in Counties Wicklow, Kildare, and Dublin, Ireland, rising in the Wicklow Mountains, about 20 mi (32 km) southwest of Dublin. Following a tortuous course laid out in preglacial times, it flows in a generally northwesterly direction from its source to the Lackan Reservoir, the site of a gorge cut through the Slievethoul ridge. The river then runs westward in the Kildare lowland and gradually turns northwestward to Droichead Nua and northeast to Celbridge and Leixlip. It then flows eastward through the city of Dublin, in which it is extensively canalized and bordered with quays. It empties into Dublin Bay, an arm of the Irish Sea, after a course of 50 mi.

Lifou, Île, English LIFU ISLAND, largest (462 sq mi [1,196 sq km]) and most populous of the Loyalty Islands in the French overseas territory of New Caledonia, southwestern Pacific Ocean. It is the central island of the group. Lifou rises no higher than 200 ft (60 m). The coral limestone creates a fertile soil but also precludes the existence of surface streams, so that fresh water can be found only in caves and wells. The inhabitants grow taro, yams, and bananas and produce copra for export. Chépénéhé, on the west coast's Baie du Sandal (Sandal Bay), is the chief town and administrative centre. Pop. (1981 est.) 8,358.

ligament, tough fibrous band of connective tissue that serves to support the internal organs and hold bones together in proper articulation at the joints. A ligament is composed of dense fibrous bundles of collagenous fibres and spindle-shaped cells known as fibroblasts, with little ground substance (a gel-like component of the various connective tissues). Ligaments may be of two major types: white ligament is rich in collagenous fibres, which are sturdy and inelastic; yellow ligament is rich in elastic fibres, which are quite tough even though they allow elastic movement. At joints, ligaments form a capsular sac that encloses the articulating bone ends and a lubricating membrane, the synovial membrane. Sometimes the structure includes a recess, or pouch, lined by synovial tissue; this is called a bursa. Other ligaments fasten around or across bone ends in bands, permitting varying degrees of movement, or act as tie pieces between bones (such as the ribs or the bones of the forearm), restricting inappropriate movement. *See also* aponeurosis; tendon.

ligancy (chemistry): *see* coordination number.

ligand, in chemistry, any atom or molecule attached to a central atom, usually a metallic element, in a coordination or complex compound. The atoms and molecules used as ligands are almost always those that are capable of functioning as the electron-pair donor in the electron-pair bond (a coordinate covalent bond) formed with the metal atom. Examples of common ligands are the neutral molecules water (H_2O), ammonia (NH_3), and carbon monoxide (CO) and the anions cyanide (CN^-), chloride (Cl^-), and hydroxide (OH^-). Occasionally, ligands can be cations (*e.g.,* NO^+, $N_2H_5^+$) and electron-pair acceptors. The ligands in a given complex may be identical, as the CO ligands in $Fe(CO)_5$ and the H_2O ligands in $Ni(H_2O)_6^{2+}$, or different, as the CO and NO ligands in $Co(CO)_3(NO)$. Attachment of the ligand to the metal may be through a single atom, in which case it is called a unidentate ligand, or through two or more atoms, in which case it is called a bidentate or polydentate ligand.

ligand field theory, in chemistry, one of several theories that describe the electronic structure of coordination or complex compounds, notably transition metal complexes, which consist of a central metal atom surrounded by a group of electron-rich atoms or molecules called ligands. The ligand field theory deals with the origins and consequences of metal–ligand interactions as a means of elucidating the magnetic, optical, and chemical properties of these compounds.

Attributed mainly to the works of the U.S. physicist J.H. Van Vleck, the ligand field theory evolved from the earlier crystal field theory, developed for crystalline solids by the U.S. physicist Hans Albrecht Bethe. Bethe's theory considers the metal–ligand linkage as a purely ionic bond; *i.e.,* the bond between two particles of opposite electrical charges. It further assumes that the electronic structure of the metal atom is altered by the electrical field generated by the surrounding negative charges (the ligand field). In particular, the effects of the ligand field on the five *d* orbitals of an inner electron shell of the central atom are considered. (The *d* orbitals are regions within an electron shell with certain preferred orientations in space; in transition metals these orbitals are only partly occupied by electrons.) In the isolated metal atom, the *d* orbitals are of the same energy state and have equal probabilities of being occupied by electrons. In the presence of the ligand field these orbitals may be split into two or more groups that differ slightly in energy; the manner and the extent of orbital splitting depend on the geometric arrangement of the ligands with respect to the orbitals and on the strength of the ligand field.

The change in energy state is accompanied by a redistribution of electrons; in the extreme, those orbitals promoted to a higher energy state may be left unoccupied, and those orbitals brought to a lower energy state may become completely filled by pairs of electrons with opposite spin. Molecules that contain unpaired electrons are attracted to a magnet and are called paramagnetic; the state of pairing or unpairing of electrons in metal complexes is correctly predicted from the concept of orbital splitting. The colours of metal complexes are also explained in terms of the split *d* orbitals: because the energy differences among these orbitals are comparatively small, electronic transitions are readily achieved by absorption of radiation in the visible range.

The ligand field theory goes beyond the crystal field theory, however. The chemical bond between the metal and the ligands and the origins of orbital splitting are ascribed not only to electrostatic forces but also to a small degree of overlap of metal and ligand orbitals and a delocalization of metal and ligand electrons. Introduction of these modifications into the quantum-mechanical formulation of the crystal field theory improves the agreement of its quantitative predictions with experimental observations. In another theory, called the molecular orbital theory—also applied to coordination compounds—complete mixing of metal and ligand orbitals (to form molecular orbitals) and complete delocalization of electrons are assumed.

In some contexts, the term ligand field theory is used as a general name for the whole gradation of theories from the crystal field theory to the molecular orbital theory.

ligase, also called SYNTHETASE, any one of a class of about 50 enzymes that catalyze reactions involving the conservation of chemical energy and provide a couple between energy-demanding synthetic processes and energy-yielding breakdown reactions. They catalyze the joining of two molecules, deriving the needed energy from the cleavage of an energy-rich phosphate bond (in many cases, by the simultaneous conversion of adenosine triphosphate [ATP] to adenosine diphosphate [ADP]). A ligase catalyzing the formation of a carbon-oxygen bond between an amino acid and transfer RNA is called amino acid–RNA ligase. Carbon–nitrogen (C—N) bonds are formed by the action of such enzymes as amide synthetases and peptide synthetases.

Ligdan, also spelled LINGDAN, LEGDAN, or LIKDAN (d. 1634, Tibet), last of the paramount Mongol khans (ruled 1604–34).

Ligdan was a member of the Chahar royal family in which the Mongol supreme khanate was vested. He lived at a time when the Mongols were abandoning their traditional shamanism to convert to Tibetan Buddhism. He had Buddhist temples constructed and religious texts translated from Tibetan into Mongolian.

Ligdan's authority as khan was not recognized beyond his own tribe, and his attempts to maintain a degree of control over nearby Mongols were ignored. He was known as a formidable fighter, however, and was feared by his neighbours. Attacks from enemy Mongol tribes and clans and from the Manchus who were coming to power in China forced him and many of the Chahars to flee westward. Ligdan died before he could reconsolidate his position, and the Chahar line ended.

liger, offspring of a lion and a tigress. The liger is a zoo-bred hybrid, as is the tigon, the result of mating a tiger with a lioness. It is probable that neither the liger nor the tigon occurs in the wild, as differences in the behaviour and habitat of the lion and tiger make interbreeding unlikely. The liger and the tigon possess features of both parents, in variable proportions, but are generally larger and darker than either. It is thought that most, if not all, male ligers and tigons are sterile; the females, however, on occasion, may be able to produce young.

Liger (*Leo leo* x *Leo tigris*)
Sally Anne Thompson—Animal Photography

Ligeti, György (b. May 28, 1923, Diciosânmartin [now Tîrnăveni], Transylvania, Rom.), a leading composer of the branch of avant-garde music concerned principally with shifting masses of sound and tone colours.

Ligeti, of Hungarian ancestry, studied and taught music in Hungary until 1956. Later he was associated with centres of new music in Cologne and Darmstadt, Ger., Stockholm, and Vienna, where he composed electronic music (*e.g., Artikulation,* 1958) as well as music for performers. In the early 1960s he caused a sensation with his *Future of Music—A Collective Composition* (1961) and his *Poème symphonique* (1962). The former consists of the composer regarding the audience from the stage and the audience's reactions to this; the latter is written for 100 metronomes, operated by 10 performers.

Most of Ligeti's music after the late 1950s involved radically new approaches to music composition. Specific musical intervals, rhythms, and harmonies are often not distinguishable but act together in a multiplicity of sound events to create music sometimes of remarkably smooth stillness, sometimes of dynamic anguished motion. Good examples of these effects occur in *Atmosphéres* (1961) for orchestra and *Requiem* (1963–65) for soprano, mezzo-soprano, two choruses, and orchestra. In *Aventures* (1962) and *Nouvelles Aventures* (1962–65), Ligeti attempts to obliterate the differences between vocal and instrumental sounds. In these works the singers hardly do any "singing" in the traditional sense.

In Ligeti's cello concerto (1966), the usual concerto contrast between soloist and orchestra is minimized in music of mainly very long lines and slowly changing, very nontraditional textures. Other works include *Clocks and Clouds* (1973), for female chorus and orchestra, and *San Francisco Polyphony* for orchestra (1974).

Liggett Group Inc., U.S. conglomerate with major interests in making tobacco products, spirits and wines, and pet foods. Headquarters are in Durham, N.C.

In 1849 J.E. Liggett and Brother was established in St. Louis, Mo., by John Edmund Liggett (1826–97) as an outgrowth of a family concern dating to 1822. George S. Myers entered the business in 1873, and in 1878 the company was incorporated as Liggett & Myers Company. By 1885 it was the world's largest manufacturer of plug chewing tobacco, at a time in the United States when chewing was by far the most popular use of tobacco. Not until the 1890s did the company begin producing cigarettes.

From 1899 to 1911 Liggett & Myers was part of the American tobacco trust (*see* American Brands, Inc.), but it reemerged after dissolution of the trust by the U.S. Court of Appeals and was reincorporated in 1911 as Liggett & Myers Tobacco Company, headquartered in Durham.

Until 1964 the company engaged exclusively in making tobacco products (with such familiar brands as Chesterfield and L&M cigarettes), but in that year it began diversifying with the purchase of Allen Products Company, makers of pet foods. Two years later it acquired controlling interest in Paddington Corporation and Carillon Importers Ltd., importers of spirits and wines (*e.g.,* J&B scotch, Grand Marnier liqueur, Campari aperitif). In 1968 the corporate name was changed to Liggett & Myers Incorporated; in 1976 it was again changed, to Liggett Group Inc. In 1977 Diversified Products Corporation, makers of sporting goods, merged with the Liggett Group.

In 1980 the Liggett Group was acquired by a British-based conglomerate, Grand Metropolitan PLC, which sold it to American financier Bennett S. LeBow in 1986. LeBow led the company through a merger in 1990, when it was renamed Brooke Group Ltd. The company pioneered the development of low-priced, generic cigarettes while marketing more expensive, classic brands, such as Chesterfield, Eve, and Lark.

light, electromagnetic radiation that can be detected by the human eye. In terms of wavelength, electromagnetic radiation occurs over an extremely wide range, from gamma rays with a wavelength of 3×10^{-14} centimetre to long radio waves measured in millions of kilometres. In that spectrum the wavelengths visible to humans occupy a very narrow band, from about 7×10^{-5} centimetre (red light) down to about 4×10^{-5} centimetre (violet). The spectral regions adjacent to the visible band are often referred to as light also, infrared at the one end and ultraviolet at the other. The speed of light in a vacuum is a fundamental physical constant, the currently accepted value of which is exactly 299,792,458 metres per second, or about 186,282 miles per second (299,792 kilometres per second).

Light is treated in a number of articles in the MACROPAEDIA. For the basic properties of light, *see* Light; Optics, Principles of. For more general electromagnetic phenomena, *see* Electromagnetic Radiation; Radiation. For the dual nature of light (as wave and as particle) and the current quantum mechanical understanding of optical phenomena, *see* Mechanics. For the fundamental role of light in relativity theory, *see* Relativity. For the role of light in physiological processes, *see* Sensory Reception; Perception, Human; Photosynthesis. For optical instrumentation and methods of analysis, *see* Analysis and Measurement, Physical and Chemical; Microscopes; Telescopes. For practical and engineering applications, *see* Photography.

Light, Francis (b. *c.* 1740, Suffolk, Eng.—d. Oct. 21, 1794, Penang Island [now in Malaysia]), British naval officer who was responsible for acquiring Penang (Pinang) Island in the Strait of Malacca as a British naval base.

Light served in the Royal Navy from 1759 until 1763. In command of a merchant ship, he went in 1771 to the northern Malay state of Kedah, where he won the confidence of the sultan, Mohammed. About that time England, at war with France, was looking for a suitable naval outpost along the Malay Peninsula. By March 1786 the East India Company, apparently at Light's urging, settled on Penang as the site. Light conducted the negotiations with Mohammed's son, Sultan Abdullah of Kedah, who was threatened by the powerful states of Siam (Thailand) and Myanmar (Burma). Abdullah agreed to English occupation in exchange for support against other Southeast Asian powers.

Penang was annexed on Aug. 11, 1786, but the British allowed Siam to take over control of Kedah early in the 19th century. Light governed the settlement, which was declared a free port. His generous land grants and encouragement of trade attracted a number of immigrants, particularly Chinese, and the area soon prospered.

light bulb, electric incandescent lamp based on a glowing metallic filament enclosed within a glass shell filled with an inert gas such as nitrogen. *See* incandescent lamp; lamp.

light curve, in astronomy, graph of the changes in brightness with time of a star, particularly of the variable type. The light curves of different kinds of variable stars differ in

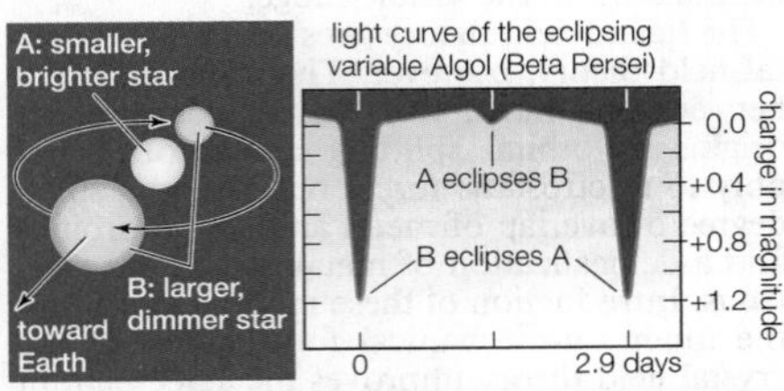

Light curve of the eclipsing-variable star Algol (Beta Persei); sharp dips occur when the fainter component star eclipses the brighter one

EB Inc.

the degree of change in magnitude (*i.e.,* the amount of light flux observed), in the degree of regularity from one cycle to the next, and in the length of the cycle—*i.e.,* the period. Variations in magnitude range from barely detectable to the billionfold increase in brightness of a supernova, while periods vary from milliseconds for some pulsars to a supernova's single explosion.

light-emitting diode (LED), in electronics, a semiconductor diode that emits infrared or visible light (electroluminescence) when charged with an electric current.

A brief treatment of light-emitting diodes follows. For full treatment, *see* MACROPAEDIA: Electronics: Light-emitting diode.

Visible LEDs are used in many electronic devices as indicator lamps and, when arranged in a matrix, as alphanumeric displays. Infrared LEDs are applied in optoelectronics, such as in autofocus cameras and television remote controls, and as light sources in some long-range optical-fibre communication systems. LEDs are formed by the so-called III-V compound semiconductors related to gallium arsenide. Compared to a laser diode, an LED also consumes little power but has a simpler configuration and wider bandwidth.

light meter: *see* exposure meter.

light opera: *see* comic opera.

light quantum: *see* photon.

light rail transit, system of railways usually powered by overhead electrical wires and used for local transportation in metropolitan areas. Light rail vehicles (LRVs) are a technological outgrowth of streetcars (trams). Light rail transit lines are more segregated from street traffic than are tramways (particularly in congested urban areas) but less so than are rapid transit (heavy rail) lines. *See* mass transit.

light verse, poetry on trivial or playful themes that is written primarily to amuse and entertain and that often involves the use of nonsense and wordplay. Frequently distinguished by considerable technical competence, wit, sophistication, and elegance, light poetry constitutes a considerable body of verse in all Western languages.

The Greeks were among the first to practice light verse, examples of which may be found in the Greek Anthology. Roman poets, such as Catullus, singing of his love's sparrow, and Horace, inviting friends to share his wine, set patterns in light poetry that were followed to the end of the 19th century.

Medieval light verse, mainly narrative in form, was often satirical, bawdy, and irreverent but nonetheless sensible and essentially moral, as can be seen in the 12th-century Latin songs of wandering students (goliards), the often indecent French fabliaux, and mock epics such as the *Roman de Renart*.

French light poetry of the 14th and 15th centuries was written largely in ballades and rondeaux, challenging such poets as Clément Marot and Pierre de Ronsard to great displays of virtuosity. A vein of light melancholy runs through the witty verse of many English Renaissance poets, from Sir Thomas Wyat to Richard Lovelace. The more cheerful poetry of Ben Jonson and Robert Herrick sometimes celebrated food and simple pleasures.

Late 17th-century examples include Samuel Butler's *Hudibras* (1663), which satirized the English Puritans, and the *Fables* (1668, 1678–79, 1692–94) of Jean de La Fontaine, which create a comprehensive picture of society and minutely scrutinize its behaviour.

The great English light poem of the 18th century is Alexander Pope's *The Rape of the Lock* (1712–14), a mock epic in which the polite society of his day is shown by innuendo to be a mere shadow of the heroic days of old. Lord Byron's verse novel *Don Juan* (1819–24), sardonic and casual, combined the colloquialism of medieval light verse with a sophistication that inspired a number of imitations.

Light verse proliferated in the later 19th century with the rise of humorous periodicals. Among the best-known light works of the period are the limericks of Edward Lear's *Book of Nonsense* (1846), W.S. Gilbert's *Bab Ballads* (1869), and the inspired nonsense of Lewis Carroll's *Hunting of the Snark* (1876). The American poet Charles G. Leland exploited the humorous possibilities of immigrant jargon in *The Breitmann Ballads* (first published under that title in 1871).

In the 20th century the distinction between light and serious verse has been obscured by the flippant, irreverent tone used by many modern poets, the nonsense verse of the Dadaists, Futurists, and Surrealists, and the primitivistic techniques of such writers as the Beat poets and E.E. Cummings. In spite of their seeming lightness, the works of such poets as Vladimir Mayakovsky, W.H. Auden, Louis MacNiece, Theodore Roethke, and Kenneth Fearing are usually seriously intended; they may begin by being amusing but often end in terror or bitterness. Though light verse was occasionally produced by major poets—for example, Ezra Pound's delightful Middle English parody "Ancient Music" ("Winter is icummen in") and T.S. Eliot's *Old Possum's Book of Practical Cats* (1939)—it has come to be associated with exclusive or frequent practitioners of the genre: in the United States, Ogden Nash, Dorothy Parker, Phyllis McGinley, and Morris Bishop; in England, Sir John Betjeman and Hilaire Belloc; and in Germany, Christian Morgenstern and Erich Kästner.

light-year, in astronomy, the distance traveled by light moving in a vacuum in the course of one year, at its accepted velocity of 299,792,458 metres per second (186,282 miles per second). A light-year equals about 9.46053×10^{12} km (5.878×10^{12} miles), or 63,240 astronomical units. About 3.262 light-years equal one parsec (*q.v.*).

lighter, shallow-draft boat or barge, usually flat-bottomed, used in unloading (lightening) or loading ships offshore. Use of lighters requires extra handling and thus extra time and expense and is largely confined to ports without enough traffic to justify construction of piers or wharves. Lighters are also used in transporting freight for short distances, as around harbours. Lighters have been developed that can be loaded, cargo and all, on specially designed ships in a combination called LASH (lighter aboard ship).

lighthouse, structure, usually with a tower, built onshore or on the seabed to serve as an aid to maritime coastal navigation. From the sea a lighthouse may be identified by the distinctive shape or colour of its structure, by the colour or flash pattern of its light, or by the coded pattern of its radio signal.

A brief treatment of lighthouses follows. For full treatment, *see* MACROPAEDIA: Public Works.

The first known lighthouse was the Pharos of Alexandria, which stood some 350 feet (110 m) high. During the first few centuries AD the Phoenicians and Romans also built lighthouses at numerous sites, ranging from the Black Sea, along the Mediterranean and Atlantic coasts, to Britain. After the fall of the Roman Empire in the 5th century, there was little maritime trade or travel, and no lighthouses were built in Europe until the revival of commerce in the 12th century. The French and Italians built the earliest of these lighthouses, followed by the Hanseatic League, which constructed a number of such structures along the Scandinavian and German coasts.

Dungeness Lighthouse (constructed 1961), Dungeness, Kent, Eng.
Ace Distributors Ltd.

The modern lighthouse dates from the early 18th century. Initially these towers were made of wood, but wooden towers were often washed away in severe storms. The first lighthouse made of interlocking masonry blocks was built on the treacherous Eddystone Rocks reef in England in 1759. This structure, designed by the engineer John Smeaton, was also the first to employ the classic curved hyperbolic design. Following the success of Smeaton's innovations, a large number of lighthouses were built on the open sea.

Interlocking masonry blocks remained the principal material of lighthouse construction until they were replaced by concrete and steel in the 20th century. There are now three major kinds of offshore lighthouse structures. The first rests on a hollow, steel cylinder (caisson) that is partly sunk into the seabed and then filled with concrete. The second utilizes a concrete base that sinks to the bottom of the water, thus anchoring the lighthouse tower that rises from this base. The third, resembling an offshore oil rig, consists of a large deck supported by tubular steel piles driven into the seabed; the tower rises from the deck. Most lighthouses also have landing pads for helicopters.

The standard illuminant of modern lighthouses (as well as lightships and buoys) is the electric lamp. The most common type is the electric-filament lamp, which requires as much as 1.5 kilowatts to as little as 5 watts in small buoys. Refinements in lenses and reflectors have made it possible for a 250-watt bulb to be boosted to several hundred thousand candlepower, or candelas. The maximum intensity now sought in lighthouse beams is in the range of 100,000 candelas; this gives a beam that can be seen from 20 nautical miles (37 km) in clear weather.

Sirens and horns are commonly used to provide audible warnings when a lighthouse and its beacon are obscured by bad weather. But because the range of their sound is also highly dependent on weather conditions, many lighthouses are also fitted with radio and radar beacons, which either amplify a ship's radar or emit signals of their own that can be detected by navigators.

Radio and satellite-based navigation systems have greatly reduced the need for large lighthouses in sighting land, although smaller structures are still important aids to navigating crowded coastal waters and shipping lanes. Almost all lighthouses are now completely automated, eliminating the expense of maintenance by resident crews. Modern computerized lighthouses analyze the weather, activate foghorns and other equipment, and transmit signals to remote control stations ashore.

lightning, the visible discharge of atmospheric electricity that occurs when a region of the atmosphere acquires an electrical charge, or potential difference, sufficient to overcome the resistance of the air.

A brief treatment of lightning follows. For full treatment, *see* MACROPAEDIA: Climate and Weather.

Lightning is usually associated with cumulonimbus clouds (thunderclouds) but also occurs in nimbostratus clouds, in snowstorms and dust storms, and sometimes in the dust and gases emitted from erupting volcanoes. During a thunderstorm, a lightning flash can occur within a cloud, between clouds, between a cloud and air, or from cloud to ground.

Lightning occurs because regions of net charge are generated by charge-separation processes that produce an electric dipole structure in a cloud. The charges within a thundercloud are distributed between a large net-positive charge in the upper region of the cloud, a large net-negative charge in the lower region, and a small net-positive charge in the lowest part of the cloud. Charges reside on water drops, ice particles, or both. If the surrounding air has a net charge, an air discharge from the cloud may occur.

The flash of cloud-to-ground lightning is initiated by the neutralization of the small net-positive charge in the lowest region of the cloud. A cloud-to-ground flash comprises at least two strokes: a leader stroke and a return stroke. A leader stroke carrying a negative charge passes from cloud to ground. (Occasionally, however, the leader stroke is from ground to cloud—especially with very high structures such as church steeples, multistory buildings, or tall trees.) The leader stroke is not very bright and is often stepped and has many branches extending out from the main channel. As it nears the ground, it induces an opposite charge, concentrated at the point to be struck, and a return stroke carrying a positive charge from ground to cloud is generated through the channel. The two strokes generally meet about 50 m (164 feet) above the ground. At this juncture, the cloud is short-circuited to the ground and a highly luminous return stroke of high current passes through the channel to the cloud.

A typical lightning flash involves a potential difference between cloud and ground of several hundred million volts, with peak currents on the order of 20,000 amperes. Temperatures in the channel are on the order of 30,000 K (50,000° F). The entire process is very rapid; the leader stroke reaches the juncture point or the ground in about 20 milliseconds, and the return stroke reaches the cloud in about 70 microseconds.

The thunder associated with lightning is caused by the rapid heating of air to high temperatures along the whole length of the lightning channel. The air thus heated expands at supersonic speeds, but within a metre or two the shock wave decays into a sound wave, which is then modified by the intervening medium of air and topography. The result is a series of claps and rumbles.

Although lightning strikes are dangerous because of their high-voltage discharges, the tendency of strikes to occur at high points enables lightning rods of conductive metal to draw the strikes and conduct them harmlessly into the ground. By moving indoors or by sheltering in a low, depressed area, such as a ditch, exposed persons can avoid being struck.

Consult
the
INDEX
first

lightning bug: *see* firefly.

lightning rod, metallic rod (usually copper) that protects a structure from lightning damage by intercepting flashes and transmitting their current to the ground. Because lightning tends to strike the highest object in the vicinity, the rod is placed at the apex of the structure; it is connected to the ground by low-resistance cables. In the case of a building, the soil is used as the ground; on a ship, the water is used. A lightning rod affords protection because it diverts the current from the nonconducting parts of the structure, allowing it to follow the path of least resistance and pass harmlessly through the rod and its cables. It is the high resistance of the nonconducting material that causes it to be heated by the passage of electric current, leading to fire and other damage. A lightning rod provides a cone of protection whose ground radius approximately equals its height above the ground.

lights, ancient (English property law): *see* ancient lights.

Lights, Feast of (Judaism): *see* Ḥanukka.

lightship, marine navigation and warning beacon stationed where lighthouse construction is impractical. The first lightship was the *Nore* (1732), stationed in the estuary of the River Thames in England. Modern lightships are small, unattended vessels equipped with fog signals, radio beacons, and gimbal devices for keeping the navigational light beam horizontal in rough weather. Their names are marked in large letters for easy daytime recognition.

The chief advantage of lightships is their mobility, which makes them valuable in marking shifting hazards and traffic lanes in coastal waters and harbour approaches.

Ligne, Charles-Joseph, prince de (b. May 23, 1735, Brussels, Austrian Netherlands [now in Belgium]—d. Dec. 13, 1814, Vienna, Austria), Belgian military officer and man of letters whose memoirs and correspondence with leading European figures such as Jean-Jacques Rousseau and Voltaire had an important influence on Belgian literature.

The son of Claude Lamoral, prince de Ligne, head of a family long established in Hainaut and in the Holy Roman Empire, de Ligne married Marie-Françoise de Liechtenstein in 1755. After serving with distinction for Austria in the Seven Years' War (1756–63), he became a trusted adviser of the Holy Roman emperor Joseph II, who sent him on missions to Catherine II the Great of Russia in 1780 and 1786. He traveled with Catherine in 1787, and in 1788–89 he fought for Russia and Austria in the Russo-Turkish War of 1787–92.

Ligne, detail of a painting by Leclercq; in the collection of the Prince de Ligne, Beloeil

By courtesy of the Prince de Ligne, Beloeil; photograph, © A.C.L., Brussels

De Ligne's memoirs and letters reflect his experiences as a favourite at the leading European courts and salons until his exile following the Belgian rebellion of 1789. His works include *Mélanges militaires, littéraires et sentimentaires,* 34 vol. (1795–1811; "Miscellaneous Military, Literary, and Sentimental Memoirs"), *Fragments de l'histoire de ma vie* (1927; "Fragments of the History of My Life"), and *Letters and Memoirs of the Prince de Ligne* (translated by Leigh Ashton, 1927).

ligneous thyroiditis, also called STRUMA FIBROSA: *see* Riedel thyroiditis.

lignin, complex oxygen-containing organic substance that, with cellulose, forms the chief constituent of wood. It is second only to cellulose as the most abundant organic material on Earth, though it has found relatively few industrial uses other than as a fuel. It is a mixture of complex, apparently polymeric compounds of poorly known structure. Lignin is concentrated in the cell walls of wood and makes up 24–35 percent of the oven-dry weight of softwoods and 17–25 percent of hardwoods. It is removed from wood pulp in the manufacture of paper, usually by treating with agents such as sulfur dioxide, sodium sulfide, or sodium hydroxide. Lignin has a number of industrial uses as a binder for particleboard and similar laminated or composite wood products; as a soil conditioner; as a filler or an active ingredient of phenolic resins; and as an adhesive for linoleum. Vanillin (synthetic vanilla) and dimethyl sulfoxide are also made from lignin.

lignite, brown to black coal that has been formed from peat under moderate pressure; it is one of the first products of coalification and is intermediate between peat and subbituminous coal. Dry lignite contains about 60 to 75 percent carbon. It has been estimated that about 45 percent of the world's total coal reserves are lignitic, but these reserves have not been exploited to any great extent because lignite is inferior to higher-rank coals (*e.g.,* bituminous coal) in heating value, storage stability, and other properties. In some areas, however, the scarcity of fuel has led to extensive developments, especially in eastern Germany, where the production of lignite far exceeds that of bituminous coal. Schemes for its use, particularly by briquetting, have received attention in Australia, New Zealand, Canada, the United States, and elsewhere. The fuel is used by local utility, industrial, and domestic consumers close to the mine site.

There are two types of raw lignite: one is brown and amorphous; the other, black and pitchlike. Raw lignite has a high water content, amounting to as much as 60 percent in the brown varieties; upon weathering, a proportion of this water is given up, and disintegration, or crumbling, of the material occurs, which reduces the value of lignite as a fuel. Lignite also tends to disintegrate during combustion, and hence the losses through a grate may be relatively high. It requires special care in storing, is uneconomical to transport long distances, and is liable to spontaneous combustion. Against these drawbacks, many lignite beds lie close to the surface and are of great thickness, sometimes more than 30 m (100 feet); they are thus easily worked and the cost of production is low. *See also* brown coal.

lignum vitae, any of several trees of the genus *Guaiacum,* of the family Zygophyllaceae, particularly *G. officinale,* native to the New World tropics.

Guaiacum officinale occurs from the southern United States to northern South America. It grows about 9 m (30 feet) tall and reaches a diameter of about 25 cm (10 inches). The evergreen leaves are opposite, divided into leaflets (arranged along an axis), and leathery in texture. The flowers are bright blue when first open but gradually fade to white. The yellow, heart-shaped fruit is about 2 cm (0.8 inch) long.

(Top) trunk and (bottom) leaves and fruit of lignum vitae (*Guaiacum officinale*)

(Top) W.M. Stephens—Bruce Coleman/EB Inc.; (bottom) Walter Dawn

The tree is the source of a very hard, heavy wood that is brownish green in colour. It is used to make pulleys, shafts, axles, and bowling balls. The wood is relatively waterproof because of its high fat content. The resin, called guaiacum, is obtained from the wood by distillation; it is used to treat respiratory disorders.

Ligo feast, in Baltic religion, the major celebration honouring the sun goddess, Saule (*q.v.*).

Ligorio, Pirro (b. *c.* 1510, Naples—d. October 1583, Ferrara [Italy]), Italian architect, painter, landscaper, and antiquarian who designed the Villa d'Este at Tivoli (1550–69), which still stands in its original state. Built for Ligorio's patron, Cardinal Ippolito d'Este, the villa has a planted landscape and a vast terraced garden with spectacular fountains leading up to the huge house. Ligorio also built the Casino of Pope Pius IV (Casina di Pio IV) in the Vatican Gardens (1558–62) and the Rotunda with Baldassare Peruzzi (1481–1536). He decorated his works with profuse stucco ornament; the Casino is a good example of his decoration. Ligorio also published a work on Roman antiquities and compiled an influential collection of Roman inscriptions, many of which were later found to be fradulent.

The Casino of Pius IV, Vatican City, by Pirro Ligorio, 1558–62

Anderson—Alinari from Art Resource/EB Inc.

Liguori, Saint Alfonso Maria de', Alfonso also spelled ALPHONSUS (b. Sept. 27, 1696, Marianella, Kingdom of Naples—d. Aug. 1, 1787, Pagani; canonized 1839; feast day August 1), Italian doctor of the church, one of the chief 18th-century moral theologians, and founder of the Redemptorists, a congregation dedicated primarily to parish and foreign missions. In 1950 he was named patron of moralists and confessors by Pope Pius XII.

After practicing law for eight years, he was ordained a priest in 1726. In 1732 he founded the Congregation of the Most Holy Redeemer, or the Redemptorists, at Scala. Dissension within the congregation culminated in 1777 when he was deceived into signing what he thought was a royal sanction for his rule. Actually, the document was a new rule devised by one of his enemies, thus causing the followers of the old rule to break away. In 1762 Pope Clement XIII made him bishop of Sant' Agata del Goti near Naples; he resigned in 1775 because of ill health. He was declared a doctor of the church by Pope Pius IX in 1871.

Liguori's extensive works fall into three genres: moral theology, best represented by his celebrated *Theologia moralis* (1748); ascetical and devotional writings, including *Visits to the Blessed Sacrament, The True Spouse of Jesus Christ* (for nuns), *Selva* (for priests), and *The Glories of Mary*—one of the most widely used manuals of devotion to the Virgin Mary; and dogmatic writings on such subjects as papal infallibility and the power of prayer. By the middle of the 20th century, his works had gone through several thousand editions and had been translated into 60 languages. In theology Liguori is known as the principal exponent of equiprobabilism, a system of principles designed to guide the conscience of one in doubt whether he is free from or bound by a given civil or religious law.

Liguria, the third smallest of the *regioni* of Italy, bordering the Ligurian Sea, in the northwestern part of the country. It comprises the *provincie* of Genoa, Imperia, La Spezia, and Savona.

Shaped like a crescent reaching from the mouth of the Roia River to that of the Magra and from the French frontier to Tuscany, Liguria is dominated by the Maritime Alps as far as the Cadibona Pass and by the Ligurian Apennines east of that point. The narrow, picturesquely indented coastal fringe, the Italian Riviera, is customarily divided into a western section, the Ponente Riviera, and an eastern section, the Levante Riviera, the point of division being the apex of the Ligurian arc at Voltri, near Genoa. Most of the population is concentrated within this coastal area.

The region, which derived its name from the Ligurians, its pre-Roman inhabitants, came under the domination of Rome in the 1st century BC. After brief Lombard and Frankish rule, the city of Genoa began to emerge as a leading power as early as the 11th century AD. By 1400 the city had gained control of the entire region and become one of the principal maritime and commercial powers of Europe. Despite numerous conflicts with its competitors, especially Venice, Genoa kept its independence until 1796, when it was seized by Napoleon Bonaparte for France. The Congress of Vienna (1815) gave Liguria to the kingdom of Piedmont-Sardinia. Liguria played a leading part in the Risorgimento (movement for Italian independence) and contributed significantly to the union of Italy in 1860. Genoa became the major port of the new unified Italy, rivaling Marseille in France.

Because of the shelter from winter winds afforded by the mountains, Liguria is particularly favoured in growing early vegetables, flowers (especially in the western section), olives, and wine grapes, and its mild climate draws an active tourist trade in the numerous coastal resorts.

Industries are concentrated in and around Genoa (the regional and provincial capital), around Savona, and along the shores of the Gulf of La Spezia. At Genoa and La Spezia are Italy's leading shipyards; La Spezia is Italy's major naval base, and Savona is a major centre of the Italian iron industry. Chemical, textile, and food industries are also important. Area 2,092 square miles (5,418 square km). Pop. (2000 est.) 1,625,870.

Ligurian, Latin LIGUS, or LIGUR, plural LIGURES, any member of a collection of ancient peoples who inhabited the northwestern Mediterranean coast from the mouth of the Ebro River in Spain to the mouth of the Arno River in Italy in the 1st millennium BC.

No ancient texts speak of Ligurians in southern Gaul as nations or attribute definite racial characteristics to them. They were apparently an indigenous collection of Neolithic peoples living in village settlements in remote places, and it was probably to loose political groupings of these people that ancient authors attached the name. Such authors as Strabo and Diodorus Siculus described them as a rough and strong people whose piracy the Romans deplored. These views, however, appear in late texts and refer to the Celticized Ligurians (Celtoligures) between the Rhône and Arno rivers. Strabo declared that they were a different race from the Gauls or Celts, and Diodorus mentioned that they lived in villages and made a difficult living from the rocky, mountainous soil. In any event, their reputed boldness caused them to be in great demand as mercenaries. They served the Carthaginian commander Hamilcar in 480 BC and the Sicilian Greek colonies in the time of Agathocles and openly sided with Carthage in the Second Punic War (218–201 BC). Steps were not taken for their final reduction by Rome until 180 BC, when 40,000 Ligurians were deported to Samnium and settled near Beneventum (Benevento).

The name Ligurian, or Ligures, has been used by modern archaeologists to designate a stratum of Neolithic remains in the region from northeastern Spain to northwestern Italy.

Ligurian language, language spoken by the Ligurians in northwestern Italy (and perhaps also in southern France and northeastern Spain) in pre-Roman and early Roman times. It is apparently an Indo-European language. Some scholars have maintained that Ligurian is closely related to the Italic and Celtic languages, holding an intermediate linguistic position between them. The language is known primarily from a small number of glosses in classical writings.

Ligurian Republic, French RÉPUBLIQUE LIGURIENNE, Italian REPUBBLICA LIGURE, republic created by Napoleon Bonaparte on June 15, 1797, organizing the conquered city of Genoa and its environs. The government was modeled on that of the Directory in France, and the republic was tied to France by alliance. In 1803 it became also a military district, closely linked to France, and its chief of state became appointable by Napoleon. In May 1805 the Ligurian Republic was absorbed into the French Empire.

Ligurian Sea, Latin MARE LIGUSTICUM, Italian MARE LIGURE, French MER LIGURIENNE, arm of the Mediterranean Sea indenting the northwestern coast of Italy. It extends between Liguria and Tuscany (north and east) and the French island of Corsica (south). It receives many rivers that originate in the Apennines, and it reaches a depth of more than 9,300 feet (2,850 m) northwest of Corsica. The sea includes the Gulf of Genoa in the north and is connected through the Tuscan Archipelago in the southeast with the Tyrrhenian Sea.

Liholiho: *see* Kamehameha II.

Liholiho, Alexander: *see* Kamehameha IV.

Lihue, city, seat of Kauai county, in southeastern Kauai Island, Hawaii, U.S. It is the island's chief port and its cultural and business centre. Sugarcane became the locality's economic mainstay with the foundation of the Lihue Sugar Plantation (1849) by German colonists. The Germans built a Lutheran church (1883), a fusion of classical New England architecture and Bavarian Baroque. The city is served by an airport to the northeast and the deepwater Nawiliwili Harbor, 1 mile (1.6 km) southeast. Lihue is equipped with a highly mechanized plant from which raw sugar is shipped to U.S. mainland refineries.

In ancient times, Hawaiian chiefs would prove their courage by diving over the cliff at Wailua Falls, 5 miles (8 km) north. At nearby Niumalu, the Alakoko Fishpond was formed by a 900-foot (274-metre) stone wall at a bend in the Huleia Stream; the wall, 4 feet (1.2 m) wide and 5 feet (1.5 m) above water level, was reputedly built by the legendary *menehunes* ("little people"), who supposedly accomplished great construction feats. Kauai Community College (1928) is in the city. Pop. (2000) 5,674.

lijia, Wade-Giles LI-CHIA, system of social organization in Ming-dynasty China. *See* pao-chia.

Likasi, formerly (until 1966) JADOTVILLE, city, southeastern Congo (Kinshasa). It lies along the Likasi River, 86 miles (138 km) northwest of Lubumbashi, to which it is connected by road and rail. In 1892 Belgians discovered copper deposits at Likasi and at Kambove, 15 miles (24 km) northwest. Likasi was founded in 1917 and was designated an urban district in 1943. It is now one of the nation's most important mineral-processing centres, with plants for refining copper and cobalt. There are also chemical factories (sulfuric acid, glycerin) and a brewery. The city has an archaeological and mineral museum. Pop. (1994 est.) 299,118.

likembe: *see* lamellaphone.

likin, Chinese (Wade-Giles) LI-CHIN, or (Pinyin) LIJIN, special tax paid by merchants and traders in mid-19th-century China. Likin ("a tax of one-thousandth") was levied on goods in transit or as a sales tax in shops where goods were sold.

The tax originated in 1853 in the central Chinese province of Kiangsu as a method of financing troops to aid in suppressing the great Taiping Rebellion (1850–64). With the great volume of trade carried on in China after the opening of the country to the industrial West in the second half of the 19th century, it generated considerable revenue, and by 1860 the likin had spread to virtually every province in China. Within a few years the central government began to demand that a portion of the likin revenues be made available to the imperial treasury, and it soon became one of the major financial supports of the Ch'ing dynasty (1644–1911/12), relieving some of the burden on the overtaxed peasantry.

The tax was a constant source of contention with Western trading countries, which resented the petty levies their goods were subjected to in the interior of China because of the likin. In 1928 China agreed to abolish the likin in return for the restoration of tariff autonomy, which had been taken from China in the series of "unequal treaties" signed in the 19th century after the Opium Wars.

Likoma Island, island in Lake Nyasa, Malaŵi, just northwest of Cóbuè, Mozambique. Located near the lake's eastern shore, the rocky and barren island has an area of 7 square miles (18 square km). There is some fishing and limited cultivation of grain; cassava and corn (maize) are imported. The Universities' Mission to Central Africa (Church of England) established a station there in 1885 as a base for operations against the slave trade and built an imposing cathedral (completed 1911). Likoma village is on the southeastern shore. Pop. (1998) 8,074.

Likud, in full LIKUD-LIBERALIM LEUMI (Hebrew: "Unity-National Liberals"), right-wing Israeli political party. It was founded in September 1973 and first came to power in 1977, with Menachem Begin as prime minister. Thereafter, Likud alternated in government with the Israel Labour Party (*q.v.*), forming coalitions with minor parties, especially those with a conservative religious or nationalist ideology. Because of the country's political fragmentation and unique security needs, Labour and Likud have sometimes entered into so-called "unity governments" with each other.

At its founding in 1973, the Likud coalition was dominated by the Gahal bloc, which consisted of the Herut ("Freedom") party and the Liberal Party (Miflaget ha-Liberali). The Herut had its roots in Russian Jewish Zionism of the 1920s and '30s and was formally organized in 1948, the year of Israel's independence, in the merger of preindependence groups such as the Irgun Zvai Leumi, some of which had been considered terrorist organizations by the British mandate authorities. Begin, a Polish-born Jew, had been leader of the Irgun. The other member of the Gahal bloc, the Liberal Party, was formed in 1961 in the merger of the General Zionist Party (which was active from 1948 to 1961) and the smaller Progressive Party. Staunchly Zionist, it advocated retention of all territories conquered by Israel in the 1967 Arab-Israeli War. The other partners in Likud were relatively small, though they were often influential.

During Begin's prime ministry (1977–83), Israel signed a peace treaty with Egypt and launched a controversial invasion of Lebanon. Although his peace initiative was popular, it alienated many party stalwarts who opposed the return of any territories. In 1983 Begin was succeeded as prime minister and party leader by Yitzḥak Shamir, who governed in coalition with the Labour Party from 1984 to 1990. Likud was ousted from government by a Labour-led coalition in 1992, and in 1993 Shamir was succeeded as party leader by Benjamin Netanyahu, who led Likud back to power in 1996. Netanyahu was defeated in 1999 by Labour's Ehud Barak, but in 2001 Barak was defeated by Likud's Ariel Sharon, who subsequently formed a unity government with Labour.

Ideologically, Likud is both conservative and nationalist; it is generally seen as uncompromising in matters of national security.

lilac, any of about 30 species of fragrant and beautiful northern spring-flowering garden shrubs and small trees constituting the genus *Syringa* of the family Oleaceae. Lilacs are native to eastern Europe and temperate Asia.

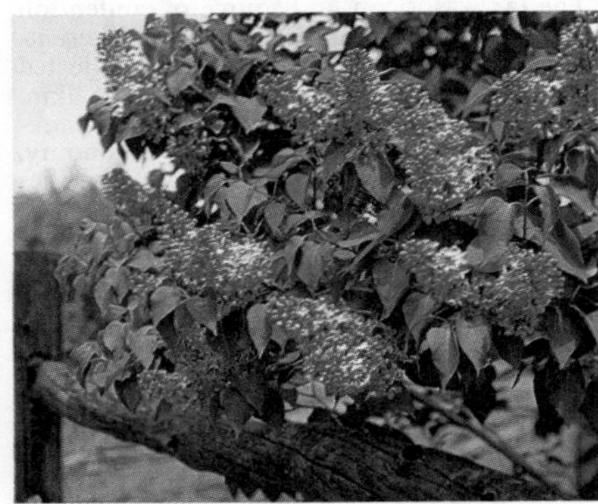

Common lilac (*Syringa vulgaris*)
By courtesy of the State of New Hampshire; photograph, Ernest Gould

Their deep green leaves enhance the attractiveness of the large, oval clusters of colourful blooms. The fruit is a leathery capsule.

The common lilac (*S. vulgaris*), from southeastern Europe, is widely grown in temperate areas. There are several hundred named varieties with single or double flowers in deep purple, lavender, blue, red, pink, white, and pale, creamy yellow. The common lilac reaches approximately 6 m (20 feet) and produces many suckers (shoots from the stem or root). It may be grown as a shrub or hedge or, by clearing away the suckers, as a small tree.

The weaker-stemmed Persian lilac (*S. persica*), ranging from Iran to China, droops over, reaching about 2 m in height. Its flowers usually are pale lavender, but there are darker and even white varieties.

Other decorative species are the dwarf Korean lilac (*S. velutina*), about 3 m tall, with lavender-pink flowers; the 4-metre-tall nodding lilac (*S. reflexa*) of China, with pinkish flowers; the Hungarian lilac (*S. josikaèa*), about 3 m tall, with scentless bluish purple flowers; and the daphne lilac (*S. microphylla*), about 1.5 m tall, from China, with small leaves, deep red buds, and pale pink flowers. The Chinese lilac, or Rouen lilac (*S. chinensis*), is a thickly branched hybrid, a cross of the Persian and common lilacs.

The name syringa was formerly used for the mock orange of the family Saxifragaceae. Species of the genus *Ceanothus* of the family Rhamnaceae are known as summer lilacs, a term also applied to the butterfly bush of the family Loganiaceae.

Lilburne, John (b. 1614?, Greenwich, near London, Eng.—d. Aug. 29, 1657, Eltham, Kent), English revolutionary, leader of the Levelers, a radical democratic party prominent during the English Civil Wars.

Coming from a family of gentry, Lilburne was apprenticed from about 1630 to 1636 to a London cloth merchant. Meanwhile, he joined the Puritan opposition to the Anglican High Church policies of King Charles I, and by 1638 he had adopted Separatist principles hostile to the notion of a state church. He helped to smuggle into England Puritan pamphlets that had been printed in the Netherlands. These illegal activities led to his arrest and trial before the Star Chamber in 1638; he was fined, publicly whipped, pilloried, and imprisoned until liberated by the Long Parliament (on a motion by Oliver Cromwell) in November 1640.

Upon the outbreak of the first Civil War between Charles and Parliament in 1642, Lilburne was commissioned a captain in the Parliamentarian army. He was taken prisoner at Brentford in November 1642 but was exchanged after narrowly missing being tried for treason. In April 1645 Lilburne, by then a lieutenant colonel, chose to resign from the army rather than subscribe to the Solemn League and Covenant with Scotland, which committed Parliament to reform the Church of England along Presbyterian lines.

Thereafter Lilburne's career was fused with the history of the Levelers. "Free-born John," as he was called, became a master propagandist, demanding, in his pamphlets, religious liberty, extension of the suffrage to craftsmen and small-property owners, and complete equality before the law. Lilburne was fierce in his criticism of Parliament and the army for failing to meet the Levelers' demands. As a result, he spent most of the period from August 1645 to August 1647 in prison. After the army seized power in 1648, the Levelers were crushed. Nevertheless, Lilburne maintained his immense popularity with Londoners. A London jury acquitted him of high treason in 1649, and a second acquittal, in 1653, led to a great popular demonstration that alarmed the government of Oliver Cromwell. Lilburne was therefore kept in prison until 1655, by which time he had converted to the Quaker faith. He died two years later.

Lili Marleen, English LILI, or LILLI, MARLENE, German song popular during World War II among both German and Allied soldiers. Hans Leip (1893–1983) began writing the lyrics in 1914 or 1915, reputedly while standing guard duty one night under a lamppost ("*Vor der Kaserne vor dem grossen Tor stand eine Laterne*"; "Underneath the lantern by the barrack gate"). "Lili Marleen" was a composite of his own girlfriend Lili and a comrade's girlfriend Marleen. Leip did not finish the verses for publication until 1937, when, as a poem, it appeared in his collection *Die Kleine Hafenorgel* ("A Little Harbour Organ"); a year later, music for it was composed by Norbert Schultze (b. 1911). The song did not become popular until after Aug. 18, 1941, when it was first broadcast to Allied troops in North Africa on Nazi propaganda radio. The song, first sung by a German cabaret singer, Lale Andersen, became especially famous in the version recorded by the German-American movie star Marlene Dietrich.

Liliaceae, the lily family of the flowering plant order Liliales, with about 280 genera and some 4,000 species of herbs and shrubs, native primarily to temperate and subtropical regions. Members of the family usually have six-segmented flowers and three-chambered

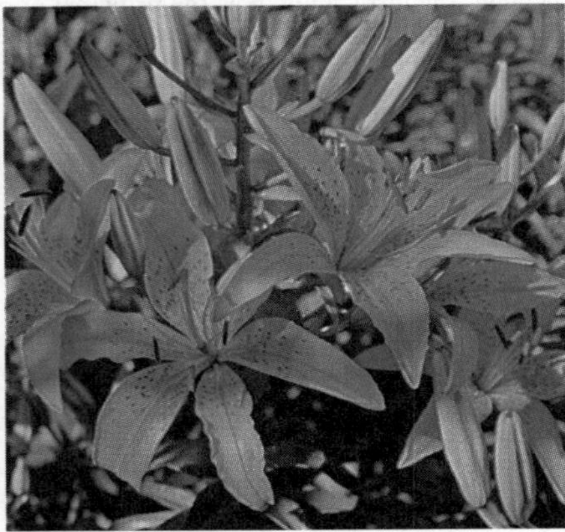

Lilium umbellatum
Sven Samelius

capsular fruits; occasionally the fruits are berries. The leaves usually have parallel veins and are clustered at the base of the plant but may alternate along the stem or be arranged in whorls. Most species have an underground storage structure, such as a stem, bulb, corm, or tuber.

The family is important for its many garden ornamentals and houseplants, especially *Aspidistra,* bellwort (*Uvularia*), bluebell (*Endymion*), *Colchicum,* day lily (*Hemerocallis*), *Dracaena, Erythronium,* fritillary (*Fritillaria*), *Galtonia,* grape-hyacinth (*Muscari*), herb Paris (*Paris*), hyacinth (*Hyacinthus*), lily (*Lilium*), lily of the valley (*Convallaria*), *Ornithogalum,* plantain lily (*Hosta*), snowdrop (*Galanthus*), Solomon's seal (*Polygonatum*), squill (*Scilla*), ti (*Cordyline*), torch lily (*Kniphofia*), *Trillium,* tuberose (*Polianthes*), tulip (*Tulipa*), *Veratrum,* and *Zygadenus.*

Liliales, an order of flowering plants, exemplified by the lily. The 15 families, more than 400 genera, and 8,000 species constituting this assemblage are largely perennial herbs; some are climbers, shrubs, or even trees. Members of this order are important as sources of food; in the production of drugs, chemicals, and commercial fibres; and as ornamental plants.

A brief treatment of Liliales follows. For full treatment, *see* MACROPÆDIA: Angiosperms.

In addition to possessing the linear leaves with parallel venation that are common to most monocots, members of the Liliales are characterized by bulbs or rhizomes (horizontal underground stems), leaves clustered near ground level, and showy bisexual flowers (possessing both male and female parts).

Although distributed throughout the world, Liliales species are most common in subtropical and temperate regions. The greatest number of species and individuals are found in southern Africa, North America, western Asia, and Australia. One liliaceous *Tofieldia* ranges to northern Greenland.

Many members of the order thrive best in rich garden soil, but its large number of species and wide geographic range make generalization difficult. Many species of *Agave* inhabit desert areas of northern Mexico, and several species of *Aloe* are native in arid South Africa. One *Leucocoryne* of the Chilean desert can survive several rainless years, while the water hyacinth (*Eichhornia crassipes*) is aquatic.

The Liliaceae, the largest family in the order, comprises some 280 genera and 4,000 species. Liliaceae is a very diverse family, however, and authorities differ as to its taxonomic composition. Species of *Lilium* are some of the most stately of garden plants. Some kinds, such as the Easter lily (*L. longiflorum*), which originated in Japan, can be forced into flower in greenhouses; the varieties *croftii* and *eximum* are also commercially important. Species native to eastern North America include the leopard and Turk's-cap lilies; Humboldt and chaparral lilies are found along the Pacific coast.

In contrast to lily bulbs, which consist of a basal stem and many overlapping scales, bulbs of the tulip (*Tulipa*) possess cylindrical leaf-bases that bulge as new leaves are added in the centre. *Tulipa gesnerana* of eastern Europe and Asia Minor is a prominent ancestor of the modern tulips developed by breeding and selection over several centuries.

Additional significant ornamental genera of the Liliaceae include the spring-flowering *Crocus* and *Hyacinthus* and the summer-flowering *Hemerocallis* (daylily), now available in thousands of cultivars; its buds are edible. Also important are *Amaryllis, Hippeastrum,* and *Narcissus.* The succulent *Aloe* of tropical Africa, with its elongate, succulent (fleshy) leaves, is a favoured houseplant and is used medicinally.

Important food plants in the Liliaceae include the onion (*Allium cepa*), native to western Asia, garlic (*A. sativum*), the leek (*A. ampeloprasum*), and the chive (*A. schoenoprasum*), as well as asparagus (*Asparagus officinalis*).

The Agavaceae family contains 18 genera and some 600 species distributed throughout the world, principally in semiarid tropical regions. The genera *Agave* (300 species) and *Yucca* (40 species) are found in North America and northern South America.

Agaves include some of the largest members of the Liliales; the flower stalk of the century plant (*Agave americana*) may reach 6 m (20 feet) in height. These slow-growing plants flower once and die. Several species of *Agave* are cultivated for henequen and sisal fibres derived from their leaves. The bulky, asparagus-like inflorescence (flower cluster) of plantation-grown plants yield a rich juice that is fermented and distilled into tequila.

Many yuccas are small plants, but the Joshua tree (*Yucca brevifolia*) attains a height of 12 m in California. Several other genera of this family are treelike. Yuccas contain saponins, compounds that foam when mixed with water; they are one of the original sources of natural detergents.

Some species of the Dioscoreaceae family produce the tuberous roots, rich in starch, that are staple foods in many tropical nations. The yampee, or cush-cush (*Dioscorea trifida*), originated in South America and the West Indies. *D. alata,* the white yam of India and the Malay Peninsula, is widely cultivated for its enlarged roots. Elephant's-foot (*Dioscorea* [or *Testudinaria*] *elephantipes*), grown in Africa, is used as a famine food. Roots of all these plants contain poisonous alkaloids that are destroyed by boiling. Mexican species of *Dioscorea* are harvested in the wild for the manufacture of drug hormones.

As the scales (leaf-bases) of underground lily bulbs mature, buds may arise at their base to become bulblets. As the parent scales disintegrate, these bulblets grow into new individuals. Similar offsets and buds on creeping rhizomes give rise to new plants in many Liliales. The onion (*Allium cepa*) produces bulblets in place of flowers atop the flowering stalk. The European wild-garlic (*A. vineale*) is a prolific producer of bulblets and has become a noxious weed even in North America. In the zephyr lily (*Zephyranthes*), seeds develop in the ovary without fertilization—they are, in essence, internal buds. In addition to these vegetative means of propagation, most members of the lily order produce seeds in the conventional manner.

Even though the six showy perianth parts of a lily flower may appear alike, three of them (sepals) arise at a slightly lower level than the petals. Six stamens produce copious pollen. The pistil consists of three joined carpels (specialized leaves) that are differentiated into a long, basal inferior ovary containing many ovules; and the style, which ends in an expanded stigma.

In many species, the rate of growth of pollen tubes in the style is controlled biochemically, so that pollen of a different flower reaches the ovules first. This insures cross-pollination, a factor in maintaining generic vigour of species. Pollen is carried by bees, other insects, and hummingbirds. Following pollination and fertilization, the ovule becomes the seed and the ovary the fruit. A dry capsule that splits open at maturity is the most common fruit in the Liliales, although some genera, such as asparagus, produce fleshy berries.

Liliencron, Detlev, Baron (Freiherr) **von,** in full FRIEDRICH ADOLF AXEL DETLEV LILIENCRON (b. June 3, 1844, Kiel, Holstein [Germany]—d. July 22, 1909, Alt-Rahlstedt, near Hamburg), German writer, noted for his fresh and unconventional verse.

The son of an impoverished family of baronial descent, Liliencron entered the Prussian army in 1863. He served as a regular officer during the Seven Weeks' War (1866) and the Franco-German War (1870–71). He later used experiences from these campaigns in his poems and stories. In 1875 Liliencron left the

Liliencron
Historia Photo

army because of debts; after spending some time in America, he entered the civil service in 1878. From 1887 he struggled to make a living as a full-time writer.

In 1883 Liliencron published his first book, *Adjutantenritte und andere Gedichte* ("Rides of the Adjutant and Other Poems"). The poems in this collection broke with established literary conventions; it has been called a landmark in the development of Naturalism in Germany.

Liliencron also wrote several dramas, none of which were successful, and published several collections of stories and short novels, notably *Kriegsnovellen* (1895; "War Stories"). But he is best known for his lyric poems, published in several collections between 1883 and 1909. The best of these poems are characterized by a vividness of expression and accuracy of detail. Liliencron's insights and observations are original, and he portrays nature with a new realism and immediacy. His loosely constructed satiric epic *Poggfred, ein kunterbuntes Epos* (1896; "Poggfred, a Topsy-Turvy Epic") achieved some success.

Lilienthal, David E., in full DAVID ELI LILIENTHAL (b. July 8, 1899, Morton, Ill., U.S.—d. Jan. 15, 1981, New York, N.Y.), American businessman and government official, who was codirector (1933) and first chairman (1941) of the Tennessee Valley Authority (TVA) and first chairman of the Atomic Energy Commission (AEC).

After graduation from Depauw University (Greencastle, Ind.) and Harvard Law School (1923), Lilienthal practiced law, engaging especially in cases of labour and public utilities. His winning a telephone-rate case that resulted in a refund of $20,000,000 to Chicago subscribers brought him to the attention of the governor of Wisconsin, who made him a member of the Wisconsin Public Service Commission in 1931. In this capacity he reorganized the utilities statutes for that state in such a way that they became a model for six other states.

Such accomplishments drew the attention of President Franklin D. Roosevelt, and when the TVA flood-control project was approved by Congress, Roosevelt named Lilienthal one of the three codirectors of the TVA's power program in 1933. In 1941 Lilienthal was appointed chairman of the project.

By becoming the first chairman of the Atomic Energy Commission in 1947, Lilienthal assumed power over the U.S. nuclear-development program, which had previously been supervised by the U.S. Army. As chairman, he was committed to improving and expanding nuclear-power plants, to building up a stockpile of atomic bombs, and to developing nuclear weapons.

Lilienthal resigned from the AEC in 1950 and in 1953 became chairman and chief executive officer of Development and Research Corp., where he continued formulating a resource development program that included dams, irrigation, electric power, and flood control. His books included *Big Business, a New Era* (1953), *Change, Hope and the Bomb* (1963), and *Atomic Energy, a New Start* (1980).

Lilienthal, Otto (b. May 23, 1848, Anklam, Prussia [now in Germany]—d. Aug. 10, 1896, Berlin), German aeronautical pioneer on whose work such later engineers as Octave Chanute and the Wright brothers drew heavily.

After graduation from the trade school at Potsdam and the Berlin Trade Academy, Lilienthal experimented with flying models with flapping wings and wing gliders. His book *Der Vogelflug als Grundlage der Fliegekunst* (1889; "The Flight of Birds as the Basis of the Act of Flying") and his essays on flying machines (1894) were recognized as basic works in aeronautics. From an artificial hill near Lichterfelde, he made more than 2,000 flights in monoplane and biplane gliders he designed. He died after his craft crashed in flight at Stölln near Rhinow, Ger.

Lilith, female demon of Jewish folklore; her name and personality are derived from the class of Mesopotamian demons called *lilû* (feminine: *lilītu*). In rabbinic literature Lilith is variously depicted as the mother of Adam's demonic offspring following his separation from Eve or as his first wife, who left him because of their incompatibility. Three angels tried in vain to force her return; the evil she threatened, especially against children, was said to be counteracted by the wearing of an amulet bearing the names of the angels. A cult associated with Lilith survived among some Jews as late as the 7th century AD.

Liliuokalani, original name LYDIA KAMAKAEHA, also called LYDIA PAKI LILIUOKALANI, or LILIU KAMAKAEHA (b. Sept. 2, 1838, Honolulu, Hawaii [now in the United States]—d. Nov. 11, 1917, Honolulu), first and only reigning Hawaiian queen and the last Hawaiian sovereign to govern the islands, which were annexed by the United States in 1898. Queen Liliuokalani bitterly fought annexation, championing the *Oni pa'a* ("Stand Firm") movement; she inspired an insurrection against Sanford B. Dole's Provisional Republic in 1895. A talented musician, she is renowned for her song "Aloha Oe."

Liliuokalani's mother, Keohokalole, was an adviser of King Kamehameha III. Reared in the missionary tradition deemed appropriate for Hawaiian princesses, she received a thoroughly modern education, which was augmented by a tour of the Western world. At the death of her younger brother, Prince Regent W.P. Leleiohoku in 1877, she was named heir presumptive, and in 1891 she succeeded her older brother, David Kalakaua, on the throne.

Liliuokalani regretted the loss of power the monarchy had suffered under Kalakaua and tried to restore something of the traditional autocracy to the Hawaiian throne. She had earlier made her position clear by opposing the renewed Reciprocity Treaty of 1887, signed by King Kalakaua, granting privileged commercial concessions to the United States and ceding to them the port of Pearl Harbor. This attitude forever alienated her from Hawaii's *haole*—foreign businessmen—who, after her accession, tried to abrogate her authority.

Queen Liliuokalani
By courtesy of the Bernice P. Bishop Museum

Led by Sanford Dole, the Missionary Party asked for her abdication in January 1893 and, declaring the queen deposed, announced the establishment of a provisional government pending annexation by the United States. To avoid bloodshed, Liliuokalani surrendered, but she appealed to the U.S. president, Grover Cleveland, to reinstate her. Cleveland ordered the queen restored, but Dole defied the order, claiming that Cleveland did not have the authority to interfere. In 1895 an insurrection in the queen's name, led by royalist Robert Wilcox, was suppressed by Dole's group, and Liliuokalani was kept under house arrest on charges of treason. On Jan. 24, 1895, to win pardons for her supporters who had been jailed following the revolt, she agreed to sign a formal abdication. She withdrew from public life and in 1898 wrote her memoirs, *Hawaii's Story by Hawaii's Queen.*

Lille, city, capital of Nord *département* and of the Nord-Pas-de-Calais *région,* northern France, on the Deûle River, 136 miles (219 km) north-northeast of Paris, and 9 miles (14 km) from the Belgian frontier by road.

Lille (often written L'Île ["the island"] until the 18th century) began as a village between arms of the Deûle River. Count Baldwin IV of Flanders fortified it in the 11th century. The medieval town was destroyed or changed hands several times. Louis XIV besieged and claimed it in 1667. After being captured by the Duke of Marlborough in 1708, it was finally ceded to France in 1713 by the Treaty of Utrecht. Lille was damaged and also occupied by the Germans during World Wars I and II.

With Tourcoing and Roubaix, Lille forms one of the largest conurbations in France. Its commercial and industrial activities have been stimulated by its proximity to the northern countries of the European Economic Community and by its good communications location. It is an important railway junction, and it is served by an airport, by the motorway from Belgium to Paris and the Mediterranean, and by the canalized river Deûle. Lille's Chamber of Commerce dates from the 18th century. It has a commission for regional economic development, a branch of the Bank of France, and has an annual international commercial fair (begun 1925). The city has a state university (transferred from Douai in 1887 and reorganized in 1970), a Roman Catholic university, commercial and technical schools, and a branch of the Pasteur Institute.

Lille is the traditional textile centre of France. Other industries include an iron and steel works, machinery manufacturing, and food-processing and chemical plants. The boulevard de la Liberté, running southeast-northwest, divides the old town in the north, which used to be cramped within the city walls, from the new town in the south, with its wide and regular streets. At the northwestern end of the boulevard stands the imposing pentagonal military citadel (1667–70), the best preserved of all the military buildings designed by the engineer Sébastien Le Prestre de Vauban (1633–1707). The fortifications around the old city have been destroyed, but the majestic archway, the Porte de Paris (1682), still stands. The old hospital Hospice Comtesse, founded in 1236, was rebuilt in the 15th and 17th centuries. The Vieille Bourse, a 17th-century building in typically Flemish style, stands near the square named for General Charles de Gaulle, a native son. The museum has one of the richest art collections in France, with paintings dating from the 15th to the 20th century. Throughout the entire heart of the city private houses have been demolished and replaced by modern multistory buildings. Between the three cities of the conurbation, a new town, called Villeneuve d'Ascq, was built to be the regional administrative centre. Pop. (1990) 178,301.

Lille I, II, and III, Universities of, French UNIVERSITÉS DE LILLE I, II, ET III, coeducational, autonomous, state-financed institutions of higher learning at Lille, in northern France; they were founded in 1970 under the 1968 law reforming French higher education, to replace the former University of Lille, founded in 1560 at Douai and suppressed by the French Revolution. After the Revolution faculties of letters, medicine, and other fields were established in Lille and Douai. They were all transferred to Lille in 1887 and were reconstituted as a university in 1896. Louis Pasteur was dean of the university's science faculty from 1854 to 1857. Pasteur began his studies of fermentation at Lille.

Lille I specializes in science and technology; Lille II, law and health sciences (medicine, pharmacy, dentistry, physical education); Lille III, human sciences, literature, and arts (history, languages and letters, philosophy and psychology). Within the separate universities, teaching and research are organized into separate units, each enjoying academic and administrative independence.

Lille lace, bobbin-made lace made since the 16th century in the town of Lille, formerly in Flanders but now in northwestern France. It was notable for its very fine net background, with a hexagonal mesh in which the thread was twisted, rather than plaited. The net was often scattered with small square dots. Patterns were of conventional curving flowers and scrolls. Lille lace was much sought after at the end of the 18th century.

French Lille lace, beginning of the 19th century; in the Museum Boymans-van Beuningen, Rotterdam
By courtesy of the Museum Boymans-van Beuningen, Rotterdam

Lillebonne, town, northwestern France, Seine-Maritime *département,* Haute-Normandie *région,* north of the Seine River and east of Le Havre. The Romans called it Juliobona. Under Roman rule in the 2nd century it had baths and a great theatre; materials from the theatre were used to build fortifications during the Middle Ages. Tradition holds that William the Conqueror was in his castle at Lillebonne in 1066 when he made his decision to invade England. The castle was rebuilt in the 12th century, but today only ruins remain. Textiles, rubber, and chemicals are the chief industries of the town. Pop. (1990) 9,426.

Lillehammer, town, seat of Oppland *fylke* (county), southeastern Norway, lying where the Lågen (river) flows into Lake Mjøsa (the largest lake in Norway) in the southern end of Gudbrands Valley (*q.v.*). Lillehammer was chartered in 1827. Industries include textiles, lumber, and paper and food processing. A gateway to picturesque Gudbrands Valley, it is a year-round resort. The open-air Maihaugen folk museum features Norwegian art and architecture. The authors Bjørnstjerne Bjørnson and Sigrid Undset lived near Lillehammer. Bjørnson's home and farm, about 10 miles (16 km) northwest, is a national memorial. The town was the site of the 1994 Winter Olympics. Pop. (1992 est.) mun., 23,055.

Lilli burlero, also spelled LILLIBULLERO, 17th-century English political song that played a part in driving James II from the throne in 1688. Written in 1687 by Thomas (afterward Marquess of) Wharton, the verses were intended to discredit the administration in Ireland of Richard Talbot, Earl of Tyrconnell. Among the many verses extremely popular throughout the country, two were as follows:

Dare was an old prophesy found in a bog,
Lilli burlero, bullen a-la
"Ireland shall be ruled by an ass and a dog."
Lilli burlero, bullen a-la
Lero, lero, lilli burlero, lero, lero,
bullen a-la,
Lero, lero, lilli burlero, lero, lero,
bullen a-la.
And now dis prophesy is come to pass,
Lilli burlero, etc.
For Talbot's de dog and Ja . . s is de ass.
Lilli burlero, etc.

The earliest known printed version of the tune now associated with the words appeared in Robert Carr's *Delightful Companion* (1686), for recorder or flute. The words, with the tune printed above, were issued on a single sheet in 1688; it was reprinted in a number of different collections during the next 100 years.

Lilli Marlene (song): *see* Lili Marleen.

Lillie, Beatrice (Gladys), byname BEA LILLIE, married name (from 1925) LADY PEEL (b. May 29, 1894, Toronto, Ont., Can.—d. Jan. 20, 1989, Henley-on-Thames, Oxfordshire, Eng.), sophisticated-comedy star of British and American revues, perhaps the foremost theatrical comedienne of the 20th century.

Making her stage debut in London in 1914 as a sentimental-ballad singer, Lillie proved her comic genius in a series of revues produced by André Charlot during World War I. In 1924 she made her first New York City appearance in a revue, establishing her reputation as an international celebrity. She appeared in at least one comedy revue a year from 1914 to 1939. After her film debut in the silent *Exit Smiling* (1926), she made other occasional screen appearances. After World War II she appeared in the revue *Inside U.S.A.* (1948–50) and toured in a one-woman show entitled *An Evening with Beatrice Lillie* (1952 and revised later productions). Her last stage performances were in *Auntie Mame* (1958, London) and *High Spirits* (1964, New York City), the musical version of Noël Coward's *Blithe Spirit.*

Beatrice Lillie
Brown Brothers

In 1920 she married Sir Robert Peel (d. 1934), who succeeded as 5th Baronet Peel in 1925. Her autobiography, *Every Other Inch a Lady,* was published in 1973.

Lillie, Frank Rattray (b. June 27, 1870, Toronto, Ont., Can.—d. Nov. 5, 1947, Chicago, Ill., U.S.), American zoologist and embryologist, known for his discoveries concerning the fertilization of the egg (ovum) and the role of hormones in sex determination.

Lillie spent most of his career at the University of Chicago (1900–47), where he served as professor of embryology (1906–35), chairman of the zoology department (1910–31), and dean of the biological sciences division (1931–35). In his researches, Lillie found that the animal ovum is coated with a gelatinous substance composed of carbohydrate and protein, which he termed fertilizin. Its specific interaction with a substance surrounding sperm cells, called antifertilizin, causes the sperm to adhere to and penetrate the egg. The process is thought to ensure fertilization of the ovum only by sperm of its own species.

Lillie also demonstrated that bovine "freemartinism" is a classic example of hormonal intersexuality in which a male fetus influences the development of its female twin. Cattle twins may consist of two males, two females, or a male and a "freemartin," an apparent female possessing a male's internal reproductive system. Knowing that sex hormones flow freely between fetal cattle twins, Lillie concluded that the freemartin is a genetic female masculinized by androgenic hormones from the male.

Throughout much of his life, he was associated with the Marine Biological Laboratory, Woods Hole, Mass., serving as its director (1908–26) and president of the corporation and board of trustees (1926–42). He was the founder and first president of the Woods Hole Oceanographic Institution (1930–39). His books include *Development of the Chick* (1908) and *Problems of Fertilization* (1919).

Lillo, George (b. Feb. 4, 1693, London, Eng.—d. Sept. 3, 1739, London), English dramatist of pioneer importance in whose domestic tragedy *The London Merchant: or, the History of George Barnwell* (1731) members of the middle class replaced the customary aristocratic or royal heroes. The play greatly influenced the rise of bourgeois drama in Germany and France, as well as in England.

Lillo was the son of a Dutch jeweler, and his first piece was a ballad opera (produced in 1730). Inspired by the Elizabethan drama of passion (*e.g.,* the anonymous *A Yorkshire Tragedy*), *The London Merchant* tells of a London apprentice who thrice robs his master and finally murders his uncle.

Lilongwe, city, capital (since 1975) of Malaŵi. It is located on the inland plains and is the nation's second largest city. An agricultural market centre for the fertile Central Region Plateau, it was selected by President H. Kamuzu Banda in 1965 as an economic growth point for northern and central Malaŵi. Lilongwe's development as the new national capital began in 1968.

The city is spread between two centres, the old city, which functions as a service and distribution centre, and Capital Hill, 3 miles (5 km) away, which houses the government buildings and embassies. Development projects of the 1970s and '80s included a new international airport, rail connections to Salima (east) and the Zambian border (west), industrial areas in the northern part of the city, and a development program for the fertile tobacco lands of the Central Region Plateau. Pop. (1998) 435,964.

Lilongwe Plain: *see* Central Region Plateau.

lily, the common name applied to herbaceous flowering plants belonging to the genus *Lilium* of the family Liliaceae. The genus contains between 80 and 100 species, native to the temperate areas of the Northern Hemisphere. Lilies are prized as ornamental plants, and they have been extensively hybridized.

The word lily is also used in the common names of many plants of other genera that resemble true lilies. These include the day lily (*Hemerocallis*) and various species of the family Amaryllidaceae.

The true lilies are erect perennial plants with leafy stems, scaly bulbs, usually narrow leaves, and solitary or clustered flowers. The flowers consist of six petallike segments, which may form the shape of a trumpet, with a more or less elongated tube, as in the Madonna lily (*Lilium candidum*) and Easter lily (*L. longiflorum*). Alternatively, the segments may be reflexed (curved back) to form a turban shape, as in the Turk's cap lily (*L. martagon*); or they may be less strongly reflexed and form an open cup or bowl shape, as in *L. umbellatum* and *L. auratum.* The flowers of some species are quite fragrant, and they occur in a wide variety of colours. Plants of most species range in height from 30 to 120 cm (1–4 feet); plants of certain species, however, exceed 2.5 m (8 feet) in height.

Lilies are among the oldest cultivated plants. In Asia Minor, during the 2nd millennium BC, the bulb of the Madonna lily was cultivated for use in a medicinal ointment; the ancients raised the bulbs of this species for food. The Greeks and Romans grew it for ornamental and medicinal purposes. During the Middle Ages the Madonna lily was associated with the Virgin Mary as a symbol of purity; it is often included in paintings of her. In East Asia various species of lily were grown as food and ornamental plants from an early date.

Lilies are usually raised from bulbs, but they can be grown from seed. Different species vary in the amount of sunlight they require. Most prefer a porous, loamy soil, and good drainage is essential. Most species bloom in July or August. The flowering periods of certain species begin in late spring; others bloom in late summer or early autumn.

Lily, William, Lily also spelled LILYE (b. 1468?, Odiham, Hampshire, Eng.—d. Feb. 25, 1522, London), English Renaissance scholar and classical grammarian, a pioneer of Greek learning in England and one of the authors of an extremely popular Latin grammar that, with corrections and revisions, was used as late as the 19th century.

Lily entered the University of Oxford in 1486 and, after graduating in arts, went on a pilgrimage to Jerusalem. On his return he put in at Rhodes, where he became acquainted with many Greeks, and then went on to Italy, where he attended lectures in Rome and Venice. After his return he settled in London (where he became a close friend of Sir Thomas More), became a private teacher of grammar, and is believed to have been the first to teach Greek in that city. In 1510 John Colet, dean of St. Paul's, who was then founding the school of St. Paul's, appointed Lily its first high master.

Lily's Grammar, as the work came to be known, was first published around 1540 and was actually a combined version of two shorter Latin syntaxes that Lily had written some years before. Henry VIII and his successor, Edward VI, ordered the book to be used in all English grammar schools, whereupon it became known as the "King's Grammar." *Lily's Grammar* came to be severely criticized by schoolmasters, however, because it provided the rules for the Latin language in that same language, rather than in English. Consequently, English translations of the rules and the syntax were added to the grammar by a number of 17th-century grammarians.

Later editions incorporating recognized emendations were published at the University of Cambridge (1634 and 1640) and at Oxford (1636 and 1687). John Ward's edition (1732) was commonly used in 18th-century English schools. Revised in 1758 and appropriated by Eton College as *The Eton Latin Grammar,* Lily's grammar was superseded 10 years later by the *Public School Latin Grammar.*

lily of the valley (*Convallaria majalis*), fragrant perennial herb and only species of the genus *Convallaria* of the family Liliaceae, native to Eurasia and eastern North America. Lily of the valley has nodding, white, bell-shaped flowers that are borne in a cluster on one side of a leafless stalk. The glossy leaves, usually two, are located at the base of the plant. The fruit is a red berry, and the rootstock creeps horizontally below the ground. Lily of the valley is cultivated in shaded garden areas in many temperate parts of the world. The plants often grow closely together, forming a dense mat.

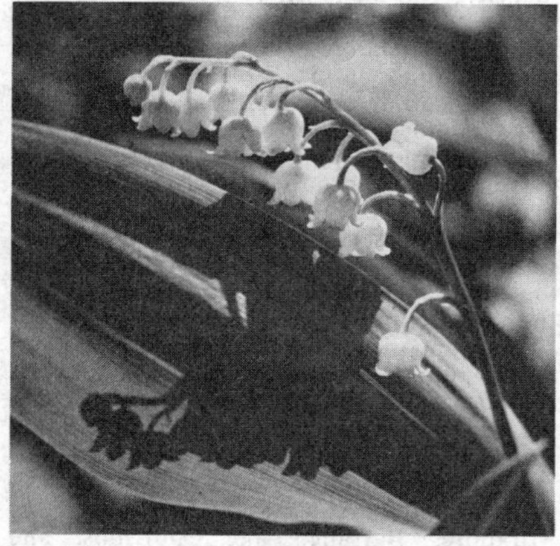

Lily of the valley (*Convallaria majalis*)
Walter Chandoha

lily-trotter (bird): *see* jacana.

Lima, department of central Peru and site of the national capital of Lima. The department stretches from the Pacific Ocean in the west to the Cordillera Occidental of the Andes in the east. There is little rainfall along its coastal section, and irrigation is possible only where rivers descend from the Andes. Fog often blankets the coast, especially from June to October; where the fog touches the mountain slopes, from about 2,500 to 4,000 feet (760 to 1,200 m) above sea level, there is a lush growth of herbaceous annual plants known as *lomas,* on which cattle are fed. Above the *lomas* zone there is a regular rainy season from October to April.

The department is Peru's most populous one. It contains, in a single agglomeration centred on Lima and extending into the adjoining constitutional province of Callao (Lima's separately administered port), nearly one-third of Peru's population. Specifically, the metropolitan area comprises the city of Lima proper, numerous nearby urbanized districts within Lima department, and the urbanized areas of Callao constitutional province.

Outside the Lima-Callao metropolitan area, most residents of the department are farmers and herders. Crops of the irrigated lowlands include sugarcane, cotton, and vegetables. There is some fishing off the coast at Callao and Huacho, and salt is produced from the evaporation of seawater at Huacho and Chilca. In the mountains there are copper mines at Casapalca and coal mines at Oyón. The department is crossed from northwest to southeast by the Pan-American Highway and is connected with highland centres by air, railroad, and highway. Area 13,437 square miles (34,802 square km). Pop. (2000 est.) 7,475,495.

Lima, city, capital of Lima department and of Peru. Located near the central Peruvian coast just inland from the Pacific Ocean, Lima is the country's commercial and industrial centre. The city is surrounded by the Peruvian coastal desert and overshadowed by the neighbouring Andes Mountains. Area city, 27 square miles (70 square km); urban agglomeration, 11,093 square miles (28,732 square km). Pop. (1998 est.) urban agglomeration, 7,060,600.

The following article treats briefly the modern city of Lima. Fuller treatment is provided in the following MACROPAEDIA articles. For history and contemporary life and for a map, *see* Lima; for additional perspective on the city in its national context, *see* Peru.

Central Lima is situated about 8 miles (13 km) inland from its Pacific port at Callao, on the south bank of the Rímac River. Suburbs extend in all directions, but urban growth to the east is limited by the Andes. Although Lima is located in the tropical zone, the cooling effect of the offshore Peru (Humboldt) Current creates a temperate climate, with an average temperature of about 62° F (17° C) in winter and about 75° F (24° C) in summer. Despite high humidity, annual precipitation averages only 1 to 2 inches (25 to 50 mm).

Lima's principal industries produce textiles, plastics, pharmaceuticals, chemicals, and man-made fibres. Heavy industry is also important, as are services. There are many banks, financial firms, and insurance companies in the city. The main commercial districts are in the southern part of the metropolitan area.

The boundaries of the old city—once marked by the ruins of its walls—are defined by the Avenues Alfonso Ugarte to the west, Unión to the east, and Miguel Grau to the south and by the Rímac River to the north. The metropolitan area extends southwestward to the residential suburbs and seaside resort towns of Miraflores, Barranco, and Chorrillos. The urban agglomeration includes most of Lima department and Callao. Industrial activity is concentrated along the east-west corridor from Vitarte to Callao and north to south along the Pan-American Highway. The main commercial districts are in the southern part of the metropolitan area. In Miraflores and San Isidro, in the area surrounding the city, squatter towns known as *barriadas* (slum neighbourhoods) and *pueblos jóvenes* ("young towns") have arisen. The constant migration of rural people to the city has caused a shortage of housing and of services.

Lima has a blend of colonial styles with modern architecture, but the frequency of earthquakes in the area has precluded the building of tall skyscrapers. Examples of Spanish colonial architecture include the cathedral, the temples of San Francisco, and the Palace of the Tagle Tower.

The most important university in Lima is the National University of San Marcos (1551). Academies of language and of history are the principal cultural centres in the city. Other institutions include the House of Peruvian Culture, a school of fine arts, a national symphony orchestra, a national conservatory of music, and also a national theatre. The area's many museums include those featuring collections of art, archaeological artifacts, historical items, and pre-Columbian objects made of gold. The National Library and the National Archives of Peru have the country's leading library collections.

A well-developed highway network radiates in all directions from the old city, connecting with the Pan-American Highway in the north and south and the Central Highway in the east. The Central Railway of Peru, the highest standard-gauge railway in the world, climbs the Andes from Lima northeast to La Oroya. The railway line to Callao (opened in 1851) is the oldest in South America. Callao is also the site of Lima's international airport.

Lima, city, seat (1831) of Allen county, northwestern Ohio, U.S. The city is situated on the Ottawa River, 88 miles (142 km) northwest of Columbus. Laid out in 1831, its name (from Lima, Peru) was chosen by lot by being drawn from a hat. Oil was discovered nearby in 1885, and by the beginning of the 20th century Lima was the centre of oil fields, which are now largely exhausted; however, the city remains an important pipeline and refining centre. Lima's economy is now highly diversified and includes the manufacture of machinery, electric motors, aerospace equipment, and chemicals. The Lima Campus of Ohio State University, east of the city, is also the site of Lima Technical College (1971). Inc. town, 1842; city, 1920. Pop. (2000) city, 40,081; Lima MSA, 155,084.

Lima, Jorge de (b. April 23, 1895, União dos Palmares, Braz.—d. Nov. 15, 1953, Rio de Janeiro), Brazilian poet and novelist who became one of the foremost representatives of regionalist poetry in Brazil in the 1920s.

Raised on a sugar plantation in northeastern Brazil, Lima practiced as a medical doctor. His earliest verses show the marked influence of the French Parnassian poets, but the volume *O Mundo do Menino Impossível* (1925; "The World of the Impossible Child") signals his break with European tradition and his adherence to the Modernist movement in Latin-American literature. He became an active collaborator with Gilberto Freyre and others in the northeastern regionalist movement and produced a great deal of "Afro-Brazilian" poetry in that vein throughout the 1930s.

Following his religious conversion in 1935, Lima sought to "restore poetry in Christ" and added metaphysical and expressionist poetry and fiction to his literary production. His best known collections of poems include *A Túnica Inconsútil* (1938; "The Seamless Tunic"), *Poemas Negros* (1947; "Black Poems"), and *Invenção de Orfeu* (1952; "The Invention of Orpheus"). In fiction, he is best known for *Calunga* (1935) and *A Mulher Obscura* (1939; "The Obscure Woman").

Lima, Manuel dos Santos (b. Jan. 28, 1935, Silva Porto, Angola), Angolan poet, dramatist, and novelist whose writing is rooted in the struggle for liberation of Angola from Portuguese colonialism.

Lima represented Angola in 1956 at the first International Congress of Black Writers and Artists in Paris and again at the Congress of Afro-Asian Writers in Cairo in 1962. He was a member of the Organizing Committee of the Popular Movement for the Liberation of Angola and a military leader of the Popular Army for the Liberation of Angola. These experiences provided nourishment for his writing. He later moved to Montreal, where he taught French.

Lima's first novel, *As Sementes da Liberdade* (1965; "The Seeds of Liberty"), was published in Rio de Janeiro, and his second, *As Lagrimas e o Vento* (1975; "Tears and Wind"), in Lisbon. The latter work is a fictional account of the war of liberation that resulted in independence. Lima also published a volume of poems, *Kissange* (1961), and a play, *A Pele do Diabo* (1977; "The Skin of the Devil"), as well as a political fable, *Os anões e os mendigos* (1984; "Dwarfs and Beggars").

Lima Barreto, Afonso Henriques de (b. May 13, 1881, Rio de Janeiro—d. Nov. 1, 1922, Rio de Janeiro), Brazilian novelist, journalist, short-story writer, and an aggressive social critic, who re-created in caricatural fashion the city and society of Rio de Janeiro at the turn of the century.

Lima Barreto was an active journalist throughout his adult life. His often vitriolic social analysis and criticism are more direct and less refined than was the case with his older contemporary Joachim Maria Machado de Assis. A lifelong *carioca* (resident of Rio), he depicts in his novels the main events of the new republic in Brazil (principally the 1890s and the first decade of the 20th century) and the life of that period. His ironic humour is evident in the creation of melancholic, quixotic protagonists who are unable to cope with mechanized urban society, militarism, and governmental organization.

Lima Barreto's best known novels include *Vida e Morte de M.J. Gonzaga de Sá* (1919; "Life and Death of M.J. Gonzaga de Sá"), *Recordações do Escrivão Isaías Caminha* (1909; "Memoirs of the Notary Public Isaiah Caminha"), *O Triste Fim de Policarpo Quaresma* (1915; "The Sad End of Polycarp Lent"), *Numa e a Ninfa* (1915; "Numa and the Nymph"), and *Clara dos Anjos* (composed in 1904 but published posthumously). His life was cut short by alcoholism.

lima bean, any of a variety of legumes of the species *Phaseolus limensis* widely cultivated for their edible seeds. *See* bean.

Liman von Sanders, Otto (b. Feb. 17, 1855, Stolp, Pomerania—d. Aug. 22, 1929, Munich), German general largely responsible for making the Ottoman army an effective fighting force in World War I and victor over the Allies at Gallipoli.

Liman began his military career in 1874 and rose to the rank of lieutenant general. In 1913 he was appointed director of a German military mission charged with reorganizing the Turkish army. Up to the outbreak of World War I, he did much to improve its fighting capabilities, which had been impaired by reverses during the Balkan Wars.

In March 1915 Liman was given command of the 5th Turkish Army at Gallipoli. Assisted by Turkish commanders, he succeeded in forcing the British and Australian invasion force to evacuate the Dardanelles, thus preventing an Allied seizure of Constantinople (now Istanbul). In March 1918 he headed the 4th, 7th, and 8th Turkish armies in Syria and Palestine.

For a time he held up the British advance but was forced to withdraw to Aleppo. After the armistice, he organized the repatriation of German soldiers who had served in Turkey during the war.

Limasawa, small island of historic importance near the island of Leyte, east-central Philippines. Located about 4 miles (6 km) off the southern tip of the island of Leyte just outside the mouth of Sogod Bay, Limasawa rises to about 700 feet (200 m). On this island, Ferdinand Magellan first made extended contact with Filipino natives on March 28, 1521. There also the first Roman Catholic mass was celebrated (March 31, 1521) in the Philippines. The island is inhabited by Visayan peoples who practice subsistence agriculture and fishing.

Limassol, Greek LEMESÓS, Turkish LIMASOL, city and chief port of the Republic of Cyprus. The city lies on Akrotiri Bay, on the southern coast, southwest of Nicosia; it is the island's second largest city and is also its chief tourist centre.

Limassol's rise from a humble market town between the ancient settlements of Amathus and Curium took place at the end of the Byzantine Empire, when Richard I the Lion-Heart landed there in 1191 and was married to Berengaria of Navarre in the chapel of a castle fortress, now a regional museum and one of only two surviving buildings of the period. After the Genoese seizure of Famagusta in 1372, the port's fortunes increased; but damage from numerous incursions between 1414 and 1426, the Turkish invasion of 1570, and a disastrous earthquake had reduced its population to 150 by 1815. Its resurgence dates from the end of the 19th century, when the island came under British administration.

Limassol's harbour facilities, which were extended in the 1960s to improve its shallow-water location, were increased by a new port (operational in 1974) that was able to provide berthing spaces for large vessels. The Turkish intervention (1974) in northern Cyprus and the closing of the island's main port at Famagusta made Limassol the chief port of the Republic of Cyprus. The port has also taken over much of the trade that once passed through Beirut. In the 1970s and '80s Limassol also became home to many thousands of prosperous Arab refugees from Lebanon and immigrants from Saudi Arabia and Kuwait. Limassol's bustling port exports wines, beverages, fruits, and vegetables. Bricks, tiles, shoes, textiles, furniture, cement, buttons, and soft drinks are manufactured; fruit is canned; and chrome and asbestos are processed. Legumes, vegetables, oranges, lemons, grapefruits, nuts, and apples are grown on the adjacent coastal plain, and goats and cattle are raised as well. The Troödos Mountains lie inland from the plain. Limassol city is linked by roads with Moni, Akrotíri, and Episkopi. Pop. (1982) city, 74,782; (1989 est.) metropolitan area, 120,000.

Limavady, Irish LÉIM AN MHADAIDH, town, seat, and district (established 1973), formerly in County Londonderry, Northern Ireland. Limavady town is on the River Roe 17 miles (27 km) east of the old city of Londonderry. Its name, meaning "the dog's leap," is derived from a gorge south of town over which a dog of ancient times carried a message of impending danger. Limavady dates from the Plantation of Ulster in the early 17th century; it was settled by Protestant Scots who built the town's numerous Georgian homes and archways. The town is an important market centre and has industries making synthetic textiles and prefabricated buildings.

Limavady district covers an area of 240 square miles (622 square km) south of Lough (inlet of the sea) Foyle and is bordered by the districts of Londonderry to the west, Strabane and Magherafelt to the south, and Coleraine to the east. The glacially scoured Sperrin Mountains in southern Limavady descend to rolling hills and fertile lowlands in the River Roe Valley in the centre of the district and then to the flat shores of Lough Foyle in the north. Sheep graze in the mountains and hills, and cattle are raised on the farms in the valley, where barley and potatoes are also grown. Pop. (1981) town, 8,015; (1988 est.) district, 30,000.

limb darkening, in astrophysics, gradual decrease in brightness of the disk of the Sun or of another star as observed from its centre to its edge, or limb. This phenomenon is readily apparent in photographs of the Sun. The darkening is greatest for blue light, amounting to a drop of as much as 90 percent from the Sun's photosphere to its outer atmospheric regions. Such limb darkening occurs because the solar atmosphere increases in temperature with depth. At the centre of the solar disk, an observer sees the deepest and warmest layers that emit the most light. At the limb, only the upper, cooler layers that produce less light can be seen. Observations of solar limb darkening are used to determine the temperature structure of the Sun's atmosphere. Information derived from such observations is applied in studying other stars.

Limbe, formerly VICTORIA, port, southwestern Cameroon. It lies along Ambas Bay of the Gulf of Guinea, at the southern foot of Mount Cameroon, just south of Buea. Limbe is Cameroon's second largest port, after the much larger nearby port of Douala. It is dependent upon migrant labour and the export produce of nearby plantations: coffee, cocoa, palm oil and kernels, tea, bananas, and rubber.

The town was founded in 1858 by Baptist missionaries, and several historical monuments dating from the colonial 1890s have been preserved. A hospital and an airport serve the town, which also has beaches and boating facilities. Pop. (1987 est.) 42,511.

limbo, in Roman Catholic theology, the border place between heaven and hell where dwell those souls who, though not condemned to punishment, are deprived of the joy of eternal existence with God in heaven. The word is of Teutonic origin, meaning "border," or "anything joined on." The concept of limbo probably developed in the European Middle Ages. Two distinct kinds of limbo have been supposed to exist: (1) the *limbus patrum* ("father's limbo"), which is the place where the Old Testament saints were thought to be confined until they were liberated by Christ in his "descent into hell"; and (2) the *limbus infantum,* or *puerorum* ("children's limbo"), which is the abode of those who have died without actual sin but whose original sin has not been washed away by Baptism. This "children's limbo" included not only dead unbaptized infants but also the mentally defective.

The question of the destiny of infants dying unbaptized presented itself to Christian theologians at a relatively early period. Generally speaking, it may be said that the Greek Fathers of the Church inclined to a cheerful view and the Latin Fathers to a gloomy view. Indeed, some of the Greek Fathers expressed opinions that are almost indistinguishable from the Pelagian view that children dying unbaptized might be admitted to eternal life, though not to the Kingdom of God. St. Augustine recoiled from such Pelagian heresies and drew a sharp antithesis between the state of the saved and that of the damned. Later theologians followed Augustine in rejecting the notion of any final place intermediate between heaven and hell, but they otherwise were inclined to take the mildest possible view of the destiny of the irresponsible and unbaptized.

The Roman Catholic church in the 13th and 15th centuries made several authoritative declarations on the subject of limbo, stating that the souls of those who die in original sin only (*i.e.,* unbaptized infants) descend into hell but are given lighter punishments than those souls guilty of actual sin. The damnation of infants and also the comparative lightness of their punishment thus became articles of faith, but the details of the place such souls occupied in hell or the nature of their actual punishment remained undetermined. From the Council of Trent (1545–63) onward, there were considerable differences of opinion as to the extent of the infant souls' deprivation, with some theologians maintaining that the infants in limbo are affected with some degree of sadness because of a felt privation, and other theologians holding that the infants enjoy every kind of natural felicity, as regards their souls now and their bodies after the Resurrection. The concept of limbo has remained similarly undefined and problematical in modern Roman Catholic doctrine.

Limbu, the second most numerous tribe of the indigenous people called Kiranti, living in Nepal on the easternmost section of the Himalayas between the Arun River and the border of Sikkim state, India. Of Mongolian stock, they number an estimated 200,000 and speak a Tibeto-Nepalese dialect of Kiranti. Limbu villages are found 2,500 to 4,000 feet (800 to 1,200 m) above sea level and consist of 30–100 stone houses surrounded by dry-cultivated fields. Divided into patrilineal clans, the families are led by a headman, or *subba,* who is often a returned Gurkha soldier. Maintaining a self-sufficient economy, the Limbu grow rice, wheat, and corn (maize) on terraced and irrigated fields; land is planted once a year. In addition, buffalo are kept, and goats, chickens, and sheep are raised for meat. Although influenced by Buddhism from Tibet as well as by rituals from nearby lamaseries, the Limbu observe a traditional religion, worshiping a chief god, Niwa Buma, and mountain and river deities. Each Limbu household additionally honours an ancestor god and has a religious leader (a *shamba,* or a *fedangba*) to conduct family rituals.

Limburg, historic region of the Low Countries that was one of many small states resulting from the division of the duchy of Lower Lorraine in the second half of the 11th century.

The name Limburg was finally applied when the rival houses of Limburg (heirs of the first count, Walram of Arlon) and Louvain made peace in 1155. The territory along the Meuse River became known as Limburg, and the much larger territory to the west became known as Brabant.

The direct male line of the house of Arlon continued to rule Limburg until 1282. When war broke out between Count Reinald of Guelders (who had married into the rights of Limburg) and Adolph V of Berg (who had been granted those same rights by the Holy Roman emperor), Adolph was not strong enough to contest his rights militarily and sold them to John I of Brabant. After five years of war against Reinald and his ally, John was victorious. Limburg was united with Brabant under his rule but maintained its separate institutions and laws. In 1430 the duchy of Limburg was united with the rest of the Netherlands under Philip III, duke of Burgundy. As a part of the Burgundian inheritance, Limburg passed to the house of Habsburg in 1482.

With the Peace of Westphalia (1648), Limburg was divided in two—the northern part being ceded by Spain to the United Provinces of the Netherlands. In 1714, when the Peace of Rastatt was effected, the southern part of Limburg passed to the Austrian Habsburgs and formed part of the Austrian Netherlands until the French conquest in 1795. While under French rule, Limburg became a section of two *départements,* Ourthe and Meuse-Inferieure. Its name was restored in 1815 when it, with a few additions, formed a province of the new Kingdom of The Netherlands. The territory was traded off several times in the ensuing diplomatic discussions between The Netherlands, Belgium, and Luxembourg. In 1866 Limburg was finally integrated into The Netherlands.

Limburg, French LIMBOURG, *province,* northeastern Belgium. It is bounded by The Netherlands on the north and east, where the Meuse River marks the frontier. Limburg consists of three administrative *arrondissements* (Hasselt, Maaseik, and Tongeren). Largely Flemish-speaking, it was formerly part of the feudal duchy of Limburg, which was divided between Belgium and The Netherlands in 1839.

The Kempen heathland in the north is characterized by gentle eminences of sand dune and moor separated by shallow marshy depressions, with pine plantations covering about one-quarter of the surface. In some areas the soil has been fertilized to produce rye, oats, potatoes, vegetables, and fodder; livestock also are raised. Rich coalfields in the Kempen have been developed since World War I, producing much of Belgium's coal. Zinc and other nonferrous refineries, chemical works, and glassworks are located on isolated heathland sites, and there is diversified industry around Hasselt (*q.v.*), the capital. The construction of the Albert Canal (1930–39) from Antwerp to Liège also stimulated the economic growth of this formerly poor region.

The Demer Valley at the southern edge of the Kempen supports dairy farming and, along its margin, prosperous market gardening. In the southern part of Limburg, sandy loams of the northern Hesbaye Plateau support fruit, grains, sugar beets, and vegetables. Industries of the region are related to agriculture—sugar refining and food processing. Limburg's principal population centres are Genk (*q.v.*), Maaseik, and Tessenderloo in the Kempen; Hasselt; and Sint-Truiden and Tongeren (*q.v.*) in the Hesbaye.

The province is served by the Albert, Schelde-Meuse Junction, and Zuidwillemsvaart canals and by several railway lines. There are also several natural reserves in the Kempen region. Area 935 square miles (2,422 square km). Pop. (1991) 750,435.

Limburg, *provincie,* southeastern Netherlands. It is bounded on the northwest by Noordbrabant *provincie,* on the north by Gelderland *provincie,* on the east by Germany, and on the south and southwest by the Belgian provinces of Limburg and Liège. It is drained by the Geul, Gulp, Roer, and Maas (Meuse) rivers, the latter forming part of the province's southwestern boundary and bisecting its northern portion.

Formerly part of the duchy of Limburg, which was divided in 1648 between the United Provinces of the Netherlands and the Spanish Netherlands, the area was united in 1815 to the Kingdom of The Netherlands. The Dutch-Belgian treaty of 1839 divided the territory into the Dutch and Belgian provinces of Limburg.

The province's hilly southern part, extending to Sittard, is a loess-covered rock plateau with a coalfield under some parts. Wheat, rye, sugar beets, and fruit are cultivated, and there is some dairy farming. Until the early 1970s, coal mining was important around Heerlen, Kerkrade, and Geleen; Bonn and Stein are river ports. Maastricht, the provincial capital, is the chief industrial centre. In the sandy regions of the rest of the province, farming is mostly mixed, although there is more arable land (mostly producing rye). Pigs and poultry production are also important, and there is market gardening around Venlo. Industry is mainly concentrated around the larger centres, such as Roermond, Sittard, Venlo, and Weert, and includes the manufacture of light metals, clothing, hosiery, and chemicals. East of the Maas, between Venlo and Roermond, is an important brickmaking and tile-making district. Area 838 square miles (2,170 square km). Pop. (1990 est.) 1,103,960.

Limburg, Pol, Herman, and Jehanequin de, Limburg also spelled LIMBOURG (all b. after 1385, Nijmegen, Brabant [now in The Netherlands]—d. by 1416), three Flemish brothers who were the most famous of all late Gothic illuminators. They synthesized the achievements of contemporary illuminators into a style characterized by subtlety of line, painstaking technique, and minute rendering of detail. The sons of a sculptor, Arnold van Limburg, they were also the nephews of Jean Malouel, court painter to the Duke of Burgundy, and are sometimes known by the name "Malouel." The brothers worked together, and although the most celebrated appears to have been the eldest brother, Pol, it is difficult to distinguish their individual styles.

The illustration for May from the *Très Riches Heures du duc de Berry,* manuscript illuminated by the Limburg brothers, 1416; in the Musée Condé, Chantilly, Fr.

By courtesy of the Musee Conde, Chantilly, Fr.; photograph, Giraudon—Art Resource

About 1400 the brothers were apprenticed to a goldsmith in Paris, and between 1402 and 1404 Pol and Jehanequin were working for the Duke of Burgundy in Paris, possibly on the illustration of a *Bible moralisée* now in the Bibliothèque Nationale, Paris. Some time after Burgundy's death in 1404, they entered the service of his brother, the Duke de Berry, and it was for him that their most lavishly illustrated books of hours (the popular form of private prayer book of the period) were produced. The *Belles Heures* (or *Les Heures d'Ailly;* now in The Cloisters, New York) show the influence of the Italianate elements of the contemporary French artist Jacquemart de Hesdin's illuminations. The *Très Riches Heures du duc de Berry* (Musée Condé, Chantilly, Fr.), considered their greatest work, is one of the landmarks of the art of book illumination and ranks among the supreme examples of the International Gothic style. It is essentially a court style, elegant and sophisticated, combining naturalism of detail with overall decorative effect. An awareness of the most progressive international currents of the time, particularly those deriving from Italy, suggests that at least one of the brothers visited there. The *Très Riches Heures* was left unfinished in 1416 but was completed about 1485 by Jean Colombe.

The Limburg brothers were among the first to render specific landscape scenes with accuracy. Their art did much to determine the course that Early Netherlandish art was to take during the 15th century.

Limburger, semisoft surface-ripened cow's-milk cheese that has a rind of pungent odour and a creamy-textured body of strong flavour. Limburger originated in the Belgian province of Liège and was first sold at markets in Limbourg. By the late 20th century, most Limburger was produced in Germany and the United States.

The characteristic form of Limburger is in small bricks, squares, or cubes. Its thin-skinned reddish rind is formed by corynebacteria that ripen the cheese into a soft, spreadable paste. The celebrated odour develops as the cheese ripens, becoming quite rank within a few weeks. The flavour of Limburger is pronounced but not as strong as the odour, which can be detected at a considerable distance when the cheese is exposed.

limburgite, dark-coloured volcanic rock that resembles basalt but normally contains no feldspar. It is associated principally with nepheline-basalts and leucite-basalts; it also occurs with monchiquite, from which it is not easily distinguished. Limburgite may occur as flows, sills, or dikes and sometimes contains many cavities.

Limburgite consists essentially of olivine and augite with a brown, glassy groundmass in which a second generation of small augite crystals is commonly found. The principal accessory minerals are titaniferous iron oxides and apatite; in some limburgites, hornblende and biotite are found as large, scattered crystals, in others soda-orthoclase or anorthoclase. Rocks of this group are found in considerable quantities, as in the Rhine district of Germany; Bohemia, Czech Republic; Haddington, Lothian region, Scotland; the Auvergne region, France; Spain; Kilimanjaro, Africa; and Brazil.

lime (*Citrus aurantifolia*), tree widely grown in tropical and subtropical areas and its edible acid fruits. The tree seldom grows more than 5 m (16 feet) high and if not pruned becomes shrublike. Its branches spread and are irregular, with short, stiff twigs, small leaves, and many small, sharp thorns. The leaves are pale green; the small white flowers are usually borne in clusters. The fruit is about 3 to 4 cm (1 to 1.5 inches) in diameter, oval to nearly globular in shape, often with a small apical nipple; the peel is thin and greenish yellow when

Lime (*Citrus aurantifolia*)

Grant Heilman

the fruit is ripe. The pulp is tender, juicy, yellowish green in colour, and decidedly acid. Limes exceed lemons in both acid and sugar content. There are, however, some varieties so lacking in citric acid that they are known as sweet limes. These are grown to some extent in Egypt and other tropical countries.

Limes probably originated in the Indonesian archipelago or the nearby mainland of Asia. The Arabs may have taken limes, as well as lemons, from India to the eastern Mediterranean countries and Africa around AD 1000. Limes were introduced to the western Mediterranean countries by returning crusaders in the 12th and 13th centuries. Columbus took citrus-fruit seed, probably including limes, to the West Indies on his second voyage in 1493, and the trees soon became widely distributed in the West Indies, Mexico, and Florida.

Brazil leads in lime production, producing around 700,000 metric tons per year. Mexico produces about 530,000 tons annually and the U.S. about 44,000, mainly in southern Florida. Limes are grown throughout the West Indies and to a limited extent in practically all citrus-growing areas.

Tahiti lime trees resemble lemon trees and are larger and more vigorous than the Mexican, with larger and darker coloured leaves. The fruit is larger and more elongated than the Mexican lime, the peel is thicker, and the fruit is nearly seedless.

The lime fruit is a key ingredient in certain pickles and chutneys. Juice of the lime is used to flavour drinks, food, and confections. Limeade and other lime-flavoured drinks have a flavour and bouquet quite distinct from those made from lemons. The juice may be concentrated, dried, frozen, or canned. Lime oil is processed mainly in the West Indies. Citrate of lime and citric acid are also prepared from the fruit.

Limes contain vitamin C (ascorbic acid) and were formerly used in the British Navy to prevent scurvy; hence the nickname "Limey."

The basswood, or linden, tree (a species of *Tilia*) is also called lime in England.

To make the best use of the Britannica, consult the INDEX *first*

lime, calcium oxide, an alkaline inorganic compound of calcium (*q.v.*).

lime painting: *see* fresco painting.

Limehouse, neighbourhood in the borough of Tower Hamlets in the East End of London, on the north bank of the River Thames. Many seamen's hostels, churches, and public houses still enhance the character of the district, although the nearby docks have closed. (The sometimes pejorative term "Limey" for Englishman, often thought to derive from the many sailors of Limehouse, probably derives from the unrelated term "lime-juicer," from the maritime use of lime juice as an anti-scorbutic.) Urban redevelopment has removed the residents of the Chinatown at Pennyfields, but several Chinese restaurants remain. The parish church of St. Anne's, completed in 1724, was designed by Nicholas Hawksmoor. The name of the district derives from the limekilns that were on the riverbank at least as early as the 16th century and that used coal brought by sea from Newcastle.

Limeira, city, east central São Paulo state, Brazil, on the headwaters of the Ribeirão (stream) do Tatu, a tributary of the Rio Piracicaba. Known at various times as Tatuibi, Rancho de Limeira, and Nossa Senhora das Dores de Tatuibi, it was elevated to city status in 1863. Limeira processes local crops (sugarcane, rice, cotton, coffee, oranges) and manufactures automobile parts, machinery, hats, and matches. Goods are transported by road, rail, and air to São Paulo, the state capital, 80 mi (130 km) southeast, and to neighbouring urban centres. Pop. (2000 prelim.) 248,632.

limelight, first theatrical spotlight, also a popular term for the incandescent calcium light invented by Thomas Drummond in 1816. Drummond's light, which consisted of a block of calcium heated to incandescence in jets of burning oxygen and hydrogen, provided a soft, very brilliant light that could be directed and focussed. It was first employed in a theatre in 1837 and was in wide use by the 1860s. Its intensity made it useful for spotlighting and for the realistic simulation of effects such as sunlight and moonlight. Limelights placed at the front of the balcony could also be used for general stage illumination, providing a more natural light than footlights. The expression "in the limelight" originally referred to the most desirable acting area on the stage, the front and centre, which was brilliantly illuminated by limelights.

The greatest disadvantage of limelight was that each light required the almost constant attention of an individual operator, who had to keep adjusting the block of calcium as it burned and to tend to the two cylinders of gas that fuelled it. Electric lighting in general and the electric arc spotlight replaced the limelight late in the 19th century.

Limerick, Irish LUIMNEACH, county, southwestern Ireland, in the province of Munster, with an area of 1,037 sq mi (2,686 sq km). Its northern boundary, with County Clare, is the River Shannon and its estuary. The River Maigue bisects the county and flows north into the Shannon. On the west the boundary with County Kerry runs through plateaus 1,000–2,000 ft high (300–600 m). On the east the boundary with Tipperary runs from the Shannon to Slievefelim (1,524 ft [465 m]), then across the Golden Vale southward to the Galtee mountains to the summit of Galtymore (3,018 ft [920 m]). The southern boundary, with Cork, follows the Ballyhoura Hills, a continuation of the line of the Galtees. Lowland Limerick is mainly a rolling landscape with a variety of glacial drifts diversified by hills, including a number of isolated volcanic hills. The peat bog that formerly covered parts of the lowland has been largely removed, and pastoral farming dominates. The farms are about 50–80 ac (20–32 ha) in size. There are remains of round towers at Ardpatrick and Dysert, of prehistoric monuments at Lough Gur, and of numerous monasteries in the city of Limerick and elsewhere.

A county council meets at Limerick, and there is a county manager; Limerick city is a county borough. The largest town of the west of Ireland, Limerick is a distributing centre for an area far wider than the county, but the county's many villages are mainly shopping centres and have fairs. Much of Limerick lies within the Golden Vale, famed for its rich pastures and dairy products. In many areas almost all the land is under grass and hay, for the main wealth lies in the dairy herds. Pigs are raised, and bacon curing is an old industry of Limerick city. Manufactures include aluminum castings, automotive parts, concrete pipes, and office equipment. Pop. (1996) excluding Limerick county borough, 113,003.

Limerick, Irish LUIMNEACH (Bare Land), county borough, port, and chief town of County Limerick, Ireland, occupying both banks and King's Island of the River Shannon at the head of its estuary. The Norse, who sacked the early settlement in 812, made it the principal town of their kingdom of Limerick; they were expelled at the end of the 10th century by the Irish hero Brian Boru. From 1106 to 1174 it was the seat of the kings of Thomond, or North Munster. Richard I granted it a charter in 1197. King John (reigned 1199–1216) granted it to William de Burgh, who founded English Town and erected a strong castle. In the 15th century its fortifications were extended to include Irish Town, and it became one of the strongest fortresses of the kingdom. After an unsuccessful siege by William III, its resistance was ended in 1691 by the treaty of Limerick. In 1609 it had received a charter constituting it a county of a city and also incorporating a society of merchants. Fragments of the old walls remain.

Thomond Bridge over the River Shannon and King John's Castle at Limerick, Ireland

G.F. Allen—Bruce Coleman

Under the Local Government Act of 1888, Limerick became a county borough with a city council. The city is divided into English Town (on King's Island), Irish Town, and Newtown Pery (founded 1769), the first including the ancient nucleus of the city and the last, the principal modern streets. The main stream of the Shannon is crossed by the Thomond and the Sarsfield, or Wellesley, bridges. The Protestant Cathedral of St. Mary was originally built in 1142–80. The modern Roman Catholic Cathedral of St. John is in Early Pointed style. Communication with the Atlantic Ocean is open, while inland navigation is facilitated by a canal. Quays extend on each side of the river, along which lie a graving (dry) dock and a wet dock. Main imports are grain, timber, oil, and coal; exports are chiefly fish and agricultural produce. Industries include flour milling, bacon curing, and milk processing. Limerick is the centre of the Shannon salmon fisheries. The city benefitted from the establishment of the nearby Shannon hydroelectric power station. The National Institute for Higher Education at Limerick, begun in 1972, is part of the National University of Ireland. A teachers' training college, Thomond College of Education, is also at Limerick. Pop. (1996) 52,039.

limerick, a popular form of short, humorous verse, often nonsensical and frequently ribald. It consists of five lines, rhyming *aabba,* and the dominant metre is anapestic, with two feet in the third and fourth lines and three feet in the others. The origin of the limerick is unknown, but it has been suggested that the name derives from the chorus of an 18th-century Irish soldiers' song, "Will You Come Up to Limerick?" To this were added impromptu verses crowded with improbable incident and subtle innuendo.

The first collections of limericks in English date from about 1820. Edward Lear, who composed and illustrated those in his *Book of Nonsense* (1846), claimed to have gotten the idea from a nursery rhyme beginning "There was an old man of Tobago." A typical example from Lear's collection is this verse:

There was an Old Man who supposed
That the street door was partially closed;
But some very large rats
Ate his coats and his hats,
While that futile Old Gentleman dozed.

Toward the end of the 19th century, many noted men of letters indulged in the form. W.S. Gilbert displayed his skill in a sequence of limericks that Sir Arthur Sullivan set as the familiar song in *The Sorcerer* (1877):

My name is John Wellington Wells,
I'm a dealer in magic and spells,
In blessings and curses,
And ever-fill'd purses,
In prophecies, witches, and knells.

The form acquired widespread popularity in the early years of the 20th century, and limerick contests were often held by magazines and business houses. The true limerick addict, however, turned to more complicated verse, such as this anonymous tongue twister:

A tutor who taught on the flute
Tried to teach two tooters to toot.
Said the two to the tutor,
"Is it harder to toot, or
To tutor two tooters to toot?"

Others wrote limericks in French or Latin, exploited the anomalies of English spelling, or used the form for pithy observations upon serious philosophical concerns.

Limerick, Thomas Dongan, 2nd earl of: *see* Dongan, Thomas.

Limerick lace, strictly speaking not lace at all but embroidered machine-made net the appearance of which approximates true lace. It was made at Mount Kennet, near Limerick, in Ireland, having been introduced there by an English lace manufacturer in 1829. Designs similar to those of contemporary lace were embroidered in tambour stitch (a form of chain stitch) and in needlerun stitches, versions of needlepoint filling stitches. The word Limerick is sometimes used loosely to refer to embroidered net in general.

limes (Latin: "path"), plural LIMITES, in ancient Rome, the strip of open land along which troops advanced into unfriendly territory. The word, therefore, came to mean a Roman military road, fortified with watchtowers and forts. Finally, *limes* acquired the sense of frontier, either natural or artificial; towers and forts tended to be concentrated along it, and the military road between them was often replaced by a continuous barrier.

The *limes* as a continuous barrier can best be seen in Great Britain and Germany. The Rhine and Danube rivers were adopted from AD 9 as the natural frontiers of the Roman Empire. Later in the 1st century the Romans extended their control into the Black Forest area; under the emperors Hadrian (117–138) and Antoninus Pius (138–161) a *limes* was established, consisting of a continuous nine-foot palisade running, in its final form, more than 300 miles across the angle between the two rivers. The palisade was later replaced by stone and earth walls. The Alemanni broke through the *limes* in *c.* 260 and the Roman frontier was withdrawn to the Rhine and Danube once more. The *limites* in Great Britain were Hadrian's Wall between the Rivers Tyne and Solway and, farther north, the turf wall of Antoninus Pius between the Rivers Forth and Clyde.

The *limes* as a system of fortifications was employed on other frontiers during the 2nd century AD and assumed various forms according to the differing geographical and military conditions. In what is now Romania a *limes* of Trajanic-Hadrianic times has been traced in the Dobruja area; lines of forts to the east and west of this area, however, do not appear to have been linked by ramparts. In Anatolia a continuous barrier was neither practicable nor necessary, as the Romans controlled the roads and river crossings. In Syria, however, an elaborate *limes* system was established, not only to control the mobile native population and the caravan routes but also for defense against Parthian or Sāsānian attacks. The main part of this line held until the Arab conquest in the 7th century. Control of nomads was also necessary in North Africa. The network system of roads, forts, and watchtowers was adopted, but the defenses also included a continuous barrier, a ditch, and either a stone or earth wall.

limestone, sedimentary rock composed mainly of calcium carbonate ($CaCO_3$), usually in the form of calcite or aragonite. It may contain considerable amounts of magnesium carbonate (dolomite) as well; minor constituents also commonly present include clay, iron carbonate, feldspar, pyrite, and quartz.

A brief treatment of limestones follows. For full treatment, *see* MACROPAEDIA: Minerals and Rocks.

Most limestones have a granular texture. Their constituent grains range in size from 0.001 millimetre (0.00004 inch) to visible particles. In many cases, the grains are microscopic fragments of fossil animal shells.

Limestone has two origins: (1) biogenic precipitation from sea water (autochthonous limestone), the primary agents being lime-secreting organisms and foraminifera; and (2) mechanical transport and deposition of preexisting limestones (allochthonous limestone), forming clastic deposits.

Limestone has long fascinated earth scientists because of its rich fossil content. Much knowledge of the Earth's chronology and development has been derived from the study of fossils embedded in limestone and other carbonate rocks. Limestone also has considerable commercial importance. Limestones enriched in phosphate by the chemical action of ocean waters constitute a principal source of raw materials for the fertilizer industry. When heated to temperatures of 900° to 1,000° C (1,650° to 1,800° F), limestones will dissociate calcium carbonate and yield carbon dioxide and lime, the latter having major applications in the manufacture of glass and in agriculture. Certain varieties of limestone also serve as a building stone; they are widely used for flooring, exterior and interior facings, and monuments.

Limfjorden, strait (110 mi [180 km] long) across northern Jutland, Denmark, connecting the North Sea and the Kattegat and separating the Vendsyssel and Thy regions from the mainland. Actually a series of fjords dotted with inlets and islands, it opens into a lagoon (15 mi wide) in its middle course, then becomes narrow from Ålborg to the Kattegat. Shallow in parts (maximum depth 50 ft [15 m]), it has been deepened to aid shipping. Its western outlet at Thyborøn was open during the Viking period but silted up in the Middle Ages creating freshwater lakes, which drained into the Kattegat from the eastern end. In 1825 the tide of the North Sea broke through the western part, and the Thyborøn Kanal was cut in 1875 to keep the outlet open.

Limfjorden, Denmark
Erik Friis—Photo Trends

In addition to being a thoroughfare for shipping, it is noted for its oysters and mussels, and the ash and clay of the surrounding region supplies special lightweight building bricks (*moler*). The largest island is Mors and the chief ports are Ålborg, Nørresundby, Løgstør, Nykøbing Mors, and Thisted.

limit, mathematical concept based on the idea of closeness, used primarily to assign values to certain functions at points where no values are defined, in such a way as to be consistent with nearby values. For example, the function $(x^2-1)/(x-1)$ is not defined when x is 1, because division by zero is not a valid mathematical operation. For any other value of x, the numerator can be factored and divided by the $(x-1)$, giving $x+1$. This is equivalent to the quotient for all values of x except 1, in which it is equal to 2, in contrast to the quotient that has no value. This value of 2 is then assigned to the function $(x^2-1)/(x-1)$ not as its value when x equals 1, but as its limit when x approaches 1.

One way of defining the limit of a function $f(x)$ at a point x_0, written as

$$\lim_{x\to x_0} f(x),$$

is by the following: if there is a continuous (unbroken) function $g(x)$ such that $g(x)=f(x)$ in some interval around x_0, except possibly at x_0 itself, then

$$\lim_{x\to x_0} f(x)=g(x_0).$$

The following more basic definition of limit, independent of the concept of continuity, can also be given:

$$\lim_{x\to x_0} (x)=L$$

if, for any desired degree of closeness ε, one can find an interval around x_0 so that all values of $f(x)$ calculated here differ from L by an amount less than ε (*i.e.,* if $|x-x_0|<\delta$, then $|f(x)-L|<\varepsilon$). This last definition can be used to determine whether or not a given number is in fact a limit, but it is the first definition that gives a method for finding it. The calculation of limits, especially of quotients, usually involves manipulations of the function so that it can be written in a form in which the limit is more obvious, as in the above example of $(x^2-1)/(x-1)$.

Limits are the method by which the derivative (*q.v.*), or rate of change, of a function is calculated, and are used throughout analysis as a way of making approximations into exact quantities, as when the area inside a curved region is defined to be the limit of approximations by rectangles.

limitations, statute of, legislative act restricting the time within which legal proceedings may be brought, usually to a fixed period after the occurrence of the events that gave rise to the cause of action. Such statutes are enacted to protect persons against claims made after evidence has been lost, memories have faded, or witnesses have disappeared.

Statutes of limitations appeared early in Roman law and form the basis of the limitations provided in the codes of civil-law countries. In England limitations on actions to recover landed property were not instituted until the 16th century and those on personal actions until the 17th. Civil actions commonly are limited in different degrees by general statutes that classify the actions into broad groups. Although the periods prescribed are arbitrary, they bear a rough relation to the times for which reliable evidence of the respective transactions may be expected to endure. The initiation actions for recovery of real property and actions on contracts under seal are commonly limited to periods of from 10 to 20 years. Actions on oral or simple written contracts usually are limited to periods of from three to six years and those for personal injury to three years or less. There is considerable variation in the periods that are prescribed in different jurisdictions. In Germany, for example, there is a general 30-year limitation on civil actions, but in some specific actions, such as tort and interest claims, the period may be only two or three years.

In addition to general statutes of limitations, a large number of special laws limit the period within which particular actions by or against particular parties may be brought. Actions for slander, for claiming forfeitures or penalties, and those against certain public officials frequently are restricted by short periods of limitation, usually less than six months. Proceedings involving the administration of estates are subject to short limitation periods, normally measured from the appointment of the executor or administrator.

General statutes of limitations uniformly include provisions allowing persons who are legally disabled by infancy, imprisonment, or insanity at the time a cause of action arises to initiate the action within some fixed period after the disability has been removed. In cases of fraud when the injured party is for some time unaware of the existence of a cause of action, activation of the statute is delayed until such a time as the facts reasonably might have been discovered. Similarly, the period of the statute does not go into effect during the time that the defendant is outside the jurisdiction and thus beyond the reach of its courts.

In civil actions, statutes of limitations have been held not to apply to a government suing in its own courts, by virtue of its sovereignty. In many instances, however, legislatures have waived this governmental immunity by express statutory enactments.

General statutes limiting the period within which prosecutions for crimes must be begun are common in civil-law countries and in the United States. In the United States the periods normally are shorter than in continental Europe, and the limitations are restricted to misdemeanours and, sometimes, minor felonies. As with civil actions, the period prescribed in a criminal statute of limitations does not run in the case of a defendant who has fled or concealed himself in order to avoid prosecution. In England there is no general statute of limitations applicable to criminal actions, although statutes defining certain actions as criminal frequently have included time limits for their prosecution.

limited liability, condition under which the loss that an owner (shareholder) of a business firm may incur is limited to the amount of capital invested by him in the business and does not extend to his personal assets. Acceptance of this principle by business enterprises and governments was a vital factor in the development of large-scale industry, because it enabled business concerns to mobilize large amounts of capital from a wide variety of investors who were understandably unwilling to risk their entire personal fortunes in their investments.

Joint-stock companies in which members had transferable shares of joint or common stock had become widespread in England in the 17th century to meet the requirements of the new trading companies operating in remote lands in which the financial and political risks were greater. A speculative panic in 1720 resulted in a severe setback to joint-stock enterprise, however, and legislation passed that year made it much more difficult for such companies to obtain charters.

To meet the need for larger amounts of capital in industry, limited partnerships became popular. Known as the *société en commandite* in France and *Kommanditgesellschaft* in Germany, the limited-partnership arrangement required at least one partner to be totally liable as in a regular partnership (*q.v.*) and allowed other partners to be liable only for the amounts invested by them in the business. Limited partnerships were common on the European continent and in the United States in the 18th and early 19th centuries, and in England many unincorporated joint-stock companies were in existence by 1825.

The legal inadequacies regarding extended partnerships and unincorporated joint-stock companies and the need for larger and larger amounts of capital gradually led to the acceptance of the corporate form of enterprise. In England the Joint-Stock Companies Act (1844) made incorporation possible merely by registration, and between 1844 and 1862 the full joint-stock company with limited liability for all shareholders became widespread. The formation of corporate enterprises was also made simpler in France and Germany during the 1860s and '70s. From this point forward, the limited-liability company was established as the most important form of commercial association in modern economies. *See also* corporation.

Limmen Bight, inlet of the Gulf of Carpentaria, in the northeast coast of Northern Territory, Australia. It extends for 85 miles (135 km) between the islands of Groote Eylandt (north) and the Sir Edward Pellew Group (southeast) and includes Maria Island. The bight receives the Roper, Towns, and Limmen Bight rivers. Abel Tasman, the Dutch mariner, sighted the bight in 1644, and its coast was charted in the early 1800s by the English navigator Matthew Flinders.

limner, in the visual arts, during the European Middle Ages, a manuscript illuminator; from the 16th century, a painter of miniatures; and in American usage, until the early 19th century, an itinerant painter and sometimes any painter. Itinerant painters were often trained craftsmen for whom portrait painting was a natural extension of their work as house painters or as coach and sign painters.

Frequently these limners prepared in advance stock portrait canvases, fully painted except for the face, which accounts for the recurrence of odd proportions, particularly in child portraits. The subjects sometimes extended beyond portraits to landscapes, meticulously painted views of farms, incidents from the life of George Washington, biblical subjects, and even still lifes. Most of the artists remain anonymous; some of their names were recorded, however, and among the best known

"Reverend Ebenezer Devotion," oil painting by limner Winthrop Chandler, 1770; owned by the Brookline Historical Society, Brookline, Mass.

Brookline Historical Society, Brookline, Massachusetts

are Winthrop Chandler, James Peale, Edward Hicks, and George Mark Washington.

Limnocharitaceae, family of the water plantain order Alismales, containing 4 genera and about 12 species of tropical, freshwater plants. Two species—*Hydrocleys nymphoides* and *Limnocharis flava,* both native to tropical America—are cultivated in ponds and aquariums.

limnology, subsystem of hydrology that deals with the scientific study of fresh waters, specifically those found in lakes and ponds. The discipline also includes the biological, physical, and chemical aspects of the occurrence of lake and pond waters. Limnology traditionally is closely related to hydrobiology, which is concerned with the application of the principles and methods of physics, chemistry, geology, and geography to ecological problems.

Límnos (Greece): *see* Lemnos.

Limnoscelis, extinct genus of primitive reptiles, among the earliest of the disputed labyrinthodont reptilian forms, that occurs as fossils in Early Permian rocks (those 258 to 286 million years old) of North America. It has been presented as a stem form from which the more advanced reptiles may have derived; another theory has *Limnoscelis* as an abnormal labyrinthodont amphibian. *Limnoscelis* was about 1.5 m (5 feet) long, with a robust skeleton and a rather long and solid skull. An opening for the pineal organ, which was in effect a third eye, was present between the parietal bones of the skull roof. The nostrils were placed well forward, and the margins of the jaws contained numerous sharp teeth. The anteriormost teeth were larger than the others and labyrinthine in internal structure. Teeth also were present on the bones of the palate. The body and tail were long, and the limb girdles were

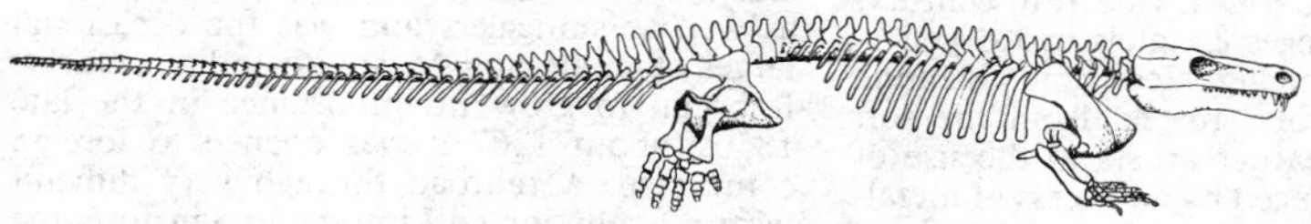

Skeleton of *Limnoscelis*

Reprinted from *Vertebrate Paleontology* by A.S. Romer, by permission of the University of Chicago, copyright 1933, 1945, 1966; all rights reserved

massive. In life, the limbs were splayed outward from the body in a sprawling pose, a relatively primitive reptilian condition.

Limoges, city, capital of Haute-Vienne *département* and of the Limousin region, south central France (formerly in the province of Limousin), south-southwest of Paris, on the right bank of the Vienne River.

Capital of the Lemovices, a Gallic tribe, Limoges was an important Roman centre, with its own Senate and currency. Christianity was brought to the town by St. Martial in the 3rd century. Legends of his miracles spread rapidly, and his shrine became a stopping place for pilgrims on the road to Santiago de Compostela in northwest Spain, one of the most important shrines in Christendom. In the 9th century an abbey was built at the crypt and tomb of St. Martial, very close to Limoges; the settlement that grew around it under the Abbot's control soon rivalled the other city, which was controlled by the Bishop. The two towns were on opposing sides during the Hundred Years' War between England and France (1337–1453) and remained separate until 1792.

Until the 16th century, Limoges was frequently devastated by fire, plague, and famine. It recovered its former prosperity in the 18th century, especially after introduction of porcelain manufacture in the second half of the century.

The porcelain factories have been modernized to use natural gas and have developed new production techniques. Uranium is mined in the region. Other industries include the manufacture of leather products, cotton textiles, and machinery. It is a railway junction on the main Paris-Toulouse line and a trade centre for stock farming.

The two medieval towns, now merged into and overgrown by the modern city, can still be recognized by their narrow winding streets, which are in contrast to the spacious roads of the newer neighbourhoods. The 13th-century cathedral of Saint-Étienne has an elegant, partly octagonal bell tower, typical of the Gothic churches of the region. The church of Saint-Michel-des-Lions (14th–15th century) has a tower 198 ft (65 m) high, with a spire surmounted by a big bronze ball; it also has fine 15th-century stained-glass windows. The 18th-century Palais de l'Évêché now houses the municipal museum, which has a large collection of old enamels. The Musée National de Céramique Adrien-Dubouché has a collection of ceramics and porcelain. Limoges is the seat of the Université de Limoges (founded 1808; suppressed 1840; reopened 1965) and is a bishopric. Pop. (1982) 137,809.

Limoges painted enamel, any of the enamelled products made in Limoges, Fr., and generally considered the finest painted enamelware produced in Europe in the 16th and 17th centuries. Limoges enamels are largely the work of a few families such as the Pénicaud, Limosin, and Reymond families. The earliest examples show religious scenes in the late Gothic style. But around 1520, Italian Renaissance motifs appeared and became especially characteristic of the work of Leonard Limosin and Pierre Reymond. Painting in grisaille, or monochromatic painting intended to look like sculpture, was introduced at Limoges and became a speciality of Jean III Pénicaud. By the last quarter of the 16th century, the quality of Limoges enamels had degenerated, and the enamellers Jean and Suzanne de Court in particular turned from the soft harmonies of the earlier artists to the use of bright colours enhanced by an excess of metallic foil called paillons, for gaudy rich effects. The Laudin family dominated the production of the ware in the 17th century and were the

"Cupid and Psyche," Limoges painted enamelwork by Pierre Courteys, mid-16th century; in the Walters Art Gallery, Baltimore

By courtesy of the Walters Art Gallery, Baltimore

last major enamellers at Limoges. *See also* Limosin, Leonard; Pénicaud family.

Limoges ware, porcelain, largely servicewares, produced in Limoges, Fr., from the 18th century. Faience (tin-glazed earthenware) of mediocre quality was produced there after 1736, but the manufacture of hard-paste, or true, porcelain dates only from 1771. The manufacturers took advantage of being near Saint-Yrieix, the largest source of clay and china stone in France. In 1784 the factory was acquired as an adjunct of the Royal factory at Sèvres, and the decoration of the two wares were similar. Other factories opened after 1797, and Limoges became a mass exporter of porcelain to the U.S. under the name Haviland ware, which now is produced there as well.

Limón, province, eastern Costa Rica, bounded on the north by Nicaragua, on the east by the Caribbean Sea, and on the southeast by Panama. Although the territory of 3,600 sq mi (9,300 sq km) rises in the south into the Cordillera de Talamanca and contains Chirripó, the highest peak in Costa Rica (12,530 ft [3,819 m]), it is predominantly an area of coastal lowlands. With the heavy rainfall (about 100 in. [2,500 mm] annually), sugarcane and two corn (maize) crops a year can be cultivated. Once dominated by banana plantations of the United Fruit Company, the region suffered from Panama disease in the 1930s, but a disease-resistant variety of banana has been introduced. Limón is the provincial capital. There is a large population of more than 30,000 English-speaking Jamaicans who originally went there generations ago to work on the banana plantations. Pop. (1983 est.) 153,638.

Limón, capital, Limón province, eastern Costa Rica, on an open roadstead of the Caribbean Sea near the landfall sighted by Columbus in 1503. The waters are deep enough for large ships, and a sandbar offers some protection for the port. In the colonial era, the port was used by Spanish merchants as well as smugglers and was the occasional target of pirate and Mosquito Indian attacks. It began to grow in importance in the late 1850s; about 1867 it was opened to foreign commerce. A railroad through very difficult terrain finally joined Limón and San José, the national capital, in 1890. The banana industry was developed along the tracks to provide a cash cargo, and from 1900 to the 1930s the United Fruit Company dominated the area. Although banana production subsequently fell drastically because of Panama disease, it has increased again with the introduction of a disease-resistant variety of banana. Limón handles more freight yearly than any other Costa Rican port (40 percent of the country's exports, chiefly to the United States and Europe), yet it is not accessible from the capital by highway. It does, however, have an airport. Pop. (1983 est.) 53,641.

Limón, Bahía, English LIMON BAY, natural harbour of the Caribbean Sea, in Panama at the north end of the Panama Canal. Approximately $4^1/_2$ mi (7 km) long and $2^1/_2$ mi wide, it is protected from storms by breakwaters at its entrance. The bay serves as a waiting area for ships about to enter the canal. On its eastern shore are the twin cities of Cristóbal and Colón, the Atlantic terminus of the canal.

Limón, José (Arcadio) (b. Jan, 12, 1908, Culiacán, Sinaloa, Mex.—d. Dec. 2, 1972, Flemington, N.J., U.S.), Mexican-born U.S. modern dancer and choreographer who expanded the repertoire of modern dance in works that explored the strengths and weaknesses of the human character.

Discouraged by his progress as an art student, Limón in 1930 began to study dance with Doris Humphrey and Charles Weidman; he became one of the leading dancers of their company in New York City until 1940. After

Limón, 1965

Martha Swope

World War II he established his own company, with Humphrey as artistic director. His first major work, *The Moor's Pavane* (1949; music by Henry Purcell), conveyed the jealousy, rage, and remorse of Shakespeare's *Othello* within the framework of a stately court dance. Much of Limón's choreography was developed from natural gesture and expressed, as he said, "human grandeur, dignity, and nobility" through themes drawn from history, literature, and religion. His dances were also characterized by well-defined structure and form. Other successful works include *Missa Brevis* (1958; music by Zoltán Kodály), which portrayed the sustaining faith of survivors of World War II bombings, and *La Malinche* (1949), based on a Mexican legend. Limón and Pauline Koner, guest artist with his company for several years, created many of the leading roles in his dances.

Limón's company was the first to be sponsored by the U.S. State Department's International Cultural Exchange Program, performing in South America in 1954; subsequently the company toured Europe, Central America, and the Far East, in addition to annual tours of the U.S. Limón has also danced and choreographed for the National Academy of Dance in Mexico. The José Limón Dance Company survived the death of its founder and continues to perform on both national and international scenes.

limonene, a colourless liquid abundant in the essential oils of pine and citrus trees and used as a lemonlike odorant in industrial and household products and as a chemical intermediate.

Limonene exists in two isomeric forms (compounds with the same molecular formula—in this case, $C_{10}H_{16}$—but with different structures), namely *l*-limonene, the isomer that rotates the plane of polarized light counterclockwise, and *d*-limonene, the isomer that causes rotation in the opposite direction. In the extraction of citrus juices *d*-limonene is obtained as a by-product, and it also occurs in caraway oil; *l*-limonene is present in pine needles and cones; *dl*-limonene, or dipentene, the mixture of equal amounts of the *l*- and *d*-isomers, is a component of turpentine.

Dipentene may be sulfurized to produce additives that improve the performance of lubricating oils under heavy loads; *d*-limonene is commercially converted to *l*-carvone, which has a caraway-seed flavour.

limonite, one of the major iron minerals, hydrated ferric oxide ($Fe_2O_3 \cdot H_2O$). It was originally considered one of a series of such oxides; later it was thought to be the amorphous

Limonite (left) from Ironwood, Mich., and (right) from Montgomery, Pa.

By courtesy of the Field Museum of Natural History, Chicago; photograph, John H. Gerard—EB Inc.

equivalent of goethite and lepidocrocite, but X-ray studies have shown that most so-called limonite is actually goethite.

The name limonite properly should be restricted to impure hydrated iron oxide (with variable water content) that is colloidal, or amorphous, in character. Often brown and earthy, it is formed by alteration of other iron minerals, such as the hydration of hematite or the oxidation and hydration of siderite or pyrite. It probably bears the same relationship to iron oxides that wad and gummite do to manganese and uranium oxides. *Compare* goethite.

Consult the INDEX *first*

Limosin, Léonard, Limosin also spelled LIMOUSIN (b. *c.* 1505, Limoges, Fr.—d. *c.* 1577), French painter especially known for the revealing realism of his portraits painted in enamel.

Limosin was the most accomplished member of one of the best-known families of enamelers working in Limoges during the 16th century. His early works were influenced by German Renaissance art; in fact, his earliest authenticated work (1532) is a series of 18 enamel plaques of the "Passion of the Lord," after a series of prints by the German artist Albrecht Dürer. This Germanic influence was later counterbalanced by that of Francesco Primaticcio, Giovanni Rosso, Giulio Romano, and Antonio Solario, Italian Mannerist painters who worked for Francis I in the mid-16th century on decorating the royal château of Fontainebleau.

In 1530 Limosin entered the service of Francis I as painter and *valet de chambre,* a position he retained under Henry II. For both monarchs he produced many finely characterized portraits in enamel, among them enamel

"Portrait of Anne, duc de Montmorency," enamel painting by Léonard Limosin; in the Louvre, Paris

Giraudon—Art Resource/EB Inc.

plaques depicting Henry's mistress Diane de Poitiers in various poses and characters. He executed many plates, vases, ewers, and cups, as well as decorative paintings.

Although Limosin is best known for his richly coloured enamels, as well as his use of grisaille enamel (monochromatic enamel painting to give the illusion of sculpture), he was also an accomplished oil painter who acquired a great reputation in his day. His last signed works bear the date 1574. The most renowned of Limosin's 2,000 enamels that are not portraits are two votive tablets with 23 plaques each that he made in 1553 for the Sainte-Chapelle in Paris.

Limousin, *région,* encompassing the central French *départements* of Corrèze, Haute-Vienne, and Creuse and coextensive with the former province of Limousin (*q.v.*). The capital is Limoges. The *région* has an area of 6,541 square miles (16,942 square km) and is bounded by the *départements* of Indre and Cher to the north, Allier, Puy-de-Dôme, and Cantal to the east, Lot to the south, Dordogne to the southwest, Charente to the west, and Vienne to the northwest.

Limousin took its name from the tribe of the Lemovices, under whom the area formed

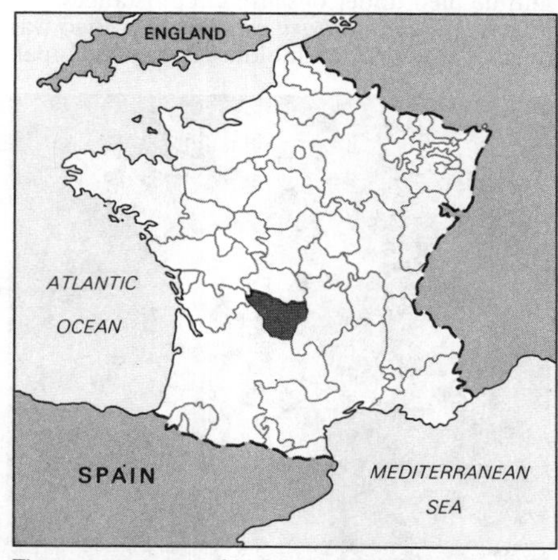

The *gouvernement* of Limousin in 1789

a *civitas,* or tribal association, of Gaul. Controlled by the Romans from about 50 BC, the *civitas* was a part of the province of Aquitania. Under the Merovingians (6th–8th century AD), the *pagus Lemovicinus* (*i.e.,* the district of the Lemovices) was disputed by rival kings; under the Carolingians (8th–10th century), it was included in the kingdom of Aquitaine. From the Merovingian period to the 12th century, its monasteries, especially Saint-Martial at Limoges, were major cultural centres.

In the 10th century Limousin was divided into a number of feudal units. The northern part was set up as the county of Marche; other sections were annexed by the neighbouring counts of Auvergne, Angoulême, and Poitou. By the mid-11th century the viscounts of Limoges, Comborn, Turenne, and Ventadour had control of the remaining territory and recognized the overlordship of the Duke of Aquitaine.

From the 12th to the 15th century, Limousin was one of the areas disputed between the English and the French. The marriage of Eleanor of Aquitaine to the future Henry II of England (1152) brought suzerainty of Limousin to the English, but Philip II Augustus recovered the province in the early 13th century. During the course of the Hundred Years' War (1337–1453), Limousin was ceded to the English by the Treaty of Calais (1360) and reconquered by the French king Charles V from 1370 to 1374. After further disruptions during the war, Limousin remained under the suzerainty of the French kings. Royal control became direct when the viscounty of Limoges was added to the domain (1607) and when Turenne was purchased in 1738.

The *gouvernement* of Limousin, organized in the 17th century, was much reduced in size from the original province, including only the territory of the four medieval viscounties. The three *départements* of the area, dating from the French Revolution, joined in the 1960s to form the *région* of Limousin.

Limousin belongs to the Massif Central and enjoys an oceanic climate. Annual precipitation is high, ranging from 30 to 50 inches (750 to 1,200 mm).

The population, which decreased by more than one-third between 1891 and 1980, has been depleted by emigration of the young. Emigrants have left behind an aging population, with the result that the birth rate lags behind the national average. The population is predominantly rural. Haute-Vienne has grown at the expense of Creuse and Corrèze, with the industries of Limoges accounting for much of the increase.

Emigration from the countryside has resulted in the consolidation of farms and in the extension of wasteland and abandoned land; afforestation is also increasing. Farms in Creuse rely on migrant workers from Mayenne and Sarthe. Absentee ownership of farmland is widespread. Animal husbandry predominates; cattle and sheep are largely raised for meat. Wheat and fodder are cultivated in the south.

The industrial sector is underdeveloped outside Limoges, where automobiles and electrical equipment are manufactured. Bessines-sur-Gartempe in Haute-Vienne is a leading producer of uranium; hydroelectric power from the Dordogne River is exported. The region is linked by highway to Paris and Toulouse and by railway to Bordeaux, Clermont-Ferrand, and Lyon. Tourism is underdeveloped and centres on eastern Corrèze. Pop. (1990) 722,-850.

limpet, any of various snails having a flattened shell. Limpets belonging to the subclass Prosobranchia (class Gastropoda) are marine; most cling to rocks near shore. A common American species is the Atlantic plate limpet (species *Acmaea testudinalis*) of cold waters; the common species of Britain and northern Europe is *Patella vulgata.* Keyhole limpets, of the prosobranch family Fissurellidae, have a slit or hole at the apex of the shell.

Limpets belonging to the subclass Pulmonata live in brackish and fresh water. For slipper limpet, *see* slipper shell.

limpkin, also called COURLAN, or CRYING BIRD (species *Aramus guarauna*), large swamp bird of the American tropics, sole member of the family Aramidae (order Gruiformes). The

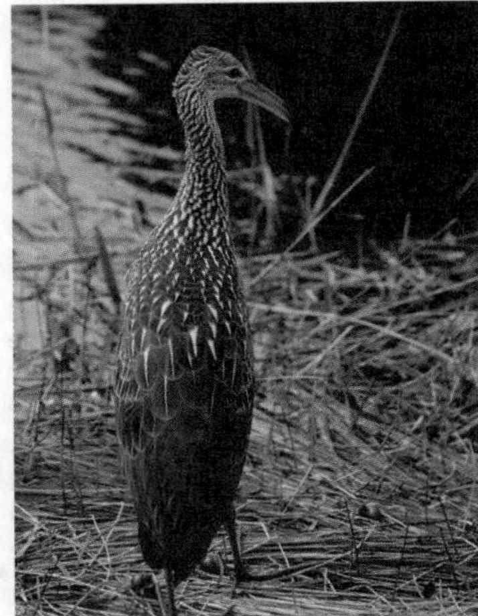

Limpkin (*Aramus guarauna*)
Martin W. Grosnick—Ardea London

bird is about 70 cm (28 inches) long and is coloured brown with white spots. The limpkin's most distinctive characteristics are its loud, prolonged, wailing cry and its halting gait. The species ranges the lowlands from the southeastern United States, Puerto Rico, and Hispaniola south to central Argentina.

The limpkin is found along borders of wooded streams, bayous, and sloughs, or in open marshes and sometimes in uplands, where it runs through brush with long strides or perches on small trees. The limpkin flies like a crane, with short concave wings slowly flapping, neck extended, and legs dangling. It feeds on mollusks, crustaceans, aquatic insects, frogs, and worms. In the Florida Everglades it feeds chiefly on large, greenish, freshwater snails (*Ampullaria*). These, carried to its nest or favourite feeding perch and held firmly in one foot, are struck several powerful blows with the bill, which is then forced into the shell to pull out the snail. The limpkin's nest of leaves, twigs, and Spanish moss is found among grasses or shrubs, or in a low tree over or near water. Its eggs, four to six, rarely eight, are buff, splashed with brown and drab.

Limpopo River, river in southeast Africa that rises as the Crocodile (Krokodil) River in the Witwatersrand, South Africa, and flows on a semicircular course first northeast and then east for about 1,100 miles (1,800 km) to the Indian Ocean. From its source the river flows northward to the Magaliesberg Mountains, cutting the Hartbeespoort Gap, site of an irrigation dam. It then flows across the fertile Bushveld basin to open granite country, where it is joined on the left bank by the Marico River. From there it is known as the Limpopo. (The name may be related to *uku popozi,* meaning "to rush.") Turning northeastward, the river forms the border for about 250 miles (400 km) between the Transvaal and Botswana, receiving seasonal tributaries. After swinging eastward between the Transvaal and Zimbabwe, the Limpopo receives the Shashi River and flows about 150 miles (240 km) to Mozambique, where it reaches the fall line. In this zone the river drops about 800 feet (250 m), with most of the drop concentrated in 27 miles (43 km) of rapids, especially those at Malala, Molukwe, and Quiqueque. The Limpopo is unnavigable until its confluence with the Olifants River, 130 miles from the coast. Though partially blocked by a sandbar at its outlet, the river can be entered by coastal steamers at high tide. The Limpopo is dammed about 62 miles from its mouth near Guijá, where an agricultural settlement has been developed.

Lin, Maya (b. Oct. 5, 1959, Athens, Ohio, U.S.), American architect and sculptor who is best known for her design of the Vietnam Veterans Memorial in Washington, D.C.

The daughter of intellectuals who had fled China in 1948, Lin received her bachelor's degree in 1981 from Yale University in New Haven, Conn., where she studied architecture and sculpture. During her senior year she entered a nationwide competition sponsored by the Vietnam Veterans Memorial Fund to create a design for a commemorative monument. Lin's award-winning design consisted of a polished black granite V-shaped wall inscribed with the names of the approximately 58,000 men and women who were killed or missing in action. This minimal plan was in sharp contrast to the traditional format for a memorial, which usually entailed figurative, heroic sculpture. The design aroused a great deal of controversy, reflecting the lack of resolution of the national conflicts over the war, as well as the lack of consensus over what constituted an appropriate memorial at the end of the 20th century. Eventually a traditional statue depicting three servicemen with a flag was commissioned to stand at the entrance to the memorial. Once Lin's monument was dedicated in Washington, D.C., on Veterans Day 1982, however, it became a popular and moving tourist attraction.

After returning to academia for a time, Lin went on to create other large-scale works, including a minimal granite monument commemorating the Civil Rights Movement that was dedicated in Montgomery, Ala., in 1989. In 1995 a feature-length film, *Maya Lin: A Strong Clear Vision,* won the Oscar for best documentary.

Lin Biao, Wade-Giles romanization LIN PIAO (b. Dec. 5, 1907, Huang-kang, Hupeh province, China—d. Sept. 13, 1971?, Mongolian People's Republic?), Chinese military leader who, as a field commander of the Red Army, contributed to the Communists' 22-year struggle for power and held many high government and party posts. He played a prominent role in the Cultural Revolution, but in 1971 he allegedly sought to seize power from Mao Zedong; his plot was discovered and he died under obscure circumstances.

Early life and military career. Lin Biao was born of a modest landholding family in Hupeh

Lin Biao, 1967
Eastfoto

province in central China. He received his primary education in the village school, then entered middle school in Wuchang, the provincial capital, in 1921. While in middle school, he was deeply affected by the social and cultural upheaval then taking place in his country. He soon became interested in socialism and communism, and in 1925, after his graduation from middle school, he joined the Socialist Youth League.

Also in 1925, Lin Biao went south to Canton to enroll in the Whampoa Academy and there began his military career. China at this time suffered from the twin evils of warlordism and imperialism; *i.e.,* internal disunity and foreign encroachment. In order to fight the warlords and curb the imperialists, the Nationalists, led by Sun Yat-sen until his death in March 1925, had secured the assistance of the Soviet Union and the cooperation of the Chinese Communist Party and were then preparing a military expedition from their base in Canton. The Whampoa Academy, headed by Sun's successor, Chiang Kai-shek, was to train the officers for the revolutionary army. Lin Biao had been at the academy less than a year when Chiang launched the Northern Expedition in July 1926. Nevertheless, despite the brevity of his formal training, Lin quickly demonstrated his military prowess. A few months later, when the expedition reached the Yangtze River in central China, he had risen from deputy platoon leader to battalion commander. But, when Chiang then turned savagely against his Communist allies in 1927, Lin forsook his mentor and fled with the Communists.

In the spring of 1928, Lin Biao joined Mao Zedong in the hills of south-central China and established himself at once as one of the ablest and most active commanders in Mao's small but growing Red Army. From 1928 to 1934 he helped to enlarge the Communist-controlled territory in Kiangsi province and defended it against repeated attacks by the Nationalists. In 1932 he was promoted to corps commander. When the Communists were finally driven from their Kiangsi base in 1934 by the Nationalists, Lin's First Army Corps formed the vanguard of the epic retreat known as the Long March, which a year later brought them into the northern province of Shensi, where they were able to regroup. By then the 28-year-old Lin was already a legendary figure with a reputation of never having lost a battle. In Shensi he became the president of the Red Army Academy and was among the handful of commanders who ranked just below the important military leaders Zhu De and Peng Dehuai.

In 1937 the bitter civil war between the Nationalists and the Communists ended temporarily as the two sides formed a united front against the common foe, Japan. In September 1937, just after the outbreak of war, Lin Biao, in command of one of the Red Army's three divisions, scored an important early victory over the Japanese invaders. He was wounded in battle the following spring and retired from the field for the rest of the war. When his wound did not heal, he went to the Soviet Union for medical treatment and stayed three years. After his return to China in 1942, he served briefly as a member of the Communist liaison team with the Nationalists. In 1943 he resumed the presidency of the Military and Political Academy in the Communist capital of Yenan. As the war with Japan neared its end in 1945, he was elected for the first time to the Communist Party's 44-member Central Committee.

When World War II ended, the civil war in China resumed. Returning to the field once more, Lin Biao went to Manchuria, in northeastern China, as commander of what later became the Fourth Field Army. In a brilliant display of Maoist strategy, he first abandoned the cities of Manchuria to the Nationalists and concentrated instead on securing the support of the peasants in the countryside. Using guerrilla warfare, he then patiently and methodically whittled away at his numerically superior enemy. Gradually, he isolated the Nationalists in the cities and eventually forced garrison after garrison to surrender. By the end of 1948, his army, which had originally numbered 100,000, had grown to 800,000, and he had captured all of Manchuria. Lin's victory in Manchuria ensured the rapid collapse of Chiang Kai-shek's Nationalists in the rest of China. His own forces, moving south, captured Peking in January 1949, Wu-han in May, and Canton in October.

Positions in the People's Republic. With the establishment of the People's Republic in October 1949, Lin Biao was appointed to many high posts in the government and the party. At first he was both administrative head and party chief of the six-province "Central-South" region of China. In 1954, when the central government was reorganized, he was named a vice premier of the State Council (or Cabinet) and a vice chairman of the National Defense Council. Among army officers he ranked only behind the aging Zhu De and Peng Dehuai, then the minister of defense. In 1955 he was elevated within the party to the Central Committee's 13-man Politburo and then in May 1958 to the Politburo's 7-man Standing Committee. But throughout these early years of Communist rule Lin, who may have been in chronic ill-health, seldom appeared in public and was probably only occasionally active at his various posts.

In late 1958 Lin Biao suddenly began to assume a more active and important role in the army and the party. In September 1959 he succeeded Peng Dehuai as minister of defense, after Peng was ousted for opposing Mao's economic and defense policies. Lin then inaugurated a reformation of the army that both intensified the political education of its soldiers and upgraded their military training. As a result, Lin's army in the early 1960s became an example of how, according to Mao's teachings, professional expertise could be combined with political consciousness, and the army even became a model for the rest of society, including the party itself, to emulate. This movement to "learn from the People's Liberation Army" eventually developed in 1965 into the extensive purge of the party known as the Great Proletarian Cultural Revolution, whose principal casualty was Liu Shaogi, the party organizer who for more than 20 years had been Mao's second in command. In August 1966 the 58-year-old Lin Biao replaced Liu as the future successor to Mao; this position was formalized in April 1969, when Lin was so designated by the new constitution. From 1966 to 1971 the army effectively took over the role previously played by the party in ruling China.

By 1971, however, Lin and the army may have amassed more political authority than Mao thought desirable. In a desperate move to avoid being purged, Lin and others of the military high command plotted a coup that failed. The Chinese government later announced that Lin Biao was killed on Sept. 13, 1971, in an airplane crash in Mongolia as he was fleeing to the Soviet Union after having plotted unsuccessfully to assassinate Mao. Since then he has been posthumously criticized as a rightist reactionary and a traitor to the cause of Chinese Communism. Speculation that Lin was in fact assassinated by the Chinese leadership was reinforced in 1990 when Mongolian officials cast doubt on the Chinese government's claim that Lin had been among those killed in the 1971 airplane crash. The actual circumstances of Lin's death—and of the power struggle that immediately preceded it—remain an unresolved mystery in the history of Communist China.

Assessment. Throughout his life, Lin Biao was more a doer than a thinker. His writings are few and uninspiring. They deal primarily with questions of military strategy and tactics, especially the latter (of which he was a master), or with the importance of political indoctrination. As a leader, Lin lacked Mao's wit and charisma and Zhou Enlai's charm and urbanity. In contrast to these other two members of the ruling triumvirate in the late 1960s, Lin seemed almost colourless. Even as a military commander he was characterized more by caution and deliberation than by dash and flamboyance. (E.J.M.R.)

BIBLIOGRAPHY. The best account of Lin's life is a study by Thomas W. Robinson, *A Politico-military Biography of Lin Piao* (1971–). Michael Y.M. Kau (ed.), *The Lin Piao Affair: Power Politics and Military Coup* (1975), discusses the circumstances of Lin's death and contains a compendium of documents including a translation of Lin's official biography as of 1969.

Lin-fen, Pinyin LINFEN, city, southern Shansi *sheng* (province), China. Lin-fen is situated on the east bank of the Fen River about 140 miles (220 km) south of T'ai-yüan.

The Fen River valley was one of the earliest centres of Chinese civilization, being the site of well-developed prehistoric (Paleolithic and Neolithic) cultures and of Shang (about 1766–1122 BC) settlements. The antiquity of Lin-fen was proverbial, even in early times, when it was believed to have been the capital of the legendary sage-emperor Yao. In the 7th century BC it was the site of P'ing-yang fief during the Warring States period. Under the unified empire of the Han dynasty (206 BC–AD 220) it became a county (*hsien*) of the same name. In 248 it became a commandery (district under the control of a commander). From 309 to 318 it was the capital of the minor dynasty of Ch'ien Chao.

After various administrative changes the county was first given the name Lin-fen in 581, whereas P'ing-yang remained the name of the commandery of which it was the administrative centre. Under the T'ang dynasty (618–907) the prefecture based on Lin-fen was called Chin. During the late T'ang and the Five Dynasties (907–960), because of the city's strategic location commanding the approaches to T'ai-yüan, it became an important garrison and was often under military administration. During the Ming (1368–1644) and Ch'ing (1644–1911) dynasties, it was the centre of the superior prefecture of P'ing-yang. The Ming built very strong walls, some 4 miles (6 km) in circumference; and in early Ch'ing times settlement extended beyond the walls.

In 1853, however, the northern expedition of the Taiping armies passed through the city, leaving a trail of destruction; further damage was caused in the 1860s during the Nien Rebellion. In the late 19th century the city sharply declined in importance; and, after the beginning of the Chinese republic in 1911, it was reduced to the status of a county town. In the late 1930s it had fewer than 10,000 inhabitants, and a great part of the area within the walls was wasteland. At that time it was a medium-sized market centre, dealing in local grain and cotton; it was notable mainly for its great cattle fair held every spring, which attracted traders from southern Shensi and western Honan provinces, as well as from southern Shansi.

The arrival in 1935 of the railway from T'ai-yüan through the Fen River valley and the later development of highways centring on Lin-fen increased its commercial importance. The city was completely devastated by the Japanese in World War II. Rich coal deposits had been discovered in the area before the war, and afterward local coal production increased steadily. In the late 1950s food processing and the manufacture of agricultural implements began, and by the 1960s the city had begun to develop a considerable industrial output. Pop. (1989 est.) 172,700.

Lin-kuei (China): *see* Kuei-lin.

Lin Shu, Pinyin LIN SHU (b. Nov. 8, 1852, Fu-chou, Fukien province, China—d. Oct. 9, 1924, Peking), translator who first made available to Chinese readers more than 171 works of Western literature, even though he himself had no firsthand knowledge of any foreign language and had never traveled abroad. Working through oral interpreters, Lin Shu translated fiction from England, the United States, France, Russia, Switzerland, Belgium, Spain, Norway, Greece, and Japan into flowing classical Chinese. He was opposed to the use of vernacular Chinese, which was urged by the new breed of Chinese writers then emerging and whom Lin Shu ridiculed in satirical short stories. Because of the second-hand nature of Lin Shu's translations—indeed, many are translations of translations—they are not completely accurate and have been severely criticized for their errors. Lin Shu's skilled use of the Chinese literary language has been highly praised, however, and his translations remain important for their role in introducing Western literature to China.

Consult the INDEX *first*

Lin Tse-hsü, Pinyin LIN ZEXU (b. Aug. 30, 1785, Hou-kuan, Fukien province, China—d. Nov. 22, 1850, Ch'ao-chou, Kwangtung province), leading Chinese scholar and official of the Ch'ing (Manchu) dynasty, known for his role in the events leading up to the Anglo-Chinese Opium War (1839–42). He was a proponent of the revitalization of traditional Chinese thought and institutions, a movement that became known as the Self-Strengthening Movement.

Rise as administrator. Lin's father was a teacher, who, though poor, was determined that his sons should have the grounding in the Confucian Classics that alone could advance them in the governmental bureaucracy. Lin Tse-hsü, the second son, proved immensely capable and passed the initial examinations in 1804. He then was selected as an aide to the governor of his native province, an informal apprenticeship that served to balance the abstract, moral, and largely literary content of his early education. In 1811 Lin passed the highest of the examinations, the *chin-shih,* and joined the Hanlin Academy, which advised the emperor and helped him to draft documents. In 1820 Lin took up his first regular administrative post and rose through a number of the most responsible offices in the bureaucracy. After starting in the salt monopoly, he supervised water-control systems in several localities, administered the collection of taxes, and served a term as a local judge, during which he earned the respectful nickname "Lin the Clear Sky." Lin's quick rise showed him to be an effective organizer and ambitious bureaucrat.

Role in the Opium War. Following the traditional period of mourning and retirement at the death of his father, a time that also served for reflection and literary activity, Lin returned to official life in the upper reaches of the government. When, in the middle of the 1830s, the Tao-kuang emperor became alarmed over the growth of the opium trade carried on by British and Chinese smugglers—both for the obvious moral reasons and for the more practical one that even illegal imports had to be paid for with the export of Chinese silver—Lin submitted a memorial condemning a suggestion that the trade be legalized. In support of his position he cited the measures by which he had suppressed the drug traffic in the provinces of which he was then governor general. The emperor, who for almost two decades had vainly attempted to enforce the ban on the importation of opium, responded by appointing Lin imperial commissioner in late 1838, vesting him with extraordinary powers. After an unusual 19 personal audiences with the emperor, Lin proceeded to Canton, the hub of the trade. His diary for this period survives and conveys a vivid picture of a Chinese official of the time at work: making the arduous journey from Peking; perspiring in the heat of Canton's subtropical climate as he kowtows before the very written instructions of the emperor; peremptorily summoning the British merchants and officials; vainly trying to make the corrupt Chinese officials, grown soft on the profits and use of opium, perform their duties; and composing an ode of apology to the god of the sea for defiling his ocean with confiscated opium.

Lin was only too successful. He forced foreign merchants to surrender their stocks of opium for destruction and put pressure on them to guarantee that they would cease importing the cargo. Yet, when the British retaliated by ravaging large parts of South China, the emperor, who had personally approved Lin's tough policies, quickly dismissed him. Although exiled to the northwest frontier, Lin served quietly and loyally, was soon called back to important service, and was rewarded with the title of grand guardian of the heir apparent for pacifying rebel Muslims in the province of Yunnan. He died in 1850, on his way to help suppress the Taiping Rebellion.

Assessment. Lin's significance goes beyond his career. He belonged to a small but later influential group of reform officials and scholars whose slogan was "find in antiquity the sanction for present-day reform." This "Statecraft school" pioneered in the compilation of practical information for use in governing on many subjects, including geography and the knowledge of the history of foreign countries. Yet when Lin, one of the most experienced and best-informed men of his day, went to Canton, he had no idea that his success in stopping the opium trade would only open up his country to the humiliating and ruinous penetration by foreign interests that was to hasten its downfall. He simply drew on the precedents of generations of officials whose policy against the Central Asian tribes had been to play them off against each other and to whom commercial considerations were somewhat petty matters; he did not comprehend the significance of the British demands for free trade and international equality, which were based on their concept of a commercial empire. This concept was a radical challenge to the Chinese world order, which knew only an empire and subject peoples; at his arrival in Canton, Lin still thought of the British as dependent on the Chinese and believed that they would perish from constipation without Chinese tea and rhubarb. In a famous letter to Queen Victoria, written when he arrived in Canton, Lin asked whether she would allow the importation of a substance as poisonous as opium into her own country and asked her to forbid her subjects to bring it into his.

Lin relied on aggressive moral tone, meanwhile proceeding relentlessly against British merchants in a manner that could only insult their government. The only lesson Lin drew from China's humiliation was that it was necessary to learn more about these "barbarians" and to import their technology. He could neither comprehend the implications of the European challenge nor overcome the weakness and conservative opposition of his contemporaries. Later, the so-called Self-Strengthening Movement adopted Lin's program of reform; still later generations of revolutionaries abandoned Chinese culture in order to save China but accepted Lin as a national hero because of his courage and example in opposing the British. (C.W.H.)

BIBLIOGRAPHY. Hsin-pao Chang, *Commissioner Lin and the Opium War* (1964, reissued 1970); and Arthur Waley, *The Opium War Through Chinese Eyes* (1958, reissued 1968).

Lin-tzu, Pinyin LINZI, town, central Shantung *sheng* (province), China. It is situated on the west bank of the Tzu River, a tributary of the Hsiao-ch'ing River, some 19 miles (30 km) east of Po-shan (Tzu-po) city.

While modern Lin-tzu is little more than a local market town and a collecting centre for the agricultural produce of the surrounding district on the railway between Tsinan (Chi-nan) and Tsingtao, it, nevertheless, has considerable historical importance. In Chou times (*c.* 1122–221 BC) it was the capital of the state of Ch'i from 869 BC onward. Ch'i was one of the most powerful of the feudal kingdoms, and by the 4th and 3rd centuries BC Lin-tzu was the greatest city in China, with a population said to have numbered 70,000 households (perhaps 350,000 persons). As the capital of the richest and most advanced of the Chinese states, it also became the intellectual and cultural capital of eastern China. Even after the unification of the empire it remained an important city and was the chief administrative centre of Shantung throughout Han times (206 BC–AD 220), when it was the seat of Ch'i province.

During the civil wars of the late 3rd century, however, and during the invasions of the 3rd and 4th centuries AD, it was devastated and fell into ruins. In the 5th century the Northern Wei state moved the seat of Ch'i province to I-tu, and in the 6th century Lin-tzu for a while lost even the status of a county seat. It was revived at a site some distance to the southwest under the Sui (581–618) and until the later years of the Ch'ing dynasty (1644–1911) remained the seat of a county, usually subordinated to Po-shan.

The existing city walls, which date to Sui times, are only 1.5 miles (2.4 km) in circumference. To the north, however, on the west bank of the Tzu Shui, are the ruins of ancient Lin-tzu, with massive walls 12 miles (19 km) in circumference. In the southwestern corner is another walled enclosure, which is thought to be the site of the royal palace of Ch'i. Outside the walls are many other remains connected with Lin-tzu's historic role, including the four huge tombs of the kings of the T'ien family, the Ch'i ruling house. Pop. (mid-1980s est.) fewer than 10,000.

Lin-yi (ancient Indochinese kingdom): *see* Champa.

Lin Yü-t'ang, Pinyin LIN YUTANG (b. Oct. 10, 1895, Lun-chi, Fukien province, China—d. March 26, 1976, Hong Kong), prolific writer of a wide variety of works in Chinese and English and founder in the 1930s of several Chinese magazines specializing in social satire and Western-style journalism.

The son of a Chinese Presbyterian minister, Lin Yü-t'ang was educated for the ministry but renounced Christianity in his early '20s and became a professor of English. In 1919 he traveled to the United States and Europe for advanced study at Harvard University and the University of Leipzig. On his return to China, he continued to teach and served as the editor of several English-language journals. He also contributed essays to Chinese literary magazines.

The peak of Lin Yü-t'ang's literary career in China came in 1932, when he established the *Lun-yü pan-yüeh-kan* ("Analects Fortnightly"), a type of Western-style satirical magazine totally new to China at that time. The fortnightly was highly successful, and he soon introduced two more publications.

In 1935 Lin published the first of his many English-language books, *My Country and My People.* An immediate success, it was widely translated and for years regarded as a standard text on China. The following year he moved to New York City to meet the popular demand for his historical accounts and novels, which he produced in rapid succession. *The Wisdom of China and India* appeared in 1942.

Although he returned to China briefly in 1943 and again in 1954, Lin Yü-t'ang both times became involved in disputes, often stemming from his stand in favour of literature as self-expression rather than as pure propaganda and social education, as argued by most of the Chinese Communist literary critics. After his second unsuccessful trip to China, he remained in the United States, writing more books on Chinese history and philosophy. He made highly acclaimed English translations of Chinese literary masterpieces, such as *Famous Chinese Short Stories Retold* (1952).

Lin Zexu (Chinese leader): *see* Lin Tse-hsü.

Linaceae, the flax family, comprising about 14 genera of herbaceous plants and shrubs, in the order Linales, of cosmopolitan distribution. The genus *Linum* includes flax (*q.v.*), perhaps the most important member of the family, grown for linen fibre and linseed (*q.v.*) oil and as a garden ornamental. *Reinwardtia* species are primarily low shrubs, grown in greenhouses and outdoors in warm climates; *R. indica,* the yellow flax, is notable for its large yellow flowers, borne in profusion in late fall and early winter.

Linacre, Thomas (b. *c.* 1460, Canterbury, Kent, Eng.—d. Oct. 20, 1524, London), English physician, classical scholar, founder and first president of the Royal College of Physicians of London.

Educated at the University of Oxford (1480–84), Linacre traveled extensively through Italy (1485–97), studying Greek and Latin classics under several noted scholars, and medicine at the University of Padua (M.D., 1496). Returning to England, he was appointed (1500) tutor to Prince Arthur, son of Henry VII, and served as physician (1509–20) to Henry VIII. He conducted a highly successful practice in London, numbering among his patients the humanist Desiderius Erasmus; Sir Thomas More, the author of *Utopia;* and Cardinal Wolsey, chief adviser to Henry VIII.

Distressed by the indiscriminate practice of medicine by barbers, clergymen, and anyone else inclined toward the art, Linacre obtained from Henry VIII in 1518 letters patent for the institution of a body of regular physicians empowered to decide who should practice medicine in greater London. This body, the Royal College of Physicians of London, also possessed authority to examine and license physicians throughout the kingdom and to inflict fines and imprisonment on offenders, with the exception of Oxford and Cambridge graduates. Linacre left medical practice in 1520, when he was ordained a Roman Catholic priest.

Linares, capital of Linares *provincia,* Maule *región,* central Chile, lying inland, 60 miles (100 km) from the Pacific coast, in the fertile Central Valley. Founded in 1755 as San Javier de Bella Isla, it was renamed San Ambrosio de Linares in 1794, and its present name became official in 1875. The city is a commercial and agricultural centre dealing in wine grapes, grains, fruits, vegetables, and livestock and has dairies, tanneries, and flour mills. Both the Pan-American Highway and the main north-south railroad pass through Linares, and a branch line leads to the Termas (hot springs) de Panimávida, 17 miles northeast. Pop. (1990 est.) mun. 70,528.

Linares, town, north-central Jaén *provincia,* situated in the *comunidad autonóma* ("autonomous community") of Andalusia, southern Spain, in the southern foothills of the Sierra Morena just northwest of the Río Guadalimar. The town is connected by branch railways with the lead mines on its northwestern outskirts. Mining and the manufacture of gunpowder, dynamite and blasting materials, and rope are the main economic activities. The smelting of lead, the manufacture of lead sheets and pipes, and the production of by-product silver from the lead ores are carried on. The local lead is of high quality.

Just to the south is the village of Cazlona, with remains of the ancient Iberian settlement of Cástulo. Spain's famous bullfighter Manolete (Manuel Rodríguez) was killed in the Linares bullring (1947). Pop. (2001 est.) 57,796.

Lincoln, city (district), administrative and historic county of Lincolnshire, England. It stands 200 feet (60 metres) above sea level on an impressive site at the point where the River Witham cuts a deep gap through the limestone

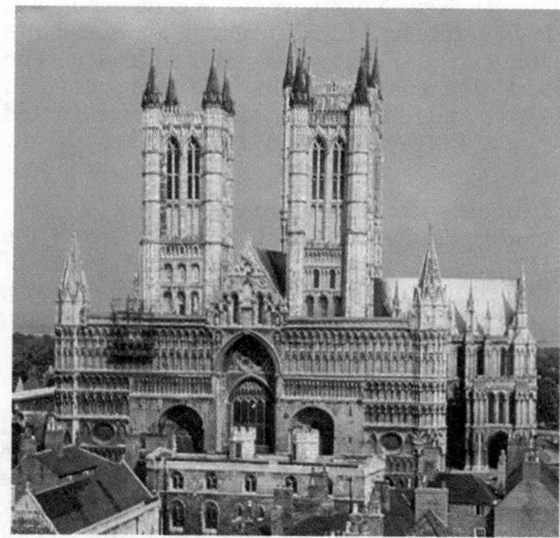

Lincoln cathedral, Lincolnshire
Ray Manley—Shostal/EB Inc.

escarpment of Lincoln Edge. Lincoln is the market centre for a major arable agricultural district, and many of its industries are agriculturally based, including food processing; it also has manufacturing of heavy machinery. Major eastern English road and rail routes converge on Lincoln, contributing to its importance.

Lincoln was a significant Roman town; called Lindum, it lay on the line of Fosse Way and Ermine Street and served as a fortress for the 9th Legion. By 71 CE it had become a *colonia*, serving as a settlement for retired legionary soldiers. The town walls were first established in this period, and relics of these still remain, including Newport Arch. Exchequer Gate, Potter Gate, and Stonebow are medieval gates built much later. The many other Roman finds include a public fountain, cemeteries, baths, and kilns, and the museum has an extensive collection of Roman antiquities.

Lincoln became one of the five boroughs under Danish rule in eastern England, and by the late Middle Ages it was one of England's major towns. Henry II gave the city its first charter in 1154, and citizens gained many privileges and a freedom somewhat similar to that of the City of London. Lincoln's importance continued when it was made a staple (trading) town dealing in wool, leather, and skins, activities that contributed to its prosperity at the end of the 13th century.

Many of Lincoln's famous buildings are medieval. Lincoln Castle, standing on the Lincoln Edge opposite the cathedral, dates from 1068 and contains Norman fragments. The castle keep dates from the 12th century. The cathedral, also Norman, stands on an elevated site overlooking the city. Built of local limestone, it is severely weathered on the outside, but inside it contains noted examples of Gothic architecture. The surrounding cathedral close contains the polygonal Chapter House (1225), the earliest English example of its kind. Area 14 square miles (36 square km). Pop. (2001) 85,616.

Lincoln, city, seat (1853) of Logan county, central Illinois, U.S., about 30 miles (48 km) northeast of Springfield. Founded in 1853, it was named for Abraham Lincoln, then a Springfield attorney, who handled the legalities of its founding and christened it with the juice of a watermelon. It was the only U.S. community named for Lincoln during his lifetime and with his knowledge and cooperation. Lincoln also tried cases in Postville, a settlement founded in 1835 and chosen as county seat in 1839, which, in the 1860s, became a part of Lincoln. A replica of the Postville Courthouse is maintained as a state historic site; another site preserves the Mount Pulaski Courthouse (1848).

Lincoln is a trading centre for a rich agricultural area (corn [maize], soybeans, and livestock) and has some manufacturing. The city is the seat of Lincoln (junior) College (1865) and Lincoln Christian College and Seminary (1944). Edward R. Madigan State Park is nearby. Inc. 1857. Pop. (2000) 15,369.

Lincoln, city, capital and second largest city of Nebraska, U.S., and seat (1869) of Lancaster county, in the southeastern part of the state, about 60 miles (95 km) southwest of Omaha. Oto and Pawnee Indians were early inhabitants. Settlers were drawn to the area in the 1850s by the salt flats located nearby, but a plan to establish salt mining was soon abandoned. Because the Platte River made access to Omaha, the territorial capital, difficult from the south, the site that is now Lincoln was chosen as the state capital in 1867 (the year of Nebraskan statehood) and was officially founded that year. A legislator who opposed the capital's move from Omaha named the new site for President Abraham Lincoln in an unsuccessful attempt to get the "South Platters," many of whom had favoured the Confederacy in the American Civil War, to vote against the change of location.

The Burlington and Missouri River Railroad arrived in 1870, and Lincoln became a railroad junction; by the 1890s, the city had 19 different rail routes. Havelock, University Place, College View, and Bethany, previously separate towns, were annexed by Lincoln during 1926–30.

The state capitol, Lincoln, Neb.
Philip Gould/Corbis

Lincoln is a regional centre of government, commerce, finance, arts, education, and health care. It has extensive rail connections and an airport. Area agriculture produces soybeans, corn, sorghum, wheat, hogs, and poultry. Lincoln is a major grain market with milling, grain storage, meatpacking, and farm-equipment distribution business. Manufactures include industrial rubber products, motorcycles, watercraft, software, scientific instruments, wireless communication equipment, bricks, and pharmaceuticals. The city is also an insurance centre. Government-operated institutions, including several correctional facilities, also contribute to the economy.

Lincoln's educational institutions include the University of Nebraska (1869), Union College (1891; Seventh-day Adventist), Nebraska Wesleyan University (1887; Methodist), and a campus of Southeast Community College (1973). Cultural organizations include the Lincoln Symphony Orchestra and the Lincoln Community Playhouse. The state capitol, completed in 1932 and Lincoln's third, was designed by American architect Bertram Grosvenor Goodhue; its central tower, rising 400 ft (120 m) from a massive three-story base, is a highly visible landmark. The legislature that meets there became unicameral in 1937 (unique in the United States).

In the early 20th century the political life of the city was dominated by William Jennings Bryan, who lived there from 1887 to 1921. Fairview (1903), the Bryan house on the grounds of Bryan LGH Medical Center East, has been restored. Lincoln is the site of the Nebraska State Fair (August). The Spring Creek Prairie preserves more than 500 acres (200 hectares) of unplowed tallgrass prairie southwest of the city. Inc. village, 1869; city, 1871. Pop. (2000) city, 225,581; Lincoln MSA, 250,291.

Lincoln, Abraham, byname HONEST ABE, THE RAILSPLITTER, or THE GREAT EMANCIPATOR (b. Feb. 12, 1809, Hodgenville, Ky., U.S.—d. April 15, 1865, Washington, D.C.), 16th president of the United States (1861–65), who preserved the Union during the American Civil War and brought about the emancipation of the slaves.

A brief account of the life and works of Abraham Lincoln follows; for a full biography, *see* MACROPAEDIA: Lincoln.

Of humble origins, Lincoln was a self-educated lawyer in frontier Illinois in the 1830s and '40s. In 1842 he married Mary Todd, who bore him four children (Robert Todd, Edward Baker, William Wallace, and Thomas ["Tad"]).

Before he began to be prominent in national politics, Lincoln had made himself one of the most distinguished and successful lawyers in Illinois. He was noted not only for his shrewdness and practical common sense, which enabled him always to see to the "nub" of any legal case, but also for his invariable fairness and utter honesty. After serving a term in Congress (1847–49), Lincoln became a Republican in 1856. Two years later he engaged in a series of debates with Stephen A. Douglas in an attempt to gain Douglas' seat in the U.S. Senate. Despite his defeat at the polls, the debates made him a nationally known figure, and he was elected to the presidency in 1860. His period as president was wholly taken up with the war against the secessionist southern states. As a war measure, Lincoln proclaimed the slaves in the rebellious states free in 1863. Assassinated by John Wilkes Booth as he sat in Ford's Theatre in Washington, D.C., just days after the Union victory in 1865, he came to be regarded as a hero and martyr by later generations of Americans.

Lincoln, Benjamin (b. Jan. 24, 1733, Hingham, Mass.—d. May 9, 1810, Boston), Continental army officer in the American Revolution who rendered distinguished service in the northern campaigns early in the war, but was forced to surrender with about 7,000 troops at Charleston, S.C., May 12, 1780.

A small-town farmer, Lincoln held local offices and was a member of the Massachusetts militia (1755–76). In May 1776 he was appointed major general in the Continental Army and in 1778 was placed in command of Continental forces in the South. He was widely criticized for the Charleston defeat, although no formal action was taken against him. Released in a prisoner exchange, he participated in the Yorktown campaign in 1781, then served the Continental Congress as secretary of war (1781–83). Shays's Rebellion (brought on in Massachusetts in 1786 by business depression and heavy taxes) was quelled by militiamen led by Lincoln. He was elected lieutenant governor of Massachusetts (1788) and was collector for the port of Boston (1789–1809).

Lincoln, Robert Todd (b. Aug. 1, 1843, Springfield, Ill., U.S.—d. July 26, 1926, Manchester, N.H.), eldest and sole surviving child of Abraham Lincoln who became a millionaire corporation attorney and served as U.S. secretary of war and minister to Great Britain during Republican administrations.

Raised in Springfield, Ill., as his father rose from local to national prominence, Lincoln later attended Phillips Exeter Academy and Harvard, graduating from the latter in 1864. He attended Harvard Law School for four months but left when commissioned a captain in the U.S. Army and assigned to Gen. Ulysses S. Grant's staff.

Following Robert E. Lee's surrender and his father's assassination, Lincoln completed his legal education in Chicago and in 1867 was admitted to the bar. His practice prospered as he obtained major railroads and corporations as clients.

In 1881 Lincoln joined James A. Garfield's administration as secretary of war and remained at that Cabinet post under Chester A. Arthur until 1885. He then returned to private law practice in Chicago until Pres. Benjamin Harrison appointed him minister to Britain in 1889. Both periods of public service were largely uneventful.

He was back at his law practice in 1893, serving, among other notable corporations, the Pullman Company. When George Pullman died in 1897, Lincoln ran the company, first as acting executive and later as president. He retired in 1911 but remained chairman of the board at Pullman as well as director of several other Chicago-based corporations and financial institutions. Near the end of his life he deposited his father's papers in the Library of Congress with the stipulation that they remain sealed for 21 years after his death.

Lincoln Battalion (Spanish Civil War): *see* Abraham Lincoln Battalion.

Lincoln–Douglas Debates, series of seven debates between Democratic Sen. Stephen A. Douglas and Republican challenger Abraham Lincoln during the 1858 Illinois senatorial campaign, largely concerning the issue of slavery extension into the territories.

The slavery extension question had seemingly been settled by the Missouri Compromise nearly 40 years earlier. The Mexican War, however, had added new territories, and the issue flared up again in the 1840s. The Compromise of 1850 provided a temporary respite from sectional strife, but the Kansas–Nebraska Act of 1854—a measure Douglas sponsored—brought the slavery extension issue to the fore once again. Douglas' bill in effect repealed the Missouri Compromise by lifting the ban against slavery in territories north of the 36°30′ latitude. In place of the ban, Douglas offered "popular sovereignty," the doctrine that the actual settlers in the territories and not Congress should decide the fate of slavery in their midst.

The Kansas–Nebraska Act spurred the creation of the Republican Party, formed largely to keep slavery out of the western territories. Both Douglas' doctrine of popular sovereignty and the Republican stand on free soil were seemingly invalidated by the Dred Scott decision of 1857, in which the Supreme Court said that neither Congress nor the territorial legislature could exclude slavery from a territory.

When Lincoln and Douglas debated the slavery extension issue in 1858, therefore, they were addressing the problem that had divided the nation into two hostile camps and that threatened the continued existence of the Union. Their contest, as a consequence, had repercussions far beyond determining who would win the senatorial seat at stake.

When Lincoln received the Republican nomination to run against Douglas, he said in his acceptance speech that "A house divided against itself cannot stand" and that "this government cannot endure permanently half slave and half free." Douglas thereupon attacked Lincoln as a radical, threatening the continued stability of the Union. Lincoln then challenged Douglas to a series of debates, and the two eventually agreed to hold joint encounters in seven Illinois congressional districts.

The debates, each three hours long, started on August 21 and concluded on October 15. Douglas repeatedly tried to brand Lincoln as a dangerous radical who advocated racial equality and disruption of the Union. Lincoln emphasized the moral iniquity of slavery and attacked popular sovereignty for the bloody results it had produced in Kansas.

At Freeport, Ill., on August 27, Lincoln challenged Douglas to reconcile popular sovereignty with the Dred Scott decision. Douglas replied that settlers could circumvent the decision by not establishing the local police regulations—*i.e.*, a slave code—that protected a master's property. Without such protection, no one would bring slaves into a territory. This became known as the "Freeport Doctrine."

Douglas' position, while acceptable to many Northern Democrats, angered the South and led to the division of the last remaining national political institution, the Democratic Party. Although he retained his seat in the Senate, narrowly defeating Lincoln when the state legislature (which then elected U.S. senators) voted 54 to 46 in his favour, Douglas' stature as a national leader of the Democratic Party was gravely diminished. Lincoln, on the other hand, lost the election but won acclaim as an eloquent spokesman for the Republican cause.

In 1860 the Lincoln–Douglas debates were printed as a book and used as an important campaign document in the presidential contest that year, which once again pitted Republican Lincoln against Democrat Douglas. This time, however, Douglas was running as the candidate of a divided party and finished a distant second in the popular vote to the triumphant Lincoln.

Lincoln Memorial, stately monument in Washington, D.C., honouring Pres. Abraham Lincoln and "the virtues of tolerance, honesty, and constancy in the human spirit." Designed by Henry Bacon on a plan similar to that of the Parthenon in Athens, the structure includes 36 columns (each 44 ft [13.4 m] high) of Colorado marble surrounding the building, one for each state that comprised the Union in Lincoln's time. The colossal (19-ft) seated statue of Lincoln, composed of Georgia white marble and resting on a pedestal of Tennessee marble, was designed by Daniel Chester French and carved by the Piccirilli brothers of New York; it dominates the interior and looks eastward across a reflecting pool at the Washington Monument and Capitol. On the South Wall is inscribed Lincoln's Gettysburg Address and on the North Wall his Second Inaugural Address. Above are two paintings by Jules Guerin representing "Reunion and Progress" and the "Emancipation of a Race." The cornerstone was laid in 1915 and the completed Memorial was dedicated on Memorial Day, May 30, 1922.

Lincoln Park Zoological Gardens, zoo in the city of Chicago noted for its excellent collection of great apes living together in family groups. The 14-hectare (35-acre) park is operated by the Chicago Park District with the aid of the Lincoln Park Zoological Society. Opened in 1874, the zoo is among the oldest in the United States and is undergoing a modernization program that is scheduled for completion by the late 1980s. Major strengths of the zoo's collection are the cats, edentates (*e.g.*, sloths and anteaters), and South American primates.

Lincoln Tunnel, vehicular tunnel under the Hudson River, from Manhattan Island (39th Street), New York City, to Weehawken, N.J. It is 8,200 feet (2,500 metres) long and lies about 100 ft below the river's surface. The first tube was opened in 1937, the second in 1954, and the third in 1957. It is operated by the Port Authority of New York and New Jersey.

Lincolnshire, county in eastern England, extending along the North Sea coast from the Humber Estuary to The Wash. The area of the county is 2,284 sq mi (5,915 sq km), and it comprises seven districts: East Lindsey, North Kesteven, South Kesteven, West Lindsey, South Holland, the borough of Boston, and the city of Lincoln.

Lincolnshire contains two prominent upland areas, which cross it from north to south. The more westerly, and narrower, is Lincolnshire Edge, a limestone escarpment rising abruptly on its western side and on which the city of Lincoln is situated. Separated from the Edge by a clay lowland are the Lincolnshire Wolds, an area of rolling chalk hills. Between the Wolds and the coast lies an area known as the Lincoln Marsh; this merges at its southern end into the low-lying area of the Fens, which surrounds The Wash and which has been the scene of drainage and reclamation efforts at least since Roman times.

The upland areas of Lincolnshire provided dry defensive sites for prehistoric settlement, and the latter increased in density as trade across the North Sea with Europe developed. There was extensive Roman settlement in the county. The main artery of Ermine Street followed the line of the Lincoln Edge, intersecting with the Fosse Way at Lincoln. The Anglo-Saxons, who followed the Romans, used the River Trent as a route for penetration from the sea and established the kingdom of Lindsey. Danish influence was also widespread; the county contains two Danish boroughs—Lincoln and Stamford—and also many villages established by the Danes.

Medieval Lincolnshire became prosperous by its farming, as is attested by a number of large churches, abbeys, and monasteries. With the Industrial Revolution, however, and the shift of population to cities and coalfields, the county in the 19th century began to find itself outside the main lines of circulation across England. Partly isolated by the deep indentations of the Humber and The Wash at its northern and southern boundaries, the county had to rely exclusively on its agriculture and the processing industries that it brought into being. With its deeply rural countryside and small market towns, the centre of the county presents something of a reminder of rural England in a past era. Along the coast, however, a new source of economic vitality has arisen thanks to the tourist industry. Seaside towns like Skegness and Mablethorpe and caravan sites (trailer camps) form an almost unbroken line across the shore except at a few places, most notably at Gibraltar Point, where nature reserves have been established.

Grain, sugar beet, and vegetable crops are the main farm products of the county. Pop. (1986 est.) 567,300.

Lind, James (b. 1716, Edinburgh—d. July 13, 1794, Gosport, Hampshire, Eng.), physician, "founder of naval hygiene in England," whose recommendation that fresh citrus fruit and lemon juice be included in the diet of seamen resulted in the eradication of scurvy from the British Navy.

A British naval surgeon (1739–48) and a physician at the Haslar Hospital for men of the Royal Navy, Gosport (1758–94), Lind observed thousands of cases of scurvy, typhus, and dysentery and the conditions on board ship that caused them. In 1754, when he

James Lind, engraving by I. Wright after a portrait by Sir George Chalmers, 1783
Archiv fur Kunst und Geschichte, Berlin

published *A Treatise on Scurvy,* more British sailors were dying from scurvy during wartime than were killed in combat.

Nearly two centuries earlier the Dutch had discovered the benefits of citrus fruits and juices to sailors on long voyages. In his *Treatise* and in *On the Most Effectual Means of Preserving the Health of Seamen* (1757), Lind recommended this dietary practice. When it was finally adopted by the Royal Navy in 1795, scurvy disappeared from the ranks "as if by magic." Lind recommended shipboard delousing procedures, suggested the use of hospital ships for sick sailors in tropical ports, and arranged (1761) for the shipboard distillation of seawater for drinking. He also wrote *An Essay on Diseases Incidental to Europeans in Hot Climates* (1768).

Lind, Jenny, original name JOHANNA MARIA LIND (b. Oct. 6, 1820, Stockholm—d. Nov. 2, 1887, Malvern, Worcestershire, Eng.), Swedish-born operatic and oratorio soprano admired for her vocal control and agility and for the purity and naturalness of her art.

Lind made her debut in *Der Freischütz* at Stockholm in 1838 and in 1841 studied with Manuel García in Paris. Giacomo Meyerbeer wrote the part of Vielka for her in *Ein Feldlager in Schlesien* (Berlin, 1844), and in 1847 she sang in London the role of Amelia in *I Masnadieri,* written for her by Giuseppe Verdi. She first appeared in London in Meyerbeer's *Robert le Diable* (May 4, 1847); Henry Chorley reported that the town "went mad about the Swedish nightingale."

Her range extended from the B below middle C to high G. A skilled coloratura singer who often wrote her own cadenzas, she also sang simple songs with great appeal. Eventually her sincere piety made her determine to leave the stage. Success in oratorio and recital made it easier for her to do so, and her final appearance in opera was in 1849, in *Robert*

Jenny Lind
By courtesy of the New-York Historical Society

le Diable. The following year she toured the United States under P.T. Barnum's auspices, and in 1852 she married her accompanist, Otto Goldschmidt. She and her husband lived first in Dresden, Ger., and from 1856 in England. In 1870 she appeared in Goldschmidt's oratorio *Ruth* at Düsseldorf, and in 1875 she led the sopranos in the Bach choir in London, founded by Goldschmidt. Her last appearance was in 1883. From 1883 to 1886 she taught at the Royal College of Music, London.

Lindahl, Erik Robert (b. Nov. 21, 1891, Stockholm—d. Jan. 6, 1960), Swedish economist who was one of the members of the famous "Stockholm school" of economics that developed, during the late 1920s and early 1930s, from the macroeconomic theory of Knut Wicksell.

Lindahl held positions at the universities of Lund, Gothenburg, and Uppsala (1942–60). His main work in English is *Studies in the Theory of Money and Capital* (1939). One of his most important achievements was the development of the sequence analysis in economics, which influenced Gunnar Myrdal's concepts of saving and investment.

Lindahl and the Swedish economists Myrdal and Bertil Ohlin developed Wicksell's monetary theory, applying it to conditions other than full employment. Lindahl developed the benefit principle in taxation, described in his book *Die Gerechtigkeit der Besteuerung* (1919; "The Justness of Taxation"). Lindahl also carried on Wicksell's development of the Austrian economic school theory of capital. He was interested in the development of economic accounting systems that would have general validity, and he made statistical studies of income and prices.

Lindane, trade name for an insecticide composed of the most toxic of the isomers of benzene hexachloride (*q.v.*).

Lindau, city, Bavaria *Land* (state), extreme southern Germany, on an island in Lake Constance, connected to the mainland by two bridges, southeast of Friedrichshafen. It was the site of a Roman camp, Tiberii, and of a Benedictine abbey founded in 810. Fortified in the 12th century, it became an imperial free city in 1275 and was a prosperous merchant town along the trade route from Italy. The abbey was an ecclesiastical principality of the Holy Roman Empire from 1466 until it was secularized in 1802. The town was ruled by Austria in 1804 and passed to Bavaria in 1805. The communities of the "Garden City" on the lake's north shore were incorporated with Lindau in 1922. The city retains a medieval and Baroque appearance. Among notable landmarks are the old town hall (1422–36; remodeled 1578), the collegiate church of the old abbey (1751), St. Stephen's Church (1180), and the 19th-century Bavarian lion at the entrance to the small harbour. A renowned summer resort and tourist centre, Lindau is also a customs station. There is a lake steamer service to Austria and Switzerland. Pop. (1989 est.) 23,699.

The Mang Tower and the harbour at Lindau, on Lake Constance, Germany
Malak/Shostal Assoc.

Lindbergh, Charles A(ugustus) (b. Feb. 4, 1902, Detroit—d. Aug. 26, 1974, Maui, Hawaii, U.S.), American aviator, one of the best-known figures in aeronautical history, remembered for the first nonstop solo flight across the Atlantic, from New York to Paris, on May 20–21, 1927.

Lindbergh's early years were spent chiefly in Little Falls, Minn., and in Washington, D.C., where for 10 years his father represented the 6th district of Minnesota in the Congress. His formal education ended during his second year at the University of Wisconsin, in Madison, when his growing interest in aviation led to enrollment in a flying school in Lincoln, Neb., and the purchase of a World War I Curtiss Jenny, with which he made stunt-flying tours through Southern and Midwestern states. After a year at the army flying schools in Texas (1924–25), he became an airmail pilot (1926), flying the route from St. Louis, Mo., to Chicago. During this period he obtained financial backing from a group of St. Louis businessmen to compete for the $25,000 prize offered for the first nonstop flight between New York and Paris. In the monoplane *Spirit of St. Louis* he made the flight in 33½ hours on May 20–21, 1927. Overnight Lindbergh became a folk hero on both sides of the Atlantic and a well-known figure in most of the world. There followed a series of goodwill flights in Europe and America.

In Mexico, Lindbergh met Anne Morrow, daughter of the United States ambassador, Dwight Morrow. They were married in May

1929. She served as copilot and navigator for him on many flights, and together they flew to many countries of the world. During this period, Lindbergh acted as technical adviser to two airlines, Transcontinental Air Transport and Pan American Airways, personally pioneering many of their routes.

Lindbergh, 1927
By courtesy of the Library of Congress, Washington, D.C.

In March 1932 the Lindberghs' two-year-old son, Charles Augustus, Jr., was kidnapped from their home near Hopewell, N.J., and murdered. Partly because of Lindbergh's worldwide popularity, this became the most celebrated crime of the 1930s, and it was a major subject of newspaper attention until April 1936, when Bruno Richard Hauptmann was executed after being convicted of the kidnap-murder. The publicity was so distasteful to the Lindberghs that they took refuge in Europe. After 1936, when he visited German centres of aviation, Lindbergh repeatedly warned against the growing air power of Nazi Germany. His decoration by the German government in 1938 led to considerable criticism, as did the speeches advocating American neutrality in World War II he made in 1940–41 after his return to the United States. Criticism of his public statements by President Franklin D. Roosevelt led Lindbergh to resign his Air Corps Reserve commission in April 1941.

When the United States entered the war, however, Lindbergh, as a civilian, threw himself into the war effort, serving as a consultant to the Ford Motor Company and to the United Aircraft Corporation. In the latter capacity he flew 50 combat missions during a tour of duty in the Pacific; and later, after the end of the war in Europe, he accompanied a navy technical mission in Europe investigating German aviation developments.

Following World War II, Lindbergh and his family lived quietly in Connecticut and then in Hawaii. He continued as consultant to Pan American World Airways and to the U.S. Department of Defense. He was a member of the National Advisory Committee for Aeronautics and served on a number of other aeronautical boards and committees. He received many honours and awards, in addition to the Medal of Honor that had been awarded to him by special act of Congress in 1927. For his services to the government he was appointed brigadier general in the Air Force Reserve by President Dwight D. Eisenhower in 1954. His book *The Spirit of St. Louis,* describing the flight to Paris, was published in 1953 and gained him a Pulitzer Prize. He was also the author of *We* (1927), *Of Flight and Life* (1948), and, with the French surgeon and biologist Alexis Carrel, *The Culture of Organs* (1938), concerning researches on which he and Carrel had collaborated. His *Wartime Journals* (1970) is a record (not initially intended for publication) of his life during the years 1938–45.

BIBLIOGRAPHY. Lindbergh's world views and values are the focal point of his memoirs, *Autobiography of Values* (1978), ed. by William Jovanovich and Judith A. Schiff. Lindbergh describes his famous airplane flight in *The Spirit of St. Louis* (1953, reprinted 1987), and in *"We"* (1927, reissued 1955), which also tells the story of his youth. See also *The Wartime Journals of Charles A. Lindbergh* (1970), which covers the period from March 1938 to June 1945. Two biographies are Walter S. Ross, *The Last Hero: Charles A. Lindbergh,* rev. ed. (1976); and Brendan Gill, *Lindbergh Alone* (1977). Perry D. Luckett, *Charles A. Lindbergh: A Bio-Bibliography* (1986), is also useful.

Lindblad, Bertil (b. Nov. 26, 1895, Örebro, Swed.—d. June 26, 1965, Stockholm), Swedish astronomer who contributed greatly to the theory of galactic structure and motion and to the methods of determining the absolute magnitude (true brightness, disregarding distance) of distant stars.

After serving as an assistant at the observatory in Uppsala, Swed., Lindblad joined the Stockholm Observatory and in 1927 was appointed director, a post he held until 1965. He planned the observatory's relocation in 1931 to nearby Saltsjöbaden and modernized its facilities.

By the early 1920s the Dutch astronomer Jacobus C. Kapteyn and others had made statistical studies establishing that generally stars appear to move in one of two directions in space. In 1926 Lindblad successfully explained this phenomenon (called star streaming) as an effect of rotation of the Milky Way and thus became the first to offer substantial evidence that the Galaxy rotates. This theory was definitely proved soon after by Jan Oort of The Netherlands.

Lindblad also pioneered in studies to determine the absolute magnitude of distant stars from the stellar spectra (the characteristic individual wavelengths of light). Establishing his own spectral classification system, he used it to determine absolute magnitudes and, thence, the distance and transverse velocities of many distant stars.

Lindblad was president of the International Astronomical Union (1948–52).

Linde, Carl (Paul Gottfried) von (b. June 11, 1842, Berndorf, Bavaria [Germany]—d. Nov. 16, 1934, Munich, Ger.), German engineer whose invention of a continuous process of liquefying gases in large quantities formed a basis for the modern technology of refrigeration and provided both impetus and means for conducting scientific research at low temperatures and very high vacuums.

Linde, 1932
Ullstein Bilderdienst

While an assistant professor of machine design at the newly established Technische Hochschule in Munich from 1868, he developed a methyl ether refrigerator (1874) and an ammonia refrigerator (1876). Though other refrigeration units had been developed earlier, Linde's were the first to be designed with the aim of precise calculations of efficiency.

In 1895 he set up a large-scale plant for the production of liquid air. Six years later he developed a method for separating pure liquid oxygen from liquid air that resulted in widespread industrial conversion to processes utilizing oxygen (*e.g.,* in steel manufacture).

Lindegren, Erik (Johan) (b. Aug. 5, 1910, Luleå, Swed.—d. May 31, 1968, Stockholm), Swedish modernist poet who made a major contribution to the development of a new Swedish poetry in the 1940s.

Lindegren attended the University of Stockholm and established himself as a literary reviewer for a number of leading newspapers and magazines. The appearance of Lindegren's second volume of poetry, *Mannen utan väg* (1942; *The Man Without a Way*), marked the beginning of the poetry of the '40s. Using unconventional imagery and syntax, the poetry in this volume can best be understood in terms of its visions of the stupidities and horrors of the contemporary human scene. Lindegren's two later volumes of poetry, *Sviter* (1947; "Suites") and *Vinteroffer* (1954; "Winter Sacrifice"), continue to reveal the strength of his commitment to modernism, though they are more lyrical.

In 1947 Lindegren and Karl Vennberg (also a modernist poet) edited the anthology *40-talslyrik* ("Poetry of the 1940s"), including verse from more than a score of young poets whose work reflected the ideas and moods of the decade. Lindegren made notable translations of T.S. Eliot's *Murder in the Cathedral,* William Shakespeare's *Hamlet,* the poetry of the French writers Saint-John Perse, Paul Éluard, and Paul Valéry, and the prose of William Faulkner and Graham Greene. He also translated the librettos of several operas and, during the last 10 years of his life, himself wrote texts for performance.

Lindeman Island, island in the Cumberland Islands, across Whitsunday Passage from northeastern Queensland, Australia. A rocky, coral-fringed continental island of the Great Barrier Reef, it has an area of 6 square miles (16 square km) and rises to 800 feet (240 m) at Mount Oldfield. Lindeman was the first island (1923) of the Cumberland group to be developed as a resort and has been designated a national park.

Lindemann, (Carl Louis) Ferdinand von (b. April 12, 1852, Hannover, Hanover [Germany]—d. March 1, 1939, Munich, Ger.), German mathematician who proved that the number π is transcendental—*i.e.,* it does not satisfy any algebraic equation with rational coefficients. This proof established that the classical Greek construction problem of squaring the circle (constructing a square with an area equal to that of a given circle) by compass and straightedge is insoluble.

Lindemann became professor of mathematics at the University of Königsberg, Ger. (now Kaliningrad, Russia), in 1883 and at the University of Munich in 1893. His work in mathematics was primarily in geometry and analysis. He published his famous proof in an article entitled "Über die Zahl π" (1882; "Concerning the Number π").

Linden, city, northeastern Guyana, on the Demerara River upstream from Georgetown. The former towns of Mackenzie, Wismar, and Christianborg, which were unified as Linden (1971), grew up around the large mining camp that was established by the Aluminum Company of Canada, and later nationalized as The Guyana Bauxite Company. Bauxite mined in the vicinity is brought to Linden for processing and then loaded onto oceangoing vessels at the camp. There is a bridge across the Demerara, and Georgetown can be reached by road. Linden also has an airport. Pop. (1992 est.) 27,200.

linden, any of several trees of the genus *Tilia* (family Tiliaceae), native to the Northern Hemisphere. Of the approximately 30 species, a few are outstanding as ornamental and shade trees. They are among the most graceful of deciduous trees, with heart-shaped, coarsely toothed leaves, fragrant cream-coloured flowers, and small globular fruit hanging from a narrow leafy bract.

Leaves and fruit hanging from the bract of the European linden, or common lime (*Tilia europaea*)
John Markham

The American linden, basswood, or whitewood (*T. americana*), a large shade tree, reaching 40 m (130 feet) in height, provides wood for beehives, crating, furniture, and excelsior. It is a popular bee tree, linden honey being pale and of distinctive flavour. Small-leaf, or little-leaf, linden (*T. cordata*), a European tree, is widely planted as a street tree. The hybrid Crimean linden (*T. euchlora,* a cross between *T. cordata* and *T. dasystyla*), which grows up to 20 m (66 feet), has yielded a graceful pyramidal variety, the Redmond linden (*T. euchlora* variety 'Redmond'), having a single straight trunk.

The European linden, or common lime (*T. europaea*), is a natural hybrid between the bigleaf linden (*T. platyphyllos*) and little-leaf linden. A delicate tea is made from its dried flowers. Silver linden (*T. tomentosa*) is distinguished by its white-silvery underleaf; pendent silver linden (*T. petiolaris*) is valued for its weeping habit.

Carolina linden (*T. caroliniana*) and white basswood (*T. heterophylla*), from the eastern United States, are native on moist soils.

Linden, Pieter Cort van der: *see* Cort van der Linden, Pieter (Wilhelm Adriaan).

Lindenthal, Gustav (b. May 21, 1850, Brünn, Austria—d. July 31, 1935, Metuchen, N.J., U.S.), Austrian-born American civil engineer known for designing Hell Gate Bridge across New York City's East River.

After gaining experience working on railways and bridges in Austria and Switzerland, Lindenthal immigrated to the United States (1871). He served as a construction engineer at the Philadelphia Centennial Exposition (1874–77) and then went to Pittsburgh as a consulting engineer in railway and bridge construction.

In 1890 he moved to New York City, where he became commissioner of bridges (1902–03). There he designed and acted as consulting engineer for the Hell Gate Railway bridge, which opened for traffic in March 1917. At that time Hell Gate was the longest (977 feet [298 m]) steel arch in the world. Lindenthal designed the Queensboro (cantilever) Bridge, also over the East River, and was a consulting engineer for railroad tunnels under the Hudson and East rivers.

Lindet, Jean-Baptiste-Robert (b. 1743, Bernay, France—d. Feb. 17, 1825, Paris), member of the Committee of Public Safety that ruled Revolutionary France during the Jacobin dictatorship (1793–94). He organized the provisioning of France's armies and had charge of much of the central economic planning carried out by the committee.

At the outbreak of the Revolution in 1789, Lindet was a well-to-do lawyer in Bernay. He was elected to the Revolution's Legislative Assembly (October 1791–September 1792) and accepted a seat in the Assembly's successor, the National Convention. During the trial of King Louis XVI, Lindet drafted a report on Louis's counterrevolutionary "crimes" (December 1792) and voted with the majority for the king's death (January 1793). He became a member of the first Committee of Public Safety on April 6, 1793. Siding with the Montagnards (deputies from the Club of the Jacobins), he proclaimed that strict economic controls had to be imposed if the republic was to survive in its war with the major European powers. He helped the Montagnards expel their moderate Girondist rivals from the Convention on June 2, and on July 10 he was reelected to the second, predominantly Jacobin, Committee of Public Safety. In October Lindet assumed direction of the Central Food Committee, which was to requisition food and supplies for the troops. Soon the efficient bureaucratic apparatus he set up was regulating much of the production and distribution of agricultural and industrial goods.

Essentially a moderate, Lindet looked forward to the eventual elimination of controls, disapproved of the use of terror against counterrevolutionaries, and showed little sympathy for the demands of the Parisian lower classes. Although he frequently supported the opponents of the committee's chief spokesman, Robespierre, he took no part in the conspiracy that brought about Robespierre's downfall on 9 Thermidor (July 27, 1794). During the ensuing Thermidorian reaction against the Jacobin regime, Lindet withdrew from the Committee of Public Safety (October 1794). He was appointed minister of finance under the Directory in June 1799, but he retired from politics when Napoleon seized power in November. He spent the rest of his life practicing law in Paris.

Lindgren, Astrid (b. Nov. 14, 1907, Vimmerby, Swed.—d. Jan. 28, 2002, Stockholm), influential Swedish writer of children's books.

Lindgren's great popularity began in 1945 with the creation of *Pippi Långstrump* ("Pippi Longstocking"), the first of three books with Pippi as its main character. This strangely dressed girl living alone with her horse and ape, having great wealth and enormous physical strength, stands totally apart from the conformist demands of everyday life and incarnates every child's dream of freedom and power. The Pippi books also exhibit the infectious humour for which Lindgren is known. The books have been translated into numerous languages, and more than 35 feature-length films have been devoted to Pippi.

An equally popular character is found in *Emil in Lönneberga* (1963), which was followed by a sequel in 1970. Emil is another uninhibited child of nature depicted in a setting from Lindgren's home province around the turn of the century. Other well-known characters include the children from Bullerbyn, portrayed in three books from the 1940s and 1950s, and *Nils Karlsson-Pyssling* (1949), a poetic tale of a lonely child and his world of imaginary creatures. In *Mio, min Mio* (1954) and *Bröderna Lejonhjärta* (1973; "The Brothers Lionheart") she turned with equal success to the world of folklore.

Lindgren received the gold medal of the Swedish Academy (1971).

Lindgren, Waldemar (b. Feb. 14, 1860, Kalmar, Swed.—d. Nov. 3, 1939, Brighton, Mass., U.S.), Swedish-born American economic geologist who helped establish that veins of metal and similar deposits are created by hot solutions derived from molten rock below, not by water seepage from above.

Lindgren immigrated to the United States in 1883 and was associated with the U.S. Geological Survey from the following year until 1912. Extensive studies of ore deposits in the western states enabled him to determine with unprecedented accuracy the physical and chemical conditions of ore formation. He established the igneous sources of many minerals and clarified the methods by which ores are deposited, notably the replacement of certain minerals by others.

He is noted for a system of classification, devised in 1913, that separates ore deposits into magmatic segregates, contact metamorphic deposits, pegmatites, veins and veinlike deposits of differing degrees of intensity in temperature and pressure (hypothermal, mesothermal, epithermal), and sedimentary deposits.

He became chief geologist of the Geological Survey in 1911 but resigned to become professor of economic geology and chairman of the department of geology at the Massachusetts Institute of Technology, Cambridge. He published nearly 200 books and papers, and his *Mineral Deposits* (4th ed., 1933) became the leading advanced text in its field.

Lindisfarne (England): *see* Holy Island.

Lindisfarne Gospels, manuscript (MS. Cotton Nero D.IV.; British Museum, London) illuminated in the late 7th or 8th century in the Hiberno-Saxon style. The book was probably made for Eadfrith, the bishop of Lindisfarne from 698 to 721. Attributed to the Northumbrian school, the Lindisfarne Gospels show the fusion of Irish, classical, and Byzantine elements of manuscript illumination.

Lindley, John (b. Feb. 5, 1799, Catton, Northumberland, Eng.—d. Nov. 1, 1865, London), British botanist whose attempts to formulate a natural system of plant classification greatly aided the transition from the artificial (considering the characters of single parts) to the natural system (considering all characters of a plant).

In 1819 Lindley arrived in London where, with the help of the botanist Sir William Jackson Hooker, he obtained a position as an assistant librarian. In 1822 he became garden assistant secretary at the Horticultural Society for which, in 1830, he organized the first flower shows to be held in England. He then served as the first professor of botany at the University of London (University College), where he remained until 1860.

John Lindley, engraving, 1865, after a photograph
The Mansell Collection

Lindley's investigation in 1838 of the conditions at the Kew Gardens in London led him to recommend that the gardens be turned over to the nation and used as the botanical headquarters for the United Kingdom. His famous collection of orchids was eventually housed in the Kew herbarium. His *Theory and Practice of Horticulture* (1842) is considered to be one of the best books ever written on the physiological principles of horticulture. He developed his own natural system of plant classification for his best-known book, *The Vegetable Kingdom* (1846). Although his system was never adopted by other botanists, it did much to enhance the popularity of the natural system in England.

Lindley, William (b. Sept. 7, 1808, London, Eng.—d. May 22, 1900, Blackheath, London), British civil engineer who helped renovate the German city of Hamburg after a major fire.

Lindley engaged in railway work on the European continent and settled in Hamburg as engineer in chief to the Hamburg-Bergedorf Railway (1838–60). On May 5, 1842, a fire broke out in Hamburg, raging for three days. Lindley organized strong measures to check it, including blowing up the town hall. He was afterward appointed consulting engineer to the burned city, and he surveyed it and drew up a plan for its complete rebuilding. He constructed a system of sewers, waterworks (1844–48), gasworks (1846), and public baths and washhouses, and he planned extensions to the port that were carried out in 1854.

He left Hamburg in 1860, working in many other cities as consulting engineer (1865–79). He constructed a sewerage system for Frankfurt am Main that was widely imitated in Europe and America. He also worked in Warsaw, Budapest, Düsseldorf, Galaţi (Romania), and Basel and carried out works in Helgoland for the British government.

Lindos, also spelled LINDUS, Greek LÍNDHOS, town on the eastern coast of Rhodes and the site of one of the three city-states of Rhodes before their union (408 BC). Lindos was the site of Danish excavations (1902–24, resumed 1952) that uncovered the Doric Temple of Athena Lindia on the acropolis, propylaea

Temple of Athena Lindia, Lindos
Bernard G. Silberstein from Rapho/Photo Researchers

(entrance gates), and a stoa (colonnade). Also discovered was a chronicle of the temple compiled in 99 BC by a local antiquarian, listing mythical and historical dedications from many parts of the Mediterranean. Residents of the town today are largely engaged in catering to the area's active tourist industry. Pop. (1981) 661.

Lindsay, town, seat (1861) of Victoria county, southeastern Ontario, Canada. It lies along the Scugog River, 21 miles (34 km) west-northwest of Peterborough. Laid out in 1825 as Purdy's Mills (after William Purdy, who built the first mills), it was renamed for one of the original land surveyors. The town's growth has been due partly to the Trent Canal (1833) and the improvement of the waterway between Sturgeon and Scugog lakes, including the locks at Lindsay. The town is a gateway to the Kawartha Lakes recreation area and has lumbering and farming interests and light industries. The town's annual Kawartha Summer Theatre features professional stock companies. Inc. 1857. Pop. (1991) 16,696.

Lindsay, Sir David: *see* Lyndsay, Sir David.

Lindsay, Howard; and Crouse, Russel (respectively b. March 29, 1889, Waterford, N.Y., U.S.—d. Feb. 11, 1968, New York, N.Y.; b. Feb. 20, 1893, Findlay, Ohio, U.S.—d. April 3, 1966, New York, N.Y.), team of American playwrights and producers who coauthored an unbroken string of humorous, successful plays and collaborated on theatrical productions. Their partnership was notable both for its continual successes and for the way the two men complemented each other's talents.

Prior to meeting Crouse, Lindsay had already gained experience as an actor, director, and playwright, traveling for 42 weeks in the production of *Polly of the Circus.* Crouse's early experience was primarily journalistic, although he did write a libretto for *The Gang's All Here* (1931), which ran for only two weeks. He also wrote several nostalgic books in the early 1930s about 19th-century America.

While trying to salvage a play in 1933, producer Vinton Freedley paired the talents of Lindsay and Crouse. The result was *Anything Goes* (1934) and a partnership that was to expand and mature over the following years. Their longest-playing drama was a 1939 production based on Clarence Day's book *Life With Father,* which ran for 7½ years (3,213 performances) and in which Lindsay played Father opposite his real-life wife, Dorothy Stickney. When Lindsay and Crouse were offered *Arsenic and Old Lace* in 1940, they tried their hands at theatrical production, and the result was another success. In 1946 the pair won the Pulitzer Prize in drama for *State of the Union* (1945), which was a satire of American politics. Sections of this play were rewritten every day to correspond to actual events. They also wrote the libretto for the play *The Sound of Music* (1959).

Lindsay and Crouse's work had a universal appeal, created by a blend of Lindsay's theatrical knowledge and Crouse's sharp wit. Together they had a gift for transforming ideas into extremely popular musicals and plays.

Lindsay, Norman (Alfred William) (b. Feb. 23, 1879, Creswick, Vic., Australia—d. Nov. 29, 1969, Sydney), Australian artist and novelist especially known for his political cartoons and sensual book illustrations.

At 16 Lindsay began to draw for a Melbourne newspaper, and in 1901 he moved to New South Wales. He was for many years the chief cartoonist of the *Sydney Bulletin.* His major characteristics of imaginative power, grim strength, and a certain coarseness of style are apparent in his illustrations for editions of the works of Theocritus, Giovanni Boccaccio, Giovanni Giacomo Casanova, Gaius Petronius Arbiter, and François Rabelais and for his own novel *The Cautious Amorist* (1932). Mainly done in an Art Nouveau manner, the erotic nature of these illustrations was considered scandalous in Australia, as was his first novel *Redheap* (1931), which was banned. Among other published works are *Saturdee* (1933), *Pan in the Parlour* (1934), *Age of Consent* (1938), and *The Cousin from Fiji* (1945). He was joint founder of the Endeavour press.

Lindsay, Vachel, in full NICHOLAS VACHEL LINDSAY (b. Nov. 10, 1879, Springfield, Ill., U.S.—d. Dec. 5, 1931, Springfield), American poet who—in an attempt to revive poetry as an oral art form of the common people—wrote and read to audiences compositions with powerful rhythms that had an immediate appeal.

Vachel Lindsay
Culver Pictures

After three years at Hiram College, Hiram, Ohio, Lindsay left in 1900 to study art in Chicago and New York City. He supported himself in part by lecturing for the YMCA and the Anti-Saloon League. Having begun to write poetry, he wandered for several summers throughout the country reciting his poems in return for food and shelter.

He first received recognition in 1913, when *Poetry* magazine published his poem on William Booth, founder of the Salvation Army. His poems of this kind are studded with vivid imagery and express both his ardent patriotism and his romantic appreciation of nature. Lindsay's poetry depicted with evocative clarity such leaders of American cults and causes as Alexander Campbell (a founder of the Disciples of Christ), Johnny Appleseed, John Peter Altgeld, and William Jennings Bryan. Lindsay recited his poetry in a highly rhythmic and syncopated manner that was accompanied by dramatic gestures in an attempt to achieve contact with his audience. Among the 20 or so poems that audiences demanded to hear—so often that Lindsay grew weary of reciting them—were "General William Booth Enters into Heaven," "The Congo," and "The Santa Fe Trail." His best volumes of verse include *Rhymes To Be Traded for Bread* (1912), *General William Booth Enters into Heaven and Other Poems* (1913), *The Congo and Other Poems* (1914), and *The Chinese Nightingale and Other Poems* (1917). Both Lindsay's poetic powers and his faculty of self-criticism steadily declined during the 1920s, and he lost his popularity. He committed suicide by drinking poison.

BIBLIOGRAPHY. Edgar Lee Masters, *Vachel Lindsay: A Poet in America* (1935, reissued 1969).

Lindsey, an Anglo-Saxon kingdom, probably coterminous with the modern districts of East Lindsey and West Lindsey, in Lincolnshire. It was an area of early settlement by the Angles and was ruled by its own kings until the late 8th century. In the mid-7th century Northumbria had controlled Lindsey but in 678 finally lost it to the midland kingdom of Mercia. The Danes raided Lindsey in 841, wintered at Torksey in 873, and settled there soon afterward. Lindsey seems to have been recaptured by the Anglo-Saxons in 918, but place-name evidence shows Danish settlement there to have been very intense and that Lindsey supported the Danish invaders Sweyn and Canute in the early 11th century.

The Roman missionary Paulinus converted Lindsey to Christianity about 631, and it had a diocese from 677 to the time of the Danish settlement. In the mid-10th century the diocese was apparently joined to that of Dorchester on Thames (Dorchester, Oxfordshire); after the Norman Conquest (1066), the see was transferred from Dorchester to Lincoln.

Lindsey, Ben B., byname of BENJAMIN BARR LINDSEY (b. Nov. 25, 1869, Jackson, Tenn., U.S.—d. March 26, 1943, Los Angeles, Calif.), American judge, international authority on juvenile delinquency, and reformer of legal procedures concerning offenses by youths and domestic-relations problems. His controversial advocacy of "companionate marriage" was sometimes confused with the "trial marriage" idea of the philosopher Bertrand Russell.

Lindsey was admitted to the Colorado bar in 1894. He wrote the statute establishing a juvenile court in Denver, and from 1900 to 1927 he presided over that tribunal, which was the model for similar courts throughout the United States. He applied the now generally accepted theories that the juvenile offender should be protected as a ward of the court, that treatment of the youth's problem rather than punishment should be the objective, and that equity rather than criminal procedure should be employed. In addition, he secured the passage of contributory delinquency laws against irresponsible parents.

After moving to California, Lindsey was elected judge of the Los Angeles Superior Court in 1934. In that city he helped establish a conciliation court to deal with divorce cases when there was some chance of reconciling the parties; he served as judge of that court from 1939 until his death.

An outspoken foe of political machines, Lindsey was an unsuccessful candidate for governor of Colorado in 1906 and a member of the Progressive (Bull Moose) Party's national committee in 1912. He wrote numerous books, the most widely discussed of which was *The Companionate Marriage* (1927; with Wainwright Evans), in which he argued for birth control to prevent parenthood until a marriage was solidly established and for divorce by mutual consent (but not if children were involved).

line-and-wash drawing, also called PEN-AND-WASH DRAWING, in the visual arts, a drawing marked out by pen or some similar instrument and then tinted with diluted ink or watercolour. In 13th-century China, artists used transparent ink washes to create delicate atmospheric effects. The line-and-wash technique was practiced in Europe from the Renaissance, and in the early 15th century Cennino Cennini gave detailed instructions for reinforcing a pen drawing with the brush. The technique entered into common use in the 16th century and reached its height in the 17th century in the works of Rembrandt, Claude Lorrain, Nicolas Poussin, and a host of Italian artists. The technique was freely used to make preparatory sketches for paintings, with the pen line providing accurate detail and the coloured washes (or brushstrokes) suggesting tone, volume, and atmosphere.

The line-and-wash technique was also used in the topographical drawings of the 18th century and in drawings of buildings, and it was widely recommended in textbooks on sketching. By the early 19th century an emphasis on spontaneity and the free expression of emotion had led to the increasing use of direct colour with little or no underdrawing. Line-and-wash drawing nevertheless continued to attract many artists and is still a common form of graphic expression. *See also* wash drawing.

line integral, also called CONTOUR INTEGRAL, in mathematics, integral of a function of several variables, defined on a line or curve C with respect to arc length s:

$$\int_C f(x,y)\,ds = \lim \sum_{i=1}^{n} f(x_i,y_i)\,\Delta_i s$$

as the maximum segment $\Delta_i s$ of C approaches 0. The line integrals

$$\int_C f(x,y)\,dx \text{ and } \int_C f(x,y)\,dy$$

are defined analogously. Line integrals are used extensively in the theory of functions of a complex variable.

Line Islands, chain of coral atolls in the central Pacific Ocean, some of which belong to the Republic of Kiribati and some of which are claimed as unincorporated territories belonging to the United States.

The Line Islands extend 1,600 miles (2,600 km) northwestward from French Polynesia. They have a land area of 193 square miles (500 square km) and are divided into Northern, Central, and Southern groups. The Northern Line Islands politically comprise Teraina (Washington) Island and Tabuaeran (Fanning) and Kiritimati (Christmas) atolls, all parts of Kiribati from its independence (1979), and Kingman Reef, Palmyra Atoll, and Jarvis Island, all unincorporated territories of the United States. The Central and Southern Line Islands, comprising Malden and Starbuck islands (the Central group) and Vostok and Flint islands, with Caroline Atoll (the Southern group), are also original parts of Kiribati. There is no permanent habitation except on Kiritimati and Tabuaeran atolls and on Teraina Island. Pop. (1990) 4,782.

line of force (physics): *see* force, line of.

lineage, descent group reckoned through only one parent, either paternal (patrilineage) or maternal (matrilineage). All members of such a group trace their common ancestry to a single person. A lineage is exclusive in its membership and is normally corporate, its members exercising rights in common and being collectively subject to obligations. A lineage may comprise any number of generations but commonly is traced through 5 or 10.

Lineage structure may be regarded as a branching process, as when two or three founders of small lineages are represented as brothers. The groups thus constitute a single larger lineage in which the smaller groups are segments. This structure may lend stability to a society; since the lineages are considered permanent groups, political and religious relationships are perpetuated over time through the preservation of the lineal segments.

In societies lacking central political authority, territorial groups often organize themselves around lineages; as these are usually exogamous, marriage becomes a means of bridging the various groups.

Linear A and Linear B, linear forms of writing used by certain Aegean civilizations during the 2nd millennium BC.

Linear A is attested in Crete and on some Aegean islands from approximately 1850 BC to 1400 BC. Its relation to the so-called hieroglyphic Minoan script is uncertain. It is a syllabic script written from left to right. The approximate phonetic values of most syllabic signs used in Linear A are known from Linear B, but the language written in Linear A remains unknown. It must have been a pre-Hellenic language of Minoan Crete. Its eventual relation with the Eteocretan language of the 1st millennium BC is also unknown.

Linear A tablet from Ayía Triádha, Crete, Late Minoan I
Hirmer Fotoarchiv, Munchen

Linear B is an adapted form of Linear A, which was borrowed from the Minoans by the Mycenaean Greeks, probably about 1600 BC. Its language is the Mycenaean Greek dialect. Linear B script is attested on clay tablets and on some vases, both dating from about 1400 BC to roughly 1200 BC. The script was exclusively used for the economic administration of the Mycenaean palaces, such as those at Knossos and Khaniá in Crete, and Mycenae, Pylos, Thebes, and Tiryns in continental Greece. Linear B's 90 syllabic signs express open syllables (*i.e.,* syllables ending in a vowel), generally beginning without a consonant or with only one consonant; because of this, the script is unable to represent groups of consonants or final consonants clearly. For instance, *sperma* 'seed' is spelled *pe-ma,* and *stathmos* 'stable' is spelled *ta-to-mo.*

Linear B inscribed tablet, *c.* 1400 BC, from the Palace of Minos, Knossos, Crete
Hirmer Fotoarchiv, Munchen

The Linear B texts are extremely important for Greek linguistics. They represent the oldest known Greek dialect, elements of which survived in Homer's language as a result of a long oral tradition of epic poetry. Linear B was deciphered as Greek in 1952 by Michael Ventris.

linear accelerator, also called LINAC, type of particle accelerator (*q.v.*) that imparts a series of relatively small increases in energy to subatomic particles as they pass through a sequence of alternating electric fields set up in a linear structure. The small accelerations add together to give the particles a greater energy than could be achieved by the voltage used in one section alone.

In 1924 Gustaf Ising, a Swedish physicist, proposed accelerating particles using alternating electric fields, with "drift tubes" positioned at appropriate intervals to shield the particles during the half-cycle when the field is in the wrong direction for acceleration. Four years later, the Norwegian engineer Rolf Wideröe built the first machine of this kind, successfully accelerating potassium ions to an energy of 50,000 electron volts (50 kiloelectron volts).

Linear machines for accelerating lighter particles, such as protons and electrons, awaited the advent of powerful radio-frequency oscillators, which were developed for radar during World War II. Proton linacs typically operate at frequencies of about 200 megahertz (MHz), while the accelerating force in electron linacs is provided by an electromagnetic field with a microwave frequency of about 3,000 MHz.

The proton linac, designed by the American physicist Luis Alvarez in 1946, is a more efficient variant of Wideröe's structure. In this accelerator, electric fields are set up as standing waves within a cylindrical metal "resonant cavity," with drift tubes suspended along the central axis. The largest proton linac is at the Clinton P. Anderson Meson Physics Facility in Los Alamos, N.M., U.S.; it is 875 m (2,870 feet) long and accelerates protons to 800 million electron volts (800 megaelectron volts). For much of its length, this machine utilizes a structural variation, known as the side-coupled cavity accelerator, in which acceleration occurs in on-axis cells that are coupled together by cavities mounted to their sides. These coupling cavities serve to stabilize the performance of the accelerator against changes in the resonant frequencies of the accelerating cells.

Electron linacs utilize traveling waves rather than standing waves. Because of their small mass, electrons travel at close to the speed of light at energies as low as 5 megaelectron volts. They can therefore travel along the linac with the accelerating wave, in effect riding the crest of the wave and thus always experiencing an accelerating field. The world's longest electron linac is the 3.2-kilometre (2-mile) machine at the Stanford (University) Linear Accelerator Center, Menlo Park, Calif., U.S.; it can accelerate electrons to 50 billion electron volts (50 gigaelectron volts). Much smaller linacs, both proton and electron types, have important practical applications in medicine and in industry. (Ch.Su.)

linear equation, statement that a first-degree polynomial—that is, the sum of a set of terms, each of which is the product of a constant and the first power of a variable—is equal to zero. Specifically, a linear equation in n variables is of the form $a_0 + a_1x_1 + \cdot \cdot \cdot + a_nx_n = 0$, in which $x_1, \ldots, x_n$ are variables and $a_0, \ldots, a_n$ are scalars. If there is more than one variable, the equation may be linear in some and not in the others. Thus the equation $x + y = 3$ is linear in both x and y, whereas $x + y^2 = 0$ is linear in x but not in y. Any equation of two variables, linear in each, represents a straight line in Cartesian coordinates; in the absence of a constant term, the line passes through the origin.

A set of equations that has a common solution is called a system of simultaneous equations. For example, in the system

$$2x - y = 1$$
$$x + 2y = 8$$

both equations are satisfied by the solution $x = 2$, $y = 3$. The point (2,3) is the intersection of the straight lines represented by the two equations. *See also* Cramer's rule.

A linear differential equation is of first degree with respect to the dependent variable (or variables) and its (or their) derivatives. As a simple example, note $dy/dx + Py = Q$, in which P and Q can be constants or may be functions of the independent variable, x, but do not involve the dependent variable, y.

linear motor, power source providing electric traction in a straight line, rather than rotary, as in a conventional motor; it is useful in such applications as high-speed ground transportation. In one form designed for rail vehicles, a continuous stationary conductor is fastened to the roadbed and a double stator is suspended between the wheels in the centre of the vehicle, straddling the stationary conductor. Electric energy is generated on the vehicle or is picked up by trolley from a power line paralleling the track. This energy is fed to the double stator to produce traction in a linear direction.

Linear motors may be used to actuate belt conveyors, shuttles in textile looms, and other devices requiring a linear motion. An electromagnetic pump is a linear motor in which the solid conductor is replaced by a conducting fluid such as a liquid metal. The force on the conducting fluid produces the pumping action.

linear programming, mathematical modeling technique useful for guiding quantitative decisions in business planning, industrial engineering, and—to a lesser extent—in the social and physical sciences.

Applications of the method of linear programming were first seriously attempted in the late 1930s by the Soviet mathematician Leonid Kantorovich and by the American economist Wassily Leontief in the areas of manufacturing schedules and of economics, respectively, but their work was ignored for decades. During World War II, linear programming was used extensively to deal with transportation, scheduling, and allocation of resources subject to certain restrictions such as costs and availability. These applications did much to establish the acceptability of this method, which gained further impetus in 1947 with the introduction of the American mathematician George Dantzig's simplex method, which greatly simplified the solution of linear programming problems. However, as increasingly more complex problems involving more variables were attempted, the number of necessary operations expanded exponentially and exceeded the computational capacity of even the most powerful computers. Then, in 1979, the Russian mathematician Leonid Khachian discovered a polynomial-time algorithm—*i.e.,* the number of computational steps grows as a power of the number of variables, rather than exponentially—thereby allowing the solution of hitherto inaccessible problems.

The solution of a linear-programming problem reduces to finding the optimum value (largest or smallest, depending on the problem) of the linear expression (called the objective function):

$$f = c_1x_1 + \ldots + c_nx_n$$

subject to a set of constraints expressed as inequalities:

$$a_{11}x_1 + \ldots + a_{1n}x_n \le b_1$$
$$\vdots$$
$$a_{m1}x_1 + \ldots + a_{mn}x_n \le b_m \text{ with } \forall\, x_i \ge 0.$$

The a's, b's, and c's are constants determined by the capacities, needs, costs, profits, and other requirements and restrictions of the problem. The basic assumption in the application of this method is that the various relationships between demand and availability are linear; that is, none of the x_i is raised to a power other than 1. In order to obtain the solution to this problem it is necessary to find the solution of the system of linear inequalities (that is, the set of n values of the variables x_i that simultaneously satisfies all the inequalities). The objective function is then evaluated by substituting the values of the x_i in the equation that defines f.

ling (*Molva molva*), in zoology, commercially valuable marine fish of the cod family (Gadidae), found in deep northern waters near Iceland, the British Isles, and Scandinavia. The ling is a slim, long-bodied fish with small scales, a long anal fin, and two dorsal fins, the second being much longer than the first. A large, mottled, brown or greenish fish, the ling may grow to a length of about 2 m (almost 7 feet). It is related to two other deepwater European fishes: the Spanish, or Mediterranean, ling (*M. macrophthalma,* or *M. elongata*) and the blue ling (*M. dypterygia,* or *M. byrkelange*).

ling (botany): *see* heather.

Ling Canal, Chinese (Wade-Giles) LING CH'Ü, or (Pinyin) LING QU, canal in northern Chuang autonomous *ch'ü* (region) of Kwangsi, China. Ling Canal was constructed to connect the headwaters of the Hsiang River flowing north into Hunan *sheng* (province), with the Li River, one of the headwater tributaries of the Kuei River, a tributary of the Hsi River leading eventually to Canton. Near the city of Hsing-an in northern Kwangsi, these two rivers are separated by a low divide broken by a saddle. A contour canal was built leading water diverted from the Hsiang River along some 3 miles (5 km) of gentle gradient into the Li River. Below the point at which the water for the canal was diverted, another canal, the Pei Canal, some 1.5 miles (2.4 km) long, diverted the waters of the Hsiang itself to provide a better channel. The main section of the canal joining the two rivers was called the Nan Canal. The course of the Li River, unsuited in its natural state for navigation, was canalized for some 17 miles (27 km) to its junction with the Kuei River.

This canal was first constructed about 215 BC to supply the armies of the Ch'in dynasty (221–206 BC) in their campaigns against the state of Nan Yüeh in Kwangtung province, providing a water route from the Yangtze River and Ch'ang-sha in Hunan to Canton. It was kept in repair and used regularly during the Han period (206 BC–AD 220), at least from 140 BC to AD 50. During this period the route through Hunan was the chief route from central to southern China. Early in the 9th century the Ling Canal fell into disrepair and became impassable. In 825 the canal was rebuilt with a system of locks, but in the 11th or 12th century these were replaced by a series of 36 improved locks that made it possible for larger boats to pass through. The canal is still in use although it can take only relatively small craft.

ling lung ware, Pinyin LING LONG, Chinese porcelain made in the late Ming dynasty (reign of Wan-li, 1572–1620) and characterized by pierced ornamentation. *Ling lung* ware is generally limited to small objects such as cups, brushpots, and covered jars. The decoration is sometimes biscuit (unglazed porcelain), either left white or enhanced with touches of gilding or coloured glazes. Much *ling lung* ware was made for the export trade by the Ching-te-chen kilns (in Kiangsi), whose potters protested against the imperial order to make this *kuei kung* ("devil's work"), as *ling lung* was also called in China. The term is thought to refer to the devilish skill needed to produce such porcelain openwork, but it is possible that it refers to the foreign markets for which it was destined. Although *ling lung* was also made during the reign of the Ch'ing emperor K'ang-hsi (1661–1722) and for the

Ling lung perfume bowl and cover, Wan-li period, Ming dynasty; in the Victoria and Albert Museum, London

By courtesy of the Victoria and Albert Museum, London

rest of the 18th century, the best wares are of late Ming vintage.

Ling Qu (China): *see* Ling Canal.

liṅga, also spelled LIṄGAM (Sanskrit: "sign," "distinguishing symbol"), in Hinduism, the phallus, symbol of the god Śiva, worshipped as an emblem of generative power. The *liṅga* is the main object of worship in Śaivite temples and private family shrines throughout India. Anthropomorphic representations of Śiva are less commonly worshipped. The *yoni,* which is the symbol of the female sexual organ (and thus of the goddess Śakti, consort of Śiva), often forms the base of the erect *liṅga;* the two together are a reminder to the devotee that the male and female principles are forever inseparable and that together they represent the totality of all existence.

Sandstone *liṅga*, *c.* 900; in the British Museum
Reproduced by courtesy of the trustees of the British Museum

Scholars believe that the cult of the *liṅga* has been followed by some non-Aryan peoples of India since antiquity, and short, cylindrical pillars with rounded tops have been found in Harappan remains. The Vedic Aryans appeared to have disapproved of *liṅga* worship, but literary and artistic evidence shows that it was firmly established by the 1st–2nd century AD. The process of conventionalizing its representation began during the Gupta period, so that in later periods its original phallic realism was to a considerable degree lost.

Worship of the *liṅga* is performed with offerings of fresh flowers, pure water, young sprouts of grass, fruit, leaves, and sun-dried rice. The purity of the materials and the cleanliness of the worshipper are particularly stressed. Among the most important of all *liṅga*s are the *svāyambhuva* ("self-originated") *liṅga*s, which are believed to have come into existence by themselves at the beginning of time; nearly 70 are worshipped in various parts of India. Images of *liṅga*s created by hand range from simple ones made of sandal paste or of river clay for a particular rite, and then disposed of, to more elaborate ones of wood, precious gems, metal, or stone. The canons of sculpture lay down exact rules of proportion to be followed for the height, width, and curvature of the top. The *mukhaliṅga* has from one to five faces of Śiva carved on its sides and top. Another common icon in South India is the *liṅgōdbhavamūrti,* which shows Śiva emerging out of a fiery *liṅga.* This is a representation of the sectarian myth that the gods Vishnu and Brahmā were once arguing about their respective importance when Śiva appeared in the form of a blazing pillar to quell their pride. Brahmā took the form of a swan and flew upward to see if he could find the top of the pillar, and Vishnu took the form of a boar and dived below to find its source, but neither was successful, and both were compelled to recognize Śiva's superiority.

Liṅgāyat, also called VĪRAŚAIVA, member of a Hindu sect with a wide following in South India that worships Śiva as the only deity. The followers take their name ("*liṅga*-wearers") from the small representations of a *liṅga,* a phallic figure symbolizing Śiva, which both the men and women always wear hanging by a cord around their necks, in place of the sacred thread worn by most orthodox upper caste Hindu men.

The sect is generally regarded as having been founded by Basava in the 12th century, but some scholars believe that he furthered an already existing creed. Philosophically, their qualified spiritual monism and their conception of bhakti (devotion) as an intuitive and loving knowledge of God show the influence of the 11th/12th-century thinker Rāmānuja. It is in their cult and social observances that their split with orthodoxy is most apparent.

The Liṅgāyats' earlier overthrow of caste distinctions has been modified in modern times, but the sect continues to be strongly anti-Brahmanical and opposed to worship of any image other than the *liṅga.* In their rejection of the authority of the Vedas, the doctrine of transmigration of souls, child marriage, and ill treatment of widows, they anticipated much of the viewpoint of the social-reform movements of the 19th century.

Lingayen Gulf, large inlet of the South China Sea that indents the western coast of central Luzon, Philippines, for 36 mi (56 km). It is 26 mi wide at its entrance between Santiago Island (west) and San Fernando Point (east). Santiago, Cabarruyan, and Hundred Islands (site of Manleluang Spring National Park) lie within the gulf. Dagupan, a chartered city on its southern shore, is the principal commercial centre, and the port of Lingayen, the provincial capital, lies at the Agno River Delta. During World War II Japan (December 1941) and the United States (January 1945) landed forces on the shores of the gulf.

lingcod (*Ophiodon elongatus*), commercially popular species of fish in the family Hexagrammidae (order Scorpaeniformes). A voracious predator, the lingcod has a large mouth and canine-like teeth for eating fishes and other aquatic prey, including squid. The species is strictly marine, occurring along the Pacific coast of North America.

Lingcods are popular game and commercial fish that may reach a length of 1.5 metres (5 feet). They have well-developed fins and tails. Although the meat has a greenish colour, it is considered highly edible. The lingcod belongs to the greenling (*q.v.*) group of fishes.

Lingdan (Mongol chief): *see* Ligdan.

Linggadjati Agreement, also called CHERIBON AGREEMENT (drafted Nov. 15, 1946), treaty between the Dutch and the Republic of Indonesia, concluded on Linggadjati hill near Cheribon (modern Cirebon, formerly Tjirebon, western Java). Soon after the capitulation of the Japanese in World War II, the independence of the Republic of Indonesia was declared, on Aug. 17, 1945, by the Indonesian nationalists. The Dutch attempted to restore their rule in Indonesia and hence came into conflict with the republican government, whose influence was still confined to Java and Sumatra. Upon the departure of the Allied troops, the Dutch and the republic began negotiations, which led to the Linggadjati Agreement that was signed in Batavia (modern Jakarta) on March 25, 1947.

The main content of the agreement was that The Netherlands recognized the republic as the de facto authority in Java (including Madura) and Sumatra. Both governments were to cooperate in the formation of a sovereign, democratic, and federal United States of Indonesia, comprising the entire territories of the Dutch East Indies, including the Republic of Indonesia, Kalimantan (Borneo), and the Great East. Both governments were to cooperate in establishing a Netherlands–Indonesian Union with the Dutch queen as its head. Both the United States of Indonesia and the Netherlands–Indonesian Union were to be formed not later than Jan. 1, 1949. The two governments agreed to settle by arbitration any dispute that might arise and that they could not settle by themselves. The agreement was intended to lay down broad principles, leaving the details to be worked out later. Each party interpreted the agreement to suit its interests, however, and eventually open conflict developed between the Dutch and Indonesian governments.

Lingones, Celtic tribe that originally lived in Gaul in the area of the Seine and Marne rivers. Some of the Lingones migrated across the Alps and settled near the mouth of the Po River in Italy around 400 BC. These Lingones were part of a wave of Celtic tribes that included the Boii and Senoni; the Lingones may have helped sack Rome in 390 BC.

The Italian Lingones were an agricultural people highly skilled in metalworking and in weaving. After periodic war between the Celts and the Romans in Italy, they submitted in 224 BC. No further record of them exists after the Gallic Wars of the 190s. The Gallic Lingones were allies of Julius Caesar when he conquered Gaul. The emperor Otho gave them Roman citizenship in 69 AD.

lingua franca, auxiliary or compromise language used between groups having no other language in common. Examples are English and French for diplomatic purposes, Swahili in eastern Africa, Hindi and English in India, Melanesian Pidgin in the South Pacific, and Bazaar Malay in the East Indian archipelago. The term lingua franca ("Frankish language") was perhaps first applied to a jargon or pidgin based on southern French and Italian, developed by crusaders and traders for use in the eastern Mediterranean during the Middle Ages. In the post-Renaissance period of European exploration, many other such contact languages developed—*e.g.,* Indo-Portuguese (Ceylon), Annamite-French (Indochina), Papiamento (based on Spanish, spoken in Curaçao), and several types of Pidgin English—all of these based on the languages of the European colonizing nations. Insofar as a European language was simplified or distorted in pronunciation or grammar, it became a pidgin. When such a pidgin or other lingua franca replaced the original language of a speech community, it became a creole (*q.v.*).

lingua-geral, lingua franca developed in Brazil under Portuguese influence in the 16th and 17th centuries as a medium of communication between Europeans and Indians and between Indians of different languages. *Língua-geral* was a modification of the Tupinambá Indian language.

Linguet, Simon-Nicolas-Henri (b. July 14, 1736, Reims, Fr.—d. June 27, 1794, Paris), French journalist and lawyer whose delight in taking views opposing everyone else's earned him exiles, imprisonment, and finally the guillotine.

He attended the Collège de Beauvais, winning the three highest prizes there in 1751. Received at first into the ranks of the Philosophes, he soon went over to their opponents and thenceforth attacked whatever was considered modern and enlightened. His early writings include *Histoire du siècle d'Alexandre le Grand* (1762), in which he declared that Nero caused far fewer deaths than Alexander, and *Le Fanatisme des philosophes* (1764), a violent attack on the most widely held doctrines of the Enlightenment.

He was admitted as an advocate in the Paris Parlement in 1764, and his greatest masterpiece of pleading was his *Mémoire* of 1772 on behalf of the Comte de Morangiès, accused of trying to defraud his creditors. His attacks on other lawyers, however, led to his expulsion from the bar in 1775. He went into exile, travelled in Switzerland, Holland, and England and launched the *Annales politiques, civiles et littéraires du XVIIIe siècle* (1777–92). Soon after his return to France he began an attack on the Duc de Duras and was imprisoned in the Bastille (1780–82). On his release he went back to England, where he published *Mémoires sur la Bastille* (1783). Proceeding to Brussels, he obtained titles of nobility and 1,000 ducats from the Holy Roman emperor Joseph II; yet, in 1789 he argued in favour of the Belgian insurgents against Joseph's regime.

During the French Revolution, Linguet presented several eloquent petitions, including one to the Constituent Assembly in defense of the inhabitants of San Domingo against the "white tyrants" in 1791. He retired to Marnes, near Ville d'Avray, in 1792. Arrested there, he was eventually tried and condemned to death in Paris for having "flattered the despots of Vienna and London."

Among his more important works are the following: *Théorie des lois civiles* (1767), an attack on Montesquieu; *Histoire impartiale des Jésuites* (1768); and *Histoire des révolutions de l'empire romain* (2nd ed., 1766–68).

Linguistic philosophy: *see* Analytic philosophy.

linguistics, the study of language as system. It involves an investigation of the nature, structure, constituent units, and modification of any such system.

A brief treatment of linguistics follows. For full treatment, *see* MACROPAEDIA: Linguistics.

Linguistics is called theoretical when it attempts to establish a theory of the underlying structure of language, and is called applied when linguistic concepts are put to use for pedagogical purposes. Linguists may use either a synchronic approach to language study (*i.e.*, describe a particular language at a particular time) or a diachronic approach (*i.e.*, trace the development of a particular language through its history). Theoretical linguistics tends to isolate the structure of language from actual language production and therefore favours the synchronic approach when describing a language. Theoretical linguistics does not take into account language acquisition, usage, or any other aspects of language that are studied by scholars in such specialized fields of linguistics as psycholinguistics, sociolinguistics, and anthropological linguistics. Findings from these fields often become useful tools in the hands of applied linguists.

Greek philosophers of the 5th century BC were the first in the West to be concerned with linguistic theory. For the philosophers, controversial linguistic issues revolved around the origin of the human language and the grammatical structure of Greek. In the 1st century BC, the first complete Greek grammar was written by Dionysus Thrax, an Alexandrian. It was so influential that it served as a model for Roman grammarians, whose work, in turn, became the basis for grammars of the vernacular languages written during the Middle Ages and Renaissance. Except for occasional groups of dissenting scholars, such as the speculative grammarians of the 13th and 14th centuries, most scholars confined their work to a study of Latin and Greek or to the creation of prescriptive grammars of vernacular languages in order to teach "correct" usage. After the Renaissance, however, interest in the grammars of the world's languages started to grow. The fruits of that interest led to important discoveries that helped establish linguistics as a science in the 19th century.

The historical linguists of the 19th century developed the comparative method of diachronic description, which consisted of comparing different languages in terms of their grammar, vocabulary, and phonology in the hope of finding a common ancestral language. This the historical linguists did accomplish when they discovered that Sanskrit, Greek, and Latin were related, that most of the languages of Europe had family relationships, and that all these languages descended from a common language called Proto-Indo-European. It was also shown that, through the centuries, systematic changes in pronunciation were responsible for the differentiation of languages.

The Swiss linguist, Ferdinand de Saussure, was largely responsible for changing the course of linguistic study in the late 19th and early 20th centuries. Although a comparative or historical linguist in his early work, Saussure broke new ground by drawing the distinction between diachronic and synchronic linguistics and by introducing another distinction between *langue* (language) and *parole* (speech). For Saussure, *langue* referred to the unobservable underlying structure of language and *parole* was the outward manifestation of that structure. With the posthumous publication of his *Cours de Linguistique Générale* (1916), in which these distinctions were made public, a new era of linguistic study called structuralism began. Saussure redefined the goal for linguistics: to describe the nature of *la langue*. Although the structuralists who followed Saussure, such as the U.S. linguists Edward Sapir and Leonard Bloomfield, differed as to what linguistics should specifically study and for what reasons, there was a concerted effort among structuralists to insist that language study be based on empirical evidence. Structuralists also moved away from previous prescriptive approaches by looking at language the way it is, not the way someone thinks it should be.

By the 1950s, weaknesses in structuralism were being identified by some linguists. They pointed out that, because structural linguists had never fully accepted Saussure's implied notion that the human language system is a mental property, they had to limit their subject matter to observable phenomena only. As a result, some of them tended to ignore those aspects of language that cannot be observed and to overlook those things that characterize all languages.

The U.S. linguist Noam Chomsky challenged the structuralist approach by saying that universal patterns are present in all languages. Because he was interested in understanding how the mind works through studying language, Chomsky stressed the "mentalistic" theory of language that structuralists had rejected. The goals of linguistics changed once again as a result of Chomsky's work. He claimed that linguistics should study a native speaker's unconscious knowledge of his or her own language (competence), not the speaker's actual production of language (performance).

Because Chomsky thought that a description of the rules that make up a native speaker's *competence* could account for an infinite number of examples of *performance*, he wanted to write a grammar that would identify those unconscious rules. Unlike the structuralists, then, who collected samples of language produced by native speakers and then classified them, Chomsky developed transformational grammar, a set of rules that could generate structural descriptions for all the grammatical sentences of a language, and he tested results against actual language samples.

Transformational grammar has been continually evolving since Chomsky first introduced it in *Syntactic Structures* in 1957. From the 1970s on, many transformationalists focussed their attention on the relation between syntax and semantics, an issue that was largely ignored by Chomsky until 1965.

lingulid, any member of a group of brachiopods, or lamp shells, that includes very ancient extinct forms as well as surviving representatives. First known from Cambrian rocks (about 500,000,000 to 570,000,000 years old), they probably originated during Precambrian time. The lingulids are small, inarticulate brachiopods; their shells are unhinged and consist

Lingulid

By courtesy of the trustees of the British Museum (Natural History); photograph, Imitor

of chitinous (fingernail-like) material. A modern genus, *Lingula,* is found in normal marine environments but is most common in muddy, brackish water that is poor in oxygen and generally unsuited to most organisms. The genus *Lingulella* is a fossil form known from the Cambrian and was similar in appearance and structure to the modern *Lingula. Lingulepis,* a related genus more or less restricted to the Late Cambrian, differs from other lingulids in appearance; it is more teardrop in form. The lingulids are useful fossils for the environmental information that they provide; they are of little use for stratigraphic correlations. The lingulids were an important component of Cambrian brachiopod faunas.

link-and-link stitch (knitting): *see* purl stitch.

Link Trainer, airplane cockpit replicated, with full instruments and controls, in such a way that it can be used in a ground location for pilot training. The cockpit responds to the controls as though it were an airplane in flight. The Link Trainer was the first effective flight simulator (*q.v.*).

linkage, in mechanical engineering, a system of solid, usually metallic, links (bars) connected to two or more other links by pin joints (hinges), sliding joints, or ball-and-socket joints so as to form a closed chain or a series of closed chains. When one of the links is fixed, the possible movements of the other links relative to the fixed link and to one another will depend on the number of links and the number and types of joints. With four pin-connected links, for example, the links all move in parallel planes, and regardless of which link is fixed, the other links have constrained motion; *i.e.,* they move in a fixed and determinate way relative to the fixed link. By varying the relative lengths of the links, this four-bar linkage becomes a useful mechanism for converting uniform rotary to non-uniform rotary motion or continuous rotary to oscillatory motion; it is the most commonly used linkage mechanism in machine construction.

linkage group, in genetics, all of the genes on a single chromosome. They are inherited as a group; that is, during cell division they act and move as a unit rather than independently. The existence of linkage groups is the reason some traits do not comply with Mendel's law of independent assortment (recombination of genes and the traits they control); *i.e.,* the principle applies only if genes are located on different chromosomes. Variation in the gene composition of a chromosome can occur when a chromosome breaks, and the sections join with the partner chromosome if it has broken in the same places. This exchange of genes between chromosomes, called crossing over, usually occurs during meiosis, when the total number of chromosomes is halved.

Sex linkage is the tendency of a characteristic to be linked to one sex. The X chromosome in *Drosophila* flies and human beings, for example, carries a complete set of genes; the Y chromosome has only a few genes. Eggs of females carry an X chromosome; sperm of males may carry an X or a Y. An egg fertilized by a sperm with an X chromosome results in a female; one fertilized by a sperm with a Y chromosome results in a male. In offspring with the XY chromosome pair, any trait carried by the X chromosome will appear unless there is a corresponding gene (allele) on the Y chromosome. Examples of sex-linked traits in man are red–green colour blindness and hemophilia. These traits are controlled by genes on the X chromosome and thus occur much more frequently in men than in women because there is no allele on the Y chromosome to offset them. *See also* sex chromosome.

linkage isomerism, the existence of coordination compounds having the same atomic composition but differing in the attachment to the central atom of a ligand group; certain such groups, called ambident ligands, contain more than one atom by which they may bind to the central atom: the nitrogen-oxygen group NO_2, for example, binds through its nitrogen atom in nitro compounds but through one of its oxygen atoms in nitrito compounds.

Linked Ring, association of English photographers formed in 1892, one of the first groups to promote the idea that photography is an art. Henry Peach Robinson (*q.v.*) was notable among the founding members.

The Linked Ring called its annual exhibitions salons, a name that was borrowed from the world of painting and demonstrated its artistic motivation. The members of the group refused to exhibit photographs that, in their judgment, failed to further "the development of the highest form of art of which photography is capable." They also made innovations in the display of photographs. Instead of crowding photographs onto a wall from ceiling to floor, as was usually done, the Linked Ring photographers displayed their work at eye level, and their galleries were decorated with flowers and pastel designs drawn on the walls and occasionally on the frames. This self-consciously artistic attitude was subsequently adopted by European groups, such as the Photo-Club de Paris. In America, the Photo-Secession Group (*q.v.*) promulgated similar ideas.

Linklater, Eric (Robert) (b. March 8, 1899, Dounby, Orkney Islands, Scot.—d. Nov. 7, 1974, Aberdeen), British novelist, poet, and historical writer noted for his satiric wit.

Linklater began studying medicine at Aberdeen University but switched to English literature. After service in the Black Watch in World War I, during which he was wounded, he turned to journalism, becoming assistant editor of the *Times of India* (1925–27). He taught English at Aberdeen and in 1928–30 visited the United States on a Commonwealth Fellowship. That visit produced the first of his "innocent abroad" novels, *Juan in America* (1931). During World War II Linklater commanded the Orkney Fortress and worked in the War Office. After the war he became rector of Aberdeen University (1945–48).

Linklater's early novels include *White-Maa's Saga* (1929), *The Men of Ness* (1932), and *Magnus Merriman* (1934). He was a prolific writer, and his 30th book, *The Voyage of the Challenger* (1972), a nonfictional account of the expedition of HMS *Challenger* in 1872–76, has all the verve that his early works displayed. Linklater wrote three volumes of autobiography, *The Man on My Back* (1941), *A Year of Space* (1953), and *Fanfare for a Tin Hat* (1970).

Linköping, city and capital of Östergötland *län* (county), southeastern Sweden, on the Stång River near its outflow into Rox Lake. The site has been settled since the Bronze Age. During the Middle Ages it attained commercial importance and was surpassed as a cultural and religious centre only by Uppsala and Lund. Several important diets were held there during the reign of Gustav I Vasa. In 1598 at Linköping the battle against King Sigismund III Vasa preserved the Evangelical Lutheran Church in Sweden and secured the Swedish throne for the Vasa dynasty. Two years later four of Sigismund's partisans were beheaded on Stora Torget (Main Square), an event known as "the Linköping Massacre." After a fire in 1700 the city declined.

The "Fountain of the Folkungs" by Carl Milles, Linköping, Swed.
Refot

Industrial development came with the building of the Göta and Kinda canals and the Stockholm–Malmö railway. The city is a rail junction, with aircraft, freight car, and automobile industries. The University of Linköping, affiliated with the University of Stockholm, was founded in 1970. Pop. (1989 est.) mun., 119,167.

Linlithgow, royal burgh (1389) and seat of West Lothian district, Lothian region, Scotland. It contains one of Scotland's four royal palaces, which now stands roofless. The building of the palace was begun by James I of Scotland, and it subsequently became a favourite abode of Scottish kings: Mary, Queen of Scots, and her father, James V, were both born there. The castle was burned down in 1746.

Extensive rebuilding has developed the town as a residence for commuters to the nearby industrial towns of Grangemouth and Bathgate. Its own industries include papermaking and whisky distilling. Pop. (1981) 9,544.

Linlithgow, Victor Alexander John Hope, 2nd Marquess of, EARL OF HOPETOUN, VISCOUNT OF AITHRIE, LORD HOPE, BARON HOPETOUN OF HOPETOUN, BARON NIDDRY OF NIDDRY (b. Sept. 24, 1887, Abercorn, West Lothian, Scot.—d. Jan. 5, 1952, Abercorn), British statesman and longest serving viceroy of India (1936–43) who suppressed opposition to British presence there during World War II. He succeeded to the marquessate in 1908.

During World War I (1914–18) Linlithgow served on the western front. In 1922 he was appointed a civil lord of the Admiralty, and, when the first Labour government was formed in 1924, he was selected deputy chairman of the Conservative and Unionist Party organization. Exposed to India's problems as chairman of the royal commission on agriculture in India (1926–28) and of the select committee on Indian constitutional reform, he succeeded Lord Willingdon as viceroy in 1936. According to the Government of India Act of 1935, the provinces were to be governed by ministries responsible to the elected legislatures. The Indian nationalist Congress Party, with clear majorities in five of the 11 provinces, was unwilling to take office without assurance that the governors would not use their reserve powers to override the ministries. Because Linlithgow overcame these fears, provincial autonomy functioned smoothly, but he failed to secure consent of the princes, which was necessary for establishment of the federal structure provided by the statute.

Linlithgow
Keystone

In September 1939 Linlithgow broadcast an appeal for unity in the war against Germany before consulting the Indian political parties, offending the Congress Party leaders, who then asked their provincial ministers to resign. The Congress Party leaders also refused Linlithgow's offer of representation in his executive council; nevertheless, he enlarged the council's number of Indian members. Added to the Japanese threat to British control of India during World War II was the attempt in August 1942 at a mass civil-disobedience campaign by the Congress Party, which was dissatisfied by Britain's refusal to grant independence to India. Linlithgow interned its leaders and suppressed resistance to the government. By the date of his retirement in 1943, a completely volunteer army of more than 2,000,000 men, plus considerable contingents from the Indian states, had joined the British military efforts.

linnaeite, a cobalt sulfide mineral (Co_3S_4) or any member of a series of similar substances with the general formula $(Co,Ni)_2(Co, Ni, Fe, Cu)S_4$. The other known members of the series are siegenite, $(Co,Ni)_3S_4$ with Co:Ni = 1:1; carrollite, Co_2CuS_4; violarite, Ni_2FeS_4; and polydymite, Ni_3S_4. The linnaeites are usually associated with other metal sulfides in hydrothermal veins. A typical occurrence is the Siegen district, Germany. The members of this series crystallize in the isometric system; they all have spinellike structures. For chemical formulas and detailed physical properties, *see* sulfide mineral (table).

Linnaeus, Carolus (Latin), also called CARL LINNAEUS, Swedish CARL VON LINNÉ (b. May 23, 1707, Råshult, Småland, Swed.—d. Jan. 10, 1778, Uppsala), Swedish botanist and explorer who was the first to frame principles for defining genera and species of organisms and to create a uniform system for naming them.

Linnaeus, detail of a portrait by A. Roslin, 1775; in the Svenska Porträttarkivet, Stockholm
By courtesy of the Svenska Portrattarkivet, Stockholm

Linnaeus was the son of a curate. His love of flowers developed at an early age; when only eight years old he was nicknamed "the little botanist." He studied at the universities of Lund and Uppsala and received his degree in medicine from the latter.

At Uppsala he met the veteran botanist Olof Celsius, who had a profound influence on Linnaeus' subsequent career. Linnaeus was appointed lecturer in botany in 1730 and two years later conducted explorations in Lapland for the Uppsala Academy of Sciences. The results of his journey were published in Amsterdam in 1737 as the *Flora Lapponica* and in English by Sir J.E. Smith as *Lachesis Lapponica* (1811). His reputation was firmly established by this work and, even more, by the appearance in 1735 of his *Systema Naturae* and of the *Genera Plantarum* two years later (the *Species Plantarum* was not published until 1753). For purposes of nomenclature of flowering plants and ferns, the first edition of the *Species Plantarum* has been internationally agreed upon as the starting point, together with the fifth edition of the *Genera Plantarum,* published in 1754.

The *Systema Naturae,* which Linnaeus had shown to the botanist Jan Fredrik Gronovius in manuscript, so impressed Gronovius that he published it at his own expense. Linnaeus' system was based mainly on flower parts, which tend to remain unchanged during the course of evolution. Although artificial, as Linnaeus himself recognized, such a system had the supreme merit of enabling students rapidly to place a plant in a named category. It came into use at a period when the richness of the world's vegetation was being discovered at a rate that outstripped more leisurely methods of investigation. So successful was his method in practice that its very ease of application proved to be the greatest obstacle to its replacement by the more natural systems that superseded it.

In 1736 Linnaeus visited England, where he met the botanist and physician Sir Hans Sloane in London and Johann Jakob Dillenius, the first professor of botany at Oxford. He returned to Holland to complete his work on the famous *Hortus Cliffortianus* and in Paris visited the three Jussieu brothers, distinguished botanists with whom he established a close friendship. Soon afterward, he went once again to Sweden, and in 1738 he settled in Stockholm as a practicing physician, a profession in which he attained considerable success. In 1739 he married Sara Moraea, the daughter of a physician. Two years after his marriage he was appointed to the chair of medicine at Uppsala, but a year later he exchanged this for the chair of botany, his true calling. An inveterate classifier, he not only systematized the plant and animal kingdoms but even classified the mineral kingdom and drew up a treatise on the kinds of diseases known in his day.

His later years were taken up by teaching and the preparation of other works: *Flora Suecica* (1745) and *Fauna Suecica* (1746); two volumes of observations made during journeys in Sweden, *Västgöta resa* (1747) and *Skånska resa* (1751); *Hortus Upsaliensis* (1748); his *Philosophia Botanica* (1751); and the important *Species Plantarum* (1753), in which the specific names are fully set forth. In 1755 he declined an invitation from the King of Spain to settle in that country with a liberal salary and full liberty of conscience. In 1761 he was granted a Swedish patent of nobility, antedated to 1757, from which time he was styled Carl von Linné. An apoplectic attack in 1774 left him greatly weakened, and he died four years later.

The Linnaean manuscripts, and his herbarium and collections of insects and shells, purchased by Sir J.E. Smith in 1783, are carefully preserved by the Linnean Society at Burlington House, London. (E.J.S.)

BIBLIOGRAPHY. The most comprehensive work on Linnaeus is T.M. Fries, *Linné, Lefnadsteckning,* 2 vol. in 11 parts (1903; *Linnaeus,* 1923), including a selective but extensive bibliography. Other studies recommended are: B.D. Jackson, *Linnaeus* (1923); Wilfred Blunt, *The Compleat Naturalist: A Life of Linnaeus* (1971); and James L. Larson, *Reason and Experience: The Representation of Natural Order in the Work of Carl von Linné* (1971).

Linnankoski, Johannes, pseudonym of VIHTORI PELTONEN (b. Oct. 18, 1869, Askola, Russian Finland—d. Aug. 10, 1913, Helsinki), novelist, orator, and champion of Finnish independence from Russia; his works were instrumental in forming Finnish national consciousness in the early 20th century.

Linnankoski
By courtesy of the Embassy of Finland, Washington, D.C.

Linnankoski was of peasant origin and largely self-taught. His finest novel, *Pakolaiset* (1908; "The Fugitives"), is about peasant life. More popular in his day was *Laulu tulipunaisesta kukasta* (1905; *The Song of the Blood-Red Flower,* 1920), a lyrical fantasy relating the amorous adventures of a young lumberjack. The story was the basis for three successful Finnish films.

Linné, lunar crater the reported disappearance of which in the 19th century caused scientific controversy and stimulated study of the Moon. In 1866 Julius Schmidt, director of the Athens Observatory, announced that the crater, formerly easily seen, was gone, and only a white spot was visible where it had been. Schmidt and other skilled observers had until 1843 agreed that Linné (named for the Swedish botanist Carolus Linnaeus) was a deep crater about 10 kilometres (6 miles) in diameter. Apparently, no careful observations were made of the site between 1843 and 1866. In 1903, however, there came to light a drawing made in 1788 in which Linné was also shown as a white spot; this cast doubt on the reality of the reported change. Modern observations show a crater about 1.6 kilometres (1 mile) wide, near the centre of a light-coloured mound at about 28° north, 12° east. The appearance of the formation varies considerably with the angle of sunlight. Whether any structural change or occasional obscuring emission of gas has occurred is uncertain.

Linnebach lantern, also called LINNEBACH PROJECTOR, theatrical lighting device by which silhouettes, colour, and broad outlines can be projected as part of the background scenery. Originally developed in the 19th century by the German lighting expert Adolf Linnebach, it is a concentrated-filament, high-intensity lamp placed in a deep box painted black inside. One side of the box is open and contains a glass or mica slide carrying the design to be projected; it can be projected from behind onto a translucent screen or from the front of the stage onto a backdrop. The device has been refined to include a wide-angle-lens system that prevents the radical distortion of the image. Advances in projection equipment replaced the Linnebach lantern after the mid-20th century.

linnet (*Carduelis,* sometimes *Acanthis, cannabina*), seed-eating European finch of the family Carduelidae (order Passeriformes). It is 13 centimetres (5 inches) long and brown streaked, with a white-edged forked tail; the crown and breast of the male is red. It is a hedgerow singer, and flocks forage for seeds in open country.

Linnet (*Carduelis cannabina*)
Stephen Dalton from the Natural History Photography Agency—EB Inc.

The house finch (*see* rosefinch) of the United States is often called linnet.

Consult the INDEX *first*

linocut, also called LINOLEUM CUT, type of print made from a sheet of linoleum into which a design has been cut in relief. This process of printmaking is similar to woodcut (*q.v.*), but since linoleum is easier to work than wood, linocuts yield a greater variety of effects than do woodcuts. Linocut designs can be cut in large masses, engraved to give supple white lines, or worked in numerous ways to achieve many different textures. The ease with which linoleum is worked makes it admirably suited to large decorative prints, using broad areas of flat colour.

The linocut process, introduced in the beginning of the 20th century, was long despised by many artists as not sufficiently demanding of technical skill. After Pablo Picasso and Henri

"Bust of a Woman After Lucas Cranach the Younger," colour linocut by Pablo Picasso, 1958

By courtesy of the Museum of Modern Art, New York City, gift of Mr. and Mrs. Daniel Saidenberg

Matisse used the technique to advantage in the 1950s, however, many other artists adopted it.

linoleum, smooth-surfaced floor covering made from a mixture of oxidized linseed oil, gums and resins, and other substances, applied to a felt or canvas backing.

In the original process for manufacturing linoleum, a thin film of linseed oil was allowed to oxidize. Since oxidation proceeds mainly on the surface, fresh oil was continually applied to the surface of the oxidized film. After weeks of exposure, during which the thickness of the oil film reached an inch or more, the oxidized oil was fluxed with a natural resin. Cork and other fillers were mixed with the resin and oxidized oil.

This process was eventually replaced by a faster method in which linseed oil is oxidized in large cylindrical kettles where the oil is stirred at elevated temperatures. The oxidization is continued until the oil barely flows at reaction temperature; then the oil is blended with resin in heated kettles and the mixture is exposed to hot air. The plastic material of high viscosity that forms is blended with wood flour and whiting. The binder, fillers, and pigments are mixed, then calendered into sheet form between rollers and applied to a backing of felt or canvas saturated with asphalt. The backed linoleum is hung in tall buildings or stoves, which are heated to harden the linoleum. The hardening process may take weeks.

Modern manufacturing methods are used to produce plain and inlaid, or printed, decorative patterns. Inlaid patterns are made by cutting squares out of two differently coloured linoleum sheets and attaching them to the backing material. Marble effects are achieved by mixing blends of two or more colours, and other effects are obtained by granulating mixes of variously coloured sheets, applying these crumbled materials through stencils to a backing, and then pressing them into sheet form again.

Linoleum is resilient, warm, unaffected by reasonable floor temperatures, and does not readily support combustion. It is specially hardened to resist indentation and is not susceptible to damage from fats, oils, greases, or organic solvents, but moisture and certain alkalies will attack it after prolonged contact.

Linoproductus, genus of extinct articulate brachiopods (lamp shells) found throughout the midcontinent region of North America as fossils in Early Carboniferous to Permian rocks (from about 360 to about 286 million years ago). The genus *Linoproductus* is a distinctive invertebrate form distinguished by its strongly convex pedicle valve and its slightly concave brachial valve. Fine ribbing is present on the convex shell.

Linos (Greek mythology): *see* Linus.

Linosa Island, Italian ISOLA DI LINOSA, one of the Pelagie Islands, which are part of Italy. The islands lie in the Mediterranean Sea between Malta and Tunis, about 30 miles (48 km) north-northeast of Lampedusa Island.

Linosa is administered as part of Agrigento *provincia,* Sicily, and has an area of 2.1 square miles (5.4 square km). The island is moderately fertile, although it suffers from a lack of freshwater. Agriculture and fishing are the principal activities. Its port and population centre is the village of Linosa. Pop. (2000 est.) Lampedusa and Linosa mun., 5,937.

Linotype (trademark), typesetting machine by which characters are cast in type metal as a complete line, rather than as individual characters as on the Monotype typesetting machine. It was patented in the United States in 1884 by Ottmar Mergenthaler. Linotype, which has now largely been supplanted by photocomposition, was most often used when large amounts of straight text matter were to be set.

In Linotype, the operator selects a magazine containing brass matrices to mold an entire font of type of the size and face specified in the copy at hand. A keyboard is manipulated (or driven by paper or magnetic computer tape) to select the matrices needed to compose each line of text, including tapered spacebands, which automatically wedge the words apart to fill each line perfectly. Each matrix is transported to an assembling unit at the mold.

The slugs produced by the machine are rectangular solids of type metal (an alloy of lead, antimony, and tin) as long as the line or column measure selected. Raised characters running along the top are a mirror-image of the desired printed line. After hot-metal casting, a distributing mechanism returns each matrix to its place in the magazine. The slug of type, air-cooled briefly, is then placed in a "stick" for insertion in the proper position into the press form being assembled or made up.

Lins, city, west-central São Paulo *estado* ("state"), Brazil. It is located in the highlands at 1,299 feet (396 m) above sea level, south of the Tietê River. Formerly known as Santo Antônio do Campestre and as Albuquerque Lins, the settlement was given town status in 1913 and was made the seat of a municipality in 1919.

Coffee is the principal crop for the region, which also produces rice, corn (maize), peanuts (groundnuts), cassava, *feijão* (beans), and cotton. Industrial products include liquor, processed foods, wax, dyes, ceramics, and shoes. Lins also has an airfield. Pop. (2000 prelim.) mun., 65,954.

Lins do Rego Cavalcanti, José (b. June 3, 1901, Pilar, Paraíba, Brazil—d. Sept. 13, 1957, Rio de Janeiro), novelist of Brazil's Northeastern school of realists, best known for his five-book Sugar Cane Cycle, which described the clash between the old feudal order of plantation society and the new ways introduced by industrialization.

Lins do Rego grew up on a plantation, and the first work of the cycle, *Menino de Engenho* (1932; "Plantation Lad"), is based on his own boyhood and family. It was followed in quick succession by *Doidinho* (1933; "Daffy Boy"), *Bangüê* (1934; "Old Plantation"), *O Moleque Ricardo* (1935; "Black Boy Richard"), and *Usina* (1936; "The Sugar Refinery"). The first three volumes of the cycle were published in English translation as *Plantation Boy* (1966). The author returned to the plantation setting with *Fogo Morto* (1943; "Dead Fire"), now considered to be his masterwork.

Having studied law, Lins do Rego briefly practiced in the 1920s and thereafter was a bank and tax inspector.

linsang, any of three species of long-tailed, catlike mammals belonging to the civet family (Viverridae). The African linsang (*Poiana richardsoni*), the banded linsang (*Prionodon linsang*), and the spotted linsang (*Prionodon pardicolor*) vary in colour, but all resemble elongated cats. They grow to a length of 33–43 cm (13–17 inches), excluding a banded tail almost as long, and have slender bodies, relatively narrow heads, elongated muzzles, retractile claws, and dense, close fur.

The banded linsang occurs in Malaysia and the Indonesian archipelago, while the spotted linsang is found in tropical uplands in northern India and Myanmar (Burma), southern China, and Nepal. The African linsang, or oyan, lives in western and central Africa. All three species inhabit dense forests and jungles. The two Asian species are strictly carnivorous, but the African linsang eats plant materials as well. All three species are nocturnal and arboreal. They usually produce two litters annually, each containing two or three young.

Linschoten, Jan Huyghen van (b. 1563, Haarlem, Holland [now in The Netherlands]—d. Feb. 8, 1611, Enkhuizen, Neth.), Dutch traveler and explorer who sailed via the Cape of Good Hope to Portuguese Goa (in India) in 1583 and later explored the Arctic Ocean.

As bookkeeper to the archbishop of Goa, Linschoten spent six years (1583–89) in India. After his return to the Netherlands, he wrote two books containing valuable information about the peoples and customs of the country; these books were influential in stimulating early Dutch and English trade expeditions to India and the East Indies.

Linschoten was interested in finding a shorter route to India, and in 1594 he sailed with the Dutch navigator Willem Barents in search of a northeast passage to the Orient via the Arctic. After reaching Novaya Zemlya, Barents returned to the Netherlands, while Linschoten sailed into the Kara Sea before being forced back by bad weather. In 1595 he and Barents took seven ships into the Kara Sea but were again compelled to turn back because the sea had already frozen over. In 1601 Linschoten published his journal of these explorations, which inspired interest among the Dutch and the English in the search for a northern route to India.

linseed, also called FLAXSEED, seed of a variety of the common flax, *Linum usitatissimum,* grown for its yield of linseed oil and meal. This variety of flax has shorter straw, more branches, and more seeds than other varieties that are grown primarily for linen fibre. It is cultivated principally in Argentina, Canada, the United States, Russia, and Ukraine.

Linseed was used as food by the ancient Greeks and Romans. In modern times, its main food use is as livestock feed. After the oil is removed from linseed by compression, the remaining meal, high in protein and minerals, is heated and pressed into cakes for livestock.

Linseed is borne in globular capsules, each with 10 long, flat, elliptical seeds with slight projections at one end. The seeds are typically about 3 to 4 mm (0.1 to 0.15 inch) long. They are usually brown and are smooth and shiny, with a mucilaginous substance in their outer layer that makes them sticky when wet. The whole seed usually contains from 33 to 43 percent oil by weight of air-dried seed.

Linseed oil is golden yellow, brown, or amber in colour. It is classified as a drying oil because it thickens and becomes hard on exposure to air. It is slightly more viscous than most vegetable oils and is used in the production of paints, printing inks, linoleum, varnish, and oilcloth. Linseed oil was formerly a common vehicle in exterior house paints, but its chief remaining use in this field is in artists' oil paints, which are made by grinding raw pigment into the oil.

The chief commercial grades of linseed oil are raw, refined, boiled, and blown. Raw oil is the slowest-drying. Refined oil is raw oil with the free fatty acids, gums, and other extraneous materials removed. The boiled and blown grades dry most quickly and form the hardest films.

lintel (architecture): *see* post-and-lintel system.

Linth, Hans Conrad Escher von der: *see* Escher (von der Linth), Hans Conrad.

Linton, Ralph (b. Feb. 27, 1893, Philadelphia, Pa., U.S.—d. Dec. 24, 1953, New Haven, Conn.), American anthropologist who had a marked influence on the development of cultural anthropology.

As an undergraduate at Swarthmore College, Philadelphia, Linton pursued archaeological interests, taking part in expeditions to New Mexico, Colorado, and Guatemala (1912 and 1913). Following his graduation (1915) he examined a prehistoric site in New Jersey, the subject of his first professional writings. He returned to the Southwest again (1916 and 1919), but a two-year stay in the Marquesas Islands, beginning in 1920, diverted his interest from archaeology to ethnology. He became curator of American Indian and Oceanic collections at the Field Museum of Natural History, Chicago (1922–28). He received his Ph.D. from Harvard University (1925) and made a one-man expedition to Madagascar and East Africa (1925–27) that resulted in his major ethnological work, *The Tanala, a Hill Tribe of Madagascar* (1933).

Ralph Linton

By courtesy of *The Capital Times*, Madison, Wis.

He was a professor at the University of Wisconsin, Madison (1928–37), Columbia University (1937–46), and Yale University (1946–53). *The Study of Man* (1936) is frequently regarded as his most important theoretical work. It is an influential synthesis of theories from anthropology, psychology, and sociology. In *The Cultural Background of Personality* (1945), he advanced the idea of "status personalities," common elements that form the basic personality type in a culture. His final major work, *The Tree of Culture* (1955), elaborated on human origins and the biological and primate influences on cultural behaviour.

Linus, also spelled LINOS, in Greek mythology, the personification of lamentation; the name derives from the ritual cry *ailinos,* the refrain of a dirge. Two principal stories, associated with Argos and Thebes, respectively, arose to explain the origin of the lament.

According to the Argive story, Linus, child of Apollo (god of light, truth, and prophecy) and Psamathe (daughter of Crotopus, king of Argos), was exposed at birth and was torn to pieces by dogs. In revenge, Apollo sent a

Linus slain by Heracles, detail of a red-figured kylix in the style of Douris, early 5th century BC; in the State Collections of Classical Art and Glyptothek, Munich

By courtesy of the Staatliche Antikensammlungen und Glyptothek, Munich

Poine, or avenging spirit, which destroyed the Argive children. The hero Coroebus killed the Poine, and a festival, Arnis, otherwise called dog-killing day (*kunophontis*), was instituted, in which stray dogs were killed, sacrifice offered, and mourning made for Linus and Psamathe.

In the Theban version, Linus was the son of Urania, Muse of astronomy, and the musician Amphimarus, and he was himself a great musician. He invented the Linus song but was put to death by Apollo for presuming to be his rival.

A later, half-burlesque story related that Linus was the Greek hero Heracles' music master and was killed by his pupil, whom he tried to correct.

Linus, SAINT (b. Tuscany?—d. AD 76/79; feast day September 23), pope from about 67 to 76 or 79, who may have been the immediate successor to St. Peter. St. Irenaeus identifies him with the Linus in 2 Timothy 4:21 and writes that "the blessed Apostles passed on the sacred ministry of the episcopacy to Linus." Although his martyrdom is doubtful, he is among the martyrs named in the canon of the mass.

Linz, city, capital of Oberösterreich *Bundesland* (federal state), north-central Austria. Linz lies along the Danube River 100 miles (160 km) west of Vienna. It originated as the Roman fortress of Lentia and became an important medieval trading centre. By the 13th century it had all of the outward characteristics of a city but none of a city's rights. It became the provincial capital in the 15th century during the residence of the Holy Roman emperor Frederick III and was noted for its fairs. The see of a Roman Catholic bishop since 1785, Linz has become an important cultural centre, with the Johannes Kepler University (1966), schools of art and music, a college-level Academy of Industrial and Art Design (1947), a seminary, scientific institutes, museums and art galleries, libraries, archives, an opera house, and theatres.

The city is rich in historic buildings, which include the old castle, St. Martin's Church (first mentioned 799), the early Baroque town hall, the 13th-century main square with a monument to the Holy Trinity, the City Parish Church (13th century, remodeled 1648), the old cathedral (1669–78), the Minorite (Franciscan) Church (13th century, remodeled 1752–58), and the 16th-century Landhaus ("State House"). Also notable are the monastic churches (Capuchin, Ursuline, Carmelite), the neo-Gothic New Cathedral (1862–1924), and the 19th-century fortifications built by Archduke Maximilian d'Este. The bridge (renewed 1938–39) across the Danube leads to the Urfahr quarter on the left bank beneath the Pöstling Hill (1,768 feet [539 m]).

Lying on a direct rail route between the Baltic and Adriatic seas, as well as on the Danube, Linz has extensive docks and a busy river-transit trade. After 1938 it developed into an important industrial centre with ironworks and steelworks and a nitrogen-fixation plant. War damage necessitated their reconstruction after 1945. The city's manufactures also include machinery, electrical equipment, textiles, glass, furniture, beverages, shoes, rubber, and tobacco products. Pop. (2001) 183,504.

Linzi (China): *see* Lin-tzu.

lion (*Panthera leo*), large, powerfully built cat of the family Felidae that is the second largest of the big cats (after the tiger). The proverbial "king of beasts," the lion has been, since earliest times, one of the best-known of wild animals. It is now found mainly in parts of Africa south of the Sahara. About 200 lions, constituting an Asiatic race, live under strict protection in the Gīr Forest National Park in Gujarāt state, India. The preferred habitats of lions are grassy plains and open savanna.

Lion (*Panthera leo*)

R.I.M. Campbell/Bruce Coleman Ltd.

The lion is a well-muscled cat with a long body, short legs, and large head. It varies considerably between the sexes in both size and appearance. A full-grown male is about 1.8–2.1 m (6–7 feet) long, excluding the 1-m (3-foot) long tail; stands about 1.2 m (4 feet) high at the shoulder; and weighs 170–230 kg (370–500 pounds). The female, or lioness, is smaller, with a body length of 1.5 m (5 feet), a shoulder height of 0.9–1 m (3–3.5 feet), and a weight of 120–180 kg (265–390 pounds). The lion's coat is short and varies in colour from buff yellow, orange-brown, or silvery gray to dark brown, with a tuft on the tail tip that is usually darker than the rest of the coat. Lionesses are more consistently tawny or sandy in colour. The male's outstanding characteristic is his mane, which varies in different individuals. It may be entirely lacking; it may fringe the face; or it may be full and shaggy, covering the back of the head, neck, and shoulders and continuing onto the throat and chest to join a fringe along the belly. In some lions the mane and fringe are very dark, almost black, and give the animals a majestic appearance.

Lions are unique among cats in that they live in a group, or pride. A pride consists of several generations of lionesses, all of whom are related, their cubs, and one or two adult male lions who defend the pride's territory and mate with the females. The adult males are outsiders who may hold the pride for a few months to several years, depending on their ability to defend it against other outsider males. A pride may have as few as 4 or as many as 37 members, but about 15 is the average size. Each pride has a well-defined territory; where prey is abundant, its area may be as small as 20 square km (8 square miles), but if game is sparse, the territory may be up to 400 square km (150 square miles) in area. Male cubs are expelled from the pride at about 3 years of age and become nomads until they are old enough (at age 5) to try and take over another pride. Many adult males remain nomads for life, however. Some female cubs remain within the pride when they attain sexual maturity, but others are forced out and join other prides. The members of a pride typically spend the day in several scattered groups, though these may unite to hunt or to share in a kill.

Lions proclaim their territory by roaring and by scent marking. The lion's well-known roar is generally uttered in the evening before a night's hunting and again before getting up at dawn. Males also proclaim their presence by urinating on bushes, trees, or simply on the ground, leaving pungent scent markings in the process. Defecation and rubbing against bushes leave other scent markings.

Lions prey on a large number of animals ranging in size from gazelles and baboons upward to buffalo and hippopotamuses, but they prefer to hunt such medium- to large-sized hoofed animals as wildebeest, zebra, and impala and other antelopes. Lions readily eat any meat they can find, including carrion and

A lioness with cubs
Erwin and Peggy Bauer/Bruce Coleman Ltd.

fresh kills that they scavenge from hyenas through the use of force or intimidation. It is the lionesses of a pride who do most of the hunting. When hunting, the cats pay no attention to the wind's direction, which can carry their scent to their prey, and they also tire after running only short distances; a high proportion of their hunts thus end in failure. When hunting, lionesses (and lions) patiently stalk prey using every bit of available cover and then run it down in a short, rapid rush. After leaping on the prey, the lioness lunges at its neck and bites until the animal is strangled. Other members of the pride quickly crowd around to feed on the kill, with males obtaining the most meat in the resulting scuffles and the smaller cubs acquiring little or none. Lionesses sometimes hunt in groups, with members of a pride encircling a herd of prey animals or approaching them from opposite directions and then closing in to try for a kill in the resulting panic.

Lions and lionesses typically gorge themselves on a kill and then rest for several days in its vicinity. After consuming more than 34 kg (75 pounds) of meat at a single meal, an adult male can rest for a week before resuming the hunt. If prey is abundant, both sexes typically spend 20 hours a day resting, sleeping, or sitting and only hunt for 2 or 3 hours a day.

Both sexes are polygamous and breed throughout the year, but females are usually restricted to the one or two adult males of a pride for their breeding partners. In captivity lions often breed every year, but in the wild they usually breed no more than once in two years. The gestation period is about 108 days, and the litter size varies from one to six cubs, with two to four on average. The newborn cub is helpless and blind and has a thick, dark-spotted coat, the markings of which usually disappear with maturity. Cubs are able to follow their mothers at around 3 months of age and are weaned by 6 or 7 months. They begin participating in kills by 11 months but probably cannot survive on their own until they are 2 years old. They reach sexual maturity at three or four years of age. There is a high mortality rate among cubs, and wild adults seldom live more than 8 or 10 years, chiefly owing to attacks by humans, other lions, or the effects of kicks and gorings from intended prey animals. In captivity lions may live 25 years or more, however.

During the late Pleistocene Epoch (1,600,000 to 10,000 years ago), lions had an extremely wide geographic distribution and ranged over all of North America and Africa, most of the Balkans, and across Anatolia and the Middle East into India. They disappeared from North America about 10,000 years ago, from the Balkans about 2,000 years ago, and from Palestine during the Crusades. By the late 20th century their numbers had dwindled to a few tens of thousands, and those outside of national parks were rapidly losing their habitat to agriculture. Their future protection in Tanzania's Serengeti and other national parks seemed secure, however, partly because of the animals' tourist appeal.

In captivity, the lion has been induced to mate with other big cats. The offspring of a lion and a tigress is called a liger; that of a tiger and a lioness, a tigon; that of a leopard and a lioness, a leopon. The cat known as the American, Mexican, or mountain lion is a New World member of the genus *Felis* (*see* puma).

Lion (constellation): *see* Leo.

Lion, Gulf of, French GOLFE DU LION, gulf of the Mediterranean Sea, extending along the coast of southern France from the Spanish border (west) to Toulon (east). The gulf receives the Tech, Têt, Aude, Orb, Hérault, Vidourle, and Petit and Grand Rhône rivers. When cold-air masses flow past the Alps and sweep southward down the Rhône River valley, the gulf experiences a dry, cold, northerly wind known locally as the mistral.

The gulf coastline includes the easternmost spurs of the Pyrenees, several lagoons, the Rhône River delta, and limestone hills near the city of Marseille. Many canals and waterways (especially, the Rhône River) link coastal areas with the hinterland. The Gulf of Fos, which receives the outlet from the Berre Lagoon, and the bay of Marseille are part of the Gulf of Lion. The major ports along the gulf are Marseille and Sète. The coast of Languedoc, west of the Rhône delta, has been transformed by the creation of new towns that are centres of tourism and recreation.

lion-fish, also called TURKEY FISH, or FIRE-FISH (*Pterois*), any of several species of showy Indo-Pacific fish of the scorpion fish family,

Lion-fish (*Pterois volitans*)
Toni Angermayer

Scorpaenidae (order Scorpaeniformes). Lion-fish are noted for their venomous fin spines, which are capable of producing painful, though rarely fatal, puncture wounds. The fishes have enlarged pectoral fins and elongated dorsal fin spines, and each species bears a particular pattern of bold, zebralike stripes. When disturbed, the fish spread and display their fins and, if further pressed, will present and attack with the dorsal spines. One of the best-known species is *Pterois volitans,* an impressive fish sometimes kept by fish fanciers. It is striped with red, brown, and white and grows to about 30 cm (12 inches) long.

Also known as fire-fish or lion-fish are several smaller Indo-Pacific scorpaenids of the genus *Dendrochirus,* such as the greenish to pinkish *D. barberi* of Hawaii and the reddish *D. zebra* of the Orient.

Lion of Fo, also called LION OF BUDDHA, DOG OF FO, or SHIH-SHIH (Chinese: "Stone Lion"), in Chinese art, stylized figure of a snarling lion, the original significance of which was that of a guardian presence in a Buddhist temple. Lions of Fo are often in pairs, the male playing with a ball and the female with a cub. They occur in many types of Chinese pottery and in Western imitations.

Lionel OF ANTWERP: *see* Clarence, Lionel of Antwerp, Duke of.

Lionne, Hugues de (b. Oct. 11, 1611, Grenoble, France—d. Sept. 1, 1671, Paris), French secretary of state for foreign affairs from 1663 to 1671 who laid the diplomatic groundwork that enabled King Louis XIV to initiate wars of conquest against the Spanish (War of Devolution, 1667–68) and the Dutch (1672–78).

Lionne, detail from an engraving by Nicolas I de Larmessin, 1664
Giraudon—Art Resource

Born into the lower nobility, Lionne was the nephew of the French diplomat Abel Servien. He received training in international politics at an early age, and he was made an adviser for foreign affairs when Cardinal Jules Mazarin became chief minister on the accession of the four-year-old Louis XIV in 1643. While Mazarin was in temporary exile during the aristocratic uprising known as the Fronde (1648–53), Lionne remained in Paris as his agent. In 1659 Lionne negotiated the Treaty of the Pyrenees, which ended a 24-year war with Spain by arranging a marriage between Louis XIV and Marie-Thérèse, daughter of the Spanish king Philip IV. Lionne was responsible for the treaty's *moyennant* ("on condition") clause by which Marie-Thérèse renounced her claims to the Spanish throne in return for a large dowry.

When Louis personally took control of the government upon the death of Mazarin in 1661, Lionne was made a minister in the king's exclusive inner council (Conseil d'en Haut). Two years later he purchased the office of secretary of state for foreign affairs. The death of Philip IV and the accession of the sickly young Charles II to the Spanish throne in 1665 gave Lionne and Louis an opportunity to advance French interests at the expense of Spain. Because the Spanish dowry had not been paid, Lionne declared Marie-Thérèse's renunciation void and claimed that most of the Spanish Netherlands had devolved upon her. French troops invaded the Spanish Netherlands in May 1667, and in the ensuing months Lionne obtained support for France from the electors of Brandenburg and Bavaria. In January 1668 he concluded with the Holy Roman emperor Leopold I a secret pact for the partitioning of the Spanish inheritance between France and Austria on the death of Charles II. Nevertheless, the English and Dutch soon pressured Louis into accepting a peace that gave France control of only a few towns in the Netherlands. Lionne immediately set about isolating the Dutch in preparation for a French invasion of the United Provinces. He formed an alliance with England in 1670, but he died before the conclusion of treaties with Sweden and Austria enabled Louis to launch the Dutch invasion in 1672. The collapse of Lionne's network of alliances prevented Louis from subduing the Dutch.

Lions Clubs, International Association of, civilian service club organized in Dallas, Texas, U.S., in 1917 to foster a spirit of "generous consideration" among peoples of the world and to promote good government, good citizenship, and an active interest in civic, social, commercial, and moral welfare. Because it adopted more lenient membership rules than other service clubs and did not impose a rigid quota on membership from each business and profession, it soon became the largest of all service club organizations.

Lions' activities include general community welfare projects, aid to the blind, and promotion of knowledge and support of the United Nations. The Lions Clubs, with members in some 150 countries, are headquartered in Oakbrook, Ill., U.S.

Liopelma, single genus of the Leiopelmatidae family of small frogs (order Anura). The genus contains three species, which are confined to mountainous areas in New Zealand.

These frogs possess numerous primitive characteristics and are considered to be closely related to the tailed frog (*Ascaphus Truei*) of the northwestern United States. The eggs are laid in moist habitats out of the water and develop into frogs without going through a tadpole stage.

Lios Mor (Ireland): *see* Lismore.

Lios na gCearrbhach (Northern Ireland): *see* Lisburn.

Liotard, Jean-Étienne (b. Dec. 22, 1702, Geneva—d. June 12, 1789, Geneva), Swiss painter noted for his pastel portraits.

After studying in Paris, Liotard was taken to Naples by a patron and went to Rome in 1735 to paint the portraits of Pope Clement XII and several cardinals. In 1738 he accompanied another patron, Lord Duncannon, to Constantinople. He travelled to Vienna in 1743 to paint the portraits of Empress Maria Theresa and her family, earning the nickname of "the Turkish painter" by his eccentric adoption of Oriental costume. He visited England from 1753 to 1755 and painted portraits of the Princess of Wales and other notables. He went to Holland to work in 1756. On another visit to England begun in 1772, he exhibited at the Royal Academy in 1773 and 1774, returning to Geneva in 1776, where he spent his final years. A versatile artist, in addition to his graceful and delicate pastel drawings he achieved distinction for his enamels, copperplate engravings, and glass painting. He wrote a *Treatise on the Art of Painting* and was himself an art collector.

"Self-portrait," pastel by Jean-Étienne Liotard; in the Staatliche Kunstsammlungen, Dresden

By courtesy of the Staatliche Kunstsammlungen, Dresden; photograph, G. Reinhold

Liouville, Joseph (b. March 24, 1809, Saint-Omer, Fr.—d. Sept. 8, 1882, Paris), French mathematician known for his work in analysis, the theory of numbers, and differential geometry, and particularly for his discovery of transcendental numbers—*i.e.,* numbers that are not the roots of algebraic equations having rational coefficients.

Liouville became professor at the École Polytechnique, Paris, in 1833. In 1836 he founded and became editor of the *Journal de Mathématiques Pures et Appliquées,* sometimes known as *Journal de Liouville,* which did much to raise and maintain the standard of French mathematics throughout the 19th century. Most of the papers of the eminent French mathematician Évariste Galois were first published by Liouville in 1846.

A boldly original mathematician, Liouville investigated (1832–33) criteria for the analytic character of integrals of algebraic functions. He was the first to prove (1844) the existence of transcendental numbers, and he constructed an infinite class of such numbers. He also worked in differential equations and boundary-value problems. His methods in the latter, now known as the Stürm–Liouville theory, became of major importance in 20th-century mathematical physics as well as in the theory of integral equations. In differential geometry, he contributed notably to the theories of applicability of surfaces and conformal transformations. The Liouville theorem concerning the measure-preserving property of the Hamiltonian dynamics is basic to statistical mechanics and measure theory.

In number theory Liouville made contributions to numerical functions, quadratic representations, and general formulas in parity functions. Although nearly all this work was published without indication of the means by which he had obtained his striking results, proofs have since been provided. In analysis Liouville was the first to deduce the theory of doubly periodic functions from general theorems (including his own) in the theory of analytic functions of a complex variable. His works include about 400 items, more than 200 on the theory of numbers alone.

lip fern, ferns of the genus *Cheilanthes* (family Adiantaceae), about 180 species of tropical and temperate regions. Most are small, sturdy, often evergreen plants that thrive in dry and rocky areas. The leaves arise directly from the rootstocks and are often covered with dense hairs. Spore-bearing structures (sporangia) occur at the ends of veins and are protected by the leaf margins, which curl over them.

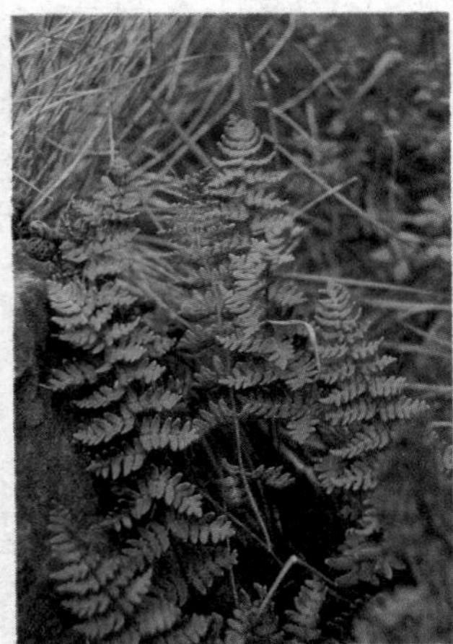

Lip fern (*Cheilanthes*)

A.J. Jermy

lip ring, lip plug, and lip plate, objects, usually ring-shaped, inserted into the lips to alter their shape, used as decoration by certain primitive peoples. The lip plug is also known as a labret.

In South America at the time of the Spanish conquests, lip plugs, usually made of stone, gold, or rock crystal, were worn by the indigenous peoples. In several parts of Africa, especially in Zaire, Tanzania, and the upper reaches of the Nile, and in South America among the Botocudo, enormous plates and plugs are inserted into holes cut in the upper and lower lips. The lip studs and pins of the Nilotic peoples of Uganda, Kenya, and The Sudan—usually small and made of ivory, rock crystal, or stone—are inserted through the upper or lower lip or both. Sometimes lip rings are finely worked; those of the Haida Indians of the Queen Charlotte Islands, British Columbia, for example, are made of wood delicately inlaid with abalone shell.

Lipa, chartered city, Batangas province, southwestern Luzon, Philippines. Formerly a Spanish military headquarters, it is a market town for a fruit-growing region. Lipa was rebuilt (including its cathedral) after a disastrous volcanic eruption in 1754 and again after its virtual destruction under Japanese occupation in World War II. Industries include clothing manufacture and some agricultural processing. The site of a military air base and a citrus experimental station, Lipa is linked to other parts of the island by railway and road. Inc. 1947. Pop. (2000) 218,447.

Lipalian interval, in geology, time span suggested in an attempt to explain the sudden appearance of abundant life forms in the earliest known Cambrian rocks (approximately 570,000,000 years old), in contrast to their absence in the latest Precambrian strata (no more than about 800,000,000 years old). Unlike Precambrian indications of life, Cambrian faunas are comparatively highly developed and diverse, characteristics that indicate a long period of development and evolution in which most of the major phyla are represented. Among the many solutions offered to explain the sudden appearance of abundant life forms in the earliest Cambrian rocks was one posited by the U.S. paleontologist Charles D. Walcott, who suggested that living forms rapidly evolved during the time between the deposition of the youngest Precambrian and the oldest Cambrian sediments and that no record of this interval, the Lipalian interval, exists because the rocks have been eroded or remain undiscovered. Walcott was supported in his views by the fact that an almost worldwide Precambrian-Cambrian unconformity does indeed exist. Even more remarkable is the clear distinction between the virtually barren Precambrian horizons and the productive Cambrian strata, because many localities are now recognized throughout the world in which no break exists in the sedimentary record from the latest Precambrian (sometimes termed Eocambrian) to the earliest Cambrian.

Lipari Islands (Italy): *see* Eolie Islands.

lipase, any of a group of fat-splitting enzymes found in the blood, gastric juices, pancreatic secretions, intestinal juices, and adipose tissues. Lipases hydrolyze triglycerides (fats) into their component fatty acid and glycerol molecules.

Initial lipase digestion occurs in the lumen (interior) of the small intestine. Bile salts reduce the surface tension of the fat droplets so that the lipases can attack the triglyceride molecules. The fatty acid and glycerol molecules are then taken up into the epithelial cells that line the intestinal wall, where they are resynthesized into triglycerides for transport to muscles and adipose tissues. At these sites lipases in the bloodstream hydrolyze the triglycerides, and the resulting fatty acids and glycerol are taken up by the cells of these tissues. In the adipose tissues triglycerides are re-formed for storage until the energy needs of the animal increase under conditions of stress or exercise. Lipases in the cells of adipose tissues break down the triglycerides so that fatty acids can reenter the bloodstream for transport to energy-requiring tissues.

Lipchitz, Jacques, original name CHAIM JACOB LIPCHITZ (b. Aug. 10 [Aug. 22, New Style], 1891, Druskininkai, Lithuania, Russian Empire—d. May 26, 1973, Capri, Italy), Russian-born French sculptor whose style was based on the principles of Cubism; he was a pioneer of nonrepresentational sculpture.

Jacques Lipchitz, photograph by Arnold Newman, 1946

As a youth Lipchitz studied engineering in Vilnius, Lithuania. When he moved to Paris in 1909, however, he was wonder struck by French avant-garde art, especially Cubism, and began to study sculpture as an avenue to understanding modern art. After a brief term of service (1912–13) in the Imperial Russian Army, he returned to Paris and soon began to translate the pictorial experiments of Cubist painters into three-dimensional sculpture, as, for example, in "Sailor with a Guitar" (1914; Albright-Knox Art Gallery, Buffalo, N.Y., U.S.). Lipchitz worked exclusively in solid blocks of material or in low-relief still lifes to simulate the polychromatic prisms of Cubist paintings.

About 1925, however, Lipchitz began to produce a series of sculptures collectively known as "transparents." These open-spaced, curvilinear bronzes, such as "Harpist" (1928; Mrs. T. Catesby Jones Collection, New York City), greatly influenced the course of sculpture in the following quarter century. Such transparents as "The Couple" (1928–29; Rijksmuseum Kröller-Müller, Otterlo, The Netherlands) attempt to express emotion instead of merely solving a sculptural problem as had his earlier works.

By 1941, when he moved to New York City, Lipchitz had established an international reputation. His new obsession with spiritual questions coincided with a revived desire to give his pieces solidity, notably in such massive works as "The Prayer" (1943) and "Prometheus Strangling the Vulture II" (1944–53; Walker Art Center, Minneapolis, Minn., U.S.). His last large work, "Bellerophon Taming Pegasus," was completed in 1966 and was installed at Columbia University, New York City, in 1977.

Lipetsk, *oblast* (province), western Russia. It is situated on the rolling hills of the Central Russian Upland and, in the east, the low Oka-Don Plain. The Don and Voronezh rivers cross the centre of the *oblast* from north to south. The local agriculture has caused most of the natural oak forest cover and grass steppe to be ploughed up, resulting in severe gully erosion. Agriculture supports a large rural population and is intensively developed; rye, wheat, corn (maize), oats, sugar beets, potatoes, sunflowers, and hemp are grown, while livestock husbandry is less developed. Apart from Lipetsk city, the administrative centre, most local industry processes agricultural products. Area 9,300 square miles (24,100 square km). Pop. (1993 est.) 1,241,000.

Lipetsk, city and administrative centre of Lipetsk *oblast* (province), western Russia. It lies along both banks of the Voronezh River in the Don Basin. A fortified settlement existed on the site in the 13th century, until its destruction by Tatars in 1284. The town was founded in 1703 as an ironworking centre by Peter I the Great. It also served as a spa resort; its natural springs and mineral-laden mud were valued as curatives. An ironworks dating from 1897 and another from 1934 were converted in the 1960s into huge iron- and steelworks. The city, favourably located owing to its proximity to Kursk Magnetic Anomaly iron ore and Donets Basin coking coal, is the centre of the major industrial region of Central Chernozem. Nitrogenous fertilizers are made from coke by-products in the city, and there are also engineering, chemical, cement, and foodstuffs industries. Pop. (1993 est.) 466,000.

lipid, any member of a varied class of water-insoluble, colourless organic compounds present in the tissues of plants and animals, from which they can be extracted by organic solvents such as ether, naphtha, or chloroform.

A brief treatment of lipids follows. For full treatment, *see* MACROPAEDIA: Biochemical Components of Organisms; Chemical Compounds.

The main types of lipids are the neutral lipids (or triglycerides, *i.e.,* fatty-acid esters of the alcohol glycerol), the phospholipids (or phosphoglycerides, *i.e.,* fatty-acid esters of glycerol and phosphoric acid), the sphingolipids (complex lipids derived from alcohols such as sphingosine), the sterols (such as cholesterol), carotenoids, and prostaglandins.

Fatty acids are long carbon-hydrogen chains with a carboxyl (COO−) group at one end. The hydrocarbon chain can be saturated with hydrogens or contain some double bonds (unsaturated). Triglycerides, representing the many edible fats and oils, are formed by combining three fatty acid chains with one glycerol molecule through ester linkages between the carboxyl groups of the fatty acids and the three hydroxyl groups of glycerol. The fluidity of a lipid depends on the length of the fatty acid chains and their degree of saturation; short and unsaturated chains are more fluid and have lower melting points.

Of the lipids, triglycerides are most often used by animals to store energy. Layers of neutral lipids deposited beneath the skin can also insulate animals against cold, since fats transfer heat poorly. If an animal eats more fats or carbohydrates than it can immediately use, fatty acids combine with glycerol to form triglycerides, which are stored in the adipose tissues of the animal. If needed, these stored neutral lipids can be readily broken down (hydrolyzed) by enzymes called lipases to give glycerol and fatty acids; the latter can be carried in the bloodstream to target tissues (*e.g.,* skeletal muscles) where they are further broken down to release energy. Mammals must ingest one or more specific fatty acids (linoleic, linolenic, and arachidonic, for instance) in order to synthesize certain essential lipids.

Triglycerides make excellent food reserves; they are insoluble and can be stored as droplets in cells. Plants such as the castor-oil plant store lipids in their seeds. Mammals store fats in specialized adipose cells; large fat globules fill up most of the cell. Triglycerides are good fuel molecules because they are reduced—they contain proportionally more hydrogen atoms to be oxidized than does sugar. And they can be stored in a relatively anhydrous (water-free) state because they are less polar than protein or carbohydrate. The liver can convert fats into glucose, the brain's only source of energy, when carbohydrates are not available for breakdown, as for instance during fasting. A side effect is the increased production of acidic ketone bodies, a condition known as ketosis.

Phospholipids are important constituents of cellular membranes. They are the principal components of myelin, the sheath that surrounds the axons of neurons (nerve cells) and allows them to conduct nerve impulses properly. Phospholipids contained in platelets in the blood are involved in the formation of blood clots. Sphingolipids that are found in the nervous tissue and brain are necessary for the normal functioning of the nervous system.

Sterols (or steroids) and carotenoids differ from the other lipids discussed in that they are not hydrolyzed by potassium hydroxide to give water-soluble products. Steroids and carotenoids are said to be not saponifiable. Sterols such as cholesterol are present in many cell membranes and play important roles in the synthesis of many biologically active compounds, including bile acids, vitamin D, and certain hormones—such as cortisol, estrogen, testosterone, glucocorticoids, and mineralocorticoids. Carotenoids provide yellow and orange pigments in many plants and also function in photosynthesis. Prostaglandins, cyclic derivatives of linoleic acid, have complex effects on metabolism and apparently often act as local hormones.

Consult
the
INDEX
first

---

lipid storage disease, any of a group of relatively rare hereditary disorders of fat metabolism, characterized by the accumulation of distinctive types of lipids, notably cerebrosides, gangliosides, or sphingomyelins, in various body structures. Each type of lipid accumulates as a result of a defect in one of the several organic catalysts or enzymes that normally metabolize it inside the cell.

In Gaucher's disease, abnormal amounts of cerebrosides accumulate in the liver, spleen, bone marrow, and lymph nodes. The defective enzyme is glucocerebrosidase. The excess lipids, stored in the large distended Gaucher cells that are typical of the disease, interfere with cell function and produce two distinctive syndromes: (1) An acute cerebral form chiefly affects infants, who appear normal at birth but soon become apathetic and retarded in their development; enlargement of their abdomen is followed by severe nervous system symptoms, and death usually occurs during the first year of life. (2) A more chronic form that may become evident at any age is characterized by an enlargement of the spleen, by anemia, and by a patchy brown pigmentation of the skin; the bones show characteristic changes in shape, and interference with calcification may result in fractures and deformities.

Niemann-Pick disease has many clinical features in common with Gaucher's disease, but in this case the deposition of lipids in the body is more widespread and the lipids involved are sphingomyelins. The defective enzyme is sphingomyelinase. The disease is usually apparent during the first year of life, and affected children seldom live beyond their fourth year.

In Tay-Sachs disease, or amaurotic (blind) idiocy, gangliosides are deposited in body tissues, chiefly those of the central nervous system, which deteriorates, resulting in severe mental deficiency. Characteristic early symptoms of Tay-Sachs disease include extreme sensitivity to noise, muscle weakness, and the appearance of a cherry-red spot on the small, highly sensitive area near the centre of the retina, this red spot being sometimes also seen in Niemann-Pick disease. Progressive loss of vision eventually results in blindness. Affected children generally die at about three years of age. Niemann-Pick disease and Tay-Sachs disease are both seen more frequently among individuals of Jewish ancestry than among others.

In Fabry's disease, characteristic symptoms include the appearance of many purplish papules (small, solid elevations) on the skin, enlargement of the heart, poor kidney function, opacity of the cornea, and dilated blood vessels. These symptoms result from the deposition of the lipid ceramide trihexoside, closely related to the sphingomyelins, in the affected body structures. The defective enzyme is ceramide trihexosidase. Fabry's disease is sex-linked, affecting chiefly males, who generally die of kidney failure complicated by cardiovascular disease. Except for alleviating the symptoms, there is no specific treatment for any of the lipid storage diseases.

Lipizzaner, also spelled LIPPIZANER, also called LIPIZZAN, breed of horse that derived its name from the Austrian imperial stud at Lipizza, near Trieste, formerly a part of the Austro-Hungarian Empire. The founding of the breed dates to 1580, and detailed breeding records date from 1700. The ancestry is Spanish, Arabian, and Berber. The six strains (Pluto, Conversano, Neapolitano, Favory, Maestoso, and Siglavy) are named from their foundation sires.

Lipizzaners are of comparatively small stature with a long back, a short, thick neck, and powerful conformation. They average 14.3 to 15.2 hands (about 59 to 62 inches, or 150 to 157 cm) high and weigh from 1,000 to 1,300 pounds (450 to 585 kg). The head, with a Roman nose, lacks the refinement of most light breeds, but they have attractive, expressive eyes. The colour is usually gray; bay and brown occur rarely. They are found to a limited extent in countries that were originally a part of the Austro-Hungarian Empire, and a few have been exported to the United States. The best known Lipizzaners are those trained at the Spanish Riding School in Vienna.

Lipizzaner
Sally Anne Thompson

Lipmann, Fritz Albert (b. June 12, 1899, Königsberg, Ger. [now Kaliningrad, Russia]—d. July 24, 1986, Poughkeepsie, N.Y., U.S.), German-born American biochemist, who received (with Sir Hans Krebs) the 1953 Nobel Prize for Physiology or Medicine for the discovery of coenzyme A, an important catalytic substance involved in the cellular conversion of food into energy.

Lipmann, 1953
EB Inc.

Lipmann earned an M.D. degree (1924) and a Ph.D. degree (1927) from the University of Berlin. He conducted research in the laboratory of the biochemist Otto Meyerhof at the University of Heidelberg (1927–30) and then did research at the Biological Institute of the Carlsberg Foundation (Carlsbergfondets Biologiske Institut), Copenhagen (1932–39), and at the Cornell Medical School, New York City (1939–41).

At Massachusetts General Hospital, Boston (1941–57), where he directed the biochemistry research department, and as professor of biological chemistry at the Harvard Medical School (1949–57), Lipmann found a catalytically active, heat-stable factor in pigeon liver extracts. He subsequently isolated (1947), named, and determined the molecular structure (1953) of this factor, coenzyme A (or CoA), which is now known to be bound to acetic acid as the end product of sugar and fat breakdown in the absence of oxygen. Coenzyme A is one of the most important substances involved in cellular metabolism; it helps in the conversion of amino acids, steroids, fatty acids, and hemoglobins into energy. Lipmann taught or conducted research at the Rockefeller Institute, now Rockefeller University, New York City, from 1957 until his death.

lipoprotein, any member of a group of substances containing both lipid (fat) and protein. They occur in both soluble complexes—as in egg yolk and mammalian blood plasma—and insoluble ones, as in cell membranes. The lipoproteins in blood plasma have been intensively studied because they are the mode of transport for cholesterol (*q.v.*) through the bloodstream and lymphatic fluid.

Cholesterol is insoluble in the blood, and so it must be bound to lipoproteins in order to be transported. Two types of lipoprotein are involved in this function: low-density lipoproteins (LDLs) and high-density lipoproteins (HDLs). LDLs transport cholesterol from its site of synthesis in the liver to the body's cells, where the cholesterol is separated from the LDL and is then used by the cells for various purposes. HDLs probably transport excess or unused cholesterol from the body's tissues back to the liver, where the cholesterol is broken down to bile acids and is then excreted. About 70 percent of all cholesterol in the blood is carried by LDL particles, and most of the remainder is carried by HDLs. LDL-bound cholesterol is primarily responsible for the atherosclerotic buildup of fatty deposits on the blood vessel walls, while HDL particles may actually reduce or retard such atherosclerotic buildups and are thus beneficial to health.

Body cells extract cholesterol from the blood by means of tiny coated pits (receptors) on their surfaces; these receptors bind with the LDL particles (and their attached cholesterol) and draw them from the blood into the cell. There are limits to how much cholesterol a body cell can take in, however, and a cell's capture of LDL particles inhibits the making of more LDL receptors on that cell's surface, thus lowering its future intake of cholesterol. Fewer receptors on the body cells means that less cholesterol is ingested by the cells and that more remains in the bloodstream, thus increasing the risk of cholesterol accumulating in the interior walls of blood vessels.

Several hereditary genetic disorders, called hyperlipoproteinemias, involve excessive concentrations of lipoproteins in the blood. Other such diseases, called hypolipoproteinemias, involve abnormally reduced lipoprotein levels in the blood.

Lipot (Hungarian personal name): *see under* Leopold.

Lippe, one of the smallest of the former German states, forming, since 1946–47, the northeastern corner of the *Land* (state) of North Rhine-Westphalia; the rather smaller Schaumburg-Lippe, now in the southern part of the *Land* of Lower Saxony, was founded in the 1640s under a separate branch of the House of Lippe. Both were until 1990 in West Germany. The Lippe lands lie north and south of the east–west bend of the middle Weser River and extend southwestward to the Teutoburg Forest.

The medieval lords of Lippe had their original possessions around Lippstadt on the Lippe River, west of Paderborn. Simon V of Lippe (died 1536) assumed the title of count in 1528. In the Reformation, Lippe became Lutheran (1538) and later, Calvinist (1605). Dynastic divisions occurred in the early 17th century; but the Lippe-Detmold line, princes from 1720, reunited most of the Lippe lands except for those held by Schaumburg-Lippe.

Schaumburg, or Schauenburg, northeast of Rinteln, was the seat of a dynasty of counts from *c.* 1100 to 1640. Hesse-Kassel and Brunswick acquired some of those lands; but Philip of Lippe-Alverdissen, brother of the last countess of Schaumburg, retained others to form a principality with its capital at Bückeburg. Both states joined the Confederation of the Rhine, under the aegis of Napoleon I, in 1807, and the German Confederation in 1815. Schaumburg-Lippe adhered to the fiscal union of the northeastern German states in 1837, the Zollverein (German Customs Union) in 1854, the North German Confederation in 1866 (Lippe joining in 1867), and the German Empire in 1871. Under the constitution of the Weimar Republic (1919–33) the princely regimes in both states gave place to republican governments, which were suppressed during the Nazi era.

Lippe River, river, a right-bank tributary of the Rhine, that flows through North Rhine-Westphalia *Land* (state) in Germany. Rising near Bad Lippspringe on the western edge of the Teutoburger Wald, the Lippe follows a westerly course of 155 miles (250 km) and flows into the Rhine near Wesel. The river lies along the northern border of the Ruhr industrial region. By the aid of locks it is navigable downstream from Lippstadt for boats and barges drawing less than 4 ft (1.2 m). The Lippe was once used for the transport of coal, timber, and agricultural produce to and from Westphalia, but in 1929 it was replaced by a canal that follows its course from the Dortmund-Ems-Kanal to the Rhine. The Lippe supplies water to the canal system of the Ruhr region, and during the 1960s the canal along the river was extended to east of Hamm.

Lippershey, Hans, also called JAN LIPPERSHEIM, or HANS LIPPERSHEIM (b. *c.* 1570, Wesel, Ger.—d. *c.* 1619, Middelburg, Neth.), spectacle maker from the United Netherlands, traditionally credited with inventing the telescope (1608).

On Oct. 2, 1608, he formally offered his invention, which he called a *kijker* ("looker"), to the Estates of Holland for use in warfare. The Estates granted him 900 florins for the instrument but required its modification into a binocular device. His telescopes were made available to Henry IV of France and others before the end of 1608. The potential importance of the instrument in astronomy was recognized by, among others, Jacques Bovedere of Paris; he reported the invention to Galileo, who promptly built his own telescope.

Lippi, Filippino (b. *c.* 1457, Prato, Republic of Florence—d. April 18, 1504, Florence), early Renaissance painter of the Florentine school whose works influenced the Tuscan Mannerists of the 16th century.

The son of Fra Filippo Lippi and his wife, Lucrezia Buti, he was a follower of his father and of Botticelli. After Fra Filippo Lippi's death,

"The Vision of St. Bernard," tempera on panel by Filippino Lippi; in the Badia, Florence
SCALA—Art Resource/EB Inc.

Filippino entered the workshop of Botticelli. By 1473 he had finished his apprenticeship. The style of Filippino's earliest works stems from that of Botticelli, but Filippino's use of line is less sensitive and subtle than Botticelli's. In a group of paintings executed about 1480–85 he developed a harder and more individual style. Among the most notable works of this period is the "Journey of Tobias" in the Galleria Sabauda, Turin, Italy. He was employed, along with Botticelli, Perugino, and Ghirlandajo, on the frescoed decoration of Lorenzo de' Medici's villa at Spedaletto and at the end of 1482 was commissioned to complete work left unfinished by Perugino in the Palazzo della Signoria in Florence. No trace of either work survives. Soon after (probably 1483–84) he was entrusted with the completion of the frescoes in the Brancacci Chapel in the Carmine, which had been left unfinished on Masaccio's death in 1428.

His most popular picture, the beautiful altarpiece of "The Vision of St. Bernard" (Badia, Florence), has been variously assigned to the years 1480 and 1486. In Rome Filippino decorated the Caraffa Chapel in Sta. Maria sopra Minerva. Nothing in Filippino's earlier works prepares for the vein of inspiration that he struck in the Caraffa Chapel, which became one of his most influential works.

On his return from Rome (probably 1491) Filippino Lippi executed a fresco of the "Sacrifice of Laocoön" for the villa of Lorenzo de' Medici at Poggio a Caiano, in which some of the decorative devices used in the Caraffa Chapel are again employed, and resumed work in the Strozzi Chapel (completed 1502), the frescoes of which anticipate Tuscan Mannerism of the 16th century.

Lippi, Fra Filippo (b. *c.* 1406, Florence—d. Oct. 8/10, 1469, Spoleto, Papal States), Florentine painter in the second generation of Renaissance artists. While exhibiting the strong influence of Masaccio (*e.g.*, in "Madonna and Child," 1437) and Fra Angelico (*e.g.*, in "Coronation of the Virgin," *c.* 1445), his work achieves a distinctive clarity of expression. Legend and tradition surround his unconventional life.

Life and works. After the death of both his father and mother, the young Filippo Lippi stayed with an aunt in Florence for some years, and in 1421 he pronounced the vows of a Carmelite monk at Sta. Maria del Carmine. The Brancacci chapel of this monastery was at this time being decorated with frescoes by Masaccio. These frescoes, which were to be among the most glorious and influential paintings of the Renaissance, were Lippi's first important contact with art.

In 1432 Lippi left the monastery after having painted some frescoes in the church and in the cloister. According to the Renaissance biographer Giorgio Vasari, who wrote a lively and fanciful profile of the painter, Lippi was abducted with some companions by the Moors on the Adriatic, held as a slave for 18 months, and then freed after he painted a portrait of his owner. It is known that in 1434 the artist was at Padua. None of the works executed in the period at Padua is known, but the effect of his presence may be recognized in the paintings of others there, such as Mantegna.

In 1437 Lippi returned to Florence, protected by the powerful Medici family, and was commissioned to execute several works for convents and churches.

The qualities he acquired during his years of travel are affirmed with clarity in two works of 1437, immediately after he returned from Padua: "The Virgin and Child Between SS. Frediano and Augustin" and the "Madonna and Child." In both of these altarpieces, the influence of Masaccio is still evident, but it is absorbed into a different style, having the pictorial effect of bas-relief, rendered more evident by lines, so that it resembles the reliefs of the sculptors Donatello and Jacopo della Quercia. In these works, the colour is warm, toned down with shadings, approaching the limpid chromatics of his great contemporary Fra Angelico. Still further testimony of Lippi's development is the painting "The Annunciation," formerly believed to be a late work but now dated between 1441 and 1443. It is composed in a new way, using the newly discovered effects of perspective and skillful contrasts between colour and form; the suggested movement of the light garments of the two frightened girls at the door is rendered with such sensitivity as to anticipate Botticelli.

A famous altarpiece of the same time, Lippi's well-known "Coronation of the Virgin," is a complex work crowded with figures. The celebrated altarpiece is so sumptuous in appearance that it seems to have been painted in competition with Angelico; it marks a historic point in Florentine painting in its success in uniting as one scene the various panels of a polyptych.

The altarpieces are characterized by a solemnity of composition that is absent from the paintings in which he developed a typical motive of 15th-century Florentine art: the Madonna with the Child at her breast. The masterpiece of these is "Madonna with Child and Scenes from the Life of Mary," a circular painting now in the Pitti Palace in Florence; it is a clear and realistic mirror of life, transfigured in a most intimate way, and it had a great effect on Renaissance art.

"The Madonna and Child with Two Angels," by Fra Filippo Lippi, *c.* 1465; in the Uffizi, Florence
Alinari—Art Resource/EB Inc.

A second "Coronation of the Virgin," executed about 1445, displays a marked change in the style of Lippi—from the plastic values suggested by his study of Masaccio to the serene chromatics of Angelico.

In 1442 Lippi had been made rector of the church of S. Quirico at Legnaia. His life, however, became constantly more eventful, and tradition has given him the reputation (borne out in great part by documents) of a man dominated by love affairs and impatient of methodical or tranquil conduct. His adventures culminated in 1456 in his romantic flight from Prato, where he was painting in the convent of the nuns of Sta. Margherita, with a young woman of the convent, Lucrezia Buti. The Pope later gave permission to the former priest-painter to marry her, and from this union was born a son, Filippo, called Filippino, who was to be one of the most noted Florentine painters of the second half of the 15th century.

The bright and active city of Prato, a short distance from Florence, was the second home of Filippo Lippi. He returned to Prato often, staying there for long periods, painting frescoes and altarpieces. Accompanied by Fra Diamante, who had been his companion and collaborator since he was a young man, Lippi began to redecorate the walls of the choir of the cathedral there in 1452. He returned in 1463 and again in 1464, remaining in the city this time until 1467. At the centre of his activity in Prato stand the frescoes of the cathedral, with the four Evangelists and scenes from the lives of St. John the Baptist and St. Stephen. Perhaps the most solemn scene of the life and death of St. Stephen is the burial; at the sides of the funeral bed of the saint stand a crowd of prelates and illustrious persons in mourning, among them Cardinal Carlo de' Medici, Fra Diamante, and the artist himself.

In 1467 Lippi and Fra Diamante left for Spoleto, where he had received a commission, through the Medici family, for another vast undertaking: the decorations and frescoes of the choir of the cathedral, which included the "Nativity," the "Annunciation," the "Death of Mary," and—in the centre of the vault of the apse—the "Coronation." These frescoes were Lippi's final work; they were interrupted by his death, for which there are two documented dates—in the monks' necrology of Sta. Maria del Carmine in Florence and the archives of Spoleto. The Medici had a splendid sepulchre, designed by his son, erected for him in the cathedral of Spoleto.

Assessment. Posthumous judgments of Filippo Lippi were often coloured by the traditions of his adventurous life. Moreover, his works have been criticized from time to time for their borrowings from other painters; nevertheless, it has also been recognized that his art was not diminished but rather enriched and rendered more balanced by what he took from Masaccio and Fra Angelico. He was constantly seeking the techniques to realize his artistic vision and the new ideas that made him one of the most appreciated artists of his time.

The 20th-century critic Bernard Berenson, who maintained that Lippi's true place as an artist was among the "painters of genius," also described him as "a high-class illustrator," intending by this to underline the importance of expressive content and the presentation of reality in his works. Later critics have recognized in Lippi a "narrative" spirit that reflected the life of his time and translated into everyday terms the ideals of the early Renaissance.

(V.M.)

MAJOR WORKS. "The Reform of the Carmelite Rule" (fresco, 1432; Sta. Maria del Carmine, Florence); "Madonna of Humility" (*c.* 1432; Castello Sforzesco, Milan); "Madonna and Child" (1437; Galleria Nazionale d'Arte Antica, Rome); "The Virgin and Child Between SS. Frediano and Augustin" (1437; Louvre, Paris); "Madonna and Child Enthroned" (*c.* 1437; Metropolitan Museum of Art, New York City); "Annunciation" (*c.* 1437–40; S. Lorenzo, Florence); "The Coronation of the Virgin" (1441–47; Uffizi, Florence); "The Madonna Enthroned with Saints" (1441–42; Uffizi); "Virgin and Child" (1441–42; Museo Mediceo, Florence); "The Annunciation" (1441–43; Galleria Nazionale d'Arte Antica); "Annunciation" (*c.* 1442–47; Alte Pinakothek, Munich); "St. Lawrence Enthroned with SS. Cosmo and Damian and Alessandro Alessandri and Two of His Sons; St. Benedict; St. Anthony Abbott" ("Alessandri Altarpiece"; *c.* 1442–47; Metropolitan Museum of Art); "Adoration of the Magi" (*c.* 1445–47; National Gallery of Art, Washington, D.C.); "Coronation of the Virgin" (*c.* 1445; Vatican Museum, Rome); "St. Bernard's Vision of the Virgin" (1447; National Gallery, London); choir frescoes (1452–64; cathedral, Prato, Italy); "Madonna with Child and Scenes from the Life of Mary" (1452; Pitti Palace, Florence); "The Virgin Enthroned and Two Saints" (1453; Museo Comunale, Prato); "The Adoration of the Child with St. Hilary" (*c.* 1455; Uffizi); "Seven Saints" (1458–60; National Gallery, London); "The Virgin Adoring the Child" (*c.* 1460; Staatliche Museen Preussischer Kulturbesitz, Berlin); "The Adoration of the Child with St. Bernard" (*c.* 1463; Uffizi); "The Madonna and Child with Two Angels" (*c.* 1465; Uffizi); choir and apse frescoes (commissioned 1466, begun 1467–69; cathedral, Spoleto, Italy).

BIBLIOGRAPHY. Mary Pittaluga, "Fra Filippo Lippi," in the *World Encyclopedia of Art,* vol. 9, col. 257–261 (1964), a biographical and critical synopsis with modern bibliography; and *Filippo Lippi* (1949), includes a critical evaluation (in Italian) of the artist and precise attributions; Edward C. Strutt, *Fra Filippo Lippi* (1901), the first systematic biography with comments on the principal works; Bernard Berenson, *The Study and Criticism of Italian Art,* 2nd Series (1902), and *Italian Pictures of the Renaissance* (1932), contain important critical evaluations of the artist; I.B. Supino, *Fra Filippo Lippi* (1902), in Italian; Henriette Mendelsohn, *Fra Filippo Lippi* (1909), in German; Giuseppe Fiocco, *La pittura toscana del Quattrocento* (1945); Robert Oertel, *Fra Filippo Lippi* (1942), a critical study (in German) with attributions; Mario Salmi (ed.), *Filippo Lippi: Gli affreschi nel duomo di Prato* (1944), with illustrations of particular frescoes and comments and notes.

Lippisch, Alexander M(artin) (b. Nov. 2, 1894, Munich, Ger.—d. Feb. 11, 1976, Cedar Rapids, Iowa, U.S.), German-American aerodynamicist whose designs of tailless and delta-winged aircraft in the 1920s and 1930s were important in the development of high-speed jet and rocket airplanes.

Lippisch designed the world's first successful rocket-propelled airplane (a tailless glider fitted with two solid-fuel rockets, flown June 11, 1928, in the Rhön Mountains, Germany) and was largely responsible for the first operational liquid-fuel rocket aircraft (the Messerschmitt Me 163 Komet fighter, first used by the Luftwaffe in 1944). After World War II Lippisch moved to the United States and in 1965 established the Lippisch Research Corporation, Cedar Rapids, Iowa. He was an early proponent of the delta-wing configuration.

Lippizaner (horse): *see* Lipizzaner.

Lippman, Yom-Tob: *see* Zunz, Leopold.

Lippmann, Gabriel (b. Aug. 16, 1845, Hollerich, Luxembourg—d. July 13, 1921, at sea, en route from Canada to France), French physicist who received the Nobel Prize for Physics in 1908 for producing the first colour photographic plate. He was known for the innovations that resulted from his search for a direct colour-sensitive medium in photography.

Though born of French parents in Luxembourg, Lippmann grew up in Paris and was

Gabriel Lippmann
H. Roger-Viollet

a bright but unruly student. Despite the fact that he never received his teacher's certificate, he was appointed professor of mathematical physics at the Sorbonne in 1883. He later was appointed head of the Sorbonne's Laboratories of Physical Research (1886).

Lippman's scientific talents were varied, but he was best known for his contributions in the fields of optics and electricity. He did early, important studies of piezoelectricity (precursors of Pierre Curie's work) and of induction in resistanceless, or superconductive, circuits (precursors of Heike Kamerlingh Onnes' validations). He also invented the coleostat, an instrument that allowed for long-exposure photographs of the sky by compensating for the Earth's motion during the exposure.

In 1891 Lippmann revealed a revolutionary colour-photography process, later called the Lippmann process, that utilized the natural colours of light wavelengths instead of using dyes and pigments. He placed a reflecting coat of mercury behind the emulsion of a panchromatic plate. The mercury reflected light rays back through the emulsion to interfere with the incident rays, forming a latent image that varied in depth according to each ray's colour. The development process then reproduced this image, and the result, when viewed, was brilliantly accurate. This direct method of colour photography was slow and tedious because of necessarily long exposure times, and no copies of the original could be made. It never achieved popularity, therefore, but it was an important step in the development of colour photography.

Lippmann, Walter (b. Sept. 23, 1889, New York, N.Y., U.S.—d. Dec. 14, 1974, New York), American newspaper commentator and author who in a 60-year career made himself one of the most widely respected political columnists in the world.

While studying at Harvard (B.A., 1909), Lippmann was influenced by the philosophers William James and George Santayana. He helped to found (1914) *The New Republic* and served as its assistant editor under Herbert David Croly. Through his writings in that liberal weekly and through direct consultation, he influenced Pres. Woodrow Wilson, who is said to have drawn on Lippmann's ideas for the post-World War I settlement plan (Fourteen Points) and for the concept of the League of Nations. Lippmann was briefly (1917) an assistant to Secretary of War Newton D. Baker. Wilson sent him to take part in the negotiations for the Treaty of Versailles (1919).

After writing editorials (1921–29) for the reformist *World,* Lippmann served as its editor (1929–31) and then moved to the *New York Herald Tribune.* On Sept. 8, 1931, his column, "Today and Tomorrow," first appeared; eventually, it was syndicated in more than 250 newspapers in the United States and about 25 other nations and won two Pulitzer Prizes (1958, 1962). In preparing his commentaries, he traveled throughout the world. His first book, *A Preface to Politics* (1913), was mildly socialistic, but *Drift and Mastery* (1914) was anti-Marxist, and in *The Good Society* (1937) he repudiated socialism entirely. During World War II he warned against a postwar return of the United States to an isolationist policy. *Essays in the Public Philosophy* (1955) evoked some criticism for its natural-law theory.

In perhaps his most influential book, *Public Opinion* (1922; reissued 1956; paperback ed., 1965), Lippmann seemed to imply that ordinary citizens can no longer judge public issues rationally, since the speed and condensation required in the mass media tend to produce slogans rather than interpretations. In *The Phantom Public* (1925) he again treated the problem of communication in politics; while continuing to doubt the possibility of a true democracy, he nonetheless rejected government by an elite.

Lippold, Richard (b. May 3, 1915, Milwaukee, Wis., U.S.—d. Aug. 22, 2002, Roslyn, N.Y.), American sculptor of intricate, abstract wire constructions.

He studied at the University of Chicago and trained in industrial design at the School of the Art Institute of Chicago. After graduating in 1937, he established an industrial-design studio in Milwaukee.

In 1942, under the influence of Naum Gabo and Constructivism, he began creating delicate, weblike sculptures from brass, nickel, gold, and silver wire. Stretched taut between focal points and axes, these reflective rays describe an ideal and infinitely inclusive geometry. In some pieces (*e.g.,* "Gemini II," 1968), metal tubes or other forms are threaded onto the wires in complex patterns. Most of Lippold's works are designed for suspension by anchor wires in the upper reaches of large rooms; "Variations in a Sphere No. 10: The Sun" (1953–56; gold wire), commissioned by the Metropolitan Museum of Art, New York City, is a major example. Constructions from the 1960s appeared in all kinds of public buildings: "Flight" (Pan American Building, New York City, 1963); "Baldacchino" (St. Mary's Cathedral, San Francisco, 1967); "Ad Astra" (Mall Entrance of the Space Museum, Washington, D.C., 1976); and in the Atrium Tower Building, New York City, 1981.

Consult the INDEX *first*

Lipps, Theodor (b. July 28, 1851, Wallhalben, Bavaria [Germany]—d. Oct. 17, 1914, Munich), German psychologist best known for his theory of aesthetics, particularly the concept of *Einfühlung,* or empathy, which he described as the act of projecting oneself into the object of a perception.

At the University of Bonn (1877–90) Lipps wrote a comprehensive account of psychology of the time, *Grundtatsachen des Seelenlebens* (1883; "Fundamental Facts of the Inner Life"). After serving as professor at the University of Breslau (1890–94), he was appointed to the faculty at the University of Munich (1894–1914), and in 1897 he wrote *Raumästhetik und geometrisch-optische Täuschungen* ("Spatial Aesthetics"), an experimental study of optical illusions that influenced much contemporary research on this subject.

According to Lipps's concept of empathy, a person appreciates another person's reaction by a projection of the self into the other. In his *Ästhetik,* 2 vol. (1903–06; "Aesthetics"), he made all appreciation of art dependent upon a similar self-projection into the object.

Lippstadt, city, North Rhine-Westphalia *Land* (state), northwestern Germany. It lies along the Lippe River, on the slopes of the Teutoburger Wald. Lippstadt was probably founded by the lords of Lippe in 1168, and it joined the Hanseatic League in 1280. Half of the town passed to the county of Mark, which in 1614 was acquired by Brandenburg. In 1850 the prince of Lippe-Detmold sold his share to Prussia when this joint lordship ceased.

Lippstadt has several 13th-century churches, old half-timbered houses, and a town hall dating from 1773, and there is a fine Rococo hall in the Hotel Köppelmann. The moated castles of Overhagen, Eringerfeld, Heringhausen, and Körtlinghausen are nearby. The city is a rail junction, with iron foundries and metalworking, and textile manufacturing. Pop. (1989 est.) 60,396.

Lipscomb, William Nunn, Jr. (b. Dec. 9, 1919, Cleveland), American physical chemist who won the Nobel Prize for Chemistry in 1976 for his research on the structure and bonding of boron compounds and the general nature of chemical bonding.

Lipscomb graduated from the University of Kentucky in 1941 and earned his Ph.D. in 1946 from the California Institute of Technology. He worked as a physical chemist in the Office of Science Research and Development from 1942 to 1946 and then joined the University of Minnesota as assistant professor. By 1959, when he left the university, he was professor and chief of the physical chemistry division. He then became professor of chemistry at Harvard University, where he served as chairman of the department of chemistry from 1962 to 1965. By developing X-ray techniques that later proved useful in many chemical applications, Lipscomb and his associates were able to map the molecular structures of numerous boron hydride compounds (boranes) and their derivatives.

Lipscomb wrote *Boron Hydrides* (1963) and *Nuclear Magnetic Resonance Studies of Boron and Related Compounds* (1969).

Lipset, Seymour Martin (b. March 18, 1922, New York City), American sociologist and political scientist whose work in class structures, comparative politics, and systems of elites and political parties brought him international renown.

After receiving his B.S. from City College of New York (1943), Lipset was a lecturer at the University of Toronto (1946–48) and then an assistant professor at the University of California at Berkeley (1948–50). He took his doctorate at Columbia University (1949), where he remained on the graduate faculty (1950–56) and served as assistant director of the Bureau of Applied Social Research (founded by Paul Lazarsfeld) from 1954 to 1956. Lipset was a professor of sociology at Berkeley for the next 10 years and was director of its Institute of International Studies from 1962 to 1966. He was a professor at Harvard University from 1966 until he became a professor of political science and sociology in the Hoover Institute of Stanford University from 1975.

Lipset was a prolific author. Among his numerous books were *Agrarian Socialism* (1950; revised 1968) and *Union Democracy* (1956; with others). He wrote *Political Man* (1960; revised 1981), which won the MacIver Award. His other books include *Revolution and Counter Revolution* (1968); *The Politics of Unreason* (1970; with Earl Raab revised 1978), which won the Myrdal Award; *Rebellion in the University* (1972; reprinted 1976); and *The Divided Academy* (1975; with E.C. Ladd). These books developed his theory of elite systems and politics. He also edited *Emerging Coalitions in American Politics* (1978) and *The Confidence Gap: Business, Labor, and Government in the Public Mind* (1983; with William Schneider), a study of the decline of confidence of the American public in all major institutions, covering the period from the mid-1960s to the early 1980s.

Lipset's work had great influence in the field of sociology, with his books translated into 18 languages.

Lipsius, Justus (Latin), Flemish JOEST LIPS (b. Oct. 18, 1547, Overijse, near Brussels—d. March 23/24, 1606, Louvain, Brabant), Flemish humanist, classical scholar, and moral and political theorist.

Justus Lipsius, oil painting by an unknown artist, 1585; in the Musée Plantin-Moretus, Antwerp
A.C.L., Brussels

Appointed to the chair of history and philosophy at Jena in 1572, Lipsius later accepted the chair of history and law at the new University of Leiden (1578) and that of history and Latin at Louvain (1592). His first scholarly publication, the *Variae lectiones* of 1569, was in the traditional field of textual criticism. He quickly established himself as the leading editor of Latin prose texts, and his editions of Tacitus (first in 1574) and of Seneca (1605) were long renowned as models of their kind and are still worthy of attention. Lipsius was also a leader in the anti-Ciceronian stylistic movements of his time. His Latin style, terse and epigrammatic, owes a large debt to Tacitus. Force of personality and style also distinguish his vast correspondence conducted in Latin. Lipsius was noted for his antiquarian and historical studies and still more for his essays in moral and political theory. His 1604 introduction to Stoic thought remained the most intelligent and complete assessment of that philosophy for more than two centuries, although it was chiefly Roman, not Greek, Stoicism that inspired it. For him the ancient philosophers and historians were no mere subjects for research: they were guides to practical morality. He considered himself a Stoic, and his interest in Seneca lies at the root of his tract *De constantia* (1584). Similarly, his interest in Tacitus inspired his political theory, the *Politicorum libri sex* of 1589.

Lipsius, Richard Adelbert (b. Feb. 14, 1830, Gera, Prussia—d. Aug. 19, 1892, Jena, Ger.), German Protestant theologian who clarified the origin and authorship of early Christian literature, particularly the apocryphal acts of various apostles in his *Die Apokryphen, Apostelgeschichten und Apostellegenden* (1883–87; "Apocrypha, Acts, and Legends of the Apostles"). He also investigated the history of the early papacy and held that St. Peter never lived in Rome. His moderately liberal theology was principally expressed in his *Philosophie und Religion* (1885), in which he integrated aspects of Kantian Idealism with systematic theology.

Lipton, Seymour (b. Nov. 6, 1903, New York City—d. Dec. 5, 1986, Glen Cove, N.Y., U.S.), American sculptor known for his forceful metal sculptures of abstract organic forms.

Lipton attended City College of New York, studied dentistry at Columbia University (1923–27), and had no formal art training. He embarked on his artistic career in 1932 as a figurative sculptor, primarily in wood; when he shifted to abstract work after 1945, his major material became sheet metal.

The play between external and internal forms dominates Lipton's later work. His characteristically massive, textured pieces twist, curve, and seem frozen on the verge of opening. They are frequently suggestive of and titled after animals and plants.

His commissioned works include sculptures at Philharmonic Hall at Lincoln Center, New York City (1964), and Dulles International Airport, Washington, D.C. (1964).

Lipton, Sir Thomas Johnstone, 1ST BARONET (b. May 10, 1850, Glasgow—d. Oct. 2, 1931, London), British merchant who built the Lipton tea empire and also won fame as a yachtsman.

Lipton, whose Irish parents ran a small grocery, immigrated to the United States in 1865. After five years at various jobs, he returned to Glasgow and opened a small provision shop, whose success led him to open other shops

Sir Thomas Johnstone Lipton
BBC Hulton Picture Library

throughout the United Kingdom. To supply his retail shops on the most favourable terms, Lipton purchased extensive tea, coffee, and cocoa plantations in Ceylon and provided his own packing house for hogs in Chicago. He also acquired fruit farms, jam factories, bakeries, and bacon-curing establishments in England. In 1898 his business was organized into Lipton, Ltd. He was knighted in the same year and in 1902 was created a baronet. A keen yachtsman, Lipton raced his "Shamrock" yachts five times unsuccessfully for the America's Cup between 1899 and 1930.

liquefied natural gas, abbreviation LNG, natural gas (primarily methane) that has been liquefied for ease of storing and transporting. LNG takes up about 1/600 the space that natural gas does in its gaseous form, and it can be easily shipped overseas. LNG is produced by cooling natural gas below its boiling point, −162° C (−259° F), and is stored in double-walled cryogenic containers at or slightly above atmospheric pressure. It can be converted back to its gaseous form by simply raising the temperature.

LNG is more practical than liquefied petroleum gas (*q.v.*) or other liquid gases, particularly for use in large volumes, because it has the same chemical composition as natural gas. This fact and the growing demand for natural gas have stimulated LNG production. Moreover, LNG technology has made it possible to utilize natural gas from remote areas of the world where it previously had no commercial use and was flared (burned). Special tankers transport LNG from such countries as Algeria, Borneo, and Indonesia to markets in Europe, Japan, and the United States.

liquefied petroleum gas, also called LP GAS, or LPG, any of several liquid mixtures of the volatile hydrocarbons propene, propane, butene, and butane. It was used as early as 1860 for a portable fuel source, and its production and consumption for both domestic and industrial use have expanded ever since. A typical commercial mixture may also contain ethane and ethylene as well as a volatile mercaptan, an odorant added as a safety precaution.

LPG is recovered from "wet" natural gas (gas with condensable heavy petroleum compounds) by absorption. The recovered product has a low boiling point and must be distilled to remove the lighter fractions and then be treated to remove hydrogen sulfide, carbon dioxide, and water. The finished product is transported by pipeline and by specially built seagoing tankers. Transportation by truck, rail, and barge has also developed, particularly in the United States.

LPG reaches the domestic consumer in cylinders under relatively low pressures. The largest part of the LPG produced is used in central heating systems and the next largest as raw material for chemical plants; LPG is also used as an engine fuel. *Compare* liquefied natural gas.

liqueur, flavoured and sweetened distilled liquor, with alcohol content ranging from 24 percent to 60 percent by volume (48–120 U.S. proof). Liqueurs are produced by combining a base spirit, usually brandy, with fruits or herbs and are sweetened by the addition of a sugar syrup composing more than 2½ percent of the total beverage by volume.

The word liqueur is derived from the Latin *liquefacere,* meaning "to make liquid." Liqueurs were probably first produced commercially by medieval monks and alchemists. They have been called balms, crèmes, elixirs, and oils and have been used over the centuries as medicines and tonics, love potions, and aphrodisiacs.

Fruit liqueurs are produced by the infusion method, in which fruit is steeped in the spirit, which absorbs aroma, flavour, and colour. Plant liqueurs, naturally colourless, are produced by either percolation or distillation. Percolation is accomplished in an apparatus much like a coffee percolator. Leaves or herbs are placed in the top section, and the base spirit in the bottom section is pumped up over the flavouring material, extracting and carrying down the flavour constituents. The distillation method uses plants, seeds, roots, or herbs as flavouring material. They are softened in the base spirit, then combined with additional spirits and distilled. After the base spirit is completely flavoured, it is sweetened and filtered. Plant liqueurs are frequently coloured with vegetable colourings. Liqueurs may be aged or bottled immediately.

Generic liqueurs, marketed under accepted common names, frequently vary according to brand because of formula differences. They include apricot liqueur; crème d'ananas, flavoured with pineapple; crème de cacao, flavoured with cocoa and vanilla beans; crème de framboises, made from raspberries; crème de menthe, mint-flavoured; crème de noyaux, with bitter-almond flavour derived from fruit stones; crème de violette, also called parfait amour, with oils from both violets and vanilla beans; Curaçao, with flavour from the dried peel of the green oranges of the island of Curaçao; Danziger Goldwasser, spicy and containing tiny gold specks; kümmel, flavoured with caraway seed; prunelle, with plum flavour; sloe gin, flavoured with the fruit of the blackthorn bush; and Triple Sec, a colourless Curaçao.

Proprietary brands, usually prepared from secret formulas, are made by individual producers, who market their products under registered brand names. French proprietary brands include Bénédictine, a plant liqueur first produced in 1510 from one of the most closely guarded of all formulas; Chartreuse, made from a formula developed in 1607, including yellow and green plant liqueurs, both with spicy and aromatic flavour; Cointreau, a proprietary brand of Triple Sec; Grand Marnier, produced in the Cognac region, an orange Curaçao; and Vieille Cure, a plant liqueur made in Bordeaux. Italian liqueurs include Liquore Galliano and Strega, both with spicy flavours. British brands include Drambuie, with Scotch whisky as a base and flavoured with honey, made from a French formula taken to Scotland in 1745; and Irish Mist, a spicy liqueur made with Irish whiskey and honey. Cherry Heering is a cherry liqueur produced in Denmark. Liqueurs manufactured in the United States include Forbidden Fruit, made with brandy and grapefruit; and Crème Yvette, with violet flavour and colour. Coffee-flavoured brands include Kahlúa, from Mexico; and Tia Maria, using rum as the base spirit, from Jamaica. O Cha, with the flavour of green tea, and Midori, with the flavour of melon, are from Japan. Van der Hum is a spicy and aromatic product made in South Africa.

Liqueurs, sweet in flavour and with ingredients promoting digestion, are popular after-dinner drinks. They may be served straight, poured over ice, or mixed in an endless variety of combinations that may include liquors, brandies, and cream. Liqueurs are also used as flavourings in various dessert dishes.

liquid, in physics, one of the three principle states of matter; it is intermediate between gases and crystalline solids.

A brief treatment of the liquid state follows. For full treatment, *see* MACROPAEDIA: Matter: Its Properties, States, Varieties, and Behaviour.

Solids are characterized by low potential energies that result from powerful cohesive forces and bind the constituent molecules together, usually in an orderly pattern. In direct contrast, gases have high potential energies, resulting from weak cohesive forces, that allow free motion and a completely random molecular distribution. A liquid, with its intermediate potential energies and moderate cohesive forces, has neither the orderliness of a crystalline solid nor the randomness of a gas. Its molecules are not capable of unrestricted motion throughout the total volume; rather they are preserved in an orderly array over a few molecular diameters.

Other distinguishing features of liquids include an ability to flow under the action of very small shear stresses. Moreover, liquids in contact with their own vapours or air possess a surface tension that, unless opposed by external forces, causes the interface to assume the configuration of minimum area. In the absence of gravity and other forces, the stable form of a mass of liquid is spherical. Surfaces between a liquid and a solid or another immiscible liquid (*i.e.,* one that is incapable of mixing) are also characterized by interfacial tensions, which determine whether the liquid in question will spread on the other material. The electrical properties of liquids are determined by the density of charge carriers. With the exception of liquid metals, molten salts, and solutions of salts in ionizing solvents, the electrical conductivities of liquids are small. In molten salts and solutions of salts the current is carried by the ions of the salt, whereas in liquid metals it is carried by electrons.

liquid, in phonetics, a consonant sound in which the tongue produces a partial closure in the mouth, resulting in a resonant, vowel-like consonant, such as English *l* and *r.* Liquids may be either syllabic or nonsyllabic; *i.e.,* they may sometimes, like vowels, act as the sound carrier in a syllable. The *r* in "father" or Czech *krk* "neck" and the *l* in "rattle" are syllabic; the *r* in "rim" and the *l* in "lock" are nonsyllabic.

liquid crystal, a substance that flows as a liquid but maintains some of the ordered structure characteristic of a crystal. Certain organic substances when heated will not melt directly but will turn from a crystalline solid to a liquid-crystal (mesomorphic) state. Upon further heating, a temperature is reached at which a true (isotropic) liquid is formed. The liquid-crystal state has some characteristics of a crystal and some of a liquid but generally has properties that are unique.

Because the molecular forces producing liquid crystalline states are very weak, the structures are easily affected by changes in mechanical stress, electromagnetic fields, temperature, and chemical environment. Three main categories have been recognized: smectic, nematic, and cholesteric.

Smectic liquid crystals consist of flat layers of cigar-shaped molecules with their long axes oriented perpendicularly to the plane of the layer. Each layer is one or two molecules thick, and the positions of the molecules within each layer can be ordered or random, depending upon the substance. The sheets flow freely over each other; the molecules within each layer, however, remain oriented and do not move between layers.

Nematic liquid crystals are also oriented with their long axes parallel; but they are not separated into layers, and they behave like toothpicks in a box, maintaining their orientation but free to move in any direction. Nematic substances can be aligned by electric and magnetic fields, resulting in a number of characteristics such as the ability in some cases to be electrically switched from clear to opaque. This peculiarity gives rise to many technical applications such as in image display systems.

Cholesteric liquid crystals form in thin layers, each one molecule thick; and within each layer the molecules are arranged with their long axes in the plane of the layer and parallel to each other, as a two-dimensional nematic structure. One of their unusual optical properties is circular dichroism, a phenomenon in which a beam of light is split, one wavelength becoming circularly polarized while the other wavelengths are reflected. Thus, when white light falls on cholesteric liquid crystals, the reflected light is an iridescent colour characteristic of the angle of the incident beam as well as of the temperature. The ability to react to minute variations in temperature by changing colour has many applications, such as the determination of temperature variations over surfaces such as the skin.

liquid crystal display (LCD), optoelectronic device first introduced in the late 1960s and now used in displays for many electronic devices. By applying a low voltage to specific portions of a liquid crystal solution, its crystals can be realigned to produce visual images on a LCD. LCDs are much lighter and consume less power than other display technologies, making them ideal for portable electronic devices.

A brief treatment of liquid crystal display follows. For full treatment, *see* MACROPAEDIA: Electronics: Liquid crystal displays.

LCDs utilize either nematic or smectic liquid crystals. The molecules of nematic liquid crystals align themselves with their axes in parallel. Smectic liquid crystals arrange themselves in layered sheets; within different smectic phases, the molecules may take on different alignments relative to the plane of the sheets. The backlight of LCDs typically accounts for more than 80 percent of the display's power consumption. For mobile use, battery lifetime is of great importance, and displays that can be viewed in ambient light without backlighting, known as reflective displays, are highly desirable.

liquid-drop model, in nuclear physics, description of atomic nuclei formulated (1936) by Niels Bohr and used (1939) by him and John A. Wheeler to explain nuclear fission.

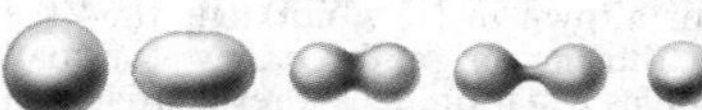

Nuclear fission according to the liquid-drop model
Encyclopædia Britannica, Inc.

According to the model, the nucleons (neutrons and protons) behave like the molecules in a drop of liquid. If given sufficient extra energy (as by the absorption of a neutron), the spherical nucleus may be distorted into a dumbbell shape and then split at the neck into two nearly equal fragments, releasing energy. Although inadequate to explain all nuclear phenomena, the theory underlying the model provides excellent estimates of average properties of nuclei.

liquidation, discharge of a debt or the determination by agreement or litigation of the amount of a previously unliquidated claim. At the dissolution of a solvent corporation or unincorporated association, the assets are usually liquidated (turned into money) rather than distributed in kind. An insolvent concern, on the other hand, may be liquidated in a receivership (*q.v.*), in which a court-appointed receiver sells the assets and distributes the proceeds; in general assignments for the benefit of creditors; in bankruptcy; or in the administration of a decedent's estate.

liquidity preference, in economics, the premium that holders of wealth demand for exchanging ready money or bank deposits for safe, nonliquid assets such as government bonds. As originally employed by John Maynard Keynes, liquidity preference referred to the demand for money as an asset. He hypothesized that the amount of money held for this purpose would vary inversely with the rate of interest. Post-Keynesian analysis of liquidity preference has identified other factors that influence the demand for money, including income levels, wealth and the many forms in which it is held, and the yields of those various forms of wealth.

liquor, distilled: *see* distilled liquor.

lira, plural LIRE, the former monetary unit of Italy, equal to 100 centesimi. The lira was introduced in Europe by Charlemagne, who based it on the pound (*libra*) of silver. No lira coins were struck during the Middle Ages, and the lira remained strictly a money of account. By the 16th century several of the Italian states actually struck lira coins, but they varied considerably in weight. One of the states that used the lira was the kingdom of Sardinia, and this monetary unit was adopted in all of Italy when it became unified under Sardinian leadership. In 1862 the lira, which up to then had been divided into 20 solidi, was redefined, and the decimal system was introduced.

In 2002 the lira ceased to be legal tender after the euro, the European Union's monetary unit, became Italy's sole currency.

lira, in music, a pear-shaped bowed instrument with three to five strings. Closely related to the medieval rebec and, like the rebec, a precursor of the medieval fiddle, the lira survives essentially unchanged in several Balkan folk instruments, among them the Bulgarian *gadulka,* the Aegean lira, and the Balkan Slavic *gusla.* Its tuning and range vary.

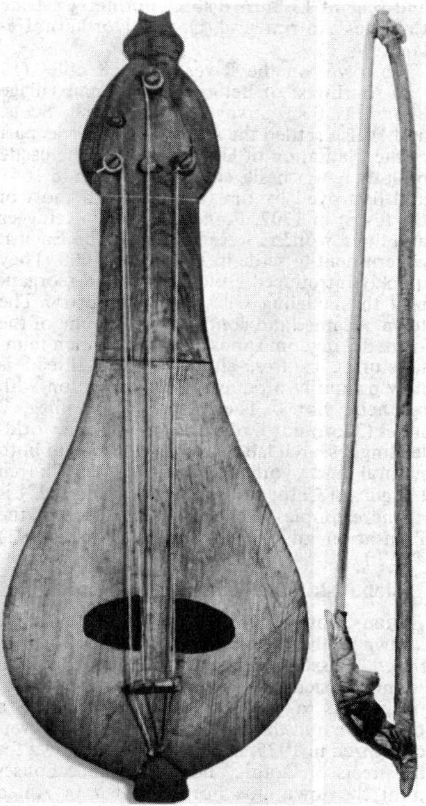

Greek lira and bow; in the Pitt Rivers Museum, Oxford
By courtesy of the Pitt Rivers Museum, Oxford

The word lira, a misapplication of *lyra,* the ancient Greek lyre played with a plectrum, had appeared by the 9th century for the Byzantine form of the Arab *rabāb,* the ancestor of all European bowed instruments. The Byzantine lira spread westward through Europe, where its precise evolution is unclear; writers in the 11th and 12th centuries often used the words fiddle and lira interchangeably. Unlike the *rabāb* and rebec but like the medieval fiddle, the lira has rear tuning pegs set in a flat peg disk. The lira, or *lira da braccio,* an Italian predecessor of the violin, was a 15th-century fiddle with three to five melody strings plus two off-the-fingerboard drone strings. Its bass version was the *lira da gamba,* or *lirone.*

Liri River, Latin LIRIS, river in central Italy, made up of two streams, the Rapido (or Gari) and the Liri, and having a total length of 98 mi (158 km) and a drainage basin of 1,911 sq mi (4,950 sq km). It has its sources near Cappadocia, in the Monti Simbruini east of Rome, and flows south and southeast through a long, narrow, scenic valley in its upper course as far as Arce, where it enters its wide lower valley and receives the waters of the Sacco (left bank) and Melfa (right) rivers. Near San Giorgio it is joined by the Rapido and there becomes the Garigliano River, turning southwest to empty into the Tyrrhenian Sea near Minturno, forming the boundary between Lazio (Latium) and Campania regions in its lower course.

During the winter of 1943–44, as part of the Allied drive toward Rome, heavy fighting took place along the Rapido and Liri, the Allied forces finally crossing in April 1944.

Liriope, genus of small marine jellyfish of the class Hydrozoa (phylum Cnidaria). Its medusoid body is characteristically hemispherical and measures up to about 30 mm (1.2 inches) in diameter. Eight short tentacles hang down from the edges of the body, and a shorter stalk-like structure, the manubrium, containing the mouth, extends downward from the centre. It is believed that only one, if highly variable, species exists (*Liriope tetraphylla*). It is found in the warm parts of the Atlantic and Indo-Pacific oceans. The liriope does not begin as a sessile (attached) form; the fertilized eggs develop directly into small medusae. Lacking a sessile stage, liriopes do not need a solid substrate during their life cycle and so are not restricted to coastal waters. They sometimes occur in great shoals near the surface.

Lisa, Manuel (b. Sept. 8, 1772, New Orleans—d. Aug. 12, 1820, St. Louis, Mo., U.S.), U.S. fur trader who helped to open up the Missouri River area to commerce in the early 19th century.

Of Spanish descent, Lisa automatically gained citizenship when Louisiana was purchased by the United States in 1803. Entering the fur trade out of St. Louis at an early age, he soon became one of the leading traders on the upper Mississippi. He was granted a monopoly of trade with the Osage Indians in 1802, but this ended with the transfer of national dominion two years later. He led a number of river expeditions and in 1807 established a trading post at the mouth of the Bighorn River (located in present Montana). The following year he built Ft. Raymond there for trade with the Crow Indians; later called Manuel's Fort, it was the first such outpost on the upper Mississippi.

In 1811 a "race" famous in Missouri River folklore occurred when the river barge of a search party led by Lisa overtook at the Niobrara River a flotilla sent out three weeks earlier by John Jacob Astor's trading company. After meeting, the two parties cooperated, and Lisa's return to home base was uneventful.

Near what later became the site of Omaha, Neb., Lisa established Ft. Lisa, which from 1813 to 1822 was the most important post on the Missouri, controlling trade with the Omaha, Pawnee, Oto, and other neighbouring Indians. In 1814 Lisa was appointed subagent for all tribes on the Missouri above the mouth of the Kansas River.

Lisboa, administrative district, west central Portugal, bounded by the Atlantic Ocean (west and south) and by the Tagus River and its estuary (southeast). It has an area of 1,066 sq mi (2,762 sq km). Principal occupations outside Lisbon (*q.v.*), the district and national capital, are agriculture and fishing, ironworking, and tourism. A disastrous flood in November 1967 caused over 450 deaths and much damage in the district. Pop. (1993 est.) 2,048,000.

Lisboa, António Francisco: *see* Aleijadinho.

Lisbon, Portuguese LISBOA, city, seat of Lisboa *distrito* ("district") and capital of Portugal. It is the country's chief port and largest city and stands 8 miles (13 km) upstream from the westernmost point of the European continent, where the Tagus (Tejo) River flows into the Atlantic Ocean. Area city, 34 square miles (87 square km). Pop. (2001) city, 556,797; urban aggl. 3,447,173.

A brief treatment of Lisbon follows. For full treatment, *see* MACROPAEDIA: Lisbon.

At Lisbon the Tagus widens to form a 7-mile-(11-kilometre-) wide bay called the Sea of Palha. On both sides of the river the land rises to gently rolling hills. The Baixa, the city centre and commercial heart of Lisbon, lies on the north bank of the Tagus near the water's edge; it was completely rebuilt after a devastating earthquake in 1755. Many other features of the historic city also have been preserved. Traces of the Moorish walls remain. The Avenida da Liberdade, which is the city's main promenade, has retained its wide, blue-mosaic sidewalks graced with palms and shade trees, fountains, and ornamental waters. A formal garden is located at its upper end, and outdoor cafés enhance the avenue. Most of the city's churches, decorated in Baroque, Rococo, or rocaille styles, were restored after the 1755 earthquake. The 14th-century Carmo (Carmel) Church, however, was left as it was, and the roofless shell is now an archaeological museum. The Castle of St. George (São Jorge) overlooks the city from the hill where Lisbon was first founded. The Tower of Belém and the Jerônimos Monastery are among other architectural monuments.

In the 20th century Lisbon emerged as a bustling metropolis, its growth spurred by tourism and commerce. The 4-story buildings of the Avenida da Liberdade and its ancillary streets (Avenidas Novas) have, for example, been almost totally replaced by 10-story buildings in more modern styles. The municipality also has built new neighbourhoods in the north and northwest sectors, and other building has pushed westward toward Belém. For the city's hosting of the World's Fair in 1998, many new facilities were built, including Europe's largest oceanarium and the cable-stayed Vasco da Gama Bridge.

The part of greater Lisbon along the south bank of the Tagus has become Portugal's most important manufacturing centre; the production of cement, steel, cork, and plastics and the storage of grain are important activities. Other industries include the production of soap, munitions, steel, glass, and electronic equipment and the refining of petroleum.

The University of Lisbon (founded 1288) is the principal centre of higher education; other educational institutions include the Higher Technical Institute and a teaching hospital. The city's museums have collections of modern, antique, sacred, decorative, and folk arts.

Public transportation is provided by a subway, supplemented by cable cars. Rail lines connect to the port and to other points in Portugal and Spain. Lisbon's international airport is located 4.5 miles (7 km) north of the city.

Lisbon, University of, Portuguese UNIVERSIDADE DE LISBOA, coeducational state institution of higher learning at Lisbon. The modern university, restored in 1911, traces its history, together with that of the University of Coimbra, to the medieval University of Lisbon founded in 1288. King Dinis of Portugal endowed a *studium generale,* a place of study accepting scholars from all over Europe and conferring a recognized degree. The university subsequently was moved several times to Coimbra and back to Lisbon. It remained in Lisbon from 1377 to 1537, when it again migrated, this time permanently, to Coimbra.

In 1911 the present sister university was founded in Lisbon. Modern faculties include science, letters, law, pharmacy, medicine, and psychology and educational science.

Lisburn, district, Northern Ireland. Established in 1973, the district is bordered by the city (district) of Belfast and district of Antrim to the north and by the districts of Craigavon to the west, Banbridge to the south, and Down and Castlereagh to the east. The chief town and seat of the district is Lisburn. Recently established industrial estates and residential suburbs are located at Dunmurry and around Lisburn town. Pigs, poultry, and barley are raised in rural areas. Hillsborough Castle at the town of Hillsborough, south of Lisburn town, accommodates members of the British royal family when they visit Northern Ireland. Area 171 square miles (444 square km). Pop. (1999 est.) 111,300.

Lisburn, Irish LIOS NA GCEARRBHACH, town and seat of Lisburn district, formerly astride Counties Antrim and Down, Northern Ireland.

The town, on the River Lagan 8 miles (13 km) southwest of Belfast, was a small village known as Lisnagarvey before English, Scots, and Welsh settled the site in the 1620s as part of the Plantation of Ulster scheme. The castle built there was besieged by native Irish in 1641 and destroyed by fire (together with most of the town) in 1707. French Huguenot refugees and linen workers were invited by the English government to settle in Lisburn in 1698. They quickly introduced Dutch looms and reorganized the fledgling Ulster linen industry. The town became (and continues to be) one of the United Kingdom's most important linen manufacturing centres, although linen thread is now primarily produced in combination with synthetic fibres. The village of Lambeg, 2 miles (3 km) north of Lisburn, houses a world-leading research laboratory on the uses of both natural and synthetic fibres. Christ Church (Anglican) Cathedral (originally built 1623) is a fine example of church architecture of the Plantation of Ulster period. Pop. (1991) 42,110.

Lisichansk (city, Ukraine): *see* Lysychansk.

Lisieux, town, formerly capital of the district known as the Pays d'Auge, Calvados *département,* Basse-Normandie *région,* northern France. Lisieux has become a world centre of pilgrimage to the shrine of St. Theresa, a Carmelite nun there who died in 1897 and was canonized in 1925. Lisieux was also known for its streets of Gothic and Renaissance houses until the town was burned down in Allied bombing raids in 1944 during World War II. The 12th- to 13th-century cathedral, partly rebuilt in the 16th and 17th centuries, was one of the few buildings that escaped destruction. A museum devoted to the history of old Lisieux also contains prehistoric and Gallo-Roman exhibits.

In Roman times the town was called Noviomagus Lexoviorum. An episcopal see from the 6th to the 18th century, Lisieux was a place of refuge for Henry II's exiled archbishop of Canterbury, Thomas Becket. Taken from the English and reunited to France in 1203, the town was a frequent subject of dispute during the Hundred Years' War (1337–1453) and later. The pilgrimage sites in Lisieux include the Chapelle du Carmel, where St. Theresa is buried, and the imposing Sainte-Thérèse Basilica, built in Romano-Byzantine style, begun in 1929 and consecrated in 1954. Formerly a leather and wool centre, the town now has plants manufacturing electronic equipment, wood products, pharmaceuticals, and processed food. It is also a local service and administrative centre. Pop. (1999) 23,166.

The Sainte-Thérèse Basilica, in Lisieux, Fr.
Ray Halin—Photo Researchers

Lisitsky, Lazar Markovich (Russian painter): *see* Lissitzky, El.

Liski, also spelled LISKY, formerly (until 1943) SVOBODA, or (1965–90) GEORGIU-DEZH, city and administrative centre of Liski *rayon* (sector), Voronezh *oblast* (province), western Russia, situated on the banks of the Don River. It is a main railway junction, with shops for servicing locomotives; its food industries include meat-packing and flour milling. It became a city in 1937 and underwent various name changes. Pop. (1993 est.) 55,500.

Lisle, village, Du Page county, northeastern Illinois, U.S., western suburb of Chicago. It was founded in 1832 by James and Luther Hatch, settlers from New Hampshire, and named for a town in New York. In 1864 the Chicago, Burlington, and Quincy Railroad chose Lisle as a station. It is a residential area and a centre for high-technology industries, such as computer software, electronics, and telecommunications. Immediately north is the Morton Arboretum, an outdoor park with more than 3,600 varieties of systematically arranged trees, shrubs, and vines, covering 1,700 acres (690 hectares). The arboretum was established in 1922 by Joy Morton (1855–1934), whose father, Julius Sterling Morton, inaugurated Arbor Day. Lisle is the seat of St. Procopius Abbey (founded 1885 by Bohemian Benedictines) and Benedictine University (1887). Inc. 1956. Pop. (2000) 21,182.

Lismore, city, northeastern New South Wales, Australia, on the north arm of the Richmond River. It is situated 18 miles (29 km) inland from the Pacific Ocean and has its outport at Ballina. Ward Stephens first settled the site in 1843; it was later occupied by William Wilson and named by him, probably for the Scottish island of Lismore. It is a farm processing centre (butter, bacon, sugar) and has had considerable light industrial development, including sawmilling, engineering, steel fabrication, and clothing manufacture. It became a village in 1856, a municipality in 1879, and a city in 1946. Pop. (2001 prelim.) 30,083.

Lismore, Irish LIOS MOR, market town, County Waterford, Ireland. It lies in the Blackwater valley, at the southern foot of the Knockmealdown Mountains. A monastery was founded in Lismore by St. Cartagh about 633. In the 9th and 10th centuries it was plundered by the Norsemen. The baronial castle, erected by Prince John, later king of England, in 1185, was the residence of the bishops of Lismore until the 14th century; in 1581 the manor was granted to Sir Walter Raleigh, and from him it passed to Richard Boyle in 1602. Robert Boyle, one of the

The baronial castle of Lismore, County Waterford

Eric Carle—Shostal

founders of modern chemistry, was born in the manor in 1627. In 1753 the castle passed to the 4th Duke of Devonshire, whose successor still retains it. Lismore has some river trade and is the centre of a salmon fishery. Pop. (2002 prelim.) 729.

Lismore, island in the entrance of Loch (lake) Linnhe, Argyll and Bute district, Strathclyde region, Scotland. It is about 9.5 miles (15 km) long and less than 2 miles (3 km) wide. A Columban (early Celtic Christian) monastery was founded on the island about 592. In the 13th century it became the seat of the bishop of Argyll. A small cathedral has been restored and is used as the parish church of the small island community.

Lismore, The Book of the Dean of, miscellany of Scottish and Irish poetry, the oldest collection of Gaelic poetry extant in Scotland. The chief compilers were Sir James MacGregor (*c.* 1480–1551), dean of Lismore (now in Argyll and Bute district, Strathclyde region), and his brother Duncan.

The manuscript, preserved in the National Library of Scotland, begins with a fragmentary Latin genealogy of MacGregor chiefs and contains the *Chronicle of Fortingall* to 1579 and a Latin list of Scottish kings to 1542. It concludes with a series of heroic tales and ballads from both the Ulster (Ulaid) cycle and Fenian cycle (*qq.v.*) of Irish legend, and it also contains miscellaneous poems by 44 Scottish and 21 Irish authors. The poems are written in literary Gaelic, in spelling based on vernacular usage, with phonetic additions to the Gaelic alphabet, probably common in part of the Scottish Highlands.

Lispector, Clarice (b. Dec. 10, 1925, Chechlnik, Ukraine, U.S.S.R.—d. Dec. 9, 1977, Rio de Janeiro, Braz.), novelist and short-story writer, one of Brazil's more important 20th-century literary figures. Her works depict a highly personal, almost existentialist view of the human dilemma and are written in a prose style characterized by a simple vocabulary and an elliptical sentence structure. In contrast to the regional or national social concerns expressed by many of her Brazilian contemporaries, her artistic vision transcends time and place; her characters, in elemental situations of crisis, are frequently female and only incidentally modern or Brazilian.

Lispector's first novel, *Perto do Coração Selvagem* (1944; "Near to the Savage Heart"), published when she was 19 years old, won critical acclaim for its sensitive interpretation of adolescence. In her later works, such as *A Maçã no Escuro* (1961; *The Apple in the Dark*), *A Paixão Segundo G.H.* (1964; "The Passion According to G.H."), and *Água Viva* (1973; "Living Water"), her characters, alienated and searching for meaning in life, gradually gain a sense of awareness of themselves and accept their place in an arbitrary, yet eternal, universe.

Lispector's finest prose is found in her short stories. Collections such as *Laços de Família* (1960; *Family Ties*) and *A Legião Estrangeira* (1964; "The Foreign Legion") focus on personal moments of revelation in the everyday lives of the protagonists and the lack of meaningful communication among individuals in a contemporary urban setting.

Lissa (Croatia): *see* Vis.

Lissajous figure, also called BOWDITCH CURVE, pattern produced by the intersection of two sinusoidal curves the axes of which are at right angles to each other. First studied by the American mathematician Nathaniel Bowditch in 1815, the curves were investigated independently by the French mathematician Jules-Antoine Lissajous in 1857–58. Lissajous used a narrow stream of sand pouring from the base of a compound pendulum to produce the curves.

If the frequency and phase angle of the two curves are identical, the resultant is a straight line lying at 45° (and 225°) to the coordinate axes. If one of the curves is 180° out of phase with respect to the other, another straight line is produced lying 90° away from the line produced where the curves are in phase (*i.e.,* at 135° and 315°).

Otherwise, with identical amplitude and frequency but a varying phase relation, ellipses are formed with varying angular positions, except that a phase difference of 90° (or 270°) produces a circle around the origin. If the curves are out of phase and differing in frequency, intricate meshing figures are formed.

Of particular value in electronics, the curves can be made to appear on an oscilloscope, the shape of the curve serving to identify the characteristics of an unknown electric signal.

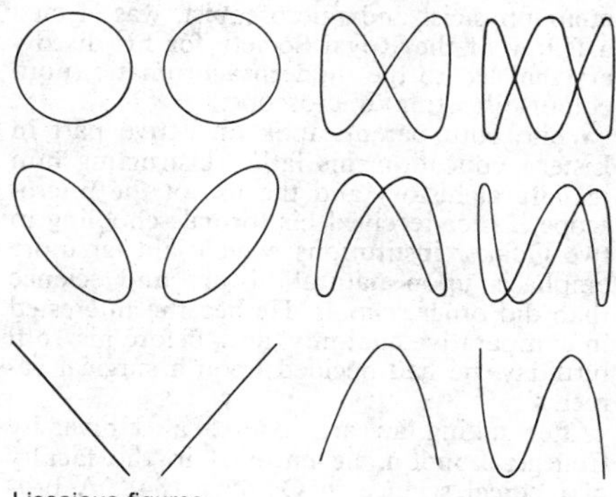

Lissajous figures

For this purpose, one of the two curves is a signal of known characteristics. In general, the curves can be used to analyze the properties of any pair of simple harmonic motions that are at right angles to each other.

Lisse, *gemeente* (commune), Zuidholland *provincie,* western Netherlands. It lies in the centre of the flower fields between Haarlem and Leiden. With Hillegom it is one of the two great commercial centres of The Netherlands' bulb-growing district and is the site of the State Bulb School and Laboratory. The annual (March to May) flower exhibition (started in 1950), held on a former country estate around the 17th-century De Keukenhof Castle, consists of gardens covering 65 acres (26 hectares). Pop. (2001 est.) 22,002.

Lissitzky, El, byname of ELIEZER, or ELIZAR, LISSITZKY, Russian in full LAZAR MARKOVICH LISITSKY (b. Nov. 10 [Nov. 22, New Style], 1890, Pochinok, near Smolensk, Russia—d. Dec. 30, 1941, Moscow), Russian painter, typographer, and designer, a pioneer of nonrepresentational art in the early 20th century. His innovations in typography, advertising, and exhibition design were particularly influential.

Lissitzky studied architecture at Darmstadt, Ger., and, during World War I, at Moscow. In 1919 Marc Chagall appointed him teacher at the revolutionary school of art in Vitebsk. Kasimir Malevich, the painter and founder of the Suprematist movement, which advocated the supremacy of pure geometric form over representation, also taught there, and he greatly influenced Lissitzky. In 1919 Lissitzky began to work on a series of abstract geo-

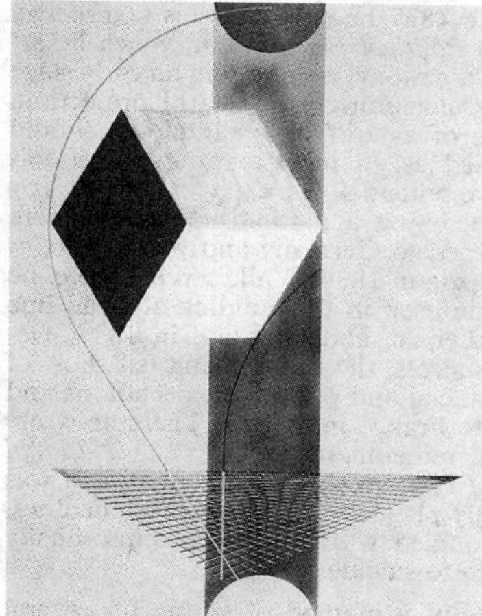

"Construction 99 (Proun 99)," oil painting by El Lissitzky, early 20th century; in Yale University Art Gallery

By courtesy of Yale University Art Gallery, gift of the Collection Societe Anonyme

metric paintings that he named "Proun," an acronym for the Russian words translated as "Projects for the Affirmation of the New." These paintings were a major contribution to the Constructivist art movement. In 1921 he became professor at the state art school in Moscow, but he left his country at year's end, when the Soviet government turned against modern art. He went to Germany, where he met the artist-designer László Moholy-Nagy, who transmitted Lissitzky's ideas on art to western Europe and the United States through his teaching at the Bauhaus.

Between 1925 and 1928 Lissitzky lived in Hannover, where he cofounded a number of periodicals propagating the most progressive artistic tendencies of the 1920s. In the winter of 1928–29 he returned to Moscow, where he continued to be an innovative force. His experiments in spatial construction led him to devise new techniques in exhibiting, printing, photomontage, and architecture, which have had much influence in western Europe.

List, (Georg) Friedrich (b. Aug. 6, 1789, Reutlingen, Württemberg—d. Nov. 30, 1846, Kufstein, Austria), German-U.S. economist who advocated tariff protection to stimulate national industrial development. Largely self-educated, List rose to prominence as

Friedrich List, lithograph by F. Kriehuber

Bruckmann—Art Reference Bureau

founder and secretary of an association of middle and south German industrialists that favoured abolition of the tariff barriers dividing the German states.

Exiled in 1825 for his liberal views, List went to the United States, where he became editor of a German-language newspaper in Reading, Pa. In 1827 he published his *Outlines of American Political Economy*, in which he argued that a national economy in an early stage of industrialization requires tariff protection. The costs of a tariff, he maintained, should be regarded as an investment in a nation's productive potentialities.

After becoming a naturalized U.S. citizen, List returned to Germany and was U.S. consul at Leipzig in 1834. While serving there, he involved himself in the building of a rail line between Leipzig and Dresden, in 1837. Despite its success, the undertaking fell short of List's financial and personal expectations and he went to France in despair. There he wrote his most remembered book, *The National System of Political Economy* (1841). List was perennially plagued with financial difficulties, which, coupled with other problems, finally drove him to suicide.

list system, a method of voting for several electoral candidates, usually members of the same political party, with one mark of the ballot. It is used to elect the parliaments of many western European countries, including Switzerland, Italy, the Benelux countries, and Germany. Electors vote for one of several lists of candidates, usually prepared by the political parties. Each party is granted seats in proportion to the number of popular votes it receives. There are several rules for computing the number of seats awarded to a party, the best known being the "d'Hondt rule" and the "largest-remainder rule." Seats are usually awarded to candidates in the order in which their names appear on the lists. Although ordinarily the list system forces the voters to cast their votes for parties rather than for individual candidates, a number of variations on the system permit voter preferences for individuals to be taken into account. The Swiss system, one of the most extreme variations, is marked by *panachage,* the ability of the voter to mix candidates from several party lists if he so desires.

Lista (y Aragón), Alberto (b. Oct. 15, 1775, Triana, Spain—d. Oct. 5, 1848, Seville), Spanish poet and critic considered to be the foremost member of the second Sevillian school of late 18th-century writers who espoused the tenets of Neoclassicism.

At the age of 20, Lista held the chair of mathematics at a college in Seville; later (1807) he assumed the chair of rhetoric and poetry at the University of Seville. After spending four years (1813–17) in France, he returned to Spain and founded the periodical *El censor* and the Free University of Madrid. He spent most of his life trying to educate people in the Neoclassic principles of good taste, emphasizing the need for balance between form and content. His *Poesías* (1822, 1837; "Poems") show faint influences of the Romantic movement. Among his best known works are *El imperio de la estupidez* (1798; "The Empire of Stupidity"), a critical work in the manner of Alexander Pope's *Dunciad*; *Ensayos literarios y críticos* (1844; "Literary and Critical Essays"); and *Lecciones de literatura española* (1836; "Lessons in Spanish Literature"), the published form of his lectures at the University of Madrid in 1822.

Lister, Joseph, BARON LISTER, OF LYME REGIS, also called (1883–97) SIR JOSEPH LISTER, BARONET (b. April 5, 1827, Upton, Essex, Eng.—d. Feb. 10, 1912, Walmer, Kent), British surgeon and medical scientist who was the founder of antiseptic medicine and a pioneer in preventive medicine. While his method, based on the use of antiseptics, is no longer employed, his principle—that bacteria must never gain entry to an operation wound—remains the basis of surgery to this day. He was made a baronet in 1883 and raised to the peerage in 1897.

Joseph Lister, 1857
By courtesy of the Wellcome Trustees, London

Education. Lister was the second son of Joseph Jackson Lister and his wife, Isabella Harris, members of the Society of Friends, or Quakers. J.J. Lister, a wine merchant and amateur physicist and microscopist, was elected a fellow of the Royal Society for his discovery that led to the modern achromatic (non-colour-distorting) microscope.

While both parents took an active part in Lister's education, his father instructing him in natural history and the use of the microscope, Lister received his formal schooling in two Quaker institutions, which laid far more emphasis upon natural history and science than did other schools. He became interested in comparative anatomy, and, before his 16th birthday, he had decided upon a surgical career.

After taking an arts course at University College, London, he enrolled in the faculty of medical science in October 1848. A brilliant student, he was graduated a bachelor of medicine with honours in 1852; in the same year he became a fellow of the Royal College of Surgeons and house surgeon at University College Hospital. A visit to Edinburgh in the fall of 1853 led to Lister's appointment as assistant to James Syme, the greatest surgical teacher of his day, and in October 1856 he was appointed surgeon to the Edinburgh Royal Infirmary. In April he had married Syme's eldest daughter. Lister, a deeply religious man, joined the Scottish Episcopal Church. The marriage, although childless, was a happy one, his wife entering fully into Lister's professional life.

When three years later the Regius Professorship of Surgery at Glasgow University fell vacant, Lister was elected from seven applicants. In August 1861 he was appointed surgeon to the Glasgow Royal Infirmary, where he was in charge of wards in the new surgical block. The managers hoped that hospital disease (now known as operative sepsis—infection of the blood by disease-producing microorganisms) would be greatly decreased in their new building. The hope proved vain, however. Lister reported that, in his Male Accident Ward, between 45 and 50 percent of his amputation cases died from sepsis between 1861 and 1865.

Work in antisepsis. In this ward Lister began his experiments with antisepsis. Much of his earlier published work had dealt with the mechanism of coagulation of the blood and role of the blood vessels in the first stages of inflammation. Both researches depended upon the microscope and were directly connected with the healing of wounds. Lister had already tried out methods to encourage clean healing and had formed theories to account for the prevalence of sepsis. Discarding the popular concept of miasma—direct infection by bad air—he postulated that sepsis might be caused by a pollen-like dust. There is no evidence that he believed this dust to be living matter, but he had come close to the truth. It is therefore all the more surprising that he became acquainted with the work of the bacteriologist Louis Pasteur only in 1865.

Pasteur had arrived at his theory that microorganisms cause fermentation and disease by experiments on fermentation and putrefaction. Lister's education and his familiarity with the microscope, the process of fermentation, and the natural phenomena of inflammation and coagulation of the blood impelled him to accept Pasteur's theory as the full revelation of a half-suspected truth. At the start he believed the germs were carried solely by the air. This incorrect opinion proved useful, for it obliged him to adopt the only feasible method of surgically clean treatment. In his attempt to interpose an antiseptic barrier between the wound and the air, he protected the site of operation from infection by the surgeon's hands and instruments. He found an effective antiseptic in carbolic acid, which had already been used as a means of cleansing foul-smelling sewers and had been empirically advised as a wound dressing in 1863. Lister first successfully used his new method on Aug. 12, 1865; in March 1867 he published a series of cases. The results were dramatic. Between 1865 and 1869, surgical mortality fell from 45 to 15 percent in his Male Accident Ward.

In 1869, Lister succeeded Syme in the chair of Clinical Surgery at Edinburgh. There followed the seven happiest years of his life when, largely as the result of German experiments with antisepsis during the Franco-German War, his clinics were crowded with visitors and eager students. In 1875 Lister made a triumphal tour of the leading surgical centres in Germany. The next year he visited America but was received with little enthusiasm except in Boston and New York City.

Lister's work had been largely misunderstood in England and the United States. Opposition was directed against his germ theory rather than against his "carbolic treatment." The majority of practicing surgeons were unconvinced; while not antagonistic, they awaited clear proof that antisepsis constituted a major advance. Lister was not a spectacular operative surgeon and refused to publish statistics. Edinburgh, despite the ancient fame of its medical school, was regarded as a provincial centre. Lister understood that he must convince London before the usefulness of his work would be generally accepted.

His chance came in 1877, when he was offered the chair of Clinical Surgery at King's College. On Oct. 26, 1877, Lister, at King's College Hospital, for the first time performed the then-revolutionary operation of wiring a fractured patella, or kneecap. It entailed the deliberate conversion of a simple fracture, carrying no risk to life, into a compound fracture, which often resulted in generalized infection and death. Lister's proposal was widely publicized and aroused much opposition. Thus, the entire success of his operation carried out under antiseptic conditions forced surgical opinion throughout the world to accept that his method had added greatly to the safety of operative surgery.

More fortunate than many pioneers, Lister saw the almost universal acceptance of his principle during his working life. He retired from surgical practice in 1893, after the death of his wife in the previous year. Many honours came to him. Created a baronet in 1883, he was made Baron Lister of Lyme Regis in 1897 and appointed one of the 12 original members of the Order of Merit in 1902. He was a gentle, shy, unassuming man, firm in his purpose because he humbly believed himself to be directed by God. He was uninterested in social success or financial reward. In person he was handsome, with a fine athletic figure, fresh complexion, hazel eyes, and silver hair. For some years before his death, however, he was almost completely blind and deaf. Lister wrote no books but contributed many papers to professional journals. These are contained in *The Collected Papers of Joseph, Baron Lister*, 2 vol. (1909). (F.F.C.)

BIBLIOGRAPHY. The authoritative biography is Rickman John Godlee, *Lord Lister* (1917). Other biographies include Rhoda Truax, *Joseph Lister, Father of Modern Surgery* (1944); and Richard B. Fisher, *Joseph Lister, 1827–1912* (1977).

Consult the INDEX *first*

Lister, Joseph Jackson (b. Jan. 11, 1786, London, Eng.—d. Oct. 24, 1869, West Ham, Essex), English amateur opticist whose discoveries played an important role in perfecting the objective lens system of the microscope, elevating that instrument to the status of a serious scientific tool.

Lister discovered a method of combining lenses that greatly improved image resolution by eliminating certain chromatic and spherical aberrations. In 1830 he began grinding his own lenses, developing techniques that he taught to optical instrument makers in London. Using his newly developed lenses, Lister was the first to determine the true form of the red corpuscle in mammalian blood. In recognition of his achievements, Lister was made a fellow of the Royal Society in 1832. He was the father of the surgeon Joseph Lister.

Lister, Samuel Cunliffe: *see* Masham (of Swinton), Samuel Cunliffe Lister, 1st Baron.

listeriosis, disease caused by the bacterium *Listeria monocytogenes*. The bacterium has been isolated from humans and from more than 50 species of wild and domestic animals, including mammals, birds, fish, crustaceans, and ticks. It has also been isolated from environmental sources such as animal silage, soil, plants, sewage, and stream water.

Evidence suggests that most humans with listeriosis may be infected by soil-contaminated food. The disease normally develops in persons whose immune systems are weak or impaired, such as newborn infants, pregnant women, the elderly, and those whose immune systems have been compromised by an underlying disease or by immunosuppressive drugs. The disease may appear as a mild influenzalike illness and go unrecognized. In adults meningitis is the most commonly recognized clinical manifestation of listeriosis; the bacterium can also cause endocarditis (inflammation of the heart lining), septicemia (blood poisoning), skin lesions, and other conditions. Intrauterine infection of the fetus may result in miscarriage, premature birth, or stillbirth; if the infant is born alive, it may develop septicemia or meningitis. Listeriosis responds to treatment with antibiotics.

Sheep, cattle, goats, horses, pigs, and other domesticated animals are susceptible to the infection, which may result in encephalitis, septicemia, and spontaneous abortion. In animals listeriosis is also known as circling disease, because some infected animals walk in circles.

Liston, Sonny, byname of CHARLES LISTON (b. May 8, 1917?, St. Francis county, Ark., U.S.—d. Dec. 31?, 1970, Las Vegas, Nev.), American boxer who was world heavyweight boxing champion from Sept. 25, 1962, when he knocked out Floyd Patterson in the first round in Chicago, until Feb. 25, 1964, when he stopped fighting Cassius Clay (afterward Muhammad Ali) before the seventh round at Miami Beach, Fla. Liston was noted for his punching power and durability.

Liston, the son of a tenant farmer, served two long terms in prison, where he is said to have learned to box. Although he gave his birth year as 1932, there is evidence that he began his ring career as early as 1934, at the age of 17, under the name of Charles ("Sailor") Liston. If that is true, he was 45 years old when he won the championship.

From 1953 (his first recorded fight) through 1970 Liston, who stood 6 feet 1 inch tall and weighed 215 pounds, had 54 bouts, winning 39 by knockouts and losing only 4. He defended his title successfully only once, scoring another first-round knockout over Patterson; but in his next bout he complained of an injury after six rounds and refused to continue fighting against Clay. In a rematch with Clay on May 25, 1965, Liston was knocked out in the first round.

Liszt, Franz, Hungarian FERENC LISZT (b. Oct. 22, 1811, Raiding, Hung.—d. July 31, 1886, Bayreuth, Ger.), Hungarian piano virtuoso and composer. Among his many notable compositions are his 12 symphonic poems, two (completed) piano concerti, several sacred choral works, and a great variety of solo piano pieces.

Youth and early training. Liszt's father, Ádám Liszt, was an official in the service of Prince Nicolas Eszterházy, whose palace in Eisenstadt was frequented by many celebrated musicians. Ádám Liszt was a talented amateur musician who played the cello in the court concerts. By the time Franz was five years old he was already attracted to the piano and was soon given lessons by his father. He began to show interest in both church and Gypsy music. He developed into a religious child, also because of the influence of his father, who during his youth had spent two years in the Franciscan order.

Liszt, lithograph by Joseph Kriehuber, 1846

By courtesy of the Museo Teatrale alla Scala, Milan

Franz began to compose at the age of eight. When only nine he made his first public appearance as a concert pianist at Sopron and Pozsony (now Bratislava, Slovakia). His playing so impressed the local Hungarian magnates that they put up the money to pay for his musical education for the next six years. Ádám obtained leave of absence from his post and took Franz to Vienna, where he had piano lessons with Karl Czerny, a composer and pianist who had been a pupil of Ludwig van Beethoven, and studied composition with Antonio Salieri, the musical director at the Viennese court. He gave several concerts in Vienna, with great success. The legend that Beethoven attended one of Liszt's concerts and kissed the prodigy on the forehead is considered apocryphal—but Liszt certainly met Beethoven.

Liszt moved with his family to Paris in 1823, giving concerts in Germany on the way. He was refused admission to the Paris Conservatoire because he was a foreigner; instead, he studied with Anton Reicha, a theorist who had been a pupil of Joseph Haydn's brother Michael, and Ferdinando Paer, the director of the Théâtre-Italien in Paris and a composer of light operas. Liszt's Paris debut on March 7, 1824, was sensational. Other concerts quickly followed, as well as a visit to London in June. He toured England again the following year, playing for George IV at Windsor Castle and also visiting Manchester, where his *New Grand Overture* was performed for the first time. This piece was used as the overture to his one-act opera *Don Sanche,* which was performed at the Paris Opéra on Oct. 17, 1825. In 1826 he toured France and Switzerland, returning to England again in the following year. Suffering from nervous exhaustion, Liszt expressed a desire to become a priest. His father took him to Boulogne to take seabaths to improve his health; there Ádám died of typhoid fever. Liszt returned to Paris and sent for his mother to join him; she had gone back to the Austrian province of Styria during his tours.

Liszt now earned his living mainly as a piano teacher, and in 1828 he fell in love with one of his pupils. When her father insisted that the attachment be broken off, Liszt again became extremely ill; he was considered so close to death that his obituary appeared in a Paris newspaper. After his illness he underwent a long period of depression and doubt about his career. For more than a year he did not touch the piano and was dissuaded from joining the priesthood only through the efforts of his mother. He experienced much religious pessimism. During this period Liszt took an active dislike to the career of a virtuoso. He made up for his previous lack of education by reading widely, and he came into contact with many of the leading artists of the day, including Alphonse de Lamartine, Victor Hugo, and Heinrich Heine. With the July Revolution of 1830 resulting in the abdication of the French king Charles X and the coronation of Louis-Philippe, he sketched out a *Revolutionary Symphony.*

Between 1830 and 1832 he met three men who were to have a great influence on his artistic life. At the end of 1830 he first met Hector Berlioz and heard the first performance of his *Symphonie fantastique.* From Berlioz he inherited the command of the romantic orchestra and also the diabolic quality that remained with him for the rest of his life. He achieved the seemingly impossible feat of transcribing Berlioz' *Symphonie fantastique* for the piano in 1833, and he helped Berlioz by transcribing other works of his and playing them in concert. In March 1831 he heard Niccolò Paganini play for the first time. He again became interested in virtuoso technique and resolved to transfer some of Paganini's fantastic violin effects to the piano, writing a fantasia on his *Campanella.* At this time he also met Frédéric Chopin, whose poetical style of music exerted a profound influence on Liszt.

Years with Marie d'Agoult. In 1834 Liszt emerged as a mature composer with the solo piano piece *Harmonies poétiques et religieuses,* based on a collection of poems by Lamartine, and the set of three *Apparitions.* The lyrical style of these works is in marked contrast to his youthful compositions, which reflected the style of his teacher Czerny. In the same year, through the poet and dramatist Alfred de Musset, he met the novelist George Sand and also Marie de Flavigny, Countess d'Agoult, with whom he began an affair. In

1835 she left her husband and family to join Liszt in Switzerland; their first daughter, Blandine, was born in Geneva on December 18. Liszt and Madame d'Agoult lived together for four years, mainly in Switzerland and Italy, though Liszt made occasional visits to Paris. He also taught at the newly founded Geneva Conservatory and published a series of essays, "On the Position of Artists," in which he endeavoured to raise the status of the artist—who up to then had been regarded as a kind of superior servant—to that of a respected member of the community.

Liszt commemorated his years with Madame d'Agoult in the first two books of solo piano pieces collectively named *Années de pèlerinage* (1837–54; *Years of Pilgrimage*), which are poetical evocations of Swiss and Italian scenes. He also wrote the first mature version of the *Transcendental Études* (1838, 1851); these are works for solo piano based on his youthful *Étude en 48 exercices*, but here transformed into pieces of terrifying virtuosity. He transcribed for the piano six of Paganini's pieces—five studies and *La campanella*—and also three Beethoven symphonies, some songs by Franz Schubert, and further works of Berlioz. He made these transcriptions to make the work of these men more available and thus spread the appreciation of their music, which was still greatly neglected at that time. Liszt also wrote a number of fantasias on popular operas of the day and dazzled audiences with them at his concerts.

His second daughter, Cosima, was born in 1837 and his son, Daniel, in 1839, but toward the end of that year his relations with Madame d'Agoult became strained and she returned to Paris with the children. Liszt then returned to his career as a virtuoso to raise money for the Beethoven Memorial Committee in Bonn for the completion of its Beethoven monument.

For the next eight years Liszt traveled all over Europe, giving concerts in countries as far apart as Ireland, Portugal, Turkey, and Russia. He continued to spend his summer holidays with Madame d'Agoult and the children on the island of Nonnenwerth in the Rhine River until 1844; then they finally parted, and Liszt took the children to Paris. Liszt's brilliance and success were at their peak during these years as a virtuoso. Everywhere he was received with great adulation; gifts and decorations were showered on him, and he had numerous mistresses, including the dancer Lola Montez and Marie Duplessis. Nevertheless, he still continued to compose, writing songs as well as piano works.

His visit to Hungary in 1839–40, the first since his boyhood, was an important event. His renewed interest in the music of the Gypsies laid the foundations for his *Hungarian Rhapsodies* and other piano pieces composed in the Hungarian style. He also wrote a cantata for the Beethoven Festival of 1845, his first work for chorus and orchestra, and some smaller choral works.

Compositions at Weimar. In February 1847 Liszt met the princess Carolyne Sayn-Wittgenstein at Kiev and later spent some time at her estate in Poland. She quickly persuaded him to give up his career as a virtuoso and to concentrate on composition. He gave his final concert at Yelizavetgrad (Kirovograd) in September of that year. Having been director of music extraordinary to the Weimar court in Germany since 1843, and having conducted concerts there since 1844, Liszt decided to settle there permanently in 1848. He was later joined by the princess, who had unsuccessfully tried to obtain a divorce from her husband. They resided together in Weimar, and Liszt now had ample time to compose, as well as to conduct the court orchestra in operas and concerts. This was the period of his greatest production: the first 12 symphonic poems, *A Faust Symphony* (1854; rev. 1857–61), *A Symphony to Dante's Divina Commedia* (1855–56), the *Piano Sonata in B Minor* (1852–53), the *Piano Concerto No. 1 in E Flat Major* (1849; rev. 1853 and 1856), and the *Piano Concerto No. 2 in A Major* (1839; rev. 1849–61). (A third piano concerto, in E flat, composed in 1839, was left unperformed during his lifetime and was not discovered until 1988.) During the period in Weimar Liszt also composed the *Totentanz* for piano and orchestra, revised versions of the *Transcendental* and *Paganini Études* and of the first two books of the *Années de pèlerinage,* choral works, and numerous others. Some of these works had been sketched out in the 1840s or earlier, but, even so, his productivity in this period remains astonishing.

The avant-garde composers of the day regarded Weimar as the one city where modern composers could be heard, and many of them came to Liszt as pupils. The so-called New German school hoisted the banner of modernism, which naturally annoyed the more academic musicians. Some members of the Weimar court also were upset by Liszt's continued support of the composer Richard Wagner, who had had to flee in 1849 with Liszt's help from Germany to Switzerland because of his political activism. The straitlaced citizens of Weimar also objected strongly to the princess openly living with Liszt, and the grand duchess of Weimar was under pressure from her brother, Nicholas I of Russia, to ban Princess Sayn-Wittgenstein from all court functions. Furthermore, the grand duke who originally appointed Liszt died in 1853, and his successor took little interest in music. Liszt resigned five years later, and, though he remained in Weimar until 1861, his position there became more and more difficult. His son, Daniel, had died in 1859 at the age of 20. Liszt was deeply distressed and wrote the oration for orchestra *Les Morts* in his son's memory. In May 1860 the princess had left Weimar for Rome in the hope of having her divorce sanctioned by the pope, and in September, in a troubled state of mind, Liszt had made his will. He left Weimar in August of the following year, and after traveling to Berlin and Paris, where he saw Marie d'Agoult, he arrived in Rome. He and the princess hoped to be married on his 50th birthday. At the last moment, however, the pope revoked his sanction of the princess' divorce; they both remained in Rome in separate establishments.

Eight years in Rome. For the next eight years Liszt lived mainly in Rome and occupied himself more and more with religious music. He completed the oratorios *Die Legende von der heiligen Elisabeth* (1857–62) and *Christus* (1855–66) and a number of smaller works. He hoped to create a new kind of religious music that would be more direct and moving than the rather sentimental style popular at the time. Liszt was one of the few 19th-century musicians to be interested in Gregorian plainsong, but his efforts were frowned on by the ecclesiastical authorities, and much of his sacred music remained unpublished until many years after his death.

In 1862 his daughter Blandine died at the age of 26. Liszt wrote his variations on a theme from the J.S. Bach cantata *Weinen, Klagen* (*Weeping, Mourning*) ending with the chorale *Was Gott tut das ist wohlgetan* (*What God Does Is Well Done*), which must have been inspired by this event. The princess' husband died in 1864, but there was no more talk of marriage, and in 1865 Liszt took the four minor orders of the Roman Catholic church, though he never became a priest. In 1867 he wrote the *Hungarian Coronation Mass* for the coronation of the emperor Francis Joseph I of Austria as king of Hungary. This commission renewed his links with his native land. Meanwhile, his daughter Cosima, who, at the age of 19, had married Liszt's favourite pupil, Hans von Bülow, was having an affair with Richard Wagner. She had an illegitimate child by Wagner, which led to a quarrel between the two composers that lasted until 1872.

Last years. In 1869 Liszt was invited to return to Weimar by the grand duke to give master classes in piano playing, and two years later he was asked to do the same in Budapest. From then until the end of his life he divided his time between Rome, Weimar, and Budapest. After a reconciliation with Wagner in 1872, Liszt regularly attended the Bayreuth festivals. He appeared occasionally as a pianist in charity concerts and continued to compose. His music began to lose some of its brilliant quality and became starker, more introverted, and more experimental in style. His later works anticipate the harmonic style of Claude Debussy, and one late work called *Bagatelle Without Tonality* anticipates Béla Bartók and even Arnold Schoenberg.

In 1886 Liszt left Rome for the last time. He attended concerts of his works in Budapest, Liège, and Paris and then went to London—his first visit there in 45 years—where several concerts of his works were given. He then went on to Antwerp, Paris, and Weimar. He played for the last time at a concert in Luxembourg on July 19. Two days later he arrived in Bayreuth for the festival. His health had not been good for some months, and he went to bed with a high fever, though he still managed to attend two Wagner performances. His final illness developed into pneumonia, and his condition was not helped by the callous behaviour of Cosima, who left him alone in order to supervise the running of the festival. He died on July 31.

Assessment. Liszt was not only the greatest piano virtuoso of his time but also a composer of enormous originality and a principal figure in the Romantic movement. As a composer he radically extended the technique of piano writing, giving the instrument not only brilliance but a full and rich, almost orchestral sound. Most of his compositions bear titles and are representations of some natural scene or of some poetic idea or work of literature or art. Liszt extended the harmonic language of his time, even in his earlier works, and his later development of chromatic harmony helped lead eventually to the breakdown of tonality and ultimately to the atonal music of the 20th century. Liszt also invented the symphonic poem for orchestra and the method of "transformation of themes," by which one or two themes in different forms can provide the basis for an entire work—a principle from which Wagner derived his system of so-called leitmotifs in his operas.

As a pianist Liszt was the first to give complete solo recitals, and he did a great deal to encourage the performance of music by Bach, Beethoven, Schubert, Berlioz, Wagner, and Robert Schumann by transcribing their works for piano and playing them in his concerts at a time when they were insufficiently appreciated. He also helped younger composers, including Edvard Grieg, Mily Balakirev, Aleksandr Borodin, and Claude Debussy; and he taught a number of pupils who themselves became famous virtuosos.

Apart from his more than 700 compositions, Liszt was the author of books on Frédéric Chopin, Hungarian Gypsy music, Wagner's *Lohengrin* and *Tannhäuser,* John Field's nocturnes, the lieder of Robert Franz, and the Goethe Foundation in Weimar. His published essays and correspondence fill many volumes. A controversial figure in his time, he was attacked for his innovations, and his rivals were jealous of his brilliance and panache. For a long time he was regarded merely as a superficial composer of brilliant trifles, but in recent years his true stature has been seen more clearly as that of a composer who revolutionized the music of his time and anticipated numerous later developments. As Princess Sayn-Wittgenstein said, "Liszt has flung his spear far into the future." (H.Se./Ed.)

BIBLIOGRAPHY. Useful biographical sources in English are Sacheverell Sitwell, *Liszt,* rev. ed. (1955, reissued 1988); Alan Walker (ed.), *Franz Liszt: The Man and His Music* (1970); Eleanor Perényi, *Liszt: The Artist as Romantic Hero* (1974); Alan Walker, *Franz Liszt* (1983–); Ronald Taylor, *Franz Liszt: The Man and the Musician* (1986); Klára Hamburger, *Liszt* (1987); and Ernst Burger, *Franz Liszt: A Chronicle of His Life in Pictures and Documents* (1989).

Consult the INDEX *first*

Līṭānī River, Arabic NAHR AL-LĪṬĀNĪ, Latin LEONTES, chief river of Lebanon, rising in a low divide west of Baalbek and flowing southwestward through the Al-Biqāʿ Valley between the Lebanon and Anti-Lebanon mountains. Near Marj ʿUyūn it bends sharply west and cuts a spectacular gorge up to 900 feet (275 m) deep through the Lebanon Mountains to the Mediterranean south of Sidon. The river's lower course is known as Qāsimīyah. Although the river's total length is only about 90 miles (145 km), its waters irrigate one of Lebanon's most extensive farming regions, Al-Biqāʿ (*q.v.*). The Litani River Authority, established in 1954, was to have provided for an increase in irrigated land, generation of electricity, and development of recreational areas; however, the main achievement of the project was later limited to the establishment of electrical power plants.

Litchfield, town (township), Litchfield county, western Connecticut, U.S. It includes the boroughs of Litchfield and Bantam. The town, settled and incorporated in 1719, was named for Lichfield, Eng., and during the American Revolution it became a supply point and rest stop for American troops en route to Boston. Judge Tapping Reeve established the country's first law school there in 1784; its students included the U.S. vice presidents Aaron Burr and John C. Calhoun. The judge's house (1773) and school are preserved. The town was the birthplace of Ethan Allen, Revolutionary leader of the Green Mountain Boys, and Harriet Beecher Stowe, author of *Uncle Tom's Cabin* (1852).

Litchfield is now the centre of a resort and agricultural (poultry, dairy products, and fruit) area. The town's light manufactures include electrical equipment, lumber, and metal furniture. The Litchfield Historical Society Museum houses collections of Indian and American crafts. Pop. (1988 est.) 1,500.

Litchfield, Paul W(eeks) (b. July 26, 1875, Boston, Mass., U.S.—d. March 18, 1959, Akron, Ohio), American industrialist who was president (1926–40) and chairman of the board (1930–58) of Goodyear Tire & Rubber Company, a firm that he helped develop into a worldwide operation.

Litchfield graduated from the Massachusetts Institute of Technology in 1896 in chemical engineering. His first job in the rubber industry was with a bicycle-tire manufacturer. In 1900 he became superintendent at the Akron plant of Goodyear Tire & Rubber Company and thereafter ascended rapidly, becoming president in 1926 and chairman of the board four years later.

At Goodyear Litchfield established a research and development department that produced the first practical airplane tire, long-haul conveyor belts, hydraulic disc brakes for airplanes, the first pneumatic truck tire, and a bullet-sealing fuel tank for military airplanes. Goodyear built a research centre in 1943 for almost $1,500,000 to centralize the work of 250 research scientists.

Litchfield expanded Goodyear's foreign operations, setting up plants, factories, and plantations in Java, the Philippines, Mexico, and Sumatra, as well as in South America, Europe, and Africa. An advocate of flying, Litchfield began an aeronautics department for Goodyear in 1910 and launched the company into lighter-than-air craft production. It produced observation balloons, zeppelins, and dirigibles, many of which set size and altitude records. During World War II, the company had 37,000 workers producing aircraft and airplane parts, making it one of the 10 largest such producers in the country. Litchfield authored books on air power, trucks, employee relations, and business. His autobiography, *Industrial Voyage,* was published in 1954.

litchi, also spelled LYCHEE, LICHI, or LEECHEE, fruit of *Litchi chinensis,* a tree of the family Sapindaceae, believed native to southern China and adjacent regions. The handsome tree develops a compact crown of foliage, bright green the year round. The leaves are compound, composed of two to four pairs of elliptic to lanceolate leaflets that are 50–75 mm (2–3 inches) long. The flowers, small and inconspicuous, are borne in loose, diverse terminal clusters, or panicles, sometimes 30 cm (12 inches) in length.

Litchi (*Litchi chinensis*)
Donald P. Watson—EB Inc.

The fruits, produced in clusters, are oval to round, strawberry red in colour, and about 25 mm (1 inch) in diameter. The brittle outer covering encloses white, translucent, watery flesh and one large seed. The fruit is eaten fresh, canned, or dried, as the litchi nut of commerce. The flavour of the fresh pulp is musky; when dried, it is acidic and very sweet.

Litchi has been the favourite fruit of the Cantonese since ancient times. Its introduction into the Western world came when it reached Jamaica in 1775. The first litchi fruits in Florida—where the tree has attained commercial importance—are said to have ripened in 1916. To a lesser extent the tree has been cultivated around the Mediterranean, in South Africa, in numerous parts of India, and in Hawaii.

The tree is propagated by seed and by air layering. When moved to a permanent orchard, litchi are set 7.5–10.5 m (24.5–34.5 feet) apart. They require very little pruning and no unusual attention, though they should have abundant moisture around the roots most of the time. The trees come into production at three to five years of age.

literary criticism, a discipline concerned with a range of enquiries about literature that have tended to fall into three broad categories: philosophical, descriptive, and evaluative. Criticism asks what literature is, what it does, and what it is worth.

A brief treatment of literary criticism follows. For full treatment, *see* MACROPAEDIA: Literature, The Art of.

The Western critical tradition begins with Plato in the 4th century BC. In his *Republic* he attacked the poets on two fronts: their art was merely imitative, and it appealed to the worst rather than to the best in human nature. These are the charges that Aristotle countered a generation later in his *Poetics* by claiming for literature a level of imaginative truth that transcends that of imitation, and by arguing that it excited the emotions simply in order to allay them. The taxonomy of literary forms that Aristotle developed and the principles of composition he affirmed were of signal importance to the literature of Renaissance Europe. As late as 1674 Nicolas Boileau was still, in his *L'Art Poétique,* recommending observance of the Aristotelian rules, or unities, of time, action, and place.

European literary criticism from the Renaissance on has for the most part focused on the same two issues that underlie the debate between Plato and Aristotle: the moral worth of literature and the nature of its relationship with reality. At the end of the 16th century Sir Philip Sidney returned to the question in his *Defence of Poesie,* arguing that it was the special property of literature to express moral and philosophical truths in a way that rescued them from abstraction and made them immediately graspable. A century later, John Dryden, in *Of Dramatick Poesie, An Essay* (1668), put forward the less idealistic view that the business of literature was primarily to offer an accurate representation of the world "for the delight and instruction of mankind." This remains the assumption of the great critical works of 18th-century England, underlying both Alexander Pope's *Essay on Criticism* (1711) and the extensive work of Samuel Johnson.

In the late 18th century, literary criticism began to reflect the influence of the growing Romantic movements in England and Germany. William Wordsworth's assertion in his Preface to the second edition of the *Lyrical Ballads* (1800) that the object of poetry is "truth . . . carried alive into the heart by passion" marks a significant change from the ideas of the mid-century. Other important statements of critical theory in the Romantic period were Samuel Taylor Coleridge's *Biographia Literaria* (1817), which drew heavily on the work of such German theorists as F.W.J. Schelling and A.W. Schlegel, and Percy Bysshe Shelley's *Defence of Poetry* (written 1821). The later 19th century saw a development in one direction toward an aesthetic theory of art for art's sake, which enjoyed considerable influence in France and England, and in another direction toward the view, expressed by Matthew Arnold, that the cultural role of literature should be to take over the sort of moral and philosophical functions that had previously been fulfilled by religion.

For the future of literary criticism, however, the most important change during the final years of the century was the gradual establishment of literature as an academic discipline. In the 20th century there has been a massive increase in the volume of literary criticism. An early product of this in the English-speaking world was I.A. Richards' *Principles of Literary Criticism* (1924), which became influential as the basis of "Practical Criticism." From this developed the "New Criticism" of the 1940s and '50s, which was associated with such American critics as John Crowe Ransom and Cleanth Brooks. The premise of the New Critics, that a work of literature should be studied as a separate and self-contained entity, set them in opposition both to biographical criticism and to those schools of criticism—Marxist, psychoanalytical, historical, and the like—that had their roots in the 19th century and that set out to examine literature from perspectives external to the text.

The late 20th century saw a radical reappraisal of traditional modes of literary criticism. Building on the work of the Russian Formalist critics of the 1920s and the examinations of linguistic structure carried out by the Swiss philologist Ferdinand de Saussure, literary theorists began to question the overriding importance of the concept of "the author" as the source of the text's meaning. Structuralist and poststructuralist critics, such as Roland Barthes and Jacques Derrida of France, instead directed attention toward the ways in which meaning is created by the determining structures of language and culture.

literary sketch, short prose narrative, often an entertaining account of some aspect of a culture written by someone within that culture for readers outside of it—for example, anecdotes of a traveler in India published in an English magazine. Informal in style, the sketch is less dramatic but more analytic and descriptive than the tale and the short story. A writer of a sketch maintains a chatty and familiar tone, understating his major points and suggesting, rather than stating, conclusions.

One common variation of the sketch is the character sketch, a form of casual biography usually consisting of a series of anecdotes about a real or imaginary person.

The sketch was introduced after the 16th century in response to growing middle-class interest in social realism and exotic and foreign lands. The form reached its height of popularity in the 18th and 19th centuries and is represented by such famous sketches as those of Joseph Addison and Richard Steele in *The Spectator* (1711–12). They created characters such as Mr. Spectator, Sir Roger de Coverley, Captain Sentry, and Sir Andrew Freeport, representatives of various levels of English society, who comment on London manners and morals. *The Sketch Book of Geoffrey Crayon, Gent.* (1819–20) is Washington Irving's account of the English landscape and customs for readers in the United States.

literati painting (Chinese art): *see* wen-jen-hua.

literati painting (Japanese art): *see* Nan-ga.

literature, a body of written works. The name is often applied to those imaginative works of poetry and prose distinguished by the intentions of their authors and the excellence of their execution. Literature may be classified according to a variety of systems, including language, national origin, historical period, genre, and subject matter.

Literature is treated in a number of articles in the MACROPAEDIA. For the nature and scope of literature, major literary genres and techniques, and trends in literary criticism, *see* Literature, The Art of; Rhetoric. For a general history of the literary tradition of the West, *see* Literature, The History of Western. For surveys of the major literatures of the world, *see* American Literature; Australia and New Zealand, Literatures of; Belgian Literature; Canadian Literature; Celtic Literature; Chinese Literature; Dutch Literature; English Literature; French Literature; German Literature; Greek Literature; Hebrew Literature; Hungarian Literature; Italian Literature; Japanese Literature; Korean Literature; Latin-American Literature; Latin Literature; Polish Literature; Portuguese Literature; Russian Literature; Scandinavian Literature; Spanish Literature; Yiddish Literature. *See also* the literature sections of African Arts; Islāmic Arts; Oceanic Arts; South Asian Arts; Southeast Asian Arts.

For the literatures of still other nations and those written in a historically important language or dialect, *see* MICROPAEDIA: Anglo-Norman literature; Armenian literature; Bulgarian literature; Coptic literature; Estonian literature; Ethiopian literature; Finnish literature; Georgian literature; Indian literature; Latvian literature; Lithuanian literature; Provençal literature; Romanian literature; South African literature; Swiss literature; etc.

For a description of the place of literature in the circle of learning and for a list of both MACROPAEDIA and MICROPAEDIA articles on the subject, *see* PROPAEDIA: Part Six, Division II.

litharenite, sandstone (*i.e.,* sedimentary rock composed of grains 0.06–2 mm [0.0024–0.08 inch] in diameter) containing over 25 percent rock fragments. Litharenites most often are of gray or salt-and-pepper colour because of the inclusion of dark rock fragments, mainly slate, phyllite, or schist but also andesite or basalt. Litharenites formed by rapid deposition in areas subject to crustal deformation.

litharge, also called LITHARGITE, one of two mineral forms of lead(II) oxide (PbO). It is found with the other form, massicot, as dull or greasy, very heavy, soft, red crusts in the oxidized zone of lead deposits, as at Cucamonga Peak and Fort Tejon, Calif., U.S., and near Hailey, Idaho, U.S. For mineralogic properties, *see* oxide mineral (table). Synthetic lead(II) oxide is called litharge, though it is a mixture of litharge and massicot.

Lithgow, city, east-central New South Wales, Australia, on the western slopes of the Blue Mountains. Founded in 1824 and named after former state auditor-general William Lithgow, it became a municipality in 1889 and a city in 1945; in 1977 it was amalgamated with Blaxland Shire to form the City of Greater Lithgow. It lies at the heart of the western coalfield (although most of the mines in the Lithgow Valley have been worked out), extending from the Grose River valley to Kandos and Ulan. In 1858 this coal was used to power local woolen and flour mills and was also the basis for the founding in the late 19th century of iron- and steel- and copper-refining industries.

Lithgow's enterprises include the Australian Commonwealth Small Arms Factory (opened in 1912), woolen and flour mills, and the manufacture of textiles and ceramics. The city, linked to Sydney (86 miles [137 km] southeast) by rail and the Great Western Highway, has a technical college and is close to the Zigzag, an unused railroad right-of-way that in the 1970s was partially restored as a tourist attraction. Pop. (1991) 11,968.

Lithgow, William (b. 1582, Lanark, Lanarkshire, Scot.—d. *c.* 1645, Lanark), Scottish traveler and writer.

Lithgow was the son of a merchant and began his travels in his youth. He visited the Orkney and Shetland islands, Germany, Bohemia, and the Low Countries, arriving in Paris in 1609. The following year he went to Rome and began the first of his major journeys, having traveled by 1613 to Greece, the Middle East, Egypt, Malta, western Europe, and England. Between 1614 and 1618 he visited North Africa and central Europe and in 1619 went to Ireland and Spain (where he was tortured by the Inquisition). He traveled throughout Scotland in 1627–29.

Lithgow's major literary work is *The Totall Discourse of the Rare Adventures and Painefull Peregrinations of Long Nineteene Yeares Travayles* (1632; reprinted 1906), which, though written in a florid style, contains much cultural and economic detail. He also produced six poems about his travels and pamphlets on the siege by Frederick Henry of Orange of the Netherlands city of Breda (published 1637), on a survey of London (1643), and on the siege of Newcastle (1645) during the English Civil Wars.

lithia mica (mineral): *see* lepidolite.

lithification, complex process whereby freshly deposited loose grains of sediment are converted into rock. Lithification may occur at the time a sediment is deposited or later. Cementation is one of the main processes involved, particularly for sandstones and conglomerates. In addition, reactions take place within a sediment between various minerals and between minerals and the fluids trapped in the pores; these reactions, collectively termed authigenesis, may form new minerals or add to others already present in the sediment. Minerals may be dissolved and redistributed into nodules and other concretions, and minerals in solution entering the sediment from another area may be deposited or may react with minerals already present. The sediment may be compacted by rearrangement of grains under pressure, reducing pore space and driving out interstitial liquid.

lithiophilite, common phosphate mineral similar to triphylite (*q.v.*).

lithium (Li), chemical element of Group Ia in the periodic table, the alkali metal group, lightest of the solid elements. The metal itself—which is soft, white, and lustrous—and several of its alloys and compounds are produced on an industrial scale.

A brief treatment of lithium follows. For full treatment, *see* MACROPAEDIA: Chemical Elements: *Alkali metals.*

Occurrence, uses, and properties. Discovered (1817) by Johan August Arfwedson in the mineral petalite, lithium is found also in economically exploitable quantities in such minerals as spodumene, lepidolite, amblygonite, and petalite; it constitutes about 0.002 percent of the Earth's crust. Chemical treatment of the ores provides lithium hydroxide, carbonate, or sulfate, which can be converted to other compounds. Lithium metal is made by electrolyzing a molten mixture of lithium chloride and potassium chloride. The metal, which can be drawn into wire and rolled into sheets, is softer than lead but harder than the other alkali metals and has the body-centred cubic crystal structure. Lithium and its compounds impart a crimson colour to a flame, the basis of a test for its presence. Lithium floats on water, reacting with it to yield lithium hydroxide (LiOH) and hydrogen gas. It is commonly kept coated with petrolatum because it reacts with the moisture in the air.

Natural lithium exists as two isotopes: lithium-7 (92.5 percent) and lithium-6 (7.5 percent); five radioactive isotopes have been prepared—lithium-5, lithium-8, lithium-9, lithium-10, and lithium-11—all having half-lives of less than one second. Lithium was used (1932) as the target metal in the pioneering work of John Cockcroft and Ernest Walton in transmuting nuclei by artificially accelerated atomic particles; each lithium nucleus that absorbed a proton became two helium nuclei. The bombardment of lithium-6 with slow neutrons produces helium and tritium.

Aluminum, lead, and other soft metals can be made harder by alloying them with small proportions of lithium.

Compounds. Lithium is chemically active, readily losing one of its three electrons to form compounds containing the Li^+ cation. Many of these differ markedly in solubility from the corresponding compounds of the other alkali metals.

A number of the lithium compounds have practical applications. Lithium hydride (LiH), a gray, crystalline solid produced by the direct combination of its constituent elements at elevated temperatures, is a ready source of hydrogen, instantly liberating that gas upon treatment with water. It also is used to produce lithium aluminum hydride ($LiAlH_4$), which quickly reduces aldehydes, ketones, and carboxylic esters to alcohols.

Lithium hydroxide (LiOH), commonly obtained by the reaction of lithium carbonate with lime, is used in making lithium salts (soaps) of stearic and other fatty acids; these soaps are widely used as thickeners in lubricating greases. Lithium hydroxide is also used as an additive in the electrolyte of alkaline storage batteries and as an absorbent for carbon dioxide. Other industrially important compounds include lithium chloride, LiCl, and lithium bromide, LiBr. They form concentrated brines capable of absorbing aerial moisture over a wide range of temperatures; these brines are commonly employed in large refrigerating and air-conditioning systems. Lithium fluoride, LiF, is used chiefly as a fluxing agent in enamels and glasses. Of greater significance is lithium carbonate, Li_2CO_3. Not only is it utilized in the preparation of other lithium compounds but it has been found to be effective in the treatment of the mental disorder manic-depressive psychosis.

Organolithium compounds, in which the lithium atom is not present as the Li^+ ion but is attached directly to a carbon atom, are useful in making other organic compounds. Butyllithium, C_4H_9Li, which is used in the manufacture of synthetic rubber, is prepared by the reaction of butyl bromide, C_4H_9Br, with metallic lithium.

atomic number	3
atomic weight	6.941
melting point	180.5° C
boiling point	1,342° C
specific gravity	0.534 g/cm³ (20° C)
valence	1
electronic config.	2-1 or $1s^22s^1$

lithium, in pharmacology, drug that is the primary treatment for bipolar disorder. Given primarily in its carbonate form, lithium is highly effective in dissipating a manic episode and in calming the individual, although its action in this regard may take several weeks. When given on a long-term maintenance basis, lithium can prevent both manic and depressive mood swings or can drastically reduce their severity. It can also suppress the psychotic features sometimes exhibited in individuals with bipolar disorder. The drug's mode of action is unknown. Side effects of its use include increased urination, tremors, diarrhea, nausea, drowsiness, and, at higher concentrations, convulsions, coma, and death. *See* manic depression.

litho-offset: *see* offset printing.

lithography, planographic printing process that makes use of the immiscibility of grease and water.

In the lithographic process, ink is applied to a grease-treated image on the flat printing surface; nonimage (blank) areas, which hold moisture, repel the lithographic ink. This inked surface is then printed—either directly on paper, by means of a special press (as in most fine-art printmaking), or onto a rubber cylinder (as in commercial printing).

The process was discovered in 1798 by Alois Senefelder of Munich, who used a porous Bavarian limestone for his plate (hence lithography, from Greek *lithos,* "stone"). The secret of lithographic printing was closely held until 1818, when Senefelder published *Vollständiges Lehrbuch der Steindruckerey* (*A Complete Course of Lithography*).

Fine-art lithography. The method of preparing stones for hand printing, which is still the lithographic method preferred by artists, has remained substantially unchanged since Senefelder's time. The materials and procedures of the 19th-century lithographer are duplicated in almost every respect by the contemporary hand printer. Although stone is the preferred printing surface in fine art, zinc and aluminum plates are also used, and, like stone, the metal plates can be reground.

As described earlier, an image is drawn with tusche and litho crayon, and the printing surface is fixed, moistened, and inked in preparation for printing. The printing itself is done on a press that exerts a sliding or scraping pressure. Because it undergoes virtually no wear in printing, a single stone can yield an almost unlimited number of copies, although in art printmaking only a specific number of prints are pulled, signed, and numbered before the stone is "canceled" (defaced).

"The Striped Blouse," transfer lithograph printed in colour, by Pablo Picasso, 1949 (64.8 cm × 50.16 cm)

Collection, The Museum of Modern Art, New York City, Abby Aldrich Rockefeller Fund; © S.P.A.D.E.M., Paris, 1987

Lithography became a popular medium among the artists who worked in France during the mid-1800s; Francisco de Goya (in voluntary exile in France), Théodore Géricault, and Eugène Delacroix were among the first lithographers. Honoré Daumier was far more prolific, however, making about 4,000 designs, ranging from newspaper caricatures to major prints. Daumier was one of the first lithographers to make use of the process called transfer lithography, by which the tusche drawing is made on paper instead of on the lithographic stone. The drawing is then fixed to the stone and printed in the usual way. This method, which is more convenient than working on stone, retains the paper's texture in the final print. In the second half of the 19th century, Edgar Degas and Édouard Manet worked in lithography, and Odilon Redon made it his principal means of expression.

Colour lithographs, called chromolithographs, or oleographs (*q.v.*), were developed in the second half of the 19th century. Although popular, they were of generally poor quality. In the hands of Henri de Toulouse-Lautrec, however, colour lithography in the 1890s reached new heights (*see* photograph), and his example was enthusiastically followed by Paul Gauguin, Pierre Bonnard, and Édouard Vuillard. The subtle views of the Thames River that the American expatriate artist James McNeill Whistler rendered, in the late 19th century, in transfer lithography contrast markedly to the straightforward and robust lithographs commercially produced in the United States in the mid-19th century by Currier & Ives.

In the 20th century the Norwegian Edvard Munch; the German Expressionists, especially Max Beckmann, Ernst Kirchner, and Käthe Kollwitz; José Clemente Orozco, Diego Rivera, and Rufino Tamayo of Mexico; the Americans Rockwell Kent, Ben Shahn, and Robert Rauschenberg; the Frenchmen Henri Matisse and Georges Rouault; and, above all, the Spaniard Pablo Picasso have imbued the medium with great vitality and power.

Commercial lithography. After about 1825 many firms that utilized the lithographic process were established for producing a variety of commercial work and for distributing topical, historical, and religious subjects to a wide audience. The best known of these publishers was Currier & Ives of New York City. The firm's popular lithographs were printed in black ink and were often hand coloured by an assembly line of women, each of whom applied a separate tint of watercolour.

Some good early work was done in colour lithography (using coloured inks) by Godefroy Englemann in 1837 and Thomas S. Boys in 1839, but the method did not come into wide commercial use until 1860. It then became the most popular method of colour reproduction for the rest of the 19th century. These commercial prints were made by preparing a separate stone by hand methods for each colour (tint) to be used and printing one colour in register over another. Sometimes as many as 30 stones were used for a single subject.

The steam-driven lithographic press was perfected by Hughes & Kimber of England in about 1865. It was introduced into the United States in 1866. These presses utilized automatic rollers to moisten and ink the stone, while the paper was pressed into contact by a revolving cylinder.

In 1853 the method known as offset lithography (or offset printing) was first patented by John Strather of England. The principle was not practically applied until the 1870s, when rubber offset rollers were used on flat-bed presses for printing on metals. In 1860 the phototransfer process was patented, enabling a photographic image on sensitized paper to be inked and transferred to the printing surface.

Lithograph poster for Whiting's Standard Papers by Will Bradley, *c.* 1900 (50.48 cm × 23.019 cm)

Collection, The Museum of Modern Art, New York City; Exchange

Six years later the first lithographic halftone screen was used in England. Offset methods for printing on paper were developed in the United States shortly after 1900.

In the offset process—by far the most popular method in use—the inked image is first printed on a rubber cylinder, which then offsets, or transfers, the image to paper or other materials. Because of the flexibility of the rubber cylinder, offset lithography can be used to print on tin, wood, cloth, leather, and rough or smooth paper. It is used mainly to produce printed matter in large quantities, including calendars, greeting cards, booklets, letterheads, books, magazines, newspapers, maps, posters, billboards, stamps, labels on cans, packaging, and other advertising matter.

Lithographic printing on a modern rotary offset press can produce high-quality, finely detailed impressions at high speed. It can reproduce any material that can be photographed in the platemaking process. As a result, it accounts for more than 40 percent of all printing, packaging, and publishing carried out; that percentage is more than twice the percentage produced by any other single printing process.

lithography, offset: *see* offset printing.

lithophane, biscuit, or unglazed, white porcelain decorated with a molded or impressed design, usually reproducing a painting, that

Hanging lamp with painted biscuit porcelain lithophanes impressed with reproductions of paintings, Germany, 1850–70; in the Blair Museum of Lithophanes and Carved Waxes, Toledo, Ohio

By courtesy of the Blair Museum of Lithophanes and Carved Waxes, Toledo, Ohio

was meant to be seen by transmitted light. Only a few examples were painted.

Lithophanes were produced from about 1830 to about 1900, mostly in Germany, by the Royal Factory at Berlin and by Meissen. In England the main producers appear to have been Minton and Copeland. Most lithophanes were plaques, ranging from miniatures to larger sizes that were framed and hung with the light (either natural or artificial) behind them; some examples were set in the bottom of tankards, where they could be seen when the vessel was emptied. The paintings reproduced are mostly of the sentimental Victorian kind; a list from Minton in 1850 cites as subjects a penitent, a guardian angel, and a mother with dying child.

lithophone (musical instrument): *see* stone chimes.

lithops, also called LIVING STONE, FLOWERING STONE, or STONEFACE (genus *Lithops*), any of a group of about 50 species of succulent plants of the carpetweed family (Aizoaceae), native to southern Africa. The plants are virtually stemless, the thickened leaves being more or less buried in the soil with only the tips visible. Two leaves grow during each rainy season and form a fleshy, roundish structure that is

Lithops

A to Z Botanical Collection

slit across the top. The old leaves then shrivel. Living stones spread sideways, and one plant may have the appearance of several stones. They are cultivated worldwide as indoor plant curiosities.

Lithuania, officially REPUBLIC OF LITHUANIA, Lithuanian LIETUVA, or LIETUVOS RESPUBLIKA, country of northeastern Europe. Lithuania is bounded on the north by Latvia, on the east and south by Belarus, and on the southwest by Russia's Kaliningrad *oblast* (province) and by Poland. It is bounded on the west by the Baltic Sea. The capital is Vilnius. Area 25,213 square miles (65,301 square km). Pop. (1993 est.) 3,798,000.

A brief treatment of Lithuania follows. For full treatment, *see* MACROPAEDIA: Baltic States.

For current history and for statistics on society and economy, *see* BRITANNICA BOOK OF THE YEAR.

Physical and human geography. The Lithuanian landscape consists of low-lying plains alternating with hilly uplands of glacial drift left by Ice Age glaciers. The lakes and hills of the Baltic Highlands lie in the eastern and southeastern parts of the country. The rivers of Lithuania meander slowly westward to the Baltic Sea.

Ethnic Lithuanians make up about four-fifths of the population. They speak an East Baltic language that is most closely related to Latvian. Most ethnic Lithuanians are Roman Catholic. There are smaller numbers of Russians, Poles, and Belorussians.

Lithuania

Lithuania's agricultural economy traditionally provided food products for the Russian market. From the 1940s on, Lithuania industrialized rapidly, but agriculture remains important, and about one-fifth of the economically active population still engages in farming. Livestock breeding is the leading branch of agriculture, with emphasis on dairy farming and pigs. Also important is the cultivation of cereals, flax, sugar beets, potatoes, and fodder crops.

Lithuanian planners have divided the republic into four economic regions. Eastern Lithuania has a diversified and expanding industrial sector that comprises metalworking, general manufacturing, woodworking, and light industry. The region also contains a number of health resorts. The southern region has more than half of the republic's waterpower resources and has metalworking, general-manufacturing, and food-processing industries. Farming is intensive in the south, especially in livestock raising and sugar beets. Northern Lithuania has little industry but is important farming country, notable for its winter wheat, flax, and sugar beets. The western region is known for its shipbuilding and repairing and for fish processing. Horses are raised, as are dairy cattle and pigs.

Lithuania is highly dependent on imported raw materials and fuels. Major exports include machinery, light industrial products, and food products. Most of Lithuania's trade is conducted with the countries of the former Soviet Union, notably Russia.

Under the constitution adopted in 1992, the highest legislative body is the Diet (Lithuanian: Seimas). Its members are elected for a term of four years by universal suffrage; just over half are elected directly from single-seat districts, and the remainder are elected by proportional representation. The head of state is the president, who is directly elected for a term of five years; he may not serve more than two consecutive terms. The president appoints the prime minister, who is responsible for forming the government.

The court system consists of the Supreme Court, the Court of Appeal, district courts, and local courts. The Constitutional Court determines the constitutionality of acts of the government.

History. The Lithuanian tribes united in the mid-13th century under the leadership of Mindaugas. His successors ruled the united Lithuania as grand dukes, and one of them, Gediminas, expanded Lithuania into an empire that dominated much of eastern Europe from the 14th to the 16th century. (*See* Lithuania, grand duchy of.) In 1386 the reigning Lithuanian grand duke also became the king of Poland, and these two countries remained closely associated for the next 400 years. Lithuania became in effect the subordinate member of the Polish-Lithuanian state, and it remained so until the Third Partition of Poland (1795) placed Lithuania under Russian rule.

Lithuania was subjected to an intensive campaign of Russification from 1864 to 1905. Lithuanian nationalist feelings nevertheless grew in the early 20th century, and in 1918, while Lithuania was occupied by the Germans, the Lithuanians proclaimed an independent state for themselves. After much fighting between Russian Bolshevik, Polish, and Lithuanian forces, the Soviet Union signed a peace treaty with newly independent Lithuania in 1920. Lithuania had a democratically elected coalition government until 1926, at which time a military coup partially curtailed the nation's parliamentary democracy. In 1939 Lithuania was forced to accept Soviet military bases on its soil, and in 1940 the Soviet Red Army occupied Lithuania, which was soon incorporated into the Soviet Union.

Nazi Germany occupied Lithuania from 1941 until the Red Army liberated the area in 1944, and in the following years Lithuania's economy was collectivized and forcibly integrated into that of the Soviet Union. The Lithuanian people retained strong memories of their two decades as an independent nation, however, and, when Mikhail Gorbachev began the liberalization of the Soviet regime in the mid-1980s, Lithuanian nationalism resurfaced in demands for greater independence from Moscow in Lithuania's management of its internal affairs. In 1990 Lithuania declared its independence from the Soviet Union, and it attained full independence in 1991.

In the ensuing decade, Lithuania transitioned to a market economy. In 2004 it formally became a member of both the North Atlantic Treaty Organization and the European Union.

Lithuania, grand duchy of, state—incorporating Lithuania proper and present-day Belarus, and East Slavic western Ukraine—which became one of the most influential powers in eastern Europe (14th–16th century). Pressed by the Teutonic and Livonian Knights, the Lithuanian tribes united under Mindaugas (d. 1263) and formed a strong, co-

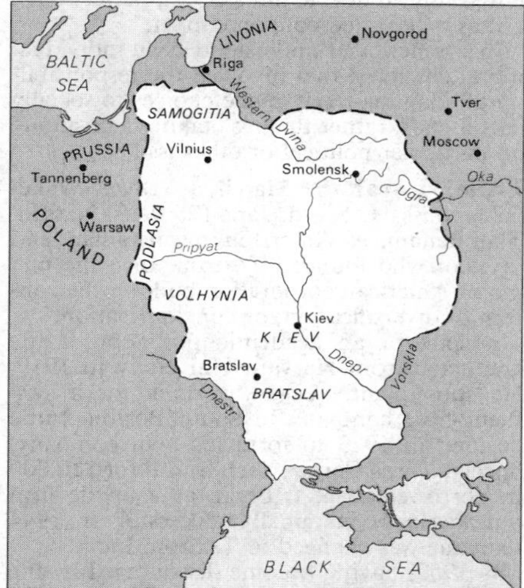

The grand duchy of Lithuania, about 1396

From G. Vernadsky, *The Mongols and Russia;* Yale University Press, 1953

hesive grand duchy during the reign of Gediminas (1316–41), who extended its frontiers across the upper Dvina River in the northeast to the Dnepr (Dnieper) River in the southeast and to the Pripet Marshes in the south. After Gediminas' death, two of his sons succeeded him: Kęstutis ruled Lithuania proper, preventing encroachments by the German knights and their allies, while Algirdas, the titular grand duke, continued his father's expansionist policies and, by conquering vast former Kievan Rus and Tatar territories, stretched his domain from the Baltic to the Black Sea.

Influenced greatly by their Belarusian and Ukrainian subjects, the Lithuanians not only reorganized their army, government administration, and legal and financial systems on Slavic models but also allowed the East Slavic nobility to retain its Orthodox religion, its privileges, and its local authority.

The Lithuanians, however, also remained involved with their western neighbours; in 1385, under pressure from the hostile Teutonic Knights, the grand duke Jogaila (reigned 1377–1434) concluded a pact with Poland (Union of Krewo), agreeing to accept the Roman Catholic faith, marry the Polish queen, become king of Poland, and unite Poland and Lithuania under a single ruler. Jogaila took the Polish name Władysław II Jagiełło.

Polish influence subsequently began to replace Belarusian and Ukrainian influence in Lithuania. The grand duchy, however, retained its autonomy, and, under the rule of Vytautas, Jogaila's cousin and former political rival, who was named viceroy in 1392, it expanded to the Ugra and Oka rivers in the east, assumed a dominant role in Tatar and East Slavic political affairs, and became the most powerful state in eastern Europe. In 1410 Lithuania, led by Vytautas, also joined Poland and defeated the Teutonic Knights (Battle of Tannenberg), gaining control of the northwestern territory of Samogitia (confirmed in 1422) and permanently reducing the German threat to Lithuania.

After Vytautas' death (1430), Lithuania continued to have its own rulers, who were nominally subordinate to the Polish king but maintained Lithuania's autonomy and its authority in eastern European affairs. When the Poles chose the 19-year-old Lithuanian grand duke Casimir as their king (1447), the two countries became somewhat more closely associated. Casimir, however, in an attempt to guarantee Lithuania's independent status, granted a charter to the Lithuanian boyars who had proclaimed him grand duke (1447), verifying the nobles' rights and privileges, giving them extensive authority over the peasantry, and thereby increasing their political power.

The authority of the grand duke subsequently declined, and, without its strong ruler, Lithuania was unable to prevent the Tatars from continually raiding its southern lands; nor could it stop Muscovy from annexing the principalities of Novgorod (1479) and Tver (1485), which had maintained close relations with Lithuania, from seizing one-third of Lithuania's East Slavic lands (1499–1503), and from capturing Smolensk (1514), which Lithuania had held since 1408.

During the 16th century Lithuania made major economic advances, including agrarian reforms, and generally appeared to maintain itself as a strong, dynamic state. When the wars between Muscovy and Lithuania were resumed in the Livonian War (*q.v.;* 1558–83), however, Lithuania's resources were strained, and it was forced to appeal to Poland for help. The Poles refused unless the two states were formally united. Lithuanian resistance to a union was strong, but, when Sigismund II Augustus (grand duke of Lithuania 1544–72; king of Poland 1548–72) attached one-third of Lithuania's territories (Volhynia, Kiev, Bratslav, and Podlasia) to Poland, the Lithuanians had to accept the Union of Lublin (1569).

Under the terms of the union, Lithuania officially remained a distinct state, constituting an equal partner with Poland in a Polish-Lithuanian confederation. Nevertheless, it soon became the subordinate member of the new state. Its gentry adopted Polish customs and language; its administration organized itself on Polish models and pursued Polish policies. Although the peasants retained their Lithuanian identity, Lithuania was politically an integral part of Poland from 1569 until the end of the 18th century, when the partitions of Poland placed it in the Russian Empire.

Lithuanian language, Lithuanian LIETUVIU KALBA, East Baltic language most closely related to Latvian; it is spoken primarily in Lithuania, where it has been the official language since 1918. It is the most archaic Indo-European language still spoken.

A Lithuanian literary language has been in existence since the 16th century, the earliest document being translations of the Lord's Prayer, a creed, and the Ave Maria, made about 1525. This language, used solely for writings of a religious character, differs in many respects from modern Lithuanian; thus, it has longer forms of some grammatical endings than does modern literary Lithuanian, has two more cases, shows stronger influences from Slavic in its vocabulary and syntax, and differs from the modern standard language in accentuation. Most of these characteristics survived through the first half of the 17th century.

Three literary dialects were in use in the 19th century: a Low Lithuanian dialect along the Baltic Sea coast, an East High Lithuanian poetic dialect, and a West High Lithuanian dialect, used primarily in the region bordering East Prussia. The modern standard literary language, written in a 32-letter Latin alphabet, is based on the West High Lithuanian dialect of the scholar Jonas Jablonskis (1861–1930), who is considered to be its father.

Like all Baltic languages, Lithuanian has preserved many archaic features from the ancestral Proto-Indo-European language.

Lithuanian literature, body of writings in the Lithuanian language. In the grand duchy of Lithuania, which stretched in the 14th and 15th centuries from the Baltic to the Black Sea, the official language was Ruthenian (Slavonic heavily infused with vernacular Ukrainian and Belarusian elements), and later Latin. In the 16th century the temporary spread of Protestantism, and thereafter the Counter-Reformation, led to the writing of religious works in the vernacular.

The first known Lithuanian printed book was the catechism of M. Mažvydas (1547). Later there appeared the religious writings of J. Bretkūnas, or J. Bretke. In 1701 the New Testament was published and, in 1727, the entire Scriptures. Until the 18th century, books were mostly of a religious character. Among publications outside this category, the first Lithuanian dictionary, K. Širvydas' *Dictionarium trium linguarum* (1629), is noteworthy.

The 18th century produced more books of secular tendency, including grammars, dictionaries, and the first collections of folk songs. The most significant work of the period was the poem of Kristijonas Donelaitis called *Metai* (1818; "The Four Seasons"); it is written in hexameters, shows German influence, and depicts village life throughout the year.

During the first half of the 19th century there arose a new movement to create a Lithuanian literary language and foster a new Romantic interest in the early history of the country. In the literature of the period, notably in the poetry of Simanas Stanevičius and Dionyzas Poška, a surge of Western influence appeared in the wake of the French Revolution. Despite a Russian prohibition of the printing of Lithuanian writings in Latin letters, this renaissance was continued by Bishop Motiejus Valančius, noted for religious and educational works, and by Bishop Antanas Baranauskas, a poet whose greatest work was *Anykščių šilelis* (1858–59; *The Forest of Anykščiai*). The literature of this era sought to rally Lithuanians against the political control of Russia and the cultural influence of Poland.

The first modern Lithuanian periodical, *Aušra* ("Dawn"), founded in 1883 by Jonas Basanavičius, gave its name to the literature of the ensuing generation. One of the poems of Vincas Kudirka, a leading publicist and short-story writer, became the national anthem of independent Lithuania. The most famous Lithuanian poet, Jonas Mačiulis (pseudonym Maironis), was noted for both dramatic and lyric poetry and has been called "the poet-prophet of the Lithuanian renaissance." Other distinguished names were Vilius Storasta (pseudonym Vydūnas), philosopher, poet, and dramatist; J. Biliūnas, a sensitive short-story writer; and Juozas Tumas (called Vaižgantas), a literary critic.

In 1918 Lithuania regained independence. Writers began to concentrate on developing national culture and a greater degree of sophistication in literature. Vincas Krėvė-Mickevičius, novelist and dramatist, was regarded by some as the greatest Lithuanian writer, and Jurgis Baltrušaitis achieved distinction as a lyrical poet. Other prominent figures were Vincas Mykolaitis, who pioneered the modern Lithuanian romance; Balys Sruoga and Kazys Binkis, both poets and dramatists; and Ignas Šeinius, novelist and short-story writer.

When Lithuania was occupied by the Soviet Union in 1940 and again in 1944, writers were compelled to follow the communist line. Those Lithuanian writers working in the West tried to further the development of the national literature. New modes of expression were successfully attempted in the philosophical poetry of Alfonsas Nyka-Niliūnas, in the idylls of J. Mekas, and in the novels of Marius Katiliškis. The genres most favoured have been the short story and the lyric.

BIBLIOGRAPHY. Rimvydas Šilbajoris, *Perfection of Exile: Fourteen Contemporary Lithuanian Writers* (1970); Aleksis Rubulis, *Baltic Literature* (1970); Rimvydas Šilbajoris (ed.), *Mind Against the Wall: Essays on Lithuanian Culture Under Soviet Occupation* (1983).

Litke, Fyodor Petrovich, Count (Graf) (b. Sept. 17 [Sept. 28, New Style], 1797, St. Petersburg, Russia—d. Oct. 8 [Oct. 20], 1882, St. Petersburg), Russian explorer and geographer who explored the Arctic and who exerted a considerable influence on Russian science in general and geography in particular.

In 1812 Litke joined the imperial navy, participating in a voyage around the world (1817–19). During the four summers of 1821–24, he mapped the west coast of Novaya Zemlya, an archipelago in the Russian Arctic, conducted the first scientific exploration there, and also studied the adjacent southwestern part of the Barents Sea. In 1826–29 he again circumnavigated the world on a scientific expedition in the sloop *Senyavin,* conducting surveys and gathering scientific collections in the Bering Strait and in the western Pacific on the Bonin and Caroline islands. In 1845 he helped to found the Russian Geographical Society, which he headed until 1873, except for the years 1850–57. He wrote accounts of each of his major expeditions.

litmus, mixture of coloured organic compounds obtained from several species of lichen that grow in The Netherlands, particularly *Lecanora tartarea* and *Roccella tinctorum.* Litmus turns red in acidic solutions and blue in alkaline solutions and is the oldest and most commonly used indicator of whether a substance is an acid or a base.

Treatment of the lichens with ammonia, potash, and lime in the presence of air produces the various coloured components of litmus. By 1840 litmus had been partially separated into several substances named azolitmin, erythrolitmin, spaniolitmin, and erythrolein. These are apparently mixtures of closely related compounds that were identified in 1961 as derivatives of the heterocyclic compound phenoxazine.

Archil (orchil, or orseille) is a mixture of dyes similar to litmus that are obtained from the same lichens by a different method. The manufacture of archil, which produces a violet shade on wool or silk, was introduced into Europe from the Orient about 1300.

litoptern (order Litopterna), any of various extinct hoofed mammals that first appeared in the Paleocene Epoch (which began approximately 66 million years ago) and became extinct during the Pleistocene Epoch (which ended about 10,000 years ago). The group's members were restricted to South America. In many ways the evolution of the litopterns paralleled that of hoofed mammals in the Northern Hemisphere; two distinct lines of litoptern evolution are discernible in the fossil record. One line, the proterotheres, strongly resembled the evolution of the horse. Their limbs were adapted to running and were similar in form and function to those of horses; the skull was long and low, with cheek teeth resembling those of horses. The proterotheres became extinct in the Pliocene Epoch (which ended approximately 1.6 million years ago), about the time that true horses appeared in South America.

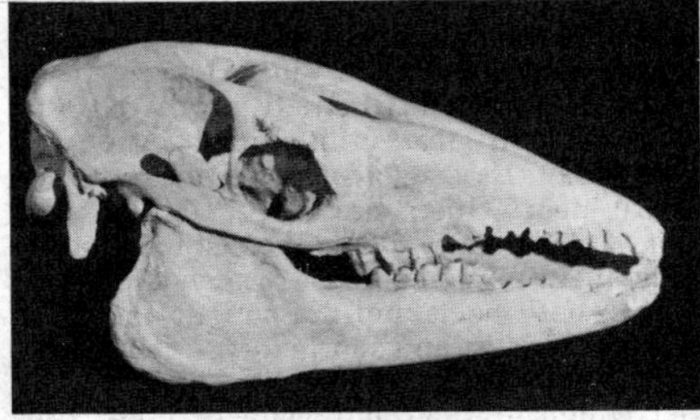

Skull of a macrauchenid litoptern

By courtesy of the trustees of the British Museum (Natural History); photograph, Imitor

The other line of litoptern evolution is a group known as the macrauchenids, which resembled camels in many ways. The nasal opening of the skull was set far back and probably supported a short proboscis, or trunk. Some of the macrauchenids survived the intrusion of more advanced mammals from North America and persisted well into the Pleistocene Epoch, when they became extinct.

It seems clear that the horselike litopterns succumbed to competition for similar resources by the true horses over the course of the Pliocene, but the macrauchenids were better adapted to their environment, probably swampy areas, and thus were able to compete for a while with the newly introduced North American forms.

Consult the INDEX *first*

litotes, a figure of speech, conscious understatement in which emphasis is achieved by negation; examples are the common expressions "not bad!" and "no mean feat." Litotes is a stylistic feature of Old English poetry and of the Icelandic sagas, and it is responsible for much of their characteristic stoical restraint. The term meiosis means understatement generally, and litotes is considered a form of meiosis.

litre, unit of volume in the metric system, equal to one cubic decimetre (0.001 cubic metre), or 0.264172 U.S. gallon. From 1901 to 1964 the litre was defined as the volume of one kilogram of pure water at 4° C (39.2° F) and standard atmospheric pressure; in 1964, the original, present value was reinstated.

litter, portable bed or couch, open or enclosed, that is mounted on two poles and carried at each end on the shoulders of porters

Litter, about 1850; in the Science Museum, London

By courtesy of the Science Museum, London, Crown copyright reserved

or by animals. Litters, which may have been adapted from sledges that were pushed or dragged on the ground, appear in Egyptian paintings and were used by the Persians; they are mentioned in the Book of Isaiah. Litters were also common in the Orient, where they were called palanquins. In ancient Rome, litters were reserved for empresses and senators' wives, and plebeians were forbidden to travel in them. By the 17th century, litters were plentiful in Europe; protection and privacy were provided by canopies held up by poles and by curtains or leather shields. The introduction of spring-mounted coaches ended the need for litters except as transport for the sick and wounded.

littera da brevi (calligraphy): *see* cancellaresca corsiva.

littérature engagée (French: "engaged literature"), literature of commitment, popularized in the immediate post-World War II era, when the French existentialists, particularly Jean-Paul Sartre, revived the idea of the artist's serious responsibility to society. The idea is an application to art of a basic existentialist tenet: that a person defines himself by consciously engaging in willed action. The position was a reaction against the creed of "art for art's sake" and against the "bourgeois" writer, whose obligation was to his craft rather than his audience. In his introductory statement to *Les Temps Modernes* (1945), a review devoted to *littérature engagée,* Sartre criticized Marcel Proust for his self-involvement and referred to Gustave Flaubert, whose private means allowed him to devote himself to a perfectionist art, as a "talented coupon clipper."

Engagement was understood as an individual moral challenge that involved the responsibility of adapting freely made choices to socially useful ends, rather than as "taking a position" on particular political or other issues.

Little, Royal (b. March 1, 1896, Wakefield, Mass., U.S.—d. Jan. 12, 1989, Nassau, The Bahamas), American businessman and investor who founded Textron, Inc., the first major American corporation built on the concept of diversification, or conglomeration.

In spite of an academic probation, Little graduated from Harvard University in 1919. He subsequently began working for a synthetic-fibre company in South Boston. Little decided in 1923 to form his own company, Special Yarns Corp., which he did for $10,000 in borrowed cash. It began as a textile firm but was only marginally successful. In 1944 its name was changed to Textron, Inc.

By 1952, having become discouraged by the low rate of return on capital investment in the textile industry, Little reorganized his company and started it on a broad program of unrelated diversification. He had bought 40 firms by 1960, when he retired as chairman of the firm. Textron came to oversee the manufacture of a wide range of products, such as watchbands, chain saws, helicopters, radar antennas, snowmobiles, electronic equipment, and roller bearings. The company eventually became one of the largest conglomerates in the United States, and its success spurred other corporations to broadly diversify their industrial activities.

Little Alfold, Hungarian KIS-ALFÖLD, English LITTLE HUNGARIAN PLAIN, extensive basin occupying the northwestern part of Transdanubia in northwestern Hungary, and extending into Austria and Slovakia (where it is called Podunajská Lowland). It has an area of approximately 3,000 square miles (8,000 square km). It is bounded on the south and east by the highlands of Transdanubia (Bakony and Vértes), to the west by the foothills of the Austrian Alps, and to the north by the Carpathians in Slovakia. The major drainage direction is west-east via the Danube River. The Rába River and its tributaries drain the Hungarian section through Győr, and in Slovakia the Váh River system enters the Danube at Komárno (Komárom).

Some of the Little Alfold is exceptionally rich agricultural land that produces wheat, corn (maize), rye, barley, sugar beets, potatoes, fodder crops, table vegetables, and tobacco; the basin has orchards and vineyards. Livestock breeding—dairy cattle, pigs, horses, and poultry—is also important. The climate is relatively dry, but abundant water comes from the surrounding highlands.

Only in its middle and north-central parts is the Little Alfold properly a plain; on the margins are degraded alluvial fans and low hills. The major settlement in the area is Győr. Submergence and basin formation of the Little Alfold began several million years ago. Deposition and local submergence has continued on a smaller scale, and the Little Alfold is subsiding very slightly.

Little America, principal American base in Antarctica, lying on the northeastern edge of Ross Ice Shelf near Kainan Bay. First set up in 1928 as the headquarters for the polar explorations of Richard E. Byrd, it was reused and enlarged by Byrd on his return expedition in 1933–35. In 1940 Byrd established a camp 7 miles (11 km) northeast, later named Little America III, that served as the western base for a government-sponsored exploration of Marie Byrd Land before World War II. After the war Little America IV, consisting of an airstrip and 60 tents, was set up nearby as a headquarters for Operation High Jump (1946–47), an expedition designed to explore and document Antarctica's coastline as well as to extend U.S. sovereignty to the continent.

When an expedition next returned (1956) in preparation for the International Geophysical Year (1957–58), parts of the earlier Little America camps were found to have vanished because of calving of the ice shelf. Consequently, Little America V was set up several miles northeast, near Kainan Bay, to serve as a supply base and terminus of a 630-mile- (1,014-kilometre-) long "highway" to Byrd Station in the continent's interior.

Little Armenia, also called LESSER ARMENIA, or ARMENIA MINOR, kingdom established in Cilicia, on the southeast coast of Anatolia, by the Armenian Rubenid dynasty in the 12th century. The Rubenids ruled first as barons and then, from 1199 to 1226, as kings of Cilicia. Thereafter the family of Oshin, another Armenian noble, ruled as the Hethumid dynasty until 1342. After initial trouble with the Byzantine Empire, Little Armenia established itself and developed contacts with the West. Frankish culture, disseminated by Frankish families traveling on Crusades, had considerable influence on the development of Little Armenia. The kingdom was also important for being on the route of Venetian and Genoese trade with the East. It was conquered by the Muslim Mamlūks in 1375.

little auk (bird): *see* dovekie.

Little Barrier Island, island in the northern end of Hauraki Gulf, eastern North Island, New Zealand, lying 15 miles (24 km) across Jellicoe Channel from the mainland. Cradock Channel separates it from Great Barrier Island to the east. Of volcanic origin, the island has a total land area of 11 square miles (28 square km). Its generally wooded surface rises steeply to 2,370 feet (722 m) in Mount Hauturu, the flanks of which are cut by deep ravines.

Captain James Cook named the island in 1769, and it was bought by the British government in the 1880s. The island is a wildlife sanctuary without permanent inhabitants; visitors must procure a permit to land from the Department of Conservation.

Little Bighorn, Battle of the, also called CUSTER'S LAST STAND (June 25, 1876), much-discussed battle at the Little Bighorn River in Montana Territory, U.S., between federal troops led by Lieutenant Colonel George A. Custer and a band of Northern Plains (Dakota [Eastern Sioux] and Northern Cheyenne) Indians; Custer and all his men were slain.

Events leading up to the confrontation were typical of the irresolute and confusing policy of the U.S. government toward American Indians. Although the Second Treaty of Fort Laramie (1868), in effect, had guaranteed to the Indians exclusive possession of the Dakota territory west of the Missouri River, white miners in search of gold were settling in lands sacred to the Dakota Indians. Unwilling to remove the settlers, unable to persuade the Dakota to sell the territory, and feeling that the occasional Indian raid on a white settlement effectively released them from the treaty, the U.S. government issued an order to the Indian agencies that all the Indians return to the designated reservations by Jan. 31, 1876, or be deemed hostile. The improbability of getting this message to the hunters, coupled with its rejection by many of the Plains Indians, made confrontation inevitable.

In June of 1876, the government sent in troops under the command of Brigadier General Alfred H. Terry to locate and rout the Indians. Terry, taking the main body of men up the Yellowstone River, hoped to block the movement of the Indians at the mouth of the Little Bighorn River, while Custer and the 7th Cavalry were to travel up the Rosebud River and cross the Little Bighorn River, thus, it was hoped, trapping the Indians between the two groups. Some three days into his march, Custer abandoned the plan when he rather suddenly encountered a large group of Sioux and Cheyenne encamped nearby. Envisioning a three-pronged attack, he ordered Captain Frederick Benteen and Major Marcus Reno to lead troops on either side of the river, while he would advance to the northwest and surprise the encampment from the north. Reno, who attacked first (and long before Custer reached the northern edge of the camp), was clearly overwhelmed by the Indians, and he retreated across the river, losing his strategic edge. He was joined by Benteen's fresh troops, and the combined forces dug in and continued to fight. At Reno's retreat, however, the major force of Indians, by then alerted to Custer's presence, rode to the attack and completely vanquished Custer and his men within an hour, leaving more than 200 dead.

The outcome of the battle, while it proved to be the height of Indian power, so stunned and enraged white Americans that government troops flooded the area, forcing the Indians to surrender. The Little Bighorn Battlefield National Monument commemorates the battle.

Little Brothers of Jesus and Little Sisters of Jesus, Roman Catholic religious congregations inspired by the example of Charles-Eugène de Foucauld, a French military officer and explorer who experienced a religious conversion in 1886, while serving in Morocco. He later lived as a hermit among the Tuareg tribesmen in the Sahara Desert before he was shot and killed by a band of Senusi tribesmen in 1916.

The Little Brothers were founded in 1933 by René Voillaume in southern Oran, Alg.; the Little Sisters were founded in September 1939 at Touggourt, Alg., by Sister Madeleine of Jesus. Both congregations live in small groups, called fraternities, in ordinary dwellings among the poor labouring classes. They hold the same type of jobs as their neighbours hold. Their hope is that their presence among the people will influence an acceptance of Christianity.

Little Caucasus, also called LESSER CAUCASUS, Russian MALY KAVKAZ, range of folded mountains in the southern part of the Caucasus region, connected with the main Caucasus Mountains by means of the Likhsky Mountains, which form the divide between the basins of the Rioni and Kura rivers. The range covers portions of Georgia, Armenia, and Azerbaijan. To the south the Little Caucasus, which runs northwest-southeast, merges almost imperceptibly with the Armenian Highland, which covers much of the southern part of Armenia and adjacent areas of Turkey and Iran. The western ranges are intensively folded and are much affected by volcanic action; the central and eastern portions are slightly less folded. Few peaks in the range exceed an elevation of 8,000 feet (2,400 m).

Little Dipper, The, constellation of seven stars of the larger constellation Ursa Minor (*q.v.*).

Little Entente, mutual defense arrangement among Czechoslovakia, Yugoslavia, and Romania during the period between World Wars I and II. Based on several treaties (1920–21), it was directed against German and Hungarian domination in the Danube River basin and toward the protection of the members' territorial integrity and political independence. During the 1920s the three nations sought economic and political cooperation and negotiated alliances with France.

After Adolf Hitler assumed power in Germany (1933), the members of the Little Entente created a Permanent Secretariat and a Permanent Council, composed of their foreign ministers, that met three times a year to direct a common policy. Nevertheless, during the 1930s the three states increasingly adopted independent foreign policies, especially after Germany occupied the Rhineland (1936) and the French support, upon which the entente relied, lost much of its value.

The entente lost its remaining political significance when Yugoslavia and Romania denied (April 1937) a request by Czechoslovakia, then threatened by Germany, that the entente pledge full military aid to a member that was the victim of aggression. The entente finally collapsed when Germany annexed the Sudeten area of Czechoslovakia (September 1938).

Little Genesis: *see* Jubilees, Book of.

Little Karoo, Karoo also spelled KARROO, also called SOUTHERN KAROO, Afrikaans KLEIN KAROO, or SUIDERLIK KAROO, intermontane plateau basin in Western Cape province, South Africa, lying between the east-west oriented Groot-Swart Mountains (north), the Lange Mountains (southwest), and the Outeniqua Mountains (southeast), with the discontinuous Kammanassie Mountains running between those ranges. The Little Karoo, which lies south of the Great Karoo and the main Karoo, is about 150 miles (245 km) long and averages 30 miles (48 km) from north to south. It contains the basins of the Gourits, Groot, Touws, Olifants, and Kammanassie rivers, whose valleys (1,000–2,000 feet [300–600 m] above sea level) are the only habitable parts. Rainfall varies from 16 inches (400 mm) in the mountains to 5 inches (130 mm) in the valleys.

Irrigation permits intensive cultivation of lucerne (alfalfa). Merino sheep and angora goats yield high-quality wool and mohair. The valleys also produce grains and apricots, apples, and peaches, sometimes processed into brandies and dessert wines. The stalactite Cango Caves are 17 miles (27 km) north of the principal town, Oudtshoorn, an ostrich farming centre.

Little League, international baseball organization for children and youth, started in 1939 in Williamsport, Pa., U.S., by Carl E. Stotz. The league originally included boys aged 8 to 12; girls were admitted beginning in 1974. The Little League now includes a senior division for youth aged 13 to 15 and a big-league division for ages 16 to 18.

Among teams of the junior division the game is played on a field two-thirds the size of a professional baseball diamond, and games are six innings rather than nine. Of a team's nine members, two must be under 11 years old; and no more than seven in the regular lineup may be 12. Leagues comprise 4 to 12 teams that play a season of about 15 games, the winners then engaging in local and regional playoffs to qualify for the World Series.

The great period of expansion for Little League ball began following World War II; and in the 1990s there were more than 2.5 million players in the United States and some 30 other countries. In 1974 World Series teams from foreign countries were banned from the Little League World Series but were restored from 1976. Throughout the 1970s the World Series was dominated by Asian teams, notably Taiwan.

A number of similar organizations have also been successful, including the Babe Ruth League (Little Bigger League, 1952–53), for boys and girls 13 through 18. The Babe Ruth leagues were founded in 1952 in Trenton, N.J., and have been established in most sections of the United States and Canada. Playing rules and infield dimensions are those of professional baseball. Also played under these conditions is American Legion Baseball for teenagers, founded in 1925.

little magazine, any of various small periodicals devoted to serious literary writings, usually avant-garde and noncommercial. They were published from about 1880 through much of the 20th century and flourished in the United States and England, though French writers (especially the Symbolist poets and critics, 1880–*c.* 1900) often had access to a similar type of publication and German literature of the 1920s was also indebted to them. The name signifies most of all a noncommercial manner of editing, managing, and financing. A little magazine usually begins with the object of publishing literary work of some artistic merit that is unacceptable to commercial magazines for any one or all of three reasons—the writer is unknown and therefore not a good risk; the work itself is unconventional or experimental in form; or it violates one of several popular notions of moral, social, or aesthetic behaviour.

Foremost in the ranks of such magazines were two American periodicals, *Poetry: a Magazine of Verse* (founded 1912), especially in its early years under the vigorous guidance of Harriet Monroe, and the more erratic and often more sensational *Little Review* (1914–29) of Margaret Anderson; a group of English magazines in the second decade of the 20th century, of which the *Egoist* (1914–19) and *Blast* (1914–15) were most conspicuous; and Eugene Jolas' *transition* (1927–38). In all but the last of these, a major guiding spirit was the U.S. poet and critic Ezra Pound; he served as "foreign correspondent" of both *Poetry* and the *Little Review,* manoeuvred the *Egoist* from its earlier beginnings as a feminist magazine (*The New Freewoman,* 1913) to the status of an avant-garde literary review, and, with Wyndham Lewis, jointly sponsored the two issues of *Blast.* In this case, the little magazines showed the stamp of a single vigorous personality; similar strong and dedicated figures in little magazine history were the U.S. poet William Carlos Williams (whose name appears in scores of little magazines, in one capacity or another); the British critic and novelist Ford Madox Ford, editor of the *Transatlantic Review* (1924–25) and contributor to many others; and Gustave Kahn, a minor French poet but a very active editor associated with several French Symbolist periodicals.

There were four principal periods in the general history of little magazines. In the first, from 1890 to about 1915, French magazines served mainly to establish and explain a literary movement; British and U.S. magazines served to disseminate information about and encourage acceptance of continental European literature and culture. In the second stage, 1915–30, when other magazines, especially in the United States, were in the vanguard of almost every variation of modern literature, a conspicuous feature was the expatriate magazine, published usually in France but occasionally elsewhere in Europe by young U.S. and British critics and writers. The major emphasis in this period was upon literary and aesthetic form and theory and the publication of fresh and original work, such as that of Ernest Hemingway (in the *Little Review, Poetry, This Quarter,* and other publications), T.S. Eliot (in *Poetry,* the *Egoist, Blast*) James Joyce (in the *Egoist,* the *Little Review, transition*), and many others. The third stage, the 1930s, saw the beginnings of many leftist magazines, started with specific doctrinal commitments that were often subjected to considerable editorial change in the career of the magazine. *Partisan Review* (1934) was perhaps the best known example of these in the United States, as was the *Left Review* (1934–38) in England.

The fourth period of little magazine history began about 1940. One of the conspicuous features of this period was the critical review supported and sustained by a group of critics, who were in most cases attached to a university or college. Examples of this kind of periodical were, in the United States, *The Kenyon Review,* founded by John Crowe Ransom in 1939, and in Great Britain, *Scrutiny,* edited by F.R. Leavis (1932–53). This and related kinds of support, such as that of publishers maintaining their own reviews or miscellanies, represented a form of institutionalism which was radically different from the more spontaneous and erratic nature of the little magazines of earlier years.

Little Octobrist, Russian OKTYABRYONOK, plural OKTYABRYATA, member of a Communist organization for children aged nine and under, closely associated with the Komsomol (*q.v.*) for youth aged 14 to 28.

little owl (*Athene noctua*), brownish bird about 20 centimetres (about 8 inches) long, belonging to the family Strigidae (order Strigiformes). Little owls occur in Europe, central Asia, and northern Africa and have been introduced into New Zealand. They are active during the day and often perch in the open.

Little owl (*Athene noctua*)
D. Middleton—Bruce Coleman Ltd.

They usually nest in buildings or natural holes and eat insects and small mammals, birds, and reptiles. Two other species (*A. brama* and *A. blewitti*) are found in India and southeast Asia.

Little Poland Uplands, Polish WYŻYNA MAŁOPOLSKA, lakeland area, southern Poland, having an area of 10,000 sq mi (25,000 sq km). Located south of the Middle Polish Lowlands, it embraces the territory from the Częstochowa–Kraków scarplands (Polish Jura) to the Vistula River. The region includes the Silesian Uplands (the Silesian–Cracovian upthrust), the Nida Basin, and the Góry Świętokrzyskie (Holy Cross Mountains), which rise to 2,008 ft (612 m), all within the provinces of Kraków, Częstochowa, Kielce, and Piotrków Trybunalski. The northern and central parts of the uplands are drained by the Vistula River; the eastern part is drained by the San River, a tributary of the Vistula.

The topography of the region is the result of mountain glaciers and continental ice sheets that advanced from the north. There are contrasting areas of sand, glacial till, and loess blown from the northern areas during postglacial times. There are extensive loess deposits, particularly in the Carpathian foothills and on the Lublin Plateau. Fertile brown and black soils have developed on the loess base and yield crops of rye, potatoes, and oats. The land is sandy and marshy at the confluence of the Vistula and San rivers. Meadows and forests are present throughout the uplands. The Little Poland Uplands contain rich deposits of coal in the west (the Silesian Uplands), constituting one of the leading bituminous coalfields of Europe. There are also deposits of iron ore, zinc, and lead in the region.

Eleven closely linked cities in Katowice province form the core of the Upper Silesian metropolitan conurbation, Katowice town being the largest centre. Closely connected economically to the Katowice region is the area around Kraków containing Nowa Huta (Lenin Steelworks), Poland's largest industrial establishment; it uses Silesian coal and Russian iron ore. Other important cities in the region are Kielce, Częstochowa, Piotrków Tribunalski, and Lublin.

Little Rock, city, capital of Arkansas, U.S., seat of Pulaski County, on the Arkansas River in the foothills of the Ouachita Mountains in the central part of the state. Bernard de la Harpe, a Frenchman exploring the Arkansas River in 1722, saw on the riverbank two conspicuous rock formations, which he named La Petite Roche and La Grande Roche. Near the smaller rock was a Quapaw Indian settlement, which La Harpe made his trading post. The "little rock" later became the abutment for a railway bridge. The "big rock," 2 mi (3 km) further upstream, was the site of an army post, and later a hospital for veterans was built there.

In 1812 William Lewis, a trapper, built his home at the "little rock." In 1819 Arkansas became a territory, with its capital at Arkansas Post. The site of Little Rock was surveyed in 1821, and the territorial capital was moved there the same year. The capitol building where the legislature met from 1821 to 1836 is preserved in the Territorial Capitol Restoration, along with a block of buildings of the period, including the Old State House (designed by Gideon Shyrock and the second of Little Rock's three state capitols) and the first printshop of the *Arkansas Gazette.* Little Rock was strongly anti-Union at the outbreak of the Civil War, and the Federal arsenal was seized by state authorities in 1861. In September 1863 Federal troops under Gen. Frederick Steele occupied the city, and a pro-Union government was set up.

In the 1880s Little Rock became an important transportation centre with the expansion of the railways. Industry in the metropolitan area experienced planned, diversified growth beginning in the 1940s, mainly because of the proximity of raw materials (timber, oil, gas, coal, and bauxite). The city became a river

State Capitol, Little Rock, Ark.
By courtesy of the Arkansas Department of Parks and Tourism Commission; photograph, Harold Phelps

port in 1969 with the opening of a system of locks and dams on the Arkansas River. There are large railroad shops at North Little Rock (*q.v.*) across the river. Little Rock is the chief market for the surrounding agricultural region. The Arkansas Livestock Showgrounds are centred around the T.H. Barton Coliseum.

In 1957 the city was the focus of world attention over the issue of the right of nine black students to attend Central High School under a gradual desegregation plan adopted by the city school board in accordance with the 1954 decision of the U.S. Supreme Court holding racial segregation unconstitutional. The result was a test of power between the federal and state governments. Gov. Orval E. Faubus ordered state militia to prevent blacks from entering the school, but the state was enjoined from interfering by U.S. Pres. Dwight D. Eisenhower, who sent federal troops to maintain order. Within the next decade desegregation was accomplished in all public schools.

The city's educational institutions include the University of Arkansas at Little Rock (1927; formerly Little Rock University); Philander Smith College (1868); the University of Arkansas Medical Center (1956); Arkansas Baptist College (1884); and the state schools for the blind and deaf. MacArthur Park surrounds the Arkansas Arts Center and Gen. Douglas MacArthur's birthplace. Little Rock Air Force Base (1955) is northeast, near Jacksonville. Inc. town, 1831; city, 1836. Pop. (2000) city, 183,133; Little Rock–North Little Rock MSA, 583,845.

Little Saint Bernard Pass, Italian COLLE DEL PICCOLO SAN BERNARDO, French COL DU PETIT-SAINT-BERNARD, pass (7,178 ft [2,188 m]) situated just southwest of the Italian border in Savoie *département* of southeastern France; it lies between the Mont Blanc Massif (north) and the Graian Alps (*q.v.*; south-southeast). The road across the pass connects Bourg-Saint-Maurice (7 miles [11 km] southwest) in the Isère River Valley, France, with Morgex (10 miles northeast) in the Valle d'Aosta, Italy. Until the Treaty of Paris in 1947 the pass lay on the French–Italian border.

Just southwest of the pass is a hospice founded in the 11th century by St. Bernard of Aosta (Italy).

According to some scholars, Hannibal led the Carthaginian Army over the Little St. Bernard Pass on his way toward Rome in 218 BC. The pass was the principal route over the Alps into Gallia Comata, a province of Gaul, until Montgenèvre Pass (*q.v.*) was opened in 77 BC. The ancient name, Alpis Graia, interpreted to mean "Greek pass," was associated with the legend that the Greek hero Hercules, returning from Spain with the oxen of the three-bodied giant Geryon, crossed the Alps by this route, though the legend better suits a route through the Maritime Alps.

Little Sisters of Jesus: *see* Little Brothers of Jesus and Little Sisters of Jesus.

Little Tennessee River, river rising in the Blue Ridge Mountains of northeastern Georgia, U.S., and flowing about 150 miles (240 km) north and northwest, through southwestern North Carolina and across Tennessee to the Tennessee River just below Fort Loudoun Dam. Tennessee Valley Authority dams on the Little Tennessee include Calderwood in Tennessee and Cheoah and Fontana dams in North Carolina. Fort Loudoun, built in 1756–57 on the river's southern bank, was named for the earl of Loudoun, British colonial commander; it was destroyed by Indians in 1760.

little theatre, movement in U.S. theatre to free dramatic forms and methods of production from the limitations of the large commercial theatres by establishing small experimental centres of drama. The movement was initiated at the beginning of the 20th century by young dramatists, stage designers, and actors who were influenced by the vital European theatre of the late 19th century; they were especially impressed by the revolutionary theories of the German director Max Reinhardt, the designing concepts of Adolphe Appia and Gordon Craig, and the staging experiments at such theatres as the Théâtre-Libre of Paris, the Freie Bühne in Berlin, and the Moscow Art Theatre. Community playhouses such as the Toy Theatre in Boston (1912), the Little Theatre in Chicago (1912), and the Little Theatre, New York City (1912) were centres of the experimental activity. Some groups owned or leased their own theatres; a few, such as the Washington Square Players (1915), the predecessor of the Theatre Guild (1918), became important commercial producers. By encouraging freedom of expression, staging the works of talented young writers, and choosing plays solely on the basis of artistic merit, the little theatres provided a valuable early opportunity for such playwrights as Eugene O'Neill, George S. Kaufman, Elmer Rice, Maxwell Anderson, and Robert E. Sherwood.

Little Turtle (b. *c.* 1752, near Fort Wayne, Ind.—d. July 14, 1812, Fort Wayne, Ind., U.S.), Native American, leader of the Miami tribe, who achieved fame during the turbulent period when the U.S. Congress launched a punitive campaign against the Indians who were raiding settlers in the Northwest Territory. In 1790 he routed Gen. Josiah Harmar's poorly trained militia. The next year he decimated the well-trained garrison of Gen. Arthur St. Clair, who had arrived in the territory to build a series of forts between the Ohio River and Lake Erie. Not until Gen. Anthony Wayne took to the field in 1793 was Little

Little Turtle, mixed-media painting by Ralph Dille after a portrait by Gilbert Stuart, 1797; in the collection of the Chicago Historical Society

By courtesy of the Chicago Historical Society

Turtle subdued—at Ft. Recovery (on the site of St. Clair's defeat) and at Fallen Timbers (near present Maumee, Ohio). In August 1795 Little Turtle signed the Treaty of Greenville, by which a loose confederacy of Indians ceded to the U.S. much of Ohio and parts of Illinois, Indiana, and Michigan. Thereafter, he advocated peace and succeeded in keeping the Miami from joining the Shawnee Confederacy of Tecumseh. *See also* Fallen Timbers, Battle of.

Littleton, Mark (U.S. author): *see* Kennedy, John P(endleton).

Littleton, Sir Thomas, Littleton also spelled LYTTELTON, or LUTTELTON (b. 1422, probably at Frankley, Worcestershire, Eng.—d. Aug. 23, 1481, Frankley), jurist, author of *Littleton on Tenures* (or *Treatise on Tenures*), the first important English legal text neither written in Latin nor significantly influenced by civil (Roman) law. An edition (1481 or 1482?) by John Lettou and William de Machlinia was doubtless the first book on English law to be printed. In the 20th century his work was still occasionally cited as authoritative.

Throughout a turbulent period in English history, Littleton held several high offices: sheriff of Worcestershire; recorder of Coventry, Warwickshire; justice of assize (trial judge) on the Northern Circuit; and judge of the Court of Common Pleas (appointed by King Edward IV, 1466). In 1475 he was created a Knight of the Bath.

Intended for the instruction of his second son, Richard, Littleton's *Treatise* subtly differentiates various kinds of medieval English land tenure. It was written in law French, a specialized form of Anglo-Norman.

Littlewood, Joan (Maud) (b. Oct. 6, 1914, London, Eng.—d. Sept. 20, 2002, London), influential British theatrical director who rejected the standardized form and innocuous social content of the commercial theatre in favour of experimental productions of plays concerned with contemporary social issues.

After studying at the Royal Academy of Dramatic Art, Littlewood founded in the 1930s Theatre Union, which specialized in open-air productions, and the Theatre of Action. In 1945, in Manchester, she founded Theatre Workshop—for working-class audiences—which in 1953 moved to the Theatre Royal, Stratford, in the East End of London. The productions were at first mainly of Shakespeare and other classics, with some topical plays written or adapted by her husband, Ewan MacColl, a folk singer and political dramatist. Gradually the group developed a more definite style. Influenced by Bertolt Brecht, she encouraged audience participation, allowed onstage improvisation, altered the text, and used techniques originally developed in the music hall. Her later productions were collective in that the actors shared in planning the presentations. After the success in 1955 of MacColl's dramatic version of *The Good Soldier Schweik,* by Jaroslav Hašek, her influence grew. *Oh! What a Lovely War* (1963), an original evocation and criticism of World War I using popular songs of the period, projected newspaper headlines, and other devices to emphasize its message, became perhaps her most famous production. Other outstanding plays, full of vitality, noisy, and broadly humorous, yet with subtle characterization, include *The Quare Fellow* (1956) and *The Hostage* (1958) by Brendan Behan and *A Taste of Honey* (1958) by Shelagh Delaney. Her theatre workshop company was disbanded in 1964, and Joan Littlewood afterward became interested in projects less narrowly theatrical. In the early 1970s, however, Theatre Workshop was reformed under her direction. She was also active in the creation of Children's Environments, Bubble Cities linked with Music Hall around the Theatre Royal, Stratford (1968–75). Thereafter she left England to work in France. Her autobiography, *Joan's Book,* was published in 1994.

Litton Industries, diversified American multinational company that became a subsidiary of the Northrop Grumman Corp. in 2001. Founded in 1953 by Charles Bates ("Tex") Thornton (1913–81), Litton provides products and services that range from electronic and electrical components and equipment to aerospace and marine systems and equipment. Among Litton's popularly known brand-name products are Litton microwave ovens and Royal and Triumph typewriters. It also is a major defense contractor.

When chartered on Nov. 2, 1953, the company was named Electro Dynamics Corporation. In 1954 Thornton acquired Litton Industries, Inc., an electron-tube manufacturer in San Carlos, Calif. (originally founded in 1932), and adopted the name of the acquired company. In the same year, he established Litton's headquarters in Beverly Hills. Over the years there were dozens of further acquisitions, such as Ingalls Shipbuilding Company in 1962. In 1983 the company purchased International Laser Systems, Inc. A number of companies were bought and later sold, including Stouffer Foods Corporation (1967–73), the construction business of Rust Engineering Company (1967–72), and Monroe Systems office-equipment division (1958–83).

From 1934 to 1941 Thornton had worked for several federal agencies, had served as a civilian planner in the Pentagon during World War II, and had been an industrial planner for the Ford Motor Company (1946–48) and for Howard Hughes in the Hughes Aircraft Company and Hughes Tool Company (1948–53).

littoral zone, marine ecological realm that experiences the effects of tidal and longshore currents and breaking waves to a depth of 5 to 10 m (16 to 33 feet) below the low tide level, depending on the intensity of storm waves. The zone is characterized by abundant dissolved oxygen, sunlight, nutrients, generally high wave energies and water motion, and, in the intertidal subzone, alternating submergence and exposure. The geological nature of shorelines and nearshore bottoms is exceedingly varied. Consequently, the littoral fauna taken as a whole involves an enormous number of species and every major phylum, although the number of individuals may vary widely with locality. Coral reefs, rocky coasts, sandy beaches, and sheltered embayments each possess specialized, intricately interrelated floral and faunal littoral populations.

The types of living things that inhabit a littoral zone depend to a considerable extent on the type of bottom and on the degree of the zone's exposure to wave action. Exposed sandy coasts generally develop sparse populations, especially between the tide lines, while the few organisms inhabiting wave-swept rocky shores are generally firmly cemented or anchored to the substratum. Bays and inlets that are protected from violent wave action often develop rich populations, however. Protected rocky shores are generally covered with seaweeds, mussels, barnacles, and so on, with various kinds of crabs and worms crawling among them. Protected sandy and muddy bottoms teem with burrowing mollusks, worms, and echinoderms.

Littré, (Maximilien-)Paul-Émile (b. Feb. 1, 1801, Paris—d. June 2, 1881, Paris), French language scholar, lexicographer, and philosopher whose monumental *Dictionnaire de la langue française,* 4 vol. (1863–73; "Dictionary of the French Language"), is one of the outstanding lexicographic accomplishments of all time. A close friend of the philosopher Auguste Comte, Littré did much to publicize Comte's ideas.

Educated in medicine as well as English, German, Greek, Latin, and Sanskrit and Sanskrit philology, Littré was an ardent democrat who took part in the insurrection against King Charles X in 1830. In the decade that followed, he began preparation of a 10-volume translation of the writings of Hippocrates, completed in 1862. About the time the first volume appeared (1839), he became acquainted with the writings of Comte and was soon a fervent disciple, publishing many works on Positivism. After Comte lost his teaching position at the École Polytechnique, Paris (1842), Littré became one of his principal financial supporters. After 1852 he diverged from Comte's increasingly mystical views but waited until after Comte's death to publish his points of disagreement both in *Paroles de philosophie positive* (1859; "Words of Positivist Philosophy") and in another work (1863), in which he traced the origin of Comte's ideas and analyzed his philosophical system and its effects.

When finally completed, Littré's dictionary, begun in 1844, proved to be of incomparable value for its precise definitions and historical grasp of the growth of the French language. The dictionary gives an authoritative interpretation of the use of each word, based on the various meanings the word had held in the past. After some controversy because of his materialist views, he was elected to the Académie Française (1871) and in 1875 was elected a senator for life.

Littre gland: *see* urethral gland.

Lituites, genus of extinct cephalopods (primitive animals related to the modern pearly nautilus) found as fossils in marine rocks of the Ordovician Period (430,000,000 to 500,000,000 years ago). The distinctive shell of *Lituites* is composed of serially arranged chambers.

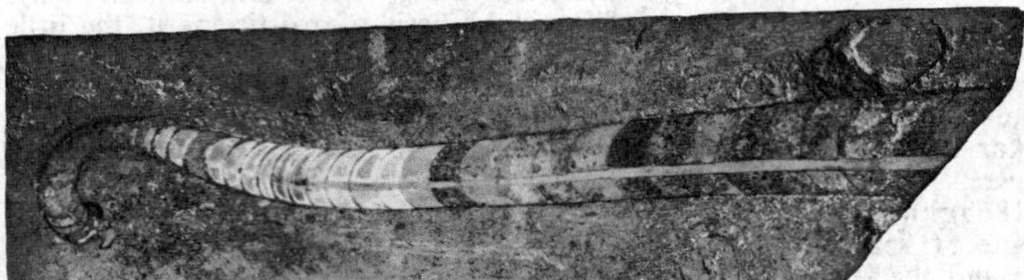

Lituites

By courtesy of the trustees of the British Museum (Natural History); photograph, Imitor

The shell begins with a tightly coiled portion that gradually straightens out after a few whorls; the anterior portion of the shell, the largest part, is straight in form and expands toward the front. The sutures between the chambers appear as simple lines around the shell.

liturgical drama, in the Middle Ages, type of play acted within or near the church and relating stories from the Bible and of the saints. Although they had their roots in the Christian liturgy, such plays were not performed as essential parts of a standard church service. The language of the liturgical drama was Latin, and the dialogue was frequently chanted to simple monophonic melodies. Music was also used in the form of incidental dance and processional tunes.

The earliest traces of the liturgical drama are found in manuscripts dating from the 10th century. Its genesis may perhaps be found in the chant "Quem quaeritis" ("Whom do you seek"), a trope to the Introit of the Easter mass. In *Regularis concordia* (mid-10th century), Aethelwold, bishop of Winchester described in some detail the manner in which the "Quem quaeritis" trope was performed as a small scene during the Matins service on Easter morning. The dialogue represents the well-known story of the three Marys approaching the tomb of Christ: "Whom do you seek?" "Jesus of Nazareth." "He is not here. He has arisen as was prophesied. Go. Announce that he has arisen from the dead."

The liturgical drama gradually increased in both length and sophistication and flourished particularly during the 12th and 13th centuries. The most popular themes were derived from colourful biblical tales (Daniel in the lion's den, the foolish virgins, the story of the Passion and death of Jesus, etc.) as well as from the stories of the saints (as the Virgin Mary and St. Nicholas). Eventually, the connection between the liturgical drama and the church was severed completely, as the plays came under secular sponsorship and adopted the vernacular. *See also* miracle play; morality play; mystery play.

liturgical hours (religious service): *see* divine office.

Liturgical Movement, a 19th- and 20th-century effort in Christian churches to restore the active and intelligent participation of the people in the liturgy, or official rites, of the Christian religion. The movement sought to make the liturgy both more attuned to early Christian traditions and more relevant to modern Christian life. The process involved simplifying rites, developing new texts (in the case of Roman Catholicism, translating the Latin texts into the vernacular of individual countries), and reeducating both laity and clergy on their role in liturgical celebrations. The Liturgical Movement made use of patristic and biblical studies, Christian archaeology, and the increased availability of early Christian literature and liturgical texts.

In the Roman Catholic Church, the movement can be traced back to the mid-19th century, when it was initially connected with monastic worship, especially in the Benedictine communities in France, Belgium, and Germany. After about 1910, it spread to Holland, Italy, and England and subsequently to the United States. About the time of World War II, the movement spread into parishes and became more pastoral in tone in France and Germany. Revisions of liturgy attempted to bring the rites more in accord with early Christian liturgical understanding and practices and yet to take into account the present needs of church members. Early changes included an emphasis on frequent reception of communion at mass and some revisions in the church calendar.

Pope Pius XII played a significant role with the 1947 encyclical *Mediator Dei,* in which he stressed the importance of liturgy and the need for people to participate. The actual reform of rites began with Holy Week revisions in 1951 and 1955. The second Vatican Council (1962–65) endorsed the aims of the movement and recommended that Roman Catholics should actively take part in the liturgy; legislated the use of the vernacular for liturgies, overturning the traditional use of Latin as the sole liturgical language; and ordered the reform of all sacramental rites, a task completed in the 1970s. A new lectionary and calendar (the *Ordo Missae*) appeared in 1969, and a definitive Roman Missal was published in 1970.

Protestant churches have also revised texts and updated archaic expressions in their liturgical rites, often taking advantage of the broader ecumenical studies. The United Presbyterian Church published a liturgy for congregational use, the *Worshipbook,* in 1970. In 1978 the Lutheran Church in the United States published its revised *Lutheran Book of Worship,* offering more individual choices in liturgy and also an expanded variety of musical styles. In 1979 the Episcopal Church adopted a revised *Book of Common Prayer,* which offered a choice of texts, one preserving the traditional language.

liturgical music, also called CHURCH MUSIC, music written for performance in a religious rite of worship; the term is most commonly associated with the Christian tradtion. Developing from the musical practices of the Jewish synagogues, which allowed the cantor an improvised charismatic song, early Christian services contained a simple refrain, or responsorial, sung by the congregation. This evolved into the various Western chants, the last of which, the Gregorian, reached its apogee in the Carolingian Renaissance. From the 10th century there also emerged a vast number of hymns.

Polyphony was at first restricted to major feasts. Solo ensembles of virtuoso singers were accompanied by the organ or, possibly, a group of instruments. By about 1200 the early polyphonic style culminated in the spectacular organa of the Notre-Dame school composers Léonin and Pérotin.

The 14th century saw a proliferation of locally produced verbal tropes set to music by more or less trained composers, often in relatively simple homophonic (chordal) manner. In French circles, however, isorhythm (use of complex underlying rhythmic repetitions) was applied to the motet and also to sections of the mass. The first few polyphonic settings of the ordinary of the mass as a unified whole date from this century.

Late medieval church music became progressively more direct in method and expression. Subtleties of rhythm gave way to a strong feeling for tonality, order, and symmetry. The liturgical music of the Burgundian Guillaume Dufay, John Dunstable and Leonel Power in England, and their contemporaries was written for princely chapels and court ceremonies, rather than for abbey and cathedral.

During the Renaissance the use of small choirs rather than soloists for polyphonic music was established. Although the a cappella (unaccompanied) choir style is associated with this era, church choirs were sometimes accompanied by organ and other instruments. The Netherlanders Jakob Obrecht and Jean d'Okeghem, succeeded by the celebrated Josquin des Prez, brought clarity and lyricism to an art that had sometimes leaned toward the sombre. In the next generation the Italian Giovanni Pierluigi da Palestrina, the Fleming Orlando di Lasso, the Spaniards Tomás Luis de Victoria and Cristóbal de Morales, and the Englishman William Byrd provided outstanding contributions.

The Renaissance also witnessed the growth of liturgical organ music, which was used originally when there was no choir capable of singing polyphony. The organist alternated harmonized settings of plainsong hymns, canticles, and masses with plainsong verses that were sung by the choir or by the congregation. The rise of the verse anthem in England and of the Baroque motet in Italy (genres that included elaborate vocal solos) stimulated the organist's ability to improvise accompaniments. In Venice, Andrea and Giovanni Gabrieli and their followers made dramatic use of spatial contrasts and opposing forces of strings, winds, and voices.

In Germany the chorale, or hymn melody, was an important ingredient of motets, organ music, and, later, cantatas. Heinrich Schütz, Franz Tunder, and Dietrich Buxtehude led music to assume the greatest importance in church services, culminating in the liturgical music of J.S. Bach.

In the Classical era, anthems, motets, and masses—often of routine quality—continued to be written. The great composers of the era often set liturgical texts with the concert hall, rather than the church, in mind. The resounding, spirited, and church-intended masses of Joseph Haydn and the other early Viennese masters remained a local product.

The masses of Ludwig van Beethoven, Franz Schubert, and Anton Bruckner, the motets of Gioacchino Rossini and Johannes Brahms, the organ music of César Franck and Max Reger, and the requiems of Hector Berlioz and Giuseppe Verdi belong to the extremely varied development of church music in the 19th century. An attempt to revive the 16th-century style drew some composers of church music away from the earlier Romantic flamboyance. In the 20th century such composers as Ralph Vaughan Williams, William Walton, Benjamin Britten, Oliver Messiaen, Francis Poulenc, Igor Stravinsky, and Krsztof Penderecki helped show new paths for the ancient forms.

liturgy of the hours: *see* divine office.

Litvínov, industrial commune, northern Severočeský *kraj* (region), northwestern Czech Republic. Located at the foot of the Krušné Hory (Ore Mountains), the commune was created in 1950 from the villages of Horní Litvínov, Dolní Litvínov, Chudeřín, Lipětín, and Rauchengrund and has become part of the Most-Záluží-Litvínov industrial complex. Brown coal (lignite) is mined, and there is metallurgical industry in the city of Litvínov; it also has chemical and petrochemical complexes. Záluží has a petroleum refinery. Litvínov also is a major producer of cotton textiles and clothing. Pop. (1991 prelim.) 29,-085.

Consult the INDEX *first*

Litvinov, Maksim Maksimovich, original name MEIR WALACH (b. July 17 [July 5, Old Style], 1876, Białystok, Pol.—d. Dec. 31, 1951, Moscow, Russian S.F.S.R.), Soviet diplomat and commissar of foreign affairs (1930–39), who was a prominent advocate of world disarmament and of collective security with the Western powers against Nazi Germany before World War II.

Having been influenced by Marxism while serving in the Imperial Russian Army, Litvinov joined the Russian Social-Democratic Workers' Party in 1898. He was arrested for his revolutionary activity in 1901 but escaped and fled to Great Britain (1902). Aligned with the Bolshevik faction after 1903, Litvinov was involved in party activities throughout Europe.

Litvinov
Tass—Sovfoto

With the Bolshevik seizure of power in Russia (October 1917), Litvinov was appointed diplomatic representative in London. Arrested in October 1918 for engaging in propaganda activities, he was released the following January in exchange for Robert Bruce Lockhart, the British journalist who led a special mission to the Soviet Union in 1918. Litvinov then returned to Russia and joined the Commissariat for Foreign Affairs. He achieved prominence when he led the Soviet delegation to the preparatory commission for the League of Nations' World Disarmament Conference (1927–30) and proposed sweeping disarmament programs. Having become commissar for foreign affairs (July 21, 1930), he was the principal Soviet delegate to the World Disarmament Conference held at Geneva in 1932. He also led the Soviet delegation to the World Economic Conference in London (1933) and conducted negotiations for establishing diplomatic relations between the Soviet Union and the United States (1934).

When the power of Nazi Germany became a threat, Litvinov urged the League of Nations to make plans for collective resistance against Germany (1934–38) and negotiated anti-German treaties with France (signed May 2, 1935) and Czechoslovakia (signed May 16, 1935). The Western democracies' appeasement of Germany eventually prompted the Soviet leaders to change their policy and dismiss Litvinov, who was Jewish and closely identified with the anti-German position (May 3, 1939), before concluding the German-Soviet Treaty of Nonaggression (August 1939). Litvinov returned to active duty in 1941 after the Germans invaded the Soviet Union, serving first as ambassador to the United States (November 1941–August 1943), then as deputy commissar for foreign affairs. He retired in August 1946.

Litvonian Highland (Latvia): *see* Vidzeme.

Litwos: *see* Sienkiewicz, Henryk.

Liu An (Chinese philosopher): *see* Huai-nan-tzu.

Liu Bei (Chinese ruler): *see* Liu Pei.

Liu Ch'e: *see* Wu-ti (156 BC–87 BC).

Liu Chi: *see* Kao-tsu (256–195 BC).

Liu Ch'i: *see* Ching-ti (d. 141 BC).

Liu Chin, Pinyin LIU JIN (d. 1510, Peking, China), eunuch who dominated the Chinese government during the early rule of Cheng-te (reigned 1505–21) of the Ming dynasty.

The emperor was an eccentric pleasure-seeker, and Liu Chin gradually gained control of the government. Corruption spread, offices were bought and sold, and excessive taxes were levied. Liu and seven other eunuchs who shared power with him became known collectively as the Eight Tigers (*pa hu*) because of the way they terrorized the country. But the people became dissatisfied, and rebellions erupted.

Finally, a group of officials forced the emperor to banish Liu. When Liu's house was searched, it was found to contain a fortune in gold, silver, and gems as well as a number of false seals. At last the emperor realized the extent of the eunuch's corruption and had him executed.

Liu-chou, formerly MA-P'ING, Pinyin LIUZHOU, or MAPING, city in central Kwangsi Chuang autonomous *ch'ü* (region), southern China.

Liu-chou, the second largest city in Kwangsi, is a natural communication centre, being situated at the confluence of several tributaries that form the Liu River, which flows southward into a tributary of the Hsi River. In recent times Liu-chou has become the focus of a highway system and is linked by rail northeastward to Kuei-lin and Heng-yang (in Hunan), southwestward to Nan-ning and the Vietnamese border at P'ing-hsiang, northwestward to Kuei-yang (in Kweichow province) and Szechwan province, and southeastward to the port of Chan-chiang (in Kwangtung province).

Until comparatively recent centuries, the area was occupied by non-Chinese peoples. The county of T'an-chung was founded there in the 1st century BC; renamed Ma-p'ing in 591, it became the seat of a prefecture under the T'ang dynasty (618–907) and of a superior prefecture (Liu-chou) after 1368. In the Middle Ages, however, it was little more than a frontier garrison and trading post, often used as a place of exile. Through the centuries it has frequently been a centre of rebellion—for example, in the risings led by Ch'en Chin in 1004–08, by Chou Chien in the late 15th century, and by Wei Chin-t'ien in the second quarter of the 16th century. Only in the 17th century did the area become dominated by Chinese settlers.

Liu-chou has always been a centre for the collection of agricultural products, timber, and vegetable and tung oil from north central Kwangsi and southern Kweichow and has had handicraft industries based on local products. It has been renowned for the production of coffins as well as for papermaking, tobacco curing, and textile manufacturing. There are also plants for oil extraction and grain milling.

Since 1949 there has been considerable industrial expansion; new installations include large lumber-processing and woodworking factories as well as chemical plants (extracting sulfur and producing alcohols). Liu-chou supports a large engineering industry, producing agricultural machinery and gasoline and diesel engines; there is also a large locomotive repair works. In the late 1950s a steel and iron plant was built, using rich local iron ores and coal from the Ho-shan mines (on the railway to the southeast). In the 1960s Liu-chou, in addition to becoming a major manufacturer of tractors, also developed a large fertilizer plant and began to produce cement. There is a large thermal power station, and there are also several hydroelectric installations in the district. Pop. (1982) 581,980.

Liu Chuang: *see* Ming Ti (AD 29–76).

Liu E, also spelled LIU O, Pinyin LIU E, or LIU O, courtesy name (Wade–Giles romanization) T'IEH-YÜN (b. Oct. 18, 1857, Liu-ho [Tan-t'u], China—d. Aug. 23, 1909, Tihua, Sinkiang), Chinese government functionary and economic promoter famed for his major literary work, *Lao Ts'an yu-chi* (1904–07; *The Travels of Lao Ts'an*).

The son of a provincial official, Liu engaged variously in government work related to flood control, famine relief, and railroad construction until he became disillusioned with Imperial attitudes about reform and turned to the promotion of private economic development. Liu's experience in these projects as well as his contacts with foreigners convinced him of China's need to modernize using Western technology and business methods. His desire to see China develop indirectly shaped much of the novel *The Travels of Lao Ts'an*, a social satire exposing the limitations of the old elite and officialdom. Written in the traditional mode of vernacular novels, this work stands preeminent among the satirical fiction that dominated the literature of the late Ch'ing dynasty. Despite the popular success of the work, which was serialized in journals and newspapers, Liu was framed on a charge of malfeasance and exiled to Sinkiang, where he died in disgrace the following year.

Liu Hsiu: *see* Kuang-wu Ti (4 BC–AD 57).

Liu K'un-i, Pinyin LIU KUNYI (b. Jan. 21, 1830, Hsin-ning, Hunan Province, China—d. Oct. 6, 1902, Peking), official and modernizer in the later years of the Ch'ing dynasty (1644–1911/12).

A principal figure in quelling the great Taiping Rebellion in South China between 1850 and 1864, Liu became one of the leading provincial viceroys who dominated China after the uprising. He advised the government on its relations with Western powers, and his administration attempted to end corruption and waste. He was one of the first Chinese officials to purchase Western guns and ships for his troops and to build Western-style arsenals and shipyards.

In the late 1890s he kept South China free of the Boxers (secret societies whose motto was "Protect the country, destroy foreigners"). He was not so successful, however, in preventing the spread of the Boxers in North China and could not eliminate their growing influence on the central government. In 1900, when the dynasty decided to support the antiforeignism of the Boxers and declared war on all foreign powers in China, Liu joined with the other South China provincial governors and ignored the dynasty's orders. This action served to confine the Boxer Rebellion to North China and minimize the number of foreigners killed. As a result, when the Western powers crushed the Boxer Rebellion, they were amenable to lenient terms for China in the final peace settlement.

In 1902, Liu, together with the scholar-general Chang Chih-tung (1837–1909), submitted to the throne several influential memorandums calling for the reform and transformation of the traditional Chinese state along Western lines; only a part of their comprehensive program was adopted by the country's Ch'ing rulers, and that proved to be too little and too late to save the dynasty from being overthrown in 1911.

Consult the INDEX *first*

Liu-p'an Mountains, Wade–Giles romanization LIU-P'AN SHAN, Pinyin LIUPAN SHAN, mountain range in northern China extending southward from the Ningsia Hui Autonomous Region across the eastern panhandle of Kansu Province and into western Shensi Province. The range is formed by the tilted western edge of the structural basin that underlies the Loess Plateau (a plateau covered with wind-deposited silt) of Shensi and that continues northward to form the Ho-lan Shan (mountains) west of the Huang Ho (river) in the Yin-ch'uan region of Ningsia Hui. The range is a sharply defined one, with a general elevation of more than 6,500 ft (2,000 m); individual peaks reach 9,826 ft. To the south, the mountains are separated from the far higher Tsinling Shan, which extend from west to east, by the major fault line forming the valley of the Wei Ho. The main axis of the Liu-p'an Mountains can be traced from southeast to northwest, from north of Pao-chi in Shensi, crossing Kansu and entering into Ningsia Hui, beyond which it swings into a nearly north–south axis. The name Liu-p'an Mountains properly belongs to this higher northern section, while the southern section is called the Lung Shan (also Kuan Shan, Lung-t'ou, or Lung-pan).

The range forms a sharp watershed between two tributary systems of the Wei Ho—the Hu-lu Ho system to the west and the Ching Ho system to the east. It has provided an important cultural barrier, dividing the southern basin of Shensi (the Wei Valley area, which is one of the cradles of sedentary Chinese culture) from the arid pasture lands of Kansu. The only important passes through the range are the Wei Valley in the south (the Lung Kuan [pass] or Ta-chen Kuan) and the route in the north between P'ing-liang and Ching-ning (both in Kansu). The area is very dry, much eroded, and heavily dissected by its rivers. Because of their elevation, the mountains receive somewhat more rain than the surrounding plateau areas, and there remain some patches of pine forest in the higher parts. The rest of the area is covered by grassland.

Liu Pang: *see* Kao Tsu (256 BC–195 BC).

Liu Pei, Pinyin LIU BEI, posthumous name, or *shih*, CHAO-LIEH TI, or HSIEN CHU (b. AD 162, Chihli, now Hopeh Province, China—d. 223, Szechwan Province), ruler of one of the three kingdoms into which China was divided at the end of the Han dynasty (206 BC–AD 220).

Although Liu claimed descent from one of the early Han emperors, he grew up in poverty. Distinguishing himself in battle in the great Yellow Turban Rebellion that broke out at the end of the Han, he eventually became one of the leading Han generals and a rival of the other great general, Ts'ao Ts'ao. After P'ei, the son of Ts'ao Ts'ao, usurped the Han throne in 220, Liu Pei occupied the area in central China around Szechwan and founded his own dynasty. Liu retained the name Han for his new dynasty, and his is usually known as the Shu, or Minor, Han to distinguish it from the Great Han dynasty. As one of the heroes of the 14th-century Chinese historical novel *San Kuo chih yen-i* (*Romance of the Three Kingdoms*), Liu has been celebrated and romanticized in Chinese history. The dynasty that he founded, however, never expanded much beyond Szechwan and lasted only from 221 to 263 or 264.

Liu Ping-chi (Chinese emperor): *see* Hsüan Ti.

Liu Shaoqi, Wade–Giles romanization LIU SHAO-CH'I (b. 1898, Ning-hsiang district, Hunan Province, China—d. Nov. 12, 1969, K'ai-feng, Honan Province), chairman of the People's Republic of China (1959–68) and chief theoretician for the Chinese Communist Party (CCP), who was considered Mao Zedong's heir apparent until he was purged in the late 1960s. Liu was active in the Chinese labour movement from its inception, and he was influential in formulating party and, later, governmental strategy. He played an important role in Chinese foreign affairs after the Communists had gained control of the country.

Liu Shaoqi
Eastfoto

Early life and career. Liu was the youngest son of a rich peasant landowner. He attended middle school, went to normal school in Ch'ang-sha, and in 1918 studied French in North China. Two years later, Liu joined the Socialist Youth League and subsequently journeyed to Moscow, where he enrolled in the University for Toilers of the East and became a member of the newly formed CCP. Liu's education and his extensive experience abroad later made him one of the most cosmopolitan of the Chinese leaders.

In 1922 Liu returned to China, where he helped organize the First National Labour Congress in May. Soon after this he was assigned to the Secretariat of the Hunan provincial party organization as an aide to Mao Zedong. Late that year Liu went to the An-yüan colliery to organize miners for what was to become a successful strike. From this time onward he became increasingly more involved in the labour movement—as leader of a sympathy strike in February 1923, as vice chairman of the All-China Federation of Labour in May 1925, and as secretary general of the Third National Labour Congress in 1926.

The year 1926 marked the high point of the Chinese labour movement. When the Nationalist Party (Kuomintang) and the CCP split in April 1927, Liu and his comrades found the urban component of the Chinese Communist movement decimated by Nationalist forces, and so they fled underground. In late April, Liu was elected to the Fifth Central Committee of the CCP.

After the turbulence of 1927, Liu's ascendancy in the party was rapid; he was named director of the workers' department in mid-1928, and in the following year he assumed the post of secretary of the Manchurian Provincial Party Committee, a post he later relinquished (early 1931) in order to go to Shanghai. By 1931 the centre of gravity of the Chinese Communist movement had shifted away from the cities to rural areas, but Liu remained in Shanghai, underground, taking part in movements in opposition to the Japanese invasion of Manchuria and encroachment in North China.

In late 1932 Liu joined Mao Zedong's forces in Kiangsi Province and was named head of the All-China Federation of Labour; by 1934 he had gained a seat on the Politburo (Political Bureau) of the Sixth Central Committee. Shortly after his elevation to the Politburo, he left Mao's forces, who were in the midst of their Long March, and went to Peking to agitate further against the Japanese. In early 1936 Liu was designated secretary of the party's North China Bureau. When the war with Japan had spread to most of China, he was put in charge of the Central Plain Bureau of the CCP, and in this position he worked closely with the Communist New Fourth Army operating in Central China.

In mid-1939 in Yenan (the Communist headquarters), Liu delivered a famous series of lectures called "How To Be a Good Communist." In these talks he drew upon all his organizational experience as a labour leader and underground figure to define the demands to be made upon all party members; at this point Liu began to assume the role of chief theoretician for the party. He delivered another important talk in July 1941, entitled "On Intraparty Struggle," which further enhanced his position as the party's theoretical spokesman.

In 1943 Liu was named secretary of the Central Secretariat and vice chairman of the People's Revolutionary Military Council, making him one of the most powerful men in the Chinese Communist hierarchy. By June 1945 he was clearly spokesman for party affairs, and at the Seventh Party Congress he delivered the major address, entitled "On the Party." During the closing days of World War II, Mao Zedong and Chiang Kai-shek were engaged in talks at Chungking, and Liu served as acting chairman in Mao's absence. By Oct. 1, 1949, the Communists controlled much of China, the People's Republic of China had been established, and Liu had been named vice chairman of the new government.

Experience with Soviet leadership. Once the Chinese Communists had achieved power, Liu's cosmopolitan outlook and experience with the Soviet leadership enabled him to act as initial spokesman for Peking's new hard-line foreign policy, and it also gave him a central role in the formation of China's industrialization plans; both endeavours were dependent on Moscow in 1949. For these reasons Liu headed the Sino-Soviet Friendship Association in 1949–54 and led the Chinese delegation to the Soviet 19th Party Congress in October 1952.

In August 1954, at the First National People's Congress, Liu was elected chairman of the Standing Committee. His influence was not confined to state organs, however, but extended also into the party, where in late 1953 and early 1954 he led a purge of regional power holders. Subsequently his position in the party grew, and by 1956 he was clearly Mao Zedong's heir apparent.

During the second session of the Eighth Party Congress in May 1958, Liu outlined the strategy for the second five-year economic plan (called the Great Leap Forward), which was to lay the foundation for the rapid industrialization of China. Shortly after the initiation of the Great Leap Forward, however, it became apparent that industrialization could not be achieved as rapidly as hoped, and a policy of retrenchment was called for. Partly as a result of the failures of the Great Leap, Mao relinquished his position as chairman of the People's Republic of China, though he remained party chairman, and Liu assumed the chairmanship in April 1959. During this period, Liu tried to revitalize agriculture by initiating policies that permitted peasants to cultivate private plots and spurred them on with monetary incentives; both were policies to which Mao later strongly objected.

In his new post as head of state, Liu began to play a more prominent role in foreign affairs, receiving state visitors from Indonesia, the Soviet Union, Pakistan, Ghana, Cuba, North Vietnam, Cambodia, and North Korea. In addition, he traveled abroad rather extensively during 1959–66. Upon reaching this pinnacle, however, Liu became one of the most important figures to be purged in the Great Proletarian Cultural Revolution (1966–69). Many persons associated with him, such as Peng Zhen, mayor of Peking, and Deng Xiaoping, a member of the Politburo, were also purged, decimating what had been viewed as a highly cohesive Chinese leadership. In October 1968 Liu was stripped of party positions and labeled China's Khrushchev, and, by April 1969, a new constitutionally designated successor to Mao had been chosen—Lin Biao, head of the armed forces. In the autumn of 1971 Lin Biao disappeared, and it was announced that he—"a conspirator and arch-traitor"—had died in an airplane crash while fleeing from an attempt to assassinate Mao.

During 1974 rumours of Liu's death gained wide circulation, and on October 31 a Communist newspaper in Hong Kong confirmed the fact. No details of date or place of death were revealed, however, until May 1980, when the *Beijing Review* reported that Liu had died on Nov. 12, 1969, in K'ai-feng, northern Honan Province.

Possible causes of Liu's fall. The causes of Liu's fall (and events leading to Lin's death) are not clear. For several years the names of Liu, Deng, and Lin were linked, and the three were condemned in the party press as "capitalist roaders" intent on defeating the revolution. After Mao's death, on Sept. 9, 1976, however, his widow, Jiang Qing, and her so-called Gang of Four undertook a coup that was quickly aborted. Hua Guofeng, a relatively junior member of the hierarchy, achieved party leadership, and Deng Xiaoping was rehabilitated. Then, in February 1980, the 11th Central Committee of the CCP decided "to completely rehabilitate" Liu, calling him a "great Marxist and proletarian revolutionary," and to remove the labels of "renegade, traitor, and scab" formerly attached to him. Lin was then identified with the Gang of Four and charged with "concocting false evidence" and subjecting Liu to "political frame-up and physical persecution" while overthrowing other leaders on the charge of being Liu's agents.

While little is known of Liu's first four spouses, his fifth wife, Wang Guangmei, achieved great notoriety during the Cultural Revolution for her "bourgeois" life-style. Liu had at least eight children, none of whom achieved political prominence. (R.C.N.)

BIBLIOGRAPHY. Donald W. Klein and Anne B. Clark, *Biographic Dictionary of Chinese Communism, 1921–1965* (1971), a monumental, two-volume set that gives an excellent discussion of Liu's life; Liu Shao-ch'i, *The Collected Works of Liu Shao-ch'i,* 3 vol. (1968–69), is an anthology of Liu's major statements; "Fifth Plenary Session of 11th C.C.P. Central Committee," *Beijing Review,* No. 10 (March 10, 1980), pp. 3–10, which documents official rehabilitation measures.

Liu Shih (Chinese emperor): *see* Yüan Ti.

Liu Ta (Chinese emperor): *see* Chang Ti.

Liu-t'iao Pien (China): *see* Willow Palisade.

Liu Tsung-yüan, Pinyin LIU ZONGYUAN (b. 773, Tung-kuan', Shansi Province, China—d. 819, Liu-chou, Kwangsi Province), Chinese poet, prose writer, and supporter of his contemporary, the poet and essayist Han Yü, in the movement to liberate writers from the highly formalized *p'ien-wen,* the "parallel prose" style cultivated by the Chinese literati for nearly 1,000 years.

A talented writer from his youth, Liu Tsung-yüan served as a government official for most of his life, acting with integrity and courage, despite his politically motivated exile to minor positions in isolated regions of China. Liu joined Han Yü in condemning the artificialities and restrictions of the *p'ien-wen* style and in urging a return to the simplicity and flexibility of the classical prose style of ancient times. In pursuit of this goal, Liu Tsung-yüan produced many examples of clear and charming prose.

Liu Yüan, Pinyin LIU YUAN (d. 310, China), Hsiung-nu invader who took the title of king of Han in 304. Liu's invasion is seen as the start of the "barbarian" inundation of China that continued until 589.

Liu was the ruler of the Hsiung-nu people of northern Shansi Province. He entered China at the request of one of the princes of the Western Chin dynasty (265–316), who was engaged in a civil war known as the Revolt of the Eight Kings. Conquering much of northern Shansi, Liu proclaimed himself the emperor of a new Han dynasty. Liu's dynasty, renamed the Chao by his son and successor, was overthrown in 329.

Liubertsy (Russia): *see* Lyubertsy.

Liudolf, also spelled LUDOLF (b. 930—d. Sept. 6, 957, Pombia, near Novara, Italy), duke of Swabia and son of the Holy Roman emperor Otto I, against whom he led a revolt.

Liudolf, Otto's son by his marriage to the English princess Eadgyth, was made duke of Swabia by his father in 950. In 952, feeling his inheritance rights threatened by Otto's second marriage (to Adelaide of Burgundy) and by the influence of his uncle, Henry, duke of Bavaria, Liudolf joined with Conrad the Red of Lotharingia and Frederick, archbishop of Mainz, to raise a rebellion in Germany. He exacted concessions from Otto in 953 and, when these were repudiated, seized the city of Regensburg and welcomed Magyar invaders into Germany. Liudolf held out until 955, when, deserted by Conrad and Frederick, he surrendered and was reconciled with his father.

Liudolfing DYNASTY: *see* Saxon dynasty.

Liutiaobian (China): *see* Willow Palisade.

Liutprand, also spelled LIUDPRAND, Italian LIUTPRANDO (d. 744), Lombard king of Italy whose long and prosperous reign was a period of expansion and consolidation for the Lombards.

From his position as a Lombard chief, Liutprand gained the throne in 712, when revolution ended a succession of weak kings. He used to his advantage the Iconoclastic Controversy (727), a rebellion in Byzantine Italy caused by Emperor Leo III's condemnation of image worship. Pope Gregory II sought the support of the Lombard dukes of Spoleto and Benevento, while Liutprand contracted an alliance with the exarch (Byzantine governor) of Ravenna (730). Liutprand's forces, aided by the Byzantines, invaded the Duchy of Spoleto and attacked Rome. The Pope left the city for a personal confrontation with Liutprand, a pious Catholic, who was then forced by his conscience to yield.

In 739 Liutprand seized four cities of the Duchy of Rome. Pope Gregory III, successor to Gregory II, appealed to Charles Martel, the Frankish ruler of Gaul, but Charles, who had been Liutprand's ally against the Saracens in Provence, refused aid. When Liutprand threatened Rome once again in 742, a new pope, Zacharias, met with Liutprand in person at Terni, north of Rome, and again Liutprand's expansionism was thwarted by an appeal to his religious faith.

Liutprand emended King Rothari's Edict of 643, which served as the code of Lombard law; his revision added 153 articles and abolished the *guidrigild,* a fine of money, like the Germanic *wergild,* levied to compensate for personal injury or murder.

Liuvigild (Visigothic king of Spain): *see* Leovigild.

Liuzhou (China): *see* Liu-chou.

live-bearer, any of the numerous live-bearing topminnows of the family Poeciliidae (order Atheriniformes), found only in the New World and most abundantly in Mexico and Central America. Most of the many species are rather elongated, and all are small, the largest growing to only about 15 centimetres (6 inches) long.

Live-bearers resemble the related killifish (family Cyprinodontidae) but differ in their mode of reproduction and in the possession, by the males, of a specialized organ (gonopodium) derived from the anal fin and used to place the sperm in the body of the female. The family is also noted for the sometimes considerable differences between the sexes, the female often being larger and less brightly coloured. The young may number from a few to 100 or more, and several broods may result from one mating.

One-spot live-bearer (*Poecilia vivipara*)
Painting by Karen Allan

Live-bearers are usually omnivorous; some, such as the mosquito fish (*q.v.*), feed heavily on mosquito larvae and are used to control these pests. Many live-bearers are popular aquarium fishes; among the best known are the guppy, molly, platy, and swordtail (*qq.v.*).

live-forever (plant): *see* houseleek.

live oak, any of several species of North American ornamental and timber trees belonging to the red oak group of the genus *Quercus* in the beech family (Fagaceae).

Specifically, the term refers to the southern live oak (*Quercus virginiana*), a massive evergreen tree native to Cuba and the Atlantic and Gulf coastal plains. It often grows to a height of 15 metres (50 feet) or more on hummocks and ridges but may be shrubby on barren coastal soils. The trunk divides near the ground into several limbs that may extend horizontally as much as two to three times the height of the tree. The elliptical leaves, usually unlobed, are dark green and glossy above, whitish and hairy below. A valuable timber tree, southern live oak is also planted as a shade and avenue tree in the southern U.S. It grows rapidly on good soil but is not as long-lived as was once thought: the oldest known specimens range in age from 200 to 300 years. Live oak derives its name from the fact that it is evergreen and durable: lumbered or injured trees send up many sprouts, which also produce sprouts if cut themselves. The heavy, strong wood was once used in shipbuilding.

California live oak (*Q. agrifolia*) and interior live oak (*Q. wislizenii*), native to western North America, have holly-like leaves. They are usually shrubby but may reach 15 to 25 m or more; the California live oak is planted as an ornamental in other areas of the world for its rounded shape.

A member of the white oak group, the canyon live oak (*Q. chrysolepsis*), a timber tree occasionally more than 27 m tall, is often called goldencup oak for its egg-shaped acorns, each enclosed at the base in a yellow, woolly cup. The thick, leathery leaves remain on the tree three to four years.

Livens, Johannis: *see* Lievens, Jan.

liver, the largest organ in the vertebrate body, composed of a spongy mass of wedge-shaped lobes that has many metabolic and secretory functions.

A brief treatment of the liver follows. For full treatment, *see* MACROPAEDIA: Digestion and Digestive Systems.

For a depiction of the liver in human anatomy, shown in relation to the other parts of the body, see the colour Trans-Vision in the PROPAEDIA: Part Four, Section 421.

Functionally the most complex of the body's organs, the liver secretes bile, a digestive fluid; metabolizes proteins, carbohydrates, and fats; stores glycogen, vitamins, and other substances; synthesizes blood-clotting factors; removes wastes and toxic matter from the blood; regulates blood volume; and destroys old red blood cells.

To perform many of its varied functions, the liver is uniquely and closely connected with both the intestine and the gallbladder (*q.v.*). From the intestine the portal vein carries venous blood to the liver to be processed before returning to the heart. From the liver a duct system carries bile to the common bile duct, which empties into the duodenum of the intestine and which connects with the gallbladder for storage and subsequent release of bile.

Liver tissue consists of a mass of cells tunnelled through with bile ducts and blood vessels. Hepatic cells make up about 60 percent of the tissue and carry on more metabolic functions than any other group of cells in the body. A second group of cells, called Kupffer cells, line the smallest channels of the liver's vascular system and play a role in blood formation, antibody production, and ingestion of foreign particles and cellular debris.

The human liver secretes about 800 to 1,000 millilitres (about a quart) each day of bile, which contains bile salts needed for the digestion of fats in the diet. Bile is also the medium for excretion of certain metabolic waste products, drugs, and toxic substances. Bile secreted into the common bile duct enters the gallbladder, where it is concentrated and stored. The presence of fat in the duodenum stimulates the flow of bile out of the gallbladder and into the intestine. Worn-out red blood cells are destroyed in the liver, spleen, and bone marrow. A pigment, bilirubin, formed in the process of hemoglobin breakdown, is released into the bile, creating its characteristic greenish-orange colour, and is excreted from the body through the intestine.

The liver cells synthesize a number of enzymes. As blood flows through the liver, both from the portal vein and from the hepatic artery, the cells and enzymes filter out and modify many substances and particles. Nutrients entering the liver from the intestine are changed into forms usable by the body cells or are stored for future use. Fats are converted into fatty acids and then into carbohydrates or ketone bodies and transported by the blood to the tissues, where they are further metabolized. Sugars are converted into glycogen, which remains stored in the liver until it is needed for energy production, when it is reconverted into glucose and released into the bloodstream. The liver manufactures blood serum proteins, including albumin and several clotting factors, and supplies them to the blood. In its role as a blood purifier, the liver metabolizes nitrogenous waste products from body processes and detoxifies poisonous substances, preparing them for elimination in the urine or feces.

A common sign of impaired liver function is jaundice, a yellowness of the eyes and skin arising from excessive bilirubin in the blood. Jaundice can result from an abnormally high level of red blood cell destruction (hemolytic jaundice), defective uptake or transport of bilirubin by the hepatic cells (hepatocellular jaundice), or a blockage in the bile duct system (obstructive jaundice). Failure of hepatic cells to function can result from hepatitis, cirrhosis, tumours, vascular obstruction, or poisoning. Symptoms may include weakness, low blood pressure, easy bruising and bleeding, tremor, apathy, brain wave changes, and accumulation of fluid in the abdomen. Tests of liver function help in identifying disease, estimating liver damage, and evaluating treatment. Blood tests can reveal abnormal levels of bilirubin, cholesterol, serum proteins, urea, ammonia, and various enzymes. Injecting the dye bromsulfalein (BSP) and measuring its time of retention in the blood is another gauge of liver function. The condition of liver tissue can be examined microscopically by performing a needle biopsy.

Acute viral hepatitis is an inflammation of the liver that includes hepatitis A, usually spread by fecal contamination of food or drink, and hepatitis B, commonly transmitted by injection with unsterile instruments or by transfusion of contaminated blood or plasma. A third category of viral hepatitis, called non-A, non-B hepatitis, is caused by at least one (and probably two) other viral agents. Non-A, non-B infection is a common cause of post-transfusion hepatitis. In all forms of viral hepatitis, the illness may last two to six weeks, and fatigue often persists for as long as six months. The disease is ordinarily self-limiting; treatment includes bed rest and abstention from alcohol. Prevention of outbreaks requires careful sanitation as well as sterile injection and transfusion procedures.

Cirrhosis of the liver is an irreversible chronic disease characterized by the replacement of functioning liver tissue with bands and lumps of scar tissue. It can be brought about by viral hepatitis, chronic alcoholism, obstruction of the bile channels or the hepatic vein, heart failure, deposition of iron or copper, or some forms of metabolic disease. Cirrhosis causes hepatic cell failure and abnormally high pressure in the portal vein, leading to enlargement of the spleen and rupture of blood vessels. Treatment requires eliminating the primary cause, if possible. An alcoholic with cirrhosis, for example, can show striking improvement with bed rest and total avoidance of alcohol.

The liver is subject to a variety of other disorders and diseases. Abscesses can be caused by acute appendicitis; those occurring in the bile ducts may result from gallstones or may follow surgery. The parasite that causes amebic dysentery in the tropics can produce liver abscesses as well. Various other parasites prevalent in different parts of the world also infect the liver. Cancers of the liver are common, most of them secondary tumours originating elsewhere in the body. Glycogen-storage diseases, a group of hereditary disorders, generate a buildup of glycogen in the liver and an insufficient supply of glucose in the blood. Certain drugs may damage the liver, producing jaundice.

liver cancer, any of several forms of disease characterized by tumours in the liver. Most malignant liver tumours are hepatomas, also called hepatocellular carcinomas (HCCs). HCCs begin in the functional cells of the liver and account for 85 percent of all liver cancers worldwide. The remaining cancers develop from blood vessels (hemangiosarcomas), small bile ducts (cholangiosarcomas), or immature liver cells (hepatoblastomas).

The causes of liver cancer vary and in many cases remain unknown, but several risk factors have been identified. Previous infection with hepatitis B or hepatitis C viruses is linked to liver cancer, as is cirrhosis of the liver. Exposure to several chemicals also increases cancer risk; these include vinyl chloride (used in plastics manufacturing), aflatoxin (a poison produced by a fungus of spoiled peanuts and certain grain products), and arsenic. Use of anabolic steroids and oral contraceptives may increase the risk of liver cancer. Gallstones, chronic inflammation of the colon or gallbladder, and certain parasitic infections are also risk factors.

Symptoms of liver cancer include abdominal pain or swelling, loss of appetite, unexplained weight loss, an early sense of fullness during meals, or jaundice.

Early diagnosis of liver disorders usually involves blood tests. If cancer is suspected, a biopsy will be done either during surgery or by inserting a thin needle into the liver. The cancer is further diagnosed by means of imaging techniques such as computed tomography (CT) scans, magnetic resonance imaging (MRI), and ultrasound. An X-ray procedure called angiography may be used to examine blood vessels in and around the liver. The liver may be examined directly with a laparoscope, a flexible tube with a lens on the end that is inserted through an incision in the abdomen.

The three-year survival rate for persons with liver cancer is fairly high if the cancer is localized and can be completely removed by surgery. If the cancer is localized but inoperable, or if the cancer is in more advanced stages, the rate is lower. Overall survival from liver cancer is lower than that from many other types of cancer because it is not usually detected in its early stages.

Surgery can cure liver cancer, but only when the cancer is limited to a region small enough to permit its removal while leaving enough of the liver behind to perform normal functions. Surgery is not curative for cancers that have spread beyond the liver and is not usually recommended for patients with cirrhosis. When surgery is not an option, some local tumours can be destroyed either by being frozen or by being injected with alcohol. Other cancers may be starved by blocking nearby blood vessels. Chemotherapy may be used to treat liver cancer, especially if the cancer has spread to distant tissues. A chemotherapeutic agent may, in some cases, be administered directly into the main artery that feeds the liver; this allows direct delivery of cancer-destroying drugs to the liver.

The risk of liver cancer can be reduced by taking steps to eliminate key risk factors. Hepatitis B infection can be prevented by vaccination against the virus and by avoiding unprotected sexual contact or contact with human blood. Hepatitis C can also be avoided by eliminating direct exposure to blood. Alcohol consumption should be limited, and anabolic steroids should never be used without the advice of a physician.

liver fluke, any of certain parasitic flatworms that invade the liver of the host animal. *See* fluke.

liverleaf (plant): *see* hepatica.

Livermore, city, Alameda county, western California, U.S. It is situated on the eastern edge of the Livermore-Amador Valley, 33 miles (53 km) southeast of Oakland. Located partly on the site of the Rancho Las Positas of Robert Livermore (d. 1858), it developed after the arrival of the Central Pacific Railroad (1869). It became a shipping-processing point for valley produce, including cattle, roses, and particularly (since the 1880s) dry white wines. The establishment in 1952 of the Lawrence Radiation Laboratory (renamed Lawrence Livermore Laboratory in 1971 and Lawrence Livermore National Laboratory in 1979) by the University of California spurred the city's technological growth (atomic ordnance, nuclear research, medicine). Del Valle Dam and Reservoir are nearby. Inc. town, 1876; city, 1900. Pop. (1999 est.) 75,515.

Liverpool, town, Queens county, southeastern Nova Scotia, Canada. It lies at the mouth of the Mersey River, 88 miles (142 km) west-southwest of Halifax. The site was called Ogumkiqueok by the Indians, and Port Rossignol (1604) by Pierre du Gua, sieur de Monts, an early colonizer. Under French occupancy it was known as Port Senior, or Port Saviour; but, when New England settlers arrived in 1759, it was renamed for Liverpool, Eng. During and after the U.S. War of Independence, the harbour was a base for privateers equipped by local seamen who joined battle against the Americans. In 1781 the town was subjected to a retaliatory attack by an American expedition from Salem; and during the War of 1812, the *Liverpool Packet,* sailing out of Liverpool, was said to have captured 100 American merchantmen.

Paper, fish, and timber are the town's major products, and marine building and refitting has, since World War II, become an important industry. The home of Colonel Simeon Perkins, a Nova Scotian diarist, built in 1766, has been restored as a museum. Inc. 1897. Pop. (1996) 3,048.

Liverpool, fifth largest city of England, a seaport, and the nucleus of the metropolitan county of Merseyside in the historic county of Lancashire. The city proper, which is a metropolitan borough of Merseyside, forms an irregular crescent along the north shore of the Mersey estuary a few miles from the Irish Sea.

The first significant date in the history of Liverpool is 1207, when King John of England granted a charter for a planned new town there. The town's medieval growth was slow, but in the 18th century it expanded rapidly as a result of profitable trade with the Americas and the West Indies and became the second most important port in Britain. A major element in the general trading pattern was the Liverpool Triangle—the exchange of manufactured goods from the Mersey hinterland for slaves in West Africa who were then traded for sugar, molasses, and spices in the West Indies.

The first dock in Liverpool was built in 1715. By the end of the century four others were established along the Mersey, and the port even outranked London in dock space. In 1830 the Liverpool and Manchester Railway, the first in England to link two major cities, was opened. A rail network providing easy and cheap access to all major British industrial centres was soon created, and steam ferry links between Liverpool and the Wirral, across the Mersey River, were established. This growth was accompanied by high levels of immigration from surrounding areas and from Ireland, especially during and after the Irish famine (1845–48).

By the beginning of the 20th century Liverpool had become the centre of 7 miles (11 km) of docks extending along the Mersey from Hornby (1884) in the north to Herculaneum (1866) in the south. Additional improvements were made to the docks, but after World War II Liverpool declined as an exporting and passenger port. This change can be attributed mainly to the decreasing significance, in the economic life of Britain, of Liverpool's industrial hinterland and its traditional trade with the United States and West Africa. Low capital investment and unemployment in the docks have intensified the situation.

Liverpool continues to exert a great degree of dominance over the surrounding metropolitan region. Although the traditional industries of transport, communication, distribution, and shipping have declined, they are still important in the economic life of the city.

Architectural landmarks include the 18th-century Town Hall and the 19th-century St. George's Hall; the Neo-Gothic Anglican cathedral, founded in 1904 and completed in 1978; and the Roman Catholic Metropolitan Cathedral (1967), of strikingly modern design. The Merseyside County Museum and Library, the Walker Art Gallery, the Picton Library, and the University of Liverpool (chartered 1881) are among the many cultural institutions. There is also a well-known symphony orchestra in the city. Pop. (1998 est.) city, 461,500; metropolitan area, 1,409,400.

Consult
the
INDEX
first

Liverpool, Charles Jenkinson, 1st Earl of, BARON HAWKESBURY OF HAWKESBURY (b. April 26, 1727, Winchester, Hampshire, Eng.—d. Dec. 17, 1808, London), politician who held numerous offices in the British government under King George III and was the object of widespread suspicion as well as deference because of his reputed clandestine influence at court. It was believed that he in some way controlled the relationship between the king and Lord North, prime minister (1770–82) during the American Revolution.

The son of an army officer, Jenkinson in 1760 became private secretary to the 3rd Earl of Bute, favourite of George III, and in 1763, having been elected to Parliament, was appointed joint secretary of the Treasury. He was leader of the "king's friends" in the House of Commons after the retirement of Bute from active politics. Chosen vice treasurer for Ireland (1773), he became a member of the Privy Council. Later he was master of the Royal Mint (1775–78) and, during the American Revolution, secretary at war (1778–82), in which capacity he carried out Lord North's policies.

Jenkinson's reputation improved during the first prime ministry (from 1783) of the younger William Pitt, to whom he was a valuable adviser. In 1786 he was appointed chancellor of the duchy of Lancaster and president of the Board of Trade. A member of the Cabinet from 1791, he became an invalid about 1801, ceased to attend Cabinet meetings, and by the middle of 1804 had resigned all his offices. He was created Baron Hawkesbury in 1786 and Earl of Liverpool in 1796.

Liverpool, Robert Banks Jenkinson, 2nd Earl of, BARON HAWKESBURY OF HAWKESBURY (b. June 7, 1770, London—d. Dec. 4, 1828, Fife House, Whitehall, London),

2nd Earl of Liverpool, detail of an oil painting by Sir Thomas Lawrence; in the National Portrait Gallery, London

British prime minister from June 8, 1812, to Feb. 17, 1827, who, despite his long tenure of office, was overshadowed by the greater political imaginativeness of his colleagues, George Canning and Viscount Castlereagh (afterward 2nd Marquess of Londonderry), and by the military prowess of the Duke of Wellington.

Entering the House of Commons in 1790, Jenkinson soon became a leading Tory, serving as a member of the Board of Control for India (1793–96), master of the Royal Mint (1799–1801), foreign secretary (1801–04), home secretary (1804–06, 1807–09), and secretary for war and the colonies (1809–12). As foreign secretary he negotiated the short-lived Treaty of Amiens (signed March 27, 1802) with Napoleonic France.

After the assassination of Prime Minister Spencer Perceval (May 11, 1812), Liverpool reluctantly took his place, hoping to find and train a more brilliant successor. The War of 1812 with the United States and the final campaigns of the Napoleonic Wars were fought during his premiership. At the Congress of Vienna (1814–15), he strenuously urged the international abolition of the slave trade; within a few years the other European powers accepted this view.

In 1819 he strengthened the British monetary system by restoring the gold standard. Throughout his tenure he insisted that ecclesiastical and other appointments be justified by merit rather than by influence. Less enlightened was his attitude toward civil disturbances following industrial and agricultural failures: he suspended the Habeas Corpus Act for Great Britain in 1817 and for Ireland in 1822 and imposed other repressive measures in 1819. His position on proposals to repeal the Corn Laws (import duties on foreign foodstuffs) and to grant political rights to Roman Catholics was equivocal. After nearly 15 years in office, he was forced to retire because of a paralytic stroke.

Liverpool delft, tin-glazed earthenware made from about 1710 to about 1760 in Liverpool, Eng., which, along with Bristol and London (Southwark and Lambeth), was one of the three main centres of English delftware. Some of the wares produced at Liverpool are similar to those of Bristol and London: teapots and coffeepots; sauceboats and punch bowls; tiles; puzzle jugs; and the so-called bricks—rectangular blocks with holes on the top that were used as pen-and-ink stands and perhaps as flower holders. Among the wares typical of Liverpool are puzzle jugs with inscribed verses, bell-shaped mugs copied from pewter models, and trinket trays. The decoration often consists of pseudo-Chinese motifs. Two other specialties of Liverpool are shallow char-pots, crudely decorated with fish, and tiles with transfer prints done by John Sadler and Guy Green, generally in black or red, though sometimes in polychrome, with subjects such as famous actors and actresses of the time.

Liverpool delft punch bowl, *c.* 1760; in the Victoria and Albert Museum, London

By courtesy of the Victoria and Albert Museum, London; photograph, EB Inc.

Liverpool porcelain, soft-paste porcelain, rather heavy and opaque, produced between 1756 and 1800 in various factories of Liverpool, Eng., largely for export to America and the West Indies. The earliest factory was Richard Chaffers and Co., whose steatitic, or soaprock, porcelain, produced from 1756, resembles Worcester porcelain. Most of the plates made by the factory are octagonal, and some tea and coffee sets are six-sided. Liverpool porcelain was also produced by Philip Christian (1765–76), who took over the factory when Chaffers died in 1765. "Biting snake" handles, palm columns, and leaf-molded teapots are characteristic of this porcelain. Also attributed to Pennington is a "sticky" blue, so called because a very shiny glaze makes the particularly bright cobalt-blue enamel appear freshly painted.

liverwort (class Hepatopsida, or Hepaticae), any of more than 8,000 species of small, nonvascular, spore-producing land plants constituting part of the division Bryophyta. They include the thallose liverworts that show branching, ribbonlike gametophytes, and the leafy liverworts (mainly in the order Jungermanniales). The seven orders of liverworts are segregated primarily on gametophyte structures, with sporophyte features also supporting the classification.

Conocephalum conicum, sometimes known as great scented liverwort; asexual plants (sporophytes) rise on long stalks from the leaflike thallus of the sexual plants (gametophytes)

A to Z Botanical Collection—EB Inc.

Liverworts are distributed worldwide, though most commonly in the tropics. Thallose liverworts grow commonly on moist soil or damp rocks, while leafy liverworts are found in similar habitats as well as on tree trunks in damp woods. The thallus of thallose liverworts resembles a lobed liver—hence the common name liverwort ("liver plant"). Filamentous structures called rhizoids anchor most liverworts to their substrata, except for the few genera that are aquatic.

Sexual (gametophyte) and asexual (sporophyte) generations characterize a liverwort life cycle. The gametophyte generation develops from a germinating spore. Sperm from the male reproductive organ (antheridium) travel through an aqueous environment, and one sperm fertilizes an egg that is still retained in the female reproductive organ (archegonium). The sporophyte develops from this embryo and forms a sporangium at its apex. Spores are released when the sporangium ruptures, marking the start of a new gametophytic generation. Asexual reproduction occurs by means of gemmae, which are produced by the gametophytic generation or by separation of branches of that plant body, resulting in new plants.

Liverworts are not economically important to humans but do provide food for animals, facilitate the decay of logs, and aid in the disintegration of rocks by their ability to retain moisture.

The most ancient liverwort fossil genus, *Hepaticites,* a member of the order Metzgeriales, dates to the Devonian period of the Paleozoic era (408 to 360 million years ago). It resembles a thallose liverwort.

livery company, any of various craft or trade associations of the City of London, Eng., most of which are descended from medieval guilds. Certain grades of members are privileged to wear a special "livery," or distinctive clothing in the form of a fur-trimmed gown.

In the late 20th century there were more than 80 livery companies. Most were incorporated by royal charter between the 14th and the 17th century, but the Weavers gained a charter as early as the 12th century; and such companies as the Master Mariners, the Solicitors, the Farmers, the Air Pilots & Air Navigators, the Furniture Makers, and the Scientific Instrument Makers have come into existence since 1925. The incorporation in 1960 of the Tobacco Pipe Makers & Tobacco Blenders was a revival of a former company that fell into desuetude in the 19th century. The companies vary a great deal in detail, and the range of their wealth and influence is wide. Nearly every one of the companies once controlled the craft or trade indicated by its name; most were concerned with skilled crafts such as the Goldsmiths and the Carpenters, while several dealt with victualing trades, as, for example, the Bakers and the Vintners. Most of the companies have now lost control over their trades; but the Fishmongers still possess powers of search and inspection in Billingsgate fish market, the Goldsmiths continue to "hallmark" gold and silver, and the Gunmakers still "proof" small arms.

Most of the companies are governed by a small self-appointing body known as a court of assistants presided over by a master (or prime warden) and wardens. Few of the companies restrict their membership to persons following the particular calling represented by the company's name, but the Apothecaries' society confines its senior membership to medical men, the Brewers' company is limited to the brewing trade, and the Solicitors, Master Mariners, and Air Pilots admit only persons qualified in those specialties. By the custom of London, admission to the basic grade of membership of a company—known as the freedom of the company—is by patrimony, servitude (apprenticeship to a freeman of the company), or redemption (purchase). An order of precedence was settled by the court of aldermen in Henry VIII's reign in the 16th century, and the first "twelve great" companies are the Mercers, Grocers, Drapers, Fishmongers, Goldsmiths, Skinners, Merchant Taylors, Haberdashers, Salters, Ironmongers, Vintners, and Clothworkers.

At the zenith of their power in the Middle Ages, the guilds controlled their members by the exercise of powers conferred by charter or ordinances—powers, that is, to regulate apprenticeship and conditions of employment, to examine workmanship and destroy defective goods, and to enforce rules by fines and penalties. The ultimate sanction was that only those free of the City of London could ply their trade, and the freedom of the city was obtainable only through membership of a guild.

Changing economic and political conditions from the 16th century onward resulted in a gradual but steady loss of power and influence. Repeated attempts to adapt the constitution and powers of the medieval guild to the new pattern of society failed; friction began to develop between the governing bodies of the livery companies and the growing ranks of artisans who resented the restrictions inherent in the apprenticeship system. By about 1787 most of the companies finally abandoned any pretense of controlling their respective trades. However, at the close of the 19th century there was a widespread movement on the part of the livery companies to revive interest in their respective crafts and trades and to devote corporate funds, where these existed, to charity and technical education in various schools and university colleges. Benevolence and the relief of distress were always a principal concern of the old guilds, and the livery companies of today continue this tradition.

Livesay, Dorothy, in full DOROTHY KATHLEEN MAY LIVESAY (b. Oct. 12, 1909, Winnipeg, Man., Can.—d. Dec. 29, 1996, Victoria, B.C.), Canadian lyric poet whose sensitive and reflective works spanned six decades.

Livesay attended several schools, including the Sorbonne in Paris (1931–32), where a study of French Symbolist poets influenced her own work. A second formative element was her experience in Montreal as a social worker during the Depression, and an affinity for the social gospel of such poets of the 1930s as C. Day Lewis, Stephen Spender, and W.H. Auden. Notable among her collections are *Day and Night* (1944), *Poems for People* (1947), *Call My People Home* (1950), *Selected Poems* and *New Poems* (both 1957), *The Unquiet Bed* (1967), and *Phases of Love* (1983). Her *Collected Poems* appeared in 1972. Among Livesay's prose works are the children's book *Beginnings: A Winnipeg Childhood* (1975; originally published as *A Winnipeg Childhood*) and *The Husband* (1990), a novella. A memoir, *Journey with My Selves,* was published in 1991. Livesay received numerous awards, including the Governor General's award for poetry (1944, 1947). In 1987 she was made an Officer of the Order of Canada.

livestock, farm animals, with the exception of poultry. In Western countries the category encompasses primarily cattle, sheep, pigs, goats, horses, donkeys, and mules; other animals, such as buffalo, oxen, or camels, may predominate in the agriculture of other areas.

A brief treatment of livestock follows. For information on individual species, *see* cow, goat, horse, etc. For full treatment, *see* MACROPAEDIA: Farming and Agricultural Technology.

Cattle (genus *Bos*) make up the largest livestock group worldwide, comprising some 277 identifiable breeds. Among those prominent in beef production are Hereford, Shorthorn, and Angus. The chief dairy cattle breeds are Holstein-Friesian, Brown Swiss, Ayrshire, Jersey, and Guernsey. Cattle feed primarily on pasture by grazing. They are sometimes used as draft animals.

Sheep (genus *Ovis*) were among the first animals to be domesticated, perhaps as early as 10,000 BC. They are almost as abundant as cattle worldwide; more than 200 breeds are recognized. Closely related to goats, sheep are raised primarily for the fleece or wool of their coats, for meat (mutton and lamb), and, to a lesser degree, for milk. Like cattle, sheep graze for their food.

Pigs, or domestic swine (family Suidae), have been raised for their meat (pork) since ancient times. There are more than 300 breeds worldwide. In the United States, the term hog is used for swine weighing more than 120 pounds (50 kilograms), and the animals, regardless of breed, are classified for marketing purposes as lard, bacon, or pork types, the lard types being the heaviest. Corn is usually the basic feed for pigs, although wheat, sorghum, oats, and barley are often included in their diet.

Goats (genus *Capra*) are raised for their milk and its by-products and for meat, hides, and wool. The numerous breeds comprise three major groups: the prick-eared (*e.g.*, Swiss); the eastern (*e.g.*, Nubian); and the wool (*e.g.*, Angora [mohair] and Cashmere). Goats eat pasture grass, alfalfa or other hays, and feeds made from grain.

Horses (genus *Equus*), first intensively domesticated in Central Asia, are bred not only as livestock but also for riding, show, and racing. As livestock, horses are used for farm work or for riding, the latter especially on large cattle ranches. The numerous breeds may be classified according to place of origin (*e.g.*, Clydesdale, Arabian), by their principal use (*e.g.*, riding, draft), or by outward appearance (light, heavy, pony). Horses feed on grass and other pasture growths, and their diets are usually supplemented with hays, grain (primarily oats), and other nutritive feeds.

Donkeys, also called asses, and mules, the hybrids formed by crossbreeding a jackass and a female horse, are used as work animals on many farms. Sure-footed and strong, they are often employed as saddle mounts as well.

For international statistical data on livestock, *see* the *Britannica World Data* section in the BRITANNICA BOOK OF THE YEAR.

Livia Drusilla, also called (from AD 14) JULIA AUGUSTA (b. Jan. 30, 58 BC—d. AD 29), Caesar Augustus' devoted and influential wife who counseled him on affairs of state and who, in her efforts to secure the imperial succession for her son Tiberius, was reputed to have caused the deaths of many of his rivals, including Marcus Claudius Marcellus, Gaius and Lucius Caesar, Agrippa Posthumus, and Germanicus.

Livia Drusilla, marble bust; in the Vatican Museum
Alinari—Art Resource/EB Inc.

Her father was Marcus Livius Drusus Claudianus, an adoptive son of the tribune of 91, Marcus Livius Drusus. She married her cousin Tiberius Claudius Nero and in 42 bore him Tiberius, the future emperor. She was still pregnant with her second son, Nero Claudius Drusus, when early in 38, Octavian (later Augustus) arranged for her to divorce Nero and marry him. Her second marriage was childless. After the death of Augustus (Aug. 19, AD 14), she was adopted in Augustus's will, assumed the name Julia Augusta, and played a major role in the cult of the deified Augustus.

Livia's power and ambition proved embarrassing to Tiberius after his accession. He forbade her to accept certain honours and even refused to carry out the terms of her will. She was, however, deified (42) by her grandson Claudius. Surviving portraiture confirms her reputation for dignified beauty.

living, standard of, in social science, the scale of aspirations or desires of an individual or group for goods and services. Alternatively, the term is applied specifically to a measure of the consumption of goods and services that a particular person or group can achieve. This includes not only privately purchased items but also collectively consumed goods and services such as those provided by public utilities and governments.

Standard of living is thus to be distinguished from personal economic welfare, which refers to the consumption standards that actually have been achieved. It is also to be distinguished from disposable income (*q.v.*) since it includes items that lead to an increased sense of well-being but are not under the individual's direct control, such as publicly provided services and the quality of the environment. Some social scientists maintain that a person's standard of living (in terms of his aspirations) is strongly influenced by the consumption pattern of his income peers, in which case an individual's standard of living may be expected to change as incomes change.

In speaking of the standard of living of a group of people, such as a country, care must be taken to distinguish between the average value of some measure of actual consumption standards and the dispersion around that average. If, for example, the average value increases over time, but at the same time the rich become richer and the poor poorer, it may not be correct to conclude that the group is collectively better off. Accordingly, comparison of standards of living among countries that exhibit widely differing degrees of dispersion can be extremely difficult. In practice there are wide disparities both within countries and among countries. By most criteria, the differences in living standards between developed and less developed countries are vastly more acute than the differences that exist within countries with developed economies.

These general problems are evident regardless of what quantitative indicators are taken as measuring rods for the standard of living. Apart from income, useful indicators may include an index of consumption of certain foodstuffs such as protein, a measure of life expectancy, and access to basic amenities like a safe water supply. These indices also involve serious problems of comparability among nations and regions, however, especially since even the most basic data, such as reliable population estimates, may be unavailable for some very poor countries.

Besides omitting important components that do not appear in marketable form and therefore are not included in conventional national income accounts, the use of a dollar measure of real income or consumption as a guide to living standards involves important technical difficulties. Even the items that are measurable in monetary terms may have been valued at distorted prices. International comparisons using official exchange rates can be particularly misleading, especially where the foreign exchange market is manipulated by governments. Comparisons over time need to be adjusted for differences in price levels, but this is not always a simple matter. If relative prices of various goods and services differ substantially between two countries, it is particularly difficult to compare standards of living, interpreted as consumption levels.

For international statistical data and indicators on standard of living, *see* the *Britannica World Data* section in the BRITANNICA BOOK OF THE YEAR.

Living Newspaper, theatrical production consisting of dramatizations of current events, social problems, and controversial issues, with appropriate suggestions for improvement. The technique was used for propaganda in the

U.S.S.R. from the time of the Revolution in 1917. It became part of the Epic theatre tradition initiated by Erwin Piscator and Bertolt Brecht in Germany in the 1920s. The Living Newspaper was initiated in the United States in 1935 as part of the Federal Theatre Project. One of its major supporters was Elmer Rice, a dramatist and producer who believed in the value of drama as an instrument of social change. It became the most effective new theatre form developed by the Project, vividly dealing, in flashing cinematic techniques, with the realities of agriculture, housing, and economics. Outstanding productions were *Triple-A Plowed Under,* dealing with the Supreme Court's invalidation of the Agricultural Adjustment Administration (AAA), and *One-Third of a Nation,* dramatizing the plight of that part of the nation who, in President Roosevelt's words, were "ill-housed, ill-clad, and ill-nourished." Criticism of the Living Newspaper for alleged communist leanings contributed to the cancellation of the Federal Theatre Project in 1939.

living-rock cactus, any of several cactus plants comprising the genus *Ariocarpus,* family Cactaceae, and especially *A. fissuratus fissuratus.* The six species almost entirely lack spines but are woolly covered. They are native to Texas and Mexico and live on limestone-rich soil.

Mexican living-rock cactus (*Ariocarpus fissuratus*)
L.N. and Anella Dexter

All the species are low-growing and have a rosette of tubercles (projections) that are flattened in *A. fissuratus* and *A. kotschoubeyanus.* In the other four species, pointed tubercles protrude up and out. Water is stored against the dry winter in the thickened taproot and in mucilage canals and reservoirs.

The summer rains bring flowers of magenta, white, yellow, or cream that measure 2 to 5 cm (1 to 2 inches) in diameter. Fruits ripen just before the next summer's rain.

Ariocarpus species contain sufficient alkaloids, principally hordenine, to make them mildly hallucinogenic.

living stone (plant): *see* Lithops.

Living Theatre, The (1951–70), theatrical repertory company known for its innovative production of experimental drama, often on radical themes, and for its confrontations with tradition, authority, and audiences. It was formed in New York City by Julian Beck and Judith Malina. The group struggled during the 1950s, producing little-known, new, and experimental plays by Gertrude Stein, Luigi Pirandello, Alfred Jarry, T.S. Eliot, Jean Cocteau, August Strindberg, and others. Its first big success came with its 1959 production of *The Connection,* Jack Gelber's drama of drug addiction. In 1961 the company made a successful tour of Europe with *The Connection* and with plays by Bertolt Brecht and William Carlos Williams.

On returning to New York City, the political views of the members of the troupe—nonviolent protest and anarchism—came to the fore in their work. In 1963 they produced Kenneth H. Brown's *The Brig,* a play that depicted military discipline as dehumanizing. The U.S. Internal Revenue Service demanded payment of a large sum in admissions taxes that the constantly impoverished group had collected and had used to pay production costs while vainly seeking tax exempt status. Beck and Malina were tried and convicted of tax law violation and jailed briefly, and The Living Theatre was closed.

In 1964 the company took up "voluntary exile" in Europe. Now influenced by Oriental mysticism, gestalt therapy techniques, and an Artaudian desire to abolish the distinction between art and life, The Living Theatre moved toward deliberately shocking and confronting its audiences in such works as *Paradise Now,* in which the actors performed rituals, provoked arguments, and carried on until members of the audience left. In 1970 the troupe split into several groups and dispersed.

Livingston, new town, West Lothian district, Lothian region, Scotland. Scotland's fourth new town, Livingston was designated in 1962 with the dual purpose of accommodating overflow population from Glasgow (30 miles [50 km] west) and providing a major industrial growth point in West Lothian. Situated on the Glasgow–Edinburgh motorway in an area of declining primary and heavy industry, Livingston will eventually house a population of 100,000 (most of them from Glasgow) and function as a district centre. Once dependent on coal mining and oil shale, the town now has a wider economic base in four industrial estates and new service employment. Pop. (1982 est.) 37,900.

Livingston, city, seat of Park county, south-central Montana, U.S. It lies along the Yellowstone River and is surrounded by divisions of the Gallatin National Forest. Originally called Clark's City, it was founded in 1882 as a division headquarters of the Northern Pacific Railway and was renamed for Crawford Livingston, a railroad executive. Large locomotive repair shops were built, and agriculture and ranching developed concurrently with mining activities. Livingston holds an annual roundup and is the site of the National Fresh Water Trout Derby. Tourism (including dude ranches) is significant to its economy. The northern entrance to Yellowstone National Park is 28 miles (45 km) south. Inc. 1889. Pop. (1990) 6,701.

Livingston, Edward (b. May 28, 1764, Columbia county, N.Y. [U.S.]—d. May 23, 1836, Dutchess county, N.Y.), American lawyer, legislator, and statesman, who codified criminal law and procedure.

Livingston was admitted to the bar in 1785 and began to practice law in New York City. He was a Republican representative in Congress from 1795 to 1801, when he was appointed U.S. district attorney for New York state. In the same year he was elected mayor of New York City. As district attorney, he was held responsible for public funds that had been lost through the dishonesty of one of his clerks. As a consequence, he resigned both his offices in 1803 and moved to Louisiana. He established a large law practice in New Orleans, and he prepared a provisional code of judicial procedure that was in force in Louisiana from 1805 to 1825. In 1821, a year after he became a member of the state legislature, he wrote a code of criminal law and procedure. Although not adopted by the legislature, this code gained wide influence in Europe and the United States.

Livingston served again in Congress (1823–29) and as a U.S. senator (1829–31). From 1831 to 1833 he was secretary of state under President Andrew Jackson, in which position he prepared the anti-nullification proclamation of 1832, concerning South Carolina's opposition to the protective tariff. He was minister plenipotentiary to France from 1833 to 1835.

Edward Livingston, portrait by John Trumbull, 1805; in the City of New York collection
By courtesy of the Art Commission of the City of New York

Livingston, Henry Brockholst (b. Nov. 25, 1757, New York, N.Y. [U.S.]—d. March 18, 1823, Washington, D.C.), associate justice of the United States Supreme Court from 1806 to 1823.

Livingston joined the Continental Army at the age of 19 and saw action with Benedict Arnold and as an aide to General Philip John Schuyler and General Arthur St. Clair before accompanying his brother-in-law, John Jay, on his mission to solicit aid from Spain in 1779. On his return voyage he was captured by the British and, upon being paroled, studied law at Albany, being admitted to the bar in 1783. He had a successful practice in New York City until 1802, when he was appointed to the state Supreme Court. In 1806 Livingston was named to the U.S. Supreme Court by President Thomas Jefferson. There he was overshadowed by Chief Justice John Marshall and wrote no major opinions on constitutional questions.

Livingston, Robert (b. Dec. 13, 1654, Ancrum, Roxburghshire, Scot.—d. Oct. 1, 1728, Clermont, N.Y. [U.S.]), early American landowner, politician, and merchant who founded the prominent Livingston family of New York state and laid the basis of his family's material fortune.

Livingston was the son of a Scottish Presbyterian minister who emigrated to Rotterdam in Holland in 1663. Young Livingston himself emigrated to New England in 1673 and settled in the frontier village of Albany, N.Y., in 1674. There his fluency in English and Dutch proved useful to him as an intermediary between speakers of those languages, and he was soon appointed the town clerk and secretary of New York's board of commissioners for Indian affairs. He married advantageously and built up influence with successive governors of New York. He also was able to purchase the Indian claims to large tracts of land along the Hudson River, thereby eventually acquiring an estate of 160,000 acres (65,000 hectares) in New York. In 1686 he secured a patent raising his landholdings to the status of a manor (Livingston Manor). He also became prominent in New York politics, serving as secretary for Indian affairs (1696–1721), member of the governor's council (1698–1702), and as a member (1709–26) and the speaker (1718–25) of New York's provincial assembly.

Livingston's grandson William and his great-grandsons Edward, Robert R., and Henry Brockholst Livingston became prominent figures in American political life.

Livingston, Robert R. (b. Nov. 27, 1746, New York, N.Y. [U.S.]—d. Feb. 26, 1813, Clermont, N.Y.), early American leader who served as a delegate to the Continental Congress, first secretary of the Department of Foreign Affairs (1781–83), and minister to France (1801–04).

Born into a wealthy and influential New York family, Livingston was admitted to the bar in 1770. Devoted to the idea of liberty, he worked on numerous committees of the Continental Congress at Philadelphia (1775–76, 1779–81, 1784–85), especially in the areas of finance and foreign and judicial affairs. He was a member of the committee that drafted the Declaration of Independence, and, after helping to draft New York state's first constitution (1777), he served as the state's first chancellor (1777–1801).

With the inauguration of the federal government under the Articles of Confederation (1781), Livingston was appointed secretary of the Department of Foreign Affairs, in which post he established vital administrative precedents and organized the conduct of foreign affairs on a businesslike basis. He insisted on greater independence for American delegates to the Paris Peace Conference (1782–83) but reprimanded them for negotiating without the full concurrence of France.

Robert R. Livingston, portrait by Charles Willson Peale, *c.* 1782; in Independence National Historical Park, Philadelphia

By courtesy of the Independence National Historical Park Collection, Philadelphia

On April 30, 1789, under the new Constitution, Chancellor Livingston administered the oath of office in New York City to the nation's first president, George Washington. During the 1790s he gradually associated himself with the anti-Federalists and in 1801 was appointed by President Thomas Jefferson to represent the United States in France. In that capacity he rendered his most distinguished service by helping effect the Louisiana Purchase (1803)—one of the country's greatest diplomatic coups.

In retirement Livingston became enthusiastically involved with steam-navigation experiments, and in partnership with the inventor Robert Fulton, he received a steamboat monopoly in New York waters. Their first successful steam vessel, operating on the Hudson River in 1807, was named the *Clermont* after Livingston's ancestral home.

BIBLIOGRAPHY. George Dangerfield, *Chancellor Robert R. Livingston of New York, 1746–1813* (1960), examines his life in the context of colonial New York landowners.

Livingston, William (b. Nov. 30, 1723, Albany, N.Y. [U.S.]—d. July 25, 1790, Elizabeth, N.J.), first Revolutionary governor of New Jersey.

A graduate of Yale, Livingston was admitted to the New York bar in 1748 and served briefly in the New York legislature (1759–60). His chief political influence was exerted through pamphlets and newspaper articles, first in the short-lived *Independent Reflector* (1752–53), which he founded, and later in the *New York Mercury.* With the historian William Smith, he prepared a digest of the laws of New York for the period 1691–1756 (2 vol., 1752–62).

Moving to New Jersey in 1772, he represented that colony in the First and Second Continental Congresses (1774–76) but left Philadelphia in June 1776 to command the New Jersey troops. Chosen in 1776 as the state's first governor, he was regularly reelected to that office until his death. He was a delegate to the federal Constitutional Convention of 1787, and the following year led his state to an early ratification of the new constitution.

William Livingston, etching by A. Rosenthal, 1888, after a painting by an unknown artist

By courtesy of the Library of Congress, Washington, D.C.

Livingston's brother Philip (1716–78) was a member of the First Continental Congress and a signer of the Declaration of Independence.

Livingstone, also called MARAMBA, town, extreme southern Zambia. It lies on the northern bank of the Zambezi River at the Zimbabwe border. The first European settlement in the area was upriver at the Old Drift Ferry Station in the 1890s; the town's present site was occupied in 1905 with the completion of Victoria Falls Bridge and the railway line. Livingstone was the capital of Northern Rhodesia from 1907 to 1935, and became the country's first municipality in 1927. Situated on the main railway system of southern Africa, it is a distribution point for agricultural products and timber. The town's secondary industries include automobile assembly, sawmilling, blanket weaving, and the making of furniture. Livingstone has an international airport, and tourism is based on nearby Victoria Falls, Lake Kariba, Livingstone Game Park, and Kafue and Wankie national parks. A small hydroelectric power station is located on Zambia's side of Victoria Falls. The Livingstone Museum has a collection of ethnological, archaeological, and historical exhibits, including those related to the explorer-missionary David Livingstone. Pop. (1988 est.) 98,460.

Livingstone, David (b. March 19, 1813, Blantyre, Lanarkshire, Scot.—d. May 1, 1873, Chitambo, Barotseland [now in Zambia]), Scottish missionary and explorer who exercised a formative influence upon Western attitudes toward Africa.

Early life. Livingstone grew up in a distinctively Scottish family environment of personal piety, poverty, hard work, zeal for education, and a sense of mission. His father's family was from the island of Ulva, off the west coast of Scotland. His mother, a Lowlander, was descended from a family of Covenanters, a group of militant Presbyterians. Both were poor, and Livingstone was reared as one of seven children in a single room at the top of a tenement building for the workers of a cotton factory on the banks of the Clyde. At the age of 10 he had to help his family and was put to work in a cotton mill, and with part of his first week's wages he bought a Latin grammar. Brought up in the Calvinist faith of the established Scottish church, Livingstone, like his father, joined an independent Christian congregation of stricter discipline when he came to manhood. By this time he had acquired those characteristics of mind and body that were to fit him for his African career.

In 1834 an appeal by British and American churches for qualified medical missionaries in China made Livingstone determine to become a medical missionary. To prepare himself, while continuing to work part-time in the mill, he studied Greek, theology, and medicine for two years in Glasgow. In 1838 he was accepted by the London Missionary Society. The Opium War (1839–42) put an end to his dreams of going to China, but a meeting with Robert Moffat, the notable Scottish missionary in southern Africa, convinced him that Africa should be his sphere of service. On Nov. 20, 1840, he was ordained as a missionary; he set sail for South Africa at the end of the year and arrived at Cape Town on March 14, 1841.

Initial explorations. For the next 15 years, Livingstone was constantly on the move into the African interior: strengthening his missionary determination; responding wholeheartedly to the delights of geographical discovery; clashing with the Boers and the Portuguese, whose treatment of the Africans he came to detest; and building for himself a remarkable reputation as a dedicated Christian, a courageous explorer, and a fervent antislavery advocate. Yet so impassioned was his commitment to Africa that his duties as husband and father were relegated to second place.

From Moffat's mission at Kuruman on the Cape frontier, which Livingstone reached on July 31, 1841, he soon pushed his search for converts northward into untried country where the population was reputed to be more numerous. This suited his purpose of spreading the Gospel through "native agents." By the summer of 1842, he had already gone further north than any other white man into the difficult Kalahari country and had familiarized himself with the local languages and cultures. His mettle was dramatically tested in 1844, when, during a journey to Mabotsa to establish a mission station, he was mauled by a lion. The resulting injury to his left arm was complicated by another accident, so that he could never again support the barrel of a gun steadily with his left hand and was obliged to fire from his left shoulder and to take aim with his left eye.

David Livingstone, oil painting by F. Havill after photographs; in the National Portrait Gallery, London

By courtesy of the National Portrait Gallery, London

On Jan. 2, 1845, Livingstone married Moffat's daughter, Mary, and she accompanied him on many of his journeys until her health and the family's needs for security and education forced him to send her and their four children back to Britain in 1852. Before this first parting with his family, Livingstone had already achieved a small measure of fame when, as surveyor and scientist of a small expedition, he had assisted in the discovery of Lake Ngami on Aug. 1, 1849, and was awarded a gold medal and monetary prize by the British Royal Geographical Society. This was the beginning of his lifelong association with the society, which continued to encourage his ambitions as an explorer and to champion his interests in Britain.

Opening the interior. With his family safely in Scotland, Livingstone was ready to push Christianity, commerce, and civilization—the trinity that he believed was destined to open up Africa—northward beyond the frontiers of South Africa and into the heart of the continent. In a famous statement in 1853 he made his purpose clear: "I shall open up a path into the interior, or perish." On Nov. 11, 1853, from Linyanti at the approaches to the Zambezi and in the midst of the Makololo peoples whom he considered eminently suitable for missionary work, Livingstone set out northwestward with little equipment and only a small party of Africans. His intention was to find a route to the Atlantic coast that would permit legitimate commerce to undercut the slave trade and that would also be more suitable for reaching the Makololo than the route leading through Boer territory. (In 1852 the Boers had destroyed his home at Kolobeng and attacked his African friends.) After an arduous journey that might have wrecked the constitution of a lesser man, Livingstone reached Luanda on the west coast on May 31, 1854. In order to take his Makololo followers back home and to carry out further explorations of the Zambezi, as soon as his health permitted he began the return journey Sept. 20, 1854. He reached Linyanti nearly a year later on Sept. 11, 1855. Continuing eastward on November 3, Livingstone explored the Zambezi regions and reached Quelimane in Mozambique on May 20, 1856. His most spectacular visit on this last leg of his great journey was to the thundering, smokelike waters on the Zambezi at which he arrived on Nov. 17, 1855, and with typical patriotism named Victoria Falls after his queen. Livingstone returned to England on Dec. 9, 1856, as a national hero. News from and about him during the previous three years had stirred the imagination of English-speaking peoples everywhere to an unprecedented degree.

Livingstone recorded his accomplishments modestly but effectively in his *Missionary Travels and Researches in South Africa* (1857), which quickly sold more than 70,000 copies and took its place in publishing history as well as in that of exploration and missionary endeavour. Honours flowed in upon him. His increased income meant that he was now able to provide adequately for his family, which had lived in near poverty since returning to Britain. He was also able to make himself independent of the London Missionary Society. After the completion of his book, Livingstone spent six months speaking all over the British Isles. In his Senate House address at Cambridge on Dec. 4, 1857, he foresaw that he would be unable to complete his work in Africa, and he called on young university men to take up the task that he had begun. The publication of *Dr. Livingstone's Cambridge Lectures* (1858) roused almost as much interest as his book, and out of his Cambridge visit came the Universities' Mission to Central Africa in 1860, on which Livingstone set high hopes during his second expedition to Africa.

The Zambezi expedition. This time Livingstone was away from Britain from March 12, 1858, to July 23, 1864. He went out originally as British Consul at Quelimane "for the Eastern Coast and independent districts of the interior, and commander of an expedition for exploring eastern and central Africa, for the promotion of Commerce and Civilization with a view to the extinction of the slave-trade." This expedition was infinitely better organized than Livingstone's previous solitary journeys. It had a paddle steamer, impressive stores, 10 Africans, and 6 Europeans (including his brother Charles and an Edinburgh doctor, John Kirk). That Livingstone's by then legendary leadership had its limitations was soon revealed. Quarrels broke out among the Europeans and some were dismissed. Disillusionment with Livingstone set in among members both of his own expedition and of the abortive Universities' Mission that followed it to central Africa. It proved impossible to navigate the Zambezi by ship, and Livingstone's two attempts to find a route along the Rovuma River bypassing Portuguese territory to districts around Lake Nyasa (Malawi) also proved impractical. Livingstone and his party had been the first Britons to reach (Sept. 17, 1859) these districts that held out promise of colonization. To add to Livingstone's troubles, his wife, who had been determined to accompany him back to Africa, died at Shupanga on the Zambezi on April 27, 1862. His eldest son, Robert, who was to have joined his father in 1863, never reached him and went instead to the United States, where he died fighting for the North in the Civil War on Dec. 5, 1864.

The British government recalled the expedition in 1863, when it was clear that Livingstone's optimism about economic and political developments in the Zambezi regions was premature. Livingstone, however, showed something of his old fire when he took his little vessel, the "Lady Nyassa," with a small, untrained crew and little fuel, on a hazardous voyage of 2,500 miles across the Indian Ocean and left it for sale in Bombay. Furthermore, within the next three decades the Zambezi expedition proved to be anything but a disaster. It had amassed a valuable body of scientific knowledge, and the association of the Lake Nyasa regions with Livingstone's name and the prospects for colonization that he envisaged there were important factors for the creation in 1893 of the British Central Africa Protectorate, which in 1907 became Nyasaland, and in 1966 the republic of Malawi.

Back in Britain in the summer of 1864, Livingstone, with his brother Charles, wrote his second book, *Narrative of an Expedition to the Zambesi and Its Tributaries* (1865). Livingstone was advised at this time to have a surgical operation for the hemorrhoids that had troubled him since his first great African journey. He refused; and it is probable that severe bleeding hemorrhoids were the cause of his death at the end of his third and greatest African journey.

The quest for the Nile. Livingstone returned to Africa, after another short visit to Bombay, on Jan. 28, 1866, with support from private and public bodies and the status of a British Consul at large. His aim, as usual, was the extension of the Gospel and the abolition of the slave trade on the East African coast, but a new object was the exploration of the central Africa watershed and the possibility of finding the ultimate sources of the Nile. This time Livingstone went without European subordinates and took only African and Asian followers. Trouble, however, once more broke out among his staff; and Livingstone, prematurely aged from the hardships of his previous expeditions, found it difficult to cope with. Striking out from Mikindani on the east coast, he was compelled by Ngoni raids to give up his original intention of avoiding Portuguese territory and reaching the country around Lake Tanganyika by passing north of Lake Nyasa. The expedition was forced south, and in September some of Livingstone's followers deserted him. To avoid punishment when they returned to Zanzibar, they concocted the story that Livingstone had been killed by the Ngoni. Although it was proved the following year that he was alive, a touch of drama was added to the reports circulating abroad about his expedition.

Drama mounted as Livingstone moved north again from the south end of Lake Nyasa. Early in 1867 a deserter carried off his medical chest, but Livingstone pressed on into central Africa. On Nov. 8, 1867, he discovered Lake Mweru, and on July 18, 1868, Lake Bangweulu. Assisted by Arab traders, Livingstone reached Lake Tanganyika in February 1869. Despite illness, he went on and arrived on March 29, 1871, at his ultimate northwesterly point, Nyangwe, on the Lualaba leading into the Congo River. This was farther west than any European had penetrated.

Returning to Ujiji on the eastern shore of

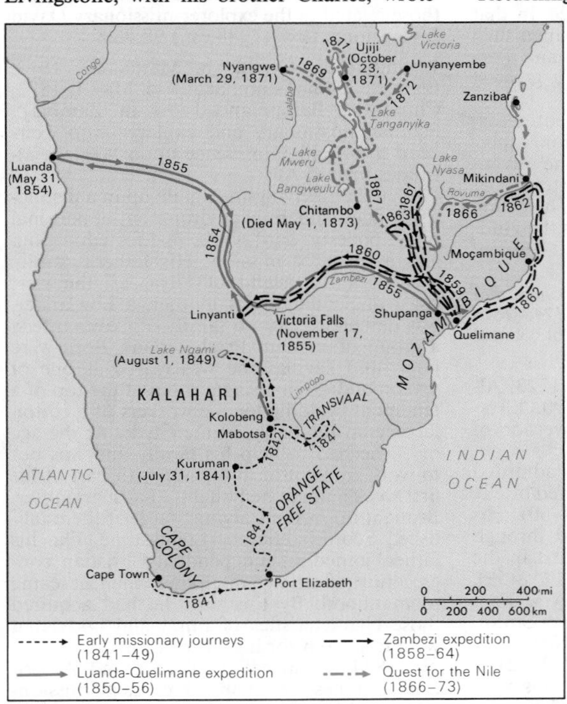

The expeditions of David Livingstone

Lake Tanganyika on Oct. 23, 1871, Livingstone was a sick and failing man, and the arrival of Henry M. Stanley, a correspondent of the *New York Herald* who had been sent to search for Livingstone, provided him with desperately needed food and medicine. Livingstone felt strong enough to join Stanley in exploring the northern reaches of Lake Tanganyika and then accompanied him to Unyanyembe, 200 miles eastward. But he refused all of Stanley's pleas to leave Africa with him, and on March 14, 1872, Stanley departed for England to add, with journalistic fervour, to the saga of David Livingstone.

Replenished by Stanley's supplies, Livingstone moved south again, obsessed by his quest for the Nile sources and his desire for the destruction of the slave trade. But his illness overcame him. In May 1873, at Chitambo in the Ilala district of what is now Zambia, Livingstone's African servants found him dead, kneeling by his bedside as if in prayer. In order to embalm Livingstone's body, they removed his heart and viscera and buried them in African soil. In a difficult journey of nine months, they carried his body to the coast. It was taken to England and, in a great Victorian funeral, was buried in Westminster Abbey on April 18, 1874. *The Last Journals of David Livingstone* were published in the same year.

Influence. In his 30 years of travel and Christian missionary work in southern, central, and eastern Africa—often in places where no European had previously ventured—Livingstone may have influenced Western attitudes toward Africa more than any other individual before him or since. His discoveries—geographic, technical, medical, and social—provided a complex body of knowledge that is still being explored. In spite of his paternalism and Victorian prejudices, Livingstone believed wholeheartedly in the African's ability to advance into the modern world. He was, in this sense, a forerunner not only of European imperialism in Africa but also of African nationalism. (G.A.S.)

BIBLIOGRAPHY. The following books by David Livingstone himself are fundamental: *Missionary Travels and Researches in South Africa* (1857); *Dr. Livingstone's Cambridge Lectures,* ed. by W. Monk (1858); *Narrative of an Expedition to the Zambesi and Its Tributaries and of the Discovery of Lakes Shirwa and Nyassa, 1858–1867* (1865); *The Last Journals of David Livingstone in Central Africa, from 1865 to His Death,* 2 vol., ed. by H. Waller (1874).

The most useful biography of Livingstone is George Seaver, *David Livingstone: His Life and Letters* (1957). A much older work, still useful for personal details, is W.G. Blaikie, *The Personal Life of David Livingstone* (1880). Various aspects of Livingstone's life and work are examined in: Reginald Coupland, *Livingstone's Last Journey* (1945); Frank Debenham, *The Way to Ilala* (1955), valuable for Livingstone as a geographer; Michael Gelfand, *Livingstone the Doctor, His Life and Travels: A Study in Medical History* (1957); I. Schapera (ed.), *David Livingstone: Family Letters, 1841–1856,* 2 vol. (1959), *Livingstone's Private Journals, 1851–1853* (1960), and *Livingstone's African Journal, 1853–1856,* 2 vol. (1963); George Shepperson (ed.), *David Livingstone and the Rovuma* (1965); J.P.R. Wallis (ed.), *The Zambezi Expedition of David Livingstone, 1858–1863* (1956); James Stewart, *The Zambesi Journal, 1862–1863* (1952); and George Martelli, *Livingstone's River: A History of the Zambezi Expedition, 1858–1864* (1970). The following articles are also useful: R.C. Bridges, "The Sponsorship and Financing of Livingstone's Last Journey," *African Historical Studies,* 1:79–104 (1968), and George Shepperson, "David Livingstone the Scot," *The Scottish Historical Review,* 39:113–121 (1960).

Livingstone, Sir Richard Winn (b. Jan. 23, 1880, Liverpool—d. Dec. 26, 1960, Oxford), classical scholar and university administrator who championed the classical liberal arts curriculum.

Livingstone's parents were an Anglican vicar and the daughter of an Irish baron, and he was educted at Winchester and then New College at Oxford, where he took honours in Latin verse and other subjects. He stayed at Oxford until 1924 as a fellow, tutor, and librarian of Corpus Christi College. During these years he also served (1920) on the prime minister's committee on the classics and was co-editor (1920–22) of the *Classical Review.*

In 1924 Livingstone assumed the position of vice chancellor at Queen's University in Belfast. Under his administration, which lasted until 1933, he greatly enhanced the university's stature and its financial support. In 1931 he was knighted.

From 1933 to the end of his academic career, Livingstone was back at Oxford. As president of Corpus Christi College he instituted summer schools for colonial administrators and expanded educational opportunities for adults. He also played a major role in establishing a residential college for women. He was vice chancellor from 1944 to 1947.

Livingstone retired from academic life in 1950 and filled the final decade of his life with writing and lecturing. He vigorously defended the value of a liberal arts education, with particular emphasis on the classics.

His lifelong commitment to classical literature was apparent in the many books he wrote and edited: *The Greek Genius and its Meaning to Us* (1912), *A Defence of Classical Education* (1916), *The Legacy of Greece* (1921), *The Pageant of Greece* (1923), *The Mission of Greece* (1928), *The Future in Education* (1941), *Portrait of Socrates* (1938), and *The Rainbow Bridge* (1959).

Livingstone Falls, French CHUTES DE LIVINGSTONE, series of 32 rapids and cataracts on the Congo River, extending for about 220 mi (354 km) between Kinshasa and Matadi in Zaire and partially along the border of Congo (Brazzaville). The total drop of the falls is about 850 ft (260 m), despite only minor rapids over an 87-mi stretch to Isangila. The falls, beginning 100 mi inland from the coast, prevent navigation from the mouth of the river to the interior but provide, in return, a tremendous potential for hydropower, as manifested in the giant Inga hydroelectric scheme just above Matadi. Other dams have been built (mainly on Congo tributaries). The falls, named for the Scottish explorer-missionary David Livingstone, were crossed in 1877 by Henry Morton Stanley, who charted the course of the Congo River.

Livius, Titus (Roman historian): *see* Livy.

Livius Andronicus, Lucius (b. *c.* 284 BC, Tarentum, Magna Graecia—d. *c.* 204 BC, Rome?), founder of Roman epic poetry and drama.

He was a Greek slave, freed by a member of the Livian family; he may have been captured as a boy when Tarentum surrendered to Rome in 272 BC. A freedman, he earned his living teaching Latin and Greek in Rome.

His main work, the *Odyssia,* a translation of Homer's *Odyssey,* was possibly done for use as a schoolbook. Written in rude Italian Saturnian metre, it had little poetic merit to judge from the less than 50 surviving lines and from the comments of Cicero and Horace. It was, however, the first major poem in Latin, the first example of artistic translation, and the subject matter happily chosen for introducing Roman youth to the Greek world.

In 240, as part of the Ludi Romani (the annual games honouring Jupiter), Livius produced a translation of a Greek play, probably a tragedy, and perhaps also a comedy. After this, the first dramatic performance ever given in Rome, he continued to write, stage, and sometimes perform in both tragedies and comedies, after 235 in rivalry with Gnaeus Naevius (*q.v.*). Only one fragment is known from each of his three remaining comedies; fewer than 40 lines of the nine tragedies have survived. Their titles show that he translated mainly the three great tragedians, Aeschylus, Sophocles, and Euripides.

In 207, to ward off menacing omens, he was commissioned to compose an intercessory hymn to be sung, in procession, to Aventine Juno. As a reward for the success of this intervention, a guild of poets and actors, of which he became president, was granted a domicile in the temple of Minerva on the Aventine.

Livonia, German LIVLAND, lands on the eastern coast of the Baltic Sea, north of Lithuania; the name was originally applied by Germans in the 12th century to the area inhabited by the Livs, a Finno-Ugric people whose settlements centred on the mouths of the Western Dvina and Gauja rivers, but eventually it was

Livonia proper, *c.* 1560

From W. Shepherd, *Historical Atlas;* Barnes & Noble Books, New York

used to refer to nearly all of modern Latvia and Estonia. During the 13th century greater Livonia, which was inhabited by several Baltic and Finnish tribes, was conquered and Christianized by the Order of the Brothers of the Sword (founded 1202; after 1237, the Order of Teutonic Knights of Livonia). The conquered territory was organized into the Livonian confederation, which consisted of ecclesiastical states, free towns, and regions ruled directly by the knights. After 1419, when the various political elements combined to form a common legislative diet, the Knights and their vassals emerged as the dominant estate. They prospered, in particular by supplying grain for the Baltic Sea trade, but they were not politically united among themselves; and mutual suspicion and conflicting interests prevented them from overcoming their rivalry with the other estates (*i.e.,* the bishops and the autonomous cities). By the middle of the 16th century the problems of religious disunity resulting from the spread of Protestantism and of peasant discontent had also become acute in Livonia.

When Russia invaded the area (beginning the Livonian War, 1558–83) in an effort to prevent Poland-Lithuania from gaining dominance over it, the Livonian Knights were unable to defend themselves. They disbanded their order and dismembered Livonia (Union of Wilno, 1561). Lithuania incorporated the knights' territory north of the Western Dvina River (*i.e.,* Livonia proper); Courland, the area south of the Western Dvina, became a Polish fief. Sweden, which also had acquired an interest in the area, seized northern Estonia. This territorial distribution remained in effect until 1621, when Sweden took the cities of Riga and Jelgava (Mitau, the capital of Courland) and subsequently won all Estonia as well as northern Latvia (*i.e.,* the region of

Vidzeme or Livonia) from the Polish-Lithuanian state (Truce of Altmark, 1629).

Sweden retained these territories for almost a century, defending them from both Poland (Polish-Swedish War, 1654–60) and Russia (Russo-Swedish War, 1654–61). In 1721, however, after the Great Northern War, Sweden ceded them to Russia (Treaty of Nystad), which also, as a result of the partitions of Poland, annexed Latgale (1772)—the southeastern section of Livonia that had been retained by Poland in 1629—and Courland (1795). Historic Livonia was then divided into three governments within the Russian Empire: Estonia (*i.e.,* the northern part of ethnic Estonia), Livonia (*i.e.,* the southern part of ethnic Estonia and northern Latvia), and Courland. After the October Revolution in Russia (1917), Latvia and Estonia proclaimed their independence; they were incorporated into the Soviet Union in 1940, though under German occupation from 1941 to 1944.

Livonia, city, western suburb of Detroit, Wayne county, southeastern Michigan, U.S. It originated in 1834 as Livonia Township (named for Livonia, N.Y.) and was basically a farming community for more than a century. After World War II it rapidly experienced planned industrial and residential growth. It is the site of Madonna College (1937), Schoolcraft (junior) College (1961), and the Detroit Race Course. Inc. city, 1950. Pop. (1990) 100,850.

Livonian Order, also called LIVONIAN KNIGHTS: *see* Brothers of the Sword, Order of the.

Livonian War (1558–83), prolonged military conflict, during which Russia unsuccessfully fought Poland, Lithuania, and Sweden for control of greater Livonia—the area including Estonia, Livonia, Courland, and the island of Oesel—which was ruled by the Livonian branch of the Teutonic Knights (Order of the Brothers of the Sword).

In 1558 Ivan IV of Russia invaded Livonia, hoping to gain access to the Baltic Sea and to take advantage of the weakness of the Livonian Knights; he seized Narva and Dorpat and besieged Reval. The Knights, unable to withstand the Russian attack, dissolved their Order (1561); they placed Livonia proper under Lithuanian protection and gave Courland to Poland, Estonia to Sweden, and Oesel to Denmark.

Ivan was then obliged to wage war against Sweden and Lithuania to retain his conquests in Livonia. Initially successful, the Russians captured Polotsk, in Lithuanian Belorussia (1563), and occupied Lithuanian territory up to Vilna. In 1566 the Russian *zemsky sobor* ("assembly of the land") refused a Lithuanian peace proposal. But as the war progressed, Russia's position deteriorated; during the 1560s Russia experienced severe internal social and economic disruptions while Lithuania became stronger, forming a political union with Poland (1569) and acquiring a new king, Stephen Báthory (1576).

Báthory launched a series of campaigns against Russia, recapturing Polotsk (1579) and laying siege to Pskov. In 1582 Russia and Lithuania agreed upon a peace settlement (Peace of Yam Zapolsky), whereby Russia returned all the Lithuanian territory it had captured and renounced its claims to Livonia. In 1583 Russia also made peace with Sweden, surrendering several Russian towns along the Gulf of Finland (its only access to the Baltic Sea) and giving up its claims to Estonia.

Livorno, English LEGHORN, French LIVOURNE, Latin LIBURNUM, or LIBURNI PORTUS, city, capital of Livorno *provincia,* Toscana (Tuscany) *regione,* central Italy. It lies on the Ligurian Sea at the western edge of a cultivated coastal plain and is enclosed east and south by a circle of low hills, the Livornesi Hills.

Originally a small fishing village, it first became important when it was given by the countess Matilda of Tuscany to the Pisan church (1103), and it was fortified by the Pisans in the 14th century. It was sold in 1399 to the Visconti family, in 1407 to the Genoese, and in 1421 to the Florentines. Its greatest importance dates from the rule of the Florentine Medici family. Cosimo I initiated the construction of the Medici Harbour in 1571; and Ferdinand I, grand duke of Tuscany from 1587 to 1609, gave asylum to many refugees—Roman Catholics from England, Jews and Moors from Spain and Portugal, and others—and launched the community as a commercial centre. Among the princes of Habsburg-Lorraine who succeeded the Medicis, the last, Leopold II (1747–92), is of particular importance; he enlarged the city, gave privileges to foreign merchants, and had the great curved breakwater built to protect the port from the open sea. Livorno flourished as a free port from 1675 until it became part of the Kingdom of Italy in 1860. Much of the city has been rebuilt according to the original general plan after sustaining severe damage by bombing during World War II.

The city is intersected and bordered by canals connecting with the sea and the Arno River (north). Notable landmarks include the Fortezza Vecchia (1521–34) and the Fortezza Nuova (1590; Old and New Forts); the monument to Ferdinand I, a marble statue of the grand duke (1595); and the famous bronze statues of "The Four Moors" ("I Quattro Mori"; 1623–24) by Pietro Tacca. The cathedral (1595) was entirely reconstructed in 1954–59. Other points of interest are the old Protestant cemetery (burial place of the 18th-century English novelist Tobias Smollett) and the two villas where the poets Percy Bysshe Shelley and Lord Byron stayed in 1819 and 1822, respectively. The Giovanni Fattori Civic Museum possesses works of Fattori and other Tuscan artists as well as modern paintings. In the same building is the fine Francesco Domenico Guerrazzi Communal Library. The scenic coastal avenue (Viale Italia) to the southern suburbs of Ardenza and Antignano is marked by numerous bathing places, the civic aquarium, and the Italian Naval Academy.

The port, one of Italy's largest, has regular services to points on the Mediterranean and beyond and is well served by rail, road, and air (by Pisa airport). Its extensive commercial activities include imports of crude mineral oils, coal, cereals, phosphates and fertilizers, silica sand, and metal minerals; and exports include mineral and derived oils, marble, plate glass, wine, tomato preserves, olive oil, sodium carbonate and sodium hydrate, and copper and its alloys. Livorno has a large shipbuilding yard and smaller yards for ship repair. Industries include metallurgical plants (aluminum, copper), a petroleum refinery, steelworks, and chemical manufactures. Pop. (1988 est.) mun., 173,114.

A list of the abbreviations used in the MICROPAEDIA *will be found at the end of this volume*

Livy, Latin in full TITUS LIVIUS (b. 59/64 BC, Patavium, Venetia, Italy—d. AD 17, Patavium), with Sallust and Tacitus, one of the three great Roman historians. His history of Rome became a classic in his own lifetime and exercised a profound influence on the style and philosophy of historical writing down to the 18th century.

Early life and career. Little is known about Livy's life and nothing about his family background. Patavium, a rich city, famous for its strict morals, suffered severely in the Civil Wars of the 40s. The wars and the unsettled condition of the Roman world after the death of Caesar in 44 BC probably prevented Livy from studying in Greece, as most educated Romans did. Although widely read in Greek literature, he made mistakes of translation that would be unnatural if he had spent any length of time in Greece and had acquired the command of Greek normal among his contemporaries. His education was based on the study of rhetoric and philosophy, and he wrote some philosophical dialogues that do not survive. There is no evidence about early career. His family apparently did not belong to the senatorial class, however distinguished it may have been in Patavium itself, and Livy does not seem to have embarked on a political or forensic profession. He is first heard of in Rome after Octavian (later known as the emperor Augustus) had restored stability and peace to the empire by his decisive naval victory at Actium in 31 BC. Internal evidence from the work itself shows that Livy had conceived the plan of writing the history of Rome in or shortly before 29 BC, and for this purpose he must have already moved to Rome, because only there were the records and information available. It is significant that another historian, the Greek Dionysius of Halicarnassus, who was to cover much the same ground as Livy, settled in Rome in 30 BC. A more secure age had dawned.

Most of his life must have been spent at Rome, and at an early stage he attracted the interest of Augustus and was even invited to supervise the literary activities of the young Claudius (the future emperor), presumably about AD 8. But he never became closely involved with the literary world of Rome—the poets Horace, Virgil, and Ovid, as well as the patron of the arts, Maecenas, and others. He is never referred to in connection with these men. He must have possessed sufficient private means not to be dependent on official patronage. Indeed, in one of the few recorded anecdotes about him, Augustus called him a "Pompeian," implying an outspoken and independent turn of mind. His lifework was the composition of his history.

Livy's history of Rome. Livy began by composing and publishing in units of five books, the length of which was determined by the size of the ancient papyrus roll. As his material became more complex, however, he abandoned this symmetrical pattern and wrote 142 books. So far as it can be reconstructed, the shape of the history is as follows (books 11–20 and 46–142 have been lost):

1–5 From the foundation of the city until the sack of Rome by the Gauls (386 BC)
6–10 The Samnite wars
11–15 The conquest of Italy
16–20 The First Punic (Carthaginian) War
21–30 The Second Punic War (until 201 BC)
31–45 Events until the end of the war with Perseus (167 BC)
46–70 Events until the Social War (91 BC)
71–80 Civil wars until the death of Marius (86 BC)
81–90 Civil wars until the death of Sulla (78 BC)
91–103 Events until the triumph of Pompey in 62 BC
104–108 The last years of the Republic
109–116 The Civil War until the murder of Caesar (44 BC)
117–133 From the death of Caesar to the Battle of Actium
134–142 From 29 to 9 BC

Apart from fragments, quoted by grammarians and others, and a short section dealing with the death of the orator and politician Cicero from Book 120, the later books after Book 45 are known only from summaries. These were made from the 1st century AD onward, because the size of the complete work made it unmanageable. There were anthologies of the speeches and also concise summaries, two of which survive in part, a 3rd-century papyrus from Egypt (containing summaries of Books 37–40 and 48–55) and a 4th-century summary of contents (known as the *Periochae*) of the whole work. A note in the *Periochae* of Book 121 records that that book (and presumably those that followed) was published after Augustus' death in AD 14. The implication is that the last 20 books dealing with the events from the Battle of Actium until 9 BC were an afterthought to the original plan and were also too politically explosive to be published with impunity in Augustus' lifetime.

The sheer scope of the undertaking was formidable. It presupposed the composition of three books a year on average. Two stories reflect the magnitude of the task. In his letters the statesman Pliny the Younger records that Livy was tempted to abandon the enterprise but found that the task had become too fascinating to give it up; he also mentions a citizen of Cádiz who came all the way to Rome for the sole satisfaction of gazing at the great historian.

Livy's historical approach. The project of writing the history of Rome down to the present day was not a new one. Historical research and writing had flourished at Rome for 200 years, since the first Roman historian Quintus Fabius Pictor. There had been two main inspirations behind it—antiquarian interest and political motivation. Particularly after 100 BC, there developed a widespread interest in ancient ceremonies, family genealogies, religious customs, and the like. This interest found expression in a number of scholarly works: Titus Pomponius Atticus, Cicero's friend and correspondent, wrote on chronology and on Trojan families; others compiled lengthy volumes on Etruscan religion; Marcus Terentius Varro, the greatest scholar of his age, published the encyclopaedic work *Divine and Human Antiquities.* The standard of scholarship was not always high, and there could be political pressures, as in the attempt to derive the Julian family to which Julius Caesar belonged from the legendary Aeneas and the Trojans; but the Romans were very conscious and proud of their past, and an enthusiasm for antiquities was widespread.

Previous historians had been public figures and men of affairs. Fabius Pictor had been a praetor, the elder Cato had been consul and censor, and Sallust was a praetor. So, too, many prominent statesmen such as Sulla and Caesar occupied their leisure with writing history. For some it was an exercise in political self-justification (hence, Caesar's *Gallic War* and *Civil War*); for others it was a civilized pastime. But all shared a common outlook and background. History was a political study through which one might hope to explain or excuse the present.

Livy was unique among Roman historians in that he played no part in politics. This was a disadvantage in that his exclusion from the Senate and the magistracies meant that he had no personal experience of how the Roman government worked, and this ignorance shows itself from time to time in his work. It also deprived him of firsthand access to much material (minutes of Senate meetings, texts of treaties, laws, etc.) that was preserved in official quarters. So, too, if he had been a priest or an augur, he would have acquired inside information of great historical value and been able to consult the copious documents and records of the priestly colleges. But the chief effect is that Livy did not seek historical explanations in political terms. The novelty and impact of his history lay in the fact that he saw history in personal and moral terms. The purpose is clearly set out in his preface:

> I invite the reader's attention to the much more serious consideration of the kind of lives our ancestors lived, of who were the men and what the means, both in politics and war, by which Rome's power was first acquired and subsequently expanded, I would then have him trace the process of our moral decline, to watch first the sinking of the foundations of morality as the old teaching was allowed to lapse, then the final collapse of the whole edifice, and the dark dawning of our modern day when we can neither endure our vices nor face the remedies needed to cure them.
>
> What chiefly makes the study of history wholesome and profitable is this, that in history you have a record of the infinite variety of human experience plainly set out for all to see, and in that record you can find for yourself and your country both examples and warnings.

Although Sallust and earlier historians had also adopted the outlook that morality was in steady decline and had argued that people do the sort of things they do because they are the sort of people they are, for Livy these beliefs were a matter of passionate concern. He saw history in terms of human personalities and representative individuals rather than of partisan politics. And his own experience, going back perhaps to his youth in Patavium, made him feel the moral evils of his time with peculiar intensity. He punctuates his history with revealing comments:

> Fortunately in those days authority, both religious and secular, was still a guide to conduct and there was as yet no sign of our modern scepticism which interpets solemn compacts to suit its own convenience (3.20.5). Where would you find nowadays in a single individual that modesty, fairness and nobility of mind which in those days belonged to a whole people? (4.6.12).

In looking at history from a moral standpoint, Livy was at one with other thinking Romans of his day. Augustus attempted by legislation and propaganda to inculcate moral ideals. Horace and Virgil in their poetry stressed the same message—that it was moral qualities that had made and could keep Rome great.

The preoccupation with character and the desire to write history that would reveal the effects of character outweighed for Livy the need for scholarly accuracy. He showed little if any awareness of the antiquarian research of his own and earlier generations; nor did he seriously compare and criticize the different histories and their discrepancies that were available to him. For the most part he is content to take an earlier version (from Polybius or a similar author) and to reshape it so as to construct moral episodes that bring out the character of the leading figures. Livy's descriptions of the capture of Veii and the expulsion of the Gauls from Rome in the 4th century BC by Marcus Furius Camillus are designed to illustrate his piety; the crossing of the Alps shows up the resourceful intrepidity of Hannibal. Unfortunately, it is not known how Livy dealt with the much greater complexity of contemporary history, but the account of Cicero's death contains the same emphasis on character displayed by surviving books.

It would be misplaced criticism to draw attention to his technical shortcomings, his credulity, or his lack of antiquarian curiosity. He reshaped history for his generation so that it was alive and meaningful. It is recorded that the audiences who went to his recitations were impressed by his nobility of character and his eloquence. It is this eloquence that is Livy's second claim to distinction.

Together with Cicero and Tacitus, Livy set new standards of literary style. The earliest Roman historians had written in Greek, the language of culture. Their successors had felt that their own history should be written in Latin, but Latin possessed no ready-made style that could be used for the purpose: for Latin prose had to develop artificial styles to suit the different genres. Sallust had attempted to reproduce the Greek style of Thucydides in Latin by a tortured use of syntax and a vocabulary incorporating a number of archaic and unusual words, but the result, although effective, was harsh and unsuitable for a work of any size. Livy evolved a varied and flexible style that the ancient critic Quintilian characterized as a "milky richness." At one moment he will set the scene in long, periodic clauses; at another a few terse, abrupt sentences will mirror the rapidity of the action. Bare notices of archival fact will be reported in correspondingly dry and formal language, whereas a battle will evoke poetical and dramatic vocabulary, and a speech will be constructed either in the spirit of a contemporary orator such as Cicero or in dramatically realistic tones, designed to recapture the atmosphere of antiquity. "When I write of ancient deeds my mind somehow becomes antique," he wrote.

The work of a candid man and an individualistic thinker, Livy's history was deeply rooted in the Augustan revival and owed its success in large measure to its moral seriousness. But the detached attempt to understand the course of history through character (which was to influence later historians from Tacitus to Lord Clarendon) represents Livy's great achievement. (R.M.Og.)

BIBLIOGRAPHY. *Texts.* Books 1–10, 21–35 have been edited and published in the "Oxford Classical Series"; the other books are in course of preparation. The complete text of surviving books and fragments has been published in the "Teubner Series."

Translations. Books 1–5 and 21–30 have been translated by A. de Selincourt and published in the "Penguin Classics," with complete text and translation in the "Loeb Classical Library."

Commentaries. Books 1–5 by R.M. Ogilvie (1965), with bibliography. Individual books have been edited with commentaries in the "Macmillan Series." Complete commentary on the surviving books by W. Weissenborn, rev. by H.J. Muller (1878–1910).

Studies. P.G. Walsh, *Livy: His Historical Aims and Methods* (1961), with bibliography; J. Briscoe *et al., Livy* (1971); T.J. Luce, *Livy: The Composition of His History* (1977).

Lixus, ancient site located north of the modern seaport of Larache, Morocco, on the right bank of the Oued Loukkos (Lucus River). Originally settled by Phoenicians during the 7th century BC, it gradually grew in importance, later coming under Carthaginian domination. After the destruction of Carthage, Lixus fell to Roman control and was made an imperial colony, reaching its zenith during the reign of the emperor Claudius I (AD 41–54).

Some ancient Greek writers located at Lixus the mythological garden of the Hesperides, the keepers of the golden apples.

Liyong, Taban lo (b. 1938, Gulu, Acholi, Uganda), prolific author whose experimental works and provocative opinions stimulated literary controversy in East Africa.

Liyong was reared in Uganda and attended National Teachers College in Kampala, its capital, before continuing his undergraduate studies at Knoxville College in Tennessee and Howard University in Washington, D.C. He went on to earn a master of fine arts degree at the University of Iowa in Iowa City, specializing in creative writing. After returning to Uganda in 1968 he worked at the University of Nairobi in Kenya for several years, first as a research fellow in the Institute of African Studies, then as a lecturer in the literature department. From 1975 to 1977 he served as chairman of the literature department at the University of Papua New Guinea, after which he returned to The Sudan as a senior public relations officer at the University of Juba.

Liyong's work includes highly imaginative short narratives (*Fixions,* 1969), unorthodox free verse (*Franz Fanon's Uneven Ribs,* 1971; *Another Nigger Dead,* 1972; and *Ballads of Underdevelopment,* 1976), argumentative and amusing personal essays (*Meditations in Limbo,* 1970; *The Uniformed Man,* 1971; and *The Meditations of Taban lo Liyong,* 1978), bold literary criticism (*The Last Word,* 1969), and half-serious quasi-political commentary (*Thirteen Offensives Against Our Enemies,* 1973), and he edited collections of oral lore (*Eating Chiefs,* 1970, and *Popular Culture of East Africa,* 1973) and an English translation of Ham Mukasa's *Sir Apolo Kagwa Discovers Britain* (1973). His aim seems to be to startle the reader out of complacency by presenting challenging new ideas in an original manner. His lighthearted approach to a number of serious issues has led some critics to dismiss him as a glib and irresponsible clown, but his work remains refreshingly unpredictable, always with something interesting to offer.

lizard, suborder name SAURIA, any of about 3,700 species of vertebrates that together with the snakes (suborder Serpentes) make up 95 percent of living reptiles. Although most diverse and abundant in the tropics, they are also found from the Arctic Circle to southern Africa, South America, and Australia.

A brief treatment of lizards follows. For full treatment, *see* MACROPAEDIA: Reptiles.

Lizards share with snakes the presence of ectodermal scales, paired male copulatory organs (hemipenes), and flexible skulls. Typical lizards have moderately cylindrical bodies, four well-developed legs, a tail slightly longer than the head and body, and movable lower eyelids. They range in size from 3 to more than 300 centimetres (1 inch to 10 feet), but most are about 30 cm (12 in.) long. Ornamentation includes crests on the head, back, or tail, spines, brightly coloured throat fans, and throat frills.

Like fish and amphibians, lizards are cold-blooded animals; *i.e.,* the temperature of the environment regulates their body temperature, although a few species have the ability to store the Sun's warmth for extended periods of time. Most lizards lay eggs, which they bury in the ground; in the embryo, a special tooth is formed for rupturing the shell. A number of species, however, bear live young. Members of most species feed on insects and rodents, but some, such as the iguana, are herbivorous.

lizard beetle, also called LANGURIID BEETLE, any member of the approximately 400 species of the insect family Languriidae (order Coleoptera). Most species occur in Asia and North America. Lizard beetles are narrow and long, between 5 and 10 millimetres (0.2 to 0.4 inch).

The adults, reddish in colour with dark wing covers (elytra), feed on plants. The larvae of the clover stem borer (*Languria mozardi*) may become serious pests in clover fields. Members of many species make squeaking sounds using well-developed stridulatory organs on top of the head.

Consult the INDEX *first*

lizard orchid (*Himantoglossum hircinum*), unusual-looking plant of the family Orchidaceae, occurring sporadically in a variety of dry European habitats. Each greenish-purple flower bears several long, slightly twisted lobes. The two side lobes resemble the hindlegs of a lizard, the long central part of the lip is similar to a tail, and the petals and sepals form the head and body.

Lizard orchid flowers are clustered on a spike about 10 to 50 centimetres (4 to 20 inches)

Lizard orchid (*Himantoglossum hircinum*)
E.L. Crowson—J.E. Downward

long. The plant has a goatlike odour and a rather untidy appearance.

Lizard Peninsula, also called THE LIZARD, peninsula in Kerrier district, county of Cornwall, England. It is the southernmost part of the island of Great Britain. The coastal scenery is magnificent, with offshore rocks, rugged cliffs up to 250 ft (75 m) high, and small coves. Inland there is level, open landscape. The local serpentine rock is used for building. At Poldhu a monument marks the spot where, in 1901, Marconi sent and received the first transatlantic radio message. There are several villages on the peninsula.

lizardfish, any of about 36 species of marine fish of the family Synodontidae, found primarily in the tropics. Lizardfish are elongated with rounded bodies and scaly heads.

Lizardfish (*Synodus*)
A. Power—Bruce Coleman Inc.

They grow to a maximum length of about 50 centimetres (20 inches) and are characteristically mottled or blotched to blend with their surroundings. Most lizardfish live in shallow water. They tend to frequent sandy or muddy areas, and sometimes lie partly buried in the bottom. They are carnivorous and prey on fish, holding the catch with their many sharp teeth. They are sometimes taken by fishermen but are not generally considered good to eat.

Lizardi, José Joaquín Fernández de: *see* Fernández de Lizardi, José Joaquín.

lizard's tail, also called WATER DRAGON, (*Saururus cernuus*), member of the lizard's-tail family (Saururaceae), found in marshy areas of eastern North America. The plant has creeping stems, or runners. Erect branches about 60 to 150 centimetres (2 to 5 feet) tall

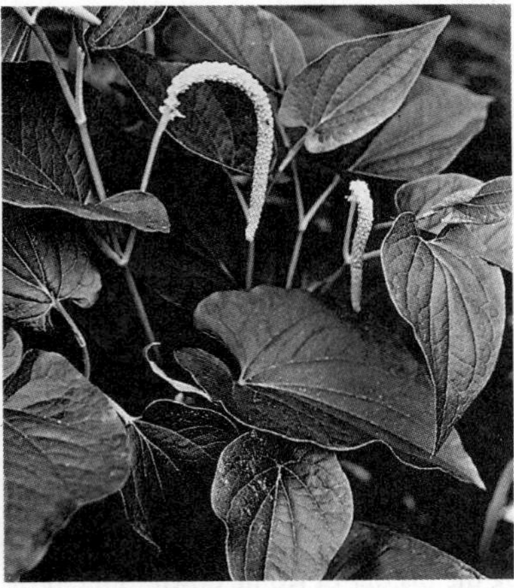

Lizard's tail (*Saururus cernuus*)
Kitty Kohout—Root Resources

bear heart-shaped leaves on long stalks. Small, white flowers grow in a spike with a drooping tip (the lizard's tail).

Ljouwert (The Netherlands): *see* Leeuwarden.

Ljubljana, German LAIBACH, Italian LUBIANA, capital city and economic, political, and cultural centre of Slovenia, on the Ljubljanica River. The city lies in a natural depression surrounded by high peaks of the northern Dinaric Alps. Heavy fogs are frequent. The Roman city of Emona (1st century BC) was located there. A strategic city on the route to Pannonia, commanding the Ljubljana Gap, it was destroyed by barbarians about the 5th century AD. After the Slavs rebuilt it as Luvigana, it was damaged by Magyars in the 10th century. In the 12th century the city passed to the dukes of Carniola. In 1270 it was taken by Otakar II of Bohemia, and in 1277 it came under the Habsburgs as Laibach.

From 1461, Ljubljana was the seat of a bishop. Taken by the French in 1809, it became the government seat of the Illyrian Provinces until 1813. In 1821 the Congress of Laibach, a meeting of members of the Holy Alliance, was held there. The building of the southern railway from Vienna in 1849 stimulated development of Ljubljana, which became a centre of Slovene nationalism under Austrian rule. Foreign rule ended in 1918, when it became part of Yugoslavia. It remained the Slovenian capital after Slovenia's independence in 1992.

Ljubljana is dominated by a medieval

Ljubljana along the Ljubljanica River, Slovenia
Salmer—Plessner International

fortress. The old quarter of the city lies between the fortress and the river. Only a few old buildings of Austrian Baroque style survived the violent earthquake of 1895. In the newer part of the city is the large Tivoli Park. Most buildings of historic interest date from the 18th century. Ljubljana has a museum, an art gallery, an opera house, the University of Ljubljana (founded in 1595), a Faculty of Theology (1919), art academies, the Slovene Academy of Sciences and Arts, and a metallurgical institute.

Ljubljana is an important centre of rail and road communications to Austria. Manufactures include turbines for hydroelectric stations, as well as natural and synthetic textiles, alumina, paper and newsprint, footwear, leather, electrical consumer goods, chemicals, and soap. Pop. (2000 est.) 270,986.

Ljusnan, river in central Sweden. After rising in the Norwegian border mountains it flows for 270 miles (430 km) in a generally southeasterly direction through the provinces of Härjedalen and Hälsingland past the towns of Sveg, Ljusdal, and Bollnäs to the Gulf of Bothnia at Ljusne. With a drainage area of 7,650 square miles (19,800 square km), it is the largest river in Hälsingland and one of the most important rivers in Sweden. It is a source of hydroelectric power and is known for its salmon.

llama (*Lama glama*), South American member of the camel family, Camelidae (order Artiodactyla), closely related to the alpaca, guanaco, and vicuña, which are known collectively as lamoids. Unlike camels, lamoids do not have the characteristic camel humps; they are slender-bodied animals and have long legs and necks, short tails, small heads, and large, pointed ears. Gregarious animals, they graze on grass and other plants. When annoyed, they spit. Lamoids are able to interbreed and to produce fertile offspring.

Most herds of llamas are maintained by the Indians of Bolivia, Peru, Ecuador, Chile, and Argentina. The llama is primarily a pack animal but is also used as a source of food, wool, hides, tallow for candles, and dried dung for fuel. The largest of the lamoids, it averages 120 cm (47 inches) at the shoulder. A 113-kilogram (250-pound) llama can carry a load of 45–60 kg and average 25 to 30 km (15 to 20 miles) travel a day. The llama's high thirst tolerance, endurance, and ability to subsist on a wide variety of forage makes it an important transport animal on the bleak Andean plateaus and mountains. The llama is a gentle animal, but, when overloaded or maltreated, it will lie down, hiss, spit and kick, and refuse to move. Llamas breed in the (Southern Hemispheric) late summer and fall, from November to May. The gestation period lasts about 11 months, and the female gives birth to one young. Although usually white, the llama may be solid black or brown, or it may be white with black or brown markings.

The llama and the alpaca (*L. pacos*) are domestic animals not known to exist in the wild state. They appear to have been bred from guanacos during or before the Inca Indian civilization to be used as beasts of burden.

Depending on the authority, the llama, alpaca, and guanaco may be classified as distinct species or as races of *Lama glama.* Because of certain structural features, the vicuña is sometimes classified into a separate genus from the other lamoids and is known as *Vicugna vicugna.*

Llamas are normally sheared every two years, each yielding about 3–3.5 kg of fibre. Llama fleece consists of the coarse guard hairs of the protective outer coat (about 20 percent) and the short, crimped (wavy) fibre of the insulating undercoat. The coarse fleece is inferior to the wool of the alpaca. The hair's colour is usually variegated, generally in shades of brown, although there are some pure blacks and whites. Cleaning reduces the final yield of fleece to about 66–84 percent of the original weight. Individual locks of hair appear wavy; the fairly downy fibres have about two to four crimps per centimetre, but the coarse hairs are fairly straight. The hair's length ranges from 8 to 25 cm, the coarse hairs being longest. Llama fibre is used, alone or in blends, for knitwear and for woven fabrics made into outerwear. It is used locally for rugs, rope, and fabric.

Llandaff, Welsh LLANDAF, part of the city of Cardiff, Cardiff district, South Glamorgan county, Wales; it was formerly a separate town. It lies along the west bank of the River Taff, about 2 miles (3.2 km) northwest of Cardiff city centre. The cathedral of the ancient diocese of Llandaff in the Church in Wales originated in a 6th-century foundation by the Celtic St. Teilo, but the present structure was begun by Bishop Urban in the early 12th century. The *Book of Llandaff,* compiled under Bishop Urban, was a record of privileges and grants made to the see in recognition of its ecclesiastical status. The cathedral lost a great deal of its revenue after the Reformation and fell into decay; in the 18th century the southwest tower and part of the roof collapsed, and a small church was erected inside the ruins. Considerable restoration of the original building occurred during the 19th century and, again, following severe damage in an air raid in World War II. Jacob Epstein's "Christ in Majesty" dominates the nave. An annual music festival is held in the cathedral.

Cathedral of Llandaff, South Glamorgan, from the southeast
Justin B. Ingram—Bruce Coleman Inc.

Llandaff Castle, the home of the medieval bishops, was destroyed about 1403–04 by the Welsh insurgent leader Owen Glendower; but the ruined gatehouse remains. Nearby are the Cathedral School, a theological college, and Howell's School for Girls. Retaining much of a village atmosphere at its centre, Llandaff has become an attractive residential section of Cardiff.

Llandeilan Series, the fourth of six divisions (in ascending order) comprising the Ordovician System; it represents all those rocks on a global basis deposited during the Llandeilan Age, between 458 and 468 million years ago. The name is derived from the town of Llandeilo in Dyfed, Wales, which serves as the traditional British type area.

At its maximum, the series locally attains a thickness of approximately 760 m (2,500 feet) and consists of shales, limestones, and sandy beds. The base of the type succession, however, is unconformable with underlying Llanvirnian strata and thus unsuitable as a global stratotype section. No global stratotype section and point (GSSP) has yet been defined by the International Commission on Stratigraphy, under the authority of the International Union of Geological Sciences. Nearby, above the base of the British type section, is a graptolite fauna within the *Glyptograptus teretiusculus* biozone. The base of this biozone has been taken as the base of the Llandeilan Series, pending a more precise definition. In principle, the top of the Llandeilan Series is defined by the base of the overlying Caradocian Series.

Llandovery Series, lowermost of four main divisions in the Silurian System, representing all those rocks on a global basis deposited during the Llandovery Epoch, between 428 and 438 million years ago. The name is derived from the type district around the town of Llandovery in Dyfed, southern Wales, where about 1,200 m (4,000 feet) of fossiliferous shales, sandstones, and gray mudstones occur.

The base of the Llandovery Series is coincident with the base of the Silurian System. As formally defined in 1985 under the authority of the International Commission on Stratigraphy (International Union of Geological Sciences), the global stratotype section and point (GSSP) for this boundary is established 1.6 m (5.2 feet) above the base of the Birkhill Shale Formation on the north side of the Linn Branch stream at Dob's Linn, near Moffat in southern Scotland. The boundary point, or "golden spike," is marked by the base of the graptolite biozone of *Parakidograptus acuminatus* fixed by the first occurrence of that species together with the graptolite *Akidograptus ascensus.* Other key reference districts for the Llandovery Series are located in the Oslo region of southern Norway and on Anticosti Island in Quebec, Canada. Shelly facies in all three districts are characterized by brachiopods belonging to the genera *Stricklandia, Pentamerus,* and *Eocoelia.* The top of the Llandovery Series is defined by the base of the overlying Wenlock Series. The Llandovery Series is subdivided into three worldwide stages: the Rhuddanian, Aeronian, and Telychian stages.

Llandrindod Wells, Welsh LLANDRINDOD, town and resort, seat of Radnorshire district and of Powys county, Wales. It developed as a spa, based on medicinal waters first discovered about 1696, and with the coming of the railroad in the 19th century it became widely popular. The spa declined after World War II and closed in the 1960s, but it reopened in 1983. The town is an active tourist centre, with a number of hotels, spacious streets, parks, museums, and a 14-acre (6-hectare) boating lake. To the northwest lie the remains of the Roman fort of Castell Collen. Pop. (1991) 4,362.

Llandudno, seaside resort, seat of Aberconwy district, Gwynedd county, Wales, on the Irish Sea. It fronts Llandudno Bay, between the limestone headlands of Great Orme and Little Orme. Traces of prehistoric and Roman occupation have been found on Great Orme, the summit of which (679 feet [207 m]) is accessible by tramway, cable lift, road, and nature trail; wild goats live on its slopes. There are caves around the base of Little Orme (463 feet [141 m]).

The town, set in a former fishing and copper-mining region, was developed around the railroad in the second half of the 19th century as an elegant, dignified resort characterized by wide boulevards and gracious Victorian buildings. It was there that Charles Dodgson (Lewis Carroll) told Alice Liddell the stories on which he based *Alice in Wonderland.* Llandudno in modern times has become somewhat commercialized and crowded with holiday-seekers. It is now the largest town in Gwynedd. Pop. (1991) 14,573.

Llanelli, town, district, and district seat, Dyfed county, Wales. The old, established settlement's most significant growth dates from the late 18th century, when it became a centre of nonferrous metal manufacture (lead; copper after 1804; and, after 1847, tinplate, which came to dominate the local economy). It also became a port for the anthracite coalfield. Gradually these industrial interests have declined. The docks were closed in 1951, and the old tinplate mills were all closed. Afterward, however, the large new cold-reduction mill at Trostre, using steel strip from Port Talbot, made Llanelli one of the three present-day centres of the South Wales tinplate industry. The town also has a small steel fabrication industry. Pop. (1991) 44,953.

Llanelli, district and borough, Dyfed county, Wales. It was created in 1974 and covers rolling hills and coastline along Carmarthen Bay. It is bordered by the districts of Carmarthen and Dinefwr to the north and by the Lliw Valley to the west and south. Near the western edge of the district lies Kidwelly, one of the oldest boroughs (established 1115) in Wales. Its castle was built by Roger of Salisbury in 1106 as one of a network of strongholds to maintain Norman control of South Wales. Kidwelly manufactures optical glass and silica bricks. The coastal town of Burry Port, primarily a yachting centre, once exported coal. The first seaplane to cross the Atlantic Ocean, piloted by Amelia Earhart, landed in Burry Port. A power station was recently built there, and in 1980 Country Park opened at Pembrey. The district and borough were dissolved in 1996 when the region became part of the county of Carmarthenshire.

Llanelwy (Wales): *see* Saint Asaph.

Llangefni, town, seat of Ynys Môn district, Gwynedd county, Wales. Situated on the River Cefni almost in the middle of the Isle of Anglesey, the town originated as a market centre for the agricultural activity on the island. The Moriah Calvinistic Methodist Church, one of the town's several Nonconformist churches, commemorates John Elias (1774–1841), a well-known pulpit orator of the Welsh Methodist Revival who fled to Llangefni when forced to take refuge from an angry mob in Beaumaris. Llangefni has remained a bustling market centre, and livestock are brought from all over the island for trading every Wednesday and Thursday. Industry consists mostly of the manufacture of agricultural implements. The road from Holyhead to Bangor passes just south of Llangefni. Pop. (1991) 4,643.

Llangollen, market town, Glyndŵr district, Clwyd county, Wales, in the valley of the River Dee. It is the home of the international musical eisteddfod (Welsh festival of the arts) founded in 1946 to promote international goodwill, and it also has a thriving tourist trade, located as it is on a main route into the North Wales mountains. Historic local features include Valle Crucis Abbey (established AD 1200), Eliseg's Pillar (a remarkable 9th-century stone cross), Castell-Dinas-Bran (a 13th-century Welsh prince's stronghold gateway), and a 14th-century bridge across the Dee. Pop. (1991) 3,267.

Llanilltud Fawr (Wales): *see* Llantwit Major.

Llano Estacado, also called STAKED PLAINS, portion of the High Plains of the United States, along the Texas–New Mexico border. It covers an area of about 30,000 square miles (78,000 square km) and is bounded by the Canadian River valley (north), the "break of the plains" (east), the Edwards Plateau (south), and the Mescalero Ridge overlooking the Pecos River (west). Strikingly level in appearance and averaging 3,000–4,000 feet (900–1,200 m) above sea level, the semiarid plain is occasionally broken by localized water-retaining depressions. Its potentially fertile soils, though handicapped by meagre rainfall, high evaporation rates, and periodic droughts, support grazing, dry-land farming of wheat and grain sorghums, and irrigated cotton production. Production of petroleum and natural gas is also important. Lubbock and Amarillo, Tex., are the most important cities in the region; but a less than salubrious climate and isolation combine to restrict population growth.

Llanos (Spanish: "Plains"), wide grasslands stretching across northern South America and occupying western Venezuela and northeastern Colombia. The Llanos has an area of approximately 220,000 square miles (570,000 square km) and is delimited by the Andes Mountains to the north and west, the Guaviare River and the Amazon River basin to the south, and the lower Orinoco River and the Guiana Highlands to the east.

The elevations of the Llanos rarely exceed 1,000 feet (300 m) and rise from the Llanos Bajos ("Low Plains") west of the Orinoco River to the Llanos Altos ("High Plains") below the Andes. The Llanos Altos form extensive platforms between rivers and rise 100 to 200 feet (30 to 60 m) above the valley floors. The Llanos is drained by the Orinoco and its western tributaries, including the Guaviare, Meta, and Apure rivers. Annual precipitation is concentrated between April and November and ranges from 45 inches (1,100 mm) in Ciudad de Nutrias in the central plains to 180 inches (4,570 mm) in Villavicencio near the Andes. Mean daily temperatures in the Llanos exceed 75° F (24° C) throughout the year.

Most of the Llanos is treeless savanna that is covered with swamp grasses and sedges in the low-lying areas and with long-stemmed and carpet grasses in the drier areas. Trees are concentrated along rivers and in the Andean piedmont; trees scattered on the open savanna include scrub oak and dwarf palm. Various birds and burrowing rodents are the only wildlife indigenous to the savanna. Most mammals nest in the gallery forests and feed on the grassland; among these are included several species of deer and rabbit, as well as anteater, armadillo, tapir, jaguar, and capybara, which is the world's largest living rodent.

The raising of cattle has long been the mainstay of the Llanos' economy, since Spanish colonial days. Since the 1950s there has also been considerable small farming. The economic importance of the region has been greatly enhanced by the oil fields in the Venezuelan Llanos at El Tigre and Barinas.

Llanquihue, Lake, Spanish LAGO LLANQUIHUE, lake in Llanquihue and Osorno *provincias,* Los Lagos *región,* southern Chile. The largest and, with neighbouring Todos los Santos, the best known of Chilean lakes, Llanquihue has an area of about 330 square miles (860 square km) and is 22 miles (35 km) long and 25 miles (40 km) wide with depths of 5,000 feet (1,500 m). Its western shores are bordered by farmlands; to the east rise forested Andean foothills. In the distance stand the snowcapped volcanoes Osorno and Calbuco, and beyond them on the Argentine border towers the great, glaciated Mount Tronador (11,660 feet [3,554 m]). The setting of the lake and good fishing have made the lakeside towns, especially Puerto Varas, Llanquihue, and Puerto Octay, popular resorts. Sawmills and a beet-sugar factory are also on its shores. Its outlet is the Maullín River, which flows into the Pacific Ocean.

Llantrisant, town, Taft-Ely district, Mid Glamorgan county, Wales. Situated on a ridge between two steep hills overlooking the Ely River valley and the Vale of Glamorgan, Llantrisant ("Church of Three Saints") takes its name from the saints Illtyd, Gwyno, and Dyfod, to whom the village church is dedicated. Iron Age settlement is evidenced by the well-preserved ramparts of the hill-fort Caerau, located to the east of the community. The Normans ousted the community's native Welsh ruler and built a castle there about 1245; England's King Edward II and Hugh Despenser were held in the castle in 1326 after being betrayed by a monk of Neath Abbey. During the 18th and 19th centuries, Llantrisant's importance was overshadowed by the mining and industrial communities to the north, but as the coal industry declined, there was a general drift of population away from the northern valleys to the newly created industry in villages and towns in the south. Government-funded building and industry provided new employment opportunities in Llantrisant, and development was greatly aided by the transfer of the Royal Mint from Tower Hill, London, to Llantrisant in 1967. The M4 Motorway extends through the region from Cardiff to Port Talbot and connects Llantrisant with other industrially developing areas in what has been called an emerging "linear city." Pop. (1991) 9,136.

Llantwit Major, Welsh LLANILLTUD FAWR, town, Vale of Glamorgan district, South Glamorgan county, Wales. Prehistoric and Roman remains have been discovered in and near the town. Its medieval importance lay in its monastic college (founded *c.* AD 500 by the Celtic St. Illtud), which was a famous centre of learning and of ecclesiastical influence for the Celtic church. The monastery was eventually closed at the Dissolution (1536–39), having by then become a cell of Tewkesbury Abbey, but its gatehouse and dovecote remain. The parish church dates from the 12th and 15th centuries and the town hall from the 15th. Llantwit Major is now a shopping centre and a resort, as well as a residential community for commuters to a nearby air base and to industrial towns such as Barry and Bridgend. Pop. (1991) 12,909.

Llanvirn Series, sequence of Ordovician rocks first studied in North Wales (the Ordovician Period lasted from 505 to 438 million years ago). The Llanvirn precedes the Llandeilo Series and follows the Arenig Series. In the type region, the Llanvirn consists of approximately 760 m (2,500 feet) of mudstones and shales, as well as volcanic lavas and tuffs. Two Llanvirn graptolite fossil zones, shorter spans of time, are generally recognized: a lower zone of the species *Didymograptus bifudus* and an upper zone of *D. murchisoni.* Rocks correlated with the Llanvirn of Wales have a worldwide distribution. In the Baltic region, shales predominate and zonation has been achieved with both trilobites (extinct marine arthropods) and graptolites. Important Llanvirn sequences are known from eastern Europe, northern Africa, China, Australia and New Zealand, and South America. Different regional names are applied to rocks that have been correlated with the Llanvirn in these areas.

Llewelyn, also spelled LLEWELLYN (Welsh name): *see under* Llywelyn, except as below.

Llewellyn, Richard, byname of RICHARD DAFYDD VIVIAN LLEWELLYN LLOYD (b. Dec. 8, 1906, St. David's, Pembrokeshire, Wales—d. Nov. 30, 1983, Dublin, Ire.), Welsh novelist and playwright, known especially for *How Green Was My Valley* (1939; filmed 1941), a best-selling novel about a Welsh mining family. It was followed by *Up, Into the Singing Mountain* (1960), *And I Shall Sleep . . . Down Where the Moon Is Small* (1966), and *Green, Green My Valley Now* (1975).

Educated in Wales and London, Llewellyn went to Italy to learn hotel management but began working in the motion-picture industry in various capacities. After a time in the army, more film work, and some journalism, he wrote two successful mystery plays, *Poison Pen* (1938) and *Noose* (1947). Among his other novels are *None But the Lonely Heart* (1943; filmed 1944) and *A Few Flowers for Shiner* (1950). *A Night of Bright Stars* (1979), Llewellyn's 20th novel, is a fictionalized account of the Brazilian aeronautic pioneer Alberto Santos Dumont.

Llivia, town and enclave of Spanish territory in the French *département* of Pyrénées-Orientales, administratively part of the Spanish Catalan province of Gerona. The Roman Julia Livia, it lay within the ancient district of Cerdagne, or Cerdaña (*q.v.*) (the upper basin of the Río Segre), of which it was capital until 1177. In 1659, by the Treaty of the Pyrenees, 33 Cerdagne villages were ceded to France, and the political enclave was created with a neutral road across French territory to Puigcerdá, a Spanish fortified town. Notorious during the 17th and 18th centuries as a smuggling centre, it now trades in agricultural products. Pop. (1999 est.) 961.

Lliw Valley, district, West Glamorgan County, Wales. It was created in 1974, covers an area of 82 sq mi (214 sq km), and extends from the River Tawe in the east to the Loughor River Estuary in the west, reaching into the foothills of the Black Mountains in the north. Lliw Valley district borders the districts of Llanelli to the west, Dinefwr and Brecknock to the north, Neath to the east, and Swansea to the south. Loughor, situated on the River Loughor at the southern end of the valley, was first settled by the Romans as a military station known as *Leucarum.* The Normans also recognized the strategic value of the river crossing; there they built a castle, which was destroyed by the Welsh prince Gruffydd ap Rhys in 1115 (rebuilt 1215). Pontardulais, on the western edge of the district, was the centre of the bloody Rebecca Riots during the agrarian troubles of the 1840s.

Most of the towns and villages in the area grew up around the collieries and foundries established in South Wales during the 18th and 19th centuries. The area continues to be dominated by its metallurgical industries; one of the largest nickel refineries in the world is located at Clydach. In recent years attempts have been made to diversify both industry and agriculture. Gorseinon, with a newly developed magnetic tape industry, and Pontardawe are the chief population centres and function mainly as residential settlements for workers who commute to nearby Swansea. The district ceased to exist in 1996 when it was divided between the county of Swansea and the county borough of Neath Port Talbot.

Lloyd, Harold (b. April 20, 1893, Burchard, Neb., U.S.—d. March 8, 1971, Hollywood), U.S. motion-picture comedian who was the highest paid star of the 1920s and one of the cinema's most popular personalities.

The son of an itinerant commercial photographer, Lloyd finally settled in San Diego, Calif., where in 1913 he started playing minor parts in one-reel comedies. He mastered the art of the comic chase in the short time he was a member of Mack Sennett's Keystone comedy troupe. In 1915 Lloyd joined the new acting company formed by Hal Roach, a former actor who had turned producer. During this period he experimented with a comic character, the bewhiskered Willie Work. The most consistently successful of his early films, however, were those of the Lonesome Luke series. Beginning with *Just Nuts* (1915), Luke quickly became a popular U.S. screen character.

By 1918 the figure of the ordinary white-faced man in round glasses had replaced Luke as Lloyd's screen trademark. He developed his humour from plot and situation and was the first comedian to use physical danger as a source of laughter. Lloyd performed his own stunts and was known as the screen's most daring comedian. In *Safety Last* (1923), an outstanding success, he hung from the hands of a clock several stories above a city street; in *Girl Shy* (1924) he took a thrilling ride atop a runaway streetcar; in *The Freshman* (1925), one of the most successful of all silent pictures, he stood in for the football tackling dummy.

Lloyd's peak of popularity was reached during the period of silent films, when emphasis was on visual rather than verbal humour, although he made many films after the coming of sound. His last was *Mad Wednesday* (1947). He was honoured with a special Academy Award in 1952 for his contribution to motion-picture comedy. In 1962 Lloyd released *Harold Lloyd's World of Comedy,* a compilation of scenes from his old movies, and *Harold Lloyd's Funny Side of Life.* The reception given to both demonstrated the timelessness of Lloyd's silent comedy. Adam Reilly's *Harold Lloyd: The King of Daredevil Comedy* (1977) includes a filmography and interpretative essays by five critics.

Lloyd, Henry Demarest (b. May 1, 1847, New York City—d. Sept. 28, 1903, Chicago), U.S. journalist whose exposés of the abuses of industrial monopolies are classics of muckraking journalism.

Lloyd was educated at Columbia College and admitted to the bar in 1869. After reform activity in New York City, in 1872 he joined the staff of the *Chicago Tribune,* where he worked for 13 years at the literary, financial, and editorial desks. "The Story of a Great Monopoly," his documented study of methods used by the Standard Oil Company and the railroads to eliminate competitors, had a sensational effect when it appeared in *The Atlantic Monthly* (March 1881). It alerted the public to the need for antitrust legislation and served as a model for the new genre of muckraking journalism. His attack on monopolies was later expanded into his most important book, *Wealth Against Commonwealth* (1894).

Henry Demarest Lloyd
By courtesy of the Library of Congress, Washington, D.C.

After 1885 Lloyd devoted full time to public affairs as a supporter of free trade and of the rights of labour and of the consumer. In the 1890s he visited Europe and New Zealand to study social experiments, chiefly in the area of the reconciliation of industrial conflicts. Defeated in 1894 as a congressional candidate of the independent National People's Party, he withdrew from active politics but supported the Socialists.

Lloyd, Marie, original name MATILDA ALICE VICTORIA WOOD (b. Feb. 12, 1870, London—d. Oct. 7, 1922, London), foremost English music-hall artiste of the late 19th century, who became well known in the London, or Cockney, low comedy then popular. She first appeared in 1885 at the Eagle Music Hall under the name Bella Delmare. Six weeks later she adopted her stage name.

T.S. Eliot wrote that her deep popular appeal stemmed from her ability to capture and express the spirit of the English common people. In her songs and sketches she introduced to the public a series of studies in Cockney humour, sympathetic to the little man and often risqué. Her best acts included "Everything in the Garden's Lovely," "Oh, Mr. Porter," and "One of the Ruins that Cromwell Knocked About a Bit."

Marie Lloyd
By courtesy of the Victoria and Albert Museum, London

Lloyd, (John) Selwyn (Brooke), also called (1976–78) JOHN SELWYN BROOKE SELWYN-LLOYD, BARON SELWYN-LLOYD OF WIRRAL (b. July 28, 1904, Liverpool—d. May 17, 1978, Preston Crowmarsh, Oxfordshire, Eng.), British Conservative politician who was foreign secretary during Britain's diplomatic humiliation in the Suez crisis of 1956 and later chancellor of the exchequer under Prime Minister Harold Macmillan.

Lloyd studied law at Cambridge and was called to the bar in 1930. After World War II army service, he was elected to the House of Commons, in which he served from 1945 to 1976. An effective parliamentarian, he became known as one of the "Young Turks" of the Conservative Party. When his party returned to power in 1951, Lloyd became minister of state for foreign affairs. After short terms as minister of supply (1954–55) and minister of defense (1955), he became foreign secretary (1955–60). During that term the invasion of Egypt was undertaken by Prime Minister Anthony Eden (October 1956) in alliance with France, following the Egyptian seizure of the Suez Canal. Soviet and U.S. opposition to this move soon led to a United Nations-conducted cease-fire and withdrawal of troops. Because of these events and his own ill health, Eden resigned in late 1956; Lloyd, however, was retained in his post by Harold Macmillan, the new prime minister.

In July 1960 Lloyd was appointed chancellor of the exchequer but soon proved unable to cope with inflation and balance of payments difficulties, and in July 1962 he was purged along with other senior Cabinet members. Lloyd rejected an offer of a peerage and took his place as a Conservative backbencher in the Commons. In 1963 he joined the Cabinet of the new prime minister, Sir Alec Douglas-Home, as lord privy seal, serving until 1964, when his party was defeated. With the Conservative victory in 1970, Lloyd was elected speaker of the House of Commons, a post he held until he accepted a life peerage as Baron Selwyn-Lloyd in 1976. He was the author of *Mr. Speaker, Sir* (1976).

Lloyd George, David, also called (1945) 1ST EARL LLOYD-GEORGE OF DWYFOR, VISCOUNT GWYNEDD OF DWYFOR (b. Jan.

17, 1863, Manchester—d. March 26, 1945, Ty-newydd, near Llanystumdwy, Caernarvonshire, Wales), British prime minister (1916–22) who dominated the British political scene in the latter part of World War I. He was raised to the peerage in the year of his death.

Early life. Lloyd George's father was a Welshman from Pembrokeshire and had be-

Lloyd George, 1908
EB Inc.

come headmaster of an elementary school in Manchester. His mother was the daughter of David Lloyd, a Baptist minister. His father died in June 1864, leaving Mrs. George in poverty. She moved to Llanystumdwy in Caernarvonshire, where her brother Richard, a shoemaker and Baptist minister, supported her and her children; and it was from him that David Lloyd George imbibed many of his formative beliefs. His uncle enabled him to embark at the age of 14 on the career of a solicitor; he became articled (1879) to a firm at Portmadoc, passing his final examination in 1884. In Wales, as in Ireland, an anglicized and Anglican Tory "ascendancy" class of landed gentry dominated a Celtic people of different race and religion. The causes of the Liberal Party, the Welsh nation, and Nonconformity were inseparable in the atmosphere in which Lloyd George was raised, and he first made his name by a successful battle in the courts to establish the right of Nonconformists to burial in the churchyard of their parish. Ironically, he who came to be the standard-bearer of the oppressed religious sects had lost his faith even as a boy.

As a young man, Lloyd George had the romantic good looks that ensured success with women. After numerous love affairs, he was married in 1888 to Margaret Owen, who bore him two sons and three daughters. The marriage cannot be described as happy. Lloyd George was incapable of fidelity, and his affairs with other women were notorious. His wife stood by him on many occasions, but in the end his behaviour was too much for even her long-suffering tolerance.

Lloyd George entered Parliament in 1890, winning a by-election at Caernarvon Boroughs, the seat he retained for 55 years. He soon made a name for himself in the House of Commons by his audacity, charm, wit, and mastery of the art of debate. During the 10 years of Liberal opposition that followed the election of 1895, he became a leading figure in the radical wing of the party. He bitterly and courageously opposed the South African War and in 1901 was nearly lynched in Birmingham, the stronghold of Joseph Chamberlain and Conservative imperialism. With the arrival of peace, Lloyd George worked up a great agitation in Wales against tax-aided grants to church schools established by Balfour's Education Act (1902).

Arthur J. Balfour resigned in December 1905, and Sir Henry Campbell-Bannerman formed a Liberal administration, appointing Lloyd George to the Cabinet as president of the Board of Trade. In that office, he was responsible for important legislation: the Merchant Shipping Act (1906), improving seamen's living conditions, but also endangering their lives by raising the Plimsoll line on newly constructed ships; the Patents and Designs Act (1907), preventing foreign exploitation of British inventions; and the Port of London Act (1908), setting up the Port of London Authority. He also earned a high reputation by his patient work in settling strikes. He suffered a cruel bereavement in November 1907, when his daughter Mair died of appendicitis at the age of 17. Years afterward, the sight of her portrait could plunge him into tears.

Chancellor of the Exchequer. Campbell-Bannerman's health failed in 1908. He was succeeded as prime minister by the chancellor of the Exchequer, Herbert Henry Asquith, who appointed Lloyd George to take his own place. This was a notable promotion and made him at least a strong competitor for the premiership after Asquith. By this time, the Liberal Party's fortunes were beginning to languish. The House of Lords had blocked much of its social reform legislation, and the radical wing of the party was concerned that its thunder might be stolen by the nascent Labour Party unless the deadlock could be broken. At the same time, the demand for more battleships to match the German naval program threatened the finances available for social reform. It was to meet these difficulties that Lloyd George framed the famous "People's Budget" of 1909, calling for taxes upon unearned increment on the sale of land and on land values, higher death duties, and a supertax on incomes above £3,000. Moreover, it seemed for a time that the House of Lords' veto on progressive legislation would be bypassed, since the custom of the constitution forbade the upper house from interfering with the budget. In fact, however, the Conservative majority in the House of Lords, against the advice of some of its wiser members, decided to reject it. The consequences of this rejection were two general elections, a major constitutional crisis, and the ultimate passage of the Parliament Act of 1911, which severely curtailed the powers of the upper house. The principal burden of all this fell upon Asquith, but Lloyd George gave him vigorous support in a series of notable philippics against the aristocracy and the rich. The most famous of all was his speech at Limehouse, where he denounced the rapacity of the landlord class, especially the dukes, in unforgettable language.

In 1913 he faced one of the gravest personal crises in his career. In April 1912, along with Rufus Isaacs, the attorney general, he had purchased shares in the Marconi Wireless Telegraph Company of America at a rate well below that available to the general public. The American Marconi company was legally independent of the British concern, but the two companies were closely connected, and the latter's shares had recently boomed as a result of the government's decision to accept its proposal to construct a chain of radio stations throughout the empire. Lloyd George and Isaacs denied, in somewhat ambiguous language, any transactions in the shares of "the Marconi company," a denial that technically referred only to the British company but was generally assumed to cover the American as well. A select committee of the House of Commons revealed the facts and, although by a party majority it acquitted the ministers of blame, Lloyd George's reputation was damaged.

Social reform and the outbreak of war. Lloyd George's major achievement during the years immediately before the war was in the field of social insurance. Inspired by a visit to Germany (1908), where he studied the Bismarckian scheme of insurance benefits, Lloyd George decided to introduce health and unemployment insurance on a similar basis in Britain. This he did in the National Insurance Act of 1911. The measure inspired bitter opposition and was even unpopular with the working class, who were not convinced by Lloyd George's slogan "ninepence for fourpence," the difference in these two figures being the employer's and the state's contribution. Lloyd George, undeterred, piloted his measure through Parliament with great skill and determination. He thus laid the foundations of the modern welfare state and, if he had done nothing else, would deserve fame for that achievement.

Though much of the government's time during these years was occupied by the Irish question, Lloyd George played little part in it and, on the whole, left foreign policy to his colleagues. It was, therefore, something of a surprise when, in July 1911, after careful consultation with Asquith and Sir Edward Grey, he issued a formidable warning to Germany over the Moroccan crisis. When the question of entry into the war convulsed the Cabinet in late July and early August 1914, he seemed at first to incline to the isolationist section. For a brief moment he contemplated retirement. But the tide of events swept him to the other side. As chancellor, he plunged into the financial problems posed by the war.

Minister of munitions and secretary of state for war. Throughout the remainder of 1914 and the early months of 1915, Lloyd George was a vigorous advocate of increased munitions production. Here he came into sharp conflict with Lord Kitchener in the War Office. The resignation of Admiral Fisher in 1915 forced Asquith to reconstruct the government on a coalition basis and admit the Conservatives. In the new administration, Lloyd George became minister of munitions. In this capacity, he made one of the most notable contributions to the victory of the Allies. His methods were unorthodox and shocked the civil service, but his energy was immense. He imported able assistants from big business and used his eloquence to induce the cooperation of organized labour. When, in the summer of 1916, the great Battle of the Somme began, supplies were forthcoming.

Lloyd George acquired definite views on war strategy at an early stage. He doubted the possibility of breaking through on the Western Front and advocated instead a flank attack from the Near East. He was thus at loggerheads with the view of the official military hierarchy, cogently pressed by Sir Douglas Haig and Sir William Robertson, that the war could only be won in the West. On June 5, 1916, Kitchener was drowned on his way to Russia, when his ship struck a German mine. A last-minute accident—acute developments in the Irish situation—alone had prevented Lloyd George from travelling with him. After some hesitation, Asquith appointed him to the vacant position at the War Office.

Lloyd George held the post for five months, but Robertson as chief of the imperial general staff possessed nearly all the important powers of the war minister. Lloyd George chafed under these restrictions, the more so because he disagreed with Robertson on issues of strategy. Thus frustrated, he began to survey the whole direction of the war with increasing skepticism; and he did not conceal his doubts from his friends who, by the end of November, had become convinced that Asquith should delegate the day-to-day running of the war to a small committee whose chairman should be Lloyd George. There was undoubtedly widespread uneasiness at Asquith's conduct of affairs, particularly in the Conservative Party. Asquith was manoeuvred into resigning on

December 5 and was replaced two days later by Lloyd George. He was supported by the leading Conservatives, but the most prominent Liberal ministers resigned with Asquith.

Prime minister. Lloyd George was now 54 and at the height of his powers. His energy, eloquence, and ability had already made him the leading statesman of the day, and his accession to the premiership was highly popular in the country generally. He immediately substituted a small War Cabinet of five, which was to be in constant session, for the body of 23 that had hitherto conducted affairs. The result was a general speeding up of decisions.

One of Lloyd George's most notable efforts was in combating the submarine menace, which, in early 1917, threatened to starve Britain into submission. He achieved this by forcing the adoption of the convoy system upon a reluctant Admiralty. The food shortage resulting from the submarine war was acute. Drastic action had to be taken to step up agricultural production, and eventually a system of food rationing had to be introduced (1918). In these matters Lloyd George was at his best, contemptuous of red tape, determined to take action and to make his will prevail.

It was in the field of grand strategy that he was least successful. Lloyd George remained profoundly skeptical of the ability of the British high command to conduct even a "Western" strategy successfully. Without warning Haig or Robertson in advance, he confronted them at the Calais Conference of February 1917 with a plan to place the British army under French command for General Robert-Georges Nivelle's forthcoming offensive. Haig and Robertson deeply distrusted Lloyd George from that moment onward. The Nivelle offensive was a total failure, and Lloyd George was, as a result, on shaky ground when he endeavoured to resist Haig's proposals for a major British campaign in Flanders in the summer. After much hesitation, he gave way, and on July 31, 1917, the ill-fated Passchendaele offensive began. Although it may have forestalled a possible German attack on the French, Passchendaele, with enormous loss of life, achieved none of its main objectives. Lloyd George was now convinced of the incompetence of the British high command.

He still dared not take action against them openly. Instead, he began what Sir Winston Churchill called "a series of extremely laborious and mystifying maneuvers," with the object of creating a unified command under someone other than Haig. In February 1918 Robertson offered his resignation, which Lloyd George accepted, but Haig remained as commander in chief. Such was Lloyd George's distrust of Haig that, during the winter of 1917–18, he had deliberately kept him short of troops for fear that he might renew the attack. The result was that the German commander, General Erich Ludendorff, came near to launching a successful offensive against the British sector in March 1918. The emergency caused a unified command under Marshal Ferdinand Foch to be established (April), and by May the situation had stabilized.

The tide now turned, and the Western Allies launched a series of successful attacks upon the exhausted Germans. The Armistice of November 1918 presented Lloyd George with a dilemma. Should he allow a return to peacetime party politics or continue the coalition? There was little doubt of the answer. The leader of the Conservatives, Bonar Law, was willing to cooperate. A somewhat perfunctory offer to include Asquith was declined. The ensuing election in December gave the coalitionists an overwhelming victory. The rift between Lloyd George and Asquith's supporters was now wider than ever, however, and Lloyd George was now largely dependent on Conservative support.

As one of the three chief statesmen at Versailles, Lloyd George must bear a major responsibility for the peace settlement. He pursued a middle course between Georges Clemenceau and Woodrow Wilson. But, throughout, Lloyd George was under pressure to pursue the more draconian policy of Clemenceau. It is to his credit that the final settlement was not far worse than it was. The treaty was well received in Britain, and in August 1919 the king conferred on Lloyd George the Order of Merit.

A major domestic problem was Ireland, where the Sinn Fein refused to recognize the British Parliament. From 1919 to 1921 a civil war raged. In the summer of 1921, Lloyd George, with full agreement of his Conservative colleagues, reversed the policy of repression in Ireland and began the negotiations that culminated in Irish independence in December 1921. The more rigid Tories never forgave this "surrender," as they deemed it. In 1922 Lloyd George ran into trouble over the so-called honours scandal, when accusations were made that peerages and other honours were being sold for large campaign contributions. Tory discontent was rife, when a crisis occurred that drove Lloyd George from power forever. This was the Çanak incident, in which it seemed to critics that the reckless foreign policy of the government had led Britain to the verge of an unnecessary war with Turkey. When the Conservative leaders decided to appeal to the country on a coalition basis once again, a party revolt ensued. Bonar Law, who had retired because of ill health in 1921, returned to the political scene. On Oct. 19, 1922, a two-to-one majority of Conservative members of Parliament endorsed his and Stanley Baldwin's plea to fight as an independent party. Lloyd George at once resigned.

Later years and assessment. The long twilight of Lloyd George's career was a melancholy anticlimax. The feud with the Asquithians was never healed, and from 1926 to 1931 he headed an ailing Liberal Party. He devoted himself thereafter to writing his *War Memoirs* (1933–36) and *The Truth About the Peace Treaties* (1938). In 1940 Winston Churchill invited him to join his War Cabinet, but Lloyd George declined, ostensibly on grounds of age and health. Just two months before his death, he was elevated to the peerage as Earl Lloyd-George of Dwyfor.

Lloyd George possessed eloquence, extraordinary charm and persuasiveness, a capacity to see the heart of problems whose complexity baffled lesser men, a profound sympathy with oppressed classes and races, and a genuine hatred of those who abused power, whether based on wealth or caste or military might. But there was an obverse side to these virtues: his love of devious methods, his carelessness over appointments and honours, and a streak of ruthlessness that left little room for the cultivation of personal friendship.

Lloyd George, for all his greatness, aroused in many persons a profound sense of mistrust, and it was in the upper-middle class, represented in politics by Stanley Baldwin and Neville Chamberlain, that he inspired the most acute misgivings. They were both determined to exclude him from office, and it would be wrong to ascribe his long years in the political wilderness solely to the declining fortunes of the Liberal Party. Lloyd George was thus never able to recover the position he had lost in 1922. It was one of the tragedies of the interwar years that, in an era not notable for political talent, the one man of genius in politics should have had to remain a spectator. But his earlier achievements make his place in history secure: he laid the foundations of the welfare state and led Britain to victory in World War I. (B.)

BIBLIOGRAPHY. Biographical studies include Albert J. Sylvester, *The Real Lloyd George* (1947); Thomas Jones, *Lloyd George* (1951); Frank Owen, *Tempestuous Journey: Lloyd George, His Life and Times* (1954); and John Grigg, *The Young Lloyd George* (1973), *Lloyd George: The People's Champion, 1902–1911* (1978), and *Lloyd George: From Peace to War, 1912–1916* (1985).

Lloyd Webber, Sir Andrew (b. March 22, 1948, London, Eng.), English composer whose eclectic rock-based works helped revitalize British and American musical theatre in the late 20th century.

Lloyd Webber studied at Magdalen College, Oxford, and at the Royal College of Music. While a student he began collaborating with Timothy Rice, who wrote the lyrics to Lloyd Webber's music. Their first notable venture was *Joseph and the Amazing Technicolor Dreamcoat* (1968), a pop oratorio for children that earned worldwide popularity in a later full-length version. It was followed by the rock opera *Jesus Christ Superstar* (1971), a popular though controversial work that blended classical forms with rock music to tell the story of Jesus' life. This show was one of the longest-running musicals in British theatrical history. Lloyd Webber's last major collaboration with Rice was on *Evita* (1978), a musical about Eva Perón, the wife of the Argentine dictator Juan Perón.

In his next major musical, *Cats* (1981), Lloyd Webber set to music verses from a children's book by T.S. Eliot. *Cats* became the longest-running musical in the history of British theatre, and in 1997 the Broadway production of the play eclipsed the record set by *A Chorus Line* to become the longest-running show ever on Broadway; on Sept. 10, 2000, *Cats* closed after 7,485 performances. With lyricists Charles Hart and Richard Stilgoe, Lloyd Webber then composed a hugely popular musical version of *The Phantom of the Opera* (1986). His other musicals included *Song and Dance* (1982), *Starlight Express* (1984), and *Aspects of Love* (1989). He was knighted in 1992.

Lloyd Webber's best musicals were flashy spectacles that featured vivid melodies and forceful and dramatic staging. He was able to blend such disparate genres as rock and roll, English music-hall song, and operatic forms into music that had a wide popular appeal.

Lloyds Bank, one of the largest comprehensive commercial banks in the United Kingdom, with subsidiary banks in other countries. It is also a major insurance company. It is headquartered in London.

The bank was established as Taylor and Lloyd in 1765 and renamed Lloyds and Company in 1853. With the amalgamation of Moilliet and Sons in 1865, the firm was incorporated as Lloyds Banking Company Ltd., a joint-stock company. Since 1865 the bank has absorbed more than 50 other banks. It adopted the name Lloyds Bank Ltd. in 1889. In 1995 Lloyds merged with TSB to create the present company, Lloyds TSB Group PLC.

In 1973 Lloyds Bank acquired practically all of the stock of Lloyds and BOLSA International Bank, Ltd. BOLSA (Bank of London and South America) had been formed in 1923 with the merger of two Latin-American banks. BOLSA had acquired the business of the Anglo-South American Bank in 1936, giving it interests in France, Spain, and Portugal as well as in most Latin-American countries. During the next few years Lloyds further expanded its geographic base; in the early 21st century, 20 percent of its sales were outside the United Kingdom.

Lloyd's of London, formally CORPORATION OF LLOYD'S, international insurance marketing association in London, consisting of more than 20,000 individual underwriting members who accept insurance for their own account and risk. The corporation—which provides generally high-risk, specialized marine, automobile, aviation, and nonmarine insurance services—sets strict financial rules and other regulations but does not itself assume liability.

The members are formed into several hundred syndicates, each comprising from a few to several hundred members. These syndicates are represented at Lloyd's by underwriting agents, and it is they who accept insurance business on behalf of the syndicate members. The syndicate system was developed to handle the greatly increased insured values of the 20th century, for it permits an insurance risk

The market floor with galleries above in Lloyd's Building, London

Jonathan Player—*The New York Times*

to be spread over a number of individuals; when a claim is made, each underwriter is responsible only for his portion of it. Syndicate members who do not underwrite personally are known as "names." Traditionally, names had unlimited personal liability for the business transacted for them by their underwriting agents. After record losses in the late 1980s and early '90s bankrupted some names and hurt many others, this policy was modified. From 1993, personal losses were limited to 80 percent of a name's total permitted annual premium income over a period of four years. Losses exceeding the limit would be paid from a pool funded by an annual levy on all names. That same year Lloyd's voted to allow corporate and institutional investors to participate in its underwriting business for the first time.

Lloyd's history traces to 1688, when Edward Lloyd kept a coffeehouse in Tower Street (or, from 1692, in Lombard Street). There, merchants, bankers, and seafarers assembled to transact business informally. It also became a popular meeting place for underwriters—those who would accept insurance on ships for the payment of a premium. In 1696, for a short period, Edward Lloyd published *Lloyd's News,* giving news of shipping movements and other matters of interest; this was the forerunner of *Lloyd's List,* first published in 1734.

Gradually, the underwriters at Lloyd's formed an association and, in 1774, moved their operations to the royal exchange. In 1928 Lloyd's moved to Leadenhall Street and, in 1957, to a new building in Lime Street. In 1986 Lloyd's moved to a new building adjoining Leadenhall Market; the new Lloyd's Building was a dramatic structure with a soaring interior atrium.

In 1871 control over the affairs of the association by its committee was consolidated by an act of incorporation (Lloyd's Act, 1871), which gave it the power to make its own bylaws, to acquire real and personal property, and to perform all acts in its corporate name. By the act of 1871 the association was restricted to marine insurance, but by an act of 1911 it was empowered to carry on insurance of every description. Following a series of financial scandals in the late 1970s and early '80s, Parliament passed a new constitution (Lloyd's Act, 1982) to replace the original act. To avoid the conflict of interests, the newer act regulated the amount of interest that a broker may have in an underwriter. It also established a formal governing body to write and amend bylaws and to set up a disciplinary committee and an internal appeals court.

Lloyd's Register of Shipping, world's first and largest ship-classification society, begun in 1760 as a registry for ships likely to be insured by marine insurance underwriters meeting at Lloyd's coffeehouse in London. It is concerned with the establishment of construction and maintenance standards for merchant ships and the provision of a technical service to assist owners in maintaining such standards. Its *Register Book,* begun in 1764, is issued annually and lists all merchant ships of 100 or more tons gross. The society also publishes yacht registers and statistical summaries on shipbuilding, fleets, and marine casualties.

Llull, Ramon, also called RAYMOND LULLY (b. 1232/33, Ciutat de Majorca [now Palma]?, Majorca [now in Spain]—d. 1315/16, Tunis or near Majorca), Catalan mystic and poet whose writings helped to develop the Romance Catalan language and widely influenced Neoplatonic mysticism throughout medieval and 17th-century Europe. He is best known in the history of ideas as the inventor of an "art of finding truth" (*ars inveniendi veritatis*) that was primarily intended to support the Roman Catholic faith in missionary work but was also designed to unify all branches of knowledge.

Reared at the royal court of Majorca, Llull developed characteristics of a troubadour in his chivalrous upbringing. He wrote a manual of chivalry, which appeared in a 15th-century English version edited by William Caxton, the first English printer. From the large Moorish population in Majorca he acquired a knowledge of Arabic, which he used in some of his writings. His milieu also aroused in him an interest in Islāmic Ṣūfī mysticism and the Eastern contemplative spirit.

Having married, Llull at about the age of 30 experienced mystical visions of Christ on the Cross, after which he abandoned courtly life and devoted himself to missionary work. Influenced by the pacifist spirituality of Francis of Assisi, he traveled throughout North Africa and Asia Minor attempting to convert Muslims to Christianity.

About 1272, after another mystical experience on Majorca's Mount Randa in which Llull related seeing the whole universe reflecting the divine attributes, he conceived of reducing all knowledge to first principles and determining their convergent point of unity. Borrowing certain tenets from the 11th-century Scholastic theologian Anselm of Canterbury, he wrote his principal work; this is collectively known as the *Ars magna* (1305–08; "The Great Art") and includes the treatises *Arbor scientiae* ("The Tree of Knowledge") and *Liber de ascensu et descensu intellectus* ("The Book of the Ascent and Descent of the Intellect"). Llull attempted to place Christian apologetics on the level of rational discussion, mainly to meet the needs of disputation with the Muslims. Llull used logic and complex mechanical techniques (the *Ars magna*) involving symbolic notation and combinatory diagrams to relate all forms of knowledge, including theology, philosophy, and the natural sciences as analogues of one another and as manifestations of the godhead in the universe. Llull thus used original logical methods in an attempt to prove the dogmas of Christian theology. The *Ars magna*'s apologetic applications receded into the background after Llull's death, and it was as a universal system and compendium of knowledge that the *Ars* remained influential until long after the Renaissance.

Llull devoted his life to the spread of his *Ars* and attempted to interest rulers and popes in his projects. King James II of Aragon was persuaded to establish a school at Majorca for the study of Oriental languages so that the *Ars* could be disseminated throughout the Islāmic world.

According to legend, Llull was stoned in North Africa at Bejaïa (Bougie) or Tunis and died a martyr at sea before reaching Majorca, where he was buried. Charges of confusing faith with reason led to the condemnation of Llull's teaching by Pope Gregory XI in 1376. In the 19th century, however, the Roman Catholic church showed more sympathetic interest and approved of his veneration. Current interest centres on his mystical writings, particularly the *Llibre d'amic e amat* (*The Book of the Lover and the Beloved*). In Catalan culture his allegorical novels *Blanquerna* (*c.* 1284) and *Felix* (*c.* 1288) enjoy wide popularity. Llull's works in Catalan were critically edited by M. Obrador, S. Galmes, *et al.*, 21 vol. (1905–52).

Llwyd, Morgan (b. 1619, Merioneth, Wales—d. June 3, 1659, Wrexham, Denbighshire), Puritan writer whose *Llyfr y Tri Aderyn* (1653; "The Book of the Three Birds") is considered the most important original Welsh work published during the 17th century. One of the most widely read of Welsh classics, the work is in two parts, on the theory of government and on religious liberty. The book is in the form of a discourse conducted among the eagle (Oliver Cromwell, or the secular power), the raven (the Anglicans, or organized religion), and the dove (the Nonconformists, or the followers of the inner light).

Llwyd came from a gentry family and probably received his early education at Wrexham, Denbighshire. In the English Civil Wars he served as a chaplain in the Parliamentary army. He was identified with the first Dissenting church in Wales. His other works include *Llythyr ir Cymryu Cariadus* (1653; "Letter to the Beloved Welsh"). A selection of his works was published by the University of Wales in two volumes (1899, 1905).

Llyr, in Celtic mythology, leader of one of two warring families of gods; according to one interpretation, the Children of Llyr were the powers of darkness, constantly in conflict with the Children of Dôn, the powers of light. In Welsh tradition, Llyr and his son Manawydan, like the Irish gods Lir and Manannân, were associated with the sea. Llyr's other children included Brân (Bendigeidfran), a god of bards and poetry; Branwen, wife of the sun god Matholwch, king of Ireland; and Creidylad (in earlier myths, a daughter of Lludd).

Hearing of Matholwch's maltreatment of Branwen, Brân and Manawydan led an expedition to avenge her. Brân was killed in the subsequent war, which left only seven survivors, among them Manawydan and Pryderi, son of Pwyll. Manawydan married Pryderi's mother, Rhiannon, and was thereafter closely associated with them.

Llywarch Hen (fl. 6th century), central figure in a cycle of poems composed by a 9th-century storyteller in Powys (Wales). Set against the background of the struggle of the Welsh of the kingdom of Powys against the Anglo-Saxons of Mercia, the poems speak of heroic virtues, express laments for fallen heroes, and grieve for the misfortunes of old age and the transitoriness of earthly things. In these tales, prose was used for narrative and description and verse for dialogue and soliloquy, but the verse passages are all that remain. They are written in three-line stanzas (*englynion*), for the most part, and are preserved in *The Red Book of Hergest,* a manuscript of the 15th century. The poems have been edited and translated several times in the 20th century.

Llywelyn, also spelled LLEWELYN, name of Welsh princes grouped below chronologically and indicated by the symbol •.

•**Llywelyn** AP IORWERTH, byname LLYWELYN THE GREAT (d. April 11, 1240, Aberconway, Gwynedd, Wales), Welsh prince, the most outstanding native ruler to appear in Wales before the region came under English rule in 1283.

Llywelyn was the grandson of Owain Gwynedd (d. 1170), a powerful ruler of Gwynedd in northern Wales. While still a child, Llywelyn was exiled by his uncle, David. He deposed David in 1194 and by 1202 had brought most of northern Wales under his control. In 1205 he married Joan, the illegitimate daughter of England's King John (reigned 1199–1216). Nevertheless, when Llywelyn's attempts to extend his authority into southern Wales threatened English possessions, John invaded Wales (1211) and overran most of Gwynedd. The prince soon won back his lands. He secured his position by allying with John's powerful baronial opponents, and his actions helped the barons influence the king's signing of Magna Carta (1215).

Two years after the accession of King Henry III (reigned 1216–72), the English acknowledged that Llywelyn controlled almost all of Wales, but by 1223 they had forced him to withdraw to the north behind a boundary between Cardigan, Dyfed, and Builth, Powys. Many Welsh princes in the south, however, still accepted his overlordship. In his last years the aged Llywelyn turned his government over to his son David (prince of Gwynedd). When Llywelyn died, a chronicler described him as prince of Wales, which he was in fact, if not in law.

•**Llywelyn** AP GRUFFUDD (d. Dec. 11, 1282, near Builth, Powys, Wales), prince of Gwynedd in northern Wales who struggled unsuccessfully to drive the English from Welsh territory. He was the only Welsh ruler to be officially recognized by the English as prince of Wales, but within a year after his death Wales fell completely under English rule.

Although Llywelyn ap Gruffudd's grandfather, Llywelyn ap Iorwerth (d. 1240), had made Gwynedd the centre of Welsh power, the state nearly collapsed during the brief reign of his son David ap Llywelyn (1240–46). When David died in 1246, Llywelyn and his brother Owain divided the remaining territory. In 1255 Llywelyn seized Owain's lands and set out to assert once again Gwynedd's hegemony over Wales.

Taking advantage of the conflict between King Henry III of England and his barons, Llywelyn proclaimed himself prince of Wales and received the homage of the other Welsh princes (1258). In 1262 he took up arms against the English lords of southern Wales and allied himself with Henry III's chief baronial opponent, Simon de Montfort, who seized power in England in 1264. Montfort was killed in 1265, and two years later Llywelyn signed a treaty by which he recognized Henry's overlordship; in return, he was authorized to receive homage from the other Welsh princes. Nevertheless, upon the death of Henry III and the accession of Edward I (1272), Llywelyn again defied the English. Edward invaded Wales and subjugated Llywelyn in 1276–77, but in 1282 Llywelyn and his brother David raised a rebellion for national independence. The uprising collapsed soon after Edward's forces killed Llywelyn in a skirmish near Builth. David was killed in 1283.

Llywelyn y Glyn: *see* Lewis Glyn Cothi.

LNG: *see* liquefied natural gas.

Lo-ho, also called T'A-HO, Pinyin LUOHE, or TAHE, city in central Honan *sheng* (province), China. Lo-ho is situated on the Sha River, which flows southeastward to the Huai River at the point where it is crossed by the main Peking–Han-k'ou railway. It is a focus not only for rail and river transport but also for the local road network.

Originally it was merely a small village and a minor landing place on the river, subordinate to the ancient county town of Yen-ch'eng some 3 miles (5 km) to the northwest. Its growth dates from the construction of the railway in 1905. Situated between Yen-ch'eng and the station, Lo-ho before World War II rapidly grew into a local market and a collecting centre for agricultural produce, particularly cotton, soybeans, and wheat, which were transported to Han-k'ou. It was also a commercial centre with a sizable business community and a distribution point for foreign goods. By 1949 it had outgrown its neighbour Yen-ch'eng and was constituted as a municipality. It is the site of an electric-lightbulb factory. Pop. (1990) 126,438.

Lo-Johansson, Ivar, in full KARL IVAR LO-JOHANSSON (b. Feb. 23, 1901, Ösmo, Sweden—d. April 11, 1990, Stockholm), Swedish writer and social critic who in more than 50 "proletarian" novels and short-story collections depicted the lives of working-class people with great compassion.

Lo-Johansson was first recognized in the mid-1930s for his detailed and realistic depiction of the plight of landless Swedish peasants, known as *statare,* in two volumes of short stories, *Statarna I–II* (1936–37; "The Sharecroppers"), and in his novel *Jordproletärerna* (1941; "Proletarians of the Earth"). These works are based on his own recollections but are at the same time an indictment of existing social conditions. In their combination of political tract and novel, and their use of the collective as a central focus, the books served as models for many documentary portrayals of the Swedish labour movement. Perhaps more importantly, these books helped spur extensive land reforms in Sweden, including the abolition of indentured farm labour in 1945.

Lo-Johansson gave intense expression to individual human suffering, as in his characterization of a farm servant's wife in *Bara en mor* (1939; "Only a Mother"). The conflict between individualism and collectivism emerges in his autobiographical cycle of eight novels from the 1950s, with *Analfabeten* (1951; "The Illiterate") as the first and *Proletärförfattaren* (1960; "The Proletarian Writer") as the last volume of the series. In the 1970s he used short stories in his cycle of tales on the seven deadly sins, and in the 1980s he wrote a series of memoirs.

Lo Kuan-chung, Pinyin LUO GUANZHONG (b. *c.* 1330, T'ai-yüan?, Shansi province, China—d. *c.* 1400, Hangchow?, Chekiang province), Chinese writer to whom has been attributed such classic Chinese novels as *San Kuo chih yen-i* (*Romance of the Three Kingdoms*) and *Shui-hu chuan* (*Water Margin,* also known to English readers as *All Men Are Brothers*).

Almost nothing is known about the life of Lo Kuan-chung. His authorship of *San Kuo chih yen-i* and *Shui-hu chuan* (the latter jointly with Shih Nai-an), however, has increasingly been disputed. The first work is a historical narrative that exists today in a version of 120 chapters, while the second is a semihistorical picaresque novel of 100 chapters, written in the colloquial style, about a band of outlaws. Both works enjoy continued popularity among Chinese readers.

Lo-lang (ancient Korean colony): *see* Nang-nang.

Lo-yang, Pinyin LUOYANG, formerly called HONAN-FU, commonly known as HONAN, city in northwestern Honan *sheng* (province), China. It was important in history as the capital of nine ruling dynasties and as a Buddhist centre. Lo-yang is divided into an east town and a west town.

Lo-i (modern Lo-yang) was founded at the beginning of the Chou dynasty (late 12th century BC), near the present west town, as the residence of the imperial kings. It became the Chou capital in 771 BC and was later moved to a site northeast of the present east town; it was named Lo-yang because it was north (*yang*) of the Lo River, and its ruins are now distinguished as the ancient city of Lo-yang.

The city of the Han period (206 BC–AD 220) was located approximately on the site of the ancient Lo-i but was called Lo-yang. This name alternated with the name Honan-fu until modern times. Lo-yang did not become the Han capital until the 1st century AD, at the beginning of the Eastern Han period, though its economic importance had been recognized earlier. In AD 68 the Pai-ma-ssu ("White Horse Temple"), one of the earliest Buddhist foundations in China, was built about 9 miles (14 km) east of the modern east town.

During the 4th century Lo-yang changed hands several times between the rulers of Eastern Chin, Later Chao, and Yen, and it did not prosper again until 494, when it was revived by Hsiao-wen ti of the Northern Wei dynasty (386–534). The Northern Wei emperors ordered the construction of cave temples at Lung-men, south of the city. This inaugurated one of the greatest centres of Chinese Buddhism, the surviving sculptures of which are of prime importance to the history of Chinese art. As the eastern capital of the T'ang dynasty (618–907), Lo-yang was expanded and the part now constituting the east town was created. After a rebellion in the mid-8th century, however, Lo-yang fell into an economic decline, which lasted until the mid-20th century. A tractor plant and other factories were built after 1949, and Lo-yang soon became a leading industrial and commercial centre. Cotton, wheat, and other crops grown in the region are processed in the city. It is the hub of several highways and lies on the Longhai railroad (connecting Su-chou with Sian). Pop. (1990) 759,752.

Loa River, Spanish RÍO LOA, river, the longest in Chile, in Antofagasta and Tarapacá regions. It rises in the Andes at the base of Miño Volcano, near the Bolivian border, and flows southwest through the mountains, emerging at the oasis of Calama; it then veers westward and northward across the Atacama Desert. About 45 miles (70 km) north of Tocopilla it turns westward again, crosses the coastal mountain range, and empties into the Pacific Ocean after a course of 275 miles (about 440 km). Although it is not navigable, its waters irrigate Calama and other oases, provide Antofagasta region with drinking water, and are used to generate hydroelectric power for nearby copper and nitrate mines.

loach, any of the small, generally elongated freshwater fishes of the family Cobitidae. More than 200 species are known; most are native to central and southern Asia, but three are found in Europe and one in northern Africa. A typical loach has very small scales and three to six pairs of whiskerlike barbels around its mouth. In some species, such as the spined loach (*Cobitis taenia*) of Eurasia, there is also a short, movable spine near each eye.

Loaches are hardy, usually nocturnal fishes that inhabit both still and flowing waters. They use their barbels to comb the bottom for worms, insect larvae, and other food. In low and stagnant ponds, they may swallow air at the surface, their intestines then absorbing the oxygen and thus aiding respiration.

Several Asian loaches are popular aquarium fishes. Among these are the clown loach (*Botia macracanthus*), an orange fish about 13–30 centimetres (5–12 inches) long and

Clown loach (*Botia macracanthus*)
Jane Burton—Bruce Coleman Ltd.

marked with three vertical black bands, and the coolie loach (*Acanthophthalmus kuhlii*), a pinkish, eel-like species about 8 centimetres long, marked with many vertical black bands. Other loaches include the stone (*Nemachilus barbatula*) and spined loaches, both mottled, yellow and brown fishes about 13 centimetres long found in Europe and northern Asia. The European weatherfish (*Misgurnus fossilis*) is a yellowish fish about 25 centimetres long, banded and speckled with brown; like the similar Japanese weatherfish (*M. anguillicaudatus*), it is named for its heightened activity during periods of rapid change in barometric pressure, such as occur before a storm.

loading, in communications technology, addition of inductance to an antenna or at periodic intervals to a transmission line to improve operating characteristics. Loading coils in telephone lines may be spaced as close as one mile. Counteracting the effects of capacitance, they make line impedance approach the equivalence of pure resistance.

Radio antennas that are too short to be resonant at their operating frequency can be made to approach resonance by inserting a coil in series in the antenna circuit. Automobile radios generally include loading coils because whip antennas are much too short to resonate at broadcast frequencies. Some telephone and telegraph cables are provided with continuous loading by being wrapped with a spiral of magnetic material.

Loanda (Angola): *see* Luanda.

Loango, Kingdom of, also called BRAMA KINGDOM, former African state in the basin of the Kouilou and Niari rivers (now largely in southwestern Congo). Founded by the Vili people, (Bavili), probably before 1485, it was one of the oldest and largest kingdoms of the region. By 1600 it was importing ivory and slaves from the interior along well-established trade routes that extended as far inland as Malebo Pool.

Administration was orderly but decentralized. The men in line for succession to the crown served as provincial governors, rotating provinces in a set sequence each time a king died. Other territorial officials held office for life. By the 18th century, power had become fragmented. A long interregnum began in 1786, and when a king was finally enthroned he lacked any real authority.

Loasaceae, mostly tropical American plant family of about 15 genera and more than 250 species, many with painfully stinging hairs but beautiful and often bizarre flowers in red, orange, yellow, or white. Loasaceae species are frequently twining and mostly herbaceous. The genus *Loasa,* with about 100 species from Mexico to the Andes, has nettle-like stinging hairs that can result in discomfort for days; its oddly formed flowers have five pouchlike yellow petals covering united stamens that form coloured nectaries. The closely related *Caiophora* (or *Cajophora*), with about 65 tropical American species, like the *Loasa,* mostly grows in rocky slopes of cool Andean areas.

The clusters of red-orange, pouchlike petals of *C. lateritia* measure about 5 centimetres (2 inches) across, on a twining plant up to 6 metres (about 20 feet) long. Species of the genus *Mentzelia* have nonstinging but hooked hairs. Some have satiny orange blooms smaller than the 6-cm, cupped, five-petalled flowers of blazing star (*M. lindleyi*) of western North America. The yellow, fragrant blooms of blazing star open in the early evening. The two species of *Kissenia,* the only non-American genus, are native to West Africa, East Africa, and western Asia.

Lobachevskian geometry: *see* hyperbolic geometry.

Lobachevsky, Nikolay Ivanovich (b. Dec. 1 [Nov. 20, old style], 1792, Nizhny Novgorod, Russia—d. Feb. 24 [Feb. 12, O.S.],

Lobachevsky, detail of a portrait by an unknown artist
Novosti Press Agency

1856, Kazan), Russian mathematician who, with János Bolyai of Hungary, is considered the founder of non-Euclidean geometry.

Lobachevsky was the son of an impecunious government official. His entire life centred around the University of Kazan, beginning at age 14, when he entered as a student. In 1811 he received the M.A. degree and then taught, from 1816 as extraordinary professor and from 1822 as ordinary professor.

His administrative talents were soon recognized; in 1820 he became dean of the faculty of mathematics and physics, in 1825 university librarian, and in 1827 rector of the university, a position he held, with repeated reelections, until 1846. In all of his duties, he exercised remarkable organizing and educational skill in rescuing the university from the chaotic conditions into which it had drifted. The previous administration had reflected the spirit of the later years of Tsar Alexander I, who was distrustful of modern science and philosophy, particularly that of the German philosopher Immanuel Kant, as evil products of the French Revolution and a menace to orthodox religion. The results at Kazan during the years 1819–26 were factionalism, decay of academic standards, dismissals, and departure of some of the best professors, including Johann Martin Christian Bartels, friend of the German mathematician Carl Friedrich Gauss, and Lobachevsky's teacher of mathematics.

In 1826 a more tolerant period was inaugurated with the accession of Tsar Nicholas I, and Lobachevsky became the leading innovator at the university, restoring academic standards and faculty harmony. He was active in saving lives during the cholera epidemic of 1830, in rebuilding several university buildings after a devastating fire in 1842, and in popularizing science and modernizing primary and secondary education in the region of Kazan. Although burdened with this work, in addition to a heavy administrative teaching load, he still found time for extensive mathematical research.

In 1826 Lobachevsky announced and in 1829 published his theory of non-Euclidean geometry. This form of geometry is not based on Euclid's parallel postulate, according to which one and only one line can be drawn through a point in a plane parallel to a given line in the plane. In showing that a non-Euclidean geometry was logically possible, he demonstrated that Euclid's parallel postulate could not be deduced as a consequence of his other postulates. Lobachevsky's discovery, corroborated by Bolyai's work published in 1832, was the final solution of a problem that had baffled mathematicians for 2,000 years.

Lobachevsky's ideas were rooted in his opposition to Kant's transcendental Idealism, which maintains that such ideas as space, time, and extension are a priori, and that the mind imposes order on sense experience. For him space was an a posteriori concept, derived by the human mind from external experience.

In addition to geometry, Lobachevsky also did distinguished work in the theory of infinite series, especially trigonometric series, integral calculus, and probability; in algebra he found, in 1834, a method for approximating the roots of algebraic equations, often called after the Swiss mathematician Carl Heinrich Gräeffe (1837).

His fame, like that of Bolyai, was posthumous. During his lifetime, few were impressed by his geometry, and the leading Russian mathematician of his day, Mikhail Vasilevich Ostrogradsky, who was well known in western Europe, could not appreciate it. Moreover, Lobachevsky's first publications, in Russian—in 1829 in a local general periodical and in 1835–39 in the Kazan academic transactions—were little known abroad. But Lobachevsky, in contrast to Bolyai, refused to be discouraged. With characteristic perseverance he continued the publication of his ideas not only in Russian but also in French and German. In 1837 his "Géométrie imaginaire" ("Imaginary Geometry") appeared in *Crelle's Journal* (Berlin), and in 1840 his book *Geometrische Untersuchungen zur Theorie der Parallellinien* (Eng. trans., *Geometrical Researches on the Theory of Parallels*) was published. There was no general recognition of his work, despite the praise bestowed on it by Gauss, the leading mathematician of Europe, who had reached, but never published, the same conclusions.

Toward the end of his life, nearly blind and grieved by domestic losses, Lobachevsky in 1855 once more presented his theory in French in the book *Pangéométrie,* also appearing in Russian. Acceptance of non-Euclidean geometry, however, had to wait until, under the influence of the German mathematician Bernhard Riemann's ideas on the principles underlying geometry in 1866, the Italian mathematician Eugenio Beltrami in 1868 and the German mathematician Felix Klein in 1871 demonstrated the consistency and general applicability of this geometry. (D.J.S.)

BIBLIOGRAPHY. The collected works of Lobachevsky were published in Russian, 5 vol. (1946–51). The *Geometrische Untersuchungen* of 1840 was translated by G.B. Halsted as *Geometrical Researches on the Theory of Parallels,* new ed. (1914). It was republished in Roberto Bonola, *Non-Euclidean Geometry* (1911, reprinted 1955), a good book for the study of this geometry, with biographical and bibliographical references. Halsted also published (1897) translations of Lobachevsky's early Russian papers from the German translation in F. Engel, *N.I. Lobatschewskij: Zwei geometrische Abhandlungen,* 2 vol. (1898–99)—vol. 2 contains an extensive biography. Much biographical and bibliographical information is presented in A. Vucinich, "Nicolai Ivanovich Lobachevskii: The Man Behind the First Non-Euclidean Geometry," *Isis,* 53:465–481 (1962).

Lobamba, densely populated rural area, central Swaziland, southern Africa. According to traditional Swazi customs, Lobamba is the residence of the *Ndlovukazi* ("She Elephant"; the Queen Mother) and is thereby the spiritual home of the Swazi nation; in addition, it is the legislative capital of the country. Situated in the eastern Ezulwini valley in the Middle Veld, Lobamba lies 11 miles (18 km) south of Mbabane, the modern administrative and judicial capital of Swaziland, and almost at the country's geographic centre. Lobamba stands on the site of a previous royal village, called Nkanini.

As the principal royal *kraal* (an enclosed dwelling area belonging to a family) of the Swazi, Lobamba is the site of parliamentary buildings, an official residence of the king, the offices of the Swazi National Council, the National Archives and Museum, and the National Stadium. The two most important cultural events of Swaziland, the sacred *Incwala* (National Ceremony) and the *Umhlanga* (Reed Dance), are held annually at Lobamba. The Mlilwane (Little Fire) game sanctuary and the Gilbert Reynolds Memorial Garden are situated about 6 miles (10 km) northwest. Pop. (latest est.) 5,746.

Lobanov-Rostovsky, Aleksey Borisovich, Knyaz (Prince) (b. Dec. 30 [Dec. 18, Old Style], 1824, Voronezh province, Russia—d. Aug. 30 [Aug. 18], 1896, Shepetovka, Russia), diplomat and statesman who, while serving as Russia's foreign minister (1895–96), brought northern Manchuria into Russia's sphere of influence.

Having begun his diplomatic career in 1844, Lobanov held posts in Berlin and Paris before becoming Russia's minister in Constantinople in 1859. He retired in 1863 but resumed his career in 1878, serving as ambassador at Constantinople (1878–79), London (1879–82), Vienna (1882–94), and Berlin (1894–95) and becoming one of Russia's most influential diplomats in Europe.

On March 10 (Feb. 26, Old Style), 1895, Lobanov was appointed foreign minister. During his tenure he firmly supported the Franco-Russian alliance that had been concluded in 1894, sought friendly relations with Germany and Austria-Hungary, and also settled a long-standing dispute with Bulgaria that had begun in 1886 when Russia refused to recognize Ferdinand of Saxe-Coburg as prince of Bulgaria.

Lobanov directed most of his attention, however, to East Asia, where Japan had recently won a war against China (1894–95); as a result China had been compelled to cede Formosa, the Pescadores Islands, and the Liaotung (south Manchurian) Peninsula to Japan (Treaty of Shimonoseki; April 17, 1895). Although Lobanov was personally willing to let this settlement remain in effect, provided that Russia was compensated with a port in Korea, he was opposed by the powerful minister of finance Sergey Witte and overruled by Emperor Nicholas II (reigned 1894–1917). Consequently, Lobanov enlisted the diplomatic aid of France and Germany, and in April 1895 the three countries forced Japan to withdraw its claim to the Liaotung Peninsula. Lobanov then concluded a secret agreement with China (June 3, 1896) whereby Russia promised to protect China from foreign aggression in exchange for the right to build the Chinese Eastern railroad, which would extend the Trans-Siberian Railway line across northern Manchuria to Vladivostok on Russia's east coast and effectively place the railroad's territory under Russian control.

A few months later Lobanov died while traveling from Kiev to meet the German emperor William II in Silesia.

Lobato, José Bento Monteiro: *see* Monteiro Lobato, José Bento.

Lobatse, also spelled LOBATSI, town, southeastern Botswana. It lies on a main road and a rail line about 45 miles (72 km) southwest of Gaborone, the national capital. Lobatse is the site of the Botswana Meat Commission, which operates one of the largest meat processing plants in Africa. In addition, the town has a tannery, a canning factory, and a soap factory. Lobatse is also the seat of the High Court of Botswana and the headquarters of the Department of Geological Survey. Pop. (1997 est.) 29,872.

lobbying, any attempt by individuals or private interest groups to influence the decisions of government; in its original meaning it referred to efforts to influence the votes of legislators, generally in the lobby outside the legislative chamber. Lobbying in some form is inevitable in any political system.

Lobbying, which has gained special attention in the United States, takes many forms. Group representatives may appear before legislative committees. Public officials may be "buttonholed" in legislative offices, hotels, or private homes. Letters may be written or telephone calls made to public officials, and campaigns may be organized for this purpose. Organizations may provide favoured candidates with money and services. Massive public-relations campaigns employing all the techniques of modern communication may be launched to influence public opinion. Extensive research into complex legislative proposals may be supplied to legislative committees by advocates of various and often conflicting interests. Substantial election campaign contributions or other assistance may be supplied to favoured legislators or executives. The persons who lobby in these ways may be full-time officials of a powerful trade or agricultural association or labour union, individual professional lobbyists with many clients who pay for their services, or ordinary citizens who take the time to state their hopes or grievances. Cities and states, consumer and environmental protection and other "public interest" groups, and various branches of the federal government also maintain staff lobbyists in the United States.

The right "to petition the government for a redress of grievances" is protected in the First Amendment to the U.S. Constitution. The federal government and the majority of U.S. states regulate lobbying. Most laws, such as the Federal Regulation of Lobbying Act (1946), require that lobbyists register and report contributions and expenditures and that groups whom they represent make similar reports. The efficacy of these laws is doubtful. Especially difficult to regulate is any kind of indirect lobbying—such as group activity designed to influence government by shaping public opinion.

Consult the INDEX *first*

lobed comb jelly, any of several, mostly small, marine invertebrates of the order Lobata (phylum Ctenophora). The transparent, gelatinous animals are found drifting in most oceans, especially in surface waters near the shore. Lobed comb jellies (*e.g., Mnemiopsis, Bolinopsis*) are carnivorous, preying on tiny aquatic animals. Their tentacles, used in feeding, are smaller than those of other ctenophores, and the two oral lobes (structures surrounding the mouth) are greatly enlarged.

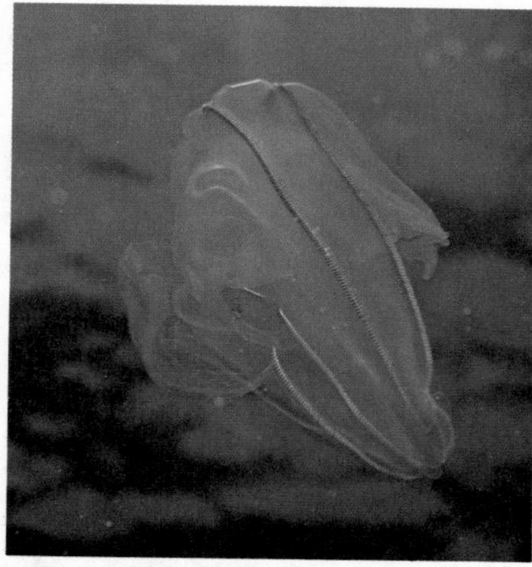

Lobed comb jelly (*Lobata*)
Douglas Faulkner

Lobedu (people): *see* Lovedu.

L'Obel, Matthias de, L'Obel also spelled LOBEL, also called MATTHAEUS LOBELIUS (b. 1538, Lille, Fr.—d. March 3, 1616, Highgate, London, Eng.), French physician and botanist whose *Stirpium adversaria nova* (1570; written in collaboration with Pierre Pena) was a milestone in modern botany. It argued that botany and medicine must be based on thorough, exact observation.

L'Obel studied at the University of Montpelier (France) with Guillaume Rondolet. The *Stirpium adversaria,* a collection of data about some 1,200 plants that L'Obel had observed and gathered, tried to classify plants into families according to the form of their leaves. L'Obel's rough notions of genus and family were later developed by Carolus Linnaeus; a few of L'Obel's plant groups are still recognized. *Plantarum seu stirpium historia,* 2 vol. (1576), comprised the second edition of the *Stirpium adversaria,* together with the *Stirpium observationes,* an appendix with 1,486 engravings by botanists such as Pietro Mattioli, Rembert Dodoens, and Charles de l'Ecluse.

L'Obel lived in the Low Countries from 1571, leaving in 1584 for England, where he became botanist and physician to King James I.

Lobeliaceae, the lobelia family of the bellflower order (Campanulales), containing about 25 genera and more than 750 species of flowering plants, native to both hemispheres. Some are grown for their attractive, two-lipped flowers, including annual and perennial herbs, shrubs, and trees. The family is included by some authorities in the bellflower family (Campanulaceae), from which it differs by its irregularly shaped flowers.

Postlike and shaggy-tree forms are found on mountains in Africa. These include *L. gibberoa,* 9 m (30 feet) tall, in wetter forests 1,200 to 2,700 m in elevation; *L. aberdarica,* 2 m tall, occurring at elevations of 2,100 to 3,400 m and as high as 4,600 m; and *L. telekii,* in which a shaggy appearance results from hairy foliage, an adaptation to dry and cold weather. Trailing lobelia (*L. erinus*), native to southern Africa, is usually blue flowered and green foliaged, but pink, white and blue, and white flowered forms are known, and bronze-coloured foliage occurs as well. The little flowers are flylike in shape. Tall and shrubby, *L. laxiflora,* from Mexico and Central America, produces spikes of long-stalked, toothlike, orange and yellow flowers. It is widespread on the forest edges of mountain slopes. Some of the ornamental lobelias come from the genera

Downingia, Hypsela, Centropogon, Isotoma, Monopsis, Palmerella, and *Pratia. See also* cardinal flower; Indian tobacco.

Lobengula (b. *c.* 1836, Mosega, Transvaal—d. January 1894, near Bulawayo, Rhodesia), second and last king of the South African Ndebele (Matabele) nation. Lobengula, the son of the founder of the Ndebele kingdom, Mzilikazi, was unable to preserve the independence of his people in the face of growing pressure from British and Boer settlers.

Though Mzilikazi died in 1868, Lobengula only succeeded to the throne in 1870, after a period of serious civil war. Feeling that his throne was threatened, he attempted to form an alliance with the British to forestall both internal and external dangers, granting first farming (1886) and then mineral (1888) concessions to the British authorities in South Africa and to Cecil Rhodes's British South Africa Company in Rhodesia. Not satisfied with these concessions, and anxious to exploit gold fields near Bulawayo, the company undertook a military expedition that destroyed the kingdom in October 1893.

Lobi, people residing in the western region of Burkina Faso (formerly Upper Volta) and in the Côte d'Ivoire (Ivory Coast) and speaking a Gur language of the Niger-Congo family. They are farmers and hunters, growing millet and sorghum as staples. Traditionally, the Lobi governed themselves through the clan system, with no formal political organization.

Religious beliefs were purely animistic until Islāmic influence entered the area around the 14th century. Polygyny is practiced. In 1897, France annexed the Lobi lands, but because of the Lobi's effective use of poisoned arrows the population was not subdued until 1903.

Lobo, Francisco Rodrigues: *see* Rodrigues Lobo, Francisco.

lobotomy, surgical procedure in which the nerve pathways in a lobe or lobes of the brain are severed from those in other areas. The procedure formerly was used as a radical therapeutic measure to help grossly disturbed patients with schizophrenia, bipolar disorder, and other mental illnesses. Lobotomy was introduced in 1935 by two Portuguese neurophysicians, António Egas Moniz and Almeida Lima. The practice was soon widely adopted, largely because there were few other viable therapeutic measures at the time for treating chronically agitated, delusional, self-destructive, or violent patients.

The prefrontal lobotomy involved severing the nerve pathways in the two frontal lobes of the brain, after entry to the brain had been achieved by boring two holes in the skull. This method was soon replaced by the transorbital lobotomy, in which a picklike instrument was forced through the back of the eye sockets to pierce the thin bone that separates the eye sockets from the frontal lobes; the pick's point was then inserted into the frontal lobes where the connections between the lobes were severed. A lobotomy was favoured for those patients who did not respond to electroshock treatments; the emphasis was on making such patients more manageable. A large proportion of such lobotomized patients exhibited reduced tension or agitation, but many also showed such effects as increased apathy, passivity, lack of initiative, poor ability to concentrate, and a generally decreased depth and intensity of their emotional response to life.

Lobotomies were performed on a wide scale during the 1940s and up until about 1956, when antipsychotics, antidepressants, and other medications that were much more effective in treating mentally disturbed patients and alleviating their distress came into use. Lobotomies are no longer performed; however, psychosurgery, the surgical removal of specific regions of the brain, is occasionally used to treat patients whose symptoms have resisted treatment to all other approaches.

lobster, any of numerous marine crustaceans (order Decapoda) constituting the families Homaridae (or Nephropsidae), true lobsters; Palinuridae, spiny lobsters, or sea crayfish; Scyllaridae, slipper, Spanish, or shovel lobsters; and Polychelidae, deep-sea lobsters. All are marine and benthic (bottom-dwelling), and most are nocturnal. Lobsters scavenge for dead animals but also eat live fish, small mollusks and other bottom-dwelling invertebrates, and seaweed. Some species, especially of true and spiny lobsters, are commercially important.

The lobster has a rigid, segmented body covering (exoskeleton) and five pairs of legs, one or more pairs of which are often modified into pincers (chelae) with the chela on one side usually larger than that on the other. The eyes are on movable stalks, and there are two pairs of long antennae. Several pairs of swimming legs (swimmerets) are on the elongated abdomen. A flipper-like tail is used for swimming; flexure of the tail and abdomen propel the animal backward.

The true lobsters (Homaridae) have claws on the first three pairs of legs, with very large claws on the first pair. They have a distinct rostrum, or snout, on the carapace, which covers the head and thorax, or midsection. The American lobster (*Homarus americanus*) and the Norway lobster, also known as Dublin Bay prawn and scampi (*Nephrops norvegicus*), are the most valuable and are often marketed alive; the heavily muscled abdomen and claws are the parts eaten. True lobsters are found in all but polar seas and the greater depths. *H. gammarus,* the European lobster, a dark greenish animal, occurs on rocky bottoms of the European Atlantic coast and the Mediterranean Sea. *H. capensis,* of the waters around South Africa, grows to 10 or 13 cm (4 to 5 inches) and is of little commercial value.

H. americanus, found in waters from Labrador to North Carolina, sometimes dwells in shallow water but is more abundant in deeper water down to 200 fathoms (1,200 feet [366 m]). Lobsters caught in shallow water weigh about 0.45 kg (about one pound) and are about 25 cm (about 10 inches) long. They are caught usually in lobster pots—cages baited with dead fish. In deeper water, they weigh about 2.5 kg (about 5.5 pounds) and are often caught by trawling. Exceptionally large specimens may weigh 20 kg (40 pounds). The American lobster is often marketed alive. It is commonly blackish green or brownish green above and yellow orange, red, or blue underneath. The red colour of lobsters is caused by immersion in hot water.

Females are ready to lay eggs when about five years old. Sperm are transferred from males to females in summer, but fertilization does not occur until spring. A female lays 3,000 or more eggs, which remain attached to her swimmerets until they hatch several months later. Unlike adults, the young, about 1 cm (0.4 inch) long, swim freely for about 12 days and then descend to the bottom, where they remain. Some lobsters may live for 50 years. Young lobsters are preyed upon especially by dogfish, skates, and cod. The principal enemy of the adult lobster is man.

Unlike true lobsters, spiny lobsters (Palinuridae), so called because of their very spiny bodies, do not have large claws. Usually only the abdomen is eaten and is marketed as lobster tail. The antennae are strongly developed. Most species live in tropical waters; *Palinurus elephas,* however, is found from Great Britain to the Mediterranean Sea. Two palinurid species are commercially important in America: *Palinurus interruptus,* the California spiny lobster of the Pacific coast, and *P. argus,* the West Indian spiny lobster, from Bermuda to Brazil. *P. interruptus* attains lengths of about 40 cm (16 inches); *P. argus* about 45 cm (18 inches). *Jasus lalandei,* the commercially important South African rock lobster, occurs in waters around South Africa.

The mainly tropical slipper lobsters (Scyllaridae) are rather flat and clawless, with antennae flattened into broad plates. Most species are short and small and of little economic importance. Deep-sea lobsters (Polychelidae) are soft, weak animals with claws; some are blind. None is commercially important.

(Top) Spiny lobster (*Palinurus*); (bottom) American lobster (*Homarus americanus*)

(Top) Douglas P. Wilson; (bottom) John H. Gerard

lobster pot, in commercial fishing, portable trap to capture lobster, either half-cylindrical or rectangular and constructed of laths, formerly wooden but now usually plastic. An opening permits the lobster to enter, but not to escape, through a tunnel of netting. Pots are usually constructed with two compartments, called the "chamber" and the "parlour." The lobster enters the chamber first, and then, through another tunnel of netting (or a self-closing door), the parlour, in which bait is placed. The more widely used rectangular pot is about 76 to 102 cm (30 to 40 inches) in length. The pots are usually dropped to the ocean floor in strings of 10 or 15, marked by a buoy for later retrieval.

local colour, style of writing derived from the presentation of the features and peculiarities of a particular locality and its inhabitants. The name is given especially to a kind of American literature that in its most characteristic form made its appearance just after the Civil War and for nearly three decades was the single most popular form of American literature, fulfilling a newly awakened public interest in distant parts of the country and, for some, providing a nostalgic memory of times gone by. It concerned itself mainly with depicting the character of a particular region, concentrating especially upon the peculiarities of dialect, manners, folklore, and landscape that distinguish the area. The frontier novels of James Fenimore Cooper have been cited as precursors of the local-colour story, as have the New York Dutch tales of Washington Irving. The California Gold Rush provided a vivid and exciting background for the stories of Bret Harte (*q.v.*), whose "The Luck of Roaring Camp" (1868), with its use of miners' dialect, colourful characters, and Western background, is among the early local-colour stories.

Harte was not the only local colourist to begin as a humorist. His unavailing efforts to solicit quality writing eventually led him to simply mock with overblown verse the mentality of the uncritical western writers. His lead in the satiric vein was followed by a number of men—George Horatio Derby and the master of dialect spelling, Robert Henry Newell, among them. Other writers of the "Old Southwest" (*i.e.,* Alabama, Tennessee, Mississippi, and later Missouri, Arkansas, and Louisiana) joined in the satirical, broadly humorous style. Samuel Clemens, later known as Mark Twain, apprenticed with Harte during this period. His adaptation of the local-colour story—and the humorist subgenre—to the tall tale and life on the Mississippi River make his antecedents clear.

Many other well-known authors first achieved success with vivid evocations of their own localities: Harriet Beecher Stowe, Rose Terry Cooke, and Sarah Orne Jewett wrote of New England; George Washington Cable, Joel Chandler Harris, and Kate Chopin described the Deep South; Thomas Nelson Page romanticized Virginia plantation life; Lafcadio Hearn, before he began his Japanese adventures, wrote of New Orleans; Edward Eggleston wrote of Indiana frontier days; Mary Noailles Murfree told stories of the Tennessee mountaineers; and O. Henry was a brilliant chronicler of both the Texas frontier and the streets of New York City. Among the writers who inherited and drew upon the local-colour traditions may be numbered Willa Cather, William Faulkner, and Grace Paley.

Local Group, in astronomy, the group of more than 20 galaxies to which the Milky Way Galaxy belongs. About half are elliptical galaxies, with the remainder being of the spiral or irregular type. As in other clusters of galaxies, members are probably kept from separating by their mutual gravitational attraction. The Milky Way system is near one end of the volume of space occupied by the Local Group, and the great Andromeda galaxy (M31) is near the other end, about 2,000,000 light-years away.

Locarno (Italian), German LUGGARUS, town, Ticino canton, southern Switzerland. It is situated at the northern end of Lago Maggiore, near the mouth of the Maggia River, west of Bellinzona. The site was settled in prehistoric times, and the town was first mentioned in 789. A possession of the dukes of Milan from 1342, it was taken by the Swiss in 1513. It became part of the newly formed Ticino canton in 1803 and, with Lugano and Bellinzona, was one of the three capitals of that canton until 1878. An Italianate town, it counts among its landmarks the 14th-century castle of the dukes of Milan, now a museum; the Pretorio, or law court, in which the Pact of Locarno, an attempt to guarantee the peace in western Europe, was initiated in 1925; and several old churches, including the pilgrimage church of Madonna del Sasso (founded 1480, extended 1616). Locarno is a noted health and tourist resort with a warm Mediterranean climate and numerous hotels and other tourist facilities. There are machinery and electrochemical factories. The population is Italian speaking and Roman Catholic. Pop. (1990) 14,430.

Pilgrimage church, Madonna del Sasso, Locarno, Switz.

Josef Muench

Locarno, Pact of (Dec. 1, 1925), series of agreements whereby Germany, France, Belgium, Great Britain, and Italy mutually guaranteed peace in western Europe. The treaties were initialed at Locarno, Switz., on October 16 and signed in London on December 1.

The agreements consisted of (1) a treaty of mutual guarantee between Germany, Belgium, France, Great Britain, and Italy; (2) arbitration agreements between Germany and Belgium and between Germany and France; (3) a note from the former Allies to Germany explaining the use of sanctions against a covenant-breaking state as outlined in article 16 of the League of Nations Covenant; (4) treaties of guarantee between France and Poland and between France and Czechoslovakia.

The treaty of guarantee provided that the German-Belgian and Franco-German frontiers as fixed by the Treaty of Versailles were inviolable; that Germany, Belgium, and France would never attack each other except in "legitimate defense" or in consequence of a League of Nations obligation; that they would settle their disputes by pacific means; and that in case of an alleged breach of these undertakings, the signatories would come to the defense of the party adjudged by the League to be the party attacked and also in case of a "flagrant violation." The treaties between France and Poland or Czechoslovakia provided for mutual support against unprovoked attack. A further consequence of the pact was the evacuation of Allied troops from the Rhineland in 1930, five years ahead of schedule.

The clear meaning of Locarno was that Germany renounced the use of force to change its western frontiers but agreed only to arbitration as regards its eastern frontiers, and that Great Britain promised to defend Belgium and France but not Poland and Czechoslovakia.

In March 1936 Germany sent troops into the Rhineland, which had been demilitarized by the Treaty of Versailles, declaring that the situation envisaged at Locarno had been changed by the Franco-Soviet alliance of 1935. France regarded the German move as a "flagrant violation" of Locarno, but Great Britain declined to do so, and no action was taken. Germany made no effort to arbitrate its dispute with Czechoslovakia in 1938 or with Poland in 1939.

Locatelli, Pietro, in full PIETRO ANTONIO LOCATELLI (b. Sept. 3, 1695, Bergamo, Rep. of Venice—d. March 30, 1764, Amsterdam), Italian violinist and composer, one of the first great violinists who practiced virtuosity for virtuosity's sake, thereby extending the technical vocabulary of the violin. He is perhaps best known for his *L'Arte del violino*, a group of 12 violin concertos issued with 24 capriccios ad libitum for solo violin.

At age 14 he was a member of the instrumental ensemble of Santa Maria Maggiore in Bergamo. At 16 he went to Rome, perhaps to study with violinist-composer Arcangelo Corelli, though he may well have studied with a number of other eminent musicians in and around the city at that time. Locatelli toured widely, refining his skills. Ultimately, about 1729, he settled in Amsterdam, where he gave up public performance in favour of regular concerts for a group of wealthy amateurs. There, too, within the strong Dutch music publishing tradition, he published his works. His playing was particularly admired for its double stops (playing two strings at once), and he frequently used special tunings for special effects. Some of the bravura passages in his studies and caprices, which anticipate those of Paganini in their concentration on technical feats, slight the musical content for the technical effect. As a composer, Locatelli was most drawn to the sonata and concerto forms. Both reveal him to have been capable of elegant and expressive melody.

Consult the INDEX *first*

location theory, in economics and geography, theory concerned with the geographic location of economic activity; it has become an integral part of economic geography, regional science, and spatial economics. Location theory addresses the questions of what economic activities are located where and why. The location of economic activities can be determined on a broad level such as a region or metropolitan area, or on a narrow one such as a zone, neighbourhood, city block, or an individual site.

Johann Heinrich von Thünen, a Prussian landowner, introduced an early theory of agricultural location in *Der isolierte Staat* (1826) (*The Isolated State*). The Thünen model suggests that accessibility to the market (town) can create a complete system of agricultural land use. His model envisaged a single market surrounded by farmland, both situated on a plain of complete physical homogeneity. Transportation costs over the plain are related only to the distance traveled and the volume shipped. The model assumes that farmers surrounding the market will produce crops which have the highest market value (highest rent) that will give them the maximum net profit (the location, or land, rent). The determining factor in the location rent will be the transportation costs. When transportation costs are low, the location rent will be high, and vice versa. This situation produces a rent gradient along which the location rent decreases with distance from the market, eventually reaching zero. The Thünen model also addressed the location of intensive versus extensive agriculture in relation to the same market. Intensive agriculture will possess a steep gradient and will locate closer to the market than extensive agriculture. Different crops will possess different rent gradients. Perishable crops (vegetables and dairy products) will possess steep gradients while less perishable crops (grains) will possess less steep gradients.

In 1909 the German location economist Alfred Weber formulated a theory of industrial location in his book entitled *Über den Standort der Industrien* (*Theory of the Location of Industries,* 1929). Weber's theory, called the location triangle, sought the optimum location for the production of a good based on the fixed locations of the market and two raw material sources, which geographically form a triangle. He sought to determine the least-cost production location within the triangle by figuring the total costs of transporting raw material from both sites to the production site and product from the production site to the market. The weight of the raw materials and the final commodity are important determinants of the transport costs and the location of production. Commodities that lose mass during production can be transported less expensively from the production site to the market than from the raw material site to the production site. The production site, therefore, will be located near the raw material sources. Where there is no great loss of mass during production, total transportation costs will be lower when located near the market.

Once a least-transport-cost location had been established within the triangle, Weber attempted to determine a cheap-labour alternate location. First he plotted the variation of transportation costs against the least-transport-cost location. Next he identified sites around the triangle that had lower labour costs than did the least-transport-cost location. If the transport costs were lower than the labour costs, then a cheap-labour alternative location was determined.

Another major contribution to location theory was Walter Christaller's formulation of the central place theory, which offered geometric explanations as to how settlements and places are located in relation to one another and why settlements function as hamlets, villages, towns, or cities.

William Alonso (*Location and Land Use: Toward a General Theory of Land Rent*, 1964) built upon the Thünen model to account for intra-urban variations in land use. He attempted to apply accessibility requirements to the city centre for various types of land use (housing, commercial, and industry). According to his theory, each land use type has its own rent gradient or bid rent curve. The curve sets the maximum amount of rent any land use type will yield for a specific location. Households, commercial establishments, and industries compete for locations according to each individual bid rent curve and their requirements for access to the city centre. All households will attempt to occupy as much land as possible while staying within their accessibility requirements. Since land is cheaper at the fringe of the city, households with less need for city centre accessibility will locate near the fringe; these will usually be wealthy households. Poor households require greater accessibility to the city centre and therefore will locate near the centre, competing with commercial and industrial establishments. This will tend to create a segregated land use system, because households will not pay commercial and industrial land prices for central locations.

The Thünen, Weber, Alonso, and Christaller models are not the sole contributors to location theory, but they are its foundation. These theories have been expanded upon and refined by geographers, economists, and regional scientists.

Where the same name may denote a person, place, or thing, the articles will be found in that order

---

Loch (of Drylaw), Henry Brougham Loch, 1st Baron (b. May 23, 1827, Scotland?—d. June 20, 1900, London), British soldier and administrator who served as high commissioner in South Africa and governor of Cape Colony from 1889 to 1895, a period of mounting tension between the British and the Boers.

A career soldier, Loch began his service in India (1844–53) and fought in the Crimean War (1853–56) and in the second and third China wars (1857–58 and 1860). After 1860 he held civil appointments. From 1863 to 1882 he was governor of the Isle of Man. He thus earned knighthood (1880) and an appointment as governor of Victoria (1884).

Loch was sent to Cape Colony five years later to act as governor and high commissioner in South African affairs. A staunch imperialist, he thought the British government should assert itself more directly rather than permit men like Cecil Rhodes to determine the character of British expansion. When Rhodes and his British South Africa Company became involved in the Matabele War in 1893, it was with reluctance that Loch approved the use of British forces to support the company's troops. As high commissioner, Loch could not avoid being drawn into the problems of the Uitlanders, who were mainly British residents in the Transvaal with strong grievances against the Boer government of Paul Kruger.

After two official visits to the Transvaal (1893 and 1894), Loch was convinced that the Kruger regime could be easily overthrown with outside help. His "Loch plan" called for a quick raid from the Bechuanaland border when an opportune situation developed. After Loch's return to England in April 1895, Rhodes seems to have adopted his scheme, which led to the abortive Jameson Raid into the Transvaal in December 1895. Loch, who meanwhile had been created Baron Loch, in 1896 thought it necessary to defend himself in the House of Lords against the charge that he had promised Uitlanders in Johannesburg armed intervention if they staged an insurrection.

Loch Cuan (Northern Ireland): *see* Strangford Lough.

Loch Éirne (Northern Ireland): *see* Erne, Lough.

Loch Garman (Ireland): *see* Wexford.

Loch nEathach (Northern Ireland): *see* Neagh, Lough.

Lochaber, district, Highland region, northwestern Scotland, created by the reorganization of 1975 from parts of the former counties of Inverness and Argyll. The district, area 1,724 sq mi (4,465 sq km), includes the islands of Rhum, Eigg, Canna, and Muck and mountain country rising to Ben Nevis (4,406 ft, or 1,343 m), the highest mountain in the British Isles. It is cut by Glen More nan Albin. Crofting (subsistence farming), cattle and sheep raising, and fishing are the chief occupations. Fort William, with an aluminum works, is the seat of the district authority. Mallaig is a herring fishery port with a ferry service to Skye. Pop. (1982 est.) 19,468.

Lochalsh (Scotland): *see* Skye and Lochalsh.

Loches, town, Indre-et-Loire *département,* Centre region, west central France, southeast of Tours, on the left bank of the Indre River. The town is dominated by the medieval citadel, which is surrounded by 1.5 mi (2 km) of old walls. It embraces three separate buildings: the Royal Lodge (mainly 15th century), the Collégiale Saint-Ours (10th–11th century), and a ruined fortress with an 11th-century keep and a 15th-century tower cut into the rock. Fortified in the 6th century, Loches was fought over by the French and English during the 12th and 13th centuries. It became a royal residence and a state prison in the 15th century, when Louis XI imprisoned his enemies there in iron cages. Today it is a centre for agricultural trade. Recently developed industry includes food preparations and electronics. To the northeast of the town is the Forêt de Loches, about 8,900 ac (3,600 ha) in area. Pop. (1982) 5,847.

The Royal Lodge (15th century), Loches, Fr.
Toni Schneiders—Bruce Coleman Inc.

Lochgilphead, burgh and holiday resort, Argyll and Bute district, Strathclyde region, Scotland, at the head of Loch (lake) Gilp, an inlet of Loch Fyne, by the side of the Crinan Canal (built 1793–1801). The burgh developed from an older herring fishing village and now shares the district's administrative offices with Inveraray and Dunoon. Pop. (1981) 2,460.

Lochmaben, royal burgh (1298), Annandale and Eskdale district, Dumfries and Galloway region, Scotland, situated near several small lochs in Annandale valley. Robert I the Bruce of Scotland (ruled 1306–29) had close associations with the town and, according to local tradition, was born in Lochmaben Castle. In 1290 a peel tower (small fortified tower) was erected by Edward I of England. In 1330 a stone castle was built, which remained in English hands until 1385. Pop. (1981) 1,714.

Lochnagar, scenic mountain of coarse red granite, Grampian region, Scotland, south of the River Dee. The mountain ridge, popularized in the 19th century by Lord Byron's poem "Lachin y Gair," has 11 summits over 3,000 ft (900 m), the highest being Cac Carn Beag (3,786 ft [1,154 m]). The name Lochnagar (Goat Lake) was originally applied only to the small loch at the foot of the eastern ridge.

Lochner, Stefan (b. *c.* 1400, Meersburg am Bodensee, Bishopric of Constance—d. 1451, Cologne), late Gothic painter, considered to be the greatest representative of the school of Cologne. He is known primarily for his highly mystical religious paintings.

Little is known of his early life, but he is thought to have studied in the Netherlands, possibly under Robert Campin (tentatively identified with the Master of Flémalle), whose influence is evident in the treatment of the drapery and the careful rendering of detail in what may be Lochner's earliest extant painting, "St. Jerome in His Cell" (heirs of Edith von Schröder Collection).

Lochner settled in Cologne about 1430. The earliest work he did there was an altarpiece for the church of St. Laurenz (centrepiece with the "Last Judgment" now in Wallraf-Richartz-Museum, Cologne; the wings are dispersed). The abundance of minute observation reflects his continued interest in Netherlandish art. But in the central panel he bound the various themes into a unified composition through the use of a dominating rhythmic design.

In the later 1430s Lochner must have been in the Netherlands again, where he encountered the art of van Eyck. The first work to reflect this influence is the "Madonna with the Violet" (*c.* 1443; Erzbischöfliches Diözesan-Museum, Cologne). Van Eyck's influence is most noticeable in Lochner's chief work, the great town hall altarpiece much admired by Dürer.

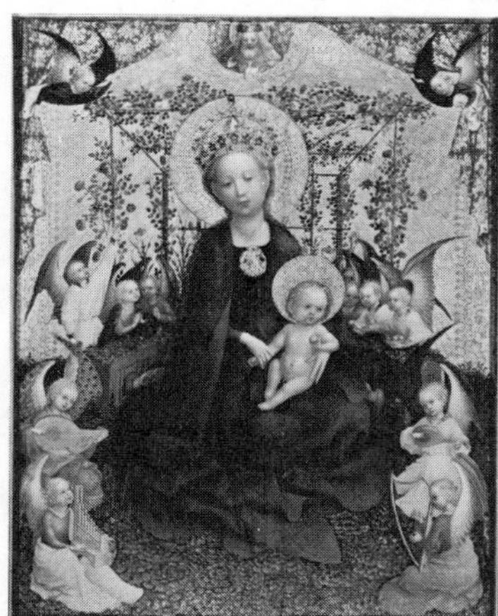

"Madonna of the Rose Bower," painting on wood by Stefan Lochner; in the Wallraf-Richartz-Museum, Cologne
By courtesy of the Wallraf-Richartz-Museum, Cologne

In this "Altar of the Patron Saints," now in Cologne cathedral, Lochner adds to the idealism of the older painters of the Cologne school with a wealth of naturalistic observation in the figures, while the sculpture-like draperies lend them a monumental dignity. In 1447 he became a member of the town council, and from the same year dates the splendid "Presentation in the Temple" (Hessisches Landesmuseum, Darmstadt), which was originally in St. Katharinen. The exquisite "Madonna of the Rose Bower" (Wallraf-Richartz-Museum, Cologne) was painted soon afterward.

Lochner became one of Cologne's greatest painters, combining naturalism with a masterful sense of colour and design into a festal solemnity of representation. His work forms perhaps the most successful visual interpretation of late medieval German mysticism before Grünewald. Book illumination was also done in his workshop.

lock, mechanical device for securing a door or receptacle so that it cannot be opened except by a key or by a series of manipulations that can be carried out only by a person knowing the secret or code.

Early history. The lock originated in the Near East; the oldest known example was found in the ruins of the palace of Khorsabad near Nineveh. Possibly 4,000 years old, it is of the type known as a pin-tumbler or, from its widespread use in Egypt, an Egyptian lock. It consists of a large wooden bolt, which secures the door, through which is pierced a slot with several holes in its upper surface. An assembly attached to the door contains several wooden pins positioned to drop into these holes and grip the bolt. The key is a large wooden bar, something like a toothbrush in shape; instead of bristles it has upright pegs that match the holes and the pins. Inserted in the large keyhole below the vertical pins it is simply lifted, raising the pins clear and allowing the bolt, with the key in it, to be slid back (Figure 1A). Locks of this type have been found in Japan, Norway, and the Faeroe Islands and are still in use in Egypt, India, and Zanzibar. An Old Testament reference, in Isaiah, "And I will place on his shoulder the key of the house of David," shows how the keys were carried. The falling-pin principle, a basic feature of many locks, was developed to the full in the modern Yale lock (Figure 2).

In a much more primitive device used by the Greeks, the bolt was moved by a sickle-shaped key of iron, often with an elaborately carved wooden handle. The key was passed through a hole in the door and turned, the point of the sickle engaging the bolt and drawing it back. Such a device could give but little security. The Romans introduced metal for locks, usually iron for the lock itself and often bronze for the key (with the result that keys are found more often today than locks). The Romans invented wards—*i.e.,* projections around the keyhole, inside the lock, which prevent the key from being rotated unless the flat face of the key (its bit) has slots cut in it in such a fashion that the projections pass through the slots. For centuries locks depended on the use of wards for security, and enormous ingenuity was employed in designing them and in cutting the keys so as to make the lock secure against any but the right key (Figure 1B). Such warded locks have always been comparatively easy to pick, since instruments can be made that clear the projections, no matter how complex. The Romans were the first to make small keys for locks—some so small that they could be worn on the fingers as rings. They also invented the padlock, which is found throughout the Near and Far East, where it was probably independently invented by the Chinese.

In the Middle Ages, great skill and a high degree of workmanship were employed in making metal locks, especially by the German metalworkers of Nürnberg. The moving parts of the locks were closely fitted and finished, and the exteriors were lavishly decorated. Even the keys were often virtual works of art. The security, however, was solely dependent on elaborate warding, the mechanism of the lock being developed hardly at all. One refinement was to conceal the keyhole by secret shutters, another was to provide blind keyholes, which forced the lock picker to waste time and effort. The 18th-century French excelled in making beautiful and intricate locks.

Development of modern types. The first serious attempt to improve the security of the lock was made in 1778 when Robert Barron, in England, patented a double-acting tumbler lock. A tumbler is a lever, or pawl, that falls into a slot in the bolt and prevents it being moved until it is raised by the key to exactly the right height out of the slot; the key then slides the bolt. The Barron lock (see Figure 1C) had two tumblers and the key had to raise each tumbler by a different amount before the bolts could be shot. This enormous advance in lock design remains the basic principle of all lever locks.

But even the Barron lock offered little resis-

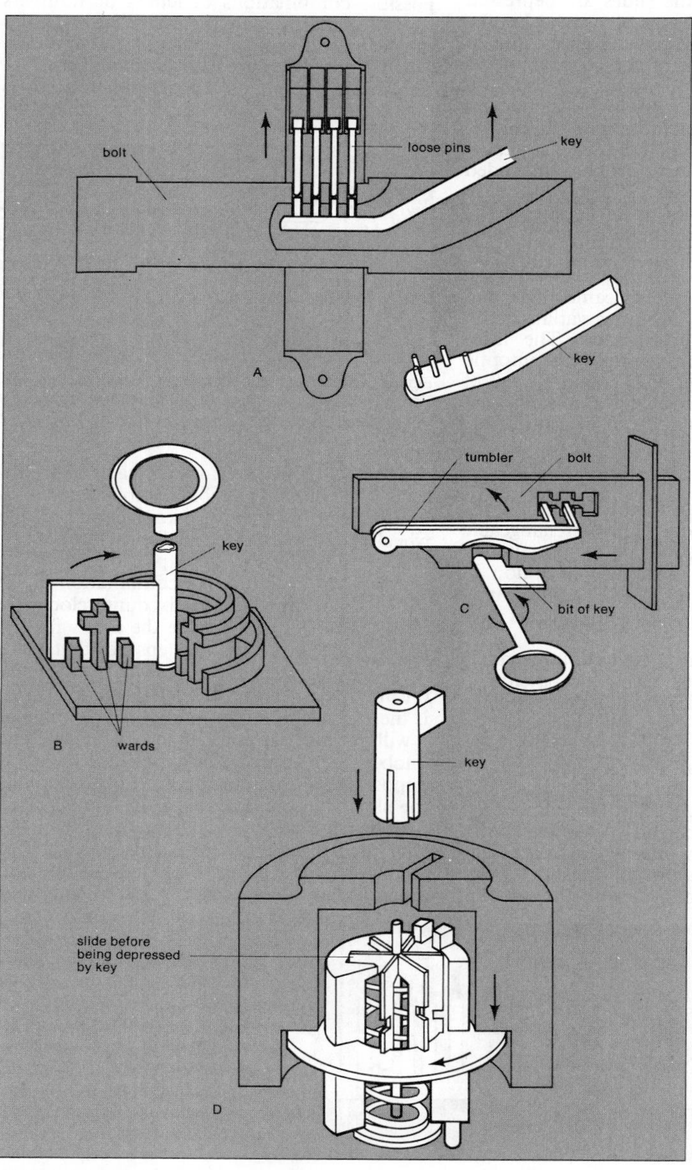

Figure 1: *Early locks*
(A) Ancient Egyptian lock; (B) warded lock and key; (C) Barron tumbler lock, 1778; (D) Bramah lock, 1784
After F.P. Gillman

tance to the determined lock picker, and in 1818 Jeremiah Chubb of Portsmouth, Eng., improved on the tumbler lock by incorporating a detector, a retaining spring that caught and held any tumbler which, in the course of picking, had been raised too high. This alone prevented the bolt from being withdrawn and also showed that the lock had been tampered with.

In 1784 (between Barron's lock and Chubb's improvements on it) a remarkable lock was patented in England by Joseph Bramah. Working on an entirely different principle, it used a very small light key, yet gave an unprecedented amount of security. Bramah's locks are very intricate (hence, expensive to make), and for their manufacture Bramah and his young assistant Henry Maudslay (later to become a famous engineer) constructed a series of machines to produce the parts mechanically. These were among the first machine tools designed for mass production. The Bramah key is a small metal tube that has narrow longitudinal slots cut in its end. When the key is pushed into the lock, it depresses a number of slides, each to the depth controlled by the slots. Only when all the slides are depressed to exactly the right distance can the key be turned and the bolt thrown (Figure 1D). So confident was Bramah of the security of his lock that he exhibited one in his London shop and offered a reward of £200 to the first person who could open it. For more than 50 years it remained unpicked, until 1851 when a skilled American locksmith, A.C. Hobbs, succeeded and claimed the reward.

The lock industry was in its heyday in the mid-19th century. With the rapidly expanding economy that followed the Industrial Revolution, the demand for locks grew tremendously.

In this period lock patents came thick and fast. All incorporated ingenious variations on the lever or Bramah principles. The most interesting was Robert Newell's Parautoptic lock, made by the firm of Day and Newell of New York City. Its special feature was that not only did it have two sets of lever tumblers, the first working on the second, but it also incorporated a plate that revolved with the key and prevented the inspection of the interior, an important step in thwarting the lock picker. It also had a key with interchangeable bits so that the key could be readily altered. Newell displayed an example in London in the Great Exhibition of 1851. Despite many attempts, there is no record that it has ever been picked.

In 1848 a far-reaching contribution was made by an American, Linus Yale, who patented a pin tumbler lock working on an adaptation of the ancient Egyptian principle. In the 1860s his son Linus Yale, Jr., evolved the Yale cylinder lock, with its small, flat key with serrated edge, now probably the most familiar lock and key in the world. Pins in the cylinder are raised to the proper heights by the serrations, making it possible to turn the cylinder. The number of combinations of heights of the pins (usually five), coupled with the warding effect of the crooked key and keyhole, give an almost unlimited number of variations (see Figure 2). It has come to be almost universally used for outside doors of buildings and automobile doors, although in the 1960s there was a trend toward supplementing it on house doors with the sturdy lever lock.

In the 1870s a new criminal technique swept the United States: robbers seized bank cashiers and forced them to yield keys or combinations to safes and vaults. To combat this type of crime, James Sargent of Rochester, N.Y., in 1873 devised a lock based on a principle patented earlier in Scotland, incorporating a clock that permitted the safe to be opened only at a preset time.

The keyless combination lock derives from the "letter-lock," in use in England at the beginning of the 17th century. In it a number of rings (inscribed with letters or numbers) are threaded on a spindle; when the rings are turned so that a particular word or number is formed, the spindle can be drawn out because slots inside the rings all fall in line. Originally, these letter locks were used only for padlocks and trick boxes. In the last half of the 19th century, as developed for safes and strong-room doors, they proved to be the most secure form of closure. The number of possible combinations of letters or numbers is almost infinite and they have no keyholes into which an explosive charge can be placed. Furthermore, they are easy to manufacture.

A simple combination lock with four rings (tumblers, in the U.S.) and 100 numbers on the dial (*i.e.,* 100 positions for each ring) presents 100,000,000 possible combinations. Figure 3 shows how the single knob can set all the wheels; in this case the lock has three rings, or wheels, giving 1,000,000 possible combinations. If, for example, the combination is 48, 15, 90, the knob is turned counterclockwise until the 48 comes opposite the arrow for the fourth time, a process that ensures that there is no play between the other wheels. The slot on the first wheel (on the left in the diagram) is then in the correct position for opening and it will not move in subsequent operations. The knob is then turned clockwise until the 15 is opposite the arrow for the third time; this sets the slot of the middle wheel in line with the first. Finally, the knob is turned counterclockwise to bring the 90 for the second time to the arrow. All three slots are then in line and a handle can be turned to withdraw the bolts.

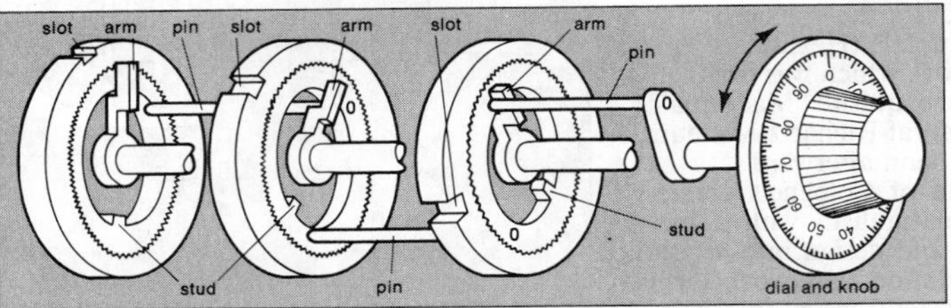

Figure 3: *Combination safe lock*
The lock cannot be opened until the slots on the three wheels are in line; movement of the dial is transmitted to each wheel by a system of pins (in practice much shorter than shown), arms, and studs

The combination can easily be changed, for the serrations shown on each wheel enable the slot to be set to a different position relative to the stud for that wheel.

It is frequently necessary, particularly in hotels and office buildings, for a manager or caretaker to have a master key that will open all the locks in the building. To design a set of single locks each of which can be opened by its own key, and also by the master key, requires a coordinated arrangement of the warding. The master key is so shaped as to avoid the wards of all the locks. Another method involves two keyholes, one for the normal key, the other for the master key, or two sets of tumblers or levers, or in the case of Yale locks, two concentric cylinders.

Present status of locks and safes. Over the years, locks have been constructed with many specialized functions. Some have been designed to resist being blown open, others to shoot or stab intruders or seize their hands. Locks have been made that can be opened or closed by different keys but can be unlocked only by the key that closed them. So-called unpickable locks are usually devised to prevent a thief from exploring the positions of the lock parts from the keyhole or from sensing with his picking tool slight changes of resistance when pressure is applied to the bolt. The basic types, however, remain the Bramah, lever, Yale, and combination locks, though innumerable variations have been made, sometimes combining features of each. The Swiss Kaba lock, for example, employs the Yale principle but its key, instead of having a serrated edge, has flat sides marked with deep depressions into which four complete sets of pin-tumblers are pressed. The Finnish Abloy lock is a compact combination lock, but the rings, instead of being turned separately by hand, are moved to the correct positions by a single turn of a small key.

Magnetic forces can be used in locks working on the Yale principle. The key has no serrations; instead, it contains a number of small magnets. When the key is inserted into the lock, these magnets repel magnetized spring-loaded pins, raising them in the same way that the serrations on a Yale-type key raise them mechanically. When these pins are raised the correct height, the cylinder of the lock is free to rotate in the barrel.

The importance of locks as a protection against professional thieves declined after World War II, during which the knowledge and use of explosives was widely disseminated. As most safe locks and strong-room locks became almost unpickable, criminals tended to ignore the locks and to use explosives to blow them off. An attempt to blow up the mechanism of a lock by detonating an explosive in the keyhole can be foiled by introducing a second series of bolts, not connected to the lock mechanism, but automatically inserted by springs when an explosion occurs; the safe then cannot be opened except by cutting through the armour.

Another method used by criminals is to burn away the plating or hinge of a safe by an electric arc or an oxyacetylene flame, an op-

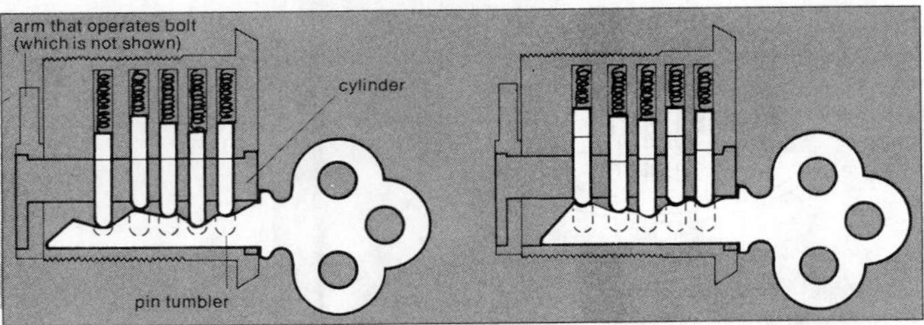

Figure 2: *Contemporary version of the Yale lock*
(Left) All pins lifted to proper height by correct key, which can be turned to open lock, and (right) pins lifted to incorrect height by wrong key, lock will not open
After F.P. Gillman

eration requiring many hours' work. To resist this type of entry, safe makers produced even more resistant materials and new methods of construction to carry away the heat of the cutting flame.

lock, enclosure or basin located in the course of a canal or a river (or in the vicinity of a dock) with gates at each end, within which the water level may be varied to raise or lower boats. Where the required lift is of considerable height, a series of connected but isolable basins, or locks, is used. On the Trollhätte Canal, Sweden, three locks overcome a total rise of 77 feet (23 m). Single locks of greater rise are known (*e.g.,* a 50-foot [15-metre] rise lock on the canal bypassing the Falls of St. Anthony in Minnesota). The mitred canal gate, angled into the downward force of the stream and replacing the earlier vertical lift gate, may have been invented by Leonardo da Vinci for the San Marco Lock in Milan, making possible the interconnection, formerly prevented by their different levels, of the Martesana Canal and the Naviglio Grande.

Lock Haven, city, seat (1839) of Clinton county, north-central Pennsylvania, U.S. It lies along the West Branch of the Susquehanna River, in the Bald Eagle Mountains, 26 miles (42 km) southwest of Williamsport. Founded in 1834 by Jeremiah Church, a land speculator, it was laid out on the site of the frontier post, Fort Reed, and developed as a lumbering centre. It was named for the Pennsylvania Canal lock and the huge lumber boom that made it a "haven" for lumberjacks from nearby logging camps. The city's manufactures include small aircraft, paper, textiles, and clay and metal products. Lock Haven State College was founded in 1870. Kettle Creek and Bald Eagle State parks and the Bucktail Natural Area are nearby. Inc. borough, 1840; city, 1870. Pop. (1990) 9,230.

Locke, Alain (LeRoy) (b. Sept. 13, 1886, Philadelphia—d. June 9, 1954, New York City), American educator, writer, and philosopher, best remembered as the leader and chief interpreter of the Harlem Renaissance (*q.v.*).

Alain Locke
By courtesy of Howard University, Washington, D.C.

Graduated in philosophy from Harvard University (1907), Locke was the first black Rhodes scholar, studying at Oxford (1907–10) and the University of Berlin (1910–11). He received his Ph.D. in philosophy from Harvard (1918). For almost 40 years, until retirement in 1953 as head of the department of philosophy, Locke taught at Howard University, Washington, D.C.

Locke stimulated and guided artistic activities and promoted the recognition and respect of blacks by the total American community. Having studied African culture and traced its influences upon Western civilization, he urged black painters, sculptors, and musicians to look to African sources for identity and to discover materials and techniques for their work. He encouraged black authors to seek subjects in black life and to set high artistic standards for themselves. He familiarized American readers with the Harlem Renaissance by editing a special Harlem issue for *Survey Graphic* (March 1925), which he expanded into *The New Negro* (1925), an anthology of fiction, poetry, drama, and essays.

Locke edited the *Bronze Booklet* studies of cultural achievements by blacks. For almost two decades he annually reviewed literature by and about blacks in *Opportunity* and *Phylon,* and from 1940 until his death he regularly wrote about blacks for the *Britannica Book of the Year.* His many works include *Four Negro Poets* (1927), *Frederick Douglass, a Biography of Anti-Slavery* (1935), *Negro Art—Past and Present* (1936), and *The Negro and His Music* (1936). He left unfinished materials for a definitive study of the contributions of blacks to American culture. His materials formed the basis for M.J. Butcher's *The Negro in American Culture* (1956).

A humanist who was intensely concerned with aesthetics, Locke termed his philosophy "cultural pluralism" and emphasized the necessity of determining values to guide human conduct and interrelationships. Chief among these values was respect for the uniqueness of each personality, which can develop fully and remain unique only within a democratic ethos.

Locke, Bobby, byname of ARTHUR D'ARCY LOCKE (b. Nov. 20, 1917, Germiston, Transvaal, S.Af.—d. March 9, 1987, Johannesburg), South African golfer who won the British Open four times.

A meticulous putter who was considered among the best in golf, Locke won the Vardon Trophy for lowest scoring average among male professional golfers in 1946, 1950, and 1954. Nine times the winner of the South African Open championship (1935, 1937–40, 1946, 1950–51, and 1955) and six times the winner of the South African Professional championship, he was considered, with Gary Player, to be one of South Africa's greatest golfers.

The son of Irish immigrants, he won his first tournament at the age of 14. He served as a South African Air Force bomber pilot in World War II. After the war his victories included the Canadian Open (1947), the French Open (1952–53), and the German Open (1954). Before the war he twice was leading amateur in the British Open and won it in 1949, 1950, 1952, and 1957. Noted for his steady play, he finished in the top 10 in all but three of the 25 tournaments he entered in 1948. He wrote *Bobby Locke on Golf* (1953).

Locke, David Ross: *see* Nasby, Petroleum V(esuvius).

Locke, John (b. Aug. 29, 1632, Wrington, Somerset, Eng.—d. Oct. 28, 1704, Oates, Essex), English political and educational philosopher who laid the epistemological foundations of modern science. He was the initiator of the Age of Enlightenment and Reason in England and France, an inspirer of the U.S. Constitution, and is still a powerful influence on the life and thought of the West.

A brief treatment of John Locke follows. For full treatment, *see* MACROPAEDIA: Locke.

Locke was educated at Westminster School and Oxford, where he was fascinated with experimental science. After gaining diplomatic experience abroad (1665), Locke became physician and adviser (1667) to Lord Ashley (later 1st earl of Shaftesbury) and collaborated with such scientists as Robert Boyle. He was elected to the Royal Society (1668) and was attracted by the liberal ideas of the Cambridge Platonists and Latitudinarians.

By 1675 Locke suffered from asthma, and, believing at this time that his ailment was phthisis and hoping to improve his health, he went to France late in the year. He spent his time partly in Montpellier, where there was a good medical school; partly in Paris, where he made friends with several scholars and scientists who influenced his developing empiricism; and partly traveling about France. He particularly studied that country's great works of civil engineering, its methods of cultivation, and Louis XIV's treatment of his Protestant subjects, whose rights, granted them by the Edict of Nantes, were being diminished legally or by chicanery. He also worked on what was to be his major book, the *Essay Concerning Human Understanding* (1689), and wrote short essays on various philosophical subjects.

The fall of Shaftesbury and his adherents, now called Whigs, and the accession of James II forced Locke to live in Holland from 1683 to 1689. He was declared a traitor (1685) but returned to England in 1689 after William of Orange became king. In 1691 Locke retired to Essex, where he continued to write, prepare fresh editions of the *Essay,* superintend a French translation (by P. Coste, 1700), and answer criticism.

Locke, Matthew (b. *c.* 1630, Exeter, Devon, Eng.—d. August 1677, London), leading English composer for the stage in the period before Henry Purcell.

By 1661 Locke had been appointed composer in ordinary to the king. After his conversion to Roman Catholicism he was appointed organist to the queen. With Christopher Gibbons he wrote the music for James Shirley's masque *Cupid and Death* (1653), possibly the most elaborate masque of the period. He also wrote part of the music for Sir William Davenant's *The Siege of Rhodes* (1656), which is usually considered the first English opera. Other stage works were music for Thomas Shadwell's *Psyche* (1673), for Davenant's version of *Macbeth* (1663), and for Shadwell's version of *The Tempest* (1674). In *The Tempest* Locke used for the first time in English music directions such as "soft" and "louder by degrees" and included tremolos for stringed instruments.

Matthew Locke, portrait by an unknown artist; in the collection of the Faculty of Music, University of Oxford
By courtesy of the Faculty of Music, University of Oxford

Locke's instrumental music, which is harmonically less daring than his vocal music, is considered among the finest of the 17th century; an example is the *Little Consort of Three Parts* (1656) for viols. He also wrote music for the coronation festivities of Charles II and anthems for the Chapel Royal. His treatise *Melothesia* (1673) was one of the earliest English works to deal with "Certain General Rules for playing upon a Continued Bass."

Lockhart, John Gibson (b. July 14, 1794, Wishaw, Lanarkshire, Scot.—d. Nov. 25, 1854, Abbotsford, near Melrose, Roxburghshire), Scottish critic, novelist, and biographer, best remembered for his *Life of Sir Walter Scott* (1837–38; enlarged 1839), one of the great biographies in English.

Lockhart, the son of a Presbyterian minister descended from the landed gentry, studied at the universities of Glasgow and Oxford and began the practice of law in Edinburgh in

1816. He was too reserved for the law, however, and turned to writing.

Lockhart became one of the main contributors to the Tory-oriented *Edinburgh Monthly Magazine* (later *Blackwood's Edinburgh Magazine*) from the time of its founding in 1817.

Lockhart, detail of an oil painting by H.W. Pickersgill, 1830

By courtesy of the John Murray (Publishers) Ltd., London

With others, he wrote the "Translation from an Ancient Chaldee Manuscript," which lampooned Scottish celebrities in a parody of Old Testament style; this article made *Blackwood's* an immediate succès de scandale. Another article mainly written by Lockhart, "On the Cockney School of Poetry," was the first of a series of attacks on the English poets John Keats and Percy Bysshe Shelley.

In 1818 Lockhart met Sir Walter Scott, the "elder statesman" of European Romanticism. Lockhart married Scott's daughter Sophia in 1820, became, through his influence, editor (1825–53) of the Tory *Quarterly Review,* and inherited Scott's Abbotsford estate. Though attacked by contemporaries for exposing Scott's faults, Lockhart's *Life* is now regarded as an idealized portrait, depicting Scott's success in brilliant colour.

During his long tenure at *The Quarterly Review,* Lockhart contributed much sound literary criticism, giving judicious praise to William Wordsworth, Samuel Taylor Coleridge, Shelley, and Lord Byron. Early in his editorship (1828) he produced a biography of Robert Burns that showed sympathetic insight into that Scottish poet's life. Other works include a "daring" novel about a clergyman's surrender to sexual temptation, *Adam Blair* (1822).

Lockheed Martin Corporation, major American diversified company with core business concentrations in aerospace products including aircraft, space launchers, satellites, and defense systems. It was formed in 1995 from the merger of Lockheed Corporation and Martin Marietta Corporation. In 1996 the company acquired Loral Corporation's defense electronics and systems. Headquarters are in Bethesda, Md.

Lockheed Corporation was formed in 1926 as Lockheed Aircraft Company by Allan Lockheed (originally Loughead). With John K. Northrop as chief designer, the company developed the Vega, a streamlined wooden monoplane that set many speed and endurance records. In 1929 the firm was sold to Detroit Aircraft Corporation, which went bankrupt in 1932. A group of investors soon bought Lockheed's assets, and the company's fortunes were revived after the introduction in 1934 of its Electra, a twin-engine, all-metal airliner.

With the advent of World War II, Lockheed began a long association with the U.S. military by producing the P-38 Lightning fighter-interceptor. In 1943 it formed a highly secret division, Advanced Development Projects (ADP), popularly known as the "Skunk Works," under the leadership of the designer Clarence L. ("Kelly") Johnson. After the war, ADP became the leading U.S. military aircraft developer, producing the F-104 Starfighter and the U-2 and SR-71 Blackbird spy planes. Later its stealth aircraft research culminated in the F-117A Nighthawk fighter. Lockheed also built antisubmarine aircraft and such transports as the turboprop-driven C-130 Hercules and the huge jet-powered C-5 Galaxy.

In the civilian sector after World War II, Lockheed introduced the propeller-driven Constellation and the Super Constellation airliners, but its production of the L-1011 TriStar jetliner (first flown 1970) was troubled by the bankruptcy of the plane's engine maker, Rolls-Royce, in 1971. Delays to the L-1011, combined with other problems, placed Lockheed in severe financial straits. The plane and its manufacturer were saved only through massive loan guarantees from the U.S. government and the nationalization of Rolls-Royce by the British government.

Lockheed's work in missile development, beginning in the 1950s, resulted in the Polaris, Poseidon, and Trident submarine-launched ballistic missile systems for the U.S. Navy. In the space sector, its activities included the development of the Agena rocket. It also was responsible for the construction and systems integration of the Hubble Space Telescope. In the early 1990s it acquired the Fort Worth (Texas) Division of General Dynamics, whose major product was the F-16 fighter. In partnership with Boeing, it contracted to build the F-22 Raptor stealth fighter for the U.S. Air Force. In 1995, as Lockheed Martin, it formed a joint venture, International Launch Services, with the Russian firms Energia and Khrunichev to market commercial space-launch services worldwide.

Martin Marietta has its roots in Martin Company, formed in 1928 by Glenn L. Martin. The firm's M-130 flying boat was a pre-World War II mainstay for transoceanic Clipper service. In the 1950s it began work on ballistic missiles, including the Titan, which it later developed into a series of space launchers. In 1961 Martin Company merged with American-Marietta Company (incorporated 1930), a leading supplier of construction materials.

Martin Marietta's contributions in the space sector included the construction of the landers for the Viking missions to Mars and the Venus-mapping Magellan spacecraft; it also designed and produced the U.S. space shuttle's external fuel tank. In the early 1990s it acquired General Electric's aerospace business and the space systems division of General Dynamics, producer of the Atlas launcher and Centaur upper-stage rocket.

lockjaw (disease): *see* tetanus.

lockout, tactic used by employers in labour disputes in which the employer withholds employment, usually by locking employees out of work facilities. In modern times the lockout is seldom used, usually being resorted to when a labour union strikes a single employer who is a member of an employers' association whose members have agreed to close their work facilities when one member is struck.

In the 1880s and '90s, when unions of silver and lead miners in Nevada, Colorado, Idaho, and Utah were fighting for an eight-hour day and higher pay, employers often used the lockout. During this period it was also often used against the Knights of Labor in industries that included meatpacking, cigar making, knitting, and laundering. The lockout was central to the demise of that labour organization.

Lockwood, Belva Ann, *née* BENNETT (b. Oct. 24, 1830, Royalton, N.Y., U.S.—d. May 19, 1917, Washington, D.C.), feminist and lawyer who was the first woman admitted to practice law before the U.S. Supreme Court.

After a career in teaching, Lockwood pursued a legal education and earned a law degree in 1873 from the National University Law School. She was admitted to the District of Columbia bar in 1873 but was not allowed to speak before the U.S. Supreme Court because of "custom." Lockwood successfully lobbied Congress for a bill permitting women to practice before the federal courts, and in 1879 she became the first woman admitted to practice before the U.S. Supreme Court.

Lockwood was one of the most effective legal advocates of women's rights of her time. She contributed to the passage of laws granting women equal property rights and equal guardianship of children, and she prepared amendments granting suffrage to women in the statehood bills for Oklahoma, New Mexico, and Arizona. In 1884 and 1888 she ran for the U.S. presidency as the candidate of the National Equal Rights Party. In her later years she also became a staunch advocate of peace arbitration.

Lockyer, Sir Joseph Norman (b. May 17, 1836, Rugby, Warwickshire, Eng.—d. Aug. 16, 1920, Salcombe Regis, Devon), British astronomer who in 1868 discovered in the Sun's atmosphere a previously unknown element that he named helium.

Lockyer

BBC Hulton Picture Library

Lockyer became a clerk in the War Office in 1857, but his interest in astronomy eventually led to a career in that field. He initiated in 1866 the spectroscopic observation of sunspots, and in 1868 he found that solar prominences are upheavals in a layer around the Sun, which he named the chromosphere. Also in 1868, he and Pierre Janssen, working independently, discovered a spectroscopic method of observing solar prominences without the aid of an eclipse to block out the glare of the Sun. Lockyer identified the element helium in the solar spectrum 27 years before that element was found on the Earth.

Between 1870 and 1905, Lockyer conducted eight expeditions to observe solar eclipses. He also built a private observatory at Sidmouth and theorized on stellar evolution. A prolific writer, he founded the science periodical *Nature* in 1869 and edited it until a few months before his death. He was knighted in 1897.

Locmariaquer, village and seaside resort, on the coast of the Gulf of Morbihan, Morbihan *département,* Bretagne *région,* western France, south of Auray. It is famous for its megalithic monuments, notably the Fairies' Stone, a huge, broken standing stone, originally 66 feet (20 m) high—the greatest known menhir (upright monumental stone) in existence. Behind it is the Merchants' Table, composed of three carved slabs and 17 supporting stones. Pop. (1990) 1,316.

Locofoco Party, in U.S. history, radical wing of the Democratic Party, organized in New York City in 1835. Made up primarily of workingmen and reformers, the Locofocos were opposed to state banks, monopolies, paper money, tariffs, and generally any financial policies that seemed to them antidemocratic and conducive to special privilege. The Locofocos received their name (which was later derisively applied by political opponents to all Democrats) when party regulars in New

York turned off the gas lights to oust the radicals from a Tammany Hall nominating meeting. The radicals responded by lighting candles with the new self-igniting friction matches known as locofocos, and proceeded to nominate their own slate.

Never a national party, the Locofocos reached their peak when President Van Buren urged and Congress passed (July 4, 1840) the Independent Treasury Act; it fulfilled the primary Locofoco aim: complete separation of government from banking. After 1840 Locofoco political influence was largely confined to New York, and by the end of the decade many Locofocos were allied with the Barnburner Democrats, who eventually left the party over the slavery extension issue.

locomotion, in ethology, any of a variety of movements among animals that results in progression from one place to another.

A brief treatment of locomotion follows. For full treatment, *see* MACROPAEDIA: Behaviour, Animal.

All locomotion systems require both propulsion and control mechanisms that vary with the animal's habitat, which may be aquatic, fossorial (underground), terrestrial, or aerial (including arboreal). In all of these situations, the forces of gravity and drag that resist upward and forward movement, respectively, are found in different degrees. Most animals have evolved muscular systems to counteract these forces as well as skeletons that prevent their bodies from collapsing.

Animal locomotion is classified as either appendicular, accomplished by special appendages, or axial, achieved by changing the body shape. In passive locomotion, an animal depends on the environment for mobility; the remora, for example, attaches itself to another fish. Aquatic protozoans (one-celled animals) move by ciliary or flagellar appendages, both acting like oars, or by pseudopods, footlike appendages into which the body empties itself and then extends the appendage again. Aquatic invertebrates move along the bottom by ciliary movement or muscular contraction; by walking, like crabs and lobsters; or by the contract–anchor–extend method, which is best developed in leeches. Swimming may be accomplished by either hydraulic propulsion (jellyfish and scallops) or undulation (eels and fishes). Undulatory locomotion is also used by aquatic vertebrates that have walking appendages (salamanders and lizards), but most aquatic tetrapods move by the appendicular motion of hind legs or flippers. Most aquatic birds are propelled by webbed feet.

Fossorial animals move by building tunnels. Soft-bodied invertebrates burrow by peristaltic action (worms) or the contract–anchor–extend method (clams). Some invertebrates, chiefly mollusks, can bore through rock by chemical or mechanical means. Fossorial vertebrates may be amphibians, reptiles (usually with axial locomotion), or mammals that rely mostly on strongly developed forelegs and claws.

Terrestrial locomotion among invertebrates has developed mainly in the arthropods (*e.g.,* insects, spiders, and crustaceans). Because the legs of these animals provide support as well as locomotion, limb movements must be synchronized in order to maintain the animal's balance. Locomotion takes place in two stages: the propulsive or retractive stage, in which the body pivots forward over the stationary leg and foot, and the recovery or protractive stage, beginning with foot lift-off and ending with footfall, in which the body remains stationary. Saltatory, or leaping, animals (rabbits, kangaroos, and many insects) have hind legs about twice as long as their most anterior front legs. Crawling animals move by peristaltic or contract–anchor–extend motion, except for those without limbs.

Each group of arboreal animals has a unique method of climbing, but all have strong grasping ability and are able to maintain their centre of gravity near the object being climbed. Grasping is achieved by prehensile tails or toes or by scales that enable the animal to cling to the surface. Climbing birds hold on with their feet and brace themselves with stiffened tail feathers; some use their bills. Arboreal leaping is mechanically similar to the terrestrial type, while brachiation (swinging) is accomplished by the forelegs. Gliding may be either gravitational, used by amphibians, reptiles, and mammals, or soaring, which is confined to birds. Lift-off is achieved by flapping, and height is regulated by air currents. Soaring is either static, at relatively high levels over land, or dynamic, at lower levels and usually over water.

True flight, developed in insects, birds, and mammals, is achieved by the forward thrust of lateral appendages and is independent of gravitational pull or air currents. Thrust is produced by simultaneous rotation of left and right wings in a circle or figure eight. The wing movement of insects is caused by pulsations of the thorax rather than by muscles. Patterns of flight and wing movements are distinctive for each species. Hovering flight is found in some birds, mainly hummingbirds, but most birds and bats use propulsive flight.

locomotive, any of various self-propelled vehicles used for hauling railroad cars on tracks.

A brief treatment of locomotives follows. For full treatment, *see* MACROPAEDIA: Transportation.

The three main sources of power for locomotives are steam, electricity, and oil. The first locomotive to do actual work, the "New Castle" built in 1803 by Richard Trevithick for a Welsh tramroad, was too heavy for the iron rails of the time. The first practical locomotive was built in 1812 by John Blenkinsop, an inspector at the Middleton colliery near Leeds, Eng. Two vertical cylinders drove two shafts that in turn were geared to a toothed wheel that meshed with a rack rail.

By 1829 the English engineer George Stephenson had developed a locomotive, the "Rocket," that was the prototype for the modern steam locomotive. Instead of the single-flue boiler that had been used until then, Stephenson created a multiple fire-tube boiler. The "Rocket" also exhausted steam and created a draft in its firebox in the manner of modern locomotives. Its pistons were connected to a single pair of driving wheels that were flanged on the inside to keep them from sliding off the rails. In the United States John Stevens ran the first locomotive in 1825 on a three-rail track, the centre rail engaging a toothed wheel on the engine.

From the single pair of driving wheels on the "Rocket," locomotives were soon developed with four coupled wheels, relying for traction on the simple friction produced between the wheels and the rails by the weight of the engine. Until well after 1865, an engine with four driving wheels and four pilot (or leading) wheels to guide it around curves was the dominant locomotive type in the United States; it was known as the American Standard. Like all steam locomotives, it heated water to boiling, then channelled the resulting steam into a cylinder. The great force of escaping steam drove a piston that was linked to the driving wheels, causing them to revolve and to move the locomotive and the rest of the train.

In the 20th century steam locomotives became huge, sophisticated machines capable of moving freight trains of 200 cars at 75 miles (120 kilometres) per hour. The drive wheels became as much as seven feet (two metres) in diameter, and on the largest engines their number was increased to 16. Smaller "trailing" wheels behind the drivers supported even larger fireboxes that heated water in immense horizontal boilers. Smaller locomotives, especially in Europe, carried their own fuel (coal or sometimes oil), but most carried their fuel and water in a car coupled behind them.

Steam locomotives were simple and could withstand much wear and tear; but they required extensive servicing after relatively short trips, tended to kink rails because of their pounding motion, and needed separate crews for each engine. Their thermal efficiency was seldom greater than about 6 percent because of incomplete combustion and heat losses. For these reasons, the steam locomotive is practically extinct. Only in China and in some parts of India and sub-Saharan Africa are steam locomotives still in daily use.

Even as steam locomotives were being developed, designers were experimenting with the idea of using electricity for motive power. Batteries were tried as early as 1835, but it was not until 1879 that the first practical electric locomotive was run at an exhibition in Berlin. In the United States the Baltimore and Ohio Railroad ran an electric locomotive under Baltimore harbour in 1895; in Italy electric locomotives were operating on main lines by 1902.

Unlike steam and diesel-electric locomotives, which produce their own power, electric locomotives simply convert the electric power that is generated elsewhere. They can thus develop more power than their rated capacity for short times when subject to increased loads, such as climbing a steep grade or starting a heavy train. Because of their simpler machinery, they require less maintenance, their maintenance costs are much lower, and they last longer than diesel-electrics.

In order to be economical, however, electric traction requires the availability of cheap electricity. The traffic density must also be heavy enough to justify the high cost of maintaining generating facilities and the overhead wires or trackside rail that carry electric current to the locomotive. In the Scandinavian countries and Italy more than one-half of the railroad route miles are electrified, and in France about one-third. In the United States, however, only about 1 percent of the railroad routes are electrified; these are mostly in the Northeast between major cities.

The diesel-electric locomotive uses a diesel engine to run a generator that produces electricity for traction motors geared directly to the axles of the engine. Diesel switching engines were in use by 1925. Main-line diesel service was launched in Germany in 1932, with a two-car, streamlined train that was capable of running at an average speed of 77 miles per hour. In 1935 passenger engines were in use in the United States, and by 1939 the first freight units were being built.

Although the use of steam locomotives was prolonged by World War II, after the war diesels quickly supplanted steam, first in North America and then in Europe. The thermal efficiency of diesels is about four times as great as that of steam locomotives, and they thus require substantially less fuel for equivalent power. They can accelerate more quickly, run at higher speeds with less damage to the track, and require less servicing than steam engines. Diesels also function with the efficiency of electric locomotives (within the limits of their power-generating capacity) but do not require the capital investment in substations and electrical-distribution networks needed by electrics. Especially attractive to railroad management is the diesel's flexibility: Many units can be combined according to the power needed for a particular train with only one crew required for all the units.

There has also been a substantial amount of experimentation with turbines as alternate sources of motive power. One successful model is a passenger train powered by aircraft-type turbines that went into service in the United

States and Canada in 1969. Other trains have been developed that use gas turbines and turbine-electric combinations.

Consult the INDEX *first*

locoweed, any of several species of poisonous plants of the genera *Astragalus* and *Oxytropis*, in the pea family (Fabaceae), native to the prairies of north central and western North America. Locoweeds pose a danger to livestock, horses, and other grazing animals, because they contain a toxin that affects muscle control, producing frenzied behaviour, impaired vision, and sometimes death. Most locoweeds, however, are unpalatable to livestock and are eaten only when other forage is

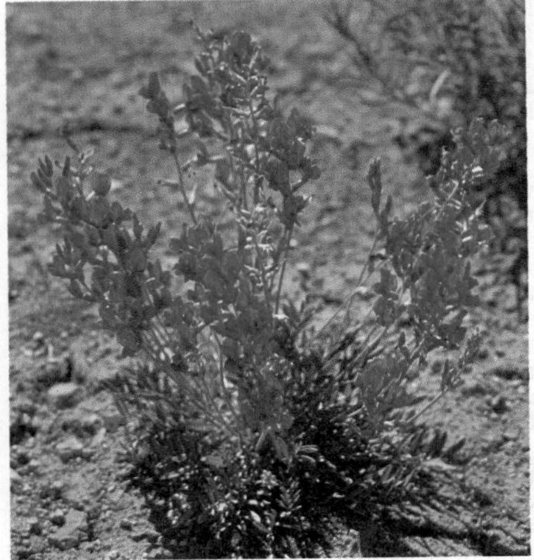

Locoweed (*Astragalus*)
Arthur H. Bilsten—EB Inc.

unavailable. The level of toxicity appears to depend on soil conditions; decaying locoweeds release toxins sometimes taken up by otherwise harmless forage crops.

Many species are low-growing plants, up to 45 centimetres (1½ feet) high, of variable hairiness with fernlike leaves and spikes of pealike flowers. A few are especially dangerous: woolly locoweed (*Astragalus mollissimus*), with woolly leaves and violet flowers; *A. wootonii*, with whitish flowers; crazyweed, or purple loco (*Oxytropis lambertii*), with pink to purplish flowers; and the showy oxytropis (*O. splendens*), bearing silvery hairs and rich lavender-pink flowers.

Locri Epizephyrii, also called LOCRI, ancient city on the eastern side of the "toe" of Italy, founded by Greeks *c.* 680 BC; the inhabitants used the name of Locri Epizephyrii to distinguish themselves from the Locri of Greece.

Persephone being carried off to the underworld, terra-cotta plaque from the sanctuary of Persephone at Locri Epizephyrii, first half of the 5th century BC; in the Museo Nazionale di Taranto, Italy
Leonard Von Matt—EB Inc.

Locri Epizephyrii was the first Greek community to have a written code of laws, given by Zaleucus *c.* 660 BC. Locri Epizephyrii founded colonies, repelled the attacks of Croton during the 6th century, and worked against Athenian intervention in the west during the Peloponnesian War. Dionysius I of Syracuse married a Locrian, increased the city's territory, and enlarged its walls, but the city lost its freedom. Locri Epizephyrii continually changed allegiance between Rome and its enemies until the Romans under Scipio Africanus captured the city in 205 BC. Sicilian Muslims destroyed the city in 915.

Excavations in 1889–90, and resumed in 1954, disclosed a Doric temple, a sanctuary of Persephone, and numerous 5th-century-BC terra-cotta native plaques (*pinakes*). The discovery of prehistoric objects confirmed the accounts by Thucydides and Polybius that the Greeks were not the first settlers.

locust, species of short-horned grasshopper (orthopteran family Acrididae) that often increases greatly in number and migrates long distances in destructive swarms. In Europe the word locust connotes large size; smaller acridids are called grasshoppers. In North America the names locust and grasshopper are used for any acridid. A cicada (order Homoptera) also may be called a locust; the 17-year "locust" actually is the periodic, or 17-year, cicada (*see* cicada). The grouse (or pygmy) locust is a member of the family Tetrigidae (*see* pygmy grasshopper).

A phase theory has been developed to account for the sporadic appearance and disappearance of locust swarms. According to the theory a plague species has two phases; one solitary, the other gregarious. The phases can be distinguished by differences in coloration, form, physiology, and behaviour of the species. A solitary phase nymph, for example, adjusts its coloration to match that of its surroundings; it does not collect in groups, has low metabolic and oxygen-intake rates, and is sluggish. A gregarious phase nymph, on the other hand, has black and yellow (orange) coloration in a fixed pattern, gathers in large groups, has high metabolic and oxygen intake rates, and is active and nervous. Adult locusts differ more in form than in colour. The solitary phase has shorter wings, longer legs, and a narrower pronotum, or dorsal sclerite (with higher crest and larger head), than the gregarious. The adult of this phase has a more saddle-shaped pronotum, broader shoulders, and long wings.

When a nymph of a solitary phase locust matures in the presence of many other locusts, it changes toward a gregarious type; if crowding is sufficiently dense and of long enough duration the gregarious migratory phase results. The young of a gregarious phase locust, on the other hand, reverts to the solitary phase if it matures in isolation. The solitary phase is the normal state of the species; the gregarious phase is a physiological response to violent fluctuations in the environment. Migratory swarms do not form in regions favourable for the growth of a species; instead they form in regions, called marginal regions, in which suitable habitats are scarce. A succession of favourable seasons enables a restricted population to expand in numbers so that individuals are forced into marginal areas. When unfavourable environmental conditions occur in the marginal regions the enlarged populations are forced to return to the small, permanently habitable areas; crowding results.

A gregarious phase locust is restless and irritable; it flies spontaneously on warm, dry days when its body temperature is high. The muscular activity of flight further raises its temperature. A swarm ceases flying only when environmental conditions change; *e.g.*, rain falls, temperature decreases, or darkness occurs. In 1869 desert locust swarms reached England, probably from West Africa, and a flight across the Red Sea in 1889 was estimated as about 2,000 square miles in size.

The range of the migratory locust (*Locusta migratoria*) is wider than that of any other acridid. It is found in grasslands throughout

(Left) Gregarious phase and (right) solitary phase of the desert locust (*Schistocerca gregaria*)
By courtesy of the Anti-Locust Research Centre, London

Africa, most of Eurasia south of the Taiga Forest, the East Indies, tropical Australia, and New Zealand. The desert locust (*Schistocerca gregaria*) inhabits dry grasslands and deserts from Africa to the Punjab and can fly upward to about 5,000 feet in huge towers. The smaller Italian and Moroccan locusts (*Calliptamus italicus* and *Dociostaurus maroccanus*) cause extensive plant damage in the Mediterranean area; the second species can be found as far east as Turkestan. In South Africa the brown and red locusts (*Locustana pardalina* and *Nomadacris septemfasciata*) are extremely destructive. In Central and South America the chief migratory species is the South American locust (*Schistocerca paranensis*); the nonmigratory *S. americana* (found in the United States) may be a solitary phase of this genus. The Rocky Mountain locust and the migratory grasshopper (*Melanoplus spretus* and *M. sanguinipes*, respectively) destroyed many prairie farms in Canada and the United States in the 1870s. Many other species occasionally increase sufficiently in numbers to be called plagues.

Once developed, a locust plague is almost impossible to stop or control. Control measures include destroying egg masses laid by invading swarms; digging trenches to trap nymphs; using hopperdozers, wheeled screens, that cause locusts to fall into troughs containing water and kerosene; using poison baits; and dusting and spraying swarms and breeding grounds from aircraft.

In 1945 the Anti-Locust Research Centre was begun in London; its purpose is to record and project locust outbreaks and migrations, to issue warnings to threatened countries, and to plan and supervise control measures. The centre also conducts research on the life cycle of the locust and other characteristics.

locust, in botany, any tree of the genus *Robinia* within the pea family (Fabaceae). About 20 species are known, all occurring in eastern North America and Mexico. The best

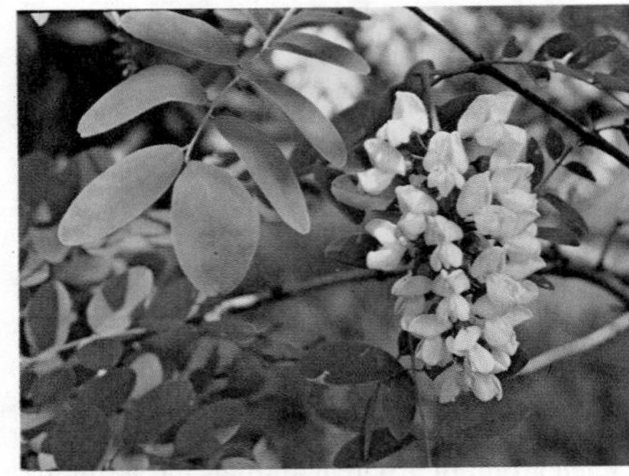

Black locust (*Robinia pseudoacacia*)
John H. Gerard—EB Inc.

known is the black locust (*R. pseudoacacia*), often called false acacia, or yellow locust. It is widely cultivated in Europe as an ornamental. It grows to 24 m (80 feet) high and bears long, compound leaves with 6 to 20 oblong leaflets. The fragrant white flowers hang in loose clusters. There are many varieties, some thornless. It has long been used for erosion control and as a timber tree.

The so-called honey locust (*q.v.*), also of the pea family, is a North American tree commonly used as an ornamental and often found in hedges.

locust bird, any of various African birds that eat grasshoppers and locusts, especially the black-winged pratincole (*see* pratincole). In India the rose-coloured starling is called locust bird.

Lóczy, Lajos (b. Nov. 2, 1849, Poszony, Hung.—d. May 13, 1920, Balatonarács), Hungarian geologist who first scientifically described the mountains bordering the Tibetan

Lóczy, detail of an oil painting by Aladár Edvi Illés; in the Hungarian Geographical Society, Budapest
Gyorgy Lajos—INTERFOTO MTI

Plateau that connect the Kunlun Mountains with the north–south-oriented belt of mountains and gorges in central China.

From 1877 to 1880 Lóczy traveled through India and China as geologist to the expedition of Count Béla Széchenyi, which he described in his major work, *Wissenschaftliche Ergebnisse der Reise in Ostasien, mit B. Széchenyi* (1899; "The Scientific Results of the Expedition Through Eastern Asia with B. Széchenyi"). In 1889 he became professor of geology at the University of Budapest and in 1908 director of the Hungarian Geological Institute. He completed geologic researches in China, Hungary, and, during World War I, Serbia. His research of the steppe formations of the Gobi (desert) and the northern Huang Ho (Yellow River) territory was very important. He also published a monograph on Lake Balaton, in Hungary, explaining the formations of the region. His posthumously published works include a new geologic map of pre-World War I Hungary and a book on the geology of west Serbia, which revolutionized the geologic map of Serbia.

Lod, also called LYDDA, city, central Israel, on the Plain of Sharon southeast of Tel Aviv–Yafo. Of ancient origin, it is mentioned several times in the Bible: in a New Testament account (Acts 9:32), the apostle Peter healed the paralytic at Lod. The city was a well-known centre of Jewish scholars and merchants from the 5th century BC until the Roman conquest in AD 70. It was the Roman colony of Diospolis after AD 200 and the traditional site of the martyrdom of St. George, patron saint of England; the alleged tomb of the legendary saint is still shown. An important city after the Arab conquest of Palestine in the 7th century AD, it was held (1099–1191) by the crusaders, who named it St. Jorge de Lidde.

In modern times, Lod was part of the territory allocated to the potential Arab state in Palestine according to the United Nations partition resolution of Nov. 29, 1947. When the resolution was rejected by the Arab states, Lod was occupied by the invading Arab Legion of Jordan. The Israel Defense Forces attacked and captured the city on July 12, 1948; since then it has been part of Israel and has been largely resettled with Jewish immigrants, who now make up about four-fifths of the population.

Lod is a major Israeli transportation hub, with an important railway and road junction, but principally because of David Ben-Gurion International Airport—Israel's only terminus for overseas flights—located 5 miles (8 km) north. There, one of Israel's largest industries is located—servicing and repairing civilian aircraft of many nationalities and building commercial and military jet aircraft. Lod also manufactures paper and cardboard, food preserves, and electrical appliances. Inc. 1949. Pop. (1987 est.) 41,300.

Loddon River, river, central Victoria, Australia, rising in the Eastern Highlands 50 miles (80 km) northwest of Melbourne and flowing northwest and north for more than 200 miles (320 km), past Kerang, joining with the Little Murray and then with the Murray near Swan Hill. Inconstant in volume, the Loddon has been dammed for several reservoirs, including Cairn Curran and Tullaroop, to form part of the Goulburn Irrigation System. Visited (1836) by Thomas Mitchell, it is named after the Loddon River, Hampshire, England.

lode, in mining, ore body disseminated within definite boundaries in unwanted rock. *See* vein.

loden coat, jacket of Tyrolean origin, made of loden cloth, which was first handwoven by peasants living in Loderers, Austria, in the 16th century. The material comes from the

Man wearing a loden coat, Bavaria
Tom Hollyman—Photo Researchers/EB Inc.

coarse, oily wool of mountain sheep and is thick, soft, and waterproof.

Loden cloth is dyed in several colours, but bluish green is the most common. The jacket sometimes has a stiff, standup collar and is trimmed with braid or silver buttons.

lodestone (mineral): *see* magnetite.

Lodewijk (Dutch personal name): *see under* Louis.

lodge, originally an insubstantial house or dwelling, erected as a seasonal habitation or for some temporary occupational purpose, such as woodcutting. In this sense the word is currently used to describe accommodations for sportsmen during hunting season and for recreationists, such as skiers.

The lodge became a more permanent type of house as the lands around European mansions were developed as parks. The lodge was the cottage of the gamekeeper, caretaker, gatekeeper, or gardener and might be at the park's entrance or elsewhere on the grounds, usually displaying some architectural relation to the main buildings. Lodges could be of considerable size in royal parks and be occupied by important persons. Lord John Russell, for example, lived in Pembroke Lodge at Richmond Park, London, by permission of Queen Victoria, for more than 30 years.

Lodge, Henry Cabot (b. May 12, 1850, Boston, Mass., U.S.—d. Nov. 9, 1924, Cambridge, Mass.), Republican U.S. senator for

Henry Cabot Lodge, 1918
By courtesy of the Library of Congress, Washington, D.C.

more than 31 years (1893–1924); he led the successful congressional opposition to his country's participation in the League of Nations following World War I.

Lodge received in 1876 the first Ph.D. in political science to be granted by Harvard University. He remained at Harvard for the next three years as instructor in American history and retained an active interest in this field throughout his life, editing scholarly journals and writing or editing works on major figures and events in the nation's history. He launched his political career in the state legislature (1880–81) and in the U.S. House of Representatives (1887–93) and then was elected to the U.S. Senate.

With the entrance of the United States into World War I (1917), he called for united support of the war effort. Initially he endorsed an international peacekeeping mechanism in an address before the League to Enforce Peace (May 1916), but, when a world organization with compulsory arbitration was advocated by President Woodrow Wilson, Lodge felt that the nation's sovereignty was at stake and that it would be fatal to bind the nation to international commitments that the United States would not or could not keep. When in 1919 the Republicans gained control of the Senate, Lodge became chairman of the Foreign Relations Committee. He was thus in a position to mastermind the strategy of opposition to adoption of the Treaty of Versailles, including the League of Nations covenant. He adopted a dual course of action: first, delaying tactics to allow enthusiasm for the League to wane; second, introducing a series of amendments (the Lodge reservations) that would require the approval of Congress before the United States would be bound by certain League decisions. Thus, Lodge became the main leader of the U.S. isolationists. Wilson refused to accept the Lodge reservations, feeling that they would destroy the basic intent of the League. The treaty was defeated in the Senate, and the onus of rejection fell on the Wilsonians.

The landslide election of Republican Warren G. Harding in 1920 was considered a vindication of the Lodge position, and with enhanced prestige he went on to serve as one of four

U.S. delegates to the Washington Conference on the Limitation of Armaments (1921).

BIBLIOGRAPHY. John A. Garraty, *Henry Cabot Lodge, a Biography* (1953, reissued 1968), presents the standard views. William C. Widenor, *Henry Cabot Lodge and the Search for an American Foreign Policy* (1980), contends that Lodge's actions were based on consistent beliefs about appropriate American foreign policy.

Lodge, Henry Cabot (b. July 5, 1902, Nahant, Mass., U.S.—d. Feb. 27, 1985, Beverly, Mass.), U.S. senator and diplomat who ran unsuccessfully for the vice presidency of the United States in 1960.

He was the grandson of Senator Henry Cabot Lodge (1850–1924) and a member of a politically dedicated family that included six U.S. senators and a governor of Massachusetts. Lodge began his career in politics, after several years as a journalist, with two terms as a Republican in the Massachusetts legislature (1933–36), followed by service in the U.S. Senate (1937–44, 1947–52). He lost his Senate seat in 1952 to Representative John F. Kennedy. In that year he had been active in promoting the presidential candidacy of Dwight D. Eisenhower, who subsequently appointed Lodge permanent U.S. representative to the United Nations.

In July 1960 he was nominated for the vice presidency on the unsuccessful Republican ticket headed by Richard M. Nixon. Lodge served as U.S. ambassador to South Vietnam (1963–64, 1965–67) and ambassador to West Germany (1968–69), and he was chief negotiator at the talks in Paris on peace in Vietnam (1969). He then served as special envoy to the Vatican (1970–77). Lodge's writings include *Cult of Weakness* (1932), *The Storm Has Many Eyes* (1973), and *As It Was* (1976).

BIBLIOGRAPHY. William J. Miller, *Henry Cabot Lodge* (1967), is an authorized biography.

Lodge, Sir Oliver Joseph (b. June 12, 1851, Penkhull, Staffordshire, Eng.—d. Aug. 22, 1940, Lake, near Salisbury, Wiltshire), British physicist who perfected the coherer, a radio-wave detector and the heart of the early radiotelegraph receiver.

Lodge became assistant professor of applied mathematics at University College, London, in 1879 and was appointed to the chair of physics at University College, Liverpool, in 1881. During his tenure in Liverpool, he conducted experiments in the propagation and reception of electromagnetic waves. In 1890 a French physicist, Édouard Branly, showed that loose iron filings in a glass tube coalesce, or "cohere," under the influence of radiated electric waves. To this basic design Lodge added a "trembler," a device that shook the filings loose between waves. Connected to a receiving circuit, this improved coherer detected Morse code signals transmitted by radio wave and enabled them to be transcribed on paper by an inker. Lodge's device, first demonstrated before the Royal Institute in 1894, quickly became the standard detector in early wireless telegraph receivers. It was outmoded the following decade by magnetic, electrolytic, and crystal detectors. Lodge also obtained patents in 1897 for the use of inductors and capacitors to adjust the frequency of wireless transmitters and receivers.

In 1900 Lodge was chosen the first principal of the new Birmingham University, and he was knighted in 1902. After 1900 he became prominent in psychical research, believing strongly in the possibility of communicating with the dead.

Lodge, Thomas (b. *c.* 1557, London?, Eng.—d. 1625, London), English poet, dramatist, and prose writer whose innovative versatility typified the Elizabethan age. He is best remembered for the prose romance *Rosalynde,* the source of William Shakespeare's *As You Like It.*

He was the son of Sir Thomas Lodge, who was lord mayor of London in 1562. The younger Lodge was educated at Merchant Taylors' School and at Trinity College, Oxford, and he studied law at Lincoln's Inn, London, in 1578. Lodge's earliest work was an anonymous pamphlet (*c.* 1579) in reply to Stephen Gosson's attack on stage plays. His next work, *An Alarum Against Usurers* (1584), exposed the ways in which moneylenders lured young heirs into extravagance and debt. He then engaged in varied literary activity for a number of years. His *Scillaes Metamorphosis* (1589), an Ovidian verse fable, is one of the earliest English poems to retell a classical story with imaginative embellishments, and it strongly influenced Shakespeare's *Venus and Adonis.* Lodge's *Phillis* (1593) contains amorous sonnets and pastoral eclogues from French and Italian originals. In *A Fig for Momus* (1595), he introduced classical satires and verse epistles (modeled after those of Juvenal and Horace) into English literature for the first time. Aside from *Rosalynde: Euphues Golden Legacie* (1590), which provided the plot for Shakespeare's comedy, Lodge's most important romance was *A Margarite of America* (1596), which combines Senecan motives and Arcadian romance in an improbable love story between a Peruvian prince and a daughter of the king of Muscovy. His other romances are chiefly notable for the fine lyric poems scattered through them. Lodge continued to write moralizing pamphlets such as *Wits Miserie, and the Worlds Madnesse* (1596), and in 1594 he published two plays: *The Wounds of Civill War* and (with Robert Greene) *A Looking Glasse for London and England.*

To escape poverty Lodge took part in unprofitable freebooting voyages to the Canary Islands in 1588 and to South America in 1591. In 1597 he became a Roman Catholic, and he graduated in medicine from the University of Avignon in 1598. He received another M.D. degree from Oxford in 1602 and thereafter practiced medicine in London and in Brussels, where he took refuge as a recusant following exposure of the Gunpowder Plot (1605). He was back in England by 1612, became a distinguished physician in London, and died there while fighting the plague in 1625. His later works include *A Treatise of the Plague* (1603) and two major translations: *The Works of Lucius Annaeus Seneca* (1614) and *The Famous and Memorable Works of Josephus* (1620), both of which went through many editions.

Much of Lodge's work before 1600 was surreptitious translation, but in this regard he shows a real talent for creative selection and assimilation from classical, French, and Italian sources. His reputation remains based chiefly on his poetry and his romances. Of his pamphlets, *Wits Miserie* and the *Alarum* are memorable for their cameos of London life, reminiscent of the writings of Thomas Nashe.

Lodi, town, capital of Lodi *provincia,* Lombardia (Lombardy) *regione,* northern Italy. It lies on the right bank of the Adda River, southeast of Milan. The original settlement (5th century BC) on the site of the present suburb of Lodi Vecchio obtained Roman citizenship in 89 BC as Laus Pompeia. Destroyed in the communal struggles of 1111 and by the Milanese in 1158, it was refounded on the present site by the emperor Frederick I Barbarossa but later joined the Lombard League against him. In the 14th century it lost its independence to Milan, with which its history was thereafter linked. On May 10, 1796, Napoleon gained control of Lombardy by defeating the Austrians at the Battle of Lodi.

The town's notable buildings include the 12th-century Romanesque cathedral; the Church of the Incoronata (1488–94); and the Lombard-Gothic-style Church of San Francesco (1289), with fine 13th–15th-century frescoes. Lodi is an important agricultural and industrial centre noted for its cheese, ceramics, wrought iron, and wool products. Pop. (1993 est.) mun., 42,277.

Lodi, city, San Joaquin county, central California, U.S. Lodi lies along the Mokelumne River at the junction of the San Joaquin and Sacramento valleys just north of Stockton. It originated as Mokelumne Station (1869) on the Central Pacific (later part of the Southern Pacific) Railroad. In 1873 it was renamed, presumably for a famous racehorse of the time. Since 1881 Lodi has been known for its wines, notably Tokay. It is also a packing and processing centre for cereals, fruits, and vegetables from the surrounding agricultural area and has light industry. Camanche Dam and Reservoir is 15 miles (24 km) east, and Micke Grove Park and Zoo is nearby. Inc. 1906. Pop. (1994 est.) 52,423.

To make the best use of the Britannica, consult the INDEX *first*

Lodī DYNASTY, (1451–1526), last ruling family of the Delhi sultanate of India. This dynasty was of Afghan origin.

The first Lodī ruler was Bahlūl Lodī (reigned 1451–89), the most powerful of the Punjab (Pañjāb) chiefs, who replaced the last king of the Sayyid dynasty in 1451. Bahlūl was a vigorous leader, holding together a loose confederacy of Afghan and Turkish chiefs with his strong personality. Starting with only the control of the region adjacent to Delhi, Bahlūl extended the effective boundaries of his empire to the borders of Bengal. This expansion involved the conquest of the powerful kingdoms of Mālwa and Jaunpur. Though twice besieged in Delhi, he finally defeated and partially annexed Jaunpur in 1479.

Bahlūl's second son, Sikandar (reigned 1489–1517), continued his father's expansion policy. He gained control of Bihār and founded the modern city of Āgra on the site known as Sikandarābād. His reign was clouded only by a reputation for religious bigotry.

Sikandar's eldest son, Ibrāhīm (reigned 1517–26), attempted to enhance the royal authority. His harshness built up discontent, however, which led the governor of the Punjab, Dawlat Khān Lodī, to invite the Mughal ruler of Kabul, Bābur, to invade India. Ibrāhīm was killed at the First Battle of Pānīpat (April 21, 1526), whereupon the loose aristocratic confederacy of the Lodīs dissolved.

Lodi, Battle of (May 10, 1796), small but dramatic engagement in Napoleon Bonaparte's first Italian campaign, in which he earned the confidence and loyalty of his men, who nicknamed him "The Little Corporal" in recognition of his personal courage. It was fought at the Lodi Bridge, over the Adda River, 19 miles (31 km) southeast of Milan, between 5,000 troops of Napoleon's Army of Italy and K.P. Sebottendorf's 10,000 troops, the rear guard of Jean-Pierre Beaulieu's Austrian army. After knocking the kingdom of Sardinia (Piedmont) out of the war in April, Napoleon turned northeastward against Beaulieu. Beaulieu refused to stand and fight, afraid to lose his army in a major battle. The retreating Austrians' rear guard continued to hold the Lodi Bridge, however. Napoleon set up artillery to blast the Austrian guns and defenses across the Adda River and sent columns to ford the Adda above and below Lodi; then he and generals Louis-Alexandre Berthier and André Masséna led a massed infantry column to charge across the bridge. Despite 400 casualties in the savage melee on the bridge, the column swept forward to bayonet the Austrians away from their guns. Then other French columns attacked the Austrians from both flanks, forcing them to retire. Austrian losses were 153 men killed and 1,700 captured. Napoleon's reports portrayed the battle as a minor epic, though Beaulieu had made good his escape.

Lodi, Peace of (April 9, 1454), treaty between Venice and Milan ending the war of succession to the Milanese duchy in favour of Francesco Sforza. It marked the beginning of a 40-year period of relative peace, during which power was balanced among the five states that dominated the Italian peninsula—Venice, Milan, Naples, Florence, and the Papal States.

Venice, faced with a threat to its commercial empire by the Ottoman Turks, was eager for peace in Italy. Sforza, a condottiere (mercenary general) who had been proclaimed duke by the people of Milan, also was eager to end the costly war. By the terms of the peace, Sforza was recognized as ruler of Milan, and Venice regained its considerable holdings in northern Italy, including Brescia and Bergamo. The other belligerents (Milan's allies—Florence, Mantua, and Genoa—and Venice's allies—Naples, Savoy, and Montferrat) had no choice but to acquiesce to the peace.

In conjunction with the treaty, a 25-year mutual defensive pact was concluded to maintain existing boundaries, and an Italian League (Lega Italica) was set up. The states of the league promised to defend one another in the event of attack and to support a contingent of soldiers to provide military aid. The league, officially proclaimed by Pope Nicholas V on March 2, 1455, was soon accepted by almost all the Italian states. Although the league was often renewed during the 15th century, the system was not entirely effective in preventing war, and individual states continued to pursue their own interests against others. The league definitely lapsed after the French invasion of the peninsula in 1494.

Łódź, former (1975–99) *województwo* (province), central Poland, now part of Łódzkie (*q.v.*) province.

Łódź, city, capital of Łódzkie *województwo* (province), central Poland. It lies on the northwestern edge of the Łódź Highlands, in the watershed of the Vistula and Oder rivers, 81 miles (130 km) southwest of Warsaw.

Łódź is mentioned in 14th-century records as a village, and it acquired municipal rights in 1798, but it remained an insignificant settlement that had only 799 inhabitants by 1820. That year the Congress Kingdom of Poland decided to make it a centre for the textile industry and invited foreign weavers and artisans to settle there. Congress Poland was ruled by Russia, and, after customs barriers between Russia and Congress Poland were lifted in 1850, a great market for Łódź's manufactures opened up in the Russian Empire. By the end of the 19th century Łódź had become the leading centre in Poland for the production of cotton textiles. Its other industries included the processing of wool, silk, jute, hemp, and leather and the manufacture of clothing, metals, chemicals, and paper. The town's rapid expansion resulted in a population of 500,000 inhabitants by 1913. When Łódź became part of newly independent Poland after World War I, it lost its large Russian market. The city survived German occupation during World War II with relatively little damage, and its textile mills and other plants were reactivated after 1945.

In the early 21st century Łódź was still the nation's second largest city and a major centre of Poland's textile industry, producing a large portion of the nation's cotton goods as well as processing wool, silk, and artificial fibres. Because it did not develop extensively until the late 19th century, Łódź has a modern industrial appearance and very few distinguished buildings. During its rapid territorial expansion, Łódź absorbed nearby villages and suburbs, giving the city an unplanned and somewhat chaotic layout; some districts are a maze of factories, apartment blocks, former mansions of factory owners, and workers' cottages. Łódź is an important railway junction on the Warsaw-Wrocław rail line. A notable educational centre, Łódź contains institutions of higher education and several museums, music centres, and theatres. Łódź is also the centre of the Polish film industry and of a flourishing art community. Pop. (2002) 789,318.

Łódzkie, *województwo* (province), central Poland. It is made up of the former provinces (1975–98) of Łódź, Piotrków, and Sieradz, as well as portions of Skierniewice, Płock, Częstochowa, Radom, Kalisz, and Konin. The mostly flat land is largely devoted to agriculture, despite the province's mild, dry climate and poor soils. The chief crops are rye, potatoes, sugar beets, fodder, vegetables, and fruit. The provincial capital, Łódź, long has been an important industrial centre. Major industries in the province are textiles and clothing, pharmaceuticals, rubber, food and beverage processing, machine manufacturing, ceramics, and logging. Łódź is a cultural centre as well and the heart of the Polish film industry. A large community of Jews in Łódź was decimated during the Holocaust. Other cities include Piotrków Trybunalski, Pabianice, Tomaszów Mazowiecki, and Bełchatów, site of a huge lignite-fueled power plant. Area 7,035 square miles (18,219 square km). Pop. (2003 est.) 2,603,700.

Loeb, Jacques (b. April 7, 1859, Mayen, near Koblenz, Prussia [now in Germany]—d. Feb. 11, 1924, Hamilton, Bermuda), German-born American biologist noted chiefly for his experimental work on artificial parthenogenesis (reproduction without fertilization).

Jacques Loeb
By courtesy of Bryn Mawr College, Pennsylvania

Loeb received his medical degree from the University of Strasbourg in 1884 and worked in biology in Würzburg, Strasbourg, and Naples, before relocating to the United States in 1891. There he was a professor, successively at Bryn Mawr (Pa.) College, the University of Chicago, and the University of California, Berkeley. In 1910 he became a member of the Rockefeller Institute for Medical Research (now Rockefeller University), New York City, a position he held until his death. A good deal of his experimental work was done at the Marine Biological Laboratory at Woods Hole, Mass.

Popular interest, attended by some controversy, accompanied his parthenogenesis experiments, beginning in 1899, when he succeeded in bringing about the development of sea urchin larvae from unfertilized eggs by exposing them to controlled changes in their environment. This work was later extended to the production of parthenogenetic frogs, which he raised to sexual maturity. Loeb's work was significant in showing that the initiation of cell division in fertilization was controlled chemically and was in effect separate from the transmission of hereditary traits.

Loeb also is remembered for his work on the physiology of the brain, animal tropisms (involuntary orientations), regeneration of tissue, and the duration of life. He argued in favour of mechanism, the belief that the phenomena of life can be explained in terms of physical and chemical laws. He also contributed to the theory of colloidal behaviour of proteins.

Loeb, Richard A.: *see* Leopold, Nathan F., Jr., and Loeb, Richard A.

Loeffler, Charles Martin, in full CHARLES MARTIN TORNOW LOEFFLER (b. Jan. 30, 1861, Mulhouse, France—d. May 19, 1935, Medfield, Mass., U.S.), American composer whose works are distinguished by a poetic lyricism in an Impressionist style.

As a youth, Loeffler studied violin and music theory in Berlin and Paris. He went to the United States in 1881 and joined the Boston Symphony Orchestra as a violinist the following year. He resigned in 1903 to devote himself to composition. Almost all of his symphonic works were first performed by the Boston Symphony. His most enduring work, *A Pagan Poem* (1907; after an eclogue of Virgil) for piano and orchestra, uses Impressionistic harmonies to evoke pagan antiquity. Among other works are the symphonic poem *Memories of My Childhood,* subtitled *Life in a Russian Village* (1924), *La Mort de Tintagiles* (1905; after Maeterlinck), *Evocation* (1931; for women's voices and orchestra), *Canticum Fratris Solis* (1925; for voice and chamber orchestra), *Music for Four Stringed Instruments* (1917), and the *Fantastic Concerto* (1894; for cello and orchestra), as well as a number of songs, piano pieces, and other chamber music.

loellingite, an iron arsenide mineral ($FeAs_2$) that usually occurs with iron and copper sulfides in hydrothermal vein deposits. It typically occurs with impurities of cobalt, nickel, and arsenic, as at the Andreas-Berg, in the Erzgebirge of Germany; Andalusia, Spain; and Franklin, N.J., in the United States. Loellingite is classified in a group of iron, cobalt, and nickel arsenides that form orthorhombic crystals and are assigned to the sulfide minerals, though they contain very little sulfur. For detailed physical properties, *see* sulfide mineral (table).

loess, an unstratified, geologically recent deposit of silty or loamy material that is usually buff or yellowish brown in colour and is chiefly deposited by the wind. Loess is a sedimentary deposit composed largely of silt-size grains that are loosely cemented by cal-

Loess complex on the right bank of the Danube River in the Great Alföld, showing the vertical fracturing that is typical in loess deposits
By courtesy of Marton Pecsi, Geographical Research Institute, Hungarian Academy of Sciences, Budapest

cium carbonate. It is usually homogeneous and highly porous and is traversed by vertical capillaries that permit the sediment to fracture and form vertical bluffs. The word loess, with connotations of origin by wind-deposited accumulation, is of German origin and means "loose." It was first applied to Rhine River valley loess about 1821.

Loess covers extensive areas in Asia, Europe, and North America. Most widespread in today's temperate zones and in the marginal semiarid zones of the deserts, loess covers about 10 percent of the land surface of the Earth. Loess usually exhibits a surface cover of fertile soil that is conducive to intensive agriculture. The capacity of loess to retain vertical or even overhanging walls is especially evident on the Loess Plateau in China, where some loess bluffs stand 150 m high and contain innumerable cellarlike dwellings excavated by the local inhabitants. In semiarid regions people such as the Pueblo Indians made houses and fortresslike closed edifices from loess-based adobe.

Physical and chemical properties. The dominant grain-size fraction of loess, called the loess fraction, ranges from 0.02 to 0.05 mm (0.0008 to 0.002 inch) and includes grains of coarse and medium-grained dust. Grain-size analyses by various methods indicate that the abundance of this fraction is about 50 weight percent. Clay-sized particles (less than 0.005 mm [0.0002 inch]) make up another 5 to 10 percent. In some loess regions, the grain-size distribution shifts toward finer grains with increasing distance from the source of dust (*e.g.,* eastward from Sand Hills, Neb.).

Loess typically exhibits a low moisture content of 10 to 15 percent that increases as porosity decreases. Its porosity is 50 to 55 percent, decreasing slightly downward to a depth of about 10 m (33 feet). Below this depth, porosity varies as a function of the grain-size distribution. If the loess is enriched with clay, then the porosity may decrease to 34 to 45 percent. The porosity of sandy loess is about 60 percent.

Loess contains 60 to 70 percent quartz with extremes of 40 and 80 percent. Feldspars and micas make up 10 to 20 percent and carbonates 5 to 35 percent. About 2 to 5 percent of the silt is composed of such heavy minerals as amphiboles, apatite, biotite, chlorite, disthene (cyanite), epidote, garnet, glauconite, pyroxenes, rutile, sillimanite, staurolite, tourmaline, and zircon. Grains are typically slightly weathered. In the finest grain-size fractions (below 0.002 mm [0.00008 inch]), such clay minerals as montmorillonite, illite, and kaolinite predominate over the detrital (fragmental) constituents. Clay minerals may be formed by various processes during and after the accumulation of loess.

The mineralogical composition of loess is fairly uniform, but there are some local deviations due to differences in grain size and area of origin. The area of origin of the dust fraction is revealed by the heavy mineral assemblage, and research has shown that the dust sources may be local, neighbouring, or distant.

The chemical composition of loess most often falls within the following percentage ranges: silica, SiO_2, 50 to 60; alumina, Al_2O_3, 8 to 12; iron oxide as Fe_2O_3, 2 to 4; iron oxide as FeO, 0.8 to 1.1; titanium dioxide, TiO_2, and manganese oxide, MnO, about 0.5; lime, CaO, 4 to 16; and magnesium oxide, MgO, 2 to 6.

The characteristic carbonate content of loess depends on the nature of the dust source, on geochemical and biological processes that occur during and after deposition, and on precipitation and leaching by groundwater. Carbonates are present in loess in a variety of forms, primarily as incrustations on quartz grains and clay-particle aggregates and as small granules and shell fragments. Secondary concentrations include concretions of nodules (Loess-doll) and layers of lime accumulation (caliche). Lime forms frequent tubular incrustations along decayed plant roots, fissure fillings, and similar avenues in loess.

Loess is a rather ill-consolidated sediment of low compressive strength. It is stable, however, as long as it remains dry. Parting surfaces are vertical because capillary incrustations of lime, developed around the roots of a grassy plant cover, lend a vertical texture to loess.

Soaked and loaded loess, however, is liable to collapse and slumping. Wetting decreases cohesion between grains by two-thirds, and the angle of internal friction also decreases (*e.g.,* from 32° to 20°). Groundwater flow in loess will carry away fine, insoluble mineral particles, and this mechanical separation in loess can be accompanied by solution of mineral particles. This process gives rise to depressions, sinkholes, loess wells, and collapse ravines and is much accelerated by gully erosion.

Distribution and classification. The world's largest loess-covered areas lie between latitudes 55° and 24° N: in China on the banks of the Huang Ho; on the margins of the continental deserts of Inner Asia; in Central Asia in Kazakhstan, Uzbekistan, the foreland of the Tien Shan, and east of the Caspian Sea; and in Siberia along Lake Baikal and the Lena River and in vast regions in the southern parts of the catchment areas of the Ob and Yenisey rivers. In Europe there is an extensive, uninterrupted loess cover in the South Russian Plain, large spots and belts in the Danube Basin, along the Rhine, along the margin of the former inland ice cap in the German-Polish plain, and in the Paris Basin. In North America loess covers the plains of the Platte, Missouri, Mississippi, and Ohio rivers and the Columbia Plateau. In the Southern Hemisphere, between latitudes 30° and 40° S, the most significant loess regions include the "pampas loesses" of Uruguay and Argentina and parts of New Zealand.

Loess blankets may cover a variety of relief forms; they occur most often in plains; on river valley slopes, flats, and rises; on pediments in the forelands of mountains; and on alluvial fans. On mountain slopes and intermontane basins, loess occurs to a maximum elevation of 400–600 m in Europe, 1,000–2,000 m in Inner Asia, and up to 4,000 m in China.

The lithological classification of loess is based on physical and chemical properties, and the conditions of origin are partly or entirely neglected. In addition to true or typical loess, loessial and loesslike deposits also are quite frequent in occurrence. The proportions of silt and other fractions and constituents (clay, sand, lime), as well as colour, porosity, strength, and plasticity of loessial deposits, differ significantly from comparable properties of true loess. Loessial deposits include sandy loess, loessial sand, loess loam, clayey loess, and loess that is altered during soil-forming processes. Loesslike deposits, on the other hand, include sediments that resemble typical loess only in certain features (mineralogical composition, dominant dust fraction, colour, etc.). These deposits occur within or on the margins of loess regions and are most often mixed with other types of sediment. The group of loesslike deposits is not rigidly circumscribed; it usually is understood to include loess loam, loess mud, loess-containing rock debris, and stratified loess.

Genetic classifications of loess, in contrast to this lithological classification, are based on the origin of the silt and on the processes that have brought about its accumulation. This requires knowledge of the circumstances of loess formation, which involves many complications and, in all its ramifications, is termed the loess problem.

Environmental conditions in the areas of loess formation are revealed by pollen and the shell remains of snails, among other animals. Pollen analysis reveals only the broad outlines of ancient plant ecology, but pollen assemblages indicate that cool grasslands, steppes, wooded steppes, and wooded tundras and tundras were among the preferred environments of loess deposition. These climatic zones lay south of the margins of the extensive Pleistocene ice sheets, significantly displaced from their normal (non-Ice Age) position, together with the zone of westerly winds.

Origin and age. For more than a century a number of partly conflicting and partly complementary hypotheses have been put forward to explain the origin of the silt fraction of loess. The mineral constituents of loess (quartz and feldspar, for example) are reduced to minute particles by weathering action, principally in semiarid and arid regions. But the source of dust may also be a silty, sandy unconsolidated sediment of Tertiary age (formed from 66.4 to 1.6 million years ago), as, for instance, the Ogallala Group of the United States. The sand and silt may have been size sorted by the wind, which then transported and deposited the silt. Dust storms derived from such rock units are frequent even today in the continental deserts of Asia; the silt content of "continental loesses" is derived in this manner.

Another significant source of dust may have been the marginal zone of the Pleistocene ice sheet over Europe and North America. During the several ice advances, or glaciations, huge amounts of glacial till, rich in silt, could accumulate in the zone. The silt fraction could then be carried away by the westerly winds and deposited on the lee side of some relief feature; this is sometimes called the theory of glacial loess.

Silt may also be removed from its site of origin of first deposition and be sorted by fluvial processes. Abundant silt is borne by rivers and deposited in times of flood in basins and on alluvial fans that border mountain regions. Some of the silt is then removed from broad floodplains by winds; this results in a double sorting, once by water and once by wind, and hence a more sharply defined typical grain size. In this case loess accumulation is not necessarily connected with a glaciation; indeed, most of the alluvial loesses do not date back to a glaciation.

The reason for conflicting opinions on loess formation is that the silt fraction may have been deposited or reworked by any of the various processes; and, depending on environment and other circumstances, the dominant process may change through time.

There is a consensus that the accumulated dust fraction must have undergone diagenesis (physical and chemical changes after deposition) in order to turn into loess. Diagenesis includes the weathering of fine grains of lime, aluminum silicates, and other substances by hydration in arid climates. In near-surface silt the finest clay particles are cemented by migrating solutions of calcium carbonate and iron oxides and colloidal iron compounds; the quartz grains acquire crusts or coatings of lime or iron, and adjacent grains are cemented together. As a result of these processes, some of the finer particles also attain loess fraction size of 0.01 to 0.05 mm. It has been proved that a grain size of about 0.05 mm is the most favourable for thriving grassy vegetation. Essentially, diagenesis turns sediment deposited in the form of dust into a loosely cemented siltstone.

The peculiar features of loess are thus developed during a process of loess genesis that is akin to that of soil formation. This circumstance served as a basis for the pedogenic (soil origin) theory of loess formation, which basically held that loess is a product of weathering and pedogenesis under semiarid conditions in grasslands and wooded steppes.

It would be difficult to explain the formation of a thick loess blanket subdivided by several horizons of paleosols in this way, however. More reasonable would be a polygenetic origin, in which dust can accumulate as the result of any process alternating in time and space, with loess formation resulting from pedogenetic processes acting under favourable climatic conditions.

These pedogenetic processes may take place in three different ways. Epigenesis is an accumulation of a mineral mass without loess properties, perhaps with a high silt and lime content, which under weathering and soil formation acquires loess properties and is transformed into loess. In syngenesis, the accumulation of a mineral mass that is mainly of eolian origin and the acquisition of all loess properties occurs simultaneously, under the influence of soil formation. In protogenesis the accumulated mineral matter already has all the main loess properties because transport occurred subsequent to weathering and soil formation.

The optimum conditions of loess formation are thought to have existed along the border of the continental ice sheet, in such areas as the cold steppes, wooded steppes, loess tundras, and in the steppes bordering the continental deserts. Under conditions other than optimum, the accumulated dust would likely turn into a loesslike deposit differing from typical loess, namely loess loam, limeless loess, brown earth, or reddish loam, or, alternatively, into a soil.

The formation of loess packets is correlated with the cold, dry climatic phases of the Pleistocene glaciations in regions marginal to the ice. The climatic phases, and the occasions of loess formation, recurred three to five times as within the last glaciation.

A list of the abbreviations used in the MICROPAEDIA *will be found at the end of this volume*

Loess Plateau, Wade-Giles romanization HUANG-T'U KAO-YÜAN, Pinyin HUANGTU GAOYUAN, highland area in north-central China, covering much of Shansi, north Honan, Shensi, and eastern Kansu provinces and the middle part of the Huang Ho (Yellow River) basin. Averaging 3,300 feet (1,000 m) in elevation and covering 154,000 square miles (400,000 square km), it is the world's largest loess plateau. The region is overlain by a mantle of fine-grained, wind-deposited, yellowish alluvium known as loess, which is also carried in suspension by the Huang Ho. The loess layers average 165–260 feet (50–80 m) in thickness and mask the detailed relief of the underlying surfaces. The loess is highly subject to erosion; factors include sparse vegetation, heavy concentrations of rainfall in summer, and gullying. The government has conducted programs to control erosion by afforestation terracing on an extensive scale to permit better agricultural use of the land. Grain is the major crop on the plateau.

Loesser, Frank (Henry) (b. June 29, 1910, New York, N.Y., U.S.—d. July 28, 1969, New York City), American composer, librettist, and lyricist, who achieved major success writing for Broadway musicals, culminating in the 1962 Pulitzer Prize-winning *How to Succeed in Business Without Really Trying.*

Self-taught despite his piano-teacher father's efforts to discourage his youthful interest in popular song, Loesser dropped out of the City College of New York and worked at various nonmusical jobs before becoming a music publisher's staff lyricist in the late 1920s. Little of his work was published until "I Wish I Were Twins" (1934) was recorded by Fats Waller. In 1936 Loesser moved to Hollywood, where he became an accomplished lyricist, collaborating with Hoagy Carmichael on "Small Fry" and "Two Sleepy People" and with Joseph J. Lilley on "Jingle, Jangle, Jingle." Other composers for whom he wrote lyrics included Burton Lane, Jule Styne, Arthur Schwartz, Frederick Hollander, and Jimmy McHugh.

Loesser's first melody with lyrics was "Praise the Lord and Pass the Ammunition," the first big hit song of World War II. During the war he wrote for soldier-produced shows at army camps and composed the official song of the infantry, "What Do You Do in the Infantry?" From 1947 Loesser enjoyed major successes on Broadway and in Hollywood, often with songs employing an urban, postwar vernacular. His song "On a Slow Boat to China" was a leading hit of 1948. *Where's Charley?* (1948), a musical comedy version of the farce *Charley's Aunt,* and *Guys and Dolls* (1950), based on the stories of Damon Runyon, both received Tony Awards and were made into successful motion pictures (1952 and 1955, respectively). *The Most Happy Fella* (1956) contained elements of opera, but Loesser returned to his earlier formula in *How to Succeed.*

In Hollywood Loesser's composing work included the score for the film *Hans Christian Andersen* (1952), starring Danny Kaye. The song "Baby It's Cold Outside" won a 1949 Academy Award.

Loew, Marcus (b. May 7, 1870, New York, N.Y., U.S.—d. Sept. 5, 1927, New York City), American motion-picture executive and pioneer motion-picture theatre owner whose consolidation and expansion of his business interests helped establish Hollywood as the centre of the film industry.

Loew was the son of an Austrian immigrant and left school at the age of nine to help support his family, later finding modest prosperity in the fur business. Attracted by the new popularity of moving pictures, Loew owned a chain of nickelodeons by 1905, and thereafter he acquired many leading theatres for combined vaudeville and motion-picture exhibition. In 1920 Loew's, Inc., purchased a production company named Metro Pictures Corporation; and in 1924 the Goldwyn Pictures Corporation, from which Samuel Goldwyn had resigned, was absorbed. The following year the name became Metro-Goldwyn-Mayer (MGM), Inc., after Louis B. Mayer Pictures joined the group. Loew amassed an enormous fortune, and after his death MGM became the largest producer of motion pictures in the world.

Loewe, (Johann) Carl (Gottfried) (b. Nov. 30, 1796, Löbejün, near Halle, Brandenburg [Germany]—d. April 20, 1869, Kiel, Prussia), German composer and singer who is best-known for his songs, particularly his dramatic ballads.

Loewe began to compose while still a choirboy in Köthen and completed his musical training in Halle. He frequently toured Europe singing his songs with great success, and in Vienna he was called "the north German Schubert." Although he wrote operas, oratorios, and much instrumental music, today he is almost exclusively known for his songs. Among these the most-admired include settings of Goethe's *Erlkönig,* the Scottish folk ballad "Edward," "Herr Oluf," "Archibald Douglas," and "Tom der Reimer."

Loewe, Frederick (b. June 10, 1901, Berlin, Ger.—d. Feb. 14, 1988, Palm Springs, Calif., U.S.), German-born American composer and collaborator with Alan Jay Lerner (*q.v.*) on a series of hit musical plays, including the phenomenally successful *My Fair Lady* (1956; filmed 1964).

Loewe, whose father was a Viennese actor and operetta tenor, was a child prodigy, playing piano at age 5, composing for his father's presentations at 7, and at 13 becoming the youngest soloist to appear with the Berlin Philharmonic Orchestra. He received advanced musical instruction from Ferruccio Busoni and Eugène d'Albert. Loewe wrote a popular song, "Katrina," at age 15, and more than 1,000,000 copies of the sheet music for it were eventually sold.

Loewe arrived in the United States in 1924 and worked in a variety of odd jobs for the next 10 years. In 1934 he contributed music to the play *Petticoat Fever,* and by 1936 he was writing music for Broadway revues, but he received little acclaim. Loewe collaborated with lyricist Earle Crooker on the musical plays *Salute to Spring* (1937) and *Great Lady* (1938), but they also failed to gain attention.

In 1942 Loewe met Alan Jay Lerner at the Lambs, a theatrical club in New York City, and asked him to work on revising *Salute to Spring* for a Detroit producer. They continued their collaboration through two failures, *What's Up?* (1943) and *The Day Before Spring* (1945), before achieving success on Broadway with *Brigadoon* (1947). This was followed by *Paint Your Wagon* (1951), *My Fair Lady,* the film *Gigi* (1958), and *Camelot* (1960). Personal differences between Loewe and Lerner surfaced during the writing of *Camelot,* and they suspended their collaboration for more than a decade. They reunited to adapt *Gigi* for the stage (1973) and to write the score for the film *The Little Prince* (1974).

The score of *My Fair Lady* was among the most successful ever to emerge from the American musical theatre. More than 5,000,000 copies of the Broadway-cast recording were sold, and, of Loewe's 16 very different melodies, "I Could Have Danced All Night," "On the Street Where You Live," and "I've Grown Accustomed to Her Face" underwent innumerable arrangements and renditions. His music ranged from high romance ("If Ever I Would Leave You" from *Camelot* and "On the Street Where You Live" from *My Fair Lady*) to lighthearted melodies ("The Night They Invented Champagne" and "Thank Heaven for Little Girls" from *Gigi*) to subtle settings for nearly spoken songs ("Why Can't the English?" from *My Fair Lady*).

Loewi, Otto (b. June 3, 1873, Frankfurt am Main, Ger.—d. Dec. 25,1961, New York, N.Y., U.S.),German-born America physician and pharmacologist who, with Sir Henry Dale, received the Nobel Prize for Physiology or Medicine in1936 for their discoveries relating to the chemical transmission of nerve impulses.

After Loewi graduated in medicine (1896) from the German University (now the University of Strasbourg), he studied and taught in European universities, becoming professor of pharmacology at Graz, Austria, in 1909. In 1940 he went to the United States; he was made research professor at the School of Medicine of New York University, New York City, where he remained until his death.

His neurological researches (1921–26) provided the first proof that chemicals were involved in the transmission of impulses from one nerve cell to another and from neuron to the responsive organ. He and his colleagues, by stimulating the nerves in the heart of a frog, slowed the heart's rate of contraction. The fluid perfusing this heart was allowed to perfuse a second heart in which the nerves were not stimulated; the second heart slowed in rate also, indicating the presence of a reactive substance in the fluid. This substance was shown to be acetylcholine, whose physiological properties Dale had described comprehensively in 1914. Acetylcholine was subsequently isolated from animal tissue by Dale and Harold Dudley in 1929.

In addition to researches on the nervous system, Loewi studied diabetes and the action of the drugs digitalis and epinephrine. He devised Loewi's test for the detection of pancreatic disease.

Loewy, Raymond (b. Nov. 5, 1893, Paris—d. July 14, 1986, Monaco), French-born American industrial designer who, through his accomplishments in product design beginning in the 1930s, helped to establish industrial design as a profession.

Raymond Loewy
EB Inc.

Loewy studied electrical engineering at the University of Paris, graduating in 1910. His studies in advanced engineering at the École de Lanneau were interrupted by World War I, in which he served in the French Army; he received his degree in 1918.

Loewy went to the United States in 1919 and worked as a fashion illustrator for *Vogue* magazine and later as a designer of window displays for New York City department stores. Loewy's first major success came when he redesigned the Gestetner copier, giving it a form that was to remain unchanged for 40 years. He started his own design organization in 1929. His design in 1934 of a refrigerator for Sears, Roebuck and Co. was a great commercial triumph and won first prize at the Paris International Exposition of 1937. During the 1930s and '40s Loewy designed a wide variety of household products with rounded corners and simplified outlines. In 1945 he formed Raymond Loewy Associates with five partners; it became the largest industrial design firm in the world.

In the years that followed, Loewy's vision of beauty through the use of "streamlined," highly functional forms shaped modern industrial design in the United States, and the images of his work permeated the nation's lifestyle. Working closely with client engineers, he made notable designs for Studebaker automobiles, locomotives and passenger cars for the Pennsylvania Railroad, and buses for Greyhound. He also made important contributions to the design of such products as electric shavers, toothbrushes, ball-point pens, office machines, soft-drink bottles, radios, and packages, including that for Lucky Strike cigarettes. Perhaps his best-known design was that of the Coca-Cola bottle.

In the 1960s and '70s Loewy applied his expertise and his formula of sleek and simplified lines to objects used in aerospace technology. He designed *Air Force One* for President John F. Kennedy, and from 1967 to 1973 he worked for the U.S. National Aeronautics and Space Administration, producing interior designs for the Apollo and Skylab orbiters.

Loewy wrote *The Locomotive* (1937), *Never Leave Well Enough Alone* (1951), and *Industrial Design* (1979).

Loewy, Salomon: *see* Sulzer, Salomon.

Löffler, Friedrich August Johannes (b. June 24, 1852, Frankfurt an der Oder, Prussia [Germany]—d. April 9, 1915, Berlin), German bacteriologist who, with Edwin Klebs, in 1884 discovered the organism that causes diphtheria, *Corynebacterium diphtheriae,* commonly known as the Klebs–Löffler bacillus. Simultaneously with Émile Roux and Alexandre Yersin, he indicated the existence of a diphtheria toxin. His demonstration that some animals are immune to diphtheria was a basic feature in Emil von Behring's work in antitoxin development.

The son of an army surgeon, Löffler studied medicine at Würzburg University and at the Friedrich Wilhelm University in Berlin before serving in the army during the Franco-German War (1870–71). He obtained his medical degree at Berlin in 1874 and, after a period of service as an army doctor, became an assistant in the Imperial Health Office (1879–84), Berlin, where he was an associate of Robert Koch. He was professor of hygiene from 1888 at the University of Greifswald, where he served as rector from 1903 to 1907, and in 1913 he became director of the Robert Koch Institute for Infectious Diseases in Berlin.

Löffler also discovered the cause of swine erysipelas and swine plague (1885) and, with Wilhelm Schütz, identified the causative organism of glanders, *Pfeifferella* (*Malleomyces*) *mallei* (1882). With Paul Frosch he found that foot-and-mouth disease is caused by a virus—the first time the cause of an animal disease was attributed to a virus—and developed a serum against it.

Lofoten, island group, in the Norwegian Sea, Nordland *fylke* (county), northern Norway. Lying off the mainland entirely within the Arctic Circle, the group comprises the southern end of the Lofoten–Vesterålen archipelago and includes five main islands (Austvågøya, Gimsøya, Vestvågøya, Flakstadøya, and Moskenesøya) extending about 70 miles (110 km) from north to south. In addition, there are many small islands and skerries (rocky islets and reefs). The total length of the archipelago is about 110 miles (175 km), and the area is about 550 square miles (1,425 square km). A broad and deep fjord, the Vesterålsfjorden, lies between Lofoten and the mainland. The islands, composed of volcanic rocks (gneiss and granite), are the highly eroded tops of a partially submerged mountain range. The highest peak is Higravstind (3,809 feet [1,161 m]) on Austvågøya. North of the Arctic Circle, the islands are washed by the warm North Atlantic Current, which tempers their climate.

The Lofoten have been continuously inhabited since at least 1120, when King Øystein built a church and lodgings for fishermen near Kabelvåg, on Austvågøya. Fishing has always been predominant, and until the late 19th century, when tourists arrived on the islands, it was almost the only economic activity. Cod, along with some haddock, are the principal catch. The main fishery season extends from February through April, when thousands of men from all over Norway come to the area to land and process the cod catch. Local industries are related to fishing (cod-liver-oil processing and fertilizer manufacture from fish parts). Some potatoes and berries are grown, but the scanty soils will not support even the hardiest grains.

Svolvær, on Austvågøya, is the chief town and main port of the islands. Between Moskenesøya and the islet of Mosken flows the famed Moskenstraumen tidal channel, also called the Maelström (*q.v.*), with its treacherous reversing currents. Many artists come to the Lofoten group to depict the highly scenic landscapes; the famed Norwegian painter Gunnar Berg (1863–93) was born in Svolvær. Pop. (latest est.) deanery, 26,241.

loft, in architecture, upper space within a building, or a large undivided space in a building used principally for storage in business or industry. In churches the rood loft is a display gallery above the rood screen, and a choir or organ loft is a gallery reserved for church singers and musicians. In theatres a loft is the area above and behind the proscenium.

In comparison with an attic, a loft is usually opened on one side, similar to a balcony, as with a hayloft—the space under the roof of a barn. Sleeping lofts are often constructed in smaller dwellings to give more space. In many modern cities where living space is at a premium, industrial lofts are converted into residences, with tenants subdividing the open area to fit their needs.

Lofthuus, Christian Jensen (baptized May 15, 1750, Risør, Nor.—d. June 13, 1797, Christiania [now Oslo]), leader of a reform movement who sought redress for the grievances of Norway's peasantry from the absolutist Danish-Norwegian court. His imprisonment and death made him a martyr for Norwegian agrarian reform.

Lofthuus first journeyed to Denmark in June 1786 to present the peasants' grievances on taxes, official corruption, and exploitation to the crown prince. Told to return to Norway and to demonstrate public support, an action that could have led to his arrest for agitating against the crown, Lofthuus gathered a petition committee and attempted to return to Denmark in November 1786. The issuance of an arrest warrant, however, caused him to seek refuge in the more remote peasant villages. While southern Norway's peasants prepared to organize resistance to his arrest, he was taken into custody in March 1787 and imprisoned in the fortress of Akershus in Christiania. A peasant rising, which was quickly put down, led, however, to some reforms in 1788. Lofthuus died in prison.

Lofting, Hugh (b. Jan. 14, 1886, Maidenhead, Berkshire, Eng.—d. Sept. 26, 1947, Santa Monica, Calif., U.S.), English-born American author of a series of children's classics about Dr. Dolittle, a chubby, gentle, eccentric physician to animals, who learns the language of animals from his parrot, Polynesia, so that he can treat their complaints more efficiently. Much of the wit and charm of the stories lies in their matter-of-fact treatment of the doctor's bachelor household in Puddleby-on-the-Marsh, where his housekeeper, Dab-Dab, is a duck and his visitors and patients are animals.

Lofting attended a Jesuit boarding school in Derbyshire from the age of eight. He studied at the Massachusetts Institute of Technology, Cambridge, in 1904–05 and completed his studies in civil engineering at the London Polytechnic in 1906–07. His work took him to Africa, the West Indies, and Canada, but in 1912 he decided to become a writer and settled in New York City. He lived most of his life in the United States, but the ambience of all his books is English. Since Dr. Dolittle was originally created to entertain Lofting's children in letters he sent from the front during World War I, it is not surprising that he was a firm opponent of war, violence, and cruelty. After serving in Flanders and France, Lofting was wounded and invalided out. *The Story of Dr. Dolittle,* the first of his series, appeared in 1920 and won instant success. He wrote one Dr. Dolittle book a year until 1927, and these seven are generally considered the best of the series—certainly the sunniest. *The Voyages of Dr. Dolittle* (1922) won the Newbery Medal as the best children's book of the year.

Wearying of his hero, Lofting tried to get rid of him by sending him to the moon (*Dr. Dolittle in the Moon,* 1928), but popular demand compelled him to write *Dr. Dolittle's Return* in 1933. The last of the series, *Dr. Dolittle and the Secret Lake,* was 13 years in the writing and was published posthumously in 1948.

A motion picture, *Doctor Dolittle* (1967), heightened the already worldwide interest in his books, and several were reissued with new illustrations—Lofting's own apt and charming drawings had accompanied the original publications. *Dr. Dolittle; A Treasury* (1967) collected outstanding episodes from the series.

Lofting also wrote books in which the doctor did not appear, including *The Story of Mrs. Tubbs* (1923) and its sequel, *Tommy, Tilly, and Mrs. Tubbs* (1934).

log, also called MARITIME LOG, instrument for measuring the speed of a ship through water. The first practical log, developed in the 16th century, consisted of a pie-shaped log chip with a lead weight on its curved edge that caused it to float upright and resist towing. When the log was tossed overboard, it remained more or less stationary while an attached line (marked off with equally spaced knots) was let out behind the vessel for a measured interval of time (measured with a sandglass). The line and log were then hauled aboard and the speed of the ship determined by dividing the length of the line by the time interval.

In the 19th century the log chip was replaced by a towed rotor or propeller connected by a line to automatic speed- and distance-measuring equipment. Two logs in use today are the pitometer log and the bottom log. The pitometer uses a pitot tube projecting through the bottom of the ship. The tube has one forward-facing and two side-facing orifices. When the ship is moving, pressure in the forward-facing tube exceeds the pressure in the side tubes; this differential is transmitted to equipment that translates it into a speed measurement. In the bottom log, which also protrudes through the bottom of the ship, a water-driven impeller turns a small electric generator, the current from which is proportional to the speed of the ship. This current is similarly used to produce a speed measurement.

log cabin, small house built of logs notched at the ends and laid one upon another with the spaces filled with plaster, moss, mortar, mud, or dried manure. Log cabins are found especially in wooded areas, where the construction material is easily at hand. In North America they were built by early settlers and by hunters, loggers, and other wilderness dwellers. They have also been built in Europe, particularly in the Scandinavian countries.

Although the designs vary, a common style features a sloping, single-gabled timbered roof and small windows. The interior is usually simple, with one room, perhaps partitioned, over which a loft might be built. Modern summer cottages may be built of logs (or given log-cabin siding) to achieve a rustic effect.

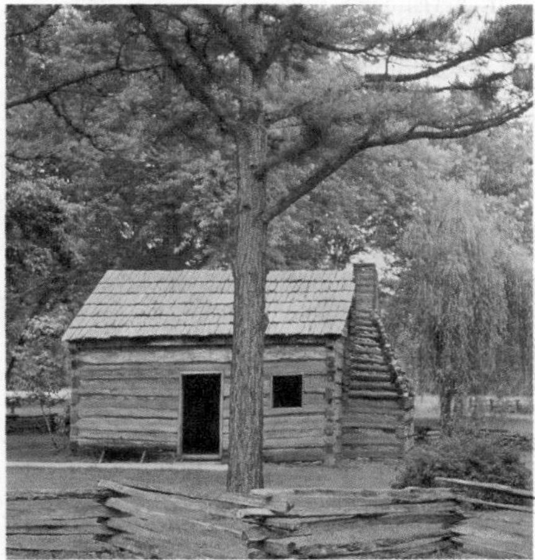

Log cabin, Abraham Lincoln's boyhood home, Knob Creek, Ky., originally built early 19th century
Wettach—Shostal/EB Inc.

Logan, city, seat of Cache county, northern Utah, U.S. It lies along the Logan River (named for Ephraim Logan, a trapper), in the Cache Valley, 35 miles (56 km) northeast of Ogden. The city is built on terraces of prehistoric Lake Bonneville at the mouth of Logan Canyon, 4,535 feet (1,382 m) above sea level, in the Wasatch Mountains. The Cache Valley was settled in 1856 by Mormons, and Logan was laid out in 1859. The Utah Northern Railroad (later part of the Union Pacific) reached the site in 1873. The city's agricultural economy (grains, sugar beets, cheese, livestock) is supplemented with small manufactures (pianos and organs, textiles, and farm equipment). Utah State University was founded there as an agricultural college in 1888. The city's Mormon Temple was completed in 1884, and the Tabernacle in 1878. The Wasatch-Cache National Forest is nearby. Inc. 1866. Pop. (1990) 32,762.

Logan, city, seat (1824) of Logan county, southwestern West Virginia, U.S. It lies along the Guyandotte River, 40 miles (64 km) southwest of Charleston, near the Kentucky border. Laid out in 1827 and known as Lawnsville, it was chartered in 1852 and was renamed Aracoma. In 1907 it was rechristened for Logan, an Indian leader. By 1850 it was a centre for logging operations and by the early 1900s for coal mining. The Appalachian area around Logan was made famous by the notorious mountain-family feud between the Hatfields (of Logan county) and the McCoys (of Pike county, Ky.). The Logan area was the scene of a major disaster in 1972 when coal-mine waste waters burst a makeshift dam on Buffalo Creek and inundated mining communities, killing 118 people. The coal industry, including the manufacture of mining equipment, remains the city's main economic activity. Chief Logan State Park is nearby. Pop. (1990) 2,206.

Logan, Harvey: *see* Curry, Kid.

Logan, James (b. Oct. 20, 1674, Lurgan, County Armagh, Ire.—d. Oct. 31, 1751, Stenton, Pa. [U.S.]), British-American colonial statesman and merchant who was also prominent in British-colonial intellectual life.

After receiving instruction in classical and modern languages from his schoolmaster father, Logan worked in commerce in Bristol, Eng., prior to becoming secretary to William Penn in 1699. Later that year Logan joined his employer and fellow Quaker in journeying to Pennsylvania. Logan was appointed provincial secretary in 1701 and then advanced to other political posts in the proprietary colony. It was as president of the Governor's Council from 1736 to 1738 that he in effect was Pennsylvania's chief executive owing to the absence of a governor. Logan, who represented the colony's aristocratic proprietary party, also served as a Philadelphia alderman, and in October 1722 he was elected mayor of the city. He entered the colony's judicial sphere in 1726 as a justice for Philadelphia County, then became a judge of the Court of Common Pleas, and in 1731 was made chief justice of Pennsylvania's Supreme Court. Logan was able to make use of his political influence and social connections to become wealthy through land speculation and the Indian trade.

Logan wrote several scientific works, but his primary contribution was in botany; he published a treatise, *Experimenta at Meletemata de Plantarum Generatione,* describing experiments on the impregnation of plant seeds. He also wrote on ethics and philology, and he translated several Latin classics for publication, including *M.T. Cicero's Cato Major, or His Discourse on Old Age.* Logan had a personal library of more than 3,000 volumes, which he contributed to start the Philadelphia Public Library.

Logan, James, also called JOHN LOGAN, original name, TAH-GAH-JUTE (b. *c.* 1725, probably at Shamokin [now Sunbury], Pa. [U.S.]—d. 1780, near Lake Erie), prominent Indian leader, whose initial excellent relations with white settlers in Pennsylvania and the Ohio Territory deteriorated into a vendetta after the slaughter of his family in 1774.

Logan's mother was a Cayuga Indian; his father was Chief Shikellamy, who was purportedly a white Frenchman who had been captured as a child and raised by the Oneida. Chief Shikellamy became a friend of the secretary of the Pennsylvania colony, James Logan, whose name the chief's son assumed.

Logan moved to the Ohio River valley after the French and Indian War (1754–63). He was never a chief but achieved renown among many Indian tribes, at first because of his friendship with the white settlers. Logan was converted to an intense hatred of all white men in 1774, when his entire family was treacherously slaughtered by a frontier trader named Daniel Greathouse during the Yellow Creek Massacre. In the ensuing conflict, which is known as Lord Dunmore's War, Logan was a prominent leader of Indian raids on white settlements, and he took the scalps of more than 30 white men. But when the defeated Indians finally gathered at Chillicothe, Ohio, to make peace after the Battle of Point Pleasant (Oct. 10, 1774), Logan sent a message containing his refusal to participate in the negotiations. His memorable statement of his grievances was widely circulated through the colonies and was recorded for posterity by Thomas Jefferson. The statement remains known as "Logan's Lament."

Logan continued his attacks on white settlers and associated himself with the Mohawk auxiliaries of the British during the American War of Independence. He was by then a violent alcoholic and died in an altercation.

Logan, John A(lexander) (b. Feb. 9, 1826, Jackson County, Ill., U.S.—d. Dec. 26, 1886, Washington, D.C.), U.S. congressman, Union general during the American Civil War (1861–65), and originator of Memorial Day.

Logan graduated in law from the University of Louisville (Kentucky) in 1851. He served as a Democratic congressman (1859–61) from Illinois, resigning his seat to join the Union Army as colonel of the 31st Illinois Infantry, which he had organized. He served under General Ulysses S. Grant until the capture of Vicksburg (July 1863), rising to the rank of major general of volunteers. In 1864 Logan succeeded General James McPherson as commander of the Army of the Tennessee but was later relieved of his command, apparently because General William T. Sherman felt Logan did not pay enough attention to logistics.

John Logan
By courtesy of the Library of Congress, Washington, D.C.

After the war, Logan, by then a Republican, represented Illinois in the U.S. House of Representatives (1867–71) and the Senate (1871–77, 1879–86). He helped found (1865) the Grand Army of the Republic (GAR), an organization of Union Army veterans, and was its head for three successive terms. In 1868, as commander in chief of the GAR, he inaugurated the observance of Memorial, or Decoration, Day when he asked GAR members to decorate soldiers' graves with flowers on May 30.

Logan, Joshua, in full JOSHUA LOCKWOOD LOGAN 3RD (b. Oct. 5, 1908, Texarkana, Texas, U.S.—d. July 12, 1988, New York City), American stage and motion-picture director, producer, and writer.

Logan was active in theatricals while attending Princeton University, where he studied from 1927 to 1931, and he studied acting under Konstantin Stanislavsky in Moscow on a scholarship. He made his Broadway debut as an actor in 1932 and soon began working as an assistant stage manager and then as a director. His initial directorial successes on Broadway were *On Borrowed Time* (1938), *I Married an Angel* (1938), and *By Jupiter* (1942), and he began a fruitful collaboration with the composer Richard Rodgers in the latter play. After serving in the U.S. Air Force during World War II, Logan directed the highly successful musical *Annie Get Your Gun* (1946), which was produced by Rodgers and Oscar Hammerstein and composed by Irving Berlin. Logan cowrote and directed *Mister Roberts* (1948) and then cowrote, coproduced, and directed the musical *South Pacific* (1949), which won the Pulitzer Prize for drama. Among the other popular plays that he directed were *Happy Birthday* (1945), *John Loves Mary* (1946), *Picnic* (1953), *Fanny* (1954), and *The World of Suzie Wong* (1958). Logan directed the highly acclaimed motion-picture version of *South Pacific* (1958) as well as several other popular films, among them *Bus Stop* (1956), *Sayonara* (1957), *Fanny* (1961), *Camelot* (1967), and *Paint Your Wagon* (1969).

Logan, Mount, mountain, highest point (19,524 feet [5,951 m]) in Canada and second in North America only to Mount McKinley. Located in the St. Elias Mountains of southwestern Yukon Territory, the peak towers about 14,000 feet (4,300 m) above the Seward Glacier at the Alaska border to the south and is a focal point of Kluane National Park, an 8,500-square-mile (22,000-square-kilometre) rugged wilderness. The actual ridge crest of the mountain is about 10 miles (16 km) across, while the entire mass is more than 20 miles (32 km) long. An expedition under A.H. MacCarthy and H.F. Lambert on June 23, 1925, became the first to reach the summit. The peak was named after Sir William Logan (1798–1875), founder of the Geological Survey of Canada.

Logan, Sir William Edmond (b. April 20, 1798, Montreal—d. June 22, 1875, Llechryd, Cardiganshire, Wales), one of the foremost Canadian geologists of the 19th century.

Logan was educated at the University of Edinburgh and began working for his uncle in London in 1818. From 1831 until 1838 he managed his uncle's coal and copper-smelting interests in Swansea, Glamorganshire, and in this capacity he prepared geologic maps of the Welsh coalfields. Logan's observations of the close association of underlying clay layers and fossil tree roots with local coal beds provided decisive evidence for the theory that coal beds are formed in place.

In 1842, when the Geological Survey of Canada was formed, Logan was made its director, and he served in this capacity until 1869. His chief work for the Geological Survey was his monumental *Report on the Geology of Canada* (1863), a compilation of 20 years of research. Another of Logan's important achievements was his recognition that the Paleozoic (from 570 million to 245 million years ago) rocks of northeastern North America were divided by a prominent zone of thrust faulting running along the valley of the St. Lawrence River and then trending south along the Hudson River valley and southwest across Pennsylvania. This line is known as Logan's Line. The Paleozoic strata west of Logan's Line are relatively undisturbed, while those lying east of the line have been greatly deformed. Logan was knighted in 1856.

loganberry (*Rubus loganobaccus*), bramble fruit of the family Rosaceae that originated in the United States, at Santa Cruz, Calif., in 1881. Raised from seed, it is thought to be a hybrid between the wild blackberry of the Pacific coast and the red raspberry. It is grown in large quantities in Oregon and Washington and also cultivated in England and Tasmania. The loganberry, or Logan, is a vigorous, nearly trailing, blackberry-like plant with compound leaves of three to five leaflets and prickly canes. Its deep, wine-red, tart, high-flavoured berries separate from the stem as do blackberries. The fruit is canned, frozen for preserve or pie stock, or made into wine.

Loganberry (*Rubus loganobaccus*)
Job Kuijt

Loganiaceae, family of flowering plants in the order Gentianales, containing about 21 genera with more than 500 species of woody vines, shrubs, or trees native primarily to tropical areas of the world. Members of the family bear leaflike appendages at the base of the leafstalks and have terminal flower clusters. The ring of petals on each flower has four or five overlapping lobes. The fruit is a capsule containing winged or wingless seeds.

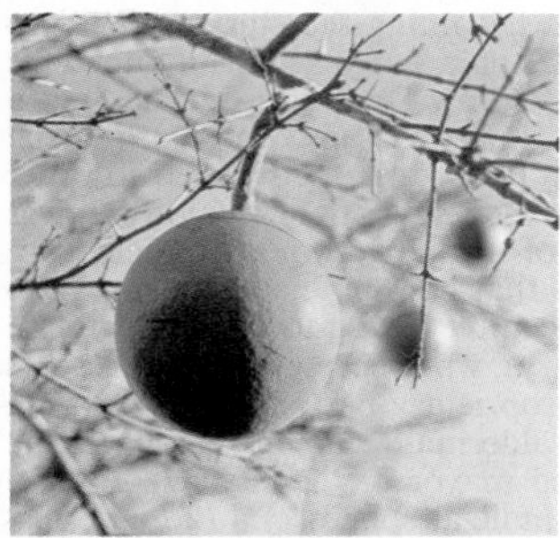

(Top) fruit of *Strychnos*; (bottom) flowers of Carolina jasmine (*Gelseminum sempervirens*)
(Top) Gordon L. Maclean, (bottom) Jack Dermid

Carolina, or yellow, jasmine, or jessamine (*Gelsemium sempervirens*), an ornamental evergreen vine, bears fragrant clusters of yellow flowers that are pinkish orange behind the petal lobes. Several species of butterfly bush (*q.v.; Buddleia*) and pinkroot (*Spigelia marilandica*) also are cultivated as ornamentals. Poisonous alkaloids found in the bark and seeds of plants of the genus *Strychnos* are used in arrow poisons such as curare (*q.v.*) and in drugs that stimulate the heart and central nervous system. *Buddleia* is now considered by many botanists to belong to the family Budlejaceae, and *Spigelia* and *Strychnos* occasionally are placed in the families Spigeliaceae and Strychnaceae respectively.

logarithm, the exponent or power to which a base must be raised to yield a given number.

A brief treatment of logarithms follows. For full treatment, *see* MACROPAEDIA: Arithmetic.

An example of a logarithm is as follows. In the expression $b^x = N$, if b is the base and equal to 10 and N a number, equal to 100, then x is equal to 2 and is said to be the logarithm of 100 to the base 10. This is written: $\log 100 = 2$, in which it is understood that log means logarithm to the base 10. The latter is also called a common logarithm. Logarithms that employ the base e, in which $e = 2.71828\ldots$ are called natural, or Napierian, logarithms; the notation used is ln, to distinguish natural logarithms from common logarithms (log).

When a common logarithm of a number is written as the sum of an integer and a positive decimal (*e.g.,* 2.3147), the integer—called the characteristic—serves to locate the decimal point in the number, and the decimal—called the mantissa—indicates the digits in the number. The latter are determined from tables of logarithms, which relate mantissas to numbers. When the number is greater than or equal to 1, the characteristic is 1 less than the number of digits to the left of the decimal point; when the number is less than 1, the characteristic is negative and is 1 more than the number of zeros following the decimal point. For example, the number 365.0 has the characteristic 2; the number 0.005 has the characteristic −3.

Logau, Friedrich, Freiherr von (baron of), pseudonym SALOMON VON GOLAW (b. June 1604, Brockuth, near Nimptsch, Silesia [now in Poland]—d. July 24, 1655, Liegnitz [now Legnica, Poland]), German epigrammatist noted for his direct, unostentatious style.

Logau was of noble descent and became an orphan early. He spent his life in service to the petty courts of Brieg and Liegnitz. Logau resented the forced lowliness of his position, and he directed much of his satirical wit at courtly life, particularly at the falsity of foreign (primarily French) cultural customs he saw adopted by the nobility, and at their misguided contempt for the German language. His terse epigrams support the ideals of genuine noblemen and loyal German patriots and decry the futility of bloody rivalries among religious groups. Pointed yet rarely didactic, Logau's writing is remarkably direct and unadorned for his time. The first collection of epigrams, *Erstes Hundert Teutscher Reimensprüche* (1638; "First Hundred German Proverbs in Rhyme"), was enlarged and polished, appearing in 1654 as *Salomons von Golaw Deutscher Sinn-Getichte Drey Tausend*, 3 vol. ("Salomon von Golaw's Three Thousand German Epigrams"; reissued 1872 as *Friedrichs von Logau sämmtliche Sinngedichte*). Logau's epigrams were forgotten until a century after his death, when they were published in 1759 by G.E. Lessing and C.W. Ramler as *Friedrichs von Logau Sinngedichte*.

loggia, room, hall, gallery, or porch open to the air on one or more sides; it evolved in the Mediterranean region, where an open sitting room with protection from the sun was desirable. Ancient Egyptian houses often had a loggia on their roofs or an interior loggia facing upon a court.

In medieval and Renaissance Italy the loggia was often used in conjunction with a public square, as in the Loggia dei Lanzi (begun 1376) in Florence by Benci di Cione and Simone di Francesco. The loggia was also an essential feature of a villa and often had outstanding decoration—*e.g.,* the frescoes of Raphael in the Villa Farnesina loggia at Rome.

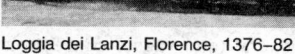

Loggia dei Lanzi, Florence, 1376–82
Alinari—Art Resource/EB Inc.

logging, process of harvesting trees, sawing them into appropriate lengths (bucking), and transporting them (skidding) to a sawmill. The different phases of this process vary with local conditions and technology.

In the 19th century logging was a hand process, and in some parts of the world it has remained one. In colder regions, trees are felled by ax in winter and conveyed by a sled drawn by oxen, mules, or horses to a frozen river. After the spring thaw, the logs are floated downriver to a sawmill.

In mechanized modern logging, trees are felled by crosscut saw or power-driven chain saw or, for trees of relatively young plantations, by a machine that cuts the entire tree in one bite. Trees are then cut into standard lengths and skidded to the mill by truck or tractor or conveyed to a central point by cable, either high above ground (high-lead and overhead skidding) or along the ground (groundline skidding). Helicopters and balloons are also used to transport logs.

Local conditions may dictate uncommon logging methods. In India, teakwood trees are killed by girdling (making a circular cut around the tree through the outer bark and cortex to interrupt the circulation of water and nutrients) and harvested several years later. Then, as is also common in Nigeria, they may be floated down the river by raft. In several Asian countries, timber may be transported by elephant. *See also* forestry.

logia (Greek: "sayings," "words," or "discourses"), hypothetical collection, either written or oral, of the sayings of Jesus, which might have been in circulation around the time of the composition of the Synoptic Gospels (*i.e.,* those of Matthew, Mark, and Luke). Most biblical scholars agree that Matthew and Luke based their written accounts largely on The Gospel According to Mark. The versions of Matthew and Luke, however, both share a good deal of material that is absent from Mark. This shared material is largely made up of sayings attributed to Jesus, an ostensible coincidence that has led biblical scholars to hypothesize the existence of an undetermined source, perhaps the logia, from which the shared material is drawn.

Matthew and Luke, however, share narrative material as well as the sayings of Jesus. Scholars have therefore hypothesized the existence of a kind of proto-gospel that incorporates the logia. Experts have called this hypothetical source Q (from German *Quelle,* "source"). The existence of Q, sometimes called the lost source, is theoretical; some scholars, although believing that Q exists, contend that the logia is an entirely different entity.

The first references to the logia were made by Papias, a 2nd-century bishop of Hierapolis in Asia Minor, in his work *Logiōn kyriakōn exēgēseis* ("Interpretation of the Logia of the Lord"), and by other early Christian writers, such as Polycarp, a 2nd-century bishop of Smyrna in Asia Minor. According to Eusebius, a 4th-century church historian, Papias wrote that the Apostle Matthew arranged the logia of Jesus in an orderly form in Hebrew.

Some scholars contend that the logia was a collection of Old Testament oracles predicting the coming of the Messiah, but this view has been challenged. Though the logia may not have been part of the theoretical lost source known as Q or of the Old Testament messianic oracles, it is generally assumed that early Christians either wrote down or transmitted orally the sayings of Jesus, much as Jews of the period collected the sayings of respected rabbis, and that this material was used by both Matthew and Luke.

logic, the study of the principles of reasoning, and especially of drawing inferences. This study may be carried on at a very abstract level, as in formal logic, or it may focus on the practical art of right reasoning, as in applied logic.

A brief treatment of logic follows. For full treatment, *see* MACROPAEDIA: Logic, The History and Kinds of.

A basic notion of logic is validity. An argument or inference is said to be valid if the conclusion follows necessarily from the premises—*i.e.,* if it is impossible for the premises to be true and the conclusion false. Valid arguments do not increase the amount of information the reasoner has but only draw out, in the conclusion, information that is latent or implicit in the premises. Valid arguments whose premises are true are called sound. Valid arguments are also called deductive arguments, though occasionally the term "deductive" is used to refer to an argument that is intended to be valid, though it may not be. Unlike deductive arguments, inductive arguments are those in which the conclusion provides additional information not already contained in the premises. Such arguments are also called ampliative. Because the conclusion contains new information, inductive arguments are always invalid. This does not mean, however, that all inductive arguments are bad. A good inductive argument is one in which the premises are true or likely to be true, and the truth of the premises makes the conclusion to a certain degree likely or reasonable. A typical form of inductive argument is generalization, in which a conclusion about all or most cases of a certain type is drawn from premises about a limited number of such cases.

In its narrowest sense, deductive logic comprises the logic of propositions, also called sentential logic, and the logic of predicates, which concerns properties or relations. In its widest sense, it embraces various general features of language (such as syntax and semantics), metalogic (the methodology of formal systems), theories of modalities (the analyses of the notions of necessity, possibility, impossibility, and contingency), and the study of paradoxes and logical fallacies. Both the narrow and the wide senses may be called formal or pure logic, in that they construct and analyze an abstract body of symbols, rules for combining these symbols into formulas, and rules for manipulating these formulas. When certain meanings are attached to these symbols and formulas, and this machinery is adapted and deployed over issues treated in a certain range of special subjects, logic is said to be applied. The analysis of questions that transcend the concerns of either pure or applied logic, such as the examination of the meaning and implications of the concepts and assumptions of either discipline, is the domain of the philosophy of logic.

Logic was developed independently and brought to some degree of systematization in China (5th to 3rd century BC) and India (from the 5th century BC through the 17th century AD). Logic as it is known in the West comes from Greece. Building on an important tradition of mathematics and rhetorical and philosophical argumentation, Aristotle in the 4th century BC worked out the first system of the logic of noun expressions. The logic of propositions originated in the work of Aristotle's pupil Theophrastus and in that of the 4th-century Megarian school of dialecticians and logicians and the school of the Stoics. After the decline of Greek culture, logic reemerged first among Arab scholars in the 10th century. Medieval interest in logic dated from the work of St. Anselm of Canterbury and Peter Abelard. Its high point was the 14th century, when the Scholastics developed logic, especially the analysis of propositions, well beyond what was known to the ancients. Rhetoric and natural science largely eclipsed logic during the Renaissance. Modern logic began to develop with the work of the philosopher and mathematician G.W. Leibniz, who attempted to create a universal calculus of reason. Great strides were made in the 19th century in the development of symbolic logic, leading to the highly fruitful merging of logic and mathematics in formal analysis.

Modern formal logic is the study of inference and propositional forms. Its simplest and most basic branch is that of the propositional calculus. In this logic, propositions or sentences are treated as simple and unanalyzable; attention is focused on how they are related to other propositions by propositional connectives (such as "if . . . then," "and," "or," "it is not the case that," etc.) and formed into arguments. By representing propositions with symbols called variables and connectives with symbolic operators, and by deciding on a set of transformation rules (axioms that define validity and provide starting points for the derivation of further rules called theorems), it is possible to model and study the abstract characteristics and consequences of this formal system in a way similar to the investigations of pure mathematics. A logical system that treats predicates rather than propositions as basic is known as a lower predicate calculus. This system includes, in addition to the logical connectives mentioned above, certain symbols known as quantifiers—"(∃x)", read as "There exists an individual x such that . . ." and (∀x), read as "For all individuals x such that . . ."—and typically also identity. A major step in modern logic is the discovery that it is possible to examine and characterize other formal systems in terms of the logic resulting from their elements, operations, and rules of formation; such is the study of the logical foundations of mathematics, set theory, and logic itself.

Logic is said to be applied when it systematizes the forms of sound reasoning or a body of universal truths in some restricted field of thought or discourse. Usually this is done by adding extra axioms and special constants to some preestablished pure logic such as propositional logic or the lower predicate calculus. Examples of applied logics are practical logic, which is concerned with the logic of choices, commands, and values; epistemic logic, which analyzes the logic of belief, knowing, and questions; the logics of physical application, such as temporal logic and mereology (the logic of classes); and the logics of correct argumentation, fallacies, hypothetical reasoning, and so on.

Varieties of logical semantics have become the central area of study in the philosophy of logic. Some of the more important contemporary philosophical issues concerning logic are the following: What is the relation between logical systems and the real world? What are the limitations of logic, especially with regard to some of the assumptions of its wider senses and the incompleteness of first-order logic? What consequences stem from the nonrecursive nature of many mathematical functions?

logic of quantifiers: *see* predicate calculus.

Logical Atomism, theory, developed primarily by the British logician Bertrand Russell and the Austrian-born philosopher Ludwig Wittgenstein, proposing that language, like other phenomena, can be analyzed in terms of aggregates of fixed, irreducible units or elements. Logical Atomism supposes that a perfect one-to-one correspondence exists between an "atom" of language (an atomic proposition) and an atomic fact; thus, for each atomic fact there is a corresponding atomic proposition. An atomic proposition is one that asserts that a certain thing has a certain quality (*e.g.:* "This is red."). An atomic fact is the simplest kind of fact and consists in the possession of a quality by some specific, individual thing. Therefore, on the assumption that language mirrors reality, it can be proposed that the world is composed of facts that are utterly simple and comprehensible.

Through mathematical logic laid down in *Principia Mathematica* (1910–13; with Alfred North Whitehead), Russell sought to show that philosophical arguments could be solved in much the same way mathematical problems are solved. He rejected Hegel's monism, maintaining that it led to a denial of relations between things. For Russell, atomic propositions are the building blocks from which, using logical connectives, the more complex molecular propositions are constructed.

Logical Positivism, also called LOGICAL EMPIRICISM, a philosophical doctrine formulated in Vienna in the 1920s, according to which scientific knowledge is the only kind of factual knowledge and all traditional metaphysical doctrines are to be rejected as meaningless.

A brief treatment of Logical Positivism follows. For full treatment, *see* MACROPAEDIA: Philosophical Schools and Doctrines.

The Logical Positivist school differs from earlier empiricists and positivists (David Hume, Ernst Mach) in holding that the ultimate basis of knowledge rests upon public experimental verification rather than upon personal experience. It differs from Auguste Comte and J.S. Mill in holding that metaphysical doctrines are not false but meaningless—that the "great unanswerable questions" about substance, causality, freedom, and God are unanswerable just because they are not genuine questions at all. This last is a thesis about language, not about nature, and is based upon a general account of meaning and of meaninglessness. All genuine philosophy (according to the group that came to be called the Vienna Circle) is a critique of language; and (according to some of its leading members) its result is to show the unity of science—that all genuine knowledge about nature can be expressed in a single language common to all the sciences.

The Vienna Circle, which launched its first manifesto in 1929, had its origin in discussions among physicists and mathematicians before World War I. The general conclusion was reached that the empiricism of Mill and Mach was inadequate since it failed to explain mathematical and logical truths, or to account satisfactorily for the apparently a priori element in natural science. In 1922 Hans Hahn at Vienna University laid before his students the *Tractatus Logico-Philosophicus* of Ludwig Wittgenstein, published in the previous year. This work introduced a new general theory of meaning, derived in part from the logical inquiries of Giuseppe Peano, Gottlob Frege, Bertrand Russell, and A.N. Whitehead, and gave the Vienna group its logical foundation. Most of the group's members moved to the United States at the outset of World War II. In the meantime disciples had been found in many other countries, including Poland and England, where A.J. Ayer's *Language, Truth, and Logic* (1936; rev. ed., 1946) provided an excellent introduction to the views of the group.

In England, however, the direct influence of Wittgenstein proved much more powerful. Wittgenstein had visited England before World War I and had spent some time at Cambridge; while there he discussed logic with Bertrand Russell. The *Tractatus Logico-Philosophicus* expresses and generalizes the conclusions that he had reached upon philosophical questions. In 1929 Wittgenstein returned to Cambridge and worked there (with a few intermissions) until 1947. During this later period Wittgenstein himself subjected the doctrines of the *Tractatus* to fundamental criticism and produced what was in effect a new account of philosophy. His *Philosophical Investigations* (German text with English trans., 1953) appeared posthumously.

logical relation, those relations between the elements of discourse or thought that constitute its rationality, in the sense either of (1) reasonableness or (2) intelligibility. A statement may be perfectly intelligible without being based upon any good evidence or reason, though of course no statement can be reasonable without its being intelligible. Logical relations are contrasted by most philosophers with causal relations within reality, thought, or discourse.

Statements or propositions are logically related in the sense of reasonableness if the truth or falsity of one requires truth or falsity in the other. Thus, "John has a high IQ and is immensely popular" is logically related to "John has a high IQ," because if the latter is false the former must be false, whereas if the former is true the latter must be true. Similarly, "All living things require oxygen" and "No living things require oxygen" are logically related in that if one is true the other must be false. The more important logical relations are implication (as in the first example above) and equivalence; and, as displayed in the square of opposition (*see* opposition, square of), contrariety (as in the second example), contradiction, subcontrariety, and subimplication.

A type of relation between the elements of thought and discourse that has almost always been regarded by philosophers as much more significant for their concerns than those that condition reasonableness is the kind that must be maintained if the discourse is to be intelligible or understandable, *i.e.,* if it is to be about, and be recognized as being about, some definite object or event or state of affairs. These logical relations often are thought of as holding between concepts, as opposed to whole propositions. Clear cases may be drawn from certain rules of grammar. Thus, no string of mere prepositions and adverbs—as "to quickly brightly away through . . ."—yields an intelligible assertion. A similar but not identical unintelligibility is present in "Prudence is light blue in odour." Many relations, however, have to do, not with grammar, but with the context—often the extra-linguistic context—in which an expression or thought occurs. Thus, if a person looks out the window and says, "It is raining, but I do not believe it"; or if after telling you he has no auto he wishes to sell you his car; or if he asks you to close a door that both of you know is already closed, in each of these examples it is not clear what he is saying or doing.

A still more general (and vague) conception of logical relation is that it is any relation in which a logician may have a peculiar professional interest. Relations of names to their objects, of functions to their arguments (as of an equation to its x's, y's, a's, and b's), or of metalanguages (discourse on languages) to their object languages, are examples here. But on questions relating to the nature and range of logic as a theoretical discipline, because of widespread disagreement on these issues among competent professionals, little of accepted substance can be said about logical relations in this third sense. Nonetheless, the adjective logical lies at the centre of interest, disagreement, and confusion in 20th-century British and American philosophy.

Logician, also called DIALECTICIAN, any member of a school of Chinese philosophers of the Warring States period (475–221 BC). In Chinese the school is called Ming-chia (Pinyin Mingjia), "School of Names," because one of the problems addressed by the Logicians was the correspondence between name and actuality. In addition, they discussed such problems as existence, relativity, space, time, quality, and causes. The school was small and had little influence on subsequent Chinese intellectual history, but it was the only Chinese philosophical school devoted primarily to logical and epistemological problems. Hui Shih (*c.* 380–*c.* 305 BC) and Kung-sun Lung (b. 380 BC) were the most prominent members of the school.

logicism, school of mathematical thought introduced by the 19th–20th-century German mathematician Gottlob Frege and the British mathematician Bertrand Russell, which holds that mathematics is actually logic. Logicists contend that all of mathematics can be deduced from pure logic, without the use of any specifically mathematical concepts, such as number or set. *Compare* formalism; intuitionism. *See also* mathematics, foundations of.

logistic system (philosophy): *see* formal system.

logistics, in military science, all the activities of armed-force units in roles supporting combat units, including transport, supply, signal communication, medical aid, and the like.

A brief treatment of logistics follows. For full treatment, *see* MACROPAEDIA: War, The Theory and Conduct of.

The word logistics stems from the Greek word *logistikos,* "skilled in calculating." "Logista" was the title of administrative officials in the Roman and Byzantine armies. A cognate French word, *loger,* means the billeting of soldiers, and in the late 17th century the French staff officer responsible for the quartering and movement of troops was the *maréchal des logis,* or quartermaster general. His staff was linked with a branch of the French military engineers, the *ingénieurs géographes,* whose task was to make maps and draw up memoranda of operational areas for use in planning the movement and maintenance of armies. Henri, Baron de Jomini, an early 19th-century authority on Napoleonic warfare, in his book *Précis de l'art de la guerre* (1836), defined logistics as "the practical art of moving armies" in which he included reconnaissance, engineer, and staff work. The purpose was to produce a logistical approach to battle and so to achieve strategic and tactical mobility and surprise.

Jomini's logistic theories had little influence on military thought in Europe, and the term itself fell into disuse. It was revived in 1882 by then U.S. captain (later admiral) Alfred Thayer Mahan, who defined logistics as the support of armed forces by the economic and industrial mobilization of a nation.

From 1918 the U.S. armed forces increasingly used logistics to describe the activities of the Ordnance Department and Quartermaster Corps, embracing a wide range of staff duties including supply, transportation, construction, and medical service. The term was seldom used elsewhere until World War II. In the British Royal Army, administration covered all activities connected with the interior economy of units in peace and their supply, movement, and maintenance in war. Neither logistics nor administration was used by European armies. The French *intendance,* "management of supply," led to the title of *intendant general* for the officer in continental armies responsible for supply.

With the complexity of modern war the term logistics has acquired a wider meaning. It is concerned not only with the movement and maintenance of forces and the evacuation and hospitalization of personnel but also with the design, development, acquisition, storage, and distribution of material—in other words, the procurement of weapons, their associated systems, and all other materials of war. The term administration is increasingly used to denote personnel management and the day-to-day handling of matters affecting pay, discipline, and morale.

The complexity of modern war imposes many strains on the logistic planners who must recognize the speed and depth of operations, the vulnerability of lines of communication to air and ground attack, and the vast organization needed for the maintenance of modern forces. Also, the evolution of modern warfare—with its complicated vehicles, aircraft, naval vessels, communications systems, and weapons, combined with the ability to mobilize large populations—has escalated military demands for supplies, provisions, and products. The effort to supply the war machines of belligerent powers has taken over more and more of their national economies and required greater numbers of transport, service, and supply personnel under direct military authority. In World War II, for instance, it was estimated that only 3 out of 10 men in the U.S. Army served in a combat role.

logogram, written or pictorial symbol intended to represent a whole word. Writing systems that make use of logograms include Chinese, Egyptian hieroglyphic writing, and early cuneiform writing systems. No known writing system is totally logographic; all such systems have both logograms and symbols representing particular sounds or syllables.

Logone River, principal tributary of the Chari (Shari) River of the Lake Chad Basin, draining northeastern Cameroon and Chad. It is formed by the Mbéré River and its tributary the Vina (Wina, Mba, Bini) of northern Cameroon and by the Pendé of northwestern Central African Republic. The two headstreams join 28 miles (45 km) south-southeast of Laï, Chad, to form the Logone, which then flows 240 miles (390 km) northwest to N'Djamena, Chad, and combines with the Chari.

Trapping fish in the Logone River, Chad
Bonnotte—De Wys Inc.

There are extensive papyrus swamps and marshes along much of the Logone. During the rainy season, it is linked to the Benue River system through the Lake Fianga and Tikem swamps (Chad) and the Mayo Kébi River in Cameroon. The regular loss of a portion of Lake Chad's water supply to the Benue system is a serious problem for the arid region. The Logone is seasonally navigable below Bongor, Chad, for small steamers and provides rich fishing grounds.

logos (Greek: "word," "reason," or "plan"), plural LOGOI, in Greek philosophy and theology, the divine reason implicit in the cosmos, ordering it and giving it form and meaning. Though the concept defined by the term logos is found in Greek, Indian, Egyptian, and Persian philosophical and theological systems, it became particularly significant in Christian writings and doctrines to describe or define the role of Jesus Christ as the principle of God active in the creation and the continuous structuring of the cosmos and in revealing the divine plan of salvation to man. It thus underlies the basic Christian doctrine of the preexistence of Jesus.

The idea of the logos in Greek thought harks back at least to the 6th-century-BC philosopher Heracleitus, who discerned in the cosmic process a logos analogous to the reasoning power in man. Later, the Stoics, philosophers who followed the teachings of the thinker Zeno of Citium (4th–3rd century BC), defined the logos as an active rational and spiritual principle that permeated all reality. They called the logos providence, nature, god, and the soul of the universe, which is composed of many seminal logoi that are contained in the universal logos. Philo of Alexandria, a 1st-century-AD Jewish philosopher, taught that the logos was the intermediary between God and the cosmos, being both the agent of creation and the agent through which the human mind can apprehend and comprehend God. According to Philo and the Middle Platonists, philosophers who interpreted in religious terms the teachings of the 4th-century-BC Greek master philosopher Plato, the logos was both immanent in the world and at the same time the transcendent divine mind.

In the first chapter of The Gospel According to John, Jesus Christ is identified as "the Word" (Greek *logos*) incarnated, or made flesh. This identification of Jesus with the logos is based on Old Testament concepts of revelation, such as occurs in the frequently used phrase "the Word of the Lord"—which connoted ideas of God's activity and power—and the Jewish view that Wisdom is the divine agent that draws man to God and is identified with the word of God. The author of The Gospel According to John used this philosophical expression, which easily would be recognizable to readers in the Hellenistic (Greek cultural) world, to emphasize the redemptive character of the person of Christ, whom the author describes as "the way, and the truth, and the life." Just as the Jews had viewed the Torah (the Law) as preexistent with God, so also the author of John viewed Jesus, but Jesus came to be regarded as the personified source of life and illumination of mankind. The Evangelist interprets the logos as inseparable from the person of Jesus and does not simply imply that the logos is the revelation that Jesus proclaims.

The identification of Jesus with the logos, which is implied in various places in the New Testament but stated specifically in the Fourth Gospel, was further developed in the early church but more on the basis of Greek philosophical ideas than on Old Testament motifs. This development was dictated by attempts made by early Christian theologians and apologists to express the Christian faith in terms that would be intelligible to the Hellenistic world and to impress their hearers with the view that Christianity was superior to, or heir to, all that was best in pagan philosophy. Thus, in their apologies and polemical works, the early Christian Fathers stated that Christ as the preexistent logos (1) reveals the Father to mankind and is the subject of the Old Testament manifestations of God; (2) is the divine reason in which the whole human race shares, so that the 6th-century-BC philosopher and others who lived with reason were Christians before Christ; and (3) is the divine will and word by which the worlds were framed.

logothete, in Byzantine government from the 7th to the 14th century, any of several officials who shared a variety of responsibilities ranging from the assessment and collection of taxes to the direction of foreign policy. The logothete of the drome, who was charged with presenting gifts to foreign embassies, eventually became the sovereign's chief adviser on foreign affairs. Theoctistus, logothete of the drome under Empress Theodora (regent 842–856), was one of the most powerful men ever to hold the office.

By the 12th and 13th centuries an official called the grand logothete headed the entire civil service. In this capacity he sometimes even represented the emperor's religious interests. In July 1274 at the second Council of Lyon the grand logothete George Acropolites accepted Roman Catholic orthodoxy and papal supremacy in the name of Emperor Michael VIII Palaeologus (1259–82). In the 14th and 15th centuries, the offices of the logothetes became empty titles.

logrolling: *see* birling.

Logroño, former name of a province in Spain known from 1980 as La Rioja (*q.v.*).

Logroño, city, capital of La Rioja *provincia* and *comunidad autónoma* ("autonomous community"), north-central Spain on the Ebro River. Originating in Roman times, it owed its growth during the European Middle Ages to its position on the pilgrim route to Santiago de Compostela as much as to its production of wool. An ancient walled town, Logroño has both old and modern quarters. Notable landmarks include the churches of Santiago el Real (16th century), Santa María la Redonda (15th–17th century), and Santa María del Palacio (11th century), and the Instituto, a museum of art reproductions. A trade centre in an agricultural and wine-growing district, Logroño is known for its Rioja wine. Industries include food processing, sawmilling, and the manufacture of furniture and textiles. Pop. (1986 est.) mun., 115,922.

Logue, Christopher (b. Nov. 23, 1926, Portsmouth, Hampshire, Eng.), English poet and one of the leaders in the movement to bring poetry closer to the popular experience. His own pungent verse has been read to jazz accompaniment, sung, and printed on posters. It is engaged politically and owes much to the work of the earlier 20th-century German poet and playwright Bertolt Brecht and to the English ballad tradition.

Logue served in the British army from 1944 to 1948 and lived in France from 1951 to 1956. His first book of poetry, *The Weakdream Sonnets* (1955), was published there. One of the first English appreciators of Pablo Neruda, he adapted 20 of that Chilean writer's poems as *The Man Who Told His Love* (1958). These adaptations also appeared in the collection *Songs* (1959). Subsequent volumes include *Songs from the Lily-White Boys* (1960), *Logue's A.B.C.* (1966), *New Numbers* (1969), and *Fluff* (1984). Among his poster poems are "I Shall Vote Labour" (1966), "Kiss Kiss" (1968), and "Black Dwarf" (1968). He worked on a remarkably fresh adaptation of the *Iliad,* three sections of which have been published: *Patrocleia* (1962), *Pax* (1967), and *War Music* (1981). Logue's long and varied list of works includes plays, screenplays, documentaries, and numerous children's books in addition to poetry and translation. He also acted in several television, movie, and stage roles.

logwood (species *Haematoxylon campechianum*), tree of the pea family (Fabaceae), native to Central America and the West Indies. The name is sometimes applied also to *Condalia obovata,* a tree of the buckthorn family (Rhamnaceae) native to southwestern North America. *H. campechianum* grows 9–15 m (30–50 feet) tall and has a short, crooked trunk. The leaves are pinnately compound (feather-formed), with rather oval leaflets. The small yellow flowers grow in a cluster from the leaf axil (upper angle between branch and leaf stem). The wood is heavy and extremely hard. A black dye, also called logwood, is obtained from the heartwood.

Loheiya, Al- (Yemen): *see* Luḥayyah, Al-.

Lohengrin, the knight of the swan, hero of German versions of a legend widely known in variant forms from the European Middle Ages onward. It seems to bear some relation to the northern European folktale of "The Seven Swans," but its actual origin is uncertain. The basic story tells of a mysterious knight who arrives—in a boat drawn by a swan—to help a noble lady in distress. He marries her but forbids her to ask his origin; she later forgets this promise, and he leaves her, never to return.

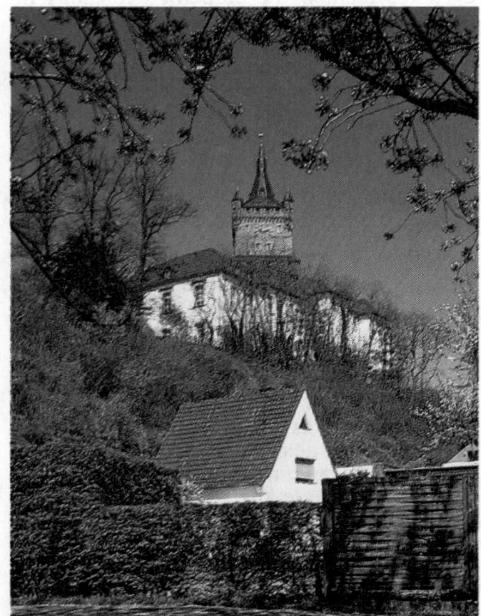

The tower of Swans' Castle (Schwanenburg), Kleve, Ger., associated with the legend of Lohengrin

Stief Pictures, Frankfurt

The first German version of this old legend—which itself probably derives from a fairy tale of seven brothers who are persecuted by a wicked grandmother and then metamorphosed into swans—appeared in Wolfram von Eschenbach's *Parzival* (*c.* 1210), a poem chiefly concerned with the theme of the Holy Grail. In this account the swan knight's name was Loherangrîn, and he was the son of Parzival (Perceval), the Grail hero, and heir to Parzival's title; he arrived in a swan-drawn boat from the castle of the Grail to aid Elsa of Brabant, married her, and in the end returned to the Grail castle.

An anonymous Middle High German poem, *Lohengrin* (*c.* 1275–90), set the story in the historical context of the reign of the German king Henry I the Fowler (876?–936), and its author elaborated the realistic elements of the story at the expense of much romantic material. A contemporary poem known as the *Wartburgkrieg* presented the story of Lohengrin as an entry in a story-telling competition; it was the contribution of von Eschenbach, who recited it in the famous singers' contest held at Wartburg (a castle overlooking the town of Eisenach) by the landgrave of Thuringia, Hermann I (*c.* 1156–1217). Other German medieval versions of the story include Konrad von Würzburg's *Schwanritter* ("Swan Knight") and an anonymous 15th-century epic called *Lorengel.* The latter was the chief source used by the 19th-century composer and librettist Richard Wagner for his opera *Lohengrin* (first performed on Aug. 28, 1850, at Weimar, Ger.).

In a French version of the legend, the *Chevalier au cygne,* the knight of the swan (here called Helyas) married Beatrix of Bouillon, the story being arranged and elaborated to glorify the house of Bouillon. Godfrey of Bouillon, a leader of the First Crusade, was held to be the son of a mysterious swan knight. English versions of the legend, composed in the late 14th and early 16th centuries, were strongly influenced by this French account.

Through its alignment with a historical period and its integration with the Wartburg story, the Lohengrin legend became part of German popular tradition. In particular, the legend came to be associated with the town of Cleves (modern Kleve, Ger.), the rulers of which took the swan as their crest; the swan tower of the castle, as well as a statue of the knight and his swan, perpetuate the legend's memory there.

Loi-kaw, town, east-central Myanmar (Burma), on the Pilu River, a tributary of the Salween River. Situated in hilly forested country, Loi-kaw has timber and silk-processing industries and is the site of an important hydroelectric power plant. The Loi-kaw Area Irrigation Project is an important undertaking along the Pilu River. The town has an airstrip and is linked by a circuitous road to Toungoo, 70 miles (110 km) southwest. Pop. (1983) 36,478.

loincloth, usually, a rectangular piece of cloth draped around the hips and groin. One of the earliest forms of clothing, it is derived, perhaps, from a narrow band around the waist from which amuletic and decorative pendants were hung. From about 3000 BC, the Egyptians wore *schenti* of woven material that was wrapped around the body several times and tied in front or belted. Sometimes the *schenti* was pleated or partially pleated and sometimes stiffened to project in front.

Man wearing a loincloth (*schenti*), King Akhenaton and Queen Nefertiti, XVIII dynasty, 1539–1292 BC; in the Louvre, Paris

By courtesy of Musee du Louvre, Paris

Cretan loincloths from around 2000 BC were highly patterned and decorated. Loincloths are still worn in the 20th century in some tropical and subtropical areas of the world.

Consult
the
INDEX
first

Loir-et-Cher, *département,* Centre *région,* north-central France, created from the southwestern part of the historic province of Orléanais and small parts of Maine and Touraine. Its area of 2,449 square miles (6,343 square km) is bisected by the Loire River, while the Loir River flows through Vendôme and Montoire-sur-le-Loir in the northwest and the Cher through Mennetou-sur-Cher and Montrichard in the south. Blois (*q.v.*), the departmental capital, Chambord, Chaumont, and Beaugency have historic châteaus that attract thousands of visitors annually to the Loire River valley.

The château at Chaumont-sur-Loire, Loir-et-Cher *département,* France

Bruno Barbey—Magnum

The *département* is mainly agricultural: mixed farming is practiced in the wooded Perche hill country northwest of the Loir. The so-called Petite Beauce, which is the southern prolongation of the Beauce Plain (the main granary of France), is situated between the Loir and the Loire rivers. The lush Loire valley is cultivated for vines, fruit, and vegetables. In the reclaimed marshland of Sologne, famed for its game, asparagus has become an important crop.

The *département* as a whole has benefited from the decentralization of industry away from Paris. Some industries have been developed in the Blois region. A nuclear station has been built in Saint-Laurent-des-Eaux on an artificial island in the Loire, northeast of Blois. The wool industry, formerly dispersed across the local countryside, has been concentrated at Romorantin-Lanthenay. Romorantin and Vendôme are picturesque, historic towns. The *département* has three *arrondissements*—Blois, Romorantin-Lanthenay, and Vendôme—and is in the educational division of Orléans. Pop. (1990) 305,937.

Loir River, river of northwest-central France, an affluent of the Sarthe River, that rises north of Illiers in Eure-et-Loir *département.* The Loir flows generally west-southwest, passing through the western extreme of the Little Beauce in its upper course and by Châteaudun. Beyond Vendôme it enters the picturesque Loir valley, where there is evidence of troglodyte habitation. Flowing through La Flèche, it joins the Sarthe north of Angers. The river stretches 193 miles (311 km), some 70 miles (114 km) of which are navigable. It drains a basin of about 2,700 square miles (7,000 square km), and its average annual discharge is 35 cubic m/s.

Loire, *département,* Rhône-Alpes *région,* east-central France, comprising chiefly the ancient Forez region with parts of the historic Lyonnais and Beaujolais provinces. One of the most industrialized areas in France, Loire lies in the eastern part of the Massif Central and is traversed south to north for more than 70 miles (110 km) by the Loire River. Saint-Étienne (*q.v.*), the departmental capital, is situated in a coal basin between the Loire River and the Rhône River (which borders the *département* for 7 miles [11 km]). Firminy, Le Chambon, Saint-Chamond, and other industrial towns are strung out for 30 miles (48 km) southwest and northeast of Saint-Étienne. Roanne, in the north, is another industrial centre.

Mount Pilat, 4,698 feet (1,432 m), rises southeast of Saint-Étienne between the industrial basin and the Rhône. The Lyonnais Mountains lie to the northeast of Saint-Étienne. In its course to the north, the Loire flows west of Saint-Étienne through the Forez Plain, which extends between mountain chains almost the entire length of the *département.* The Forez Mountains, capped by Pierre-sur-Haute (5,261 feet [1,634 m]), stretch two-thirds of the way, and the Madeleine Mountains continue northward. On the east, the Lyonnais Mountains are continued to the north by the Beaujolais Range.

The climate is cold and harsh in the extensively forested mountain regions but more clement in the valleys. Much of the marshy and waterlogged Forez Plain has been reclaimed for pastoral farming. Cereals are grown and cattle raised in the Roannais Plain, and cattle farming is practiced in the Lyonnais and Beaujolais heights. Coal production in the Saint-Étienne field, which comprised 35 percent of France's output in the 19th century, has dwindled to an insignificant amount. Heavy industries—steelworks, coking plants, metalworks, armaments, bicycles, and hardware—have had to specialize to remain competitive. Looms throughout the *département* supply the Lyon textile industry. Uranium fields have been discovered at Saint-Priest-la-Prugne, southwest of Roanne. Ancient villages with medieval churches and châteaus abound. The *département* has three *arrondissements,* Saint-Étienne, Roanne, and Montbrison (the former capital of the Forez county); it is in the educational division of Lyon. Area 1,846 square miles (4,781 square km). Pop. (1990) 746,288.

Loire-Atlantique, *département,* Pays de la Loire *région,* western France, on the Bay of Biscay astride the estuary of the Loire River. Two-thirds of its area lies north of the Loire, which flows east to west for 80 miles (130 km) across the *département.* Until 1957 known as Loire-Inférieure, it was created from the southern part of the province of Brittany, including the historic district of Retz, south of the Loire. The climate is humid, mild, and more favourable than the soil for agriculture, which produces cereals, forage, vegetables, and fruits. Vineyards produce the popular dry white Muscadet wine. Industry—building materials, chemicals, metals, textiles, food processing, and tanning—is concentrated largely in the regions of Nantes (*q.v.*), the capital, and its shipbuilding port, Saint-Nazaire. The Vilaine River follows the northern border for 20 miles (32 km) before entering the sea in neighbouring Morbihan *département.* The Vilaine is linked by the Nantes-to-Brest Canal to the Erdre, a northern tributary flowing into the Loire at Nantes.

The *département,* most of which lies less than 150 feet (45 m) above sea level, has 85 miles (137 km) of rocky, sandy coastline broken by the Loire estuary. Saint-Nazaire at the mouth of the Loire contrasts sharply with La Baule-Escoublac, a fashionable seaside resort on a fine sweep of sand 10 miles (16 km) west. The marshlands to the north, dominated by the medieval fortified town of Guérande, have been drained for pasture, but farther inland La Grande-Brière marshes, noted for duck shooting, are still flooded in winter. Still farther inland beyond the Sillon de Bretagne, a line of hillocks running northwest from Nantes, the meadowland is used for mixed farming. The *département* rises in the northeast to the hilly region of Châteaubriant, an ancient fortified town.

South of the Loire the shallow Grande-Lieu Lake, surrounded by swamps, is a favourite fishing and hunting area. The Sèvre Nantaise River, which enters the *département* in the southeast, joins the Loire at Nantes. The 17 miles (27 km) of coast south of the Loire estuary, known as the Côte de Jade because of the green colour of the sea, is dotted with resorts. It has four *arrondissements*—Nantes, Ancenis, Châteaubriant, and Saint-Nazaire—and is in the educational division of Nantes. Area 2,631 square miles (6,815 square km). Pop. (1990) 1,052,183.

Loire River, longest river in France, rising in the southern Massif Central and flowing north and west for 634 miles (1,020 km) to the Atlantic Ocean, which it enters south of the Bretagne (Brittany) peninsula. Its major tributary is the Allier, which joins the Loire at Le Bec d'Allier. Its drains an area of about 45,000 square miles (117,000 square km). The picturesque valley is dotted with châteaus.

The river rises at about 4,500 feet (1,370 m) above sea level, at the foot of the Gerbier de Jonc in the Cévennes near the Mediterranean coast. In its upper course it flows through a succession of downfaulted, flat-floored basins set in the highlands of the Massif Central. Crossing them, its valley narrows to gorges. After being joined by the Allier, the greatly enlarged stream flows across the limestone platform of Berry, and its valley becomes only a slight groove.

The upper course of the Loire tends to flow north toward the centre of the Paris Basin, but it then swings in a great curve past Orléans and flows westward to the sea by its long estuary at Nantes.

The Loire Basin has a temperate maritime climate, with no consistent dry season and with heavy precipitation, including winter snowfall, in the highlands that occupy its upper basin. The area of its headwaters is also subject to violent autumn storms from the Mediterranean. The river is usually highest in late winter, but there is no reliable rule; floods may occur in any month, though normally not in July and August.

In its middle course, the river occupies a shallow but steep-sided groove. Its once-marshy floodplain is protected from flooding by *levées* ("embankments") built progressively from the 12th to the 19th century. Effective agricultural reclamation began in the 14th century and was stimulated by the presence of the French court in the 15th and 16th centuries, when the middle Loire valley sustained a strip of land intensively cultivated for cash crops. In the 18th century, before the French Revolution, it reached the peak of its prosperity. The river was the great highway for movement of goods, and the cities on its banks were busy ports. During the period of developing river traffic in the 17th and 18th centuries, canal links were built connecting the Loire navigation with the Seine system of navigable waterways, which allowed products to be carried to Paris. These connecting canals are too narrow for modern vessels, and their use is limited. Left behind by modern developments, the Loire countryside remains predominantly rural, Old World, and little affected by modern industry.

Loiret, *département,* Centre *région,* central France, created mainly from the eastern part of historic Orléanais province and situated in the Paris Basin. The Loire River enters in the southeast and describes a sweeping arch, flowing through Gien, Sully, Orléans (*q.v.*), the capital, and Beaugency. The *département* takes its name from the short Loiret River, which rises south of Orléans from springs fed by the Loire and joins the main stream 8 miles (13 km) to the west. The Essonne and the Loing, both tributaries of the Seine, flow through the northeast. The Seine is linked to the Loire and its lateral canal by the Loing and Briare canals, constructed in the 17th century and still in use, mostly for coal transport.

Loiret has a temperate climate, with an average of 120 days of rain a year. Its highest point is a hill 825 feet (251 m) above sea level on the wooded Sologne plateau, which extends south of the Loire. The lowest point, 174 feet (53 m), is in the undulating Gâtinais country in the northeast, in which mixed farming and beekeeping are practiced. In the section of the Beauce Plain in the northwest, wheat, barley, and corn (maize) are cultivated. The great forest of Orléans, in the centre, slopes gradually down to the gentle Loire Valley, which is cultivated intensely; its vineyards account for nearly one-half of France's vinegar production. Loiret has, in particular, benefited from the decentralization of industry away from Paris. Its industry is mainly in the Orléans region, but tires are made in Montargis. Pottery long has been made in Gien, which, like Sully and Beaugency, is a historic town with an ancient château.

The abbey church of Saint-Benoît-sur-Loire is near the basilica of Germigny-des-Prés, which dates in part from the 9th century and has a Byzantine mosaic unique in France. In Bignon (now Le Bignon-Mirabeau) was born the Revolutionary politician Honoré Mirabeau. Orléans, Montargis, and Pithiviers give their names to the three *arrondissements* of Loiret, which is in the educational division of Orléans. Area 2,616 square miles (6,775 square km). Pop. (1990) 580,612.

Loisy, Alfred Firmin (b. Feb. 28, 1857, Ambrières, Fr.—d. June 1, 1940, Ceffonds), French biblical scholar, linguist, and philosopher of religion, generally credited as the founder of Modernism, a movement within the Roman Catholic church aimed at revising its dogma to reflect advances in science and philosophy.

Loisy trained at the Institut Catholique in

Paris, where he was influenced by the historian L.-M.-O. Duchesne, a pioneer in the application to church history of archaeology and other sciences. After being ordained in 1879, he became a lecturer in Oriental languages at the institute. Loisy, however, was deeply committed to historical and critical methods in his studies of the Bible and, particularly, to the introduction of new 19th-century developments in scholarship. He proposed a greater freedom of biblical interpretation in the development of religious doctrine, a position that brought him into conflict with the conservative popes Leo XIII and Pius X. In 1893 he was dismissed from the institute for his heretical views.

Loisy's *L'Évangile et l'Église* (1902; *The Gospel and the Church*) became the cornerstone of Modernism. Ostensibly a reply to the rationalist approach to religion of the German Protestant historian Adolph von Harnack, whose theories were antithetical to those of Loisy, the book was actually a reinterpretation of the Catholic faith. Noting that critical science demonstrated that Jesus considered himself a prophet, with no thought of a church or sacraments following from his teachings, Loisy argued that the role of the church was to preach a message of hope, not an absolute, unchanging doctrine. New discoveries could thus be incorporated into the body of religion without conflicting with established dogma, thus allowing the church to reflect the times.

Loisy's book produced a storm of condemnation in conservative theological circles, and in 1903 it was placed, along with four of his other works, on the church's *Index of Forbidden Books*. Pope Pius X's encyclical *Pascendi Dominici Gregis* (1907), which condemned Modernism as heresy, was aimed chiefly at Loisy and was the last of a series of papal censures dating from 1893. Although Loisy had reluctantly submitted to the first censure, Leo XIII's encyclical *Providentissimus Deus* (on biblical scholarship), he refused to bow to this latest pressure and was excommunicated in 1908.

Loisy continued to teach, occupying the chair of history of religions at the Collège de France from 1909, and to develop his philosophy, regarding Christian religion and the Bible more as a system of humanistic ethics than as a historical verification of divine revelation. He also undertook comparative studies of pre-Christian religious phenomena and their influence on the formation of Christianity. Unlike other Modernists censured by the church, Loisy did not protest his excommunication and never recanted his views.

Loíza River, Spanish RÍO GRANDE DE LOÍZA, river in eastern Puerto Rico, rising in the Sierra de Cayey south of San Lorenzo. Flowing about 40 miles (65 km) between the humid foothills of the Cayey and the Sierra de Luquillo, it emerges through swamps to empty into the Atlantic Ocean near Loíza Aldea. In its floodplain and on the surrounding terraces, sugarcane, tobacco, bananas, and vegetables are grown. In 1948 the Loíza River Project was initiated with the construction of a hydroelectric dam just south of Trujillo Alto. Its reservoir, Embalse de Loíza, is the major source of San Juan's water supply. The last 8 miles (13 km) of the river from Santa Bárbara have been straightened and made navigable.

Loja, principal city of far southern Ecuador, on a small plain at the northwestern foot of the Cordillera de Zamora of the Andes, near the junction of the Zamora and Malacatos rivers. Founded in the mid-16th century by the Spanish captain Alonso de Mercadillo, the town was destroyed by an earthquake a century later and subsequently rebuilt. It was, for a time during Spanish colonial rule, a world centre for cinchona (a source of quinine) production. A small hydroelectric project began operation in 1897, making Loja the first city in Ecuador to have electricity.

The city's economy is largely based on regional agricultural trade (sugarcane, coffee, cereals, and cinchona). Industries include tanning and textile weaving and the manufacture of light consumer goods. Many of the public buildings are of fine marble and building stone from nearby quarries.

Loja is on the Pan-American Highway and is connected by air with the principal cities of Ecuador. It is the seat of a Roman Catholic diocese (1862), of the National University of Loja (founded 1869 as a law school; elevated to university status 1943), and of a technical university (1971). Pop. (1989 est.) 38,482.

Lok Sabhā (Hindi: "House of the People"), the lower chamber of India's bicameral parliament. Under the constitution of 1950, it is elected for a term of five years by universal suffrage for citizens 18 and older. Members are elected directly from territorial constituencies in the states. In the early 1990s the Lok Sabhā had 543 elected members; 13 of these represented the union territories. Two additional members were appointed by the president to represent the Anglo-Indian community. The upper chamber is the Rājya Sabhā ("Council of States"). It has a maximum of 250 members, most of whom are elected indirectly by state legislatures; 12 of them are nominated by the president.

The president of India, who is elected for a five-year term by an electoral college consisting of all elected members of parliament and of state legislatures, is more a constitutional sovereign than a chief executive. The real power resides in the prime minister, who heads the Council of Ministers—ministers who are members of the cabinet and other ministers of state and deputy ministers. The council is responsible to the Lok Sabhā.

loka (Sanskrit: "world"), in Hindu cosmography, the universe or any particular division of it. The most common division of the universe is the *tri-loka,* or three worlds (heaven, earth, atmosphere; later, heaven, world, netherworld). Each of the *tri-loka*s is again divided into seven regions, variously described and listed depending upon the source. Sometimes, instead of the *tri-loka,* 14 worlds are enumerated: 7 above earth and 7 below. Whatever the division, it illustrates a basic Hindu concept, that of innumerable hierarchically ordered worlds.

lokapāla, in Hindu and Buddhist mythology, any of the guardians of the four cardinal directions. They are known in Tibetan as *'jig-rtenskyong,* in Chinese as *t'ien-wang,* and in Japanese as *shi-tennō.* The Hindu protectors, who ride on elephants, are Indra, who governs the east, Yama the south, Varuṇa the west, and Kubera the north. Kubera, also referred to as Vaiśravaṇa, is common to both Hindu and Buddhist traditions. The other Buddhist *lokapāla*s are Dhṛtarāṣṭra (east), Virūḍhaka (south), and Virūpākṣa (west).

The four are mentioned in the earliest Buddhist writings as participating in all the important events of the Buddha's life. They received him at his birth, held up the hooves of his horse when he left the palace to renounce the world, and offered him four bowls of food that miraculously became one bowl following his fast under the Bo tree. The four became popular deities in Tibet, China, and Japan, as well as among the southern Hīnayāna Buddhists, though only Kubera is worshiped singly. They are usually depicted fully armed, standing on demons.

In India Kubera is called king of the *yakṣa*s and is shown coloured yellow, holding a banner in the right hand and a mongoose in the left. In China he is called To-wen (in Japan, Bishamon; in Tibet, Rnam-thos-sras) and symbolizes autumn.

The guardian of the east, Dhṛtarāṣṭra, in India is known as the king of the celestial musicians, the *gandharva*s. He is coloured white and has as his symbol a stringed instrument. In China he is called Ch'ih-kuo (in Japan, Jikoku; in Tibet, Yul-'khor-bsrung) and is associated with summer. The guardian of the south, Virūḍhaka, in India is king of the giant *kumbhaṇḍa*s (pot-bellied gnomes). He is coloured blue or green and carries a sword. In China he is called Tseng-chang (in Japan, Kōmoku; in Tibet, 'Phags-skyes-po) and symbolizes spring. The guardian of the west, Virūpākṣa, in India commands the serpents (*nāga*s). He is coloured red and has as his symbol a small shrine, or a jewel, and a serpent. In China he is called Kwang-mu (in Japan, Zōchō; in Tibet, Klu) and is associated with winter.

Lokāyata (philosophical school): *see* Cārvāka.

Lokeren, municipality (*gemeente*), East Flanders (Oost-Vlaanderen) *province,* northern Belgium, on the Durme River, just east-northeast of Ghent (Gent). Notable buildings include the Church of St. Lawrence (1721), the town hall (1761), and several Flemish Renaissance houses. Lokeren was granted a weekly market in 1555. By the 1940s the town had an almost complete Belgian monopoly of *couperie de poils*—the shearing of rabbits and the preparation of their fur for use in felt manufacture. Other industries include textile and rope manufacture. Pop. (1992 est.) mun., 35,100.

Loki, in Norse mythology, a cunning trickster who had the ability to change his shape and sex. Although his father was the giant Fárbauti, he was included among the Aesir (a tribe of gods). Loki was represented as the companion of the great gods Odin and Thor, helping them with his clever plans but sometimes causing embarrassment and difficulty for them and himself. He also appeared as the enemy of the gods, entering their banquet uninvited and demanding their drink; he was the principal cause of the death of the god Balder. Loki was punished by being bound to a rock, thus in many ways resembling the Greek figures Prometheus and Tantalus. Loki created a female, Angerboda (Angrboda: "Distress Bringer"), and produced three evil progeny: Hel, the goddess of death; Jörmungand, the evil serpent surrounding the world; and Fenrir (Fenrisúlfr), the wolf.

The figure of Loki remains obscure; there is no trace of a cult, and the name does not appear in place-names.

Lokoja, town and river port, capital of Kogi state, south-central Nigeria, on the west bank of the Niger River opposite the mouth of the Benue River. British merchants established a trading post at the Benue-Niger confluence in the late 1850s; and in 1860 William Balfour Baikie, the Scottish explorer, founded Lokoja. Besides being an important commercial settlement, the site (originally ceded in 1841 to the British by the Ata [King] of Idah, 50 miles [80 km] south) was selected for the first British consulate in the interior (1860–69) and for the military headquarters for Sir George Goldie's Royal Niger Company (1886–1900). Formerly the capital of Kabba province, Lokoja was part of Kwara from 1967 to 1991, when it became the capital of the newly formed state of Kogi.

The modern town is a collecting point for cotton, leather, and palm oil and kernels, which are shipped to the Niger delta ports of Burutu and Warri for export. The town is also a trade centre for the yams, cassava, corn (maize), sorghum, beans, fish, palm produce, shea nuts, and cotton produced by the local Igbira people. Fulani herdsmen from the north drive their cattle across the Niger to Lokoja in the dry season. Cotton ginning and weaving and palm- and shea-kernel processing are important local activities. There are limestone and iron deposits in the vicinity, and nearby Mount Patti, the original site of Lokoja, is a 1,349-foot- (411-metre-) high mass of oolitic iron ore. The town has a hydroelectric power generating plant. It is situated on the local highway between Kabba and Ayangbe and has ferry service across the Niger River. Pop. (1991) 39,500.

Lolland, island, Storstrøm *amtskommune* (county commune), Denmark, in the Baltic Sea. It is separated from southern Sjælland (Zealand) by Smålandsfarvandet Sound. Lolland has an area of 480 square miles (1,243 square km). Third largest island of the Danish archipelago, its irregular coastline is broken by Sakskøbing and Nakskov fjords. There are forests in the north and east, and the marshy southern coastal regions are protected from flooding by sand dunes and dikes. The island's fertile clay loams support tobacco and a thriving sugar-beet industry. Ålholm Castle in Nysted was a royal residence in the 12th century and now houses a Veteran Car Museum. Many fine manor houses and estates survive from as early as the 15th century, chief among them Knuthenborg (1866) and Christianssæde (1690). The principal towns are Nakskov, Maribo, Sakskøbing, Rødby, and Nysted. Rødbyhavn is the site of a major ferry line to Germany. Pop. (2001 est.) 70,383.

Lollard, in late medieval England, a follower, after about 1382, of John Wycliffe, a University of Oxford philosopher and theologian whose unorthodox religious and social doctrines in some ways anticipated those of the 16th-century Protestant Reformation. The name, used pejoratively, derived from the Middle Dutch *lollaert* ("mumbler"), which had been applied earlier to certain European continental groups suspected of combining pious pretensions with heretical belief.

At Oxford in the 1370s, Wycliffe came to advocate increasingly radical religious views. He denied the doctrine of transubstantiation and stressed the importance of preaching and the primacy of Scripture as the source of Christian doctrine. Claiming that the office of the papacy lacked scriptural justification, he equated the pope with Antichrist and welcomed the 14th-century schism in the papacy as a prelude to its destruction. Wycliffe was charged with heresy and retired from Oxford in 1378. Never brought to trial, he continued to write and preach until his death in 1384.

The first Lollard group centred (*c.* 1382) on some of Wycliffe's colleagues at Oxford led by Nicholas of Hereford. The movement gained followers outside of Oxford, and the anticlerical undercurrents of the Peasants' Revolt of 1381 were ascribed, probably unfairly, to the influence of Wycliffe and the Lollards. In 1382 William Courtenay, archbishop of Canterbury, forced some of the Oxford Lollards to renounce their views and conform to Roman Catholic doctrine. The sect continued to multiply, however, among townspeople, merchants, gentry, and even the lower clergy.

The accession of Henry IV in 1399 signaled a wave of repression against heresy. In 1401 the first English statute was passed for the burning of heretics. The Lollards' first martyr, William Sawtrey, was actually burned a few days before the act was passed. In 1414 a Lollard rising led by Sir John Oldcastle was quickly defeated by Henry V. The rebellion brought severe reprisals and marked the end of the Lollards' overt political influence.

Driven underground, the movement operated henceforth chiefly among tradespeople and artisans, supported by a few clerical adherents. About 1500 a Lollard revival began, and before 1530 the old Lollard and the new Protestant forces had begun to merge. The Lollard tradition facilitated the spread of Protestantism and predisposed opinion in favour of King Henry VIII's anticlerical legislation during the English Reformation.

From its early days the Lollard movement tended to discard the scholastic subtleties of Wycliffe, who probably wrote few or none of the popular tracts in English formerly attributed to him. The most complete statement of early Lollard teaching appeared in the *Twelve Conclusions,* drawn up to be presented to the Parliament of 1395. They began by stating that the church in England had become subservient to her "stepmother the great church of Rome." The present priesthood was not the one ordained by Christ, while the Roman ritual of ordination had no warrant in Scripture. Clerical celibacy occasioned unnatural lust, while the "feigned miracle" of transubstantiation led men into idolatry. The hallowing of wine, bread, altars, vestments, and so forth was related to necromancy. Prelates should not be temporal judges and rulers, for no man can serve two masters. The *Conclusions* also condemned special prayers for the dead, pilgrimages, and offerings to images, and they declared confession to a priest unnecessary for salvation. The *Twelve Conclusions* covered all the main Lollard doctrines except two: that the prime duty of priests is to preach and that all men should have free access to the Scriptures in their own language. The Lollards were responsible for a translation of the Bible into English, by Nicholas of Hereford, and later revised by Wycliffe's secretary, John Purvey.

Lomami River, river in Congo (Kinshasa), a major tributary of the Congo River. It rises in the Katanga highlands of southern Congo and flows northward some 930 miles (1,500 km) to join the Congo at Isangi, some 70 miles (113 km) west of Kisangani.

Lomas de Zamora, *cabecera* (county seat) and *partido* (county) of Gran (Greater) Buenos Aires, Arg. It lies immediately south of the city of Buenos Aires, in Buenos Aires *provincia.* The name and origin of the *partido* and *cabecera* date from the late 16th century, when Juan de Zamora, one of the founders of Buenos Aires, was granted a large landholding on the *lomas* ("slopes") in the vicinity. In 1861 the *partido* of Lomas de Zamora was officially established. Besides Lomas de Zamora *cabecera* (officially declared the seat of the *partido* in 1864), the major localities are Banfield, Temperley, Villa Turdera, and Llavallol. In 1865 the Church of Our Lady of Peace was built in Lomas de Zamora. The national normal school was founded there in 1902, and the National University of Lomas de Zamora (1972) is located in the city.

Prior to 1910, when it was given city status, Lomas de Zamora was a residential town with a large British colony. Since 1940 it has become an industrial centre, with chemical, electrical-manufacturing, and cement industries. The *cabecera* and *partido* are completely within the Gran Buenos Aires urban area. Pop. (1999 est.) *cabecera,* 609,621.

Lomax, Alan (b. Jan. 15, 1915, Austin, Texas, U.S.—d. July 19, 2002, Safety Harbor, Fla.), American ethnomusicologist, one of the most dedicated and knowledgeable folk-music scholars of the 20th century.

After study at Harvard University, the University of Texas at Austin (B.A., 1936), and Columbia University, Lomax toured the prisons of the American Deep South with his father, John Lomax, also a noted student of folk song, recording folk-song performances for the Archive of American Song of the Library of Congress. During this tour they discovered the great blues singer Huddie Ledbetter ("Leadbelly"). Later, Lomax was responsible for introducing to American audiences other folk and blues artists, including Woody Guthrie, Muddy Waters, Josh White, and Burl Ives. In 1938 he made a series of recordings with the jazz pianist Jelly Roll Morton. From 1951 to 1958 he was in Europe, recording hundreds of folk songs in Great Britain, Italy, and Spain.

A profound folklorist who was also interested in the historical and social origins of jazz, Lomax wrote an outstanding biography of Jelly Roll Morton, *Mr. Jelly Roll* (1950). *The Folk Songs of North America in the English Language* was published in 1960. His work in cantometrics (the statistical analysis of singing styles correlated with anthropological data), which he developed with Victor Grauer, is the most comprehensive study of folk song as yet undertaken. *Cantometrics: A Handbook and Training Method* appeared in 1976. In 1997 the Alan Lomax Collection debuted on Rounder Records. The series featured more than 100 albums of music recorded by Lomax.

Lombard, Latin LANGOBARDUS, plural LANGOBARDI, member of a Germanic people who from 568 to 774 ruled a kingdom in Italy.

The Lombards were one of the Germanic tribes that formed the Suebi, and during the 1st century AD their home was in northwestern Germany. Though they occasionally fought with the Romans and with neighbouring tribes, the main body of the Lombards seems to have pursued a settled, pastoral existence until the beginnings of their great southward migrations in the 4th century. By the end of the 5th century they had moved into the area roughly coinciding with modern Austria north of the Danube River.

In 546 a new Lombard royal dynasty was begun by Audoin. At that time, it seems, the Lombards began to adapt their tribal organization and institutions to the imperial military system of the period, in which a hierarchy of dukes, counts, and others commanded warrior bands formed from related families or kin groups. For two decades the Lombards waged intermittent wars with the Gepidae, who were finally destroyed (*c.* 567) by Audoin's successor, Alboin.

About this time the Lombards decided to migrate into Italy, which had been left almost defenseless after the Byzantine Empire's armies had overthrown the Ostrogothic kingdom there. In the spring of 568 the Lombards crossed the Julian Alps. Their invasion of northern Italy was almost unopposed, and by late 569 they had conquered all the principal cities north of the Po River except Pavia, which fell in 572. At the same time, they occupied areas in the central and southern parts of the peninsula. Shortly afterward, Alboin was murdered, and the 18-month rule of his successor, Cleph, was marked by the ruthless treatment of the Italian landowners.

On the death of Cleph, no successor was chosen; instead, the dukes exercised authority in their particular city-territories. The 10-year "rule of the dukes" was later viewed as one of violence and disorder. In 584, threatened by a Frankish invasion that the dukes had provoked, the Lombards made Cleph's son Authari king; when he died in 590 he was succeeded by Agilulf, duke of Turin, who was able to recover most portions of Italy that had been lost to a Frankish-Byzantine alliance.

When Authari became king the dukes surrendered half their estates for the maintenance of the king and his court. Pavia, where the royal palace was located, became the centre of administrative organization. The Lombards converted from Arianism to orthodox Christianity in the latter part of the 7th century.

After the brutal Aripert II (reigned 700–712), a new dynasty took the Lombard throne. Its second representative, Liudprand (reigned 712–744), was probably the greatest of the Lombard kings. Until 726 he seems to have been concerned exclusively with the internal condition of his kingdom. Later, however, he steadily reduced the area of Italy still under Byzantine rule. Coins and documents from his court confirm the impression of a strong and effective monarch.

The invasion of papal territories by the Lombard kings Aistulf (reigned 749–756) and Desiderius (reigned 756–774) compelled Pope Adrian I to seek aid from the Frankish king Charlemagne. The Franks entered Italy in 773, and after a year's siege Pavia fell to their armies. Desiderius was captured, and Charlemagne became king of the Lombards as well as of the Franks. Lombard rule in Italy thus came to an end.

The Lombards gave their name to the northern Italian region that was their stronghold, now known as Lombardy.

Lombard, Carole, original name JANE ALICE PETERS (b. Oct. 6, 1908, Fort Wayne, Ind., U.S.—d. Jan. 16, 1942, in flight near Las Vegas, Nev.), American actress and comedienne who starred in some of the most successful comedies of the 1930s.

Her first screen role was as a 13-year-old tomboy in *A Perfect Crime* (1921), and after graduating from junior high school she became a professional actress in Hollywood, appearing in small parts and in comedy shorts from 1925 on. She appeared in her first sound picture in 1930, and she developed her comic talents until her performance opposite John Barrymore in *Twentieth Century* (1934) established her as a star. She later appeared in some of the best 1930s screwball comedies (comedies with slangy, fast-paced dialogue, irreverent humour, and zany characters). Her major film appearances were in *My Man Godfrey* (1936), *Nothing Sacred* (1937), *They Knew What They Wanted* (1940), *Mr. and Mrs. Smith* (1941), and *To Be or Not To Be* (1942). She was married to the actors William Powell (1931; divorced 1933) and Clark Gable (from 1939). She died at age 34 in a plane crash while on tour to sell war bonds.

Lombard, Peter: *see* Peter Lombard.

Lombard League, Italian LEGA LOMBARDA, Italian league that, in the 12th and 13th centuries, resisted attempts by the Holy Roman emperors to reduce the liberties and jurisdiction of the communes of Lombardy in northern Italy. Originally formed for a period of 20 years on Dec. 1, 1167, the Lombard League initially consisted of 16 cities, later expanded to 20, including Milan, Venice, Mantua, Padua, Brescia, and Lodi. It was backed from its beginning by Pope Alexander III, who saw in it a welcome ally against his enemy the Holy Roman emperor Frederick I Barbarossa. Frederick suffered several military setbacks at the hands of the league, notably the Battle of Legnano (1176), and, after a six-year truce (1177–83), agreed to the Peace of Constance, by which he retained the fealty of the Lombard cities but granted them communal liberties and jurisdiction.

The Lombard League was renewed in 1198 and again in 1208. Not until 1226, however, when Frederick II reasserted imperial authority in northern Italy, did it again become a powerful factor in Italian politics for a long period. The new league was formed for 25 years by Milan, Bologna, Brescia, Mantua, Padua, Vicenza, and Treviso. They were soon joined by Piacenza, Verona, Lodi, and other cities, as well as by Boniface II of Montferrat and Godfrey of Biandrate. They received the support of the papacy and effectively opposed Frederick's reorganization of northern Italy. The league passed out of existence after Frederick's death in 1250.

Lombardi, Vince, byname of VINCENT THOMAS LOMBARDI (b. June 11, 1913, Brooklyn, N.Y., U.S.—d. Sept. 3, 1970, Washington, D.C.), coach in American professional football who became a national symbol of single-minded determination to win. In nine seasons (1959–67) as head coach of the previously moribund Green Bay Packers, he led the team to five championships of the National Football League (NFL) and, in the last two seasons, to victory in the first two Super Bowl games against the American Football League titleholder.

At Fordham University, New York City, Lombardi was one of the group of linemen known as the "Seven Blocks of Granite." After completing his undergraduate education (1937), he studied law at Fordham, briefly played minor-league professional football, and then (1939) entered high-school football coaching. Afterward he served as an assistant coach at Fordham (1947–48), at the United States Military Academy, West Point, N.Y. (1949–53), and with the New York Giants of the NFL (1954–58). Hired as head coach and general manager of the Packers in February 1959, Lombardi imposed an unusually strenuous regimen (some critics described it as Spartan or fanatical) on his players, most of whom had been accustomed to defeat. In his second year Green Bay led the Western Conference of the NFL. Subsequently the Packers won the league championship in 1961–62 and 1965–67 and defeated Kansas City and then Oakland in the Super Bowl games following the 1966 and 1967 seasons.

Retiring as coach, Lombardi served the Packers in 1968 as general manager. He then went to the Washington Redskins of the NFL as head coach, general manager, and part owner, and in 1969 he led the team to its first winning season in 14 years. He died of cancer shortly before the 1970 season.

Lombardo, Guy, in full GUY ALBERT LOMBARDO (b. June 19, 1902, London, Ont., Can.—d. Nov. 5, 1977, Houston, Texas, U.S.), Canadian-born American dance-band leader whose New Year's Eve radio and television broadcasts with his Royal Canadians became an American tradition for 48 years. Derided by some music critics as the "king of corn," Lombardo gained long-lasting popularity by conducting what was billed as "the sweetest music this side of heaven." With his brother Carmen playing lead saxophone, his band introduced more than 300 songs and sold more than 250,000,000 recordings.

Guy Lombardo was the eldest son of musically inclined parents and trained as a violinist. His career was launched through an engagement in Cleveland that led to his being represented by the then-fledgling Music Corporation of America (MCA). He first broadcast nationally from Chicago in 1927, and by 1929 he was the winter attraction at New York City's Roosevelt Grill, a booking repeated for more than 30 years. After the Grill closed, Lombardo moved to the Waldorf-Astoria Hotel, continuing the televised New Year's Eve broadcasts, begun in 1954, that climaxed with the playing of "Auld Lang Syne." He became a naturalized U.S. citizen in 1937.

Guy Lombardo, *c.* 1940s

Beginning as a nonet, the Royal Canadians numbered 16 by 1968. Long tenure was common in the orchestra. Dewey Bergman was Lombardo's arranger from the orchestra's inception in London, Ont., in 1923 until he died in 1971. Guy's and Carmen's siblings Lebert (lead trumpeter), Rose Marie, and Victor and their brother-in-law Ken Garner were all band members.

Lombardo, Pietro (b. *c.* 1435, Carona, duchy of Milan [Italy]—d. June 1515, Venice), leading sculptor and architect of Venice in the late 15th century, known for his significant contribution to the Renaissance in that city. He was the father of Tullio and Antonio, both respected sculptors of the time.

Lombardo's early work shows a Florentine influence, but his mature style is clearly affected by Northern ideas. His first known work was the Monument of Antonio Roselli (1464–67) in the Church of San Antonio in Padua, where he also designed the Casa Olzignan. About 1467 he moved to Venice, where he spent the remainder of his life, producing numerous monuments and buildings.

Two of Lombardo's most significant tombs in Venice are in the Church of Santi Giovanni e Paolo: the Malipiero Monument (*c.* 1463) and the Doge Pietro Mocenigo Monument (*c.* 1476–81), which is decorated with 15 life-size marble figures. On the latter and numerous other works, Lombardo was assisted by his sons, and they sometimes executed entire projects under his supervision—*e.g.,* the Onigo Monument (1490); San Nicolò, Treviso.

Lombardo was architect and chief sculptor for the Church of Santa Maria dei Miracoli (1481–89), which is considered one of the finest Renaissance buildings in Venice. In 1482 he executed the tomb of Dante in Ravenna and in 1485 began work on his most distinguished monument, the Zanetti tomb in the cathedral at Treviso, for which most of the carving was done by Tullio and Antonio. From 1498 until 1515 he served as master mason of the Palazzo Ducale (Doges' Palace) in Venice.

Lombardy, Italian LOMBARDIA, *regione* of northern Italy. It is bordered on the north by Switzerland and by the Italian *regioni* of Emilia-Romagna (south), Trentino–Alto Adige and Veneto (east), and Piedmont (west). Administratively, Lombardy consists of the *provincie* of Bergamo, Brescia, Como, Cremona, Lecco, Lodi, Mantova, Milano, Pavia, Sondrio, and Varese. The capital is Milan.

Lombardy is divided physically into three parts from north to south—a mountainous Alpine and pre-Alpine zone; a zone of gently undulating foothills; and a zone of alluvial plains sloping gently to the Po River in the south. The Alpine division reaches a height of 13,284 feet (4,049 m) in the Bernina. The foothill zone is partly composed of morainic material and contains a number of scenic lakes. The *regione* is drained southward by many rivers, all of them tributaries of the Po, including the Ticino, the Adda, and the Oglio, with its affluents the Mella and Chiese, and the Mincio. The *regione* abounds in lakes and contains all or part of Lakes Garda (Italy's largest lake), Maggiore, Lugano, Como, Iseo, Idro, and Varese and the lakes of the Brianza (Pusiano, Annone, Alserio, and Segrino). The climate is generally continental, with hot summers and cold winters, and rainfall varies from about 24 inches (610 mm) annually in the area near the Po River to 80 inches (2,032 mm) in the mountainous regions.

Lombardy was inhabited by Celtic peoples from the 5th century BC and was conquered by Rome after the Second Punic War (218–201 BC), upon which it became part of Cisalpine

Gaul. The region suffered heavily in the barbarian invasions that ended the western Roman Empire, and from AD 568 to 774 it was the centre of the kingdom of the Lombards, a Germanic people who gave their name to the region. (*See* Lombard.) The Lombard kingdom ended in 774, and Lombardy became part of the empire of the Frankish king Charlemagne. Frankish rule continued until 887, and after the breakup of the Carolingian empire a number of independent units, mostly towns ruled by counts or bishops, emerged in Lombardy.

These towns' growing prosperity by the 11th century was based on the role of the middle Po valley as a transit point for trade between the Mediterranean and the trans-Alpine lands. A number of Lombard towns—Milan, Cremona, Brescia, and Bergamo—were able to throw off their feudal rulers and evolve into communes (self-governing municipalities) that became the commercial leaders of Europe at the time. These communes reached the height of their power in the 12th century, when, in an effort to resist encroachments by the emperor Frederick I Barbarossa, they formed the Lombard League (*q.v.*); the league defeated the emperor at the Battle of Legnano in 1176 and forced him to recognize its members' autonomy in the Peace of Constance (1183).

Conflicts within the Lombard communes between Guelfs and Ghibellines were only resolved in the 13th and 14th centuries by the rise of overlords or despots, some of whom, such as the Visconti and Sforza in Milan and the Bonacolsi and Gonzaga in Mantua, founded local dynasties. Milan became the strongest city in Lombardy early in the 14th century and went on to establish its rule over most of the neighbouring towns, though it had to yield Brescia and Bergamo to Venice and the city of Mantua remained independent. Lombardy lost territory to the Swiss, Venetians, and other neighbours in the early 16th century, and in the chaotic wake of the French invasions of Italy, the duchy of Milan came under Spanish Habsburg rule in 1535. Mantua remained independent until 1713, when both it and Milan passed to the Austrian Habsburgs. Austrian rule yielded to that of France from 1796 to 1814. In 1815 Lombardy was restored to Austria as part of a new Lombardo-Venetian kingdom. In 1859 a Franco-Piedmontese army expelled the Austrians from Lombardy, which joined newly unified Italy.

Lombardy has the largest population of any Italian region, though it covers less than one-tenth of the country's area. The population is concentrated in the industrial cities of the upper plains and foothills, with secondary concentrations in the rich farmlands in the south. Lombardy is the leading industrial and commercial *regione* of Italy. Milan, the chief city, is one of the largest industrial centres of Italy. It makes iron and steel, automobiles and trucks, and machinery and is also a centre of banking and wholesale and retail trade. Lombardy's other major cities include Brescia, Bergamo, Cremona, Pavia, Como, Mantua, and Monza. Their varied manufactures include electrical appliances, textiles, furniture, processed foods, chemicals, and leather.

Lombardy is also Italy's leading agricultural area. The region's highly productive agriculture is centred on the irrigated plains of the Po River valley, which produce rice, wheat, corn (maize), sugar beets, and fodder crops for beef and dairy cattle. The higher plains produce cereals, vegetables, fruit trees, and mulberries. The foothill region produces fruit, vines, and olives, and the Alps afford excellent grazing for cattle, pigs, and sheep.

Milan is the hub of northern Italy's rail network and has direct rail links with Switzerland, France, and Germany via passes and tunnels through the Alps. Lombardy is linked to other regions of Italy by an excellent system of railroads, highways, and expressways. Area 9,211 square miles (23,857 square km). Pop. (2001) 8,922,463.

Lombi (Zaire): *see* Boma.

Lomblen Island, Indonesian PULAU LOMBLEN, also called KAWULA, or KAWOELA, largest of the Solor Islands, in the Lesser Sundas, Nusa Tenggara Timur *provinsi* ("province"), Indonesia. Lomblen lies between the Flores Sea (north) and the Savu Sea (south), about 25 miles (40 km) east of Flores and just east of Adonara Island. Lomblen is irregular in shape, with a southwest-northeast length of about 50 miles (80 km) and a width east-west of about 20 miles (32 km). It is mountainous, rising to 5,394 feet (1,644 m) in the northeast; the coastal areas have patches of fertile soil as a result of volcanic ash deposits. The island is densely inhabited by the Solorese peoples, who cultivate corn (maize), bananas, papayas, and rice and engage in deep-sea fishing. There are coconut plantations along the coasts. Area 499 square miles (1,292 square km).

Lombok, island, Nusa Tenggara Barat *provinsi* ("province"), Indonesia. It is one of the Lesser Sunda Islands, lying due east of Bali across the Lombok Strait and due west of Sumbawa across the Alas Strait. To the north is the Java Sea, to the south the Indian Ocean.

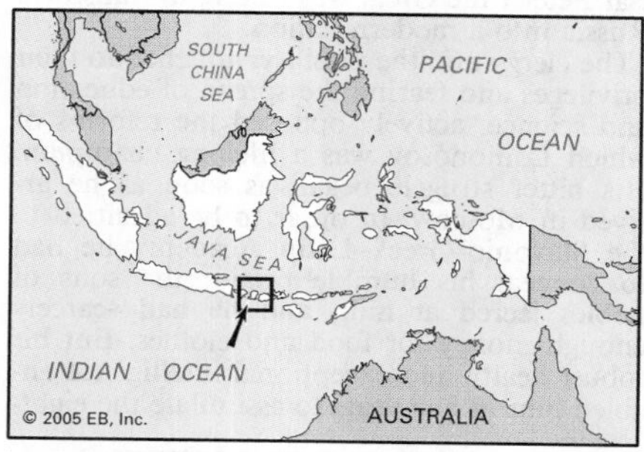

Lombok

The island is divided for nearly its entire length by two mountain chains. The southern chain, a range of limestone hills, rises to 2,350 feet (716 m), but the northern chain reaches 12,224 feet (3,726 m) at Mount Rinjani. None of the small rivers is navigable. Cliffs often rise precipitously from the sea, but there are good anchorages in bays on the western and eastern coasts.

Lombok Strait, which has depths exceeding 3,600 feet (1,100 m), has been called the edge of the Asian continental shelf, a contention supported by the marked differences between the plant and animal life of Bali and Lombok. Some intermingling of species is taking place, and Lombok represents the beginning of a transitional area in which Asian forms of life are being supplanted gradually by Australian forms. Vegetation includes a great palm, and there are monkeys, deer, and wild pigs.

The population of Lombok is composed largely of Sasaks of Malay origin, although there are Chinese in the urban area around Mataram, some Balinese in the west, and some Sumbawanese in the east. The Sasak are Muslim, though there is a strong animist element to their religion. Agriculture is by far the dominant occupation, with paddy rice, soybeans, tubers, peanuts (groundnuts), tobacco, coconuts, and vegetables the chief crops. The central lowland strip of the island, between the two elevated coastal areas, is the centre of rice cultivation and of population. Mataram, the provincial capital, is the largest city. The chief port is Lembar, on the western coast.

As early as 1640 Lombok was under the sultan of Makasar (Macassar). Eventually, the Balinese seized control and established four kingdoms on the island; one of them, Mataram, entered into a contract with the Dutch that lasted from 1843 to 1872, when Mataram's interference in politics on Bali caused the Dutch to step in and, in 1894, impose direct rule themselves. Area 2,098 square miles (5,435 square km).

Lombroso, Cesare (b. Nov. 6, 1835, Verona, Austrian Empire [now in Italy]—d. Oct. 19, 1909, Turin, Italy), Italian criminologist whose views, though now largely discredited, brought about a shift in criminology from a legalistic preoccupation with crime to a scientific study of criminals.

Lombroso studied at the universities of Padua, Vienna, and Paris, and from 1862 to 1876 he was professor of psychiatry at the University of Pavia. In 1871 he became director of the mental asylum at Pesaro, and in 1876 he became professor of forensic medicine and hygiene at the University of Turin, where he subsequently held appointments as professor of psychiatry (1896) and then of criminal anthropology (1906).

Lombroso tried to discern a possible relationship between criminal psychopathology and physical or constitutional defects. His chief contention was the existence of a hereditary, or atavistic, class of criminals who are in effect biological throwbacks to a more primitive stage of human evolution. Lombroso contended that such criminals exhibit a higher percentage of physical and mental anomalies than do noncriminals. Among these anomalies, which he termed stigmata, were various unusual skull sizes and asymmetries of the facial bones. Lombroso's theories were widely influential in Europe for a time, but his emphasis on hereditary causes of crime was later strongly rejected in favour of environmental factors. Lombroso tried to reform the Italian penal system, and he encouraged more humane and constructive treatment of convicts through the use of work programs intended to make them more productive members of society. Among his books are *L'uomo delinquente* (1876; "The Criminal Man") and *Le Crime, causes et remèdes* (1899; *Crime, Its Causes and Remedies*).

Lomé, city, capital of Togo. Lomé lies on the Gulf of Guinea (Atlantic coast) in the extreme southwestern corner of the country. Selected as the colonial capital of German Togoland in 1897, it became important as an administrative, commercial, and transport centre. A modern town was laid out, and a 1,380-foot (420-metre) jetty was built to facilitate the export of raw materials. Three railways fan out from Lomé to the hinterland: northwest to Palimé, north to Sokodé, and east along the coast to Aného. Modernization of the port was begun in the 1960s, and a deep-water harbour, completed in 1968, can handle 1,500,000 tons of goods annually. This has

Independence monument in Lomé, Togo
Paul Almasy

greatly facilitated the shipping of phosphates and other major exports, such as cocoa, coffee, copra, cotton, and palm products. The Lomé oil refinery was opened in 1978, and in that same year construction began on a thermal power plant. The Maison du Peuple, opened in 1972, has a 3,000-seat conference hall and is the national headquarters for Togo's only political party. An international airport is nearby. The Université du Bénin was founded in 1965 at Lomé. Pop. (1999 est.) urban agglomeration, 790,000.

Loménie de Brienne, Étienne-Charles de (b. Oct. 9, 1727, Paris—d. Feb. 19, 1794, Sens, Fr.), French ecclesiastic and minister of finance on the eve of the French Revolution. His unusual intelligence and aristocratic connections secured his rapid advancement in the church: he became bishop of Condom in 1760 and archbishop of Toulouse in 1763. He was placed in control of finance in 1787 through the influence of Marie-Antoinette and because of his role in the first assembly of notables (1787). But he proved unable to cope with the worsening financial crisis. The Parlement of Paris opposed his plans for imposition of a land tax on the privileged orders. In June 1788 his demand for an enlarged voluntary tax from the assembly of the clergy was only partially granted, and he was compelled in July to submit to demands for the summons of the States General. In August, having virtually declared national bankruptcy, he resigned in favour of Jacques Necker and was then made archbishop of Sens and, later in 1788, cardinal. Loménie de Brienne was one of the few prelates who took the oath to the Civil Constitution of the Clergy of 1790. His former position as a court favourite, however, made him a suspect during the Reign of Terror, and he died in prison at Sens.

Loménie de Brienne, engraving by J.-F. Janinet after a painting by P. Cossard

By courtesy of the Bibliotheque Nationale, Paris

Lomi, Orazio (Baroque painter): *see* Gentileschi, Orazio.

Lomond, Loch, largest of the Scottish lakes, lying across the southern edge of the Highlands. It forms part of the boundary between Strathclyde and Central regions. The scenery ranges from rugged, glaciated mountains above 3,000 ft (900 m) in the north to softer, well-wooded hills and islands in the south. It extends about 24 mi (39 km), widening south in the shape of a triangle. Although its surface is only 23 ft above sea level, its glacially excavated floor reaches a depth of 623 ft. It drains by the short River Leven into the Firth of Clyde at Dumbarton. Within very easy reach of the metropolitan region of Glasgow, it is a favourite resort for the urban dwellers. The chief lakeside resort settlements are Balloch, Ardlui, Inversnaid, Balmaha, Luss, Rowardennan, and Tarbet. At Inveruglas is a hydroelectric power station.

Lomonosov, formerly (until 1948) ORANIENBAUM, town, St. Petersburg *oblast* (province), northwestern Russia, on the Gulf of Finland. Founded in 1710 by Prince Menshikov, it was a summer retreat of the Russian royal family. The palace of Peter I the Great (1714) and the Chinese Palace, designed by the Italian architect Antonio Rinaldi (1762–68), suffered grave damage in World War II but have been restored. Pop. (1991 est.) 42,000.

Lomonosov, Mikhail Vasilyevich (b. Nov. 19 [Nov. 8, old style], 1711, near Kholmogory, Russia—d. April 15 [April 4, O.S.], 1765, St. Petersburg), Russian poet, scientist, and grammarian who is often considered the first great Russian linguistic reformer. He also made substantial contributions to the natural sciences, reorganized the St. Petersburg Imperial Academy of Sciences, established in Moscow the university that today bears his name, and created the first coloured glass mosaics in Russia.

Lomonosov was the son of a poor fisherman. At the age of 10 he too took up that line of work. When the few books he was able to obtain could no longer satisfy his growing thirst for knowledge, in December 1730, he left his native village, penniless and on foot, for Moscow. His ambition was to educate himself to join the learned men on whom the tsar Peter I the Great was calling to transform Russia into a modern nation.

The clergy and the nobility, attached to their privileges and fearing the spread of education and science, actively opposed the reforms of which Lomonósov was a lifelong champion. His bitter struggle began as soon as he arrived in Moscow. In order to be admitted to the Slavonic-Greek-Latin Academy he had to conceal his humble origin; the sons of nobles jeered at him, and he had scarcely enough money for food and clothes. But his robust health and exceptional intelligence enabled him in five years to assimilate the eight-year course of study; during this time he taught himself Greek and read the philosophical works of antiquity.

Lomonosov, detail of an oil painting; in the M.V. Lomonosov Museum of the Science Academy, St. Petersburg

Photo Larousse

Noticed at last by his instructors, in January 1736 Lomonosov became a student at the St. Petersburg Academy. Seven months later he left for Germany to study at the University of Marburg, where he led the turbulent life of the German student. His work did not suffer, however, for within three years he had surveyed the main achievements of Western philosophy and science. His mind, freed from all preconception, rebelled at the narrowness of the empiricism in which the disciples of Isaac Newton had bound the natural sciences; in dissertations sent to St. Petersburg, he attacked the problem of the structure of matter.

In 1739, in Freiberg, Lomonosov studied firsthand the technologies of mining, metallurgy, and glassmaking. Also friendly with the poets of the time, he freely indulged the love of verse that had arisen during his childhood with the reading of Psalms. The "Ode," dedicated to the Empress, and the *Pismo o pravilakh rossiyskogo stikhotvorstva* ("Letter Concerning the Rules of Russian Versification") made a considerable impression at court.

After breaking with one of his masters, the chemist Johann Henckel, and many other mishaps, among which his marriage at Marburg must be included, Lomonosov returned in July 1741 to St. Petersburg. The Academy, which was directed by foreigners and incompetent nobles, gave the young scholar no precise assignment, and the injustice aroused him. His violent temper and great strength sometimes led him to go beyond the rules of propriety, and in May 1743 he was placed under arrest. Two odes sent to the empress Elizabeth won him his liberation in January 1744, as well as a certain poetic prestige at the Academy.

While in prison he worked out the plan of work that he had already developed in Marburg. The *276 zametok po fizike i korpuskulyarnoy filosofi* ("276 Notes on Corpuscular Philosophy and Physics") set forth the dominant ideas of his scientific work. Appointed a professor by the Academy in 1745, he translated Christian Wolff's *Institutiones philosophiae experimentalis* ("Studies in Experimental Philosophy") into Russian and wrote, in Latin, important works on the *Meditationes de Caloris et Frigoris Causa* (1747; "Cause of Heat and Cold"), the *Tentamen Theoriae de vi Aëris Elastica* (1748; "Elastic Force of Air"), and the *Theoria Electricitatis* (1756; "Theory of Electricity"). His friend, the celebrated German mathematician Leonhard Euler, recognized the creative originality of his articles, which were, on Euler's advice, published by the Russian Academy in the *Novye kommentari.*

In 1748 the laboratory that Lomonosov had been requesting since 1745 was granted him; it then began a prodigious amount of activity. He passionately undertook many tasks and, courageously facing ill will and hostility, recorded in three years more than 4,000 experiments in his *Zhurnal laboratori,* the results of which enabled him to set up a coloured glass works and to make mosaics with these glasses. *Slovo o polze khimi* (1751; "Discourse on the Usefulness of Chemistry"), the *Pismo k I.I. Shuvalovu o polze stekla* (1752; "Letter to I.I. Shuvalov Concerning the Usefulness of Glass"), and the "Ode" to Elizabeth celebrated his fruitful union of abstract and applied science. Anxious to train students, he wrote in 1752 an introduction to the physical chemistry course that he was to set up in his laboratory. The theories on the unity of natural phenomena and the structure of matter that he set forth in the discussion on the *Slovo o proiskhozhdeni sveta* (1756; "Origin of Light and Colours") and in his theoretical works on electricity in 1753 and 1756 also matured in this laboratory.

Encouraged by the success of his experiments in 1760, Lomonosov inserted in the *Meditationes de Solido et Fluido* ("Reflections on the Solidity and Fluidity of Bodies") the "universal law of nature"—that is, the law of conservation of matter and energy, which, with the corpuscular theory, constitutes the dominant thread in all his research.

To these achievements were added the composition of *Rossiyskaya grammatika* and of *Kratkoy rossiyskoy letopisets* ("Short Russian Chronicle"), ordered by the Empress, and all the work of reorganizing education, to which Lomonosov accorded much importance.

From 1755 he followed very closely the development of Moscow State University (now Moscow M.V. Lomonosov State University), for which he had drawn up the plans. Appointed a councillor by the Academy in 1757, he undertook reforms to make the university an intellectual centre closely linked with the life of the country. To that end, he wrote several scholarly works including *Rassuzhdeniye o bolshoy tochnosti morskogo puti* (1759; "Discussion of the Great Accuracy of the Maritime Route"); *Rassuzhdeniye o proiskhozhdenii ledyanykh gor v severnykh moryakh* (1760; "Discussion of the Formation of Icebergs in the Northern Seas"); *Kratkoye opisaniye raznykh puteshestviy po severnym moryam . . .* (1762–63; "A Short Account of the Various Voyages in the Northern Seas"); and *O sloyakh zemnykh* (1763; "Of the Terrestrial Strata"), which constituted an important contribution both to science and to the development of commerce and the exploitation of mineral wealth.

Despite the honours that came to him, he continued to lead a simple and industrious life, surrounded by his family and a few friends. He left his house and the laboratory erected in his garden only to go to the Academy. His prestige was considerable in Russia, and his scientific works and his role in the Academy were known abroad. He was a member of the Royal Swedish Academy of Sciences and of that of Bologna. His theories concerning heat and the constitution of matter were opposed by the empiricist scientists of Germany, although they were analyzed with interest in European scientific journals.

The persecutions he suffered, particularly after the empress Elizabeth's death in 1762 (1761, Old Style) exhausted him physically, and he died in 1765. The empress Catherine II the Great had the patriotic scholar buried with great ceremony, but she confiscated all the notes in which were outlined the great humanitarian ideas he had developed. Publications of his works were purged of the material that constituted a menace to the system of serfdom, particularly that concerned with materialist and humanist ideas. Efforts were made to view him as a court poet and an upholder of monarchy and religion rather than as an enemy of superstition and a champion of popular education. The authorities did not succeed in quenching the influence of his work, however. The publication of his *Polnoye sobraniye sochineny* ("Complete Works") in 1950–83 by Soviet scholars has revealed the full contributions of Lomonosov, who has long been misunderstood by historians of science. (L.-A.L.)

BIBLIOGRAPHY. Biographies and studies include Boris N. Menshutkin, *Russia's Lomonosov* (1952, reissued 1970; originally published in Russian, 1937); Luce Langevin, *Lomonossov* (1967); Henry M. Leicester (trans.), *Mikhail Vasil'evich Lomonosov on the Corpuscular Theory* (1970); and G.E. Pavlova and A.S. Fedorov, *Mikhail Vasil'evich Lomonosov: His Life and Work* (1984).

Lomonosov Ridge, major submarine ridge of the Arctic Ocean. The ridge is 1,100 miles (1,800 km) long. From Ellesmere Island on the continental shelf of North America, the ridge extends north to a point near the North Pole and then continues south to a point near the continental shelf of the New Siberian Islands. The ridge divides the Arctic Ocean into two major basins, and it influences water circulation, marine life, and ice movement. The ridge crest, which at its highest point is at a depth of 3,200 feet (975 m), rises 6,000–11,000 feet (1,800–3,400 m) from the basin floor. The basin on the Atlantic side is more than 13,000 feet (4,000 m) deep, whereas the adjacent basin is about 11,000 feet deep. An aseismic ridge (characterized by no associated earthquake activity), it is asymmetrical in shape and has gentle relief over its surface.

At one time it was believed that the Lomonosov Ridge was a continuation of the mid-oceanic ridge, with an associated seismic belt. It has been shown, though, that the seismic belt lies 250 miles (400 km) toward the Barents Sea from the ridge. Thus, the Lomonosov Ridge is not a part of the mid-oceanic ridge system.

Lompoc, city, Santa Barbara county, southwestern California, U.S. It lies along the Santa Ynez River in the coastal Lompoc valley, 155 miles (250 km) northwest of Los Angeles. Originally inhabited by Chumash Indians, the area was part of a Spanish land grant established in 1787. The city was founded (1874) as a farming community by the Lompoc Valley Land Company, which bought and subdivided the Ranchos Lompoc and Misión Vieja.

Lompoc (Chumash Indian: "Little Lake" or "Lagoon") now has a diversified economy based on agriculture, oil production (since 1904), the mining and processing of diatomite, the flower-seed market of the valley (with an annual festival), and the vast aerospace complex at Vandenberg Air Force Base (just north). The air base also includes the California Spaceport, which offers orbital launches and payload processing for businesses and the government.

The city's many murals are popular attractions. The Lompoc Museum contains exhibits on the area's regional history. Jalama Beach, just south of the city, is a popular surfing spot. La Purísima Mission State Historic Park, 3 miles (5 km) northeast of the city, contains many restored buildings of the Franciscan Misión la Purísima Concepción de María Santísima, established in 1787. Inc. 1888. Pop. (2003 est.) city, 41,167; (2000) Santa Barbara–Santa Maria–Lompoc MSA, 399,347.

Łomża, former (1975–98) *województwo* (province), northeastern Poland, now part of Podlaskie and Mazowieckie (*qq.v.*) provinces.

Łomża, city, Podlaskie *województwo* (province), northeastern Poland. The city was first chronicled in the 14th century and received its city rights in 1428. Located on the Narew and Komżyczka rivers in the western plains of Podlaskie province, it lies midway between the cities of Ostrołęka and Białystok. The local economy is dependent upon food processing and textile manufacturing. During World War II, Łomża city was almost totally destroyed. An extensive postwar building and restoration program has produced a cultural centre and the Kurpie Museum; the 16th-century Gothic cathedral was also restored. Pop. (2002) 63,936.

Lon Nol (b. Nov. 13, 1913, Prey Vêng, Camb.—d. Nov. 17, 1985, Fullerton, Calif., U.S.), soldier and politician whose overthrow of Prince Norodom Sihanouk (1970) involved Cambodia in the Indochina war and ended in the takeover (1975) of the country by the communist Khmer Rouge.

Lon Nol entered the French colonial service in 1937 and became a magistrate, then a provincial governor and head of the national police (1951). He joined the army in 1952 and fought against intruding Vietnamese communist guerrillas in Cambodia as an area commander. After again serving as a provincial governor, he became Cambodian army chief of staff (1955) and commander in chief (1960) under the country's leader, Prince Norodom Sihanouk. He was deputy premier (1963), minister of defense (1968–69), and twice premier (1966–67 and from 1969) under Sihanouk.

Lon Nol was a prime architect of the U.S.-supported coup in March 1970 that overthrew Sihanouk, and he became the most prominent leader in the new government, serving as its premier until 1972. Abandoning Sihanouk's policy of neutrality in the Vietnam War, Lon Nol established close ties with both the United States and South Vietnam, permitting their forces to operate on Cambodian territory. On March 10, 1972, Lon Nol assumed total power over Cambodia, and two days later, he installed himself as president of the country. In the meantime, the communist Khmer Rouge movement was gathering strength in the Cambodian countryside, despite a covert U.S. air campaign against the insurgents. On April 1, 1975, with Khmer Rouge communist guerrillas only a few miles from the capital, Lon Nol left the country and settled in the United States.

London, city, seat of Middlesex county, southeastern Ontario, Canada. It lies at the forks of the Thames River, midway between Lakes Ontario (east) and St. Clair (west) and Lakes Huron (north) and Erie (south).

Its name and site were chosen in 1792 for the location of a capital of Upper Canada, but the plans failed to materialize, and settlement did not take place until 1826. Serving as a British garrison town during the mid-19th century, London developed into an important transportation and industrial centre as a result of its interlake location. It lies at the hub of extensive rail and highway networks radiating into the surrounding agricultural region, which produces fruit, vegetables, grain, and dairy products. London's industries include the manufacture of food products, brass and steel products, diesel locomotives, textiles, electrical appliances, and clothing. The city is a seat of Anglican and Roman Catholic dioceses, as well as the University of Western Ontario (founded in 1878) and its affiliated schools. Inc. village, 1840; town, 1848; city, 1854. Pop. (2001) city, 336,539; metropolitan area 432,451.

London, city, capital of the United Kingdom and the centre of the Commonwealth. It lies astride the River Thames in southeastern England, 50 miles (80 km) from the river's estuary on the North Sea. The city was once the industrial, commercial, and political hub of a wealthy and extensive empire; it continues to be the United Kingdom's main centre of population, commerce, and culture.

A brief treatment of London follows. For full treatment (including a map), *see* MACROPAEDIA: London.

The chalk basin within which London is built is filled with younger sediments including solid rock, sands, clays, terraced pebble gravels, and Thames alluvium. The climate within the basin is relatively mild, with January to July mean temperatures ranging from 37.4° to 72.5° F (3° to 22.5° C); rainfall amounts to 21 inches (533 mm) a year.

Founded by the Romans as Londinium in the 1st century AD, the town experienced tremendous growth in trade and population during the late 16th and early 17th centuries. Extensive building projects were initiated after the Great Fire of 1666, and London became the dominant centre not only of the nation but of its expanding empire. During the 19th century, the problems caused by rapid industrialization, such as pollution and disease, were slowly remedied through advances in public health and other services. Heavy damage from aerial bombings during World War II brought the greatest setback in the history of modern London. Reconstruction and new development restored much of the city's grandeur, and relocation of manufacturing and shipping outside the city shrank its population and hastened its transition to a centre of international trade and finance. Tourism and retail trade are other major sectors of the city's economy; and, because London is the nation's capital, government services are also an important sector.

The City of London, about 1 square mile (2.7 square km) in area, is the core of an area called Inner, or Central, London, which contains the City of London and 13 of the 33 boroughs of Greater London. The central point in the City of London is an open space from which eight streets radiate. On the southern side is Mansion House, residence of the lord mayor of London. Lombard Street, the traditional banking street, is nearby, as are the Bank of England headquarters, the Royal Exchange, and the Stock Exchange. To the east is the fortress-castle known as the Tower of London, whose core dates from the late 11th century and is surrounded by constructions from many periods of English architecture. To the west lie the Inns of Court, longtime chambers and offices of barristers and lawyers-in-training, and the Royal Courts of Justice, or Law Courts. The City of London and the City of Westminster are linked by the Strand, an avenue upon which are located two of London's oldest churches, St. Clement Dane's and St. Mary-le-Strand.

The City of Westminster, which stretches along the River Thames, is one of the country's wealthiest boroughs and is famed for its commitment to historic renovation. It includes Westminster Abbey and Westminster Cathedral, Buckingham Palace, the principal government offices, important shopping districts, New Scotland Yard, luxury hotels, the Tate Gallery, and the National Gallery. Retail shopping areas are concentrated around Oxford Street. Kensington High Street and Knightsbridge are also major shopping districts. The shops spread west and south toward King's Road in Chelsea.

London's East End, containing neighbourhoods such as Aldgate and Whitechapel, now constitutes the borough of Tower Hamlets. The area is historically associated with the Cockney dialect and became an infamous slum during the 19th century. The East End was the most heavily bombed area of London during World War II and subsequently benefited from extensive rehabilitation.

Parks, gardens, and churchyards abound in Inner London. The most celebrated parklands are the six royal parks that sweep through London's West End: St. James's Park, oldest of the six central royal parks, bordered on the north by the half-mile-long Mall that terminates at the Queen Victoria Memorial; Buckingham Palace Gardens, bordered on the east by the royal residence; Green Park, plainest of the royal parks but fringed on the east by lavish, once-private buildings; Hyde Park, with its famous Speakers' Corner for soapbox orators; the more elegant Kensington Gardens, with the Victorian Gothic Albert Memorial and an 80-acre (32-hectare) cultural centre; and Regent's Park, home of the Zoological Gardens and Regent's (Grand Union) Canal.

Squares and variously shaped commons are prominent features of London's landscape. Of note are Grosvenor Square, site of the F.D. Roosevelt Memorial, and Trafalgar Square, which features a statue of Lord Nelson, hero of the Battle of Trafalgar (1805); the National Gallery borders the square.

London's other major cultural institutions include the British Museum, which houses collections of antiquities, prints, and manuscripts and the national library; the Victoria and Albert Museum of decorative arts; and the music and arts complex located on the South Bank of the Thames, begun in 1951 for the Festival of Britain.

The development of the city's outlying areas was promoted by the opening of the world's first electric underground railway in 1890. Major roads and rail lines radiate in all directions. Dock activity and river traffic are controlled by the Port of London Authority. The London (Heathrow) International Airport is located in the western reaches of Greater London. Area City, 1 square mile (2.7 square km); Inner London, 124 square miles (321 square km); Greater London, 610 square miles (1,579 square km). Pop. (1994 est.) City, 5,200; Inner London, 2,434,400; Greater London, 6,967,-400.

London, Artur, in full ARTUR GERARD LONDON (b. Feb. 1, 1915, Ostrava, Moravia, Austria-Hungary [now in Czech Republic]—d. Nov. 8, 1986, Paris, France), Czechoslovak Communist official who wrote a powerful autobiographical account of his own political trial.

A Communist from the age of 14, London joined the International Brigades in the Spanish Civil War in 1936. During World War II he worked for the French Resistance from August 1940 until 1942, when he was arrested by the Germans and deported to Mauthausen concentration camp. After the war he returned to France. In 1947 he sought treatment in Switzerland for the tuberculosis he had contracted at Mauthausen.

After his return to Czechoslovakia, London joined the Communist regime as undersecretary for foreign affairs in 1949. In January 1951 he was arrested in a purge directed largely at former members of the International Brigades; he was accused of espionage activities and was imprisoned in Hungary. In November 1952 London and 13 other defendants, including former Communist Party secretary-general Rudolf Slánský, were put on trial. The proceedings had strong overtones of anti-Semitism: Slánský, London, and most of the other defendants were Jewish and were charged with being Zionist agents. Having undergone torture in prison and hopeful of light sentences by cooperating with the prosecution, all defendants confessed to their indictments. London was sentenced to life imprisonment. As a result of the Soviet leader Nikita Khrushchev's policies of de-Stalinization, London's case was reviewed; he was released in 1956 and was later rehabilitated. He left Czechoslovakia in 1963 and returned to France, where, with his wife, Lise, he wrote *L'Aveu* in 1968 (published in English as *The Confession*), an account of his ordeal. The book was made into a film under the same name in 1970 by Costa-Gavras.

London, City of, municipal corporation and borough, London, Eng. The City Corporation is Britain's oldest local government; it has the status of a county, with powers that exceed those of London's 32 other boroughs (collectively called Greater London), notably the control of its own police force. Sometimes called "The Square Mile," the City arcs along the left (north) bank of the River Thames from the Temple Bar to the Tower of London. Near its centre stand St. Paul's Cathedral, the Bank of England, the Royal Exchange (which no longer functions), the Stock Exchange, and the rest of London's financial district. There also are the Guildhall, Mansion House (the residence of the lord mayor), and the College of Arms. West of St. Paul's are the heart of the legal profession, the Temple and the Law Courts; and Fleet Street, once the hub of London's newspaper establishment. Area 1 square mile (2.7 square km). Pop. (1998 est.) 5,000.

London, Fritz Wolfgang (b. March 7, 1900, Breslau, Ger. [now Wrocław, Pol.]—d. March 30, 1954, Durham, N.C., U.S.), German-American physicist who, with Walter Heitler, devised (1927) the first quantum mechanical treatment of the hydrogen molecule.

London was educated at the universities of Bonn, Frankfurt, Göttingen, Munich (Ph.D., 1921), and Paris. He was a Rockefeller research fellow at Zürich and Rome and a lecturer at the University of Berlin. From 1933 to 1936 he was a research fellow at the University of Oxford and then went to the University of Paris as master and director of research.

In 1939 he immigrated to the United States to become professor of theoretical chemistry at Duke University, Durham, N.C., and from 1953 he was James B. Duke professor of chemical physics there. He became a U.S. citizen in 1945. His publications include two volumes on *Superfluids* (1950, 1954).

London's theory of the chemical binding of homopolar molecules marked the beginning of modern quantum mechanical treatment of the hydrogen molecule and is considered one of the most important advances in modern chemistry. With his brother, Heinz London, he developed (1935) the phenomenological theory of superconductivity, providing a new foundation for the understanding of molecular forces and clarifying the connection between pure quantum phenomena and many of the most striking facts of chemistry.

London, Great Fire of (1666): *see* Great Fire of London.

London, Great Plague of (1664–66): *see* Great Plague of London.

London, Jack, pseudonym of JOHN GRIFFITH CHANEY (b. Jan. 12, 1876, San Francisco, Calif., U.S.—d. Nov. 22, 1916, Glen Ellen, Calif.), American novelist and short-story writer whose works deal romantically with elemental struggles for survival. He is one of the most extensively translated of American authors.

Deserted by his father, a roving astrologer, London was raised in Oakland, Calif., by his spiritualist mother and his stepfather, whose surname, London, he took. At 14 he quit school to escape poverty and gain adventure. He explored San Francisco Bay in his sloop, alternately stealing oysters or working for the government fish patrol. He went to Japan as a sailor and saw much of the United States as a hobo riding freight trains and as a member of Kelly's industrial army (one of the many protest armies of unemployed born of the panic of 1893). He saw depression conditions, was jailed for vagrancy, and in 1894 became a militant socialist. London educated himself at public libraries with the writings of Charles Darwin, Karl Marx, and Friedrich Nietzsche, usually in popularized forms, and created his own amalgam of socialism and white superiority. At 19 he crammed a four-year high school course into one year and entered the University of California at Berkeley, but after a year he quit school to seek a fortune in the Klondike gold rush of 1897. Returning the next year, still poor and unable to find work, he decided to earn a living as a writer.

London studied magazines and then set himself a daily schedule of producing sonnets, ballads, jokes, anecdotes, adventure stories, or horror stories, steadily increasing his out-

Jack London writing *The Sea Wolf,* 1903

Jack London State Historic Park

Tower of London
Aerofilms Ltd., London

put. The optimism and energy with which he attacked his task are best conveyed in his autobiographical novel *Martin Eden* (1909), perhaps his most enduring work. Within two years stories of his Alaskan adventures began to win acceptance for their fresh subject matter and virile force. His first book, *The Son of the Wolf* (1900), gained a wide audience. During the remainder of his life he produced steadily, completing 50 books of fiction and nonfiction in 17 years. Although he became the highest-paid writer in the United States, his earnings never matched his expenditures. He sailed a ketch to the South Pacific, telling of his adventures in *The Cruise of the Snark* (1911). In 1910 he settled on a ranch near Glen Ellen, Calif., where he built his grandiose Wolf House. He maintained his socialist beliefs almost to the end of his life.

Jack London's hastily written output is of uneven quality. His Alaskan stories *Call of the Wild* (1903), *White Fang* (1906), and *Burning Daylight* (1910) are outstanding. In addition to *Martin Eden,* he wrote two other autobiographical novels of considerable interest: *The Road* (1907) and *John Barleycorn* (1913). Other important works are *The Sea Wolf* (1904), which features a Nietzschean superman hero, and *The Iron Heel* (1907), a fantasy of the future that is a terrifying anticipation of fascism. London's reputation declined in the United States in the 1920s when a brilliant new generation of postwar writers made the prewar writers seem lacking in sophistication, but his popularity has remained high throughout the world, especially in Russia, where a commemorative edition of his works published in 1956 was reported to have been sold out in five hours. A three-volume set of his letters, edited by Earle Labor *et al.*, was published in 1988.

BIBLIOGRAPHY. In addition to personal accounts by the writer's wife, Charmian London, *The Book of Jack London,* 2 vol. (1921); and daughter, Joan London, *Jack London and His Times* (1939, reprinted 1968); biographies include Russ Kingman, *A Pictorial Life of Jack London* (1979); and Andrew Sinclair, *Jack: A Biography of Jack London* (1977). London's short stories are examined in Earle Labor, *Jack London* (1974); and James I. McClintock, *White Logic* (1975). See also Robert Barltrop, *Jack London: The Man, the Writer, the Rebel* (1976); and Charles N. Watson, Jr., *The Novels of Jack London* (1983).

London, Tower of, byname THE TOWER, royal fortress and London landmark, on the north bank of the River Thames, on the east side of the City of London. Immediately after his coronation (Christmas, 1066), William I the Conqueror began to erect fortifications there to dominate the indigenous mercantile community and to control access to the Pool of London, the major port area before the construction of docks farther downstream in the 19th century. The central keep—known as the White Tower—was begun about 1078 close inside the Roman City wall and was built of limestone from Caen in Normandy. During the 12th and 13th centuries the fortifications were extended beyond the City wall, the White Tower becoming the nucleus of a series of concentric defenses enclosing an inner and an outer ward.

The inner "curtain" has 13 towers, of which the best known are the Bloody Tower, the Beauchamp Tower, and the Wakefield Tower. The outer curtain, with six towers and two bastions, is surrounded by the moat, originally fed by the Thames but drained since 1843. The wall outside the moat has embrasures for cannons, some of which are still fired on state occasions. The whole complex of buildings covers 18 acres (7 hectares). The only entrance from the land is at the southwest corner, from the City; when the river was still a major highway of London, the 13th-century watergate was much used. Its nickname, Traitors' Gate, derives from the prisoners brought through it to the Tower, which was long used as a state prison. Many prisoners were murdered or executed there, either on Tower Green or, outside the castle, in public on Tower Hill. The armouries that now occupy the White Tower, as well as a later 17th-century brick building alongside, house arms and armour from the early Middle Ages to modern times.

The Tower was a royal residence until the 17th century. In its time it has also housed the Royal Mint, the ordnance store, the public records, and the Royal Menagerie (the Lion Tower). Most of these functions have been dispersed to other places. Until 1994 the British crown jewels and regalia were kept in the underground Jewel House; they are now housed in a more spacious aboveground facility. During the 1990s restoration work was carried out in various parts of the Tower, notably in the medieval apartments in Wakefield and St. Thomas's towers.

A military garrison is maintained within the Tower, which with its precincts constitutes a "liberty" outside the jurisdictions of the lord mayor and the bishop of London. It is held for the sovereign by a constable, who is now always a field marshal. There is a resident governor, who occupies the 16th-century Queen's House on Tower Green and is in charge of the yeoman warders, or "beefeaters," as they are popularly called. They still wear a Tudor uniform and live within the Tower. By the Tower is Tower Bridge (1894), the only central-city bridge across the Thames below London Bridge.

London, University of, a federation of more than 50 British institutions of higher learning, located primarily in London. It also examines and grants degrees to students not enrolled in any of its constituent schools.

The university was a product of the Liberal movement of the 19th century. Following a call by poet Thomas Campbell in 1825 for a university to provide education for the class between the "mechanics" and the "enormously rich," liberals and religious dissenters founded London University (now University College) in 1828. Its application for a royal charter was refused because the college admitted Roman Catholics, Jews, and other non-Anglicans. In 1831 King's College was founded under Anglican auspices, but its charter was blocked by the dissenters. In 1836 the University of London was created as an administrative entity that would hold no classes of its own but would examine and confer degrees on students of the other two colleges. Under the Supplemental Charter of 1849, it became possible for students enrolled in any institution of higher learning anywhere in the British Empire to be examined by the university and awarded a University of London degree. Students from institutions as different as the University of Oxford and the Working Men's College of London thereby could become recipients of London degrees. In 1858 students who were not enrolled in any institution were allowed to become degree candidates.

By the early 20th century many other institutions had become affiliated with the university, including Bedford College, the first British university to grant degrees to women; the London School of Economics and Political Science, now an internationally respected centre for the study of social science; and three institutions that later became the Imperial College of Science and Technology.

In 1900 the university was authorized to begin offering its own courses. Students attending the university or its affiliated schools were dubbed "internal students"; those who sat for university examinations but were enrolled elsewhere were "external students."

London Bridge, any of several successive structures spanning the River Thames between Borough High Street, Southwark, and King William Street in the City of London. The Old London Bridge of nursery-rhyme fame was built by Peter of Colechurch between 1176 and 1209, replacing the last of

Old London Bridge, lithograph after a manuscript illumination of *c.* 1500 in the British Library (Royal M.S.S.16.F.ii.XV.)
Reproduced by permission of the British Library; photograph, J.R. Freeman & Co. Ltd.

several timber bridges built in late Roman and early medieval times. Its 19 arches of varying breadths mounted on piers of different sizes were so narrow as to turn the river into a series of races during tidal flow. The widest arch was 34 feet (10.4 metres), the narrowest 15 ft. On the largest pier, in the middle of the river, stood a chapel. A defensive tower fronted a drawbridge partway across while another stood on the Southwark shore. Three years after completion the bridge was severely damaged by fire, the first of many calamitous incidents. Despite these, it remained for centuries a choice residential and business site, its roadway loaded with houses and shops, many of which projected out over the river. It remained the sole crossing of the Thames at London until the 1740s, when Westminster Bridge was built, despite opposition from city merchants. Extensively rebuilt by Charles Labelye in the 1750s, the ancient structure was demolished and replaced in the 1820s by New London Bridge, designed by John Rennie, Sr., and built by his son John Jr. New London Bridge spanned the river with only five arches, with a centre span of 150 ft. In the 1960s it was in turn replaced, but its masonry facing, dismantled and shipped across the Atlantic, was reerected on a core of reinforced concrete at Lake Havasu City, Ariz., as a tourist attraction.

London Bridge, children's singing game in which there are several players (eight or more), two of whom join hands high to form an arch (the bridge). The other players march under the bridge, each holding onto the waist of the player in front. Either the bridge or all players sing: "London Bridge is falling down, / Falling down, falling down, / London Bridge is falling down, / My fair lady." At the last word, the arms of the bridge are lowered to capture the last player through. The song continues with more stanzas.

In the modern game, which dates back to 17th-century England and to the 16th-century continental European "fallen bridges" games, as the players are captured, they are kept in an area called the Tower of London, and at the end of the game they are chased by the bridge. The first two caught form the next bridge. In the earlier game, captured players went to alternate sides, forming two teams, and a tug-of-war followed. In the original game, each prisoner paid a forfeit, possibly a vestigial remnant of the old folk superstition that a bridge would only stand after the death of a sacrifice.

The song has numerous variant stanzas, sung while the prisoners are being captured, such as "Build it up with iron bars"; "Iron bars will bend and break"; and "Get a man to watch all night." The name of the game also varies in different locations: broken bridges (Scotland); *Die Goldene Brücke* (Germany); *Le Pont-Levis* (France); and Charlestown Bridge (New England).

London Clay, major division of Eocene rocks in the London Basin of England (the Eocene Epoch began about 54,000,000 years ago and lasted about 16,000,000 years); it immediately underlies much of the city of London. The London Clay overlies the Reading Beds, underlies the Bagshot Sands, and is included in the Ypresian Stage, the lowermost division of Eocene rocks and time. In the London Basin the London Clay is as much as 200 metres (600 feet) thick and is brown, bluish, or gray. In the regions of Greater London and Surrey, the upper portions of the London Clay consist of alternating clays and sands that are sometimes known as the Claygate Beds.

Although animal fossils are not especially abundant in the London Clay, a diverse faunal assemblage has been discovered through comprehensive sampling at a number of localities. Mollusks dominate the animal assemblage, but fishes, brachiopods, worms, foraminifera, crabs, and cirripedes also occur. The diverse and abundant fossil plant assemblage discovered in the London Clay has proved to be of exceptional importance. Terrestrial plants, including trees and leaves, were swept out to sea by currents or storms, became waterlogged, and sank into the soft sediments at the bottom of the basin. Logs are preserved, as are the seeds and fruits of palms, dicots, and conifers; the large fruits of the modern palm genus *Nypa,* currently restricted to the deltas and swamps of India, are exceptionally abundant. The plant and animal assemblages are indicative of warm, probably tropical climatic conditions that prevailed in western Europe during the Eocene. The discovery of crocodile remains in the London Clay further confirms this interpretation.

London Company, also called VIRGINIA COMPANY OF LONDON, commercial trading company chartered by England's King James I in April 1606 with the object of colonizing the eastern American coast between latitudes 34° and 41° N. Its shareholders were London men, and it was distinguished from the Plymouth Company (*q.v.*), which was chartered at the same time and composed largely of Plymouth men.

The London Company quickly (in December 1606) sent out three ships with 120 colonists, led by Capt. John Smith and Bartholomew Gosnold. In May 1607 the colonists reached Virginia and founded Jamestown at the mouth of the James River. After some initial hardships, the colony took root; and the London Company itself was reconstituted on a broader legal basis. It obtained two new charters, one in 1609 and one in 1612, which appropriated to it a great belt of territory 400 miles (640 kilometres) wide extending through the American continent to the Pacific Ocean. It also obtained large rights of government, authorizing it to appoint and hold full control of the resident governor, his resident council, and other officers. In 1619 the company established continental America's first true legislature—a two-part legislature, one part consisting of the governor and his council, named by the company in England, and the other a house made up of two burgesses from each settlement.

Despite increasing prosperity in Virginia over the following years, the company's role came under attack as internal disputes among the shareholders grew and because the King himself was offended both by the trend toward popular government in Virginia and by the colony's efforts to raise tobacco, a "noisome" product of which the King disapproved. A petition submitted to the King calling for an investigation of conditions in the colony led to a trial before the King's Bench in May 1624. The court ruled against the company, which was then dissolved, and Virginia was transformed into a royal colony.

London Dock Strike (1889), influential strike by workers in the Port of London that won them the famous "dockers' tanner" (a pay rate of sixpence per hour) and revitalized the British Trades Union movement.

Following a minor dispute at the South-West India Dock (Aug. 13, 1889), labour activists Ben Tillett, Tom Mann, and John Burns announced (August 19) the formation of a dockers' union. From August 20 the entire Port of London was closed, and Burns led orderly processions of strikers throughout London. A crisis (August 29) caused by shortage of relief funds was averted by financial support organized in Australia; nearly £30,000 was hastily remitted, and this, with the £49,000 soon subscribed in Britain, assured the strike's indefinite continuance. From September 5 the employers began negotiations, the principal mediator being the Roman Catholic archbishop of Westminster, Cardinal H.E. Manning. Agreement was reached on September 10; with their "tanner" and most other demands conceded, the dockers resumed work on September 16. Their success inspired the formation of many new unions of largely unskilled labourers, while membership of already-existing unions rose dramatically.

London Festival Ballet, British dance troupe. Organized in 1949 by Alicia Markova and Anton Dolin with a corps de ballet drawn chiefly from the Cone-Ripman School in London and at Tring, Hertford, the troupe holds an annual London season at the Royal Festival Hall and conducts world tours. Its repertoire includes classical ballets and such newer works as Michael Charnley's *Symphony for Fun* and Nureyev's *The Sleeping Beauty.* The company was originally named Festival Ballet, which was changed to London's Festival Ballet and then in 1968 it became London Festival Ballet. John Field was made artistic director in 1979.

London group, English artists' group founded in November 1913, with Harold Gilman as president, for the purpose of joint exhibition. The group was noted during the first months of its existence for the diversity of its membership and the controversy that attended its exhibitions. It was formed, primarily for convenience, by several English artists' alliances, the most important of which was the Camden Town group under the leadership of Gilman, Walter Sickert, and Spencer Gore. These artists, along with their allies Charles Ginner and Lucien Pissarro, advocated painting the urban and working classes and favoured the light palette and high-key colour of the Impressionists and Postimpressionists.

Some considerably more radical painters, whose work was strongly influenced by Cubist and Futurist geometrics and colour, also joined the London group. These included Wyndham Lewis and Edward Wadsworth, who called themselves Vorticists in 1914–15, and David Bomberg, an independent Cubist painter. The radical and conservative artists coexisted in the London group until late 1915, when most of the radicals left London to serve in the war. Their abstract work had provoked heated controversy at the first and second exhibitions of the London group.

London Naval Conference (Jan. 21–April 22, 1930), conference held in London to discuss naval disarmament and to review the treaties of the Washington Conference of 1921–22. Hosted by Great Britain, it included representatives of the United States, France, Italy, and Japan. At the end of three months of meetings, general agreement had been secured on the regulation of submarine warfare and a five-year moratorium on the construction of capital ships. The limitation of aircraft carriers, provided for by the Washington Five-Power Treaty (1922), was extended. The United States, Great Britain, and Japan signed, on April 22, a treaty limiting battleship tonnage in the ratios of 10:10:7. France and Italy, opposed respectively to the concept of ratios and to the acceptance of any inequality, declined to sign.

The treaties were to run until 1936. In December 1935, in accord with the treaty of 1930, another naval conference met in London. Japan, however, withdrew; and the naval treaty, signed on March 25, 1936, provided for little more than consultation. In December 1938 Italy acceded to certain provisions, but the outbreak of war in September 1939 cancelled all such treaties.

London Prize Ring rules, set of rules governing bareknuckle boxing, which were adopted in 1838 and revised in 1853. They superseded those drawn up by Jack Broughton, known as the father of English boxing, in 1743. Under the London rules, bouts were held in a "ring" 24 feet (7.3 metres) square enclosed by ropes. A knockdown ended the round, followed by a 30-second rest and an additional 8 seconds to regain the centre of the ring. Butting, gouging, hitting below the waist, and kicking were banned. Although the Marquess of Queensberry rules, which called for glove matches, appeared in 1867, professional bareknuckle fights continued. In 1889 John L. Sullivan beat Jake Kilrain in 75 rounds to defend his heavyweight championship, the last heavyweight championship bout held under London rules.

London Stock Exchange, a marketplace for securities based in London. It was formed in 1773 by several stockbrokers who had been doing business informally in neighbourhood coffeehouses. In 1801 a group of the members raised money for the construction of a building in Chapel Court, Bartholomew Lane, and rules for the exchange were established the following year; the rules subsequently have been amended several times. In 1973 the exchange merged with several regional stock exchanges in Great Britain. It is governed by a council of its members.

London Zoo, zoo in Regent's Park, London. It has one of the most comprehensive animal collections in the world and the largest zoological library of any zoo. The London Zoo is administered by the Zoological Society of London.

The zoo opened in 1828, and its initial collections were augmented by the additions of the royal menagerie from Windsor in 1830 and the menagerie from the Tower of London soon afterward. It opened the world's first reptile house (1849) and public aquarium (1853). The zoo was severely affected during World War II, when its animals were killed or removed; its edible fish ended up on London tables. In 1955 a reconstruction program was begun, and within 10 years a footbridge, the Elephant and Rhino Pavilion, a walk-through aviary, and an animal hospital were built. A pavilion for small mammals followed in 1967. In 1972 the zoo added the Sobell Pavilion for apes and monkeys; the structure also houses the zoo's giant pandas and the Zoo Studies Centre. A summer children's zoo, originally established in 1938, was reopened in 1994.

The 36-acre (15-hectare) zoo exhibits thousands of specimens. It has had outstanding success breeding Père David's deer, as well as the pygmy hippopotamus, musk ox, Chilean flamingo, and polar bear. Chi-Chi, the famous giant panda, arrived there from China in 1958.

In 1931 the Zoological Society of London opened a country branch, Whipsnade Wild Animal Park, in Dunstable, Bedfordshire. Resembling a large country estate, this 600-acre (240-hectare) zoo displays and breeds large numbers of animals. It also houses two major research units, the Wellcome Institute of Comparative Physiology and the Nuffield Institute of Comparative Medicine.

Londonderry, former (until 1973) county, Northern Ireland. It was bounded by the Atlantic Ocean (north), the River Bann (east), former County Tyrone (south), and the River Foyle (west). It had an area of 801 square miles (2,075 square km), roughly triangular in shape. The former county's principal physical features are the glacially eroded Sperrin Mountains formed by ancient mica schists and rising to more than 2,000 feet (600 m). To the north, extensive plateaus of basaltic lava, covered with peat bog, overlie chalk and igneous formations. The lava escarpments are flanked by drift-covered hills and river valleys with wide deltaic terraces. To the south and east sandstones cap older rocks and meet igneous rock and intrusive granite of north Tyrone at Slieve Gallion (1,737 feet). The climate is temperate with an annual rainfall of 40–50 inches (1,000–1,250 mm).

There is evidence of prehistoric settlement in the Mesolithic site at Toome Bay on Lough (lake) Neagh and in the massive Neolithic burial chambers scattered over the Londonderry area. Raths (circular earthworks) are also numerous. The area was relatively unaffected by Viking and Norman invaders and until the 17th century had little contact with England. The shiring of Ulster was undertaken in 1585, when the area was described as the County of Coleraine. Following the defeat of the Irish earls and the confiscation of their lands in 1609, English colonization was undertaken by livery companies of the City of London and the Honourable Irish Society (founded 1610). A charter of 1613 established the county of Londonderry, which comprised the old county, O'Neill lands of Loughinsholin, and small parts of Donegal and Antrim. New towns were established and populated with Scots and English planters. Many of the original buildings of the settlement towns were destroyed in the 1641 rebellions and in the wars of the late 17th century. The early 18th century saw the mass migration of dissenting Presbyterians to New England. During World War II, Lough (inlet of the sea) Foyle assumed strategic importance as a naval base. In the 1973 administrative reorganization of Northern Ireland, the county was divided into the districts of Limavady, Londonderry, and Magherafelt, and portions of Coleraine and Cookstown districts.

Londonderry, locally and historically DERRY, Irish DOIRE, city and the larger district that encompasses it, formerly in the even larger County Londonderry, Northern Ireland. The old city and adjacent urban and rural areas were administratively merged in 1969 and later became one of Northern Ireland's 26 districts during the United Kingdom's local government reorganization in 1973. Steeped in the region's political turmoil, controversy surrounds the city's name. The British government officially refers to the city and district as Londonderry City, and since 1984 the nationalist-controlled city council has called itself the Derry City Council. Derry comes from the Irish word *doire,* meaning "oak grove."

Londonderry with the Craigavon Bridge, on the River Foyle, Northern Ireland
Roy Rainford—Robert Harding Picture Library

Centred on a hill on the west bank of the River Foyle, the old city is partially contained by well-preserved city walls (completed in 1618) 1.2 miles (2 km) in circumference. It is about 4 miles (6 km) upstream from where the Foyle widens into the broad Atlantic inlet of Lough Foyle. St. Columba established a monastery on the site in the mid-6th century, but the settlement was destroyed by Norse invaders, who reportedly burned it down seven times before 1200. Later the town served as a strategic point in the Tudor wars against the native Irish. In 1600 an English force seized Derry, demolishing Irish churches and the monastery. Shortly thereafter (in 1613) James I of England granted Derry to the citizens of London who laid out the new city, built stout walls, and brought in Protestant (both English and Scottish) settlers. The place was thereafter officially known as Londonderry. The new city was unsuccessfully besieged several times in the 17th century, particularly by the forces of James II in 1688–89. St. Columba's (Anglican) Cathedral, originally built in 1633, contains many relics of the siege of 1688–89.

The modern city's growth dates from the 1850s, when linen shirt making became important. Clothing manufacture continues to be a significant industry; other local factories process foods and manufacture chemicals and other light industrial products. Londonderry served as a naval base during World Wars I and II; its contemporary port facilities, however, are of minor importance. A civil rights campaign seeking equal rights for Roman Catholics was inaugurated in Northern Ireland in 1968, and in 1969 street violence occurred in Londonderry. Disturbances using firearms and bombs continued into the 1980s.

The district includes rolling lowlands and valleys that gradually rise to the wooded slopes of the Sperrin Mountains in the southeast. It is bordered by Limavady to the east and Strabane to the south, the Irish republic to the west, and Lough Foyle to the north. Salmon are commercially fished in the tidal portions of the River Foyle; and sheep, barley, and poultry are raised by farmers in the district. A comprehensive modernization program has resulted in extensive redevelopment within the old city; several industrial estates have also been established at the mouth of the River Foyle, along with new outlying residential areas, and a second bridge has been built across the Foyle. Area district, 148 square miles (380 square km). Pop. (1998 est.) district, 105,800.

Londonderry, Robert Stewart, 2nd marquess of: *see* Castlereagh, Robert Stewart, Viscount.

Londrina, city, northern Paraná state, southeastern Brazil. Founded in 1930 by a small

Praça Rocha Pombo, a garden square in Londrina, Braz.
Dilson Martins—EB Inc.

group of Japanese and German settlers, it rapidly became the commercial, political, and cultural centre of the state's northern pioneer zone. Its industries include the processing of coffee, cotton, rice, fruit, and livestock products, as well as paper milling and liquor distilling. A large coffee factory serves the surrounding coffee-growing district. The State University of Londrina (1971) is located in the city. Londrina is connected by rail with São Paulo, 300 miles (480 km) east, and with Curitiba, the state capital, and the Atlantic port of Paranaguá by a 300-mile (480-kilometre), two-lane highway running southeastward to the coast. Pop. (1991 prelim.) mun., 388,331.

Lone Ranger, renegade lawman in the American West, a fictional character of American radio and television programs, books, films, and comics.

In all media the Lone Ranger fictions are similar. John Reid was born in 1850 and was the sole survivor of a group of Texas Rangers who were ambushed by outlaws who killed five rangers, including his older brother, Daniel. The Indian Tonto found him and nursed him to health. Reid then donned a black mask made from his dead brother's vest, mounted his stallion, Silver, and roamed the West as the Lone Ranger to aid those in need, to fight evil, and to establish justice.

The character was created in the Lone Ranger radio program by George W. Trendle and Fran Striker. First aired on radio station WXYZ in Detroit, Mich., on Jan. 30, 1933, the radio program was carried by more than 400 American stations by the end of the decade. It was radio that made the Lone Ranger's theme song, Gioacchino Rossini's "William Tell Overture," a familiar tune in every child's repertoire, and it was radio that made "Hi-yo Silver, Away!" a familiar playground exclamation.

The Lone Ranger's first movie serial appeared in 1938. In 1949 the radio show moved to television, and the sounds were linked to images and actors who became equally familiar. Clayton Moore played the Lone Ranger for all but a few episodes, and Jay Silverheels became the embodied Tonto. The television show was syndicated for four years, then picked up by the Columbia Broadcasting System, on which it ran until 1958. The show continued to run in syndication, and in 1980 an entirely new movie, *The Legend of the Lone Ranger,* appeared.

long (Chinese dragon): *see* lung.

Long, Crawford Williamson (b. Nov. 1, 1815, Danielsville, Ga., U.S.—d. June 16, 1878, Athens, Ga.), American physician traditionally considered the first to have used ether as an anesthetic in surgery.

After serving in hospitals in New York City, Long returned to Georgia, where he set up practice in Jefferson. There he observed that persons injured in "ether frolics" (social gatherings of people who were in a playful state of ether-induced intoxication) seemed to suffer no pain, and in 1842 he painlessly removed a tumour from the neck of a patient to whom he had administered ether. He continued to use ether in other cases but did not publish any report of its use until 1849. Three years earlier William Morton, a dental surgeon, had demonstrated the use of ether in a similar type of surgery. Despite Morton's claims to the discovery and the publicity that attended his demonstration, Long's priority in actual practice is recognized.

Long, George Washington de: *see* De Long, George Washington.

Long, Huey (Pierce) (b. Aug. 30, 1893, near Winnfield, La., U.S.—d. Sept. 10, 1935, Baton Rouge, La.), flamboyant and demagogic governor of Louisiana and U.S. senator whose social reforms and radical welfare proposals were ultimately overshadowed by the unprecedented executive dictatorship that he perpetrated to ensure control of his home state.

Huey Long
UPI

In spite of an impoverished background, young Long managed to obtain enough formal schooling to pass the bar examination in 1915. He was politically ambitious and won election to the state railroad commission at age 25. In this post his calls for the equitable regulation of the state utility companies and his attacks on Standard Oil earned him widespread popularity. He ran for the Louisiana governorship in 1924 and was defeated, but in 1928 he won the governorship through the heavy support of the discontented rural districts. His picturesque if irreverent speech, fiery oratory, and unconventional buffoonery soon made him nationally famous, and he was widely known by his nickname, "Kingfish." Long made a genuine contribution with an ambitious program of public works and welfare legislation in a state whose road system and social services had been sadly neglected by the wealthy elite that had long controlled the state government. Always the champion of poor whites, he effected a free-textbook law, launched a massive and very useful program of road and bridge building, expanded state university facilities, and erected a state hospital where free treatment for all was intended. He was opposed to excessive privileges for the rich, and he financed his improvements with increased inheritance and income taxes as well as a severance tax on oil—earning him the bitter enmity of the wealthy and of the oil interests.

Long's folksy manner and sympathy for the underprivileged diverted attention from his ruthless autocratic methods. Surrounding himself with gangsterlike bodyguards, he dictated outright to members of the legislature, using intimidation if necessary. When he was about to leave office to serve in the U.S. Senate (1932), he fired the legally elected lieutenant governor and replaced him with two designated successors who would obey him from Washington. In order to fend off local challenges to his control in 1934, he effected radical changes in the Louisiana government, abolishing local government and taking personal control of all educational, police, and fire job appointments throughout the state. He achieved absolute control of the state militia, judiciary, and election and tax-assessing apparatus, while denying citizens any legal or electoral redress.

In the Senate (1932–35) he sought national power with a Share-the-Wealth program ("every man a king"), which was tempting to a depression-shocked public. Had Long been able to unite the various nationwide radical movements, a private poll taken in the spring of 1935 estimated that he would have won up to 4 million votes in the next year's presidential election, thus wielding a balance of power between the two major parties.

Long was at the height of his power when assassinated by Carl Austin Weiss, the son of a man whom he had vilified. The Long political dynasty was carried on by his brother, Earl K. Long, who served as governor (1939–40, 1948–52, 1956–60), and his son, Russell B. Long, who served in the U.S. Senate from 1948 to 1987.

BIBLIOGRAPHY. T. Harry Williams, *Huey Long* (1969, reissued 1981); William Ivy Hair, *The Kingfish and His Realm: The Life and Times of Huey P. Long* (1991).

Long Beach, city, port, Los Angeles county, California, U.S., on San Pedro Bay. Originally an Indian trading camp, the site was part of the Rancho Nieto (1784) and later of the Ranchos Los Alamitos and Cerritos. Laid out in 1881 by W.E. Willmore as Willmore City, it was promoted as a seaside resort and was incorporated (1888) and renamed for its 8.5-mile (13.5-kilometre) beach. Reincorporated as a city in 1897, it surrounds the independent city of Signal Hill.

Industrial and harbour development was stimulated by the discovery of oil in 1921 at Signal Hill, and Long Beach expanded with the post-World War II growth of the Los Angeles metropolitan area. It possesses tideland oil rights, and offshore city derricks are concealed as skyscrapers on landscaped islands. Land subsidence caused by the draining of oil pools has been contained by injections of seawater. In 1933 a severe earthquake caused widespread damage.

Connected to the Los Angeles harbour by the Cerritos Channel, Long Beach is the site of a U.S. naval station and shipyard and possesses extensive docking and storage facilities. Long Beach City College opened in 1927 and California State University at Long Beach in 1949. The historic British transatlantic liner *Queen Mary* has, since 1969, been moored in the harbour and functions as a maritime museum, convention centre, and hotel. The Long Beach Museum of Art has a permanent collection of modern art as well as changing exhibits. The city's diversified industries include the production of aircraft and ships, as well as oil refining, food processing, and marine research. Pop. (1992 est.) city, 445,405; (1990) Los Angeles–Long Beach PMSA, 8,863,164.

To make the best use of the Britannica, consult the INDEX *first*

Long Beach, island and township in Ocean county, eastern New Jersey, U.S. It lies 4–6 miles (6–10 km) offshore and shelters Barnegat Bay and Little Egg Harbor (both part of the Atlantic Intracoastal Waterway) from the ocean.

Extending 19 miles (30 km) southward from historic Barnegat Lighthouse (1858; 172 feet [52 m] high and near the scene of more than 200 shipwrecks in sailing-ship days), the narrow island includes a string of resorts, notably Loveladies (where there is a Foundation of Arts and Sciences), Harvey Cedars (Long Beach's oldest town, settled by whalers after the War of 1812), Surf City, Ship Bottom (bridged to the mainland), Brant Beach, and Beach Haven (near the southern tip), which is known for its Surflight Summer Theatre. The island is a popular place for summer cottages and art colonies and has facilities for bathing, surfing, fishing, and boating. Pop. (1980) island, 9,182; (1990) township, 3,407.

Long Beach, first nuclear-powered surface warship, launched by the U.S. Navy in 1959. Displacing 14,000 tons, the *Long Beach* was classed as a cruiser but had a substantially larger below-deck space than conventionally powered ships of the same tonnage because of the compactness of its nuclear plant. It carried guided-missile armament and antisubmarine weapons and devices and was capable of remaining at sea for as much as six months at a time.

Long Branch, city, Monmouth county, eastern New Jersey, U.S. It lies along the Atlantic Ocean, 50 miles (80 km) south of New York City. Settled in 1668 on land purchased from the Lenni Lenape Indians, it was named for its location on the Long Branch of the South Shrewsbury River. Its development as a coastal resort began in the 1780s. During the gilded Victorian Age it was frequented by many notables, including Lillie Langtry, Lillian Russell, and "Diamond Jim" Brady. It became the summer capital of U.S. presidents Ulysses S. Grant, James Garfield, and Woodrow Wilson. After Garfield was shot in Washington, D.C., a spur line was laid from the Elberon Railway Station to the porch of Francklyn Cottage, where he was taken to recover. He died there on Sept. 19, 1881.

With the establishment of textile and electronics industries and the foundation in 1933 at West Long Branch of Monmouth College, Long Branch has become a year-round residential city. Long Branch includes the communities of Elberon, North Long Branch, and West End. Inc. 1904. Pop. (1990) 28,658.

long-distance running, in track and field (athletics), races ranging from 5,000 m through 10,000, 20,000, 25,000, and 30,000 m and up to the marathon (*q.v.*) at 26 miles, 385 yards, as well as cross-country for men. Before the second half of the 20th century, races were run in English-speaking countries at the roughly equivalent distances of 3, 6, 10, and 15 miles.

Like the middle-distance races, long-distance races are run at a strategic pace, but less seldom than in the former races is a final spurt needed by the winning racer. Women rarely ran in races beyond 3,000 metres until the second half of the 20th century, but they became more frequent competitors in the marathon from the 1970s on. Some middle-distance runners also succeeded as long-distance runners. For world records, *see* Sporting Record: *Athletics*. *See also* Olympic Games.

long-eared bat, also called LUMP-NOSED BAT, or BIG-EARED BAT (*Plecotus*), any of five

Long-eared bat (*Plecotus phyllotis*)
Roger W. Barbour

species of small, usually colony-dwelling bats of the family Vespertilionidae. Long-eared bats are found in the Old World and in North America. They are approximately 5–7 cm (2–3 inches) long without the 3.5–5.5-centimetre (1.4–2.2-inch) tail and weigh 5–20 g (1/6–2/3 ounce). They have soft, brown fur, and some species have glandular lumps on the muzzle. The ears, which may be 4 cm (1.6 inches) long, are folded when the bats rest. Long-eared bats fly slowly and frequently hover to pick insects from leaves or walls. They hibernate in winter.

long-eared owl (*Asio otus*), nocturnal bird of prey of the family Strigidae (order Strigiformes). Common to woodlands of northern Europe and America, it is recognized by its long ear tufts. Long-eared owls are brownish above, mottled and streaked. They have white underparts with dark streaks. These owls are

Long-eared owl (*Asio otus*)
Schrempp—Annan Photo Features

about 30 cm (about 1 foot) long. They eat mice, birds, fish, frogs, and insects.

long-faced style of Buli (African art): *see* Buli style.

long-horned beetle, also called LONGICORN, or WOOD-BORING BEETLE, any member of the approximately 25,000 species of the insect family Cerambycidae (order Coleoptera). These beetles occur throughout the world but are most numerous in the tropics. They range in size from 2 to 152 mm (less than 1/8 to about 6 inches); the length may be double or triple those sizes when the antennae are included.

Many adults (*e.g., Clytus arietes* of Europe) visit flowers and mimic wasps with their yellow, black, and orange coloration and patterns. Some tropical species of *Clytus* mimic ants. The African *Pterognatha gigas* resembles a patch of moss or lichen with a few strands sticking out (its antennae).

(Top) Elderberry longhorn (*Desmocerus palliatus*), (bottom) prionid beetle (*Derobrachus*)
(Top) Mary W. Ferguson, (bottom) Stephen Collins

The yellowish or white larvae are often known as roundheaded borers because the front part of the plump larva is expanded to give it a rounded appearance. The strong jaws of the larvae bore through trees for two years or more, destroying timber. When ready to pupate the larva bores a tunnel to the outside, pupates within the tree, and as a new adult uses this tunnel as its exit. The long-horned beetle family is divided into several subfamilies, including the following:

The prionids (subfamily Prioninae) have leathery, brownish wing covers (elytra), and the margins of the prothorax (region behind the head) are toothlike and expanded laterally. Included in this group is the pine-living genus *Parandra* (sometimes separated into the family Spondylidae) and the broad-necked prionus (*Prionus laticollis*), whose larvae live in grape, apple, poplar, and other tree roots.

The cerambycids (subfamily Cerambycinae) include the ribbed pine borer (*Rhagium cineatum*), which has a narrow thorax with a spine on each side and three lengthwise ridges on its wing covers. It lives in pine trees during the larval stage.

The lepturids (subfamily Lepturinae) include the elderberry longhorn (*Desmocerus palliatus*), also called the cloaked knotty-horn beetle because it looks as if it has a yellow cloak on its shoulders and has knotted antennae. It feeds on leaves and flowers of the elderberry bush, and its larvae bore into the pithy stems.

The lamiids (subfamily Lamiinae) include the sawyer (*Monochamus*), a gray-brown beetle about 30 mm (1.2 inches) long, not including the long antennae. The larvae live in pines and firs and bore tunnels up to 10 mm (0.3 inch) in diameter. The roundheaded apple tree borer (*Saperda candida*) is one of the worst apple pests. The twig girdler (*Oncideres cingulata*) deposits eggs in twigs and then girdles, or cuts, a groove around the twig. Eventually the twig dies and breaks off; the larvae develop inside the dead twig.

long-horned grasshopper, any member of the cricket-like orthopteran insect family Tet-

Long-horned grasshopper (*Tettigonia viridissima*)
S.C. Bisserot

tigoniidae (about 3,000 species), distinguished from the true cricket (family Gryllidae) by hearing organs located on the front legs, hairlike antennae as long as or longer in length than the body, a sword-shaped ovipositor (in females) for laying eggs, and wing covers that differ in shape. Most long-horned grasshoppers spend the winter in the egg stage. When the male rubs his wing covers together, he produces a song, one song being characteristic for each species.

The family Tettigoniidae includes the katydid, the meadow grasshopper, the cone-headed grasshopper, and the shield-backed grasshopper (*qq.v.*). All members of this family, with the exception of the shield-backed grasshopper, are green in colour, have long wings, and inhabit trees, bushes, or shrubs. The shield-backed grasshopper subfamily, which includes the Mormon and coulee crickets, is brown or gray in colour and lives on the ground or in low vegetation; most species are wingless or have reduced wings.

Long Island, island that comprises the southeasternmost part of New York state, U.S. The island lies roughly parallel to the south shore of Connecticut, from which it is separated on the north by Long Island Sound. Long Island's western end forms part of the harbour of New York City. The island has four counties; from west to east they are Kings, Queens, Nassau, and Suffolk.

Kings County is also the New York City borough of Brooklyn, and Queens County is the borough of Queens. The western third of Long Island is almost entirely given over to the urban and suburban sprawl extending from New York City, but the island's eastern two-thirds are still partly rural in character and are largely composed of flat, fertile farmlands and long, sandy beaches.

Long Island extends 118 miles (190 km) east-northeast from the mouth of the Hudson River. It is from 12 to 23 miles (19 to 37 km) wide and has an area of 1,723 square miles (4,463 square km). Its eastern end is divided into two narrow peninsulas; the northern peninsula is about 25 miles (40 km) long and culminates in Orient Point, while the southern peninsula is about 40 miles (64 km) long and ends in Montauk Point, Long Island's eastern extremity. Bays along the island's northern shore include Flushing, Little Neck, Manhasset, Cold Spring, Huntington, Smithtown, and Port Jefferson. Long Island's southern shore is lined by an almost continuous series of sandbars and sand spits that shelter several bays, including Jamaica Bay (*q.v.*), from the ocean. This ribbon of sand widens at certain points to form little islands, several of which have become popular bathing beaches. Rockaway Beach, Long Beach, Jones Beach, and Oak Island Beach derive their existence from it. The long peninsula called Fire Island (*q.v.*), or Great South Beach, forms part of the Fire Island National Seashore.

The island, until settled by Europeans, was inhabited by Indians, generally of Delaware stock. It was originally part of the territory administered by the Plymouth Company, and in 1635 its title was presumably conveyed to the earl of Stirling (Sir William Alexander) by Charles I. Despite English claims, the island later became part of the territory claimed by the Dutch West India Company. Breuckelen (Brooklyn), Amersfort (Flatlands), Midwout (Flatbush), and Nieuw Utrecht (New Utrecht) were established by the company between 1636 and 1660. Towns founded by English settlers included Southampton (1640), Southold (1640), Hempstead (1644), Gravesend (1645), Flushing (1645), Newtown (1655), and Jamaica (1656). By the Treaty of Hartford (1650) between New Netherlands and the United Colonies of New England, a demarcation line was drawn from Oyster Bay to the ocean, recognizing the island as Dutch to the west and English to the east.

In March 1664 Long Island was part of the area given to the duke of York by Charles II, and in August the English conquest of New Amsterdam and the Dutch territory was effected. Long Island became a part of Yorkshire and was governed by laws that were promulgated at Hempstead in March 1665. The county system was introduced in 1683 with the creation of Suffolk, Queens, and Kings counties. During the American Revolution, Long Island was a hotbed of activity by both Loyalists and Patriots, and its coastal area was raided by privateers and military units. The island was a major source of food and wood during the war, and the Battle of Long Island was the first engagement in the campaign of 1776.

The completion of the Long Island Rail Road to Greenport in 1844 enabled the island to become a major market-gardening centre whose produce could be shipped to New York City. Fishing, whaling, and oystering also remained important, but during the second half of the 19th century the island became an attractive watering place for New York's wealthy elite. Great estates and mansions were built along the north shore, and along the south shore eastward from New York City, summer hotels that attracted thousands of summer vacationers were constructed. Coney Island, Jones Beach, and the many other beaches, harbours, yacht basins, golf courses, and parklands on the island now make it a playground for millions of visitors each summer.

New York City's continual growth during the 20th century caused Long Island's population to climb precipitately; Nassau and Suffolk counties, respectively, doubled and quadrupled their populations between 1950 and 1970, although they subsequently stabilized. Hundreds of thousands of Long Islanders commute to work in New York City each day, but the island has itself become a major manufacturing centre, with the making of aircraft and electrical equipment being especially significant industries. Long Island is served on both its north and south shores and through the central part of the island by the Long Island Rail Road, which carries more commuters than any other railroad in the country. A highly developed and efficient system of express highways connects the island to Manhattan and the other boroughs of New York City through the use of several major bridges and tunnels carrying automobile and subway traffic. Pop. (1990) 6,861,474.

Long Island, Battle of (Aug. 27, 1776), in U.S. War of Independence, successful British action in Brooklyn, N.Y., against the American Continental Army. The battle initiated the British campaign of 1776 to seize control of New York and thereby isolate New England from the rest of the colonies. After the British evacuation from Boston in March, the British general Lord Howe moved to occupy New York City under the protection of a British fleet that commanded the surrounding waters. To protect his left flank, the defending American general, George Washington, stationed one-third of his troops (numbering no more than 20,000 trained soldiers) on the Long Island side of the East River, where they erected fortifications.

From his encampment on Staten Island, Howe attacked Washington's isolated wing by landing 20,000 men at Gravesend Bay, Long Island, on August 22. After four days' reconnaissance, Howe drove the Americans back and inflicted heavy losses (1,200 American prisoners were taken, and about 400 men on each side were killed or wounded). Howe might have captured Washington's entire force on Long Island at this point, but instead he elected to lay siege. The following week Washington took advantage of this delay to retreat across the river to Manhattan, a successful move that helped repair low American morale.

Long Island Rail Road Company, American railroad on Long Island, N.Y., and one of the few in the world still operating under its original name. Incorporated in 1834, it opened its main line to Greenport, at the eastern end of Long Island, in 1844. Over the years it acquired other Long Island railroads: the North Shore Branch in 1921, a line to Rockaway Beach in 1922, the New York, Brooklyn, and Manhattan Beach Railway in 1925, and the Glendale and East River Railroad in 1928.

Early in the century the Pennsylvania Railroad Company gained control of the Long Island, and it operated out of Pennsylvania Station in Manhattan. In 1966 the Pennsylvania sold it to the state of New York, and since 1968 it has been run by the state's Metropolitan Transportation Authority (MTA).

The railroad has the distinction of having a number of railway firsts: the first railroad in the world to operate a steel-car fleet (1905), the first to discard all wooden passenger equipment (1927), and the first steam road to make practical use of electricity for power (1905). It also is the only American railroad in its class the passenger revenue of which exceeds its freight revenue.

Long Island Sound, semienclosed arm of the North Atlantic Ocean, lying between the New York–Connecticut (U.S.) shore to the north and Long Island to the south. Covering 1,180 square miles (3,056 square km), it is 90 miles (145 km) long and 3–20 miles (5–32 km) wide and is limited on the east by Orient Point (Long Island) and Plum, Gull, and Fishers islands and on the west by the narrow Throgs Neck, which leads into Upper New York Bay via the East River. Two glacial advances have deepened the sound's water to more than 100 feet (30 m); near its eastern limits it reaches a maximum depth of 330 feet (100 m). The mean tidal range is from less than 3 feet (1 m) in its eastern reaches to more than 6 feet (about 2 m) in the west. The sound's drainage basin is nearly 13 times its area, and the annual volume of incoming fresh water is about 35 percent of the total. Most of the drainage of the Housatonic, Connecticut, and Thames rivers flows out rapidly through the open eastern end of the sound and thus has little effect on the salinity. The sound's waters are rich in plankton and bottom-dwelling organisms, making it favourable for young fish but deterring most commercially valuable fish. Except for menhaden processed for fish meal, the sound alone does not support an important fishery. The major sport fishing is for weakfish and bluefish. Lobsters, crabs, and clams are caught along the Connecticut shores, and oyster farms are found from Bridgeport, Conn., eastward. The sound is part of the Atlantic Intracoastal Waterway, and around its shores are many residential communities and yachting resorts.

long jump, also called BROAD JUMP, track-and-field sport consisting of a horizontal jump for distance. It was formerly performed from both standing and running starts, as separate events, but the standing long jump is no longer included in major competitions. The running long jump was an event in the Olympic Games of 708 BC.

Standard equipment for the long jump includes a runway at least 40 m (131 feet) in length with no outer limit, a takeoff board planted level with the surface at least 1 m (3 feet) from the end of the runway, and a sand-filled landing area at least 2.75 × 10 m (9 × 33 feet).

The jumper usually begins his approach run about 30 m (100 feet) from the takeoff board and accelerates to reach maximum speed at takeoff while gauging his stride to arrive with one foot on and as near as possible to the edge of the board. If a contestant steps beyond the edge (scratch line), his jump is disallowed; if he leaps from too far behind the line, he loses valuable distance.

The most commonly used techniques in flight are the tuck, in which the knees are brought up toward the chest, and the hitch kick, which is in effect a continuation of the run in the air. The legs are brought together for landing, and, since the length of the jump is measured from the edge of the takeoff board to the nearest mark in the landing area surface made by any part of the body, the jumper attempts to fall forward.

In international competition the eight contestants who make the longest jumps in three preliminary attempts qualify to make three final attempts. The winner is the one who makes the single longest jump in the final competition. In 1935 Jesse Owens of the United States set a record of 8.13 m (26.6 feet) that was not broken until 1960. For world records, *see* Sporting Record: *Athletics*. *See also* Olympic Games.

Long Lake (Saskatchewan, Canada): *see* Last Mountain Lake.

long-legged fly, any insect of the family Dolichopodidae (order Diptera). These tiny, metallic blue or green flies prey on smaller insects and are found around damp, marshy places.

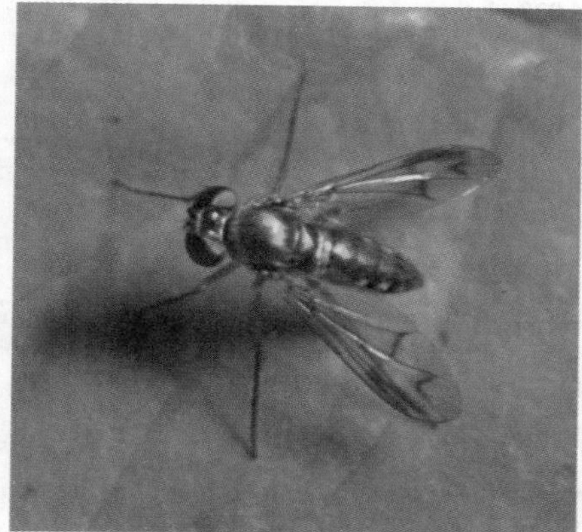

Long-legged fly (*Condylostylus sipho*)
Richard Parker

The male has conspicuous genitalia at the end of the abdomen; cuplike structures on his legs go over the female's eyes during mating. Many species perform unusual mating dances. The elongated larvae have almost no external head structure; they are found in mud, decaying vegetation, and water.

Long March (1934–35), the 6,000-mile (10,000-kilometre) historic trek of the Chinese Communists, which resulted in the relocation of the Communist revolutionary base from Southeast China to Northwest China and in the emergence of Mao Zedong as the undisputed party leader. Fighting Nationalist forces under Chiang Kai-shek throughout their journey, the Communist troops crossed 18 mountain ranges and 24 rivers to reach the northwestern province of Shensi. The heroism attributed to the Long March inspired many young Chinese to join the Chinese Communist Party during the late 1930s and early 1940s.

Routes of the Long March, 1934–35
Adapted from *An Outline History of China*. Joint Publishing Co., Hong Kong, in association with China Books and Periodicals, Inc., San Francisco

Between 1930 and 1934 Chiang Kai-shek launched a series of five military encirclement campaigns against the Chinese Communists in an attempt to annihilate their base area (the Kiangsi Soviet) on the Kiangsi–Fukien border in southeastern China. The Communists successfully fought off the first four campaigns using tactics of mobile infiltration and guerrilla warfare developed by Mao. In the fifth campaign Chiang mustered about 700,000 troops and established a series of cement blockhouses around the Communist positions. The Chinese Communist Central Committee, which had removed Mao from the leadership early in 1934, abandoned his guerrilla warfare strategy and used regular positional warfare tactics against the better-armed and more numerous Nationalist forces. As a result the Communist forces suffered heavy losses and were nearly crushed.

On Oct. 15, 1934, the remaining 85,000 troops, 15,000 administrative personnel, and 35 women broke through the Nationalist lines at their weakest points and fled westward. Mao, at the time of the Communists' departure, was not in control of events; Zhu De was the commander of the army, and Zhou Enlai was the political commissar of the party. The first three months of the march were disastrous for the Communists: subjected to constant bombardment from Chiang's air force and repeated attacks from his ground troops, they lost more than half of their army. Morale was low when they arrived in Tsun-i, in the southwestern province of Kweichow, but at a conference in Tsun-i in January 1935 Mao was able to gather enough support to establish his dominance of the party.

The march then headed toward Northwest China, near the safety of the Soviet border and close to the territory occupied by the Japanese in northeastern China. In June 1935 a force under Chang Kuo-t'ao, a longtime Communist leader, joined the main army, and at Mao-erh-kai in western Szechwan a power struggle ensued between Mao and Chang. Chang's group, accompanied by Zhu De, headed toward the extreme southwestern part of China. The main body under Mao proceeded toward northern Shensi, where the Communist leaders Gao Gang and Liu Zhidan had built up another Soviet area. Mao arrived at this destination in October 1935 along with only about 8,000 survivors. Along the route some Communists had left the march to mobilize the peasantry; but most of the missing had been eliminated by fighting, disease, and starvation. Among the missing were Mao's two small children and his younger brother, Mao Zetan.

Mao's troops joined the local Red Army contingent of 7,000 men, and other units (including that of Zhu De) swelled their total strength by late 1936 to about 30,000 troops. In December 1936 the Communists moved to the nearby district of Yen-an in Shensi, where they remained throughout the war with the Japanese. The Long March decisively established Mao's leadership of the Chinese Communist Party, and it enabled the embattled Communists to reach a base area beyond the direct control of the Nationalists. From their base at Yen-an the Communists grew in strength and eventually defeated the Nationalists in the struggle to control mainland China.

long moss (plant): *see* Spanish moss.

Long Mountains (Norway): *see* Langfjellet.

Long Parliament, session of the English Parliament summoned in November 1640 by King Charles I; it has been so named to distinguish it from the Short Parliament of April–May 1640. The duration of the Long Parliament has been held to have extended either until April 1653, when its remaining members were forcibly ejected by the Cromwellian army, or until March 1660, when its members, finally restored, passed an act for its dissolution. Legally the act of 1660 was as invalid as the ejection of 1653, because it lacked royal assent. An act of the Convention Parliament of April–December 1660 can be said to have finally dissolved the Long Parliament, though the Convention was itself not a lawful parliament because it had not been summoned by the king; its acts were reinforced by later legislation.

Charles I summoned both the Short and Long Parliaments in 1640 because only the Parliament could raise the money he needed to wage the second Bishops' War against the Scots, who were resisting his attempts to impose episcopacy on them. Because of disputes he dismissed the Short Parliament hastily; the Scots then invaded northern England, and, in order to buy them off, a fresh recourse to Parliament was unavoidable. The Long Parliament proved much more intransigent than the Short, however. During its first nine months it brought down the king's advisers, swept away the machinery of conciliar government developed by the Tudors and early Stuarts, made frequent sessions of Parliament a statutory necessity, and passed an act forbidding its own dissolution without its members' consent. Tension between the king and Parliament steadily increased, notably upon Charles' abortive attempt to arrest five of its members in January 1642, and the Civil War broke out later that year. After the king was finally defeated in the field (1646), the army exercised political power, and in December 1648 Colonel Thomas Pride expelled all but about 60 members of the Long Parliament ("Pride's Purge"). The surviving group, known to historians as the Rump, brought Charles I to trial and execution in 1649; it was forcibly ejected in 1653. After the Protectorate of Oliver Cromwell, the Rump was restored in May 1659 and expelled in October. It was reestablished in December 1659, and, after those excluded in 1648 had joined it, it dissolved itself; the newly elected Convention Parliament then opened negotiations for the restoration of Charles II.

long-period variable star, any intrinsically variable star whose light fluctuations are fairly regular and require many months or several years to complete one cycle. They are, without exception, red giant and supergiant stars. Those in one fairly distinct group with periods of about 200 days belong generally to the larger class of stars called Population II (older stars found mainly in the galactic core and halo). Another group, that of variables with periods of a year or more, mostly belong to Population I (younger stars found generally in the spiral arms of a galaxy).

A long-period variable may change a hundredfold in brightness, but the variation in energy output is much smaller because at the low temperature of such a star most energy is released at infrared wavelengths rather than as light. Long-period variables are sometimes called Mira stars, after Mira Ceti (Omicron Ceti) in the constellation Cetus, the first star recognized to be variable.

Long Point, peninsula in Lake Erie, Norfolk county, southern Ontario, Canada. It lies about 45 miles (70 km) southwest of Port Colborne, which is the Lake Erie terminus of the Welland Canal. Formerly an island separated from the mainland by a small channel, it is now a narrow peninsula jutting nearly 20 miles (32 km) eastward into the lake. Long Point consists mainly of uninhabited sand dunes, but Long Point Provincial Park (356 acres [144 hectares]) is often frequented by hunters, campers, and fishermen attracted to the peninsula because of its wildlife. Despite the peninsula's having been the site of a lighthouse since 1830, numerous shipwrecks have occurred along its shoals.

Long Range Mountains, highest range on the island of Newfoundland, Canada, extending about 250 miles (400 km) northward from Cape Ray along the western shore. The mountains have an average elevation of nearly 2,200 feet (670 m) and a maximum height of 2,670 feet (814 m) in the Lewis Hills, southwest of Corner Brook. Their relatively uniform summits represent the remnants of an ancient peneplain that has undergone periods of uplift and erosion. Gros Morne (2,644 feet), northeast of Bonne Bay, is the central mountain feature of the 750-square-mile (1,942-square-kilometre) Gros Morne National Park, with its numerous lakes, fjords, and wooded valleys and coast. The Humber is the only major river that rises in the range, and it traverses the mountains in a semicircular course to the west coast. The mountains are densely forested and support large pulp- and paper-milling operations such as the one in Corner Brook. The southern section around Table Mountain (1,699 feet [518 m]) is notorious for violent winds (measured at up to 120 miles [193 km] per hour) funneled from the open sea.

long-range navigation: *see* loran.

Long Xuyen, city, southern Vietnam. It is located on the west bank of the Hau Giang (Bassac) River, a channel of the Mekong. Fishing, the breeding of fish, and rice and fruit growing are major occupations near Long Xuyen. The city is connected by road to Can Tho and Chau Doc. Pop. (1992 est.) 132,681.

Longabaugh, Harry: *see* Sundance Kid.

longan, also spelled LUNGAN (*Euphoria longana*), tropical fruit tree, of the soapberry family (Sapindaceae), native to Asia and introduced into other warm regions of the world. The tree grows to 9–12 m (30–40 feet). The flowers are small and yellowish white. The almost spherical, yellowish brown, edible fruit, which is also called longan, has a white and juicy pulp.

Longan (*Euphoria longana*)
Douglas David Dawn

longbow, bow commonly 6 feet (1.8 m) tall and the predominant missile weapon of the English in the Hundred Years' War and on into the 16th century. It was probably of Welsh origin. The best longbows were made of yew, might require a force of 100 pounds (45 kg) to draw, and shot arrows a cloth yard (about 37 inches, or 94 cm) long, with an effective range of about 200 yards (180 m). The longbow played an important role in the battles of Crécy, Poitiers, and Agincourt.

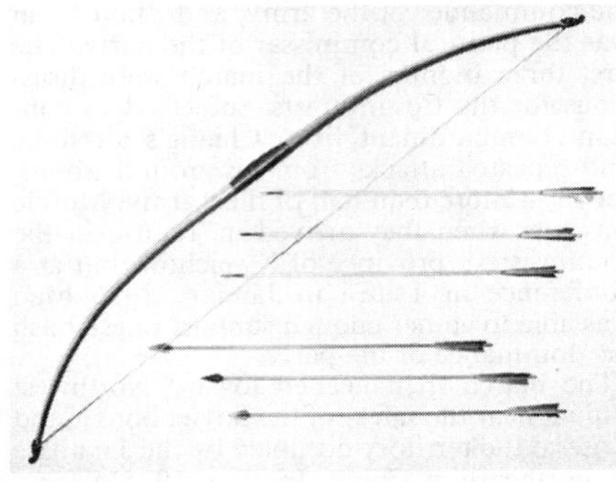

Longbow and arrows, English, 14th century (reproduction)
By courtesy of the West Point Museum Collections, United States Military Academy

longcase clock, also called GRANDFATHER CLOCK, tall pendulum clock enclosed in a wooden case that stands upon the floor and is typically from 6 to 7.5 feet (1.8 to 2.3 m) in height. The first longcase clocks were referred to as coffin clocks, because of their elongated style and door opening in front. Later, the name grandfather clock became popular after the popular song "My Grandfather's Clock," written in 1876 by Henry Clay Work. The first longcase clocks featured a classical architectural appearance, but a variety of styles enjoyed popularity over the years.

Longchamp, William (d. Jan. 31, 1197, Poitiers, France), ecclesiastical statesman who governed England in 1190–91, while King Richard I (reigned 1189–99) was away from the kingdom during the Third Crusade.

Of Norman origin, Longchamp was made chancellor of England and bishop of Ely when Richard ascended the throne. After Richard's departure on Crusade, he became joint justiciar with Hugh de Puiset, bishop of Durham (March 1190). Longchamp soon drove Hugh from office, and in June 1190 he was appointed papal legate by Pope Clement III. Although he was able and completely loyal to Richard, Longchamp's overbearing manner and anti-English prejudices earned him the hostility of the English people. Hoping to profit by this situation, Richard's brother John (later King John, 1199–1216) rebelled and forced Longchamp to flee to France. Early in 1193 Longchamp visited Richard, who was being held prisoner in Germany, and arranged for the king to be ransomed. John's rebellion collapsed upon Richard's return to England (March 1194). Richard retained Longchamp as chancellor and employed him on diplomatic missions.

Longden, Johnny, byname of JOHN ERIC LONGDEN (b. Feb. 14, 1907, Wakefield, Yorkshire, Eng.—d. Feb. 14, 2003, Banning, Calif., U.S.), British-born American jockey who, in a career of 40 years (1927–66), established a world record in Thoroughbred racing with 6,032 victories (some sources give 6,026). This mark was surpassed in 1970 by Willie Shoemaker. On May 15, 1952, Longden became the first jockey in the United States to ride 4,000 winners and the second in the world to do so. (Two years earlier, Gordon Richards of England achieved that feat.) On Feb. 28, 1957, Longden became the first to ride 5,000 winners.

Longden emigrated with his family from England to Canada in 1912, and he began his racing career in Utah in 1927. In 1943 he rode Count Fleet to victory in the Triple Crown events of U.S. Thoroughbred racing (the Kentucky Derby, the Preakness Stakes, and the Belmont Stakes). For three seasons (1938 and 1947–48) he led American jockeys in races won. After his retirement from riding, he became a Thoroughbred trainer and breeder. One of his horses, Majestic Prince, won the Kentucky Derby in 1969.

Longfellow, Henry Wadsworth (b. Feb. 27, 1807, Portland, Mass. [now in Maine], U.S.—d. March 24, 1882, Cambridge, Mass.), the most popular American poet in the 19th century.

Longfellow attended private schools and the Portland Academy. He graduated from Bowdoin College in 1825. At college he was attracted especially to Sir Walter Scott's romances and Washington Irving's *Sketch Book,* and his verses appeared in national magazines. He was so fluent in translating that on graduation he was offered a professorship in modern languages provided that he would first study in Europe.

On the continent he learned French, Spanish, and Italian but refused to settle down to a regimen of scholarship at any university. In 1829 he returned to the United States to be a professor and librarian at Bowdoin. He wrote and edited textbooks, translated poetry and prose, and wrote essays on French, Spanish, and Italian literature, but he felt isolated. When he was offered a professorship at Harvard, with another opportunity to go abroad, he accepted and set forth for Germany in 1835. On this trip he visited England, Sweden, and The Netherlands. In 1835, saddened by the death of his first wife, whom he had married in 1831, he settled at Heidelberg,

Longfellow
Historical Pictures Service, Chicago

where he fell under the influence of German Romanticism.

In 1836 Longfellow returned to Harvard and settled in the famous Craigie House, which was later given to him as a wedding present when he remarried in 1843. His travel sketches, *Outre-Mer* (1835), did not succeed. In 1839 he published *Voices of the Night,* which contained the poems "Hymn to the Night," "The Psalm of Life," and "The Light of the Stars" and achieved immediate popularity. That same year Longfellow published *Hyperion,* a romantic novel idealizing his European travels. In 1841 his *Ballads and Other Poems,* containing such favourites as "The Wreck of the Hesperus" and "The Village Blacksmith," swept the nation. The antislavery sentiments he expressed in *Poems on Slavery* (1842), however, lacked the humanity and power of John Greenleaf Whittier's denunciations on the same theme. Longfellow was more at home in *Evangeline* (1847), a narrative poem that reached almost every literate home in the United States. It is a sentimental tale of two lovers separated when British soldiers expel the Acadians (French colonists) from what is now Nova Scotia. The lovers, Evangeline and Gabriel, are reunited years later as Gabriel is dying.

Longfellow presided over Harvard's modern-language program for 18 years and then left teaching in 1854. In 1855, using Henry Rowe Schoolcraft's two books on the Indian tribes of North America as the base and the trochaic metrics of the Finnish epic *Kalevala* as his medium, he fashioned *The Song of Hiawatha* (1855). Its appeal to the public was immediate. Hiawatha is an Ojibwa Indian who, after various mythic feats, becomes his people's leader and marries Minnehaha before departing for the Isles of the Blessed. Both the poem and its singsong metre have been frequent objects of parody.

Longfellow's long poem *The Courtship of Miles Standish* (1858) was another great popular success. But the death in 1861 of his second wife after she accidentally set her dress on fire plunged him into melancholy. Driven by the need for spiritual relief, he translated the *Divine Comedy of Dante Alighieri,* producing one of the most notable translations to that time, and wrote six sonnets on Dante that are among his finest poems.

The *Tales of a Wayside Inn,* modeled roughly on Geoffrey Chaucer's *Canterbury Tales* and published in 1863, reveals his narrative gift. The first poem, "Paul Revere's Ride," became a national favourite. Written in anapestic tetrameter meant to suggest the galloping of a horse, this folk ballad recalls a hero of the American Revolution and his famous "midnight ride" to warn the Americans about the impending British raid on Concord, Mass. Though its account of Revere's ride is historically inaccurate, the poem created an American legend. Longfellow published in 1872 what he intended to be his masterpiece, *Christus: A Mystery,* a trilogy dealing with Christianity from its beginning. He followed this work with two fragmentary dramatic poems, "Judas Maccabaeus" and "Michael Angelo." But his genius was not dramatic, as he had demonstrated earlier in *The Spanish Student* (1843). Long after his death in 1882, however, these neglected later works were seen to contain some of his most effective writing.

During his lifetime Longfellow was loved and admired both at home and abroad. In 1884 he was honoured by the placing of a memorial bust in Poets' Corner of Westminster Abbey in London, the first American to be so recognized. Sweetness, gentleness, simplicity, and a romantic vision shaded by melancholy are the characteristic features of Longfellow's poetry. He possessed great metrical skill, but he failed to capture the American spirit like his great contemporary Walt Whitman, and his work generally lacks emotional depth and imaginative power. Some years after Longfellow's death a violent reaction set in against his verse as critics dismissed his conventional high-minded sentiments and the gentle strain of Romanticism that he had made so popular. This harsh critical assessment, which tried to reduce him to the status of a mere hearthside rhymer, was perhaps as unbalanced as the adulation he had received during his lifetime. Some of Longfellow's sonnets and other lyrics are still among the finest in American poetry, and *Hiawatha,* "The Wreck of the Hesperus," *Evangeline,* and "Paul Revere's Ride" have become inseparable parts of the American heritage. Longfellow's immense popularity helped raise the status of poetry in his country, and he played an important part in bringing European cultural traditions to American audiences.

BIBLIOGRAPHY. Edward Wagenknecht, *Longfellow: A Full-Length Portrait* (1955), and *Henry Wadsworth Longfellow: His Poetry and Prose* (1986); Cecil Brown Williams, *Henry Wadsworth Longfellow* (1964); Newton Arvin, *Longfellow: His Life and Work* (1963, reprinted 1977).

Longfellow-Evangeline State Commemorative Area, historic site just north of St. Martinville, in St. Martin's parish, southern Louisiana, U.S. The site lies on Bayou Teche, southwest of Baton Rouge. Established in 1934, it occupies an area of 157 acres (64 hectares). Its chief feature is Acadian House Museum, which is believed to have been the home of Louis Arceneaux after he was exiled from Nova Scotia. Arceneaux served as the prototype of Evangeline's lover, Gabriel, in Henry Wadsworth Longfellow's poem *Evangeline* (1847). Built in 1765 of hand-hewn timbers, the three-story cottage and adjoining kitchen have been completely restored. Another building houses the Acadian Craft Shop.

Longford, Irish AN LONGFORT, county in the province of Leinster, central Ireland. It is bounded by Counties Leitrim and Cavan to the northwest and northeast, respectively, by Westmeath on the southeast, and by Roscommon on the west. The main features of drainage are the valleys of the Rivers Shannon, Erne, and Inny and Loughs (lakes) Gowna and Ree. The surface of the county, generally a part of lowland Ireland, rises from the Shannon to 200–400 feet (60–120 m), but there are isolated hills and ranges. The lowland is thickly plastered with glacial drifts and has large areas of bog.

Longford, whose early name was Annaly, or Anale, was a principality of the O'Farrells and was originally part of the county of Meath. In the 12th century it was granted by Henry II to Hugh de Lacy, who started an English colony there. On the division of Meath into two counties in 1543, Annaly was included in Westmeath. By 1569 it was a shire under the name of Longford.

One-tenth of the county's farmland is given to crops, mainly oats and potatoes. Most farms occupy less than 30 acres (12 hectares), and their main concern is the pasturing of cattle, chiefly for export to the richer and larger farms of County Meath. Some dairying is carried on. One-quarter of the county's population lives in towns, of which the largest is Longford, the county seat. Area 403 square miles (1,044 square km). Pop. (1991) 30,296.

longhair, also called PERSIAN, breed of domestic cat noted for its long, soft, flowing coat. Long-haired cats were originally known as Persians, or Angoras. These names were later discarded in favour of the name longhair, although the cats are still commonly called Persians in the United States. The longhair, a medium-sized or large cat with a cobby (stocky), short-legged body, has a broad, round head, a snub nose, and a short, heavily haired tail. The large, round eyes may be blue, orange, golden, green, or copper-coloured, depending on the colour of the cat. The soft, finely textured coat forms a heavy ruff about the neck.

The longhair is bred in a number of colour varieties. The solid, or self, colours are white, black, blue, red, and cream. Patterned coats include shaded silver and black (smoke); silver, brown, blue, or red with darker markings (tabby); white finely ticked with black (chinchilla); cream, red, and black (tortoiseshell); calico, or tortoiseshell and white; blue-gray and cream intermingled (blue cream); and bicoloured. The colours of tortoiseshells, calicos, and blue creams are genetically linked with the sex of the cat. Almost all are females, and most of the few males are sterile. Blue-eyed white cats may be deaf.

White longhair
John Gajda

Longhairs with Siamese markings (*i.e.,* pale body and dark face, ears, legs, and tail) are Himalayans, or colourpoints. Similarly marked longhairs with white paws are called Birmans. Peke-faced longhairs have short, pushed-in, Pekingese-like faces.

Longhair cats, although generally considered more languorous than short-haired cats, are, like shorthairs, noted for playfulness, affection, and the ability to defend themselves if necessary.

The Maine coon cat, or Maine cat, named in the mistaken belief that it is part raccoon and part cat, is a type of long-haired cat found in the New England region of the United States. It is large, generally aggressive, and longer in the muzzle and body than the longhair but has a shorter, less heavy coat. It may be any of a variety of colours.

Longhena, Baldassare (b. 1598, Venice [Italy]—d. 1682, Venice), major Venetian architect of the 17th century.

Longhena was a pupil of Vincenzo Scamozzi and completed Scamozzi's Procuratie Nuove (1584–1640) in the Piazza San Marco in Venice. Among his churches are the cathedral at Chioggia (1624–47), Santa Maria degli Scalzi, Venice (1656–80), with the facade by Giuseppe Sardi, and the facade of the Chiesa dell'Ospedaletto, near SS. Giovanni e Paolo (1670–78). His two famous palaces, both on the Grand Canal, are the Palazzo Pesaro (now the Museum Correr; 1659–1710) and the Palazzo Rezzonico (1660s–1752/56; top floor by G. Massari). Longhena's staircase in the Monastery of San Giorgio Maggiore (1643–45), where two parallel flights of stairs join a common landing, became a fundamental design elaborated in the rest of Italy and Europe.

Longhena's masterpiece, the Church of Santa Maria della Salute (1631/32–1687) at the entrance to the Grand Canal in Venice, was commissioned by the republic in thanksgiving to God for deliverance from the plague of 1630. Longhena's unique design called for an octagonal church with a huge dome; sculptured figures standing on spirals act as its buttresses. The columns and arches are placed so as to guide the visitor's eyes to the chapels and other units of design,

Sta. Maria della Salute, Venice, by Longhena
SCALA—Art Resource/EB Inc.

almost as if it were a theatre, and Longhena has been credited with founding this type of scenographic architecture of the 18th century.

Longhi FAMILY, also spelled LONGO: *see* Lunghi family.

Longhi, Alessandro (b. June 12, 1733, Venice—d. 1813, Venice), painter, etcher, and biographer of Venetian artists, the most important Venetian portrait painter of his day.

The son of the painter Pietro Longhi, he was given his first training by his father, who quite soon put him to study under the portrait painter Giuseppe Nogari. In 1759 he was elected a member of the Venetian academy, for which he painted one of his rare allegorical pictures, "Painting and Merit." In 1762 Longhi issued his book *Compendio delle Vite de' Pittori Veneziani Istorici piu rinomati del presente secolo con sui ritratti dal naturale delineati ed indisi*, one of the most important source books for the history of Venetian 18th-century painting. Both portraits and text were printed from plates he etched. Longhi's facilely rendered portraits are largely generalized likenesses lacking any acuity of character observation. He mainly portrayed the leading Venetian luminaries and dignitaries of his day in a style that drew upon his father's Rococo manner and 16th-century traditions of Venetian Renaissance portraiture.

Longhi, Pietro, original name PIETRO FALCA (b. 1702, Venice—d. May 8, 1785, Venice), painter of the Rococo period known for his small scenes of Venetian social and domestic life.

He was the son of a silversmith, Alessandro Falca, in whose workshop he received his first training. Later he worked under the Veronese historical painter Antonio Balestra, but his one important work of this sort, the monumental ceiling of the "Fall of the Giants" (completed 1734) for the Palazzo Sagredo, was an artistic and critical failure. It is likely that because of this he left Venice for a time and studied at Bologna under the genre painter Giuseppe Maria Crespi. After his return to Venice he devoted himself to painting everyday scenes from the life of the city's upper class and bourgeoisie, somewhat in the manner of Nicolas Lancret but in a more ironic vein. He was also undoubtedly influenced by Dutch

"Exhibition of a Rhinoceros at Venice," oil on canvas by Pietro Longhi, *c.* 1751; in the National Gallery, London
By courtesy of the trustees of the National Gallery, London; photograph, J.R. Freeman & Co. Ltd.

genre painting, of which there was at least one important collection in Venice at that date. Longhi's genre pictures provide a varied and detailed documentation of contemporary Venetian life and events (*e.g.,* "The Dancing Master" [Accademia, Venice] and "Exhibition of a Rhinoceros at Venice" [1751; National Gallery, London]). Popular for their charm and seeming naivete, his paintings have a Rococo sense of the intimate and manifest the interest in social observation characteristic of the Enlightenment. His works, like those of Antoine Watteau, were based on carefully observed figure drawings, a large number of which survive. He also painted landscapes and occasional portraits. Many of his paintings were engraved. He was elected to the Venetian Academy at its foundation in 1756.

longhouse, traditional dwelling of the Iroquois Indians of the northeastern United States, particularly northern New York, until the 19th century, when they abandoned it as a

Iroquois longhouse
From Rugg, *History of American Civilization;* courtesy of Ginn and Company

residence. The term has also been used to describe the dwellings of other North American Indians; and it is applied today to the building on an Iroquois reservation that is designated as church and meeting hall, though its form is entirely different from the traditional longhouse residence.

The traditional Iroquois longhouse is thought to have been built by constructing a long rectangular box out of poles 2 to 3 inches (5 to 7.5 centimetres) in diameter. A domed roof was placed down the entire length of the building by bending saplings from posts on one side over to the opposite side. The whole was then covered by tying bark onto the frame. Separate doors were provided for men and women, one at each end of the house.

Excavations of many longhouses in New York state testify to the design and structure of these houses. They ranged from 40 to 334 feet (12 to 102 metres) in length but were always about 22 or 23 feet wide. Each was subdivided into numerous stalls by walls built out from the two long side walls about every seven feet, leaving a long, open centre aisle from one end of the house to the other. It is supposed that each family had a stall for its use; but as there was no wall shutting off each stall from the central aisle, there was virtually no privacy. For cooking, four stalls, two on each side, shared a central fire built in the aisle; an opening was left in the roof to serve as a chimney.

Life in the longhouse had ended by 1800, but the meeting room of the contemporary tribe continues to be called the longhouse. Today, however, it is generally built with clapboard sides, and the interior, which has no stalls, functions as a large meeting hall. Separate doorways for males and females are still provided.

The dwelling gave its name to the Longhouse Religion, founded by a Seneca, Handsome Lake. *See* Handsome Lake cult.

Longhouse Religion: *see* Handsome Lake cult.

longicorn: *see* long-horned beetle.

Longimanus: *see* Artaxerxes I.

Longinus, also called DIONYSIUS LONGINUS, or PSEUDO-LONGINUS (fl. early 1st century AD), name sometimes assigned to the author of *On the Sublime* (Greek *Peri Hypsous*), one of the great, seminal works of literary criticism. The earliest surviving manuscript, from the 10th century, first printed in 1554, ascribes it to Dionysius Longinus. Later it was noticed that the index to the manuscript read "Dionysius or Longinus." The problem of authorship embroiled scholars for centuries, attempts being made to identify him with Dionysius of Halicarnassus, Cassius Longinus, Plutarch, and others. The solution has been to name him Pseudo-Longinus.

On the Sublime apparently dates from the first century AD, because it was a response to a work of that period by Caecilius of Calacte, a Sicilian rhetorician. There are 17 chapters on figures of speech, which have occupied critics and poets ever since they were written. About a third of the manuscript is lost.

Longinus defines sublimity (Greek *hypsos*) in literature as "the echo of greatness of spirit," that is, the moral and imaginative power of the writer that pervades his work. Thus for the first time greatness in literature is ascribed to qualities innate in the writer rather than his art.

The author suggests that greatness of thought, if not inborn, may be acquired by emulating great authors such as his models (chief among them Homer, Demosthenes, and Plato). Quotations that were chosen to illustrate the sublime and its opposite occasionally also preserve work that would otherwise now be lost; *e.g.,* one of Sappho's odes. *See also* sublime.

Longinus, Gaius Cassius: *see* Cassius Longinus, Gaius.

Longinus, Johannes: *see* Długosz, Jan.

Longinus, Quintus Cassius: *see* Cassius Longinus, Quintus.

longitude (geography): *see* latitude and longitude.

longitudinal wave, wave consisting of a periodic disturbance or vibration that takes place in the same direction as the advance of the wave. A coiled spring that is compressed at one end experiences a wave of compression that travels its length, followed by a stretching; a point on any coil of the spring will move with the wave and return along the same path, passing through the neutral position and then reversing its motion again. Sound mov-

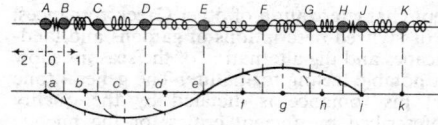

A longitudinal wave and its transverse representation

From *Physics* by Erich Hausmann and Edgar P. Slack © by Litton Educational Publishing, Inc. Reprinted by permission of Van Nostrand Reinhold Company

ing through air also compresses and rarefies the gas molecules in the direction of travel of the sound wave as they vibrate back and forth. The *P* (primary) seismic waves are also longitudinal. In a longitudinal wave, each particle of matter vibrates about its normal rest position and along the axis of propagation, and all particles participating in the wave motion behave in the same manner, except that there is a progressive change in phase (*q.v.*) of vibration—*i.e.,* each particle completes its cycle of reaction at a later time. The combined motions result in the advance of alternating regions of compression and rarefaction in the direction of propagation.

A mechanical model is helpful in explaining longitudinal waves. At the top of the figure, small masses *A, B, C,* etc. are joined together by coiled springs to represent a transmitting medium that has properties of both inertia and elasticity. Because mass *B* has inertia, motion of *A* toward the left (arrow 2) extends the spring it is attached to and motion to the right (arrow 1) compresses it. A corresponding motion will be communicated to *B* through the spring, except that there will be a slight lag in phase. Mass *B* will impart its motion to its partner *C,* and so on, the impulse travelling from *A* to *K* and the lag progressively increasing. At the instant shown, *A* and *J* are out of phase by 360°; *A* is starting its second vibration, whereas *J* is just beginning its first.

A transverse representation of a longitudinal wave is shown at the bottom of the figure. Here vertical lines are drawn through the rest positions (indicated by *a,b,c,* etc.), with lengths proportional to the distances that the masses have moved from equilibrium (their amplitudes). Lines are drawn upward from the axis when displacement is to the left and downward when to the right. A smooth curve drawn through the ends of the vertical lines gives a transverse curve. This transverse curve shows that there is one compression and one rarefaction per half cycle, represented here as *ae* and *ej, aj* being one wavelength. Frequency would be represented by the number of complete cycles executed by any of the masses per second.

Longjumeau, Andrew of (French diplomat to Central Asia): *see* Andrew of Lonjumel.

Longmen caves (cave temples): *see* Lungmen caves.

Longmont, city, Boulder county, northern Colorado, U.S., on St. Vrain Creek between the South Platte River and foothills of the Rocky Mountains, at an elevation of 5,000 ft (1,524 m), 30 mi (48 km) northwest of Denver. Founded in 1871 as a farming community of the Chicago-Colorado Colony Company, it was named for Maj. Stephen H. Long, discoverer of Longs Peak, 28 mi (45 km) west. The Colorado Central Railroad arrived in 1873, and Longmont grew as a processing and shipping point for livestock and farm crops from the surrounding lands irrigated by the Colorado-Big Thompson water-diversion project. Industries include sugar beet processing, vegetable canning, and the manufacture of automotive filters, chemicals, pickup campers, and electronic equipment. Roosevelt National Forest (including Rocky Mountain National Park) is to the west. Inc. town, 1885; city, 1961. Pop. (1990) city, 51,555; Boulder-Longmont PMSA, 225,339.

Longmyndian, major division of Late Precambrian rocks and time in the southern Shropshire region of England (the Precambrian began about 3.8 billion years ago when the Earth's crust formed and ended 570 million years ago). Named for prominent exposures in the Longmynd Plateau region, Longmyndian rocks consist of steeply angled and even overturned unfossiliferous mudstones, sandstones, conglomerates, and volcanic rocks. Two major subdivisions are recognized: the Western Longmyndian and the underlying Eastern Longmyndian. The Western Longmyndian consists of the Wentnor Series, purple sandstones, conglomerates, and some greenish siltstones and shales; thicknesses of about 4,800 metres (15,700 feet) of Wentnor rocks have been measured. The Eastern Longmyndian is subdivided into the overlying Minton Series and the underlying Stretton Series. The Minton Series, about 1,200 metres in thickness and made up of purple and green shales, sandstones, and conglomerates, is separated from the underlying Stretton Series by an unconformity representing a period of erosion rather than depositon. The Stretton Series, grayish and greenish siltstones, sandstones, shales, and volcanic rocks, is as much as 3,500 metres thick. Rocks underlying the Stretton Series and possibly related to the Longmyndian are known as the Eastern and Western Uriconian, geographically separated from each other but similar in lithology and probably broadly contemporaneous. The Eastern and Western Uriconian consist of lavas, tuffs, and intrusive igneous bodies; they are separated from the overlying Stretton Series by a prominent unconformity. Elsewhere, in the Charnwood Forest and Midlands regions, a sequence of rocks occurs that may favourably be compared to the Stretton Series of the Eastern Longmyndian; three subdivisions have been recognized: the lowermost Blackbrook Series, overlain in turn by the Maplewell Series and the Brand Series. These rocks, collectively known as the Charnian, consist largely of volcanic rocks (most prominent in the Maplewell Series and least in the Brand Series) and of sedimentary conglomerates, sandstones, siltstones, and slates.

Charnian sedimentary rocks contain impressions of a Precambrian organism known as *Charnia*; these are especially prominent in the higher levels of the Maplewell Series. Similar if not identical forms are known to occur in Australia. The zoological affinities of *Charnia* are uncertain; opinions have ranged from including the form in the Coelenterata (corals, hydras, and jellyfish) to the algae.

Longomontanus, Christian, byname of CHRISTIAN SEVERIN (b. Oct. 4, 1562, Longberg, Den.—d. Oct. 8, 1647, Copenhagen), Danish astronomer and astrologer who is best known for his association with, and published support for, Tycho Brahe. Longomontanus used Tycho's data to compile the *Astronomia danica* (1622), an exposition of the Tychonic system, which holds that the Sun revolves around the Earth and the other planets revolve around the Sun. He began the construction of the Copenhagen Observatory in 1632 but died before its completion.

Longshan culture (China): *see* Lung-shan culture.

longship, also called VIKING SHIP, type of sail and oar vessel that predominated in northern European waters for more than 1,500 years and played an important role in history. Ranging from 45 to 75 feet (14 to 23 metres) in length, and clinker-built (with overlapped planks), the longship carried a single square sail and was exceptionally sturdy in heavy seas. Its ancestor was, doubtless, the dugout, and the longship remained double-ended; fully developed examples have been found dating from 300 BC. It carried the Vikings on their piratical raids of the 9th century and bore Leif Eriksson to America in 1000; it was also used by Dutch, French, English, and German mer-

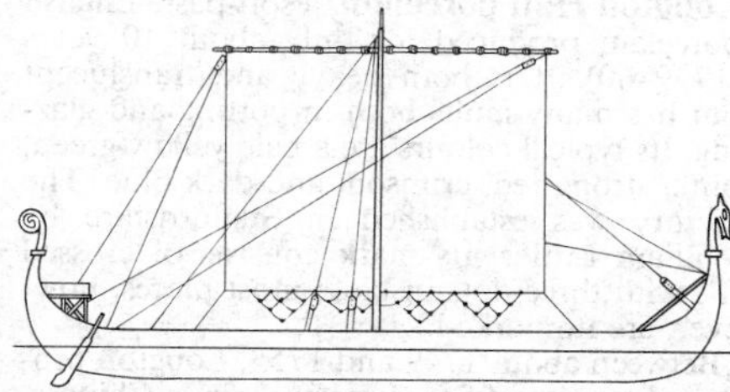

Longship of the type used by William the Conqueror, as shown in the Bayeux tapestry

From Bjorn Landstrom, *The Ship*, illustration copyright 1961 by Bjorn Landstrom; reproduced by permission of Interbook Publishing AB, Stockholm, Sweden

chants and warriors. Some of the 11th-century versions shown in the Bayeux tapestry have their masts supported by shrouds, implying that their square sails could be manipulated enough to sail with the wind abeam. The introduction of the stern rudder in about 1200 led to the differentiation of bow and stern and the transformation of the longship.

Longstreet, James (b. Jan. 8, 1821, Edgefield District, S.C., U.S.—d. Jan. 2, 1904, Gainesville, Ga.), Confederate officer during the American Civil War. A graduate of the U.S. Military Academy at West Point, N.Y. (1842), he resigned from the U.S. Army when his native state seceded from the Union (December 1860); he was made a brigadier general in the Confederate Army. He fought in the first and second battles of Bull Run, called First and Second Manassas by the Confederates (July 1861; August–September 1862); was a division commander in the Peninsular Campaign (March–July 1862); and at Antietam (September 1862) and Fredericksburg (November–December 1862) commanded what was soon called the I Corps in the Army of Northern Virginia. Promoted to lieutenant general (1862), Longstreet participated in the Battle of Gettysburg as Gen. Robert E. Lee's second in command. His delay in attacking and his slowness in organizing "Pickett's Charge," his critics argue, were responsible for the Confederate defeat at Gettysburg; others, however, place the blame on Lee, citing his inability to cope with unwilling officers. In September 1863 he directed the attack at Chickamauga that broke the Federal lines. He was severely wounded in the Wilderness Campaign. In November 1864, although with a paralyzed right arm, he resumed command of his corps. He surrendered with Lee at Appomattox.

After the war he became unpopular in the South—partly because of his admiration for Pres. Ulysses S. Grant and partly because he joined the Republican Party. He served as U.S. minister to Turkey (1880–81) and com-

Longstreet

By courtesy of the National Archives, Washington, D.C.

missioner of Pacific railways (1898–1904). His reminiscences, *From Manassas to Appomattox,* appeared in 1896.

Longton Hall porcelain, a soft-paste English porcelain produced for only about 10 years (1749–60). It is both heavy and translucent but has many faults both in potting and glazing. Its typical colours are a pale yellow-green, pink, strong red, crimson, and dark blue. The factory was established in Staffordshire by William Littler. Its mark consists of crossed L's with three dots in blue; most pieces, however, are unmarked.

Between about 1749 and 1753, Longton produced a series of figures derived from Chinese, Meissen, and Chelsea originals and known as "snowmen" because of their blurred outline (the result of overthick glazing). The factory also made tableware that was molded instead of thrown and was decorated in cobalt, or "Littler's blue." Between 1754 and 1757 Littler's blue softened into powder blue, and tureens, sauceboats, and platters emerged from Longton Hall in the shape of cauliflowers, cabbages, and lettuces. During this period, William Duesbury, who subsequently founded Derby, enameled some Longton Hall ware. Figures, frequently based on those produced at Plymouth, were fairly numerous. In the last period, from about 1758 to 1760, Littler made a vain attempt to avert financial ruin by concentrating on producing tableware in blue and white as well as teapots and mugs decorated with transfer prints. Among the figures then produced, the "Four Continents" are considered the finest of all those made at Longton Hall.

Longueuil, city, Montérégie region, southern Quebec province, Canada, on the St. Lawrence River, opposite Montreal city. The city was founded in 1657 by Charles Le Moyne. Reached by the Montreal and Sorel Railway in 1880, it grew to become an important residential and industrial suburb of Montreal; after annexing Montreal South in 1961, it nearly quadrupled its population. Longueuil is the eastern terminus of Montreal's Metro (subway system) as well as of the Jacques-Cartier Bridge, which gives access to the islands of Sainte-Hélène and Notre-Dame. In 1969 the city of Jacques-Cartier was merged with Longueuil. Inc. town, 1874; city, 1920. Pop. (1991) 129,874.

Longueville, Anne-Geneviève de Bourbon-Condé, Duchess (duchesse) **de** (b. Aug. 28, 1619, Vincennes, France—d. April 15, 1679, Paris), French princess remembered for her beauty and amours, her influence during the civil wars of the Fronde, and her final conversion to Jansenism.

Anne-Geneviève de Bourbon-Condé was the only daughter of Henri II de Bourbon, Prince de Condé, and Charlotte de Montmorency. She was born in the prison of Vincennes, into which her father and mother had been thrown for opposition to Marshal d'Ancre, the favourite of Marie de Médicis, who was then regent in the minority of Louis XIII. She was educated with great strictness in the convent of the Carmelites in the Rue Saint-Jacques at Paris. Her early years were clouded by the execution of the Duke de Montmorency, her mother's only brother, but later her parents made their peace with Cardinal de Richelieu; introduced into society in 1635, she soon became one of the stars of the Hôtel Rambouillet, at that time the centre of all that was learned, witty, and gay in France.

In 1642 she married the Duke de Longueville, governor of Normandy, a widower twice her age. The marriage was not happy.

After Richelieu's death her father became chief of the council of regency during the minority of Louis XIV, her brother (the Great Condé) won the great victory of Rocroy in 1643, and the duchess became involved in political affairs. About 1646 she fell in love with the Duke de la Rochefoucauld, the author of the *Maximes,* who made use of her love to obtain influence over her brother and thus win honours for himself. The duchess was the guiding spirit of the uprising known as the first Fronde. She brought over Armand, Prince de Conti (her second brother), and her husband to the *frondeurs,* but she failed to attract Condé himself, whose loyalty to the court overthrew the first Fronde. The second Fronde was for the most part her work, and in it she played the most prominent part in attracting to the rebels first Condé and later Turenne.

In 1652, the last year of the war, the duchess was accompanied into Guyenne by the Duke de Nemours, and her intimacy with him gave La Rochefoucauld an excuse for abandoning her. Thus abandoned, and in disgrace at court, she betook herself to religion. She lived chiefly in Normandy until 1663, when her husband died and she came to Paris. There she became more and more Jansenist in opinion and became the great protectress of the Jansenists. Her famous letters to the pope are part of the history of Port Royal, and as long as she lived the nuns of Port Royal des Champs were left in safety. Her elder son resigned his title and estates and became a Jesuit under the name of the Abbé d' Orléans, while the younger, after leading a debauched life, was killed leading the attack in the passage of the Rhine in 1673. As her health failed, the duchess hardly ever left the convent of the Carmelites in which she had been educated.

Consult the INDEX *first*

Longueville, Henri II d'Orléans, Duke (duc) **de,** DUKE DE COULOMMIERS (b. April 27, 1595—d. May 11, 1663), noted rebel in the French civil wars of the Fronde, whose second wife was the celebrated Anne-Geneviève de Bourbon-Condé, Duchess de Longueville (*q.v.*).

After taking part in the conspiracy against Cardinal de Richelieu in 1626, Longueville distinguished himself in the wars in Italy and Germany. His first wife, Louise de Bourbon-Soissons, having died in 1637, he then married in 1642 Anne-Geneviève of the princely house of Condé, who eventually drew him into the intrigues of the Fronde. By 1648 his campaigns had made him virtually sovereign in Normandy. Back in Paris early in 1649, he engaged in renewed rebellions later that year and was arrested (Jan. 18, 1650), along with the princes Condé and Conti. Freed, he became irritated by the pride of Condé and the adulteries of his wife and quit the rebel cause. He spent the rest of his life governing Normandy.

Longumeau, Andrew of (French diplomat): *see* Andrew of Lonjumel.

Longus (fl. 2nd–3rd century AD), Greek writer, author of *Daphnis and Chloe,* the first pastoral prose romance (*see* pastoral literature) and one of the most popular of the Greek erotic romances.

The story concerns Daphnis and Chloe, two foundlings brought up by shepherds in Lesbos, who gradually fall in love and finally marry. The author is less concerned with the complications of plot, however, than with describing the way that love developed between his hero and heroine, from their first naïve and confused feelings of childhood to full sexual maturity. Longus' penetrating psychological analysis contrasts strongly with the inept characterization of other Greek romances. His stylized descriptions of gardens and landscapes and the alternating of the seasons show a notable feeling for nature. The general tone of his romance is dictated by the quality prescribed by ancient critics for the bucolic genre—*glykytēs,* a "sweetening" of the pastoral life.

Longview, city, seat (1871) of Gregg county, eastern Texas, U.S., near the Sabine River, 65 miles (105 km) west of Shreveport, La. It is the centre of a metropolitan and industrial area that includes Marshall, Kilgore, and Gladewater. The area was settled in the early 19th century and was developed after 1850 by planters. The townsite was named in 1870 by surveyors for the Texas and Pacific Railroad, who were impressed by the long-distance view. Incorporated in 1872, the community became a trading centre for beef cattle, hogs, and horses raised in the river valley. The discovery of oil in the 1930s ushered in a period of industrial expansion and rapid population growth.

The city, characterized by its great concentration of oil derricks, is a business focus for the extensive East Texas oil field and has oil refineries and pipelines, machine shops, breweries, and food-processing plants. Manufactures include steel, transportation, farm, and earth-moving equipment, aircraft components, and clothing. Institutions include the Caddo Indian Museum and LeTourneau University (1946). Lake Cherokee (impounded on Cherokee Bayou for flood control, irrigation, and recreation) is 12 miles south. Pop. (1992 est.) city, 73,082; Longview-Marshall MSA, 203,936.

Longview, city, Cowlitz county, southwestern Washington, U.S., at the confluence of the Cowlitz River with the Columbia, 50 miles (80 km) north of Portland, Ore. A planned community, it was founded in 1922 by R.A. Long of the Long-Bell Lumber Company on the site of old Monticello, where a convention met to seek creation of Washington Territory in 1852.

Longview was developed as one of the world's great lumber centres; it maintains paper, wood, aluminum, paint, and food-processing industries. Its deepwater port also serves the adjoining city of Kelso. Lower Columbia College was established there in 1934. Inc. 1924. Pop. (1990) 31,499.

Longwell, Chester R., in full CHESTER RAY LONGWELL (b. Oct. 15, 1887, Spalding, Mo., U.S.—d. Dec. 15, 1975, Palo Alto, Calif.), American geologist, known for his studies of the western United States.

After serving as a member of the Oklahoma Geological Survey from 1916 to 1920, Longwell joined the U.S. Geological Survey and became a faculty member at Yale University. In 1956 he became a research associate at Stanford University; he later became a professor there.

Longwell's work included field research and geologic mapping, studies of Basin and Range geology and structure, and Precambrian, Mesozoic, and Cenozoic geologic history. He was a coauthor of *Physical Geology* (1932) and *Introduction to Physical Geology* (1955).

Longwood Gardens, botanical gardens in Kennett Square, near Philadelphia, Pa., U.S., operated by the Longwood Foundation, Inc., which, in cooperation with the U.S. Department of Agriculture, sponsors expeditions to many parts of the world in search of ornamental plants for introduction into the United States. The 1,000-acre (400-hectare) gardens, containing collections of tropical and subtropical plants, originated with the plantings of exotic trees begun by Joshua and Samuel Peirce about 1800. The property, known as Peirce's Park, was acquired in 1906 by Pierre Samuel du Pont, who developed its conservatories in 1921 and created the foundation in 1937.

Longworth, Alice Roosevelt, née ALICE ROOSEVELT (b. Feb. 12, 1884, New York, N.Y., U.S.—d. Feb. 20, 1980, Washington, D.C.), daughter of President Theodore Roosevelt, known for her wit and her political influence.

When her father became president in 1901, Alice Roosevelt became the centre of national attention. In 1906 she married Ohio Representative Nicholas Longworth. She devoted much of her time to political activity, attending Senate debates, campaigning for favoured candidates, and serving the Republican Party in various official capacities.

Mrs. Longworth had a pillow in her home embroidered with the legend "If you can't say something good about someone, sit right here by me." It was a sentiment that she practiced. Her most scathing remarks were reserved for political figures: she said that Warren G. Harding was "just a slob"; that Calvin Coolidge "looked as if he had been weaned on a pickle"; and that Franklin D. Roosevelt, a distant cousin, was "one-third sap and two-thirds Eleanor." During the 1930s she wrote columns of Washington comment for the *Ladies' Home Journal* and other magazines, and in 1933 she published a book of memoirs, *Crowded Hours.*

Longwy, town, Meurthe-et-Moselle *département,* Lorraine *région,* northeastern France, on the Chiers River, near the borders of Belgium and Luxembourg. A part of the former Duchy of Bar, Longwy was annexed by France in 1678. Its 17th-century fortifications in the old quarter (Longwy-Haut) were designed by the military engineer Sébastien Le Prestre de Vauban. The town was successfully assaulted by the Prussians in 1792 and 1815 and by the Germans in 1870 and 1914. Longwy is a centre of heavy industry in an iron-mining area. The uncertain future of the iron industry has necessitated an effort to replace it with other industry. Pop. (1982) 17,317.

Longxi (China): *see* Chang-chou.

Longyan (China): *see* Lung-yen.

Lonjumel, Andrew of (French diplomat to Central Asia): *see* Andrew of Lonjumel.

Lönnbohm, Armas Eino Leopold (Finnish poet): *see* Leino, Eino.

Lönnrot, Elias (b. April 9, 1802, Sammatti, Swedish Finland—d. March 19, 1884, Sammatti, Russian Finland), folklorist and philologist who created the Finnish national epic, the *Kalevala* (1835, enlarged 1849), from short ballads and lyric poems collected from oral tradition. He also published *Kanteletar* (1840–41; "Old Songs and Ballads of the Finnish People") and collections of proverbs, riddles, and incantations.

Lönnrot received a medical degree from the University of Helsinki (1832). In 1833 he became a district medical officer at Kajaani, in a remote part of eastern Finland, near Russian Karelia, where he remained for 20 years. During this time he made field trips among the Lapps, the Estonians, and the Finnish tribes of northwestern Russia and collected evidence of the relationship of the Baltic branches of the Finno-Ugric languages as well as folk poetry. Believing that the short poems he collected were fragments of a continuous epic of which no full version survived, he joined a number of them together with connective material of his own and imposed upon this a unifying plot. Though his method is frowned upon by many scholars, the influence of the *Kalevala* (*q.v.*) on Finnish national consciousness, art, and culture has been immense.

Lönnrot was professor of Finnish language and literature at the University of Helsinki (1853–62). As a leader of the national revival movement, he promoted Finnish as a national language (Swedish had previously been predominant) and paved the way for the birth of modern Finnish literature.

Lons-le-Saunier, town, capital of Jura *département,* Franche-Comté *région,* eastern France, south-southeast of Dijon. Located at 846 feet (258 m) above sea level in the valley of the Solvan, it is surrounded by vine-clad hills. It is a pleasant spa, owing its original Roman name, Salinarius, to the local salt mines. It manufactures optical instruments, cheese, and sparkling wines. The Church of Saint-Désiré has an 11th-century crypt. On the avenue called the Promenade de la Chevalerie there is a statue by Frédéric-Auguste Bartholdi, the 19th-century French sculptor (who designed the Statue of Liberty in New York Harbor), of Rouget de Lisle, a native of the town, who composed the French national anthem, "La Marseillaise." The museum in the Hôtel de Ville has a collection of the composer's songs. Pop. (1982) 19,996.

Lonsdale, Frederick Leonard, original name LIONEL FREDERICK LEONARD (b. Feb. 5, 1881, St. Helier, Jersey, Channel Islands, U.K.—d. April 4, 1954, London, Eng.), British playwright and librettist whose lightweight comedies of manners have survived because of their tight construction and epigrammatic wit.

Lonsdale established himself as a librettist of musical comedies, chief among them being *The King of Cadonia* (1908), *The Balkan Princess* (1910), and *The Maid of the Mountains* (1916). During the 1920s, however, he began to produce his most characteristic work, reminiscent of the plays of Somerset Maugham. The most successful of them were *Aren't We All* (1923), *The Last of Mrs. Cheyney* (1925), *On Approval* (1927), *Canaries Sometimes Sing* (1929), and *Once is Enough* (1938).

Lonsdale, Gordon Arnold, original name KONON TROFIMOVICH MOLODY (b. Aug. 27, 1924, Cobalt, Ont., Can.—d. October 1970?, near Moscow, Russian S.F.S.R.), spy for the U.S.S.R. who in March 1961 was sentenced to 25 years in prison by a British court.

Lonsdale's family moved to Poland in 1932, where he served, under various aliases, in the underground during World War II. He served in the Soviet military administration in Berlin after the war and then attended a university until 1950, when, posing as a German, he went to the United States to conduct intelligence activities for the Soviet Union.

In 1954 he was transferred to Great Britain, where, posing as a Canadian businessman named Gordon Arnold Lonsdale, he organized a group that gathered submarine detection secrets from the Underwater Detection Establishment at Portland, Dorset. Arrested on Jan. 7, 1961, he was tried for espionage with four other persons and imprisoned until April 22, 1964, when he was exchanged for the British intelligence agent Greville Wynne. His autobiography, *Spy,* was published in 1965.

Lonsdale, Dame Kathleen, *née* YARDLEY (b. Jan. 28, 1903, Newbridge, County Kildare, Ire.—d. April 1, 1971, London, Eng.), British crystallographer who developed several X-ray techniques for the study of crystal structure. She was the first woman to be elected (1945) to the Royal Society of London.

From 1922 to 1927 and from 1937 to 1942, she was research assistant to Sir William Henry Bragg at University College and the Royal Institution, London. In 1929 her use of X rays definitely established the regular hexagonal arrangement of carbon atoms in the molecules of benzene compounds. Later she developed an X-ray technique with which she obtained an accurate measurement (to seven figures) of the distance between carbon atoms in diamond. She also applied crystallographic techniques to medical problems, in particular to the study of curarelike drugs and bladder stones.

Dame Kathleen Lonsdale, 1948
BBC Hulton Picture Library

She became professor of chemistry at University College, London, in 1949. In 1956 she was created Dame of the British Empire.

Lonsdale, William (b. Sept. 9, 1794, Bath, Somerset, Eng.—d. Nov. 11, 1871, Bristol, Gloucestershire), English geologist and paleontologist whose studies of fossil corals suggested the existence of an intermediate system of rocks, the Devonian System, between the Carboniferous System (286 to 360 million years old) and the Silurian System (408 to 438 million years old).

Educated for the military, Lonsdale served in the British army at the battles of Salamanca (1812) and Waterloo (1815) and retired as a lieutenant. In 1829 he became assistant secretary and curator of the Geological Society of London at Somerset House. In that same year he published the results of a survey begun two years earlier on the oolitic strata (rocks composed of rounded particles resembling fish eggs) of Bath. Later he was engaged in a survey of the oolitic strata of Gloucestershire (1832).

Lonsdale became the foremost authority in England on corals, and he described fossil forms from the Tertiary (1.6 to 66.4 million years old) and Cretaceous (66.4 to 144 million years old) strata of North America and from older strata of Great Britain and Russia. In 1837 he suggested from a study of the fossils of the South Devon limestones that they would prove to be of an age intermediate between the Carboniferous and Silurian systems. This suggestion was adopted by British geologists Adam Sedgwick and Roderick Impey Murchison in 1839 and may be regarded as the basis on which they founded the Devonian System.

Lonsdale Belt, British boxing award originated in 1909 by Lord Lonsdale, president of the National Sporting Club. The first belt went to a lightweight, Freddie Welsh. A belt was originally given to the champion in each division and was passed on as the title changed hands. From 1929 the belts were awarded by the British Boxing Board of Control, becoming the property of a champion who won three title fights in a division, not necessarily in succession. Perennial European, British, and Commonwealth heavyweight champion Henry Cooper won three Lonsdale belts.

Loo, formerly LANTERLOO (from French *lanturlu,* the refrain of a popular 17th-century song), game of cards of the Euchre (*q.v.*) family, invariably played for a stake. The players may number from five to about nine, each for himself. The pack of 52 cards is used. Popularity of the game faded in the 20th century.

In the simplest form of the game, three cards are dealt to each player and the next is turned for trump. The player to the left of the dealer leads, and one-third of the pool goes to the winner of each trick. The pool is formed by antes before each deal and may be increased by payments for loo (failure to win a trick) and fines for irregularities.

Looe, town ("parish"), Caradon district, county of Cornwall, England. It is divided into East and West Looe by the River Looe, which

Seven-arched bridge across the river at Looe in Cornwall, with characteristic houses
Tourist Photo Library

forms the harbour on the English Channel. East Looe beach is sandy, while the Hannafore beach, on the other side of the river, is largely rocky. Remains of a Celtic chapel and Benedictine priory have been found. A charter of incorporation was granted in 1587. West Looe (also known as Porpighan) was incorporated in 1325 and again in 1374. The harbour is now used mainly for pleasure craft, and shark angling has become a major tourist attraction. Fish processing also takes place there. Pop. (1991) 5,002.

loofah (plant): *see* dishcloth gourd.

Lookout Mountain, narrow southwestern ridge of the Cumberland Plateau and a segment of the Appalachian Mountains, U.S., extending south-southwestward for 75 miles (120 km), from Moccasin Bend, Tenn., on the Tennessee River across northwestern Georgia to Gadsden, Ala. Most peaks along the ridge rise to 2,000 feet (600 m); the loftiest is High Point (2,392 feet [730 m]), near La Fayette, Ga. At the northeastern end, a steep-incline railway ascends to the top of a peak, site of the town of Lookout Mountain, with excellent scenic views. In the interior of the peak are caves with a 145-foot- (45-metre-) high waterfall (Ruby Falls), and atop are the gardens and strange rock formations known as Rock City. During the American Civil War, the "Battle Above the Clouds" was fought in 1863 on and around this summit.

Lookout Mountain, Battle of, also called BATTLE ABOVE THE CLOUDS, in the American Civil War, one of the battles that ended the Confederate siege of Union troops at Chattanooga, Tenn. *See* Chattanooga, Battle of.

loom, machine for weaving cloth. The earliest looms date from the 5th millennium BC and consisted of bars or beams fixed in place to form a frame to hold a number of parallel threads in two sets, alternating with each other. By raising one set of these threads, which together formed the warp, it was possible to run a cross thread, a weft, or filling, between them. The block of wood used to carry the filling strand through the warp was called the shuttle.

The fundamental operation of the loom remained unchanged, but a long succession of improvements were introduced through ancient and medieval times in both Asia and Europe. One of the most important of these was the introduction of the heddle, a movable rod that served to raise the upper sheet of warp. In later looms the heddle became a cord, wire, or steel band, several of which could be used simultaneously.

The drawloom, probably invented in Asia for silk weaving, made possible the weaving of more intricate patterns by providing a means for raising warp threads in groups as required by the pattern. The function was at first performed by a boy (the drawboy), but in the 18th century in France the function was successfully mechanized and improved further by the ingenious use of punched cards. Introduced by Jacques de Vaucanson and Joseph-Marie Jacquard, the punched cards programmed the mechanical drawboy, saving labour and eliminating errors. In England, meanwhile, the inventions of John Kay (flying shuttle), Edmund Cartwright (power drive), and others contributed to the Industrial Revolution, in which the loom and other textile machinery played a central role. Modern looms retain the basic operational principles of their predecessors but have added a steadily increasing degree of automatic operation.

Counterparts of these looms were used in many other cultures. A backstrap loom was known in pre-Columbian America and in Asia, and the Navajo Indians wove blankets on a two-bar loom for centuries.

loon, also called DIVER (*Gavia*), any of four species of diving birds constituting the family Gaviidae (order Gaviiformes). These birds were formerly included, along with the grebes, to which they bear a superficial resemblance, in the order Colymbiformes (*q.v.*). Loons range in length from 60 to 90 cm (2 to 3 feet). Characteristics include a strong, tapered bill; small pointed wings; webs between the front three

Common loon, or great northern diver (*Gavia immer*)
Wayne Lankinen—Bruce Coleman Ltd.

toes; and legs placed far back on the body, making walking awkward. Loons have thick plumage, mainly black or gray above and white below. During the breeding season the dorsal plumage is patterned with white markings, except in the red-throated loon (species *Gavia stellata*), which, during the summer, is distinguished by a reddish brown throat patch. In winter the red-throated loon develops white speckling on the back, while the other species lose these markings.

Almost wholly aquatic, loons can swim long distances underwater and can dive from the surface to a depth of 60 m (200 feet). They are generally found singly or in pairs, but some species, especially the Arctic loon, or black-throated diver (*G. arctica*), winter or migrate in flocks. The voice is distinctive, including guttural sounds and the eerie, wailing cries, which in North America gave rise to the common name loon. They feed mainly on fishes, crustaceans, and insects. The nest is usually a heap of vegetation at the water's edge, in which two (or rarely three) olive-brown, spotted eggs are laid. The parents share the task of incubation. The chicks hatch in about 30 days and, as soon as their down is dry, enter the water with the parents. Although loons are strong fliers, all but the small red-throated loon need a broad expanse of water for takeoff. Thus, except for *G. stellata,* they are limited to large lakes.

The common loon, or great northern diver (*G. immer*), is the most abundant loon in North America; its counterpart across Eurasia is the similar white- (or yellow-) billed diver (*G. adamsii*). The red-throated and arctic loons are virtually circumpolar in distribution, the latter being most abundant on the Pacific coast of North America.

Loop, The, 35-block area of downtown Chicago, Illinois, U.S. The area was probably so named because elevated railroad tracks form a loop around it; the term is now sometimes used to refer to downtown Chicago generally. The Loop includes a portion of State Street, a major shopping district, with some of the nation's largest department stores, and La Salle Street (often called Chicago's Wall Street), the location of several large financial institutions, including the Midwest Stock Exchange and the Chicago Board of Trade. The Loop was the site of the Home Insurance Building (completed 1885; demolished 1931), generally considered to be the first metal-frame building. Several other buildings constructed during the late 19th century also introduced innovative techniques. Sears Tower, at 1,454 feet (443 m), was the world's tallest building upon its completion in 1974.

loop of Henle, long, U-shaped portion of the tubule that conducts urine within each nephron (*q.v.*) of the kidney of reptiles, birds, and mammals. The principal function of the loop of Henle appears to be the recovery of water and sodium chloride from the urine.

The liquid entering the loop is the solution of salt, urea, and other substances passed along by the proximal convoluted tubule, from which most of the dissolved components needed by the body—particularly glucose, amino acids, and sodium bicarbonate—have been reabsorbed into the blood. The first segment of the loop, the descending limb, is permeable to water, and the liquid reaching the bend of the loop is much richer than the blood plasma in salt and urea. As the liquid returns through the ascending limb, sodium chloride diffuses out of the tubule into the surrounding tissue, where its concentration is lower. In the third segment of the loop, the tubule wall can, if necessary, effect further removal of salt, even against the concentration gradient, in an active-transport process requiring the expenditure of energy. In a healthy person the reabsorption of salt from the urine exactly maintains the bodily requirement: during periods of low salt intake, none is allowed to escape in the urine, but, in periods of high salt intake, the excess is excreted.

looper: *see* measuring worm.

Loos, Adolf (b. Dec. 10, 1870, Brno, Moravia, Austria-Hungary [now in Czech Republic]—d. Aug. 23, 1933, Kalksburg, near Vienna, Austria), Austrian architect whose planning of private residences strongly influenced European Modernist architects after World War I. Frank Lloyd Wright credited Loos with doing for European architecture what Wright was doing in the United States.

Educated in Dresden, Ger., Loos practiced in

Vienna, although he spent extended periods in the United States (1893–97) and in Paris (1924–28). Loos was opposed to both Art Nouveau and Beaux-Arts historicism, and as early as 1898 he announced his intention to avoid the use of unnecessary ornament. His first building, the Villa Karma, Clarens, near Montreux, Switz. (1904–06), was notable for its geometric simplicity. It was followed by the Steiner House, Vienna (1910), which has been referred to by some architectural historians as the first completely modern dwelling; the main (rear) facade is a symmetrical, skillfully balanced composition of rectangles. His essays from this period, denouncing ornament and decoration, were equally influential. Loos's best-known large structure is the Goldman and Salatsch Building, Vienna (1910), in which a little classical exterior detail is offset by large areas of blank, polished marble. A resident of France from 1922, he built a house in Paris for the Dada writer Tristan Tzara in 1926.

BIBLIOGRAPHY. Ludwig Münz and Gustav Künstler, *Adolf Loos: Pioneer of Modern Architecture* (1966) and Benedetto Gravagnuolo, *Adolf Loos, Theory and Works* (1982), are documentary studies of Loos's theory, work, and writing.

Loos, Anita (b. April 26, 1893, Sissons [now Mount Shasta], Calif., U.S.—d. Aug. 18, 1981, New York, N.Y.), American novelist and Hollywood screenwriter celebrated for her novel *Gentlemen Prefer Blondes* (1925), which became the basis of a popular play, two musicals, and two films. By the time of her death it had run through 85 editions and translations into 14 languages.

Loos was a child actress, playing on the stage in San Francisco, Los Angeles, and San Diego, Calif., as well as in early films. The film of her first scenario, *The New York Hat,* was produced in 1912 by D.W. Griffith and starred Mary Pickford and Lionel Barrymore. By the age of 20 Loos was a professional screenwriter, and she eventually worked on more than 60 silent films, including *Intolerance* (1916), *A Virtuous Vamp* (1919), *The Perfect Woman* (1920), *Polly of the Follies* (1922), and *Learning to Love* (1925). The publication of *Gentlemen Prefer Blondes* in 1925 gave her instant international fame and made equally famous the central character of the book, Lorelei Lee, the archetypal "dumb blonde" with a penchant for rich men and the diamonds that they could offer. Loos's stage adaptation of *Gentlemen Prefer Blondes* premiered in New York in 1926 and was followed by a Broadway musical version (starring Carol Channing) in 1949 and a film version (starring Marilyn Monroe) in 1953.

Loos's later screenwriting credits included such films as *San Francisco* (1936), *Saratoga* (1937), *The Women* (1939), *Blossoms in the Dust* (1941), and *I Married an Angel* (1942). She also wrote autobiographical books, notably *A Girl Like I* (1966) and *Kiss Hollywood Good-By* (1974).

loosestrife, any of the ornamental plants of the family Lythraceae, especially the genera *Lythrum* and *Decodon,* and two genera of the family Primulaceae, *Lysimachia* and *Steironema.*

Purple loosestrife (*Lythrum salicaria*), native to Eurasia and now common in eastern North America, grows 0.6 to 1.8 m (2 to 6 feet) high on riverbanks and in ditches. It has a branched stem bearing whorls of narrow, pointed, stalkless leaves and ending in tall, tapering spikes of red-purple flowers. Purple loosestrife was introduced into North America early in the 19th century. It is now considered a noxious weed in many parts of the United States and Canada, where it forms dense colonies and crowds out native wetland vegetation that provides food and habitat for wildlife.

Swamp loosestrife, water willow, or wild oleander (*Decodon verticillatus*) is a perennial herb native to swamps and ponds of eastern North America. The Eurasian yellow loosestrife (*Lysimachia vulgaris*), an erect plant 0.6 to 1.2 m high, is common on riverbanks in England and grows in eastern North America. The branched stem bears tapering leaves in pairs or whorls and terminal clusters of deep-yellow flowers. Yellow pimpernel, or wood loosestrife (*L. nemorum*), a low plant with slender, spreading stem and solitary, yellow flowers, is common in England. Fringed loosestrife (*Steironema ciliatum*), a yellow-flowered perennial, is native to moist parts of North America and common in Europe.

Purple loosestrife (*Lythrum salicaria*)
Kitty Kohout from Root Resources

Looy, Jacobus van (b. Sept. 12, 1855, Haarlem, Neth.—d. Feb. 24, 1930, Haarlem), Dutch author and painter who personified the close association between art and literature in the late 19th century.

Van Looy, drawing by Jan Pieter Veth, 1896; in the Teylers Museum, Haarlem, Neth.
By courtesy of the Iconographisch Bureau, The Hague, and of the Teylers Museum, Haarlem, Neth.

Looy wrote first in the direct, personal, "1880" style, as in his popular novel *De dood van mijn poes* (1889; "The Death of My Cat"). The influence of the Symbolism of the time is seen in his early story *De nachtcactus* (1888; "The Night Cactus"), with the flower representing ephemeral desire that blooms for one night and then dies. In his later work *Feesten* (1902; "Celebrations"), he appears more objective, describing scenes from lower-middle-class life; and in his autobiographical *Jaapje* (1917), *Jaap* (1923), and *Jacob* (1930), he shows his genius for impressionistic word-painting.

Lop Buri, also spelled LOPBURI, town, south-central Thailand, north of Bangkok. Lop Buri is a rice-collecting centre situated on the Lop Buri River and on the country's main north-south highway and railway. Founded as Lavo in the 5th–7th century, it was incorporated into the Khmer empire of Angkor in the 10th or 11th century and became an important provincial capital. It later became an active centre within the kingdom of Ayutthaya (founded 1351) and was the summer capital of the Ayutthaya king Narai (reigned 1657–88). Thereafter the town declined, and many of its buildings decayed.

One of Thailand's major historical sites, the town retains numerous buildings from the early periods. The Prang Sam Yod ("Three-Spired Sanctuary"), the symbol of the Lop Buri region, was built by the Khmers. The Phra Narai Rachanives Palace is now a museum. The Royal Reception House was built by King Narai to receive the Chevalier de Chaumont, the first French ambassador to Thailand (1685). Other places of interest include the temple complex of Wat Phra Si Ratana Maha That (1157), the remains of the Nakhon Kosa temple, and the ruins of the 17th century Jesuit San Paolo Church.

The surrounding area is drained by the Lop Buri River, which is an eastern tributary of the Chao Phraya River. Rice is the principal crop. Pop. (1993 est.) town, 31,898.

Lop Nor, Wade-Giles romanization LO-PU PO, Pinyin LOP NUR, former saline lake in northwestern China that is now a salt-encrusted lake bed. It lies within the Tarim depression of the eastern Takla Makan Desert, in the Uighur Autonomous Region of Sinkiang, and is one of the most barren areas of China.

The former lake, occupying roughly 770 square miles (2,000 square km) in the 1950s, ceased to exist by about 1970 upon completion of irrigation works and reservoirs on the middle reaches of the Tarim River, one of its former tributaries. According to carbon-14 dating conducted by Chinese scientific teams in 1980 and 1981, a lake of variable dimensions had constantly existed in the area for about 20,000 years, even though the local climatic conditions have long been arid to extremely arid. The Lop Nor area is experiencing increased wind erosion and salt-encrustation. Salt crust now covers 8,000 square miles (21,000 square km), and *yardang* (irregularly shaped salt ridges) occupy nearly 1,200 square miles (3,100 square km).

The Lop Nor area has not had permanent habitation since about 1920, when Uighur bands fled the depression after a plague decimated them. Native animals include a few wild Bactrian camels. Since 1964 the area has been intermittently used as a test site for Chinese underground and atmospheric nuclear explosions. The generic term *nor* is derived from the Mongolian word *nuur* 'lake.'

Lope DE VEGA: *see* Vega, Lope de.

Lopes, Fernão (b. *c.* 1380—d. *c.* 1460), Portuguese historian, the first and greatest of the Portuguese royal chroniclers and the most accomplished writer of 15th-century Portuguese prose. He occupies a special place in medieval historiography because he held that the surest way of arriving at historical truth was through the evidence of historical documents.

Nothing certain is known of Lopes' early life, and his name is first mentioned in 1418, when he was already keeper of the royal archives—a post he long held. In 1434 King Duarte appointed Lopes to write the chronicles of Portugal from the monarchy's origins to the time of John I. The new chronicler prepared himself for his task by studying the contents of the royal archives and by traveling around the kingdom examining monastic and other records, looking at epitaphs and familiarizing himself with the topography of towns and battlefields. When he retired (1454), his history had been completed up to 1411. The last contemporary reference to him is dated 1459.

All his chronicles up to the death of Alfonso IV (1357) disappeared from sight early in the 16th century after they had been utilized by Rui de Pina, though what may be an incomplete transcription of them has since been found. There remain intact the short *Crónica de D. Pedro I,* the much more elaborate *Crónica de D. Fernando,* and the massive *Crónica de D. João I,* which, though unfinished, runs to nearly 400 chapters. This last was the first of Lopes' works to be printed (1644).

Lopes used documents systematically, sometimes quoting them *in extenso* in his text but, more often, building up a continuous narrative from what he read, particularly in the chancery registers. Since much of this documentary material has now disappeared, the value of Lopes' work as a primary source for Portuguese medieval history can hardly be exaggerated. Fernão Lopes wrote in a rich, slightly archaic, easy-flowing language with a distinct popular flavour, and his style was quite characteristic of the period.

Lopes, Manuel (b. Dec. 23, 1907, Santo Antão, Cape Verde Islands), African poet and novelist who portrayed the struggle of his people to live in a land besieged by drought, famine, and unemployment.

Lopes studied at the University of Coimbra in Portugal, then returned to Cape Verde. In 1944 he took up work for Western Telegraph, and in 1951 he was transferred to the Azores. Subsequently, he worked in Portugal, where he continued to live even after retirement.

Lopes was one of the founders of the journal *Claridade,* which in 1936 gave birth to modern Cape Verdean literature. Lopes' story "O Galo que Cantou na Baía" (1936; "The Cock that Crowed in the Bay") is the first prose narrative in Cape Verde rooted in a social reality that includes traditional folk elements. Two prize-winning novels, *Chuva Braba* (1956; "Torrential Rains") and *Os Flagelados do Vento Leste* (1960; "Victims of the East Wind"), reflect both the anguish and the hope of his people.

Lopes published essays on Cape Verdean culture, as well as two volumes of poetry, *Poemas de Quem Ficou* (1949; "Poems of One Who Remained Behind") and *Crioulo e Outros Poemas* (1964; "Creole and Other Poems"). His poems examine themes of Cape Verdean life, including the conflict between the desire to escape and the need to remain.

Lopes da Silva, Baltasar, Baltasar also spelled BALTAZAR, pseudonym OSVALDO ALCÂNTARA (b. April 23, 1907, Vila da Ribeira Brava, São Nicolau, Cape Verde Islands), African poet, novelist, and short-story writer who was instrumental in the shaping of modern Cape Verdean literature. Lopes was educated at the University of Lisbon, where he took a degree in law and in Romance philology. He then returned to Cape Verde and became a high school teacher and later rector of the Liceu Gil Eanes in São Vicente (retired 1972).

His one novel, *Chiquinho* (1947), written in Portuguese, recreates the experiences of a Cape Verdean who grows up to understand that, in his land, life is a prolonged tragedy given meaning by the assertion of human courage, unselfishness, and dignity. *Chiquinho,* marking the beginning of realism in the Cape Verdean novel, is now a classic.

His poems have been published in journals in Cape Verde, Portugal, and Brazil. As a creative writer, Lopes da Silva was one of the three founders in 1936 of the journal *Claridade* ("Clarity"). His published nonfiction includes *Cabo Verde Visto por Gilberto Freire* (1956), a study of Cape Verdean culture. He also edited an anthology of contemporary Cape Verdean fiction (1960).

López, Carlos Antonio (b. Nov. 4, 1790, Asunción, Río de la Plata—d. Sept. 10, 1862, Asunción, Paraguay), second dictator of Paraguay, who ended his country's isolation, sought to modernize Paraguay, and became deeply involved in international disputes.

López was the son of poor parents, reportedly of Indian and Spanish descent. After attending the San Carlos Seminary in Asunción, he taught there until it was closed by the dictator José Gaspar Rodríquez de Francia. López, who had married into one of the country's leading families, was exiled to his *estancia* (ranch). In 1841, a year after Rodríguez de Francia's death, López became the principal of the two consuls ruling the country. Governing Paraguay constitutionally until 1844, he then suspended the constitution and dismissed his fellow consul, making himself dictator. An exceedingly corrupt ruler, who owned half his

Carlos Antonio López, portrait by Nessi
By courtesy of the Organization of American States

country's land and never bothered to make a distinction between his own and his country's revenue, he placed most of Paraguay's commerce in the hands of his family.

López was credited, however, despite his dislike of foreigners, with trying to stimulate his country's economy by encouraging European artisans and professionals to immigrate to develop industry and the army. He was also somewhat more lenient toward his political opponents than was his predecessor, and in 1844 he released all political prisoners. He officially abolished slavery and torture, though both were still prevalent at his death. Harsh toward the clergy, he nevertheless attempted to improve elementary education.

López established diplomatic relations with many European powers and with the United States, but under him Paraguay's relations were never smooth. Difficulties with the United States almost resulted in war, and Lopez interfered in the Argentine civil war of 1845–46, when the Argentine president Juan Manuel de Rosas refused to recognize Paraguay's independence.

López, Francisco Solano (b. July 24, 1827, Asunción, Paraguay—d. March 1, 1870, Concepción province), dictator of Paraguay responsible for the Paraguayan War (also known as the War of the Triple Alliance), in which Paraguay was practically destroyed by Brazil, Argentina, and Uruguay.

López, the eldest son of the dictator Carlos Antonio López, seized power upon his father's death (Sept. 10, 1862) and quickly established his own supremacy with the help of the army. Showing little understanding of his country's need to remain neutral in squabbles between the two South American giants, Brazil and Argentina, early in 1863 he allowed himself to be drawn into boundary disputes with both countries and to become entangled in a civil war raging in Uruguay in which Brazil and Argentina were involved. He evidently hoped to play the role of arbitrator in the dispute

Francisco Solano López
By courtesy of the Library of Congress, Washington, D.C.

and thereby take centre stage in Latin-American politics. As a result of complicated diplomatic intrigues, however, López found himself at war with Brazil in December 1864. By demanding the right to place troops in the Argentine province of Corrientes, he violated Argentina's desire to remain neutral and provoked the alliance of Brazil, Argentina, and Uruguay against Paraguay on May 1, 1865.

Although López had successfully invaded the Brazilian province of Mato Grosso in late 1864, his invasion of Uruguay in 1865 was a disaster. The allies defeated him at Tuyutí in May 1866, captured the fortress of Humaitá in July 1867, and forced López to withdraw into northern Paraguay, where he was killed.

López de Ayala, Pedro (b. 1332, Vitoria, Castile—d. 1407, Calahorra, Navarre), Spanish poet and court chronicler who observed firsthand the happenings of his time and, unlike earlier chroniclers, recorded them objectively. His *Crónicas* (standard ed., 1779–80) are marked by this personal observation and vivid expression, making them among the first great Spanish histories.

Ayala had a long and distinguished civil career under four Castilian monarchs, Peter I, Henry II, John I, and Henry III. Holding such posts as captain of the Castilian fleet (1359), ambassador to France (1379–80 and 1395–96), and royal chancellor of Castile (1398 until his death), he spent his lifetime in close association with leading men and events. As a poet, he is chiefly remembered for his *Rimado de palacio* (*c.* 1400), one of the last works in *cuaderna vía* (Spanish narrative verse form consisting of 4-line stanzas, each line having 14 syllables and identical rhyme), an autobiographical satire on contemporary society. Ayala's translations from Livy, Boccaccio, and others gave him a reputation as the first Castilian humanist.

López de Legazpi, Miguel (Spanish explorer): *see* Legazpi, Miguel López de.

López de Mendoza, Íñigo, marqués de Santillana: *see* Santillana, Íñigo López de Mendoza, marqués de.

López Mateos, Adolfo (b. May 26, 1910, Atizapán de Zaragoza, Mex.—d. Sept. 22, 1969, Mexico City), Mexican president (1958–64) who expanded industrial development and agrarian reform.

A librarian and teacher of Spanish-American literature, López began his public career with an assignment to the UN. He was elected federal senator (1946–52) and later appointed secretary-general of the Partido Revolucionario Institucional (PRI). As minister of labour, he was skilled in mediating disputes and helped draft the U.S.–Mexico migrant-labour treaty. Though accusations of corruption clouded his six-year term as president, López increased industrialization, extended agrarian reform laws, and initiated a literacy campaign.

López Michelsen, Alfonso (b. June 30, 1913, Bogotá), president of Colombia, 1974–78.

The son of Alfonso López Pumarejo, who was twice president of Colombia (1934–38 and 1942–45), López Michelsen was educated in Bogotá, Paris, London, and Brussels, with postgraduate studies at Georgetown University and the University of Chile. Returning to Colombia from voluntary exile in Mexico in 1958, he organized a new party of dissident Liberals, the Liberal Revolutionary Movement (MRL), to oppose the National Front. The National Front was a coalition of Liberals and Conservatives established in 1957 to end a decade of violent civil strife. The pact between the two major established parties had guaranteed the peaceful alternation of presidential terms between them but also, in López' opinion, stifled any real political competition and leadership.

López Michelsen ran unsuccessfully for president in 1962 but gained a seat in the Senate, to which he was reelected in 1966. In 1967 he led the MRL back into the Liberal Party and was appointed governor of the new department of César by President Alberto Lleras Camargo. In August 1968 he became minister of foreign relations, in which capacity he formed closer cultural and commercial ties with the Soviet Union and worked for better relations with other Latin-American countries. With the termination in 1974 of the National Front agreement to alternate national elective offices, López was elected president in a landslide victory in the first competitive presidential election in Colombia in 16 years. On taking office, López took steps to curb inflation and raised taxes on high incomes, but the elimination of price subsidies and a rise in unemployment led to a surge in labour unrest, land seizures by peasants, and guerrilla activity. In 1975 López Michelsen declared a state of siege. By the end of his term, López' government was being accused of corruption involving the illegal-drug trade and of taking repressive measures to deal with a wave of political violence. López lost the 1982 presidential election to the Conservative candidate.

López Ortega, Domingo (bullfighter): *see* Ortega, Domingo.

López Portillo (y Pacheco), José (b. June 16, 1920, Mexico City, Mex.—d. Feb. 17, 2004, Mexico City), lawyer, economist, and writer who was president of Mexico from 1976 to 1982.

López Portillo attended the National Autonomous University of Mexico and the University of Chile. He then practiced law and later was professor of law, political science, and public administration at the National University of Mexico before beginning his political career. He held various administrative positions under Presidents Gustavo Díaz Ordaz and Luis Echeverría before becoming minister of finance in 1971. In this position he modernized tax-collection procedures, pursued tax evaders, and reduced public spending.

As president of Mexico López Portillo followed a more conservative approach than that of his predecessor, deemphasizing land redistribution and favouring the creation of nonagricultural jobs, exploitation of oil and natural gas, tax concessions to stimulate industrial development, and attraction of foreign investment. He continued Echeverría's population-control program, which achieved a modest reduction in the country's high birth rate. López Portillo's most significant political reform was to increase the size of the Chamber of Deputies to 400 members, with a minimum of 100 seats reserved for opposition parties. This measure was designed to permit more minority participation in Mexican politics, which had been dominated by the Institutional Revolutionary Party since 1929.

López Portillo mounted an ambitious program for the exploitation of huge, newly discovered petroleum reserves in Veracruz and Tabasco states by Petróleos Mexicanos (PEMEX), the state-owned Mexican oil agency. The program resulted in the rapid expansion of Mexico's oil exports, but much of the resulting wealth was squandered on inefficient state-run enterprises or was pocketed by government and labour-union officials. By the end of López Portillo's term in 1982, rampant government corruption and unrestrained government borrowing had resulted in a huge foreign debt and the discrediting of his administration.

On the international front, López Portillo adopted a somewhat conciliatory approach toward supplying the United States with oil and gas while exerting pressure for the easing of U.S. trade and immigration restrictions. In 1978 Mexico reopened diplomatic relations with Spain after a 38-year hiatus. In 1983 President Miguel de la Madrid dissociated himself from López Portillo's administration, accusing it of aggravating the "grotesque" maldistribution of wealth and defrauding PEMEX.

López Rega, José (b. Oct. 17, 1916—d. June 9, 1989, Buenos Aires), Argentine politician and political confidante who was virtual prime minister during the regime of President Isabel Martínez de Perón.

A retired police corporal and longtime right-wing Peronista leader, López Rega acted as private secretary to Juan Perón during the latter's exile in Spain. López Rega returned to Argentina with Perón in 1973. When Perón was again elected president (1973), his faithful secretary was appointed minister of social welfare and police commissioner, both positions giving him broad powers. López Rega engineered the nomination of Perón's third wife, Isabel, as vice president, and, when she became president in 1974 upon the death of her husband, he was given even more power, including the coordination of all the secretariats within the presidency. An astrologist who reportedly exercised a Rasputin-like authority over Perón's widow, López Rega loaded the cabinet with his political allies in September 1974 and instituted an unpopular program of fiscal conservatism. By the spring of 1975 inflation had soared because his protégé, economy minister Celestino Rodrigo, had devalued the peso by 50 percent and decontrolled prices. Under constant attack by leftist Peronistas who denounced him as a fascist and counterrevolutionary, López Rega was accused by Peronista congressional deputies in July 1975 of being the instigator of the Argentine Anticommunist Alliance, one of the first right-wing death squads to be formed in Argentina in the 1970s. On July 11 he resigned and left for Spain after having been hurriedly designated ambassador extraordinary by Isabel Perón. At year's end, under pressure from the military, President Perón stripped him of this position. López Rega spent the next 10 years in hiding. In 1986 he was arrested in the United States and extradited to Argentina, where he died while awaiting trial.

López Velarde, Ramón (b. June 15, 1888, Jerez, Mex.—d. June 19, 1921, Mexico City), postmodernist Mexican poet who incorporated French Symbolist techniques into the treatment of purely Mexican themes.

López Velarde studied law and was a journalist and civil servant. His first book of poems, *La sangre devota* (1916; "Devout Blood"), treats the simplicity of country life, the tension between sensuality and spirituality, and the poet's love for his cousin Fuensanta (Josefa de los Ríos); the language is often complex and full of daring imagery. In *Zozobra* (1919; "Anguish") the themes of his previous work are treated with greater intensity. The death of Fuensanta in 1917 elicited the feelings of loss and anguish and the expressions of profound sensuality found in the poems. *El son del corazón* (1932; "The Sound of the Heart") collected the poems not published at the time of López Velarde's death.

Although his poetry did not gain recognition during his lifetime, López Velarde came to be considered one of the greatest Mexican poets of the century. His influence on avant-garde poets in Mexico is unquestionable. He is also the author of the essay collections *El minutero* (1933; "The Minute Hand"), *El don de febrero* (1952; "The Gift of February"), and *Prosa política* (1953; "Political Prose"), dealing with some of the same preoccupations of his poetry in a highly poetic style.

López y Fuentes, Gregorio (b. Nov. 17, 1895, Huasteca, Veracruz, Mex.—d. Dec. 10, 1966, Mexico City), novelist who was one of the most important chroniclers of the Mexican Revolution and its effects.

In his youth he spent much time in his father's general store, where he came in contact with the Indians, farmers, and labourers of the region, whose lives he would later describe with deep insight. After unsuccessful efforts at poetry and novels, he began to draw upon his experiences in the Revolution. His first success, *Campamento* (1931; "Encampment"), was followed by several others dealing with aspects of the Revolution, including *Tierra* (1932; "Earth"), a novel about the Mexican revolutionary Emiliano Zapata; *¡Mi general!* (1934; "My General!"), a work on the lives of generals after the Revolution; and *El indio* (1935; "The Indian"), a fictional study of the life of Mexico's indigenous race, his most celebrated work.

lophophorate, any of several invertebrate animals that possess a lophophore, a fan of ciliated tentacles around the mouth. Currents of water carrying food particles toward the mouth are drawn by movements of the cilia. The lophophorates include the moss animals (phylum Bryozoa), lamp shells (Brachiopoda), and phoronid worms (Phoronida).

lophophore hypothesis, viewpoint that conodonts, small toothlike structures found as fossils in marine rocks over a long span of geologic time, are actually parts of and supports for a lophophore organ used for respiration and for gathering or straining minute organisms to be used as food. Lophophores are frilled or fringed organs possessed by many kinds of animals, including brachiopods and bryozoans. The animals that had conodonts, it is hypothesized, were probably distinct from any known group.

Lophophyllum, extinct genus of solitary marine corals found as fossils especially characteristic of the Late Carboniferous epoch (between 320 million and 286 million years ago) in North America. *Lophophyllum,* included in the horn corals (so named because of the hornlike form of the individual), probably preferred warm, clear, shallow marine waters.

Lophospira, genus of extinct gastropods (snails) found as fossils in marine rocks of

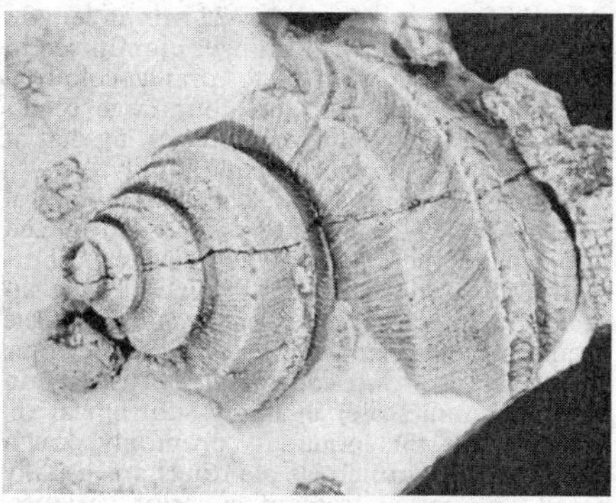

Lophospira, of Ordovician age, from Canada

By courtesy of the trustees of the British Museum (Natural History); photograph, Imitor

Ordovician to Devonian age (505 million to 360 million years old). The shell consists of a series of whorls arranged much like a series of ascending steps, each successive whorl smaller than the one below it. The apex of the shell is closed by a small cone-shaped whorl.

lopolith, igneous intrusion associated with a structural basin, with contacts that are parallel to the bedding of the enclosing rocks. In an ideal example, the enclosing sediments above and below the lopolith dip inward from all sides toward the centre, so that the lopolith is concave upward. Lopoliths, which can be several miles to several hundred miles in diameter, with thicknesses up to several thousand feet, are some of the largest igneous intrusions known. Many large ones are composed dominantly of basic rocks; a classic example is the Bushveld Igneous Complex of South Africa, which is composed of both granite and basic rocks. Many other lopoliths are either composite or differentiated. The feeder of a lopolith is assumed to be relatively small and probably is centrally located; it may connect the lopolith with a larger magma chamber at greater depth.

Lopukhina, Yevdokiya Fyodorovna (tsarina): *see* Eudoxia.

loquat (*Eriobotrya japonica*), subtropical tree of the rose family (Rosaceae), related to the apple and other well-known fruit trees of the temperate zone. Ornamental in appearance and rarely more than 10 metres (33 feet) in height, the evergreen loquat is frequently planted in parks and gardens. The leaves, clustered toward the ends of the branches, are thick and stiff, elliptic to lanceolate in form,

Loquat (*Eriobotrya japonica*)
G.R. Roberts

200–250 millimetres (8–10 inches) in length, with coarsely serrate margins. The small, fragrant, white flowers are arranged in dense terminal panicles. The fruits are borne in large, loose clusters; individually they are round, obovoid, or pear-shaped, 25–75 mm in length, with a tough, yellow to bronze, plumlike skin enclosing juicy, whitish to orange-coloured flesh surrounding three or four large seeds. The flavour is agreeably tart, suggesting that of several other fruits of the same family.

Though its native home is probably central eastern China, the loquat tree was introduced into Japan, where it was much developed horticulturally and is still highly valued. Some superior Japanese varieties reached Europe, the Mediterranean area, and a few other regions. The loquat is grown commercially (usually on a rather small scale) in many subtropical regions. While the loquat is commonly grown from seeds, commercial plantings are usually based on grafted trees of superior varieties. The tree is propagated by shield budding and cleft grafting; loquat seedlings or quince rootstocks grown from cuttings can be used, the latter if a dwarf tree is desired. They grow well on various soils, from sandy loams to clays, and come into bearing at three or four years.

Lorain, city, Lorain county, northern Ohio, U.S. It is located on Lake Erie at the mouth of the Black River, north-northwest of and adjacent to Elyria and about 25 miles (40 km) west of Cleveland.

Moravian missionaries camped briefly on the site in 1787, but the first permanent settler was Nathan Perry, from Vermont, who built a trading post there in 1807. First known as Black River, it was incorporated as the village of Charleston in 1836 and was renamed in 1874 for the county (which had taken its name from the province of Lorraine, Fr.) when it was rechartered as a city. The coal and iron-ore trade was established after a rail line was completed east to Cleveland in 1872 and grew after the Poe Lock at Sault Ste. Marie, Mich., opened in 1896. Industrial development began after 1894, when a steel mill was built on the Black River.

Lorain has remained a major Midwestern shipping centre handling coal, iron ore, and limestone. Industries include automobile and truck assembly and the manufacture of steel bars and tubing, power shovels, cranes, bearings, gypsum products, and clothing. Novelist and Nobel laureate Toni Morrison and textile artist Lenore Tawney are natives of Lorain. Pop. (2003 est.) city, 67,955; (2000) Cleveland-Lorain-Elyria PMSA, 2,250,871.

Lorain, John (b. 1753, England—d. 1823, Philipsburg, Pa., U.S.), U.S. farmer, merchant, agricultural writer, and the first person to create a hybrid by combining two types of corn. His experiments anticipated the methods employed in the century following his death.

Lorain apparently went to the North American colony of Maryland when he was a child. After managing a farm there for many years; he moved in 1795 to Germantown, Pa. From 1810 to 1813 he contributed articles to the journal of the Philadelphia Society for the Promotion of Agriculture; in 1812 he described his experiments—the earliest known—on crossing flint corn and gourd seed corn to form a hybrid with higher productivity than either parent. In 1812 he moved to Philipsburg, Pa., where, in addition to farming, he kept a store and served as postmaster and justice of the peace. In 1825 Lorain's widow published his book *Nature and Reason Harmonized in the Practice of Husbandry,* which contains detailed descriptions of his experiments with hybrids and his attempts to combine the best qualities of different corns into one strain.

Loralai, town in Quetta division, Balochistān province, Pakistan. The town lies just north of the Loralai River, at an elevation of 4,700 feet (1,430 m) above sea level, about 100 miles (160 km) east of Quetta. Founded in 1886, it is connected by road to Quetta and to Dera Ghāzi Khān, 130 miles (210 km) to the east. Cattle, sheep, and goat grazing is the main occupation in the surrounding valleys; there is also some cultivation. The chief crops are wheat, millet, rice, corn (maize), and fruit (grapes, apricots, pomegranates, and melons). Pashtun are the predominant ethnic group. Pop. (1998) 31,900.

loran, abbreviation of LONG-RANGE NAVIGATION, land-based system of radio navigation, first developed at the Massachusetts Institute of Technology during World War II for military ships and aircraft located within 600 miles (about 1,000 km) of the American coast. In the 1950s a more accurate (within 0.3 mile), longer-range (over 2,000 miles) system, known as Loran-C, operating in the 90–110 kilohertz range, was developed for civilian use, and the original loran (renamed Loran-A) was phased out. Eventually, Loran-C was extended to cover most of the continental United States and, in cooperation with Canada and Russia, Canadian waters and the Bering Sea. Other countries have deployed loran-like systems, and it is still used by many marine craft, but the precision (typically within 30 feet) of satellite-based navigational aides, such as GPS (*q.v.*), has relegated land-based navigational systems to the status of backup systems.

Loran is a pulsed hyperbolic system. This means that hyperbolic lines of position are determined by noting differences in time of reception of synchronized pulses from widely spaced transmitting stations. A primary station broadcasts an uninterrupted series of pulses of fixed duration and at a fixed rate (*e.g.*, of 50 microseconds' duration at a rate of 25 pulses per second). A secondary station, 200–300 miles away, automatically transmits its own signals, maintaining a frequency and pulse duration in accord with those of the primary station. The secondary station maintains a fixed time difference between its reception of the primary signal pulse and the sending out of its own. The noted time difference of arrival of the two pulses locates the craft somewhere on a curve (hyperbola) every point of which is located at a constant difference in distance between the stations (*e.g.*, three miles farther from the primary than from the secondary). Tuning in another secondary station locates the craft on another hyperbola, so that its position can be fixed at the intersection of the two.

Lorant, Stefan (b. Feb. 22, 1901, Budapest [Hungary]—d. Nov. 14, 1997, Rochester, Minn., U.S.), Hungarian-born U.S. editor, author, and pioneer in photojournalism.

Lorant attended the Academy of Economics in Budapest and then worked as a director, cameraman, and editor of films in Vienna and Berlin. From 1926 to 1933 he was editor in chief of the renowned *Münchner Illustrierte Presse* and in this position did much to influence and develop the new field of photojournalism, which at that time had its greatest practitioners and patrons in Germany. After a brief imprisonment in a Nazi concentration camp, Lorant went to England (1934), where he created three of the country's most popular picture magazines—*Weekly Illustrated* (founder and editor, 1934), *Lilliput* (editor in chief, 1937–40), and *Picture Post* (1938–40). He came to the United States in 1940 (naturalized in 1948).

Lorant's influence on photojournalism was enormous. In addition to promoting the careers of such photographers as Felix Man, Alfred Eisenstaedt, and Robert Capa, he formulated many of the most basic precepts of the profession. He believed that photojournalists should not arrange a picture but record events as they occur. An innovative magazine editor, he instituted picture layouts with photos contrasting in size and mood, set on facing pages, a practice now standard in journalism. He felt that pictures should be organized so that they told a story and not appear just as a collection of snapshots.

In the U.S., Lorant is perhaps best known for his works on the presidency. His *Lincoln: His Life in Photographs* (1941; rev. ed. 1957) created the genre of the pictorial biography. Other works include *The New World* (1946; rev. ed. 1965), *F.D.R.* (1950), *The Presidency* (1951), and *Lincoln: A Picture Story of His Life* (1952; rev. ed. 1969). He also wrote two autobiographical works, *I Was Hitler's Prisoner* (1935) and *My Years in England* (1982).

Loranthaceae, one of the mistletoe families of the sandalwood order (Santalales), having approximately 65 genera and about 850 species of parasitic flowering trees or shrubs. Some authorities also consider the 11 genera and about 450 species of the family Viscaceae, including the commonly known mistletoes of the genera *Arceuthobium* and *Phoradendron* in North America and of the genera *Viscum* in Europe, to be part of the Loranthaceae family.

The striking Australian Christmas tree (*Nuytsia floribunda*) belongs to the family Loranthaceae. The Old World tropical genus *Loranthus,* with about 500 species, is the largest genus in this family. Nearly all of the Loranthaceae are limited to the tropics. The plants range in size from small herbs to trees up to 10 m (about 33 feet) high; the smaller species are usually woody parasites on tree branches, while the larger species are root parasites. The unlobed leaves are usually evergreen, sometimes thick and fleshy, and arranged in pairs, each leaf opposite the other on the branch. The green leaves contain some chlorophyll, which allows the plants to manufacture food, but all Loranthaceae are parasitic to a certain extent and form connections (haustoria) to their hosts to obtain water and nutrients. The flowers are usually bisexual, and the fruits are almost always one-seeded berries. The berries are eaten by birds, who distribute the seeds by depositing them on trees or shedding them in droppings.

Lorca, town, Murcia province and autonomous community (region), southeastern Spain. It is situated along the Río Guadalentín in a semiarid and steppelike area that is surrounded by rugged mountains. The town, which sits on both banks of the river, was the Ilurco (Ilukro) of the Romans and the Lurka of the Moors. It was the scene of numerous battles between Christian and Moorish forces and was finally recaptured by Alfonso X the Wise in 1243, after which it became a Christian stronghold. The old part of Lorca surrounded the remains of its Moorish castle. The new sector is centred on the Calle (street) de la Corredera and contains houses with coats of arms on their walls dating from the 18th century, as well as the church of Santa María Real de las Huertas, which was allegedly built on the spot where Alfonso pitched his first tent before retaking the town.

The municipality includes the industrial area of San Cristóbal and the San Juan farming district (cereals, fruit growing). Local pasturelands support cattle, sheep, mules, and donkeys, and livestock fairs are held in the Santa Quiteria suburb. Irrigation has been practiced since Moorish times; water rights are sold annually in the Casa del Alporchón. Pop. (1999) mun., 70,689.

Lorca, Federico García: *see* García Lorca, Federico.

lord, in Great Britain, a general title for a prince or sovereign or for a feudal superior (especially a feudal tenant who holds directly from the king, *i.e.,* a baron). It today denotes a peer of the realm, a member of the House of Lords, which includes the lords temporal and the lords spiritual.

The prefix lord is ordinarily used as a less formal alternative to the full title (whether held by right or by courtesy) of marquess, earl, or viscount and is always so used in the case of baron (particularly in the peerage of Scotland, where it remains the only correct usage at all times). Where the name is territorial, the "of" is dropped—thus "the marquess of A.," but "Lord A." The younger sons of a duke or marquess have, by courtesy, the title of lord prefixed to their Christian name and surname, *e.g.,* Lord John Russell.

In the case of a diocesan bishop his proper title is the Lord Bishop of A., whether he be a spiritual peer or not. Some high officials of the Cabinet have the word lord prefixed to their titles, *e.g.,* first lord of the Treasury (the prime minister), lord high chancellor, lord president of the council, lord privy seal. In certain cases the members of a board that has taken the place of an office of state are known as lords commissioners, *e.g.,* lords of the Treasury, civil or naval lords of the Admiralty.

The form of address "my lord" is properly used not only for bishops and those of the nobility to whom the title "lord" is applicable but also for all judges of the high court in England and lord provosts. *See also* lady.

lord chancellor, also called LORD HIGH CHANCELLOR, British officer of state who presides over the House of Lords and is the head of the judiciary and custodian of the great seal. He is a Cabinet minister, having control of all judicial appointments in the country except those reserved to the prime minister.

The office dates back to Edward the Confessor (1042–66), who, in making the appointment, followed the model of the Carolingian court. Until the 14th century the chancellor was invariably a priest and served as royal chaplain, the king's secretary in secular matters, and keeper of the royal seal. All of the secretarial work of the royal household was handled by the chancellor and his staff of chaplains; the accounts were kept under the justiciar and treasurer, writs were drawn up and sealed, and the royal correspondence was carried on. This combination of duties, characteristic of the primitive administrative systems of the early Middle Ages, has remained with the chancellorship in modern times, although most of the office's power, exemplified in the administrations of such great chancellors as Thomas Becket (d. 1170) and Thomas Wolsey (d. 1530), ceased to exist centuries ago.

Much of the reason that the English chancellor did not develop into the head of government, as did his counterpart in the Holy Roman Empire, lies in the growth of his judicial duties. All petitions addressed to the king passed through the chancellor's hands, and by the reign of Henry II the chancellor's time was already largely taken up with judicial work. The office acquired a more definitely judicial character in the reign of Edward III, when the chancellor's court ceased to follow the king. It was at this time also that all petitions that were matters of grace were definitely committed to the king rather than to the strict and cumbersome common-law courts, thereby beginning the chancellor's equity jurisdiction (*see* equity). The chancellor's court was the direct precursor of the Court of Chancery, which, by the Judicature Act of 1873, was fused into the High Court of Justice. The Chancery Division of the latter is primarily responsible for its equitable jurisdiction. The lord chancellor is nominally president of the whole court and of the Chancery Division; he is also a member of the Court of Appeal and presides over it when present.

The important judicial work of contemporary chancellors is, however, almost exclusively confined to the House of Lords and the Judicial Committee of the Privy Council; when the chancellor is present, he presides over both tribunals, though because of the weight of administrative business since 1939, modern chancellors have had less time for their judicial duties.

The position of the chancellor as speaker, or prolocutor, of the House of Lords dates from the time of the English Norman kings, when the ministers of the *curia regis* ("king's court") sat ex officio in the *commune concilium* ("great council") and Parliament. When the other officials ceased to attend Parliament, the chancellor continued to do so. He now attends by virtue of his office, but since the early 18th century he has invariably been a peer. As speaker of the House of Lords, he differs considerably in his powers and duties from the speaker of the House of Commons. He puts the question but has no power to rule upon points of order. Like the speaker of the House of Commons, he may take part in debates and, unlike his modern counterpart in Commons, often does so.

The chancellor also has certain powers of ecclesiastical patronage. Consequently there remains a statutory prohibition against the appointment of Roman Catholics to the office. It is the only office in England still restricted on a religious basis.

lord chief justice, in England and Wales, the head of the Queen's (or King's) Bench Division of the High Court of Justice and next in rank to the lord chancellor. Appointed by the crown on the nomination of the prime minister, he usually presides over the Court of Criminal Appeal and is an ex officio member of the Court of Appeal. He is invariably raised to the peerage on appointment and so is able to take part in the appellate work of the House of Lords; and, although, like all other judges except the lord chancellor, he must not form public associations with any political party, the lord chief justice may intervene in debates on legal and judicial problems. His title derives from the Judicature Act of 1873.

Lord Dunmore's War (1774), Virginia-led attack on the Shawnee Indians of Kentucky, removing the last obstacle to colonial conquest of that area. During the early 1770s the Shawnee watched with growing distress the steady encroachment upon their rich Kentucky hunting grounds by white trappers, traders, speculators, and settlers. In early 1774 the Virginia militia seized Fort Pitt and renamed it Fort Dunmore for their royal governor, John Murray, 4th earl of Dunmore. Securing frontiersmen behind colonial forts, Lord Dunmore joined Colonel Andrew Lewis in carrying the aggression against the Indians, who they felt threatened white settlers. The Moravian-influenced Delaware Indians remained peaceful, but the inflamed Shawnee sprang to the defense of their homelands. The major confrontation occurred October 10 at the Battle of Point Pleasant, in which the Shawnee under Chief Cornstalk were decisively defeated. To protect their families from attack, Shawnee chiefs quickly agreed in the Treaty of Camp Charlotte to relinquish their hunting grounds to the white settlers.

Lord Dunmore was widely accused of commencing the war to divert Virginians from differences with the royal administration of that colony, and for this reason the fighting at Point Pleasant has sometimes been called the first battle of the Revolution.

lord high chancellor (British officer of state): *see* lord chancellor.

lord high steward, an honorific office that came to England with the Norman ducal household. From 1153 it was held by the earls of Leicester and then of Lancaster until it came into the hands of John of Gaunt, duke of Lancaster, who assumed control over the minor King Richard II and strengthened the office. By the Duke's order the minutes were kept of proceedings held before him on the claims to take part in the coronation ceremonies. The resulting judgments became precedents for the court of coronation claims held before the steward. (In the 20th century this court was still held before coronations but was presided over by commissioners.) In 1397 John of Gaunt established another notable tradition by presiding as lord high steward at the trial before Parliament of the Earl of Arundel and others. The lord high stewardship ceased to be a permanent post in 1421 with the death of Thomas of Lancaster, duke of Clarence. Thereafter a steward was appointed only to preside over the Court of Claims, to perform certain ceremonial duties at the following coronation, and, in certain cases, to preside over those members of the House of

Lords who were acting in their capacity as judges at the trial of a peer. The Criminal Justice Act of 1948 abolished the privilege of peers in relation to criminal proceedings, and the judicial function of the lord high steward thus ended.

Lord Howe Island, island dependency of New South Wales, Australia, situated in the southwestern Pacific Ocean, 436 miles (702 km) northeast of Sydney. It has an area of 7 square miles (17 square km). It was discovered in 1788 and named after Admiral Lord Howe by Lieutenant Henry Lidgbird Ball of the British navy. The island's main income derives from tourism. Pop. (1996) 369.

Lord Ordainer (English history): *see* Ordainer.

lord steward, also called LORD STEWARD OF THE HOUSEHOLD, in England, an official of the royal household, whose duties were originally domestic and who was known as the "chief steward" of the household. The office was of considerable political importance under the Tudors and Stuarts. In 1924 it ceased to be a political appointment and since then it has been filled at the discretion of the sovereign. In theory the lord steward is responsible for the day-to-day management and financial affairs of the royal household; in practice these functions are carried out by the master of the household. Thus, the duties of the lord steward are now purely ceremonial, though he is still the first dignitary of the court and is always a peer and a privy councillor.

Lords, House of, the upper chamber of Great Britain's bicameral legislature. Originating in the 11th century, when the Anglo-Saxon kings consulted witans (councils) composed of religious leaders and the monarch's ministers, it emerged as a distinct element of Parliament (*q.v.*) in the 13th and 14th centuries. It currently comprises the following elements: (1) the Lords Spiritual, including the archbishops of Canterbury and York and the bishops of Durham, London, and Winchester, as well as 21 other bishops holding sees in England; (2) from November 1999, 92 hereditary peers; (3) from January 1980, all life peers and peeresses created under the Life Peerages Act of 1958; and (4) the Law Lords, consisting of the judges of the Supreme Court of Judicature (the Court of Appeal and the High Court of Justice), who act as Britain's final court of appeal. The total number of persons qualified to sit in the House of Lords is in excess of 670.

The powers of the modern House of Lords are extremely limited—necessarily so, since the permanent and substantial majority enjoyed there by the Conservative Party would otherwise be incompatible with the principles of representative government. The House of Lords' powers are defined in the Parliament Act of 1911 and 1949. Under the 1911 act, all bills specified by the speaker of the House of Commons as money bills (involving taxation or expenditures) become law one month after being sent for consideration to the House of Lords, with or without the consent of that house. Under the 1949 act, all other public bills (except bills to extend the maximum duration of Parliament) not receiving the approval of the House of Lords become law provided that they are passed by two successive parliamentary sessions and that a period of one year has elapsed between the bill's second reading in the first session and its third reading in the second session. On rare occasions the 1949 act has been used to pass controversial legislation lacking the Lords's support—including the War Crimes Act of 1991, which enabled Britain to prosecute alleged war criminals who became British citizens or residents of Britain. The act has discouraged the House of Lords from opposing bills strongly supported by the House of Commons. The Salisbury convention of 1945, which prevents the Lords from rejecting a bill at second reading (the principle stage at which parliamentary bills are debated) if it fulfills any pledge in the government's election manifesto, has further constrained the Lords' power.

Despite these limitations, the House of Lords has played a significant role in Parliament. Its most useful functions are the revision of bills that the House of Commons has not formulated in sufficient detail and the first hearing of noncontroversial bills that are then able, with a minimum of debate, to pass through the House of Commons. It is further argued by some observers that the House of Lords serves a valuable function by providing a national forum of debate free from the constraints of party discipline. Although the defeat of major government legislation by the house has been relatively rare, it sometimes does defy the government, especially Labour Party governments. For example, the Labour government of 1974–79 was defeated 230 times by the House of Lords.

In 1998 the Labour government of Tony Blair introduced legislation to deprive hereditary peers (by then numbering 750) of their 700-year-old right to sit and vote in the upper chamber. A compromise, however, allowed 92 of them—who were elected by their fellow peers—to remain as temporary members. The measure, which went into effect in late 1999, was seen as a prelude to wider reform.

Lord's Cricket Ground, the headquarters and home ground of the Marylebone Cricket Club, long the world's foremost cricket organization, and the scene of Test matches between England and visiting national teams and of matches of the Middlesex County Cricket Club, Oxford versus Cambridge, and Eton versus Harrow. Various cup finals and one-day international matches also take place there. The original Lord's was established in 1787 at Dorset Square, St. Marylebone, southwest of Regent's Park, London, by Thomas Lord. In 1811 it was moved to St. John's Wood Estate and in 1814 to the present site, at St. John's Wood Road west of Regent's Park. Lord's is also the headquarters of the International Cricket Council, the world governing body, and of the Cricket Council and the Test and County Cricket Board, which control English cricket.

Lord's Prayer, Latin ORATIO DOMINICA, also called PATER NOSTER (Latin: "Our Father"), prayer taught by Jesus to his disciples, and the principal prayer used by all Christians in common worship. It appears in two forms in the New Testament, the shorter version in Luke 11:2–4 and the longer version, part of the Sermon on the Mount, in Matthew 6:9–13. In both contexts it is offered as a model of how to pray. Many scholars believe the version in Luke to be closer to the original, the extra phrases in Matthew's version having been added in liturgical use.

The Lord's Prayer resembles other prayers that came out of the Jewish matrix of Jesus' time and contains three common Jewish elements: praise, petition, and a yearning for the coming Kingdom of God. It consists of an introductory address and seven petitions. The Matthean version used by the Roman Catholic church is as follows:

Our Father who art in Heaven,
Hallowed be thy name;
Thy kingdom come;
Thy will be done
On earth as it is in heaven.
Give us this day our daily bread;
And forgive us our trespasses
As we forgive those who trespass against us;
And lead us not into temptation,
But deliver us from evil.

The English version of the Lord's Prayer used in many Protestant churches is the following (though some translations eliminate such archaisms as "thy" and "art," replacing them with "your" and "are"):

Our Father who art in Heaven,
Hallowed be thy name;
Thy kingdom come;
Thy will be done
On earth as it is in heaven.
Give us this day our daily bread;
And forgive us our debts
As we have forgiven our debtors;
And lead us not into temptation,
But deliver us from evil.
For thine is the kingdom
And the power
And the glory,
Forever.

The concluding doxology (short formula of praise) in the Protestant version was probably added early in the Christian era, since it occurs in some early manuscripts of the Gospels.

In 1977 the Church of England adopted a new version of the Lord's Prayer, closely following a version proposed by the International Consultation on English Texts (ICET), an interdenominational commission working to bring up to date prayers and texts used in English-language churches. The new version is:

Our Father in Heaven,
Hallowed be your Name,
Your kingdom come,
Your will be done,
On earth as in Heaven.
Give us today our daily bread.
Forgive us our sins
As we forgive those
Who sin against us.
Lead us not into temptation
But deliver us from evil.
For the kingdom, the power,
And the glory are yours
Now and for ever
Amen.

A number of other churches adopted texts based on the ICET version.

Biblical scholars disagree about Jesus' meaning in the Lord's Prayer. Some view it as "existential," referring to present human experience on earth, while others interpret it as eschatological, referring to the coming Kingdom of God. The prayer lends itself to both interpretations, and further questions are posed by the existence of different translations and the problems inherent in the process of translation. In the case of the term "daily bread," for example, the Greek word *epiousion,* which modifies "bread," has no known parallels in Greek writing and may have meant "for tomorrow." The petition "Give us this day our daily bread" may thus be given the eschatological interpretation "Give us today a foretaste of the heavenly banquet to come." This interpretation is supported by Ethiopic versions and by St. Jerome's reference to the reading "bread of the future" in the lost Gospel According to the Hebrews. The eschatological interpretation suggests that the Lord's Prayer may have been used in a eucharistic setting in the early church.

Lord's Supper (Christianity): *see* Eucharist; Last Supper.

Loredan, Pietro (d. 1439, Venice [Italy]), Venetian nobleman and admiral who became one of the city's popular heroes. His naval achievements ensured Venice's supremacy over its trading rivals in the Mediterranean and made it the dominant power in northeast Italy in the 15th century.

As captain of the Venetian fleet he defeated the Ottoman Turks, who had been threatening Venetian shipping, in a decisive battle near Gallipoli in June 1416. His sound naval strategy led to the defeat of the fleet of the rival city of Genoa, near Rapallo, in 1431. Five years later he was general of the republic in its war against the Marchese of Mantua.

Elected generalissimo in 1438, he reconquered the Venetian fortresses along the Po River, ensuring Venice's dominance in that area. Loredan, however, was ultimately defeated in his power struggle with the doge Francesco Foscari, a longtime enemy of his family, with whom Loredan had contended for the dogeship in 1433. Loredan was murdered in 1439. His death was attributed, probably without foundation, to Foscari's son Jacopo.

Lorelei, German LORELEY, large rock on the bank of the Rhine River near Sankt Goarshausen, Ger. The rock produces an echo and is associated with the legend of a beautiful maiden who threw herself into the Rhine in despair over a faithless lover and was transformed into a siren who lured fishermen to destruction. The essentials of the legend were claimed as his invention by German writer Clemens Brentano in his novel *Godwi* (1800–02). Lorelei has been the subject of a number of literary works and songs; the poem *Die Loreley* by Heinrich Heine was set to music by more than 25 composers.

Loren, Sophia, original name SOFIA SCICOLONE (b. Sept. 20, 1934, Rome, Italy), internationally popular Italian film actress best known for her portrayals of passionate, earthy women. At first noticed only for her statuesque proportions, she was later recognized as a talented actress of great emotional depth.

An illegitimate child, Loren spent her childhood in a poor, war-torn suburb of Naples. At 15, after winning second place in a local beauty contest, she became a model and film extra in Rome. Two years later she starred in a semidocumentary, *Africa sotto i mari* (1952; "Africa Under the Sea"). Dozens of later films as varied as the comedy *L'oro di Napoli* (1954; "The Gold of Naples") and the adaptation of the opera *Aida* (1954) brought her European fame and, eventually, international stardom. Though most of Loren's Hollywood films are unremarkable, she won critical attention for her portrayal of the pessimistic, wily girl in *Desire Under the Elms* (1958) and as the widow of a gangster in *The Black Orchid* (1959). She achieved immense respect as an actress in a film directed by Vittorio De Sica, *La ciociara* (1961; "The Peasant"; *Two Women*), for which she won an American Academy Award for her performance as a devoted mother of a teenaged girl in wartime Italy. Her later films include *Ieri, oggi, domani* (1964; *Yesterday, Today, and Tomorrow*), *Matrimonio all'italiana* (1964; *Marriage—Italian Style*), *Sunflower* (1970), *The Priest's Wife* (1971), *Man of La Mancha* (1972), *Il Viaggio* (1974; *The Voyage*), and *Una Giornata Particolare* (1977; *A Special Day*).

Sophia Loren in *Boccaccio '70* (1962)
Brown Brothers

Loren's marriage in 1957 to the producer Carlo Ponti, who guided her early film career, was interrupted in 1962 by a highly publicized charge of bigamy resulting from the stringent Italian divorce laws. After an annulment, they were remarried in 1966.

Lorena, city, southeastern São Paulo *estado* ("state"), Brazil. It lies along the Paraíba do Sul River, at 1,719 feet (524 m) above sea level. Formerly known as Pôrto de Guaipacaré and Freguesia de Nossa Senhora da Aparecida, it was given town status in 1782 and was made the seat of a municipality in 1788. The city is a trade centre for an agricultural hinterland in which rice, corn (maize), *feijão* (beans), potatoes, sugarcane, coffee, and fruits are cultivated. It has a sugar refinery and such varied manufactures as chemical products, concrete tubing, and furniture. Situated midway between the cities of São Paulo and Rio de Janeiro, Lorena is easily accessible by rail and road and also has an airfield. Pop. (1991 prelim.) 67,766.

Lorengau, town, northeastern Manus Island, in the Admiralty Islands, Papua New Guinea. It lies on Seeadler Harbour. Captured by the Japanese in 1942, the settlement was retaken by Allied forces in 1944 and eventually became part of a large U.S. naval and air base. As a port, the town handles the local copra production. Pop. (1990 prelim.) 4,547.

Lorentz, Hendrik Antoon (b. July 18, 1853, Arnhem, Neth.—d. Feb. 4, 1928, Haarlem), Dutch physicist and joint winner (with Pieter Zeeman) of the Nobel Prize for Physics in 1902 for his theory of electromagnetic radiation, which, confirmed by findings of Zeeman, gave rise to Albert Einstein's special theory of relativity.

Hendrik Antoon Lorentz
By courtesy of the Nobelstiftelsen

Lorentz was appointed professor of mathematical physics at Leiden University in 1878. In his doctoral thesis (1875) he refined the electromagnetic theory of James C. Maxwell of England so that it more satisfactorily explained the reflection and refraction of light. His work in physics was wide in scope, but his central aim was to construct a single theory to explain the relationship of electricity, magnetism, and light. Although, according to Maxwell's theory, electromagnetic radiation is produced by the oscillation of electric charges, the charges that produce light were unknown. Since it was generally believed that an electric current was made up of charged particles, Lorentz later theorized that the atoms of matter might also consist of charged particles and suggested that the oscillations of these charged particles (electrons) inside the atom were the source of light. If this were true, then a strong magnetic field ought to have an effect on the oscillations and therefore on the wavelength of the light thus produced. In 1896 Zeeman, a pupil of Lorentz, demonstrated this phenomenon, known as the Zeeman effect, and in 1902 they were awarded the Nobel Prize.

Lorentz' electron theory was not, however, successful in explaining the negative results of the Michelson-Morley experiment, an effort to measure the velocity of the Earth through the hypothetical luminiferous ether by comparing the velocities of light from different directions. In an attempt to overcome this difficulty he introduced in 1895 the idea of local time (different time rates in different locations). Arriving at the notion that moving bodies approaching the velocity of light contract in the direction of motion, Lorentz in 1904 developed the Lorentz transformations. These mathematical formulas describe the increase of mass, shortening of length, and dilation of time that are characteristic of a moving body and form the basis of Einstein's special theory of relativity. In 1912 Lorentz became director of research at the Teyler Institute, Haarlem, though he remained honorary professor at Leiden, where he gave weekly lectures.

Lorentz, Pare (b. Dec. 11, 1905, Clarksburg, W.Va., U.S.—d. March 4, 1992, Armonk, N.Y.), American filmmaker whose government-sponsored documentaries focused attention on the waste of human and natural resources in the United States in the 1930s.

Lorentz was a well-known movie critic in New York City when, in 1935, he was requested to set up a federal government film program that would effectively highlight the problems of American agriculture. A film-production unit was formed under the sponsorship of the Resettlement Administration (later, it became part of the Department of Agriculture), and the following year Lorentz' *The Plow That Broke the Plains* (1936) was released. A classic among documentary films, it recounts, with a harmonious blend of poetic images, narrative, and music, the agricultural misuse of the Great Plains that resulted in the Dust Bowl of the 1930s. Lorentz then wrote and directed *The River* (1937) for the Department of Agriculture. This history of the Mississippi River basin and the effect of the Tennessee Valley Authority on the area further realized the potential of the documentary as a powerful impetus to social change. The two films were commercially and artistically successful both in the United States and abroad and stirred widespread discussion not only of the problems presented but also of the documentary approach to filmmaking.

Lorentz' film unit became the United States Film Service in the late 1930s and was expanded to produce motion pictures and shorts for various government agencies. Lorentz directed *The Fight for Life* (1940), the compelling and starkly realistic story of the struggle of a young doctor against disease and death during pregnancy and childbirth in a city slum.

Pare Lorentz, 1938
AP/Wide World Photos

The United States Film Service was disbanded by Congress in 1941. Lorentz made films for the United States Army Air Forces during World War II. In 1946, with Stuart Schulberg, he produced for the War Department a stark documentary account of Nazi activities recounted in the Nürnberg trials. The film played to capacity audiences for two years in Germany but was not released in the United States until 1979.

Consult the INDEX *first*

Lorentz–FitzGerald contraction, also called SPACE CONTRACTION, in relativity physics, the shortening of an object along the direction of its motion relative to an observer. Dimensions in other directions are not contracted. The concept of the contraction was proposed by the Irish physicist George FitzGerald in 1889, and it was thereafter independently developed by Hendrik Lorentz of The Netherlands. The Michelson–Morley experiment in the 1880s had challenged the postulates of classical physics by proving that the speed of light is the same for all observers, regardless of their relative motion. FitzGerald and Lorentz attempted to preserve the classical concepts by demonstrating the manner in which space contraction of the measuring apparatus would reduce the apparent constancy of the speed of light to the status of an experimental artifact.

In 1905 the German-American physicist Albert Einstein reversed the classical view by proposing that the speed of light is indeed a universal constant and showing that space contraction then becomes a logical consequence of the relative motion of different observers. Significant at speeds approaching that of light, the contraction is a consequence of the properties of space and time and does not depend on compression, cooling, or any similar physical disturbance. *See also* time dilation.

Lorentz transformations, set of equations in relativity physics that relate the space and time coordinates of two systems moving at a constant velocity relative to each other. Required to describe high-speed phenomena approaching the speed of light, Lorentz transformations formally express the relativity concepts that space and time are not absolute; that length, time, and mass depend on the relative motion of the observer; and that the speed of light in a vacuum is constant and independent of the motion of the observer or the source. *See also* Galilean transformations.

Lorenz, Konrad (b. Nov. 7, 1903, Vienna—d. Feb. 27, 1989, Altenburg, Austria), Austrian zoologist, founder of modern ethology, the study of animal behaviour by means of comparative zoological methods. His ideas contributed to an understanding of how behavioral patterns may be traced to an evolutionary past, and he was also known for his work on the roots of aggression. He shared the Nobel Prize for Physiology or Medicine in 1973 with the animal behaviourists Karl von Frisch and Nikolaas Tinbergen.

Lorenz was the son of an orthopedic surgeon. He showed an interest in animals at an early age, and he kept animals of various species—fish, birds, monkeys, dogs, cats, and rabbits—many of which he brought home from his boyhood excursions. While still young, he provided nursing care for sick animals from the nearby Schönbrunner Zoo. He also kept detailed records of bird behaviour in the form of diaries.

In 1922, after graduating from secondary school, he followed his father's wishes that he study medicine and spent two semesters at Columbia University, in New York City. He then returned to Vienna to study.

During his medical studies Lorenz continued to make detailed observations of animal behaviour; a diary about a jackdaw that he kept was published in 1927 in the prestigious *Journal für Ornithologie.* He received the M.D. degree in Vienna in 1928 and was awarded the Ph.D. degree in zoology in 1933. Encouraged by the positive response to his scientific work, Lorenz established colonies of birds, such as the jackdaw and greylag goose, published a series of research papers on his observations of them, and soon gained an international reputation. In 1935 Lorenz described learning behaviour in young ducklings and goslings. He observed that at a certain critical stage soon after hatching, they learn to follow real or foster parents. The process, which is called imprinting, involves visual and auditory stimuli from the parent object; these elicit a following response in the young that affects their subsequent adult behaviour. Lorenz demonstrated the phenomenon by appearing before newly hatched mallard ducklings and imitating a mother duck's quacking sounds, upon which the young birds regarded him as their mother and followed him accordingly.

In 1936 the German Society for Animal Psychology was founded. The following year Lorenz became coeditor in chief of the new *Zeitschrift für Tierpsychologie,* which became a leading journal for ethology. Also in 1937, he was appointed lecturer in comparative anatomy and animal psychology at the University of Vienna. From 1940 to 1942 he was

Lorenz
Hermann Kacher

professor and head of the department of general psychology at the Albertus University at Königsberg.

From 1942 to 1944 he served as a physician in the German army and was captured as a prisoner of war in the Soviet Union. He was returned to Austria in 1948 and headed the Institute of Comparative Ethology at Altenberg from 1949 to 1951. In 1950 he established a comparative ethology department in the Max Planck Institute of Buldern, Westphalia, becoming codirector of the Institute in 1954. From 1961 to 1973 he served as director of the Max Planck Institute for Behaviour Physiology, in Seewiesen. In 1973 Lorenz, together with Frisch and Tinbergen, was awarded the Nobel Prize for Physiology or Medicine for their discoveries concerning animal behavioral patterns. In the same year, Lorenz became director of the department of animal sociology at the Institute for Comparative Ethology of the Austrian Academy of Sciences in Altenberg.

Lorenz's early scientific contributions dealt with the nature of instinctive behavioral acts, particularly how such acts come about and the source of nervous energy for their performance. He also investigated how behaviour may result from two or more basic drives that are activated simultaneously in an animal. Working with Tinbergen of The Netherlands, Lorenz showed that different forms of behaviour are harmonized in a single action sequence.

Lorenz's concepts advanced the modern scientific understanding of how behavioral patterns evolve in a species, particularly with respect to the role played by ecological factors and the adaptive value of behaviour for species survival. He proposed that animal species are genetically constructed so as to learn specific kinds of information that are important for the survival of the species. His ideas have also cast light on how behavioral patterns develop and mature during the life of an individual organism.

In the latter part of his career, Lorenz applied his ideas to the behaviour of humans as members of a social species, an application with controversial philosophical and sociological implications. In a popular book, *Das sogenannte Böse* (1963; *On Aggression*), he argued that fighting and warlike behaviour in man have an inborn basis but can be environmentally modified by the proper understanding and provision for the basic instinctual needs of human beings. Fighting in lower animals has a positive survival function, he observed, such as the dispersion of competitors and the maintenance of territory. Warlike tendencies in humans may likewise be ritualized into socially useful behaviour patterns. In another work, *Die Rückseite des Spiegels: Versuch einer Naturgeschichte menschlichen Erkennens* (1973; *Behind the Mirror: A Search for a Natural History of Human Knowledge*), Lorenz examined the nature of human thought and intelligence and attributed the problems of modern civilization largely to the limitations his study revealed. (E.H.H./Ed.)

BIBLIOGRAPHY. Lorenz's works, other than those mentioned earlier, include *King Solomon's Ring: New Light on Animal Ways* (1952, reissued 1980; originally published in German, 1949); *Man Meets Dog* (1953, reissued 1980; originally published in German, 1949), both entertaining semipopular accounts of Lorenz's experiences with animals and his views on animal behaviour; and *The Foundations of Ethology* (1981; originally published in German, 1978), a comprehensive restatement and assessment of the major themes of his work. Lorenz's life and his general approach to the study of behaviour are well described in Alec Nisbett, *Konrad Lorenz* (1976).

Lorenzetti, Ambrogio (b. *c.* 1290, Siena, Republic of Siena—d. 1348), younger brother of Pietro Lorenzetti, who ranks in importance with the greatest of the Italian Sienese painters, Duccio and Simone Martini. Only six documented works of Ambrogio, apparently covering a period of merely 13 years, have survived.

"Annunciation," panel by Ambrogio Lorenzetti, 1344; in the Pinacoteca Nazionale, Siena, Italy
SCALA—Art Resource

They include four scenes from the legend of St. Nicholas of Bari in the Uffizi, Florence, which are parts of an altarpiece painted about 1332 in Florence; the "Good and Bad Government" wall decorations of 1337–39 in the Sala della Pace in the Palazzo Pubblico, Siena, and the signed and dated panels of the "Presentation of Christ in the Temple" (1342) in the Uffizi and of the "Annunciation" (1344) in the Pinacoteca Nazionale, Siena.

It is not known who Ambrogio's teacher was, but his early works indicate that he early received his main inspiration from the art of Duccio, his brother Pietro, and Giotto. Already his representations reveal a realistic individualism and an intense preoccupation with significant composition and form. These characteristics are most evident in the "Allegories" in the Palazzo Pubblico, the most important Sienese fresco decoration. In it Ambrogio is seen as an acute observer, an empirical explorer of linear and aerial perspective, a student of classical works of art, and a political and moral philosopher. His desire to depict spatial depth convincingly led him to an increasingly accurate rendering of space in his paintings and almost to one-point perspective in his last work, the "Annunciation." With his profound interest in perspective and in classical antiquity, Ambrogio anticipated the Renaissance. The art of the Lorenzettis was widely imitated in Siena during the third quarter of the 14th century, and many works by close followers are still commonly attributed to one or the other brother.

Lorenzetti, Pietro (b. *c.* 1280/90, Siena?, Republic of Siena—d. *c.* 1348, Siena), Italian Gothic painter of the Sienese school who with his brother Ambrogio was the principal exponent of Sienese secular art in the years before the Black Death. Little is known of

"Birth of the Virgin," panel by Pietro Lorenzetti, 1342; in the Museo dell'Opera del Duomo, Siena, Italy
SCALA—Art Resource/EB Inc.

Lorenzetti's life, and the attribution and dating of many of the works associated with him remains hazardous.

He was probably a pupil of Duccio, whose influence is seen in the graceful linearity and rich colour of Lorenzetti's earliest documented work, the altarpiece (1320) in the Pieve di Sta. Maria, in Arezzo. But the altar's centrepiece, a "Madonna and Child," replaces Duccio's frigidly hierarchical conception of the subject with an intimate depiction of an affectionate mother caressing her mischievously playful baby. Those features, combined with the wealth of decorative detail (recalling Simone Martini) and the plasticity of the figures (derived from Giovanni Pisano), lend the painting a vivacity rare in contemporary Sienese art.

Sometime during 1330–40, Lorenzetti worked on a number of frescoes in the lower church of S. Francesco, in Assisi. The "Deposition," in its clarity of composition and the monumentality of the sculpture-like draperies, shows a sensitive response to the art of Giotto. Lorenzetti's figures achieve corporeality by means of strong, only partly blended colours. The "Madonna and Child" in the same cycle, however, returns to the intimacy of the Arezzo altarpiece in the Child's exuberance and the Madonna's reproving look and abrupt gesture toward St. Francis. It is in such scenes as the "Last Supper" that he departs most strikingly from Giotto. He abandons Giotto's unity of time and place and compositional clarity in favour of carefully rendered minutiae and nonessential anecdote. That love of detail intrudes upon the otherwise Giottesque "Crucifixions" in S. Francesco, Siena, and Museo Diocesaro, Cortona.

Lorenzetti's mature style is epitomized in the triptych "Birth of the Virgin" (1342; Museo dell'Opera del Duomo, Siena), his last major work. That he used the decorative detail and familial anecdotes as the theme of a major altarpiece is illustrative of his nonhierarchical, humanizing tendencies. Perhaps the most notable feature of the "Birth" is its sophisticated handling of perspective and the logical placement of figures within space. The arches and colonnettes of the triptych frame form the foreground of the painted picture space, and one of the figures is painted in such a way that it appears to be standing behind one of the colonnettes. This constitutes one of the most advanced perspective studies of its time.

Lorenzini, Carlo: *see* Collodi, C.

Lorenzo MONACO (Italian: Lorenzo the Monk), original name PIERO DI GIOVANNI (b. *c.* 1370/71, Siena, Republic of Siena—d. *c.* 1425, Florence), Italian painter in the International Gothic style whose work combined the rhythmic, graceful flow of line and decorative feeling of the Sienese school with the Florentine traditions of the followers of Giotto. He took the vows of the Camaldolese order in 1391 and lived mostly at the monastery of Sta. Maria degli Angeli, in Florence.

His large polyptych "Madonna and Child" (1406–10; Uffizi, Florence) and the "Coronation of the Virgin" (1413; Uffizi, Florence) reflect his typically blond palette, his predilection for swirling draperies and rhythmic, curvilinear forms, and his knowledgeable use of light. Lorenzo's feeling for decorative composition and expressive line is especially evident in his small predella pieces, such as the three small fragments at the Accademia in Florence, representing the "Nativity," the "Life of a Hermit," and a stormy seascape. Such late works as his "Adoration of the Magi" (*c.* 1422; Uffizi, Florence) show Lorenzo's mature sense of design. During the final years of his life, he was influenced by the naturalism of Lorenzo Ghiberti, as can be seen in his frescoes of the "Life of the Virgin" and the "Annunciation

"Nativity," predella panel of "Coronation of the Virgin" by Lorenzo Monaco, *c.* 1413; in the Uffizi, Florence
SCALA—Art Resource/EB Inc.

Altarpiece" (1420–24; both in the Bartolini Chapel, Sta. Trinità, Florence). He was also a miniaturist, but no illuminations have been assigned to him with certainty.

Lorenzo THE MAGNIFICENT: *see* Medici, Lorenzo de'.

Lorestān, also spelled LURISTAN, *ostān* (province), western Iran, with an area of 12,117 sq mi (31,383 sq km). It is bounded by the *ostāns* of Kermānshāhān on the northwest, Hamadān and Markazī (Tehrān) on the northeast, Īlām on the west-southwest, Khūzestān on the south, and Eṣfahān on the east. It is also a historical region (the name means Land of the Lurs) extending from the Iraqi frontier and Kermanshah and separating the Khūzestān lowland from interior uplands.

Extensive mountains stretch northwest–southeast; between the higher ranges are well-watered pockets with lush pastures. Oak forest covers the outer slopes, together with elm, maple, walnut, and almond trees. The Lurs are of aboriginal stock with strong Iranian and Arab admixtures, speak a Persian dialect, and are Shīʿah Muslims. Under the Pahlavis the Lurs were settled, and only a few retain their pastoral nomadism. Lorestān was inhabited by Iranian Indo-European peoples, including the Medes, *c.* 1,000 BC. Cimmerians and Scythians intermittently ruled the region from about 700 to 625. The Luristan Bronzes, noted for their eclectic array of Assyrian, Babylonian, and Iranian artistic motifs, date from this turbulent period. The bronzes were found mainly in tombs near Bakhtarān (now in Bakhtarān, formerly Kermānshāhān, *ostān*). Cyaxares, ruler of the Medes, drove out the Scythians in about 620. Under Cyrus the Great, Lorestān was incorporated into the growing Achaemenid Empire in about 540 and successively was part of the Seleucid, Parthian, and Sāsānid dynasties.

Little Lorestān, the northern part, was governed by independent princes of the Khorshīdī dynasty, called *atabegs*, from 1155 to the beginning of the 17th century, when the last *atabeg,* Shāh Vardī Khān, was removed by the Ṣafavid ʿAbbās I the Great and government of the territory was given to the chief of a rival tribe, with the title of *vālī;* his descendants retained the title.

The southern part of Lorestān, or Great Lorestān, is composed of Bakhtīārī, Kuhgalu, and Mamaseni districts. Great Lorestān was independent under the Faḍlawayh (Fazlaveye) *atabegs* from 1160 until 1424; its capital was Idaj, now only mounds and ruins at Malamir.

Lorestān *ostān* proper stretches between the Dez valley (used by the Trans-Iranian Railway) and the Upper Karkheh River, and northward to near Imāmshahr and Nehāvend. Agriculture is the mainstay of the economy; crops include rice, wheat, barley, cotton, oilseeds, sugar beets, vegetables, and fruits. Industries produce cement, sugar, processed foods, carded wool, and ginned cotton. Iron ore and molybdenum are mined. Roads and railways link Khorramābād, the capital of the *ostān,* with Borūjerd and Alīgūdarz. Pop. (1983 est.) 1,074,000.

Lorestān Bronze (metalwork): *see* Luristan Bronze.

Loreto, town and episcopal see, Ancona province, Marche region, central Italy, on the Musone River just south of Ancona and near the Adriatic coast. It is a noted pilgrimage resort famous for the Santa Casa, or Holy House of the Virgin. According to tradition, the Santa Casa, threatened with destruction by the Turks in 1291, was carried from Nazareth by the ministry of angels and deposited on a hill at Tersatto in Dalmatia; there an alleged appearance of the Virgin and miraculous cures attested to its sanctity. In 1294 it was similarly transported across the Adriatic to a laurel grove (*lauretum,* whence Loreto) near Recanati and in 1295 from there to its present site.

Papal bulls were issued in favour of the shrine. Pope Innocent VII established a special mass for the feast of the Transportation of the Holy House (December 10). Benedict XV declared the Madonna di Loreto to be the patron of aviators (1920). The chief festival is held on September 8, the Nativity of Our Lady.

The Holy House is enclosed by a lofty marble screen designed by Donato Bramante and reposes in the Santuario della Santa Casa, a late Gothic structure begun in 1468 and continued by Giuliano da Maiano, Giuliano da Sangallo, Bramante, and other architects, who altered the original plan, which was again revived in 1886 by Giuseppe Sacconi. The facade of the basilica was completed under Pope Sixtus V (1585–90), whose colossal statue stands in the middle of the entrance steps. Over the main door is a life-size bronze statue of the Virgin and Child by Girolamo Lombardo; the three superb late 16th-century bronze doors are also by Lombardo, his sons, and his pupils. The interior of the church has mosaics of Domenichino, Guido Reni, Barrocci, and Carlo Maratti and frescoes by Melozzo da Forlì and Luca Signorelli. The Santa Casa itself is of plain stone, 28 ft (9 m) by 12½ ft and 13½ ft in height, with a niche containing a small black image of the Virgin and Child in Lebanon cedar. Adjacent to the sanctuary on the Piazza della Madonna is the Palazzo Apostolico. The rest of the town is virtually a long narrow street lined with shops for the sale of religious objects. Pop. (1990 est.) mun., 10,618.

Loreto, department (formed 1866) of eastern Peru, bounded by Colombia (northeast), Ecuador (northwest), and Brazil (east). Largest of Peru's departments, it occupies 134,432 sq mi (348,177 sq km), more than one-fourth the total area of the country.

Loreto lies almost entirely in the Amazonian rain forest at an average elevation of about 500 ft (152 m). The climate is hot and humid, with heavy rainfall. The Ucayali River and its tributaries drain the south, and the Marañón River and its affluents the west. Below Nauta, the Ucayali and Marañón unite to form the Amazon, which is joined downstream by the Río Napa, flowing from the north. Ocean steamers can reach Nauta; smaller vessels can penetrate much farther inland.

Important exports of Loreto include rubber, Brazil nuts, skins and hides, and hardwoods. Rice, sugarcane, bananas, manioc, and other tropical plants are cultivated. The population is concentrated along the river banks, especially in Iquitos (*q.v.*), the departmental capital. Little-known Indians inhabit the interior. Transportation is mainly by river, although now, in Ucayali department, Iquitos and Yurimaguas have airports, and several towns have landing strips. In 1980 the department of Ucayali was created from the former southern part of Loreto. Pop. (1990 est.) 654,100.

Loria, Ruggiero di: *see* Lauria, Ruggiero di.

lorica, a tubular, conical, or vaselike structure secreted by some protozoans (*e.g., Stentor*) and many rotifers. Many species incorporate sand grains and other particles into the lorica for reinforcement. The loose-fitting lorica, closed at one end, has a large opening at the anterior end through which part of the organism (or its appendages) may be extended. The lorica is of taxonomic importance among Protozoa. *See also* test.

Lorient, maritime town, Morbihan *département,* Bretagne region, western France, southeast of Quimper, and west-southwest of Paris, situated on the right bank of the Scorff River at its confluence with the Blavet on the Bay of Biscay. Almost completely destroyed by bombing in 1944, the town was rebuilt after World War II.

The fishing port of Kéroman (one of the most important in France), to the south of the town, sends special rail deliveries to Paris and Bordeaux. Nearby, the submarine base built by the Germans during World War II is used for French submarines. The arsenal, on the banks of the Scorff, specializes in the construction of prefabricated naval vessels. The commercial and naval ports are of minor national importance. Main industries include textiles, furniture, paint production, fish canning, and the manufacture of navigational equipment for pleasure craft.

The medieval hamlet of Blavet took the name of Port-Louis when a citadel was built on the site under Louis XIII, king of France (reigned 1610–43). In 1664, Louis XIV (reigned 1643–1715) authorized a merchant company to settle there; and the town was named L'Orient in reference to the Eastern countries with which it traded. The town prospered and was further enlarged when another major trading company settled there in 1719. After France lost its possessions in India, commerce declined. Louis XVI (reigned 1774–92) bought the port and established a royal arsenal there. Pop. (1990) 59,271.

lorikeet, any of numerous parrots of the subfamily Loriinae. *See* parrot.

Lorillard Company, in full P. LORILLARD COMPANY, oldest tobacco manufacturer in the United States, dating to 1760, when a French immigrant, Pierre Lorillard, opened a "manufactory" in New York City. It originally made pipe tobacco, cigars, plug chewing tobacco, and snuff. Tobacco for "roll-your-own" cigarettes was introduced in 1860, and cigarettes were being manufactured by the 1880s. From the 1890s to 1911 it was a part of the giant tobacco trust, the American Tobacco Company (*see* American Brands, Inc.), but once more became independent when the U.S. Court of Appeals dissolved the trust.

Lorillard's chief cigarettes have been Old Gold (introduced in 1926) and Kent (1952).

The company, now called Lorillard, is a division of the conglomerate Loews Corporation and is headquartered in New York City. The major factory is in Greensboro, N.C.

Lorimer, George Horace (b. Oct. 6, 1867, Louisville, Ky., U.S.—d. Oct. 22, 1937, Wyncote, Pa.), U.S. editor of *The Saturday Evening Post,* during whose long tenure (May 17, 1899–Jan. 1, 1937) the magazine attained its greatest success, partly because of his astute judgment of popular U.S. tastes in literature.

After working for Philip D. Armour's meat-packing company in Chicago (1887–95) and failing in his own wholesale grocery business,

Lorimer

By courtesy of the Library of Congress, Washington, D.C.

Lorimer went to Boston and became a newspaper reporter. When Cyrus H.K. Curtis bought *The Saturday Evening Post* in 1897, he hired Lorimer as literary editor and then made him editor in chief. In 1932 Lorimer became president of the Curtis Publishing Company.

In the *Post* he published works by some of the best U.S. writers of the time: Stephen Crane, Frank Norris, Theodore Dreiser, Jack London, Willa Cather, Ring Lardner, F. Scott Fitzgerald, and Sinclair Lewis. In addition, he brought such European authors as Joseph Conrad and John Galsworthy to U.S. readers. It was sometimes believed, however, that he accidentally found excellence while seeking mere novelty; the poet Ezra Pound remarked (in *Guide to Kulchur*) that "Lorimer honestly didn't know that there ever had been a civilization."

loris, any of the tailless Indo-Malay primates, family Lorisidae, of the genera *Loris* (slender loris) and *Nycticebus* (slow loris). Lorises are found in forested regions and may be recognized by their soft, gray or brown fur; huge

Slender loris (*Loris tardigradus*)

Tierbilder Okapia, Frankfurt am Main

eyes encircled by dark patches; and shortened index fingers. They are arboreal and nocturnal, curling up to sleep by day. They move with great deliberation and often hang by their feet with their hands free to gain holds on branches or to grasp food.

The slender loris (*L. tardigradus*) of India and Sri Lanka is about 20–25 centimetres (8–10 inches) long and has long, slender limbs, small hands, a rounded head, and a pointed muzzle. It feeds on insects and small animals and apparently is solitary. The female usually bears a single young after about 160–170 days' gestation.

The two species of slow lorises are more robust and have shorter, stouter limbs, more rounded snouts, and smaller eyes and ears. They are found in Southeast Asia and the Malay Peninsula. The smaller species (*N. pygmaeus*) is about 20 cm long; the larger (*N. coucang*) is about 27–38 cm long. Slow lorises are slower moving than slender lorises and feed on insects, small animals, fruit, and vegetation. The females bear one (sometimes two) young after about 190 days' gestation.

Loris, Heinrich: *see* Glareanus, Henricus.

Loris-Melikov, Mikhail Tariyelovich, Graf (Count) (b. Jan. 1, 1826 [Dec. 20, 1825, old style], Tiflis, Russia—d. Dec. 24 [Dec. 12, O.S.], 1888, Nice, Fr.), military officer and statesman who, as minister of the interior at the end of the reign of the emperor Alexander II (ruled 1855–81), formulated reforms designed to liberalize the Russian autocracy.

Loris-Melikov was the son of an Armenian merchant. He attended the Lazarev School of Oriental Languages and the Guards' Cadet Institute in St. Petersburg before he joined a hussar regiment in 1843. Assigned to the Caucasus in 1847, he served as governor of the Terek region (1863–75) and, while commanding an army corps in Turkey during the Russo-Turkish War of 1877–78, scored notable military victories. For his heroism, he was made a count.

After serving briefly as governor-general of the plague-ridden lower Volga region (1879), Loris-Melikov was transferred to the provinces of central Russia, where he recommended to the emperor a modest scheme of administrative and economic reforms, aimed at alleviating the causes of social discontent and, thereby, combating revolutionary terrorism. Impressed by his suggestions, Alexander appointed him chairman of a special commission that was given authority to use the entire government apparatus to suppress the revolutionary movement and also to prepare a reform program for the country. Six months later Alexander abolished the commission and named Loris-Melikov the new minister of the interior (November 1880).

In this position Loris-Melikov devised a program of moderate reforms that included provisions for locally elected representatives to give the government advice on certain current problems. Although the project was approved in principle by Alexander, the emperor was assassinated (March 13 [March 1, O.S.], 1881) before it was formally enacted. When his successor, Alexander III, rejected the reform program and firmly committed himself to the preservation of the autocracy, Loris-Melikov resigned (May 19 [May 7], 1881), retiring to Nice.

Lorrain, Claude (painter): *see* Claude Lorrain.

Lorraine, German LOTHRINGEN, *région,* encompassing the northeastern French *départements* of Vosges, Meuse, Meurthe-et-Moselle, and Moselle and roughly coextensive with the historical region of Lorraine. The capital is Metz. The region has an area of 9,092 square miles (23,547 square km) and is bounded by the *départements* of Ardennes and Marne to the west, Haute-Marne and Haute-Saône to the south, and Haut-Rhin and Bas-Rhin to the east. Germany, Luxembourg, and Belgium lie to the north.

The *gouvernement* of Lorraine and Bar in 1789

By the treaty of Verdun (AD 843), the three sons of the Carolingian emperor Louis I the Pious divided the Frankish territory into three parts: Francia Occidentalis went to Charles II the Bald, Francia Orientalis to Louis the German, and Francia Media, the zone extending from the Low Countries to Italy, to the emperor Lothair I. This Francia Media was partitioned by Lothair I in 855 between his sons: the elder, Louis II, received Italy and the imperial title; the younger, Lothair, received the northern area, henceforward known as Lothair's kingdom, or Lotharingia.

This kingdom was bounded on the north by the North Sea; on the east by a line from the mouth of the Ems River to Wesel and then by the Rhine southward to the confluence of the Aare River (but with a westward recession of the frontier that left Mainz, Worms, and Speyer to the Germans); on the south by the Aare and by the Jura Mountains; and on the west by the Saône River (from a point just south of the Doubs confluence) and the Ornain, Meuse, and Schelde rivers.

After King Lothair died without heirs in 869, sovereignty over the area was repeatedly contested until 925, when it was finally conquered by the German king Henry I, who created the duchy of Lotharingia. His successor, Otto I, eventually entrusted the duchy to his brother, Bruno, archbishop of Cologne.

In 959 Bruno divided Lotharingia into two parts, the southern Upper Lorraine and the northern Lower Lorraine, with their boundary running from a point on the Rhine north of Andernach westward and southwestward to a point on the Meuse north of Mézières. Lower Lorraine thus included most of the historic Netherlands belonging to the German kingdom between the Rhine, middle Meuse, and Schelde rivers, while Upper Lorraine included the Ardennes, the Moselle valley, and the upper Meuse valley. From the time of Bruno's death (965), the two duchies remained separate, except for the years 1033–44. By the early 12th century the duchy of Lower Lorraine was being rivaled by the growing countships of Limburg, Hainaut, Louvain, and Namur; and in 1190 the reigning duke dropped the title Duke of Lothier (*i.e.,* Lower Lorraine) and took that of Duke of Brabant, as Henry I (d. 1235).

With the dissolution of the Lower duchy, the Upper duchy came to be called simply Lorraine. It remained with one Gerard of Châtenois and his male descendants from 1048 to 1431. The authority of these dukes was offset not only by the temporal power of the three bishoprics within their frontiers, namely Metz, Toul, and Verdun, but also by the rise of great feudal dynasties: the counts of Luxembourg challenged the dukes in the north; the counts of Bar were dangerous vassals in the west; and from 1070 a junior branch of the ducal house held the countship of Vaudémont in the southwest. The dukes, who had their capital at Nancy, therefore sought the protection of their suzerains, the German kings or emperors, but, from 1250 on, these sovereigns were too weak to protect Lorraine from French and Burgundian encroachments. Lorraine, united with Bar and Vaudémont in 1480, nevertheless survived and even rose to the zenith of its prosperity in the late 16th century.

French domination of the area dates from the 17th century, when control of the duchy became vital in the struggles between the French kings and the Habsburgs, who ruled the Holy Roman Empire. The French had already established a foothold by taking Metz, Toul, and Verdun in 1552, and they occupied the duchy a number of times in the devastating wars of the 17th century. Lorraine was given to Stanisław I, the former king of Poland and father-in-law of the French king Louis XV, by the treaties ending the War of the Polish Succession (1738). On Stanisław's death in 1766, Lorraine was incorporated into France as an administrative *généralité* under an intendant (royal governor), with Nancy as its capital. It was broken up into *départements* during the French Revolution (1790).

Part of Lorraine, along with Alsace, was joined to the German Reich after the French defeat in the Franco-German War of 1870–71 but was returned to France at the end of World War I.

Lorraine contains some of the largest iron-ore deposits in Europe. The ore is low-grade, however, and major development of the Lorraine field took place only after the Franco-German War, when the Thomas-Gilchrist process enabled its ores to be used in steelmaking. In subsequent decades the Lorraine ore field was rapidly developed on both sides of the frontier and came to account for the bulk of French production. Despite the attractions of jobs in the mines and mills of Lorraine, it, like most regions of France, lost population during the 20th century. The population is heavily concentrated along the Moselle River between Nancy and Thionville. Vosges, western Meuse, and southern Meurthe-et-Moselle remain largely rural.

Emigration from the countryside has encouraged the spread of animal husbandry. Dairying dominates agriculture, with the result that barley has supplanted wheat as the region's leading cereal. Viticulture is largely limited to the area around Toul. Forests cover more than one-third of the land.

The production of coal, which is concentrated around Forbach, declined sharply after 1960. Iron is mined around Briey (Meurthe-et-Moselle), Longwy, and Thionville; production has been undermined by imports of high-grade ores, with the result that metalworking industries have contracted. Salt is mined in Meurthe-et-Moselle around Dombasle-sur-Meurthe.

Lorraine is linked by railroad to Berlin, Amsterdam, Brussels, Basel, and Milan and has benefited from the establishment of the European Economic Community in 1957. The regional park of Lorraine was opened in 1974 and occupies parts of Meuse, Meurthe-et-Moselle, and Moselle. Lorraine is part of the Paris Basin except for the massif (mountain mass) of the Vosges in the east. Pop. (1990) 2,305,726.

To make the best use of the Britannica, consult the INDEX *first*

Lorraine, CARDINALS OF, Roman Catholic cardinals belonging to the house of Guise (a junior branch of the ducal house of Lorraine), grouped below chronologically and indicated by the symbol •. For other cardinals of the house of Guise, *see* Guise, cardinals of.

• Lorraine, Jean de Lorraine, 1st cardinal (1er cardinal) **de** (b. April 9, 1498, Bar, Fr.—d. May 18, 1550, Nogent-sur-Yonne), French cardinal of the celebrated family of Guise, a noted patron of arts and letters. His older brother was Claude de Lorraine, 1st Duke de Guise.

Jean became coadjutor of the bishop of Metz at the age of three and cardinal at 20. In the course of his life, the cardinal held many archbishoprics, bishoprics, and abbeys, some of which he subsequently conferred on his nephews. He was dissolute and extravagant, lavishing vast sums of money on entertainments at the Hôtel de Cluny, his Paris residence; as a patron of scholars, writers, and artists, including Erasmus, Clément Marot, and Benvenuto Cellini, and as an almsgiver, he had few equals. By his munificence he helped to build up a clientele for the Guises at court. The cardinal served King Francis I as councillor and diplomat but toward the end of Francis' reign fell from favour and retired to Rome. His hopes of becoming pope were never fulfilled. He died at Nogent-sur-Yonne in 1550 as he was returning from Italy.

• Lorraine, Charles de Lorraine, 2nd cardinal (2^e^ cardinal) **de** (b. Feb. 15, 1524, Joinville, Fr.—d. Dec. 26, 1574, Avignon), one of the foremost members of the powerful Roman Catholic house of Guise and perhaps the most influential Frenchman during the middle years of the 16th century. He was intelligent, avaricious, and cautious.

The second son of Claude, 1st Duke de Guise, and Antoinette de Bourbon, Charles was from the first destined for the church and studied theology at the College of Navarre in Paris. He attracted notice for his oratorical skills, and in 1538 King Francis I made him archbishop of

2e cardinal de Lorraine, detail from a drawing by François Clouet; in the Musée Condé, Chantilly, France
Giraudon—Art Resource

Reims. Soon after King Henry II's accession, he became cardinal de Guise (1547). When his uncle Jean died in 1550, he took over his title of cardinal de Lorraine as well as his numerous benefices, which included the see of Metz and the abbeys of Cluny and Fécamp. His ecclesiastical patronage was extensive. He was easily the wealthiest prelate in France.

The cardinal was also very important politically: as a member of the king's council he actively supported the policy of French intervention in Italy, and in 1559 he helped negotiate the Peace of Cateau-Cambrésis. With the weak Francis II as king, he was, with his brother François, Duke de Guise, virtual head of government in 1559–60. Their policy provoked the Huguenots' abortive conspiracy of Amboise, and with the accession of Charles IX (1560), the regent, Catherine de Médicis, in hopes of reducing the Guise influence, brought Michel de L'Hospital into the government. The cardinal became less influential in state affairs but continued to exert religious influence over Catherine.

Although he persecuted the Huguenots, he proposed a French national council to seek a compromise with them. Rather than an expression of toleration, this was a means of threatening Pope Pius IV in order to secure liberties and privileges for the Gallican (French) church. In 1561 he defended the Catholic viewpoint against the Calvinist Theodore Beza at a colloquy at Poissy. In 1562–63 he championed the Gallican cause at the Council of Trent, but in 1564 he was unable to secure the promulgation of the council's decrees in France. He retired from court in 1570.

Lorre, Peter, original name LÁSZLÓ LOEWENSTEIN (b. June 26, 1904, Rózsahegy, Hung.—d. March 23, 1964, Hollywood, Calif., U.S.), Hungarian-born American motion-picture actor who projected a sinister image as a lisping, round-faced, soft-voiced villain in thrillers.

A player of bit parts with a German theatrical troupe from 1921, Lorre achieved international fame as the psychotic child murderer in the German classic film *M* (1931), directed by Fritz Lang. His portrayal is considered one of the screen's greatest criminal characterizations. Three years later he made his English-language film debut in *The Man Who Knew Too Much* and then his first Hollywood appearance in *Mad Love* (1935). It was followed by other roles as malevolent, sadistic characters in such films as *Crime and Punishment* (1935), *The Maltese Falcon* (1941), *Casablanca* (1942), and *The Beast with Five Fingers* (1946). He also played the Japanese detective in the Mr. Moto series (1937–39). His later films sometimes burlesque his traditional chilling presence. During the 1950s and '60s, Lorre made frequent television appearances.

lorry: *see* truck.

Lorsch, village, Hesse *Land* (state), central Germany, north of Mannheim. It is best known for the ruins of its medieval abbey, from which excavations in 1932 uncovered fragments of an early pictorial stained-glass window, perhaps dating from the Carolingian period (8th–9th century). Lorsch is the burial place of Louis the German and Louis the Younger, both 9th-century kings of Saxony, and the village is mentioned in the 13th-century German epic *Nibelungenlied* as the burial place of Siegfried. Pop. (1993 est.) 11,407.

Lortzing, Albert, in full GUSTAV ALBERT LORTZING (b. Oct. 23, 1801, Berlin, Prussia [Germany]—d. Jan. 21, 1851, Berlin), composer who established the 19th-century style of light German opera that remained in favour until the mid-20th century.

Lortzing's parents were actors, and he was largely self-taught as a musician. He produced a one-act vaudeville, *Ali Pascha von Janina,* in 1828; a play with music, *Der Pole und sein Kind* (1832; "The Pole and His Child"); and in 1832 wrote (but did not produce) *Szenen aus Mozarts Leben* ("Scenes of Mozart's Life"), with music selected from the works of Wolfgang Amadeus Mozart. From 1833 to 1844 he sang as a tenor in Leipzig. His most successful opera was *Zar* (originally *Czaar*) *und Zimmermann* (1837; "Tsar and Carpenter"), based on an episode from the life of Peter the Great. Other operas include *Undine* (1845), a romantic opera in the style of Carl Maria von Weber and Heinrich August Marschner, *Der Waffenschmied* (1846; "The Military Blacksmith"), and *Rolands Knappen* (1849). His style derives from that of the German *Singspiel* and from the early 19th-century French opéra comique, which enjoyed a great vogue in Germany.

lory, any of numerous parrots of the subfamily Loriinae. *See* parrot.

Los, Îles de (Guinea): *see* Los Islands.

Los Alamos, city, seat (1949) of Los Alamos county, north-central New Mexico, U.S. It lies on the Pajarito Plateau (elevation 7,300 feet [2,225 m]) of the Jemez Mountains, 35 miles (56 km) northwest of Santa Fe. The site was named Los Alamos (Spanish for "the cottonwoods") by Ashley Pond, founder of the Los Alamos Ranch School for Boys (1918–43).

In 1942 Los Alamos was chosen by the U.S. government (because of its comparative isolation and natural facilities) as the location for the Atomic Research Laboratory then known as the Manhattan Project, which developed the first nuclear-fission, or atomic, bomb. After World War II, the Los Alamos Scientific Laboratory (later called Los Alamos National Laboratory) developed the first thermonuclear-fusion, or hydrogen, bomb. The laboratory, which is operated by the University of California under contract with the federal government, conducts solar and nuclear research and utilizes more than 300 buildings and a 77-square mile (199-square km) area.

A modern city was built by the government to house employees of the laboratory. It was made "open" in 1957, and in 1962 there was a transfer of property from federal to private ownership. The city has a science museum and a history museum. Bandelier National Monument, site of Anasazi ruins, is nearby. Los Alamos was incorporated with a consolidated city-county government in 1969. Pop. (2000) 11,909.

Los Angeles, formerly LOS ANJELES, capital of Bío-Bío *provincia,* Bío-Bío *región,* south-central Chile. It is located on a tributary of the Bío-Bío River in the southern part of the Central Valley. Founded in 1739 and elevated to city status in 1852, Los Angeles was swept by fire in 1820, has suffered earthquake damage repeatedly, and was destroyed several times in the long struggle with the Araucanian Indians. It is now an agricultural processing centre handling dairy products, wheat, sugar beets, fruit, and lumber produced mainly in the valley. The city is on the Pan-American Highway; it is linked to Concepción 60 miles (97 km) northwest by road and rail and to the main north-south railroad by a 13-mile branch line. Pop. (1999 est.) 109,606.

Los Angeles, city, seat, since 1850, of Los Angeles county, southern California, U.S., the second largest city in the country. Area city, 466 square miles (1,207 square km); metropolitan area (PMSA), 4,070 square miles (10,541 square km). Pop. (2000) city, 3,694,820; Los Angeles–Long Beach PMSA, 9,519,338; Los Angeles–Riverside–Orange County CMSA, 16,373,645.

A brief treatment of Los Angeles follows. For full treatment, *see* MACROPAEDIA: Los Angeles.

Originally founded by Spanish settlers in 1781 as El Pueblo de la Reyna de los Angeles (the Town of the Queen of the Angels), Los Angeles became a U.S. city when taken (bloodlessly) by U.S. forces in the Mexican War in 1846. The town prospered in the wake of the northern California gold rush of 1849, and vast Spanish and Mexican land grants were quickly broken up, fenced, and settled by large numbers of Americans arriving from the east. Aided by a railroad rate war and the rapid development of port facilities, the population of Los Angeles more than quadrupled between 1880 and 1890, and it tripled in size in the first decade of the 20th century. The sprawling metropolis has at the same time acquired contemporary urban problems, such as severe air and water pollution, clogged freeways, energy shortages, extensive slum areas, overcrowded schools, and budgetary shortfalls, but the city was still growing at the beginning of the 21st century.

Los Angeles spreads over a broad coastal plain between the San Gabriel Mountains and the Pacific Ocean, enclosing within its boundaries independent municipalities such as Beverly Hills and Culver City. The Santa Monica Mountains bisect the city, separating Hollywood, Beverly Hills, and Pacific Palisades from the southern boundary of the San Fernando Valley. Coastal mountain ranges to the north and east act as buffers against extreme summer heat and winter cold, and even in the hottest months humidity tends to be low and the nights cool. Brushfires occur sporadically, and earthquakes are relatively frequent but are not often of major intensity.

Although Los Angeles county was once the nation's wealthiest agricultural county, significant agricultural production has declined. Several thousand acres of farmland were sacrificed to freeways and housing between 1950 and 1965 to accommodate the area's dramatic population growth. Major industries now include tourism; banking; insurance; health-care services; the manufacture of aerospace equipment, pharmaceutical supplies, glass, rubber, and cement; petroleum exploitation and refining; food processing; and electronics. The high-technology sector is also important. Los Angeles is the nation's motion-picture capital and plays an important role in the radio, television, and recording industries.

City planners in Los Angeles have long been eager to give the city a "real" downtown, but the downtown area remains mainly a financial centre, largely separate from the city's daily life. Neighbourhood living conditions range from expansive town-house complexes and shopping centres in the San Fernando Valley to congested urban slums in the African American neighbourhoods of south-central Los Angeles and the Hispanic neighbourhoods of East Los Angeles, as well as Asian-American enclaves on the eastern and western edges of the downtown area. Hollywood, long a part of Los Angeles (since 1910), has lost much of the glamour that it had in earlier years.

Public parks include Griffith Park, which spreads over more than 4,000 acres (1,600 hectares) of mountainous area and contains the city's zoo and Will Rogers State Historic Park. The missions of San Gabriel Arcángel (1771) and San Fernando Rey de España (1797) have been preserved, and the plaza where the city got its start is part of the El Pueblo de Los Angeles Historic Monument; the latter also contains the city's first church and Olvera Street, an important attraction that has many Mexican shops and cafés. The city's Central Library (1926) was the last building designed by Bertram Goodhue. Art museums include the Los Angeles County Museum of Art and the Museum of Contemporary Art.

Major institutions of higher education include the University of Southern California (USC; 1880), Occidental College (1887), and the University of California at Los Angeles (UCLA; 1919). The California Institute of Technology (1891) is in nearby Pasadena.

Unlike other large American cities, Los Angeles does not have an efficient public transportation system (a light rail and subway system opened in 1990), and the vast majority of its residents operate private automobiles over the extensive network of freeways that dominate the city. Los Angeles (in and around San Pedro) has one of the most active international ports in the country. Airports include a municipal airport and the private Hughes airport, two airports serving the San Fernando Valley, and the Los Angeles International Airport in southwestern Los Angeles.

Los Angeles County Museum of Art, museum complex with distinguished collections of Asian (Indian, Tibetan, Nepalese), Islāmic, medieval, European, and modern art. The largest building, the four-level Ahmanson Gallery, houses the permanent collection, the adjoining Frances and Armand Hammer Wing displays temporary exhibitions, and the Leo S. Bing Center contains a library (with more than 60,000 volumes) and auditorium. The Robert O. Anderson Building, housing the museum's modern-art collection, opened in 1986. The Textile and Costumes Research Center is the strongest in the western United States. Established in 1913, the museum was part of the Los Angeles County Museum of History, Science and Art until 1961, when it became an independent institution. It moved to its present location in 1965.

Los Angeles Times, morning daily newspaper published in Los Angeles that in the 1960s began to develop from a regional daily into one of the world's great newspapers.

It was established in 1881, and in 1884 Harrison Gray Otis purchased and incorporated the *Times* under a public corporation, The Times-Mirror Company (the hyphen was later dropped from the name). The paper prospered, soon becoming an important power in conservative politics in California and a major voice in the southern part of the state. Although its news coverage reflected its political bias, the *Times* won widespread respect for its contributions to the development of southern California and for its technological and other innovations. The *Times* launched the United States' first newspaper-owned radio station in 1922. In 1928 it began to use airplanes to deliver newspapers to other cities.

The *Los Angeles Times* was long dominated by the Chandler family, beginning when Harry Chandler succeeded his father-in-law, Otis, as publisher in 1917. Norman Chandler took over from his father in 1944, and in 1948 he introduced an afternoon tabloid, the *Los Angeles Mirror,* which was discontinued in 1962. Norman resigned as publisher in 1960 to devote full attention to the corporation, his son Otis Chandler taking over the *Times.*

When Otis Chandler became publisher, the paper's writing, editing, and editorial policy underwent a striking metamorphosis, noticeably under editor Nick Williams (1958–71). From its traditional ultraconservative stance, the *Times* developed into a model of balanced, fair, and comprehensive journalism. This was accomplished in large part by upgrading and enlarging its staff, opening new *Times* bureaus in the United States and abroad, and developing thorough coverage of important events. In 1964 The Times Mirror Company became listed on the New York Stock Exchange, the first general-interest newspaper corporation to do so. The parent company of the *Times* also publishes other newspapers, books, and magazines and owns broadcasting and multimedia concerns. In 2000 the Chandlers, who owned the majority of Times Mirror stock, sold the company to the Tribune Company.

Los Angeles Zoo, The, byname GRIFFITH PARK ZOO, zoological park founded in 1912 in Los Angeles as the Griffith Park Menagerie. It is a completely outdoor zoo that has holdings of the emperor tamarin, mountain tapir, and California condor. The Los Angeles Zoo was also the first to breed the tarictic hornbill. Comprising a main zoo and a children's zoo, it occupies 46 hectares (113 acres) of Griffith Park, a large city-owned park. The main zoo has about 2,000 specimens of 500 species.

Los Baños, resort town, southwestern Luzon, Philippines. Near the southern shore of Laguna de Bay, it was named Los Baños ("The Baths") for the thermal springs that flow from the base of Mount Makiling. The waters are piped into the town's numerous hotels.

Los Baños was the site of a U.S. air base and later of a Japanese concentration camp that was captured by U.S. forces on Feb. 23, 1945. It is the site of the College of Agriculture of the University of the Philippines. In the 1960s the International Rice Research Institute, headquartered there, developed IR8, a high-yielding strain that has been called a miracle rice. Pop. (2000) mun., 82,027.

Los Dos Caminos, city, northwestern Miranda *estado* ("state"), northern Venezuela, just east of Caracas. Nestled in the central highlands, the city was formerly a commercial centre in a fertile agricultural area producing coffee, cacao, and sugarcane. With the growth of the national capital, it has become a residential suburb in the Caracas metropolitan area. The Humboldt Planetarium, a national park, and La Carlota Airport are located in the southern portion of the city. Expressways lead to downtown Caracas, approximately 8 miles (13 km) to the west. Pop. (2000) 74,701.

Los Glaciares National Park, Spanish PARQUE NACIONAL LOS GLACIARES, national park in Santa Cruz *provincia,* southwestern Argentina, in the Andes surrounding the western extensions of Lakes Argentino and Viedma, at the Chilean border. It has an area of 625 square miles (1,618 square km) and was established in 1937. The park has two distinct regions—forests and grassy plains in the east and needlelike peaks, lakes, large glaciers, and snowfields in the west. Mount Fitzroy (11,073 feet [3,375 m]) is the highest point in the park. Wildlife includes guanacos, chinchillas, pudu and guemal (two species of small deer), condors, and rheas.

Los Islands, French ÎLES DE LOS, small archipelago in the Atlantic Ocean, off Conakry, the capital of Guinea, West Africa. They provide protection for the port of Conakry and include Tamara (Factory), Kassa, Roume (Crawford), Blanche (White), and De Corail (Coral) and several smaller islets. Tamara, the largest (8 miles [13 km] long and 1–2 miles [1.6–3 km] wide), has the highest point of elevation (499 feet [152 m]). Only Tamara and Kassa have sizable settlements (Fotoba and Cité de Kassa). The group, named for the sacred idols (*los idolos*) found there by early Portuguese navigators, are of volcanic origin and are covered with palm trees.

Bauxite mining began on Kassa in 1949, but supplies were depleted in 1966. Tamara's deposits were worked from 1967 until they were exhausted in 1972.

In 1812 the British established a garrison on Tamara to control slave trading and piracy; and in 1818 Sir Charles MacCarthy, governor of Sierra Leone, obtained the islands from the Baga tribe. They were ceded to the French in 1904 and became part of independent Guinea in 1958.

Los Lagos, *región,* southern Chile, bordering Argentina to the east and facing the Pacific Ocean to the west. Created in 1974, it comprises Valdivia, Osorno, Llanquihue, Palena, and Chiloé *provincias,* with an area of 25,868 square miles (66,997 square km). In the north are the forested coastal mountain range, the westward-extending lowlands of the Valdivia and Bueno river systems, the southern end of

Lake Todos los Santos, Los Lagos region, Chile
Arthur Griffin

the fertile Central Valley, and, rising above these, the Andean cordillera. In the south the landforms of central Chile are transformed. The Andean cordillera dominates the *región*'s southeast mainland, its elevation is much reduced, and its peaks rise between glacial valleys to become fjordlike estuaries. The sunken Central Valley becomes the 30-mile- (48-kilometre-) wide Corcovado Gulf. The coastal mountain range of the north is submerged, its tips emerging from the Pacific as the large Chiloé Island and the innumerable archipelagos and islands (chiefly Guafo and the Guaitecas) to its east and south.

German colonizers, who began arriving in the mid-19th century, stimulated economic growth in the north. Agriculture is the economic mainstay, and potatoes, beef, dairy products, wheat, oats, and fruit are produced. Lumber production in Valdivia *provincia* is of major economic importance to the nation. Local industry is concerned for the most part with processing farm and forest products, but there are also iron and steel smelters, foundries, and fish canneries. Tourism provides a major source of income, for the northern area has many lakes, including Calafquen, Panguipulli, Riñihue, Ranco, Puyehue, and Chile's largest lake, Llanquihue. The Pan-American Highway and the main north-south railway terminate at Puerto Montt (*q.v.*), the regional capital.

The topography of the southern part of the *región,* and its colder, rainy climate, has kept this area relatively poor. The chief agricultural product is potatoes; lumbering is important, and the fishing potential has been developing rapidly. Population is sparse, mostly Indian, and concentrated on Chiloé Island. Transportation is almost solely by water. Pop. (1999 est.) 1,050,600.

Los Mochis, city, northwestern Sinaloa *estado* ("state"), northwestern Mexico. It lies on the coastal plain, inland from Topolobampo Bay on the Gulf of California. The creation of the Fuerte River irrigation district in the 1950s led to the growth of Los Mochis as an agricultural (corn [maize], cotton, sugarcane, tomatoes, and other crops and cattle and pigs) centre. Among the city's industries are large sugar refineries and a cannery. Tourism is an additional economic asset; Los Mochis is a popular winter holiday resort and headquarters for fishing and hunting. It is just off the Nogales–Mexico City highway and is linked by railroad and highway to the port of Topolobampo. The city also has an airport. Pop. (1990) 162,659.

Los Pijiguaos, bauxite deposit and associated mining development, on the Pijiguaos Plateau, in western Bolívar state, Venezuela. Discovered in 1974, this large, high-quality, laterite-type deposit underlies some 2,000 square miles (5,000 square km) and is located approximately 25 miles (40 km) east of the Orinoco River, which is an economical source of transportation and hydroelectric power. Commercial production began in 1987 and reached nearly 3 million metric tons in 1993. Proven reserves amount to 500 million metric tons. The bauxite is transported down the Orinoco River to be processed at alumina plants in Puerto Ordaz, in greater Ciudad Guayana, some 300 miles (500 km) to the northeast.

Los Teques, city, capital of Miranda *estado* ("state"), north-central Venezuela. It occupies a strategic pass in the northern coastal range, just southwest of Caracas. Named after local Indians, the city was the birthplace of their chief, Guaicaipuro (died *c.* 1560), known for his staunch resistance to the Spanish conquistadors who searched for legendary gold in the surrounding hills. The city subsequently became a residential and resort area for Caracas but by the 1970s had developed industrially, benefiting from inexpensive land and easy access to raw materials imported via nearby Puerto Cabello. Pop. (1990) 140,617.

Los Tuxtlas (Mexico): *see* San Andrés Tuxtla.

Loschmidt, Joseph, in full JOHANN JOSEPH LOSCHMIDT (b. May 15, 1821, Putschin, Bohemia, Austrian Empire [now in Czech Republic]—d. July 8, 1895, Vienna, Austria), German chemist who made advances in the study of aromatic hydrocarbons.

The son of poor peasants, Loschmidt gained an education through the help of his village priest, and by 1839 he was a student at the German University in Prague. Moving to Vienna in 1841, he completed his university studies in 1843 but was unable to obtain a teaching post. His attempts to succeed in business ended in bankruptcy in 1854, and he decided to return to his studies in the natural sciences. In 1856 Loschmidt qualified as a teacher and obtained a post at the Vienna Realschule. He turned to research in chemistry and theoretical physics and soon began publishing scientific papers. He was appointed an assistant professor of physical chemistry at the University of Vienna in 1868 and went on to become an important figure in Vienna's scientific community.

Loschmidt was the first to use double and triple lines to graphically represent the double and triple bonds in organic molecules. He recognized that most "aromatic compounds" (*i.e.,* aromatic hydrocarbons, so called because they were obtained from pleasantly fragrant substances) could be derived from benzene by replacing one or more hydrogen substituents by other atoms or groups. The term "aromatic" thus came to be applied to any hydrocarbon that has the benzene ring as part of its structure, regardless of the question of aroma. Loschmidt was the first to state that in alcohols containing several OH groups, each OH group is attached to a different carbon atom. He partly explained the structures of several organic and inorganic compounds, among them benzene, toluene, and ozone, and he also recognized that an element could have several valences. Loschmidt made perhaps the first accurate calculations of the size of air molecules and of the number of molecules in a gram-mole (the quantity now commonly called the Avogadro constant). He arrived at a size of somewhat less than 10^{-7} cm for the diameter of the molecules in air, which is relatively close to the accepted figure of 0.5×10^{-7} cm.

Losey, Joseph, in full JOSEPH WALTON LOSEY (b. Jan. 14, 1909, La Crosse, Wis., U.S.—d. June 22, 1984, London, Eng.), American motion-picture director, whose highly personal style was often manifested in films centring on intense and sometimes violent human relationships.

Losey, 1971
AP/Wide World Photos

After graduating from Dartmouth College (B.A., 1929) and Harvard University (M.A., 1930), Losey wrote book and theatre reviews. In 1935, while working as a European-based reporter for *Variety,* the newspaper of the entertainment industry, he attended classes conducted by Sergey Eisenstein, the foremost Soviet film director and theorist. During the 1930s and '40s Losey directed stage productions on Broadway and for the WPA Federal Theatre Project. One of his greatest artistic successes was the 1947 presentation of Bertolt Brecht's *Galileo Galilei.*

Losey directed educational and documentary films in the late 1930s and in 1945 won an Academy Award nomination for the short subject *A Gun in His Hand.* Gradually, he came to direct full-length features, which were personal statements on controversial topics—*e.g.,* pacifism (*The Boy with Green Hair,* 1948), racial prejudice (*The Lawless,* 1950), and police corruption (*The Prowler,* 1951). Blacklisted in Hollywood in 1952 along with numerous others accused of Communist affiliations, Losey went to England, where he worked anonymously until the release of *The Gypsy and the Gentlemen* in 1958. Many of his films were written by the British playwright Harold Pinter, including *The Servant* (1963), *Accident* (1967), and *The Go-Between,* which won the grand prize at the Cannes Film Festival in 1971. They brought him international recognition especially among the French critics. Later films include *The Assassination of Trotsky* (1972), *A Doll's House* (1973), *Mr. Klein* (1976), *Don Giovanni* (1979), and *La Truite* (1982; *The Trout*).

Loskop Dam Nature Reserve, nature preserve in Eastern Transvaal province, South Africa, on the Olifants River, north of Middelburg. The reserve has an area of 57 square miles (148 square km) and lies around a dam on the Olifants River in a scenic valley that has been restocked with animals once indigenous to the area. These include the eland and other species of antelope, giraffe, zebra, wildebeest, white rhinoceros, and more than 200 species of birds, including the ostrich, fish eagle, goliath heron, and other waterfowl. The Loskop Reservoir, impounded by the dam on the river, is well stocked with fish.

Lossiemouth, North Sea fishing port and holiday resort, Moray district, Grampian region, Scotland. The town developed from several old fishing villages including Seatown, Branderburgh—built around a new harbour (1830) and now Lossiemouth's business centre—and the later settlement of Stotfield. Lossiemouth was Elgin's port in the 15th century but declined along with the fishing industry until its prosperity was revived by the tourist trade and the proximity of British Royal Air Force bases at Fulmar and Kinloss. Fishing is the chief occupation. J. Ramsay MacDonald, first Labour prime minister of the United Kingdom, was born there. Pop. (1981) 6,848.

Lossky, Nikolay Onufriyevich (b. Nov. 24 [Dec. 6, New Style], 1870, Kreslavka, near Vitebsk, Russia—d. Jan. 24, 1965, Sainte-Geneviève-des-Bois, France), Russian intuitionist philosopher who studied the nature of cognition, causation, and morals. His philosophy was a compound of many influences, especially Leibnizian monadology and Bergsonian intuitionism.

Lossky graduated from the University of St. Petersburg, received a doctorate in 1907 under Wilhelm Wundt in Germany, and then taught at St. Petersburg until 1921. The following year he was exiled by the Soviet government for his religious beliefs. He taught at the Russian University in Prague for many years before becoming a professor at the University of Bratislava (1942–45). After World War II, in 1946, he emigrated to the United States to become professor at St. Vladimir Russian Orthodox Seminary in New York City (1947–50). His important works include *Osnovnye ucheniya psikhologi s tochki zreniya volyuntarizma* (1903; "The Fundamental Doctrines of Psychology from the Point of View of Voluntarism"), *Obosnovaniye intuitivizma* (1906; *The Intuitive Basis of Knowledge*), *Mir kak organicheskoe tseloe* (1917; *The World as an Organic Whole*), *Chuvstvennaya intellektualnaya i misticheskaya intuitsiya* (1938; "Sensory, Intellectual, and Mystical Intuition"), and *Bog i mirovonye zlo* (1941; "God and Cosmic Evil").

Losso (people): *see* Lamba.

Lost Colony, early British settlement on Roanoke Island, N.C. (U.S.), that mysteriously disappeared between the time of its founding (1587) and the return of the expedition's leader (1590). In hopes of securing permanent trading posts for Britain, Sir Walter Raleigh had initiated explorations of the islands off North Carolina as early as 1584. Because of the Indian threat, the first Raleigh-sponsored settlement on Roanoke Island lasted only a short period (1585–86). The next year approximately 100 settlers under Governor John White attempted to colonize the same site. Returning to England for supplies, White was delayed by the Spanish Armada. By the time he got back to the island in August 1590, everyone had vanished. The only trace of the "lost colony" was the word Croatoan carved on one tree and the word Cro on another. The group may have been annihilated by hostile Indians, but there is just as valid speculation that it may have moved among a friendly tribe. In any event, the mystery of the "lost colony" has never been solved. *See* Roanoke Island.

Lost Generation, in general, the post-World War I generation, but specifically a group of

U.S. writers who came of age during the war and established their literary reputations in the 1920s. The term stems from a remark made by Gertrude Stein to Ernest Hemingway, "You are all a lost generation." Hemingway used it as an epigraph to *The Sun Also Rises* (1926), a novel that captures the attitudes of a hard-drinking, fast-living set of disillusioned young expatriates in postwar Paris. The generation was "lost" in the sense that its inherited values were no longer relevant in the postwar world and because of its spiritual alienation from a U.S. that, basking under President Harding's "back to normalcy" policy, seemed to its members to be hopelessly provincial, materialistic, and emotionally barren. The term embraces Hemingway, F. Scott Fitzgerald, John Dos Passos, e.e. cummings, Archibald MacLeish, Hart Crane, and many other writers who made Paris the centre of their literary activities in the '20s. They were never a literary school. In the 1930s, as these writers turned in different directions, their works lost the distinctive stamp of the postwar period. The last representative works of the era were Fitzgerald's *Tender Is the Night* (1934) and Dos Passos' *The Big Money* (1936).

lost-wax process, also called CIRE-PERDUE, method of hollow metal casting in which a layer of wax corresponding to the desired shape is encased within two heat-proof layers; the process is also used for small solid castings, using a solid wax form. In both variations, the wax is melted and drained off, and molten metal is poured into the resulting cavity. Common on every continent except Australia, the cire-perdue method dates from the 3rd millennium BC and has sustained few changes since then.

To cast a clay model in bronze, a mold is made from the model, and the inside of this negative mold is brushed with melted wax to the desired thickness of the final bronze. After removal of the mold, the resultant wax shell is filled with a heat-resistant mixture. Wax tubes, which provide ducts for pouring bronze during casting, are fitted to the outside of the wax shell, which may be modelled or adjusted by the artist. Metal pins are hammered through the shell into the core to secure it. Next, the prepared wax shell is completely covered in layers of heat-resistant plaster, and the whole is inverted and placed in an oven. During heating, the plaster dries and the wax runs out through the ducts created by the wax tubes. The plaster mold is then packed in sand, and molten bronze is poured through the ducts, filling the space left by the wax. When cool, the outer plaster and core are removed, and the bronze may receive finishing touches. *See also* investment casting.

Lostwithiel, parish (town), Restormel district, county of Cornwall, England, built on a medieval grid plan by the River Fowey, spanned there at the lowest bridge point by a 14th-century bridge. The town developed near Restormel Castle, which dates from *c.* 1100. It is the best preserved British castle of its period. Much of it, however, is of the 13th century, when Lostwithiel was capital of the duchy of Cornwall and one of the four stannary, or coinage, towns (Helston, Lostwithiel, Truro, and Liskeard), where all smelted tin was taxed and tested for quality. The remains of the stannary offices (*c.* 1280) are in Quay Street. Pop. (1971) 1,905.

Lot, *département,* Midi-Pyrénées region, southwestern France, created from the major part of the Quercy district in the historic province of Guyenne. Its 2,019 sq mi (5,228 sq km) extend from the western part of the Massif Central into the Aquitaine Basin. The Lot River cuts east–west in a deep valley through arid limestone plateaus known as the Causses and meanders around Cahors (*q.v.*), Lot's capital, one of the most ancient towns in France. The Lot is joined from the northwest by the Célé, which flows through the market town of Figeac, the only other locality with more than 10,000 inhabitants. The Dordogne River flows across the northeast.

Warm, humid winds predominate in the winter, but icy mountain winds blow across the plateaus in spring and autumn. Agriculture—vegetables, cereals, fruit trees, tobacco—flourishes in the sheltered valleys in which most of the villages and towns are situated; vines grow on the lower slopes. On the plateaus, sometimes called the Petits Causses, cattle and sheep are raised, and truffles are found. Industry is not very well developed: there is an aeronautical factory at Figeac, but little else.

Lot has continued to suffer from an exodus of rural inhabitants despite the increasing number of tourists, who are attracted by the beauty of the countryside and its ancient towns and villages. The famous Gouffre de Padirac, a sinkhole with an underground river, lies near Rocamadour, a pilgrimage centre. Pech-Merle, a cave with prehistoric wall paintings, is located east of Cahors. Murat, king of Naples, was born in Labastide-Murat (formerly La Bastide-Fortunière); the statesman Léon Gambetta, in Cahors. Lot has three *arrondissements*: Cahors, Figeac, and Gourdon; it is in the educational division of Toulouse. Pop. (1999) 160,034.

Lot, Ferdinand (b. Sept. 20, 1866, Paris—d. July 20, 1952, near Paris), French historian of the early Middle Ages and the later Roman Empire. He is best known for his important monographs on the transition from Roman to medieval civilization.

Lot taught at the École Pratique des Hautes Études (1900), later becoming professor at the University of Paris (1909). His work on the diplomatic and narrative texts of the high Middle Ages appeared as *Études sur le règne de Hughues Capet et la fin du Xᵉ siècle* (1904; "Studies on the Reign of Hugh Capet and the End of the 10th Century"). He also wrote *Les Invasions barbares et le peuplement de l'Europe* (1937; "The Barbaric Invasions and the Populating of Europe"); *L'Art Militaire et les armées du Moyen Âge* (1946; "Military Art and the Armies of the Middle Ages"); and many other works on medieval philology, demography, and Romanesque literature. He received many honours, including membership in the Académie des Inscriptions et Belles-Lettres and the Legion of Honour.

Lot-et-Garonne, *département,* Aquitaine region, southwestern France, created from parts of the historic provinces of Guyenne and Gascony (*qq.v.*). Lying in a plain in the centre of the Aquitaine Basin, it has an area of 2,069 sq mi (5,358 sq km). It is crossed southeast–northwest by the Garonne River, which flows through Agen, its capital, and is joined by the Lot River before flowing through Tonneins and Marmande. The climate is largely maritime. Agriculture prospers: cereals are grown, cattle are raised, and dairy farming is practiced. Fruit growing is a speciality, and the *département* is noted for its plums from which the confections *prunes d'agen* are made. The vineyards produce good wines (Duras, Marmande), and the region is one of the main tobacco-growing centres of France. Industry has been little developed. Agen, Marmande, Nérac, and Villeneuve-sur-Lot, all towns with medieval buildings, give their names to the four *arrondissements.* The *département* is in the educational division of Bordeaux. Pop. (1999) 305,396.

Lot Kamehameha (Hawaiian king): *see* Kamehameha V.

Lot River, river, rising in the Cévennes mountains, near Mont Lozère, in Lozère *département,* southern France, flowing about 300 mi (480 km) generally west to join the Garonne River near Aiguillon, draining a basin of about 4,400 sq mi (11,400 sq km). In its sinuous course, the Lot crosses the Causses (limestone plateaus) in a deep gorge. It flows west from Mende, past Entraygues-sur-Truyère, where it receives its most important tributary, the Truyère, which in its upper course is dammed for generating hydroelectric power.

The Lot River continues through the Aveyron coalfield near Decazeville and past Cahors (the old capital of Quercy) and the medieval town of Villeneuve-sur-Lot before entering the Garonne. It is canalized and navigable upstream from the Garonne for 160 mi (260 km) but is little used.

Lota, major coal-mining centre, Concepción province, Bío-Bío region, southern Chile, on the Golfo (gulf) de Arauco. Although it was founded in 1662, sustained development did not begin until 1852, when Matías Cousiño, the industrialist, began a coal-mining enterprise. Completion of a railway from Concepción, 20 mi (32 km) north, in 1888 stimulated growth. Other industries in Lota include a brick and refractories plant and a copper smelter; it is a coaling station for coastal vessels. Operating and administrative facilities and a planned company town are found in Lota Alto (Upper Lota); Lota Bajo (Lower Lota) is the commercial and residential community. Renowned in Chile for its scenic beauty is the local Isidora Cousiño Park. Pop. (1992) 50,123.

Isidora Cousiño Park, Lota, Chile
Peter L. Gould

Lotario (Italian personal name): *see under* Lothair.

Loṭf ʿAlī Khān Zand (b. 1769, Shīrāz, Zand Iran—d. 1794, Tehrān), last ruler of the Zand dynasty of Iran, who was defeated in the civil war of 1779–94. With the death of Loṭf ʿAlī Khān's grandfather, Karīm Khān Zand, a 15-year civil war ensued between his descendants and Āghā Moḥammad Khān Qājār. Although the Zand forces were weakened by internal dissensions and rivalries, Loṭf ʿAlī Khān's father, Jaʿfar Khān, proclaimed himself sovereign in the Zand capital of Shīrāz in 1785.

Given charge of the Zand armies in the provinces of Lārestān and Kermān by his father, Loṭf ʿAlī Khān was forced to abandon these provinces on Jaʿfar's death (1789) and return to Shīrāz, where a rival had proclaimed himself king. Executing his rival, he had himself proclaimed king; and during the next four years he undertook several campaigns against Āghā Moḥammad Khān Qājār, who possessed superior troops. After the governor of Shīrāz treacherously abandoned the city to Qājār forces in 1791, Loṭf ʿAlī Khān was never able to secure a new base of operations and was constantly on the move. His inability to control significant territory and the consequent loss of revenues doomed the Zand cause to failure. An able and gallant soldier, he won several tactical victories over his opponent after the loss of Shīrāz; but the balance of power favoured the Qājārs, who could afford to lose minor battles.

The final act of the civil war came in 1794, when Qājār forces broke a four-month resistance to take the city of Kermān. Loṭf ʿAlī Khān managed to flee, but he was captured and delivered to Āghā Moḥammad Khān, who had him tortured to death.

Lothair, name of rulers grouped below by country and indicated by the symbol •.

See also Chlotar.

Foreign-language equivalents:

French .... Lothaire
German .... Lothar
Italian .... Lotario

France

•Lothair (b. 941—d. March 2, 986), Carolingian king of France from 954 to 986, the eldest son of Louis IV. He was elected king without opposition after his father's death but was dominated first by Hugh the Great and then, from 956 to 965, by his uncle, Bruno, archbishop of Cologne, whose support was invaluable but who used his influence also in the interests of Otto I, his brother, the German king, and of Hugh Capet and the other sons of Hugh the Great, Bruno's nephews.

After Bruno's death, Lothair's position deteriorated. Although his relations with Hugh Capet were generally good, he had only a tiny domain and was much distracted by feudal conflict. Also, a persistent desire to get Lorraine from the German allegiance brought disastrous consequences: his support of a revolt there (976) against Otto II impelled the latter to give the duchy of Lower Lorraine to Lothair's refractory brother, Charles; Lothair's plan to capture Otto's family at Aachen (978) miscarried and provoked a retaliatory raid into France; and a third invasion of Lorraine (985) not only failed in its purpose but determined the powerful Archbishop Adalbero of Reims to support Hugh Capet against Lothair. Lothair was, however, preparing yet another expedition into Lorraine when he died, to be succeeded by his son, Louis V.

Germany/Holy Roman Empire

•Lothair I (b. 795—d. Sept. 29, 855, Abbey of Prüm, Ger.), Frankish emperor whose attempt to gain sole rule over the Frankish territories was checked by his brothers.

Lothair I, miniature from his psalter, 9th century; in the British Library (MS. Add. 37768)

The eldest son of the emperor Louis I the Pious and a grandson of Charlemagne, Lothair was made King in Bavaria after Louis succeeded Charlemagne in 814, and in 817 he was made joint emperor. Under the *Ordinatio imperii,* a decree issued by Louis in 817 to provide for the unity of the empire after his death, Lothair's younger brothers, Pepin and Louis (later called the German), were to receive their own kingdoms, Aquitaine and Bavaria, but were to remain under the general suzerainty of Lothair.

Ruler in Italy from 822, Lothair was crowned emperor by Pope Paschal I in 823. He issued the *Constitutio Romana* (824), affirming imperial sovereignty over Rome and demanding an oath of fealty from the pope. When in 829 Louis I, under the influence of his second wife, Judith, revised the *Ordinatio imperii* to grant part of the empire previously granted to Lothair to his son by Judith, Charles (later called the Bald), Lothair broke with the imperial government. A palace revolution forced his reappointment as co-emperor in 830, but he was again deposed shortly afterward.

In 833 discontent with the rule of Louis the Pious ended in a revolt of the three elder sons, led by Lothair, and Lothair replaced the deposed Louis. Louis was restored to power the following year, however, and Lothair's rule was restricted to Italy.

When Pepin died in December 838, Louis I drew up a new partition scheme, dividing the empire, aside from Bavaria and neighbouring areas, which were left to Louis the German, between Lothair and Charles the Bald, with Lothair taking the eastern portion. Lothair was to have the title of emperor, but without the suzerainty over the other princes that had been granted by the *Ordinatio imperii* of 817.

On Louis I's death (840), Lothair again claimed his rights under the *Ordinatio* of 817, but his brothers, Louis the German and Charles the Bald, defeated him at the Battle of Fontenoy (841). The Treaty of Verdun (August 843) left Lothair the Middle Realm of the Frankish dominions, from the North Sea to Italy, while Louis received the eastern and Charles the western territory. The imperial title fell to Lothair.

After granting the government of Italy to his eldest son, Louis II, as early as 844, Lothair partitioned his realm between Louis (emperor from 850) and his two other sons, Lothair and Charles, in 855. Then he abdicated and became a monk.

•Lothair (II) (b. *c.* 835—d. Aug. 8, 869, Piacenza, Italy), Frankish king of the area known as Lotharingia whose attempts to have his marriage dissolved so that he could marry his mistress caused much controversy and led to a bitter struggle between himself and Pope Nicholas I.

Lothair was the second son of the Frankish emperor Lothair I, ruler of the middle portion of the former empire of Charlemagne. Upon the death of Lothair I in 855, his realm was divided among his three sons, young Lothair receiving the area west of the Rhine from the North Sea to the Alps, which became known as Lotharingia (*Lotharii regnum,* or Lothair's kingdom, the modern Lorraine). When his younger brother, Charles of Provence, died in 863, Charles's kingdom was divided between the two surviving brothers: Louis II took Provence proper, and Lothair received the area around Vienne and Lyon.

In 855 Lothair had been forced by his father to marry Theutberga, a sister of Hicbert, the lay abbot of St. Maurice. Theutberga, however, remained childless, and from 857 the King tried to have the marriage dissolved and to take his mistress Waldrada, by whom he had had children, as his legitimate wife and queen. He accused his wife of incest with her brother, but her champion prevailed in the ordeal by boiling water, and Lothair was forced to take her back.

Lothair then induced two subservient archbishops, Günther of Cologne and Theutgaud of Trier, to start ecclesiastical proceedings against his wife. Two synods at Aachen dissolved the marriage and in 862 gave Lothair permission to marry Waldrada. He obtained the papal legate's confirmation of this decision, probably through bribery, at a synod at Metz (June 863). Pope Nicholas I, however, reversed these decisions and took the unprecedented step of deposing archbishops Günther and Theutgaud (October 863). In August 865 another papal legate forced Lothair to take Theutberga back again.

In 867 Pope Nicholas I was succeeded by the more pliable Adrian II, and Lothair forced Theutberga to ask the new pope for a divorce herself. Lothair was received by the Pope in 869 and was promised that the question would be considered at a council. He died shortly thereafter, while on his way home.

•Lothair II (or III) (b. early June 1075—d. Dec. 3/4, 1137, Breitenwang, now in Austria), German king (1125–37) and Holy Roman emperor (1133–37). He is reckoned as Lothair III by those who count not only Lothair I, but also his son Lothair in their numeration of German kings. Lothair II's election as king in 1125 represented a triumph for the principle of elective monarchy over that of hereditary succession, on which the claims of his Hohenstaufen opponents were based.

Lothair, the son of Gebhard, count of Supplinburg, was born a few days before his father was killed in battle on June 9, 1075. He succeeded to extensive lands around Helmstedt, in Saxony, and in 1088 became involved in an uprising against the Holy Roman emperor Henry IV. By his marriage in 1110 to Richenza, heiress of both the Nordheim and the Brunswick houses, Lothair became the most powerful noble in Saxony and the wealthiest prince in northern Germany.

Having supported the German king Henry V against his father, Henry IV, in 1104, Lothair was appointed duke of Saxony by Henry V when Duke Magnus, the last of the Billung dynasty, died in 1106. Lothair's independent attitude, however, soon brought him into conflict with the King. From 1112 to 1115 he was intermittently involved in revolts against Henry, and his forces defeated the King at the Battle of Welfesholz in 1115.

In 1125 Henry V died, and Lothair was elected German king and crowned at Aachen. Civil war between Lothair's supporters and the heirs of the House of Hohenstaufen, the brothers Conrad and Frederick, duke of Swabia, broke out. In 1127 Conrad was elected king by his adherents. The fall of the Hohenstaufen strongholds Nürnberg and Speyer two years later ended effective resistance, although the Hohenstaufens carried on the struggle for several more years while Conrad maintained his fictitious title.

In 1130 Lothair's support was solicited by two rival candidates for the papacy, Innocent II and Anacletus II. In March 1131 Lothair received Innocent at Liège, and, accompanied by Innocent, he marched with his army into Italy in 1132–33. Although part of Rome was held by Anacletus, Lothair was crowned Holy Roman emperor in June 1133. He then received as papal fiefs the vast estates of Matilda of Tuscany.

In 1134, after his return to Germany, Lothair resumed the campaign against the Hohenstaufens. Frederick of Hohenstaufen soon submitted. Peace was proclaimed at the Diet of Bamberg (March 1135), at which Swabia was returned to Frederick. In September 1135 Conrad made peace with Lothair under similar lenient conditions.

Lothair, in addition, encouraged the extension of German authority and the spread of Christianity in the districts east of the Elbe. In 1135 Eric II of Denmark declared himself a vassal of Lothair, and the Polish prince Bolesław III promised tribute and received Pomerania and Rügen as German fiefs.

As the result of an agreement with the Byzantine emperor John Comnenus, Lothair launched a second Italian expedition in 1136–

37, driving the forces of Roger II of Sicily from the southern part of the Italian peninsula. He died on his way back to Germany.

BIBLIOGRAPHY. W. Bernhardi, *Lothar von Supplinburg* (1879); and H. Hirsch, *Die Urkunden Lothar II. und der Kaiserin Richenza* (1927).

ITALY

•**Lothair I:** *see* Lothair I (Germany/Holy Roman Empire).

•**Lothair II** (d. 950, Turin, Lombardy), king of Italy in the chaotic post-Carolingian period who ruled as co-king with his father, Hugh of Provence, from 931 until Hugh's exile and death in 947. Lothair remained in Italy when his father, harassed by the powerful Lombard Berengar II of Ivrea, fled to Provence. Marrying 16-year-old Adelaide, daughter of Rudolf II of Burgundy (later wife of Emperor Otto I), in the hope of strengthening his position, Lothair found himself playing the role of a figurehead, while Berengar exercised the real power in Italy. Lothair died in 950, possibly poisoned by Berengar.

Lothair OF SEGNI (pope): *see* Innocent III.

Lothaire (French personal name): *see under* Lothair; Chlotar.

Lothar (German personal name): *see under* Lothair; Chlotar.

Lotharingia: *see* Lorraine.

Lothian, also called LYONNESSE, a primitive province of Scotland lying between the rivers Tweed and Forth. The name, of Welsh origin but uncertain meaning, is retained in the names of the modern Scottish council areas of East and West Lothian and Midlothian and the historic region of Lothian. Occupied in the 3rd and 4th centuries by a British tribe called by the Romans the Votadini, the area seems by the mid-7th century to have been conquered by the Angles settled in northern England. Kenneth I MacAlpin, first king of the Picts and of the Scots, made southward attacks in the mid-9th century, and from *c.* 975 Lothian was held by Scottish kings. King Edward III of England acquired it in 1333, and it was only gradually won back by the Scots, the border town of Berwick-upon-Tweed remaining, from 1482, in English hands.

Lothian, former administrative region of southeastern Scotland. The region was formed from the historic counties of West Lothian, Midlothian, and East Lothian in 1975. It was the next most populous Scottish region after Strathclyde. In 1996 it was divided into the council areas of East Lothian, area 263 sq mi (681 sq km); Midlothian, area 137 sq mi (355 sq km); West Lothian, area 184 sq mi (476 sq km); and the City of Edinburgh, with an area of 100 sq mi (260 sq km). Edinburgh was the seat of the regional authority.

Much of the region lies along the eastern coast of the central rift valley of Scotland. Between the Lammermuir Hills to the south and the post-glacial raised beaches of the eastern coast and Firth of Forth to the east and north lie fertile deposits of glacial clays above rocks rich in coal seams. The Lothians, being thus well endowed for both agriculture and industry, have been an important area of Scotland from very early times. The fertile glacial soils of the coastal lowlands, together with low rainfall and long hours of sunshine, led to the concentration on arable farming. Barley, grown mainly for whisky distilling and beer brewing, is now the chief cash crop, but wheat, oats, seed potatoes, and fodder crops for winter fattening of livestock are all important. Farms are generally large, prosperous, and highly mechanized. The proximity of the large urban markets has encouraged dairy farming and market gardening, as well as increased production of pigs and poultry. Sheep farming prevails on the Lammermuir Hills inland.

Industry in the Lothians was established by the 12th century, when salt was produced at Preston Pans. Coal seams were early exploited to provide fuel to evaporate the brine, and by the mid-17th century the small ports of Musselburgh, Cockenzie, and Port Seton were thriving outlets for the locally produced salt, coal, and grain. By the 19th century coal mining had reached the height of its prosperity in West Lothian and Midlothian, and oil was being produced from crushed oil shale at Pumpherston. This early oil industry declined in the 20th century. Coal mining extended into East Lothian by the mid-20th century but thereafter underwent a precipitous decline, and by the 1990s no large coal mines remained in the Lothians. A nuclear power station began operation in 1988 at Torness, on the southern shore of the Firth of Forth. The decline of mining prompted the establishment of light engineering and vehicle assembly plants such as that at Bathgate. Further expansion of light industry is taking place, particularly electronics, which now employs more workers in Scotland than shipbuilding, coal mining, or the iron and steel industry. There are notable concentrations of electronics industry at Dalkeith and Livingston, which form part of the Scottish computer-making region known as "Silicon Glen." Software development became increasingly important in the area, and by the 1990s the service sector as a whole employed a majority of the region's workforce.

Edinburgh, the Scottish capital, together with its port of Leith, has dominated the area since medieval times as the principal commercial, market, and cultural centre. Surrounding small towns such as Penicuik, once a paper-making centre, now serve largely as dormitory suburbs for Edinburgh. The new town of Livingston in West Lothian was designated in 1964 to provide a new focus for economic growth. It is now the largest town in the Lothians apart from Edinburgh. The historic burgh of Linlithgow (*q.v.*) is the administrative centre for the council area of West Lothian; Haddington for East Lothian; and Dalkeith for Midlothian. Pop. (1994 est.) 758,600.

Lothringen: *see* Lorraine.

Loti, Pierre, pseudonym of LOUIS-MARIE-JULIEN VIAUD (b. Jan. 14, 1850, Rochefort, Fr.—d. June 10, 1923, Hendaye), novelist whose exoticism made him popular in his time and whose themes anticipated some of the central preoccupations of French literature between World Wars.

Loti's career as a naval officer took him to the Middle and Far East, thus providing him with the exotic settings of his novels and reminiscences. Following his naval schooling and training, he was promoted ship's lieutenant in 1881 and during 1885–91 saw service in Chinese waters. His subsequent promotions led to an appointment as ship's captain in 1906.

After the publication of his first novel, *Aziyadé* (1879), he rapidly developed a parallel literary career, winning the respect of critics and the devotion of a large public. With such successes as *Pêcheur d'Islande* (1886) and *Madame Chrysanthème* (1887) to his credit and with the approval of such exacting critics as Ferdinand Brunetière, Anatole France, Paul Bourget, and Jules Lemaître, the way was made smooth for his reception into the Académie Française in 1891.

Loti, engraving after a drawing by Gaston Vuillier, *c.* 1891

By courtesy of the Bibliotheque Nationale, Paris

Each year there was a new book, sometimes a novel—*Ramuntcho* (1897), *Les Désenchantées* (1906)—often treating objectively the love affairs with which he tried to satisfy his dreams and melancholy at every landfall, and sometimes a volume in which he himself figured—*Le Roman d'un enfant* (1890), *Prime Jeunesse* (1919), *Un Jeune Officier pauvre* (1923)—which reflected most fully his passionate nature.

An exceptionally gifted observer, he was able to return from his voyages with a rich store of pictorial images and embody them in simple, musical prose. But this literary impressionism served a deeper strain in his nature; death, as much as love, lies at the heart of his work, revealing a profound despair at the passing of sensuous life.

This despair was tempered by his tenderness and compassion for the human condition, and such books as *Le Livre de la pitié et de la mort* (1890) and *Reflets sur la sombre route* (1889) are perfect examples of his candid art—an art so simple that Lemaître asserted that it was impossible to discover "how it was done."

Where the same name may denote a person, place, or thing, the articles will be found in that order

lotic ecosystem: *see* riverine ecosystem.

Lotichius Secundus, Petrus (b. Nov. 2, 1528, Niederzell, near Schlüchtern, Hesse—d. Oct. 22, 1560, Heidelberg, Lower Palatinate), one of Germany's outstanding neo-Latin Renaissance poets.

Lotichius studied in Frankfurt, Marburg, and Wittenberg. He participated in the Protestant defense of Magdeburg (1547) and later studied at Montpellier and Padua, where he received his medical degree. Appointed professor of medicine and botany at Heidelberg (1557), he remained there until his death.

Lotichius' elegies, poems, and eulogies were first published in 1551; the complete works, with dedicatory epistle by the scholar-poet Joachim Camerarius, appeared in 1561. The verses, written in Latin, are indebted to Catullus and Ovid and show feeling for the countryside; his love lyrics have an autobiographical directness and exhibit 16th-century sensibilities.

Lotophagoi (Greek mythology): *see* Lotus Eater.

Lots, Feast of (Judaism): *see* Purim.

lottery, procedure for distributing something (usually money or prizes) among a group of people by lot or chance. The type of lottery considered here is a form of gambling in which a usually large number of people purchase chances, called lottery tickets, and the winning tickets are drawn from a pool composed of all tickets sold (sweepstakes) or offered for sale. The value of the prizes is the amount remaining after expenses—including the profits for the promoter, the costs of promotion, and the taxes or other revenues—are deducted from the pool. In most large-scale lotteries a very large prize is offered along with many smaller ones. Lotteries have a very wide appeal as a means for raising money; they are simple to organize, easy to play, and, in general, popular but controversial.

The practice of determining the distribution

of property by lot is traceable to ancient times. Among dozens of Biblical examples, that in the Old Testament (Numbers 26:55–56) has the Lord instructing Moses to take a census of the people of Israel and to divide the land among them by lot. The Roman emperors Nero and Augustus used lotteries to give away property and slaves during Saturnalian feasts and other entertainments. Modern lotteries of a similar type include those used for military conscription, commercial promotions in which property is given away by a random procedure, and the selection of jury members from lists of registered voters. Under the strict definition of a gambling type of lottery, however, payment of a consideration (property, work, or money) must be made for a chance of receiving the prize.

Early history. The first European lotteries appeared in 15th-century Burgundy and Flanders with towns attempting to raise money to fortify defenses or aid the poor. Francis I of France permitted the establishment of lotteries for private and public profit in several cities between 1520 and 1539. The first public lottery to have paid money as prizes is believed to be *La Lotto de Firenze* in Florence in 1530. This was such a successful enterprise that the practice quickly spread to other Italian cities. When the Italian nation was united, the first national lottery was created in 1863, with regular (weekly) drawings organized for the purpose of providing income for the state. *Lotto,* the Italian National Lottery, is regarded as the basis for such modern gambling games as policy, the numbers game, lotto, keno, and bingo.

Queen Elizabeth I chartered a general lottery in England in 1566 to raise money for repairing harbours and other public purposes. In 1612 the Virginia Company obtained permission from James I for a lottery to help in financing the settlement of Jamestown in the New World. While several lotteries organized by the company did not erase a desperate need for funds and although businessmen in some English towns complained of difficulties related to them, they were nevertheless thought to be the "first and most certaine" way to obtain funds. Lotteries accounted for almost half of the yearly income of the company by 1621, when, as a result of bitter dissension within the company itself, the company's lotteries were finally prohibited by the House of Commons. In 1627 a series of lotteries was licensed to raise money for the building of an aqueduct for London, and, in fact, except for a ban from 1699 to 1709, lotteries were held in England until 1826.

Some important problems developed in the manner of conducting lotteries in England in the 17th and 18th centuries. For most of that period lotteries were the only form of organized gambling available to the people. They were intensively advertised by such promotions as torchlight processions in the streets. Contractors would often manage to purchase tickets at less than the standard prices for subsequent resale at excessive markups, and a type of side bet was popularized called insurance—a small wager that a ticket would or would not be drawn in the regular lottery. The state could not derive revenues from either of the latter two practices, but dishonest private operators could. Also, it was claimed that lotteries encouraged mass gambling and that drawings were fraudulent. Their abuses strengthened the arguments of those in opposition to lotteries and weakened their defenders, but, before they were outlawed in 1826, the government and licensed promoters had used lotteries for all or portions of the financing of such projects as the building of the British Museum and the repair of bridges, plus many projects in the American colonies, such as supplying a battery of guns for the defense of Philadelphia and rebuilding Faneuil Hall in Boston.

The Continental Congress in 1776 voted to establish a lottery to try to raise funds for the American Revolution. The scheme was abandoned, but over the next 30 years the practice continued of holding smaller public lotteries, which were seen as mechanisms for obtaining "voluntary taxes" and helped build several American universities: Harvard, Dartmouth, Yale, King's College (now Columbia), William and Mary, Union, and Brown. Privately organized lotteries also were common in England and America as means to sell products or properties for more money than could be obtained from a regular sale. By 1832 lotteries had become very popular indeed; the *Boston Mercantile Journal* reported that 420 had been held the previous year in eight states.

Abuses by private organizers continued, however, and once again voices of opposition began to dominate. In 1827 postmasters and their assistants were barred from selling lottery tickets. Most of the states began legislating antilottery laws. In 1868 Congress declared it unlawful to use the mail for letters or circulars concerning lotteries "or other similar enterprises on any pretext whatever." The opinion of the Supreme Court in 1878 held lotteries to have "a demoralizing influence upon the people."

The postal rules did not have an immediate effect in eliminating lotteries; the most successful lottery in America was organized in Louisiana in 1869 and ran continuously for 25 years. Agents for the Louisiana Lottery were located in every city in the United States: the total sales per month were $2,000,000 at its peak; monthly drawings generated prizes up to $250,000, and twice-yearly prizes could go as high as $600,000. In 1890 President Benjamin Harrison and Congress agreed in condemning lotteries as "swindling and demoralizing agencies" and prohibited the interstate transportation of lottery tickets. The Louisiana Lottery, the last state lottery in the United States until 1963, was killed, but not until it had acquired both enormous profits for its (private) promoters and a reputation for bribery and corruption.

The history of lotteries in several European countries was roughly similar to those of England and America but not to that of Italy. In France, lotteries became increasingly popular after their introduction by Francis I in the 1500s. Their general appeal lasted until the 17th century, when Louis XIV and several members of his court managed to win the top prizes in a drawing—an event that seems to have generated some suspicion and resulted in the king's returning the money for redistribution. French lotteries were abolished in 1836. Almost a century later (1933) a new *Loterie nationale* was established, closed just before World War II and later reopened.

In the 1930s, the Irish Hospitals' Sweepstakes was established and a pattern set for the modern, highly organized lotteries of the 20th century. The pattern of the sweepstakes, however, was not very different from the state lotteries of Georgian England or 19th-century Europe.

Modern lottery operations. The basic elements of lotteries are usually quite simple. First, there must be some means of recording the identities of the bettors, the amounts staked by each, and the number or other symbol on which the money is bet. The bettor may write his name on a ticket that is deposited with the lottery organization for subsequent shuffling and possible selection in the drawing. Or the bettor may buy a numbered receipt, in the knowledge that this number will be entered into a pool of numbers, the bettor having the responsibility of determining later if his ticket was among the winners. Another procedure requires only that the bettor inform a representative of the lottery which number, usually up to three digits, he guesses will be drawn, and the representative is trusted to appear later with the prize, if any is won. This is the usual procedure in the numbers game (*q.v.*), which has been popular for several decades in several large U.S. cities. The numbers game is defined in U.S. state laws as an illegal lottery. (*See also* policy). Bolita, a lottery similar to policy, is played in Puerto Rico and, in the United States, among Cuban and Puerto Rican groups. The drawing is of one numbered ball from a sack of balls numbered 1 to 100.

A second element of all lotteries is the drawing, a procedure for determining winning numbers. This may take the form of a pool or collection of tickets or their counterfoils from which the winners are extracted. The tickets must first be thoroughly mixed by some mechanical means, such as shaking or tossing; this is a randomizing procedure designed to insure that chance and only chance determines the selection of winners. Computers have increasingly come into use for this purpose because of their capacity for storing information about large numbers of tickets and also for generating random numbers for identifying the winners.

Promoters of public, especially of large-scale, lotteries may exploit the opportunity to make the drawing and mixing process as colourful and dramatic as possible. The drawings held by the Irish Sweepstakes until it ceased operation in 1987 could be combined with horse racing. In that lottery two drawings were held, one to identify winning numbers and another to associate those numbers with the names of horses entered in a major race; the success of the individual horses then determined the final order of the prizes.

A third element common to all lotteries is the existence of a mechanism for collecting and pooling all the money placed as stakes. This is usually accomplished by a hierarchy of sales agents who pass money paid for the tickets up through the organization until it is "banked." A practice common in many national lotteries is to divide tickets into fractions, usually tenths. Each fraction if and when it is sold separately costs slightly more than its share of the total cost of an entire ticket. Many people then buy whole tickets, in effect at a premium or discounted price, for marketing in the streets where customers can place relatively small stakes on the fractions. In a large-scale lottery, the use of the regular mail system is desirable for communicating information and transporting tickets and stakes. In the United States and some other countries, however, postal rules prohibit use of the mails. Postal prohibitions apply also to international mailings of lotteries. Though post-office authorities are diligent, it is clear that much smuggling and other violation of interstate and international regulations occurs.

A fourth requirement is a set of rules determining the frequencies and sizes of the prizes. Costs of organizing and promoting the lotteries must be deducted from the pool, and a percentage normally goes as revenues and profits to the state or sponsor. Of the remainder available for the winners, a decision must be made on whether to pay few large prizes or many smaller ones. Potential bettors seem to be attracted to lotteries that offer very large prizes, but in some cultures they also demand a chance to win smaller ones (which, typically, are wagered again in the next round). Authorities on lotteries disagree about which of these choices is better for the welfare of the people and the economic success of the lottery. The amount of the pool returned to the bettors tends to be between 50 percent and 60 percent. The numbers game usually returns 54 percent to winners.

Distribution of modern lotteries. Countries that have state lotteries or license large-scale private ones are many African and Near Eastern states, most European countries, Russia itself, most Latin American countries, Japan, Australia, and several countries on the Asian mainland, but not the People's Republic of China and India (which permits "small" lotteries). The list also included in the United States: New Hampshire, New York, and New Jersey in the 1960s; Connecticut, Massachusetts, Michigan, Pennsylvania, Maryland, Maine, Rhode Island, Illinois, Delaware, Ohio, and Vermont in the 1970s; and the District of Columbia, Washington, and Colorado in the 1980s. Communist countries attempted for a few decades to reject public gambling institutions as decadent and anti-Marxist, but later only privately organized gambling was in disfavour.

Australia, however, has been called the real home of the state lottery. There, all the states except South Australia conduct lotteries for financing public programs and projects. New South Wales, which had lotteries as early as 1849, has the largest, with sales of more than 1,000,000 tickets a week; it has financed, among other things, the spectacular Sydney Opera House. New South Wales also raffles houses, cars, and other prizes on a scale unequalled anywhere else. (R.D.H.)

lotto (game): *see* bingo.

Lotto, Lorenzo (b. *c.* 1480, Venice—d. 1556, Loreto, Papal States), late Renaissance Italian painter known for his perceptive portraits and mystical paintings of religious subjects. In the earlier years of his life he lived at Treviso, and, although he was influenced by the Venetians Giovanni Bellini and Antonello da Messina, he always remained somewhat apart from the main Venetian tradition. His earliest dated pictures, the "Madonna and St. Peter Martyr" (1503) and the "Portrait of Bishop Bernardo de' Rossi" (1505), both in Naples, have unmistakable Quattrocento traits in the treatment of the drapery and landscape and in the cool tonality.

Between 1508 and 1512, Lotto was in Rome, where he was influenced by Raphael, who was painting the Stanza della Segnatura in the Vatican palace. In the "Entombment" (1512) at Jesi and the "Transfiguration" (*c.* 1513) at Recanati, Lotto abandoned the dryness and cool colour of his earlier style and adopted a fluid method and a blond, joyful colouring.

After 1513 Lotto lived primarily in Bergamo, where his style matured. His most successful works of this period are the altarpieces in S. Bernardino and S. Spirito, which show a new inventiveness, a greater competence in rendering light and shade, and a preference for opulent colours. The compositions of his Bergamo works are more self-assured, and the "Susanna and the Elders" (1517; Contini Bonacossi Collection, Florence) exhibits his growing faculty for narrative painting.

In 1526 or 1527 Lotto returned to Venice, where he was briefly influenced by the glowing palette and grand compositional schemes of Titian. This is best seen in his "St. Nicholas of Bari in Glory" (1529; Church of the Carmini, Venice). But Lotto's main interest was in the forceful depiction of emotions and psychological insights. This is evident in his many portraits and especially in the "Annunciation" (*c.* 1527; Sta. Maria sopra Mercanti Recanati), with its agitated figures, swirling drapery, dramatic lighting, and neglect of perspective.

In Venice, Lotto had been snubbed by the circle of Titian, and in 1529 he moved to the Marches, where he could paint without censure. In this period his work became even more emotional, and many works, such as the "Madonna of the Rosary" (1539; Cingoli) and the "Crucifixion" (1531; Monte San Giusto), exhibit a highly charged mysticism in their nervous, crowded compositions and lurid colouring. His numerous portraits of this period are among his most incisively descriptive of the sitter's character; and the "Madonna Enthroned with Four Saints" (*c.* 1540; Sta. Maria della Piazza, Ancona) shows Lotto at the height of his narrative power.

Lotto was back in Venice in 1540, and his "St. Antonino Giving Alms" (1542; SS. Giovanni e Paolo, Venice) shows a renewed interest in Titian. But in 1549 he returned to the Marches, and his life became increasingly unsettled. He had a nervous, irritable temperament and seemed unable to stay long in one place or to sustain permanent relationships. In his old age he was destitute and was forced to paint numbers on hospital beds to earn a living. In 1554, partially blind, he entered the Santa Casa in Loreto as an oblate member to escape his critics and his debts. There he began one of his most sensitive masterpieces, the "Presentation in the Temple," which remained unfinished at his death.

Lotto carpet, pile floor covering, handwoven in Turkey, so called because it appears in several of the works of the 16th-century Venetian painter Lorenzo Lotto. They are characterized by a lacy arabesque repeated field pattern, usually in yellow upon a red ground. This pattern was a 16th- and 17th-century favourite for carpets apparently produced somewhere along the Aegean coast of Anatolia and repeated in much more geometric draftsmanship in small rugs from Transylvania or elsewhere in European Turkey.

Lotto carpet from Anatolia, 17th century; in the Metropolitan Museum of Art, New York City

By courtesy of the Metropolitan Museum of Art, New York City; photograph, Otto E. Nelson

The pattern was taken up in the 17th century at Cuenca, in Spain, for carpets the colour scheme of which consists of yellows and oranges; and it was copied in several other European countries. Many counterfeits of the Turkish carpets exist, particularly of the Balkan type.

Lotuko, also spelled LOTUHO, LOTUXO, or LATUKA, people of the southern Sudan, living near Torit, who speak an Eastern Sudanic language of the Chari-Nile branch of the Nilo-Saharan family. They grow millet, maize, peanuts (groundnuts), and tobacco and have many cattle. They live in large, fortified villages, often with several hundred huts and divided into quarters. They lack a centralized chieftaincy but recognize the rule of hereditary rainmakers, each of whom has ritual and political authority over one of the nine rain areas. There are a number of patrilineal clans with a distribution that is distinct from that of the rain areas.

The rainmakers control an elaborate age-set system. There are annual initiation rites for those who have reached puberty: four annual groups are together initiated into sets based upon village clusters, and, when this is completed, all members are initiated into wider sets, based on rain areas. Every 16 years there is a last initiation that involves the lighting of a new fire by friction. At this time, after a mock battle between elders and youth, the initiates carry the flame of the rainmakers' new fire to each village.

Lotuko rainmakers dancing

George Roger—Magnum

Another important office is that of the diviner, who can counter witchcraft and whose power is hereditary. Lotuko believe in a supreme being, Naijok, who is a power associated with the dead.

lotus, any of several different plants. The lotus of the Greeks was the species *Ziziphus lotus* of the buckthorn family (Rhamnaceae), a bush native in southern Europe. It has large fruits containing a mealy substance that can be used for making bread and fermented drinks. In ancient times the fruits were an article of food among the poor, and a wine made from the fruit was thought to produce contentment and forgetfulness.

The Egyptian lotus is a white water lily (*q.v.*), *Nymphaea lotus* (family Nymphaeaceae). The blue lotus (*N. caerulea*) was the dominant lotus in Egyptian art. The sacred lotus of the Hindus is an aquatic plant (*Nelumbo nucifera*) with white or delicate pink flowers; the lotus of eastern North America is *Nelumbo pentapetala*, a similar plant with yellow blossoms (*see* Nelumbonales). The lotus tree, known to the Romans as the Libyan lotus, was probably *Celtis australis,* the nettle tree of southern Europe, a member of the elm family (Ulmaceae), with fruits like small cherries, first red and then black at maturity.

The *Lotus* is also a genus of the pea family (Fabaceae or Leguminosae), containing about 100 species distributed in temperate regions of Europe, Asia, Africa, and North America. It is represented in Great Britain, for example, by *L. corniculatus,* bird's-foot trefoil, a low-growing ground cover with clusters of small bright yellow flowers that are often streaked with crimson. In North America 20 or more species of *Lotus* occur and are called such common names as deervetch, deerclover, and bastard indigo. They are grazed by animals.

The lotus, in the water-lily form, is a persistent ornament in architecture. A well-known example is its use in decorating the capitals of columns, a practice dating from ancient Egyptian times. The lotus is also the basis of the Assyrian sacred tree and the Phoenician stela capitals, which were the antecedent of the Ionic order of architectural design.

In addition to artistic uses, the lotus, since ancient times, has symbolized fertility and related ideas, including birth, purity, sexuality, rebirth of the dead, and, in astrology, the rising sun.

lotus bird: *see* jacana.

Lotus-Eater, Greek plural LOTOPHAGOI, Latin plural LOTOPHAGI, in Greek mythology, one of a tribe encountered by the Greek hero Odysseus on the Libyan coast, after a north wind had driven him and his men from Cape Malea. The local inhabitants, whose distinctive practice is indicated by their name, invited Odysseus' scouts to eat of the mysterious plant. Those who did so were overcome by a blissful forgetfulness; they had to be dragged back to the ship and chained to the rowing-benches, or they would never have returned to their duties.

The Greeks called several non-narcotic plants *lōtos,* but the name may have been used in this case for the opium poppy, the ripe seed pod of which resembles the pod of the true lotus. The phrase "to eat lotus" is used metaphorically by numerous ancient writers to mean "to forget," or "to be unmindful."

Consult the INDEX *first*

Lotus Sūtra, Sanskrit SADDHARMAPUṆḌARĪKA-SŪTRA ("Lotus of the Good Law [or True Doctrine] Sūtra"), one of the earlier Mahāyāna Buddhist texts venerated as the quintessence of truth by the Japanese Tendai (Chinese T'ien-t'ai) and Nichiren sects. The *Lotus Sūtra* is regarded by many others as a religious classic of great beauty and power and one of the most important and most popular works in the Mahāyāna tradition, the form of Buddhism predominant in East Asia. In China it is called the *Miao-fa lien-hua ching* or *Fa-hua Ching* and in Japan, *Myōhō-renge-kyō* or *Hoke-kyō*.

In the *Lotus Sūtra* the Buddha has become the divine eternal Buddha, who attained perfect Enlightenment endless eons ago. His nature as the supreme object of faith and devotion is expressed partly through the language of wondrous powers (*e.g.,* his suddenly making visible thousands of worlds in all directions, each with its own Buddha). In keeping with this exalted Buddhology, the Hīnayāna goals of emancipation and sainthood are reduced to inferior expedients: here all beings are invited to become no less than fully enlightened Buddhas through the grace of innumerable bodhisattvas ("Buddhas-to-be").

The *sūtra,* composed largely in verse, has a total of 28 chapters and contains many charms and mantras (sacred chants). It was first translated into Chinese in the 3rd century AD and became extremely popular in China and Japan, where common belief held that the simple act of chanting it would bring salvation. The 25th chapter, which describes the glory and special powers of the great bodhisattva of compassion, Avalokiteśvara (Chinese Kuan-yin; Japanese Kannon), has had an important separate life under the name of *Kuan-yin Ching* (Japanese *Kannon-gyō*).

Lotuxo (people): *see* Lotuko.

Lotze, Rudolf Hermann (b. May 21, 1817, Bautzen, Saxony [Germany]—d. July 1, 1881, Berlin), German philosopher who bridged the gap between classical German philosophy and 20th-century idealism and founded Theistic Idealism.

While studying for doctorates in medicine and philosophy at the University of Leipzig (1834–38), he began interpreting physical processes as essentially mechanistic. After a short medical practice, he concentrated his efforts on philosophy by teaching at Leipzig (1842–44) and becoming professor of philosophy at the universities of Göttingen (1844–80) and Berlin (1881).

He first became known as a physiologist in his polemic against vitalism. Although he regarded physical and psychic sciences equally, he espoused a natural order to the creation of the universe as determined by a supreme being. His religious philosophy affected modern thought by emphasizing the problem of delineating value from existence. The foundation for his theories is documented in *Logik* (1843), *Mikrokosmos,* 3 vol. (1856–64), and *Metaphysik* (1879).

Louang Namtha, formerly HOUAKHONG, town, northwestern Laos. The town is situated about 10 miles (16 km) south of the Chinese border and about 50 miles (80 km) east of the border with (Myanmar) Burma, in the upper Tha River valley. It is linked to eastern Myanmar and Louangphrabang (95 miles [153 km] southeast) by highways.

The surrounding region is predominantly mountainous, with the uplands being occupied by Lao-Theng (Lao-Theung; Mountain Mon-Khmer) peoples such as the Lamet and Khün, who constitute the majority of the populace of this area. Other minor mountain peoples are the Lolo and Akha (Ko) groups. The lowlands are inhabited by rice-farming Lü peoples closely related to the predominant valley Lao.

The Tha River, for which the town is named, rises on the Chinese border and joins the Mekong southeast of Ban Houayxay (Fort Carnot). In addition to teak and other forest products, there are unexploited lignite and copper deposits on the Tha River, as well as alluvial gold, sapphires, and zircons on the watercourses near Ban Houayxay.

Louangphrabang, formerly spelled LUANG PRABANG, town, northern Laos. A port on the Mekong River, Louangphrabang lies 130 miles (210 km) north-northwest of Vientiane, the national capital.

From 1353 Louangphrabang, then called Muong Swa, was the capital of the kingdom of Lan Xang. Around 1563 the royal court was removed to Vientiane, and Muong Swa was renamed Luang Prabang in honour of the Pra Bang, a Sinhalese gold Buddha brought to the town probably in 1356. At the partition of Lan Xang in 1707, Luang Prabang became the capital of a new kingdom of the same name. In the reorganization of Laos in 1946–47, the kingdom of Luang Prabang was divided. Louangphrabang remained the royal residence and the religious centre of Laos, but Vientiane was made the nation's administrative capital.

Despite its former royal status, Louangphrabang remains a relatively small town lacking modern industries. Under royal patronage, before the Communist takeover in 1975, lacquering, goldsmithing, and silversmithing crafts survived. Shop trade was largely in the hands of the Indian and Chinese minorities. There are several teacher-training schools. Among its more than 20 Buddhist pagodas is the Phu Si, alleged to enshrine Buddha's footprint.

The region surrounding the town is one of the driest in Indochina. About half the populace of the region are valley Lao, who raise corn (maize), rice, and poultry. The uplands are inhabited largely by the Khmu of the Lao-Theng (Lao-Theung; Mountain Mon-Khmer) group, the highest areas by Meo (Miao, or Hmong) people. Pop. (1985) 68,400.

Loubet, Émile(-François) (b. Dec. 31, 1838, Marsanne, Fr.—d. Dec. 20, 1929, Montélimar), statesman and seventh president of the French Third Republic, who contributed to the break between the French government and the Vatican (1905) and to improved relations with Great Britain.

A lawyer, Loubet entered the Chamber of Deputies in 1876, championing the republican cause and working especially for free, obligatory, and secular primary education. He entered the Senate in 1885 and from December 1887 to March 1888 was minister of public works. His tenure as premier and minister of the interior, beginning in February 1892, ended in November as a result of the financial scandal following the collapse of the French Panama canal company, the Campagnie Universelle du Canal Interocéanique, though for a short time he continued to serve as minister of the interior under his successor.

In 1899 Loubet became president of the republic. Known to favour settlement of the case of Alfred Dreyfus, the Jewish army officer whose conviction for treason on questionable evidence in 1894 had divided French society, he summoned René Waldeck-Rousseau to form a ministry to resolve the Dreyfus affair and appealed to all republicans to rally behind it. Dreyfus, brought back from the penal colony of Devil's Island (off the coast of South America), was again convicted by a court-martial; but Loubet, by remitting the sentence and canceling the order for deportation, signaled the victory of republican forces against those of the royalists, the Roman Catholic clergy, and the army.

Loubet's presidency also marked the complete separation between the French state and the church. In 1905, amid violent controversy, any relationship of the Roman Catholic Church, as well as that of the Protestant and Jewish faiths, to the state was dissolved.

Active also in foreign relations, Loubet visited foreign leaders, including Nicholas II of Russia, Edward VII of Great Britain, and Victor Emmanuel III of Italy—a visit that infuriated Pope Pius X. Loubet smoothed relations with England in April 1904 by signing the Anglo-French entente (Entente Cordiale), which settled their colonial differences.

Loubomo, formerly DOLISIE, commune (town), southern Congo, and an important transport centre for western Zaire and southern Gabon. It lies 70 miles (110 km) northeast of Pointe-Noire (the Atlantic coastal terminus of the Congo's railway and highway network), near the junction of the main Brazzaville–Pointe-Noire railway with a branch north to the Gabon border, and is also the southern terminus of major highways from Cameroon and Gabon. Loubomo also has an airport. It is a mining (gold and lead) and market (leather, sisal, and cattle) centre. The town also has small industries producing wood veneer, sawed lumber, and carbonated beverages. Pop. (1992 est.) 83,605.

louderback, a fault block that is gently tilted (usually 15 degrees or less) and is capped by a lava flow. These slopes are especially evident wherever lavas, resistant to erosion in dry climates, flowed onto the surfaces before they were tilted. Louderbacks are common in the Basin and Range Province (occupying almost all of Nevada, the western half of Utah, southeastern California, and the southern part of Arizona, as well as northwestern Mexico), where they are used for relative dating of the strata and faulting. Occasionally the surrounding area is greatly eroded, leaving the louderbacks as relatively flat-topped mesas.

loudness, in acoustics, attribute of sound that determines the intensity of auditory sensation produced. The loudness of sound as perceived by human ears is roughly proportional to the logarithm of sound intensity: when the intensity is very small, the sound is not audible; when it is too great, it becomes painful and dangerous to the ear. The amount of sound energy that the ear can tolerate is nearly 2×10^{12} times greater than the amount that is just perceptible. This range varies from person to person and with the frequency of the sound.

A unit of loudness, called the phon, has been established; one phon is equal to a difference in sound intensity of one decibel. The number of phons of a given sound is equal to the number of decibels (*q.v.*) of a pure 1,000-hertz tone judged by the listener to be equally loud. The increase in loudness of any sound is said to be one phon when judged equal to the increase of one decibel in intensity for a 1,000-hertz tone.

Because loudness does not appear to increase proportionately with the number of phons (*e.g.,* 60 phons does not seem twice as loud as 30 phons), another more practical unit of loudness, the sone, is used. One sone is defined as the loudness of a tone having a loudness level of 40 phons. On this scale, a sound that is perceived as twice as loud as this reference sound would have a loudness of two sones. In equation form, expressing sones as S and phons as P, $\log_{10}S = 0.03(P - 40)$, approximately.

Loudon, John Claudius (b. April 8, 1783, Cambuslang, Lanarkshire, Scot.—d. Dec. 14, 1843, London), Scottish landscape gardener and architect. Loudon was the most influential horticultural journalist of his time, and his writings helped shape Victorian taste in gardens, public parks, and domestic architecture.

Loudon, oil painting by John Linnell the Elder, 1840–41

By courtesy of the Linnean Society of London

With his wife, the author Jane Webb Loudon (1807–58), he wrote and published his widely read *The Suburban Gardener and Villa Companion,* which set the style for the smaller gardens kept by England's expanding middle class.

Loudon went to school in Edinburgh and then served as apprentice to a nurseryman and landscape gardener at Easter Dalry, Scot. He moved to London in 1803 and quickly established himself as a successful landscape gardener. His prodigious publishing activity began in 1806 with his first book on gardening, which was followed by numerous others covering all aspects of horticulture, landscape design, and related subjects.

Loudon advocated irregular, picturesque gardens that were simultaneously intended as settings for botanical study. He called his style the "Gardenesque," in contrast to the more visually and artistically oriented Picturesque. With its rather moralistic aim of combining instruction and pleasure, Loudon's style became the dominant influence on Victorian taste in gardens. The epitome of his approach is the concept of the arboretum—a place where trees and shrubs are cultivated for the purpose of observation and study—exemplified by his most important work, the Derby Arboretum (1839–41).

Loudon's involvement with architecture arose naturally out of his interest in landscape. He made himself a specialist in rural vernacular building types by writing his *Encyclopaedia of Cottage, Farm, and Villa Architecture* (1833).

Loudonia, genus of perennial plants belonging to the water milfoil family (Haloragaceae), found in dry areas of southern Australia. Three species are known, all with stiff, smooth stems, growing to about 30 cm (1 foot) in height and bearing masses of yellow flowers and two- or four-winged fruits. *L. behrii,* called golden pennants because of the way its thin, delicate fruits wave in the breeze, occurs in South Australia, western Victoria, and New South Wales. *L. aurea* and *L. roei* are restricted to South Australia and Western Australia. *L. aurea,* which has inflated yellow fruits that explode when compressed, is called the popflower.

loudspeaker, also called SPEAKER, in sound reproduction, device for converting electrical energy into acoustical signal energy that is radiated into a room or open air. The term signal energy indicates that the electrical energy has a specific form, corresponding, for example, to speech, music, or any other signal in the range of audible frequencies (roughly 20 to 20,000 hertz). The loudspeaker should preserve the essential character of this signal energy in acoustical form. This definition of a loudspeaker excludes such devices as buzzers, gongs, and sirens, in which the acoustical signal energy does not correspond in form to the electrical signal. The part of the speaker that converts electrical into mechanical energy is frequently called the motor, or voice coil. The motor vibrates a diaphragm that in turn vibrates the air in immediate contact with it, producing a sound wave corresponding to the pattern of the original speech or music signal.

A single loudspeaker cannot fully reproduce the entire frequency range of recorded sound, so it is customary to divide the frequency spectrum into parts that are reproduced by different kinds of speakers designed for a particular frequency range. The low-frequency speaker is called a woofer, and the high-frequency speaker is called a tweeter. In many sound reproduction systems a third, or midrange, speaker is also used, and in some systems there are separate "subwoofers" and "supertweeters" to reproduce the extremities of the audible spectrum.

Louga, town, northwestern Senegal, West Africa. Louga is a cattle-market centre and has road and rail links with the port city of Saint-Louis to the northwest and Dakar to the southwest. Pop. (1994 est.) 67,154.

Loughborough, locality, Charnwood district, county of Leicestershire, England. It is situated near the River Soar and on the Loughborough Canal, 11 miles (17 km) northwest of Leicester. There was a settlement on the site of Loughborough before the Roman invasion of Britain, but remains from the time of Roman occupation are scanty. Loughborough is mentioned in Domesday Book, and grants for markets and fairs were made to it in the 13th century, when the wool trade was an important activity in the area. Lacemaking later became the chief industry, but when the lacemaking machines of John Heathcoat in Loughborough were destroyed by the Luddites in 1816, the industry lost much of its local importance. Loughborough is the market centre of a fertile agricultural district, and its main industries include electrical engineering and bell founding. The Loughborough College of Technology became the nucleus of a new university in 1966. Pop. (1991) 46,867.

Louganis, Greg, in full GREGORY EFTHIMIOS LOUGANIS (b. Jan. 29, 1960, San Diego, Calif., U.S.), American diver generally considered the greatest in the history of the sport.

As a child Louganis trained in dancing, tumbling, and acrobatics, skills that would later earn him a reputation as a graceful, effortless diver. In 1976, at age 16, Louganis won an Olympic silver medal in the platform event. In 1979 he won gold medals in both the springboard and platform events at the Pan-American Games and was a favourite to win at the 1980 Olympics but was unable to compete because of the U.S. boycott. In 1983 Louganis set 3-metre springboard records with a 99-point dive and a 755.49-point total. His platform record of 717.41 points came in 1986.

At the 1984 Olympic Games in Los Angeles, Louganis won gold medals in the 3-metre springboard and 10-metre platform. At the 1988 Olympics in Seoul, South Korea, he hit the back of his head on the diving board during the springboard competition, requiring several stitches. The next day, however, he completed his dives and won the event. The following week he won a gold medal in the 10-metre platform. After those Games he retired, having won an unprecedented 47 national and 13 world championships.

In 1994 Louganis revealed that he was gay and the following year disclosed that he had AIDS. His autobiography, *Breaking the Surface*, was published in 1995.

Loughrea, Irish BAILE LOCHA RIACH (Gray Lake), market town, County Galway, Ireland. It lies along the northern shore of Lough (lake) Rea, 116 miles (185 km) west of Dublin. It has a Roman Catholic cathedral (1900–05) and the remains of a medieval castle and friary and of the town fortifications. Near Loughrea are a dolmen (a prehistoric stone-slab monument), souterrains (underground passages and chambers), and ruined towers. Crannogs, or prehistoric stockaded islands, were discovered in the lake. Pop. (1991) 3,271.

Louis, name of rulers grouped below by country and indicated by the symbol •.

Foreign-language equivalents:

Czech	Ludvík
Dutch	Lodewijk
French	Louis
German	Ludwig
Hungarian	Lajos
Italian	Luigi
Polish	Ludwik
Portuguese	Luís
Spanish	Luis

ANJOU-MAINE

•**Louis I** (b. July 23, 1339, Vincennes, Fr.—d. Sept. 20, 1384, Bisceglie, Apulia, Kingdom of Sicily), duke of Anjou, count of Maine, count of Provence, and claimant to the crown of Sicily and Jerusalem, who augmented his own and France's power by attempting to establish a French claim to the Sicilian throne and by vigorously fighting the English in France.

A son of John II of France, Louis in 1356 fought ably at Poitiers against the English. He was sent to England as one of the hostages under the Treaty of Brétigny (1360) but soon escaped. In 1360 his father created the hereditary duchy of Anjou for him, having already given him the county of Maine (1356).

Having been made lieutenant general of the provinces of Languedoc and Guyenne by his brother Charles V, who had become king of France in 1364, Louis spent many years fighting the English and harshly subduing those areas sympathetic to the English, especially Brittany.

Upon his brother's death (1380) Louis became regent. Primarily interested in extending his own personal realm, he agreed to support the antipope Clement VII, who promised him Itria, a kingdom to be created in central Italy. In 1380 Joan I, queen of Sicily and an ally of Clement, adopted Louis as her heir. A rival claimant, Charles of Durazzo, took over Sicily and had Joan murdered before Louis could come to her aid. He was, nevertheless, crowned king of Sicily and Jerusalem by

Clement at Avignon (May 1382). Moving into southern Italy against Charles, Louis died before a decisive battle had been fought.

• **Louis II** (b. Oct. 7, 1377, Toulon, Fr.—d. April 29, 1417, Angers), duke of Anjou, count of Maine and Provence (1384–1417), king of Naples, Sicily, and Jerusalem, who attempted, with only temporary success, to enforce the Angevin claims to the Neapolitan throne initiated by his father, Louis I.

In 1389 Louis inherited his father's titles and was crowned king of Naples by the antipope Clement VII, although Naples was, in fact, ruled by Ladislas of the Durazzo branch of the Angevin family. Louis occupied Naples in 1390–99, until driven out by Ladislas. He then withdrew to Provence.

In 1409 Louis abandoned Pope Benedict XIII and recognized the antipope Alexander V, who named him king of Naples once more. He entered Rome to fight the Neapolitan army, which occupied the city, and then began an unsuccessful campaign to retake Naples (1409–10). Called to Rome again, this time by the antipope John XXIII, Louis finally defeated Ladislas at Roccasecca (May 11, 1411). He failed to follow up this victory, however, and, losing the support of the Pope, who had switched allegiance to Ladislas, he was forced to return to France to administer his lands. There he instituted the Parliament of Aix (1415) and increased the privileges of universities in Aix and Angers.

• **Louis III** (b. Sept. 25, 1403, Anjou, Fr.—d. Nov. 15, 1434, Cosenza, Italy), duke of Anjou and Touraine, count of Maine and Provence, and titular king of Naples and Sicily (1417–34). Advancing Angevin claims to the throne of Naples, Louis struggled with the Aragonese claimant Alfonso V, sometimes supported, sometimes opposed by the childless Queen Joan II of Naples (ruled 1414–35).

Succeeding his father, Louis II of Anjou, as claimant to the Neapolitan throne, Louis was crowned king of Naples by Pope Martin V in September 1419. Louis gathered a considerable army, including the famed *condottiere* (mercenary commander) Muzio Attendola Sforza, and sailed to Naples to conquer the kingdom. Joan, however, recognized as her heir Alfonso V of Aragon (1421), who arrived to defend Naples against Louis.

Alfonso prevented Louis from taking the whole kingdom. When he also usurped some of the royal power from Joan, however, she renounced him and adopted Louis (1423), naming him governor of the duchy of Calabria. Later, in April 1433, the capricious Joan disinherited Louis, only to readopt him in June. Louis' forces had nevertheless gained most of the kingdom and were about to drive out Alfonso when Louis died suddenly, leaving his brother René of Anjou as his successor.

Consult the INDEX *first*

BAVARIA

• **Louis I** (b. Dec. 23, 1174, Kelheim, Bavaria—d. Sept. 15, 1231, Kelheim), second Wittelsbach duke of Bavaria, who greatly increased his family's territory and influence.

Succeeding his father, Otto I, as duke in 1183, Louis enlarged the Bavarian domains and founded the cities of Landshut, Landau, Iser, and Straubing. In the struggle between Otto IV (of Brunswick) and Frederick of Hohenstaufen (Emperor Frederick II) for the throne of the Holy Roman Empire, he sided first with Otto, then switched to Frederick, who gave him control of the Rhenish Palatinate for his son (also named Otto) in 1214. He participated in the Fifth Crusade in Egypt (1221), and from 1225 to 1228 he was Frederick II's regent in Germany. Louis rebelled against Frederick's son Henry in 1228 and was murdered three years later, perhaps at the Emperor's instigation.

• **Louis I** (b. Aug. 25, 1786, Strasbourg, Fr.—d. Feb. 29, 1868, Nice), king of Bavaria from 1825 to 1848, a liberal and a German nationalist who rapidly turned conservative after his accession, best known as an outstanding patron of the arts who transformed Munich into the artistic centre of Germany.

Louis, the well-educated eldest son of King Maximilian I, was a fervent German nationalist as a youth and served only reluctantly at Napoleon's headquarters in the wars against Prussia and Russia (1806–07) and Austria (1809). In Bavaria he came to head the anti-French party, and at the Congress of Vienna (1814–15) he unsuccessfully advocated the return of Alsace and Lorraine to Germany. The liberal Bavarian constitution of 1818 bears his stamp, and he was to resist repeatedly the demands of Metternich, the Austrian statesman, for basic changes in that document. In church questions, however, Louis was more conservative, opposing his father's secularization of monasteries. He played an active part in the downfall of Bavaria's leading minister, Maximilian, Graf von Montgelas (1817), whom he blamed for these anti-ecclesiastical policies.

Louis I, detail from an oil painting by Wilhelm von Kaulbach; in the Bayerische Staatsgemäldesammlungen, Munich

By courtesy of the Bayerische Staatsgemaldesammlungen, Munich

Louis' liberal reputation assured him of general acclaim upon his accession, but he was soon to disappoint his subjects. The King frequently feuded with the Diet, and after the revolutions of 1830 in Europe he came to distrust all democratic institutions. The Öttingen-Wallerstein ministry (1831–37) was a shift to the right, and the subsequent government under Karl von Abel (from 1837) steered a strictly reactionary and clericalist course, restoring many monasteries and proceeding to erode the liberal constitution.

Culturally, however, Louis' reign was brilliant. An enthusiastic patron of the arts, he collected the works that formed the nucleus of Munich's two best known museums, the Glyptothek and Alte Pinakothek. His large-scale planning of Munich created the city's present layout and classic style. He commissioned many representative buildings, among them the Ludwigskirche, Staatsgalerie, Propyläen, Siegestor, Feldherrnhalle, and Odeon.

On the outbreak of the revolutions of 1848, Louis, whose passion for the dancer Lola Montez (*q.v.*) had reduced his popularity even further, abdicated in favour of his son Maximilian II.

• **Louis II,** byname MAD KING LUDWIG, German DER VERRÜCKTE KÖNIG LUDWIG (b. Aug. 25, 1845, Nymphenburg Palace, Munich—d. June 13, 1886, Starnberger See, Bavaria), eccentric king of Bavaria from 1864 to 1886 and an admirer and patron of the composer Richard Wagner. He brought his territories into the newly founded German Empire

Louis II, detail from a portrait by Ferdinand Piloty; in the Bayerische Staatsgemäldesammlungen, Munich

By courtesy of the Bayerische Staatsgemaldesammlungen, Munich

(1871) but concerned himself only intermittently with affairs of state, preferring a life of increasingly morbid seclusion and developing a mania for extravagant building projects.

Louis was the elder son of King Maximilian II of Bavaria and Marie of Prussia. Politically a romantic conservative, he came to the throne after his father's death in 1864 before he had completed his studies. Louis entered the Seven Weeks' War (1866) on the side of Austria but, on his defeat, signed an alliance with Prussia (1867) and, through his prime minister, Chlodwig, Fürst von Hohenlohe-Schillingsfürst, worked for a reconciliation between Germany's two great powers. A German patriot, he resisted the overtures of Napoleon III for a Franco-Austrian-Bavarian alliance and immediately joined Prussia in the war of 1870–71 against France. In December 1870, on the initiative of Bismarck, Louis addressed a letter to Germany's princes calling for the creation of a new empire. His fears for the independence of his crown were allayed by a number of special privileges for Bavaria, although his demands for a substantial territorial increase and the alternation of the imperial title between Prussia and Bavaria remained unfulfilled. Disappointed with the empire, alarmed by the Bavarian population's Pan-German enthusiasm, and weary of feuding with his ministers over his moves to strengthen the church, he retired more and more from politics, devoting himself increasingly to his private pursuits.

Soon after his accession, the King called Richard Wagner to Munich. After little more than a year, however, he was forced to expel the composer because of governmental and popular objection to the friendship and Wagner's own improprieties, though Louis remained a lifelong patron of the musician. The King worshipped the theatre and the opera, and henceforth concerned himself almost exclusively with his artistic endeavours, developing an extravagant mania for building in the Bavarian mountains that he loved. The palace at Herrenchiemsee (Herrn-Insel), constructed from 1878 to 1885 and never completed, was a copy of Versailles; the Linderhof castle (1869–78) was patterned after the Trianon palace; and Neuschwanstein, the most fantastic, was a fairy-tale castle precariously situated on a crag and decorated with scenes from Wagner's romantic operas.

In the early 1880s the King withdrew from society almost completely. Finally, on June 10, 1886, he was declared insane by a panel of doctors. His uncle Prince Luitpold became regent. Removed to Schloss Berg near the Starnberger See by the psychiatrist Bernhard von Gudden, he drowned himself in the lake on June 13. Gudden also perished attempting to save the King's life. Further biographical information may be found in Wilfrid Blunt, *The Dream King: Ludwig II of Bavaria* (1970).

• **Louis III,** German in full LUDWIG LEOPOLD JOSEPH MARIA ALOYS ALFRED (b. Jan. 7, 1845, Munich—d. Oct. 18, 1921, Sárvár, Hung.), last king of Bavaria, from 1913 to 1918, when the revolution of November 7–8 brought the rule of the Wittelsbach dynasty to an end.

In 1868 he married Maria Theresa, daughter of the archduke Ferdinand of Austria-Este. In December 1912, on the death of his father, the regent Luitpold, Louis took over the regency for his insane cousin, King Otto I. On Nov. 5, 1913, although Otto was still alive, Louis assumed the royal title himself.

The new king was interested chiefly in improving agriculture and transportation but also continued the traditional Wittelsbach patronage of the arts. In World War I he took as little part as was possible, though from 1917 he opposed the military policies of Erich Ludendorff, de facto head of the imperial German army.

Louis III, drawing by F. Gärtner, 1915; in the Staatliche Graphische Sammlung, Munich

By courtesy of the Staatliche Graphische Sammlung, Munich

The Bavarian revolution, led by the Socialist Kurt Eisner, was a complete surprise to Louis. Although he did not abdicate, he released his civil and military officers from their oath of loyalty on Nov. 13, 1918. Greatly embittered, he died in exile.

BOHEMIA

• **Louis:** *see* Louis II (Hungary).

FLANDERS

• **Louis I,** also called LOUIS OF NEVERS, French LOUIS DE NEVERS, Dutch LODEWIJK VAN NEVERS (b. *c.* 1304—d. Aug. 25, 1346, near Crécy, Fr.), count of Flanders and of Nevers (from 1322) and of Réthel (from 1325), who sided with the French against the English in the opening years of the Hundred Years' War.

Grandson and heir of Robert of Bethune, count of Flanders, Louis was brought up at the French court and married Margaret of France. His sympathies were entirely French, and he made use of French help in his contests with the Flemish communes.

Under Louis of Nevers, Flanders was practically reduced to the status of a French province. In his time the long contest between Flanders and Holland for the possession of the island of Zeeland was brought to an end by a treaty signed on March 6, 1323, by which West Zeeland was assigned to the count of Holland, the rest to the count of Flanders. The latter part of the reign of Louis of Nevers was remarkable for the successful revolt of the Flemish communes, then rapidly advancing to great material prosperity under Jacob van Artevelde. Artevelde allied himself with Edward III of England in his contest with Philip VI of Valois for the French crown, while Louis of Nevers espoused the cause of Philip. Louis fell at the Battle of Crécy (1346).

• **Louis II,** also called LOUIS OF MÂLE, French LOUIS DE MÂLE, Dutch LODEWIJK VAN MALE (b. Nov. 29, 1330, Mâle Castle, near Bruges, Flanders—d. Jan. 30, 1384, Saint-Omer, Flanders), count of Flanders, Nevers, and Réthel (1346–84), who, by marrying his daughter Margaret to the Burgundian duke Philip the Bold (1369), prepared the way for the subsequent union of Flanders and Burgundy.

The reign of Louis of Mâle was one long struggle with the Flemish communes, headed by the town of Ghent, for political supremacy. Louis was as strong in his French sympathies as his father, Louis I of Nevers, and relied upon French help in enforcing his will upon his refractory subjects, who resented his arbitrary methods of government and the heavy taxation imposed upon them by his extravagance and love of display. Had the great towns with their organized gilds and great wealth held together in their opposition to the Count's despotism, they would have proved successful, but Ghent and Bruges, always keen rivals, broke out into open feud. The power of Ghent reached its height under Philip van Artevelde in 1382. He defeated Louis, took Bruges, and was made regent of Flanders. But the triumph of the White Hoods, as the popular party was called, was of short duration. On Nov. 27, 1382, Artevelde suffered a crushing defeat from a large French army at Roosebeke and was himself slain. Louis of Mâle died two years later, leaving his only daughter Margaret, duchess of Burgundy. Flanders then became a portion of the great Burgundian domain.

FRANCE

• **Louis I:** *see* Louis I (Germany/Holy Roman Empire).

• **Louis II,** byname LOUIS THE STAMMERER, French LOUIS LE BÈGUE (b. 846—d. April 10, 879, Compiègne, Fr.), king of Francia Occidentalis (the West Frankish kingdom) from 877 until his death.

Louis, the son of King Charles II the Bald, was made king of Aquitaine under his father's tutelage in 867. Charles became emperor in 875 and two years later left Louis as regent while he defended Italy for Pope John VIII. Louis was elected king of the West Franks in December 877. At a council at Troyes in 878, the Pope attempted to force Louis to take up the role of defender of the papacy, but Louis refused. Louis and his cousin Louis the Younger, ruler of the East Frankish kingdom, agreed to maintain the division of Lotharingia that their respective fathers had negotiated in the Treaty of Mersen in 870. Louis had hoped to redistribute offices of state but was frustrated by the Frankish magnates, who had accepted him as king on the condition that he respect their possessions and rights.

• **Louis III** (b. 863—d. Aug. 5, 882, Saint-Denis, Fr.), king of France (*i.e.,* Francia Occidentalis, the West Frankish kingdom) from 879 to 882, whose decisive victory over the Northmen in August 881, at Saucourt, Ponthieu, briefly stemmed the incursions of the Scandinavian invaders into northern France.

After the death of their father, Louis II the Stammerer, on April 10, 879, Louis and his brother Carloman agreed at Amiens in 880 to a partition of the kingdom, by which Louis received Francia and Neustria. Invasions instigated by dissident West Frankish nobles and by Louis the Younger, one of the East Frankish kings, were bought off by the cession of western Lotharingia (Treaties of Verdun, 879, and of Ribémont, 880). In 880–881 Louis and his brother made a concerted but unsuccessful campaign against the usurper Boso of Provence.

The pagan Northmen, whose frequent raids had turned to conquest, were the greatest menace faced by Louis III; Amiens, Arras, Cambrai, and the famous monasteries of Saint-Bertin and Corbie were all sacked in 880–881. Louis's victory at Saucourt (the memory of which was preserved in the *chanson de geste* called *Gormont et Isembart*) inflicted heavy losses on the Vikings, but the able and energetic king, not yet 20, died in the following year.

• **Louis IV,** byname LOUIS D'OUTREMER (Louis from Overseas) (b. 921—d. Sept. 10, 954, Reims, Fr.), king of France from 936 to 954 who spent most of his reign struggling against his powerful vassal Hugh the Great.

When Louis's father, Charles III the Simple, was imprisoned in 923, his mother, Eadgifu, daughter of the Anglo-Saxon king Edward the Elder, took Louis to England. He was recalled to France in 936 and crowned on June 19 at Laon by Artand, archbishop of Reims, who became Louis's chief supporter against Hugh the Great. Louis proved not to be the puppet monarch that Hugh had anticipated; he even moved from Paris to Laon to avoid Hugh's influence. When Hugh and Herbert of Vermandois seized Reims and attacked Laon in 940, Louis valiantly defended his city; but because of Louis's earlier interference in Lorraine the German king, Otto I, sent aid to the rebels. Louis appeared to be totally defeated in 941, but he made peace with Otto in November 942 at Vise on the Meuse, and Hugh and he were reconciled after Herbert, Hugh's chief supporter, died in 943.

In 945, while intervening in Norman politics, Louis was captured and handed over to Hugh, who imprisoned him for a year. On his release, Louis closely allied himself with Otto to retake Reims in 946. In 949 Louis again received control of Laon, and Hugh, excommunicated by French and German synods and by the Pope, made a peace in 951 that lasted until Louis's death.

• **Louis V,** byname LOUIS LE FAINÉANT (Louis the Do-Nothing) (b. 967—d. May 21/22, 987), king of France and the last Carolingian monarch.

Crowned on June 8, 979, while his father Lothair was still alive, he shortly afterward married Adelaide, widow of an Aquitanian count, and was established as king in Aquitaine. His frivolity, however, and his rejection of his wife, who finally ran away, brought him into discredit. Sole king on his father's death in 986, he disregarded the advice of his mother, Queen Emma, and Archbishop Adalbero of Reims, who wanted him to seek friendship with the German king Otto III. Just as he was about to have the Archbishop tried for treason, Louis died as the result of a hunting accident. His unpopular uncle Charles of Lower Lorraine, the only surviving member of the Carolingian dynasty, was passed over in favour of Hugh Capet as Louis's successor, thus initiating the Capetian line of French monarchs.

• **Louis VI,** byname LOUIS THE FAT, French LOUIS LE GROS (b. 1081—d. Aug. 1, 1137), king of France from 1108 to 1137; he brought power and dignity to the French crown by his recovery of royal authority over the feudal nobles in his domains of the Île-de-France and the Orléanais.

Louis was designated by his father, Philip I, as his successor in 1098 and was already effectively the ruler well before Philip's death in 1108. He quickly recognized that his priority must be to bring the unruly barons of the royal lands under firm control, and he spent much of his reign in conflict with such men as Hugh de Puiset. His success won him the respect of his greater vassals and was crucial to later Capetian expansion. From his pacification program Louis developed several important concepts for future kings: for example, that the king was a vassal of no man.

Louis had a good relationship with the church and clergy. He has been presented by some historians as the father of communes or towns, but in fact he recognized towns only out of circumstance rather than from principle.

Louis's major wars were against King Henry I of England during the periods 1104–13 and 1116–20. When Charles the Good, count of Flanders, was assassinated in 1127, Louis supported William Clito, who became the successor; even though William was eventually toppled, Louis's actions demonstrated the new strength of the monarchy. In 1124 he was able to muster forces from many parts of France to counter a threatened invasion by the Holy Roman emperor Henry V. Louis's last major achievement was to arrange a marriage between his son Louis VII and Eleanor, heiress of William X, duke of Aquitaine. Abbot Suger of Saint-Denis, a most trusted adviser, is the primary historian for Louis's reign.

• **Louis VII,** byname LOUIS THE YOUNGER, French LOUIS LE JEUNE (b. *c.* 1120—d. Sept. 18, 1180, Paris), Capetian king of France who pursued a long rivalry, marked by recurrent warfare and continuous intrigue, with Henry II of England.

In 1131 Louis was anointed as successor to his father, Louis VI, and in 1137 he became the sole ruler at his father's death. Louis married Eleanor, daughter of William X, duke of Aquitaine, in 1137, a few days before his effective rule began, and he thus temporarily extended the Capetian lands to the Pyrenees. Louis continued his father's pacification program by building the prestige of the kingship through an administrative government based on trustworthy men of humble origin and by consolidating his rule over his royal domains rather than by adding new acquisitions. From 1141 to 1143 he was involved in a fruitless conflict with Count Thibaut of Champagne and the papacy. But thereafter his relations with the popes were good; Alexander II, whom he supported against Frederick Barbarossa, took refuge in France. But the major threat to his reign came from Geoffrey, count of Anjou and, briefly, of Normandy, and Geoffrey's son Henry, who later (1154) became King Henry II of England as well as ruler of both Anjou and Normandy. After Louis repudiated his wife Eleanor for misconduct on March 21, 1152, she married Henry, who then took over control of Aquitaine. Ironically, this act was probably to Capetian advantage because Aquitaine might have drained the resources of Louis's kingdom while bringing him little revenue. After the death of Louis's second wife, he married Alix of Champagne, whose Carolingian blood brought added prestige to the monarchy (1160); their son became Philip II Augustus.

Louis might have defeated Henry if he had made concerted attacks rather than weak assaults on Normandy in 1152. Anglo-Norman family disputes saved Louis's kingdom from severe incursions during the many conflicts that Louis had with Henry between 1152 and 1174. Louis was helped by the quarrel (1164–70) between Henry and Thomas Becket, archbishop of Canterbury, and a revolt (1173–74) of Henry's sons. Suger, abbot of Saint-Denis, who acted as regent in 1147–49 while Louis was away on the Second Crusade, is the primary historian for Louis's reign.

• **Louis VIII,** byname LOUIS THE LION, or THE LION-HEART, French LOUIS LE LION, or LOUIS COEUR-DE-LION (b. Sept. 5, 1187, Paris—d. Nov. 8, 1226, Montpensier, Auvergne, Fr.), Capetian king of France from 1223 who spent most of his short reign establishing royal power in Poitou and Languedoc.

Coronation of Louis VIII and Blanche of Castile, manuscript illumination by an unknown artist, 15th century; in the Bibliothèque Nationale, Paris

By courtesy of the Bibliotheque Nationale, Paris

On May 23, 1200, Louis married Blanche of Castile, daughter of Alfonso VIII of Castile, who effectively acted as regent after Louis's death. In 1212 Louis seized Saint-Omer and Aire to prevent a powerful Flanders from being on the flank of his county of Artois. In 1216, after the barons rebelling against King John of England had offered the English throne to Louis in return for his aid, Louis went to England to aid the rebels. Initially he was successful, but eventually he was defeated at sea and suffered defections. In 1217, when peace was concluded at Kingston, Louis was secretly paid 10,000 marks. In 1224, now king, he seized Poitou and, in 1226, he launched a successful crusade against the Albigensian heretics, capturing the major fortress of Avignon before returning toward Paris because of illness.

Louis was the first Capetian to grant appanages on a large scale and to have a reversion clause that made alienation of royal property more difficult. Louis also developed other particular rights for the kingship, such as the concept that fealty was sworn not only to the individual king but also to the kingship. His eldest son, Louis IX (afterward St. Louis), peacefully succeeded him while his other sons received appanages.

• **Louis IX,** also called SAINT LOUIS (b. April 25, 1214, Poissy, Fr.—d. Aug. 25, 1270, near Tunis; canonized Aug. 11, 1297, feast day August 25), king of France from 1226 to 1270, the most popular of the Capetian monarchs. He led the Seventh Crusade to the Holy Land in 1248–50 and died on another crusade to Tunisia.

Early life. Louis was the fourth child of King Louis VIII and his queen, Blanche of Castile, but, since the first three died at an early age, Louis, who was to have seven more brothers and sisters, became heir to the throne. He was raised with particular care by his parents, especially his mother.

Experienced horsemen taught him riding and the fine points of hunting. Tutors taught him biblical history, geography, and ancient literature. His mother instructed him in religion herself and educated him as a sincere, unbigoted Christian. Louis was a boisterous adolescent, occasionally seized by fits of temper, which he made efforts to control.

When his father succeeded Philip II Augustus in 1223, the long struggle between the Capetian dynasty and the Plantagenets of England (who still had vast holdings in France) was still not settled, but there was a temporary lull, since the English king, Henry III, was in no position to resume the war. In the south of France the Albigensian heretics, who were in revolt against both church and state, had not been brought under control. Finally, there was ferment and the threat of revolt among the great nobles, who had been kept in line by the firm hand of Philip Augustus.

Louis VIII managed to bring these external and internal conflicts to an end. In 1226 Louis VIII turned his attention to quelling the Albigensian revolt, but he unfortunately died at Montpensier on Nov. 8, 1226, on returning from a victorious expedition. Louis IX, who was not yet 13, became king under the regency of his redoubtable mother.

Accession to the throne. The Queen Mother's first concern was to take Louis to Reims to be crowned. Many of the most powerful nobles refrained from participating in the ceremony, but Blanche was not a woman to be discouraged by adversity. While continuing her son's education she vigorously attacked the rebellious barons, particularly Hugh of Lusignan and Peter of Dreux (Pierre Mauclerc), duke of Brittany. Without support from King Henry III of England the baronial coalition collapsed, and the Treaty of Vendôme gave Blanche a brief respite.

She took advantage of it to put an end to the Albigensian revolt. Louis's troops were sent into Languedoc, where they forced Raymond VII, count of Toulouse, to concede defeat. On April 11, 1229, the King imposed the Treaty of Paris on Raymond, in accordance with the terms of which Raymond's daughter was to marry the King's brother Alphonse, and, after their deaths, all of Languedoc would revert to the royal domain. As a political debut it was a magnificent success. When the students at the University of Paris revolted for a trivial reason, Louis, on his mother's advice, closed the university and ordered the students and professors to disperse, thereby strengthening the royal authority.

The problem of the Plantagenet holdings in France remained. Supported by Peter of Dreux, Henry III landed in Brittany and attempted an expedition in the west of France. Louis IX, though only 15, personally commanded the troops. He ordered the château at Angers to be rebuilt and pushed toward Nantes, where Henry was based. There was not even a battle, for, after a futile ride to Bordeaux, Henry withdrew. Truces were renewed, and Peter of Dreux submitted to Louis's authority.

Louis IX, carrying the hand of justice, detail from the *Ordonnances de l'Hotel du Roi*, late 13th century; in the Archives Nationales, Paris

Giraudon—Art Resource/EB Inc.

When Blanche laid down the reins of government in 1234, the kingdom was temporarily at peace. Louis IX could now think about marriage. He was a splendid knight whose kindness and engaging manner made him popular. And he was a just king: although he exacted what was due him, he had no wish to wrong anyone, from the lowest peasant to the richest vassal. He often administered justice personally, either in the great hall of the Palais de la Cité, which he later endowed with a magnificent chapel, or in his Vincennes manor, where he assembled his subjects at the foot of an oak, a scene often recalled by his biographer Jean de Joinville, the seneschal of Champagne. He was also a pious king, the protector of the church and friend of those in holy orders. In 1228 he founded the noted Abbey of Royaumont. Although respectful of the pope, he staunchly resisted unreasonable papal demands and protected his clergy.

Blanche had selected Margaret, daughter of Raymond Berenger IV, the count of Provence, as Louis's wife. The marriage was celebrated at Sens, May 29, 1234, and Louis showed himself to be an eager and ardent husband, which made Blanche intensely jealous of her daughter-in-law. Louis and Margaret had 11 children.

After subduing Thibaut of Champagne, Louis IX had to set out again for Aquitaine. This time the rebel was Hugh of Lusignan, who had married the widowed mother of Henry III. Once again Henry descended on the Continent, this time at Royan, with a powerful force. The majority of the nobles in the west of France united with him. An almost bloodless encounter at the bridge of Taillebourg in 1242 resulted in defeat for the English, and Henry returned to London. With each truce slightly more progress was made toward gaining a peace that would put a permanent end to the Hundred Years' War between France and England.

Leadership of the Seventh Crusade. After his victory over the English, Louis IX fell seriously ill with a form of malaria at Pontoise-lés-Noyon. It was then, in December 1244, that he decided to take up the cross and go to free the Holy Land, despite the lack of enthusiasm among his barons and his entourage. The situation in the Holy Land was critical; Jerusalem had fallen into Muslim hands on Aug. 23, 1244, and the armies of the Sultan of Egypt had seized Damascus. If aid from the West was not forthcoming, the Christian kingdom of the east would soon collapse. In Europe the times had never been more propitious for a crusade. There was a respite in the great struggle between the Holy Roman Empire and the papacy; moreover, Louis IX's forceful attitude toward the Holy Roman emperor, Frederick II, had dampened the latter's enthusiasm for war. The kingdom of France was at peace, and the barons agreed to accompany their sovereign in the Sixth Crusade.

The preparations were long and complex. After entrusting the regency to his mother, Louis IX finally embarked from Aigues-Mortes on Aug. 25, 1248. He took his wife and children with him, since he preferred not to leave the mother and daughter-in-law alone together. His fleet comprised about 100 ships carrying 35,000 men. Louis's objective was simple: he intended to land in Egypt, seize the principal towns of the country, and use them as hostages to be exchanged for Syrian cities.

The beginning was promising. After wintering in Cyprus, the expedition landed near Damietta, Egypt, in June 1249. The King was one of the first to leap onto land, where he planted the oriflamme of St. Denis on Muslim territory. The town and port of Damietta were strongly fortified, but on June 6 Louis IX was able to enter the city. He then pushed on toward Cairo, but the rain-swollen waters of the Nile and its canals stopped him for several months. It was necessary to capture the citadel of al-Manṣūrah. After several attempts, a pontoon bridge was finally built, and the battle took place on Feb. 8, 1250. The outcome of the struggle was for a long time undecided, and the King's brother Robert of Artois was killed. Louis finally gained control of the situation through his energy and self-possession.

But the army was exhausted. The Nile carried thousands of corpses away from al-Manṣūrah, and plague struck the survivors. The King had to issue orders for the agonizing retreat toward Damietta. Louis IX, stricken in turn, dragged himself along in the rear guard of his disintegrating force. The Egyptians harassed the fleeing army and finally captured it on April 7, 1250.

After long negotiations, the King and his principal barons were freed for a high ransom, and Louis rejoined his wife at Acre. The crusaders would have preferred to return to France, but the King decided instead to remain. In four years he was to transform a military defeat into a diplomatic success, conclude advantageous alliances, and fortify the Christian cities of Syria. He returned to his kingdom only upon learning of his mother's death.

Achievement of peace and administrative reforms. The saintly Louis enjoyed immense prestige throughout western Christendom. He took advantage of this to open negotiations for a lasting peace with the English king, Henry III, who had become his brother-in-law. The discussions extended over several years, but the treaty was finally signed in Paris on May 28, 1258. The terms of the treaty were generous with regard to the Plantagenets. Although Louis could have stripped Henry III of all his continental holdings, he left him Aquitaine and some neighbouring territories. In return, the King of England acknowledged himself to be Louis's vassal. In Louis's eyes this was the most important point, for in the 13th century the power of a sovereign was measured less by the extent of his possessions than by the number and importance of his vassals. A just and equitable ruler, Louis also wanted to create goodwill between his children and those of the Plantagenets. The King's reputation for impartiality was so great that he was often called upon to arbitrate disputes outside France, as he once did in a violent dispute between Henry III and his barons.

He took advantage of his authority to reorganize the administration of his kingdom. Some of his officials, profiting by his absence, had abused their power. Louis IX appointed royal investigators charged with correcting abuses on sight and with hearing complaints. Two well-known ordinances, in 1254 and 1256, carefully outlined the duties and responsibilities of officials in the royal domain, and Louis closely supervised their activities. Royal officials were forbidden to frequent taverns or to gamble, and business activities such as the purchase of land or the marriage of their daughters could be carried out only with the King's consent. Further ordinances forbade prostitution, judicial duels, and ordeal by battle. The King imposed strict penalties on counterfeiting, stabilized the currency, and compelled the circulation of royal coinage. In general, his measures strengthened royal justice and administration and provided a firm base for French commercial growth.

Louis should not, however, be portrayed as a stained-glass figure. Like all men he had faults. He was quick-tempered and sometimes violent, and he had to struggle against his gluttony. He made his decisions alone but knew how to choose wise counsellors, and his sincere piety did not prevent him from curbing the abuses of the clergy, sometimes brutally.

The King devoted attention to the arts and to literature. He directed the construction of several buildings in Paris, Vincennes, Saint-Germain, and Corbeil (to house relics of the "True Cross"). He encouraged Vincent of Beauvais, his chaplain, to write the first great encyclopaedia, *Speculum majus.* During his reign foreign students and scholars flocked to the University of Paris.

The King was very high spirited. Nothing would be more inaccurate than to imagine him entirely steeped in piety. After meals he gladly descended into his gardens, surrounded by his intimates, and discussed diverse topics with them. There, each one indulged in quodlibet, or in talking about anything that pleased him.

Death and canonization. But throughout the latter part of his reign he was obsessed by the memory of the Holy Land, the territory of which was rapidly shrinking before the Muslim advance. In 1269 he decided once again to go to Africa. Perhaps encouraged by his brother Charles of Anjou, he chose Tunisia as the place from which to cut the Islāmic world in half. It was a serious mistake for which he must take responsibility, and he eventually had to bear the consequences of it. Ill and weak, he knew that he risked dying there.

The expedition landed near Tunis at the beginning of July 1270 and at first won a succession of easy victories. Carthage was taken. But once again plague struck the army, and Louis IX could not withstand it. After having entrusted the future of the kingdom of France to his son Philip, to whom he gave excellent instructions (*enseignements*), asking him especially to protect and assist the poor, who were the humblest of his subjects, he died in August 1270.

The crusade dissolved, and Louis's body was brought back to France. All along the way, through Italy, the Alps, Lyon, and Cluny, crowds gathered and knelt as the procession passed. It reached Paris on the eve of Pentecost in 1271. The funeral rites were solemnly performed at Notre-Dame de Paris, and the coffin went to rest in the abbey of Saint-Denis, the tomb of the kings of France.

Without awaiting the judgment of the Roman Catholic Church, the people considered Louis IX to be a saint and prayed at his tomb. Pope Boniface VIII canonized Louis IX, the only king of France to be numbered by the Roman Catholic Church among its saints, in 1297. (J.Le.)

BIBLIOGRAPHY. Among contemporary sources are Jean de Joinville, who lived close to the King for 25 years and wrote down his recollections between 1305 and 1309; and Queen Margaret's confessor, Guillaume de Saint-Pathus, *Vie de Saint Louis,* written in 1302–03.

Modern works include Henri Wallon, *Saint Louis et son temps,* 2 vol. (1875), old but still useful. Jacques Levron, *Saint Louis; ou, l'apogée du Moyen Age* (1969), is a good recent study with an extensive bibliography. A number of books were published on the 700th anniversary of Louis IX's death. The most valuable of them, ed. by Régine Pernoud, is a collection of articles by about 30 French and foreign historians: *Le Siècle de Saint Louis* (1970).

•Louis X, byname LOUIS THE STUBBORN, French LOUIS LE HUTIN (b. Oct. 4, 1289, Paris—d. June 5, 1316, Vincennes, Fr.), Capetian king of France from 1314 and king of Navarre from 1305 to 1314, who endured baronial unrest that was already serious in the time of his father, Philip IV the Fair.

The eldest son of Philip and Joan of Navarre, he took the title of king of Navarre on his mother's death (April 4, 1305). But when he succeeded his father as king of France (Nov. 30, 1314), he resigned Navarre to his next brother, the future Philip V of France. In 1305 Louis married Margaret, daughter of Robert II, duke of Burgundy; in the last months of Philip IV's reign, she was convicted of adultery and was later strangled in prison (1315).

Louis then married (July 1315) Clémence, daughter of Charles I, of Hungary.

Louis's main policies were designed to allay baronial discontent and to gain support and money for a projected campaign against Flanders. Charters were granted to groups of nobles in almost every province of France.

Louis X, detail of a miniature from a manuscript, *c.* 14th century; in the Bibliothèque Nationale, Paris

Giraudon—Art Resource/EB Inc.

Louis bought the support of the clergy by similar means; but whereas they gained for the church some real privileges, the use of ambiguous formulas made the baronial charters virtually worthless. Louis also sold the serfs their liberty, the beginning of the eventual end of serfdom.

Louis restored the office of chancellor and dismissed and imprisoned many of his father's unpopular ministers and advisers, among them Enguerrand de Marigny. Louis's posthumous son, John I, lived only five days and was succeeded by Louis's brother Philip V.

Where the same name may denote a person, place, or thing, the articles will be found in that order

---

• **Louis XI** (b. July 3, 1423, Bourges, Fr.—d. Aug. 30, 1483, Plessis-les-Tours), king of France (1461–83) of the House of Valois who continued the work of his father, Charles VII, in strengthening and unifying France after the Hundred Years' War. He reimposed suzerainty over Boulonnais, Picardy, and Burgundy, took possession of France-Comté and Artois (1482), annexed Anjou (1471), and inherited Maine and Provence (1481).

Early life and exile. Louis was the son of Charles VII of France by his consort Mary of Anjou. When Louis was born, the English were ruling a large part of France, and he spent most of his childhood at the Loches in Touraine. Ugly and fat, Louis grew up in austere seclusion to become secretive, ruthless, and superstitious; yet, he was also devout, intelligent, and well informed, a cunning diplomat and a bold warrior who was able to command loyalty. Known as the "universal spider" because of his incessant machinations and intrigue, he could still claim to personify the French national consciousness; as he was later to say to his rebellious vassals, "I am France."

Louis was married to Margaret, daughter of James I of Scotland, in 1436—an unhappy union formed solely for political reasons. In 1439 the King sent him to superintend the defense of Languedoc against the English and then to act as royal lieutenant in Poitou. Louis, however, was impatient to reign and was induced by malcontent princes to put himself at their head in 1440 during the revolt known as the Praguerie, named after a contemporary disturbance in Bohemia. Charles VII pardoned his rebellion and installed him as ruler of the Dauphiné.

Louis took part in his father's campaigns of 1440–43 against the English, and in 1443 he forced the English to raise their siege of Dieppe. When the Anglo-French truce of 1444 left numbers of mercenary troops unemployed, he led a large body of them to attack Basel, in ostensible support of the German king Frederick V (later Holy Roman emperor as Frederick III) in his quarrel with the Swiss confederacy. Failing to take Basel, Louis attacked the Habsburg possessions in Alsace since Frederick would not grant him the promised winter quarters.

Meanwhile, Charles VII had invaded Lorraine and was holding court at Nancy. When Louis rejoined him there, Charles was completely under the influence of Agnès Sorel and Pierre de Brézé. Father and son became wholly estranged after the death (1445) of the dauphine Margaret, to whom the father had been attached. Detected in a plot against Brézé, Louis was exiled to Dauphiné. He was never to see his father again.

In Dauphiné, Louis served his apprenticeship as a ruler. He set up a central chancellery, reconstituted the local administration, founded the University of Valence, instituted a *parlement*, reduced the nobles to obedience, and confirmed the privileges of the towns. He also started to exploit the country's mines and forests and to promote its trade. Exercising full sovereignty, he pursued a foreign policy sometimes at variance with his father's. After concluding a secret alliance with Savoy for a partition of the Duchy of Milan, Louis, recently widowed, married Charlotte, daughter of Duke Louis of Savoy, despite Charles VII's prohibition (1451). Subsequently, however, Louis fell out with Savoy, and in 1456, when Charles approached Louis's frontiers with an army and summoned him to his presence, he fled to the Netherlands to the court of Philip the Good, duke of Burgundy.

King of France. Installed as Philip's guest, Louis could acquaint himself thoroughly with the working of the great Burgundian state, the ruin of which he was later to seek. (Charles VII remarked that Philip was feeding the fox that would eat his hens.) At the same time, Louis kept himself posted by spies with every detail of his father's illness, thus laying himself open to the unsubstantiated accusation that he had hastened his death by poison. At last, after five years of impatient exile, Louis became king of France when Charles died in 1461.

His first act was to strike at Charles VII's ministers. Pierre de Brézé and Antoine de Chabannes were imprisoned, but they and some of their more serviceable colleagues were subsequently reinstated. Relying largely on men drawn from the lower nobility or from the middle class, Louis formed a circle of loyal advisers who helped him to impose his authority, to enlarge the royal domain, and to develop the wealth of the kingdom.

Louis XI's major preoccupation was with the princes and great vassals of the kingdom, who were ready to form alliances with one another or with England against him. Former officers of Charles VII stirred up hostility against the King's new men; Jean II, duc de Bourbon, and Francis II of Brittany emerged as the leaders of the malcontent nobility; Philip the Good's son and future successor, Charles the Bold of Burgundy, supported the King's enemies; and the King's own brother, Charles de France, at first duc de Berry, became a tool of the rebels.

In 1465 the malcontent princes formed the League of the Public Weal to make war against Louis. All France seemed on the verge of anarchy, but the lesser gentry refused to rise against the King and the bourgeoisie rallied to him. After some fighting, the league was brought to an end by treaties with the Burgundians and with Brittany, but Louis had to yield much: the Somme towns were given back to the Burgundians, and Normandy was granted, in exchange for Berry, to Charles de France, so that all northern France, from Brittany to Burgundian Artois, was linked in the hands of the former rebels. In 1466, however, the King reoccupied Normandy.

Charles the Bold, having become duke of Burgundy on Philip the Good's death (1467), allied himself with Francis of Brittany and with Edward IV of England, but in 1468 Louis invaded Brittany and detached Francis from the alliance. He then went to his disastrous interview with Charles the Bold at Péronne (October 1468). During the negotiations Charles learned of an insurrection in Liège, fomented by the French king's agents. Furious, he put Louis under house arrest, forced him to make far-reaching concessions, and finally took him to Liège to witness the suppression of the revolt.

After his humiliation at Péronne, Louis attempted to nullify the Anglo-Burgundian alliance by assisting the ousted House of Lancaster against Edward IV, but the final defeat of the Lancastrians (May 1471) put an end to his hope. Having already attacked Burgundy, Louis found himself facing a new host of enemies, including not only Charles the Bold, Edward IV, and Francis of Brittany but also, in the southwest, Charles de France, to whom Louis had granted the Duchy of Guyenne in 1469, Jean V d'Armagnac, and John II of Aragon, who hoped to recover Roussillon. But, after Charles de France died in 1472, both Charles the Bold and Francis of Brittany signed truces; the royal army overran Armagnac, and France and Aragon agreed to suspend hostilities in Roussillon. Charles the Bold then began scheming for a partition of France between Burgundy, England, and other states, but Louis soon concluded truces with or bought off Charles's allies.

After 1475 it remained for Louis to destroy the power of Burgundy. He subsidized the Swiss confederates and René II of Lorraine in their war against Charles the Bold, and Charles was defeated and killed in battle at Nancy on Jan. 5, 1477. Louis thereupon proceeded to dismember the Burgundian state, eager to reunite its French fiefs to the royal domain and to take as much else as he could. Charles's daughter Mary, however, married the Austrian archduke Maximilian, who defended her inheritance against Louis. Finally, by the Treaty of Arras (1482), Louis retained full sovereignty over the Duchy of Burgundy, Picardy, and Boulonnais and possession of Franche-Comté and Artois as the dowry of Margaret of Austria, daughter of Mary and Maximilian, fiancée of his infant son and heir, the future Charles VIII.

Louis regarded war as a precarious enterprise and made it only with reluctance, though he

Louis XI, limestone sculptured head from Toul, Fr.; in the Art Institute of Chicago

By courtesy of the Art Institute of Chicago

maintained the standing army that Charles VII had instituted. Diplomacy and inheritance were the means that he preferred for extending the royal domain. Even so, Louis pursued an active policy in Spain and in Italy. After Charles the Bold's death there was no one to prevent Louis from exercising a virtual protectorate over Savoy, where his sister Yolande was regent, and he made himself the arbiter of the affairs of northern Italy.

Domestic achievements. In France itself, having broken the resistance of the princes, Louis could impose his authority everywhere. Louis XI, in referring to the abstract concept of the crown, expressed a modern idea of the state. He reaffirmed tradition by making the feast of "Saint" Charlemagne a holiday and by founding the knightly Order of Saint Michael. Yet, in his time, the subordination of subject to sovereign definitely replaced the feudal ties of personal fidelity. Centralization developed. A section of the royal council administered the justice formerly "reserved" by a lord. The role of the administrative departments was expanded, and the officers of the king, owning their offices, began to constitute an influential class. A network of messengers allowed Louis XI to be abreast of all developments, and he frequently travelled throughout his kingdom. A new concordat with the Pope, concluded in 1472, allowed him to control the appointment of bishops. He augmented the royal revenues by raising taxes on his own authority. The meetings of notables and the assemblies of the estates had only a consultative role. Nevertheless, Louis XI sought the support of the bourgeoisie, some of whom were among his most trusted advisers. Considering wealth to be an element of power, he encouraged the guilds and promulgated numerous ordinances for industry. He encouraged the exploitation of mines, introduced the silk industry to Lyon and Tours, established printing at the Sorbonne (1470), stimulated Rouen's commerce with England and the Hanseatic towns, and promoted the fairs of Lyon. He also planned to create a company for the spice trade in the Mediterranean.

Of delicate health, Louis XI was a tireless worker, and overwork may have precipitated the cerebral arteriosclerosis that finally affected him. For his last two or three years he lived in seclusion at Plessis-les-Tours, in Touraine, where he died in 1483. (M.J.Mo.)

BIBLIOGRAPHY. For general studies, see Christopher Hare, *The Life of Louis XI* (1907); O.W. Mosher, *Louis XI, King of France, As He Appears in History and in Literature* (1925); Pierre Champion, *Louis XI,* 2 vol. (1927; Eng. trans. 1929); Joseph Calmette, *Autour de Louis XI* (1947); and for an analysis of the character of the King, Jean Dofournet, *La Destruction des mythes dans les mémoires de Ph. de Commynes* (1966). Paul Murray Kendall, *Louis XI, the Universal Spider* (1970), is a lively as well as scholarly biography, making use of new material from Italian diplomatic records. James Cleugh, *Chart Royal* (1970), a well-researched biography, includes a select multilingual bibliography.

•**Louis XII,** also called (until 1498) DUC (duke) D'ORLÉANS, byname FATHER OF THE PEOPLE, French PÈRE DU PEUPLE (b. June 27, 1462, Blois, Fr.—d. Jan. 1, 1515, Paris), king of France from 1498, noted for his disastrous Italian wars and his domestic popularity.

Son of Charles, duc d'Orléans, and Marie de Clèves, Louis succeeded his father as duc in 1465. In 1476 he was forced to marry the saintly but misshapen Jeanne of France, daughter of his second cousin King Louis XI. During the minority of King Charles VIII he launched a revolt and was imprisoned (1488). Restored to royal favour, he commanded troops at Asti during Charles VIII's invasion of Italy (1494–95).

After becoming king of France on the death of Charles, he annulled his marriage in order to marry Charles's widow, Anne of Brittany, and thereby reinforce the personal union of her duchy and his kingdom. His next concern was to make good his claim to the duchy of Milan. His army, spreading terror deliberately, drove his rival Ludovico Sforza from Milan in the summer of 1499, but Sforza reoccupied it the following winter.

Louis XII, portrait by Jean Perréal; in Windsor Castle, New Windsor, Berkshire
Giraudon—Art Resource/EB Inc.

Pursuing Charles VIII's claims to the kingdom of Naples, Louis concluded the Treaty of Granada (1500) with Ferdinand II of Aragon for a partition of that kingdom, which was conquered in 1501; but a year later the two kings were at war over the partition, and by March 1504 the French had lost all of Naples. By the Treaty of Blois of September 1504, instigated by Anne of Brittany, the Habsburg emperor Maximilian I recognized Louis as duke of Milan in return for a promise that Milan and also Burgundy should go to Maximilian's grandson, the future Charles V, and his fiancée, Claude of France, daughter of Louis XII and Anne, unless Louis should have a son; meanwhile Claude was the natural heiress to Brittany. The French were enraged, however, at the possibility of losing Brittany, and representatives of the three estates were assembled by Louis at Tours in May 1506 to insist on Claude's betrothal to his heir presumptive, Francis of Angoulême.

Crossing the Alps again to subdue rebels in Genoa, Louis met Ferdinand at Savona in June 1507 to consolidate a new entente formalized in 1508 as the League of Cambrai against Venice, with the inclusion of Maximilian and Pope Julius II. Gradually, the League fell apart, and in the end most of its members joined England in a Holy League against France, invading it at several points. Louis XII's overambitious enterprises ended in catastrophe. Diplomatically, he had been outwitted twice by Ferdinand and once by Julius; and his deception of Maximilian over Claude's marriage had been repaid by Maximilian's final desertion of him.

In France itself Louis XII was highly popular. From the time of the assembly at Tours (1506) he was known as "the Father of the People." He simplified and improved the administration of justice; sought to protect his lowest subjects against oppression; financed his wars, up to 1509, without increase in direct taxation; and kept his kingdom free from civil war and, until the end of the reign, from invasion.

•**Louis XIII,** byname LOUIS THE JUST, French LOUIS LE JUSTE (b. Sept. 27, 1601, Fontainebleau, Fr.—d. May 14, 1643, Saint-Germain-en-Laye), king of France from 1610 to 1643, who cooperated closely with his chief minister, the Cardinal de Richelieu, to make France a leading European power.

The eldest son of King Henry IV and Marie de Médicis, Louis succeeded to the throne upon the assassination of his father in May 1610. The Queen Mother was regent until Louis came of age in 1614; but she continued to govern for three years thereafter. As part of her policy of allying France with Spain, she arranged the marriage (November 1615) between Louis and Anne of Austria, daughter of the Spanish king Philip III. By 1617 the King, resentful at being excluded from power, had taken as his favourite the ambitious Charles d'Albert de Luynes, who soon became the dominant figure in the government. Louis exiled his mother to Blois; and in 1619–20 she raised two unsuccessful rebellions. Although Richelieu (not yet a cardinal), her principal adviser, reconciled her to Louis in August 1620, the relationship between the King and his mother remained one of thinly disguised hostility.

At the time of Luynes' death (December 1621) Louis was faced with a Huguenot rebellion in southern France. He took to the field in the spring of 1622 and captured several Huguenot strongholds before concluding a truce with the insurgents in October. Meanwhile, in September Richelieu had become a cardinal. Louis still distrusted Richelieu for his past association with Marie de Médicis, but he began to rely on the Cardinal's political judgment. In 1624 he made Richelieu his principal minister.

Although Louis had displayed courage on the battlefield, his mental instability and chronic ill health undermined his capacity for sustained concentration on affairs of state. Hence Richelieu quickly became the dominant influence in the government, seeking to consolidate royal authority in France and break the hegemony of the Spanish and Austrian Habsburgs. Immediately after the capture of the Huguenot rebel stronghold of La Rochelle in October 1628, Richelieu convinced the King to lead an army into Italy (1629); but his campaign increased tensions between France and the Habsburgs, who were fighting the Protestant powers in the Thirty Years' War. Soon the pro-Spanish Catholic zealots led by Marie de Médicis began appealing to Louis to reject Richelieu's policy of supporting the Protestant states. During the dramatic episode known as the Day of the Dupes (Nov. 10–12, 1630), the Queen Mother demanded that Louis dismiss Richelieu. After some hesitation, the King decided to stand by his minister; Marie de Médicis and Gaston, duc d'Orléans, Louis's rebellious brother, withdrew into exile. Thereafter Louis adopted the Cardinal's merciless methods in dealing with dissident nobles.

Louis XIII, engraving by Jaspar Isac, 1633
By courtesy of the Bibliotheque Nationale, Paris

In May 1635, France declared war on Spain; and by August 1636 Spanish forces were advancing on Paris. Richelieu recommended evacuation of the city; but Louis, in a surprising display of boldness, overruled him. The King rallied his troops and drove back the invaders. Late in 1638 he suffered a crisis of conscience over his alliances with the Protestant powers, but Richelieu managed to overcome his doubts. Meanwhile, Anne of Austria, who had long been treated with disdain by her husband, had given birth (September 1638) to their first child, the dauphin Louis (the future Louis XIV).

In 1642, Louis's young favourite, the Marquis de Cinq-Mars, instigated the last major conspiracy of the reign by plotting with the Spanish court to overthrow Richelieu; revelation of Cinq-Mars's treason made Louis more dependent than ever on the Cardinal. By the time Richelieu died in December 1642, substantial victories had been won in the war against the Spaniards, and Louis was respected as one of the most powerful monarchs in Europe. The King succumbed to tuberculosis five months later. He was succeeded by his son Louis XIV.

• **Louis XIV,** byname LOUIS THE GREAT, LOUIS THE GRAND MONARCH, or THE SUN KING, French LOUIS LE GRAND, LOUIS LE GRAND MONARQUE, or LE ROI SOLEIL (b. Sept. 5, 1638, Saint-Germain-en-Laye, Fr.—d. Sept. 1, 1715, Versailles), king of France (1643–1715) who ruled his country, principally from his great palace at Versailles, during one of its most brilliant periods and who remains the symbol of absolute monarchy of the classical age. Internationally, in a series of wars between 1667 and 1697, he extended France's eastern borders at the expense of the Habsburgs and then, in the War of the Spanish Succession (1701–14), engaged a hostile European coalition in order to secure the Spanish throne for his grandson.

Louis XIV, detail of a portrait by Hyacinthe Rigaud, 1701; in the Louvre, Paris
Giraudon—Art Resource/EB Inc.

Early life and marriage. Louis was the son of Louis XIII and his Spanish queen, Anne of Austria. He succeeded his father on May 14, 1643. At the age of four years and eight months, he was, according to the laws of the kingdom, not only the master but the owner of the bodies and property of 19 million subjects. Although he was saluted as "a visible divinity," he was, nonetheless, a neglected child given over to the care of servants. He once narrowly escaped drowning in a pond because no one was watching him. Anne of Austria, who was to blame for this negligence, inspired him with a lasting fear of "crimes committed against God."

Louis was nine years old when the nobles and the Paris Parlement (a powerful law court), driven by hatred of the prime minister Cardinal Jules Mazarin, rose against the crown in 1648. This marked the beginning of the long civil war known as the Fronde, in the course of which Louis suffered poverty, misfortune, fear, humiliation, cold, and hunger. These trials shaped the future character, behaviour, and mode of thought of the young king. He would never forgive either Paris, the nobles, or the common people.

In 1653 Mazarin was victorious over the rebels and then proceeded to construct an extraordinary administrative apparatus with Louis as his pupil. The young king also acquired Mazarin's partiality for the arts, elegance, and display. Although he had been proclaimed of age, the King did not dream of disputing the Cardinal's absolute power.

The war begun in 1635 between France and Spain was then entering its last phase. The outcome of the war would transfer European hegemony from the Habsburgs to the Bourbons. A French king had to be a soldier, and so Louis served his apprenticeship on the battlefield.

In 1658 Louis faced the great conflict between love and duty, a familiar one for princes of that period. He struggled with himself for two years over his love for Mazarin's niece, Marie Mancini. He finally submitted to the exigencies of politics and in 1660 married Marie-Thérèse of Austria, daughter of the King of Spain, in order to ratify peace between their two countries.

The childhood of Louis XIV was at an end, but no one believed him capable of seizing the reins of power. No one suspected his thoughts. He wrote in his *Mémoires:*

> In my heart I prefer fame above all else, even life itself . . . Love of glory has the same subtleties as the most tender passions . . . In exercising a totally divine function here on earth, we must appear incapable of turmoils which could debase it.

The young king. Mazarin died on March 9, 1661. The dramatic blow came on March 10. The King informed his astonished ministers that he intended to assume all responsibility for ruling the kingdom. This had not occurred since the reign of Henry IV. It cannot be overemphasized that Louis XIV's action was not in accordance with tradition; his concept of a dictatorship by divine right was his own. In genuine faith, Louis viewed himself as God's representative on earth and considered all disobedience and rebellion to be sinful. From this conviction he gained not only a dangerous feeling of infallibility but also considerable serenity and moderation.

He was backed up first by the great ministers Jean-Baptiste Colbert, the Marquis de Louvois, and Hugues de Lionne, among whom he fostered dissension, and later by men of lesser capacity. For 54 years Louis devoted himself to his task eight hours a day; not the smallest detail escaped his attention. He wanted to control everything from court etiquette to troop movements, from road building to theological disputes. He succeeded because he faithfully reflected the mood of a France overflowing with youth and vigour and enamoured of grandeur.

Despite the use of pensions and punishments, the monarchy had been unable to subdue the nobles, who had started 11 civil wars in 40 years. Louis lured them to his court, corrupted them with gambling, exhausted them with dissipation, and made their destinies dependent on their capacity to please him. Etiquette became a means of governing. From that time, the nobility ceased to be an important factor in French politics, which in some respects weakened the nation.

Patronage of the arts. Louis's great fortune was in having among his subjects an extraordinary group of men in every area of activity. He knew well how to make use of them. He was the protector of writers, notably Molière and Jean Racine, whom he ordered to sing his praises, and he imposed his own visions of beauty and nature on artists. France's appearance and way of life were changed; the great towns underwent a metamorphosis, the landscape was altered, and monuments arose everywhere. The King energetically devoted himself to building new residences. Little remains of his splendid palaces at Saint-Germain and Marly, but Versailles—cursed as extravagant even as it was under construction and accused of having ruined the nation—still stands.

Versailles was approximately the price of a modern airport; it was an object of universal admiration and enhanced French prestige. All the power of the government was brought to bear in the construction of Versailles. Louis XIV was not wrong, as some have claimed, to remove himself from unhealthful and tumultuous Paris, but he erred in breaking with the wandering tradition of his ancestors. The monarchy became increasingly isolated from the people and thereby assumed a decidedly mythical quality.

While Louis watched his buildings going up, Colbert, who supervised the construction, obtained from him the means to carry out an economic revolution aimed at making France economically self-sufficient while maximizing exports. Manufacturers, the navy and merchant marine, a modern police organization, roads, ports, and canals all emerged at about the same time. Louis attended to every detail, while at the same time giving dazzling entertainment and carrying on a tumultuous love affair with Louise de La Vallière.

In 1667 he invaded the Spanish Netherlands, which he regarded as his wife's inheritance, thus beginning a series of wars that lasted for a good part of his reign. Louis himself on his deathbed said, "I have loved war too much," but his subjects, who often complained of his prudence and moderation, would not have understood had he not used force to strengthen the frontiers of France. After a brilliant campaign, the King had to retreat (1668) in the face of English and especially Dutch pressure. He never forgave the Dutch and swore to destroy their Protestant mercantile republic. To this end he allied himself with his cousin Charles II of England and invaded the Netherlands in 1672. The long war that ensued ended in 1678, in the first treaty of Nijmegen with Louis triumphant.

Zenith and decline. The Sun King was at his zenith. Almost alone he had defeated a formidable coalition (Spain and the Holy Roman emperor had joined the Dutch against him) and dictated terms to the enemy. He had extended the frontier of France in the north by annexing part of Flanders and in the east by seizing Lorraine and the Franche-Comté. His fleet equaled those of England and Holland. Paris called him "the Great." In his court he was an object of adoration, and as he approached the age of 40 he could view himself as far surpassing all other men.

At the same time, great changes were occurring in his private life. In 1680 the Marquise de Montespan, who had replaced Mme de La Vallière as Louis's mistress in 1667, was implicated in the Affair of the Poisons, a scandal in which a number of prominent people were accused of sorcery and murder. Fearful for his reputation, the King dismissed Mme de Montespan and imposed piety on his entourage. The ostentation, gambling, and entertainments did not disappear, but the court, subjected to an outward display of propriety, became suffused with boredom. Hypocrisy became the rule.

The King had openly renounced pleasure,

but the sacrifice was made easier for him by his new favourite, the very pious Mme de Maintenon. She was the widow of the satirist Paul Scarron and the former governess of the King's illegitimate children.

In 1682 the seat of government was transferred to Versailles. The following year marked a turning point in the life and reign of Louis XIV. The Queen died, and the King secretly married Mme de Maintenon, who imperceptibly gained in political influence. He remained devoted to her; even at the age of 70 she was being exhorted by her confessor to continue to fulfill her conjugal duties, according to letters still extant.

Colbert also died, leaving the way free for the bellicose Louvois. The repulse of a Turkish invasion of his Austrian domains left the Emperor free to oppose France in the West. In 1688-89 the fall of the Stuarts and William of Orange's accession to the throne of England further reversed the situation to the detriment of France.

Revocation of the Edict of Nantes. To his traditional enemies Louis now added the entire Protestant world. His mother had inculcated in him a narrow and simplistic religion, and he understood nothing of the Reformation. He viewed French Protestants as potential rebels. After having tried to convert them by force, he revoked the Edict of Nantes, which had guaranteed their freedom of worship, in 1685. The revocation, which was accompanied by a pitiless persecution, drove many artisans from France and caused endless misfortune.

Thus began the decline.

England, the Dutch, and the Emperor united in the Grand Alliance to resist Louis's expansionism. The resulting war lasted from 1688 to 1697. Despite many victories, Louis gave up part of his territorial acquisitions when he signed the Treaty of Rijswijk, for which the public judged him harshly. He reconciled himself to another painful sacrifice when he recognized William of Orange as William III of England, in violation of his belief in the divine right of the Stuart king James II to William's throne.

Three years later, in 1700, Charles II, the last Habsburg king of Spain, died, bequeathing his kingdoms to Louis's grandson, Philip of Anjou (Philip V). Louis, who desired nothing more than peace, hesitated but finally accepted the inheritance. He has been strongly criticized for his decision, but he had no alternative. With England against him, he had to try to prevent Spain from falling into the hands of the equally hostile Holy Roman emperor Leopold I, who disputed Philip's claim.

Final years. In the War of the Spanish Succession the anti-French alliance was reactivated by William of Orange before his death. The disasters of the war were so great that, in 1709, France came close to losing all the advantages gained over the preceding century. Private griefs were added to Louis's public calamities. Almost simultaneously he lost his son, the Grand Dauphin, two of his grandsons, the ducs de Bourgogne and Berry, his great grandson, the Duc de Bretagne, and the Duchesse de Bourgogne, who had been the consolation of his declining years.

An excess of flattery from within and an excess of malediction from without had created an artificial image of the King. He was viewed as an idol who would collapse under the blows of ill fortune, but the opposite occurred. Having first been the embodiment of a triumphant nation, Louis surpassed himself by bearing his own suffering and that of his people with unceasing resolution.

Finally, a palace revolution in London, bringing the pacific Tories to power, and a French victory over the imperial forces at the Battle of Denain combined to end the war. The treaties of Utrecht, Rastatt, and Baden, signed in 1713–14, cost France its hegemony but left its territory intact. It retained its recent conquests in Flanders and on the Rhine, which were so much in the order of things that neither later defeats nor revolutions would cause it to lose them.

Louis XIV died in 1715, at the age of 77. His body was borne, amid the jeers of the populace, to the Saint-Denis basilica.

His heir, the last son of the Duc de Bourgogne, was a five-year-old child who was not expected to live. Louis had distrusted his nephew, the Duc d'Orléans, and wanted to leave actual power in the hands of the Duc du Maine, his son by Mme de Montespan. In attempting to accomplish this, he had drawn up a will that was to help destroy the monarchy. The Parlement of Paris, convened to nullify the will after his death, rediscovered a political power that it used to prevent all reforms during the ensuing reigns, thus making the Revolution inevitable.

Assessment. During his lifetime, Louis was flattered ceaselessly by his subjects, while foreign journals compared him to a bloodthirsty tiger. Voltaire portrayed his grandeur in his *Age of Louis XIV*. The Duc de Saint-Simon, a member of his court whose *Mémoires* show equal proportions of literary genius and insincerity, dealt with him quite harshly, without denying his admiration for him. Later judgments of Louis varied according to the author's political views.

Louis XIV was the foremost example of the monarchy that brought France to its pinnacle. He has been accused of having dug the grave of that monarchy, particularly through his religious policy, his last will, and his isolation of the court from the people. These mistakes could have been corrected. His irremediable error was to have concentrated all the machinery of the state in his own person, thus making of the monarchy a burden beyond human strength.

His reign, compared by Voltaire to that of the Roman emperor Augustus, had both its strong and its weak points. Despite his victories and conquests, France lost her primacy under him. Yet the brilliance of his reign made up for his military policies. The aristocracy of Europe adopted the language and customs of the France where the Sun King had shone, although resentments lingered for a long time.

The King identified with his office to such an extent that it is difficult to find the individual. His harshness and courage, despotism and stoicism, prodigious pride and passion for order, megalomania and religion, intolerance and love of beauty can be understood only as a function of the exigencies of governing. He wanted France to be powerful, prosperous, and magnificent but was not overly concerned with the well-being of the French people. His armies committed atrocities, but the horrors of today have eclipsed them, and under his reign one did not see whole nations reduced to slavery, mass deportations, and genocide. When an Italian chemist offered him the first bacteriological weapon, he gave him a pension on condition that he never divulge his invention.

Louis was sometimes a tyrant, but in the words of Voltaire: "His name can never be pronounced without respect and without summoning the image of an eternally memorable age." (P.Er.)

BIBLIOGRAPHY. Louis XIV, *Mémoires* (Eng. trans., *Memoirs of Lewis the Fourteenth, Written by Himself and Addressed to His Son,* 2 vol., 1806), is very important for an understanding of the psychology of Louis XIV. There are many French editions of this work. Contemporary accounts include: the Duchess d'Orléans (Madame Palatine), *Correspondance complète,* 2 vol. (1857); *Mémoires* of the Duc de Saint-Simon; the *Journal* of Dangeau; and Ezechiel Spanheim, *Relation de la cour de France en 1690* (1704; *Account of the Court of France,* 1900). Voltaire, *Le Siècle de Louis XIV,* 2 vol. (1751; *The Age of Louis XIV*), an admirably written and well-documented study, remains an important source. Jacques Roujon, *Louis XIV* (1943), is a very objective and complete work. Two of the best books written on this period in the past century are Philippe Erlanger, *Louis XIV* (1965; Eng. trans. 1970); and John B. Wolf, *Louis XIV* (1968). Pierre Goubert, *Louis XIV and Twenty Million Frenchmen* (1970), is a popularized but well-researched treatment of Le Grand Siècle.

•**Louis XV,** byname LOUIS THE WELL-BELOVED, French LOUIS LE BIEN-AIMÉ (b. Feb. 15, 1710, Versailles, Fr.—d. May 10, 1774, Versailles), king of France from 1715 to 1774, whose ineffectual rule contributed to the decline of royal authority that led to the outbreak of the Revolution in 1789.

Louis was the great-grandson of King Louis XIV (ruled 1643–1715) and the son of Louis, duc de Bourgogne, and Marie-Adélaïde of Savoy. Because his parents and his only surviving brother had all died in 1712, he became king at the age of five on the death of Louis XIV (Sept. 1, 1715). Until he attained his legal majority in February 1723, France was governed by a regent, Philippe II, duc d'Orléans. In 1721 Orléans betrothed Louis to the infanta Mariana, daughter of King Philip V of Spain. After the death of Orléans (December 1723), Louis appointed as his first minister Louis-Henri, duc de Bourbon-Condé, who

Louis XV, detail of a portrait by Hyacinthe Rigaud; in the Château de Versailles
Giraudon—Art Resource/EB Inc.

cancelled the Spanish betrothal and married the King to Marie Leszczyńska, daughter of the dethroned king Stanisław I of Poland. Louis's tutor, the bishop (later cardinal) André-Hercule de Fleury, replaced Bourbon as chief minister in 1726; and the dynastic connection with Poland led to French involvement against Austria and Russia in the War of the Polish Succession (1733–38).

Louis XV's personal influence on French policy became perceptible only after Fleury's death in 1744. Although he proclaimed that he would henceforth rule without a chief minister, he was too indolent and lacking in self-confidence to coordinate the activities of his secretaries of state and give firm direction to national policy. While his government degenerated into factions of scheming ministers and courtiers, Louis isolated himself at court and occupied himself with a succession of mistresses, several of whom exercised considerable political influence. Already Pauline de Mailly-Nesle, marquise de Vintimille, Louis's mistress from 1739 to 1741, had sponsored the war party that brought France into the inconclusive War of the Austrian Succession (1740–48) against Austria and Great Britain.

In September 1745 the king took as his official mistress (*maîtresse en titre*) Jeanne-Antoinette Poisson, Marquise de Pompadour, whose political influence lasted until her death in 1764.

Louis was not, however, a totally passive monarch. His desire to determine the course of international affairs through intrigue caused him to set up, about 1748, an elaborate system of secret diplomacy known as *le Secret du roi.* Secret French agents were stationed in major European capitals and ordered by the king to pursue political objectives that were frequently opposed to his publicly announced policies. At first Louis employed his secret diplomacy in an unsuccessful attempt to win the elective Polish crown for a French candidate (a goal he officially renounced). Soon he expanded the network of agents, intending to form an anti-Austrian alliance with Sweden, Prussia, Turkey, and Poland. Because his official ministers knew nothing of *le secret,* Louis's foreign policy became paralyzed with confusion. In 1756 the king, prompted by Madame de Pompadour, temporarily abandoned the objectives of his secret diplomacy and concluded an alliance with Austria. France and Austria then went to war with Great Britain and Prussia (Seven Years' War, 1756–63), but Louis's continental commitments to the Austrians prevented him from concentrating his country's resources on the crucial colonial struggle with Great Britain, a country with greater maritime power and overseas resources. As a result, by 1763 France had lost to the British almost all her colonial possessions in North America and India. Although Madame de Pompadour's favourite, Étienne-François, Duke de Choiseul (foreign minister from 1758 to 1770), restored France's military strength, the failure of Louis's secret diplomacy in Poland enabled Russia, Austria, and Prussia to partition Poland (1772) and virtually eliminate French influence in central Europe. Although Louis had been popular as *le Bien-Aimé* (the Well-Beloved) in his youth, he had gradually earned the contempt of his subjects.

During the later years of Louis XV's reign, an attempt was made to strengthen the waning authority of the crown by withdrawing from the Parlements the privilege of obstructing royal legislation. This privilege, which had been suspended by Louis XIV, had been restored to the Parlements during the regency. The judicial magistrates had later consolidated their position as opponents of the crown by claiming, in the absence of the States General, to be defenders of the fundamental laws of the kingdom and by uniting the provincial Parlements in a close union with the Parlement of Paris. In this manner they had overthrown the financial system of John Law, had helped to procure the expulsion of the Jesuits in 1764, and had, for a time, disrupted the provincial administration of Brittany. The Parlements also stood resolutely in the way of financial reform. In 1771 the chancellor, René de Maupeou, determined to strike at this abuse by restricting the Parlement of Paris to purely judicial functions and by abolishing the sale of judicial offices. In spite of some popular opposition, the new judicial system functioned effectively until the king's death and might have saved the Bourbon monarchy from the path that led to revolution if his successor had not gratuitously abandoned the reform. Apart from this reform, Louis XV's long reign had been marked by a decline in the crown's moral and political authority, as well as by reverses in foreign and military affairs. The king died in 1774, hated as much as Louis XIV had been.

BIBLIOGRAPHY. G.P. Gooch, *Louis XV: The Monarchy in Decline* (1956, reprinted 1976); I.D.B. Pilkington, *The King's Pleasure: The Story of Louis XV* (1957); Olivier Bernier, *Louis the Beloved* (1984).

• **Louis XVI,** also called (until 1774) LOUIS-AUGUSTE, DUC (duke) DE BERRY (b. Aug. 23, 1754, Versailles, Fr.—d. Jan. 21, 1793, Paris), the last king of France (1774–92) in the line of Bourbon monarchs preceding the Revolution of 1789. The monarchy was abolished on Sept. 21, 1792; later he and his queen consort, Marie-Antoinette, were guillotined on charges of counterrevolution.

Early life and accession. Louis was the third son of the dauphin Louis and his consort Maria Josepha of Saxony. At first known as the Duke de Berry, he became the heir to the throne on his father's death in 1765. His education was entrusted to the Duke de La Vauguyon (Antoine de Quélen de Caussade), who made little effort to ensure that he should be properly trained for his responsibilities. Louis nevertheless possessed an excellent memory, acquired a sound knowledge of Latin and English, and took an interest in history and geography. In 1770 he married the Austrian archduchess Marie-Antoinette, daughter of Maria Theresa and the Holy Roman emperor Francis I.

On the death of his grandfather Louis XV, Louis succeeded to the French throne on May 10, 1774. At that time he was still immature, lacking in self-confidence, austere in manner, and, because of a physical defect (later remedied by an operation), frigid in his relations with his young wife. Well-disposed toward his subjects and interested in the conduct of foreign policy, Louis had not sufficient strength of character or power of decision to combat the influence of court factions or to give the necessary support to reforming ministers, such as Anne-Robert-Jacques Turgot or Jacques Necker (*qq.v.*), in their efforts to give great stability to the tottering finances of the ancien régime. The prestige of the monarchy was also compromised early in his reign by the decision in August 1774 to restore the powers of the Parlements (judicial bodies supporting the interests of the aristocracy) whose political authority had been withdrawn in 1771. Louis XVI's reign before 1789 coincided with the increasing strength of the aristocratic reaction. It was aristocratic opposition to the fiscal, economic, and administrative reforms of the controller general of finance, Charles-Alexandre de Calonne, in 1787 that forced the king, in July 1788, to summon the States General, the representatives of the clergy, nobility, and commoners, for the following year and thus set in motion the Revolution.

Louis's reaction to the Revolution. After 1789 Louis XVI's incapacity to rule, his irresolution, and his surrender to reactionary influences at court were partially responsible for the failure to establish in France the forms of a limited constitutional monarchy. Louis had at first rightly regarded the Revolution as the product of aristocratic intransigence and should, therefore, have grasped the opportunity of forming an alliance between the crown and the middle-class reformers. Instead he allowed himself, in the spring of 1789, to be dominated by the reactionary court faction surrounding his younger brother Charles, Count d'Artois (later King Charles X) and to be converted to the policy of defending the privileges of the clergy and nobility in the States General. He continued to believe, even after the increasingly radical trend of popular movements in Paris and the provinces during the summer had demonstrated the futility of such hopes, that the Revolution would burn itself out.

Louis XVI, detail of a portrait by J.-S. Duplessis; in the Château de Versailles

Giraudon—Art Resource/EB Inc.

By this time the fundamental weakness of the king's character had become evident: lethargic in temperament, lacking political insight and therefore incapable of appreciating the need to compromise, Louis continued to divert himself by hunting and with his personal hobbies of making locks and doing masonry. He dismissed Necker in early July 1789 and showed his reluctance to sanction the achievements of the National Assembly (as the States General was now called) such as the Declaration of the Rights of Man and of the Citizen and the "destruction" of the feudal regime in August.

Attempt to flee the country. Louis's resistance to popular demands was one of the causes of the forcible transfer of the royal family from Versailles to the Tuileries Palace in Paris on October 6. Yet he made still more mistakes, refusing to follow the secret advice tendered to him after May 1790 by the royalist deputy, the Count de Mirabeau, abdicating his responsibilities, and acquiescing in the disastrous attempt to escape from the capital to the eastern frontier on June 21, 1791. Caught at Varennes and brought back to Paris, he lost credibility as a constitutional monarch. Thenceforward he seems to have been completely dominated by the queen, who must bear the chief blame for the court's subsequent political duplicity.

From the autumn of 1791 the king tied his hopes of political salvation to the dubious prospects of foreign intervention. At the same time he encouraged the Girondin faction in the Legislative Assembly in their policy of war with Austria, in the expectation that French military disaster would pave the way for the restoration of his authority. Prompted by Marie-Antoinette, Louis rejected the advice of the moderate constitutionalists, led by Antoine Barnave, to implement faithfully the constitution of 1791, which he had sworn to maintain, and committed himself to a policy of subterfuge and deception.

The outbreak of the war with Austria in April 1792, the suspected machinations of the queen's "Austrian committee," and the publication of the manifesto by the Austrian commander, the Duke of Brunswick, threatening the destruction of Paris if the safety of the royal family were again endangered, led to the capture of the Tuileries by the people of Paris and provincial militia on Aug. 10, 1792. It also led to the temporary suspension of the king's powers by the Legislative Assembly and the proclamation of the First French Republic on September 21. In November proof of Louis XVI's secret dealings with Mirabeau and of his counterrevolutionary intrigues with the foreigners was found in a secret cupboard in the Tuileries. On December 3 it was decided that Louis, who together with his family had been imprisoned since August, should be brought to trial for treason. He himself appeared twice before the Convention (December 11 and 23).

Condemnation to death. Despite the last-minute efforts of the Girondins to save him, Citizen Capet, as he was then called, was found guilty by the Convention and condemned to death on Jan. 18, 1793, by 387 votes (including 26 in favour of a debate on the possibility of postponing execution) against 334 (including 13 for a death sentence with the proviso that it should be suspended). When a final decision on the question of a respite was taken on January 19, Louis was condemned to death by 380 votes against 310. He was guillotined in the Place de la Révolution in Paris on Jan. 21, 1793. Louis XVI's courage on June 20, 1792, when the royal palace was invaded by the Paris mob after his dismissal of the Girondin ministry, and his dignified bearing during his trial and at the moment of execution did something to redeem, but did not reestablish, his reputation. (Al.G.)

BIBLIOGRAPHY. S.K. Padover, *Life and Death of Louis XVI* (1939; new ed., 1963), is virtually the only serious biography available in English. J. Droz, *Histoire du règne de Louis XVI,* 3 vol. (1858), though old-fashioned and written from an exclusively political angle, is still worth consultation on the attempts of the central government to reform the ancien régime. It has been superseded in that respect by D. Dakin, *Turgot and the Ancien Régime in France* (1939); G. Lefebvre, *Quatre-vingt-neuf* (1939; *The Coming of the French Revolution, 1789,* 1947); and J. Egret, *La Pré-Révolution Française, 1787–1788* (1962). The most recent scholarly studies of royal policy after the flight to Varennes are: J. Chaumie, *Le Réseau d'Antraigues et la Contre-Révolution, 1791–1793* (1965), which throws an entirely new light on the royal web of counterrevolutionary intrigue; A. Soboul, *Le Procès de Louis XVI* (1966), which gives a succinct analysis of the issues raised by the King's trial and execution, along with documentary material from the French archives; and M. Reinhard, *La Chute de la Royauté* (1969), which is likely to remain the definitive account of the final overthrow of the Bourbon monarchy. Vincent Cronin, *Louis and Antoinette* (1975), is a lively, well-written dual biography that attempts a more favourable than usual assessment of the King's character.

•**Louis (XVII),** also called (1789–93) LOUIS-CHARLES, DUC (duke) DE NORMANDIE, or LOUIS-CHARLES DE FRANCE (b. March 27, 1785, Versailles, Fr.—d. June 8, 1795, Paris), titular king of France from 1793. Second son of King Louis XVI and Queen Marie-Antoinette, he was the royalists' first recognized claimant to the monarchy after his father was executed during the French Revolution.

Louis XVII, portrait by A. Kucharski; in the Petit Trianon de Versailles, France
Giraudon—Art Resource/EB Inc.

Baptized Louis-Charles, he bore the title duc de Normandie until he became dauphin (heir to the throne) on the death of his eight-year-old elder brother, Louis-Joseph, in June 1789, shortly after the outbreak of the Revolution. With the overthrow of the monarchy in the popular insurrection of Aug. 10, 1792, Louis-Charles was imprisoned with the rest of the royal family in the Temple in Paris. Louis XVI was beheaded on Jan. 21, 1793, and French émigrés (nobles in exile) immediately proclaimed Louis-Charles the new king of France.

Since France was at war with Austria and Prussia, Louis XVII became a valuable pawn in negotiations between the revolutionary government and its enemies. On July 3, 1793, he was taken from his mother and put under the surveillance of a cobbler, Antoine Simon. Marie-Antoinette was guillotined on Oct. 16, 1793, and in January 1794 Louis was again imprisoned in the Temple. The harsh conditions of his confinement rapidly undermined his health. His death was a severe blow to the constitutional monarchists, who had once again become a powerful political force. An inquest established that Louis had succumbed to scrofula (tuberculosis of the lymph glands).

The secrecy surrounding the last months of Louis XVII's life gave rise to rumours. Some said that he was not dead but had escaped from the Temple. Others alleged that he had been poisoned. During the next few decades, more than 30 persons claimed to be Louis XVII. A. Castelot's *Louis XVII* was published in 1960.

•**Louis XVIII,** also called (until 1795) LOUIS-STANISLAS-XAVIER, COMTE (count) DE PROVENCE (b. Nov. 17, 1755, Versailles, Fr.—d. Sept. 16, 1824, Paris), king of France by title from 1795 and in fact from 1814 to 1824, except for the interruption of the Hundred Days, during which Napoleon attempted to recapture his empire.

Louis was the fourth son of the dauphin Louis, the son of Louis XV, and received the title comte de Provence; after the death of his two elder brothers and the accession of his remaining elder brother as Louis XVI in 1774, he became heir presumptive. The birth of two sons to Louis XVI, however, temporarily put a stop to his royal ambitions. When the Revolution broke out in 1789, he remained in Paris, possibly to exploit the situation as a royal candidate; but he fled the country in June 1791.

With little concern for the safety of Louis XVI and Marie-Antoinette, who were held captive in Paris, the Comte de Provence issued uncompromising counterrevolutionary manifestos, organized émigré associations, and sought the support of other monarchs in the fight against the Revolution. When the King and Queen were executed in 1793, he declared himself regent for his nephew, the dauphin Louis XVII, at whose death, in June 1795, he proclaimed himself Louis XVIII.

Between 1795 and 1814 Louis wandered throughout Europe, sojourning in Prussia, England, and Russia, promoting the royalist cause, however hopeless it seemed after Napoleon's proclamation as emperor in 1804. Although financially hard pressed, he refused to abdicate and accept a pension from Bonaparte. After Napoleon's defeats in 1813, Louis issued a manifesto in which he promised to recognize some of the results of the Revolution in a restored Bourbon regime. When the Allied armies entered Paris in March 1814, the brilliant diplomatist Talleyrand was able to negotiate the restoration, and on May 3, 1814, Louis was received with jubilation by the war-weary Parisians.

On May 2, Louis XVIII officially promised a constitutional monarchy, with a bicameral parliament, religious toleration, and constitutional rights for all citizens. The resulting Charte Constitutionnelle was adopted on June 4, 1814. Louis's constitutional experiments were cut short, however, by the return of Napoleon from Elba. After Marshal Michel Ney defected to Napoleon on March 17, 1815, the King fled to Ghent. He did not return until July 8, after Waterloo.

Louis XVIII, engraving by P. Audouin
By courtesy of the Bibliotheque Nationale, Paris

Louis XVIII's reign saw France's first experiment in parliamentary government since the Revolution. The King was invested with executive powers and had "legislative initiative," whereas a largely advisory parliament voted on laws and approved the budget. The legislature, though, had a strong right-wing, royalist majority. Influenced by his favourite, Élie Decazes, who became prime minister in 1819, the King opposed the extremism of the ultras, who were determined to wipe out every vestige of the Revolution, and he dissolved the parliament in September 1816. After 1820, however, the ultras exercised increasing control and thwarted most of Louis's attempts to heal the wounds of the Revolution. At his death he was succeeded by his brother, the comte d'Artois, as Charles X.

GERMANY/EAST FRANKS

•**Louis II,** byname LOUIS THE GERMAN, German LUDWIG DER DEUTSCHE (b. *c.* 804, Aquitaine?, Fr.—d. Aug. 28, 876, Frankfurt), king of the East Franks, who ruled lands from which the German state later evolved.

Louis II, miniature from a manuscript; in the Vatican Library (Reg. Lat. 438)
By courtesy of the Biblioteca Apostolica Vaticana

The third son of the Carolingian emperor Louis I the Pious, Louis the German was assigned Bavaria at the partition of the empire in 817. Entrusted with the government of Bavaria in 825, he began his rule the following year. Louis took part in the revolts against his father (830–833) and joined his half-brother, Charles the Bald, in opposing the claim of his brother, Lothair I, to imperial suzerainty over the whole empire after their father's death in 840. By the Treaty of Verdun (August 843), Charles, Lothair I, and Louis divided the western, middle, and eastern parts of the empire, respectively, between them. Louis received the territory of the Franconians, the Swabians, the Bavarians, and the Saxons, together with the Carolingian provinces to the east.

In 853 a group of nobles opposing Charles the Bald, then king of the West Franks, appealed to Louis for help; in 854 Louis sent his son Louis the Younger to Aquitaine, and in 858 went west himself to try to depose Charles; both expeditions failed. At the Peace of Coblenz (860) Louis renounced his claims to Charles's dominions.

When Lothair I died in 855, his lands were divided among his sons, one of whom, Lothair, received Lotharingia (Greater Lorraine). This Lothair had no legitimate children, and Louis the German and Charles the Bald agreed (865 and 867/868) on the partition of their nephew's dominions between themselves on his death. When Lothair died (869), however, Charles broke the agreements by annexing Lotharingia. Louis invaded Lotharingia (870), and the country was divided between Louis and Charles by the Treaty of Mersen (Meerssen), under which Louis received Friesland and an extremely large expansion of this territory west of the Rhine.

Louis in 865 and 872 divided his territories between his sons Carloman, Louis the Younger, and Charles III the Fat. Quarrels and discontent at the partitions led to revolts by one or another of the sons between 861 and 873.

Although Louis the German supported Frankish Catholic missions in Moravia, he could not maintain control in that area and lost a war that led to the founding of Greater Moravia, independent after 874.

Louis the German unsuccessfully sought the imperial dignity and the succession in Italy for his line after the death of Lothair I's son, the emperor Louis II; but though Louis II declared (874) in favour of Carloman, eldest son of Louis the German, as the next emperor (August 875), Charles the Bald had himself crowned by Pope John VIII after Louis II's death in August 875. Meanwhile, Louis the German unsuccessfully attempted to invade Charles's possessions in Lotharingia. At the time of his death, Louis the German was again preparing for war against Charles.

• **Louis III,** byname LOUIS THE YOUNGER, German LUDWIG DER JÜNGERE (b. *c.* 830—d. Jan. 20, 882, Frankfurt), king of part of the East Frankish realm who, by acquiring western Lotharingia (Lorraine) from the West Franks, helped to establish German influence in that area.

A son of Louis the German, king of the East Franks, Louis the Younger invaded Aquitaine on his father's orders in 854. For some time Charles the Bald, Louis the German's half brother and king of the West Franks, had been attempting to conquer the Aquitanian kingdom, and in 852 he imprisoned Pepin II of Aquitaine, his nephew, who had fallen into his hands. In the following year the Aquitanian magnates sent envoys to Louis the German, offering the crown either to him or to one of his sons. It was at that time that Louis agreed to send Louis the Younger to Aquitaine with an army. The expedition was, however, unsuccessful. Pepin escaped from prison, and upon his return the Aquitanians abandoned the cause of Louis the Younger, who was forced to return to Bavaria.

Under arrangements made by his father in 865 and 872, Louis the Younger received Franconia, Thuringia, and Saxony after his father's death (August 876). When Charles the Bald attempted to seize eastern Lotharingia (*i.e.,* that part of Lotharingia that had belonged to Louis the German), Louis the Younger defeated him at Andernach (October 876) and incorporated it into his own dominions. By invading the West Frankish kingdom, he acquired western Lotharingia in the treaties of Verdun (879) and Ribémont (880).

• **Louis IV,** byname LOUIS THE CHILD, German LUDWIG DAS KIND (b. 893, Altötting, Bavaria—d. Sept. 24, 911, Frankfurt), East Frankish king, the last of the East Frankish Carolingians. During his reign the country was ravaged by frequent Magyar raids, and local magnates (the ancestors of the later ducal dynasties) brought Bavaria, Franconia, Swabia, and Saxony under their sway.

A son of the East Frankish king Arnulf, Louis was declared heir to the kingdom in 897, and after Arnulf's death (899) was crowned king in 900. Later that year a party of Lotharingians, after defeating their king, Zwentibold (Louis' half brother), in an uprising, acknowledged Louis as their sovereign.

Although in theory the boy king was himself the ruler, the government was, in fact, controlled by Archbishop Hatto I of Mainz. The kingdom was, however, too weak to check the raids of the Magyars, which became increasingly frequent after 900. In 910 they defeated a large royal army near Augsburg. Louis died the following year.

Louis IV, seal, *c.* 9th century; in the Bayerisches Nationalmuseum, Munich

By courtesy of the Bayerisches Nationalmuseum, Munich; photograph, Foto Marburg

GERMANY/HOLY ROMAN EMPIRE

• **Louis I,** byname LOUIS THE PIOUS, or THE DEBONAIR, French LOUIS LE PIEUX, or LE DÉBONNAIRE, German LUDWIG DER FROMME (b. 778, Chasseneuil, near Poitiers, Aquitaine—d. June 20, 840, Petersaue, Ger.), son of the Frankish ruler Charlemagne; he was crowned as co-emperor in 813 and became emperor in 814 on his father's death. Twice deprived of his authority by his sons (Lothair, Pepin, Louis, and Charles), he recovered it each time (830 and 834), but at his death the Carolingian empire was in disarray.

Louis was the fifth child of Charlemagne's second wife, Hildegard the Swabian. From 781 until 814 Louis ruled Aquitaine with some success, though largely through counsellors. When Charlemagne died at Aachen in 814 and was succeeded by Louis, by then his only surviving legitimate son, Louis was well experienced in warfare; he was 36, married to Irmengard of Hesbaye, and was the father of three young sons, Lothair, Pepin, and Louis (Louis the German); he had inherited vast lands, which seemed to be under reasonable control; there was no other claimant to the throne; and on Sept. 11, 813, shortly before his father's death, Louis had been crowned in Aachen as heir and co-emperor.

Louis' first task was to carry out the terms of Charlemagne's will. According to the Frankish chronicler Einhard, Louis did this with great scrupulousness, although other contemporary sources tell a different story.

Louis next began to allocate parts of the empire to the various members of his family, and here began the difficulties and disasters that were to beset him for the remainder of his life. In August 814 he made Lothair and Pepin nominal kings of Bavaria and Aquitaine. He also confirmed Bernard, the son of his dead brother Pepin, as king of Italy, which position Charlemagne had allowed him to inherit in 813. But when Bernard revolted in 817, Louis had him blinded, and he died as a result of it. Louis sent his sisters and half sisters to nunneries and later put his three illegitimate half brothers—Drogo, Hugo, and Theodoric—into monasteries.

At the assembly of Aachen in July 817, he confirmed Pepin in the possession of Aquitaine and gave Bavaria to Louis the German; Lothair he made his co-emperor and heir. Charlemagne had been in his 70s and within a few months of death before naming his heir, and for Louis to give such premature expectations to a youth of 22 was to ask for trouble. Moreover, Louis did not anticipate that he would become father of another child: the empress Irmengard died in 818; and four months later Louis married Judith of Bavaria, who, in June 823, bore him a son, Charles (Charles the Bald), to whom the Emperor gave Alemannia in 829.

Backed by his two brothers, Lothair rose in revolt and deposed his father. The assembly of Nijmegen in October 830, however, restored Louis to the throne; and, the following February, at the assembly of Aachen, in a second partition, Lothair was given Italy. In 832 Louis took Aquitaine away from Pepin and gave it to Charles. The three brothers revolted a second time, with the support of Pope Gregory IV, and at a meeting near Sigolsheim, in Alsace, once more deposed their father. In March 834 Louis was again restored to the throne and made peace with Pepin and with Louis the German. Later in 834, Lothair rose again, but alone, and had to retreat into Italy. Encouraged by his success, Louis made over more territories to his son Charles at the assemblies of Aachen and Nijmegen (837–838)—a move the three brothers accepted but

Louis I, portrait from *De laudibus sanctae crucis* by Rabanus Maurus, Fulda, 830–840 (Codex 652); in the Österreichische Nationalbibliothek, Vienna

By courtesy of the Osterreichische Nationalbibliothek, Vienna with bad grace. In 839 Louis the German revolted but was driven back into Bavaria.

Meanwhile, Pepin had died (December 838), and, at the assembly of Worms (May 30, 839), a fourth partition was made, the empire being divided between Lothair and Charles, with Bavaria left in the hands of Louis the German. Toward the end of 839 Louis the German marched his troops for the last time against his father, who once more drove him back. The Emperor called an assembly at Worms on July 1, 840. Before it could meet, however, Louis the Pious died at Petersaue, an island in the Rhine near Ingelheim. He was 62 and had ruled for nearly 27 years. He was buried in the Church of St. Arnulf in Metz by Bishop Drogo, his half brother.

The empire he had inherited in peace, Louis left in disarray. He had engaged in no serious external conflict, although the Danes and others had continued to make inroads into the empire. From 829 his four sons had been a constant source of disruption; the quarrels among Lothair, Louis the German, and Charles the Bald were to continue for decades after his death. In many ways Louis seems to have been an estimable person. He was presumably given the epithet the Pious because of his devoutness, his liberality to the church, his interest in ecclesiastical affairs, and the good education he had received. Contemporary historians vary little in their judgment: the Astronomer of Limousin stresses his continued courage in the face of adversity; Thegan, bishop of Trier, gives a long and admiring description of his person, his talents, his Christian charity, his devoutness, and his skill as a hunter; and the poem of Ermoldus Nigellus is full of adulation.

Like his father, Charlemagne, Louis the Pious is depicted in several of the chansons de geste of the 12th century, notably the *Chanson de Guillaume,* the *Couronnement de Louis,* and the *Charroi de Nîmes:* he appears as a kindly ruler but a weak and vacillating one.

(L.T.)

BIBLIOGRAPHY. An excellent study of Louis I in English is that of René Poupardin in the *Cambridge Medieval History,* vol. 3, ch. 1 (1922), with bibliography.

• **Louis II** (b. *c.* 822—d. Aug. 12, 875, near Brescia, Lombardy), Frankish emperor (850–875) who, as ruler of Italy, was instrumental in checking the Arab invasion of the peninsula.

The eldest son of the Frankish emperor Lothair I, who ruled the "middle realm" of what had once been Charlemagne's empire, Louis took over the administration of Italy on his father's behalf in 844 and was crowned king of the Lombards in Rome on June 15 of that year. In April 850 he was crowned emperor. When his father divided his realm in September 855, Italy was allotted to Louis. After Lothair's death a few weeks later, Louis was sole emperor, a dignity which at that time implied rule over only part of the Carolingian dominions, without suzerainty over the whole.

In 859 Louis II acquired territory from his brother Lothair II, king of Lotharingia (Lorraine), and at the death of his other brother, King Charles of Provence, in 863, he received a large part of that kingdom.

Louis II's most important task was the war against the Arabs, who had seized Bari and various other places in southern Italy. In 866 he began an extensive campaign that, with the help of the Byzantine fleet, culminated in the conquest of the Arab headquarters at Bari (February 871). In August 871, however, the Emperor was made prisoner by Adelchis, duke of Benevento. The Duke feared that Louis would attempt to assert his sovereignty, and he extracted from his prisoner a promise not to reenter the southern part of the peninsula.

Adelchis soon set Louis free, but after obtaining from the Pope a dispensation from his oath, the Emperor returned to southern Italy. Although he won another victory, near Capua, in 872, his power and energy no longer sufficed for a decisive blow against the Arabs. He gave up his hopes and withdrew to northern Italy, where he died shortly thereafter. His only child was a daughter, and the elder male line of the Carolingian dynasty thus expired with him.

• **Louis III,** byname LOUIS THE BLIND, French LOUIS L'AVEUGLE (b. *c.* 880/882, Autun?, Fr.—d. September 928, Arles, Fr.), king of Provence and, from 901 to 905, Frankish emperor whose short-lived tenure marked the failure to restore the Carolingian dynasty to power in Italy.

Louis was a son of Boso, king of Provence, and Irmingard, daughter of the Frankish emperor Louis II, the last of the elder male line of the Carolingian dynasty. The emperor Charles III the Fat took Louis under his protection on Boso's death in 887, and, although Charles was deposed that same year, Louis was recognized as king of Provence in 890. In 900 Louis was called to Italy by a group of nobles who were opposed to the rule of the Italian king Berengar of Friuli; in October, Louis was elected king of the Lombards at Pavia and, a few months later, in February 901, received the imperial crown from Pope Benedict IV at Rome. In 902, however, Berengar captured Louis, who was forced to leave the country.

Louis attempted to reconquer Italy in 904. He secured the submission of Lombardy but in July 905 was captured at Verona by Berengar, who blinded him and sent him back to Provence, where he remained until his death.

• **Louis IV,** byname LOUIS THE BAVARIAN, German LUDWIG DER BAYRISCH (b. 1283?, Munich—d. Oct. 11, 1347, Munich), duke of upper Bavaria (from 1294) and of united Bavaria (1340–47), German king (from 1314), and Holy Roman emperor (1328–47), first of the Wittelsbach line of German emperors. His reign was marked by incessant diplomatic and military struggles to defend the right of the empire to elect an emperor independently of the papacy, to consolidate his own position, and to improve the status of his family.

Early life. As the younger son of Louis II, count Palatine and duke in Upper Bavaria, Louis had no claim to the crown by birth. On his father's death in 1294, the 11-year-old boy was made a ward of his brother Rudolf, who was then 20, and of his mother, Mechthild, a Habsburg and a daughter of King Rudolf I. Louis immediately found himself involved in high politics; his brother took the side of King Adolf of Nassau and his mother that of her brother, Albert I of Austria, who was attempting to depose Adolf. Keeping her son out of Munich, she sent him to her brother's court in Vienna, where he was reared, together with his Habsburg cousins, Frederick and Leopold. This circumstance no doubt had a lasting effect on Louis, though he never let political decisions be influenced by family ties. Albert's victory over Adolf of Nassau at Göllheim (July 2, 1298) allowed Louis to assume the share in the government that was his by law but that his older brother had hitherto withheld from him. The rivalry between the brothers, which had flared up again after the assassination of King Albert (1308), ended in 1310 with a partition of territories, which Louis was able to impose on the strength of being the guardian of his Lower Bavarian cousins. But the traditionally anti-Austrian attitude of Lower Bavaria led to a quarrel with the Habsburgs. Having assured himself of his brother's goodwill by means of a compromise (June 21, 1313), Louis gained a decisive victory over the Habsburgs at Gammelsdorf (November 9), while the succession to the German crown, fallen vacant with the emperor Henry VII's unexpected death on August 24, was still the subject of negotiations.

The empire had become an elective monarchy, but counts no longer figured among the candidates. The houses of Habsburg and Luxembourg (Luxemburg), risen to the rank of major German powers as a result of acquiring Austria (1282) and Bohemia (1310), respectively, contended for the throne; had it not been divided into warring lines, the House of Wittelsbach might have been a third contender. On the strength of his victory, Louis, in 1314, became the candidate of the Luxembourgs, who had failed to gain the crown for John of Bohemia, the late emperor's son. The Habsburgs, however, would not acknowledge Louis, though he was grandson of King Rudolf; in the double election of Oct. 19–20, 1314, Louis gained little advantage from the fact that his claims were rather more substantial than those of the anti-king, Frederick III of Austria, crowned on the same day, November 25. Military successes enabled Louis to wrest exclusive control over Upper Bavaria and the Rhenish Palatinate from his brother, who had voted against him; but a permanent settlement with the latter's descendants could be made only after the death of Rudolf, his widow Mathilde of Nassau, and his oldest son, Adolf. The dynastic Compact of Pavia (1329), dividing the House of Wittelsbach into a Bavarian and a Palatinate line, enabled Louis to gain the latter line's support in matters of imperial policy. He failed, however, to achieve a lasting understanding with his Lower Bavarian cousins; that conflict was not settled until this line became extinct in 1340.

Struggle with the Habsburgs. Louis's most pressing problem was the struggle with the Habsburgs. The decisive battle was fought on Sept. 28, 1322, at Mühldorf, where Louis gained victory, taking prisoner King Frederick with his brothers. By April 1323 he could risk investing his oldest son, Louis, still a minor, with the Margravate of Brandenburg, which had been in abeyance since 1319. Territorial aspirations motivated the conclusion of a hereditary alliance with the House of Wettin as well as Louis' second marriage, to Margaret of Holland (1324), which in 1345 led to the accession of Holland and its dependencies. These successes did not sit well with John of Bohemia, who refused to be pacified either by the donation of Upper Lusatia in 1320 or by the marriage of Duke Henry the Elder of Lower Bavaria with a Luxembourg the following year, or by the acquisition, by way of collateral, of the Egerland. Luxembourg finally allied itself with France, and this move, in turn, led to an increased hostility toward Louis on the part of the Pope, who was wholly under French influence.

Pope John XXII had taken advantage of the contest for the crown of Germany to appoint Robert of Naples imperial vicar in Italy *vacante imperio* (in the absence of a Holy Roman emperor) and to threaten the Italian Ghibellines with heresy proceedings. When Louis's own imperial vicar forced the Pope and Robert to raise the siege of Milan, the heresy proceedings were extended to Louis himself, who was excommunicated in March 1324. This interdiction, never lifted, exposed Louis' adherents to a conflict of conscience while providing his enemies with a convenient excuse for disobedience. In the eyes of the Curia and of his other enemies, he was thenceforth merely Ludovicus Bavarus, Louis the Bavarian, by which name he lives on in history.

Louis hit back with several proclamations of his own, notably the so-called Sachsenhausen Appellation of May 22, 1324, in which the charge of heresy was turned against the Pope. The argumentation ill-advisedly dealt with constitutional problems touching on the empire as well as with doctrinal points. Louis quickly acknowledged this as a mistake and softened its effect, but at this time the Austrians also joined the alliance of France and Luxembourg (July 27, 1324). Louis broke up the hostile combination by agreeing to share the rule with his prisoner Frederick; even so, he overcame Duke Leopold's objections only by further agreeing (Jan. 7, 1326) to abdicate altogether, provided that the Pope gave his approbation to Frederick's sole rule. There was little likelihood of that because the Curia was interested in perpetuating the rivalry for the German crown. Its reaction proved to Frederick that he had been callously used; he now became a loyal co-ruler with Louis.

Acceptance of the imperial crown. When Duke Leopold died in February 1326, Louis boldly opposed the Pope in Italy itself. Supported by the Ghibellines, he accepted the iron crown of Lombardy in Milan (May 31, 1327) and the imperial crown in Rome (Jan. 11, 1328), offered by the representatives of the Roman populace. This unusual move could be considered an emergency measure because the Pope had refused to crown the designated emperor, declaring him a heretic on purely political grounds.

Louis let himself be persuaded to depose the Pope formally by a decree of April 18, 1328, and to countenance the appointment of an antipope whose incompetence furnished John XXII with an easy triumph. Moreover, Louis' forces were insufficient to subjugate Robert of Naples or to institute a stable order in Italy, for which he lacked the necessary prerequisite of a firm hold on Germany. Turning to the north again, he celebrated Christmas of 1329 in Trent, whence he had departed for Italy in February 1327.

King Frederick died on Jan. 13, 1330. The problem of shared rule was thus solved. Yet Louis' German enemies had not been idle. John of Bohemia had arranged the marriage of his younger son, John Henry, with Margaret, the heiress of Carinthia-Tirol, in 1330. This caused Louis to enter into a secret covenant with the Habsburgs regarding the partition of this strategically important inheritance (May 31, 1331). He thus encircled John of Bohemia, forcing him to withdraw from Italy, where he had ensconced himself in the guise of an imperial vicar. In order to confuse his enemies, Louis issued a new decree of abdication, hedged with countless provisos, on Nov. 19, 1333; this time he proposed to renounce the throne in favour of his Lower Bavarian cousin Henry. The death of Duke Henry of Carinthia-Tirol in 1335 compelled Louis to invest the Habsburgs with Carinthia, by way of carrying out his part of the secret compact; he also granted them southern Tirol in order to save at least the northern part for himself. But the Habsburgs, in their eagerness to secure Carinthia, concluded an agreement behind his back with Luxembourg, which thus acquired the whole of the Tirol. As a result, the influential archbishop of Mainz came over to Louis' side (June 29, 1337), and Edward III of England made a treaty with him (August 26), thus proving that Louis was a desirable ally on the international plane.

The Germans, tired of the incessant quarrels over the crown, were disconcerted by the Pope's intransigence. Through their city magistrates and other representatives, they pressed for legitimization of Louis' rule and the rejection of papal interference. When Louis issued a statement of principle regarding the accession to the imperial throne before the Frankfurt Diet (*Fidem catholicam* of May 17, 1338), he had the support not only of the cities but also of the empire's ecclesiastical lords. He relied upon this support in promulgating a basic electoral law (*Licet juris*) in Frankfurt (August 3) and again in Coblenz, where he met the King of England and bestowed on him an imperial vicarate on the Lower Rhine. The promulgation of that law, however, remained an empty gesture because the electoral princes, while assembled at Rhens on July 16, had rejected the Pope's claims without declaring themselves in favour of Louis and withheld their approval. The conflict over the crown and the charge of heresy thus continued to smolder. By isolating John of Bohemia and issuing a formal waiver of his own claims to the Tirol, Louis managed nonetheless to force John to renounce all claims to Italy, to declare himself a vassal, and to acknowledge Louis emperor in 1339.

Seeing that the entire clergy of the empire, except for the border bishoprics of Liège and Cambrai, had submitted to his rule and that the English held out the prospect of subsidies, Louis had reason to hope that he could confront the French in battle and thereby make the Pope yield. When Edward III declared war on France on Sept. 1, 1339, and had himself acknowledged as king of France in Ghent on Jan. 27, 1340, Louis was in a position to arbitrate between England and France. But the Tirolean question spoiled everything. In November 1341 Margaret expelled her Luxembourg husband; whereupon Louis, declaring that the marriage had not been consummated and was therefore void, married her with ill-considered haste to his widowed son, Louis of Brandenburg, on Feb. 10, 1342. This created an unfavourable impression throughout the empire. Worse, it led to the final rupture with Luxembourg and to Charles of Moravia declaring himself a candidate for the imperial crown now that the King of France, at war with England, was eliminated as a pretender. Louis vainly attempted to propitiate the Luxembourgs by the cession of Lower Lusatia and by the offer of one of his daughters in marriage. They negotiated with him but at the same time encouraged the new, intensely nationalistic French pope to renew the heresy proceedings against him and to demand a new election (August 1343). Once more Louis countered by offering to abdicate, this time in favour of his son, Louis of Brandenburg-Tirol (September 1343). The Luxembourgs maintained the negotiations until Charles of Moravia, who had granted excessive concessions to the Pope, gained all electoral votes except the two of the House of Wittelsbach and thus was elected king (July 1346). Preparing himself for the war that had become inevitable, Louis died of a heart attack while bear hunting near Munich in the autumn of 1347.

The Tirolean question. Louis had wanted to raise his family to a royal status like that of the houses of Habsburg and Luxembourg. But he failed to achieve the major prerequisite—the welding of his family into a uniform body motivated by a single political will. He strove for this unity with all the diplomatic and juridical means at his disposal, and the Upper Bavarian law code of 1346 (first formulated about 1335) remains a monument to these efforts. For, while Charles IV did what he could to erase Louis' memory within the empire, Charles's famous edict, the Golden Bull of 1356, represents only the final codification of fundamental imperial laws that had actually evolved under Louis. This codification enabled the empire to stand up to the juridically minded church of Avignon.

Louis possessed courage and tenacity without being rigid. He won men over by a jovial and chivalrous demeanour, and his suppleness, coupled with diplomatic skill, charmed them even as a certain mercurial quality made him appear unfathomable. He was a political man, whose guiding principle remained the *honor imperii.* Even in his darkest hours he brooked no interference with the imperial rights. It would be unfair to judge him solely by the yardstick of success. It was Louis' fate to come up repeatedly against adversaries who were talented and powerful. (H.Li.)

BIBLIOGRAPHY. Important summaries reflecting modern research are given by Herbert Grundmann, "Der Kampf um das Reichsrecht unter Ludwig dem Bayern," in Bruno Gebhardt, *Handbuch der deutschen Geschichte,* 9th ed., vol. 1, pp. 518–554 (1970); and on Louis IV as ruler, in articles by Max Spindler and Heinz Angermeier in the *Handbuch der bayerischen Geschichte,* ed. by Spindler, vol. 2, pp. 104–137, 144–181 (1969), both with bibliographies. An important work in English is W.T. Waugh, "Lewis the Bavarian," *Cambridge Medieval History,* vol. 7, ch. 4 (1932).

HOLLAND

• **Louis:** *see* Bonaparte, Louis.

HUNGARY

• **Louis I,** byname LOUIS THE GREAT, Hungarian LAJOS NAGY, Polish LUDWIK WIELKI (b. March 5, 1326—d. Sept. 10, 1382, Nagyszombat, Hung.), king of Hungary from 1342 and of Poland (as Louis) from 1370, who, during much of his long reign, was involved in wars with Venice and Naples.

Louis was crowned king of Hungary in succession to his father, Charles I, on July 21, 1342. In 1346 he was defeated by the Venetians at Zara (now Zadar, Croatia), an Adriatic port city that had been under Hungarian protection. In 1347 he led an expedition against the kingdom of Naples to avenge the murder (1345) of his younger brother, Andrew, consort of Joan I of Naples, whose new husband, Louis of Taranto, was a suspected accomplice in the murder. Louis I occupied Naples in 1348, but a plague soon forced him to retire; a later invasion (1350) also led to no permanent results.

In 1351 Louis I confirmed the Golden Bull of 1222, a charter of liberties, which he modified somewhat by the law of entail, providing that estates of nobles were to be inherited by the male line and could neither be cut up nor given away. If a line died out entirely, the estate was to revert to the crown. Also serfs were to pay their lords one-ninth of their produce. These steps made Louis virtually independent of the Diet financially.

Louis' second war against Venice (1357–58) was more successful than his first ventures. Under the Treaty of Zara (February 1358), most of the Venetians' Dalmatian towns went to Hungary. In the east he protected his expanded domains by defeating the Turks in northern Bulgaria.

King Casimir III of Poland, who died without sons, named Louis as his successor, and he was crowned king of Poland on Nov. 17, 1370. The Poles, however, never let him exert much real authority over them, though in 1374 they recognized his daughter Maria and her betrothed husband, Sigismund of Luxembourg, as their future queen and king.

Louis' attention again turned to Italy when the Western Schism broke out (1378). Louis helped his protégé Charles of Durazzo conquer Naples and supplant its queen, Joan, who declared herself in favour of the antipope Clement VII. Meanwhile, Louis undertook a third war against Venice and won virtually all of Dalmatia (Treaty of Turin, Aug. 18, 1381).

King Louis I died in the following year. Maria (with Sigismund), whom he had intended to rule Poland, succeeded him in Hungary, and his other daughter, Jadwiga, became queen of Poland instead of Hungary.

Consult the INDEX *first*

• **Louis II** (b. July 1, 1506—d. Aug. 29, 1526, Mohács, Hung.), king of Hungary and of Bohemia from 1516, who was the last of the Jagiełło line to rule those countries and the last king to rule all of Hungary before the Turks conquered a large portion of it.

Louis II. portrait by an unknown artist after a portrait by Titian; in the Museum of Fine Arts, Budapest

By courtesy of the Museum of Fine Arts, Budapest

The only son of Vladislas II of Hungary and Bohemia, Louis was sickly as a child but intelligent. To assure the succession, he was crowned king of Hungary (June 4, 1508) and of Bohemia (May 11, 1509), and became king on his father's death (March 1516). He was declared of age to rule on Dec. 11, 1521. He married Maria of Austria the following January 13, and both pursued a life of riotous pleasure, soon disqualifying the teenage king from affairs of state.

The Ottoman Turks attacked Hungary in the summer of 1526, and Louis, with an inadequate force, advanced against them. He was routed at Mohács on the Danube (Aug. 29, 1526) and is said to have drowned fleeing the battlefield. After that defeat, Hungary was divided between the Turks and the Austrian Habsburgs.

Naples

• **Louis,** byname LOUIS OF TARANTO, Italian LUIGI DI TARANTO (b. 1320, Naples—d. May 26, 1362, Naples), count of Provence (1347–62), as well as prince of Taranto and Achaia, who by his marriage to Queen Joan I of Naples (1343–82) became king of Naples after a struggle with King Louis I of Hungary.

Louis, who is believed to have played a major role in the murder of Andrew of Hungary, Joan's first husband (September 1345), married Joan in August 1347. When Andrew's brother Louis I of Hungary invaded the kingdom, occupying Naples (1348), the royal couple fled to Avignon, where they received the protection of Pope Clement VI. The Hungarian king left Naples, which Joan and Louis reoccupied briefly before a second Hungarian invasion forced them to flee to Gaeta. Louis' final departure allowed them to return for good in 1352. In the presence of the grand seneschal Niccolò Acciaiuoli (1310–65), their major supporter and counsellor, they were crowned in Naples by a papal legate.

Having usurped the royal power from Joan, Louis regained much of the island of Sicily, including the capital of Palermo. A barons' revolt, however, forced him to return to the mainland, where he defeated his enemies. His sudden death prevented his return to Sicily.

• **Louis I–III:** *see* Louis I–III (Anjou/Maine).

Navarre

• **Louis:** *see* Louis X (France).

Poland

• **Louis:** *see* Louis I (Hungary).

Portugal

• **Louis** (b. Oct. 31, 1838, Lisbon—d. Oct. 19, 1889, Cascais, Port.), king of Portugal whose reign (1861–89), in contrast to the first half of the century, saw the smooth operation of the constitutional system, the completion of the railway network, the adoption of economic and political reforms, and the modernization of many aspects of Portuguese life.

The second son of Queen Maria II and her consort, Ferdinand II, Louis succeeded on the early death of his more brilliant elder brother, Peter V. He married Maria Pia, daughter of the King of Italy, in 1862. The reign began inauspiciously amidst financial difficulties.

In 1868 the question of the Spanish succession caused a crisis when Napoleon III favoured the succession of King Louis or his father Ferdinand. Louis weakly allowed Marshal Saldanha to seize power, but the aged hero was soon forced to resign. Unlike his predecessor, Louis preferred the conservative Regenerator Party, which, under the minister António Maria de Fontes Pereira de Mello, pursued a policy of economic development and deficit financing. The Progressists accused the King of partisanship and thus favoured the emergence of republicanism. King Louis took a hand in treaties with Britain concerning Mozambique and India and helped to settle other territorial disputes through arbitration. He translated Shakespeare and other works into Portuguese.

Spain

• **Louis** (b. Aug. 25, 1707, Madrid—d. Aug. 31, 1724, Madrid), king of Spain in 1724, son of Philip V.

Louis was born during the War of the Spanish Succession, which disputed his French father's succession to the Spanish throne; thus, his birth was celebrated by the French and the Spanish. Louis XIV of France was his godfather. In 1709 he was recognized as heir presumptive, being named príncipe (prince) de Asturias, and succeeded to the throne on Jan. 15, 1724, upon the abdication of his father. On February 9 he was formally proclaimed king. He fell ill, however, probably of smallpox, on August 19 and died 12 days later. Philip V returned to the throne.

louis, also called LOUIS D'OR, gold coin circulated in France before the Revolution. The franc (*q.v.*) and livre were silver coins that had shrunk in value to such an extent that by 1740 coins of a larger denomination were needed. The French kings therefore had gold coins struck and called after their name Louis, or louis d'or ("gold Louis"). After the Revolution, Napoleon continued the practice but called the coins "napoleons." They had a value of 20 francs.

Louis, SAINT: *see* Louis IX *under* Louis (France).

Louis COEUR-DE-LION: *see* Louis VIII *under* Louis (France).

Louis DE FRANCE, byname LE GRAND DAUPHIN, or MONSEIGNEUR (b. Nov. 1, 1661—d. April 14, 1711, Meudon, Fr.), son of Louis XIV and Marie-Thérèse of Austria; his death preceded his father's (1715), and the French crown went to his own grandson, Louis XV. In 1688 he received nominal command of the French armies in Germany, led by Vauban, but throughout his life he depended on the favours of his strong-willed father and acquired a reputation for timidity, subservience, and—despite an education under the philosopher Bossuet—general mediocrity.

He married (1680) Marie-Anne-Christine-Victoire of Bavaria (d. 1690) and had three sons: Louis, duc de Bourgogne (1682–1712), who himself was dauphin for two years (1711–12) and was the father of Louis XV; Philippe, duc d'Anjou (1683–1746), who became King Philip V of Spain; and Charles, duc de Berry (1686–1714).

Louis D'OUTREMER: *see* Louis IV *under* Louis (France).

Louis LE BÈGUE: *see* Louis II *under* Louis (France).

Louis LE FAINÉANT: *see* Louis V *under* Louis (France).

Louis OF NASSAU, Dutch LODEWIJK VAN NASSAU (b. Jan. 10, 1538, Dillenburg, Nassau—d. April 14, 1574, Mook, near Nijmegen, Neth.), nobleman who provided key military and political leadership in the early phases (1566–74) of the Netherlands' revolt against Spanish rule and who served as a valued ally of his older brother William, prince of Orange (William I the Silent).

A Lutheran from birth, Louis lived in Brussels after 1556, where he became active in the opposition movement of lesser noblemen against the Spanish government. In 1566 he wrote the original draft of the noblemen's petition to the governess, Margaret of Austria, duchess of Parma, for an end to religious persecution, and he began to negotiate for aid from Protestant leaders in France and the Rhineland. After the arrival of Spain's new captain general, the Duke of Alba, in 1567, Louis went into exile with other Protestant rebels, including the Gueux (Beggars), a party of lesser nobles.

Louis of Nassau, panel portrait by an unknown artist, 1574; in the Orange Nassau Museum, Delft, Neth.

By courtesy of the Iconographisch Bureau, The Hague

Louis returned in April 1568 to lead an invasion of the northern Netherlands, which is considered the beginning of the Eighty Years' War, the war of the Netherlands' independence from Spain. He defeated Spanish troops at Heiligerlee, east of Groningen (May 23), where his brother Adolph was killed, but was decisively beaten by Alba's forces at Jemgum on the Ems (July 21). After fighting alongside his brother William of Orange in another disastrous campaign in the south, he retreated to France, where he established excellent relations with the Huguenot leader Gaspard de Coligny and, through him, with the French king Charles IX.

Inspired by Gueux victories at Brill (Brielle) and Flushing (Vlissingen) in early 1572, Louis launched another invasion of the Netherlands, capturing Mons in Hainaut on May 23, where he was, however, besieged by Spanish troops on June 3. He capitulated on September 19 after the St. Bartholomew's Day massacre (August 24) of Protestants in Paris had ended any prospect of French aid and after a relief effort by William of Orange had been repulsed. Yet while the brothers were engaging Spanish troops in the south, other rebels in the north had been able to reconquer all of Holland except Amsterdam.

To relieve renewed Spanish pressure on Holland in 1574, Louis tried to lead troops he had assembled in Germany across the Meuse. But his forces were crushed in April by Sancho de Ávila's army at Mook, where both Louis and his younger brother Henry were mortally wounded in battle.

Louis OF TARANTO: *see* Louis *under* Louis (Naples).

Louis THE BAVARIAN: *see* Louis IV *under* Louis (Germany/Holy Roman Empire).

Louis THE BLIND: *see* Louis III *under* Louis (Germany/Holy Roman Empire).

Louis THE CHILD: *see* Louis IV *under* Louis (Germany/East Franks).

Louis THE DEBONAIR: *see* Louis I *under* Louis (Germany/Holy Roman Empire).

Louis THE FAT: *see* Louis VI *under* Louis (France).

Louis THE GERMAN: *see* Louis II *under* Louis (Germany/East Franks).

Louis THE GOOD: *see* Bourbon, Louis II, 3[e] duc de.

Louis THE GRAND MONARCH: *see* Louis XIV *under* Louis (France).

Louis THE GREAT: *see* Louis I *under* Louis (Hungary); Louis XIV *under* Louis (France).

Louis THE JUST: *see* Louis XIII *under* Louis (France).

Louis THE LION, also called LOUIS THE LION-HEART: *see* Louis VIII *under* Louis (France).

Louis THE PIOUS: *see* Louis I *under* Louis (Germany/Holy Roman Empire).

Louis THE STAMMERER: *see* Louis II *under* Louis (France).

Louis THE STUBBORN: *see* Louis X *under* Louis (France).

Louis THE WELL-BELOVED: *see* Louis XV *under* Louis (France).

Louis THE YOUNGER: *see* Louis III *under* Louis (Germany/East Franks).

Louis, Joe, byname of JOSEPH LOUIS BARROW, also called THE BROWN BOMBER (b. May 13, 1914, Lexington, Ala., U.S.—d. April 12, 1981, Las Vegas, Nev.), American boxer who was world heavyweight champion from June 22, 1937, when he knocked out James J. Braddock in eight rounds in Chicago, until March 1, 1949, when he retired undefeated. During his reign, the longest in the history of the heavyweight division, he successfully defended the title 25 times, scoring 21 knockouts. His service in the U.S. Army during World War II no doubt prevented him from defending his title many more times.

Joe Louis, 1946
EB Inc.

Louis began his boxing career in Detroit. He won the U.S. Amateur Athletic Union 175-pound championship in 1934 and also was a Golden Gloves titleholder. He had his first professional fight on July 4, 1934, and within 12 months had knocked out Primo Carnera, the first of six previous or subsequent heavyweight champions who were his victims; the others were Max Baer, Jack Sharkey, Braddock, Max Schmeling, and Jersey Joe Walcott. Louis sustained his first professional loss in 1936 at the hands of Schmeling, but in 1938, after having beaten Braddock and taken the title, Louis defeated Schmeling with a vengeance in the first round of their rematch.

Louis was at his peak in the period 1939–42. From December 1940 through June 1941 he defended the championship seven times. After the war he was less active, and in 1949 he retired as the undefeated champion long enough to allow Ezzard Charles to earn recognition as his successor. Louis returned as challenger for the championship but lost a 15-round decision to Charles on Sept. 27, 1950. In Louis' last fight of consequence, he was knocked out in eight rounds by future champion Rocky Marciano on Oct. 26, 1951. From 1934 to 1951, Louis had 71 bouts, winning 68, 54 by knockouts. He was an extremely accurate and economical knockout puncher.

After his second retirement he was faced with a vast accumulation of improperly paid federal income tax bills, owing to poor management of his financial affairs. Late in life he became a greeter for Caesar's Palace in Las Vegas, Nev.

Louis, Morris, original name MORRIS BERNSTEIN (b. Nov. 24, 1912, Baltimore, Md., U.S.—d. Sept. 7, 1962, Washington, D.C.), American painter associated with the New York school of Abstract Expressionism who is notable for his distinctly personal use of colour, often in brilliant bands or stripes.

Louis studied painting at the Maryland Institute, Baltimore (1929–33), and from 1937 to 1940 he worked as an easel painter in the Works Projects Administration (WPA) Federal Art program. His early work was Cubistic, but his style changed abruptly in 1952 following his exposure to the Abstract Expressionist paintings of Jackson Pollock. In 1953 he was deeply impressed by Helen Frankenthaler's method of staining an untreated canvas with poured paint, and his later work took the form of stained vertical waves of colour, of which "Iris" (1954) is an example. After 1961 he painted in striking parallel streams of colour that flowed across the bottom corners of his pictures. In his last works he used vertical, straight stripes of colour.

Louis, Victor, original name NICOLAS LOUIS (b. May 10, 1731, Paris, Fr.—d. July 2, 1800, Paris), one of the most active of late 18th-century French Neoclassical architects, especially noted for theatre construction.

After at least seven unsuccessful attempts, Louis won the Prix de Rome in 1755. While in Rome (1756–59), he offended the director of the Academy there, Charles Joseph Natoire, and this social misstep resulted in his subsequent exclusion from the Academy of Architecture and from participation in royal building projects. However, after an unproductive sojourn in Poland (1765), he returned to France and began receiving commissions. The Intendance (governor's residence) at Besançon (begun 1771) was his first important building, and this was followed by his masterpiece, the Grand-Théâtre in Bordeaux, the largest theatre in pre-Revolutionary France. With its impressive colonnade of 12 huge Corinthian columns and its elegant Neoclassical vestibule and symmetrical staircase lit by a glass dome, this building became the model for subsequent French theatre buildings and was the prototype for Charles Garnier's Paris Opera House.

Louis's next important commission was to enclose the garden of the Palais-Royal in Paris. He designed a large structure with a remarkably uniform facade of repeated pilasters and bays over a continuous ground-floor arcade. At one corner of the building he built a theatre, the Théâtre-Français, which became the home of the Comédie-Française. His final project, a grandiose public square in Bordeaux, was interrupted by the Revolution, which effectively ended his career.

A list of the abbreviations used in the MICROPAEDIA *will be found at the end of this volume*

Louis XIII style, visual arts produced in France during the reign of Louis XIII (1601–43). Louis was but a child when he ascended the throne in 1610, and his mother, Marie de Médicis, assumed the powers of regent. Having close ties with Italy, Marie introduced much of the art of that country into her court. The Mannerist influences from Italy and from Flanders were so great that a true French style did not develop until the second quarter of the century. At that time the Italian influences of the painter Caravaggio were assimilated into a new interest in genre scenes, notably in the work of Georges de la Tour and the brothers Le Nain—Antoine, Louis, and Mathieu. The main French tradition in painting, however, was carried on under the influence of the Italian Carracci brothers by Simon Vouet. It was Vouet who trained the academic painters of the next generation, though the work of Nicolas Poussin proved to be the greater influence on later French painting.

Sculpture in France during this period was not of outstanding quality. Those working in this area included Jacques Sarrazin and Jean Warin, competent craftsmen but lacking the great talents that flourished under Louis XIV.

Perhaps the most prolific area for the arts under Marie de Médicis and Louis XIII was the field of architecture. Salomon de Brosse, the chief architect, designed both the Palais de Justice at Rennes and, for Marie de Médicis, the Palais du Luxembourg in Paris (begun 1615). As in the other arts, the Italian influence was felt, notably in the work of Jacques Lemercier, who designed works for the powerful Cardinal de Richelieu, including the Church of the Sorbonne in Paris (begun 1635). It was not, however, until the next king's rule that French architecture reached its greatest heights, as in the work of François Mansart.

The furniture of the Louis XIII period, typically massive and solidly built, is characterized by carving and turning (shaping on a lathe). Common decorative motifs found on it include cherubs, ornate scrollwork, cartouches (ornamental frames), fruit-and-flower swags, and grotesque masks.

Louis XIV style, visual arts produced in France during the reign of Louis XIV (1638–1715). The man most influential in French painting of the period was Nicolas Poussin. Although Poussin himself lived in Italy for most of his adult life, his Parisian friends commissioned works through which his classicism was made known to French painters. In 1648 the painter Charles Le Brun, assisted by the king, founded the Royal Academy of Painting and Sculpture, an organization that dictated style to such a degree that it virtually controlled the fortunes of all French artists for the remainder of the reign. French sculpture reached a new zenith at this time, after the mediocrity of the first half of the

Model of a Louis XIV-style antechamber to a reception suite in the palace of Versailles, late 17th century; in the Art Institute of Chicago

By courtesy of Thorne Rooms in Miniature, the Art Institute of Chicago

century. François Girardon was a favourite of the King and did several portrait sculptures of him, as well as the tomb of the cardinal de Richelieu. Antoine Coysevox also received royal commissions, including the tomb of Cardinal Mazarin, while Pierre Puget, whose work showed strong Italian Baroque influences, was not so well favoured at court.

At the Gobelins factory, founded by Louis for the production of *meubles de luxe* and furnishings for the royal palaces and the public buildings, a national decorative arts style evolved that soon spread its influence into neighbouring countries. Furniture, for example, was veneered with tortoise shell or foreign woods, inlaid with brass, pewter, and ivory, or heavily gilded all over; heavy gilt bronze mounts protected the corners and other parts from friction and rough handling and provided further ornament. The name of André-Charles Boulle is particularly associated with this style of furniture design. Common decorative motifs of the period include shells, satyrs, cherubs, festoons and garlands, mythological themes, cartouches (ornamental frames), foliated scrolls, and dolphins.

The ability of the King to form a strong "national" style was exhibited particularly in the field of architecture. The year 1665 was crucial for the history of French art, for it was in that year that Gian Lorenzo Bernini arrived in Paris to design a new facade for the Louvre. It was decided, however, that the Italian Baroque style was incompatible with the French temperament, and the Louvre was completed according to the new tenets of French classicism.

The Louvre was the project of Louis's minister Colbert; the King's interest lay at Versailles, where in the 1660s he began to renovate an ancient hunting lodge, and the resultant palace dazzled the world. Never before had a single man attempted any architectural plan on such a large scale. The result is a masterpiece of formal grandeur, and, because the arts were all under the rigid control of the state, each element at Versailles was overseen and designed to be in keeping with the whole. Versailles, though usually thought of by the French as Classical, can be considered the ultimate Baroque composition, in which motion is always present but always contained.

Not the least important element at Versailles was the landscaping. André Le Nôtre, the greatest artist in the history of European landscape architecture, worked with the King, designing vistas, fountains, and many other outdoor arrangements. Versailles had an enormous impact on the rest of Europe, both artistic and psychological, but the whole complex was so large that even the extremely long life of Louis XIV did not hold enough years to see it completed.

Louis XV style, in the decorative arts, the Rococo style that is characterized by the superior craftsmanship of 18th-century cabinetmaking in France. The artists of this style produced exquisite Rococo decor for the enormous number of homes owned by royalty and nobility during the reign of Louis XV. Emphasis was laid on the ensemble, so that painters and sculptors were a part of the decorative arts. Some of the famous names connected with the finest in Louis XV Rococo style are those of the painter François Boucher; the sculptor, painter, and decorator Jean-Louis-Ernest Meissonier; the German craftsman J.-F. Oeben, whose intricate floral marquetry and ingenious mechanical specialities are extraordinary; and Pierre Migeon, a favourite of Mme de Pompadour. The full range of richness in decorative techniques is represented in this period—superb carving, ornamentation in all sorts of metal, all types of inlaid work in woods, metal, mother-of-pearl, and ivory, as well as the pinnacle of achievement in lacquered chinoiserie.

Model of a Louis XV-style boudoir, 1740–60; in the Art Institute of Chicago

By courtesy of Thorne Rooms in Miniature, the Art Institute of Chicago

It was the fashion to have at least two complete sets of furniture, for summer and winter, for each home. The furniture combines usefulness with elegance. Chairs have curved legs, floral decorations, and comfortably padded seats and backs, yet sacrifice nothing in design. In addition to nature and Orientalia, fantasy played a large part in motifs, with curious animals and exotic landscapes adorning all surfaces. Rare woods such as tulip, lemon tree, violet, and king woods were used for sumptuous effects, and richly veined and tinted marbles were also imported. The art of polishing reached its peak in this period, even rivalling objects from the Far East. At its most extreme the Rococo mode became deliberately asymmetrical, although contriving always to maintain a harmonious balance within the larger scheme of decor.

Louis XVI style, also spelled LOUIS SEIZE, visual arts produced in France during the reign (1774–93) of Louis XVI, which was actually both a last phase of Rococo and a first phase of Neoclassicism. The predominant style in architecture, painting, sculpture, and the decorative arts was Neoclassicism, a style that had come into its own during the last years of Louis XV's life, chiefly as a reaction to the excesses of the Rococo but partly through the popularity of the excavations at ancient Herculaneum and Pompeii, in Italy, and partly on the basis of Jean-Jacques Rousseau's call for "natural" virtue and honest sentiment. One of the most dramatic episodes in the stylistic oscillation from Rococo to Neoclassicism was played out in 1770 at Mme du Barry's Pavillon de Louveciennes. A series of large painted canvases by the Rococo painter Jean-Honoré Fragonard depicting the "Progress of Love" were removed almost as soon as they were installed and replaced with a series commissioned from Joseph-Marie Vien, a Neoclassicist. Vien's pupil Jacques-Louis David was the most important painter of the reign of Louis XVI; his severe compositions recalling the style of the earlier painter Nicolas Poussin are documents extolling republican virtues. During the Revolution, David was a deputy and voted for the execution of the King.

The foremost sculptor of the reign of Louis XVI was Jean-Antoine Houdon (1741–1828). He portrayed a number of the most prominent men of his day, often in classical togas. His nude "Diana," of which there are several versions, attempts to evoke the feeling of the Classical Greek nude.

The lavish court style of Louis and Marie Antoinette, his young queen, gave impetus to the highly skilled *ébénistes,* or cabinetmakers, of the period. Whereas the general style of furniture was again Neoclassic (*i.e.,* straight, simple lines and classical motifs), the workmanship was as complicated and as finely performed as in any period to date. Jean-Henri Riesener and Bernard van Risenburgh were two of the foremost cabinetmakers, filling commissions for Mme du Barry as well as for the Queen. Many of the *ébénistes,* including Riesener, were German craftsmen who, nevertheless, contributed to the tradition of French furniture. Other makers of luxury items benefited

Model of a Louis XVI-style boudoir, *c.* 1780; in the Art Institute of Chicago
By courtesy of Thorne Rooms in Miniature, the Art Institute of Chicago

from the excesses of the court, chief among them the porcelain manufactory at Sèvres.

Louis-Charles DE FRANCE: *see* Louis XVII *under* Louis (France).

louis d'or (monetary unit): *see* louis.

Louis-Napoléon: *see* Napoleon III.

Louis of Nevers: *see* Louis I *under* Louis (Flanders).

Louis-Philippe, also called (1793–1830) LOUIS-PHILIPPE, DUKE (duc) D'ORLÉANS, byname CITIZEN KING, French ROI CITOYEN (b. Oct. 6, 1773, Paris, France—d. Aug. 26, 1850, Claremont, Surrey, Eng.), king of the French from 1830 to 1848; basing his rule on the support of the upper bourgeoisie, he ultimately fell from power because he could not win the allegiance of the new industrial classes.

Louis-Philippe was the eldest son of Louis-Philippe Joseph de Bourbon-Orléans, Duke de Chartres, and Adélaïde de Bourbon-Penthièvre. At first styled Duke de Valois, he became Duke de Chartres when his father inherited the title Duke d'Orléans in 1785. On the outbreak of the French Revolution

Louis-Philippe, detail of a portrait by F.X. Winterhalter; in the Château de Versailles, France
Giraudon—Art Resource

in 1789, Louis-Philippe joined the group of progressive nobles who supported the Revolutionary government. He became a member of the Jacobin Club in 1790, and, when France went to war with Austria in April 1792, he joined the Army of the North, receiving a commission as lieutenant general in September. Within a year, however, in April 1793, he joined his commander, Charles-François Dumouriez, in deserting to the Austrians. He took refuge in Switzerland and taught under an assumed name at the college at Reichenau. He became Duke d'Orléans on the execution of his father by the Jacobin government in November 1793. After living in the United States for more than two years, Louis-Philippe decided to return to Europe. When he arrived in England in early 1800 and found that there was no hope of rallying opposition to Napoleon, he reconciled the house of Orléans with the elder branch of the Bourbon family, headed by Louis XVIII, the exiled titular king of France.

After a long residence at Twickenham in England, Louis-Philippe joined the Neapolitan royal family at Palermo, Sicily, in 1809; on November 25 he married Marie-Amélie, a daughter of King Ferdinand IV of Naples. He returned to France on the First Restoration of King Louis XVIII (1814) and regained possession of that portion of the Orléans estates that had not been sold after his emigration. When Napoleon again seized power in March 1815, he fled to England. After the Second Restoration of Louis XVIII (July 1815), Louis-Philippe was a consistent adherent of the liberal opposition.

In 1830 Charles X's attempt to enforce repressive ordinances touched off a rebellion (July 27–30) that gave Louis-Philippe his long-awaited opportunity to gain power. He was elected lieutenant general of the kingdom by the legislature on July 31, two days before Charles abdicated the throne. On August 9 Louis-Philippe accepted the crown.

The revolution that brought Louis-Philippe to power constituted a victory for the upper bourgeoisie over the aristocracy; the new ruler was titled Louis-Philippe, king of the French, instead of Philip VII, king of France. He consolidated his power by steering a middle course between the right-wing extreme monarchists (the Legitimists) on the one side and the socialists and other republicans (including the Bonapartists) on the other. The numerous rebellions and attempts on his life caused the king increasingly to resort to repressive measures; by the end of the 1830s his opponents had been either silenced or driven underground.

Meanwhile, Louis-Philippe was strengthening France's position in Europe. He cooperated with the British in forcing the Dutch to recognize Belgian independence. The industrial and agricultural depression of 1846 aroused widespread popular discontent at a time when the king had already embittered the lower bourgeoisie through his refusal to extend to them the franchise. Faced with an insurrectionary movement of proletarian and middle-class elements, Louis-Philippe abdicated on Feb. 24, 1848, and withdrew to Surrey in England, where he died.

Louis Seize (visual arts): *see* Louis XVI style.

Louisbourg, formerly spelled LOUISBURG, town, Cape Breton county, northeastern Nova Scotia, Canada, on the east side of Cape Breton Island, overlooking the Atlantic Ocean, 25 miles (40 km) southeast of Sydney.

Founded in 1713 by French settlers from Placentia, Newfoundland, and named for Louis XIV, it became an important fishing and shipbuilding centre and capital of the French colony of Île Royale. It was later heavily fortified, becoming one of France's chief strongholds in North America. In 1745, when Britain was opposing France in the War of the Austrian Succession (King George's War), Louisbourg was attacked by a force from New England under Sir William Pepperell, with British naval support. The garrison surrendered after a siege of 48 days. In 1748 Louisbourg was restored to France by the Treaty of Aix-la-Chapelle. The town recovered, and by 1752 it was carrying on a lively commerce with Europe, continental North America, and the West Indies and had a population of over 4,000, including 1,500 soldiers. In 1758, during the Seven Years' War, a large British army and fleet under General Jeffrey (later Lord) Amherst and Admiral Edward Boscowen again besieged and captured Louisbourg. The British then evacuated the French population, and in 1760 they demolished the fortifications after having used Louisbourg as a base for their conquest of Canada.

Restored fortress of Louisbourg, Nova Scotia
© E. Otto/Comstock Photofile Limited

An area of 23 square miles (60 square km), including the modern town and the ruined fortress across the harbour to the southwest, was declared a national historic park in 1940; restoration of a large part of the area was begun in 1961. About one-fifth of the restoration had been completed by 1980. The present-day town of Louisbourg, inhabited by persons mostly of pre-Loyalist, Loyalist, and Highland Scottish descent, is a fishing port, with fish-processing and packing plants. Pop. (1991) 1,261.

Louise OF SAVOY, French LOUISE DE SAVOIE (b. Sept. 11, 1476, Pont d'Ain, France—d. Sept. 22, 1531, Grez, near Fontainebleau), mother of King Francis I of France, who as regent twice during his reign played a major role in the government of France.

The daughter of Philip II the Landless, duke of Savoy, and Marguerite de Bourbon, Louise married Charles de Valois-Orléans, comte d'Angoulême; they had two children, Margaret, future queen of Navarre and patron of Humanists and Reformers, and Francis, who became heir presumptive to the French crown on the accession of Louis XII in 1498.

In 1515 Francis ascended the throne and Louise, devoted to her son, took an active part in government. Created duchesse d'Angoulême, she was appointed regent when Francis undertook his first expedition to Italy (1515–16). When her niece Suzanne de Bourbon died in 1521 and left her estate to her husband Charles, the constable duke de Bourbon, Louise claimed the estate for herself, doing much to push Charles to treason (1523).

Regent again in 1525–26, during the king's second Italian expedition, Louise was able to detach Henry VIII of England from his alliance with the Holy Roman emperor Charles V. She was also active in negotiations to free her son from captivity in Spain, and, with Margaret of Austria, she negotiated the Treaty of Cambrai, or "Ladies' Peace," in 1529 between Francis and Charles V.

Louisiade Archipelago, island group of Papua New Guinea, 125 miles (200 km) southeast of the island of New Guinea. Stretching for more than 100 miles (160 km), it occupies 10,000 square miles (26,000 square km) of the southwestern Pacific. Of the nearly 100 islands, the largest—Sudest (Tagula), Misima, and Rossel—are volcanic, mountainous, and fringed with reefs, but most are small coral formations. The archipelago was visited by the Spanish navigator Luis Vaez de Torres in 1606. It was named (1768) by Louis-Antoine de Bougainville after Louis XV of France. Later visitors included Admiral Bruni d'Entrecasteaux (1793) and Captain Owen Stanley (1849). Occupied by Japanese forces in 1942, the islands are near the site of the Battle of the Coral Sea.

Louisiana, constituent state of the United States of America bordering the Gulf of Mexico in the south-central region of the country.

A brief treatment of Louisiana follows. For full treatment, *see* MACROPAEDIA: United States of America: *Louisiana.*

Louisiana is bounded by the states of Mississippi on the east, Arkansas on the north, and Texas on the west. The capital is Baton Rouge. The boot-shaped state extends about 275 miles (440 km) from north to south and for about 300 miles (480 km) from east to west along the coast.

The earliest inhabitants were Indians, whose occupancy has probably spanned 16,000 years. Archaeological sites have been excavated dating to 700 BC. At the time of initial European settlement, Caddo and Choctaw groups lived in hunting and gathering camps and in farming villages.

The French explorer Robert Cavelier de La Salle descended the Mississippi River in 1682 and claimed the entire river basin for France. The city of New Orleans was established in 1718 by Jean-Baptiste Le Moyne de Bienville. When Louisiana became a French crown colony in 1731, its population was about 8,000, including black slaves. Colonization increased significantly in the 1760s with the arrival of the French-speaking Acadians (Cajuns) who had been expelled from Nova Scotia by the British. Spain controlled the territory from 1762 until 1800, when it passed again to the French. Louisiana was acquired by the United States as part of the Louisiana Purchase from France in 1803. The Territory of Orleans, which consisted essentially of the present area of the state, was established in 1804. Louisiana entered the Union as the 18th state in 1812.

In the first half of the 19th century, Louisiana experienced an economic boom generated by slave labour on the flourishing cotton and sugarcane plantations. Natural cleavages asserted themselves in the political affairs of the state as the interests of first French and Americans, and later planters and farmers, clashed in the political process. Despite the objection of a large portion of its population, Louisiana seceded from the Union at the beginning of the American Civil War in 1861. Effective separation was short-lived as New Orleans was occupied by Union troops by 1862. Readmission to the Union occurred in 1868. When the Reconstruction period, severely administered by Northern radicals, was over, the planter-elite emerged in control of the government and economy. The enactment of the 1898 constitution legally denied nearly all blacks the right to vote, and a rigid policy of racial segregation developed that rendered blacks almost powerless until the mid-1960s. From 1928 until 1960 political power in the state was held by governor Huey P. Long and his successor and brother, Earl K. Long. The Longs were populists who tended toward demagoguery; they were not, however, anti-black.

Louisiana can be divided into two main physical regions: (1) the Mississippi flood plain with its great delta, natural levees, and moderate relief; and (2) the Gulf coastal plain with its terraces and low hills. Along the coast is a wide fringe of swampland with slow-flowing bayous and large, shallow lakes.

The Louisiana climate is subtropical, with average annual temperatures ranging from 64° F (18° C) in the extreme north to 71° F (21° C) at the mouth of the Mississippi River. Rainfall averages about 48 inches (1,220 mm) at Shreveport and 64 inches (1,625 mm) at New Orleans. The growing season ranges from 220 days in the north to 320 days in the south. Soil conditions are generally well-suited for agriculture, especially in the areas of the state that are covered by rich alluvium deposited by the overflowing of its rivers and bayous.

The peoples of Louisiana exhibit a greater diversity than in most states of the Deep South. French is still spoken in many parishes, especially in the southwest. The state has long been an immigration point for Europeans, Latin Americans, and, more recently, Asians. By 1990 only the District of Columbia and the state of Mississippi had a higher proportion of black population than Louisiana. More than two-thirds of the total population is urban. The New Orleans metropolitan statistical area contains about 30 percent of the state's total population.

Agriculture is led by soybeans, cotton, beef cattle, poultry, dairy products, and sugarcane. Extensive "tree farming" projects and shrimp fishing fleets add to the state's economy. Petroleum and natural gas are by far the most important mineral resources. Sulfur and salt are extracted from geological formations found in association with the oil. Chemicals, refined petroleum, paper, transport equipment, and processed food are among the most important manufactured items.

The port of New Orleans is the country's second-ranked port, moving much of the nation's petroleum and grain. Baton Rouge, another busy port, lies at the head of deep channel navigation on the Mississippi. The Intracoastal Waterway runs the entire length of the Gulf coast. Pipelines carry crude oil to refineries and loading terminals, or natural gas to markets. Railroads, highways, and airways crisscross the state. New Orleans International Airport is a major connection point with Latin America and the Caribbean.

Tourism has developed as a major industry around the traditions of the French Quarter of New Orleans with its annual Mardi Gras festival, and around the statewide antebellum plantation museums, gardens, and parks. A major world's fair was held in New Orleans in 1984. The New Orleans Superdome stadium holds sporting events of national interest.

Louisiana's cultural and folk-art traditions have long influenced music, art, literature, and cuisine in the rest of the country. New Orleans actively supports its arts and philanthropic institutions. The Roman Catholic and Baptist churches have long held sway over the social and cultural life of much of the state's population. Along with the Louisiana State University system, the state administers several other colleges and universities. Area 47,752 square miles (123,677 square km). Pop. (2000) 4,468,976.

Louisiana Creole, language spoken in Louisiana by persons of mixed French, African, and Indian descent. Louisiana Creole, which is closely related to Haitian Creole, should not be confused with either Louisiana provincial standard French, spoken by the descendants of the French upper classes in and around New Orleans, nor with the language of the Cajuns; both of the latter are dialects of French, with some archaic or provincial features, whereas Louisiana Creole is a creole language based on French. *Compare* Cajun; Haitian Creole. *See also* creole.

Louisiana Purchase, western half of the Mississippi River basin purchased in 1803 from France by the United States; at less than three cents per acre for 828,000 square miles (2,144,520 square km), it was the greatest land bargain in U.S. history. The purchase doubled

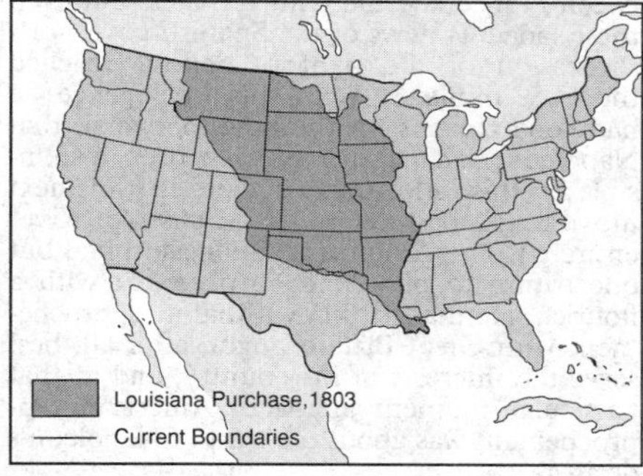

Louisiana Purchase

the size of the United States, greatly strengthened the country materially and strategically, provided a powerful impetus to westward expansion, and confirmed the doctrine of implied powers of the federal Constitution.

The Louisiana Territory had been the object of Old World interest for many years before 1803. Explorations and scattered settlements in the 17th and 18th centuries had given France control over the river and title to most of the Mississippi valley.

The first serious disruption of French control over Louisiana came during the Seven Years' War. In 1762 France ceded Louisiana west of the Mississippi River to Spain and in 1763 transferred virtually all of its remaining possessions in North America to Great Britain. This arrangement, however, proved temporary. French power rebounded under the subsequent military leadership of Napoleon Bonaparte, and on Oct. 1, 1800, Napoleon induced a reluctant King Charles IV of Spain to agree, for a consideration, to cede Louisiana back to France. King Charles gave at least his verbal assent on the condition that France would never alienate the territory to a third power. With this treaty of retrocession, known as the Treaty of San Ildefonso (confirmed March 21, 1801), would go not only the growing and commercially significant port of New Orleans but the strategic mouth of the Mississippi River.

Reports of the supposed retrocession soon were received by official Washington with deep misgivings. During the preceding 12 years, Americans had streamed westward into the valleys of the Cumberland, Tennessee, and Ohio rivers. The very existence of these new settlers depended on their right to use the Mississippi River freely and to make transshipment of their exports at New Orleans. By terms of the Treaty of San Lorenzo, Spain, in 1795, had granted to the United States the right to ship goods originating in American ports through the mouth of the Mississippi without paying duty and also the right of deposit, or temporary storage, of American goods at New Orleans for transshipment. But in 1802 Spain in effect revoked the right of deposit, and so it was in an atmosphere of growing tension in the West that President Thomas Jefferson was confronted with the prospect of a new, wily, and more powerful keeper of the strategic window to the Gulf of Mexico.

Jefferson instructed Robert R. Livingston, the U.S. minister at Paris, to take two steps: (1) to approach Napoleon's minister, Charles Maurice de Talleyrand, with the object of preventing the retrocession in the event this act had not yet been completed; and (2) to try to purchase at least New Orleans if the property had actually been transferred from Spain to France. Direct negotiations with Talleyrand, however, appeared to be all but impossible. For months Livingston had to be content with tantalizing glimmerings of a possible deal between France and the United States. But even these faded as news of the Spanish governor's revocation of the right of deposit reached the U.S. minister. With this intelligence he had good reasons for thinking the worst: that Napoleon Bonaparte may have been responsible for this unfortunate act and that his next move might be to close the Mississippi River entirely to the Americans. Livingston had but one trump to play, and he played it with a flourish. He made it known that a rapprochement with Great Britain might, after all, best serve the interests of his country, and at that particular moment an Anglo-American rapprochement was about the least of Napoleon's desires.

There are good reasons to believe that French failure in Santo Domingo, the imminence of renewed war with Great Britain, and financial stringencies may all have prompted Napoleon in 1803 to offer for sale to the United States the entire Louisiana Territory. At this juncture, James Monroe arrived in Paris as Jefferson's minister plenipotentiary; and even though the two American ministers possessed neither instructions nor authority to purchase the whole of Louisiana, the negotiations that followed, with Barbé-Marbois acting for Napoleon, moved swiftly to a conclusion.

A treaty was signed on May 2 but was antedated to April 30. By its terms the Louisiana Territory, in the form France had received it from Spain, was sold to the United States. For this vast domain the United States agreed to pay $11,250,000 outright and assumed claims of its citizens against France in the amount of $3,750,000. Interest payments incidental to the final settlement made the total price $27,267,622.

Precisely what the United States had purchased was unclear. The wording of the treaty was vague; it did not clearly describe the boundaries. It gave no assurances that West Florida was to be considered a part of Louisiana; neither did it delineate the southwest boundary. The American negotiators were fully aware of this.

But before the United States could establish fixed boundaries to Louisiana there arose a basic question concerning the constitutionality of the purchase. Did the Constitution of the United States provide for an act of this kind? The president, in principle a strict constructionist, thought that an amendment to the Constitution might be required to legalize the transaction; but, after due consideration and considerable oratory, the Senate approved the treaty by a vote of 24 to 7.

The setting of fixed boundaries awaited negotiations with Spain and Great Britain. The exasperating dispute with Spain over the ownership of West Florida and Texas was finally settled by the purchase of the Floridas from Spain in 1819 and the establishment of a fixed southwest boundary line. This line followed the Sabine River from the Gulf of Mexico to the parallel of 32° N; ran thence due north to the Red River, following this stream to the meridian 100° W; thence north to the Arkansas River and along this stream to its source; thence north or south, as the case might be (the source of the Arkansas was not then known), to the parallel of 42° N and west along this line to the Pacific Ocean. The northern boundary was amicably established by an Anglo-American convention in 1818. It established the 49° parallel N between the Lake of the Woods and the Rocky Mountains as the American-Canadian border. The Rocky (then referred to as "Stony") Mountains were accepted as the western limit of the Louisiana Territory, and the Mississippi River was considered for all practical purposes the eastern boundary of the great purchase. Much of the territory turned out to contain rich mineral resources, productive soil, valuable grazing land, forests, and wildlife resources of inestimable value. Out of this empire were carved in their entirety the states of Louisiana, Missouri, Arkansas, Iowa, North Dakota, South Dakota, Nebraska, and Oklahoma; in addition, the area included most of the land in Kansas, Colorado, Wyoming, Montana, and Minnesota.

A list of the abbreviations used in the MICROPAEDIA *will be found at the end of this volume*

Louisville, largest city in Kentucky, U.S., and the seat of Jefferson county, opposite the Falls of the Ohio River. Louisville is the centre of a metropolitan area including Jefferson county, Ky., and Clark and Floyd counties, Ind. Bridges spanning the Ohio link the city with New Albany and Jeffersonville, Ind.

The first recorded visit to the area by white men was on July 8, 1773, when Captain Thomas Bullitt arrived to survey the lands with a commission from William and Mary College in Virginia. George Rogers Clark settled (May 1778) on Corn Island (since swept away by floods) opposite Beargrass Creek and organized a base for the conquest of the British-held Old Northwest. Most of the settlers who came with him moved ashore the following winter and established Fort-on-Shore (Fort Nelson) within the present city limits. The town was organized in 1779 and incorporated and named (1780) for Louis XVI of France.

By 1811 Louisville had become an important frontier and river-flatboat trading place, and its development was further stimulated that year when Captain Nicholas Roosevelt docked the *New Orleans,* the first successful steamboat to ply Ohio-Mississippi waters. The city had become a major river port by 1820, and further stimulation came about with the construction (1825–30) of the canal around the 25-foot- (7.6-metre-) high Falls. Louisville's commercial influence extended over a vast area of the South and the Middle West. During the American Civil War, Louisville served as a military headquarters and a major Union supply depot. The city escaped the ravages of war and became an important way station for slaves seeking freedom in Indiana, across the river. A vigorous campaign to reclaim the South's trade followed the war. In the 1880s the Louisville and Nashville Railroad was extended to Jacksonville, Fla.

The city's economy was boosted during World War I with the building of nearby Camp Zachary Taylor and, later, with the enlargement of Fort Knox. Periodic flooding of the Ohio necessitated extensive protection work; a destructive flood in 1937 caused widespread damage. The city is a leading producer of bonded bourbon whiskey and cigarettes. Manufacture of the famed Louisville Slugger baseball bats has been moved across the Ohio River to Indiana. Other products include synthetic rubber, paint and varnish, aluminum items, automobiles, pottery, and printed matter. The American Printing House for the Blind (1858), which publishes books in Braille, is located in Louisville. The University of Louisville was founded in 1798 as Jefferson Seminary. The city is also the seat of two Roman Catholic institutions—Spalding University (1814) and Bellarmine College (1950). Southern Baptist (1859) and Presbyterian (1853) theological seminaries are also in the city. The J.B. Speed Art Museum and the Louisville Museum of Natural History and Science are also notable institutions.

As the scene of the annual Kentucky Derby (*q.v.*), held every May at Churchill Downs since 1875, the city's name has become synonymous with horse racing. The Kentucky State Fair, one of the oldest agricultural fairs in the United States, features an annual horse show that closely rivals the Derby in interest. Many historical buildings, including the homes of George Rogers Clark and President Zachary Taylor, are open to the public. The sternwheeler *Belle of Louisville* holds its annual race with the *Delta Queen* during the Kentucky Derby Festival. Inc. city, 1828. Pop. (1990) city, 269,063; Louisville MSA, 952,662.

Loukaris, Kyrillos: *see* Lucaris, Cyril.

Loup River, river, rising in three branches (North Loup, Middle Loup, and South Loup rivers) in east-central Nebraska, U.S., and flowing east past Fullerton and Genoa to join the Platte River in Platte county just southeast of Columbus. The Loup River itself is 68 miles (109 km) long; including the North Loup, it is 300 miles (485 km) in length. Diversion Dam, southwest of Genoa, and Sherman Dam on Oak Creek are part of the Loup power project. The river's name is derived from the French (meaning "wolf") used to designate the Skidi Indians, the local branch of the Pawnee Indian tribe.

louping ill, also called LEAPING ILL, viral disease mainly of sheep, causing inflammation of the brain and spinal cord. It is transmitted by bites of the castor-bean tick, species *Ixodes ricinus.* The disease is most common in northern England and Scotland and is called louping (or leaping) ill because infected sheep leap about. Other mammals, including humans, are susceptible, as are woodland birds. There is no specific treatment, but vaccines confer immunity.

Lourdes, pilgrimage town, southwestern France, Hautes-Pyrénées *département,*

The basilica on the left bank of the Gave de Pau at Lourdes, Fr.

Yan—Photo Researchers/EB Inc.

Provence-Alpes-Côte-d'Azur region, southwest of Toulouse. Situated at the foot of the Pyrenees and now on both banks of a torrent, the Gave de Pau, the town and its fortress formed a strategic stronghold in medieval times. During the Hundred Years' War the French captured it from the English in 1406 after an 18-month siege. The medieval castle, on the right bank of the Gave de Pau, has an interesting 14th-century keep. From the reign of Louis XIV (1643–1715) to the beginning of the 19th century, the castle was used as a state prison.

The contemporary importance of Lourdes, however, dates from 1858. In that year, from February 11 to July 16, Bernadette Soubirous, a 14-year-old girl, had numerous visions of the Virgin Mary in the nearby Massabielle grotto, on the left bank of the stream. The visions were declared authentic by the Pope in 1862, and the cult of Our Lady of Lourdes was authorized. The underground spring in the grotto, revealed to Bernadette, was declared to have miraculous qualities; and since then Lourdes has become a major pilgrimage centre. Almost 3,000,000 pilgrims, about 50,000 of them sick or disabled, go there annually. The basilica, built above the grotto in 1876, eventually became overcrowded by the increasing number of pilgrims, and in 1958 an immense pre-stressed concrete underground church, seating 20,000, was inaugurated. Pop. (1982) 17,252.

Lourenço Marques (city and province, Mozambique): *see* Maputo.

Lourenço Marques, Baía de (Mozambique): *see* Delagoa Bay.

lourie (bird): *see* turaco.

louse, plural LICE, a member of one of some 3,300 species of small, wingless, parasitic insects of the order Phthiraptera. There are two main suborders of lice, the Mallophaga and the Anoplura. The former, also known as biting, or chewing, lice, are parasitic on birds and various types of mammals. They feed on the softer parts of feathers, scales, skin, and hair and occasionally on dried blood. The Anoplura, also known as sucking lice, are parasitic only on mammals, including humans. These lice live exclusively on the blood of their hosts. A third suborder, Rhynchophthirina, consists of two species that parasitize elephants and African warthogs.

A brief treatment of lice follows. For full treatment, *see* MACROPAEDIA: Insects.

The body of a louse is flattened and is divided into head, thorax, and abdomen. The eyes, antennae, and mouthparts are all located on the head. The eyes are occasionally absent; when present they are sensitive only to light and dark. The antennae are short. The structure of the mouth depends on the type of louse. Mallophaga have mouthparts suitable for biting and chewing. Anoplura have three retractable stylets that can be thrust into the skin; blood is sucked into the mouth while a special substance is added to prevent coagulation. The thorax is small and bears three pairs of short legs that end in claws or hooks, enabling the louse to grip its host securely. The abdomen is flat and nearly transparent.

Lice spend their entire lives on the body of the host animal, with the sole exception of the human body louse, which lives in clothing. The eggs are cemented to the hair or plumage of the host and are known as nits. Many eggs are laid, and under the right conditions lice multiply rapidly; it has been estimated that a single female can produce 5,000 offspring in about eight weeks. The nits hatch in about one to two weeks. The nymphs undergo a gradual and partial metamorphosis in the course of three molts, reaching adult form in about a month.

Species of lice are parasitic on specific host species, and little evidence of transfer from one host species to another is known. Among host species, infestation is virtually universal in the wild. In domesticated animals, heavy infestations cause much irritation; animals may scratch and rub against objects to relieve the irritation, injuring their fur or hide in the process and sometimes causing secondary infections. In moving from one host animal to another, lice may spread many diseases, including tapeworm in dogs and murine typhus in rats.

The lice that infest human beings are mainly *Pediculus humanus*, with varietal or subspecific names according to sites of infestation; colloquially they are referred to as head lice (*P.h. capitis*) or body lice (*P.h. corporis*). The pubic, or crab, louse (*Phthirus pubis*) also affects humans. Louse infestations tend to be widespread under conditions of overcrowding and inadequate hygiene. Head lice spread by direct personal contact and through the sharing of hats, combs, etc. Body lice also spread by person-to-person contact and through shared clothing and bedding. The transmission of pubic lice is primarily venereal. Louse infestations provoke substantial irritation and may lead to secondary infections, particularly impetigo in children. In addition, the body louse is a major carrier of the organisms that cause relapsing fever, trench fever, and typhus. Louse infestations can be quickly cured with shampoos, soaps, and lotions that contain benzene hexachloride; the disinfection of clothing, bedding, and other shared articles is necessary to prevent the spread of the parasites.

louse fly, any insect of the parasitic family Hippoboscidae (order Diptera) characterized by piercing mouthparts used to suck blood from warm-blooded animals. Genera occur in both winged and wingless forms. The winged louse flies, parasitic on birds, are usually dark brown in colour, flat in shape, and leathery in appearance.

The most common wingless species, the sheep ked (*Melophagus ovinus*), is about 6 millimetres (0.2 inch) long, red-brown in colour, and parasitic on sheep. Each female produces from 10 to 20 larvae at the rate of about one per week. The sheep ked cannot survive if separated from its host for more than several days. The parasite is of considerable economic importance because it stains wool, reducing its market value. Some insecticides are useful in control.

Louse fly
E.S. Ross

The louse flies *Lipoptena depressa* and *Neolipoptena ferrisi* are found on deer. They sometimes attach to each other in chains; the first sucks blood from the host, the second from the first, and so on.

lousewort, herbaceous plant of the genus *Pedicularis* (family Scrophulariaceae, *q.v.*), which contains about 500 species found throughout the Northern Hemisphere but especially on the mountains of Central and eastern Asia. Louseworts have bilaterally symmetrical flowers, sometimes highly irregular. For example, the little elephant (*P. groenlandica*) presents the aspect of head, trunk, and ears of an elephant in its pink flowers, which are 2.5 centimetres (1 inch) long.

Lousewort (*Pedicularis lanceolata*)
Kitty Kohout from Root Resources—EB Inc.

The plants are semiparasitic on the roots of other plants. For this reason they are difficult to cultivate in the home garden.

Louth, Irish LÚ, county, province of Leinster, Ireland. The smallest county in Ireland, with an area of 317 sq mi (821 sq km), it is bounded on the north by Northern Ireland, on the east by the Irish Sea, on the south and west by County Meath, and on the northwest by County Monaghan. Most of Louth is part of a central lowland, generally about 200 ft (60 m) above sea level, and occurrences of glacial drift are found everywhere. Only one-eighth of the county is unimproved land, of which the largest stretch is in the mountains of the Carlingford Peninsula in the northeast. Many patches of peat bog have been cleared and the land used for pasture and crops.

The kingdom of Oriel, established in the 4th century and comprising Louth, Monaghan, and Armagh, was conquered by Anglo-Norman invaders, and in 1185 Prince John annexed the barony of Louth to the English crown. Under Richard II, late in the 14th century, Louth was included in the English Pale. The towns of Drogheda and Dundalk became important, and parliaments were sometimes held in them. In Tudor times (16th century) Dundalk was often a marshalling place for armies that advanced north into Ulster through the Dundalk gap. Notable relics of the monastic period of the Celtic Church are in Mellifont and Monasterboice; castles of the Anglo-Norman era are relatively numerous.

Two-thirds of the population lives in towns, especially Dundalk and Drogheda (*q.v.*), both urban districts. Dundalk is the county town (seat), and there is a county manager. Local agriculture is transitional between the small farm regimes of Counties Down and Armagh and the large grazing farms of County Meath. Pop. (1981) 88,514.

Loutherbourg, Philip James de, Loutherbourg also spelled LUTHERBOURG, or LAUTERBOURG, also called PHILIPP JAKOB II, or JACQUES PHILIPPE II (b. Oct. 31, 1740, Fulda, Abbacy of Fulda—d. March 11, 1812, Chiswick, Middlesex, Eng.), early Romantic painter, illustrator, printmaker, and scenographer, especially known for his paintings of landscapes and battles and for his innovative scenery designs and special effects for the theatre.

First trained under his father, a miniature painter from Strasbourg, about 1755 he worked in Paris under Charles Van Loo, the Tischbeins, and finally Francesco Casanova. He was received into the French Royal Academy of Painting and Sculpture in 1767, and at the official Salon exhibitions he won the praise of Denis Diderot.

In 1771 he went to London with an introduction to the actor-manager David Garrick, who hired him in 1773 as his regular adviser on scenic effects at Drury Lane Theatre. Loutherbourg created elaborate Romantic settings that were designed to bathe the entire stage in an atmosphere of picturesque illusion. He worked as a theatrical designer until 1785, and his set designs decidedly influenced his English-period paintings, which came to look like arrangements of stage scenery. Loutherbourg had a marked talent for ingenious dramatic effects in his paintings of landscapes, seascapes, and naval battles.

He was made a member of the British Royal Academy in 1780. The following year he turned his talents to the immediately successful Eidophusikon, a moving panorama combined with dramatic lighting effects and music. He illustrated Macklin's Bible and an edition of the works of Shakespeare. His Romantic landscapes influenced J.M.W. Turner and other English artists.

Louvain (French), Flemish LEUVEN, municipality and capital of Flemish Brabant *province,* Flemish Region, central Belgium. It lies along the Dyle (Dijle) River and is connected by canal with the Scheldt (Schelde). The city is about 16 miles (26 km) east of Brussels. It was founded in the 9th century around a fortress

Catholic University library, Louvain, Belg.
Visbach Decovisie BV/Benelux Press

built by a German emperor against the Normans, and it became important in the 11th century as the residence of the counts of Louvain, afterward (1190) the dukes of Brabant.

Louvain was a cloth-weaving centre and one of the largest cities in Europe in the 14th century, when a feud began between its citizenry and nobility. In 1379, 17 nobles were massacred in the town hall, bringing down the vengeance of the duke, to whom the citizens made abject surrender in 1383. Soon thereafter the city declined as many weavers fled to Flanders and England; the duke moved to Vilvoorde, and Brussels replaced Louvain as the capital of Brabant. What it lost in trade, Louvain partly recovered as a seat of learning, for in 1425 the Catholic University of Louvain was founded. The first university in the Netherlands, it became renowned for its Roman Catholic teaching. Louvain suffered considerable damage in World Wars I and II. During the German invasion of 1914, the university's famous library and the Cloth Workers' Hall (1193) were burned.

Louvain is still a major cultural centre and is also an agricultural market. Its industries include food processing, brewing, and the manufacture of leather goods, machinery, and chemicals, as well as sawmilling and bell founding.

The three-story town hall is one of the richest and most detailed examples of pointed Gothic and was built by Mathieu de Layens, the master mason, from 1448 to 1463. The Church of St. Peter, which originally dated from the early 11th century, was twice destroyed before being rebuilt as a Gothic structure (1425–97), and it was again damaged in both world wars. The church contains two fine paintings by Dirck Bouts and ironwork and brasswork—much of it by Quentin Massys. Other notable medieval buildings include the "Round Table" (former meeting place of the merchant guilds), churches of St. Gertrude, St. Quentin, Saint-Michel, and St. James, two monasteries, and a *béguinage* (retreat for secular nuns) with a church of 1305; the *béguinage* has been the property of Louvain's Catholic University since 1962. At nearby Heverlee is the 16th-century château of Arenberg; Leefdaal has one of similar vintage. Pop. (1993 est.) mun., 85,592.

Louvain, Catholic University of, either of two Belgian universities established in 1970 but both descended from a renowned institution of higher learning founded in 1425 in Louvain. In the one university (Katholieke Universiteit te Leuven) the language of instruction is Netherlandic (Flemish), and its site remains in Louvain. In the other university (Université Catholique de Louvain) the language of instruction is French, and the site is a newly created town, Louvain-la-Neuve ("New Louvain"), about 15 miles (24 km) south-southwest of old Louvain.

The original university was founded by Pope Martin V at the behest of Duke John (Jean) IV of Brabant, who modeled its constitution after the University of Paris. In 1517 the Dutch scholar Desiderius Erasmus became involved with the founding of Louvain's Trilingual College, "the school of the new learning in Europe," for the study of Greek, Latin, and Hebrew. During the 16th century Justus Lipsius and Gerard Mercator were also on the faculty. At that time Louvain was the chief centre of anti-Reformation thought. The forces of the French Revolution suppressed the university in 1797, but in 1834 the Belgian episcopate reestablished it as a French-language, Roman Catholic university.

The university's famous library was burned during the German invasion in 1914, and a new library was built (1921–28) with American funds and books donated by many nations. The library was again destroyed by fire during the German invasion in 1940 but was subsequently restored.

In the 1930s Louvain began to teach some courses in Flemish. Although the Belgian government had previously forbidden the use of Flemish in universities, it changed its policy in 1932 in response to growing pressure from Belgium's sizable Flemish-speaking population. In 1969, after student riots, ethnic protests, and government upheavals, the Catholic University of Louvain was reorganized into separate Flemish- and French-language divisions. Each of the two divisions was given separate legal status in 1970, and the first faculties were installed in Louvain-la-Neuve in 1972.

louver, also spelled LOUVRE, arrangement of parallel, horizontal blades, slats, laths, slips of glass, wood, or other material designed to regulate airflow or light penetration. Louvers are often used in windows or doors in order to allow air or light in while keeping sunshine or moisture out. They may be either movable or fixed. The name louver was originally applied to a turret or domelike lantern set on roofs of medieval European buildings for ventilation; the arrangement of boards now called a louver was one means of closing the apertures of this turret against weather. This original use of louvers is still current as covering for the intake and exhaust system of some ventilation and air-conditioning units.

A louvered window is one having louvered construction, whether of glass or some other material. A louvered door has some part of it filled with louvers to allow air to pass while the door is closed. Closet doors sometimes have louvers. A louvered ceiling has a system of louvers dropped below light sources in order to shield or conceal them.

Louvet, Jean-Baptiste, in full JEAN-BAPTISTE LOUVET DE COUVRAY (b. June 12, 1760, Paris, France—d. Aug. 25, 1797, Paris), French literary figure prominent as a Girondin during the Revolution.

While working as a bookseller, Louvet won fame as the author of a licentious novel published from 1786 to 1791; the work was reprinted many times as *Les Amours* [or, in some editions, *Les Aventures*] *du chevalier de Faublas* ("The Loves [The Adventures] of the Chevalier de Faublas"). In 1793 Louvet married a former jeweler's wife, Marguerite Denuelle, whom he had abducted and whom he named Lodoïska; she shared in all the future vicissitudes of his life.

Louvet became involved in the early stages of the French Revolution. He joined the Jacobin Club and, as a member of the Jacobins' correspondence committee, launched a poster newssheet, *La Sentinelle,* in March 1792, to combat the court's policy. The newssheet was soon subsidized by the Ministry of the Interior, then under J.-M. Roland, and its success helped Louvet's election to the Convention as deputy for Loiret.

He joined the Girondins in the Convention and participated in their attack on Robespierre (Oct. 29, 1792). He retorted to Robespierre's reply with a pamphlet, "À Maximilien Robespierre et à ses royalistes," which was full of misrepresentations. At King Louis XVI's trial, he voted for the death sentence with a suspension.

After the overthrow of the Girondins (June 2, 1793), Louvet fled Paris to escape the guillotine, but the Thermidorian Reaction that ended the Terror allowed him to return in October 1794. Readmitted to the Convention on March 8, 1795, he remained a republican while many other Girondins turned royalist. He protested against the excesses of the reaction after the rising of Prairial (May 1795). Under the Directory, he represented Haute-Vienne in the Council of Five Hundred.

Louvois, François-Michel Le Tellier, marquis de (baptized Jan. 18, 1639, Paris, France—d. July 16, 1691, Versailles), secretary of state for war under Louis XIV of France and his most influential minister in the period 1677–91. He contributed to the reorganization of the French army.

Early life. Louvois was the son of one of the wealthiest and most powerful officials in France, Michel Le Tellier, secretary for war and a creature of Jules, cardinal Mazarin, Louis XIV's chief minister. Indeed, after the cardinal's death many observers thought that Le Tellier would succeed his patron as first minister. Realizing that the king wanted no ambitious man to challenge his authority, Le Tellier subtly effaced himself while grooming his son as his replacement. His method was simple: he personally directed Louvois's education while planting the suggestion in the king's mind that the monarch deserved the credit for recognizing his son's administrative talents. The task was no easy one; Louvois was not a brilliant scholar, and he received no more than a superficial education at the Jesuit college of Clermont. He was, moreover, dissolute and seemed well on the road to becoming a wastrel. If the secretaryship was to remain in the family—Louvois had acquired no more than the right of succession in 1655—he had to be reformed. Consequently, his father brought him into the war department and subjected him to an iron discipline that led the youth to the point of rebellion. Yet he

Louvois, detail of a portrait by Pierre Mignard; in the Musée des Beaux-Arts, Reims, Fr.
Giraudon—Art Resource, New York City

emerged hardworking, supremely confident of his own ability, and with extensive experience in military administration.

Career as minister. As his knowledge increased, so did his position: in 1662 he obtained the right to exercise his father's functions in the latter's absence or incapacity. The same year, he improved his social position by marrying Anne de Souvré, daughter of the marquis de Courtenvaux. In 1665 the king granted Louvois the right to handle all the duties of Le Tellier's office and to sign all papers, but only in his father's presence. His first important test came in the War of Devolution (1667–68) between France and Spain over Louis XIV's claim to the Spanish Netherlands, when Louvois accompanied the king into battle. Although this campaign revealed a disturbing lack of supplies, Louvois learned his lessons well, and his competence became unquestioned. Nevertheless, Le Tellier continued to guide his son until 1677, when the father accepted the position of chancellor of France. Until this date, Louis XIV had in fact two secretaries of war, father and son, who cooperated closely. Indeed, the son consulted his father until the latter's death in 1685.

Louvois's successful career was tarnished by two acts: the dragonnades leading up to the revocation in 1685 of the Edict of Nantes, which had granted French Protestants certain liberties, and the destruction of the Palatinate. Historians have accused Louvois of originating the dragonnades, the quartering of troops in Protestant households with the intention of forcing conversion to Roman Catholicism. Recent research, however, has shown that he was not responsible for this measure. Instead, they were the work of ambitious subordinates, who saw that overstepping the letter of the law led to royal favour. Yet, although Louvois had no strong religious feelings himself, he was guilty of complicity. As an astute politician, he recognized Louis XIV's interest in religious unity and went along with the king's wishes. Personally, he disliked the methods of the dragonnades, for they encouraged a lack of discipline among the troops.

Louvois bore much more responsibility for the destruction of the Palatinate (1688), to which Louis XIV laid claim, thus leading to the War of the League of Augsburg. Louvois had never been afraid of using force in enemy territory, and now military necessity seemed to demand the destruction of the Rhineland to prevent it from being used as a base for the invasion of France. He encouraged the destruction of the major cities of the Palatinate: Worms, Speyer, Mannheim, and Heidelberg. Yet Louvois alone cannot bear the entire blame; the king also approved the measure.

Louvois's relationship with the king was often strained, particularly during the last years of Louvois's life. Louis XIV had always tried to play off his officials against one another, preventing any servant from becoming too powerful. With the death of Colbert in 1683, however, Louvois increasingly dominated affairs of state. War seemed to perpetuate itself, and every campaign made the war minister indispensable, while Louis XIV's resentment grew as Louvois asserted himself. Finally, during the difficult years of the War of the League of Augsburg (1689–97), rumours circulated at court of Louvois's imminent disgrace, and, according to contemporaries, only his sudden death in July 1691 saved him from imprisonment in the Bastille. Most historians, however, reject this theory. Certainly, Louis XIV valued Louvois's military talents too highly to remove him in the middle of a war.

Assessment. Most historians have allotted to Louvois all the glory for perfecting the French military machine. In reality, Le Tellier was the innovator; Louvois was only the brilliant administrator who brought his father's reforms to fruition. Yet Louvois had done his work well. After his death the French army remained one of the most formidable in Europe. (D.C.B.)

BIBLIOGRAPHY. Standard works include Camille Rousset, *Histoire de Louvois et de son administration politique et militaire*, 3rd ed., 4 vol. (1863–65); and particularly Louis André, *Michel Le Tellier et Louvois* (1942), as well as his earlier work, *Michel Le Tellier et l'organisation de l'armée monarchique* (1906). Jacques Roujon, *Louvois et son maître* (1934), is a popular and less satisfactory study.

Louvre Museum, French MUSÉE DU LOUVRE, official name GREAT LOUVRE, French GRAND LOUVRE, national museum and art gallery of France, housed in part of a large palace in Paris that was built on the right-bank site of the 12th-century fortress of Philip Augustus. In 1546 Francis I, who was a great art collector, had this old castle razed and began to build on its site another royal residence, the Louvre, which was added to by almost every subsequent French monarch. Under Francis I, only a small portion of the present Louvre was completed, under the architect Pierre Lescot. This original section is today the southwestern part of the Cour Carrée. In the 17th century, major additions were made to the building complex by Louis XIII and Louis XIV. Cardinal de Richelieu, the chief minister of Louis XIII, acquired great works of art for the king. Louis XIV and his minister, Cardinal Mazarin, acquired outstanding art collections, including that of Charles I of England. A committee consisting of the architects Claude Perrault and Louis Le Vau and the decorator and painter Charles Le Brun planned that part of the Louvre which is known as the Colonnade.

Louvre Museum, with pyramid designed by I.M. Pei
© Mary Ann Hemphill/Photo Researchers

The Louvre ceased to be a royal residence when Louis XIV moved his court to Versailles in 1682. The idea of using the Louvre as a public museum originated in the 18th century. The comte d'Angiviller helped build and plan the Grande Galerie and continued to acquire major works of art. In 1793 the revolutionary government opened to the public the Musée Central des Arts in the Grande Galerie. Under Napoleon the Cour Carrée and a wing on the north along the rue de Rivoli were begun. In the 19th century two major wings, their galleries and pavilions extending west, were completed, and Napoleon III was responsible for the exhibition that opened them. The completed Louvre was a vast complex of buildings forming two main quadrilaterals and enclosing two large courtyards.

The Louvre building complex underwent a major remodeling in the 1980s and '90s in order to make the old museum more accessible and accommodating to its visitors. To this end, a vast underground complex of offices, shops, exhibition spaces, storage areas, and parking areas, as well as an auditorium, a tourist bus depot, and a cafeteria, was constructed underneath the Louvre's central courtyards of the Cour Napoléon and the Cour du Carrousel. The ground-level entrance to this complex was situated in the centre of the Cour Napoléon and was crowned by a controversial steel-and-glass pyramid designed by the American architect I.M. Pei. The underground complex of support facilities and public amenities was opened in 1989. In 1993, on the museum's 200th anniversary, the rebuilt Richelieu wing, formerly occupied by France's Ministry of Finance, was opened; for the first time, the entire Louvre was devoted to museum purposes. The new wing, also designed by Pei, had more than 230,000 square feet (21,368 square m) of exhibition space, housing collections of European painting, decorative arts, and Islāmic arts. Three glass-roofed interior courtyards display French sculpture and ancient Assyrian artworks.

The Louvre's painting collection is one of the richest in the world, representing all periods of European art up to Impressionism. The Louvre's collection of French paintings from the 15th to the 19th century is unsurpassed in the world, and it also has many masterpieces by Italian Renaissance painters and Flemish and Dutch painters of the Baroque period.

The department of medieval, Renaissance, and modern art objects displays the treasures of the French kings—bronzes, miniatures, pottery, tapestries, jewelry, and furniture—while the department of Greek and Roman antiquities (which includes Etruscan art) features architecture, sculpture, mosaics, bronzes, jewelry, and pottery. The department of Egyptian antiquities was established in 1826 to organize the collections acquired during Napoleon's Egyptian campaign. The department of Oriental antiquities is most important for its collection of Mesopotamian art. In 1954 a section of Christian antiquities was established to group Early Christian, Byzantine, and Coptic works including ivories, glass, ceramics, textiles, gold, and Greek and Russian icons.

Louÿs, Pierre, pseudonym of PIERRE LOUIS (b. Dec. 10, 1870, Ghent, Belgium—d. June

Louÿs
H. Roger-Viollet

4, 1925, Paris, France), French novelist and poet whose merit and limitation were to express pagan sensuality with stylistic perfection.

Louÿs frequented Parnassian and Symbolist circles and was a friend of the composer Claude Debussy. He founded short-lived literary reviews, notably *La Conque* (1891). His *Chansons de Bilitis* (1894), prose poems about Sapphic love, purporting to be translations from the Greek, deceived even experts. *Aphrodite* (1896), a novel depicting courtesan life in ancient Alexandria, made him famous. His best novel is *La Femme et le pantin* (1898; *Woman and Puppet*), which is set in Spain. Louÿs's popularity, which rested more on his eroticism than on purely aesthetic grounds, has faded.

lovage (*Levisticum officinale*), herb of the family Apiaceae (Umbelliferae) native to southern Europe. It is cultivated for its stalks and foliage, which are used for tea, as a vegetable,

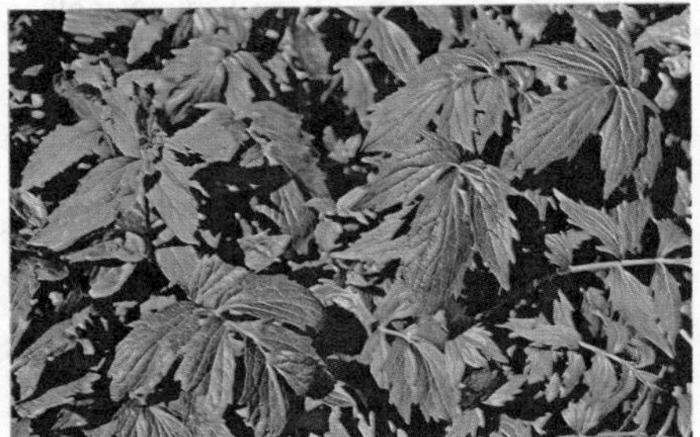

Lovage (*Levisticum officinale*)
Walter Chandoha

and to flavour foods, particularly meats. Its rhizomes (underground stems) are used as a carminative and its seeds as flavouring in confectionery and liqueurs. Lovage has a sweet flavour similar to that of celery. Its essential oil is obtained from the flowering tops for use in perfumery and flavouring.

Lovale (people): *see* Luvale.

Lovat, Simon Fraser, 11th Lord (b. *c.* 1667—d. April 9, 1747, London, Eng.), Scottish Jacobite, chief of clan Fraser, noted for his violent feuds and changes of allegiance.

Grandson of the 7th Lord Lovat, Simon Fraser persuaded the weak 9th Lord Lovat to settle the liferent of his estates on his father in 1696, but the destination of the estates had already been settled in favour of Lovat's daughters. After the death of the 9th lord, Simon Fraser forcibly married the dowager Lady Lovat and thus incurred a long and bitter feud with her kinsmen, the Murrays of Atholl. As a consequence, in 1698 Simon was tried and sentenced to death, but through the intercession of the Earl of Argyll he won a pardon from William III. It was not a complete pardon, however, and in 1701 Fraser was tried for the "rapt" of Lady Lovat. For failing to stand trial he was once more outlawed. After spending some time in London he crossed to France, where he soon made contact with the court of the exiled Stuarts.

Simon Fraser returned to Scotland in 1703 on a Jacobite mission that he betrayed to the Duke of Queensberry, head of the Scottish ministry. Fraser's treachery leaked out, and on his return to France he was held captive for 10 years. He escaped and in 1715 returned to Scotland, where he rendered good service to the government. For this he was pardoned and granted a liferent of the coveted estates. Not content with this, he strove to gain the full title, successfully securing the Lovat title in 1730 and complete possession of the estates in 1733.

Lovat hoped for greater rewards if the Stuarts were restored, and he was largely instrumental in founding (1739) the Jacobite Association. In 1740 he was secretly created duke of Fraser by James Edward, the Old Pretender. But Prince Charles Edward's failure to bring arms and troops with him in 1745 nonplussed Lovat. He forced his son Simon to join the rebels while he himself pretended loyalty to George II. After the Jacobite victory at Prestonpans, however, Lovat openly espoused the Stuart cause, although he played no appreciable part in the rebellion. After the Jacobite defeat at Culloden he urged Charles Edward, the Young Pretender, to continue the campaign; but all was lost, and Lovat was eventually captured. He was condemned by the House of Lords on March 18, 1747, and, with a great show of bravado to the last, was executed on Tower Hill, London.

Love Canal, neighbourhood in Niagara Falls, N.Y., U.S., that was the site of the worst environmental disaster involving chemical wastes in U.S. history.

Love Canal was originally the site of an abandoned canal that became a dumping ground for nearly 22,000 tons of chemical waste (including polychlorinated biphenyls, dioxin, and pesticides) produced by the Hooker Chemicals and Plastics Corporation in the 1940s and '50s. In the following years, the site was filled in and given by the company to the growing city of Niagara Falls, which allowed housing to be built on it. In 1978, however, state officials detected the leakage of toxic chemicals from underground into the basements of homes in the area.

Subsequent investigations established an abnormally high incidence of chromosomal damage among the area's residents, presumably caused by their long-term exposure to the toxic chemical wastes. Much of Love Canal was then evacuated, the abandoned land being purchased by the state of New York. The canal was capped and fenced off, and the buildings around it were razed. After protracted litigation, 1,300 former residents of Love Canal agreed to a $20,000,000 settlement of their claims against the Occidental Chemical Corporation, which had taken over Hooker in the late 1960s, and the city of Niagara Falls. Occidental faced the prospect of massive payments for cleanup costs associated with the site.

In the early 1990s New York state ended its cleanup and declared parts of the Love Canal area safe to live in. The area north of the dump site was renamed Black Creek Village, and the state began to auction off houses there.

To make the best use of the Britannica, consult the INDEX *first*

---

love grass, any of the tufted annual and perennial grasses of the genus *Eragrostis* (family Poaceae). About 250 species are native to tropical and temperate regions of the world.

Plains love grass (*E. intermedia*), sand love grass (*E. trichodes*), and weeping love grass (*E. curvula*) are forage species in southern North America. Weeping love grass, native to South Africa, was introduced elsewhere as an ornamental and now is used to reclaim abandoned or eroded areas formerly under cultivation. Stink grass (*E. cilianensis*), a weedy, coarse annual native to the Mediterranean regions and introduced into many other areas, has a musty odour produced by glands on its leaves and can be poisonous to livestock if consumed in large amounts.

love-in-a-mist (*Nigella damascena*), an annual herbaceous plant of the buttercup family (Ranunculaceae). Native to the Mediterranean region, it is now grown in gardens throughout temperate regions of the world. It grows 45 to 60 cm (18 to 24 inches) tall and has lacelike leaves. The delicate flowers, blue or white and

Love-in-a-mist (*Nigella damascena*)
Valerie Finnis

about 4 cm across, are set within a circlet of threadlike green bracts. Pinks and purples are seen in certain hybrids. The globular fruit is sometimes tinged with purple.

love seat, wide chair capable of, if not necessarily designed for, accommodating two people, whose intentions are implied in the name. The makers of early examples, in the late 17th and the 18th centuries, probably were not motivated by the amorous considerations with which later generations have credited them; their concern was allowing more space for the ample dresses of the period.

French love seat (causeuse), part of a drawing-room suite made for Saint-Cloud in Louis XVI style, upholstered in Beauvais tapestry by Michel Victor Cruchet, 1855; in the Mobilier National, Paris
Giraudon/Art Resource, New York City

From the beginning of the 19th century onward, however, chairs of this size were being produced under the name love seat, or courting chair. To emphasize the presumptions of duality, the two sections were sometimes divided (by an S-shape plan, for example) in a manner more symbolic than effective.

lovebird, any of nine species of small parrots, genus *Agapornis* (subfamily Psittacinae), of Africa and Madagascar. Lovebirds are noted for pretty colours and the seemingly affectionate proximity of pairs. (That one will die grieving if bereft of its mate is unproved.) The nine species are 10 to 16 cm (4 to 6 inches) long, chunky, and short-tailed; most have a red bill and prominent eye-ring. Sexes look alike. In the wild, large flocks forage in woods and scrublands for seeds and may damage crops. Some species nest in tree holes; the female carries nest material tucked into her rump feathers and runs bits of grass or leaf through her bill to soften them. The 4 to 6 eggs are incubated for about 20 days.

Popular in small aviaries, lovebirds are not easy to tame. However, they may be taught to perform tricks and to mimic human speech to a limited extent. They are hardy and long-lived but pugnacious toward other birds and have loud, squawky voices.

Lovebirds (*Agapornis personata*)
Toni Angermayer

The black-masked lovebird, *A. personata,* of Tanzania is green with a blackish brown head and a yellow band across the breast and hindneck; a common mutation in captivity is blue and whitish. The largest species is the rosy-faced lovebird, *A. roseicollis,* of Angola to South Africa.

Birds erroneously called lovebirds include the budgerigar (*see* parakeet) and the parrotlet (*Forpus* species), of tropical American forests.

Lovech, town, north-central Bulgaria, on the Osŭm (Ossăm) River. A rapidly developing industrial town, its manufactures include bicycles, motorcycles, automobiles, agricultural machinery, and leather goods. Once a prehistoric settlement, it was later a Roman town and then a large Turkish centre. In the twilight of the Turkish era in the 19th century, Lovech played a leading role in anti-Turkish sentiment. The national hero and revolutionary Vasil Levsky was hanged at nearby Kakrina; the Vasil Levsky house museum commemorates his life. Other historic attractions are a covered bridge that is a facsimile of an older wooden structure destroyed by fire, the Stratesh Hill, and the Devetashka Cave. The last, a prehistoric dwelling and now a park, contains a large cave with stalagmites, stalactites, an underground river, and a waterfall. Pop. (1992 est.) 51,945.

Lovecraft, H.P., in full HOWARD PHILLIPS LOVECRAFT (b. Aug. 20, 1890, Providence, R.I., U.S.—d. March 15, 1937, Providence), American author of fantastic and macabre short novels and stories, one of the 20th-century masters of the Gothic tale of terror.

Lovecraft was interested in science from childhood, but lifelong poor health prevented him from attending college. He made his living as a ghostwriter and rewrite man and spent most of his life in seclusion and poverty. His fame as a writer increased after his death.

Lovecraft, about 1934
By courtesy of Brown University Library, Providence, Rhode Island

From 1923 on, most of Lovecraft's short stories appeared in the magazine *Weird Tales.* His Cthulhu Mythos series of tales describe ordinary New Englanders' encounters with horrific beings of extraterrestrial origin. In these short stories, Lovecraft's intimate knowledge of New England's geography and culture is blended with an elaborate original mythology. His other short stories deal with similarly terrifying phenomena in which horror and morbid fantasy acquire an unexpected verisimilitude. *The Case of Charles Dexter Ward* (1928), *At the Mountains of Madness* (1931), and *The Shadow Over Innsmouth* (1936) are considered his best short novels. Lovecraft was a master of poetic language, and he attained unusually high literary standards in his particular fictional genre.

Lovedu, also spelled LOBEDU, also called BALOVEDU, a Bantu-speaking people of Northern province, S.Af. Their immediate neighbours include the Venda and the Tsonga. Agriculture is their major economic activity, with corn (maize), millet, squash, and peanuts (groundnuts) cultivated by hoe. Animal husbandry is a secondary means of food production. Cattle are also a form of currency in some social and economic transactions, and in many common daily activities beer is traditionally used to make compensation. For the Lovedu the accumulation of goods is frowned upon, and produce is consumed rather than marketed.

A Lovedu village typically consists of 20 to 80 small structures used for dwelling, work, and social activities. Such a settlement is formed to accommodate several generations of related males but also includes many individuals related through other kinship ties.

Lovedu kinship, politics, economy, and religion are united in the person of the Rain Queen. Her lineage is traced to Karanga (Shona) immigrants from what is now southern Zimbabwe. The Rain Queen is believed to provide the rain crucial to agriculture through rituals and appeals to her divine ancestors. The Lovedu expect a queen's death to result in natural disasters such as drought, famine, and disease.

Christianity has been embraced only slowly among the Lovedu, but its influences have reached deeply inside Lovedu culture, as such traditional practices as polygyny, spirit possession, and drumming and dancing have come to be deemed unsuitable. Lovedu labourers migrate from their localities to raise money for tax payments, working in South African mines and in industry.

Lovejoy, Arthur O., in full ARTHUR ONCKEN LOVEJOY (b. Oct. 10, 1873, Berlin, Ger.—d. Dec. 30, 1962, Baltimore, Md., U.S.), American philosopher best known for his work on the history of ideas and theory of knowledge.

The son of a Boston minister and his German wife, Lovejoy received his B.A. from the University of California, Berkeley (1895), and his M.A. from Harvard University (1897) before studying at the Sorbonne. After teaching at Stanford University (1899–1901), Washington University (1901–07), and the University of Missouri (1908–10), he joined the faculty at Johns Hopkins University in 1910 and, at the time of his death, was emeritus professor of philosophy there. He founded the *Journal of the History of Ideas* after his retirement in 1938, and he was a cofounder of the American Association of University Professors.

Lovejoy's most famous work, *The Great Chain of Being: A Study of the History of an Idea* (1936), which was an expansion of lectures he had delivered at Harvard in 1933, traced the history of the "principle of plenitude" (*i.e.,* that all possibilities are to be realized) from the time of the early Greeks to the 18th century. *Essays in the History of Ideas* (1948), which treated such general ideas as Romanticism, evolutionism, naturalism, and primitivism, further stamped Lovejoy as America's chief historian of ideas. His major philosophical work, *The Revolt Against Dualism* (1930), was an attempt to defend epistemological dualism against 20th-century monism. His last works were *Reflections on Human Nature* (1961) and *The Reason, the Understanding, and Time* (1961), which dealt with Romanticism. *See also* Great Chain of Being.

Lovejoy, Elijah P., in full ELIJAH PARISH LOVEJOY (b. Nov. 9, 1802, Albion, Maine, U.S.—d. Nov. 7, 1837, Alton, Ill.), American newspaper editor and martyred Abolitionist who died in defense of his right to print antislavery material in the period leading up to the American Civil War (1861–65).

In 1827 Lovejoy moved to St. Louis, Mo., where he established a school and entered journalism. Six years later he became editor of the *St. Louis Observer,* a Presbyterian weekly in which he strongly condemned slavery and supported gradual emancipation. Missouri was a slave state, and in 1835 a letter signed by a number of important men in St. Louis requested him to moderate the tone of his editorials. He replied in an editorial reiterating his views and his right to publish them. Threats of mob violence, however, forced him to move his press across the Mississippi River to Alton, in the free state of Illinois. Despite its new location, his press was destroyed by mobs several times in one year. Finally, on the night of Nov. 7, 1837, a mob attacked the building, and Lovejoy was killed in its defense. The news of his death stirred the people of the North profoundly and led to a great strengthening of Abolitionist sentiment.

Elijah P. Lovejoy
By courtesy of the Library of Congress, Washington, D.C.

Lovek, the principal city of Cambodia after the sacking of Angkor by the Siamese king Boromoraja II in 1431. In the 14th and 15th centuries Cambodia was in a state of eclipse and was relegated to the role of a minor state. After the virtual destruction of Angkor, Lovek was chosen as a new capital because of its more readily defensible terrain. It was located halfway between Phnom Penh and the lower end of the Tonle Sap (Great Lake). King Ang Chan (1516–66) chose Lovek as his official capital and erected his palace there in 1553.

In the 14th and 15th centuries Cambodia and the Tai state of Ayutthaya were involved in almost constant warfare. In 1587 the Ayutthaya leader Naresuan (also called Phra Naret) attacked the Cambodians and drove to the walls of Lovek before a lack of supplies forced an end to the campaign. In 1594 Naresuan succeeded in capturing Lovek, taking many Cambodian captives to repopulate areas of Siam ravaged in the wars with Myanmar (Burma). A usurper took control of the city until the Cambodian kings, with Portuguese and Spanish help, were returned to the city.

Lovek's importance waned in the 17th century. A new capital was established south of Lovek at Oudong by King Chey Chetta II in 1618, after Cambodia won a degree of independence from Siam.

Lovel, Francis Lovel, Viscount: *see* Lovell, Francis Lovell, Viscount.

Lovel and Holland, John Perceval, 1st Baron: *see* Egmont, John Perceval, 2nd earl of.

Lovelace, Augusta Ada King, countess of, *née* LADY BYRON (b. Dec. 10, 1815, Piccadilly Terrace, Middlesex [now in London]—d. Nov. 29, 1852, Marylebone, London), English mathematician, an associate of Charles Babbage, for whose prototype of a digital computer she created a program. She has been called the first computer programmer.

She was the daughter of the 6th Lord Byron (the famous poet) and Annabella Milbanke Byron, who legally separated two months after her birth. Her father then left Britain forever, and his daughter never knew him personally. She was educated privately by tutors and then self-educated but was helped in her advanced studies by Augustus De Morgan, the first professor of mathematics at the University of London. On July 8, 1835, she married William King, 8th Baron King; and, when he was created an earl in 1838, she became countess of Lovelace.

She became interested in Babbage's machines as early as 1833 and, most notably, in 1843 came to translate and annotate an article written by the Italian mathematician and engineer Luigi Federico Menabrea, "Notions sur la machine analytique de Charles Babbage" (1842; "Elements of Charles Babbage's Analytical Machine"). Her detailed and elaborate annotations (especially her description of how the proposed "Analytical Engine" could be programmed to compute Bernoulli numbers) were excellent; "the Analytical Engine," she said, "*weaves algebraic patterns,* just as the Jacquard-loom weaves flowers and leaves."

A biography, Doris Langley Moore's *Ada, Countess of Lovelace: Byron's Legitimate Daughter,* was published in 1977.

Lovelace, Richard (b. 1618—d. 1657, London), English poet, soldier, and Royalist whose graceful lyrics and dashing career made him the prototype of the perfect Cavalier.

Lovelace was probably born in the Netherlands, where his father was in military service. He was educated at Charterhouse and Oxford, and at age 16 or possibly a little later he wrote *The Scholar,* a comedy acted at Whitefriars,

Lovelace, oil painting by an unknown artist; in Dulwich College Picture Gallery, London

By courtesy of Dulwich College Picture Gallery, London

of which the prologue and epilogue survive. He took part in the expeditions to Scotland (1639–40) at the time of the rebellions against Charles I. During this period he wrote *The Soldier,* a tragedy never acted and now lost.

Returning to his estates in Kent, Lovelace was chosen to present (1642) a Royalist petition to a hostile House of Commons. For this he was imprisoned in the Gatehouse, London, where he wrote "To Althea, from Prison," which contains the well-known lines: "Stone walls do not a prison make/Nor iron bars a cage." He passed much of the next four years abroad and was wounded fighting for the French against the Spaniards at Dunkerque in 1646. In 1648 he was again imprisoned. During his imprisonment, Lovelace prepared *Lucasta* (1649) for the press.

The antiquarian and historian Anthony à Wood says he died in misery and poverty in 1658, but an elegy on him was printed in 1657. He had certainly sold much of his estates, but none of the elegies supports the story of his unhappy death.

The only other publication of his work was *Lucasta; Posthume Poems of Richard Lovelace, Esq.* (1659), edited by his brother Dudley, including *Elegies,* and dated 1660.

Loveland, city, Larimer county, northern Colorado, U.S., on the Big Thompson River, east of the Front Range of the Rocky Mountains, 45 mi (72 km) north of Denver. Founded in 1877 during construction of the Colorado Central Railroad, it was soon populated by unlucky gold miners who turned to farming. Named in honour of W.A.H. Loveland, president of the railroad, it was incorporated in 1881. Loveland is a processing and shipping centre for local farm products (sugar beets, alfalfa, vegetables, small grains, cherries, and livestock); manufactures include toys, electronic instruments, and mobile homes. The city is a tourist base for nearby Estes Park, Roosevelt National Forest, and Rocky Mountain National Park. Pop. (1990) city, 37,352; Fort Collins–Loveland MSA, 186,136.

Lovell, Sir (Alfred Charles) Bernard (b. Aug. 31, 1913, Oldland Common, Gloucestershire, Eng.), English radio astronomer, founder and director (1951–81) of England's Jodrell Bank Experimental Station.

Life and work. Lovell attended the University of Bristol, from which he received the Ph.D. degree in 1936. After a year as an assistant lecturer in physics at the University of Manchester, he became a member of the cosmic-ray research team at that institution, working in this capacity until the outbreak of World War II in 1939, when he published his first book, *Science and Civilization.* During World War II, Lovell worked for the Air Ministry, doing valuable research in the use of radar for detection and navigation purposes for which he was awarded the Order of the British Empire in 1946.

On returning to the University of Manchester in 1945 as a lecturer in physics, Lovell acquired a surplus army radar set for use in his research on cosmic rays. Because interference from the surrounding city hampered his efforts, he moved the equipment, which included a searchlight base, to Jodrell Bank, an open field located about 20 miles south of Manchester. Shortly thereafter, authorities at the university agreed to provide him with a permanent establishment at the site, which already belonged to the university's botany department, and to sponsor the construction of his first radio telescope, for which he used the searchlight base as a mounting.

Lovell's initial investigations with the instrument involved the study of meteors. About 15 years earlier, when radio waves had been bounced off meteors during certain meteor showers, some astronomers had noted that the number of meteors observed visually was much smaller than the number of radio echoes

Sir Bernard Lovell, 1964

Camera Press

received, an indication that the showers actually consisted of more meteors than could be seen. To determine if the echoes were meteoric in origin, Lovell used his new radio telescope to observe a particularly intense meteor shower on the night of Oct. 9–10, 1946. As the shower first increased and later decreased in intensity, radio signals from the instrument's transmitter were directed toward the shower. Throughout the evening, not only did the number of optical sightings coincide with the number of radio echoes being received, but the timing of the two rates was also as predicted, conclusively proving that the echoes were caused by the meteors. Having established this fact, Lovell could now apply radio techniques to meteor showers previously unknown because they occurred during daylight hours. Further experiments showed that orbits of meteors are elliptical, confirming the belief that these bodies are members of the solar system and are not of interstellar origin.

In recognition of his work and growing reputation, Lovell was appointed by the University of Manchester to the position of senior lecturer in 1947 and reader in 1949; from 1951 to 1980 he was professor of radio astronomy at the university. During this time, he had already begun planning and building a bigger and more sophisticated radio telescope, which, when it was completed in 1957, was the world's largest of its kind, with a diameter of 250 feet. The structure rotates horizontally at 20° per minute, and the reflector itself moves vertically at 24° per minute. While work on the telescope was in progress, Lovell published *Radio Astronomy* (1952), *Meteor Astronomy* (1954), and *The Exploration of Space by Radio* (1957).

Lovell frankly admitted that it was mainly the prospect of using the new radio telescope to track the first Sputnik, scheduled for launch by the Soviet Union on Oct. 4, 1957, that spurred his efforts to complete the instrument by that time. By supplying a much-needed boost to the prestige of the project at a time when it was being seriously threatened by rapidly rising costs, this application of the instrument guaranteed its success and Lovell's personal fame. Ever since, the giant radio telescope at Jodrell Bank has been a vital tool for pinpointing the exact locations of Earth satellites, space probes, and manned space flights, as well as for collecting data transmitted by instruments in some of these vehicles.

Because of the widespread publicity given to Jodrell Bank and its director, coupled with the latter's reputation as a popularizer of science, the British Broadcasting Corporation in 1958 invited Lovell to give a series of radio talks, known as the Reith Lectures, which were published in 1959 as *The Individual and the Universe.* When Lovell was knighted (1961) for his pioneering work in radio astronomy, 20 investigations—mostly on radio emissions originating thousands of millions of light years away—were in progress at Jodrell Bank. Some of this work is discussed in his book *The Exploration of Outer Space* (1962). His research has since been concerned mainly with cosmology; radio emissions from outer space, including those from pulsars (discovered in 1968); the measurement of the angular diameters of distant quasars; and flare stars.

Lovell received a number of honorary degrees from various academic institutions as well as honorary membership in several academies and organizations. He was elected a fellow of the Royal Society in 1955, receiving its Royal Medal in 1960. From 1969 to 1971 he was president of the Royal Astronomical Society, and he received the Society's Gold Medal in 1981. (M.A.H./Ed.)

BIBLIOGRAPHY. A good summary of Lovell's scientific work is given in *McGraw-Hill Modern Scientists and Engineers,* vol. 2, pp. 247–249 (1980). See also Shirley Thomas (ed.), *Men of Space,* vol. 8, pp. 24–28 (1968); and Patrick M.S. Blackett, *A Biographical Memoir* (1976). The building and accomplishments of the Jodrell Bank telescope are described in full by Lovell himself in his *Story of Jodrell Bank* (1968), and in *Out of the Zenith: Jodrell Bank 1957–1970* (1973). Later works by Lovell include *The Origins and International Economics of Space Exploration* (1973); *Man's Relation to the Universe* (1975); *In the Center of Immensities* (1978); and *Emerging Cosmology* (1981).

Lovell, Francis Lovell, Viscount, also called (from 1465) 9TH LORD LOVELL OF TICHMARSH, Lovell also spelled LOVEL (b. 1454—d. 1487?), English politician, supporter of King Richard III in the dynastic struggles of the 1480s; he led the first rebellion against Richard's enemy and successor Henry VII and took part in the later rising of the impostor Lambert Simnel (*q.v.*).

A son of John, 8th Baron Lovell of Tichmarsh (d. 1465), Francis Lovell was knighted by Richard, duke of Gloucester (later Richard III), during an expedition to Scotland in 1480 and was created viscount in January 1483. Throughout the reign of Richard III (June 1483–August 1485), Lovell was the King's chamberlain.

He fought for the King against the Earl of Richmond (afterward Henry VII) at Bosworth Field (Aug. 22, 1485) and, after the defeat and death of Richard, fled to sanctuary in Colchester. The following year he escaped to lead a potentially dangerous but ill-organized revolt in Yorkshire against Henry VII. When the rebellion was put down, he went to the Netherlands and, in May 1487, to Ireland with John de la Pole, earl of Lincoln, and a force of German mercenaries in support of Lambert Simnel, the impostor "King Edward VI." They crossed to England but were defeated by Henry VII's army at East Stoke, Nottinghamshire, in June 1487.

Lovell was seen fleeing after this battle but was never heard of again. In 1708 there was found in a secret vault in Lovell's house at Minster Lovell, Oxfordshire, the skeleton of a man seated at a table, on which were writing materials and a book. It is thought that Lovell died there in hiding.

Lovell, James A(rthur), Jr. (b. March 25, 1928, Cleveland), U.S. astronaut, commander of the nearly disastrous Apollo 13 flight to the Moon in 1970.

Lovell, a graduate (1952) of the U.S. Naval Academy, Annapolis, Md., became a test pilot and, at the time (1963) he was selected for the manned space program, was serving as a flight instructor and safety officer. He accompanied Frank Borman on the record-breaking 14-day flight of Gemini 7. Launched Dec. 4, 1965, Gemini 7 was joined in space by Gemini 6, launched 11 days later and manned by Walter M. Schirra, Jr., and Thomas P. Stafford, for the first successful space rendezvous. Lovell joined Edwin E. Aldrin for the last flight of the Gemini series, Gemini 12, which was

James A. Lovell, Jr., 1969

By courtesy of the National Aeronautics and Space Administration

launched on Nov. 11, 1966, and remained in orbit for four days.

Apollo 8 was launched on Dec. 21, 1968, and carried Lovell, Borman, and William Anders on the first manned flight around the Moon. This flight was the first of three preparatory to the Moon landing of Apollo 11.

With astronauts Fred W. Haise, John L. Swigert, Jr., and Lovell aboard, Apollo 13 lifted off on April 11, 1970, headed for the Fra Mauro Hills on the Moon. On April 13, approximately 205,000 miles (330,000 kilometres) from Earth, an explosion ruptured an oxygen tank in the service module. The resulting shortage of power and oxygen forced the abandonment of the Moon mission. Apollo 13's crew changed course to swing once around the Moon and then return to Earth. With the successful return of Apollo 13 on April 17, Lovell had completed over 715 hours of space travel.

In 1971 Lovell became a deputy director of the Johnson Space Center, Houston, Texas. He retired from the Navy and the space program in 1973 but remained in Houston as a corporation executive.

Lovelock, Jack, byname of JOHN EDWARD LOVELOCK (b. Jan. 5, 1910, Cushington, N.Z.—d. Dec. 28, 1949, New York City), New Zealand athlete famous for an unexpected victory in the 1,500-metre (metric-mile) race in the 1936 Olympic Games. The world record he set on that occasion—3 min 47.8 sec—endured until 1941.

After studying at the University of Otago, N.Z., Lovelock went to Oxford University in 1931 as a Rhodes scholar. The next year he set a British record of 4 min 12 sec for the mile. On July 15, 1933, at Princeton, N.J., he ran the mile in the world record time of 4 min 7.6 sec. In the 1936 Olympics in Berlin, the favourite in the metric-mile event was the U.S. runner Glenn Cunningham, who had broken Lovelock's world mile record in 1934. On August 6, however, Lovelock used his greater mastery of pace to defeat Cunningham and the rest of an exceptional field of milers.

An orthopedic surgeon in New York City from 1947, Lovelock was killed in a subway accident.

Lover, Samuel (b. Feb. 24, 1797, Dublin—d. July 6, 1868, St. Helier, Isle of Jersey), Anglo-Irish novelist, songwriter, and painter. Privately educated, Lover fled his father's stockbroking office and became a successful painter, largely of portraits. He also wrote songs, notably "Rosy O'More" (1826), which he also developed as a novel (1837) and a play (1837). His best known novel is *Handy Andy* (1842). After failing eyesight forced him to give up painting, he gave successful entertainments using his own writings in both Great Britain and North America.

Lovett, William (b. May 8, 1800, Newlyn, Cornwall, Eng.—d. Aug. 8, 1877, London), Chartist leader in England, the person mainly responsible for drafting the People's Charter of 1838, demanding electoral reform.

A cabinetmaker in London after 1821, he was self-educated in economics and politics and a follower of the utopian socialist Robert Owen. In 1829 he became honorary secretary to the British Association for the Promotion of Co-operative Knowledge, an organization that proved to be extremely important in the development of working-class radicalism. In 1836 Lovett and a number of other London radicals founded the London Workingmen's Association, which issued the People's Charter two years later.

Lovett's moderation made it difficult for him to work with the more militant Chartist leader Feargus O'Connor; thus his role in Chartism was limited, although in 1839 he was secretary of a Chartist national convention. Arrested after Chartist disturbances in Birmingham while the convention was in progress there, he was sentenced to a year's imprisonment in Warwick jail. There he and John Collins, a fellow prisoner, wrote *Chartism: A New Organization of the People.* (*See also* Chartism.)

In 1841 Lovett established the National Association for Promoting the Political and Social Improvement of the People, to which he devoted most of his energies. He wrote (after

Lovett, detail of an engraving

The Mansell Collection

1857) a number of textbooks for working-class students. His autobiography was published in 1876.

loving cup, large, two-handled cup, often made of silver, that may take many forms. In the past, at weddings, banquets, or meetings, a loving cup might be shared by a number of persons for ceremonial drinking, symbolizing friendship and unity. Loving cups are often given as trophies to winners of games or other

English loving cup with cover, silver gilt, by Paul de Lamerie (1688–1751); in the Metropolitan Museum of Art, New York City

By courtesy of the Metropolitan Museum of Art, New York, bequest of Alfred Duane Pell, 1925

competitions. The French *coupe de mariage* is a somewhat shallow form of loving cup.

low (meteorology): *see* cyclone.

Low, Sir David (Alexander Cecil) (b. April 7, 1891, Dunedin, N.Z.—d. Sept. 19, 1963, London, Eng.), New Zealand-born British journalist, one of the great modern political cartoonists and caricaturists.

A self-taught artist, Low was already contributing cartoons to a local weekly paper at the age of 11. At 17 he set out as a full-time free-lance artist, combining this work from 1911 with a post on the *Bulletin* of Sydney, Australia. Having acquired a certain notoriety with some highly successful and impudent cartoons of Australia's Labor prime minister "Billy" Hughes (*The Billy Book,* 1918), Low was invited to England by the *Daily News* in 1919. He found himself on the *Star,* however, remaining there until 1927, when he joined the *Evening Standard* at the invitation of Lord Beaverbrook. Thriving in opposition to this paper's right-wing political views, Low produced his best work. He reached his peak with the political cartoons of the years before and during World War II, which earned him world fame and the special hatred of Adolf Hitler. His Colonel Blimp also was born in the *Evening Standard.* The dramatic simplicity of his conception and the almost Oriental facility of his brushwork combined with telling effect, especially when dealing with the black-and-white issues of fascism and oppression. Much work on these themes is contained in *The Years of Wrath* (1949).

"The Conference Excuses Itself," cartoon by David Low, published in the London *Evening Standard,* May 23, 1937

By permission of the Low Trustees and the London *Evening Standard*

Thirty collections of Low's works were published between 1908 and 1960. His *Autobiography* appeared in 1956. He left the *Evening Standard* for the *Daily Herald* in 1950, but the situation was unsatisfactory and in 1953 he joined *The Guardian,* with which he had long been associated. He was knighted in 1962.

Low, Sir Hugh (b. May 10, 1824, Clapton, London, Eng.—d. April 18, 1905, Alassio, Italy), first successful British administrator in the Malay Peninsula, whose methods became models for subsequent British colonial operations in Malaya.

Before going to the Malay Peninsula, Low had spent an uneventful 30 years as a colonial civil servant on the small island of Labuan, a crown colony off the northwest coast of Borneo. There he acquired administrative experience, fluency in Malay, and a reputation as a naturalist. In April 1877, he became resident of Perak. By the terms of the Pangkor Engagement (1874), the resident was an adviser whose decisions were binding in all matters except for custom or religion. The first resident had been murdered by Malays in 1874, precipitating a war that had left nearly all high Malay officials dead or in exile. Low's appointment marked a return to civil authority.

In his 12 years in Perak, Low firmly established a peaceful British administration. He created a state council that included the principal Malay, Chinese, and British leaders, and he made use of prominent Malays at most levels of his administration. While he was careful to allow the Malays no real independence, he was notably successful in molding an effective administration from the racial and cultural amalgam he found in the state.

Low, Juliette, *née* JULIETTE MAGILL KINZIE GORDON (b. Oct. 31, 1860, Savannah, Ga., U.S.—d. Jan. 18, 1927, Savannah), founder of the Girl Scouts of America.

Juliette Low was married in 1886 to William Mackay Low (d. 1905). During travels in England, she met General Sir Robert Baden-Powell, who had founded the Boy Scouts. Her interest in the Girl Guides, the British female counterpart of the Boy Scouts, led her to organize the first Girl Guides in the United States in 1912 in Savannah. The movement grew rapidly, and Low worked to establish a national organization; in 1915, she founded the Girl Scouts of America.

As president of the Scouts, Low traveled throughout the United States, donating and soliciting funds and organizing troops. In 1919 she represented the United States at the first International Council of Girl Guides and Girl Scouts. By the time of her death in 1927, there were over 140,000 Girl Scouts in troops in every U.S. state.

Low, Seth (b. Jan. 18, 1850, Brooklyn, N.Y., U.S.—d. Sept. 17, 1916, Bedford Hills, N.Y.), American municipal reformer, university builder, and philanthropist who during his tenure as president of Columbia College transformed it from a small college on a crowded city block into a large university with an impressive campus on Morningside Heights.

Low was graduated as valedictorian of Columbia College in 1870, thereupon entering his father's prosperous importing business and becoming a leader in the silk trade. Low was twice elected mayor of Brooklyn, and his administration (1881–85) was noted for its civil service reform, administrative efficiency, public school reorganization, and advocacy of home rule.

Low served as president of Columbia from 1890 to 1901. By absorption or alliance he brought the College of Physicians and Surgeons, Barnard College, Teachers College, and other Columbia affiliates more closely into the university system. He also organized the University Council and the graduate faculties of philosophy and pure science.

His philanthropy was marked by his gift of an imposing central building on the new campus, by his support of professorships, and by his aid, through Frederick Barnard, of education for women. In 1899 he was a delegate to the first Hague Peace Conference.

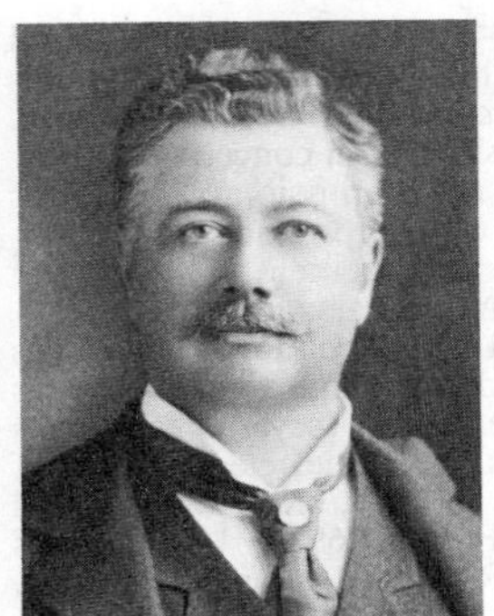

Seth Low

By courtesy of the Library of Congress, Washington, D.C.

Elected mayor of New York City in 1901 on an anti-Tammany fusion ticket, Low eliminated paternalism and demonstrated municipal administration on business principles. Failing reelection in 1903, he nonetheless continued outstanding public service, furthering education for blacks as chairman of the trustees of Tuskegee Institute (Alabama) from 1907 until his death.

BIBLIOGRAPHY. Benjamin R.C. Low, *Seth Low* (1925, reprinted 1971); Gerald Kurland, *Seth Low: The Reformer in an Urban and Industrial Age* (1971).

low comedy, dramatic or literary entertainment with no underlying purpose except to provoke laughter by boasting, boisterous jokes, drunkenness, scolding, fighting, buffoonery, and other riotous activity. Used either alone or added as comic relief to more serious forms, low comedy has origins in the comic improvisations of actors in ancient Greek and Roman comedy. Low comedy can also be found in medieval religious drama, in the works of William Shakespeare, in farce and vaudeville, in the antics of motion-picture comedians, and in television.

Low Countries, also called BENELUX COUNTRIES, coastal region of northwestern Europe, consisting of Belgium, The Netherlands, and Luxembourg (*qq.v.*). These are together known as the Benelux countries, from the initial letters of their names. The Low Countries are bordered by Germany to the east and France to the south. In 1947 the three nations formed the Benelux Customs Union, which broadened over the years into what a 1960 treaty confirmed as the Benelux Economic Union.

The Low Countries are so called because much of their land along the North Sea coast and for some distance inland is either below sea level or just slightly above it. More than a quarter of the total land area of The Netherlands is below sea level, for instance. Natural sand dunes and a system of man-made sea walls and dikes protect the polders (artificially drained flat country largely below sea level) from flooding. The Prince Alexander Polder north of Rotterdam is the lowest point in the Low Countries and lies 22 feet (6.7 m) below sea level. The principal rivers of the Low Countries include the Schelde, Meuse (Maas), and branches of the lower Rhine. An extensive network of shipping canals and waterways links the major rivers. More than 3,000 square miles (8,000 square km) of fertile farmland have been reclaimed from the deltas of the Schelde, Meuse, and Rhine rivers and from the Zuiderzee, which was formerly a shallow arm of the North Sea cutting deep into the northwestern coast of The Netherlands.

Ethnically, the Low Countries form a transitional zone between the ancient Germanic and Latin heritages of western Europe. Netherlandic (a Germanic language) is spoken in The Netherlands (where it is known as Dutch) and in northern Belgium (where it is known as Flemish), while French (a Romance language) and its Walloon dialects are spoken in southern Belgium. In Luxembourg, Letzenburgish, a German dialect, is the spoken language of the majority. Most of the population of Belgium and Luxembourg is Roman Catholic, while religious adherence in The Netherlands is equally divided between Roman Catholics and Protestants.

The population density of the Low Countries is among the highest in Europe and in the world. All three countries are highly urbanized, and some nine-tenths of the region's total population resides in cities or urbanized communities. Brussels and Antwerp (in Belgium) and Amsterdam, Rotterdam, and The Hague (in The Netherlands) are among Europe's major cities.

The Low Countries are one of the world's more highly industrialized regions and have market economies that are heavily dependent upon external trade. In order to help secure and protect their trade, they were early pioneers in economic integration, forming the Belgium-Luxembourg Economic Union (BLEU) in 1921, followed after World II by Benelux. That union allows for the free movement of people, goods, capital, and services between the three countries; coordinates their policy in economic, financial, and social fields; and pursues a common foreign-trade policy. In 1958 the three nations of the Low Countries were among the six founding members of the European Economic Community (EEC; now in the European Union).

Conquered by the Romans in the 1st century BC, the Low Countries remained under Roman occupation until the early 5th century AD, when the area came under the control of the Franks. After the collapse of the Frankish Carolingian empire in the mid-9th century, a number of political units emerged in the area of the Low Countries, including the county of Flanders, the duchy of Brabant, the county of Holland, and the bishopric of Liège. The rule of the dukes of Burgundy and then of the house of Habsburg during the 15th and early 16th centuries brought a degree of unity and stability to the area. A revolt began against the rule of Spanish Habsburgs in 1568, and the predominantly Protestant northern provinces formed a Dutch republic, the United Provinces, 12 years later. Spain formally recognized Dutch independence in 1648. Throughout the 17th century the United Provinces was one of the great commercial powers of Europe.

The Low Countries came under the rule of revolutionary France in 1795, and in 1814 they were reunited as the independent Kingdom of The Netherlands. But the mostly Catholic southern provinces, which had remained under Habsburg rule during the 17th and 18th centuries (to 1795), revolted against the north and formed the independent kingdom of Belgium in 1831. Luxembourg, for much of its history a principality of the Holy Roman Empire, was set up as a grand duchy in 1815 to be ruled as a separate state by the kings of The Netherlands. That union ended in 1890.

During World War I The Netherlands remained neutral, while Belgium and Luxembourg were occupied by German forces. All the Low Countries were overrun by the Germans in World War II. After the war, all three countries abandoned their policies of neutrality and became founding members of NATO, proceeding from there to the customs union that became the expanded Benelux Economic Union in 1960. The Low Countries are constitutional and hereditary monarchies with parliamentary forms of government.

lowboy, a small dressing table with four or six legs and two or three drawers, resembling in some ways the lower portion of a highboy

Mahogany lowboy in the Chippendale style, Philadelphia, 1760–75; in the Metropolitan Museum of Art, New York City

By courtesy of the Metropolitan Museum of Art, New York City, Kennedy Fund, 1918

(*q.v.*). Lowboy and highboy were often made to match. In the versions made until about 1750, the legs are joined by stretchers, but after that date they usually assume a cabriole shape.

Lowden, Frank Orren (b. Jan. 26, 1861, Sunrise City, Minn., U.S.—d. March 20, 1943, Tucson, Ariz.), American lawyer and politician, governor of Illinois (1917–21), and a leading contender for the Republican presidential nomination in 1920 and 1928.

Lowden attended law school in Chicago and within a few years of graduating had become a prominent and prosperous corporate attorney. Throughout his legal and political career, he remained devoted to agriculture, practicing scientific farming on his large Illinois estate. Following his election to the House of Representatives in 1906, he became a spokesman for agricultural interests and sponsored legislation designed to aid farmers.

Lowden served in the House until 1911. In 1917 he was elected governor of Illinois, an office that brought him to national attention. Lowden vigorously advocated the United States' entry into World War I, launched an extensive program to build roads and canals throughout Illinois, and instituted a series of progressive tax reforms. By 1920 he had become a party leader, but at the Republican convention that year he became hopelessly deadlocked with General Leonard Wood for the presidential nomination. On the ninth ballot, both Lowden and Wood were forced to give way to Warren G. Harding.

Lowden was offered but declined the Republican vice presidential nomination in 1924. Four years later, he was again frustrated in his attempt to capture his party's presidential nomination—this time by Herbert Hoover. He never again held public office, but he remained active throughout the Great Depression, advocating federal assistance to farmers.

Lowe, Doug, byname of DOUGLAS GORDON ARTHUR LOWE (b. Aug. 7, 1902, Manchester, Eng.—d. March 30, 1981), English middle-distance runner who won gold medals in the 800-metre races at the 1924 Olympic Games in Paris and at the 1928 Games in Amsterdam.

Lowe was a champion runner at Highgate School and also at the University of Cambridge, where he studied law. He came in fourth in the 1,500-metre race at the 1924 Olympics. After his final Olympics performance, he went to Berlin to race Otto Peltzer, who had beaten him at London in 1926 while setting a world record of 51.6 sec; in Berlin he defeated Peltzer. With Arthur Porritt (later Lord Porritt), he wrote *Athletics* (1929), which had training hints and described attitudes toward running in their day. Lowe was a tactical runner, more interested in winning than in fast time, and he used a finishing kick to advantage. Lowe was called to the bar in 1928, made queen's counsel in 1964, and named recorder of the Crown Court (1972–77).

Lowe, Sir Hudson (b. July 28, 1769, Galway, County Galway, Ire.—d. Jan. 10, 1844, London, Eng.), British general, governor of St. Helena when Napoleon I was held captive there; he was widely criticized for his unbending treatment of the former emperor.

Lowe held several important commands in the war with France from 1793. He was knighted in 1814. He arrived on the island of St. Helena, Napoleon's last place of exile, in April 1816. Many persons, notably the

Sir Hudson Lowe, engraving

BBC Hulton Picture Library

duke of Wellington, considered the choice ill advised, for Lowe was a conscientious but unimaginative man who took his responsibility with excessive seriousness. Overwhelmed by the magnitude of the charge given him, Lowe adhered rigorously to orders and treated Napoleon with extreme punctiliousness. After October 1816, the news that rescue operations were being planned by Bonapartists in the United States caused Lowe to impose even stricter regulations. The next month he deported the comte de Las Cases, Napoleon's confidant and former imperial chamberlain, for writing letters about Lowe's severity.

When, late in 1817, Napoleon first showed symptoms of his fatal illness, Lowe did nothing to mitigate the emperor's living conditions. Yet Lowe recommended that the British government increase its allowance to Napoleon's household by one-half. After the emperor's death (May 5, 1821), Lowe returned to England, where he received the thanks of King George IV but was met with generally unfavourable opinion. He later commanded the British forces on Ceylon (1825–30) but was not appointed governor of that island when the office fell vacant in 1830.

Lowe, Robert: *see* Sherbrooke, Robert Lowe, Viscount.

Lowell, city, co-seat (with Cambridge) of Middlesex county, northeastern Massachusetts, U.S. It lies at the junction of the Concord and Merrimack rivers, 25 miles (40 km) northwest of Boston. The site was originally settled in 1653 as a farming community known as East Chelmsford. Beginning in the early 19th century, this village grew to become a major cotton-textile-manufacturing centre because of an abundance of waterpower from the Merrimack's Pawtucket Falls (32 feet [10 m]) and the completion of the Middlesex Canal link to Boston in 1803. By 1824 the locality was crisscrossed by a canal system that served numerous cotton-textile mills along the Merrimack River. The community was incorporated as a town in 1826 and was named for Francis Cabot Lowell, pioneer textile industrialist. The town's growth was further sustained by the completion of the Boston and Lowell Railroad in 1835.

By the mid-19th century, Lowell had become one of the nation's major industrial cities; it was called the "spindle city" and the "Manchester of America" because of its large textile industries. As such it aroused the interest of such European writers as Charles Dickens and Anthony Trollope, who recorded their impressions of it. Its peak as a textile centre was reached about 1924. Following a period of decline and eventual relocation of the textile mills to Southern states, the city's economy became more diversified and now includes electronic, chemical, ordnance, publishing, leather, and clothing industries.

The birthplace of the artist James Abbott McNeill Whistler in Lowell is preserved as an art gallery. The University of Lowell was formed in 1975 by the merger of Lowell State College (1894) and Lowell Technical Institute (1895). Lowell National Historical Park, commemorating the first U.S. textile mills, was established in 1978. Inc. city, 1836. Pop. (1990) city, 103,439; Lowell PMSA, 273,067.

Lowell, A(bbott) Lawrence (b. Dec. 13, 1856, Boston, Mass., U.S.—d. Jan. 6, 1943, Boston), American lawyer and educator, president of Harvard University from 1909 to 1933, who led the university in significant academic growth.

A. Lawrence Lowell

By courtesy of the Library of Congress, Washington, D.C.

A member of a prominent Boston family, Lowell was the brother of the astronomer Percival Lowell and of the poet Amy Lowell. He graduated from Harvard (A.B. 1877, LL.B. 1880) and practiced law in Boston for 17 years before turning to teaching at Harvard. In 1909 he succeeded Charles William Eliot as president. Within a few years he modified Eliot's "free elective" system; devised general examinations to offset the effect of fragmented, isolated courses; and set up a tutorial plan to supplement undergraduate lectures. During his administration student enrollment more than doubled, the faculty nearly trebled, endowments increased from $22 million to $130 million, and new professional schools of architecture, business administration, education, and public health were added. Beginning in 1930 he reorganized the Harvard undergraduate body of about 3,200 students into seven separate, self-contained residential houses. His influence on American education in general is typified by *Conflicts of Principle* (1932; rev. ed., 1956) and *At War with Academic Tradition in America* (1934).

Lowell, Amy (b. Feb. 9, 1874, Brookline, Mass., U.S.—d. May 12, 1925, Brookline), American critic, lecturer, and a leading poet of the Imagist school.

A member of the prominent Lowell family of Boston (her brothers were A. Lawrence Lowell and Percival Lowell), she was educated by her mother and in private schools and traveled widely. At 28 she began to devote herself seriously to poetry, but she published nothing until 1910. Her first volume, *A Dome of Many-Coloured Glass* (1912), was succeeded by *Sword Blades and Poppy Seed* (1914), which included her first poems in free verse and what she called "polyphonic prose." *A Critical Fable* (1922), an imitation of her kinsman James Russell Lowell's *Fable for Critics,* was published anonymously and stirred widespread speculation until she revealed her authorship.

Later Lowell's vivid and powerful personality and her independence and zest made her conspicuous, as did her scorn of convention in such defiant gestures as smoking cigars. Having been displaced by her as the leader of the Imagists, Ezra Pound promptly restyled them the "Amygists" in tribute to her domineering qualities. A bold experimenter in form and technique, she remained conservative at the core, retaining conventional verse forms and in her last years severing connections with all radical schools of poetry. "Lilacs" and "Patterns" are among her most frequently anthologized poems. Her other works include *Six French Poets* (1915); *Tendencies in Modern American Poetry* (1917); *Can Grande's Castle* (1918); a two-volume biography, *John Keats* (1925); *What's O'Clock* (1925); *East Wind* (1926); and *Ballads for Sale* (1927). The *Complete Poetical Works* were published in 1955. She also wrote critical articles for periodicals and frequently lectured.

BIBLIOGRAPHY. Biographies include Horace Gregory, *Amy Lowell* (1958, reissued 1969); Jean Gould, *Amy* (1975); and Richard Benvenuto, *Amy Lowell* (1985).

Lowell, Francis Cabot (b. April 7, 1775, Newburyport, Mass., U.S.—d. Aug. 10, 1817, Boston), American businessman, a member of the gifted Lowell family of Massachusetts and the principal founder of what is said to have been the world's first textile mill in which were performed all operations converting raw cotton into finished cloth.

While visiting the British Isles (1810–12) Lowell closely studied the textile industries of Lancashire and Scotland. On returning to the United States, he joined Patrick Tracy Jackson (his brother-in-law) and Nathan Appleton in founding the Boston Manufacturing Company, Waltham, Mass. (1812; factory built 1813–14). With the inventor Paul Moody he devised an efficient power loom as well as spinning apparatus. The working conditions in his mill and the workers' housing that he built were exemplary for the period.

Lowell, James Russell (b. Feb. 22, 1819, Cambridge, Mass., U.S.—d. Aug. 12, 1891, Cambridge), American poet, critic, essayist, editor, and diplomat whose major significance probably lies in the interest in literature he helped develop in the United States. He was a highly influential man of letters in his day, but his reputation declined in the 20th century.

A member of a distinguished New England family, Lowell graduated from Harvard in 1838 and in 1840 took his degree in law, though his academic career had been lackluster and he did not care to practice law for a profession. In 1844 he was married to the gifted poet Maria White, who had inspired his poems in *A Year's Life* (1841) and who would help him channel his energies into fruitful directions.

In 1845 Lowell published *Conversations on Some of the Old Poets,* a collection of critical essays that included pleas for the abolition of slavery. From 1845 to 1850 he wrote about 50 antislavery articles for periodicals. Even more effective in this regard were his *Biglow Papers,* which he began to serialize June 17, 1846, and the first series of which were collected in book form in 1848. In these satirical verses, Lowell uses a humorous and original New England dialect to express his opposition to the Mexican War as an attempt to extend the area of slavery. The year 1848 also saw the publication of Lowell's two other most important pieces of writing: *The Vision of Sir Launfal,* an enormously popular long poem extolling the brotherhood of man; and *A Fable for Critics,* a witty and rollicking verse evaluation of contemporary American authors. These books, together with the publication that year of the second series of his *Poems,* made Lowell the most popular new figure in American literature.

James Russell Lowell

By courtesy of the Library of Congress, Washington, D.C.

The death of three of Lowell's children was followed by the death of his wife in 1853. Henceforth his literary production comprised mainly prose essays on topics of literature, history, and politics. In 1855 his lectures on English poets before the Lowell Institute led to his appointment as Smith professor of modern languages at Harvard University, succeeding Henry Wadsworth Longfellow. After a yearlong visit to Italy and Germany in 1855–56 to study, he held this professorship for the next 20 years. In 1857 he married Frances Dunlap, who had cared for his only remaining child, Mabel; and in that year he began his four years' editorship of the new *Atlantic Monthly,* to which he attracted the major New England authors. Lowell wrote a second series of *Biglow Papers* for the *Atlantic Monthly* that were devoted to Unionism and that were collected in book form in 1867. After the American Civil War he expressed his devotion to the Union cause in four memorial odes, the best of which is "Ode Recited at the Harvard Commemoration" (1865). His essays such as "E Pluribus Unum" and "Washers of the Shroud" (1862) also reflect his thought at this time.

Disillusioned by the political corruption evident in President Ulysses S. Grant's two administrations (1869–77), Lowell tried to provide his fellow Americans with models of heroism and idealism in literature. He was editor with Charles Eliot Norton of *North American Review* from 1864 to 1872, and during this time appeared his series of critical essays on such major literary figures as Dante, Chaucer, Edmund Spenser, John Milton, William Shakespeare, John Dryden, William Wordsworth, and John Keats. These and other critical essays were collected in the two series of *Among My Books* (1870, 1876). His later poetry includes *The Cathedral* (1870), a long and ambitious but only partly successful poem that deals with the conflicting claims of religion and modern science.

President Rutherford B. Hayes rewarded Lowell's support in the Republican convention in 1876 by appointing him minister to Spain (1877–80) and ambassador to Great Britain (1880–85). Lowell won great popularity in England's literary and political circles and served as president of the Wordsworth Society, succeeding Matthew Arnold. After his second wife died in 1885, Lowell retired from public life.

Lowell was the archetypal New England man of letters, remarkable for his cultivation and charm, his deep learning, and his varied literary talents. He wrote his finest works before he was 30 years old, however, and most of his subsequent writings lack vitality. The totality of his work, though brilliant in parts, ultimately suffers from a lack of focus and a failure to follow up on his undoubted early successes.

Lowell, Josephine Shaw, *née* SHAW (b. Dec. 16, 1843, West Roxbury, Mass., U.S.—d. Oct. 12, 1905, New York, N.Y.), American charity worker and social reformer, an advocate of the doctrine that charity should not merely relieve suffering but that it should also rehabilitate the recipient.

She was born to wealthy Bostonians who numbered among their friends such well-known figures as James Russell Lowell and Margaret Fuller. Traveling abroad with her parents for nearly five years, she attended school in Paris and Rome and completed her education in New York City and Boston. In 1863 she married Colonel Charles Russell Lowell (a nephew of James Russell Lowell), of the 2nd Massachusetts Cavalry, who was wounded at Cedar Creek, Va., and died in 1864.

Lowell's involvement in charity concerns began after the American Civil War, when she became active in the National Freedmen's Relief Association of New York. In 1876 she became the first woman appointed a commissioner of the New York Charities Commission, a post that she held until 1889. Her investigations there led to the establishment of the first custodial asylum for feebleminded women in the United States in 1885 and to the House of Refuge for Women (later the State Training School for Girls) in 1886. She was also responsible for the presence of matrons in police stations, a practice established in 1888.

In 1882 Lowell was a founder of the New York Charity Organization Society, a group devoted to the cooperation of charitable agencies. She guided the society for 25 years; during that time she wrote a number of papers on the theoretical foundations of relief work, especially the influential *Public Relief and Private Charity* (1884).

She was also a founder of the Consumers' League of New York (1890), the Woman's Municipal League (1894), and the Civil Service Reform Association of New York State (1895). In addition to *Public Relief and Private Charity,* Lowell published some 40 reports and addresses on welfare topics. She was also involved in such issues as the labour movement and the anti-imperialist movement.

Lowell, Percival (b. March 13, 1855, Boston, Mass., U.S.—d. Nov. 12, 1916, Flagstaff, Ariz.), American astronomer who predicted the existence of the planet Pluto and initiated the search that ended in its discovery.

A member of the distinguished Lowell family of Massachusetts (he was brother to A. Lawrence Lowell and Amy Lowell), he devoted himself (1883–93) to literature and travel, much of the time in the Far East, which he described in *Chosön* (1886), *The Soul of the Far East* (1888), *Noto* (1891), and *Occult Japan* (1895). During part of this time he was counselor and foreign secretary to the Korean Special Mission to the United States.

Percival Lowell
By courtesy of the Lick Observatory Archives, Santa Cruz, Calif.

In the 1890s, inspired by Giovanni Schiaparelli's discovery of "canals" on Mars, Lowell decided to devote his fortune and energy to the study of Mars. After careful consideration of desirable sites, he built a private observatory at Flagstaff, Ariz. Lowell championed the now-abandoned theory that intelligent inhabitants of a dying Mars constructed a planet-wide system of irrigation, utilizing water from the polar ice caps, which melt annually. He thought the canals were bands of cultivated vegetation dependent on this irrigation. Among his many books on this subject is *Mars and Its Canals* (1906). Lowell's theory, long vigorously opposed, was finally put to rest by information received from the U.S. spacecraft Mariner 4 when it flew past Mars in July 1965.

Early in the 20th century Lowell made an elaborate mathematical study of the orbit of Uranus. He attributed certain irregularities to the action of an unseen planet beyond Neptune and calculated its probable position. In 1905 he organized a systematic search for the planet by the staff of his observatory, and in 1915 he published his "Memoir on a Trans-Neptunian Planet." Fourteen years after his death the search culminated successfully in the discovery of Pluto.

Lowell, Robert (Traill Spence), Jr. (b. March 1, 1917, Boston, Mass., U.S.—d. Sept. 12, 1977, New York, N.Y.), American poet noted for his complex, autobiographical poetry.

Robert Lowell
Jill Krementz

Lowell grew up in Boston. James Russell Lowell was his great-granduncle, and Amy, Percival, and A. Lawrence Lowell were his distant cousins. Although he turned away from his Puritan heritage—largely because he was repelled by what he felt was the high value it placed on the accumulation of money—he continued to be fascinated by it, and it forms the subject of many of his poems. Lowell attended Harvard University, but, after falling under the influence of the Southern formalist school of poetry, he transferred to Kenyon College in Gambier, Ohio, where John Crowe Ransom, a leading exponent of the Fugitives, was teaching. Lowell graduated in 1940 and that year married the novelist Jean Stafford and was converted temporarily to Roman Catholicism.

During World War II, he was sentenced, for conscientious objection, to a year and a day in the federal penitentiary at Danbury, Conn., and he served five months of his sentence. His poem "In the Cage" from *Lord Weary's Castle* (1946) comments on this experience, as does in greater detail "Memories of West Street and Lepke" in *Life Studies* (1959). His first volume of poems, *Land of Unlikeness* (1944), deals with a world in crisis and the hunger for spiritual security. *Lord Weary's Castle,* which won the Pulitzer Prize in 1947, exhibits greater variety and command. It contains two of his most praised poems: "The Quaker Graveyard in Nantucket," elegizing Lowell's cousin Warren Winslow, lost at sea during World War II, and "Colloquy in Black Rock," celebrating the feast of Corpus Christi.

After being divorced in 1948, Lowell married the writer and critic Elizabeth Hardwick the next year (divorced 1972). In 1951 he published a book of dramatic monologues, *Mills of the Kavanaughs.* After a few years abroad, Lowell settled in Boston in 1954. His *Life Studies* (1959, which won the National Book Award for poetry, contains an autobiographical essay, "91 Revere Street," as well as a series of 15 confessional poems. Chief among these are "Waking in Blue," which tells of his confinement in a mental hospital, and "Skunk Hour," which conveys his mental turmoil with dramatic intensity.

Lowell's activities in the civil-rights and anti-war campaigns of the 1960s lent a more public note to his next three books of poetry: *For the Union Dead* (1964), *Near the Ocean* (1967), and *Notebook 1967–68* (1969). The last-named work is a poetic record of a tumultuous year in the poet's life and exhibits the interrelation between politics, the individual, and his culture. Lowell's trilogy of plays, *The Old Glory,* which views American culture over the span of history, was published in 1965 (rev. ed. 1968). His later poetry volumes include *The Dolphin* (1973), which won him a second Pulitzer Prize, and *Day by Day* (1977). His translations include *Phaedra* (1963) and *Prometheus Bound* (1969); *Imitations* (1961), free renderings of various European poets; and *The Voyage and Other Versions of Poems by Baudelaire* (1968).

In his poetry Lowell expressed the major tensions—both public and private—of his time with technical mastery and haunting authenticity. His earlier poems, dense with clashing images and discordant sounds, convey a view of the world whose bleakness is relieved by a religious mysticism compounded as much of doubt as of faith. Lowell's later poetry is composed in a more relaxed and conversational manner.

Lower Austria: *see* Niederösterreich.

Lower Burma, historical and geographic division of Burma (Myanmar), referring to the southern coastal and delta region on the Bay of Bengal and the Andaman Sea (as opposed to Upper Burma). It was the centre of the Mon kingdoms based at Pegu and was acquired by the British Indian government in 1826 and 1852. Under the British, Lower Burma rapidly developed into the country's principal rice-growing and exporting region. Yangôn (*q.v.*) is the largest city.

Lower California (Mexico): *see* Baja California.

Lower Canada, in Canadian history, the region in Canada now known as Quebec. Known as Lower Canada from 1791 to 1841, the region became known as Canada East (*q.v.*) with the Act of Union of 1841. *See also* Quebec.

Lower Egypt, Arabic MIṢR BAḤRĪ, geographic and cultural division of Egypt consisting primarily of the triangular Nile River delta region and bounded generally by the 30th parallel north in the south and by the Mediterranean Sea in the north. Characterized by broad expanses of fertile soil, Lower Egypt contrasts sharply with Upper Egypt, where the centres of habitation along the Nile valley are never far from the desert. Lower Egypt in late predynastic times constituted a political entity separate from Upper Egypt. But Menes (fl. 3100 BC) traditionally joined the two regions, that unification being recognized in the royal title, "King of Upper and Lower Egypt."

Lower Himalayas (Asia): *see* Lesser Himalayas.

Lower Hutt, city, Wellington local government region, southern North Island, New Zealand, about 9 miles (14 km) northeast of Wellington. It is the major business centre for the highly urbanized Hutt River valley and is within the Wellington urban area. Its heavy-industrial facilities include auto-assembly plants and oil installations; plastics, paint, footwear, and glass factories; rail workshops; and engineering plants. The city is also home to many research organizations, including major units of New Zealand's Department of Scientific and Industrial Research and the head office of the New Zealand Geological Survey. Pop. (1991) 94,540.

Lower Saxony, German NIEDERSACHSEN, constituent *Land* (state) of Germany. The second largest *Land* in size, it occupies an important band of territory across the northwestern part of the nation. Lower Saxony stretches from The Netherlands border in the west to the border of Mecklenburg–West Pomerania and Saxony-Anhalt Länder in the east. The neck of land occupied by Schleswig-Holstein, Hamburg, and, farther north, Denmark borders it on the north, while to the south are the *Länder* of North Rhine–Westphalia (containing the industrial zone of the Ruhr), Hesse, and Thuringia. Its capital is Hannover.

Lower Saxony was established on Nov. 1, 1946, by the British military government, which merged the former Prussian province of Hanover with the states of Braunschweig, Oldenburg, and Schaumburg-Lippe.

The land. With the exception of a small highland area to the south, the landscapes of the state are dominated by the great North German Plain. Much of the *Land*'s northern half consists of sandy lowlands of heath, bog, and polder, interspersed with scattered forests. In the northwest the East Frisian Islands—12 islands in the North Sea—and about 325 square miles (840 square km) of coastal land are actually below sea level and are protected from inundation by dikes similar to those nearby in The Netherlands. More than half of Lower Saxony is drained by the Weser River and its tributaries, the Fulda and the Werra, although the major settlement of Bremerhaven (at the mouth of the Weser) and Bremen itself (40 miles [64 km] up the river) form a separate political entity that is the smallest of the German *Länder.* At the mouths of the Weser and other rivers flowing into the North Sea, fertile marshes are found, mostly supporting a pasture economy. In the *Land*'s northeastern region there is a less fertile area of land partly covered with forests. This contains the Lüneburger Heath, which is noted for its old-fashioned red farmhouses and the ancient megalithic structures known as "graves of giants." It is now a celebrated nature preserve. In the south-central part of the *Land* are two sizable lakes: Steinhuder Lake (12 square miles) and Dümmer Lake (6 square miles). The highland area occupies the southern portions of the *Land* and contains the Weser, Deister, and Harz Mountains. The important Mittelland (Midland) Canal runs east-west across the south-central part of Lower Saxony.

The sandy lowlands of the north are sparsely populated in comparison to the south-central belt. The troughlike valleys of the forested southern uplands provide good-quality agricultural land, as do their foothills farther north. The latter form part of a treeless belt of rich, often windblown, soils known as the Börde, which runs in a narrow east-west zone across the *Land.* In addition to supporting an arable farming population, this area, situated on the boundary between plain and upland, became a historical nucleus for the growth of a string of small towns. Lower Saxony's climate offers mild winters, moderately warm summers, and a steady year-round rainfall ranging from 24 to 35 inches (600 to 900 mm).

The people. The population of Lower Saxony regards itself as Lower German, linked by a common ancient Saxon origin and use of the Lower German dialect known as Plattdeutsch. The latter, a dialect closely related to Dutch, Frisian, and English, is quite distinct from the official High German. Some regional literature is still produced in this form, and it remains the language of the home in much of the state. This feeling of cultural unity helps to bind together such diverse areas as the parts of ancient Hanover east of the Weser, the younger regions of Braunschweig, Emsland, Osnabrück, and South Oldenburg (which were formerly under Westphalian influence), and the Frisian portions of northern Oldenburg and Ostfriesland. About four-fifths of the population is Protestant, with a Roman Catholic minority in the state's western part.

In 1939 the population of Lower Saxony as presently defined amounted to 4,500,000. By 1946 the influx of refugees from other areas of war-torn Europe had caused an increase to 6,200,000, and this in spite of war losses. By 1950 the population had reached 6,744,000. During the 1950s more than 340,000 refugees were transferred to other states of the Federal Republic of Germany that were able to offer better living conditions. By the middle of 1968 the population passed the 7,000,000 mark. This growth was mainly caused by natural increase and, to a certain degree, by immigration. The major cities of Lower Saxony are Hannover, Braunschweig, Osnabrück, Oldenburg, Salzgitter, Göttingen, and Wilhelmshaven.

The economy. Agriculture, the traditional mainstay of the local economy, remains more important in Lower Saxony than in most other German states, with farms producing wheat, rye, oats, potatoes, and dairy and beef cattle. A substantial portion of the land is covered by forests, with small portions of uncultivated moors and wasteland. Manufacturing and services now form the base of the economy, however, and Hannover and Braunschweig are major centres with diversified industries. The *Land*'s chief manufactures include trucks and other motor vehicles, heavy machinery, rubber goods, chemicals, radio and other electronics equipment, and dyes and inks. Lower Saxony also has considerable reserves of iron ore and smaller amounts of coal and oil.

Transportation. Lower Saxony is well provided with transport facilities, and Hannover is the most important road and rail junction in northwestern Germany. The state's importance in the regional economy of Germany was enhanced by the building of such inland waterways as the Mittelland Canal, the Dortmund-Ems Canal, and a host of others. In addition, the major rivers, notably the Weser and the Elbe, are navigable for considerable distances. Many tens of millions of tons of goods pass through the ports of Wilhelmshaven, Emden, Nordenham, and Brake each year, an indication of Lower Saxony's importance in regional and world trade. The state's main airport is Hannover-Langenhagen. The scenic beauties of the Lüneburger Heath and the southern uplands, together with the seaside resorts of the northwest, attract a considerable tourist traffic.

Government and social conditions. The governmental structure of Lower Saxony is composed of a prime minister, state chancellory, and eight ministries. The *Land* is divided into four governmental districts (Braunschweig, Hannover, Lüneburg, and Weser-Ems). Lower Saxony entered the late 20th century with several political parties, the Social Democrats (left-wing), the Christian Democrats (centre right), the Free Democrats (centre left), and the Greens (left-wing). Justice is administered by means of a constitutional court, courts of appeal, regional courts, and local courts. Public primary, middle, and secondary schools are available to students, as are special schools. University education is offered by the Georg August University of Göttingen (1737), the institutes of the Max Planck Society for the Advancement of Science, technical universities at Hannover and Braunschweig, and a number of smaller institutes.

Cultural life. In common with other German *Länder,* Lower Saxony has a thriving and well-subsidized cultural life. There are state theatres at Hannover, Oldenburg, and Braunschweig. Hannover, the state's cultural capital, boasts three other theatres, among them the Landesbühne, which gives performances in more than 40 towns in the region. Other notable theatres are, in Wilhelmshaven, the Landesbühne Niedersachsen-Nord; in Göttingen, the Deutsches Theater; in Hildesheim, the Stadttheater; and in Celle, the Schlosstheater, whose plays are performed in a fine Baroque building dating from 1674. In addition, several hundred cinemas cater to more popular tastes. The *Hannoversche Allgemeine Zeitung* is the leading state newspaper. Hannover is also the centre of the agricultural and forestry press. A famous cultural periodical, *Westermanns Monatshefte,* is edited from Braunschweig. Radio and television are broadcast by the Norddeutscher Rundfunk (NDR), based in Hamburg but with studios at Hannover and Oldenburg. Area 18,282 square miles (47,351 square km). Pop. (1992 est.) 7,475,800.

Lower Southampton, town ("township"), Bucks county, southeastern Pennsylvania, U.S. It is a northeastern residential suburb of Philadelphia. Settled in 1686 by Quakers known as the Friends of Southampton, it was part of Southampton township (1703) until 1928, when Upper Southampton and Lower Southampton were created. Communities within the township include Feasterville, Siles, Trevose, and Neshaminy Falls. Pop. (1992 est.) 20,072.

Lower Tauern (mountains, Austria): *see* Niedere Tauern.

Lower Tunguska River (Russia): *see* Nizhnyaya Tunguska River.

Lowes, John Livingston (b. Dec. 20, 1867, Decatur, Ind., U.S.—d. Aug. 15, 1945, Boston, Mass.), American scholar of English literature and persuasive teacher, known for his scholarly method in tracing authors' sources and his allusive style of speaking and writing.

Lowes received his A.B. degree from Washington and Jefferson College (Washington, Pa.) in 1888 and taught mathematics there until 1891, when he received his M.A. degree. After teaching ethics at Hanover College, in Indiana, Lowes in 1902 began graduate studies in English at Harvard (Ph.D., 1905). He taught English at Swarthmore College (Pennsylvania, 1905–09) and at Washington University (St. Louis, Mo., 1909–18) and then joined the Harvard faculty, where he remained until his retirement in 1939.

Lowes's first book was *Convention and Revolt in Poetry* (1919), an account of innovations and the ensuing reactions to them in the history of English poetry. His masterpiece is *The Road to Xanadu* (1927), which traced the origins of the inspiration and wordings in Samuel Taylor Coleridge's "The Rime of the Ancient Mariner" and "Kubla Khan" in sources indicated by records of the poet's reading in his notebooks. The book was popular among scholars and poetry readers. Other works by Lowes include *Of Reading Books and Other Essays* (1930) and *The Art of Geoffrey Chaucer* (1931).

Lowestoft, locality, Waveney district, county of Suffolk, England, originating as a Danish settlement on Lowestoft Ness, the most easterly point in the United Kingdom. From

1757 until 1802, Lowestoft china, a soft-paste porcelain, was manufactured in the town. The present harbour was built in 1831 by linking Lake Lothing with the sea. After the railway came in 1847, the town grew rapidly both as a fishing port and as a seaside resort. Lowestoft has also attracted some light industry. Pop. (1981) 59,875.

Lowestoft porcelain, English phosphatic soft-paste ware, resembling Bow porcelain, produced in Lowestoft, Suffolk, from 1757 to 1802; the wares are of a domestic kind, such as pots, teapots, and jugs. Generally on a small scale and light in weight, they are decorated in white and blue or in a polychrome that utilizes a bright brick red. After 1770 transfer printing was used. The shapes were copied from silverwork or from Bow and Worcester porcelain.

Lowestoft has no factory mark; but certain idiosyncrasies help to identify it, such as inside glazing of coffeepots and, on teapots, blue strokes painted at the junctures of handle and spout with the body. Some Lowestoft pieces bear dates, names of owners, or the words "A Trifle from Lowestoft," and specimens with

Lowestoft soft-paste porcelain mug inscribed "A Trifle from Lowestoft," *c.* 1790; in the Victoria and Albert Museum, London

By courtesy of the Victoria and Albert Museum, London; photograph, EB Inc.

the mark of Meissen or Worcester are not uncommon. Porcelain made and decorated in China for export to Europe and America was confused with Lowestoft and is still erroneously called "Oriental Lowestoft" in the United States.

Lowie, Robert H(arry) (b. June 12, 1883, Vienna, Austria—d. Sept. 21, 1957, Berkeley, Calif., U.S.), Austrian-born American anthropologist whose extensive studies of North American Plains Indians include exemplary research on the Crow. He also influenced anthropological theory through such works as *Culture and Ethnology* (1917), *Primitive Society* (1920), and *Social Organization* (1948).

Lowie studied under Franz Boas at Columbia University, New York City, receiving his Ph.D. in 1908. From then until 1921 he was affiliated with the American Museum of Natural History, New York City, and, under the direction of Clark Wissler, undertook many of his major field trips to the Plains Indians, including the northern Shoshone, Blackfoot, and Crow. His most original ethnographic contributions appear in 18 monographs on the tribes he studied. Besides writing a study, *The Crow Indians* (1935), he also collected three volumes of Crow language texts. His book *Primitive Society* had a major impact on anthropology, dominating theory of social organization for nearly 30 years. Broad in scope, the work considered kinship, justice, property, government, and other topics and made much of the concept of cultural diffusion.

Lowie was professor of anthropology at the University of California, Berkeley, from 1921 to 1950, and he maintained a lifelong interest in psychology and dealt with it at some length in *The History of Ethnological Theory* (1937). Included among the ideas he advanced was the suggestion that religion and mythology may originate in dreams that have some kind of

Lowie

Neg. #125303, by courtesy of the Department of Library Services, American Museum of Natural History, New York City

biological basis. He also conjectured that cultural selection as an aspect of natural selection may partly determine genes as advantageous or damaging.

Later in life he wrote about German culture in *The German People* (1945) and *Toward Understanding Germany* (1954), the latter dealing with the effect of war on personality. Other works include *Robert H. Lowie, Ethnologist: A Personal Record* (1959) and 33 papers (1911–57) in *Selected Papers in Anthropology* (1960), edited by Cora Dubois.

Lowin, John, Lowin also spelled LOWINE, LOWEN, LOWYN, or LEWEN (baptized Dec. 9, 1576, Cripplegate, London, Eng.—buried March 18, 1659, or March 16, 1669, London), English actor, a colleague of William Shakespeare.

Lowin, the son of a carpenter, worked as a goldsmith's apprentice for eight years and then joined Worcester's Men as an actor in 1602. By 1603 he was a member of the King's Company. He is known to have specialized in the roles of comic soldiers as well as downright villains. He created Bosola in John Webster's *The Duchess of Malfi.* Shakespeare is said to have coached him in the part of Henry VIII. Lowin was also remembered for his Falstaff and the Jonsonian parts of Morose (*Epicoene*), Volpone, and Mammon (*The Alchemist*). After the death of John Heminge, Lowin became, with Joseph Taylor, comanager of the King's Company. As such, he received payments for the company's appearances in court performances. He also acquired shares as a

Lowin, 1640

Ashmolean Museum, Oxford

housekeeper in the Globe and Blackfriars theatres. At the outbreak of the English Civil Wars, after the theatres' closing, Lowin became an innkeeper at Brentford.

Lowlands, also called SCOTTISH LOWLANDS, natural region of central Scotland, south of a line drawn from Dumbarton to Stonehaven (north of which is the Highlands). Much of the area, which has a characteristic structure of sedimentary rocks with coal deposits, lies within the basins of the Rivers Forth and Clyde. The coal has formed the basis for concentrated industrial activity in the Lowlands, where 80 percent of the population of Scotland lives.

Lowndes, Marie Adelaide, *née* BELLOC, pen name MRS. BELLOC LOWNDES (b. 1868, France—d. Nov. 14, 1947, Eversley Cross, Hampshire, Eng.), English novelist and playwright best known for murder mysteries that were often based on actual murder cases.

The sister of the poet and essayist Hilaire Belloc, she received little formal education, but, because of the prominence of her family in intellectual circles, she was acquainted with the leading literary figures of the day. Lowndes published her first story at 16 and her first novel 20 years later. After a series of historical and fictional character studies—*e.g., The Heart of Penelope* (1904) and *Barbara Rebell* (1905)—she wrote *The Chink in the Armour* (1912), a psychological study of a murder-plot victim. *The Lodger,* published the following year, was a fictional treatment of the Jack the Ripper murders. Her numerous works, spanning the first 40 years of the 20th century, include a series featuring the detective Hercules Popeau and an autobiography, *"I, Too, Have Lived in Arcadia"* (1941).

Lowry, Laurence Stephen (b. Nov. 1, 1887, Manchester, Eng.—d. Feb. 23, 1976, Glossop, Derbyshire), English painter noted for industrial landscapes that express the bleakness and loneliness of modern urban life.

Lowry studied intermittently at art schools in Manchester and Salford from 1905 to 1925, and he rose from rent collector to become chief cashier at a Manchester real estate company in his long employment there from 1910 to 1952. In 1915 he became interested in depicting the industrial landscapes of Salford, Manchester, and other locations in the East Midlands. Over the next 20 years he developed a unique subject matter of urban landscapes, with a background of chimneys and other industrial structures before which crowds of drably dressed figures move in a state of curious isolation. The colour in his paintings is similarly drab but can create powerful and subtle tonal relationships. The naive elements in his style are belied by strong compositions and skillful drawing. Lowry received little public recognition until 1939, when he had his first one-man show in London. Critical opinion remains divided over his actual stature, but the originality of his artistic vision is generally accepted.

Lowry, (Clarence) Malcolm (b. July 28, 1909, Birkenhead, Cheshire, Eng.—d. June 27, 1957, Ripe, Sussex), English novelist, short-story writer, and poet whose masterwork is *Under the Volcano* (1947; reissued 1962). It was begun in 1936 and is redolent of that period, when the world itself seemed to be lurching toward self-destruction.

Lowry was the son of a prosperous cotton broker who assisted him with an inadequate allowance. From the age of 9 until a successful operation at 13, Lowry was nearly blind from ulceration of the corneas. He was educated at Leys School, near Cambridge, and, in rebellion against his conventional bourgeois upbringing, shipped to China as a cabin boy before going on with his education. At the University of Cambridge he wrote *Ultramarine* (1933; reissued 1963), a novel based on his sea voyage.

After obtaining his B.A. at Cambridge in 1932, Lowry lived in London and then Paris, where he married an American woman. He went without her to the United States in 1935, gravitated toward the movie colony in Hollywood, and then reunited with his wife before going to Cuernavaca, Mex., the scene of *Under the Volcano.* The technique of the book's narrative, with flashbacks and juxtaposition of contrasting thoughts and images, owes much to the cinema.

Returning to Hollywood, Lowry met Margerie Bonner, a writer who became his second wife. They settled in a primitive cabin in Dollarton, near Vancouver, B.C., where he did the extensive rewriting that led to the acceptance of *Under the Volcano* for publication. It was received with some critical praise but went largely unnoticed by the public and assumed the status of an underground classic until his reputation burgeoned after his death.

The Lowrys left Canada for Europe in 1954, living first in Italy and then in England. A collection of short stories, *Hear Us O Lord from Heaven Thy Dwelling Place,* appeared in 1961, and *Selected Poems* the next year. His *Selected Letters,* edited by his wife and Harvey Breit, was published in 1965. An unfinished novel, *Dark as the Grave Wherein My Friend Is Laid* (1968), throws some light on his writing.

BIBLIOGRAPHY. Douglas Day, *Malcolm Lowry* (1973, reissued 1984); M.C. Bradbrook, *Malcolm Lowry: His Art & Early Life* (1974); Tony Bareham, *Malcolm Lowry* (1989).

Lowveld (southern Africa): *see* Bushveld.

Lowyn, John, Lowyn also spelled LOWEN, or LEWEN: *see* Lowin, John.

loxodrome, also called RHUMB LINE, or SPHERICAL HELIX, curve cutting the meridians of a sphere at a constant nonright angle. Thus, it may be seen as the path of a ship sailing always oblique to the meridian and directed always to the same point of the compass. Pedro Nunes, who first conceived the curve (1550), mistakenly believed it to be the shortest path joining two points on a sphere (*see* great circle route). Any ship following such a course would, because of convergence of meridians on the poles, travel around the Earth on a spiral that approaches one of the poles as a limit. On a Mercator projection such a line (rhumb line) would be straight. Rhumb lines are used to simplify small-scale charting.

Loxonema, genus of extinct gastropods (snails) found as fossils in rocks of Ordovician to Early Carboniferous age (505 to 320 million years ago). *Loxonema* has a distinctive high-spired, slender shell with fine axial ornamentational lines. A distinct lip is present at the base of the aperture of the main whorl.

Loxonema hamiltoniae, Devonian in age, from Marilla, N.Y.

By courtesy of the Buffalo Museum of Science, Buffalo, N.Y.

Loxton, town, southeastern South Australia. It lies along the Murray River and is the service centre for an extensive, irrigated fruit-raising area. Major European settlement of the region began in 1894, and the town of Loxton, named after William Loxton, a boundary rider at a nearby sheep station (ranch), was proclaimed in 1907. Wheat, wool, fruit, and grapes are produced in the area, and the town has a winery, engineering works, and fruit-packing factories. The soldier-settlement (farming) area at Loxton, established by government loans to former servicemen and completed in 1948, is the largest in the state. A historical village at Loxton, featuring the lifestyle of early settlers, was opened in 1973. The island conservation parks of Kapunda, Media, and Rilli are nearby, and the state capital, Adelaide, lies about 150 miles (240 km) to the southwest. Pop. (1991) 3,322.

Loy, Myrna, original name MYRNA WILLIAMS (b. Aug. 2, 1905, Raidersburg, near Helena, Mont., U.S.—d. Dec. 14, 1993, New York, N.Y.), American motion-picture actress.

She was the daughter of a rancher and moved to Los Angeles in 1918, working first as a dancer in a chorus line, then as a bit player in the 1925 production of *Ben-Hur.* Her small role as an exotic mistress fixed her film style for the next decade. In her subsequent and increasingly important roles, Loy personified the foreign vamp for American audiences. It was not until she appeared in the successful comedy/mystery *The Thin Man* (1934) that she was able to break out of her screen mold. With her performance as Nora Charles she received both critical and popular acclaim, and a number of sequels were made.

During World War II Loy worked with the American Red Cross, and following the war she served as a representative to UNESCO. After 1945 she remained active in films, theatre, and television; however, she played mostly character roles after 1960. Her many films included *The Best Years of Our Lives* (1946), *Mr. Blandings Builds His Dream House* (1948), *The Red Pony* (1949), *Lonelyhearts* (1958), *The April Fools* (1969), and *Just Tell Me What You Want* (1980).

Loyal Forty-seven Rōnin, The (Japanese play cycle): *see* Chūshingura.

Loyal League (American Civil War): *see* Union League.

Loyal Publication Society, either of two groups, one in New York and one in New England, that during the American Civil War published pamphlets and broadsides supporting the Union and blasting Copperheads, or Southern sympathizers.

In addition to distributing materials "of unquestionable loyalty," the societies were active in both state and national politics, allied with the Republican Party. Their main purpose, however, was propagandistic, and the larger Loyal Publication Society of New York ultimately published 900,000 copies of 90 pamphlets. The smaller New England Loyal Publication Society, based in Boston, worked with its counterpart in New York in distributing a wide variety of pro-Union tracts.

Loyalist, also called TORY, colonist loyal to Great Britain during the American Revolution. Loyalists constituted about one-third of the population of the American colonies during that conflict. They were not confined to any particular group or class, but their numbers were strongest among the following groups: officeholders and others who served the British crown and had a vested interest in upholding its authority; Anglican clergymen and their parishioners in the North, who had likewise taken vows of allegiance and obedience to the king; Quakers, members of German religious sects, and other conscientious pacifists; and large landholders, especially in the North, and wealthy merchant groups in the cities whose businesses and property were affected by the war. The most common trait among all Loyalists was an innate conservatism coupled with a deep devotion to the mother country and the crown. Many Loyalists at first urged moderation in the struggle for colonial rights and were only driven into active Loyalism by radical fellow colonists who denounced as Tories all who would not join them. Loyalists were most numerous in the South, New York, and Pennsylvania, but they did not constitute a majority in any colony. New York was their stronghold and had more than any other colony. New England had fewer Loyalists than any other section.

The Loyalists did not rise as a body to support the British army, but individuals did join the army or form their own guerrilla units. New York alone furnished about 23,000 Loyalist troops, perhaps as many as all the other colonies combined. The Loyalist fighters aroused a vengeful hatred among the Patriots (as the American Revolutionaries called themselves), and when taken in battle they were treated as traitors. George Washington detested them, saying as early as 1776 that "they were even higher and more insulting in their opposition than the regulars."

Congress recommended repressive measures against the Loyalists, and all states passed severe laws against them, usually forbidding them from holding office, disenfranchising them, and confiscating or heavily taxing their property. Beginning in March 1776, approximately 100,000 Loyalists fled into exile. (This was between 3 and 4 percent of the total number of settlers in the colonies, which is estimated at 2,500,000–3,000,000 during the Revolutionary period.) The largest portion of those who fled ultimately went to Canada, where the British government provided them with asylum, compensating them for losses in property and income and paying pensions to Loyalist officers. Public sentiment in the United States against the Loyalists died down significantly after government began under the new U.S. Constitution in 1789, and the remaining state laws against them were repealed after the War of 1812.

Loyalty Islands, French ÎLES LOYAUTÉ, limestone coral group in the French overseas territory of New Caledonia, southwestern Pacific Ocean. Comprising the islands of Ouvéa, Lifou, and Maré (*qq.v.*), the group has a total area of 761 square miles (1,970 square km) and nowhere rises higher than 300 feet (90 m). The islands were sighted by Europeans early in the 19th century and were long a focus of Anglo-French conflict. Annexed by France in 1853, they were attached administratively to New Caledonia in 1946.

Yams, taro, bananas, and coconuts are grown, with copra as the chief export. The Loyalty islanders, who are Melanesian, speak several languages. Pop. (1989 prelim.) 17,912.

Loyd, Sam, byname of SAMUEL LOYD (b. Jan. 31, 1841, Philadelphia, Pa., U.S.—d. April 10, 1911, New York, N.Y.), American puzzlemaker who was best known for composing chess problems and games, including Parcheesi.

Loyd studied engineering and took a license as a steam and mechanical engineer, but he engaged in a variety of business enterprises until he was able to earn a living exclusively from his chess problems and puzzles.

Loyd began inventing chess problems when he was 14 years old, and three years later he was recognized as the foremost American at this skill. From 1860 he was problem editor of the magazine *Chess Monthly,* edited by leading Chess master Paul C. Morphy. He contributed to *American Chess-Nuts* in 1868 and in 1878 published his own book of problems, *Chess Strategy.* He later moved from Chess problems to puzzles and games, inventing The Trick Donkeys, Pigs in Clover, and Parcheesi. His son joined him in his puzzle adventures, and about 1896, they began publishing a puzzle column that was widely syndicated in newspapers and magazines. The Loyd puzzles are remarkable for their disguised use of simple algebraic formulas.

Loyola, Saint Ignatius of, Spanish SAN IGNACIO DE LOYOLA, baptized IÑIGO (b. 1491, Loyola, Castile—d. July 31, 1556, Rome; canonized March 12, 1622; feast day July 31), Spanish theologian and one of the most influential figures in the Catholic Reformation

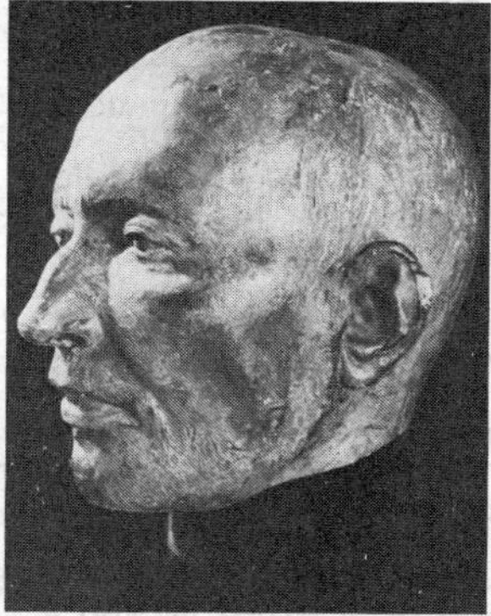

St. Ignatius of Loyola, death mask
By courtesy of the Archivum Romanum Societatis Iesu

of the 16th century, founder of the Society of Jesus (Jesuits) in Paris in 1534.

Early life. He was born in the ancestral castle of the Loyolas in the Basque province of Guipúzcoa. The youngest son of a noble and wealthy family, Ignatius became, in 1506, a page in the service of a relative, Juan Velázquez de Cuéllar, treasurer of the kingdom of Castile. In 1517 Ignatius became a knight in the service of another relative, Antonio Manrique de Lara, duke of Nájera and viceroy of Navarre, who employed him in military undertakings and on a diplomatic mission.

While defending the citadel of Pamplona against the French, Ignatius was hit by a cannonball on May 20, 1521, sustaining a bad fracture of his right leg and damage to his left. This event closed the first period of his life, during which he was, on his own admission, "a man given to the vanities of the world, whose chief delight consisted in martial exercises, with a great and vain desire to win renown" (*Autobiography,* 1). Although his morals were far from stainless, Ignatius was in his early years a proud rather than sensual man. He stood just under five feet two inches in height and had in his youth an abundance of hair of a reddish tint. He delighted in music, especially sacred hymns.

Spiritual awakening. It is the second period of Ignatius' life, in which he turned toward a saintly life, that is the better known. After treatment at Pamplona, he was transported to Loyola in June 1521. There his condition became so serious that for a time it was thought he would die. When out of danger, he chose to undergo painful surgery to correct blunders made when the bone was first set. The result was a convalescence of many weeks, during which he read a life of Christ and a book on the lives of the saints, the only reading matter the castle afforded. He also passed time in recalling tales of martial valour and in thinking of a great lady whom he admired. In the early stages of this enforced reading, his attention was centred on the saints. The version of the lives of the saints he was reading contained prologues to the various lives by a Cistercian monk who conceived the service of God as a holy chivalry. This view of life profoundly moved and attracted Ignatius. After much reflection, he resolved to imitate the holy austerities of the saints in order to do penance for his sins.

In February 1522 Ignatius bade farewell to his family and went to Montserrat, a place of pilgrimage in northeastern Spain. He spent three days in confessing the sins of his whole life, hung his sword and dagger near the statue of the Virgin Mary as symbols of his abandoned ambitions, and, clothed in sackcloth, spent the night of March 24 in prayer. The next day he went to Manresa, a town 30 miles from Barcelona, to pass the decisive months of his career, from March 25, 1522, to mid-February 1523. He lived as a beggar, ate and drank sparingly, scourged himself, and for a time neither combed nor trimmed his hair and did not cut his nails. Daily he attended mass and spent seven hours in prayer, often in a cave outside Manresa.

The sojourn at Manresa was marked by spiritual trials as well as by joy and interior light. While sitting one day on the banks of Cardoner River, "the eyes of his understanding began to open and, without seeing any vision, he understood and knew many things, as well spiritual things as things of the faith" (*Autobiography,* 30). At Manresa, he sketched the fundamentals of his little book *The Spiritual Exercises.* Until the close of his studies at Paris (1535), he continued to make some additions to it. Thereafter there were only minor changes until Pope Paul III approved it in 1548. *The Spiritual Exercises* is a manual of spiritual arms containing a vital and dynamic system of spirituality. During his lifetime, Ignatius used it to give spiritual retreats to others, especially to his followers. The booklet is indeed an adaptation of the Gospels for such retreats.

The remainder of the decisive period was devoted to a pilgrimage to Jerusalem. Ignatius left Barcelona in March 1523 and, travelling by way of Rome, Venice, and Cyprus, reached Jerusalem on September 4. He would have liked to have settled there permanently, but the Franciscan custodians of the shrines of the Latin church would not listen to this plan. After visiting Bethany, the Mount of Olives, Bethlehem, the Jordan, and Mount of Temptation, Ignatius left Palestine on October 3 and, passing through Cyprus and Venice, reached Barcelona in March 1524.

Period of study. "After the pilgrim had learned that it was God's will that he should not stay in Jerusalem, he pondered in his heart what he should do and finally decided to study for a time in order to be able to help souls" (*Autobiography,* 50). So Ignatius, who in his *Autobiography* refers to himself as the "pilgrim," describes his decision to acquire as good an education as the circumstances permitted. He probably could have reached the priesthood in a few years. He chose to defer this goal for more than 12 years and to undergo the drudgery of the classroom at an age when most men have long since finished their training. Perhaps his military career had taught him the value of careful preparation. At any rate, he was convinced that a well-trained man would accomplish in a short time what one without training would never accomplish.

Ignatius studied at Barcelona for nearly two years. In 1526 he transferred to Alcalá. By this time he had acquired followers, and the little group had assumed a distinctive garb; but Ignatius soon fell under suspicion of heresy, was imprisoned and tried. Although found innocent, he left Alcalá for Salamanca. There not only was he imprisoned but his companions were also apprehended. Again he won acquittal but was forbidden to teach until he had finished his studies. This prohibition induced Ignatius to leave his disciples and Spain.

He arrived in Paris on Feb. 2, 1528, and remained there as a student until 1535. He lived on alms, and in 1528 and 1529 he went to Flanders to beg from Spanish merchants. In 1530 he went to England for the same purpose. In Paris, Ignatius soon had another group of disciples whose manner of living caused such a stir that he had to explain himself to the religious authorities. This episode finally convinced him that he must abstain from public religious endeavour until he reached the priesthood.

During his long stay in the French capital, Ignatius won the coveted M.A. of the famous university. He also gathered the companions who were to be cofounders with him of the Society of Jesus, among them Francis Xavier, who became one of the order's greatest missionaries. On Aug. 15, 1534, he led the little band to nearby Montmartre, where they bound themselves by vows of poverty, chastity, and obedience, though as yet without the express purpose of founding a religious order.

Ordination. Early in 1535, before the completion of his theological studies, Ignatius left Paris for reasons of health. He spent more than six months in Spain and then went to Bologna and Venice where he studied privately. On Jan. 8, 1537, his Parisian companions joined him in Venice. All were eager to make the pilgrimage to Jerusalem, but war between Venice and the Turkish Empire rendered this impossible. Ignatius and most of his companions were ordained on June 24, 1537. There followed 18 months during which they acquired experience in the ministry while also devoting much time to prayer. During these months, although he did not as yet say mass, Ignatius had one of the decisive experiences of his life. He related to his companions that on a certain day, while in prayer, he seemed to see Christ with the cross on his shoulder and beside him the Eternal Father, who said, "I wish you to take this man for your servant," and Jesus took him and said, "My will is that you should serve us." On Christmas Day 1538 Ignatius said his first mass at the Church of St. Mary Major in Rome. This ends the third period of his life, that of his studies, which were far from a formality. Diego Laínez, a cofounder of the Society of Jesus and an intelligent observer, judged that despite handicaps Ignatius had as great diligence as any of his fellow students. He certainly became in the difficult field of ascetic and mystical theology one of the surest of Catholic guides.

Founding of the Jesuit order. The final period of Loyola's life was spent in Rome or its vicinity. In 1539 the companions decided to form a permanent union, adding a vow of obedience to a superior elected by themselves to the vows of poverty, chastity, and obedience to the Roman pontiff that they had already taken. In 1540 Pope Paul III approved the plan of the new order. Loyola was the choice of his companions for the office of general.

The Society of Jesus developed rapidly under his hand. When he died there were about 1,000 Jesuits divided into 12 administrative units, called provinces. Three of these were in Italy, a like number in Spain, two in Germany, one in France, one in Portugal, and two overseas in India and Brazil. Loyola was, in his last years, much occupied with Germany and India, to which he sent his famous followers Peter Canisius and Francis Xavier. He also dispatched missionaries to the Congo and to Ethiopia. In 1546 Loyola secretly received into the society Francis Borgia, duke of Gandía and viceroy of Catalonia. When knowledge of this became public four years later it created a sensation. Borgia organized the Spanish provinces of the order and became third general.

Loyola left his mark on Rome. He founded

the Roman College, embryo of the Gregorian University, and the Germanicum, a seminary for German candidates for the priesthood. He also established a home for fallen women and one for converted Jews.

The Jesuit Constitutions. Although at first Loyola had been somewhat opposed to placing his companions in colleges as educators of youth, he came in the course of time to recognize the value of the educational apostolate and in his last years was busily engaged in laying the foundations of the system of schools that was to stamp his order as largely a teaching order.

Probably the most important work of his later years was the composition of the *Constitutions* of the Society of Jesus. In them he decreed that his followers were to abandon some of the traditional forms of the religious life, such as chanting the divine office, physical punishments, and penitential garb, in favour of greater adaptability and mobility; they also renounced chapter government by the members of the order in favour of a more authoritative regime, and their vows were generally of such a nature that separation from the order was easier than had been usual in similar Catholic groups. The Society of Jesus was to be above all an order of apostles "ready to live in any part of the world where there was hope of God's greater glory and the good of souls." Loyola insisted on long and thorough training of his followers. Convinced that women are better ruled by women than by men, after some hesitation he resolutely excluded a female branch of the order. The special vow of obedience to the pope was called by Loyola "the cause and principal foundation" of his society.

While general of the order, Loyola was frequently sick. In January 1551 he became so ill that he begged his associates, though to no purpose, to accept his resignation as superior. Despite his condition he continued to direct the order until his death in July 1556. Since his days at Manresa, Loyola had practiced a form of prayer that was later published in *The Spiritual Exercises* and appears to have rivaled that of the greatest mystics.

Ignatius Loyola was beatified by Pope Paul V in 1609 and canonized by Pope Gregory XV in 1622. In 1922 he was declared patron of all spiritual retreats by Pope Pius XI. His achievements and those of his followers form a chapter in the history of the Roman Catholic church that cannot be neglected by those who desire to understand that institution. English translations of Ignatius' two most important works are *The Spiritual Exercises of St. Ignatius,* trans. by L.J. Puhl (1951); and *The Constitutions of the Society of Jesus: Translated, with an Introduction and a Commentary,* by G.E. Ganss (1970). (E.A.R./Ed.)

BIBLIOGRAPHY. The most authoritative life in English is P. Dudon, *St. Ignace de Loyola* (1949). Other excellent biographies are Francis Thompson, *St. Ignatius Loyola,* rev. and ed. by J.H. Pollen (1962); J. Brodrick, *St. Ignatius of Loyola: The Pilgrim Years* (1956); and T. Maynard, *St. Ignatius and the Jesuits* (1956), a simpler work. L. von Matt and H. Rahner, *St. Ignatius of Loyola* (1956), is a pictorial biography. Special aspects of Ignatius' thought are examined by H. Rahner, *The Spirituality of St. Ignatius Loyola* (1953); and G.E. Ganss, *St. Ignatius' Idea of a Jesuit University* (1956).

Lozère, *département,* Languedoc-Roussillon *région,* southern France, in the southeastern part of the Massif Central astride the Atlantic-Mediterranean watershed. One of the smallest *départements,* the most mountainous and the least populated, it has an area of 1,995 square miles (5,167 square km). It was created from the district of Gévaudan and from dependencies of the former dioceses of Alès and Uzès, all in the historic province of Languedoc. The name was derived from Mount Lozère, 5,574 feet (1,699 m), the site of a national park southwest of the old cathedral town of Mende (*q.v.*), the departmental capital and the only sizable locality.

Lozère is divided into three distinct regions: in the southeast, the Cévennes mountains, capped by Montagne de l'Aigoual, 5,134 feet (1,565 m), site of a national park; in the southwest, the high plateaus, or Causses, of Sauveterre and Méjan, separated by the magnificent Tarn Gorges; and in the northern half, the wooded granite mountains of the Haut Gévaudan. All the rivers and streams—more than 400—have their sources in the *département* itself. The Allier River, which rises in the Maure de la Gardille range, flows for 25 miles (40 km) along the northeastern border; the Tarn River rises south of Mount Lozère; and the Lot River rises south of the Montagne du Goulet and flows east through Mende. Several small rivers, including the Chassezac, one of the wildest torrents in France, flow into the Rhône Basin via the Ardèche River and the Gard River.

The climate of Lozère is wet, severe, and characterized by sharp contrasts. The area has little industry, and farming, devoted almost entirely to sheep and cattle, is difficult except in the valleys. Increasing tourism has not arrested the exodus of the rural populace. The *département* is divided into the *arrondissements* of Mende and Florac and is in the educational division of Montpellier. Pop. (1988 est.) 72,200.

Consult
the
INDEX
first

Lozi, also called MALOZI, or BAROTSE, formerly ALUYI, a complex of about 25 peoples of about 6 cultural groups inhabiting western Zambia, the area formerly known as Barotseland in Zambia and speaking Benue-Congo languages of the Niger-Congo family.

Formerly, the groups were all called Barotse as subjects of the paramount chief of the dominant Barotse tribe; the Barotse nation extended into other parts of Zambia, Angola, and the Caprivi strip of Namibia. The Barotse tribe, originally known as the Aluyi, was conquered in 1838 by the Kololo of South Africa; in Kololo speech "Aluyi" became "Barotse." In 1864 the Aluyi defeated the Kololo, and "Barotse" has since become "Lozi" ("Malozi"), referring to both the dominant tribe and all its subjects. The dominant tribe occupies the floodplain of the Zambezi River, and the people move between two sets of villages, in the plain and on the margin, in response to the annual flooding. They have made skillful use of varying water levels and of different soil and grass conditions to develop an elaborate economy of agriculture, animal husbandry, and fishing. The necessity for cooperation to exploit these resources has produced real social cohesion among the Lozi, but they have always been short of labour and have constantly imported people from their subject tribes and serfs from raided foreigners. These serfs had substantial rights in Lozi law, within a social hierarchy of aristocrats, commoners, and serfs. Authority was divided among various rulers at the main and other capitals, and in an elaborate system of councils at each capital.

LPG, also called LP GAS: *see* liquefied petroleum gas.

LSD, abbreviation of LYSERGIC ACID DIETHYLAMIDE, also called LYSERGIDE, potent synthetic hallucinogenic drug that can be derived from the ergot alkaloids (as ergotamine and ergonovine, principal constituents of ergot, the grain deformity and toxic infectant of flour caused by the fungus of grasses, *Claviceps purpurea*). LSD usually is prepared in the laboratory by chemical synthesis. Its basic chemical structure is similar to that of the ergot alkaloids. LSD also is related structurally to several other drugs (*e.g.,* bufotenine, psilocybin, harmine, and ibogaine); all can block the action of serotonin (the indole amine transmitter of nerve impulses) in brain tissue.

LSD produces marked deviations from normal behaviour, which probably are consequences of its ability to inhibit the action of serotonin, though the mechanism of the drug remains uncertain. Because of that ability LSD was used experimentally in medicine as a psychotomimetic agent to induce mental states that were believed to resemble those of actual psychotic diseases (primarily the schizophrenias).

After administration, LSD can be absorbed readily from any mucosal surface, even from the ear, and acts within 30 to 60 minutes. Its effects usually last for 8 to 10 hours; occasionally some effects persist for several days. Two serious side effects are prolongation of and transient reappearance of the psychotic reaction.

Since LSD is not an approved drug, its therapeutic applications are regarded as experimental. In the 1960s LSD was proposed for use in the treatment of neuroses, especially for patients who were recalcitrant to more conventional psychotherapeutic procedures. LSD also was tried as a treatment for alcoholism and was used to reduce the suffering of terminally ill cancer patients. The drug also was studied as an adjunct in the treatment of narcotic addiction, of autistic children, and of the so-called psychopathic personality. None of these claims were substantiated by the early 1990s, and researchers found no clinical value in the use of LSD.

The use of LSD outside of the laboratory may be dangerous. Mood shifts, time and space distortions, and impulsive behaviour are complications especially hazardous to an individual who takes the drug. The individual may become increasingly suspicious of the intentions and motives of those around him and may act aggressively against them.

Legitimate use of LSD declined markedly in the mid-1960s. In the United States, manufacture, possession, sale, transfer, and use of LSD came under the restrictions of the Drug Abuse Control Amendment of 1965. In 1966 the only authorized manufacturer of LSD in the United States withdrew the drug from the market and transferred its supplies to the federal government. Research projects have continued under the supervision of the National Institute of Mental Health, a governmental agency. Black market LSD accounts for much of the remaining use of the drug.

LTH (luteotropic hormone): *see* prolactin.

Lu, Pinyin LU, one of the vassal states of ancient China that originated during the Western Chou, but came to prominence in the Warring States period of the Eastern Chou (770–221 BC). One of the smaller of the warring states, Lu is known as the birthplace of Confucius. The famous *Ch'un-ch'iu* ("Spring and Autumn [Annals]") is a chronological record of the major events that occurred at the court of the state of Lu between 722 and 481 BC. For almost 2,000 years this work has been revered as one of the great Chinese Classics, mainly because it has been claimed that Confucius edited the work. As a result of the continued interest in the *Ch'un-ch'iu,* more is known about Lu than about most of the other states of the period.

The rulers of Lu, which was located in the southern portion of the present Chinese province of Shantung, traced their ancestry back to the founders of the Chou dynasty (11th century BC). It is thought that Lu began as a vassal state of the Chou; Lu rulers continued to acknowledge the traditions and customs of the Western Chou court as late as the time of Confucius (551–479 BC). It was in this milieu that Confucius developed his teachings that the solution to the problems of the present was for men to return to the wisdom of the past. The rulers of Lu, however, did not heed Confucius' advice and never employed him in a responsible government position. In 249 BC the state was finally extinguished by Chu, one of the larger of the warring kingdoms then fighting for supremacy in China.

Lú (Ireland): *see* Louth.

Lu-an (China): *see* Ch'ang-chih.

Lü Buwei (Chinese minister): *see* Lü Pu-wei.

Lu Chi, Pinyin LU JI (b. 261, southern China—d. 303, China), renowned Chinese literary critic and the first important writer to emerge from the kingdom of Wu (222–280).

Grandson of the great Lu Hsun, one of the founders of the Wu kingdom, and fourth son of Lu K'ang, the Wu commander in chief, Lu Chi remained in obscurity for 10 years after the Wu kingdom was subjugated by the Chin dynasty (265–317). In 290 Lu Chi traveled to Lo-yang, the imperial capital, where he was warmly received by the literary elite and appointed president of the national university. He eventually rose to higher official posts and became a member of the nobility; but because of his later involvement in political plots to overthrow the emperor and attack the capital, Lu Chi was executed in 303.

Although Lu Chi left a considerable body of lyric poetry in imitative style, he is better known as a writer of *fu,* an intricately structured form of poetry mixed with prose. A prime specimen of this form is his *Wen fu* ("On Literature"), a subtle and important work of literary criticism that defines and demonstrates the principles of composition with rare insight and precision.

Lu-chiang, also spelled LU-KANG, town and port in Chang-hua *hsien* (county), western coastal Taiwan, situated west of the city of Chang-hua, with which its fortunes have been closely linked. Formerly one of the chief ports of Taiwan, it absorbed many immigrants from

The Temple of Matsu in Lu-chiang, Taiwan
© George Y.F. Chan

the Chinese mainland cities of Amoy and Foochow in the late 17th and early 18th centuries. At one time, early in the 19th century, it is said to have had a population of 100,000. The central area of Taiwan, however, for which Lu-chiang was the chief port, declined in importance in the 19th century with the rapid growth of agriculture in the south and with the move of the administration in 1891 from T'ai-nan farther south to Taipei in the north. Taiwan's trade moved away to the new ports of Chi-lung and Kao-hsiung, which had better harbours and rail connections with the interior. By the early 1970s, Lu-chiang's commercial role, too, had largely been taken over by Chang-hua. It is now important for salt manufacturing and for such handicrafts as hat making. Pop. (1982 est.) 73,459.

Lu Chiu-yüan, Pinyin LU JIUYUAN, courtesy name (*tzu*) TZU-CHING, literary name (*hao*) TS'UN-CHAI, also called MASTER HSIANG-SHAN (b. 1139, Kiangsi, China—d. Jan. 10, 1193, China), Idealist Neo-Confucian philosopher of the Southern Sung and rival of his contemporary, the great Neo-Confucian rationalist Chu Hsi. Lu's thought was revised and refined three centuries later by the Ming dynasty Neo-Confucianist Wang Yang-ming. The name of their school is Hsin Hsüeh, often called the Lu-Wang school, after its two great proponents. It was opposed to the other great school (and the one that was dominant), the Li Hsüeh, often called the Ch'eng-Chu after its leading philosophers, Ch'eng I and Chu Hsi.

Lu held a number of government posts, but he devoted most of his life to teaching and lecturing. In contrast to Chu Hsi's emphasis on "constant inquiry and study," Lu taught that the highest knowledge of the Way (Tao) comes from the constant practice of inner reflection and self-education. In this process, man develops his original goodness, for human nature is basically good, or regains his goodness if it has been corrupted and lost through material desires (*wu yü*).

After his death, Lu's works were collected and published under the title of *Hsiang-shan Hsien-sheng ch'üan-chi* ("Complete Works of Master Hsiang-shan"). In 1217 he was canonized as Wen-an, and in 1530 a tablet in his honour was placed in the central Confucian temple of the Ming dynasty.

BIBLIOGRAPHY. Studies of his philosophy include Siu-chi (Hsui-chi) Huang, *Lu Hsiang-shan, a Twelfth Century Chinese Idealist Philosopher* (1944, reprinted 1978); and Carsun Chang, *The Development of Neo-Confucian Thought,* vol. 1 (1957).

Lu-chou (Anhwei province, China): *see* Ho-fei.

Lu-chou, Pinyin LUZHOU, city in southern Szechwan *sheng* (province), China. A river port at the junction of the Yangtze River and the T'o River, Lu-chou's communications were further improved during World War II, when a highway was built south across the mountains to K'un-ming in Yunnan province to connect Szechwan to the Burma Road. Lu-chou, although an ancient city, remains essentially a river port.

The first county there, Chiang-yang, was founded in the 2nd century BC and became the seat of a commandery in AD 25. Under the Sui dynasty (581–618) the county was renamed Lu-ch'uan and became the seat of the *chou* (prefecture) of Lu. This name was kept until 1912, when it became Lu county. Until the completion of the Ch'eng-tu–Nei-chiang–Ch'ung-ch'ing–I-pin rail network in the mid-1950s, which bypassed the city, Lu-chou was the main port outlet for such commodities as the salt and chemicals of Tzu-kung, the sugar of Nei-chiang, and the agricultural goods of the region to the north. It was also a transshipment place for grain, tea, tobacco, hides, and meat from northern Yunnan. The completion of the railway has, however, taken away some of its former trade, which now goes direct to Chungking (Ch'ung-ch'ing) by rail, while much of the export trade from Nei-chiang has been diverted to I-pin.

With the exception of a small ammonia fertilizer plant built in the 1960s, Lu-chou has no major industry and has, therefore, declined since the early 1950s, although it remains a major market and commercial centre for the densely peopled and fertile plain of the lower T'o River. Pop. (1988 est.) 248,700.

Lü Dongbin (in Chinese mythology): *see* Lü Tung-pin.

Lu Hsiang-shan (Chinese philosopher): *see* Lu Chiu-yüan.

Lu Hsing, Pinyin LU XING, in Chinese mythology, one of three stellar gods known collectively as Fu-Shou-Lu. He was honoured as a deity who could make people happy through increased salaries or promotions that brought prosperity (*lu*).

In life, Lu Hsing was a scholar who bore the name Shih Fen. In the 2nd century BC he was

Lu Hsing, wood sculpture; in the Musée Guimet, Paris
By courtesy of the Musee Guimet, Paris

a favourite of Emperor Ching and was made a high official at the royal court. His family prospered through imperial generosity. Perhaps because the Chinese have many gods of wealth and happiness, Lu Hsing is not nearly so widely honoured as is Shou Hsing, the god of longevity.

Lu Hsün, Pinyin LU XUN, pen name (*pi-ming*) of CHOU SHU-JEN (b. Sept. 25, 1881, Shao-hsing, Chekiang province, China—d. Oct. 19, 1936, Shanghai), writer commonly considered the greatest in Chinese literature of the 20th century.

Although he originally studied to be a doctor, Lu Hsün became associated with the nascent Chinese literary movement in 1918, when, at the urging of friends, he published his famous short story "A Madman's Diary." Modeled after Nikolay Gogol's tale of the same title, the tale is a condemnation of traditional Confucian culture which the madman narrator sees as a "man-eating" society. The first Western-style story written wholly in Chinese, it was a tour de force that attracted immediate attention and helped gain acceptance for the short-story form as an effective literary vehicle. "The True Story of Ah Q" (in Chinese, 1921; Eng. trans. in *Ah 2 and Others*) is a representative work. A mixture of humour and pathos, it is a repudiation of the old order; it added the word Ah Qism to the modern Chinese language as a term characterizing the Chinese penchant to rationalize defeat as a "spiritual victory." Other stories in *Na-han* (1923; "Call to Arms"), the work that established his reputation as the leading Chinese writer, *P'ang-huang* (1926; "Hesitation"), and his various symbolic prose-poems, reminiscences, and retold classical tales all reveal a modern sensibility informed by a sardonic humour and biting satire.

Although Lu Hsün is better known for his works of fiction, he was also a master of the prose essay, a vehicle he utilized more and more toward the end of his life. His *Chung-kuo hsiao-shuo shih-lueh* ("Outline History of Chinese Fiction") and companion compilations of classical fiction remain standard works. Translations, largely from the Russian, also occupy a large place in his complete works.

Forced by political circumstances to flee Peking in 1926, he eventually found sanctuary in the Shanghai International Settlement. Increasingly pessimistic about the political future of China, in the 1930s he began to see the Chinese communists as the only salvation for his country. Although he himself refused to join the party, he became a fellow traveler, recruiting many of his fellow writers and countrymen to the communist cause. Considered a revolutionary hero by present-day Chinese communists, Lu Hsün was adopted posthumously as the exemplar of Socialist Realism by the Chinese communist movement.

Lu Ji (Chinese author): *see* Lu Chi.

Lu Jiuyuan (Neo-Confucianist philosopher): *see* Lu Chiu-yüan.

Lu-kang (Taiwan): *see* Lu-chiang.

Lü-liang Mountains, Chinese (Wade-Giles) LÜ-LIANG SHAN, or (Pinyin) LÜLIANG SHAN, range in Shansi province, China. The name Lü-liang Mountains is generally used for the whole system of ranges in the west and southwest of Shansi, separating the north-south section of the Huang Ho (Yellow River) to the west from the valley of its tributary, the Fen River, to the east. Properly, however, the name designates the northern part of this range, lying to the west of the Fen River basin at T'ai-yüan, where the name also refers to one of several adjacent peaks (Mount Lü-liang). The highest peak in the range, Kuan-ti Mountain, reaches 9,288 feet (2,831 m). The southern part of the range, which has a more marked southwest-northeast axis, is properly called the Huo-yen Range.

The ranges have a mean elevation of 5,000 to 6,500 feet (1,500 to 2,000 m), the highest area being in the north. The higher areas of the chain are free of loess (wind-deposited silt), but the western side of the chain, reaching down to the Huang Ho valley, is covered with loess and has the heavily dissected landscape characteristic of the loess areas of Shensi province. Structurally, the ranges were formed by a series of downwarps (the sinking of rock strata to produce the valleys between adjacent ranges), with the north-south and northeast-southwest axes of the ranges broken up by a series of fault troughs, formed through the mountain-building processes of the Jurassic Period (208 to 144 million years ago). Many of the rocks in these ranges are of the Carboniferous and Permian periods (*i.e.,* about 248 to 354 million years old) and contain rich coal reserves, which are mined on a large scale at Fen-hsi. The ranges originally supported a sparse forest, but most of the area is now covered with grass and low scrub.

Lu Mountains, Chinese (Wade-Giles and Pinyin) LU SHAN, famous mountain area in northern Kiangsi province, southeastern China. Situated to the south of Chiu-chiang and west of Hsing-tzu, it looks north over the Yangtze River valley and east over the P'o-yang Lake. It forms the eastern extremity of the Mu-fu Mountains. Its highest peak, K'uang-lu, or K'uang Mountain, is about 4,836 feet (1,474 m) above sea level. The Lu Mountains were venerated as a holy area from ancient times, when they were called the K'uang Mountains. In early times they were the home of many prominent Buddhists, and they were the intellectual centre of Taoism from the 6th to the 8th century. The Lu Mountains also have associations with many famous poets and literary figures—among them Li Po, Pai Chü-i, and Su Tung-p'o, who referred to it as K'uang-lu. Before World War II the mountains still had some 300 temples and Taoist shrines and were a popular summer resort for Western residents of Shanghai and the coastal cities, and the area has continued to thrive as a resort, with many convalescent homes and rest homes for workers. The mountain area has also been the subject of geological studies of glaciers of the Quaternary Period (the past 1.6 million years).

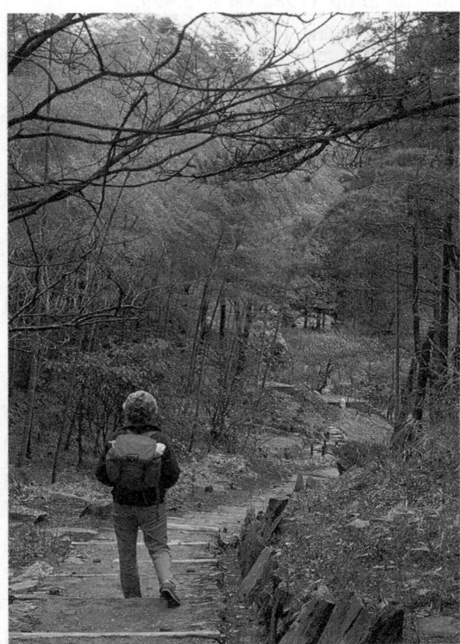

A path in the Lu Mountains, Kiangsi province, China
Heather Angel

The Lu Mountains form a horst-style fault block, integrating mountains, rivers, and lakes into a unified scenic landscape. Designated a UNESCO World Heritage site in December 1996, it is famous worldwide for its grandeur, unusual shape, and elegance. The Lu Shan scenic area extends over 117 square miles (302 square km), being protected by an outlying zone of 193 square miles (500 square km).

Lü P'ei-lin (Chinese philosopher): *see* T'ai Hsü.

lü pipes, Chinese musical instrument consisting of 12 bamboo pipes closed at one end. The bamboo pipes are cut into graduated lengths. When blown across their open ends, they produce the 12 *lü*, or fundamental pitches, of the untempered scale (*i.e.,* a scale whose semitones are not all of equal size). This is the oldest specific music-theory system known. Although the pitches are the same as those of the Greek and early Western systems, they are generated by a different method; the tones of Chinese music are produced by the so-called overblown-fifths method, whereas Western music uses the divisions of a string.

The term *lü* means "rule" or "law." When used in a music context, it refers to standard pitches as well as pipes for tuning. *Lü* pipes were most often made of bamboo but could be of bronze or, in a few cases, jade. Each pipe is closed at the bottom and is played by blowing across the top. Each of the 12 pipes produces one of the 12 chromatic pitches in an octave.

As these origins do in most ancient cultures, the invention of the *lü* pipes occurs in legend. The fifth chapter of the compendium known as *Lü-shih Ch'un Ch'iu* (*c.* 239 BC; "The Spring and Autumn [Annals] of Master Lü"), states that Huang-ti (The Yellow Emperor) sent his minister, Ling Lun, to a faraway western region to gather bamboo tubes of equal thickness to make tuning pipes. Ling Lun cut a 3.9-inch (9.9-cm) length of bamboo between two knots, blew it, and named it the Huang Chung ("Yellow Bell"), or tonic pitch. He then, according to legend, cut 11 shorter pipes, determining their relative pitch by listening to the cries of male and female phoenixes.

The veracity of the story cannot be known, but the legend at least confirms that the Chinese had discovered the division of the octave into 12 pitches at a very early period. Using the ratio 3:2, Ling Lun produced the graduated tones of the other pipes. The second pipe was two-thirds the length of the first and produced a note one-fifth higher than the first. The third pipe was cut two-thirds the length of the second and produced a note one-fifth higher than the second. When played as a scale, the 12 tones became the 12 chromatic pitches of the octave. This method, called the principle of the overblown fifth, was the foundation of the ancient Chinese musical scale. It differs from that of South Asia, the Middle East, and the West, which use divisions of a string to determine an octave's tones.

In 1986 several broken bamboo *lü* pipes were excavated from a tomb of the Warring States period (475–221 BC) in Hupeh. Four of these pipes have pitch names marked on them.

Lü Pu-wei, Pinyin LÜ BUWEI (d. 235 BC, Szechwan province, China), Chinese statesman, minister of the state of Ch'in, one of the small feudal kingdoms into which China was divided between 770 and 221 BC. Under Lü's clever management the state of Ch'in, in northwest China, engulfed many of its neighbouring states, and by the end of Lü's ministry, China was well on the way to unification.

Originally a merchant, Lü used his influence to have one of the princes of Ch'in declared the heir apparent to the throne. And when the prince fell in love with one of Lü's concubines, Lü relinquished her, even though she was rumoured to be pregnant at the time. In return for these favours, the prince, when he became ruler of Ch'in, made Lü minister of state, a position he continued to hold after the ruler died and the concubine's son Cheng, or Ying, formally acceded to the throne in 246 BC.

Implicated in a revolt against the boy emperor in 238 BC, Lü was banished from the capital. Accused of involvement in a second plot, he was again banished, this time to the present-day central province of Szechwan, where he is said to have ended his life by poison. Calling himself Shih huang-ti ("First Sovereign Emperor"), Cheng completed the unification of China begun by Lü and founded the Ch'in dynasty (221–206 BC).

While serving as minister, Lü engaged a number of scholars to produce an encyclopaedia of knowledge. The result was the first expertly arranged, full-length book, the famous *Lü-shih Ch'un Ch'iu* ("The Spring and Autumn [Annals] of Master Lü"), a compendium of folklore and pseudoscientific and Taoist writings.

Lu Shan (China): *see* Lu Mountains.

Lü-shun, Pinyin LÜSHUN, also called LÜ-SHUN-K'OU, formerly PORT ARTHUR, former city and naval port in Liaoning *sheng* (province), China. It is currently an administrative district of Ta-lien (*q.v.*). Situated at the southern tip of the Liaotung Peninsula, Lü-shun has a good deepwater harbour that is ice-free throughout the year. It is in an extremely important strategic position, commanding the entrance to the Po Hai (Gulf of Chihli) and access to Tientsin.

Historically the former city was an important port of entry for southern Manchuria (now known as the Northeast), and it was used as a staging post in the 2nd century BC by colonists of the Han dynasty (206 BC–AD 220) in northern Korea and by the T'ang dynasty (618–907) in campaigns in the 7th century. During the 15th and 16th centuries, under the Ming dynasty (1368–1644), it was a fortified port for Chinese settlements in the Liaotung area. It was captured by the Manchus in 1633 and became the headquarters of a coastal defense unit under the Ch'ing dynasty (1644–1911). In 1878 it was chosen as the chief base for the Peiyang fleet, China's first modern naval force, and was again fortified.

Captured by the Japanese in the Sino-Japanese War of 1894–95, it was leased to Japan under the Treaty of Shimonoseki, which ended the war, but after the intervention of the Western powers that followed, it was returned to China. Russia, however, which was anxious to acquire an ice-free port on the Pacific, occupied the Liaotung Peninsula in 1897 after the Germans had taken Chiao-chou (Kiaochow) on the southern side of the Shantung Peninsula. In 1898 Russia acquired a lease of the Liaotung Peninsula and the right to build a railway connecting with the Chinese Eastern Railway at Harbin, and thus with the Trans-Siberian Railroad. The Russians constructed a heavily fortified naval base for their Pacific fleet at Port Arthur, began the development of a commercial port in nearby Dalny (Dairen; now Ta-lien), and in 1903 completed the rail link to Harbin. During the Russo-Japanese War of 1904–05, Port Arthur was one of the principal Japanese objectives. In May 1904 the Japanese army cut off the Liaotung Peninsula from the mainland and seized the port of Dairen. The Russian forces withdrew to their supposedly impregnable base at Port Arthur, which was eventually taken by the Japanese.

The Treaty of Portsmouth (1905), which concluded the war, transferred Port Arthur to Japan. The Japanese renamed it Ryojun and made it the administrative and military headquarters of their Kwantung Provincial Government (later transferred to Dairen) and of the Kwantung army command (later transferred to Mukden [now Shen-yang]). The naval base was strengthened, becoming a base for Japanese military operations not only in Manchuria but also in northern China. The Yalta Conference had envisioned the return of the Liaotung territory to the Soviet Union after World War II, and, under a treaty of friendship and alliance concluded in Moscow in 1945 between China and the Soviet Union, it was agreed that the Port Arthur naval base should be used jointly by the two countries for 30 years, but that the Soviet Union should be responsible for its defense, and that the Russians should have control of the peninsula, apart from the port of Dairen. Soviet forces finally withdrew from Port Arthur in 1955, after which it became an important Chinese naval base.

In 1950, Lü-shun was annexed by Ta-lien to form the city of Lü-ta. In 1981 Lü-ta was renamed Ta-lien, and Lü-shun subsequently became a city district. It is now a major tourist attraction of the Liaotung Peninsula.

Lü-ta, Pinyin LUDA, city (1950–81) and port of Liaoning *sheng* (province), China, that encompassed the former cities of Lü-shan and Ta-lien, in 1981 renamed Ta-lien (*q.v.*).

Lü Tsu (Chinese mythology): *see* Lü Tung-pin.

Lü-tsung (Buddhist philosophy): *see* Ritsu.

Lü Tung-pin, Pinyin LÜ DONGBIN, original name LÜ YEN, literary name (*hao*) CH'UN YANG-TZU, also called LÜ TSU, in Chinese mythology, one of the Pa Hsien, the Eight Immortals of Taoism, who discoursed in his Stork Peak refuge on the three categories of merit and the five grades of genies (spirits). He is said to have been a Taoist priest during the Five Dynasties (907–960) and early Sung (960–1279) periods and is depicted in art as a man of letters carrying a magic sword and a fly switch.

Lü Tung-pin, wood sculpture, 18th century; in the Guimet Museum, Paris

By courtesy of the Guimet Museum, Paris

One of many legends relates that Lü rewarded an old woman for her honesty by magically transforming her well water into wine. Another well-known legend recounts Lü's three attempts to convert the singsong girl White Peony from her wayward life.

Lü is the most renowned of the Eight Immortals and as Lü Tsu ("Patriarch Lü") is credited with founding a Taoist sect that absorbed Nestorian influence. The Taoist canon contains dozens of treatises attributed to Lü, among them *The Secret of the Golden Flower*. *See also* Pa Hsien.

Lu Xing (Chinese mythology): *see* Lu Hsing.

Lu Xun (Chinese author): *see* Lu Hsün.

Lu Xun jinianguan (Shanghai museum): *see* Lu Hsün's Museum.

Lü Yen (Chinese mythology): *see* Lü Tung-pin.

Lu Yu, Pinyin LU YOU, literary name (*hao*) FANG-WENG, courtesy name (*tzu*) WU-KUAN (b. 1125, Shan-yin [now Shao-hsing, Chekiang province], China—d. 1210, Shan-yin), one of the most important and prolific Chinese writers of the Southern Sung dynasty, who left behind a collection of nearly 10,000 poems as well as numerous prose pieces.

Primarily a poet, Lu gained renown for his simple, direct expression and for his attention to realistic detail, features that set his writing apart from the elevated and allusive style characteristic of the prevailing Kiangsi school of poetry. As a conservative in matters of form, however, he wrote a number of poems in the *ku-shih* ("old poetry") mode and excelled at the *lü-shih* ("regulated poetry") form, the sharply defined tonal and grammatical patterns of which had been perfected by the great masters of the T'ang dynasty (618–907).

Lu is most admired for the ardour of his patriotic poems; in these he protested the Juchen invasion of Sung in 1126, the year after his birth, and chided the Southern Sung court for its passive attitude toward the invaders and its failure to drive them out and reconquer its lost northern territories. Because of his hawkish views, expressed at a time when the displaced court was controlled by a peace faction, Lu failed to advance in his career as an imperial official. Four times demoted for his outspoken opinions, Lu finally resigned his civil-service commission and retired to his country estate.

During retirement Lu devoted most of his poetry to the appreciation and celebration of rural life. Like the poet T'ao Ch'ien, whom he took as his model, Lu depicted the rural countryside in domestic detail, evoking its moods and scenes through fresh and precise imagery.

Lualaba River, headstream of the Congo River. Its 1,100-mile (1,800-kilometre) course lies entirely within Congo (Kinshasa), central Africa. It rises on the Katanga (Shaba) plateau at about 4,600 feet (1,400 m), near Musofi, Congo. Its upper course descends to the Manika Plateau and is marked by falls and rapids. Its drop to the Kamolondo Trough (1,500 feet in 45 miles [457 m in 72 km]) is harnessed for generating hydroelectric power at Nzilo Dam, near Nzilo Falls (formerly Delcommune Falls).

In the trough the Lualaba becomes navigable at Bukama for 400 miles (644 km). During this stretch the river expands into a series of marshy lakes (including Upemba and Kisale) that are periodically flooded and encumbered with papyrus and floating vegetation. Tributaries include the Lufira, Luvua, and Lukuga rivers.

The Lualaba River in the gorges of Nzilo, above Busanga, Congo

By courtesy of Gecamines, Lubumbashi, Congo

Below Kongola the river enters a deep, narrow gorge, the Portes d'Enfer, in which navigation is impossible. The river is thereafter navigable for 68 miles [109 km] between Kasongo and Kibombo but is again broken by rapids to Kindu-Port-Empain. Although the final stretch of river between Kindu-Port-Empain and Boyoma (formerly Stanley) Falls is periodically shallow and lined with rocky bluffs, it can be negotiated by boats. The seven cataracts of Boyoma Falls mark the end of the Lualaba and the beginning of the Congo River proper.

Luan River, Wade-Giles romanization LUAN HO, Pinyin LUAN HE, formerly LEI RIVER, Wade-Giles and Pinyin LEI SHUI, river in

Hopeh province, China. The Luan River rises in northern Hopeh and flows northward into the Inner Mongolia Autonomous Region through steep gorges; its headstream is called the Shan-tien River. It passes north of the ancient Mongol capital Shang-tu (K'ai-p'ing), from which this section of the upper course is named the Shang-tu River, and the town of To-lun. Its course then swings to the southeast, where it is joined by its tributary the Hsiao-luan River. The Luan then flows southeastward across the mountains of northeast Hopeh. Near Ch'eng-te (Jehol) it is joined by the Je, Liu, and Pao rivers. It passes through the Great Wall of China at Hsi-feng K'ou and then flows into the eastern fringes of the North China Plain. In its lower course it receives the Ch'ing-lung River. From Lo-t'ing it divides into a number of distributaries, discharging into the Po Hai (Gulf of Chihli) through a delta some 30 miles (50 km) wide. The Luan is 545 miles (877 km) long and flows through an area of 17,220 square miles (44,600 square km). In ancient times the Luan was called the Ju (Ru) River.

The river's upper stream is precipitous, with many rapids. Below Ch'eng-te, however, it is navigable for small craft during the summer. Because of this it was important during earlier times as the only water route into the Ch'eng-te region for military supplies, and it was also used as a trade route from parts of Hopeh (then in the former province of Chihli) to the regions beyond the Great Wall. Because of steep hills and deep ravines at its upper reaches, the river overflows its banks during the rainy season. The flow of water is much-reduced in winter, and for some months the river is icebound. Its upper basin, which was forest-covered until the 19th century, has suffered from soil erosion caused by deforestation and unsuitable methods of cultivation.

Several reservoir and canal projects have been finished along the Luan River since the 1950s. These projects have increased the supply of water for industrial and agricultural use and augmented hydroelectric output. At the same time, flood control capabilities have been enhanced.

Luanda, also spelled LOANDA, formerly SÃO PAULO DE LUANDA, city, northern Angola, on the Atlantic coast. The capital of Angola, it is the country's largest city and second busiest seaport. Founded in 1576 by Paulo Dias de Novais, it became the administrative centre of the colony in 1627 and was a major outlet for slave traffic to Brazil. The old fortress of São Miguel overlooks Luanda Island beyond the port.

Luanda has a warm, equable climate. It has an international airport, is the seat of a Roman Catholic archdiocese and of the state-controlled University of Luanda (founded 1962), and is linked by rail inland to Malange (378 miles [608 km] east). Coffee, cotton, diamonds, iron, and salt are the chief exports. Skyscrapers and wide avenues give the city a modern appearance. Many Mbundu live in the city, and a sizable Cuban community, including both soldiers and civilians, has largely replaced the Portuguese population who left en masse shortly before Angola achieved independence in 1975. The higher part of the city consisting of the outlying districts is generally poverty-ridden, and the lower is commercial and industrial. Petroleum was discovered nearby in 1955, and there is a refinery at the north end of Luanda Bay.

The surrounding region fronts a tropical coastal plain that gives way to a tableland dissected and drained by the Kwanza River and other coastal streams. Cambambe Dam (1963) on the Kwanza supplies power to the city of Luanda, 110 miles (177 km) northwest. Coffee, cotton, sugarcane, oilseeds, and palm oil and kernels are produced in the region; cattle raising is locally important. Pop. (1999 est.) 2,555,000.

Fortress of São Miguel, Luanda, Angola

stern—Black Star/EB Inc.

Luang Lake, Thai THALE LUANG, one of three coastal lakes that comprise Lake Songkhla, a coastal lagoon (*thale*), southern Thailand, on the east coast of the Malay Peninsula. Together with Noi Lake and Sap Songkhla Lake, Thale Luang is Thailand's largest inland waterway, approximately 50 miles (80 km) long and up to 15 miles (24 km) wide. Luang Lake, which is a fertile fishing ground, contains several islands. The lake complex also has two bird sanctuaries and is connected to the Gulf of Thailand at Songkhla town on its southern shore.

Luang Prabang (Laos): *see* Louangphrabang.

Luangwa River, Portuguese RIO ARUÂNGUA, river rising on the Malawi–Zambia border, southern Africa. From its source near Isoka, Zambia, it flows 500 miles (800 km) south-southwest, skirting the Muchinga Mountains to join the Zambezi River between Luangwa (formerly Feira), Zambia, and Zumbo, Mozambique. Along its lower course the Luangwa forms part of the Zambia–Mozambique border.

The Luangwa River valley, which forms the southern extension of the East African Rift System, is particularly noted for its wildlife. Four conservation areas—the Luambe, Lukusuzi, North Luangwe, and South Luangwe national parks—have been designated. The smallest of the four, Luambe National Park covers about 95 square miles (247 square km) and is situated between North and South Luangwa parks. Lukusuzi, on the eastern side of the valley, is the remotest of the four parks and is slightly higher in altitude. By far the most popular of the parks is South Luangwa, which covers nearly 3,500 square miles (9,050 square km). The park is open throughout the year, and tourism, notably in the form of walking safaris, is widespread. Its main camp is located at Mfuwe, where a number of trails begin. Entry to the North Luangwa park, which is about half the size of South Luangwa, is restricted, and the park is relatively undeveloped. The parks are accessible by air or road.

The North and South Luangwa parks are situated along some 120 miles (193 km) of the Luangwa River rift valley, a wide area of alluvial flats containing Karoo sediments and dissected into ridges. They rise gently westward to about 2,500 feet (765 m) at the foot of the 4,600-foot (1,400-metre) Muchinga escarpment. Their vegetation consists of growth characteristic of miombo (woodland), savanna, thickets, and floodplain grassland bordered by riparian forest. The meandering river has changed course many times, leaving dry beds and oxbow pools rich in vegetation nestled between high ranges of mountains. The parks' abundant and varied animal life includes vervet monkey, baboon, leopard, lion, elephant, zebra, black rhinoceros, hippopotamus, kudu, eland, buffalo, puku, Cookson's wildebeest, wild dog, hyena, cheetah, giraffe, and sable and roan antelope. The more than 400 species of birds include storks, geese, cranes, and carmine bee-eaters. The Luangwa River also provides a habitat for the Nile crocodile.

The parks were established as game reserves in the late 1930s and were made national parks in 1972. In the years following independence, tourism declined and the poaching of great numbers of animals was a serious threat to wildlife populations, particularly those of the rhinoceros and the elephant. Beginning in the late 1980s and early 1990s, conservation efforts were renewed in an effort increase tourism in the country. Poaching to nonetheless remains a problem in remoter regions of the valley.

Luanshya, municipality, central Zambia, southern Africa. Known as "the garden town of the copper belt," Luanshya is the service centre for the adjacent Roan Antelope mine. The terminus of a rail branch from Ndola (21 miles [34 km] northeast), Luanshya is also connected by road to other copper-belt towns and has an airfield. Besides copper mining, industry includes steel production, general machine shops, and a variety of factories. Pop. (1990) 146,275.

Luapula River, river in south-central Africa, rising in the Bangweulu Swamps (one of the world's largest wetlands) lying east of Lake Bangweulu in eastern Zambia. For most of its 350-mile (560-km) course the river forms part of the boundary between Zambia and Congo (Kinshasa). The Luapula slopes gently through most of its southward- then westward-trending upper course, but it descends a series of falls as it veers northward.

Much of the swampy area around Lake Bangweulu is fringed with white sand beaches. The mouth of the Chambeshi River, of which the Luapula is a continuation, is hidden in a vast sea of papyrus. The Luapula is navigable only below Johnston Falls, from which it flows a distance of about 100 miles (160 km) to its mouth in Lake Mweru. Roads that run almost parallel to the Luapula River link Mansa, a regional capital, with Mwenda and Kawambwa. Ferries operate on a number of tributaries of the river.

luau, a modern Hawaiian banquet. Luau originally denoted only the leaves of the taro plant, which are eaten as a vegetable; it came to refer to the dishes prepared with the leaves and then to the feasts at which the dishes were eaten. The term designates the modern, informal feast, as distinct from the ancient ceremonial banquets that were ritualized and attended only by men.

The standard luau is eaten at a low table that is covered with *ti* leaves and decorated with fruits and flowers. Traditional dishes include poi (*q.v.*), pig baked whole in an underground oven, *lau lau* (*luau* leaves and pork wrapped in a *ti* leaf and steamed), *lomi lomi* salmon (marinated raw fish), baked sweet potatoes, fish or chicken cooked in coconut milk, shellfish, and sweets. Dancing and music accompany the feast.

Luba, also called BALUBA, Bantu-speaking cluster of peoples of south-central Congo (Kinshasa). Numbering more than 9.3 million at the beginning of the 21st century, they inhabit a wide area extending throughout much

Female Luba ancestral statue of carved wood; in the Musée de l'Homme, Paris
By courtesy of the Musee de l'Homme, Paris

of southern Congo. The name Luba applies to a variety of groups that, though of different origins, speak closely related Bantoid languages, exhibit many common cultural traits, and share a common political history founded on the beginnings (15th century) and breakdown (19th century) of the Luba-Lunda states. Three main subdivisions may be recognized: the Luba-Katanga (also called Luba-Shaba, or Central Luba), the Luba-Kasai (Luba-Lulua, or Western Luba), and the Luba-Hemba (Hemba, or Eastern Luba) of northern Katanga and southern Kivu. All are historically, linguistically, and culturally linked with other Congo peoples. The Luba-Katanga branch is also connected with the early founders of the Lunda state.

The Luba are savanna and forest dwellers who practice hunting, food gathering, and agriculture (cassava, corn [maize]); keep small livestock; and live in villages of a single street, with rectangular thatched-roof huts along either side. They fish the Congo and its main tributaries intensively. In the 16th and 17th centuries, most of the Luba were ruled by a paramount chief (*mulopwe,* pl. *bulopwe*), although smaller independent chiefdoms already existed. The breakdown of the empire resulted in the development of either smaller chiefdoms or small autonomous local lineage groups. Luba practice circumcision and girls' initiation. Scarification was practiced at one time and is evident in the art created by the Luba. Associations exist for hunting, magic, and medicine.

Sickness is believed to have a spiritual cause discernible by divination. Nonroyal individuals practice a form of divination known as *kashekesheke* (or, by northern Luba and others, *katatora*). In this ritual, a 3-to-6-inch hollow-bodied female figure (*kakishi*) is prepared (anointed or rubbed with an aromatic substance) by the diviner and held by both the diviner and the questioner; the nature of the figure's movement (or its lack of movement) sheds light on the question at hand. Diviners also use dreams to provide answers to their clients. The Luba have a strong belief in a supreme being, and they worship ancestral spirits (*bafu*) and natural spirits.

Luba art, like that of most African peoples, is created to serve various practical functions. In addition to the *kakishi* and other items used for a variety of divination ceremonies, Luba art consists generally of ceremonial axes, headrests, stools, and masks. The Luba-Katanga and the Luba-Hemba, renowned as woodcarvers, are especially known for their carvings of anthropomorphic figures, which appear on masks, headrests, and stools. The axes, produced by blacksmiths, are worn over the shoulder by important officials and represent power and wealth. Stools, which also symbolize power, figured prominently in investiture ceremonies for kings. During the ceremony, the king's stool was placed on top of a leopard skin, so that the king's feet would not touch the ground. Headrests allow women particularly to rest comfortably when they are wearing elaborately designed hair styles. *See also* Buli style.

Luba-Lunda states, a complex of states that flourished in Central Africa (in the present-day Democratic Republic of the Congo) from the late 15th to the late 19th century. The Luba state was situated east of the Kasai River around the headwaters of the Lualaba River, and the Lunda state east of the Kwango River around the headwaters of the Kasai River. A later state, Kazembe, was located to the southeast.

Luba traditions record no large or powerful states until the late 15th century, when the warrior Kongolo entered the region, subdued several small chiefdoms, and founded a centralized state, with its capital at Mwibele. Around this central state a number of satellites proliferated; by the 17th century they had spread into the southern Congo basin and to what are now parts of Angola and Zambia. The largest of these satellites was Lunda, to the south and west of the Luba state and soon surpassing it in territory. Its founder, known by the title of Mwata Yamvo (ruler), was a Luba nobleman who married a Lunda princess. The Lunda state expanded westward in the middle of the 18th century and imposed its rule on peoples living near the Kwango River.

Largest of all the Luba-Lunda states was Kazembe (*q.v.*), which was founded early in the 18th century, when the last major expansion of the Luba-Lunda complex took place; migrants from Lunda moved southeastward, establishing a capital in the Luapula River valley to the south of Lake Mweru (in present-day Zambia).

From the outset the Luba-Lunda states were indirectly connected with the Portuguese in Angola, who supplied cloth and other goods in return for slaves and ivory. The Kazembe Lunda, who established their state with the aid of Portuguese arms, soon were exchanging their ivory at the Portuguese trading stations on the Zambezi River. Kazembe continued to flourish until late in the 19th century, when it was colonized by the British.

The once-independent states now are part of the Democratic Republic of the Congo, but the Lunda people continue to recognize a Lunda ruler with ceremonial authority. The last Luba ruler, Kasongo Nyembo, led the state from 1891 until 1917.

Lubango, formerly SÁ DA BANDEIRA, city, southwestern Angola, about 100 miles (160 km) east of Namibe (formerly Moçâmedes), to which it is linked by rail. The city was originally established in 1885 as a settlement for colonists from the Madeira Islands. It lies at an elevation of 5,774 feet (1,760 m) in a valley of the Huíla Plateau and is surrounded by a scenic park spreading up the mountain slopes. The city, once the major centre of Portuguese settlement in the interior of southern Angola, is built in a Portuguese style of architecture, with a cathedral, commerce hall, industrial hall, and secondary school. Pop. (latest est.) 105,000.

Lubbock, city, seat (1891) of Lubbock county, northwestern Texas, U.S., some 120 miles (190 km) south of Amarillo; it is the commercial hub of the South Plains. Formed in 1890 from Old Lubbock and Monterey and named for Colonel Tom S. Lubbock, a signer of the Texas Declaration of Independence, it developed as a ranching centre, but artesian well water brought mixed farming to the plains that now support cotton and grain as well as cattle.

Since the arrival of the Santa Fe Railroad, Lubbock has grown to be one of the country's leading inland cotton markets and the centre of a highly diversified agricultural-industrial complex. Petroleum, agricultural, and earth-moving equipment, cottonseed oil, and engineering products are major commodities. Lubbock experienced rapid growth after World War II, its population increasing nearly fivefold from 1940 to 1970. One of the costliest tornadoes in Texas history hit the city in May 1970, causing widespread damage and rendering thousands homeless. Two years later the city allowed the purchase and consumption of alcohol, ending nearly a century of prohibition and its distinction as the largest "dry" city in the United States.

Educational institutions include Texas Tech University (1923), with a museum and the National Ranching Heritage Center on its campus, and Lubbock Christian University (1957). The Texas Tech University Health Sciences Center and other modern hospitals have made Lubbock a regional hub for medical care. Mackenzie State Park and Buffalo Lakes provide recreational facilities. The Lubbock Lake National Historic and State Archeological Landmark, north of the city, preserves archaeological ruins dating from more than 10,000 years ago. The annual Panhandle South Plains Fair is a notable regional event. The Buddy Holly Center (1999) includes a permanent exhibition on the rock musician's life and music, as well as an art gallery and the Texas Musicians Hall of Fame. Inc. 1909. Pop. (2002 est.) city, 206,481; (2000) Lubbock MSA, 227,890.

Lubec, town, Washington county, eastern Maine, U.S. It lies along the Atlantic coast, just south of Eastport. The town includes the communities of Lubec, North Lubec, South Lubec, and West Lubec. Settled about 1780, it was part of Eastport until separately incorporated in 1811. It was named for Lübeck, Germany. Lubec has developed as a commercial centre for a resort and fishing area; sardines and locally farmed salmon are processed there. The Quoddy Head State Park (the easternmost point in the continental United States) has a lighthouse originally built in 1808 (rebuilt 1858). A bridge connects Lubec with Roosevelt Campobello International Park on Campobello Island, where President Franklin D. Roosevelt had his summer home. Inc. 1811. Area 33 square miles (86 square km). Pop. (2000) 1,652.

Lübeck, in full HANSESTADT LÜBECK ("Hanseatic City of Lübeck"), city and major seaport of the *Land* (state) of Schleswig-Holstein, northern Germany. It is located on the Trave and Wakenitz rivers, about 9 miles (14 km) from the Baltic Sea. In the Middle Ages it was one of the main commercial centres of northern Europe and the chief city of the Hanseatic League (an association of towns for the protection of trading interests).

An earlier settlement in the area was named Liubice; located at the confluence of the Schwartau and Trave rivers, 4 miles (6 km) downstream from the present city centre, it

Spires of the Marienkirche, Lübeck, Ger.
By courtesy of the Museen fur Kunst und Kulturgeschichte, Lubeck, Ger.

was the seat of a Slavic principality and had a castle and harbour. The German city was founded by Count Adolf II of Holstein in 1143. This settlement was destroyed by fire in 1157, but a new city was built there by Henry III, duke of Saxony, in 1159. It developed rapidly as the main trading point between the raw-material-producing countries of northern and eastern Europe and the manufacturing centres in the west.

For a short time (1201–26) Lübeck belonged to Denmark, but in 1226 it was made a free imperial city by Frederick II. During this time Lübeck developed a form of self-government with its own laws and constitution. The "laws of Lübeck" were later granted to more than 100 cities in the Baltic area, and the example of Lübeck greatly influenced the economy and appearance of those cities. In 1358 the Hanseatic League made Lübeck its administrative headquarters. This event took place a mere eight years after the city's population had been devastated by the Black Death. Subsequent decades brought increasing wealth to the city, but there were also periods of civil unrest (1380–84 and 1408–16) in which the artisans' and craftsmen's guilds actively opposed the city council, which was controlled by the merchants. The opening of the Stecknitz Canal in 1398 greatly facilitated the shipping of salt from Lüneburg. By the early 15th century, Lübeck was the second largest city (after Cologne) in northern Germany, with some 22,000 inhabitants.

Sweeping changes came with the Protestant Reformation (1529–30). The city council was expelled, and the revolutionary Jürgen Wullenwever became burgomaster of Lübeck. Wullenwever waged an unsuccessful war against Denmark, Sweden, and the Netherlands, which brought about a decline in the city's economy and in its regional political influence. Although the Hanseatic League was dissolved in 1630, Lübeck remained the most important harbour on the Baltic Sea. It was neutral during the Thirty Years' War, but during the French Revolutionary and Napoleonic Wars (1792–1815) the city's trade was completely ruined, for it was caught between economic pressures exerted by the rival powers. Lübeck was under French rule from 1811 to 1813 and after 1815 was a member state of the German confederation.

From 1866 Lübeck belonged to the North German Confederation and from 1871 to the German Empire. The city's economy was restored with the construction of the Elbe-Lübeck Canal in 1900. Its status as a separate, self-governing entity, dating from 1226, ended in 1937, when the Nazi regime made it part of the Prussian province of Schleswig-Holstein. In World War II, a large part of the historic inner city was destroyed by a British bombing raid (March 28, 1942), but the area was restored during postwar reconstruction. At the end of the war, the city's population swelled tremendously with the arrival of 100,000 German refugees who had fled the Soviet advance in the east.

Lübeck is the largest Baltic harbour of Germany, and the port is a major employer in the city. Paper and wood products, fruit, grain, automobiles, salt, and fertilizer are among the cargoes handled, and there is a significant amount of ferry traffic. Other industries include shipbuilding, metalworking, and food processing; services related to finance, communications, and the tourist trade have become increasingly important.

The novelist Thomas Mann was born to a patrician family in Lübeck, which forms the setting for his novel *Buddenbrooks* (1900).

The inner city was designated a World Heritage site by UNESCO in 1987; it retains a distinctive medieval character in its narrow cobblestone streets and its faithfully restored houses and shops, along with its ecclesiastical and municipal structures. Among Lübeck's outstanding monuments are the Marienkirche (St. Mary's Church, a 13th–14th-century brick structure in the Gothic style), the Romanesque cathedral (begun in 1173 under Henry III), and the magnificent Rathaus (town hall) built in a combination of Gothic and Renaissance style. Waterways and parklands outline the inner city, where the moat and ramparts once shielded it from attack. Two towered gates are remnants of the medieval fortifications: the Burgtor (1444), which received a new roof in 1685, and the famous Holstentor (1478), which has housed the municipal museum since 1950. Pop. (2002 est.) 213,496.

Lubecki, Ksawery Drucki (b. Dec. 28, 1779, St. Petersburg, Russia—d. May 23, 1846, St. Petersburg), Polish statesman who restored the

Lubecki, detail from a portrait by Marie Gouvier Prévot, 1825; in the National Museum, Warsaw
By courtesy of the National Museum, Warsaw

finances of the remnant of Poland that was constituted as the "Congress Kingdom" under the tsar of Russia after the Napoleonic Wars.

A member of a princely family descended from the ancient Russian ruling house of Rurik, Lubecki began his career as an officer in the Russian army. From 1813 to 1815 he was a member of the provisional government of the Russian-occupied Duchy of Warsaw; later (1817–21) he successfully negotiated in Berlin and Vienna the settlement of the Polish foreign debt.

Appointed minister of the treasury of the Russian-controlled Congress Kingdom of Poland when its finances were in a critical state (1821), Lubecki restored public confidence by restraining abuses and efficiently collecting overdue taxes; in three years he balanced the budget. Using budget surpluses, Lubecki developed state mines and foundries and helped the growing textile industry. In addition, he created the Land Credit Society (1825) and the Bank of Poland (1828).

While steadily defending Polish autonomy, Lubecki, a conservative, tried to keep the Polish revolutionary movement of 1830 within legal limits. He ended up being a passive witness to the defeat of the Polish rebellion of 1830 and to the merging of the Congress Kingdom of Poland into the Russian Empire. He spent the rest of his life in St. Petersburg, where in 1832 he was appointed a member of the State Council.

Lubelskie, *województwo* (province), eastern Poland. It comprises the former provinces (1975–98) of Lublin, Biała Podlaska, Chełm, and Zamość Toruń, as well as portions of Siedlce and Tarnobrzeg. The province's elevation rises from north to south, with marshlands and peat bogs in the north trending into uplands in the centre and then hills in the south. The Vistula and Bug are the main rivers, and lakes abound. The province is one of the least-developed in Poland, with an emphasis on agriculture. Cereals, potatoes, and sugar beets are grown; pigs and cattle are raised; and Arabian horses are bred. Lublin is the provincial capital, and the historic towns of Zamość and Kazimierz Dolny are frequent tourist destinations. During the German occupation in World War II, the area was home to several concentration camps, including Majdanek. Area 9,664 square miles (25,114 square km). Pop. (2003 est.) 2,194,900.

L'ubercy (Russia): *see* Lyubertsy.

Lubiana (Slovenia): *see* Ljubljana.

Lubin, David (b. June 10, 1849, Kłodawa, Pol., Russian Empire—d. Jan. 1, 1919, Rome, Italy), Polish-born American merchant and agricultural reformer whose activities led to the founding (1905) of the International Institute of Agriculture as a world clearinghouse for data on crops, prices, and trade to protect the common interests of farmers of all nations.

Migrating with his family to England in 1853 and to New York City in 1855, where he became a goldsmith and jeweler, Lubin went to California in 1865 and for a few years sought gold there and in Arizona. He returned to California in 1874 and started a dry-goods business. After prospering as a merchant and farmer in California, Lubin helped to lead fruit growers in organizing for better treatment from the railroads. Later he became an energetic though unsuccessful advocate of tariff protection for American farmers. A trip to Europe in 1896 led to a more international outlook, and he then proposed his Institute—a proposal that was ignored by Great Britain, the United States, and France. Victor Emmanuel III of Italy, however, encouraged Lubin to organize the Institute in Rome and helped establish it by calling a conference resulting in a treaty that eventually was ratified by 77 nations. Lubin remained the American delegate to the Institute for the rest of his life.

BIBLIOGRAPHY. Olivia Rossetti Agresti, *David Lubin: A Study in Practical Idealism,* 2nd ed. (1941); Azriel Louis Eisenberg, *Feeding the World: A Biography of David Lubin* (1965).

Lubitsch, Ernst (b. Jan. 28, 1892, Berlin, Ger.—d. Nov. 30, 1947, Hollywood, Calif., U.S.), German-American motion-picture director who was best known for sophisticated comedies of manners.

He studied acting and in 1911 joined the

company of Max Reinhardt, the famous German stage director. He played minor stage roles until shortly before World War I, when he became an actor in and a director of one-reel film comedies.

His elaborate costume features in the early post-World War I period were the first German productions to be shown abroad. Some of the more important of these films, especially admired for their innovative camera work, were *Madame Du Barry* (1919; *Passion*), *Anna Boleyn* (1920; *Deception*), *Das Weib des Pharao* (1921; *The Loves of Pharaoh*), and *Sumurun* (1920; *One Arabian Night*).

Lubitsch's reputation as a director was firmly established by comedies such as *Die Puppe* (1919; *The Doll*) and *Die Austernprinzessin* (1919; *The Oyster Princess*). In 1923 he was commissioned to direct the actress Mary Pickford in *Rosita* (1923), a grand-scale Hollywood costume drama. He was the first important German director to emigrate to the United States, and his success attracted many others. During the next five years he developed a readily identifiable style that became known as the "Lubitsch touch." It was a combination of understatement and graceful wit that resulted in a sophisticated comedy with implied sexual overtones. Among early films in this style were his silent comedies *Forbidden Paradise* (1924), *The Marriage Circle* (1924)—the film that revolutionized set design by making it an integral part of the action—*Lady Windermere's Fan* (1925), *Kiss Me Again* (1925), and *So This Is Paris* (1926). Lubitsch produced as well as directed the last three of these films, and he continued to work as a producer throughout his career.

In *The Love Parade* (1929) and *Monte Carlo* (1930), his first talking pictures, Lubitsch freed the camera from its soundproof box by filming sequences without dialogue and dubbing in the sound later. In the Maurice Chevalier and Jeanette MacDonald musicals of the 1930s, Lubitsch was the first director to introduce songs as a natural part of the plot. Although *Broken Lullaby* (1932), Lubitsch's one dramatic film of this period, was successful for its brilliant camera work, his most consistently successful films were such comedies as *Trouble in Paradise* (1932), *The Merry Widow* (1934), *Ninotchka* (1939), *The Shop Around the Corner* (1940), *To Be or Not to Be* (1942), *Heaven Can Wait* (1943), *Cluny Brown* (1946), and *That Lady in Ermine* (1948), completed after his death.

Lübke, Heinrich (b. Oct. 14, 1894, Enkhausen, Ger.—d. April 6, 1972, Bonn, W.Ger.), politician who served as president of the German Federal Republic (1959–69).

Lübke
Karsh—Camera Press from Pictorial Parade

Lübke studied at several German universities, and after serving in World War I he was able to unify many small German farmers' organizations into the German Farmers Federation. He served as the federation's director from 1926 to 1933. Politically inactive throughout the National Socialist era (1933–45), Lübke helped to organize the Christian Democratic Party in Westphalia after World War II and was a member of the North Rhine–Westphalia Landtag (provincial diet) from 1946 to 1952. Between 1947 and 1952 he also served as the North Rhine–Westphalia minister of food, agriculture, and forestry. During 1949–50 and later from 1953 to 1959, he sat in the federal Bundestag (lower house of parliament), and in 1953 he entered the cabinet of Chancellor Konrad Adenauer as federal minister of food, agriculture, and forestry. In this post he played an important role in modernizing West German agriculture. In 1959 he was chosen to be Christian Democratic candidate for the federal presidency after Adenauer had declined to run. He was elected president in July 1959 and was reelected in 1964. Though his powers as president were constitutionally limited, he acquired considerable popularity for his dignified demeanour and discretion and at times effectively intervened in domestic political affairs, especially during the last period of Adenauer's chancellorship. He resigned from office in early 1969.

Lublin, city, capital of Lubelskie *województwo* (province), eastern Poland, on the Bystrzyca River. Founded as a stronghold in the late 9th century, the settlement grew up around the castle, receiving town rights in 1317. It served as a joint meeting ground for Poland and Lithuania, and in 1569 the Union of Lublin between the two kingdoms was signed there. Lublin reached its economic peak during the late 16th century. In 1795 it passed to Austria and in 1815 to Russia. The first independent temporary Polish government was proclaimed there in 1918. In 1941 the Nazis established Majdanek (*q.v.*) concentration and extermination camp in the southeastern Lublin suburb of that name. After World War II, Lublin was made the provisional seat of the Polish Committee of National Liberation and served briefly as the seat of the national government.

Located on the route between Kraków, Warsaw, and Russia, Lublin is the industrial and cultural centre for southeastern Poland. Agricultural machinery, chemicals, automobiles and trucks, foodstuffs (especially sugar), and beer are produced. The city houses the Catholic University and the Marie Skłodowska-Curie University, as well as schools of medicine, agronomy, and engineering, and supports many museums, theatres, and music centres. Its notable landmarks include the medieval castle, which was restored in 1954; its chapel houses the Lublin Museum. There is a museum and memorial park at the site of the concentration camp. Pop. (2002) 357,110.

Lublin, Union of (1569), pact between Poland and Lithuania that united the two countries into a single state. After 1385 (in the Union of Krewo) the two countries had been under the same sovereign. But Sigismund II (Sigismund Augustus; reigned 1548–72) had no heirs; and the Poles, fearing that when he died the personal union between Poland and Lithuania would be broken, urged that a more complete union be formed. After the Livonian War began (1558) and Muscovy presented a serious threat to Lithuania, many of the Lithuanian gentry also desired a closer union with Poland and in 1562 made a proposal for merging the two states. The dominant Lithuanian magnates, however, feared that a merger would diminish their power and blocked the proposal as well as subsequent initiatives. When representatives from both countries at a meeting of the Sejm (legislature) at Lublin (January 1569) failed to reach an accord, Sigismund II annexed the Lithuanian provinces of Podlasie and Volhynia (including the regions of Kiev and Bracław), which together constituted over one-third of Lithuania's territory. Although the Lithuanian magnates wanted to oppose Poland, the gentry declined to enter a new war, forcing negotiations for forming a union to be resumed in June. On July 1, 1569, the Union of Lublin was concluded, uniting Poland and Lithuania into a single, federated state, which was to be ruled by a single, jointly selected sovereign. Formally, Poland and Lithuania were to be distinct, equal components of the federation, each retaining its own army, treasury, civil administration, and laws; the two nations agreed to cooperate with each other on foreign policy and to participate in a joint Diet. But Poland, which retained possession of the Lithuanian lands it had seized, had greater representation in the Diet and became the dominant partner.

Union of Lublin

The Polish–Lithuanian state remained a major political entity until it was partitioned toward the end of the 18th century.

Lubnān ash-Sharqī (Lebanon): *see* Anti-Lebanon Mountains.

Lubny, also spelled LUBNI, city, Poltava *oblast* (province), Ukraine. Lubny is a port on the Sula River. Established in the late 10th century as a fortified Rus town, Lubny was destroyed by the Mongols in 1239 and was not rebuilt until the latter 16th century. In 1658–1781 it was a regimental centre in the Hetmanate, an autonomous hetman state, before coming under direct Russian administration. The city's industries include textiles, furniture, and construction. There are colleges of forestry and medicine and a monastery. Pop. (2001) 52,572.

Articles are alphabetized word by word, not letter by letter

lubrication, introduction of any of various substances between sliding surfaces to reduce wear and friction. Nature has been applying lubrication since the evolution of synovial fluid, which lubricates the joints and bursas of vertebrate animals. Prehistoric people used mud and reeds to lubricate sledges for dragging game or timbers and rocks for construction. Animal fat lubricated the axles of the first wagons and continued in wide use until the petroleum industry arose in the 19th century, after which crude oil became the chief source of lubricants. The natural lubricating capacity of crude oil has been steadily improved through the development of a wide variety of products designed for the specific lubricating needs of the automobile, the airplane, the diesel locomotive, the turbojet, and power machinery of every description. The improvements in petroleum lubricants have in turn made possible the increase in speed and capacity of industrial and other machinery.

There are three basic varieties of lubrication: fluid-film, boundary, and solid.

Fluid-film lubrication. Interposing a fluid film that completely separates sliding surfaces results in this type of lubrication. The fluid may be introduced intentionally, as the oil in the main bearings of an automobile, or unintentionally, as in the case of water between a smooth rubber tire and a wet pavement. Although the fluid is usually a liquid, it may also be a gas. The gas most commonly employed is air.

To keep the parts separated, it is necessary that the pressure within the lubricating film balance the load on the sliding surfaces. If the lubricating film's pressure is supplied by an external source, the system is said to be lubricated hydrostatically. If the pressure between the surfaces is generated as a result of the shape and motion of the surfaces themselves, however, the system is hydrodynamically lubricated. This second type of lubrication depends upon the viscous properties of the lubricant.

Boundary lubrication. A condition that lies between unlubricated sliding and fluid-film lubrication is referred to as boundary lubrication, also defined as that condition of lubrication in which the friction between surfaces is determined by the properties of the surfaces and properties of the lubricant other than viscosity. Boundary lubrication encompasses a significant portion of lubrication phenomena and commonly occurs during the starting and stopping of machines.

Solid lubrication. Solids such as graphite and molybdenum disulfide are widely used when normal lubricants do not possess sufficient resistance to load or temperature extremes. But lubricants need not take only such familiar forms as fats, powders, and gases; even some metals commonly serve as sliding surfaces in some sophisticated machines.

A lubricant primarily controls friction and wear, but it can and ordinarily does perform numerous other functions, which vary with the application and usually are interrelated.

Control functions. The amount and character of the lubricant made available to sliding surfaces have a profound effect upon the friction that is encountered. For example, disregarding such related factors as heat and wear but considering friction alone between two oil-film lubricated surfaces, the friction can be 200 times less than that between the same surfaces with no lubricant. Under fluid-film conditions, friction is directly proportional to the viscosity of the fluid (see Table 1). Some lubricants, such as petroleum derivatives, are twofold. When machinery is idle, the lubricant acts as a preservative. When machinery is in use, the lubricant controls corrosion by coating lubricated parts with a protective film that may contain additives to neutralize corrosive materials. The ability of a lubricant to control corrosion is directly related to the thickness of the lubricant film remaining on the metal surfaces and the chemical composition of the lubricant.

Lubricants also can assist in controlling temperature by reducing friction and carrying off the heat that is generated. Effectiveness depends upon the amount of lubricant supplied, the ambient temperature, and the provision for external cooling. To a lesser extent, the type of lubricant also affects surface temperature.

Other functions. Various lubricants are employed as hydraulic fluids in fluid transmission devices. Others can be used to remove contaminants in mechanical systems. Detergent-dispersant additives, for instance, suspend sludges and remove them from the sliding surfaces of internal-combustion engines.

In specialized applications such as transformers and switchgear, lubricants with high dielectric constants act as electrical insulators. For maximum insulating properties, a lubricant must be kept free of contaminants and water. Lubricants also act as shock-damping fluids in energy-transferring devices (*e.g.*, shock absorbers) and around such machine parts as gears that are subjected to high intermittent loads.

A wide variety of lubricants are available. The principal types are reviewed here.

Liquid, oily lubricants. Animal and vegetable products were certainly man's first lubricants and were used in large quantities. But, because they lack chemical inertness and because lubrication requirements have become more demanding, they have been largely superseded by petroleum products and by synthetic materials. Some organic substances such as lard oil and sperm oil are still in use as additives because of their special lubricating properties.

Petroleum lubricants are predominantly hydrocarbon products extracted from fluids that occur naturally within the Earth. They are used widely as lubricants because they possess a combination of the following desirable properties: (1) availability in suitable viscosities, (2) low volatility, (3) inertness (resistance to deterioration of the lubricant), (4) corrosion protection (resistance to deterioration of the sliding surfaces), and (5) low cost.

Table 1: Characteristics of three typical lubricants

lubricant	relative viscosity (air = 1)	typical minimum film thickness in bearing applications (in.)	typical unit load in bearing applications (lb per sq in.)
air	1	0.00005–0.0004	1–10
water	33	0.0004–0.001	25–75
oil	1,000	0.002–0.004	200–500

available in a great range of viscosities and thus can satisfy a broad spectrum of functional requirements. Under boundary lubrication conditions, the effect of viscosity on friction becomes less significant than the chemical nature of the lubricant. Delicate instruments, for example, must not be lubricated with fluids that would attack and corrode the finer metals.

Wear occurs on lubricated surfaces by abrasion, corrosion, and solid-to-solid contact. Proper lubricants will help combat each type. They reduce abrasive and solid-to-solid contact wear by providing a film that increases the distance between the sliding surfaces, thereby lessening the damage by abrasive contaminants and surface asperities. The role of a lubricant in controlling corrosion of surfaces is

Synthetic lubricants generally can be characterized as oily, neutral liquid materials not usually obtained directly from petroleum but having some properties similar to petroleum lubricants. In certain ways they are superior to hydrocarbon products. Synthetics exhibit greater stability of viscosity with temperature changes, resistance to scuffing and oxidation, and fire resistance. Since the properties of synthetics vary considerably, each synthetic lubricant tends to find a special application. A few of the more common classes of synthetics and typical uses of each are shown in Table 2.

Another form of oily lubricant is grease, a solid or semisolid substance consisting of a thickening agent in a liquid lubricant. Soaps of aluminum, barium, calcium, lithium, sodium, and strontium are the major thickening agents.

Table 2: Synthetic lubricants and typical applications

synthetic lubricant	typical uses
dibasic acid esters	instrument oil, jet turbine lubricant, hydraulic fluid
phosphate esters	fire-resistant hydraulic fluid, low-temperature lubricant
silicones	damping fluid, low-volatility grease base
silicate esters	heat transfer fluid, high-temperature hydraulic fluid
polyglycol ether compounds	synthetic engine oil, hydraulic fluids, forming and drawing compounds
fluorol compounds	nonflammable fluid, extreme oxidation-resistant lubricant

Nonsoap thickeners consist of such inorganic compounds as modified clays or fine silicas, or such organic materials as arylureas or phthalocyanine pigments. Lubrication by grease may prove more desirable than lubrication by oil under conditions when (1) less frequent lubricant application is necessary, (2) grease acts as a seal against loss of lubricant and ingress of contaminants, (3) less dripping or splattering of lubricant is called for, or (4) less sensitivity to inaccuracies in the mating parts is needed.

Solid lubricants. A solid lubricant is a film of solid material composed of inorganic or organic compounds or of metal.

There are three general kinds of inorganic compounds that serve as solid lubricants:

1. Layer-lattice solids: materials such as graphite and molybdenum disulfide, commonly called molysulfide, have a crystal lattice structure arranged in layers. Strong bonds between atoms within a layer and relatively weak bonds between atoms of different layers allow the lamina to slide on one another. Other such materials are tungsten disulfide, mica, boron nitride, borax, silver sulfate, cadmium iodide, and lead iodide. Graphite's low friction is due largely to adsorbed films; in the absence of water vapour, graphite loses its lubricating properties and becomes abrasive. Both graphite and molysulfide are chemically inert and have high thermal stability.

2. Miscellaneous soft solids: a variety of inorganic solids such as white lead, lime, talc, bentonite, silver iodide, and lead monoxide are used as lubricants.

3. Chemical conversion coatings: many inorganic compounds can be formed on a metallic surface by chemical reaction. The best known such lubricating coatings are sulfide, chloride, oxide, phosphate, and oxalate films.

Solid organic lubricants are usually divided into two broad classes:

1. Soaps, waxes, and fats: this class includes metallic soaps of calcium, sodium, lithium; animal waxes (*e.g.*, beeswax and spermaceti wax); fatty acids (*e.g.*, stearic and palmitic acids); and fatty esters (*e.g.*, lard and tallow).

2. Polymeric films: these are synthetic substances such as polytetrafluoroethylene and polychlorofluoroethylene. One major advantage of such film-type lubricants is their resistance to deterioration during exposure to the elements. Thus, ½-inch- (1.3-centimetre-) thick plates of polymeric film are used in modern prestressed concrete construction to permit thermal movement of beams resting atop columns. Such expansion and contraction of the structural members is facilitated by the long-lived polymeric film plate.

Thin films of soft metal on a hard substrate can act as effective lubricants, if the adhesion to the substrate is good. Such metals include lead, tin, and indium.

Gaseous lubricants. Lubrication with a gas is analogous in many respects to lubrication with a liquid, since the same principles of fluid-film lubrication apply. Although both gases and liquids are viscous fluids, they differ in two important particulars. The viscosity of gases is much lower and the compressibility much greater than for liquids. Film thicknesses and load capacities therefore are much lower with a gas such as air (*see* Table 1). In equipment that handles gases of various kinds, it is often desirable to lubricate the sliding surfaces with gas in order to simplify the apparatus and reduce contamination from the lubricant.

Viscosity. Of all the properties of fluid lubricants, viscosity is the most important, since it determines the amount of friction that will be encountered between sliding surfaces and whether a film can be built up thick enough to avoid wear from solid-to-solid contact. Viscosity customarily is measured by a viscometer, which determines the flow rate of the lubricant under standard conditions; the higher the flow rate, the lower the viscosity. The rate is expressed in centipoises, reyns, or seconds Saybolt universal (SSU), depending respectively on whether metric, English, or commercial units are used. In most liquids, viscosity drops appreciably as the temperature is raised. Since little change of viscosity with fluctuations in temperature is desirable to keep variations in friction at a minimum, fluids often are rated in terms of viscosity index. The less the viscosity is changed by temperature, the higher the viscosity index.

Pour point. The pour point, or the temperature at which a lubricant ceases to flow, can become the determining factor in selecting one lubricant from among a group with otherwise identical properties.

Flash point. The flash point, or the temperature at which a lubricant momentarily flashes in the pressure of a test flame, aids in evaluating fire-resistance properties. Like the pour-point factor, the flash point may in some instances become the major consideration in selecting the proper lubricant, especially in lubricating machinery handling highly flammable material.

Oiliness. Oiliness generally connotes relative ability to operate under boundary lubrication conditions. The term relates to a lubricant's tendency to wet and adhere to a surface. There is no formal test for the measurement of oiliness; determination of this factor is chiefly through subjective judgment and experience. The most desirable lubricant for a specific use need not necessarily be the oiliest; *e.g.,* long-fibre grease, which is low in oiliness as compared with machine oils, is usually preferable for packing rolling bearings.

Lubumbashi, formerly (until 1966) ÉLISABETHVILLE, second largest city in the Democratic Republic of the Congo. The main industrial centre of the mining district of southeastern Congo, it lies 110 miles (180 km) northwest of Ndola, Zambia. Lubumbashi is also the name of a small local river.

The town was established by Belgian colonists in 1910 as a copper-mining settlement and was designated an urban district in 1942. Most regional mining companies are headquartered in Lubumbashi, which is the transportation centre for mineral products (copper, cobalt, zinc, cadmium, germanium, tin, manganese, and coal) from the towns of Likasi, Kolwezi, Kipushi, and others. In addition to mineral exploitations, local industries include printing, brewing, flour milling, and the production of confectionery, cigarettes, brick, and soap. Lubumbashi has a civic auditorium, a national museum, a Roman Catholic cathedral, and the Society of Congo Historians, as well as the University of Lubumbashi (1955). The city has decent road and rail transport, and Luano international airport is nearby. Lubumbashi was the centre of disaffection in Katanga during that former province's attempted secession from the republic in the years (1960–63) immediately following independence. Pop. (1994 est.) 851,381.

Lubuskie, *województwo* (province), west-central Poland. It comprises the former provinces (1975–98) of Lublin, Biała Podlaska, Chełm, and Zamość Toruń, as well as portions of Siedlce and Tarnobrzeg. The province's elevation rises from north to south, with marshlands and peat bogs in the north trending into uplands in the centre and then hills in the south. The Vistula and Bug are the main rivers, and lakes abound. The province is one of the least-developed in Poland, with an emphasis on agriculture. Cereals, potatoes, and sugar beets are grown; pigs and cattle are raised; and Arabian horses are bred. Lublin is the provincial capital, and the historic towns of Zamość and Kazimierz Dolny are frequent tourist destinations. During the German occupation in World War II, the area was home to several concentration camps, including Majdanek. Area 5,399 square miles (13,984 square km). Pop. (2003 est.) 1,008,000.

Luca (Italy): *see* Lucca.

Lucan, Latin in full MARCUS ANNAEUS LUCANUS (b. AD 39, Corduba [now Córdoba], Spain—d. 65, Rome [Italy]), Roman poet and republican patriot whose historical epic, the *Bellum civile,* better known as the *Pharsalia* because of its vivid account of that battle, is remarkable as the single major Latin epic poem without intervention of the gods.

Lucan was the nephew of the philosopher-statesman Lucius Annaeus Seneca (Seneca the Younger). Trained by the Stoic philosopher Cornutus and later educated in Athens, Lucan attracted the favourable attention of the emperor Nero owing to his early promise as a rhetorician and orator. Shortly, however, Nero became jealous of his ability as a poet and halted further public readings of his poetry. Already disenchanted by Nero's tyranny and embittered by the ban on his recitations, Lucan became one of the leaders in the conspiracy of Piso (Gaius Calpurnius) to assassinate Nero. When the conspiracy was discovered, he was compelled to commit suicide by opening a vein. According to Tacitus, he died repeating a passage from one of his poems describing the death of a wounded soldier.

The *Bellum civile,* his only extant poem, is an account of the war between Julius Caesar and Pompey, carried down to the arrival of Caesar in Egypt after the murder of Pompey, when it stops abruptly in the middle of the 10th book. Lucan was not a great poet, but he was a great rhetorician and had remarkable political and historical insight, though he wrote the poem while still a young man. The work is naturally imitative of Virgil, though not as dramatic. Although the style and vocabulary are usually commonplace and the metre monotonous, the rhetoric is often lifted into real poetry by its energy and flashes of fire and appears at its best in the magnificent funeral speech of Cato on Pompey. Scattered through the poem are noble sayings and telling comments, expressed with vigour and directness. As the poem proceeds, the poet's republicanism becomes more marked, no doubt because as Nero's tyranny grew, along with Lucan's hatred of him, he looked back with longing to the old Roman Republic. It has been said that Cato is the real hero of the epic, and certainly the best of Lucan's own Stoicism appears in the noble courage of his Cato in continuing the hopeless struggle after Pompey had failed.

Lucan's poetry was popular during the Middle Ages. Christopher Marlowe translated the first book of the *Bellum civile* (1600), and Samuel Johnson praised Nicholas Rowe's translation (1718) as "one of the greatest productions of English poetry." The English poets Robert Southey and Percy Bysshe Shelley in their earlier years preferred him to Virgil. His work strongly influenced French classical dramatist Pierre Corneille.

Lucan, George Charles Bingham, 3rd Earl of (b. April 16, 1800, London, Eng.—d. Nov. 10, 1888, London), British soldier who commanded the cavalry division, including the famous Light Brigade, at the Battle of Balaklava (*q.v.*) in the Crimean War.

The eldest son of the 2nd Earl of Lucan, Lord Bingham was educated at Westminster and was commissioned an ensign in 1816, rose to lieutenant colonel by 1826 (a rank he held until 1837), and served with the Russians in the Balkans (1828). He was a member of Parliament from 1826 to 1830 and succeeded as Earl of Lucan in 1839.

Having been appointed a major general in 1851, he applied for a command at the outbreak of the Crimean War in 1854 and was given a cavalry division consisting of two brigades—the Heavy Brigade under James Yorke Scarlett and the Light Brigade under his brother-in-law, the Earl of Cardigan. Despite the relationship, Lucan and Cardigan disdained each other.

In the Battle of Balaklava, Lord Raglan of the British staff issued two orders through an aide-de-camp, intending to disrupt a Russian withdrawal by means of an attack by the Light Brigade. A combination of circumstances resulted in a fatal confusion in relaying the final order, and Lucan sent the Light Brigade, followed by two regiments of the Heavy Brigade, toward the stronger, rather than the weaker, Russian positions. The brigade was decimated, and Lucan himself was wounded in the leg.

Lucan was recalled to England in 1855 and asked for a court-martial, which was refused. He received no more military employment but was promoted to general in 1865 and field marshal in 1887, a year before his death.

Lucania, ancient territorial division of southern Italy corresponding to most of the modern region of Basilicata, with much of the province of Salerno and part of that of Cosenza. Before its conquest by the Lucanians, a Samnite tribe, about the mid-5th century BC, it formed part of the Greek-dominated region of Oenotria. Discoveries of elaborately painted graves at Paestum, a city taken by the Lucanians about 400, suggest that by the 4th century BC the tribe had developed a culture of great vitality. Although they allied with Rome in 298, the Lucanians opposed and were defeated by that power in the Pyrrhic War (280–275), the Second Punic War (218–201), and the Social War (90–88). Repeated devastations of the area led to its decline.

Lucaris, Cyril, Greek KYRILLOS LOUKARIS (b. Nov. 13, 1572, Candia, Crete, republic of Venice [now in Greece]—d. June 27, 1638, aboard a ship in the Bosporus [Turkey]), patriarch of Constantinople who strove for reforms along Protestant Calvinist lines. His efforts generated broad opposition both from his own communion and from the Jesuits.

Lucaris pursued theological studies in Venice and Padua, and while studying further in Wittenberg and Geneva he came under the influence of Calvinism and developed a strong distaste for Roman Catholicism. In 1596 the patriarch of Alexandria, Meletios Pegas, sent Lucaris to Poland to lead the Orthodox opposition to the Union of Brest-Litovsk, which had sealed a union of the Orthodox metropolitanate of Kiev with Rome. For six years Lucaris served as rector of the Orthodox academy in Vilnius (now in Lithuania). In 1602 he was elected patriarch of Alexandria, and in 1620 he was elected patriarch of Constantinople.

As patriarch, Lucaris sought to further his Calvinistic purposes by sending young Greek theologians to universities in Holland, Switzerland, and England. It was one of these students, Metrophanes Kritopoulos, the future patriarch of Alexandria, who discovered the *Confession of Faith,* which had been written by Lucaris in Latin and published in Geneva in 1629. In its 18 articles Lucaris professed virtually all the major doctrines of Calvinism; predestination, justification by faith alone, acceptance of only two sacraments (instead of seven, as taught by the Eastern Orthodox Church), rejection of icons, rejection of the infallibility of the church, and so on. In the Orthodox church the *Confession* started a controversy that culminated in 1672 in a convocation by Dosítheos, patriarch of Jerusalem, of a church council that repudiated all Calvinist doctrines and reformulated Orthodox teachings in a manner intended to distinguish them from both Protestantism and Roman Catholicism.

Lucaris was forced to resign five times through the interventions of French and Austrian ambassadors to the Ottoman sultan Murad IV (reigned 1623–40). His return to patriarchal office was effected on each occasion by the help of British and Dutch diplomats. He was ultimately denounced before the sultan as a traitor attempting to incite the Cossacks against the Turks, and Lucaris was condemned to death and strangled by his Ottoman guards.

Lucas VAN LEYDEN, also called LUCAS HUYGHENSZ(OON) (b. 1489/94, Leiden [Neth.]—d. before Aug. 8, 1533, Leiden), northern Renaissance painter and one of the greatest engravers of his time.

Lucas was first trained by his father, Huygh Jacobszoon; later, he entered the workshop of Cornelis Engelbrechtsz(oon), a painter of Leiden. Lucas is more highly regarded today as a printmaker than as a painter. He was extraordinarily precocious. Even such early prints as "Muhammed and the Monk Sergius" (1508) are compositionally clear and direct and show great technical skill. Such engravings as "Susanna and the Elders" (1508), "St. George Liberating the Princess" (*c.* 1508–09), and his famous series "The Circular Passion" (1510) are notable for their accurate rendering of space and subtly composed landscapes. In 1510, under the influence of Albrecht Dürer, Lucas produced two masterpieces of engraving, "The Milkmaid" and "Ecce Homo," the latter much admired by Rembrandt. Their sureness of line and modeling complement their strong, simple compositions and place them among the most forceful engravings of their time. But engravings such as the "Adoration of the Magi" (*c.* 1512), cluttered with awkward figures and architectural backgrounds, indicate a decline in conceptual power that lasted until about 1519, when he engraved the "Dance of the Magdalene." This work also has a large number of figures, but they are tranquil and are lucidly composed in small groupings.

In 1521 Lucas met Dürer in Antwerp and again fell under his influence, as can be seen in the "Passion" series of the same year. Lucas may have learned the technique of etching from Dürer, for he produced a few etchings after their meeting. But Lucas himself is thought to have developed the technique of etching on copper, instead of iron, plates. The softness of the copper made it possible to combine etching and line engraving in the same print. His well-known portrait of the emperor Maximilian (1521) is one of the earliest examples of the use of that technique. Lucas was also among the first to employ aerial perspective in prints. Impressed with the Italianate style of Jan Mabuse, Lucas produced engravings, such as "The Poet Virgil Suspended in a Basket" (1521), characterized by a contrived monumentality. Such late prints, which often show the influence of the Italian engraver Marcantonio Raimondi, are generally considered to be his least successful.

Lucas' paintings are of uneven quality and seldom attain the power of his best engravings. The most notable of his early works is doubtless his "Self-Portrait" (*c.* 1508). It shows remarkable objectivity and is given a bizarre cast by its garish red-orange background. The loose, spontaneous technique used in this work is unusual for its time. Such early works as "The Chess Players" (*c.* 1508) reveal a predilection for narrative painting and characterization, which he used often at the expense of compositional unity. That was largely overcome in his "Moses Striking the Rock" (1527), the "Worship of the Golden Calf," and above all in his masterpiece, the "Last Judgment" (commissioned 1526), in which the composition is unified by the clear, dominant rhythm of the figures and the logically rendered space.

"St. George Liberating the Princess," engraving by Lucas van Leyden, *c.* 1508–09 (16.4 × 11.8 cm)

Lucas, George (b. May 14, 1944, Modesto, Calif., U.S.), American motion-picture director, producer, and screenwriter.

Lucas became interested in filmmaking while in high school and later gained admission to the film department of the University of Southern California (B.A., 1966). Lucas' first full-length feature film was *THX 1138* (1971), a grim fantasy about a robotized, dehumanized society in the distant future. His second film, *American Graffiti* (1973), a sympathetic recollection of adolescent American life in the early 1960s, was a surprise success at the box office.

Lucas spent the next four years writing and then shooting *Star Wars* (1977), an intergalactic swashbuckler with colourful characters, realistic extraterrestrial settings, and an array of breathtaking special effects. The film was immediately popular and went on to become one of the most profitable motion pictures in history. Its success spawned a host of other science-fiction films using the newly developed computer-based special-effects that *Star Wars* had used so effectively. In 1978–79, Lucas formed the production company Lucasfilms, Ltd., which contained a number of divisions, including Industrial Light and Magic, regarded as the most prestigious special-effects workshop in American film.

Lucas served as executive producer of two additional episodes in the Star Wars saga, *The Empire Strikes Back* (1980) and *The Return of the Jedi* (1983), and of the popular Indiana Jones series directed by Steven Spielberg. Working exclusively as a producer throughout the 1980s and most of the '90s, Lucas had a few minor successes (*Willow,* 1988) and spectacular failures (*Howard the Duck,* 1986). In 1997 he added new computerized effects to the Star Wars films and re-released them to great acclaim. These films generated interest for one of the most highly-anticipated films of the decade, *Star Wars: Episode I—The Phantom Menace* (1999), the first release in a proposed new trilogy. For this film, which received mixed reviews but reaped enormous profits, Lucas returned to the director's chair for the first time in more than 20 years.

Lucas, Robert E., Jr. (b. Sept. 15, 1937, Yakima, Wash., U.S.), American economist who won the 1995 Nobel Prize for Economics for developing and applying the theory of rational expectations, an econometric hypothesis which suggests that individuals may affect the expected results of national fiscal policy by making private economic decisions based on past experiences and anticipated results. His work, which gained prominence in the mid-1970s, questioned the influence of John Maynard Keynes in macroeconomics and the efficacy of government intervention in domestic affairs.

Lucas graduated from the University of Chicago with degrees in history (A.B., 1959) and economics (Ph.D., 1964). He taught at Carnegie Mellon University, Pittsburgh, Pa., from 1963 to 1974 before returning to Chicago to accept a professorship of economics in 1975. Lucas' *Studies in Business-Cycle Theory* (1981) reprints his research from the 1970s, and *Models of Business Cycles* (1987) provides an overview of his economic theory.

The rational expectations hypothesis was first formulated in 1961 by John F. Muth to explain how traditional models of Keynesian economics fail to predict prices in speculative markets. One such model, the Phillips curve, proposes that a government can lower the rate of unemployment by stimulating inflation and thereby encouraging companies, which anticipate higher revenues, to raise wages and attract more workers. Lucas' critique of the Phillips curve shows that inflation may continue to rise in the long run without a corresponding drop in unemployment because higher production costs and higher consumer prices can eventually offset higher revenues and higher wages, thereby dampening the expectations of both companies and workers.

Lucca, Latin LUCA, city, capital of Lucca *provincia,* Toscana (Tuscany) *regione,* north-central Italy. It lies in the valley of the Serchio River and is almost surrounded by hills, with the Apuan Alps to the north and west.

Lucca was a Ligurian and later an Etruscan town, and the Romans probably established a colony there in 180 BC (mentioned by the Roman historian Livy). The rectangular Roman plan is preserved in Lucca's central streets, and remains of the walls, forum, and amphitheatre have been found. Lying at the junction of roads to Parma, Florence, Rome, Pisa, and Luni, the town was apparently fairly prosperous and was an early episcopal see. After AD 476 it was ruled successively by the Goths, the Byzantines, and the Lombards, becoming the residence of one of the three Lombard dukes in Tuscany. Frankish counts replaced the dukes after 774, but the population appears to have remained largely Lombardian. Lucca was the principal city in Tuscany in the 9th and 10th centuries, when its counts became the margraves of Tuscany, and it commanded one of the principal roads between Lombardy and Rome, the Via Francigena. The city began to lose importance in the late 10th century to Florence, which replaced Lucca as the Tuscan capital when the house of Canossa succeeded to the margravate. In 1118 the town was granted a charter of liberties, mainly economic, and the commune of Lucca was probably established soon afterward. Despite numerous conflicts with its powerful neighbours and ambitious noble houses, Lucca largely maintained its independence until it fell to the French in 1799. From 1805 until 1814, Lucca was ruled as a principality by Élisa Baciocchi, a sister of Napoleon. Assigned by the Congress of Vienna (1815) to the Spanish infanta María Luisa, widow of the former king Louis of Etruria, it passed in 1824 to her son Charles Louis, who ceded it to Tuscany in 1847. It was united to the kingdom of Italy in 1860.

Cathedral of San Martino, Lucca, Italy
SCALA—Art Resource

Many of the archiepiscopal city's numerous churches follow, with their own local variations, a distinctive style found in nearby Pisa; often basilican or Romanesque in structure, many have rich Gothic exterior decorations and some have quadrangular campaniles. Particularly notable are the Cathedral of San Martino (probably founded in the 6th century; rebuilt 1060–70; completed 13th–14th century); San Frediano (rebuilt 1112–47), retaining traces of an 8th-century structure; San Michele in Foro (begun 1143); and Santa Maria Forisportam, begun in the 13th century. Lucca is noted for its well-preserved ramparts (1561–1650) and has many fine 16th-century palaces, notably the Palazzo Pretorio and the Palazzo della Prefettura, the former grand ducal palace, now housing the National Art Gallery. There are several other art collections, libraries, and archives. Lucca, long an important musical centre, was the home of the composers Luigi Boccherini and Giacomo Puccini.

A road and rail centre, the city is the market town of a rich agricultural region that exports high-quality olive oil. Silk has been manufactured since about the end of the 11th century. Other industries include flour milling and the production of tobacco, paper, textiles, jute goods, and wine. The Serchio is used for waterpower, and an aqueduct (1823–32) carries the water supply from the Pisan mountains. Pop. (1990 est.) mun., 86,676.

Lucca, Republic of, also called LUCCAN REPUBLIC, French RÉPUBLIQUE LUCQUOISE, Italian REPUBBLICA LUCCHESE, republic established by Napoleon Bonaparte in Lucca and its environs on Dec. 27, 1801, after his second successful conquest of Italy, driving out the Austrians. It lasted less than four years; in June 1805 he granted Lucca to his sister Élisa Bonaparte as a principality, part of the new French Empire.

Luce, Clare Boothe, in full ANN CLARE BOOTHE LUCE, *née* BOOTHE (b. March 10, 1903, New York, N.Y., U.S.—d. Oct. 9, 1987, Washington, D.C.), American playwright, politician, and celebrity, noted for her satiric sense of humour and for her role in American politics of the 1940s to the '60s.

Privately educated in Garden City and Tarrytown, N.Y., she was associate editor of *Vogue* in 1930 and associate editor and managing editor of *Vanity Fair* during 1930–34. Some of her satirical articles for *Vanity Fair* were collected in *Stuffed Shirts* (1931). She was divorced from her first husband, George Tuttle Brokaw, in 1929, and she married magazine publisher Henry R. Luce in 1935.

After an earlier play failed, Luce wrote *The Women* (1936), a comedy that ran for 657 performances on Broadway; *Kiss the Boys Goodbye* (1938), a satire on American life; and *Margin for Error* (1939), an anti-Nazi play. All three were adapted into motion pictures.

She was elected to the U.S. House of Representatives as a Republican from Connecticut, serving in the 78th and 79th congresses in 1943–47. She was influential in the Republican Party nationally. In 1953 President Dwight D. Eisenhower appointed her ambassador to Italy, but she resigned in 1956 because of ill health. In 1959 and again in 1964 her political involvement brought her into the public

Clare Boothe Luce
Camera Press

eye, but thereafter she withdrew from politics, living in Phoenix, Ariz., until the death of her husband, and in Honolulu, Hawaii. In 1981 Luce became a member of President Ronald W. Reagan's Foreign Intelligence Advisory Board. In 1983 she was presented with the Presidential Medal of Freedom.

Luce, Henry R., in full HENRY ROBINSON LUCE (b. April 3, 1898, Tengchow, Shantung province, China—d. Feb. 28, 1967, Phoenix, Ariz., U.S.), American magazine publisher who built a publishing empire on *Time, Fortune,* and *Life* magazines. Luce became one of the most powerful figures in the history of American journalism. His publications, founded as means of educating what Luce considered a poorly informed American public, had many imitators. *Time,* a "weekly

Henry Luce
By courtesy of Time Inc.

newsmagazine," sought to present news in narrative form. The magazine also stressed world events, an area that Luce believed was neglected in American newspapers and magazines. Presenting each story in a specific section or department, *Time* generally suggested what readers should think with regard to the subjects covered. Luce publications frequently utilized library research materials to make stories and articles more complete. Reporters and editors worked together on stories in what was called "group journalism."

Luce was one of four children born to a Presbyterian missionary family, and his first decade was spent in China. At age 10, Luce was sent to a British boarding school at Chefoo (Yen-t'ai) in north China. From there he went alone to England and then to the United States to attend preparatory school and Yale University. There he edited the school paper, was elected to Phi Beta Kappa, and graduated in 1920, styled "most brilliant" in his class.

At Yale he met Briton Hadden, with whom Luce launched *Time* magazine. The magazine attracted attention because of its lively layout, stylistic eccentricities, mostly introduced by Hadden, and its emphasis on personalities. In four years *Time* was making a profit. In 1929, the year in which Hadden died, Luce brought out the business magazine *Fortune,* and in 1936 the picture magazine *Life* appeared for the first time. *Life* immediately became one of the most popular magazines ever published. It ceased regular publication in 1972–78, partly because of rising costs. Luce held the title of editor-in-chief of all Time, Inc. publications from 1929 until 1964, when he became editorial chairman.

Other Luce magazines included *House & Home,* established in 1952 and later sold to McGraw-Hill Publishing Company, and *Sports Illustrated,* a weekly sports magazine launched in 1954. Luce launched the radio series "The March of Time" in 1931 and theatre newsreels of the same name in 1935.

Luce married the American playwright Clare Boothe in 1935. Both were forceful and articulate and conservative in politics. Each had a major influence on the Republican Party and on national political affairs.

Luce, Stephen Bleecker (b. March 25, 1827, Albany, N.Y., U.S.—d. July 28, 1917, Newport, R.I.), principal founder and first president of the Naval War College for postgraduate studies, the world's first such institution.

Stephen Luce, *c.* 1888
By courtesy of the U.S. Navy

Starting his career in 1841 as a midshipman, Luce rose through the ranks to become a rear admiral (1886). From the beginning of his naval life, he wished to improve the education of seamen; to that end he published *Seamanship* (1863), which became a standard text.

Luce gradually became convinced of the need for postgraduate training for naval officers. After years of lobbying, his idea was realized in the establishment in 1884 of the Naval War College in Newport, R.I. Luce, then a commodore, was appointed president of the college, a post he retained until his retirement in 1889. He continued as a special adviser, however, until 1910. It was through Luce's sponsorship that Captain Alfred Thayer Mahan, in his lectures at the Naval War College, expounded the theories of sea power that gained worldwide recognition in the 1890s and early 1900s. Other countries, including Japan, England, and Germany, later founded similar institutions.

Lucena, city, south-central Luzon, Philippines. Situated near the head of Tayabas Bay of the Sibuyan Sea, its importance as a settlement predated the arrival of the Spaniards. It is a major fishing port and a regional wholesale distributing point and has food-processing plants (particularly for coconut). Lucena is served by major road and rail facilities. The Banahaw and San Cristobal Mountains National Park is located there. Inc. city, 1961. Pop. (1990 prelim.) 151,000.

Lucerne, German LUZERN, *canton,* central Switzerland. Lucerne is drained by the Reuss and Kleine Emme rivers and occupies the northern foothills of the Alps, which rise to 7,710 feet (2,350 m) at the Brienzer Rothorn. Comprising the territories acquired by its capital, the city of Lucerne (*q.v.*), it was part of the Helvetic Republic after 1798 and resumed its status as an independent *canton* in 1803, by Napoleon's Act of Mediation. After attempting to pursue a separatist policy, which led to its defeat by federal troops, in 1848 Lucerne again entered the Swiss Confederation as a full member.

Of the total surface area, about 90 percent is productive land. The main sources of income are field crops, fruit, cattle, industry, and tourism, the latter concentrated in the area around the capital. Manufactures include textiles, machinery, metallurgical goods, paper, wood, tobacco, electrical equipment, stone, glass, and ceramics. There is also boatbuilding and automobile assembly. Much transit traffic between Germany and Italy crosses the *canton.* The population is mainly German speaking and Roman Catholic. Area 576 square miles (1,493 square km). Pop. (1992 est.) 324,044.

Lucerne, German LUZERN, capital of Lucerne *canton,* central Switzerland, on the Reuss River, where it issues from the northwestern branch of Lake Lucerne (German: Vierwaldstätter See; French: Lac des Quatre Cantons), southwest of Zürich. The city's name was derived from the Benedictine monastery of St. Leodegar (Luciaria), founded in the 8th century. From the nearby fishing village grew a city, probably chartered about 1178, whose inhabitants were originally serfs of the monastery. After the opening of the St. Gotthard Pass (*c.* 1230), Lucerne developed into an important trade centre between the upper Rhine and Lombardy. In 1291 the monastery and city were purchased by Rudolf IV of Habsburg (also called Rudolf I of Germany), against the will of the citizens, who desired independence. Political instability under Rudolf's successors led Lucerne in 1332 to join the alliance formed by the cantons of Uri, Schwyz, and Unterwalden in 1291. The group won independence after the Battle of Sempach (1386) against the Habsburg army. By 1415 Lucerne had acquired most of the territory of the present canton, by either treaty, armed occupation, or purchase. It became the leader of the Catholic cantons at the Reformation and was the seat of the papal nuncio from 1579 to 1874. The city's aristocratic regime was compelled to abdicate in 1798 under the onslaught of the Napoleonic armies. Lucerne was for a time the capital of the Helvetic Republic, resuming its status as the cantonal capital in 1803.

Divided into two parts by the Reuss River, which is crossed by seven bridges within the town, Lucerne has one of the most picturesque settings in Switzerland. The Spreuerbrücke (1407), now the oldest bridge, is roofed and decorated with some 56 paintings, scenes from the Dance of Death, dating from the early 17th century. Until its destruction by fire in 1993, the Kapellbrücke (1333; "Chapel Bridge") was the oldest bridge. It was similarly decorated. The old town on the right bank is distinguished by well-preserved 14th-century town walls (Musegg) with nine watchtowers, quaint alleys, and squares with medieval, Renaissance, and Baroque houses. Notable buildings are the old town hall (1602–06), housing the historical museum; Am Rhyn House (1617); St. Peter's Chapel (1178; altered 1750); the Hofkirche (an 8th-century cathedral and collegiate church of St. Leodegar); and the Mariahilf Church (1676–81). Other landmarks are Bertel Thorvaldsen's "Lion of Lucerne" monument (1819–21), in memory of the Swiss guards slain while defending the Tuileries in Paris in 1792; the Glacier Garden, a relic of the Ice Age excavated in 1872–75; and the comprehensive Swiss Transport Museum (1959). On the left bank are the cantonal government building, Regierungsgebäude, or Ritterscher Palast (1557–64; a Jesuit college 1577–1804); the State Archives (1729–31), with a Rococo Marian chamber and library and the Central Library (1951), housing the numismatic, natural history, and Helvetica collections; the St. Francis Xavier (Jesuit) Church (1667–77); the 14th-century Gothic Franciscan Church with Rococo transepts; the Corporation Building (1675); the new town hall (1913); the Richard Wagner Museum (1933); the modern St. Anthony's Chapel (1954); and the Art Gallery and Congress Hall (Kunst- und Kongresshaus; 1932–33).

In addition to various cantonal and municipal schools, there are the central Swiss Transport School, the Swiss Catholic School of Sacred Music, the Central Swiss Technical College, and the Swiss Schools of Bakery and of Hotel Keeping. Lucerne is also the seat of the Supreme Cantonal Court, a commercial tribunal, a criminal court, a juvenile court, and the Federal Insurance Court.

Because of its magnificent surroundings, temperate climate, and easy access by road and rail, Lucerne has become one of the largest and most important tourist resorts in Switzerland. Steamer services on the lake connect with various mountain railways and cableways, and there is a direct narrow-gauge rail connection with the winter-sports centre of Engelberg. Facilities include a casino, beaches, rowing and sailing regattas, horse-racing and show-jumping competitions, an annual international music festival, and a traditional pre-Lenten carnival. Lucerne's commercial and industrial activities depend largely on the tourist trade. The population is German speaking and largely Roman Catholic. Pop. (1991 est.) 59,370.

lucerne (botany): *see* alfalfa.

Lucerne, Lake, also called LAKE OF LUCERNE, or LAKE OF THE FOUR CANTONS, German VIERWALDSTÄTTER SEE, French LAC LUCERNE, or LAC DES QUATRE CANTONS, principal lake of central Switzerland, surrounded by the *cantons* of Lucerne, Nidwalden, Uri, and Schwyz. The lake is named after the city of Lucerne, which lies at its western end. The lake is most beautifully situated between steep limestone mountains, the best-known being the Rigi (north) and Pilatus (west), at an elevation of 1,424 feet (434 m). The lake's area is 44 square miles (114 square km); it is about 24 miles (39 km) long, with a maximum width of 2 miles (3 km) and a maximum depth of 702 feet (214 m). Great promontories such as Horw (west), Bürgenstock (south), Maggenhorn (north), and Seelisberg (south) project into its waters, giving it an irregular shape. The Reuss River enters the lake near Flüelen (southeast) and leaves it at Lucerne, and the lake receives the rivers Muota (northeast) and the Engelberger Aa and the Sarner Aa (south).

Lake Lucerne is composed of four main basins (with two side basins), which represent four glaciated valleys, topographically distinct and connected only by narrow and tortuous channels. The most easterly basin, Lake Uri (Urner See), extends north from Flüelen to Brunnen, where it meets Lake Gersau (or Buochs), formed by the extension into the lake of the Muota Delta. Another narrow passage between the two "noses" (*nasen*) of the Bürgenstock and the Rigi leads west to the basin of Weggis. This expanse forms the eastern arm of the "Cross of Lucerne." The western arm is Lake Lucerne, the northern arm is Lake Küssnacht, and the southern arm is that of Hergiswil, which is prolonged southwestward by Lake Alpnach, to which it is joined by a narrow channel.

Situated at the heart of the first four cantons of the Swiss Confederation, the lake has numerous historical associations. Lake Uri's eastern shore is the site of the legendary Swiss patriot William Tell's leap from the boat in which the bailiff Gessler was taking him to prison (marked by the Chapel of Tell). The legendary meeting place of the founders of the Confederation, the meadow of Rütli, is on the west bank. The Everlasting League of 1315 was formed at Brunnen, and the Hollow Way (Hohle Gasse), the scene of the legendary murder of Gessler by William Tell, runs south along Lake Küssnacht. Lucerne is the principal lakeside town in a region noted for its summer resorts.

Luchaire, Achille, in full DENIS-JEAN-ACHILLE LUCHAIRE (b. Oct. 24, 1846, Paris, France—d. Nov. 4, 1908, Paris), definitive historian of the Capetians (the royal house of France from 987 to 1328) and of Pope Innocent III (1198–1216).

In 1879 Luchaire became a professor at Bordeaux and in 1899 professor of medieval history at the University of Paris; he was a member of the Academy of Moral and Political Science from 1895 until his death.

His most important works include *Histoire des institutions monarchiques de la France sous les premiers Capétiens* (1883; "History of the French Monarchical Institutions Under the Early Capetians"), *Manuel des institutions françaises: période des Capétiens directs* (1892; "French Institutions Under the Direct Capetian Line"), *Louis VI le Gros, annales de sa vie et de son règne* (1890; "Louis VI the Fat, Annals of His Life and Reign"), and *Étude sur les actes de Louis VII* (1885). His later works include *Innocent III,* 6 vol. (1904–08), an elaborate study of the pope's life and the social climate and events of his day, and *La Société française au temps de Philippe-Auguste* (1909). He also contributed essays on the 13th century to Ernest Lavisse's monumental *Histoire de France* (1900–11).

Luchana, Baldomero Espartero, Count (conde) **de:** *see* Espartero, Baldomero.

Lucia, SANTA: *see* Lucy, Saint.

Lucian, Greek LUCIANOS, Latin LUCIANUS, or LUCINUS (b. *c.* AD 120, Samosata, Commagene, Syria [now Samsat, Tur.]—d. after 180, Athens [Greece]), ancient Greek rhetorician, pamphleteer, and satirist, author of *Dialogues of the Gods* and *Dialogues of the Dead.*

One is entirely dependent on Lucian's writings for information about his life, but he says little about himself—and not all that he says is to be taken seriously. Moreover, since the chronology of his works is very obscure, the events of his life can only be reconstructed in broad outline, and the order and dating of these events are matters of mere probability.

As a boy Lucian showed a talent for making clay models and was therefore apprenticed to his uncle, a sculptor. They quarreled, and Lucian soon left home for western Asia Minor, in whose cities he acquired a Greek literary education. He became particularly familiar with the works of Homer, Plato, and the comic poets. So successfully did he master the Greek language (he was raised speaking Aramaic) and culture that he began a career as a public speaker, traveling from city to city giving model speeches and public lectures to display his eloquence and probably also pleading in court. After touring Greece he went to Italy and then to Gaul (modern France). To this period of his life belong many of his surviving declamations on mythological and other stock themes and his rhetorical prologues.

Lucian was evidently successful as a rhetorician, but he seems never to have reached the first rank in his profession. It may have been disillusion with the emptiness of his career that led him to give up his wandering life and settle in Athens in the late '50s of the 2nd century. In Athens he was able to extend his knowledge of Greek literature and thought far beyond anything required of a rhetorician.

In this early Athenian period Lucian gave up public speaking and took to writing critical and satirical essays on the intellectual life of his time, either in the form of Platonic dialogues or, in imitation of Menippus, in a mixture of prose and verse. Lucian's writings apparently sustained the reputation he had won as a public speaker.

Thanks to the patronage of his Roman friends, he obtained a lucrative post in Alexandria as *archistator,* a kind of chief court usher. After some years he returned to Athens and took up public speaking again. The date and circumstances of his death are unknown.

Of the 80 prose works traditionally attributed to Lucian, about 10 are spurious. The writings of Lucian are outstanding for their mordant and malicious wit, embodying a sophisticated and often embittered critique of the shams and follies of the literature, philosophy, and intellectual life of his day. Lucian satirized almost every aspect of human behaviour. One of his favourite topics is man's failure to realize the transience of greatness and wealth. This Cynic theme permeates his dialogue *Charon,* while in the *Dialogues of the Dead* and other pieces, the Cynic philosopher Menippus is made to jibe at kings and aristocrats, reminding them how much more they have lost by death than he. In *Timon* Lucian recounts how Timon, after impoverishing himself by his generosity and becoming a hermit, is restored to wealth, once again to be surrounded by toadies to whom he gives short shrift. Other human frailties Lucian satirized are the folly of bargaining with the gods by sacrifices, crying over spilt milk when bereaved, and the love of telling or listening to strange tales. In *True History,* which starts by warning the reader that its events are completely untrue and impossible, Lucian describes a voyage that starts on the sea, continues in the skies, and includes visits to the belly of a whale and to the Elysian fields; the tale is a satirical parody of all those fantastic travelers' tales that strain human credulity. In *Nigrinus* Lucian makes a Platonic philosopher censure the evils of Rome, contrasting the pretentiousness, lack of culture, and avarice of the Romans with the quiet, cultured life of the Athenians.

Lucian is particularly critical of those whom he considers impostors. In *Alexander* Lucian attacks the popular magician and wonder-working charlatan Alexander the Paphlagonian and gives an account of the various hoaxes by which Alexander was amassing wealth as a priest of Asclepius and a seer. Another contemporary personage dubbed by Lucian as an impostor was the Cynic philosopher Peregrinus, who commited public suicide by setting fire to himself on a pyre at the Olympic Games of AD 165.

Lucian regarded the worst charlatans of all to be those philosophers who failed to practice what they preached. *Banquet* gives an amusing account of an imaginary wedding feast given by a patron of the arts. Among the guests are representatives of every philosophical school, who all behave outrageously and start fighting over delicacies to take home when the party comes to an end. Hypocritical philosophers are also attacked in *Fisher,* in which the founders of the philosophical schools return to life to indict Lucian for writing *The Auction of Lives,* which was itself a lighthearted work in which Zeno, Epicurus, and others are auctioned by Hermes in the underworld but fetch next to nothing. Lucian's defense is that he was attacking not the founders of the schools but their present unworthy successors. The philosophers acquit Lucian and call to trial their modern disciples, who refuse to have their lives examined until Lucian "fishes" for them from the Acropolis using a bait of gold and figs. He soon has a fine catch of philosophers, who are renounced by the founders of the schools and hurled to their deaths from the Acropolis.

Lucian follows the lead of Xenophanes, Plato, and others also in complaining about the absurd beliefs concerning the Olympian gods. Thus the discreditable love affairs of Zeus with mortal women play a prominent part in *Dialogues of the Gods,* and in *Zeus Confuted* and *Tragic Zeus* the leader of the gods is powerless to intervene on earth and prove his omnipotence to coldly skeptical Cynic and Epicurean philosophers. Lucian's interest in philosophy was basically superficial, however, and his attitude to philosophical studies is best seen in *Banquet,* where, after noting how much worse the philosophers are behaving than the ordinary guests, he cannot help reflecting that book learning is worthless if it does not improve one's conduct.

Lucian's best work in the field of literary criticism is his treatise *How to Write History.* In this work he stresses the impartiality, detachment, and rigorous devotion to truth that characterize the ideal historian. He also comments on the ideal historical style and provides amusing descriptions of contemporary historians who imitate Thucydides by introducing plagues and funeral orations into their narratives. Less attractive are his attacks on contemporary rhetoricians. His *Teacher of Orators* contains ironical advice on how to become a successful orator by means of claptrap and impudence, while in *Word-Flaunter* he attacks a contemporary rhetorician who is excessively fond of using an archaic and recondite vocabulary.

Lucian's primary literary models for his works were the satires of Menippus, which mocked institutions, ideas, and conventions in a mixture of prose and verse. But Lucian improved on the Menippean satire by creating his own harmonious blend of Platonic dialogue and comic fantasy, and he raised it to the level of art by his broad, fluent, and seemingly effortless command of the Attic Greek language and literary style. The only thing that had real value in his eyes and that provided him with a standard of judgment was classical Greek literature. In this turning toward a half-imaginary, idealized past, Lucian was at one with his age. His own classicizing style served as a model for writers of the later Roman Empire and for the Byzantine period.

BIBLIOGRAPHY. Studies of his life and works include Jennifer Hall, *Lucian's Satire* (1981); Graham Anderson, *Studies in Lucian's Comic Fiction* (1976); Christopher Robinson, *Lucian and His Influence in Europe* (1979); C.P. Jones, *Culture and Society in Lucian* (1986); and R. Bracht Branham, *Unruly Eloquence: Lucian and the Comedy of Traditions* (1989).

Lucian OF ANTIOCH, SAINT (b. *c.* 240, Samosata, Commagene, Syria [now Samsat, Tur.]—d. Jan. 7, 312, Nicomedia, Bithynia, Asia Minor [now İzmit, Tur.]), Christian theologian-martyr who originated a theological tradition at Antioch that was noted for biblical linguistic scholarship and for a rationalist approach to Christian doctrine.

In his principal work, Lucian analyzed the Greek text of both the Old and New Testaments, creating a tradition of manuscripts known as the Lucianic Byzantine, or Syrian, text. Until the development of 19th-century biblical criticism, its clarity made it the common text. By comparative study of the Greek and Hebrew grammatical styles in their Semitic background, Lucian proposed to limit the symbolical interpretation characteristic of the Alexandrian (Egyptian) allegorical tradition by emphasizing the primacy of the literal sense, whether expressed directly or metaphorically.

Such analytical methods influenced Antiochene theological formulations by Lucian's students and colleagues relative to doctrines on Christ and the divine Trinity. Later critics, including Alexander of Alexandria, during the Council of Nicaea in 325, associated Lucian's school with the condemned theological revisions of Arius and his attack on the absolute divinity of Christ. Lucian, in 269, had also been implicated with the denounced teachings—known as Monarchianism—of the Antiochene bishop Paul of Samosata. Church authorities subsequently accepted Lucian's conciliatory statement of belief in 289 and, posthumously, in 341 at a church council in Antioch. Lucian's influence permanently oriented Christian theology toward a historical realist approach in its debate with classical non-Christian thought.

Lucian's martyrdom by torture and starvation for refusing to eat meat ritually offered to the Roman gods during the early-4th-century persecution of the Roman emperor Maximinus elicited praise from his antagonists.

Luciano, Lucky, byname of CHARLES LUCIANO, original name SALVATORE LUCANIA (b. Nov. 11, 1896, Lercara Friddi, Sicily, Italy—d. Jan. 26, 1962, Capodicino Airport, Naples), the most powerful chief of American organized crime in the early 1930s and a major influence even from prison, 1936–45, and after deportation to Italy in 1946.

Luciano immigrated with his parents from Sicily to New York City in 1906 and, at the age of 10, was already involved in mugging, shoplifting, and extortion; in 1916 he spent six months in jail for selling heroin. Out of jail, he teamed up with Frank Costello and Meyer Lansky and other young gangsters; he earned his nickname "Lucky" for success at evading arrest and winning craps games. In 1920 he joined the ranks of New York's rising crime boss, Joe Masseria, and by 1925 had become Masseria's chief lieutenant, directing bootlegging, prostitution, narcotics distribution, and other rackets. In October 1929 he became the rare gangster to survive a "one-way ride"; he was abducted by four men in a car, beaten, stabbed repeatedly with an icepick, had his throat slit from ear to ear, and was left for dead on a Staten Island beach—but survived. He never named his abductors. (Soon after, he changed his name to Luciano.)

The bloody gang war of 1930–31 between Masseria and rival boss Salvatore Maranzano was anathema to Luciano and other young racketeers who decried the publicity and loss of business, money, and efficiency. On April 15, 1931, Luciano lured Masseria to a Coney Island restaurant and had him assassinated by four loyalists, Vito Genovese, Albert Anastasia, Joe Adonis, and Bugsy Siegel. Six months later, on September 10, he had Maranzano murdered by four Jewish gunmen loaned by Meyer Lansky. Luciano had carefully nurtured his contacts with all the young powers in gangdom and had become *capo di tutti capi* ("boss of all the bosses"), without ever accepting or claiming the title. By 1934 he and the leaders of other crime "families" had developed the national crime syndicate or cartel.

Then, in 1935, New York special prosecutor Thomas E. Dewey bore down on Luciano, gathering evidence of his brothel and call-girl empire and related extortion. In 1936 he was indicted, tried, and convicted and was sentenced to Clinton Prison at Dannemora, N.Y., for a 30-to-50-year term.

From his cell Luciano continued to rule and issue orders. In 1942, after the luxury line "Normandie" blew up in New York Harbor, Navy intelligence sought Luciano's help in tightening waterfront security. (The crime syndicate's power extended to the longshoremen's union.) Luciano gave the orders; sabotage on the docks ended; and in 1946 his sentence was commuted and he was deported to Italy, where he settled in Rome. In 1947 he moved to Cuba, to which all the syndicate heads came to pay homage and cash. But the pressure of public opinion and the U.S. narcotics bureau forced the embarrassed Cuban regime to deport him. He ended up in Naples, where he continued to direct the drug traffic into the United States and the smuggling of aliens to America. He died of a heart attack in Naples in 1962 and was buried in St. John's Cathedral Cemetery, Queens, N.Y.

Lucidor (Swedish poet): *see* Johansson, Lars.

Lucifer (Latin: Lightbearer), Greek PHOSPHORUS, or EOSPHOROS in classical mythology, the morning star (*i.e.,* the planet Venus at dawn); personified as a male figure bearing a torch, Lucifer had almost no legend, but in poetry he was often herald of the dawn. In Christian times Lucifer came to be regarded as the name of Satan before his fall. It was thus used by John Milton (1608–74) in *Paradise Lost,* and the idea underlies the proverbial phrase "as proud as Lucifer."

Lucifer, also called LUCIFER CALARITANUS (d. *c.* 370), bishop of Cagliari, Sardinia, who was a fierce opponent of the heresy of Arianism (*q.v.*). To further his rigorously orthodox views, he founded the Luciferians, a sect that survived in scattered remnants into the early 5th century.

Lucifer's opposition to Arianism was tested during the reign of the Roman emperor Constantius II. Himself an Arian, the Emperor had the chief opponent of the heresy, Bishop St. Athanasius the Great, of Alexandria, condemned at a church council at Arelate (later Arles, Fr.), Gaul, in 353. Pope Liberius, disturbed by the council's bias, asked Lucifer to request a new and impartial imperial council. The result was the Council of Milan (355), at which Athanasius, despite a vigorous defense by Lucifer, was again condemned. Lucifer refused to endorse this decision and was banished to the East, where he wrote five harsh polemical tracts against the emperor. These are of scholarly interest because of their many biblical quotations in Old Latin.

When Constantius died in 361, Lucifer's exile was ended by an edict issued the next year by the new emperor, Julian the Apostate. Lucifer then went to Antioch, where the church was shattered by factions supporting two men as the rightful bishop. Lucifer deepened the controversy into a schism by consecrating one of the candidates, Paulinus, as bishop. The supporters of his rival, Meletius, did not believe Lucifer had this authority according to canon law, and the church in Antioch remained split until the death of Meletius in 381.

Meanwhile, Lucifer had unalterably opposed a council held in Alexandria in 362 by Athanasius, which had decided to pardon Arians who renounced their views, and he withdrew to his see in Sardinia. There he formed the Luciferians, who promulgated his opinions that all clerics who had been involved in Arianism should be deposed and that any bishop accepting them should be excommunicated. The sect had small groups of adherents in Spain, Gaul, and Rome before it collapsed. It was attacked by St. Jerome in his polemic *Altercatio Luciferiani et orthodoxi* ("The Dispute of the Luciferian and the Orthodox").

luciferin, in biochemistry, any of several organic compounds whose oxidation in the presence of the enzyme luciferase produces light. Luciferins vary in chemical structure; the luciferin of luminescent bacteria, for example, is completely different from that of fireflies. For each type luciferin, there is a specific luciferase. *See also* bioluminescence.

Lucilius, Gaius (b. *c.* 180 BC, Suessa Aurunca, Campania, Italy—d. *c.* 103 or 102 BC, Neapolis), effectively the inventor of poetical satire who gave to the existing, formless Latin *satura* (meaning "a mixed dish") the distinctive character of critical comment that the word satire still implies.

Lucilius was a Roman citizen of good family and education, a friend of learned Greeks, and well acquainted with Greek manners, which afforded him some targets for his wit; he was on familiar terms with the general Scipio Aemilianus, under whom he served in Spain, and with other great figures of his time. He spent the greater part of his life in Rome, beginning to write from the wealth of his experiences only after middle life.

His works were collected in a posthumous edition of 30 books. Only about 1,300 lines survive, mostly written in the hexameters that were to influence the development of the later Roman satirists Horace, Persius, and Juvenal.

An egoist of ebullient nature, pungent wit, and strong opinions, Lucilius used the satiric form for self-expression, fearlessly criticizing public as well as private conduct and displaying the originality of his genius by using themes of daily life: politics, social life, luxury, marriage, business, and travel.

Lucite, also called PLEXIGLAS, British PERSPEX, trademark name of polymethyl methacrylate, a synthetic organic compound of high molecular weight made by combination of many simple molecules of the ester methyl methacrylate (monomer) into long chains (polymer); this process (polymerization) may be effected by light or heat, although chemical catalysts are usually employed in manufacture of the commercial product.

The material has high dimensional stability and good resistance to weathering and to shock; it is colourless and highly transparent, but can be tinted or rendered opaque by the addition of other substances. It is usually fabricated by molding into solid articles or casting into sheets. An object made of polymethyl methacrylate displays the unusual property of keeping a beam of light reflected within its surfaces and thus carrying the beam around bends and corners of a pipe, bundle of threads, or sheet and reflecting it out through the ends or edges. It is widely used in aircraft canopies and windows, boat windshields, and the like, and for making ornaments, medallions, and lenses for cameras and automobile stoplights and taillights. It is also used in medicine in devices for illuminating and visually inspecting interior organs.

Lucius (ancient Roman personal name, or praenomen): *see under* gens or family name or honorific (*e.g.,* under Seneca for Lucius Annaeus Seneca), except as below.

Lucius I, SAINT (d. March 5, 254; feast day March 4), pope from June 253 to March 254.

He succeeded St. Cornelius on June 25, 253. He was exiled to Civitavecchia, Italy, by the Roman emperor Gallus but later was allowed to return to Rome by Gallus' successor, Valerian. According to Bishop St. Cyprian of Carthage, Lucius continued the liberal policy Cornelius had established toward apostates who renounced Christianity because of the persecution of the Roman emperor Decius. Thus Lucius opposed and condemned the Novatian Schism, a rigorist movement against penitent apostates, inspired by the antipope Novatian. Lucius is honoured in Denmark as the patron saint of Copenhagen. Lucius' martyrdom in the Valerian persecution is unproven.

Lucius II, original name GHERARDO CACCIANEMICI (b. Bologna, Papal States—d. Feb. 15, 1145, Rome), pope from 1144 to 1145.

He was made cardinal by Pope Honorius II in 1124 and papal chancellor by Pope Innocent II, whom he aided against the antipope Anacletus II. He was elected to succeed Celestine II on March 12, 1144. When King Roger II of Sicily invaded papal lands and forced Lucius to accept his truce, Anacletus' brother, the patrician Giordano Pierleoni, led the Romans to proclaim a constitutional republic free from papal civil rule. Lucius opposed this bid for Roman independence, led an unsuccessful assault against the rebels, and presumably died from injuries suffered in the conflict.

Lucius III, original name UBALDO ALLUCINGOLI (b. 1097?, Lucca, Tuscany—d. Nov. 25, 1185, Verona), pope from 1181 to 1185.

A Cistercian monk whom Pope Innocent II had made cardinal in 1141, Lucius was bishop of Ostia (consecrated 1159) and papal counsellor when elected on Sept. 1, 1181, to succeed Alexander III. As pope, Lucius was forced to leave Rome because the Romans had earlier declared their city a republic free from papal interference.

At the Synod of Verona in 1184, Lucius, in agreement with the Holy Roman emperor Frederick I Barbarossa, decreed the excommunication of heretics and their protectors; after ecclesiastical trial, heretics who refused to recant were transferred to civil authorities for punishment—usually death by burning. Lucius' synod activated the strict decrees of the third Lateran Council (1179); founded the medieval Inquisition; and instigated the church's attack against the Cathari, a heretical sect that held that good and evil had separate creators. Apart from Frederick's promise to renew the Crusades, relations between Emperor and Pope were strained.

Łuck (Ukraine): *see* Lutsk.

Luckman, Sid, byname of SIDNEY LUCKMAN (b. Nov. 21, 1916, Brooklyn, N.Y., U.S.—d. July 5, 1998, North Miami Beach, Fla.), quarterback in U.S. professional football who, during his 12 seasons (1939–50) in the National Football League (NFL), directed with exceptional success the revolutionary T-formation offense of the Chicago Bears. The forward passing feats of Luckman and of his greatest adversary, quarterback Sammy Baugh of the Washington Redskins, terminated a long era in professional football in which offensive systems were based largely on rushing (running with the ball) from the single-wing formation.

A graduate of Columbia University (1939), Luckman became the Bears' starting quarterback in his second NFL season, 1940. On December 8 of that year he participated in the Bears' 73–0 victory over Washington in the most one-sided championship game in NFL history. With Luckman at quarterback, the Bears won additional championships in 1941, 1943, and 1946. For the 1943 season he was selected as the most valuable player in the NFL. On November 14 of that year he set a league record by passing for seven touchdowns in a single regular season game, and on December 26 he established an NFL championship game record by throwing five touchdown passes as the Bears defeated Washington, 41–21.

After his retirement from active play, Luckman became a successful businessman in Chicago and a part-time assistant coach of the Bears. He was inducted into the Football Hall of Fame in 1965.

Consult the INDEX *first*

Lucknow, city, capital of Uttar Pradesh state, northern India, on the Gomati River, at the junction of numerous roads and rail lines. The city is a marketplace for agricultural products (mangoes, melons, and various grains are grown locally), and its industries include food

The Rumi Darwaza, or Turkish Gate, Lucknow, Uttar Pradesh, India

© Ann & Bury Peerless—Slide Resources & Picture Library

processing, manufacturing, handicrafts, and railroad shops.

Lucknow became important in 1528, when it was captured by Bābur, the first Mughal ruler of India. Under Akbar, his grandson, the city became part of Oudh province. Āṣaf-ud-Dawlah, who became nawab of Oudh in 1775, transferred his capital from Faizābād to Lucknow. When the Indian Mutiny broke out in 1857, Sir Henry Lawrence, the British commissioner, and the European inhabitants of Lucknow were besieged for several months until rescued by British troops. The British then abandoned the city until the following year, when they regained control over India.

Lucknow contains notable examples of architecture. The Great Imāmbārā (1784) is a single-storied structure where Shīʿite Muslims assemble during the month of Muḥarram. The Rumi Darwaza, or Turkish Gate, was modeled (1784) after the Sublime Porte (Bab-i-Hümayun) in Istanbul. The best-preserved monument is the Residency (1800), the scene of the defense by British troops during the 1857 Mutiny. A memorial commemorating the Indians who died during the uprising was erected in 1957.

Among Lucknow's educational institutions are the University of Lucknow (1921), a music academy, an institute of Muslim theology, the Central Drug Research Institute (1951), an arts and crafts college, and a state museum. The city also has a botanical and a national zoological garden. Pop. (2001 prelim.) 2,207,-340; metropolitan area, 2,226,933.

Lucknow Pact (December 1916), agreement made by the Indian National Congress and the All-India Muslim League and adopted by the Congress at its Lucknow session on December 29 and by the league on Dec. 31, 1916. The meeting at Lucknow marked the reunion of the moderate and radical wings of the Congress and was dominated by B.G. Tilak, the Marāthā leader. This session and the pact that came from it marked nationalist beginnings that resulted in the Non-cooperation Movement of Mohandas Gandhi, 1920–22. The pact dealt both with the structure of the government of India and with the relation of the Hindu and Muslim communities.

On the former count, the proposals were an advance on G.K. Gokhale's "political testament." Four-fifths of the provincial and central legislatures were to be elected on a broad franchise, and half the executive council members, including those of the central executive council, were to be Indians elected by the councils themselves. Except for the provision for the central executive, these proposals were largely embodied in the Government of India Act of 1919. The Congress also agreed to separate electorates for Muslims in provincial council elections and for weightage in their favour (beyond the proportions indicated by population) in all provinces except the Punjab and Bengal, where they gave some ground to the Hindu and Sikh minorities. This pact paved the way for Hindu-Muslim cooperation in the Khilafat Movement and Gandhi's Noncooperation Movement from 1920.

Lucretia, legendary heroine of ancient Rome. According to tradition, she was the beautiful and virtuous wife of the nobleman Lucius Tarquinius Collatinus. Her tragedy began when she was raped by Sextus Tarquinius, son of Lucius Tarquinius Superbus, the tyrannical Etruscan king of Rome. After exacting an oath of vengeance against the Tarquins from her father and her husband, she stabbed herself to death. Lucius Junius Brutus then led the enraged populace in a rebellion that drove the Tarquins from Rome. The event (traditionally dated 509 BC) marks the foundation of the Roman Republic. Lucretia's story is recounted in Shakespeare's narrative poem *The Rape of Lucrece.*

Lucretius, in full TITUS LUCRETIUS CARUS (fl. 1st century BC), Latin poet and philosopher known for his single, long poem, *De rerum natura* (*On the Nature of Things*). The poem is the fullest extant statement of the physical theory of the Greek philosopher Epicurus; it also alludes to his ethical and logical doctrines.

Life. Apart from Lucretius' poem almost nothing is known about him. What little evidence there is, is quite inconclusive. Jerome, a leading Latin Church Father, in his chronicle for the year 94 BC (or possibly 96 or 93 BC), stated that Lucretius was born in that year and that years afterward a love potion drove him insane; and in lucid intervals having written some books, which Cicero afterward emended, he killed himself in his 44th year (51 or 50 BC). Aelius Donatus, a grammarian and teacher of rhetoric, in his "Life" of Virgil noticed that Virgil put on the *toga virilis* (the toga of an adult) in his 17th year, on his birthday (*i.e.,* 54 or 53 BC), and that Lucretius died that same day. But Donatus contradicted himself by stating that the consuls that year were the same as in the year of Virgil's birth (*i.e.,* Crassus and Pompey, in 55 BC). This last date seems partly confirmed by a sentence in Cicero's reply to his brother in 54 BC (*Ad Quintum fratrem* 2, 9, 3), which suggests that Lucretius was already dead and also that Cicero may have been involved in the publication of his poem: "The poems of Lucretius are as you write in your letter—they have many highlights of genius, yet also much artistry." Excepting the single mention in Cicero, the only contemporary who named Lucretius was a Roman historian, Cornelius Nepos (*Atticus* 12, 4), in the phrase "after the death of Lucretius and Catullus," and the only contemporary whom Lucretius named was one Memmius, to whom he dedicated his poem, probably Gaius Memmius (son-in-law of Sulla, praetor of 58 BC, and patron of Catullus and Gaius Helvius Cinna), for whose friendship Lucretius "hopes."

De rerum natura. The title of Lucretius' work translates that of the chief work of Epicurus, *Peri physeōs* (*On Nature*), as also of the didactic epic of Empedocles, a pluralist philosopher of nature, of whom Lucretius spoke with admiration only less than that with which he praised his master Epicurus.

Lucretius distributed his argument into six books, beginning each with a highly polished introduction. Books I and II established the main principles of the atomic universe, refuted the rival theories of the pre-Socratic cosmic philosophers Heracleitus, Empedocles, and Anaxagoras, and covertly attacked the Stoics, a school of moralists rivaling that of Epicurus. Book III demonstrated the atomic structure and mortality of the soul and ended with a triumphant sermon on the theme "Death is nothing to us." Book IV described the mechanics of sense perception, thought, and certain bodily functions and condemned sexual passion. Book V described the creation and working of this world and the celestial bodies and the evolution of life and human society. Book VI explained remarkable phenomena of the earth and sky, in particular, thunder and lightning. The poem ends with a description of the plague at Athens, a sombre picture of death contrasting with that of spring and birth in the invocation to Venus, with which it opened.

Argument of the poem. The argument in outline is as follows:

1. No thing is either created out of or reducible to nothing. The universe has an infinite extent of empty space (or void) and an infinite number of irreducible particles of matter (or atoms)—though their kinds are finite. Atoms differ only in shape, size, and weight and are impenetrably hard, changeless, everlasting, the limit of physical division. They are made up of inseparable minimal parts, or units. Larger atoms have more such parts, but even the larger are minute. All atoms would have moved everlastingly downward in infinite space and never have collided to form atomic systems had they not swerved at times to a minimal degree. To these indeterminate swerves is due the creation of an infinite plurality of worlds; they also interrupt the causal chain and so make room for free will. All things are ultimately systems of moving atoms, separated by greater or smaller intervals of void, which cohere more or less according to their shapes. All systems are divisible and therefore perishable (except the gods), and all change is explainable in terms of the addition, subtraction, or rearrangement of changeless atoms.

2. The soul is made of exceedingly fine atoms and has two connected parts: the *anima* distributed throughout the body, which is the cause of sensation, and the *animus* in the breast, the central consciousness. The soul is born and grows with the body, and at death it is dissipated like "smoke."

3. Though the gods exist, they neither made nor manipulate the world. As systems of exceedingly fine atoms, they live remote, unconcerned with human affairs, examples to men of the ideal life of perfect happiness (absence of mental fear, emotional turmoil, and bodily pain).

4. Men know by sense perception and argue by reason according to certain rules. Though the senses are infallible, reason can make false inferences. Objects can be seen because they discharge from their surface representative films, which strike the eye just as smells strike the nose. Separate atoms are in principle imperceptible, having no dischargeable parts. The senses perceive the properties and accidents of bodies; reason infers the atoms and the void, which exists to explain the perceived movement of bodies.

5. Men naturally seek pleasure and avoid pain. Their aim should be so to conduct their

lives that they get, on balance, the maximum of pleasure and the minimum of pain. They will succeed in this only if they are able, through philosophy, to overcome the fear of death and of the gods.

Literary qualities of the poem. The linguistic style and spirit of the poem are notable. The problem of Lucretius was to render the bald and abstract Greek prose of Epicurus into Latin hexameters at a time when Latin had no philosophic vocabulary. He succeeded by applying common words to a technical use. Thus, he used *concilium* ("assembly of people") for a "system of atoms" and *primordia* ("first weavings") for the "atoms" that make up the texture of things. When necessary, he invented words. In poetic diction and style he was in debt to the older Latin poets, especially to Quintus Ennius, the father of Roman poetry. He freely used alliteration and assonance, solemn and often metrically convenient archaic forms, and old constructions. He formed expressive compound adjectives of a sort rejected by Augustan taste—*e.g.,* "the light-sleeping hearts of dogs," "forest-breaking winds." He imitated or echoed Homer; the dramatists Aeschylus and Euripides; Callimachus, a poet and critic; the historian Thucydides; and the physician Hippocrates. His hexameters stand halfway between those of Ennius, who introduced the metre into Latin, and Virgil, who perfected it. There is also some incoherence of rhythm, as well as harsh elisions and examples of unusual prosody.

The influence of Lucretius on Virgil was pervasive, especially in Virgil's *Georgics;* and it is in clear allusion to Lucretius that Virgil wrote "Happy is the man who can read the causes of things" (*Georgics* II, 490).

Lucretius spoke in austere compassion for the ignorant, unhappy human race. His moral fervour expressed itself in gratitude to Epicurus and in hatred of the seers who inculcated religious fears by threats of eternal punishment after death, of the Etruscan soothsayers with their lore of thunder and lightning, of the false philosophers—Stoics with their belief in divine providence or Platonists and Pythagoreans who taught the transmigration of immortal souls. The first appearance of *religio* in the poem is as a monster that thrusts its fearful head from the regions of the sky. Epicurus, not intimidated by these spectres, had ranged beyond the "flaming ramparts of the world" through the infinite universe, broken into the citadel of nature, and brought back in triumph the knowledge of what can and what cannot be, of that "deep-set boundary stone" that divides the separate properties of things, the real from the not real. And "so religion is crushed beneath our feet and his [Epicurus'] victory lifts us to the skies." (A.F.We.)

BIBLIOGRAPHY. Introductions are James H. Nichols, Jr., *Epicurean Political Philosophy: The De Rerum Natura of Lucretius* (1976); and Diskin Clay, *Lucretius and Epicurus* (1983). D.R. Dudley (ed.), *Lucretius* (1965), is a collection of essays by eminent scholars on various aspects of the poem. Analyses of form, imagery, and philosophy include Richard Minadeo, *The Lyre of Science: Form and Meaning in Lucretius' De Rerum Natura* (1969); David West, *The Imagery and Poetry of Lucretius* (1969); and Charles Segal, *Lucretius on Death and Anxiety: Poetry and Philosophy in De Rerum Natura* (1990).

Lucullus, Lucius Licinius (b. *c.* 117 BC—d. 58/56), Roman general who fought Mithradates VI Eupator of Pontus from 74 to 66 BC.

He served Lucius Cornelius Sulla as quaestor in 88, took part in his march on Rome, and was his proquaestor in the East from 87 until his return to Italy. He was aedile in 79 and (by special dispensation) praetor in 78.

In 74, when Lucullus was consul, the Roman province of Bithynia was invaded by Mithradates, king of Pontus. Lucullus was appointed governor of Cilicia and later of Asia and commanded Roman forces in the war against Mithradates. With five legions he drove his opponent from Cyzicus in the winter of 74–73 and defeated him at Cabira in 72. By 70 the war seemed to be over. Lucullus' able financial administration alleviated the crisis caused by the war in the province of Asia and earned him the hostility of those Roman businessmen whose profits were cut by his reforms on behalf of the provincials.

Mithradates then gained the alliance of his son-in-law, Tigranes, king of Armenia. Lucullus attacked Armenia, defeated Tigranes, and captured his capital, Tigranocerta, in 69. Three mutinies by Lucullus' troops in 68–67, however, forced him to curtail operations. Mithradates recovered much of his lost territory, and Lucullus' enemies carried legislation (Lex Manilia) requiring him to hand over his command to Gnaeus Pompey.

Lucullus was prevented from celebrating his triumph at Rome until 63. Afterward he retired to enjoy a life of great extravagance. The adjective *Lucullan,* meaning "luxurious," derives from his name.

Lucy, SAINT, Italian SANTA LUCIA (d. 304, Syracuse, Sicily; feast day December 13), virgin and martyr who was one of the earliest Christian saints to achieve popularity, having a widespread following before the 5th century. She is the patron saint of the city of Syracuse (Sicily). Because of various traditions associating her name with light, she came to be thought of as the patron of sight and was depicted by medieval artists carrying a dish containing her eyes.

According to apocryphal texts, Lucy came from a wealthy Sicilian family. Spurning marriage and worldly goods, however, she vowed to remain a virgin in the tradition of St. Agatha. An angry suitor reported her to the local Roman authorities, who sentenced her to be removed to a brothel and forced into prostitution. This order was thwarted, according to legend, by divine intervention; Lucy became immovable and could not be carried away. She was next condemned to death by fire, but she proved impervious to the flames. Finally, her neck was pierced by a sword and she died.

In actuality, Lucy was probably a victim of the wave of persecution of Christians that occurred late in the reign of the Roman emperor Diocletian. References to her are found in early Roman sacramentaries and, at Syracuse, in an inscription dating from AD 400. As evidence of her early fame, two churches are known to have been dedicated to her in Britain before the 8th century, at a time when the land was largely pagan.

One of the patron saints of virgins, St. Lucy is venerated on her feast day, December 13, by a variety of ceremonies. In Sweden, St. Lucia's Day marks the beginning of the Christmas celebration. On that day the eldest daughter of the family traditionally dresses in a white robe and wears as a crown an evergreen wreath studded with candles.

Lucy, Richard de (d. July 14, 1179, Lesnes Abbey, Kent, Eng.), chief justiciar (judiciary officer) of England under King Henry II (reigned 1154–89). He was involved in the king's struggle against the archbishop of Canterbury, Thomas Becket, and he virtually controlled the country during Henry's protracted absences resulting from family rebellions that challenged the king's royal power.

Richard came from Lucé, near Domfront, Normandy. He probably entered the English royal service under King Henry I. As a supporter of King Stephen in the civil war that broke out in 1139, Lucy in 1143 became county justiciar and sheriff of Essex. About 1155 Henry II made him and Robert de Beaumont, 2nd Earl of Leicester, chief justiciars; after Leicester's death in 1168 Lucy held the office alone.

As one of Henry II's chief councillors, Lucy helped formulate much important legislation, including reforms of property law and of judicial procedure. He was singled out by Henry's enemies as the main author of the Constitutions of Clarendon (1164), which maintained—contrary to Becket's stand—that clerics convicted of felony in ecclesiastical courts should be punished by lay authority instead of by the church. Lucy was excommunicated by Becket in 1166 and again in 1169, and Becket's murder by the king's henchmen in 1170 resulted in part from his refusal to lift such sentences of excommunication. In 1173–74, while Henry was fighting the rebels in Normandy, Anjou, and the north of England, Lucy helped greatly to maintain Henry's rule throughout the rest of the king's domains.

Shortly before his death Lucy resigned (1179) his office and entered Lesnes Abbey, which he had founded the previous year in penance for his part in the events leading to Becket's murder.

Lucy, Sir Thomas (b. April 24, 1532, Charlecote, near Stratford-on-Avon, Warwickshire, Eng.—d. July 7, 1600, Charlecote), English squire whom William Shakespeare may possibly have caricatured as Justice Shallow in *2 Henry IV,* and in *The Merry Wives of Windsor.*

At 16 Lucy married an heiress, Joyce Acton, daughter of Thomas Acton of Sutton, Worcestershire, and rebuilt Charlecote, the family house, with her fortune. Lucy was knighted in 1565. He sat in two sessions of Parliament as knight of the shire for Warwick, was a justice of the queen's peace and a member of the council for the Marches of Wales (to superintend the Welsh borders), and became a hunter of recusants (usually Roman Catholic dissenters from the Church of England). In 1588 he was a commissioner for musters against the Spanish Armada.

It was said that he prosecuted the young Shakespeare for stealing deer in Charlecote park, though the story gained currency only long after Shakespeare's death.

lud, among the Votyaks and Zyryans, a sacred grove where sacrifices were performed. The *lud,* surrounded by a high board or log fence, generally consisted of a grove of fir trees, a place for a fire, and tables for the sacrificial meal. People were forbidden to break even a branch from the trees within the enclosure, which was watched over by a special guardian whose position was hereditary. In some areas women and children were banned from the grove altogether. The sacrificial ceremonies performed annually in the groves were usually centred on some ancient tree dedicated to a deity. The grove was so sacred that no unseemly behaviour was allowed in its vicinity, and those with legitimate business at the enclosure had to bathe before entering it. Each family had its own *lud,* and, in addition, there were great *lud*s at which the entire clan met for sacrificial feasts. All food had to be consumed on the premises, and the hides of the sacrificed animals were hung on the trees.

Similar sacrificial groves existed among most of the Finno-Ugrian peoples. In the *keremet* of the Mordvins, sacrifices were made both upward to the sun or downward to the night. In groves of deciduous trees the high gods were worshiped, whereas the lower spirits lived in the fir groves. In the Cheremis *keremet* only the native language could be spoken because the deities would have been offended by foreign speech. Some of the groves were specifically dedicated to heroic ancestors, and carved images were reported present in the groves by the earliest travelers to the area.

The Finnish *hiisi* and Estonian *hiis* were apparently comparable groves, though little information exists on actual sacrifices or other ceremonies in them. In Ingria sacred groves were still in use during the latter part of the 19th century, where prayers and offerings were directed to Ukko, a thunder god, and Sämpsä, a god of vegetation.

Lüda (China): *see* Lü-ta.

Luddite, member of the organized bands of 19th-century English handicraftsmen who rioted for the destruction of the textile machinery that was displacing them. The movement began in the vicinity of Nottingham toward the end of 1811 and in the next year spread to Yorkshire, Lancashire, Derbyshire, and Leicestershire.

The "Ludds," or Luddites, were generally masked and operated at night. Their leader, real or imaginary, was known as King Ludd, after a probably mythical Ned Ludd. They eschewed violence against persons and often enjoyed local support. In 1812 a band of Luddites was shot down under the orders of a threatened employer named Horsfall (who was afterward murdered in reprisal). The government of Robert Banks Jenkinson, 2nd Earl of Liverpool, instituted severe repressive measures culminating in a mass trial at York in 1813, which resulted in many hangings and transportations. Similar rioting in 1816 was caused by the depression that followed the Napoleonic Wars; but the movement was soon ended by vigorous repression and reviving prosperity.

Ludendorff, Erich (b. April 9, 1865, Kruszewnia, near Poznań, Prussian Poland—d. Dec. 20, 1937, Munich, Ger.), Prussian general who was mainly responsible for Germany's military policy and strategy in the

Ludendorff, *c.* 1930
Archiv fur Kunst und Geschichte, Berlin

latter years of World War I. After the war he became a leader of reactionary political movements, ultimately joining the Nazi Party.

Early life. Ludendorff was the son of an impoverished landowner and cavalry captain. His mother was a member of an aristocratic military family. Ludendorff was educated in the cadet corps, became an infantry officer, and, because of his outstanding military qualities, was soon promoted to the general staff.

In 1908 he was put in charge of the 2nd (German) department in the army general staff, the institution generally known as the "great general staff," which was responsible for preparing contingency deployment and mobilization plans. Under the chief of the general staff, General Helmuth von Moltke, Ludendorff played a significant part in the revision of the Schlieffen Plan. This plan envisaged a gigantic outflanking movement involving the infringement of Belgian neutrality with the aim of crushing France with one blow. Moltke and Ludendorff decided to secure more firmly the extended southern flank between Switzerland and Lorraine. They also discarded the idea of forcing a way through southern Holland and instead made preparations for the surprise capture of Liège, the most important fortress in eastern Belgium, often characterized as "impregnable."

In Germany, supreme political and military power was traditionally wielded by the commander in chief and the emperor, and general staff officers were not expected to engage in politics. Ludendorff, however, violated this tradition by campaigning for a strengthening of the army, both in personnel and equipment, which the general staff considered essential in view of the general armaments race in Europe. His contact with extreme nationalist political circles favouring increased armament convinced him that, if policy was influenced by "strong men," a vigorous conduct of war was assured.

The excessively active departmental chief irritated the military authorities, and in 1913 Ludendorff was transferred to the infantry as regimental commander. When war broke out in 1914 he was appointed quartermaster in chief (supply and maintenance) of the 2nd Army in the west.

Military career during World War I. It was not until two Russian armies threatened to overrun the German 8th Army in East Prussia that Ludendorff was appointed chief of staff of the 8th Army. Ludendorff, dynamic but occasionally harsh and in times of crisis often nervous, was assigned to the elderly General Paul von Hindenburg, who was renowned for his iron nerves. Ludendorff regarded the problems with which he and his commander in chief were faced as difficult but never insoluble.

The spectacular victory of Hindenburg and Ludendorff over the Russians in August 1914 at Tannenberg, in East Prussia, a battle that brought Hindenburg worldwide renown, was followed by the German defeat on the Marne in the west that signaled the failure of Ludendorff's revised Schlieffen Plan. For two years Hindenburg and Ludendorff fought the Russians in the east. Ludendorff's plan of a general offensive against Russia by means of a temporary reduction of the German forces in the west did not receive approval by the supreme army command in the summer of 1915.

Only in August 1916, after the failure of the German offensive at Verdun and in view of the Allied onslaught on both the eastern and western fronts, did the emperor finally appoint the two generals to assume supreme military control. They attempted to conduct a sort of total war by mobilizing the entire forces of the home front, which was already suffering from the effects of the British blockade. Ludendorff staked everything on a single card, the stubborn pursuit of a "victorious peace" that was to secure German territorial gains in east and west. In 1917 he approved the unrestricted submarine warfare against the British that led to the entry of the United States into the war against Germany but not to England's collapse. After the tsar had been deposed in March 1917, Ludendorff gave his blessing to the return of the Russian Bolshevik emigrants (including the as yet unknown V.I. Lenin), in the hope of persuading the Russians to conclude peace. Hindenburg and Ludendorff, who now exercised a sort of military semidictatorship, also brought about the dismissal of Chancellor Theobald von Bethmann Hollweg in the delusory hope that "a strong man" could be found to assume the leadership of the *Reich.*

On March 21, 1918, Ludendorff opened a general offensive on the Western Front with the object of smashing the Anglo-French armies and forcing a decision in Europe before the Americans landed. But he had overestimated the strength of the German armies; the offensive failed, and when, in the autumn of 1918, the collapse of the German allies—Austria-Hungary, Bulgaria, and Turkey—was imminent, Ludendorff demanded immediate negotiations for an armistice. For a while, the nerves of the hopelessly overworked general gave way, and a psychiatrist had to be summoned to supreme headquarters. When Ludendorff realized the severity of the armistice conditions, he insisted that the war be carried on. When he saw that the political leaders were not prepared to do this, he offered his resignation, which William II accepted on Oct. 26, 1918. At the same time, the emperor, much to Ludendorff's distaste, ordered Hindenburg to remain at his post. A titan of willpower and energy who had attempted the impossible was suddenly torn away from his sphere of activity; the shock was immense. Ludendorff met the revolution that broke out in November 1918 with complete resignation and went into exile in Sweden for several months.

While, according to Prussian custom, general staff officers accepted joint responsibility for all decisions made, they had to preserve strict anonymity. Ludendorff, however, whose ambition was as immense as his strategic gifts, at the close of the lost war claimed to have been the sole real "commander" of World War I. He asserted that he had been deprived of victory by sinister forces that had been operating behind the scenes; he was, he claimed, like Siegfried in the heroic Germanic sagas, a victim of a stab in the back. By propagating the legend that the German army, undefeated in the field, was sabotaged by the "home front," he did a great deal to poison public life in the Weimar Republic.

Postwar political activities. During the next 20 years Ludendorff led a bizarre life. Adopting the role of the betrayed and misunderstood commander, he took part in the unsuccessful coups d'état of Wolfgang Kapp in 1920 and of Adolf Hitler in 1923, and in 1925 he ran for president against his former commander in chief, Hindenburg, whom he now bitterly hated. From 1924 to 1928 he was a National Socialist member of Parliament.

Consistently pursuing a purely military line of thought, Ludendorff developed, after the war, the theory of "total war," which he published as *Der Totale Krieg* (*The Nation at War*) in 1935. In the first half of the 19th century, the great military theorist of the Prussian general staff, Carl von Clausewitz, had advanced the doctrine of war as an extension of politics by different means. Ludendorff advocated the diametrically opposite view that politics should serve the conduct of war, for which the entire physical and moral forces of the nation should be mobilized, because, according to him, peace was merely an interval between wars.

Ludendorff had always had a weakness for the female sex; his first wife, a striking beauty, divorced her husband in order to marry Ludendorff. In 1926, however, he insisted on dissolving this marriage and married the neurologist and popular philosopher Mathilde von Kemnitz. Ludendorff succumbed completely to this eccentric woman, who regarded him as the real "commander in chief" of the Germans and had developed a belief in the activities of "supernational powers"—Jewry, Christianity, Freemasonry. From then on he joined with his second wife in fighting against these imaginary foes who were supposed to have deprived him and Germany of victory. Both preached a German "divine faith." Over this faith he quarreled both with the old officer corps and with Hitler and his National Socialists. Just as he had not permitted the emperor to make him a count, he now forbade Hitler to promote him to field marshal. Apart from a group of fanatical followers, he was henceforth completely isolated. When, during the 1930s, he began to utter warnings against Hitler's tyranny, he found no echo. At his death in 1937, many old soldiers mourned him, but most had long ceased to understand him. (W.Go.)

BIBLIOGRAPHY. D.J. Goodspeed, *Ludendorff* (1966); Roger Parkinson, *Tormented Warrior: Ludendorff and the Supreme Command* (1978); Robert B. Asprey, *The German High Command at War: Hindenburg and Ludendorff Conduct World War I* (1991).

Lüdenscheid, city, North Rhine–Westphalia *Land* (state), west-central Germany, in the hilly, wooded Sauerland region between the Lenne and Volme rivers. A Frankish settlement in the 9th century and chartered in 1278, it became a centre of the iron industry during the Middle Ages and was a member of the Hanseatic League. It passed with Cleves-Mark to Brandenburg in 1609 and to Prussia in 1815. It was partially destroyed by fire in 1723. The parish church of the Saviour, with a tower dating from 1072, is in the centre of the old town, and the moated castle of Neuenhof is a historic landmark. An industrial and metalworking centre, Lüdenscheid manufactures aluminum, metal products, plastics, and synthetics. Pop. (1999 est.) 81,300.

Lüderitz, formerly ANGRA PEQUENA, town on the Atlantic coast of Namibia (formerly South West Africa). The Portuguese navigator Bartolomeu Dias stopped there in 1487 and named the bay Angra Pequena. Long neglected, it became the first German settlement in South West Africa when a Hamburg merchant, Franz Adolf Lüderitz, began trading operations and persuaded the German government in 1883 to place the territory under German protection. In 1908, during construction of a railway, diamonds were discovered in the Namib Desert hinterland. Lüderitz then became a booming mining town in what the South African government later established as a huge prohibited zone, *Sperrgebiet,* where no one may enter without permit, for diamond mining was strictly controlled by the South African government.

Lüderitz itself is not restricted and is a centre of rock-lobster fishing and processing. Ships at the port are served by lighters (small barges). The town receives fresh water from a saltwater-condensing plant. Roads and rail link it to Windhoek, the capital of Namibia, and to the Republic of South Africa. There is a small museum displaying tools of various Khoisan peoples and other archaeological and historical finds. Pop. (1991) 7,700.

Ludhiāna, city, central Punjab state, northwestern India. The city stands on the Sutlej River's old bank, 8 miles (13 km) south of its present course, and is on the Grand Trunk Road from Delhi to Amritsar at a junction of several rail lines. The city lies about 170

Winnowing wheat near Ludhiāna, Punjab, India
Baldev

miles (270 km) northwest of Delhi. Founded in 1480 by members of Delhi's ruling Lodī dynasty, from which its name is derived, Ludhiāna is a major agricultural market and industrial centre. The city's largest industry is hosiery manufacturing, but the production of cotton textiles, steel, and machinery and the processing of agricultural products are also economically important. Ludhiāna is the site of Punjab Agricultural University (founded 1962) and a number of other colleges, as well as of a U.S. Presbyterian mission that operates a medical college and a hospital.

The area about Ludhiāna is about 80 percent cultivated, much of it irrigated by the Sirhind Canal. The crops grown include wheat, corn (maize), cotton, and peanuts (groundnuts). Pop. (2001 prelim.) 1,395,053.

ludi publici (Latin: "public games"), ancient Roman spectacles, primarily consisting of chariot races and various kinds of theatrical performances, usually held at regular intervals in honour of some god; they are distinct from the gladiatorial contests (associated with funeral rites). A special magistrate presided over them. Oldest and most famous were the Ludi Romani, or Magni, dedicated to Jupiter and celebrated each year in September. Like the Ludi Apollinares (for Apollo) and the Ludi Cereales (for Ceres), they centred on the chariot races of the Circus Maximus. A special feature of the Megalensia, or Megalesia, held in April and dedicated to Cybele, the Great Mother, were the *ludi scaenici,* consisting of plays and farces.

Ludi Saeculares: *see* Secular Games.

ludi scaenici (Latin: "stage games"), in ancient Rome, theatrical performances associated with the celebration of public games (*ludi publici*), in which Greek dramatic forms were first used by the Romans. Although originally performed at the Ludi Romani (for which Livius Andronicus wrote the first Latin tragedy and the first Latin comedy in 240 BC), the *ludi scaenici* became the characteristic feature of the Megalensia, or Megalesia, the festival of the goddess Cybele (established in 204 BC). They originally included serious dramas but later, under the Roman Empire, were almost wholly devoted to farces and pantomime. The Ludi Saeculares (Secular Games) were celebrated only once in a century.

Ludington, city, seat (1855) of Mason county, western Michigan, U.S. It is on Lake Michigan at the mouth of the Pere Marquette River, 58 miles (93 km) north of Muskegon. Settled in the 1840s, it was originally known as Marquette for Jacques Marquette, the Jesuit explorer who died there in 1675 (a memorial cross near the harbour marks the site). It was later (1871) named for James Ludington, a local lumberman. The city is a Great Lakes port with passenger, rail, and auto-ferry service to points in Wisconsin. Manufactures include wood and metal products, watchcases, and highway and railway equipment. Ludington State Park is 8 miles (13 km) north. Inc. city, 1873. Pop. (2000) 8,357.

Ludlow, town ("parish"), South Shropshire district, county of Shropshire, England, on the River Teme. A castle, occupying a commanding position, was probably begun in 1085 by Roger de Lacy; it fell into ruin in the 18th century. The planned town was laid out in 12th-century grid fashion some time after the castle was built; the town's first charter was granted in 1189. The burgesses owed most of their privileges to their allegiance to the house of York. In 1461, when King Edward IV ascended the throne, the castle became royal property, and the town received a royal charter. Because of its strong position, Ludlow was the final Shropshire fortress to yield (1646) to Parliamentary forces during the English Civil Wars.

The greater portion of the old town wall, together with one of the original seven gates, still remains. The town has many fine half-timbered buildings and several Georgian houses. The parish church of St. Lawrence is of great size with a lofty central tower and some 14th- and 15th-century glass; the ashes of A.E. Housman, the poet, are buried in the churchyard. The medieval Ludford bridge over the Teme has been declared an ancient monument. Ludlow is a thriving market town, noted for the sale of Hereford cattle. It is also a tourist centre. Apart from light engineering, industries are mostly agricultural. Pop. (1998 est.) 10,100.

Ruins of the medieval castle overlooking the town of Ludlow, Shropshire
By courtesy of British Information Services

Ludlow, town (township), Hampden county, south-central Massachusetts, U.S. It is located on the Chicopee River, within the Springfield metropolitan area. Settled around 1751, it was known as Stony Hill until 1775, when it was renamed (probably for Ludlow, Eng.), incorporated, and set off from Springfield because of difficulties in crossing the river that separated the two places. Formerly an independent milling town, Ludlow now relies on food-processing and manufacturing (machinery and plastic products). Indian Leap, a rocky cliff on the Chicopee, was the site where, according to local history, a band of Indians, led by Roaring Thunder, jumped into the water to escape their pursuers during King Philip's War (1675–76). Pop. (2000) 21,209.

Ludlow, Edmund (b. *c.* 1617, Maiden Bradley, Wiltshire, Eng.—d. November 1692, Vevey, Switz.), radical republican who fought for Parliament against the Royalists in the English Civil Wars and later became one of the chief opponents of Oliver Cromwell's Protectorate regime. His memoirs provide valuable information on republican opposition to Cromwell and on the factional struggles of the period between the collapse of the Protectorate (May 1659) and the Restoration of King Charles II (1660).

The son of a knight from Wiltshire, Ludlow studied at Trinity College, Oxford, and at the Inner Temple, London, and joined the Parliamentarian army at the outbreak of the Civil Wars. He fought against the Royalists in a number of campaigns before leaving the war to accept a seat in Parliament (1646). Ludlow helped the Independents (radical Puritans) expel the Presbyterians (moderate Puritans) from Parliament in 1648, and he was one of the judges who condemned King Charles I to death in January 1649. In the following month he joined the Council of State of the newly created Commonwealth. From November 1651 to October 1652 Ludlow was commander of the Cromwellian army that crushed Royalist resistance in Ireland and pursued the policy of transplantation of the Irish. After Cromwell made himself lord protector in 1653, Ludlow went into open opposition, claiming that Cromwell had betrayed republican principles; this resulted in his brief imprisonment at Beaumaris Castle. He played a leading role in the events that followed the end of the Protectorate, and upon the Restoration he escaped to Switzerland (August 1660). The memoirs Ludlow wrote while in exile were published six years after his death.

Ludlow; portrait by an unknown artist

By courtesy of the trustees of the British Museum; photograph, J.R. Freeman & Co., Ltd.

Consult the INDEX *first*

Ludlow Series, the third of four main divisions (in ascending order) comprising the Silurian System; it represents all those rocks on a global basis deposited during the Ludlow Epoch, some 421 to 414 million years ago. The name is derived from the type district, located immediately west of the town of Ludlow in Shropshire, Eng., where about 350 m (1,150 feet) of siltstone and limestone strata occur. The base of the Ludlow Series was formally defined in 1980 on authority of the International Commission on Stratigraphy (International Union of Geological Sciences) with a global stratotype section and point (GSSP) in the quarry at Pitch Coppice on the south side of the Ludlow-Wigmore Road, 4 km (2.5 miles) southwest of Ludlow. The boundary point is coincident with the base of the Lower Elton Formation, which is equated with the base of the graptolite biozone *Neodiversograptus nilssoni.* Among the shelly fauna typical of the Ludlow Series—found in places as widely separated as the Midwestern United States and the Altai Mountains of Russia—are many species of brachiopods belonging to the genus *Kirkidium.* The top of the Ludlow Series is defined by the base of the overlying Pridoli Series. The Ludlow Series is divided into two worldwide stages: the Gorstian and Ludfordian stages.

Ludlul bel nemeqi (Akkadian: "Let Me Praise the Expert"), in ancient Mesopotamian religious literature, a philosophical composition concerned with a man who, seemingly forsaken by the gods, speculates on the changeability of men and fate. The composition, also called the "Poem of the Righteous Sufferer" or the "Babylonian Job," has been likened to the biblical Book of Job.

Ludmila, SAINT (b. *c.* 860, near Mělník, Bohemia [now in Czech Republic]—d. Sept. 15, 921, Tetin Castle, near Poděbrady; feast day September 16), Slavic martyr and patron of Bohemia, where she pioneered in establishing Christianity. She was grandmother of St. Wenceslas, the future prince of Bohemia.

Ludmila married Borivoj, the first Czech prince to adopt Christianity. After their baptism by Archbishop St. Methodius of Sirmium, apostle of the Slavs, they built Bohemia's first Christian church, near Prague. Borivoj tried to induce his people to accept Christianity, but he was unsuccessful. After Borivoj died, Borivoj and Ludmila's son, Ratislav, married Drahomíra, Wenceslas' mother.

Entrusted with the care of Wenceslas, Ludmila brought him up as a Christian. After Ratislav's death, Bohemia was administered by anti-Christians, who opposed Ludmila and resented her influence over Wenceslas, whom she urged to take over the government and to maintain Christianity. Wenceslas' ascension to the throne about 921 worsened Ludmila's relations with the opposing party, particularly with Drahomíra, who, as regent, favoured the pagans. An ensuing feud between Ludmila and Drahomíra ended when agents entered Tetin Castle and strangled Ludmila, a deed that has traditionally been ascribed to Drahomíra's instigation.

Oral tradition honoured Ludmila with martyrdom. Soon the first legends arose—a "prologue on St. Ludmila" in Church Slavonic and a Latin life based on it. The best-known legend is the 10th-century Latin life of Wenceslas and Ludmila written by the monk Christian. J. Pekař's *Die Wenzels und Ludmila-Legenden und die Echtheit Christians* ("The Legends of Wenceslas and Ludmila and the Authenticity of Christian") appeared in 1906.

Ludo (board game): *see* Pachisi.

Ludvík (Czech personal name): *see under* Louis.

Ludwig (German personal name): *see under* Louis, except as below.

Ludwig, Carl F.W., in full CARL FRIEDRICH WILHELM LUDWIG (b. Dec. 29, 1816, Witzenhausen, near Kassel, Hesse-Kassel [Germany]—d. April 23, 1895, Leipzig, Ger.), a founder of the physicochemical school of physiology in Germany.

A professor of physiology at the universities of Marburg (1846–49), Zürich (1849–55), Vienna (1855–65), and Leipzig (1865–95), Ludwig is best known for his study of the cardiovascular system. He invented (1847) a device known as a kymograph to record changes in arterial blood pressure; a simple stromuhr (1867), or flowmeter, to measure the rate of blood flow through arteries and veins; and a mercurial blood-gas pump for the separation of gases from the blood, which led to an understanding of the role played by oxygen and other gases in the purification of blood.

Carl F.W. Ludwig, detail of an engraving

H. Roger-Viollet

Ludwig was the first to keep animal organs alive in vitro (outside the animal's body) by perfusing frog hearts with a solution approximating the composition of blood plasma (1856); to locate a blood vessel regulatory mechanism in the medulla oblongata (at the base of the brain); and to measure blood pressure in the capillaries. He discovered the depressor and accelerator nerves of the heart and, with the American physiologist Henry Bowditch, formulated (1871) the "all-or-none law" of cardiac muscle action, stating that the heart muscle, under whatever stimulus, will contract to the fullest extent or not at all.

Modern theories of urine and lymph formation stem from Ludwig's paper (1844) on urine secretion, postulating that the surface layer, or epithelium, of the kidney tubules (known as glomeruli) serves as a passive filter in urine production, the rate of which is controlled by blood pressure. He also introduced the measurement of nitrogen in the urine as an indication of the approximate rate of protein metabolism in the entire animal and was first to show that human digestive glands may be influenced by secretory nerves. Ludwig is considered one of the great physiology teachers; nearly 200 of his students, including Bowditch and the American physician William Welch, became prominent scientists.

Ludwig, Emil (b. Jan. 25, 1881, Breslau, Ger. [now Wrocław, Pol.]—d. Sept. 17, 1948, near Ascona, Switz.), German writer who is internationally known for his many popular biographies.

Emil Ludwig

Bavaria-Verlag

Ludwig was trained in law but at 25 began writing plays and poems. After serving as foreign correspondent for a German newspaper during World War I, he wrote a novel (*Diana,* originally published as two works, 1918–19; Eng. trans., 1929). In 1920 he published a biography of J.W. von Goethe, which established him as a writer in the "new school" of biography that emphasized the personality of the subject.

Ludwig's work has elicited a mixed response. His biographies appearing in English translation include: *Napoleon* (1927); *Bismarck* (1927); *William Hohenzollern* (1927); *Goethe* (1928); *The Son of Man* (1928), a highly controversial biography of Christ; *Lincoln* (1929); *Hindenburg* (1935); *Cleopatra: The Story of a Queen* (1937); *Roosevelt: A Study in Fortune and Power* (1938); *Three Portraits: Hitler, Mussolini, Stalin* (1940); and *Beethoven* (1943). *Othello* (1947) is an imaginative retelling of William Shakespeare's tragedy.

Ludwig, Otto (b. Feb. 11, 1813, Eisfeld, Thuringia [Germany]—d. Feb. 25, 1865, Dresden, Saxony), German novelist, playwright, and critic, remembered for his realistic stories, which contributed to the development of the *Novelle.* He coined the expression *poetischer Realismus* ("poetic Realism"), later used to describe the writing of many of his contemporaries.

Although expected to follow a mercantile career, Ludwig early became interested in poetry and music and in 1838 produced an opera, *Die Köhlerin*. He studied under Felix Mendelssohn at Leipzig (1839), but ill health and shyness caused him to forsake his musical career. He moved to Dresden and turned to literary studies, writing stories and dramas.

Ludwig's psychological drama *Die Erbförster* (1850) was only partially successful, though it attracted immediate attention. His more enduring work includes a series of stories on Thuringian life, characterized, as were the dramas, by attention to detail and careful psychological analysis. The most notable are *Die Heiteretei und ihr Widerspiel* (1851; *The Cheerful Ones and Their Opposites*) and *Zwischen Himmel und Erde* (1855; *Between Heaven and Earth*). His *Shakespeare-Studien* (1891) showed him to be a discriminating critic, but his preoccupation with literary theory proved something of a hindrance to his success as a creative writer.

Ludwigsburg, city, Baden-Württemberg *Land* (state), southwestern Germany. It lies along the Neckar River, just north of Stuttgart. It was founded by Duke Eberhard Ludwig of Württemberg around his palace (1704–33), the largest Baroque castle in Germany, with 18 main buildings and more than 450 rooms. The city was chartered in 1718 and was later enlarged by Duke Charles Eugene. Set in a scenic park, Ludwigsburg Palace contains a portrait gallery of the rulers of Württemberg and also their burial vault, a state art gallery and archives, the castle and regional museums, and a theatre. Also notable are two other castles, Favorite (1718) and Monrepos (1760). A rail junction, the city manufactures machinery, iron and wire goods, organs, and china. Pop. (1995 est.) 86,213.

Ludwigshafen, in full LUDWIGSHAFEN AM RHEIN, city, Rhineland-Palatinate *Land* (state), southwestern Germany. Ludwigshafen is a port on the west (left) bank of the Rhine River. Founded in 1606 as a bridgehead (Rheinschanze) opposite Mannheim, it was renamed for King Ludwig (Louis) I of Bavaria in 1843 and was chartered in 1859. The city was severely bombed during World War II and has been rebuilt in modern style. The Neoclassical pilgrimage church of Mariä Himmelfahrt (1774–77) is in the Oggersheim district of the city, where Friedrich Schiller, the poet and dramatist, lived after fleeing from Stuttgart.

Ludwigshafen is a rail junction, commercial centre, and the gateway to the wine-growing region of the Rhine. The city is noted for its large chemical industry, which was established in the 1860s. Steel and machinery are also manufactured, and trade in iron, coal, and agricultural products was fostered by the opening of the harbour in 1897. The Southwest Stadium (1951) has made the city a sports centre. Pop. (1995 est.) 167,883.

Lueger, Karl (b. Oct. 24, 1844, Vienna, Austria—d. March 10, 1910, Vienna), politician, cofounder and leader of the Austrian Christian Social Party, and mayor of Vienna who transformed the Austrian capital into a modern city.

Lueger, from a working-class family, studied law at the University of Vienna. Elected to the capital's municipal council as a liberal in 1875, he soon became popular for his exposure of corruption. Though he was not himself an anti-Semite and regarded German nationalism with skeptical antipathy, Lueger did not hesitate to exploit the prevalent anti-Semitic and nationalistic currents in Vienna for his own demagogic purposes. He had his largest following among artisans and the lower-middle class. Lueger was elected to the Austrian Reichsrat (parliament) in 1885 and in 1889 was one of the founders of the Christian Social Party, remaining one of the party's most effective leaders until his death.

Lueger opposed Austro-Hungarian dualism and advocated a federal state. When the Christian Social Party won two-thirds of the seats in the Viennese municipal council in 1895, he

Lueger
By courtesy of the Bild-Archiv, Österreichische Nationalbibliothek, Vienna

was elected mayor; but the emperor, Francis Joseph I, regarding Lueger as a social revolutionary, refused to confirm his appointment for two years. From 1897 on, Lueger served as mayor of Vienna. He incorporated the suburbs; brought streetcars, electricity, and gas under the city government; and developed parks and gardens, schools, and hospitals. Under his administration, Vienna became an efficient, modern metropolis.

It was largely because of Lueger's efforts that universal suffrage was introduced in Austria (January 1907). The Christian Social Party's platform of federation to solve the empire's nationalities problem was also decisively influenced by him.

Luena (people): *see* Luvale.

Luening, Otto, in full OTTO CLARENCE LUENING (b. June 15, 1900, Milwaukee, Wis., U.S.—d. Sept. 2, 1996, New York, N.Y.), American composer, conductor, and flutist noted for his innovative experiments in composition employing the tape recorder.

Luening's father moved their family from Milwaukee to Munich in 1912 and to Zürich in 1917. Luening studied at conservatories in Munich and Zürich and with the composer Ferruccio Busoni. He moved back to the United States in 1920 and held teaching positions at the Eastman School of Music, the University of Arizona, and Bennington College. From 1944 to 1970 Luening taught

Luening
By courtesy of the B.M.I. Archives

at Columbia University, where he headed an innovative opera-production group that presented a total of about 40 new operas. In 1952 he began to experiment with the possibilities of magnetic tape recordings, and that year he collaborated with the composer Vladimir Ussachevsky in presenting the first concert of music for tape recorder in the United States (at the Museum of Modern Art in New York City). In the 1950s and '60s Luening, either alone or in collaboration with Ussachevsky, composed a variety of works in which electronic sounds are integrated with the traditional orchestra. Among their pieces is the *Rhapsodic Variations for Tape Recorder and Orchestra* (1953), in which the tape recorder is given a solo role. In 1959 the two men founded what became the Columbia-Princeton Electronic Music Center in New York City, which Luening codirected until 1980.

Though he was a tireless advocate of contemporary music, Luening also composed a considerable body of elegant, conservative music for traditional instruments. Among such works are the *Symphonic Fantasia No. 1* (1922–24) and the *Louisville Concerto* (1951).

luffa: *see* dishcloth gourd.

Lufira River, tributary of the Lualaba River, which is itself a headstream of the Congo (Zaïre) River, in Zaire. The Lufira rises in the Shaba plateau south of Likasi, Zaire, and flows 300 miles (500 km) northeast and north-northwest across the Bia Mountains to join the Lualaba through Lake Kisale. The Lufira was dammed near Likasi to form a 160-square-mile (410-square-kilometre) lake, providing storage for a power station. It provides power for the smelting industry of Likasi and the copper zone between Kambove and Lubumbashi.

Lufkin, city, seat (1890) of Angelina county, in the Piney Woods region of eastern Texas, U.S. The city is situated near the Angelina River and between the Davy Crockett and Angelina national forests, 108 miles (174 km) northwest of Beaumont.

Founded in 1882 when the Houston, East, and West Texas Railroad was surveyed, the new settlement was named for E.P. Lufkin, son-in-law of the railroad's general manager. It developed as a sawmilling centre, and it now serves as the headquarters for the national forests of Texas. The Museum of East Texas and the Texas Forestry Museum are located in the city of Lufkin. Lufkin's economy is based on forestry, agriculture, and manufacturing. It is the home of Angelina College (1966). Inc. 1890. Pop. (1994 est.) 31,660.

Lufthansa, in full DEUTSCHE LUFTHANSA AG, German airline organized in Cologne, W.Ger., on Jan. 6, 1953, jointly by the federal government, the German National Railway, and the state of North Rhine-Westphalia; later it accepted private investors. It was the successor to Deutsche Luft Hansa, or DLH, which was founded in 1926, suspended service at war's end in 1945, and was formally liquidated in 1951. The new airline, initially called Aktiengesellschaft für Luftverkehrsbedarf, or Luftag, adopted the old name, run together, in 1954; but, whereas the old company had been familiarly called DLH, the new one was popularly called Lufthansa.

DLH, the greatest airline in prewar Europe, had resulted from the merger of Deutscher Aero Lloyd (formed 1924) and Junkers Luftverkehr (formed 1921), which together controlled a large network of lines throughout Germany and central Europe, with extensions to London, Moscow, Stockholm, Helsinki, Budapest, and the Persian Gulf. By 1931 DLH was serving Paris, Barcelona, Rome, and Oslo and accounted for a third of all passenger travel and air transport in Europe. The German-built Junkers Ju 52/3m, used by other airlines as well as by DLH, became the most familiar aircraft in European airports, until it was gradually surpassed by American-made airliners in the late 1930s. In 1934 DLH began the world's first scheduled transoceanic flights—between Germany and South America—but its other experiments in transatlantic and trans-Asian routes were cut short by the outbreak of World War II.

Lufthansa, only two months after inaugurating scheduled services within West Germany in April 1955, began transatlantic flights to New York City. In the same year, scheduled service began to Paris, London, Madrid, and Lisbon, and special flights began to Moscow. In 1956 the first flights were made to Montreal, Chicago, Rio de Janeiro, São Paulo, Buenos Aires, Baghdad, and Tehrān (discontinued in 1981), followed by initial flights to India in 1958 and Bangkok in 1959. By the late 20th century the vast network of Lufthansa radiated from Frankfurt am Main to such distant cities as Santiago de Chile, Mexico City, Los Angeles, Anchorage, Tokyo, Hong Kong, Sydney, and Johannesburg, as well as to scores of airports throughout Europe and the Middle East.

Lugalbanda, one of the major figures in the surviving Sumerian epics and the hero of the tale called the "Lugalbanda Epic," or "Lugalbanda and Enmerkar." *See* Enmerkar.

Lugalzagesi, also spelled LUGALZAGGISI (reigned *c.* 2375–50 BC), *ensi* ("sacred king") of the southern Mesopotamian city of Umma, who first conquered the major cities of Lagash (*c.* 2375 BC) and Kish, then overcame the Sumerian cities of Ur and Uruk (he alone represents the 3rd dynasty of Uruk). After uniting all of Sumer, he extended his dominion to the Mediterranean coast; but, after a reign of 25 years, he lost his empire to the ascendant dynasty of Sargon, the powerful Semitic ruler of Akkad.

Lugano (Italian), German LAUIS, largest town in Ticino *canton,* southern Switzerland. It lies along Lake Lugano, northwest of Como, Italy; to the south is Mount San Salvatore (2,992 feet [912 m]), and to the east is Mount Brè (3,035 feet [925 m]). First mentioned in the 6th century, it was occupied in 1499 by the French and was taken in 1512 by the Swiss. The centre of Lugano canton of the Helvetic Republic from 1798 to 1803, it was then included in the newly formed Ticino canton and, with Locarno and Bellinzona, was one of the three cantonal capitals until 1878. In 1888 it became the seat of a bishop with jurisdiction over Italian-speaking Switzerland. During the struggle of 1848–66 to expel the Austrians from Lombardy, Lugano served as the headquarters for the Italian nationalist leader Giuseppe Mazzini.

Lugano is Italian in appearance and character. The town's main landmarks are the 13th-century Cathedral of San Lorenzo; the former Franciscan Church of Santa Maria degli Angioli (*c.* 1499), with frescoes by Bernardino Luini; and the Villa Favorita (1687) in the suburb of Castagnola, housing one of Europe's greatest private art collections.

Lugano lies along the St. Gotthard railway line. The town's chief sources of revenue are tourism and international finance, but there is some industry, including the manufacture of chocolate, cigarettes, silk, and machinery. The population is Italian-speaking and largely Roman Catholic. Pop. (1987 est.) 27,462.

Lugano, Lake, Italian LAGO DI LUGANO, or LAGO CERESIO, lake between Lakes Maggiore and Como with an area of 19 square miles (49 square km), of which the middle 12 square miles (31 square km) are in Ticino *canton* (Switzerland) and the northeastern and southwestern ends in the Lombardy *regione* (Italy). It lies at 889 feet (271 m) above sea level, among the outer spurs of the Alps that divide the Ticino River basin from that of the Adda, and is irregular in shape, with a western arm almost cut off from the main lake. Lake Lugano's greatest length is about 22 miles (35 km), greatest width 2 miles (3 km), and maximum depth 945 feet (288 m). It is fed by numerous small mountain streams and is drained by the short Tresa River into Lake Maggiore. Between Melide, Switz., south of the town of Lugano, and Bissone on the eastern shore, the lake is so shallow that a great stone dam has been built across it to carry the St. Gotthard railway line and road.

Lake Lugano, near Lugano, Switz.
R.G. Everts—Rapho/Photo Researchers

Except around the Bay of Lugano, the lake's wooded shores are more precipitous and desolate than those of the larger Italian Alpine lakes, and its northeastern arm is bounded by steep, rocky mountains. The chief town on the lake is Lugano, Switz.

Lugansk (*oblast* and city, Ukraine): *see* Luhansk.

Lugard, F.D., in full FREDERICK JOHN DEALTRY LUGARD, BARON LUGARD OF ABINGER (b. Jan. 22, 1858, Fort St. George, Madras, India—d. April 11, 1945, Abinger, Surrey, Eng.), administrator who played a major part in Britain's colonial history between 1888 and 1945, serving in East Africa, West Africa, and Hong Kong. His name is especially associated with Nigeria, where he served as high commissioner (1900–06) and governor and governor-general (1912–19). He was knighted in 1901 and raised to the peerage in 1928.

Born in India of missionary parents, Lugard was educated in England and, after briefly attending the Royal Military College at Sandhurst, joined the Norfolk Regiment. Posted to India and swept into the British imperial advance of the 1880s, he served in the Afghan, Suakin (Sudan), and Burma (Myanmar) campaigns. An officer with a promising career ahead of him in British India, he experienced a catastrophic love affair with a married woman. Highly strung and undermined by Burma fever, he sought oblivion by following the explorer David Livingstone's lead in fighting Arab slave raiders in eastern Africa. In 1888 he was severely wounded while leading an attack upon a slaver's stockade near Lake Nyasa. But he had found his life's work in service for Africa and for Britain—work that he saw as having a mutually beneficial purpose.

His next enterprise was under the imperial British East Africa Company, one of the chartered companies that preceded imperial annexation in Africa. Leaving Mombasa in August 1890, he led a caravan for five months along an almost untrodden route of 800 miles (1,300 km) to the advanced kingdom of Buganda. Here he found a complex struggle going on among animists, Muslims, Protestants, and Roman Catholics—the latter two groups converted by British and French missionaries who had reached Buganda earlier by a southern route—and the nominal king, or kabaka. Within 18 months—not without a brief use of his one operative Maxim gun—Lugard imposed peace, carried out an immense march to the west, and won a treaty of allegiance from the kabaka. Hearing that his company meant to abandon Uganda because of mounting expenses, he hurriedly returned to England to fight a successful two-pronged campaign to defend, first, the retention of Uganda in addition to imperial annexation and, second, his own reputation against accusations of harshness and injustice.

In 1894–95 Lugard accepted another dangerous mission, this time for the Royal Niger Company, to race the French in a treaty-making exploration on the Middle Niger. He succeeded in that enterprise in spite of great hardships—including a poisoned arrow in his head. From the Niger he went, again at some risk to his life, to the semidesert of the Bechuanaland Protectorate for the private British West Charterland Company, which was prospecting for diamonds. There he was tracked down by a runner sent by the colonial secretary, Joseph Chamberlain, to offer him his first official government appointment. He was to create a British-officered African regiment that he was to employ in a second attempt to fend off the French, who then were competing with the British right across Africa from the Niger to the Nile. This was to become the famous West African Frontier Force. Lugard's success in this difficult undertaking led to his appointment as high commissioner for Northern Nigeria.

Lugard, detail of a painting by W.J. Carrow, 1936; in the National Portrait Gallery, London
By courtesy of the National Portrait Gallery, London

Most of this vast region of 300,000 square miles (800,000 square km) was still unoccupied and even unexplored by Europeans. In the south were pagan tribes and in the north, historic Muslim city-states with large walled cities whose emirs raided the tribal territories to the south for slaves. In three years, by diplomacy or the swift use of his small force, Lugard established British control, though in hastening to take the major states of Kano and Sokoto he forced the hands of his more cautious home government. Only two serious local revolts marred the widespread acceptance and cooperation that Lugard obtained. His policy was to support the native states and chieftainships, their laws and their courts, forbidding slave raiding and cruel punishments and exercising control centrally through the native rulers. This system, cooperative in spirit and economical in staff and expense, he elaborated on in his detailed political memorandums. It greatly influenced British administration in Africa and beyond. Though sometimes misapplied or overprolonged, it helped bridge the gap between tribal systems and the new movements toward democracy and unity. Lugard's main fault as an administrator was an unwillingness to delegate responsibility, but the variety of the conditions and the vast distances acted as a check on this fault. If some of his officers were critical, the majority greatly respected their chief, and a number of "Lugard's men" went on to govern other territories in Africa.

In 1902 Lugard married Flora Shaw, a beautiful and famous woman, herself a great traveler, an authority upon colonial policy, and a member of the staff of *The Times* of London. A very deep devotion and partnership grew up between them. Because she could not stand the Nigerian climate, Lugard felt obliged to leave Africa and to accept the governorship of Hong Kong, which he held from 1907 to 1912. No greater contrast could be imagined than that between the vast untamed expanse of Northern Nigeria and the small island of Hong Kong with its highly civilized Chinese and sophisticated commercial British community. But the bushwhacker from Africa achieved a surprising degree of success and, on his own initiative, founded the University of Hong Kong.

He could not, however, resist the great opportunity offered to him in 1912 to unite the two parts of Nigeria into one vast state. The south and north showed wide contrasts in their original character and in their traditions of British rule. It was an immense task to unify their administration. Lugard did not attempt a complete fusion of their systems and retained a degree of dualism between south and north. He found the south, especially the sophisticated Africans of Lagos and the southeast, less easy to understand than the northerners, and in 1918 he had to deal with a serious outbreak in the important city-state of Abeokuta. Nor did he find it easy to extend the principles of indirect rule to the loosely organized societies of the Igbo (Ibo) and other southeastern tribes. His tenure of office also was made more difficult by World War I, with its interruption of communications, its resultant shortages of staff, and the war with the Germans in the Cameroons along his eastern frontier. Yet, in the main, Lugard carried through an immense task of unification, which was officially declared on Jan. 1, 1914. Historians must judge the event by the decision of the Nigerians to obtain their independence in 1960 as a united state and to defend it against the attempted Igbo secession to set up an independent state, Biafra, in the late 1960s.

In 1919 he retired, but only to a life of unceasing activity in his role as the leading authority on colonial government. He wrote his classic *Dual Mandate in British Tropical Africa,* published in 1922. In 1928 he became Baron Lugard of Abinger and spoke with authority in the House of Lords on colonial subjects. He became British member of the Permanent Mandates Commission and of the International Committees on Slavery and Forced Labour and chairman of the International Institute of African Languages and Cultures. To the end of his life, deeply saddened by the death of his wife in 1929, he worked almost incessantly in his secluded house on a survey of matters affecting the interests of native races both inside and outside the British Empire.

Though to modern critics of colonialism there may seem much to criticize in his ideas and actions, there can be no questioning the great range and effectiveness of the three periods of his work: in the opening up of Africa; in its government at a most formative stage in its history; and as elder statesman working during his so-called retirement almost up to his death. (M.Pm.)

BIBLIOGRAPHY. Harry A. Gailey, *Lugard and the Abeokuta Uprising: The Demise of Egba Independence* (1982) is a useful discussion. Margery Perham, *Lugard,* 2 vol. (1955–60, reprinted 1968), is a major study, based upon Lugard's own voluminous papers, official sources, the writer's travels and researches in the African regions where Lugard operated, and a close association between the author and Lugard during the last 15 years of his life. The same author's *Native Administration in Nigeria* (1937, reprinted 1962), gives the longer background against which Lugard's work can be set. C.L. Temple, *Native Races and Their Rulers,* 2nd. ed. (1968); and C.W.J. Orr, *The Making of Northern Nigeria,* 2nd ed. (1965), books by two of Lugard's senior officials, reflect contrasting views. D.J.M. Muffett, *Concerning Brave Captains* (1964); and I.F. Nicolson, *The Administration of Nigeria, 1900–1960* (1969), also by officials who served in Nigeria, represent a reaction against the almost universal approval of Lugard's achievements in Nigeria.

Lugbara, people living mainly in northwestern Uganda and the adjoining area of Congo (Kinshasa). They speak a Central Sudanic language of the Nilo-Saharan language family.

They are settled agriculturists, subsisting primarily by shifting hoe cultivation. Millet is the traditional staple; much cassava and tobacco are also grown. Many Lugbara migrants work as sharecroppers for Ganda (Baganda) landowners in southern Uganda.

Marriage entails a substantial bride-price in livestock or iron implements. Polygyny is the rule. The Lugbara lack centralized political authority, and what formal authority exists is exercised by rainmakers and the heads of large family groups. Government-appointed chiefs are set over large areas. The majority of Lugbara still practice ancestor worship; they believe in a creator god, Adroa. They are one of the peoples least affected by modern changes in Uganda, maintaining a strong sense of their own identity.

Lugdunensis, also spelled LUGUDUNENSIS, also called GALLIA LUGDUNENSIS, a province of the Roman Empire, one of the "Three Gauls" called the Gallia Comata. It extended from the capital of Lugdunum (modern Lyon) northwest to all the land between the Seine and the Loire rivers to Brittany and the Atlantic Ocean. It included what came to be Paris.

The area was conquered by Julius Caesar during the Gallic Wars (58–50 BC) and became a Roman province under the emperor Augustus. It included most of the region that the Greeks, from their colonies on the Mediterranean coast, had called Celtica (Celtica south of the Loire was detached and combined with other districts to form the province of Aquitania, or Aquitaine). The area was too large and strong to lose its individuality; it was also too rural and too far from the Mediterranean to be Romanized as fully and quickly as neighbouring Narbonensis. Even the Celtic language lingered on in forest districts into the 4th century AD and persisted in Brittany into modern times. Town life, however, grew. The villages of the tribes became practically, though not officially, municipalities, and many of these towns reached considerable size and contained magnificent public buildings. But they attest their tribal relations by their appellations, which are commonly drawn from the name of the tribe and not of the town itself; to this day Amiens, Paris, and others perpetuate the memory of tribes like the Ambiani and the Parisii.

lugeing, form of small-sled racing. The sled, called a luge, is of wood or wood-and-iron construction, with wide runners faced with steel. It is ridden in a sitting position and steered with the feet and a hand rope. Dating back to the 16th century, lugeing is a traditional winter sport in Austria and is also popular in Germany and Poland. It has been governed by the International Luge Federation since 1957. With single- and double-seater events, the first European luge championships were held in 1914 at Reichenfels, Austria, and

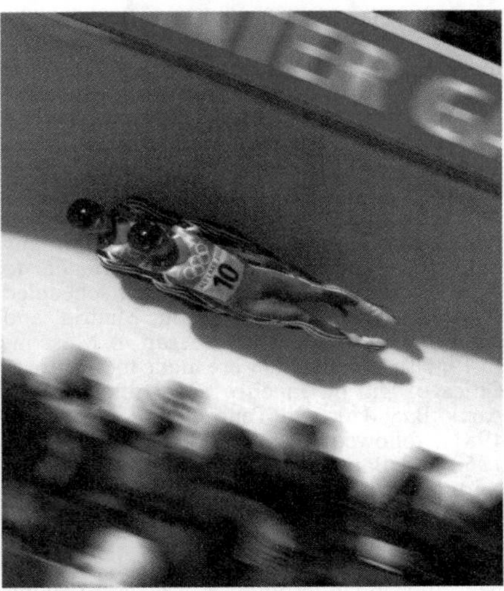

Austrians Andreas and Wolfgang Linger compete at the 2002 Olympics in Utah
Ezra Shaw—Getty Images

the first world titles were contested at Oslo in 1955. Lugeing was included in the Olympic Winter Games for the first time in 1964. Speeds above 90 miles (145 km) per hour are not uncommon. *See* Olympic Games; *see also* tobogganing.

Lugeon, Maurice (b. July 10, 1870, Poissy, France—d. Oct. 23, 1953, Lausanne, Switz.), Swiss geologist who provided the first comprehensive interpretation of the Alps as a whole.

Lugeon moved with his parents to Lausanne, Switz., in 1876 and graduated in 1893 from the university, where he later accepted a professorship (1898). He had first encountered field geology when, as a boy of 15, he accompanied an assistant in the official survey of a portion of the Prealps mountains south of Lake Geneva.

Lugeon
Boyer—H. Roger-Viollet

In 1901, in a paper before the French Geologic Society, Lugeon presented his synthesis of all the distinct and seemingly disparate elements of Alpine geology. He demonstrated that the north front of the Alpine chain is composed of large superimposed nappes (folded sheets of rock thrust over the rocks beneath). His theory that the mountains near the Simplon Pass on the Swiss-Italian border were large recumbent folds pushed toward the north was confirmed after the completion of the Simplon Tunnel (1905) allowed a geologic profile of the region to be taken.

Lugeon's work was closely connected with that of Hans Schardt, a Swiss geologist who had recognized that the Prealps were composed of folds that had advanced for tens of kilometres over the preexisting rock and who had proposed that this motion was caused by the gravitational creep or plastic flow of rock layers down gentle slopes. Lugeon became the chief proponent of Schardt's ideas and applied them in his interpretation of the entire Alpine chain. Lugeon also won international renown as a consultant on dam sites and wrote *Barrages et géologie* (1933; "Dams and Geology"), which summarized his work in this field.

Luger pistol, also called PARABELLUM PISTOL, semiautomatic German hand weapon first manufactured in 1900 for both military and commercial use. It was made in 7.65- and 9-millimetre calibres and had a toggle-joint breech mechanism. On recoil after firing, the mechanism opened to receive a new cartridge from an eight-round, removable box magazine in its grip.

Many different models of the Luger were developed after its invention by George Luger, an Austrian, in 1898. The Luger was the standard pistol of the German armed forces from 1908 to 1938. Other countries that have used the weapon in their armed forces at one time or another include Brazil, Bulgaria, Finland, Iran, Norway, Switzerland, and Turkey.

Luggarus (Switzerland): *see* Locarno.

Lugné-Poe, Aurélien-François-Marie (b. Dec. 27, 1869, Paris, Fr.—d. June 19, 1940, Villeneuve-lès-Avignon), French actor-theatrical producer who introduced the works of several great contemporary playwrights, particularly Maurice Maeterlinck and Paul Claudel.

After studies at the Paris Conservatoire, Lugné-Poe acted first at the Théâtre-Libre and then at the Théâtre d'Art, later managing (1892–1929) the celebrated Théâtre de l'Oeuvre, where he staged the plays of Henrik Ibsen, August Strindberg, and Gerhart Hauptmann, among others. He produced Oscar Wilde's highly controversial *Salomé* and, in 1912, premiered Claudel's *L'Annonce faite à Marie* (*The Tidings Brought to Mary*). A brilliant promoter of budding playwrights, he made significant contributions to the development of the French theatre by producing modern masterpieces by continental authors.

Lugo, town, Ravenna *provincia,* Emilia-Romagna *regione,* northern Italy, just west of Ravenna. The arcaded marketplace, called the Pavaglione, and a 14th-century castle converted into the town hall are notable. The town was the scene of heavy fighting in World War II. An agricultural and commercial centre, Lugo produces wine, paper, footwear, and soap. Pop. (1990 est.) mun., 32,725.

Lugo, *provincia,* in the *comunidad autónoma* ("autonomous community") of Galicia, northwestern Spain bordering the Bay of Biscay on the north. It was formed in 1833. Its 60-mile (100-kilometre) coastline, extending from Ribadeo to the Barquero Estuary, is dotted with small ports and fishing villages. The interior of the province is crossed by the Cantabrian Mountains, interspersed with valleys dotted with hamlets, while the Miño River crosses southwest toward the Atlantic Ocean. Local medicinal springs account for some tourism, but the principal sources of income are agriculture and fishing. Lugo is the main Spanish producer of rye and potatoes, but cattle and pig breeding are more important economically. Industrial development received a strong impetus in 1980 with the opening of Spain's first aluminum plant at San Cebrian, including a major port facility and reservoir. Besides Lugo city, the provincial capital, the most important towns are Mondoñedo (episcopal see), Monforte de Lemos, and Vivero. Area 3,785 square miles (9,803 square km). Pop. (1988 est.) 407,881.

Lugo, town, capital of Lugo *provincia,* in the *comunidad autónoma* ("autonomous community") of Galicia, northwestern Spain on the Miño River, southeast of La Coruña. Originating as the Roman Lucus Augusti, the walls of which remain as a public walk, the town was occupied by Suebi (Suevi), Moors, and Normans and was recaptured by King Alfonso III of Asturias and Leon in the 10th century. Notable landmarks include the Gothic Church of San Francisco, the cloister of which is a national monument, and the Romanesque cathedral (begun 1129) with Gothic, Baroque, and Neoclassical additions. Lugo is a commercial centre with agricultural fairs and markets and meat-packing plants. Pop. (1988 est.) 78,795.

The Roman walls in the city of Lugo, Spain, with the cathedral in the background
J. Allan Cash

Lugoj, city, Timiş *judeţ* (county), western Romania, on the banks of the Timiş River, 33 miles (53 km) east-southeast of Timişoara and almost 220 miles (350 km) northwest of Bucharest. The town grew up on the site of a Roman fortified camp, which in turn was built near a Dacian fortress of the 1st century BC. German influence on the settlement was strong during the Middle Ages, with a German town developing on the north bank of the river and a Romanian town on the south. The town played a significant role in the nationalist movement. Lugoj is the seat of an Orthodox bishopric and has several old churches. The modern city is a centre for the textile and wood-processing industries. Silk is the specialty of the textile works. Other industries include leatherworking, food processing, wine making, and the manufacture of agricultural machinery. Pop. (1989 est.) 54,350.

Lugol's solution, antiseptic introduced into medicine in 1829 by the French physician Jean Lugol. An effective bactericide and fungicide, Lugol's solution is a transparent brown liquid prepared by dissolving, first, 10 parts of potassium iodide, then 5 parts of iodine, in 85 parts of water. It is less irritating than iodine tincture (a solution in alcohol) when applied to open wounds.

Lugones, Leopoldo (b. June 13, 1874, Villa María del Río Seco, Arg.—d. Feb. 19, 1938, Buenos Aires), Argentine poet, literary and social critic, and cultural ambassador, considered by many the outstanding figure of his age in the cultural life of Argentina. He was a strong influence on the younger generation of writers that included the prominent short-story writer and novelist Jorge Luis Borges. His influence in public life set the pace for national development in the arts and education.

Lugones began as a socialist journalist, settling in Buenos Aires, where in 1897 he helped found *La montaña* ("The Mountain"), a socialist journal, and became an active member of the group of Modernist experimental poets led by the Nicaraguan Rubén Darío. Lugones' first important collection of poems, *Las montañas del oro* (1897; "Mountains of Gold"), reveals his affinity with the goals of Modernism in its use of free verse and exotic imagery, devices that he continued in *Los crepúsculos del jardín* (1905; "Twilights in the Garden") and *Lunario sentimental* (1909; "Sentimental Lunar Almanac").

Between 1911 and 1914 Lugones lived in Paris, editing the *Revue Sudaméricaine* ("South American Review"), but he returned to Argentina at the outbreak of World War I. A change in his political outlook from the radical socialism of his youth to an intense conservative nationalism was paralleled in his art by a rejection of Modernism in favour of a treatment of national themes in a realistic style. This change, already foreshadowed in the prose sketches of *La guerra gaucha* (1905; "The Gaucho War"), was fully revealed in the poems of *El libro de los paisajes* (1917; "The Book of Landscapes"), which extolled the beauty of the Argentine countryside. Lugones continued to develop native themes in such prose works as *Cuentos fatales* (1924; "Tales of Fate"), a collection of short stories, and the novel *El ángel de la sombra* (1926; "The Angel of the Shadow").

Lugones was director of the National Council of Education (1914–38), and he represented Argentina in the Committee on Intellectual Cooperation of the League of Nations (1924). He was also noted for several volumes of Argentine history, for studies of Classical Greek literature and culture, and for his Spanish translations of the *Iliad* and the *Odyssey.*

An introverted man who thought of himself primarily as a poet, Lugones was genuinely uneasy about the prominence that he had achieved and the public responsibilities that it entailed. He became a fascist in 1929. Under great emotional strain in later years, he committed suicide.

Lugosi, Bela, original name BÉLA BLASKO (b. Oct. 20, 1884, Lugos, Hung. [now Lugoj, Rom.]—d. Aug. 16, 1956, Los Angeles, Calif., U.S.), motion-picture actor famous for his sinister portrayal of the elegantly mannered vampire, Count Dracula, in the horror classic *Dracula* (play 1927, film 1931).

Lugosi studied at the Academy of Theatrical Art, Budapest. He made his stage debut in 1902 and from 1913 to 1919 was a member of the National Theatre in Budapest, where he also acted in several Hungarian films under the name Arisztid Olt. He went to Germany in 1919 and acted in films there until he immigrated to the United States in 1921. There he organized and was a producer, director, and star in the Hungarian dramatic company that presented a stage version of *Dracula* in New York and on tour in 1927. He

Lugosi as Count Dracula
Culver Pictures

made his Hollywood film debut in *The Silent Command* (1923) and became internationally famous as the star of *Dracula,* the picture that was the prototype of Hollywood vampire films and that typecast Lugosi as a portrayer of monsters. His better-known films include *The Black Cat* (1934), *Mark of the Vampire* (1935), *The Wolf Man* (1941), and *The Ape Man* (1943).

Lugosi's decline into poverty and obscurity was accompanied by a growing dependence on narcotics. In 1955 he voluntarily committed himself to the state hospital at Norwalk, Calif., as a drug addict; he was released later that year. At his death, according to his expressed wishes, Lugosi was buried wearing the long black cloak that he used in *Dracula.*

Lugudunensis (Roman province): *see* Lugdunensis.

Luguru, also called RUGURU, or WALUGURU, a Bantu-speaking people of the hills, Uluguru Mountains, and coastal plains of east-central Tanzania. The Luguru are reluctant to leave the mountain homeland that they have occupied for at least 300 years, despite the relatively serious population pressure in their area and the employment opportunities in the city and on estates. In the late 20th century the Luguru numbered about 1.2 million.

The mountains receive abundant rainfall, and with intensive agriculture (upland rice, sorghum, corn [maize], cassava), including some irrigation from streams, Luguru lands can support upward of 800 people per square mile (300 per square kilometre) in some places. In the lower plains surrounding the Uluguru Mountains many other groups have settled, and generally the Luguru comprise peoples of diverse origins. A common language and culture evolved or was adopted by these settlers, but rough terrain and raiding by neighbours north and south have limited communication among villages.

In the mid-19th century an important east-west caravan route was established around the northern edge of the Uluguru Mountains. The Luguru were periodically raided for slaves by a man named Kisabengo, who founded a fortified village where caravans stopped for supplies and obtained porters; first called Simbamwene, this became the town of Morogoro, which is an important trade centre in modern Tanzania.

The Luguru observe matrilineal descent and recognize about 50 exogamous, noncorporate clans, which are then divided into some 800 lineages identified with lands, leaders, and insignia (stools, staffs, drums). Historically they rarely had a political organization higher than the lineage level, the exception being when a rainmaker might rise in prominence and demand tribute. Neighbouring peoples also sought out Luguru rainmakers. German colonizers imposed a more formal organization, which was continued after World War I, when the British administration chose two "sultans" from among Luguru lineage heads; later subchiefs, headmen, and court officials were named. At independence this system was reorganized, and in 1962 the Tanganyikan government abolished all traditional chiefdoms. The mountain Luguru are now mainly Roman Catholic, while the lowland Luguru are Muslim.

Besides growing crops for their own subsistence, the Luguru export produce to local towns and to Dar es-Salaam. Coffee is grown with some success in the mountains; no cattle are kept because of tsetse fly infestation. Some of the largest sisal estates in Tanzania are in lowlands surrounding Luguru lands, and many non-Luguru have come to work on them. Luguru also sell these people foodstuffs.

Lugus, also called LUG, or LUGH (Celtic: "Lynx," or "Light"?), in ancient Celtic religion, one of the major gods. He is one of the deities whom Julius Caesar identified with the Roman god Mercury (Greek: Hermes). His cult was widespread throughout the early Celtic world, and his name occurs as an element in many continental European and British place-names, such as Lyon, Laon, Leiden, and Carlisle (formerly Luguvallium, "Strong in the God Lugus").

According to Irish tradition, Lug Lámfota ("Lug of the Long Arm") was the sole survivor of triplet brothers all having the same name. At least three dedications to Lugus in plural form, Lugoues, are known from the European continent, and the Celtic affinity for trinitarian forms would suggest that three gods were likewise envisaged in these dedications. Lug's son, or rebirth, according to Irish belief, was the great Ulster hero, Cú Chulainn ("Culann's Dog").

In Wales, as Lleu Llaw Gyffes ("Lleu of the Dexterous Hand"), he was also believed to have had a strange birth. His mother was the virgin goddess Aranrhod ("Silver Wheel"). When her uncle, the great magician Math, tested her virginity by means of a wand of chastity, she at once gave birth to a boy child, who was instantly carried off by his uncle Gwydion and reared by him. Aranrhod then sought repeatedly to destroy her son, but she was always prevented by Gwydion's powerful magic; she was forced to give her son a name and provide him with arms; finally, as his mother had denied him a wife, Gwydion created a woman for him from flowers.

Lug was also known in Irish tradition as Samildánach ("Skilled in All the Arts"). The variety of his attributes and the extent to which his calendar festival Lugnasad on August 1 was celebrated in Celtic lands indicate that he was one of the most powerful and impressive of all the ancient Celtic deities.

lugworm (genus *Arenicola*), any of several marine worms (class Polychaeta, phylum Annelida) that burrow deep into the sandy sea bottom or intertidal areas and are often quite large. Fishermen use them as bait. Adult lugworms of the coast of Europe (*e.g., A. marina*) attain lengths of about 23 cm (9 inches). The lugworm of the coasts of North America (*A. cristata*) ranges in length from 7.5 to 30 cm.

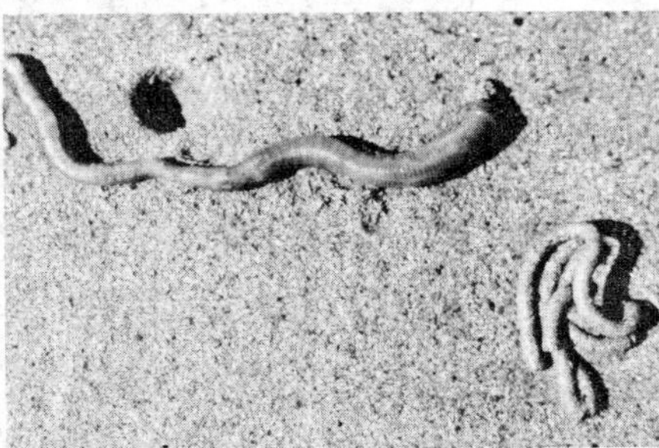

European lugworm (*Arenicola marina*) with coiled cast (bottom right)

Leslie Jackman from the Natural History Photographic Agency

The body is segmented, or ringed. The head end is dark red; behind it the body is fatter and lighter in colour. Toward the tail the body becomes thinner and yellowish red. The middle of the body has bristles and about 12 pairs of feathery gills.

Lugworms feed on decayed organic matter and ingest sand along with the food particles. At low tide their coiled casts (masses of excrement) may often be seen piled above their burrows. Their burrows may extend as deep as 60 cm (2 feet). The animals are hermaphroditic; *i.e.,* functional reproductive organs of both sexes occur in the same individual. The eggs of one individual, however, are fertilized by the sperm of another.

Luhan, Mabel Dodge, in full MABEL GANSON DODGE LUHAN (b. Feb. 26, 1879, Buffalo, N.Y., U.S.—d. Aug. 13, 1962, Taos, N.M.), American writer whose candid autobiographical volumes contain much information about well-known Americans of her era.

Luhan's life and writing revolved around the literary, artistic, and political celebrities she gathered about her both in New York and abroad. She later settled in an artists' colony in Taos amid the Pueblo Indians, whom she loved for their simple lifestyle. There her home again became a gathering place for celebrated artists and writers. She devoted herself to recording her relationships with such figures as Gertrude Stein, John Reed, and Walter Lippmann, with little regard for propriety or privacy.

The volumes of Luhan's *Intimate Memories* are *Background* (1933), *European Experiences* (1935), *Movers and Shakers* (1936), and *Edge of Taos Desert* (1937). *Lorenzo in Taos* (1932) provides insight into D.H. Lawrence, and *Taos and Its Artists* (1947) introduces 49 artists and their work.

Luhansk, Russian LUGANSK, formerly (1938–58, 1970–89) VOROSHILOVGRAD, *oblast* (province), Ukraine. It occupies an area in the extreme east of the republic, on the Donets River. North of the river is dry, rolling steppe; south of it are the low hills of the Donets Ridge, originally in forest-steppe but now, like the northern part, almost wholly under the plow. The *oblast* covers the eastern part of the Donets Coal Basin and industrial area, and its economy is dominated by coal mining, iron and steel production, heavy engineering, and chemicals. About five-sixths of the population is urban. Agriculture is well developed and is largely concerned with grain production. Sunflowers also are important, and there is much market gardening around the cities. Area 10,300 square miles (26,700 square km). Pop. (1991 est.) 2,871,100.

Luhansk, Russian LUGANSK, formerly (1935–58, 1970–89) VOROSHILOVGRAD, city and administrative centre of Luhansk *oblast* (province), Ukraine. It lies along the Lugan River at the latter's confluence with the Olkhovaya River. The city dates from 1795, when a state iron foundry was established there to supply ordnance to the Black Sea fleet. Luhansk grew with the development of the Donets Coal Basin in the 1890s. The major branch of industry is heavy engineering, dominated by a huge diesel-locomotive works. Steel tubes, coal-mining equipment, spare parts for motor vehicles, and precision instruments also are made; coal is mined in the city. There are also food and timberworking industries. Luhansk has teacher-training, medical, agricultural, and machine-building institutes. Pop. (1991 est.) 503,900.

Luḥayyah, Al-, also spelled LUHAIYAH, or LOHEIYA, town, western Yemen, on the Red Sea coast. Situated on the coastal plain known as the Tihāmah, it is one of the country's minor ports. It was founded in the mid-15th century, and tradition connects its origin with a local holy man, Sheikh Salei, around whose dwelling and tomb the town is supposed to have developed. By the end of the 18th century it was a walled and fortified town. After being held by the Ottomans from about 1800 to World War I, in 1918 it was taken by the British, who gave it, with the rest of the Yemeni Tihāmah, to the Idrīsī rulers of Asir, to the north. Recovered by Yemen in 1925, the town and coastal plain were occupied in 1934 by the Saudis, who returned them to Yemen by the terms of the Treaty of aṭ-Ṭā'if of that year.

The port is a shallow open roadstead, 4 miles (6 km) southwest of the town, that is partially protected by the offshore island of Al-Urmak. Once a Yemeni coffee export centre, the town and port have declined greatly in the last 200 years; the formerly strong fort is in ruins. Traffic is limited to coastal shipping; Yemen's international seaborne trade is now centred at the modern facilities at Aḥmadī, the port of al-Ḥudaydah. Pop. (latest est.) 2,656.

Luhya, also called LUYIA, or ABALUHYA, ethnolinguistic cluster of several acephalous, closely related Bantu-speaking peoples including the Bukusu, Tadjoni, Wanga, Marama, Tsotso, Tiriki, Nyala, Kabras, Hayo, Marachi, Holo, Maragoli, Dakho, Isukha, Kisa, Nyole, and Samia of Western Province, western Kenya. The term Luhya, which is short for Abaluhya (loosely, "those of the same hearth"), was first suggested by a local African mutual-assistance association around 1930; by 1945, when in the postwar colonial period it was found to be politically advantageous to possess a supertribal identity, the Luhya had emerged as a national group.

United as Luhya, members of various small groups were able to gain the same recognition, voice, and presence in Kenyan politics that was enjoyed by the larger groups in Kenya. The Luhya constituted the second-largest ethnic grouping in Kenya in the 1980s.

Most Luhya groups lack traditional chieftainships, being organized into more or less politically autonomous patrilineal lineages, each associated with a stretch of land. With land shortage there has been considerable tribal interspersal. Luhya grow corn (maize), cotton, and sugarcane as cash crops; cultivate millet, sorghum, and vegetables as staple crops; and also keep some livestock. They participate in trade and other activities in areas adjacent to the great waterway of Lake Victoria. Many Luyha have migrated to urban areas seeking work.

Luichow Peninsula, Wade–Giles romanization LEI-CHOU PAN-TAO, Pinyin LEIZHOU BANDAO, peninsula, some 75 mi (120 km) from north to south and 30 mi east to west, jutting out from the coast of Kwangtung Province, China, and separated by a narrow 10-mi-wide strait from Hai-nan Island (Hai-nan Tao). The peninsula is curved, forming a large bay on the east coast, in which two large islands—Nao-chou and Tung-hai—protect Chan-chiang Kang (bay), on which the city of Chan-chiang is situated. Administratively, the peninsula forms part of Chan-chiang Prefecture (*ti-ch'ü*). The peninsula forms part of the eastern limit of the Gulf of Tonkin, and it takes its name from the ancient city of Lei-chou (now Hai-k'ang) on the eastern coast, which was, until the rise of Chan-chiang in the 20th century, the chief city and the seat of the prefecture of Lei-chou.

From 1898 to 1946 the French held a lease on an area of 325 sq mi (842 sq km) on the eastern coast, including the bay and the two large islands. Usually referred to as Kwangchowan, the French called it Kouang-Tchéou-Wan. Its capital was at Chan-chiang, renamed Fort Bayard by the French. Occupied by the Japanese in World War II, it was retroceded to China by France in 1946.

The peninsula consists of undulating upland with a generally low relief, dropping in steps to the sea. It is mostly formed of basalt and recent sedimentary rocks, with the cones of numerous extinct volcanoes about 825 ft (250 m) high in the northern and southern sections of the peninsula. The climate is sharply differentiated between the eastern section, which receives more than 40 in. (1,000 mm) of rainfall annually, and the west, which receives considerably less. The whole area is much drier than the neighbouring mainland or Hainan Island, and the climate generally is tropical with no true winter conditions; average January temperatures vary between 61° and 64° F (16° and 18° C), and June temperatures between 86° and 91° F (30° and 33° C). There is thus a high rate of evaporation. Forest belts have been planted since 1955 to reduce wind velocity across the peninsula and thus evaporation.

The area was originally forested, but almost all of the forest cover, except on the hills of the north, has long since been destroyed. As a result, uncultivated areas have suffered seriously from soil erosion and are mostly covered with a type of rough savanna grassland, with shrubs and thickets growing in the valleys. The soil layer, always thin, has been completely washed away in places, often after grassland fires or overgrazing have destroyed the protective vegetation cover. In general, the area is rather poor, with little more than 20 percent of the land under cultivation. On more than a quarter of the cultivated area the crop is sweet potatoes; there is less rice grown than is usual in other parts of Kwangtung. There are some mineral deposits (*e.g.*, manganese and mercury).

The main cities are Chan-chiang and Hai-k'ang on the east coast and Hsü-wen, with its port, Hai-an, at the southern tip of the peninsula. A north–south railway connects Chan-chiang with Lien-chiang. After 1958 the Youth Canal was built from Ho-ti Shui-k'u (reservoir) near Lien-chiang southward through the outskirts of Chan-chiang to Hai-k'ang; another branch runs to the west coast.

Luigi (Italian personal name): *see under* Louis.

Luiken, Johannes: *see* Luyken, Jan.

Luini, Bernardino, Luini also spelled LUVINI (d. 1532, Milan), Renaissance painter of Lombardy, best known for his mythological and religious frescoes.

Little is known of Luini's life; the earliest surviving painting that is certainly his work is a fresco (1512) of the "Madonna and Child" at the Cistercian monastery of Chiaravalle, near Milan. It shows the dependence upon the style of the Lombardian painter Il Bergognone (*c.* 1455–after 1522), which Luini retained throughout his life. The majority of his panel paintings depict the Virgin.

Luini was influenced by Leonardo da Vinci during the latter's second stay in Milan (1506–13), as is seen in the facial types and the composition of Luini's "Holy Family" (Pinacoteca Ambrosiana, Milan). Of his frescoes, many of which are now detached and dispersed, the most notable are the "Story of Europa" (*c.* 1520; Berlin) and the "Story of Cephalus and Procris" (*c.* 1520; National Gallery of Art, Washington, D.C.) from either the Casa Rabia or the Villa Pelucca (both in Milan) and the "Story of Moses" and various mythological subjects from the Villa Pelucca (Brera, Milan).

Luís (Portuguese personal name): *see under* Louis.

Luis (Spanish personal name): *see under* Louis.

Luís (Pereira de Sousa), Washington (b. Oct. 26, 1869, Macaé, Braz.—d. Aug. 4, 1957, São Paulo), president of Brazil (1926–30) who was unable to strengthen his country's debilitated economy on the eve of the Great Depression.

Reared in the state of São Paulo and identified with it as a career politician for more than 30 years, Luís held numerous public offices, including those of mayor of São Paulo and of state governor (1920–24). After being elected president of Brazil on Nov. 15, 1926, he initiated a vast highway construction program, but he was greatly hampered by an enormous foreign debt and the collapse of the coffee market. Attempts were made to limit the production of coffee, but with the coming of the world economic decline in 1929, Brazil was left with huge and unsellable reserves. Near the end of his term he made the flagrant political mistake of attempting to ensure the election of another São Paulo politician as his successor. His candidate, Júlio Prestes, won in a controlled election in 1930; but the supporters of the opposition candidate, Getúlio Vargas, organized a successful coup d'état and deposed Luís on Oct. 24, 1930, just before he was to complete his term. The last president of the "old" republic, he left for exile in Europe, returning to Brazil only in 1946.

Luiseño, group of Indians who spoke a Uto-Aztecan language and inhabited a large area south and east of Los Angeles and north of San Diego, Calif. They were named after the Spanish mission San Luis Rey de Francia.

Although some Luiseño lived on the coast, where they fished and gathered mollusks, the great majority were hill people who gathered acorns and other seeds, fruits, and roots and hunted various game with bow and arrow or snares. In the warm climate the men wore nothing, and the women wore an apron front and back. They lived in villages of semi-subterranean earth-covered lodges. They were apparently organized in small groups of kinsmen clustered into clans or near clans, which had territorial, political, and economic functions; and there were parallel and closely related religious societies to which everyone belonged and which had both ceremonial and political functions. Several family groupings had chiefs, and in most areas there was apparently a chief of chiefs.

The Luiseño were mystics; and their conception of a great, all-powerful, avenging god was uncommon for aboriginal North America. In deference to this god, Chingichnish, they held a series of initiation ceremonies for boys, some of which involved a drug made from the jimsonweed (*Datura stramonium*) which was drunk to inspire visions or dreams of the supernatural. Intoxication was central to this jimsonweed cult. Equally important were mourning ceremonies, a series of funerary observances and anniversary commemorations of the dead. Shamans, or medicine men, were important in curing disease. Over 1,000 Luiseño descendants remained in the late 20th century.

Luisetti, Hank, byname of ANGELO ENRICO LUISETTI (b. June 16, 1916, San Francisco), American collegiate basketball player who introduced the one-handed shot. He also combined all skills on both offense and defense, including dribbling and passing behind his back.

Luisetti, at 6 ft 2½ in., played basketball at Galileo High School (San Francisco, 1931–34) and at Stanford University (Palo Alto, Calif.; 1935–38). He was the first collegiate player to score 50 points in a game—his career total points were 1,596 in four years. His team won three Pacific Conference championships and popularized the fast-break offense and a combination of man-to-man and zone defense. He served in the Navy in World War II and, afterward, played and coached amateur basketball into the early 1950s. He later became a travel company executive. He was elected to the Basketball Hall of Fame in 1959.

Luish language: *see* Luwian language.

Luisian Stage, major division of Miocene rocks and time in the Pacific Coast region of North America (the Miocene Epoch began about 26,000,000 years ago and lasted about 19,000,000 years). The Luisian Stage, which precedes the Mohnian Stage and follows the Relizian Stage, was named for exposures studied in San Luis Obispo County, Calif. Three subdivisions of the Luisian Stage are recognized, based on characteristic fossil foraminiferans—single-celled organisms having calcareous shells. The Luisian Stage is approximately equivalent in age to the Helvetian Stage recognized in Europe and elsewhere.

Luitpold (b. March 12, 1821, Würzburg, Bavaria—d. Dec. 12, 1912, Munich), prince regent of Bavaria from 1886 to 1912, in whose reign Bavaria prospered under a liberal government and Munich became a cultural centre of Europe.

The third son of King Louis (Ludwig) I, Luitpold chose a military career and fought on Austria's side against Prussia in the Seven Weeks' War (1866). During the later years of his nephew Louis II's reign, he served as the king's deputy, and, when it became clear that Louis was mentally unbalanced, Luitpold acted as regent, a post he continued to hold under Otto, his insane younger nephew. The regent's patriarchal rule and his firm application of liberal principles soon won the public's approval. Electoral reforms (1906), combined with the introduction of ministerial responsibility, made Bavaria the most democratically governed kingdom in Germany. Despite his reservations about the German emperor William II's policies, Luitpold remained strictly loyal to the German government. The 26 years of Luitpold's regency were regarded as a golden age for Bavaria. Munich, the capital, flourished under Luitpold's patronage and came to be regarded as a centre of culture. The prince regent was a friend of many artists, and he spent large sums for cultural and artistic purposes and created the Künstlerhaus as a meeting place and exhibition centre. On Luitpold's death, his eldest son became regent and then king as Louis III.

Luitpold, detail from a portrait by Friedrich August von Kaulbach, 1902; in the Bayerische Staatsgemäldesammlungen, Munich

By courtesy of the Bayerische Staatsgemaldesammlungen, Munich

Luján, city and national pilgrimage site on the Luján River, in the Pampa of northern Buenos Aires province, Argentina. The city was named for the conquistador Pedro Luján, who died there (1536) in a battle with the indigenous Indians.

The basilica at Luján, Arg.

E. Comesana—Shostal/EB Inc.

According to tradition, in 1630 a statue of the Virgin, being transported by oxcart between churches, became stuck at what is now Luján in spite of strenuous efforts to move it. This event was taken as a sign by devout Roman Catholics that the Virgin willed she should stay there, giving reason for the establishment of a religious shrine and pilgrimage site. A commemorative chapel was built, and a settlement (declared a city in 1755) grew up around it. A neo-Gothic basilica encloses the original chapel and statue of the Virgin, whose feast day on May 21 attracts large numbers of pilgrims. Luján is also the site of the provincial Historical and Colonial Museum housed in late 18th-century public buildings. Pop. (1999 est.) 74,766.

Lukács, György (b. April 13, 1885, Budapest—d. June 4, 1971, Budapest), Hungarian Marxist philosopher, writer, and literary critic who influenced the mainstream of European Communist thought during the first half of the 20th century. His major contributions include the formulation of a Marxist system of aesthetics that opposed political control of artists and defended humanism and an elaboration of Marx's theory of alienation within industrial society.

Lukács

Interfoto MTI Budapest—Eastfoto

Born into a wealthy Jewish family, Lukács became a Marxist, joining the Hungarian Communist Party in 1918. After the overthrow of Béla Kun's short-lived Hungarian Communist regime in 1919, in which Lukács served as commissar for culture and education, he moved to Vienna, where he remained for 10 years. He edited the review *Kommunismus* and was a member of the Hungarian underground movement. In his book *Geschichte und Klassenbewusstsein* (1923; *History and Class Consciousness*), he developed his own unique Marxist philosophy of history and laid the basis for his critical literary tenets by linking the development of form in art with the history of the class struggle. In his later critiques of literature, Lukács showed himself partial to the great bourgeois realist novelists of the 19th century, a preference that was denounced by proponents of the official Soviet doctrine of Socialist Realism.

Lukács was in Berlin from 1929 to 1933, save for a short period in 1930–31, at which time he attended the Marx-Engels Institute in Moscow. In 1933 he left Berlin and returned to Moscow to attend the Institute of Philosophy. He moved back to Hungary in 1945 and became a member of parliament and a professor of aesthetics and the philosophy of culture at the University of Budapest. In 1956 he was a major figure in the Hungarian uprising, serving as minister of culture during the revolt. He was arrested and deported to Romania but was allowed to return to Budapest in 1957, where, stripped of his former power and status, he devoted himself to a steady output of critical and philosophical works. Lukács wrote more than 30 books and hundreds of essays and lectures. Among his other works are *Die Seele und die Formen* (1911; *Soul and Form*), a collection of essays that established his reputation as a critic; *Der historische Roman* (1955; *The Historical Novel*); and books on Johann Wolfgang von Goethe, G.W.F. Hegel, Vladimir Lenin, Karl Marx and Marxism, and aesthetics.

Luke, SAINT (fl. 1st century AD), in Christian tradition, the author of the third Gospel and the Acts of the Apostles, a companion of the Apostle Paul, and the most literary of the New Testament writers. Information about his life is scanty. His writing style indicates a cultivated literary background. Tradition based on Gospel references has regarded him as a physician and a Gentile. He was a coworker of Paul and probably accompanied him on several missionary journeys.

Life and times. Luke is first mentioned in the letters of the Apostle Paul as the latter's "coworker" and as the "beloved physician." The former designation is the more significant one, for it identifies him as one of a professional cadre of itinerant Christian "workers," many of whom were teachers and preachers. His medical skills, like Paul's tentmaking, may have contributed to his livelihood; but his principal occupation was the advancement of the Christian mission.

If Luke was the author of the third Gospel and the Acts of the Apostles, as is very probable, the course and nature of his ministry may be sketched in more detail. He excludes himself from those who were eyewitnesses of Christ's ministry. His participation in the Pauline mission, however, is indicated by the use of the first person in the "we" sections of Acts. They reveal that Luke shared in instructing persons in the Christian message and possibly in performing miraculous healings.

The "we" sections are analogous in style to travel reports found elsewhere in writings of the Greco-Roman period. They place the author with Paul during his initial mission into Greece—*i.e.,* as far as Philippi, in Macedonia (*c.* AD 51). It is there that Luke later rejoins Paul and accompanies him on his final journey to Jerusalem (*c.* AD 58). After Paul's arrest in that city and during his extended detention in nearby Caesarea, Luke may have spent considerable time in Palestine working with the apostle as the occasion allowed and gathering materials for his future two-volume literary work, the Gospel and the Acts. In any case, two years later he appears with Paul on his prison voyage from Caesarea to Rome and again, according to the Second Letter of Paul to Timothy 4:11, at the time of the apostle's martyrdom in the imperial city (*c.* AD 66).

Further direct information about Luke is scanty in the New Testament, but certain inferences may be drawn. The literary style of his writings and the range of his vocabulary mark him as an educated man. The distinction drawn between Luke and other colleagues "of the circumcision" (Letter of Paul to the Colossians 4:11) has caused many scholars to conclude that he was a Gentile. If so, he would be the only New Testament writer clearly identifiable as a non-Jew. This conclusion, however, rests upon a doubtful equation of those "of the circumcision" with Jewish Christians. Actually, the phrase probably refers to a particular type of Jewish Christian, those who strictly observed the rituals of Judaism. It offers no support, therefore, to the view that

Luke was a Gentile. His intimate knowledge of the Old Testament and the focus of interest in his writings favour, on balance, the view that he was a Jewish Christian who followed a Greek life-style and was comparatively lax in ritual observances.

Writings from the latter half of the second century provide further information. A number of them—St. Irenaeus' *Against Heresies*, the Anti-Marcionite Prologue to the Gospel, and the *Muratorian Canon* listing the books received as sacred by the Christians—identify Luke as the author of the third Gospel and Acts. The Prologue begins:

> Luke is a man from Antioch, Syria, a physician by profession. He was a disciple of the apostles, and later he accompanied Paul until his martyrdom. Having neither wife nor child, he served the Lord without distraction. He fell asleep in Boeotia at the age of 84, full of the Holy Spirit. Moved by the Holy Spirit, Luke composed all of this Gospel in the districts around Achaia . . .

The assertion that St. Luke was "a man from Antioch, Syria" who wrote "moved by the Holy Spirit"—that is, as a prophet—receives a measure of support from the Lukan writings: the city of Antioch figures prominently in Acts, and there is a special interest in contemporary (Christian) prophets and prophecy. Whether Luke is to be identified, as some scholars believe, with the prophet Lucius mentioned in Acts 13:1 and with St. Paul's "fellow worker" (and kinsman) in the Letter of Paul to the Romans 16:21 is more questionable, although not impossible. Less than certain also is the comment of the prologue placing

St. Luke drawing a picture of the Virgin, detail of a painting by Jan Gossaert, called Mabuse; in the Kunsthistorisches Museum, Vienna

By courtesy of the Kunsthistorisches Museum, Vienna

the writing of the Gospel and Luke's death in Greece; but, on the whole, it is more probable than the later traditions locating his literary work in Alexandria (or Rome) and his death in Bithynia. The identification of St. Luke as "a disciple of the Apostles," although true in a general sense, probably reflects the concern of the 2nd-century church to place all canonical Christian writings under an apostolic umbrella. Later notions that Luke was one of the 70 disciples appointed by the Lord, that he was the companion of Cleopas, and that he was an artist appear to be legendary. In liturgical tradition Luke's feast day is October 18.

Luke's writings. Luke had a cultivated literary background and wrote in good idiomatic Greek. The Gospel bearing his name and the Acts of the Apostles were probably written during or shortly after the Jewish revolt (AD 66–73), although a somewhat later date is not inconceivable. Together they make up more than a fourth of the New Testament, and in them Luke is revealed to be not only Christianity's first historian but also a theologian of unusual perception. Some scholars have also associated Luke with the Pastoral Letters and the Letter to the Hebrews, either as author or as amanuensis, because of linguistic and other similarities with the Gospel and the Acts.

Some scholars, on the other hand, doubt that Luke is in fact the author of the two New Testament books traditionally ascribed to him. In some respects the issue is similar to that raised about the authorship of the works of Shakespeare or, in the classical field, of Plato's letters. But it is unlike the Shakespearean controversy in that no alternative author has been suggested and is unlike the problem of Plato's letters in that no larger Lukan corpus is available for comparison. Those questioning Luke's authorship point to the fact that the theological emphases of his Gospel and the Acts differ considerably from those of Paul's writings and that the description of the Council of Jerusalem (Acts 15) is divergent from the description of the conference in the Letter of Paul to the Galatians 2. These objections are based upon the assumption that Luke was the disciple of Paul (and would, therefore, reflect his theology) and upon the traditional identification of Acts 15 with the conference in Galatians 2. Both of these premises, however, are quite probably mistaken. A more serious objection is the difference between the portrait of Paul in Acts and the impression one receives of him in his letters. But it has sometimes been exaggerated, and it does not in any case exceed the variation that might be expected between a sometime colleague's impressions of a man and the man's own letters. The Gospel and Acts were, in all likelihood, tagged with the name Luke when they were deposited in the library of the author's patron, Theophilus (Luke 1:3). Within a century there was a widespread and undisputed tradition identifying that Luke with an otherwise insignificant physician and colleague of Paul. The tradition is on the whole consistent with the literary and historical character of the documents, and one may be reasonably certain that it is correct.

Jesus' parting words, "It is not for you to know times [of the consummation of this age] . . . but you shall receive power . . . and you shall be my witnesses . . ." (Acts 1:7ff), provide a guideline for Luke's theology. Thus, he called the church back from overeager speculation about the precise time of the Lord's return and the end of the age to its proper task of faithful mission in the lengthening interim. By the selection and interpretation of his sources, he charted the path by which the church would understand both its own uniqueness in the world and also its continuing relationship to Judaism and to the world. His work was no small achievement, and through the centuries it has served the church well. (E.E.E.)

BIBLIOGRAPHY. C.K. Barrett, *Luke the Historian in Recent Study* (1961), a brief and readable survey of a number of contemporary writers; "The Identity of the Editor of Luke and Acts," pp. 205–359, in F.J.F. Jackson and K. Lake (eds.), *The Beginnings of Christianity*, vol. 2, pt. 1, *The Acts of the Apostles* (1922), an extensive presentation and analysis of biblical and post-biblical traditions about St. Luke; E.E. Ellis (ed.), *The Gospel of Luke* (1967), a short summary of the background, life, and theology of the evangelist in the light of recent research; also useful, I.H. Marshall, *Luke: Historian and Theologian* (1970), and L.E. Keck and J.L. Martyn (eds.), *Studies in Luke-Acts* (1966).

Luke, Gospel According to, third of the four New Testament Gospels (narratives recounting the life and death of Jesus Christ), and, with Mark and Matthew, one of the three Synoptic Gospels (*i.e.*, those presenting a common view). It is traditionally credited to Luke, "the beloved physician" (Col. 4:14), a close associate of the Apostle Paul. Luke's Gospel is clearly written for Gentile converts: it traces Christ's genealogy, for example, back to Adam, the "father" of the human race, rather than to Abraham, the father of the Jewish people. The date and place of composition are uncertain; many date the Gospel to AD 63–70, others somewhat later.

Like Matthew, Luke derives much of his Gospel from that of Mark, generally following Mark's sequence and incorporating about 50 percent of Mark's material into his work. The Gospels of Luke and Matthew, however, share a good deal of material not found in Mark, suggesting that the two evangelists may have had access to another common source.

Despite its similarities to the other Synoptic Gospels, however, Luke's narrative contains much that is unique. It gives details of Jesus' infancy found in no other Gospel: the census of Caesar Augustus, the journey to Bethlehem, Jesus' birth, the adoration of the shepherds, Jesus' circumcision, the words of Simeon, and Jesus at age 12 in the temple talking with the doctors of the Law. It also is the only Gospel to give an account of the Ascension. Among the notable parables found only in Luke's Gospel are those of the good Samaritan and the prodigal son.

Luke's Gospel is also unique in its perspective. It resembles the other synoptics in its treatment of the life of Jesus; but it goes beyond them in narrating the ministry of Jesus, widening its perspective to consider God's overall historical purpose and the place of the church within it. Luke, and its companion book, Acts of the Apostles, portray the church as God's instrument of redemption on Earth in the interim between the death of Christ and the Second Coming. The two books combined provide the first Christian history, outlining God's purpose through three historical epochs: the epoch of the Law and the prophets, which lasted from ancient Israel to the time of John the Baptist; the epoch of Jesus' ministry; and the epoch of the church's mission, from the Ascension to the return of Christ.

Lukin, Lionel (b. May 18, 1742, Little Dunmow, Essex, Eng.—d. Feb. 16, 1834, Hythe, Kent), pioneer in the construction of the modern "unsinkable" lifeboat.

While he was working as a London coachbuilder, Lukin began experimenting with a Norwegian yawl in 1784, testing his alterations in the River Thames. In 1785 he patented his method of constructing small boats that would not sink even when filled with water. He used watertight compartments, cork, and other lightweight materials. He also invented a raft for rescuing persons under ice, an adjustable reclining bed for hospital patients, and a rain gauge.

Luks, George (Benjamin) (b. Aug. 13, 1867, Williamsport, Pa., U.S.—d. Oct. 29, 1933, New York City), one of a group of U.S. painters popularly known as the Ashcan School because of their realistic treatment of urban scenes.

Luks studied first at the Pennsylvania Academy of Fine Arts, Philadelphia, and later in Germany, London, and Paris. Returning to the United States in 1894, he became an illustrator for the Philadelphia *Press*. During that period he met the teacher and painter Robert Henri and the newspaper illustrators John Sloan and William Glackens. Luks served in Cuba in 1896 as a correspondent artist for the Philadelphia *Bulletin* during the Cuban struggle for independence from Spain. After returning to the United States, he worked as a cartoonist for the New York *World.* He also began to paint realistic pictures of New Yorkers; notable examples are "The Spielers"

"The Spielers," oil on canvas by George B. Luks, 1905 (91.44 cm × 66.04 cm); in the Addison Gallery of American Art, Andover, Mass.

(1905; Addison Gallery of American Art, Andover, Mass.), possibly his best-known work, and "The Wrestlers" (1905; Museum of Fine Arts, Boston).

In 1908, with Henri, Sloan, Glackens, and other painters, Luks formed a group called the Eight, whose exhibition in New York that year is considered a key event in the early history of modern painting in the United States.

Lukuga (Zaire): *see* Kalemie.

Lukuga River, tributary of the Lualaba River in eastern Zaire. It issues from the western shore of Lake Tanganyika at Kalemie, Zaire, and flows 200 miles (320 km) west to the Lualaba River 25 miles (40 km) north of Kabalo. There are low-grade coal deposits along its tributaries, north of Kalemie and Moluba (former Greinerville). It is Lake Tanganyika's only outlet.

Lule River, Swedish LULEÄLV, river in the *län* (county) of Norrbotten, northern Sweden. It flows southeast from the Norwegian border for 280 miles (450 km) to the Gulf of Bothnia at Luleå. Between the river's two main headstreams, the Stora (Big) Lule and the Lilla (Little) Lule, is Mount Sarek National Park, rising to 6,854 feet (2,089 m) at Mount Sarek. The headstreams have numerous lakes, some of which are dammed for hydroelectricity. Along the main river's course are several high falls, including Stora Falls and those at Porjus and Harsprånget; several major power stations supply the nearby iron mines and railway and feed power farther south.

Luleå, city and seaport, seat of Norrbotten *län* (county), northern Sweden. The city lies at the mouth of the Lule River, where it enters the Gulf of Bothnia. Gustavus II Adolphus founded the town in 1621, 7 miles (11 km) farther up the river; it was moved to its present site in 1649. In 1887 it was almost entirely destroyed by fire.

Luleå is the seat of a Lutheran bishopric. It is also an educational centre, with more than 10 schools offering various kinds of professional training. The Gammelstad Church (built *c.* 1400) is now the provincial museum. Industries include iron smelting, shipbuilding, engineering, and lumbering. The city's port, Svartöstaden, handles iron-ore exports during the ice-free months and is one of Sweden's largest export harbours. There are rail and air links. Pop. (1993 est.) mun., 68,924.

Luli, Greek ELULAIOS (fl. 705 BC), Phoenician king of the cities of Tyre and Sidon who rebelled against Assyrian rule following the death of the Assyrian king Sargon II (705). Concurrent with the insurrection of Babylon under Merodach-Baladan, Luli joined with Shabaka of Egypt and Hezekiah of Judah in a revolt against Sennacherib, Sargon's successor. After subjugating the Babylonians in 703–702, Sennacherib led an army against Luli, who abandoned Tyre and fled to Cyprus.

Luling (China): *see* Chi-an.

Lullubi, ancient group of tribes that inhabited the Sherizor plain in the Zagros Mountains of western Iran. A warlike people, they were especially active during the reign of the Akkadian king Naram-Sin (reigned *c.* 2254–*c.* 2218 BC) and at the end of the dynasty of Akkad (2334–2154 BC). The Lullubi were apparently subjugated by Naram-Sin, who commemorated his triumph on a masterpiece of Mesopotamian sculpture, the Naram-Sin stele;

The great stele of Naram-Sin, from Susa, *c.* 2250 BC; in the Louvre

the tribes, however, soon regained their independence and resumed harassment of southern Mesopotamia, helping to bring an end to the Akkadian empire. Later overshadowed by their more powerful neighbours, the Lullubi remained a source of unrest almost to the end of Mesopotamian history.

Lully, Jean-Baptiste, Italian GIOVANNI BATTISTA LULLI (b. Nov. 28, 1632, Florence [Italy]—d. March 22, 1687, Paris, France), Italian-born French court and operatic composer who from 1662 completely controlled French court music and whose style of composition was imitated throughout Europe.

Born of Italian parents, Lully gallicized his name when he became a naturalized Frenchman. His early history is obscure, but he probably was taken to France by the Duke de Guise. He entered the service of Mlle de Montpensier and became a member of her string band but was dismissed for having composed some scurrilous verses and music. He joined the court band of Louis XIV in 1652 as a violinist and soon became composer of dance music to the king and leader of the newly formed Petit-Violons du Roi. In 1658 he began to compose music for the court ballets, and from 1664 to 1671 he collaborated

Lully, detail of a portrait by an unknown artist, 17th century; in the Musée Condé, Chantilly, France

with Molière in such works as *Le Mariage forcé, La Princesse d'Élide,* and *Le Bourgeois Gentilhomme.* From 1672 until the time of his death he worked with the librettist Philippe Quinault on operatic and ballet works varying from the classical *Atys* (1676) and *Isis* (1677) to the heroic *Roland* (1685) and the pastoral *Le Temple de la paix* (1685). He died of an infected wound in his foot caused by his long conducting stick.

Lully was a man of insatiable ambition whose rise from violinist in Louis XIV's court band was meteoric and was accomplished by brazen and merciless intrigue. He held royal appointments as musical composer to the king (from 1661) and as music master to the royal family (from 1662). He then acquired from Pierre Perrin and Robert Cambert their patents of operatic production, and by 1674 no opera could be performed anywhere in France without Lully's permission. In 1681 he received his *lettres de nationalisation* and his *lettres de noblesse.* He also became one of the *secrétaires du roi,* a privilege usually held only by the French aristocracy.

At the outset Lully's operatic style was thought similar to that of the Italian masters Francesco Cavalli and Luigi Rossi. He quickly assimilated the contemporary French idiom, however, and is credited with creating a new and original style. In his ballets he introduced new dances, such as the minuet, and used a higher proportion of quicker ones, such as the bourrée, gavotte, and gigue; he also introduced women dancers to the stage. The texts in both his ballets and operas were French. His operas were described as "tragedies set to music," owing to their highly developed dramatic and theatrical aspects.

Lully established the form of the French overture and abandoned the recitativo secco style favoured by the Italians. This last he replaced by an accompanied recitative noted for its great rhythmic freedom and careful word setting. He developed a style of declamation that was well-suited to the French language; this innovation led to a lessening of the demarcation between the recitative and the aria, so that French opera acquired much more continuity. The arias themselves, however, retain many Italian characteristics. Each is written in a particular style and mood: *chanson à couplets, air-complainte* (*arioso*), and *air déclamé.* His operas frequently end with a chaconne movement, and in this he was followed by both Jean-Philippe Rameau and Christoph Gluck.

Among Lully's other works are several sacred compositions, including the famous *Miserere* and 17 motets; dances for various instruments; suites for trumpets and strings, a form that became very popular in England during the Stuart Restoration (from 1660); and the *Suites de Symphonies et Trios.*

Lully, Raymond (Catalan mystic): *see* Llull, Ramon.

Lulonga River, stream formed by the union of the Lopori and the Maringa rivers near Basankusu in north-central Congo (Kinshasa), central Africa. It flows 125 miles (200 km) west and southwest to its confluence with the Congo River north of Lulonga. It is navigable for steamboats along its entire course.

Luluabourg (Congo [Kinshasa]): *see* Kananga.

lumbago, pain in the small of the back; it is most common among middle-aged persons. Lumbago can be caused by a sprain (with bleeding into the muscles and torn ligaments), by overexertion in lifting, by a fall or jar, or by a sudden twisting movement of the back. Rest in bed, application of heat, massage, and use of analgesic ointments can bring relief. The lumbago may be of the type in which there are lumpy deposits in the sheaths around the muscles. In this instance, pain may follow overuse of the muscle or exposure to cold and drafts. Heat and exercise bring temporary relief. Pain in the loins may indicate lumbago associated with injury to an intervertebral disk. Ischemic lumbago results from artery insufficiency.

lumbar puncture, also called SPINAL TAP, direct aspiration (fluid withdrawal) of cerebrospinal fluid (CSF) through a hollow needle. The needle is inserted in the lower back, usually between the third and fourth lumbar vertebrae, into the subarachnoid space of the spinal cord where the CSF is located. Lumbar puncture is generally performed to obtain pressure measurements and to withdraw CSF in order to secure a sample of CSF for cellular, chemical, and bacteriologic examination; to administer spinal anesthetics or antibiotics; to inject air or a radiopaque or water-soluble contrast medium substance for myelography; or to inject a radioactive substance to assist in the diagnosis of CSF leak or hydrocephalus.

Lumberton, city, seat (1788) of Robeson county, southern North Carolina, U.S., on the Lumber (Lumbee) River about 30 miles (50 km) south of Fayetteville. Founded about 1787 by John Willis, an officer of the American Revolution, it began as a shipping point for lumber and naval supplies floated downriver to Georgetown, S.C. The city's economic development has been based on lumbering, tobacco curing, textile and apparel manufacturing, and the marketing of farm produce. Pembroke, 10 miles (16 km) northwest, is a centre of Croatan (Lumbee) Indian settlement. The University of North Carolina at Pembroke (1887), formerly Pembroke State University, began as an educational centre for Native Americans, but after 1953 it was open to all students. Inc. 1852. Pop. (2000) 20,795.

Lumbinī, grove near the southern border of modern-day Nepal where, according to Buddhist legend, Queen Mahā Māyā stood and gave birth to the future Buddha while holding onto a branch of a *sal* tree. There are two references to Lumbinī as the birthplace of the Buddha in the Pāli scripture, the first in a narrative poem attached to the *Nālaka Sutta* and the other in the *Kathāvatthu,* but the earliest canonical accounts of the birth are in Sanskrit scriptures, the *Mahāvastu* (ii.18) and the *Lalitavistara* (ch. 7), neither of which can be dated earlier than the 3rd or the 4th century AD. The discovery of an inscription recording the visit of Aśoka, Maurya emperor of India from about 273 to 232 BC, to the spot he considered the birthplace makes it probable, however, that the legend was established at least as early as the 3rd century BC. The site is a popular place of Buddhist pilgrimage.

Lumbwa (people): *see* Kipsikis.

lumen, unit of luminous flux, or amount of light, defined as the amount streaming outward through one steradian (a unit of solid angle, part of the volume of space illuminated by a light source) from a uniform point source having an intensity of one candela. It is used in calculations regarding artificial lighting.

Lumet, Sidney (b. June 25, 1924, Philadelphia, Pa., U.S.), American motion-picture, television, and stage director noted for his psychological dramas and other films. He was one of the most prolific and important American cinematic directors of the second half of the 20th century.

The son of a Jewish actor, Lumet made his acting debut in New York City's Yiddish theatre as a child and was appearing in plays on Broadway by the late 1930s. After serving in World War II, he began directing plays and was hired by the Columbia Broadcasting System as a television staff director in 1950. He became one of the most capable directors of American television dramas of the 1950s. The first motion picture he directed, *Twelve Angry Men* (1957), foreshadowed his lasting preoccupation with urban environments, crime, and the resolution of difficult moral conflicts by complex individuals.

Sidney Lumet
© Corbis/Sygma

Lumet established himself as a master of the motion-picture psychodrama with such powerful films as *The Fugitive Kind* (1960), film versions of Arthur Miller's *A View From the Bridge* (1962) and Eugene O'Neill's *Long Day's Journey Into Night* (1962), *Fail Safe* (1964), and *The Pawnbroker* (1965). He turned to directing lighter films in the late 1960s but returned to making tense urban dramas with *The Anderson Tapes* (1971), *Serpico* (1973), and *Dog Day Afternoon* (1975). *Network* (1976), a brilliant satirical study of commercial television, was one of his best films. He continued to examine the complexities of human emotion in such later films as *Equus* (1977), *Deathtrap* (1982), *Prince of the City* (1981), and *The Verdict* (1982).

The main characters in Lumet's most memorable films usually become enmeshed in some type of moral or emotional crisis, whether it be the obsessive pursuit of justice or truth or the passions aroused by jealousy or guilt, and his films trace his characters' varying and often tragic attempts to resolve their conflicts. His central characters are often lonely, disillusioned individuals who nevertheless act according to the idealistic dictates of their conscience.

Lumière, Auguste and Louis (respectively b. Oct. 19, 1862, Besançon, Fr.—d. April 10, 1954, Lyon; b. Oct. 5, 1864, Besançon—d. June 6, 1948, Bandol), French inventors and pioneer manufacturers of photographic equipment who devised an early motion-picture camera and projector called the Cinématographe ("cinema" is derived from this name). Their film *La Sortie des ouvriers de l'usine Lumière* (1895; "Workers Leaving the Lumière Factory"), shown in Paris, is considered the first motion picture.

Sons of a painter turned photographer, the two boys displayed brilliance in science at school in Lyon, where their father had settled. Louis worked on the problem of commercial-

Louis Lumière
Archives Photographiques, Paris—J.P. Ziolo

ly satisfactory development of film; at 18 he had succeeded so well that with his father's financial aid he opened a factory for producing photographic plates, which gained immediate success. By 1894 the Lumières were producing some 15,000,000 plates a year. That year the father, Antoine, was invited to a showing of Thomas Edison's Kinetoscope in Paris; his description of the peephole machine on his return to Lyon set Louis and Auguste to work on the problem of combining animation with projection. Louis found the solution, which was patented in 1895. At that time they attached less importance to this invention than to improvements they had made simultaneously in colour photography. But on Dec. 28, 1895, a showing at the Grand Café on the boulevard des Capucines in Paris brought wide public acclaim and the beginning of cinema history.

Auguste Lumière
Boyer—H. Roger-Viollet

The Lumière apparatus consisted of a single camera used for both photographing and projecting at 16 frames per second. Their first films (they made more than 40 during 1896) recorded everyday French life—*e.g.,* the arrival of a train, a game of cards, a toiling blacksmith, the feeding of a baby, soldiers marching, the activity of a city street. Others were early comedy shorts. The Lumières presented the first newsreel, a film of the French Photographic Society Conference, and the first documentaries, four films about the Lyon fire department. Beginning in 1896, they sent a trained crew of innovative cameraman-projectionists to cities throughout the world to show films and shoot new material.

luminescence, a process by which some materials emit light when they are relatively cool. Familiar examples of luminescence are the light emissions from: electronically excited gases in neon lamps and lightning; tiny inorganic crystals used as coatings in luminescent watch dials, television and radar kinescopes, fluorescent lamps, and X-ray fluoroscope screens; and certain organic materials undergoing oxidation in fireflies and glowworms. Because they luminesce at room temperature such materials emit what is sometimes loosely called cold light, to distinguish it from the temperature-dependent light emitted by incandescent sources.

A brief treatment of luminescence follows. For full treatment, *see* MACROPAEDIA: Light.

The process of luminescence is started by exciting some material, usually with ultraviolet radiation, X-rays, electrons, alpha particles, electric fields, or energy liberated during some chemical reactions. Suitable materials convert one or more of these invisible input energies to light. Few luminescent materials are efficient enough for practical use. The efficient ones are custom-made to convert a particular input energy to light of a particular colour and intensity. The colour is determined by the material, while the intensity depends on the material and the input energy. Every kind of atom, when alone, will luminesce; and each kind of atom exhibits characteristic spectral lines, which have been interpreted in terms of quantum theory.

According to quantum theory an isolated atom or ion can exist indefinitely in an unexcited state (called the ground state) or it can be excited and exist for short periods in one or another of various discrete excited states. In other words, a given kind of atom can exist briefly in one of several separate and distinct states of higher energy, but not in intermediate states. Each state has an energy level that corresponds to a different configuration of the electrons in the atom. When the excited atom drops from a higher to a lower energy level, the difference in energy between the two sharply defined levels is radiated as a discrete bit (quantum) of light that is called a photon.

A lone excited atom loses its excess energy by radiation, in the absence of collisions with other atoms. An excited atom in a molecule, however, can dissipate excess energy by converting it to increased agitation of all the atoms that are bound together in the molecule. Spectroscopic analysis of light from luminescing molecules shows that the energy levels of the constituent atoms are altered and proliferated into many additional closely spaced levels as a result of vibrations and rotations of the atomic ensemble. A multiatom ensemble generally has lower efficiency of luminescence than an isolated atom because the assemblage can convert excitation energy into atomic motion, which in condensed matter is thermal agitation (heat).

The probability of dissipating input energy as heat is enormously increased on going from an isolated atom to one bound to myriads of others in an elemental liquid or solid. Most elemental liquids and solids, therefore, are nonluminescent. Mercury is an efficient luminescent gas but is a nonluminescent liquid. There are some nonelemental liquids, however, that have relatively high luminescence efficiencies. In benzene C_6H_6 (which luminesces as a gas, a liquid, and a solid) the hexagonal benzene molecule emits ultraviolet radiation in all three physical states. Crystals are generally the most efficient sources of luminescence, because their ordered structures provide stable arrangements of atoms and permit relatively efficient ingress and internal transport of input energy, and emission of photons.

The terms phosphorescence and fluorescence are often used instead of luminescence. While the distinction does not hold absolutely, the two terms are commonly used to designate luminescence that persists after the activating radiation has ceased (phosphorescence) versus luminescence that ceases within about 10^{-8} seconds after the activating radiation does so (fluorescence).

Instances of luminescence may also be distinguished by the manner in which it is produced. Thus, chemiluminescence proceeds from chemical reactions, as the oxidation of luminol by hydrogen peroxide; bioluminescence (*q.v.*), a subcategory of chemiluminescence, occurs in living creatures such as fireflies or glowworms; triboluminescence occurs when crystals of certain substances, such as sugar, are crushed. Similarly, thermoluminescence, photoluminescence, electroluminescence, and radioluminescence are stimulated by heat, light, electric discharge, and radiation, respectively.

Luminism, painting style emphasizing a particular clarity of light that was characteristic of the works of a group of independent American painters of the third quarter of the 19th century, directly influenced by the Hudson River School. The name, however, was not coined until 1954 by John Baur, director of the Whitney Museum of American Art, New York City.

The most important painters in the Luminist style were FitzHugh Lane and Martin Heade; other members of the group included George Tirrell, Henry Walton, and J.W. Hill. Paintings by the Luminists are almost always landscapes or seascapes, particularly the latter, and are distinguished by smooth, slick finish; cold, clear colours; and meticulously detailed objects, modelled by light.

The paintings typically include land, water, and sky, with the sky occupying about one-half of the composition, which is often in the form of a rather long rectangle. The works show a geometric organization, the edges of specific objects aligned parallel to the canvas edges. The treatment of atmosphere is completely different from that of the French Impressionists and other outdoor painters (*see* Impressionism). Rather than the uniform, engulfing atmosphere of Impressionist paintings, there are deep spaces and subtle changes. The space and the objects so clearly defined by strong contrasts of light often produce an effect of timelessness; the deep, often stilted perspective helps to create a silent and sometimes mysterious world.

Although not an organized movement, later landscapists, such as George Loring Brown, adopted certain characteristics of the Luminists and therefore are sometimes classified with them. Many untrained, or naïve, painters, of the late 19th and early 20th centuries, especially, were influenced by such elements of Luminism as the hard linearism, depth, and clear modelling based on light.

luminous intensity, the quantity of visible light that is emitted in unit time per unit solid angle. The unit for the quantity of light flowing from a source in any one second (the luminous power, or luminous flux) is called the lumen. The lumen is evaluated with reference to visual sensation. The sensitivity of the human eye is greatest for light having a wavelength of 555 nanometres (10^{-9} metre); at this wavelength there are 685 lumens per watt of radiant power, or radiant flux (the luminous efficiency), whereas at other wavelengths the luminous efficiency is less. The unit of luminous intensity is one lumen per steradian, which is the unit of solid angle—there are 4π steradians about a point enclosed by a spherical surface. This unit of luminous intensity is also called the standard candle, or candela, one lumen per steradian.

luminous moss, also called ELFIN-GOLD (*Schistostega pennata;* formerly *S. osmundacea*), light-reflecting plant of the order Bryales, native to the Northern Hemisphere. It forms green mats in caves, holes in wood or earth, or cavities between rocks or under tree roots. A luminous moss is about one centimetre (1/2 inch) or more tall. The lower part of the caulid (stem) is bare, and the upper part has two rows of phyllids (leaves), causing the plant to resemble a small fern frond. Male plants have budlike reproductive organs. The small capsule (spore case) of the female plant resembles a pinhead. The golden-green appearance of the moss is caused by reflection of light from chlorophyll grains in lens-shaped cells of the protonema (the structure that produces the sexual plant by budding).

luminous paint, paint that glows in the dark because it contains a phosphor, a substance that emits light for a certain length of time after exposure to an energy source, such as ultraviolet radiation. Zinc sulfide and calcium sulfide are such phosphors.

Some luminous paints contain a source of radiant energy, such as salts of radium. These paints glow indefinitely and are used for painting dials and signs to be read at night.

lump-nosed bat: *see* long-eared bat.

Lumpenproletariat (German: "rabble proletariat"), according to Karl Marx in *The Communist Manifesto*, the lowest stratum of the industrial working class, including also such undesirables as tramps and criminals. The members of the *Lumpenproletariat*—this "social scum," said Marx—are not only disinclined to participate in revolutionary activities with their "rightful brethren," the proletariat, but also tend to act as the "bribed tools of reactionary intrigue."

Consult the INDEX *first*

lumpsucker, also called LUMPFISH, any of certain marine fish of the family Cyclopteridae (order Scorpaeniformes), found in cold northern waters. Lumpsuckers are thickset, short-bodied, scaleless fish with skins that are either smooth or studded with bony tubercles. Like the snailfish, which are often included in the family, they are characterized by a strong sucking disk on the undersurface. The disk is formed from the pelvic fins and is used by the fish in holding firmly to the sea bottom.

Lumpsucker (*Cyclopterus lumpus*)
Painting by Gilbert Emerson

Lumpsuckers are carnivorous, slow-moving fish. A notable species is *Cyclopterus lumpus,* known in Europe as sea hen or hen fish because the male guards and cares for the eggs, without eating, until they hatch in about six or seven weeks. This fish is found in the Arctic and on both sides of the North Atlantic. It is a large lumpsucker and attains a maximum length and weight of about 60 centimetres (2 feet) and 5 to 6 kilograms (11–13 pounds).

Lumumba, Patrice (Hemery) (b. July 2, 1925, Onalua, Belgian Congo—d. January 1961, Katanga, Congo), African nationalist leader, the first prime minister of the Democratic Republic of the Congo (modern Zaire; June–September 1960). Forced out of office during a political crisis, he was assassinated a short time later.

Lumumba was born in the village of Onalua in Kasai Province, Belgian Congo. He

Lumumba
Agence Dalmas

was a member of the small Batetela tribe, a fact that was to become significant in his later political life. His two principal rivals, Moise Tshombe, who led the breakaway of the Katanga province, and Joseph Kasavubu, who later became the nation's president, both came from large, powerful tribes from which they derived their major support, giving their political movements a regional character. In contrast, Lumumba's movement emphasized its all-Congolese nature.

After attending a Protestant mission school, Lumumba went to work in Kindu-Port-Empain, where he became active in the club of the *évolués* (educated Africans). He began to write essays and poems for Congolese journals. He also applied for and received full Belgian citizenship. Lumumba next moved to Léopoldville (now Kinshasa) to become a postal clerk and went on to become an accountant in the post office in Stanleyville (now Kisangani). There he continued to contribute to the Congolese press.

In 1955 Lumumba became regional president of a purely Congolese trade union of government employees that was not affiliated, as were other unions, to either of the two Belgian trade-union federations (socialist and Roman Catholic). He also became active in the Belgian Liberal Party in the Congo. Although conservative in many ways, the party was not linked to either of the trade-union federations, which were hostile to it. In 1956 Lumumba was invited with others to make a study tour of Belgium under the auspices of the Minister of Colonies. On his return he was arrested on a charge of embezzlement from the post office. He was convicted and condemned one year later, after various reductions of sentence, to 12 months' imprisonment and a fine.

When Lumumba got out of prison, he grew even more active in politics. In October 1958 he founded the Congolese National Movement (Mouvement National Congolais; MNC), the first nationwide Congolese political party. In December he attended the first All-African People's Conference in Accra, Ghana, where he met nationalists from across the African continent and was made a member of the permanent organization set up by the conference. His outlook and terminology, inspired by pan-African goals, now took on the tenor of militant nationalism.

In 1959 the Belgian government announced a program intended to lead in five years to independence, starting with local elections in December 1959. The nationalists regarded this program as a scheme to install puppets before independence and announced a boycott of the elections. The Belgian authorities responded with repression. On October 30 there was a clash in Stanleyville that resulted in 30 deaths. Lumumba was imprisoned on a charge of inciting to riot.

The MNC decided to shift tactics, entered the elections, and won a sweeping victory in Stanleyville (90 percent of the votes). In January 1960 the Belgian government convened a Round Table Conference in Brussels of all Congolese parties to discuss political change, but the MNC refused to participate without Lumumba. Lumumba was thereupon released from prison and flown to Brussels. The conference agreed on a date for independence, June 30, with national elections in May. Although there was a multiplicity of parties, the MNC came out far ahead in the elections, and Lumumba emerged as the leading nationalist politician of the Congo. Maneuvers to prevent his assumption of authority failed, and he was asked to form the first government, which he succeeded in doing on June 23, 1960.

A few days after independence, some units of the army rebelled, largely because of objections to their Belgian commander. In the confusion, the mineral-rich province of Katanga proclaimed secession. Belgium sent in troops, ostensibly to protect Belgian nationals in the disorder. But the Belgian troops landed principally in Katanga, where they sustained the secessionist regime of Moise Tshombe.

The Congo appealed to the United Nations to expel the Belgians and help them restore internal order. As prime minister, Lumumba did what little he could to redress the situation. His army was an uncertain instrument of power, his civilian administration untrained and untried; the United Nations forces (whose presence he had requested) were condescending and assertive, and the political alliances underlying his regime very shaky. The Belgian troops did not evacuate, and the Katanga secession continued.

Since the United Nations forces refused to help suppress the Katangese revolt, Lumumba appealed to the Soviet Union for planes to assist in transporting his troops to Katanga. He asked the independent African states to meet in Léopoldville in August to unite their efforts behind him. His moves alarmed many, particularly the Western powers and the supporters of President Kasavubu, who pursued a moderate course in the coalition government and favoured some local autonomy in the provinces.

On September 5 President Kasavubu dismissed Lumumba. The legalities of the move were immediately contested by Lumumba. There were thus two groups now claiming to be the legal central government. On September 14 power was seized by the Congolese army leader Colonel Joseph Mobutu, (president of Zaire as Mobutu Sese Seko), who later reached a working agreement with Kasavubu. In October the General Assembly of the United Nations recognized the credentials of Kasavubu's government. The independent African states split sharply over the issue.

In November Lumumba sought to travel from Léopoldville, where the United Nations had provided him with protection, to Stanleyville, where his supporters had control. He was caught by the Kasavubu forces and arrested on December 2. On Jan. 17, 1961, he was delivered to the Katanga secessionist regime, where he was murdered. His death caused a scandal throughout Africa, and, retrospectively, his enemies proclaimed him a "national hero."

The reasons that Lumumba provoked such intense emotion are not immediately evident. His viewpoint was not exceptional. He was for a unitary Congo and against division of the country along tribal or regional lines. Like many other African leaders, he supported pan-Africanism and the liberation of colonial territories. He proclaimed his regime one of "positive neutralism," which he defined as a return to African values and rejection of any imported ideology, including that of the Soviet Union.

Lumumba was, however, a man of strong character who intended to pursue his policies, regardless of the enemies he made within his country or abroad. The Congo, furthermore, was a key area in terms of the geopolitics of Africa, and because of its wealth, its size, and its contiguity to white-dominated southern Africa, Lumumba's opponents had reason to fear the consequences of a radical or radicalized Congo regime. Moreover, in the context of the Cold War, the Soviet Union's support for Lumumba appeared at the time as a threat to many in the West. (I.W./Ed.)

BIBLIOGRAPHY. Overviews of his life and career are provided by Robin McKown, *Lumumba: A Biography* (1969); and Thomas Kanza, *The Rise and Fall of Patrice Lumumba: Conflict in the Congo,* expanded ed. (1977). G. Heinz and H. Donnay, *Lumumba: The Last Fifty Days* (1970), is a detailed reconstruction of the last critical period of his life.

Lumumba University (Moscow): *see* Patrice Lumumba People's Friendship University.

Lumut, port, West Malaysia (Malaya), at the mouth of the Dindings River, on the Strait of Malacca. Lumut lies about 48 miles (77 km) southwest of the tin-mining town of Ipoh. It is the main town of the Dindings coastal district and the best sheltered deepwater port in Malaysia. A Royal Malaysian Navy facility with dry-dock equipment is located there. Nearby Pangkor Island and its resort hotels are connected by ferry with Lumut. Pop. (1991) 1,736.

Lun yü (Chinese: "Conversations"), English ANALECTS, one of four Confucian texts that, when published together in 1190 by the Neo-Confucian philosopher Chu Hsi, became the great Chinese classic known as *Ssu shu* (*q.v.*; "Four Books").

Lun yü is considered by scholars to be the most reliable source of the doctrine of the ancient sage Confucius (551–479 BC) and is usually the first Confucian text studied in schools. It covers practically all the basic ethical concepts of Confucius—*e.g., jen* ("benevolence"), *chün-tzu* ("the superior man"), *t'ien* ("Heaven"), *chung yung* (doctrine of "the mean"), *li* ("proper conduct"), and *cheng ming* ("adjustment to names"). The last inculcates the notion that all phases of a person's conduct should correspond to the true significance of "names"—*e.g.,* marriage should be true marriage, not concubinage.

Among many direct quotations attributed to Confucius is one explaining filial piety (*hsiao*). If *hsiao* means nothing more than providing for parents, said Confucius, even dogs and horses do that; *hsiao* does not exist without genuine respect for parents. *Lun yü* also contains homely glimpses of Confucius as recorded by his disciples.

In general, *Lun yü* is unsystematic, occasionally repetitive, and sometimes inaccurate historically.

Luna, any of a series of unmanned Soviet lunar probes.

Luna 2 (launched Sept. 12, 1959) was the first spacecraft to strike the Moon, and Luna 3 (Oct. 4, 1959) made the first circumnavigation of the Moon and returned the first photographs of its far side. Luna 9 (Jan. 31, 1966) made the first successful lunar soft landing. Luna 16 (Sept. 12, 1970) was the first unmanned spacecraft to carry lunar soil samples back to Earth. Luna 17 (Nov. 10, 1970) soft-landed a robot vehicle for exploration. It also contained television equipment, by means of which it transmitted live pictures of several kilometres of the Moon's surface. Luna 22 (May 29, 1974) orbited the Moon 2,842 times while conducting space research in its vicinity. Luna 24 (Aug. 9, 1976) returned with lunar soil samples taken from a depth of seven feet (about two metres) below the surface.

Luna, Álvaro de (b. *c.* 1390, Cañete, Castile [Spain]—d. June 2 or 22, 1453, Valladolid), constable of Castile, ruler of Castile during much of the reign of the weak John II.

Luna was the illegitimate son of a noble of

Aragonese descent and the only distinguished statesman during a dismal period in Castilian history. He was a skilled politician, a far-sighted legislator, a competent soldier, and a minor poet and wit. His weakness was that, born without inherited wealth, he used his position to accumulate estates and money. Luna secured the favour of John II at a very early age, but his period of real power began when he rescued the king from the tutelage of rebel nobles (1420) and was appointed constable (1423).

For many years his main efforts were concerned with saving the crown from armed factions of dissident magnates who sought to control it. These twice succeeded in ousting Luna (1427 and 1438), but they proved incapable of governing effectively, and Luna was summoned back to power. The chief rebel leaders were the sons of Ferdinand I of Aragon, who were Castilian magnates in their own right. When they were routed at Olmedo (1445), where Luna as constable led the loyalist vanguard, the rebellions were at last at an end.

However, in 1447 John II married Isabella of Portugal, who determined to destroy Luna's power over her husband. In 1453, Isabella, supported by their son, the future Henry IV, persuaded the king to arrest Luna and have him publicly executed at Valladolid—an event which seems to have led to the king's death, of remorse, a year later.

Lunacharsky, Anatoly Vasilyevich (b. Nov. 23 [Nov. 11, Old Style], 1875, Poltava, Ukraine, Russian Empire—d. Dec. 26, 1933, Menton, Fr.), Russian author, publicist, and politician who, with Maksim Gorky, did much to ensure the preservation of works of art during the civil war of 1918–20.

Deported in 1898 for his revolutionary activities, Lunacharsky joined the Bolshevik group of the Social Democratic Party and started to work on the editorial board of the Bolshevik journal *Vpered* ("Forward"). He disseminated Social Democratic propaganda and organized lectures for Russian students and political refugees in foreign countries. During the Russian Revolution of 1905, Lunacharsky was arrested and imprisoned. In 1909 he joined Gorky on Capri, where, together with A. Bogdanov, they started an advanced school for a select elite of Russian factory workers, but Lenin's opposition to this project quickly ended it. Lunacharsky was preoccupied with the place of religion in the Bolsheviks' proposed new social order, and in 1909 he published a book titled *Outlines of a Collective Philosophy*.

Lunacharsky
Novosti Press Agency

In March 1917 he joined Lenin and Trotsky in Russia and was appointed peoples' commissar for education. This position enabled him to preserve many historic buildings and works of art from wanton destruction. His interest in the theatre encouraged a number of dramatic experiments and innovations. In 1933 Lunacharsky was appointed Soviet ambassador to Spain. Of his many dramatic works, three were translated into English and collected in *Three Plays* (1923).

lunar calendar, any dating system based on a year consisting of synodic months—*i.e.,* complete cycles of phases of the Moon. In every solar year (or year of the seasons), there are about 12.37 synodic months. Therefore, if a lunar-year calendar is to be kept in step with the seasonal year, a periodic intercalation (addition) of days is necessary.

The Sumerians were probably the first to develop a calendar based entirely on the recurrence of lunar phases. Each Sumero-Babylonian month began on the first day of visibility of the new Moon. Although an intercalary month was used periodically, intercalations were haphazard, inserted when the royal astrologers realized that the calendar had fallen severely out of step with the seasons. Starting about 380 BC, however, fixed rules regarding intercalations were established, providing for the distribution of seven intercalary months at designated intervals over 19-year periods. Greek astronomers also devised rules for intercalations to coordinate the lunar and solar years. It is likely that the Roman republican calendar was based on the lunar calendar of the Greeks.

Lunar calendars remain in use among certain religious groups today. The Jewish calendar, which supposedly dates from 3,760 years and three months before the Christian Era (BCE) is one example. The Jewish religious year begins in autumn and consists of 12 months alternating between 30 and 29 days. It allows for a periodic leap year and an intercalary month. Another lunar calendar, the Muslim, dates from the Hegira—July 15, AD 622, the day on which the prophet Muḥammad began his migration from Mecca to Medina. It makes no effort to keep calendric and seasonal years together.

lunar caustic, fused, molded form of silver nitrate (*q.v.*).

lunar deity, any god or goddess related to or associated with the moon and its cycles. *See* moon worship.

Lunar Orbiter, any of a series of five unmanned U.S. spacecraft placed in orbit around the Moon from 1966 to 1967. The orbiters obtained 1,950 wide-angle and high-resolution photographs of much of the Moon's surface, including the polar regions and the far side, some from as close as 28.5 miles (45.6 km) above the surface. These pictures enabled the selection of five primary landing sites for the manned Apollo missions and also made possible the construction of lunar maps with as much as 100 times the detail available from Earth-based telescopic observations. *See also* Moon exploration.

Lunceford, Jimmie, byname of JAMES MELVIN LUNCEFORD (b. June 6, 1902, Fulton, Miss., U.S.—d. July 12, 1947, Seaside, Ore.), American jazz dance-band leader whose rhythmically appealing, well-disciplined orchestra performed arrangements by trumpeter Sy Oliver and others to popular acclaim from 1934 to 1945 and influenced both swing and post-World War II dance bands.

Lunceford, during his youth, acquired proficiency on all reed instruments, but he seldom played with his band because he preferred to conduct. He taught and organized a student orchestra in a Memphis, Tenn., high school before beginning his professional career as a bandleader in 1929. Practiced showmanship, precise ensembles, and a medium two-beat swing tempo rather than exciting soloists were the Lunceford band's trademarks. The band's most popular songs included "Organ Grinder's Swing" (1936) and "For Dancers Only" (1937). The Lunceford band was considered to be on a par with bands led by Duke Ellington, Count Basie, and Benny Goodman during the 1930s, and in 1940 the ensemble won a celebrated "battle of the bands" from a field of 28 groups, among them Basie's, Goodman's, and Glenn Miller's. Arranger Oliver left Lunceford in 1939, and by 1942 the band's popularity had declined. Following Lunceford's death while on tour, pianist Edwin Wilcox and saxophonist Joe Thomas led the band for several years.

Lund, city, in the *län* (county) of Malmöhus, southern Sweden, northeast of Malmö. It was founded in about 1020 by the Danish king Canute and became the seat of a bishopric in 1060 and the seat of the archbishop of all Scandinavia in 1103; today it is the seat of a Lutheran bishopric. During the Middle Ages it played an important part in Danish affairs. It was reduced in importance after the Reformation and the Swedish conquest in 1658 but developed rapidly after 1850.

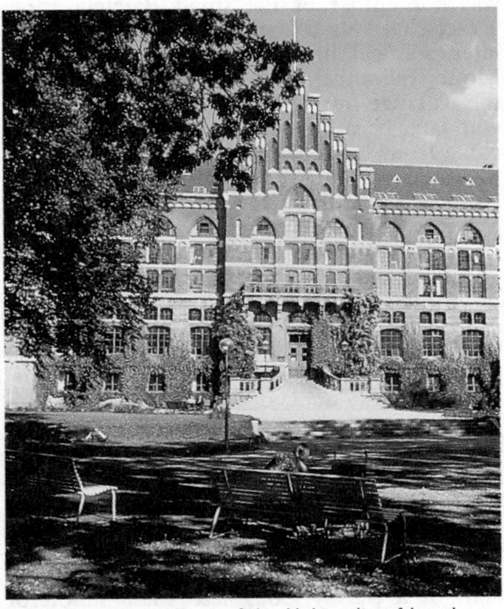

Library on the campus of the University of Lund, founded 1671 by Charles XI
Harry Dittmer/TIOFOTO

The city centre is dominated by the 12th-century Romanesque cathedral. Among the city's museums are the Cultural History Museum, the Archives of Decorative Art, and the Art Exhibition Hall. Known as the cultural centre of southern Sweden, Lund has the second oldest university in Sweden, founded in 1666 by Charles XI. The various educational institutions and hospitals of the city employ a considerable part of the population, but there are also important industries, including packaging, printing, textile weaving, and the manufacture of food-industry equipment. Pop. (1991 est.) mun., 87,681.

Lunda, any of several Bantu-speaking peoples scattered over wide areas of the southeastern part of Zaire, eastern Angola, and northern and northwestern Zambia. The various regional groups—the Lunda of Musokantanda in Zaire, Kazembe, Shinje, Kanongesha, Ndembu, Luvale (Luena, Balovale), Chokwe, Luchazi, Songo, and Mbunda—are all of Congo origin and broke away from the central Lunda kingdom in the southern Congo. (*See* Luba-Lunda states.) In southwestern Zaire they have spread to the Kwango River, where they form the political authority among the Yaka and other peoples. Most Lunda live in savanna country intersected by belts of forest along the rivers. Food gathering and hunting are important among many groups, fishing less so. All groups practice shifting hoe cultivation of cassava, millet, peanuts (groundnuts), beans, and corn (maize), and all keep small livestock; some groups keep a few cattle. Local trade is widespread; the Lunda of Kazembe have been well known as traders of ivory and slaves.

Descent systems differ: among the southern Lunda, Luvale, and Luchazi, descent is matrilineal; among the northern Zambian Lunda, it is patrilineal; the system of the Kapanga Lunda uses both lines. Marriage payments are low; widow inheritance and cross-cousin marriage are practiced.

Lunda villages are small and compact. Among the Lunda of Kapanga, the central political organization is very complex. The Lunda religions are based upon a supreme being who is either a sky or an earth god. The worship of ancestors is also practiced.

Lunda empire, historic Bantu-speaking African state founded in the 16th century in the region of the upper Kasai River (now in northeastern Angola and western Zaire). Although the Lunda people had lived in the area from early times, their empire was founded by invaders coming west from Luba. Between 1600 and 1750, bands of Lunda adventurers established numerous satellites (*see* Kasanje; Kazembe; Luba-Lunda states). The Lunda empire consisted of a centralized core, a ring of provinces closely tied to the capital, an outer ring of provinces that paid tribute but were otherwise autonomous, and a fringe of independent kingdoms that shared a common Lunda culture. The imperial boundaries were thus only loosely defined.

Lunda traded with both the Arabs on the Indian Ocean and, from about 1650, the Portuguese on the Atlantic. The leading exports were ivory and slaves; imports included cloth and guns. The empire reached the height of its power by the 1850s. Thereafter its might was eroded by the incursions of the neighbouring Chokwe. Portuguese troops arrived from Angola in the west in 1884 and Belgians from the Congo Free State in the northeast in 1898. Lunda was partitioned between them. Guerrilla warfare against the Congo Free State continued until 1909, when the Lunda leaders were captured and executed.

Lundeberg, Christian (b. July 14, 1842, Valbo, Swed.—d. Nov. 10, 1911, Stockholm), industrialist and politician who presided over the 1905 Swedish government, which negotiated an end to the Swedish-Norwegian union.

A leading ironmaster, Lundeberg was active in industrial organizations and local government before entering the upper chamber of the Riksdag (parliament) in 1885. He served as deputy speaker of that body from 1899 to 1908 and as speaker from 1908 to 1911. After 1888 he was undisputed leader of the conservative groups in parliament. In parliament and in the council of state (as chairman from 1896 to 1900 and from 1902 to 1904) he vigorously fought for a strong defense position and for maintenance of the Swedish-Norwegian union.

When separation of the two states became inevitable in 1905, King Oscar II appointed Lundeberg prime minister of a coalition government to negotiate a separation that would be satisfactory to Sweden. Lundeberg, amidst an atmosphere of crisis in both countries, succeeded in drawing up terms of separation acceptable to everyone involved. With the dissolution of the union, the Lundeberg government resigned in October 1905.

Lundi River, river in southeastern Zimbabwe rising at Gweru in the Highveld and flowing southeast to Hippo Valley at the confluence with the Shashe River in the Middleveld. It continues across the Lowveld and joins the Sabi River near the Chivirigo (Chivirira) Falls at the Mozambique border, after a course of 260 miles (418 km), to form the Save River. Among the Lundi's great network of tributaries are the Ingezi, Tokwe, Mtilkwe, and Chiredzi rivers. In its upper reaches the river is arrested by Gwenora Dam, and its lower section is incorporated into the Sabi-Limpopo Irrigation Project.

Lundkvist, Artur, in full ARTUR NILS LUNDKVIST (b. March 3, 1906, Oderljunga, Swed.—d. Dec. 11, 1991, Stockholm), Swedish poet, novelist, and literary critic.

Lundkvist grew up in a rural community, where he felt himself an outcast because of his appreciation for literature. He left school at age 10 and thereafter educated himself. He moved to Stockholm when he was 20 and published his first books of poems *Glöd* (1928; "Glowing Embers") and *Svart stad* (1930; "Black City"). In the 1930s he became one of the foremost representatives of the Vitalist movement and participated in the group Fem Unga ("Five Young Men"). His affirmation of life and his idealization of man's instincts and passions took the form of a sexual mysticism not unlike that espoused by the English novelist D.H. Lawrence. In the shadow of World War II Lundkvist's writings became marked by pessimism and by a longing for a new kind of human solidarity. The surrealistic imagery found in his earlier poetry had been toned down by the time that *Korsväg* ("Crossroads") was published in 1942. *Det talande trädet* (1960; "The Talking Tree") and *Flykten och överlevandet* (1977; "Escape and Survival") are a combination of poetry and prose. *Vallmor från Taschkent* (1952; "Poppies from Tashkent") and *Så lever kuba* (1965; "This is the Way Cuba Lives") are travel books.

No Swedish critic or writer introduced more literature from abroad than did Lundkvist through his criticism, essays, and translations. In 1934–35, as coeditor and founder of the literary magazine *Karavan,* with Gunnar Ekelöf, Lundkvist introduced T.S. Eliot, D.H. Lawrence, and William Faulkner to Swedish readers. In 1968 he was elected to the Swedish Academy. In 1983, as one of the most influential members of the academy's jury for selecting the Nobel Prize for Literature, Lundkvist disputed the award of the literature prize to William Golding and generated a controversy by saying that the prize should have gone to Claude Simon (who received the award in 1985).

Lundy, small island in the Bristol Channel, 11 miles (18 km) off the north coast of the county of Devon, southwestern England. Mainly composed of granite, with high cliffs (notably Shutter Rock at the southwestern end), Lundy reaches a summit of 466 feet (142 m) and has an area of 1.5 square miles (4 square km). The exception to granite composition lies in the southeast, where Devonian slates have weathered to give the one landing cove. This is sheltered by Rat Island, on which the once-common black rat survives. Lundy lends its name to a weather-forecasting area that extends to the Scilly Isles and the southeastern tip of Ireland. The puffin and many other seabirds breed on Lundy.

The Old Lighthouse, its outbuilding, and a cemetery on Beacon Hill, Lundy, Eng.
Britain on View (BTA/ETB)

Long a base for privateers and smugglers, Lundy was owned by the British crown from 1150 until 1647, when it was sold to Lord Saye and Sele. The church was built in 1896 by the Heaven family, owners of Lundy from 1836 to 1918. Lundy was acquired by the National Trust in 1969. The name is from the Norse *lunde,* meaning "puffin." Pop. (1981) 52.

Lundy, Benjamin (b. Jan. 4, 1789, Sussex County, N.J., U.S.—d. Aug. 22, 1839, Lowell, Ill.), American publisher and leading Abolitionist in the 1820s and '30s.

Lundy, detail of a lithograph after a painting
By courtesy of the Library of Congress, Washington, D.C.

Lundy's dedication to the Abolitionist cause began while he was working as an apprentice saddlemaker in Wheeling, Va., where he was first exposed to the slave trade. In 1815 he organized the Union Humane Society, an antislavery association, in Ohio. In 1821 he founded a newspaper, the *Genius of Universal Emancipation,* which he edited at irregular intervals in various places until 1835, when he began publication of another newspaper, *The National Enquirer* (later the *Pennsylvania Freeman*), in Philadelphia. Much of his time was spent traveling in search of suitable places where freed slaves could settle, such as Canada and Haiti. From 1836 to 1838 he worked closely with U.S. Representative John Quincy Adams against the annexation of Texas, which would provide an opportunity for the extension of slavery. He moved to Illinois in 1839 and reestablished the *Genius,* which he published until his death.

Lundy's Lane, Battle of (July 25, 1814), engagement fought a mile west of Niagara Falls, ending a U.S. invasion of Canada during the War of 1812. After defeating the British in the Battle of Chippewa on July 5, 1814, U.S. troops under General Jacob Brown established themselves at Queenston. On the night of July 24–25, a British force under General Phineas Riall moved forward to Lundy's Lane. On the 25th he was reinforced by troops from Kingston under the British commander in chief, General Gordon Drummond. The U.S. troops advanced, and the battle began at 6 PM. For hours on end, each side hurled desperate charges against the other in the dusk and darkness. The losses on both sides were the heaviest in the entire war. With fewer than 3,000 men, the British had 878 casualties, 84 of whom were killed; the Americans suffered 853 casualties, with 171 killed. Drummond,

Riall, Brown, and the American general Winfield Scott were all severely wounded, and Riall was taken prisoner.

By midnight, the U.S. troops, too exhausted to attack again, fell back, leaving Drummond's men in possession of the field. The British troops, in turn, were too exhausted to pursue. Neither side won a decisive victory, but the action stopped the advance of the Americans, who withdrew to Ft. Erie the next day.

Lune, River, river rising near Newbiggin, county of Cumbria, England, and flowing 45 mi (72 km) westward and then southward to empty into the Irish Sea a few miles south of Heysham in Lancashire. The river drains part of the northern Pennines, and its entry to the sea at Sunderland Point is marked by extensive sand flats at low tide. Lancaster—an important crossing point—is the major town.

Lüneburg, *Regierungsbezirk* (administrative district), northeastern Lower Saxony *Land* (state), north-central Germany. Lüneburg is bordered by the *Länder* of Schleswig-Holstein and Hamburg to the north and Mecklenburg-West Pomerania and Saxony-Anhalt to the east, the *Regierungsbezirke* of Braunschweig and Hannover (Hanover) to the south, and Weser-Ems, Bremen *Land,* and the North Sea to the west. The largest of four districts in Lower Saxony, it occupies an area of 5,925 sq mi (15,346 sq km) and is coextensive with portions of the former German state of Hannover and the larger historic region of Saxony. Its contemporary boundaries were created in 1977 by an administrative reorganization merging the smaller *Regierungsbezirke* of Stade (west) and Lüneburg (east). Lüneburg *Regierungsbezirk* takes its name from that of the second largest city and administrative seat of the district.

Lüneburg lies on an extensive low plateau built of glacial sand and gravel deposits, set between the parallel courses of the lower Elbe River to the north and the valley of the Aller and Weser rivers to the south. It merges westward into the alluvial plains and marshlands bordering the North Sea and the Elbe and Weser estuaries, among them the regions of Wursten, Hadeln, Kehdingen, and Altes Land. To the east the plateau slopes into the lower Altmark territory of eastern Germany. Celle, the largest city of the district, is located at the southern fringe on the Aller River, while Lüneburg lies on the steeper northeast edge.

The western third of the plateau is composed of the Stade *Geest,* dry sandy heath and wooded land interspersed with low-lying peat bogs. Pastureland used for cattle and sheep farming dominates the landscape, which averages between 35 and 165 ft (10 and 50 m) in elevation. The eastern two-thirds of the plateau, known as the Lüneburger Heide (Luneburg Heath), has an average altitude of 260 to 330 ft. Great expanses of heather and juniper bushes are topped by morainic hills; the highest, the Wilseder Berg, rises to 554 ft (169 m). The traditional sources of income are sheep and cattle farming, forestry, and beekeeping. More recently the production of potatoes and rye has expanded with the introduction of artificial fertilizers to the sandy soils. More fertile sandy-loam soils in the lowland surrounding Uelzen, a town on the Elbe-Seiten-Kanal, support sugar beet and wheat crops. Natural gas fields are found west of Uelzen. Much of the plateau's least productive land is planted in conifer plantations. Tourism is growing as the Lüneburger Heide becomes an increasingly popular holiday resort, especially among the people of Hamburg. The region's most beautiful scenery can be seen during the August flowering season in the 77-sq-mi (200-sq-km) Lüneburger Heide Nature Reserve near the village of Wilsede.

The population density of Lüneburg *Regierungsbezirk* is quite low, averaging 246 persons per sq mi (95 per sq km); many areas of the Lüneburger Heide have fewer than 50 persons per sq mi (20 per sq km). The majority of the population are descendants of the western Saxons and speak a Low German dialect. Nearly 90 percent of the people are Protestants. The Lüneburger Heide is notable for its traditional redbrick heath farmhouses and for the numerous *Hünengräber* (ancient megalithic structures) known as "graves of giants." Pop. (1989 est.) 1,450,666.

Lüneburg, city, Lower Saxony *Land* (state), north-central Germany, on the Ilmenau River at the northeastern edge of the Lüneburger Heide (heath). Known as Luniburc in AD 956, it expanded in the 12th century under Henry the Lion, duke of Saxony. Chartered in 1247, it was the residence of the dukes of Brunswick-Lüneburg until 1371. A powerful member of the Hanseatic League, it was incorporated into Hanover in 1705 and became part of Prussia in 1866. Virtually undamaged in World War II, Lüneburg has some fine examples of brick buildings in northern German Gothic style. Notable landmarks include the town hall (13th–18th century), with its council chamber and royal hall; St. John's and St. Nicholas' churches, from the 13th and 14th centuries; the Sand, an impressive square of Gothic and Renaissance houses; and the ducal palace (1693–96), overlooking the marketplace. Stimulated industrially after 1900, its manufactures include chemicals and wood products. There is trade in foodstuffs, metal and coal, and salt (worked since the 10th century), and it is a tourist and health resort with saline springs and mud baths. Pop. (1989 est.) 60,053.

Old mill and former water tower (right) on the Ilmenau River, Lüneburg, Ger.

E. Landschak—ZEFA

Consult the INDEX *first*

Lüneburger Heide, English LÜNEBURG HEATH, region, Lower Saxony *Land* (state), north-central Germany, between the Aller and Elbe rivers. Its main character is that of a broad saddleback running for 55 mi (89 km) in a southeast–northwest direction with a mean elevation of about 250 ft (75 m) and a high point, Wilseder Berg, of 554 ft. Its soil is quartz sand, chiefly covered with heather and brushwood. In the north and in the deep valleys are extensive forests of oak, birch, and beech; in the south, fir and larch forests have been planted. The heather is mixed with broom, gorse, and juniper, the latter often forming small pyramidal cypress-like trees. Though the climate is raw and rich soil is rare, the heath is not infertile. The main products are potatoes, bilberries, cranberries, and honey. There is controlled grazing of sheep (the famous Heidschnucke breed). The district is also remarkable for numerous megaliths, huge undressed stones popularly called *Hünegräber* ("graves of giants"), and a countryside with many picturesque farmhouses built in the typical old Lower Saxon style in red brickwork and oak beams with thatched roofs. Large parts of the heath are under the protection of the federal German government as a preserve. Interlaced with footpaths, it is popular hiking country. It is also crossed by important rail and road routes.

Lüneburger Heide, Germany

Eberhard W. Haase

Lüneburger Heide was the site of the German surrender (May 4, 1945) to Field Marshal Bernard (later Lord) Montgomery, commander of the British-Canadian forces in northern Europe.

Lünen, city, North Rhine-Westphalia *Land* (state), northwestern Germany, on the Lippe River and the Seitenkanal, just north of Dortmund. Founded 1336–40 and chartered in 1341 by the count of Mark, it passed to Brandenburg in 1609 and to Prussia in 1701. A nearby castle, Schloss Kappenberg (1708), was a former Premonstratensian monastery and the last seat of the statesman Freiherr vom Stein; it is now the Dortmund Museum. Two other castles, Buddenberg and Schwansbell, are in local parks. The city is a rail junction, port, and coal-mining centre and has iron foundries, aluminum plants, copper refineries, and a large electric power station. Pop. (1989 est.) 85,584.

Lunenburg, town, seat of Lunenburg county, southeastern Nova Scotia, Canada, on Lunenburg Bay, an inlet of the Atlantic Ocean, 57 mi (92 km) west-southwest of Halifax. The townsite was once occupied by the Indian village of Malliggeak or Merliguesche (Milky Bay) and later by a French fishing community. In 1656 it was granted to Charles de Saint-Étienne de La Tour, governor of Acadia, by Oliver Cromwell, the lord protector of England; but there was no permanent settlement until Hanoverians from Lüneburg, Ger., and Swiss immigrants arrived in the early 1750s. During the American Revolution, Lunenburg was sacked by an American fleet from Boston.

Now an important fishing port, it was the home of the "Bluenose," undefeated North Atlantic Fishing Fleet champion and winner of several international schooner races (1921–46); the "Bluenose," which was lost on a reef off Haiti in 1946 is pictured on the obverse of the Canadian dime, and its trophies are displayed in the Lunenburg Fisheries Museum. Apart from fishing and fish processing, economic activities focus on shipbuilding (wooden trawlers, small boats, marine engines, sails) and market gardening. The Nova Scotia Fisheries Exhibition and Fishermen's Reunion is held at Lunenburg each September.

Historic buildings include St. John's Anglican Church (1754) and Zion Evangelical Lutheran Church (1776), with a bell that was taken from Fort Louisburg on Cape Breton Island in 1758. Inc. 1888. Pop. (1996) 2,599.

lunette, arching aperture in a wall or concave ceiling. It may be crescent-shaped or semicircular. The word is the French diminutive of *lune,* "moon." Lunettes may function as windows, they may form a cove for ornament or statuary, or they may be simply a section of wall framed by an arch or vault. In the last case, the area will sometimes be decorated with a mural.

An early example of lunette windows is in the Basilica of Constantine, Rome (AD 310–313), where they are set in the upper part of the nave over the aisle vaults. Giacomo da Vignola's Gesù church, Rome (1568–84), the prototype of many Baroque churches, features lunettes set into the base of the nave's barrel vault. In the 19th century lunettes were frequently used in large halls, either terminating wagon-headed ceilings or set into coves beneath a plane ceiling.

Lunéville, town, in the Meurthe-et-Moselle *département,* Lorraine *région,* eastern France, east-southeast of Nancy, at the confluence of the Vezouze and Meurthe rivers. Incorporated in the duchy of Lorraine in the 15th century, it was joined to France in 1766. The Treaty of Lunéville between France and Austria was signed there in 1801. The 18th-century planned town has a fine château, inspired by Versailles, and a church built in a Rococo style. Main industries include the production of china, textiles, and railway equipment. Pop. (1999) 20,200.

lung, Pinyin LONG (Chinese: "dragon"), in Chinese mythology, a type of majestic beast that dwells in rivers, lakes, and oceans and roams the skies. Originally a rain divinity, the Chinese dragon, unlike its malevolent European counterpart (*see* dragon), is associated with heavenly beneficence and fecundity. Rain rituals as early as the 6th century BC involved a dragon image animated by a procession of dancers; similar dances are still practiced in traditional Chinese communities to secure good fortune.

Ancient Chinese cosmogonists defined four types of dragons: the Celestial Dragon (T'ien Lung), who guards the heavenly dwellings of the gods; the Dragon of Hidden Treasure (Fu Tsang Lung); the Earth Dragon (Ti Lung), who controls the waterways; and the Spiritual Dragon (Shen Lung), who controls the rain and winds. In popular belief, only the latter two were significant; they were transformed into the Dragon Kings (Lung Wang), gods who lived in the four oceans, delivered rain, and protected seafarers.

Generally depicted as a four-legged animal with a scaled, snakelike body, horns, claws, and large, demonic eyes, the *lung* was considered the king of animals, and his image was appropriated by Chinese emperors as a sacred symbol of imperial power.

lung, in air-breathing vertebrates, either of the two large organs of respiration located in the chest cavity and responsible for aerating the blood. In humans each lung is encased in a thin membranous sac called the pleura, and each is connected with the trachea (windpipe) by its main bronchus (large air passageway) and with the heart by the pulmonary arteries. The lungs are soft, light, spongy, elastic organs that normally, after birth, always contain some air. If healthy, they will float in water and crackle when squeezed; diseased lungs sink, as do lungs of infants who are born dead.

In the inner side of each lung, about two-thirds of the distance from its base to its apex, is the hilum, the point at which the bronchi, pulmonary arteries and veins, lymphatic vessels, and nerves enter the lung. The main bronchus subdivides many times after entering the lung; the resulting system of tubules resembles an inverted tree. The diameters of the bronchi diminish eventually to less than 1 mm (0.04 inch). The branches 3 mm and less in diameter are known as bronchioles, which lead to minute air sacs called alveoli (*see* pulmonary alveolus), where the actual gas molecules of oxygen and carbon dioxide are exchanged between the respiratory spaces and the blood capillaries.

Each lung is divided into lobes separated from one another by a tissue fissure. The right lung has three major lobes; the left lung, which is slightly smaller because of the asymmetrical placement of the heart, has two lobes. Internally, each lobe further subdivides into hundreds of lobules. Each lobule contains a bronchiole and affiliated branches, a thin wall, and clusters of alveoli.

In addition to respiratory activities, the lungs perform other bodily functions. Through them, water, alcohol, and pharmacologic agents can be absorbed and excreted. Normally, almost a quart of water is exhaled daily; anesthetic gases such as ether and nitrous oxide can be absorbed and removed by the lungs. Fat (lipid) in the bloodstream is frequently removed and stored in the alveolar cells. The lungs can store glycogen (animal starch) and metabolize it; this process aids the liver in the regulation of carbohydrates (starches).

A person not engaged in vigorous physical activity uses only about one-twentieth of the total available gaseous-exchange surface of the lung. Pressure inside the lungs is equal to that of the surrounding atmosphere. The lungs always remain somewhat inflated because of a partial vacuum between the membrane covering the lung and that which lines the chest. Air is drawn into the lungs when the diaphragm (the muscular portion between the abdomen and the chest) and the intercostal muscles contract, expanding the chest cavity and lowering the pressure between the lungs and chest wall as well as within the lungs.

The lungs are frequently involved in infections and injuries. Some infections can destroy vast areas of a lung, rendering it useless. Healed lung tissue becomes a fibrous scar unable to perform respiratory duties. There is no functional evidence that lung tissue, once destroyed, can be regenerated.

For a depiction of the lungs in human anatomy, shown in relation to other parts of the body, *see* the colour Trans-Vision in the PROPAEDIA: Part Four, Section 421.

lung cancer, uncontrolled growth of cells in the lungs. In the early 20th century it was considered relatively rare, but by the end of the century lung cancer was the leading cause of cancer-related death among men in more than 25 developed countries. In the United States it has surpassed breast cancer as the leading cause of death from cancer among women. This rapid increase is due mostly to the increased use of cigarettes since World War I.

Lung cancer occurs primarily in persons between 45 and 75 years of age. In countries with a prolonged history of cigarette smoking, between 80 and 90 percent of all cases are caused by smoking. Heavy smokers have a greater likelihood of developing the disease than do light smokers, and the risk is also greater for those who started smoking at a young age. Passive inhalation of cigarette smoke (secondhand smoke) is linked to lung cancer in nonsmokers. Other risk factors include exposure to radon gas and asbestos; uranium and pitchblende miners, chromium and nickel refiners, welders, and workers exposed to halogenated ethers also have an increased incidence, as do some workers in hydrocarbon-related processing, such as coal processors, tar refiners, and roofers.

Tumours can begin anywhere in the lung, but symptoms do not usually appear until the disease has reached an advanced stage or spread to another part of the body. The most common symptoms include shortness of breath, a persistent cough or wheeze, chest pain, bloody sputum, unexplained weight loss, and susceptibility to lower respiratory infections. In cases where the cancer has spread beyond the lungs, visible lumps, jaundice, or bone pain may occur. Lung cancer may be diagnosed by needle biopsy, in which a sample of lung tissue is removed for analysis, or by viewing the lungs directly with a bronchoscope. Noninvasive methods include X rays, computed tomography (CT) scans, positron emission tomography (PET) scans, and magnetic resonance imaging (MRI). Most cases are usually diagnosed well after the disease has spread (metastasized) from its original site. For this reason, lung cancer has a poorer prognosis than many other cancers. Even when it is detected early, the five-year survival rate is about 50 percent.

Once diagnosed, the tumour's type and degree of invasiveness are determined. There are two basic forms: small-cell carcinoma, which accounts for 20–25 percent of all cases, and non-small-cell carcinoma, which is responsible for the remainder. Small-cell carcinoma (SCLC), also called oat-cell carcinoma, is rarely found in people who have never smoked. SCLC is the most aggressive type of lung cancer; because it tends to spread quickly before symptoms become apparent, the survival rate is very low.

Non-SCLCs consist primarily of three types of tumour: adenocarcinoma, squamous cell carcinoma, and large-cell carcinoma. Adenocarcinoma accounts for some 25 to 30 percent of cases worldwide, and it is one of the most common types of lung cancer in the United States. Tumours often originate in the smaller, peripheral bronchi. Symptoms at the time of diagnosis often reflect invasion of the lymph nodes, pleura, and both lungs or metastasis to other organs. Some 25 to 30 percent of primary lung cancers are squamous cell carcinomas, also called epidermoid carcinomas; this tumour often develops in the larger bronchi of the central portion of the lungs. Squamous cell carcinoma tends to remain localized longer than other types and thus is generally more responsive to treatment. About 10 percent of all lung cancers are large-cell carcinomas. These carcinomas can begin in any part of the lung and tend to grow very quickly.

As with most cancers, treatments for lung cancer include surgery, chemotherapy, and radiation. The choice of treatment depends on the patient's general health, the stage or extent of the disease, and the type of cancer. Surgery involves the removal of a cancerous segment (segmentectomy), a lobe of the lung (lobectomy), or the entire lung (pneumonectomy). Although removal of an entire lung does not prohibit otherwise healthy people from ultimately resuming normal activity, the already poor condition of many patients' lungs results in long-term difficulty in breathing after surgery. Radiation may be used alone or in conjunction with surgery—either before surgery to shrink tumours or following surgery to destroy small amounts of cancerous tissue. Side effects include vomiting, diarrhea, fatigue, or additional damage to the lungs. Chemotherapy uses chemicals to destroy cancerous cells, but these chemicals also attack normal cells to varying degrees, causing side effects similar to radiation therapy.

The probability of developing lung cancer can be greatly reduced by avoiding smoking. Smokers who quit also reduce their risk significantly. Testing for radon gas and avoiding exposure to coal products, asbestos, and other airborne carcinogens also lowers risk.

Lung-ch'i (China): *see* Chang-chou.

lung congestion, distention of blood vessels in the lungs and filling of the alveoli with blood as a result of an infection, high blood pressure, or cardiac insufficiencies (*i.e.*, inability of the heart to function adequately). The alveoli in the lungs are minute air sacs where carbon dioxide and oxygen exchange occurs.

Active congestion of the lungs is caused by infective agents or irritating gases, liquids, and particles. The alveolar walls and the capillaries in them become distended with blood. Passive congestion is due either to high blood pressure in the capillaries, caused by a cardiac disorder, or to relaxation of the blood capillaries followed by blood seepage.

Left-sided heart failure—inability of the left side of the heart to pump sufficient blood into the general circulation—causes back pressure on the pulmonary vessels delivering oxygenated blood to the heart. The blood pressure becomes high in the alveolar capillaries, and they begin to distend. Eventually the pressure becomes too great, and blood escapes through the capillary wall into the alveoli, flooding them. Mitral stenosis, narrowing of the valve between the upper and lower chambers in the left side of the heart, causes chronic passive congestion. Iron pigment from the blood that congests the alveoli spreads throughout the lung tissue and causes deterioration of tissue and formation of scar tissue. The walls of the alveoli also thicken and gas exchange is greatly impaired. The affected person shows difficulty in breathing, there is a bloody discharge, and the skin takes on a bluish tint as the disease progresses.

Passive congestion due to relaxation of the blood vessels occurs in bedridden patients with weak heart action. Blood accumulates in the lower part of the lungs, although there is usually enough unaffected lung tissue for respiration. The major complication arises in mild cases of pneumonia, when the remaining functioning tissue becomes infected.

Pulmonary edema is much the same as congestion except that the substance in the alveoli is the watery plasma of blood, rather than whole blood, and the precipitating causes may somewhat differ. Inflammatory edema results from influenza or bacterial pneumonia. In mechanical edema the capillary permeability is broken down by the same type of heart disorders and irritants as in congestion. It can occur, for unknown reasons, after reinflation of a collapsed lung. After an operation, if too great a volume of intravenous fluids is given, the blood pressure rises and edema ensues. Excessive irradiation and severe allergic reactions may also produce this disorder.

The lungs become pale, wet, enlarged, and heavy. It may take only one or two hours for two to three quarts of liquid to accumulate; in acute cases, it can be fatal in 10 to 20 minutes. A person with pulmonary edema experiences difficulty in breathing, with deep gurgling rattles in the throat, his skin turns blue, and, because he is too weak to clear the fluids, he may actually drown in the lung secretions.

lung infarction, death of one or more sections of lung tissue due to deprivation of an adequate blood supply. The section of dead tissue is called an infarct. The cessation or lessening of blood flow results ordinarily from an obstruction in a blood vessel that serves the lung. The obstruction may be a blood clot that has formed in a diseased heart and has travelled in the bloodstream to the lungs, or air bubbles in the bloodstream (both of these are instances of embolism), or the blockage may be by a clot that has formed in the blood vessel itself and has remained at the point where it was formed (such a clot is called a thrombus). Ordinarily, when the lungs are healthy, such blockages fail to cause death of tissue because the blood finds its way by alternative routes. If the lung is congested, infected, or inadequately supplied with air, however, lung infarctions can follow blockage of a blood vessel.

Because neither the lung tissue nor the pleural sac surrounding the lungs has sensory endings, infarcts that occur deep inside the lungs produce no pain; those extending to the outer surface cause fluids and blood to seep into the space between the lungs and the pleural sac. The sac distends with the excess fluid and there may be difficulty in inflating the lungs. When pain is present it indicates pleural involvement. The pain may be localized around the rib cage, shoulders, and neck, or it may be lower, near the muscular diaphragm that separates the chest cavity from the abdomen. One explanation for the pain is that it is from tension on the sensitive nerve endings in the membrane lining the chest. Pain is most severe on inhalation.

The symptoms of infarcts are generally spitting up of blood, coughing, fever, moderate difficulty in breathing, increased heartbeat, pleural rubbing, diminished breath sounds, and a dull sound heard when the chest is tapped. The blood shows an increase in number of white blood cells and sedimentation rate (clumping of red blood cells).

Infarcts that do not heal within two or three days generally take two to three weeks to heal. The dead tissue is replaced by scar tissue.

Lung-men caves, Pinyin LONGMEN, series of Chinese cave temples carved into the rock of a high river bank south of the city of Lo-yang, in Honan Province. The temples were begun late in the Northern Wei dynasty (386–535), in the Six Dynasties period, and construction continued sporadically through

Stone sculptures in the Pin-yang Cave (Cave 3), Lung-men, Honan Province; Northern Wei dynasty (AD 386–535)

Jimbunkagaku Kenkyusho, Kyoto

the 6th century and the T'ang dynasty (618–907). Following the transfer of the Northern Wei capital from P'ing-ch'eng (the present Ta-t'ung, Shansi Province) south to Lo-yang in 494, a new series of cave temples was begun, based on the precedent of an ambitious series constructed in the preceding decades at Yün-kang (*see* Yün-kang caves).

The Northern Wei caves at Lung-men (including the often-cited Ku-yang cave and the Pin-yang cave), however, are more intimate in scale, more complex in iconography, and more preciously and elegantly crafted to create ethereal effects in the hard stone. The Buddha images—clothed in the costume of the Chinese scholar, with a sinuous cascade of drapery falling over an increasingly flattened figure—provide the type form for what is known as the Lung-men style, in contrast to the blockier Yün-kang style (*see* Northern Wei sculpture). Work at the site, which continued in a minor and sporadic way through later times, culminated in the T'ang dynasty with the construction of a cave shrine, known as Feng-hsien Ssu, of truly monumental proportions, carved out over the three-year period 672–675. The square plan measures about 100 feet (30 metres) on each side, and a colossal seated Buddha figure upon the back wall, flanked by attendant figures, is more than 35 ft high.

lung plague, also called CONTAGIOUS PLEUROPNEUMONIA, an acute bacterial disease producing pneumonia and inflammation of lung membranes in cattle, buffalo, sheep, and goats. It is caused by *Mycoplasma mycoides*. *See also* mycoplasma.

Lung-shan culture, Pinyin LONGSHAN, Neolithic culture of central China, named for the site in Shantung Province where its remains were first discovered by C.T. Wu. Dating from about 3000 BC to the mid-2nd millennium BC, it is characterized by fine burnished ware in wheel-turned vessels of angular outline; abundant gray pottery; rectangular polished stone axes; walls of compressed earth; and a method of divination by heating cattle bones and interpreting the cracks. Lung-shan Black Pottery ware has been found in northern Honan, Anhwei, and as far away as the Kwantung Peninsula in the northeast.

lung squeeze (medicine): *see* thoracic squeeze.

Lung-yen, Pinyin LONGYAN, town, Fukien Province (*sheng*), China. Lung-yen is a county (*hsien*) seat and the administrative centre of Lung-yen Prefecture (*ti-ch'ü*), in the mountainous region of southwest Fukien. It is situated on a branch of the Chiu-lung Chiang (river), at the centre of a fertile agricultural basin ringed by wooded hills. A highway network connects it with Chang-chou and Amoy on the coast, Chang-p'ing and San-ming in central Fukien to the north, and the Kwangtung and Kiangsi provincial borders to the south and west. Lung-yen (Dragon Rock) was established as a county seat in 736. In the 1930s it became the centre of the short-lived Communist-type Min-hsi regime. Since 1960 Lung-yen has been joined by a branch rail line to the Amoy–Ying-t'an (Kiangsi) railway, which it joins at Chang-p'ing. Both Lung-yen and Chang-p'ing are centres of coal mining, with deposits of high-grade anthracite. The area around Lung-yen also has rich reserves of iron ore, as well as of manganese, tungsten, copper, lead, zinc, and molybdenum. Pop. (mid-1970s est.) 10,000–50,000.

lungan (tree): *see* longan.

lungfish, any of six species of air-breathing fishes placed with a number of extinct forms in the subclass Dipnoi (order Dipnoi of some authorities). Lungfishes are found in rivers and lakes of South America, Africa, and Australia.

A brief treatment of lungfishes follows. For full treatment, *see* MACROPAEDIA: Fishes.

The South American lungfish (*Lepidosiren paradoxa*) and the African lungfishes (four

Young African lungfish (*Protopterus annectans*) with larval gill filaments above the pectoral fins

By courtesy of the New York Zoological Society

species of *Protopterus,* considered a single species by some authorities) are placed in the family Lepidosirenidae. The members of this family are slim, elongated, eel-like fishes with small scales and two lungs. The pectoral and pelvic fins are slender filaments and are used by the fishes to sense their surroundings. The South American lungfish grows about 1 m (40 inches) long. The largest of the African lungfishes is *P. aethiopicus,* a mottled yellow, East African species that may grow about 2 m long. Both the South American and African lungfishes build nests for spawning, and in both instances the nests are guarded by the male. In dry periods, the South American species buries itself in the mud and aestivates (becomes dormant) until water returns. The African species also aestivate, but do so in cocoons that are secreted by their bodies and that harden into leathery cysts.

The Australian lungfish (*Neoceratodus forsteri*), placed in the family Ceratidae, is found in Queensland, Australia. Unlike the other lungfishes, it has a single lung, large scales, and paddle-like pectoral and pelvic fins. It may reach a length of about 1.25 m (49 inches) and a weight of 10 kg (22 pounds). Considered more primitive than the South American and African forms, the Australian lungfish lays its eggs among aquatic plants but does not build a nest and does not aestivate during droughts.

Lunghi FAMILY, Lunghi also spelled LONGHI, or LONGO, a family of three generations of Italian architects who were originally from Viggiu, near Milan, but worked in Rome. Martino Lunghi the Elder (d. 1591) was a

Facade of the church of San Girolamo degli Schiavoni, Rome, by Martino Lunghi
Alinari—Art Resource/EB Inc.

Mannerist architect who was commissioned by Pope Sixtus V (1585–90) to build the church of San Girolamo degli Schiavoni (1588–90) and continued work on the Chiesa Nuova (Santa Maria in Vallicella, Rome; 1599–1605 and on), which had been started by Matteo di Citta di Castello.

His son, Onorio Lunghi (1569–1619), began his major work, San Carlo al Corso, Rome, one of the largest churches in that city, in January 1612; and when he died in 1619, his son, Martino Longhi the Younger (1602–57), continued the work. Onorio Longhi also designed the large oval chapel in San Giovanni in Laterano, Rome, in the early 1630s.

Martino Longhi the Younger worked on San Carlo al Corso (1612–79) until he returned to Milan in 1656, but his unique work was the facade of Santi Vincenzo ed Anastasio in the Piazza di Trevi (1646–50). He also started the church of Santo Antonio de'Portoghesi in 1638 but left it unfinished when he returned to Milan. The staircase (*c.* 1640) in Bartolommeo Ammannati's Palazzo Caetani (now Ruspoli) is another of his important Roman works.

Lunglei, also spelled LUNGLEH, town, south-central Mizorām state, northeastern India. One of the most populous towns in the Mizo Hills, it is located 131 miles (211 km) south of Aizawl. Rice is the principal crop in the agricultural economy. Cottage industries produce handloomed cloth, furniture, agricultural equipment, woven textiles, and bamboo and cane work.

The surrounding region consists of rugged, north–south-aligned hill ranges with an elevation of from 500 feet (150 m) to 900 feet (275 m). The major streams are the Dhaleśwarī and the Tuivai, both cutting the hill ranges almost at right angles to form steep, narrow valleys. The natural vegetation consists of extensive bamboo jungles. Crops include paddy rice, oilseeds, cotton, peanuts (groundnuts), pumpkins, and corn (maize). Timber, beeswax, rubber, catechu, and gum are also collected. Industries include handloom weaving, blacksmithing, carpentry, cane and bamboo working, and the making of traditional clothing. The Lushai people are the major ethnic group of the region. They live in settlements on the hillsides above the river valleys. Most of the inhabitants are Christians. Pop. (1981) 17,205.

Lungwebungu River, largest headwater tributary of the Zambezi River, in southwest central Africa. It rises in the central plateau of Angola as the Lungué-Bungo River to flow east and southeast into Zambia. There it joins the Zambezi 65 miles (105 km) north of Mongu, after a course of 400 miles (645 km).

lungworm, any of the parasitic worms of the superfamily Metastrongyloidea (class Nematoda, phylum Aschelminthes) that infest the lungs and air passages of mammals, including dolphins and whales. Examples include those of the genus *Metastrongylus* that live in pigs and of the genus *Dictyocaulus* in sheep. Many species of lungworms are of veterinary importance. Members of the genus *Angiostrongylus,* normally occurring as parasites in rats, are known to be pathogenic in humans. The life cycle of lungworms can be direct or involve intermediate hosts, such as snails and slugs. Lungworms should not be confused with lung flukes, such as those of the genus *Paragonimus,* which are trematodes.

lungwort, any plant of the genus *Pulmonaria* of the family Boraginaceae, especially *P. officinalis,* an herbaceous, hairy perennial plant, widespread in open woods and thickets of Europe. It is grown as a garden flower for its drooping, pink flowers that turn blue and for its often white-spotted leaves.

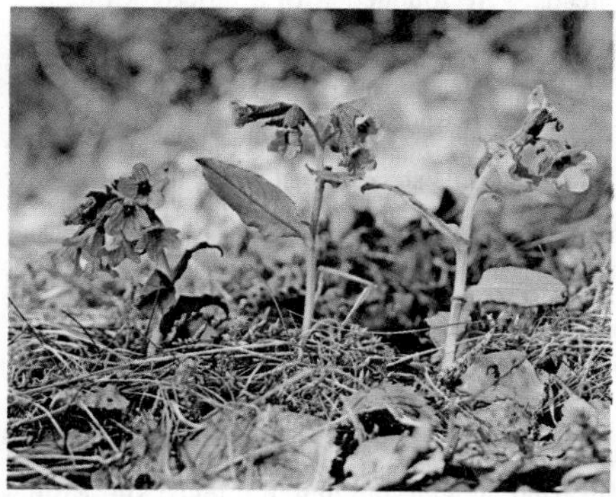

Lungwort (*Pulmonaria*)
Sven Samelius

The lungwort's basal leaves are heart-shaped and the stem leaves clasping and oval. The flowering stems, topped by drooping clusters of cylindrical flowers, reach 30 cm (12 inches). *P. longifolia,* with smaller flowers and narrow leaves, grows in similar terrain.

lungwort (lichen): *see* tree lungwort.

Lūni, river in Rājasthān state, western India. Rising on the western slopes of the Arāvalli Range near Ajmer town, where it is known as the Sāgarmati, the river flows generally southwestward through the hills and across the plains of the region. It then enters a patch of desert before it finally dissipates into the wastes of the northeastern part of the marsh called the Rann of Kutch in Gujarāt state. A seasonal river, it receives much of the drainage of the southwest slopes of the Arāvalli Range; the Jowai, Sukri, and Jojari rivers are its main tributaries. The Lūni derived its name from the Sanskrit Lāvaṇavāri ("Salt River") and is so called because of its excessive salinity. With a course of some 330 miles (530 km), the Lūni is the only major river of the area, and it serves as an essential source of irrigation waters.

Consult
the
INDEX
first

Lunn, Sir Arnold (Henry Moore) (b. April 18, 1888, Madras, India—d. June 2, 1974, London), British slalom skier and international authority on skiing who in 1922 introduced slalom gates (paired poles between which the skier must pass on his downward descent) and thereby created the modern Alpine slalom race.

Lunn was introduced to skiing as a boy by his father, a Methodist minister who founded a travel agency that promoted skiing in Switzerland. At the University of Oxford he founded the Oxford Ski Club and later the Ski Club of Great Britain (1903), the Alpine Ski Club (1908), and the Kandahar Ski Club (1924). He helped organize the Anglo-Swiss University match of 1925 to popularize the slalom course. In 1930 he convinced the Fédération Internationale de Ski (FIS) to recognize competition in the slalom as well as in the downhill, and in 1936 he assisted in the organization of the events for the Winter Olympic Games. He served as a member of the FIS executive committee (1934–49) and as chairman of the International Downhill Ski Racing Committee (1946–49). Lunn was editor of British Ski Yearbook from 1919 for more than 50 years and wrote many books on skiing, mountaineering, philosophy, and Christianity. He was knighted in 1952 for service to British skiing and Anglo-Swiss relations.

Lunsar, town, west-central Sierra Leone, western Africa. A traditional trade centre of the Marampa–Masimera chiefdom for rice and palm oil and kernels, it developed after 1933 with the exploitation of iron ore, mined at Marampa, 4 miles (6 km) east. The Marampa mine closed down in 1975. The town has a number of institutions, including a government health centre, a Roman Catholic hospital, a Young Muslims' Association, and several schools. Pop. (1984 est.) 23,791.

Lunt, Alfred; and Fontanne, Lynn, Fontanne's original name LILLIE LOUISE FONTANNE (respectively b. Aug. 19, 1892, Milwaukee, Wis., U.S.—d. Aug. 3, 1977, Chicago; b. Dec. 6, 1887, Essex, Eng.—d. July 30, 1983, Genesee Depot, Wis., U.S.), American husband-and-wife acting team who performed together in more than two dozen theatrical productions, from *Sweet Nell of Old Drury* (1923) to *The Visit* (1958). They were long associated with the playwright Noël Coward, whose play *Design for Living* (1933) was written for them. They eventually earned a reputation as the greatest husband-and-wife team in the history of the theatre.

Lunt attended Carroll College (Waukesha, Wis.) and Harvard College but left school for an acting career, making his debut in a Boston repertory company in 1912 and thereafter taking several dramatic and vaudeville roles; these culminated in a critical success in the title role of Booth Tarkington's *Clarence* (1919) on Broadway. Meanwhile, Fontanne had studied under Ellen Terry in England, made her road-show debut in 1905, and won her first London role in 1909 in the Drury Lane Pantomime and her first New York City role in 1910. Between revisits to England, she became a mild success on Broadway, where she and Lunt met in 1917 and again in 1919; during the summer of the latter year they appeared in their first plays together. While Lunt was on a road tour with *Clarence* in 1921, Fontanne won praise as the star of the comedy *Dulcy.* They were married on May 26, 1922.

In 1924 they joined the Theatre Guild and with *The Guardsman* of that year were celebrated enthusiastically as the bright couple of the Broadway stage. Their superlative performances, especially in comedies focusing on marital infidelity, brought many triumphs for the Theatre Guild, under whose auspices they appeared until 1929. The couple constantly strove for perfection and rehearsed almost continuously to attain the effortless rapport that was their hallmark. Although they were considered at their best in comedies by George Bernard Shaw, Noël Coward, and Terence Rattigan, Fontanne and Lunt appeared in several dramas as well. Among their plays were *Arms and the Man* (1925), *The Goat Song* (1926), *The Doctor's Dilemma* (1927), *Elizabeth the Queen* (1930), *Idiot's Delight* (1936), *Amphitryon 38* (1938), and *The Pirate* (1942). They appeared separately in two Eugene O'Neill plays, he in *Marco Millions* (1928) and she in *Strange Interlude* (1928). They also appeared together in films and on television. Over the years from the 1930s, Lunt himself directed a number of plays, as well as two operas for the Metropolitan Opera Company.

The Lunts were almost inseparable both on and off the stage during their 55-year marriage. In 1958 the old Globe Theatre in New York City was renamed the Lunt-Fontanne Theater in their honour.

Luo, also called KAVIRONDO, people living in the flat country near Lake Victoria in western Kenya and northern Uganda. They constitute the third largest ethnic group in Kenya (about 11 percent), after the Kikuyu, with whom they shared major political power in the first years after Kenya achieved independence, and the Luhya. The Luo speak an Eastern Sudanic language of the Chari-Nile branch of the Nilo-Saharan family.

Luo are settled agriculturists who also keep many cattle. They are found throughout East Africa as agricultural labourers and tenant farmers and as urban workers.

Traditionally, each Luo group is an autonomous political unit, controlled by a dominant clan or lineage. The Luo traditionally believed in a supreme creator, whom they called Nyasi (Nyasaye), and had a strong ancestor cult. Today most Luo are Christians.

Luo Guanzhong (Chinese novelist): *see* Lo Kuan-chung.

Luohe (China): *see* Lo-ho.

Luorawetlan (people): *see* Chukchi.

Luorawetlan languages, also spelled LUORAVETLAN, family of languages including Chukchi, Koryak, Itelmen, Aliutor, and Kerek, spoken in northeastern Siberia. The Luorawetlan language family is placed with the Yeniseian languages, Yukaghir, and Nivkh within the Paleo-Siberian languages, which are not genetically related. The largest languages of the Luorawetlan family are Chukchi and Koryak.

Luoyang (China): *see* Lo-yang.

Lupemban industry, also called LUPEMBIAN INDUSTRY, a sub-Saharan African stone tool industry dating from the late Pleistocene, beginning about 40,000 years ago. The Lupemban industry was derived from and replaced the Sangoan industry, which is found in forested areas of sub-Saharan Africa. The Lupemban industry is characterized by fairly small, well-shaped tools: chisels, adzes, planes (probably demonstrating intensive woodworking), sidescrapers, and blades. The most characteristic Lupemban tool is an elongate, lanceolate bifacial point that is often very finely and beautifully flaked.

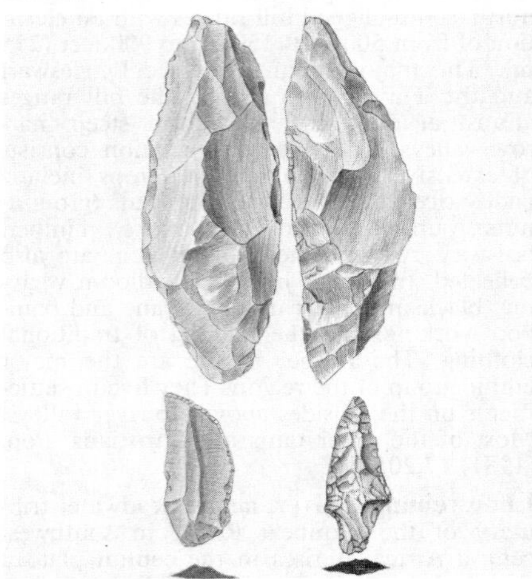

Lupemban stone tools
(Top) bifacial point, (bottom left) backed knife, (bottom right) projectile point
From F. Bordes, *The Old Stone Age,* copyright 1968 by McGraw-Hill Book Co. and Weidenfeld and Nicolson Ltd.; used with permission

Lupercalia, ancient Roman festival that was conducted annually on February 15 under the superintendence of a corporation of priests called Luperci. The origins of the festival are obscure, although the likely derivation of its name from *lupus* (Latin: "wolf") has variously suggested connection with a primitive deity who protected herds from wolves and with the legendary she-wolf who nursed Romulus and Remus. As a fertility rite, the festival is also associated with the god Faunus (*q.v.*).

Each Lupercalia began with the sacrifice by the Luperci of goats and a dog, after which two of the Luperci were led to the altar, their foreheads were touched with a bloody knife, and the blood wiped off with wool dipped in milk; then the ritual required that the two young men laugh. The sacrificial feast followed, after which the Luperci cut thongs from the skins of the victims and ran in two bands around the Palatine hill, striking with the thongs at any woman who came near them. A blow from the thong was supposed to render a woman fertile. In AD 494 the Christian church under Pope Gelasius I appropriated the form of the rite as the Feast of the Purification.

Lupescu, Magda, original name MAGDA WOLFF (b. 1896?, Iaşi, Rom.—d. June 28/29, 1977, Estoril, Port.), Romanian adventuress who, as mistress of King Carol II of Romania, exerted a wide-ranging influence on Romanian public affairs during the 1930s.

The facts concerning her early life are uncertain, but it is known that her father was Jewish and her mother Roman Catholic. She was evidently married to an army officer named Tampeanu when, in the early 1920s, she began her liaison with Prince Carol, the heir-apparent to the Romanian throne. When Carol refused to end the relationship, he was forced to renounce his rights of succession and go into exile (1925). He later agreed to end the affair and became reconciled with his former wife, Princess Helen of Greece, in order to reclaim his crown; but in 1930, shortly after his return to Romania as king, he installed Lupescu in Bucharest.

She soon came to wield an influence that was considered stronger than that of any government minister. The National Peasant Party leader Iuliu Maniu railed against the "sinister Jewish influence at the palace" that was "responsible for almost every evil in this country." Her Jewish origins marked her especially for vilification by the principal Romanian fascist organization, the Iron Guard. She fled the country with Carol after his abdication in September 1940. Upon her marriage to the former king in July 1947, he conferred on her the title Princess Elena. After the death of Carol (1953) she continued to live in Estoril, Port.

Lupin (China): *see* Man-chou-li.

lupine, any member of a genus (*Lupinus*) of herbaceous and partly woody plants in the pea family (Fabaceae). Lupines are widely distributed in the Mediterranean area but are especially numerous on the prairies of western North America. About 200 species are known. Many are grown in the United States as ornamentals, and a few species are useful as cover and forage crops.

The herbaceous lupines, up to 1.25 m (4 feet) tall, have low, palmately divided leaves and an upright flower spike. Through hybridization and selection some highly ornamental varieties have been developed. Especially popular in gardens are the Russell hybrids, about 1 m high, with long, dense flower spikes in a wide range of colours. The Texas bluebonnet is a lupine. In Europe and elsewhere tall species of lupines (*e.g.,* white lupine, or wolf bean, *Lupinus alba*) are planted as a nitrogen-collecting winter cover crop.

The term lupine (sometimes spelled lupin), from the Latin for "wolf," derives from the mistaken belief that these plants depleted, or "wolfed," minerals from the soil. The contrary is true, however; lupines aid soil fertility by fixing nitrogen from the air in a soil form useful for other plants.

Wild lupine (*L. perennis*) and Nuttal's lupine (*L. nuttallii*), both with blue flower spikes, are found in dry open woods and fields of eastern North America. Spreading lupine (*L. diffusa*) and hairy lupine (*L. villosus*) are distributed throughout the southern United States. *L. polyphyllus,* from the Pacific Northwest, is becoming abundant in the northeastern United States and adjacent Canada.

Lupine (*Lupinus*)
F.K. Anderson

Lupino FAMILY, one of England's most celebrated theatrical families.

The earliest traceable Lupino—who spelled his name Luppino—flourished probably in Italy, *c.* 1612, and billed himself as Signor Luppino. His descendant, George William (1632–93), a singer, reciter, and puppet master, went to England as a political refugee. His son,

George Charles (1662–1725), was a performer and puppeteer at the age of eight. After the Restoration the Luppino family was granted a license to play in the service of King Charles II. John Rich—the theatre manager and actor who originated the English pantomime—had as an apprentice a boy called George Richard Eastcourt Luppino (1710–87), whose son Thomas Frederick (1749–1845), the first to spell the family name Lupino, became a scenic artist and dancer.

The family tree shows nearly all descendants to have been connected with the stage. George Hook Lupino (1820–1902) had 16 children, at least 10 of whom became professional dancers, two marrying into the family of the well-known actress Sara Lane, manager (1871–99) of the Britannia Theatre, London. Almost the last of the old-style clowns was George Hook's eldest son, George (1853–1932), born in a dressing room of the Theatre Royal, Birmingham, who was immediately carried onto the stage in swaddling clothes. He died at the age of 79, shortly after his last performance as the clown in a harlequinade, with his son Barry as Harlequin. His two brothers, Arthur (1864–1908) and Henry Charles (called Harry) (1865–1925), were well-known music-hall performers at the turn of the century. Arthur, an incomparable animal impersonator, was chosen by Sir James Barrie to be Nana, the dog, in the premiere (1904) of his play *Peter Pan.*

Of George Lupino's children, Barry (1884–1962), besides being an actor, was the family archivist and Stanley (1894–1942) was a popular comedian who played variety for several years at the Drury Lane Theatre, London. Barry Lupino served some years as company comedian at the Britannia and then made extensive tours that included Australia (1913), South Africa, and the Far East. He excelled in pantomime and musical comedy, and he wrote or was coauthor of about 50 pantomimes, made numerous tours of the United States, and appeared in several films. Stanley, best remembered for his performances in revue and musical comedy, wrote plays, novels, and *From the Stocks to the Stars* (1934), a collection of reminiscences. His nephew Henry George (1892–1959), taking Sara Lane's name, was known under the stage name of Lupino Lane. Lane became a well-known cockney comedian and toured extensively in variety, musical comedy, and pantomime. In 1937 he scored a tremendous success as Bill Snibson in the British musical *Me and My Girl,* in which he created the "Lambeth walk," a ballroom dance supposedly representing the strut of the cockney residents of the Lambeth section of London.

Stanley Lupino's daughter Ida (1916–95) made her British motion-picture debut in 1932 in *Her First Affair.* She later moved to the United States and first appeared there on film in 1934. She acted in such films as *They Drive by Night* (1940), *The Sea Wolf* (1941), and *High Sierra* (1941). She was voted Best Actress by the New York film critics for her role in *The Hard Way* (1942). Subsequently turning to independent production, she directed several motion pictures in which she also often acted. Ida Lupino also wrote for, directed, and acted in television.

Lupton, Thomas Goff (b. Sept. 3, 1791, London, Eng.—d. May 18, 1873, London), English mezzotint engraver and miniatures painter, who introduced to the art of engraving soft steel plates that permitted a printing of up to 1,500 mezzotints of excellent quality. The copper plates formerly used were very soft and could produce only 50 prints of similar quality.

Lupton was apprenticed to an engraver by his father, who was a goldsmith. After spending a number of years learning the techniques of mezzotint engraving and receiving recognition for his crayon portraits exhibited at the Royal Academy, Lupton turned his interest to improving the engraving plate. He experimented with plates of nickel, tutenag (an impure zinc alloy), and steel before he produced a satisfactory steel plate. It was well received, and from 1823 steel engravings superseded copper engravings. Lupton's works include copies of landscape series by J.M.W. Turner as well as engraved portraits after oil paintings by eminent contemporary British painters.

Lupus (English ecclesiastic): *see* Wulfstan.

lupus erythematosus, either of two distinct inflammatory diseases—discoid lupus erythematosus and systemic lupus erythematosus. In rare instances (5–10 percent of the cases), the discoid type develops into the systemic, according to some but not all investigators.

Discoid lupus erythematosus is a disease of the skin that affects women more often than men. Distinct reddened patches covered with grayish brown scales may appear on the upper cheeks and the nose, on the scalp, the lips, or the lining of the cheeks. The lesions on the outside of the cheeks and on the nose often are in a butterfly pattern. In treatment the affected skin is protected against sunlight and other powerful radiation that exacerbates the disease. Antimalarial drugs sometimes bring about improvement.

Systemic lupus erythematosus, also called disseminated lupus erythematosus, or SLE, may affect any organ or structure of the body, especially the skin, the joints, the kidneys, the heart, the serous membranes (membranes that exude moisture, such as those of the joints or those lining the abdomen), and the lymph nodes. The course of the disease is marked by varying acute episodes and remissions, and prospects of survival depend largely on the type and extent of organ involvement; patients with kidney and central nervous system involvement generally face a graver prognosis than patients whose illness involves mainly the joints. The skin lesions may resemble the lesions of discoid lupus erythematosus. Among the features that lead to identification of the disease are the typical skin lesions, the characteristic way in which the skin reacts to sunlight, the inflammation of the joints that does not cause deformity, the inflammation of the kidneys, and the presence in the blood of autoantibodies that bind to the nucleic acid and protein constituents of cell nuclei. The chemical binding action triggers the inflammatory process. The first of these typical autoantibodies to be recognized was named the lupus erythematosus cell factor. Treatment of systemic lupus erythematosus is directed toward relief of pain, controlling the inflammation, and limiting as far as possible the damage to vital organs.

Luque, city, southern Paraguay. Founded in 1635, Luque rose to prominence as the temporary national capital during the bloody Paraguayan War (1864–70) with Argentina, Brazil, and Uruguay. Oranges, sugarcane, tobacco, cotton, and livestock produced in the area supply the markets of nearby Asunción, to which it is accessible by railroad and highway. Factories in Luque manufacture guitars and harps. Luque also contains soap factories, distilleries, tile and brick factories, and processing plants. Pop. (1992 prelim.) 83,591.

Lur, member of a mountain Muslim people of western Iran, speaking a distinct language closely related to Persian. The Lurs are thought to be of aboriginal stock, with strong Iranian, Arabic, and other admixtures.

The Lurs and their neighbours, the Bakhtyārī, are partly agricultural and partly pastoral tribes. Lush grazing pastures between the mountain ranges enabled the Lurs to maintain themselves as pastoral nomads until the 20th century, when they developed agriculture largely in response to economic and political pressures from outside. Lurs on the western frontier, south of Kermanshah, Iran, were once almost independent under their own vālīs (viceroys) until Reza Shah Pahlavi brought them under control of the central government and deported some sections to

Nomadic Lurs
Paul Almasy

Khorāsān. The economic and political life of the Lurs resembles that of their northern Kurdish neighbours. The traditional authority of the tribal chiefs remains a more viable force among nomadic groups than among those who are more fully settled. As with the Kurds and Bakhtyārī, women among the Lurs have traditionally had greater freedom than other Arab or Iranian women.

lur, also spelled LURE, bronze horn, or trumpet, found in prehistoric Scandinavian excavations. It has a conical bore, is 5 to 8 feet (1.5 to 2.5 m) long in a bent S-shape resembling a mammoth tusk, and ends in a flat metal disk.

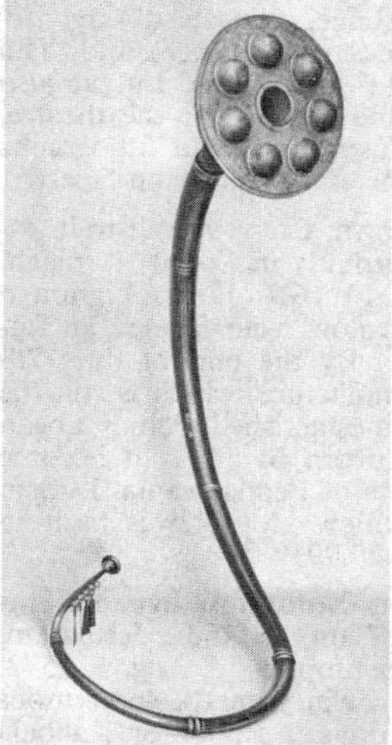

Lur, Late Bronze Age; in the National Museum, Copenhagen
By courtesy of the Nationalmuseet, Copenhagen

The mouthpiece of the lur is permanently affixed. *Lurs* are usually found in pairs and were probably played ritually.

Luray Caverns, series of limestone caves in Page county, northwestern Virginia, U.S., near the town of Luray (headquarters of the Shenandoah National Park). Covering 64 acres (26 hectares), the caverns, discovered in 1878, were formed millions of years ago by underground rivers and seepage of acid-bearing water through layers of limestone and clay. In time the clay was washed away, leaving only the limestone shell. Long after the formation of the caverns and the development of stalactites from dripping limewater, they were filled with glacial mud. The acid-charged mud eroded the dripstone and altered its shape. When the mud was later removed by flowing water, the older eroded forms remained alongside the new growth, resulting in a striking display of many-hued stalactites, stalagmites, columns, and cascades. The caverns comprise a group of chambers, 30 to 140 feet (9 to 43 m) in height, with indirect lighting and connected by corridors, stairways, and bridges. The inside temperature is a constant 54° F (12° C). The Luray Singing Tower, at the entrance to the caverns, is a 117-foot high carillon with 47 bells ranging from 12.5 pounds (5.7 kg) to 7,640 pounds (3,466 kg).

Consult the INDEX *first*

Lurçat, Jean (b. July 1, 1892, Bruyères, Fr.—d. Jan. 6, 1966, Saint-Paul, Fr.), French painter and designer who is frequently called the most instrumental figure in reviving the art of designing and weaving tapestries in the 20th century.

Although his first tapestries were executed and exhibited in 1917, it was not until 1936 that Lurçat turned from being primarily a painter to designing tapestries. In 1939 he and the painters Toussaint Dubreuil and Marcel Gromaire went to Aubusson, a French town historically associated with tapestry weaving since at least the 16th century, and established a centre for the making of modern tapestries in cooperation with the master weaver François Tabard. Among the most notable of the more than 1,000 tapestries Lurçat designed are the "Four Seasons" (1940), the "Apocalypse Tapestry" (1948; in the Church of Notre-Dame de Toute-Grâce, Plateau d'Assy, *département* of Haute-Savoie, France), and "The Song of the World" (1957–64). Lurçat also did set and costume designs for the theatre, ceramics, book illustrations, and lithographs and wrote poetry, as well as books on tapestry.

Lurgan, market town, Craigavon district (established 1973), formerly in County Armagh, Northern Ireland. In 1610 James I granted land to John Brownlow, who formed an English colony there. By the end of the 17th century, linen manufacture, which is still the chief industry, was established. James Logan emigrated from Lurgan in 1699 to become one of the founders of Pennsylvania. Lurgan Castle (now Brownlow House) was built in 1836. Pop. (1981) 20,991.

Luria, Isaac ben Solomon, byname HA-ARI (Hebrew: The Lion) (b. 1534, Jerusalem, Palestine, Ottoman Empire—d. Aug. 5, 1572, Safed, Syria [now Zefat, Israel]), eponymous founder of the Lurianic school of Kabbala (Jewish esoteric mysticism).

Luria's youth was spent in Egypt, where he became versed in rabbinic studies, engaged in commerce, and eventually concentrated on study of the *Zohar,* the central work of Kabbala. In 1570 he went to Safed in Galilee, where he studied under Moses ben Jacob Cordovero, the greatest Kabbalist of the time, and developed his own Kabbalistic system. Although he wrote few works beyond three famous hymns, Luria's doctrines were recorded by his pupil Ḥayyim Vital, who presented them in a voluminous posthumous collection.

Luria's father was an Ashkenazi (a German or Polish Jew), while his mother was a Sephardi (of Iberian-North African Jewish stock). Legend has it that the prophet Elijah appeared to his father and foretold the birth of the son, whose name was to be Isaac. As a child, Luria was described as a young genius, "a Torah scholar who could silence all opponents by the power of his arguments," and also as possessed of divine inspiration.

The main source for his life story is an anonymous biography, *Toledot ha-Ari* ("Life of the Ari"), written or perhaps edited some 20 years after his death, in which factual and legendary elements are indiscriminately mingled. According to the *Toledot,* Luria's father died while Isaac was a child, and his mother took him to Egypt to live with her well-to-do family. While there, he became versed in rabbinic studies, including Halakha (Jewish law), and even wrote glosses on a famous compendium of legal discussions, the *Sefer ha-Halakhot* of Isaac ben Jacob Alfasi. He also engaged in commerce during this period.

While still a youth, Luria began the study of Jewish mystical learning and lived for nearly seven years in seclusion at his uncle's home on an island in the Nile River. His studies concentrated on the *Zohar* (late 13th–early 14th century), the central and revered work of the Kabbala, but he also studied the early Kabbalists (12th–13th century). The greatest Kabbalist of Luria's time was Moses ben Jacob Cordovero of Safed (modern Ẕefat), in Palestine, whose work Luria studied while still in Egypt. During this period he wrote a commentary on the *Sifra di-tzeniʿuta* ("Book of Concealment"), a section of the *Zohar.* The commentary still shows the influence of classical Kabbala and contains nothing of what would later be called Lurianic Kabbala.

Early in 1570 Luria journeyed to Safed, the mountain town in the Galilee that had become a centre of the Kabbalistic movement, and he studied there with Cordovero. At the same time, he began to teach Kabbala according to a new system and attracted many pupils. The greatest of these was Ḥayyim Vital, who later set Luria's teachings down in writing. Luria apparently expounded his teachings only in esoteric circles; not everyone was allowed to take part in these studies. While he devoted most of his time to the instruction of his pupils, he probably made his living in trade, which prospered at that time in Safed, situated as it was at the crossroads between Egypt and Damascus.

At the time of Luria's arrival in Safed, the group of Kabbalists gathered there around Cordovero had already developed a unique style of living and observed special rituals, going out, for instance, into the fields to welcome the sabbath, personified as the Sabbath Queen. With Luria's arrival, new elements were added to these excursions, such as communion with the souls of the zaddikim (men of outstanding piety) by means of special *kawwanot* (ritual meditations) and *yiḥudim* ("unifications") that were in essence a kind of lesser redemption whereby the souls were lifted up from the *kelipot* ("shells"; *i.e.,* the impure, evil forms) into which they were banned until the coming of the Messiah.

The strong influence of Luria's personality helped to bring about in Safed an atmosphere of spiritual intensity, messianic tension, and the fever of creation that accompanies the sense of a great revelation. Deep devoutness, asceticism, and withdrawal from the world marked the Kabbalists' way of life. Luria apparently looked upon himself as the Messiah ben Joseph, the first of the two messiahs in Jewish tradition, who is fated to be killed in the wars (of Gog and Magog) that will precede the final redemption. In Safed there was an expectation (based on the *Zohar*) that the Messiah would appear in Galilee in the year 1575.

Even though he did not distinguish himself as a writer, as is evident from his own remarks about the difficulty of writing, Luria composed three hymns that became widely known and part of the cultural heritage of the Jewish people. These are hymns for the three sabbath meals, which became part of the Sephardic sabbath ritual and were printed in many prayer books. The three meals were linked by means of mystical "intention" or meditation (*kawwana*) to three *partzufim* (aspects of the Godhead). The hymns are known as "Azamer be-she-vaḥim" ("I Will Sing on the Praises"), "Asader seʿudata" ("I Will Order the Festive Meal"), and "Bene hekh-ala de-khesifin" ("Sons of the Temple of Silver"). They are mystical, erotic songs about "the adornment (or fitting) of the bride"—*i.e.,* the sabbath, who was identified with the community of Israel—and on the other *partzufim: arikh anpin* (the long-suffering: the countenance of grace) and *zeʿir anpin* (the impatient: the countenance of judgment).

During his brief sojourn in Safed—a scant two years before his death—Luria managed to construct a many-faceted and fertile Kabbalistic system from which many new elements in Jewish mysticism drew their nourishment. He set down almost none of his doctrine in writing, with the exception of a short text that seems to be only a fragment: his commentary on the first chapter of the *Zohar*—"Be-resh hormanuta de-malka"—as well as commentaries on isolated passages of the *Zohar* that were collected by Ḥayyim Vital, who attests to their being in his teacher's own hand. Luria died in an epidemic that struck Safed in August 1572.

What is called Lurianic Kabbala is a voluminous collection of Luria's Kabbalistic doctrines, recorded after his death by Ḥayyim Vital and appearing in two versions under different editorship. Because of this work, Lurianic Kabbala became the new thought that influenced all Jewish mysticism after Luria, competing with the Kabbala of Cordovero. Vital laboured much to give Lurianic Kabbala its form as well as to win legitimization for it.

Lurianic Kabbala propounds a theory of the creation and subsequent degeneration of the world and a practical method of restoring the original harmony. The theory is based on three concepts: *tzimtzum* ("contraction," or "withdrawal"), *shevirat ha-kelim* ("breaking of the vessels"), and *tiqqun* ("restoration"). God as the Infinite (En Sof) withdraws into himself in order to make room for the creation, which occurs by a beam of light from the Infinite into the newly provided space. Later the divine light is enclosed in finite "vessels," most of which break under the strain, and the catastrophe of the "breaking of the vessels" occurs, whereby disharmony and evil enter the world. Hence comes the struggle to rid the world of evil and accomplish the redemption of both the cosmos and history. This event occurs in the stage of *tiqqun,* in which the divine realm itself is reconstructed, the divine sparks returned to their source, and Adam Qadmon, the symbolic "primordial man," who is the highest configuration of the divine light, is rebuilt. Man plays an important role in this process through various *kawwanot* used during prayer and through mystical intentions involving secret combinations of words, all of which is directed toward the restoration of the primordial harmony and the reunification of the divine name.

The influence of Luria's Kabbala was far-reaching. It played an important role in the movement of the false messiah Shabbetai Tzevi in the 17th century and in the popular Ḥasidic (mystical-pietistic) movement a century later. (R.S.-U.)

BIBLIOGRAPHY. Useful studies include Gershom G. Scholem, "Isaac Luria and His School," in his *Major Trends in Jewish Mysticism,* 3rd rev. ed., pp. 244–286 (1954), and Solomon Schechter, "Safed in the Sixteenth Century: A City of Legists and Mystics," in his *Studies in Judaism,* 2nd Series, pp. 202–285 (1908).

Luria, Ruggiero di (Italian admiral): *see* Lauria, Ruggiero di.

Luria, Salvador (Edward) (b. Aug. 13, 1912, Turin, Italy—d. Feb. 6, 1991, Lexington, Mass., U.S.), Italian-born American biologist who (with Max Delbrück and Alfred Day Hershey) won the Nobel Prize for Physiology or Medicine in 1969 for research on bacteriophages, viruses that infect bacteria.

Luria graduated from the University of Turin in 1935 and became a radiology specialist. He fled Italy for France in 1938 and went to the United States in 1940 after learning the techniques of phage research at the Pasteur Institute in Paris. Soon after his arrival, he met Delbrück, through whom he became involved with the American Phage Group, an informal scientific organization devoted to solving the problems of viral self-replication. Working with a member of the group in 1942, Luria obtained an electron micrograph of phage particles, which confirmed earlier descriptions of them as consisting of a round head and a thin tail.

In 1943 Luria and Delbrück published a paper showing that, contrary to the current view, viruses undergo permanent changes in their hereditary material. Luria also proved that the simultaneous existence of phage-resistant bacteria with phage-sensitive bacteria in the same culture was a result of the selection of spontaneous bacterial mutants. In 1945 Hershey and Luria demonstrated the existence not only of such bacterial mutants but also of spontaneous phage mutants.

Luria became Sedgwick professor of biology at the Massachusetts Institute of Technology in 1964. In 1974 he became director of the Center for Cancer Research at MIT. He was an author of a college textbook, *General Virology* (1953), and a popular text for the general reader, *Life: The Unfinished Experiment* (1973).

Luristan (Iran): *see* Lorestān.

Luristan Bronze, Luristan also spelled LORESTĀN, any of the horse trappings, utensils, weapons, jewelry, belt buckles, and ritual and votive objects of bronze probably dating from roughly 1500–500 BC that have been excavated since the late 1920s in the Harsin, Khorramābād, and Alishtar valleys of the Zagros Mountains in the Lorestān region of western Iran, especially at the site of Tepe Sialk. Their precise origin is unknown. Scholars believe that they were created either by the Cimmerians, a nomadic people from southern Russia who may have invaded Iran in the 8th century BC, or by such related Indo-European peoples as the early Medes and Persians.

Bronze standard with ibexes, from Luristan (Lorestān), Iran, probably 10th–9th century BC; in the University Museum of the University of Pennsylvania, Philadelphia

By courtesy of the University Museum, Philadelphia

Lurton, Horace H(armon) (b. Feb. 26, 1844, Newport, Ky., U.S.—d. July 12, 1914, Atlantic City, N.J.), associate justice of the United States Supreme Court (1910–14).

Lurton enlisted in the Confederate army at the outbreak of the war and was twice taken prisoner, but he was paroled by President Abraham Lincoln the second time upon his mother's appeal, pleading illness. After the war he finished his studies and established a successful legal practice in Clarksville, Tenn., until elected to the state Supreme Court in 1886. During 1898–1910 he also taught law at Vanderbilt University. In 1893 President Grover Cleveland named Lurton to the sixth federal Circuit Court of Appeals, in which Lurton made a strong impression on William Howard Taft, then presiding judge. Lurton succeeded Taft in this position in 1900; and, after Taft became president, he took the first opportunity to elevate Lurton to the U.S. Supreme Court (1910). The appointment by a Republican of a Southern Democrat caused considerable surprise, as did the fact that Lurton was 66 years old at the time, the oldest justice ever to be appointed.

Lurton was a constitutional conservative and opposed the concept that social changes be brought about through judicial interpretation.

Lusaka, city and capital of Zambia. It is situated in the south-central part of the country on a limestone plateau 4,198 feet (1,280 m) above sea level. In the 1890s the area in which Lusaka is situated was taken over by the British South Africa Company from the local chiefs in the course of the formation of Northern Rhodesia, with control passing to the British Colonial Office in 1924. Lusaka became the capital of Northern Rhodesia in 1935. The city figured prominently in the movement for independence and was where the Federation of African Societies founded the Northern Rhodesian Congress in 1948. After the federation of Northern and Southern Rhodesia took place in 1953, Lusaka was a hub of the civil-disobedience movement (1960) that led to the creation of the independent state of Zambia, of which Lusaka became the capital.

Lusaka's newer government section contrasts with the old township along the railway line. Although basically reliant on its agricultural environs, and a major collecting point for corn (maize) and tobacco, Lusaka has a mixed economy that includes cement, textile, and shoe manufacture, and food processing. An international airport and the University of Zambia (founded 1965) are just outside the city, and the Munda Wanga Botanical Gardens are nearby. The city lies at the junction of the Great North Road (to Tanzania) and the Great East Road (to Malaŵi) and has rail connections to Livingstone, Ndola, and Tanzania.

The surrounding area consists mostly of flat grassland that supports ranches and farms. Termite mounds 10 to 20 feet (3 to 6 m) high are a regular feature of the landscape. Farming and stock rearing are the principal economic activities in the region, and products include corn, beef, hides, dairy products, and tobacco. The Nyanja and Soli are the major ethnic groups in the area, and there are minorities of Europeans and Asians. Pop. (1990) 982,-362; (1999 est.) urban agglom., 1,577,000.

Lusatia, German LAUSITZ, Sorbian LUZIA (from *luz,* "meadow"), central European territory of the Sorbs (Lusatians, or Wends), called Sorben (or Wenden) by the Germans. Historic Lusatia was centred on the Neisse and upper Spree rivers, in what is now eastern Germany, between the present-day cities of Cottbus (north) and Dresden (south).

In the 9th century the area settled by the Sorbs, a Slavic people, extended westward to the Saale River and marked the eastern frontier of the Frankish empire. It was conquered by the Germans in 928 and lost by them in 1002 to the Poles, who incorporated it into Poland in 1018. It was reconquered by the Germans in 1033 and was subsequently absorbed by the German states of Meissen and Brandenburg. Lusatia was then subjected to a ruthless Germanization, and severe economic restrictions were placed on the Sorb inhabitants. The Sorbs obtained some relief after 1368–70, when the area was made part of the Bohemian crownlands by the Holy Roman emperor Charles IV.

Lusatia became part of Saxony in 1635 under the Peace of Prague at the conclusion of the Thirty Years' War. In 1815 it was partitioned, with Lower (*i.e.,* southern) Lusatia being transferred to Prussia and Upper (northern) Lusatia remaining under the rule of Saxony. Lower Lusatia was subjected to an intensive Germanization campaign by Prussia, and its western section was completely Germanized and the number of Sorbian speakers greatly reduced. The eastern section experienced a similar process after 1871. The region's Sorb inhabitants were suppressed again by Adolf Hitler in the late 1930s. After World War II, the western and central portions of Lusatia were incorporated into East Germany in 1949, and the Sorbs were guaranteed the right to use their language and to maintain their distinctive culture. The eastern portion became part of Poland.

Lusatian languages: *see* Sorbian languages.

Lusatian Mountains, Czech LUŽICKÉ HORY, German LAUSITZER GEBIRGE, mountain group, situated in extreme northern Bohemia, Czech Republic; it is part of the Sudeten mountains (Czech: Sudety). The group extends from the Ještěd ridge in the east (3,320 feet [1,012 m]) to the gorge of the Elbe (Labe) River at Děčín in the west and also into Poland and Germany. Sandstone is the group's most common constituent rock, but there are also volcanic rock formations in conical hills. The Lusatian Mountains are separated from the Jizera Mountains (Jizerské hory) by the Neisse (Nisa) River.

Luscinus, Gaius Fabricius: *see* Fabricius Luscinus, Gaius.

Lushai, also spelled LUSHEI (people): *see* Mīzo.

Lushai Hills (India): *see* Mizo Hills.

Lusignan FAMILY, noble family of Poitou (a province of western France) that provided numerous crusaders and kings of Jerusalem, Cyprus, and Lesser Armenia. A branch of the family became counts of La Marche and Angoulême and played a role in precipitating the baronial revolt in England against King Henry III. The castle of Lusignan is associated with the medieval legend of Mélusine.

Hugh (Hugues) I, lord of Lusignan, was a vassal of the counts of Poitiers in the 10th century. Early members of the family participated in the Crusades, but it was Hugh VIII's sons who established the family fortunes.

Hugh VIII's eldest son and successor, Hugh IX the Brown (d. 1219), held the countship of La Marche. In 1200 his fiancée, Isabella of Angoulême, was taken for wife by his feudal lord, King John of England. This outrage caused Hugh to turn to the king of France, Philip II Augustus, forming an alliance that culminated in John's loss of his continental possessions.

John, in an attempt to pacify Hugh, gave his daughter Joan as fiancée to Hugh X (d. 1249), but the marriage never took place. Instead, after John's death, Hugh X married his widow, Isabella, in 1220. Hugh and Isabella fluctuated in their loyalty to John's successor (Isabella's son), Henry III. When Louis IX of France granted Poitou as a countship to his brother Alphonse, Hugh at first supported him. Isabella's anger caused a turnabout and, eventually, brought about a disastrous revolt supported by Henry III. In this revolt Hugh lost his principal strongholds, but Louis IX pardoned the Lusignans, and they swore loyalty again.

Nine children were born to Isabella and Hugh X, five of whom went to England at the invitation of their half brother, Henry III. There they were rewarded with lands, riches, and distinctions at the expense of the English barons, who eventually revolted against Henry and forced the exile of the Lusignan brothers from England in 1258. Hugh XIII (d. 1303) pledged La Marche and Angoulême to Philip IV the Fair of France.

Two other sons of Hugh VIII became kings of Jerusalem and Cyprus. Guy (*c.* 1129–94), through his marriage to Sibyl, the sister of King Baldwin IV of Jerusalem, got the kingdom in 1186 but lost his capital city in wars with the Muslims (1187) and finally exchanged his empty title for the sovereignty of Cyprus (1192).

Guy's brother Amalric (Amaury) II (d. April 1, 1205) succeeded to the crown of Cyprus and became king of Jerusalem in 1197 by marrying Sibyl's sister Isabella after the death of her two previous husbands. Amalric was the founder of a dynasty of sovereigns of Cyprus lasting until 1475, when Cyprus was ceded to Venice. His descendants after 1269 regularly enjoyed the title of king of Jerusalem. Among the most famous members of the house who ruled in Cyprus was Peter I (Pierre I; d. 1369), who set forth on various expeditions against the Muslims in a last attempt to gain the Holy Lands. He was assassinated by discontented nobles in Cyprus.

Lusitani, an Iberian people living in what is now Portugal who resisted Roman penetration in the 2nd century BC. It is uncertain to what extent the Lusitani were Celticized, though they may have been related to the Celtic Lusones of northeastern Iberia. They first clashed with the Romans in 194 BC and joined the Celtiberians in a war against the Roman presence that lasted until 179 BC.

War broke out again in 153 BC, and under the leadership of Viriathus, an excellent strategist who managed to unite many Celtiberian tribes against the Romans, the Lusitani inflicted a series of defeats (*c.* 147–*c.* 139) on Roman troops from their military camp on the Hill of Venus (Sierra S. Vincente in Spain). After Viriathus was assassinated by his aides at Roman instigation, the Lusitanians were subdued. The name Lusitania was given to a Roman province later established (27 BC) in central Portugal.

Lusitania, British ocean liner, the sinking of which by a German submarine on May 7, 1915, contributed indirectly to the entry of the United States into World War I. The 32,000-ton ship was returning from New York to Liverpool, with 1,959 passengers and crew on board. The sinkings of merchant ships off the south coast of Ireland and reports of submarine activity there prompted the British Admiralty to warn the *Lusitania* to avoid the area and to recommend adopting the evasive tactic of zigzagging, changing course every few minutes at irregular intervals to confuse any attempt by U-boats to plot her course for torpedoing. The ship's crew chose to ignore these recommendations, and on the afternoon of May 7, 1915, the vessel was attacked. A torpedo struck and exploded amidships on the starboard side, followed by a heavier explosion, probably of the ship's boilers. Within 20 minutes the vessel had sunk, and 1,198 people were drowned. The loss of the liner and so many of its passengers, including 128 U.S. citizens, aroused a wave of indignation in the United States, and it was fully expected that a declaration of war would follow, but the U.S. government clung to its policy of neutrality.

The *Lusitania* was also carrying a cargo of rifle ammunition and shells (together about 173 tons), and the Germans, who had circulated warnings that the ship would be sunk, felt themselves fully justified in attacking a vessel that was furthering the war aims of their enemy. The German government also felt that, in view of the vulnerability of U-boats while on the surface and the British announcement of intentions to arm merchant ships, prior warning of potential targets was impractical. On May 13, 1915, the U.S. government sent a note to Berlin expressing an indictment of the principles on which the submarine war was being fought, but this note and two following ones constituted the immediate limit of U.S. reaction to the *Lusitania* incident. Later, in 1917, however, the United States did cite German submarine warfare as a justification for American entry into the war.

lussatite, a widespread silica mineral, the fibrous variety of low-temperature cristobalite (*compare* opal) that occurs with opal and chalcedony near the surface of low-temperature hydrothermal deposits. Originally found in the bitumen veins at Lussat, Fr. (whence its name), it also occurs in the Czech Republic, Austria, and Hungary. For detailed physical properties, *see* silica mineral (table).

Lussy, Melchior (b. 1529, Stans, Switz.—d. Nov. 14, 1606, Stans), Roman Catholic partisan and champion of the Counter-Reformation in Switzerland who was one of the most important Swiss political leaders in the latter half of the 16th century.

Representative of the Catholic cantons at the Council of Trent and at the courts of four popes—Paul IV, Pius IV, Gregory XIII, and Gregory XIV—Lussy devoted much of his life to the furtherance of papal interests. Serving in the army of the Papal States (1557) and later in that of Venice (1560), he secured a substantial fortune from the sale of Swiss mercenaries into the pope's service. Lussy was a personal friend of Charles Borromeo, cardinal archbishop of Milan, and played a major role in implementing the reforms of Trent in Catholic Switzerland. In his native Unterwalden, he ruled as a virtual dictator. He also served on numerous diplomatic missions, most frequently in the cause of Catholicism.

Lustenau, town, Vorarlberg *Bundesland* (federal state), western Austria, on the Rhine River, just west of Dornbirn. First mentioned in 887, it later became an imperial free city (until 1803) and passed to Austria in 1814. A customs station on the Swiss border, Lustenau has a well-known embroidery industry and manufactures textiles and metal products. Pop. (1991) 18,579.

lustration (from Latin *lustratio,* "purification by sacrifice"), any of various processes in ancient Greece and Rome whereby individuals or communities rid themselves of ceremonial impurity (*e.g.,* bloodguilt, pollution incurred by contact with childbirth or with a corpse) or simply of the profane or ordinary state, which made it dangerous to come into contact with sacred rites or objects. The methods varied from sprinkling with or washing in water, through rubbing with various substances, such as blood or clay, to complicated ceremonies, some of which involved confession of sins. Fumigation was also used.

When a community was to be purified, either from collective guilt or from the accumulated ill luck and ill-doing of a period of time, different processes were used from culture to culture. The usual Greek method, for instance, seems to have been to lead through the village certain persons or animals capable of absorbing the pollution and then to lead them out of the city. In Rome, purifying materials were led or carried around the person or community in question. Many noteworthy public rites were of this kind, such as the Lupercalia (around the Palatine hill) and the *amburbium* ("around the city").

lustre, in mineralogy, the appearance of a mineral surface in terms of its light-reflective qualities. Lustre depends upon a mineral's refractive power, diaphaneity (degree of transparency), and structure. Variations in these properties produce different kinds of lustre, whereas variations in the quantity of reflected light produce different intensities of the same lustre. The kind and intensity of lustre is the same for crystal faces of like symmetry but may be different on those with different symmetry.

The kinds of lustre are usually described as follows (the prefix "sub-," as in submetallic, is used to express imperfect lustre of the kind): metallic (the lustre of metals—*e.g.,* gold, tin, copper; minerals with a metallic lustre are usually opaque and have refractive indices near 2.5); adamantine (nearly metallic lustre of diamond and other transparent or translucent minerals with high refractive indices [between 1.9 and 2.5] and relatively great density—*e.g.,* cerussite and other compounds of lead); vitreous (the lustre of broken glass—the most common lustre in the mineral kingdom; it occurs in translucent and transparent minerals with refractive indices between 1.3 and 1.8, as in quartz); resinous (the lustre of yellow resins—*e.g.,* sphalerite); greasy (the lustre of oiled surfaces—*e.g.,* nepheline, cerargyrite); pearly (like pearl or mother-of-pearl—*e.g.,* talc; surfaces parallel to a perfect cleavage exhibit this lustre, which results from the repeated reflections from minute cleavage cracks); silky (like silk—*e.g.,* satin spar; minerals with a fibrous structure have this lustre); dull, or earthy (without lustre—*e.g.,* chalk).

lustred glass, art glass in the Art Nouveau style. It is a delicately iridescent glass with rich colours. Lustred glass was first produced in the United States by Louis Comfort Tiffany during the late 1800s for use as windowpanes. The intention of the inventor of Tiffany lustred glass, Arthur J. Nash, was to recreate artificially the natural iridescent sheen produced by the corrosion of ancient buried glassware, such as that unearthed near Roman ruins. In 1893 Tiffany founded the Stourbridge Glass Company in Long Island, N.Y., to produce decorative lustred glassware, including drinking glasses, bowls, vases, lamps, and jewelry. Because of the tremendous popularity of this glassware, known by the trade name Favrile glass, the Stourbridge firm and other Tiffany companies continued to make thousands of lustred glass articles annually until 1933.

Bowl of Favrile lustred glass by Louis Comfort Tiffany, *c.* 1900; in the Corning Museum of Glass, Corning, N.Y.

By courtesy of the Corning Museum of Glass, Corning, N.Y.

Although Tiffany lustred glass was inspired by the metallized glassware produced in the 1870s in Paris and Vienna, it differed from the European variety in that it had a pearl-like sheen rather than a mirrorlike finish. This variation resulted largely from differences in the type and colour of the glass to which the metallic lustre pigments were applied. On transparent glass, such as was used in Europe, the effect is a brilliant iridescence, but on opaque glass, which Tiffany employed, the effect is a soft, satiny sheen. Lustre applied to glass that is both transparent and yellow in colour produces gold, while transparent cobalt-blue glass sandwiched between two layers of transparent yellow glass turns to a deep and iridescent blue when lustred.

Among Tiffany's more intricately and lavishly lustred wares is a textured variety. The textured surface was created by rolling glass, while still hot, over multicoloured crushed glass and by inducing and breaking bubbles on its surface. In another elaborate form of lustred ware, the opaque glass body is decorated with threads or patches of both transparent and coloured glass that produce contrasting effects of brilliance and subdued sheen when coated with a metallic compound.

See also Art Nouveau.

lustreware, type of pottery ware decorated with metallic lustres by techniques dating at least from the 9th century. One technique of Middle Eastern origin, which produced the famous Hispano-Moresque pottery in Spain and Italian and Spanish majolica, involved a multistaged process that produced a kind of staining of the ware. In a second type of lustreware, which was cheaper and less complicated, pigments containing salts of gold and platinum were used. Although inspired by the late 18th-century Spanish majolica dishes, it was an English invention that found its widest and most economical application throughout the 19th century.

Lustreware
(Top) Persian lustreware jug from Rayy, Iran, *c.* 1200; (bottom) pearlware jug decorated in platinum ("poor man's silver") lustre and underglaze blue, Staffordshire, England, early 19th century; both in the Victoria and Albert Museum, London
By courtesy of the Victoria and Albert Museum, London

Among the lustres produced in Spain were golden-greenish–tinged and tarnished-copper lustres, which in the 17th century tended to be replaced by bright-red copper lustres; in 16th-century Italy, ruby-red or golden-yellow lustres with nacreous reflections predominated. Because of a scarcity of gold during the Napoleonic Wars, most potters turned to a silver lustre that was produced with platinum chloride and was known as "poor man's silver" for its resemblance to the more expensive Sheffield plate.

Lūt Desert, Persian DASHT-E LŪT, also spelled DASHT-I LŪT, desert in eastern Iran. It stretches about 200 miles (320 km) from northwest to southeast and is about 100 miles wide. In the east a great massif of dunes and sand rises, while in the west an extensive area of high ridges is separated by wind-swept corridors. In its lowest, salt-filled depression—less than 1,000 feet (300 m) above sea level—the summer heat and low humidity are believed to be unsurpassed anywhere.

lute, plucked, stringed musical instrument popular in 16th- and 17th-century Europe. The lute that was prominent in European popular art and music of the Renaissance and Baroque periods originated as the Arab *ʿūd.* This instrument was brought to Europe in the 13th century by way of Spain and by returning crusaders and is still played in Arab countries. Like the *ʿūd,* the European lute has a deep, pear-shaped body, a neck with a bent-back pegbox, and strings hitched to a tension, or guitar-type, bridge glued to the instrument's belly. European lutes have a large, circular sound hole cut into the belly and ornamented with a perforated rose carved from the belly's wood.

The earliest European lutes followed the Arab instruments in having four strings plucked with a quill plectrum. By the mid-14th century the strings had become pairs, or courses. During the 15th century the plectrum was abandoned in favour of playing with the fingers, movable gut frets were added to the fingerboard, and the instrument acquired a fifth course. By the 16th century the classic form of the lute was established, with its six courses of strings (the top course a single string) tuned to G–c–f–a–d′–g′, beginning with the second G below middle C. Playing technique was systematized, and the music was written in tablature (a system of notation in which a staff of horizontal lines represented the courses of the lute), and letters or figures placed on the lines denoted the fret to be stopped and the strings to be plucked by the right hand.

By 1600 the great Bolognese and Venetian schools of lute makers had arisen, including Laux and Sigismond Maler, Hans Frei, Nikolaus Schonfeld, and the Tieffenbruckers. By the fine workmanship and tonal proportions of their instruments, they contributed much to the popularity of the lute and paved the way for its extensive and noble literature of solo music (fantasias, dance movements, chanson arrangements), song accompaniments, and consort music by such composers as Luis Milán and John Dowland.

After about 1600, modified tunings were introduced by French lutenists. At the same time, the lute itself was altered by the addition of bass strings, or diapasons, which required the enlargement of the neck and head of the instrument. Such modified instruments were called archlutes and included the chitarrone and the theorbo (*qq.v.*).

A smaller archlute, known as the theorbo-lute (so called because it resembled the theorbo), or French lute, was used by the 17th-century French school of lutenists, including Jacques and Denys Gaultier. This instrument's repertory required a highly mannered and ornamented style of performance and a new technique of broken chords and slurred notes that exerted a marked influence on 17th-century harpsichord composers.

By the 18th century, keyboard instruments eclipsed the lute in popularity. Twentieth-century lutenists such as Julian Bream and Walter Gerwig successfully revived the lute and its repertory.

Angel playing a lute, from "Presentation in the Temple," painted altarpiece by Vittore Carpaccio, 1510; in the Accademia, Venice
SCALA—Art Resource

Generically, "lute" refers to any chordophone whose strings are parallel to its belly, or soundboard, and run along a distinct neck. In this sense, instruments such as the Indian sitar are classified as lutes. Lutes that are bowed rather than plucked are called fiddles.

luteinizing hormone (LH), also called INTERSTITIAL-CELL STIMULATING HORMONE (ICSH), one of two gonadotropic hormones (*i.e.,* hormones concerned with the regulation of the gonads, or sex glands) that is produced by the pituitary gland. LH is a glycoprotein and operates in conjunction with follicle-stimulating hormone (FSH). Following the release of the egg (ovulation) in the female, LH promotes the transformation of the graafian follicle (a small egg-containing vesicle in the ovary) into the corpus luteum, an endocrine gland that secretes progesterone. In the male, LH stimulates the development of the interstitial cells of the testes, which secrete testosterone, a male sex hormone. The production of LH is cyclical in nature (especially in the female). *See also* follicle-stimulating hormone; menstruation.

luteotropic hormone, also called LUTEOTROPIN: *see* prolactin.

Lutero, Giovanni: *see* Dosso Dossi.

Lutetian Stage, the second of four stages in the Eocene Series, representing all those rocks deposited on a global basis during the Lutetian Age (52 to 43.6 million years ago). Together with the overlying Bartonian Stage, the Lutetian Stage constitutes the Middle Eocene.

The stage's name is derived from Lutetia, the ancient Latin name for Paris, France, whose surrounding area is usually considered the type district for the stage. Traditionally, the base of the Calcaire Grossier formation has been used to define the base of the Lutetian Stage; however, no global stratotype section and point (GSSP) has been defined. The Lutetian Stage often is taken to embrace three foraminiferal biozones (in ascending order): *Hantkenina aragonensis, Globigerinatheka subconglobata,* and *Morozovella lehneri.*

lutetium (Lu), chemical element, rare-earth metal of transition Group IIIb of the periodic table; the hardest and densest rare-earth element, last member of the lanthanide series. Lutetium was discovered (1907–08) by Carl Auer von Welsbach and Georges Urbain, working independently. Urbain derived the name for the element from Lutetia, which was the ancient Roman name for Paris. The name Urbain gave it to honour Paris, his native city, became widely accepted, except in Germany, where it was commonly called cassiopeium until the 1950s. One of the rarest of the rare earths, lutetium occurs in rare-earth minerals such as xenotime and euxenite. Though it composes only about 0.003 percent of the commercially important mineral monazite, it has proved feasible to extract it as a by-product. Separation and purification are accomplished by ion-exchange techniques. Lutetium is also found in the products of nuclear fission. The metal has been prepared by thermoreduction of the anhydrous halides by alkali or alkaline-earth metals. It has the highest melting point of the rare-earth elements. Natural lutetium consists of two isotopes: stable lutetium-175 (97.41 percent) and radioactive lutetium-176 (2.59 percent, 3×10^{10}-year half-life). The radioactive isotope is used to determine the age of meteorites relative to that of the Earth. Few other uses have been found for lutetium.

The element behaves as a typical trivalent rare earth, forming a series of white salts such as lutetium oxide, sulfate, and chloride.

atomic number	71
atomic weight	174.970
melting point	1,656° C
boiling point	3,315° C
specific gravity	9.835 (25° C)
valence	3
electronic config.	2-8-18-32-9-2 or (Xe)$4f^{14}5d^{1}6s^{2}$

Luṭfī as-Sayyid, Aḥmad (b. Jan. 15, 1872, Egypt—d. March 5, 1963, Egypt), journalist and lawyer, a leading spokesman for Egyptian modernism in the first half of the 20th century.

Luṭfī studied law and accepted a job in the legal department of the central government. In March 1907 he founded a newspaper, *al-Jarīdah,* to present the views of the Ummah Party, representing the moderate wing of Egyptian nationalism. With the advent of World War I (1914–18), British authorities in Egypt imposed a rigid censorship, and Luṭfī resigned his position as editor of *al-Jarīdah.* At the end of the war he served on an Egyptian delegation that negotiated with Britain for the end of the British occupation of Egypt. Bickering among the various Egyptian factions during these talks hardened Luṭfī's determination to avoid direct political involvement, and he concerned himself instead with the needs of the people and the affairs of the University of Cairo.

In Luṭfī's view Egypt suffered from a deficiency in national character, most notably evidenced in the servility of the people before governmental authority. He believed that the root of the problem lay in the fact that Egypt had always had an autocratic government, which encouraged a low level of social and political independence. He thus wanted to train the public to bear the responsibilities of government. He favoured the liberation of women from their traditional inferior status in Islāmic society, and he advocated the assimilation of the technical progress of Western civilization. He also sought for remedies in the education of the population, from the peasant to the urban bureaucrat. Until his retirement in 1942 Luṭfī devoted his energies to encouraging Egyptian social and moral growth.

Luther, Hans (b. March 10, 1879, Berlin, Ger.—d. May 11, 1962, Düsseldorf, W.Ger.), German statesman who was twice chancellor (1925, 1926) of the Weimar Republic and who helped bring Germany's disastrous post-World War I inflation under control.

After studying law at Berlin, Kiel, and Geneva, Luther joined the local civil service in Berlin. From 1907 to 1913 he was stationed at Magdeburg. In 1913 he was elected secretary to the German Städtetag, which was a nationwide council of various city government representatives. In 1918 he was elected mayor (burgomaster) of Essen. There he gained a reputation as one of the best local administrative officials in the western part of Germany. Luther was appointed minister of food and agriculture under Chancellor Wilhelm Cuno in December 1922. Under Cuno's successor, Gustav Stresemann (October 1923), Luther was named finance minister and successfully met the task of stabilizing the inflated national currency—with the help of Hjalmar Schacht, later Adolf Hitler's minister of economics. He kept his finance ministry post in the Wilhelm Marx ministry that followed, and at this time he took part in negotiating a new war-reparations settlement for Germany—the Dawes Plan (1924).

After the elections of December 1924 Marx was unable to form a new Cabinet, and so Luther was appointed chancellor of Germany in January 1925. As chancellor, Luther carried through significant taxation and trade measures, but his most important achievement came when he joined with his foreign minister, Stresemann, in securing Germany's adhesion to the various treaties known as the Locarno Pact (December 1925). Resigning immediately after the Locarno signings, he was quickly recalled (January 1926) to form a short-lived minority Cabinet that fell in May 1926. In 1930 he succeeded Schacht as president of the Reichsbank (Germany's central bank), and in 1933–37 he was German ambassador to the United States. He resigned in the latter year and lived in retirement throughout World War II. In the postwar years he taught at the Munich Academy of Political Sciences and served as an informal adviser to the West German government.

Luther, Martin (b. Nov. 10, 1483, Eisleben, Saxony [Germany]—d. Feb. 18, 1546, Eisleben), German preacher, biblical scholar, and linguist whose Ninety-five Theses, an attack on various Roman Catholic ecclesiastical abuses, precipitated the Protestant Reformation.

A brief treatment of Martin Luther follows. For full treatment, *see* MACROPAEDIA: Luther.

Luther, the son of a miner who wanted him to become a lawyer, attended the University of Erfurt (B.A., 1502; M.A., 1505). In 1505 he joined the monastic order of the Augustinian eremites, and he was ordained a priest in 1507. From 1508 to 1546 he taught at the newly founded University of Wittenberg. He received a doctorate in theology in 1512 and was appointed to the chair of biblical theology at Wittenberg that same year. The exposition of the Bible to his students was a task that called forth his best gifts and energies. In between lectures, so to speak, he began the Protestant Reformation.

In his search for salvation, Luther minutely attempted to fulfill the rule of his order. Nonetheless, he soon found himself struggling against uncertainties and doubts. His spiritual dilemma stemmed from his increasing difficulties with medieval Roman Catholic theology. The turning point for him came when he discovered the message of grace, according to which the sinner is saved by God through faith alone—not by his own actions. The great courses of lectures that Luther delivered at this time on the Psalms (1513–15), Romans (1515–16), Galatians (1516–17), and Hebrews (1517–18) show the growing richness and maturity of his thought. Meanwhile, his other duties had accumulated. From 1511 he had been preaching in his monastery, and in 1514 he became preacher in the parish church. This pulpit became the place from which Luther expounded profoundly and beautifully the Scriptures for the common people and related them to the practical context of their lives. Within his order he had become prior and then in May 1515 district vicar over 11 other houses. Thus, he became involved in practical administration and pastoral care.

Luther, however, observed so much that he found wrong with the Roman Catholic church and the world that "for the purpose of eliciting truth" he drew up the Ninety-five Theses (in Latin). After nailing the Theses onto the door of the Wittenberg Castle Church on Oct. 31, 1517, Luther passed them on to his university colleagues. The translation of the Theses into German immediately widened the debate to a larger audience. The opinions expressed in the Theses were tentative, and Luther himself was not committed to some of them. The Theses did not deny papal prerogative, though by implication they criticized papal policy; still less did they attack such established teaching as the doctrine of purgatory. But they did stress the spiritual, inward character of the Christian religion. The invention of printing enabled copies of the Theses to be circulated far and wide, so that what might have been a mere local issue became a public controversy discussed in ever-widening circles.

The Reformation that was triggered soon spread over northern Europe. Luther's personal discovery of the doctrine of "justification by faith" alone (*c.* 1515–16 or 1518–19) led to a reformation of medieval doctrine and, along with other factors, to the rise of the Protestant churches. Luther was a prolific writer: his commentarial, polemical, and practical devotional works became the hallmark of Reformation writings, and his translation of the Bible into the vernacular German influenced German literature.

Luther v. Borden (1849), U.S. Supreme Court decision growing out of the 1842 conflict in Rhode Island called the "Dorr Rebellion."

In the spring of 1842, Rhode Island had two governors and two legislatures. One government was committed to retaining the old colonial charter, which severely limited voting rights, as the state's constitution. The other government, led by Thomas W. Dorr and providing for white manhood suffrage, took control over northwestern Rhode Island. The Dorr government eventually took military action, but its attempt to seize a state arsenal proved unsuccessful. Meanwhile, the more conservative government declared martial law. A suit arising from the conflict reached the Supreme Court.

The Court evaded the issue as to which Rhode Island government was legitimate. Chief Justice Roger B. Taney's opinion said that the president and Congress must make that decision, the Congress, under Article IV Section 4 of the Constitution, having the power to guarantee republican government in the states and to recognize lawful state governments. Taney did state, however, that existing state authority (the conservative government) was legally empowered to use martial law in the face of a violent insurrection.

Lutheran: *see* Lutheranism.

Lutheran Church in America, Lutheran church in North America that in 1988 merged with two other Lutheran churches to form the Evangelical Lutheran Church in America (*q.v.*).

Lutheran Church in Württemberg, independent Lutheran church established in the duchy of Württemberg in 1534 during the Protestant Reformation in Germany. A strong Lutheran church throughout the centuries, it was influenced in the 17th and 18th centuries by Pietism, the Lutheran-based movement that emphasized personal religious experience and reform. It became independent of the state after Germany became a republic at the end of World War I. During the Nazi period (1933–45) the church remained independent and successfully resisted the efforts of the national government to gain control of all the churches.

A bishop, elected for life, is the head of the church. Congregations belong to conferences that are combined into districts. The church is a member of the Evangelical Church in Germany (EKD), a federation of Lutheran, Reformed, and United (Reformed and Lutheran) churches. It is also a member of the World Council of Churches and the Lutheran World Federation. It did not enter the United Evangelical Lutheran Church of Germany (VELKD), a union of German Lutheran territorial churches organized in 1948.

Lutheran Church–Missouri Synod, a conservative Lutheran church in the United States, organized in Chicago in 1849 by German immigrants from Saxony (settled in Missouri) and Bavaria (settled in Michigan and Indiana) as the German Evangelical Lutheran Synod of Missouri, Ohio, and Other States. C.F.W. Walther, a seminary professor and pastor ordained in Germany, was president of the church from 1847 to 1850 and from 1864 to 1878. The church grew rapidly through an active educational and evangelistic program, by absorbing entire congregations and synods, and by meeting newly arrived German immigrants in port cities to guide them into its congregations. "German" was dropped from the name in 1917, and in 1947 the present name was adopted.

The Missouri Synod has often been involved in controversy with other Lutheran groups because of its insistence on strict conformity with its interpretation of "pure doctrine" based on the Bible and the Lutheran confessions. Until the 1960s it refused association and cooperation with all groups that it considered doctrinally in error. In 1872 it formed a loose federation (the Evangelical Lutheran Synodical Conference) with several small conservative Lutheran groups. In 1967, however, the conference dissolved when the Missouri Synod joined with the American Lutheran Church, the Lutheran Church in America, and the Synod of Evangelical Lutheran Churches (which in 1971 became part of the Missouri Synod) to form the Lutheran Council in the United States of America (LCUSA), a cooperative agency; the Missouri Synod, however, subsequently withdrew.

Beginning in 1969, when conservative elements regained policy-making positions, the Missouri Synod experienced internal strife that led to a mass exodus of faculty and students from Concordia Seminary in 1974 and the formation two years later of the Association of Evangelical Lutheran Churches by 100,000 Missouri Synod dissidents. At issue in the dispute was congregational autonomy versus synodical authority and the nature of the church's mission. The new denomination also ordained women, while the Missouri Synod did not. In 1982 the new group voted to join with two other Lutheran bodies to begin planning the formation of what became, in 1988, the Evangelical Lutheran Church in America (ELCA).

The Missouri Synod is governed through a biennial general convention and several elected officers, including a president. Congregations are grouped in geographical districts. The church supports an extensive educational system that includes parochial schools, colleges, and seminaries. Headquarters and Concordia Theological Seminary are in St. Louis, Mo.

Lutheran Church of Oldenburg, independent Lutheran church in Oldenburg, Ger. Pastors who had accepted the Lutheran faith were established in Oldenburg during the Protestant Reformation in Germany, and in 1573 an order for church government and the Lutheran confessions were accepted for the church. Until the German Republic was established after the end of World War I (1918), the church was governed by the secular head of state. After 1918 it became independent of the state, and the system of church government was reorganized. During the Nazi period (1933–45) the church attempted to resist the efforts of the secular government to control it, and after the end of World War II it experienced a period of renewal.

The head of the church is the bishop. Congregations belong to districts, each of which is headed by a superintendent. The church is a member of the Lutheran World Federation and of the Evangelical Church in Germany (EKD), a federation of Lutheran, Reformed, and United (Lutheran and Reformed) territorial churches; but it did not become part of the United Evangelical Lutheran Church of Germany, a union of Lutheran territorial churches (1948).

Lutheran Council in the United States of America (LCUSA), cooperative agency for four Lutheran churches whose membership included about 95 percent of all Lutherans in the U.S., established Jan. 1, 1967, as a successor to the National Lutheran Council (NLC). The member churches were the Lutheran Church in America, the American Lutheran Church, the Lutheran Church–Missouri Synod, and the Synod of Evangelical Lutheran Churches.

The NLC, organized in 1918, had served eight Lutheran churches as a cooperative organization and had developed various programs, including social service, missions, public relations, service to military personnel, service to students, and overseas aid. When it seemed probable in the late 1950s that the eight member churches of the NLC would merge into two churches (subsequently the American Lutheran Church [1960] and the Lutheran Church in America [1963]), it became necessary to restructure the NLC.

In 1959 the Missouri Synod accepted an invitation to consider a more inclusive Lutheran agency, and consultations in 1960 and 1961 led to agreements to establish the LCUSA. This was a breakthrough in cooperation among Lutherans in the United States, because the conservative Missouri Synod had previously refused to consider joining a cooperative agency unless doctrinal agreement had been reached by all participants. It agreed, however, to join the LCUSA when it was assured that all participants would take part in doctrinal discussions as part of the program of the council. Subsequently, the small (21,000 members in the late 1960s) Synod of Evangelical Lutheran Churches also agreed to join in forming the new council. In 1977 the Missouri Synod withdrew from the council.

The LCUSA continued much of the work of the NLC, with the added emphasis on doctrinal and theological discussions and study.

Lutheran Synodical Conference, cooperative agency organized in 1872 by several conservative U.S. Lutheran groups. Its members accepted strict conservative interpretations of the Bible and the Lutheran confessions and insisted that fellowship among Lutheran groups could take place only after agreement was reached on doctrine and church practices. Over the years some of the original members left the Synodical Conference because of doctrinal differences, and some merged into other groups, while some new groups joined the conference. One of the founding churches and always the largest member was the Lutheran Church–Missouri Synod.

In the 1950s controversies developed within the conference when the Missouri Synod adopted a more open attitude toward more liberal Lutheran groups. In 1963 the Wisconsin Synod and the Evangelical Lutheran Synod (formerly the Norwegian Synod) withdrew from the Synodical Conference, leaving only the Missouri Synod and the small Synod of Evangelical Lutheran Churches as members. The council dissolved in 1967 with the formation of the Lutheran Council in the United States of America (LCUSA).

A list of the abbreviations used in the MICROPAEDIA *will be found at the end of this volume*

Lutheran World Federation (LWF), international cooperative agency of Lutheran churches, organized at Lund, Swed., in 1947. It developed from the Lutheran World Convention, which held conventions in 1923, 1929, and 1935. The effectiveness of the Lutheran World Convention during the war years was hampered because it had no constitution or defined organization. At the Lund conference in 1947 the Lutheran World Convention was reorganized into the Lutheran World Federation and a constitution was adopted.

The LWF is a free association of churches, whose combined membership approaches 55,000,000, and it cannot dictate to or interfere in the autonomy of the member churches. In its early years it was extensively involved in aiding refugees and others who had suffered because of World War II. Its various activities include mission, social welfare, and educational programs. Through theological study and discussion it encourages Lutheran fellowship and unity and ecumenical activities.

Since its founding in 1947 the LWF has held world assemblies, which are called by the president at intervals ranging from five to seven years. The president and other members of the executive committee are elected by the world assembly. The executive committee meets annually and is responsible for electing the general secretary, who is a full-time employee of the organization. Headquarters are in Geneva.

Lutheranism, the branch of the Western Christian church that adopted the religious principles of Martin Luther, as opposed to those of the Roman Catholic Church and of the followers of John Calvin, the Anglican Communion, and the sectaries of the Reformation period. Lutheran churches often term themselves Evangelical as distinct from Reformed, but these uses are not always strictly applied.

A brief treatment of Lutheranism follows. For full treatment, *see* MACROPAEDIA: Protestantism: *Lutheran churches.*

Lutheranism cannot be defined or understood without some reference to the personal experience and the biblical studies of Luther, which came to voice in 1517 in his famous Ninety-five Theses for debate over indulgences and in his attack on the theology and sacramental practice of the late medieval church of the West. In 1521 Luther was excommunicated; his followers accepted the designation "Lutheran" in part against his will and in spite of the fact that it was filled, in many instances, with implications of derision and sectarianism. The Lutheran movement spread from the University of Wittenberg through much of Germany and into Scandinavia, where it was established by law.

The theological vigour of Luther's generation gave way to an arid orthodoxy in the late 16th and 17th centuries. This in turn precipitated a pietist reaction that asserted the need for living faith in addition to right doctrine (*see* Pietism). The Pietists encouraged missionary and charitable work in addition to devotional practice. Eighteenth-century Lutheranism was marked by Rationalist influences. Orthodoxy was reasserted during the next century, notably by the Danish bishop and poet N.F.S. Grundtvig. Grundtvig's contemporary and countryman Søren Kierkegaard criticized orthodoxy and the state church through a highly personalized philosophy that was to form the basis of Existentialism.

In America, Lutherans were among the earliest colonists to settle in New Netherland and New Sweden (on the Delaware River), and they were followed by German colonists who settled especially in the present Middle Atlantic states, the Shenandoah Valley, Georgia, and Nova Scotia, Canada. Because of some geographic and much linguistic isolation and because the majority of American Protestantism was at first of Reformed background, Lutheranism did not play a major role in shaping the early political and religious complexion of the nation.

The geographic spread of Lutheranism in the United States was extended by migrations to the western frontier and by the large immigrations during the 19th and early 20th centuries of Germans, Norwegians, Swedes, Danes, and Finns. Many of these immigrants settled in the Midwest, and from there later pushed on to the far West. Since immigrants brought with them from Europe a variety of languages and customs, they organized in congregations and later synods according to their national origins. It was largely the prolongation of linguistic and ethnic barriers that prevented Lutheran union until well into the 20th century, when the barriers broke down and advance into intra-Lutheran ecumenical relations became rapid.

Lutheran doctrinal statements are usually said to include nine separate formulations that together form the Book of Concord. Three belong to the early Christian church—the Apostles' Creed, the Nicene Creed in its western form, and the so-called Athanasian Creed. Six derive from the 16th-century Reformation—the Augsburg Confession, the Apology for the Augsburg Confession, the Schmalkald Articles, Luther's two Catechisms, and the Formula of Concord. Only the three early creeds and the Augsburg Confession are recognized by all Lutherans. Luther's Catechisms have met almost universal acceptance, but many Lutheran churches rejected the Formula of Concord because of its strict and detailed doctrinal statements. The Augsburg Confession and Luther's Small Catechism may properly be said to define Lutheranism inclusively in its doctrinal aspect, though Lutherans may be divided on many issues raised since the Augsburg Confession of 1530.

The largest and one of the oldest of non-Roman Catholic, non-Orthodox families of Christians, Lutheranism is represented in most areas of the world, but its particular geographic orientation has been in northern and western Europe and in younger countries settled by Germans and Scandinavians. It has been represented with less strength in Switzerland, the Low Countries, and Scotland, where Reformed confessions predominated, and it has been a secondary influence in the British empire and the Commonwealth of Nations, where the Anglican communion has prevailed. Because of early and persistent efforts of continental missionary societies and later separate Lutheran denominations, Lutheranism has been significantly represented in the mission fields and in the formation of what were formerly called the younger churches.

Lutheranism acknowledges no world headquarters, but the vast majority of the world's Lutherans cooperate in the Lutheran World Federation, which has offices in Geneva.

Lutherbourg, Philip James de (Romantic painter): *see* Loutherbourg, Philip James de.

lutite, any fine-grained sedimentary rock consisting of clay- or silt-sized particles (less than 0.063 mm [0.0025 inch] in diameter) that are derived principally from nonmarine (continental) rocks. Laminated lutites and lutites that are fissile—*i.e.,* easily split into thin layers—are called shales. Nonfissile lutites composed primarily of clay-sized particles (less than 0.0039 mm in diameter) are called claystones, those composed primarily of silt-sized particles are termed siltstones, and those composed of indeterminate mixtures are sometimes named mudstones. The nomenclature is imprecise, however, and the terms lutite, claystone, mudstone, siltstone, and shale have overlapping usages.

Luton, town and unitary authority, geographic and historic county of Bedfordshire, England. It lies along England's chief superhighway (M1), 30 miles (48 km) northwest of London. Long famous for the manufacture of straw hats, Luton is now an industrial town dominated by the motor vehicle industry. The hat industry still prospers, with felt hats as the principal product. South of the town, the mansion of Luton Hoo houses the Wernher collection of porcelain, enamel, and other art treasures. Area 17 square miles (43 square km). Pop. (1998 est.) 183,300.

Lutosławski, Witold (b. Jan. 25, 1913, Warsaw, Pol.—d. Feb. 7, 1994, Warsaw), outstanding Polish composer of the 20th century.

Lutosławski studied theory and composition at the Warsaw Conservatory and mathematics at the University of Warsaw, subsequently taking an active role in Polish musical life. His early works tend to be conservative in style, basically within the system of traditional Western tonality, sometimes using material from Polish folk tunes. The *Symphonic Variations* (1938) and *Variations on a Theme of Paganini* for two pianos (1941) demonstrate Lutosławski's early dependence on traditional forms.

Lutosławski spoke of his *Funeral Music* (1958) for string orchestra as marking a turning point in his style; dedicated to the memory of the Hungarian composer Béla Bartók, it is a 12-tone work that received recognition from the United Nations Educational, Scientific, and Cultural Organization's Tribune Internationale des Compositeurs. It was followed by Lutosławski's first use of aleatory (chance) operations in combination with conventional effects, in *Venetian Games,* written for the Venice Festival of 1961. In this work Lutosławski used non-staff, optically suggestive notation to guide the performer in the various improvisatory operations.

Lutosławski is best known for his orchestral works. Other works include piano pieces, children's songs, choral works, and a string quartet (1964). He was honoured with a government prize in 1955, soon after composing his *Concerto for Orchestra,* based on folk themes. Lutosławski's later works include *Symphony No. 2* (1967), *Concerto for Cello and Orchestra* (1970), *Symphony No. 3* (1983), and *Chain 2* (1985).

Lutsk, also spelled LUCK, Polish ŁUCK, German LUCK, city and centre of Volyn *oblast* (province), Ukraine, on a defensive site at a bend in the Styr River. It is an old city, probably founded about AD 1000 by Prince Vladimir of Kiev. It then became a part of the Principality of Galicia-Volhynia and until the late 18th century was in Lithuania-Poland, when it fell into Russian hands. Lutsk belonged to Poland again in 1919–39. The older part of the city contains the 14th-century Lyubart Castle and much old architecture. Three monasteries date from the 16th to the 18th century.

Today Lutsk is an industrial centre specializing in scientific instruments, food, and other light industries. Trucks are manufactured, and an automobile plant was constructed in the late 1970s to build the Volynyanka, a multipurpose vehicle for rural use. A teacher-training institute and a medical school are also located there. Pop. (1998 est.) 217,900.

Luttelton, Sir Thomas: *see* Littleton, Sir Thomas.

Lüttich (city, Belgium): *see* Liège.

Lutuli, Albert (John Mvumbi), Lutuli also spelled LUTHULI (b. 1898, Rhodesia—d. July 21, 1967, Stanger, S.Af.), Zulu chief, teacher and religious leader, and president of the African National Congress (1952–60) in South Africa. He was the first African to be awarded the Nobel Prize for Peace (1960), in recognition of his nonviolent struggle against racial discrimination.

Albert John Mvumbi (Zulu: "Continuous Rain") Lutuli was born in Rhodesia, where his father, John Bunyan Lutuli, a missionary interpreter, had gone from Zululand. After his father's death, the 10-year-old Albert returned to South Africa and learned Zulu traditions and duties in the household of his uncle, the chief of Groutville, a community associated with an American Congregational mission in Natal's sugar lands. Educated through his mother's earnings as a washerwoman and by a scholarship, he was graduated from the American Board Mission's teacher-training college at Adams, near Durban, and became one of its first three African instructors. In 1927 Lutuli married Nokukhanya Bhengu, a teacher and granddaughter of a clan chief.

In 1936 Lutuli left teaching to become the elected chief of the community of 5,000 at Groutville. Though confronted by land hunger, poverty, and political voicelessness, he did not yet recognize the need for political action. In those early years he was, variously, secretary of the Natal African Teachers' Association and of the South African Football Association, founder of the Zulu Language and Cultural Society, and member of the Christian Council Executive, of the Joint Council of Europeans and Africans, and of the Institute of Race Relations in Durban.

Lutuli's first political step in joining the African National Congress (ANC) in 1945 was motivated by friendship with its Natal leader; far more significant was his election to the Natives Representative Council (an advisory body of chiefs and intellectuals set up by the government), at the very time in 1946 when troops and police were crushing a strike of African miners at the cost of eight lives and nearly a thousand injured. Lutuli immediately joined his people's protest against the council's futility. When he toured America in 1948 as a guest of the Congregational Board of Missions, he warned that Christianity faced its severest test in Africa because of racial discrimination. On his return home he found that

Lutuli, 1961
PHOTOWORLD—FPG

the Afrikaner Nationalists had newly come to power with their policy of apartheid.

At this crucial time, Lutuli was elected president of the Natal African National Congress. Since its founding in 1912 the ANC's efforts to achieve human rights by deputation, petition, or mass protests had met with increasing repression. In 1952, stimulated by young black intellectuals, the ANC joined the South African Indian Congress in a countrywide campaign to defy what were deemed unjust laws; 8,500 men and women went voluntarily to prison. As a result of Lutuli's leadership in Natal, the government demanded that he resign from the ANC or from chieftainship. He refused to do either, stating, "the road to freedom is via the cross." The government deposed him. Not only did he continue to be affectionately regarded as "chief" but his reputation spread. In that same year, 1952, the ANC elected him president general. Henceforth, between repeated bans (under the Suppression of Communism Act), he attended gatherings, visited towns, and toured the country to address mass meetings (despite a serious illness in 1954).

In December 1956 Lutuli and 155 others were dramatically rounded up and charged with high treason. His long trial failed to prove treason, a Communist conspiracy, or violence, and in 1957 he was released. During this time Lutuli's quiet authority and his inspiration to others profoundly impressed distinguished foreign observers, leading to his nomination for the Nobel Prize. Nonwhite people responded in large numbers to his call for a stay-at-home strike in 1957; later, whites also began attending his mass meetings. In 1959 the government confined him to his rural neighbourhood and banned him from gatherings—this time for five years—for "promoting feelings of hostility" between the races.

In 1960, when police shot down Africans demonstrating against the pass laws at Sharpeville, Lutuli called for national mourning, and he himself burned his pass. (Too ill to serve the resulting prison sentence, he paid a fine.) The government outlawed the ANC and its rival offshoot, the Pan-Africanist Congress.

In December 1961 Lutuli was allowed to leave Groutville briefly when, with his wife, he flew to Oslo to receive the Nobel Prize. His acceptance address paid tribute to his people's nonviolence and rejection of racialism despite adverse treatment, and he noted how far from freedom they remained despite their long struggle. A week later, throughout South Africa, a sabotage group called the Spear of the Nation attacked installations; the policy of nonviolence had at last been abandoned, and Lutuli, back in enforced isolation, was an honoured elder statesman, dictating his autobiography and receiving only those visitors permitted by the police.

On July 21, 1967, as he made a habitual crossing of a railway bridge near his small farm, Chief Lutuli was struck by a train and died. (D.M.B.)

BIBLIOGRAPHY. Albert Lutuli, *Let My People Go* (1962), a comprehensive autobiography; Mary Benson, *Chief Albert Lutuli of South Africa* (1963), a short biography, and *South Africa: Struggle for a Birthright*, rev. ed. (1969), Lutuli's life in the history of the African National Congress; Colin and Margaret Legum, *The Bitter Choice: Eight South Africans' Resistance to Tyranny* (1968), contains an essay on Lutuli.

Lutyens, Sir Edwin (Landseer) (b. March 29, 1869, London—d. Jan. 1, 1944, London), English architect noted for his versatility and range of invention along traditional lines. He is known especially for his planning of New Delhi and his design of the Viceroy's House there.

After studying at the Royal College of Art, London, he was articled in 1887 to a firm of architects but soon left to set up in practice on his own. In his early works (1888–95) he assimilated the traditional forms of local Surrey buildings. Lutyens' style changed when he met the landscape gardener Gertrude Jekyll, who taught him the "simplicity of intention and directness of purpose" she had learned from John Ruskin. At Munstead Wood, Godalming, Surrey (1896), Lutyens first showed his personal qualities as a designer. This house, balancing the sweep of the roof with high buttressed chimneys and offsetting small doorways with long strips of windows, made his reputation. A brilliant series of country houses followed in which Lutyens adapted varied styles of the past to the demands of contemporary domestic architecture.

North court of the Viceroy's House (now Rāshtrapati Bhavan, or Presidential Palace), New Delhi, by Sir Edwin Lutyens, completed 1930

About 1910 Lutyens' interest shifted to larger, civil projects, and in 1912 he was selected to advise on the planning of the new Indian capital at Delhi. His plan, with a central mall and diagonal avenues, may have owed something to Pierre-Charles L'Enfant's plan for Washington, D.C., and to Christopher Wren's plan for London after the Great Fire, but the total result was quite different: a garden-city pattern, based on a series of hexagons separated by broad avenues with double lines of trees. In his single most important building, the Viceroy's House (1913–30), he combined aspects of classical architecture with features of Indian decoration. Lutyens was knighted in 1918.

After World War I Lutyens became architect to the Imperial War Graves Commission, for which he designed the Cenotaph, London (1919–20), the Great War Stone (1919), and military cemeteries in France. His vast project for the Roman Catholic cathedral at Liverpool was incomplete at his death.

A.S.G. Butler and Christopher Hussey's *The Architecture of Edwin Lutyens* was published in 1950, and a biography by Hussey appeared in 1953.

Lützen, Battle of (Nov. 16, 1632), military engagement of the Thirty Years' War in which Gustavus II Adolphus of Sweden lost his life; it was fought by the Swedes to help their North German allies against the forces of the Holy Roman emperor Ferdinand II. Having received the information that Albrecht von Wallenstein, the imperial commander, had sent Gottfried Heinrich, Graf zu Pappenheim, with a portion of his army on a separate mission, Gustavus Adolphus, with Bernhard of Saxe-Weimar, offered Wallenstein battle outside Lützen in Saxony. Foggy weather delayed the Swedish attack, and though Pappenheim, returning with his cavalry, was mortally wounded, Wallenstein's forces were almost victorious. When the Swedish king was killed, however, Bernhard assumed command of his army, retrieved the situation along the line, and captured the entire imperial artillery. The arrival of Pappenheim's infantry allowed Wallenstein to retreat in good order.

Lützow, Adolf, Freiherr von (baron of) (b. May 18, 1782, Berlin—d. Dec. 6, 1834, Berlin), Prussian major general and a famous, though largely ineffectual, guerrilla leader during the Napoleonic Wars of 1813–15.

Lützow entered the Prussian Army in 1795 and was present at the decisive defeat of the Prussian forces by the French at Auerstädt (1806). He retired in 1808 and participated in Ferdinand von Schill's abortive popular rising against the French the next year. In 1811 Lützow reentered the Prussian Army. At the outbreak of the Wars of Liberation (1813), he received permission from Gerhard von Scharnhorst (the Prussian chief of staff) to organize a mounted free corps (called the Lützowsche Freikorps), composed mainly of non-Prussian volunteers, to operate behind the French lines. The formation eventually numbered about 3,000 and became popularly known as the Schwarze Schar ("Black Band") after its uniform, which was a symbol of mourning for enslaved Germany. The armistice of June 4, 1813, caught Lützow's group on the wrong side of the demarcation line, and it was practically annihilated. Reorganizing his unit, he again fought partisan actions, during which he was repeatedly wounded. At Ligny (June 16, 1815) Lützow led the 6th Uhlans in an abortive charge which ended in their being routed by the French cavalry. He was captured, but escaped at Waterloo on June 18. He remained in the Prussian Army after the war.

Lützow, lithograph, 1815

Luvale, also spelled LUBALE, or LOVALE, also called LWENA, or LUENA, Bantu-speaking people of northwestern Zambia and southeastern Angola. In terms of history, language, material culture, and religion, the Luvale are closely related to the Lunda and Ndembu to the northeast, who extend northward into southern Zaire. They are also culturally similar to the Kaonde to the east, and to the Chokwe and Luchazi, important groups of eastern Angola. Luvale have long differentiated themselves from Lunda, however; the politics of tribalism has led to strife between the two groups several times since the 1940s. Conflict between them is especially acute over prime agricultural lands, in an area of generally poor soils, and both groups, in turn, oppose their powerful Lozi neighbours to the south.

Seeking slaves for the Portuguese, Ovimbundu (Mbundu) traders from Angola encountered the Luvale in the upper Zambezi during the late 18th century. In exchange for guns and cloth, beads, and other trade goods, the Luvale raided their neighbours to procure slaves for the Ovimbundu. Their activities were only stopped by British conquest in the early 20th century.

The Luvale differ from other northwestern Zambian peoples in their strong lineage and clan structures. Commoner lineage groups play important social and political roles and are largely independent of the Luvale chiefs, whose formal powers are apparently limited. Matrilineal descent is observed and cross-cousin marriage preferred. Male initiation (*mukanda*) is an important experience, a rite of passage by which full manhood and attendant responsibilities are attained.

The Luvale are renowned fishermen; each year they export dried catfish to mining centres of the Copperbelt. They also have an active hunting tradition, although game has become scarce in much of their region, and they keep cattle. Cassava and corn (maize) are staple crops, with peanuts (groundnuts) and yams important as well.

The Luvale migrate to labour centres as far away as South Africa. Stigmatized as rustics, they have often been allowed access to only the most menial of jobs. Luvale is one of the eight official languages of Zambia.

Luvua River, tributary of the Lualaba River in southeastern Zaire. It issues from the northern end of Lake Mweru, on the Zaire-Zambia border, and flows about 220 miles (350 km) northwest past Kiambi to its confluence with the Lualaba River opposite Ankoro. The river is navigable by shallow-draft boats for 100 miles (160 km) in its lower course below Kiambi but contains rapids on its middle course. At Piana Mwanga the falls have been harnessed to generate electricity for the mines at Manono and Kitotolo.

Luwian, also called LUITE, member of an extinct people of ancient Anatolia. The Luwians were related to the Hittites and were the dominant group in the Late Hittite culture. Their language is known from cuneiform texts found at the Hittite capital, Boğazköy. (*See* Luwian language.)

Luwiya is mentioned as a foreign country in the Hittite laws (about 1500 BC). It probably coincided roughly with Arzawa, a large region composed of several principalities in western or southwestern Anatolia, and Kizzuwadna, a district occupying the Cilician Plain. Both Arzawa and Kizzuwadna were independent kingdoms during the Old Hittite period (*c.* 1700–*c.* 1500 BC) but later became vassals of the Hittite empire. Linguistic evidence testifies to the cultural penetration of the Hittite empire by Luwians.

After the downfall of the Hittite empire (*c.* 1180 BC), hieroglyphic inscriptions in Luwian became common in southeastern Anatolia and northern Syria, an indication of Luwian expansion into regions not previously held by them, where they formed the "Syro-Hittite," or Late Hittite, principalities. Most of the documentation on these states comes from the annals of Assyrian kings, who repeatedly raided them until Sargon II (reigned 721–705 BC) incorporated them as provinces into his empire.

The religious beliefs of the Hittites and the Luwians were similar. The chief god in both systems was a god of thunderstorm and rain, called Tarhum (Tarhund) in Luwian. The moon god had the same name, Arma, in both languages. The presence of Luwian magical rituals in the Hittite capital indicates that Luwians had a certain reputation as magicians. The Luwians assimilated the general characteristics of Hittite civilization, making it difficult to determine distinctly Luwian cultural traits. The art of the small Luwian states of the 1st millennium BC combines Hittite motifs with others of general Middle Eastern origin, its style being influenced by that of the Aramaeans and, later, of the Assyrians. The importance of the Luwians lies in their preservation of Hittite tradition for almost 500 years after the downfall of the Hittite empire.

Luwian language, also called LUVIAN, or LUISH, extinct Indo-European language primarily of the southern part of ancient Anatolia. It was closely related to Hittite, Palaic, and Lydian and was a forerunner of the Lycian language. Modern knowledge of Luwian comes primarily from passages introduced by the adverb *luwili* ("in Luwian") in cuneiform tablets discovered in the ruins of the Hittite archives at Boğazköy (in modern Turkey); these passages were spoken in the rituals of some deities. The pioneering work on Cuneiform Luwian was done by Emil Forrer in 1922.

In addition to Luwian passages in the cuneiform tablets, a number of inscriptions occur in a hieroglyphic system of writing that originated with the early Hittite stamp seals of the 17th and 18th centuries BC. Hieroglyphic Luwian (often called Hieroglyphic Hittite) texts have been found dating from as late as the last quarter of the 8th century BC. Most of the work of deciphering the language was completed in the 1930s, although more was learned about the meaning of the writing after the discovery in 1947 of the Karatepe bilingual inscriptions, written in both Hieroglyphic Luwian and Phoenician. Hieroglyphic Luwian is thought to represent an eastern dialect of Luwian, while Cuneiform Luwian represents a central dialect. The Lycian language (*q.v.*) of about 600–200 BC, written in an alphabetic script, is believed to be descended from a West Luwian dialect. *See also* Hittite language.

lux, unit of illumination in the International System of measurement (SI). One lux (Latin for "light") is the amount of illumination provided when one lumen is evenly distributed over an area of 1 square m. This is also equivalent to the illumination that would exist on a surface all points of which are one metre from a point source of one international candle (candela). One lux is equal to 0.0929 footcandle.

Luxembourg, *province,* southeastern Belgium. It has an area of 1,715 square miles (4,441 square km) and is drained by three tributaries of the Meuse River: the Ourthe, Semois, and Lesse rivers. The province is bounded by the Grand Duchy of Luxembourg (east), France (south), and the provinces of Namur (west) and Liège (north). It is divided into five administrative *arrondissements* (Arlon, Bastogne, Marche-en-Famenne, Neufchâteau, and Virton). Formerly part of the Grand Duchy of Luxembourg, it became a Belgian province in 1831. Its northeastern part around Bastogne suffered severe damage during World War II, especially in the Battle of the Bulge (1944–45).

Three-quarters of the province lies within the highlands of the Ardennes (*q.v.*), and the rest, about 400 square miles (1,000 square km) in the south, comprises Belgian Lorraine, a part of the Paris Basin. The Ardennes Plateau rises to 1,968 feet (600 m) at the Baraque de Fraiture in the northeast and to 1,837 feet in the St. Hubert Forest. More than one-third of the plateau's area is wooded with oak, birch, and beech in the valleys and spruce and Scots pine on the heights. The plateau's thin acid soils and uncertain climate limit its agricultural use largely to pasturage for pigs and cattle, along with some dairying and cultivating of oats, rye, clover, and potatoes. Tobacco is grown extensively, with heavy fertilization, in the alluvial flats of the Semois River valley. An extensive tourist industry has developed in the Ardennes, where some timber export and limited quarrying of quartzite and slate are also carried out. Belgian Lorraine is composed of sandstone and limestone hills separated by lower areas of clays, marls, and shales. It is still nearly half wooded, with less than one-third of the area in pasture or cropland (wheat, potatoes, and fodder). There are also cattle, pig, dairy, and fruit farms.

The industry of the province is concentrated in the southeast around the previously active iron mines of Belgian Lorraine, which supplied the blast furnaces at Musson and Halanzy and the steelworks at Athus. Principal population centres are the market and resort towns of Houffalize, La-Roche-en-Ardenne, St. Hubert, Libramont, and Vielsalm in the Ardennes; Florenville, Bouillon, and Chiny in the Semois River valley; and Arlon (*q.v.;* the capital) and Virton in the southeast. There are two nature reserves in the Ardennes—Rouge Ponce (established 1969) and the Plateau des Tailles (1968). Historic landmarks include the ruined castle at Bouillon and the restored Cistercian Abbey of Orval near Florenville. Pop. (1990 est.) 230,827.

Luxembourg, officially GRAND DUCHY OF LUXEMBOURG, French GRAND-DUCHÉ DE LUXEMBOURG, German GROSSHERZOGTUM LUXEMBURG, one of the smallest nations in Europe, situated in the northwestern sector of the continent. Luxembourg covers an area of 998 square miles (2,586 square km). Its maximum length (north to south) is 51 miles (82 km) and maximum width (east to west) 35 miles (56 km). The capital is the city of Luxembourg. The country is bordered by Belgium (north and west), France (south), and Germany (east). Its eastern boundary with Germany is formed by the Our, Sûre, and Moselle rivers. The population in 1991 was estimated at 380,000.

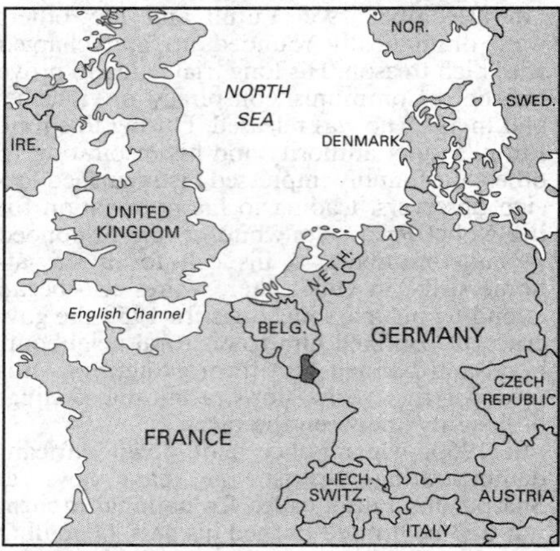

Luxembourg

A brief treatment of Luxembourg follows. For full treatment, *see* MACROPAEDIA: Luxembourg.

For current history and for statistics on society and economy, *see* BRITANNICA BOOK OF THE YEAR.

The land. Luxembourg is divided into two distinct physiographic regions: the Oesling (Ösling), which occupies the northern one-third of the country; and the Bon Pays, or Gutland (French and German, respectively: "Good Land"), which makes up the southern two-thirds. The Oesling is an eastward extension of the densely forested Ardennes Mountains (average elevation 1,500 feet [450 m]), which form a high plateau dissected by deep river valleys. Buurgplaatz (1,835 feet) in the extreme north is the highest point in the country. The relatively thin and infertile soils in the Oesling have been developed for agriculture by the use of basic-slag fertilizer and now produce barley, oats, rye, and potatoes. Beef cattle are raised on the pastures of the hill slopes, and there is some dairying in the sheltered valleys. The rolling plateau of the Bon Pays, with an average elevation of 800 feet (250 m), is a northeastern continuation of the Paris Basin and is marked by sandstone ridges that formed one of Europe's richer iron-ore deposits until their depletion late in the 20th century. Agricultural land is more fertile in the Bon Pays than in the north, and wheat, fruit, and grapes are cultivated with a high degree of mechanization. Forests, covering less than one-third of the total land area, are mostly deciduous.

Luxembourg's temperate climate is transitional between the maritime and continental types and has mild summers and winters and a high degree of humidity. The average annual precipitation is 32 inches (810 mm).

The people. People of French and German ethnic orientation predominate in modern-day Luxembourg. The extremely low birth rate among native Luxembourgers has resulted in a labour shortage that has been alleviated by immigration. Many of the immigrants come from Portugal, Italy, and other southern European countries. Many immigrants and foreign workers are employed in the steel industry, in foreign-owned banks, or in intra-European organizations headquartered in Luxembourg city. French, German, and Luxembourgian (Letzeburgesch), a Germanic tongue, are the grand duchy's official languages. The population is predominantly Roman Catholic, with some Protestants (mostly Lutherans) and a small Jewish minority. The bulk of the population is concentrated in Luxembourg city and in the smaller cities of the southwest, which has been the grand duchy's industrial heartland since the late 19th century.

The economy. Luxembourg has a developed market economy that is largely based on heavy industry and on international trade and banking. Luxembourg's income per capita is one of the highest in the world.

Manufacturing industries account for more than one-tenth of the gross domestic product (GDP) and employ about one-tenth of the workforce. With the encouragement of the government, the steel industry was restructured in the late 20th century to better cope with increased foreign competition and decreased worldwide demand for steel. In 2002 Aciéries Réunies de Burbach-Eich-Dudelange (ARBED), which dominated the country's steel industry, officially merged with two other European companies, Aceralia and Usinor, to form Arcelor, one of the world's largest steel producers. Also contributing to the country's manufacturing sector are American-based and other multinational companies that have opened plants in Luxembourg to produce motor-vehicle tires, chemicals, and other goods.

Luxembourg's deposits of iron ore in the southwest are largely depleted, and their associated foundries now depend on iron ore from France; coke and petroleum must also be imported. Luxembourg meets most of its energy needs with imported petroleum and other fossil fuels.

More than 160 banks have branches in Luxembourg city, which had become one of the more important financial centres in western Europe by the late 20th century. The European Investment Bank of the European Union (EU) is headquartered in Luxembourg city, as is the European Court of Justice.

Agriculture accounts for a very small percentage of the GDP and of the workforce. Farms tend to be small and highly mechanized, and agricultural output meets all but a small fraction of domestic demand. Pastures cover one-fourth of the land, and livestock and their by-products account for the bulk of agricultural production, followed by wheat, barley, and other cereal grains. The Moselle River valley produces some notable wines.

The General Confederation of Labour, organized in 1919, is Luxembourg's main labour union. Numerous workers commute from France, Belgium, and Germany. The grand duchy's external trade is dominated by the EU, in particular by Germany, Belgium, and France, which together account for about three-fifths of Luxembourg's exports and about three-fourths of its imports. Luxembourg belongs to the Benelux Economic Union.

Government and social conditions. Luxembourg is a constitutional monarchy with a parliamentary form of government. Its constitution vests legislative power in a unicameral Chamber of Deputies, whose members are directly elected to five-year terms. A Council of State is appointed by the grand duke and functions as a second legislative chamber whose powers are mainly advisory. Executive power is vested in the grand duke but is exercised by a prime minister and his ministerial council, who are responsible to the Chamber of Deputies. The judiciary is headed by the Superior Court of Justice, whose members are appointed by the grand duke.

Luxembourg's comprehensive social welfare system covers virtually the entire population. The programs provide health insurance, pensions, compensation for work injury, family allowances, and unemployment relief. Luxembourg has a high standard of living, and the average life expectancy is 75 years for men and 81 years for women. The population is almost entirely literate, and education is compulsory from age 6 to 15. In primary schools, instruction is given in both German and French; language courses are heavily emphasized throughout the educational system. There are no four-year colleges or universities in Luxembourg, so many young Luxembourgers study abroad.

Luxembourg has two of the oldest daily newspapers in Europe, founded in 1848 and 1880, and one of the highest circulation rates in the world. Radio-Television-Luxembourg, a privately owned broadcasting company, is heard well outside Luxembourg's own borders. Luxembourg's other main cultural institution is the Grand Ducal Institute, which promotes the arts and humanities and sponsors exhibits on languages, folklore, arts and letters, and natural sciences.

History. At the time of Roman conquest (57–50 BC), the area of Luxembourg was inhabited by a Belgic tribe, the Treveri. After AD 400, Germanic tribes invaded the region, which became part of the Frankish kingdom of Austrasia and later of Charlemagne's empire. Luxembourg became an independent entity in 963 when Siegfried, count of Ardennes, exchanged his lands for a small Roman castle lying along the Alzette River. This castle became the nucleus of what would become Luxembourg city, and the castle gave its name, Lucilinburhuc ("Little Fortress"), to Luxembourg as a whole. Siegfried's successors enlarged their little domain by conquests, treaties, marriages, and inheritance. Conrad, a descendant of Siegfried, took the title count of Luxembourg in 1060. Henry IV, count of Luxembourg, became Holy Roman emperor in 1312 as Henry VII, and Emperor Charles IV, another member of the Luxembourg dynasty, made the county a duchy in 1354.

In 1441 Luxembourg was ceded to the house of Burgundy, and in 1477 it became a dominion of the Habsburgs. In the mid-16th century it became part of the Spanish Netherlands. Following the War of the Spanish Succession (1701–14), Luxembourg passed from Spanish to Austrian Habsburg rule.

The Congress of Vienna (1815) made Luxembourg a grand duchy and awarded it to William I, prince of Orange-Nassau and king of The Netherlands. In 1830, when the Belgians revolted against William I, so did most of Luxembourg. Following the revolt, the western, French-speaking portion of Luxembourg was detached and became part of Belgium. The remainder of the grand duchy stayed in possession of The Netherlands' ruling house of Nassau as that dynasty's personal possession. In 1867 the European powers made the duchy an independent state with its sovereignty vested in the house of Nassau. The Great Powers also guaranteed Luxembourg's perpetual neutrality in European politics.

Technological progress in the 1870s enabled Luxembourg to begin using its iron-ore deposits to build what would become a great steel industry, and the country evolved in the following decades from an agricultural into an industrialized nation. In 1914 Luxembourg's neutrality was violated by Germany, which invaded and occupied the grand duchy until the end of World War I in 1918. In 1921 Luxembourg concluded an economic union with Belgium. During World War II the grand duchy was again occupied by German troops. Luxembourg was liberated in 1944 and subsequently abandoned its neutrality, joining the North Atlantic Treaty Organization in 1949. Perhaps more important, the grand duchy was a founding member of the Benelux Economic Union in 1944, as well as of the European Coal and Steel Community (1952) and the European Economic Community (1957; now part of the European Union). Luxembourg, which was also a founding member of the European Union, continued to pursue a fuller integration of Europe into the 21st century.

Luxembourg, also called LETZEBURG, city and capital of Luxembourg, in the south-central part of the country. Luxembourg city is situated on a sandstone plateau into which the Alzette River and its tributary, the Petrusse, have cut deep, winding ravines. Within a loop of the Alzette, a rocky promontory called the Bock (Bouc) forms a natural defensive position where the Romans and later the Franks built a fortress, or castle, around which the medieval town developed. The purchase of this castle in AD 963 by Siegfried, count of Ardennes, marked the beginning of Luxembourg as an independent entity, and the castle's old name, Lucilinburhuc ("Little Fortress") is the origin of the name Luxembourg.

The old town, with the grand ducal palace (1572), the town hall (1830–38), and the Cathedral of Notre Dame (1613–23; a Gothic structure), occupies the plateau. The city eventually spread westward, and the suburbs of

Cathedral of Notre Dame and a portion of the fortress wall in Luxembourg city

S.E. Hedin—Ostman Agency

Grund, Clausen, and Pfaffenthal developed in lower-lying sections across the Alzette from the old town. These different sections are linked by several bridges.

The city's cathedral contains the tomb of John the Blind, king of Bohemia and count of Luxembourg (d. 1346). The old castle was gradually elaborated by the Spaniards, Austrians, French, and Dutch to become the strongest in Europe after Gibraltar and was garrisoned by the Prussians as a bulwark of the German Confederation from 1815 to 1866. It was dismantled in 1867. Scenic parks, in which are situated the studios of the Radio-Television-Luxembourg broadcasting company, have replaced earlier fortifications on the western fringe of the old town. There are also several museums, notably the Luxembourg State Museums. At Hamm, to the east, is a military cemetery with the graves of more than 5,000 U.S. soldiers, including that of General George S. Patton.

At Eich, a northern suburb, iron foundries stand on the site of the first ironworks (1845) to use the ore from the southern part of the country. Highly diversified industrial concerns are concentrated in the suburbs. Luxembourg has long been an important road and railway focus, and in the 20th century it became a thriving financial centre as well, with many banks. Luxembourg is the seat of the European Investment Bank, the European Court of Justice, and several major administrative offices of the European Community (EC). Pop. (1999 est.) 79,800.

Luxembourg, François-Henri de Montmorency-Bouteville, duc de (duke of) (b. Jan. 8, 1628, Paris, Fr.—d. Jan. 4, 1695, Versailles), one of King Louis XIV's most successful generals in the Dutch War (1672–78) and the War of the Grand Alliance (1689–97).

The posthumous son of François de Montmorency-Bouteville, he was reared by a distant relative, Charlotte de Montmorency, princesse de Condé. Although Bouteville was hunchbacked and physically weak, the princesse's son Louis II de Bourbon, prince de Condé (later known as the Great Condé), prepared him for a military career. In 1648 he distinguished himself fighting under Condé against the Spanish at the Battle of Lens. In 1650, during the second phase of the aristocratic uprising known as the Fronde (1648–53), Bouteville joined Condé's supporters in a revolt against Cardinal Jules Mazarin, who controlled the government of the young king Louis XIV. The uprising collapsed in 1653, and Bouteville then entered the Spanish army. He was pardoned and permitted to return to France in 1659. Through his marriage to an heiress, he acquired the title Duke de Luxembourg two years later. Condé procured a commission for him as lieutenant general in 1668.

Duc de Luxembourg, engraving by G. Edelinck after a painting by Hyacinthe Rigaud
By courtesy of the Bibliotheque Nationale, Paris

When Louis XIV invaded the United Provinces of the Netherlands in June 1672, Luxembourg was sent to command an army in the electorate of Cologne. In the winter of 1672 he was assigned to hold the captured Dutch city of Utrecht. The French position in Holland deteriorated rapidly, and in late 1673 the duke executed a masterful retreat from Utrecht in the face of the numerically superior forces of William of Orange. He was created a marshal of France in July 1675 and given command of the Army of the Rhine the following year. After being forced to surrender Philippsburg to Charles V, Duke of Lorraine, Luxembourg took revenge by devastating part of Flanders in 1677–78. On Aug. 14, 1678, he defeated William of Orange at Saint-Denis, near Mons, in a victory that brought him more criticism then honours, since it took place four days after the conclusion of peace.

By the time Luxembourg returned to Paris, his name had been associated with the scandals that developed into the sensational criminal case known as the Affair of the Poisons. In March 1679 Louis XIV had him imprisoned on a charge of sorcery; on his acquittal 14 months later he was exiled from Paris and Versailles. Recalled to court as captain of the king's guards in 1681, Luxembourg was made commander in chief of the royal armies shortly after France went to war with the other major European powers in 1689. He prevented an invasion of France by crushing the army of George Frederick, prince of Waldeck, at Fleurus, in the Spanish Netherlands, on July 1, 1690. During the next four years Luxembourg consistently outmaneuvered his major opponent, William of Orange, who had ascended the English throne as King William III. The duke took Mons in April 1691, covered the successful siege of Namur from May to July 1692, and defeated William in major battles at Steenkerke (Aug. 3, 1692) and Neerwinden (July 29, 1693). He sent so many captured flags to be hung in the cathedral in Paris that wits called him the tapissier ("upholsterer") of Notre Dame. In 1694 he returned in high honour to Versailles, where he died.

Luxembourg State Museums, French MUSÉES DE L'ÉTAT LUXEMBOURG, national museum of Luxembourg, housed in a late Gothic and Renaissance mansion in Luxembourg city. The museum has collections of Gallo-Roman art, coins, medieval sculpture, armour, and contemporary art as well as sections devoted to natural history. The museum also has an exhibit entitled "The Fortress of Luxembourg" with models. In addition there are sections devoted to geology, mineralogy, and astronomy, including a planetarium.

Luxemburg, Rosa, byname BLOODY ROSA, German BLUTIGE ROSA (b. March 5, 1871, Zamość, Pol., Russian Empire [now in Poland]—d. Jan. 15, 1919, Berlin, Ger.), Polish-born German revolutionary and agitator who played a key role in the founding of the Polish Social Democratic Party and the Spartacus League, which grew into the Communist Party of Germany. As a political theoretician Luxemburg developed a humanitarian theory of Marxism, stressing democracy and revolutionary mass action to achieve international socialism. She was murdered during the Spartacus Revolt of January 1919.

Rosa Luxemburg was the youngest of five children of a lower middle-class Jewish family in Russian-ruled Poland. She became involved in underground activities while still in high school. Like many of her radical contemporaries from the Russian Empire who were faced with prison, she emigrated to Zürich (1889), where she studied law and political economy, receiving a doctorate in 1898. In Zürich she became involved in the international socialist movement and met Georgy Valentinovich Plekhanov, Pavel Axelrod, and other leading representatives of the Russian social democratic movement, with whom, however, she soon began to disagree. Together with a fellow student, Leo Jogiches, who was to become a lifelong friend and sometime lover, she challenged both the Russians and the established Polish Socialist Party because of their support of Polish independence. Consequently, she and her colleagues founded the rival Polish Social Democratic Party, which was to become the nucleus of the future Polish Communist Party. The national issue became one of Luxemburg's main themes. To her, nationalism and national independence were regressive concessions to the class enemy, the bourgeoisie. She consistently underrated nationalist aspirations and stressed socialist internationalism. This became one of her major points of disagreement with Vladimir Lenin and his theory of national self-determination.

Rosa Luxemburg
Interfoto—Friedrich Rauch, Munich

In 1898, after marrying Gustav Lübeck to obtain German citizenship, she settled in Berlin to work with the largest and most powerful constituent party of the Second International, the Social Democratic Party of Germany. Almost at once, she jumped into the revisionist controversy that divided the party. In 1898 the German revisionist Eduard Bernstein had argued that Marxist theory was essentially outdated and that socialism in highly industrialized nations could best be achieved through a gradualist approach, using trade-union activity and parliamentary politics. This, Luxemburg denied categorically in *Sozialreform oder Revolution?* (1889; *Reform or Revolution*), in which she defended Marxist orthodoxy and the necessity of revolution, arguing that parliament was nothing more than a bourgeois sham. Karl Kautsky, the leading theoretician of the Second International, agreed with her, and revisionism consequently became a socialist heresy both in Germany and abroad, though it continued to make headway, especially in the labour movement.

The Russian Revolution of 1905 proved to be the central experience in Rosa Luxemburg's life. Until then, she had believed that Germany was the country in which world revolution was most likely to originate. She now believed it would catch fire in Russia. She went to Warsaw, participated in the struggle, and was imprisoned. From these experiences emerged her theory of revolutionary mass action, which she propounded in *Massenstreik, Partei und Gewerkschaften* (1906; *The Mass Strike, the Political Party, and the Trade Unions*). Luxemburg advocated the mass strike as the single most important tool of the proletariat, Western as well as Russian, in attaining a socialist victory. The mass strike, the spontaneous result of "objective conditions," would radicalize the workers and drive the revolution forward. In contrast to Lenin, she deemphasized the need for a tight party structure, believing that organization would emerge naturally from the struggle. For this, she has been repeatedly chastised by orthodox communist parties.

Released from her Warsaw prison, she taught at the Social Democratic Party school in Berlin (1907–14), where she wrote *Die Akkumulation des Kapitals* (1913; *The Accumulation of Capital*). In this analysis, she described imperialism as the result of a dynamic capitalism's expansion into underdeveloped areas of the world. It was during this time also that she began to agitate for mass actions and broke completely with the established Social Democratic party leadership of August Bebel and Kautsky, who disagreed with her incessant drive toward proletarian radicalization.

The Social Democratic Party backed the German government at the outbreak of World War I, but Rosa Luxemburg immediately went into opposition. In an alliance with Karl

Liebknecht and other like-minded radicals, she formed the Spartakusbund, or Spartacus League, which was dedicated to ending the war through revolution and the establishment of a proletarian government. The organization's theoretical basis was Luxemburg's pamphlet *Die Krise der Sozialdemokratie* (1916; *The Crisis in the German Social Democracy*), written in prison under the pseudonym Junius. In this work she agreed with Lenin in advocating the overthrow of the existing regime and the formation of a new International strong enough to prevent a renewed outbreak of mass slaughter. The actual influence of the Spartacus group during the war, however, remained small.

Released from prison by the German revolution (November 1918), Luxemburg and Liebknecht immediately began agitation to force the new order to the left. They exercised considerable influence on the public and were a contributing factor in a number of armed clashes in Berlin. Like the Bolsheviks, Luxemburg and Liebknecht demanded political power for the workers' and soldiers' soviets but were frustrated by the conservative Socialist establishment and the army. In late December 1918, they became founders of the German Communist Party, but Luxemburg attempted to limit Bolshevik influence in this new organization. In fact, her *Die russische Revolution* (1922; *The Russian Revolution*) chastised Lenin's party on its agrarian and national self-determination stands and its dictatorial and terrorist methods. Luxemburg always remained a believer in democracy as opposed to Lenin's democratic centralism. She was never able, however, to exercise a decisive influence on the new party, for she and Liebknecht were assassinated in 1919 by reactionary troops.

(H.D.S.)

BIBLIOGRAPHY. The best biography is J.P. Nettl, *Rosa Luxemburg,* 2 vol. (1966), also published in an abridged ed. (1969, reissued 1989). See also Elżbieta Ettinger, *Rosa Luxemburg: A Life* (1986); Paul Frölich, *Rosa Luxemburg: Her Life and Work* (1970), by one of her contemporaries; and Norman Geras, *The Legacy of Rosa Luxemburg* (1976, reissued 1985).

Luxemburgian language, also called LUXEMBOURGISH, LETZEBURGISCH, LETZEBUERGESCH, or LUXEMBOURGEOIS, dialect of German that is spoken exclusively in Luxembourg. Luxemburgian is a Moselle-Franconian dialect of the West Middle German group. This old language has been enriched by many French words and phrases, and the resulting dialect is spoken by all classes of people in Luxembourg. The population of Luxembourg is generally bilingual or trilingual, with most people speaking Luxemburgian and either French or German, or all three. French and German became official languages of the nation in 1830. Luxemburgian was made the third official language in 1939. Luxemburgian is mostly used orally, while French is the language most commonly used in government and the courts and German is the language most commonly used in newspapers. All three languages are used in the country's schools.

Consult the INDEX *first*

Luxor, also called EL-AKSUR, or AL-UQṢUR, market town in Qinā *muḥāfaẓah* (governorate), Upper Egypt, which has given its name to the southern half of the ruins of the ancient Egyptian city of Thebes (*q.v.*).

The ancient ruins. The southern part of Thebes grew up around the Great Temple of Amon. The modern name, in Arabic Al-Uqṣur, means "the palaces," or perhaps, after the Roman *castra* (remains of which have been found in the neighbourhood), "the forts." Here, close to the Nile and parallel with the bank of the river, King Amenhotep III (reigned 1390–53 BC) of the late 18th dynasty built a beautiful temple dedicated to Amon-Re, king of the gods, his consort Mut, and their son Khons.

A small pavilion is all that is left of earlier building on the site, though there was probably a temple there earlier in the 18th dynasty

Great Temple of Amon, Luxor, Egypt, seen from the southwest, with the Nile River in the background
Hirmer Fotoarchiv, Munchen

if not before. Amenhotep III's Great Temple of Amon was completed by Tutankhamen and Horemheb and added to by Ramses II; smaller additions were made to it in Ptolemaic times. The temple's hypostyle hall was at one time converted into a Christian church, and the remains of another Coptic church can be seen to the west of it.

The original part of the Great Temple of Amon consisted of a large peristyle court and a complex of halls and chambers beyond. In one hall is a granite shrine of Alexander the Great. The great peristyle forecourt is surrounded on three sides by a double row of graceful papyrus-cluster columns, their capitals imitating the umbels of the papyrus plant in bud. An entrance flanked by the towers of a pylon was planned for the north end, but this design was altered, and, instead, the most striking feature of the temple, a majestic colonnade of 14 pillars, 52 feet (16 m) high, was added. This colonnade, which also has papyrus-umbel capitals, may have been intended for the central nave of a hypostyle hall similar to that at Karnak, but the side aisles were not built; instead, enclosing walls were built down either side. Ramses II added an outer court, decorated with colossal statues of himself between the pillars of a double colonnade, and a lofty pylon on which he depicted festival scenes and episodes from his wars in Syria. In front of the pylon were colossal images of the pharaoh and a pair of obelisks, one of which still stands; the other was removed in 1831 and reerected in the Place de la Concorde in Paris.

In the outer court of the temple is the mosque of Sheikh Yūsuf al-Ḥaggāg, the local Muslim saint. His feast is celebrated with a boat procession resembling an ancient rite, the "Beautiful Festival of Ope," during which, on the 19th day of the second month, Amon was said to come from Karnak on his state barge to visit his other temple at Luxor, escorted by the people of Thebes in holiday attire. Reliefs on the walls of the great colonnade depict preparations for the procession of sacred barks during the festival.

Later history. When Thebes declined politically, Luxor remained the populated part of the town, which huddled around the Ramesside pylon. A Roman legion had its headquarters inside the 18th-dynasty temple, and Coptic churches were built around the temple and in the Ramesside court. In the Fāṭimid period, a mosque dedicated to Sheikh Yūsuf al-Ḥaggāg, who is reputed to have introduced Islām to Luxor, was built over the foundations of the church in the court.

The modern market town for the surrounding agricultural district has grown north, south, and east of the temple. It has a number of churches, as about half of the population is Christian, and mosques. There is also a railway station on the Cairo-Aswan railroad, an airport, and ferry service to the western bank. Numerous tourist facilities and a new local museum have been built in recent years. Pop. (1986 est.) 147,900.

luxury tax, excise levy on goods or services considered to be luxuries rather than necessities. Modern examples are taxes on jewelry and perfume. Luxury taxes may be levied with the intent of taxing the rich, as in the case of the late 18th- and early 19th-century British

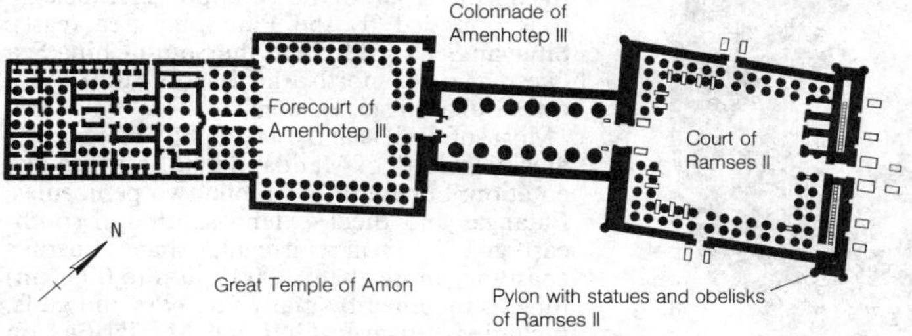

The Great Temple of Amon, Luxor, Egypt, 18th–19th dynasty
(Top) Papyrus-cluster columns of the peristyle forecourt of the Great Temple of Amon (seen from the southwest), built by Amenhotep III, *c.* 1390 BC; (bottom) plan of the temple complex
(Top) Hirmer Fotoarchiv, Munchen; (bottom) adapted from J. Hawkes, *Atlas of Ancient Archaeology* (1974); McGraw-Hill Book Co., Inc.

taxes on carriages and manservants; or they may be imposed in a deliberate effort to alter consumption patterns, either for moral reasons or because of some national emergency. In modern times, the revenue productivity of luxury taxes has probably overshadowed the moral argument for them. Furthermore, the progressive nature of the early taxes began to be lost as more lower-income people's "luxuries" were taxed in the interest of generating additional revenue; an example is the amusement tax. To avoid moralistic implications, economists now identify as necessities any goods with low demand elasticity, which include such "luxuries" as tobacco and beer.

Luyia (people): *see* Luhya.

Luyken, Jan, also called JOHANNES LUIKEN (b. April 16, 1649, Amsterdam, Neth.—d. April 5, 1712, Amsterdam), Dutch lithographer and poet whose work ranges from hedonistic love songs to introspective religious poetry.

Luyken, lithograph by Pieter Sluiter after a design by Arnold Houbraken
By courtesy of the Iconographisch Bureau, The Hague

As a young man, Luyken published *De duyste lier* (1671; "German Lyric"), a volume of erotic poetry. He was married in 1672 and baptized in the Baptist church the following year. Influenced by the writings of the German mystic Jakob Böhme, Luyken embraced pietistic Christianity. He worked as a book illustrator but became increasingly ascetic and began to withdraw from society. His later poetry, including *Jezus en de ziel* (1678; "Jesus and the Soul"), was inspired by his mystical vision of life. Luyken left Amsterdam in 1699 but returned in 1705. He died in poverty.

Luynes, Charles d'Albert, Duke (duc) **de** (b. Aug. 5, 1578—d. Dec. 15, 1621, Longueville, Fr.), French statesman who, from 1617 to 1621, dominated the government of young King Louis XIII.

Luynes, engraving by Balthasar Moncornet, 17th century
Giraudon—Art Resource

The son of Honoré d'Albert, Seigneur (lord) de Luynes, he became the king's falconer in 1611. Since Louis was neglected and deprived of political influence by his mother, the queen regent Marie de Médicis, he readily became dependent on the ambitious Luynes. Luynes was already a councillor of state and governor of Amboise when he sponsored the plot that led to the murder of Marie's powerful favourite, the Marquis d'Ancre, on April 24, 1617. The king then exiled his mother to Blois and made Luynes his chief minister. Luynes initiated a rapprochement with England and attempted by diplomacy to establish a balance of power between the Catholic Habsburgs and the Protestants in Germany and Bohemia. In 1619–20 he put down two rebellions of the great nobles led by Marie.

Meanwhile, Luynes had married (1617) Marie de Rohan-Montbazon, the future Duchess (duchesse) de Chevreuse, whose conspiracies were later to disturb Louis's reign. In 1619 he became Duke de Luynes and governor of Picardy. Despite his military incompetence, he was appointed constable (commander in chief) of France by Louis in March 1621 and launched a campaign against the Huguenot (French Protestant) rebels of southern France. He failed to capture the stronghold of Montauban and died soon thereafter.

Since he had prevented Richelieu, the ablest of Marie de Médicis' partisans, from becoming a cardinal in January 1621, Richelieu consistently denigrated Luynes in his writings. Although many historians have shared Richelieu's assessment, others have pointed out that the duke's efforts to break the power of the nobility and the Huguenots foreshadowed the policies followed by Richelieu after he became chief minister in 1624.

Luzern (canton and city, Switzerland): *see* Lucerne.

Luzhou (China): *see* Lu-chou.

Luzia (central European territory): *see* Lusatia.

Lužické hory (central Europe): *see* Lusatian Mountains.

Lužnice River, German LAINSITZ, river in Niederösterreich *Bundesland* ("federal state"), Austria, and Jihočeský *kraj* (region), Czech Republic. The Lužnice rises in the Freiwald forest of Austria as the Lainsitz River. It flows northward, soon crossing into the Czech Republic and passing through the Třeboň lake region to Tábor, at which point it narrows into a gorge and turns 120° to flow southwestward into the Vltava (Moldau). The total length of the river is 129 miles (208 km); the area of its drainage basin is 1,631 square miles (4,224 square km).

Luzon, largest and most important of the Philippine islands, with an area of 40,420 square miles (104,688 square km). It is the site of Manila, the nation's capital and major metropolis, and of Quezon City. Located on the northern part of the Philippine archipelago, it is bounded by the Philippine Sea (east), Sibuyan Sea (south), and the South China Sea (west). To the north, the Luzon Strait separates Luzon from Taiwan.

Most of the island, a roughly rectangular area, lies north of Manila in a north-south orientation; but south of Manila two peninsulas, Batangas and Bicol, extend south and southeast, giving Luzon its irregular shape. Luzon's coastline, more than 3,000 miles (5,000 km) long, is indented by many fine bays and gulfs, including Lingayen Gulf and Manila Bay on the west and Lamon Bay and Lagonoy Gulf on the east. Luzon (meaning "big light") represents 35 percent of the land area of the Philippines, and its greatest dimensions are 460 by 140 miles (740 by 225 km). There is a predominant north-south trend in its rivers and relief features. The important ranges are the Cordillera Central in the north; the Sierra Madre, following much of the east coast; and

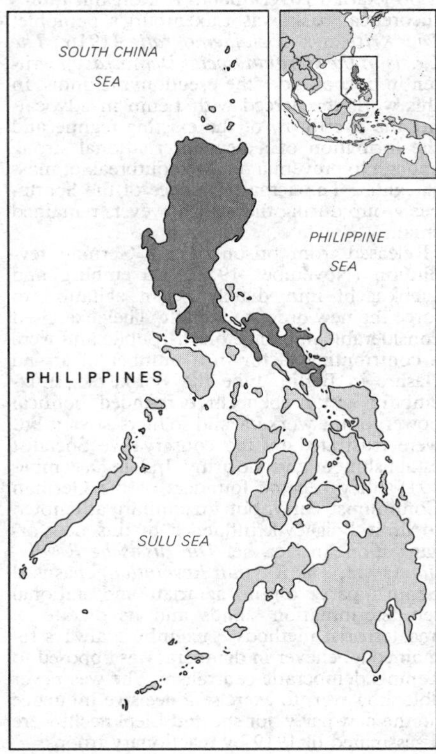

Luzon

the Zambales Mountains on the central-western coast. Mount Pulog (9,612 feet [2,930 m]) is the island's highest peak. Isolated volcanic cones such as the near-perfect and still-active Mayon Volcano (8,077 feet) are on Bicol Peninsula. Taal Lake is a crater lake, and Laguna de Bay is the largest (344 square miles [891 square km]) lake in the Philippines. The major rivers are Cagayan, Abra, Agno, Pampanga, and Bicol.

Terraced rice paddies in Banaue, Luzon, Phil.
Steve Vidler/Leo de Wys, Inc.

In 1991 Mount Pinatubo in the Zambales Mountains, some 55 miles (90 km) northwest of Manila, erupted. The eruption altered the geography of the island's central plain, disrupting agriculture and displacing hundreds of thousands of people.

Luzon leads the nation both in industry (concentrated near Manila) and in agriculture (rice, corn [maize], coconuts, sugarcane, mangoes, bananas). A central plain stretching 100 miles (160 km) north of Manila is the major grain-producing region. Farther north are the spectacular rice terraces of the Ifugao mountaineers. There are extensive coconut plantations on the Bondoc and Bicol peninsulas. Iron, gold, manganese, and copper are mined. Forest areas yield excellent hardwoods.

In addition to Manila and Quezon City, the main cities are Pasay, Cabanatuan, Legaspi, Baguio, Batangas City, and Laoag. About 50 percent of the Filipino population lives on Luzon. Pop. (1990 prelim.) including adjoining islands, 30,660,000.

Luzon Strait, strait extending for more than 200 miles (320 km) between the islands of Taiwan (north) and Luzon, Philippines (south). It connects the South China Sea (west) with the Philippine Sea (east). The strait is a series of channels, dotted with islands in its southern reaches—*i.e.,* the Batan and Babuyan island groups. The main channels are Bashi (north), Balintang (central), and Babuyan (south). It is on a main shipping route.

Luzzatto, Moshe Ḥayyim (b. 1707, Padua, Venetian republic [Italy]—d. May 6, 1747, Acre, Palestine [now ʿAkko, Israel]), Jewish cabalist and writer, one of the founders of modern Hebrew poetry.

Luzzatto wrote lyrics and about 1727 the drama *Migdal ʿoz* ("Tower of Victory"), but he early turned to cabalist studies, eventually becoming convinced that he was receiving divine revelation and, finally, that he was the Messiah. After being expelled by the Italian rabbis, he moved to Amsterdam (1736), where he wrote his morality play *La-yesharim tehilah* (*Praise for Uprightness*) and an ethical work, *Mesilat yesharim* (1740; *The Path of the Upright*), which still ranks as a classic.

Luzzatto, Samuel David, also called by acronym SHEDAL (b. Aug. 22, 1800, Trieste [Italy]—d. Sept. 30, 1865, Padua), Jewish writer and scholar.

In his writings, which are in Hebrew and Italian, Luzzatto presents an emotional and antiphilosophical concept of Judaism, and his Hebrew poetry is also pervaded by national spirit. His chief merit as a scholar lies in biblical exegesis, Hebrew philology, and the history of Hebrew literature. His extensive correspondence in Hebrew was published in 1882–94 and in other languages in 1890. His autobiography in Italian appeared in 1882.

Lviv, Russian LVOV, *oblast* (province), western Ukraine. It extends from the crestline of the Carpathian Mountains, across the upper Dniester River valley and the Roztochchya Upland to the Bug River basin. There is much variation in soil and vegetation—mixed forest in the north, forest-steppe on the upland, meadows along the Dniester, and dense forest on the Carpathian slopes, yielding to meadows on the gently rounded summits. Much of the region has been cleared for agriculture, which is intensively developed. Rye, wheat, corn (maize), and sugar beets are the main crops. Cattle and sheep raising are important in the high summer pastures of the mountains.

There is considerable timberworking in the mountains, and furniture making is widespread; Zhydachiv has the largest paper mill in Ukraine. Mineral exploitation is also significant. Near Boryslav is a small but locally important oil field, and at Dashava and Rudky are large deposits of natural gas, which is piped to the city of Lviv (the *oblast* headquarters) and used locally. The region produces native sulfur, and potassium salts are also mined. Area 8,400 square miles (21,800 square km). Pop. (1991 est.) 2,771,300.

Lviv, Russian LVOV, Polish LWÓW, German LEMBERG, city and administrative centre of Lviv *oblast* (province), Ukraine, on the Roztochchya Upland. Founded in the mid-13th century by Prince Daniel Romanovich of Galicia, Lviv has historically been the chief centre of Galicia, a region now divided between Ukraine and Poland. Its position controlling east-west routes and passes across the Carpathians has given it a stormy history. Polish control was established in 1349. The town was seized by the Cossacks in 1648 and the Swedes in 1704. It was given to Austria on the first partition of Poland in 1772 and occupied by Russia in 1914–15. The government of a short-lived western Ukrainian republic arose in Lviv in late 1918, but the Poles drove Ukrainian troops out of the city and regained control. Lviv was seized by the Soviet Union in 1939 and, after German occupation, annexed by the Soviets in 1945.

Modern Lviv retains its nodal position, with nine railways converging on the city. As a result, industrial development has been considerable: engineering products manufactured in the city include buses, agricultural machinery, loading machinery, bicycles, and television sets; there is also a wide range of consumer goods and foodstuffs industries.

Lviv is also a major publishing and cultural centre, especially of Ukrainian culture, which flourished there in tsarist times when it was suppressed in Russian Ukraine. The university, which was founded in 1661 and named for the Ukrainian poet and journalist Ivan Franko under the Soviet regime, is one of the institutions of higher education and research in the city. Pop. (1993 est.) 810,000.

Lvov, Georgy Yevgenyevich, Prince (Knyaz) (b. Oct. 21 [Nov. 2, New Style], 1861, Popovka, near Tula, Russia—d. March 7, 1925, Paris, France), Russian social reformer and statesman who was the first head of the Russian provisional government established during the February Revolution (1917).

An aristocrat who held a degree in law from the University of Moscow, Lvov worked in the civil service until 1893, when he resigned. He became a member of the Tula *zemstvo* (local government council), and during the Russo-Japanese War (1904–05) he organized voluntary relief work in the Orient. In 1905 he joined the newly founded liberal Constitutional Democratic (Kadet) Party, was elected to the first Duma (Russian parliament; convened May 1906), and in 1906 was informally nominated for a ministerial post.

During World War I Lvov became chairman of the All-Russian Union of Zemstvos (1914) and a leader of Zemgor (the Union of Zemstvos and Towns; 1915), which provided relief for the sick and wounded and procured supplies for the army. Although his activities were often obstructed by bureaucratic officials who objected to voluntary organizations that encroached upon their areas of responsibility,

Lvov

Lvov's groups made significant contributions to the war effort, and he won the respect of many political liberals and army commanders. When the imperial government fell, he became the prime minister (with Tsar Nicholas II's subsequent approval) of the provisional government (March 2 [March 15], 1917).

Lvov also served as minister of the interior, but his government, composed initially of liberals and, after May 5 (May 18), of moderate socialists as well, was unable to satisfy the increasingly radical demands of the general population. In July, after a major left-wing demonstration threatened to overthrow the provisional government, Lvov resigned his posts (July 7 [July 20]), allowing Aleksandr Kerensky to succeed him as prime minister. When the Bolsheviks seized power in October, Lvov was arrested, but he escaped and eventually settled in Paris.

Lwena (people): *see* Luvale.

LWF: *see* Lutheran World Federation.

Lwoff, André, in full ANDRÉ-MICHAEL LWOFF (b. May 8, 1902, Ainay-le-Château, France—d. Sept. 30, 1994, Paris), French biologist who contributed to the understanding of lysogeny, in which a bacterial virus, or bacteriophage, infects bacteria and is transmitted to subsequent bacterial generations solely through the cell division of its host. His discoveries brought him (with François Jacob and Jacques Monod) the Nobel Prize for Medicine or Physiology in 1965.

Lwoff, born of Russian-Polish parents, was educated at the University of Paris. He spent most of his research career at the Pasteur Institute in Paris, serving on the board of directors from 1966 to 1972. From 1959 to 1968 he was also a professor of microbiology at the Sorbonne in Paris. When he retired from the Pasteur Institute in 1968, he served as director of the Cancer Research Institute at nearby Villejuif until 1972.

Lwoff, 1965

In his prizewinning research, Lwoff showed that, after infection, the virus is passed on to succeeding generations of bacteria in a noninfective form called a prophage. He demonstrated that under certain conditions this prophage gives rise to an infective form that causes lysis, or disintegration, of the bacterial cell; the viruses that are released upon the cell's destruction are capable of infecting other bacterial hosts. Lwoff also discovered that vitamins serve both as growth factors for microbes and as coenzymes. Among his written works are *Problems of Morphogenesis in Ciliates* (1950) and *Biological Order* (1962).

During World War II Lwoff won the Medal of the Resistance for work in the French underground. He was made an officer of the Legion of Honour.

Lwów (Ukraine): *see* Lviv.

Ly DYNASTY (Vietnamese history): *see* Later Ly dynasty.

Ly Bon, also called LY BAN, LI BI, or LY BI, reign name LI NAM-VIET DE BON, or LI NAM DE (b. Giao-chao province, northern Vietnam—d. 549, Laos), founder of the first Vietnamese dynasty mentioned in extant historical records, and Vietnam's first great champion of independence.

Ly Bon led a successful revolt against the Chinese governor of Giao-chao province in 542 and captured the capital at Long Bien. Two years later he proclaimed himself emperor and assumed his royal name. The earliest surviving Vietnamese historical records (13th–14th century) indicate that he controlled a vast territory, covering most of what is now northern and central Vietnam, and his authority was recognized throughout the Red River delta in the north and southward to the frontiers of the Champa kingdom. He named his newly founded empire Van Xuan, implying that it would last "One Thousand Springs." The Chinese regained power, however, defeating Ly Bon in 547 at the northern village of Chu Dien. Seeking refuge, Ly Bon fled to Laos, but he was killed by local tribesmen who decapitated him and sent his head to the Chinese.

Though short-lived, Ly Bon's kingdom formed the nucleus of the future Dai Viet, the first truly independent Vietnamese state. Shortly thereafter two other Viets attempted to gain control over Giao-chao: Ly Xuan (589–590) and Ly Phat Tu (late 590s–603). These three together constitute what has been called the Earlier Ly dynasty to distinguish it from that established by Ly Thai To in 1009 (the Later Ly dynasty; *q.v.*).

Lyadov, Anatoly, in full ANATOLY KONSTANTINOVICH LYADOV, Lyadov also spelled LIADOV (b. April 29 [May 11, New Style], 1855, St. Petersburg, Russia—d. Aug. 15 [Aug. 28], 1914, Palimovka, Novgorod), Russian composer whose orchestral works and poetic, beautifully polished piano miniatures earned him a position of stature in Russian Romantic music.

The son of the conductor of the imperial opera, Lyadov entered the conservatory in 1870, studying composition with Nikolay Rimsky-Korsakov, but was expelled for idleness in 1876. Readmitted in 1878, he later occupied various teaching posts in the conservatory and the imperial chapel. From 1897 he was much occupied with the arrangement of folk songs collected by the Imperial Geographical Society. Until 1900 he mainly composed piano pieces. Turning to orchestral music he wrote two of his most successful pieces, *Kikimora* and *The Enchanted Lake,* which were based on sketches for a fantastic opera he never finished.

Lyallpur (Pakistan): *see* Faisalābād.

lyase, in physiology, any member of a class of enzymes that catalyze the addition or removal of the elements of water (hydrogen, oxygen), ammonia (nitrogen, hydrogen), or carbon dioxide (carbon, oxygen) at double bonds. For example, decarboxylases remove carbon dioxide from amino acids and dehydrases remove water. *See* enzyme.

Lyautey, Louis-Hubert-Gonzalve (b. Nov. 17, 1854, Nancy, Fr.—d. July 21, 1934, Thorey), French statesman, soldier, marshal of France, and devoted believer in the civilizing virtues of colonialism, who built the French protectorate over Morocco.

Despite a childhood spinal injury, Lyautey was an outstanding student and entered the Saint-Cyr Military Academy in 1873. After serving with a cavalry regiment at Châteaudun, he went to Algeria in 1880. On his return to France two years later he was promoted to captain. Though he was a staunch royalist, his Legitimist beliefs prevented him from sympathizing with the royal House of Orléans, and he preferred instead to serve the existing republican regime.

Lyautey
By courtesy of the Bibliotheque Nationale, Paris

In 1894 Lyautey was sent to Indochina, where, at Tonkin, he met Joseph Gallieni, whose notion of conquest as a means of civilization he adopted. Despite his liking for Tonkin, Lyautey responded immediately when Gallieni summoned him to Madagascar, which he conquered in two years. In 1902 he returned to France to take command of the 14th Regiment of Hussars at Alençon. In 1904 the governor general of Algeria, Célestin Jonnart, obtained for Lyautey the post of commandant of the subdivision of Aïn Sefra. When Morocco protested to France over Lyautey's encroachments on Moroccan territory in order to round off the frontier, Jonnart protected him, and Lyautey reduced the frontier tribes to obedience. From 1906, as commandant at Oran, he continued with persistence to push the frontier westward.

In 1910 Lyautey was recalled to France to command the army corps at Rennes but in 1912 was appointed resident general in Morocco, over which the French protectorate had just been proclaimed. After routing insurgent tribes in Fès, he replaced the sultan Moulay Hafid by his more reliable brother Moulay Yusuf. In the task of conquering and pacifying the whole country, however, Lyautey showed respect for local institutions and impressed the Arabs with his sense of grandeur and his competence. Recalled to France to be minister of war (1916–17), he thereafter returned to Morocco, remaining until his resignation in 1925. A member of the French Academy from 1912, Lyautey was made a marshal of France in 1921.

lycanthropy (from Greek *lykos,* "wolf"; *anthropos,* "man"), mental disorder in which the patient believes that he is a wolf or some other nonhuman animal. Undoubtedly stimulated by the once widespread superstition that lycanthropy is a supernatural condition in which men actually assume the physical form of werewolves or other animals, the delusion has been most likely to occur among people who believe in reincarnation and the transmigration of souls. Usually, a person is deemed to take the form of the most dangerous beast of prey of the region: the wolf or bear in Europe and northern Asia, the hyena or leopard in Africa, and the tiger in India, China, Japan, and elsewhere in Asia; but other animals are mentioned too. Both the superstition and the psychiatric disorder are linked with belief in animal guardian spirits, vampires, totemism, witches, and werewolves. The folklore, fairy tales, and legends of many nations and peoples show evidence of lycanthropic belief.

Stories of men turning into beasts go back to antiquity. In parts of ancient Greece, werewolf myths, presumably stemming from prehistoric times, became linked with the Olympian religion. In Arcadia, a region plagued by wolves, there was a cult of the Wolf-Zeus. Mount Lycaeus was the scene of a yearly gathering at which the priests were said to prepare a sacrificial feast that included meat mixed with human parts. According to legend, whoever tasted it became a wolf and could not turn back into a man unless he abstained from human flesh for nine years.

The Romans also knew of this superstition. Anyone who was supposed to have been turned into a wolf by means of magic spells or herbs was called *versipellis* ("turnskin") by the Romans.

Stories about the werewolf (in French, *loup-garou*) were widely believed in Europe during the Middle Ages. Outlaws and bandits played on these superstitions by sometimes wearing wolfskins over their armour. At that time people were unusually prone to develop the delusion that they themselves were wolves; suspected lycanthropists were burned alive if convicted. Only rarely was their condition recognized as a psychological disturbance. Although the superstition is no longer common, traces still linger in some primitive and isolated areas. *See also* werewolf.

Lycaon, in Greek mythology, a legendary king of Arcadia. Traditionally, he was an impious and cruel king who tried to trick Zeus, the king of the gods, into eating human flesh. The god was not deceived and in wrath caused a deluge to devastate the earth.

The story of Lycaon was apparently told in order to explain an extraordinary ceremony, the Lycaea, held in honour of Zeus Lycaeus at Mount Lycaeus.

Lycaonia, ancient region in the interior of Anatolia north of the Taurus Mountains, inhabited by a wild and warlike aboriginal people who pastured sheep and wild asses on the bleak central highlands. Little is known about the early Lycaonians. They seem to have escaped Persian domination but afterward shared the fate of many Anatolian states, passing under the rule of Alexander the Great, the Seleucids, the Attalids of Pergamum, and, finally, the Romans. Under Roman administration, Lycaonian territory was attached to Galatia to the north and Cappadocia to the east. The country was traversed by one of the great highroads across Anatolia, along which were clustered its urban centres. Iconium was its capital and principal city since Seleucid times. Lycaonia, visited by St. Paul, was Christianized early, and by the 4th century it possessed a more completely organized ecclesiastical system than any other region of Anatolia.

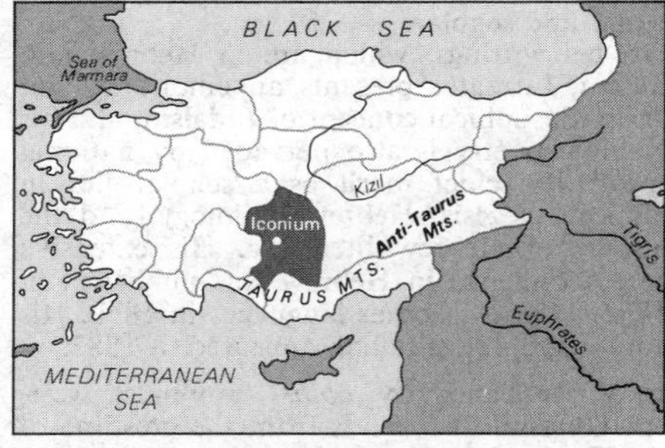

The district of Lycaonia under the Roman Empire
From W. Shepherd, *Historical Atlas*, Harper & Row, Publishers (Barnes & Noble Books), New York; revision copyright © 1964 by Barnes & Noble, Inc.

Lycaste, genus of about 45 species of tropical American orchids, family Orchidaceae, that grow on other plants or in soil. The sepals of *Lycaste* flowers are larger than the petals.

Lycaste xytriophora
Walter Dawn

Each thick, egg-shaped pseudobulb (swollen stem) has one to three large, folded leaves that fall before the long-lasting flowers die. A number of flower stalks grow from the base of each pseudobulb.

lycée, in France, an upper-level secondary school preparing pupils for the *baccalauréat* (the degree required for university admission). The first lycée was established in 1801, under the educational reforms of Napoleon Bonaparte. Lycées formerly enrolled the nation's most talented students in a course of instruction lasting seven years. These lycées were divided into three types having different areas of specialization: classical studies, modern studies, and scientific-technological studies.

In the late 20th century, however, the lycée system was reorganized; lycées became three-year courses for students aged 15 to 18, and these lycées were divided into just two curricular types. The more common of the two is the general and technological upper-secondary school (LEGT; *lycée d'enseignement général et technologique*); this is the successor to the traditional academic upper-secondary school. Students entering the LEGT choose one of three basic streams (humanities, science, or technology) their first year and then concentrate on somewhat more specialized fields of learning (*e.g.,* literary-philosophical, or mathematical and physical sciences) for the last two years. There is a common core of subjects in the first two years of the LEGT, however, aside from the student's major area of study.

The second type of lycée is the vocational upper-secondary school (LEP; *lycée d'enseignement professionel*), which offers a range of technical-vocational studies that give access to corresponding studies in higher education. Students entering the LEP choose courses of study leading to one of 30 or so technical *baccalauréats.*

Lyceum, Athenian school founded by Aristotle in 335 BC in a grove sacred to Apollo Lyceius. Owing to his habit of walking about the grove while lecturing his students, the school and its students acquired the label of Peripatetics (Greek *peri,* "around," and *patein,* "to walk"). The *peripatos* was the covered walkway of the Lyceum. Most of Aristotle's extant writings comprise notes for lectures delivered at the school as edited by his successors.

lyceum movement, early form of organized adult education, of widespread popular appeal in the northeastern and midwestern United States. The first lyceum was founded in 1826 in Millbury, Mass., by Josiah Holbrook, a teacher and lecturer. The lyceum movement was named for the place where Aristotle lectured to the youth of ancient Greece. The lyceums were voluntary local associations that gave people an opportunity to hear debates and lectures on topics of current interest. The American lyceums multiplied rapidly, numbering 3,000 by 1834.

As conceived by Holbrook, each lyceum was to contribute to the spread of learning, especially of the natural sciences. In communities hungry for knowledge, the idea caught fire and soon expanded to include home-talent productions of essays, discussions, debates, and lectures. A major topic in early years was the establishment of public schools.

At first the lyceums were local ventures with speakers supplied by the community, but by 1840 they had become professionalized institutions with outside lecturers to whom fees were paid. Among the well-known speakers who traveled from state to state were Ralph Waldo Emerson, Frederick Douglass, Henry David Thoreau, Daniel Webster, Nathaniel Hawthorne, and Susan B. Anthony. Many of Emerson's essays were originally written as lyceum lectures.

Lyceums flourished up to the American Civil War and thereafter blended indistinguishably into the chautauqua movement (*q.v.*). In their heyday the American lyceums contributed to the broadening of school curricula and the development of local museums and libraries in the United States.

Lyceum Theatre, London playhouse in Wellington Street, off the Strand. A hall called the Lyceum stood on the site from 1772. A new building, called the Royal Lyceum and English Opera House, opened in 1834 to become the most notable theatre in London under the management of Sir Henry Irving, who was there with his company from 1871 to 1902. Extensively rebuilt in 1904, it then became a music hall and the home of melodrama and pantomime.

lych-gate, also spelled LICH-GATE, also called CORPSE GATE (Middle English *lyche,* "body"; *yate,* "gate"), roofed-in gateway to a churchyard in which a bier might stand while the introductory part of the burial service was read. The most common form of lych-gate was a simple shed composed of a roof with two gabled ends, covered with tiles or thatch. Lych-gates existed in England in the 7th century, but comparatively few early ones survive because they were almost always of wood.

lychee (fruit): *see* litchi.

Lychnis, genus of ornamental plants, of the pink family (Caryophyllaceae), with about 35 species, native primarily to the North Temperate Zone. Members of the genus are commonly called catchfly, or campion, names that also are used for related plants of the genus

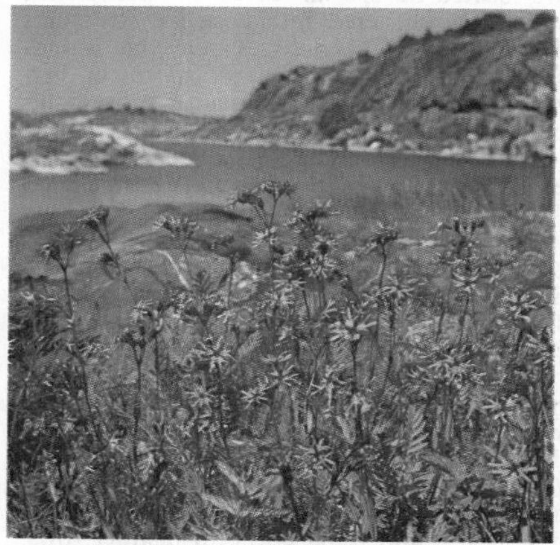

Cuckoo-flower (*Lychnis flos-cuculi*)
Ingmar Holmasen

Silene of the same family. The name catchfly refers to the sticky, hairy stems of some *Lychnis* species. Some of the more popular garden plants of the genus include the cuckoo-flower, or ragged robin (*L. flos-cuculi*); scarlet lightning, or Maltese cross (*L. chalcedonica*); flower of Jove (*L. flos-jovis*); and mullein pink, or rose campion (*L. coronaria*). The five-petaled flowers range in colour from white or pink to red or purple.

Consult
the
INDEX
first

Lycia, ancient maritime district of southwestern Anatolia (now Turkey). Lycia lay along the Mediterranean coast between Caria and Pamphylia, and extended inland to the ridge of the Taurus Mountains. In Egyptian, Hittite, and Ugaritic records of the 14th and 13th centuries BC, the Lycians are described as wedged between the Hittites on the north and the Achaean Greeks on the coast. Known as Luka, they participated in the Sea Peoples' attempt to invade Egypt in the late 13th century. Nothing more is known of the Lycians until the 8th century BC, when they reappear as a thriving maritime people confederated in at least a score of cities that made up the Lycian League. Neither Phrygia nor Lydia were able to bring Lycia under its control, but the country eventually fell to Cyrus' general Harpagus after a heroic resistance. Under Achaemenian Persia and later under the rule of the Romans, Lycia enjoyed relative freedom and was able to preserve its federal institutions until the time of Augustus. It was annexed to Roman Pamphylia in AD 43 and became a separate Roman province after the 4th century. Archaeological discoveries made on sites at Xanthus, Patara, Myra, and other of its cities have revealed a distinctive type of funerary architecture.

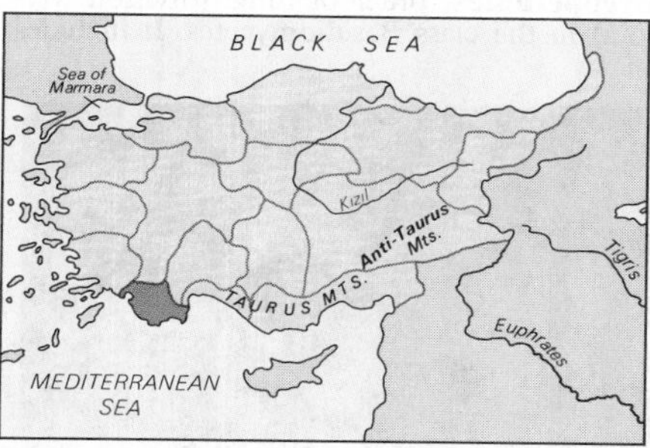

Lycia
From W. Shepherd, *Historical Atlas,* Harper & Row, Publishers (Barnes & Noble Books), New York; revision copyright © 1964 by Barnes & Noble, Inc.

Lycian alphabet, writing system of the Lycian people of southwest Asia Minor, dating from the 5th–4th centuries BC. The Lycian alphabet is clearly related to the Greek, but the exact nature of the relationship is uncertain. Several letters appear to be related to symbols of the Cretan and Cyprian writing systems. The script has 29 letters (6 vowels), with several sounds not represented in Greek. The most important inscription in Lycian occurs on a pillar discovered at Kınık; it is as yet undeciphered. Other inscriptions, often bilingual in Greek and Lycian, concern funerary materials.

Inscription in Lycian
From H. Pedersen, *The Discovery of Language: Linguistic Science in the Nineteenth Century,* John W. Spargo, tr., published by Indiana University Press, 1962; copyright 1931 and 1959 by the President and Fellows of Harvard College

Lycian language, extinct language of southwestern Asia Minor (now Turkey), written in an indigenous Lycian alphabet based on a West Greek prototype. Inscriptions in the language date from about 500 BC to about 200 BC. Until 1945 scholars had believed Lycian to be closely related to either Greek or Iranian, but in 1945 Holger Pedersen, a Danish linguist, published a convincing monograph indicating that Lycian belonged to the Anatolian group. Later, other scholars, among them the Frenchman Emmanuel Laroche, showed Lycian to be related to Luwian. It is now believed that Lycian descended from a West Luwian dialect. *See also* Luwian language.

lycopene, an organic compound belonging to the isoprenoid series and responsible for the red colour of the tomato, the hips and haws of the wild rose, and many other fruits. Lycopene is an isomer of the carotenes, the yellow colouring matter, both having the same molecular formula, $C_{40}H_{56}$, but differing in structure. Lycopene was isolated from the black bryony (*Tamus communis*), a European yam, in 1873, and from tomatoes in 1875.

Lycoperdales, order of fungi (division Mycota) in the class Basidiomycetes. It includes

(Top) Earthstar (*Geastrum hygrometricus*) and (bottom) puffball (*Lycoperdon perlatum*)

(Top) R.H. Runde, (bottom) Walter Chandoha

about 270 species, among them earthstars and puffballs, which are found in soil or on decaying wood in grassy areas and woods. Many puffballs, named for the features of the fruiting body (basidiocarp), are edible before maturity, at which time the internal tissues become dry and powdery. Puffs of spores discharge when the fruiting structure is disturbed. *Calbovista subsculpta,* an edible puffball, is found along old road beds and in pastures.

Lycoperdon is a genus of 50 cosmopolitan species of small common puffballs. *L. perlatum* (*gemmatum*) has spotlike scars on the surface and is edible only when young. These fungi are found in the woods or on sawdust in summer and autumn.

Calvatia is a genus of about 35 species that are especially common in temperate regions. The giant puffball (*C. gigantea*), edible while young and white inside, is found in late summer on wet humus or soil. The fruiting body may be as large as 120 cm (4 feet) across and contain 10^{13} spores.

Another genus is *Geastrum* (*Geaster*), consisting of about 30 widespread species of earthstars with an expanded starlike base. They are found among dead leaves in woods in summer and autumn.

A problematic group of puffballs and earthstars, the Sclerodermatales, is sometimes placed within the order Lycoperdales, but some authorities accord it status as a separate order. Individuals of these species, found in soil and rotting wood, form puffball-like fruiting bodies with a hard outer wall and a dark-coloured interior when mature. The genus *Tulostoma* contains about 50 species usually found in dry regions.

Lycophron OF CHALCIS (fl. late 3rd century BC), Greek poet and scholar best known because of the attribution to him of the extant poem *Alexandra.*

Invited to work in the Alexandrian library (*c.* 285 BC), Lycophron there wrote a treatise on comedy and numerous tragedies, of which only a few fragments survive. The *Alexandra* is in form a messenger's speech in which the prophecies of Cassandra are reported. The poem carries the cult of erudition and obscurity to extremes, the material is recondite, the vocabulary is exotic, the style is affected, and the names of gods and men are disguised by cult title or riddling periphrasis. Considerable historical interest attaches to the references to Rome and the West, which have been thought to be more in keeping with the historical situation in 197 BC than with that a century earlier. On this ground it has sometimes been argued that the *Alexandra* is by a later author than the tragedian Lycophron.

Lycophyta, a division of spore-bearing vascular plants that contains the club mosses and their allies. They are distributed worldwide and are grouped in four genera and about 1,200 species.

A brief treatment of lycophytes follows. For full treatment, *see* MACROPAEDIA: Ferns and Other Lower Vascular Plants.

Lycophytes are small plants that may grow erect, as creepers, or upon rocks or trees. Branching is usually dichotomous. They have true roots, stems, and leaves and are capable of photosynthesis. The sporangia (spore cases) are located on special leaves, or sporophylls, which are clustered into conelike structures called strobili. Lycophytes may be homosporous (having one kind of spore) or heterosporous (having two kinds of spores, microspores and megaspores).

The order Lycopodiales is divided into two extant genera: *Phylloglossum,* restricted to Australia and New Zealand, and *Lycopodium* (club mosses), which are primarily tropical but are frequent in temperate regions as well. Some botanists divide *Lycopodium* into 4–12 genera. The order Selaginellales is represented by one living genus, *Selaginella* (spike mosses). Spike mosses are heterosporous and have organs on the stem called rhizophores, which form roots upon contact with the soil. The order Isoetales comprises one living genus, *Isoetes* (quillworts), which is characterized by a compact, cormlike stem; long, narrow, quill-like leaves; and roots borne in distinct rows. Members are found mostly in cooler climates.

Like other vascular plants (*i.e.,* plants with special systems for food and water conduction), lycophytes alternate between asexual (sporophyte) and sexual (gametophyte) reproduction. Gametophytes in club mosses germinate from a single type of spore. The sperm-producing antheridia and the egg-producing archegonia are both located on the gametophyte, and fertilization occurs when a sperm travels to an egg in the archegonium. A sporophyte then grows out and separates from the gametophyte, which eventually dies. Upon reaching maturity, the sporophyte sheds its spores, and the cycle is repeated. Spike mosses and quillworts produce separate male and female gametophytes, both of which undergo most of their development inside the sporangia. The gametophytes are later shed onto the soil, and, after fertilization, a sporophyte is produced. Quillworts generally produce many more spores than spike mosses.

Extinct lycophytes were especially numerous in the Devonian and Carboniferous periods (408 to 286 million years ago). Members of the genera *Lepidodendron* and *Sigillaria* developed into trees over 30 m (100 feet) in height, with leaves sometimes 1 m (3 feet) long. The remains of these extinct trees make up most of the world's coal beds.

Lycurgus (fl. 7th century BC?), traditionally, the lawgiver who founded most of the institutions of ancient Sparta.

Scholars have been unable to determine conclusively whether Lycurgus was a historical person and, if he did exist, which institutions should be attributed to him. In surviving ancient sources, he is first mentioned by the Greek writer Herodotus (5th century BC), who claimed that the lawgiver belonged to Sparta's Agiad house, one of the two houses (the other being the Eurypontid) that held Sparta's dual kingship. According to Herodotus, the Spartans of his day claimed that Lycurgus' reforms were inspired by the institutions of Crete. The historian Xenophon, writing in the first half of the 4th century BC, apparently believed that Lycurgus had founded Sparta's institutions soon after the Dorians invaded Laconia (*c.* 1000 BC) and reduced the native Achaean population to the status of serfs, or helots.

By the middle of the 4th century BC, it was generally accepted that Lycurgus had belonged to the Eurypontid house and had been regent for the Eurypontid king Charillus. On this basis Hellenistic scholars dated him to the 9th century BC. In his *Life of Lycurgus,* the Greek biographer Plutarch pieced together popular accounts of Lycurgus' career. Plutarch described Lycurgus' journey to Egypt and claimed that the reformer had introduced the poems of Homer to Sparta.

In the light of the conflicting opinions about Lycurgus held by writers before 400 BC, some modern scholars have concluded that Lycurgus was not a real person. They point out that the Greeks tended to discuss the origins of political and social institutions in terms of the personal intentions of a single founder. Nevertheless, many historians believe that a man named Lycurgus should be associated with the drastic reforms that were instituted in Sparta after the revolt of the helots in the second half of the 7th century BC. Those scholars claim that, in order to prevent another helot revolt, Lycurgus devised the highly militarized communal system that made Sparta unique among the city-states of Greece. If that view is correct, it is probable that Lycurgus also delineated the powers of the two traditional organs of the Spartan government, the *gerousia* (council of elders, including the two kings) and the *apella* (assembly).

Lycurgus (b. *c.* 390 BC—d. *c.* 324), Athenian statesman and orator noted for his efficient financial administration and vigorous prosecutions of officials charged with corruption.

Lycurgus supported Demosthenes' opposition to Macedonian expansion. During the 12 years (338–326) following the Athenian defeat by Macedonia at Chaeronea, he controlled the state finances and is said to have doubled the annual public revenues. He reformed the constitution of the army, remodeled the fleet, repaired dockyards, and finished the arsenal designed by the architect Philo. Lycurgus carried out an extensive building program, including the reconstruction in stone of the Dionysiac theatre. He also had official copies made of the plays of the three great tragic dramatists, Aeschylus, Sophocles, and Euripides.

An austerely pious and patriotic man, he felt it his mission to raise the level of public and private morals. Of his 15 speeches existing in ancient times, only one, "Against Leocrates," has survived complete; in it, Lycurgus indicts Leocrates for fleeing Athens in the panic that followed the Battle of Chaeronea. The speech is an impersonal homily on patriotism in a style that, although showing traces of Isocrates' influence, is marred by careless sentence structure and unnecessarily long quotations from historical and poetical sources.

Lycus (river, Lebanon): *see* Kalb, Nahr al-.

Lydd, parish (town), Shepway district, county of Kent, England. Nearby is the complex shingle spit of Dungeness, on the coast of the English Channel, where a nuclear power station has been built. Until the 14th century the town was on an island and was a member of the Cinque Ports (*q.v.*), but it now lies 3 mi (5 km) from the sea. Its parish church includes Saxon work and has a tower that is a widely known landmark. Nearby Ferryfield Airport has car ferry services to the European mainland. Pop. (1981 prelim.) 4,721.

Lydda (Israel): *see* Lod.

Lydgate, John (b. *c.* 1370, Lidgate, Suffolk, Eng.—d. *c.* 1450, Bury St. Edmunds?), English poet, known principally for long moralistic and devotional works.

In his *Testament* Lydgate says that while still a boy he became a novice in the Benedictine abbey of Bury St. Edmunds, where he became a priest in 1397. He spent some time in London and Paris; but from 1415 he was mainly at Bury, except during 1421–32 when he was prior of Hatfield Broad Oak in Essex.

Lydgate had few peers in his sheer productiveness; 145,000 lines of his verse survive. His only prose work, *The Serpent of Division*

Lydgate, detail from a manuscript, 15th century; in the British Library (Harley Ms. 4826)

Reproduced by permission of the British Library

(1422), an account of Julius Caesar, is brief. His poems vary from vast narratives such as *The Troy Book* and *The Falle of Princis* to occasional poems of a few lines. Of the longer poems, one translated from the French, the allegory *Reason and Sensuality* (*c.* 1408) on the theme of chastity, contains fresh and charming descriptions of nature, in well-handled couplets. *The Troy Book*, begun in 1412 at the command of the prince of Wales, later Henry V, and finished in 1421, is a rendering of Guido delle Colonne's *Historia troiana*. It was followed by *The Siege of Thebes*, in which the main story is drawn from a lost French romance, embellished by features from Boccaccio.

Lydgate admired the work of Chaucer intensely and imitated his versification. In 1426 Lydgate translated Guillaume de Deguilleville's *Le Pèlerinage de la vie humaine* as *The Pilgrimage of the Life of Man*, a stern allegory; between 1431 and 1438 he was occupied with *The Falle of Princis*, translated into Chaucerian rhyme royal from a French version of Boccaccio's work. He also wrote love allegories such as *The Complaint of the Black Knight* and *The Temple of Glass*, saints' lives, versions of Aesop's fables, many poems commissioned for special occasions, and both religious and secular lyrics.

His work is uneven in quality, and the proportion of good poetry is small. Yet with all his faults, Lydgate at his best wrote graceful and telling lines. His reputation long equalled Chaucer's, and his work exercised immense influence for nearly a century.

Lydia, ancient land of western Anatolia, extending east from the Aegean Sea and occupying the valleys of the Hermus and Cayster rivers. The Lydians were said to be the originators of gold and silver coins. During their brief hegemony over Asia Minor from the middle of the 7th to the middle of the 6th century BC, the Lydians profoundly influenced the Ionian Greeks to their west.

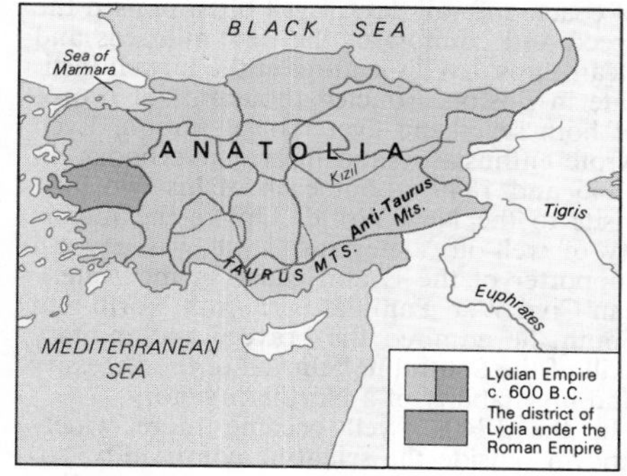

Lydia

From W. Shepherd, *Historical Atlas*, Harper & Row, Publishers (Barnes & Noble Books), New York; revision copyright © 1964 by Barnes & Noble, Inc.

In the 7th century BC Lydia filled the vacuum left by the Cimmerian destruction of Phrygia and established a dynasty at Sardis under the legendary king Gyges. The kingdom reached its zenith under Alyattes (*c.* 619–560), who parried a Median threat, pushed back the Cimmerians, and extended his rule in Ionia. The kingdom seemed destined to reach even greater heights under Alyattes' son, the wealthy Croesus, when the Persians under Cyrus brought the Lydian monarchy to a final and dramatic end (*c.* 546–540).

The Lydians were a commercial people, who, according to Herodotus, had customs like the Greeks and were the first people to establish permanent retail shops. Their invention of metallic coinage, which the Greeks quickly adopted, played an important part as a catalyst in the commercial revolution that transformed Greek civilization in the 6th century BC.

Lydian language, extinct Indo-European language of ancient Lydia, in the central part of the western coast of Anatolia. The texts, most of which have been found by U.S. excavators at the Lydian capital Sardis, date back to the 5th or 6th century BC, although the majority of them stem from the 4th century BC. The East Greek alphabet was the prototype for that of the Lydian texts. In 1936 Lydian was proven to be an Indo-European language by the Italian scholar Piero Meriggi, and Onofrio Carruba gave strong evidence in 1959 that Lydian should be placed in the Anatolian subgroup of Indo-European languages because Lydian shares many common features with Hittite, Luwian, and Palaic.

Lydian mode, in music, fifth of the eight medieval church modes. *See* church mode.

lye, the alkaline liquor obtained by leaching wood ashes with water, commonly used for washing and in soapmaking; more generally, any strong alkaline solution or solid, such as sodium hydroxide or potassium hydroxide (*see* sodium; potassium).

Lyell, Sir Charles, BARONET (b. Nov. 14, 1797, Kinnordy, Forfarshire, Scot.—d. Feb. 22, 1875, London), Scottish geologist largely responsible for the general acceptance of the view that all features of the Earth's surface are produced by physical, chemical, and biological processes through long periods of geological time. The concept was called uniformitarianism (initially set forth by James Hutton). Lyell's achievements laid the foundations for evolutionary biology as well as for an understanding of the Earth's development. He was knighted in 1848 and made a baronet in 1864.

Life. Lyell was born at Kinnordy, the stately family home at the foot of the Grampian Mountains in eastern Scotland. His principal childhood associations, however, were with the New Forest near Southampton, Eng., where his parents moved before he was two years old. His father, a naturalist who later turned to more literary pursuits, kept the study well stocked with books on every subject, including geology. The eldest of 10 children, Charles attended a series of private schools, where he was not a particularly diligent student; he much preferred rambles in the New Forest and his father's instruction at home to those places, with their schoolboy pranks and pecking orders whose spirit he never really shared. His first scientific hobby was collecting butterflies and aquatic insects, an activity pursued intensively for some years, even though labelled unmanly by local residents. His observations went far beyond those of any ordinary boy, and later this instinct for collecting and comparing led to important discoveries.

Lyell, detail of a replica in oil by L. Dickinson, 1883; in the National Portrait Gallery, London

By courtesy of the National Portrait Gallery, London

At 19 Lyell entered Oxford University, where his interest in classics, mathematics, and geology was stimulated, the latter by the enthusiastic lectures of William Buckland, later widely known for his attempt to prove Noah's Flood by studies of fossils from cave deposits. Lyell spent the long vacations between terms travelling and conducting geological studies. Notes made in 1817 on the origin of the Yarmouth lowlands clearly foreshadow his later work. The penetrating geological and cultural observations Lyell made while on a continental tour with his family in 1818 were as remarkable as the number of miles he walked in a day. In December 1819 he earned a B.A. with honours and moved to London to study law.

Career. Lyell's eyes were weakened by hard law study, and he sought and found relief by spending much time on geological work outdoors. Among these holidays was a visit to Sussex in 1822 to see evidence of vertical movements of the Earth's crust. In 1823, on a visit to Paris, he met the renowned naturalists Alexander von Humboldt and Georges

Cuvier and examined the Paris Basin with the French geologist Louis-Constant Prévost. In 1824 Lyell studied sediments forming in freshwater lakes near Kinnordy. When in London, Lyell participated in its vigorous intellectual life, meeting such literati as Sir Walter Scott and taking active part in several scientific societies.

New approach to geology. Prodded to finish his law studies, Lyell was admitted to the bar in 1825, but with his father's financial support he practiced geology more than law, publishing his first scientific papers that year. Lyell was rapidly developing new principles of reasoning in geology and began to plan a book which would stress that there are natural (as opposed to supernatural) explanations for all geologic phenomena, that the ordinary natural processes of today and their products do not differ in kind or magnitude from those of the past, and that the Earth must therefore be very ancient because these everyday processes work so slowly. With the ambitious young geologist Roderick Murchison, he explored districts in France and Italy where proof of his principles could be sought. From northern Italy Lyell went south alone to Sicily. Poor roads and accommodations made travel difficult, but in the region around Mt. Etna he found striking confirmation of his belief in the adequacy of natural causes to explain the features of the Earth and in the great antiquity even of such a recent feature as Etna itself.

The results of this trip, which lasted from May 1828 until February 1829, far exceeded Lyell's expectations. Returning to London, he set to work immediately on his book, *Principles of Geology,* the first volume of which was published in July 1830. A reader today may wonder why this book filled with facts purports to deal with principles. Lyell had to teach his principles through masses of facts and examples because in 1830 his method of scientific inquiry was novel and even mildly heretical. A remark of Charles Darwin shows how brilliantly Lyell succeeded: "The very first place which I examined . . . showed me clearly the wonderful superiority of Lyell's manner of treating geology, compared with that of any other author, whose work I had with me or ever afterwards read."

During the summer of 1830 Lyell travelled through the geologically complex Pyrenees to Spain, where the closed, repressed society both fascinated and repelled him. Returning to France, he was astonished to find King Charles X dethroned, the tricolour everywhere, and geologists able to talk only of politics. Back in London he set to work again on the *Principles of Geology,* finishing Volume II in December 1831 and the third and final volume in April 1833. His steady work was relieved by occasional social or scientific gatherings and a trip to a volcanic district in Germany close to the home of his sweetheart, Mary Horner, in Bonn, whom he married in July 1832, taking a long honeymoon and geological excursion in Switzerland and Italy. Mary, whose father had geological leanings, shared Charles's interests. For 40 years she was his closest companion; the happiness of their marriage increased because of her ability to participate in his work.

During the next eight years the Lyells led a quiet life. Winters were devoted to study, scientific and social activities, and revision of *Principles of Geology,* which sold so well that new editions were frequently required. Data for the new editions were gathered during summer travels, including two visits to Scandinavia in 1834 and 1837. In 1832 and 1833 Lyell delivered well-received lectures at King's College, London, afterward resigning the professorship as too time-consuming.

Scientific eminence. Publication of the *Principles of Geology* placed him among the recognized leaders of his field, compelling him to devote more time to scientific affairs. During these years he gained the friendship of men like Darwin and the astronomer Sir John Herschel. In 1838 Lyell's *Elements of Geology* was published; it described European rocks and fossils from the most recent, Lyell's specialty, to the oldest then known. Like the *Principles of Geology,* this well-illustrated work was periodically enlarged and updated.

In 1841 Lyell accepted an invitation to lecture and travel for a year in North America, returning again for nine months in 1845–46 and for two short visits in the 1850s. During their travels, the Lyells visited nearly every part of the United States east of the Mississippi River and much of eastern Canada, seeing almost all of the important geological "monuments" along the way, including Niagara Falls. Lyell was amazed at the comparative ease of travel, although they saw many places newly claimed from the wilderness. A veteran of coach and sail days, Lyell often praised the speed and comfort of the new railroads and steamships. Lyell's lectures at the Lowell Institute in Boston attracted thousands of people of both sexes and every social station. Lyell wrote enthusiastic and informative books, in 1845 and 1849, about each of his two long visits to the New World. Unlike the majority of well-off Victorians, Lyell was a vocal supporter of the Union cause in the American Civil War. Familiar with both North and South, he admired the bravery and military skill of the South but believed in the necessity and inevitability of a Northern victory.

In the 1840s Lyell became more widely known outside the scientific community, socializing with Lord John Russell, a leading Whig; Sir Robert Peel, founder of Scotland Yard; and Thomas Macaulay, the historian of England. In 1848 Lyell was knighted for his scientific achievements, beginning a long and friendly acquaintance with the royal family. He studied the prevention of mine disasters with the English physicist Michael Faraday in 1844, served as a commissioner for the Great Exhibition in 1851–52, and in the same year helped to begin educational reform at Oxford University—he had long objected to church domination of British colleges. Lyell's professional reputation continued to grow; during his lifetime he received many awards and honorary degrees, including, in 1858, the Copley Medal, the highest award of the Royal Society of London; and he was many times president of various scientific societies or functions. Expanding reputation and responsibilities brought no letup in his geological explorations. With Mary, he travelled in Europe or Britain practically every summer, visiting Madeira in the winter of 1854 to study the origin of the island itself and of its curious fauna and flora. Lyell especially liked to visit young geologists, from whom he felt "old stagers" had much to learn. After exhaustive restudy carried out on muleback in 1858, he proved conclusively that Mt. Etna had been built up by repeated small eruptions rather than by a cataclysmic upheaval as some geologists still insisted. He wrote Mary that "a good mule is like presenting an old geologist with a young pair of legs."

In 1859 publication of Darwin's *Origin of Species* gave new impetus to Lyell's work. Although Darwin drew heavily on Lyell's *Principles of Geology* both for style and content, Lyell had never shared his protégé's belief in evolution. But reading the *Origin of Species* triggered studies that culminated in publication of *The Geological Evidence of the Antiquity of Man* in 1863, in which Lyell tentatively accepted evolution by natural selection. Only during completion of a major revision of the *Principles of Geology* in 1865 did he fully adopt Darwin's conclusions, however, adding powerful arguments of his own that won new adherents to Darwin's theory. Why Lyell was hesitant in accepting Darwinism is best explained by Darwin himself: "Considering his age, his former views, and position in society, I think his action has been heroic."

After 1865 Lyell's activities became more restricted as his strength waned, although he never entirely gave up outdoor geology. His wife, 12 years his junior, died unexpectedly in 1873 after a short illness, leaving Lyell to write, "I endeavour by daily work at my favourite science, to forget as far as possible the dreadful change which this has made in my existence." He died in 1875, while revising his *Principles of Geology* for its 12th edition, and was buried in Westminster Abbey.

Assessment. Lyell typified his times in beginning as an amateur geologist and becoming a professional by study and experience. Unlike most geologists then and now, however, he never considered observations and collections as ends in themselves but used them to build and test theories. The *Principles of Geology* opened up new vistas of time and change for the younger group of scientists around Darwin. Only after they were gone did Lyell's reputation begin to diminish, largely at the hands of critics who had not read the *Principles of Geology* as carefully as had Darwin and attributed to Darwin things he had learned from Lyell. Lyell is still underestimated by some geologists who fail to see that the methods and principles they use every day actually originated with Lyell and were revolutionary in his era. The lasting value of Lyell's work and its importance for the modern reader are clear in Darwin's assessment:

> The great merit of the *Principles* was that it altered the whole tone of one's mind, and therefore that, when seeing a thing never seen by Lyell, one yet saw it partially through his eyes.

(R.W.Ma.)

BIBLIOGRAPHY. Katherine M. Lyell (ed.), *Life, Letters, and Journals of Sir Charles Lyell, Bart.*, 2 vol. (1881), is the best source of Lyell's own observations. Charles Lyell, *Principles of Geology, Being an Attempt to Explain the Former Changes of the Earth's Surface by Reference to Causes Now in Operation,* 3 vol. (1830–33, reprinted 1969), and *Principles of Geology, or The Modern Changes of the Earth and Its Inhabitants,* 11th ed., 2 vol. (1872), are the two best editions to consult and compare. T.G. Bonney, *Charles Lyell and Modern Geology* (1895), is a perceptive 19th-century view. See also M.J.S. Rudwick, "Lyell on Etna, and the Antiquity of the Earth," in C.J. Schneer (ed.), *Toward a History of Geology* (1969); and *Sir Charles Lyell's Scientific Journals on the Species Question* (1970), written by the leading student of Lyell's life and work, L.G. Wilson, who also provided the definitive biography *Charles Lyell. The Years to 1841: The Revolution in Geology* (1972).

Lyell, Mount, mining area, western Tasmania, Australia. The site, discovered in the 1880s, derives its name from a 2,900-ft (880-m) peak in the west coast range, which was named after Charles Lyell, the 19th-century English geologist. First mined for gold and later silver, the area currently yields about 90 percent of the state's copper. After 1968, vast new underground deposits were developed. Most of the workers reside nearby in Queenstown. The ore is railed north to the port of Burnie, from which most is shipped to Japan and the remainder sent to Port Kembla, N.S.W.

lygaeid bug, any insect of the family Lygaeidae (order Heteroptera), which includes, among its more than 3,000 species, many important crop pests. Lygaeid bugs range from 3 to 15 millimetres (0.1 to 0.6 inch) in length, although they are usually less than 10 mm. They vary from brown to brightly patterned with red, white, or black spots and bands. The large milkweed bug (*Oncopeltus fasciatus*) is distinguished by its broad red and black bands.

The family is sometimes called the chinch bug family because one species, the destruc-

Milkweed bug (*Oncopeltus fasciatus*)
E.S. Ross

tive chinch bug (*q.v.*), feeds on the sap of plants. Other important members of the family include the Old World, or Egyptian, cotton stainer (*Oxycarenus hyalinipennis*) and the Australian *Nysius vinitor,* both of which are destructive to fruit trees, and *Geocoris punctipes,* which preys on mites, termites, and other small plant-feeding insects.

Lyly, John (b. 1554?, Kent, Eng.—d. November 1606, London), author considered to be the first English prose stylist to leave an enduring impression upon the language. As a playwright he also contributed to the development of prose dialogue in English comedy.

Lyly was educated at Magdalen College, Oxford, and went to London about 1576. There in 1578 he soared to fame with the publication of two prose romances, *Euphues, or the Anatomy of Wit* (1578) and *Euphues and His England* (1580), that made him the most fashionable English writer in the 1580s. *Euphues* is a romantic intrigue told in letters interspersed with general discussions on such topics as religion, love, and epistolary style. Lyly's preoccupation with the exact arrangement and selection of words, his frequent use of similes drawn from classical mythology, and his artificial and excessively elegant prose inspired a short-lived Elizabethan literary style called "euphuism." The *Euphues* novels introduced a new concern with form into English prose.

Lyly abandoned the novel after 1580 and devoted himself almost entirely to writing comedies. In 1583 he gained control of the first Blackfriars Theatre, in which his earliest plays, *Campaspe* and *Sapho and Phao,* were produced. All of Lyly's comedies except *The Woman in the Moon* were presented by a children's company that was periodically favoured by Queen Elizabeth. His plays' dates of first performance are as follows: *Campaspe* and *Sapho and Phao,* 1583–84; *Gallathea,* 1585–88; *Endimion,* 1588; *Midas,* 1590; *Love's Metamorphosis,* 1590; *Mother Bombie,* 1590; and *The Woman in the Moon,* 1595. All but one of these are in prose. The finest is *Endimion,* which some critics hold a masterpiece despite its preciosity.

Lyly's comedies mark an enormous advance upon those of his predecessors in English drama. Their plots are drawn from classical mythology and legend, and their characters engage in euphuistic speeches redolent of Renaissance pedantry; but the charm and wit of the dialogues and the light and skillful construction of the plots set standards that younger and more gifted dramatists could not ignore.

Lyly's popularity waned with the rise of Thomas Kyd, Christopher Marlowe, and William Shakespeare, and his appeals to Queen Elizabeth for financial relief went unheeded. He had hoped to succeed Edmund Tilney in the court post of master of the revels, but Tilney outlived him, and Lyly died a poor and bitter man.

Lyme disease, tick-borne bacterial disease that was first conclusively identified in 1975 and is named for the town in Connecticut, U.S., in which it was first observed. The disease has been identified in every region of the United States and in Europe, Asia, Africa, and Australia.

Lyme disease is caused by the spirochete (corkscrew-shaped bacterium) *Borrelia burgdorferi.* The spirochete is transmitted to the human bloodstream by the bite of various species of ticks. In the northeastern United States, the carrier tick is usually *Ixodes dammini;* in the West, *I. pacificus;* and in Europe, *I. ricinus.* Ticks pick up the spirochete by sucking the blood of deer or other already-infected animals. *I. dammini* mainly feeds on white-tailed deer and white-footed mice, especially in areas of tall grass, and is most active in summer. The larval and nymphal stages of this tick are more likely to bite humans than are the adult and are hence more likely to cause human cases of the disease.

In humans the disease progresses in three stages. The first and mildest stage is characterized by a circular rash in a bull's-eye pattern that appears anywhere from a few days to a month after the tick bite. The rash is often accompanied by such flu-like symptoms as headaches, fatigue, chills, loss of appetite, fever, and aching joints or muscles. The majority of persons who contract Lyme disease experience only these first-stage symptoms, and never become seriously ill. A minority, however, will go on to the second stage of the disease, which begins two weeks to three months after infection. This stage is indicated by arthritic pain that migrates from joint to joint and by disturbances of memory, vision, locomotion, or other neurological symptoms. The third stage of Lyme disease, which generally begins within two years of the bite, is marked by crippling arthritis and by neurological symptoms that resemble those of multiple sclerosis. Symptoms vary widely, however, and some victims experience facial paralysis, meningitis, memory loss, mood swings, and an inability to concentrate.

Because Lyme disease often mimics other disorders, its diagnosis is sometimes difficult, especially when there is no record of the distinctive rash. The early treatment of Lyme disease by means of antibiotics (usually tetracycline for adults and penicillin for children) is important in order to prevent progression of the disease to a more serious stage. More powerful antibiotics are used in the latter case, though symptoms may recur periodically thereafter.

lyme grass: *see* wild rye.

Lyme Regis, town ("parish"), West Dorset district, county of Dorset, England. It is built on a steep-sided hill above a small harbour and shingle beach. The harbour is flanked by a jetty to the east and a massive curved wall, known as The Cobb, to the west. Three manors of Lyme are mentioned in Domesday Book (1086). Edward I granted a charter in 1284 making the community a free borough with a merchant guild. At that time it was engaged in trade with France, and by 1311 it had become an important English port. Further charters were granted by later English monarchs. The picturesque town contains many Georgian houses, and the chief industry is tourism. Pop. (1981) 3,464.

Consult the INDEX *first*

---

lymph, pale fluid that bathes the tissues of an organism, maintaining fluid balance, and removes bacteria from tissues; it enters the blood system by way of lymphatic channels and ducts.

Prominent among the constituents of lymph are lymphocytes and macrophages, the primary cells of the immune system with which the body defends itself from invasion by foreign microorganisms. Lymph is conveyed from the tissues to the venous bloodstream via the lymphatic vessels. On the way, it is filtered through the lymphatic organs (spleen and thymus) and lymph nodes.

Pressure within the walls of lymph vessels is lower than that in blood vessels. Lymph flows more slowly than blood. The cell walls of lymph vessels are more permeable than those of the capillary walls of blood vessels. Thus, proteins that may have been delivered to the tissues by the bloodstream but that are too big to reenter the capillaries, along with waste products and large proteins synthesized in the local tissue cells, enter the lymphatic vessels for return to the bloodstream.

The lymphatic vessels of vertebrates generally empty into the bloodstream near the location at which the cardinal veins enter the heart. In mammals, lymph enters the bloodstream at the subclavian vein, via the thoracic duct. From their terminal ducts to their sources between the cells of the tissues, the lymph vessels divide and subdivide repeatedly, becoming narrower at each division. A system of valves in the larger vessels keeps the lymph flowing in one direction.

In mammals, lymph is driven through the lymphatic vessels primarily by the massaging effect of the activity of muscles surrounding the vessels. Animals lower than mammals have muscular swellings called lymph hearts at intervals of the lymphatic vessels to pump lymph through them.

All multicellular animals distinguish between their own cells and foreign microorganisms and attempt to neutralize or ingest the latter. Macrophages (literally, "big eaters") are motile cells which surround and ingest foreign matter. All animals above the level of bony fishes have concentrations of lymphoid tissue, which consists of macrophages and lymphocytes (white blood cells that react to chemically neutralize foreign microorganisms). The spleen, thymus, and lymph nodes of mammals consist of lymphoid tissue; further concentrations of it are found throughout the body in places (such as the gut wall, or the tonsils and adenoids of humans) where foreign microorganisms might have easiest ingress.

Bacteria and other particles that find their way into body tissues are taken up by the lymph and carried into the lymph nodes, where the bands of lymphatic tissue crossing the lymph sinuses impede their passage. Lymphocytes proliferate in response to the foreign invader, some cells remaining in the node and others migrating to other nodes elsewhere in the body. Some of these cells produce antibodies against the invading bacteria, while others take part in a direct attack on the foreign material, surrounding and engulfing it.

Although the primary function of the lymphatic system is to return proteins and fluids to the blood, this immune function accounts for the tendency of many infections and other disease processes to cause swelling of the lymph nodes. Bacteria, allergenic particles, and cancerous cells from elsewhere in the body that have collected in the nodes stimulate lymphocyte proliferation, thereby greatly enlarging the node. Interference with lymphatic flow may cause an accumulation of fluid in the tissues that are drained by the blocked vessel, producing tissue swelling known as lymphedema.

Other and more serious conditions affecting the lymphatic system include various forms of malignancy, either lymphocytic leukemia or lymphoma, depending on the nature of lymphatic proliferation. Dramatic increases in circulating lymphocytes characterize acute lymphocytic leukemia, a highly fatal disease that occurs most frequently in children; less rapid increases in circulating lymph cells occur in chronic lymphocytic leukemia, which is more common in those over 45. In both conditions, the accumulation of lymphocytes in the bloodstream is accompanied by anemia.

Gross enlargement of the lymph nodes through malignant proliferation of lymph cells characterizes Hodgkin's disease and other forms of lymphoma.

Lymph node enlargement may occur in syphilis, infectious mononucleosis, amyloidosis, and tuberculosis, as may local lymph node swelling in other infectious processes.

lymph node, any of the small, rounded masses of lymphoid tissue surrounded by a capsule of connective tissue that occur in association with the lymphatic vessels. Lymph nodes consist of a reticulum of connective-tissue fibres in the meshes of which are contained numerous small, round cells, each of which has a large, round, deeply staining nucleus and which, when carried off by the flow of lymph through the node, becomes a lymphocyte.

Lymph nodes expose microorganisms and other substances circulating in the lymph to infection-fighting phagocytic cells and lymphocytes. Great numbers of lymph nodes are distributed along the lymphatic vessels. Lymph channels leading to the nodes conduct lymph slowly into and out of the node. As the lymph is filtered through the node, it is exposed to many phagocytic cells—cells that can engulf microorganisms or other foreign materials. Foreign materials in the lymph are particularly exposed to lymphocytes, which attack the invaders directly or synthesize antibodies against them. Another function of the node is to add lymphocytes and antibodies to the lymph as it passes through, ensuring that the capacity for immune response pervades the entire lymphatic system.

Under normal conditions lymph nodes are small and hidden; when inflamed by bacterial invasion, they may enlarge to 1 to 2 cm (0.4 to 0.8 inch) in human beings. Besides the many lymph nodes distributed along the lymphatic circulatory system throughout the body, there are clusters of lymph nodes in certain regions such as the neck, groin, and armpits. Lymph nodes commonly play a role in the spread of cancer. Since lymphatic vessels are ubiquitous in the body, malignant tumours frequently invade them. Cells that break away from the tumour are carried to the lymph nodes, where they are entrapped and begin to grow, thereby establishing secondary tumours. For this reason many lymph nodes must be removed during surgical treatment of cancer in order to ensure the tumour's complete removal.

lymph nodule, small, localized collection of lymphoid tissue, usually located in the loose connective tissue beneath wet epithelial (covering or lining) membranes, as in the digestive system, respiratory system, and urinary bladder. Lymph nodules form in regions of frequent exposure to microorganisms or foreign materials and contribute to the defense against them. The nodule differs from a lymph node in that it is much smaller and does not have a well-defined connective-tissue capsule as a boundary. It also does not function as a filter, because it is not located along a lymphatic vessel. Lymph nodules frequently contain germinal centres—sites for localized production of lymphocytes. In the small intestine, collections of lymph nodules are called Peyer's patches. The tonsils are also local regions where the nodules have merged together.

lymphedema, an abnormal condition in which drainage of the lymphatic system is blocked, allowing fluid to build up in the tissues. Lymphedema can be either primary or secondary in form. Primary lymphedema occurs most commonly as simple congenital lymphedema, which is present at birth but is not familial (hereditary). Similar familial forms are seen in such disorders as Milroy's disease and Noonan's syndrome. The lymphedema in all these types usually involves both legs below the knees and begins as a painless swelling in the foot that moves up to the leg as it progresses. Although the swelling is initially painless, it may impair leg function in extreme cases and be cosmetically undesirable. Primary lymphedema is more common in women and is treated by regular elevations of the affected limbs and external compression with elastic stockings. In very severe cases, surgical drainage of the obstructed lymph channels may be necessary. In its secondary form, lymphedema most commonly results from infection, and it also can occur after the surgical removal of lymph nodes or after radiation treatments used to fight cancer. If caused by infection, it can be treated with antibiotics.

lymphocyte, type of leukocyte (white blood cell) that is of fundamental importance in the immune system. In humans, lymphocytes make up 20–25 percent of the total number of leukocytes.

The two primary types of lymphocytes are B lymphocytes and T lymphocytes, or B cells and T cells. Both originate from stem cells in the bone marrow and travel in the blood to lymphoid tissues, such as the spleen, tonsils, and lymph nodes. Most T cells are long-lived, their life span averaging 2 to 4 years, while most B cells are short-lived, with an average life span of a week to a few months.

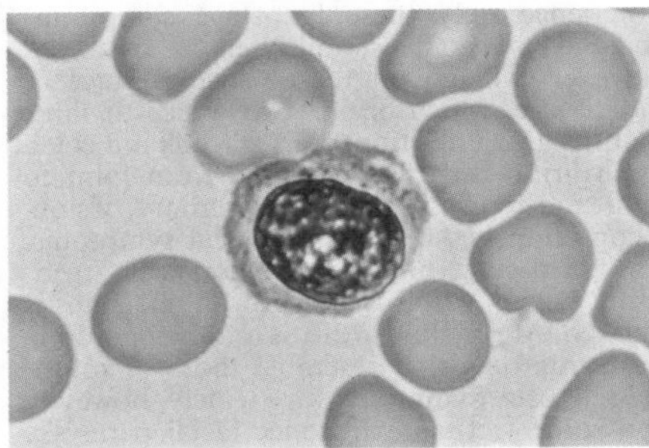

Human lymphocyte (phase contrast microphotograph)
Manfred Kage—Peter Arnold

Through receptor molecules on their surfaces, lymphocytes are able to bind to antigens (foreign substances or microorganisms that the host recognizes as "nonself") and help remove them from the body. Each lymphocyte bears receptors that bind to a specific antigen. The ability to respond to virtually any antigen comes from the fact that the body contains millions of lymphocytes, with many carrying unique receptors.

Once stimulated by binding to an antigen, such as a bacterium or a virus, a B cell multiplies into a clone of identical cells. Some of these cloned B cells differentiate into plasma cells that produce antibody molecules. These antibodies are closely modeled after the receptors of the precursor B cell, and, once released into the blood and lymph, they bind to the target antigen and initiate its neutralization or destruction (*see* antibody). Antibody production continues for several days, until the antigen has been overcome. Other B cells, called memory cells, are stimulated to multiply but do not differentiate into plasma cells; they provide the immune system with long-lasting memory and a heightened sensitivity to a particular type of antigen should it return to the host.

Before arriving in the lymphoid tissues, T cells mature in the thymus, where they multiply and differentiate into helper, suppressor, and cytotoxic T cells. Once stimulated by the appropriate antigen, helper T cells secrete lymphokines, which stimulate the differentiation of B cells into plasma cells, thereby promoting antibody production. Suppressor T cells act to diminish this reaction, hence their name. Cytotoxic T cells, which are activated by the leukokine interleukin 2, bind to and kill infected cells (especially those infected by viruses). *See also* leukocyte.

lymphogranuloma venereum, also called LYMPHOGRANULOMA INGUINALE, CLIMATIC BUBO, or NICOLAS-FAVRE DISEASE, infection of lymph channels and lymph nodes by the microorganism *Chlamydia trachomatis.* Like chlamydia, which is a venereal disease caused by *C. trachomatis,* lymphogranuloma venereum is acquired in sexual intercourse. The disease produces swollen lymph nodes, ulcerations, enlargement of genital organs, and rectal stricture. It is a relatively common disease, occurring throughout most of the world, especially in tropical and subtropical areas. Incidence of the infection is about the same for both sexes, and all races are affected. It is endemic in the southern United States, particularly among the poor.

The primary lesion, usually on the genitalia, appears from 5 to 21 days after infection. The lesion is often so transitory as to escape notice, and the first manifestation of the disease may be a hot, tender swelling of lymph glands (buboes) in the inguinal region (groin), appearing from 10 to 30 days after exposure. In the female the initial symptoms frequently occur on the rectum.

Fever, chills, headache, and joint pains may be present. Abscess formation with drainage of pus from the inguinal lymph nodes is usual. Later manifestations of the disease include secondary ulceration and elephantiasis (great enlargement) of the genitalia in both sexes, polypoid growths about the anus, inflammation, ulceration, and stricture of the rectum, and (rarely) arthritis, conjunctivitis, and nervous-system involvement. The course of the disease varies from asymptomatic infection to extreme debilitation with chronic invalidism as the result of chronic late manifestations.

Effective treatment is limited. Periodic follow-up blood tests for syphilis are advisable.

lymphoid tissue, cells, tissues, and organs that compose the immune system. Among the elements of lymphoid tissue are the bone marrow, thymus, spleen, and lymph nodes. Lymphoid tissue has several different structural organizations related to its particular function in the immune response. The most highly organized lymphoid tissues are the thymus and lymph nodes, which are well-defined encapsulated organs with easily identifiable architectures. In the spleen (a soft, purplish organ lying high in the abdomen), the lymphoid tissue is a cylinder of loosely organized cells surrounding small arteries. In the bone marrow this tissue is mixed with the blood-forming cells, and no organization is apparent. The most diffuse component of the lymphoid tissue is found in the loose connective-tissue spaces beneath most wet epithelial membranes, such as those that line the gastrointestinal tract and the respiratory system. In these spaces many cells of the lymphoid system wander and become exposed to invading microorganisms and antigenic (foreign) material. They can establish localized centres of cell production in response to such invasions. These are referred to as nodules and are not to be confused with nodes, an entirely different structure. Some nodules become relatively permanent structures, such as the tonsils, appendix, and Peyer's patches, which are in the lining of the small intestine. Most nodules appear and disappear in response to local needs.

Several types of cells are included in the lymphoid system. Reticular cells are the structural component, since they produce and maintain the thin networks of fibres that are a framework for most lymphoid organs. Macrophages are cells that engulf foreign materials and probably alter them to initiate the immune response. These cells may be fixed, as in lymph nodes, or may wander in the loose connective-tissue spaces. The most common cell type in the lymphoid tissue is the lymphocyte. Like macrophages, lymphocytes are formed from stem cells in the bone marrow and then circulated in the blood to the lymphoid tissue. T lymphocytes mature in the thymus before proceeding to the other lymphoid organs, such as the spleen. B lymphocytes mature in the bone marrow and proceed directly to the lymphoid organs. Both kinds play a key role in immune responses to infectious microorganisms.

lymphoma, any of a group of malignant diseases, usually starting in the lymph nodes or in the lymphoid tissues (including the lung, the gut, or the skin). They are generally classified into two types, Hodgkin's disease (*q.v.*) and non-Hodgkin's lymphoma, each category being further subdivided. Hodgkin's disease is a cancerous disease involving enlargement of the lymph nodes and spleen and severe anemia. Burkitt's lymphoma is a cancer of the lymphatic system most commonly found in African children; research suggests it may be caused by or linked in some way to a virus called the Epstein-Barr virus. The other non-Hodgkin's lymphomas, which are referred to in a number of ways, may be further described by the morphology of the cells and may be either diffuse or nodular. Generally speaking, the nodular type of disease follows a slower course than the diffuse type. Diffuse large-cell (histiocytic) lymphomas are highly invasive, able to involve the skin, liver, lung, kidneys, and even the brain. Diagnosis of either major form of lymphoma requires analysis of biopsy material, usually from the lymph nodes.

lymphoreticuloma: *see* Hodgkin's disease.

Lynch, Benito (b. June 25, 1885, Buenos Aires, Arg.—d. Dec. 23, 1951, La Plata), Argentine novelist and short-story writer whose tales of Argentine country life examined in a simple and direct style the psychology of ordinary persons at everyday activities. Lynch thus brought a new realism to the tradition of the gaucho novel, a genre that portrays the people of the South American grasslands.

Of Irish ancestry, Lynch lived as a boy on a cattle ranch in the province of Buenos Aires, gaining an intimate knowledge of the rural life that he later used as the subject for most of his writings. His first important novel, *Los caranchos de la Florida* (1916; "The Vultures of La Florida"), deals with the conflict between a father, master of a cattle ranch, and his son, who has returned after study in Europe.

Lynch diverged from the usual dramatic or sensational myth of the gaucho. His simple, ironic approach is displayed in *Raquela* (1918) and in the novel generally considered his best, *El inglés de los güesos* (1924; "The Englishman of the Bones"), a tragic story of love between a young English anthropologist and a gaucho girl. Lynch also wrote several collections of short stories.

Lynch, John (Mary) (b. Aug. 15, 1917, Cork, County Cork, Ire.—d. Oct. 20, 1999, Dublin), Irish politician who was prime minister of Ireland from 1966 to 1973 and from 1977 to 1979.

Lynch studied law and entered the civil service (Department of Justice) in 1936. He eventually decided on an active legal career, was called to the bar (1945), resigned from the civil service, and practiced on the Cork circuit. He entered politics as a member of the opposition in 1948 and worked closely with Eamon De Valera. After his party, Fianna Fáil, came to power in 1951, he was a parliamentary secretary in 1951–54, minister for the *Gaeltacht* (Gaelic-speaking districts) in 1957, minister for education in 1957–59, minister for industry and commerce in 1959–65, and minister for finance in 1965–66.

When Sean Lemass announced his retirement as *taoiseach* (prime minister) in 1966, the result was an inner-party conflict over the succession that led to Lynch's selection as a compromise candidate. In November he became head of Fianna Fáil and prime minister.

In 1972 Lynch secured a successful referendum on Ireland's entry into the European Economic Community, and on Jan. 1, 1973, Ireland became a member. Though favouring the unity of Ireland and Northern Ireland, Lynch took a tough attitude toward the terrorist activities of the Provisional Irish Republican Army, arresting several members over the years. Defeated in the 1973 elections, his party returned to power after the 1977 elections. In December 1979, however, discouraged about his party's prospects, Lynch resigned his leadership.

Lynch, John R(oy) (b. Sept. 10, 1847, Concordia Parish, La., U.S.—d. Nov. 2, 1939, Chicago, Ill.), black politician after the American Civil War who served in the Mississippi state legislature and U.S. House of Representatives and was prominent in Republican Party affairs of the 1870s and '80s.

Born a slave, Lynch was freed during the American Civil War and settled in Natchez, Miss. There he learned the photography business, attended night school, and in 1869 entered public life as justice of the peace for Natchez county.

In November 1869 Lynch was elected to the Mississippi House of Representatives, and he was reelected in 1871. Although blacks never were in the majority in the Mississippi legislature, Lynch was chosen speaker of the House in 1872. That same year he was elected to Congress, and he was reelected in 1874. But by 1876 Reconstruction was over, and Lynch was defeated for a third term. In 1880 he ran again and was declared the loser, but he contested the decision and eventually was returned to his congressional seat. In the House he backed civil-rights legislation.

Lynch retired to his plantation in Adams county, Mississippi, in 1883. In 1889 he returned to public office when President Benjamin Harrison appointed him fourth auditor of the U.S. Treasury for the Navy Department. Always active in the Republican Party, Lynch served as a delegate to the national Republican conventions of 1872, 1884, 1888, 1892, and 1900. He was temporary chairman in 1884—the first black to preside over a national convention of a major U.S. political party.

In *The Facts of Reconstruction* (1913), Lynch attempted to dispel the erroneous notion that Southern state governments after the Civil War were under the control of blacks.

Lynchburg, city, Campbell and Bedford counties, central Virginia, U.S. It is situated on the James River, in the foothills of the Blue Ridge Mountains. The city grew from a ferry landing settled in 1757 by Quakers; it was named for John Lynch, the ferry operator who owned the original townsite. During the American Revolution, John's patriot brother, Charles, set up an irregular court and imposed savage penalties on Tories, giving rise to the expression "lynch law." The town flourished after the James River and Kanawha Canal (1840) connected it with Richmond, Va., 156 miles (251 km) east, and after the arrival of the railroad in 1852. During the American Civil War, Lynchburg was a Confederate supply base and the scene of General Jubal A. Early's victory over General David Hunter's Union troops (June 1864); the restored Fort Early commemorates the event.

Following the war Lynchburg developed as a shoe- and iron-manufacturing centre. Its importance as a market for dark tobacco (for chewing) decreased with the increased use of bright tobacco (for cigarettes). Lynchburg's modern economy includes manufacturing and agriculture (tobacco, corn [maize], and other grains).

The city is the seat of Virginia Seminary and College (1888; Baptist), Randolph-Macon Woman's College (1891; Methodist), Lynchburg College (1903; Disciples of Christ), Central Virginia Community College (1966), and Liberty Baptist (1971). Inc. town, 1805; city, 1852. Pop. (1990) city, 66,049; Lynchburg MSA, 142,199.

lynching, form of mob violence in which a mob executes a presumed offender, often also torturing him and mutilating his body, without trial, under the pretense of administering justice. The term "lynch law" refers to a self-constituted court that imposes sentence on a person without due process of law. Both terms are derived from the name of Charles Lynch, a Virginia planter and patriot who, during the American Revolution, headed an irregular court formed to punish Loyalists.

Summary and irregular justice have been practiced in many countries under unsettled conditions whenever informally organized groups have attempted to supplement or replace legal procedure. The fehmic courts of medieval Germany had some aspects of lynching, as did the gibbet law and Cowper justice of border districts in England. The Santa Hermandad institution in medieval Spain and pogroms directed against Jews in Russia and Poland were similar, though in these cases there was support from legally constituted authorities.

Statistics of reported lynching in the United States indicate that, between 1882 and 1951, 4,730 persons were lynched, of whom 1,293 were white and 3,437 were black. Lynching continued to be associated with racial disputes during the 1950s and '60s when civil rights workers and advocates were threatened and in some cases killed by mobs.

Lynd, Robert (Staughton); and Lynd, Helen, Helen Lynd *née* MERRELL (respectively b. Sept. 26, 1892, New Albany, Ind., U.S.—d. Nov. 1, 1970, Warren, Conn.; b. March 17, 1894, La Grange, Ill.—d. Jan. 30, 1982, Warren, Ohio), American sociologists, husband and wife who collaborated on the *Middletown* books, which became classics of sociological literature as well as popular successes. They are said to have been the first to apply the methods of cultural anthropology to the study of a modern Western city.

Robert Lynd edited the trade magazine *Publishers Weekly* (1914–18) and later worked for book-publishing firms in New York City. He directed a sociological study of small cities for the Institute of Social and Religious Research (1923–26), served as an official of the Social Science Research Council (1927–31), and taught sociology at Columbia University (from 1931). He was the sole author of *Knowledge for What?* (1939). He and Helen Merrell were married on Sept. 3, 1921. Helen Lynd taught at Sarah Lawrence College, Bronxville, N.Y. (1929–64), and her independent writings included *On Shame and the Search for Identity* (1958) and *Toward Discovery* (1965).

On the basis of field observations of social stratification in Muncie, Ind., the Lynds wrote *Middletown: A Study in Contemporary American Culture* (1929) and *Middletown in Transition: A Study in Cultural Conflicts* (1937). An innovation was the Lynds' treatment of the middle class as a tribe in the anthropological sense. *Middletown in Transition* is devoted to analyzing the social changes induced by the Great Depression of the 1930s.

Lyndsay, Sir David, Lyndsay also spelled LINDSAY (b. *c.* 1490—d. before April 18, 1555), Scottish poet of the pre-Reformation period who satirized the corruption of the Roman Catholic church and contemporary government. He was one of the company of gifted courtly poets (*makaris*) who flourished in the golden age of Scottish literature. His didactic writings in colloquial Scots were characterized by a ribald buffoonery and a combination of moralizing and humour.

Born into an aristocratic family, Lyndsay was appointed attendant and companion to

Lyndsay, drawing after a woodcut on the title page of Lyndsay's *Workes,* 1634

By courtesy of the trustees of the British Museum; photograph, J.R. Freeman & Co. Ltd.

the infant prince (born 1512), the son of King James IV. Dismissed from court 12 years later, when his charge, then James V, fell under the control of the Douglas faction, he returned to the king's service in 1528. An influential diplomat, Lyndsay represented the king on important missions to the courts of Henry VIII, Charles V, Francis I (after James's death in 1542), and other European monarchs. Most of his verse, with a work on heraldry, was written during his prosperous years at court.

Lyndsay's *Ane Satyre of the Thrie Estaits* is the only surviving complete Scottish morality play. Originally entitled "the mysdemeanours of Busshops Religious persones and preists within the Realme" (1540), it was enlarged with coarse comedy and performed in 1552 at Cupar, Fife, and again on the slopes of the Calton Hill, Edinburgh. It is a dramatic representation of the crucial issues of the mid-century in religion, government, and social life, with all classes of society mirrored, admonished, and entertained.

The Dreme (completed 1528), Lyndsay's earliest surviving work in verse, is an allegory of the contemporary condition of Scotland, with a delightfully personal epistle to the king. *The Testament and Complaynt of Our Soverane Lordis Papyngo* (completed 1530), written to celebrate the king's escape from the Douglases, is a mixture of satire, comedy, and moral instruction in which the king's dying parrot gives advice to the king and court; and his *An Answer quhilk Schir David Lyndsay maid to the Kingis Flyting* (1536) is a ribald example of the game of poetic abuse ("flyting") practiced by Celtic poets. *The Complaynt and Publict Confessioun of the Kingis Auld Hound callit Bagsche* (*c.* 1536) is a short didactic piece, satirizing court life through the mouth of a dog, a device later revived by Robert Burns.

Lynen, Feodor (b. April 6, 1911, Munich, Ger.—d. Aug. 8, 1979, Munich), German biochemist who, for his research on the metabolism of cholesterol and fatty acids, was a corecipient (with Konrad Bloch) of the 1964 Nobel Prize for Physiology or Medicine.

Lynen was trained at the University of Munich. After several years as a lecturer in the chemistry department there (1942–47), he became a professor. While at Munich he worked on the intermediary metabolism of the living cell, research that led him to the demonstration of the first step in a chain of reactions resulting in the biosynthesis of sterols and fatty acids: the acetylation of coenzyme A. In 1954 Lynen became director of the Max Planck Institute for Cell Chemistry in Munich.

Lynen was highly regarded in the scientific community. His work on the biosynthesis of sterols and fatty acids was cited by the Nobel Prize committee as a contribution to pure chemistry and to the search for a remedy for heart disease caused by cholesterol.

Lynmouth (England): *see* Lynton and Lynmouth.

Lynn, city, Essex county, northeastern Massachusetts, U.S. It lies on Nahant Bay and Lynn Harbor (inlets of Massachusetts Bay), just northeast of Boston. Settled in 1629 as Saugus, it was renamed in 1637 for Lynn Regis, Eng. Tanning and shoemaking were early colonial activities, and the first iron-smelting works in the American colonies was built there in 1643. After the introduction of the shoe-sewing machine in 1848 and factory production methods, it became the country's leading shoe centre. A more diversified economy has prevailed since the 1930s, which now focuses on services (mainly health care and telecommunications). Lynn is the site of extensive manufacturing facilities of the General Electric Company, producing jet engines and electrical instruments.

Recreational areas include Lynn Woods, a large municipal park with wilderness areas. The city has a campus of North Shore Community College (1965). The Mary Baker Eddy House, where the Christian Science movement originated in the 1860s, is in the adjacent town of Swampscott. Lynn is connected to the peninsular resort town of Nahant by Lynn Beach, a 1.5-mile- (2.4-km-) long sand spit. Inc. town, 1629; city, 1850. Pop. (2002 est.) 89,590.

Lynn Canal, narrow scenic passage, 3 to 12 miles (5 to 19 km) wide, in the eastern North Pacific Ocean, southeastern Alaska, U.S. It lies within the Alexander Archipelago and extends north from Chatham Strait for 60 miles (100 km). It is the northernmost fjord to penetrate the Coast Mountains, which rise on its eastern side. The canal was named (1794) by Captain George Vancouver for his birthplace, King's Lynn, Eng. Just south of Haines, the navigable canal divides into two inlets, the westernmost to the mouth of the Chilkat River, the easternmost through Taiya Inlet to the port of Skagway, terminus of the Inside Passage from Washington state.

Lynn Lake, mining village, northwestern Manitoba, Canada, in the subarctic Reindeer Lake region. It developed after copper and nickel deposits were discovered in the vicinity of Lynn Lake in 1941. The Sherritt Gordon Mining Company, following the abandonment of its copper-mining operations at Sherridon (120 miles [193 km] south) in 1951, in collaboration with the provincial government, moved the Sherridon townsite by tractor-train over the frozen northland to Lynn Lake. It was later connected to The Pas (south) by a rail branch (1953) and by air. Lynn Lake produces much of the province's nickel-ore output and manufactures ammonium sulfate fertilizer. Gold and silver are also mined locally. Pop. (2001) 699.

lynnhaven, edible variety of oyster (*q.v.*).

Lynton and Lynmouth, town ("parish"), North Devon district, administrative and historic county of Devon, Eng. Lynmouth lies at the mouth of the East Lyn and West Lyn rivers, and Lynton stands on a cliff 500 feet (150 metres) above. Lynmouth's small harbour on the Bristol Channel, with its Rhenish tower, was reconstructed after a disastrous flood in August 1952. Both villages are summer resorts in Exmoor National Park. Pop. (2001) 1,738.

lynx (genus *Lynx*), short-tailed cat (family Felidae), found in the forests of Europe, Asia, and northern North America. The Canada lynx (*Lynx canadensis*) and bobcat (*L. rufus*) live in North America. The two other lynx species are the Eurasian (*L. lynx*) and Iberian

Lynx (*Lynx lynx*)

Philip Wayre

(*L. pardinus*) lynx, the latter being an endangered species now found only in the mountains of southern Spain.

Lynx are long-legged, large-pawed cats with tufted ears, hairy soles, and a broad, short head. The coat, which forms a bushy ruff on the neck, is tawny to cream-coloured and somewhat mottled with brown and black; the tail tip and ear tufts are black. In winter the fur is dense and soft, up to 10 cm (4 inches) long, and is sought for trimming garments. Lynx range in size from 80 to 100 cm long, without the 10–20-cm tail, and stand about 60 cm tall at the shoulder. Weight is from 10 to 20 kg (22 to 44 pounds).

Nocturnal and silent, except during the mating season, lynx live alone or in small groups. They climb and swim well and feed on birds and small mammals. The Eurasian lynx will take larger prey such as deer. The Canada lynx depends heavily on the snowshoe hare for food, and its population increases and decreases regularly every 9 or 10 years, relative to the population of its prey. Lynx breed in late winter or early spring, and a litter of one to four young is born after a gestation period of about two months.

lynx spider, any member of the family Oxyopidae (order Araneida). They are distributed

Lynx spider (*Peucetia viridans*)

Jack Dermid

worldwide and in North America are most common in southern regions. The eyes are arranged in a hexagon, and the abdomen usually tapers to a point. Lynx spiders are usually found on vegetation seeking insect prey. They do not build a nest or web but capture their prey by pouncing upon them.

lyochrome (pigment): *see* flavin.

Lyon, also spelled LYONS, capital of Rhône *département*, east-central France, set on a hilly site at the confluence of the Rhône and Saône rivers. A Roman military colony called Lugdunum was founded there in 43 BC, and it subsequently became the capital of the Gauls. Lyon reached its peak of classical development in the 2nd century AD, during which time Christianity was introduced. In 177 the Christian community was persecuted by the Roman emperor Marcus Aurelius, and in 197 Lucius Septimius Severus decimated Lyon. In 1032 Lyon was incorporated into the Holy Roman Empire, but the real power lay with the city's archbishops, whose influence caused important ecumenical councils to be held there in 1245 and again in 1274. Lyon was annexed to the kingdom of France in 1312.

The Renaissance ushered in a period of economic prosperity and intellectual brilliance. The establishment, in 1464, of commercial fairs together with the arrival in the city of Italian merchant bankers enabled Lyon to flourish. By the 17th century it was the silk-manufacturing capital of Europe. Printing was introduced as early as 1473, and Lyon soon became one of the most active printing centres in Europe.

The French Revolution brought uneasy times. The collapse of the domestic market and the closing of foreign markets brought a slump in the silk industry, and in 1793 the city was besieged by republican forces of the Montagnards. In the 19th century prosperity returned, bringing about considerable industrial expansion. Urban development began only in the 1950s, after the periods of stagnation and depression between 1920 and the end of World War II.

Lyon is spread over a narrow peninsula between the Rhône and Saône rivers and on their opposite banks. A zone of factory and residential suburbs encircles the city. On the right bank of the Saône, Vieux Lyon (Old Lyon) remains as one of the finest surviving architectural complexes of the Renaissance era. The peninsula is now the heart of the business district. The east bank of the Rhône is divided between a wealthy area, the Brotteaux, and a district with factories and workers' houses extending east toward the fringing communities of Villeurbanne and Bron. To the south, along the Rhône, Feyzin and Saint-Fons constitute one of the largest oil-refining complexes in France.

The city now has a diversified economy. The textile industry is dominated by the manufacture of rayon and silk, but the production of chemicals has become the key industry. Originally connected with the treatment of textiles, it was given fresh impetus by the manufacture of dyes, synthetic fibres, and oil products. The important metallurgical industry includes a wide variety of processes, varying from foundries to the construction of mechanical, electrical, and electronic equipment. The construction, food, and printing industries are prosperous.

Lyon is the seat of a university and is the most important educational centre outside Paris. Cultural life is reflected in the riches of the local museums, which include a textile collection, the archaeological museum at Fourvière, a museum of fine arts, and a museum of printing and banking. The collections of the municipal library are noted for their specimens of items from the first 50 years of printing and for their rare books. City theatres include the Opéra, the Célestins (a municipal theatre), and some avant-garde companies that have gained national recognition. Music and drama festivals, held every year in June in the Roman theatre at Fourvière, provide a reminder of the long history of the city. Pop. (1982) city, 410,455; metropolitan area, 1,170,000.

Lyon, Amy: *see* Hamilton, Emma, Lady.

Lyon, Butcher of (Nazi leader): *see* Barbie, Klaus.

Lyon, Corneille de (b. *c.* 1500, The Hague—d. 1574?), highly reputed portrait painter of 16th-century France, few of whose works have survived.

Early in his life Corneille went to France, where in 1524 he became attached to the royal court in Lyon. In 1541 he was appointed official painter of the Dauphin (the future king Henry II). When Henry II ascended the throne in 1547, Corneille became his painter and chief valet. He became a naturalized French citizen. The artist's major work of this period was a series of portraits of the French court. In 1564 Catherine de Médicis visited the artist and was struck by the lifelike quality of her own portrait. In that same year Corneille received a gift of money from Charles IX, whom he served as royal painter. One of the last known facts about him is his rejection of Protestantism to become a Roman Catholic in 1569. After 1574 there is no record of him.

Very few existing works bear the de Lyon signature. A series of royal portraits in the Louvre are uncertainly attributed to him.

Lyon, councils of, 13th and 14th ecumenical councils of the Roman Catholic Church. In 1245 Pope Innocent IV fled to Lyon from the besieged city of Rome. Having convened a general council attended by only about 150 bishops, the Pope renewed the church's excommunication of the Holy Roman emperor Frederick II and declared him deposed on the four counts of perjury, disturbing the peace, sacrilege, and suspicion of heresy. During the council the Pope also urged support for Louis IX, king of France, who was making preparations for the Seventh Crusade.

The second Council of Lyon was convened by Pope Gregory X in 1274 after Michael VIII Palaeologus, the Byzantine emperor, gave assurances that the Orthodox Church was prepared to reunite with Rome. By acknowledging the supremacy of the pope, Michael hoped to gain financial support for his wars of conquest. Accordingly, a profession of faith, which included sections on purgatory, the sacraments, and the primacy of the pope, was approved by the Orthodox representatives and some 200 Western prelates, and reunion was formally accepted. The Greek clergy, however, soon repudiated the reunion. The council also formulated and approved strict regulations to ensure the speedy election of future popes, and it placed restrictions on certain religious orders.

Lyon, Mary (Mason) (b. Feb. 28, 1797, near Buckland, Mass., U.S.—d. March 5, 1849, South Hadley, Mass.), U.S. pioneer in the field of higher education for women and founder and first principal of Mount Holyoke Female Seminary, the forerunner of Mount Holyoke College.

Mary Lyon, detail of an oil painting by an unknown artist; in the collection of Mount Holyoke College, South Hadley, Mass.

By courtesy of Mount Holyoke College, South Hadley, Mass.

She began to teach when she was 17, and in 1817, with earnings from spinning and weaving, she went to Sanderson Academy, Ashfield, Mass. She supported herself there and at the other academies she attended by teaching. Her success as teacher and administrator and the demand for the young women she trained led to her plan for a permanent instructional institution for women. Aided by Edward Hitchcock, the geologist, with whom she had studied, she won the necessary financial support. In 1835 a site was selected near the village of South Hadley; the school was incorporated in 1836 as Mount Holyoke Female Seminary. On Nov. 8, 1837, it opened with Mary Lyon as principal. She served in this post until her death.

Lyon faience, tin-glazed earthenware produced at Lyon, from the 16th century to 1770. Originally made by Italian potters, 16th-century Lyon faience remained close to its Italian prototype, the so-called *istoriato* Urbino maiolica, the subjects of which are either historical, mythological, or biblical. Such, for instance, is a large, circular dish (British Museum) inscribed "Lyon, 1582," the overall decoration of which was obviously inspired by an illustration in Jean de Tournes's Bible, published in Lyon in 1554. The dish is possibly the work of an Italian, Giulio Gambini, who later became a partner at Nevers. In the 17th century Lyon's output seems to have consisted almost entirely of drug jars and *faience blanche,* or plain white faience. In about 1733 Joseph Combe tried to revive the manufacture of more sumptuous wares, but Lyon's faience remained derivative, this time of Moustiers, the birthplace of Combe. Later in the century it was almost indistinguishable from that of Turin; it had the same medley of Chinese and architectural motifs, interspersed with exotic birds, plants, and insects, the only difference being that instead of the red used at Turin, the Lyon potters used a yellow ochre. Except for a few signatures, Lyon faience bears no proprietary marks.

Lyonia, genus of about 45 species of shrubs, of the heath family (Ericaceae), notable for its attractive white or pinkish flowers and dense foliage. All occur in North America and Asia. All species except *L. lucida,* the tetterbush, are deciduous. The leaves are alternate, have short stalks, and are smooth-edged or finely toothed. The flowers are usually bell-shaped or urn-shaped.

Commonly cultivated species—all of which grow best in damp or swamp soil—include *L. ligustrina,* the maleberry, which grows 3.6 metres (12 feet) tall; *L. lucida,* which grows 1.2–1.8 m tall; and *L. mariana,* the staggerbush, which grows 1.8 m tall. Staggerbush is poisonous to livestock.

Lyonnais, historic and cultural region encompassing the eastern French *départements*

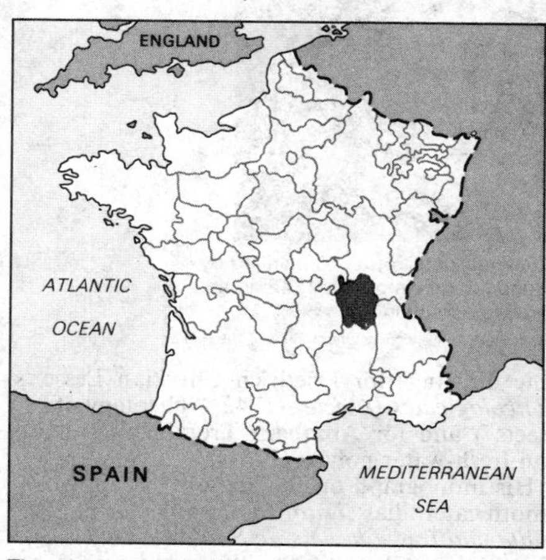

The *gouvernement* of Lyonnais in 1789

of Loire and Rhône and coextensive with the former province of Lyonnais.

As a former province or *gouvernement* of the *ancien régime,* Lyonnais was bounded on the north by Burgundy; on the east by Dombes, Bresse, and Dauphiné; on the south by Languedoc; and on the west by Auvergne and Bourbonnais. The older Lyonnais comprised the territory dependent on Lyon west of the Saône and Rhône rivers as far as the Lyonnais Mountains, east of the Rhône in the immediate vicinity of Lyon, and east of the Saône north of Lyon. It included the country around Vimy (Neufville-sur-Saône), which had the right to vote its own taxes and so was called the Franc-Lyonnais. The province was formed in the 16th century when Beaujolais and Forez were merged with the older Lyonnais. The entire region was converted into the *département* of Rhône-et-Loire in 1790 and was divided into Rhône and Loire in 1793.

The Rhône, Saône, and Loire rivers flow through this highly industrialized region. The city of Lyon has long been a centre of the silk and cloth industries; metallurgy, chemicals, vehicles, armaments, and food-processing are also significant. Cereals, sugar beets, and cattle are the principal agricultural products.

Though it adjoins the Rhône River valley, Lyonnais itself comprises the crystalline uplands of the Massif Central; its average elevation is about 2,300–2,950 feet (700–900 m). Farms in the Massif Central are ordinarily small, though emigration from the countryside has increased the consolidation of farmland. Small farms are owned and worked by families, and adjoining land is often leased. Open fields predominate in the plains. Farmsteads tend to be dispersed.

Roman Catholicism predominates and is particularly strong in Lyon, a major centre of missionary activities. There is a sizable Calvinist enclave in Lyon, and numerous Lutherans have emigrated to Lyonnais from Alsace since 1870. Lyon has a large Jewish community. The regional dialect is rarely spoken. French is spoken with a droning and nasal accent and is interspersed with various local words.

Lyonnet, Pierre, also called PIETER LYONET (b. July 22, 1708, Maastricht, Neth.—d. Oct. 10, 1789, The Hague), Dutch naturalist and engraver famed for his skillful dissections and illustrations of insect anatomy.

Trained as an attorney, Lyonnet was a respected biologist and spent most of his time engraving objects of natural history. He made

Lyonnet, detail of an oil painting by Hendrik van Limborch, 1742; in a private collection

By courtesy of the Iconographisch Bureau, The Hague

the drawings for Friedrich Christian Lesser's *Théologie des Insectes* (1742; "Theology of Insects") and for Abraham Trembley's treatise on fresh-water polyps (1744).

His monograph on the anatomy of the goat-moth caterpillar, *Traité anatomique de la Chenille, qui ronge le bois de Saule* (1760), is one of the most beautifully illustrated works on anatomy ever published. His drawings, engraved on copper plates, distinguished more than 4,000 separate muscles and showed details of nerves and tracheae never before recorded. The publication of his work caused a sensation, bringing charges of embellishment and the use of fanciful detail. In the second edition (1762) he replied to his critics by supplying drawings of his instruments and a description of his methods.

Lyot, Bernard(-Ferdinand) (b. Feb. 27, 1897, Paris, Fr.—d. April 2, 1952, Cairo, Egypt), French astronomer who invented the coronagraph (1930), an instrument which allows the observation of the solar corona when the Sun is not in eclipse.

Before Lyot's coronagraph, observing the corona had been possible only during a solar eclipse, but this was unsatisfactory because total eclipses occur only rarely and the duration of such eclipses is too short (no more than seven minutes) to allow prolonged scientific observation of the corona. Merely blocking out the Sun's radiant disk was insufficient to view the comparatively dim corona because of the diffusion of the Sun's light by the atmosphere, whose brightness rendered the delicate corona invisible. But by going to the Pic du Midi Observatory high in the French Pyrenees, where the high altitude resulted in less atmospheric diffusion, and by equipping his coronagraph with an improved lens and a monochromatic filter that he had developed, Lyot succeeded in making daily photographs of the Sun's corona. In 1939, using his coronagraph and filters, he shot the first motion pictures of the solar prominences.

Lyot was elected to the Academy of Sciences in 1939; in the same year, he was awarded the Gold Medal of the Royal Astronomical Society.

Lyotard, Jean-François (b. Aug. 10, 1924, Versailles, Fr.—d. April 21, 1998, Paris), French philosopher and leading figure in the intellectual movement known as postmodernism.

In his youth, Lyotard considered becoming a monk, a painter, and a historian. After receiving his philosophy degree from the Sorbonne in 1950, he taught for two years in Constantine, Algeria, where he witnessed firsthand the oppressive atmosphere of colonialism. During the 1950s Lyotard was active in the anti-Stalinist socialist group Socialisme ou Barbarie ("Socialism or Barbarism"), and his political writings vehemently criticized French colonial involvement in Algeria. In 1969 he began teaching philosophy at the University of Paris VIII (Vincennes and St. Denis).

In his first major philosophical work, *Discourse/Figure* (1971), Lyotard distinguished between the meaningfulness of linguistic signs and the meaningfulness of plastic arts such as painting and sculpture. He argued that, because rational thought or judgment is discursive whereas works of art are inherently symbolic, certain aspects of artistic meaning will always be beyond rational understanding. In *Libidinal Economy* (1974), Lyotard contended that "desire" always escapes the generalizing and synthesizing activity inherent in rational thought and that reason and desire stand in a relationship of constant tension.

In *The Postmodern Condition* (1979), Lyotard characterized the postmodern era as one that has lost faith in the grand "metanarratives" in terms of which thinkers since the time of the Enlightenment have attempted to construct comprehensive explanations of historical experience. Disillusioned with metanarratives such as "reason," "truth," and "progress," the postmodern age has turned to smaller, narrower *petits récits* ("little narratives"), such as the history of everyday life or of marginalized groups. In *The Differend: Phrases in Dispute* (1983), Lyotard compared discourses to the "language games" developed in the later work of Ludwig Wittgenstein (1889–1951), characterizing them as discrete systems of rule-governed activity involving language. Because there is no common set of assumptions in terms of which their conflicting claims or viewpoints can be adjudicated (there is no universal "reason" or "truth"), discourses are for the most part incommensurable. The basic imperative of postmodern politics is then to create communities in which the integrity of different language games is respected—communities based on heterogeneities, conflict, and "dissensus."

(R.B.W.)

lyre, stringed musical instrument having a yoke, or two arms and a crossbar, projecting out from and level with the body. The strings run from a tailpiece on the bottom or front of the instrument to the crossbar. Most lyres are plucked, but a few are bowed. Box lyres are instruments having a boxlike wooden body with a wooden soundboard; in some instances the arms are hollow extensions of the body, as in

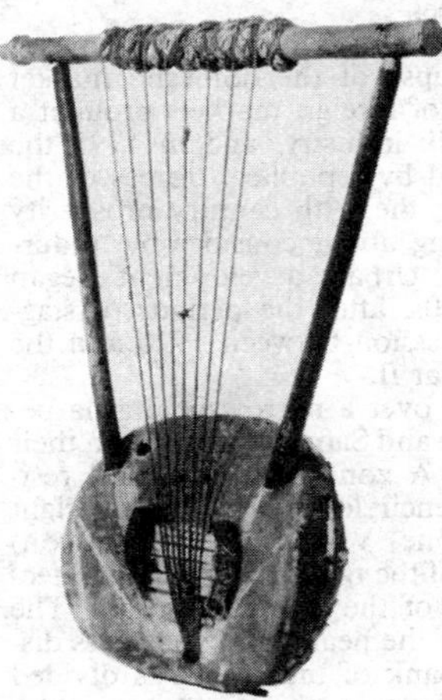

East African bowl lyre; in the Pitt Rivers Museum, Oxford

By courtesy of the Pitt Rivers Museum, Oxford

the ancient Greek kithara. Bowl lyres have a rounded body with a curved back—often of tortoiseshell—and a skin belly; the arms are invariably constructed separately, as in the Greek *lyra.*

Box lyres were widespread in the ancient Middle East. Giant lyres placed on the ground and played by seated musicians appear in Sumerian reliefs (3rd millennium BC); some exceeded 40 inches (100 cm) in height, although smaller lyres were also used. Typically ornamented with a carved bull on one side, the Sumerian lyres were played in upright position with the fingers of both hands. They were asymmetrical, having one longer arm.

Small asymmetrical lyres predominated after Sumerian times. Most were held vertically or at an angle and were played with a plectrum; Babylonia also had a small horizontally held lyre. Egyptian lyres included (from *c.* 2000 BC) an asymmetrical, plectrum-plucked instrument held horizontally and (from *c.* 1000 BC) a smaller symmetrical lyre played upright. The Hebrew *kinnor* was also a box lyre. Except for the Sumerian instruments, the Middle Eastern and Greek lyres were tuned by thong or cloth bulges into which the ends of the strings were wound and which could be shifted or tightened to increase string tension. Sumerian lyres were tuned by wooden wedges inserted into the winding bulges.

As an attribute of Apollo, the god of prophecy and music, the lyre to the ancient Greeks symbolized wisdom and moderation. Greek lyres fell into two types, exemplified by the *lyra* and kithara. The kithara was apparently of Asiatic origin, the *lyra* either indigenous or of Syrian provenance. Both shared the same playing technique, tuning, and stringing, the number of strings varying from 3 or 4 in Homer's time to as many as 12 by the 5th century BC; the classical number was 7. Normally used to accompany singing, they were played by a plectrum held in the right hand, the left-hand fingers damping unwanted notes and occasionally plucking or stopping a string to produce a higher note. In solo playing, both hands apparently plucked with the fingers. The *lyra* was the instrument of the amateur, the kithara, of the professional singer. Latinized to "cithara," it was adopted by the Romans.

In medieval Europe new varieties of lyre emerged that, like the kithara, were box lyres, although their precise relation to the lyres of classical antiquity is not known. The European lyres, often called rotta, varied from straight-sided to gently waisted. In most cases the body and yoke were cut from a single piece of wood. Tuning pegs replaced the wound thongs of the ancient lyres. Around the 12th century bowed lyres appeared; they are still played in Finland and Estonia under the name bowed harp. One bowed lyre was the Welsh crwth, which by the 13th century had gained a fingerboard running from the crossbar to the soundbox. Plucked lyres in which rattling pebbles are placed survive among the Ostyak and Vogul, Finno-Ugric peoples of Siberia.

The lyres of modern East Africa probably reflect ancient diffusion of the instrument via Egypt. Box lyres survive only in Ethiopia and among the Sebei, a Nilo-Hamitic people of Uganda. The Ethiopian *begenna* is a plectrum-plucked instrument normally used to accompany singing. Like the Sumerian lyres, it is tuned by wooden wedges. African bowl lyres vary from the Ethiopian *masonquo* and *krar* to the *ndongo* and *odi* of Uganda and similar instruments in the Congo. In some cases the sound is made to buzz either by running the strings close to the skin or by placing a rattling object on the skin under the strings. Observation of the playing techniques and tuning of the African lyres affords insight into the probable tuning and playing techniques of the ancient Greek lyres, notably because in significant instances such observation corresponds with pictorial evidence and with some interpretations of Greek technical terminology.

Consult the INDEX *first*

lyrebird, either of two species of Australian birds (family Menuridae, order Passeriformes) named for the shape of their tail when spread in courtship display. The name also aptly suggests a musician. Inhabiting forests of southeastern Australia, lyrebirds are ground dwellers, and their brown bodies rather resemble those of chickens. In the so-called superb lyrebird (*Menura superba*, or *M. novaehollandiae* of many authors), the male's tail consists of eight pairs of ornate feathers, which resemble a lyre when erect. There are six pairs of filmy, whitish feathers; one pair of 60–75 centimetre (24–30 inch) feathers that forms the arms of the "lyre" are broad and curled at the tip and are silvery on one side and marked with golden-brown crescents on the other. There are also two equally long "wires," narrow, stiff, slightly curved feathers that correspond to a lyre's strings; they are situated in the centre of the curved "arms." With a total length of about one metre (39 inches), the male lyrebird is the longest of passerine birds.

When the male displays in small clearings, which he makes at several places in the forest, he brings his tail forward so that the white plumes form a canopy over his head and the lyrelike feathers stand out to the side. In this position he sings, while prancing in rhythm,

Superb lyrebird (*Menura superba*)
John Warham

far-carrying melodious notes interspersed with perfect mimicry of other creatures and even of mechanical sounds. Its breeding season is rainy winter, when insect food is abundant. Its nest is a large mound of sticks, usually on the ground, that contains a spacious chamber for the single egg. Nest building and incubation are done by the female, which resembles the male except in tail development.

Albert's lyrebird (*M. alberti*) is a much less showy bird than the superb lyrebird, but an equally good mimic. It is rarely seen because its range is restricted to deep rain forest.

Lyrebirds were formerly thought to be related to pheasants or to the birds-of-paradise. With the scrub-birds (Atrichornithidae) the lyrebirds now occupy a suborder, Menurae, distinct from all other passerine birds.

lyretail, any of a half dozen species of fishes in the genus *Aphyosemion* of the family Cyprinodontidae (order Atheriniformes). All are freshwater species of tropical Africa. They attain lengths of five centimetres (two inches). Female lyretails are drab olive or beige, but the males are brilliantly splashed and spotted with reds, yellows, and blues. The tail is fan-shaped with extended filaments at the top and bottom giving the appearance of a lyre. The Cape Lopez lyretail (*A. arnoldi*), one of the first species discovered, is a popular aquarium fish, as are the others. Lyretails belong to the killifish (*q.v.*) group.

lyric, a verse or poem that is, or supposedly is, susceptible of being sung to the accompaniment of a musical instrument (in ancient times, usually a lyre) or that expresses intense personal emotion in a manner suggestive of a song. Lyric poetry expresses the thoughts and feelings of the poet and is sometimes contrasted with narrative poetry and verse drama, which relate events in the form of a story. Elegies, odes, and sonnets are all important kinds of lyric poetry.

In ancient Greece an early distinction was made between the poetry chanted by a choir of singers (choral lyrics) and the song that expressed the sentiments of a single poet. The latter, the *melos,* or song proper, had reached a height of technical perfection in "the Isles of Greece, where burning Sappho loved and sung," as early as the 7th century BC. That poetess, together with her contemporary Alcaeus, were the chief Doric poets of the pure Greek song. By their side, and later, flourished the great poets who set words to music for choirs, Alcman, Arion, Stesichorus, Simonides, and Ibycus, who were followed at the close of the 5th century by Bacchylides and Pindar, in whom the tradition of the dithyrambic odes reached its highest development.

Latin lyrics were written by Catullus and Horace in the 1st century BC; and in medieval Europe the lyric form can be found in the songs of the troubadours, in Christian hymns, and in various ballads. In the Renaissance the most finished form of lyric, the sonnet, was brilliantly developed by Petrarch, Shakespeare, Edmund Spenser, and John Milton. Especially identified with the lyrical forms of poetry in the late 18th and 19th centuries were the Romantic poets, including such diverse figures as Robert Burns, William Blake, William Wordsworth, John Keats, Percy Bysshe Shelley, Lamartine, Victor Hugo, Goethe, and Heinrich Heine. With the exception of some dramatic verse, most Western poetry in the late 19th and the 20th century may be classified as lyrical.

Lyrical Ballads (1798), collection of poems by Samuel Taylor Coleridge and William Wordsworth; its appearance is often designated by scholars as a signal of the beginning of the English Romantic movement. The work included Coleridge's "Rime of the Ancient Mariner" and Wordsworth's "Tintern Abbey," as well as many controversial common-language poems by Wordsworth, such as "The Idiot Boy." The "Preface" to the second edition (1800) contains Wordsworth's famous definition of poetry as the "spontaneous overflow of powerful feelings" and his theory that poetry should be written in "the language really used by men."

Lysander (d. 395 BC, Haliartus, Boeotia), Greek military and political leader who won the final victory for Sparta in the Peloponnesian War and, at its close, wielded great power throughout Greece.

Nothing is known of his early career. In his first year as admiral he won a sea battle off Notium (406) and obtained support of the Persian viceroy, Cyrus the Younger. Because Spartan law forbade a second term, Lysander nominally was second in command, though the actual Spartan leader, in the destruction of the Athenian fleet in the Battle of Aegospotami (*q.v.*), September 405 BC; this action closed the grain route through the Hellespont, thereby starving Athens into surrender (April 404). Lysander instigated establishment of the oligarchy of the Thirty Tyrants in Athens, and many of Athens' former allies came to be ruled by boards of 10 (decarchy) of his partisans, often reinforced with garrisons under a Spartan commander (harmost). In 403 Lysander was sent to support the Thirty at Athens against Thrasybulus' democratic revolt. He was nearly successful, but a reversal of policy in Sparta led to a settlement that allowed the restoration of democracy at Athens. This was a defeat for Lysander; his decarchies probably were abolished and most likely he suffered a political eclipse. He helped Agesilaus II succeed to the throne of Sparta in 399 but subsequently was rejected by the monarch. At the outbreak of the Corinthian War (395–387), Lysander led an army of Sparta's northern allies into Boeotia and was killed while attacking Haliartus.

Lysenko, Trofim Denisovich (b. 1898, Karlovka, Ukraine, Russian Empire—d. Nov. 20, 1976, Kiev, Ukrainian S.S.R.), Soviet biologist and agronomist, the controversial "dictator" of Communistic biology during Stalin's regime. He rejected orthodox genetics in favour of "Michurinism" (named for the Russian horticulturist I.V. Michurin), which was begun by an uneducated plant breeder fashioning explanations for his hybrid creations. After Michurin's death in 1935, Lysenko led the movement and transformed it into an assault on orthodox genetics.

Lysenko was graduated from the Uman School of Horticulture in 1921 and was stationed at the Belaya Tserkov Selection Station in the same year. After his 1925 graduation from the Kiev Agricultural Institute, with the degree of doctor of agricultural science, he

Lysenko, 1938
Sovfoto

was stationed at the Gyandzha Experimental Station until 1929. From 1929 to 1934 he held the office of senior specialist in the department of physiology of the Ukrainian All-Union Institute of Selection and Genetics in Odessa; from 1935 to 1938 he was scientific director and then director of the All-Union Selection and Genetics Institute at Odessa.

The Soviet chiefs began to support Lysenko during the agricultural crisis of the 1930s. On the basis of rather crude and unsubstantiated experiments, Lysenko promised greater, more rapid, and less costly increases in crop yields than other biologists believed possible. Under Stalin, Lysenko became director of the Institute of Genetics of the Academy of Sciences of the U.S.S.R. (1940–65) and president of the then powerful V.I. Lenin All-Union Academy of Agricultural Sciences. By 1948, when education and research in standard genetics were virtually outlawed, some geneticists had suffered secret arrest and death of undisclosed causes.

Lysenko's doctrines and claims varied with the amount of power that he held. Between 1948 and 1953, when he was the total autocrat of Soviet biology, he claimed that wheat plants raised in the appropriate environment produce seeds of rye, which is equivalent to saying that dogs living in the wild give birth to foxes. His fundamental, continuing argument was that theoretical biology must be fused with Soviet agricultural practice. After Stalin's death, this principle caused Lysenko some embarrassment, for efforts to improve Soviet agriculture brought the abandonment of measures to which his name and fame were tied. His "grassland" system of crop rotation was abandoned in favour of cultivation with mineral fertilizers, and a hybrid corn program based on the U.S. example was pursued (Lysenko halted the program in the mid-1930s, for he was opposed to the inbreeding with which it must begin). During Nikita Khrushchev's premiership, opposition to Lysenko's programs was tolerated, and Lysenko lost titular control of the Lenin Agricultural Academy. After Khrushchev's political demise, in 1964, Lysenko's doctrines were discredited, and intensive efforts made toward the reestablishment of orthodox genetics in the U.S.S.R. Deposed as director of the Institute of Genetics early in 1965, Lysenko seemed to be at the end of his mutable career. He and his followers, however, long retained their degrees, their titles, and their academic positions and remained free to support their aberrant trend in biology.

lysergic acid diethylamide, also called LYSERGIDE (hallucinogenic drug): *see* LSD.

Lysias (b. *c.* 445 BC—d. after 380 BC), Greek professional speech writer, whose unpretentious simplicity became the model for a plain style of Attic Greek.

Lysias was the son of Cephalus, a wealthy native of Syracuse who settled in Athens. Plato, at the opening of the *Republic,* had drawn a charming picture of Cephalus and his sons Lysias and Polemarchus. After studying rhetoric in Italy, Lysias returned to Athens in 412. It was possibly then that he taught rhetoric. In 404, during the reign of the Thirty Tyrants, he and his brother Polemarchus were seized as aliens. Polemarchus was killed, but Lysias escaped to Megara, where he helped the cause of exiled Athenian democrats. On the restoration of Athenian democracy in 403, he returned to Athens and began writing speeches for litigants.

His surviving forensic speeches often deal with crimes against the state—murder, malicious wounding, sacrilege, and taking bribes. A particularly delightful speech, "For the Cripple," defends a cripple's right to a state pension. In this and other works Lysias displays his characteristic adaptability in suiting his composition to the character of the speaker; and, though the tone of his professional writing was quiet, he was capable of passionate oratory, as exemplified in his own longest and most famous speech, "Against Eratosthenes," denouncing one of the Thirty Tyrants for his part in the reign of terror that followed the collapse of Athens in 404.

Lysicrates, Choragic Monument of, only extant example of the ancient Greek architectural structure known as the choragic monument (*q.v.*).

Lysimachus (b. *c.* 360 BC—d. 281), Macedonian general, satrap (provincial governor), and king who, as one of the *diadochoi* ("successors") to Alexander the Great, came to rule strategic parts of the divided Macedonian Empire.

Lysimachus was one of Alexander's bodyguards during the conquest of Asia, and, in the distribution of satrapies that followed Alexander's death (323), he was assigned to govern Thrace. Occupied there for many years in wars against the local peoples, Lysimachus took little part in the struggles among Alexander's other successors in Greece and Asia. Not until 302, when he bore the brunt of the campaign that ended in the overthrow of the successor Antigonus Monophthalmus, king of Asia, at the Battle of Ipsus (301), did Lysimachus emerge as a power of the first rank. Through this victory he added the greater part of Asia Minor to his European possessions and began to consolidate his power in both areas against the threat posed by Antigonus' son, Demetrius I Poliorcetes. In 285 Lysimachus drove Demetrius from Macedonia, which had been taken by Demetrius in 294.

The last period of Lysimachus' life was darkened by the intrigues of his third wife, Arsinoe II, daughter of Ptolemy I Soter, king of Egypt. In order to gain the succession for her own sons, she had her husband execute his eldest son, Agathocles, on a charge of conspiring with Seleucus I, the Syrian king, to commit treason. During the disorders that followed Agathocles' death, Seleucus seized the opportunity to invade Asia Minor, where he killed Lysimachus in the decisive battle of Corupedium in Lydia, in 281.

lysine, an amino acid released in the hydrolysis of many common proteins but present in small amounts or lacking in certain plant proteins; *e.g.,* gliadin from wheat, zein from corn (maize). First isolated from casein (1889), lysine is one of several so-called essential amino acids for warm-blooded animals; *i.e.,* they cannot synthesize it and require dietary sources. (It is formed in plants, algae, and fungi by two distinct biosynthetic pathways.) Human populations dependent on grains as a sole source of dietary protein suffer from lysine deficiency.

Lysippus (fl. 4th century BC, Sicyon, Greece), Greek sculptor, head of the school at Argos and Sicyon in the time of Philip of Macedon and especially active during the reign of Philip's son Alexander the Great (336–323 BC). Lysippus was famous for the new and slender proportions of his figures and for their lifelike naturalism.

Originally a worker in metal, he taught himself the art of sculpture by studying nature and the "Doryphorus" ("Spearbearer") of Polyclitus, whose canon of ideal male proportions he modified by creating a smaller head and slimmer body that increased his figures' apparent height.

Lysippus is said by the Roman writer Pliny the Elder (1st century AD) to have made more than 1,500 works, all of them in bronze. Of these, not one has been preserved, nor is there a completely reliable copy. There are, however, a few copies that may be ascribed to him with some certainty. The best and most reliable is that of the "Apoxyomenos" (Vatican museum), a young male athlete, scraping and cleaning his oil-covered skin with a strigil. The original "Apoxyomenos" is known to have been transported to Rome at the time of the emperor Tiberius (reigned AD 14–37), who placed it before Agrippa's bath. The Vatican copy of the "Apoxyomenos" is tall, slender, and elegantly shaped, the head small in proportion to the body. There is a precision of detail, especially in the hair and the eyes.

Lysippus' portraits of Alexander the Great are many; he sculpted Alexander from boyhood onward, and Alexander would have no other sculptor portray him. The most noteworthy is the herm (bust on a tapering pedestal) of Alexander in the Louvre, with an ancient inscription attributing it to Lysippus. The bronze statue of Alexander in the Louvre and the head of Alexander in the British Museum are similar in style to the "Apoxyomenos."

Other key works attributed to Lysippus include the "Agias" of Pharsalus, a statue of a victor in the pancratium (athletic games for boys); "Troilus" (an Olympic victor, 372 BC); "Coridas" (a Pythian victor in the pancratium, 342 BC); the colossal bronze statue of Zeus at Tarentum; the colossal bronze seated Heracles at Tarentum, later sent to Rome and then to the hippodrome at Constantinople, where it was melted down in 1022; and the chariot of the sun at Rhodes (Apollo on a four-horse chariot).

The bronze Zeus of Lysippus, which is described by the 2nd-century-AD traveller Pausanias as having stood in the marketplace at

"Apoxyomenos," Roman marble copy of Greek bronze by Lysippus, *c.* 310 BC; in the Vatican Museum
Anderson—Alinari from Art Resource

Sicyon, survives in miniature on a bronze coin from the time of the 3rd-century Roman emperor Caracalla; it is similar in style to the "Apoxyomenos." Lysippus' colossal, but exhausted and melancholy, Heracles at Sicyon was the original of the Farnese Heracles, signed by Glycon as copyist. The Glycon copy has many copies extant, including one in the Pitti Palace, Florence, with an inscription naming Lysippus as the artist.

Lysis OF TARENTUM (fl. *c.* 400 BC), Greek philosopher and member of the Pythagorean school in southern Italy.

Lysis left Italy for Greece about 390 BC, after escaping a massacre of the Pythagoreans at Croton. Settling in Thebes, he became the teacher of Epaminondas (*c.* 420–362 BC), the Greek military commander and strategist. The nature of Lysis' writing is not known, but one source suggests that some works attributed to Pythagoras were actually written by Lysis.

lysogeny, type of life cycle that takes place in a bacteriophage following its infection of certain types of bacteria. In this cycle, the genome (the collection of genes in the nucleic-acid core of a virus) of the bacteriophage stably integrates into the chromosome of the host bacterium and replicates in concert with it. No progeny viruses are produced in the process. Instead, the infecting virus lies dormant within the bacterium's chromosome until the bacterium is exposed to certain stimuli, such as ultraviolet light. Following this induction event, the virus enters a life cycle in which its genome is excised from the host chromosome and begins to multiply, forming new progeny viruses. Ultimately the bacterial host is destroyed (lysed) and the virus particles are released into the environment and infect new bacterial cells.

lysosome, subcellular organelle that is found in all eucaryotic cells and is responsible for the cell's digestion of macromolecules, old cell parts, and microorganisms. Each lysosome is surrounded by a membrane that maintains an acidic environment within the interior. Lysosomes contain a wide variety of hydrolytic enzymes (acid hydrolases) that break down macromolecules such as nucleic acids, proteins, and polysaccharides. These enzymes are active only in the lysosome's acidic interior; their acid-dependent activity protects the cell from self-degradation in case of lysosomal leakage or rupture, since the pH of the cell is neutral to slightly alkaline.

Lysosomes originate by budding off from the membrane of the trans-Golgi network. Materials to be digested are transported to the lysosomes by three main pathways: endocytosis, autophagocytosis, and phagocytosis. In endocytosis, extracellular macromolecules are taken up into the cell to form membrane-bound vesicles called endosomes that fuse with lysosomes. Autophagocytosis is the process by which old organelles are removed from a cell; they are enveloped by internal membranes that then fuse with lysosomes. Phagocytosis is carried out by specialized cells (*e.g.,* macrophages) that engulf large extracellular particles such as dead cells or foreign invaders (*e.g.,* bacteria) and target them for lysosomal degradation. Many of the products of lysosomal digestion, such as amino acids and nucleotides, are recycled back to the cell for use in the synthesis of new cellular components.

Lysosomal storage diseases are genetic disorders in which a genetic mutation affects the activity of one or more of the acid hydrolases. In such diseases, the normal metabolism of specific macromolecules is blocked and the macromolecules accumulate inside the lysosomes, causing severe physiological damage or deformity. Hurler's syndrome, which involves a defect in the metabolism of mucopolysaccharides, is a lysosomal storage disease.

lysozyme, enzyme found in the secretions (tears) of the lacrimal glands of animals and in nasal mucus, gastric secretions, and egg white. Discovered in 1921 by Sir Alexander Fleming, lysozyme catalyzes the breakdown of certain carbohydrates found in the cell walls of certain bacteria (*e.g.,* cocci). It thus functions, in the case of lacrimal fluid, to protect the cornea of the eye from infection.

lyssa (disease): *see* rabies.

Lysva, city, Perm *oblast* (province), Russia. It lies along the Lysva River in the mid-Urals. First recorded in the mid-17th century, the settlement acquired an iron-smelting factory as an economic base in 1785 and became a town in 1926. Its steel industry was modernized after the October Revolution (1917), and the city is a metallurgical centre producing tinplate and quality steels. Pop. (1993 est.) 78,300.

Lysychansk, Russian LISICHANSK, also spelled LISIČANSK, city, Luhansk *oblast* (province), eastern Ukraine, on the Donets River. In 1721 the first discovery of coal in the Donets Basin was made there at the Cossack village of Lisya Balka, which dated from 1710. Modern industries include coal mining, underground gasification of coal, chemicals (especially soda making), and glassmaking. A petroleum refinery was opened in the 1970s. The city is part of a metropolitan area that includes Syeverodonetsk and Rubizhne, the three towns together constituting one of Ukraine's largest chemical complexes. Pop. (1993 est.) 127,000.

Lyttelton, town and port, Canterbury local government region, eastern South Island, New Zealand. It is situated within the Christchurch urban area and on Lyttelton Harbour, an inlet of the southwest Pacific extending 8 miles (13 km) into the north shore of Banks Peninsula. The harbour's entrance is flanked by Godley Head on the north and Adderley Head on the south. Sealers and whalers were using the harbour late in the 18th century. It was known as Port Cooper in the 1830s and appears as Port Victoria on a map of 1849. The town, first laid out in 1849, was renamed nine years later in honour of Lord George Lyttelton, chairman of the Canterbury Association. Because the development of Christchurch (7 miles [11 km] northwest) was hampered by shortages of building materials and money, Lyttelton for a time served as the chief settlement of Canterbury. It was constituted a municipality in 1862 and a borough in 1868.

Lyttelton is the port for Christchurch, to which it is linked by rail lines and roads piercing the Port Hills through tunnels, which also give it access to the Canterbury Plains. With a low-water depth of 32 feet (10 m), the harbour can accommodate large ships bringing in petroleum products, fertilizers, iron, and steel and taking out wool, dairy products, wheat, frozen meats, and timber. Space is very limited within the town, with most level areas devoted to wharfage, storage, rail yards, offices, and bulk-oil terminals. There is some industry, including ship repair and construction yards, engineering works, and clothing factories. There are residential areas on the surrounding hills. Pop. (1989 est.) 3,180.

Lyttelton (of Frankley), George Lyttelton, 1st Baron (b. Jan. 17, 1709, Hagley, Worcestershire, Eng.—d. Aug. 22, 1773, Hagley), British Whig statesman and writer, patron of novelist Henry Fielding and poet James Thomson.

The son of a prominent Whig family, Lyttelton was an early political associate of his brother-in-law, William Pitt (later Earl of Chatham), in the so-called Boy Patriot circle, which opposed the Robert Walpole ministry. Elected to the House of Commons in 1735, he was a lord of the Treasury (1744–54) under Henry Pelham and chancellor of the Exchequer under the Duke of Newcastle (1755–56). His refusal to oppose Newcastle caused him to break with Pitt, and for a time Lyttelton was Newcastle's only important supporter in the House of Commons. In 1756 he became Baron Lyttelton, and thereafter he sat in the House of Lords.

Acquainted with the leading literary figures of his day, Lyttelton wrote a poetic epistle to Alexander Pope and a description of James Thomson included in the poet's *The Castle of Indolence* (1748). Henry Fielding dedicated his novel *Tom Jones* (1749) to him, and Tobias Smollett satirized him as Gosling Scragg in *The Adventures of Peregrine Pickle* (1751). John Lord Harvey rather maliciously accused Lyttelton of having "a great flow of words that were always uttered in lulling monotony."

Lyttelton, Sir Thomas: *see* Littleton, Sir Thomas.

Lytton, BARONS AND EARLS, titled British nobility grouped below chronologically and indicated by the symbol •.

• Lytton (of Knebworth), Edward George Earle Bulwer-Lytton, 1st Baron (b. May 25, 1803, London, Eng.—d. Jan. 18, 1873, Torquay, Devonshire), British politician, poet, and critic, chiefly remembered, however, as a prolific novelist. His books, though dated, remain immensely readable, and his experiences lend his work an unusual historical interest.

Bulwer-Lytton was the youngest son of General William Bulwer and Elizabeth Lytton. After leaving the University of Cambridge, he visited Paris and Versailles. Back in England, he met Rosina Doyle Wheeler, an Irish woman, whom he married in 1827. He published an unsuccessful novel during the same year, but *Pelham* (1828), the adventures of a dandy, inaugurated his career as a fluent, popular novelist. The couple's extravagant style of living necessitated a large output of work, and the strain made Bulwer-Lytton an irritable and negligent husband. After many violent quarrels, he and Rosina were legally separated in 1836. Bulwer-Lytton's political career began in 1831, when he entered Parliament as Liberal member for Lincoln. In 1841 he retired in protest against repeal of the Corn Laws. This, together with his friendship with Benjamin Disraeli, converted him into a Tory, and in 1852 he returned to the House as member for Hertfordshire.

Bulwer-Lytton's literary activity had, meanwhile, been immense. His popularity was largely a result of his skill in anticipating and satisfying changes in public taste. He flirted quite successfully with the theatre, though his plays have not endured. Having started as a novelist with *Pelham,* which combined Gothic romance with a setting of the fash-

Baron Lytton, detail of an oil painting by H.W. Pickersgill, *c.* 1831; in the National Portrait Gallery, London

ionable world, he then embarked on a series of historical novels, weighted with meticulous detail, the most notable of which were *The Last Days of Pompeii,* 3 vol. (1834), and *Harold, the Last of the Saxon Kings* (1848). In *Eugene Aram,* 3 vol. (1832), he made use of current fascination with criminals and the underworld. He turned to realism and the portrayal of English society in *The Caxtons,* 3 vol. (1849), and *My Novel* (1853). Bulwer-Lytton also published several volumes of poetry, a satirical novel in verse (containing an attack on Alfred, Lord Tennyson, the poet laureate), and an unsuccessful long epic, *King Arthur* (1848). He was created a peer in 1866.

Contemporary literary critics, notably William Makepeace Thackeray, attacked him unmercifully, especially in *Fraser's Magazine,* and his reputation declined sharply in the 20th century.

• Lytton, (Edward) Robert Bulwer-Lytton, 1st Earl of, VISCOUNT KNEBWORTH OF KNEBWORTH, 2ND BARON LYTTON OF KNEBWORTH, pseudonym OWEN MEREDITH (b. Nov. 8, 1831, London, Eng.—d. Nov. 24, 1891, Paris, France), British diplomat and viceroy of India (1876–80) who also achieved, during his lifetime, a reputation as a poet.

Lytton, son of the 1st Baron Lytton, began his diplomatic career as unpaid attaché to his uncle Sir Henry Bulwer, then minister at Washington, D.C. His first paid appointment was at Vienna (1858), and in 1874 he was appointed minister at Lisbon. He inherited his father's barony in 1873.

In November 1875 Prime Minister Benjamin Disraeli appointed Lytton governor-general of India. During his service there, Lytton was concerned primarily with India's relations with Afghanistan. At the time of his appointment, Russian influence was growing in Afghanistan, and Lytton had orders to counteract it or to secure a strong frontier by force. When negotiations failed to persuade the Afghans to expel the Russians, Lytton resorted to force, precipitating the Second Afghan War of 1878–80.

Lytton resigned his post in 1880 and was created Earl of Lytton and Viscount Knebworth that same year. Though Afghanistan received the most attention during Lytton's viceroyalty, he also did much for Indian administration. He supervised effective measures for famine relief, abolished internal customs barriers, decentralized the financial system, proclaimed Queen Victoria empress of India, and reserved one-sixth of the civil-service posts for Indians. Lytton ended his career as British minister to France (1887–91).

To his contemporaries, Lytton was better known as a poet than as a diplomat or administrator. His first collections—*Clytemnestra . . . and Other Poems* (1855), verse narratives imitative of Browning, and *The Wanderer* (1858), autobiographical lyrics—were well received, as was *Lucile* (1860), a witty and romantic novel in verse. In 1883 he also published two volumes of the *Life, Letters and Literary Remains* of his father, Edward George Earle Bulwer-Lytton.

• Lytton, Victor Alexander George Robert Bulwer-Lytton, 2nd Earl of, VISCOUNT KNEBWORTH OF KNEBWORTH, 3RD BARON LYTTON OF KNEBWORTH (b. Aug. 9, 1876, Simla, India—d. Oct. 26, 1947, Knebworth, Hertfordshire, Eng.), British governor of Bengal (1922–27) and chairman of the League of Nations mission to Manchuria, which produced the so-called Lytton Report (1932), condemning Japan's aggression there. (*See* Lytton Commission.)

Bulwer-Lytton was born in India when his father, the 1st earl, was viceroy there; and he succeeded to his father's titles while still a schoolboy. He was educated at Eton and at Trinity College, Cambridge, and secured his first government posts, in the Admiralty, during World War I. In 1920 he became parliamentary undersecretary to the India Office and in 1922 became governor of Bengal, serving for the next few years as occasional viceroy while the appointed viceroy was on leave.

His League of Nations mission to Manchuria in 1932 was widely praised but led to no effective sanctions against Japan. From then on, Lytton chaired various bodies but none of great import. He retired in 1945.

Lytton, Sir Henry Alfred, original name HENRY ALFRED JONES (b. Jan. 3, 1865, London, Eng.—d. Aug. 15, 1936, London), British comic actor best known for his leading roles in Gilbert and Sullivan operettas. The mainstay of the D'Oyly Carte Opera Company for nearly 30 years, Lytton was so distinguished that his stage jubilee celebration was attended by the British prime minister and his two predecessors.

Jones had only appeared in amateur theatrical productions when he joined the chorus of Richard D'Oyly Carte's repertory company in 1884 to be with his wife, the actress Louie Henri. Three years later at the Savoy Theatre in London, the understudy "H.A. Henri" came to prominence in *Ruddigore.* At Gilbert's suggestion he adopted the name Lytton and went on to portray more than 30 Gilbert and Sullivan characters, including Ko-Ko (*The Mikado*), Jack Point (*The Yeoman of the Guard*), and Lord Chancellor (*Iolanthe*). His pleasant voice, sense of comic timing, and poise made him popular in London and on tour throughout Great Britain, Canada, and the United States. His memoirs were published as *The Secrets of a Savoyard* (1922) and *A Wandering Minstrel* (1933). Lytton was knighted in 1930.

Lytton Commission (1931–32), investigation team that was led by V.A.G.R. Bulwer-Lytton, 2nd Earl of Lytton, and was appointed by the League of Nations to determine the cause of the Japanese invasion of Manchuria begun on Sept. 18, 1931.

After extensive research and a six-week stay in Manchuria (Northeast Provinces), the commission submitted its report in September 1932. It found both parties guilty, blaming the Chinese for their anti-Japanese propaganda and refusal to compromise but branding Japan as an aggressor. Japan, which had meanwhile created the puppet state of Manchukuo out of its new possessions, not only rejected the commission's findings but also resigned from the League of Nations, thus removing itself from the sanctions of that international body and destroying any hope for reconciliation between the two nations. Friction between China and Japan continued until it resulted in all-out war in 1937.

Lyubertsy, also spelled L'UBERCY, or LIUBERTSY, city, Moscow *oblast* (province), Russia. It lies in the greenbelt, southeast of Moscow city. Before the October Revolution in 1917 it was an agricultural centre, but its position at an important railway junction made it an attractive site for industry. In the early Soviet period, the electrification of the Moscow railway made the city a dormitory settlement for the capital, and it experienced rapid growth. Its industries include machine building, oil refining, and consumer goods. Pop. (1993 est.) 163,700.

Lyubimov, Yury Petrovich, Lyubimov also spelled LIUBIMOV (b. Sept. 30 [Sept. 17, Old Style], 1917, Yaroslavl, Russia), Soviet theatre director and actor noted for his two decades of somewhat experimental productions for the Taganka Theatre in Moscow.

Lyubimov served from 1940 to 1946 in the Soviet army, joining the company of the Yevgeny Vakhtangov Theatre upon his release. In 1953 he began teaching at the B.V. Shchukin Drama School, from which he had graduated in 1939, and in 1964 he became the chief director of the Taganka Theatre. Because his productions did not avoid raising philosophical or political issues that questioned the Communist Party line, the Taganka became a gathering place for intellectuals and dissidents. In 1984, while he was in London, he was stripped of his citizenship. Thereafter he was a guest director for many theatre and opera companies throughout the United States and western Europe.

M, abbreviation of Messier catalog (*q.v.*), an astronomical listing.

M1 rifle: *see* Garand rifle.

M16 rifle, also called AR-15, assault rifle adopted as a standard weapon by the U.S. Army in 1967. The M16 superseded the M14 rifle. It is gas-operated and has both semiautomatic (*i.e.,* autoloading) and fully automatic capabilities. Weighing less than 8 pounds (3.6 kg) and equipped with a 20-round or 30-round magazine, the M16 is 39 inches (99 cm) long and fires 5.56-millimetre (.223-calibre) ammunition at the rate of 700–950 rounds per minute. Both U.S. and South Vietnamese forces used it during the Vietnam War.

Ma, Yo-Yo (b. Oct. 7, 1955, Paris, France), French-born American cellist known for his extraordinary technique and rich tone. His frequent collaborations with musicians and artists from other genres and media reinvigorated classical music and expanded its audience.

Born to Chinese parents, Ma was a child prodigy. At age five he gave his first public recital. He made his Carnegie Hall debut at age nine. He studied at the Juilliard School before graduating from Harvard University (1977) with a degree in humanities.

Ma received an unusually large number of commissions from contemporary composers. He frequently performed as part of a trio with pianist Emanuel Ax and violinist Young-Uck Kim and as part of a quartet with Ax and violinists Isaac Stern and Jaime Laredo. Ma and Ax received high acclaim for their recordings of the sonatas of Ludwig van Beethoven (1985) and Johannes Brahms (1991). Of special interest to Ma were the six suites for unaccompanied cello by Johann Sebastian Bach, which he first played as a young boy. He recorded the suites in 1983 and again in 1998. Accompanying the latter release was a series of six interpretative films on which Ma collaborated with artists from several disciplines.

In addition to his conventional repertoire, Ma also recorded with improvisational singer Bobby McFerrin on *Hush* (1992) and with bluegrass musicians on *Appalachia Waltz* (1996) and *Appalachian Journey* (2000). On *Soul of the Tango* (1997), he recorded the tangos of Astor Piazzolla. He also played on the soundtrack for the movie *Crouching Tiger, Hidden Dragon* (2000) and in 2003 collaborated with Latin American musicians on *Obrigado Brazil.* In 1998 Ma founded the Silk Road Project, an arts organization that explored the cultural traditions along the Silk Road, an ancient trade route that linked China with the West. Soon after, he established the Silk Road Ensemble, and the group's first recording, *Silk Road Journeys: When Strangers Meet,* was released in 2001. A prolific musician, Ma recorded more than 50 albums between 1983 and 2003, and during this time he received 15 Grammy Awards.

Ma-an-shan, Pinyin MA'ANSHAN, new city and industrial centre in southeastern Anhwei *sheng* (province). Ma-an-shan is situated on the south bank of the Yangtze River some 22 miles (35 km) downstream from Wu-hu, near the border of Kiangsu *sheng,* opposite Ho-hsien. The city is on the railway between Wu-hu and Nan-ching (Nanking).

The region along the southern bank of the Yangtze between Ma-an-shan and T'ung-ling (about 150 miles [240 km] upstream) has long been a mining area. The development of a modern metallurgical industry was made possible by the opening of the Huai-nan coalfield in the mid-1930s and by the construction of the Huai-nan–Ho-fei–Yü-ch'i-k'ou railway. After 1938, under Japanese occupation, a small steelworks and an iron-smelting plant were established. They were, however, destroyed late in World War II, and the local iron mines—most of whose production had been shipped to Japan—were abandoned.

After 1949 the smelting plant was restored, and it resumed production in 1953. During the First Five-Year Plan (1953–57), Ma-an-shan rapidly grew into a major industrial centre. In the early 1950s Ma-an-shan's iron production was increased to supply the steel industry in Shanghai. Under the Second Five-Year Plan (1958–62), it was decided to develop Ma-an-shan into an integrated iron and steel complex. Sulfur is also mined in the area. Pop. (1999 est.) 393,174.

Ma Duanlin (Chinese historian): *see* Ma Tuan-lin.

Ma-Hsia school, Pinyin MAXIA, group of Chinese landscape artists that used a style of painting named after Ma Yüan and Hsia Kuei, two great painters of the Southern Sung Academy, of which they were members in the last quarter of the 12th century AD and the beginning of the 13th. The aim of their landscapes was to create a feeling of limitless space, a vast atmospheric void out of which a few elements, such as mountain peaks and twisted trees, emerge with subdued drama. Ma and Hsia are credited with the fullest expression of this tendency in Chinese painting.

Ma-Hsia school compositions are of a type, called "one corner," that is asymmetrical, with the design weight off to one side and the rest of the silk or paper left bare or slightly tinted. Ink tones are simplified to increase the dramatic impact of brushwork of a type called "ax stroke," for the similarity of its brush marks to the marks left on wood by an ax or chisel. In general, there is a preference for angular line expressed in abrupt, staccato brush strokes.

Ma-p'ing (China): *see* Liu-chou.

Ma River, Vietnamese SONG MA, river, northern Vietnam, one of the longest of the region, rising in the northwest. It flows southeastward through Laos for about 50 miles (80 km), cutting gorges through uplands to reach the plains region at which northern Vietnam begins to narrow. The river enters the Gulf of Tonkin, 65 miles (105 km) south of Hanoi, after a course of 250 miles (400 km). Like the Red River (Song Hong) to the north, it has an irregular regime with maximum flow toward the end of the summer. The Ma River delta differs, however, from that of the Red River because of its narrowness and the presence of sandy soil. Thanh Hoa town lies about 9 miles (14 km) upstream from the river mouth. Sampans can navigate 60 miles (100 km) upstream to Phan Y.

Ma Tuan-lin, Pinyin MA DUANLIN (b. 1254?, Le-p'ing [now in Kiangsi province], China—d. 1324), Chinese historian who wrote the *Wen hsien t'ung k'ao* ("General Study of the Literary Remains"), a huge encyclopaedia of general knowledge. This work, with the works of two other historians of the Sung dynasty (960–1279), Cheng Ch'iao (1108–66) and Ssu-ma Kuang (1019–86), is considered one of the greatest institutional histories ever written on China and, as such, was a model for many later historians. Ma insisted that a knowledge of institutional history was just as necessary to the Confucian official as knowledge of the Confucian Classics.

Ma-ubin, town, southern Myanmar (Burma). The town is a river port on the west bank of the main Irrawaddy distributary and is protected by flood-control embankments. It is linked with Yangon (Rangoon), 40 miles (65 km) east, by the Twante Canal and is the site of a diesel electric plant. The surrounding area occupies a largely swampy portion of the Irrawaddy River delta. It has a southern coastline along the Andaman Sea. Rice growing and fishing are the primary economic activities. Pop. (1993 est.) 42,000.

Ma-wang-tui, Pinyin MAWANGDUI, Chinese archaeological site uncovered in 1963 and located near Ch'ang-sha, Hunan province, southeastern China. It is the burial place of a high-ranking official, the marquess of Tai, who lived in the 2nd century BC, and of his immediate family. He was one of many petty nobles who governed small semiautonomous domains under the Han dynasty. The tombs were discovered during the construction of a hospital.

The almost perfectly preserved body of the marquess's wife was found in tomb number one; it subsequently was placed on exhibit in a specially designed museum in Ch'ang-sha. In the same tomb, an exquisite banner was discovered in 1972 that shows the noblewoman on her journey to heaven. This banner has become important for the information that it provides about ancient Chinese religious beliefs and practices. Also uncovered at Ma-wang-tui were lacquers and silks that have shed light on artistic styles of the Han period.

Ma Yüan, Pinyin MA YUAN, courtesy name (*tzu*) WEN YUAN (b. 14 BC, Mou-ling, now in Shensi province, China—d. AD 49, Hunan), Chinese general who helped establish the Eastern Han dynasty (AD 25–220) after the usurpation of power by the minister Wang Mang ended the Western Han dynasty (206 BC–AD 25).

Ma began his career in the service of Wang Mang, but when revolts erupted throughout the countryside in opposition to Wang's policies, Ma joined the minister's enemies. He eventually took service under Kuang-wu ti (reigned AD 25–57/58), a member of the Han imperial family, who made himself emperor and reestablished the Han dynasty.

In AD 35 Ma was appointed governor of South China, and he reinstituted Chinese rule in the area as far south as present-day northern Vietnam. In 45 Ma was sent to the northern frontier, where he helped subdue the Hsiungnu tribes of Central Asia. After his death he was enshrined as a god and, until modern times, was worshiped as the wave-quelling god of Kwangsi province in South China. Ma Yüan was a noted judge of horses and wrote a book on that subject.

Ma Yüan, Pinyin MA YUAN (b. *c.* 1160/65, Ch'ien-t'ang [now Hang-chou], Chekiang province, China—d. 1225), Chinese landscape painter whose work, together with that of Hsia Kuei, formed the basis of the Ma-Hsia school of painting. Ma occasionally painted flowers, but his genius lay in landscape painting, his

"Early Spring: Bare Willows and Distant Mountains," fan painting by Ma Yüan, ink and slight colour on silk, late 12th–early 13th century; in the Museum of Fine Arts, Boston

By courtesy of the Museum of Fine Arts, Boston, Chinese and Japanese Special Fund

lyrical and romantic interpretation becoming the model for later painters. He was a master of "one-corner" painting, in which visual interest is focused in a corner of the work.

Early life and works. Ma was born into a family of court painters: his great-grandfather Ma Fen had been *tai-chao* (*i.e.*, painter in attendance) at the Northern Sung court about 1119–25; both his grandfather Ma Hsing-tzu and his father, Ma Shih-jung, held the same rank at the Southern Sung court in the middle decades of the 12th century. Ma Yüan began his career under the emperor Hsiao-tsung, became *tai-chao* under Emperor Kuang-tsung, and received the highest Chinese honour, the Golden Belt, under Emperor Ning-tsung. His son Ma Lin, the last of the Ma artistic dynasty, rose to be painter-in-waiting, *chih-hou*. Apart from these bare facts, practically nothing is known about Ma's life. Being neither a scholar nor an official, he did not leave a body of his own writings, and he did not earn a biography in the dynastic history. He seems, however, to have been in high favour at court, particularly under Ning-tsung, who, with his empress, Yang Mei-tzu, wrote poems or short inscriptions inspired by a number of his paintings.

Ma occasionally painted flowers and figure subjects. A group of small, delicate flower paintings in the National Palace Museum in Taipei, Taiwan, are attributed to him. Typically, a single spray of blossoms lies poised in empty space across the square album leaf. One of these works is signed, and two bear couplets written by Yang. There are also three paintings of Zen masters in simple landscape settings—two of them in Tenryū Temple, Kyōto, Japan, the third in the Tokyo National Museum—which, though not signed, bear inscriptions considered to be in the handwriting of Yang. They all have certain similar features of technique that have led some Japanese authorities to attribute them to Ma.

Landscape painting. It was in landscape painting that Ma's genius lay. He executed a number of large landscape screens, all of which are now lost. He also painted tall, hanging scrolls in which, according to an early Chinese writer, "there are steep mountains rising imposingly, with streams winding around them and waterfalls partly hidden among the trees." The author also wrote that Ma made his pine trees "very tall and strong as if they were made of iron wire; sometimes he painted them with a stump brush; the effect is vigorous, beautiful, and elegant." Typical of this kind of picture is the tall, unsigned "Rain over Trees on a Rocky Shore" in the Seikadō Foundation in Tokyo. The monumental composition, the expressive use of monochrome ink, and the powerful angularity of the brushwork, in which the artist hacked out the facets of his rocks by means of a slanting "ax-cut" stroke, are features that first had been developed by Li T'ang, the senior landscapist in the Imperial Academy in the last years of the Northern Sung dynasty. Although Li may not have lived long enough to see the Sung court reestablished at Lin-an (now Hang-chou) in 1136, his influence there was profound, and his style of landscape painting became the orthodox manner for Southern Academy painters, being transmitted down to Ma through a follower, Hsiao Chao, and through Ma's own forebears.

Later works and influence. By the late 12th century, however, this style was changing, and the new elements that were appearing reflected the nostalgic and somewhat precious atmosphere of the exiled court at Lin-an. In some hanging scrolls attributed to Ma, and in many of the exquisite small album and fan paintings, the mountains are pushed to one side, creating a "one corner" composition; between the distant mountains and the strongly accented foreground rocks, where a scholar may be sitting enjoying the view, lies a vast expanse of empty space with but a suggestion of mist or water. Many of Ma's pictures are romantic night scenes. A particularly moving hanging scroll of this kind, attributed to him and bearing a long poem composed by the emperor and written by Yang, is the unsigned version of the "Banquet by Lantern Light" in the National Palace Museum in Taipei.

Such paintings are redolent of a poetic melancholy that hints at the decay of Sung culture, and the pictorial expression of this feeling is often rather conventional. The one-sided composition, the jutting pine tree silhouetted against empty space, the meditating scholar, and the brilliant brush technique of Ma all lent themselves easily to imitation. His style was popular with late Sung painters, men and women, professionals and amateurs, and it is often difficult to separate the genuine fans and album leaves by Ma from those of his followers. Among the best of the surviving works are "Early Spring" and "Two Sages and an Attendant Beneath a Plum Tree," both in the Museum of Fine Arts, Boston; "Watching the Deer by a Pine-Shaded Stream," in the Mr. and Mrs. Dean Perry Collection, Cleveland, Ohio; and "On a Mountain Path in Spring," a signed album leaf bearing a couplet written by the emperor Ning-tsung, in the National Palace Museum in Taipei.

Finally, a small group of hand scrolls shows another facet of Ma's genius. Most striking, and most likely to be from his hand, is the picture "The Four Sages of Shang-shan" (recluses who lived at the beginning of the Han dynasty), in the Cincinnati Art Museum in Ohio. Although damaged and poorly restored, the picture presents a dramatic contrast between the vital handling of the landscape and raging torrent and the extreme delicacy and precision of the figures of the scholars and their attendants, qualities that suggest the hand of a great master. The scroll is signed and bears 40 colophons or seals of the various owners, including one by the noted Yüan-dynasty scholar-painter Ni Tsan (1301–74). A signed long scroll of mountains and pine trees in deep winter snow in the Imperial Museum in Peking (Beijing), though roughly painted, is an extremely impressive work that may be a product of Ma's old age.

The romantic landscape style of the Southern Sung academicians such as Ma, his son Ma Lin, and Hsia Kuei went out of fashion after the fall of the dynasty in 1279. It was revived in the Ming dynasty (1368–1644) as a form of decorative academicism by professional painters of the so-called Che school. The style was not greatly admired by gentlemen and connoisseurs, who considered it too brilliantly professional for their taste. As a result, few high-quality paintings of the Ma-Hsia school survived in China outside the imperial collection. Their work, however, found favour in Japan, where it was a powerful influence in forming the style of the great ink painters Shūbun (early 15th century) and Sesshū and of the early masters of the Kanō school during the Muromachi period (1338–1573). (M.Su.)

BIBLIOGRAPHY. Osvald Siren, *Chinese Painting: Leading Masters and Principles,* 7 vol. (1956–58, reissued 1974), is the standard history of Chinese painting. Ma Yüan's work is discussed in S. Shimada and Y. Yonezawa, *Painting of Sung and Yüan Dynasties* (1952); Kojiro Tomita, *Portfolio of Chinese Paintings in the Museum: Han to Sung Periods,* 2nd ed. (1938), from the collection of the Boston Museum of Fine Arts; Sherman E. Lee, *Chinese Landscape Painting,* 2nd rev. ed. (1962); Laurence Sickman (ed.), *Chinese Calligraphy and Painting in the Collection of John M. Crawford, Jr.* (1962); James Francis Cahill, *Chinese Painting, XI–XIV Centuries* (1960); and Michael Sullivan, *A Short History of Chinese Art,* rev. ed. (1967, reissued 1970).

Maʿadi (people): *see* Madi.

Maʿādī, Al-, predynastic Egyptian site located just south of modern Cairo in Al-Qāhirah *muḥāfaẓah* (governorate) in Lower Egypt. The settlement at Al-Maʿādī was approximately contemporary with the widespread Gerzean culture (*c.* 3400–*c.* 3100 BC) of Upper Egypt. Al-Maʿādī was apparently a peasant village with a separate cemetery; the settlement was characterized by rectangular huts, splay-footed vases, globular, rimmed-neck vessels, and large storage jars similar to those found at Gerzean sites. Copper was occasionally used, and Upper Egyptian stone vase types have been found. In addition to Al-Maʿādī's connections with the culture of Upper Egypt, its position on the southern leg of the Syro-Egyptian trade route also brought it under the cultural influence of Syria and Palestine.

maʿamadot (Hebrew: "stands," or "posts"), 24 groups of Jewish laymen that witnessed, by turns of one week each, the daily sacrifice in the Second Temple of Jerusalem as representatives of the common people. Gradually *maʿamadot* were organized in areas outside Jerusalem, so that the people could hold special services in their villages while their representatives were present in the Temple. Some scholars view these village *maʿamadot* as the first step toward regular synagogue worship.

Though public sacrifices were terminated when Jerusalem was destroyed in AD 70, daily prayers called *maʿamadot* are still recited privately by many pious Jews.

Maʿān, town, southern Jordan. It is a regional trade centre for the sparsely settled southern part of the country, which is inhabited mainly by the Ḥuwayṭat and other Bedouin tribes. Maʿān is the chief road and rail junction of southern Jordan. The town lies on the Hejaz-Jordan Railway, which runs north-south and connects to Damascus (Syria) in the north. The part of the rail line south of Maʿān that formerly reached Medina (now in Saudi Arabia) was largely destroyed by Arab guerrillas led by the English leader T.E. Lawrence (Lawrence of Arabia) in World War I; it has been replaced by the Desert Highway, which roughly follows the route of the former rail line in its Jordanian section. An all-weather road runs from the port of Al-ʿAqabah north to Maʿān and there connects to Jordan's main north-south highway, which leads to Amman, the capital. Maʿān and Al-ʿAqabah are also connected by rail via Baṭn al-Ghūl.

After World War I the status of Maʿān and all of southern Jordan was disputed between the emirate of Transjordan (later the kingdom of Jordan) and the kingdom of the Hejaz to the south. When King Ibn Saʿūd conquered the Hejaz (now part of Saudi Arabia) in 1925, the British placed the entire Maʿān area under Transjordan's authority. The de facto annexation was not recognized by the Saudis until 1965, when a treaty was signed fixing the frontier and placing Maʿān and its environs well within Jordan. From the town, travelers set out to visit the ancient ruins of Petra, 19 miles (30 km) northwest. Pop. (1994) 22,989.

maarib, also spelled MAARIV, plural MAARIBIM, or MAARIVIM, Hebrew MAʿARIV ("who brings on twilight"), Jewish evening prayers recited after sunset; the name derives from one of the opening words of the first prayer. Maarib consists essentially of the Shema, with its accompanying benedictions, and the amidah. The Shema expresses the central theme of Jewish worship: "Hear, O Israel: The Lord our God is one Lord" (Deuteronomy 6:4), while the amidah is composed of a series of benedictions. The amidah is recited by the congregation but is not repeated by the reader because in ancient times some argued that its recitation was optional. Maarib has other elements also, some of which vary from place to place. Certain Ashkenazic (German-rite) congregations, for example, include special liturgical poems composed during the European Middle Ages in the maarib service on festivals.

The institution of evening prayer is traditionally ascribed to Jacob. Unlike shaharith (morning prayers) and minhah (afternoon prayers), maarib (sometimes also called *ʿarvit,* from the Hebrew *ʿerev,* "evening") is not a substitute for former Temple sacrifices.

Maʿarrī, al-, in full ABŪ AL-ʿALĀʾ AḤMAD IBN ʿABD ALLĀH AL-MAʿARRĪ (b. December 973, Maʿarrat an-Nuʿmān, near Aleppo, Syria—d. May 1057, Maʿarrat an-Nuʿmān), great Arab poet, known for his virtuosity and for the originality and pessimism of his vision.

Al-Maʿarrī was a descendant of the Tanūkh tribe. A childhood disease left him virtually blind. He studied at the Syrian cities of Aleppo, Antioch, and Tripoli and soon began his literary career, supported by a small private income. His early poems were collected in *Saqṭ az-zand* ("The Tinder Spark"), which gained great popularity.

After about two years in Baghdad, al-Maʿarrī returned to northern Syria in 1010, partly because of his mother's ill health. In Baghdad he had been well received at first in prestigious literary salons; but when he refused to sell his panegyrics, he was unable to find a dependable patron. He renounced material wealth and retired to a secluded dwelling, living there on a restrictive diet. Al-Maʿarrī enjoyed respect and authority locally, and many students came to study with him. He also maintained an active correspondence.

Al-Maʿarrī wrote a second, more original collection of poetry, *Luzūm mā lam yalzam* ("Unnecessary Necessity"), or *Luzūmīyāt* ("Necessities"), referring to the unnecessary complexity of the rhyme scheme. The skeptical humanism of these poems was also apparent in *Risālat al-ghufrān* (Eng. trans. by G. Brackenbury, *Risalat ul Ghufran, a Divine Comedy,* 1943), in which the poet visits paradise and meets his predecessors, heathen poets who have found forgiveness. These later works aroused some Muslim suspicions. *Al-Fuṣūl wa al-ghāyāt* ("Paragraphs and Periods"), a collection of homilies in rhymed prose, has even been called a parody of the Qurʾān. Although an advocate of social justice and action, al-Maʿarrī suggested that children should not be begotten, in order to spare future generations the pains of life.

Maas, Nicolas: *see* Maes, Nicolaes.

Maas River (Europe): *see* Meuse River.

Maasai (people): *see* Masai.

Maastricht, *gemeente* (commune) and capital, Limburg *provincie,* southeastern Netherlands. It lies along the Maas (Meuse) River at the junction of the Juliana, Liège-Maastricht, and Zuid-Willems canals. Maastricht is the principal city in the southeastern appendix of The Netherlands and is only 2 miles (3 km) from the Belgian border.

It was the site of the Roman settlement Trajectum ad Mosam ("Ford on the Maas") and was later the seat of a bishop from 382 to 721. The town was held by the dukes of Brabant after 1204, coming under the joint sovereignty of Brabant and the prince-bishops of Liège in 1284 and of Liège and the Dutch Estates-General in 1632. It was taken by the Spanish in 1579, by Prince Frederick Henry of Orange in 1632, and by the French in 1673, 1748, and 1794, but it successfully resisted the Belgians in 1830–32. Portions of its old fortifications—Helpoort (1229), the Pater Fink Tower, and 16th- and 17th-century bastions—remain. Attacked on the first day of the German invasion of the Low Countries in 1940, Maastricht was the first Dutch town to be liberated, in 1944. During a 1991 meeting of the European Communities that was held in Maastricht, an accord was signed calling for the establishment of a European Union, with common policies on economics, foreign affairs, security, and immigration.

Maastricht's landmarks include the St. Servatius Bridge (*c.* 1280) over the Maas, the Dinghuis, or former courthouse (*c.* 1475), and the town hall (1658–64). The cathedral, dedicated to St. Servatius, was founded by Bishop Monulphus in the 6th century; it is the oldest church in The Netherlands, although rebuilt and enlarged from the 11th to the 15th century. The Protestant Church of St. John, with a 246-foot (75-metre) tower, originally served as its parish church. The much-restored Church of Our Lady has remnants of 10th-century crypts. There are many other medieval churches, as well as fine houses in regional Renaissance and French styles. Maastricht is the site of the University of Limburg (1976), a music conservatory, a symphony orchestra, art academies, and several museums.

To the south are the sandstone (marl) quarries of St. Pietersberg, comprising more than 200 miles (322 km) of underground man-made passages worked from Roman times to the 19th century. They served to hide peasants and cattle during the wars with Spain and art treasures and refugees during World War II. There are four castles in the neighbourhood of Maastricht.

An early trade was carried on in cloth, leather, hardware, and building materials. Until the coming of the railways in 1853, however, Maastricht did not reap the full advantages of its central position between the mining and industrial cities of Heerlen and Kampen (both in The Netherlands), Aachen (Ger.; also called Aix-la-Chapelle), and Liège (Belg.). Its manufactures now include pottery, glass, crystal, cement, paper, tobacco products, steel, and chemicals. Tourism and art printing are important, and there is a trade in beer, grain, vegetables, and butter. Pop. (1994 est.) 118,102; metropolitan area, 164,153.

Maastricht Treaty: *see* European Union, Treaty on.

Maastrichtian Stage, also spelled MAESTRICHTIAN, uppermost of six main divisions in the Upper Cretaceous Series, representing all those rocks on a global basis deposited during the Maastrichtian Age (74.5 to 66.4 million years ago). The stage's name is derived from the city of Maastricht in the southeastern Netherlands, whose surrounding area serves as the classic type district for rocks of this age. The Maastrichtian Stage is extensively represented by chalk formations in northern Europe and in England, for example, the Trimingham Chalk and part of the Norwich Chalk. No global stratotype section and point (GSSP) for the base of the stage has been approved. However, the first appearance of the fossil ammonite *Hoploscaphites constrictus* is often taken as the base of this stage. The biozones of the calcareous microfossils *Micula mura, Lithraphidites quadratus,* and *Broinsonia parca* and of the planktonic foraminifera *Abathomphasus mayaroensis/Racemigulembelina fructicosa* are also considered to indicate rocks of the stage. The Maastrichtian Stage overlies the Campanian Stage and is itself overlain by the Danian Stage of the Tertiary System.

Maʿat, also spelled MAYET, in ancient Egyptian religion, the personification of truth, justice, and the cosmic order. The daughter of the sun god Re, she was associated with Thoth, god of wisdom.

The ceremony of judgment of the dead (called the "Judgment of Osiris," named for Osiris, the god of the dead) was believed to focus upon the weighing of the heart of the deceased in a scale balanced by Maʿat (or her hieroglyph, the ostrich feather), as a test of conformity to proper values. The Hall of Double Justice where this occurred was so called from Maʿat's frequent appearances there as two identical goddesses.

In its abstract sense, *maʿat* was the divine order established at creation and reaffirmed at the accession of each new king of Egypt. In setting *maʿat,* "order," in place of *izfet,* "disorder," the king played the role of the sun god, the god with the closest links to Maʿat. Maʿat stood at the head of the sun god's bark

Maʿat, bronze figure of the 26th dynasty; in the British Museum

By courtesy of the trustees of the British Museum

as it traveled through the sky and the underworld. Although aspects of kingship and of *maʿat* were at times subjected to criticism and reformulation, the principles underlying these two institutions were fundamental to ancient Egyptian life and thought and endured to the end of ancient Egyptian history.

Maazel, Lorin, in full LORIN VARENCOVE MAAZEL (b. March 6, 1930, Neuilly, France), conductor and violinist who, as music director of the Cleveland Orchestra from 1972 to 1982, was only the second American to have served as principal conductor of a major American orchestra.

Maazel grew up in Los Angeles and began his first musical instruction at the age of five. Although he began conducting as early as the age of nine, he made his adult debut in 1953 in Italy, where he was researching Baroque music on a Fulbright scholarship. Thereafter he held conducting appointments with the Deutsche Oper, West Berlin (1965–71), the West Berlin Radio Symphony Orchestra (1965–75), the New Philharmonia Orchestra of London (1970–72; 1976–80), the Cleveland Orchestra (1972–82), the French National Orchestra (from 1977), the Pittsburgh Symphony (from 1986), and the Bavarian Radio Symphony Orchestra (from 1993). In 1982–1984 he was artistic director of the Vienna State Opera, the first American to hold the post.

Maazel was equally at home in operatic and orchestral music, and his repertoire ranged from the 18th century to the most recent works. Undemonstrative on the podium, he combined clarity with great emotional depth. He also appeared frequently as a violinist.

Mab, also called QUEEN MAB, in English folklore, the queen of the fairies. Mab is a mischievous but basically benevolent figure. In William Shakespeare's *Romeo and Juliet,* she is referred to as the fairies' midwife, who delivers sleeping men of their innermost wishes in the form of dreams. In Michael Drayton's mock-epic fairy poem *Nymphidia* (1627), she is the wife of the fairy king Oberon and is the queen of the diminutive fairies. Mab is similarly mentioned as a pixielike fairy in works by Ben Jonson, John

Milton, and Robert Herrick. Her place as queen of the fairies in English folklore was eventually taken over by Titania.

Mabillon, Jean (b. Nov. 23, 1632, near Reims, Fr.—d. Dec. 27, 1707, Paris), French monastic scholar, antiquarian, and historian who pioneered the study of ancient handwriting (paleography).

He entered Saint-Rémi Abbey, Reims, in 1653 and became a Benedictine monk the following year. He was ordained priest (1660)

Mabillon, engraving by Loir after a painting by Hallé
Harlingue—H. Roger-Viollet

at Corbie, Fr., before moving in 1664 to St. Germain-des-Prés, Paris, headquarters of the Maurists, a congregation of French Benedictine scholars. He worked there for 20 years, coediting in 1667 the works of Abbot St. Bernard of Clairvaux and *Lives* of the Benedictine saints (9 vol., 1668–1701).

With the aid of his colleagues, Mabillon wrote *De Re Diplomatica* (1681; supplement, 1704), in which he established the principles for determining the authenticity and dates of medieval manuscripts. *De Re Diplomatica* founded the science of diplomatics—the critical study of the formal sources of history—and practically created Latin paleography, the science fundamental to European diplomatics. *De Re Diplomatica* challenged the Jesuit Daniel Papebroch—who had declared that nearly all Merovingian documents were spurious and that no authentic charters survived from times before AD 700—and caused a major controversy between the Benedictines and the Jesuits.

In 1691 Mabillon had to defend the Maurists' mode of living against Abbot de Rancé of La Trappe, Fr. (founder of the reformed Cistercians called Trappists), who favoured manual work for monks. The ensuing dispute caused Mabillon to write (1691–92) *Traité des études monastiques* ("Treatise on Monastic Studies") and *Réflexions sur la réponse de M. l'abbé de la Trappe* ("Reflections on the Reply of the Abbot of La Trappe"); both works embodied the Maurists' ideas and program for ecclesiastical studies. Generally considered the greatest of the Maurists, Mabillon died amid the colossal production of the Benedictine *Annals,* 4 vol. (1703–07; vol. 5, posthumously, 1713; vol. 6, the work of other authors, 1739).

BIBLIOGRAPHY. T. Ruinart, *Abrégé de la vie de D.J.M.* (1709), reprinted in 1933 as *Mabillon;* Henri Leclercq, *Life,* 2 vol. (1953–57); J.U. Bergkamp, *Dom Jean Mabillon and the Benedictine Historical School of Saint-Maur* (1928).

Mabini, Apolinario (b. July 23, 1864, Talaga, Phil.—d. May 13, 1903, Manila), Filipino theoretician and spokesman of the Philippine Revolution, who wrote the constitution for the short-lived republic of 1898–99.

Born into a peasant family, Mabini studied at San Juan de Letran College in Manila and won a law degree from the University of Santo Tomás in 1894. In an insurrection organized in August 1896 by nationalists, he joined the forces of the patriot general Emilio Aguinaldo and soon became his right-hand man. When the Spanish–American War broke out in 1898, Mabini urged cooperation with the United States as a means to gain freedom from Spain. At a convention held at the market town of Malolos in September and October 1898, an independent republic was proclaimed with Aguinaldo as its president; Mabini drew up its constitution, which resembled that of the United States. When the United States announced, however, that it would annex the Philippines, Mabini joined Aguinaldo in a renewed struggle for independence. He was captured by U.S. troops in December 1899 and, because he refused to swear allegiance to the United States, was exiled to Guam, not being allowed to return home until a few months before his death. Mabini wrote *La revolución filipina,* which was published in 1931.

Mabinogion, collection of 11 medieval Welsh tales based on mythology, folklore, and heroic legends. The tales provide interesting examples of the transmission of Celtic, Norman, and French traditions in early romance. The name Mabinogion derives from a scribal error and is an unjustified but convenient term for these anonymous tales.

The finest of the tales are the four related stories known as "The Four Branches of the *Mabinogi,*" or "The Four Branches" (dating, in their present form, from the late 11th century), the only tales in which the word Mabinogi (meaning "Matters Concerning [the Family of?] Maponos") appears. Of great interest to Welsh studies are "The Four Independent Native Tales," which show minimal continental influence and include "Culhwch and Olwen" (*q.v.*), "Lludd and Llefelys," "The Dream of Macsen," and "The Dream of Rhonabwy." The tales "Owein and Luned" (or "The Lady of the Fountain"), "Geraint and Enid," and "Peredur Son of Efrawg" parallel the French romances *Yvain, Erec,* and *Perceval* of Chrétien de Troyes.

The Welsh text was edited by Ifor Williams, as *Pedeir Keinc y Mabinogi,* in 1930 (revised reprint 1959); an English translation, *The Mabinogion,* was published in 1949 (rev. ed. 1974); and a new translation was included in *The Mabinogi and Other Medieval Welsh Tales* (1977) by Patrick K. Ford.

Mabuse, Jan, original name JAN GOSSAERT, or JENNI GOSSART, also called JAN MALBODIUS (b. *c.* 1478, County of Hainaut—d. *c.* 1532, Breda, Brabant [now in Neth.]), Flemish painter who was one of the first artists to introduce the style of the Italian Renaissance into the Low Countries.

He derived the name Mabuse from his family home, Maubeuge, in northern France. He is most likely to be identified with one Jennyn van Hennegouwe, who is registered as a master in the Guild of St. Luke at Antwerp in 1503. His most important early work extant is the "Adoration of the Kings" (National Gallery, London), which is painted in the ornate style of the Antwerp school. Other early works, such as "Jesus, the Virgin, and the Baptist" (Prado, Madrid), reflect his interest in the works of Jan van Eyck and Albrecht Dürer. Another early work, famous for its sense of mood, is the "Agony in the Garden" (Staatliche Museen Preussischer Kulturbesitz, Berlin).

In 1508 Mabuse accompanied his employer, Philip of Burgundy, to Italy, where he was strongly impressed by the art of the High Renaissance. After his return from Italy in 1509, he continued to study Italian art through the engravings of Marcantonio Raimondi and Jacopo de' Barbari. Mabuse's subsequent work shows a continuous effort to develop a fully Italianate style. This is evident in such works as the "Neptune and Amphitrite" (1516; Staatliche Museen Preussischer Kulturbesitz) and the "Hercules and Deianira" (1517; Barber Institute, Birmingham, Eng.), in which his early, complex designs have given way to a comparatively simple and direct conception.

Sculpturesque nudes become common in Mabuse's later paintings, but they seldom avoid the stiff, lapidary quality of his earlier figures. In his "Danae" (Alte Pinakothek, Munich), Mabuse employs an elaborate architectural setting as a foil for the seminude figure, a device he frequently used. Throughout his life, he retained the jewellike technique and careful observation that were traditional in Netherlandish art.

"Danae," oil on panel by Jan Mabuse, 1527; in the Alte Pinakothek, Munich
By courtesy of the Alte Pinakothek, Munich

Mabuse was also a renowned portrait painter. His portraits, such as the "Charles de Bourgogne" (Staatliche Museen Preussischer Kulturbesitz), "Eleanor of Austria" (*c.* 1525; H.A. Wetzlar Collection, Amsterdam), and "Jean Carondelet" (1517; Louvre, Paris), reveal his facility for psychological perception and are particularly notable for their expressive depiction of hands.

Mac FAMILY, Vietnamese clan that established a dynasty ruling the Tonkin area of northern Vietnam from 1527 to 1592.

The Mac family began as ministers to the Le kings of the Vietnamese Later Le dynasty (1428–1787). By the early 16th century, however, the Later Le rulers had become virtually powerless, and in 1527 Mac Dang Dung, the head of the family, usurped the throne. Eight years later the powerful Nguyen family reestablished the Le monarchs and drove the Mac family out of central and southern Vietnam. They were, however, able to establish their own kingdom in the north, which was recognized as an independent state by the Chinese protectors of the region. Weakened by internal dissension, in 1592 the Mac lost most of their territory to the Trinh family, who also formerly served as ministers to the Later Le dynasty. Nevertheless, the Mac, with the support of the Chinese, managed to retain a small amount of territory on the Vietnamese–Chinese border until 1677.

Mac-Mahon, Marie-Edme-Patrice-Maurice, comte de (count of), DUC DE (duke of) MAGENTA (b. July 13, 1808, Sully, Fr.—d. Oct. 17, 1893, Loiret), marshal of France and second president of the Third French Republic. During his presidency the Third Republic took shape, the new constitutional laws of 1875 were adopted, and important precedents were established affecting the relationship between executive and legislative powers.

A descendant of an Irish family that fled to France during the time of the Stuarts, Mac-Mahon began his army career in 1827 in Algeria and distinguished himself in the

Mac-Mahon, lithograph by J.-B.-A. Lafosse, 1876

By courtesy of the Bibliotheque Nationale, Paris

storming of Constantine (1837) and in the Crimean War (1853–56). The climax of his military career came in the Italian campaign of 1859, when his victory at Magenta resulted in his being created duc de Magenta. In 1864 he became governor general of Algeria. Commanding the I Army Corps in Alsace during the Franco-German War (1870–71), he was wounded and defeated at the Battle of Wörth. After a short convalescence at Sedan, Mac-Mahon was appointed head of the Versailles Army, which defeated the Paris Commune revolt in May 1871.

When Adolphe Thiers resigned as president of the republic on May 24, 1873, French rightists turned to Mac-Mahon as his successor; he was elected president the same day. On Nov. 20, 1873, the National Assembly passed the Law of the Septennate, conferring upon him presidential power for seven years. The Marshal assumed his presidential duties somewhat reluctantly, for he disliked publicity and lacked an understanding of the complex political issues of his day.

During Mac-Mahon's term the constitutional laws of 1875 were promulgated. The National Assembly dissolved itself, and the elections of 1876 returned a large majority of republicans to the new chamber. The first crisis came in December 1876, when the republican chamber compelled Mac-Mahon to invite the moderate republican Jules Simon to form a government. The conservative Senate disapproved of Simon because he had purged some rightist officials, and, on May 16 (*le seize mai*), 1877, Mac-Mahon posted a letter to Simon that was tantamount to dismissal. Premier Simon's resignation precipitated the crisis of *le seize mai.* When Mac-Mahon commissioned conservative Albert de Broglie to form a ministry and won the Senate's assent to dissolve the chamber (June 25, 1877), the question of whether the President or Parliament would control the government was squarely posed.

The new elections to the chamber returned a majority of republicans, and the de Broglie ministry was given a vote of "no confidence." The succeeding ministry, headed by Rochebouët, also collapsed. By Dec. 13, 1877, Mac-Mahon gave in to the extent of accepting a ministry led by conservative republican Jules Dufaure and composed mostly of republicans. On Jan. 5, 1879, the republicans gained a majority in the Senate, and Mac-Mahon resigned on January 28. The constitutional crisis during his presidency was resolved in favour of parliamentary as against presidential control, and thereafter during the Third Republic the office of president became largely an honorific post.

macadam, form of pavement invented by John McAdam of Scotland in the 18th century. McAdam's road cross section was composed of a compacted subgrade of crushed granite or greenstone designed to support the load, covered by a surface of light stone to absorb wear and tear and shed water to the drainage ditches. In modern macadam construction crushed stone or gravel is placed on the compacted base course and bound together with asphalt cement or hot tar. A third layer to fill the interstices is then added and rolled. Cement-sand slurry is sometimes used as the binder.

McAdam, John Loudon (b. Sept. 21, 1756, Ayr, Ayrshire, Scot.—d. Nov. 26, 1836, Moffat, Dumfriesshire), Scottish inventor of the macadam road surface.

In 1770 he went to New York City, entering the countinghouse of a merchant uncle; he returned to Scotland with a considerable fortune in 1783. There he purchased an estate at Sauhrie, Ayrshire. McAdam, who had become a road trustee in his district, noted that the local highways were in poor condition. At his own expense he undertook a series of experiments in road making.

In 1798 he moved to Falmouth, Cornwall, where he continued his experiments under a government appointment. He recommended that roads should be raised above the adjacent ground for good drainage and covered,

McAdam, engraving by Charles Turner

By courtesy of the trustees of the British Museum; photograph, J.R. Freeman & Co. Ltd.

first with large rocks, and then with smaller stones, the whole mass to be bound with fine gravel or slag. In 1815, having been appointed surveyor general of the Bristol roads, he put his theories into practice. To document his work, McAdam wrote *Remarks on the Present System of Road-Making* (1816) and *Practical Essay on the Scientific Repair and Preservation of Roads* (1819).

As the result of a parliamentary inquiry in 1823 into the whole question of road making, his views were adopted by the public authorities, and in 1827 he was appointed Surveyor General of Metropolitan Roads in Great Britain. Macadamization of roads did much to facilitate travel and communication. The process was quickly adopted in other countries, notably the United States.

Consult the INDEX *first*

macadamia (*Macadamia*), any of about 10 species of ornamental evergreen tree belonging to the family Protaeceae, producing an edible, richly flavoured dessert nut.

Macadamias originated in the coastal rain forests and scrubs of what is now Queensland in northeastern Australia. The macadamias grown commercially in Hawaii and Australia are principally of two species, the smooth-shelled *Macadamia integrefolia* and the rough-shelled *M. tetraphylla*; the two tend to hybridize beyond distinction. Because of the successes of the Hawaiian nut industry, other subtropical regions have planted macadamia orchards. Large acreages are planted in South Africa, Zimbabwe, and Malawi and parts of South and Central America.

As an orchard crop, the macadamia needs rich, well-drained soil and 130 centimetres (50 inches) of rain annually. Macadamia trees commonly grow to 18.3 metres (60 feet) high and 15.2 m wide. The everbearing trees have shiny, leathery leaves that are 20–30 cm long. Fragrant pink or white flower clusters are succeeded by bunches of one to 20 fruits. The

Macadamia (*Macadamia ternifolia*)

Walter Dawn

shiny, round, 25-millimetre (1-in.) nuts have a thick, leathery husk called a pericarp that splits along one side during the ripening process. Because it is difficult to tell precisely when the nut is ripe, the macadamias are not harvested until they drop to the ground. The mature nuts are then gathered by hand and machine-hulled, dried, and stored for processing. In Hawaiian factories, the nuts are roasted, usually in oil, salted, and packed. Some of the crop is used by bakers in confections. The nuts are a good source of calcium, phosphorus, iron, and vitamin B; they contain 73 percent fat. Because macadamias are difficult to propagate, slow to bear, and limited in range of cultivability, production has not kept pace with increased demand, thus rendering the product costly.

McAdoo, William G(ibbs) (b. Oct. 31, 1863, near Marietta, Ga., U.S.—d. Feb. 1, 1941, Washington, D.C.), U.S. secretary of the treasury (1913–18), a founder and chairman (1914) of the Federal Reserve Board, and director general of the U.S. railroads during and shortly after World War I (1917–19). He directed four fund-raising drives that raised $18,000,000,000 to help finance the Allied war effort.

McAdoo began his career as a lawyer in Chattanooga, Tenn. He moved to New York City (1892), where he organized and headed two companies (later consolidated as the Hudson and Manhattan Railway Company) that built tunnels under the Hudson River. He supported Democrat Woodrow Wilson in the 1910 gubernatorial election in New Jersey and in the 1912 presidential campaign. As

McAdoo

By courtesy of the Library of Congress, Washington, D.C.

treasury secretary, he became one of Wilson's most trusted officials. In 1914, after the death of his first wife, McAdoo married the President's daughter, Eleanor Randolph Wilson, in a White House ceremony.

He emerged from the Wilson administration the acknowledged leader of the Democratic Party, yet lost the presidential nomination three times. From 1933 to 1938 he served as U.S. senator from California.

Macaire, title often assigned to a French medieval epic poem, or chanson de geste, after one of its chief characters. Blanchefleur, wife of the aged and infirm emperor Charlemagne, having repulsed the advances of Macaire, is accused of infidelity and sentenced to perpetual exile. Ultimately her innocence is proved, she pardons her husband, and is reunited with him.

The same story was developed in another chanson, known as *La Reine Sebile,* the text of which has been reconstructed from 13th-century fragments discovered in England, Belgium, and Switzerland. This poem was the basis for a popular Spanish prose romance called the *Historia de la Reyna Sebilla.* It is not certain whether *Macaire* or *La Reine Sebile* is the older poem, though the existence of an epic romance on these folklore themes (a queen unjustly suspected of infidelity; a dog that avenges its master's death) was attested in France as early as the first half of the 13th century. The same story, separated from its Charlemagne context, was worked over many times in France from the 14th century onward.

McAlester, city, seat (1907) of Pittsburg county, southeastern Oklahoma, U.S., south of Eufaula Reservoir and Dam and the South Canadian River. It originated as a trading post, built in 1870 by James McAlester (later lieutenant governor of the state) in Choctaw territory at the intersection of the Texas and California trails. The arrival of the railroad in 1872 stimulated the working of local coal deposits. McAlester has aerospace-aviation and marine industries and is the site of the U.S. Army Ammunition Depot. Oil, gas, agriculture, clothing manufacture, and food processing are additional economic factors. The city is the site of the Oklahoma State Penitentiary, McAlester Consistory Temple (home of the Scottish Rite Masons), and the International Temple of the Order of the Rainbow for Girls (founded 1922). Inc. 1906. Pop. (1990) 16,370.

McAllen, city, Hidalgo county, southern Texas, U.S., in the irrigated Lower Rio Grande Valley, 7 mi (11 km) from the International Bridge to Reynosa, Mex., and 52 mi west-northwest of Brownsville. With Edinburg and Pharr, it forms a metropolitan complex. Founded in 1905, it was named for John McAllen, a Scottish settler whose ranch was the townsite. A leading winter resort, McAllen is a hub of oil and gas production. It is also a processing centre for citrus fruits, vegetables, and cotton, and a port of entry for trade with Mexico. Inc. town, 1910; city, 1927. Pop. (2000) city, 106,414; McAllen-Edinburg-Mission MSA, 569,463.

McAllister, (Samuel) Ward (b. December 1827, Savannah, Ga., U.S.—d. Jan. 31, 1895, New York City), U.S. lawyer and social leader who originated the phrase "the Four Hundred" to designate New York City's society leaders. McAllister was shortening an invitation list for Mrs. William Astor when he boasted, in 1892, that there were "only about 400 people in New York society." The phrase quickly became a popular idiom.

Moving to California with his father to establish a law firm in 1850, McAllister made a fortune by 1852. He retired from the bar and devoted himself to social life. He lived in Europe for several years, returning to spend most of his time at Newport, R.I. In the early 1870s he established "the Patriarchs," a group of heads of old New York families. The Patriarchs accepted or rejected aspirants to New York's "high society." McAllister contributed articles to newspapers and magazines, becoming known as an authority on the social graces. His book *Society As I Have Found It* was published in 1890.

MacAlpin, Kenneth: *see* Kenneth I.

Macao (South China): *see* Macau.

Macapá, city, capital of Amapá state, northern Brazil, on the northern channel (Canal do Norte) of the Amazon Delta, situated on a small plateau of firm ground 50 ft (15 m) above sea level, just on the Equator. It was given city status in 1856. Macapá is the commercial, manufacturing, and transportation centre of the state, exporting high-grade manganese (including silicomanganese and ferromanganese), gold, iron, and tin ores and lumber from its hinterland. Automobiles, oils, rubber, pelts from jungle animals, and fish from both the river and ocean are exported from Macapá's port, Pôrto Sontana. The city has air links with Belém in Pará state and with Rio de Janeiro, and local roads and a railroad lead to the manganese mines at Serra do Navio. Pop. (2000 prelim.) 270,077.

Macapagal, Diosdado (b. Sept. 28, 1910, Lubao, Phil.—d. April 21, 1997, Makati), Filipino reformist president of the Republic of the Philippines from 1961 to 1965.

After receiving his law degree, Macapagal was admitted to the bar in 1936. During World War II he practiced law in Manila and aided the anti-Japanese resistance. After the war he worked in a law firm and in 1948 served as second secretary to the Philippine Embassy in Washington, D.C. The following year he was elected to a seat in the Philippine House of Representatives, serving until 1956. During this time he was Philippine representative to the United Nations General Assembly three times. From 1957 to 1961 Macapagal was a member of the Liberal Party and vice president under Nacionalista president Carlos Garcia. In the 1961 elections, however, he ran against Garcia, forging a coalition of the Liberal and Progressive parties and making a crusade against corruption a principal element of his platform. He was elected by a wide margin.

While president, Macapagal worked to suppress graft and corruption and to stimulate the Philippine economy. He placed the peso on the free currency-exchange market, encouraged exports, and sought to curb income tax evasion, particularly by the wealthiest families, which cost the treasury millions of pesos yearly. His reforms, however, were crippled by a House of Representatives and Senate dominated by the Nacionalistas, and he was defeated in the 1965 elections by Ferdinand Marcos.

In 1972 he chaired the convention that drafted the 1973 constitution only to question in 1981 the validity of its ratification. In 1979 he organized the National Union for Liberation as an opposition party to the Marcos regime.

macaque (*Macaca*), any of about 12 species of gregarious, diurnal monkeys, belonging to the family Cercopithecidae, found primarily in Asia. Macaques are robust animals with arms and legs of about the same length. Their fur is generally a shade of brown or blackish and their muzzles, like those of baboons, are dog-like but are rounded in profile and bear the nostrils on the upper surface. The tail varies among species and may be long, of moderate length, short, or absent. Size differs between the sexes and among the species; males range in head and body length from about 41–70 centimetres (16–28 inches) and in weight

Japanese macaque (*Macaca fuscata*)
Painting by Al P. Nielsen

from about 3.5–8.3 kilograms (8–18 pounds) in crab-eating macaques to a maximum of about 18 kilograms in the Japanese macaques.

Macaques live in troops of varying size. The males, which lead and maintain discipline, live within a more well-defined dominance order than do females. Macaques are somewhat more arboreal than baboons but are equally at home on the ground; they are also able to swim. They live in forests, plains, and among cliffs and rocky terrain. They are omnivorous and possess large cheek pouches in which they carry extra food. Breeding occurs all year round. The single young are born after about six months' gestation and become adult at four years. Macaques are considered highly intelligent but may be bad-tempered as adults.

Celebes, or moor, macaques (*M. maurus*) are short-tailed lowland macaques sometimes placed in the genus *Cynomacaca.* Crab-eating macaques (*M. fascicularis* or *M. irus*) are long-tailed monkeys with whiskery brown faces; they fish for crabs and other crustaceans and were used extensively in studies leading to development of the polio vaccine. Lion-tailed macaques, or wanderoos (*M. silenus,* sometimes *Silenus silenus*), are black with gray ruffs and tufted tails; an endangered species, they are found only in a small area of South India. Pig-tailed macaques (*M. nemestrina*) carry their short, furry tails curved over the back. Inhabitants of lowland forests, they are trained by Malays to pick ripe coconuts. Stump-tailed macaques (*M. speciosa*) are strong, shaggy-haired, mountain dwellers with pink or red faces and very short tails; like the Japanese macaques they are sometimes placed in the genus *Lyssodes.* Japanese macaques (*M. fuscata*) are also large, muscular, and shaggy-haired; they have pink faces and short, furry tails. Monkeys of this species were important in myths and folktales and provided the models for the Buddhist saying and its representation: "see no evil, hear no evil, speak no evil."

Other well known species commonly called by names other than "macaque" are the bonnet monkey, rhesus monkey, and Barbary ape (*qq.v.*). The Celebes black ape (*q.v.*) is sometimes known as the Celebes crested macaque.

McArdle's disease, also called GLYCOGENOSIS TYPE V, hereditary deficiency of the enzyme glycogen phosphorylase in muscle cells. In the absence of this enzyme, muscles cannot break down animal starch (glycogen) to meet the energy requirements of exercise. Muscle activity is thus solely dependent on the availability of glucose (blood sugar) and other nutrients in the circulating blood. Victims of McArdle's disease are chronically weak because their muscles are incapable of prolonged exertion; even moderate exercise produces muscle cramping and severe pain. Unlike other types of glycogenosis, the disease is not fatal, and the missing enzyme does not impair the functioning of other body systems. McArdle's disease is inherited as a recessive trait.

Macarius, Russian MAKARY (b. *c.* 1482—d. Jan. 12, 1564 [Dec. 31, 1563, old style], Moscow), Russian metropolitan (archbishop) of Moscow and head of the Russian Church during the period of consolidation of the Muscovite Empire.

A monk of the monastery of St. Paphnutius in Borovsk, southwest of Moscow, Macarius became archbishop of Novgorod in 1526. After his elevation in 1542 as metropolitan of Moscow and of all Russia, Macarius gathered a council of theologians and began to effect his policy of integrating sacred and secular powers through ecclesiastical support of an autocratic monarchy.

Having established the first printing press in Russia, Macarius collected and revised annalistic and legendary records in an attempt to assign to Russia a God-chosen and unique place in Christian history. Under his direction, Moscow's synods of 1547 and 1549 canonized more than 40 Russian saints to centralize the scattered local devotions and further the independent identity of Pan-Russian Christianity. He composed the first *Minei-Cetii,* the first major collection of the lives of Russian saints for daily meditation and worship, arranging them in 12 volumes, one for each month of the year. His *Stepennaya Kniga* ("Book of Generations") is a comprehensive history of Russian ruling families and a compendium of earlier chronicles.

Macarius' ecclesiastico-political reform was consolidated by the Stoglavy Sobor (Council of the Hundred Chapters) at Moscow in 1551, when his new codification of Russian church law, administration, and rites was approved by the assembly of bishops. The Russianizing of Orthodoxy also had its aesthetic consequence in the development of a Muscovite religious art form. Macarius influenced Tsar Ivan to push the expansion of Russia toward the East, leading to the capture of the Tatar territory of Kazan (1552) and Astrakhan (1556), thereby opening the way to Siberia and a new field of missionary activity.

Macarius BULGAKOV: *see* Bulgakov, Macarius.

Macarius MAGNES (fl. early 5th century), Eastern Orthodox bishop and polemicist, author of an apology for the Christian faith, a document of signal value for its verbatim preservation of early philosophical attacks on Christian revelation.

Of Macarius' origin and career, nothing is known except that he is probably identified with the bishop of Magnesia, later Manisa, Tur., who, at the Synod of the Oak in 403, contended with an episcopal friend of the eminent 4th-century reform patriarch of Constantinople, John Chrysostom. His importance, however, stems from his theological defense of Christianity by the obscurely titled *Apokritikos ē monogenēs pros Hellēnas,* 5 books (*c.* 400; "Response of the Only-Begotten to the Greeks"), commonly called the *Apocriticus.* Its doctrine is basically derived from the Cappadocian school, one of the foremost cultural centres of the early Greek Church. Ironically, its chief claim to historical notice is its accurate presentation of the pagan viewpoint.

Through the literary device of an imaginary five-day dispute in dialogue form with an unbelieving critic, the *Apocriticus* precisely reproduces the best known forms of anti-Christian propaganda contemporary with the author. The pagan criticism, according to scholarly consensus, derived from the learned 15-book argument *Against the Christians* by the 3rd-century Greek philosopher Porphyry; the loss of this work renders the *Apocriticus* of even greater value.

The critic questions biblical texts, particularly concerning Christ's Incarnation and Resurrection. The 16th-century Jesuit F. Torres (Latin Turrianus) adduced the work in his theological controversy with the Lutherans on the sacrament of Christ's body. About half of the *Apocriticus* text has survived through the edition of C. Blondel (1876). An English version was produced by T.W. Crafer in 1919.

Macarius THE EGYPTIAN, also called MACARIUS THE GREAT (b. *c.* AD 300, Upper Egypt—d. *c.* AD 390, Scete Desert, Egypt; feast day January 15), monk and ascetic who, as one of the Desert Fathers, advanced the ideal of monasticism in Egypt and influenced its development throughout Christendom. A written tradition of mystical theology under his name is considered a classic of its kind.

About the age of 30 Macarius retired to the desert of Scete, where for 60 years he lived as a hermit among the scattered settlements of other solitaries. He won the confidence of numerous followers who, because of his unusual judgment and discernment, called him "the aged youth."

He was ordained priest *c.* 340 after gaining a reputation for extraordinary powers of prophecy and healing. In his priestly function of presiding at the monks' worship, Macarius also acquired fame for his eloquent spiritual conferences and instructions. Contemporary commentators referred to his proficiency in asceticism and contemplative experience, rivalling in influence the monastic patriarch of the East, Saint Anthony of Egypt.

About 374 Bishop Lucius of Alexandria banished Macarius to an island in the Nile for his determined opposition to Arianism, the heretical doctrine holding that Christ was essentially a composite of created natures, human and spiritual (demigod). He returned from exile and remained in the desert until his death.

The only literary work ascribed to Macarius is a letter, *To the Friends of God,* addressed to younger monks. His spiritual doctrine is not the cultivated speculative thought circulated by the eminent 3rd-century theologian Origen of Alexandria, but, as with the doctrine of the monk Anthony, it is a learning derived from primitive monasticism's "book of nature." The essence of his spiritual theology is the doctrine (with Neoplatonic traces) of the mystical development of the soul that has been formed in the image of God. By physical and intellectual labour, bodily discipline, and meditation, the spirit can serve God and find tranquillity through an inner experience of the divine presence in the form of a vision of light.

A body of literature incorrectly ascribed to Macarius alone is found in later manuscripts. The most popular of these "Macarian writings" is a collection of 50 *Spiritual Homilies.* They possibly were recorded in expanded form by a monastic colleague and attributed to Macarius after his death.

The Macarian literature appealed to certain Lutheran devotional writers, such as Johann Arndt in the 16th century and Arnold Gottfried in the early 18th century. John Wesley, the 18th-century founder of the Methodist Church, published an English version of 22 of the *Spiritual Homilies,* which influenced his hymn writing.

The Macarian literature is contained in *Patrologia Graeca* (ed., J.-P. Migne; vol. 34, 1857–66). An English version of the *Spiritual Homilies,* more complete than Wesley's, is A.J. Mason's *Fifty Spiritual Homilies of St. Macarius the Egyptian* (1921). The later status of the Macarian writings, augmented by recent research, is given by W. Jaeger in *Two Rediscovered Works of Ancient Christian Literature: Gregory of Nyssa and Macarius* (1954).

macaroni, small tubular form of pasta (*q.v.*).

macaroni, in art, Late Paleolithic finger tracings in clay, the oldest form of art known. Innumerable examples appear on the walls and ceilings of limestone caves associated with human habitation in France and Spain, the oldest dating from about 30,000 BC. They range from simple scratchings and jumbled aimless lines to deliberate meanders and arabesques and outline drawings of animals.

It is thought that these macaroni, like the numerous foot and handprints pressed into the clay of the caves, were inspired by animal tracks; they were perhaps first made in emulation of the similar claw marks of cave bears, with only a later realization of their potential for delineating form and design.

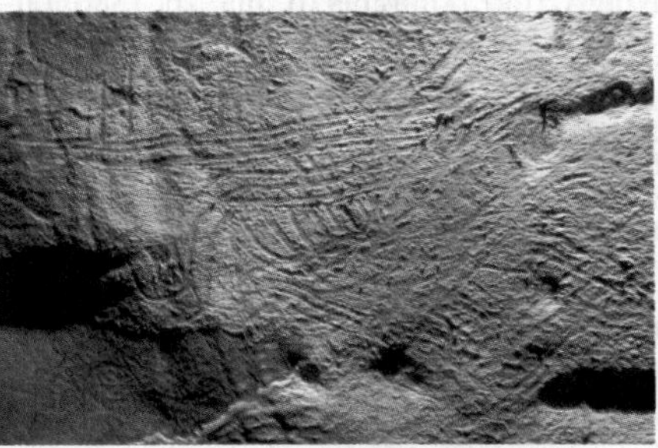

Macaroni from Pech-Merle, in the *département* of Lot, France

Jean Vertut, France

macaronic, originally, comic Latin verse form characterized by the introduction of vernacular words with appropriate but absurd Latin endings: later variants apply the same technique to modern languages. The form was invented in the early 16th century by Teofilo Folengo, a dissolute Benedictine monk who applied Latin rules of form and syntax to an Italian vocabulary in his burlesque epic of chivalry, *Baldus* (1517; *Le maccherone,* 1927–28). He described the macaronic as the literary equivalent of the Italian dish, which, in its 16th-century form, was a crude mixture of flour, butter, and cheese. The *Baldus* soon found imitators in Italy and France, and some macaronics were even written in mock Greek.

The outstanding British poem in this form is the *Polemo-Middinia inter Vitarvam et Nebernam* (published 1684), an account of a battle between two Scottish villages, in which William Drummond subjected Scots dialect to Latin grammatical rules. A modern English derivative of the macaronic pokes fun at the grammatical complexities of ancient languages taught at school, as in A.D. Godley's illustration of declension in "Motor Bus":

Domine defende nos
Contra hos Motores Bos

("Lord protect us from these motor buses").

The form has survived in comic combinations of modern languages. The German-American medleys of Charles G. Leland in his *Hans Breitmann's Ballads* (first published under that title in 1884) are examples of the modern macaronic, in particular his warning "To a Friend Studying German":

Vill'st dou learn die Deutsche Sprache?
Den set it on your card
Dat all de nouns have shenders,
Und de shenders all are hard.

macaroon, cookie or small cake made of sugar, egg white, and almonds, ground or in paste form, or coconut. The origin of the macaroon is uncertain. The name is applied generally to many cookies having the chewy, somewhat airy consistency of the true macaroon.

Cake flour is often used as a base for the essential ingredients of macaroons. These are worked together and flavoured with vanilla and salt. The resulting dough is squeezed through a pastry bag onto a cookie sheet and allowed to stand. Prior to baking, it is often glazed with gum arabic or decorated with chopped almonds, walnuts, raisins, or cherry bits. Macaroon crumbs are often added to ice creams, pie fillings, and puddings. Frangipane is a cream filling made by flavouring butter and crushed macaroons with lemon extract, rum, sherry, or brandy.

MacArthur, Douglas (b. Jan. 26, 1880, Little Rock, Ark., U.S.—d. April 5, 1964, Washington, D.C.), U.S. general who commanded the Southwest Pacific Theatre in World War II, administered postwar Japan during the Allied occupation that followed, and led United Nations forces during the first nine months of the Korean War.

Early life. MacArthur was the third son of Arthur MacArthur, later the army's senior ranking officer, and Mary Hardy MacArthur,

Douglas MacArthur, 1945
By courtesy of the Bureau of Archives, MacArthur Memorial; photograph, U.S. Signal Corps

an ambitious woman who strongly influenced Douglas. He was graduated from West Point in 1903 with the highest honours in his class and served the next 10 years as an aide and a junior engineering officer, following this with four years on the general staff. He spent several months with the U.S. troops that occupied Veracruz, Mex., in 1914.

On the 42nd Division's staff in 1917–19, MacArthur was variously chief of staff, brigade commander, and divisional commander during combat operations in France during World War I and in the Rhine occupation that followed. During the 1920s he initiated far-reaching reforms while superintendent at West Point, served on William ("Billy") Mitchell's court-martial, held two commands in the Philippines, commanded two U.S. corps areas, and headed the 1928 American Olympic Committee.

Having advanced in rank to brigadier general in 1918 and to major general seven years later, MacArthur was promoted to general when he was selected as army chief of staff in 1930. His efforts as military head for the next five years were largely directed toward preserving the army's meagre strength during the Depression. MacArthur was widely criticized in mid-1932 when he sent regular troops to oust the Bonus Army of veterans from Washington. In 1935–41 he served as Philippines military adviser (and field marshal), endeavouring, despite inadequate funds, to build a Filipino defense force. He retired from the U.S. Army in December 1937.

MacArthur married Louise Cromwell Brooks in 1922, but the childless union ended in divorce seven years later. In 1937 he married Jean Faircloth; Arthur, their only child, was born in Manila the next year.

Duty in World War II. Recalled to active duty in July 1941, MacArthur conducted a valiant delaying action against the Japanese in the Philippines after war erupted in December. He was ordered to Australia in March 1942 to command Allied forces in the Southwest Pacific Theater. He soon launched an offensive in New Guinea that drove the Japanese out of Papua by January 1943. In a series of operations in 1943–44, MacArthur's troops seized strategic points in New Guinea from Lae to Sansapor, while capturing the Admiralties and western New Britain. The simultaneous northward movement of South Pacific forces in the Solomons, over whom MacArthur maintained strategic control, neutralized Rabaul and bypassed many Japanese units.

After winning a decision to invade the Philippines next rather than Formosa, MacArthur attacked Morotai, Leyte, and Mindoro in autumn 1944. Not until the Leyte operation did he have overwhelming logistical support; his earlier plans had been executed despite inadequacies of personnel and matériel and with little assistance from the Pacific Fleet. MacArthur seriously questioned his superiors' decision to give priority to the European war over the Pacific conflict and to the Central Pacific Theater over his Southwest Pacific area.

His largest, costliest operations occurred during the seven-month Luzon campaign in 1945. That spring he also undertook the reconquest of the southern Philippines and Borneo. Meanwhile, he left the difficult mopping-up operations in New Guinea and the Solomons to the Australian Army. He was promoted to general of the army in December 1944 and was appointed commander of all U.S. army forces in the Pacific four months later. He was in charge of the surrender ceremony in Tokyo Bay on Sept. 2, 1945.

As Allied commander of the Japanese occupation in 1945–51, MacArthur effectively if autocratically directed the demobilization of Japanese military forces, the expurgation of militarists, the restoration of the economy, and the drafting of a liberal constitution. Significant reforms were inaugurated in land redistribution, education, labour, public health, and women's rights. While he was in Japan, MacArthur also headed the army's Far East command.

UN command in Korean War. When the Korean War began in 1950, MacArthur was soon selected to command United Nations forces there. After stemming the North Korean advance near Pusan, he carried out a daring landing at Inch'ŏn in September and advanced into North Korea in October as the North Korean Army rapidly disintegrated. In November, however, massive Chinese forces attacked MacArthur's divided army above the 38th parallel and forced it to retreat to below Seoul. Two months later MacArthur's troops returned to the offensive, driving into North Korea again. On April 11, 1951, President Harry S. Truman relieved MacArthur of his commands because of the general's insubordination and unwillingness to conduct a limited war. Returning to the United States for the first time since before World War II, MacArthur at first received widespread popular support; the excitement waned after a publicized Senate investigation of his dismissal.

In 1944, 1948, and 1952, conservative Republican groups tried in vain to obtain MacArthur's nomination for the presidency. MacArthur accepted the board chairmanship of the Remington Rand Corporation in 1952; thereafter, except for these duties and rare public appearances, he lived in seclusion in New York City. He died in Washington, D.C., in 1964 and was buried at Norfolk, Va.

In personality MacArthur was enigmatic and contradictory. To many he seemed imperious, aloof, egotistical, and pretentious. To others, especially his headquarters staff, he appeared warm, courageous, unostentatious, and even humble. Most authorities agree that he possessed superior intelligence, rare command ability, and zealous dedication to duty, honour, and country. (D.C.J.)

BIBLIOGRAPHY. Two comprehensive studies are D. Clayton James, *The Years of MacArthur,* 3 vol. (1970–85), a study by a U.S. historian; and William Manchester, *American Caesar: Douglas MacArthur, 1880–1964* (1978, reissued 1983), a massive, sympathetic examination of the general's character and personality. Other studies of his life and career include Frazier Hunt, *The Untold Story of Douglas MacArthur* (1954, reissued 1977), by an admiring correspondent; Charles A. Willoughby and John Chamberlain, *MacArthur, 1941–1951* (1954); Courtney Whitney, *MacArthur: His Rendezvous with History* (1956, reprinted 1977), by a general close to MacArthur; Gavin Long, *MacArthur As Military Commander* (1969), a candid Australian view; Carol Morris Petillo, *Douglas MacArthur, the Philippine Years* (1981), a psychobiography; and Paul P. Rogers, *The Good Years: MacArthur and Sutherland* (1990), and *The Bitter Years: MacArthur and Sutherland* (1991), detailing the periods 1941–42 and 1943–45, respectively.

Macarthur, John (christened Sept. 3, 1767, Stoke Damerel, Devonshire, Eng.—d. April 11, 1834, Camden, New South Wales), agriculturist and promoter who helped found the Australian wool industry, which became the world's largest.

In 1789 Macarthur went to Australia as a lieutenant in the New South Wales Corps. By 1793 he had become a large landholder, having attained power as inspector of public works and paymaster of the corps. In the conflict between Governor Philip King and the corps over its monopoly on trade and labour supply, Macarthur shot King's representative in a duel in 1801. He was sent to England in an abortive attempt to bring him to trial. While there, he interested English manufacturers in the prospect of establishing a wool industry in Australia, to which he returned in 1805 with a grant of 5,000 acres and a mandate for developing wool production.

In 1808 Macarthur inspired the Rum Rebellion against Governor William Bligh, who had sought to limit the landholdings and rum monopoly of the corps. Exiled to England for the next eight years, Macarthur studied the English wool market and again returned to Australia, where he, with his wife and sons, promoted the activities of the Australian Agricultural Company, formed in London in 1824 to develop the colony's wool industry. By 1830 he had enlarged his grazing estate, Camden Park, to more than 60,000 acres, becoming the dominant force in the wool trade. Between 1825 and 1832 he served two terms on the Legislative Council as spokesman for the Exclusionists, conservative large landowners. His mind failed, and in 1832 he was removed from the council by the governor, Sir Richard Bourke.

McArthur River, river in northeastern Northern Territory, Australia, rising about 45 miles (70 km) south of Anthony Lagoon, along the scarp that marks the northern edge of the Barkly Tableland, and flowing northwest for 150 miles (240 km) across rugged country to Port McArthur on the Gulf of Carpentaria. Swamp and jungle border its lower course, which is navigable by barge for 40 miles (64 km). The river, fed by Tooganginie Creek and the Kilgour and Clyde rivers, often floods in the summer. It was visited in 1845 by the explorer Ludwig Leichhardt, who named it after James and William McArthur (Macarthur), sheep ranchers of Camden, N.S.W., and was first navigated in 1883.

Macartney, George Macartney, Earl, VISCOUNT MACARTNEY OF DERVOCK, BARON OF LISSANOURE, BARON MACARTNEY OF PARKHURST AND OF AUCHINLECK, LORD MACARTNEY (b. May 3, 1737, Lissanoure, County Antrim, N.Ire.—d. March 31, 1806, Chiswick, Surrey, Eng.), first British emissary to Peking.

A member of an old Scots-Irish family, Macartney studied at Trinity College, Dublin (M.A., 1759). He was knighted and appointed envoy extraordinary to Russia in 1764 and, on his return, entered Parliament, becoming chief secretary for Ireland (1769–72). In 1775 he became governor of the Caribbee Islands (Grenada, the Grenadines, and Tobago), he was created an Irish baron in 1776, and from 1780 to 1786 he served as governor of Madras. After being created a viscount (1792), he was sent to China to negotiate additional trading rights for Britain. Instead of granting Macartney's trade requests, the Chinese asserted that their empire was self-sufficient and that they granted the little trade that they did only as a special favour. The emperor and his court considered Macartney's presents to be "tribute presents," and the whole mission was viewed imperially as one of "submission."

Macartney was created a viscount in the Irish peerage in 1792 and an earl in 1794; he was raised to the British peerage as Baron Macartney in 1796, just before his appointment as governor of the newly acquired colony of the Cape of Good Hope, in southern Africa. He retired in 1798 in ill health.

His marriage had no surviving issue, and his titles became extinct upon his death.

Macas, town, southeastern Ecuador. It lies on the Upano River along the eastern slopes of the Andes, at an elevation of 3,445 feet (1,050 m). Founded by the Spanish captain José Villanueva Maldonado in the mid-16th century as the city of Sevilla del Oro ("Golden Seville"), it was a large settlement for several decades and prospered by the exploitation of nearby alluvial gold deposits. After its destruction by a Jívaro Indian insurrection in 1599, it was refounded as Macas but never again regained its former size or importance. The town is now a local agricultural trade centre for cassava, bananas, papayas, coffee, and cacao. Pop. (1983 est.) 3,433.

Macassar (Indonesia): *see* Ujung Pandang.

Macassar Strait (Pacific Ocean): *see* Makassar Strait.

Macau, also spelled MACAO, Chinese (Wade-Giles) AO-MEN, or (Pinyin) AOMEN, special administrative region (Wade-Giles *t'e-pieh hsing-cheng-ch'ü;* Pinyin *tebie xingzhengqu*) of China, on the country's southern coast. It is located on the western side of the Pearl River estuary, at the head of which is the Chinese port of Canton, and it stands opposite the special administrative region of Hong Kong, which is on the eastern side of the estuary. It comprises a small, narrow peninsula projecting from the Chinese mainland *sheng* (province) of Kwangtung and includes the islands of Taipa and Coloane. The city of Macau occupies almost the entire peninsula. The name is derived from the Chinese A-mangao, or "Bay of A-ma," for A-ma, the patron goddess of sailors. Area 6.5 square miles (23.6 square km). Pop. (2000 est.) 440,000.

For current history and for statistics on society and economy, *see* BRITANNICA BOOK OF THE YEAR.

Both the peninsula and the islands consist of small granite hills surrounded by limited areas of flatland. No part of Macau is of any great height; the highest point, 571 feet (174 m), is on the island of Coloane. There are no permanent rivers, and water either is collected during rains or is imported from the mainland.

Macau lies just within the tropics. Four-fifths of Macau's total annual rainfall of between 40 and 100 inches (1,020 and 2,540 mm) falls within the summer rainy season, from April to September, when the southwest monsoon blows. Besides being rainy, the summer months are also hot, humid, and unpleasant. Winters, on the other hand, can be delightful.

The natural vegetation was evergreen monsoonal forest before the hills were stripped for firewood and construction. Small, restricted patches of farmland exist on the islands, and the rural settlements are small. The chief crops are vegetables.

The first Portuguese ship anchored in the Pearl River estuary in 1513, and further Portuguese visits followed regularly. Official trade with China began in 1553. Four years later Portuguese paying tribute to China settled in Macau, which became the official entrepôt for trade with China and Japan. The first Portuguese governor was appointed in the 17th century, but the Portuguese remained largely under Chinese control. Even though China's trade with the outside world was gradually centralized in Canton toward the end of the 18th century, merchants were allowed into Canton only during the trading season—from November to May—and the international merchant community established itself at Macau. By the mid-19th century Hong Kong had eclipsed Macau in trade, and Macau never again became a major entrepôt.

There were always relatively few Portuguese in Macau; ethnic Chinese now make up the overwhelming majority of the territory's population. Buddhism and Christianity—largely Roman Catholicism—are the predominant religions.

Except for fish in the Pearl River estuary, Macau has few natural resources. It is, however, a free port, and trade is important. It relies on other parts of China for food and inexpensive consumer goods. Textiles and garments are the most important exports, but Macau also exports machinery and mechanical appliances, fireworks, toys, Chinese wines, incense sticks, camphorwood chests, artificial flowers, and electronics. Macau has long had a reputation for gold smuggling. Tourism is an important factor in Macau's economy, and the colony in effect serves as the playground of nearby Hong Kong. Regular hydrofoil connections carry tourists from Hong Kong to Macau's numerous gambling casinos, bars, massage parlors, and other attractions. Also the traditional but slower river ferries still ply between Macau and Hong Kong. Internal transport is good, and there are local ferries between the peninsula and the islands.

In accordance with a 1987 agreement between Portugal and China, modeled on the agreement three years earlier between Britain and China concerning Hong Kong, Macau was returned to Chinese rule in December 1999. The chief executive heads the government but is under central Chinese authority. The Legislative Council comprises up to 30 members serving 4-year terms.

Macaulay, Catharine, *née* SAWBRIDGE, also called (from 1778) CATHARINE MACAULAY GRAHAM (b. April 2, 1731, Wye, Kent, Eng.—d. June 22, 1791, Binfield, near Windsor, Berkshire), British historian and radical political writer.

She was privately educated, and her readings in Greek and Roman history inculcated in her an enthusiasm for libertarian and republican ideals. Following her marriage to the Scottish physician George Macaulay in 1760, she be-

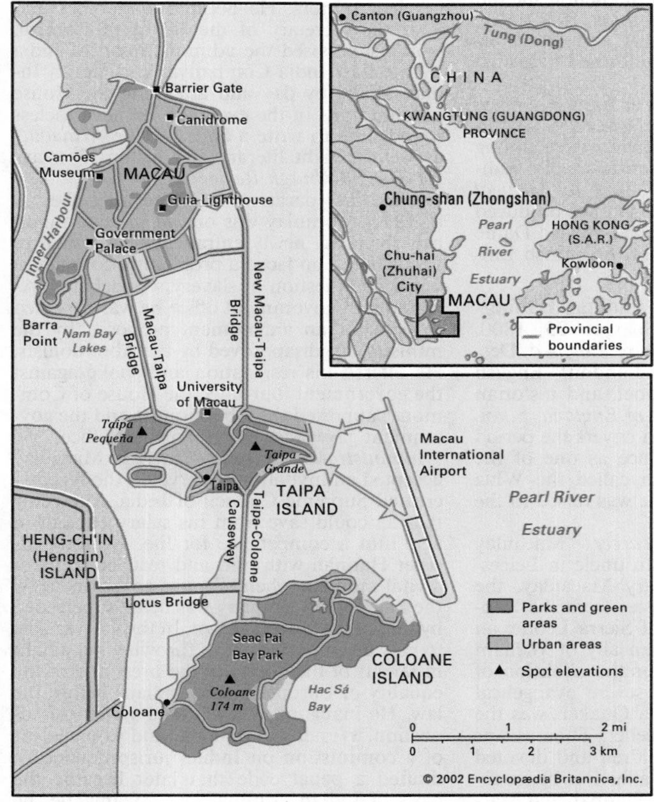

Macau

gan her *History of England from the Accession of James I to That of the Brunswick Line,* published in eight volumes between 1763 and 1783, in which she championed the Parliamentary cause, condemned Oliver Cromwell as a tyrant, and found her own republican ideals reflected in the parliamentarian John Hampden. The *History* was widely read in spite of the controversies generated by its clear republican sympathies.

Widowed in 1766, she moved in 1774 to Bath, where she attracted many admirers. In addition to espousing popular sovereignty and the moderate distribution of land in her works, Macaulay also took up the cause of the American colonists by attacking the Quebec Act and British colonial taxation in her *Address to the People of England, Scotland and Ireland* (1775). On a visit to Paris at the peak of her fame in 1777, she met Jacques Turgot and Benjamin Franklin; but her marriage the following year to William Graham, the 21-year-old brother of a quack physician, disgraced her in some circles. Nevertheless, on a trip to America in 1784–85, she and her husband were guests of George Washington at Mount Vernon. Her last political tract, *Observations on the Reflections of The Right Hon. Edmund Burke on the Revolution in France* (1790), defended the French Revolution, finding the unicameral National Assembly superior even to the American polity.

Macaulay, Dame (Emilie) Rose (b. Aug. 1, 1881, Rugby, Warwickshire, Eng.—d. Oct. 30, 1958, London), author of novels and travel books characterized by intelligence, wit, and lively scholarship.

Daughter of a university instructor, she grew up in an intellectually stimulating and liberal-minded home environment. She first attracted attention as a social satirist with a series of novels, *Potterism* (1920), *Dangerous Ages* (1921), *Told by an Idiot* (1923), *Orphan Island* (1924), *Crewe Train* (1926), and *Keeping Up Appearances* (1928). After 1930 she wrote fewer novels, though the fiction she did produce, such as *Going Abroad* (1934), *The World My Wilderness* (1950), and *The Towers of Trebizond* (1956), conformed to a high standard.

Some Religious Elements in English Literature (1931) and *They Were Defeated* (1932), a study of the poet Robert Herrick, were among her best works of literary criticism. In addition to travel books, *They Went to Portugal* (1946) and *Fabled Shore* (1949), she produced three volumes of verse. She was created Dame Commander of the Order of the British Empire in 1958.

Macaulay (of Rothley), Thomas Babington Macaulay, Baron (b. Oct. 25, 1800, Rothley Temple, Leicestershire, Eng.—d. Dec. 28, 1859, Campden Hill, London), English Whig politician, essayist, poet, and historian best known for his *History of England,* 5 vol. (1849–61); this work, which covers the period 1688–1702, secured his place as one of the founders of what has been called the Whig interpretation of history. He was raised to the peerage in 1857.

Early life and political career. Macaulay was born in the house of an uncle in Leicestershire. His father, Zachary Macaulay, the son of a Presbyterian minister from the Hebrides, had been governor of Sierra Leone; an ardent philanthropist and an ally of William Wilberforce, who fought for the abolition of slavery, he was a man of severe evangelical piety. Macaulay's mother, a Quaker, was the daughter of a Bristol bookseller. Thomas was the eldest of their nine children and devoted to his family, his deepest affection being reserved for two of his sisters, Hannah and Margaret. When eight years old he had written

Thomas Macaulay, detail of an oil painting by J. Partridge, 1840; in the National Portrait Gallery, London

By courtesy of the National Portrait Gallery, London

a compendium of universal history and also "The Battle of Cheviot," a romantic narrative poem in the style of Sir Walter Scott. After attending a private school, in 1818 he went to Trinity College, Cambridge, where he held a fellowship until 1831 and where he gained a reputation for inexhaustible talk and genial companionship in a circle of brilliant young men. In 1825 the first of his essays, that on Milton, published in *The Edinburgh Review,* brought him immediate fame and the chance to display his social gifts on a wider stage; he was courted and admired by the most distinguished personages of the day.

He studied law and was called to the bar in 1826 but never practiced seriously. When his father's commercial interests failed, he undertook the support of his whole family by writing and teaching and obtained a minor government post. He aspired to a political career, and in 1830 he entered Parliament as member for Calne in Wiltshire.

During the debates that preceded the passage of the Reform Act (1832), he eloquently supported the cause of parliamentary reform and was regarded as a leading figure in an age of great orators. He became a member and later the secretary of the Board of Control, which supervised the administration of India by the East India Company. Working on Indian affairs by day and attending the House of Commons in the evenings, he nevertheless found time to write a ballad, "The Armada," as well as eight literary and historical essays for *The Edinburgh Review.*

In the first parliament elected after the act of 1832, Macaulay was one of the two members from the newly enfranchised borough of Leeds. He soon faced a problem of conscience when the question of slavery was debated. As a holder of government office he was expected to vote for an amendment proposed by the ministry but disapproved by the Abolitionists. He offered his resignation and spoke against the government, but since the House of Commons supported the Abolitionists and the government gave way, he remained in office.

Administration in India. In 1834 Macaulay accepted an invitation to serve on the recently created Supreme Council of India, foreseeing that he could save from his salary enough to give him a competence for life. He took his sister Hannah with him and reached India at a vital moment when effective government by the East India Company was being superseded by that of the British crown. In this he was able to play an important part, throwing his weight in favour of the liberty of the press and of the equality of Europeans and Indians before the law. He inaugurated a national system of education, Western in outlook, and as president of a commission on Indian jurisprudence he drafted a penal code that later became the basis of Indian criminal law. Meanwhile, he suffered two personal blows: his sister Margaret died in England, and in 1835 his sister Hannah left him to marry a promising young servant of the East India Company, Charles Trevelyan.

Later life and writings. Macaulay returned to England in 1838 and entered Parliament as a member for Edinburgh. He became secretary for war in 1839, with a seat in Lord Melbourne's Cabinet, but the ministry fell in 1841, and he found the leisure to publish his *Lays of Ancient Rome* (1842) and a collection of *Critical and Historical Essays* (1843). He was made paymaster general when Lord John Russell became prime minister in 1846 but spoke only five times in the parliamentary session of 1846–47. In the latter year he lost his seat at Edinburgh, where he had neglected local interests. He had, in fact, lost much of his interest in politics and retired into private life with a sense of relief, settling down to work on his *History of England.* His composition was slow, with endless corrections both of matter and style; he spared no pains to ascertain the facts, often visiting the scene of historical events. The first two volumes appeared in 1849 and achieved an unprecedented success, edition after edition selling well both in Britain and in the United States. When the Whigs returned to power in 1852 he refused a seat in the Cabinet but was returned to Parliament by Edinburgh and took his seat. Soon afterward he developed a heart disease and thenceforth played little part in politics. The third and fourth volumes of his *History* were published in 1855 and at once attained a vast circulation. Within the generation of its first appearance more than 140,000 copies had been sold in the United Kingdom, and sales in the United States were correspondingly large. The work was translated into German, Polish, Dutch, Danish, Swedish, Hungarian, Russian, Bohemian, French, and Spanish.

In 1856 Macaulay left Albany in Piccadilly, where he had lived since 1840, and moved to Holly Lodge, Campden Hill, then a district of lawns and trees. In the following year he was raised to the peerage, with the title of Baron Macaulay of Rothley. His health was now visibly failing; he never spoke in the House of Lords, and he accepted that he would live scarcely long enough to complete the reign of William III in his *History.* He died at Campden Hill and was buried in Westminster Abbey. The fifth volume of his *History,* edited by his sister Hannah, was published in 1861.

Character. Macaulay's exceptional gifts of mind were never, as they have been for many men of genius, a source of calamity or mental anguish. Had he wished, he could have risen to high political place, perhaps to the highest; instead, he chose to devote his powers to the portrayal of England's past. His command of literature was unrivalled. That of Greece and Rome, stored in his extraordinary memory, was familiar from college days, and to it he added the literature of his own country, of France, of Spain, and of Germany. He had limitations. In later life he never gave expression to any religious conviction, and he had no appreciation of spiritual, as distinct from ethical, excellence. All religious and philosophical speculation was alien to his mind, and he showed no interest in the discoveries of science as distinct from technology. Of art he confessed himself ignorant, and to music he was completely deaf. At games, sports, and physical skills—even those of shaving or tying a cravat—his incompetence was complete. In appearance he was short and stocky, with plain features that reflected a powerful mind and a frank and open character.

Macaulay never married. His great capacity for affection found its satisfaction in the attachment and close sympathy of his sisters, particularly of Hannah, later Lady Trevelyan, who remained in almost daily contact with him even after her marriage, and whose children were to him as his own. He had a keen relish for the good things of life and welcomed fortune as the means of obtaining them for himself and others, but there was nothing mercenary or selfish in his nature; when affluent, he gave away with an open hand, often rashly, and his last act was to dictate a letter to a poor curate and sign a check for £25.

Assessment. Macaulay's *History of England* brought him a secure, if diminished, place among English historians as the founder, with his contemporary Henry Hallam, of what is now known as the Whig interpretation of history. Fostered in the traditions of sturdy evangelical piety and liberal reform, he saw the origin and triumph of these values in the Revolution of 1688, which firmly established the supremacy of Parliament and restricted the monarchy to a constitutional status. He planned to write the history of England from 1688 to 1820 (the death of George III) but died before he had completed it. Macaulay's work is thus an account of that revolution, with a narration of the years preceding and following it. In stressing the unique importance for England of the revolution and, by implication, the superior virtues of those who brought it about, traditionally the Whig Party (though the Tories were also involved), Macaulay popularized a view of English history that was notably followed by his nephew Sir George Otto Trevelyan and his great-nephew George Macaulay Trevelyan and that affected the teaching of history as late as World War II.

His essays helped to mold the outlook of a generation of Englishmen and to give to many their first vivid glimpse of the past, together with a conviction that their own institutions would serve the best interests of developing countries under their care. His style, clear, emphatic, and insensitive, with short sentences forming a self-contained paragraph, came to be for half a century the characteristic English style in higher journalism and exposition of all kinds. Macaulay's reputation, immense during the last decade of his life, fell steadily in the 50 years that followed. His undisguised political partisanship, his arrogant assumption that English bourgeois standards of culture and progress were to be forever the norm for less favoured nations, and the materialism of his judgments of value and taste all came under heavy fire from such near-contemporary critics as Thomas Carlyle, Matthew Arnold, and John Ruskin. Moreover, a revolution in the realm of historical studies, already accomplished in Germany during Macaulay's lifetime but never appreciated by him, soon affected English historiography. Wide as was Macaulay's reading, his approach was largely uncritical, as his enthusiasm often carried him away. By taste and training an orator, his writing was special pleading rather than impartial presentation. Yet, despite these severe limitations, his greatness is incontrovertible, and, regarded solely as a work of art, the status of his *History* remains unassailed. In the grasp and range of his knowledge, in his powers of vivid and sustained narrative, and in his marshalling of topics to serve a great design, his *History* is unsurpassed among the work of English historians, save, perhaps, by *The History of the Decline and Fall of the Roman Empire* of Edward Gibbon. (M.D.K.)

BIBLIOGRAPHY. The standard edition of Macaulay's complete works is that originally edited by Lady Trevelyan, in the Albany edition, 12 vol. (1898). John Clive and Thomas Pinney, *Thomas Babington Macaulay: Selected Writings* (1972), include further material. For the *History,* see Sir Charles H. Firth, *A Commentary on Macaulay's History of England* (1938, reprinted 1964); and for his speeches, G.M. Young, *Speeches by Lord Macaulay* (1935). There is no complete or critical edition of his *Essays.*

The Life and Letters of Macaulay, 2 vol. (1876; enlarged 1908, and with full index 1959; reprinted 1978), by his nephew, Sir George Otto Trevelyan, is acknowledged as one of the best biographies in the English language. Of shorter, derivative studies J.A.C. Morison, *Macaulay* (1882); and Sir Arthur Bryant, *Macaulay* (1932; 2nd rev. ed., 1979), deserve mention. John Clive has used previously unpublished material for *Thomas Babington Macaulay: The Shaping of the Historian* (1973). Scholarly research on Macaulay, long dormant, awoke in the second half of the 20th century. A complete edition of his letters, now preserved at Trinity College, Cambridge, edited by Thomas Pinney, had reached 1848 in four volumes in 1977. Two good bibliographic sources are *The New Cambridge Bibliography of English Literature,* vol. 2 (1969); and Bryant (*op. cit.*).

McAuley, Catherine Elizabeth (b. Sept. 29, 1787, County Dublin, Ire.—d. Nov. 11, 1841, Dublin), founder of the Religious Sisters of Mercy (R.S.M.), a congregation of nuns engaged in education and social service.

With a legacy from her Protestant foster parents, McAuley, a Roman Catholic, commissioned a large building in Dublin. On Sept. 24, 1827, she opened it as the House of Mercy, an institution for the education of orphans and the poor. She and two companions took their vows on Dec. 12, 1831, officially forming the Religious Sisters of Mercy, with Catherine as superior until her death. In 1839 Mother McAuley established the congregation's first non-Irish house in London. Thenceforth, the Sisters of Mercy became one of the largest English-speaking congregations. Roland Burke Savage's *Catherine McAuley, the First Sister of Mercy* appeared in 1949, followed by Sister M. Bertrand Degnan's *Mercy unto Thousands* (1957).

McAuley, James Phillip (b. Oct. 12, 1917, Lakemba, N.S.W., Australia—d. Oct. 15, 1976, Hobart, Tasmania), Australian poet noted for his classical approach, great technical skill, and academic point of view.

Educated at the University of Sydney, he taught for a while, served with Australian forces in World War II, and then became a senior lecturer at the Australian School of Pacific Administration, editor of *Quadrant,* a literary journal, and professor of English at the University of Tasmania.

His first volume of poetry, *Under Aldebaran* (1946), was followed by *A Vision of Ceremony* (1956); *Captain Quiros* (1964), a verse narrative of the settlement and Christianization of Australia; *Surprises of the Sun* (1969); *Collected Poems, 1936–70* (1971); *Music Late at Night: Poems, 1970–1973* (1976); and *A World of Its Own* (1977). McAuley's prose works include a volume of literary criticism, *The End of Modernity* (1959); a critical interpretation of an earlier Australian poet, *Christopher Brennan* (1973); and *A Map of Australian Verse* (1975).

McAuliffe, Anthony C(lement) (b. July 2, 1898, Washington, D.C.—d. Aug. 11, 1975, Washington), U.S. Army general who commanded the force defending Bastogne, Belgium, in the Battle of the Bulge (December 1944) during World War II.

Graduating from the U.S. Military Academy at West Point, N.Y. (1919), McAuliffe was commissioned in the field artillery and held routine service and school appointments in peacetime. At the time of the Normandy invasion (June 1944), he was artillery commander of the 101st Airborne Division. He was in command of the entire division when the Germans counterattacked in the Ardennes; his stout defense of Bastogne checked the German drive and contributed directly to the final defeat of the Germans. His terse reply to a Nazi ultimatum to surrender at Bastogne was "Nuts!"

McAuliffe, 1955
By courtesy of the U.S. Army

After the war McAuliffe held various command and staff appointments. He retired in May 1956 to enter industry.

macaw, any of about 18 species of tropical American parrots of the subfamily Psittacinae (family Psittacidae). Macaws are the most colourful of large parrots. Their very long tails are unique in the family, and their big sickle-shaped beaks are equalled only by those of cockatoos. Macaws eat much fruit and also crack nuts open with their extremely powerful beaks, using their blunt tongues to extract the nut meat. They are bare-faced and may blush when excited. Sexes look alike. As pets, they need flying space and something to chew on. Easily tamed, macaws get along well with other parrots but may bite other animals and human strangers. A few have lived 65 years. Some learn to mimic, in a soft voice, but most screech—as they do in the wild.

Macaw (*Ara ararauna*)
John C. Stevenson—Animals Animals

Best known species in aviaries is the scarlet macaw, *Ara macao,* from Mexico to southern Brazil—a 90-centimetre (36-inch) bright-red bird with blue and yellow wings, blue and red tail, and white face.

The hyacinthine macaw, *Anodorhynchus hyacinthinus,* of similar length but heavier body, is deep blue with yellow eye-ring and bill-base; in Brazil south of the Amazon, it sometimes nests in holes in riverbanks.

Macbeth (d. Aug. 15, 1057, near Lumphanan, Aberdeen, Scot.), king of Scots from 1040, the legend of whose life was the basis of Shakespeare's *Macbeth.* He was probably a grandson of King Kenneth II (ruled 971–995), and he married Gruoch, a descendant of King Kenneth III (ruled 997–1005). About 1031 Macbeth succeeded his father, Findlaech (Sinel in Shakespeare), as *moarmaer,* or chief, in the province of Moray, in northern Scotland. Macbeth established himself on the throne after killing his cousin King Duncan I in battle near Elgin—not, as in Shakespeare, by murdering Duncan in bed—on Aug. 14, 1040. Both Duncan and Macbeth derived their rights to the crown through their mothers.

Macbeth's victory in 1045 over a rebel army, near Dunkeld (in modern Tayside region) may account for the later references (in Shakespeare and others) to Birnam Wood, for the village of

Birnam is near Dunkeld. In 1046 Siward, Earl of Northumbria, unsuccessfully attempted to dethrone Macbeth in favour of Malcolm (afterward King Malcolm III Canmore), eldest son of Duncan I. By 1050 Macbeth felt secure enough to leave Scotland for a pilgrimage to Rome. But in 1054 he was apparently forced by Siward to yield part of southern Scotland to Malcolm. Three years later Macbeth was killed in battle by Malcolm, with assistance from the English.

Macbeth was buried on the island of Iona, regarded as the resting place of lawful kings but not of usurpers. His followers installed his stepson, Lulach, as king; when Lulach was killed on March 17, 1058, Malcolm III was left supreme in Scotland.

McBride, Patricia (b. Aug. 23, 1942, Teaneck, N.J., U.S.), American ballerina, best known for her performances with the New York City Ballet.

McBride began her dance training when she was seven years old. At age 13 she began classes in New York City with Sonia Doubrovinskaya and at the School of American Ballet, making her debut in 1957 with Andre Eglevsky's Petit Ballet Company.

McBride performed with the New York City Ballet as an apprentice, entered the corps de ballet in 1959, became a soloist a year later, and was made principal dancer in 1961. McBride's radiant technique inspired roles in many ballets, perhaps most notably in George Balanchine's *Tarantella* (1964) and *Jewels* (1967). Her performance in *Who Cares?* (1970) was widely acclaimed. Later dances included *Dybbuk Variations* (1974) and *Le Bourgeois Gentilhomme* (1978). After 30 years with the New York City Ballet, she retired in 1989.

McBride, Sir Richard (b. Dec. 15, 1870, New Westminster, B.C., Can.—d. Aug. 6, 1917, London, Eng.), statesman who was premier of British Columbia from 1903 to 1915.

McBride entered the British Columbian legislature in 1898 and was appointed minister of mines in 1900. After one year as leader of his

Sir Richard McBride
By courtesy of the Provincial Archives, Victoria, B.C.

party in opposition, he became Conservative premier for the province in 1903.

As premier he introduced the two-party system of government and coped with the rapid growth of population and industry in British Columbia. His commitment to extending the Pacific Great Eastern Railway put the province considerably in debt. McBride resigned in 1915 because of ill health and served as agent general for British Columbia in London until his death. He was knighted in 1912.

MacBride, Seán (b. Jan. 26, 1904, Paris, Fr.—d. Jan. 15, 1988, Dublin, Ire.), Irish statesman, who was awarded the Nobel Prize for Peace in 1974 for his efforts on behalf of human rights.

MacBride was the son of the Irish actress and patriot Maud Gonne and her husband, Major John MacBride, who was executed in

Seán MacBride, 1978
United Nations/Photo by Y. Nagata

1916 for his part in the Easter Rising of that year against the British. Educated in Paris and Ireland, Seán MacBride, like his parents, was a fighter for Irish liberty and an opponent of the partition, and at age 24 he was chief of staff of the Irish Republican Army. He worked as a journalist and then became a lawyer.

Eventually accepting the fact of partition and the futility of warfare, he was elected to the Dáil Éireann (House of Representatives) in 1947 and remained until 1958 as a member of the Clann na Poblachta ("Republican Party"), which he had founded in 1936. He was minister for external affairs in 1948–51. In 1950 he was president of the Council of Foreign Ministers of the Council of Europe, and he was vice president of the Organisation for European Economic Co-operation in 1948–51. MacBride was active in a number of international organizations concerned with human rights, among them the International Prisoners of Conscience Fund (trustee) and Amnesty International (chairman, 1961–75), and he served as secretary-general of the International Commission of Jurists. In 1973 he became United Nations assistant secretary-general and commissioner for South West Africa/Namibia, posts he held until 1977. In 1977 he was appointed president of the International Commission for the Study of Communication Problems, set up by UNESCO.

Maccabaeus (surname): *see under* Maccabeus.

Maccabees, also spelled MACHABEES (fl. 2nd century BCE, Palestine), priestly family of Jews who organized a successful rebellion against the Seleucid ruler Antiochus IV and reconsecrated the defiled Temple of Jerusalem.

Historical context of the Maccabees. The name Maccabee was a title of honour given to Judas, a son of Mattathias and the hero of the Jewish wars of independence, 168–164 BCE. Later, the name the Maccabees was extended to include his whole family, specifically Mattathias (his father) and Judas' four brothers—John, Simon, Eleazar, and Jonathan. Its use was also extended to John Hyrcanus, Simon's son, who was next in succession.

There is no unanimity about the meaning of the title Maccabee. The Hebrew may be read as "Hammer," "Hammerer," or "Extinguisher." Since Judas held the initative in the long war against the Syrians, he was probably regarded in the same light as King Edward I of England, who was known as the "Hammer of the Scots."

Throughout the 2nd century BCE, the city-state of Jerusalem-Judah lay between the two great powers of Egypt and Syria. The Ptolemies ruled in Egypt and the Seleucids in Syria. These were residual states that had been left when Alexander the Great's empire had broken up about 20 years after his death. Antiochus IV ruled Syria from 175 to 164/163 BCE. He carried the substitute name of Epiphanes, a Greek word meaning "god manifest." A conqueror of overweening pride, as he is described in the Book of Daniel in the Bible, he set out to seize Judaea (or Judah), which until then had been a province of Egypt. He aimed incidentally to rid the world of the annoying (and, to him, peculiar), exclusive, "nonconformist" religion of the Jewish people. In order to unify his vast and racially heterogeneous empire, which stretched as far as the Caspian Sea, he planned to create one religion for all.

In Antiochus' day the Syrians were devotees of the culture of Greece. Antiochus sought to continue what he regarded as the "civilizing" colonization process of Alexander. For him culture meant the pursuit of the "good." The restless, inquiring, creative spirit of Greece—what might today be called the scientific spirit—was based on the assumption that "man is the measure of all things." The Jewish view of life, on the other hand, was totally in opposition to that of the Hellenism that had spread throughout the Middle East. It, too, was a total way of life, one lived in accordance with what the Jewish people believed was revelation. They regarded Hellenism as a form of nature worship. They saw it as the spiritual continuation of the religion of the Canaanites, who had presented their views against Israel's for all the centuries since the days of Joshua. They were aghast that Antiochus encouraged the Semitic peoples of the Mediterranean coast to regard him as the ancient god Baal of the Canaanites. The Canaanite gods, they asserted, were merely the mythologizing of the anger, hate, lust, envy, and greed of unregulated human hearts.

Israel, its prophets proclaimed, was the chosen instrument of the transcendent God, whose name was Yahweh. Yahweh was utterly "other" than man, that is to say, he was "holy." It was God who had created man, not man the gods, and Israel was God's chosen instrument to be "a light to lighten the nations" (Isaiah). To make the meaning of its special relationship to Yahweh evident to the world was therefore Israel's reason for being. Its task was to put the revelation of God into purposeful use by producing an ordered human society that was ruled by God's justice and love and not by man's force and greed.

Prohibition of Jewish religious practices. This conception of revealed religion and of loyalty to the Word of God, rather than to a human king, Antiochus could not appreciate, particularly since he himself delighted in the name God Manifest. In order to extirpate the faith of Israel, therefore, he attacked Israel's religious practices. He thus forbade the observance of the Sabbath and of the traditional feasts, for these had been ordained by a "jealous," or intolerant, God. All sacrifices were to come to an end. He forbade the reading of the Law of Moses and gave orders to search out and burn any copies that could be found. He forbade the practice of circumcision, for it was this that set the Jews off from other peoples as the one "people of God." In place of these practices Antiochus encouraged the development of cultural clubs called gymnasia, in which people gathered to study, to learn, and to enjoy each other's company. After competing in various forms of athletics, men and women used to soak themselves in hot baths. But because the pursuit of the "good" included a delight in the body beautiful, such activities were performed naked. A circumcised Jew taking part in the games in a gymnasium could not therefore hide where his loyalty lay. Finally, in 168 BCE, Antiochus invaded Jerusalem and desacralized the Holy of Holies in the Temple. This was the one place on earth about which Yahweh said "My name" (the expression of his Person) "shall be there" (I Kings).

A number of Jews, under their leader Jason, the high priest, took the easy way of conformity with the new universal trends. But with Antiochus' impious act, a strong general reaction set in. Thus, when, later in the same year, Antiochus again entered Jerusalem, this time plundering and burning and setting up his citadel, the Acra, on the hill overlooking the Temple courts, he went too far, for his final act of spite, on Dec. 25, 167 BCE, was to rededicate the Temple in Jerusalem to the Olympian god Zeus.

Jewish resistance. The home of Mattathias, a priest in the village of Modi'im (now an important archaeological site), 17 miles (27 km) northwest of Jerusalem, quickly became the centre of resistance. With him were his five sons, John Gaddi, Simon Thassi, Judas Maccabeus, Eleazar Avaran, and Jonathan Apphus. Josephus, the Jewish historian, gives Mattathias' great-grandfather the surname Asamonaios. From this title comes the name Hasmonean that was applied to the dynasty that descended from the Maccabees in the following century. Mattathias sparked the resistance movement by striking a Jew who was preparing to offer sacrifice to the new gods and by killing the king's officer who was standing by. Then he and his family took to the hills. Many joined them there, especially the Hasideans, a pious and strict group deeply concerned for the Law of Moses. These at first refused to fight on the Sabbath and at once lost a thousand lives. Mattathias then insisted that all groups of resisters should fight if required on the holy sabbath. The guerrilla war that followed was as much a civil war as a war of national resistance. Mattathias treated all degrees of collaborators with the same bitterness as he did the Syrian enemy.

After the death of Mattathias (*c.* 166 BCE), Judas Maccabeus, the third son, became the leader of the resistance movement. In his first battle he seized the sword of Apollonius, governor of Samaria, the general leading the opposing army. But he was also a man of faith in the God of his fathers. He saw himself as a charismatic, divinely appointed leader, like Gideon of old. He would pause in his guerrilla tactics to assemble his men to "watch and pray" and to read the Torah (the divinely revealed Law of Moses) together. Judas saw his task as that of the successor of Moses and Joshua. "Remember how our fathers were saved at the Red Sea," he told his men, "when Pharaoh with his forces pursued them" (I Maccabees 4:9). Then they would blow their trumpets, as in the days of Joshua, and engage the enemy with renewed vigour.

Moreover, Judas could be as cruel as Joshua was. After the manner of his time and also of his enemies, he was ready to exterminate all the males of a conquered city. Some of his activities are in accord with what today would be called the "rules for holy war" as found scattered in sections of Deuteronomy and as developed in great detail in one of the scrolls from the Dead Sea, written within the century following Judas, and now entitled *The War of the Sons of Light Against the Sons of Darkness.*

Ḥanukka: reconsecration of the sanctuary. In December 164 BCE, three years after Antiochus had defiled it, Judas recaptured Jerusalem, all except the Acra. Judas then had "blameless priests" cleanse the Holy Place and erect a new altar of unhewn stones. They then reconsecrated the sanctuary. The Hebrew word for this act, Ḥanukka ("Dedication"), is the name still used for the Jewish eight-day Festival of Lights that commemorates the event. Beginning on Kislev 25 in the Jewish religious year, it occurs near or at the same time as the Christian celebration of Christmas.

Judas next continued the war elsewhere—in Galilee and even in Transjordan. His name was greatly honoured "in all Israel and among the Gentiles" (I Maccabees 5:63). The Syrians, in the war against him, fastened wooden towers on elephants' backs, and each beast then charged into battle with a thousand armoured warriors surrounding it. Eleazar, Judas' second-youngest brother, lost his life in 163 BCE when he stabbed an elephant from underneath. In dying, the beast fell on top of him and crushed him.

When Antiochus Epiphanes died in 164 BCE, others administered the kingdom because his son, Antiochus Eupator, was still a minor. Lysias, the Syrian general, was now the real power. A peace of a sort was agreed between Judas and the Syrian general, who was having trouble elsewhere, and the Jews secured liberty of conscience and worship. The war, however, soon resumed. Judas sent a delegation to Rome at one point to seek for help. This marked the first step toward the eventual takeover by Rome. Judas was killed in battle after more than five years of leadership.

The succession of Jonathan. Jonathan, his brother, succeeded him as general. Jonathan more than sustained the dignity of Judas. King Alexander Balas (also known as Alexander Epiphanes), now in control, made peace with Jonathan, calling him his "friend." In 153 or 152 BCE he elected Jonathan as high priest in Jerusalem. Thus was born the high priestly Hasmonean line. The strict upholders of the Law, however, were alienated, because the Law held that no man should be high priest who was not of priestly descent from Aaron. From now on this group formed a strong opposition party, later to be known as the most conservative section of the Pharisees (the religious group whose interpretations and applications of the law, written and oral, became accepted tradition in later Judaism).

The war continued. The Acra was still in enemy hands, and Jonathan sought to wall it off from the city. He died by treachery and was succeeded by his brother Simon, a man of character and prudence as well as a born leader who had quietly and loyally served under his other brothers. On his own initiative Simon brought peace and security to Jerusalem. He was the second Hasmonean high priest. In 135/134 BCE he was assassinated.

The rule of Hyrcanus I. The succession of the Maccabees was maintained by Simon's son John, known later as Hyrcanus I. He remained as high priest in Jerusalem until his death in 104 BCE. His was a long and disturbed reign, but he consolidated and extended Jewish control, bringing Samaria into subjection and even forcing the Idumaeans (the descendants of the ancient Edomites who lived southeast of the Dead Sea) to accept Judaism. That is how the Idumaean king Herod of Jesus' day was a Jew by religion.

John Hyrcanus' reign marked a turning point in the history of the Maccabees. The movement that had begun with intense conviction and deep patriotic zeal had so completely succeeded that all memory of its first wild enthusiasm had gone. John in spirit had become a Sadducee, an upper-class conservative who accepted only the Written Law as divinely revealed and authoritative. In outlook he was worldly, agnostic, and urbane, utterly unlike his grandfather. (G.A.F.K./Ed.)

BIBLIOGRAPHY. *The Apocrypha and Pseudepigrapha of the Old Testament in English,* vol. 1, *Apocrypha,* ed. by R.H. Charles (1913, reprinted 1978), includes introductions and critical explanatory notes on the first two Books of the Maccabees. Other commentaries include John Christopher Dancy, *A Commentary on I Maccabees* (1954), a popular yet detailed guide; and Jonathan A. Goldstein, *I Maccabees* (1976), and *II Maccabees* (1983), both in "The Anchor Bible" series. Histories of the times may be found in Elias Bickerman, *The Maccabees: An Account of Their History from the Beginnings to the Fall of the House of the Hasmoneans* (1947); Robert H. Pfeiffer, *History of New Testament Times, with an Introduction to the Apocrypha* (1949, reprinted 1972); William R. Farmer, *Maccabees, Zealots, and Josephus: An Inquiry into Jewish Nationalism in the Greco-Roman Period* (1956); and D.S. Russell, *Between the Testaments* (1960, reissued 1977).

Maccabees, The Books of the, Maccabees also spelled MACHABEES, four books, none of which is in the Hebrew Bible but all of which appear in some manuscripts of the Septuagint. The first two books only are part of canonical scripture in the Septuagint and the Vulgate (hence are canonical to Roman Catholicism and Eastern Orthodoxy) and are included in the Protestant Apocrypha.

The First Book of the Maccabees. I Maccabees presents a historical account of political, military, and diplomatic events from the time of Judaea's relationship with Antiochus IV Epiphanes of Syria (reigned 175–164/163 BC) to the death (135/134 BC) of Simon Maccabeus, high priest in Jerusalem. It describes the refusal of Mattathias to perform pagan religious rites, the ensuing Jewish revolt against Syrian hegemony, the political machinations whereby Demetrius II of Syria granted Judaea its independence, and the election of Simon as both high priest and secular ruler of the Judaean Jews.

I Maccabees is the only contemporary source for the civil wars in Judaea, and the only surviving one for Judaean-Syrian relations after the reign of Antiochus IV. The historical integrity of the book, which was compiled from official written sources, oral tradition, and eyewitness reporting, is attested to by the absence of almost all of the conventions of the Hellenistic rhetorical school of historiography and by its uncritical use by the later Jewish historian Josephus.

The author of I Maccabees, likely the Hasmonean court historian, wrote his history during the high priesthood (135/134–104 BC) of John Hyrcanus I, son and successor of Simon.

The Second Book of the Maccabees. II Maccabees focuses on the Jews' revolt against Antiochus and concludes with the defeat of the Syrian general Nicanor in 161 BC by Judas Maccabeus, the hero of the work. In general, its chronology coheres with that of I Maccabees. An unknown editor, the "Epitomist," used the factual notes of a historian, Jason of Cyrene, to write this historical polemic. Its vocabulary and style indicate a Greek original.

The Third Book of the Maccabees. III Maccabees has no relation to the other three books of Maccabees, all of which deal with the revolt of Judaea against Antiochus IV Epiphanes. It purports to be a historical account of the repression and miraculous salvation of Egyptian Jewry during the reign (221–205 BC) of Ptolemy IV Philopator. Ptolemy supposedly threatened the Jews with loss of citizenship after Palestinian Jews refused to permit him to enter the sanctuary of the Temple of Jerusalem. He relented after angels intervened on behalf of the Jews.

The Fourth Book of the Maccabees. IV Maccabees has scanty historical information and belongs to the Maccabees series only because it deals with the beginning of the persecution of Jews by Antiochus IV Epiphanes. It possibly was written during the reign of the emperor Caligula (AD 37–41). Throughout the early Christian period, IV Maccabees was wrongly attributed to the 1st-century-AD Jewish historian Josephus.

The work's main religious theme is that the martyr's sufferings vicariouly expiated the sins of the entire Jewish people.

The Maccabees books were preserved only by the Christian church. Augustine wrote in *The City of God* that they were preserved for their accounts of the martyrs. This suggests that in antiquity, IV Maccabees, dealing almost exclusively with martyrdom, may have been the most highly regarded.

Maccabees, Feast of (Judaism): *see* Ḥanukka.

Maccabeus, Jonathan, also called APPHUS, Maccabeus also spelled MACCABAEUS (d. 143/142 BC), Jewish general, a son of the priest

Mattathias, who took over the leadership of the Maccabean revolt after the death of his elder brother Judas. A brilliant diplomat, if not quite so good a soldier as his elder brother, Jonathan refused all compromise with the superior Seleucid forces, taking advantage of their internal troubles to free Judaea again from external rule. In 143/142, however, he was lured into a trap and killed; he was then succeeded as leader of the revolt by his youngest brother, Simon.

Maccabeus, Judas, also called JUDAH MACCABEE, Maccabeus also spelled MACCABAEUS (d. 161/160 BC), Jewish guerrilla leader who defended his country from invasion by the Seleucid king Antiochus IV Epiphanes, preventing the imposition of Hellenism upon Judaea, and preserving the Jewish religion.

The son of Mattathias, an aged priest who took to the mountains in rebellion when Antiochus attempted to impose the Greek religion on the Jews, Judas took over the rebel leadership on his father's death and proved to be a military genius, overthrowing four Seleucid armies in quick succession and restoring the Temple of Jerusalem. This deed is celebrated in the Jewish festival of lights, Hanukka. On Antiochus' death in 164 BC, the Seleucids offered the Jews freedom of worship, but Judas continued the war, hoping to free his nation politically as well as religiously. Although he himself was killed two years later, his younger brothers took over the fight, finally securing the independence of Judaea.

Maccabiah Games, international games held in Palestine (later Israel) from 1932, sponsored by the World Maccabi Union, an international Jewish sports organization founded in 1921. Events held are such Olympic events as athletics (track-and-field), swimming, water polo, fencing, boxing, wrestling, soccer, basketball, tennis, table tennis, and volleyball and such non-Olympic events as karate.

The Games are open to Jewish athletes from all over the world. The first two Games were held in 1932 and 1935, the latter drawing 1,700 competitors from 27 countries. The anti-Semitic climate of the 1930s led to the permanent settlement of many Maccabiah competitors, coaches, and trainers in Palestine. The Games resumed in 1950 and from 1953 were held every four years. A permanent Maccabiah village was built for competitors and their staffs. By the 1980s the Games attracted 3,600 competitors from 35 countries.

MacCaig, Norman, in full NORMAN ALEXANDER MACCAIG (b. Nov. 14, 1910, Edinburgh, Scot.—d. Jan. 23, 1996, Edinburgh), one of the most important Scottish poets of the 20th century.

After graduation from the University of Edinburgh, MacCaig held various teaching positions, mostly in Edinburgh. His early published works, which he later disavowed, were *Far Cry* (1943) and *The Inward Eye* (1946). In *Riding Lights* (1955), his characteristic poetic voice—recalling the polished Metaphysical elegance of John Donne—was first revealed. Many of his images were taken from the natural world, and his poetry was noted for its wit, humour, apt observation, and command of metaphor. He considered life on a small scale in a number of volumes of verse, including *The Sinai Sort* (1957), *A Common Grace* (1960), *A Round of Applause* (1962), *Measures* (1965), *Rings on a Tree* (1968), and *A Man in My Position* (1969). A volume of his collected poems was published in 1985.

McCardle, Ex Parte (1869), refusal of the U.S. Supreme Court to hear a case involving the Reconstruction Acts. The court's refusal marked the apogee of Radical Republican power to determine national policy.

William H. McCardle was a Mississippi editor who was arrested and jailed for sedition after criticizing both the local Union military commander and Congress. He was denied the benefit of habeas corpus but sought to take advantage of the Radicals' recently passed Habeas Corpus Act, designed to protect newly freed slaves against Southern state courts.

The Habeas Corpus Act provided for appeal to the U.S. Supreme Court in any case where a person was denied constitutional rights. McCardle, after being denied a writ from a federal circuit court, appealed to the Supreme Court on the basis that the military commission in Mississippi was unconstitutional.

The Supreme Court agreed to hear McCardle's appeal, and the Radical Republicans envisioned a repetition of *Ex Parte Milligan,* in which the court limited the jurisdiction of military tribunals. Fearing that the court might declare the Reconstruction Acts (which mandated military occupation of the South) unconstitutional, the Radicals passed a law stripping the court of its power of judicial review with regard to Reconstruction measures. President Andrew Johnson vetoed the bill, but Congress overrode the veto.

In 1869 the court dismissed McCardle's appeal on the grounds that it now lacked jurisdiction over such matters. Congress had thus established its supremacy over both the federal executive and judicial branches.

McCarey, Leo, in full THOMAS LEO MCCAREY (b. Oct. 3, 1898, Los Angeles, Calif., U.S.—d. July 5, 1969, Santa Monica), American motion-picture writer, producer, and director who made light, nostalgic comedies and romances.

McCarey graduated from the University of California law school, practiced briefly, tried songwriting unsuccessfully, and broke into films in 1918 as assistant to Tod Browning. From 1923 to 1928 McCarey worked with Hal Roach, learning the art of creative comedy and directing many shorts, including several early Laurel and Hardy films.

McCarey's most popular films were made in the 1930s and '40s. He directed *Duck Soup* (1933), starring the Marx Brothers, the light comedy *Going My Way* (1944), which won seven Academy Awards, and its successful sequel, *The Bells of Saint Mary's* (1945). Believing films should serve as dream worlds, McCarey created unfailingly entertaining motion pictures. His other award-winning films include *The Awful Truth* (1937) and *Love Affair* (1939). His last picture was *Satan Never Sleeps* (1962).

MacCarthy, Sir Desmond, in full SIR DESMOND CHARLES OTTO MACCARTHY (b. May 20, 1877, Plymouth, Devon, Eng.—d. June 8, 1952, Cambridge, Cambridgeshire), English journalist who, as a weekly columnist for the *New Statesman* known as the "Affable Hawk," gained a reputation for erudition, sensitive judgment, and literary excellence.

MacCarthy was associated with the Bloomsbury group. He began his career as a freelance journalist, quickly moving to editorial work at the *New Quarterly* (1907–10) and *Eye Witness* (1911–13; later *New Witness*). In 1913 he became a drama critic for the *New Statesman*. During World War I he served with the Red Cross attached to the French army (later described in *Experience;* 1935). He continued with the *New Statesman* as drama critic (1913–44), literary editor (1920–27), and weekly columnist (1920–29) and became senior literary critic to the *Sunday Times* in 1928. He was also editor of *Life and Letters* for five years.

Believing that literary criticism "must be in great part a Natural History of Authors," MacCarthy was most revealing when his approach was biographical rather than purely literary. He was open to original visions of reality in literature and helped promote unknown or new authors (including the then-obscure Henrik Ibsen and Anton Chekhov). He gave literary talks for the British Broadcasting Company. His seven volumes of collected writings include *Portraits* (1931), *Drama* (1940), and *Shaw* (1951). MacCarthy was knighted in 1951.

McCarthy, Eugene J., in full EUGENE JOSEPH MCCARTHY (b. March 29, 1916, Watkins, Minn., U.S.), U.S. senator whose entry into the 1968 race for the Democratic presidential nomination ultimately led President Lyndon B. Johnson to drop his bid for reelection.

McCarthy graduated from St. John's University (Collegeville, Minn.) in 1935, then taught high school while working on his master's degree at the University of Minnesota. He returned as a faculty member to St. John's (1940–43) and subsequently served in the War Department's military intelligence division until the end of World War II.

After the war McCarthy again taught school, eventually becoming chairman of the sociology department at the College of St. Thomas in St. Paul, Minn. In 1948 he ran successfully on Minnesota's Democratic-Farmer-Labor Party ticket for the U.S. House of Representatives, where he remained for 10 years, compiling a decidedly liberal voting record.

In 1958 McCarthy was elected to the Senate, where he remained a relatively unknown figure nationally until Nov. 30, 1967. On that day, he announced his intention to challenge President Lyndon B. Johnson in the Democratic state presidential primaries. Although in 1964 he had supported the Gulf of Tonkin Resolution (which gave the president broad powers to wage the Vietnam War), by 1967 McCarthy had become an outspoken critic of the war.

At first McCarthy's challenge was not taken seriously, but his candidacy soon attracted the growing numbers of Democrats who opposed further American involvement in the Vietnam War. After the Minnesota senator, with his trenchant wit and scholarly, understated manner, captured 20 of the 24 New Hampshire delegates in the March 1968 primary, Johnson made the dramatic announcement of his withdrawal from the race.

McCarthy went on to sweep three primaries but then lost four of the next five to Senator Robert F. Kennedy. Following Kennedy's assassination, McCarthy lost the nomination at the convention in Chicago to Vice President Hubert H. Humphrey, who had declined to run in a single primary.

In 1970 McCarthy decided not to run for reelection to the Senate. Humphrey won his seat, and McCarthy turned to a career of writing and lecturing. In 1972 he conducted a lacklustre campaign for the Democratic presidential nomination, which was won by Senator George S. McGovern. Four years later he made a much more vigorous, but again unsuccessful, attempt to win the presidency as an independent.

In 1980 he endorsed Ronald Reagan for the presidency, and in 1982 he made an unsuccessful bid for the Senate seat from Minnesota.

McCarthy, Joseph R., in full JOSEPH RAYMOND MCCARTHY (b. Nov. 14, 1908, near Appleton, Wis., U.S.—d. May 2, 1957, Bethesda, Md.), U.S. senator who dominated the early 1950s by his sensational but unproved charges of Communist subversion in high government circles. In a rare move, he was officially censured for unbecoming conduct by his Senate colleagues (Dec. 2, 1954), thus ending the era of McCarthyism.

A Wisconsin attorney, McCarthy served for three years as a circuit judge (1940–42) before enlisting in the Marines in World War II. In 1946 he won the Republican nomination for the Senate in a stunning upset primary victory over Senator Robert M. LaFollette, Jr.; he was elected that autumn and again in 1952.

McCarthy was a quiet and undistinguished senator until February 1950, when his public charge that 205 Communists had infiltrated the State Department created a furor and catapulted him into headlines across the country. Upon subsequently testifying before the Senate Committee on Foreign Relations, he proved unable to produce the name of a single "card-carrying Communist" in any government department. Nevertheless, he gained increasing popular support for his campaign of accusations by capitalizing on the fears and frustrations of a nation weary of the Korean War and appalled by Communist advances in eastern Europe and China. McCarthy proceeded to instigate a nationwide, militant anti-Communist "crusade"; to his supporters, he appeared as a dedicated patriot and guardian of genuine Americanism, to his detractors, as an irresponsible, self-seeking witch-hunter who was undermining the nation's traditions of civil liberties.

Joseph McCarthy

By courtesy of the National Archives, Washington, D.C.

McCarthy was reelected in 1952 and obtained the chairmanship of the Government Committee on Operations of the Senate and of its permanent subcommittee on investigations. For the next two years he was constantly in the spotlight, investigating various government departments and questioning innumerable witnesses about their suspected Communist affiliations. Although he failed to make a plausible case against anyone, his colourful and cleverly presented accusations drove some persons out of their jobs and brought popular condemnation to others. The persecution of innocent persons on the charge of being Communists and the forced conformity that this practice engendered in American public life came to be known as McCarthyism. Meanwhile, less flamboyant government agencies actually did identify and prosecute cases of Communist infiltration.

McCarthy's increasingly irresponsible attacks came to include President Dwight D. Eisenhower and other Republican and Democratic leaders. His influence waned in 1954 as a result of the sensational, nationally televised, 36-day hearing on his charges of subversion by U.S. Army officers and civilian officials. This detailed television exposure of his brutal and truculent interrogative tactics discredited him and helped to turn the tide of public opinion against him.

When the Republicans lost control of the Senate in the midterm elections that November, McCarthy was replaced as chairman of the investigating committee. Soon after, the Senate felt secure enough to formally condemn him on a vote of 67 to 22 for conduct "contrary to Senate traditions," and McCarthy was largely ignored by his colleagues and by the media thereafter.

M'Carthy, Justin (b. Nov. 22, 1830, Cork, County Cork, Ire.—d. April 24, 1912, Folkestone, Kent, Eng.), Irish politician and historian who first made his name as a novelist with such successes as *Dear Lady Disdain* (1875) and *Miss Misanthrope* (1878) but then published his *History of Our Own Times* (1879–1905), which won general recognition.

Justin M'Carthy, oil painting by Harold Waite; in the National Gallery of Ireland, Dublin

By courtesy of the National Gallery of Ireland, Dublin

M'Carthy began his career as a journalist, but in 1879 he entered Irish politics and became vice chairman of the new Home Rule Party under Charles Stuart Parnell. In a crisis over the leadership, M'Carthy became chairman of the anti-Parnellites. In the 1892 general election his party won an overwhelming success, but he had no great political ambitions and in 1896 resigned the leadership to John Dillon. Although his health broke down and he became nearly blind, he continued writing by dictation.

McCarthy, Mary (Therese) (b. June 21, 1912, Seattle, Wash., U.S.—d. Oct. 25, 1989, New York, N.Y.), American novelist and critic noted for bitingly satiric commentaries on marriage, sexual expression, the impotence of intellectuals, and the role of women in contemporary urban America. She frequently used autobiographical details in her fiction, which is noted for its wit and acerbity in analyzing the finer moral nuances of intellectual dilemmas.

After receiving a B.A. degree from Vassar College in 1933, McCarthy began writing book reviews for the *Partisan Review* and other periodicals. She served on the editorial staff of the *Partisan Review* from 1937 to 1948. She married four times, the second time, in 1938, to the noted American critic Edmund Wilson, who encouraged her to begin writing fiction.

Her first novel, *The Company She Keeps* (1942), a loosely arranged collection of somewhat autobiographical stories, concerns a fashionable woman who experiences divorce and psychoanalysis. *The Oasis* (British title, *Source of Embarrassment;* both 1949) is a short novel about the failure of a utopian community of ineffectually idealistic intellectuals. *The Groves of Academe* (1952) is a satiric examination of American higher education during the Joseph McCarthy era. *The Group* (1963), her most popular work of fiction, follows the lives of eight graduates of Vassar (McCarthy's own college) as they resist or succumb to the intellectual fads of the 1930s and early '40s. *Birds of America* (1971) is a post-World War II version of the 19th-century international novel in which American innocence is confronted with European sophistication. *Cannibals and Missionaries* (1979) is about the hijacking of a liberal committee flying to Iran to investigate the shah's atrocities. McCarthy was a longtime member of the staff of the *Partisan Review,* and, for that publication and others, she wrote extensively on art, theatre, travel, and politics. She also wrote two autobiographies, *Memories of a Catholic Girlhood* (1957) and *How I Grew* (1987).

BIBLIOGRAPHY. Carol Gelderman, *Mary McCarthy: A Life* (1988), was written with McCarthy's cooperation.

MacCarthy Island, also called JANGJANGBURE, originally LEMAIN ISLAND, island, in the Gambia River, 176 miles (283 km) upstream from Banjul, central Gambia. It was ceded in 1823 to Captain Alexander Grant of the African Corps, who was acting for the British crown. Designated as a site for freed slaves, the island was renamed for Sir Charles MacCarthy, British colonial governor (1814–24). In the 1830s peanut (groundnut) cultivation was introduced by the Wesleyan Mission at the port town of Georgetown (*q.v.*) on the island. The island is 6 miles (10 km) long and 1.5 miles (2.5 km) wide and is chiefly inhabited by Malinke (Mandingo) people. Pop. (latest census) 2,510.

McCarty, Maclyn (b. June 9, 1911, South Bend, Ind., U.S.), American biologist who, with Oswald T. Avery and Colin M. MacLeod, provided the first experimental evidence that the genetic material of living cells is composed of deoxyribonucleic acid (DNA).

McCarty attended Stanford University and Johns Hopkins School of Medicine (M.D., 1937) before joining William S. Tillett at New York University in 1940. Tillett not only introduced McCarty to the study of pneumococcic bacteria but also arranged for him to work with Avery in his laboratory at the Rockefeller Institute (now Rockefeller University), New York City. McCarty became a member of the institute in 1950 and, 15 years later, its vice president and physician in chief.

McCarty's classic experiments with Avery and MacLeod, published in 1944, involved the transformation of certain types of pneumococcus into distinctly different types. The transformation occurred when cell-free material, extracted from one type of bacterium encased in smooth capsules in the living state, was mixed with living bacteria of a second type lacking capsules. The second type would then produce a capsule characteristic of the first type, with which it had been mixed. The results of this research indicated that the substance responsible for the change was DNA.

McCay, Winsor (b. Sept. 26, 1869, Spring Lake, Mich., U.S.—d. July 26, 1934), American artist who was a pioneer of cartoon films.

After working as a cartoonist on several newspapers, including the *New York Herald,* he made an animated film of his comic strip hero Little Nemo, inspired by the work of Emile Cohl and J. Stuart Blackton, which proved to be a great success.

This cartoon film was followed by *Gertie the Dinosaur* (1909), the final version of which included 10,000 drawings, and by many other short cartoons, which McCay used in his vaudeville act. His first feature-length animated films were *The Sinking of the Lusitania* (1918) and *The Flying House* (1920).

Macchiaioli, group of 19th-century Florentine and Neopolitan painters who reacted against the rule-bound Italian academies of art and looked to nature for instruction. The Macchiaioli felt that patches (Italian *macchia*) of colour were the most significant aspect of painting. The effect of a painting on the spectator was to derive from the painted surface itself, rather than from any ideological message or narrative. The Macchiaioli used a sketch technique to record their initial impressions of nature—often as seen from a distance—by means of colour and light. Their theory was similar to that of the French Impressionists, but it was even more concerned with colour structure.

During a short period of 20 years the Macchiaioli produced startlingly fresh and vivid paintings. The most outstanding artist of the group was the Florentine Giovanni Fattori (1825–1908), who attained brilliant effects of light and colour by the use of strong colour patches. Other important painters included Telemaco Signorini (1853–1901), the critic and theoretician of the group, who used colour with great sensitivity in his usually socially significant scenes; Silvestro Lega (1826–95), who combined a clearly articulated handling of colour patches with a poetic feeling for his subject; and Raffaello Sernesi (1838–66) and Giuseppe Abbati (1836–68), also artists of great originality in their use of colour.

macchie (Mediterranean vegetation): *see* maquis.

McClellan, George B(rinton) (b. Dec. 3, 1826, Philadelphia, Pa., U.S.—d. Oct. 29, 1885, Orange, N.J.), general who skillfully reorganized Union forces in the first year of the American Civil War (1861–65) but drew wide criticism for repeatedly failing to press his advantage over Confederate troops.

McClellan
By courtesy of the U.S. Signal Corps

Graduating second in his class at the U.S. Military Academy, West Point, N.Y. (1846), McClellan served in the Mexican War (1846–48) and taught military engineering at West Point (1848–51). He was then assigned to conduct a series of surveys for railroad and military installations, concluding with a mission to the Crimea (1855–56) to report on European methods of warfare.

McClellan resigned his commission in 1857 to become chief of engineering for the Illinois Central Railroad and, in 1860, president of the Ohio and Mississippi Railroad. Although a states' rights Democrat, he was nevertheless a staunch Unionist, and, a month after the outbreak of the American Civil War (April 1861), he was commissioned in the regular army and placed in command of the Department of the Ohio with responsibility for holding western Virginia. By July 13 the Confederate forces there were defeated, and McClellan had established a reputation as the "Young Napoleon of the West."

After the disastrous Union defeat at the First Battle of Bull Run the same month, McClellan was placed in command of what was to become the Army of the Potomac. He was charged with the defense of the capital and destruction of the enemy's forces in northern and eastern Virginia. In November he succeeded General Winfield Scott as general in chief of the army. His organizing abilities and logistical understanding brought order out of the chaos of defeat, and he was brilliantly successful in whipping the army into a fighting unit with high morale, efficient staff, and effective supporting services. Yet he refused to take the offensive against the enemy that fall, claiming that the army was not prepared to move. President Abraham Lincoln was disturbed by McClellan's inactivity and consequently issued his famous General War Order No. 1 (Jan. 27, 1862), calling for the forward movement of all armies. "Little Mac" was able to convince the president that a postponement of two months was desirable and also that the offensive against Richmond should take the route of the peninsula between the York and James rivers in Virginia.

In the Peninsular Campaign (April 4–July 1, 1862), McClellan was never really defeated and actually achieved several victories. But he was overly cautious and seemed reluctant to pursue the enemy. Coming to within a few miles of Richmond, he consistently overestimated the number of troops opposing him, and, when Confederate forces under General Robert E. Lee began an all-out attempt to destroy McClellan's army in the Seven Days' Battles (June 25–July 1), McClellan retreated. Lincoln's discouragement over McClellan's failure to take Richmond or to defeat the enemy decisively led to the withdrawal of the Army of the Potomac from the peninsula.

Returning to Washington as news of the Union defeat at the Second Battle of Bull Run (August 29–30) was received, McClellan was asked to take command of the army for the defense of the capital. Again exercising his organizing capability, he was able to rejuvenate Union forces. When Lee moved north into Maryland, McClellan's army stopped the invasion at the Battle of Antietam (September 17). But he again failed to move rapidly to destroy Lee's army, and, as a result, the exasperated president removed him from command in November.

In 1864 McClellan was nominated for the presidency by the Democratic Party, though he repudiated its platform, denouncing the war as a failure. On election day he resigned his army commission and later sailed for Europe. Returning in 1868, he served as chief engineer of the New York Department of Docks (1870–72) and in 1872 became president of the Atlantic and Great Western Railroad. He served one term as governor of New Jersey (elected 1877) and spent his remaining years traveling and writing his memoirs.

BIBLIOGRAPHY. Stephen W. Sears, *George B. McClellan: The Young Napoleon* (1988), explores the personality traits that led to the general's battlefield incompetence.

Macclesfield, district (borough), county of Cheshire, England. The district includes a narrow strip of the Pennines in the east that is part of the Peak District National Park. The principal town, Macclesfield, is the centre of the silk industry. The manufacture of silk-covered buttons began in the 16th century, and silk throwing was introduced in 1756, when the first silk mill was built. By the end of the 18th century the silk industry was flourishing, and it is still important, although the district's industrial structure has been broadened. Other towns in the district include residential towns for Manchester commuters such as Poynton, Wilmslow, Alderley Edge, and Knutsford. Knutsford, which is the original "Cranford" in Elizabeth Gaskell's novel of that name (1853), has some industry, including nuclear-energy engineering laboratories. Area of district, 203 square miles (525 square km). Pop. (1981) town, 48,071; (1991 prelim.) district, 147,000.

McClintock, Barbara (b. June 16, 1902, Hartford, Conn., U.S.—d. Sept. 2, 1992, Huntington, N.Y.), American scientist regarded as one of the most important figures in the history of genetics. Her discovery during the 1940s and '50s of mobile genetic elements won her the Nobel Prize for Physiology or Medicine in 1983.

McClintock studied plant genetics at Cornell University in Ithaca, N.Y., receiving her doctorate in botany in 1927. She taught for several years before taking a research position with the Carnegie Institution of Washington, D.C. She remained at Carnegie's Cold Spring Harbor (N.Y.) Laboratory for more than 50 years.

By observing and experimenting with variations in the coloration of kernels of corn (maize), McClintock discovered that genetic information is not stationary. She isolated two control elements in genetic material and found that not only did they move but also the change in position affected the behaviour of neighbouring genes. She suggested that these transposable elements were responsible for the diversity in cells during an organism's development.

Although the importance of her research was not recognized for many years, it has since been seen as pioneering work that has significantly increased the knowledge of genetic function and organization.

BIBLIOGRAPHY. McClintock's character and scientific contributions are explored by Evelyn Fox Keller, *A Feeling for the Organism* (1983).

McClintock, Sir Francis Leopold (b. July 8, 1819, Dundalk, County Louth, Ire.—d. Nov. 17, 1907, London, Eng.), British naval officer and explorer who discovered the tragic fate of the British explorer Sir John Franklin and his 1845 expedition to the North American Arctic. Before his own successful search of 1857–59, McClintock took part in three earlier efforts to find Franklin. On the second and third of these (1850–51 and 1852–54), his improvements in the planning and execution of sledge journeys greatly advanced the possibilities of Arctic exploration.

The first information suggesting that Franklin's party had perished around King William Island, now in Canada's Northwest Territories, was obtained from Eskimo in 1854. When the British government refused to equip another search expedition, Franklin's widow equipped the *Fox,* with McClintock in command. He found the graves of some of Franklin's crew as well as remains from Franklin's ships and some of his belongings. He also received an old Eskimo woman's account of how Franklin's starving men died in their tracks as they sought to journey southward on foot. The most important evidence that McClintock recovered was a written record of Franklin's expedition up to April 25, 1848. McClintock's account of his journey, *The Voyage of the "Fox" in the Arctic Seas: A Narrative of the Fate of Sir John Franklin and His Companions,* was published in 1859, and he was knighted in 1860.

Sir Francis Leopold McClintock, detail of an oil painting by Stephen Pearce; in the National Portrait Gallery, London
By courtesy of the National Portrait Gallery, London

McCloskey, John (b. March 10, 1810, Brooklyn, N.Y., U.S.—d. Oct. 10, 1885, New York, N.Y.), second archbishop of New York, who was the first American churchman to be appointed cardinal.

Educated at Mount St. Mary's College, Emmitsburg, Md., McCloskey was ordained priest in 1834. After graduate study at the Gregorian University, Rome, he returned to New York City (1837) as rector of St. Joseph's Church. In 1841 he organized and became first president of St. John's College (later Fordham University). Becoming archbishop of New York in 1864, he renewed construction of St. Patrick's Cathedral, suspended during the American Civil War, and dedicated the edifice in 1879. Named cardinal by Pope Pius IX in 1875, he went to Rome in 1878 and assisted in the

McCloskey, *c.* 1876
Religious News Service

coronation of Pope Leo XIII, who formally gave him the cardinal's hat. McCloskey is buried in St. Patrick's Cathedral.

McCloy, John J(ay) (b. March 31, 1895, Philadelphia, Pa., U.S.—d. March 11, 1989, Stamford, Conn.), American diplomat and lawyer. He was an adviser to every U.S. president from Franklin D. Roosevelt to Ronald Reagan.

McCloy graduated from Harvard Law School in 1921. Thereafter he practiced law on Wall Street. His work on the "Black Tom" case, in which he proved that German agents had caused an explosion at a munitions factory, attracted the attention of Secretary of War Henry L. Stimson, who in 1941 persuaded President Roosevelt to appoint McCloy assistant secretary of war. In this capacity McCloy helped secure Congressional approval of the Lend-Lease Act and oversaw the internment of some 120,000 Japanese-Americans, a policy he continued to defend even as the U.S. government disavowed it in the 1980s. He was also later criticized for having opposed a plan to bomb the railroads leading to Auschwitz. McCloy was one of the few civilians aware of the decision to use the atomic bomb against Japan. His argument that the United States should issue a warning, hence an opportunity to surrender, to Japan was overruled.

Between 1947 and 1949 McCloy was president of the International Bank for Reconstruction and Development (World Bank). From 1949 to 1952 he was high commissioner for Germany, in which capacity he created a civilian government and laid the groundwork for rebuilding West Germany's industry and commerce. From 1953 he was chairman of several corporations and foundations, including the Chase Manhattan Bank (1953–60) and the Ford Foundation (1958–65), and began his long association (1953–89, chairman 1953–70) with the Council on Foreign Relations. In 1961, as President John F. Kennedy's principal arms adviser, he negotiated terms for the resumption of East-West disarmament talks and drafted the bill that led to the establishment of the U.S. Arms Control and Disarmament Agency. He was a member of the Warren Commission appointed in 1963 to investigate Kennedy's assassination. He continued to serve as an adviser on foreign affairs until shortly before his death.

McClung, Clarence E(rwin) (b. April 6, 1870, Clayton, Calif., U.S.—d. Jan. 17, 1946, Swarthmore, Pa.), American zoologist whose study of the mechanisms of heredity led to his 1901 hypothesis that an extra, or accessory, chromosome was the determiner of sex. The discovery of the sex-determining chromosome provided some of the earliest evidence that a given chromosome carries a definable set of hereditary traits. He also studied how the behaviour of chromosomes in the sex cells of different organisms affects their heredity.

McClung was educated at the University of Kansas (Ph.D., 1902), where he became a professor and later dean of the medical school. In 1912 he went to the University of Pennsylvania as head of the zoological laboratories, a position he held until his retirement in 1940.

McClure, Sir Robert John Le Mesurier (b. Jan. 28, 1807, Wexford, County Wexford, Ire.—d. Oct. 17, 1873, London, Eng.), Irish naval officer who followed the Arctic waterway linking the Atlantic and Pacific oceans and thereby completed the first crossing of the Northwest Passage.

In 1850 McClure took command of the *Investigator,* one of two ships sent to find the British explorer Sir John Franklin, missing in the North American Arctic since 1845. From

McClure, detail from an engraving
BBC Hulton Picture Library

the Pacific, McClure entered the Bering Strait and, heading eastward north of Alaska, found two entrances to the Northwest Passage around Banks Island, now part of the Northwest Territories of Canada. The *Investigator* became trapped in the ice of Mercy Bay just north of Banks Island, compelling him to abandon the ship, but his party was rescued by two ships at nearby Melville Island. The rescue ships were in turn abandoned, and the party proceeded on foot to Beechey Island, and thence home by ship. McClure was knighted in 1854.

M'Clure Strait, eastern arm of the Beaufort Sea of the Arctic Ocean. It is about 170 miles (270 km) long and 60 miles (90 km) wide. In western Franklin District, Northwest Territories, Canada, it extends west of Viscount Melville Sound and lies between Melville and Eglinton islands (north) and Banks Island (south). The strait is part of the Northwest Passage route through the Canadian Arctic archipelago. It is named for the British explorer Sir Robert McClure (or M'Clure).

MacColl, Ewan, original name JAMES MILLER (b. Jan. 25, 1915, Auchterarder, Scot.—d. Oct. 22, 1989, London, Eng.), British singer, songwriter, and playwright.

MacColl's parents were singers and taught him many folk songs. He left school at 14, taking a variety of blue-collar jobs and working as a singer and actor. In 1945 he and Joan Littlewood founded Theatre Workshop; he was the company's artistic director until 1953 and wrote a number of plays for it. MacColl was a leading figure in the British folk-song revival of the 1950s and '60s. He and his third wife, American musician Peggy Seeger, pioneered a type of documentary, the "radio-ballad," combining recorded interviews with songs and narration. The two published several collections of folk songs, including *Till Doomsday in the Afternoon* (1986). Among MacColl's best-known songs is "The First Time Ever I Saw Your Face."

McConnell, Francis John (b. Aug. 18, 1871, Trinway, Ohio, U.S.—d. Aug. 18, 1953, Lucasville, Ohio), American Methodist bishop, college president, and social reformer.

McConnell entered the Methodist ministry in 1894, and after serving as pastor of churches in Massachusetts and New York he became president of De Pauw University, Greencastle, Ind. (1909–12). Elected bishop in 1912, he served in Mexico and in Pittsburgh, Pa., U.S., where he studied industrial conditions. As chairman of the Commission of Inquiry of the Interchurch World Movement, he supported the investigation that resulted in the *Report on the Steel Strike of 1919,* which was influential in abolishing the 12-hour day and the 7-day week in the steel industry. McConnell wrote many books, including *The Christlike God* (1927) and *Evangelicals, Revolutionists, and Idealists* (1942).

MacCool, Finn: *see* Fenian cycle.

McCormack, John (b. June 14, 1884, Athlone, County Westmeath, Ire.—d. Sept. 16, 1945, near Dublin), Irish tenor who was considered to be one of the finest singers of the first quarter of the 20th century.

McCormack won the prize at the National Irish Festival (the Feis Ceoil) in Dublin in 1903. Later he studied in Italy. He made his London operatic debut in 1907 at Covent Garden as Turiddu in Pietro Mascagni's *Cavalleria rusticana.* He appeared at the Manhattan Opera House, New York City, in 1909 as Alfredo in Giuseppe Verdi's *La traviata.* Subsequently he sang with opera companies in Chicago and Boston and with the Metropolitan Opera Company, New York City. In 1911 he toured Australia with Nellie Melba in Italian opera. He later turned to the concert stage and became a fine singer of German lieder. Most popular with his recital audiences were the Irish folk songs he invariably included in

John McCormack
AP/Wide World

the program. He was admired for the beauty of his voice and for his careful musicianship. He became a U.S. citizen in 1919 and was made a count in the papal peerage in 1928.

McCormack, John W(illiam) (b. Dec. 21, 1891, Boston, Mass., U.S.—d. Nov. 22, 1980, Dedham, Mass.), American politician who served as speaker of the U.S. House of Representatives from 1962 to 1970.

McCormack had little formal education. He read law while working as an office boy and passed the bar examination at the age of 21. He joined the Democratic Party and won his first election to public office at age 25. He served for two years in the Massachusetts House of Representatives and for three years in the state senate. In 1928 he was elected to the U.S. House of Representatives and remained a member of Congress for the next 42 years. In 1940 he became House majority leader, and in 1962 he succeeded Sam Rayburn as Speaker of the House. McCormack was known as a loyal Democrat and a skillful debater; he supported civil-rights bills, antipoverty programs, and wage-and-hour laws. He opposed communism and defended U.S. involvement in Vietnam. He retired in 1970.

McCormick, Cyrus Hall (b. Feb. 15, 1809, Rockbridge county, Va., U.S.—d. May 13, 1884, Chicago, Ill.), American industrialist and inventor who is generally credited with the development (from 1831) of the mechanical reaper.

McCormick was the eldest son of Robert McCormick, a farmer, blacksmith, and inventor. McCormick's education, in local schools, was limited. Reserved, determined, and serious-minded, he spent all of his time in his father's workshop.

The elder McCormick had invented several practical farm implements but, like other inventors in the United States and England,

Cyrus McCormick
Culver Pictures

had failed in his attempt to build a successful reaping machine. In 1831 Cyrus, aged 22, tried his hand at building a reaper. Resembling a two-wheeled, horse-drawn chariot, the machine consisted of a vibrating cutting blade, a reel to bring the grain within its reach, and a platform to receive the falling grain. The reaper embodied the principles essential to all subsequent grain-cutting machines.

For farmers in the early 19th century, harvesting required a large number of labourers, and, if they could be found, the cost of hiring them was high. When McCormick's reaper was tested on a neighbour's farm in 1831, it offered the hope that the yield of the farmer's fields would soon not be limited to the amount of labour available. The machine had defects, not the least of which was a clatter so loud that slaves were required to walk alongside to calm the frightened horses.

McCormick took out a patent in 1834, but his chief interest at that time was the family's iron foundry. When the foundry failed in the wake of the Bank Panic of 1837, leaving the family deeply in debt, McCormick turned to his still-unexploited reaper and improved it. He sold 2 reapers in 1841, 7 in 1842, 29 in 1843, and 50 the following year.

An 1844 visit to the prairie states in the Midwest convinced McCormick that the future of his reaper and of the world's wheat production lay in this vast fertile land rather than in the rocky, hilly East. In 1847, with further patented improvements, he opened a factory in the then small, swampy, lakeside town of Chicago in partnership with the mayor, William Ogden, who capitalized the venture with $50,000 of his own money. The first year, 800 machines were sold. More were sold the next year, and McCormick was able to buy out Ogden.

McCormick's main rival was Obed Hussey, whose machine proved to be inferior as a reaper but superior as a mower. When McCormick's basic patent expired in 1848, competing manufacturers—Hussey among them—tried to block renewal. The ensuing legal battle was but one of many in McCormick's career. He was involved in endless litigation not only with rival manufacturers and infringers but also with the New York Central Railroad, which he sued for $20,000 damages following an altercation over an $8.75 overcharge on his wife's baggage. He fought this particular case up to the Supreme Court three times—and won, even though it took 20 years. He did not win his 1848 patent renewal battle, however. Except for improvements on the reaper patented after 1831, the basic machine passed into the public domain. McCormick then set out to beat his manufacturing competitors another way: by outselling them.

Pockets stuffed with order blanks, McCormick rode over the plains selling his reaper to farmers and would-be farmers. To increase sales, he used innovations such as mass production, advertising, public demonstration, warranty of product, and extension of credit to his customers. Soon the factory expanded, and the company had a traveling sales force. By 1850 the McCormick reaper was known in every part of the United States, and at the Great Exhibition of 1851 in London it was introduced to European farmers. Although mocked by *The Times* of London as "a cross between an Astley Chariot, a wheelbarrow, and a flying machine," the reaper took the Grand Prize. In 1855 it won the Grand Medal of Honour at the Paris International Exposition. There followed a long series of prize honours and awards that made the McCormick reaper known to farmers throughout the world.

By 1856 McCormick was selling more than 4,000 machines a year. In the 1858 account of his marriage to Nancy (Nettie) Fowler, the *Chicago Daily Press* referred to him as the "massive Thor of industry." Business did not absorb all of his energy, however. He became active in the Democratic Party and in the Presbyterian church, establishing the McCormick Theological Seminary in Chicago.

In 1871 the Chicago fire gutted his factory. Then—more than 60 years old, his fortune long since made—he rebuilt. When he died, his business was still growing. In 1902 the McCormick Harvesting Company joined with other companies to form International Harvester Company, with McCormick's son, Cyrus, Jr., as its first president. (M.Wi.)

BIBLIOGRAPHY. Reuben Gold Thwaites, *Cyrus Hall McCormick and the Reaper* (1909); Herbert N. Casson, *Cyrus Hall McCormick: His Life and Work* (1909, reprinted 1971); Cyrus McCormick, *The Century of the Reaper* (1931, reprinted 1972).

McCormick, Robert R(utherford) (b. July 30, 1880, Chicago, Ill., U.S.—d. April 1, 1955, Wheaton, Ill.), American newspaper editor and publisher, popularly known as Colonel McCormick, whose idiosyncratic editorials made him the personification of conservative journalism in the United States. Under his direction the *Chicago Tribune* achieved the largest circulation among American standard-sized newspapers and led the world in newspaper advertising revenue.

A grandnephew of the inventor Cyrus Hall McCormick and grandson of Joseph Medill, editor and publisher of the *Chicago Tribune* (1855–99), McCormick served as a Chicago alderman (1904–05) and as president of the Chicago Sanitary District Board (1905–10). As an officer with the American Expeditionary Force in France during World War I, he was awarded the Distinguished Service Medal.

Colonel McCormick, 1947
Chicago Tribune

McCormick was named president of the Chicago Tribune Company in 1911, and he shared the functions of editor in chief and publisher with his cousin Joseph Medill Patterson from 1914 until 1925, when he became sole editor and publisher. McCormick acquired or established forestlands, paper mills, hydroelectric installations, and shipping companies (all to supply the *Tribune* with newsprint) as well as radio and television facilities and additional newspapers: the tabloid New York *Daily News* (1919, directed solely by Patterson from 1925); and the Washington *Times-Herald* (1949, sold to the Washington *Post* 1954).

A strident if rather idiosyncratic conservative, McCormick attacked Prohibition, the New Deal administration of President Franklin D. Roosevelt, the Fair Deal of President Harry S. Truman, and the Marshall Plan for European recovery after World War II.

McCoy FAMILY: *see* Hatfield and McCoy families.

McCoy, (Charles) Kid, original name NORMAN SELBY (b. Oct. 13, 1873, Rush county, Ind., U.S.—d. April 18, 1940, Detroit, Mich.), American professional boxer whose trickery and cruelty in the ring made him a semilegendary figure in boxing history.

A former sparring partner of welterweight champion Tommy Ryan, McCoy pleaded with Ryan for a title match as a benefit for himself, asserting that he was in ill health and needed money. Ryan, deceived, did not train seriously for the fight; McCoy, who was in excellent condition, knocked the champion out in 15 one-sided rounds to win the title (March 2, 1896). Growing into the middleweight class (then 158 pounds [72 kg]), McCoy never defended the welterweight championship. On April 22, 1903, he lost a 10-round decision to Jack Root in the first light-heavyweight (175-pound [80-kilogram]) championship bout. He also fought outstanding heavyweights.

An inveterate gambler, McCoy is thought to have bet against himself occasionally, as in his knockout defeat by James J. Corbett in 1900. He was married 10 times to eight women and served eight years in a penitentiary as a consequence of the death of one of his wives. Reduced to poverty, he committed suicide.

McCrae, Hugh (Raymond) (b. Oct. 4, 1876, Melbourne, Vic., Australia—d. Feb. 17, 1958, Sydney), Australian poet, actor, and journalist best known for his sophisticated, romantic, highly polished lyrics.

McCrae studied art and was apprenticed to an architect, but he soon left this profession for free-lance journalism, selling his work in Melbourne and New York City. In the United States in 1914 he tried unsuccessfully to make his way as a free-lance journalist and actor and later returned to Australia, where he became a successful author and occasional actor.

His first book of verse, *Satyrs and Sunlight: Sylvarum Libri* (1909), appeared in a revised edition in 1928, which contains much of his best work. *Colombine* (1920) was followed by *Idyllia* (1922). Other works include *The Mimshi Maiden* (1938), *Poems* (1939), *Forests of Pan* (1944), and *Voice of the Forest* (1945).

McCrea, Joel (Albert) (b. Nov. 5, 1905, South Pasadena, Calif., U.S.—d. Oct. 20, 1990, Woodland Hills, Calif.), American motion-picture actor of the 1930s and '40s.

The son of a utility company executive, McCrea graduated from Pomona College in 1928 and worked as a stunt man and bit player in Hollywood before playing his first leading role in 1930, in *The Silver Horde*. He appeared in 38 more films during the 1930s, among which were *The Most Dangerous Game* (1932), *Pri-*

vate Worlds (1935), *These Three* (1936), *Dead End* (1937), *Wells Fargo* (1937), and *Union Pacific* (1939). Among his most important roles were those in the comedies *Primrose Path* (1940), *Sullivan's Travels* (1941), *The Palm Beach Story* (1942), and *The More the Merrier* (1943). Other notable performances were in Alfred Hitchcock's *Foreign Correspondent* (1940) and *Buffalo Bill* (1944). After 1946 McCrea acted almost exclusively in westerns, chief among which were *The Virginian* (1946), *Colorado Territory* (1949), *The Outriders* (1950), and *Stranger on Horseback* (1955). His last major film appearance was in the classic western *Ride the High Country* (1962).

McCrea's typical screen persona, that of a dependable, even-tempered man speaking in a resonant American twang, suited him to star in a great variety of films ranging from romantic comedies to serious dramas and action-adventure films.

MacCready, Paul Beattie (b. Sept. 29, 1925, New Haven, Conn., U.S.), American aerodynamicist who headed a team that designed and built both the first man-powered aircraft and the first solar-powered aircraft capable of sustained flights.

MacCready was a national champion model-plane builder in the 1930s and received his pilot's license at the age of 16. He graduated with a B.S. degree in physics from Yale University in 1947 and earned an M.S. degree in physics (1948) and a Ph.D. in aeronautics (1952) from the California Institute of Technology.

MacCready started sailplaning in 1947 and was U.S. soaring champion in 1948, 1949, and 1953 and international champion in 1956. He was head of his own firm, AeroVironment, in Pasadena, Calif., working on the improvement of air quality, the conservation of energy, and the derivation of power from wind and water.

On Aug. 23, 1977, at Shafter Airport near Bakersfield, Calif., MacCready's *Gossamer Condor,* pedaled and piloted by 137-pound (62-kilogram) Bryan Allen, a bicyclist and hang-glider enthusiast, completed the course required to win the Kremer Prize of £50,000 ($95,000), clearing a 10-foot- (3-metre-) high start-and-finish line while making a figure-eight flight around two pylons set half a mile apart. The total distance flown was 1.15 miles (1.85 km) in 6 min 27.05 s, at a top speed of 11 miles per hour (18 km/h). The 70-pound (32-kilogram) plane had a 96-foot (29-metre) wingspan.

A subsequent, more streamlined MacCready plane, the *Gossamer Albatross,* was pedaled and piloted by Allen from near Folkestone, Kent, Eng., to Cape Gris-Nez, Fr., a distance of 23 miles (37 km), in 2 h 49 min, on June 12, 1979. This flight won the £100,000 Kremer Prize for the first man-propelled flight across the English Channel. The plane had a wingspan of 93 feet 10 inches (28.6 m), weighed 70 pounds, and was constructed of Mylar, polystyrene, and carbon-fibre rods.

On July 7, 1981, the *Solar Challenger,* a solar-powered plane designed by MacCready, flew from the Pointoise Cormeilles airport, near Paris, to the Manston Royal Air Force Base, in Kent, Eng., a distance of 160 miles (258 km), in 5 hr 23 min at an average speed of about 30 miles per hour (48 km/h) and a cruising altitude of 11,000 feet (3,350 m). The pilot was Stephen Ptacek, weighing 122 pounds (55 kg). The plane, powered by 16,128 solar cells connected to two electric motors, weighed 210 pounds (95 kg) and had a wingspan of 47 feet (14.3 m).

MacCready was international president of the International Human Powered Vehicle Association (founded 1975), which is dedicated to maximizing the speed of the bicycle.

McCullers, Carson, *née* LULA CARSON SMITH (b. Feb. 19, 1917, Columbus, Ga., U.S.—d. Sept. 29, 1967, Nyack, N.Y.), American writer of novels and stories that depict the inner lives of lonely people.

At the age of 17, she went to New York City to study music and attended Columbia University. She married the writer Reeves McCullers in 1937, was divorced from him in 1940, and remarried him in 1945. Her first, and in the opinion of many her finest work, the novel *The Heart Is a Lonely Hunter,* appeared in 1940. The book concerns four inhabitants of a small town in Georgia—an adolescent girl with a passion to study music; an unsuccessful socialist agitator; a black physician struggling to maintain his personal dignity; and a widower who owns a café. The novel *A Member of the Wedding* (1946) is about a 13-year-old motherless girl, Frankie, who yearns to go on her brother's honeymoon. McCullers adapted it into a successful stage play in 1950, and it was made into a film in 1952. Another novel, *Reflections in a Golden Eye* (1941), a highly coloured psychological horror story of sexual perversion and domestic tragedy in a peacetime Southern army camp, was also made into a film, and *The Ballad of the Sad Café,* a novelette published with short stories in 1951, was dramatized by Edward Albee in 1963. Paralyzed on the left side from the age of 29, Carson McCullers spent her last years in a wheelchair.

McCulloch, Hugh (b. Dec. 7, 1808, Kennebunk, Maine, U.S.—d. May 24, 1895, near Washington, D.C.), American financier, comptroller of the currency, and secretary of the Treasury.

Having taught school and studied law in Boston, McCulloch moved in 1833 to Fort Wayne, Ind., where he practiced law. He soon turned to banking, becoming cashier and manager of the Fort Wayne branch of the old State Bank of Indiana (1835–56) and president of the new State Bank (1857–63). He won a reputation for prudent bank management during the panics of 1837 and 1857. As comptroller of the currency (1863–65) he successfully implemented the National Bank Act of 1863, authorizing the issuance of national bank notes by national banks. As secretary

Hugh McCulloch
By courtesy of the Library of Congress, Washington, D.C.

of the Treasury (1865–69) under Presidents Abraham Lincoln and Andrew Johnson, McCulloch attempted to return the United States to the gold standard by withdrawing from circulation paper money issued during the Civil War. He was thwarted, however, by public opposition to the plan. In 1870 he went to England as a member of the banking house of Jay Cooke, McCulloch and Company. He again served briefly as secretary of the Treasury under President Chester A. Arthur (October 1884–March 1885).

McCulloch, Sir James (b. 1819, Glasgow, Scot.—d. Jan. 31, 1893, Ewell, Surrey, Eng.), prime minister of Victoria, Australia, whose first government (1863–68) was cited as the most stable ministry in the province up to that time.

McCulloch went to Australia in 1853 to open a branch office in Melbourne for his mercantile firm. In 1854 he was nominated to the Legislative Council and in 1856 was elected to the Legislative Assembly for Wimmera. When he failed to form a ministry in 1857, he became minister of trade and customs and treasurer in 1859.

In his first ministry, McCulloch championed the popular struggle for protective tariffs against the resistance of the Legislative Council, and he eventually won. He was again prime minister in July 1868–September 1869; April 1870–June 1871; and 1875–77. Soon after his 1877 defeat he returned to England. He was knighted in 1870.

McCulloch, John R(amsay) (b. March 1, 1789, Whithorn, Wigtownshire, Scot.—d. Nov. 11, 1864, London, Eng.), Scottish-born economist and statistician whose work as a publicist did much to assure general acceptance of the economic principles of his contemporary, the economist David Ricardo.

A student of political economy, McCulloch wrote articles for *The Edinburgh Review* (1816–37), edited the leading liberal newspa-

John McCulloch, detail of a portrait by Daniel Macnee, 1840; in the National Portrait Gallery, London
By courtesy of the National Portrait Gallery, London

per, *The Scotsman* (1818–20), and taught political economy at University College, London (1828–32). In 1832 he published his *Dictionary of Practical, Theoretical, and Historical Commerce and Commercial Navigation,* later largely incorporated into his *Statistical Account of the British Empire* (1837), both authoritative reference works.

McCulloch's *Discourse on the Rise, Progress, Peculiar Objects and Importance of Political Economy* (1824) has been considered the first formal history of economic thought. His annotated editions of Adam Smith's *Wealth of Nations* (1828) and of *Works of David Ricardo* (1846) and his bibliographic work, *The Literature of Political Economy* (1845), were pioneer studies in economic historiography.

McCulloch v. Maryland, U.S. Supreme Court case decided in 1819, in which Chief Justice John Marshall affirmed the constitutional doctrine of Congress' "implied powers." It determined that Congress had not only the powers expressly conferred upon it by the Constitution but also all authority "appropriate" to carry out such powers. In the specific case the court held that Congress had the power to incorporate a national bank, despite the Constitution's silence on both the creation of corporations and the chartering of banks. It was concluded that since a national bank would facilitate the accomplishment of purposes expressly confided to the federal government, such as the collection of taxes and the maintenance of armed forces, Congress had a choice of means to achieve these proper ends. The doctrine of implied powers became a powerful force in the steady growth of federal power.

McCutcheon, John T(inney) (b. May 6, 1870, South Raub, Ind., U.S.—d. June 10, 1949, Lake Forest, Ill.), U.S. newspaper cartoonist and writer particularly noted for cartoons in which Midwestern rural life was treated with gentle, sympathetic humour.

After receiving his degree in 1889 from Purdue University, Lafayette, Ind., McCutcheon went to Chicago, where he became a cartoonist on the *Chicago Morning News.* In the 14 years he was with the paper, its name changed from *News* to *News-Record* to *Chicago Record* and finally to *Record-Herald.* He frequently illustrated the stories of the humorist George Ade. McCutcheon's first political cartoons were published during the presidential campaign of 1896. As a correspondent he covered the Spanish American War, the Philippine insurrection, and the Boer War.

At the *Record* McCutcheon began a series of pictures and text describing life in the fictional Illinois town he called Bird Center. The series, continued when he joined the *Chicago*

John T. McCutcheon's Pulitzer Prize cartoon, drawn 1931

By courtesy of the *Chicago Tribune*

Tribune in 1903, stressed the wholesome values of small-town life. A collection of the Bird Center cartoons was published in 1904. In 1909 he went on a big-game hunt in Africa with the naturalist Carl Akeley, and for part of the time he was with Pres. Theodore Roosevelt's safari, which he reported for the *Tribune.* He later covered World War I, from the German and later from the Allied fronts.

As a cartoonist McCutcheon portrayed the American scene for the *Tribune* for more than 40 years. Perhaps his most famous cartoon was "Injun Summer," first printed on Sept. 30, 1907. The top half of the drawing shows a small boy and his grandfather looking over an Indiana cornfield; in the bottom half shocks of corn were transformed into tepees and the field into an Indian camp by the boy's imagination. "Injun Summer" became a regular fall feature in the *Tribune.* He received a Pulitzer Prize in 1932 for a cartoon dealing with bank failure. *John McCutcheon's Book* (1948), by Franklin J. Meine and John Merryweather, contained a collection of McCutcheon's drawings; his autobiography is *Drawn from Memory* (1950).

MacDiarmid, Alan G. (b. April 14, 1927, Masterson, N.Z.), New Zealand-born American chemist who, with Hideki Shirakawa and Alan J. Heeger, was awarded the Nobel Prize for Chemistry in 2000 for their discovery that certain plastics can be chemically modified to conduct electricity almost as readily as metals.

MacDiarmid earned Ph.D.'s in chemistry at the University of Wisconsin at Madison (1953) and the University of Cambridge (1955). He then joined the faculty of the University of Pennsylvania, becoming full professor in 1964 and Blanchard Professor of Chemistry in 1988.

During a visit to Japan in the mid-1970s, MacDiarmid met Shirakawa, who reported that he and his colleagues had synthesized polyacetylene, a polymer that was known to exist as a black powder, into a metallic-looking material that still behaved as an insulator. In 1977 the two men and Heeger, collaborating at the University of Pennsylvania, decided to introduce impurities into the polymer much as in the doping process used to tailor the conductive properties of semiconductors. Doping with iodine increased polyacetylene's electrical conductivity by a factor of 10 million, which made it as conductive as some metals. The discovery led scientists to uncover other conductive polymers. These polymers contributed to the emerging field of molecular electronics and were predicted to find application in computers.

MacDiarmid, Hugh, pseudonym of CHRISTOPHER MURRAY GRIEVE (b. Aug. 11, 1892, Langholm, Dumfriesshire [now in Dumfries and Galloway], Scot.—d. Sept. 9, 1978, Edinburgh), preeminent Scottish poet of the first half of the 20th century and leader of the Scottish literary renaissance.

The son of a postman, MacDiarmid was educated at Langholm Academy and the University of Edinburgh. After serving in World War I he became a journalist in Montrose, Angus, where he edited three issues of the first postwar Scottish verse anthology, *Northern Numbers* (1921–23). In 1922 he founded the monthly *Scottish Chapbook,* in which he advocated a Scottish literary revival and published the lyrics of "Hugh MacDiarmid," later collected as *Sangschaw* (1925) and *Penny Wheep* (1926). Rejecting English as a medium for Scottish poetry, MacDiarmid scrutinized the pretensions and hypocrisies of modern society in verse written in "synthetic Scots," an amalgam of elements from various middle Scots dialects and folk ballads and other literary sources. He achieved notable success both in his lyrics and in *A Drunk Man Looks at the Thistle* (1926), an extended rhapsody. Later, as he became increasingly involved in metaphysical speculation and accepted Marxist philosophy, he wrote Scotticized English in *To Circumjack Cencrastus* (1930) and archaic

Hugh MacDiarmid

Mark Gerson—Camera Press

Scots in *Scots Unbound* (1932), then returned to standard English in *Stony Limits* (1934) and *Second Hymn to Lenin* (1935). His later style was best represented in *A Kist of Whistles* (1947) and *In Memoriam James Joyce* (1955). Autobiographical volumes include *Lucky Poet* (1943) and *The Company I've Kept* (1966). His *Complete Poems* appeared in 1974. MacDiarmid became professor of literature to the Royal Scottish Academy (1974) and president of the Poetry Society (1976).

McDivitt, James A(lton) (b. June 10, 1929, Chicago), U.S. astronaut and business executive. McDivitt joined the U.S. Air Force in 1951 and flew 145 combat missions in Korea. In 1959 he graduated first in his engineering class at the University of Michigan, Ann Arbor. He was an experimental test pilot at Edwards Air Force Base, California, when he was chosen as an astronaut in 1962. McDivitt was the command pilot of Gemini 4 (launched June 3, 1965); a flight that included the first space walk by a U.S. astronaut, and was commander of Apollo 9 (launched March 3, 1969). He was then manager of the Apollo spacecraft program until he retired from the Air Force in 1972 with the rank of brigadier general and entered private business.

MacDonagh, Donagh (b. 1912—d. Jan. 1, 1968, Dublin, Ire.), poet, playwright, and balladeer, prominent representative of lively Irish entertainment in the mid-20th century.

MacDonagh was the son of Thomas MacDonagh, a poet and leader of the Easter Rising (1916). After attending the National University of Ireland, Dublin, MacDonagh practiced law (1936–46) and was a district judge (1946–68). His varied literary career includes comedies such as *Happy as Larry* (1946) and *God's Gentry* (1951) and poetry such as *Veterans and Other Poems* (1941). Also an authority on the traditional Irish ballad, MacDonagh was a popular radio and stage performer in the 1940s and '50s. With E.S. Lennox Robinson, he edited *The Oxford Book of Irish Verse* (1958).

Macdonald, Flora (b. 1722, Milton, South Uist, Outer Hebrides, Scot.—d. March 5, 1790, Kingsburgh House, Skye, Inner Hebrides), Scottish Jacobite heroine who helped Charles Edward, the Young Pretender, the Stuart claimant to the British throne, escape from Scotland after his defeat in the Jacobite

Flora Macdonald, detail of an oil painting by Allan Ramsay; in the Ashmolean Museum, Oxford

By courtesy of the Ashmolean Museum, Oxford

rebellion of 1745–46. She was immortalized in Jacobite ballads and legends.

The Pretender suffered his final defeat of the war at Culloden in April 1746, and, pursued by the English, he took refuge in the Hebrides, where Flora was visiting some friends. She allowed him to join her party disguised as Betty Burke, an Irish spinning maid, and obtained permission from the English for the group to sail to Skye (also in the Hebrides). At Skye, Flora and the Pretender parted, but the English learned of her role in the escape. She was imprisoned in the Tower of London but was pardoned in 1747. Three years later she married Allan Macdonald of Kingsburgh, and in 1774 they emigrated to North Carolina. Allan was captured while fighting for the British in the American Revolutionary War, and Flora returned alone to Scotland in 1779. She was later joined by her husband. Alexander MacGregor's *Life of Flora Macdonald* (1882) has frequently been reprinted.

Macdonald, George (b. Dec. 10, 1824, Huntly, Aberdeen, Scot.—d. Sept. 18, 1905, Ashtead, Surrey, Eng.), novelist of Scottish

George Macdonald, engraving
BBC Hulton Picture Library

life, poet, and writer of Christian allegories of man's pilgrimage back to God, who is remembered chiefly, however, for his allegorical fairy stories, which have continued to delight children and their elders. He became a Congregational minister, then a free-lance preacher and lecturer. In 1855 he published a poetic tragedy, *Within and Without,* and after that he made literature his profession. Of his literature for adults, *Phantastes: A Faerie Romance for Men and Women* (1858) and *Lilith* (1895) are good examples. Although his best known book for children is *At the Back of the North Wind* (1871), his best and most enduring works are *The Princess and the Goblin* (1872) and its sequel, *The Princess and Curdie* (1873).

Macdonald, Jacques (-Étienne-Joseph)-Alexandre, DUC (duke) DE TARENTE (b. Nov. 17, 1765, Sedan, Fr.—d. Sept. 25, 1840, Courcelles), French general who was appointed marshal of the empire by Napoleon.

Marshal Macdonald, detail from a portrait by Jacques-Louis David; in the Musée National Bonnat, Bayonne
Giraudon—Art Resource/EB Inc.

The son of a Scottish adherent of the exiled British Stuart dynasty, who had served in a Scots regiment in France, he joined the French Army and was a colonel when the wars of the French Revolution broke out. He was promoted to general in 1793 and to general of division in 1796.

In May 1798 Macdonald was sent to Italy, where he became governor of Rome and occupied Naples in March 1799; however, his forces were decisively routed by the Russian general A.V. Suvorov at Trebbia, Italy, on June 17–19, 1799, while he was marching north to relieve Gen. Victor Moreau at Genoa. After the coup d'etat of 18 Brumaire (Nov. 9, 1799), in which Napoleon became first consul, Macdonald commanded the right wing of the Army of the Rhine. In 1800 he won Napoleon's admiration and praise for his winter crossing of the Splügen Pass from Switzerland into Lombardy, an operation that has been compared to Napoleon's own crossing of the St. Bernard Pass and one that contributed to the Treaty of Lunéville between France and Austria (1801).

Macdonald's involvement in the anti-Bonapartist intrigues of General Moreau in 1804 led to his discharge, and he was not recalled to active duty until 1809, when Napoleon judged his military talents indispensable. After contributing to the Austrian defeat at Wagram in July 1809, he was made marshal of the empire and duc de Tarente. He served in Austria in 1809–10 and in Catalonia in 1810–11, but he played no active part in the Russian campaign, being posted in Courland (Latvia). He was defeated by the Prussian marshal Blücher in Silesia at the Battle of Katzbach (1813) and barely escaped with his life at the decisive French defeat at Leipzig (October 1813).

Although he was reluctant to recognize the abdication of Napoleon, he served Louis XVIII loyally and did not rejoin Napoleon during the Hundred Days. After the Second Restoration of the Bourbons, he was appointed major general of the Royal Guard and named to the Legion of Honour.

Macdonald, Sir James Ronald Leslie (b. Feb. 8, 1862, Aberdeen, Aberdeenshire, Scot.—d. June 27, 1927, Bournemouth, Hampshire, Eng.), British soldier, engineer, and explorer who carried out a geographical exploration of British East Africa (now Kenya and Uganda) while surveying for a railroad and later mapped the previously untravelled mountains from East Africa to the Sudan.

After serving as an engineer in the British Army in India, Macdonald was appointed chief engineer (1891) for the projected Uganda railroad between Mombasa (on the Kenya coast) and Lake Victoria (in western Uganda). Made acting commissioner of the Uganda Protectorate in 1893, he resumed his duty in India (1894). In 1897 he was recalled to Africa during Lord Kitchener's campaign to reconquer the Sudan. In that year he undertook to map the territory between Lake Victoria and Fashoda. His work was interrupted by a mutiny of Muslim troops in Uganda, but he was able to complete the mission in 1899.

Macdonald subsequently served in China, India, and Mauritius. He was knighted in 1904.

Macdonald, Sir John (Alexander) (b. Jan. 11, 1815, Glasgow—d. June 6, 1891, Ottawa), the first prime minister of the Dominion of Canada (1867–73, 1878–91), who led Canada through its period of early growth. Though accused of devious and unscrupulous methods, he is remembered for his achievements.

Sir John Macdonald
National Film Board of Canada Phototheque

Macdonald emigrated from Scotland to Kingston, in what is now Ontario, in 1820. He was called to the bar in 1836. After the British Parliament united Upper and Lower Canada as Canada West (now in Ontario) and Canada East (now in Quebec) in the Act of Union of 1840, Macdonald was elected to the assembly of the Province of Canada as a Conservative for Kingston in 1844. From 1848 to 1854, while his party was in opposition, Macdonald worked at promoting the British America League, designed to unify Canada and strengthen its ties to Great Britain. Growing sympathy for reform led him to bring about a coalition government in 1854 with Sir George Étienne Cartier (*q.v.*), leader of Canada East, out of which developed the Liberal-Conservative Party, with Macdonald its leader. He became prime minister of the Province of Canada in 1857. In June 1864 Macdonald and Cartier joined with their chief opponent, George Brown, in order to further the scheme of confederation of British North America. After conferences in Charlottetown, P.E.I.; Quebec; and London, the British North America Act was passed (1867), creating the Dominion of Canada, and Macdonald became its first leader. He was created Knight Commander of the Bath in that year in recognition of his services to the British Empire.

Under Macdonald's leadership, the dominion quickly expanded to include the provinces of Manitoba (1870), British Columbia (1871), and Prince Edward Island (1873). The Pacific Scandal of 1873, in which the government was accused of taking bribes in regard to the Pacific railway contract, forced Macdonald to resign; but he returned as prime minister five years later and served until his death. Commercial policy was the main issue of the general election of 1878. The Liberals supported free trade; but after several years of depression the country preferred Macdonald's policy of trade protectionism, which he applied swiftly and thoroughly once he had returned to power. He also aided in the completion of the Pacific railway. During his final years, he dealt with challenges to Canadian unity, including a rebellion in the northwest. His guiding principle was always loyalty to the Commonwealth and independence from the United States; he remained true to his declaration, "A British subject I was born; a British subject I will die."

Macdonald, John Sandfield (b. Dec. 12, 1812, St. Raphael, Upper Canada—d. June 1, 1872, Cornwall, Ont., Can.), prime minister of the province of Canada from 1862 to 1864 and first premier of Ontario from 1867 to 1871.

Macdonald was called to the bar in 1840, and the next year he was elected to the Canadian Parliament for Glengarry, a seat he held for 16 years. He supported constitutional government and in 1849–51 served as solicitor general. He held the posts of speaker of the house (1852–54) and attorney general (1858). He was called by Gov. Gen. Lord Monck to form a ministry in 1862 and held office as prime minister of Canada for two years. Macdonald opposed Canadian confederation, but after the Dominion of Canada was created in 1867, he accepted the post of first premier of Ontario and helped settle the relationship of provincial to federal government. When his government was defeated in 1871, Macdonald resigned.

MacDonald, (James) Ramsay (b. Oct. 12, 1866, Lossiemouth, Moray, Scot.—d. Nov. 9, 1937, at sea en route to South America), first Labour Party prime minister of Great Britain, in the Labour governments of 1924 and 1929–31 and in the national coalition government of 1931–35.

The son of an unmarried maidservant, Mac-

Ramsay MacDonald
Central Press Photos Ltd.

Donald ended his elementary education at the age of 12, but he continued at school for another six years, working as a pupil-teacher.

In 1885 he went to work in Bristol, where the activities of the Social Democratic Federation acquainted him with left-wing ideas. Travelling to London the following year, he joined the Fabian Society, was employed in menial office jobs, and worked for a science degree in his spare time until his health broke down. In 1894 he joined the newly founded Independent Labour Party, and the next year he was defeated as a candidate of that party for the House of Commons.

In 1900 he became the first secretary of the Labour Representation Committee (LRC), the true predecessor of the Labour Party. In 1906 he was one of 29 LRC members to win election to the Commons; the LRC thereupon transformed itself into the Labour Party. Five years later he succeeded Keir Hardie as parliamentary leader of the party. He was forced to resign in favour of Arthur Henderson in 1914 after stating that Great Britain was morally wrong in declaring war on Germany. Although he nonetheless insisted that the nation should make every effort to win the war, he lost much of his popularity and was defeated for reelection in 1918. On returning to Parliament in 1922, he was chosen to lead the Labour opposition.

After the election of 1923 the Conservatives remained the largest party in Parliament, but for the first time they were outnumbered by the Labourites and the Liberals combined. H.H. Asquith, leader of the Liberals and a former prime minister, offered to support MacDonald. On Jan. 22, 1924, MacDonald became prime minister and also foreign secretary. Under his leadership that year, Great Britain granted recognition to the Soviet regime in Russia; the Geneva Protocol for security and disarmament (approved by the League of Nations Assembly on Oct. 2, 1924) was initiated; and the threat of violence in Ireland was averted when the British government agreed to cancel the debt owed by the Irish Free State, in return for the Free State's abandonment of its demand for the six northern counties.

A bungled prosecution of J.R. Campbell, a Communist newspaper editor, led to an adverse vote in the Commons. Because of that rebuff and various other factors, the Conservatives regained a majority, and MacDonald resigned Nov. 4, 1924. At the general election of 1929, however, Labour for the first time achieved the largest number of seats, and MacDonald returned as prime minister on June 5. He negotiated an Anglo–U.S. naval limitation treaty (1930), while his foreign secretary, Arthur Henderson, was organizing the World Disarmament Conference at Geneva. At home, the effects of the worldwide economic depression proved beyond the understanding of MacDonald and most of his Cabinet. On Aug. 24, 1931, he offered his resignation, but the next day his Labour colleagues were dismayed to learn that he was remaining in office as head of a coalition, with Conservative and Liberal support. His ability to lead the government was waning, however, and the lord president of the council, Stanley Baldwin, a former Conservative prime minister, became effective head of the government. Finally, on June 7, 1935, MacDonald exchanged offices with Baldwin. He resigned the lord presidency on May 28, 1937, and died later that year on a voyage to South America.

The first volume of Lord Elton's *Life of James Ramsay MacDonald*, covering his career until 1919, appeared in 1939; the second volume was never published. L. MacNeill Weir wrote *The Tragedy of Ramsay MacDonald* (1938). A major biography is David Marquand's *Ramsay MacDonald* (1977).

McDonald Observatory, observatory founded in 1939 by the University of Texas, on the legacy of the Texas financier William J. McDonald, on Mount Locke near Fort Davis, Texas. Its four operating telescopes—all reflectors—include the 9.2-metre (362-inch) Hobby-Eberly Telescope (dedicated 1997), with a segmented primary mirror; the 2.7-metre (107-inch) Harlan J. Smith Telescope; the 2.1-metre (82-inch) Otto Struve Telescope, the facility's original reflector and for years the world's second largest telescope; and a 0.8-metre (30-inch) telescope.

Until 1963 McDonald Observatory was operated jointly with the University of Chicago. Discoveries credited to the observatory include those of Nereid, a moon of Neptune, and Miranda, a moon of Uranus. Principal research has emphasized stellar composition and evolution and the properties of galaxies. Other research specialties include high-speed photometry and lunar laser and satellite ranging.

Macdonald-Wright, Stanton (b. July 8, 1890, Charlottesville, Va., U.S.—d. Aug. 22, 1973, Pacific Palisades, Calif.), painter and teacher, one of the first American Abstract painters, who in 1913–14 founded with Morgan Russell the movement known as Synchromism (*q.v.*), which proclaimed colour to be the basis of expression in painting.

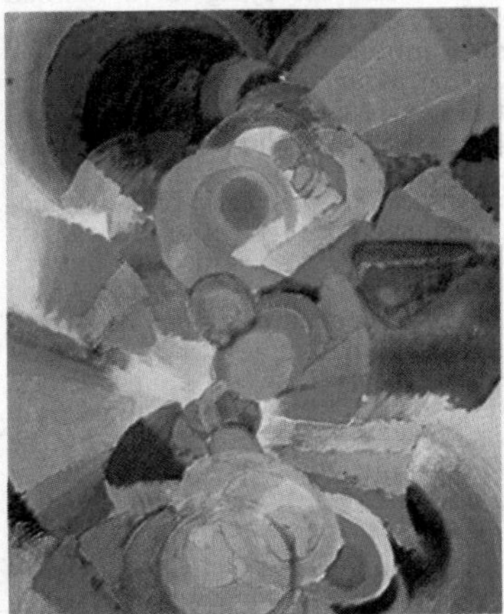

"Abstraction on Spectrum (Organization 5)," oil on canvas by Stanton Macdonald-Wright, 1914; in the Des Moines Art Center, Iowa

By courtesy of the Des Moines Art Center, Iowa, Nathan Emory Coffin Memorial Collection

In 1907 Macdonald-Wright went to Paris to study, and there he became intrigued with the colour theory of the optical scientists Chevreul and Helmholtz and with the formal abstractions of the Cubist painters.

Early Synchromist pictures were renderings of traditional subjects in a representational manner but with vibrant colours. Eventually Macdonald-Wright's pictures became absolute colour abstractions. By 1920, however, his art was no longer avant-garde and had become a compromise between Synchromist abstraction and a traditional representational style. His attention eventually turned toward filmmaking, writing, and teaching art history at the University of California. During the Depression he was again active as a painter and directed and executed WPA projects in the realistic style of American Regionalism. Of these, his murals for the Santa Monica City Hall and Public Library (1935) are most notable.

MacDonnell, Randal: *see* Antrim, Randal MacDonnell, 1st marquess of.

MacDonnell, Sorley Boy, Irish SOMHAIRLE BUIDHE MACDONNELL (b. *c.* 1505, probably Dunluce Castle, near Ballycastle, County Antrim, Ire.—d. 1590, Dunanynie Castle, County Louth), Scots-Irish chieftain of Ulster, foe and captive of the celebrated Shane O'Neill.

From an ancestor who had married Margaret Bisset, heiress of the district on the Antrim coast known as the Glynns (or Glens), MacDonnell inherited a claim to the lordship of that territory; and he was one of the most powerful of the Scottish settlers in Ulster whom the English government tried to bring into subjection. He took an active part in the tribal warfare between his own clan and the MacQuillins and, by defeating the latter at Glenshesk in 1558, acquired the lordship of the Route. He was now too powerful to be neglected by Queen Elizabeth I and her ministers, who were also being troubled by Shane O'Neill. Elizabeth aimed at fomenting the rivalry between the two men and came to terms sometimes with the one and sometimes with the other. Shane O'Neill defeated Sorley Boy near Coleraine in 1564; in 1565 he invaded the Glynns and at Ballycastle won a decisive victory, in which James MacDonnell and Sorley Boy were taken prisoners. James soon afterward died, but Sorley Boy remained O'Neill's captive until 1567, when Shane was murdered by the MacDonnells at Cushendun.

After the massacre of his family by the English in 1575, Sorley Boy made a successful raid on Carrickfergus and reestablished his power in the Glynns and the Route. His position was further strengthened by an alliance with Turlough Luineach O'Neill and by a formidable immigration of followers from the Scottish islands. In 1585 he regained possession of Dunluce Castle. Elizabeth's representative, Sir John Perrot, reluctantly opened negotiations with Sorley Boy, who in 1586 made submission. He obtained a grant to himself and his heirs of all the Route country between the rivers Bann and Bush, with certain other lands to the east, and was made constable of Dunluce Castle. For the rest of his life he gave no trouble to the English government.

McDonnell Douglas Corporation, former aerospace firm, with headquarters in St. Louis, Mo., that was a major U.S. producer of jet fighters, commercial aircraft, and space vehicles. It merged with Boeing Company in 1997.

McDonnell Douglas was formed in 1967 through the merger of Douglas Aircraft Company with McDonnell Aircraft Corporation. Douglas Aircraft originated in 1921 as Douglas Company, established by the American aircraft designer Donald Douglas. The company was restructured in 1928 as Douglas Aircraft Company, and a few years later it began building its "DC" (Douglas Commercial) series of passenger planes. The twin-engine DC-3 (first flown 1935) became the model for future commercial aircraft through its unprecedented comfort, reliability, speed, and low maintenance cost. With its military derivative, the C-47 transport, the DC-3 was the best-selling commercial airframe in history.

During World War II, Douglas Aircraft contributed some 29,000 warplanes, one-sixth of the U.S. airborne fleet. After the war it dominated the commercial air routes with its piston-engine DC-6 and DC-7 airliners. Its postwar military products included the carrier-based A4D Skyhawk bomber and the Nike and Thor missiles, the latter of which was modified for use as a space launcher. In 1965 Douglas first flew its DC-9 jetliner, which became its most successful transport since the DC-3.

McDonnell Aircraft was founded in 1939 by the American aeronautical engineer James Smith McDonnell. After an initial struggle, the company grew rapidly as a maker of airplane parts. Because of its research into jet propulsion, it received a U.S. Navy contract to build the FH-1 Phantom, which, in 1946, became the first jet aircraft used on an aircraft carrier. With the success of its F-4 Phantom II fighter (1958), McDonnell grew quickly to become a major U.S. defense supplier. In the 1960s it built the first American manned spacecraft—the Mercury and Gemini space capsules.

In the mid-1960s McDonnell sought to enter the commercial aircraft market. At the same time, despite the success of the DC-9, the financial condition of Douglas Aircraft was deteriorating. In 1967 McDonnell purchased Douglas and took the name McDonnell Douglas Corporation. It subsequently introduced several notable aircraft, including the DC-10 jetliner and the F-15 Eagle and F/A-18 Hornet fighters. In 1984 McDonnell Douglas purchased Hughes Helicopters, Inc., from the estate of Howard Hughes. The loss of a contract to build a next-generation fighter prototype for the U.S. armed forces in 1996 and continued poor sales of its commercial aircraft led McDonnell Douglas to its merger with Boeing the following year.

MacDonnell Ranges, mountain system in south central Northern Territory, Australia, a series of bare quartzite and sandstone parallel ridges that rise from a plateau 2,000 ft (600 m) above sea level and extend east and west of the town of Alice Springs for about 230 mi (380 km). They reach a maximum elevation of 4,954 ft at Mt. Ziel and are the source of the Finke, Todd, and Plenty rivers and Ellery Creek. Some streams have carved spectacular gorges (Simpson Gap, Standley Chasm) that contain luxuriant vegetation. One striking feature is the coloration of the stone, which constantly varies as the direction of the sun changes. The MacDonnells are the best watered district in central Australia. They were explored in 1860 by the Scot John McDouall Stuart and were named after Sir Richard MacDonnell, governor of South Australia (1855–62). In 1872 the Overland Telegraph Line was built across the ranges through Heavitree Gap near Alice Springs.

The MacDonnell Ranges west of Alice Springs, Northern Territory, Australia

By courtesy of the Australian National Travel Association

Macdonough, Thomas (b. Dec. 31, 1783, The Trap, Del., U.S.—d. Nov. 10, 1825, at sea en route from the Mediterranean Sea to New York City), U.S. naval officer who won one of the most important victories in the War of 1812 at the Battle of Plattsburg (or Lake Champlain) against the British.

Entering the navy as a midshipman in 1800, Macdonough saw service during the U.S. war with Tripoli (1801–05). When war broke out with England, his major assignment was to cruise the lakes between Canada and the United States. When enemy ground forces threatened Plattsburg, N.Y.—the U.S. Army headquarters on the northern frontier—Macdonough's foresight and painstaking preparation for battle paid off. On Sept. 11, 1814, his 14-ship fleet met the British in the harbour and after several hours of fighting forced the 16-vessel squadron to surrender, thus saving New York and Vermont from invasion.

Macdonough, detail from an engraving by T. Gimbrede after a portrait by John Wesley Jarvis

By courtesy of the U.S. Navy

The victory brought Macdonough the thanks of the U.S. Congress and promotion to captain. More important, it left the British no grounds for territorial claims in the Great Lakes area at the peace negotiations that followed. In failing health, he died en route home after serving on various European assignments.

McDougall, William (b. Jan. 25, 1822, near York, Upper Canada—d. May 29, 1905, Ottawa), one of the fathers of Canadian Confederation who later served unsuccessfully as lieutenant governor of the Northwest Territories.

McDougall practiced law as a solicitor, being called to the bar in 1862. As one of the leaders of the "Clear Grit," or radical wing of the Reform Party, he founded in 1850 the *North American,* a newspaper that expressed the radicals' political views. This paper was absorbed by *The Globe* (Toronto) in 1857, when McDougall became an associate of *The Globe*'s publisher George Brown, the Liberal Party leader. The following year McDougall was elected to the legislature of the united province of Canada. He was appointed commissioner of crownlands in the John Sandfield Macdonald–Louis Victor Sicotte administration in 1862, and in 1864 he became provincial secretary.

McDougall attended the Charlottetown, P.E.I.; Quebec; and Westminster conferences leading to Confederation, which was achieved in 1867, when the British Parliament passed the British North America Act. As one of the leading liberals in the first Dominion government, McDougall was minister of public works in 1867–69, during which time he accompanied Sir George Ètienne Cartier to England to arrange the acquisition of Hudson's Bay Company land for the Dominion of Canada. McDougall took up the post of lieutenant governor of Rupert's Land and the Northwest Territories in 1869, but his attempts to exert his authority met with resistance from the Red River settlers, who repelled him at Pembina.

McDougall was removed from office in 1869 and soon lost political influence. After retiring from public life, he resumed his legal practice in 1873.

McDougall, William (b. June 22, 1871, Chadderton, Lancashire, Eng.—d. Nov. 28, 1938, Durham, N.C., U.S.), British-born U.S. psychologist influential in establishing experimental and physiological psychology and author of *An Introduction to Social Psychology* (1908; 30th ed. 1960), which did much to stimulate widespread study of the basis of social behaviour.

Soon after becoming a fellow of St. John's College, Cambridge, McDougall joined the Cambridge Anthropological Expedition to the Torres Strait, between Australia and New Guinea, and there administered psychological tests to the native inhabitants. He then went to Germany, where, at the University of Göttingen, he conducted research on colour vision. His interest in psychical research also dates from that period. An assistant at the experimental laboratory, University College, London (1901), he was appointed reader in mental philosophy at the University of Oxford (1904), where he wrote *Physiological Psychology* (1905), demonstrating the value of a thoroughgoing biological approach in place of the traditional philosophical approach.

McDougall's well-known *Introduction to Social Psychology* developed a Darwinian theory of human behaviour based on the assumption of inherited instinct, or tendency, to note particular stimuli and to respond to them for the purpose of attaining some goal. Should response be delayed, an emotional reaction follows. Diversification and stabilization of response result from learning. A classic work, *Body and Mind* (1911), subtitled *A History and Defense of Animism* represented the kind of espousal of unpopular causes that increasingly tended to isolate McDougall from colleagues.

Opposed to mechanistic interpretations of human behaviour, he wrote *The Group Mind* (1920), an attempt to interpret national life and character that was intended as a sequel to his *Social Psychology.* Its poor reception was partly responsible for his move that year to the United States and a professorship at Harvard University. Maintaining that the basic human activity is searching for goals, he alienated himself from the dominant U.S. behaviourists, who confined psychology to observable evidence of organismic activity. In an attempt to demonstrate inheritance of acquired characteristics, he published *Outline of Psychology* (1923) and *Outline of Abnormal Psychology* (1926). Finding his situation at Harvard unsatisfactory, in 1927 he moved to Duke University, Durham, N.C. There he developed a psychology department and continued various research, including work in parapsychology.

MacDowell, Edward (Alexander) (b. Dec. 18, 1860, New York City—d. Jan. 23, 1908, New York City), U.S. composer known especially for his piano pieces in smaller forms. As one of the first to incorporate native materials into his works, he helped establish an independent American musical idiom.

MacDowell first studied in New York with Teresa Carreño and then at the Conservatoire (1876–78) in Paris. In 1878 he went to Germany to study composition with Joachim Raff at the Frankfurt Conservatory and later taught piano at Darmstadt. In 1882 Raff introduced MacDowell to Liszt, who arranged for him to play his *Modern Suite No. 1* at Zürich. In 1884 he went to the U.S., where he married his former pupil, Marian Nevins (1857–1956). He returned with her to Wiesbaden and remained there until 1887. The following year he settled in the U.S. In 1889 he played in New York City the first performance of his *Second Piano Concerto in D Minor,* his most successful larger work, one that retains popularity throughout the world.

In 1896 he was invited to establish a department of music at Columbia University, New York City. As a result of disagreement with the university, he resigned in 1904, becoming the subject of much unpleasant publicity, which may have contributed to his mental collapse. He eventually receded to infantilism from which he never recovered. A public appeal for funds was made on his behalf in 1906. Shortly before his death, his wife organized the MacDowell Colony at their residence in Peterborough, N.H., as a permanent institution in the form of a summer residence for American composers and writers.

MacDowell's music is said to derive from the contemporary Romantic movements in Europe, his lyrical style suggesting Grieg, his harmony, Schumann and sometimes Liszt. Almost all his works have literary or pictorial associations. His early symphonic poems include *Hamlet and Ophelia* (1885), *Lancelot and Elaine* (1888), *Lamia* (1889), and *The Saracens* (1891). More distinctive is his orchestral *Indian Suite* (1892), based on Indian tunes. His songs, though derivative, are lyrical; but he is considered at his best in his piano music, particularly in small pieces, when he shows the gifts of a sensitive miniaturist. The best of his piano works are thought to be the suites *Sea Pieces* (1898) and *Fireside Tales* (1902) and the imaginative evocations of the American scene in the albums *Woodland Sketches* (1896) and *New England Idylls* (1902). His four piano sonatas, *Tragica* (1893), *Eroica* (1895), *Norse* (1900), and *Keltic* (1901), are cited as ambitious attempts at programmatic music in classical forms.

mace, spice consisting of the dried aril, or lacy covering, of the nutmeg fruit of *Myristica fragrans,* a tropical evergreen tree. Mace has a slightly warm taste and a fragrance similar to that of nutmeg. It is used to flavour bakery, meat, and fish dishes; to flavour sauces and vegetables; and in preserving and pickling.

Nutmegs showing the aril from which mace is produced
W.H. Hodge

In the processing of mace, the crimson-coloured aril is removed from the nutmeg that it envelops and is flattened out and dried for 10 to 14 days; its colour changes to pale yellow, orange, or tan. Whole dry mace consists of flat pieces—branched or segmented, smooth, horny, and brittle—about 40 mm (1.6 inches) long.

Mace, James, byname JEM MACE (b. April 8, 1831, Beeston, Norfolk, Eng.—d. Nov. 30, 1910, Jarrow, Durham), professional boxer and English heavyweight champion who is considered by some authorities to have been world champion. He was the first fighter of consequence to show interest in the Queensberry Rules.

Traveling as a youth with a show booth in which he played the violin and gave boxing exhibitions, Mace attracted the attention of a showman and former boxer. He began to fight in earnest in the early 1850s. Throughout his life he combined innkeeping and circus performing with fighting. Mace weighed only 160 pounds (73 kg), but he overcame his lack of bulk with speed and an effective left jab. He was the model of scientific boxing in England, as James J. Corbett later was in the United States. Mace won the English middleweight championship in 1860. He then won the English heavyweight title in 1861 and lost it the next year but once more was recognized as champion when his conqueror, Tom King, refused to fight him again.

Boxing as an international sport was advanced by Mace's visit to North America in 1870–71. On May 10, 1870, at Kennerville, La., he defeated Tom Allen in 10 rounds in a match advertised as the world championship. Mace is thus regarded as the last world heavyweight champion under London Prize Ring Rules. He retired late in 1871, but on Feb. 7, 1890, at almost 59, he lost to the world heavyweight contender Charley Mitchell in three rounds in an attempt to regain the English title. At a time when most prizefighters were considered highly dubious persons, Mace was universally respected for his integrity.

Macedo, José Agostinho de (b. Sept. 11, 1761, Beja, Port.—d. Oct. 2, 1831, Pedrouços), Portuguese didactic poet, critic, and pamphleteer notable for his acerbity.

Macedo took vows as an Augustinian in 1778. Because of his turbulent character he spent much time in prison and was constantly transferred from one community to another. In 1792 he was unfrocked but obtained a papal brief that gave him the status of a secular priest. He was soon recognized as the leading pulpit orator of the day and in 1802 was appointed one of the royal preachers.

The best of his didactic poems are *A Meditação* ("The Meditation") and *Newton* (1813). He also founded and wrote for a large number of journals, and the tone and temper of these and of his political pamphlets caused one of his biographers to call him the "chief libeler" of Portugal. His malignity reached its height in a satiric poem, *Os Burros* (1812–14; "The Asses"), in which he pilloried, by name, men and women of all grades of society, living and dead. From about 1823 he was the virulent champion of the absolutist reaction.

Macedonia, ancient kingdom centred on the plain in the northeastern corner of the Greek peninsula, at the head of the Gulf of Thérmai. In the 4th century BC it achieved hegemony over Greece and conquered lands as far east as the Indus River, establishing a short-lived empire that introduced the Hellenistic Age of ancient Greek civilization.

The cultural links of prehistoric Macedonia were mainly with Greece and Anatolia. A people of unknown ethnic origins who called themselves Macedonians are known from about 700 BC, when they pushed eastward from their home on the Haliacmon (Aliákmon) River under the leadership of King Perdiccas I and his successors. By the 5th century BC the Macedonians had adopted the Greek language and had forged a unified kingdom. Athenian control of the coastal regions forced Macedonian rulers to concentrate on bringing the uplands and plains of Macedonia under their sway—a task finally achieved by their king Amyntas III (reigned *c.* 393–370/369).

Two of Amyntas' sons, Alexander II and Perdiccas III, reigned only briefly. Amyntas' third son, Philip II, assumed control in the name of Perdiccas' infant heir; but having restored order he made himself king (reigned 359–336) and raised Macedonia to a predominant position in Greece.

Philip's son Alexander III (reigned 336–323; *see* Alexander III the Great) overthrew the Achaemenian (Persian) Empire and expanded Macedonia's dominion to the Nile and Indus rivers. On Alexander's death at Babylon his generals divided up the satrapies (provinces) of his empire and used them as bases in a struggle to acquire the whole. From 321 to 301 warfare was almost continual. Macedonia itself remained the heart of the empire, and its possession (along with the control of Greece) was keenly contested. Antipater (Alexander's regent in Europe) and his son

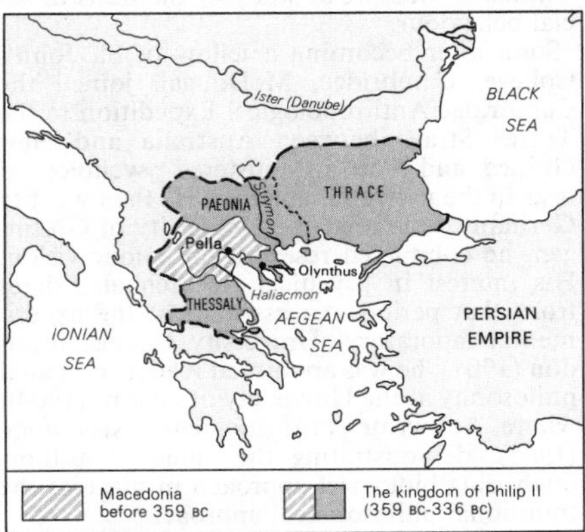

Ancient Macedonia

Cassander managed to retain control of Macedonia and Greece until Cassander's death (297), which threw Macedonia into civil war. After a six-year rule (294–288) by Demetrius I Poliorcetes, Macedonia again fell into a state of internal confusion, intensified by Galatian marauders from the north. In 277 Antigonus II Gonatas, the capable son of Demetrius, repulsed the Galatians and was hailed as king by the Macedonian army. Under him the country achieved a stable monarchy—the Antigonid dynasty, which ruled Macedonia from 277 to 168.

Under Philip V (reigned 221–179) and his son Perseus (reigned 179–168), Macedonia clashed with Rome and lost. (*See* Macedonian Wars.) Under Roman control Macedonia at first (168–146) formed four independent republics without common bonds. In 146, however, it became a Roman province with the four sections as administrative units. Macedonia remained the bulwark of Greece, and the northern frontiers saw frequent campaigning against neighbouring tribes. Toward AD 400 it was divided into the provinces of Macedonia and Macedonia *secunda,* within the diocese of Moesia.

Macedonia, Bulgarian MAKEDONIYA, Modern Greek MAKEDHONÍA, Serbo-Croatian and Macedonian MAKEDONIJA, region in the south-central part of the Balkan Peninsula that comprises northern and northeastern Greece, the southwestern corner of Bulgaria, and the independent Republic of Macedonia.

Land. Macedonia's traditional boundary on the east is the lower Néstos (Mesta in Bulgaria) River and the western slopes of the Rhodope Mountains, which straddle the Greek-Bulgarian frontier. On the north the boundary is marked by the Široka, Skopska Crna Gora, and Šar mountains, bordering southern Serbia. On the west the boundary is marked by the Korab range and by Lakes Ohrid and Prespa, which straddle the Albanian-Macedonian border. The region is bordered on the southwest by the Pindus Mountains and on the south by the valley of the Aliákmon River, which reaches the Gulf of Salonika near Mount Olympus. Including the Chalcidice Peninsula, this stretch of land covers about 25,900 square miles (67,100 square km). About 50 percent lies in Greece, with its centre at the port of Thessaloníki, and 10 percent in Bulgaria, with its centre at Blagoevgrad. The Republic of Macedonia, with its capital at Skopje, occupies the rest.

The Macedonian region ranges from the high plateaus and mountain peaks of Bulgaria and the Macedonian republic to the wide, flat, and almost treeless floodplains of the lower Vardar and Struma rivers in Greece (where the rivers are known as the Axiós and Strimón, respectively). Since ancient times, Macedonia has had strategic importance as a crossroads linking the Adriatic and Aegean coasts with the Bosporus and the Danube River, respectively. The Byzantine and Ottoman empires, both based in Constantinople (now Istanbul, Turkey), considered it essential to hold Macedonia, and in the 19th century the region figured largely in Austria's *Drang nach Osten* ("Drive to the East") toward Constantinople and in Russia's attempts to secure passage to the Mediterranean through the Dardanelles. When the national consciousness of the Balkan peoples began to waken, the European Great Powers found that drawing international frontiers along strategic or economic lines could not easily be reconciled with ethnic considerations, and the Macedonian Question became a problem of international magnitude.

History. Macedonia owes its name to the ancient kingdom of Macedonia (or Macedon). Centred in the southern part of the region, this kingdom seems to have been largely Greek-speaking, with Thracian and Illyrian admixtures. By the 4th century BC, it had extended its rule northward into the Balkan Peninsula and throughout the Mediterranean. In the 2nd century BC, Macedonia was made into a Roman province.

When the Roman Empire was divided in the 4th century AD into eastern and western halves, Macedonia was in the eastern part, which became the Byzantine Empire. By that time the population of Macedonia had been largely Christianized. Macedonia's Greek ethnic composition was overturned by the invasion of Slavic peoples into the Balkans in the 6th and 7th centuries AD. Most of the region subsequently fell under the sway of the first Bulgarian empire in the 9th century. The Bulgarians were Christianized during this period by disciples of Saints Cyril and Methodius, whose adaptation of Greek characters to a Slavonic dialect spoken in southern Macedonia eventually became the Cyrillic alphabet. For the rest of the Middle Ages parts of the region were variously ruled by the Byzantine Empire, the second Bulgarian empire, and the Serbian empire. The groundwork was thus laid for the conflicting national claims to Macedonia that emerged in the modern era.

Macedonia fell under the sway of the Ottoman Empire in the late 14th century, and the area was subsequently colonized by significant numbers of Muslim Turks and Albanians, thus further complicating the region's ethnic fabric. In the late 15th century sizable numbers of Sephardic Jews who had been expelled from Spain settled in the towns of Macedonia (especially Thessaloníki), where they competed with the Greeks for local trade.

In 1878, after winning the Russo-Turkish War of 1877–78, Russia by the Treaty of San Stefano compelled the Ottomans to grant independence to Bulgaria and give that revived nation all of Macedonia except Thessaloníki and the Chalcidice Peninsula. This settlement was soon overturned by the major European powers, who in the Treaty of Berlin that year returned Macedonia to Turkey, allowing it to keep its Christian administration. For the next three decades Macedonia was coveted by the Greeks, the Bulgarians, and the Serbs, with each claiming closer ethnic or historical ties to Macedonia than the others. The liberation of Macedonia from the Turks was desired by all non-Muslim Macedonians, however, and to this end the Internal Macedonian Revolutionary Organization (IMRO) was started in 1893 with a program of "Macedonia for the Macedonians."

In 1912 Bulgaria, Serbia, and Greece put aside their differences and formed the Balkan League in order to wrest the region from the Turks. They promptly achieved this goal in the First Balkan War (1912–13) but then quarreled with each other over how to divide up Macedonia among themselves. The Serbs, Greeks, and Montenegrins, helped by the Romanians, then fought and won the Second Balkan War (1913) against Bulgaria. The ensuing treaty in 1913 assigned the southern half, or "Aegean Macedonia," to Greece and most of the northern half ("Vardar Macedonia") to Serbia; a much smaller portion, "Pirin Macedonia," went to Bulgaria. Bulgaria sided with the Central powers in World War I and thus was able to occupy all of Macedonia. But the Central powers' defeat in that war resulted in another reduction of Bulgaria's portion of Macedonia, so that it retained only its present-day Pirin share. Vardar Macedonia was incorporated with the rest of Serbia into the new Kingdom of the Serbs, Croats, and Slovenes (renamed Yugoslavia in 1929).

During the period from 1912 to 1923, several population shifts occurred in Macedonia. The largest of these took place under the terms of the Treaty of Lausanne (1923), when 375,000 Turks left Aegean Macedonia and were replaced by 640,000 Greek refugees from Turkey. When the Balkan Peninsula was overrun and partitioned by the Axis powers during World War II, Bulgaria again occupied almost all of Macedonia except for Thessaloníki; this was occupied by the Germans, who sent four-fifths of the city's Jews to their deaths. After the defeat of the Axis in 1945, the internal frontiers of Macedonia were restored roughly to their previous lines. Yugoslav Macedonia was elevated to a separate republic within the communist federation. In 1991 the Macedonian republic declared its independence from Yugoslavia.

Macedonia, modern Greek MAKEDHONÍA, traditional region of Greece, comprising the northern and northeastern portions of that country. Greek Macedonia has an area of about 13,200 square miles (34,200 square km). It is bounded by Albania to the west, independent Macedonia and Bulgaria to the north, the Greek region of Thrace to the east, the Aegean Sea to the southeast, and the Greek regions of Thessaly and Epirus to the south. The principal city of the region is Thessaloníki (formerly Salonika).

Present-day Greek Macedonia was formerly part of the larger region of Macedonia that was dominated by the Ottoman Empire between 1371 and 1912. Greek Macedonia was created as a result of the Second Balkan War in 1913. The region was occupied by Bulgarian troops during most of World War I and by Bulgarians and German troops in World War II, but each time it was returned to Greek sovereignty at the war's end. Macedonia was the site of bitter fighting between leftists and royalists in the Greek Civil War (1946–49).

Most inhabitants of the region are ethnic Greeks and are heavily concentrated around the city of Thessaloníki, which is Greece's second largest city, the largest port after Piraeus, and the administrative, industrial, and commercial centre of northern Greece. Fewer than 20,000 Muslims remain in the region, these being mostly Pomaks, a Turkicized people speaking a Bulgarian dialect. Vlachs are concentrated in the cities of Thessaloníki and Sérrai, Macedonians (who speak their own South Slavic language) are clustered along the northern border, and there are also small enclaves of Gypsies and Albanians.

Most of the interior of Greek Macedonia is hilly or mountainous and reaches elevations of about 6,500 feet (2,000 m). The coastal areas along the Aegean Sea and the river valleys of the region constitute the only significant lowlands in all of Macedonia. The plain of Dráma and the valleys of the Strimón and Axiós rivers are the richest farmland in Greece and produce rice, olives, cotton, and tobacco. Fruit and grapes are widely grown, and wine and ouzo are produced. The processing of tobacco and other agricultural commodities and the weaving of textiles are the chief manufacturing industries. Thessaloníki has an international airport and is linked by roads and railways to Athens, Yugoslavia, and Bulgaria. Tourism centres on the Chalcidice Peninsula and the island of Thasos. Mount Olympus and the monastic site of Mount Athos also lie within the region.

Macedonia, officially REPUBLIC OF MACEDONIA, Macedonian MAKEDONIJA, or REPUBLIKA MAKEDONIJA, country of the southern Balkans (from 1918 to 1991 part of Yugoslavia). It is bordered to the north by Serbia and Montenegro, to the east by Bulgaria, to the south by Greece, and to the west by Albania. The capital is Skopje. Area 9,928 square miles (25,713 square km). Pop (2004 est.) 2,035,000.

A brief treatment of Macedonia follows. For full treatment, *see* MACROPAEDIA: Balkan States.

For current history and for statistics on society and economy, *see* BRITANNICA BOOK OF THE YEAR.

Physical and human geography. Much of the Macedonian republic is situated on a plateau lying between 2,000 and 3,000 feet (600 and 900 m) above sea level and studded with mountains reaching 8,000 feet (2,500 m). The general relief is composed mainly of schists, volcanic rocks, and partly infilled tectonic basins. Most of Macedonia's drainage is oriented southward by the Vardar River's passage toward the Aegean Sea. Because of the dryness of the climate and overactive forest clearance and grazing in the past, the land has a distinctive steppelike character. In the southwest, faulting and downwarping have resulted in the formation of Lakes Ohrid and Prespa, which drain northward toward the Adriatic Sea via the Crni Drim River.

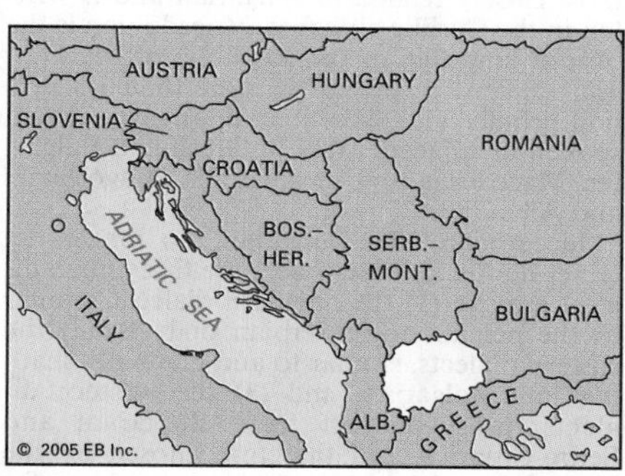

Macedonia

The climate approaches the continental type, having warm, mildly rainy summers and cold winters with snowfall.

More than half of the people are Slavic Macedonians, whose South Slavic language is more akin to Bulgarian than to Serbo-Croatian. About one-fifth of the people are Albanians, who live mostly in the northwest. There are also Turkish, Roma (Gypsy), Aromanian (Macedo-Romanian), Serbian, and Croatian minorities.

A land with few mineral resources, Macedonia is one of the poorest countries in Europe. Wheat, tobacco, rice, fruit, vegetables, and wine grapes are the leading crops; sheepherding and dairying are important. Major metallurgical plants were set up during the socialist Yugoslav era in Skopje; other manufactures include textiles, pharmaceuticals, and construction materials.

Macedonia's constitution of 1991 established a legislature of 120 members elected by majority vote. A directly elected president forms the government by selecting a prime minister with the approval of the legislature.

History. The Republic of Macedonia occupies part of the larger region of Macedonia dominated by the Ottoman Empire from 1371 to 1912. The north and centre of this region was annexed by Serbia in 1913 and thus became part of the Kingdom of Serbs, Croats, and Slovenes (subsequently renamed Yugoslavia) when that nation was formed in 1918. When Yugoslavia was partitioned by the Axis powers in 1941 during World War II, Josip Broz Tito organized a Macedonian section of the Partisans (a communist-led Yugoslav resistance movement). After the liberation of Yugoslavia by the Partisans in 1944–45, Yugoslav Macedonia became part of the re-formed Yugoslav state and in 1946 was made one of the six constituent republics of that new socialist federation. Macedonian was recognized as the republic's national language, in place of Serbo-Croatian.

Macedonia continued to be one of the poorest of the Yugoslav republics. After Croatia and Slovenia seceded from Yugoslavia, fear of Serbian dominance drove Macedonia to declare its independence from Yugoslavia in 1991. Greece immediately objected to the name of the new republic, insisting that "Macedonia" had been used by Greeks since ancient times and that its appropriation indicated a revival of claims upon Greek Macedonia. The Macedonian republic argued in turn that Slavs had lived in the area for 14 centuries and had used the name Macedonia for hundreds of years. As a compromise, Macedonia joined the United Nations in 1993 under the name of The Former Yugoslav Republic of Macedonia. Further international recognition followed, though the name remained contentious into the 21st century.

Macedonian language, Macedonian MAKEDONSKI JAZIK, South Slavic language that is most closely related to Bulgarian and is written in the Cyrillic alphabet. Macedonian is the official language of the Republic of Macedonia, where it is spoken by more than 1.3 million people. The Macedonian language is also spoken in adjacent areas of Greek and Bulgarian Macedonia and in Australia, Yugoslavia, and Albania.

Macedonian, like Bulgarian, no longer declines nouns for case. There are three main dialect groups: (1) the northern dialects, similar to the neighbouring Serbian dialects, (2) the eastern dialects, similar to and gradually shading into Bulgarian, and (3) the western dialects, most distinct from Bulgarian and Serbo-Croatian and therefore chosen by the Yugoslav authorities in 1944 as the basis for the standard language.

Macedonian literature, literature written in the South Slavic Macedonian language.

The earliest Macedonian literature, in the medieval period, was religious and Orthodox Christian. Under Ottoman Turkish rule, Macedonian literature suffered an eclipse, but in the 19th century there appeared original lyric poetry written by Konstantin Miladinov, who, with his brother Dimitrije, compiled a notable collection of legends and folk songs that contributed to the development of a nascent Macedonian literature.

When Serbian rule supplanted Turkish rule in 1913, the Serbs officially denied Macedonian distinctiveness, considering the Macedonian language merely a dialect of Serbo-Croatian. The language was not officially recognized until Macedonia became a constituent republic of communist Yugoslavia in 1946. Nonetheless, some progress was made toward the foundation of a national language and literature, notably by Kosta P. Misirkov in his *Za Makedonskite raboti* (1903; "In Favour of Macedonian Literary Works") and in the literary periodical *Vardar* (established 1905). After World War I Kosta Racin, who wrote mainly poetry in Macedonian, propagated its use through the literary journals of the 1930s. Some writers, such as Kole Nedelkovski, worked and published abroad because of political pressure.

After World War II, under the new republic of Macedonia, the scholar Blaže Koneski and others standardized Macedonian as the official literary language. With this new freedom to write and publish in its own language, Macedonia produced many literary figures in the postwar period, including the poets Aco Šopov, Slavko Janevski, Blaže Koneski, and Gane Todorovski. Prewar playwrights, such as V. Iljoski, continued to write, and the theatre was invigorated by new dramatists, such as Kole Čašule and Tome Arsovski. Živko Čingo became one of Macedonia's best-known writers of prose.

Macedonian Revolutionary Organization, Internal: *see* Internal Macedonian Revolutionary Organization.

Macedonian Wars (3rd and 2nd centuries BC), four conflicts between the ancient Roman Republic and the kingdom of Macedonia. They caused increasing involvement by Rome in Greek affairs and helped lead to Roman domination of the entire eastern Mediterranean area.

The First Macedonian War (215–205 BC) occurred in the context of the Second Punic War, while Rome was preoccupied with fighting Carthage. The ambitious Macedonian king Philip V set out to attack Rome's client states in neighbouring Illyria and confirmed his purpose in 215 by making an alliance with Hannibal of Carthage against Rome. The Romans fought the ensuing war ineffectively, and in 205 the Peace of Phoenice ended the conflict on terms favourable to Philip, allowing him to keep his conquests in Illyria.

Philip then began harrying Rhodes, Pergamum, and other Greek city-states of the Aegean. The Second Macedonian War (200–196) was launched by the Roman Senate against Philip after he refused to guarantee to make no hostile moves against these states. Philip's forces were badly defeated by the Romans and their Greek allies in a battle at Cynoscephalae in 197. The terms of peace included the loss of most of his navy, payment of a large indemnity to Rome, and the loss of his territories outside of Macedonia. Rome subsequently established a benevolent protectorate over Greece.

Philip's son and successor, Perseus (reigned 179–168), began to make alliances with various Greek city-states and thus aroused the displeasure of Rome. So began the Third Macedonian War (171–168), which ended in 168 when the Roman army of Lucius Aemilius Paullus utterly defeated Perseus' forces at the Battle of Pydna. Perseus was taken back to Rome in chains, and Macedonia was broken up into four formally autonomous republics that were required to pay annual tribute to Rome. This arrangement produced a state of chronic disorder in Macedonia, however, and in 152 a pretended son of Perseus, Andriscus, tried to reestablish the Macedonian monarchy, thus provoking the Fourth Macedonian War (149–148). The Roman praetor Quintus Caecilius Metellus crushed the rebellion with relative ease, and in 146 Macedonia was made a Roman province. It was in fact the first province of the nascent Roman Empire.

Macedonianism, also called PNEUMATOMACHIAN HERESY, a 4th-century Christian heresy that denied the full personality and divinity of the Holy Spirit. According to this heresy, the Holy Spirit was created by the Son and was thus subordinate to the Father and the Son. (In Orthodox Christian theology, God is one in essence but three in Person—Father, Son, and Holy Spirit, who are distinct and equal.) Those who accepted the heresy were called Macedonians but were also and more descriptively known as pneumatomachians, the "spirit fighters."

Some sources attribute leadership of the group to Macedonius, a semi-Arian who was twice bishop of Constantinople, but the writings of the Macedonians have all been lost, and their doctrine is known mainly from polemical refutations by Orthodox writers, particularly St. Athanasius of Alexandria (*Letters to Serapion*) and St. Basil of Caesarea (*On the Holy Spirit*). The second ecumenical Council of Constantinople (AD 381) formally condemned the Macedonians and expanded the creed of Nicaea to affirm the Orthodox belief in the third person of the Trinity, "who with the Father and the Son together is worshiped and glorified." The Macedonian heresy was suppressed by the emperor Theodosius I.

Macedonicus, Lucius Aemilius Paullus: *see* Paullus Macedonicus, Lucius Aemilius.

Macedonius (fl. 4th century), Greek bishop of Constantinople (Istanbul) and a leading moderate Arian theologian in the 4th-century Trinitarian controversy. His teaching concerning the Son, or Logos (Greek: "the Word"), oscillated between attributing to him an "identity of essence" (Greek: *homoousios*) and "perfect similarity" with the divinity of the Father, or Godhead. After Macedonius' death about 362, a heretical Christian sect that rejected the divinity of the Holy Spirit arose; because of the similarity of their teaching to Macedonius' doctrine of the Son, they were called Macedonians (*see* Macedonianism).

About 339 Macedonius usurped the episcopal throne of Constantinople from the orthodox incumbent with the support of the Arian faction, a heretical group that denied the absolute divinity of the Son. Except for the conservative, or orthodox, ascendancy (346–351), he held office until 360. Although he maintained an ambiguous theological stance, he repressed the orthodox Nicene element in Constantinople. Owing to his semi-Arian orientation or to political differences, he lost favour with the Roman emperor Constantius II (reigned 337–361) and, at a local church council in 360, was deposed and exiled.

Maceió, capital, Alagoas *estado* ("state"), northeastern Brazil. It is situated below low bluffs on a level strip of land between the Atlantic Ocean and the Norte (or Mundaú) Lagoon, a shallow body of water extending inward for several miles. Formerly called Macayo, the city dates from 1815, when a small settlement there was made a villa. In 1839 it became capital of Alagoas (then a *provincia*) and was given city status.

Government Palace, Maceió, Braz.
Epaminondas Carneiro Lima

A lighthouse is situated on a hill in the centre of the city and serves as a conspicuous landmark, located half a mile from the sea. Colonial buildings in Maceió include the Government Palace, the Metropolitan Cathedral, and the Church of Bom Jesús dos Mártires. Maceió is the seat of the Federal University of Alagoas (founded in 1961), the Medical Society of Alagoas (1917), and the Historical Institute of Alagoas (1869). Jaraguá port, which lies just to the east, is protected by a reef; its harbour can accommodate only vessels of light draft, and oceangoing ships anchor outside the reef.

Maceió is the commercial centre of the state. The city's economy is basically industrial and includes textile mills; sugar refineries; steel, iron, and zinc foundries; distilleries; and chemical, cellulose, and cigarette factories. Oil is extracted from nearby offshore platforms, and sugar, cotton, and rum are exported. Nearby are coconut- and dende-palm plantations. The tourist industry is important, owing to the area's sheltered lagoons and numerous fine beaches. Maceió has rail and road connections with Recife (about 120 miles [190 km] northeast) and other cities. There is also domestic air service. Pop. (2000 prelim.) 794,894.

McEnroe, John, in full JOHN PATRICK McENROE, JR. (b. Feb. 16, 1959, Wiesbaden, W.Ger.), American tennis player who established himself as a leading competitor in the late 1970s and the '80s. He also was noted for his poor behaviour on court, which resulted in a number of fines and suspensions and, on Jan. 21, 1990, in his default at the Australian Open. He was the first player to be ejected from a Grand Slam event in nearly 30 years.

McEnroe grew up in Douglaston, N.Y. At the age of 18 he became the youngest man to reach the Wimbledon semifinals. He enrolled at Stanford (Calif.) University in 1977, but, after winning the U.S. collegiate title in 1978, he left school and turned professional. In his first six months as a professional, McEnroe had acquired a record of 49 wins and only 7 losses.

In 1978 McEnroe helped the United States win the Davis Cup for the first time in five years. In 1979 McEnroe's powerful volley helped him to win his first U.S. Open. He repeated his U.S. Open victory in 1980, 1981, and again in 1984. He also won the Wimbledon Singles in 1981, 1983, and 1984. With partner Peter Fleming, McEnroe won several doubles titles at the U.S. Open and Wimbledon, as well as Championship Tennis tournaments.

Macenta, town, southeastern Guinea. It is located in the Guinea Highlands (at 2,033 feet [620 m]) on the road from Nzérékoré to Guéckédou and is the chief trading centre for the tea, coffee, rice, cassava, kola nuts, and palm oil and kernels grown in the surrounding agricultural area. Macenta has a tea-processing plant (1968), an agricultural-research station, a sawmill, and several secondary schools. Pop. (1983 prelim.) 28,131.

maceral, microscopic organic component of coal consisting of an irregular mixture of different chemical compounds. Macerals are analogous to minerals in inorganic rocks, but they differ from minerals in that they have no fixed chemical composition and lack a definite crystalline structure. Macerals change progressively both chemically and physically as the rank of coal advances. (Rank constitutes position in the lignite-to-anthracite series and is primarily based on increasing carbon content and increasing fuel value.)

Macerals are classified into three major groups: vitrinite, inertinite, and exinite. Vitrinite is derived from woody plant tissue and includes the macerals collinite and telinite. Most coals have a high percentage of vitrinites. The inertinite group comprises fusinite, micrinite, sclerotinite, and semi-fusinite, which are all rich in carbon. The exinite macerals, characterized by a high hydrogen content, include alginite, cutinite, resinite, and sporinite.

Macerata, city, capital of Macerata *provincia,* in Marche *regione,* central Italy. It is situated on a hill between the Potenza and Chienti rivers, south of Ancona. The town was built in the 10th and 11th centuries near the ruins of the ancient Roman town of Helvia Recina, which was destroyed about 408 by the Visigothic king Alaric. A commune in the 12th century and the seat of a bishop from 1320, Macerata passed to the Papal States about 1445. Noteworthy buildings in the city include the Loggia dei Mercanti (1485–91), the neoclassical Sferisterio (sports arena), the cathedral (1771–90), and the Church of Santa Maria delle Vergini (1555–73), with a painting by Tintoretto. Macerata is the seat of a university with a faculty of jurisprudence, founded in 1290, and of several other learned institutions.

Macerata is an important agricultural market for cereals, and the locality is known for cattle and pig breeding, horticulture, and floriculture. The city's industries include brewing, brickmaking, and the manufacture of furniture. Pop. (1999 est.) mun., 41,907.

McEwen, Sir John (b. March 29, 1900, Chiltern, Vic., Australia—d. Nov. 21, 1980, Melbourne), farmer, politician, and prime minister of Australia from Dec. 19, 1967, to Jan. 10, 1968.

A member of the House of Representatives (1934–71), McEwen served in several ministerial posts during World War II, including deputy prime minister (1958–71), and was acting prime minister for three weeks upon the death of Prime Minister Harold Holt in 1967. McEwen was knighted in 1971.

McFadden, Daniel L. (b. July 29, 1937, Raleigh, N.C., U.S.), American economist and winner of the 2000 Nobel Memorial Prize in Economic Sciences, along with James Heckman (*q.v.*), for the development of theory and methods used in the analysis of individual or household behaviour, such as understanding how people choose where to work, where to live, or when to get married.

McFadden majored in physics (B.S., 1957) and pursued graduate studies in economics (Ph.D., 1962) at the University of Minnesota. He taught economics (1963–79) at the University of California, Berkeley, leaving to teach at Yale University (1977–78) and the Massachusetts Institute of Technology (1978–91). In 1990 he returned to Berkeley and was named the E. Morris Cox Professor of Economics. He has also served as director of the university's Econometrics Laboratory.

McFadden's work combines economic theory, statistical methods, and empirical applications toward the resolution of social problems. In 1974 he developed conditional logit analysis—a method for determining how individuals choose among finite alternatives to maximize the utility of their decisions. Through the analysis of discrete choice (*i.e.*, the choices made among a finite set of alternatives), McFadden's work has helped predict usage rates for public transportation systems, and his statistical methods have been applied to studies of labour-force participation, health care, housing (particularly for the elderly), and the environment.

Macfarquhar, Colin (b. 1745?—d. April 2, 1793, Edinburgh?, Scot.), Scottish printer, who, with Andrew Bell, founded the *Encyclopædia Britannica* in 1768.

A printer in Edinburgh and presumably the printer of the *Britannica*—for the first edition is stated to have been sold at his printing office in Nicolson Street—Macfarquhar remains an obscure figure. Even the dates and places of his birth and death are uncertain. The one certainty about his part in launching the *Britannica* is that he edited the early volumes of the third edition (1788–97).

McGee, Thomas D'Arcy (b. April 13, 1825, Carlingford, County Louth, Ire.—d. April 7, 1868, Ottawa, Ont., Can.), Irish-Canadian writer and chief political orator of the Canadian confederation movement.

Thomas D'Arcy McGee, *c.* 1862
By courtesy of the Public Archives of Canada

An Irish patriot, McGee was associated with *The Nation* (1846–48), the literary organ of the Young Ireland political movement. He was implicated in the abortive Irish rebellion of 1848 and fled to the United States, where he established two newspapers, the New York *Nation* and the *American Celt.* He gradually came to advocate peaceful reforms for Ireland, and in 1857 he moved to Canada. He was elected to the Legislative Assembly of Canada in 1858 and served there until his death. He held ministerial posts during the 1860s, and he played a leading part in the movement that resulted in 1870 in the confederation of the Canadian colonies. McGee also encouraged the development of a Canadian culture and wrote nationalist poetry. He was assassinated in Ottawa, presumably for remarks made against the Canadian Fenians, the Irish nationalists in Canada. Selections from McGee's writings appear in two edited collections: *The Poems of Thomas D'Arcy McGee* (1869) and *D'Arcy McGee: A Collection of Speeches and Addresses* (1937).

BIBLIOGRAPHY. Josephine Phelan, *The Ardent Exile* (1951), is a biography.

McGee, William John (b. April 17, 1853, Farley, Iowa, U.S.—d. Sept. 4, 1912, Washington, D.C.), American geologist and archaeologist who was noted for his pioneer studies of Pleistocene geology (1,600,000 to 10,000 years ago) of the upper Mississippi River valley and the stratigraphy of the Atlantic Coastal Plain.

McGee was in charge of the U.S. Geological Survey division of the Atlantic Coastal Plain from 1883 until 1893, when he was appointed to the Bureau of American Ethnology. In 1903 he became head of the department of anthropology of the St. Louis World's Fair and in 1905 was appointed director of the St. Louis Art Museum. From 1907 until his death, he served with the Inland Waterways Commission and the Bureau of Soils of the U.S. Department of Agriculture.

McGee's work included the application of geomorphology to the interpretation of landscape evolution, studies of hydrology, and the anthropology of American Indians. He wrote *The Geology of the Head of Chesapeake Bay* (1888), *The Seri Indians* (1898), and *Outlines of Hydrology* (1908).

McGhee, Brownie, byname of WALTER BROWN MCGHEE (b. Nov. 30, 1915, Knoxville, Tenn., U.S.—d. Feb. 16, 1996, Oakland, Calif.), American blues singer, guitarist, pianist, songwriter, and longtime partner of the vocalist and harmonica player Sonny Terry.

The son of a singer and guitarist, McGhee early learned to play the guitar and piano. He dropped out of high school in the late 1920s to perform for carnivals, minstrel shows, and dances throughout Tennessee. In the mid-1930s he led his own washboard band. McGhee first met Terry in North Carolina in 1939 and worked with him and the singer Paul Robeson in Washington, D.C., in 1940. Settling in New York City in the early 1940s, he roomed with Terry and the blues musician Leadbelly (Huddie Ledbetter), and the three performed with Woody Guthrie and others as the Headline Singers. Terry and McGhee's partnership began in 1941 and lasted (with frequent interruptions) until the late 1970s.

McGhee's first recordings were for the OKeh label in 1940; he later recorded extensively with Terry and others. He appeared in Tennessee Williams' play *Cat on a Hot Tin Roof* on Broadway (1955–57) and toured with that show. McGhee recorded several motion-picture soundtracks, including that for *A Face in the Crowd* (1957).

McGill, James (b. Oct. 6, 1744, Glasgow, Strathclyde, Scot.—d. Dec. 19, 1813, Montreal, Que., Can.), fur trader, merchant, and politician in Canada who founded McGill University in Montreal.

McGill emigrated from Scotland to Canada, where he became involved in the fur trade. About 1774 he made his headquarters at Montreal and soon became an important figure in the fur trade.

McGill represented the west ward of Montreal in the Legislative Assembly of Lower Canada (now in Quebec) in 1792–96 and 1800–04; in 1793 he was appointed a member of the Executive Council of the province. During the War of 1812 between the United States and Great Britain, he was an honorary colonel of the Montreal Infantry Volunteer Regiment. He bequeathed much of his estate to the founding of McGill University.

McGill, Ralph (Emerson) (b. Feb. 5, 1898, near Soddy, Tenn., U.S.—d. Feb. 3, 1969, Atlanta, Ga.), crusading American journalist whose editorials in the Atlanta *Constitution* had a profound influence on social change in the southern United States. He was sometimes called "the conscience of the New South," and his influence was also important in interpreting the Southern states to the North and West.

McGill attended a private secondary school and went on to Vanderbilt University, where he worked his way almost to graduation, with an interruption for World War I service in the U.S. Marine Corps. In 1922 and 1923 he worked for the *Nashville Banner,* where he was a reporter and soon became sports editor. He also contributed occasional features to the Atlanta *Constitution*. In 1931 he became the *Constitution*'s sports editor, continuing to write non-sports features from time to time.

As executive editor of the *Constitution* from 1938 to 1942, editor from 1942 to 1960, and publisher from 1960 until his death, McGill became known for his courageous campaigns against political corruption and racial injustice. He consistently opposed the Ku Klux Klan and in 1958 won a Pulitzer Prize for his enlightened editorials.

In the 1950s and '60s his editorial voice strongly supported the drive to win full civil rights for blacks in the United States. He was awarded the Presidential Medal of Freedom in 1964. His widely acclaimed book *The South and the Southerner* (1963) won the *Atlantic* magazine nonfiction prize.

McGill University, private state-supported English-language university in Montreal that is internationally known for its work in chemistry, medicine, and biology. A bequest from the estate of James McGill, a Montreal merchant, was used to found the university, which received a royal charter in 1821. Faculties of medicine and arts were the first to be established, and in 1899 Royal Victoria College was opened for women. Royal Victoria gradually merged with McGill and the university is now completely coeducational. Also incorporated in the university system is Macdonald College at Sainte-Anne de Bellevue, founded in 1905 and specializing in the agricultural sciences. McGill is one of the leading universities of Canada.

McGillivray, Alexander (b. *c.* 1759—d. Feb. 17, 1793, Pensacola, Fla. [United States]), the principal chief of the Creek Indians in the years following the American Revolution. He was largely responsible for the Creeks' retention of their tribal identity and the major part of their homeland for another generation.

In a letter to the Spanish commandant at Pensacola in 1783, McGillivray identified himself as "a Native of and a chief of the Creek Nation." The penmanship and the name made that statement seem improbable, but it was correct. McGillivray was, in fact, of mixed Indian and European blood. His father was Lachlan McGillivray, a Scottish trader. His mother was Sehoy Marchand, a French-Creek woman. By blood McGillivray was thus only one-quarter Indian. But the Creeks, with whom descent was matrilineal, had no difficulty in claiming McGillivray as Creek. As was the custom, his early upbringing was primarily by his mother and, though bilingual, was in the ways of her people.

At 14 McGillivray was sent to Charleston, S.C., for tutoring and served a short apprenticeship in a countinghouse in Savannah, Ga. He might have stayed on, but the American Revolution intervened. His father was proscribed as a Loyalist, and his properties were confiscated. Father and son decided to go home, Lachlan to Scotland and Alexander to the Creek nation, where he was given status as a chief and where the British commissioned him colonel and Indian agent. During the War of Independence the Creeks were opportunists. Some of them fought alongside the Revolutionaries, while McGillivray contributed toward keeping a larger number on the Loyalist side.

By 1782 British military defeats made it clear that the Creeks would lose their British connection. Deeply distrusting American land speculators and encroaching settlers, McGillivray put out feelers for Spanish support and suggested a council at Pensacola, West Florida. There, on June 1, 1784, he and governors Esteban Miró and Arturo O'Neill signed a treaty headed "Articles of Agreement, Trade, and Peace." Spain would extend a protectorate over the Creeks within Spanish territorial limits and would supply an adequate trade. McGillivray's more remarkable success was in persuading the Spanish that the trade should be in English goods and that a contract for the purpose should go to a British merchant, William Panton.

Over the next several years, McGillivray staunchly resisted overtures from Georgia and the United States to concede lands and trading privileges. On occasion he sent raiding parties to clear the Indian hunting grounds. Then, in 1788, Miró gave notice that Spanish support would be reduced. McGillivray indicated that in the circumstances he could not refuse discussions with commissioners sent by Georgia and the U.S. Congress.

In 1789 President George Washington sent distinguished commissioners to negotiate with the Creeks. They proposed a boundary well into the Creek hunting lands and recognition of U.S. sovereignty over the entire Creek area. Bolstered by reactivated Spanish support, McGillivray objected. Obtaining no concession, he and his companions decamped. Washington then sent another commissioner to invite McGillivray and a delegation of chiefs to come to New York City to make a treaty "as strong as the hills and as lasting as the rivers."

With the commissioner, the delegation members traveled overland to New York City, where they were welcomed by the newly formed political Society of St. Tammany. Secretary of War Henry Knox and McGillivray worked out the terms of a treaty specifying American sovereignty over Creek lands within the limits of United States territory and setting a line near the Altamaha River separating Georgian and Creek lands. McGillivray accepted a U.S. Army commission as a brigadier general and a salary of $100 a month, but he did not promise U.S. trade except in the event of war between Britain and Spain, at the time a possibility.

In 1792 McGillivray went to New Orleans, La., to establish a better understanding with the Spanish. The new treaty specified that the Creeks would order Americans off their lands and that Spain would guarantee territorial integrity within Spanish limits and provide sufficient arms and ammunition. Although the Spanish urged that the Americans be driven back, McGillivray wisely pursued a much less aggressive course.

En route home, McGillivray contracted a violent fever that immobilized him for months. He died at Pensacola in his 34th year. Panton, in whose garden he was buried, attributed his death to "gout of the stomach" and "perepneumonia." Neither Panton nor the Spaniards found a suitable replacement for him, nor did his tribesmen the Creeks, though the policies he had put into effect carried on and served the Creek nation well. (J.W.C./Ed.)

BIBLIOGRAPHY. John Walton Caughey, *McGillivray of the Creeks* (1938, reprinted 1959).

Macgillycuddy's Reeks (Irish: "ridge" or "crests"), mountain range on the Iveragh peninsula in County Kerry, southwestern Ireland. Its geological basis is a long anticlinal range of Devonian sandstones that was strongly glaciated, producing many valleys, serrated ridges, and peaks, including Carrantuohill (3,414 feet [1,041 m]), the highest mountain in Ireland.

McGinley, Phyllis (b. March 21, 1905, Ontario, Ore., U.S.—d. Feb. 22, 1978, New York, N.Y.), American poet and author of books for juveniles, best known for her light verse celebrating suburban home life.

Starting in the 1920s, McGinley wrote poetry for such magazines as *The New Yorker* and the *Atlantic.* Although her verse is often dismissed as being merely light, it is serious as well as witty. She upheld in her poetry the values she cherished, writing with delight of the suburban landscape. She wrote in masterfully controlled conventional form, and her great technical expertise gave her work the appearance of effortlessness. In 1961 she won the Pulitzer Prize in poetry for *Times Three: Selected Verse from Three Decades* (1960). Her later poetry became more free and inventive. McGinley also wrote a popular series of autobiographical essays about being a wife in the suburbs, titled *Sixpence in Her Shoe* (1964). Her works for juveniles include *The Horse Who Lived Upstairs* (1944) and *The Make-Believe Twins* (1953).

McGovern, George S(tanley) (b. July 19, 1922, Avon, S.D., U.S.), U.S. senator who was an unsuccessful reformist Democratic presidential candidate in 1972. His campaign platform advocated an immediate end to the Vietnam War and a broad program of liberal social and economic reforms at home.

After service as a pilot in World War II, for which he was awarded the Distinguished Flying Cross, McGovern earned a Ph.D. in history at Northwestern University, Evanston, Ill., and later taught at Dakota Wesleyan University, Mitchell, S.D. He was active in Democratic politics from 1948 and served in the House of Representatives (1957–60). After losing an election for a Senate seat in South Dakota in 1960, he served for two years as the director of the Food for Peace Program under President John F. Kennedy. Stressing farm-support programs, McGovern won election to the U.S. Senate in 1962 and was reelected in 1968. By then he had emerged as one of the leading opponents to the United States' continued military involvement in Indochina.

As chairman of a Commission on Party Structure and Delegate Selection prior to the Democratic National Convention in 1972, McGovern helped enact party reforms that gave increased representation to minority groups at the convention. Supported by these groups, he won the presidential nomination but alienated many of the more traditional elements in the Democratic Party. McGovern was unable to unify the party sufficiently to offer an effective challenge to the incumbent Republican president, Richard M. Nixon, who defeated him by an overwhelming margin.

McGovern was reelected to the Senate in 1974, but lost his seat in 1980 to a Republican opponent supported by right-wing groups. After lecturing as a visiting professor in foreign policy at several universities, including Northwestern University, McGovern declared himself a candidate for the 1984 Democratic presidential nomination, but decided to drop out of the race after a third-place finish in the Massachusetts primary—the only state that he had carried in the 1972 election. Although unsuccessful, his 1984 bid for the nomination did serve to reassert his status as a noted American spokesman for liberal causes.

McGovern's autobiography, entitled *Grassroots*, was published in 1978.

McGraw, John (Joseph), byname LITTLE NAPOLEON (b. April 7, 1873, Truxton, N.Y., U.S.—d. Feb. 25, 1934, New Rochelle, N.Y.), professional U.S. baseball player and manager.

McGraw, 1910
The Bettmann Archive

During the 1890s McGraw was a star infielder for the Baltimore National League club. His .391 mark of 1899 remains the highest batting average attained by any major league third baseman.

In 1901 McGraw was appointed manager of the Baltimore club in the new American League. On July 19, 1902, he returned to the National League as manager of the New York team. Until his retirement in June 1932 the Giants were generally the most feared team in the league. They won league championships in 1904, 1905, 1911, 1912, 1913, 1917, 1921, 1922, 1923, and 1924, taking World Series titles in 1905, 1921, and 1922. In his 33 years of managing, McGraw's teams won 2,840 games, a total exceeded only by that of one other manager, Connie Mack.

McGuffey, William Holmes (b. Sept. 23, 1800, Pennsylvania, U.S.—d. May 4, 1873, Charlottesville, Va.), U.S. educator who is remembered chiefly for his series of elementary school readers.

With little formal education, McGuffey mastered the school arts and began teaching in the Ohio frontier schools at the age of 13. While teaching, he continued his own education intermittently—under private tutors, at Greersburg Academy, and at Washington (Pennsylvania) College. During his 10 years (from 1826) on the faculty of Miami University, Oxford, Ohio, McGuffey took great interest in public education and assisted the teachers of the local elementary schools.

In 1835 he contracted with the Cincinnati publishers Truman and Smith to compile four school readers, the first and second of which were published in 1836 and the third and fourth in 1837. A fifth appeared in 1844. A spelling book by McGuffey's brother, Alexander Hamilton McGuffey, was published in 1846, and a sixth reader was added in 1857. The readers were graded collections of didactic tales and excerpts from great books. They became standard texts in nearly all states, eclipsing all rival textbook publications for half a century and reaching a reputed total sale of over 125 million copies.

McGuffey served as president of Cincinnati College (1836–39) and of Ohio University, Athens (1839–43). He was a founder of the common school system of Ohio. In 1845 he was elected to the chair of mental and moral philosophy at the University of Virginia, Charlottesville, a position he held until his death.

McGuire, Al, byname of ALFRED JAMES MCGUIRE (b. Sept. 7, 1928, New York City—d. Jan. 26, 2001, Milwaukee, Wis., U.S.), U.S. collegiate basketball coach, who was a master at game coaching.

McGuire learned basketball in the hard school of Queens street basketball. He later played for St. John's Preparatory School and St. John's College, both in Brooklyn, and played in the professional National Basketball Association, with the New York Knickerbockers (1951–54) and with the Baltimore Bullets (1954–55). He then turned to coaching.

McGuire served as an assistant coach at Dartmouth College (Hanover, N.H., 1955–57) before becoming head coach at Belmont Abbey College (Belmont, N.C., 1957–64), where he compiled a record of 109–64. In 1965 he joined Marquette University (Milwaukee, Wis.; also athletic director from 1971) and quickly turned its basketball program into one of the best in the country. At Marquette his teams won 295 games and lost 80 while making 11 post-season appearances, including 9 National Collegiate Athletic Association (NCAA) tournaments. Marquette won the 1970 National Invitation Tournament and the NCAA national championship in 1977, the last game McGuire coached.

After retiring in 1977 McGuire became a television commentator for collegiate games. His plain-spoken, unorthodox style proved highly popular with listeners and players alike. He announced games until March 2000, when he was forced to retire owing to failing health. McGuire was inducted into the Basketball Hall of Fame in 1992.

McGwire, Mark, in full MARK DAVID MCGWIRE (b. Oct. 1, 1963, Pomona, Calif., U.S.), American professional baseball player, considered one of the most powerful hitters in the history of the game. In 1998 he set a major league record for most home runs in a season (70), breaking Roger Maris's mark of 61.

McGwire was drafted by the Montreal Expos as a pitcher in 1981 but instead attended the University of Southern California, where he played first base, the position he maintained in the majors. Selected by the Oakland Athletics in the 1984 draft, McGwire joined the club in 1987 and quickly displayed the strength that would become his trademark. His 49 home runs that year set a rookie record and helped earn him American League Rookie of the Year honours. In 1989 his .343 postseason batting average guided Oakland to the World Series championship. Injuries, however, soon plagued McGwire, and from 1993 to 1995 he missed 290 games. Traded to the St. Louis Cardinals in 1997, he posted 58 homers.

Attempts to top Maris's 37-year-old single-season home-run record dominated the 1998 season. McGwire and the Chicago Cubs' Sammy Sosa (*q.v.*) thrilled fans with their home-run derby. On September 8, McGwire hit his shortest home run of the year (104 metres [341 feet]) to break the record. The following year, he became the second player (Sosa was the first) to hit 60 home runs in two seasons.

Mach, Ernst (b. Feb. 18, 1838, Chirlitz-Turas, Moravia, Austrian Empire—d. Feb. 19, 1916, Haar, Ger.), Austrian physicist and philosopher who established important principles of optics, mechanics, and wave dynamics and who supported the view that all knowledge is a conceptual organization of the data of sensory experience (or observation).

Mach was educated at home until the age of 14, then went briefly to gymnasium (high school) before entering the University of Vienna at 17. He received his doctorate in physics in 1860 and taught mechanics and physics in Vienna until 1864, when he became professor of mathematics at the University of Graz. Mach's interests had already begun to turn to the psychology and physiology of sensation, although he continued to identify himself as a physicist and to conduct physical research throughout his career. During the 1860s he discovered the physiological phenomenon that has come to be called Mach's bands, the tendency of the human eye to see bright or dark bands near the boundaries between areas of sharply differing illumination.

Mach left Graz to become professor of experimental physics at the Charles University in Prague in 1867, remaining there for the next 28 years. There he conducted studies on kinesthetic sensation, the feeling associated with movement and acceleration. Between 1873 and 1893 he developed optical and photographic techniques for the measurement of sound waves and wave propagation. In 1887 he established the principles of supersonics and the Mach number—the ratio of the velocity of an object to the velocity of sound.

In *Beiträge zur Analyse der Empfindungen* (1886; *Contributions to the Analysis of the Sensations,* 1897), Mach advanced the concept that all knowledge is derived from sensation; thus, phenomena under scientific investigation can be understood only in terms of experiences, or "sensations," present in the observation of the phenomena. This view leads to the position that no statement in natural science is admissible unless it is empirically verifiable. Mach's exceptionally rigorous criteria of verifiability led him to reject such metaphysical concepts as absolute time and space, and prepared the way for the Einstein relativity theory.

Mach also proposed the physical principle, known as Mach's principle, that inertia (the tendency of a body at rest to remain at rest and of a body in motion to continue in motion in the same direction) results from a relationship of that object with all the rest of the matter in the universe. Inertia, Mach argued, applies only as a function of the interaction

Mach
By courtesy of the Osterreichische Nationalbibliothek, Vienna

between one body and other bodies in the universe, even at enormous distances. Mach's inertial theories also were cited by Einstein as one of the inspirations for his theories of relativity.

Mach returned to the University of Vienna as professor of inductive philosophy in 1895, but he suffered a stroke two years later and retired from active research in 1901, when he was appointed to the Austrian parliament. He continued to lecture and write in retirement, publishing *Erkenntnis und Irrtum* ("Knowledge and Error") in 1905 and an autobiography in 1910.

Mach number, in fluid mechanics, ratio of the velocity of a fluid to the velocity of sound in that fluid, named after Ernst Mach (1838–1916), an Austrian physicist and philosopher. In the case of an object moving through a fluid, such as an aircraft in flight, the Mach number is equal to the velocity of the object relative to the fluid divided by the velocity of sound in that fluid. Mach numbers less than one indicate subsonic flow; those greater than one, supersonic flow. Fluid flow, in addition, is classified as compressible or incompressible on the basis of the Mach number. For example, gas flowing with a Mach number of less than three-tenths may be considered incompressible, or of constant density, a point of view that greatly simplifies the analysis of its behaviour. For higher Mach numbers, compressibility must be considered, as in aircraft flight, spacecraft reentry, and jet- and rocket-propulsion systems.

Macha, in Celtic religion, one of three war goddesses; it is also a collective name for the three, who were also referred to as the three Morrígan. As an individual, Macha was known by a great variety of names, including Dana and Badb ("Crow," or "Raven"). She was the great earth mother, or female principle, and a great slaughterer of men, as was another of the trinity, Morrígan, or Black Annis, who survives in Arthurian legend as Morgan le Fay. The third goddess was Nemain.

Mácha, Karel Hynek (b. Nov. 16, 1810, Prague—d. Nov. 5, 1836, Litoměřice, Bohemia, Austrian Empire), literary artist who is considered the greatest poet of Czech Romanticism.

Born of poor parents, Mácha was influenced as a student by the Czech national revival and by English and Polish Romantic literature. After wandering amid ruined castles in the Bohemian countryside and a journey to northern Italy (1834), he took up a legal post in Litoměřice in 1836 but soon succumbed to pneumonia, when not quite 26 years old.

After schoolboy attempts to write in German, Mácha had begun (1830) to write poems, sketches, and novels in Czech. Practically all his prose works remained unfinished, but they exhibit a mastery not previously attained by writers in the newly revived literary language. His best work is the lyrical epic *Máj* (1836; *May,* 1932, 1949). Coldly received at the time, *Máj* has exercised an almost magical fascination on Czech poets and critics of the 20th century. Mácha's letters and diaries, *Dílo Karla Hynka Máchy,* edited by K. Janský (3 vol., 1948–50), are an essential supplement and background to his poetry.

Machado (y Ruiz), Antonio (b. July 26, 1875, Seville—d. Feb. 22, 1939, Collioure, Fr.), outstanding Spanish poet and playwright of Spain's Generation of '98.

Machado received a doctoral degree in literature in Madrid, attended the Sorbonne, and became a secondary school French teacher. He rejected the modernism of his contemporaries and adopted what he called "eternal poetry," which was informed more by intuition than by intellect. Three stages can be distinguished in his artistic evolution. The first, typified by the poems in *Soledades* (1903; "Solitudes") and *Soledades, galerías, y otros poemas* (1907; "Solitudes, Galleries, and Other Poems"), established his links with pure romanticism. These poems are concerned largely with evoking memories and dreams and with the subjective identification of the poet with natural phenomena, especially the sunset. In his second stage Machado turned away from pure introspection, and in *Campos de Castilla* (1912; "Plains of Castile") he sought to capture the stark landscape and spirit of Castile in a severely denuded and sombre style. His later works, *Nuevas canciones* (1924; "New Songs") and *Poesías completas* (1928; "Complete Poems"), express profound Existential views and reflect on the solitude of the poet. He also wrote plays in collaboration with his brother Manuel and a collection of philosophical reflections with strong Existentialist overtones, *Juan de Mairena* (1936). A strong supporter of the Spanish Republic, Machado fled Spain when the Republic collapsed in early 1939; he died soon afterward in exile.

Machado, Bernardino Luis (b. March 28, 1851, Rio de Janeiro—d. April 29, 1944, Porto, Port.), Brazilian-born political leader who was twice president of Portugal (1915–17, 1925–26).

A professor at Coimbra University, Lisbon, from 1879, Machado was elected twice to the chamber of peers as representative of the university (1890, 1894). He was also minister of public works (1893) and created the first labour court in Portugal. In 1902, after espousing republicanism, he was elected president of the governing board of the Republican Party. With the overthrow of the monarchy (1910), he served as minister of foreign affairs (1910–11), deputy to the constituent assembly and senator (1911), and minister (later ambassador) to Brazil (1912). While he was prime minister and minister of the interior in 1914, he committed Portugal to the side of Great Britain in World War I. Elected president on Aug. 6, 1915, he was overthrown by the rightist revolution of Dec. 8, 1917. He became president again on Dec. 11, 1925, but was once more deposed (May 28, 1926) by a military revolt, which soon brought Gen. António Óscar de Fragoso Carmona to power. Machado went into exile, but in 1940 he was allowed to return home.

Machado (y Ruiz), Manuel (b. Aug. 29, 1874, Seville—d. Jan. 19, 1947, Madrid), Spanish poet and playwright, brother of Antonio Machado. The son of an Andalusian folklorist, he is best known for his popular poetry inspired by traditional folklore, as in *Cante hondo* (1912; "Singing from the Depths"). He collaborated with his brother on several verse plays, including *Desdichas de fortuna o Julianillo Valcárcel* (1926; "Miseries of Fortune; or, Julianillo Valcárcel") and *La Lola se va a los puertos* (1930; "La Lola Is Seen in Doorways").

During his youth he led a Bohemian existence, residing in Paris and becoming a leading figure in the Spanish Modernist movement. His poems of this period, *Alma* (1902; "Soul"), reveal the influence of the Symbolists and Parnassians, especially Verlaine and Rubén Darío. *El mal poema* (1909; "The Evil Poem") is one of the first attempts in Spanish poetry to convey the sordidness of city life through the use of slang and sarcasm. After his marriage in 1909 he became a librarian and achieved success as a journalist. He supported the Nationalists in the Spanish Civil War (1936–39), while his brother Antonio supported the Republicans. He was director of Madrid's municipal museum from the mid-1920s until 1944.

Machado de Assis, Joaquim Maria (b. June 21, 1839, Rio de Janeiro—d. Sept. 29, 1908, Rio de Janeiro), Brazilian poet, novelist, and short-story writer, the classic master of Brazilian literature, whose art is rooted in the traditions of European culture and transcends the influence of Brazilian literary schools.

The son of a house painter of mixed black and Portuguese ancestry, he was raised, after his mother's death, by a stepmother, also of mixed parentage. Sickly, epileptic, unprepossessing in appearance, and a stutterer, he found employment at the age of 17 as a printer's apprentice and began to write in his spare time. Soon he was publishing stories, poems, and novels in the Romantic tradition.

By 1869 Machado was a typically successful Brazilian man of letters, comfortably provided for by a government position and happily married to a cultured woman, Carolina Augusta Xavier de Novais. In that year illness forced him to withdraw from his active career. He emerged from this temporary retreat with a new novel in a strikingly original style that marked a clear break with the literary conventions of the day. This was *Memórias Póstumas de Brás Cubas* (1881; "The Posthumous Memoirs of Brás Cubas"; *Epitaph of a Small Winner,* 1952), an eccentric first-person narrative with a flow of free association and digression. The "small winner," Brás Cubas, cynically reviews his life in 160 short, often disconnected chapters and, after balancing the good and the bad, concludes that he is slightly ahead since he had no children to perpetuate the legacy of human misery. Machado's reputation now rests on this work, his short stories, and two later novels, *Quincas Borba* (1891; *Philosopher or Dog?,* 1954) and his masterpiece, *Dom Casmurro* (1899; Eng. trans., 1953), a haunting and terrible journey into a mind warped by jealousy. Translations of his shorter fiction include *The Devil's Church and Other Stories* (1977) and *The Psychiatrist and Other Stories* (1963).

Urbane, aristocratic, cosmopolitan, aloof, and cynical, Machado ignored such social questions as Brazilian independence and the abolition of slavery. He failed to share Brazilian enthusiasm for local colour and self-conscious nationalism. The locale of his fiction is usually Rio, which he takes for granted as though there were no other place. The natural world is practically nonexistent in his work. He writes with a deep-rooted pessimism and disillusionment that would be unbearable were it not disguised by flippancy and wit. He became the first president of the Brazilian Academy of Letters in 1896 and held the office until his death.

Machado y Morales, Gerardo (b. Sept. 29, 1871, Camajuaní, Cuba—d. March 29, 1939, Miami Beach), hero in the Cuban War of Independence (1895–98) who was later elected president by an overwhelming majority, only to become one of Cuba's most powerful dictators.

Leaving the army as a brigadier general after the war, he turned to farming and business but remained active in politics, heading the Liberal Party in 1920. His election to the presidency in 1924 was welcomed by most Cubans, especially the middle class, who thought a sensible businessman would restore order to Cuba's disrupted society. To counteract economic depression caused by declining sugar prices, Machado instituted a massive program of public works but was accused of enriching

Machado y Morales, 1931
By courtesy of the Library of Congress, Washington, D.C.

himself at public expense. In 1927 he seized control of the Cuban political parties. He was reelected in 1928, despite heated opposition from students and professional men, and began to rule even more dictatorially. Disorder became widespread, and in 1933 U.S. Ambassador Sumner Welles, under instructions from Pres. Franklin D. Roosevelt, tried to mediate between Machado and opposition forces, but a general strike was called, and even the army demanded Machado's ouster. He was forced into an exile (August 12) from which he never returned.

Machaire Fíolta (Northern Ireland): *see* Magherafelt.

Machala, capital of El Oro province, southwestern Ecuador, in the Pacific coastal lowlands 2 mi (3 km) from the Gulf of Guayaquil. A commercial centre for the surrounding agricultural region, the city trades in bananas, cacao, coffee, and hides. An annual banana fair is held there in the fall. Industrial development is slight, but a technical university was established in 1969. Puerto Bolívar, 4 mi southwest, is the outport of Machala and handles about one-quarter of Ecuador's banana exports. Pop. (1982 prelim.) 109,162.

Machanganaland (South Africa): *see* Gazankulu.

Machaut, Guillaume de, Machaut also spelled MACHAULT (b. *c.* 1300, Machault, Fr.—d. 1377, Reims), French poet and musician, greatly admired by contemporaries as a master of French versification and regarded as one of the leading French composers of the Ars Nova (*q.v.*) musical style of the 14th century. It is on his shorter poems and his musical compositions that his reputation rests. He was the last great poet in France to think of the lyric and its musical setting as a single entity.

Machaut, detail of a miniature from *Oeuvres de Guillaume de Machaut, c.* 1370–80; in the Bibliothèque Nationale (Ms. Fr. 1584)

By courtesy of the Bibliotheque Nationale, Paris

He took holy orders and in 1323 entered the service of John of Luxembourg, king of Bohemia, whom he accompanied on his wars as chaplain and secretary. He was rewarded for this service by his appointment in 1337 as canon of Reims cathedral. After the King's death, he found another protector in the King's daughter, Bonne of Luxembourg, wife of the future king John II of France, and in 1349 in Charles II, king of Navarre. Honours and patronage continued to be lavished by kings and princes on Machaut at Reims until his death.

In his longer poems Machaut did not go beyond the themes and genres already widely employed in his time. Mostly didactic and allegorical exercises in the well-worked courtly love tradition, they are of scant interest to the modern reader. An exception among the longer works is *Voir-Dit,* which relates how a young girl of high rank falls in love with the poet because of his fame and creative accomplishments. The difference in age is too great, however, and the idyll ends in disappointment. Machaut's lyric poems also are based on the courtly love theme but reworked into a deft form with a verbal music that is often perfectly achieved. His influence—most significantly his technical innovations—spread beyond the borders of France. In England, Geoffrey Chaucer drew heavily upon Machaut's poetry for elements of *The Book of the Duchesse.*

All of Machaut's music has been preserved in 32 manuscripts, representing a large part of the surviving music from his period. He was the first composer to write single-handedly a polyphonic setting of the mass ordinary, a work that has been recorded in modern performance. In most of this four-part setting he employs the characteristic Ars Nova technique of isorhythm (repeated overlapping of a rhythmic pattern in varying melodic forms).

Machaut's secular compositions make up the larger part of his music. His three- and four-part motets (polyphonic songs in which each voice has a different text) number 23. Of these, 17 are in French, 2 are Latin mixed with French, and 4, like the religious motets of the early 13th century, are in Latin. Love is often the subject of their texts, and all but 3 employ isorhythm. Machaut's 19 lais (*see* lai) are usually for unaccompanied voice, although two are for three parts, and one is for two parts. They employ a great variety of musical material, frequently from the popular song and dance. Of his 33 virelais (*see* virelai), 25 consist solely of a melody, and they, along with the bulk of his lais, represent the last of such unaccompanied songs composed in the tradition of the trouvères. The rest of his virelais have one or two additional parts for instrumental accompaniment, and these are typical of the accompanied solo song that became popular in the 14th century. The polyphonic songs he wrote, in addition to his motets, consist of 21 rondeaux and 41 of his 42 ballades. The wide distribution of his music in contemporary manuscripts reveals that he was esteemed not only in France but also in Italy, Spain, and much of the rest of Europe.

Machen, Arthur, pseudonym of ARTHUR LLEWELLYN JONES (b. March 3, 1863, Caerleon, Monmouthshire, Eng.—d. Dec. 15, 1947, Beaconsfield, Buckinghamshire), Welsh novelist and essayist, a forerunner of 20th-century Gothic science fiction.

Machen's work was deeply influenced by his childhood in Wales and his readings in the occult and metaphysics. He lived most of his life in poverty as a clerk, teacher, and translator. In 1902 he became an actor with Benson's Shakespearean Repertory Company. And, in 1912, approaching his 50th birthday, he joined the staff of the London *Evening News.*

The quality of Machen's writing was demonstrated early in World War I when the newspaper published the short story "The Angel of Mons" from *The Bowmen and Other Legends of War* (1915), which circulated widely as a true story and gave hope to thousands of soldiers in battle. Like Thomas Hardy, Machen responded to the spiritual power and antiquity of the British countryside. His fantasies are often set in medieval England or Wales, as in the autobiographical *The Hill of Dreams* (1907), which evokes ancient Roman forts and Welsh mysteries. Even his stories set in London are deeply romantic and nostalgic for a pre-industrial era. Other works include *The Terror* (1917), *The Great God Pan and the Inmost Light* (1894), *Far Off Things* (1922), and *Things Near and Far* (1923). Machen also translated Casanova's *Memoirs* (12 vol., 1930).

Machen, John Gresham (b. July 28, 1881, Baltimore—d. Jan. 1, 1937, Bismarck, N.D., U.S.), U.S. Presbyterian scholar (Princeton Theological Seminary) who joined in forming the doctrinally conservative Presbyterian Church in America (1936; later named the Orthodox Presbyterian Church) after his suspension from the ministry by the General Assembly of the Presbyterian Church, U.S.A., for his opposition to modern liberal revision of the 17th-century English Presbyterian creed, the Westminster Confession of Faith. Criticizing Liberal Protestantism as unbiblical and unhistorical in his *Christianity and Liberalism* (1923), he left Princeton (1929) to help found Westminster Theological Seminary in Philadelphia.

Machias, town, seat (1790) of Washington county, eastern Maine, U.S., near the mouth of the Machias River at the head of Machias Bay, 84 mi (135 km) east-southeast of Bangor. It was the site of an English trading post (1633) which was quickly destroyed by the French. For many years its sheltered coastal location was a haven for Atlantic privateers, including Rhodes the Pirate and Samuel Bellamy (the Robin Hood of American piracy), until finally settled by English colonists in 1763. Granted as a township in 1770, it was incorporated in 1784 and named for the river (Machias is an Abnaki Indian word meaning "bad little falls"). The area was a hotbed of Revolutionary activity and a liberty pole proclaiming U.S. independence was raised there. Probably the first naval engagement of the Revolutionary War took place downriver off Machiasport (once part of Machias) when the British armed schooner "Margaretta" was captured (June 1775). Colonial landmarks include Burnham Tavern (1770, now a museum) and Fort O'Brien State Memorial (harbour defense earthworks commissioned by George Washington in 1775). Machias was once an active shipbuilding and lumbering centre. Its economy now depends on tourism, timbering, granite quarrying, grist and rayon milling, truck, poultry, and dairy farming, and the University of Maine at Machias (which originated in 1909 as a state normal school). The area is noted for hunting (bear, deer) and fishing (salmon, striped bass). Cobscook Bay State Park and Moosehorn National Wildlife Refuge are nearby. Pop. (1990) 2,569.

Machiavelli, Niccolò (b. May 3, 1469, Florence—d. June 21, 1527, Florence), Italian writer and statesman, Florentine patriot, and original political theorist whose principal work, *The Prince,* brought him a reputation of amoral cynicism.

Early life. Machiavelli's family, from the 13th century onward, had been counted among the wealthy and prominent houses of the city, holding on occasion the most important offices. His father, a doctor of laws, was nevertheless among the poorest members of the family; he lived frugally, administering his little landed property near the city and supplementing his meagre income from it with small earnings from the restricted and almost clandestine exercise of his profession, since he was debarred from any public office as an insolvent debtor of the commune of Florence. Niccolò was to write later that he had "learnt to do without before he learnt to enjoy"; and this poverty may have been the reason why he did not have the education suited to his ability. In the years when young Florentines crowded to the lectures of Politian, then Italy's leading scholar of Greek and Latin, Machiavelli never embarked on the study of Greek. His father's memoirs show Niccolò working at Latin under obscure teachers: he learned more by himself in the books that were the only luxury of his home than he did at school.

Machiavelli, detail of an oil painting by Santi di Tito; in the Palazzo Vecchio, Florence

Alinari—Art Resource/EB Inc.

This kind of education saved him from the faults and excesses of Humanist erudition and preserved the originality of his thought and the unequalled force of his style, which was elevated and popular at the same time.

Under the republic. In 1498, after the changes in the Florentine government following the execution of Savonarola—the ascetic monk who tried to impose extreme political and religious reforms on the republic—and the triumph of the opposing faction, Niccolò Machiavelli was made head of the second chancery (*cancelleria*) at the early age of 29. He was then completely unknown; the tradition of his having an apprenticeship in the lower grades of the chancery from 1494 onward is not confirmed by documentary evidence, and his own statements tend to disprove it. The office to which he was appointed, though not comparable in power with that of first chancellor, was an important one. Originally it dealt only with internal affairs of the republic, but it was later merged with the secretariat of the Ten (*i Dieci*), the executive council. Machiavelli was, moreover, secretary to the magistracy, which, in the name of the Signoria, the governing council, and under its authority, directed foreign affairs and defense. The chancellors were often entrusted with diplomatic missions to Italian and foreign courts when it was not desirable to send ambassadors. Machiavelli's first important mission was to the French court in 1500. Five months spent beyond the Alps introduced to his eager mind the people and customs of a strong nation united under the rule of a single prince.

On his return to Florence, Machiavelli found much to do, as the republic was on the verge of being ruined by the ambitions of Cesare Borgia, who was then in the midst of attempting to create a principality for himself in central Italy. Besides dictating letters in the chancery, Machiavelli undertook missions whenever the need arose; he was always ready to ride off and to face danger and hardship, being fonder of action than of words. His short work *Del modo di trattare i sudditi della Val di Chiana ribellati* (1503; "On the Way to Deal with the Rebel Subjects of the Valdichiana") belongs to this period. In it, the fundamental principle of a new doctrine is enunciated for the first time: "The world has always been inhabited by human beings who have always had the same passions." He was sent twice to Cesare Borgia; and he was a witness to the bloody vengeance taken by Cesare on his mutinous captains at the town of Sinigaglia (Dec. 31, 1502), of which he wrote a famous account, *Descrizione del modo tenuto dal Duca Valentino nello ammazzare Vitellozzo . . .* ("On the Manner Adopted by the Duke Valentino to Kill Vitellozzo . . . "). That strong, sinister prince caught the imagination of the Florentine statesman with his natural bent for abstraction and theory. Implacable, resolute, ferocious, and cunning, Cesare Borgia had conquered a dominion for himself in a few months; and Machiavelli adapted Cesare's qualities and methods to his own ideal of a "new prince" who would provide a desperate remedy for the desperate ills of Italy. It is clear that this was a case of idealization and that his admiration for the Prince did not go hand in hand with admiration for the man. When Pope Alexander VI, the father of Cesare Borgia, died in 1503 and his successor, Pius III, also died shortly afterward, Machiavelli was sent to Rome for the duration of the conclave that elected Julius II, an implacable enemy of the Borgias. There, with ever-increasing scorn, Machiavelli witnessed the decline of his hero and finally celebrated Cesare's imprisonment "which he deserved as a rebel against Christ."

In Florence, meanwhile, Piero Soderini had been elected gonfalonier (chief magistrate) for life, and Machiavelli was immediately able to win his favour and become his right-hand man. This remarkable influence over the head of state encouraged him to realize his military ideas. For centuries the states of Italy had used mercenary troops in their wars, and Machiavelli had seen in practice their lack of discipline, their faithlessness, and their unbearable arrogance. Inspired both by the military enterprises of ancient Rome and by his own observations in France (where he went on a second mission early in 1504) and in Romagna (where Cesare Borgia had replaced mercenaries with levies from his own territory), Machiavelli ardently pursued the idea of giving the Florentine state a militia of its own, recruited from the peoples under its control. Age-old prejudices had to be overcome, as well as the reluctance of suspicious townsmen, to arm men from the country districts around. Having set to work immediately after his return from the Roman legation, he succeeded in persuading the gonfalonier to risk an experiment and then to have a law passed in order to establish a militia (1505). In 1506, as the importance of the new militia increased, the council of the Nine was created to control it, and Machiavelli was made secretary of this body. The territory of the republic was divided into districts, and Machiavelli himself went out to see to the levies and to carry out inspections, alternating these military tasks with those of the chancery and with a further mission (1506) to Julius II, whose armies, moving up to free the states of the Church from their various usurpers, entered Bologna in triumph.

In December 1507 the Holy Roman emperor, Maximilian I, was preparing an invasion of Italy from Germany. Florence's gonfalonier, who did not trust his own ambassador at the imperial court, accordingly sent Machiavelli on another journey beyond the Alps. On the journey Machiavelli passed through Switzerland, and three days spent in that country were enough for him to produce some brief but acute observations on it. He did the same, at greater length, for Germany, composing on the day after his return to Florence (June 17, 1508) a *Rapporto delle cose della Magna* ("Report on the State of Germany"). In this work, compiled in the course of his official duties, and likewise in the literary version made four years later under the title *Ritratto delle cose della Magna* ("Portrait . . . "), he was able to pick out with great acumen the reasons both for the strength of the German nation and for its political weaknesses. Yet all his official reports, though marvelously intuitive, are marred by a tendency to theorize; they are bold syntheses, not complete and accurate sources of information.

On his return from Germany, as the Florentines were showing new strength in an effort to recapture the city of Pisa, which had temporarily freed itself from Florentine rule, Machiavelli was able to try out the militia that he had created. He went to command his troops at the front and put all his usual enthusiasm into the task: when the Ten begged him to remain at headquarters, he answered that they must let him be with his soldiers, since behind the lines he would die of melancholy. Such was the patriotism and passion of a man who has been represented as skeptical, cautious, and cynical. Pisa capitulated on June 8, 1509, and Machiavelli with his militia had no small share in this success for Florence.

After a mission to Mantua in connection with yet another invasion by Maximilian, Machiavelli had to go again to France, in July 1510, to persuade Florence's ally Louis XII to make peace with Pope Julius II or at least not to drag Florence into a war that would bring the republic to needless ruin, emphasizing that a neutral Florence could be useful to the French. The French, however, "who knew nothing about statecraft," were not influenced by what Machiavelli had to tell them. From this mission, which resulted in the *Ritratto di cose di Francia,* he returned in October 1510 convinced that there would be a major war between the French king and the pope and that the Florentines would be involved. All of his efforts now were to arm his country. At the end of the summer of 1511 he went once more to France to persuade Louis XII to remove the schismatic council that he was sponsoring in Pisa, since this had brought upon the Florentines the rage of Julius II. As soon as he was back from France, Machiavelli himself went to Pisa and removed this council without much ceremony. For the free republic, however, the last hour had already come: the army of the pope's Holy League was on its way to punish Florence. The gonfalonier Soderini was deposed, and in 1512 the Medici returned as masters of the city.

Under the Medici. Machiavelli lost his position and was forbidden to enter the Palazzo della Signoria. Also, when a conspiracy against the Medici was found early in 1513, Machiavelli, already an object of suspicion to the new government, was accused of complicity. Thrown into prison, he maintained his innocence even under tortures that often persuaded the innocent to declare themselves guilty. His name, however, was on a list taken from the conspirators, and finally, though he was released from prison, restrictions were put on his freedom. In the meantime, Julius II had died, and Giovanni de' Medici had become Pope Leo X. Machiavelli composed for the celebrations on that occasion a pious "Canto degli spiriti beati" ("Song of the Blessed Spirits") and sought in vain to get into the good graces of the Medici.

Reduced to poverty, Machiavelli sought refuge in the little property near Florence that he had inherited from his father. There he employed his leisure in writing, between spring and autumn 1513, his two most famous works, *Il principe* (*The Prince*) and a large part of the *Discorsi sopra la prima deca di Tito Livio* ("Discourses on the First Ten Books of Livy").

Machiavelli's affections always lay with the republic, and all of his theories were intended for its betterment; but the corruption of the times, the weakness of the states of Italy, and the threat of foreign conquest made him long for that "new prince" who might give reality to his great dream of the redemption of Italy. This "redeemer," to whom he sought in vain to give a face and a name, would have had to overcome superhuman difficulties; nor could there be much choice of means in attaining such ends. Machiavelli, in *Il principe,* attempted to indicate to the prince those means that were compatible with the conditions of the time and with human nature. Even religion—for which he had a deep feeling though he was not outwardly pious—was subordinated by him to the state's iron necessity and made into a tool of power. Indeed, Machiavelli is regarded as the inventor of the "reason of state," though that expression appears for the first time 20 years after his death. *Il principe,* while its underlying ideas are the same as those of the *Discorsi,* won a greater reputation, thanks to its concision, its vigorous imagery, and the bluntness of some of its aphorisms, which were taken too literally by contemporaries and by posterity. He remarked of certain cynical precepts that he would not have proffered them if mankind had not been wicked. This bleak pessimism is certainly not refuted by the annals of his own time. Yet his longing was for a society of good and pure men; he sought it in ancient times and, in his own day, admired less civilized nations as being less corrupt. Machiavelli's great hope was that *Il principe,* dedicated to Lorenzo de' Medici, ruler of Florence from 1513, would obtain from the Medici an office to support his family and satisfy his love of action; but the hope was in vain.

From this time also dates the comedy first entitled *Commedia di Callimaco e di Lucrezia,* later *La Mandragola* (1518; "The Mandrake"), in which the wickedness and corruption of men, particularly of the clergy, are the subject of laughter—but of a bitter and painful laughter that is never an end in itself.

Machiavelli's hopes were raised when, on the death of Duke Lorenzo, the Cardinal Giulio de' Medici came to govern Florence. He was presented to the Cardinal by Lorenzo Strozzi, to whom in gratitude he dedicated the dialogue *Dell'arte della guerra* (1521; *The Arte of Warre,* 1560) which is complementary to his two political treatises.

The first employment given him by the cardinal was to go to Lucca on a matter of small importance. Presently, however, the cardinal agreed to have Machiavelli elected official historiographer of the republic, a post to which he was appointed by the University of Florence in November 1520 with a salary of 57 gold florins a year, later increased to 100. The university's terms allowed for Machiavelli's also being employed in other ways. In the meantime, he was to compose for the Medici pope Leo X a *Discorso* on the organization of the government of Florence after the death of Duke Lorenzo; in this he boldly advised the Pope to restore the city's ancient liberties. Shortly after, in May 1521, he was sent to the Franciscan chapter at Carpi.

After Pope Leo X's death (December 1521), the cardinal Giulio de' Medici, who remained sole master of Florence, was more than ever inclined to reform its government. He sought the advice of Machiavelli, who simply refurbished the *Discorso* composed for Leo X. After the death of Pope Adrian VI in September 1523, Giulio de' Medici became Pope Clement VII. Machiavelli now worked with more enthusiasm on the *Istorie fiorentine,* his official history of Florence; in June 1525 he was able to present the Pope with eight books, and he received in return 120 florins and encouragement to continue the work. The *Istorie fiorentine,* like his earlier writings, bears the impress of a powerful and original mind. In this work, written by fits and starts and wearily dragged on into his later years, Machiavelli enters on a new road, leaving behind him the traditions and methods of Humanist historiography. His love of truth often in conflict with the necessity to avoid offending his powerful patrons, he writes history more as a politician than as a historian set on discovering the truth, often accepting sources uncritically and accommodating facts to his thesis. It is not narrative exactitude that is to be sought in the *Istorie* but the power of synthesis, the brilliant coordination and organization of facts.

In April 1526 Machiavelli was elected secretary of a five-man body lately constituted to superintend the fortifications. Next, the Pope having formed the League of Cognac against the Holy Roman emperor Charles V, Machiavelli went with the army to join Francesco Guicciardini, the Pope's lieutenant, with whom he remained almost continuously until the sack of Rome by the Emperor's forces brought the war to an end in May 1527. Florence having regained its freedom by casting off the Medici, Machiavelli on his return hoped to be restored to his old post in the chancery; but the little favours that the Medici had so meagrely doled out to him caused the supporters of the free republic to forget the love that he had always had for his native city and for freedom. It was the last of his disappointments and the greatest. Machiavelli fell ill and died, with the comforts of religion, within a month.

Character and thought. Machiavelli was an upright man, a good citizen, and a good father. He was not by any means a faithful husband but lived in affectionate harmony with his wife, Marietta Corsini (whom he had married in the latter part of 1501), and had five children by her. He loved his native city "more than his own soul," and he was generous, ardent, and basically religious.

Out of a desire to shock his contemporaries, Machiavelli liked to appear more wicked than he was. This, together with certain blunt maxims in his works, gave him a reputation for immorality. The maxims became a target for attacks by the Catholic Counter-Reformation; and the word "Machiavellianism" was coined as a term of opprobrium by the French, out of hatred for all things Italian. He "was a scapegoat because he was a great man and because he was unfortunate."

As one of the founders of the philosophy of history, he well knew that he was opening "a road as yet untrodden by man." He was the first to propound the thesis of historical cycles and—starting from the principle that human nature does not change—the first to build a political science based on the study of man.

Machiavelli was a great writer because he was a great thinker. He was also a poet; his poetry, however, is to be found not so much in his verse as in his prose, which has no equal in Italian literature. It is also noteworthy that his great gifts showed themselves in nearly all the genres that he attempted: in historical writings, in political treatises, in the short story and, particularly, in comedy. (Ro.Ri./Ed.)

BIBLIOGRAPHY. Quentin Skinner, *Machiavelli* (1981), a discussion of his life and major works for the general reader; Roberto Ridolfi, *The Life of Niccolò Machiavelli* (1963, trans. from the Italian by Cecil Grayson), an informed biography; Pasquale Villari, *Niccolò Machiavelli and His Times,* 2 vol., (1878; also published in Italian in 3 vol., 1877–82), still perceptive and fundamental, especially for the numerous documents in the appendix; Leo Strauss, *Thoughts on Machiavelli* (1958, reissued 1978), representative of the school that sees Machiavelli as a teacher of evil; Gennaro Sasso, *Niccolò Machiavelli, storia del suo pensiero politico,* new ed. (1980), a complete study on this aspect of his thought; J.G.A. Pocock, *The Machiavellian Moment* (1975), an important study of the development of civic humanism with special attention to Machiavelli; *The Discourses of Niccolò Machiavelli,* trans. by Leslie J. Walker, 2 vol. (1950, reissued 1975), a basic translation.

Machida, city, Tokyo Metropolis (*to*), Honshu, Japan, on the border of Kanagawa Prefecture (*ken*). Situated on the southern slopes of the Tama Hills, the city was formed by the amalgamation of Hara-Machida and three neighbouring villages in 1958. During the Meiji era (1868–1912) Hara-Machida was a market for goods (mostly silk) destined for the port of Yokohama. In 1908 the railway between Yokohama and Hachiōji passed through the city, increasing its importance as a trade and transport hub. Machida later developed as a residential suburb of the Tokyo–Yokohama Metropolitan Area; large-scale housing was constructed, and the population almost tripled between 1960 and 1970 but slowed throughout the late 1970s. Pop. (1983 est.) 308,031.

Machilipatnam (India): *see* Masulipatam.

machine, device, having a unique purpose, that augments or replaces human or animal effort for the accomplishment of physical tasks. This broad category encompasses such simple devices as the lever, wedge, wheel and axle, pulley, and screw (*qq.v.*; the five so-called simple machines) as well as such complex mechanical systems as the modern automobile.

The operation of a machine may involve the transformation of chemical, thermal, electrical, or nuclear energy into mechanical energy, or vice versa, or its function may simply be to modify and transmit forces and motions. All machines have an input, an output, and a transforming or modifying and transmitting device.

Machines that receive their input energy from a natural source, such as air currents, moving water, coal, petroleum, or uranium, and transform it into mechanical energy are known as prime movers. Windmills, waterwheels, turbines, steam engines, and internal-combustion engines are prime movers. In these machines the inputs vary; the outputs are usually rotating shafts capable of being used as inputs to other machines, such as electric generators, hydraulic pumps, or air compressors. All three of the latter devices may be classified as generators; their outputs of electrical, hydraulic, and pneumatic energy can be used as inputs to electric, hydraulic, or air motors. These motors can be used to drive machines with a variety of outputs, such as materials processing, packaging, or conveying machinery, or such appliances as sewing machines and washing machines. All machines of the latter type and all others that are neither prime movers, generators, nor motors may be classified as operators. This category also includes manually operated instruments of all kinds, such as calculating machines and typewriters.

In some cases, machines in all categories are combined in one unit. In a diesel-electric locomotive, for example, the diesel engine is the prime mover, which drives the electric generator, which, in turn, supplies electric current to the motors that drive the wheels.

Machine components in an automobile. As part of an introduction to machine components, some examples supplied by an automobile are of value. In an automobile, the basic problem is harnessing the explosive effect of gasoline to provide power to rotate the rear wheels. The explosion of the gasoline in the cylinders pushes the pistons down, and the transmission and modification of this translatory (linear) motion to rotary motion of the crankshaft is effected by the connecting rods that join each piston to the cranks that are part of the crankshaft. The piston, cylinder, crank, and connecting rod combination is known as a slider-crank mechanism; it is a commonly used method of converting translation to rotation (as in an engine) or rotation to translation (as in a pump).

To admit the gasoline–air mixture to the cylinders and exhaust the burned gases, valves are used; these are opened and closed by the wedging action of cams (projections) on a rotating camshaft that is driven from the crankshaft by gears or a chain.

In a four-stroke-cycle engine with eight cylinders, the crankshaft receives an impulse at some point along its length every quarter revolution. To smooth out the effect of these intermittent impulses on the speed of the crankshaft, a flywheel is used. This is a heavy wheel, attached to the crankshaft, that by its inertia opposes and moderates any speed fluctuations.

Since the torque (turning force) that it delivers depends on its speed, an internal-combustion engine cannot be started under load. To enable an automobile engine to be started in an unloaded state and then connected to the wheels without stalling, a clutch and a transmission are necessary. The former makes and breaks the connection between the crankshaft and the transmission, while the latter changes, in finite steps, the ratio between the input and output speeds and torques of the transmission. In low gear, the output speed is low and the output torque higher than the engine torque, so that the car can be started moving; in high gear, the car is moving at a substantial speed and the torques and speeds are equal.

The axles to which the wheels are attached are contained in the rear axle housing, which is clamped to the rear springs, and are driven from the transmission by the drive shaft. As the car moves and the springs flex in response to bumps in the road, the housing moves relative to the transmission; to permit this movement without interfering with the transmission of torque, a universal joint is attached to each end of the drive shaft.

The drive shaft is perpendicular to the rear axles. The right-angled connection is usually made with bevel gears having a ratio such that the axles rotate at from one-third to one-fourth the speed of the drive shaft. The rear axle housing also holds the differential gears that permit both rear wheels to be driven from the same source and to rotate at different speeds when turning a corner.

Like all moving mechanical devices, automobiles cannot escape from the effects of friction. In the engine, transmission, rear axle housing, and all bearings, friction is undesirable, since it increases the power required from the engine; lubrication reduces but does not eliminate this friction. On the other hand, friction between the tires and the road and in the brake shoes makes traction and braking possible. The belts that drive the fan, generator, and other accessories are friction-dependent devices. Friction is also useful in the operation of the clutch.

Some of the devices cited above are found in machines of all categories, assembled in a multitude of ways to perform all kinds of physical tasks. The function of most of these basic mechanical devices is to transmit and modify force and motion. Other devices, such as springs, flywheels, shafts, and fasteners, perform supplementary functions.

A machine may be further defined as a device consisting of two or more resistant, relatively constrained parts that may serve to transmit and modify force and motion in order to do work. The requirement that the parts of a machine be resistant implies that they be capable of carrying imposed loads without failure or loss of function. Although most machine parts are solid metallic bodies of suitable proportions, nonmetallic materials, springs, fluid pressure organs, and tension organs such as belts are also employed.

Constrained motion. The most distinctive characteristic of a machine is that the parts are interconnected and guided in such a way that their motions relative to one another are constrained. Relative to the block, for example, the piston of a reciprocating engine is constrained by the cylinder to move on a straight path; points on the crankshaft are constrained by the main bearings to move on circular paths; no other forms of relative motion are possible.

On some machines the parts are only partially constrained. If the parts are interconnected by springs or friction members, the paths of the parts relative to one another may be fixed, but the motions of the parts may be affected by the stiffness of the springs, friction, and the masses of the parts.

If all the parts of a machine are comparatively rigid members whose deflections under load are negligible, then the constrainment may be considered complete and the relative motions of the parts can be studied without considering the forces that produce them. For a specified rotational speed of the crankshaft of a reciprocating engine, for example, the corresponding speeds of points on the connecting rod and the piston can be calculated. The determination of the displacements, velocities, and accelerations of the parts of a machine for a prescribed input motion is the subject matter of kinematics of machines. Such calculations can be made without considering the forces involved, because the motions are constrained.

Mechanism of a machine. According to the definition, both forces and motions are transmitted and modified in a machine. The way in which the parts of a machine are interconnected and guided to produce a required output motion from a given input motion is known as the mechanism of the machine. The piston, connecting rod, and crankshaft in a reciprocating engine constitute a mechanism for changing the rectilinear motion of the piston into the rotary motion of the crankshaft.

Although both forces and motions are involved in the operation of machines, the primary function of a machine may be either the amplification of force or the modification of motion. A lever is essentially a force increaser, while a gearbox is most often used as a speed reducer. The motions and forces in a machine are inseparable, however, and are always in an inverse ratio. The output force on a lever is greater than the input force, but the output motion is less than the input motion. Similarly, the output speed of a gear reducer is less than the input speed, but the output torque is greater than the input torque. In the first case a gain in force is accompanied by a loss in motion, while in the second case a loss in motion is accompanied by a gain in torque.

Although the primary function of some machines can be identified, it would be difficult to classify all machines as either force or motion modifiers; some machines belong in both categories. All machines, however, must perform a motion-modifying function, since if the parts of a mechanical device do not move, it is a structure, not a machine.

While all machines have a mechanism, and consequently perform a motion-modifying function, some machines do not have a planned force-modifying purpose; the forces that exist are caused by friction and the inertia of the moving masses and do not appear as a useful output effort. This group would include measuring instruments and clocks.

In the science of mechanics, "work" is something that forces do when they move in the direction in which they are acting, and it is equal to the product of the average force and the distance moved. If a man carries a weight along a horizontal path, he does no work according to this definition, since the force and the motion are at right angles to one another; that is, the force is vertical and the motion horizontal. If he carries the weight up a flight of stairs or a ladder, he does work, since he is moving in the same direction in which he is applying a force. Mathematically, if F equals force (in pounds or kilograms), and S equals distance (in feet or metres), work is then equal to the applied force F multiplied by the distance this force moves S; or $\text{WORK} = F \times S$.

When a force causes a body to rotate about a fixed axis, or pivot, the work done is obtained by multiplying the torque (T) by the angle of rotation.

Calculating efficiency. These concepts of work are fundamental in defining the mechanical work function of machines in terms of forces and motions, and they bring out the inseparability of forces and motions in machines. Because of friction, the work output from a machine is always less than the work input, and the efficiency, which is the ratio of the two, is always less than 100 percent.

The ratio of the output to input forces is the mechanical advantage (MA), and it defines the force-modifying function, while the ratio of the input to output motions is the velocity ratio (VR), and it defines the motion-modifying function. When the efficiency is high, these ratios are approximately equal; if the output force is 10 times the input force, the input motion must be 10 times the output motion; *i.e.,* what is gained in force is lost in motion. Friction affects the mechanical advantage but not the velocity ratio (except in some mechanisms using belts and idler pulleys).

To calculate the efficiency from the ratio of output to input work, it would be necessary to know the work done by the output and input forces over a specified distance. Since this would entail the determination of average forces over the interval, it would be inconvenient. The efficiency of a machine is more easily determined from instantaneous values of load and the rate at which the load is moving. For this purpose, power formulas are most useful.

Power is the rate at which work is done. If a man carries a 10-pound (4.5-kilogram) weight a vertical height of 12 feet (3.66 m)—*i.e.,* up a ladder or stairs—in half a minute, his power expenditure is 10×12 or 120 foot-pounds in half a minute; his rate of doing work is then 240 foot-pounds per minute.

The unit of power or rate of doing work in English-speaking countries is the horsepower (hp), which is equal to 33,000 foot-pounds per minute, so that 240 foot-pounds per minute equals $240/33{,}000 = 0.00727$ horsepower.

In dealing with simple force-amplifying machines such as the lever and the wheel and axle, it is convenient to call the input force the "effort" and the output force the "load." The mechanical advantage is then the ratio of the load to the effort, and the velocity ratio is the motion (displacement or velocity) of the effort divided by the corresponding motion of the load.

machine gun, automatic weapon of small calibre that is capable of rapid, sustained fire.

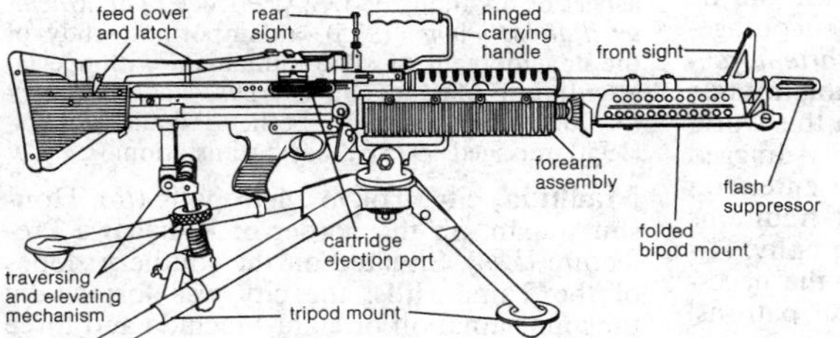

Components of a typical machine gun (U.S. M60)

The machine gun was developed in the late 19th century and has profoundly altered the character of modern warfare.

Modern machine guns are classified into three groups. The light machine gun, also called the squad automatic weapon, is equipped with a bipod and is operated by one soldier; it usually has a box-type magazine and is chambered for the small-calibre, intermediate-power ammunition fired by the assault rifles of its military unit. The medium machine gun, or general-purpose machine gun, is belt-fed, mounted on a bipod or tripod, and fires full-power rifle ammunition. Through World War II the term "heavy machine gun" designated a water-cooled machine gun that was belt-fed, handled by a special squad of several soldiers, and mounted on a tripod. Since 1945 the term has designated an automatic weapon firing ammunition larger than that used in ordinary combat rifles; the most widely used calibre is .50 inch or 12.7 mm, although a Soviet heavy machine gun fires a 14.5-millimetre round.

Most machine guns fire from 500 to 1,000 rounds per minute. The modern machine gun is a belt-fed weapon that will continue to fire as long as the trigger is held back, or until the supply of ammunition is exhausted.

From the introduction of firearms in the late European Middle Ages, attempts were made to design a weapon that would fire more than one shot without reloading, typically by a cluster or row of barrels fired in sequence. In 1718 James Puckle in London patented a machine gun that was actually produced; a model of it is in the Tower of London. Its chief feature, a revolving cylinder that fed rounds into the gun's chamber, was a basic step toward the automatic weapon; what prevented its success was the clumsy and undependable flintlock ignition. The introduction of the percussion cap in the 19th century led to the invention of numerous machine guns in the United States, several of which were employed in the American Civil War. In all of these either the cylinder or a cluster of barrels was hand cranked. The most successful was the Gatling gun, which in its later version incorporated the modern cartridge, containing bullet, propellant, and means of ignition.

The introduction of smokeless powder in the 1880s made it possible to convert the hand-cranked machine gun into a truly automatic weapon, primarily because smokeless powder's even combustion made it possible to harness the recoil so as to work the bolt, expel the spent cartridge, and reload. Hiram Stevens Maxim of the United States was the first inventor to incorporate this effect in a weapon design. The Maxim machine gun (*c.* 1884) was quickly followed by others—the Hotchkiss, Lewis, Browning, Madsen, Mauser, and other guns. Some of these utilized another property of the even burning of smokeless powder: small amounts of the combustion gas were diverted through a port to drive a piston or lever to open the breech as each round was fired, admitting the next round. As a result, during World War I the battlefield was from the outset dominated by the machine gun, generally belt-fed, water-cooled, and of a calibre matching that of the rifle. Except for synchronizing with aircraft propellers, the machine gun remained little changed throughout World War I and into World War II. Since then, innovations such as sheet-metal bodies and air-cooled, quick-changing barrels have made machine guns lighter and more reliable and quick-firing, but they still operate under the same principles as in the days of Hiram Maxim.

Most machine guns employ the gas generated by the explosion of the cartridge to drive the mechanism that introduces the new round in the chamber. The machine gun thus requires no outside source of power, and instead uses the energy released by the burning propellant in a cartridge to feed, load, lock and fire each round, and to extract and eject the empty cartridge case. This automatic operation may be accomplished by any of three ways: blowback, recoil, and gas operation.

In simple blowback operation, the empty cartridge case is hurled backward by the explosion of the cartridge and thereby pushes back the bolt, or breechblock, which in turn compresses a spring and is returned to the firing position upon that spring's recoil. The basic problem involved in blowback is to control the rearward motion of the bolt so that the gun's cycle of operation (*e.g.,* loading, firing, and ejection) takes place correctly. In recoil operation, the bolt is locked to the barrel immediately after a round is fired; both the bolt and barrel recoil, but the barrel is then returned forward by its own spring while the bolt is held to the rear by the locking mechanism until a fresh round has fallen into place in the opened breech.

More common than either of these two methods is gas operation. In this method, the energy required to operate the gun is obtained from the pressure of gas tapped off from the barrel after each cartridge explodes. In a typical gas-operated machine gun, an opening or port is provided in the side of the barrel at a point somewhere between the breech and the muzzle. When the bullet has passed this opening, some of the high-pressure gases behind it are tapped off through the hole and operate a piston or some similiar device for converting the pressure of the powder gases to a thrust. This thrust is then used through a suitable mechanism to provide the energy necessary for performing the automatic functions required for sustained fire; *e.g.,* loading, firing, and ejection.

machine tool, stationary power-driven machine that is used to shape or form parts made of metal or other materials. *See* tool.

Consult the INDEX *first*

---

machine-tractor station, Russian MASHINNO-TRAKTORNAYA STANTSIYA (MTS), in the Soviet Union, state-owned institution that rented heavy agricultural machinery (*e.g.,* tractors and combines) to a group of neighbouring kolkhozy (collective farms) and supplied skilled personnel to operate and repair the equipment. The stations, which became widespread and prominent during the collectivization drive in the early 1930s, were instrumental in the mechanization of Soviet agriculture.

The MTS were paid in kind for their services by the kolkhozy and thereby also functioned as major agencies for grain procurement for the state. In addition, they were the chief instrument used by the Communist Party to control the countryside. The MTS' political departments were given absolute control of the farms and continued to have great local political influence until they were abolished in 1953. But in exercising their influence they frequently caused confusion by rivaling the authority of the district party organizations, and they often conflicted with the kolkhoz management, which controlled the labour.

In 1958, as part of a major agricultural reform, the MTS were abolished and their equipment was sold to the kolkhozy. Some of the stations were transformed into Repair and Technical Service Stations (*Remontnotekhnicheskie stantsii;* RTS), which repaired the machinery, supplied spare parts, and continued to rent machines for special purposes—*e.g.,* road building. In 1961 the RTS were replaced by the All-Union Farm Machinery Association (*Soyuzselkhoztekhnika*).

Machkund (India): *see* Sileru River.

Machramion (ancient city): *see* Assus.

Machray, Robert (b. May 17, 1831, Aberdeen, Aberdeenshire, Scot.—d. March 9, 1904, Winnipeg, Manitoba, Can.), Scottish-born archbishop of Rupert's Land in northern and western Canada.

He studied at Aberdeen and at Sidney Sussex College, Cambridge, and became a Church of England priest in 1856. He was elected to a fellowship at Cambridge, remaining there until 1865, when he was made bishop of Rupert's Land with headquarters in Winnipeg. The diocese was then thinly populated and covered an area of 2,000,000 square miles (5,000,000 square km). The population grew, and by the end of the century his territory had been divided into eight sees with 190 clergy. When the Canadian Anglican churches were unified in 1893, Machray was made archbishop of Rupert's Land and primate of all Canada.

Mach's principle, in cosmology, hypothesis that the inertial forces experienced by a body in nonuniform motion are determined by the quantity and distribution of matter in the universe. It was so called by Albert Einstein after the 19th-century Austrian physicist and philosopher Ernst Mach. Einstein found the hypothesis helpful in formulating his theory of general relativity—*i.e.,* it was suggestive of a connection between geometry and matter—and attributed the idea to Mach, unaware that the English philosopher George Berkeley had proposed similar views during the 1700s. (Berkeley had argued that all motion, both uniform and nonuniform, was relative to the distant stars.) Einstein later abandoned the principle when it was realized that inertia is implicit in the geodesic equation of motion and need not depend on the existence of matter elsewhere in the universe.

Machu Picchu, ancient fortress city of the Incas in the Andes Mountains of south-central Peru, about 50 miles (80 kilometres) northwest of Cuzco. Perched in a narrow saddle between two sharp peaks, it escaped detection by the Spaniards and was discovered only in 1911 by Hiram Bingham of Yale University. It is one of the few pre-Columbian urban centres found nearly intact. The site, about 5 square miles (13 square kilometres) in area,

Machu Picchu
Mayes—FPG/EB Inc.

includes a temple and a citadel that were once surrounded by terraced gardens linked by more than 3,000 steps. The stonework of the buildings is not so highly refined as that of other Inca sites, and the period of occupancy is uncertain.

machzor (Judaism): *see* maḥzor.

Macià, Francesc (b. Oct. 21, 1859, Vilanueva y Geltrú, Spain—d. Dec. 25, 1933, Barcelona), Catalan leader and founder of the nationalist party Estat Català (1922), who played a major role in achieving an autonomous status for Catalonia.

In the turmoil after the collapse of Primo de Rivera's dictatorship, Macià formed the Republican Left of Catalonia, a coalition of the Catalan Republican Party, the Estat Català, and a third party. After the electoral victory over the Spanish monarchy (April 1931), Macià proclaimed the Catalan Republic and immediately started a vigorous campaign for home rule. One year later (Sept. 9, 1932) the statute of Catalonian autonomy was promulgated.

As head of the Catalan government, Macià had to face discontent on the left. In the resulting swing to the right, Macià's Republican Left was defeated in the election of Nov. 19, 1933. He died five weeks later.

Macias Nguema Biyogo (Equatorial Guinea): *see* Fernando Po.

Macina, also spelled MASINA, region, the middle course of the Niger River in Mali, between Ségou and Timbuktu (Tombouctou), where its braided channels form a vast inland delta extending 300 mi (480 km) northeast-southwest. The depression is covered by a network of lakes, swamps, and channels and is flooded during the rainy season, making the area one of the most fertile in Africa. A large dam at Sasanding supplies irrigation canals. Millet is the chief crop, and cattle and sheep are bred by the Fulani.

MacInnes, Tom, byname of THOMAS ROBERT EDWARD McINNES (b. Oct. 29, 1867, Dresden, Ont., Can.—d. Feb. 11, 1951, Vancouver, B.C.), Canadian writer whose works range from vigorous, slangy recollections of the Yukon gold rush, *Lonesome Bar* (1909), to a translation of and commentary on Lao-tzu's philosophy, irreverently titled *The Teaching of the Old Boy* (1927). His collected poems include *Complete Poems* (1923) and *In the Old of My Age* (1947). *Chinook Days* (1927), a fictionalized autobiography, also contains history and folklore of British Columbia.

McIntire, Samuel (b. January 1757, Salem, Mass.—d. Feb. 6, 1811, Salem, Mass., U.S.), U.S. architect and craftsman known as "the architect of Salem." A versatile craftsman, McIntire designed and produced furniture and interior woodwork in addition to his domestic architecture, in which he was influenced by the American architect Charles Bulfinch.

Gardner-White-Pingree House, Salem, Mass., designed by Samuel McIntire, 1804
Wayne Andrews

The house McIntire created for Jerathmeel Peirce was considered one of the finest built in New England during the post-Revolutionary period. The Salem courthouse (1785; demolished 1839) was another excellent example of his work. Bulfinch made the first designs and McIntire the final ones for the lavishly decorated Derby mansion in Salem begun in 1794 (destroyed in 1815). McIntire's furniture, more than 100 pieces of which survive, included some of the best American examples of the Sheraton style.

Macintosh, Charles (b. Dec. 29, 1766, Glasgow—d. July 25, 1843, near Glasgow), Scottish chemist, best known for his invention in 1823 of a method for making waterproof garments by using rubber dissolved in coal-tar naphtha for cementing two pieces of cloth together. The mackintosh garment was named for him.

In 1823, while trying to find uses for the waste products of gasworks, Macintosh noted that coal-tar naphtha dissolved india rubber. He then took wool cloth, painted one side of it with the rubber preparation, and placed another thickness of wool cloth on top, thereby producing a waterproof fabric. Soon after he began the manufacture of coats and other garments. But problems developed. In the process of seaming a garment, tailors punctured the fabric, allowing rain to penetrate; the natural oil in woollen cloth caused the rubber cement to deteriorate; and, in the earlier years, the garments became stiff in winter and sticky in hot weather. The mackintosh, as it came to be known, was greatly improved when vulcanized rubber, which resisted temperature changes, became available in 1839.

Mačiulis, Jonas (Lithuanian poet): *see* Maironis.

MacIver, David Randall- (archaeologist): *see* Randall-MacIver, David.

MacIver, Robert Morrison (b. April 17, 1882, Stornoway, Outer Hebrides, Scot.—d. June 15, 1970, New York City), Scottish-born sociologist, political scientist, and educator who expressed belief in the compatibility of individualism and social organization. His creative power to make distinctions between state and community led to new theories of democracy, of multi-group coexistence, and a definition for the nature of authority.

After formal education at Edinburgh and reading classics at Oxford, MacIver began teaching at the University of Aberdeen (1907). He received a doctorate from Edinburgh in 1917. MacIver accepted a political-science post at the University of Toronto, first as a professor (1915–22) and then as head of the department (1922–26), where he found a compatible intellectual climate and produced two of his early works, *Community: A Sociological Study* (1917) and *Elements of Social Science* (1921).

MacIver then chaired the department of economics and sociology at Barnard College (1927–29). Subsequently he was professor of political philosophy and sociology at Columbia University (1929–50) and was president (1963–65) and chancellor (1965–66), of the New School for Social Research, New York City.

Among his numerous writings are *Society: Its Structure and Changes* (1931), for which he received an honorary degree at the Harvard Tercentenary (1936); *Leviathan and the People* (1939); *The Web of Government* (1947; revised 1965), which received the Woodrow Wilson Prize; *The More Perfect Union* (1948); *The Pursuit of Happiness* (1955); *The Nations and the United Nations* (1959); *Power Transformed* (1964); *The Prevention and Control of Delinquency* (1966); his autobiography, *As a Tale That is Told* (1968); and *Politics and Society* (1969).

MacIver upheld the idea that societies evolve from highly communal states to ones in which individual functions and group affiliations are extremely specialized. He felt that the sociologist must avoid imposing his own values on social fact; social evolution is not necessarily equivalent to social progress, which can only be measured by personal judgment.

Mack, Connie, byname of CORNELIUS ALEXANDER McGILLICUDDY (b. Dec. 22/23, 1862, East Brookfield, Mass., U.S.—d. Feb. 8, 1956, Philadelphia), professional U.S. baseball manager and team executive, the "grand old man" of the major leagues in the first half of the 20th century. He managed the Philadelphia Athletics from 1901 through 1950, during which time they won nine American League championships and five World Series (1910–11, 1913, 1929–30). He was president of the club from 1937 through 1953. In 1937 he was elected to the Baseball Hall of Fame.

Connie Mack
AP/Wide World Photos

Mack played, chiefly as a catcher, in about 700 major league games with Washington (1886–89), Buffalo (1890), and Pittsburgh (1891–96). While a player he shortened his name so that it would fit on a scoreboard. Mack also managed Pittsburgh from Sept. 3, 1894, through the 1896 season.

In 1897 Mack joined the Milwaukee club in the Western League (renamed the American League in 1900) as playing manager. In 1901 he became manager and part owner of the Philadelphia team and helped to establish the American League as a major league. In his 53 years of managing in the big leagues, his teams won 3,776 games and lost 4,025, both all-time records.

Mack von Leiberich, Karl, Freiherr (Baron) (b. Aug. 25, 1752, Nenslingen, Bavaria—d. Oct. 22, 1828, Sankt Pölten, Austria), Austrian soldier, commander of the defeated forces at the Napoleonic battles of Ulm and Austerlitz.

In 1770 he joined an Austrian cavalry regiment, becoming an officer seven years later. He served in the brief War of the Bavarian Succession; in 1778 he was promoted to first lieutenant and in 1785 ennobled under the name of Mack von Leiberich. Against the French in the Revolutionary wars he fought first in the Netherlands and, after becoming lieutenant field marshal (1797), accepted command of the Neopolitan army in 1798. Forced to take refuge from his own men, he escaped to the French camp and was sent as a prisoner of war to Paris, whence he escaped in disguise two years later.

Mack was not employed for some years but in 1804 was made quartermaster-general of the army, with instructions to prepare for a war with France. He attempted hastily to reform the army, and in 1805 he became the real commander (under titular commander-in-chief Archduke Ferdinand) of the army that opposed Napoleon in Bavaria, but his position was ill-defined and his authority treated with slight respect by his colleagues. His miscalculations and lack of control contributed to the disastrous Austrian defeats at Ulm, where he was surrounded and forced to surrender at least 50,000 men (October 15), and then at Austerlitz (December 2), the scene of one of Napoleon's greatest victories.

After Austerlitz, Mack was tried by a court-martial, sitting from February 1806 to June 1807, and sentenced to be deprived of his rank, his regiment, and the order of Maria Theresa, and to be imprisoned for two years. He was released in 1808, and, in 1819, when the ultimate victory of the allies had obliterated the memory of earlier disasters, he was reinstated in the army as lieutenant field marshal and a member of the order of Maria Theresa.

Mackay, city, eastern coast of Queensland, Australia, at the mouth of the Pioneer River. Its deepwater artificial port has one of the world's largest bulk-handling installations. The centre of Australia's sugar industry and site of a sugar-research institute (1953), it also produces dairy foods, lumber, and alcohol. Tropical fruits are grown in the area, and tourism is significant. Founded in 1862 and named for Capt. John MacKay, who explored the region, it became a municipality in 1869 and a city in 1918. Pop. (1981) 35,361.

Mackay, Clarence Hungerford (b. April 17, 1874, San Francisco—d. Nov. 12, 1938, New York City), U.S. communications executive and philanthropist who supervised the completion of the first transpacific cable between the United States and the Far East in 1904.

Clarence Mackay, 1925

By courtesy of the Library of Congress, Washington, D.C.

His father, John William Mackay (1831–1902), one of the miners who discovered the bonanza of the Comstock Lode, organized the Commercial Cable Company in 1883, broke the monopoly held by the Western Union Telegraph Company directed by Jay Gould, and established the competing Postal Telegraph & Cable Corporation. Postal Telegraph, with Clarence Mackay as president following his father's death, laid a cable between New York and Cuba in 1907 and later established cable communication with southern Europe via the Azores and with northern Europe via Ireland. In 1928 he became the first to combine radio, cables, and telegraphs under one management. His daughter Ellin married the popular-song composer Irving Berlin in 1926.

McKay, Claude (b. Sept. 15, 1890, Jamaica, British West Indies—d. May 22, 1948, Chicago), Jamaican-born poet and novelist whose *Home to Harlem* (1928) was the most popular novel written by an American black to that time. Before going to the U.S. in 1912, he wrote two volumes of Jamaican dialect verse, *Songs of Jamaica* and *Constab Ballads* (1912).

After attending Tuskegee Institute (1912) and Kansas State Teachers College (1912–14), McKay went to New York in 1914, where he contributed regularly to the *Liberator*, then a leading journal of avant-garde politics and art. The shock of American racism turned him from the conservatism of his youth. With the publication of two volumes of poetry, *Spring in New Hampshire* (1920) and *Harlem Shadows* (1922), McKay emerged as the first and most militant voice of the Harlem Renaissance (*q.v.*). After 1922 McKay lived successively in the Soviet Union, France, Spain, and Morocco. In both *Home to Harlem* and *Banjo* (1929), he attempted to capture the vitality and essential health of the uprooted black vagabonds of urban America and Europe. There followed a collection of short stories, *Gingertown* (1932), and another novel, *Banana Bottom* (1933). In all these works McKay searched among the common folk for a distinctive black identity.

After returning to America in 1934, McKay was attacked by the Communists for repudiating their dogmas and by liberal whites and blacks for his criticism of integrationist-oriented civil rights groups. McKay advocated full civil liberties and racial solidarity. In 1940 he became a U.S. citizen; in 1942 he was converted to Roman Catholicism and worked with a Catholic youth organization until his death. He wrote for various magazines and newspapers, including the *New Leader* and the New York *Amsterdam News*. He also wrote an autobiography, *A Long Way from Home* (1937), and a study, *Harlem: Negro Metropolis* (1940). His *Selected Poems* (1953) was issued posthumously.

McKay, David O(man) (b. Sept. 8, 1873, Huntsville, Utah, U.S.—d. Jan. 18, 1970, Salt Lake City, Utah), U.S. religious leader, ninth president (1951–70) of the Church of Jesus Christ of Latter-day Saints (Mormons).

He served as a missionary in Scotland (1897–99) and then returned to Utah to become instructor and principal (1899–1908) of the Weber State Academy, now Weber State College. In 1906 he was elected a member of the Quorum of the Twelve Apostles, and in 1950 he was chosen as its president. During his 19 years as president of the church, relations between Mormons and non-Mormons improved greatly, and the church experienced extensive growth in membership.

McKay, Donald (b. Sept. 4, 1810, Nova Scotia—d. Sept. 20, 1880, Hamilton, Mass., U.S.), Canadian-born naval architect and builder of the largest and fastest of the clipper ships.

After emigrating to New York City in 1827, he worked as an apprentice to the ship carpenter Isaac Webb. In 1845 he established a shipyard at East Boston, Mass.; there he designed and built his great clipper ships. His first, the "Stag Hound," launched in 1850, was followed by many others, including the "Lightning," which established a long-standing world record of 436 nautical miles in a day, at times reaching a speed of 21 knots. His "James Baines" set an around-the-world record of 133 days and a transatlantic record of 12 days 6 hours from Boston to Liverpool. McKay's "Great Republic," the largest clipper ever built, weighed 4,555 tons.

Donald McKay, detail of a lithograph by L. Geozelier, *c.* 1853

By courtesy of the Mariners' Museum, Newport News, Va.

By 1855 the demand for clipper ships was over and McKay closed his yard. In 1863 he equipped the yard to build iron ships and constructed several such vessels for the U.S. Navy, including the warship "Nausett"; but he was not financially successful in this work. His last sailing ship, the "Glory of the Seas," built in 1869, was under sail until 1923.

MacKaye, Percy (b. March 16, 1875, New York City—d. Aug. 31, 1956, Cornish, N.H., U.S.), U.S. poet and playwright whose use of historical and contemporary folk literature furthered the development of the pageant in the U.S.

MacKaye was introduced to the theatre at an early age by his father, actor Steele MacKaye, with whom he first collaborated. Graduating from Harvard University in 1897, he studied abroad for two years and returned to the U.S. to write and lecture. In 1912 he published *The Civic Theatre,* in which he advocated amateur community theatricals. He attempted to bring poetry and drama to large participant groups and to unite the stage arts, music, and poetry by the use of masques and communal chanting. He wrote, among others, the pageants *The Canterbury Pilgrims* (published in 1903) and, as co-author, *St. Louis: A Civic Masque* (performed in St. Louis, Mo., in 1914 with 7,500 participants).

A trip to the Kentucky mountains in 1921 stimulated MacKaye's interest in folk literature. In 1929 he became advisory editor to *Folk-Say,* a journal of American folklore; he also conducted research in collaboration with his wife, Marion Morse MacKaye; and taught poetry and folklore at Rollins College in Winter Park, Fla. His most noteworthy contributions to U.S. drama and pageantry are *The Scarecrow* (1908), a historical play; *Caliban* (1916), an elaborate pageant-masque; *This Fine Pretty World* (1923), a regional play; and *The Mystery of Hamlet: King of Denmark* (1945), a study of past and present tragedy seen by a contemporary U.S. poet.

MacKaye, (James Morrison) Steele (b. June 6, 1842, Buffalo—d. Feb. 25, 1894, Timpas, Colo., U.S.), U.S. playwright, actor, theatre manager, and inventor who has been called the closest approximation to a Renaissance man produced by the United States in the 19th century.

In his youth he studied painting with Hunt, Inness, and Troyon. A pupil of Delsarte and Régnier, he was the first American to act Hamlet in London (1873). At Harvard, Cornell, and elsewhere he lectured on the philosophy of aesthetics. In New York City he founded the St. James, Madison Square, and Lyceum theatres.

MacKaye wrote 30 plays, including *Hazel Kirke*, performed many thousands of times, *Paul Kauvar,* and *Money Mad*, acting in them in 17 different roles. He organized the first school of acting in the U.S, which later became the American Academy of Dramatic Art; initiated overhead lighting (1874); invented the first moving "double stage" (1879); and invented folding theatre seats. In all, he patented over 100 theatrical inventions.

For the Chicago World's Fair of 1893, MacKaye projected the world's largest theatre, his Spectatorium (seating 12,000, with 25 moving stages), revolutionizing stage production and anticipating motion pictures. Financial difficulties prevented completion of the theatre, but a scale model was later successfully demonstrated.

His two-volume biography, *Epoch: The Life of Steele MacKaye* (1927), written by his son Percy, was reprinted in 1968.

Macke, August (b. Jan. 3, 1887, Meschede, Ger.—d. Sept. 26, 1914, Perthes-les-Hurlus, Fr.), German painter who was a leader of Der Blaue Reiter group, one of the sources of German Expressionism.

Macke was influenced, particularly in his earlier work, by his teacher Lovis Corinth, as well as by the Cubists and the Impressionists. A lyrical temperament, however, is revealed in his works, which avoid the often violent style and subject matter of his fellow Expressionists. His art combines the tradition of French painting—its sense of the grace of movement and atmosphere in landscape painting—with the cosmic sentiment of German art.

In 1914 Macke traveled to Tunis with Paul Klee, and there he painted a series of works that place the subject upon a grid of various pure colours. These paintings demonstrate the effect that Orphic Cubism had upon Macke and number among his most widely admired works. Macke was killed in action in World War I.

McKeesport, city, Allegheny county, southwestern Pennsylvania, U.S. It is situated at the junction of the Monongahela and Youghiogheny rivers, 14 miles (23 km) southeast of Pittsburgh. First settled about 1755 by David McKee, a ferry operator, the town was laid out in 1795 by his son John. In 1794 it was a centre of dissident activity during the Whiskey Rebellion (an insurrection against an excise tax on distilled liquors). Coal mining began in the area about 1830, but McKeesport did not develop appreciably until the basic ingredients of the steel industry (coal, iron, and railroads) coalesced in the late 19th century. It became part of the Pittsburgh industrial complex, with steel production as the dominant activity. McKeesport began experiencing considerable unemployment as the steel industries in the Pittsburgh area declined in the 1980s. The McKeesport campus of Pennsylvania State University opened in 1947. Inc. borough, 1842; city, 1890. Pop. (1990) 26,016.

McKellen, Sir Ian (Murray) (b. May 25, 1939, Burnley, Lancashire, Eng.), British actor of great versatility, noted for his work with the Royal Shakespeare Company.

McKellen performed on stage while attending school. He graduated (B.A.) from St. Catharine's College, Cambridge, in 1961 and made his professional debut as Roper in Robert Bolt's *A Man For All Seasons* shortly thereafter. Acting steadily throughout the 1960s, McKellen won both popular and critical acclaim in his performances as both William Shakespeare's Richard II and Christopher Marlowe's Edward II for the 1969 Edinburgh Festival. In 1971 he cofounded (with Edward Petherbridge and David Williams) a cooperative known as the Actors Company, designed to involve its members in all aspects of play production and all sorts of roles. He left the group in 1974 to join the Royal Shakespeare Company.

A versatile actor, McKellen played a range of characters from Shakespearean to contemporary, and many roles (in plays by such authors as Anton Chekhov, Frank Wedekind, and others) in between. Though his interpretations were frequently controversial, his immense talent for acting was unquestionable. He also directed several plays, wrote and performed a one-man show, called "Acting Shakespeare," and acted in a number of motion pictures, notably a film version of David Hare's *Plenty* (1985). McKellen became a Commander of the British Empire in 1979 and was knighted in 1991.

Macken, Walter (b. 1915, Galway, Ire.—d. April 22, 1967, Galway), Irish novelist and dramatist whose tales combine an honest and often harsh reflection of the realities of Irish life with a love of Ireland and a compassionate respect for its people.

Macken was an actor and stage manager in Galway, where he became actor-manager-director of the Gaelic Theatre. He was also connected with the famous Abbey Theatre in Dublin. Macken's novel *Rain on the Wind* (1950), a story of Galway life, was popular in Europe and in the United States. He later wrote a trilogy of historical novels, including *Seek the Fair Land* (1959), set in Cromwellian Ireland; *The Silent People* (1962), depicting the great Irish potato famine; and *The Scorching Wind* (1964), which brought the story up to the present day. As a dramatist Macken is chiefly known for *Mungo's Mansion,* performed in 1946 at the Abbey Theatre and in 1947 in London as *Galway Handicap.* Macken also wrote *Home is the Hero,* which was produced by the Abbey Theatre and published in 1953.

McKenna, Joseph (b. Aug. 10, 1843, Philadelphia, Pa., U.S.—d. Nov. 21, 1926, Washington, D.C.), U.S. Supreme Court justice from 1898 to 1925.

McKenna grew up in California and was admitted to the state bar in 1865. A Republican, he served as Solano county district attorney (1866–70) and in the California state legislature (1875–76). Despite the prevailing anti-Roman Catholic sentiments that contributed to two defeats at the polls, McKenna was elected in his third Congressional bid to the U.S. House of Representatives (1885–92).

In 1892 President Benjamin Harrison named him to the Ninth U.S. Circuit Court. President William McKinley called McKenna back to Washington in 1897 to join his cabinet as attorney general; later that year the president nominated him to fill a vacancy on the Supreme Court. The nomination was confirmed early in 1898 despite widespread complaints that McKenna's record on the circuit court had been undistinguished. During his 27 years on the Supreme Court bench, McKenna was considered a diligent but not otherwise notable justice.

McKenna, Reginald (b. July 6, 1863, London, Eng.—d. Sept. 6, 1943, London), British statesman who, as first lord of the Admiralty, initiated in 1909 a battleship construction program that gave Great Britain a considerable advantage over Germany in capital-ship strength at the beginning of World War I.

Reginald McKenna, detail of a portrait by Sir James Gunn

By courtesy of the Midland Bank; photograph, A.C. Cooper

In 1905, after serving for 10 years in the House of Commons, McKenna became financial secretary of the Treasury, and in 1907 he was named president of the Board of Education. Appointed first lord of the Admiralty in 1908, he urged that 18 battleships of the Dreadnought class be built, 6 in each of the years 1909–11, in order to offset the growth of the German fleet. He was opposed in this by David Lloyd George, Winston Churchill, and others who wished to build fewer ships and spend more money on social-reform programs. McKenna prevailed, however, and 18 Dreadnoughts actually were begun by the end of 1911. In that year a dispute with the war minister, Viscount Haldane, resulted in McKenna's exchanging office with Churchill, the home secretary.

As chancellor of the Exchequer from May 1915 to December 1916, during the early period of World War I, McKenna was responsible for a 40 percent personal income surtax and a 50 percent excess-profits tax (both called "McKenna duties") to sustain the war effort. He resigned when Lloyd George, whom he disliked, became prime minister. From 1919 until his death McKenna was chairman of the Midland Bank.

McKenna, Siobhan, original name SIOBHAN GIOLLAMHUIRE NIC CIONNAITH (b. May 24, 1923, Belfast, N.Ire.—d. Nov. 16, 1986, Dublin, Ire.), versatile Irish actress best known for her portrayals of such impassioned characters as Shaw's *Saint Joan* and Pegeen Mike, the lusty innkeeper in John Millington Synge's most famous play, *The Playboy of the Western World.*

Siobhan McKenna as Joan of Arc

By courtesy of the Raymond Mander and Joe Mitchenson Theatre Collection, London

A member of an amateur Gaelic theatre group, McKenna made her professional stage debut in 1940 at the Gaelic repertory theatre An Taibhdhearc in Galway, Ire. In 1951 she starred in her own Gaelic translation of *Saint Joan,* a role she repeated in English in London (1955) and in the United States (1956). She appeared with the Abbey players in Dublin in both Gaelic- and English-language plays (1943–46), then made her London debut in Paul Vincent Carroll's *White Steed* (1947). McKenna first achieved international fame for her role as Pegeen Mike in 1951 at the Edinburgh Theatre Festival. She also performed in the motion picture version of the play (1962).

In 1961 she appeared as Joan Dark in Bertolt Brecht's *Saint Joan of the Stockyards,* repeating the role in 1964. She was also memorable as Juno in Sean O'Casey's *Juno and the Paycock* and as Josie in Eugene O'Neill's *Moon for the Misbegotten.* Her one-woman readings from Irish authors were also popular.

Mackensen, August von (b. Dec. 6, 1849, Haus Leipnitz, Saxony [Germany]—d. Nov. 8, 1945, Celle, Ger.), German field marshal and one of the most successful commanders in World War I.

Beginning his army career in 1869, Mackensen served in various campaigns, received successive promotions, and, during World War I, took command of the combined German-Austrian 11th Army in western Galicia (Poland; April 1915). Then, ably assisted by his chief of staff, Hans von Seeckt, Mackensen achieved the great German breakthrough in the Gorlice-Tarnów area (Poland), for which he was promoted to field marshal (June 20, 1915). The breakthrough was the beginning of a series of victories for Mackensen: the defeat of the Russians at Brest-Litovsk and at Pinsk (August–September 1915), the overrunning of Serbia (October–November 1915),

Mackensen, 1915

By courtesy of the Staatsbibliothek Preussischer Kulturbesitz, West Berlin

and the occupation of Romania (1916–17). After the Armistice, Mackensen was interned for a year. He retired from the army in 1920 and was made a state councillor in 1933.

Mackenzie, Alexander (b. Jan. 28, 1822, Logierait, Perth, Scot.—d. April 17, 1892, Toronto), Scottish-born politician, the first Liberal prime minister of Canada (1873–78).

Mackenzie emigrated in 1842 from Scotland to Canada West (now Ontario), where

Alexander Mackenzie, portrait by an unknown artist

National Film Board of Canada Phototheque

he worked as a stone mason and established himself as a building contractor at Sarnia. His interest in reform led to his becoming editor in 1852 of the *Lambton Shield,* a local Liberal newspaper. He became friendly with George Brown, editor of *The Globe* (Toronto) and leader of the Reform Party. Mackenzie supported the confederation movement. After the Dominion of Canada was created in 1867, he was elected by Lambton to the dominion's first House of Commons, in which he led the Liberal opposition. When dual representation was abolished in 1872, he gave up his post as provincial treasurer in the Ontario Assembly.

Mackenzie became Canada's first Liberal prime minister after the fall of Sir John Macdonald's Conservative government in 1873. Lacking a strong party, however, he could not cope with the urgent economic difficulties of the time. Macdonald's protectionist policy was preferred to Mackenzie's aim of renewed reciprocity with the United States, and the Liberal government was defeated in 1878. Mackenzie also failed to complete the Pacific railway. He resigned the leadership of the opposition in 1880 but retained his seat in Parliament until his death.

Mackenzie, Sir Alexander (b. 1755?, Stornoway, Lewis and Harris, Outer Hebrides, Scot.—d. March 11, 1820, near Pitlochry, Perth), Scottish fur trader and explorer who traced the course of the 1,100-mile Mackenzie River in Canada.

Emigrating to North America, he entered (1779) a Montreal trading firm, which amalgamated with the North West Company, a rival of the Hudson's Bay Company. In what is now the province of Alberta, Mackenzie and a cousin set up a trading post, Ft. Chipewyan, on Lake Athabasca (1788). This was the starting point of his expedition of 1789, which followed the Mackenzie from the Great Slave Lake to the river's delta on the Arctic Ocean. In 1793 Mackenzie crossed the Rocky Mountains from Ft. Chipewyan to the Pacific coast of what is now British Columbia. These journeys together constitute the first known transcontinental crossing of America north of Mexico. His *Voyage from Montreal on the River St. Lawrence, Through the Continent of North America, to the Frozen and Pacific Oceans, in the Years 1789 and 1793* was published in 1801. Knighted in 1802, he lived in Scotland after 1808.

Mackenzie, Sir Alexander Campbell (b. Aug. 22, 1847, Edinburgh—d. April 28, 1935, London), Scottish composer who, with Sir Hubert Parry and Sir Charles Stanford, was associated with the revival of British music in the late 19th century.

At the age of 10 he was sent to study music in Germany at Sondershausen; later he studied at the Royal Academy of Music, London, of which he was principal from 1888 to 1924. He was knighted in 1922. His works include the cantatas *The Bride* (1881) and *Jason* (1882); the operas *Colomba* (1883) and *The Troubadour* (1886); an oratorio, *The Rose of Sharon* (1884); a *Scottish Concerto* for piano (1897); three Scottish rhapsodies; and an overture, *Britannia* (1894).

Mackenzie, Charles Frederick (b. April 10, 1825, Portmore, Peebles, Scot.—d. Jan. 31, 1862, Malo Island, Portuguese East Africa), Scottish-born Anglican priest and the first bishop in the British colonial territory of Central Africa.

Mackenzie went to Africa in 1854 as archdeacon to Bishop John Colenso of Natal. There he aroused opposition among English settlers by obeying the bishop's order to wear a surplice and sharing the bishop's desire that African Christians participate in full equality with white Christians in all church affairs.

Illness forced Mackenzie to return to England in 1859, but, at the behest of the Universities Mission to South Africa, he returned to Africa and headed its mission in the Zambezi River region the following year, being consecrated bishop on New Year's Day, 1861. Settling at Magomero (in modern Malâwi), Mackenzie worked for a year in the Manganja tribal territory despite constant illness, breakdowns in communications and supply lines, and involvements in local tribal warfare.

BIBLIOGRAPHY. H. Goodwin, *Memoir of Bishop Mackenzie,* 2nd ed. (1865); O. Chadwick, *Mackenzie's Grave* (1959).

Mackenzie, (Sir Edward Montague) Compton (b. Jan. 17, 1883, West Hartlepool, Durham, Eng.—d. Nov. 30, 1972, Edinburgh), British novelist who suffered critical acclaim and neglect with equal indifference, leaving a prodigious output of more than 100 novels, plays, and biographies.

Born into a well-known theatrical family, he was educated at Magdalen College, Oxford, and turned from the stage to literature when he was in his late 20s. Mackenzie showed a mastery of cockney humour in *Carnival* (1912) and *Sinister Street* (1913–14); a satiric sting in *Water on the Brain* (1933), attacking the British secret service, which had prosecuted him under the Official Secrets Act for his autobiographical *Greek Memories* (1932); and a love of pure fun in *The Monarch of the Glen* (1941) and *Whisky Galore* (1947). Other novels included *Poor Relations* (1919), *Rich Relatives* (1921), *Vestal Fire* (1927), and *Extraordinary Women* (1928); among his plays were *The Gentleman in Grey* (1906), *Columbine* (1920), and *The Lost Cause* (1931). The first volume of his memoirs, *My Life and Times: Octave One*, appeared in 1963, and *Octave Ten* in 1971.

An ardent Scottish nationalist, Mackenzie lived in Scotland after 1928 and aided in the foundation of the Scottish National Party. He served as rector of Glasgow University (1931–34), as literary critic for the London *Daily Mail* (1931–35), and as the founder and editor of *Gramophone* magazine (1923–62). Mackenzie was named Officer of the Order of the British Empire in 1919 and was knighted in 1952.

Mackenzie (of Rosehaugh), Sir George (b. 1636, Dundee, Scot.—d. May 8, 1691, Westminster, London), Scottish lawyer who gained the nickname "Bloody Mackenzie" for his prosecution of Covenanters; he was founder of the Advocates' Library, Edinburgh.

As king's advocate after August 1677, Mackenzie conducted, in the name of Charles II, a vigorous prosecution of Covenanters for their refusal to conform to the established church and, in consequence, has been compared to England's notorious Judge Jeffreys. As dean of the faculty of advocates, Mackenzie promoted the foundation of the Advocates' Library, now the National Library of Scotland. After he refused to concur with measures to abolish anti-Catholic laws, Mackenzie was removed from office (1686) but was later reinstated (1688). After the Revolution of 1688, he ceased to play an active political role.

Mackenzie wrote on religious issues and moral philosophy, but the bulk of his writing dealt with the law. In *Jus Regium* (1684) and other works, he advocated doctrines of royal prerogative and the support of hereditary monarchy; yet he criticized intolerance and inhumanity. Mackenzie's *Vindication of the Government of Scotland During the Reign of Charles II* (1691) is a valuable primary source for that period. Mackenzie was knighted sometime before 1668.

Mackenzie, Henry (b. Aug. 26, 1745, Edinburgh—d. Jan. 14, 1831, Edinburgh), Scottish novelist, playwright, poet, and editor, whose most important novel, *The Man of Feeling,* established him as a major literary figure in Scotland. His work had considerable influence on Sir Walter Scott, who dedicated his *Waverley* novels to him in 1814.

Henry Mackenzie, detail of an oil painting by William Stavely; in the Scottish National Portrait Gallery, Edinburgh

By courtesy of the Scottish National Portrait Gallery, Edinburgh

Mackenzie's early works include imitations of traditional Scottish ballads, but, on moving to London to study law after 1765, he began to imitate English literary styles in which "sentiment" was then becoming a powerful literary influence. His mawkish novel *The Man of Feeling* (begun 1767, published 1771) was a best-seller. Settling in Scotland from 1768, Mackenzie wrote two more novels: *The Man of the World* (1773), portraying a villainous hero, and *Julia de Roubigné* (1777), imitating Richardson's *Clarissa*. He also wrote a play, edited two periodicals, and helped found learned societies.

Consult the INDEX *first*

Mackenzie, Sir James (b. April 12, 1853, Scone, Perthshire, Scot.—d. Jan. 26, 1925, London), Scottish cardiologist, pioneer in the study of cardiac arrhythmias. He was first to make simultaneous records of the arterial and venous pulses to evaluate the condition of the heart, a procedure that laid the foundation for much future research. Mackenzie also drew attention to the question of the heart's capacity for work, paving the way for the study of the energetics of the heart muscle.

After receiving his M.D. degree at the University of Edinburgh in 1882, Mackenzie practiced medicine for more than a quarter of a century in Burnley, Lancashire, where he was also physician to Victoria Hospital.

After his move to London at the age of 54, Mackenzie established a successful practice as a consulting physician. His reputation grew rapidly. In his classic text *The Study of the Pulse* (1902), he described an instrument of his own devising that he called a "polygraph," which allowed the user to correlate the arterial and venous pulses with the beat of the heart itself. This instrument enabled Mackenzie to make important and original distinctions between harmless and dangerous types of pulse irregularities. In his ambitious text *Diseases of the Heart* (1908), Mackenzie summarized his diagnostic work on pulsation and cardiovascular disease. He also convincingly demonstrated the efficacy of the drug digitalis in the treatment of cardiac arrhythmias. During World War I he served as a consultant to the Military Heart Hospital, an institution he had been instrumental in founding. He was knighted in 1915.

Mackenzie, John (b. Aug. 30, 1835, Knockando, Moray County, Scot.—d. March 23, 1899, Kimberley, Cape Colony), British missionary who was a constant champion of the rights of Africans in South Africa and a proponent of British intervention to curtail the spread of Boer influence over the lands and tribes of the interior of South Africa.

Mackenzie went to South Africa in 1858 and began his missionary work in Bechuanaland (now Botswana). Troubled by the growing encroachments on tribal territories by Boers from the Transvaal republic to the east, he was active from 1867 in attempts to have Britain declare Bechuanaland a protectorate, claiming that the British would safeguard African rights from Boer racism. In 1884 the protectorate was established with Mackenzie as its deputy commissioner. He lost this job to Cecil Rhodes in 1885 but remained in politics, retaining a great deal of influence. In 1889 he retired to resume his missionary activities.

McKenzie, Sir John (b. 1838, Ardross, Ross, Scot.—d. Aug. 6, 1901, Shag Point, N.Z.), New Zealand statesman who, as minister of lands (1891–1900), sponsored legislation that provided land and credit to small farmers and helped to break up large estates.

McKenzie's deep antagonism toward land monopolists was rooted in his boyhood in Scotland, where he witnessed the dispossession of small farmers by Highland landlords. After immigrating to New Zealand in 1860, he farmed and served in the Otago provincial council (1871–76). Elected to Parliament as an independent in 1881, he was legislative whip for the ministry of Sir Robert Stout (1884–87) and was named minister of lands and agriculture in 1891 by Liberal Prime Minister John Ballance, who shared McKenzie's determination to create opportunities for small farmers.

In 1892 McKenzie won passage of the Lands for Settlement Act that opened up crown land for leasing and, when amended in 1894, compelled owners of large estates to sell portions of their holdings. Also in 1894 he introduced the Government Advances to Settlers Act, which greatly expanded the supply of credit available to farmers, and he sponsored a plan for unemployed workers to clear and then lease landholdings. He promoted scientific methods in agriculture, and by the time of his retirement in 1900 he had laid the foundations for the present Ministry of Agriculture. He was knighted in 1901.

Mackenzie, Sir Morell (b. July 7, 1837, Leytonstone, Essex, Eng.—d. Feb. 3, 1892, London), English physician who was at the centre of a bitter international controversy over the death of Emperor Frederick III of Germany.

Mackenzie, the leading throat specialist of the time, was called into the difficult case of

Morell Mackenzie
The Mansell Collection

the German crown prince Frederick in May 1887. Frederick's illness had been diagnosed by German physicians as throat cancer. Basing his opinion on a biopsy made by the eminent German pathologist Rudolf Virchow, Mackenzie insisted that the throat lesion was not demonstrably cancerous and that an operation was unnecessary.

Mackenzie was knighted in September 1887 and decorated with the Grand Cross of the Hohenzollern Order the following year. By November, however, the disease was confirmed to be cancer. Frederick became emperor on March 9, 1888, and died on June 15. A heated dispute erupted between Mackenzie and the German doctors. After a critical account of the case was published in Germany, Mackenzie retaliated with *The Fatal Illness of Frederick the Noble* (1888), for which he was censured by the Royal College of Surgeons.

McKenzie, Robert (Trelford) (b. Sept. 11, 1917, Vancouver, B.C., Can.—d. Oct. 12, 1981, London), Canadian-born British political scientist and television commentator on electoral politics. In the latter role, McKenzie popularized to the British public the word psephology (the study of votes) and the idea of "swing" votes, using a device he called a "swingometer" to show the shifting fortunes of the major parties during the announcement of election results.

McKenzie taught at the University of British Columbia and lectured at Harvard and Yale universities. In 1964 he joined the London School of Economics, where he became professor of political sociology. He soon became a prolific free-lance broadcaster on politics and current affairs. An academic contemporary of Pierre Trudeau, he was able to obtain the first overseas interview when Trudeau was appointed prime minister of Canada. McKenzie conducted interviews with numerous other politicians for the BBC, including former prime minister Harold Macmillan. His books include *Angels in Marble: Working Class Conservatism in Urban England* (coauthor; 1968) and *British Political Parties* (1955, 1964).

Mackenzie, Sir Thomas (b. March 10, 1854, Edinburgh—d. Feb. 14, 1930, Dunedin, N.Z.), Scottish-born explorer, businessman, and politician who was for a short time prime minister of New Zealand (1912) and who later served as High Commissioner in London during World War I.

Mackenzie's family had immigrated to New Zealand (1858), where, as a young man, he worked as a surveyor and began his own mercantile business. He served in local government and was elected to Parliament (1887). During these years Mackenzie pursued his interests in the natural history of New Zealand. He crossed from Lake Wakatipu to Martins Bay by the Harris Saddle, explored the Tautuku Forest, and led a party to estimate the height of Sutherland Falls. He later became a Fellow of the Royal Geographical Society.

Reelected to Parliament (1900), Mackenzie was an opponent of the Liberals, but by 1909 he was offered and accepted the cabinet posts of industries and commerce and of agriculture in the first ministry of Sir Joseph Ward (1909). When Ward resigned Mackenzie was elected leader of the party and served as prime minister from March 28 to July 10, 1912, when the government was defeated. Mackenzie also resigned his seat and accepted the appointment as High Commissioner in London, where he served with distinction until 1920. He was knighted in 1916. He represented New Zealand at the Peace Conference and the League of Nations and participated in a variety of international gatherings in the United States, dealing with business interests, as the representative for the London Chamber of Commerce. On his return to New Zealand Mackenzie was appointed to the Legislative Council (1921, 1928).

Mackenzie, William Lyon (b. March 12, 1795, Springfield, Angus, Scot.—d. Aug. 28, 1861, Toronto), Scottish-born journalist and political agitator who led an unsuccessful revolt against the Canadian government in 1837.

Mackenzie emigrated from Scotland to Canada in 1820 and became a general merchant. Responding to the discontent in Upper Canada (now part of Ontario), he became involved in politics. In 1824 he founded a newspaper in Queenston, the *Colonial Advocate,* in which he criticized the ruling oligarchy. Later that year he moved to York (as of 1834, Toronto); there his newspaper office was sabotaged by political opponents, but, with the damages awarded, he set up an improved plant and became leader of the radical wing of the province. Elected as a member of the provincial Parliament for York in 1828, he was expelled six times by the Tory majority, mainly because of fierce invectives against the Tories in his newspaper, only to be returned each time by the York electors. He visited England in 1832; well received by the colonial office, he caused the dismissal of several officers in Canada. While in England he wrote *Sketches of Canada and the United States,* stating Canadian grievances. In 1835 he was returned to the provincial Canadian Parliament in a reform administration. A report by Mackenzie's committee on grievances exposed the inadequacies of colonial rule and caused the British government to recall the current governor, but the new governor was the even more autocratic Sir Francis Bond Head. Mackenzie was elected mayor of the new city of Toronto in 1835; but he lost his parliamentary seat in 1836, along with other prominent reformers accused of disloyalty.

Mackenzie then began seriously to consider rebellion, and he founded a more radical newspaper, the *Constitution,* in which he supported ideas of Jacksonian democracy (the policies of U.S. President Andrew Jackson). As corresponding secretary for the extreme wing of the Reform Party, he communicated with Louis Joseph Papineau in Lower Canada (now in Quebec), who was already planning rebellion. An economic depression in 1837 brought many newcomers to Mackenzie's rural meetings; that December he assembled 800 followers near Toronto and planned to seize the governor and set up a provisional government. Inadequate organization and control resulted in failure, however, and Mackenzie escaped to the United States. When an attempt to rally his forces on Navy Island in the Niagara River collapsed, Mackenzie was charged by the United States with breaking neutrality laws and was imprisoned for 11 months. While serving time in a Rochester, N.Y., prison, he wrote *The Caroline Almanack,* expressing his disillusionment with U.S. politics.

Mackenzie was pardoned and allowed to reenter Canada in 1849. In 1851 he was elected to Parliament for Haldimand. Allied to the Radicals, he maintained his position of extreme independence and incorruptibility, refusing several government positions. He opposed the development of large-scale corporations and clung to the ideal of an agrarian democracy and small-scale industrialism. He was forced to resign in 1858 because of illness. After his death he became a symbol of Canadian radicalism.

Mackenzie Island (Caroline Islands): *see* Ulithi.

Mackenzie Mountains, northern extension of the Rocky Mountains, in the Yukon and in Inuvik and Fort Smith regions (Northwest Territories), Canada. The range extends northwestward from the British Columbia border for approximately 500 miles (800 km) to the Peel River plateau and the Porcupine River basin. The mountains serve as the watershed for the basins of the Mackenzie River (east) and Yukon River (west) and are the source for the Pelly River, a headstream of the Yukon. The Franklin Mountains, paralleling the eastern bank of the Mackenzie River for about 300 miles (480 km), are sometimes regarded as part of the range. The highest peak is Mount Sir James MacBrien (9,061 feet [2,762 m]), and many others, including Keele and Dome peaks and Mounts Hunt, Sidney Dodson, and Ida, reach elevations exceeding 8,000 feet (2,400 m).

Named for Sir Alexander Mackenzie, who explored the Mackenzie River in 1789, the mountains were generally ignored until World War II, when an oil field at Norman Wells on the Mackenzie River was developed. A 400-mile (645-kilometre) pipeline was built to Whitehorse, Yukon Territory, to fuel U.S. military bases in the Pacific Northwest. After the war, oil production was confined to local needs.

The Mackenzie Mountains Game Preserve was established in 1938, and Nahanni National Park was established in 1972 in the southern part of the range.

Mackenzie River, seasonal tributary of the Fitzroy River, eastern Queensland, Australia. Formed by the junction of the Comet and Nogoa rivers, which rise in the Eastern Highlands, it flows for 170 miles (275 km) past Comet, northeast across the Expedition Range, and then southeast, joining the Dawson River to form the Fitzroy River. Its principal tributary is the Isaac. Explored in 1844 by Ludwig Leichhardt, it was named after Sir Evan Mackenzie, a Queensland settler. Its valley supports dairy and beef cattle.

Mackenzie River, river system of northwestern North America, a major element in the drainage pattern of the continent. It issues from Great Slave Lake in the Northwest Territories of Canada and flows generally northward through Fort Smith and Inuvik regions to the Beaufort Sea of the Arctic Ocean. Its basin, with an area of 697,000 square miles (1,805,200 square km), is the largest in Canada and is exceeded on the continent only by the Mississippi-Missouri system.

A brief treatment of the Mackenzie River follows. For full treatment, *see* MACROPAEDIA: North America.

The Mackenzie itself is 1,025 miles (1,650 km) long, according to the conventional measurement from Great Slave Lake. If the Finlay River, its farthest headstream, which flows into the Peace River Reservoir west of the Rocky Mountains, is included, however, the entire river system runs for 2,635 miles (4,241 km) through the sparsely settled, lake-strewn Canadian north country. The river is generally wide, mostly from 1 to 2 miles (1.5 to 3 km) across; in its island-dotted sections it is 3 to 4 miles (5 to 6.5 km) wide.

The headwaters of the system include several large rivers that drain the vast forested plains of northeastern British Columbia and northern Alberta, among them the Liard, Peace, and Athabasca rivers. Shorter rivers flow into the system from the east, draining the low rocky hills of the Canadian Shield. The system also includes the huge Great Slave and Great Bear lakes.

The Mackenzie River basin is sparsely populated, and its natural resources are few and largely inaccessible. As a result, the unspoiled region offers abundant wildlife and spectacular scenery. The large lakes of the Mackenzie basin are a source of lake trout and whitefish. Limited lumber and agricultural products are produced, mostly in the southern part of the basin. Minerals are the economic basis of some of the larger settlements. The first oil field was discovered at Norman Wells in 1921. Others were found in the early 1970s near the Mackenzie River delta, and large reserves lie in the Athabasca Tar Sands along the Athabasca River north of Fort McMurray. Oil is carried southward by pipeline to Edmonton, Alta., where it is distributed to refineries in southern Canada and the northern United States.

The water of the Mackenzie River system was too far away from large industrial and urban markets to be used for hydroelectric power until the late 1960s, when the Peace River was dammed. There are other developed waterpower sites on the Snare and Taltson rivers.

mackerel, any of a number of swift-moving, streamlined food and sport fishes found in temperate and tropical seas around the world, allied to tunas in the family Scombridae (order Perciformes). Mackerels are rounded and torpedo-shaped, with a slender, keeled tail base, a forked tail, and a row of small finlets behind the dorsal and anal fins. They are carnivorous fishes and feed on plankton, crustaceans, mollusks, fish eggs, and small fish. They congregate in schools and swim actively in the upper 25–30 fathoms of the water in the warmer months and then descend to as deep as 100 fathoms during the winter. They spawn during the spring and early summer along coastlines. Their eggs average 1 mm (0.4 inch) in diameter, are buoyant, and drift in the uppermost five fathoms of water. Mackerels are mostly caught by nets, rather than by angling.

The common mackerel (*Scomber scombrus*) of the Atlantic Ocean is an abundant and economically important species that is sometimes found in huge schools. It averages about 30 cm (12 inches) in length and is blue-green above and silver-white below, with a series of wavy, dark, vertical lines on the upper sides. It has two well-separated dorsal fins and two small keels on either side of the tail base; it lacks an air bladder. The common mackerel occurs along both coasts of the North Atlantic Ocean, from North Carolina to Labrador and from Spain to Norway.

Allied to this species is the chub mackerel (*S. colias;* once separated into Atlantic and Pacific species). They are more finely marked than the common mackerel; the chub mackerel that is found in the Pacific Ocean is bright green with vertical stripes. It has an air bladder but is otherwise similar to the common mackerel. It is sometimes placed in the genus *Pneumatophorus.* The Pacific chub mackerel is caught in considerable numbers off the coast of California, while the Atlantic chub mackerel is widely distributed along both coasts of the North and South Atlantic.

Mackerel (*Scomber scombrus*)

Painted especially for *Encyclopaedia Britannica* by Tom Dolan, under the supervision of Loren P. Woods, Field Museum of Natural History, Chicago

The members of the genus *Scomberomorus* are related fishes that are found throughout the warm seas of the world. They are elongated with small scales, large mouths and teeth, and three keels on either side of the tail base. There are several species, among them: the barred Spanish mackerel (*S. commerson*), an Indo-Pacific fish said to weigh up to 45 kg (100 pounds); the king mackerel, or kingfish (*S. cavalla*), a western Atlantic fish about 170 cm long and weighing 36 kg or more; and the cero, or painted mackerel (*S. regalis*), an abundant, spotted Atlantic fish reportedly about 120 cm long. *Scomberomorus* members are favourite game fish, and their flesh is of excellent quality. They are taken in considerable numbers in the South Atlantic and in the Gulf of Mexico.

Other fishes known as mackerel and belonging to the family Scombridae include the Indian mackerels (*Rastrelliger*), which are rather stout, commercially valuable Indo-Australian fishes up to 38 cm long, and the frigate mackerels (*Auxis*), which are small, elongated fishes found worldwide and distinguished by a corselet of enlarged scales around the shoulder region.

The name mackerel is also used for certain species of tuna and bonito. Horse mackerel are mackerel-like carangids. Snake mackerels, or escolars, are long, slim fishes of the family Gemphylidae.

mackerel shark, (genus *Lamna*), any member of a group of sharks in the family Isuridae. The name is also used as a collective name for the family, which includes, in addition, the white shark and the mako shark groups.

Mackerel shark (*Lamna nasus*)

Painting by Richard Ellis

The genus *Lamna* includes the Atlantic mackerel shark, or porbeagle (*L. nasus*); the Pacific mackerel shark, or salmon shark (*L. ditropis*); and two other species of sharks, *L. whitleyi* and *L. phillipi,* that are of uncertain taxonomic standing.

Mackerel sharks are swift, active fishes with crescent-shaped tails and slender teeth. These sharks are gray or blue-gray above and paler below and grow to a length of about 3 m (10 feet). They inhabit temperate waters and are fished commercially for food.

McKim, Charles Follen (b. Aug. 24, 1847, Chester County, Pa., U.S.—d. Sept. 14, 1909, St. James, Long Island, N.Y.), American architect who was of primary importance in the American Neoclassical revival.

McKim was educated at Harvard and at the École des Beaux-Arts in Paris. He was trained as a draftsman by the architect H.H. Richardson while the latter was completing Trinity Church, Boston. In 1879 he joined William Rutherford Mead and Stanford White to found McKim, Mead & White, which became the most successful and influential American architectural firm of its time. Until 1887 the firm excelled at informal summerhouses built of shingles, and McKim designed one of the most significant of these, the residence at Bristol, R.I., of W.G. Low (1887).

In later years the firm was famous for championing the formal tradition of the Italian Renaissance and its classical antecedents. Among the celebrated examples of the formal planning of McKim are the Boston Public Library (1887) and in New York City the Columbia University Library (1893), the University Club (1899), the Morgan Library (1903), and the Pennsylvania Railway Station (1904–10). With D.H. Burnham and Richard Morris Hunt, he developed and oversaw the building program of the World's Columbian Exposition at Chicago in 1893, which was classically inspired. McKim designed the Agricultural Building. He also aided Burnham in reviving Pierre L'Enfant's plan for Washington, D.C., and was the originator of the American Academy in Rome.

Mackinac, Straits of, channel connecting Lake Michigan (west) and Lake Huron (east), and forming an important waterway between the Upper and Lower peninsulas of Michigan, U.S. Spanned by the Mackinac Bridge (opened 1957) and underwater gas and oil pipelines, the straits are 4 miles (6 km) wide and approximately 30 miles (48 km) long and include the passage between several islands in northwestern Lake Huron. Discovered by Jean Nicolet in 1634, the straits played a prominent role in the fur trade.

Mackinac Bridge, one of the longest and strongest suspension bridges in the world, spanning the Straits of Mackinac from the Upper to the Lower Peninsula of Michigan, U.S. Designed by David B. Steinman in the wake of the failure of the Tacoma Narrows Bridge (1940), the Mackinac Bridge was not constructed until the 1950s because of World War II. The bridge measures 8,344 feet (2,543 m) between the main anchorages. Its 3,800-foot (1,158-m) main span is stiffened by a truss 38 feet (13 m) deep, with open spaces on either side of the roadway and grid construction of the deck to permit the passage of wind gusts. Heavy pier foundations, the deepest 210 feet (64 m), were necessary to resist the ice masses that accumulate every winter in the Straits of Mackinac. In November 1955 the incomplete bridge withstood a 76-mph (122-km-per-hour) gale. Mackinac Bridge was opened to vehicle traffic in 1957.

Mackinac Bridge, seen from the water's edge, near Mackinaw City, Mich.

W. Cody/Corbis

Mackinac Island, summer resort, Mackinac county, northern Michigan, U.S. It is situated in Lake Huron near the Straits of Mackinac, and has ferry connections to St. Ignace and Mackinaw City. The island, 8 miles (13 km) in circumference and thickly forested, has been a state park since 1895. It retains an atmosphere of a bygone age; automobiles are banned.

The island was an ancient Indian burial ground called Michilimackinac (Ojibwa: "Great Turtle"). It was first visited by French explorers in the 1600s, and, because of its strategic location, the British established a fort there in 1780. After the United States took possession (1783), it became the headquarters of John Jacob Astor's American Fur Company and later developed as a resort. It was occupied by the British during the War of 1812 and regained by the United States in 1815.

Inner grounds of the restored Fort Mackinac on Mackinac Island, Mich.

Jack Zehrt—Shostal/EB Inc.

The island is bordered by limestone cliffs and rises in the east to 339 feet (103 m) above the surrounding waters; it includes Skull Cave and Arch and Sugar Loaf rocks. Old Fort Mackinac, Beaumont Memorial (dedicated to U.S. Army surgeon William Beaumont, who while serving at the fort observed human digestion through the open stomach wound of a French-Canadian trapper), and the Stuart House (1817; residence of the island's American Fur Company agent) are preserved as historical museums. The resplendently Victorian Grand Hotel dates from 1887. The annual Lilac Festival (June) marks the start of the summer resort season. The island is the terminus of the Chicago Yacht Club's Race to Mackinac, a yachting event that began in 1898 and has been run annually since 1921. Pop. (2000) 523.

Mackinaw City, village, Cheboygan and Emmet counties, northern Michigan, U.S. It lies on the Straits of Mackinac opposite St. Ignace, with which it is linked northward by the 5-mile- (8-km-) long Mackinac Bridge. The village is located at the northernmost point of Michigan's Lower Peninsula.

European settlement of the site originated in 1673 with a French trading post, which in 1715 developed as Fort Michilimackinac. During the French and Indian War, the fort was taken over (1760) by the British, but its garrison was massacred in 1763 by a Chippewa-Sauk band of Indians under Chief Minavavana. It was reoccupied by British troops the next year. In 1780–81 the British moved across the straits to a new fort on Mackinac Island, abandoning Fort Michilimackinac. A restoration of the fort, designated a national historic landmark, stands in Colonial Michilimackinac State Historical Park at the southern end of the bridge. Mackinac Maritime Park, adjacent to the fort, includes Old Mackinac Point Lighthouse (1890) and the reconstructed 18th-century wooden sloop *Welcome.*

The village of Michilimackinac (Ojibwa: "Great Turtle") was laid out in 1857 and its name shortened to Mackinaw in 1894. Its position as a control point on the straits was sustained by the arrival of the Grand Rapids and Indiana Railroad in 1881, and it was incorporated as a village in 1882. Mackinaw City is a departure point for ferries to Mackinac Island (a 40-minute crossing). Pop. (2000) 859.

Mackinaw trout: *see* lake trout.

Mackinder, Sir Halford John (b. Feb. 15, 1861, Gainsborough, Lincolnshire, Eng.—d. March 6, 1947, Parkstone, Dorset), British political geographer noted for his work as an educator and for his geopolitical conception of the globe as divided into two camps, the ascendant Eurasian "heartland" and the subordinate "maritime lands," including the other continents. He was knighted in 1920.

Mackinder was the son of a physician of Scottish descent. In 1880 he entered Christ Church, Oxford, where he studied natural sciences with a preference for biology; he obtained first-class honours in 1883 and, one year later, a second-class in modern history. He was president of the Oxford Union, the principal debating society at the university. After leaving Oxford he read for the bar at the Inner Temple, one of the law "colleges" in London, and qualified as a barrister in 1886. As a lecturer for the Oxford extension movement—formed to give educational opportunities to people unable to attend a university—he traveled widely through the country, particularly among the workingmen of the north of England, expounding what he called the "new geography." With this new, clear-cut concept of geography as a bridge between the natural sciences and the humanities, he soon won attention. His *Britain and the British Seas* (1902, 2nd ed. 1930), written with assurance and style, is a recognized landmark in British geographical literature.

At that time, a group of men at the Royal Geographical Society were making strong efforts to raise the status of geography as an academic discipline in Britain and to secure for it an adequate place in the educational system. Learning of Mackinder's success, the society invited him to address it on the new geography. He met the challenge boldly, delivering his paper on "The Scope and Methods of Geography" with great persuasiveness. In 1887 he had become reader in geography at Oxford, the first such appointment in a British university. When in 1899 the Royal Geographical Society and the university established the Oxford School of Geography, it was almost inevitable that Mackinder should be the first director. It was typical of the man

Mackinder, detail of a drawing by Sir William Rothenstein, 1933; in the collection of the London School of Economics and Political Science

By courtesy of the London School of Economics and Political Science; photograph, J.R. Freeman & Co. Ltd.

that in the same year he organized and led an expedition to East Africa, where he made the first ascent of Mt. Kenya. As he commented, in the popular view the geographer must also be "an explorer and adventurer."

Mackinder, working also at Reading and London, continued at Oxford until 1904, when he was appointed director of the recently founded London School of Economics and Political Science, a constituent body of the University of London. There, for four years, he devoted his energies to its administration and to that of the university. He played a prominent part in ensuring that the university centre was established at Bloomsbury in the heart of London and not on the periphery of the metropolis. Though he continued as reader in economic geography for another 18 years, his resignation as director marked the beginning of the third phase of his career. He entered Parliament in 1910 as Unionist (Conservative) member for the Camlachie division of Glasgow. Holding strong imperialist views, he included in his circle of friends similarly minded men, among them the politician L.S. Amery and Lord Milner, the imperial administrator. In the House, Mackinder did not make a strong impact. He retained his seat at the general election of 1918, when he described his opponent as "boldly defensive of the Russian Bolsheviks," but was defeated in 1922.

Studying the prerequisites for a stable peace settlement during World War I, he developed a thesis in political geography that he had first outlined in a paper read to the Royal Geographical Society in 1904, "The Geographical Pivot of History." In it he argued that interior Asia and eastern Europe (the heartland) had become the strategic centre of the "World Island" as a result of the relative decline of sea power as against land power and of the economic and industrial development of southern Siberia. His extended views were set out in a short book, *Democratic Ideals and Reality,* published early in 1919 while the Paris Peace Conference was in session. The role of Britain and the United States, he considered, was to preserve a balance between the powers contending for control of the heartland. As a further stabilizing factor, he urged the creation of a tier of independent states to separate Germany and Russia, much along the lines finally imposed by the peace treaty. The book included, apart from the main theme, many farsighted observations—*e.g.,* his insistence on the "one world" concept, the need for regional organizations of minor powers, and the warning that chaos in a defeated Germany would inevitably lead to dictatorship. The book attracted little attention in Britain but rather more in the United States. There was an unexpected sequel, however, for the concept of the heartland was seized upon by the German geopolitician Karl Haushofer to support his grand design for control of the World Island. Thus, during World War II there were suggestions that Mackinder, through Haushofer, had inspired Hitler. More sober evaluation disposed of this absurd notion, and, though developments have affected some of the arguments, the thesis is recognized as an important view of world strategy. In 1924, mindful of the lessons of World War I, Mackinder published his prophetic theory of the Atlantic community that became reality after World War II and assumed military form in the North Atlantic Treaty Organization (NATO). In his hypothesis—which remained largely unnoticed—Mackinder argued that the power of the Eurasian heartland could be offset by western Europe and North America, which "constitute for many purposes a single community of nations."

In 1919 Mackinder went as British high commissioner to southern Russia in an attempt to unify the White Russian forces and was knighted on his return in 1920. After the close of his academic career in 1923, he served as chairman of the Imperial Shipping Committee in 1920–45 and of the Imperial Economic Committee in 1926–31. He was made a privy councillor (an honorific office) in 1926; among the other honours he received were the Patron's Medal, Royal Geographical Society (1946), and the Charles P. Daly Medal of the American Geographical Society (1944). (G.R.C.)

BIBLIOGRAPHY. E.W. Gilbert, *Sir Halford Mackinder, 1861–1947* (1961), a detailed biographical sketch; H.J. Mackinder, *The Scope and Methods of Geography and the Geographical Pivot of History* (papers of the Royal Geographical Society, reprinted 1951), detailed discussion in the introduction by E.W. Gilbert of Mackinder's contribution to the advancement of geography and the "heartland" thesis; "Round World and the Winning of the Peace," *Foreign Affairs,* 21:595–605 (1943), a classic restatement of Mackinder's thesis; G.R. Crone, *Modern Geographers,* rev. and enlarged ed. (1970), sketch of the general background of Mackinder's work as a geographer.

McKinley, John (b. May 1, 1780, Culpeper County, Va., U.S.—d. July 19, 1852, Louisville, Ky.), American politician and associate justice of the United States Supreme Court (1837–52).

After practicing law briefly in Kentucky, where he grew up, McKinley settled in Huntsville, Alabama, then a centre of planting and political interests, in 1818. In 1820 he was elected to the Alabama state legislature and two years later, despite the support of the Georgia political machine, was defeated by one vote for the U.S. Senate. Having become a supporter of Jacksonian Democracy, he secured the Senate seat four years later, served one term, and returned to the state legislature after failing reelection. McKinley remained loyal to the Andrew Jackson forces in succeeding electoral contests and in 1837 was appointed to the U.S. Supreme Court by Pres. Martin Van Buren. He served on the court for the rest of his life and attended his duties despite increasing enfeeblement in his later years.

McKinley, Mount, highest peak (20,320 ft [6,194 m]) in North America, located near the centre of the Alaska Range, south central Alaska, U.S. Lying 130 mi (210 km) north-northwest of Anchorage in Denali National Park (*q.v.*), the mountain rises abruptly 17,000 ft above its base at the higher, more southerly of its two peaks. The upper two-thirds of its massive summit is covered with permanent snowfields that feed many glaciers, some surpassing 30 mi in length.

Mt. McKinley, Alaska
Bradford Washburn

In 1794 George Vancouver, the English navigator, sighted the mountain from Cook Inlet (Gulf of Alaska). The first attempt to climb it was made in 1903 by an attorney, James Wickersham, who was unsuccessful. A much-publicized but fraudulent claim by Frederick A. Cook, a physician, that he had reached the top inspired the conquest of the north peak in 1910 by two prospectors, William Taylor and Peter Anderson. On June 13, 1913, Hudson Stuck and Harry Karstens led a party to the south peak, the true summit.

Known to the Indians as Denali ("The High One") and to the Russians as Bolshaya Gora ("Great Mountain"), it was named Densmores Peak in 1889 after Frank Densmore, a prospector. The modern name was applied in 1896 by William A. Dickey, another prospector, in honour of William McKinley, who was elected president of the United States later that year. Efforts were undertaken in the mid-1970s to restore its original Indian name.

McKinley, William (b. Jan. 29, 1843, Niles, Ohio, U.S.—d. Sept. 14, 1901, Buffalo, N.Y.), 25th president of the United States (1897–1901); a staunch Republican who rose to national prominence by championing tariff protectionism and opposing free silver, he came to be identified with the global imperialism associated with U.S. territorial acquisitions following the Spanish–American War (1898).

William McKinley
By courtesy of the Library of Congress, Washington, D.C.

During the U.S. Civil War (1861–65) McKinley served under Col. Rutherford B. Hayes (later the 19th U.S. president, 1877–81), who made him his aide-de-camp and subsequently encouraged his political career. Two years after his admission to the bar at Canton, Ohio (1867), he entered public life as county prosecuting attorney.

Elected to Congress, where he served for 14 years (1877–91), McKinley became particularly well known for his support of high tariffs to protect U.S. industry from foreign competition; as chairman of the House Ways and Means Committee, he was the principal sponsor of the McKinley Tariff of 1890, which raised duties on many imports to the highest levels up to that time.

McKinley was defeated for reelection in 1890, but he had won the admiration of Mark Hanna, a wealthy Ohio industrialist who was active in the Republican Party. With the support of Hanna he was elected governor of Ohio and served two terms (1892–96), while Hanna laid plans to win the Republican presidential nomination for him in 1896. McKinley won the nomination easily on a platform stressing high protective tariffs and the maintenance of the gold standard. This position directly opposed that of the Democratic–Populist candidate, William Jennings Bryan, who advocated a bimetallic standard of gold and silver. The dynamic Hanna raised enormous sums of money from big business and directed a vigorous campaign; McKinley remained at home, daily addressing from his front porch streams of visitors who flocked to Canton by railroad. The Republicans won with an electoral vote of 271 to 176.

In office the new President promptly called a special session of Congress to revise customs duties upward (the Dingley Tariff). All other domestic concerns were eclipsed, however, by the nation's preoccupation with the Cuban insurrection and Spain's reported mistreatment of insurgents. McKinley hoped to avoid U.S. involvement, but after the mysterious sinking of the U.S. battleship "Maine" in the harbour at Havana (Feb. 15, 1898), sentiment in the United States increasingly demanded armed intervention and congressional leaders were anxious to satisfy the public demand for action. Despite evidence that Spain was prepared to make major concessions, McKinley referred the issue to Congress, which authorized him to intervene with armed force to secure the independence of Cuba (April 20, 1898). In the short war that followed, the United States defeated Spanish forces in Cuba and on the seas. By the end of July, Spain was seeking an armistice.

Though McKinley had not entered the war for territorial aggrandizement, he was now faced with the disposition of the former Spanish territories. He declared that Puerto Rico, the Philippines, and other strategically located islands must not be allowed to fall into unfriendly hands and must therefore be made U.S. dependencies. Despite opposition to this "imperialism" from certain Republicans, McKinley stood fast in his decision throughout the peace negotiations.

McKinley was renominated by the Republicans without opposition and, in a period of prosperity, was returned to office by a large majority in the election of 1900. With the war out of the way, he spoke throughout the country on two subjects that had been overshadowed by it: the control of trusts and—in a change from his previous position—commercial reciprocity as a stimulant to foreign trade. He ended his tour at the Pan-American Exposition at Buffalo, where he was fatally shot on Sept. 6, 1901, by Leon Czolgosz, an anarchist. McKinley was succeeded in office by his vice president, the Progressive Republican Theodore Roosevelt. A reliable biography is M.K. Leech's *In the Days of McKinley* (1959).

MacKinnon, Roderick (b. Feb. 19, 1956, Burlington, Mass., U.S.), American doctor, corecipient of the Nobel Prize for Chemistry in 2003 for his pioneering research on ion channels in cell membranes. He shared the award with Peter Agre of the United States.

MacKinnon earned an M.D. degree from Tufts University's School of Medicine in 1982. After practicing medicine for several years, he turned to basic research, beginning in 1986 with postdoctoral work on ion channels at Brandeis University. In 1996 he joined Rockefeller University as a professor and laboratory head. A year later he was appointed investigator at Rockefeller's Howard Hughes Medical Institute.

Of particular importance to the nervous system and the heart, ion channels are specialized openings in cell membranes that enable ions, such as potassium and sodium, to easily flow in and out of cells; similar structures also exist for the passage of water. MacKinnon's groundbreaking work focused on "filters" in channels that passed one type of ion while blocking others. To understand how these filters worked, he obtained sharper images of channels using X-ray diffraction. In 1998 he determined the three-dimensional molecular structure of an ion channel. He also found a molecular "sensor" in the channel that reacts to conditions around the cell, sending signals that open and close the channel at the appropriate times. His pioneering work allowed scientists to pursue the development of drugs for diseases in which ion channels play a role.

mackintosh, waterproof outercoat or raincoat, named for a Scottish chemist, Charles Macintosh (1766–1843), who invented the waterproof material that bears his name. The fabric used for a mackintosh was made waterproof by cementing two thicknesses of it together with rubber dissolved in a coal-tar naphtha solution.

Macintosh patented his fabric in 1823. The word mackintosh has become a general term for any raincoat.

Mackintosh, Charles Rennie (b. June 7, 1868, Glasgow, Scot.—d. Dec. 10, 1928, London, Eng.), Scottish architect and designer who was prominent in the Arts and Crafts Movement in Great Britain.

He was apprenticed to a local architect, John Hutchinson, and attended evening classes at the Glasgow School of Art. In 1889 he joined the firm of Honeyman and Keppie, becoming a partner in 1904.

In collaboration with three other students, one of whom, Margaret Macdonald, became his wife in 1900, Mackintosh achieved an international reputation in the 1890s as a designer of unorthodox posters, craftwork, and furniture. In contrast to contemporary fashion his work was light, elegant, and original, as exemplified by four remarkable tearooms he designed in Glasgow (1896–1904) and other domestic interiors of the early 1900s.

Glasgow School of Art library by Charles Rennie Mackintosh, 1907–09
By courtesy of the Glasgow School of Art; photograph, T. and R. Annan

Mackintosh's chief architectural projects were the Glasgow School of Art (1896–1909), considered the first original example of Art Nouveau architecture in Great Britain; two unrealized projects—the 1901 International exhibition, Glasgow (1898), and "Haus eines Kunstfreundes" (1901); Windyhill, Kilmacolm (1899–1901), and Hill House, Helensburgh (1902); the Willow Tea Rooms, Glasgow (1904); and Scotland Street School (1904–06). Although all have some traditional characteristics, they reveal a mind of exceptional inventiveness and aesthetic perception. By 1914 he had virtually ceased to practice and thereafter devoted himself to watercolour painting.

Although Mackintosh was nearly forgotten for several decades, the late 20th century saw a revival of interest in his work. The stark simplicity of some of his furniture designs, in particular, appealed to contemporary taste, and reproductions of Mackintosh chairs and settees began to be manufactured. The Mackintosh House in Glasgow was reconstructed and opened to the public as a museum in the late 1970s.

BIBLIOGRAPHY. Thomas Howarth, *Charles Rennie Mackintosh and the Modern Movement* (1952; 2nd ed., 1977), is the standard work on the architecture, well supplemented by Roger Billcliffe, *Charles Rennie Mackintosh: The Complete Furniture, Furniture Drawings, and Interior Designs* (1979).

Macklin, Charles, original name CHARLES MCLAUGHLIN (b. 1690/99, Ireland—d. July 11, 1797), Irish actor and playwright whose distinguished though turbulent career spanned most of the 18th century.

Macklin first appeared as an actor at Bristol and in 1725 went to Lincoln's Inn Fields, London. A man of violent nature, he was a pioneer against the stilted declamation of his day. He went to Drury Lane Theatre in 1733 and later was concerned in its management. In 1735 he killed another actor in the greenroom over a dispute about a wig, but, although prosecuted, he received no sentence. He set the seal on his stage career at Drury Lane on Feb. 14, 1741, when he played Shylock, rescuing the part from all the comedy with which it had long been surrounded.

Macklin, detail from an engraving by John Condé, 1792
By courtesy of the Victoria and Albert Museum, London

Macklin played many parts with distinction but was constantly involved in disputes and lawsuits. He attempted to be a restaurateur but failed and returned to the stage. Two of his plays were outstanding, *Love à la mode* (1759) and *The Man of the World* (1781). At the time of his death, he claimed to be 107 years old; he may have been a centenarian, but this is subject to dispute. The length of his association with the stage, however, made him a pillar of the English theatre.

Mackmurdo, Arthur Heygate (b. Dec. 12, 1851, London, Eng.—d. March 15, 1942, Wickham Bishops, Essex), English architect, designer, and a pioneer of the English Arts and Crafts Movement.

After studying at the Ruskin School of Art, Oxford, and traveling with John Ruskin to Italy, Mackmurdo set up practice in London. Known best for his plans for the Savoy Hotel, he also built about 12 private houses, including 25 Cadogan Square. His wide interest in social problems was reflected in other types of buildings and several projects for communal living.

Although some of his architecture shows Italian influence, its originality makes Mackmurdo a forerunner of the modern movement. Basing it upon the teachings of William Morris, he founded the Century Guild of artists (1882) to produce better furniture and decorative accessories than were then available commercially. He also designed textiles, tapestries, wallpaper, and metalwork often characterized in the early '80s by swirling plant forms, foreshadowing those of the later Art Nouveau. He began publishing *The Hobby Horse* in 1884, the first finely printed magazine on art. A friend of William Morris, he was founder member of the Society for the Protection of Ancient Buildings.

McLachlan, Alexander (b. Aug. 12, 1818, Johnstone, Renfrewshire, Scot.—d. March 20, 1896, Orangeville, Ont., Can.), Scottish-born poet, called by some the Burns of Canada for his Scots dialect poetry, much of which deals with the homesickness of Scots immigrants. McLachlan was the foremost among a number of such Scottish bards, whose themes of nostalgia for Scotland appear to be literary conventions rather than original expressions.

Apprenticed to a tailor in Glasgow as a child, he went to Canada in 1840 and engaged in farming in central Canada West (Ontario). A collected edition of his work was published as *The Poetical Works of Alexander McLachlan* (1900).

McLaren, Bruce (Leslie) (b. Aug. 30, 1937, Auckland, N.Z.—d. June 2, 1970, near Chichester, Sussex, Eng.), New Zealand-born automobile racing driver, the youngest to win an international Grand Prix contest for Formula I cars (the U.S. race in 1959, when he was 22), also noted as a designer of racing vehicles.

From 1959 to 1965 McLaren drove for Charles Cooper, a British racing car designer and builder. In 1960 he finished second to Jack Brabham of Australia for the world driving championship. In 1967 and 1969 he won the Canadian-American Challenge Cup series of road races.

In 1964 McLaren, who had studied engineering at the University of Auckland, began to design racing automobiles. Although he won the 1968 Belgian Grand Prix in one of his own cars, his fellow New Zealander Denis Clive Hulme was the most successful driver of McLaren Formula I racers. McLaren was killed in an accident while testing a car on the Goodwood track.

Maclaren, Charles (b. Oct. 7, 1782, Ormiston, Haddington, Scot.—d. Sept. 10, 1866, near Edinburgh), Scottish journalist, editor of the 6th edition (1820–23) of the *Encyclopædia Britannica* and cofounder and editor of *The Scotsman* (1817), Scotland's first independent liberal paper. He also performed editorial services for the 4th, 5th, and 7th editions of the *Britannica*.

With the help of friends, Maclaren launched *The Scotsman* in 1817. As its political editor and, later, controlling editor, he shaped the paper's policies, supporting reform at home and liberalism abroad. His services to science were recognized by election to the Royal Society of Edinburgh (1839) and to the geological societies of London and of France (1846). In 1864 he became president of the Geological Society of Edinburgh.

Maclaurin, Colin (b. February 1698, Kilmodan, Argyllshire, Scot.—d. June 14, 1746, Edinburgh), Scottish mathematician who developed and extended Sir Isaac Newton's work in calculus, geometry, and gravitation.

Maclaurin, engraving by S. Freeman; in the British Museum

By courtesy of the trustees of the British Museum; photograph, J.R. Freeman & Co. Ltd.

A child prodigy, he entered the University of Glasgow at age 11. At age 19, he was elected professor of mathematics at Marischal College, Aberdeen, and two years later he became a fellow of the Royal Society of London. At this time he became acquainted with Newton. In his most important work, *Geometrica Organica; Sive Descriptio Linearum Curvarum Universalis* (1720; "Organic Geometry, with the Description of the Universal Linear Curves"), Maclaurin developed several theorems similar to some in Newton's *Principia*, introduced the method of generating conics (the circle, ellipse, hyperbola, and parabola) that bears his name, and showed that certain types of curves (of the third and fourth degree) can be described by the intersection of two movable angles.

On the recommendation of Newton, he was made professor of mathematics at the University of Edinburgh in 1725. In 1740 he shared, with the mathematicians Leonhard Euler and Daniel Bernoulli, the prize offered by the Académie des Sciences for an essay on tides. His *Treatise of Fluxions* (1742) was written in reply to criticisms by George Berkeley of England that Newton's calculus was based on faulty reasoning. In this essay he showed that stable figures for a homogeneous rotating fluid mass are the ellipsoids of revolution, later known as Maclaurin's ellipsoids. He also gave in his *Fluxions*, for the first time, the correct theory for distinguishing between maxima and minima in general and pointed out the importance of the distinction in the theory of the multiple points of curves. The Maclaurin series, a special case of the Taylor series, was named in his honour.

In 1745, when Jacobites (supporters of the Stuart king James II and his descendants) were marching on Edinburgh, Maclaurin took a prominent part in preparing trenches and barricades for the city's defense. As soon as the rebel army captured Edinburgh, Maclaurin fled to England until it was safe to return. The ordeal of his escape ruined his health, and he died at age 48.

Maclaurin's *Account of Sir Isaac Newton's Philosophical Discoveries* was published posthumously, as was his *Treatise of Algebra* (1748). "De Linearum Geometricarum Proprietatibus Generalibus tractatus" ("A Tract on the General Properties of Geometrical Lines"), noted for its elegant geometric demonstrations, was appended to his *Algebra*.

Maclean, George (b. Feb. 24, 1801, Keith, Banffshire, Scot.—d. May 22, 1847, Cape Coast, Gold Coast), Scottish-born council president of Cape Coast, West Africa, who laid the groundwork for British rule of the Gold Coast.

An officer of the Royal African Colonial Corps, Maclean served in Sierra Leone and the Gold Coast in 1826–28, and from 1830 to 1844 he was chief administrator of the Cape Coast settlement. In this post he made peace with the Ashanti kingdom of the interior and greatly increased British power by establishing an informal protectorate over the Fanti states along the coast. Although the colony prospered under his rule, he was accused of profiteering and of failing to suppress slavery. In 1838 he married the poet and novelist Letitia Landon (known by her initials L.E.L.), and her mysterious death a few months later further damaged his reputation. Removed as council president in 1844, Maclean continued to direct relations with the Fanti states until his death.

McLean, John (b. March 11, 1785, Morris County, N.J., U.S.—d. April 4, 1861, Cincinnati, Ohio), cabinet member and U.S. Supreme Court justice (1829–61) whose most famous opinion was his dissent in the Dred Scott decision (1857). He was also perhaps the most indefatigable seeker of the presidency in U.S. history; although he was never nominated, he made himself "available" in all eight campaigns from 1832 through 1860.

After two terms in the U.S. House of Representatives (1812–16), McLean was appointed a judge in the Supreme Court of Ohio, a position he resigned in 1822 to become commissioner of the General Land Office under Pres. James Monroe. In 1823 he was named postmaster general and became noted for his efficiency and nonpartisanship in that office. After Pres. Andrew Jackson took office McLean resigned in protest over Jackson's open advocacy of the spoils system of political patronage, which undermined McLean's recent reforms. Jackson thereupon appointed him an associate justice of the U.S. Supreme Court.

McLean

By courtesy of the Library of Congress, Washington, D.C.

In *Dred Scott* v. *Sandford* (1857), McLean insisted, in a minority opinion, that a slave became free when his owner took him into a state where slavery was not legally established. In McLean's view, a free black was a citizen and thus was able to sue, in a case involving diversity of state citizenship, in a federal court. His position was reflected in the Fourteenth Amendment to the U.S. Constitution (1868).

Maclean's, semimonthly news magazine published in Toronto whose thorough coverage of Canada's national affairs and of North American and world news from a Canadian perspective has made it that country's leading magazine. It was founded in 1905 in a large-page format, presenting feature articles and fiction reflecting a conservative view of Canadian life and values. It developed a reputation for outstanding photography.

The magazine features a column of notes about newsworthy Canadians. In the 1970s *Maclean's*, like other magazines, encountered rising production and distribution costs while circulation and advertising revenue declined, but it countered by reducing its page size and revising its format.

MacLeary, Donald (Whyte) (b. Aug. 22, 1937, Glasgow, Scot.), Scottish premier danseur noted for his strong finesse and natural romanticism.

He was trained at the Royal Ballet School and joined the company in 1954. He was promoted in the next year to soloist, becoming, in 1959, the youngest premier danseur of the Royal Ballet. In partnership principally with Svetlana Beriosova, MacLeary danced classical leads, including those in *Swan Lake, La Fille mal gardée,* and *Romeo and Juliet,* and he created major roles in many modern ballets. In 1975 he became ballet master of the Royal Ballet.

MacLeish, Archibald (b. May 7, 1892, Glencoe, Ill., U.S.—d. April 20, 1982, Boston, Mass.), U.S. poet, playwright, teacher, and public official, whose concern for liberal democracy figured in much of his work, although his most memorable lyrics are of a more private nature.

Educated at Yale, after three years as an attorney in Boston, MacLeish went to France in 1923 to perfect his poetic craft. The verse he published during his expatriate years—*The Happy Marriage* (1924), *The Pot of Earth* (1925), *Streets in the Moon* (1926), and *The Hamlet of A. MacLeish* (1928)—shows the fashionable influence of Ezra Pound and T.S. Eliot. During this period he wrote his frequently anthologized poem "Ars Poetica"

(1926; "The Art of Poetry"). After returning to the United States in 1928, he published *New Found Land* (1930), which reveals the simple lyric eloquence that is the persistent MacLeish note. It includes one of his best-known poems, "You, Andrew Marvell."

In the 1930s MacLeish became increasingly concerned about the menace of fascism. *Conquistador* (1932), about the conquest and exploitation of Mexico, was the first of his "public" poems. Other poems were collected in *Frescoes for Mr. Rockefeller's City* (1933), *Public Speech* (1936), and *America Was Promises* (1939). His radio verse plays include *The Fall of the City* (1937), *Air Raid* (1938), and *The Great American Fourth of July Parade* (1975).

MacLeish served as librarian of Congress (1939–44) and assistant secretary of state (1944–45) and in various other governmental positions until 1949, when he became Boylston professor at Harvard, where he remained until 1962. He published his *Collected Poems: 1917–1952* in 1952, and his *New and Collected Poems 1917–1976* appeared in 1976. His verse drama *J.B.*, based on the biblical story of Job, was performed on Broadway in 1958. *Riders on the Earth* (1978) is a collection of essays.

MacLennan, Hugh (b. March 20, 1907, Glace Bay, Cape Breton, Nova Scotia, Can.—d. Nov. 7, 1990, Montreal, Que.), Canadian novelist and essayist whose books offer an incisive social and psychological critique of contemporary Canadian life.

A Rhodes scholar at Oxford, MacLennan received a Ph.D. from Princeton (1935) and taught Latin and history at Lower Canada College, Montreal (1935–45). He was professor of English at McGill University (1951–63). MacLennan's first novel, *Barometer Rising* (1941), is a moral fable that uses as a background the actual explosion of a munitions ship that partly destroyed the city of Halifax in 1917. His later novels include *Two Solitudes* (1945), which explores Anglo-French relations in Canada; *The Precipice* (1948), a study of differences between Canadian and U.S. citizens; and *The Watch That Ends the Night* (1959), an existentialist study of a man faced with a moral and psychological crisis. *Return of the Sphinx* (1967) is a political novel about French-Canadian nationalism. His seventh novel, *Voices in Time* (1980), is the story of a man's attempt to reconstruct the history of a Canada destroyed by nuclear holocaust.

McLennan, John Ferguson (b. Oct. 14, 1827, Inverness, Inverness, Scot.—d. June 16, 1881, Hayes Common, Kent, Eng.), Scottish lawyer and ethnologist whose ideas on cultural evolution, kinship, and the origins of religion stimulated anthropological research.

McLennan was admitted to the bar in 1857, and he became a parliamentary draftsman for Scotland in 1871. His interest in survivals of practice and behaviour from earlier cultures led him to develop a theory of social evolution, outlined in his book *Primitive Marriage: An Enquiry into the Origin of the Form of Capture in Marriage Ceremonies* (1865, reissued as *Studies in Ancient History,* 2nd series, 1896).

McLennan introduced the terms exogamy (marriage outside the group, as in bride capture between warring tribes) and endogamy (marriage within a specific group, leading to monogamy and determination of kinship through males, rather than females). He was critical of the views of the American anthropologist Lewis Henry Morgan on kinship terminology, which, McLennan contended, indicated degree of respect related to considerations of station and age rather than to consanguineous relationships. McLennan regarded totems as survivals of an earlier worship of fetishes, plants, animals, and, in course, anthropomorphic gods. His views on totemism attracted the interest of Sigmund Freud and such social scientists as Émile Durkheim, Sir James George Frazer, and Robertson Smith. McLennan also wrote *The Patriarchal Theory* (1885).

Macleod (town, Alberta, Canada): *see* Fort Macleod.

Macleod, J(ohn) J(ames) R(ickard) (b. Sept. 6, 1876, Cluny, near Dunkeld, Perth, Scot.—d. March 16, 1935, Aberdeen), Scottish physiologist noted as a teacher and for his work on carbohydrate metabolism. Together with Sir Frederick Banting, with whom he shared the Nobel Prize for Physiology or Medicine in 1923, and Charles H. Best, he achieved renown as one of the discoverers of insulin.

J.J.R. Macleod, 1920
BBC Hulton Picture Library

Macleod held posts in physiology and biochemistry at the London Hospital (1899–1902) and as professor of physiology at Western Reserve University, Cleveland, Ohio (1903–18). In 1918 he joined the University of Toronto as associate dean of medicine and subsequently became director of its physiological laboratory. It was in this laboratory that Banting and Best began investigating the secretions of the pancreas and eventually succeeded in isolating and preparing insulin in 1921. Macleod subsequently was made dean of the faculty of medicine.

His publications include *Practical Physiology* (1902) and *Physiology and Biochemistry in Modern Medicine* (1918).

MacLeod, Margaretha Geertruida: *see* Mata Hari.

Macleod, Mary, Gaelic MÀIRI NIGHEAN ALASDAIR RUAIDH (b. 1569, Rowdil, Harris, Inverness, Scot.—d. 1674, Dunvegan, Skye), Scottish-Gaelic poet who is a major representative of the emergent 17th-century poetical school, which gradually supplanted the classical Gaelic bards.

Macleod's poetry is written in simple, natural rhythms and incorporates much of the imagery of the bardic poets. It mainly deals with the heroic exploits of the Macleod family and expresses her deep emotional attachment to the family. She spent most of her life at the Macleod household of Dunvegan on the Isle of Skye, acting as nurse to successive generations of chieftains. Only a few of her poems survive; among these, her tender and nostalgic elegies for the dead Macleods are notable for their fresh style and sincerity of feeling.

Macleod, Norman (b. June 3, 1812, Campbeltown, Argyllshire, Scot.—d. June 16, 1872, Glasgow), influential liberal Presbyterian minister of the Church of Scotland who took advantage of the controversy over church reform during 1833–43 to implement policies advocated by the Free Church of Scotland (which seceded in 1843) while yet remaining within the mother church. He was also known for his ministry to the Scottish working classes.

Norman Macleod, detail of an oil painting by T. Knott; in the Scottish National Portrait Gallery, Edinburgh
By courtesy of the Scottish National Portrait Gallery, Edinburgh

In 1838 Macleod became minister of Loudoun parish in Ayr. His devotion to the working classes led to the publication in 1843 of his widely circulated *Cracks About the Kirk for Kintra Folk* (*i.e.,* "Remarks About the Church for Country Folk"). The same year, he was transferred to the parish at Dalkeith, Midlothian. As a Moderate he joined the "middle party" to help resolve the great Disruption of May 1843, in which a third of the Church of Scotland clergy and laity left to form the Free Church in an effort to force church reforms. From 1849 Macleod took charge of the *Edinburgh Christian Magazine,* and in 1860 he became editor of the monthly *Good Words,* whose popularity he maintained throughout his lifetime.

From 1864 to 1872 Macleod served as chairman of the foreign-missions committee of his church and from 1857 as chaplain to Queen Victoria. He was elected moderator of the General Assembly of the Church of Scotland in 1869. From 1851 until his death he served as pastor at the Barony Church, Glasgow, where he sought to reach nonchurchgoing workers, welcoming them to his services in their work clothes. He also established the first congregational savings bank for parishioners at Glasgow and founded a workingmen's club. Among his published works, which first appeared in *Good Words,* are *The Earnest Student* (1854), *The Gold Thread* (1861), and *Simple Truth Spoken to Working People* (1867).

MacLiammóir, Micheál (b. Oct. 25, 1899, Cork, County Cork, Ire.—d. March 6, 1978, Dublin), actor, scenic designer, and playwright whose nearly 300 productions in Gaelic and English at the Gate Theatre in Dublin enriched the Irish Renaissance by internationalizing the generally parochial Irish theatre.

Using the stage name Alfred Willmore, MacLiammóir made his debut on the London stage in 1911 playing Oliver Twist; he later played John Darling in *Peter Pan.* He traveled and studied art throughout Europe but returned to Ireland and in 1928 cofounded the Gate Theatre with the English producer Hilton Edwards. Their policy of presenting a mainly international repertoire, while also encouraging Irish playwrights to write plays less local in colour than those produced at the Abbey Theatre, enabled Irish audiences to become familiar with the plays of Aeschylus, William Shakespeare, Molière, Henrik Ibsen, Anton Chekhov, Eugene O'Neill, and Arthur Miller and called attention to such new Irish dramatists as Denis Johnston and T.C. Murray. Also with Edwards, MacLiammóir organized the Galway Theatre (Taibhdhearc na Gaillimhe) in 1928 and acted as its director from 1928 to 1931. There MacLiammóir's *Diarmuid agus Gráinne* (1928), a verse-play version, in Gaelic, of a Celtic myth about two famous lovers, was first produced.

Throughout the 1930s, '40s, and '50s, MacLiammóir periodically toured as an actor, producer, and director of a repertory company that appeared in such diverse locations as Cairo, Athens, and the major cities of Canada. MacLiammóir also played Iago in Orson Welles's film version of *Othello* (1955). He developed and performed several one-man shows, including *The Importance of Being Oscar* (1960), based on the works of Oscar Wilde, and *Talking About Yeats* (1970), centred on the writings of William Butler Yeats.

Maclise, Daniel (b. Jan. 25, 1806, Cork, County Cork, Ire.—d. April 25, 1870, London), Irish historical painter whose fame rests chiefly on a series of lithograph portraits of contemporary celebrities and on two vast frescoes that he painted in the Royal Gallery in the House of Lords.

At the age of 16 he left the employ of a local bank to enter the Cork school of art, maintaining himself by portrait sketching. He went to London in 1827 and entered the Royal Academy schools, where he carried off the highest honours. He exhibited subject pictures and portraits regularly at the Royal Academy and in 1835 was elected associate and in 1840, academician.

The 72 lithograph portraits of literary and other contemporary celebrities for which he is best known first appeared in *Fraser's Magazine* (1830–36) under the pseudonym Alfred Croquis (later published as the *Maclise Portrait Gallery,* 1871). Of the two frescoes, "The Meeting of Wellington and Blucher" was unsuccessfully begun in fresco in 1859 and completed in a new German technique in 1861. Its companion "The Death of Nelson" was executed between 1861 and 1864. Maclise painted these large murals alone, under lamentable conditions. By the time of their completion, he was exhausted and never fully regained his health. Maclise's colours are harsh, but this weakness is considered to have been largely offset by his unusually retentive visual memory, vigorous draftsmanship, and gift for large-scale composition.

McLuhan, (Herbert) Marshall (b. July 21, 1911, Edmonton, Alberta, Can.—d. Dec. 31, 1980, Toronto), Canadian communications theorist and educator, whose aphorism "the medium is the message" summarized his view of the potent influence of television, computers, and other electronic disseminators of information in shaping styles of thinking and thought, whether in sociology, art, science, or religion. He regarded the printed book as an institution fated to disappear.

McLuhan was associated with the University of Toronto from 1946 until his death. He became full professor of English literature there in 1952 and from 1963 was director of the university's Centre for Culture and Technology. He was also a popular lecturer.

His works include *The Mechanical Bride: Folklore of Industrial Man* (1951), *Understanding Media: The Extensions of Man* (1964), *The Medium Is the Massage: An Inventory of Effects* (with Quentin Fiore; 1967), *From Cliché to Archetype* (with Wilfred Watson; 1970), and *City as Classroom* (with Kathryn Hutchon and Eric McLuhan; 1977). McLuhan's critical view of 20th-century society's self-transformation made him one of the popular prophetic voices of his time.

Maclure, William (b. Oct. 27, 1763, Ayr, Ayrshire, Scot.—d. March 23, 1840, San Angel, Mex.), Scottish-born American geologist who is known for his geological map—the first true geological map of any part of North America and one of the earliest such maps compiled.

Maclure traveled to New York City in 1782 and then returned to London as a partner in an import–export firm. After amassing a considerable fortune, he returned to the United States in 1796 and became a naturalized citizen. In 1803 he went back to Europe and traveled throughout the Continent, collecting geological specimens and books. Full of enthusiasm for geology, he returned to the United States and investigated the Appalachian Mountain region. In 1809 his *Observations on the Geology of the United States* was published.

A liberal patron of science, he helped to found the Philadelphia Academy of Natural Sciences, which he also endowed with his valuable library of some 3,300 volumes.

Maclurites, extinct genus of Ordovician gastropods (snails) found as fossils and useful for stratigraphic correlations (the Ordovician Period began 500,000,000 years ago and lasted 70,000,000 years). The shell is distinctively coiled and easily recognized. *Maclurites* also had an operculum, or second shell, that covered the aperture of the larger body shell. *Maclurites* is characteristic of a group of early gastropods that first appeared in the Late Cambrian and became extinct at the end of the Ordovician.

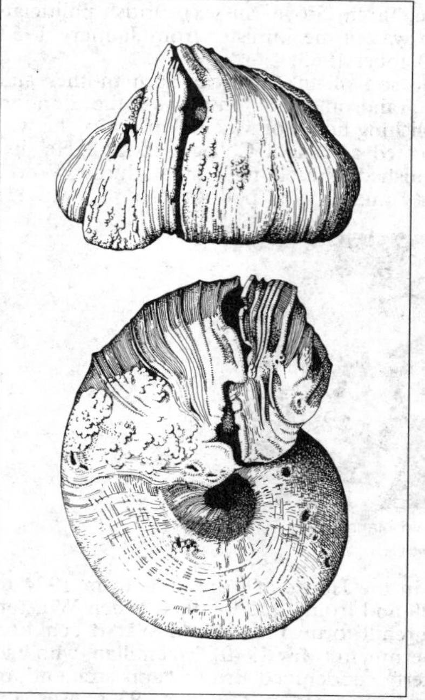

Maclurites from (top) the side and (bottom) the top

Reprinted from H. Shimer and R. Shrock, *Index Fossils of North America*, by permission of the M.I.T. Press, Cambridge, Massachusetts, Copyright 1944 by the Massachusetts Institute of Technology, Copyright renewed 1972 by the Massachusetts Institute of Technology; photograph, J. Bridge

McMahon, Sir William (b. Feb. 23, 1908, Sydney—d. March 31, 1988, Sydney), Australian politician and lawyer who was prime minister of Australia from March 1971 to December 1972.

He was educated at the University of Sydney, where he earned a degree in law. After practicing as a solicitor in Sydney he enlisted in the Australian Army in 1939 and rose to the rank of major. He served in the House of Representatives for Lowe (New South Wales) from 1949 to 1982. He held various ministerial posts in Liberal governments throughout the 1950s and '60s and headed the Treasury (1966–69) and the Ministry of Foreign Affairs (1969–71). After having served as deputy leader of the Liberal Party from 1966 to 1971, he replaced John Gorton as both party leader and prime minister in March of the latter year. He failed to save his party from defeat by the Labour Party in the next elections in late 1972. He was knighted in 1977.

McMahon Line, frontier between Tibet and Assam in British India, negotiated between Tibet and Great Britain at the end of the Simla Conference (October 1913–July 1914) and named after the chief British negotiator, Sir Henry McMahon. It runs from the eastern border of Bhutan along the crest of the Himalayas until it reaches the great bend in the Brahmaputra River where that river emerges from its Tibetan course into the Assam Valley.

Delegates of the Chinese republican government also attended the Simla Conference, but they refused to sign the principal agreement on the status and boundaries of Tibet on the ground that Tibet was subordinate to China and had not the power to make treaties. The Chinese maintained this position until the frontier controversy with independent India led to the Sino-Indian hostilities of October–November 1962. In that conflict the Chinese forces occupied Indian territory south of the McMahon Line but subsequently withdrew after a ceasefire had been achieved.

McMaster, John Bach (b. June 29, 1852, Brooklyn, N.Y., U.S.—d. May 24, 1932, Darien, Conn.), American historian whose eight-volume work on the people of the United States was innovative in the writing of social history.

The son of a former Mississippi plantation owner, McMaster grew up in New York City and worked his way through the City College of New York. Although he obtained a degree in civil engineering in 1873, he was deeply interested in American history. He worked briefly as a civil engineer in Virginia and Chicago in 1873, but he returned to New York the following year and earned a meagre living by tutoring.

McMaster was appointed assistant professor of civil engineering at Princeton University in 1877. Meanwhile, he planned to write a broad-scale history of the United States. In the summer of 1878 he led an expedition to the American West, an experience that impressed on him the pioneers' efforts and the need for a social history of the West. His inspiration materialized in 1881 with the completion of the first chapter of *A History of the People of the United States from the Revolution to the Civil War,* 8 vol. (1883–1913). Almost immediately after publication of this first extremely popular volume in 1883, he accepted an offer to teach at the Wharton School of Finance and Economy at the University of Pennsylvania, Philadelphia, where he remained until his retirement in 1919. In 1885 he wrote the second volume of his *History,* and two years later he completed another work, *Benjamin Franklin as a Man of Letters.*

In addition to writing and teaching, McMaster actively participated in the establishment in 1891 of a new School of American History at the University of Pennsylvania, the first school of its kind in the United States. His widely praised work *A School History of the United States,* published in 1897, became that same year one of the most widely used textbooks of that time. After completing his *History* in 1913, he traveled to Europe and returned to the United States to espouse American entry into World War I. He wrote an additional volume of his *History* (1927), dealing with the administration of President Abraham Lincoln.

Although McMaster has been criticized for his excessive glorification of the progress of the American people, his tendency toward exaggeration and sweeping generalization, and his casual uncited borrowing from other sources, he is credited with having placed a novel emphasis on social and economic forces in historical change and on the use of contemporary documents and newspapers as legitimate sources for historical research. He was also one of the first American scholars to stress the role of the American West in national development.

Macmillan, Daniel; and Macmillan, Alexander (respectively b. Sept. 13, 1813, Isle of Arran, Buteshire, Scot.—d. June 27, 1857, Cambridge, Cambridgeshire, Eng.; b. Oct. 3, 1818, Irvine, Ayrshire, Scot.—d. Jan. 26, 1896, London?), Scottish booksellers and publishers who, in 1843, founded Macmillan & Co., a bookshop that grew into one of the largest publishing firms in the world, producing textbooks, works of science and literature, and high-quality periodicals.

After his father's death in 1824, Daniel, aged 11, was apprenticed to a bookseller in Irvine; he moved to Glasgow in 1831 and to Cambridge two years later. From 1837 to 1843 he worked for Messrs. Seeley, London booksellers, and then bought out a bookshop in Cambridge, where he was joined by his brother Alexander; their first catalog appeared in March 1844. The shop prospered, and within two years the brothers had absorbed the business of their chief local rival. The Macmillans began publishing textbooks in 1844, met with steady success, and published their first novel, Charles Kingsley's *Westward Ho!,* in 1855. Their first best-seller was Thomas Hughes's novel *Tom Brown's School Days* (1857).

At the time of Daniel's death in 1857, the firm was still rather small, issuing about 40 titles annually. Alexander expanded the list to more than 150 annually during his 32 years of active management; he founded *Macmillan's Magazine* (1859–1907), a literary periodical, and *Nature* (1869 to date), which became a leading scientific journal. In 1867 he visited the United States to establish a branch office; the firm also expanded its activities to Canada, Australia, and India. Among the most important of the many Victorian authors published during Alexander's lifetime were Alfred Lord Tennyson, Thomas Henry Huxley, Lewis Carroll, Rudyard Kipling, and William Butler Yeats.

Frederick Orridge Macmillan, the son of Daniel, became a partner in 1876 and first chairman in 1893. Frederick's partners were his younger brothers Maurice Crawford and George Augustin Macmillan; they were succeeded by Maurice's sons Daniel de Mendi Macmillan, the chairman, and Harold Macmillan, who, in a reorganization of the company in 1964, became chairman of Macmillan & Co., the book-publishing side of the business.

McMillan, Edwin Mattison (b. Sept. 18, 1907, Redondo Beach, Calif., U.S.—d. Sept. 7, 1991, El Cerrito, Calif.), American nuclear physicist who shared the Nobel Prize for Chemistry in 1951 with Glenn T. Seaborg for his discovery of element 93, neptunium, the first element heavier than uranium, thus called a transuranium element.

McMillan was educated at the California Institute of Technology and at Princeton University, where he earned a Ph.D. in 1932. He then joined the faculty of the University of California, Berkeley, and became a full professor in 1946 and director of the Lawrence Radiation Laboratory in 1958. He retired in 1973. While studying nuclear fission, McMillan discovered neptunium, a decay product of uranium-239. In 1940, in collaboration with Philip H. Abelson, he isolated the new element and obtained final proof of his discovery. Neptunium was the first of a host of transuranium elements that provide important nuclear fuels and contributed greatly to the knowledge of chemistry and nuclear theory. During World War II he also did research on radar and sonar and worked on the first atomic bomb. He served as a member of the General Advisory Committee to the U.S. Atomic Energy Commission from 1954 to 1958.

McMillan also made a major advance in the development of Ernest Lawrence's cyclotron, which in the early 1940s had run up against its theoretical limit. Accelerated in an ever-widening spiral by synchronized electrical pulses, atomic particles in a cyclotron are unable to attain a velocity beyond a certain point, as a relativistic mass increase tends to put them out of step with the pulses. In 1945, independently of the Russian physicist Vladimir I. Veksler, McMillan found a way of maintaining synchronization for indefinite speeds. He coined the name synchrocyclotron for accelerators using this principle. McMillan was chairman of the National Academy of Sciences from 1968 to 1971.

Macmillan, Harold, in full MAURICE HAROLD MACMILLAN, 1ST EARL OF STOCKTON, VISCOUNT MACMILLAN OF OVENDEN (b. Feb. 10, 1894, London, Eng.—d. Dec. 29, 1986, Birch Grove, Sussex), British politician who was prime minister from January 1957 to October 1963.

The son of an American-born mother and the grandson of a founder of the London publishing house of Macmillan & Co., he was educated at Balliol College, Oxford. He distinguished himself in combat during World War I and entered politics after the war. He sat in the House of Commons from 1924 to 1929 and from 1931 to 1964. When Winston Churchill formed his World War II coalition government (May 1940), Macmillan, who had bitterly condemned British "appeasement" of Nazi Germany in the late 1930s, was appointed parliamentary secretary to the Ministry of Supply. After 10 months as colonial under secretary, he was sent (Dec. 30, 1942) to northwest Africa as British minister resident at Allied Forces Headquarters, Mediterranean Command. There his efforts to secure good relations with Dwight D. Eisenhower, Charles de Gaulle, and other high Allied officers improved his skills as a politician.

Harold Macmillan
Camera Press

At the end of the war in Europe, Macmillan was secretary of state for air in Churchill's "caretaker" government (May–July 1945). After the Conservatives regained power in 1951, he was successively appointed minister of housing and local government (October 1951) and minister of defense (October 1954) by Churchill and then served as foreign secretary (April–December 1955) and chancellor of the exchequer (1955–57) under Sir Anthony Eden. He was appointed prime minister on Jan. 10, 1957, following the resignation of Eden in the wake of the Suez crisis, and was elected leader of the Conservative Party 12 days later.

Macmillan immediately had to deal with a national shortage of money, and his chancellor of the exchequer, Peter Thorneycroft, resigned (January 1958) in protest against government spending. Macmillan worked to improve British-U.S. relations, which had been strained by the Suez crisis, and his old partnership with General, now President, Eisenhower was helpful in this regard. Macmillan himself supervised the conduct of foreign policy as prime minister. He had several conferences with presidents Dwight D. Eisenhower and John F. Kennedy, and he visited Nikita S. Khrushchev in Moscow (February 1959). At home, Macmillan gave firm support to Britain's array of postwar social programs. He led the Conservative Party to a resounding victory in the 1959 general election by effectively contrasting Britain's prewar unemployment with its postwar full employment under the slogan "You've never had it so good."

The Nassau agreement (December 1962) between Macmillan and Kennedy, that the United States should furnish nuclear missiles for British submarines, enraged Charles de Gaulle, who then was head of the French state and who insisted on a Europe uncontrolled by the United States. The subsequent French veto (Jan. 29, 1963) of Great Britain's entry into the European Economic Community was a severe blow to Macmillan. For most of his term Macmillan had been held in high esteem by his party. But Britain's adverse balance of payments led the government to impose a wage freeze and other deflationary measures from 1961 on, and this caused Macmillan's government to lose popularity. Another setback was an apparent Soviet espionage attempt involving John Profumo, the secretary of state for war, which ended in the latter's resignation (June 1963). Macmillan's reputation was partly rehabilitated by the successful negotiations (July 1963) among Great Britain, the United States, and the Soviet Union for the Nuclear Test-Ban Treaty, but demands continued within his own party for a new and younger leader, and, after undergoing surgery, he resigned his office on Oct. 18, 1963.

Macmillan refused a peerage and retired from the House of Commons in September 1964. He then began producing his memoirs: *Winds of Change, 1914–1939* (1966); *The Blast of War, 1939–1945* (1967); *Tides of Fortune, 1945–1955* (1969); *Riding the Storm, 1956–1959* (1971); *Pointing the Way, 1959–1961* (1972); *At the End of the Day, 1961–63* (1973); and *The Past Masters: Politics and Politicians, 1906–1939* (1975). He later accepted a peerage and was created an earl in 1984.

McMillin, Bo, byname of ALVIN N. MCMILLIN (b. Jan. 12, 1895, Prairie Hill, Texas, U.S.—d. March 31, 1952, Bloomington, Ind.), American collegiate and professional football player and coach.

McMillin excelled as a quarterback for Centre College, Danville, Ky. (1919–21). In 1921 he completed 119 of 170 passes attempted. He was named All-American in 1919.

McMillin played for the National Football League (NFL) Milwaukee Badgers (1922–23) and began collegiate coaching at Centenary College of Louisiana (Shreveport, 1922–25). He became coach at Indiana University, Bloomington, in 1934, where he remained until his retirement as a collegiate coach in 1947. He coached the NFL Detroit Lions (1948–51) and the Philadelphia Eagles briefly (1951).

McMurdo Sound, bay off Antarctica that forms the western extension of Ross Sea, lying at the edge of Ross Ice Shelf, west of Ross Island and east of Victoria Land. The channel, 92 miles (148 km) long and up to 46 miles (74 km) wide, has been a major centre for Antarctic explorations. First discovered in 1841 by the Scottish explorer Sir James Clark Ross,

Commonwealth Glacier, McMurdo Sound, Antarctica
By courtesy of the U.S. Navy

it thereafter served as one of the main access routes to the Antarctic continent. Along its shores, on Ross Island, the British explorer Robert Falcon Scott established his headquarters. That site later served as the main base for the expedition (1908) of another British explorer, Ernest Henry Shackleton, and from the 1950s it and several locations on Victoria Land served as scientific-research stations operated by the United States and New Zealand.

McMurray (town, Alberta, Canada): *see* Fort McMurray.

MacMurrough, Dermot (Irish king): *see* Dermot MacMurrough.

Macnaghten, Sir William Hay, BARONET (b. August 1793—d. Dec. 23, 1841, Kābul, Afg.), British interventionist agent in Afghanistan during the First Anglo-Afghan War (1839–42). He was created a baronet in 1840.

Macnaghten went to India in 1809, where he served as an administrator and a diplomat in Madras and Bengal, acquired a knowledge of Hindu and Muslim law, and became an expert in Oriental languages. Made an adviser to India's governor-general, Lord Auckland, in 1837, he advocated British intervention to counteract Russian influence in neighbouring Afghanistan, which led to the First Anglo-Afghan War. As political agent with the British invasion force in Kābul, he tried (unsuccessfully) to replace Afghan ruler Dōst Moḥammad Khān with his pro-British rival, Shāh Shojā'. Suspected of treachery by the Afghans, Macnaghten was captured and slain by them while he was trying to arrange the withdrawal of British forces in 1841.

McNamara, Robert S(trange) (b. June 9, 1916, San Francisco, Calif., U.S.), U.S. secretary of defense from 1961 to 1968 who revamped Pentagon operations and who played a major role in the nation's military involvement in Vietnam.

After graduating from the University of California at Berkeley in 1937, McNamara earned a graduate degree at the Harvard Business School (1939) and later joined the Harvard faculty. Disqualified by poor vision from active duty during World War II, he developed logistical systems for bomber raids and statistical systems for monitoring troops and supplies.

After the war, McNamara was one of the "Whiz Kids" hired to revitalize the Ford Motor Company. His plans, including the institution of strict cost-accounting methods and the development of both compact and luxury models, met with success, and McNamara rose rapidly in the corporate ranks. In 1960 he became the first person outside the Ford family to assume presidency of the company.

After just one month as Ford's president, however, McNamara resigned to join the Kennedy administration as secretary of defense. In his new post he successfully gained control of Pentagon operations and the military bureaucracy, encouraged the modernization of the armed forces, restructured budget procedures, and cut costs by refusing to spend money on what he believed were unnecessary or obsolete weapons systems. McNamara was also at the centre of a drive to alter U.S. military strategy from the "massive retaliation" of the Eisenhower years to a "flexible response," emphasizing counterinsurgency techniques and second-strike nuclear-missile capability.

McNamara initially supported the deepening military involvement of the United States in Vietnam. On visits to South Vietnam in 1962, 1964, and 1966, the secretary publicly expressed optimism that the National Liberation Front and its North Vietnamese allies would soon abandon their attempt to overthrow the U.S.-backed Saigon regime. He became the government's chief spokesman for the day-to-day operations of the war and acted as President Lyndon B. Johnson's principal deputy in the war's prosecution.

By 1966, however, McNamara had begun to question the wisdom of U.S. military involvement in Vietnam, and by 1967 he was openly seeking a way to launch peace negotiations. He initiated a full-scale investigation of the American commitment to Vietnam (later published as *The Pentagon Papers*), came out in opposition to continued bombing of North Vietnam (for which he lost influence in the Johnson administration), and in February 1968 left the Pentagon to become president of the World Bank.

In his 13-year tenure as head of that institution, McNamara displayed what was generally regarded as great sensitivity to the needs of Third World nations. He retired from the World Bank in 1981 but remained active in many other organizations. He addressed issues such as world hunger, East-West relations, and other policy matters. His policy papers were published in two volumes, and his book *Blundering Into Disaster: Surviving the First Century in a Nuclear Age* (1986) discusses nuclear war.

MacNeice, Louis (b. Sept. 12, 1907, Belfast, Ire.—d. Sept. 3, 1963, London, Eng.), British poet and playwright, a member, with W.H. Auden, C. Day-Lewis, and Stephen Spender, of a group whose low-keyed, unpoetic, socially committed, and topical verse was the "new poetry" of the 1930s.

MacNeice
Camera Press

After studying at the University of Oxford (1926–30), MacNeice became a lecturer in classics at the University of Birmingham (1930–36) and later in Greek at the Bedford College for Women, London (1936–40). In 1941 he began to write and produce radio plays for the British Broadcasting Corporation. Foremost among his fine radio verse plays was the dramatic fantasy *The Dark Tower* (1947), with music by Benjamin Britten.

MacNeice's first book of poetry, *Blind Fireworks,* appeared in 1929, followed by more than a dozen other volumes, such as *Poems* (1935), *Autumn Journal* (1939), *Collected Poems, 1925–1948* (1949), and, posthumously, *The Burning Perch* (1963). An intellectual honesty, Celtic exuberance, and sardonic humour characterized his poetry, which combined a charming natural lyricism with the mundane patterns of colloquial speech. His most characteristic mood was that of the slightly detached, wryly observant, ironic and witty commentator. Among MacNeice's prose works are *Letters from Iceland* (with W.H. Auden, 1937) and *The Poetry of W.B. Yeats* (1941). He was also a skilled translator, particularly of Horace and Aeschylus (*Agamemnon,* 1936).

McNeill, William H(ardy) (b. Oct. 31, 1917, Vancouver, B.C., Can.), prominent historian whose *The Rise of the West,* covering the entire span of recorded human history, had a major effect on historical theory.

McNeill attended the University of Chicago (B.A., 1938; M.A., 1939) and Cornell University (Ph.D., 1947). During World War II he served in the U.S. Army (1941–46); part of that time he was the assistant military attaché to Greece (1944–46). McNeill taught history at the University of Chicago from 1947, becoming a professor in 1957 and subsequently chairman of the department (1961–69).

His most notable work, *The Rise of the West* (1963), traces the rise, development, and interrelationships of civilizations through 5,000 years of recorded history. Dealing equally with Eastern as well as Western civilizations and discussing developments in Africa, Oceania, and Pre-Columbian America, McNeill presents his view that all cultures acted on and were acted upon by others and that the history of civilization is one of constant change and cultural diffusion. The feature that has made European civilization preeminent in the world since AD 1500 is, according to McNeill, its great instability, giving it an ever-renewing, dynamic quality that upset and overrode the ancient cultural balance of Eastern civilizations. This thesis stands in sharp contrast to the work of Arnold Toynbee, who held that civilizations rose and fell according to their own internal rhythm, without regard to any outside forces.

McNeill produced many important historical works, generally dealing with cultural influences and their means of diffusion. Other books include *Greek Dilemma: War and Aftermath* (1947), *Europe's Steppe Frontier 1500–1800* (1964), *Plagues and Peoples* (1976), *The Human Condition: An Ecological and Historical View* (1980), and *Population and Politics Since 1750* (1990).

Macocha Gorge, also called MACOCHA ABYSS, gorge in Jihomoravský *kraj* (region), Czech Republic. It is the best-known and most frequently visited feature in the Moravian Karst region and contains a labyrinth of caves and galleries and a number of magnificent stalagmites and stalactites. The gorge reaches a maximum depth of 420 feet (128 m) and is accessible through a chain of subterranean passages and caves. It is about 900 feet (275 m) in length and about 390 feet (120 m) at its widest point. Macocha Gorge probably was formed by the collapse of the roof of an underground cave. Physiographically, parts of the same system are the Catherine Cave, the largest cavern in the district, and a string of lakes, the Punkva water caves, which may be reached by boat.

Macomb, city, seat (1826) of McDonough county, western Illinois, U.S., on the east fork of the La Moine River. Settled by New Englanders in 1829 and originally called Washington, it was laid out (1830) and renamed after General Alexander Macomb, an officer in the War of 1812. The city is the site of Western Illinois University (founded there as a normal school in 1899). The economy is based on light manufacturing (pottery, porcelain products, and roller bearings) and on agriculture. Argyle Lake State Park is to the west. Inc. town, 1841; city, 1857. Pop. (1991 est.) 20,148.

Mâcon, town, capital of Saône-et-Loire *département,* Bourgogne *région,* east-central France, north of Lyon. On the right bank of the Saône River, it is a communications centre skirted by France's main motorway, the Autoroute du Sud, and traversed by the main road from the Loire region to Geneva, which crosses the restored 14th-century St. Laurent Bridge over the Saône. Called Matisco by the Romans, Mâcon was an episcopal see from 536 to 1790. The former Cathedral of Saint-Vincent was largely demolished in 1799. Old buildings include the house, now the museum, in which the 19th-century poet and politician Alphonse de Lamartine was born.

Situated near the Mâconnais and Beaujolais vineyards, which produce such renowned wines as Pouilly Fouissé, Julienas, and Moulin à Vent, it is a wine-trading centre. An international wine fair is held there annually. Mâcon is also a market for Charolais cattle and has a modern industrial zone (manufacturing mechanical equipment and motorcycles), as well as a river port by virtue of the Saône's natural navigability. Pop. (1982) 36,517.

Macon, city, seat (1823) of Bibb county, central Georgia, U.S., on the Ocmulgee River at the Fall Line. Its incorporated area extends into Jones County. The original settlement, Newtown, developed around Ft. Hawkins (1806). In 1823 a town was laid out across the river and named for Nathaniel Macon, a North Carolina agrarian legislator; it annexed Newtown in 1829. During the Civil War, Macon was a Confederate gold depository and supply depot until Gen. Howell Cobb surrendered it to the Federal cavalry commander Gen. James H. Wilson on April 20, 1865. Economic recovery, slow during Reconstruction, was stimulated during World War I with increased industrial employment. Robins Air Force Base, 17 mi (27 km) south, became an important installation during World War II. Manufacturing is well diversified and includes textiles and a brick and tile industry. Macon has for long been a processing and distributing centre for the surrounding farmland. It is the seat of Mercer University (1833), Wesleyan College (1836), Macon Junior College (1968), and the Georgia Academy for the Blind (1851). The poet Sidney Lanier (1842–81) was born there. Indian mounds are at nearby Ocmulgee National Monument. Inc. city, 1823. Pop. (1990) city, 106,612; Macon–Warner Robins MSA, 281,103.

Macon, Nathaniel (b. Dec. 17, 1758, Edgecombe, N.C.—d. June 29, 1837, Warren County, N.C., U.S.), U.S. Congressional leader for 37 years, remembered chiefly for his negative views on almost every issue of the day, particularly those concerned with a central form of government. Yet his integrity and absence of selfish motives served to strengthen his influence and to make him universally liked and respected.

Macon's long political career began in the North Carolina Senate (1781–85), shifted to the U.S. House of Representatives (1791–1815), and concluded in the U.S. Senate (1815–28). As speaker of the House (1801–07), he was one of the most important leaders of the Jeffersonian, anti-Federalist faction, who feared that individual liberties and interests would be jeopardized by a national government. At first on close terms with Thomas Jefferson, Macon associated himself briefly (1806–09) with John Randolph and a dozen other congressmen critical of Jefferson for failing to adhere to pure republican principles.

Returning to the party fold, he served as chairman of the House Foreign Relations Committee, which reported a bill, passed on May 1, 1810, restoring commerce with all nations but promising to revive non-intercourse against Great Britain or France if either nation were to reverse its restrictions on U.S. shipping. This bill was labelled Macon's Bill No. 2, although Macon opposed its adoption.

Macon, departing from his usual pattern of negative voting, approved the declaration of war against England in 1812 but opposed conscription and all taxes needed to wage war. His states' rights and sectional views became even more marked after the war. During his retirement years he engaged in political correspondence in which he stoutly defended slavery.

Maçon, Robert Le: *see* Le Maçon, Robert.

Maconde (people): *see* Makonde.

Macoraba (Saudi Arabia): *see* Mecca.

McPherson, city, seat (1873) of McPherson county, central Kansas, U.S. Laid out in 1872 on the old Santa Fe Trail, it was named for James B. McPherson, a Union general killed in the Civil War. The city is now a processing and shipping point for nearby oil fields and the surrounding diversified agricultural area. Industries include oil refining, flour milling, and the manufacture of aluminum products, plastic pipe, and mobile homes. It is the seat of McPherson College (1887), with a museum displaying the world's first synthetic diamond, and Central (junior) College (1914). McPherson State Fishing Lake is nearby. Inc. 1874. Pop. (1990) 12,422.

McPherson, Aimee Semple (b. Oct. 9, 1890, near Ingersoll, Ont., Can.—d. Sept. 27, 1944, Oakland, Calif., U.S.), controversial U.S. Pentecostal evangelist and early radio preacher whose International Church of the Foursquare Gospel brought her wealth, notoriety, and a following numbering in the tens of thousands.

Born on a farm, she inherited her religious zeal from her mother, a Salvation Army member, and began to preach her own brand of the Christian gospel at the age of 17. Her public career began in 1908 as a missionary in China with her first husband, Robert Semple, a Pentecostal evangelist. After he died, she returned to the United States with their daughter. A second marriage to Harold McPherson ended when she turned to full-time itinerant evangelism and healing. Highly successful, she settled finally in Los Angeles, where for almost 20 years she preached to large audiences in the Angelus Temple, built for her by her followers at a cost of $1,500,000. There, with the offstage help of her mother, Minnie ("Ma") Kennedy, she conducted revival services in theatrical style, sometimes dressing to express the themes of her sermons—on one occasion she wore a policeman's uniform for a speech on "God's Law."

Aimee Semple McPherson, *c.* 1926

By courtesy of the History Division, Natural History Museum of Los Angeles County

In addition to organizing (1927) and administering the International Church of the Foursquare Gospel, McPherson built a radio station, founded and headed a Bible school, edited a magazine, wrote books and pamphlets, carried on extensive social service work, and spread her gospel throughout some 200 missions. Known as "Sister Aimee," she was a dynamic and attractive woman and retained the loyalty of her followers despite a third marriage that ended in divorce, a sensational five-week disappearance in 1926, and various grave but unproved charges against her. Nevertheless, her fame, money, power, and marital relationships combined to make her a centre not only of attention but also of litigation; 45 legal actions were pending against her at one time. Her career reached its height in the late 1930s, and by 1940 the temple had begun to be a tourist attraction. After her death from an overdose of barbiturates, her son Rolf McPherson succeeded her. Her works include *This Is That* (1919), *In the Service of the King* (1927), and *Give Me My Own God* (1936). *The Story of My Life* was edited and published in her memory in 1951.

Macpherson, Sir David (Lewis) (b. Sept. 12, 1818, Castle Leathers, Inverness County, Scot.—d. Aug. 16, 1896, at sea), Scottish-born politician and railway builder who served as Canadian minister of the interior from 1883 to 1885.

David Macpherson, 1881

By courtesy of the Public Archives of Canada

Macpherson emigrated in 1835 from Scotland to Montreal, where he amassed a large fortune in shipping. He moved to Toronto in 1853 and obtained a contract to build a railway line in Canada West (now in Ontario) from Toronto to Sarnia (later part of the Grand Trunk Railway from Toronto to Montreal). He was elected member of the provincial legislative council for Saugeen in 1864, and, when the Dominion of Canada was created in 1867, he was nominated to the Senate. In 1871 he vied with Sir Hugh Allan for a charter to build the Canadian Pacific Railway. As head of the Interoceanic Railway Company, Macpherson sought government assistance; he refused to join Allan's company, which won the charter but subsequently forfeited the contract.

Macpherson was made speaker of the Senate in 1880 and minister without portfolio in the Conservative Cabinet. In 1883 he became minister of the interior, but he retired from that post in 1885, charged with incapacity in dealing with the Northwest Rebellion. Macpherson was knighted in 1884.

Macpherson, James (b. Oct. 27, 1736, Ruthven, Inverness, Scot.—d. Feb. 17, 1796, Belville, Inverness), Scottish poet whose initiation of the Ossianic controversy has obscured his genuine contributions to Gaelic studies.

His first book of poems, *The Highlander* (1758), was undistinguished; but after collecting Gaelic manuscripts and having orally transmitted Gaelic poems transcribed with the encouragement of the poet John Home and the financial support of the rhetorician Hugh Blair, he published *Fragments of ancient poetry . . . translated from the Gallic or Erse language* (1760), *Fingal* (1762), and *Temora* (1763), claiming that much of their content was based on a 3rd-century Gaelic poet Ossian. No Gaelic manuscripts date back beyond the 10th century. The authenticity of Ossian was supported by Blair, looked on with skepticism by the Scottish philosopher David Hume, admired with doubt by the English poet Thomas Gray, and denied by the panjandrum of English letters, Dr. Samuel Johnson. None of the critics knew Gaelic. Macpherson often injected a good deal of Romantic mood into the originals, sometimes closely followed them, and other times did not. His language was strongly influenced by the Authorized

Version of the Bible. The originals were published only after Macpherson's death.

McPherson, James B., in full JAMES BIRDSEYE MCPHERSON (b. Nov. 14, 1828, Sandusky county, Ohio, U.S.—d. July 22, 1864, near Atlanta, Ga.), Union general of the American Civil War about whose death General Ulysses

James B. McPherson
By courtesy of the Library of Congress, Washington, D.C.

S. Grant is reported to have said, "The country has lost one of its best soldiers, and I have lost my best friend."

After graduation from West Point at the head of the class of 1849, McPherson was commissioned in the Corps of Engineers and held minor army assignments until the outbreak of the Civil War (1861). Following several months with General H.W. Halleck in Missouri, he was assigned to General Grant's staff as chief engineer in the Tennessee campaign and, after distinguished service at the battles of Shiloh, Tenn., and Corinth, Miss., was promoted to major general of volunteers. He participated in the second advance on Vicksburg, Miss. (1863), and, after the city fell, was promoted to brigadier general in the regular army. In March 1864 he took command of the Army of the Tennessee, which moved against Atlanta under General William T. Sherman's supreme command. Shortly after reporting to Sherman, the youthful officer was killed by a Confederate skirmisher.

BIBLIOGRAPHY. Elizabeth J. Whaley, *Forgotten Hero: General James B. McPherson* (1955), is a biography.

Macpherson, Jay, in full JEAN JAY MACPHERSON (b. June 13, 1931, London, Eng.), Canadian lyric poet, member of "the mythopoeic school of poetry," who expressed serious religious and philosophical themes in symbolic verse that was often lyrical or comic.

Macpherson immigrated with part of her family to Canada in 1940; in 1954 she joined the faculty of Victoria University at the University of Toronto. Her early works, *Nineteen Poems* (1952) and *O Earth Return* (1954), were followed by *The Boatman and Other Poems* (1957, reissued with additional poems, 1968), a collection of short poems under six subtitles that established her reputation as a poet. Her lyrics, often ironic and epigrammatic and linked by recurrent mythical and legendary symbols, reflect the influences of the modern critical theories of Northrop Frye and Robert Graves, Elizabethan songs, the poetry of William Blake, Anglo-Saxon riddles, and traditional ballads. Often written in traditional verse forms, her poems repeatedly stress the importance of the imagination. *Four Ages of Man* (1962) is an illustrated account of classical myths, designed for older children. *Welcoming Disaster* (1974) is a collection of her poems from 1970 to 1974. Her study of the pastoral romance, *The Spirit of Solitude: Conventions and Continuities in Late Romance,* was published in 1982.

McPherson Range, mountain range, eastern spur of the Great Dividing Range, eastern Australia; its crest constitutes the Queensland–New South Wales border from Point Danger to Wallangara (140 miles [225 km]). Occupying a well-dissected and rainforest-covered region, the range rises to its highest point at West Barney Peak, 4,459 feet (1,359 m). In 1770 the British navigator Captain James Cook sighted the range from the coast; he named the peak he saw Mount Warning. In 1827 Captain Patrick Logan became the first European to explore the interior of the range, which was named for Major Duncan McPherson.

It was not until 1843 that a road was surveyed from the Richmond River valley westward across the mountains. The Sydney-Brisbane rail line crosses the range through a tunnel under Richmond Gap. A section of the region, the Lamington Plateau, has been made a national park.

Macquarie, Lachlan (b. Jan. 31, 1761, Ulva, Argyllshire, Scot.—d. July 1, 1824, London, Eng.), early governor of New South Wales, Australia (1809–21), who expanded opportunities for Emancipists (freed convicts) and established a balance of power with the Exclusionists, large landowners and sheep farmers.

Macquarie joined the British army as a boy and served in North America, Europe, and the West Indies between 1776 and 1784 and in India (1788–1803 and 1805–07). Appointed governor of New South Wales in 1809, he replaced the New South Wales Corps that had overthrown the previous governor, William Bligh. He began a program of public-works construction and town planning; by 1822 he had sponsored more than 200 works, many of them designed by the Emancipist architect Francis Greenway. Macquarie introduced the colony's own currency in 1813 and helped establish its first bank in 1817. He encouraged expansion of settlement and exploration, most notably the crossing of the Blue Mountains in 1813. His policy toward the Aborigines was the most liberal since that of the colony's first governor, Arthur Phillip.

Macquarie's belief in development based on Emancipist agriculture angered the colony's large landowners, headed by John Macarthur, and led to a British government investigation (1819), Macquarie's recall in 1821, and his retirement to his estate on Mull in the Inner Hebrides.

Macquarie, Lake, seaboard lagoon, New South Wales, Australia. It lies 60 miles (97 km) northeast of Sydney. Measuring 15 miles long and 5 miles wide (24 km long and 8 km wide), with 108 miles (174 km) of shoreline and an area of 45 square miles (117 square km), it was formed by sandbars closing off three small branching estuaries of the Hunter River (leaving one narrow passage open to the Pacific that is the site of the small resort and industrial town of Swansea). The lake, named after former governor Lachlan Macquarie, is the focus of recreational, commercial, and residential development. Coal is mined on the eastern and western shores. Superphosphates and sulfuric acid are produced at a plant on Cockle Creek, which enters the lake from the north. The lake's waters are used by the power station at Vales Point. A wildlife sanctuary is located on Pulbah Island.

Macquarie Harbour, inlet of the Indian Ocean indenting western Tasmania, Australia. A fault valley modified by glaciation, it extends 20 miles (32 km) northwest-southeast and is about 5 miles (8 km) wide. It receives the King River from the northeast and the Gordon from the southeast. A bar across the narrow mouth of the inlet (Hell's Gates) severely limits the use of port facilities at Strahan on Long Bay, a northern extension of the harbour. The inlet was probably visited in 1815 by an adventurer, Captain James Kelly, and was named after Lachlan Macquarie, then governor of New South Wales. In 1821 the coastal area was chosen for a penal colony to replace the one on Norfolk Island in the Pacific. Known as the Settlement (Sarah) Island Colony, it lasted until 1833, when the difficulty of supply forced its abandonment. Deserted for more than 40 years, the harbour later saw activity with gold mining in the King valley and timber cutting in the Gordon. Settlement Island and the Isle of the Condemned are now historical reserves.

Macquarie Island, island lying about 900 miles (1,450 km) southeast of Tasmania, Australia. It forms, with associated islets, a sub-Antarctic part of Tasmania. Macquarie, a volcanic mass with an area of 47 square miles (123 square km) and a general elevation of 800 feet (240 m), measures 21 by 2 miles (34 by 3 km) and has several rocky islets offshore. Rounded hills rise to 1,200–1,400 feet (365–425 m), while the coast falls steeply away. Although the island is treeless, its slopes and coastal flats are covered by heavy vegetation, and there are a few small glacial lakes. The island was sighted in 1810 by Frederick Hasselburg, an Australian sealer, who named it after Lachlan Macquarie, then governor of New South Wales. A meteorologic and geologic research station has been maintained on the island since 1948. Created a nature reserve in 1933, Macquarie is the only known breeding ground of the royal penguin, and it has a colony of fur seals, reestablished in 1956 after their near extermination in the 1830s.

macquarie pine: *see* Huon pine.

McRae, Carmen (b. April 8, 1920, New York, N.Y., U.S.—d. Nov. 10, 1994, Beverly Hills, Calif.), American jazz vocalist and pianist who outgrew an early emulation of vocalist Billie Holiday to become a distinctive stylist, known for her smoky voice and her lyrical, melodic variations—mostly on jazz standards. Her improvisations were innovative, complex, and elegant.

McRae studied classical piano as a child, worked with bandleaders Benny Carter and Count Basie in 1944, and made her recording debut as Carmen Clarke (being then married to jazz drummer Kenny Clarke) with Mercer Ellington's orchestra in 1946–47. She spent several years as an intermission pianist in small nightclubs and in nonmusical jobs until successfully recording in 1953 and 1954. From the mid-1950s, she toured extensively (being particularly popular in Japan), recorded frequently, and appeared in many musical contexts.

macramé, also spelled MACRAME (from Turkish *makrama,* "napkin," or "towel"), coarse lace or fringe made by knotting cords or thick threads in a geometric pattern. Macramé was a specialty of Genoa, where, in the 19th century, towels decorated with knotted cord were popular. Its roots were in a 16th-century technique of knotting lace known as *punto a groppo.* In the 1960s macramé became a popular craft and creative art technique in America and in Europe. It has been used to create lampshades, plant hangers, hammocks, window coverings, and wall hangings.

Macready, William Charles (b. March 3, 1793, London, Eng.—d. April 27, 1873, Cheltenham, Gloucestershire), English actor, manager, and diarist, a leading figure of the 19th-century stage in the development of techniques of acting and production.

Macready was entered at Rugby to prepare for the bar, but financial difficulties and his sense of personal responsibility caused him to abandon his education and take up—temporarily, he thought—the theatre, a profession for which he always felt an intense dislike. In 1810 he made his debut in his father's company, as Romeo, at Birmingham and rapidly acquired fame in other roles in provincial theatres. In 1816 he appeared at Covent Garden, London, and played a series of melodramatic villains. He performed with such earnestness and truth that he became firmly established, and by 1820 he was recognized as one of the finest contemporary English actors and was contested for first place only by Edmund Kean. Macready achieved his greatest fame playing such Shakespearean roles as Hamlet, Iago, Lear, Othello, and Richard II.

Macready, detail of a watercolour attributed to D. Maclise, about 1840; in the National Portrait Gallery, London
By courtesy of the National Portrait Gallery, London

Macready served as the manager of Covent Garden from 1837 to 1839 and as manager of Drury Lane from 1841 to 1843. Though his tenures as manager of these theatres were financially unsuccessful, they did allow him to extend his theory of acting to all the elements of production. He was the first to impose upon the 19th-century theatre the principle of unity: that the actors and all others connected with a performance were to be guided by the central concepts of the playwright. In an era when leading actors routinely memorized their lines in private and performed their parts any way they wished, Macready insisted upon thorough rehearsals in which all the roles were well-played and artistically coherent wih each other. Macready instituted the use of accurate costumes in historical dramas and made special efforts to obtain sets and scenery that harmonized with the plays. And finally, he rejected the corrupted versions of Shakespeare's plays that were universally used at that time and instead reverted to the original texts. All of these innovations were realized in Macready's notable revivals of Shakespeare's *As You Like It, Macbeth, King Lear, Henry V*, and *The Tempest*. The historical research behind these productions influenced English stagecraft, and the principle of theatrical unity anticipated practice in the 20th century.

Macready worked tirelessly to persuade leading literary figures of the day to turn to the writing of plays. After 1825 he moved freely in the highest literary and artistic circles of London, and the pages of his voluminous diary detail that life. Macready made several tours outside England. In 1828 he performed in Paris, and he visited the United States in 1826, 1843, and 1848–49. During Macready's last visit to America in 1849 a longstanding feud started by his rival, the American actor Edwin Forrest, erupted into tragedy. During a performance of *Macbeth* by Macready at the Astor Place Opera House in New York City, Forrest's partisans tried to storm the theatre and thus started a riot in which more than 20 persons were killed by the militia and from which Macready narrowly escaped with his life. He returned to England for his farewell performances and retired from the stage in his favourite role, Macbeth, in 1851.

Macready was an intellectual actor and was at his best in such philosophical roles as Hamlet and Richelieu. He was also capable of achieving great emotional intensity, however. Although he was a lesser actor than David Garrick and perhaps Edmund Kean at his best, Macready was more important than either in his influence on the acting style and production techniques that made possible the art of the modern theatre.

McReynolds, James (Clark) (b. Feb. 3, 1862, Elkton, Ky., U.S.—d. Aug. 24, 1946, Washington, D.C.), U.S. Supreme Court justice (1914–41) who was a leading force in striking down the early New Deal program of President Franklin D. Roosevelt.

McReynolds was admitted to the bar in 1884 and practiced law in Nashville, Tenn. He was professor of law at Vanderbilt University, Nashville, prior to his appointment as assistant attorney general (1903–07) in the administration of President Theodore Roosevelt.

As special counsel to the attorney general (1907–12) and as attorney general (1913–14) under President Woodrow Wilson, McReynolds was distinguished for his vigorous enforcement of the antitrust laws. Thus, he was widely regarded as a liberal when Wilson appointed him to the Supreme Court in 1914. Over the next 27 years, however, he became increasingly conservative and was an outspoken member of the majority that prior to 1937 succeeded in striking down many of the social-reform programs of the New Deal.

Macrinus, in full CAESAR MARCUS OPELLIUS SEVERUS MACRINUS AUGUSTUS, original name MARCUS OPELLIUS MACRINUS (b. *c.* 164, Caesarea, Mauretania [now Cherchell, Algeria]—d. June 218, in Bithynia [now in Turkey]), Roman emperor in 217 and 218, the first man to rule the empire without having achieved senatorial status.

His skills as a lawyer helped him to rise rapidly in an equestrian career (a step below the senatorial career in status) until he became a praetorian prefect under the emperor Caracalla (reigned 211–217). Macrinus is alleged to have prompted the murder of Caracalla by an army officer in April 217, while the emperor was fighting the Parthians in what is now Iran. Three days after the assassination Macrinus was proclaimed emperor by his army. He fought an inconclusive battle with the Parthians and then agreed to a peace that was unfavourable to Rome. This decision cost him the support of his Syrian troops, who transferred their allegiance to Elagabalus, the son of a cousin of Caracalla. With his remaining forces Macrinus fled toward Italy. He was overtaken, defeated in a battle near Antioch (modern Antakya, Tur.), and subsequently captured and executed.

Macrinus, marble bust; in the Uffizi, Florence
Brogi—Art Resource/EB Inc.

Macro-Algonquian languages, also spelled MACRO-ALGONKIAN, major group (phylum or superstock) of North American Indian languages; it is composed of nine families and a total of 24 languages or dialect groups. The language families included in Macro-Algonquian are Algonquian, with 13 languages; Yurok, with 1 language; Wiyot, with 1 language; Muskogean, with 4 languages; and Natchez, Atakapa, Chitimacha, Tunica, and Tonkawa, with 1 language apiece of the same name. The Macro-Algonquian languages were spoken prior to European settlement in eastern North America from Labrador and eastern Quebec down the Atlantic seacoast to North Carolina; around the Great Lakes west into Saskatchewan, Alberta, Montana, Wyoming, and Colorado; in the southeastern United States from eastern Texas to Florida and Georgia and north into Tennessee; and in an isolated area in northern California (Wiyot and Yurok).

Major languages in the phylum are the Cree, Montagnais, and Naskapi dialects of eastern Canada; the Ojibwa, Algonquin, Ottawa, and Salteaux dialects of southern Ontario; the Micmac language of eastern Canada; and the Blackfoot language of Montana and Alberta. These are all Algonquian languages. The Choctaw–Chickasaw dialects are spoken in Mississippi; and the Muskogee, or Creek, and Seminole dialects are spoken in Oklahoma, Alabama, and Florida. These languages belong to the Muskogean family.

Like many American Indian languages, the Macro-Algonquian languages are polysynthetic in their structure; that is, they form words out of many so-called bound elements (which may not be used except in combination with other such elements), which serve as nouns, verbs, adjectives, and adverbs. Thus, a single Algonquian word may carry the meaning of an entire sentence in English. These languages make great use of suffixes and, to some extent, prefixes. They also use inflection as a grammatical device and have some development of case; in addition, they make use of word-stem modification such as reduplication (doubling the stem word or syllables thereof).

Macro-Siouan languages, major grouping (phylum or superstock) of North American Indian languages; it is made up of 26 languages, grouped into 5 families: Siouan, with 12 languages; Catawba, with 1 language (extinct); Iroquoian, with 8 languages; Caddoan, with 4 languages; and Yuchi, with 1 language. Prior to European settlement, the Macro-Siouan languages were spoken in what are now the eastern United States and Canada from southern Ontario through New York state and into the southern Appalachians and in the Great Plains from Montana to Wisconsin and south into Texas and Arkansas.

The major languages of the phylum are Dakota (Sioux), spoken by Indians in the northern Great Plains region, and Crow, spoken in eastern Montana; these are of the Siouan language family. The Seneca, Cayuga, Mohawk, Oneida, and Onondaga dialects (of the Iroquois Nation tribes of the same names) are spoken in New York state. Cherokee is spoken in the southern Appalachians and Oklahoma. These are Iroquoian languages.

Characteristic of these languages is the frequent use of prefixes and of some suffixes and infixes. Infixes are sounds or sequences of sounds that are inserted within the word rather than attached to the beginning or end. For example, in Dakota the verb "to walk" is *mani*, and *-wa-*, an infix, means "I"; thus, "I walk" is *ma-wa-ni*. Some compound words are also used, and words are often composed of a series of semi-independent units. Pronouns are generally indicated by prefixes, although infixes are used sometimes, as in the example.

Macro-Sudanic languages (Africa): *see* Chari-Nile languages.

Macrobius, Ambrosius Theodosius (fl. *c.* AD 400), Latin grammarian and philosopher whose most important work is the *Saturnalia,* the last known example of the long series of symposia headed by the *Symposium* of Plato.

Little is known about his life: he may have been a praetorian prefect in Spain (399), proconsul in Africa (410), and grand chamberlain (422). The *Saturnalia,* which is dedicated to Macrobius' son Eustachius, purports to give an account of discussions in private houses on the day before the *Saturnalia* and on three days of that festival. Macrobius also wrote a commentary on Cicero's "Somnium Scipionis" ("The Dream of Scipio") from the *De Republica.* This is a Neoplatonic work in two books. Of a third work by Macrobius entitled *De differentiis et societatibus Graeci Latinique verbi* ("On the Differences and Similarities Between Greek and Latin Words") only fragments remain.

Macrocheir: *see* Artaxerxes I.

Macrocystis, genus of brown algae commonly known as kelp (*q.v.*).

macroeconomics, study of the entire economy in terms of the total amount of goods and services produced, total income earned, the level of employment of productive resources, and the general behaviour of prices. Until the 1930s most economic analysis concentrated on individual firms and industries. With the Great Depression of the 1930s, however, and the development of the concept of national income and product statistics, the field of macroeconomics began to expand. The policy goals of the discipline include economic growth, price stability, and full employment. *Compare* microeconomics.

macrofauna, in soil science, animals that are one centimetre or more long but smaller than an earthworm. Potworms, myriapods, centipedes, millipedes, slugs, snails, fly larvae, beetles, beetle larvae, and spiders are typical members of the macrofauna. Many of these animals burrow in the soil, aiding soil drainage and aeration; in addition, some organic material passes into the soil through the burrows. Most macrofauna consume decaying plant material and organic debris, but centipedes, some insects, and spiders prey on other soil animals.

macroglossia, enlargement of the tongue, due to overdevelopment of the muscle mass or the accumulation of material within the tongue. Muscular hypertrophy may be congenital, as in Down syndrome, or may develop later in life, as in acromegaly. Inadequate lymph drainage caused by infection, tumour, or other obstruction leads to enlargement of the tongue, as does deposition of glycogen in the tongue muscles in glycogen-storage disease and deposition of amyloid (a fibrous carbohydrate-protein complex) in amyloidosis.

macromolecule, any very large molecule, usually with a diameter ranging from about 100 to 10,000 angstroms (10^{-5} to 10^{-3} millimetre). The molecule is the smallest unit of the substance that retains its characteristic properties; the macromolecule is such a unit but is considerably larger than the ordinary molecule, which usually has a diameter of less than 10 angstroms (10^{-6} millimetre). Plastics, resins, many synthetic and natural fibres (*e.g.,* nylon and cotton), rubbers, and the biologically important proteins and nucleic acids are among many substances that are made up of macromolecular units.

Macromolecules are composed of much larger numbers of atoms than ordinary molecules. For example, a molecule of polyethylene, a plastic material, may consist of as many as 2,500 methylene groups, each composed of two hydrogen atoms and one carbon atom. The corresponding molecular weight of such a molecule is on the order of 35,000. Insulin, a protein hormone present in the pancreas and responsible for regulation of blood-sugar levels, has a molecular unit derived from 51 amino acids (by themselves molecules containing carbon, hydrogen, oxygen, nitrogen, and sometimes sulfur). The exact molecular weight of insulin from cattle has been determined to be 5,734.

macronucleus, relatively large nucleus believed to influence many cell activities. It occurs in suctorian and ciliate protozoans (*e.g., Paramecium*). The macronucleus is associated with one or more smaller micronuclei, which are necessary for conjugation and autogamy (reproduction by exchange between the nuclei of different individuals and of the same individuals, respectively). When these reproductive processes occur, the macronucleus degenerates. It is re-formed from nuclear material in the zygote.

macrophage system: *see* reticuloendothelial system.

Macrozamia, genus of 12 or more species of palmlike cycads (plants of the family Cycadaceae), native to Australia and grown elsewhere as ornamental and conservatory specimens. The genus includes tuberous, fernlike plants and palmlike, columnar trees that grow as high as 18 m (about 60 feet). The pith is a source of starch, but the seeds are poisonous to livestock. The cones of *Macrozamia* may grow to be about 0.6 m long and weigh more than 36 kg (about 80 pounds).

Mactan Island, coral island, central Philippines, located in the Bohol Strait off the eastern shore of the island of Cebu. Rectangular in shape, the low-lying island is part of the province of Cebu and has extensive mangrove swamps. It has an area of 24 square miles (62 square km), and it protects the harbour of Cebu City.

On April 7, 1521, Ferdinand Magellan, the Portuguese navigator, landed there; he was killed by Chief Lapulapu on April 27. The spot in the northeast where he fell is marked with a monument, and Lapulapu, regarded as the first Filipino to defeat a Western conqueror, has become a national hero.

Coconut production and fishing are the islanders' primary activities. Mactan Island has an international airport, which serves Cebu City. A 2,822-foot (860-metre) bridge (completed in 1973) connects Mactan and Cebu islands. The city of Lapu-Lapu (formerly Opon) faces Cebu City and has major port facilities, including petroleum piers. Pop. (2000) 247,083.

macula lutea, in anatomy, small yellow area on the retina of the eye. When the gaze is fixed on any object, the centre of the macula, the centre of the lens, and the object are in a straight line. In the centre of the macula is a depression, called the fovea. The nerve cells sensitive to light rays are especially numerous in the macula. In the centre of the fovea the nerve cells are exclusively of the type known as cones, which are associated with colour vision and perception of fine detail, and there are no blood vessels to interfere with vision. Consequently, in this area vision in bright light and colour perception are keenest.

Degeneration of the macula sometimes occurs in old age as a result of hardening of the blood vessels of the choroid. The disorder reduces central vision but does not interfere with peripheral vision (*see also* visual-field defect).

Macumba, Afro-Brazilian religion that is characterized by a marked syncretism of traditional African religions, European culture, Brazilian Spiritualism, and Roman Catholicism. Of the several Macumba sects, the most important are Candomblé and Umbanda.

African elements in Macumba rituals include an outdoor ceremonial site, the sacrifice of animals (such as cocks), spirit offerings (such as candles, cigars, and flowers), and ritual dances. Macumba rites are led by mediums, who fall prostrate in trances and communicate with holy spirits. Roman Catholic elements include use of the cross and the worship of saints, who are given African names such as Ogum (St. George), Xangô (St. Jerome), and Iemanjá (the Virgin Mary).

Candomblé, practiced in Bahia state, is considered to be the most African of the Macumba sects. Umbanda, practiced in urban areas such as Rio de Janeiro and São Paulo, is more sophisticated and reflects Hindu and Buddhist influence; its appeal has spread to the white middle class. Despite attempts by Christian churches to combat them, Macumba sects continue to flourish throughout Brazil.

Macy, Anne Sullivan, *née* JOANNA SULLIVAN (b. April 14, 1866, Feeding Hills, near Springfield, Mass., U.S.—d. Oct. 20, 1936, Forest Hills, N.Y.), American teacher of Helen Keller, widely recognized for her achievement in educating to a high level a person without sight, hearing, or normal speech.

Anne Sullivan, nearly blind, graduated from the Perkins Institution for the Blind in Boston in 1886. The next year she was hired as governess to Helen Keller, a six-year-old left blind and deaf by childhood illness. With patience and creativity, Sullivan within a month succeeded in teaching Keller, by means of a manual alphabet, that things had names. Sullivan thus drew out the second known blind deaf-mute child's ability to communicate; the first had been Laura Dewey Bridgman (1829–89).

In the following years Keller and Sullivan gained a national reputation as Keller mastered a full vocabulary and displayed a gifted intelligence. Sullivan accompanied Keller to Radcliffe College (Cambridge, Mass.), reading for her and spelling lectures into her hand until Keller's graduation in 1904. In 1905 Sullivan married John Albert Macy, a literary critic who had helped Helen Keller write her autobiography. The Macys separated permanently by 1913. Keller and her teacher embarked on a number of worldwide lecture trips and a vaudeville tour.

BIBLIOGRAPHY. Works about her are Nella Braddy (Nella Braddy Henney), *Anne Sullivan Macy* (1933); Helen Keller, *Teacher: Anne Sullivan Macy* (1955, reprinted 1985); William Gibson, *The Miracle Worker* (1957), originally a television play and later a Broadway play (1959) and a film (1962); and Joseph P. Lash, *Helen and Teacher* (1980).

Macy and Company, Inc., in full R.H. MACY AND COMPANY, INC., major American department store chain. Its principal outlet, the 11-story department store that occupies a city block at New York City's Herald Square (34th Street and Broadway), was for many years physically the largest single store in the country. Headquarters are in New York City.

The company grew out of a partnership founded in lower Manhattan in 1858 by Rowland H. Macy (1822?–77), whose several previous attempts at retailing had all failed. Under the close supervision of Margaret Getchell, a Macy cousin and pioneer businesswoman, the store prospered after the American Civil War, relying on extensive advertising and its reputation for value. The company's red star trademark was derived from a tattoo borne by founder R.H. Macy.

In 1887 Nathan and Isidor Straus acquired part interest in the company; by 1896 they had assumed full control. The Strauses moved the store to its present site and began purchasing or building branch stores around the country.

By the late 20th century, Macy's chain of department stores was managed through regional store groups operating in a number of states under several different names. The company was among the first retailers to place stores in suburban shopping centres, and it now owns or has interests in a number of such centres.

After Macy's was purchased in a debt-ridden buyout in 1986, a combination of questionable purchases and an economic recession forced it into bankruptcy in 1992. In 1994 it agreed to a merger with Federated Department Stores Inc., forming the United States' largest department store company.

Mad Caliph: *see* Ḥākim, al-.

mad cow disease: *see* bovine spongiform encephalopathy.

mad itch (animal disease): *see* pseudorabies.

Ma'dabā, also spelled MEDEBA, town, west-central Jordan. It is situated on a highland plain more than 2,500 feet (760 m) above sea level. The town lies 20 miles (32 km) south of Amman, along a main highway to southern Jordan.

An ancient city, Ma'dabā was mentioned in the Old Testament as being laid waste by the Israelites under Moses when the Amorites refused passage through their territory (Numbers 21). It was subsequently allocated by Joshua to the tribe of Reuben (Joshua 13:16). It later served as a Moabite stronghold, being taken by Mesha, king of Moab, after the division of the Jewish kingdom (9th century BC). Ma'dabā is mentioned in rabbinic literature as having a Jewish population. After the spread of Christianity, Ma'dabā became an important Byzantine centre. Destroyed in 1880, the town was rebuilt and resettled with Christian Arabs from al-Karak and vicinity. Wheat and barley are grown on the surrounding fertile plain.

The town is famous in historical cartography for the Ma'dabā mosaic map, the oldest known map of the Holy Land. The mosaic map, which formed the floor of one of the many ruined ancient churches in Ma'dabā, was discovered in 1884. The map dates from the 6th century AD, was originally 72 by 23 feet (22 by 7 m) in size, and showed the area from ancient Byblos (modern Jubayl, Lebanon) to Thebes (Egypt). The map language is Greek, and the geography generally follows the *Onomasticon* of Eusebius of Caesarea (*c.* AD 260–*c.* 340). The Ma'dabā map is of particular interest because of its detailed plan of Jerusalem and its numerous place-names in the Negev that are not mentioned elsewhere. By 1896, when the map came to the attention of scholars, much of it had been damaged; the extant portion extends from classical Neapolis (modern Nābulus) to Egypt. It was restored and photographed in colour by German archaeologists in 1965–66. Pop. (1994) 55,749.

Madách, Imre (b. Jan. 21, 1823, Alsósztregova, Hung.—d. Oct. 5, 1864, Alsósztregova), Hungarian poet whose reputation rests on his ambitious poetic drama *Az ember tragédiája* (1861; *The Tragedy of Man*). He is often considered to be Hungary's greatest philosophical poet.

Madách possessed keen and varied interests; he was successively a lawyer, a public servant, and a member of the Hungarian parliament (from 1861). His masterpiece, *Az ember tragédiája,* is a *Faust*-like drama in 15 acts covering the past and future of humankind. The central characters, Adam and Eve, appear throughout the play in the guise of famous historical personalities. They act out humanity's tragic destiny in their constant struggle with Lucifer. Their struggle, though not necessarily victorious, is their salvation. The distinct and consistent characterization of Adam is the play's unifying force. Though the drama was intended for reading, its production at the Budapest National Theatre in 1883 was the first of many successful performances.

Madagascar, officially REPUBLIC OF MADAGASCAR, Malagasy MADAGASIKARA, or REPOBLIKAN'I MADAGASIKARA, French MADAGASCAR, or RÉPUBLIQUE DE MADAGASCAR, nation occupying the island of Madagascar, the world's fourth largest island, lying off the southeast coast of Africa in the southwestern Indian Ocean. Madagascar island extends about 976 miles (1,570 km) from southwest to northeast and is about 355 miles (571 km) at its widest extent from east to west. It lies almost entirely within the tropics. The island of Madagascar is separated from the African coast by the 250-mile- (400-kilometre-) wide Mozambique Channel. The coastline of the island is some 2,480 miles (3,990 km) in length.

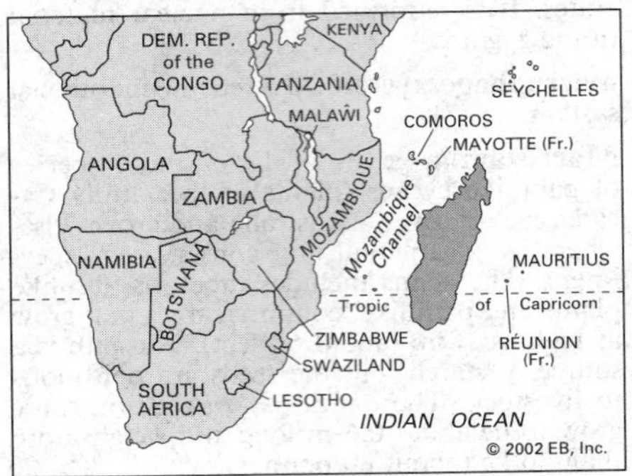

Madagascar

The capital is Antananarivo. Area, including several minor adjacent islands, 226,658 square miles (587,041 square km). Pop. (2000 est.) 15,506,000.

A brief treatment of Madagascar follows. For full treatment, *see* MACROPAEDIA: Madagascar.

For current history and for statistics on society and economy, *see* BRITANNICA BOOK OF THE YEAR.

The land. Madagascar can be divided into three parallel north-south zones: the central plateau, the narrow coastal strip in the east, and the zone of low plateaus and plains in the west. The central plateau, rising between 2,500 and 4,500 feet (800 and 1,400 m) above sea level and covering about 60 percent of the country's total area, rises abruptly from the narrow eastern coastal strip but descends more gradually to the wide plains of the west. Three principal massifs of the central plateau are (north to south) the Tsaratanana, whose volcanic summit (9,436 feet [2,876 m]) is the highest point on the island, the Ankaratra, and the Andringitra. The steep eastern slope of the plateau is drained by short, torrential rivers, while the more gently sloping western side is crossed by longer and larger rivers, such as the Betsiboka and Mangoky, which bring huge deposits of alluvium down into their lower valleys and estuaries, producing fertile sites that support Madagascar's most intensive cultivation. The eastern coast is almost straight; behind its coral beaches an almost continuous chain of lagoons connected by the Pangalanes Canal provides an inland waterway some 400 miles (650 km) in length. The western zone slopes gently toward the Mozambique Channel, its eroded sedimentary bedrock producing a succession of low hills.

Climatic conditions of the island vary considerably, from humid tropical along the east coast to temperate on the central plateau and from seasonally wet and dry along much of the west coast to desertlike conditions in the southwest. July is the coolest month, with mean monthly temperatures ranging from a low of 50° F (10° C) on the central plateau to a high of 78° F (26° C) on the northwest coast. December is the hottest month, with mean monthly temperatures ranging between 61° and 84° F (16° and 29° C). The windward east coast receives the highest amount of rainfall, reaching nearly 150 inches (3,800 mm) annually at Maroantsetra. Annual rainfall drops to 83 inches (2,100 mm) in the northwest, to 37 inches (940 mm) in the west, and to only 14 inches (360 mm) in the southwest. Tropical cyclones coming off the Indian Ocean periodically bring torrential rains and destructive floods to the island; in 1994 cyclone Geralda did extensive damage.

Though Madagascar was originally covered with evergreen and deciduous forests, much of this has been cut for fuel, building materials, and exports. Most of the island now has tall grass savanna vegetation with a few patches of deciduous and evergreen forests and some mangrove swamps along the coasts. Because of the island's isolation, some 40 species of lemurs and other zoologically unique forms have survived there. By the late 20th century, however, the destruction of their habitats had caused many of these species to be endangered or threatened.

The people. Madagascar's population consists almost entirely of the 18 to 20 Malayo-Indonesian tribal groups that inhabit the island. About half the total population is composed of the Merina, Betsmisaraka, and Betsileo groups. Since the departure of the French following independence in 1960, Madagascar's main foreign population minorities have been Comorians, Indians and Pakistanis, and Chinese. About half the population are traditional animists in religion, two-fifths are Christians (evenly divided between Roman Catholics and Protestants), and a small percentage are Muslims. Malagasy languages are spoken by all the tribal groups in several dialects, and the official dialect is Merina; French is also an official language.

Madagascar's population is growing about as rapidly as that of most African countries. Its birth rate is slightly higher than that of Africa as a whole, while its death rate is about average for the continent. Almost four-fifths of the population lives in rural areas. Although the overall population density in rural areas is relatively low, it varies greatly from place to place, often being substantially above average on the island's limited arable land, which constitutes only about 5 percent of the total land area. Madagascar's internal population migration is generally from rural areas to other rural areas, particularly from the densely populated plateau region to the underpopulated western coastal areas.

The economy. Madagascar is a developing country with a mixed economy. Agriculture dominates the economy, and the principal commodities include rice and cassava, the staple food crops, and a range of cash and export crops, particularly coffee, cloves, and vanilla. The country's agricultural output has been unable to keep pace with the growth of the population, and many staples must be imported. Madagascar's gross national product (GNP) is not growing as rapidly as the population, and its GNP per capita is among the lowest in the world.

The primary sector (agriculture, forestry, hunting, and fishing) accounts for about two-fifths of the gross domestic product (GDP). Rice is the leading cereal and is planted on one-half of the country's cultivated land. It continues to be produced primarily by subsistence, rather than commercial, farmers. Agriculture employs more than three-fourths of the workforce.

Coffee is Madagascar's leading export. The country is also the world's largest producer of vanilla and a major producer of cloves, but annual production fluctuates sharply. Cattle are the most important livestock; pigs, goats, and sheep are also raised. Animals continue to be used for religious sacrifice, and the government has been unable to modernize animal husbandry.

Forests cover approximately a fourth of the total land area. The government has regularly sponsored afforestation programs to curb the historical decline in forested area. Madagascar's territorial waters were extended to 200 nautical miles (370 km) in 1973, but the nation's fishing industry is underdeveloped.

Mining accounts for a negligible percentage of the GDP but is an important source of foreign exchange. Chromite and graphite are the leading minerals produced. Madagascar is the world's only producer of phlogopite mica.

Manufacturing is underdeveloped and represents only a little more than one-tenth of the GDP. Processed foods, paper, soap, and textiles are the leading manufactures. Lumber, fertilizers, and leather are produced for the domestic market. Two-thirds of the country's electricity is generated by hydroelectric plants, while the remainder is produced by thermal installations.

Taxes on income and profits have proved ineffective in reducing the government's huge annual deficits, which Madagascar has tried to meet by borrowing heavily from France and other countries of the European Union. In 1982, on condition of further loans and payment abatements, the government was forced to adopt a program of structural readjustment of its economy imposed by the International Monetary Fund. Greater privatization of the economy, the key element of the program, followed. Madagascar's principal trading partners are France, the United States, Japan, Germany, and Italy.

Government and social conditions. Madagascar is a multiparty republic. Its constitution, approved by national referendum in 1992, confirms the country's status as a unitary state, despite attempts to establish a federal system of government. Executive authority is divided between the president and the prime minister. The president, who is directly elected for a term of five years, repeatable once, appoints the prime minister. Legislative power is exercised by a bicameral parliament, consisting of the National Assembly and the Senate. Members of the National Assembly are directly elected for terms of four years. Two-thirds of the Senators are chosen by an electoral college, and the rest are appointed by the country's president. The judicial system is headed by the Constitutional High Court and the Supreme Court.

Health conditions in Madagascar are poor, as judged by the country's relatively high infant mortality rate and long list of endemic diseases. Health facilities are concentrated in urban areas, but a network of local clinics, supplemented by mobile health units, serves the countryside. Malaria is still found over much of the island, leprosy and tuberculosis continue to be major diseases, and debilitating parasitic diseases and venereal diseases are widespread. Life expectancy is only 56 years. Housing has been adequate, but overcrowding is increasing, in both rural areas and cities.

About four-fifths of the adult population is literate. Enrollment in the compulsory five-year primary schools is almost 65 percent of those eligible, though in secondary schools the figure is much lower. The University of Madagascar was founded in 1955.

The government has generally censored the communications media; newspapers are published in Malagasy and French.

The culture is basically Indonesian in origin, with some Bantu, Arabic, and Islāmic contributions. Folk arts, including many traditional crafts and distinctive Malagasy music and dance, have flourished in Madagascar. The Malagasy language is very rich in proverbs, and there is now an extensive written literature including poetry, legend, history, and scholarly works, as well as contemporary themes.

History. The Malagasy peoples are of mixed Malayo-Indonesian and Afro-Arab ancestry. The Indonesian element probably migrated to Madagascar about AD 700 by way of the African coast. The first European known to have visited the island was the Portuguese navigator Diogo Dias in 1500. The island was the haunt of many pirates during the late 17th and early 18th centuries.

Trade in arms and slaves allowed the development of Malagasy kingdoms. At the beginning of the 17th century the most important kingdoms, those of the Antemoro, Antesaka, Antanosy, Maroserana, Betsileo, and Merina peoples, were still confined to small areas.

The Merina were unified by the great king Andrianampoinimerina (1787–1810) and under his rule became the dominant kingdom. His son, Radama I (1810–28), gained help from the British on Mauritius, enabling him to bring under his control a large part of Madagascar.

In the early 1860s Radama II, a Merina ruler, opened up the kingdom to Europeans and signed a concession giving great powers to a French trading company. An 1868 treaty between the Merina kingdom and the French gave the French control over the northwest coast. In 1890 the British recognized Madagascar as a French protectorate, but it was not until 1895 that French troops defeated the kingdom of Merina's army. General J.S. Gallieni, Madagascar's first governor-general, abolished slavery and in 1897 exiled the Merina queen.

Following World War II, Madagascar became an overseas territory of the French Republic with parliamentary representation. In 1958 France agreed to let the territory decide its own fate, and on October 14 the autonomous Malagasy Republic was proclaimed. Philibert Tsiranana was elected the first president, and in 1960 the Malagasy Republic gained independence.

Increasing political unrest in 1972 forced Tsiranana to resign. The eventual leader was Lieutenant Commander Didier Ratsiraka, who remained in power for most of the rest of the 20th century. He withdrew from the Franc Zone and established diplomatic relations with nonwestern countries such as the People's Republic of China and the Soviet Union; relations between France and Madagascar had improved by 1990.

Urban violence and economic problems continued throughout the 1970s and '80s. Ratsiraka briefly lost the presidency in the early 1990s, but he was returned to power through presidential elections in 1996.

Presidential elections held in December 2001 were mired in controversy. Marc Ravalomanana, the eventual winner, triumphed over Ratsiraka, who finally accepted the results in mid-2002.

Consult the INDEX *first*

Madang, port on the northeastern coast of the island of New Guinea, Papua New Guinea. It lies along Astrolabe Bay of the Bismarck Sea, near the mouth of the Gogol River. Madang is the centre for a large timber industry based on the Gogol forest about 25 miles (40 km) inland and is the distributing centre for the north coast and the Central Range. It is also a communication point for the offshore islands and has a major airport. The port's economy is based on the export of copra, coconuts, coffee, and cocoa. Local industries include engineering and joinery workshops, timber milling, and the manufacture of black twist tobacco (for local use).

The town originated as Friedrich-Wilhelmshafen and served as the administrative centre for the former German colony. It was abandoned by the Germans in 1899 because of the prevalence of malaria there. Australian administration after 1914 was followed in 1942–45 by Japanese occupation of the area. Kalibobo lighthouse at the harbour entrance commemorates New Guinea coast watchers who aided the Allies during World War II. Madang is connected by a coastal road to Bogia. Pop. (2000 prelim.) 27,394.

Madanīn, also spelled MÉDENINE, town, southern Tunisia. The town lies in the semiarid plain of al-Jifārah (Jeffara). It was the capital of the Ouerghemma League of three Berber groups and was the chief town of the Southern Military Territories during the French Protectorate (1881–1955). The honeycomb-like, aboveground granaries (*ghorfas*) that belonged to the Ouerghemma are features of the locality. The town is now a trade centre for dates, olives, cereals, and esparto grass and is a road hub with links to Qābis (Gabès), 40 miles (64 km) northwest.

Ghorfas (family granaries), Madanīn, Tunisia
Art Resource

The inhabitants of the surrounding area include seminomadic shepherds and cave-dwelling cultivators of grains, olives, figs, and date palms. The densely populated Mediterranean island of Jarbah (Djerba) is nearby, and Taṭāwīn (Tataouine), south of Madanīn, is a starting point for trans-Saharan caravans. Oil fields, connected by pipeline with aṣ-Ṣukhayrah (La Skhirra) on the Gulf of Gabes, and natural-gas deposits are located at al-Burmah (El-Borma) on the Algerian border. Pop. (2000 est.) 54,500.

Madariaga y Rojo, Salvador de (b. July 23, 1886, La Coruña, Spain—d. Dec. 14, 1978, Locarno, Switz.), Spanish writer, diplomat, and historian, noted for his service at the League of Nations and for his prolific writing in English, German, and French, as well as Spanish.

The son of a Spanish army officer, Madariaga was trained at his father's insistence as an engineer in Paris but abandoned his career to become a journalist. In 1921 he joined the Secretariat of the League of Nations at Geneva as a press member and the following year was appointed head of its disarmament section. From 1928 to 1931 he was professor of Spanish studies at the University of Oxford. After the Spanish monarchy fell in 1931, the Spanish republic appointed him ambassador to the United States (1931) and then to France (1932–34), and he was Spain's permanent delegate to the League of Nations from 1931 to 1936. When the Spanish Civil War broke out in July 1936, Madariaga—"equally distant from both sides," as he wrote at the time—resigned and left for England. He became a vocal opponent of the Francisco Franco regime and did not return to Spain until April 1976, following Franco's death the previous November.

Among Madariaga's most notable essays are *Englishmen, Frenchmen, Spaniards* (1928), a study of national psychology; *Guía del lector del Quijote* (1926; *Don Quixote*), an analysis of Cervantes' classic; and *Spain* (1942), a historical essay. He also published books on various periods in Latin-American history, among them *Cuadro histórico de las Indias,* 2 vol. (1945; *The Rise and Fall of the Spanish American Empire*), and the trilogy *Christopher Columbus* (1939), *Hernán Cortés* (1941), and *Simón Bolívar* (1949), the last being the object of violent criticism for its iconoclasm. Madariaga's political writings expound his philosophy of individual liberty and the solidarity of mankind.

In addition to the essay, Madariaga cultivated other literary genres—poetry, drama, and narrative prose. His novels are based upon philosophical, political, and religious themes. Among his fictional works are *El corazón de piedra verde* (1942; *The Heart of Jade*) and *Guerra en la sangre* (1957; *War in the Blood*), novels based on Latin-American history.

Maddalena Island, Italian ISOLA MADDALENA, island, Sassari *provincia,* Italy. It lies in the Tyrrhenian Sea (of the Mediterranean) off the northeast coast of Sardinia. It has an area of 8 square miles (20 square km) and is the principal island of the Maddalena Archipelago, which includes the islands of Maddalena, Caprera, Santo Stefano, Spargi, Budelli, Santa Maria, and Razzoli. Its port, La Maddalena, is the administrative centre of a commune that includes all the islands. The harbour of La Maddalena was an important Italian naval station until its installations were destroyed by Allied bombing in World War II. Napoleon's forces had bombarded the harbour in 1793 without success, and Horatio Nelson made it his headquarters during 1803–05. The U.S. Navy's Sixth Fleet maintains a permanent support facility for nuclear submarines there. Fishing is the principal economic activity. A bridge and an embankment connect Maddalena with Caprera Island. Pop. (1987 est.) mun., 11,826.

Maddalena Pass, also called LARCHE PASS, Italian COLLE DELLA MADDALENA, or DELL'ARGENTERA, French COL DE LARCHE, or DE L'ARGENTIÈRE, gap between the Cottian Alps (north) and the Maritime Alps (south). The pass lies at 6,548 feet (1,996 m) on the French-Italian border, 12 miles (19 km) east-northeast of Barcelonnette, Fr. A road (1870) across the pass connects Cuneo, Italy, with Barcelonnette. Hannibal reputedly led his Carthaginian army over the pass toward Rome in 218 BC, and the army of King Francis I of France used the pass to enter Italy and conquer Milan in 1515.

madder, also called DYER'S MADDER, any of several species of plants belonging to the genus *Rubia* of the madder family, Rubiaceae. *Rubia tinctorum* and *R. peregrina* are native European plants, and *R. cordifolia* is native to the hilly districts of India and Java. *Rubia* is a genus of about 40 species; its members are characterized by lance-shaped leaves that grow in whorls and by small yellowish flowers that grow in clusters.

The common madder (*R. tinctorum*) and *R. cordifolia* were formerly cultivated for a red dye, alizarin, that was obtained from the ground-up roots of these plants. This dye was used for cloth and could be prepared and applied in such a way as to yield pink and purple shades as well as red. The dye properties of the madder root appear to have been known from the earliest historical times; cloth dyed with madder has been found on ancient Egyptian mummies, and madder was used for dying the cloaks of Libyan women in the time of Herodotus (5th century BC). Madder was also employed as a medicinal treatment for amenorrhea (failure to menstruate) in ancient and medieval times. Another property of alizarin is that it colours red the bones of animals that feed upon madder. This property was used by 19th-century physiologists to trace the way in which bone develops and to study the functions of the various types of cells in growing bone. In the 1860s a way was found to manufacture alizarin synthetically, and so the once-extensive use of madder as a source of alizarin dye has now practically disappeared.

Madderakka, Lapp goddess of childbirth. She is assisted by three of her daughters—Sarakka, the cleaving woman; Uksakka, the door woman; and Juksakka, the bow woman—who watch over the development of the child from conception through early childhood. Madderakka was believed to receive the soul of a child from Radien, the world ruler deity, and to give it a body, which Sarakka would then place in the mother's womb. In Norway, Juksakka and Uksakka serve functions similar to that of Sarakka. Uksakka was believed to aid in the actual childbirth; Juksakka would then take care of the child after birth. Sarakka was also thought of as the separating woman who made childbirth easier and was considered to be a deity of women in a more general sense, aiding them in women's concerns such as menstruation.

Madeira, fortified wine from the Portuguese island of Madeira in the Atlantic. Because the island was a customary port-of-call on the trade routes between Europe and the New World, this durable wine was very popular in colonial America.

Madeira wine is fortified with brandy during fermentation to raise its alcoholic content to 18–20 percent. Madeiras, ranging from dry to sweet, derive their distinctive, rich character from the volcanic soil of the island's vineyards (some of the most steeply terraced in the world) and from a unique process of aging in baking rooms, or *estufas,* for several months after fermentation. This accelerated aging process was adopted after the discovery that the wines benefited from the prolonged heat of storage that they underwent during tropical voyages. Madeira is also aged in oak casks, and wines of different ages may be blended before bottling.

Sercial is the driest Madeira, followed in increasing degree of sweetness by Verdelho, Bual (and a pale version called Rainwater), and Malmsey. Madeira is very long-lived, some varieties remaining sound and unfaded for as long as 100 years.

Madeira Islands, also called FUNCHAL ISLANDS, Portuguese ARQUIPÉLAGO DA MADEIRA, archipelago of volcanic origin in the North Atlantic Ocean, belonging to Portugal and comprising two inhabited islands, Madeira and Porto Santo, and two uninhabited groups, the Desertas and the Selvagens. The islands are the summits of mountains that have their bases on an abyssal ocean floor. Administratively they form the autonomous region of Madeira. The islands have a combined land area of 306 square miles (794 square km).

Madeira Island, the largest of the group, is 34 miles (55 km) long and has a maximum width of 14 miles (22 km) and a coastline of about 90 miles (144 km) and rises in the centre to the Ruivo de Santana Peak (6,106 feet [1,861 m]). The greater part of the interior above 3,000 feet (900 m) is uninhabited and uncultivated; communities of scattered huts are usually built either at the mouths of ravines or upon slopes that descend from the mountains to the coast.

Porto Santo Island is about 26 miles (42 km) northeast of Madeira; its main town, Vila de Porto Santo, is called locally the Vila. At each end of the island are hills, of which Facho Peak, the highest, reaches 1,696 feet (515 m). Crops include little besides wheat, grapes, and barley.

The Desertas lie about 11 miles (18 km) southeast of Madeira and consist of three islets, Chão, Bugio, and Deserta Grande, along with the Prego do Mor off the north end of Chão Island. Rabbits and wild goats live on the poor pasture and attract occasional hunters to once-inhabited Deserta Grande.

The Selvagens, or Salvage Islands, are three uninhabited rocks located 156 miles (251 km) south of Madeira, between the latter and the Canary Islands. The largest has a circumference of about 3 miles (5 km).

It has been conjectured that the Phoenicians visited Madeira. The whole archipelago, however, was undoubtedly explored before the mid-14th century by Genoese adventurers, for an Italian map (the Laurentian portolano) dated 1351 depicts the Madeiras quite clearly. A Portuguese navigator, João Gonçalves Zarco, probably sighted Porto Santo in 1418, having been driven there by a storm when exploring the coast of western Africa. When Zarco visited Madeira in 1420, the islands were without human or land-mammal habitation, and his sponsor, Henry the Navigator, at once began their colonization. The dense forests were felled and burned (the fires are said to have raged for seven years), and much land was brought into cultivation. Grape cultivation was introduced from Cyprus or Crete by the Portuguese in the 15th century. Sugarcane is said to have been brought to Madeira from Sicily about 1452. Madeira is said to have been the location of the world's first sugarcane plantation, and the island's sugar trade quickly became important. Madeira wine, which is dark brown and ranges from dry to sweet with a hard aftertaste, became an important export in the 17th century. (The wine's modern producers agitate it artificially to reproduce the effects of shipment on stormy Atlantic voyages.) The sugar and wine industries of the Madeira Islands suffered temporarily when slavery was abolished in 1775 by the order of the Portuguese statesman-reformer the Marquês de Pombal.

The Madeira Islands' economy is still based on the production of sugar, wine, and bananas. The common sweet potato and gourds of various kinds are extensively grown, as is the kalo, or taro, introduced from the Pacific islands. Most of the culinary vegetables of Europe are also grown on the islands in plentiful quantities. In addition to common temperate fruits, oranges, lemons, guavas, mangoes, loquats, custard apples, figs, pineapples, and bananas are produced, the latter being an important export. Although agriculture predominates in the Madeiran economy, handicrafts, tourism, and fishing are notable subsidiaries. Handicrafts include woodworking and wickerworking. Embroidery, which was introduced in 1850 by a Mrs. Phelps, an Englishwoman, now employs thousands of women. Pop. (1987 est.) Madeira, 264,800; Porto Santo, 4,700.

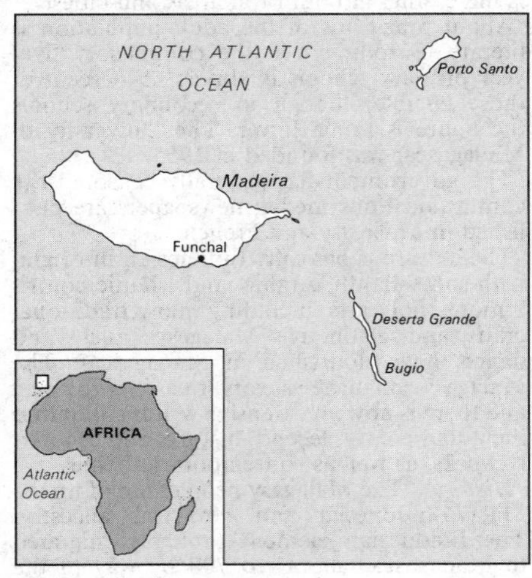

Madeira Islands

Madeira River, Portuguese RIO MADEIRA, major tributary of the Amazon. It is formed by the junction of the Mamoré and Beni rivers at Villa Bella, Bolivia, and flows northward forming the border between Bolivia and Brazil for approximately 60 miles (100 km). After receiving the Rio Abunã, the Madeira meanders northeastward in Brazil through Rondônia and Amazonas states to its junction with the Amazon River, 90 miles (145 km) east of Manaus. A distributary of the Madeira flows into the Amazon about 100 miles (160 km) farther downstream, creating the marshy island of Tupinambarama. The Madeira is 2,082 miles (3,352 km) long from the upper reaches of the Mamoré, and its general width is about ½ mile. It is navigable by seagoing vessels most of the year from its mouth on the Amazon to the Cachoeira (falls) de Santo Antônio 807 miles (1,300 km) upstream, the first of 19 falls or rapids that block further passage, near the town of Pôrto Velho, Braz.

The Estrada de Ferro (railway) Madeira-Mamoré, extending for 227 miles (365 km)

Madeira River near Pôrto Velho, Rondônia Territory, Brazil
Plessner International

between Pôrto Velho and Guajará-Mirim, provides a link with the upper course of the Madeira River. Although exploration of the Madeira Valley began in the 16th century, parts of the region were first mapped via satellite in the late 1970s. The tropical rain forest through which the river flows is almost uninhabited except for occasional settlements of Indians and mestizos who dwell along the riverbanks and gather such forest products as Brazil nuts and rubber.

Madeleine, in full ÉGLISE SAINTE-MADELEINE, English CHURCH OF ST. MARY MAGDALEN, Paris, church designed by Pierre-Alexandre Vignon in 1806. The Madeleine, in the form of a Roman temple surrounded by a Corinthian colonnade, reflects the taste for classical art and architecture that predominated in France during the Empire phase of the Neoclassical movement.

Napoleon, who had ordered its design and construction, originally intended the building to be a temple of glory celebrating his Grande Armée. This commemorative role, however, was assumed instead by the Arc de Triomphe (1806–08), and in 1816 the Madeleine was made a church by the restored Bourbon regime.

madeleine, delicate, scallop-shaped French tea cake often served with fruit or sherbet. In its preparation, flour, eggs, and sugar are beaten with a large proportion of butter, incorporating as much air as possible; then grated lemon rind and vanilla extract, and sometimes rum, are added. After baking in the customary 12-shell tin, the pastry is served plain or dusted with confectioner's sugar.

The origins of the madeleine are disputed, but it was brought to its acme, and thence to broad fame, in the 18th century by the pastry chefs of Commercy. The French author Marcel Proust immortalized the madeleine in his novel *Swann's Way* (1913), in which a taste of the cake is said to have evoked the surge of memory and nostalgia subsequently chronicled in his novel cycle *Remembrance of Things Past* (1913–27).

Madeleine, Îles de la (Canada): *see* Magdalen Islands.

mademoiselle, abbreviation MLLE, the French equivalent of "Miss," referring to an unmarried female. Etymologically it means "my (young) lady" (*ma demoiselle*).

As an honorific title in the French royal court, it came to be used (without the adjunction of a proper name) to refer to or address the daughter of the king's eldest living brother, who was himself called *monsieur*. The first to be called *mademoiselle* was Anne-Marie-Louise d'Orléans, duchesse de Montpensier, popularly called La Grande Mademoiselle, who was the daughter of Gaston, duc d'Orléans (brother of Louis XIII). A later *mademoiselle* was Marie-Louise d'Orléans, daughter of Philippe I, duc d'Orleans (brother of Louis XIV), who became queen of Spain as the wife of Charles II.

Maderna, Bruno (b. April 21, 1920, Venice—d. Nov. 13, 1973, Darmstadt, W.Ger.), Austrian composer of avant-garde and electronic music and a noted conductor.

Maderna studied with well-known teachers, including the Italian composer Gian Francesco Malipiero and the German conductor Hermann Scherchen. In 1941 he received his degree in composition at Rome from the Conservatorio di Musica Santa Cecilia. He expanded his musical activities after World War II, becoming known through his association with the Internationale Ferienkurse für Neue Musik (International Vacation Course for New Music) at Darmstadt, a centre of avant-garde musical teaching and composition. With his friend the composer Luciano Berio, Maderna founded the Studio di Fonologia Musicale at Milan Radio in Italy in 1954; the studio became a major laboratory for electronic music in Europe. With Berio he also founded a review devoted to electronic and avant-garde music, *Incontri Musicali* ("Musical Encounters"). Maderna later taught composition in Milan, at the Dartington Summer School of Music, Devon, Eng., and elsewhere.

Maderna's music showed him to be an expressive lyric composer as well as an experimenter. His *Serenata* (1954) is a colourful orchestral work noteworthy for its subtle sonorities and polyrhythms. The *Notturno* for tape (1956) and *Sintaxis* for four different, unspecified electronic timbres (tone colours) display his interest in new sonorities. His oboe concerto (1962) reveals a more conventional viewpoint, although even in this he made use of small-scale aleatoric (chance and improvisatory) operations.

Maderna conducted widely and recorded extensively, including many works of his contemporaries.

Maderno, Carlo (b. 1556, Bissone, Milan—d. Jan. 30, 1629, Rome), leading Roman architect of the early 17th century, who determined the style of early Baroque architecture.

Maderno began his architectural career in Rome assisting his uncle Domenico Fontana. His first major Roman commission, the facade of Santa Susanna (1597–1603), led to his appointment in 1603 as the chief architect for Saint Peter's. In 1607 he designed the nave and a new facade for Saint Peter's and was made architect to Pope Paul V. Maderno's additions to Saint Peter's were consonant with the spirit of the Counter-Reformation; by adding the nave he transformed Michelangelo's Greek-cross plan into a longitudinal one, thus reverting to the scheme of early Christian and Medieval cathedrals. His facade has been both criticized for impairing the effect of Michelangelo's dome and admired for its forceful grouping of huge engaged columns. The only building completely designed by Maderno is Santa Maria della Vittoria (1608–20); all his other projects, such as San Andrea della Valle and the Palazzo Barberini (1625), were either works he only began or other architects' works he finished. The Palazzo Barberini, which Maderno designed for the family of Pope Urban VIII, was completed by Francesco Borromini and Gian Lorenzo Bernini, whose works were influenced by Maderno.

Facade of Saint Peter's, Rome, by Carlo Maderno, 1607
SCALA/Art Resource, NY

Howard Hibbard's *Carlo Maderno and Roman Architecture, 1580–1630* (1972) is the definitive study.

Madero, Francisco (Indalécio) (b. Oct. 30, 1873, Parras, Mex.—d. Feb. 22, 1913, Mexico City), Mexican revolutionary and president of Mexico (1911–13) who successfully ousted the dictator Porfirio Díaz by temporarily unifying various democratic and anti-Díaz forces. He proved incapable of controlling the reactions from both conservatives and revolutionaries that his moderate reforms provoked, however.

The son of a wealthy landowning family, Madero attended Mount St. Mary's College in Emmitsburg, Md. (1886–88), followed by one semester at the University of California at Berkeley and three years at a Paris business school. He was an unimpressive man—short, slender, and pale—and a vegetarian, teetotaler, and spiritualist. Madero became a believer in a moderate form of democracy, and he helped organize the Benito Juárez Democratic Club and a political party in Coahuila (1904–05) in an unsuccessful attempt to become governor of the state. He quickly learned, however, that efforts to end the dictatorship of Porfirio Díaz would require a national democratic movement, and to this end he supported independent journalists and encouraged efforts at political organization.

Díaz inadvertently hastened events when, in 1908, he told an American journalist that Mexico was ready for democracy and that he intended to retire in 1910. This declaration prompted a flood of political literature and a flurry of political activity, including an immensely successful book by Madero, *La sucesión presidencial en 1910* (1908; "The Presidential Succession in 1910"), in which he called for honest elections, mass participation in the political process, and no reelection of Díaz. The political scene became even more hectic when Díaz changed his mind in 1909 and stated his intention to run for reelection in 1910. Madero helped organize the Antireelectionist Party and became its presidential candidate with the slogan "Effective Suffrage—No Reelection!" On the eve of the farcical election, he was arrested on charges of fomenting a rebellion and insulting the authorities. Released on bond, he escaped to San Antonio, Texas, where in October 1910 he published the Plan of San Luis Potosí, declared himself the legitimate president of Mexico, and called for an armed insurrection to begin on November 20.

Madero, *c.* 1910
Archivo Casasola

In Chihuahua his supporters Pascual Orozco and Pancho Villa kept the rebellion alive, and by February 1911 Madero was in Chihuahua with a following and an army. The Díaz government, besieged by crowds of Maderistas, undertook negotiations with the rebels. The conflagration continued to spread, however, and, after Orozco and Villa captured Ciudad Juárez (May 10, 1911), Díaz capitulated and resigned. An interim government was established under Francisco León de la Barra, the secretary of foreign relations.

The presidential election in October 1911 was a sweeping triumph for Madero. He assumed office on November 6 and was hailed throughout Mexico as the "apostle of democracy." His administration, nevertheless, culminated in personal and national disaster. Handicapped by political inexperience and excessively optimistic idealism, he failed to recognize that many of his supporters had other ends in mind. Soon Mexico had another thoroughly corrupt administration. More seriously, in his preoccupation with giving the country democratic conditions, Madero was attacked both by the entrenched supporters of the old regime who opposed any change and by revolutionary elements who were insistent on far-reaching social and economic reforms. He also had to contend with the hostility of a conservative press, the harassment of the U.S. ambassador, Henry Lane Wilson, and a series of armed rebellions.

Madero's former supporter Bernardo Reyes led the first uprising against him, which was easily suppressed. Two more conservative-inspired rebellions led, respectively, by Pascual Orozco and the former president's nephew, Félix Díaz, were put down, but Reyes and Díaz continued to plot against Madero from their jail cells. The end came when a military revolt broke out in Mexico City in February 1913. Madero had depended upon General Victoriano Huerta to command the government's troops, but Huerta conspired with Reyes and Díaz to betray Madero. The president was arrested, and while being transferred to prison he was assassinated by the escort.

In death Madero's name became a symbol of revolutionary unity in the continuing struggle against military despotism—now embodied in the Huerta regime. His martyrdom, if not his career, made him an inspiration to the democratic forces of the Mexican Revolution.

Madgaon, also called MARGÃO, town, west-central Goa state, western India. Madgaon is situated on the railway that extends from Marmagao port to Castle Rock in Karnātaka state. The third largest city in Goa, it gained importance with the development of Marmagao port, the best harbour between Bombay and Cochin. An industrial estate just outside the city, a cold-storage plant for fish, and a large agricultural-produce market have strengthened its economic position. The city is not far from Colva, considered one of India's most beautiful beaches. Pop. (1981) town, 53,076; metropolitan area, 64,858.

Mādhavācārya, also called VIDYĀRAṆYA (b. 1296?—d. ?1386, Sringeri, Kashmir, India), Hindu statesman and philosopher. He lived at the court of Vijayanagar, a southern Indian kingdom.

Mādhavācārya became an ascetic in 1377 and was thereafter known as Vidyāraṇya. He was part author of *Jīvan-muktiviveka* and *Pañcadaśī,* works of Vedānta philosophy; *Dhātu-vṛtti,* a treatise on Sanskrit grammar; *Nyāya-mālāvistara,* a work on the Mīmāṃsa system, one of the earliest orthodox systems of Vedic philosphy; and *Parāśarasmṛtivyākhyā,* an elaborate comment on the *Parāśarasmṛti.*

His younger brother Sāyaṇa, the minister of four successive Vijayanagar kings, is famous as the commentator of the Vedas. Sāyaṇa's commentaries were influenced by Mādhavācārya, who was a patron of the scholars collaborating in his brother's great work.

Madhu-keri (India): *see* Mercāra.

Madhubani, town, north-central Bihār state, northeastern India. It is situated 16 miles (26 km) northeast of Darbhanga town. Madhubani derives its name from the abundance of honey that is to be found in nearby forests (*madhu,* "honey"; *bani,* "forest"). Trade in cloth, sugarcane, mangoes, oilseeds, rice, and fish is economically important, and baskets, pottery, handloomed textiles, and wooden furniture are produced by cottage industries. Madhubani historically has been the centre of Maithilī culture.

The surrounding area is situated in the fertile tract of the Middle Ganges Plain, bordering Nepal on the north. The Balān, Kanila, and Sugarwe are the main streams. Agriculture is the principal occupation, and rice, wheat, corn (maize), pulse (legumes), sugarcane, and oilseeds are grown. Industries include rice, dal (pigeon-pea), and sugar milling. The area has a network of roads and is traversed by branches of the North Eastern Railway. Pop. (1981) 45,145.

Madhumati River, tributary of the Padma (Ganges) River, flowing through southwestern Bangladesh. It leaves the Padma just north of Kushtia and flows 190 miles (306 km) southeast before turning south across the Sundarbans to empty into the Bay of Bengal. In its upper course it is called the Garai; in its lower course it is known as the Baleswar; and its 9-mile- (14-kilometre-) wide estuary mouth is called the Hāringhāta. The Madhumati is one of the largest of the Padma distributaries in the southern part of the Gangetic Plain, and it offers the best navigation conditions of any river at the head of the Bay of Bengal.

Consult the INDEX *first*

Madhva, also called ĀNANDATĪRTHA, or PŪRṆAPRAJÑA (b. *c.* 1199, Kalyānpur, near Udipi, Karnataka, India—d. *c.* 1278, Udipi), Hindu philosopher, exponent of Dvaita (*q.v.*; dualism, or belief in a basic difference in kind between God and individual souls). His followers are called Madhvas.

Born into a Brahman family, his life in many respects parallels the life of Jesus Christ. Miracles attributed to Christ in the New Testament were also attributed to Madhva; for example, as a youth he was discovered by his parents after a four-day search discoursing learnedly with the priests of Vishnu (Viṣṇu); later, on a pilgrimage to the sacred city of Vārānasi (Benares), he is reputed to have walked on water, repeated the miracle of the loaves of bread, calmed rough waters, and become a "fisher of men." It is suggested that he may have been influenced during his youth by a group of Nestorian Christians who were residing at Kalyānpur.

Madhva set out to refute the nondualistic Advaita philosophy of Śaṅkara (d. *c.* AD 750), who believed the individual self to be a phenomenon and the absolute spirit (Brahman) the only reality. Thus, Madhva rejected the venerable Hindu theory of maya ("illusion"), which taught that only spirituality is eternal and the material world is illusory and deceptive. Madhva maintained that the simple fact that things are transient and everchanging does not mean they are not real.

Departing from orthodox Hinduism in a number of ways, he was one of a small minority of Hindu thinkers who have believed in eternal damnation, offering a concept of heaven and hell to his followers. He nevertheless offered a third alternative, a Hindu purgatory of endless transmigration of souls (reincarnation, or rebirth). Madhva's cult outlawed temple prostitutes and offered figures made of dough as a substitute for blood sacrifices, and its adherents customarily branded themselves on the shoulder with a multiarmed figure of Vishnu.

During his lifetime, Madhva wrote 37 works in Sanskrit, mostly commentaries on Hindu sacred writings and treatises on his own theological system and philosophy. He insisted that knowledge is relative, not absolute.

Madhya Bhārat Plateau, Hindi MADHYA BHĀRAT PATHĀR, plateau comprising the northern part of the Central Highlands, central India. Extending over approximately 22,000 square miles (57,000 square km) and including most of northwestern Madhya Pradesh state and central Rājasthān state, it is bounded by the East Rājasthān Uplands on the west, the Upper Ganges Plain on the north, the Bundelkhand Upland on the east, and the Mālwa Plateau on the south. The bedrock of the Madhya Bhārat Plateau consists of a uniform formation of basalt; weathering has produced rounded boulders in some places. The plateau has an average elevation of about 1,650 feet (500 m) and slopes from 1,980 feet (602 m) in the south to 990 feet (301 m) in the north. Erosion has created an almost level surface frequently punctuated by sandstone scarps. The Chambal River, rising in the northern flanks of the Vindhya Range, winds through a wide, bowl-like basin from southwest to northeast and enters a long, narrow gorge, site of the Gāndhī Sāgar Dam of the Chambal Valley Project (irrigation and hydroelectric power). The Chambal Valley has areas of severe gullying and erosion aggravated by deforestation and overgrazing of the land; its ravines are said to be used as hideouts by bandits. The soils are black and alluvial. The Bānganga, Kunwārī, Sind, Pārbati, and Kāli Sindh are the other major rivers. Savannas on the plateau, moist deciduous forests in the south, and drier deciduous forests in the north (with some teak) are common. The economy is dominated by agriculture; cereals, pulse (legumes), oilseeds, cotton, sugarcane, and tobacco are produced. Industries include sawmilling, oilseed crushing, the production of machine tools and implements, textile weaving, and the production of pottery, bricks, and cement. Deposits of iron ore, copper, lead, beryl, steatite, and limestone are worked. The transport system consists of roads and narrow-gauge railways linking Gwalior (the main industrial centre) with Kota, Morena, Bhind,

Shivpuri, and Būndi. Gwalior and Kota have airstrips.

Madhya Pradesh and Chhattīsgaṛh, constituent states of India. In 2000 Chhattīsgaṛh was carved from the eastern districts of Madhya Pradesh. Madhya Pradesh is bounded to the northwest by Rājasthān, to the north by Uttar Pradesh, to the east by Chhattīsgaṛh, to the south by Mahārāshtra, and to the west by Gujarāt. Its capital is Bhopāl. Chhattīsgaṛh is bounded to the north by Uttar Pradesh, to the northeast by Jharkhand, to the east by Orissa, to the south by Andhra Pradesh, and to the west by Mahārāshtra and Madhya Pradesh. Its capital is Raipur. Area Madhya Pradesh, 119,016 square miles (308,252 square km); Chhattīsgaṛh, 52,199 square miles (135,194 square km). Pop. (2001 prelim.) Madhya Pradesh, 60,385,118; Chhattīsgaṛh, 20,795,-956.

A brief treatment of Madhya Pradesh and Chhattīsgaṛh follows. For full treatment, *see* MACROPAEDIA: India.

Rock paintings and stone and metal implements found in the area are evidence of prehistoric habitation. The area was part of the Mauryan empire of the 4th and 3rd centuries BC and was ruled by numerous dynasties during the early centuries AD. It fell under Islāmic control in the 11th century and was annexed into the Mughal Empire in the 16th century. By 1760 the area was under Marāṭhā rule and came under British domination early in the 19th century. When India became independent in 1947, the British Indian province of Central Provinces and Berār formed Madhya Pradesh. Boundary changes followed in 1956, and the current boundaries of the two states were set in 2000.

Forested hills with steep slopes, extensive plateaus, and river valleys characterize the physiography of Madhya Pradesh. The southern portion of the state occupies the Deccan Plateau, and in the north and west it encompasses the Vindhya and Kaimur ranges, which in places rise to 1,500 feet (460 m) above sea level. There is very little land in Madhya Pradesh that is below 1,000 feet (350 m) in elevation. The Sātpura and Mahādeo ranges in the south rise above 3,000 feet (900 m), as does the Maikala Range, which forms the boundary between Madhya Pradesh and Chhattīsgaṛh. The fertile Chhattīsgaṛh Plain (*q.v.*) forms the heart of Chhattīsgaṛh state and is bounded on all sides by highlands, some of which rise to 4,000 feet (1,200 m) in elevation. The two states are the source of some of the most important rivers of India, including the Narmada, the Tāpti, and the Wainganga in Madhya Pradesh. The Chhattīsgaṛh Plain forms the upper Mahānadi River basin.

The region is heavily forested. The most economically important trees are teak, sal, bamboo, and salai. The forests have plentiful wildlife, including tigers, panthers, bears, bison, wild buffalo, and various types of deer.

The climate in both states is monsoonal, with most precipitation occurring during the cooler rainy season, from June to October. To the north and west in Madhya Pradesh, however, it is generally drier; annual precipitation averages 40 inches (1,000 mm) or less in the far west and less than 30 inches (750 mm) in the Chambal River valley to the north. In Chhattīsgaṛh precipitation averages 60 inches (1,500 mm) per year. From March until May the weather is hot and dry, with temperatures exceeding 85° F (29° C) throughout the region. Winters are usually pleasant and dry.

Hindus form the majority of the population, but there are significant minorities of Muslims, Jains, Christians, and Buddhists and a small population of Sikhs. Hindi is the official and most widely spoken language; tribal languages include Bhīlī and Goṇḍī, as well as eastern and western Hindi dialects. The second most important language is Marāṭhī. A number of tribal groups are found in the region—including the Bhīl, Baigā, Goṇḍ, Korku, Kamar, Kol, and Mariā—particularly in Chhattīsgaṛh, where tribal peoples comprise roughly one-third of the population.

Agriculture dominates the region's economy, and nearly half of all workers are cultivators or agricultural labourers. The most important crops are rice, wheat, sorghum (jowar), legumes, sugarcane, cotton, soybeans, and peanuts (groundnuts). Rice production predominates in Chhattīsgaṛh.

Both states are rich in minerals, including coal, iron ore, manganese, bauxite, limestone, dolomite, fireclay, and kaolin (china clay). The only heavy industry in Chhattīsgaṛh is the iron and steel plant at Bhilai Nagar; there is a heavy electrical factory in Madhya Pradesh at Bhopāl. Large- and medium-scale industries abound in both states, however, as do cottage industries. Well endowed with power resources, Madhya Pradesh has developed a number of hydroelectric projects. A thermal plant at Korba in Chhattīsgaṛh is the largest in India.

Inadequate transportation facilities have left the rich natural resources of the two states largely unexploited. Broad- and narrow-gauge rail lines connect the states with India's major cities, as do airports at Bhopāl, Gwalior, Khajurāho, and Indore in Madhya Pradesh and at Raipur in Chhattīsgaṛh. Many districts, however, have only limited access by road.

Tribal traditions thrive throughout the region, and a great deal of tribal mythology and folklore has been preserved. The bards of the Goṇḍ, for instance, continue to sing of the legendary deeds of Lingō-pen, the mythical originator of the Goṇḍ tribe. A number of temples, fortresses, and cave works reflect ancient times; one of the earliest monuments—the Buddhist stupa at Bhārhut in Madhya Pradesh—dates to about 175 BC. There are many universities and colleges throughout the two states.

Mādhyamika (Sanskrit: "Intermediate"), important school in the Mahāyāna ("Great Vehicle") Buddhist tradition. Its name derives from its having sought a middle position between the realism of the Sarvāstivāda ("Doctrine That All Is Real") school and the idealism of the Yogācāra ("Mind Only") school. The most renowned Mādhyamika thinker was Nāgārjuna (2nd century AD), who developed the doctrine that all is void (*śūnyavāda*). The three authoritative texts of the school are the *Mādhyamika-śāstra* (Sanskrit: "Treatise of the Middle Way") and the *Dvādaśā-dvāra-śāstra* ("Twelve Gates Treatise") by Nāgārjuna and the *Śataka-śāstra* ("One Hundred Verses Treatise"), attributed to his pupil Āryadeva.

Buddhism in general assumed that the world is a cosmic flux of momentary interconnected events (dharmas), however the reality of these events might be viewed. Nāgārjuna sought to demonstrate that the flux itself could not be held to be real, nor could the consciousness perceiving it, as it itself is part of this flux. If this world of constant change is not real, neither can the serial transmigration be real, nor its opposite, nirvana. Transmigration and nirvana being equally unreal, they are one and the same. In the final analysis, reality can only be attributed to something entirely different from all that is known, which must therefore have no identifiable predicates and can only be styled the void (sunyata).

Mādhyamika thinkers thus strongly emphasize the mutations of human consciousness to grasp the reality of that which is ultimately real beyond any duality. The world of duality could be assigned a practical reality of *vyavahāra* ("discourse and process"), but, once the ultimate meaning (*paramārtha*) of the void is grasped, this reality falls away. These ideals influenced Hindu thinkers, principally Gauḍapāda (7th century) and Śaṅkara (usually dated AD 788–820); the latter is therefore called a crypto-Mādhyamika by his adversaries.

The basic Mādhyamika texts were translated into Chinese by Kumārajiva in the 5th century, and the teachings were further systematized (as the San-lun, or Three Treatises, school) in the 6th–7th century by Chi-tsang. The school spread to Korea and was first transmitted to Japan, as Sanron, in 625 by the Korean monk Ekwan.

Consult the INDEX *first*

Madi, also spelled MAʿDI, or MAʿADI, Sudanic-speaking peoples who inhabit both banks of the Nile River in northwestern Uganda and in The Sudan. They speak a Central Sudanic language of the Chari-Nile branch of the Nilo-Saharan family. They are closely related to the Lugbara, their neighbours to the west.

Primarily hoe cultivators, with millet as their staple crop, the Madi also fish, hunt, and keep cattle; smithing is an important craft. The settlement pattern of ordinary people is one of large joint family homesteads.

The country is divided into areas under the ritual care of *vudupi* (or "owners of the land"—*i.e.,* descendants of the indigenous or preclan population of the area). *Vudupi* have a ritual relationship with the land that includes the presumed power to control wind and crop-destroying pests. The Madi also have about 25 chiefdoms with boundaries that differ from those of the ritual lands. The chief is the head of the dominant patrilineal clan that first settled in the chiefdom, later groups being assigned accessory lineages. The chiefship is a powerful office with many privileges; its authority is sanctioned by a belief that the chief's lineage ancestors will punish recalcitrant subjects. Ritual centres on the worship of ancestors.

Madina do Boé (Guinea-Bissau): *see* Boé.

Madīnah, Al-, formally AL-MADĪNAH AL-MUNAWWARAH (Saudi Arabia): *see* Medina.

Madīnah ʿĪsā, English ISA TOWN, planned community in the kingdom of Bahrain, north-central Bahrain Island, in the Persian Gulf. Conceived and underwritten by the Bahraini government as a residential settlement, it was laid out on an uninhabited site in the early 1960s; the first units were occupied in 1968. The town is named for Sheikh ʿĪsā ibn Salmān Āl Khalīfah, who ruled Bahrain when the town was established.

As a new town, Madīnah ʿĪsā has modern schools and libraries and a vehicle-free shopping centre. A stadium and Olympic-sized swimming pool are other distinctive features.

Mosque at Madīnah ʿĪsā, Bahrain
FPG

Since it was designed to attract an economic cross section of Bahrain's inhabitants, houses of varying sizes have been erected. Householders had a period of 15–20 years to pay for their new dwellings; payments of the first residents were put into a fund to permit further expansion and development. Though originally planned for an optimum 15,000 inhabitants, the project had that number in its first stage by the late 1970s, and housing was subsequently expanded. Pop. (1991) 34,509.

Madīnat al-Fayyūm (Egypt): *see* Fayyūm, al-.

Madīnat ash-Sha'b, town, southern Yemen, former administrative capital of Yemen (Aden). The town is located on the Little Aden Peninsula on the western side of At-Tawāhī Bay (Aden Harbour), across from Aden city. Founded in 1959 as Al-Ittiḥād (Arabic: "Unity"), it was at first the capital of the Protectorate of South Arabia under British rule. It was renamed after Yemen (Aden) was founded in 1967.

Madīnat Habu, also spelled MEDINET HABU, southernmost part of the necropolis region of western Thebes in Upper Egypt, although the name often refers specifically to the mortuary temple built there by Ramses III (1187–56 BC). (*See* Thebes.) This temple, which was also dedicated to the god Amon, was carved with religious scenes and portrayals of Ramses' wars against the Libyans and the Sea Peoples. It was situated within a fortified enclosure wall, with remarkable entrance towers, imitating Syrian *migdol* fortresses, on the east side. A royal palace was attached at the south of the open forecourt of this temple, while priests' dwellings and administrative units lay on either side of the temple.

The site of Madīnat Habu became an important shrine as the worship of Amon intensified in Egypt. Ramses III's walls had enclosed a small temple called Djeser-Iset that was dedicated to Amon and had been built by the earlier pharaohs Hatshepsut and Thutmose III. A series of pylons, porches, courts, and a columned hall were added to this temple by

Ruins of Madīnat Habu from the west
By courtesy of the Oriental Institute, University of Chicago

Ramses III and rulers of the 25th, 29th, and Ptolemaic dynasties and the Roman emperor Antoninus Pius. In the first millennium BC, a town called Djeme developed within the fortifications of the temple. A settlement survived there into the Coptic period.

Madīnat Rasūl Allāh (Saudi Arabia): *see* Medina.

Madioen (Indonesia): *see* Madiun.

Madison, city, seat (1811) of Jefferson county, southeastern Indiana, U.S. It lies along the Ohio River (bridged), opposite Milton, Ky. Settled about 1808 and named for President James Madison, it flourished as a river port until overshadowed by Louisville (46 miles [74 km] southwestward downstream) and Cincinnati (88 miles [142 km] upstream). Madison is now an important tobacco market and agricultural trading centre; its manufactures include road machinery, small motors, electric organs, and chemicals. Hanover College (1827) is 4 miles (6 km) west. A number of fine pre-Civil War houses, especially the J.F.D. Lanier State Memorial (mansion) and Shrewsbury House, have been preserved. The Talbot-Hyatt Pioneer Garden has a community well (*c.* 1810). The Jefferson (military) Proving Ground and Clifty Falls State Park are nearby. The annual July regatta and Governor's Cup Race for hydroplanes is held at Madison. Inc. 1838. Pop. (2000) 12,004.

Madison, borough, Morris county, northeastern New Jersey, U.S. It lies 17 miles (27 km) west of Newark. The centre of a greenhouse industry and nicknamed the "Rose City," it is the site of Drew University (1866) and the Florham-Madison Campus of Fairleigh Dickinson University. The College of St. Elizabeth (1899) is at nearby Convent Station. Sayre House (*c.* 1745) was Anthony Wayne's headquarters during the American Revolution. The community, settled in 1685 and originally called Bottle Hill after Bottle Hill Tavern, was renamed for President James Madison in 1834 and incorporated in 1889. Pop. (2000) 16,530.

Madison, city, seat of Lake county, southeastern South Dakota, U.S. It began in 1873 as a trading post for gold-seeking pioneers and was named Madison because its interlake setting resembled that of Madison, Wis. It was relocated 4 miles (6 km) west to its present site when it merged with Herman Village. Dakota (formerly General Beadle) State College was founded there in 1881. Madison is an agricultural marketing centre, and immediately west is Dakota Prairie Village, featuring pioneer memorabilia and the site of an annual Steam Threshing Jamboree and Antique Equipment Show. Lake Herman State Park, Lake Madison, and Milwaukee Lake are nearby. Inc. 1885. Pop. (2000) 6,540.

Madison, city, capital of Wisconsin, U.S., and seat of Dane county. It lies in the south-central part of the state, partly on an isthmus between lakes Mendota and Monona, which with lakes Waubesa and Kegonsa to the southeast form the "four lakes" group. Founded by James Duane Doty in 1836 (a year of frenzied land speculation in the newly created Territory of Wisconsin), it was named for President James Madison. That same year, Doty pushed a bill through the legislature to make Madison the permanent capital of Wisconsin and a county seat. The wooded site was still uninhabited, but construction of a capitol building was quickly begun there, and late in 1838 the territorial legislature held its first session in the unfinished building. Wisconsin became a state in 1848, and, through the efforts of Leonard J. Farwell, industries began to locate in the city in about 1850. The railroad arrived in 1854, and steady development ensued. Governmental operations and the University of Wisconsin (1849) account for much of the city's prosperity and stability, and there is a high proportion of professional, managerial, and technical workers. Federal agencies include the U.S. Forest Products Laboratory (1910). Wholesale and retail trade, followed by manufacturing, have broadened the city's economy.

Landscaped lakeshores and large parks, including Henry Vilas Park with the city zoo, characterize Madison, which is located in the heart of the southern Wisconsin lakelands. The skyline is dominated by the State Capitol (286 feet [87 m] high), with its white granite dome topped by a statue, "Forward"; it is

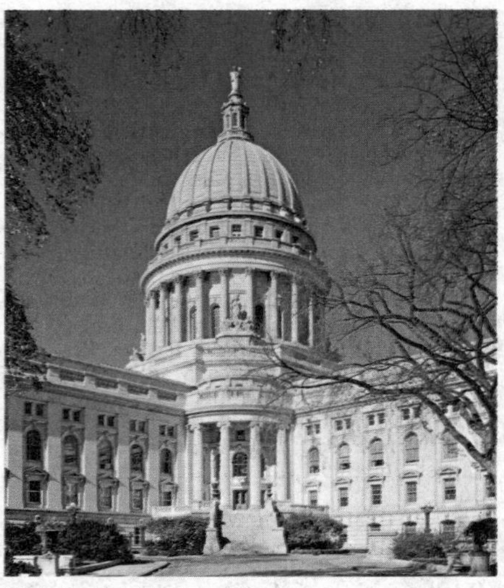

State Capitol, Madison, Wis.
Philip A. Turner

in a 13-acre (5-hectare) park. Madison is the seat of the original campus of the University of Wisconsin, Madison Area Technical College (1912), and Edgewood College (1927). Inc. village, 1846; city, 1856. Pop. (2000) city, 208,054; Madison MSA, 426,526.

Madison, James (b. March 16 [March 5, Old Style], 1751, Port Conway, Va. [U.S.]—d. June 28, 1836, Montpelier, Va., U.S.), fourth president of the United States (1809–17) and one of the founding fathers of his country. At

James Madison, detail of an oil painting by Asher B. Durand, 1833
By courtesy of The New-York Historical Society

the Constitutional Convention (1787) he influenced the planning and ratification of the U.S. Constitution and collaborated with Alexander Hamilton and John Jay in the publication of *The Federalist Papers.* As a member of the new House of Representatives, he sponsored the first 10 amendments to the Constitution. He was secretary of state under President Thomas Jefferson when the Louisiana Territory was purchased from France. The War of 1812 was fought during his presidency.

Early life and political activities. Madison was born at the home of his maternal grandmother. The son and namesake of a leading Orange county landowner and squire, he maintained his lifelong home at Montpelier, near the Blue Ridge Mountains. In 1769 he rode horseback to the College of New Jersey (Princeton University), selected for its hostility to episcopacy. He completed the four-year course in two years, finding time also to demonstrate against England and to lampoon members of a rival literary society in ribald verse. Overwork produced several years of epileptoid hysteria and premonitions of early death, which thwarted military training but did not prevent home study of public law, mixed with early advocacy of independence (1774) and furious denunciation of the imprisonment of nearby dissenters from the established Anglican Church. Madison never became a church member, but in maturity he expressed a preference for Unitarianism.

His health improved, and he was elected to Virginia's 1776 Revolutionary convention, where he drafted the state's guarantee of religious freedom. In the convention-turned-legislature he helped Thomas Jefferson disestablish the church but lost reelection by refusing to furnish the electors with free whiskey. After two years on the governor's council, he was sent to the Continental Congress in March 1780.

Five feet six inches tall, small boned, boyish in appearance, and weak of voice, he waited six months before taking the floor, but strong actions belied his mild manners. He rose quickly to leadership against the devotees of state sovereignty and enemies of Franco-U.S. collaboration in peace negotiations, contending also for the Mississippi as a western territorial boundary and the right to navigate that river through its Spanish-held delta. Defending Virginia's charter title to the vast Northwest against states that had no claim to western territories and whose major motive was to validate barrel-of-rum purchases from Indian tribes, Madison defeated the land speculators by persuading Virginia to cede the western lands to Congress as a national heritage.

Following the ratification of the Articles of Confederation in 1781, Madison undertook to strengthen the Union by asserting implied power in Congress to enforce financial requisitions upon the states by military coercion. This move failing, he worked unceasingly for an amendment conferring power to raise revenue and wrote an eloquent address adjuring the states to avert national disintegration by ratifying the submitted article. The Chevalier de la Luzerne, French minister to the United States, wrote that Madison was "regarded as the man of the soundest judgment in Congress."

The father of the Constitution. Reentering the Virginia legislature in 1784, he defeated Patrick Henry's bill to give financial support to "teachers of the Christian religion." To avoid the political effect of his extreme nationalism, he persuaded the states-rights advocate John Tyler to sponsor the calling of the Annapolis Convention of 1786, which, aided by Madison's influence, produced the Constitutional Convention of 1787.

There his Virginia Plan, put forward through Gov. Edmund Randolph, furnished the basic framework and guiding principles of the Constitution. Delegate William Pierce, of Georgia, wrote that, in the management of every great question, Madison "always comes forward the best informed Man of any point in debate." Pierce called him "a Gentleman of great modesty—with a remarkable sweet temper. He is easy and unreserved among his acquaintances, and has a most agreeable style of conversation."

Besides earning the title of father of the Constitution, Madison took day-by-day notes of debates, which furnish the only comprehensive history of the convention proceedings. To promote ratification he collaborated with Alexander Hamilton and John Jay in newspaper publication of *The Federalist Papers* (Madison wrote 29 out of 85), which became the standard commentary on the Constitution. His influence produced ratification by Virginia and led John Marshall to say that, if eloquence included "persuasion by convincing, Mr. Madison was the most eloquent man I ever heard."

Elected to the new House of Representatives, Madison sponsored the first 10 amendments to the Constitution, placing emphasis, in debate, on freedom of religion, speech, and press. His leadership in the House, which caused the Massachusetts congressman Fisher Ames to call him "our first man," came to an end when he split with Secretary of the Treasury Hamilton over methods of funding the war debts. Hamilton's aim was to strengthen the national government by cementing men of wealth to it; Madison sought to protect the interests of Revolutionary veterans.

Hamilton's victory turned Madison into a strict constructionist of the congressional power to appropriate for the general welfare. He denied the existence of implied power to establish a national bank to aid the Treasury. Later, as president, he asked for and obtained a bank as "almost [a] necessity" for that purpose, but he contended that it was constitutional only because Hamilton's bank had gone without constitutional challenge. Unwillingness to admit error was a lifelong characteristic. The break over funding turned Congress into Madisonian and Hamiltonian factions, with Fisher Ames now calling Madison a "desperate party leader" who enforced a discipline "as severe as the Prussian" (Madisonians turned into Jeffersonians after Jefferson, having returned from France, became secretary of state).

In 1794 Madison married Dolley Payne Todd, a handsome, buxom, vivacious Quaker 16 years his junior, who rejected church discipline and loved social activities.

Madison left Congress in 1797, disgusted by John Jay's treaty with England, which frustrated his program of commercial retaliation against wartime oppression of U.S. maritime commerce. The Alien and Sedition Acts of 1798 inspired him to draft the Virginia Resolutions of that year, denouncing those statutes as violations of the First Amendment of the Constitution and affirming the right and duty of the states "to interpose for arresting the progress of the evil." Carefully worded to mean less legally than they seemed to threaten, they forced him to spend his octogenarian years combatting South Carolina's interpretation of them as a sanction of state power to nullify federal law.

During eight years as Jefferson's secretary of state (1801–09), Madison used the words "The President has decided" so regularly that his own role can be discovered only in foreign archives. British diplomats dealing with Madison encountered "asperity of temper and fluency of expression." Senators John Adair and Nicholas Gilman agreed in 1806 that he "governed the President," an opinion held also by French minister Louis-Marie Turreau.

Madison's presidency. Although he was accused of weakness in dealing with France and England, Madison won the presidency in 1808 by publishing his vigorous diplomatic dispatches. Faced with a senatorial cabal on taking office, he made a senator's lacklustre brother, Robert Smith, secretary of state and wrote all important diplomatic letters for two years before removing him. Although he had fully supported Jefferson's wartime shipping embargo, Madison reversed his predecessor's policy two weeks after assuming the presidency by secretly notifying both Great Britain and France, then at war, that, in his opinion, if the country addressed should stop molesting U.S. commerce and the other belligerent continued to do so, "Congress will, at the next ensuing session, authorize acts of hostility . . . against the other."

An agreement with England providing for repeal of its Orders in Council, which limited trade by neutral nations with France, collapsed because the British minister violated his instructions; he concealed the requirements that the United States continue its trade embargo against France, renounce wartime trade with Britain's enemies, and authorize England to capture any U.S. vessel attempting to trade with France. Madison expelled the minister's successor for charging, falsely, that the President had been aware of the violation.

Believing that England was bent on permanent suppression of American commerce, Madison proclaimed nonintercourse with England on Nov. 2, 1810, and notified France on the same day that this would "necessarily lead to war" unless England stopped its molestations. One week earlier, unknown to Congress (in recess) or the public, he had taken armed possession of the Spanish province of West Florida, claimed as part of the Louisiana Purchase. He was reelected in 1812, despite strong opposition.

With his actions buried in secrecy, Federalists and politicians pictured Madison as a timorous pacifist dragged into the War of 1812 (1812–15) by congressional war hawks. In fact, he sought peace but accepted war. As wartime commander in chief he was hampered by the refusal of Congress to heed pleas for naval and military development and made the initial error of entrusting army command to aging veterans of the Revolution. The small U.S. Navy sparkled, but on land defeat followed defeat.

By 1814, however, Madison had lowered the average age of generals from 60 to 36 years; victories resulted, reversing British Cabinet policy and ending a war the principal cause of which had been removed by revocation of the Orders in Council the day before the conflict began. Contemporary public opinion in the United States, Canada, England, and continental Europe proclaimed the result a U.S. triumph. The Federalist Party was killed by its sedition in opposing the war, and the President was lifted to a pinnacle of popularity. Madison's greatest fault was delay in discharging incompetent subordinates, including Secretary of War John Armstrong, who had scoffed at the President's repeated warnings of a coming British attack on Washington and ignored presidential orders for its defense.

On leaving the presidency, Madison was eulogized at a Washington mass meeting for having won national power and glory "without infringing a political, civil, or religious right." Even in the face of sabotage of war operations by New England Federalists, he had lived up to the maxim he laid down in 1793 when he had said:

> "If we advert to the nature of republican government we shall find that the censorial power is in the people over the government, and not in the government over the people."

Later life. Never again leaving Virginia, for 19 years Madison managed his 5,000-acre (2,000-hectare) farm, cultivating it by methods regarded today as modern innovations, and, as president of the Albemarle Agricultural Society, he warned that human life might be wiped out by upsetting the balance of nature, including invisible organisms. He hated slavery, which held him in its economic chains, and worked to abolish it through government purchase of slaves and their resettlement in Liberia, financed by sale of public lands. When his personal valet ran away in 1792 and was recaptured—a situation that usually meant sale into the yellow-fever-infested West Indies—Madison set him free and hired him. Another slave managed one-third of the Montpelier farmlands during Madison's years in federal office.

Madison participated in Jefferson's creation of the University of Virginia (1819) and later served as its rector. Excessive hospitality, chronic agricultural depression, the care of superannuated slaves, and the squandering of $40,000 by and on a wayward stepson made him land-poor in old age. His last years were spent in bed, barely able to bend his rheumatic fingers, which nevertheless turned out an endless succession of letters and articles combating nullification and secession—the theme of his final "Advice to My Country." Henry Clay called him, after George Washington, "our greatest statesman." (I.Bt./Ed.)

BIBLIOGRAPHY. William T. Hutchinson *et al.* (eds.), *The Papers of James Madison,* 17 vol. (1962–91), is the most extensive collection of Madison's writings. Gaillard Hunt (ed.), *The Writings of James Madison,* 9 vol. (1900–10), comprises Madison's public papers and private correspondence; Hunt also edited *The Journal of the Debates in the Convention Which Framed the Constitution of the United States, May–September 1787, As Recorded by James Madison,* 2 vol. (1908), an almost exhaustive record of that convention. James Morton Smith (ed.), *The Republic of Letters: The Correspondence Between Thomas Jefferson and James Madison, 1776–1826,* 3 vol. (1995), includes more than 1,200 letters detailing their friendship. Madison's life is explored by Irving Brant, *James Madison,* 6 vol. (1941–61); Brant's *The Fourth President* (1970) selectively condenses the multivolume work into a single volume. Drew R. McCoy, *The Last of the Fathers: James Madison and the Republican Legacy* (1989), tells about the man after his presidential career. The following works discuss and evaluate Madison's political career: William C. Rives, *History of the Life and Times of James Madison,* 3 vol. (1859–68, reprinted 1970), concentrating on the period from the American Revolution until 1797; Sydney Howard Gay, *James Madison* (1884, reissued 1983), covering up to 1797; William Lee Miller, *The Business of May Next: James Madison and the Founding* (1992), detailing the period from 1784 to 1791; and Robert Allen Rutland, *The Presidency of James Madison* (1990), focusing on the War of 1812. Madison's political philosophy is analyzed in Stuart G. Brown, *The First Republicans: Political Philosophy and Public Policy in the Party of Jefferson and Madison* (1954, reprinted 1976); Irving Brant, *James Madison and American Nationalism* (1968); Lance Banning, *The Sacred Fire of Liberty: James Madison and the Founding of the Federal Republic* (1995); and Richard K. Matthews, *If Men Were Angels: James Madison and the Heartless Empire of Reason* (1995). (I.Bt./Ed.)

Madison River, river in southwestern Montana and northwestern Wyoming, U.S. The Madison River rises in the northwestern corner of Yellowstone National Park at the junction of the Gibbon and Firehole rivers. It flows west through Hebgen Lake (impounded by a dam) into southwestern Montana, then turns north between the Madison Range and Tobacco Root Mountains to flow through Ennis Lake, which was created by Madison Dam. After a course of 183 miles (294 km), the Madison joins the Gallatin and Jefferson rivers just northeast of Three Forks to form the Missouri River.

Madison Square Garden, indoor sports arena in New York City. The original Madison Square Garden (1874) was a converted railroad station at Madison Square; in 1891 a sports arena was built on the site, designed by Stanford White and dedicated chiefly to boxing. In 1925 a new Madison Square Garden was built at Eighth Avenue and 50th Street, with an arena suitable for basketball, hockey, and other sports; it was the site of several notable political gatherings, including the deadlocked Democratic National Convention of 1924. The present arena, opened in 1968 on the site of the former Pennsylvania Station, Eighth Avenue and 33rd Street, is a large complex containing a 20,000-seat arena for circuses, ice shows, and conventions, as well as for sports events; a 5,000-seat forum; an exposition rotunda; a bowling centre; a sports hall of fame; and a gallery of sports art. A successful renovation of the complex was completed in 1991.

Madison Square Garden, New York City

Madiun, also spelled MADIOEN, *kotamadya* (municipality) and *kabupaten* (regency) in Jawa Timur *provinsi* ("province"), eastern Java, Indonesia. The city lies on the east bank of the Madiun River. The population is mostly Indonesian and Chinese. The city was the scene of a short-lived communist rebellion, the so-called Madiun Affair, in 1948, and it maintains a site at which hundreds of soldiers killed in the Indonesian revolution are buried. The city is served by a main railway, and roads and an air service connect it to other towns.

The regency incorporates fertile plains in the north and centre, high volcanic peaks (Mount Lawu, 10,712 feet [3,265 m]) in the east and west, and limestone ranges to the south. Rice and sugarcane are the main crops, followed by corn (maize), cassava, coffee, cacao, cinchona, coconuts, and peanuts (groundnuts); teak comes from the forests. Madiun, a residency under the Dutch, was reduced in area under the Indonesian republic and became a regency. Area regency, 318 square miles (824 square km). Pop. (1995 est.) city, 171,532.

Madiun Affair, communist rebellion against the Hatta-Sukarno government of Indonesia, which originated in Madiun, a town in eastern Java, in September 1948. The Indonesian Communist Party (PKI) had been declared illegal by the Dutch following uprisings in 1926–27; it was officially reestablished on Oct. 21, 1945, when an independent Indonesia was proclaimed after World War II. The communists resumed political activities, and some of their leaders held high positions in the new republican government. In January 1948 the left-wing government was replaced by one headed by Mohammad Hatta. Hatta's government planned to demobilize those guerrilla units under communist control. The communists opposed the program; the PKI propagated the formation of a communist national front and advised the armed units to challenge the demobilization. While communist leaders were on a propaganda tour, a local communist commander in Madiun took the initiative on Sept. 18, 1948, and seized power in Madiun. The communist leaders, taken by surprise, were trapped by their own propaganda and had no alternative but to support the rebellion. The Hatta-Sukarno government took firm action. The rebellion was put down within three months, and most of the PKI leaders were killed or imprisoned.

Mädler, Johann Heinrich von (b. May 29, 1794, Berlin, Prussia [Germany]—d. March 14, 1874, Hanover, Ger.), German astronomer who (with Wilhelm Beer) published the most complete map of the Moon of the time, *Mappa Selenographica,* 4 vol. (1834–36). It was the first lunar map to be divided into quadrants, and it remained unsurpassed in its detail until J.F. Julius Schmidt's map of 1878. The *Mappa Selenographica* was accompanied in 1837 by a volume providing micrometric measurements of the diameters of 148 craters and the elevations of 830 mountains on the Moon's surface. Beer and Mädler also collaborated in publishing in 1830 the first systematic chart of the surface features of the planet Mars.

Madog AB OWAIN GWYNEDD, Madog also spelled MADOC (fl. 1170), legendary voyager to America, a son (if he existed at all) of Owain Gwynedd (d. 1170), prince of Gwynedd, in North Wales.

A quarrel among Owain's sons over the distribution of their late father's estate led Madog to sail to Ireland and then westward. In a year or so he returned to Wales and assembled a group to colonize the land he had discovered. The party sailed west in 10 ships and was not seen again. The oldest extant accounts of Madog are in Richard Hakluyt's *Voyages* (1582) and David Powel's *The Historie of Cambria* (1584). Hakluyt believed Madog had landed in Florida. In *Letters and Notes on the Manners, Customs, and Condition of the North American Indians* (1841), George Catlin surmised that Madog's expedition had reached the upper Missouri River valley and that its members were ancestors of the Mandan Indians. Most anthropologists reject the idea of pre-Columbian European contacts with American Indians, but evidence is not conclusive.

Madonna, in Christian art, depiction of the Virgin Mary; the term is usually restricted to those representations that are devotional rather than narrative and that show her in a nonhistorical context and emphasize later doctrinal or sentimental significance. The Madonna is accompanied most often by the infant Christ, but there are several important types that show her alone.

The theme of the Madonna and Child was rare in the first centuries of early Christian art (*c.* 3rd–6th century). In 431, however, the establishment of Mary's title of Theotokos ("Mother of God") definitively affirmed the full deity of Christ; thereafter, to emphasize this concept, an enthroned Madonna and Child were given a prominent place in monumental church decoration.

Byzantine art developed a great number of Madonna types. All are illustrated on icons, and one or another type was usually pictured prominently on the eastern wall of Byzantine churches below the image of Christ; the location dramatized her role as mediator between Christ and the congregation. The major types of the Madonna in Byzantine art are the *nikopoia* ("bringer of victory"), an extremely regal image of the Madonna and Child enthroned; the *hodēgētria* ("she who points the way"), showing a standing Virgin holding the Child on her left arm; and the *blacherniotissa* (from the Church of the Blachernes, which contains the icon that is its prototype), which emphasizes her role as intercessor, showing her alone in an orant, or prayer posture, with the Child pictured in a medallion on her breast. The Virgin also figured prominently as an intercessor in the group of the Deësis, where she and St. John the Baptist appear as intercessors on either side of Christ. In addition to these rather ceremonial types, the Virgin also appears in the less-frequently represented, more intimate types of the *galaktotrophousa,* in which she nurses the Child, and the *glykophilousa,* in which the Child caresses her cheek while she seems sadly to contemplate his coming Passion.

In the West, particularly with the spread of devotional images at the end of the European Middle Ages, the theme of the Madonna was developed into a number of additional types, in general less rigidly defined than those of the East but often modeled on Byzantine types. As a rule, Western types of the Madonna sought to inspire piety through the beauty and tenderness rather than the theological significance of the subject.

One of the earliest strictly Western Madonna types is a standing Gothic Madonna, a lyrical image of the smiling Virgin and playful Child,

"The Grand-Duke's Madonna," oil painting by Raphael, 1505; in the Pitti Palace, Florence
SCALA—Art Resource/EB Inc.

which was modeled on the Byzantine *hodēgētria* and found its finest expression in sculpture in the 13th century. When, in the 14th century, painted altarpieces became common, the Madonna enthroned, derived from the *nikopoia,* was a favourite subject for a time; it was particularly popular in Italy as the *maestà,* a very formal representation of the enthroned Madonna and Child surrounded by angels and sometimes saints.

More personal depictions of the figures began to emerge in the 14th century. By far the most popular type in the West throughout the Renaissance and into the Baroque period was that derived from the *glykophilousa.* Though this type has many variants, it usually depicts a Virgin of grave expression, turning her gaze away from the playful Child.

Other, less-intimate Madonna types are the Italian *sacra conversazione,* depicting a formal grouping of saints around the Madonna and Child, and the northern themes of the Madonna of the rose garden, which symbolizes Mary's virginity, and the seven sorrows of Mary, showing seven swords piercing her heart.

Three major Madonna types showing the Virgin alone have theological significance. As the Madonna of mercy, which flourished in the 15th century, the Virgin spreads her mantle protectively over a group of the faithful. The *immacolata,* which in the 17th century emphasized her Immaculate Conception, or perpetual freedom from original sin, shows her as a young girl descending from the heavens, supported by a crescent moon and crowned by stars. The Madonna of the rosary, which until the 16th century also omitted the Child, shows the Virgin giving the rosary to St. Dominic, founder of the order that spread its use.

As did most religious art, the theme of the Madonna suffered a decline in the major arts after the 17th century. Representations of the Madonna and Child, however, continued to be important in popular art into the 20th century, most following 16th- and 17th-century models; the few examples of the subject produced by "fine" artists are too individual to be classified into types. *See also* Pietà.

Madonna, original name MADONNA LOUISE CICCONE (b. Aug. 16, 1958, Bay City, Mich., U.S.), American singer and actress.

Born into a large Italian American family, Madonna studied dance at the University of Michigan and with the Alvin Ailey American Dance Theater in New York City in the late 1970s; she was also a member of Patrick Hernandez's disco revue in Paris. In the 1980s she turned to music, and her first hit, "Holiday," in 1983 provided the blueprint for her later material—an upbeat dance-club sound with sharp production and an immediate appeal. Throughout the next eight years, she scored 21 Top Ten hits in the United States and sold some 70 million albums. Her later hits include "Like a Virgin" (1984), "True Blue" (1986), "Like a Prayer" (1989), "Justify My Love" (1990), and "Ray of Light" (1998). Criticized by some as being limited in range, her sweet, girlish voice was suited to her style of music. She was also one of the first female performers to exploit the potential of the music video.

Committed to controlling her image and career, Madonna became the head of Maverick, a subsidiary of Time-Warner created by the entertainment giant as part of a $60 million deal with the performer. Her success signaled a clear message of financial control to other women in the industry, but in terms of image she was a more ambivalent role model. Her motion-picture career has been uneven, although she triumphed with her film debut *Desperately Seeking Susan* (1985) and with the title role in the film musical *Evita* (1996).

Madox, Thomas (b. 1666, England—d. Jan. 13, 1726/27), English legal antiquary and historian whose critical studies of medieval English documents establish him as the virtual founder of British administrative history and the precursor of modern English historical scholarship.

Madox studied common law (though not called to the bar) and was clerk in the office of the Exchequer, later working in the augmentation office, a prime repository of records. Under the patronage of Baron John Somers, the lord chancellor, he wrote his first work, *Formulare Anglicanum* (1702), a classified collection of charters and legal instruments of Britain from 1066 to 1547. Chosen primarily from the archives of the court of augmentation, this work is considered a landmark in the diplomatic history of post-Conquest charters.

Madox was elected to the Society of Antiquaries (1707/08) and in 1711 published his renowned work, *History and Antiquities of the Exchequer of the Kings of England . . . from the Norman Conquest to the End of the Reign of . . . Edward II,* a carefully annotated and critical history of the Exchequer and ancient law in England. He was appointed historiographer to King George I in 1714. Madox's other works are *Firma Burgi* (1722), of major importance for English municipal history, and *Baroni Anglica* (1736), a treatise on tenures.

Madras (India): *see* Tamil Nādu.

Madras, Tamil CHENNAI, capital of Tamil Nadu state, India, on the Coromandel Coast of the Bay of Bengal.

Madras is the shortened name of the fishing village Madraspatnam, where the British East India Company built a fort and trading post in 1639–40. At that time, the weaving of cotton fabrics was a local industry, and the English invited the weavers and native merchants to settle near the fort. By 1652 the factory of Fort St. George was recognized as a presidency (an administrative unit governed by a president), and between 1668 and 1749 the company expanded its control. At about 1801, by which time the last of the local rulers had been shorn of his powers, the English had become masters of southern India, and Madras had become their administrative and commercial capital.

Madras developed without a plan from its 17th-century core, formed by the fort and the Indian quarters. To the north and northwest are the industrial areas; the main residential areas are to the west and south, and the old villages are in the centre. The most distinctive buildings in the city are the seven large temples in the Dravidian style, situated in the sections of George Town, Mylapore, and Triplicane. Of the buildings of the British period, the Chepauk Palace and the University Senate House (both in the Deccan Muslim style) and the Victoria Technical Institute and the High Court buildings (both in the Indo-Saracenic style) are generally considered to be the most attractive. A number of modern high-rises have also been built.

Industries include vehicle factories, an electrical-engineering firm, rubber and fertilizer factories, and a refinery. The main commodities exported from Madras are leather, iron ore, and cotton textiles. Wheat, machinery, iron and steel, and raw cotton are imported.

There are numerous educational institutions in Madras. Professional education can be obtained in the state medical colleges, the colleges of engineering and technology, the College of Carnatic Music, the College of Arts and Crafts, and the teacher-training colleges. The city is also the site of the University of Madras (1857), which has several advanced centres of research. The Indian Institute of Technology, the Central Leather Research Institute, and the Regional Laboratories of the Council of Scientific and Industrial Research are other noteworthy scientific institutions.

Cultural institutions include the Madras Music Academy, devoted to the encouragement of Carnatic music (the music of the historic region between the southern Coromandel Coast of the Bay of Bengal and the Deccan Plateau). The Kalakshetra is a centre of dance and music, and the Rasika Ranjini Sabha, in Mylapore, encourages the theatrical arts. The suburban town of Kodambakkam, with its numerous film studios, is described as the Hollywood of southern India. Three theatres—the Children's Theatre, the Annamalai Manram, and the Museum Theatre—are popular. The Madras Government Museum has exhibitions on the history and physical aspects of Tamil Nadu. There is a small collection of East India Company antiquities in the Fort Museum and a collection of paintings in the National Art Gallery. The government of Tamil Nadu officially changed the name of the city to Chennai in 1996. Pop. (2001 prelim.) 4,216,268; urban agglom., 6,424,624.

Madras, University of, state-controlled institution of higher learning located in Madras, India. One of three affiliating universities founded by the British in 1857, Madras has developed as a teaching and research institution since the 1920s. By the mid-1970s the university comprised 11 postgraduate faculties and 22 constituent colleges and was the examining and degree-granting authority for 149 affiliated colleges throughout the state of Tamil Nadu. It is a national centre for advanced research in plant pathology, mathematical physics, biophysics, and Indian philosophy. Instruction is in English and Tamil.

madrasah (Arabic: "school"), Turkish MEDRESE, in Muslim countries, an institution of higher education. The *madrasah* functioned until the 20th century as a religious college whose curriculum stressed the study of Islāmic law. In addition to law, Arabic grammar and literature, mathematics, logic, and theology were sometimes studied. Tuition was free, and food, lodging, and medical care were provided as well. Instruction usually took place in a courtyard and consisted primarily of memorizing textbooks and the instructor's lectures. The lecturer issued certificates to his students that constituted permission to repeat his words.

Princes and wealthy families donated funds for the erection of buildings and for stipends to students and lecturers. By the end of the 12th century, *madrasah*s flourished in Damascus, Baghdad, Mosul, and most other Muslim cities.

Madre, Laguna, narrow, shallow lagoon along the shore of southern Texas, U.S., and northeastern Mexico, sheltered from the Gulf of Mexico by barrier islands, of which Padre Island (a national seashore) in Texas is the most notable. The lagoon is divided into two sections by the broad delta of the Rio Grande; the U.S. portion extends southward for 120 miles (190 km) from Corpus Christi Bay, and the Mexican portion extends northward for 100 miles (160 km) from above the mouth of the Soto la Marina River. The Gulf Intracoastal Waterway runs through the lagoon to reach its southwestern terminus at Brownsville, Texas, on the Rio Grande. The U.S. part of the lagoon is not fed by any major streams and has few outlets into the Gulf; it therefore maintains a high salinity, which occasionally rises above a critical level and kills thousands of fish. Numerous waterfowl nest in the lagoon area.

Consult the INDEX *first*

Madre de Dios River, Spanish RÍO MADRE DE DIOS, headwater tributary of the Amazon in southeastern Peru and northwestern Bolivia. It flows from the Cordillera de Carabaya, easternmost range of the Andes, in Peru, and meanders generally eastward past Puerto Maldonado to the Bolivian border. There it turns northeastward and crosses the remote tropical rain forest of northwestern Bolivia. It joins the Beni River at Riberalta in Bolivia after a course of more than 700 miles (1,100 km). Numerous tributaries, including the Manu, Colorado Arana, Pariamanu, and Tambopata, flow into the main river, the upper course of which can be navigated by small craft. Below the rapids at Puerto Heath, on the Peru-Bolivia border, the Madre de Dios again becomes an important transportation artery. Rubber is gathered from the dense tropical rain forest along the river's banks. The basin is sparsely settled and in parts of the upper course is uninhabited.

Madrid, officially COMUNIDAD DE MADRID, *comunidad autónoma* ("autonomous community") of central Spain, coextensive with the *provincia* of the same name and established by the statute of autonomy of 1983. The *provincia* was formed in 1833. It roughly coincides with the drainage of the southern slopes of the Guadarrama Mountains (7,972 feet [2,430 m]) by the Jarama, Henares, and Manzanares rivers. On the monotonous Central Plateau, the terrain is a bare, typically Castilian landscape of yellow soils and open cereal fields and was the scene of several decisive battles during the Spanish Civil War (1936–39). Pine forests, preserved on the mountain slopes, attract a new style of summer suburbia for residents of Madrid city (the provincial and national capital) and provide ski facilities in the winter. Only along the Henares and Jarama do irrigated lands give ribbons of green, intensive horticulture; on the outskirts of Greater Madrid are poultry and pig farms interspersed with the development of villas or factories along the main highways. Well-endowed with building materials, the province has granite quarries in the Guadarrama and clays to the south.

An important factor in transport and communications is the relative ease of access via passes over the central mountains, notably the Somo Mountain Pass (4,650 feet [1,417 m]) to the northeast, which is used by road and the Burgos railway. The Navacerrada Pass carries the Madrid-Segovia railway. All the great national railways converge in the province. Area 3,087 square miles (7,995 square km). Pop. (2000 est.) 5,205,408.

Madrid, city, capital of Spain, of Madrid *provincia,* and of the Madrid *comunidad autónoma* ("autonomous community"). The city is located on the undulating Central Plateau in the centre of the Iberian Peninsula and is, at 2,100 feet (635 m) above sea level, one of Europe's highest capital cities.

A brief treatment of Madrid follows. For full treatment (including a map), *see* MACROPAEDIA: Madrid.

Madrid's elevation and exposed setting make it liable to sudden variations of temperature. Because of these same circumstances, however, the city has a healthful climate and pleasant weather, except in winter, when sharp winds blow, and in July and August, when the heat can be oppressive.

Modern Madrid long made its living primarily from government, banking, insurance, and tourism and derived income as the transportation hub of the nation. After World War II, however, it became an important manufacturing city, producing automobile and truck engines, electric and electronic equipment, plastics, rubber, aircraft, and optical goods. It is also a major publishing centre.

For centuries the original town grew around the captured Moorish Alcazar, or castle, before later beginning a slow expansion eastward. In the 20th century, Madrid's growth has been achieved in abrupt stages. Although some of the pre-16th-century street patterns still exist, few buildings of that period remain. Among the rare medieval structures is the restored Casa de los Lujanez, which is in the same square as the Plaza de la Villa, the small 17th-century Madrid Town Hall. Perhaps the finest architectural feature of the city is the Plaza Mayor, a city square of the Habsburg period. The National Palace, rebuilt in the mid-1700s, is a Neoclassical building that houses one of the world's great collections of body armour as well as the swords of the conquistadores Hernán Cortés and Francisco Pizarro. Adjoining the palace on the south is Madrid's first cathedral, Nuestra Señora de la Almudena. The north-south axis, known as the Paseo, is a broad tree-lined boulevard along which are located the newest tall office buildings, luxury hotels and residences, the parliament building, embassies, and major cultural institutions.

The Prado, one of the world's major picture galleries, is devoted to works primarily from the 15th to the early 19th century; the works of Francisco de Goya and Diego Velázquez are featured. Of the city's many libraries, two are noted for their manuscripts and rare books: the National Library and the library of the Royal Palace. The main education centre is at University City; it includes the Open University (Universidad Nacional de Educación a Distancia; 1972) and the Complutensian University of Madrid (1508). The city also has academies of fine arts, history, and Spanish culture.

Madrid's prosperity has resulted in an ever-increasing number of automobiles, but subway and bus systems also provide local transportation. Railways radiate in all directions, connecting Madrid to other Spanish cities and to both coasts. The Barajas (international) Airport is located 8 miles (13 km) from the city. Area city, 234 square miles (607 square km); metropolitan area, 394 square miles (1,020 square km). Pop. (2000 est.) 2,882,860.

Madrid, Complutensian University of, original name UNIVERSITY OF ALCALÁ DE HENARES, Spanish UNIVERSIDAD COMPLUTENSE DE MADRID, or UNIVERSIDAD DE ALCALÁ DE HENARES, institution of higher learning founded in 1508 at Alcalá de Henares, in the province of Madrid, and moved in 1836 to the city of Madrid.

Founded by Cardinal Francisco Jiménez de Cisneros, as an instrument in the intellectual reform of the church, it was recognized by papal bull in 1508. The university, which taught Thomist, Scotist, and Nominalist theology and Oriental languages, attracted many outstanding scholars who cooperated in the production of the famous Complutensian Polyglot Bible (completed in 1517 and published about 1522). The Colegio de Maria de Aragon was added to the institution in 1590.

In 1836 the university was transferred to Madrid, where it became the Universidad Complutense de Madrid. (*Complutense* means "native to Complutum," the Roman settlement at the site of Alcalá de Henares.) It now embraces several other institutions, such as the Medical College of San Carlos, the Royal Institute of San Isidro, a technical college that was added in 1966, and a Jesuit school of philosophy.

Madrid (Hurtado), Miguel de la (b. Dec. 12, 1934, Colima, Mex.), president of Mexico from 1982 to 1988.

De la Madrid received a degree in law from the Universidad Nacional Autónoma de México (UNAM) in Mexico City in 1957 and a master's degree in public administration from Harvard University in 1965. He worked for the National Bank of Foreign Commerce and the Bank of Mexico, and, until 1968, he taught law at the UNAM.

A member of Mexico's ruling party, Partido Revolucionario Institucional (PRI), from 1963, de la Madrid first entered government service in the Treasury (1965). From 1970 to 1972 he worked for Petróleos Mexicanos, but he returned to government service thereafter, taking a number of economic bureaucratic posts until becoming minister of planning and budget in President José López Portillo's administration (1976–82). He was the principal author of an economic-development plan that was inspired by the revenues from vast new discoveries of Mexican petroleum.

A political conservative and friend of the business community, de la Madrid sought, as president, to combat corruption in government, in government-run industries, and in labour unions. He continued to pursue foreign policies that reflected the prevailing spirit of a more independent, worldly Mexico.

Madrid, Treaty of (Jan. 14, 1526), treaty between the Habsburg emperor Charles V (Charles I of Spain) and his prisoner Francis I, king of France, who had been captured during the Battle of Pavia in February 1525 and held prisoner until the conclusion of the treaty.

In the treaty, which was never ratified, the king of France ceded his lands in Italy, Flanders, Artois, and Tournai as well as parts of France to Charles V and contracted the marriage of his sister to Charles. The final signing of the treaty occurred in Madrid on Jan. 14, 1526, and Francis was released and allowed to return to France. On crossing the border, he announced his refusal to ratify the treaty and entered into the League of Cognac, the intent of which was to dethrone Charles V.

Madrid Codex, Latin CODEX TRO-CORTESIANUS, together with the Paris and Dresden codices, one of several richly illustrated glyphic texts of the pre-Conquest Mayan period to have survived the mass book-burnings by the Spanish clergy during the 16th century. The Madrid Codex is believed to be a product of the late Mayan period (*c.* AD 1400) and is possibly a post-Classic copy of Classic Mayan scholarship. The figures and glyphs of this codex are poorly drawn and not equal in quality to those of the other surviving codices.

The codex contains a wealth of information on astrology and on divinatory practices. It has been of particular value to historians and anthropologists interested in identifying the various Mayan gods and reconstructing the rites that ushered in new years. It shows, for example, the Muluc years celebrated by a dance on high stilts. Also illustrated are Mayan crafts such as pottery and weaving and activities such as hunting.

The Madrid Codex consists of 56 pages, inscribed on both sides, formed by folding and doubling a sheet manufactured from the bark of a fig tree. Found in two unequal sections (called the *Troano* and the *Cortesianus*) in two locations in Spain in the 1860s, the Codex is now housed in the Museum of America in Madrid.

madrigal, form of vocal chamber music that originated in northern Italy during the 14th century, declined and all but disappeared in the 15th, flourished anew in the 16th, and ultimately achieved international status in the late 16th and early 17th centuries. The origin of the term madrigal is uncertain, but it probably comes from the Latin *matricale* (meaning "in the mother tongue"; *i.e.,* Italian, not Latin). The 14th-century madrigal is based on a relatively constant poetic form of two or three stanzas of three lines each, with 7 or 11 syllables per line. Musically, it is most often set polyphonically (*i.e.,* more than one voice part) in two parts, with the musical form reflecting the structure of the poem. A typical two-stanza madrigal has an AAB form with both stanzas (AA) being sung to the same music, followed by a one- or two-line coda (B), or concluding phrase, the text of which sums up the sense of the poem.

Florence, where a new style of lyric poetry influenced the madrigalists, produced the greatest madrigal composer of the 14th century, Francesco Landini. His madrigals, along with those of his contemporaries Giovanni da Cascia, Jacopo da Bologna, and others are found in the Squarcialupi Codex, a famous illuminated manuscript.

During most of the 15th century, Italian music was dominated by foreign masters mainly from northern France and the Netherlands. In the late 15th century, however, the native tradition of music and poetry was revived by noble patronage in Florence and Mantua. The Florentine carnival song and the Mantuan frottola (*q.v.;* a type of secular song) were important forerunners of the 16th-century madrigal.

The 16th-century madrigal is based on a different poetic form from its precursor and was characteristically of higher literary quality. It included not only settings of poems called madrigals but also settings of other poetic forms (*e.g.,* canzone, sonnet, sestina, ballata). The poetic form of the madrigal proper is generally free but quite similar to that of a one-stanza canzone: typically, it consists of a 5- to 14-line stanza of 7 or 11 syllables per line, with the last two lines forming a rhyming couplet. The favourite poets of the madrigal composers were Petrarch, Giovanni Boccaccio, Jacopo Sannazzaro, Pietro Bembo, Ludovico Ariosto, Torquato Tasso, and Battista Guarini.

Unlike the 14th-century madrigal, the musical style of the new madrigal was increasingly dictated by the poem. Early in the century the madrigal more closely resembled the simple, homophonic or chordal style of the frottola. But under the influence of the polyphonic style of Franco-Flemish composers working in Italy, it became more contrapuntal, using interwoven melodies; accordingly, the text was less syllabically declaimed. Both of these early styles are represented among the works of the first generation of 16th-century madrigal composers: Costanza Festa, Philippe Verdelot, Jacques Arcadelt, and Adriaan Willaert. Important works by Festa and Verdelot appear in the first printed book of madrigals (Rome, 1530).

Willaert and his pupil Cipriano de Rore (d. 1565) brought the madrigal to a new height of expression through their sensitive handling of text declamation and the introduction of word painting. Emotional words such as "joy," "anger," "laugh," and "cry" were given special musical treatment but not at the expense of continuity. Another Willaert pupil, Andrea Gabrieli, was one of the creators of the Venetian style, in which polychoral effects and brilliant contrasts of musical texture are characteristic. Perhaps the greatest madrigal composer of the 16th century was Luca Marenzio, who brought the madrigal to perfection by achieving a perfect equilibrium between word and music. Later in the century, composers like Don Carlo Gesualdo, prince of Venosa, subjugated the music entirely to the text, leading to excesses that eventually exhausted the genre.

Although the madrigal was popular outside Italy, the only country to develop a strong native tradition was England. In 1588 Nicholas Yonge published *Musica Transalpina,* a large collection of Italian madrigals in English translation. Thomas Morley, the most popular and Italianate of the Elizabethan madrigalists, assimilated the Italian style and adapted it to English taste, which preferred a lighter mood of poetry and of music. Other English madrigalists include John Wilbye, Thomas Weelkes, Thomas Tomkins, and Orlando Gibbons.

madrigal comedy, Italian musical genre of the late 16th century, a cycle of vocal pieces in the style of the madrigal and lighter Italian secular forms, connected by a vague plot or common theme. Madrigal comedies were sung in concerts and social gatherings, not staged; in his *L'Amfiparnaso* (*The Slopes of Parnassus,* first performed 1594), Orazio Vecchi states that the scenes should reach the mind through the ear rather than the eye. The cycles were light, humorous works, often depicting animated, commonplace scenes, as in Alessandro Striggio's *Il cicalamento delle donne al bucato* (*The Chattering of the Women at the Laundry,* printed 1567).

Caricatures of various national and occupational types and momentary parodies of well-known madrigals sometimes occurred, and *L'Amfiparnaso* includes some stock characters of the commedia dell'arte. Other composers of madrigal comedies included Adriano Banchieri and Giovanni Croce.

madtom, any of several North American catfishes of the genus *Noturus,* of the family Ictaluridae. They are sometimes classified in two genera, *Noturus* and *Schilbeodes.* Generally about 5–7.5 cm (2–3 inches) long, madtoms are the smallest ictalurids and are characterized by a long adipose fin that in some species joins the rounded tail fin.

The fishes are noted for the stout, usually saw-edged spines in their pectoral fins. These spines have venom glands at the base and can produce jagged, painful wounds. Madtoms inhabit the bottoms of streams, rivers, and lake shores. Species include the stonecat (*N. flavus*), a common, yellow-brown fish usually found under stones by day, and the tadpole madtom (*N.,* or *Schilbeodes, gyrinus*), a tadpolelike catfish common in the eastern and central United States.

Stonecat (*Noturus flavus*)
Painting by C.M. Richardson

Madura, also spelled MADOERA, island, Jawa Timur *provinsi* ("province"), Indonesia, off the northeastern coast of Java and separated from Surabaya by a narrow, shallow channel. With an area of 2,042 square miles (5,290 square km), the island has an undulating surface rising to 700 feet (210 m) in the west and to more than 1,400 feet (430 m) in the east.

The climate, flora, and fauna of Madura resemble those of eastern Java, but the soil is generally dry and infertile. Kapok, copra, and coconut oil are important products, as is teak from forests in the northwest. The principal industries are cattle raising and salt panning, the latter a government monopoly. A fishing fleet of several thousand long, swift praus (sailing craft) is based at Madura. Petroleum is extracted on a small scale.

The Madurese, formerly a source of labour for estates on other islands and still known as migrant workers and traders in much of Java, tend to be shorter but of sturdier build than the Javanese. They are Muslims by religion. Bull races, usually held in September, attract

Bull racing on Madura Island, Indonesia
© Wolfgang Kaehler

huge crowds. Madura's capital is Pamekasan, in the south-central part of the island; other towns are Sumenep in the east, near which are the tombs of the Sumenep princes; Bangkalan, on the western coast, with the old palace of the sultan and an interesting mosque; and, on the southern coast, Sampang, Kamal, and Kalianget. Roads run along the northern and southern coasts and across the centre of the island but, except for the Kamal-Pamekasan road, are of poor quality.

Dutch influence was established in Madura late in the 17th century. Three regencies, established by the Dutch, were united in 1885 under a residency attached to Java. Madura became part of Indonesia in 1949. Pop. (1992 est.) 2,877,194.

Madura foot, also called MADUROMYCOSIS, or MYCETOMA, fungus infection, usually localized in the foot but occurring occasionally elsewhere on the body, apparently resulting from inoculation into a scratch or abrasion of any of a number of fungi: *Penicillium, Aspergillus,* or *Madurella,* or actinomycetes such as *Nocardia.*

The disease was first reported from the region of Madura in southern India; it occurs most frequently in tropical and subtropical areas where people go barefoot. The infection, which may remain latent for a time, forms small, subcutaneous swellings that enlarge, soften with pus, and break through the skin surface, with concurrent invasion of deeper tissues. Sulfonamide, iodide, and antibiotic therapy have been used against actinomycotic infections, but the fungi are more resistant to treatment. When tissue damage is extreme, the foot is usually amputated.

Madurai, formerly (until 1949) MADURA, city, south-central Tamil Nādu state, southeastern India, bounded on the west by Kerala state. It is the second largest, and probably oldest, city in the state. Located on the Vaigai River and enclosed by the Anai, Naga, and Pasu (Elephant, Snake, and Cow) hills, the compact old city, site of the Pāṇḍya (4th–11th century AD) capital, centres on Mīnākṣī-Sundareśvara Temple. The temple, Tirumala

Carved figures on a tower gate of the Mīnākṣī-Sundareśvara Temple in Madurai, Tamil Nādu, India
Picturepoint, London

Nayak palace, Teppakulam tank (an earthen embankment reservoir), and a 1,000-pillared hall were rebuilt in the Vijayanagar period (16th–17th century) after the total destruction of the city in 1310. The city walls were removed by the British in 1837 to enable the city to expand, and administrative and residential quarters formed north of the river.

Large-scale industry has developed in the suburbs. Predominant are cotton spinning and weaving and the manufacture of transport equipment, tobacco, and sugar. Small-scale handloom weaving of silks and cottons, which have made Madurai famous throughout history, remains important. In the early Christian era, Madurai was also well known for its Tamil *caṅkam* (literary society), and a new *caṅkam* was established in 1901. The city is the seat of Madurai-Kamaraj University (1966).

Lying southeast of the Eastern Ghāts, the surrounding region occupies part of the plain of South India and contains several mountain spurs, including the Palni and Sirumalai hills (north), the Cardamom Hills (west), and the Varushanād and Āndipatti hills (south). Between these hills in the west lies the high Kambam Valley. Eastward, the plains drop to 300 feet (90 m) above sea level but contain isolated hills. The chief river, the Vaigai, flows northeast through the Kambam Valley and east across the centre of the state.

The ancient history of the region is associated with the Pāṇḍya kings. Later it was conquered by Cōḻa, Vijayanagar, Muslim, Marāṭhā, and British rulers. In the 1940s it became known as the centre of the civil disobedience movement and remained an important seat of political leadership.

The region has never been self-sufficient in rice, despite the completion of the Periyār (1895) and Vaigai (1960) irrigation works. Its chief cash crops are peanuts (groundnuts), cotton, sugarcane, coffee, cardamom, potatoes, and pears. Pop. (2001 prelim.) city, 922,913; metropolitan area, 1,194,665.

Madurese, native population of the arid and infertile island of Madura, found today on Madura, the Kangean Islands, and the adjacent coast of northeastern Java in Indonesia. Of Deutero-Malay stock, the Madurese speak two principal dialects—West Madurese (concentrated in Pamekasan) and East Madurese (most prevalent in Sumenep)—and a minor variation in the nearby Kangean Islands. The Madurese on Madura raise cattle for export and cultivate rice by irrigation. Living in farm settlements of 10–20 nuclear families, they are grouped under a headman and have a separate religious group in charge of worship. Social organization is no longer based on kinship relations but is primarily territorial. Property is usually divided equally between husband and wife.

The Madurese on Java are a major ethnic group among the many indigenous peoples of the island. Although they are organized in a rigidly stratified class system including a hereditary nobility, ethnic and social distinctions have become blurred through intermarriage. Living in densely populated areas, they have been heavily influenced by outsiders. Many have given up cultivating rice to become fishermen or sailors. Their traditional religion has been influenced in varying degrees by Christianity and Islām.

Madurese language, an Austronesian language of the Indonesian subfamily, spoken on Madura Island, some smaller offshore islands, and the northern coast of Java, Indonesia. Dialects include Eastern, or Sumenep, and Western, including Bangkalan and Pamekasan. Sumenep is the standard dialect for educational purposes.

Madurese has more linguistic similarities to the Malay-Sumatran group than to Javanese or Sundanese, which are geographically closer. Speakers were estimated at more than 8 million in the late 20th century.

Consult the INDEX *first*

Madvig, Johan Nicolai (b. Aug. 7, 1804, Bornholm, Den.—d. Dec. 12, 1886, Copenhagen), classical scholar and Danish government official who published many works on Latin grammar and Greek syntax and helped to lay the foundation of modern textual criticism; his exemplary edition of Cicero's *De finibus bonorum et malorum* ("On Good and Evil Endings") appeared in 1839.

Madvig, drawing by Emilius-Ditlev Baerentzen, *c.* 1845; in Det Kongelige Bibliotek, Copenhagen
By courtesy of Det Kongelige Bibliotek, Copenhagen

Election to the Danish parliament (1848), appointment as minister of education (1848–52), and presidency of the parliament (1856–63) interrupted his career as professor of Latin language and literature at the University of Copenhagen (1829–80). One of his most important works was his Latin grammar of 1841. His other writings include *Die Verfassung und Verwaltung des Römischen Staates,* 2 vol. (1881–82; "The Roman Constitution and Administration") and an autobiography (1887).

Mae Hong Son, town, extreme northwestern Thailand, in the Daen Lao Range. Mae Hong Son has an airport with scheduled flights to Bangkok, Chiang Mai, Lampang, and Phrae.

The surrounding region is mountainous and densely forested. The terrain tends to isolate the region from other parts of Thailand; there are close economic and cultural ties to Myanmar (Burma), the border of which lies about 6 miles (10 km) from Mae Hong Son. The region's chief products are teak and other timber. Pop. (2000) 6,609.

Mae Nam Khong (Southeast Asia): *see* Mekong River.

Maeander River (Turkey): *see* Menderes River.

Maebara Issei, also called HIKOTARŌ, or HACHIJŪRŌ (b. April 28, 1834, Hagi, Nagato province, Japan—d. Dec. 3, 1876, Hagi), Japanese soldier-politician who helped to establish the 1868 Meiji Restoration (which ended the feudal Tokugawa shogunate and reinstated direct rule of the emperor) and who became a major figure in the new government until 1876, when he led a short-lived revolt that cost him his life.

Born into a low-ranking samurai family, Maebara as a young man studied at the Shōka-sonjuku, the private school founded in 1856 by the activist-scholar Yoshida Shōin, who later was executed for plotting against the shogunate. By 1860 Maebara had begun to participate in anti-shogun activities. He joined the 1864 uprising in his native fief of Chōshū and four years later helped lead the Chōshū forces that finally overthrew the shogunate. First appointed governor of Echigo province (now Niigata prefecture), he then became a cabinet councillor and briefly minister of war in the new imperial government.

In 1874 Maebara helped to quell the great rebellion at Saga led by his former associate Etō Shimpei. He opposed some of the government's policies, however, especially its attempts to replace samurai warriors with a peasant conscript army and its failure to invade Korea. In October 1876 Maebara decided to lead dissident Chōshū samurai against the new regime, stating that he intended to "sweep traitors from the side of the emperor." His rebellion failed, however, and he was captured and executed.

Maebashi, capital, Gumma *ken* (prefecture), Honshu, Japan, on the Kantō Plain. An old castle town, in the Muromachi period (1338–1573) it was called Umayabashi. It was the seat of the Matsudaira family during the Tokugawa period (1603–1867). The city grew rapidly after World War II as an industrial and communications centre. It continues to produce silk. Pop. (2000 prelim.) 284,156.

Maecenas, Gaius (Cilnius) (b. *c.* 70 BC—d. 8 BC), Roman diplomat, counsellor to the Roman emperor Augustus, and wealthy patron of such poets as Virgil and Horace. He was criticized by Seneca for his luxurious way of life.

The birthplace of Maecenas is unrecorded, but his mother's family, the Cilnii, had lorded it centuries earlier in Arretium (Arezzo, about 90 miles [145 km] north of Rome), and this was apparently also the hometown of his father's family. Tacitus once calls him Cilnius Maecenas (Etruscans used the mother's family name), but officially he was Gaius Maecenas. His great wealth may have been partly inherited, but he owed his position and influence to Octavian, later the emperor Augustus. Maecenas felt that, though a knight (slightly humbler than a senator but basically a nonpolitical member of the privileged class), his lineage and power overtopped any senator's, and he refused a career as one.

He was perhaps present at Philippi (the battle, in 42 BC, in which Antony, at first an

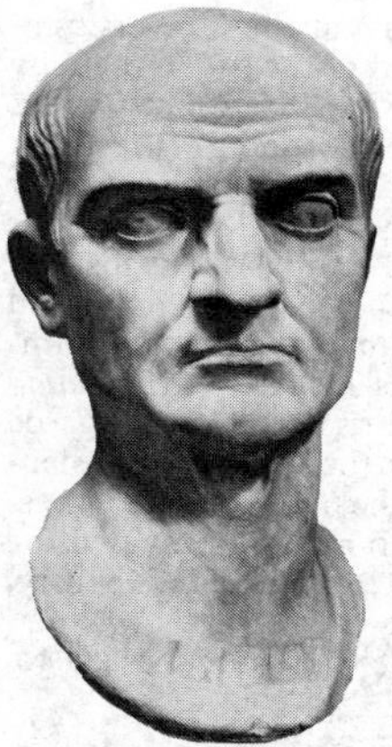

Gaius Maecenas, marble bust; in the Palazzo dei Conservatori, Rome
Alinari—Art Resource/EB Inc.

ally of Octavian, defeated Caesar's assassins Cassius and Brutus), though if he was there it was hardly as a combatant. As a counsellor he negotiated two years later the short-lived marriage of Octavian and Scribonia, designed to conciliate her kinsman the formidable Sextus Pompeius, last of the great republican generals. Before the year's end he had secured greater advantages for his leader: a treaty had ended the dangerous armed confrontation with Antony at Brundisium (modern Brindisi, on the eastern side of Italy's heel), and Antony had married Octavia, Octavian's sister. In 38–37 he persuaded Antony to come to Tarentum (Taranto, on the northernmost part of Italy's instep) and lend the warships that Octavian needed to win complete control of the West. Maecenas administered Rome and Italy, while Octavian fought Pompeius, in 36, and Antony, in 31. Although holding no office or military command, he swiftly and secretly scotched a plot to kill Octavian on his return from the East. If not on this occasion, at least in general, Maecenas kept his hands unstained by bloodshed and, in an age of ruthless violence, won praise for his mildness and humanity.

During Octavian's continued absence from Rome, Maecenas shared with Agrippa (Octavian's executive lieutenant) the position of informal vicegerent. He could use Octavian's seal and even alter his dispatches at will and continued to be deeply involved with foreign and domestic affairs after Octavian, now Augustus, had established his principate (27). He was the most trusted of advisers, holding his own in competition with the Agrippa faction.

Maecenas shared Augustus' dynastic hopes and worked for the eventual succession of Marcellus, the emperor's nephew. Meanwhile, Maecenas had recently married the beautiful, petulant Terentia. Her brother by adoption, Varro Murena, quarreled with Augustus, was disgraced, and plotted his assassination. The conspiracy was detected and Murena executed, though Maecenas had earlier revealed the plot's discovery to Terentia, thus giving his kinsman a chance to escape. Augustus had to forgive the indiscretion, but from that point on Maecenas' influence waned. Agrippa had emerged from the crises of 23 as co-regent, son-in-law, and Augustus' prospective successor. Maecenas had become a sick man, aging rapidly, though in 17 he was still sufficiently buoyant to mock Agrippa because the latter lacked a pedigree.

The domestic life of Maecenas was unhappy. Terentia tired of him and is said to have become Augustus' mistress. Maecenas died childless and left all his wealth, including his palace and gardens on the Esquiline Hill (the eastern plateau of Rome), to Augustus, with whom he had never ceased to be on friendly terms.

Maecenas impressed ancient writers by the contrast between the great energy and ability he showed in public life and the luxurious habits he flaunted as a courtier. His character as a generous patron of literature has made his name a personification of such activities. His patronage was exercised with a political object: he sought to use the genius of the poets of the day to glorify the new imperial regime of Augustus. The diversion of Virgil and Horace toward themes of public interest may be ascribed to him, and he endeavoured less successfully to do the same thing with Sextus Propertius. The relationship between Maecenas and his circle is largely a matter of conjecture, but he and Horace were certainly personal friends. It has fallen to the lot of no other patron of literature to have his name associated with works of such lasting importance as the *Georgics* of Virgil, the first three books of Horace's *Odes,* and the first book of his *Epistles.*

Maecenas himself wrote both prose and verse, but only fragments survive. His prose works on various subjects were ridiculed by Augustus, Seneca, and Quintilian for their undisciplined style.

BIBLIOGRAPHY. No trace of any formal biography of Maecenas survives from antiquity. His literary fragments are collected in R. Avallone (ed.), *Mecenate: I Frammenti* (1945). A recent biography is J.M. Andre, *Mécène, essai de biographie spirituelle* (1967). Two older works are R. Schomberg, *The Life of Maecenas: With Critical, Historical and Geographical Notes,* 2nd ed. (1766), a brief life with useful notes; and H. Richer, *Vie de Mécénas, avec des notes historiques et critiques* (1746), also brief, with copious reference to contemporary sources.

Maeda FAMILY, the daimyo, or lords, of Kaga Province (now part of Ishikawa Prefecture) in central Japan, whose domain was second only to that controlled by the powerful Tokugawa family.

Having become the dominant warrior family in west-central Japan sometime before the 16th century, the Maeda gained national prominence, as well as enlarged domains, when Maeda Toshiie (1538–99), head of the clan, allied himself with the great warrior Oda Nobunaga in his effort to reunify Japan after more than a century of civil unrest. Upon Oda's death Toshiie allied with his successor, the famed Toyotomi Hideyoshi. Before Hideyoshi died (in 1598), he appointed Maeda Toshiie as one of five regents to govern for his infant son, Hideyori.

When trouble developed among the five co-regents, Toshiie's son, Maeda Toshinaga (1562–1614), sided with Tokugawa Ieyasu, who was attempting to usurp the central power. As a reward for their services at the Battle of Sekigahara (Oct. 20, 1600), from which the Tokugawa emerged as the dominant power in Japan, the Maeda domains were considerably expanded. In terms of total taxable income, their feudal fief was second only to that of the Tokugawas, although there were other more extensive fiefs in the less fertile outlying areas.

As one of the earliest allies of the Tokugawas, the Maeda continued to maintain amicable relations with them throughout the period of Tokugawa rule, and the children of the two houses frequently intermarried. Unlike other *han,* or fiefs, the Maeda territories were never reduced, nor did the Maeda family participate in the growing opposition to Tokugawa rule in the mid-19th century. Members of the Maeda domain therefore had little influence in the new government that was established after the overthrow of the Tokugawas in 1868.

Maekawa Kunio, Maekawa also spelled MAYEKAWA (b. May 14, 1905, Niigata-shi, Japan—d. June 27, 1986, Tokyo), Japanese architect noted for his designs of community centres and his work in concrete.

After graduation from Tokyo University in 1928, Maekawa studied with the architect Le Corbusier in Paris for two years. Returning to Japan, he tried in such works as Hinamoto Hall (1936) and the Dairen Town Hall (1938) to counteract the pompous style of the Japanese imperialist regime. In the 1950s he continued to work primarily in the style of Le Corbusier. Buildings such as the Educational Centre, Fukushima (1955), the Harumi flats in Tokyo (1959), and the Setagaya Community Centre in Tokyo (1959) reflect his efforts to use concrete in a manner appropriate to the material.

Beginning with the Tokyo Metropolitan Festival Hall (1961), Maekawa displayed a warmer and more expansive style. In the Saitama Cultural Centre (1966), he brought an entirely new approach to the design of community centres. He also designed the Japanese pavilions for both the Brussels World's Fair (1958) and the New York World's Fair (1964–65).

Maelius, Spurius (d. 439 BC), wealthy Roman plebeian who allegedly tried to buy popular support with the aim of making himself king. During the severe famine of 440–439, he bought up a large store of grain and sold it at a low price to the people of Rome. This led Lucius Minucius, the patrician *praefectus annonae* ("president of the market"), to accuse Maelius of seeking to take over the government. Shortly thereafter, Maelius was killed—supposedly by a man named Gaius Servilius Ahala—and his house razed.

Maelor, Wrexham (Wales): *see* Wrexham Maelor.

Maelstrøm, Norwegian MOSKENSTRAUMEN, marine channel and strong tidal current of the Norwegian Sea, in the Lofoten islands, northern Norway. Flowing between the islands of Moskenesøya (north) and Mosken (south), it has a treacherous current. About 5 miles (8 km) wide, alternating in flow between the open sea on the west and Vestfjorden on the east, the current reaches a speed of 7 miles (11 km) per hour with the changing of the tides. Strong local winds make the passage additionally dangerous. The word maelstrom entered the English language via the fiction of the French novelist Jules Verne and the American short-story writer Edgar Allan Poe, who exaggerated the current of the channel into a great whirlpool; the word in English designates a large, fatal whirlpool, engulfing vessels and men, or a figurative application of the idea.

Maenam (river, Thailand): *see* Chao Phraya, Mae Nam.

Maerlant, Jacob van (b. 1225, Vrije van Brugge [Damme?]—d. 1291, Damme), pioneer of the didactic poetry that flourished in the Netherlands in the 14th century.

The details of Maerlant's life are disputed, but he was probably sexton at Maerlant, near Brielle on Voorne, in 1255–65?, and was employed by Albrecht van Voorne; Nicholas Cats, lord of North Beveland; and Floris V, count of Holland. About 1266 he became clerk to the court at Damme. He had an intimate knowledge of both Latin and French. His early works were versions of medieval romances—*Alexanders Geesten,* based on Gautier de Châtillon's Latin *Alexandreis;* the *Historie van den Grale Merlyn* (*c.* 1260), freely translated from Robert de Borron's early contributions to the Arthurian cycle; *Torec* (*c.* 1262); and, most important, the *Historie van Troyen* (*c.* 1264), from the *Roman de Troie* ascribed to Benoît de Sainte Maure.

When Maerlant began to write with the aim of providing instruction, he turned entirely to Latin sources, writing a scientific compilation,

Der Naturen Bloeme (1266–69?), after Thomas of Cantimpré's *De natura rerum;* a life of St. Francis (before 1273), based on Bonaventura; the *Rijmbijbel* (1271), after Petrus Comestor's *Historia Scolastica;* and, finally, his most important work, *Spieghel Historiael,* an adaptation with additions of his own of Vincent de Beauvais's *Speculum Historiale,* begun about 1282 and completed after his death by Philippe Utenbroeke and Lodewijk van Velthem. These moralizing rhymed encyclopaedic works were written to satisfy the rising class of commoners who wished for instructive reading in their own language.

His own considerable gifts as a religious poet are also fully shown in *Wapene Martijn,* a dialogue poem on the decadence of the period and moral problems, and in his fervent *Disputacie van Onser Vrouwen ende vanden Heilighen Cruce* and *Van den Lande van Oversee,* which scourges the laxity of the church and calls for a new crusade.

Maes (river, Europe): *see* Meuse River.

Maes, Nicolaes, also called NICOLAS MAAS (b. 1634, Dordrecht, Neth.—d. Nov. 24, 1693, Amsterdam), Dutch Baroque painter of genre and portraits who was a follower of Rembrandt.

"Girl at a Window," oil painting by Nicolaes Maes, *c.* 1655; in the Rijksmuseum, Amsterdam

Rijksmuseum Amsterdam

In about 1650 Maes went to Amsterdam, where he studied with Rembrandt. Before his return to Dordrecht in 1654 Maes painted a few Rembrandtesque genre pictures, with life-size figures in deep glowing colours. In the period from 1655 to 1660 Maes devoted himself to domestic genre on a smaller scale, retaining to a great extent the use of colour he had learned from Rembrandt. His favourite subjects were women spinning or reading the Bible or preparing a meal. He visited Antwerp between 1660 and 1670, after which he devoted himself almost exclusively to portraiture, abandoning intimacy and glowing colour harmonies for a careless elegance that suggests the influence of Van Dyck. The change gave rise to a theory of the existence of another Maes, of Brussels.

Maesa, Julia: *see* Julia Maesa.

Maeshowe barrow, prehistoric chambered mound located northeast of Stromness on Mainland (or Pomona) in the Orkney Islands, Scotland. The mound, probably built as a tomb for a chieftain family, was in the shape of a blunted cone, 300 feet (91 m) in circumference, and was encircled by a moat about 90 feet (27 m) from its base. The mound was probably entered from the west by a passage leading to a central apartment, the walls of which ended in a beehive roof. Maeshowe barrow has also been attributed to 10th-century Norsemen; more plausibly, a band of Norsemen at one time may have used the mound for shelter, cutting a runic record of their visit on the stones and at the same time robbing the tomb of its possessions.

Maestà (Italian: "Majesty"), double-sided altarpieces executed for the cathedral of Siena by the Italian painter Duccio. The first version (1302), originally in the Palazzo Pubblico in Siena, is now lost. The second version (Oct. 9, 1308–June 9, 1311), painted for the cathedral of Siena and one of the largest altarpieces of its time, consisted of a wide frontal panel with the Virgin and Child adored by the patrons of Siena and surrounded by saints and angels. Beneath was a predella with seven scenes from the childhood of Christ; above were pinnacles with scenes from the life of the Virgin; and on the back were scenes from the life of Christ. The main panel and the bulk of the narrative scenes are now in the Museo dell'Opera Metropolitana, Piazza del Duomo, Siena, but isolated panels from the altarpiece have found their way to the National Gallery, London; the Frick Collection, New York City; and the National Gallery of Art, Washington, D.C.

"Maestà," panel painting by Duccio, 1308–11; in the Museo dell'Opera Metropolitana, Piazza del Duomo, Siena, Italy

Alinari/Art Resource, New York City

Maestra, Sierra, mountain range in Granma and Santiago de Cuba *provincias,* southeastern Cuba. The range extends eastward from Cape Cruz, at the southern shore of the Gulf of Guacanayabo, to the Guantánamo River valley. The heavily wooded mountains rise sharply from the Caribbean coast, culminating in Turquino Peak, Cuba's highest peak, 6,470 feet (1,972 m) above sea level. The Sierra Maestra's slopes yield mahogany, cedar, ebony, and other hardwoods and are used for coffee growing. Deposits of copper, iron, manganese, silver, chromium, asphalt, and marble are found in the mountains. The area gained political prominence as the base from which Fidel Castro launched the revolution that resulted in the overthrow of Fulgencio Batista in 1959. The principal cities in the region are Santiago de Cuba and Palma Soriano.

Maestrichtian Stage: *See* Maastrichtian Stage.

Maeterlinck, Maurice, byname of MAURICE POLYDORE-MARIE-BERNARD MAETERLINCK, also called (from 1932) COUNT (comte) MAETERLINCK (b. Aug. 29, 1862, Ghent, Belg.—d. May 6, 1949, Nice, France), Belgian Symbolist poet, playwright, and essayist whose dramas are the outstanding works of the Symbolist theatre. Maeterlinck was awarded the Nobel Prize for Literature in 1911. He wrote in French and looked mainly to French literary movements for inspiration.

Maeterlinck studied law at the University of Ghent and was admitted to the bar in that city in 1886. In Paris in 1885–86 he met Villiers de L'Isle-Adam and the leaders of the Symbolist movement, and he soon abandoned law for literature. His first verse collection, *Serres chaudes* ("Hot House Blooms"), and his first play, *La Princesse Maleine,* were published in 1899. Maeterlinck made his greatest impact in the theatre. His *Pelléas et Mélisande* (1892), produced in Paris at the avant-garde Théâtre de l'Oeuvre by the director Aurélien-Marie Lugné-Poë, is the unquestioned masterpiece of Symbolist drama and provided the basis for an opera (1902) by Claude Debussy.

Set in a nebulous, fairy-tale past, the play conveys a mood of hopeless melancholy and doom in its story of the destructive passion of Princess Mélisande, who falls in love with her husband's younger brother, Pelléas. Though written in prose, *Pelléas et Mélisande* may be considered the most accomplished of all 19th-century attempts at poetic drama.

Maeterlinck, *c.* 1890

By courtesy of the City Archives of Ghent, Fondation Maeterlinck

Maeterlinck wrote many other plays, including historical dramas such as *Monna Vanna* (1902). Gradually, he tempered the influence of Symbolism by his interest in English drama, especially William Shakespeare and the Jacobeans. Only *L'Oiseau bleu* (1908; *The Blue Bird*) rivaled *Pelléas et Mélisande* in popularity. An allegorical fantasy conceived as a play for children, it portrays a search for happiness in the world. First performed by the Moscow Art Theatre (1908), this somewhat sentimental dramatic parable was highly regarded for a time, but its charm has evaporated, and the optimism of the play now seems facile. Maeterlinck's *Le Bourgmestre de Stilmonde* (1918; *The Burgomaster of Stilmonde*), a patriotic play in which he explores the problems of Flanders under the wartime rule of an unprincipled German officer, briefly enjoyed a great reputation.

In his Symbolist plays Maeterlinck uses poetic speech, gesture, lighting, setting, and ritual to create symbolic images that exteriorize his protagonists' moods and dilemmas. Often the protagonists are waiting for something mysterious and fearful that will destroy them. The profound and moving atmosphere of the plays, though lacking in intellectual complexity, is served by dialogue that is tentative, based on half-formed suggestions, at times naively repetitious, and occasionally sentimental, but sometimes possessed of great subtlety and power. Maeterlinck's plays have been widely translated, and no Belgian dramatist had greater effect on worldwide audiences.

Maeterlinck's prose writings are remarkable blends of mysticism, occultism, and interest in the world of nature. They represent the common Symbolist reaction against materialism, science, and mechanization and are concerned with such questions as the immortality of the soul, the nature of death, and the attainment of wisdom. Maeterlinck presented his mystical speculations in *Le Trésor des humbles* (1896; *The Treasure of the Humble*) and *La Sagesse et la destinée* (1898; "Wisdom and Destiny"). His most widely read prose writings, however, are two nature books, *La Vie des abeilles* (1901; *The Life of the Bee*) and *L'Intelligence des fleurs* (1907; *The Intelligence of Flowers*). These are not rigorous works of science or natural history but are instead extended essays in which Maeterlinck sets out his philosophy of the human condition. Maeterlinck was made a count by the Belgian king in 1932.

To make the best use of the Britannica, consult the INDEX *first*

Maetsuyker, Joan (b. Oct. 14, 1606, Amsterdam, Neth.—d. Jan. 4, 1678, Batavia, Dutch East Indies [now Jakarta, Indonesia]), governor-general of the Dutch East Indies from 1653 to 1678. He directed the transformation of the Dutch East India Company, then at the very height of its power, from a commercial to a territorial power.

A lawyer practicing in Amsterdam, Maetsuyker was hired by the company as a legal expert and in 1636 was sent to Batavia, where he served on the Council of Justice. In 1642 he wrote the Statutes of Batavia, the code of laws that served the Dutch during the entire period of the company's rule (1602–1867) in the East Indies.

Appointed governor of Ceylon (now Sri Lanka) in 1648, Maetsuyker paved the way for the elimination of Portuguese power there. In 1651 he was promoted to director general and in 1653 to governor-general of the East Indies, a post that he held longer than any other governor. During that quarter century the Spanish and the Portuguese were finally driven out of the Indies and their territories ceded to the Dutch. Macassar (now Ujung Pandang), the Indies' remaining important free port, was conquered and its territories taken over by the Dutch. Maetsuyker also brought most of Sumatra under Dutch supervision.

In 1674 Maetsuyker intervened in the succession to the throne of the Javanese empire of Mataram, an action that resulted in the territorial expansion of the Dutch on Java and the solid establishment of their power there.

Maéwo, also called AURORA, island of Vanuatu, in the southwestern Pacific Ocean, 65 miles (105 km) east of the island of Espiritu Santo. Volcanic in origin, it is 29 miles (47 km) long by 4 miles (6 km) wide and has an area of 104 square miles (269 square km). Maéwo's central mountain range rises to nearly 2,600 feet (795 m). Well-wooded and fertile, the island has the highest rainfall (more than 100 inches [2,500 mm] annually) in Vanuatu. Lakarere, on the northwest coast, has long been a stop for ships wanting supplies of fresh water. The east coast holds Doubtful and Deep bays. Pop. (1989) 2,362.

Maeztu, Ramiro de, in full RAMIRO DE MAEZTU Y WHITNEY (b. May 4, 1875, Vitoria, Spain—d. Oct. 29, 1936, Madrid), Spanish journalist and sociopolitical theorist.

Maeztu's mother was of English origin, his father Basque. After living in Cuba he returned to Spain and became a leading member of the Generation of '98. In 1899 he published his first book, *Hacia otra España* ("Toward Another Spain"), in which he called for Spain to break with its past and enter the European mainstream. Fluent in English, he was the London correspondent for several Spanish newspapers (1905–19) and traveled in France and Germany to cover World War I. Disillusioned by the war, he became convinced that human reason could not solve social problems. He wrote, in English, *Authority, Liberty, and Function in Light of the War,* in which he called for a reliance on authority, tradition, and the institutions of the Roman Catholic church. It was published in Spanish as *La crisis del humanismo* (1919).

On returning to Spain, Maeztu broke with his radical friends and became the most important intellectual apologist for the dictatorship of Miguel Primo de Rivera. He founded the conservative Acción Española movement and served as ambassador to Argentina in 1928. About this time he published a collection of penetrating literary essays, *Don Quijote, Don Juan y La Celestina* (1926). He was a vehement opponent of the Spanish Republic, and in his last work, *La defensa de la hispanidad* (1934; "In Defense of Spanishness"), he called for Spain to recover its 16th-century sense of Roman Catholic mission, which he considered beneficial to the conquered peoples of the old empire. Maeztu was shot by the Republicans in the early days of the Spanish Civil War.

Mafa Mucuo (China): *see* Mapam Lake.

Mafeking (South Africa): *see* Mafikeng.

Maffei, Francesco Scipione, Marchese di (marquess of) (b. June 1, 1675, Verona, republic of Venice [now in Italy]—d. Feb. 11, 1755, Verona), Italian dramatist, archaeologist, and scholar who, in his verse tragedy *Merope,* attempted to introduce Greek and French classical simplicity into Italian drama and thus prepared the way for the dramatic tragedies of Vittorio Alfieri and the librettos of Pietro Metastasio later in the 18th century.

Maffei studied at Jesuit colleges in Parma and Rome and then fought in the War of the Spanish Succession. In 1710 he was one of the founders of an influential literary journal, *Giornale dei letterati,* a vehicle for his ideas about reforming Italian drama, as was Maffei's later periodical, *Osservazioni letterarie* (1737–40). Maffei's verse tragedy *Merope* (performed and published 1713; modern ed., 1911) met with astonishing success and, because it was based on Greek mythology and the drama of Euripides and the French Neoclassical period, pointed the way for the later reform of Italian tragedy.

Maffei, engraving
By courtesy of the Biblioteca Nazionale, Florence

Maffei also wrote a number of scholarly works, librettos, occasional verse, translations of the *Iliad* and the *Aeneid,* and many plays (collected in *Teatro italiano,* 1723). His only other major work, however, aside from *Merope,* is a valuable account of the history and antiquities of his native city: *Verona illustrata,* 4 vol. (1731–32; *A Compleat History of the Ancient Amphitheatres and in particular that of Verona*).

Maffei I and II, two galaxies relatively close to the Milky Way Galaxy but unobserved until the late 1960s, when the Italian astronomer Paolo Maffei detected them by their infrared radiation. Studies in the United States established that the objects are galaxies. Lying near the border between the constellations Perseus and Cassiopeia, they are close to the plane of the Milky Way, where obscuring dust clouds in interstellar space prevent nearly all visible light emitted by external galaxies from reaching Earth.

Maffei I is a large elliptical galaxy. At about 3,000,000 light-years' distance, it is close enough to belong to what is called the Local Group of galaxies, of which the Milky Way Galaxy is a member. Maffei II has a spiral structure and is about three times farther away than Maffei I.

Mafia, hierarchically structured society of criminals of primarily Italian or Sicilian birth or extraction. The term applies to the traditional criminal organization in Sicily and also to a criminal organization in the United States.

The Mafia arose in Sicily during the late Middle Ages, where it possibly began as a secret organization dedicated to overthrowing the rule of the various foreign conquerors of the island—*e.g.,* Saracens, Normans, and Spaniards. The Mafia owed its origins and drew its members from the many small private armies, or *mafie,* that were hired by absentee landlords to protect their landed estates from bandits in the lawless conditions that prevailed over much of Sicily through the centuries. During the 18th and 19th centuries, the energetic ruffians in these private armies organized themselves and grew so powerful that they turned against the landowners and became the sole law on many of the estates, extorting money from the landowners in return for protecting the latter's crops. The Mafia survived and outlasted Sicily's successive foreign governments because the latter were often so despotic that they alienated the island's inhabitants and made tolerable the Mafia's peculiar system of private justice, which was regulated by a complicated moral code. This code was based on *omertà—i.e.,* the obligation never, under any circumstances, to apply for justice to the legal authorities and never to assist in any way in the detection of crimes committed against oneself or others. The right to avenge wrongs was reserved for the victims and their families, and to break the code of silence was to incur reprisals from the Mafia. By about 1900 the various Mafia "families" and groups of families based in the villages of western Sicily had joined together in a loose confederation, and they controlled most of the economic activities in their respective localities.

In the early 1920s Benito Mussolini's Fascist regime came close to eliminating the Mafia by arresting and trying thousands of suspected mafiosi and sentencing them to long jail terms. Following World War II, the American occupation authorities released many of the mafiosi from prison, and these men proceeded to revive the organization. The Mafia's power remained somewhat weakened in the rural areas of central and western Sicily, however, and its activities henceforth were directed more to urban Palermo—and to industry, business, and construction, as well as the traditional extortion and smuggling. During the late 1970s the Mafia in Palermo became deeply involved in the refining and transshipment of heroin bound for the United States. The enormous profits sparked fierce competition between various clans within the Mafia, and the resulting spate of murders led to renewed governmental efforts to convict and imprison the Mafia's leadership. In a 1987 "maxi-trial" 338 Sicilian mafiosi were convicted on a variety of charges.

There were, in the groups that emigrated from Sicily and Italy in the late 19th and early 20th centuries, individuals who had been part of the Mafia and who, in their new countries (particularly the United States and parts of South America), set about reproducing the criminal patterns that they had left in Europe. By the early 1930s the organized Italian criminals in the United States had wrested control of various illegal activities from rival Irish, Jewish, and other gangs, and they proceeded, after a bloody nationwide conflict in 1930–31, to organize themselves into a loose alliance with a clearly defined higher leadership. After the repeal of Prohibition in 1933, the American Mafia abandoned its bootlegging operations and settled into gambling, labour racketeering, loan-sharking, narcotics distribution, and prostitution rings. It grew to be the largest and most powerful of the U.S. syndicated-crime organizations, and it reinvested the profits accruing from crime in the ownership of such legitimate businesses as hotels, restaurants, and entertainment ventures.

Investigations conducted by U.S. government agencies in the 1950s and '60s revealed that the structure of the American Mafia was similar to that of its Sicilian prototype. (In the United States, the organization had adopted the name Cosa Nostra [Italian: "Our Affair"].) From the 1950s, Mafia operations were conducted by some 24 groups, or "families," throughout the country. In most cities where syndicated crime operated, there was one family, but in New York City there were five: Gambino, Genovese, Lucchese, Colombo, and Bonanno. The heads of the most powerful families made up a commission whose main function was judicial. At the head of each family was a "boss," or "don," whose authority could be challenged only by the commission. Each don had an underboss, who functioned as a vice president or deputy director, and a consigliere, or counselor, who had considerable power and influence. Below the underboss were the *caporegime,* or lieutenants, who, acting as buffers between the lower echelon workers and the don himself, protected him from a too-direct association with the organization's illicit operations. The lieutenants supervised squads of "soldiers," who often had charge of one of the family's legal operations (*e.g.,* vending machines, food-products companies, or restaurants) or illegal operations involving prostitution, gambling, or narcotics.

By the late 20th century the Mafia's role in U.S. organized crime seemed to be diminishing. Convictions of top officials, defections by members who became government witnesses, and murderous internal disputes thinned the ranks. In addition, the gradual breakup of insulated Italian-Sicilian communities and their assimilation into the larger American society effectively reduced the traditional breeding ground for prospective mafiosi. *See also* organized crime.

Mafia Island, island in the Indian Ocean off the eastern coast of Tanzania, eastern Africa. It lies 80 miles (130 km) southeast of Dar es-Salaam and opposite the mouth of the Rufiji River. It is 170 square miles (440 square km) in area and is separated from the mainland by a channel 10 miles (16 km) wide and 30 miles (48 km) long. The island's products include copra, limestone, and fish. The island is now part of Tanzania. Pop. (1988 prelim.) 33,054.

mafic rock, in geology, igneous rock that is dominated by the silicates pyroxene, amphibole, olivine, and mica. These minerals are high in magnesium and ferric oxides, and their presence gives mafic rock its characteristic dark colour. Mafic rock is commonly contrasted with felsic rock, in which light-coloured minerals predominate. Common mafic rocks include basalt and its coarse-grained intrusive equivalent, gabbro.

Mafikeng, formerly (until 1980) MAFEKING, town, capital of North-West province, South Africa. It was previously part of the not internationally recognized republic of Bophuthatswana, in one of that country's separated land units. It lies close to the Botswana border, about 150 miles (240 km) west of Johannesburg. Before 1980 Mafikeng was administratively within Cape Province, South Africa.

Founded in 1885 as a British military outpost, its garrison under Colonel Robert (later Lord) Baden-Powell was besieged by Boers from Oct. 12, 1899, to May 17, 1900, during the South African War; its fate excited the liveliest sympathy in England, and jubilation in London on the news of its relief led to the coining of the word "maffick." The restored fort is a national monument of South Africa. Until 1965, Mafikeng, whose name is derived from the Tswana word meaning "place of stones," was the extraterritorial headquarters of the British protectorate of Bechuanaland (now Botswana). The town is a major employer for the region, and Mmabatho, the former capital of Bophuthatswana, adjoins it on the west. Surrounded by prosperous cattle country, Mafikeng is a trade centre and supports dairy industries. Its workshops make it an important stop on the Cape Town-to-Zimbabwe railway, and a spur line connects the town to Johannesburg. Pop. (1980) 6,775.

Mafra, town, Lisboa *distrito* ("district"), west-central Portugal. It lies near the Atlantic Ocean, 18 miles (29 km) northwest of Lisbon. It is noted primarily for the National Palace (also containing a church and monastery), built (1717–35) by King John V in thanksgiving for the birth of a son and heir to

National Palace, Mafra, Port.
By courtesy of Casa de Portugal, New York

the throne. The building, which measures 700 feet (213 m) from east to west and 800 feet (244 m) from north to south, contains more than 860 rooms and has a magnificent library. The church, which is sumptuously built of marble and richly adorned with statues, low reliefs, and other objects of art, contains sculptures by the 16th-century artist Machado de Castro. In each of the towers is a carillon of 57 bells. Mafra itself is an agricultural trade centre. Limestone, basalt, granite, marble, and alabaster are quarried in the area. Pop. (1991 prelim.) 5,464.

MAG machine gun, also called FN MAG, general-purpose machine gun used primarily as a tank- or vehicle-mounted weapon, although it is also made with a butt and bipod for infantry use. Manufactured by Belgium's Fabrique Nationale d'Armes de Guerre (FN), the MAG was adopted for use by the North Atlantic Treaty Organization (NATO). It is air-cooled and gas-operated; its name is an acronym from the French phrase *mitrailleuse à gaz* ("gas-operated machine gun"). It fires a 7.62-millimetre (.31-inch) round and is fed from a metal link belt of 50 rounds. It fires automatically at a cyclic rate of 600–1,000 rounds per minute.

The MAG can be used as a medium machine gun by adding a 23-pound (10.5-kilogram) tripod. With butt and bipod, it weighs 23.9 pounds (10.8 kg). Its 21-inch (54-centimetre) barrel can be changed quickly, permitting sustained fire at a maximum effective range of 3,900 feet (1,200 m). The MAG is used by many armies around the world.

Magadan, *oblast* (province), northeastern Siberia, far eastern Russia. Magadan *oblast* is bordered by the Sea of Okhotsk to the east and southeast and by the Chukchi autonomous *okrug* to the north, Khabarovsk *kray* (region) to the southwest, and Yakut-Sakha republic to the west. Most of the *oblast* is rugged and mountainous, except for small patches of lowland along the Sea of Okhotsk. There is some poor-quality swampy forest, or taiga, of larch, fir, and birch, but most of the surface is in tundra. The climate is severely arctic. There are a number of indigenous peoples—Evens (Lamuts), Yukaghirs, Yakuts, and others, engaged chiefly in reindeer herding, fishing, and hunting. There is also a sizable Russian population. Gold is mined in the *oblast,* and there are deposits of silver, tin, and coal. Some timber is cut, and salmon and other fish are caught in the Sea of Okhotsk. Area 178,100 square miles (461,400 square km). Pop. (1993 est.) 326,500.

Magadan, port and administrative centre of Magadan *oblast* (province), far northeastern Russia. It lies at the head of Nagayevo Bay of the Gulf of Tauysk, on the northern coast of the Sea of Okhotsk. The city was founded in 1933 as the port and supply centre for the Kolyma goldfields. Engineering shops repair ships and transport and mining equipment; there are also some light industries. There are a teacher-training institute and several research institutes. Pop. (1999 est.) 121,800.

Magadha, ancient kingdom of India, situated in what is now west-central Bihār state, in northeastern India. It was the nucleus of several larger kingdoms or empires between the 6th century BC and the 8th century AD.

The early importance of Magadha may be explained by its strategic position in the Ganges River valley, enabling it to control communication and trade on the river. The river further provided a link between Magadha and the rich ports in the Ganges delta.

Under King Bimbisāra (reigned *c.* 543–*c.* 491 BC) of the Haryaṅka line, the kingdom of Aṅga (eastern Bihār) was added to Magadha. Kosala was annexed later. The supremacy of Magadha continued under the Nanda (4th century BC) and Mauryan (4th–2nd century BC) dynasties; under the Mauryan dynasty the empire included almost the entire subcontinent of India. The early centuries AD saw the decline of Magadha, but the rise of the Gupta dynasty in the 4th century brought it once more to a position of preeminence. Not only did these imperial dynasties begin by establishing their power in Magadha but in each case Pāṭaliputra (adjacent to modern Patna) was the imperial capital, thus adding to the prestige of Magadha.

Lively accounts of Pāṭaliputra and Magadha are available in the *Indica* of Megasthenes (*c.* 300 BC) and in travel diaries of the Chinese Buddhist pilgrims Fa-hsien and Hsüan-tsang

(4th–5th and 7th centuries AD). Many sites in Magadha were sacred to Buddhism. Toward the close of the 12th century, Magadha was conquered by the Muslims.

Magadi, Lake, lake, in the Great Rift Valley, southern Kenya. Lake Magadi is 20 miles (32 km) long and 2 miles (3 km) wide and is located about 150 miles (240 km) east of Lake Victoria. It occupies the lowest level of a vast depression, and its bed consists almost entirely of solid or semisolid soda. It was explored by Captain E.G. Smith in 1904, who found the outline irregular and traversed by great ridges. Several streams, both cold and hot, the latter heavily impregnated with soda, flow into the lake, while all about springs of soda water gush up through the caked crust, dyeing the waters a vivid pink. A railway from Mombasa leads to the lake, from which salt and gypsum are extracted.

Magallanes y La Antarctica Chilena, largest and southernmost *región* of Chile. Named for Ferdinand Magellan, the Portuguese navigator, it became a colonial territory in 1853 and a province in 1929. It was given its present boundaries in 1961 and established as a region in 1974. It includes the provinces of Ultima Esperanza, Magallanes, Tierra del Fuego, and Antarctica. Magallanes y La Antarctica Chilena occupies an area of 50,979 square miles (132,034 square km) and

Fort Bulnes in Magallanes y La Antarctica region, Chile
George Holton—Photo Researchers

includes the mainland west of the Argentine frontier, the numerous islands fronting the Pacific Ocean, the Archipiélago de Tierra Fuego, and the western half of Tierra del Fuego. The Chilean-claimed Antarctic region has an additional area of 480,000 square miles (1,250,000 square km). The territory west of the Andes Mountains is one of the world's most inhospitable: cool, rainy maritime conditions prevail throughout the year, and the yearly temperature range approximates 36° to 55° F (2° to 13° C). Many of the islands are barren; where forests do occur, the terrain prevents their commercial exploitation. Nevertheless, the channels, fjords, mountains, and glaciers make Magallanes a region of great scenic beauty. East of the Andes are extensive dry glacial plains covered with tussock grass, which support large sheep ranches that produce most of Chile's wool and some mutton. The development since 1945 of Chile's only oil fields in Tierra del Fuego, in the Strait of Magellan, and to the immediate north has broadened the economic base of Magallanes. Principal settlements are at Punta Arenas (*q.v.*), the regional capital; Puerto Natales; and Porvenir, on Grande Tierra del Fuego Island. Pop. (1992) excluding Chilean-claimed Antarctica, 143,486.

Magangué, city, Bolívar *departamento,* northern Colombia, on the Brazo de Loba (a branch of the Magdalena River). The original Indian village, Maganguey (Manguey), was discovered by Spanish explorers in 1532. The city was not actually founded, however, until 1610, when Diego de Carvajal expanded the indigenous settlement in the Pirinal Mountains. It later became a part of the encomienda (protected Christianized-Indian estate) of Baracoa. The present-day city has grain-processing mills, a refrigerator plant, and a fishing industry. Tropical fruits, corn (maize), coffee, and dairy products also figure in the local economy. Pop. (1985) 52,154.

Magar, also spelled MANGAR, people of Nepal and Sikkim state, India, living mainly on the western and southern flanks of the Dhaulāgiri mountain massif. They number about 390,000. The Magar speak a language of the Tibeto-Burman family. The northern Magar are Lamaist Buddhists in religion, while those farther south have come under strong Hindu influence. Most of them draw their subsistence from agriculture. Others are pastoralists, craftsmen, or day labourers. Along with the Gurung, Rai, and other Nepalese ethnic groups, they have won fame as the Gurkha soldiers of the British and Indian armies.

magatama, Korean KOGOK, chiefly Japanese jade ornament shaped like a comma with a small perforation at the thick end; it was worn as a pendant, and its form may derive from prehistoric animal-tooth pendants. There are also examples with caps made of gold or silver. In Japan, *magatama*s have been made since the Neolithic Period, but they were particularly popular during the Tumulus (Japanese Kofun) period (3rd–6th century). Along with the sword and the mirror, the *magatama* became one of the three items of Japanese imperial regalia.

In Korea, jade *magatama*s are also sporadically found at prehistoric sites, but they were in greatest vogue during the old Silla kingdom, the period corresponding to the Tumulus period in Japan. They were used as attachments to royal crowns and worn as earrings, necklaces, and the like.

magazine, also called PERIODICAL, a printed collection of texts (essays, articles, stories, poems), often illustrated, that is produced at regular intervals (excluding newspapers).

A brief treatment of magazines follows. For full treatment, *see* MACROPAEDIA: Publishing.

The modern magazine has its roots in early printed pamphlets, broadsides, chapbooks, and almanacs, a few of which gradually began appearing at regular intervals. The earliest magazines collected a variety of material designed to appeal to particular interests. One of the earliest ones was a German publication, *Erbauliche Monaths-Unterredungen* ("Edifying Monthly Discussions"), which was issued periodically from 1663 to 1668. Other learned journals soon appeared in France, England, and Italy, and in the early 1670s lighter and more entertaining magazines began to appear, beginning with *Le Mercure Galant* (1672; later renamed *Mercure de France*) in France. In the early 18th century, Joseph Addison and Richard Steele brought out *The Tatler* (1709–11; published three times weekly) and *The Spectator* (1711–12, 1714; published daily). These influential periodicals contained essays on matters political and topical that continue to be regarded as examples of some of the finest English prose written. Other critical reviews treating literary and political issues also started up in the mid-1700s throughout western Europe, and at the end of the century specialized periodicals began appearing, devoted to particular fields of intellectual interest, such as archaeology, botany, or philosophy.

By the early 19th century a different, less learned audience had been identified, and new types of magazines for entertainment and family enjoyment began to appear, among them the popular weekly, the women's weekly, the religious and missionary review, the illustrated magazine, and the children's weekly. Their growth was stimulated by the general public's broader interest in social and political affairs and by the middle and lower classes' growing demand for reading matter. Woodcuts and engravings were first extensively used by the weekly *Illustrated London News* (1842), and by the end of the 19th century many magazines were illustrated.

Magazine publishing benefited in the late 19th and 20th centuries from a number of technical improvements, including the production of inexpensive paper, the invention of the rotary press and the halftone block, and, especially, the addition of advertisements as a means of financial support. Other developments since then have included a greater specialization of topics; more illustrations, especially those reproducing colour photographs; a decline in power and popularity of the critical review and a rise in that of the mass-market magazine; and an increase in magazines for women. *See also* little magazine.

Magburaka, town, central Sierra Leone, on the Rokel River. Located on the government railway, it is a traditional trade centre (in rice, palm oil and kernels, tomatoes, and kola nuts) among the Temne people. Magburaka has government and church schools, a vocational training centre, and a government hospital. Pop. (1985 prelim.) 11,006.

Magdalen Islands, French ÎLES DE LA MADELEINE, islands in Gaspésie–Îles-de-la-Madeleine region, eastern Quebec province, Canada. They lie in the Gulf of St. Lawrence between Prince Edward Island and Newfoundland, 150 miles (240 km) southeast of Gaspé Peninsula. The group, comprising nine main islands and numerous islets, has a total area of 88 square miles (228 square km). The largest are Havre-Aubert (Amherst), Cap aux Meules (Grindstone), Loup (Wolf), and Havre aux Maisons (Alright). Fishing and fish processing are the chief occupations. The islands were discovered by the French explorer Jacques Cartier in 1534. Pop. (1991) 13,991.

Magdalena, *departamento,* northern Colombia, occupying the Caribbean lowlands and bounded by the Magdalena River on the west. Much of its area is swamp, floodplain, or high mountains (including the Sierra Nevada de Santa Marta in the northeast). The major economic activity is banana cultivation, especially in the vicinity of Santa Marta (*q.v.*), the departmental capital, which has an excellent natural harbor. Cattle are also raised in the region, and there are a number of small industries. Area 8,953 square miles (23,188 square km). Pop. (1993 est.) 994,838.

Magdalena, also called MAGDALENA CONTRERAS, or CONTRERAS, *delegación* (district), west-central Federal District, central Mexico. It lies along the Magdalena River near Cerro Ajusco. Although once simply the commercial centre for the cereals, beans, fruits, and livestock produced in the surrounding area, Magdalena gained prominence as the site of a battle (Aug. 19–20, 1847) in the Mexican War (1846–48) that enabled the U.S. general Winfield Scott to advance on Mexico City. It is now a residential and industrial neighbourhood of the federal capital, forming part of the Mexico City metropolitan area. Pop. (1990 prelim.) 195,000.

Magdalena del Mar, also called MAGDALENA NUEVA, city and *distrito* ("district") of the Lima-Callao metropolitan area of Peru, southwest of central Lima. It is bounded on the south by cliffs overlooking the Pacific Ocean. In the early 20th century the area developed as a popular resort, but it is now largely residential. The district contains the large Víctor Larco Herrera hospital complex, the Lima Cricket Club, and polo grounds. Pop. (1990 est.) district, 63,875.

Magdalena River, Spanish RÍO MAGDALENA, river, north-central Colombia. It rises at the bifurcation of the Andean Cordilleras Central and Oriental, and flows northward for 930 miles (1,497 km) to the Caribbean Sea. It receives the San Jorge, César, and Cauca rivers in the swampy floodplain of the northern lowlands. The river's mouth must be dredged to give oceangoing vessels access to

Magdalena River, Colombia
Carl Frank

the port of Barranquilla, in Atlántico department. The Magdalena is navigable by shallow-draft steamboats between Neiva, in Huila department, and the sea, interrupted only by the rapids at Honda. The course of the river is relatively straight, and although the current is fast and the depth is subject to sharp variations, it is the principal artery of riverine commerce in Colombia. It also has the greatest concentration of freshwater fishing in the country.

The Magdalena has been a major commercial artery since the Spanish conquest. From colonial times to mid-19th century, goods were carried in keelboats. Steamboats, first introduced in 1822, were profitably operated only after 1850, when a tobacco boom provided sufficient bulk cargo. In the 20th century the steamboat has been increasingly subject to competition from air, highway, and railroad transport services.

Magdalenian culture, toolmaking industry and artistic tradition of Upper Paleolithic Europe, which followed the Solutrean industry and was succeeded by the simplified Azilian; it represents the culmination of Upper Paleolithic cultural development in Europe. The Magdalenians lived some 11,000 to 17,000 years ago, at a time when reindeer, wild horses, and bison formed large herds; the people appear to have lived a semisettled life

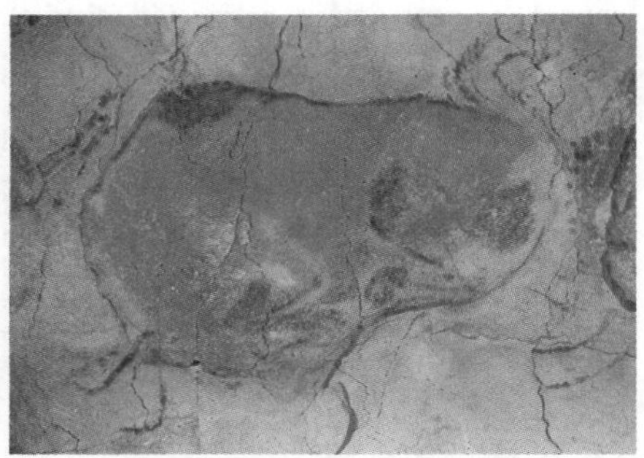

Magdalenian cave painting of a bison, Altamira, Spain
A. Held—J.P. Ziolo, Paris

surrounded by abundant food. They killed animals with spears, snares, and traps and lived in caves, rock shelters, or substantial dwellings in winter and in tents in summer. The great increase in art and decorative forms indicates the Magdalenians had leisure time. They also experienced a population explosion, living in riverside villages of 400 to 600 persons; it has been estimated that the population of France increased from about 15,000 persons in Solutrean times to over 50,000 in Magdalenian times.

Magdalenian stone tools include small geometrically shaped implements (*e.g.*, triangles, semilunar blades) probably set into bone or antler handles for use, burins (a sort of chisel), scrapers, borers, backed bladelets, and shouldered and leaf-shaped projectile points. Bone was used extensively to make wedges, adzes, hammers, spearheads with link shafts, barbed points and harpoons, eyed needles, jewelry, and hooked rods probably used as spear throwers. Bone tools were often engraved with animal images.

The widespread resumption of artistic production in the early Magdalenian Period was marked at first by a return to simple line drawing and a retreat from the Aurignacian achievements in modeling and polychromy. Generally, coarse black drawings with little concern for detail or finish characterized monumental cave art in this early phase. It may be distinguished as part of a later school by its continuation of Solutrean plastic tendencies and its correct draftsmanship in the treatment of feet and horns and of perspective in general. Later, however, as the new school consolidated itself, there was an increasing and striking naturalism in all the arts. The small arts, already at a high level in the Aurignacian era, reached a climax in the Magdalenian Period, with delicate, detailed engravings and carvings in the round; in engravings two or more animals were often represented together in a recognizable scene. The outstanding achievement of Magdalenian art, however, was the cave engraving and polychrome painting of its late phase. There was little interest in formal composition or relationships between figures, but the figures themselves, especially in painting, were remarkably beautiful, with lively realism, excellent rendering of volumes, subtle expressive poses, and sophisticated design. Some of the finest examples of this late painting are at Altamira (*q.v.*), a cave in northern Spain.

Magdalenian culture disappeared as the cool, near-glacial climate warmed at the end of the Fourth (Würm) Glacial Period (*c.* 10,000 BC), and herd animals became scarce. It has been suggested that the complexity of the later cave art represents an attempt by Magdalenian man using "sympathetic magic" to cause the animals to once more become abundant. The Azilian culture, which followed the Magdalenian, was much simplified, and there is a poverty of art; clearly the richness of Magdalenian culture owes much to the abundance of food, allowing time for leisure and the development of religion and aesthetics.

Magdeburg, city, Saxony-Anhalt *Land* (state), east-central Germany. It lies along the Elbe River, southwest of Berlin. First mentioned in 805 as a small trading settlement on the frontier of the Slavic lands, it became important under Otto I, who founded the Benedictine abbey of SS. Peter, Maurice, and Innocent there (*c.* 937). In 962 it became the seat of an archbishopric, the boundaries of which were fixed in 968, comprising the bishoprics of Havelberg, Brandenburg, Merseburg,

The cathedral at Magdeburg, Ger.
W. Krammisch—Bruce Coleman Inc./EB Inc.

Meissen, and Zeitz-Naumburg. The archbishopric played a major part in the German colonization of the Slavic lands east of the Elbe.

Although it was burned down in 1188, Magdeburg became a flourishing commercial centre in the 13th century and was a leading member of the Hanseatic League. In that century also it established an autonomous municipal administration that, known as the *Magdeburger Recht* (Magdeburg Law), was later widely adopted throughout eastern Europe. Its citizens, in almost constant conflict with the archbishops, became nearly independent of them by the end of the 15th century. Magdeburg embraced the Reformation in 1524 and was thenceforth governed by Protestant titular archbishops. During the Thirty Years' War it successfully resisted a siege by imperial forces under Albrecht von Wallenstein in 1629 but was stormed in 1631 by Johann von Tilly, who burned and sacked the city and butchered about 20,000 of the city's 30,000 inhabitants.

By the Peace of Westphalia (1648) the archbishopric became a secular duchy, passing to the electorate of Brandenburg on the death of the last administrator in 1680. In 1806 the fortress of Magdeburg surrendered to Napoleon without fighting and was included in the kingdom of Westphalia until 1813. In 1815 the city became the capital of the newly constituted Prussian province of Saxony. The fortress was dismantled in 1912.

Heavy bombing in 1945 destroyed much of the city, including the Renaissance town hall (1691). The Romanesque and Gothic Cathedral of SS. Maurice and Catherine (1209–1520) survived, and the Church of Our Lady (begun *c.* 1070), the oldest church in the city, has been restored. The Magdeburger Reiter (Magdeburg Rider), the oldest German equestrian statue (*c.* 1240), and the two accompanying female figures, can be seen in the town's museum. There are numerous schools and technical colleges and a medical academy.

The physicist Otto von Guericke, the composer Georg Telemann, and the soldier Frederick William, Baron von Steuben were born in Magdeburg.

The city's important industrial and commercial facilities have been restored and expanded since World War II. It is now a centre of food processing, particularly sugar refining and flour milling, and of metalworking and heavy engineering. A chemical industry and textile milling are also significant. Magdeburg is situated at a natural crossroads on the Elbe at the junction of six major railway lines and seven arterial highways and is linked to the Rhine River by the Mittelland Canal and with Berlin and the lower Oder River by another system of canals. During the period of German partition, it was the most important inland port of East Germany. Pop. (1990 est.) 288,355.

Magelang, *kotamadya* (municipality) and *kabupaten* (regency), Jawa Tengah *provinsi* ("province"), Java, Indonesia. Magelang regency, 436 square miles (1,130 square km) in area, is one of the most densely populated in Java, and its fertile land produces rice, tobacco, sugar, and produce for Yogyakarta. Magelang city, 25 miles (40 km) north-northwest of Yogyakarta, lies along the Progo River, which empties into the Indian Ocean. A tourist centre for those visiting the Borobuḍur, Pawon, and Mendut temples, the city has a large Roman Catholic seminary and a military academy. There are fine views of Mount Sumbing (11,060 feet [3,371 m]), an active volcano that contains an archaeologically interesting grave site. The pyramidal Buddhist "temple-mountain" of Borobuḍur, rising 100 feet (30 m) above the base, is just south of Magelang; built about AD 800, it consists of a series of galleries of bas-reliefs joined by stairways, all leading to platforms with arrangements of statues and to a large, empty *stūpa* at the peak. Pop. (1990) city, 167,842; regency, 1,015,809.

Magellan, Ferdinand, Portuguese FERNÃO DE MAGALHÃES, Spanish FERNANDO, or HERNANDO, DE MAGALLANES (b. *c.* 1480, Sabrosa, or Porto?, Port.—d. April 27, 1521, Mactan, Phil.), Portuguese navigator and explorer who sailed under the flags of both Portugal (1505–12) and Spain (1519–21). From Spain he sailed around South America, discovering

Magellan, detail of a painting by an unknown artist; in the Uffizi Gallery, Florence

Alinari—Art Resource/EB Inc.

the Strait of Magellan, and across the Pacific. Though he was killed in the Philippines, his ships continued westward to Spain, accomplishing the first circumnavigation of the world. The voyage was successfully terminated by the Basque navigator Juan Sebastián de Elcano (del Cano).

Early life. Magellan, the son of Rui de Magalhães and Alda de Mesquita, belonged to the Portuguese nobility. At an early age he became a page to Queen Leonor in Lisbon.

In early 1505 he enlisted in the fleet of Francisco de Almeida, first Portuguese viceroy in the East, whose expedition, sent by King Manuel to check Muslim sea power in Africa and India, left Lisbon on March 25. During a naval engagement at Cannanore on the Malabar Coast of India, Magellan is said by the chronicler Gaspar Correia to have been wounded. Though Correia states that during this early period of his Indian service he acquired considerable knowledge of navigation, little is known of Magellan's first years in the East until he appears among those sailing in November 1506 with Nuno Vaz Pereira to Sofala on the Mozambique coast, where the Portuguese established a fort. In 1508 he was back in India, taking part, on Feb. 2–3, 1509, in the great Battle of Diu, which gave the Portuguese supremacy over most of the Indian Ocean. Reaching Cochin in the fleet of Diogo Lopes de Sequeira, he left as one of the men-at-arms for Malacca. Magellan is mentioned as being sent to warn the commander of impending attack by Malays and during the subsequent fighting courageously saved the life of a Portuguese explorer, Francisco Serrão, who later from the Moluccas (Maluku) sent him helpful information about those islands. At a council held at Cochin on October 10, to decide on plans for recapturing Goa, he advised against taking large ships at that season, but the new viceroy, Afonso de Albuquerque, did so, the city falling on November 24; Magellan's name does not appear among those who fought. There is no conclusive evidence for the theory that during his Indian service he attained the rank of captain.

The Portuguese victories off the eastern coast of Africa and the western coast of India had broken Muslim power in the Indian Ocean, and the purpose of Almeida's expedition—to wrest from the Arabs the key points of sea trade—was almost accomplished; but without control of Malacca their achievement was incomplete. At the end of June 1511, therefore, a fleet under Albuquerque left for Malacca, which fell after six weeks. This event, in which Magellan took part, was the crowning Portuguese victory in the Orient. Through Malacca passed the wealth of the East to the harbours of the West, and in the command of the Malacca Strait the Portuguese held the key to the seas and ports of Malaysia. It remained to explore the wealth-giving Moluccas, the islands of spice. Accordingly, early in December 1511 they sailed on a voyage of reconnaissance and after reaching Banda returned with spice in 1512. The claim made by some that Magellan went on this voyage rests on unproved statements by Giovanni Battista Ramusio and Leonardo de Argensola, and the want of evidence argues against its acceptance. Even if he did, in truth, reach the Moluccas, a further voyage—which he later commanded from Spain to the Philippines—was required to complete the circle of navigation.

In 1512 Magellan was back in Lisbon; the following year he joined the forces sent against the Moroccan stronghold of Azamor and in a skirmish after its fall sustained a wound that caused him to limp for the rest of his life. Returning to Lisbon in November 1514 he asked King Manuel for a token increase in his pension, signifying a rise in rank. But unfounded reports of irregular conduct on his part after the siege of Azamor had reached the King, who, refusing his request, ordered him back to Morocco. Early in 1516 Magellan renewed his petition; the King, refusing once more, told him he might offer his services elsewhere.

Allegiance to Spain. Magellan therefore went to Spain, reaching Seville on Oct. 20, 1517. He was joined by the Portuguese cosmographer Rui Faleiro, and together they journeyed to the court at Valladolid. There, having renounced their nationality, the two men offered their services to King Charles I (later, Emperor Charles V). Magalhães henceforward became known by the Spanish version of his name—Fernando de Magallanes.

By decree of a papal bull in 1493, all new territories discovered or that should be discovered east of a line of demarcation (redrawn 1494) were assigned to Portugal, all that lay west to Spain. Magellan and Faleiro now proposed by sailing west to give practical proof of their claim that the wealth-giving Spice Islands lay west of the line of demarcation—that is, within the Spanish, not the Portuguese, hemisphere. On March 22, 1518, their proposal received royal assent; they were appointed joint captains general of an expedition directed to seek an all-Spanish route to the Moluccas. The government of any lands discovered was to be vested in them and their heirs, and they were to receive a one-twentieth share of the net profits from the venture; both were invested with the Order of Santiago. Magellan was convinced that he would lead his ships from the Atlantic to the "Sea of the South" by discovering a strait through Tierra Firme. This idea did not originate with him; others had sought a passage by which vessels sailing continuously westward would reach the East and thus avoid the Cape of Good Hope, which was controlled by the Portuguese; in the royal agreement Magellan and Faleiro were directed to find "the" strait. The officials entrusted with East Indian affairs were instructed to furnish five ships for the expedition, prepared in Seville, where an unsuccessful attempt to wreck the project was made by Portuguese agents. Magellan's flagship, "Trinidad," had as consorts "San Antonio," "Concepción," "Victoria," and "Santiago." An attack of insanity prevented Faleiro from sailing.

Magellan, who in 1517 married Beatriz Barbosa, daughter of an important official in Seville, said farewell to his wife and infant son Rodrigo before his ships left Sanlúcar de Barrameda on Sept. 20, 1519, carrying about 270 men, among whom nine countries were represented. The fleet reached Tenerife on September 26, sailing on October 3 for Brazil; becalmed off the Guinea coast, it met storms before reaching the line; on November 29 it was 27 leagues southwest of Cape St. Augustine. Rounding Cabo Frio, Magellan entered the Bay of Rio de Janeiro on December 13, then sailing south to the Río de la Plata vainly probed the estuary, seeking the strait. On March 31 he reached Port St. Julian in latitude 49° 20′ S, where on Easter day at midnight Spanish captains led a serious mutiny against the Portuguese commander. Magellan with resolution, ruthlessness, and daring quelled it, executing one of the captains and leaving another to his fate ashore when, on Aug. 24, 1520, the fleet left St. Julian.

Discovery of the Strait of Magellan. After reaching the mouth of the Santa Cruz, near which "Santiago," reconnoitring, had been wrecked earlier, Magellan started south again, on October 21 rounding the Cape of the Virgins (Cabo Vírgenes), and at approximately 52° 50′ S entered the passage that proved to be the strait of his seeking, later to bear his name. "San Antonio" having deserted, only three of his ships reached the western end of the passage; at the news that the ocean had been sighted the iron-willed admiral broke down and cried with joy.

On November 28 "Trinidad," "Concepción," and "Victoria" entered the "Sea of the South," from their calm crossing later called the Pacific Ocean. Tortured by thirst, stricken by scurvy, feeding on rat-fouled biscuits, finally reduced to eating the leather off the yardarms, the crews, driven first by the Peru Current and throughout the voyage by the relentless determination of Magellan, made the great crossing of the Pacific. Until December 18 they had sailed near the Chilean coast; then Magellan took a course northwestward; not until Jan. 24, 1521, was land sighted, probably Pukapuka in the Tuamotu Archipelago. Crossing the equinoctial line at approximately 158° W on February 13, the voyagers on March 6 made first landfall at Guam in the Marianas, where they obtained fresh food for the first time in 99 days. A *Memorial,* sent by Magellan to King Charles before leaving Spain, suggests that he knew (probably partly from Serrão's letters) the approximate position of the Moluccas; in sailing now to the Philippines instead of direct to the Spice Islands, he was doubtless dominated by the idea of early revictualing and the advantage of securing a base before visiting the Moluccas.

Leaving on March 9, Magellan steered west-southwestward to islands later called the Philippines, where at Massava he secured the first alliance in the Pacific for Spain, at Cebú the conversion to Christianity of the ruler and his chief men. Less than two months later, however, Magellan was killed in a fight with natives on Mactan Island.

Circumnavigation of the globe. After Magellan's death only two of the ships, "Trinidad" and "Victoria," reached the Moluccas; only one, "Victoria" (85 tons), returned to Spain, under command of Elcano, originally master on "Concepción," and participator in the mutiny at Port St. Julian. For bringing home, on Sept. 8, 1522, the leaking but spice-laden ship, with only 17 other European survivors and 4 Indians, "weaker than men have ever been before," Elcano received from the Emperor an augmentation to his coat of arms, a globe with the inscription "Primus circumdedisti me" ("You were the first to encircle me"). It had been left for Elcano, returning by the Cape route, to give practical proof that the Earth was round.

Magellan's accomplishment lies in his bold conception and masterly direction of the enterprise that achieved the first circumnavigation of the globe. The first navigator to cross the Pacific from east to west, he disproved the prevailing idea that a mere few days westward sailing from the New World would bring ships to the East Indies. Instead, after a crossing lasting more than three months, he brought a fleet within easy distance of them. Magellan, with a character so complex and of such extreme contradictions, will remain an enigma; psychologically he cannot have been at peace with himself. For his transference of allegiance many writers have denounced him, bearing in mind that in his time the loyalty of a Portuguese to his sovereign was second only to his loyalty to his God; others have pointed out that in offering his services to another ruler Magellan did what Christopher Columbus, Sebastian Cabot, and Amerigo Vespucci had done and that limitations imposed by nationality are irreconcilable with the advancement of knowledge. But on one thing all Portuguese are agreed: "He is ours." (M.Mi.)

BIBLIOGRAPHY. The fullest account of Magellan's remarkable voyage is that of Antonio Pigafetta, who sailed with Magellan and returned with Elcano. The text of the Italian version, translated, edited, and annotated by James Alexander Robertson, is *Magellan's Voyage Around the World,* 3 vol. (1906). *The First Voyage Round the World, by Magellan,* edited and translated by Lord Stanley of Alderley (Henry Edward Stanley) (1874, reprinted 1963), also includes the account of Pigafetta, as well as accounts by other members of the expedition.

Important introductory works on the life of Magellan include F.H.H. Guillemard, *The Life of Ferdinand Magellan and the First Circumnavigation of the Globe, 1480–1521* (1890, reprinted 1971); E.F. Benson, *Ferdinand Magellan* (1929); and Edouard Roditi, *Magellan of the Pacific* (1972).

Magellan, Strait of, Spanish ESTRECHO DE MAGALLANES, channel linking the Atlantic and Pacific oceans, between the mainland tip of South America and Tierra del Fuego island. Lying entirely within Chilean territorial waters, except for its easternmost extremity touched by Argentina, it is 350 miles (560 km) long and 2–20 miles (3–32 km) wide. It extends westward from the Atlantic between Cape Vírgenes and Cape Espíritu Santo, proceeds southwestward, and curves to the northwest at Froward Cape on the southern tip of Brunswick Peninsula to reach the Pacific Ocean after passing Cape Pillar on Desolación Island. The strait's major port is Punta Arenas, on the Brunswick Peninsula; the port is a shipping point for Chilean mutton.

The strait was first navigated (Oct. 21–Nov. 28, 1520) by Ferdinand Magellan, a Portuguese sailing for Spain, whose expedition eventually completed the first circumnavigation of the world. Although the strait follows a somewhat tortuous course among numerous islands and channels and has a cold, foggy climate, it was an important sailing-ship route before the building of the Panama Canal (completed in 1914) shortened the Atlantic-Pacific passage by several thousand miles.

Magellanic Cloud, either of two satellite galaxies of the Milky Way Galaxy, the vast star system of which the Earth is a minor component. These companion galaxies were named for the Portuguese navigator Ferdinand Magellan, whose crew discovered them during the first voyage around the world. The Magellanic Clouds are irregular galaxies that share a gaseous envelope and lie about 22° apart in the sky near the south celestial pole. One of them, the Large Magellanic Cloud (LMC), is a luminous patch about 5° in diameter, and the other, the Small Magellanic Cloud (SMC), measures less than 2° across. Although in the Southern Hemisphere the Magellanic Clouds are visible to the unaided eye, they cannot be observed from the northern latitudes. The LMC is more than 150,000 light-years from the Earth and the SMC lies roughly 200,000 light-years away.

The Magellanic Clouds were probably formed several billion years after the Milky Way system condensed from debris left behind by the big bang, a violent expansion of an intensely compressed single mass of material that is believed to have given rise to the universe. They contain numerous young stars and star clusters that were formed from nebulous clouds of pristine gas, as well as some substantially older stars. The Magellanic Clouds serve as excellent laboratories for the study of slightly retarded though very active stellar formation and evolution.

Magen David (Jewish symbol): *see* David, Star of.

Magendie, François (b. Oct. 6, 1783, Bordeaux, Fr.—d. Oct. 7, 1855, Sannois), French experimental physiologist who was the first to prove the functional difference of the spinal nerves. His pioneer studies of the effects of drugs on various parts of the body led to the scientific introduction into medical practice of such compounds as strychnine and morphine. In 1822 he confirmed and elaborated the observation by the Scottish anatomist Sir Charles Bell (1811) that the anterior roots of the spinal nerves are motor in function, while the posterior roots serve to communicate sensory impulses.

Appointed professor of medicine at the Collège de France, Paris (1831), Magendie was one of the first to observe anaphylaxis (an exaggerated reaction by an animal to the injection into its blood of a foreign protein) when he found (1839) that rabbits able to tolerate a single injection of egg albumin often died following a second injection. Founder of the first periodical of experimental physiology, *Journal de Physiologie Expérimentale* (1821), Magendie greatly influenced the intellectual development of the renowned French physiologist Claude Bernard, one of his students (1841–43). Magendie was elected to the French Academy of Sciences in 1821 and served as its president in 1837.

Magendie, detail of a lithograph by Grégoire and Deneux

Boyer—H. Roger-Viollet

Magenta, town, Milano *provincia,* Lombardia (Lombardy) *regione,* northern Italy, just west of Milan. Its name is derived from that of Marcus Maxentius, a Roman general and emperor (AD 306–312) who had his headquarters there at Castra Maxentia. The town was the site of the Battle of Magenta (June 4, 1859), fought during the Franco-Piedmontese war against the Austrians (second War of Italian Independence, 1859–61). Napoleon III and his 54,000 troops met 58,000 Austrian troops under General Franz Gyulai in a highly disorganized battle that left some 9,700 dead or injured and 4,600 missing. The narrow French victory over the Austrians was an important step toward Italian independence, for it led many districts and cities, beginning with Bologna on June 12, to throw off Austrian rule and join the cause of Italian unity. The battle is commemorated by an ossuary containing the remains of 9,000 of the dead.

Contemporary Magenta is a communications centre between Milan and Turin; its chief industries are the manufacture of matches, cotton and artificial silk, and machinery. Pop. (1988 est.) mun., 23,658.

Magenta, Marie-Edme-Patrice-Maurice Mac-Mahon, duc de (duke of): *see* Mac-Mahon, Marie-Edme-Patrice-Maurice, comte de.

maggid (Hebrew: "preacher"), plural MAGGIDIM, any of the many itinerant Jewish preachers who flourished especially in Poland and Russia during the 17th and 18th centuries. Because rabbis at that time preached only on the Sabbaths preceding Pesaḥ (Passover) and Yom Kippur (Day of Atonement), maggidim were in great demand throughout the year to instruct, encourage, and sometimes admonish their congregation. Through their preaching, the maggidim were instrumental in spreading the 18th-century pietistic movement called Ḥasidism. Rabbi Dov Baer of Mezhirich, who succeeded Ba'al Shem Ṭov as leader of the Ḥasidic movement in the 18th century, is known as the Great Maggid.

Closely associated with the maggidim were other itinerant preachers called *mokhiḥim* ("reprovers," or "rebukers"), whose self-appointed task was to admonish their listeners of severe punishments if they failed to observe the commandments. A heavenly being (or voice) that revealed secret meanings to a Jewish mystic was also called a maggid.

To make the best use of the Britannica, consult the INDEX *first*

Maggiore, Lake, Italian LAGO MAGGIORE, Latin LACUS VERBANUS, second largest lake in Italy (area 82 square miles [212 square km]), bisected by the border between Lombardy (east) and Piedmont (west). Its northern end is in the Swiss Ticino *canton.* At an elevation of 636 feet (194 m) above sea level, the lake is 34 miles (54 km) long, with a maximum width of 7 miles (11 km) and a maximum depth of 1,220 feet (370 m). The lake is traversed from north to south by the Ticino River, and its other principal affluents are the Maggia from the north, the Toce from the west, and the short Tresa from Lake Lugano on the east. Off the western shore are the famous Borromean Islands, geologic continuations of the Pallanza Promontory. Lake Maggiore is bordered by the Swiss Alps to the north and by the Lombardian Plain and has a warm, mild climate.

The greatest landowners around the lake since the 15th century have been the Borromeo family, who still own the islands and fishery rights. The lake's name, meaning "greater," refers to its being considerably larger than the neighbouring Orta and Varese lakes.

There is fishing for trout, pike, perch, and shad. Well-known lakeside resorts on the western shore are Stresa, Verbania, Arona, and Cannobio. Other towns are Luino and Laveno, on the eastern shore, and Locarno, Switz., at the northern end. Small steamers ply between them. Southwest of Verbania rises Mount Mottarone (4,892 feet [1,491 m]) between Lake Maggiore and Lake Orta.

Magh, also spelled MOGH (people): *see* Marma.

maghemite, also called GAMMA-Fe_2O_3, an iron oxide mineral. It has a composition close to ferric oxide (Fe_2O_3) and exhibits strong magnetism and remanence. Its structure is isometric, of defective spinel form, and somewhat iron-deficient. Maghemite is metastable with respect to hematite and forms a continuous metastable solid solution with magnetite; titanium can substitute for iron, giving rise to titanomaghemite. Natural maghemite forms by oxidation of magnetite. Synthetic maghemite, produced by dehydrating lepidocrocite or oxidizing magnetite at a low temperature, is used as a magnetic-recording medium.

Magherafelt, Irish MACHAIRE FÍOLTA, town, seat, and district (established 1973), formerly within County Londonderry, Northern Ireland. Magherafelt town was originally an English-company (Plantation of Ulster) town and is now the marketing centre and administrative seat of the district; Maghera town, 9 miles (14 km) to the northwest, was the birthplace of Charles Thomson (1730–1824), who served as secretary to the First and Second U.S. Continental Congresses (1774–89) and who wrote out the Declaration of Independence. Motor-vehicle components are manufactured in nearby Tobermore, and Draperstown has an important metal-fabrication industry.

Magherafelt district covers an area of 245 square miles (635 square km) and is bounded by the River Bann and Lough (lake) Neagh on the east and by the Sperrin Mountains on the west. It borders the districts of Antrim and Ballymena to the east; Coleraine to the north; Limavady, Strabane, and Omagh to the west; and Cookstown to the south. Gently rolling lowlands in the east rise gradually westward to elevations of more than 1,800 feet (550 m) above sea level in the Sperrin Mountains. The district is largely agricultural; its chief crops include potatoes, barley, flax, and oats. There is salmon fishing along the River Bann, and granite is quarried in the Sperrin Mountains. Pop. (1981) town, 5,044; (1998 est.) district, 37,900.

Maghiāna, one of the twin towns of Jhang Maghiāna (*q.v.*), Pakistan.

Maghnia, formerly MARNIA, town, northwestern Algeria, on the northern edge of the Hauts Plateau, 8 miles (13 km) east of the Moroccan border. The modern town grew around a French redoubt built in 1844 on the site of the Roman post of Numerus Syrorum. It was named for the local Muslim saint Lalla Maghnia and contains her mausoleum, probably built in the 18th century. Located within the watershed of Wadi Tafna, Maghnia is a busy agricultural centre, trading in cereals and wool from both Algeria and Morocco. There is a lead mine at Bou Beker, 18 miles (29 km) south in the Tell Atlas, and a noted mineral spring, Hammam Boughrara, 6 miles (10 km) to the northeast. Pop. (1998 prelim.) 73,274.

Maghreb, also spelled MAGHRIB (Arabic: "West"), region of North Africa bordering the Mediterranean Sea. The Africa Minor of the ancients, it at one time included Moorish Spain and now comprises essentially the Atlas Massif and coastal plain of Morocco, Algeria, Tunisia, and Libya. The weather of the Maghreb is characterized by prevailing westerly winds, which drop most of their moisture on the northern slopes and coastal plain, leaving little for the southern slopes, which maintain desert scrub fading into true desert in the Sahara to the south.

From the vastness of their mountain ranges, the native peoples of the Maghreb have resisted successive Punic, Roman, and Christian invasions. Not until the 7th and 8th centuries was the Maghreb conquered; the Arabs, who imposed on the native peoples the religion of Islām and Arabic, the language of the Qur'ān, thus absorbed the Maghreb into the Muslim civilization. Despite this absorption, most of the North African societies have preserved their cultural identity throughout the centuries.

The people of the Maghreb are ethnically Berbers and Arabs. Denizens of the Maghreb since ancient times, the Berbers probably originated in a mingling of races during the Paleolithic and Neolithic periods. The Berber stock displays a wide variety of physical characteristics, and their social and cultural characteristics are also quite diverse. Underlying all these differences, however, is a common ethnic substratum. The long succession of invaders, ranging from the Phoenicians to the Arabs and finally to the French, did not lead to much interbreeding. About one-sixth of the population of the Maghreb (most of whom live in Algeria and Morocco) still speak one of the Berber languages, but most speak some form of Arabic.

maghrebi script, maghrebi also spelled MAGHRIBI, in calligraphy, Islāmic cursive style of handwritten alphabet that developed directly from the early Kūfic angular scripts used by the Muslim peoples of the Maghreb, who were western-oriented and relatively isolated from eastern Islām. The script they developed is rounded, with exaggerated extension of horizontal elements and final open curves below the register. Maghrebi is still used in northern Africa from Morocco to Tripoli.

Magi, singular MAGUS, also called WISE MEN, in Christian tradition, the noble pilgrims "from the East" who followed a miraculous guiding star to Bethlehem, where they paid homage to the infant Jesus as king of the Jews (Matt. 2:1–12). Christian theological tradition has always stressed that Gentiles as well as Jews came to worship Jesus—an event celebrated in the Eastern church at Christmas and in the West at Epiphany (January 6). Eastern tradition sets the number of Magi at 12, but Western tradition sets their number at 3, probably based on the three gifts of "gold and frankincense and myrrh" (Matt. 2:11) presented to the infant.

The Gospel of Matthew relates how at Jerusalem they attracted the interest of King Herod I of Judaea by announcing Jesus' birth: "Where is he who has been born king of the Jews? For we have seen his star in the East, and have come to worship him" (Matt. 2:2). Herod extracted from them the place of Jesus' birth, requesting that they disclose the exact spot upon their return. They continued on to Bethlehem, where they worshipped Jesus and offered him gifts. Warned in a dream not to return to Herod, "they departed to their own country by another way" (Matt. 2:12).

Subsequent traditions embellished the narrative. As early as the 3rd century, they were considered to be kings, probably interpreted as the fulfillment of the prophecy in Ps. 72:11 ("May all kings fall down before him"). In about the 8th century the names of three Magi—Bithisarea, Melichior, and Gathaspa—appear in a chronicle known as the *Excerpta latina barbari.* They have become known most commonly as Balthasar, Melchior, and Gaspar (or Casper). According to Western church tradition, Balthasar is often represented as a king of Arabia, Melchior as a king of Persia, and Gaspar as a king of India.

Their supposed relics were transferred from Constantinople, possibly in the late 5th century, to Milan and thence to Cologne Cathedral in the 12th century. Devotion to the Magi was especially fervent in the European Middle Ages. The Magi are venerated as patrons of travelers; their feast day is July 23.

The Adoration of the Magi—*i.e.,* their homage to the infant Jesus—early became one of the most popular themes in Christian art, the first extant painting on the subject being the fresco in the Priscilla Catacomb of Rome dating from the 2nd century. In the Middle Ages the Adoration of the Magi was often associated with two other major events of Jesus' life: his Baptism, during which the voice of God publicly declared Jesus to be his son, and the wedding at Cana, at which he revealed his divinity by changing water into wine. The three events, all celebrated on the same feast day, were frequently represented together in the monumental sculpture that decorated the churches of the period.

magi (Persian priests): *see* magus.

magic, ritual performance or activity believed to influence human or natural events through access to an external mystical force beyond the ordinary human sphere. It constitutes the core of many religious systems and plays a central social role in many nonliterate cultures.

A brief treatment of magic follows. For full treatment, *see* MACROPAEDIA: Occultism.

At one time magic was considered entirely distinct from religion, as consisting of external manipulation rather than supplication and inner grace, and it is still so regarded by many religious thinkers. Contemporary anthropologists and historians of religion, however, tend to hold that since both magic and religion are

"The Adoration of the Magi," oil painting by Albrecht Dürer, 1504; in the Uffizi, Florence

concerned with the effects on human existence of outside mystical forces, they are generically similar and connected.

There are usually considered to be three main elements in magic: the spell or incantation, the rite itself, and the ritual condition of the performer. Excellent examples of spells are recorded from the earliest times and especially in Greco-Egyptian papyruses of the 1st to the 4th century AD. These include both magical recipes involving animals and animal substances and also instructions for the rites necessary to ensure the efficacy of the spells. The frequently archaic and esoteric vocabulary of incantations may represent in a symbolic sense the mysterious nature of spiritual power and in a practical sense the restriction of human access to it. Personal names are commonly used in spells by magicians to work good or harm upon individuals. This power is regarded in some societies as so strong that each individual bears two names—a "real" one that is kept a careful secret and an everyday title, through which no magic can be worked. Gods and spirits are commonly believed to have special magic names, known only to a chosen few. Along with spells may be included the material objects or "medicines" used in many societies.

The techniques of magic have generally been interpreted as supposed means to specific ends (*e.g.,* the ensuring of an enemy's defeat; the summoning of rain). Another view ascribes a more symbolic, expressive character to such activity. The magic may serve to state and maintain the formal culture and organization of the society; thus, a rainmaking ritual has also the function of stressing the importance of rain and the agricultural activities associated with it.

Even though regarded as an everyday and "natural" phenomenon in the societies it characterizes, magic is nonetheless considered as potentially dangerous and polluting, as is any sacred or religious object or activity. Both the magician and the rite itself are typically surrounded by the observance of taboos, by purification procedures, and the like. Failure to observe such precautions nullifies the magic, and the precautions indicate to the participants and witnesses the importance of the rite itself and the ends desired.

Strains of magic in the Western tradition, formerly associated with heretics, alchemists, witches, and sorcerers, persist in modern times in the activities of witches (Wiccans) and Neopagans.

magic number, in physics, in the shell models of both atomic and nuclear structure, any of a series of numbers that connote stable structure. They designate the sum of electrons in atoms or the sum of either protons or neutrons in nuclei that occupy completely filled, or closed, shells.

The magic numbers for atoms are 2, 10, 18, 36, 54, and 86, corresponding to the total number of electrons in filled electron shells. In the chemical elements of atomic number 17 to 19, for example, the chloride ion (Cl^-), the argon atom (Ar), and the potassium ion (K^+) have 18 electrons in closed-shell configurations and are chemically quite stable. The number of electrons present in the neutral atoms constituting the relatively unreactive noble gases exactly correspond to the atomic magic numbers.

The magic numbers for nuclei are 2, 8, 20, 28, 50, 82, and 126, corresponding to the total number of protons or neutrons in filled nuclear shells. Thus, tin (atomic number 50), with 50 protons in its nucleus, has 10 stable isotopes, whereas indium (atomic number 49) and antimony (atomic number 51) have only 2 stable isotopes apiece. The doubly magic alpha particle, or helium-4 nucleus, composed of two protons and two neutrons, is very stable.

magic square, square matrix often divided into cells, filled with numbers or letters in particular arrangements that were once thought to have special, magical properties. Originally used as religious symbols, they later became

S	A	T	O	R
A	R	E	P	O
T	E	N	E	T
O	P	E	R	A
R	O	T	A	S

Magic square

protective charms or tools for divination; and finally, when the original meanings were lost, people considered them mere curiosities or puzzles—except for some Western mathematicians who continue to study them as problems in number theory.

The most familiar lettered square in the Western world is the well-known SATOR square, composed of the words SATOR, AREPO, TENET, OPERA, and ROTAS. Arranged both vertically and horizontally, the meaningless phrase reads through the centre TENET, thus forming the two arms of a hidden cross. Examples of this square from the 1st century AD were found in the ruins of Pompeii, and it was still employed during the 19th century in Europe and the United States for fancied protection against fire, sickness, and other disasters.

Otherwise, numbered squares have always been far more significant, particularly in China (where they may have originated), the Arab world, and India.

In the arithmetical magic squares, the numbers are generally placed in separate cells and arranged so that each column, every row, and the two main diagonals can produce the same sum, called the constant. A standard magic square of any given number contains the sequence of natural numbers from 1 to the square of that number. Thus, the magic square of 3 contains the numbers 1 to 9. If these nine numbers are simply listed in three rows or three columns, they form the natural square of 3. A natural square has no "magical" properties, but one is often made as a first step in constructing a proper magic square. When these nine numbers in the 3×3 frame are rearranged so that they can produce a constant sum of 15, they constitute the magic square of 3.

magician, one who practices magic, sometimes considered the same as a sorcerer or witch. Conjurers are also sometimes called magicians, reflecting a historical confusion whereby legerdemain was considered to involve the supernatural. The name derives from the magus (*q.v.*), an ancient Persian priest, and the cognate *maghdim,* a Chaldean term meaning wisdom and philosophy.

Though magic may theoretically be morally neutral, and many self-styled practitioners have claimed so, magicians have throughout European history usually been feared for their powers of wreaking evil. In some societies, the magician is typically an accepted personage whose help may be sought to accomplish a goal or ward off evil. *See* magic.

Magill, Helen: *see* White, Helen Magill.

Magindanao, second largest of the Muslim cultural-linguistic groups of the Philippines. The Magindanao, numbering about 700,000 at the turn of the 21st century, live along the shores and floodlands of the Cotabato River in the southern island of Mindanao. They are chiefly rice farmers.

Like the other Filipino Muslims, they differ markedly from the Christians, who represent the overwhelming majority of the country's population. Land is owned by the clan and controlled by local leaders known as *datu*s. The customs of marriage and the family are Islāmic. All the languages of the Muslim groups are closely related to the languages of the central Philippines, which belong to the Austronesian (Malayo-Polynesian) family of languages.

Maginot, André(-Louis-René) (b. Feb. 17, 1877, Paris—d. Jan. 7, 1932, Paris), French statesman for whom a French line of elaborate fortifications against Germany was named. The Maginot Line contributed in large part to French complacency in the face of resurgent German military might after Adolf Hitler's rise to power in 1933.

Originally a member of the civil service, Maginot was elected to the French Chamber of Deputies in 1910 and became undersecretary of war three years later. Entering the army as a private at the outbreak of World War I, he received a wound that crippled him for life. He returned to politics in 1915 and served inter-

Maginot

By courtesy of the Ministere d'Etat Charge de la Defense Nationale; photograph, E.C.P.—Armees

mittently as minister for colonies, pensions, or war throughout the 1920s.

Maginot's repeated demands that France construct a line of defensive fortifications along its eastern frontiers to prevent a renewed German attack began to bear fruit in 1929, during his second term as minister of war. During that term he reorganized the army and directed the beginning of construction, on the French northeast frontier, of the Maginot Line. Maginot died in early 1932, but his project continued and was completed in 1938. *See* Maginot Line.

Consult the INDEX *first*

Maginot Line, elaborate defensive barrier in northeast France constructed in the 1930s and named after its principal creator, André Maginot, who was France's minister of war in 1929–31.

The fact that certain modern fortresses had held out against German artillery during World War I, as well as the admitted saving in military manpower, induced France to build the celebrated Maginot Line as a permanent defense against German attack. This ultramodern defensive fortification showed traces of the old circular system of fortifications, but its dominant feature was linear. The Maginot Line was, from the standpoint of the troops, a tremendous advance over previous fortifications. Its concrete was thicker than anything theretofore known and its guns heavier. In addition, there were air-conditioned areas for the troops, and the line was usually referred to as being more comfortable than a modern city. There were recreation areas, living quarters, supply storehouses, and underground rail lines connecting various portions of the line.

Strongpoints had been established in depth, capable of being supported by troops moved underground by rail.

Unfortunately, the line covered the French–German frontier, but not the French–Belgian. Thus the Germans in May 1940 outflanked the line. They invaded Belgium on May 10, continued their march through Belgium, crossed the Somme River, and on May 12 struck at Sedan at the northern end of the Maginot Line. Having made a breakthrough with their tanks and planes, they continued around to the rear of the line, making it useless.

Maginulfo (pope): *see* Sylvester (IV).

magistrates' court, in England and Wales, any of the inferior courts with primarily criminal jurisdiction covering a wide range of offenses from minor traffic violations and public-health nuisances to somewhat more serious crimes, such as petty theft or assault. Magistrates' courts with similar jurisdictions may be found in certain large municipalities in the United States.

There are several hundred such courts in England and Wales, presided over by a bench or panel of two or more lay, unpaid magistrates. They study the facts of a case and are advised on points of law by the clerk to the justices, who is responsible for the administrative functions of the court. Proceedings are held in open court, unless the magistrates sit as "examining justices," whereby they carry out inquiries preliminary to trial in serious matters that may require committal of the accused to a higher court for trial. All criminal charges are initially brought before magistrates' courts. More serious charges are subsequently committed for trial at the Crown Court.

The magistrates' courts may impose fines or brief prison sentences on those found guilty. Appeals from a magistrates' court go to the High Court or the Crown Court. The magistrates' court also sits as a juvenile court hearing cases involving care of children under 14 and dealing with children aged 14–17 with the exception, in both age groups, of homicide cases.

In the United States, magistrates are either elected or appointed and, in those areas in which they are still part of the court system, may not require legal training, although in large cities many are lawyers. A magistrates' court in the United States is sometimes called a police court, handling minor criminal matters, traffic offenses, and small civil claims.

Maglemosian industry, a tool culture of northern Europe dating from the postglacial period, approximately 9000 to 5000 BC. The Maglemosian industry was named after the bog (*magle mose,* "big bog," in Danish) at Mullerup, Den., where evidence of the industry was first recognized. The industry was created by a Mesolithic (Middle Stone Age) forest people, who settled along rivers and lakes left behind as the glaciers of the last Ice Age retreated; because their dwellings were generally at the edge of water, many products of the industry made of organic substances that ordinarily would not have survived have been preserved in waterlogged deposits. Thus more is known about the Maglemosian industry than about other tool industries of the same period. Stone microliths (tiny stone blades, edges, and points) used as arrowheads or set into the cutting edges of mattocks, axes, and adzes are common, and many bone and wood tools are known as well: bows and arrows, antler and bone spearheads, bone fishhooks, wooden paddles, and even a dugout canoe. Bark twine fishnets and bark floats have also been preserved. At its height, the Maglemosian industry was also a highly artistic one, decorative designs being found both on tools and on decorative objects, such as pendants and amulets of bone, horn, and amber.

magma, molten or partially molten rock from which igneous rocks form. It usually consists of silicate liquid, although carbonate and sulfide melts occur as well. Magma migrates either at depth or to the Earth's surface and is ejected as lava. Suspended crystals and fragments of unmelted rock may be transported in the magma; dissolved volatiles may separate as bubbles and some liquid may crystallize during movement. Several interrelated physical properties determine the characteristics of magma, including chemical composition, viscosity, dissolved gases, and temperature. As magma cools, crystals form in a systematic manner, which is most simply expressed in the form of Bowen's reaction series; early high-temperature crystals will tend to react with the liquid to form other minerals at lower temperatures. Two series are recognized: (1) a discontinuous reaction series, which from high to low temperatures is composed of olivine, orthopyroxene, clinopyroxene, amphibole, and biotite; and (2) a continuous reaction series, represented by high-temperature calcium-rich plagioclase to low-temperature sodium-rich plagioclase. Numerous variations can occur during crystallization to influence the resulting rock. Such variations include separation of early crystals from liquid, preventing a reaction; cooling of magma too rapidly for reactions to occur; and loss of volatiles, which may remove some components from the magma. Transport and emplacement of magma is strongly affected by its viscosity and by the fracture characteristics of rocks through which it moves. Viscosity is reduced by water and a lower silica content.

Magna Carta, English GREAT CHARTER, the charter of English liberties granted by King John in 1215 under threat of civil war and reissued with alterations in 1216, 1217, and 1225.

The charter meant less to contemporaries than it has to subsequent generations. The solemn circumstances of its first granting have given to Magna Carta of 1215 a unique place in popular imagination; quite early in its history it became a symbol and a battle cry against oppression, each successive generation reading into it a protection of its own threatened liberties. In England the Petition of Right (1628) and the Habeas Corpus Act (1679) looked directly back to clause 39 of the charter of 1215, which stated that "no freemen shall be . . . imprisoned or disseised [dispossessed] . . . except by the lawful judgment of his peers or by the law of the land." In the United States both the national and the state constitutions show ideas and even phrases directly traceable to Magna Carta.

Earlier kings of England—Henry I, Stephen, and Henry II—had issued charters, making promises or concessions to their barons. But these were granted by, not exacted from, the king and were very generally phrased. Moreover, the steady growth of royal administration during the 12th century weakened the barons' position vis-à-vis the crown. But the heavy taxation needed for the Third Crusade, and for the ransom of Richard I after his capture by the Holy Roman emperor Henry VI, increased his successor's difficulties. John's position was further weakened by a rival claim to the throne and by the French attack upon John's Duchy of Normandy. In 1199, 1201, and 1205, John's barons had to be promised their "rights"; his financial exactions increased after his loss of Normandy (1204), and, during his quarrel (1208–13) with Pope Innocent III, he taxed the English church heavily. It is, therefore, not surprising that after 1213 Stephen Langton, archbishop of Canterbury, directed baronial unrest into a demand for a solemn grant of liberties by the king. The document known as the Articles of the Barons was at last agreed upon and sealed by John on June 15, 1215, at Runnymede (beside the River Thames, between Windsor and Staines, now in the county of Surrey). During the next several days the document went through further modifications and refinements, and the final version of Magna Carta was accepted by the king and the barons on June 19.

Opening of the preamble to Magna Carta of 1215; in the British Library (Cotton MS Augustus II 106)

Although written continuously, the charter has been traditionally discussed as consisting of a preamble and 63 clauses. Roughly, its contents may be divided into nine groups. The first concerned the church, asserting that it was to be "free." A second group provided statements of feudal law of particular concern to those holding lands directly from the crown, and the third assured similar rights to subtenants. A fourth group of clauses referred to towns, trade, and merchants. A particularly large group was concerned with the reform of the law and of justice, and another with control of the behaviour of royal officials. A seventh group concerned the royal forests, and another dealt with immediate issues, requiring, for instance, the dismissal of John's foreign mercenaries. The final clauses provided a form of security for the king's adherence to the charter, by which a council of 25 barons should have the ultimate right to levy war upon him should he seriously infringe it.

Councillors for John's young son Henry III reissued the charter in 1216 and 1217, omitting all matters relating only to the political situation of 1215. In 1217 clauses relating to the forests were transferred to a separate forest charter. The great reissue of 1225, given by Henry III himself after his coming of age, differed little from that of 1217, and it was probably already realized that efforts to keep the charter up to date were impracticable. Thus the charter of 1225, again reissued by Henry III in 1264 and "inspected" and enrolled on his new statute rolls by Edward I in 1297, gradually became less a statement of current law than a source book of basic principles. There are four extant "originals" of the charter of 1215, one each in Lincoln Cathedral and Salisbury Cathedral, and two in the British Museum. Durham Cathedral possesses the charters of 1216, 1217, and 1225.

For a translation of the Latin text of Magna Carta, *see* pages 674–676.

Magna Graecia (Latin: "Great Greece"), Greek MEGALE HELLAS, group of ancient Greek cities along the coast of southern Italy; the people of this region were known to the Greeks as Italiotai and to the Romans as Graeci. The site of extensive trade and commerce, Magna Graecia was the seat of the Pythagorean and Eleatic systems of philosophy. Euboeans founded the first colonies, Pithecussae and Cumae, about 750 BC, and subsequently Spartans settled at Tarentum; Achaeans at Metapontum, Sybaris, and Croton; Locrians at Locri Epizephyrii; and Chalcidians at Rhegium (Reggio di Calabria). Later Greek cities in Italy were offshoots of these colonies. After the 5th century,

Magna Carta [1215]

John, by the grace of God, king of England, lord of Ireland, duke of Normandy and Aquitaine, and count of Anjou, to the archbishops, bishops, abbots, earls, barons, justiciars, foresters, sheriffs, stewards, servants, and to all his bailiffs and faithful subjects, greeting. Know that we, out of reverence for God and for the salvation of our soul and those of all our ancestors and heirs, for the honour of God and the exaltation of holy church, and for the reform of our realm, on the advice of our venerable fathers, Stephen, archbishop of Canterbury, primate of all England and cardinal of the holy Roman church, Henry archbishop of Dublin, William of London, Peter of Winchester, Jocelyn of Bath and Glastonbury, Hugh of Lincoln, Walter of Worcester, William of Conventry and Benedict of Rochester, bishops, of master Pandulf, subdeacon and member of the household of the lord pope, of brother Aymeric, master of the order of Knights Templar in England, and of the noble men William Marshal earl of Pembroke, William earl of Salisbury, William earl of Warenne, William earl of Arundel, Alan of Galloway constable of Scotland, Warin fitz Gerold, Peter fitz Herbert, Hubert de Burgh seneschal of Poitou, Hugh de Neville, Matthew fitz Herbert, Thomas Basset, Alan Basset, Philip de Aubeney, Robert of Ropsley, John Marshal, John fitz Hugh, and others, our faithful subjects:

[1] In the first place have granted to God, and by this our present charter confirmed for us and our heirs for ever that the English church shall be free, and shall have its rights undiminished and its liberties unimpaired; and it is our will that it be thus observed; which is evident from the fact that, before the quarrel between us and our barons began, we willingly and spontaneously granted and by our charter confirmed the freedom of elections which is reckoned most important and very essential to the English church, and obtained confirmation of it from the lord pope Innocent III; the which we will observe and we wish our heirs to observe it in good faith for ever. We have also granted to all free men of our kingdom, for ourselves and our heirs for ever, all the liberties written below, to be had and held by them and their heirs of us and our heirs.

[2] If any of our earls or barons or others holding of us in chief by knight service dies, and at his death his heir be of full age and owe relief he shall have his inheritance on payment of the old relief, namely the heir or heirs of an earl £100 for a whole earl's barony, the heir or heirs of a baron £100 for a whole barony, the heir or heirs of a knight 100*s*, at most, for a whole knight's fee; and he who owes less shall give less according to the ancient usage of fiefs.

[3] If, however, the heir of any such be under age and a ward, he shall have his inheritance when he comes of age without paying relief and without making fine.

[4] The guardian of the land of such an heir who is under age shall take from the land of the heir no more than reasonable revenues, reasonable customary dues and reasonable services and that without destruction and waste of men or goods; and if we commit the wardship of the land of any such to a sheriff, or to any other who is answerable to us for its revenues, and he destroys or wastes what he has wardship of, we will take compensation from him and the land shall be committed to two lawful and discreet men of that fief, who shall be answerable for the revenues to us or to him to whom we have assigned them; and if we give or sell to anyone the wardship of any such land and he causes destruction or waste therein, he shall lose that wardship, and it shall be transferred to two lawful and discreet men of that fief, who shall similarly be answerable to us as is aforesaid.

[5] Moreover, so long as he has the wardship of the land, the guardian shall keep in repair the houses, parks, preserves, ponds, mills and other things pertaining to the land out of the revenues from it; and he shall restore to the heir when he comes of age his land fully stocked with ploughs and the means of husbandry according to what the season of husbandry requires and the revenues of the land can reasonably bear.

[6] Heirs shall be married without disparagement, yet so that before the marriage is contracted those nearest in blood to the heir shall have notice.

[7] A widow shall have her marriage portion and inheritance forthwith and without difficulty after the death of her husband; nor shall she pay anything to have her dower or her marriage portion or the inheritance which she and her husband held on the day of her husband's death; and she may remain in her husband's house for forty days after his death, within which time her dower shall be assigned to her.

[8] No widow shall be forced to marry so long as she wishes to live without a husband, provided that she gives security not to marry without our consent if she holds of us, or without the consent of her lord of whom she holds, if she holds of another.

[9] Neither we nor our bailiffs will seize for any debt any land or rent, so long as the chattels of the debtor are sufficient to repay the debt; nor will those who have gone surety for the debtor be distrained so long as the principal debtor is himself able to pay the debt; and if the principal debtor fails to pay the debt, having nothing wherewith to pay it, then shall the sureties answer for the debt; and they shall, if they wish, have the lands and rents of the debtor until they are reimbursed for the debt which they have paid for him, unless the principal debtor can show that he has discharged his obligation in the matter to the said sureties.

[10] If anyone who has borrowed from the Jews any sum, great or small, dies before it is repaid, the debt shall not bear interest as long as the heir is under age, of whomsoever he holds; and if the debt falls into our hands, we will not take anything except the principal mentioned in the bond.

[11] And if anyone dies indebted to the Jews, his wife shall have her dower and pay nothing of that debt; and if the dead man leaves children who are under age, they shall be provided with necessaries befitting the holding of the deceased; and the debt shall be paid out of the residue, reserving, however, service due to lords of the land; debts owing to others than Jews shall be dealt with in like manner.

[12] No scutage or aid shall be imposed in our kingdom unless by common counsel of our kingdom, except for ransoming our person, for making our eldest son a knight, and for once marrying our eldest daughter, and for these only a reasonable aid shall be levied. Be it done in like manner concerning aids from the city of London.

[13] And the city of London shall have all its ancient liberties and free customs as well by land as by water. Furthermore, we will and grant that all other cities, boroughs, towns, and ports shall have all their liberties and free customs.

[14] And to obtain the common counsel of the kingdom about the assessing of an aid (except in the three cases aforesaid) or of a scutage, we will cause to be summoned the archbishops, bishops, abbots, earls and greater barons, individually by our letters—and, in addition, we will cause to be summoned generally through our sheriffs and bailiffs all those holding of us in chief—for a fixed date, namely, after the expiry of at least forty days, and to a fixed place; and in all letters of such summons we will specify the reason for the summons. And when the summons has thus been made, the business shall proceed on the day appointed, according to the counsel of those present, though not all have come who were summoned.

[15] We will not in future grant any one the right to take an aid from his free men, except for ransoming his person, for making his eldest son a knight and for once marrying his eldest daughter, and for these only a reasonable aid shall be levied.

[16] No one shall be compelled to do greater service for a knight's fee or for any other free holding than is due from it.

[17] Common pleas shall not follow our court, but shall be held in some fixed place.

[18] Recognitions of *novel disseisin,* of *mort d'ancester,* and of *darrein presentment,* shall not be held elsewhere than in the counties to which they relate, and in this manner—we, or, if we should be out of the realm, our chief justiciar, will send two justices through each county four times a year, who, with four knights of each county chosen by the county, shall hold the said assizes in the county and on the day and in the place of meeting of the county court.

[19] And if the said assizes cannot all be held on the day of the county court, there shall stay behind as many of the knights and freeholders who were present at the county court on that day as are

necessary for the sufficient making of judgments, according to the amount of business to be done.

[20] A free man shall not be amerced for a trivial offence except in accordance with the degree of the offence, and for a grave offence he shall be amerced in accordance with its gravity, yet saving his way of living; and a merchant in the same way, saving his stock-in-trade; and a villein shall be amerced in the same way, saving his means of livelihood—if they have fallen into our mercy: and none of the aforesaid amercements shall be imposed except by the oath of good men of the neighbourhood.

[21] Earls and barons shall not be amerced except by their peers, and only in accordance with the degree of the offence.

[22] No clerk shall be amerced in respect of his lay holding except after the manner of the others aforesaid and not according to the amount of his ecclesiastical benefice.

[23] No vill or individual shall be compelled to make bridges at river banks, except those who from of old are legally bound to do so.

[24] No sheriff, constable, coroners, or others of our bailiffs, shall hold pleas of our crown.

[25] All counties, hundreds, wapentakes and trithings shall be at the old rents without any additional payment, exept our demesne manors.

[26] If anyone holding a lay fief of us dies and our sheriff or bailiff shows our letters patent of summons for a debt that the deceased owed us, it shall be lawful for our sheriff or bailiff to attach and make a list of chattels of the deceased found upon the lay fief to the value of that debt under the supervision of law-worthy men, provided that none of the chattels shall be removed until the debt which is manifest has been paid to us in full; and the residue shall be left to the executors for carrying out the will of the deceased. And if nothing is owing to us from him, all the chattels shall accrue to the deceased, saving to his wife and children their reasonable shares.

[27] If any free man dies without leaving a will, his chattels shall be distributed by his nearest kinsfolk and friends under the supervision of the church, saving to every one the debts which the deceased owed him.

[28] No constable or other bailiff of ours shall take anyone's corn or other chattels unless he pays on the spot in cash for them or can delay payment by arrangement with the seller.

[29] No constable shall compel any knight to give money instead of castle-guard if he is willing to do the guard himself or through another good man, if for some good reason he cannot do it himself; and if we lead or send him on military service, he shall be excused guard in proportion to the time that because of us he has been on service.

[30] No sheriff, or bailiff of ours, or anyone else shall take the horses or carts of any free man for transport work save with the agreement of that freeman.

[31] Neither we nor our bailiffs will take, for castles or other works of ours, timber which is not ours, except with the agreement of him whose timber it is.

[32] We will not hold for more than a year and a day the lands of those convicted of felony, and then the lands shall be handed over to the lords of the fiefs.

[33] Henceforth all fish-weirs shall be cleared completely from the Thames and the Medway and throughout all England, except along the sea coast.

[34] The writ called *Praecipe* shall not in future be issued to anyone in respect of any holding whereby a free man may lose his court.

[35] Let there be one measure for wine throughout our kingdom, and one measure for ale, and one measure for corn, namely "the London quarter"; and one width for cloths whether dyed, russet or halberget, namely two ells within the selvedges. Let it be the same with weights as with measures.

[36] Nothing shall be given or taken in future for the writ of inquisition of life or limbs: instead it shall be granted free of charge and not refused.

[37] If anyone holds of us by fee-farm, by socage, or by burgage, and holds land of another by knight service, we will not, by reason of that fee-farm, socage, or burgage, have the wardship of his heir or of land of his that is of the fief of the other; nor will we have custody of the fee-farm, socage, or burgage, unless such fee-farm owes knight service. We will not have custody of anyone's heir or land which he holds of another by knight service by reason of any petty serjeanty which he holds of us by the service of rendering to us knives or arrows or the like.

[38] No bailiff shall in future put anyone to trial upon his own bare word, without reliable witnesses produced for this purpose.

[39] No free man shall be arrested or imprisoned or disseised or outlawed or exiled or in any way victimised, neither will we attack him or send anyone to attack him, except by the lawful judgment of his peers or by the law of the land.

[40] To no one will we sell, to no one will we refuse or delay right or justice.

[41] All merchants shall be able to go out of and come into England safely and securely and stay and travel throughout England, as well by land as by water, for buying and selling by the ancient and right customs free from all evil tolls, except in time of war and if they are of the land that is at war with us. And if such are found in our land at the beginning of a war, they shall be attached, without injury to their persons or goods, until we, or our chief justiciar, know how merchants of our land are treated who were found in the land at war with us when war broke out, and if ours are safe there, the others shall be safe in our land.

[42] It shall be lawful in future for anyone, without prejudicing the allegiance due to us, to leave our kingdom and return safely and securely by land and water, save, in the public interest, for a short period in time of war—except for those imprisoned or outlawed in accordance with the law of the kingdom and natives of a land that is at war with us and merchants (who shall be treated as aforesaid).

[43] If anyone who holds of some escheat such as the honour of Wallingford, Nottingham, Boulogne, Lancaster, or of other escheats which are in our hands and are baronies dies, his heir shall give no other relief and do no other service to us than he would have done to the baron if that barony had been in the baron's hands; and we will hold it in the same manner in which the baron held it.

[44] Men who live outside the forest need not henceforth come before our justices of the forest upon a general summons, unless they are impleaded or are sureties for any person or persons who are attached for forest offences.

[45] We will not make justices, constables, sheriffs or bailiffs save of such as know the law of the kingdom and mean to observe it well.

[46] All barons who have founded abbeys for which they have charters of the kings of England or ancient tenure shall have the custody of them during vacancies, as they ought to have.

[47] All forests that have been made forest in our time shall be immediately disafforested; and so be it done with riverbanks that have been made preserves by us in our time.

[48] All evil customs connected with forests and warrens, foresters and warreners, sheriffs and their officials, riverbanks and their wardens shall immediately be inquired into in each county by twelve sworn knights of the same county who are to be chosen by good men of the same county, and within forty days of the completion of the inquiry shall be utterly abolished by them so as never to be restored, provided that we, or our justiciar if we are not in England, know of it first.

[49] We will immediately return all hostages and charters given to us by Englishmen, as security for peace or faithful service.

[50] We will remove completely from office the relations of Gerard de Athée so that in future they shall have no office in England, namely Engelard de Cigogné, Peter and Guy and Andrew de Chanceaux, Guy de Cigogné, Geoffrey de Martigny and his brothers, Philip Marc and his brothers and his nephew Geoffrey, and all their following.

[51] As soon as peace is restored, we will remove from the kingdom all foreign knights, cross-bowmen, serjeants, and mercenaries, who have come with horses and arms to the detriment of the kingdom.

[52] If anyone has been disseised of or kept out of his lands, castles, franchises or his right by us without the legal judgment of his peers, we will immediately restore them to him: and if a dispute arises over this, then let it be decided by the judgment of

the twenty-five barons who are mentioned below in the clause for securing the peace: for all the things, however, which anyone has been disseised or kept out of without the lawful judgment of his peers by king Henry, our father, or by king Richard, our brother, which we have in our hand or are held by others, to whom we are bound to warrant them, we will have the usual period of respite of crusaders, excepting those things about which a plea was started or an inquest made by our command before we took the cross; when however we return from our pilgrimage, or if by any chance we do not go on it, we will at once do full justice therein.

[53] We will have the same respite, and in the same manner, in the doing of justice in the matter of the disafforesting or retaining of the forests which Henry our father or Richard our brother afforested, and in the matter of the wardship of lands which are of the fief of another, wardships of which sort we have hitherto had by reason of a fief which anyone held of us by knight service, and in the matter of abbeys founded on the fief of another, not on a fief of our own, in which the lord of the fief claims he has a right; and when we have returned, or if we do not set out on our pilgrimage, we will at once do full justice to those who complain of these things.

[54] No one shall be arrested or imprisoned upon the appeal of a woman for the death of anyone except her husband.

[55] All fines made with us unjustly and against the law of the land, and all amercements imposed unjustly and against the law of the land, shall be entirely remitted, or else let them be settled by the judgment of the twenty-five barons who are mentioned below in the clause for securing the peace, or by the judgment of the majority of the same, along with the aforesaid Stephen, archbishop of Canterbury, if he can be present, and such others as he may wish to associate with himself for this purpose, and if he cannot be present the business shall nevertheless proceed without him, provided that if any one or more of the aforesaid twenty-five barons are in a like suit, they shall be removed from the judgment of the case in question, and others chosen, sworn and put in their place by the rest of the same twenty-five for this case only.

[56] If we have disseised or kept out Welshmen from lands or liberties or other things without the legal judgment of their peers in England or in Wales, they shall be immediately restored to them; and if a dispute arises over this, then let it be decided in the March by the judgment of their peers—for holdings in England according to the law of England, for holdings in Wales according to the law of Wales, and for holdings in the March according to the law of the March. Welshmen shall do the same to us and ours.

[57] For all the things, however, which any Welshman was disseised of or kept out of without the lawful judgment of his peers by king Henry, our father, or king Richard, our brother, which we have in our hand or which are held by others, to whom we are bound to warrant them, we will have the usual period of respite of crusaders, excepting those things about which a plea was started or an inquest made by our command before we took the cross; when however we return, or if by any chance we do not set out on our pilgrimage, we will at once do full justice to them in accordance with the laws of the Welsh and the foresaid regions.

[58] We will give back at once the son of Llywelyn and all the hostages from Wales and the charters that were handed over to us as security for peace.

[59] We will act toward Alexander, king of the Scots, concerning the return of his sisters and hostages and concerning his franchises and his right in the same manner in which we act towards our other barons of England, unless it ought to be otherwise by the charters which we have from William his father, formerly king of the Scots, and this shall be determined by the judgment of his peers in our court.

[60] All these aforesaid customs and liberties which we have granted to be observed in our kingdom as far as it pertains to us towards our men, all of our kingdom, clerks as well as laymen, shall observe as far as it pertains to them towards their men.

[61] Since, moreover, for God and the betterment of our kingdom and for the better allaying of the discord that has arisen between us and our barons we have granted all these things aforesaid, wishing them to enjoy the use of them unimpaired and unshaken for ever, we give and grant them the under-written security, namely, that the barons shall choose any twenty-five barons of the kingdom they wish, who must with all their might observe, hold and cause to be observed, the peace and liberties which we have granted and confirmed to them by this present charter of ours, so that if we, or our justiciar, or our bailiffs or any one of our servants offend in any way against anyone or transgress any of the articles of the peace or the security and the offence be notified to four of the aforesaid twenty-five barons, those four barons shall come to us, or to our justiciar if we are out of the kingdom, and, laying the transgression before us, shall petition us to have that transgression corrected without delay. And if we do not correct the transgression, or if we are out of the kingdom, if our justiciar does not correct it, within forty days, reckoning from the time it was brought to our notice or to that of our justiciar if we were out of the kingdom, the aforesaid four barons shall refer that case to the rest of the twenty-five barons and those twenty-five barons together with the community of the whole land shall distrain and distress us in every way they can, namely, by seizing castles, lands, possessions, and in such other ways as they can, saving our person and the persons of our queen and our children, until, in their opinion, amends have been made; and when amends have been made, they shall obey us as they did before. And let anyone in the land who wishes take an oath to obey the orders of the said twenty-five barons for the execution of all the aforesaid matters, and with them to distress us as much as he can, and we publicly and freely give anyone leave to take the oath who wishes to take it and we will never prohibit anyone from taking it. Indeed, all those in the land who are unwilling of themselves and of their own accord to take an oath to the twenty-five barons to help them to distrain and distress us, we will make them take the oath as aforesaid at our command. And if any of the twenty-five barons dies or leaves the country or is in any other way prevented from carrying out the things aforesaid, the rest of the aforesaid twenty-five barons shall choose as they think fit another one in his place, and he shall take the oath like the rest. In all matters the execution of which is committed to these twenty-five barons, if it should happen that these twenty-five are present yet disagree among themselves about anything, or if some of those summoned will not or cannot be present, that shall be held as fixed and established which the majority of those present ordained or commanded, exactly as if all the twenty-five had consented to it; and the said twenty-five shall swear that they will faithfully observe all the things aforesaid and will do all they can to get them observed. And we will procure nothing from anyone, either personally or through anyone else, whereby any of these concessions and liberties might be revoked or diminished; and if any such thing is procured, let it be void and null, and we will never use it either personally or through another.

[62] And we have fully remitted and pardoned to everyone all the ill-will, indignation and rancour that have arisen between us and our men, clergy and laity, from the time of the quarrel. Furthermore, we have fully remitted to all, clergy and laity, and as far as pertains to us have completely forgiven, all trespasses occasioned by the same quarrel between Easter in the sixteenth year of our reign and the restoration of peace. And, besides, we have caused to be made for them letters testimonial patent of the lord Stephen archbishop of Canterbury, of the lord Henry archbishop of Dublin and of the aforementioned bishops and of master Pandulf about this security and the aforementioned concessions.

[63] Wherefore we wish and firmly enjoin that the English church shall be free, and that the men in our kingdom shall have and hold all the aforesaid liberties, rights and concessions well and peacefully, freely and quietly, fully and completely, for themselves and their heirs from us and our heirs, in all matters and in all places for ever, as is aforesaid. An oath, moreover, has been taken, as well on our part as on the part of the barons, that all these things aforesaid shall be observed in good faith and without evil disposition. Witness the above-mentioned and many others. Given by our hand in the meadow which is called Runnymede between Windsor and Staines on the fifteenth day of June, in the seventeenth year of our reign.

attacks by neighbouring Italic peoples, interurban strife, and malaria caused most of the cities to decline in importance.

Magna Graecia was an important centre of Greek civilization. One of its cities, Croton, reputed to have the finest physicians in the Greek world, was the home of the 6th-century athlete Milo, who was six times victor in wrestling at both the Olympic and Pythian games.

Magnani, Anna (b. March 7, 1908, Alexandria—d. Sept. 26, 1973, Rome), Italian actress, best known for her forceful portrayals of earthy, lower class women.

Deserted first by her father and then by her mother, Magnani was raised in a Roman slum by her grandparents. She attended the

Anna Magnani, 1958
EB Inc.

Academy of Dramatic Art in Rome for a short time before joining a touring repertory company. As an entertainer in Roman nightclubs, she specialized in bawdy street songs and in vaudeville. She made her film debut in *La cieca di Sorrento* (1934; *The Blind Woman of Sorrento*). In *Roma città aperta* (1945; *Open City*), the film, directed by Roberto Rossellini that heralded the Neorealist movement in Italian filmmaking, she achieved international renown. Representative of her many roles, in which she often portrayed emotions that ranged from mental torment and deep grief to exuberant comedy, were the dynamic housewife in *L'onorevole Angelina* (1947), who led a fight against black-marketeering in postwar Italy; a village idiot in *Il miracolo* (1948; *The Miracle*), who was seduced by a stranger she imagined to be her special saint; an aggressive stage mother in *Bellissima* (1951); the robust widow of a truck driver in *The Rose Tattoo* (1955), her first Hollywood film, for which she won the Academy Award for best actress; and the wife of an Italian mayor in *The Secret of Santa Vittoria* (1968).

Magnasco, Alessandro, byname LISSANDRINO, or IL LISSANDRINO (b. 1667, Genoa—d. March 12, 1749, Genoa), Italian painter of the late Baroque period distinguished for his landscapes and genre paintings.

"The Synagogue," oil on canvas by Alessandro Magnasco, 1725–30; in the Cleveland Museum of Art, Ohio
By courtesy of the Cleveland Museum of Art, Ohio, purchased from the J.H. Wade Fund

Magnasco worked in Milan, but is thought to have been influenced by the Bolognese painter Giuseppe Maria Crespi. Although he began as a portrait painter, only a self-portrait is known. His later works depicted gypsies and bandits, or religious scenes loosely painted and frequently set in romantic landscapes. Magnasco was exceedingly prolific both as a painter and a draftsman and occasionally collaborated with other painters, such as Marco Ricci, inserting figures in their landscapes. Such works as "The Synagogue" (Cleveland Museum of Art, Ohio) reveal his nervous, sketchy style and his predilection for the bizarre. His attenuated figures and unnatural, flickering light heighten the sense of the fantastic and grotesque in his art.

Magnentius, in full FLAVIUS MAGNUS MAGNENTIUS (d. Aug. 11, 353, Gaul), usurping Roman emperor from Jan. 18, 350, to Aug. 11, 353. His career forms one episode in the struggles for imperial power that occurred after the death of Constantine the Great (ruled 306–337).

Magnentius was a pagan of German descent who had achieved distinction as a soldier before having himself proclaimed emperor early in 350. Immediately he engineered the murder of Constans (sole ruler in the West from 340 to 350) and assumed control of the western half of the empire. In June 350 he crushed Nepotianus, who had declared himself emperor at Rome. But his chief opponent was Constantius II, ruler of the Eastern Empire. Failing to win recognition from Constantius, Magnentius allied himself with the commander of the Danubian troops, Vetranio, who had proclaimed himself emperor on March 1, 350. This arrangement ended quickly with the abrupt overthrow of Vetranio by Constantius. In 351 Magnentius repulsed Constantius at Atrans, and advanced into the province of Pannonia Inferior. Constantius rallied and, on Sept. 28, 351, severely defeated Magnentius at the Battle of Mursa (modern Osijek, Croatia). He then invaded Italy, whereupon Magnentius fell back to Gaul and, to avoid capture, committed suicide.

Magnes, Judah Leon (b. July 5, 1877, San Francisco—d. Oct. 27, 1948, New York City), rabbi, religious leader, prime founder and first president of the Hebrew University of Jerusalem, and a Zionist who came to favour a binational Arab–Jewish state.

A graduate of the University of Cincinnati (A.B., 1898), Magnes attended Hebrew Union College and was ordained as a rabbi in 1900. He then travelled to Germany for further studies. After receiving a Ph.D. from the University of Heidelberg in 1902, Magnes returned to the United States and in 1904 became rabbi of a Reform synagogue, Temple Israel of Brooklyn. From 1905 to 1908 he was secretary of the Federation of American Zionists. In 1906 he assumed the pulpit of the Reform temple Emanu-El in New York City. His many speaking engagements on behalf of Zionism, as well as his eloquent sermons, made him a revered figure among American Jews. He founded Qehilla (Community) to unite the disparate elements of New York Jewry; its Bureau of Jewish Education (1910–41) had a profound effect for decades. A growing dissatisfaction with Reform Jewry's latitudinarian observance of ritual and custom caused Magnes to resign from Emanu-El in 1910 and accept the pulpit of Temple B'nai Jeshurun, an Orthodox congregation.

During World War I Magnes was a pacifist and, in addition, drifted away from Zionism, whose leaders supported the Allied war effort. He joined the Joint Distribution Committee, which, unlike the Zionists, emphasized relief to Jews in Palestine rather than political activism there.

At the war's end he went to Palestine and subsequently joined one of the many committees founded by the Zionist movement to establish the Hebrew University of Jerusalem. Magnes soon became the guiding spirit of this effort. He raised funds, devised the university's academic program, and, when the institution was completed at Mt. Scopus in 1925, became chancellor. In 1935 he became the first president of the university, a post he retained until his death, which occurred while on a visit to New York.

Magnes also founded Iḥud (Unity), an association dedicated to the advancement of Arab–Jewish reconciliation, and advocated an Arab–Jewish state that would be part of an Arab Federation. He worked in Iḥud with the renowned religious philosopher Martin Buber.

magnesia, white, highly infusible oxide of magnesium (*q.v.*).

Magnesia ad Maeandrum, ancient inland city of Ionia, situated on a small tributary of the Maeander (Büyükmenderes) River about 12 miles southeast of Ephesus. According to Strabo, it was founded by some Thessalian Magnetes, who had collected fellow settlers from Crete en route. Accounted an Aeolian city, it was never, despite its early prosperity, included in the Ionian League. Destroyed in the Cimmerian invasion of *c.* 650 BC, it slowly recovered and became the residence of Oroetes, the Persian satrap, who murdered Polycrates of Samos there about 522, and later of the exiled Themistocles, who received it, with other towns, from Artaxerxes I and issued some Magnesian coins about 460. Too far inland to enter the Athenian Empire, it was transplanted some time later to a more defensible site among the eastern foothills of Mt. Thorax. The new city assumed a monumental form about 200 BC. It continued to flourish under the kings of Pergamum and the Roman Republic, and produced Hegesias, founder of the rhetorical school called "Asiatic." It resisted Mithradates VI of Pontus in 87 BC, and was rewarded with political freedom by Sulla. It appears to have declined under the empire, though on a rare bronze coin of the time of Gordian III (AD 238–244) it still calls itself the seventh city of Asia.

Magnesia ad Sipylum, city in ancient Lydia, just south of the Hermus (Gediz) River. Though lying in a rich district near prehistoric regions associated with Niobe and Tantalus, and itself going back to the 5th century BC, it is of little importance except for the battle of winter 190/189 BC, described in Livy, xxxvii, when the Romans under Lucius Scipio decisively defeated Antiochus III and threw him back permanently to the other side of the Taurus range. It suffered severely from earthquakes, notably in AD 17, and has left rather scanty remains. The modern city is Manisa (*q.v.*).

magnesioferrite, the mineral magnesium iron oxide, a member of the magnetite (*q.v.*) series of spinels.

magnesioriebeckite, magnesium-rich variety of the silicate mineral riebeckite (*q.v.*).

magnesite, the mineral magnesium carbonate ($MgCO_3$), a member of the calcite group of carbonate minerals that is a principal source of magnesium. The mineral has formed as an alteration product from magnesium-rich rocks or through the action of magnesium-containing solutions upon calcite. Notable deposits are those at Radenthein, Austria; the Liaotung Peninsula, Liaoning Province, China; and Clark County, Nev., U.S. Iron is usually present, and a complete chemical substitution series exists between magnesite and siderite in which iron replaces magnesium. Magnesite is used as a refractory material, a catalyst and filler in the production of synthetic rubber, and a material in the preparation of magnesium

Magnesite from Okanogan, Wash.
B.M. Shaub

chemicals and fertilizers. For detailed physical properties, *see* carbonate mineral (table).

magnesium (Mg), chemical element, one of the alkaline-earth metals of main Group IIa of the periodic table, the lightest structural metal. Known originally through compounds such as Epsom salts (the sulfate), magnesia (the oxide), and magnesia alba (the carbonate), the silvery white element itself does not occur free. It was first isolated in 1808 by Sir Humphry Davy, who evaporated the mercury from a magnesium amalgam made by electrolyzing a mixture of moist magnesia and mercuric oxide.

A brief treatment of magnesium follows. For full treatment, *see* MACROPAEDIA: Chemical Elements. For treatment of the refining and recovery of magnesium, *see* Industries, Extraction and Processing. For comparative statistical data on magnesium metal production, *see* MICROPAEDIA: mining (table).

Occurrence, properties, and uses. Magnesium is the eighth most abundant element in the Earth's crust (about 2.5 percent), distributed in minerals such as magnesite, dolomite, brucite, serpentine, chrysolite, meerschaum, talc, and most kinds of asbestos. Seawater contains about 0.13 percent magnesium, mostly as the dissolved chloride, which imparts the characteristic bitter taste. Magnesium is about one-sixth as plentiful as potassium in human body cells, where it is required as a catalyst for enzyme reactions in carbohydrate metabolism.

Magnesium is commercially produced by electrolysis of molten magnesium chloride ($MgCl_2$), processed mainly from seawater and by the direct reduction of its compounds with suitable reducing agents (as from calcined dolomite with ferrosilicon).

At one time, magnesium was used predominantly for photographic flash ribbon and powder, incendiary bombs, and pyrotechnic devices, because in finely divided form it burns in air with an intense white light. Because of its low density (only two-thirds that of aluminum) it has found extensive use in the aerospace industry. A part that would weigh 70 pounds (31.8 kilograms) when made of steel weighs only 15 pounds when made from magnesium. Because the pure metal has low structural strength, alloys have been developed—principally with aluminum, zinc, and manganese—to improve its hardness, tensile strength, and ability to be cast, welded, and machined. Magnesium alloys have a number of applications; they are used for parts of aircraft, spacecraft, machinery, automobiles, portable tools, and household appliances.

Magnesium occurs in nature as a mixture of three isotopes: magnesium-24 (78.70 percent), magnesium-26 (11.17 percent), and magnesium-25 (10.13 percent). It is a very strong reducing agent, reacting with most acids or with boiling water to liberate hydrogen, but is resistant to most alkalies. In compounds it always exhibits a +2 oxidation state because of the loss or sharing of its two 3*s* electrons.

Principal compounds. Magnesium carbonate, $MgCO_3$, occurs in nature as the mineral magnesite and is an important source of elemental magnesium. It can be produced artificially by the action of carbon dioxide on a variety of magnesium compounds. The odourless white powder has many industrial uses—*e.g.,* as a heat insulator for boilers and pipes and as an additive in food, pharmaceuticals, cosmetics, rubbers, inks, and glass.

Magnesium hydroxide, $Mg(OH)_2$, is a white powder produced in large quantities from seawater by the addition of milk of lime. It is the primary raw material in the production of magnesium metal. In water it forms a suspension known as milk of magnesia, which has long been used as an antacid and a laxative.

The action of hydrochloric acid on magnesium hydroxide produces magnesium chloride, $MgCl_2$, a colourless, deliquescent (water-absorbing) substance employed in magnesium metal production, in the manufacture of a cement for heavy-duty flooring, and as an additive in textile manufacture. Roasting either magnesium carbonate or magnesium hydroxide produces the oxygen compound magnesium oxide, commonly called magnesia, MgO, a white solid used in the manufacture of high-temperature refractory bricks, electrical and thermal insulators, cements, fertilizer, rubber, and plastics. It is used medically as a laxative.

Magnesium sulfate, $MgSO_4$, is a colourless, crystalline substance formed by the reaction of magnesium hydroxide with sulfur dioxide and air. A hydrate form of magnesium sulfate called kieserite, $MgSO_4 \cdot H_2O$, occurs as a mineral deposit. Synthetically prepared magnesium sulfate is sold as Epsom salt, $MgSO_4 \cdot 7H_2O$. In industry magnesium sulfate is used in the manufacture of cements and fertilizers and in tanning and dyeing; in medicine it serves as a purgative.

Among the organometallic compounds of magnesium are the important Grignard reagents, composed of an organic group (*e.g.,* alkyls and aryls), a halogen atom other than fluorine, and magnesium (*see* Grignard reagent). These are used in the production of many other kinds of organometallic compounds. Magnesium also is a constituent of chlorophyll, in which it apparently plays a role similar to that of iron in hemoglobin.

atomic number	12
atomic weight	24.312
melting point	651° C
boiling point	1,107° C
specific gravity	1.74 (20° C)
valence	2
electronic config.	2-8-2 or $1s^2 2s^2 2p^6 3s^2$

magnesium deficiency, also called HYPOMAGNESEMIA, condition in which an organism fails to receive an adequate supply of magnesium, a mineral that is essential to enzyme reactions in the metabolism of ingested carbohydrates and sometimes has the ability to replace a portion of body calcium. About three-fourths of the mineral found in the body is associated with calcium in the skeleton and tooth dentine formation, with the remainder contained in soft tissues and body fluids. Its specific function is not certain, but studies indicate magnesium probably serves as a catalyst in other physiological activities. Magnesium forms positive ions (charged particles) in solution and is essential to the electrical breakdown of nutrient and other material within the cells; it is also important to stimulation of muscles and nerves.

Magnesium deficiencies are noted in chronic kidney disease and other conditions of acidosis (pathological excess of acid), including diabetic coma. Symptoms of deficiency include weakness, dizziness, distension of the abdomen, and convulsive seizures.

The best food sources of magnesium include cereals, legumes, nuts, meats, milk, and other dairy products.

magnet, any material capable of attracting iron and producing a magnetic field outside itself. By the end of the 19th century all the known elements and many compounds had been tested for magnetism, and all were found to have some magnetic property. The most common was the property of diamagnetism, the name given to materials exhibiting a weak repulsion by both poles of a magnet. Some materials, such as chromium, showed paramagnetism, being capable of weak induced magnetization when brought near a magnet. This magnetization disappears when the magnet is removed. Only three elements, iron, nickel, and cobalt, showed the property of ferromagnetism (*i.e.,* the capability of remaining permanently magnetized).

Magnetization process. The quantities now used in characterizing magnetization were defined and named by William Thomson (Lord Kelvin) in 1850. The symbol B denotes the magnitude of magnetic flux density inside a magnetized body, and the symbol H denotes the magnitude of magnetizing force, or magnetic field, producing it. The two are represented by the equation $B = \mu H$, in which the Greek letter mu, μ, symbolizes the permeability of the material and is a measure of the intensity of magnetization that can be produced in it by a given magnetic field. The modern units of the International Standard (SI) system for B are teslas (T) or webers per square metre (Wb/m^2) and for H are amperes per metre (A/m). The units were formerly called, respectively, gauss and oersted. The units of μ are henrys per metre.

All ferromagnetic materials exhibit the phenomenon of hysteresis, a lag in response to changing forces based on energy losses resulting from internal friction. If B is measured for various values of H and the results are plotted in graphic form, the result is a loop of the type shown in the accompanying figure, called a hysteresis loop. The name describes the situation in which the path followed by the values of B while H is increasing differs from that followed as H is decreasing. With the aid of this diagram, the characteristics needed to describe the performance of a material to be used as a magnet can be defined. B_s is the saturation flux density and is a measure of how strongly the material can be magnetized.

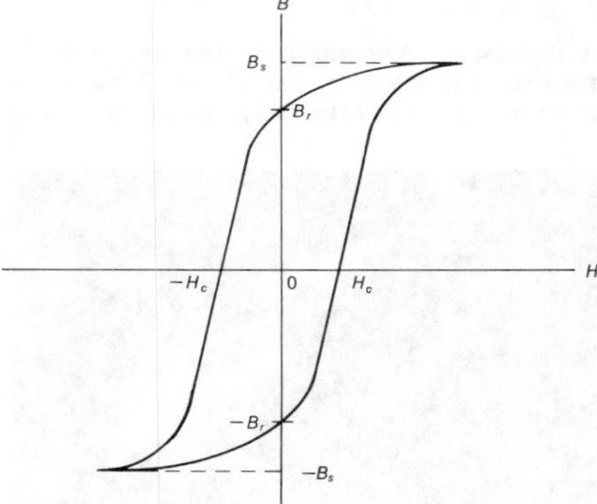

Typical hysteresis loop

B_r is the remanent flux density and is the residual, permanent magnetization left after the magnetizing field is removed; this latter is obviously a measure of quality for a permanent magnet. It is usually measured in webers per square metre. In order to demagnetize the specimen from its remanent state, it is necessary to apply a reversed magnetizing field, opposing the magnetization in the specimen. The magnitude of field necessary to reduce the magnetization to zero is H_c, the coercive force, measured in amperes per metre. For a permanent magnet to retain its magnetization without loss over a long period of time, H_c should be as large as possible. The combination of large B_r and large H_c will generally be found in a material with a large saturation flux density that requires a large field to magnetize it. Thus, permanent-magnet materials are often characterized by quoting the maximum value of the product of B and H, $(BH)_{max}$, which the material can achieve. This product $(BH)_{max}$ is a measure of the minimum volume of permanent-magnet material required to produce a required flux density in a given gap and is sometimes referred to as the energy product.

It was suggested in 1907 that a ferromagnetic material is composed of a large number of small volumes called domains, each of which is magnetized to saturation. In 1931 the existence of such domains was first demonstrated by direct experiment. The ferromagnetic body as a whole appears unmagnetized when the directions of the individual domain magnetizations are distributed at random. Each domain is separated from its neighbours by a domain wall. In the wall region, the direction of magnetization turns from that of one domain to that of its neighbour. The process of magnetization, starting from a perfect unmagnetized state, comprises three stages: (1) *Low magnetizing field.* Reversible movements of the domain walls occur such that domains oriented in the general direction of the magnetizing field grow at the expense of those unfavourably oriented; the walls return to their original position on removal of the magnetizing field, and there is no remanent magnetization. (2) *Medium magnetizing field.* Larger movements of domain walls occur, many of which are irreversible, and the volume of favourably oriented domains is much increased. On removal of the field, all the walls do not return to their original positions, and there is a remanent magnetization. (3) *High magnetizing field.* Large movements of domain walls occur such that many are swept out of the specimen completely. The directions of magnetization in the remaining domains gradually rotate, as the field is increased, until the magnetization is everywhere parallel to the field and the material is magnetized to saturation. On removal of the field, domain walls reappear and the domain magnetizations may rotate away from the original field direction. The remanent magnetization has its maximum value.

The values of B_r, H_c, and $(BH)_{max}$ will depend on the ease with which domain walls can move through the material and domain magnetization can rotate. Discontinuities or imperfections in the material provide obstacles to domain wall movement. Thus, once the magnetizing field has driven the wall past an obstacle, the wall will not be able to return to its original position unless a reversed field is applied to drive it back again. The effect of these obstacles is, therefore, to increase the remanence. Conversely, in a pure, homogeneous material, in which there are few imperfections, it will be easy to magnetize the material to saturation with relatively low fields, and the remanent magnetization will be small.

Demagnetization and magnetic anisotropy. As far as domain rotation is concerned, there are two important factors to be considered, demagnetization and magnetic anisotropy (exhibition of different magnetic properties when measured along axes in different directions). The first of these concerns the shape of a magnetized specimen. Any magnet generates a magnetic field in the space surrounding it. The direction of the lines of force of this field, defined by the direction of the force exerted by the field on a (hypothetical) single magnetic north pole, is opposite to the direction of field used to magnetize it originally. Thus, every magnet exists in a self-generated field that has a direction such as to tend to demagnetize the specimen. This phenomenon is described by the demagnetizing factor. If the magnetic lines of force can be confined to the magnet and not allowed to escape into the surrounding medium, the demagnetizing effect will be absent. Thus a toroidal (ring-shaped) magnet, magnetized around its perimeter so that all the lines of force are closed loops within the material, will not try to demagnetize itself. For bar magnets, demagnetization can be minimized by keeping them in pairs, laid parallel with north and south poles adjacent and with a soft-iron keeper laid across each end.

The relevance of demagnetization to domain rotation arises from the fact that the demagnetizing field may be looked upon as a store of magnetic energy. Like all natural systems, the magnet, in the absence of constraints, will try to maintain its magnetization in a direction such as to minimize stored energy; *i.e.,* to make the demagnetizing field as small as possible. To rotate the magnetization away from this minimum-energy position requires work to be done to provide the increase in energy stored in the increased demagnetizing field. Thus, if an attempt is made to rotate the magnetization of a domain away from its natural minimum-energy position, the rotation can be said to be hindered in the sense that work must be done by an applied field to promote the rotation against the demagnetizing forces. This phenomenon is often called shape anisotropy because it arises from the domain's geometry which may, in turn, be determined by the overall shape of the specimen.

Similar minimum-energy considerations are involved in the second mechanism hindering domain rotation, namely magnetocrystalline anisotropy. It was first observed in 1847 that in crystals of magnetic material there appeared to exist preferred directions for the magnetization. This phenomenon has to do with the symmetry of the atomic arrangements in the crystal. For example, in iron, which has a cubic crystalline form, it is easier to magnetize the crystal along the directions of the edges of the cube than in any other direction. Thus the six cube-edge directions are easy directions of magnetization, and the magnetization of the crystal is termed anisotropic.

Magnetic anisotropy can also be induced by strain in a material. The magnetization tends to align itself in accordance with or perpendicular to the direction of the in-built strain. Some magnetic alloys also exhibit the phenomenon of induced magnetic anisotropy. If an external magnetic field is applied to the material while it is annealed at a high temperature, an easy direction for magnetization is found to be induced in a direction coinciding with that of the applied field.

The above description explains why steel makes a better permanent magnet than does soft iron. The carbon in steel causes the precipitation of tiny crystallites of iron carbide in the iron that form what is called a second phase. The phase boundaries between the precipitate particles and the host iron form obstacles to domain wall movement, and thus the coercive force and remanence are raised compared with pure iron.

The best permanent magnet, however, would be one in which the domain walls were all locked permanently in position and the magnetizations of all the domains were aligned parallel to each other. This situation can be visualized as the result of assembling the magnet from a large number of particles having a high value of saturation magnetization, each of which is a single domain, each having a uniaxial anisotropy in the desired direction, and each aligned with its magnetization parallel to all the others.

Powder magnets. The problem of producing magnets composed of compacted powders is essentially that of controlling particle sizes so that they are small enough to comprise a single domain and yet not so small as to lose their ferromagnetic properties altogether. The advantage of such magnets is that they can readily be molded and machined into desired shapes. The disadvantage of powder magnets is that when single-domain particles are packed together they are subject to strong magnetic interactions that reduce the coercive force and, to a lesser extent, the remanent magnetization. The nature of the interaction is essentially a reduction of a given particle's demagnetizing field caused by the presence of its neighbours, and the interaction limits the maximum values of H_c and $(BH)_{max}$ that can be achieved. More success has attended the development of magnetic alloys.

High anisotropy alloys. The materials described above depend on shape for their large uniaxial anisotropy. Much work has also been done on materials having a large uniaxial magnetocrystalline anisotropy. Of these, the most successful have been cobalt–platinum (CoPt) and manganese–bismuth (MnBi) alloys.

Alnico alloys. High coercive force will be obtained where domain wall motion can be inhibited. This condition can occur in an alloy in which two phases coexist, especially if one phase is a finely divided precipitate in a matrix of the other. Alloys containing the three elements iron, nickel, and aluminum show just such behaviour; and permanent magnet materials based on this system, with various additives, such as cobalt, copper, or titanium, are generally referred to as Alnico alloys.

Rare-earth–cobalt alloys. Isolated atoms of many elements have finite magnetic moments (*i.e.,* the atoms are themselves tiny magnets). When the atoms are brought together in the solid form of the element, however, most interact in such a way that their magnetism cancels out and the solid is not ferromagnetic. Only in iron, nickel, and cobalt, of the common elements, does the cancelling-out process leave an effective net magnetic moment per atom in the vicinity of room temperature and above. Unfortunately, however, it loses its ferromagnetism at temperatures above 16° C (60° F) so that it is not of practical importance. Several of the rare-earth elements show ferromagnetic behaviour at extremely low temperatures, and many of them have large atomic moments. They are not, however, of great practical value.

Barium ferrites. Barium ferrite, essentially $BaO{:}6Fe_2O_3$, is a variation of the basic magnetic iron-oxide magnetite but has a hexagonal crystalline form. This configuration gives it a very high uniaxial magnetic anisotropy capable of producing high values of H_c. The powdered material can be magnetically aligned and then compacted and sintered. The temperature and duration of the sintering process determines the size of the crystallites and provides a means of tailoring the properties of the magnet. For very small crystallites the coercive force is high and the remanence is in the region of half the saturation flux density. Larger crystallites give higher B_r but lower H_c. This material has been widely used in the television industry for focussing magnets for television tubes.

A further development of commercial importance is to bond the powdered ferrite by a synthetic resin or rubber to give either individual moldings or extruded strips, or sheets, that are semiflexible and can be cut with knives. This material has been used as a combination gasket (to make airtight) and magnetic closure for refrigerator doors.

Permeable materials. A wide range of magnetic devices utilizing magnetic fields, such as motors, generators, transformers, and electromagnets, require magnetic materials with properties quite contrary to those required for good permanent magnets. Such materials must be capable of being magnetized to a high value of flux density in relatively small magnetic fields and then must lose this magnetization completely on removal of the field.

Because iron has the highest value of magnetic moment per atom of the three ferromagnetic metals, it remains the best material for applications where a high-saturation flux density is required. Extensive investigations have been undertaken to determine how to produce iron as free from imperfections as possible, in order to attain the easiest possible domain wall motion. The presence of such elements as carbon, sulfur, oxygen, and nitrogen, even in small amounts, is particularly harmful; and thus sheet materials used in electrical equipment have a total impurity content of less than 0.4 percent.

Important advantages are obtained by alloying iron with a small amount (about 4 percent) of silicon. The added silicon reduces the magnetocrystalline anisotropy of the iron and hence its coercive force and hysteresis loss. Although there is a reduction in the saturation flux density, this loss is outweighed by the other advantages, which include increased electrical resistivity. The latter is important in applications where the magnetic flux alternates because this induces eddy currents in the magnetic material. The lower the resistivity and the higher the frequency of the alternations, the higher are these currents. They produce a loss of energy by causing heating of the material and will be minimized, at a given frequency, by raising the resistivity of the material.

By a suitable manufacturing process, silicon-iron sheet material can be produced with a high degree of preferred orientation of the crystallites. The material then has a preferred direction of magnetization, and in this direction high permeability and low loss are attained. Commercially produced material has about 3.2 percent silicon and is known as cold-reduced, grain-oriented silicon steel.

Alloys of nickel and iron in various proportions are given the general name Permalloy. As the proportion of nickel varies downward, the saturation magnetization increases, reaching a maximum at about 50 percent, falling to zero at 27 percent nickel, then rising again toward the value for pure iron. The magnetocrystalline anisotropy also falls from the value for pure nickel to a very low value in the region of 80 percent nickel, rising only slowly thereafter. Highest value of permeability is at 78.5 percent nickel, which is called Permalloy A. The maximum relative permeability, which can reach a value in the region of 1,000,000 in carefully prepared Permalloy A, makes the alloy useful and superior to iron and silicon iron at low flux densities.

In addition to barium ferrite, which has a hexagonal crystal form, most of the ferrites of the general formula $MeO \cdot Fe_2O_3$, in which Me is a metal, are useful magnetically. They have a different crystalline form called spinel after the mineral spinel ($MgAl_2O_4$), which crystallizes in the cubic system. All the spinel ferrites are soft magnetic materials; that is, they exhibit low coercive force and narrow hysteresis loops. Furthermore, they all have a high electrical resistivity and high relative permeabilities, thus making them suitable for use in high-frequency electronic equipment. Their saturation magnetization, however, is low compared with the alloys, and this property limits their use in high-field, high-power transformers. They are hard, brittle, ceramic-like materials and are difficult to machine. Nevertheless, they are widely used, most importantly in computer memories.

Consult the INDEX *first*

magnetic bubble memory, any of a class of computer memory devices that store data in tiny cylindrically shaped magnetic domains in a synthetic garnet chip (*see* computer memory).

magnetic circuit, closed path to which a magnetic field, represented as lines of magnetic flux, is confined. In contrast to an electric circuit through which electric charge flows, nothing actually flows in a magnetic circuit.

In a ring-shaped electromagnet with a small air gap, the magnetic field or flux is almost

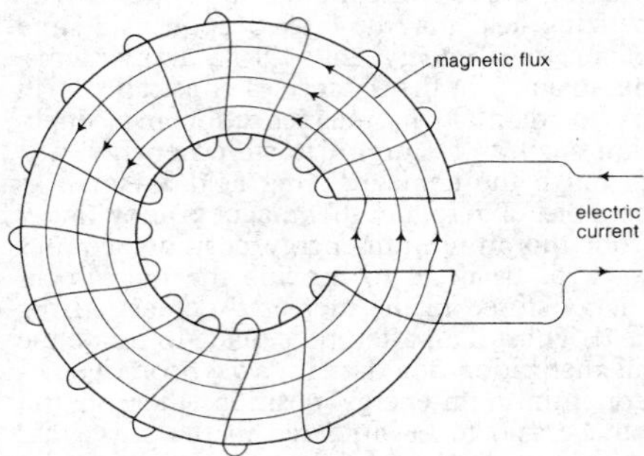

Magnetic circuit

entirely confined to the metal core and the air gap, which together form the magnetic circuit. In an electric motor, the magnetic field is largely confined to the magnetic pole pieces, the rotor, the air gaps between the rotor and the pole pieces, and the metal frame. Each magnetic field line makes a complete unbroken loop. All the lines together constitute the total flux. If the flux is divided, so that part of it is confined to a portion of the device and part to another, the magnetic circuit is called parallel. If all the flux is confined to a single closed loop, as in a ring-shaped electromagnet, the circuit is called a series magnetic circuit.

In analogy to an electric circuit in which the current, the electromotive force (voltage), and the resistance are related by Ohm's law (current equals electromotive force divided by resistance), a similar relation has been developed to describe a magnetic circuit.

The magnetic flux is analogous to the electric current. The magnetomotive force, mmf, is analogous to the electromotive force and may be considered the factor that sets up the flux. The mmf is equivalent to a number of turns of wire carrying an electric current and has units of ampere-turns. If either the current through a coil (as in an electromagnet) or the number of turns of wire in the coil is increased, the mmf is greater; and if the rest of the magnetic circuit remains the same, the magnetic flux increases proportionally.

The reluctance of a magnetic circuit is analogous to the resistance of an electric circuit. Reluctance depends on the geometrical and material properties of the circuit that offer opposition to the presence of magnetic flux. Reluctance of a given part of a magnetic circuit is proportional to its length and inversely proportional to its cross-sectional area and a magnetic property of the given material called its permeability. Iron, for example, has an extremely high permeability as compared to air so that it has a comparatively small reluctance, or it offers relatively little opposition to the presence of magnetic flux. In a series magnetic circuit, the total reluctance equals the sum of the individual reluctances encountered around the closed flux path. In a magnetic circuit, in summary, the magnetic flux is quantitatively equal to the magnetomotive force divided by the reluctance.

magnetic-core storage, any of a class of computer memory devices consisting of a large array of tiny toruses of a hard magnetic material that can be magnetized in either of two directions (*see* computer memory).

magnetic dipole, generally a tiny magnet of microscopic to subatomic dimensions, equivalent to a flow of electric charge around a loop. Electrons circulating around atomic nuclei, electrons spinning on their axes, and rotating positively charged atomic nuclei all are magnetic dipoles. The sum of these effects may cancel so that a given type of atom may not be a magnetic dipole. If they do not fully cancel, the atom is a permanent magnetic dipole, as are iron atoms. Many millions of iron atoms spontaneously locked into the same alignment to form a ferromagnetic domain also constitute a magnetic dipole. Magnetic compass needles and bar magnets are examples of macroscopic magnetic dipoles.

The strength of a magnetic dipole, called the magnetic dipole moment, may be thought of as a measure of a dipole's ability to turn itself into alignment with a given external magnetic field. In a uniform magnetic field, the magnitude of the dipole moment is proportional to the maximum amount of torque on the dipole, which occurs when the dipole is at right angles to the magnetic field. The magnetic dipole moment, often simply called the magnetic moment, may be defined then as the maximum amount of torque caused by magnetic force on a dipole that arises per unit value of surrounding magnetic field in vacuum.

When a magnetic dipole is considered as a current loop, the magnitude of the dipole mo-

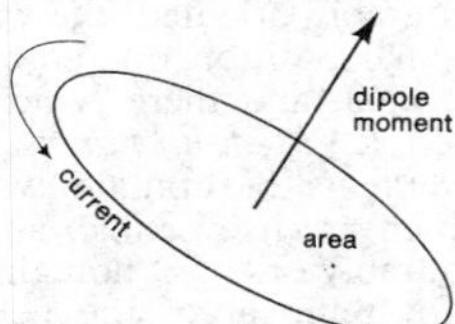

Magnetic dipole moment (proportional to current × area) associated with a current loop

ment is proportional to the current multiplied by the size of the enclosed area. The direction of the dipole moment, which may be represented mathematically as a vector, is perpendicularly away from the side of the surface enclosed by the counterclockwise path of positive charge flow. Considering the current loop as a tiny magnet, this vector corresponds to the direction from the south to the north pole. When free to rotate, dipoles align themselves so that their moments point predominantly in the direction of the external magnetic field. Nuclear and electron magnetic moments are quantized, which means that they may be oriented in space at only certain discrete angles with respect to the direction of the external field.

Magnetic dipole moments have dimensions of current times area or energy divided by magnetic flux density. In the metre–kilogram–second–ampere and SI systems, the specific unit for dipole moment is ampere-square metre. In the centimetre–gram–second electromagnetic system, the unit is the erg (unit of energy) per gauss (unit of magnetic flux density). One thousand ergs per gauss equal one ampere-square metre. A convenient unit for the magnetic dipole moment of electrons is the Bohr magneton (equivalent to 9.273×10^{-24} ampere-square metre). A similar unit for magnetic moments of nuclei, protons, and neutrons is the nuclear magneton (equivalent to 5.051×10^{-27} ampere-square metre).

magnetic field, region in the neighbourhood of a magnet, electric current, or changing electric field, in which magnetic forces are observable. Magnetic fields such as that of the

Earth cause magnetic compass needles and other permanent magnets to line up in the direction of the field. Magnetic fields force moving, electrically charged particles in a circular or helical path. This force—exerted on electric currents in wires in a magnetic field—underlies the operation of electric motors.

Around a permanent magnet or a wire carrying a steady electric current in one direction, the magnetic field is stationary and referred to as a magnetostatic field. At any given point its magnitude and direction remain the same. Around an alternating current or a fluctuating direct current, the magnetic field is continuously changing its magnitude and direction.

Magnetic fields may be represented by continuous lines of force or magnetic flux that emerge from north-seeking magnetic poles and enter south-seeking magnetic poles. The density of the lines indicates the magnitude of the magnetic field. At the poles of a magnet, for example, where the magnetic field is strong, the field lines are crowded together, or more dense. Farther away, where the magnetic field is weak, they fan out, becoming less dense. A uniform magnetic field is represented by equally spaced parallel straight lines. The direction of the flux is the direction in which the north-seeking pole of a small magnet points. The lines of flux are continuous, forming closed loops. For a bar magnet, they emerge from the north-seeking pole, fan out and around, enter the magnet at the south-seeking pole, and continue through the magnet to the north pole, where they again emerge. The SI unit for magnetic flux is the weber. The number of webers is a measure of the total number of field lines that cross a given area.

Magnetic fields may be represented mathematically by quantities called vectors that have direction as well as magnitude. Two different vectors are in use to represent a magnetic field: one called magnetic flux density, or magnetic induction, is symbolized by B; the other, called the magnetic field strength, or magnetic field intensity, is symbolized by H. The magnetic field H might be thought of as the magnetic field produced by the flow of current in wires and the magnetic field B as the total magnetic field including also the contribution made by the magnetic properties of the materials in the field. When a current flows in a wire wrapped on a soft-iron cylinder, the magnetizing field H is quite weak, but the actual average magnetic field (B) within the iron may be thousands of times stronger because B is greatly enhanced by the alignment of the iron's myriad tiny natural atomic magnets in the direction of the field. *See also* permeability, magnetic.

magnetic force, attraction or repulsion that arises between electrically charged particles because of their motion; the basic force responsible for the action of electric motors and the attraction of magnets for iron. Electric forces exist among stationary electric charges; both electric and magnetic forces exist among moving electric charges. The magnetic force between two moving charges may be described as the effect exerted upon either charge by a magnetic field created by the other.

From this point of view, the magnetic force F on the second particle is proportional to its charge q_2, the magnitude of its velocity v_2, the magnitude of the magnetic field B_1 produced by the first moving charge, and the sine of the angle theta, θ, between the path of the second particle and the direction of the magnetic field; that is, $F = q_2B_1v_2 \sin \theta$. The force is zero if the second charge is travelling in the direction of the magnetic field and is greatest if it travels at right angles to the magnetic field.

The magnetic force on a moving charge is exerted in a direction at a right angle to the plane formed by the direction of its velocity and the direction of the surrounding magnetic field.

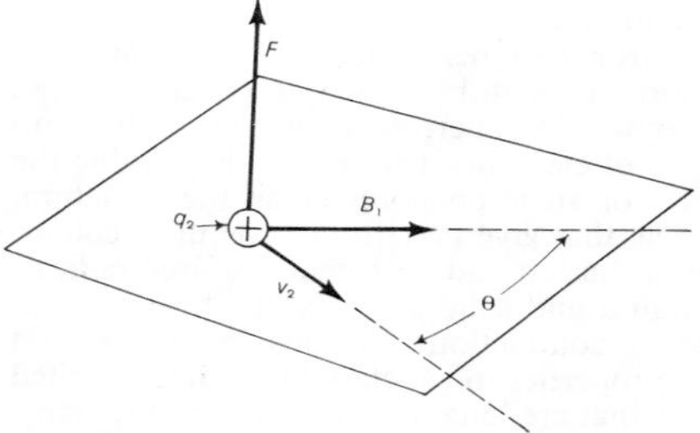

Magnetic force F is perpendicular to the plane of the velocity v_2 of the charge q_2 and the magnetic field B_1

From R.T. Weidner and R.L. Sells, *Elementary Classical Physics* (1965); Allyn and Bacon, Inc.

magnetic iron ore (mineral): *see* magnetite.

Magnetic Island, island in the Cumberland Islands, off the coast of northeastern Queensland, Australia, in Halifax Bay, an inlet of the Coral Sea. It is one of the most easily accessible islands of the Great Barrier Reef, being only 5 mi (8 km) offshore from Townsville. Coral-fringed, wooded, and hilly, it is a fragment of a drowned coastal mountain rising to 1,631 ft (497 m) above sea level at Mt. Cook. It has an area of 19 sq mi (49 sq km). The island was sighted in 1770 by the British navigator Capt. James Cook, who named it Magnetical because he believed, wrongly, that iron deposits in its hills affected his ship's compass. Now a national park, popular resort, and growing ferry-commuter suburb of Townsville, its principal communities are Arcadia, Nelly, and Picnic bays. Some pawpaws and pineapples are grown there commercially. Pop. (1981) 3,814.

magnetic mirror, static magnetic field that, within a localized region, has a shape such that approaching charged particles are repelled back along their path of approach.

A magnetic field is usually described as a distribution of nearly parallel nonintersecting field lines. The direction of these lines determines the direction of the magnetic field, and the density (closeness) of the lines determines its strength. Charged particles such as electrons tend to move through a magnetic field by following a helical path about a magnetic field line. If the field lines along the path of the particle are converging, the particle is entering a region of stronger magnetic field. The particle continues to circle about the field line, but its forward motion is retarded until it is stopped and finally forced back along its original path. The exact location at which this mirroring occurs depends only upon the initial pitch angle describing its helical path. Two such magnetic mirrors can be arranged to form a magnetic bottle that can trap charged particles in the middle.

magnetic monopole, particle with a magnetic charge, a property analogous to an electric charge. As implied by its name, the magnetic monopole consists of a single pole, as opposed to the dipole, which is comprised of two magnetic poles. As yet there is no evidence for the existence of magnetic monopoles, but they are interesting theoretically. In 1931 the English physicist P.A.M. Dirac proposed that the existence of even a single magnetic monopole in the universe would explain why electric charge comes only in multiples of the electron charge. Since the quantization of electric charge remains a great theoretical mystery, physicists have repeatedly renewed their search for monopoles whenever particle accelerators attain a new energy level or when a new source of matter is discovered. Lunar rock samples brought back by U.S. astronauts in 1969, for example, were extensively studied because it was thought that monopoles might be trapped in the surface material of the Moon. Research showed, however, that such was not the case.

magnetic permeability, relative increase or decrease in the resultant magnetic field inside a material compared with the magnetizing field in which the given material is located; or the property of a material that is equal to the magnetic flux density B established within the material by a magnetizing field divided by the magnetic field strength H of the magnetizing field. Magnetic permeability μ (Greek mu) is thus defined as $\mu = B/H$. Magnetic flux density B is a measure of the actual magnetic field within a material considered as a concentration of magnetic field lines, or flux, per unit cross-sectional area. Magnetic field strength H is a measure of the magnetizing field produced by electric current flow in a coil of wire.

In empty, or free, space the magnetic flux density is the same as the magnetizing field because there is no matter to modify the field. In centimetre–gram–second (cgs) units, the permeability B/H of space is dimensionless and has a value of 1. In metre–kilogram–second (mks) and SI units, B and H have different dimensions, and the permeability of free space (symbolized μ_0) is defined as equal to $4\pi \times 10^{-7}$ weber per ampere-metre so that the mks unit of electric current may be the same as the practical unit, the ampere. In these systems the permeability, B/H, is called the absolute permeability μ of the medium. The relative permeability μ_r is then defined as the ratio μ/μ_0, which is dimensionless and has the same numerical value as the permeability in the cgs system. Thus, the relative permeability of free space, or vacuum, is 1.

Materials may be classified magnetically on the basis of their permeabilities. A diamagnetic material has a constant relative permeability slightly less than 1. When a diamagnetic material, such as bismuth, is placed in a magnetic field, the external field is partly expelled, and the magnetic flux density within it is slightly reduced. A paramagnetic material has a constant relative permeability slightly more than 1. When a paramagnetic material, such as platinum, is placed in a magnetic field, it becomes slightly magnetized in the direction of the external field. A ferromagnetic material, such as iron, does not have a constant relative permeability. As the magnetizing field increases, the relative permeability increases, reaches a maximum, and then decreases. Purified iron and many magnetic alloys have maximum relative permeabilities of 100,000 or more.

magnetic pole, region at each end of a magnet where the external magnetic field is strongest. A bar magnet suspended in the Earth's magnetic field orients itself in a north–south direction. The north-seeking pole of such a magnet, or any similar pole, is called a north magnetic pole. The south-seeking pole, or any pole similar to it, is called a south magnetic pole. Unlike poles of different magnets attract each other; like poles repel each other.

The magnetic force between a pole of one long bar magnet and that of another was described by an inverse square law as early as 1750. If, for example, the separation between the two poles is doubled, the magnetic force diminishes to one-fourth its former value.

Breaking a magnet in two does not isolate its north pole from its south pole. Each half is found to have its own north and south poles. Magnetic forces, in fact, cannot be traced to unit magnetic poles of submicroscopic size in direct contrast to electric forces that are caused by actual discrete electric charges, such as electrons and protons. Indeed, magnetic forces themselves also fundamentally arise between electric charges when they are in motion. *See also* magnetic dipole.

magnetic recording, method of preserving sounds, pictures, and data in the form of electrical signals through the selective magnetization of portions of a magnetic material. The principle of magnetic recording was first demonstrated by the Danish engineer Valdemar Poulsen in 1900, when he introduced a machine called the telegraphone that recorded speech magnetically on steel wire.

In the years following Poulsen's invention, devices using a wide variety of magnetic recording mediums have been developed by researchers in Germany, Great Britain, and the United States. Principal among them are magnetic tape and disk recorders, which are used not only to reproduce audio and video signals but also to store computer data and measurements from instruments employed in scientific and medical research. Other significant magnetic recording devices include magnetic drum, core, and bubble units designed specifically to provide auxiliary data storage for computer systems.

Magnetic tape devices. Magnetic tape provides a compact, economical means of preserving and reproducing varied forms of information. Recordings on tape can be played back immediately and are easily erased, permitting the tape to be reused many times without a loss in quality of recording. For these reasons, tape is the most widely used of the various magnetic recording mediums. It consists of a narrow plastic ribbon coated with fine particles of iron oxide or other readily magnetizable material. In recording on tape, an electrical signal passes through a recording head as the tape is drawn past, leaving a magnetic imprint on the tape's surface. When the recorded tape is drawn past the playback or reproducing head, a signal is induced that is the equivalent of the recorded signal. This signal is amplified to the intensity appropriate to the output equipment.

Tape speeds for sound recording vary from less than 2 inches (5 centimetres) per second to as much as 15 in. (37.5 cm) per second. Video signals occupy a much wider bandwidth than do audio signals and require a much higher relative speed between the tape and the head. Data recording requires even greater speeds. The tape transport of a data-storage unit of a high-performance digital computer, for example, must be able to move the tape past the head at a rate of 200 in. (500 cm) per second.

Magnetic tape was initially designed for sound recording. German engineers developed an audio tape recording machine called the magnetophone during World War II. U.S. and British researchers adopted the basic design of this device to create a magnetic tape recorder capable of high-quality sound reproduction in the late 1940s. Within a decade magnetic tape supplanted phonograph records for radio music programming. Prerecorded tapes in the form of cartridges and cassettes for sound systems in homes and automobiles were in widespread use by the late 1960s.

Related to the audio cassette recorder is a magnetic tape recording system that serves as a telephone answering device. Messages or instructions prerecorded on tape are reproduced automatically when a telephone user's number is dialled. The answering device then actuates the recording head, which records any messages that the caller wishes to leave.

In 1956 Charles P. Ginsburg and Ray Dolby of Ampex Corporation, a U.S. electronics firm, developed the first practical videotape recorder. Their machine revolutionized television broadcasting; recorded shows virtually replaced live telecasts with a few exceptions, such as coverage of sports events. Almost all programs are videotaped during their original telecasts, and individual broadcasters then rerun the shows at times most suitable for their own viewers. An increasing number of videotape recorders are used for recording television broadcasts received in private homes. Many such units can produce home movies if connected to an accessory video camera. Commercially produced video cassettes of popular motion pictures also can be played on these recorders. *See also* videotape recorder.

Magnetic tape was introduced as a data-storage medium in 1951, when it was used in the auxiliary memory of UNIVAC I, the first digital computer produced for commercial use. For about the next 10 years nearly all computers employed magnetic tape storage units. By the 1960s, however, magnetic disk and magnetic drum auxiliary memories began replacing the tape units in large-scale scientific and business data-processing systems that require extremely fast retrieval of stored information and programs. Magnetic tape devices, particularly those using cassettes, continue to be employed as a principal form of auxiliary memory in general-purpose minicomputers and microcomputers because of their low cost and great storage capacity. About 48,000 bits of information can be stored on one inch of tape.

Magnetic tape recorders have also been widely used to record measurements directly from laboratory instruments and detection devices carried aboard planetary probes. The readings are converted into electrical signals and recorded on tape, which can be played back by researchers for detailed analysis and comparison.

Magnetic disk devices. Magnetic disks are flat circular plates of metal or plastic, coated on both sides with iron oxide. Input signals, which may be audio, video, or data, are recorded on the surface of a disk as magnetic patterns or spots in spiral tracks by a recording head while the disk is rotated by a drive unit. The heads, which are also used to read the magnetic impressions on the disk, can be positioned anywhere on the disk with great precision. For computer data-storage applications, a collection of as many as 20 disks (called a disk pack) is mounted vertically on the spindle of a drive unit. The drive unit is equipped with multiple reading/writing heads.

These features give magnetic disk devices an advantage over tape recorders. A disk unit has the ability to read any given segment of an audio or video recording or block of data without having to pass over a major portion of its content sequentially; locating desired information on tape may take many minutes. In a magnetic disk unit, direct access to a precise track on a specific disk reduces retrieval time to a fraction of a second.

Magnetic disk technology was applied to data storage in 1962. The random accessibility of data stored in disk units made these devices particularly suitable for use as auxiliary memories in high-speed computer systems. Small, flexible plastic disks called floppy disks were developed during the 1970s. Although floppy disks cannot store as much information as conventional disks or retrieve data as rapidly, they are adequate for applications such as those involving minicomputers and microcomputers where low cost and ease of use are of primary importance.

Magnetic disk recording has various other uses. Office dictating machines and transcribing units utilize the process for storing spoken messages for later use. Magnetic disk technology has also facilitated and improved a method known as "instant replay" that is widely used in live telecasts, especially of sports events. This method involves the immediate re-showing of, for example, a crucial play in a football game during a live-action broadcast. Videotape recorders were initially used for instant replay, but they proved too cumbersome. In 1967 Ampex developed a special videodisk machine that made it possible to locate and replay a desired action in less than four seconds.

Other magnetic recording devices. Such magnetic recording mediums as drums and ferrite cores have been used for data storage since the early 1950s. A more recent development is the magnetic bubble memory devised in the late 1970s at Bell Telephone Laboratories.

Auxiliary computer memories using a magnetic drum operate somewhat like tape and disk units. They store data in the form of magnetized spots in adjacent circular tracks on the surface of a metal cylinder. A single drum may carry from one to 200 tracks. Data are recorded and read by heads positioned near the surface of the drum as the drum rotates at about 3,000 revolutions per minute. Drums provide rapid, random access to stored information. They are able to retrieve information faster than tape and disk units, but cannot store as much data as either of them.

Core memories use hundreds of thousands of magnetizable ferrite cores that resemble tiny doughnuts. Through each of the cores run two or more wires, which carry electrical currents that magnetize the cores in either a clockwise or counterclockwise direction. Cores magnetized in one direction are said to represent 0, and those in the opposite direction to represent 1. The 0 and 1 correspond to the digits of the binary system, the basis for digital computer operations. Data are stored by magnetizing an array of cores in a particular combination of 0s and 1s. Core storage units allow extremely fast, random access to stored information. Unlike other magnetic memory devices that have to wait for tape reels to unwind or drums to rotate, retrieval is performed simply by sending electrical pulses to the specific array of cores holding the desired data. The pulses reverse the direction of magnetization in the cores, which includes output signals corresponding to the stored data.

The magnetic bubble memory is more economical to operate than mechanical tape, disk, or drum units and is considerably more compact. The device consists of a chip of synthetic garnet about the size of a matchbook. It stores data in tiny cylindrically shaped magnetic domains called bubbles that appear and disappear under the control of an electromagnetic field. The presence and absence of the bubbles represent information in binary form in much the same way as do the two states of magnetic cores. As each tiny garnet chip accommodates hundreds of thousands of binary digits, enormous amounts of data can be stored in a memory unit comprised of a small stack of these chips.

magnetic resonance, absorption or emission of electromagnetic radiation by electrons or atomic nuclei in response to the application of certain magnetic fields. The principles of magnetic resonance are applied in the laboratory to analyze the atomic and nuclear properties of matter.

Electron-spin resonance (ESR) was first observed in 1944 by a Soviet physicist, Y.K. Zavoysky, in experiments on salts of the iron group of elements. ESR has made possible the study of such phenomena as the structural defects that give certain crystals their colour, the formation and destruction of free radicals in liquid and solid samples, the behaviour of free or conduction electrons in metals, and the properties of metastable states (excited states that are long-lived because energy transfer from them by radiation does not occur) in molecular crystals.

Nuclear magnetic resonance (NMR) of protons was first observed in the United States in 1946 by Felix Bloch, William W. Hansen, and Martin E. Packard and independently by

Edward M. Purcell, Robert V. Pound, and Henry C. Torrey. Scientists soon observed NMR in practically all the stable nuclei with nuclear moments greater than zero (about 100 species). Later discoveries with NMR included electric quadrupole effects; an important shift of NMR frequencies in metals; and the splitting of energy levels in liquids resulting from variations in chemical structure and the influence of one nuclear spin on another.

A particle of matter that is spinning about its own axis or moving in an orbit around some external point acts like a gyroscope: it resists forces that tend to change its state of motion. The measure of this resistance is the mechanical angular momentum, which depends on the mass of the particle, its size or that of its orbit, and the angular velocity (the number of revolutions per unit time). The angular momentum is represented by a vector directed along the axis of rotation. An electric charge in such motion creates a magnetic field with strength and direction represented by a magnetic vector denoted $\boldsymbol{\mu}$. This vector, which is proportional to the magnitude of the charge (instead of the mass of a particle), measures the tendency of the charge's axis of rotation to align itself in the direction of an external magnetic field. The motion of a particle that has both mass and charge is characterized by both of these vectors, which will be collinear but may be oppositely directed, depending on the sign of the charge.

If a bar magnet that is not spinning is placed in a magnetic field, its north pole seeks the south pole of the field, and it comes to rest with its own field aligned with the external field. Work would be required to change its orientation; this means that the system can store potential energy. The energy associated with the magnet depends, therefore, on its magnetic moment, the strength of the external magnetic field, and the angle between the direction of the moment of the magnet and the direction of the external field.

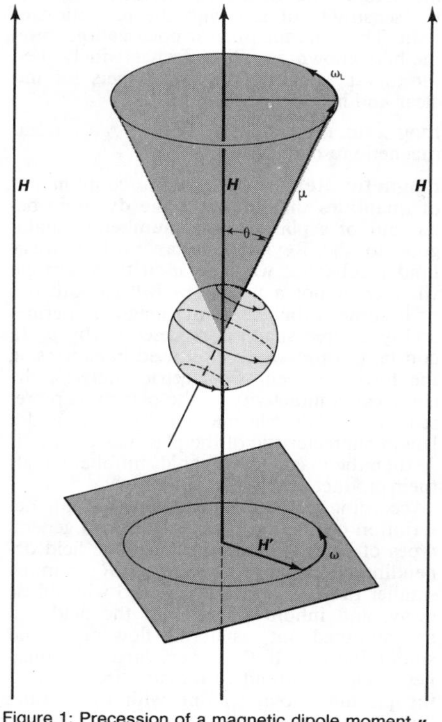

Figure 1: Precession of a magnetic dipole moment $\boldsymbol{\mu}$ in the presence of a constant field $\boldsymbol{H}$ and a rotating field $\boldsymbol{H'}$ (see text)

In Figure 1, the magnetic vector $\boldsymbol{\mu}$ of a spinning charged particle is depicted as lying along the axis of rotation. The surrounding magnetic field (symbolized by the vector $\boldsymbol{H}$) exerts a torque that tends to bring $\boldsymbol{\mu}$ and $\boldsymbol{H}$ into alignment, but this torque also interacts with the angular momentum vector; the effect of this interaction is to cause the spin axis (and the magnetic-moment vector) to undergo the so-called Larmor precession, that is, to describe a cone about the direction of the magnetic field. According to classical electrodynamics, the frequency (ω_L) of the Larmor precession (the number of rotations per second of the vector $\boldsymbol{\mu}$ about the vector $\boldsymbol{H}$) should be independent of the orientation angle (θ). But according to quantum mechanics, the orientation angle of a single particle can assume only certain discrete values because the angular momentum of the particle must be an integral multiple of a fundamental unit of angular momentum. For this reason, a rotating charged particle in a magnetic field occupies one of a limited set of discrete magnetic energy states.

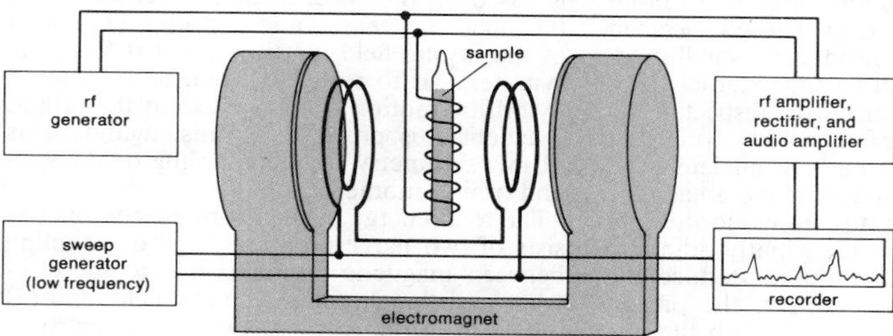

Figure 2: Magnetic resonance spectrometer (see text)

In magnetic-resonance devices, a weak oscillating field ($\boldsymbol{H'}$) is superimposed on a strong constant field ($\boldsymbol{H}$), as shown in Figure 1, and its vector rotates with an angular velocity ($\boldsymbol{\omega}$) in a plane perpendicular to the direction of the strong field. If the rate of rotation (ω) of the weak superimposed field is different from the Larmor frequency (ω_L) of the precessing particle, the two rotating fields will be out of phase; the axis of the particle will successively be attracted and repelled by the superimposed rotating field during complete revolutions and will wobble only slightly. When they are synchronized, however, a steady force will act on the axis. In this situation, called resonance, the orientation angle (and with it the magnetic energy state) of the particle will suddenly change. When a system is raised to a higher state, energy is extracted from the superimposed field, and vice versa. The use of an oscillating field to produce resonance is sometimes called "driving a resonance."

Every experiment in magnetic resonance involves detecting the resonance; *i.e.,* ascertaining that the transition has actually taken place. Magnetic resonance (MR) makes use of electromagnetic detection, in which the energy liberated or absorbed in a transition is precisely that which is measured. In an MR spectrometer (Figure 2) the amount of energy extracted from the superimposed field is continuously measured and recorded on a strip chart while the frequency of the field is slowly varied. The resulting record, or spectrum, is ordinarily a straight line—indicating that the sample is absorbing no energy—broken by peaks at the resonance frequencies. Under typical experimental conditions these peaks are so narrow (because the resonances are very sharply tuned) that they appear as lines perpendicular to the flat trace obtained over the ranges of nonresonating frequencies. These so-called magnetic resonance spectral lines are only roughly analogous to the absorption and emission lines observed in optical spectra. The interpretation of MR in bulk matter is considerably complicated by the relationship of the spins with each other and with the other degrees of freedom of the sample. This complication, however, turns out to be an asset rather than a drawback for magnetic resonance, because it is the very existence of these interactions that makes MR such a remarkable tool for the study of bulk matter.

In many kinds of atoms all of the electrons are paired; that is, the spins are oppositely directed and therefore neutralized, and there is no net spin angular momentum or magnetic moment. In other species of atoms there are one or more electrons that are not paired, and it is therefore possible for any of these atoms to acquire or lose various quantum multiples of energy. The same phenomenon occurs in many species of nuclei, so that nuclei can lie in different magnetic energy states.

For magnetic fields of the order of a few kilogauss (gauss is a unit of magnetic intensity; the horizontal intensity of the Earth's magnetic field is roughly 0.2 gauss) used in MR spectrometers, NMR frequencies fall into the radio-frequency or broadcasting range, whereas ESR frequencies occur in the microwave or radar range. For instance, the proton NMR frequency in a field of 10 kilogauss is 42.58 megahertz, and in the same field the ESR frequency of a free spin is 28,000 megahertz. The number of spins detectable by magnetic resonance varies widely with the applied field, the temperature, the nature of the sample, and for NMR the nuclear species; under the best conditions, it can be as low as 10^{18} spins for NMR and 10^{10} spins for ESR.

Nuclear magnetic resonance. In the absence of atomic motion in rigid lattices (crystals), NMR makes it possible to determine molecular structures not observable by other means. In many solids, even at low temperatures, there occur atomic diffusion and rotation of groups of atoms. These movements affect the shape of the NMR absorption peak. A study of these effects as a function of temperature can supplement other physical measurements.

In metals, the nuclei are influenced by an interaction between the spins of the conduction electrons (electrons not bound to atoms that move freely through the metal) and the applied field. This condition results in a shift of the resonant frequency from the value observed for the same nucleus when it is present in an insulator. These so-called metallic shifts provide important information on the magnetic susceptibility, the quantum mechanical wave functions that describe energy states, and the density of states of conduction electrons in the metal. In superconductors, the shape of the NMR spectral peaks provide detailed information on the penetration and internal distribution of the magnetic field. In ferromagnets or antiferromagnets (crystals in which not all electrons are paired), the NMR is influenced by the internal magnetic fields produced by the array of ordered electronic spins. In ferromagnets the shift is a measure of the lattice magnetization; in an antiferromagnet there are at least two shifts that give the magnetization of each antiferromagnetic sublattice separately, a result unattainable by conventional magnetic measurements.

For certain nuclei, the NMR spectrum reveals the existence of nuclear electric quadrupole moments (an electric quadrupole consists of a charge distribution equivalent to a special arrangement of two electric dipoles) that interact with the electric fields that exist at the nuclear sites. These interactions provide information on the microscopic distribution of electric charge around the nucleus.

The most important consequence of the extraordinary sharpness of nuclear magnetic resonance (NMR) lines in liquids is the possibility of measuring the chemical shifts—that is, the separations between NMR lines from nuclear spins of the same species but in different molecular environments. The physical origin of chemical shifts is the following: an external magnetic field polarizes the closed electron shells of the atoms and produces a small magnetic field, proportional to the external field, which shifts the NMR line with respect to its position for the bare nucleus—*e.g.,* one that is devoid of electrons. The bare nucleus itself is never observed, but the atomic diamagnetic shifts that correspond to atoms located in different molecular sites are slightly different, and it is their differences that produce the chemical shifts. As an example, the proton NMR spectrum of ethyl alcohol, with the formula CH_3-CH_2-OH, exhibits three peaks, with relative weights or intensities of 3:2:1. In more complicated molecules such spectra contain much chemical information and can help in the determination of unknown molecular structures.

The multiplicity of lines is further increased by the interaction between nuclear spins. As already mentioned in connection with motion narrowing in liquids, the usual magnetic dipolar interactions are averaged out by molecular motion and do not split the NMR spectra. There exists, however, an indirect interaction between nuclear spins, caused by the electrons, that splits the resonance line of a specific nuclear spin into many components.

High-resolution nuclear magnetic resonance has become one of the most prized tools in the fields of organic chemistry and biochemistry. On the experimental side, the requirements to be met by the equipment are severe. In order to match natural line widths of a fraction of a cycle, the applied magnetic fields must have a relative stability and homogeneity throughout the sample better than one part in 10^8. Special magnets that give uniform fields and are stabilized, devices that twirl samples in order to smooth out the magnetic inhomogeneity, and sophisticated radio-frequency detection equipment are commercially available. The trend toward higher fields (over 100 kilogauss), resulting from superconducting solenoids, improves the resolution by increasing the chemical shift splittings and the signal-to-noise ratio.

The measurement of the precession frequency of proton spins in a magnetic field can give the value of the field with high accuracy and is widely used for that purpose. In low fields, such as the Earth's magnetic field, the NMR signal is expected to be weak because the nuclear magnetization is small, but special devices can enhance the signal 100 or 1000 times. Incorporated in existing portable magnetometers, these devices make them capable of measuring fields to an absolute accuracy of about one part in 1,000,000 and detecting field variations of about 10^{-8} gauss. Apart from the direct measurement of the magnetic field on Earth or in space, these magnetometers prove to be useful whenever a phenomenon is linked with variations of magnetic field in space or in time, such as anomalies arising from submarines, skiers buried under snow, archaeological remains, and mineral deposits.

Electron-spin resonance. In contrast to nuclear magnetic resonance, electron-spin resonance (ESR) is observed only in a restricted class of substances. These substances include transition elements—that is, elements with unfilled inner electronic shells—free radicals (molecular fragments), metals, and various paramagnetic defects and impurity centres. Another difference from NMR is a far greater sensitivity to environment; whereas the resonance frequencies in NMR in general are shifted from those of bare nuclei by very small amounts because of the influence of conduction electrons, chemical shifts, spin-spin couplings, and so on, the ESR frequencies in bulk matter may differ greatly from those of free spins or free atoms because the unfilled subshells of the atom are easily distorted by the interactions occurring in bulk matter.

A model that has been highly successful for the description of magnetism in bulk matter is based on the effect of the crystal lattice on the magnetic centre under study. The effect of the crystal field, particularly if it has little symmetry, is to reduce the magnetism caused by orbital motion. To some extent the orbital magnetism is preserved against ligand fields of low symmetry by the coupling of the spin and orbital momenta.

The total energy of the magnetic centre consists of two parts: (1) the energy of coupling between magnetic moments due to the electrons and the external magnetic field, and (2) the electrostatic energy between the electronic shells and the ligand field, which is independent of the applied magnetic field. The energy levels give rise to a spectrum with many different resonance frequencies, the fine structure.

Another important feature of electron-spin resonance results from the interaction of the electronic magnetization with the nuclear moment, causing each component of the fine-structure resonance spectrum to be split further into many so-called hyperfine components. If the electronic magnetization is spread over more than one atom, it can interact with more than one nucleus; and, in the expression for hyperfine levels, the hyperfine coupling of the electrons with a single nucleus must be replaced by the sum of the coupling with all the nuclei. Each hyperfine line is then split further by the additional couplings into what is known as superhyperfine structure.

The key problem in electron-spin resonance is, on one hand, to construct a mathematical description of the total energy of the interaction in the ligand field plus the applied magnetic field and, on the other hand, to deduce the parameters of the theoretical expression from an analysis of the observed spectra. The comparison of the two sets of values permits a detailed quantitative test of the microscopic description of the structure of matter in the compounds studied by ESR.

The transition elements include the iron group, the lanthanide (or rare-earth) group, the palladium group, the platinum group, and the actinide group. The resonance behaviour of compounds of these elements is conditioned by the relative strength of the ligand field and the spin-orbit coupling. In the lanthanides, for instance, the ligand field is weak and unable to uncouple the spin and orbital momentum, leaving the latter largely unreduced. On the other hand, in the iron group, the components of the ligand field are, as a rule, stronger than the spin-orbit coupling, and the orbital momentum is strongly reduced.

The advent of ESR has marked a new understanding of these substances. Thus, it was formerly thought that in the iron group and the lanthanide group ions of the crystal were bound together solely by their electrostatic attraction, the magnetic electrons being completely localized on the transition ion. The discovery of superhyperfine structure demonstrated conclusively that some covalent bonding to neighbouring ions exists.

With few exceptions, the magnetic moments of imperfections such as vacancies at lattice sites and impurity centres in crystals that give rise to an observable ESR have the characteristics of a free electronic spin. In the study of these centres, hyperfine and superhyperfine structure provide a mapping of the electronic magnetization and make it possible to test the correctness of the model chosen to describe the defect.

The most widely studied by resonance are those of phosphorus, arsenic, and antimony, substituted in the semiconductors silicon and germanium. Studies of hyperfine and superhyperfine structure give detailed information on the status of these impurities.

Free radicals are ideally suited for study by electron-spin resonance. They can be studied in a concentrated form or in very dilute solutions. The sensitivity of ESR is particularly important for the study of very short-lived species. The ESR of free radicals in solutions gives an extreme wealth of hyperfine lines because the magnetic electron is not localized on one nucleus but interacts with several nuclei of the radical.

Combined electron-spin and nuclear magnetic resonances. When a species exhibits more than one resonance, it may be advantageous to study two or more of them simultaneously. In general, this study involves driving one resonance while detecting the other. Thus, an apparatus with two oscillating magnetic fields is employed, one for the driver and the other for the detector. Driving an NMR and detecting its effect on an ESR is known as ENDOR (electron-nuclear double resonance), whereas driving an ESR to increase a nuclear magnetization, observed by NMR, is called DNP (dynamic nuclear polarization).

Electron-nuclear double resonance is mainly used in making accurate measurements of hyperfine and superhyperfine splittings for detailed mapping of electron-spin densities. In the ENDOR method, driving an NMR resonance changes the populations of at least one of the energy levels between which an ESR transition is observable, and thus the strong ESR signal is measurably modified. ENDOR thus combines the sensitivity of ESR with the resolution of NMR. The dynamic nuclear polarization (DNP) method known as solid effect is widely used for making polarized proton targets for nuclear and high energy physics.

magnetic resonance imaging: *see* nuclear magnetic resonance.

magnetic Reynolds number, combination of quantities that indicates the dynamic behaviour of a plasma. This number is analogous to the Reynolds number of ordinary fluid mechanics, which is used to determine whether or not a fluid flow will smooth out or become turbulent. If the magnetic permeability of free space is represented by μ_0 (a constant of proportionality used in expressing the force between two electric charges), the electrical conductivity of the plasma is represented by σ, the plasma velocity by V, and a length characteristic of the plasma structure is L, then the magnetic Reynolds number equals their product, or $R_m = \mu_0 \sigma V L$.

According to the magnetohydrodynamic description of the plasma, there are two general types of behaviour for the magnetic field depending upon the value of R_m. If R_m is much smaller than 1, the magnetic field will diffuse away, and inhomogeneities in the field will be smoothed out, as in the flow of a fluid smoothing out. If R_m is very large, the magnetic-field lines tend to remain "frozen" into the plasma, moving along with the plasma flow.

magnetic storm, disturbance of the Earth's upper atmosphere brought on by solar flares—*i.e.,* bright eruptions from the visible portion of the Sun's chromosphere. The material associated with these flares consists primarily of protons and electrons with an energy of a few thousand electron volts. Called plasma, this material moves through the interplanetary medium at speeds ranging from 1,000 to

2,000 km (600 to 1,200 miles) per second, so that the ejected material reaches the Earth in approximately 21 hours. The pressure of the incoming plasma is transmitted to the outer edge of the Earth's magnetosphere; this causes an increase in the observed geomagnetic field at the ground, perhaps through hydromagnetic waves.

During these few minutes—the sudden-commencement phase—of the storm, the horizontal component of the geomagnetic field increases suddenly over the entire globe. The increase persists for two to six hours and is classified as the initial phase of the storm. One theory holds that, during the initial phase, added pressure on the Earth's magnetosphere causes the tail of the magnetosphere to be extended. In response to this unstable condition, the newly created magnetic lines in the interior of the tail contract rapidly, thereby sending plasma from the neutral sheet of the magnetosphere toward the night side of the Earth. This plasma injection results in intense auroral displays in the polar regions, while the contractions are observed on the Earth as a severe magnetic disturbance known as a polar substorm. This portion of the storm is followed by the storm's main phase, lasting 12 to 48 hours, during which the horizontal component of the field decreases, probably because of the injection or inflation of the magnetosphere by the incoming plasma. In the last stages, or recovery phase, the newly injected plasma drains slowly over several days into the interplanetary medium or the atmosphere, and the geomagnetic field approaches its prestorm condition.

magnetic survey, one of the tools used by the exploration geophysicist in his search for mineral-bearing ore bodies or even oil-bearing sedimentary structures. The essential feature is the measurement of the magnetic-field intensity and sometimes the magnetic inclination, or dip, and declination (departure from geographic north) at several stations. If the object of the survey is to make a rapid reconnaissance of an area, a magnetic-intensity profile is made only over the target area. If the object of the survey is to delineate already discovered structures, the geophysicist sets up a grid over the area and makes measurements at each station on the grid. The corrected data he records is then entered on a scale drawing of the grid, and contour lines are drawn between points of equal intensity to give a magnetic map of the target area that may clearly indicate the size and extent of the anomalous body to the trained eye of the interpreting geophysicist.

magnetic susceptibility, quantitative measure of the extent to which a material may be magnetized in relation to a given applied magnetic field. The magnetic susceptibility of a material, commonly symbolized by χ_m, is equal to the ratio of the magnetization M within the material to the applied magnetic field strength H, or $\chi_m = M/H$. This ratio, strictly speaking, is the volume susceptibility, because magnetization essentially involves a certain measure of magnetism (dipole moment) per unit volume.

Magnetic materials may be classified as diamagnetic, paramagnetic, or ferromagnetic on the basis of their susceptibilities. Diamagnetic materials, such as bismuth, when placed in an external magnetic field, partly expel the external field from within themselves and, if shaped like a rod, line up at right angles to a nonuniform magnetic field. Diamagnetic materials are characterized by constant, small negative susceptibilities, only slightly affected by changes in temperature.

Paramagnetic materials, such as platinum, increase a magnetic field in which they are placed because their atoms have small magnetic dipole moments that partly line up with the external field. Paramagnetic materials have constant, small positive susceptibilities, less than 1/1,000 at room temperature, which means that the enhancement of the magnetic field caused by the alignment of magnetic dipoles is relatively small compared with the applied field. Paramagnetic susceptibility is inversely proportional to the value of the absolute temperature. Temperature increases cause greater thermal vibration of atoms, which interferes with alignment of magnetic dipoles.

Ferromagnetic materials, such as iron and cobalt, do not have constant susceptibilities; the magnetization is not usually proportional to the applied field strength. Measured ferromagnetic susceptibilities have relatively large positive values, sometimes in excess of 1,000. Thus, within ferromagnetic materials, the magnetization may be more than 1,000 times larger than the external magnetizing field, because such materials are composed of highly magnetized clusters of atomic magnets (ferromagnetic domains) that are more easily lined up by the external field.

magnetism, phenomenon associated with the motion of electric charges. It involves magnetic fields, which are regions wherein a force is exerted on a current-carrying medium or magnetic body, and the effects of such fields.

A brief treatment of magnetism follows. For full treatment, *see* MACROPAEDIA: Electricity and Magnetism.

The magnetic properties of matter are largely determined by the behaviour of the negatively charged electrons that orbit the nuclei of atoms. The magnetic dipole moment of a single orbital electron has two components, one resulting from the spin of the electron about its own axis, the other from its orbital motion about the nucleus. Both kinds of motion may be considered as tiny circular currents—moving charges—thus linking electric and magnetic effects at a fundamental level. For most atoms and molecules, the sum total magnetic moment of all the orbital electrons is zero. When these materials are placed in a magnetic field, a small magnetic moment is induced by the interaction of the field with atomic electrons; this induced moment is opposite in direction to the applied field, and substances that exhibit this effect are called diamagnetic. In some materials whose atoms have an incomplete electron shell, each atom has a net magnetic moment which while ordinarily randomly ordered, will react to an applied field to exhibit a bulk net magnetism; such materials are called paramagnetic. In some highly ordered crystalline materials—iron, nickel, and cobalt, for instance—the spins of some of the orbital electrons in adjacent atoms become coupled, creating local magnetic domains in which the magnetization is unidirectional. Adjacent domains are magnetized in different directions, so that there is no resultant bulk magnetization. When an external field is applied, however, those domains aligned with the field grow at the expense of those that are not, and a very strong permanent magnetization results; materials exhibiting this property are called ferromagnetic. Related phenomena are antiferromagnetism and ferrimagnetism (*qq.v.*).

Magnetic fields exert forces on moving charges. Examples of this include the bending of an electron beam in a cathode-ray tube, the Hall effect in a semiconductor or conductor, and the motor force on a current-carrying conductor. The converse occurs when a conductor is moved through a magnetic field; it experiences an electromotive force which causes a current to flow through it.

The magnetic properties of the black metallic mineral magnetite, an oxide of iron found in igneous rocks, were known to the ancient Greeks. The practical application of those properties in the magnetic compass was accomplished possibly as early as the 26th century BC by the Chinese, though historians remain uncertain on this point. The first serious study of magnetism was made by Petrus Peregrinus de Maricourt in the late 1260s. He established the existence of magnetic poles and stated that like poles repel and unlike attract; he also specified the construction of a mariner's compass in detail. William Gilbert, physician to Queen Elizabeth I, observed that the Earth is a huge magnet and thus explained why a magnetic needle tends to dip its north-pointing end downward in the Northern Hemisphere. The forces between the poles of magnets were first investigated experimentally by the French physicist Charles-Augustin de Coulomb in 1785 and were found to follow an inverse square law. (Coulomb's finding corroborated the observation made by the English physicist Joseph Priestly some years earlier.) In 1824 Siméon-Denis Poisson, a French mathematician, presented a mathematical model of magnetism which still provides a sound basis for the calculation of the forces between permanent magnets.

A connection between electricity and magnetism had long been suspected, and in 1820 the Danish physicist Hans Christian Ørsted showed that an electric current flowing in a wire produces its own magnetic field. André-Marie Ampère of France immediately repeated Ørsted's experiments and within weeks was able to express the magnetic forces between current-carrying conductors in a simple and elegant mathematical form. He also demonstrated that a current flowing in a loop of wire produces a magnetic dipole indistinguishable at a distance from that produced by a small permanent magnet; this led Ampère to suggest that magnetism is caused by currents circulating on a molecular scale, an idea remarkably near the modern understanding.

The English chemist and physicist Michael Faraday demonstrated the "motor" action of a current-carrying conductor in a magnetic field in 1821 and the induction of a current in a moving conductor in a magnetic field—the dynamo effect—in 1831; he coined the term magnetic field in 1845. The electromagnet, in which an iron core enhances the field generated by a current flowing through a coil, was invented by William Sturgeon in England during the mid-1820s. It later became a vital component of both motors and generators.

The unification of electric and magnetic phenomena in a complete mathematical theory was the achievement of the Scottish physicist James Clerk Maxwell. Maxwell's field equations, published in 1864, predicted the existence of electromagnetic waves, subsequently verified by Heinrich Hertz of Germany, and showed that light was also such a wave.

Today magnetism finds many technical applications, from the humble magnetic door catch to medical imaging devices and superconducting magnets for use in high-energy particle accelerators.

magnetite, also called LODESTONE, or MAGNETIC IRON ORE, iron oxide mineral ($FeFe_2O_4$, or Fe_3O_4) that is the chief member of one of

Magnetite in talc from Chester, Vt.
E.R. Degginger—EB Inc.

the series of the spinel (*q.v.*) group. Minerals in this series form black to brownish, metallic, moderately hard octahedrons and masses in igneous and metamorphic rocks and in granite pegmatites, stony meteorites, and high-temperature sulfide veins. The magnetite series also contains magnesioferrite (magnesium iron oxide, $MgFe_2O_4$), franklinite (zinc iron oxide, $ZnFe_2O_4$), jacobsite (manganese iron oxide, $MnFe_2O_4$), and trevorite (nickel iron oxide, $NiFe_2O_4$). All are magnetic, although franklinite and jacobsite are only weakly so; magnetite, which frequently has distinct north and south poles, has been known for this property since about 500 BC. For detailed physical properties, *see* oxide mineral (table).

magneto, permanent-magnet alternating generator employed when the output of energy required is very small. It is primarily designed to generate current for the ignition of compressed gases in various types of internal-combustion engines, such as those used in aircraft, marine, tractor, and motorcycle engines. The major parts of the high-tension magneto are a permanent-magnet rotor, an armature with a primary winding containing a small number of turns of coarse wire, a secondary winding with a large number of turns of fine wire, a cam-type circuit breaker, and a capacitor. As the magnetic rotor turns, it induces in the primary winding a current that charges the capacitor. The cam breaks the circuit of the primary winding when the induced current reaches its peak, and the magnetic field around the primary winding collapses. The capacitor discharges its stored current into the primary winding, inducing a reversed magnetic field. The collapse and reversal of the magnetic field induces a high-voltage current in the secondary winding that is distributed to the spark plugs for ignition.

magnetohydrodynamic power generator, any of a class of devices that generate electric current by means of the interaction of an electrically conducting fluid and a magnetic field.

A brief treatment of magnetohydrodynamic (MHD) generators follows. For full treatment, *see* MACROPAEDIA: Energy Conversion.

Unlike conventional electric generators, MHD devices are able to achieve direct energy conversion. In a regular power plant the energy stored in a fossil fuel yields heat with which to produce steam. The steam in turn actuates a turbine to drive an electric power generator. MHD devices, in contrast, change the thermal and kinetic energy of the conducting fluid, which generally consists of ionized combustion gases from fossil fuels (chiefly coal), directly into electricity. Such an ionized gas, or plasma, passes through a duct with two opposite conducting "walls" (electrodes) and two opposite insulating walls. A powerful magnetic field is created at right angles to the duct. As the plasma flows through the duct and the magnetic field at a given speed, it produces an electrical voltage across the electrodes.

Although the basic principles of magnetohydrodynamics were established during the 19th century, the first significant experimental MHD generator was not constructed in the United States until 1938. The device, moreover, failed to operate properly owing largely to an inadequate understanding of the factors involved. By the late 1950s advances in both knowledge and technology made it possible to produce 10 kilowatts of electric power with an MHD generator. In 1973 U.S. and Soviet researchers undertook a joint project to develop a high-magnetic-field MHD generator at a test facility near Moscow. This device, equipped with a 40-ton superconducting magnet, successfully operated for 10 hours in December 1977. A later program, undertaken by the Soviet Union, involved the use of an MHD generator in conjunction with a conventional turbogenerator system for commercial power production. Various other countries, including France, Great Britain, and Japan, have been engaged in MHD research-and-development programs.

Coal-fueled MHD power plants promise greater efficiency than conventional facilities. Whereas the latter are able to convert only about 35 to 40 percent of a fuel's energy potential into electricity, installations equipped with MHD generators have the potential of achieving roughly 60 to 65 percent. One additional advantage of MHD generator facilities is that they produce less air pollution than do conventional power plants.

magnetohydrodynamics (MHD), also called MAGNETOFLUID MECHANICS, or HYDROMAGNETICS, the description of the behaviour of a plasma (*q.v.*), or, in general, any electrically conducting fluid in the presence of electric and magnetic fields.

A plasma can be defined in terms of its constituents, using equations to describe the behaviour of the electrons, ions, neutral particles, etc. It is often more convenient, however, to treat it as a single fluid, even though it differs from fluids that are not ionized in that it is strongly influenced by electric and magnetic fields, both of which can be imposed on the plasma or generated by the plasma; the equations describing the behaviour of the plasma, therefore, must involve the close relationship between the plasma and the associated fields.

The inclusion of magnetic effects gives rise to a number of quantities that have counterparts in ordinary fluid mechanics—for example, magnetic viscosity, pressure, Reynolds number, and diffusion.

magnetometer, instrument for measuring the strength and sometimes the direction of magnetic fields, including those on or near the Earth and in space. Magnetometers are also used to calibrate electromagnets and permanent magnets and to determine the magnetization of materials.

Magnetometers specifically used to measure the Earth's field are of two types: absolute and relative (classed by their methods of calibration). Absolute magnetometers are calibrated with reference to their own known internal constants. Relative magnetometers must be calibrated by reference to a known, accurately measured magnetic field.

The simplest absolute magnetometer, devised by C.F. Gauss in 1832, consists of a permanent bar magnet suspended horizontally by a gold fibre. Measuring the period of oscillation of the magnet in the Earth's magnetic field gives a measure of the field's strength.

A widely used modern absolute instrument is the proton-precession magnetometer. It measures a voltage induced in a coil by the reorientation (precession) of magnetically polarized protons in ordinary water.

The Schmidt vertical-field balance, a relative magnetometer used in geophysical exploration, uses a horizontally balanced bar magnet equipped with mirror and knife edges.

magneton, unit of magnetic moment (the product of a magnet's pole strength and the distance between its poles) used in the study of subatomic particles. The Bohr magneton, named for the 20th-century Danish physicist Niels Bohr, is equal to about 9.273×10^{-21} erg per gauss per particle. The nuclear magneton, calculated using the mass of the proton (rather than that of the electron, used to calculate the Bohr magneton) equals 1/1,836 Bohr magneton. *See* magnetic dipole.

magnetosphere, region in the atmosphere where magnetic phenomena and the high atmospheric conductivity caused by ionization are important in determining the behaviour of charged particles.

The Earth, in contrast to Mars and Venus, has a significant surface magnetic field (approximately 0.5 gauss), which, like its gravitational field, becomes weaker as the distance from the centre of the Earth increases. In the direction of the Sun, at approximately 10 Earth radii (almost 65,000 km, or 40,000 miles), the magnetic field is so weak that the pressure associated with particles escaping from the Earth's gravity is comparable to the opposing pressure associated with the solar wind—the flux mainly of protons and electrons escaping from the Sun's gravitational field. This equilibrium region, with a characteristic thickness of 100 km (60 miles), is called the magnetopause and marks the outer boundary of the magnetosphere. The lower boundary of the magnetosphere is several hundred kilometres above the Earth's surface.

On the night side, or the side away from the Sun, the forces associated with the magnetic field and the solar wind are parallel, and thus the magnetosphere extends a considerable distance, possibly even several astronomical units (one astronomical unit is the average distance between the Earth and the Sun, about 1.5×10^8 km).

In the direction perpendicular to the solar wind, the random motion of the solar-wind particles exerts a small pressure on the magnetic field, constricting the magnetosphere slightly. The net result is that the shape of the magnetosphere in gross terms is similar to that of a comet, with the Earth located near the nucleus, or head, of the "comet" and the magnetospheric "tail" trailing out well beyond the Earth, away from the Sun.

Between 10 and 13 Earth radii toward the Sun, there exists the magnetosheath, a region of magnetic turbulence in which both the magnitude and direction of Earth's magnetic field vary erratically. This disturbed region is thought to be caused by the production of magnetohydrodynamic shock waves, which in turn are caused by high-velocity solar-wind particles. Ahead of this bow shock boundary, toward the Sun, is the undisturbed solar wind.

magnetostriction, change in the dimensions of a ferromagnetic material, such as iron or nickel, produced by a change in the direction and extent of its magnetization. An iron rod placed in a magnetic field directed along its length stretches slightly in a weak magnetic field and contracts slightly in a strong magnetic field. Mechanically stretching and compressing a magnetized iron rod inversely produces fluctuations in the magnetization of the rod. This effect is utilized in nickel magnetostriction transducers that transmit and receive high-frequency sound vibrations. A bent iron rod will straighten a bit in a longitudinally directed magnetic field, and a straight rod carrying an electric current will twist slightly in a magnetic field.

magnetron, diode vacuum tube consisting of a cylindrical (straight wire) cathode and a coaxial anode, between which a dc (direct current) potential creates an electric field. A magnetic field is applied longitudinally by an external magnet. Connected to a resonant line, it can act as an oscillator. Magnetrons are capable of generating extremely high frequencies and also short bursts of very high power. They are an important source of power in radar systems and in microwave ovens.

Magnificat, in Christianity, the hymn of praise by Mary, the mother of Jesus, found in Luke 1:46–55 and incorporated into the liturgical services of the Western churches (at Vespers) and of the Eastern Orthodox churches (at the morning services). Though some scholars have contended that this canticle was a song of Elizabeth (the wife of Zechariah and the mother of John the Baptist), a relative of Mary, most early Greek and Latin manuscripts regard it as the "Song of Mary."

It is named after the first word of its first line in Latin ("Magnificat anima mea Dominum," or "My soul magnifies the Lord"). Elaborate musical settings have been created for the Magnificat. It has been chanted in all eight modes of the plainsong and has been the subject of numerous other settings.

The following are the texts of the Magnificat in the Latin Vulgate version and the English Revised Standard Version:

Magnificat anima mea Dominum
et exultavit spiritus meus in Deo
salutari meo
quia respexit humilitatem ancillae
suae
ecce enim ex hoc beatam me dicent
omnes generationes
quia fecit mihi magna qui potens est
et sanctum nomen eius
et misericordia eius in progenies et
progenies timentibus eum
fecit potentiam in brachio suo dispersit
superbos mente cordis sui
deposuit potentes de sede et
exaltavit humiles
esurientes implevit bonis et divites
dimisit inanes
suscepit Israhel puerum suum
memorari misericordiae
sicut locutus est ad patres nostros
Abraham et semini eius in saecula.

My soul magnifies the Lord,
and my spirit rejoices in God my
Savior,
for he has regarded the low estate
of his handmaiden.
For behold, henceforth all generations
will call me blessed;
for he who is mighty has done great
things for me,
and holy is his name.
And his mercy is on those who fear
him
from generation to generation.
He has shown strength with his
arm,
he has scattered the proud in the
imagination of their hearts,
he has put down the mighty from
their thrones,
and exalted those of low degree;
he has filled the hungry with good
things,
and the rich he has sent empty
away.
He has helped his servant Israel,
in remembrance of his mercy,
as he spoke to our fathers,
to Abraham and to his posterity
for ever.

magnification, in optics, the size of an image relative to the size of the object creating it. Linear (sometimes called lateral or transverse) magnification refers to the ratio of image length to object length measured in planes that are perpendicular to the optical axis. A negative value of linear magnification denotes an inverted image. Longitudinal magnification denotes the factor by which an image increases in size, as measured along the optical axis. Angular magnification is equal to the ratio of the tangents of the angles subtended by an object and its image when measured from a given point in the instrument, as with magnifiers and binoculars.

There is no theoretical limit to the amount of magnification possible in an optical system, but practical magnification is limited by the system's resolving power—*i.e.,* its ability to form distinguishable images of objects separated by small angular distances. A unit of magnification commonly used in microscopes and telescopes is the diameter, the magnification in diameters being equal to the number of times the linear dimensions of the object are increased.

Magnitogorsk, city, Chelyabinsk *oblast* (province), western Russia, on both banks of the Ural River. It was founded in 1929 to exploit the rich magnetite iron ore of Mt. Magnitnaya, just east of the city. The gigantic iron- and steelworks, several times enlarged, was one of the world's largest in 1975, with a steel capacity of about 15,000,000 tons annually. By then local ores were nearing exhaustion, and ores are now secured largely from Rudny in Kazakhstan and the Kursk Magnetic Anomaly of Kursk and Belgorod *oblasti*; coking coal is from Karaganda. There are also engineering, cement, glass, and light industries. The Ural is dammed to form two reservoirs within the city and although the steelworks and oldest part of the city lie on the left bank, most subsequent growth has been on the right bank, where air pollution is less. Magnitogorsk has teacher-training and mining-metallurgical institutes. Pop. (1991 est.) 444,500.

magnitude, in astronomy, measure of the brightness of a star or other celestial body. The brighter the object, the lower the number assigned as a magnitude. In ancient times, stars were ranked in six magnitude classes, the first magnitude class containing the brightest stars. In 1850 the English astronomer Norman Robert Pogson proposed the system presently in use. One magnitude is defined as a ratio of brightness of 2.512 times; *e.g.,* a star of magnitude 5.0 is 2.512 times as bright as one of magnitude 6.0. Thus, a difference of five magnitudes corresponds to a brightness ratio of 100 to 1. After standardization and assignment of the zero point, the brightest class was found to contain too great a range of luminosities, and negative magnitudes were introduced to spread the range.

Apparent magnitude is the brightness of an object as it appears to an observer on Earth. The Sun's apparent magnitude is −26.7, that of the full Moon is about −11, and that of the bright star Sirius, −1.5. The faintest stars visible through the largest telescopes are of (approximately) apparent magnitude 20. Absolute magnitude is the brightness an object would exhibit if viewed from a distance of 10 parsecs (32.6 light-years). The Sun's absolute magnitude is 4.8.

Bolometric magnitude is that measured by including a star's entire radiation, not just the portion visible as light. Monochromatic magnitude is that measured only in some very narrow segment of the spectrum. Narrow-band magnitudes are based on slightly wider segments of the spectrum and broad-band magnitudes on areas wider still. Because ordinary photographic plates are more sensitive to blue light than is the eye, photographic magnitude is sometimes called blue magnitude. Visual magnitude may be called yellow magnitude, because the eye is most sensitive to light of that colour. *See also* colour index.

Magnolia, city, seat (1853) of Columbia county, southwestern Arkansas, U.S., on the West Gulf Coastal Plain. Founded in 1853, it was named for the magnolia, or laurel, tree (*Magnolia grandiflora*), native to Arkansas. It evolved as a cotton town and a farm marketing and processing centre. In 1938 its economic base changed with the discovery of the Buckner oil field; the petroleum and gas industry developed, followed by light manufacturing. Magnolia is the seat of Southern Arkansas University (founded, 1909, as an agricultural school). Inc. town, 1855; city, 1949. Pop. (1990) 11,151.

magnolia, any member of the genus *Magnolia* (family Magnoliaceae; order Magnoliales), about 80 species of trees and shrubs native to North and Central America, the Himalayas, and eastern Asia. They are valued for their large and fragrant white, yellow, pink, or purple flowers and frequently handsome leaves and conelike fruits. Some are important garden ornamentals; others are local timber sources. They have evergreen or deciduous, alternate smooth-margined leaves. The flowers, usually cuplike and fragrant, are located at the branch tips and have three sepals, 6 to 12 petals arranged in two to four series, and many spirally arranged stamens. The numerous simple ovaries in the centre later form a conelike fruit. The seeds, usually reddish, often hang pendulously by slender threads.

Magnolia (*Magnolia fraseri*)
J. Horace McFarland Co.

Some of the more popular species, native to North America and relatively hardy and deciduous trees unless otherwise noted, are: laurel, or southern magnolia, or sweet bay (*M. grandiflora*), a 31-metre (102-foot) evergreen with thick, shining leaves; sweet bay (*M. virginiana*), 19 m tall with leathery leaves; big-leaf magnolia (*M. macrophylla*), 15 m with purple-based blooms; umbrella tree (*M. tripetala*), 12 m with leaves 60 cm (2 ft) long that are sometimes used as rain shields; cucumber tree (*M. acuminata*), a 30-m tree with cucumber-shaped, rosy fruits; and Thompson's magnolia (*M. tripetala* × *virginiana*), a hybrid between the umbrella tree and the laurel magnolia with fragrant blooms that have a spicy odour.

Well-known Asian species of the genus *Magnolia* include lily magnolia (*M. liliflora* or *M. quinquipeta*), a four-metre shrubby tree that has purple blossoms with white interiors and brownish fruits; yulan magnolia (*M. denudata* or *M. heptapeta*), a 60-m tree; saucer magnolia (*M. soulangeana*), a gray-barked hybrid between the lily magnolia and the yulan magnolia with flowers that may be white, pink, crimson, or purplish; Oyama magnolia (*M. sieboldii*), a 9-m tree with crimson fruits; and star magnolia (*M. stellata*) of similar height with spidery flowers.

Magnoliaceae, magnolia family of the order Magnoliales that contains 12 genera and 210 species, including many handsome, fragrant-flowering trees and shrubs. Most have simple leaves and an elongated conelike floral axis with flowers that have six tepals (sepals and petals that are not distinctly different), many spirally arranged stamens, and one, two, or many carpels (female reproductive structures). The seeds of many species hang by threads from the conelike fruits. In most species the flowers are bisexual and are borne on branch tips. The long floral axis, spiral arrangement of the flower parts, and simple vessels (water-conducting cells) in the wood all mark the family as a primitive one on the evolutionary scale. Once widely distributed in Eurasia and North America, the family is now concentrated in the southeastern United States, Mexico, Central America, the Caribbean, and in East and Southeast Asia, with only a few species in the Southern Hemisphere.

The family is important primarily for its ornamental species such as the tulip tree, or yellow poplar (*Liriodendron tulipifera*), and most members of the genus *Magnolia.* Some plants yield perfume, such as the champac (*Michelia champaca*). Others are valuable timber sources or provide ingredients used in folk medicines.

Magnoliales, the magnolia order of flowering plants, containing 166 genera and about 1,800 species in eight families. The order belongs to the class called dicotyledon (*q.v.;* characterized by two seed leaves) and consists entirely of trees and shrubs, including the ornamental magnolias. The Magnoliales are regarded as the most primitive order of angiosperms.

A brief treatment of Magnoliales follows. For full treatment, *see* MACROPAEDIA: Angiosperms.

Most trees in the group are small or medium-sized; some tall trees are found in the Magnoliaceae and Annonaceae (*qq.v.*) families. The Magnoliales are distributed mainly throughout wet tropical regions, with the greatest number of species in Southeast Asia and Africa. Some species are native to temperate zones in the Americas and East Asia. Trees belonging to the largest families in the order are used for timber, food, and ornamentation.

The Magnoliaceae family includes species that grow in temperate regions, notably the members of the genus *Magnolia.* About 80 species of magnolias have been described, and many are cultivated for their showy flowers. The southern magnolia (*Magnolia grandiflora*) is a particularly splendid evergreen, with large creamy-white blossoms. It is native to the southeastern United States and is grown as an ornamental in most warm temperate regions of the world. A hybrid species, *M. soulangiana,* is a small tree or shrub with large pink flowers that is widely cultivated for its beauty. The tulip tree (*Liriodendron tulipifera*), also in the Magnoliaceae family, is the source of American whitewood, one of the most valuable timbers in the United States.

By far the largest family in the Magnoliales order is Annonaceae, the custard apple family, whose members range throughout the tropical regions of the world. Some species in the genus *Annona* are cultivated for their edible fruits, including the custard apple (*A. reticulata*), a native of the West Indies; the sweetsop, or sugar apple (*A. squamosa*), found in the American tropics as well as in India and Pakistan; the cherimoya (*A. cherimola*) of Peru, now grown in many tropical areas; the soursop (*A. muricata*), a favourite in Cuba; and the alligator apple (*A. glabra*) of Florida.

The Annonaceae include a number of species, such as lancewood and ylang-ylang (*qq.v.*), that produce woods, flowers, and seeds of commercial value. *Polyalthia longifolia,* a tall, stately tree having religious significance in Sri Lanka and India, is planted along avenues and around temples.

The nutmeg family, Myristicaceae, consists of evergreen trees, often large, which are distributed throughout the tropics, many at lower elevations in rain forests. The spices nutmeg and mace are both derived from the seeds of *Myristica fragrans,* a native of Indonesia.

All members of the Magnoliales order are woody plants. They have simple leaves, alternately arranged, which may be evergreen. Flowers are usually bisexual (with both female and male structures), and often there is no differentiation of petals and sepals. Pollination by beetles occurs in several families.

A number of structural features found in Magnoliales are regarded by botanists as primitive: flowers often consist of numerous spirally arranged free parts on an elongated floral axis; stamens (male) are frequently broad, with pollen sacs embedded in their surfaces; carpels (female) may be only slightly modified from a leaflike structure; pollen grains usually have a single groove; and seeds contain a small embryo surrounded by abundant, food-rich endosperm. It has been suggested that either the Winteraceae or the Magnoliaceae family is the most primitive living family of flowering plants.

Magnoliidae, subclass of woody or herbaceous dicotyledonous flowering plants. Its members have regular flowers that are generally arranged separately (*i.e.,* not in inflorescences). The subclass consists of eight orders (Magnoliales, Laurales, Piperales, Aristolochiales, Illiciales, Nymphaeales, Ranunculales, and Papaverales), which together contain 39 families and about 12,000 species.

A brief treatment of the Magnoliidae follows. For full treatment, *see* MACROPAEDIA: Angiosperms.

One feature of some Magnoliidae is a spiral arrangement of the floral parts, which is a primitive feature among the flowering plants. The perianth is often not differentiated into distinct petals and sepals, and the stamens are commonly numerous and often leaflike in more primitive members, although distinct filaments and anthers are seen in others. The vast majority of species in the subclass Magnoliidae are found in the orders Magnoliales, Laurales, and Ranunculales.

Magnoliophyta, also called ANTHOPHYTA, or ANGIOSPERMAE, the division of the angiosperms, or flowering plants, which comprises the greatest number of species and occupies the widest range of habitats among all plant groups. Members range in size from the tiny duckweed (*Lemna minor*) to the enormous mountain ash (*Eucalyptus regnans*).

The division contains two classes: Magnoliopsida (dicotyledons) and Liliopsida (monocotyledons). While the formal, Latinized names tend to vary with authorities, the common English terms remain very useful, being widely known and generally accepted. *See* angiosperm.

magnon, small quantity of energy corresponding to a specific decrease in magnetic strength that travels as a unit through a magnetic substance.

In a magnetic substance, such as iron, each atom acts as a small individual magnet. These atomic magnets tend to point in the same direction, so that their magnetic fields reinforce each other. When the direction of one atomic magnet is reversed, the total magnetic strength of the group is decreased. A definite amount of energy is required to reverse such a magnet. This energy, involving the decrease in magnetic strength of the group of atoms, constitutes a magnon.

According to the laws of quantum mechanics, the reversal of a single atomic magnet is equivalent to a partial reversal of all the atomic magnets in a group. This partial reversal spreads through the solid as a wave of discrete energy transferal. This wave is called a spin wave, because the magnetism of each atom is produced by the spin of unpaired electrons in its structure. Thus, a magnon is a quantized spin wave.

As the temperature of a magnetic substance is increased, its magnetic strength decreases, corresponding to the presence of a large number of magnons.

Magnus, name of rulers grouped below by country and indicated by the symbol •.

NORWAY

•**Magnus I** OLAFSSON, byname MAGNUS THE GOOD, Norwegian MAGNUS DEN GODE (b. 1024, Norway—d. Oct. 25, 1047, Skibby, Den.), Norwegian ruler, king of Norway (1035–47) and Denmark (1042–47), who wrested hegemony in the two Scandinavian nations from descendants of Canute the Great (d. 1035), king of Denmark and England.

An illegitimate son of the Norwegian king Olaf II Haraldsson (St. Olaf), Magnus was named after the Holy Roman emperor Charlemagne (Old Norse: Karlamagnús) and was taken to Russia at the age of four with his father, who had been exiled by Canute. In 1035 the chiefs of Norway rebelled against the rule of Canute's son Sweyn (Svein) and elected Magnus king. Canute's son Hardecanute, who became king of Denmark in 1035 and England in 1040, also claimed the Norwegian throne but later accepted Magnus' sovereignty. The two rulers agreed that whoever survived would rule both Norway and Denmark.

When Hardecanute died in 1042, Magnus also became king of Denmark and appointed as his viceroy Canute's nephew Sweyn (Svein) Estridsson (later Sweyn II). Sweyn, however, soon challenged Magnus' sovereignty in Denmark. Magnus received the support of most Danes, who needed his help against the Wends (Slavs) in southern Jutland, and he repeatedly defeated Sweyn in battle. After Magnus' uncle Harald III Sigurdsson returned from Constantinople (now Istanbul) in 1045, the two men agreed to share the kingdom. Magnus died in a campaign launched by the co-rulers against Denmark in 1047, aborting his plans to claim the English throne.

•**Magnus II** HARALDSSON (b. *c.* 1048—d. 1069), joint king of Norway with his brother Olaf III Haraldsson, from 1066 until 1069. He was a son of Harald III Haraldsson.

•**Magnus III,** byname MAGNUS BAREFOOT, Norwegian MAGNUS BERRFØTT, Old Norse MAGNUS BARFOT (b. *c.* 1073, Norway—d. August 1103, Ulster, Ire.), king of Norway (1093–1103), warrior who consolidated Norwegian rule in the Orkney and Hebrides islands and on the Isle of Man (all now part of the United Kingdom). He was called Barefoot (*i.e.,* bareleg) because he often wore Scottish kilts.

After succeeding his father, Olaf III Haraldsson, Magnus initially ruled jointly with his cousin Haakon and became sole ruler on Haakon's death the following year. In 1098 he launched expeditions to the Hebrides and the Isle of Man and responded to Welsh pleas for help against the Normans by attacking Anglesey, where he defeated the Norman earls Hugh of Chester and Hugh of Shrewsbury. Magnus had attacked Sweden shortly after becoming king, but he made peace with the Swedish king Inge in 1101 and married his daughter Margaret.

Magnus made another expedition in 1102, visiting the Hebrides and Orkneys and the Isle of Man. He was killed in Ireland in August 1103 while foraging for food. Norwegian control of the Isle of Man soon ended, but earls who ruled Orkney recognized the sovereignty of the Norwegian king until 1468, and the Orkney and Hebrides dioceses became part of the Norwegian church.

•**Magnus IV,** byname MAGNUS THE BLIND, Norwegian MAGNUS DEN BLINDE (b. *c.* 1115, Norway—d. 1139, Norway), joint ruler of Norway (1130–35), with Harald IV, whose abortive attempt (1137–39) to wrest sovereignty from Inge I Haroldsson and Sigurd II, sons of Harald IV, ended the first epoch in the period of Norwegian civil wars (1130–1240).

The son of the Norwegian king Sigurd I Magnusson, Magnus succeeded to the throne jointly with Harald IV in 1130. In 1134 war broke out between the two rulers, and the following year Magnus was seized by Harald, maimed, blinded, and put in a monastery. He was liberated in 1137 by Sigurd Slembi, who had slain Harald the year before but could not gain support for his own claim to the throne and hoped, instead, to install Magnus as king. Although Magnus won the allegiance of many chieftains who honoured him as the son of Sigurd I, his forces were defeated twice by the backers of Inge and Sigurd II. In 1139 Magnus began another attack on the forces of Inge and Sigurd II, this time from Denmark in alliance with Sigurd Slembi, but he was killed in the battle.

• **Magnus V** ERLINGSSON (b. 1156, Norway—d. June 15, 1184, Fimreite, Nor.), king of Norway (1162–84) who used church support to gain the throne (1162) and become the nation's first crowned monarch (1163). After 1177 his rule was challenged by his rival Sverrir, whose forces killed Magnus in battle.

The son of Erling the Crooked, Magnus became king in 1162 when his supporters, led by his father, defeated the forces of the incumbent king, Haakon II Sigurdsson. Magnus' father served as regent until 1164 and remained the real power behind the throne until his death in 1179.

In 1163 Erling arranged with the Norwegian archbishop Eystein Erlandsson to have Magnus crowned in exchange for royal support of the Roman Catholic Church. After Magnus' supporters defeated his rivals, the Birchlegs, in 1177, the King's forces were badly defeated (1179) by the pretender Sverrir, who included the remnants of the Birchlegs among his followers. Magnus then fled to Denmark, and Sverrir became ruler of much of Norway. When Magnus attempted to regain control of the country in 1184, aided by the Danish king Canute IV, he was again defeated by Sverrir's forces and slain in battle.

• **Magnus VI,** byname MAGNUS LAWMENDER, Norwegian MAGNUS LAGABØTE (b. 1238, Norway—d. May 9, 1280, Bergen, Nor.), king of Norway (1263–80) who transformed the nation's legal system by introducing new national, municipal, and ecclesiastical codes, which also served as a model for many of the Norwegian colonies. His national code was used for more than 400 years.

Magnus succeeded his father, Haakon IV Haakonsson, in 1263 and quickly made peace with the Scottish king Alexander III, ceding to Scotland the Hebrides Islands and the Isle of Man in exchange for an initial payment and an annual rent. In 1274 Magnus introduced a new national legal code based on the existing system but replacing the provincial laws with common national laws. The new code considered crimes a public matter and replaced the custom of personal revenge with public adjudication.

Relying largely on the laws of Bergen, Magnus instituted in 1277 a new municipal code that created a city council form of government for Norwegian cities and towns. Norway's maritime commerce, based largely in the cities, attained a peak during his reign not reached again until the 19th century.

Also in 1277 Magnus came to terms with the church by concluding the Concordat of Tønsberg with Archbishop Jon the Red. The concordat, which made the church essentially independent and increased its revenue and prestige, remained an important basis of Norwegian ecclesiastical law for the next two centuries.

Magnus was the last Norwegian king whose life is narrated in the Icelandic sagas; his saga survives only in fragmentary form.

Magnus VII ERIKSSON: *see* Magnus II Eriksson (Sweden).

SWEDEN

• **Magnus I,** byname MAGNUS BARN-LOCK, Swedish MAGNUS LADULÅS (d. 1290), king of Sweden (1275–90) who helped introduce a feudal class society into Sweden.

The second eldest son of Birger Jarl (*q.v.*), he married a German princess and thereby came into contact with continental feudalism. A statute that he issued at Alsnö in 1279 created a lay upper class, the *frälse,* who, in exchange for equipping themselves for war-duty, were granted tax-free privileges and social status. Ironically, such measures also won him a reputation for protecting the common man and his property, for which Magnus received the nickname Ladulås (Barn-lock). Magnus also won the support of the church through tax relief, strengthened the privileges of German and Swedish merchants, instituted a royal advisory council, began a codification of laws, and promoted other reforms to strengthen royal authority and general administration. When he died, however, he was succeeded by his 10-year-old son Birger, who would be beset by rival brothers and magnates during a generation of unrest.

• **Magnus II** ERIKSSON (b. 1316, Norway—d. Dec. 1, 1374, Sweden), king of Sweden (1319–63) and of Norway (1319–55, as Magnus VII) who devoted himself to defending his Swedish sovereignty against rebellious nobles aided by various foreign leaders, most notably Valdemar IV Atterdag, king of Denmark.

The son of Ingeborg, daughter of the Norwegian king Haakon V, and of Duke Erik, brother of the Swedish king Birger Magnusson, Magnus was accepted as ruler of both Norway and Sweden on Haakon V's death (1319). A regency controlled his two dominions until he came of age in 1332. Since Magnus spent nearly all his time in Sweden, the leading Norwegian nobles arranged in 1343 for his son Haakon to succeed him, becoming King Haakon VI when Magnus abdicated his Norwegian throne in 1355.

Magnus soon aroused the opposition of many Swedish nobles when he imposed higher taxes to purchase the former Danish province of Skåne (in extreme southern modern Sweden). After introducing a new national law code (1350), integrating the various provincial laws, he further irritated the magnates in 1352 by curbing the economic power of the church and the landed nobility. His son Erik emerged as the champion of his opponents, who were supported by King Valdemar IV of Denmark and, after 1356, by Pope Innocent VI as well. Magnus was forced to cede to Erik about half of his Swedish kingdom, and he began to make concessions to the nobility. He then made peace with Valdemar IV and arranged (1359) the marriage of his son Haakon VI to Valdemar's daughter Margaret, paving the way for the eventual union of Norway, Sweden, and Denmark in 1397, the Kalmar Union.

Magnus renewed his attempt to check the power of the leading Swedish nobles after reuniting with Valdemar IV, who had betrayed him in 1360 in retaking Skåne. The nobles responded by offering the Swedish throne to Albert of Mecklenburg and by launching a military offensive. Taken prisoner in the ensuing hostilities, Magnus was not released until 1371, when he left for Norway.

Magnus, Johannes (b. March 19, 1488, Linköping, Swed.—d. March 22, 1544, Rome), Roman Catholic archbishop and historian, one of the most distinguished scholars of his time, who was exiled as a consequence of the Reformation.

Brother of the ecclesiastic Olaus Magnus, author of a celebrated history of Scandinavia, Johannes was made papal emissary to Scandinavia by Pope Adrian VI, his former teacher at the University of Louvain, Belg. In 1523 he investigated the dispute between the new Swedish king, Gustav I Vasa, and Archbishop Trolle of Uppsala, Swed., who was accused of supporting the claim of King Christian II of Denmark to the Swedish throne. In 1524 Pope Clement VII made Magnus administrator of the Uppsala archdiocese, but he was subsequently arrested and exiled amidst Gustav's conflicts with the papacy during the period when Sweden was veering toward Lutheranism. The Magnus brothers lived in Danzig, Pol., and, from 1541, in Rome. In 1533 Johannes was made archbishop of Uppsala, but he never lived in his see. His *Historia de omnibus gothorum sueonumque regibus* (1555; "History Concerning All the Gothic and Swedish Kings") is the primary source for the history of several Scandinavian kings.

Magnus, Olaus, Swedish OLAF MANSSON (b. October 1490, Linköping, Swed.—d. Aug. 1, 1557, Rome), Swedish ecclesiastic and author of an influential history of Scandinavia.

A Catholic priest, he went to Rome in 1523, during the Swedish Reformation, and thereafter lived in exile, first in Danzig and later in Italy, with his brother Archbishop Johannes Magnus, on whose death he was appointed Catholic archbishop of Sweden. After 1549 he was also director of St. Brigitta's, a religious house in Rome.

Olaus Magnus' *Carta marina* (1539) was the first detailed map of Scandinavia with any pretensions to accuracy. His foremost work, however, is the *Historia de gentibus septentrionalibus* (1555), a history of the northern peoples inspired by humanist historiography and imbued with patriotic warmth, which gives a picture of the countryside and people of Sweden on the threshold of a new era. It appeared in many editions and translations during the 17th century—the first English translation being the *History of the Goths, Swedes and Vandals* (1658)—and for long influenced the European idea of the Scandinavian people.

Magnus effect, generation of a sidewise force on a spinning cylindrical or spherical solid immersed in a fluid (liquid or gas) when there is relative motion between the spinning body and the fluid. Named after the German physicist and chemist H.G. Magnus, who first (1853) experimentally investigated the effect, it is responsible for the "curve" of a served tennis ball or a driven golf ball and affects the trajectory of a spinning artillery shell.

A spinning object moving through a fluid departs from its straight path because of pressure differences that develop in the fluid as a result of velocity changes induced by the spinning body. The Magnus effect is a particular manifestation of Bernoulli's theorem: fluid pressure decreases at points where the speed of the fluid increases. In the case of a ball spinning through the air, the turning ball drags some of the air around with it. Viewed from the position of the ball, the air is rushing by on all sides. The drag of the side of the ball turning into the air (into the direction the ball is travelling) retards the airflow, whereas on the other side the drag speeds up the airflow. Greater pressure on the side where the airflow is slowed down forces the ball in the direction of the low-pressure region on the opposite side, where a relative increase in airflow occurs.

Magnus Maximus: *see* Maximus, Magnus.

Magnússon, Árni (b. Nov. 13, 1663, Kvennabrekka, Ice.—d. Jan. 7, 1730, Copenhagen), Scandinavian antiquarian and philologist who built up the most important collection of early Icelandic literary manuscripts.

Magnússon graduated from the University of Copenhagen in theology in 1685, but was interested chiefly in the early history and literature of Scandinavia. He travelled extensively in Norway, Sweden, and Iceland, collecting books and manuscripts. In 1697 Magnússon was appointed secretary of the secret archives and, in 1701, professor of philosophy and Danish antiquities. From 1702 until 1710 while on a royal mission to value estates and report on economic conditions, he spent much time gathering Icelandic manuscripts. His collection was sent to Denmark in 1720. A large part of it perished in the fire of Copenhagen (1728), but the remainder passed to the University of Copenhagen, where it is still housed. Magnússon's published works were few and of minor importance.

Magnússon, Jón (b. *c.* 1610—d. 1696), Icelandic parson and author of the *Píslarsaga* ("Passion Story"), one of the strangest documents of cultural and psychic delusion in all literature.

A parson at Eyri in 1655, Magnússon was stricken by an illness he ascribed to the witchcraft of two of his parishioners, a father and son. When he did not recover, even after the "sorcerers" were burned at the stake, he in 1656 extended his accusation to a daughter of the family, who was cleared of charges and sued the parson. The *Píslarsaga,* written in protest of this suit, is an eloquent document, both in its fantastic description of Magnússon's sufferings and in its documentation of a phenomenon prevalent in many 17th-century societies, the belief in witchcraft as the cause of disease. *Píslarsaga* is a passionate denunciation of the lenient treatment of witches. As a personal exposé of Magnússon's own torment and madness, *Píslarsaga* resembles August Strindberg's *Inferno.* It was not published until 1914.

Mago, also spelled MAGON (d. *c.* 203 BC), a leading Carthaginian general during the Second Punic War (218–201 BC) against Rome. He was the youngest of the three sons of the Carthaginian statesman and general Hamilcar Barca.

In the Second Punic War Mago accompanied his brother Hannibal on the invasion of Italy and held key commands in the great victories of the first three years of that conflict. After the Carthaginian triumph at the Battle of Cannae (216), he was sent to Spain to fight alongside his other brother, Hasdrubal. There, in a battle at Ilipa (206), Mago was defeated by the Roman general Publius Cornelius Scipio (later known as Scipio Africanus). He stayed for several months in Gades (now Cádiz) before carrying the war into Liguria in Italy. In 203 he was finally defeated in Cisalpine Gaul. He died of wounds on the return voyage to Carthage.

Magog, city, Estrie region, southern Quebec province, Canada, lying along the Magog River, near the foot of Lake Memphremagog, 20 miles (32 km) north of the border with Vermont, U.S. The townsite, originally an Indian camp, was a stopping place on the trail from the Connecticut River to the St. Lawrence. It was first settled about 1776 by loyalist refugees from the American Revolution. Water-powered gristmills and sawmills were built in 1798, and a school was opened in 1818. Calico printing began in 1884. Originally called The Outlet (because of its location where the lake empties into the river), the settlement adopted an abbreviation of Memphremagog for its name in 1855, when it was incorporated as a town.

Well known as a fishing, boating, and skiing resort, it also produces textiles, clothing, dairy foods, and metal castings. Mixed farming, lumbering, and asbestos mining are local economic activities. Inc. city, 1888. Pop. (1991) 14,034.

Magog, in biblical and apocalyptic literature, a hostile power associated with Gog (*q.v.*).

Magosian industry, stone-tool technology in which an advanced Levallois technique was employed for the production of flakes for the manufacture of other tools, together with a punch technique for the production of microlithic artifacts. Projectile points were produced by pressure flaking.

The site for which the industry is named is located in northern Uganda. Other sites in central and southern Africa that are dated to the Pleistocene epoch (which occurred from 1,600,000 to 10,000 years ago) are often considered to represent the same material culture and hunting-and-gathering adaptation.

magot (primate): *see* Barbary ape.

magpie, any of several long-tailed birds belonging to the family Corvidae (order Passeriformes). The best-known species, often called

Magpie (*Pica pica*)
Bruce Coleman Ltd.

the black-billed magpie (*Pica pica*), is a 45-centimetre (18-inch) black-and-white (*i.e.,* pied) bird, with an iridescent blue-green tail. It occurs in northwestern Africa, across Eurasia, and in western North America. A bird of farmlands and tree-studded open country, it eats insects, seeds, small vertebrates, the eggs and young of other birds, and fresh carrion. It makes a large, round nest of twigs cemented with mud.

Brilliant blue or green magpies in Asia include those of the genera *Cyanopica, Cissa,* and *Urocissa.* For Australasian magpies, *see* bell-magpie.

magpie goose, also called PIED, or SEMIPALMATED, GOOSE (*Anseranas semipalmata*), large aberrant waterfowl of Australia and Papua New Guinea, the sole member of the subfamily Anseranatinae, family Anatidae (order Anseriformes). The sexes are alike in having a black-and-white body (hence "magpie"), long neck, long legs, and virtually unwebbed toes; the long hooked bill and bare face give the bird a vulturish look. It differs from other waterfowl in molting its flight feathers gradually, thereby having no flightless period. It perches high in trees but nests on the ground. Pairing is lifelong. Parent birds cooperate fully in nest building, incubation, and rearing the young.

magpie-robin, any of eight species of chat-thrushes, belonging to the family Turdidae

Dyal (*Copsychus saularis*)
Painting by Richard Keane

(order Passeriformes), found in southern Asia. They are 18 to 28 cm (7 to 11 inches) long, with pied plumage and attenuated tails—small replicas of magpies. The uptilted tail is frequently lowered and fanned. Magpie-robins hunt insects on the ground and are exceptionally fine singers. Some are popular cage and aviary birds—for example, the dyal (*Copsychus saularis,* also spelled dayal, or dhyal), a blue-black and white species, 20 cm long, prized for its rich song. Other *Copsychus* species are often called shama. The white-rumped shama (*C. malabaricus*) is a long-tailed species native to China and Southeast Asia and introduced in Hawaii.

Magritte, René (-François-Ghislain) (b. Nov. 21, 1898, Lessines, Belg.—d. Aug. 15, 1967, Brussels), Belgian artist, one of the most prominent Surrealist painters whose bizarre

Magritte (right)
Izis—Paris Match

flights of fancy blended horror, peril, comedy, and mystery. His works were characterized by particular symbols—the female torso, the bourgeois "little man," the bowler hat, the castle, the rock, the window, and others.

After studying at the Brussels Academy of Fine Arts (1916–18), Magritte became a designer for a wallpaper factory and then did sketches for advertisements. In 1922 he saw a reproduction of Giorgio de Chirico's painting "The Song of Love" (1914), an evocative and haunting juxtaposition of odd elements (a classical bust and a rubber glove among them) in a dreamlike architectural space; it had a great influence on Magritte's mature style. For the next few years he was active in the Belgian Surrealist movement. With the support of a Brussels art gallery, he became a full-time painter in 1926.

His first solo show was held in 1927. It was not well received by the art critics of the day. That same year he and his wife moved to a suburb of Paris. There he met and befriended several of the Paris Surrealists, including poets André Breton and Paul Éluard, and he became familiar with the collages of Max Ernst. In 1930 Magritte returned to Brussels, where (except for the occasional journey) he remained for the rest of his life. During the 1940s he experimented with a variety of styles, sometimes, for example, incorporating elements of impressionism, but the paintings he produced in this period were not successful by most accounts, and he eventually abandoned the experimental. For the rest of his life he continued to produce his enigmatic and illogical images in a readily identifiable style. In his last year he supervised the construction of eight bronze sculptures derived from images in his paintings.

The sea and wide skies, which were enthusiasms of his childhood, figure strongly in his paintings. In "Threatening Weather" (1928) the clouds have the shapes of a torso, a tuba, and a chair. In "The Castle of the Pyrenees" (1959) a huge stone topped by a small castle floats above the sea. Other representative fancies were a fish with human legs, a man with a bird cage for a torso, and a gentleman leaning over a wall beside his pet lion. Dislocations of space, time, and scale were common elements. In "Time Transfixed" (1939), for example, a steaming locomotive is suspended from the centre of a mantelpiece in a middle-class sitting room, looking as if it had just emerged from a tunnel. In "Golconda" (1953) bourgeois, bowler-hatted men fall like rain toward a street lined with houses.

Consult
the
INDEX
first

Magsaysay, Ramon (b. Aug. 31, 1907, Iba, Phil.—d. March 17, 1957, near Cebu), president of the Philippines (1953–57), best known for successfully defeating the communist-led Hukbalahap (Huk) movement.

The son of an artisan, Magsaysay was a schoolteacher in the provincial town of Iba on the island of Luzon. Though most Philippine political leaders were of Spanish descent, Magsaysay was of Malay stock, like most of the common people. Working his way through José Rizal College near Manila, he obtained a commercial degree in 1933 and became general manager of a Manila transportation company. After serving as a guerrilla leader on Luzon during World War II, he was appointed military governor of his home province, Zambales, when the United States recaptured the Philippines. He served two terms (1946–50) as a Liberal Party congressman for Zambales, his first experience in politics.

President Elpidio Quirino appointed Magsaysay secretary of defense to deal with the threat of the Huks, whose leader, Luis Taruc, in February 1950 established a People's Liberation Army and called for the overthrow of the government. Magsaysay then carried out until 1953 one of the most successful anti-guerrilla campaigns in modern history. Realizing that the Huks could not survive without popular support, he strove to win the trust of the peasants by offering land and tools to those who came over to the government side and by insisting that army units treat the people with respect. Reforming the army, he dismissed corrupt and incompetent officers and emphasized mobility and flexibility in combat operations against the guerrillas. By 1953 the Huks were no longer a serious threat, but Magsaysay's radical measures had made many enemies for him within the government, compelling him to resign on February 28, when he charged the Quirino administration with corruption and incompetence.

Magsaysay
AP/Wide World Photos

Although Magsaysay was a Liberal, the Nacionalista Party successfully backed him for the presidency against Quirino in the 1953 elections, winning the support of Carlos P. Romulo, who had organized a third party. Magsaysay promised reform in every segment of Philippine life, but he was frustrated in his efforts by a conservative congress that represented the interests of the wealthy. Despite initial support of Congress in July 1955, Magsaysay was unable to pass effective land-reform legislation; government indifference to the plight of the peasants then undid most of his good work in gaining the support of the people against the Huks. Nevertheless, he remained extremely popular and had a well-deserved reputation for incorruptibility.

In foreign policy, Magsaysay remained a close friend and supporter of the United States and a vocal spokesman against communism during the Cold War. He made the Philippines a member of the Southeast Asia Treaty Organization, which was established in Manila on Sept. 8, 1954. Before the expiration of his term as president, Magsaysay was killed in an airplane crash; he was succeeded by the vice president, Carlos P. Garcia.

maguey, fibre obtained from the leaf of the plant *Agave lurida,* a member of the Amaryllidaccae family and native to Mexico. It is shorter and stiffer than henequen (*q.v.*), with physical properties similar to the hard leaf fibre cantala (*q.v.*), and is used for rope and cordage.

In South America the name maguey is used for a variety of fibres as well as for the plants from which they are derived. A simple hard spindle known as a *malacate* is used to spin fairly fine yarn from the maguey and related hard fibres.

Magus (wise man): *see* Magi.

magus, plural MAGI, member of an ancient Persian clan specializing in cultic activities. The name is the Latinized form of *magoi* (*e.g.,* in Herodotus 1:101), the ancient Greek transliteration of the Iranian original. From it the word magic is derived.

It is disputed whether the magi were from the beginning followers of Zoroaster and his first propagandists. They do not appear as such in the trilingual inscription of Bīsitūn, in which Darius the Great describes his speedy and final triumph over the magi who had revolted against his rule (522 BC). Rather it appears that they constituted a priesthood serving several religions. The magi were a priestly caste during the Seleucid, Parthian, and Sāsānian periods; later parts of the Avesta, such as the ritualistic sections of the *Vidēvdāt* (*Vendidad*), probably derive from them. From the 1st century AD onward the word in its Syriac form (magusai) was applied to magicians and soothsayers, chiefly from Babylonia, with a reputation for the most varied forms of wisdom. As long as the Persian empire lasted there was always a distinction between the Persian magi, who were credited with profound and extraordinary religious knowledge, and the Babylonian magi, who were often considered to be outright imposters.

Mağusa (Cyprus): *see* Famagusta.

Magwe, town, west-central Myanmar (Burma). The town is on the Irrawaddy River opposite Minbu. It is the site of Magwe College, affiliated to the Arts and Science University at Mandalay, and has an airfield.

The surrounding area is part of the dry zone of Myanmar's central basin between the Irrawaddy to the west and the Pegu Mountains to the east. Along the river, the land undulates, with marked development of river terraces. It is seamed with nonperennial streams, only the Taungu (Yanbe) being perennial. Situated in a zone of crustal instability, the area experiences occasional earthquakes. Because the region is subject to monsoons and droughts, irrigation projects have been constructed to enable the growing of paddy rice and sesame, peanuts (groundnuts) for oil processing, and tobacco. Millet is also grown. The Pegu Mountains hold valuable forest reserves. Pop. (latest est.) 13,970.

Magyar (people): *see* Hungarian.

Magyar language: *see* Hungarian language.

Magyarország: *see* Hungary.

Magyarországi Református Egyház (Hungarian Reformed church): *see* Reformed Church of Hungary.

mah-jongg, a game of Chinese origin, played with tiles, or *p'ais,* similar in physical description to those used in dominoes but engraved with Chinese symbols and characters and divided into suits and honours. A fad in England, the United States, and Australia in the mid-1920s, the game was revived in the United States after 1935 but never regained its initial popularity. In the United States, the official body is the National Mah-Jongg League, founded in 1937.

The game is probably of 19th-century origin. Before World War I each Chinese province had its own style of play and dialect name for it. Signifying "sparrow," the name has been variously transliterated as *ma tsiang, ma chiang, ma cheuk,* and *ma ch'iau.* The sparrow or a mythical "bird of 100 intelligences" appears on one of the tiles. The name mah-jongg was coined and copyrighted by Joseph P. Babcock, an American resident of Shanghai, who is credited with introducing mah-jongg to the West after World War I. In order to promote the game in the West, he wrote a modified set of rules, gave English titles to the tiles, and added index letters and numerals familiar to card players. The game as described hereafter is prevalent in the United States; other forms of the game may be found in other Western countries.

Modern mah-jongg sets are usually made of

plastic instead of bone or ivory. A full set contains 136 or 144 tiles, depending on whether the flowers or seasons are used. Some sets include 20 flowers. The pieces are named and numbered as follows:

1. Bamboos, numbered 1 to 9, 4 of each number — 36 tiles
2. Circles, numbered 1 to 9, 4 of each number — 36 tiles
3. Characters, numbered 1 to 9, 4 of each number — 36 tiles
4. Honours, 4 red, 4 green, 4 white dragons — 12 tiles
5. Winds, 4 east, 4 south, 4 west, 4 north winds — 16 tiles

136 tiles

In addition:

6. Flowers and seasons, 4 of each or 8 of either — 8 tiles

144 tiles

The bamboos are often called sticks, or bams; the circles dots; the characters cracks, or craks. The mah-jongg set also includes a pair of dice, a quantity of tokens or chips used for scorekeeping, and a rack used to keep the tiles upright and to keep their faces hidden from other players.

The game is usually played by four individuals. The object of play, similar to that of the rummy card games, is to obtain sets of tiles. There are three kinds of sets: *chow,* a run or sequence of three tiles of the same suit in numerical order; *pung,* a sequence of three like tiles of the same suit and rank, such as three dragons of the same colour or three identical winds; and *kong,* a *pung* plus the fourth matching tile. The winner is the first player to hold a complete hand—*i.e.,* four sets and a pair of like tiles (14 tiles). The strategy of mah-jongg, like that of rummy, is both offensive and defensive: to complete a winning hand as quickly as possible; to block other players by not discarding tiles useful to them; and to build a high-scoring hand.

Players begin by drawing 13 tiles; "east wind" (who collects or pays double according to whether he or another player wins) takes 14 and begins play by discarding one. Thereafter, the other players, in counterclockwise rotation, each draw one tile, which may be the last discarded tile or a loose tile from the "wall" (comparable to stock in rummy). Any player may claim the previous discard if it completes his set. (If two or more players claim the same discard, there is a detailed order of precedence.) Losing players settle with the winner and with each other according to an accepted schedule of values for the sets or combinations of sets. A concealed set held in the hand scores differently from an exposed set on the table. Under certain rules, exceptional hands, picturesquely named "the three scholars," "four small blessings," and so on, are scored differently.

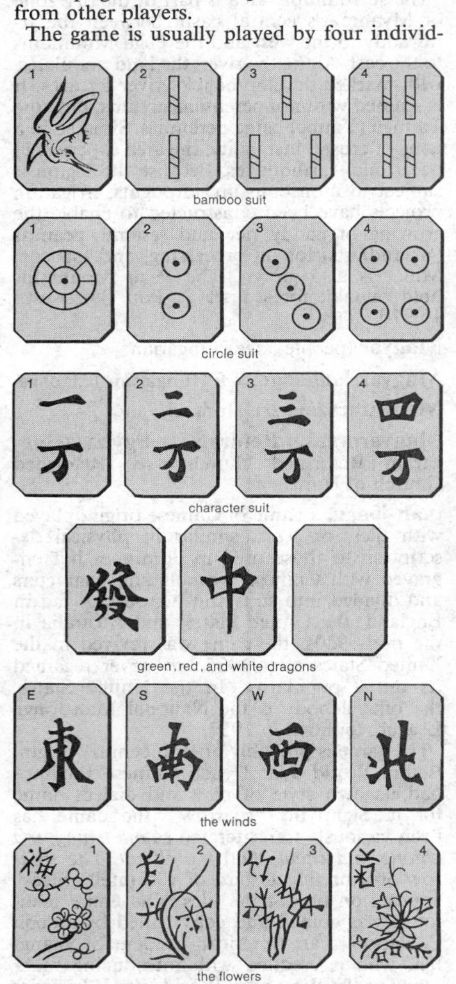

Mah-jongg tiles

Mahā Māyā, also called MĀYĀ, the mother of Gautama Buddha; she was the wife of Rāja Śuddhodana.

According to Buddhist legend, Mahā Māyā dreamt that a white elephant with six tusks entered her right side, which was interpreted to mean that she had conceived a child who would become either a world ruler or a buddha. After 10 lunar months, feeling that the time of birth was near, she went to the Lumbinī grove outside the city of Kapilavastu. While she stood upright and held onto the branch of a sal tree (in the posture adopted by mothers of all buddhas), the child came forth from her right hip. Seven days after his birth (again, in accordance with the destiny of the mothers of all buddhas) she died and was reborn again in the Heaven of the Thirty-three Gods (Tāvatiṃsa Heaven). The scenes of the conception and delivery of Gautama Buddha have been beautifully depicted in art.

Mahā Māyā dreaming of the white elephant, Gandhāra relief, 2nd century AD; in the British Museum
By courtesy of the trustees of the British Museum

Maha Sarakham, also spelled MAHASARAKHAN, or MAHASARAKHAM, town, northeastern Thailand. Maha Sarakham is located at a road junction on a bend of the Chi River. Rice is widely grown in the surrounding region, particularly in shallow river valleys, and freshwater fishing is also important. Pop. (1993 est.) 41,812.

Mahā-śivarātri (Sanskrit: "Great Night of Śiva"), the most important sectarian festival of the year for devotees of the Hindu god Śiva. The 14th day of the dark half of each lunar month is specially sacred to Śiva, but when it occurs in the month of Māgha (January-February) and, to a lesser extent, in the month of Phālguna (February-March), it is a day of particular rejoicing. The preceding day the participant observes a fast and at night a vigil during which a special worship of the linga (symbol of Śiva) is performed. The following day is celebrated with feasting, festival fairs, and, among the members of the South Indian Liṅgāyat sect, the giving of gifts to the guru (personal spiritual guide).

Mahābād, also spelled MEHĀBĀD, formerly SĀŪJBŪLĀGH, or SAVOJBOLĀGH, city, northwestern Iran. The city lies south of Lake Urmia in a fertile, narrow valley at an elevation of 4,272 feet (1,302 m). There are a number of unexcavated tells, or mounds, on the plain of Mahābād in this part of the Azerbaijan region. The region was the centre of the Mannaeans, who flourished in the early 1st millennium BC. The city is now mostly populated by Kurds. The area has been the scene of repeated political strife in modern times. Shortly after World War II, the short-lived Republic of Mahābād, with a Soviet-backed puppet government, was declared by the Kurds; the republic was overthrown when Iranian troops were sent there in 1946.

Mahābād remains a centre of Kurdish nationalism. It was under the control of Kurds for a short period in 1979, during the Iranian Revolution. The city is in one of the least economically developed parts of Iran. It is connected by road with Tabriz, Orūmīyeh (formerly Rezā'īyeh), and Mosul (Iraq). Pop. (1986) 75,238.

Mahābalipuram, also called MĀMALLAPURAM, or SEVEN PAGODAS, historic town, northeast Tamil Nādu state, southeastern India. The town lies along the Bay of Bengal 37 miles (60 km) south of Madras. The town's religious centre was founded by a 7th-century-AD Hindu Pallava king, Narasiṃhavarman, also known as Māmalla, for whom the town was named. Ancient Chinese, Persian, and Roman coins found at Mahābalipuram point to its earlier existence as a seaport. It contains many surviving 7th- and 8th-century Pallava temples and monuments, chief of which are the sculptured rock relief popularly known as "Arjuna's Penance," or "Descent of the Ganges," a series of sculptured cave temples, and a Śaiva temple on the seashore. The town's five *rathas*, or monolithic temples, are the remnants of seven temples, for which the town was known as Seven Pagodas. The town is a resort and tourist centre. It contains a college offering instruction in architecture and temple sculpture.

Mahabandula (Burmese general): *see* Bandula, Maha.

Mahābhārata (Sanskrit: "Great Epic of the Bharata Dynasty"), one of the two major Sanskrit epics of India, valued for its high literary merit and its religious inspiration. The *Mahābhārata* consists of a mass of legendary and didactic material surrounding a central heroic narrative that tells of the struggle for supremacy between two groups of cousins, the Kauravas and the Pāṇḍavas. Together with the second major epic, the *Rāmāyaṇa* ("Romance of Rāma"), it is an important source of information about the evolution of Hinduism during the period about 400 BC–AD 200. Contained within the *Mahābhārata* is the *Bhagavadgītā* (*q.v.;* "Song of the Lord"), which is the single most important religious text of Hinduism.

The poem is made up of almost 100,000 couplets—its length thus being about seven times that of the *Iliad* and the *Odyssey* combined—divided into 18 *parvan*s, or sections, to which has been added a supplement entitled *Harivaṃśa* ("Genealogy of the God Hari," *i.e.,* Krishna-Vishnu). Authorship of the poem is traditionally ascribed to the sage Vyāsa, although it is more likely that he compiled existing material. The traditional date for the war that is the central event of the *Mahābhārata* is 1302 BC, but most historians prefer a later date. The poem reached its present form about AD 400.

The story's conflict begins when because of his blindness, Dhṛtarāṣṭra, the elder of two princes, is passed over as king on his father's death in favour of his brother Pāṇḍu. Dhṛtarāṣṭra later assumes power when Pāṇḍu renounces the kingship to become a religious hermit. The sons of Pāṇḍu, the five Pāṇḍava brothers (Yudhiṣṭhira, Bhīma, Arjuna, Nakula, and Sahadeva), grow up in the court along with their cousins, the Kauravas (descendants of Kuru, a name applicable to both families, but applied for distinction to the sons of Dhṛtarāṣṭra). Because of the enmity and jealousy that develops between the cousins, the Pāṇḍavas are forced to leave the kingdom at the time of their father's death. During their exile the five jointly marry Draupadī and meet their cousin Krishna, who remains their friend and companion thereafter. They return to experience some years of prosperity in a divided kingdom but are again forced to retire to the forest for 12 years when the eldest brother, Yudhiṣṭhira, loses everything in a game of dice with the eldest of the Kauravas. The feud between the Kauravas and Pāṇḍavas culminates in a great series of battles on the field of Kurukṣetra (north of modern Delhi, in Haryana state). All the Kauravas are annihilated, and, on the victorious side, only the five Pāṇḍava brothers and Krishna survive. Krishna dies at the hands of a hunter who mistakes him for a deer, and the five brothers, along with Draupadī and a dog who joins them (Dharma, the god of justice, in disguise), set out for Indra's heaven. One by one they fall on the way, and Yudhiṣṭhira alone reaches the gate of heaven. After further tests of his faithfulness and constancy, he is finally reunited with his brothers and Draupadī to enjoy perpetual bliss.

The feud constitutes little more than a fifth of the total work and may once have formed a separate poem, the *Bhārata*. Interwoven with its episodes are the romance of Nala and Damayantī; the legend of Sāvitrī, whose devotion to her dead husband persuades Yama, the god of death, to restore him to life; descriptions of places of pilgrimages; and many other myths and legends.

Above all, the *Mahābhārata* is an exposition on dharma (codes of conduct), including the proper conduct of a king, of a warrior, of a man living in times of calamity, and of a person seeking to attain emancipation from rebirth. The several centuries during which the epic took shape were a period of transition from the religion of Vedic sacrifice to the sectarian, internalized worship of later Hinduism, and different sections of the poem express varying and sometimes contradictory beliefs. Some sections, such as the *Nārāyaṇīya* (a part of Book XIII), the *Bhagavadgītā* (Book VI), the *Anugītā* (Book XIV), and the later supplement, the *Harivaṃśa,* are important sources of early Vaiṣṇavite thought. There Krishna is identified with Lord Vishnu, and other *avatāras* (incarnations) are also described.

The *Mahābhārata* story has been retold in written and oral vernacular versions throughout South and Southeast Asia and has always enjoyed immense popularity. Its various incidents have been portrayed in stone, notably in sculptured reliefs at Angkor Wat and Angkor Thom in Cambodia, and in Indian miniature paintings.

Mahādeo Hills, sandstone hills located on the northern border of the Sātpura Range, in southern Madhya Pradesh state, central India. The hills have small plateaus and a gentle northern slope but are steep to the south, where they drop abruptly from 3,600 feet (1,100 m) to less than 900 feet (275 m). The general trend of the hills is east-northeast. The bedrock is extensively overlain by tracts of brown soil on which flourish deciduous forests. Lumbering and charcoal burning are economically important on the Mahādeo slopes. The economy of the area, however, is generally poor.

To the north, between the Sātpura and Mahādeo scarps and the Vīndhya Range, the valley floor is 20–40 miles (32–64 km) wide, and within this valley flows the Narmada River.

Mahajanga, formerly MAJUNGA, town and major port, northwestern Madagascar. It lies on the island's northwest coast, at the mouth of the Betsiboka River, whose estuary widens there into Bombetoka Bay. The town was the capital of the 18th-century kingdom of Boina.

The baobab tree of Mahajanga, Madagascar, on the Boulevard Poincaré in the harbour quarter of the town

Robin White/FotoLex

The French occupied Mahajanga in 1895 at the beginning of their conquest of Madagascar. The town's old sector is confined mainly to the harbour quarter and has some 19th-century Arabian houses. The town's modern buildings include a Roman Catholic cathedral, a Protestant meeting place, and a mosque. The University of Mahajanga, founded in 1977 as a regional centre of the University of Madagascar, became independent in 1988. A transshipment port, Mahajanga is linked by road with Antsiranana and with the national capital, Antananarivo, about 225 miles (360 km) south-southeast. An airport is nearby. Mahajanga's industries include the processing of agricultural products, meat canning, and the manufacture of soap, sugar, and cement. Immigrants from Comoros were almost as numerous in the town as the Malagasy until 1976–77, when most of the former were repatriated to Comoros following riots in Mahajanga. The Comorien population has increased again, and the town also has a substantial Indian merchant population. Fishing, cattle raising, and hardwood lumbering are important in the surrounding area, and coffee, rice, sugarcane, cashew nuts, cassava, cotton, and raffia palms are cultivated. Pop. (1993 prelim.) town, 100,807.

Mahākāla, in Tibetan Buddhism, one of the eight fierce protective deities. *See* dharmapāla.

Mahakam River, Indonesian SUNGAI MAHAKAM, also called KOETAI, or KUTAI, river rising in the mountains of central Indonesian Borneo (Kalimantan) and flowing about 400 miles (650 km) east-southeast to Makassar Strait, in a wide delta. The chief town along its course is Samarinda, capital of Kalimantan Timur (East Borneo) province, about 30 miles (48 km) above the river's mouth.

Mahalapye, village, eastern Botswana. It lies midway along the Mafikeng-Bulawayo railway and is 125 miles (200 km) northeast of Gaborone, the national capital. The name Mahalapye refers to an impala. The village is situated on a plateau with good pasturage, and its economy is based on cattle raising and extensive mixed farming of sorghum, corn (maize), and beans. Mahalapye has one of the country's meteorological stations and a branch of the National Library. Textile and small-tool manufacturing are the only important industries. Pop. (1991) 28,078.

Maḥallah al-Kubrā, Al-, also spelled MAHALLA EL-KUBRA, city, in the central Nile River delta of Lower Egypt, eastern Al-Gharbīyah *muḥāfaẓah* (governorate). It lies just west of the Damietta Branch of the Nile. Because the names of a large number of Egyptian places were compounded with *maḥallah* (Arabic: "encampment"), exact references to the town by early Arab writers are uncertain. Al-Maḥallah al-Kubrā, however, was apparently an important commercial centre after the 10th century AD. In 1836 it lost its position as capital of Al-Gharbīyah province to Ṭanṭā but continued as the seat of a smaller administrative unit.

In 1927 the Miṣr textile group established a large, modern cotton textile plant at the city, superseding domestic handloom weaving. It has since become a major centre of Egypt's textile industry. In addition to cotton products, the factory complex produces woolens, rayons, knitwear, blankets, and hosiery. It is associated with a model workers' community composed of housing estates with recreational and welfare facilities. Other mills in the city refine rice and flour. Industries in the city have been converted to natural gas brought by pipeline from the Abū Madi field in ad-Daqahlīyah *muḥāfaẓah.* The main railway from Cairo (75 miles [120 km] south-southeast) to Damietta links Al-Maḥallah al-Kubrā with Ṭanṭā, 19 miles (31 km) southwest. Pop. (1992 est.) 408,000.

maḥalwārī system, one of the three main revenue systems of land tenure in British India, the other two being the zamindar (landlord) and the ryotwari (individual cultivator). The word *maḥalwārī* is derived from the Hindi *maḥal,* meaning a house or, by extension, a district.

For revenue purposes the name was applied to any compact area containing one or more villages, which were called "estates." The revenue settlement was made with the estate—hence the term *maḥalwārī*—and there were distinct types of assessment. If a landlord, or zamindar, held the whole estate, the settlement was with him; otherwise, payment was exacted from individual cultivators.

mahāmudrā (Sanskrit: "the great seal"), in Tantric Buddhism, the final goal, the union of all apparent dualities. *Mudrā,* in addition to its more usual meaning, has in Tantric Buddhism the esoteric meaning of "female partner," which in turn symbolizes prajna ("wisdom"). The union of the Tantric initiate with his sexual partner signifies the symbolic union of the *upāya* (the "means," or method of teaching the goal) with prajna and—on the highest level—the identity of samsara (the phenomenal world) with Nirvāṇa (ultimate reality).

The intentionally ambiguous language of Tantric texts produces many difficulties in interpretation. It is not clear whether erotic terms are to be understood only symbolically or whether the spiritual process is meant to be expressed concretely in physical acts (as is the practice in certain sects of Tantric Buddhism). The transcendent meaning of the symbol, however, is always the supreme joy that comes about with the realization of mystical union.

Mahan, Alfred Thayer (b. Sept. 27, 1840, West Point, N.Y., U.S.—d. Dec. 1, 1914, Quogue, N.Y.), American naval officer and historian who was a highly influential exponent of sea power in the late 19th and early 20th centuries.

Mahan was the son of a professor at the U.S. Military Academy at West Point, N.Y. He graduated from the U.S. Naval Academy at Annapolis, Md., in 1859 and went on to serve nearly 40 years of active duty in the U.S. Navy. He fought in the Civil War, later served on the staff of Admiral J.A.B. Dahlgren, and progressed steadily in rank. In 1884 he was invited by Stephen Luce, president of the newly established Naval War College at Newport, R.I., to lecture on naval history and tactics there. Mahan became the college's president in 1886 and held that post until 1889.

Alfred Thayer Mahan, 1897

By courtesy of the Library of Congress, Washington, D.C.

In 1890 Mahan published his college lectures as *The Influence of Sea Power upon History, 1660–1783*. In this book he argued for the paramount importance of sea power in national historical supremacy. The book, which came at a time of great technological improvement in warships, won immediate recognition abroad. In his second book, *The Influence of Sea Power upon the French Revolution and Empire, 1793–1812* (1892), Mahan stressed the interdependence of the military and commercial control of the sea and asserted that the control of seaborne commerce can determine the outcome of wars. Both books were avidly read in Great Britain and Germany, where they greatly influenced the buildup of naval forces in the years prior to World War I.

Mahan retired from the U.S. Navy in 1896 but was subsequently recalled to service. In *The Interest of America in Sea Power, Present and Future* (1897), he sought to arouse his fellow Americans to a realization of their maritime responsibilities. Mahan served as president of the American Historical Association in 1902. His other major books include *The Life of Nelson* (1897) and *The Major Operations of the Navies in the War of American Independence* (1913). Before his death in December 1914, Mahan correctly foretold the defeat of the Central Powers and of the German navy in World War I.

Mahan, Larry E. (b. Nov. 21, 1943, Brooks, Ore., U.S.), professional American rodeo wrangler, the first to win five consecutive Rodeo Cowboys Association (RCA; later Professional Rodeo Cowboys Association, PRCA) all-around cowboy championships, from 1966 through 1970. His record was later surpassed by Tom R. Ferguson.

In 1962 Mahan won the all-around Oregon championship and also won the bareback bronc and bulldogging events. He joined the RCA in 1963 and soon became a consistent winner in bull riding, saddle bronc, and bareback riding. In 1965 he was the top money winner in bull riding, and in 1966 he won his first all-around title and was also the first cowboy to compete in three national finals rodeo events.

In 1967 Mahan became the first cowboy to win more than $50,000 in a single year. By the end of 1970 his career earnings were more than $280,000. Injuries early in the 1970s led to fewer appearances on the circuit, but Mahan continued to win, including another all-around title in 1973. He also ran several rodeo schools for young riders and developed a line of Western clothing. He retired from rodeo competition and owned a ranch near Phoenix, Ariz.

Mahānadi River, river in central India, rising in the hills of southeastern Madhya Pradesh state. Its upper course runs north as an insignificant stream, draining the eastern Chhattīsgarh Plain. After receiving the Seonāth River, below Baloda Bāzār, it turns east and enters Orissa state, its flow augmented by the drainage of hills to the north and south. At Sambalpur the Hīrākud Dam on the river has formed a man-made lake 35 miles (55 km) long; the dam has several hydroelectric plants. Below the dam the Mahānadi turns south along a tortuous course, piercing the Eastern Ghāts through a forest-clad gorge. Bending east, it enters the Orissa plains near Cuttack and enters the Bay of Bengal at False Point by several channels.

The Mahānadi ("Great River") follows a total course of 560 miles (900 km) and has an estimated drainage area of 51,000 square miles (132,100 square km). It is one of the most active silt-depositing streams in the Indian subcontinent. The river supplies several irrigation canals, mainly near Cuttack. Puri, at one of its mouths, is a famous pilgrimage site.

mahāpuruṣa (Sanskrit: "great man"), also called ŚALĀKĀPURUṢA, in Hindu, Jaina, and Buddhist belief, an individual of extraordinary destiny, distinguished by certain physical traits or marks (*lakṣana*s). Such men are born to become either universal rulers (*cakravartins*) or great spiritual leaders (such as buddhas or the Jaina spiritual leaders, the Tirthankaras). In the case of Gautama Buddha, soothsayers were able to recognize the signs at his birth, although all did not fully appear until he achieved Enlightenment (the *uṣṇīṣa,* or protuberance on the top of the skull, was visible only after he became a buddha). The signs have frequently been depicted in representations of the Buddha or of the Jaina Tirthankaras.

Catalogs of the distinguishing marks differ slightly between the religious traditions. In Buddhism the *lakṣana*s are enumerated as 32 major marks and 80 minor marks. The major *lakṣana*s include: (1) the *uṣṇīṣa,* or protuberance on the top of the skull; (2) hair arranged in short twists, each curl turning from left to right; (3) the *ūrṇā*, a little ball or tuft of hair between the eyebrows; (4) 40 perfectly shaped, dazzling white teeth, equal in size; (5) a large, long tongue; (6) golden-tinged skin; (7) long arms that reach to the knees when the individual is standing upright; (8) webbed fingers and toes; (9) a thousand-spoked wheel on the sole of each foot.

Jainism honours 54 "great souls" (also called *śalākāpuruṣa*s). They include the 24 Tirthankaras ("Ford-Makers"), 12 *cakravartins* ("world conquerors"), 9 *vāsudeva*s (counterparts of the Hindu god Krishna), and 9 *baladeva*s (counterparts of the Hindu god Balarāma). The birth of a great soul is always preceded by certain auspicious dreams seen by the mother. Some lists add 9 *prati-vāsudeva*s (or enemies of *vāsudeva*s), making a total of 63. The lives of the *śalākāpuruṣa*s are the subject matter of the Jaina epic and Puranic texts.

Mahar, a caste-cluster, or group of many endogamous castes, living chiefly in Mahārāshtra state, India, and in adjoining states. They mostly speak Marāṭhī, the official language of Mahārāshtra. In the early 1980s the Mahar community was believed to constitute about 9 percent of the total population of Mahārāshtra—by far the largest, most widespread, and most important of all the officially designated Scheduled Castes (formerly Untouchables or Harijans) in the region.

Traditionally, the Mahar lived on the outskirts of villages and performed a number of duties for the entire village. Their duties included those of village watchman, messenger, wall mender, adjudicator of boundary disputes, street sweeper, and remover of carcasses. They also worked as agricultural labourers and held some land, though they were not primarily farmers. In the mid-20th century, the Mahar began to migrate in large numbers to urban centres (Bombay, Nāgpur, Pune [Poona], and Sholāpur), where they were employed as masons, industrial labourers, railway workers, mechanics, and bus and truck drivers.

The Mahar were unified by the eminent 20th-century leader Bhimrao Ramji Ambedkar, who urged them to militant political consciousness and to great educational improvement. Before his death in 1956, Ambedkar and hundreds of thousands of his Mahar followers converted to Buddhism in protest against their Hindu caste status.

maharaja, also spelled MAHARAJAH, Sanskrit MAHĀRĀJA (from *mahat,* "great," and *rājan,* "king"), an administrative rank in India; generally speaking, a Hindu prince ranking above a raja. Used historically, maharaja refers specifically to a ruler of one of the principal native states of India. The feminine form is maharani (maharanee).

The title seems to have been introduced sometime in the first century BC by the Kushāns. They had been influenced by the Śaka (Scythian) and Persian-Mongolian rulers of northwestern India and preferred the honorific "great king" to "king." Candra Gupta I, the third king of the Gupta period (*c.* AD 320–540), took the title *mahārājādhirāja* ("great king of kings"), a Sanskrit rendering of the Persian *shahanshah*. Other, still more inflated honorifics followed, and during certain periods even vassal kings with relatively small holdings were known as maharajas.

Mahārāshtra, constituent state of India, the third largest in size and population. It occupies a substantial portion of the Deccan Plateau in the west-central portion of the country. It is bounded by the states of Gujarāt, Madhya Pradesh, Andhra Pradesh, Karnātaka (Mysore), and Goa, the union territory of Dādra and Nagar Haveli, and, on the west, the Arabian Sea. Its capital, Bombay (Mumbai), is an island city connected to the mainland by roads and railways; it has played a significant role in the country's social and political life.

A brief treatment of Mahārāshtra follows. For full treatment, *see* MACROPAEDIA: India.

The name Mahārāshtra first appeared in a 7th-century inscription and in a Chinese traveler's account. Between the 8th and the 13th century the people of the area were part of various Hindu kingdoms that were followed by a succession of Muslim dynasties. By the middle of the 16th century Mahārāshtra was fragmented among several independent Muslim rulers, who waged endless wars among themselves. By 1674 a Marāṭhā kingdom existed, and by the 18th century a Marāṭhā empire had been established. This empire succumbed to the British early in the following century. When India became independent in 1947, the area was known as Bombay state.

The state was split in two on a language basis in 1960, resulting in Gujarāt in the north and Mahārāshtra in the south.

Mahārāshtra presents a range of physical diversity. To the west is the narrow Konkan coastal lowland, widest near Bombay, with numerous minor hills dominating the landscape. To the east the Western Ghāts run almost continuously for 398 miles (640 km) north to south, with peaks in the north of more than 4,400 feet (1,340 m). The Deccan Plateau—containing the valleys of the Krishna, Bhīma, and Godāvari rivers—lies east of the Ghāts. In the east around Nāgpur are undulating uplands and the Wardha-Wainganga valley, part of the larger Godāvari River basin.

The climate is monsoonal, with local variations. The state experiences four seasons: March–May (hot and dry), June–September (hot and wet), October–November (warm and dry), and December–February (cool and dry). Rainfall is very heavy in Konkan, with some of the wettest spots recording 250 inches (6,350 mm) a year, diminishing to one-tenth that amount east of the Ghāts. Rainfall increases again eastward, reaching 40 to 80 inches (1,020 to 2,030 mm) in the extreme east. Coastal temperatures average only a few degrees above or below 80° F (27° C), with little variation between day and night. In the interior, daytime temperatures range from 110° F (43° C) in summer to 70° F (21° C) in winter.

Mahārāshtra contains a mixture of ethnic groups, a conglomeration of indigenous and immigrant peoples. Among them are such groups as Bhīls, Warlis, Goṇḍs, Korkus, and Gowaris, who exhibit certain affinities with Australian Aboriginals. The Kunbī Marāṭhās—supposedly descendants of waves of settlers who came from the north around the beginning of the Christian era—are most numerous. Marāṭhī, the state language, is spoken by more than 90 percent of the people; other important languages include Gujarātī, Hindi, Telugu, Kannaḍa, and Sindhī. More than four-fifths of the people are Hindus, and about two-fifths of the population live in urban areas.

The state's economy is based on agriculture, and nearly two-thirds of the population are peasants. Sorghum, millet, and pulses (legumes) dominate the cultivated area. Rice grows where rainfall exceeds 40 inches (1,020 mm), and wheat is a winter crop. Cotton, sugarcane, tobacco, and peanuts (groundnuts) are important crops in some regions, and mangoes, bananas, and oranges are also grown. Fishing is also important.

Forest products include teak and tendu leaves (for local cigarettes). Rich reserves of manganese, coal, iron ore, limestone, copper, and bauxite are found in the state. Mahārāshtra produces hydro- and thermoelectric power, and there is a nuclear-power facility at Tarapur, north of Bombay.

Mahārāshtra is more industrialized than most Indian states, its oldest and largest industry being cotton textiles. Oil refineries and petrochemical plants are found at Bombay, together with factories producing a variety of goods. The state has a railway network, five national highways that connect it with other Indian states, and airlines that provide service between Bombay and numerous domestic and foreign cities.

The state is a distinct cultural region. Its long artistic tradition is manifested in the ancient cave paintings of Ajantā and Ellora, in the remains of its medieval architecture, in its classical and devotional music, and in its theatre. The area's foremost diversion is *tamāshā,* combining music, drama, and dance.

Mahārāshtra has a number of universities, as well as medical colleges, dental colleges, agricultural universities, and engineering colleges. Area 118,800 square miles (307,690 square km). Pop. (2001 prelim.) 96,752,247.

Mahāsaṅghika (from Sanskrit *mahāsaṅgha,* "great order of monks"), early Buddhist school in India that, in its views of the nature of the Buddha, was a precursor of the Mahāyāna tradition.

Its emergence about a century after the death of the Buddha (483 BC) represented the first major schism in the Buddhist community. Although traditional accounts of the second council, at Vaiśālī (now in Bihār state), attribute the split to a dispute over monastic rules (*see* Buddhist council), later texts emphasize differences between the Mahāsaṅghikas and the original Theravādins ("followers of the Way of the Elders") regarding the nature of the Buddha and of arhatship (sainthood). The Mahāsaṅghikas believed in a plurality of buddhas who are supramundane (*lokottara*) and held that what passed for Gautama Buddha in his earthly existence was only an apparition.

The school was first located in the area of Vaiśālī and spread also to southern India, with centres at Amarāvatī and Nāgārjunakoṇḍa. Its texts were written in Prākrit. It further divided into several subsects, of which the best known was the Lokottaravāda (so called because of its views on *lokottara*).

mahāsiddha (Sanskrit: "great perfect one"), Tibetan GRUB-THOB CHEN, in the Tantric, or esoteric, traditions of India and Tibet, a person who, by the practice of meditative disciplines, has attained siddha (miraculous powers); a great magician.

Mahāsiddha, detail from a Tibetan *thang-ka* painting; in Tibet House, New Delhi
By courtesy of Tibet House, New Delhi

Both the Śaivites (followers of Śiva) of Hindu India and the Tantric Buddhists of Tibet preserve legends of 84 *mahāsiddhas* who flourished up to the 11th century. (The number 84 is a conventional, mystical number representing totality.) The lists of names vary considerably. All classes of society and both sexes are represented, and many non-Indian names appear. The prominence of the 84 *mahāsiddhas* reflects a synthesis during that period of the two religious traditions, combined with elements of Haṭha Yoga, magic, and alchemy.

The 84 *mahāsiddhas* continue to be revered in Tibet. They are the authors of most of the Tantric works on magic and are the originators of spiritual lines of descent—from master to disciple—still honoured. The most famous of the Tibetan *mahāsiddhas* is the great 8th-century Tantric master Padmasambhava.

One text lists the eight "great powers," or siddhas, as the power of shrinking to the size of an atom; of becoming light enough to fly through the air; of becoming heavy; of touching faraway objects, even as distant as the moon; of irresistible will; of supremacy over the body and mind; of having dominion over the elements; and of instantaneously fulfilling all desires. These powers are sought in order to help the yogin (spiritual adept) go on to achieve full spiritual freedom, and the texts clearly warn that the yogin who uses them for earthly gain will remain only a magician.

Mahathir bin Mohamad, in full DATUK SERI MAHATHIR BIN MOHAMAD, Mohamad also spelled MOHAMED or MUHAMMED (b. Dec. 20, 1925, Alor Setar, Kedah, Malay states [now in Malaysia]), Malaysian politician who served as prime minister from 1981 to 2003, overseeing his country's transition to an industrialized nation.

The son of a schoolmaster, Mahathir was educated at Sultan Abdul Hamid College and the University of Malaya in Singapore, where he studied medicine. After graduating in 1953 he worked as a government medical officer until 1957 and then entered private practice. He was first elected to parliament in 1964 as a member of the United Malays National Organization (UMNO), the dominant party within the ruling governmental coalition. In 1969, however, Mahathir was expelled from the UMNO after his forceful advocacy of ethnic Malay nationalism brought him into conflict with Prime Minister Tunku Abdul Rahman. (Though politically dominant, Malaysia's ethnic Malay majority was much poorer than the ethnic Chinese minority, which dominated the economy.) The New Economic Policy that the government adopted in 1971 to improve the economic situation of Malays embodied many of the ideas Mahathir had advocated.

Mahathir rejoined the UMNO in 1970, was reelected to its Supreme Council in 1972 and to parliament in 1974, and later in 1974 was appointed minister of education. In 1976 he became deputy prime minister and in June 1981 was elected president of the UMNO. He became prime minister in July of that year, the first commoner to hold that office.

Mahathir's long prime ministry gave Malaysia the political stability needed for economic growth. He welcomed foreign investment, reformed the tax structure, reduced trade tariffs, and privatized numerous state-owned enterprises. He also sought to bridge ethnic divisions by increasing general prosperity. The New Economic Policy was replaced in 1991 by the New Development Policy, which emphasized general economic growth and the elimination of poverty. Under Mahathir's leadership, Malaysia prospered economically, with a growing manufacturing sector, an expanding middle class, rising literacy rates, and increased life expectancies.

The 1997 Asian financial crisis and Malaysia's recession precipitated a split between Mahathir and his likely successor, Anwar Ibrahim. Mahathir sought to restrict foreign investment, while Anwar favoured open markets. In September 1998 Anwar was fired from his posts and arrested, and in August 2000 he was sentenced to nine years in prison. Mahathir continued to suppress Anwar's supporters and consolidate his own power. Always a controversial figure who often criticized the West, Mahathir retired as prime minister on Oct. 31, 2003.

Mahāvairocana-sūtra (Sanskrit: "Great Illuminator Sūtra"), Japanese DAINICHI-KYŌ, text of late Tantric Buddhism and a principal scripture of the large Japanese Buddhist sect known as Shingon ("True Word"). The text received a Chinese translation, under the title *Ta-jih Ching,* about AD 725, and its esoteric teachings were propagated a century later in Japan by Kūkai. These teachings, which have been called cosmotheism, centre upon Mahāvairocana (in Japanese, Dainichi Nyorai), the supreme cosmic buddha, whose body forms the universe. Through elaborate mystic rituals with a distinctly Indian flavour (even involving certain Hindu deities), one is led to realize that all one's thoughts, words, and actions are in reality Mahāvairocana's.

Mahāvaṃsa (Pāli: "Great Chronicle"), historical chronology of Ceylon (modern Sri Lanka), written in the 5th or 6th century, probably by the Buddhist monk Mahānāma. It deals more with the history of Buddhism and with dynastic succession in Ceylon than with the island's political or social history and covers the period from about the 6th century BC to the early 4th century AD.

The text—written in Pāli, the sacred language of Buddhism—is generally considered to be based on two main sources: a similar but cruder 4th-century chronicle, the *Dīpavaṃsa,* and oral tradition handed down by Buddhist monks. Because of the inclusion in the *Mahāvaṃsa* of much from these sources that is mythical or supernatural, large portions of the text are of dubious historicity. A sequel to the *Mahāvaṃsa,* known as the *Cūlavaṃsa,* continues the history of Ceylon to the 16th century.

Mahāvastu (Sanskrit: "Great Story"), important legendary life of the Buddha, produced as a late canonical work by the Mahāsaṅghika school of early Buddhism and presented as a historical introduction to the *vinaya,* the section of the canon dealing with monastic discipline. Its three sections treat the Buddha's former lives, the events from his entering the womb of Queen Mahā Māyā to his enlightenment, and his first conversions and the rise of the monastic community.

The text is exuberant in style, and in form, a labyrinth; its central narrative is frequently interrupted by Jātakas (explanations of present events by incidents in the Buddha's previous lives), Avadānas (similar tales from the previous lives of others), and doctrinal discourses. The life of the Buddha itself is presented as a profusion of miracles and wondrous events. The *Mahāvastu* reflects a growth of ideas about bodhisattvas ("buddhas-to-be") that was to continue in Mahāyāna circles, but at the same time, it preserves many ancient stories, traditions, and textual passages. The core of the work may go back to the 2nd century BC, but much material was added about the 4th century AD. *See also* Lalitavistara.

To make the best use of the Britannica, consult the INDEX *first*

Mahāvihāra, Buddhist monastery founded in the late 3rd century BC in Anurādhapura, the ancient capital of Ceylon (modern Sri Lanka). The monastery was built by the Sinhalese king Devānampiya Tissa not long after his conversion to Buddhism by the Indian monk Mahendra. Until about the 10th century, it was a great cultural and religious centre and the chief stronghold of orthodox (*i.e.,* Theravāda) Buddhism. Because of the extreme importance of Buddhism in Ceylon, the prestige of the monks of the Mahāvihāra was such that their power and influence often extended well beyond religion into the realm of secular politics. The religious authority of the Mahāvihāra was first challenged in the late 1st century BC by a heterodox group of Buddhist monks who broke away and formed the Abhayagiri-vihāra. Although an ever-present rival, this monastic order—save for brief periods of royal patronage, notably in the 3rd and 7th centuries—could not permanently usurp the favoured position of the Mahāvihāra order. The centralized authority and preeminence of the Mahāvihāra, however, gradually disintegrated until, by the 11th century, it had ceased to be a force in the religious life of Ceylon.

Mahāvīra (Sanskrit: "Great Hero"), byname of VARDHAMĀNA (b. *c.* 599 BC, Kṣatriyakuṇḍagrāma, India—d. 527, Pāvapurī), last of the 24

Mahāvira enthroned, miniature from the *Kalpa-sūtra,* 15th-century western Indian school; in the Freer Gallery of Art, Washington, D.C.

By courtesy of the Smithsonian Institution, Freer Gallery of Art, Washington, D.C.

Tirthankaras ("Ford-makers"; the saints who founded Jainism), and the reformer of the Jaina monastic community. The traditions of the two main Jaina sects record that Mahāvīra became a monk and followed an extreme ascetic life, attaining *kevala,* the stage of omniscience or highest perception. Teaching a doctrine of austerity, Mahāvīra advocated nonviolence, vegetarianism, and the acceptance of the *mahāvratas*, the five "great vows" of renunciation.

Life. Although it is traditionally accepted that Mahāvīra was born about 599 BC, this date is considered by scholars to be some 40 or more years too early, as he appears to have been a younger contemporary of the Buddha. The son of a Kshatriya (Kṣatriya; warrior caste) family, he grew up in Kṣatriyakuṇḍagrāma, a suburb of Vaiśālī (modern Basarh, Bihār state), the area of origin of both Jainism and Buddhism. His father was Siddhārtha, a ruler of the Nāta, or Jñātṛ, clan. According to one Jaina tradition his mother was named Devanandā and was a member of the Brahman (priestly) caste; other traditions name her Triśalā, Videhadinnā, or Priyakāriṇī, and place her in the Kshatriya caste.

The 6th century BC was a period of great intellectual, philosophical, religious, and social ferment in India, a period in which certain members of the Kshatriya caste opposed the cultural domination of the Brahmans, who used their positions as members of the highest caste to make demands upon the lower castes. In particular, there was growing opposition to the large-scale Vedic sacrifices (*yajña*), which involved the killing of many animals. Unnecessary killing had become objectionable to many thoughtful people of the time, with the spread of the doctrine of reincarnation, which linked animals and human beings in the same cycle of birth, death, and rebirth. Economic factors may also have encouraged the growth of the doctrine of nonviolence. The leaders of the anti-Brahman sects came to be regarded as heretical. Mahāvīra and his contemporary Siddhārtha Gautama, the Buddha, were two of the greatest leaders in this movement.

Though the traditions about the life of Mahāvīra vary according to the two Jaina sects—the Svetambaras ("White-robed") and the Digambaras ("Sky-clad"; *i.e.,* naked)—he apparently was reared in luxury, though as a younger son he could not inherit the leadership of the clan. At the age of 30, after he had married a lady of the Kshatriya caste and had a daughter, he renounced the world and became a monk. According to legend, his parents had died by practicing the rite of *sallekhana—i.e.,* voluntary self-starvation. Thus, when Mahāvīra joined the ascetic order of Pārśvanātha, to which his parents had belonged, self-denial was not foreign to him.

Perhaps beginning as a member of the order of Pārśvanātha, Mahāvīra used one garment for more than a year, but subsequently he went about naked and kept no possessions—not even a bowl for obtaining alms or drinking water. He allowed insects to crawl on his body and even bite him, bearing the pain with patience. People frequently shouted at him and hit him because of his uncouth and unsightly body. He meditated day and night and lived in various places—workshops, cremation and burial grounds, and at the foot of trees. Trying to avoid all sinful activity, he especially avoided injuring any kind of life, thus developing the doctrine of ahimsa, or nonviolence. He kept numerous fast periods and never ate anything that was expressly prepared for him. Though he wandered about continuously during most of the year, Mahāvīra spent the four months of the rainy season in villages and towns.

During his many wanderings he endured abusive language and physical injuries, always with patience and equanimity.

Mahāvīra's teachings. After 12 years of practicing such austerities, Mahāvīra attained *kevala,* the highest stage of perception. The school of Pārśvanātha apparently had been waning in appeal; Mahāvīra revived and reorganized Jaina doctrine and its monastic order, thus being credited as the founder of Jainism. Basing his doctrines, according to tradition, on the teachings of the 23rd Tirthankara, Pārśvanātha, a 9th-century-BC teacher from Banaras (Vārānasi, Uttar Pradesh), Mahāvīra systematized earlier Jaina doctrines—along with metaphysical, mythological, and cosmological beliefs—and also established the rules and guidelines for the monks, nuns, laymen, and laywomen of Jaina religious life.

Mahāvīra taught that a man can save his soul from the contamination of matter by living a life of extreme asceticism and by practicing nonviolence toward all living creatures. This advocacy of nonviolence encouraged his followers to become strong advocates of vegetarianism, which in the course of time helped to bring about a virtual end to sacrificial killing in Indian rituals. His followers were aided in their quest for salvation by accepting the five *mahāvratas* that have been attributed to Mahāvīra: renunciation of killing, of speaking untruths, of greed, of sexual pleasure, and of all attachments to living beings and nonliving things. Mahāvīra's predecessor Pārśvanātha preached only four vows.

Mahāvīra was given the title Jina, or "Conqueror" (*i.e.,* conqueror of enemies such as attachment and greed), which subsequently became a synonym for Tirthankara. He died, according to tradition, in 527 BC at Pāvā in Bihār state, leaving a group of followers who established Jainism, which, with its practice of nonviolence, has profoundly influenced Indian culture. (U.P.S./Ed.)

BIBLIOGRAPHY. Walter Schubring, *The Religion of the Jainas* (1966), describes some important aspects of Mahāvīra's personality. Padmanabh S. Jaini, *The Jaina Path of Purification* (1979), deals with the problem of the chronology and contemporaneity of Buddha and Mahāvīra. Hermann Jacobi, *Jaina Sūtras,* 2 vol. (1884–95, reprinted 1968), supplies the earliest Jaina accounts of Mahāvīra. Studies of his life and works include Bimala Churn Law, *Mahavira, His Life and Teachings* (1937); and K.C. Lalwani, *Sramana Bhagavan Mahavira: Life & Doctrine* (1975).

Mahaweli Ganga, (Sinhalese: "Great Sandy River"), river, central and eastern Sri Lanka. At 208 mi (335 km) in length, it is Sri Lanka's longest river. It rises on the Hatton Plateau on the western side of the island's hill country, flows north through a tea- and rubber-growing region, and turns east near Kandy; it then turns north across the lowlands, receives its principal tributary, the Amban Ganga, and flows past Polonnaruwa to its mouth on Koddiyar Bay, 7 mi south of Trincomalee.

With its headwaters in Sri Lanka's wet zone, the Mahaweli Ganga flows throughout the year, providing water for agriculture in the eastern dry zone. In the early 1970s a vast development project to increase the river's usefulness for irrigation and generation of electricity was under way, under the auspices of the World Bank. It is scheduled for completion by about 1990.

Mahāyāna (Sanskrit: Greater Vehicle), one of the two major Buddhist traditions and the form most widely adhered to in China, Korea, Japan, and Tibet. Mahāyāna Buddhism emerged in about the 1st century AD from the ancient Buddhist schools as a more liberal and innovative interpretation of the Buddha's teachings. Mahāyānists distinguished themselves from the more orthodox conservative schools, which they somewhat deprecatingly termed Hīnayāna (Lesser Vehicle). The Mahāyāna differ from the conservatives, represented in the modern world by the Theravādins of Sri Lanka, Burma, Thailand, Laos, and Cambodia, in their views of the nature of the Buddha and the ideal goal of a Buddhist. While Theravāda Buddhists revere the historical Gautama Buddha as a teacher of the truth, Mahāyānists attribute to the Buddha a supramundane quality and interpret the historical Buddha as an earthly manifestation of a transcendent celestial Buddha. The ideal goal toward which all Buddhists should strive is to become not, as in Theravāda Buddhism, an *arhat* or perfected saint, which Mahāyānists consider to be a limited selfish goal, but a *bodhisattva* (*q.v.*), or person who has attained to the state of Enlightenment but has postponed his Buddhahood in order to work toward the salvation of all others. Thus, compassion, the chief virtue associated with the *bodhisattva,* is accorded an equal place with wisdom, the virtue emphasized by the ancient schools. The merit accrued by a *bodhisattva* is considered transferable to others, a concept that led to such devotional movements as the Pure Land Buddhism of China and Japan.

Other major schools of Mahāyāna Buddhism with a significant modern following are Zen Buddhism, Nichiren Buddhism, and Tendai.

The Mahāyāna scriptures were composed mainly in Sanskrit, though in some cases they are known only in their Tibetan and Chinese versions, the original having been lost.

Mahāyāna-śraddhotpāda-śāstra (Sanskrit: "Treatise on the Awakening of Faith in the Mahāyāna"), relatively brief but influential exposition of the fundamentals of Mahāyāna Buddhist philosophy and faith. Though the work is said to be that of the Sanskrit poet Aśvaghoṣa, there are no extant Sanskrit copies of *The Awakening of Faith* (as it is known in the modern translation by D.T. Suzuki) and no references to it in any texts or commentaries originating in Sanskrit. A Chinese version, entitled *Ta-ch'eng ch'i-hsin lun,* first appeared about 550, but the provenance and authorship of the original are unknown.

The book contains one of the clearest presentations of the doctrine of the "three bodies" of the Buddha—the transitory physical body (*nirmāṇakāya*), the glorious body in paradise (*sambhogakāya*), and the absolute unqualified essence of the Buddha (*dharmakāya*). A number of commentaries have been written, and the work itself is a favourite authority among northern Buddhists.

Mahbūbnagar, town, administrative headquarters of Mahbūbnagar district, west central Andhra Pradesh state, southern India. Located on the Central Railway route southwest of Hyderābād, Mahbūbnagar is also a road centre. Cotton ginning and cotton pressing, as well as oilseed and rice milling, are the main industries. The town also has a college.

Mahbūbnagar district (7,112 sq mi [18,419 sq km]) is located on the Deccan Plateau and is bounded on the south by the Krishna River. Well-forested hills in the southeast yield teak, ebony, and gum arabic, while the largely sandy soils produce millet, oilseeds, and rice. It is said that the famous Golconda diamonds came from this district. Industrial centres include Nārāyanpet (which produces silks and saris), Devarkonda, and Nāgar Karnūl. Pop. (1981) town, 87,503; district, 2,444,619.

mahdī (Arabic: "divinely guided one"), in Islāmic eschatology, a messianic deliverer who will fill the Earth with justice and equity, restore true religion, and usher in a short golden age lasting seven, eight, or nine years before the end of the world. The Qurʾān (Islāmic sacred scriptures) does not mention him, and almost no reliable *ḥadīth* (saying attributed to the Prophet Muḥammad) concerning the *mahdī* can be adduced. Many orthodox Sunnī theologians accordingly question Mahdist beliefs, but such beliefs form a necessary part of Shīʿī doctrine.

The doctrine of the *mahdī* seems to have gained currency during the confusion and insecurity of the religious and political upheavals of early Islām (7th and 8th centuries). In 686, Mukhtār ibn Abū ʿUbayd, leader of a revolt of non-Arab Muslims in Iraq, seems to have first used the doctrine by maintaining his allegiance to a son of ʿAlī (Muḥammad's son-in-law and fourth caliph), Muḥammad ibn al-Ḥanafīyah, even after al-Ḥanafīyah's death. Abū ʿUbayd taught that, as *mahdī*, al-Ḥanafīyah remained alive in his tomb in a state of occultation (*ghaybah*) and would reappear to vanquish his enemies. In 750 the ʿAbbāsid revolution made use of eschatological prophecies current at the time that the *mahdī* would rise in Khorāsān in the east, carrying a black banner.

Belief in the *mahdī* has tended to receive new emphasis in every time of crisis. Thus, after the battle of Las Navas de Tolosa (1212), when most of Spain was lost for Islām, Spanish Muslims circulated traditions ascribed to the Prophet foretelling a reconquest of Spain by the *mahdī*. During the Napoleonic invasion of Egypt, a person claiming to be the *mahdī* appeared briefly in Lower Egypt.

Because the *mahdī* is seen as a restorer of the political power and religious purity of Islām, the title has tended to be claimed by social revolutionaries in Islāmic society. North Africa in particular has seen a number of self-styled *mahdī*s, most important of these being ʿUbayd Allāh, founder of the Fāṭimid dynasty (909); Muḥammad ibn Tūmart, founder of the Almohad movement in Morocco in the 12th century; and Muḥammad Aḥmad, the *mahdī* of the Sudan who, in 1881, revolted against the Egyptian administration.

Mahdī, al- (Arabic: Right-Guided One), original name MUḤAMMAD AḤMAD IBN AS-SAYYID ʿABD ALLĀH (b. Aug. 12, 1844—d. June 22, 1885, Omdurman, Sudan), creator of a vast Islāmic state extending from the Red Sea to Central Africa and founder of a movement that remained influential in The Sudan a century later. As a youth he moved from orthodox religious study to a mystical interpretation of Islām. In 1881 he proclaimed his divine mission to purify Islām and the governments that defiled it. His extensive campaign culminated in the capture of Khartoum (Jan. 26, 1885). He then established a theocratic state in the Sudan, with its capital at Omdurman.

Early life. Muḥammad Aḥmad was the son of a shipbuilder from the Dongola District of Nubia. Shortly after his birth, the family moved south to Karari, a river village near Khartoum. As a boy, Muḥammad developed a love of religious study. Instead of seeking an orthodox education, such as that offered at al-Azhar University in Cairo, and passing into the official hierarchy as a salaried judge or interpreter of Islāmic law, he remained in the Sudan. Increasingly, he tended to a more mystic interpretation of Islām, in the Ṣūfī tradition, through study of the Qurʾān—the sacred Muslim scripture—and the practice of self-denial under the discipline of a religious brotherhood.

He joined the Sammānīyah order and grew to manhood in a wholly Sudanese religious setting, purposely separating himself from the official ruling class. By now the young man had begun to attract his own disciples and, in 1870, moved with them to a hermitage on Abā Island in the White Nile, 175 miles south of Khartoum. His highly emotional and intransigent religious observance brought him into conflict with his *shaykh* (teacher), whom he reproved for worldliness. The exasperated *shaykh* expelled him from the circle of his disciples, whereupon Muḥammad Aḥmad, having vainly asked his teacher's pardon, joined the brotherhood of a rival *shaykh* within the same order.

Rise to power. The Sudan at this time was a dependency of Egypt, which was itself a province of the Ottoman Empire, and governed by the same multiracial, Turkish-speaking ruling class that governed Egypt. In appearance, education, and way of life, the rulers contrasted starkly with their Sudanese subjects, and, although the more assimilated higher officials and some of the chiefs of territories along the Nile who profited from their government connections were reconciled to the regime, the less privileged Sudanese were not. The situation was politically dangerous, for the discontented came from many different walks of life: taxpayers oppressed by fiscal injustices and enraged by the frequent floggings to which they were subject when tardy in their payments; slave traders aroused by the clumsy efforts of the government, which was hectored by the European powers, particularly Britain, to abolish the trade without delay; devout worshippers scandalized by the presence of non-Muslim Europeans as provincial governors and by their addiction to alcohol; peasants living by the Nile forced to tow government ships; warlike tribesmen, weary of the long years of enforced peace, spoiling for a fight—all these were potential enemies of the established order.

It was Muḥammad Aḥmad who converted this diversified discontent into a unified movement that for a time would transcend tribalism and weld the faithful into an unconquerable military machine. Gradually, during 1880 and the first weeks of 1881, he became convinced that the entire ruling class had deserted the Islāmic faith and that the khedive, the viceroy of Egypt, was a puppet in the hands of unbelievers and thus unfit to rule over Muslims. In March 1881 he revealed to his closest followers what he considered his divine mission—that God had appointed him to purify Islām and to destroy all governments that defiled it. On June 29 he publicly assumed the title of al-Mahdī, who, according to a tradition cherished by the oppressed throughout Islāmic history, would appear to restore Islām.

The events that followed this announcement were among the most dramatic in the history of the Nile Valley. Within less than four years al-Mahdī, who set out from Abā Island with a few followers armed with sticks and spears, ended by making himself master of almost all the territory formerly occupied by the Egyptian government, capturing an enormous booty of money, bullion, jewels, and military supplies—including Krupp artillery and Remington rifles.

By the end of 1883 al-Mahdī's ansar ("helpers," a name first given to those people in the city of Medina who helped the Prophet Muḥammad) had annihilated three Egyptian armies sent against them; the last, a force of 8,000 men with a huge camel train, commanded by General William Hicks, was butchered almost to a man. El Obeid, the present-day al-Ubayyiḍ, provincial capital of Kordofan, and Bāra, a chief town of that province, fell after being besieged by al-Mahdī. He now committed his first acts as the head of an armed theocracy on the march: taxes were collected, not as demanded by the Egyptians but as laid down by the Qur'ān. Already his fame had reached responsive ears in Arabia to the north and as far west as Bornu, now a province of northern Nigeria. A master of the art of putting his enemies always in the wrong, he supported his military operations by an intelligent and subtle propaganda. Counterpropaganda by the governor-general, ʿAbd al-Qādir Pasha Ḥilmī, a man of great resource, and by the ulama, the learned men, of Khartoum who mocked al-Mahdī's divine claims, failed miserably.

Capture of Khartoum. Al-Mahdī's crowning victory was the capture of Khartoum, on Jan. 26, 1885, after a resolute defense by its commander, Major General Charles George Gordon, who, against al-Mahdī's express order, was killed in the final assault. After many of the citizens of Khartoum had been massacred, al-Mahdī made a triumphal entry into the stricken city and led the prayers in the principal mosque. Even making allowance for the military weakness of Egypt, which during the crucial years 1881 and 1882 was torn by the nationalist revolt of Aḥmad ʿUrābī Pasha, it was an astonishing feat.

Religious empire. The withdrawal of the British expedition, which had failed to relieve Khartoum, left al-Mahdī free to consolidate his religious empire. He abandoned Khartoum, still heavy with the stench of the dead, and set up his administrative centre at Omdurman, an expanded village of mud houses and grass-roofed huts on the left bank of the Nile, opposite Khartoum. The site of the new capital had two advantages: it was higher and better-drained, hence healthier, than Khartoum, and, by governing from the exclusively Sudanese town of Omdurman, al-Mahdī avoided the evil associations of the old capital. He directed every aspect of community and personal life by proclamations, sermons, warnings, and letters. In this endeavour he was helped by the capture, intact, of the government press and an abundance of stationery. But he confined himself to the enunciation of principles; most of the routine he left to his chief officers. The political institutions, as well as the nomenclature of his government, were based insofar as practicable on those of primitive Islām. In the manner of the Prophet Muḥammad he appointed four caliphs, or deputies, to be the living successors of the four earliest caliphs in Islāmic history. Three of those appointed by al-Mahdī were Sudanese, including the caliph ʿAbd Allāh ibn Muḥammad, al-Mahdī's most trusted counselor and chief of staff; the fourth, Muḥammad al-Mahdī ibn as-Sanūsī, head of the Sanūsīyah order in the western desert, ignored al-Mahdī's invitation. Al-Mahdī referred to himself as "the successor to the apostle of God"—that is, successor to the Prophet Muḥammad, but only in the sense of continuing his work.

Al-Mahdī's rule was brief. He was taken ill, possibly of typhus, and died in June 1885, only 41 years old. At his wish his temporal functions were assumed by the caliph ʿAbd Allāh. Over his grave the caliph built a domed tomb similar in architecture to those customarily built over the remains of the more venerated holy men. Partially destroyed by gunfire during the Battle of Omdurman in 1898, it was later rebuilt by al-Mahdī's son ʿAbd ar-Raḥmān and the Mahdist community.

Assessment. Al-Mahdī made a powerful impression on his Sudanese contemporaries, and the doubters were few. Recorded recollections are capricious, but most witnesses agreed on his medium-to-tall height; his austere frame, which, according to some, fattened toward the end of his life; the soft voice that a sudden access of indignation could make terrible; the sympathetic, sensitive face; the large, piercing eyes. The pious were sure that in his person he conformed to all that was traditionally expected of a mahdi. Understandably, European captives drew a less-favourable picture.

To the British at the time of the Mahdist wars, al-Mahdī was the enemy whom they associated, though wrongly, with the killing of Gordon. The war correspondents generally reported him as an ogre, cruel when he was not lascivious, and they dubbed him the False Prophet. This caricature of al-Mahdī was reflected in a bulky literature by European authors that distorted al-Mahdī's image for an entire generation. Ironically, it was General Horatio Herbert Kitchener's conquest of the Sudan in 1896–98 that first brought Mahdists and British officials together and fostered what was to become a growing interest among European and Sudanese scholars in the study of Mahdist documents in the original Arabic. Such studies made possible a clearer view of this modern ascetic who changed the course of African history. (R.L.Hi.)

BIBLIOGRAPHY. F.R. Wingate, *Mahdiism and the Egyptian Sudan* (1891, reprinted 1968); A.B. Theobald, *The Mahdīya* (1951); P.M. Holt, *The Mahdist State in the Sudan,* 2nd ed. (1970); B. Farwell, *Prisoners of the Mahdi* (1967). Al-Mahdī's collected works in Arabic have been reprinted in a series of volumes under the auspices of the Sudan Government Central Archives, Khartoum.

Mahdist, also called ANSAR, or AL-ANṢĀR (Arabic: "Helper"), follower of al-Mahdī (Muḥammad Ahmad ibn as-Sayyid ʿAbd Allāh) or of his successor or descendants. Ansar is an old term applied to some of the companions of the prophet Muḥammad; it was revived for the followers and descendants of al-Mahdī, the Sudanese who in the late 19th century deemed himself a new prophet divinely appointed to restore Islām.

The Mahdists rose to prominence during the successful Sudanese wars and theocratic regime commanded by al-Mahdī from 1881 until his death in June 1885. His disciple ʿAbd Allāh succeeded to the temporal rule. But, following initial victories, his forces were gradually hunted down by Anglo-Egyptian armies and almost entirely destroyed in the Battle of Omdurman (*q.v.;* Sept. 2, 1898); he himself was killed in the final Battle of Umm Dibaykarat (Nov. 24, 1899). Leadership of the movement then passed to the Mahdī's son ʿAbd ar-Raḥmān (d. 1959), who, in the face of Anglo-Egyptian rule, sought to make the Ansar into a religious and political force. In 1959 he was succeeded as imam of the Ansar by his son Siddiq (d. 1961), who in turn was succeeded by a member of another branch of the family, Hadi ibn ʿAbd ar-Raḥmān. When the latter was killed fighting the leftist revolutionary government of The Sudan in 1970, most members of the Mahdī family fled into exile.

Mahdīyah, al-, also spelled MAHDIA, or MAHEDIA, town and fishing port on as-Sāḥil (coastal strip), eastern Tunisia. It lies on the narrow rocky peninsula of Cape Ifrīqīyā. The town owes its name to the mahdi (Arabic: *mahdī,* "the rightly guided one") ʿUbayd Allāh al-Mahdī, founder of the Fāṭimid dynasty, who established the town in 912 and in 921 made it his capital. Abandoned about 973, al-Mahdīyah was reestablished as a refuge capital of the Zīrid dynasty in the late 11th century. Sicilian Normans occupied the town in the mid-12th century, and thereafter it was no more than a small village and the principal place of southern as-Sāḥil. In the late 16th century it was absorbed into the Ottoman Empire. A contemporary minor port, its economic activities include olive cultivation, olive-oil milling, fishing and fish canning (sardines and mackerel), and handicraft industries. The site of a 10th-century mosque, al-Mahdīyah also contains a 16th-century Turkish fort and ruins of an ancient wall. Roads and a railway link it to Sūsah (Sousse), 20 miles (32 km) northwest. Pop. (1984) 26,602.

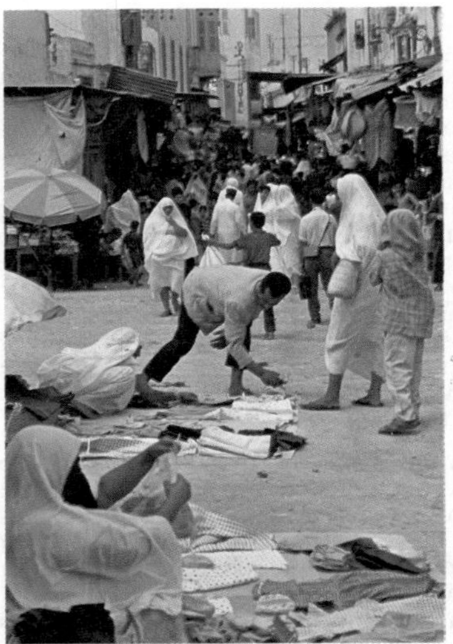

Street market in al-Mahdīyah, Tunisia
© C. Raimond-Dityvon/VIVA

Mahe, town in Pondicherry union territory, which is an enclave in northern Kerala state, southwestern India. Mahe lies on the left bank of the Naluthara River, northwest of Kozhikode (Calicut). The scene of much fighting between British and French troops in the 18th and 19th centuries, the town was captured by the French in 1726, incorporated several times into the British presidency of Madras, and finally restored to the French in 1817. It joined the Indian Union in 1954. The town is a fishing and seaside resort. Pop. (1981) town, 9,588.

Mahé Island, largest island of the Seychelles archipelago, Republic of Seychelles, in the western Indian Ocean. The island is 4 miles (6 km) wide and 16 miles (26 km) long and has an area of 57 square miles (148 square km). The island is granitic in origin and mountainous; the highest peak is Morne Seychellois, which rises to 2,969 feet (905 m) and forms part of a national park of the same

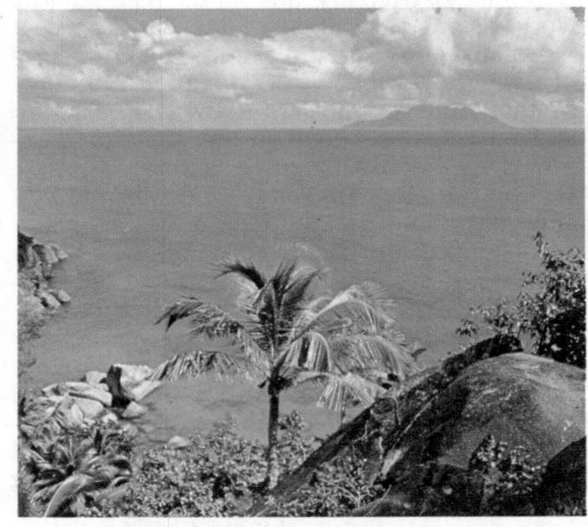

The coast of Mahé Island looking toward Silhouette Island
Gerald Cubitt

name. Port Launay Marine National Park is nearby on the northwestern side of the island, and Sainte-Anne Marine National Park is in Victoria Harbour to the northeast. A narrow coastal plain around the perimeter of the island provides most of the cropland.

Almost 90 percent of the population of the Republic of Seychelles live on Mahé, which is the site of Victoria, the republic's capital and only port. Mahé's chief exports are copra, cinnamon bark and leaf oil, patchouli, and vanilla. Tea is also grown. A paved-road system provides internal communication for the entire island, while Port Victoria and an international airport provide external communication and promote tourism. In the early 1960s a U.S. Air Force satellite-tracking station was built in the mountains in the centre of the island. Pop. (1984 est.) island and dependencies, 57,400.

Mahendra, Pāli MAHINDA (b. *c.* 270 BC, Pāṭaliputra, India—d. *c.* 204 BC, Anurādhapura, Ceylon [now Sri Lanka]), propagator of Buddhism in Ceylon. Generally believed to be the son of the Indian emperor Aśoka, he is honoured in Sri Lanka as a founding missionary of that country's majority religion.

When Aśoka, a convert to Buddhism from Hinduism, sent Mahendra and Princess Saṅghamitthā as missionaries to Ceylon about 251 BC, they converted King Tissa and the royal family, who helped them in the conversion of many of the common people. In the tradition of Aśoka, Mahendra did not propagate Buddhism by force but by works of practical piety and benevolence. Mahendra's name has not been found in any of the inscriptions of Aśoka, but his existence and works seem substantiated by the Ceylonese chronicles *Dīpavaṃsa* and *Mahāvaṃsa.* Other evidence consists of the monuments that the Sinhalese raised in his honour at the Buddhist holy city and ancient Ceylonese capital, Anurādhapura.

Mahendra, in full MAHENDRA BIR BIKRAM SHAH DEVA (b. June 11, 1920, Kathmandu, Nepal—d. Jan. 31, 1972, Bharatpur), king of Nepal from 1955 to 1972.

Mahendra ascended the throne in 1955 upon the death of his father, King Tribhuvan. The new king came into conflict with his Cabinet, which was dominated by a coalition of the Nepali Congress Party and the Ranas (a line of hereditary prime ministers). In order to assert his control, Mahendra staged a coup in 1960, dissolving the National Assembly, abrogating the constitution, and imprisoning political leaders. He had a new constitution promulgated in 1962 that in effect instituted direct rule by the Nepalese monarchy. Mahendra died in 1972 and was succeeded by his son Birendra.

Mahendravarman (king of Chenla): *see* Chitrasena.

Mahesh Yogi, Maharishi (b. 1911?, India), Hindu religious leader who introduced the practice of transcendental meditation (*q.v.;* TM) to the West.

Little is known of the Maharishi's early life. He studied physics at the University of Allahābād and worked for a time in factories. He later left for the Himalayas, where for 13 years he studied under Guru Dev, the founder of TM. When Guru Dev died in 1952, the Maharishi organized a movement to spread the teachings of TM throughout the world; his first world tour took place in 1959 and brought him to the United States.

TM is a type of meditation, practiced twice a day, in which the subject mentally recites a special mantra (sacred sound or phrase). Concentration on the repeated utterances decreases mental activity, and as a result the subject is expected to reach a higher state of consciousness. The movement grew slowly until the late 1960s, when the Beatles, an English rock-music group, and numerous other celebrities began to join his following. Since then, many have left the movement, but TM remains a popular form of relaxation, especially in the United States. The principles of transcendental meditation are discussed in the Maharishi's books *The Science of Being and Art of Living* (1963) and *Meditations of Maharishi Mahesh Yogi* (1968).

Maheshwar, also called CHOLI-MAHESHWAR, town, western Madhya Pradesh state, central India. It lies just north of the Narmada River. It is located on the ancient site of Maheśvarī, the capital of a Haihaya king, Arjuna Kārtavīrya (*c.* 200 BC), mentioned in the Sanskrit epics *Rāmāyaṇa* and *Mahābhārata.* Broad ghats—landing places with steps—sweep from the river upward toward the fort, temples, and palace of Ahalyābāi, a queen who selected Maheshwar as her capital in 1767. A 16th-century mosque is also of historical interest. On the opposite bank of the Narmada lies the early site of Navdatoli, where painted pottery and other artifacts have been excavated. An agricultural market centre, the town is also famous for its handloomed saris. Pop. (1981) town, 11,566.

Mahfouz, Naguib, also spelled NAJĪB MAḤFŪẒ (b. Dec. 11, 1911, Cairo), Egyptian novelist and screenplay writer who was awarded the Nobel Prize for Literature in 1988, the first Arabic writer to be so honoured.

The son of a civil servant, Mahfouz attended Cairo University and worked in the cultural section of the Egyptian civil service from 1934 until his retirement in 1971. His early novels, such as *Rādūbīs* (1943; "Radobis"), were set in ancient Egypt, but he had turned to describing modern Egyptian society by the time he began his major work, *Al-Thulāthiyya* (1956–57), known as "The Cairo Trilogy." Its three novels depict the lives of three generations of different families in Cairo from World War I until after the 1952 military coup that overthrew King Farouk. The trilogy provides a penetrating overview of 20th-century Egyptian thought, attitudes, and social change. In subsequent works Mahfouz offered critical views of the old Egyptian monarchy, British colonialism, and contemporary Egypt. Several of his more notable novels dealt with social issues involving women and political prisoners. His novel *Awlād ḥāratinā* (1959; *Children of Gebelawi*) was banned in Egypt for a time because of its controversial treatment of religion and its use of characters based on Muhammad, Moses, and other figures. His other better-known novels include *Al-Liṣṣ wa-al-Kilāb* (1961; *The Thief and the Dogs*), *Al-Shaḥḥādh* (1965; *The Beggar*), and *Mīrāmār* (1967; *Miramar*). His achievements as a short-story writer are demonstrated in the collection *Dunyā Allāh* (1963; *God's World*). Mahfouz wrote some 40 novels and short-story collections, as well as more than 30 screenplays and several plays.

Mahi River, stream in western India, rising in the western Vindhya Range, just south of Sardārpur, and flowing northward through Madhya Pradesh state. Turning northwest, it enters Rājasthān state and then turns southwest to flow through Gujarāt state and enter the sea by a wide estuary past Cambay after about a 360-mile (580-kilometre) course. The silt brought down by the Mahi has contributed to the shallowing of the Gulf of Cambay and the abandonment of its once-prosperous ports. The riverbed lies considerably lower than the land level and is of little use for irrigation.

Mahican, also spelled MOHICAN, Algonquian-speaking Indians of what is now the upper Hudson Valley above the Catskill Mountains in New York state, U.S. Their name means "wolf," but they were also known to the Dutch and the English as the River Indians. The Mahican consisted of five major divisions governed by hereditary sachems (chiefs) assisted by elected counselors. They lived in strongholds of 20 to 30 houses, situated on hills and enclosed by stockades, as well as in enclosed villages situated between cornfields and woodland.

When first contacted by the Dutch, the Mahican were at war with the Mohawk, and in 1664 they were forced to move from Schodack, near Albany, to what is now Stockbridge, Mass. They gradually sold their territory, and in 1736 some of them were gathered into a mission at Stockbridge and became known as the Stockbridge Indians; they were the only Mahican to preserve their cultural identity. Other groups scattered and merged with other tribes. The Stockbridge group later moved to Wisconsin. The American novelist James Fenimore Cooper drew a romanticized portrait of the declining Mahican in his book *The Last of the Mohicans* (1826).

Mahillon, Victor-Charles (b. March 10, 1841, Brussels—d. June 17, 1924, St. Jean, near Cap-Ferrat, Belgium), Belgian musical scholar who collected, described, and copied musical instruments and wrote on acoustics and other subjects.

In 1865 Mahillon entered the instrument-manufacturing firm established by his father, Charles Mahillon. He also founded a music journal, *L'Echo musical* (1869–86). As curator of the Brussels Conservatoire museum (from 1879), he formed a collection of more than 1,500 ancient, modern, and non-Western instruments. His analytical catalog of the collection (1880–1922 in 5 vol.; reprinted 1978 in 2 vol.) contains demonstrations of theories of instrument construction and a classification of instruments based on the material that produces the sound (*e.g.,* a drum is classified as a membranophone). This classification was later adopted and expanded by Erich von Hornbostel and Curt Sachs and has become the most commonly accepted system of instrument classification. He also made copies of rare instruments, notably the Bach trumpet, and organized concerts of music played on old instruments. Mahillon published *Les Éléments d'acoustique musicale et instrumentale* (1874; rev. ed. 1984; "Elements of Musical and Instrumental Acoustics") as well as numerous monographs, and he also contributed articles to the ninth edition of the *Encyclopædia Britannica.*

Mahinda (Buddhist missionary): *see* Mahendra.

Māhir Pasha, ʿAlī (b. 1882, Cairo—d. Aug. 25, 1960, Geneva), jurist and official who served three times as prime minister of Egypt.

A member of the aristocracy, Māhir Pasha took a law degree and after three years' practice became a judge in the native courts. In the years before World War I he sided with conservative Egyptian political groups who thought that it was possible to cooperate with the British (who had occupied Egypt in 1882)

Māhir Pasha, 1952
Keystone

in bringing economic and social progress to Egypt. He devoted his talents to the service of the king: in 1923 he was appointed director of the royal law school, and in the same year he played an important role in framing the new Egyptian constitution, a document that consolidated and confirmed the political pre-eminence of the monarch. In successive administrations he was at various times minister of education and minister of finance. He acquired his greatest influence in the later 1930s, when royal power was at its peak. In 1935 King Fu'ād chose him for the new position of chief of the royal cabinet, and at the end of 1935 he became prime minister in a caretaker government, serving during the next two years first as prime minister and later again as chief of the royal cabinet. He became prime minister again in 1939, and on the outbreak of World War II he took the measures against Germany that were required by the existing Anglo-Egyptian treaty. When Italy declared war in 1940, however, he refused to break diplomatic relations, and he became one of the centres in the movement to use the war as a means of undermining the British position in Egypt. Accordingly the British had him removed from office, and in April 1942 he was interned, remaining in custody until the end of the war.

Māhir Pasha remained politically inactive until the revolution of Gamal Abdel Nasser in 1952. The revolutionaries, who saw him as someone who could placate conservative political elements, secured his nomination as prime minister on July 24, 1952, one day after the revolution. In less than a year, however, ʿAlī Māhir clashed with them over their land reform policies and went into retirement.

Consult the INDEX *first*

Mahler, Alma, original name ALMA MARIA SCHINDLER, also called ALMA GROPIUS and ALMA WERFEL (b. Aug. 31, 1879, Vienna, Austria-Hungary—d. Dec. 11, 1964, New York, N.Y., U.S.), wife of Gustav Mahler, known for her relationships with celebrated men.

The daughter of the painter Emil Schindler, Alma grew up surrounded by art and artists. She studied art and became friends with the painter Gustav Klimt, who made several portraits of her. Her primary interest, however, was in music: she was a gifted pianist and studied musical composition with Alexander von Zemlinsky.

In 1902 she married Gustav Mahler, who at first discouraged her from composing; he is said to have changed his mind after hearing her songs. Mahler left a musical portrait of her in the first movement of his *Symphony No. 6,* and he dedicated *Symphony No. 8* to her. After his death in 1911 Alma had an affair with Oskar Kokoschka, who painted her many times, most notably in "The Tempest" (1914; "Die Windsbraut"). In 1915 she married the architect Walter Gropius; they were divorced after World War I. She married the writer Franz Werfel in 1929. In the late 1930s the Werfels left Nazi Germany, eventually settling in the United States.

During her lifetime Alma Mahler became friends with numerous celebrated artists, including the composer Arnold Schoenberg, the writer Gerhart Hauptmann, and the singer Enrico Caruso. The composer Alban Berg dedicated his opera *Wozzeck* (1921) to her.

Alma Mahler published two collections of Gustav Mahler's letters as well as her memoirs, *And the Bridge Is Love* (1958). She also published a number of songs.

Mahler, Gustav (b. July 7, 1860, Kaliště, Bohemia, Austrian Empire—d. May 18, 1911, Vienna, Austria), Austrian-Jewish composer and conductor noted for his 10 symphonies and various songs with orchestra, which drew together many different strands of Romanticism. Although his music was largely ignored for 50 years after his death, Mahler was later regarded as an important forerunner of 20th-century techniques of composition and an acknowledged influence on such composers as Arnold Schoenberg, Dmitry Shostakovich, and Benjamin Britten.

Early life. Mahler was the son of an Austrian-Jewish tavern keeper living in the Bohemian village of Kaliště (German: Kalischt), in the southwestern corner of the modern Czech Republic; a few months later the family moved to the nearby town of Jihlava (German: Iglau), where Mahler spent his childhood and youth. These simple facts provide a first clue to his tormented personality: he was afflicted by racial tensions from the beginning of his life. As part of a German-speaking Austrian minority, he was an outsider among the indigenous Czech population and, as a Jew, an outsider among that Austrian minority; later, in Germany, he was an outsider as both an Austrian from Bohemia and a Jew.

Mahler's life was also complicated by the tension existing between his parents. His father, a self-educated man of fierce vitality, had married a delicate woman from a cultured family, and, coming to resent her social superiority, he resorted to physically maltreating her. In consequence Mahler was alienated from his father and had a strong mother fixation, which even manifested itself physically: a slight limp was unconsciously adopted in imitation of his mother's lameness. Furthermore, he inherited his mother's weak heart, which was to cause his death at the age of 50. Finally, there was a constant childhood background of illness and death among his 11 brothers and sisters.

This unsettling early background may explain the nervous tension, the irony and skepticism, the obsession with death, and the unremitting quest to discover some meaning in life that was to pervade Mahler's life and music. But it does not explain the prodigious energy, intellectual power, and inflexibility of purpose that carried him to the heights as both a master conductor and a composer. The positive elements in his makeup stemmed no doubt from his father's side of the family, as did his great physical vitality. Despite his inherited heart trouble, he was an extremely active man—a ruthless musical director, a tireless swimmer, and an indefatigable mountain walker.

His musical talent revealed itself early and significantly. Around the age of four, fascinated by the military music at a nearby barracks and the folk music sung by the Czech working people, he reproduced both on the accordion and on the piano and began composing pieces of his own. The military and popular styles, together with the sounds of nature, became main sources of his mature inspiration. At 10 he made his debut as a pianist in Jihlava and at 15 was so proficient musically that he was accepted as a pupil at the Vienna Conservatory. After winning piano and composition prizes and leaving with a diploma, he supported himself by sporadic teaching while trying to win recognition as a composer. When he failed to win the Conservatory's Beethoven Prize for composition with his first significant work, the cantata *Das klagende Lied* (completed 1880; *The Song of Complaint*), he turned to conducting for a more secure livelihood, reserving composition for the lengthy summer vacations.

Mahler
The Mansell Collection

Career as a conductor. The next 17 years saw his ascent to the very top of his chosen profession. From conducting musical farces in Austria, he rose through various provincial opera houses, including important engagements at Budapest and Hamburg, to become artistic director of the Vienna Court Opera in 1897, at the age of 37. As a conductor he had won general acclaim, but as a composer, during this first creative period, he immediately encountered the public's lack of comprehension that was to confront him for most of his career.

Since Mahler's conducting life centred in the traditional manner on the opera house, it is at first surprising that his whole mature output was entirely symphonic (his 40 songs are not true lieder but embryonic symphonic movements, some of which, in fact, provided a partial basis for the symphonies). But Mahler's unique aim, partially influenced by the school of Richard Wagner and Franz Liszt, was essentially autobiographical—the musical expression of a personal view of the world. And for this purpose, song and symphony were more appropriate than the dramatic medium of opera: song because of its inherent personal lyricism, and symphony (from the Wagner and Liszt point of view) because of its subjective expressive power.

Musical works: first period. Each of Mahler's three creative periods produced a symphonic trilogy. The three symphonies of his first period were conceived on a programmatic basis (*i.e.,* founded on a nonmusical story or idea), the actual programs (later discarded) being concerned with establishing some ultimate ground for existence in a world dominated by pain, death, doubt, and despair. To this end, he followed the example of Ludwig van Beethoven's *Symphony No. 6 in F Major* (*Pastoral*) and Hector Berlioz' *Symphonie fantastique* in building symphonies with more than the then traditional four movements; that of Wagner's music-dramas in expanding the time span, enlarging the orchestral resources, and indulging in uninhibited emotional expression; that of Beethoven's *Symphony No. 9 in D Minor* (*Choral*) in introducing texts sung by soloists and chorus; and that of certain chamber works by Franz Schubert in introducing music from his own songs (settings of poems from the German folk anthology *Des Knaben Wunderhorn* [*The Youth's Magic Horn*] or of poems by himself in a folk style).

These procedures, together with Mahler's own tense and rhetorical style, phenomenally vivid orchestration, and ironic use of popular-style music, resulted in three symphonies of unprecedentedly wide contrasts but unified by his unmistakable creative personality and his firm command of symphonic structure. The program of the purely orchestral *Symphony No. 1 in D Major* (1888; one of its five movements was later discarded) is autobiographical of his youth: the joy of life becomes clouded over by an obsession with death in the macabre "Funeral March in the Manner of Callot" (basically a parody of popular music), which is eventually routed in the arduous and brilliant finale. The five-movement *Symphony No. 2* (1894; popular title *Resurrection*) begins with the death obsession (the first movement's "funeral ceremony") and culminates in an avowal of the Christian belief in immortality (a huge finale portraying the Day of Judgment and ending with a setting of the 18th-century German writer Friedrich Klopstock's "Resurrection" ode involving soloists and chorus). The even vaster *Symphony No. 3 in D Major* (1896), also including a soloist and chorus, presents in six movements a Dionysiac vision of a great chain of being, moving from inanimate nature to human consciousness and the redeeming love of God.

The religious element in these works is highly significant. Mahler's disturbing early background, coupled with his lack of an inherited Jewish faith (his father was a freethinker), resulted in a state of metaphysical torment, which he resolved temporarily by identifying himself with Christianity. That this was a genuine impulse there can be no doubt, even if there was an element of expediency in his becoming baptized, early in 1897, because it made it easier for him to be appointed to the Vienna Opera post. The 10 years there represent his more balanced middle period. His newfound faith and his new high office brought a full and confident maturity, which was further stabilized by his marriage in 1902 to Alma Maria Schindler, who bore him two daughters, in 1902 and 1904.

Musical works: middle period. As director of the Vienna Opera (and for a time of the Vienna Philharmonic Concerts), Mahler achieved an unprecedented standard of interpretation and performance, which proved an almost unapproachable model for those who followed him. A fanatical idealist, he drove himself and his artists with a ruthless energy that proved a continual inspiration and with a complete disregard for personal considerations that won him many enemies who worked for his dismissal. At this time too, he made a number of tours and became famous over much of Europe as a conductor. He continued his recently acquired habit of devoting his summer vacations, in the Austrian Alps, to composing, and, since, in his case, this involved a ceaseless expenditure of spiritual and nervous energy, he thereby placed an intolerable double strain on his frail constitution.

Most of the works of this middle period reflect the fierce dynamism of Mahler's full maturity. An exception is *Symphony No. 4* (1900; popularly called *Ode to Heavenly Joy*), which is more of a pendant to the first period: conceived in six movements (two of which were eventually discarded), it has a *Wunderhorn* song finale for soprano, which was originally intended as a movement for *Symphony No. 3* and which evokes a naive peasant conception of the Christian heaven. At the same time, in dispensing with an explicit program and a chorus and coming near to the normal orchestral symphony, it does foreshadow the middle-period trilogy, *Nos. 5, 6,* and *7.* These are all purely orchestral, with a new, hardedged, contrapuntal clarity of instrumentation, and devoid of programs altogether, yet each clearly embodies a spiritual conflict that reaches a conclusive resolution. *No. 5* (1902; popularly called *Giant*) and *No. 7* (1905; popularly called *Song of the Night*) move from darkness to light, though the light seems not the illumination of any afterlife but the sheer exhilaration of life on Earth. Both symphonies have five movements. Between them stands the work Mahler regarded as his *Tragic Symphony*—the four-movement *No. 6 in A Minor* (1904), which moves out of darkness only with difficulty, and then back into total night. From these three symphonies onward, he ceased to adapt his songs as whole sections or movements, but in each he introduced subtle allusions, either to his *Wunderhorn* songs or to his settings of poems by Friedrich Rückert, including the cycle *Kindertotenlieder* (1901–04; *Songs on the Deaths of Children*).

At the end of this period he composed his monumental *Symphony No. 8 in E Flat Major* (1907) for eight soloists, double choir, and orchestra—a work known as the *Symphony of a Thousand,* owing to the large forces it requires, though Mahler gave it no such title. This stands apart, as a later reversion to the expansive metaphysical tendencies of the first period, and represents a consummation of them: the first continuously choral and orchestral symphony ever composed. It could be called at once a massive statement of human aspirations and a cry for illumination, from both the religious and the humanistic points of view. The first of its two parts, equivalent to a symphonic first movement, is a setting of the medieval Catholic Pentecost hymn *Veni Creator Spiritus;* part two, amalgamating the three movement-types of the traditional symphony, has for its text the mystical closing scene of J.W. von Goethe's *Faust* drama (the scene of Faust's redemption). The work marked the climax of Mahler's confident maturity, since what followed was disaster—of which, he believed, he had had a premonition in composing his *Tragic Symphony, No. 6.* This work had revealed for the first time a superstitious element in his personality. The finale originally contained three climactic blows with a large hammer, representing "the three blows of fate which fall on a hero, the last one felling him as a tree is felled" (he subsequently removed the final blow from the score). Afterward he identified these as presaging the three blows that fell on himself in 1907, the last of which portended his own death: his resignation was demanded at the Vienna Opera, his three-year-old daughter, Maria, died, and a doctor diagnosed his fatal heart disease.

Musical works: last period. Thus began Mahler's last period, in which, at the age of 47, he became a wanderer again. He was obliged to make a new reputation for himself, as a conductor in the United States, directing performances at the Metropolitan Opera and becoming conductor of the Philharmonic Society of New York; yet he went back each summer to the Austrian countryside to compose his last works. He returned finally to Vienna, to die there, in 1911.

The three works constituting his last-period trilogy, none of which he ever heard, are *Das Lied von der Erde* (1908; *The Song of the Earth*), *Symphony No. 9* (1910), and *Symphony No. 10 in F Sharp Major,* left unfinished in the form of a comprehensive full-length sketch (though a full-length performing version has been made posthumously). The first of the three again revealed Mahler's superstition: beginning as a song cycle (to Chinese poems in German translations), it grew into "A Symphony for Tenor, Baritone (or Contralto) and Orchestra." Yet, he would not call it "Symphony No. 9," believing, on the analogy of Beethoven and Bruckner, that a ninth symphony must be its composer's last. When he afterward began the actual *No. 9,* he said, half jokingly, that the danger was over, since it was "really the tenth"; but in fact, that symphony became his last, and *No. 10* remained in sketch form when he died.

This last-period trilogy marked an even more decisive break with the past than had the middle-period trilogy. It represents a threefold attempt to come to terms with modern man's fundamental problem—the reality of death, which in his case had effectively destroyed the religious faith he had opposed to death as an imagined event. *Das Lied von der Erde*—a six-movement "song-cycle symphony" as opposed to the two-part "oratorio symphony," *No. 8*—views the evanescence of all things human in veiled poetic terms—sardonic, wistful, and grief-stricken by turns—until it finds a sad consolation in the beauty of the Earth that endures after the individual is no longer alive to see it.

In the four-movement *No. 9,* purely orchestral, the confrontation with death becomes an anguished personal one, evoking horror and bitterness in Mahler's most modern and prophetic movement, the "Rondo-Burleske," and culminating in a finale of heartbroken resignation. The finales of both these works end with an extraordinary, long-drawn disintegration of the musical texture, suggesting dissolution, and the more extreme case in *No. 9* was for long thought to be Mahler's final comment on human existence. Growing familiarity with the sketch of *No. 10,* however, has suggested that he broke through to a more positive attitude: its five movements deal with the same conflict as the two preceding works, but the resignation attained at the end of the finale is entirely serene and affirmative.

Assessment. Modern critical opinion recognizes Mahler's powerful influence during a period of musical transition. In his works may be found pervasive elements foreshadowing the radical methods employed in the 20th century: these elements include "progressive tonality" (ending a work in a different key from the initial one); dissolution of tonality (obscuring the perception of key through the constant use of chromaticism or harmonies not belonging to that key); a breakaway from harmony produced by the entire orchestra in favour of a contrapuntal texture (based on interwoven melodies) for groups of solo instruments within the full orchestra; the principle of continually varying themes rather than merely restating them; ironic quotation of popular styles and of sounds from everyday life (bird calls, bugle signals, etc.); and, on the other hand, a new way of formally unifying the symphony through the adoption of techniques subtly derived from Liszt's "cyclic" method (the carrying over of themes from one movement of a work to others).

In terms of the personal content of his art, it can be said of Mahler, more than of any other composer, that he lived out the spiritual torment of disinherited modern man in his art, and that the man is the music.

(D.V.Co.)

BIBLIOGRAPHY. Two important memoirs are Bruno Walter, *Gustav Mahler* (1958); and Natalie Bauer-Lechner, *Recollections of Gustav Mahler,* ed. and annotated by Peter Franklin (1980). The definitive biography (coupled with critical study) is Donald Mitchell, *Gustav Mahler: The Early Years,* rev. and ed. by Paul Banks and David Matthews (1980), and *Gustav Mahler: The Wunderhorn Years* (1975, reissued 1980). Other notable biographies include Kurt Blaukopf, *Gustav Mahler* (1973, reprinted 1991), a biographical portrait emphasizing Mahler's life and personality; and Edward Seckerson, *Mahler: His Life and Times* (1982). Less scholarly works for the general reader are Egon Gartenberg, *Mahler: The Man and His Music* (1978); and Michael Kennedy, *Mahler,* rev. ed. (1991), a concise treatment. Interpretations of his music include Henry A. Lea, *Gustav Mahler: Man on the Margin* (1985); Deryck Cooke, *Gustav Mahler: An Introduction to His Music,* 2nd ed. (1988), a collection of short essays on individual works; and Donald Mitchell, *Gustav Mahler: Songs and Symphonies of Life and Death* (1985), focusing on the composer's vocal music.

Mahmoud (foaled 1933), racehorse (Thoroughbred), the fastest horse ever to run in the Derby, making a record time of 2:33$^{4}/_{5}$.

Mahmoud was foaled in France by Mah Mahal and sired by Blenheim. He was owned by the Aga Khan who sent him to England to be trained by Frank Butters at Newmarket. He won all three of his races as a two-year-old, and as a three-year-old he lost the Two Thousand Guineas by a short head, but then, with Charlie Smirke as jockey, he won the Derby, setting the record. After being retired from racing and sent to stud in 1940, he was sold in the United States.

Mahmud (Arabic and Turkish personal name): *see under* Muḥammad, Mohammed, Mohammad, or Mehmet, except as below.

Mahmud, also spelled MAHMŪD, name of rulers grouped below by country and indicated by the symbol •.

GHAZNA

• **Maḥmūd,** in full YAMIN AL-DAULA ABU'L-QASIM MAḤMŪD IBN SEBÜKTIGIN (b. 971—d. April 30?, 1030, Ghazna), sultan of the kingdom of Ghazna (998–1030), originally comprising modern Afghanistan and northeastern modern Iran but, through his conquests, eventually including northwestern India and most of Iran. He transformed his capital, Ghazna, into a cultural centre rivalling Baghdad.

Life. Maḥmūd was the son of Sebüktigin, a Turkish slave, who in 977 became ruler of Ghazna. When Maḥmūd ascended the throne in 998 at the age of 27, he already showed remarkable administrative ability and statesmanship. At the time of his accession, Ghazna was a small kingdom. The young and ambitious Maḥmūd aspired to be a great monarch, and in more than 20 successful expeditions he amassed the wealth with which to lay the foundation of a vast empire that eventually included Kashmir, the Punjab, and a great part of Iran.

During the first two years of his reign Maḥmūd consolidated his position in Ghazna. Though an independent ruler, for political reasons he gave nominal allegiance to the ʿAbbāsid caliph in Baghdad, and the caliph, in return, recognized him as the legitimate ruler of the lands he occupied and encouraged him in his conquests.

Maḥmūd is said to have vowed to invade India once a year and, in fact, led about 17 such expeditions. The first large-scale campaign began in 1001 and the last ended in 1026. The first expeditions were aimed against the Punjab and northeastern India, while in his last campaign Maḥmūd reached Somnāth on the southern coast of Gujarāt.

His chief antagonist in northern India was Jaipāl, the ruler of the Punjab. When, in 1001, Maḥmūd marched on India at the head of 15,000 horse troops, Jaipāl met him with 12,000 horse troops, 30,000 foot soldiers, and 300 elephants. In a battle near Peshāwar the Indians, though superior in numbers and equipment, fell back under the onslaught of the Muslim horse, leaving behind 15,000 dead. After falling into the hands of the victors, Jaipāl, with 15 of his relatives and officers, was finally released. But the Raja could not bear his defeat, and after abdicating in favour of his son, Ānandpāl, he mounted his own funeral pyre and perished in the flames.

Ānandpāl appealed to the other Indian rajas for help. Some replied in person, others sent armies. The Indian women sold their jewels to finance a huge army. When, at last, in 1008, Maḥmūd met the formidable force thus raised, the two armies lay facing each other between Und and Peshāwar for 40 days. The Sultan finally succeeded in enticing the Indians to attack him. A force of 30,000 Khokars, a fierce, primitive tribe, charged both flanks of the Sultan's army with such ferocity that Maḥmūd was about to call a retreat. But at this critical moment Ānandpāl's elephant, panic-stricken, took flight. The Indians, believing that their leader was turning tail, fled from the battlefield strewn with their dead and dying. This momentous victory facilitated Maḥmūd's advance into the heart of India.

After annexing the Punjab, and returning with immense booty, the Sultan set about to transform Ghazna into a great centre of art and culture. He patronized scholars, established colleges, laid out gardens, and built mosques, palaces, and caravansaries. Maḥmūd's example was followed by his nobles and courtiers, and Ghazna soon was transformed into the most brilliant cultural centre in Central Asia.

In 1024 the Sultan set out on his last famous expedition to the southern coast of Kāthiāwār along the Arabian Sea, where he sacked the city of Somnāth and its renowned Hindu temple. Maḥmūd returned home in 1026. The last years of his life he spent in fighting the Central Asian tribes threatening his empire.

Significance. Maḥmūd was the first to carry the banner of Islām into the heart of India. To some Muslim writers he was a great champion of his faith, an inspired leader endowed with supernatural powers. Most Indian historians, on the other hand, emphasize his military exploits and depict him as "an insatiable invader and an intrepid marauder." Neither view is correct. In his Indian expeditions he kept his sights set mainly on the fabulous wealth of India stored in its temples. Though a zealous champion of Islām, he never treated his Indian subjects harshly nor did he ever impose the Islāmic religion on them. He maintained a large contingent of Hindu troops, commanded by their own countrymen, whom he employed with great success against his religionists in Central Asia. Conversion to Islām was never a condition of service in the Sultan's army.

Great as a warrior, the Sultan was no less eminent as a patron of art and literature. Attracted by his munificence and encouragement, many outstanding scholars settled in Ghazna, among them al-Bīrūnī, the mathematician, philosopher, astronomer, and Sanskrit scholar, and Ferdowsī, the Persian author of the great epic poem *Shāh-nāmeh.* Maḥmūd's conquest of northern India furthered the exchange of trade and ideas between the Indian subcontinent and the Muslim world. It helped to disseminate Indian culture in foreign lands. Similarly, Muslim culture, which by now had assimilated and developed the cultures of such ancient peoples as the Egyptians, the Greeks, the Romans, and the Syrians, found its way into India, and many Muslim scholars, writers, historians, and poets began to settle there. (M.Al.)

BIBLIOGRAPHY. Wolseley Haig in *The Cambridge History of India,* vol. 3 (1965), provides a reliable account of the Ghaznavid period. Ramesh Majumdar *et al., An Advanced History of India,* 3rd ed. (1967), includes a short sketch of this period. See also the relevant chapters in *A Cultural History of Afghanistan* by Mohammed Ali (1964); and S.M. Ikram and Percival Spear, *The Cultural Heritage of Pakistan* (1955).

MALACCA

• **Mahmud Shah** (d. 1528, Kampar, Sumatra), sultan of Malacca from 1488 until capture of the city by the Portuguese in 1511, after which he founded the kingdom of Johore.

At the time of Mahmud Shah's accession the city-state of Malacca was at the peak of its power and was the preeminent trade centre of Southeast Asia because of its strategic location on the Malay Peninsula, commanding the strait between it and the island of Sumatra. The *bendahara* ("chief minister") Tun Perak, architect of Malacca's greatness, was an old man, and the Malaccan court under Mahmud Shah apparently was rife with intrigue and favoritism. Mahmud Shah was not an effective ruler, but he was also a victim of circumstances. Portugal in the early 16th century was in the midst of establishing its overseas empire. Portuguese ships were in Malacca's waters before 1510, and on Aug. 15, 1511, troops commanded by Afonso de Albuquerque succeeded in capturing the city. Mahmud Shah fled across the Malay Peninsula to Pahang on the east coast, where he made a futile effort to enlist Chinese aid.

Mahmud Shah then moved south and founded the kingdom of Johore as a rival trade centre to Malacca. With his capital on the island of Bintang, or Bintan, southeast of modern Singapore, he continued to receive the tribute and allegiance from surrounding states that had been rendered him as ruler of Malacca. He became the leader of a Malay and Muslim confederacy and launched several unsuccessful attacks against Malacca. In 1526 the Portuguese responded to the threat of Mahmud Shah's forces by destroying his capital at Bintang. Mahmud Shah fled to Sumatra, but his successors went on to build Johore into a substantial empire whose power culminated in the 18th and 19th centuries.

OTTOMAN EMPIRE

• **Mahmud I** (b. Aug. 2, 1696, Edirne, Ottoman Empire—d. Dec. 13, 1754, Constantinople), Ottoman sultan who on succeeding to the throne in 1730 restored order after the Patrona Halil uprising in Constantinople; during his reign the Ottomans fought a successful war against Austria and Russia, culminating in the Treaty of Belgrade (1739).

Mahmud spent the first months of his rule eliminating the rebels, and in 1731 he suppressed a Janissary uprising. A war with Iran that lasted, with intervals, until 1746 was inconclusive. Mahmud, advised by Comte de Bonneval (Humbaraci Ahmed Paşa, a French convert to Islām), participated in political and military affairs and attempted a partial reform of the army. A patron of music and literature, he wrote poetry in Arabic.

Mahmud I, miniature by an unknown artist, 18th century; in the Topkapı Saray Museum, Istanbul

By courtesy of the Topkapi Saray Museum, Istanbul

• **Mahmud II** (b. July 20, 1785, Constantinople—d. July 1, 1839, Constantinople), Ottoman sultan (1808–39) whose westernizing reforms helped to consolidate the Ottoman Empire despite defeats in wars and losses of territory.

Mahmud was brought to the throne (July 28, 1808) in a coup led by Bayrakdar Mustafa Paşa, *aʿyān* (local notable) of Rusçuk (now Ruse, Bulg.), who had first wanted to restore Mahmud's uncle, the reform-minded sultan Selim III, until he was strangled by the conservatives. Before the year was out, however, the Janissaries revolted, killing Bayrakdar, Mahmud's grand vizier (chief minister), and delaying his reform program until the mid-1820s.

Early in his reign Mahmud faced erosion of his empire in the Balkans. The war with Russia, which had continued fitfully after a truce in 1807, was ended by the Treaty of Bucharest (May 28, 1812), ceding the province of Bessarabia to Russia. By 1815, Serbia was virtually autonomous and a Greek independence movement was stirring. The Greeks in the Morea (the Peloponnese) rebelled (1821)

Mahmud II, oil painting by Hippolyte Berteaux; in the Topkapı Saray Museum, Istanbul

By courtesy of the Topkapi Saray Museum, Istanbul

against Ottoman rule, and Mahmud summoned the assistance of Muḥammad ʿAlī Pasha, governor of Egypt. After massacres on both sides, Ottoman authority in Greece had been partly restored when the united British, French, and Russian fleets destroyed the Ottoman-Egyptian fleet in the Bay of Navarino (Oct. 20, 1827) in southern Greece. Mahmud then declared *jihād* (holy war) against the infidels. The Ottomans were defeated in the Russo-Turkish War of 1828–29, and he acknowledged Greek independence in 1830.

Earlier in the year, Mahmud had agreed to appoint Muḥammad ʿAli as governor of Syria and Tarsus (in southern Anatolia). In return for his services against the Greeks, Muḥammad ʿAlī demanded (1831) the promised governorship. When Mahmud refused, Muḥammad ʿAlī's forces under his son Ibrāhīm Pasha invaded Syria, captured Damascus and Aleppo, routed the Ottoman army at Konya (1832), and advanced on Constantinople. Mahmud sought British aid, but—with France supporting Egypt—Great Britain refused. The Sultan then turned to Russia, which sent its fleet to the Bosporus and signed a treaty of mutual defense (July 1833). Determined to take revenge, Mahmud sent his army against the Egyptians in Syria but was severely defeated at Nizip on June 24, 1839, a few days before his death.

The string of military defeats and the separatist revolts earlier had convinced Mahmud of the need for reforms in his army and administration. In 1826 he destroyed the defunct Janissary corps, thousands of its members dying in the ensuing massacre. He abolished military fiefs granted to cavalrymen (1831) and then established a new army, under his direct control, trained by German instructors.

Among his administrative reforms, Mahmud adopted the cabinet system of government, provided for a census and a land survey, and inaugurated a postal service (1834). In education, he introduced compulsory primary education, opened a medical school, and sent students to Europe. In addition, the sultan's right to confiscate the property of deceased officials was abolished, and European dress was introduced.

Mahmud Abdülbâkî: *see* Bâkî.

Mahmud Muzaffar Shah (b. 1823, Trengganu, Riau—d. July 1864, Pahang), last sultan of Riau (Riouw) and Lingga (archipelagoes south of Singapore), whose deposition cleared the way for Dutch colonial control.

Mahmud was crowned sultan in 1834, and, when the regency of his father ended in 1841, he resolved to restore the power wielded by his predecessors. He had the tacit support of the east coast Malay states to the north and particularly of Sultan Baginda Omar of Trengganu. Mahmud's claim to the throne of the Malay state of Pahang seemed threatening to the Dutch, however, and they deposed him in October 1857. Mahmud retained immense prestige among east coast Malays, and his efforts to win Malay and Thai support for his Pahang claim, although fruitless, provided occasions for further Dutch and British involvement in Malay affairs.

Mahmud Nedim Paşa (b. *c.* 1818—d. May 14, 1883, Constantinople), Ottoman diplomat and grand vizier (served 1871–72 and 1875–76) whose conservative policies and hostility to reforms permitted Sultan Abdülaziz to become an absolute monarch and thereby destroyed the westernizing reforms introduced by his predecessors.

Son of a former governor of Baghdad, Mahmud Nedim held a succession of governorships and ministries. His first tenure as grand vizier came to an end after widespread demonstrations by theological students in Constantinople and after the reform-minded administrator Midhat Paşa personally opposed his policies before the Sultan.

By 1875, Mahmud Nedim was basing all his decisions on the advice of Count Nikolay Ignatyev, the Russian ambassador to the Ottoman court. After rebellion in Bulgaria occasioned by Ignatyev's intrigues, Mahmud Nedim became so unpopular that threats were made against his life, and the Sultan had to dismiss him to mollify public opinion.

Consult the INDEX *first*

mahogany, any of several tropical hardwood timber trees, especially certain species in the family Meliaceae. One such is *Swietenia mahagoni*, from tropical America. It is a tall evergreen tree with hard wood that turns reddish brown at maturity. The leaflets of each large leaf are arranged like a feather, but there is no terminal leaflet. The small white flowers are borne in clusters, and the fruit is a five-parted woody capsule that contains squarish, winged seeds. Most commercial mahogany now comes from other genera in the family, such as the African *Khaya* and *Entandophragma.* Lauan, or Philippine, mahogany (*Shorea* species), of the family Dipterocarpaceae, is popular for furniture making and panelling.

Mahogany (*Swietenia mahagoni*)

W.H. Hodge

Mahomed, also spelled MAHOMET (Arabic and Turkish personal name): *see under* Mahmud, Mehmed, Muḥammad, or Mohammed.

Mahón, in full PUERTO DE MAHÓN, chief city of Minorca, Balearic Islands, Baleares province and autonomous community (region), Spain. It originated as the Mediterranean Portus Magonis, bearing the name of the Carthaginian general Mago. Under the Romans it was a *municipium* (privileged town). The Arab pirate Barbarossa besieged and captured the place in 1535, and in 1558 it was sacked by corsairs. The British, after their seizure of Mahón in 1708, declared it a free port in 1718. In 1756 it fell into the hands of the French, was restored to the British in 1763, recovered by the Spanish in 1781, and in 1802 finally ceded to Spain. Mahón replaced Ciudadela as the capital of Minorca during the British occupation because of its fine natural harbour of 3½ mi (6 km). At the mouth of the port are the ruins of forts San Felipe and Marlborough. Other important landmarks include the 17th-century Town Hall (Ayuntamiento) and the Casa de la Cultura, which contains an important archaeological museum and library.

Mahón's most important industries are the manufacture of shoes and imitation jewelry and pearls, and the distilling of gin; there are also handcrafts industries. The surrounding district is concerned with farming and cattle raising, and Mahón cheese is well known. Mahón is connected by road with Ciudadela, on the west side of the island, and by air and sea with Barcelona and the other islands. Pop. (1981) 22,926.

Mahon, Charles Stanhope, Lord: *see* Stanhope, Charles Stanhope, 3rd Earl.

Mahon, Philip Henry Stanhope, Viscount: *see* Stanhope, Philip Henry Stanhope, 5th Earl.

Mahone, William (b. Dec. 1, 1826, Southhampton County, Va., U.S.—d. Oct. 8, 1895, Washington, D.C.), U.S. Confederate general and railroad magnate who led Virginia's "Readjuster" reform movement from 1879 to 1882.

Born the son of a tavernkeeper in an area of large plantations, Mahone was graduated from the Virginia Military Institute in 1847 and then taught while studying engineering. He joined the Norfolk–Petersburg Railroad as an engineer in 1851, and 10 years later he was company president.

With the outbreak of the Civil War, Mahone was appointed quartermaster general of the Confederacy. But during most of the conflict, he served with the Army of Northern Virginia, eventually rising to the rank of major general. A decisive leader, much admired by his troops, Mahone was regarded as a true military hero among Southerners at the conclusion of the war.

He immediately returned to railroading at the cessation of hostilities, becoming president of the Atlantic, Mississippi and Ohio Railroad (later the Norfolk & Western) in 1867. He built a strong political base through railroad patronage, but he lost his line when it went into receivership during the 1870s.

Unable to win the Democratic gubernatorial nomination in 1877—he had never had the support of Virginia's "squirearchy" of traditionally wealthy and powerful families—Mahone organized the Readjusters in 1879. This coalition of blacks and poor whites managed to take control of the state government and run it until 1882, reducing Virginia's debt and enacting other reform measures.

In 1880 Mahone was elected to the U.S. Senate, where he served as a Republican until 1887. He thereupon built a powerful political machine in Virginia, based on his total control of the state's Republican Party. Thoroughly disliked by Southern conservatives, Mahone lost an election for governor in 1889. But he remained a potent political power in Virginia until his death.

Mahoré: *see* Mayotte.

Mahpiua Luta (Sioux Indian chief): *see* Red Cloud.

Mahra Sultanate, in full MAHRA SULTANATE OF QISHN AND SOCOTRA, former semi-independent state in the southern Arabian Peninsula, including the island of Socotra in the Indian Ocean, in what is now eastern Yemen. The mainland portion of the sultanate, on the Arabian Sea coast, had its capital in Qishn, although recent sultans preferred to reside at Tamrida (now Hadīboh) on Socotra. The sultan signed treaties in 1886 and 1888 accepting British protection for his lands; the last sultan was deposed in 1967, when the British vacated the region. The area's products include fish and frankincense.

Mahrattā (Indian people): *see* Marāṭhā.

mahseer, any of several species of edible game fishes of the genus *Barbus,* in the carp family, Cyprinidae, found in clear rivers and lakes of India and southeastern Asia. Mahseer have large, thick scales, powerful jaws, and protrusible, sometimes very fleshy, lips adapted

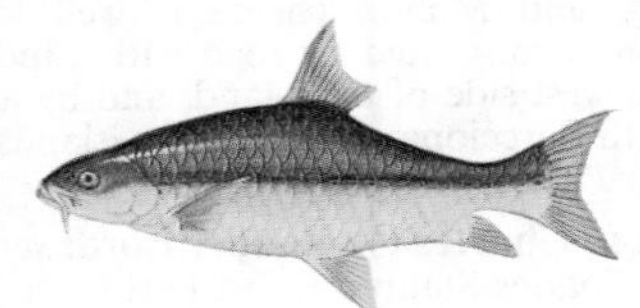

Mahseer (*Barbus tor*)

Painted especially for *Encyclopædia Britannica* by Tom Dolan, under the supervision of Loren P. Woods, Chicago Natural History Museum

for taking food from the bottom. Among the largest of Indian river fishes, mahseer attain a maximum size of some 2 m (6.5 feet), with a weight of about 90 kg (200 pounds).

mahzor, also spelled MACHZOR (Hebrew: "cycle"), plural MAHZORIM, MACHZORIM, MAHZORS, or MACHZORS, originally a Jewish prayer book arranged according to liturgical chronology and used throughout the entire year. Though cantors (hazzanim) still use such a book, mahzor has come to mean the festival prayer book, as distinguished from the siddur, the prayer book used on the ordinary sabbath and on weekdays.

Though the basic structure and prayers of the Ashkenazi (German) and Sephardic (Spanish) rites are essentially the same, the mahzorim of the various rites show considerable variety, principally owing to the adoption of different religious hymns (piyyutim) and liturgical compositions. Piyyutim composed by such celebrated medieval poets as Eleazar Kalir abound in the Ashkenazi mahzor but do not appear in Sephardic festive liturgies, which draw on the compositions of the great Spanish poets. Local ritual differences have given rise to somewhat different mahzorim within both the Ashkenazi and the Sephardic rites.

Mai-chi-shan, Pinyin MAIJISHAN, one of three major sites in northern China's Kansu *sheng* (province) where rock-cut Buddhist caves and sculpture are found. The more than 190 sculptures now visible are carved in nearly 1,000 caves and recesses on the cliff faces that are more than 400 feet (120 m) high.

A Liang-dynasty document demonstrates that monasteries probably existed at the site as early as the 5th century AD and that some of the sculptures found there may be dated at least that early. The Buddhist images continued to be made through the T'ang and Sung periods (to the early 12th century), and restorations were made to some figures during the Sung and also Ming (1368–1644) dynasties.

The historical importance of the Kansu cave sculptures, which constitute the earliest body of Buddhist sculpture in China, is their close resemblance to styles found in Central Asia and in India. Mai-chi-shan seems to contain the culminating examples of molded-clay sculpture in this early tradition. They are noted for a freedom in the treatment of drapery and other features and a certain elongation and relaxation of attitude in the figures.

Mai-Ndombe, Lake, formerly (until 1972) LAKE LEOPOLD II, lake in western Zaire, east of the Congo (Zaire) River and south-southeast of Lake Tumba. It covers approximately 890 square miles (2,300 square km) and is about 80 miles (130 km) long and up to 25 miles (40 km) wide. It empties south through the Fimi River into the Kasai. Shallow in depth and irregular in shape, with low, forested shores, it doubles or triples in size in rainy seasons. Inongo on the eastern shore is the main port. Sir Henry Morton Stanley was the first European to reach the lake, in 1882.

Maiano, Benedetto da: *see* Benedetto da Majano.

Maiasaura, genus of duck-billed dinosaurs (hadrosaurs) found as fossils in Late Cretaceous rocks (97.5 to 66.4 million years old) of North America. *Maiasaura* were bipedal, slow-moving herbivores, some 8 m (26 feet) in length; it is believed that they were migratory.

In 1978 a *Maiasaura* nesting site was discovered in the Two Medicine Formation near Choteau, Montana, U.S. The remains of an adult *Maiasaura* were found in close association with a nest of juvenile dinosaurs, each about 1 m (3.3 feet) long. Nests of hatchlings (about 0.5 m [1.6 feet] long) and nests with clutches of eggs, as well as many broken eggshells, were found nearby. These associations suggest that the nests and young dinosaurs are of the *Maiasaura* kind, and have led to the theory that duck-billed dinosaurs cared for their young. The site also demonstrates that *Maiasaura* were social animals, nesting in groups; they probably also returned to the same site year after year.

Maidanek (German Nazi extermination camp): *see* Majdanek.

maidenhair tree: *see* ginkgo.

Maidenhead, locality, Windsor and Maidenhead district, county of Berkshire, England, on the River Thames. A stone bridge (1772–77) carries the London-Bath road across the river, and the Brunel railway bridge (1837–38) has two of the widest brick spans in the world. Maidenhead Thicket and Pinkneys Green together cover 535 acres (217 hectares) of National Trust land. Along with their boating facilities and proximity to the metropolis of London, the parklands have contributed to making Maidenhead a popular residential area and summer resort. Pop. (1981) 60,461.

Maidstone, district and borough, county of Kent, southeastern England, astride the River Medway, 38 miles (61 km) southeast of London.

The name *Maidstone* is derived from the Saxon *Maeidesstana,* given as *Meddestane* in Domesday Book, and is taken to mean "the maidens' stone." At the time of the Domesday survey, the settlement, noted for its salt production, eel fishing, and flour milling, belonged to the archbishop of Canterbury. A residence of the Norman archbishops of Canterbury until the Reformation, the community grew as a market town and had a succession of charters, the last granted in 1747.

Maidstone is still a major agricultural market centre, situated in the heart of orchard country and the largest hops-growing area in England; among its industries, brewing and malting and the manufacture of agricultural implements are prominent, but the chief modern manufacture is paper. Formerly cloth making was important, boosted by an influx of Walloon weavers in 1567. The Perpendicular-style parish church, as well as many other local buildings, is built of the local limestone (Kentish rag), which has been much quarried from Roman times for shipment for major buildings in London. Hampton Court, Eton College, and the Tower of London are among the buildings for which Kentish ragstone from the Maidstone district was employed.

Assizes have been held in Maidstone since the 13th century, and it is the modern headquarters of county administration and an important shopping centre. In the European Middle Ages the shire moot (assembly) was held on Penenden Heath, which was the scene of executions and of great county meetings until the 19th century, when it was enclosed in 1882 for public recreation. Among many sites of historical and architectural interest are the medieval archbishop's palace and other ecclesiastical foundations and several Georgian buildings. Area 152 square miles (393 square km). Pop. (1991 prelim.) district, 133,200.

Maidu, group of California Indians speaking a language of Penutian stock and originally living in a territory extending eastward from the Sacramento River to the crest of the Sierra Nevada and centring chiefly in the drainage of the Feather and American rivers. Their culture existed in three primary forms dictated by differing habitats—those of the valley dwellers, foothill people, and mountaineers. The valley people were prosperous; poverty increased with elevation among the Sierra inhabitants.

The Maidu ate seeds and acorns and hunted elk, deer, bear, rabbits, ducks, and geese; they also fished for salmon, lamprey eel, and other river life. Ironically, those of the Maidu who were the least exposed to inclement conditions had the most sophisticated technology and were able to construct the most protective shelter. Thus, the valley people built large, earth-covered communal dwellings, whereas the hillmen and mountaineers made more fragile brush or bark lean-tos.

The Maidu were settled in autonomous groups, each owning its territory communally and acting as a unit, though members might be dispersed in various settlements. Among southern groups the chiefs were hereditary, but among northern groups they probably achieved their position through wealth and popularity and could be deposed.

Like many other central Californian Indians, the Maidu practiced the Kuksu cult, involving male secret societies, esoteric rites, masks and disguises, and special earth-roofed ceremonial chambers. Some of the purposes of the rituals were naturalistic—to assure good crops or plentiful game or to ward off floods and other natural disasters such as disease.

In the late 20th century, fewer than 200 Maidu remained, living in Sierran communities.

Maiduguri, also called YERWA, or YERWA-MAIDUGURI, capital and largest city of Borno state, northeastern Nigeria. It is located on the north bank of the seasonal Ngadda (Alo) River, the waters of which disappear in the *firki* ("black cotton") swamps just southwest

Pyramids of peanut (groundnut) bags, Maiduguri, Nigeria

John Moss—Photo Researchers

of Lake Chad, about 70 miles (113 km) northeast.

Modern Maiduguri actually comprises the twin towns of Yerwa and Maiduguri. In 1907 Yerwa (whose name is derived from an Arabic expression meaning "quenching the thirst," referring to the waters of the nearby river) was founded on the site of the hamlet of Kalwa and was named by *Shehu* ("Sheikh," or "Sultan") Bukar Garbai as the new traditional capital of the Kanuri people (replacing Kukawa, 80 miles [130 km] north-northeast, the former capital of the Bornu kingdom [*see* Kanem-Bornu]). Meanwhile, the market village of Maiduguri, just to the south, was selected by the British to replace nearby Mofoni (Maifoni, Mafoni) as their military headquarters; and, in 1908, they built a residency in what then became the capital of British Bornu. The combined city—locally called Yerwa—was divided into the urban district of Yerwa and the rural district of Maiduguri in 1957; but outside Borno both political units are now known simply as Maiduguri.

The arrival of the railway in 1964 reinforced Maiduguri's importance as the chief commercial centre of northeastern Nigeria. Livestock (mainly cattle but also goats and sheep), cattle hides, goatskins and sheepskins, finished leather products, dried fish, crocodile skins (the last two brought from Lake Chad), peanuts (groundnuts), and gum arabic are the city's chief exports; but there is also considerable local trade in sorghum, millet, corn (maize), rice, cotton, and indigo. There is a large cattle ranch at nearby Gombole, and poultry farming has been introduced in the surrounding countryside. The Monday market at Yerwa, a tradition brought from Kukawa, is the largest in the state; most goods are transported by donkey and, likewise in centuries-old fashion, by oxen owned by the seminomadic Shuwa Arabs.

Maiduguri's population consists mainly of Muslim Kanuri and Shuwa peoples with an admixture of Christian Nigerians from the south. Since the mid-1960s the city has become an important industrial and educational centre for Borno state. Besides food-processing facilities (abattoir, meat-refrigeration plant, peanut-oil mill, and chewing-gum factory), its industries manufacture leather goods, wooden and metal furniture, nails, aluminum and steel structural products, and asbestos cement. The government has launched a reforestation project in the area around the city, in part to provide wood for its industries.

Educational facilities include the University of Maiduguri (1975), the Ramat Polytechnic, the Borno College of Legal and Islāmic Studies, the Borno State Advanced Teachers College, and an Islāmic teacher-training college sponsored by the *shehu*. The university operates a teaching hospital, and there is also a general hospital in the city. The Lake Chad Research Institute is located in Maiduguri.

The city is dominated by the palace and the adjacent mosque of the *shehu* of Bornu, the second (after only the sultan of Sokoto) most important traditional Muslim leader in Nigeria. The city also lies astride the historic pilgrim route from Senegal to Mecca. It is the terminus for the main railway line linking northeastern Nigeria to Port Harcourt, is served by the main highway system, and is a hub for secondary highways serving the state. There is an airport located 5.5 miles (9 km) west of Maiduguri. Pop. (1991 est.) 281,900.

Maigh Eo (Ireland): *see* Mayo.

Maijishan (archaeological site): *see* Mai-chi-shan.

Maikala Range, mountain range in Madhya Pradesh state, central India, running in a north-south direction and forming the eastern base of the triangular Sātpura Range. The Maikala Range consists of laterite-capped, flat-topped plateaus (*pāts*) with an elevation of from 2,000 feet (600 m) to 3,000 feet (900 m). The Sātpura-Maikala watershed is the second largest in India. The Narmada, Son, Pāndū, Kanhār, Rihand, Bijul, Gopad, and Banās rivers run almost parallel from south to north and have carved extensive basins in the relatively soft rock formations of the Maikala Range. Vegetation varies from grass and thorny trees to deciduous trees such as teak and sal (*Shorea*).

Agriculture, the principal economic activity, is practiced mostly in the alluvial basins; crops include rice, wheat, gram (chick-pea), jowar (sorghum), barley, corn (maize), pulse (legumes), sesame seeds, and mustard seeds. Industries produce cement, ceramics, bricks, tiles, glass, dressed stone, lumber, and shellac; flour, dal (pigeon-pea), and oil are milled. Mineral deposits include coal, limestone, bauxite, corundum, dolomite, marble, slate, and sandstone. The principal ethnic groups are the Goṇḍs (numerically and historically the most important), Halbas, Bharais, Baigās, and Korkus. The chief towns are Bālāghāt, Mandla, Nainpur, and Dindori. A fort at Mandla (the capital of the Goṇḍ kings), a palace at Rāmnagar, and Kānha National Park are places of interest.

Where the same name may denote a person, place, or thing, the articles will be found in that order

Maiko National Park, reserve in eastern Zaire, about equidistant from Bukavu, in the great East African Rift valley just south of Lake Kivu, at the Rwandan border, and Kisangani, about 320 miles (515 km) to the northwest, at the great westward bend of the Congo River. The park's 3,900-square-mile (10,100-square-kilometre) expanse spans the Oso River and extends north to the Lindi River. Dense equatorial forest characterizes the park. Forest-dwellers include gorillas, elephants, leopards, and okapi. Maiko National Park has not been developed for visitors.

Maikop (Russia): *see* Maykop.

mail (armour): *see* chain mail.

mail, the postal matter consigned under public authority from one person or post office to another. *See* postal system.

mail-cheeked fish: *see* scorpaeniform.

mail-order business, also called DIRECT-MAIL MARKETING, method of merchandising in which the seller's offer is made through mass mailing of a circular or catalog or through an advertisement placed in a newspaper or magazine and in which the buyer places his order by mail. Delivery of the goods may be made by freight, express, or parcel post on a cash-on-delivery basis. Retail mail-order selling was developed primarily for rural customers, but it now includes millions of customers in urban areas.

Most mail-order businesses have been small specialty firms selling by the traditional method, but department stores also do a significant volume of business through their mail-order divisions. Most mail-order volume, however, is accounted for by a few firms selling general merchandise lines. The largest in the world in the late 20th century were Sears, Roebuck and Company and Montgomery Ward & Company, both American firms. With the development of computerized mailing lists and techniques after about 1960, many large retailers combined mail-order circularizing with billing. Book and record clubs utilized direct mail to play a major part in the marketing of books and phonograph and tape recordings.

Mail-order operations have been known in the United States in one form or another since colonial days, but not until the latter part of the 19th century did they assume a significant role in domestic trade. The completion of the continental rail network gave impetus to the development of general merchandise mail-order houses. The ability to sell a variety of merchandise to farmers, at comparatively low prices, a postal rate structure that encouraged the dissemination of mail-order papers and catalogs, and the establishment of the parcel-post system in 1913 all contributed to the expansion of mail-order operations.

Mail-order business emerged in Europe at the end of the 19th century, but its greatest development was after 1945. In the mid-1970s it was strongest in Great Britain, West Germany, Sweden, and Switzerland and was developing in France and The Netherlands. In Germany and France the tendency has been to specialize in a limited range of commodities such as textiles, cigars, or jewelry, but in Great Britain mail-order houses sell a wide variety of consumer durables under well-known brand names. The growing homogeneity of consumer tastes has encouraged European stores to expand internationally; *e.g.*, Great Universal Stores Ltd. of Great Britain has subsidiaries in Switzerland and South Africa.

Mailáth, János, Gróf (Count) (b. Oct. 5, 1786, Pest, Hung.—d. Jan. 3, 1855, Lake Starnberg, near Munich [Germany]), Hungarian writer and historian, who interpreted Magyar culture to the Germans and who wrote a sympathetic account of the Habsburg monarchy.

Mailáth, the son of Count Jozsef Mailáth, an imperial minister of state, entered government service but soon had to resign because of an injury to his eyesight. Devoting himself to literary work, he edited two important

Mailáth, lithograph by J. Ruprecht

By courtesy of the Hungarian National Museum, Budapest

collections of medieval German poetry (1818 and 1819) and wrote some German verse of his own (1824) before producing his German translations of Hungarian poems (1825 and 1829).

Writing in German, Mailáth brought out a number of major works, including his "Magyar Legends, Fables, and Tales" (1825), a five-volume "History of the Magyars" (1828–31), and his perceptive, five-volume "History of the Austrian Empire" (1834–50). He also wrote on mnemonics (1842) and on the healing power of animal magnetism (1852).

In the political ferment of the Revolution of 1848, Mailáth stood aloof, siding with neither the revolutionaries nor the conservatives. In 1848 he left Vienna for Munich, where after several years he found himself destitute. Despondent, he made a suicide pact with his daughter Henrika, who had long been his secretary. The two weighted their clothes with stones, tied themselves together at the wrists, and threw themselves into Lake Starnberg.

Mailer, Norman (b. Jan. 31, 1923, Long Branch, N.J., U.S.), American novelist who successfully developed a form of journalism that conveys actual events with the subjective richness and imaginative complexity of the novel. Both his fiction and nonfiction made a radical critique of the totalitarianism he believed inherent in the centralized power structure of 20th-century America.

Maller, 1968
Newsweek photo by Bernard Gotfryd, Copyright Newsweek, 1968

Mailer grew up in Brooklyn and graduated from Harvard University in 1943 with a degree in aeronautical engineering. Drafted into the army in 1944, he served in the Pacific until 1946. While he was enrolled at the Sorbonne, in Paris, he wrote *The Naked and the Dead* (1948), hailed immediately as one of the finest American novels to come out of World War II.

Mailer's success at 25 aroused the expectation that he would develop from a war novelist into the leading literary figure of the postwar generation. But Mailer's search for themes and forms to give meaningful expression to what he saw as the problems of his time committed him to exploratory works that had little general appeal. His second novel, *Barbary Shore* (1951), and *The Deer Park* (1955) were greeted with critical hostility and mixed reviews, respectively. His next important work was a long essay, *The White Negro* (1957), a sympathetic study of a marginal social type—the "hipster."

In 1959, when Mailer was generally dismissed as a one-book author, he made a bid for attention with the book *Advertisements for Myself,* a collection of unfinished stories, parts of novels, essays, reviews, notebook entries, or ideas for fiction. The miscellany's naked self-revelation won the admiration of a younger generation seeking alternative styles of life and art. Mailer's subsequent novels, though not critical successes, were widely read as guides to life. *An American Dream* (1965) is about a man who murders his wife, and *Why Are We in Vietnam?* (1967) is about a young man on an Alaskan hunting trip.

A controversial figure whose egotism and belligerence often antagonized both critics and readers, Mailer did not command the same respect for his fiction that he received for his journalism; *The Armies of the Night* (1968), for example, was based on the Washington peace demonstrations of October 1967, during which Mailer was jailed and fined for an act of civil disobedience. A similar treatment was given the Republican and Democratic presidential conventions in *Miami and the Siege of Chicago* (1968) and the moon exploration in *Of a Fire on the Moon* (1970).

In 1969 Mailer ran unsuccessfully for mayor of New York City. Among his other works are his essay collections *The Presidential Papers* (1963) and *Cannibals and Christians* (1966); *The Executioner's Song* (1979), a novel based on the life of convicted murderer Gary Gilmore; *Ancient Evenings* (1983), the first volume of a projected trilogy about Egypt; *Tough Guys Don't Dance* (1984), a contemporary mystery thriller; and the enormous *Harlot's Ghost* (1991).

Maillart, Robert (b. Feb. 6, 1872, Bern, Switz.—d. April 5, 1940, Geneva), Swiss bridge engineer whose radical use of reinforced concrete revolutionized masonry arch bridge design.

After studying at the Swiss Federal Institute of Technology of Zürich, where he received a degree in structural engineering in 1894, Maillart worked for several private engineering firms, collaborating for a time with the French engineer François Hennebique before organizing his own independent practice. In 1901 he built his first bridge, at Zuoz, Switz., over the Inn, an arch whose slenderness and flatness astonished the public and other engineers. Maillart's system was based on an integration of arch, roadway, and stiffening girder into a single monolithic structure, resulting in great aesthetic appeal and large economic savings. For the next 40 years he continued to embellish the Swiss Alps with a variety of graceful arches, of which perhaps the most famous is the curving Schwandbach Bridge, at Schwarzenburg, which has been described as "a work of art in modern engineering."

Maillart also built many other structures, including a number of factories and warehouses in Russia between 1912 and 1919. The Russian Revolution temporarily ruined him financially, but he returned to Switzerland to resume his career.

Maillebois, Nicolas Desmarets, Marquis de: *see* Desmarets, Nicolas.

Maillol, Aristide (b. Dec. 8, 1861, Banyuls-sur-Mer, Fr.—d. Sept. 27, 1944, near Banyuls-sur-Mer), French painter, printmaker, and one of the most important sculptors of the 20th century, whose monumental statues of female nudes restored to early 20th-century sculpture a concern for mass and rigorous formal analysis; his works paved the way for the radical experimentation of the various schools of modern abstract sculpture.

Maillol began as a painter and tapestry designer whose work reflected his great admiration for the Nabis, a group of artists whose work was composed typically of decorative patterns of colour. He was almost 40 years old when an eye disease made him decide to become a sculptor. His mature style of sculpture rejected the highly emotional sculpture of his contemporary Auguste Rodin, and he attempted to preserve and purify the tradition of sculpture derived from classical Greece and Rome. "The Mediterranean" (*c.* 1901) and "Night" (1902) show the emotional restraint, clear composition, and serene surfaces he employed in his sculpture for the rest of his life. Although most of his work depicts the mature female form, a notable exception is the lean "Cyclist" (1907–08), which greatly influenced subsequent developments in figurative expressionistic sculpture.

Maillol, *c.* 1935
Charles Leirens

After 1910 Maillol was internationally famous and received a constant flood of commissions. Because of his strict economy of aesthetic means, he managed successfully to turn out the same subject repeatedly, sometimes varying little more than the title from work to work. Only in "Action in Chains" (1906) and "The River" (*c.* 1939–43) did he vary his basic formula and represent the human form in turbulent activity.

Maillol resumed painting in 1939, but sculpture never relinquished preeminence in his affections. He also made many woodcut illustrations for fine editions of Latin poets during the 1920s and '30s, doing much to revive the art of the book.

Mailly-Nesle, Marie-Anne de: *see* Châteauroux, Marie-Anne de Mailly-Nesle, Duchess de.

Articles are alphabetized word by word, not letter by letter

Maiman, Theodore H., in full THEODORE HAROLD MAIMAN (b. July 11, 1927, Los Angeles, Calif., U.S.), American physicist who constructed the first laser, a device that produces monochromatic coherent light, or light in which the rays are all of the same wavelength and phase. The laser has found numerous practical uses, ranging from delicate surgery to measuring the distance between the Earth and the Moon.

After receiving his Ph.D. from Stanford University in 1955, Maiman accepted a position with the Hughes Research Laboratories, Miami, where he became interested in a device developed and built by Charles H. Townes and colleagues and known as a maser (acronym for "microwave [or molecular] amplification by stimulated emission of radiation"). Maiman made design innovations that greatly increased the practicability of the solid-state maser. He then set out to develop an optical maser, or laser, which is based on the maser principle but produces visible light rather than microwaves. He operated the first successful laser in 1960 and two years later established Korad Corporation for research, development, and manufacture of lasers.

Maimāna (town, Afghanistan): *see* Meymaneh.

Maimbourg, Louis (b. Jan. 10, 1610, Nancy, Fr.—d. Aug. 13, 1686, Paris), French Jesuit and historian who wrote critical works on Calvinism and Lutheranism and a defense of Gallican liberties—the belief that the Roman Catholic church in France should maintain some independence from papal control.

Maimbourg was born to a noble family. He entered the Jesuit order in 1626, was sent to Rome to study theology, and returned to Rouen, Fr., to teach humanities at its Jesuit college. Late in his life he began to publish historical works, the most famous being his *Traité historique de l'établissement et des prérogatives de l'église de Rome et de ses évêques* (1685; "Historical Treatise on the Establishment and the Prerogatives of the Church of Rome and its Bishops"), in which his defense of Gallican church liberties greatly displeased Pope Innocent XI, who ordered his expulsion from the Jesuit order. Pensioned by King Louis XIV of France, Maimbourg retired to the Abbey of Saint-Victor in Paris, where he remained until his death.

Maimbourg was a voluminous writer, and his collected *Histoires* (1686–87) include 26 volumes. Among the best known of his other works are the *Histoire du Luthéranisme* (1680; "History of Lutheranism") and the *Histoire du Calvinisme* (1682; "History of Calvinism"), both of them conventional Catholic polemics against Protestantism. Despite their emotional and inexact style, Maimbourg's works popularized the religious controversy and were useful to the French government as propaganda for the revocation of King Henry IV's Edict of Nantes (1598), which had provided religious freedom to French Protestants.

Maimon, Salomon, original name SALOMON BEN JOSHUA (b. *c.* 1754, Nieswiez, Polish Lithuania—d. Nov. 22, 1800, Nieder-Siegersdorf, Silesia), Jewish philosopher whose acute Skepticism caused him to be acknowledged by the major German philosopher Immanuel Kant as his most perceptive critic. He

Maimon, engraving by Wilhelm Arndt
By courtesy of the Staatliche Museen zu Berlin, E.Ger.

combined an early and extensive familiarity with rabbinic learning with a proficiency in Hebrew, and, after acquiring a special reverence for the 12th-century Jewish Spaniard Moses Maimonides, he took the philosopher's surname Maimon.

In 1770, before he was 20, Maimon wrote an unorthodox commentary on Maimonides' *More nevukhim* (*Guide of the Perplexed*) that earned him the hostility of fellow Jews. At 25 he left Poland for Königsberg, Prussia, and wandered over Europe until he settled in Posen, Pol., as a tutor. His material insecurity ended in 1790, when he was given residence on the estate of Count Friedrich Adolf, Graf von Kalckreuth at Nieder-Siegersdorf. During the next decade he wrote his major philosophical works, including the autobiography edited for him by K.P. Moritz as *Salomon Maimons Lebensgeschichte* (1792; *Solomon Maimon: an autobiography*, 1888) and his major critique of Kantian philosophy, *Versuch über die Transcendentalphilosophie* (1790; "Search for the Transcendental Philosophy").

Despite his defection from the ranks of Kant's disciples, Maimon evoked praise from Kant for his criticism of the master philosopher, who declared that Maimon had understood his *Critique of Pure Reason* better than had any of his other critics. Maimon's Skepticism helped to establish the critical standards for approaching Kantian philosophy.

By emphasizing the limits of pure thought, Maimon also helped to advance philosophical discussion of the connection between thought and experience and between knowledge and faith. In his view there was religious and ethical value in the pursuit of truth, even though the goal itself was not completely attainable. His other major writings are *Philosophisches Wörterbuch* (1791; "Philosophical Dictionary"), *Über die Progressen der Philosophie* (1792; "On the Progresses of Philosophy"), and *Kritische Untersuchungen über den menschlichen Geist* (1797; "Critical Investigations of the Human Spirit").

Maimonides, Moses, original name MOSES BEN MAIMON, also called RAMBAM, Arabic name ABŪ ʿIMRAN MŪSĀ IBN MAYMŪN IBN ʿUBAYD ALLĀH (b. March 30, 1135, Córdoba—d. Dec. 13, 1204, Egypt), Jewish philosopher, jurist, and physician, the foremost intellectual figure of medieval Judaism. His first major work, begun at age 23 and completed 10 years later, was a commentary on the Mishna. A monumental code of Jewish law followed in Hebrew, *The Guide of the Perplexed* in Arabic, and numerous other works, many of major importance. His contributions in religion, philosophy, and medicine have influenced Jewish and non-Jewish scholars alike.

Life. Maimonides was born into a distinguished family in Córdoba (Cordova), Spain. The young Moses studied with his learned father, Maimon, and other masters and at an early age astonished his teachers by his remarkable depth and versatility. Before Moses reached his 13th birthday, his peaceful world was suddenly disturbed by the ravages of war and persecution.

As part of Islāmic Spain, Córdoba accorded its citizens full religious freedom. But now the Islāmic Mediterranean world was shaken by a revolutionary and fanatical Islāmic sect, the Almohads (al-Muwaḥḥidūn, the Unitarians), who captured Córdoba in 1148, leaving the Jewish community faced with the grim alternative of submitting to Islām or leaving the city. The Maimons temporized by practicing their Judaism in the privacy of their homes, while disguising their ways in public as far as possible to appear like Muslims. The Maimons remained in Córdoba for some 11 years, and Maimonides continued his education in Judaic studies as well as in the scientific disciplines in vogue at the time.

When the double life proved too irksome to maintain in Córdoba, the Maimon family finally left the city about 1159 to settle in Fez, Mor. Although it was also under Almohad rule, Fez was presumably more promising than Córdoba, because there the Maimons would be strangers and their disguise would be more likely to go undetected. Moses continued his studies in his favourite subjects, rabbinics and Greek philosophy, and added medicine to them. Fez proved to be no more than a short respite, however. In 1165 Rabbi Judah ibn Shoshan, with whom Moses had studied, was arrested as a practicing Jew and was found guilty and then executed. This was a sign to the Maimon family to move again, this time to Palestine, which was in a depressed economic state and could not offer them the basis of a livelihood. After a few months they moved again, now to Egypt, settling in Fostat, near Cairo. There Jews were free to practice their faith openly, though any Jew who had once submitted to Islām courted death if he relapsed to Judaism. Moses himself was once accused of being a renegade Muslim, but he was able to prove that he had never really adopted the faith of Islām and so was exonerated.

Though Egypt was a haven from harassment and persecution, Moses was soon assailed by personal problems. His father died shortly after the arrival in Egypt. His younger brother, David, a prosperous jewelry merchant, on whom Moses leaned for support, died in a shipwreck, taking the entire family fortune with him, and Moses was left as the sole support of his family. He could not turn to the rabbinate because in those days the rabbinate was conceived of as a public service that did not offer its practitioners any remuneration. Pressed by economic necessity, Moses took advantage of his medical studies and became a practicing physician. His fame as physician spread rapidly and he soon became the court physician to the sultan Saladin, the famous Muslim military leader, and to his son al-Afḍal. He also continued a private practice and lectured before his fellow physicians at the state hospital. At the same time he became the leading member of the Jewish community, teaching in public and helping his people with various personal and communal problems.

Maimonides married late in life and was the father of a son, Abraham, who was to make his mark in his own right in the world of Jewish scholarship.

Works. The writings of Maimonides were prolific and varied. His earliest work, composed at the age of 16, was the *Millot ha-Higgayon* ("Treatise on Logical Terminology"), a study of various technical terms that were employed in logic and metaphysics. Another of his early works, like the work on logic written in Arabic, was the "Essay on the Calendar" (Hebrew title: *Maʾamar haʿibur*).

The first of Maimonides' major works, begun at the age of 23, was his commentary on the Mishna, *Kitāb al-Sirāj*, also written in Arabic. The Mishna is a compendium of decisions in Jewish law that dates from earliest times to the 3rd century. Maimonides' commentary clarified individual words and phrases, frequently citing relevant information in archaeology, theology, or science. Possibly the work's most striking feature is a series of introductory essays dealing with general philosophic issues touched on in the Mishna. One of these essays summarizes the teachings of Judaism in a creed of Thirteen Articles of Faith.

He completed the commentary on the Mishna at the age of 33, after which he began his magnum opus, the code of Jewish law, on which he also laboured for 10 years. Bearing the name of *Mishne Torah* ("The Torah Reviewed") and written in a lucid Hebrew style, the code offers a brilliant systematization of all Jewish law and doctrine. He wrote two other works in Jewish law of lesser scope: the *Sefer ha-mitzwot* ("Book of Precepts"), a digest of law for the less sophisticated reader, written in Arabic; and the *Hilkhot ha-Yerushalmi* ("Laws of Jerusalem"), a digest of the laws in the Palestinian Talmud that was written in Hebrew.

His next major work, which he began in 1176 and on which he laboured for 15 years, was his classic in religious philosophy, the *Dalālat al-ḥāʾirīn* (*The Guide of the Perplexed*), later known under its Hebrew title as the *More nevukhim*. A plea for what he called a more rational philosophy of Judaism, it constituted a major contribution to the accommodation between science, philosophy, and religion. It was written in Arabic and sent as a private communication to his favourite disciple, Joseph ibn Aknin. The work was translated into Hebrew in Maimonides' lifetime and later into Latin and most European languages. It has exerted a marked influence on the history of religious thought.

Maimonides also wrote a number of minor works, occasional essays dealing with current problems that faced the Jewish community, and he maintained an extensive correspondence with scholars, students, and community leaders. Among his minor works those considered to be most important are *Iggert Teman* (*Epistle to Yemen*), *Iggeret ha-shemad* or *Maʾamar Qiddush ha-Shem* ("Letter on Apostasy"), and *Iggeret le-qahal Marsilia* ("Letter on Astrology," or, literally, "Letter to the Community of Marseille"). He also wrote a number of works dealing with medicine, including a popular miscellany of health rules, which he dedicated to the sultan, al-Afḍal. A mid-20th-century historian, Waldemar Schweisheimer, has said of Maimonides' medical writings: "Maimonides' medical teachings are not antiquated at all. His writings, in fact, are in some respects astonishingly modern in tone and contents."

Maimonides complained often that the pressures of his many duties robbed him of peace and undermined his health. He died in 1204 and was buried in Tiberias, in the Holy Land, where his grave continues to be a shrine drawing a constant stream of pious pilgrims.

Significance. Maimonides' advanced views aroused opposition during his lifetime and after his death. In 1233 one zealot, Rabbi Solomon of Montpellier, in southern France, instigated the church authorities to burn *The Guide of the Perplexed* as a dangerously heretical book. But the controversy abated after some time, and Maimonides came to be recognized as a pillar of the traditional faith—his creed became part of the orthodox liturgy—as well as the greatest of the Jewish philosophers.

Maimonides' epoch-making influence on Judaism extended also to the larger world. His philosophic work, translated into Latin, influenced the great medieval Scholastic writers, and even later thinkers, such as Benedict de Spinoza and G.W. Leibniz, found in his work a source for some of their ideas. His medical writings constitute a significant chapter in the history of medical science. (B.Z.B.)

BIBLIOGRAPHY. Marvin Fox, *Interpreting Maimonides* (1990), treats all aspects of his life and thought. Isadore Twersky, *Introduction to the Code of Maimonides (Mishneh Torah)* (1980), is an extensive analysis of his philosophy and his ideas on religious law. Oliver Leaman, *Moses Maimonides* (1990), provides an introduction to the themes of *The Guide of the Perplexed.*

Ma'īn, ancient South Arabian kingdom that flourished in the 4th–2nd century BC in what is now northern Yemen. The Minaeans were a peaceful community of traders whose government showed features of democracy of the city-state pattern. Ma'īn fell to the Sabaeans late in the 2nd century BC.

Main Botanical Garden of the Academy of Sciences, Russian GLAVNY BOTANICHESKY SAD AKADEMI NAUK, one of the world's largest botanical gardens. Founded in 1945, it occupies a 360-hectare (889-acre) site in Moscow, Russia. About 21,000 varieties of plants are cultivated, many of which are native to Russia. One of its unique features is a large exhibit area where plants are grouped according to the geographic regions to which they are native.

The Main Botanical Garden carries on research on matters pertaining to plant introduction and acclimatization and conducts field trials of valuable new species and subspecies. For this purpose, many hundreds of plants from other continents are grown. The garden maintains a herbarium of some 267,000 reference specimens.

Main-Danube Canal, also called EUROPA CANAL, German MAIN-DONAU-KANAL, or EUROPA-KANAL, commercial waterway in Bavaria *Land* (state), southern Germany, completed in 1992. The canal, 106 miles (171 km) long, runs from Bamberg on the Main River (a tributary of the Rhine) to Kelheim on the Danube River, permitting traffic to flow between the North Sea and the Black Sea. It thus creates a 2,200-mile (3,500-kilometre) waterway that runs through 15 countries and can accommodate barges carrying up to 2,425 tons of bulk cargo.

The canal, one of the largest civil engineering projects ever undertaken, has a total of 16 locks, each about 625 feet (190 m) long, 40 feet (12 m) wide, and up to 100 feet (30 m) deep. It reaches a height of more than 1,332 feet (406 m) over the Swabian Alps, south of Nürnberg.

The idea for such a canal dates back to 793, when Charlemagne, wishing to open a route through the centre of Europe for his battle fleet, had a channel excavated between two rivers in Bavaria: the Altmühl, a tributary of the Danube, and the Schwäbische Rezat, a tributary of the Main. Heavy rains caused the banks of the channel to collapse, however, and the project was abandoned. In 1837, under Ludwig I of Bavaria, work began on a canal between Bamberg and Kelheim, following much the same route as the modern canal. The Ludwig Canal remained in use until World War II, but it was never able to compete with the railways. In 1921 the German government and the state of Bavaria formed a company to build the much larger Main-Danube Canal. Most of the construction took place between 1960 and 1992.

Main Range, also called CENTRAL RANGE, or BUFFALO RANGE, mountain range in West Malaysia, the most prominent mountain group on the Malay Peninsula. Composed of granite with some patches of altered stratified rocks, the range extends southward for 300 miles (480 km) from the Thai border, with elevations rarely less than 3,000 feet (900 m) and some peaks exceeding 7,000 feet (2,100 m; high point Mount Korbu [Kerbau], or Buffalo Mountain, 7,162 feet [2,183 m]). The heavily forested range gives rise to the Perak and Pahang river systems. From the Negeri Sembilan area, its elevation diminishes until it abuts on the coastal plain in Melaka. Its western flanks contain the rich alluvial tin fields of Larut and the Kinta and Kelang (formerly Klang) valleys. In central Malaya there are extensions eastward, which culminate in Mount Tahan (7,175 feet [2,187 m]), the highest peak in the peninsula.

Main River, Latin MOENUS, river, an important right- (east-) bank tributary of the Rhine in Germany. It is formed, near Kulmbach, by the confluence of the Weisser (White) Main, which rises in the Fichtel Mountains, and the Roter (Red) Main, which rises on the eastern slope of the Fränkische Mountains (Franconian Jura). The Main River flows southwesterly around the northern end of the Fränkische Mountains to Bamberg, where the Regnitz River enters it from the left. From there the Main flows south and east among vine-clad hills to Würzburg and then north between the forest-covered Spessart and Odenwald ranges to Gemünden, where the Fränkische Saale River enters from the right. Turning abruptly to the south, it receives the Tauber River from the left at Wertheim and continues west and then north to Aschaffenburg. From there, a generally westward course takes the river through Frankfurt am Main to its junction with the Rhine River above Mainz after a course of 326 miles (524 km). The river has been canalized upstream to Bamberg and forms part of the Main-Danube Canal (completed 1992), which links the Rhine and Danube rivers, creating a 2,200-mile (3,500-kilometre) waterway from the North Sea to the Black Sea.

Consult the INDEX *first*

Maina, also spelled MANI, peninsula of the southern Peloponnese (Pelopónnisos), in the *nomós* (department) of Laconia, Greece. The area has been set aside as a historical district by the government. The rugged, rather isolated peninsula, 28 miles (45 km) long, is an extension of the Taygetus (Taíyetos) range. It is the home of the Maniotes, an ancient people who are believed to be descended from Laconian refugees of the early Roman period. Formerly the area was known as Maina Polypyrgos ("Many-Towered Maina"), from the defensive structures built by its fierce inhabitants, who lived by raiding coastal shipping. Ruins in the district include the remains of the temple and sanctuary of Poseidon, situated at the tip of Cape Taínaron (Cape Matapan), as well as the Frankish castle (Grand Maigne), built in 1248–50 by William II de Villehardouin to pacify the region. In 1821 an uprising in the region helped trigger the War of Greek Independence. A paved road runs from Yíthion to Arcopolis and Diros, where two magnificent caves were opened to the public in 1963. However, the peninsula maintains its unspoiled medieval character with many 11th- and 12th-century Byzantine churches.

Mainard, François: *see* Maynard, François.

Maine, historic region encompassing the western French *départements* of Mayenne and Sarthe and coextensive with the former province of Maine. The two Gallo-Roman *civitates* of the Cenomani and of the Diablintes were merged in the middle of the 5th century into the single *pagus,* or district, of Le Mans. Hereditary counts, beginning with the warlord Roger in the 890s, acquired power in the province, but in the 11th century

The *gouvernement* of Maine in 1789

their countship was compressed between Normandy and Anjou. Maine fell to Anjou early in the 12th century and then, with Anjou and Normandy, to the French king Philip II Augustus at the beginning of the 13th. Later held by Naples, Maine reverted to the French crown in 1481. In the centuries before the Revolution in 1789, Maine was a province under a military governor, with his seat at Le Mans, but it was administered, with Anjou and Touraine, by the intendant of the *généralité* of Tours.

Maine comprises portions of the crystalline uplands of the Massif Armoricain and is drained southward by the Mayenne River and its tributaries. Livestock (cattle and pigs) are raised in the upland regions, while grains (wheat and corn [maize]) and forage crops are grown in the lowlands adjoining the Paris Basin. Maine is predominantly Roman Catholic, and most modern parishes date from the 13th century.

Maine, constituent state of the United States of America, lying in the New England region of the country. The capital is Augusta.

A brief treatment of Maine follows. For full treatment, *see* MACROPAEDIA: United States of America: *Maine.*

Facing the Atlantic Ocean to the east, Maine is bounded on the northwest and northeast by the Canadian provinces of Quebec and New Brunswick, respectively, and on the west and south by New Hampshire. Famed for its rocky coastline, the state extends about 320 miles (510 km) from north to south and 210 miles (340 km) from east to west. Maine is the most northeasterly state of the nation.

Algonquian Indians were the earliest-known inhabitants of Maine. European settlers found the Penobscot and Passamaquoddy tribes living along the river valleys and coasts, hunting and fishing, and planting crops.

The first European explorations may have been by Norsemen during the 10th and 11th centuries, but evidence about these expeditions is disputed. British claims to the area were based on the voyages of John Cabot to the region in the late 1490s, though evidence justifying these claims is now questioned. The French included Maine as part of the province of Acadia in 1603, and Britain included it in territory granted to the Plymouth Company in 1606. During the 17th century Britain established and maintained scattered settlements, but the area was a constant battleground until the British conquered the French in eastern Canada in 1763. Maine was governed as a district of Massachusetts from 1652 until it entered the Union as a free state under the Missouri Compromise of 1820.

Physiographically Maine lies entirely within the Appalachian system but can be divided into three main regions: (1) the Appalachian Mountain chain, an extension of the White Mountains of New Hampshire rising to 5,268 feet (1,606 m) in Maine; (2) the surrounding rugged upland region, with numerous glacier-scoured peaks, lakes, and narrow valleys; and (3) the Atlantic seaboard, with rolling hills, smaller mountains, and broad river valleys. Most of the state drains generally southward through the Kennebec and Penobscot rivers. The state is dotted with 2,500 lakes and ponds.

The Maine climate is temperate, with mild summers and cold winters. Mean summer and winter temperatures throughout the state are about 62° F (17° C) and 20° F (−7° C), respectively. Clear days range from about 100 per year in the south to only 70 in the north, and annual precipitation averages 36 to 48 inches (910 to 1,220 mm). Snowfall averages more than 100 inches (2,540 mm) in the north and at higher elevations. Soil conditions, except in the northern Aroostook valley, are not generally suitable for large-scale crop growing. Forests cover more than 85 percent of the land.

Maine was settled primarily by English and Scots-Irish Protestants, and their descendants are the major population group. The second largest ethnic group is the French, who migrated largely from Quebec seeking economic opportunities. Nonwhites make up less than 2 percent of the population. About one-half of Maine's population is classified as rural, and only a few cities have populations exceeding 25,000. More than half the population lives in the narrow coastal strip between Augusta and the New Hampshire border.

The economy of Maine is based primarily on its natural resources, although the service sector represents the largest component in the market value of the state's goods and services. Manufacturing industries based originally on low-cost water power have largely relocated to lower-wage areas. Agriculture is dominated by high-quality potatoes. The state also produces apples, blueberries, and dairy and poultry products. Maine's forests provide the basis for large timber and paper and pulp industries. Lobsters obtained from the cool waters of the rocky coast are the mainstay of the state's fishing industry. The major mineral resources are sand, gravel, limestone, and building stone. Tourists—attracted by Maine's picturesque lakes, streams, and coast—account for a large portion of retail sales and service income.

Maine's transportation facilities lie generally outside the mainstream of the country's traffic flow. Most passengers and goods are carried on the state's highways. Portland and Searsport are the major seaports. Ferries link many of the coastal islands with the mainland, and Portland and Bar Harbor have ferry service to Yarmouth, Nova Scotia.

Maine's seafaring, farming, and lumbering heritages are well preserved in museums, parks, and local traditions. The statewide University of Maine system is the most important institution of higher education. One of Maine's special attractions is Acadia National Park on Mount Desert Island and Isle au Haut, the first national park east of the Mississippi River. Area 33,265 square miles (86,156 square km). Pop. (2000) 1,274,923.

Maine, destruction of the (Feb. 15, 1898), an incident preceding the Spanish-American War in which a mysterious explosion sank the U.S. battleship *Maine* in the harbour of Havana. The destruction of the *Maine* was one of a series of incidents that precipitated the United States' intervention in the Cuban struggle for independence from Spain, which had begun in 1895. In January 1898, partly as a conciliatory gesture to the Spanish authorities there and partly to protect the lives and property of U.S. citizens presumably endangered by recent riots, the *Maine* was sent to Havana harbour. On February 15 an explosion sank the ship, carrying 260 seamen to their deaths. The exact cause of the disaster was never firmly established, though Spain offered to submit the question of its responsibility to arbitration. Nevertheless, certain U.S. newspapers seized upon the incident and coined the popular slogan, "Remember the 'Maine,' to hell with Spain!" in an effort to whip up public sentiment in favour of armed intervention, which followed in April.

The half-submerged battleship *Maine* in the harbour of Havana, 1900

By courtesy of the Library of Congress, Washington, D.C.

Maine, Sir Henry (James Sumner) (b. Aug. 15, 1822, Kelso, Roxburgh, Scot.—d. Feb. 3, 1888, Cannes, Fr.), British jurist and legal historian who pioneered in the study of comparative law, notably primitive law and anthropological jurisprudence.

While professor of civil law at the University of Cambridge (1847–54), Maine also began lecturing on Roman law at the Inns of Court, London. These lectures became the basis of his *Ancient Law: Its Connection with the Early History of Society, and Its Relation to Modern Ideas* (1861). This work influenced both political theory and anthropology, the latter primarily because of his controversial views on primitive law. To trace and define his concepts, he drew on Roman law, western and eastern European systems, laws of India, and primitive law. Though some of his statements were modified or invalidated by later research, his study helped to place comparative jurisprudence on a sound historical footing.

A member of the council of the governor-general of India (1863–69), Maine was largely responsible for the codification of Indian law. In 1869 he became the first professor of comparative jurisprudence at the University of Oxford and, in 1887, professor of international law at Cambridge. He was knighted in 1871. His other books include lectures on the *Early History of Institutions* (1875), a sequel to his *Ancient Law*.

Maine, Louis-Auguste de Bourbon, duc du (duke of) (b. March 31, 1670, probably Saint-Germain, Fr.—d. May 14, 1736, Sceaux), illegitimate son of King Louis XIV of France who attempted without success to wrest control of the government from Philippe II, Duke d'Orléans, who was the regent (1715–23) for Louis XIV's successor, Louis XV.

The eldest surviving child of Louis XIV by the Marquise de Montespan, Louis-Auguste was legitimated and granted the title Duke du Maine in 1673. He served in the War of the Grand Alliance (1689–97), and in 1714 Louis XIV designated him a prince of the blood with right of eventual succession to the throne. The king attempted to reinforce that ruling through the provisions of his will: du Maine was to be given a place in the projected regency council and made guardian of young Louis XV and commander of the royal guards. By granting du Maine such broad powers Louis hoped to restrict the authority of his legitimate nephew Orléans, who by law was to become regent for Louis XV. Nevertheless, immediately after the death of Louis XIV (Sept. 1, 1715), Orléans had the will annulled by the Parlement (high court of justice) of Paris. Assuming control of the government, he withheld command of the guards from du Maine, and in July 1717 du Maine was deprived of his status as prince of the blood. Du Maine's wife, Louise-Bénédicte de Bourbon-Condé, was enraged by the regent's actions. In 1718 she involved du Maine in a conspiracy with the Spanish ambassador, Antonio Giudice, Prince de Cellamare, to substitute Philip V of Spain (grandson of Louis XIV) as regent instead of Orléans. Orléans learned of the plot, and in December du Maine, his wife, and Cellamare were arrested. Imprisoned for a little more than a year, du Maine then retired from public life; his wife, however, maintained her salon at their château at Sceaux.

Louis-Auguste de Bourbon, duc du Maine, detail from an engraving, 1696

Giraudon—Art Resource/EB Inc.

Maine de Biran, Marie-François-Pierre, original surname GONTHIER DE BIRAN (b. Nov. 29, 1766, Bergerac, Fr.—d. July 20, 1824, Paris), French statesman, empiricist philosopher, and prolific writer who stressed the inner life of man, against the prevalent emphasis on external sense experience, as a prerequisite for understanding the human self. Born with the surname Gonthier de Biran, he adopted Maine after his father's estate, Le Maine.

After defending King Louis XVI at Versailles in October 1789 as one of the king's lifeguards at the start of the French Revolution, Maine de Biran retired to his own estate at Grateloup, near Bergerac, to study philosophy and mathematics. After the fall of Robespierre in 1794, he entered public life as an administrator in the Dordogne district. In 1813 he expressed publicly his opposition to Napoleon. After the restoration of the Bourbons in 1814, he became treasurer to the chamber of deputies in the government of King Louis XVIII.

Philosophically, Maine de Biran was known at first as one of the Idéologues, a school of

Maine de Biran, detail of a portrait by B. Duvivier
Giraudon—Art Resource/EB Inc.

philosophers who regarded all experience as being limited to the realm of sensation. In 1802 he had impressed the Institut de France with an essay upholding the views of the dominant Idéologues. A similar essay won him election to the institute in 1805. His importance, however, consists in his gradual and detailed exposition of the inadequacies of the Idéologue attitude. His diary (*Journal,* 3 vol., ed. H. Gouhier; 1954–57) discusses both his political and his philosophical activities and reveals the dilemmas of a philosopher who felt compelled to play a decisive role in politics. In the diary and in his other works he is preoccupied with the inner life, whose importance for experience the Idéologues had ignored. Already in the essay of 1802 he had suggested that the will, as well as sensation, was a necessary element for any analysis of the self. After 1805 he attached increased importance to the will, by which man could cause his body to move.

For his idea of human freedom, derived from this notion of willed movement, Maine de Biran has been considered by some to be the father of French Existentialist philosophy. His collected works, which fill 14 volumes (ed. Pierre Tisserand, 1920–49), include the *Essai sur les fondements de la psychologie* (1812; "Essay on the Fundamentals of Psychology") and *Nouveaux Essais d'anthropologie* (1823–24; "New Essays in Anthropology"). In the later essays he describes the human self as developing through a purely sensitive, animal phase, the *vie animale* ("animal life"), to a phase of will and freedom, the *vie humaine* ("human life"), and culminating in experiences that transcend humanity, the *vie de l'esprit* ("spiritual life").

BIBLIOGRAPHY. Victor Delbos, *Maine de Biran et son oeuvre philosophique* (1931); Aldous Huxley, *Themes and Variations* (1950); A. Cresson, *Maine de Biran, sa vie, son oeuvre avec un exposé de sa philosophie* (1950); Philip Hallie, *Maine de Biran: Reformer of Empiricism* (1959).

Maine-et-Loire, *département,* Pays de la Loire region, western France, created from the major part of the historic province of Anjou and a fragment of Touraine. Its 2,753-sq-mi (7,131-sq-km) area is bisected east–west by the Loire River, which is joined by the Maine River 5 mi (8 km) southwest of Angers (*q.v.*), its capital. Of the 12 principal rivers, 9 are navigable. The highest point, 630 ft (210 m), is near Cholet in the Mauges region. The *département,* essentially agricultural, has moderate rainfall at all seasons and particularly mild winters. The Loire Valley, known in the *département* as the Val d'Anjou, is a broad, fertile plain covered with market gardens, orchards, and vineyards. In the Mauges cattle-raising region in the southwest, the once flourishing cultivation of hemp has practically disappeared. In the Segré area in the west, high-grade iron ore is mined, cider apples are cultivated, and grains are grown. Cattle raising predominates in the northeast around the ancient town of Baugé. The slate quarries extending from the west to the Angers region, particularly Trélazé, account for much of France's slate production. The Rosés d'Anjou and the sparkling Saumur wines are among the better known vintages of the *département.*

Angers and Saumur on the Loire are popular tourist centres. The recumbent statues of Henry II of England, his wife, Eleanor of Aquitaine, and their son Richard I the Lion-Heart, all of whom are buried in the 12th-century Fontevrault abbey near Saumur, are of particular interest. The church of Cunault northwest of Saumur is a fine example of medieval architecture. The *département* has four *arrondissements*—Angers, Cholet, Saumur, and Segré. Pop. (1982) 675,321.

Maine River, river, Maine-et-Loire *département,* western France, 7 mi (12 km) long, formed by the confluence of the Mayenne, the Sarthe, and the Loire rivers. Within 6 mi (north) of Angers, the Loire, meandering from the east, joins the southward-flowing Sarthe River, which is linked about 2.5 mi downstream by a branch with the Mayenne River, flowing southeastward. The Sarthe and the Mayenne meet again about 3 mi further downstream at the lower point of the heart-shaped island of Saint-Aubin to form the Maine. The Maine crosses Angers in a southwesterly direction and joins the westward-flowing Loire about 5 mi below the city.

Mainichi shimbun (Japanese: "Everyday Newspaper"), national daily newspaper, one of Japan's "big three" dailies, which publishes morning and evening editions in Tokyo, Ōsaka, and three other regional centres.

The newspaper has as its origin the *Nihon Rikken Seitō shimbun* ("Japan Constitutional Government Party Newspaper"), which was first published by the Rikken Seitō in 1882. In 1888 it became the *Ōsaka mainichi shimbun.* In 1903 the newspaper came under the control of industrialist Motoyama Hikoichi, and in 1911 it commenced publication under the title *Mainichi shimbun.*

With its thorough coverage and generally progressive editorial outlook, *Mainichi* has appealed to a largely middle-class readership. It is usually ranked second to *Asahi shimbun* as regards national and international prestige, but it appears with its rival on most experts' lists of the world's greatest newspapers. It has a combined staff at its various plants of more than 6,000 people, including reporters, editors, and translators of foreign news. *Mainichi,* like other Japanese papers, publishes proportionately much more foreign news than most Western papers.

Mainit, Lake, lake on the border of Surigao del Norte and Agusan del Sur provinces, northeastern Mindanao, Philippines. It is the country's fourth largest lake and has an area of 58 sq mi (150 sq km). Its outlet is the Tubay River, which flows southward before entering Butuan Bay of the Mindanao Sea. Lake Mainit is skirted on the east by the Philippine–Japan Friendship Highway, connecting Surigao and Davao. The area has secondary forests, and rice, corn (maize), and bananas are grown.

Mainland, also called POMONA, central and largest island of the Orkney group, which lie off the northern tip of Scotland. The irregularly shaped and deeply indented island is cut into (from north and south, respectively) by the inlets of Kirkwall Bay and Scapa Flow, reducing the width to less than 2 mi (3 km) at one point. The island is low lying (Ward Hill, the highest point, only attains 881 ft [269 m]), with numerous lakes well stocked with trout. A rich and progressive agricultural area, the island shows signs of very early occupation, including the Neolithic village of Skara Brae, the great barrow (earthwork) of Maeshowe Tumulus, one of Scotland's major archaeological remains, the Standing Stones of Stenness, the Ring of Brogar stone circles, and such monoliths as the Stone of Odin.

Kirkwall, the capital of the Orkneys, and Stromness, situated on the west coast, are the only towns. The famous British naval base of Scapa Flow, where the German Navy surrendered after World War I, lies to the south. Pop. (1981) 14,279.

Mainpurī, town, administrative headquarters of Mainpurī district, Uttar Pradesh state, northern India, east of Āgra. Mainpurī and the surrounding territory were part of the kingdom of Kannauj (Kanauj) and became splintered politically when the kingdom fell. The town was conquered by the Mughal ruler Bābur in 1526; it fell to the Marāṭhās in the 18th century and was ceded to the British in 1801. It is a trade centre for agricultural products, and its principal industries are cotton ginning, oilseed milling, and lamp and glass manufacture. The town is also known for wooden sculpture and tobacco. Its most notable building is a raja's palace, the Gaṛhi.

Mainpurī district, 1,642 sq mi (4,254 sq km) in area, is situated on the alluvial plain between the Ganges and Yamuna rivers. Irrigated by the Upper and Lower Ganges canals, it contains many groves of mangoes and other trees. Main crops are wheat, gram, rice, and barley. Pop. (1981) town, 58,928; district, 1,726,202.

Maintenon, Françoise d'Aubigné, marquise de (marchioness of), byname MADAME DE MAINTENON, also called (1652–75) FRANÇOISE SCARRON, *née* FRANÇOISE D'AUBIGNÉ (baptized Nov. 28, 1635, Niort, Poitou, Fr.—d. April 15, 1719, Saint-Cyr), second wife (from either 1683 or 1697) and untitled queen of King Louis XIV of France. She encouraged an atmosphere of dignity and piety at court and founded an educational institution for poor girls at Saint-Cyr (1686).

She was born at Niort, in Poitou, perhaps in the same prison where her father, Constant,

Madame de Maintenon, detail of a portrait by Pierre Mignard; in the Louvre, Paris
Giraudon—Art Resource/EB Inc.

was then incarcerated for debt; the infant was baptized as a Roman Catholic in November 1635. Constant, the son of Agrippa d'Aubigné, a great Huguenot soldier and companion of Henry IV as well as a poet, possessed neither his father's talents nor his virtues. His child, Françoise, received a Calvinist upbringing until the age of seven at the Château de Mursay, supervised by her aunt Villette, Agrippa's favourite daughter.

Constant was freed in 1645, and the Aubigné family embarked on a journey to the West Indies, for Constant believed he had been made governor of the island of Marie-Galante. The post was not vacant, however, and Constant returned to France, leaving his family in Martinique, where they were to remain for close to two years before being able to return. Constant died in France in 1647. Françoise was entrusted once more to her aunt Villette's care, but another aunt, Mme de Neuillant, a Catholic whose daughter was Françoise's godmother, claimed the child. Françoise was forced to go to this unknown relative, who raised the child sternly.

When Françoise was 16, her mother died. Anxious to rid herself of the orphan, Mme de Neuillant arranged for her charge to live with the crippled author Paul Scarron, who was 25 years older than the girl. Françoise married him in 1652 and later said of this relationship: "I preferred to marry him rather than a convent." In addition to nursing the author, she also had to preside over his salon, where an extremely varied group was received. The marriage was probably unconsummated. The author of *Le Roman comique* was a rascal, and, although he may have formed his young wife intellectually, he also undoubtedly tried to corrupt her. Meanwhile, the men who frequented his salon did not hesitate to try their luck with his little wife, who skillfully practiced the art of flirtation until, at last, in 1660, she found herself a widow—free but without a sou. She was then 25 years old and beautiful. She was at first tempted to embark on a courtesan's life, but instead she took a room in a convent and, in this semi-retreat, lived the cultured and well-mannered life of a *précieuse*, zealous of her reputation. As the hostess of the Scarron salon, she had made powerful friends, with whose help she had obtained from Anne of Austria, the queen mother, an allowance of 2,000 pounds. Although later she was to be credited with many lovers, the widow remained discreet and was regarded as wise, rather devout, and even somewhat prudish.

In 1668 she was given a chance to improve her fortunes. One of her friends, the Marquise de Montespan, had become the King's mistress. Having supplanted the shy Louise de La Vallière, the Marquise was soon to become pregnant. As she was already married and the King did not wish a scandal, he decided that the birth was to be kept secret. For this purpose he required a trustworthy person to receive and hide the child, a delicate task requiring both ability and discretion. Scarron, displaying her prescience, agreed and thus began her surprising rise to power. The child was born in March 1669 and was followed by many others. After the third, the family moved to a house in Paris, where the King made occasional visits and met Scarron, then 36 years old. Louis XIV was three years younger.

The King recognized his illegitimate children by Montespan in December 1673. He gathered them around him, with their governess, at his residence in Saint-Germain. Because of the King's generosity, Scarron was able to purchase the Château de Maintenon in December 1674. At the beginning of 1675, Louis XIV bestowed the title of her lands upon her. In December 1679 the Marquise de Maintenon was made second lady-in-waiting to the wife of the Dauphin. She was thus able to put aside her responsibilities for the royal children and to become independent from Montespan, with whom, for some time, she had been having a stormy relationship.

After the Queen's death on July 30, 1683, Louis XIV was to have only one woman in his life: "la Scarron," as she was always called by her enemies. He married her, according to some, in October 1683 and according to others in April or May 1697. Some historians maintain that Louis XIV married Maintenon to consummate the relationship, while others believe that the King was only regularizing a liaison whose beginnings went back either to 1673 or 1678, but more likely to 1680. Whatever the date may have been, if the marriage took place in 1683, Louis XIV and his companion had a union that lasted 32 years, 16 of them before 1700, the year in which Charles II, king of Spain, died. The latter having left his kingdom to the Duke of Anjou, Louis XIV's youngest son, France then found itself engaged in a deadly war, which was to mark the beginning of the reign's decline.

The precise date of the marriage is only important for the determination of Maintenon's political role, for many have blamed her for Louis XIV's errors and faults. In reality, her influence was negligible prior to 1700 and quite prudent during the last 15 years of Louis XIV's reign. Maintenon did not have the smallest part in the Revocation of the Edict of Nantes in 1685, which denied all rights to Protestants in France. Indeed, the secret wife of Louis XIV was the only one to establish and maintain a climate of decency, dignity, and piety around her husband. Her role, all things considered, can be seen as beneficial, except for the Quietism affair, when she was to join forces with Bishop Jacques-Bénigne Bossuet in persecuting François Fénelon.

At Saint-Cyr, near Paris, she founded the Maison Royale de Saint-Louis (known simply as Saint-Cyr), an institution for the education of impoverished young women of the nobility (1686). Racine's dramatic poem *Esther* was written for performance at the school. At first Saint-Cyr was considered fashionable. There Maintenon often sought to escape the restraints of the court and to put into practice the pedagogical talents she was convinced she possessed. To this day, many recognize that she did indeed have these talents. After the death of Louis XIV in 1715, his widow took ill and eventually died in her Saint-Cyr refuge. She survived him by four years, a stranger to the new era, and died in 1719.

Hated by some, revered by others, Maintenon never ceased to kindle violent emotions. To this day she is depicted in textbooks as greedy and evil, a narrow-minded bigot. It would be true to say that she was an ambitious woman who had an exceptional destiny and did not do too badly with it. Her letters are still read with interest, and, in his exile at St. Helena, Napoleon I professed to prefer them to those of Mme de Sévigné.

BIBLIOGRAPHY. The most complete study, unfortunately not translated, is Jean Cordelier, *Madame de Maintenon, une femme au grand siècle* (1955), a tentative psychological explanation based on the factual and historical details known today. On the early years, Emile Magne, *Scarron et son milieu*, 3rd ed. (1924), furnishes interesting details. Marcel Langlois, *Madame de Maintenon* (1932), is a slightly confused, but indispensable work in spite of the contradictions that reflect the mixed feelings of the author toward his heroine. Finally, basic to all serious study are the *Lettres* of Maintenon, published in four volumes by Marcel Langlois but incomplete (1935–39). Little has been published on the subject in English; however, Mme Saint-René Taillandier, *Madame de Maintenon* (1920; Eng. trans. 1922), is worth reading.

Mainz, French MAYENCE, city, capital (1945) of Rhineland-Palatinate *Land* (state), west-central Germany, port on the left bank of the Rhine opposite Wiesbaden and the mouth of the Main River. It was the site of a Celtic settlement where the Romans established (14–9 BC) a military camp, known as Moguntiacum after the Celtic god Mogo. The town that developed became the capital of Germania Superior until the Romans abandoned the area *c.* 451. A new town arose in the 6th century, which became a bishopric (747) and the ecclesiastical centre of Germany under St. Boniface and an archbishopric (775–80).

The community grew rapidly, gaining certain rights of self-government in 1118 and becoming a free city in 1244. As "Golden Mainz," it was the centre of a powerful league of Rhenish towns in 1254. The archbishops became chancellors and electors of the Holy Roman Empire in the 14th century. Mainz is noted as the birthplace of Johannes Gutenberg, who invented the art of printing with movable type there *c.* 1440. Following an economic decline, climaxed by warfare between two rival archbishops in 1462, its citizens were deprived of their privileges. Many craftsmen were driven into exile, spreading the knowledge of the art of printing.

Although the city was occupied by the Swedes and the French during the Thirty Years' War, it remained a flourishing commercial and cultural centre until it was reoccupied in 1792 by the French. It was successfully besieged by the Prussians and Austrians (1793) but was ceded to France by the treaties of Campo Formio (1797) and Lunéville (1801). The French suppressed the archbishopric (replaced by a bishopric in 1801) and secularized the electorate in 1803. French dominance ended in 1816, when the city passed to Hesse-Darmstadt, becoming capital of the newly formed Rhenish-Hesse Province. It was a fortress of the German Confederation and later of the empire until 1918. Mainz was occupied by French troops after World Wars I and II. About 80 percent of the inner city was destroyed during World War II, but reconstruction was rapid and extensive. Mainz's right-bank suburbs were transferred to the state of Hessen in 1946.

Some remains of Roman times survive, and relics are housed in the Central Roman-Germanic Museum. St. Martin's Cathedral, originally erected 975–1009, has been repeatedly rebuilt, acquiring accretions of many later styles in addition to its original Romanesque architecture. Henry II, Conrad II, and Frederick II were crowned there. Other historic landmarks include the churches of St. Ignatius (1763–74), St. Stephen (1257–1328), and St. Peter (1748–56) and the Renaissance electoral palace (1627–78), all renovated after World War II.

A university city from 1477 until 1816, Mainz regained this status with the establishment in 1946 of Johannes Gutenberg University, with which special institutes are associated, including the Institute for Economic Research. Also in the city are the Max Planck Institute of Chemistry and the Academy of Sciences and Literature. Gutenberg is also honoured by the Gutenberg Monument (1837), the Gutenberg Museum, and the headquarters building of the International Gutenberg Society. There are museums of art, history, and natural history, as well as a diocesan museum. Mainz is the site of wine and pre-Lenten festivals.

Historically, the development of the city's commerce was hampered by its military importance and by its competition with nearby Frankfurt am Main and with Mannheim. It declined sharply under Napoleon in the early 19th century but later became the centre of the Rhenish wine trade. Although industrialization came late, its manufactures are highly diversified, including chemical and pharmaceutical products, machinery, glassware, and musical instruments. Pop. (1989 est.) 174,828.

Maio Island, Portuguese ILHA DE MAIO, island of Cape Verde, in the Atlantic Ocean, between the islands of Boa Vista and Santiago, about 400 miles (640 km) off the West African coast. It has an area of 104 square miles (269 square km) and rises to an altitude of 1,430 feet (436 m). The main economic activities are agriculture (corn [maize], beans, potatoes) and salt extraction. Porto Inglês, on the southwestern coast, is the chief town and administrative capital of Maio Island. Pop. (1990 prelim.) 4,964.

maiolica: *see* majolica.

Maipú, Battle of (April 5, 1818), during the South American wars of independence, a victory won by South American rebels, commanded by José de San Martín, leader of the resistance to Spain in southern South America, over Spanish royalists, near Santiago, Chile.

The six-hour battle left 2,000 Spaniards dead and 3,000 captured; the patriots lost about 1,000 men. It ended the struggle for Chilean independence.

Maiquetía, city, northern Distrito Federal, northern Venezuela, on the narrow strip of land between the coastal hills and the Caribbean Sea, just west of La Guaira. It is a leading port of Venezuela and a popular beach resort. Industries include a glass factory, a brewery, and a caustic-soda plant. The city is accessible by highway and expressway from Caracas, 20 miles (30 km) to the south, and it is the site of the international jet airport that serves the capital. Pop. (1990 est.) 83,367.

Mair, Simon (astronomer): *see* Marius, Simon.

Mairet, Jean (b. May 10, 1604, Besançon, Fr.—d. Jan. 31, 1686, Besançon), classical French dramatist, the forerunner and rival of Pierre Corneille. Mairet's characters, his verse, and his situations were freely borrowed by his contemporaries. Before Corneille, he brought to the stage the famous Cornelian figures Sophonisbe and Pulchérie, and he anticipated Jean Racine in two important names, Roxane and Pharnace.

Mairet worked chiefly in Paris, where he secured important patrons, notably the Duke de Montmorency and the Count de Belin. Their support enabled him to launch a series of plays catering to the growing taste and enthusiasm for classical, or "regular," drama, which observed rules of place and time and a new standard of verisimilitude and decency. Mairet imitated the *Astrée* of Honoré d'Urfé in his early, pastoral plays: *Chryséide et Arimand* (1625), *Sylvie* (1626), and *La Sylvanire, ou La Morte vivre* (1630; "The Wood Nymph, or The Living Corpse"). These works, with a comedy, *Les Galanteries du duc d'Osonne* (1632; "The Gallantries of the Duke of Osonne"), renewed conventional themes by dramatic skill and witty writing. Mairet had even greater success in applying the techniques of "regular" drama to tragedy: *Virginie* (1633), *Sophonisbe* (1634), *Le Marc-Antoine, ou La Cleopatre* (1635; "Mark Antony, or Cleopatra"), *Le Grand et dernier Solyman* (1637; "The Last Great Solomon"). Finally, after writing a series of tragicomedies, he seems to have abandoned the theatre. There are signs of his political activity, culminating in the Fronde, but nothing is known of his last years.

Maironis, pseudonym of JONAS MAČIULIS (b. Nov. 2, 1862, Pasandravys, Lithuania, Russian Empire—d. June 28, 1932, Kaunas), poet considered to be the bard of the Lithuanian national renaissance.

Maironis, a Roman Catholic priest, studied at the theological seminary in Kaunas and at the theological academy in St. Petersburg in 1888–92 and returned there as an inspector and professor of moral theology (1894–1909) after two more years at Kaunas. He then served as rector of the seminary in Kaunas until 1922, when he was elected professor of moral theology at the Lithuanian University.

In his poetry Maironis expressed the hopes and aspirations of the Lithuanian people at the time of their struggle for independence. He wrote of his love for his country: its past, countryside, language, and legends. He succeeded in replacing the traditional Lithuanian syllabic verse with accentual-syllabic verse, and his sonorous, melodic poetry achieved wide popularity in his lifetime.

All of Maironis' lyric poetry was published in the collection *Pavasario balsai* (1st ed., with 45 poems, 1895; 6th ed., with 131 poems, 1926; "Voices of Spring"). The first of three epic poems, *Jaunoji Lietuva* (1907; "Young Lithuania"), has passages of great lyric beauty. Maironis also wrote three historical dramas on the life of Vytautas the Great (1350–1430), grand duke of Lithuania.

Maisí, Cape, Spanish CABO MAISÍ, cape, Guantánamo *provincia,* eastern Cuba, jutting out from the Purial Mountains to form the easternmost extremity of the island. To the southeast, across the Windward Passage, lies Cheval Blanc Point, Haiti, at a distance of approximately 35 miles (56 km); 30 miles to the northeast is Matthew Town, on Great Inagua Island of the Bahamas.

Maison-Carrée, Roman temple at Nîmes, Fr., in remarkably good repair. According to an inscription, it was dedicated to Gaius and Lucius Caesar, adopted sons of Augustus, and dates from the beginning of the Christian era.

The Maison-Carrée, 82 feet (25 m) long by 40 feet (12 m) wide, is one of the most beautiful monuments built in Gaul by the Romans. It houses a collection of Roman sculpture and classical fragments.

Maison de Molière, La (theatre): *see* Comédie-Française.

Maistre, Casimir-Léon (b. Sept. 24, 1867, Villeneuvette, Fr.—d. Sept. 20, 1957, Paris), soldier and explorer who took part in the first thorough European exploration of Madagascar and led expeditions into previously unexplored regions of Central Africa, thereby extending French influence there.

After serving as second in command of a French mission that traversed the whole of Madagascar in 1889–90, Maistre was put in charge of an expedition (1891) to investigate the navigability of the rivers in the Congo River basin. The mission was extremely successful, for he was able to travel up the Congo and Ubangi rivers into what is now the Central African Republic, then north into present-day Chad along the Chari River from near the Sudan in the east and to Lake Chad in the west. Maistre then crossed southwest into Nigeria and followed the Benue River to the Niger, arriving on the west coast of Africa in 1893.

Maistre, Joseph de (b. April 1, 1753, Chambéry, Fr.—d. Feb. 26, 1821, Turin, kingdom of Sardinia [Italy]), French polemical author, moralist, and diplomat who, after being uprooted by the French Revolution, became a great exponent of the conservative tradition.

He studied with the Jesuits and became a member of the Savoy Senate in 1787, following the civil career of his father, a former Senate president. After the invasion of Savoy by Napoleon's Revolutionary army in 1792, he began his lifelong exile in Switzerland; there he frequented Mme de Staël's literary salon at Coppet. Appointed envoy by the king of Sardinia to St. Petersburg in 1803, he remained at the Russian court for 14 years, writing *Essai sur le principe générateur des constitutions politiques et des autres institutions humaines* (1814) and his best work (unfinished), *Les Soirées de Saint-Petersbourg* (1821), acclaiming the public executioner as the guardian of social order. On his recall he settled in Turin as chief magistrate and minister of state of the Sardinian kingdom.

Joseph de Maistre, engraving
Giraudon—Art Resource

Maistre was convinced of the need for the supremacy of Christianity and the absolute rule of both sovereign and pope. He opposed the progress of science and the liberal beliefs and empirical methods of philosophers such as Francis Bacon, Voltaire, Jean-Jacques Rousseau, and John Locke. He also wrote *Du pape* (1819) and *Lettres sur l'Inquisition espagnole* (1838), an apology for the Spanish Inquisition's punitive role, defending his absolutist convictions with rigorous logic. It was as a logical thinker, pursuing consequences from an accepted premise, that Maistre excelled; the poet Charles Baudelaire acknowledged that it was Maistre who taught him to think.

Maitani, Lorenzo (b. *c.* 1275, near Siena, republic of Siena [Italy]—d. June 1330, Orvieto, Papal States [Italy]), Italian architect and sculptor primarily responsible for the construction and decoration of the facade of Orvieto Cathedral.

Maitani established his reputation in Siena and was called to supervise the construction at Orvieto in 1308 when the unprecedented height and span of the cathedral's vaults and arches presented unforeseen difficulties. In 1310 he received the title *capomaestro* of the cathedral and became, in addition, overseer of bridges and civic buildings.

Maitani's most important contribution was the design of the cathedral's facade. Though his contributions to the facade as a sculptor are difficult to determine, it may be assumed that his sensibility dictated the overall scheme. Two of the panels attributed to Maitani, "Scenes from Genesis" and "The Last Judgment," are delicate bas-reliefs unified by an ascending vine that suggests a French Gothic influence. Sculptures generally attributed to Maitani include the bronze "Eagle of St. John" and the "Angel of St. Matthew."

Maithil Brahman, caste of Brahmans in Bihār, India (the area of the ancient kingdom of Mithilā), well known for their orthodoxy and interest in learning. The names of these Brahmans are usually followed by the appellation Miśra; many great scholars have been members of this caste, notably Vācaspati Miśra (9th century). They have no further endogamous divisions but observe a complicated pattern of marriage among five hierarchically ordered groups, each of which may take a wife from the group below it.

Maitland, city, eastern New South Wales, Australia, in the Hunter River valley. Founded as a settlement for convicts (1818–21), it was called in turn The Camp, Molly Morgan Plains, and Wallis Plains. A second town, surveyed in 1829 on higher ground on the east side of Wallis Creek and called Maitland, later became East Maitland. The older settlement continued to be called Wallis Plains until 1835, when it was renamed West Maitland. Both townships were defined in 1835; East Maitland became a municipality in 1862 and West Maitland in 1863. The city, formed in 1944 by uniting eight towns, has an area of 153 square miles (396 square km). Having suffered floods in the past, Maitland is channeling growth toward higher ground to the east and west. On the New England Highway, 20 miles (32 km) northwest of Newcastle, and an important rail junction, the region yields dairy products, pigs, vegetables, fruits, and grains. Industries include slaughtering, livestock marketing, dairy processing, light engineering, and the manufacture of ceramics, textiles, and furniture. Pop. (1986) 43,247.

Maitland, Frederic William (b. May 28, 1850, London, Eng.—d. Dec. 19, 1906, Las Palmas, Canary Islands, Spain), English jurist and historian of English law whose special contribution was to bring historical and comparative methods to bear on the study of English institutions.

Educated at Eton and at Trinity College, Cambridge (B.A., 1873; M.A., 1876), Maitland studied law at Lincoln's Inn, London, and was called to the bar (1876). After practicing in London, he became reader in English law (1884) and professor (1888) at Cambridge. His best-known work, *The History of English Law Before the Time of Edward I*, 2 vol. (1895), was written with Sir Frederick Pollock; it became a classic, widely cited simply as "Pollock and Maitland." Among Maitland's other writings are *Bracton's Note-Book* (1887), an edition of the noted 13th-century English jurist Henry de Bracton's collection of cases; *Roman Canon Law in the Church of England* (1898); and *English Law and the Renaissance* (1901). He also edited several volumes published by the Selden Society, which he and others founded (1887) for the study of English law.

Frederic Maitland, detail of an oil painting by Beatrice Lock, 1906; in the National Portrait Gallery, London

By courtesy of the National Portrait Gallery, London

Maitland, James (Scottish economist): *see* Lauderdale, James Maitland, 8th Earl of.

Maitland, John: *see* Lauderdale, John Maitland, Duke of.

Maitland (of Thirlestane), John Maitland, 1st Lord, also called 1ST LORD THIRLESTANE (b. 1545—d. Oct. 3, 1595, Thirlestane, Berwick, Scot.), lord chancellor of Scotland from 1587 to 1595 and chief adviser to King James VI (later James I of Great Britain). His father was the poet and statesman Sir Richard Maitland of Lethington, East Lothian, and his brother, William Maitland, was a prominent supporter of Mary Stuart, Queen of Scots (reigned 1542–67).

Maitland succeeded his father as keeper of the privy seal in 1567 and became a lord of session the following year. He supported the partisans of Mary Stuart in their war against the supporters of young King James VI and was briefly imprisoned upon the final defeat of the queen's cause in 1573. He was made a privy councillor in 1583 and became the king's principal adviser by 1586. Appointed chancellor in 1587, Maitland was the first person in that century to hold that office who was not a noble or a prelate. He was created Lord Maitland of Thirlestane three years later. His policy included alliance with England, compromise with the Scottish Presbyterians, and an endeavour to keep James on conciliatory terms with both. Nevertheless, his great influence aroused the jealousy of powerful nobles, one of whom, Francis Stewart, Earl of Bothwell, brought him into royal disfavour in 1592. Maitland then sponsored the "Golden Act" (1592), which sanctioned the Presbyterian hierarchy of church courts; he never recovered his former power.

John Maitland, miniature by an unknown artist, *c.* 1590; in the National Portrait Gallery, London

By courtesy of the National Portrait Gallery, London

Maitland, Sir Richard, LORD LETHINGTON (b. 1496—d. March 20, 1586), Scottish poet, lawyer, statesman, and compiler of one of the earliest and most important collections of Scottish poetry.

"Manly Maitland," as he was called in an epitaph, was the son of Sir William Maitland of Lethington. He studied law at the University of St. Andrews and in Paris, served James V, and was keeper of the Great Seal (1562–67) under Mary, Queen of Scots. Although he became blind about 1561, he remained active as a judge until 1584 and busied himself with writing and collecting Scottish poetry.

Maitland's poems reflect the troubled condition of Scotland in the 16th century. Usually dealing with social and political themes, they are either satirical or written with the meditative seriousness of an old and blind man who loves his country and who distrusts his more fanatical and intolerant contemporaries. They frequently have a laconic strength and a rhythmic expressiveness reminiscent of his English contemporary Sir Thomas Wyat. Maitland included his own poems in his valuable collection of Scottish poetry known as the Maitland Folio MS. (begun about 1570), and his daughter added others while she compiled the smaller anthology called the Maitland Quarto MS. (1586). The 183 leaves of the folio and the 138 leaves of the quarto also contain a selection of works by Robert Henryson, William Dunbar, Gavin Douglas, and other important poets of the period. Maitland's service to Scottish history and literature was commemorated by the foundation of the Maitland Club in 1828 to continue such study.

Maitland (of Lethington), William (b. *c.* 1528, probably Lethington, East Lothian, Scot.—d. June 9?, 1573, Leith), Scottish statesman and staunch supporter of Mary Stuart, Queen of Scots. In the conflict between Scotland's Protestant nobility and the Roman Catholic Mary, Maitland often defied the queen when her actions threatened to undermine her chances of remaining in power. His overriding aim was to unite the realms of England and Scotland by securing for Mary recognition as successor to England's Queen Elizabeth I.

In 1558 Maitland became secretary to the Roman Catholic, pro-French queen regent, Mary of Lorraine. He soon joined the Protestant lords against the regent, however, in order to help expel the French from Scotland. When Mary Stuart assumed control of the government in 1560, she made Maitland her secretary of state. In order to prod Elizabeth I of England into naming Mary as her successor, Maitland approved of negotiations seemingly intended to result in Mary's marriage to Don Carlos of Spain, an alliance that Elizabeth could not risk. Maitland also had a hand in the unsuccessful proposals of a marriage between Mary and Robert Dudley, Earl of Leicester.

Later, Maitland supported the murder (1566) of Mary's favourite, the Italian Catholic David Riccio, who was hated by the Protestant nobles. Maitland may also have had a hand in the murder (1567) of Mary's husband, Henry Stewart, Lord Darnley. He then opposed the queen's marriage (May 1567) to James Hepburn, 4th Earl of Bothwell, and joined the coalition of Protestant and Catholic nobles that forced Bothwell to leave Scotland.

After Mary fled to England in May 1568, Maitland remained in Scotland and worked to restore her to power. By promoting her proposed marriage to England's Duke of Norfolk in 1570, he broke with the government of James Stewart, Earl of Moray, regent for the infant Scottish king James VI. Maitland was arrested but was released upon Moray's death in 1570. In the ensuing civil war he led Mary's supporters against the king's partisans. Maitland held Edinburgh Castle until forced to surrender in May 1573; he died in prison.

Maitraka DYNASTY, Indian dynasty that ruled in Gujarāt and Saurāshtra (Kāthiāwār) from the 5th to the 8th century AD. Its founder, Bhaṭārka, was a general who, taking advantage of the decay of the Gupta empire, established himself as ruler of Gujarāt and Saurāshtra with Valabhi (modern Vala) as his capital. Although the early Maitraka kings were loosely feudatory to the Guptas, they were in fact independent. Under the powerful Śīlāditya I (*c.* late 6th century), the kingdom became very influential; its rule extended into Mālwa and Rājasthān. Later, however, the Maitrakas suffered at the hands of the Cālukyas (Chalukyas) of the Deccan and of the emperor Harṣa of Kannauj. After Harṣa's death, the Maitrakas revived, but the Arabs who had established themselves in Sind in 712 killed the last Maitraka king, Śīlāditya VI, and razed his capital about 780.

Bhaṭārka and his successors were great patrons of religious foundations. Their kingdom was an important centre of Buddhism, and, according to tradition, it was in Valabhī that the Śvetāmbara Jaina canon was codified.

Maitre de la Morte de Marie: *see* Scorel, Jan van.

Maitreya, in Buddhist tradition, the future Buddha, presently a bodhisattva residing in the Tuṣita heaven, who will descend to earth to preach anew the dharma ("law") when the teachings of Gautama Buddha have completely decayed. Maitreya is the earliest bodhisattva around whom a cult developed and is mentioned in scriptures from the 3rd century AD. He was accepted by all schools of Buddhism and is still the only bodhisattva generally honoured by the Theravāda tradition.

The name Maitreya is derived from the Sanskrit *maitrī* ("friendliness"). In Pāli the name becomes Metteyya, in Chinese Mi-lo-fo, in Japanese Miroku, and in Mongolian Maidari; in Tibetan the bodhisattva is known as Byams-pa ("kind," or "loving"). His worship was especially popular during the 4th to 7th century, and his images are found throughout the Buddhist world; many of them beautifully convey his characteristic air of expectancy and promise. He is represented in painting and sculpture both as a bodhisattva and as a buddha, and he is frequently depicted seated in European fashion or with his ankles loosely crossed.

Miroku (Maitreya) in meditation, gilt bronze figure, Japanese, Asuka period, 7th century; in the Cleveland Museum of Art

The Cleveland Museum of Art, John L. Severance Fund, 50.86

maitrī (Sanskrit), in Buddhism, the perfect virtue of sympathy. *See* brahmavihāra.

maize (agriculture): *see* corn.

Maizuru, city, Kyōto *fu* (urban prefecture), Honshu, Japan, facing Wakasa Bay. The city—then called Tanabe—developed around a castle built during the Muromachi period (1338–1573). It has one of the best natural ports on the Sea of Japan (East Sea) coast and prospered as a naval port before World War II. The naval facilities were later converted to industrial use, producing ships, textiles, chemical products, and pottery. The city is also a base for the Japanese Maritime Self-Defense Force. In 1961 Maizuru became a sister city of Nakhodka, the civil port east of Vladivostok, Siberia, and regular service between the two was initiated. Pop. (1990) 96,329.

Máj circle, group of young Czech writers of the mid-19th century whose aim was to create a new Czech literature that would reflect their liberalism and practical nationalism. They published in an almanac called *Máj* (1858; "May") after the lyrical epic poem of the same name by Karel Hynek Mácha, whom the group regarded as the forerunner of their literary revolution.

Majapahit empire, the last Indianized kingdom in Indonesia; based in eastern Java, it existed between the 13th and 16th centuries. The founder of the empire was Vijaya, a prince of Singhasāri (*q.v.*), who escaped when Jayakatwang, the ruler of Kaḍiri, seized the palace. In 1292 Mongol troops came to Java to avenge an insult to the emperor of China, Kublai Khan, by Kertanagara, the king of Singhasāri, who had been replaced by Jayakatwang. Vijaya collaborated with Mongol troops in defeating Jayakatwang; Vijaya then turned against the Mongols and expelled them from Java.

Under his rule the new kingdom, Majapahit, successfully controlled Bali, Madura, Malayu, and Tanjungpura. The power of Majapahit reached its height in the mid-14th century under the leadership of King Hayam Wuruk and his prime minister, Gajah Mada. Some scholars have argued that the territories of Majapahit covered present-day Indonesia and part of Malaysia, but others maintain that its territory was confined to eastern Java and Bali. Nonetheless, Majapahit became a significant power in the region, maintaining regular relations with China, Champa, Cambodia, Annam, and Siam (Thailand). The golden era of Majapahit was short-lived; the empire began to decline after the death of Gajah Mada in 1364, and it was further weakened after the death of Hayam Wuruk in 1389. The spread of Islām and the rise of the Islāmic states along the northern coast of Java eventually brought the Majapahit era to an end in the late 15th or early 16th century.

Majardah, Wadi, also called OUED MEDJERDA, Latin BAGRADAS, main river of Tunisia. It rises in northeastern Algeria in the Medjerda Mountains and flows northeastward for 290 miles (460 km) to the Gulf of Tunis, draining an area of about 8,880 square miles (23,000 square km) before it enters the Mediterranean Sea. Dams along the river and its tributaries provide valuable irrigation water for the surrounding plains, which are a major wheat-growing area. The river's rate of discharge varies from less than 140 cubic feet (4 cubic m) per second in summer to between 53,000 and 88,000 cubic feet (1,500 to 2,500 cubic m) in winter. Main riverine settlements include Souk-Ahras in Algeria and Jundūbah (Jendouba), Tunisia.

Majdanek, also spelled MAIDANEK, also called LUBLIN-MAJDANEK, German Nazi concentration and extermination camp on the southeastern outskirts of the city of Lublin, Pol. It was established in November 1940 and first used for Soviet prisoners of war, virtually all of whom died there of hunger and exposure. In the autumn of 1942, however, it was converted into a death camp for Jews, imported first from Bohemia and Moravia and then from Poland, The Netherlands, and Greece. In the first months, victims were shot down by mass gunfire in a nearby forest, but afterward they were herded into gas chambers built for mass executions and using Zyklon-B, which produced quick-killing hydrogen cyanide fumes. The bodies were cremated. Branch camps, such as Travniki, were added nearby.

In November 1943, after the rebellion at the extermination camp of Sobibor, most of the prisoner population at Majdanek was annihilated, and the SS tried to obliterate traces of the massacre. When the Soviet armies liberated the camp on July 24, 1944, only a few hundred prisoners remained alive. Estimates of the total numbers who died at Majdanek—whether through execution or privation—vary widely, from 200,000 to 1,500,000.

majolica, also spelled MAIOLICA, tin-glazed earthenware produced from the 15th century at such Italian centres as Faenza, Deruta, Urbino, Orvieto, Gubbio, Florence, and Savona. Tin-glazed earthenware—also made in other countries, where it is called faience, or delft—was introduced into Italy from Moorish Spain by way of the island of Majorca, or Maiolica, whence it derived the name by which it was known in Italy.

The majolica painter's palette was usually restricted to five colours: cobalt blue, antimony yellow, iron red, copper green, and manganese purple; the purple and blue were used, at various periods, mainly for outline. A white tin enamel was used also for highlights or alone on the white tin glaze in what was called *bianco sopra bianco,* "white on white."

The shapes most often employed were the albarello, or drug jar, of Middle East origin; a type of ewer evidently derived from the Greek oinochoe; and, above all, the *piatta da pompa,* or show dish, in the *istoriato,* an Italian narrative style from the early 16th century that uses the pottery body solely as support for a purely pictorial effect. Although violating aesthetic rules in their subordination of shape to decoration, such wares remain works of great skill, as well as beauty.

Majolica
(Top) Florentine majolica albarello bearing the arms of Santa Maria della Scala, second quarter of the 15th century; (bottom) Faenza majolica dish, 1510; both in the Victoria and Albert Museum, London

By courtesy of the Victoria and Albert Museum, London

Major, John (b. March 29, 1943, London, Eng.), British politician and public official who was prime minister of the United Kingdom from 1990 to 1997.

The son of a former circus performer and vaudeville manager, Major left school at age 16 to help support his family. He worked as a bank accountant for some years and eventually tried to enter politics, twice standing unsuccessfully for Parliament in 1974. He gained a seat in the House of Commons during the Conservative Party landslide of 1979, and his subsequent rise through that party's ranks was rapid, owing in part to the interested patronage of high party officials from Prime Minister Margaret Thatcher on down. He became a junior minister in 1986 and chief secretary to the Treasury in 1987, and in July 1989 Thatcher appointed him to the important Cabinet post of foreign secretary. Major had hardly been in this post three months when another Cabinet reshuffle resulted in his becoming chancellor of the Exchequer. In this post he was well placed to contend for the leadership of the Conservative Party (and the post of prime minister) in November 1990 when Thatcher unexpectedly announced her intention to resign. With Thatcher's unofficial support, Major won a three-way contest for the party leadership and consequently became prime minister of Great Britain on Nov. 28, 1990. Major shared most of Thatcher's conservative views, but as prime minister he showed himself to be more pragmatic and consensus-

John Major, 1990
AP/Wide World Photos

oriented in his approach. In April 1992, in the first general elections after his ascendancy, the Conservatives won, confirming his leadership.

Major's first years in office coincided with the longest economic recession (1990–93) in Britain since World War II. His government became increasingly unpopular despite an economic recovery in the mid-1990s that combined steady growth and drastically falling unemployment with low levels of inflation. A joint British-Irish initiative obtained a temporary ceasefire in 1995–96 by both Protestants and Roman Catholics in the long-running conflict in Northern Ireland. Major's poll ratings remained strikingly low, partly because the large tax increases undertaken by his government in 1993 were unpopular and partly because Major himself was perceived as a colourless and indecisive leader. Moreover, there was a general feeling of weariness and impatience in Britain with the Conservative Party, which had ruled uninterruptedly for 18 years and had recently weathered several scandals involving Cabinet ministers. As a result, the Conservatives lost by a landslide to a reinvigorated Labour Party led by Tony Blair in general elections held on May 1, 1997. Major resigned both the prime ministry and the party leadership soon afterward.

major histocompatibility complex (MHC), group of genes that code for certain proteins which are found on the surface of cells and which help the immune system to recognize foreign substances. MHC proteins are found in all higher vertebrates. In human beings the complex is also called the human leukocyte antigen (HLA) system.

There are two major types of MHC protein molecules—class I and class II—that span the membrane of almost every cell in an organism. In humans these molecules are encoded by several genes all clustered in the same region on chromosome 6. Each gene has an unusual number of alleles (alternate forms of a gene). As a result, it is very rare for two individuals to have the same set of MHC molecules, which are collectively called a tissue type.

MHC molecules are important components of the immune response. They allow cells that have been invaded by an infectious organism to be detected by cells of the immune system called T lymphocytes, or T cells. The MHC molecules do this by presenting fragments of proteins (peptides) belonging to the invader on the cell's surface. The T cell recognizes the foreign peptide attached to the MHC molecule and binds to it, stimulating the T cell to either destroy or cure the infected cell. In uninfected healthy cells the MHC molecule presents peptides from its own cell (self peptides), to which T cells do not normally react. However, if the immune mechanism malfunctions and T cells react against self peptides, an autoimmune disease arises.

MHC molecules were initially defined as antigens that stimulate an organism's immunologic response to transplanted organs and tissues. In the 1950s skin graft experiments carried out in mice showed that graft rejection was an immune reaction mounted by the host organism against foreign tissue. This response was elicited because the host recognized the MHC molecules on cells of the graft tissue as foreign antigens and attacked them. Thus, the main challenge to a successful transplantation is to find a host and a donor with tissue types as similar as possible.

major scale, in music, stepped arrangement of notes following the classical Greek Ionian mode (though mistaken nomenclature in the 16th century has since caused it to be referred to as the Lydian mode). In a major scale the intervals between successive notes after the first are tone, tone, semitone, tone, tone, tone, semitone. Thus, the major scale of D is D–E–F♯–G–A–B–c♯–d, and the same notes descending.

Majorca, Spanish and Catalan MALLORCA, ancient (Latin) BALEARIS MAJOR, or MAJORICA, island, Baleares *provincia* and *comunidad autónoma* ("autonomous community"), Spain. Majorca is the largest of the Balearic Islands, which lie in the western Mediterranean Sea. It is 1,405 square miles (3,640 square km) in area and contains two mountainous regions, each about 50 miles (80 km) in length and occupying the western and eastern thirds of the island; they are separated by a lowland that terminates in Palma Bay on the south and Alcudia and Pollensa bays on the north. The western mountains are the higher and rise to 4,416 feet (1,346 m) at Mayor Peak. Precipitous cliffs, often over 1,000 feet (300 m) high, characterize much of the north coast. The island's varied landscape includes pine forests, olive groves, steep gullies, intensively terraced slopes, and fertile valleys. The much less rugged hills in the southeast are known for their extensive limestone caves and subterranean lakes. The central lowland, benefiting from the shelter provided by mountains in the northwest, is a rich agricultural zone with a characteristic two-tier cultivation—olives, figs, apricots, oranges, and almond trees forming the upper tier; with a lower tier consisting of cereals, alfalfa, and legumes.

The bay at El Port, a northwestern coastal resort of Majorca
Shostal

The island's fairs and colourful ceremonies, such as those of Pollensa during Holy Week, the mountain scenery, benign climate, and the island's rich historical heritage attract thousands of visitors each year. Majorca is rich in prehistoric remains, notably talayots (rough chambered towers of stone), *taulas* (temples), and burial caves, among the most famous of which are those of San Vicente in the north, the type and carvings of which indicate a close relationship to those of southern France, near Arles. At Valldemosa is the abandoned monastery where the Polish composer Frédéric Chopin and the French writer George Sand stayed and where Chopin wrote some of his finest mazurkas and preludes.

The island's economy is based primarily on agricultural products and tourism, but stone quarries (especially of marble), superphosphate works, and light manufactures (including pottery, glassware, shoes, and rugs) and souvenirs provide some employment. Shipping services connect Majorca with the Spanish mainland and the other Balearic Islands. There are regular air services from Palma, the island and provincial capital, to Barcelona, Paris, and London. Pop. (1994 est.) 736,865.

Majorelle, Louis (b. 1859, Toul, France—d. 1926, Nancy), French artist, cabinetmaker, furniture designer, and ironworker who was one of the leading exponents of the Art Nouveau style.

Art Nouveau cabinet with marquetry and carving in various woods by Majorelle, *c.* 1900; in the Bethnal Green Museum, London
By courtesy of the Bethnal Green Museum, London; photograph, John Webb

The son of a cabinetmaker, Majorelle was trained as a painter and went in 1877 to the École des Beaux-Arts in Paris, where he studied under Jean-François Millet. After his father's death in 1879, he returned to Nancy to manage the family workshop. Concentrating on the design of furniture, Majorelle moved from 18th-century reproductions to the developing style of Art Nouveau and began (1890) to produce works conceived in that style. While still adhering to the quality of hand craftsmanship, Majorelle maintained a modern workshop that incorporated both machine- and hand-labour in wood, marquetry, bronze, cabinetry, and sculpture. Thus, he increased production and decreased price, an administrative achievement that accounts for his enormous success.

Majorelle's catalogs between 1900 and 1914 show a tremendous output: suites of furniture for individual rooms, furniture using botanical motifs or other stylistic themes, and specific pieces whose prices ranged according to custom-ordered materials. Majorelle's style incorporated a modified flowing line with polished woods, highlighted by Art Nouveau bronze mounts in the 18th-century tradition.

After World War I Majorelle continued to produce furniture in a modified, opulent Art Nouveau style, which by then was being replaced by the more severe Art Deco style. After his death Majorelle's studio was managed by his pupil Alfred Lévy.

Majorian, Latin in full JULIUS VALERIUS MAJORIANUS (d. Aug. 7, 461, Dertona, Liguria [now Tortona, Italy]), Western Roman emperor from 457 to 461, the only man to hold that office in the 5th century who had some claim to greatness.

Born of a distinguished military family, he served under the master of soldiers Aetius and helped overthrow the emperor Avitus (reigned 455–456). The real governmental power passed to Majorian's friend Ricimer, who became for 16 years the kingmaker at Rome.

Appointed master of the soldiers in 457, Majorian quickly defeated the Alemannic invaders at Bellinzona (in present Switzerland). He was proclaimed emperor, with Ricimer's support, on April 1 and set about conscientiously administering his realm. He stopped abuses in tax collection and attempted to protect the provincials from other forms of oppression.

In 458 Majorian began to build the fleet with which he hoped to recover Africa from the Vandals. After securing the support of Gaul, where a movement toward independent rule was in progress, he crossed into Spain in May 460. Most of Majorian's fleet of 300 ships was captured in the Bay of Alicante when the Vandal fleet under Gaiseric made a sudden strike on the Spanish coast. The emperor was subjected to a humiliating peace. On his return to Italy he fell into Ricimer's hands (Aug. 2, 461) and was compelled to abdicate. Five days later he was executed.

Mājūj (Islāmic myth): *see* Yājūj and Mājūj.

Majunga (Madagascar): *see* Mahajanga.

Majuro, atoll in the Ratak (eastern) chain of the Marshall Islands and capital of the Republic of the Marshall Islands, in the western Pacific Ocean. The atoll comprises 64 islets on an elliptically shaped reef 25 miles (40 km) long and has a total land area of 4 square miles (10 square km). Majuro has the largest population of any atoll or island in the Marshall Islands. The atoll's main settlement, which is situated on three islands connected by landfills—Dalap, Uliga, and Darrit—serves as the capital of the republic. The atoll has port facilities and an airport. Pop. (1999) 23,676.

majuscule, in calligraphy, capital, uppercase, or large letter in most alphabets, in contrast to the minuscule, lowercase, or small letter. All the letters in a majuscule script are contained between a single pair of (real or theoretical) horizontal lines. The Latin, or Roman, alphabet uses both majuscule and miniscule letters.

The earliest known Roman majuscule, or capital, letters are in the script known as square capitals and can be seen chiseled in the stone of numerous surviving imperial Roman monuments. Square capitals are distinguished by their slightly heavier downstrokes and lighter upstrokes, and by their use of serifs, *i.e.,* the short lines stemming at right angles from the upper and lower ends of the strokes of a letter. Square capitals set a standard for elegance and clarity in the Roman alphabet that has never been surpassed.

In contrast to square capitals, which were used mainly in stone inscriptions, the script used throughout the Roman Empire in books and official documents was rustic capitals. This letter form was freer and more curved and flowing than that of square capitals and could be more easily written because of the oblique angle at which the pen was held to form the letters. The letters were more compact, and rounded forms became elliptical. The characters lost some of the formal appearance of square capitals. Both square and rustic capitals had gradually disappeared by the late 7th century AD.

Roman cursive capitals, a running-hand script, were customarily used in the Roman Empire for notes, business records, letters, and other informal or everyday uses. This form could be written with great speed and was, therefore, often written carelessly and tended toward illegibility. It was, nonetheless, one of several forerunners of the minuscule scripts that appeared later.

Another of these forerunners was a script called uncial—a rounder, more open majuscule form influenced by cursive. Uncial was the most common script used to write books from the 4th to the 8th century AD. Half-uncial script was developed during the same period and eventually evolved into an almost entirely minuscule alphabet. The origins of lowercase letters in the modern alphabet can be traced directly to these uncial scripts. *See also* Latin alphabet; uncial.

Majuscules
(Top) Rustic capitals from a manuscript of Virgil's *Aeneid* (the "Vatican Virgil"), 4th century AD (Vatican Library, Vat. Lat. 3225); (bottom) square capitals on a Roman stela, 1st century AD, in the Walters Art Gallery, Baltimore

By courtesy of (bottom) the Walters Art Gallery, Baltimore; photograph (top), Biblioteca Apostolica Vaticana

Makālu, one of the world's highest mountains (27,766 feet [8,463 m]), in the Himalayas on the Nepalese-Tibetan (Chinese) border. It lies 14 miles (23 km) east-southeast of Mount Everest. Makālu had been observed by climbers of Mount Everest, but attempts to ascend its steep, glacier-covered sides did not begin until 1954. On May 15, 1955, two members—Jean Couzy and Lionel Terray—of a French party reached the summit, and seven more arrived within two days.

Makanalua (Hawaii, U.S.): *see* Kalaupapa.

Makapansgat, South African valley in which remains of fossil hominids have been found. It lies about 13 miles (21 km) northeast of Potgietersrus, S.Af., and about 150 miles (240 km) north of Sterkfontein, itself a well-known site of australopithecine fossils. The area consists of dolomite cliffs pierced by several caves.

A search at Limeworks Cave in 1947–62 by Raymond Dart revealed the remains of about 40 individuals of *Australopithecus africanus,* a species of gracile (slender) hominid dating from 2,500,000 to 3,000,000 years ago or more. The nearby Cave of Hearths yielded the right side of an early archaic *Homo sapiens* child's jaw, of Rhodesioid type, dating from about 100,000 to 200,000 years ago; extremely early evidence of the use of fire by humans in Africa; and tools of the transitional Acheulian-Fauresmith type. Makapansgat is probably the oldest of the known South African cave sites.

makar, also spelled MAKER (Scottish: "maker," or "poet"), plural MAKARIS, or MAKERIS, also called SCOTTISH CHAUCERIAN, any of the Scottish courtly poets who flourished from about 1425 to 1550. The best known are Robert Henryson, William Dunbar, Gavin Douglas, and Sir David Lyndsay; the group is sometimes expanded to include James I of Scotland and Harry the Minstrel, or Blind Harry.

Because Geoffrey Chaucer was their acknowledged master and they often employed his verse forms and themes, the makaris are usually called "Scottish Chaucerians"; but actually they are a product of more than one tradition. Chaucerian influence is apparent in their courtly romances and dream allegories, yet even these display a distinctive "aureate" style, a language richly ornamented by polysyllabic Latinate words.

In addition, the makaris used different styles for different types of poems. The language that they used in their poems ranges from courtly aureate English, to mixtures of English and Scots, to the broadest Scots vernacular, as their subjects range from moral allegory to everyday realism, flyting (abuse), or grotesquely comic Celtic fantasy.

Makarenko, Anton Semyonovich (b. March 1 [March 13, New Style], 1888, Belopolye, Ukraine, Russian Empire [now Bilopillya, Ukraine]—d. April 1, 1939, Moscow, Russia, U.S.S.R.), teacher and social worker who was the most influential educational theorist in the Soviet Union.

Makarenko studied at the Poltava Teachers' Institute and graduated in 1917 with honours. In the 1920s he organized the Gorky Colony, a rehabilitation settlement for children made homeless by the Russian Revolution and who roamed throughout the countryside in criminal gangs. In 1931 he was appointed head of the Dzerzhinsky Commune, a penal institution for young offenders.

Makarenko was the author of several books on education, including *Pedagogicheskaya poema* (1933–35; *The Road to Life, an Epic of Education*), which is an account of his work at the Gorky Colony, and *Kniga dlya roditeley*

(1937; *A Book for Parents*). Makarenko regarded work as basic to intellectual and moral development; all children should be assigned tasks requiring labour and should be given positions of responsibility in order to learn the limitations of their individual rights and privileges. Thus, his first principle of socialist upbringing was: "The maximum possible demands with the maximum possible respect."

Makarikari (Botswana): *see* Makgadikgadi.

Makarios III, original name MIKHAIL KHRISTODOLOU MOUSKOS (b. Aug. 13, 1913, Pano Panayia, Paphos, Cyprus—d. Aug. 3, 1977, Nicosia), archbishop and primate of the Orthodox Church of Cyprus. He was a leader in the struggle for enosis (union) with Greece during the postwar British occupation, and, from 1959 until his death in 1977, he was the president of independent Cyprus.

The son of a poor shepherd, Mouskos studied in Cyprus and at the University of Athens and later at the School of Theology of Boston University. He was ordained in 1946, became bishop of Kition (Larnaca) in 1948, and on Oct. 18, 1950, was made archbishop.

Makarios III
Camera Press

During that time Makarios became identified with the movement for enosis, the archbishop of Cyprus having traditionally played an important political role during the Turkish occupation as ethnarch, or head of the Greek Christian community. Opposing the British government's proposals for independence or Commonwealth status, as well as Turkish pressures for partition in order to safeguard the island's sizable Turkish population, Makarios met with the Greek prime minister, Alexandros Papagos, in February 1954 and gained Greek support for enosis. He was soon suspected by the British of being a leading figure in Colonel Georgios Grivas' terrorist organization. Makarios, however, preferred political bargaining to force, negotiating with the British governor in 1955–56. When these talks proved fruitless and Makarios was arrested for sedition in March 1956 and exiled, the guerrillas began a reign of terror. In February 1959 Makarios accepted a compromise that resulted in independence for Cyprus. He was elected president of the new republic on Dec. 13, 1959, with a Turkish vice president.

Makarios' administration was marred by fighting between Greeks and Turks, particularly after December 1963, and the active intervention of both Greece and Turkey. Previously a champion of exclusively Greek interests, he now worked for integration of the two communities, measures the Turks repeatedly resisted. In December 1967 he was obliged to accept a Turkish Cypriot Provisional Administration, which managed Turkish minority affairs outside the jurisdiction of the central government. Despite communal strife, he was elected president for a second term in February 1968. Talks between the two communities remained deadlocked over the question of local autonomy. In 1972 and 1973 other Cypriot bishops called for Makarios to resign, but he was returned unopposed for a third term as head of state in 1973.

In July 1974 the Greek Cypriot National Guard, whose officers were mainland Greeks, attempted a coup, planned by the ruling military junta in Athens, to achieve enosis. Makarios fled to Malta and then to London, and Turkey invaded Cyprus and proclaimed a separate state for Turkish Cypriots in the north. Makarios, vowing to resist partition of the island, returned to Cyprus in December, after the fall of the mainland Greek military junta.

Makarov, Stepan Osipovich (b. Dec. 27, 1848 [Jan. 8, 1849, New Style], Nikolayev, Ukraine, Russian Empire [now Mykolayiv, Ukraine]—d. March 31 [April 13], 1904, at sea off Port Arthur, Manchuria [now Lü-shun, China]), Russian naval commander in charge of the Pacific fleet at the start of the Russo-Japanese War in 1904.

The son of an ensign, Makarov graduated from the Maritime Academy in 1865 and was commissioned an ensign in the Russian navy in 1869. He became a brilliant and innovative naval architect, inventor, tactician, and ship designer. During the Russo-Turkish War of 1877–78, his new designs and tactics for torpedo boats were used on the Black Sea with notable success. He was a pioneering Russian oceanographer, and he also designed the first mine-laying ships intended exclusively for that purpose. His armour-piercing shells, known as Makarov tips, greatly increased the penetrating force of shells. He also designed and built the icebreaker *Ermak* to explore the Arctic.

Makarov became Russia's youngest admiral at age 41 in 1890, and he was promoted to vice admiral in 1896. He held a series of increasingly important posts during the 1890s; in February 1904 he was appointed commander of the Pacific Ocean squadron at the start of the Russo-Japanese War and acquitted himself ably until three months later, when he was killed as his flagship, *Petropavlovsk,* struck a mine and sank.

Makarova, Nataliya, in full NATALIYA ROMANOVNA MAKAROVA (b. Oct. 21, 1940, Leningrad [St. Petersburg], Russia, U.S.S.R.), Russian-born ballerina considered to be one of the greatest classical dancers.

Makarova began her training at the Leningrad Choreographic School at age 12. Upon graduation in 1959 she joined the Kirov Ballet and soon became one of their leading ballerinas. She won a gold medal at the Varna International Ballet Competition in 1965.

While performing with the Kirov in London (1970), Makarova decided to remain in the West and soon joined the American Ballet Theatre in New York City. She also became a guest artist with other companies, notably the Royal Ballet of Great Britain. Makarova's magnificent technique and acting sensibilities allowed her to excel in many different roles, although she is perhaps best known for *Giselle,* a role she danced originally with the Kirov. In 1980, disappointed that Mikhail Baryshnikov had become director of the American Ballet Theatre and not she, Makarova formed her own group, Makarova and Company, which lasted only a season. Though hampered by a knee injury, Makarova continued to dance with the American Ballet Theatre.

Makasar (Indonesia): *see* Ujung Pandang.

Makassar Strait, also spelled MACASSAR STRAIT, Indonesian SELAT MAKASAR, narrow passage of the west-central Pacific Ocean, Indonesia. Extending 500 miles (800 km) northeast–southwest from the Celebes Sea to the Java Sea, the strait passes between Borneo on the west and Celebes on the east and is 80 to 230 miles (130 to 370 km) wide. It is a deep waterway containing numerous islands, the largest of which are Laut Island and Sebuku. Balikpapan is the principal settlement along the strait on Borneo, Ujung Pandang (formerly Makasar) the largest on Celebes. In January 1942, during World War II, combined U.S. and Dutch military forces engaged a Japanese naval expedition in the strait. In five days of bitter fighting, the Allies were unable to prevent a Japanese landing at Balikpapan, the first step taken in the occupation of Dutch Borneo.

Makati, city, south-central Luzon, Philippines. A southern residential, financial, and industrial suburb of Manila, it has a large, modern manufacturing complex along its segment of the belt highway, where a number of national and foreign firms are located. Makati's Forbes Park sector, called millionaires row, has many foreign residents. Fort Andres Bonifacio (formerly Fort William McKinley) is the site of the Manila American Cemetery and Memorial, the largest cemetery maintained by the American Battle Monuments Program. Pop. (1990) mun., 453,000.

Makeevka (Ukraine): *see* Makiyivka.

Makemie, Francis (b. *c.* 1658, County Donegal, Ire.—d. 1707/08, probably near New York City [U.S.]), colonial Presbyterian leader at Accomack, Va., who joined in forming the first American presbytery (1706) that united the scattered Dissenting churches in Virginia, Maryland, Pennsylvania, and New Jersey.

During the 1680s and '90s Makemie had preached and traded in Virginia, Maryland, and the Carolinas while also seeking to unite the various struggling Protestant churches of these areas in a common cause. Anglican attempts to silence him by arrest awakened Makemie to the churches' plight, and, with the help of Increase Mather and other Boston Congregationalists, he resisted the efforts of the Church of England to suppress dissident churches. In 1707 Makemie was acquitted of the charge of preaching on Long Island without a license, and thereafter the provisions of Britain's Toleration Act were claimed by all Dissenters in the American Colonies.

Makeni, town, central Sierra Leone. Makeni grew as a trade and collecting centre among the Temne people. Palm oil and kernels and rice collected in Makeni are transported by road to Freetown, 85 miles (135 km) west-southwest. The town is known for Gara tie-dyeing, an important industrial activity of Makeni women. Pop. (1985 prelim.) 49,038.

maker (Scottish poet): *see* makar.

makeup, in the performing arts, motion pictures, or television, any of the materials used by actors for cosmetic purposes and as an aid in taking on the appearance appropriate to the characters they play. (*See also* cosmetic.)

In the Greek and Roman theatre the actors' use of masks precluded the need for makeup. In the religious plays of medieval Europe, actors playing God or Christ painted their faces white or sometimes gold, while the faces of angels were coloured bright red. During the Renaissance, popular characters in French farce wore false beards of lamb's wool and whitened their faces with flour. It is known that on the stage of Elizabethan England, actors playing ghosts and murderers powdered their faces with chalk and that those appearing as blacks and Moors were blackened with soot or burnt cork. Little attempt was made to achieve historical accuracy in either makeup or costuming until early in the 19th century.

Early stage lighting, provided first by candles and later by oil lamps, was dim and ineffectual; consequently, crudity in makeup passed unnoticed. With the introduction of gas, limelights, and, finally, electric lights into the theatre came the need for new makeup materials and more skillful techniques of application. Crude, inartistic effects could not be hidden under the revealing light of electricity. A solution was found with the use of stick greasepaint, invented in the 1860s in Germany by Ludwig Leichner, a Wagnerian opera singer. By 1890 the demand for stage makeup had warranted its manufacture on a commercial scale. Half a century later, greasepaint in stick form had given way to more easily handled creams.

On the modern stage, makeup is a necessity because powerful stage-lighting systems may remove all colour from a performer's complexion and will eliminate shadows and lines. Makeup restores this colour and defines the facial features to ensure a natural appearance. It also helps the player to look and feel the part, a consideration especially helpful in character interpretations. A theatrical makeup kit typically includes makeup base colours, rouges, coloured liners for shadow and highlighting effects, eye makeup and false eyelashes, various cleansers, powder and powder puffs, putties for making prosthetic features, adhesives, wigs, and facial hairpieces or mohair to construct them. The art of stage makeup has become so complex that most theatrical companies employ a professional makeup artist who creates and applies makeup suitable to the actors' various roles.

Stage makeup proved to be wholly unsatisfactory for the motion-picture medium. Necessarily heavy applications made it impossible to appear natural in close-ups, and the range of colours developed for theatre failed to meet the quite different requirements of motion-picture lighting and film emulsions.

The first makeup designed expressly for motion pictures was created by Max Factor in 1910. It was a light, semiliquid greasepaint available in jars in a precisely graduated range of tan tone, suitable for the lighting and orthochromatic film emulsion used during that period.

The introduction of panchromatic film and incandescent lighting on movie sets eventually made it possible to standardize the film, lighting, and colours of makeup that were most effective for motion pictures. The Society of Motion Picture Engineers conducted a special series of tests for this purpose in 1928. As a result of these experiments, Max Factor created a completely new range of makeup colours called panchromatic makeup, an achievement for which he won a special Academy of Motion Picture Arts and Sciences Award.

Motion-picture makeup is both corrective and creative. Makeup must always be applied skillfully, delicately, and subtly so that facial expression will have natural freedom. On the screen, particularly in close-ups, the face may be magnified many times larger than life size, so that every complexion flaw or crudely applied makeup artifice is clearly discernible. As a corrective art, makeup serves to (1) cover blemishes, (2) provide the face with a smooth and even colour tone for the most effective photography, (3) clearly define the facial features for more visibly expressive action, (4) make the player appear more attractive, and (5) ensure a uniform appearance before the camera. As a creative art, makeup enables the player to take on the appearance of almost any type of character. It can make the young appear to age believably and the old appear to look young again. Special makeup devices can supply the performer with any desired facial feature, from the weird effects of science fiction and horror movies to the bruises, wounds, and scars of western and war films.

The introduction of colour to motion pictures created new makeup problems. Various colour films caused existing greasepaint used on players' faces to appear yellowish or red and blue on the screen. After some experimentation, a solution was found with a successful solid (Pan-Cake) makeup that was applied with a moist sponge. Makeup charts indicate the correct colours to use for each type of colour film.

The arrival of television created new makeup problems. Light complexions looked ghostly, and dark complexions dirty. Street makeup on women either disappeared or looked dark or dowdy. Some of the colour makeup mixtures that had been developed for motion-picture makeup proved satisfactory, but others had to be modified. New problems arose when colour television came into use. A green dress might appear blue on a colour television screen and no harm was done; but a face that under lights looked natural to the human eye might be televised as green. At length, a range of television makeup shades was developed that would televise naturally on black-and-white as well as colour transmissions.

Makgadikgadi, formerly MAKARIKARI, region of sandy alkaline clay depressions (pans) in northeastern Botswana. The pans form a broad inland basin that descends gradually from 3,150 feet (960 m) in the west to 2,975 feet (900 m) and then rise more steeply to between 3,500 and 4,000 feet (1,050 and 1,200 m) eastward. They make up the lowest part of the Kalahari (desert), the elevation of which is otherwise fairly uniform (3,000 feet) and which occupies the majority of the area of Botswana. The area was occupied by a great lake at various times in the Pleistocene Epoch. The pans are flooded in normal rainy seasons by the Boteti (Botletle) River, on the west, which in turn is flooded by the Okavango River, to the north. The Makgadikgadi pans are among the largest in the world, with Ntwetwe Pan measuring approximately 75 miles (120 km) east-west and 100 miles (160 km) northeast-southwest and the smaller Sowa Pan about 45 miles (70 km) wide and 70 miles (110 km) long. In normal weather the pans consist of a series of shallow pools, sandy alkaline clays, and islands of grass and are the habitat of thousands of flamingos. Commercial exploitation of the soda deposits of the region has not been undertaken because of the lack of water supplies and electrical power, although the economic potential of the salt deposits has been fully assessed.

Makhachkala, also spelled MACHAČKALA, formerly (until 1922) PETROVSK PORT, port and capital of Dagestan republic, southwestern Russia. The city is situated along the western shore of the Caspian Sea, at the northern end of a narrow coastal plain. Founded as the Petrovskoye fortress in 1844, it became Petrovsk Port in 1857 and was renamed in 1921 after the Dagestani revolutionary Makhach. Present-day Makhachkala is a seaport linking the North Caucasus, Transcaucasus, and southern Ukraine with the western regions of Kazakhstan. It also serves as the terminal of an oil pipeline from Grozny. Its industries include machine building and chemical and textile manufacturing. Makhachkala has a branch of the Academy of Sciences, a university, and medical, agricultural, and teacher-training institutes. Pop. (1993 est.) 328,000.

maki-e (Japanese: "sprinkled picture"), lacquer ware on which the design is made by sprinkling or spraying wet lacquer with metallic powder, usually gold or silver, from a dusting tube, sprinkler canister (*makizutsu*), or hair-tipped paint brush (*kebo*). The technique was developed mainly during the Heian period (794–1185) to decorate screens, albums, *inrō*, letter boxes, and ink-slab cases. The oldest preserved piece is from 919.

Maki-e can be left to dry, as is *maki-hanashi*, or relacquered and polished (*togidashi maki-e*). It is frequently decorated with reed-style pictures (*ashide-e*) or combined with inlays of other metals or mother-of-pearl (*raden*). *Hiramaki-e* has a low-relief design, and *takamaki-e* has a high-relief design.

makimono, in Japanese art, hand scroll, or scroll painting designed to be held in the hand (as compared to a hanging scroll). *See* scroll painting.

Makin Atoll (Kiribati): *see* Butaritari Atoll.

Makira (Solomon Islands): *see* San Cristóbal.

Makiyivka, Russian MAKEYEVKA, also spelled MAKEEVKA, or MAKEYEVKA, city, Donetsk *oblast* (province), eastern Ukraine. The city was founded as Dmitriyevsk in 1899 with the establishment of a metallurgical works; the nearby small village of Makiyivka was later absorbed into the city. Dmitriyevsk subsequently developed as one of the largest coal-mining and industrial centres of the Donets Basin coalfield; in 1931 it was renamed Makiyivka. There are many coal pits in and around the city. Makiyivka's modern industries include one of the largest integrated iron and steel works in Ukraine. There are also other metalworking and coke-chemical plants and factories for pneumatic machinery, shoemaking, and food processing. The city is rather dispersed, with numerous residential communities surrounding individual industrial plants over an extensive area; it is gradually extending to form a single metropolitan area with the nearby city of Donetsk, which lies just a few miles to the southwest. Makiyivka has a large research institute in mining safety. Pop. (1993 est.) 424,000.

Housing estate for miners, Makiyivka, Ukraine
Novosti Press Agency

Maklakov, Vasily Alekseyevich (b. May 10 [May 22, New Style], 1869—d. July 15, 1957, Zürich, Switz.), liberal Russian political figure and a leading advocate of a constitutional Russian state.

Maklakov was the son of a Moscow professor. He was impressed by French political life during a visit to Paris in 1889 and spent most of his career attempting to establish a similar system in Russia. Entering the bar in 1895, he joined a moderate reform group in 1903 and played an active part in the organization of the Constitutional Democratic Party two years later, serving on its central committee. He was elected to the second state Duma (parliament) in 1907 and served in the subsequent Dumas until the Revolution of 1917. A respected orator and a voluminous writer, he tended toward conservatism, opposing alliances with revolutionaries. But he grew hostile to the government as the years passed and actively supported the Progressive Bloc, a coalition of liberal parties in the fourth Duma that called for sweeping reforms.

The provisional government sent him as ambassador to France just prior to the takeover by the Bolsheviks. Later he was prominent among Russian emigrés in Paris, writing several books on the history of social thought and the Russian liberal movement.

Makó, city, surrounded by (but administratively separate from) Makó district, Csongrád *megye* (county), southeastern Hungary. It is situated near the northern bank of the Maros River and close to the Romanian frontier. It is named after a soldier on whom the village was bestowed by King Endre II in the 13th century. The settlement was almost completely destroyed twice, once by the Turks and later by the flooding of the Maros River in 1821.

The city today is a traditional market centre surrounded by fertile farmland, known for its production of onions (exported in large quantities ever since the end of the 19th century), high grain yield, and livestock. The city has long-established milling industries and more recent textile mills and an agricultural machinery factory. Most of the buildings are in a Neo-classical style, and there are thermal baths in the centre of the city. It is a junction of secondary and minor roads. The journalist Joseph Pulitzer (1847–1911) was born in Makó. Pop. (1999 est.) 25,622.

A list of the abbreviations used in the MICROPAEDIA *will be found at the end of this volume*

---

mako shark (*Isurus*), any of certain swift, active, potentially dangerous sharks of the mackerel shark family, Isuridae. Two species are generally recognized, *I. oxyrinchus* of the Atlantic and the closely related *I. glaucus* of the Indo-Pacific.

Mako shark (*Isurus glaucus*)
Painting by Richard Ellis

Mako sharks, also known as sharp-nosed mackerel sharks and (in Australia) blue pointers, range throughout tropical and temperate seas. They are streamlined and relatively slender, with pointed snouts, crescent-shaped tails, and long, slender teeth. They are blue gray, appearing deep blue in the water, with contrasting white bellies. They grow to a length and weight of about 4 metres (13 feet) and 450 kilograms (1,000 pounds). Mako sharks prey on fishes, such as herring, mackerel, and swordfish. They are outstanding game fish, prized for their fighting qualities and repeated leaps out of the water.

Makokou, also spelled MAKOKU, town and capital of Ogooué-Ivindo province, northeastern Gabon, central Africa, on the Ivindo River where it receives the Liboumba and Mounianghi rivers. Pygmies live in the surrounding forest. The town lies in the heart of a major lumbering region, and, although it is rather isolated from the rest of the country, transportation is improving: a modern highway bridge spans the Ivindo, there is an airport, and the town is on the projected route of a northeast spur of the Trans-Gabon Railway. Pop. (1993) 9,849.

Makonde, also spelled MACONDE, Bantu-speaking people living in northeastern Mozambique and southeastern Tanzania.

Their economy rests primarily on swidden (slash-and-burn) agriculture, supplemented by hunting; corn (maize), sorghum, and cassava are the major crops. Many Makonde have migrated to other parts of the East African coast in search of employment. They are renowned for their wood carving.

The Makonde reckon descent matrilineally. Polygyny is common. Primary marriage always entails a bride-price.

Each settlement has a hereditary headman and an advisory council of elders. The Makonde lack a more embracing political structure, each settlement being independent. Though they have been under heavy Arab influence for a very long time, few have converted to Islām.

Makonnen, Tafari (Ethiopian emperor): *see* Haile Selassie I.

Makran, also spelled MEKRAN, Persian MOKRĀN, Pakistani MAKRĀN, coastal region of Baluchistan in southeastern Iran and southwestern Pakistan, constituting the Makran Coast, a 600-mi (1,000-km) stretch along the Gulf of Oman from Ra's (cape) al-Kūh, Iran (west of Jask), to Lasbela District, Pakistan (near Karāchi). The name is applied to a former province of Iran, and the Makran of Pakistan is sometimes known as Kech Makran to distinguish it from the Iranian portion.

Pakistani Makran, a former princely state that acceded in 1948, was constituted after 1955 a district (area 28,164 sq mi [72,944 sq km]) of Kalāt division. Now a part of Baluchistan Province, Pakistan, it is bounded east by Khuzdār and Lasbela districts, south by the Arabian Sea, west by Iran, and north by the Siāhān Range. Turbat is district headquarters and Panjgūr the chief town of the interior. Aside from the coastal areas, the terrain is mostly mountainous, consisting of east–west parallel ranges rising to about 7,000 ft (2,100 m) and enclosing fertile narrow valleys, including those of the Kech (upper Dasht) and Bolida. The chief spring crops (*jopag*) are wheat and barley, and the autumn crop (*eraht*) is *jowār* (sorghum). Dates, however, are the main crop; cultivation has been extended by irrigation projects. *Laghati* (compressed dates) constitute the staple food of the poor. Irrigation is provided by flooding, subterranean channels (*kārez*), riverbed pools (*kaurjo*), and springs. Sheep are also bred. Makran's 200-mi sandy coastline in Pakistan lies longitudinally with many hammerhead peninsulas. Past volcanic action is evidenced by occasional volcanoes of boiling mud along the coast. The chief ports are Gwādar, which belonged to the Sultanate of Muscat and Oman till 1958; Ormāra; and Pasni, all being difficult of approach because of off-shore sandbars. Fishing is the main coastal occupation.

Makran, the ancient Gedrosia of the Persian and Macedonian empires and the scene of Alexander the Great's retreat from India (325 BC), has been strategically significant in the history of Iran and India. The etymology of the name is uncertain, chiefly regarded either as a corruption of Māhī Khūrān (Fish Eaters), identified with the Ichthyophagoi (now represented by the Mēds) mentioned in the *Indica* of the 2nd-century-AD Greek historian Arrian, or as a Dravidian name appearing as Makara in the *Bṛhat-saṃhitā* of the 6th-century-AD astrologist Varāhamihira in a list of tribes contiguous to India on the west.

The population is predominantly Arab, the Arabs having held Makran before they conquered Sind in the 5th century. Other groups are the Darzadis, regarded as of aboriginal descent; Mēds (fishermen); and Koras (seamen). The coastal blacks are descended from imported slaves.

Makrān, also spelled MEKRĀN, division of Baluchistan province, Pakistan. Administratively it comprises Turbat, Gwādar, and Panjgūr districts and has an area of 23,460 sq mi (60,761 sq km). It is bounded by the Siāhān range (north), which separates it from Khārān district, by Kalāt and Las Bela districts (east), the Arabian Sea (south), and Iran (west). Makrān has a seacoast about 200 mi (320 km) long. The interior of the division is mountainous, with the southernmost portion of the Makrān Range lying on the coast; another of its ranges occupies the central area, while in the north the highest portion of the Makrān range is separated from Khārān district by the Siāhān range. These ranges consist of a sequence of ridges, scoured and cut by torrential watercourses that are dry except after heavy floods. The Dasht River in the west is the major river. Temperatures vary, with the dry central area having the greatest extremes; the north has cool summers and cold winters.

With the arrival of the British in 1872 a commission was sent to demarcate the Persia–Makrān boundary. In 1903 Lord Curzon landed at Pasni and appointed assistants at Panjgūr and Gwādar. With the British maintaining political control, Makrān continued as an administrative division of Kalāt until Pakistan's creation in 1947. Makrān became a part of the Baluchistan States Union in 1949.

Barley, wheat, rice, and dates are the chief agricultural products and the main sources of income. Fishing (sardines and sharks) and leatherwork are also important. Turbat, a district headquarters, has an airstrip and is located on a fair-weather road 250 mi from Kalāt. Pasni, which is about 25 mi from Turbat, was destroyed by an earthquake in 1945 and has since been rebuilt. Panjgūr is a district headquarters, to which most of the division offices of Makrān move during the summer. Jīwani is a seaport 300 mi from Karāchi; its population comprises the majority of the Baluchi Med who live in their traditional mud huts. Gwādar is an important fishing and trading centre with many commercial functions. Pop. (1981 prelim.) 652,000.

Makri rug, floor covering handwoven in or near the coastal village of Fethiye, southwest Turkey. These are rare, comparatively small rugs with rather simple, bold designs and rich, vibrant colours.

Makri rug, 19th century; in the Textile Museum, Washington, D.C.
Textile Museum Collection, Washington, D.C.; photograph, Otto E. Nelson—EB Inc.

Having an arched design, or miḥrāb, at each end of the central field, Makri rugs are not clearly prayer rugs, which normally have only one miḥrāb. They often show two or three longitudinal panels, which may have different ground colours. Each panel may contain a series of large blossoms or a rod, from which sprout pairs of winglike leaves.

maktab, also called KUTTĀB (Arabic: "school"), Muslim elementary school. Until the 20th century, boys were instructed in Qur'ān recitation, reading, writing, and grammar in *maktabs*, which were the only means of mass education. The teacher was not always highly qualified and had other religious duties, and the equipment of a *maktab* was often simple. During the 20th century, government-supported primary schools have tended to supplant the *maktab* in Muslim countries.

Makú, any of several South American Indian societies who traditionally hunted, gathered wild plant foods, and fished in the basins of the Río Negro and the Vaupés River in Colombia. The Makú comprised small bands of forest nomads. The present-day Makú are remnants of an aboriginal population who were killed or assimilated by expanding Arawak, Carib, and Tucano tribes. The Makú language is not related to others, and the several groups speak quite different dialects. It is estimated that they numbered about 2,000, but they are now on the verge of extinction.

Little is known of Makú culture. As nomadic hunters, gatherers, and fishermen, they use bows and arrows, blowguns, stone axes, and clubs. Some have recently adopted farming and live in sedentary villages.

In the Brazilian Guiana Highlands, the Makú of the Uraricoera River basin speak an isolated language. They obtain European products through trade with other Indians.

Makua language, also spelled MACUA, or MAKWA, Bantu language spoken by the Makua and Lomue peoples of northern Mozambique. (The Bantu languages form a subgroup of the Benue-Congo group of the Niger-Congo language family.) Makua had about 7,400,000 speakers in the late 20th century.

Makura no sōshi (Japanese literature): *see* Pillow Book.

Makurdi, town, capital of Benue state, east-central Nigeria. It lies on the south bank of the Benue River. Founded about 1927 when the railroad from Port Harcourt (279 miles [449 km] south-southwest) was extended to Jos and Kaduna, Makurdi rapidly developed into a transportation and market centre. In 1976, following the division of Benue-Plateau state into two states, Makurdi was selected as the capital of Benue state.

The 0.5-mile- (0.8-kilometre-) long combined rail and road bridge (1932) across the Benue River consolidated the town's position as a major transit point. It is now a major transshipment point for cattle from Nigeria's northern states. From June to November, when the Niger River has high water, Makurdi serves as a port from which goods, including locally grown sesame seeds and cotton, are shipped to Lokoja (126 miles west at the Niger-Benue confluence) and to the Niger River delta ports. The town is also a local trade centre for the yams, sorghum, millet, rice, cassava, shea nuts, sesame oil, peanuts (groundnuts), soybeans, and cotton raised by the Tiv people of the surrounding area. It is also the site of a boatyard that builds medium-size rivercraft. In the late 1970s an oil pipeline was built from the refinery near Port Harcourt to Makurdi. There are extensive limestone and marble deposits in the area around Makurdi, and a cement plant has opened at Yandev, southeast of the town.

Makurdi has the Murtala Muhammed College of Arts, Science, and Technology (1976); the Federal University of Technology; an Assembly of God commercial institute; and a government craft school. It is also served by a hospital. The Benue state radiobroadcasting service operates from the town. Makurdi is the headquarters of the Lower Benue River Basin Authority. The town is located on the main highway network and has an airport. Pop. (1991) 151,515.

Mala (Solomon Islands): *see* Malaita.

Malabar Christians: *see* Christians of Saint Thomas.

Malabar Coast, name long applied to the southern part of India's western coast, approximately from Goa southward, which is bordered on the east by the Western Ghāts range. The name has sometimes encompassed the entire western coast of peninsular India.

Rice cultivation in the Malabar Coast area of India
Harrison Forman

It now includes most of Kerala state and the coastal region of Karnātaka state. The coast consists of a continuous belt of sand dunes. Behind this are many lagoons paralleling the coast and linked by canals to form inland waterways, much used by small boats. Inland is level alluvial land, well watered by streams flowing down from the Western Ghāts. Rice and spices are the principal crops, with coconut palms on the coastal sand dunes. Fishing is also important. Cochin is the main port.

A large part of the Malabar Coast fell within the ancient kingdom of Keralaputra (Cera dynasty). The Portuguese established several trading posts there and were followed by the Dutch in the 17th century and the French in the 18th. The British gained control of the region in the late 18th century.

Malabarese Catholic Church, a Chaldean rite church of southern India (Kerala) that united with Rome after the Portuguese colonization of Goa at the end of the 15th century. The Portuguese viewed these Christians of St. Thomas, as they called themselves, as Nestorian heretics, despite their traditional alignment with Rome since about the 6th century. Although the Malabarese formally acknowledged the pope at the Synod of Diamper in 1599, the Portuguese subjected them to intense Latinization. The Malabarese reacted by breaking with Rome in 1653. Only when the Syrian bishop Sebastiani was installed in 1661 did most of the schismatic Malabarese return to the Roman Catholic church. The remainder affiliated with the Syrian Orthodox (Jacobite) patriarch of Antioch.

The Malabarese Catholics were given administrators separate from those of the Indian Catholics of the Latin rite in 1877 and in 1923 regained their own hierarchy. They use Eastern Syriac as the liturgical language.

Malabo, formerly (until 1973) SANTA ISABEL, capital of Equatorial Guinea. It lies on the northern edge of the island of Bioko (or Fernando Po) on the rim of a sunken volcano. With an average temperature of 77° F (25° C) and an annual rainfall of 75 inches (1,900 mm), it has one of the more onerous climates in the Bight of Biafra (Gulf of Guinea). Malabo is the republic's commercial and financial centre. Its harbour can dock several ships, and the main activity is the export of cocoa, timber, and coffee. It also has an international airport with air links to Bata, in continental Equatorial Guinea, and to the West African republics. The city's European population declined after the riots of 1969 and after its Nigerian contract workers returned to Nigeria in the mid-1970s. Pop. (1995 est.) 47,500.

Malacca (West Malaysia): *see* Melaka.

Malacca, Strait of, waterway connecting the Andaman Sea (Indian Ocean) and the South China Sea (Pacific Ocean). It runs between the Indonesian island of Sumatra to the west and West Malaysia and peninsular Thailand to the east and has an area of 25,000 square miles (65,000 square km). The strait is 500 miles (800 km) long and is funnel-shaped, with a width of only 40 miles (65 km) in the south that broadens northward to 155 miles (249 km) between Sabang and the Kra Isthmus. The strait derived its name from the trading port of Melaka (formerly Malacca)—which was of importance in the 16th and 17th centuries—on the Malayan coast.

In the south of the strait, water depths rarely exceed 120 feet (37 m) and are usually about 90 feet (27 m). Toward the northwest, the bottom gradually deepens until it reaches to about 650 feet (200 m) as the strait merges with the Andaman Basin. Numerous islets, some fringed by reefs and sand ridges, hinder passage at the southern entrance to the strait. The sand ridges are identified as accumulations of material that have been brought down by rivers from Sumatra.

Geologically, the strait belongs to the Sunda Shelf, which was an extensive, low-relief land surface at the beginning of Quaternary time (about 1.6 million years ago), and appears to have remained undisturbed by crustal movements since the Late Tertiary Period (about 7 million years ago). The strait attained its present configuration after having been inundated by the postglacial rise of the sea level resulting from the melting of land ice in higher latitudes.

Coastal swamps are commonly found on both sides of the strait, and a huge, low-lying swamp forest lies along the eastern coast of Sumatra. The strait is silting on both sides, and, near the mouths of large rivers, silt accretions range from about 30 feet (9 m) on the coast of Malaya to about 650 feet (200 m) annually on the east coast of Sumatra.

The climate of the strait is hot and humid and is characterized by the northeast monsoon during the (northern) winter and the southwest monsoon during the summer. The average annual rainfall varies between 76 inches (1,941 mm) and 101 inches (2,565 mm). Throughout the year, the current flows northwest through the strait. Surface-water temperatures in the strait are 87° to 88° F (30.5° to 31° C) in the east and may be as much as four degrees (F) lower in the west. The close proximity of land and the discharge of large rivers result in a low salinity for the strait.

As the link between the Indian Ocean and the South China Sea, the Strait of Malacca is the shortest sea route between India and China and hence is one of the most heavily traveled shipping channels in the world. In early times, it helped to determine the direction of major Asian migrations of peoples through the Malayan archipelago. The strait was successively controlled by the Arabs, the Portuguese, the Dutch, and the British.

The existence of oil wells on Sumatra's east coast, just off the Sunda Shelf region, has led a number of companies to prospect for petroleum in the strait in the 20th century. Besides other ships, the strait affords passage to giant oil tankers voyaging between the Middle East oil fields and ports in Japan and elsewhere in East Asia.

Malacca, sultanate of (1403?–1511), Malay dynasty that ruled the great entrepôt of Malacca (Melaka) and its dependencies and provided Malay history with its golden age, still evoked in idiom and institutions. The founder and first ruler of Malacca, Paramesvara (d. 1424, Malacca), a Sumatran prince who had fled his native Palembang under Javanese attack, established himself briefly in Tumasik (now Singapore) and settled in Malacca in the last years of the 14th century or early in the 15th. Malacca, on a fine natural harbour, commanded the main sea route between India and China through the strait that now bears its name. Paramesvara, who became a Muslim and took the title Sultan Iskandar Shah in 1414, early established tributary relations with Ming China, benefiting greatly from that kingdom's newly rearoused interest in trade with the West. By the 1430s the city had become the preeminent commercial emporium in Southeast Asia, resorted to alike by local traders, Indian, Arab, and Persian merchants, and Chinese trade missions.

Little is known of Iskandar Shah's immediate successor, but under the following ruler, Sultan Muzaffar Shah (reigned 1445–59?), the city-state became a major territorial as well as commercial power in the region and a source for the further diffusion of Islām within the Indonesian archipelago. Shortly after his succession, Muzaffar Shah refused to pay the customary tribute to Malacca's chief rival in the peninsula, the Thai kingdom of Ayutthaya, and his forces repelled two Siamese punitive expeditions in 1445 and 1456, later acquiring Selangor to the northwest as a source of food and taking control of strategic portions of the Sumatra coast across the strait.

During that period a warrior leader known as Tun Perak (d. 1498) came to the fore. In 1456 he was appointed *bendahara* (chief minister) by Muzaffar Shah. Tun Perak thereafter played a dominant role in the history of the state, securing the succession of the next three rulers—Sultans Mansur Shah, reigned about 1459–77; Ala'ud-din, 1477–88; and Mahmud Shah, 1488–1511, all of whom were related to him—and pursuing an aggressive foreign policy that saw the sultanate established as a tributary empire embracing the whole of the Malay Peninsula and much of eastern Sumatra. At the court itself, especially under Mansur Shah, the wealth of the state permitted great panoply and display and encouraged the growth of literature and learning and a lively political and religious life, later celebrated in the classical Malay chronicle *Sejarah Melayu* (*c.* 1612). The city finally fell to the Portuguese in 1511.

Malachi, The Book of, also called THE PROPHECY OF MALACHIAS, the last of 12 Old Testament books that bear the names of the Minor Prophets, grouped together as the Twelve in the Jewish canon. The author is unknown; Malachi is merely a transliteration of a Hebrew word meaning "my messenger."

The book consists of six distinct sections, each in the form of a question-and-answer discussion. With the aid of this unusual discussion technique, the prophet defends the justice of God to a community that had begun to doubt that justice because its eschatological (end of the world) expectations were still unfulfilled. The author calls for fidelity to Yahweh's Covenant. He emphasizes the necessity of proper worship, condemns divorce, and announces that the day of judgment is imminent. Faithfulness to these cultic and moral responsibilities will be rewarded; unfaithfulness will bring a curse.

The book belongs to the first half of the 5th century BC, for it clearly presupposes the reconstructed Temple (dedicated in 516 BC) but does not reflect the reconstitution of the religious community that took place under Nehemiah and Ezra about 450 BC.

malachite, a minor ore but a widespread mineral of copper, basic copper carbonate, $Cu_2CO_3(OH)_2$. Because of its distinctive bright green colour and its presence in the weathered zone of nearly all copper deposits, malachite serves as a prospecting guide for that metal. Notable occurrences are Nizhne-Tagilsk, Siberia; Chessy, Fr.; Tsumeb, Namibia;

Malachite and azurite from Bisbee, Ariz.
Floyd R. Getsinger—EB Inc.

and Bisbee, Ariz., U.S. Malachite has been used as an ornamental stone and as a gemstone. It is more abundant and widespread than azurite, with which it is usually found. For detailed physical properties, *see* carbonate mineral (table).

malachite green, also called ANILINE GREEN, BENZALDEHYDE GREEN, or CHINA GREEN, triphenylmethane dye used medicinally in dilute solution as a local antiseptic. Malachite green is effective against fungi and gram-positive bacteria. In the fish-breeding industry it has been used to control the fungus *Saprolegnia,* a water mold that kills the eggs and young fry.

Malachite green also is used as a direct dye for silk, wool, jute, and leather and to dye cotton that has been mordanted with tannin. Prepared from benzaldehyde and dimethylaniline, the dye occurs as lustrous green crystals soluble in water and in alcohol. For malachite green G, *see* brilliant green.

Małachowski, Stanisław (b. Aug. 24, 1736, Końskie, Pol.—d. Dec. 29, 1809, Warsaw, Duchy of Warsaw [now in Poland]), Polish statesman who presided over Poland's historic Four Years' Sejm, a constituent Diet that met in 1788–92.

Małachowski, detail from an oil painting by Jozef Peszka, 1790–91; in the National Museum, Warsaw
By courtesy of the National Museum, Warsaw

The son of Jan Małachowski, the royal grand chancellor, Małachowski was named marshal (speaker) of the Sejm (Diet) in 1788. He was the prime force behind a constitution, adopted in 1791, that embodied such modern western European reforms as majority rule in parliament, separation of powers, and enfranchisement of the middle classes; this constitution was abrogated at the Second Partition of Poland in 1792. In 1807–09 Małachowski served as president of the senate (government) of the Duchy of Warsaw, promoted by Napoleon.

Malachy, SAINT, Gaelic in full MÁEL MÁEDOC ÚA MORGAIR (b. 1094, Armagh, County Armagh, Ire.—d. Nov. 2/3, 1148, Clairvaux, Fr.; canonized 1190; feast day November 3), celebrated archbishop and papal legate who is considered to be the dominant figure of church reform in 12th-century Ireland.

Malachy was educated at Armagh, where he was ordained priest in 1119. Archbishop Ceallach (Celsus) of Armagh, during his absence to administer the bishopric of Dublin, appointed Malachy vicar in Armagh. There he established his reputation as a reformer by persuading the Irish Catholic church to accept Pope Gregory VII's reform then sweeping the European continent; he is also credited with having introduced the Roman liturgy into Ireland. In about 1123 Malachy was consecrated bishop in County Down, where he restored the celebrated Abbey of Bangor; the following year he was appointed bishop of Connor, County Antrim, but about 1127 violent disputes over his position compelled him to leave, and he subsequently became abbot of Iveragh, County Kerry.

Ceallach, while dying, nominated (1129) Malachy as his successor, both as abbot and as archbishop, thus breaking the time-honoured Irish custom of hereditary succession. Deferring for fear of another vehement opposition, Malachy finally was induced (1132) to accept his new prelacy. For five years he ruled the diocese and the whole province without entering the city of Armagh. He resigned in 1137. To secure the pallium (*i.e.,* symbol of metropolitan jurisdiction) for his successor at Armagh, he went in 1139 to Rome, where Pope Innocent II made him papal legate in Ireland but refused to grant the pallium. Malachy visited the celebrated abbot Bernard at Clairvaux and later introduced the Cistercians to Ireland by founding (1142) Mellifont in County Louth.

On his way to Rome to make a second application for the pallium, Malachy died at Clairvaux in the arms of Bernard. The establishment of a regular hierarchy in the Irish church—the object of his life—was realized at the Council of Kells, County Meath, in 1152. He was the first Irish Catholic to be canonized. No writings of Malachy are known to exist, but falsely ascribed to him is the Prophecy of the Popes, a 16th-century forgery consisting of a list of mottoes supposedly fitting pontiffs from the mid-12th century to the end of time.

BIBLIOGRAPHY. Ailbe J. Luddy, *Life of St. Malachy* (1930, reissued 1950); James O'Boyle, *Life of St. Malachy* (1931).

malacostracan (class Malacostraca), any member of a widely distributed crustacean group of marine, freshwater, and terrestrial invertebrates.

A brief treatment of malacostracans follows. For full treatment, *see* MACROPAEDIA: Crustaceans.

Malacostracans typically are free-living, but they do form symbiotic, commensal, or parasitic relationships with other invertebrates and marine vertebrates. They account for more than two-thirds of all extant crustacean species.

About 22,000 species have been described. The class includes some of the most highly evolved invertebrates—the lobster, crab, and shrimp (order Decapoda), the sand flea (Amphipoda), the pill bug (Isopoda), the mantis shrimp (Stomatopoda), and many other forms. Some are commercially important.

The malacostracans include the largest of all arthropods, the giant crab (*Macrocheira kaempferi*) of Japan, whose outstretched limbs may extend 3.6 m (about 12 feet) or more. The class also includes many forms smaller than 1 mm (0.04 inch). Malacostracans typically have compound eyes (*i.e.,* containing many facets). A carapace, or shield, covers the upper surface of the cephalothorax—the combined head and thorax, or midsection. The thorax has eight segments and eight pairs of appendages, the abdomen six segments and six pairs of appendages.

Málaga, *provincia,* in the *comunidad autónoma* ("autonomous community") of Andalusia, southern Spain, on the Mediterranean coast. It has an area of 2,809 square miles (7,276 square km). Its northern half belongs to the Andalusian plain, while its southern half is mountainous and rises steeply from the coast, along which there is a narrow strip of lowland. The Sierra de Alhama separates Málaga from Granada (east); and not far from the Cádiz (western) boundary the sierras of Ronda, Mijas, Tolox, and Bermeja converge to form a summit of nearly 6,500 feet (1,980 m). The principal rivers in Málaga are the Guadalhorce and the Guadiaro.

The province is largely agricultural, and fruits, vegetables, olives, and grapes are grown along the coastal lowlands and in the rich interior valleys. There are considerable mineral resources in the mountains, chiefly iron and lead. Salt is mined in the north. The warm, sunny climate of the coast (part of the Costa del Sol) has made the area popular with tourists, especially around Torremolinos and Málaga (*q.v.*) city, the provincial capital. Other attractions include the Menga, Viera, Nerja, and El Romeral caves, with their prehistoric paintings and relics, and a national hunting region in the Serranía de Ronda, north of Marbella. Besides Málaga, the most important cities in the province are Ronda and Antequera. The University of Málaga was established at El Ejido in 1972. Pop. (1999 est.) 1,258,084.

Málaga, port city and capital of Málaga *provincia,* in the *comunidad autónoma* ("autonomous community") of Andalusia, southern Spain. It lies along a wide bay of the Mediterranean Sea at the mouth of the Guadalmedina River in the centre of the Costa del Sol. It was founded by the Phoenicians in the 12th century BC, conquered successively by the Romans and the Visigoths, and taken by the Moors in 711. Under Moorish rule it became one of the most important cities in Andalusia. When the caliphate of Córdoba disintegrated, the kingdom of Málaga was founded, ruled over by emirs who named it "terrestrial paradise." After several unsuccessful attempts, the Christians took the city on Aug. 19, 1487.

The Alcazaba, a Moorish castle converted to a museum, Málaga city, Spain
Sven Samelius

The Guadalmedina River, which before the construction of the dam at Agujero caused frequent severe flooding, flows through Málaga from north to south, while above the city towers Mount Gibralfaro (558 feet [170 m]), crowned by an ancient Arab fortress. The cathedral, in the centre of the old city, was begun in 1528 on the site of a mosque; the interior, main facade, and one of the towers were completed in 1782, but the second tower remains unfinished. Other important churches are those of Santo Cristo de la Salud, Sagrario, and Victoria, the latter being notable for the macabre decorations on the tomb of the counts of Luna. The Provincial Museum of Art has a collection of 17th-century masterpieces, as well as modern works, including some by Pablo Picasso, who was born in the city at No. 16, Plaza de la Merced. The Moorish castle, the Alcazaba, has been reconstructed as a museum and garden, but the Gibralfaro fortress remains in its original form.

Málaga is the foremost Spanish Mediterranean port after Barcelona. The port's main exports are iron ore, dried fruit, almonds, olive oil, oranges, lemons, olives, canned anchovies, and the famous Málaga sweet wine; principal imports are petroleum, corn (maize), chemicals, iron and steel. Málaga's industries include the manufacture of building materials and foodstuffs; there are also breweries, fertilizer plants, textile mills, and pipes carrying crude oil from the port to the refinery at Puertollano.

Sheltered by the surrounding sierras, Málaga's mild climate makes it a popular resort. Nearby are a number of narrow beaches; some, such as Marbella and Fuengirola, have pine woods reaching to the seashore. Pop. (1999 est.) mun., 530,553.

Málaga, sweet, usually red, fortified wine that originated in the southern Spanish Mediterranean coastal province from which it takes its name. The term may also be applied generically to any of a variety of heavy, sweet red wines, including certain kosher wines served at Jewish celebrations. The best Spanish Málaga is made from muscat grapes and from the variety known as Pedro-Ximénez, the latter usually sun-dried to concentrate sweetness.

Malagasy languages, a cluster of languages spoken on Madagascar and adjacent islands and belonging to the Austronesian (Malayo-Polynesian) family of languages. The various Malagasy dialects are all closely related, having diversified only in the last 2,000 years when Madagascar was settled by an Indonesian people. The languages contain some words of Bantu, Swahili, Arab, English, and French origin. Since 1820 the Merina dialect, written in the Roman alphabet, has been the official language of the island.

Malagasy Republic: *see* Madagascar.

Malaita, also called MALA, volcanic island in the Solomon Islands, southwestern Pacific Ocean. It lies 30 miles (50 km) northeast of Guadalcanal across Indispensable Strait. The island is about 115 miles (185 km) long and 22 miles (35 km) across at its widest point, is mountainous (rising to Mount Ire [Mount Kolourat; 4,718 feet, or 1,438 m] in the centre), and is covered with dense forests. It is separated from Maramasike Island at its southeastern end by a narrow channel.

The development of sugar plantations in Queensland (Australia) and Fiji in the mid-19th century led to a sometimes brutal recruitment of the local Melanesian inhabitants, provoking reprisals by the islanders and the establishment of a British protectorate in 1893. After World War II a strongly anti-European movement known as "Marching Rule" came into being and aimed to dominate local affairs. A rapprochement in the 1950s between the government and the leaders culminated in the formation of an organized local council for the first time.

Coastline of Malaita, Solomon Islands, showing Sinerangu Harbour
Hugo Zemp

The population engages in copra production, rice and cacao cultivation, and boatbuilding. There is an airstrip at Auki on the west coast. Pop. (1986 est.) Malaita, Maramasike, and other adjacent islands, 77,900.

Malakāl, town, east-central Sudan. It lies along the right bank of the White Nile just below the latter's confluence with the Sobat River, 430 miles (690 km) south of Khartoum. The Junqalī project, a joint Sudanese-Egyptian plan aimed at increasing agricultural production, diverts the waters of the White Nile from the As-Sudd swamps by means of a 224-mile (360-kilometre) canal that starts from the mouth of the Sobat River near Malakāl. The town is linked by road with Nāṣir and Ar-Rank. A ferry service on the Sobat River originates from Malakāl, which also has a domestic airport. Pop. (1993) 73,000.

Malakbel (Hebrew: "Angel of Baal"), West Semitic sun god and messenger god, worshiped primarily in the ancient Syrian city of Palmyra; he was variously identified by the Greeks with Zeus and with Hermes and by the Romans with Sol. His name may have been of Babylonian origin, and he was considered the equivalent of the Babylonian sun god Shamash. Engravings on the four sides of a marble altar from Palmyra depict the four annual stages in the life of Malakbel, symbolizing the yearly sequence of the sun. Most other representations portray Malakbel with Aglibol, the moon god.

Malakoff, town, Hauts-de-Seine *département,* Paris *région,* north-central France. A southwestern industrial suburb of Paris, it has an electrical-engineering school and manufactures electrical equipment, chemicals, pharmaceuticals, and precision instruments. The town was created in 1883 and was named for the fortress of Malakhov at Sevastopol, which was captured by the French (Sept. 8, 1855) during the Crimean War. Pop. (1990) 31,135.

Malakoff, Aimable-Jean-Jacques Pélissier, duc de (duke of): *see* Pélissier, Aimable-Jean-Jacques.

Malakula, also spelled MALEKULA, French MALLICOLO, second largest island (781 square miles [2,023 square km]) of Vanuatu, in the southwestern Pacific Ocean. Volcanic in origin, it is 55 miles (90 km) long by 23 miles (37 km) wide and lies 20 miles (32 km) south of Espiritu Santo, across the Malo (Bougainville) Strait. Its central mountain range rises to Mount Penot, 2,884 feet (879 m). Harbours on the fertile eastern coast include Port Stanley, Bushman's Bay (former British administrative headquarters), and Port Sandwich (site of the former French headquarters at Lamap). Copra and coffee are exported, and there are a hospital and several airstrips. Pop. (1987 est.) Malakula and small adjacent islands, 18,850.

Malalas, John (b. *c.* 491, Antioch?, Syria, Byzantine Empire [now in Turkey]—d. *c.* 578), Byzantine chronicler of Syrian origin.

Malalas' *Chronographia* in 18 books is a compilation of history from the Creation certainly to 565, perhaps to 574, but the single extant manuscript ends with events of 563. The greater part of it stresses the importance of Antioch and has a Monophysite flavour. The last part of Book 18 appears to have been produced later by an Orthodox author, perhaps in Constantinople. It was written in the popular Greek of unlearned Christian circles, and, although often inaccurate and uncritical, it is of some value as a source for the first half of the 6th century. Some scholars identify John Malalas with John III Scholasticus, patriarch of Constantinople from 565 to 577, who had earlier been a lawyer in Antioch.

Malāmatīyah, a Ṣūfī (Muslim mystic) group that flourished in Sāmānid Iran during the 8th century. The name *Malāmatīyah* was derived from the Arabic verb *la'ma* ("to be ignoble," or "to be wicked"). Malāmatī doctrines were based on the reproach of the carnal self and a careful watch over its inclinations to surrender to the temptations of the world. They often referred to the Qur'ānic verse "I [God] swear by the reproachful soul" as the basis for their philosophy. This verse, they said, clearly praised a self that constantly reproached and blamed its owner for the slightest deviation from the world of God. The reproachful self in Malāmatī terminology was the perfect self.

The Malāmatīyah found value in self-blame, believing that it would be conducive to a true detachment from worldly things and to disinterested service of God. They feared the praise and respect of other persons. Piety, the Malāmatī believer said, is a private affair between man and God. A Malāmatī believer further concealed his knowledge as a precaution against acquiring fame and strove to make his faults known, so that he would always be reminded of his imperfection. Toward others they were as tolerant and forgiving as they were strict and harsh on themselves.

While other Ṣūfīs revealed their *aḥwāl* (states of ecstasy) and their joy over progressing from one *maqām* (spiritual stage) to the next, the Malāmatīyah kept their achievements and their feelings concealed. Ṣūfīs wore particular clothes, organized various orders, and assumed all sorts of titles; the Malāmatīyah were steadfast in concealing their identities and belittling their achievements. In fact, Malāmatī doctrines were so different from those of most Ṣūfī groups that a few scholars did not consider the Malāmatīyah to be Ṣūfīs.

Malamud, Bernard (b. April 26, 1914, Brooklyn, N.Y., U.S.—d. March 18, 1986, New York, N.Y.), American novelist and short-story writer who made parables out of Jewish immigrant life.

A son of Russian Jews, Malamud was educated at the City College of New York (B.A., 1936) and Columbia University (M.A., 1942). He taught at high schools in New York City (1940–49), at Oregon State University (1949–61), and at Bennington College, Vt. (1961–66, 1968–86).

His first novel, *The Natural* (1952), is a fable about a baseball hero who is gifted with miraculous powers. *The Assistant* (1957) is about a young Gentile hoodlum and an old Jewish grocer. *The Fixer* (1966) takes place in tsarist Russia. The story of a Jewish handyman unjustly imprisoned for the murder of a Christian boy, it won Malamud a Pulitzer Prize. His other novels are *A New Life* (1961), *The Tenants* (1971), *Dubin's Lives* (1979), and *God's Grace* (1982).

Malamud's genius is most apparent in his short stories. Though told in a spare, compressed prose that reflects the terse speech of their immigrant characters, the stories often burst into emotional, metaphorical language. Grim city neighbourhoods are visited by magical events, and their hardworking residents are given glimpses of love and self-sacrifice. Malamud's short-story collections are *The Magic Barrel* (1958), *Idiots First* (1963), *Pictures of Fidelman* (1969), and *Rembrandt's Hat* (1973). *The Stories of Bernard Malamud* appeared in 1983.

Malamute (dog): *see* Alaskan Malamute.

Malan, Daniel F(rançois) (b. May 22, 1874, near Riebeeck West, Cape Colony [now Cape of Good Hope, S.Af.]—d. Feb. 7, 1959, Stellenbosch, S.Af.), statesman and politician who is best remembered for forming the first exclusively Afrikaner government of South Africa and for instituting apartheid (the enforced segregation of nonwhites from whites).

Malan
By courtesy of the Information Service of South Africa

Malan was educated at Victoria College, Stellenbosch, and at the University of Utrecht, Neth., where he received a doctorate in divinity in 1905. He returned to the Cape to enter the ministry of the Dutch Reformed Church. Always a vigorous exponent of Afrikaner aspirations and the use of the Afrikaans language, Malan left the pulpit in 1915 to edit *Die Burger,* a Cape Town newspaper that backed the National Party led by J.B.M. Hertzog.

On entering Parliament in 1918, Malan soon demonstrated considerable talent, especially as a forceful speaker. The following year, he became a member of the delegation that went to the Versailles Peace Conference to request independence for South Africa on the basis of self-determination. In 1924 he joined Hertzog's Cabinet as minister of the interior. While holding that post, he instituted laws that established a South African nationality and a flag, and he succeeded in having Afrikaans recognized as an official language of the Union, replacing Dutch (Netherlandic), from which it had evolved. (Formerly only English and Dutch had been used officially.) When Hertzog's National Party merged with Jan Smuts's South African Party in 1934, Malan left the government and founded the Purified Nationalist Party, which became the official opposition.

Because Hertzog regarded World War II as no concern of South Africa, he fell from power and soon became reconciled with Malan, who also favoured neutrality. Together they formed the reunited National Party in 1939. When Hertzog withdrew from the party in December 1940, Malan assumed leadership. With patience and considerable skill, Malan welded together a reunited National Party that won 43 seats in the House of Assembly in the 1943 election. By appealing to Afrikaner racial sentiments, the Nationalists in alliance with the smaller Afrikaner Party won a narrow majority in the House of Assembly in the election of 1948. This enabled Malan to form the first exclusively Afrikaner government of South Africa.

The primary concern of Malan's new government was to implement the policy of apartheid. The government's attempt to remove the Coloureds (people of mixed race) from the common voting rolls of Cape Province in 1951 was declared invalid by the Suprme Court in 1952, however, and the crisis was still unresolved when, after increasing his party's parliamentary majority in the 1953 general election, Malan retired in 1954. His successors implemented the apartheid policies begun in his administration.

Malan, François Stephanus (b. March 12, 1871, Wellington, Cape Colony [now Cape of Good Hope, S.Af.]—d. Dec. 31, 1941, Cape Town, S.Af.), politician who was a leader of the moderate Dutch political parties in South Africa. He was a constant supporter of political rights for Africans.

Malan was a leader of the Afrikaner Bond (a political party of Dutch South Africans) and editor (1895) of its newspaper. He was originally antagonistic to British colonial influence, and he supported the Boer republics in the South African War (1899–1902). Malan was won over, however, to the British offer of reconciliation at the end of the war, and his support for the first union government was an essential factor in reestablishing peace in South Africa. He was minister of education (1910–21) and acting prime minister (1918–19). He defended the right of Africans to vote and opposed the draft union constitution (1909), which seriously curtailed African suffrage, and the special legislation (1936) that virtually abolished it.

Malang, *kotamadya* (municipality) and *kabupaten* (regency), Jawa Timur *provinsi* ("province"), Indonesia. Malang regency has an area of 3,391 square miles (8,782 square km). It is principally agricultural and known for its production of vegetables, fruits, and flowers. Malang is located on a plateau between Mount Kawi (8,697 feet [2,651 m]) and the Tengger Mountains, and the city enjoys a comfortable climate. The Indonesian parliament met there temporarily during Indonesia's struggle for independence from Dutch rule. Malang's industries include the manufacture of soap, ceramics, and cigarettes. There are good road and rail connections to the provincial capital, Surabaya. Among the tourist attractions in the surrounding area are the palace ruins of the ancient kings of Dinaya, Tumapel, and Singhasāri. Malang is now the headquarters of an Indonesian army division, and an Indonesian air force base is just east of the city. Pop. (1984 est.) city, 560,000; (1980) regency, 2,045,939.

malanggan style, one of the most sophisticated styles of carving in the South Pacific Islands, with a technical virtuosity, vocabulary of fantastic motifs, and range of colour unique in Oceanic art. Although *malanggan* carvings have been found in other areas of Melanesia, they are indigenous to northwestern New Ireland.

Malanggan carvings take the form of friezes, masks, and sculpture, in either horizontal or vertical form, depicting continuous narrative. The precise uses of the narrative carvings have not yet been determined, but it appears that they are certainly used in ritual ceremonies for deceased persons of notoriety and social position and probably also in initiation rites of young men. In both such events, one of their functions is to enhance the prestige of those responsible for the arduous preparation of the festivals, which often last for months.

The narrative sculpture consists of a single piece of softwood that has been carved in openwork and painted red, black, yellow, and white. The carvings include references to specific persons who played a role in the life of the deceased, as well as metaphorical references to animals and historical events. Usually appearing in the centre of the carving is a circular form representing "the big fire," a motif that has been interpreted as the Sun or as the hearth of the deceased man's home.

Painted wood *malanggan* frieze from Fessoa Plantation, northwestern New Ireland; in the Museum of Ethnology and the Swiss Folklore Museum, Basel, Switz.
Holle Bildarchiv, Baden-Baden, Ger.

Mythological beings appear juxtaposed with representations of the planets and elements, weapons, tools, and symbols of mythical battles. The richness and diversity of the motifs appear to be boundless. The images are often intertwined and placed on top of each other. In contrast to the narrative sculpture, *malanggan* masks are limited to symbolizing mythological personages. The wealth of motifs employed, however, is unlimited. The masks, like the narrative carvings, are directly associated with the rituals for departed souls.

Malanje, also spelled MALANGE, town, north-central Angola. The town developed in the mid-19th century as an important *feira* (open-air market) on the country's principal plateau, between Luanda, now the national capital, 250 miles (400 km) to the west and the Kwango valley, inhabited by the Mbundu people, 125 miles (200 km) to the east. Situated at an elevation of 4,373 feet (1,333 m), the town has a high-altitude tropical climate. The environs of Malanje included the principal cotton-producing area of Angola prior to independence in 1975. The withdrawal of the Portuguese and later civil wars (which partially destroyed the town) severely hampered the production of

Duque de Bragança Falls on the Lucala River, Malanje, Angola
By courtesy of the Provincia de Angola

cotton as well as that of coffee and corn (maize).

The surrounding area occupies the well-watered northern slopes of Angola's central plateau and is drained mainly by the Kwanza River and its tributaries. The region is noted for its 350-foot- (107-metre-) high Duque de Bragança Falls on the Lucala River, the Luando Game Reserve in the south, the Milando animal reserve in the north, and the Pungo Andongo stones, giant black monoliths associated with tribal legend. Most of the region's inhabitants are members of the Mbundu peoples. The chief economic activities are stock raising (mainly goats) and the cultivation of cotton, corn, fruits and nuts, cassava, sisal, and tobacco. Mineral resources include manganese and gold. Malanje is the terminus of the Luanda Railway, which connects it with the Atlantic coast. Pop. (1984 est.) town, 35,000.

Malankarese Catholic Church, an Antiochene-rite member of the Eastern Catholic church, composed of former members of the Syrian Orthodox (Jacobite) Church of Kerala, India, who united with Rome in 1930.

The Syrian Orthodox Church came into existence in 1653, when the Christians of St. Thomas—as the Indian Christians of Malabar (now Kerala) called themselves—broke with Rome after severe Latinization by Portuguese missionaries. Most of the schismatics returned to the Roman Catholic church in 1661, but a small body of dissenters continued as the Syrian Orthodox Church. These Jacobites made several unsuccessful attempts to reunite with Rome in the 18th century. In 1930, through the efforts of Bishop Ivanios, reunion was achieved. The Malankarese Catholics retain the Antiochene liturgy that they adopted as Jacobites, with the characteristic translation of the Syriac into the vernacular Malayalam language.

Malaparte, Curzio, pseudonym of KURT ERICH SUCKERT (b. June 9, 1898, Prato, Italy—d. July 19, 1957, Rome), journalist, dramatist, short-story writer, and novelist, one of the most powerful, brilliant, and controversial of the Italian writers of the fascist and post-World War II periods.

Malaparte was a volunteer in World War I and then became active in journalism. In 1924 he founded the Roman periodical *La Conquista dello stato,* and in 1926 he joined Massimo Bontempelli in founding *900,* an influential, cosmopolitan literary quarterly whose foreign editorial board included James Joyce and Ilya Ehrenburg; he later became coeditor of *Fiera Letteraria,* then editor of *La Stampa* in Turin.

An early convert to fascism, he became, next to Gabriele D'Annunzio, the most powerful writer associated with the party. His political views were voiced in his own literary magazine, *Prospettive* (1937), and in many articles written for fascist periodicals. He also wrote a particularly controversial and influential discussion of violence and means of revolution published in French, *Technique du coup d'état* (1931; *Coup d'État, the Technique of Revolution;* Italian trans., *Tecnica del colpo di stato*). His early fiction—*Avventure di un capitano di Sventura* (1927); *Sodoma e Gomorra* (1931); and *Sangue* (1937)—also showed a fascist slant.

During the 1940s Malaparte repudiated fascism and was expelled from the party. During World War II he was involved with the Allied armies, both as a correspondent and, later, as a liaison officer during the Allied occupation of Naples. His reports from the Russian front were published as *Il Volga nasce in Europa* (1943; *The Volga Rises in Europe*). He then acquired an international reputation with two passionately written, brilliantly realistic war novels: *Kaputt* (1944); and *La pelle* (1949; *The Skin*), a terrifying, surrealistically presented series of episodes showing the suffering and degradation that the war had brought to the people of Naples.

While continuing to write articles and fiction, Malaparte wrote three realistic dramas, based on the lives of Marcel Proust (*Du côté de chez Proust,* performed 1948) and Karl Marx (*Das Kapital,* performed 1949) and on life in Vienna during the Soviet occupation (*Anche le donne hanno perso la guerra,* performed 1954; "The Women Lost the War Too"). He also wrote the screenplay for a film, *Il Cristo proibito* (1951) and, in addition to other works, published a volume titled *Racconti italiani* (1957; "Italian Tales"). His complete works were published 1957–71.

malapropism, verbal blunder in which one word is replaced by another similar in sound but different in meaning. Although William Shakespeare had used the device for comic effect, the term derives from Richard Brinsley Sheridan's character Mrs. Malaprop, in his play *The Rivals* (1775). Her name is taken from the term *malapropos* (French: "inappropriate") and is typical of Sheridan's practice of concocting names to indicate the essence of a character. Thinking of the geography of contiguous countries, she spoke of the "geometry" of "contagious countries," and hoped that her daughter might "reprehend" the true meaning of what she is saying. She regretted that her "affluence" over her niece was very small.

Malar, Lake, Swedish MÄLAREN, lake in eastern Sweden, located just west of Stockholm, which lies at the lake's junction with Salt Bay, an arm of the Baltic Sea. At one time Lake Malar was a bay of the Baltic, and seagoing vessels using it were able to sail far into the interior of Sweden. Because of movements of the Earth's crust, however, the rock barrier at the mouth of the bay had become so shallow by about 1200 that ships had to unload near the entrance, and the bay became a lake.

With an area of 440 square miles (1,140 square km) and extending about 75 miles (120 km) across Sweden, it is the country's third largest lake. Together with Lake Hjalmar, it drains an area of 8,160 square miles (21,130 square km). Normally its surface is only 1 foot (0.3 m) above sea level, and its outflow is sometimes reversed. Navigable channels connect it with Lake Hjalmar to the southwest, while the Södertälje Canal and two channels at Stockholm connect it with the Baltic to the east.

Its more than 1,200 islands, with a total area of 189 square miles (489 square km), and its deeply indented, wooded shoreline have made the lake area a popular residential and resort region. There are many towns in addition to Stockholm along its shores, a number of them of historical interest. Near Mariefred is the castle of Gripsholm, begun in 1537 by Gustav I Vasa, and known today for its portrait collection. In the episcopal palace at Strängnäs, Gustav I Vasa was elected king of Sweden in 1523. The island of Drottningholm (Queen's Island) has a 17th-century palace that is a royal summer residence with a fine park and formal gardens. The château of Skokloster, south of Uppsala, on the northern arm of Lake Malar, has a remarkable collection of trophies, including an armoury, from the Thirty Years' War (1618–48).

malar bone: *see* zygomatic bone.

malaria, a serious, acute and chronic relapsing infection in humans, characterized by periodic attacks of chills and fever, anemia, splenomegaly (enlargement of the spleen), and often fatal complications. Malaria also is found in apes, monkeys, rats, birds, and reptiles. It is caused by various species of protozoa (one-celled organisms) called sporozoans (subphylum Sporozoa) that belong to the genus *Plasmodium.* These parasites are transmitted to humans by the bite of various species of mosquitoes belonging to the genus *Anopheles*.

Malaria is one of the most ancient infections known. It was noted in some of the West's earliest medical records in the 5th century BC, when Hippocrates differentiated malarial fevers into three types according to their time cycles of recurring fevers. It is not known when malaria first made its appearance in the Americas, but it is highly probable that it was a post-Columbian importation; some rather severe epidemics were first noted in 1493.

The association between swampy or marshy areas and the disease has long been recognized, but the roles of the mosquito and of the malarial parasite were not known until the beginning of the 20th century. In 1880 the French army surgeon Alphonse Laveran became the first person to describe the malarial parasite and to recognize it as the cause of malaria. In 1897–98 the British physician Sir Ronald Ross proved that bird malaria is transmitted by *Culex* mosquitoes, and he described the entire life cycle of that parasite in the mosquito. In 1898 the Italian investigators Amico Bignami, Giovanni Battista Grassi, and Giuseppe Bastianelli first experimentally infected humans with malaria by mosquitoes, described the full development of the parasite in humans, and noted that human malaria is transmitted only by anopheline mosquitoes. The disease can also be transmitted unnaturally by common use of the hypodermic needle, as among drug addicts, or occasionally by blood transfusion from infected donors.

Malaria occurs throughout the tropical and subtropical regions of the world and is the most prevalent of all serious infectious diseases. In the late 20th century, annual cases worldwide were estimated at 250 million, with 2 million deaths resulting. Incomplete or faulty reports from Africa make even those rough estimates unreliable, however. Though malaria can occur in temperate regions, it is most common in the tropics and subtropics, where climatic conditions are favourable for the mosquitoes that transmit the disease throughout the year. In many parts of sub-Saharan Africa, entire human populations are infected more or less constantly. Malaria is also common in Central America, the northern half of South America, and in South and Southeast Asia. The disease also occurs in countries bordering on the Mediterranean, in the Middle East, and in East Asia.

Anopheline mosquitoes are the only known vectors of malaria in humans, and about 60 different species perform this function throughout the world. These mosquitoes undergo an aquatic larval stage, pupate, and then hatch into flying adults. The females require a meal of blood to produce fertile eggs, and females of some species prefer human to animal blood. The female mosquito ingests the malarial parasite by biting a human already infected with the parasite.

The malarial parasite has a complicated double life cycle, with a sexual reproductive cycle while it lives in the mosquito and an asexual reproductive cycle while in the human host. While in its asexual, free-swimming stage, the malarial parasite known as a sporozoite is injected into the human bloodstream by a mosquito, passing through the skin along with the mosquito's saliva. After invading the liver of its human host, the sporozoite eventually enters a red blood cell, where it goes through ring-shaped and amoeba-like forms before fissioning (dividing) into smaller forms called merozoites. The red blood cell containing these merozoites then ruptures, releasing them into the bloodstream (and also causing the chills and fever that are typical symptoms of the disease). The merozoites can then infect other red blood cells, and their cycle of development is repeated.

A small proportion of the merozoites, however, become gametocytes, or germ cells, and can go through a sexual reproductive cycle once back in a mosquito. After a mosquito ingests them from an infected human host, the separate male and female gametocytes in the mosquito's stomach form gametes that unite to form a single-celled zygote, which grows to become an oocyst. This oocyst eventually divides, releasing a multitude of asexual, free-swimming sporozoites that migrate to the mosquito's head and salivary glands, where they are ready to pass into the human bloodstream during the mosquito's next bite. The entire asexual reproductive cycle is then repeated.

A remarkable feature of the asexual reproductive cycle is that the parasites grow and divide synchronously, and the resulting mass fissions (into merozoites) produce the regularly recurring attacks, or paroxysms, that are typical of malaria. A malarial attack normally lasts 4 to 10 hours and consists successively of a stage of shaking and chills; a stage of fever, with the temperature reaching 105° F, and severe headache; and then a stage of profuse sweating during which the temperature drops back to normal. Between attacks, the temperature may be normal or below normal. In the early days of the infection, the attacks may occur every day, but they soon begin appearing at regular intervals of either 48 hours (called tertian malaria) or 72 hours (called quartan malaria). The first attack usually occurs from 8 to 25 days after a person has been bitten by an infected mosquito.

Four species of *Plasmodium* are known to cause malaria in humans: *P. falciparum, P. vivax, P. malariae,* and *P. ovale*. The most common of these malarial types, accounting for about 50 percent of all cases, is falciparum (subtertian, or malignant tertian) malaria, which has the most severe symptoms and is the most frequently fatal; it accounts for as many as 95 percent of all deaths from malaria. Falciparum malaria requires higher temperatures for optimal development and is confined more closely to the tropical areas. In western Africa, for example, it exists almost to the exclusion of the other varieties. Once a person has recovered from falciparum malaria, however, relapses rarely if ever occur. Vivax (tertian) malaria accounts for about 40 percent of all cases and is widespread mainly because of its ability to withstand therapy and to recur frequently for a period of several years, though the initial acute phase lasts only two to three weeks. The two less common types of malaria are quartan malaria (caused by *P. malariae*) and ovale tertian malaria (caused by *P. ovale*). Infections with one or more species can occur simultaneously, however. Furthermore, a double brood of tertian parasites can segment on alternate days, giving a daily or quotidian fever.

Besides attacks, persons with malaria commonly suffer from anemia (owing to the destruction of red blood cells by the parasites), enlargement of the spleen (the organ responsible for ridding the body of degenerate red blood cells), and general weakness and debility. In falciparum malaria, the parasitized blood cells tend to stick together, and some of the smaller blood vessels may be blocked as a result. Falciparum malaria may also cause other complications, such as blackwater fever (*q.v.*).

Malaria can be reliably diagnosed upon finding the parasites in stained blood smears examined under a microscope. An effective treatment for malaria was known long before the cause of the disease was understood: the bark of the cinchona tree, whose most active principle, quinine, was used to alleviate malarial fevers from 1700 until World War II, when more effective synthetic drugs were developed. Chief among these newer drugs are chloroquine, pyrimethamine, sulfadoxine, and primaquine phosphate, all of which can destroy the malarial parasites while they are living inside red blood cells. In their initial decades of use, chloroquine and related drugs could relieve symptoms of an attack that had already started, prevent attacks altogether, and even wipe out the plasmodial infection entirely. By the late 20th century, however, some vivax strains as well as most falciparum strains had become resistant to the drugs, which were thus rendered ineffective. As a result, the incidence of malaria began to increase after having steadily declined for decades. Both one's natural resistance, as occurs among those who are carriers of one gene for the sickle-cell trait, and one's immunity acquired through previous exposure will reduce susceptibility to malaria.

The basic method of prevention is to eliminate the breeding places of *Anopheles* mosquitoes by draining and filling marshes, swamps, stagnant pools, and other large or small bodies of standing fresh water. Insecticides have proved potent in controlling mosquito populations in affected areas. Window screens and mosquito netting are widely used to secure interior spaces from the mosquitoes, which are mainly active at night.

malarial hemoglobinuria: *see* blackwater fever.

Malaspina FAMILY, feudal family powerful in northern Italy in the Middle Ages. Descended from Marquis Oberto I, who was created count palatine by the Holy Roman emperor Otto I, the family at first controlled Tuscany, eastern Liguria, and the March of Lombardy. Early in the 11th century the Este, Pallavicino, and Massa-Corsica family branches separated from the Malaspina. The situation of Malaspina lands, in the mountainous regions of the Apennines, controlling the great highways connecting the Ligurian and Tuscan ports with north Italian cities, made the Malaspina powerful and helped them resist the encroachments of neighbouring cities. Repeated partition of their territory, first between two lines, the Spino Secco and the Spino Fiorito, then among many smaller subdivisions, gradually undermined their resistance to the pressure of the great communes. In the 14th century, however, they remained a leading feudal house under Franceschino Malaspina, host to Dante in 1306 during his exile, and under Spinetta Malaspina (d. 1352), who succeeded in extending the family territories. But in the 15th and 16th centuries, most of the Malaspina dominions passed under Genoese and Florentine control. One branch of the family prospered, Spinetta Malaspina's great-grandnephew Antonio Alberigo acquiring Massa (1421) and Carrara (1428), east of Genoa, his dominions later becoming the principate (1568) and the duchy (1633) of Massa.

Malatesta FAMILY, Italian family that ruled Rimini, south of Ravenna, in the European Middle Ages and led the region's Guelf (papal) party. Originating as feudal lords of the Apennine hinterland, the family became powerful in Rimini in the 13th century, when Malatesta da Verucchio (d. 1312) expelled Ghibelline (imperial party) leaders in 1295 and became lord of the city. Possibly the best-known episode in Malatesta history centres on his son Gianciotto (d. 1304), who killed his wife, Francesca da Polenta, and his brother Paolo for adultery, an event recorded by Dante. By the time of the arrival of the papal legate

Cardinal Albornoz in the area in 1353, the Malatesta had extended their power as far as Ascoli, 100 miles (160 km) south. Albornoz forced them to surrender many of their conquests but allowed them to remain as papal vicars in Rimini and other nearby cities (1355).

The Malatesta were active in the 14th- and 15th-century wars of the Visconti family of Milan. Carlo Malatesta (d. 1429) governed the Milanese state for a time after the death of Gian Galeazzo Visconti, while his brother Pandolfo (d. 1427) seized Brescia (1404) and Bergamo (1408) but had to relinquish them in 1421. Carlo was associated with Pope Gregory XII at the end of the Great Schism, and he presented Gregory's formal renunciation of the papacy at the Council of Constance in 1416. Carlo's nephew, Sigismondo Pandolfo Malatesta (1417–68), often regarded as the prototype of the Italian Renaissance prince, was a soldier who earned a reputation as a patron of writers and artists. Malatesta power was diminished by the end of the Great Schism (1417) and the growing power of the papacy. In 1461 Pope Pius II launched a crusade against Sigismondo and deprived the Malatesta of most of their dominions. After Sigismondo's death, his son Roberto il Magnifico (d. 1482) seized Rimini (1469) from his half brother Sallustio, though at the price of increased dependence on Venice. Meanwhile, the Malatesta family lost all popular support in Rimini. Forced to flee in 1500, when Cesare Borgia marched on the city, they tried three times (in 1503, 1522, and 1527–28) to return and met defeat on each occasion.

Malatesta, Errico, Errico also spelled ENRICO (b. Dec. 14, 1853, Santa Maria Capua Vetere, Kingdom of Naples [Italy]—d. July 22, 1932, Rome), Italian anarchist and agitator, a leading advocate of "propaganda of the deed," the doctrine urged largely by Italian anarchists that revolutionary ideas could best be spread by armed insurrection.

Malatesta became politically active while still in his teens, joining the First International in 1871. A dynamic speaker and propagandist, he soon became a leader in the anarchist movement and helped organize anarchist revolutionary groups in Romania, Italy, Spain, and elsewhere in Europe, in Egypt, and in North and South America, including Argentina. Imprisoned for a total of about 12 years during his long career, he was sentenced to death three times and spent some 35 years in exile. Though often associated with the Russian anarchist Peter Kropotkin, Malatesta laid more emphasis on the organization of revolutionaries and workers as a means of achieving anarchist political goals. Accordingly, he helped organize workers' congresses in France, Belgium, and Switzerland at which he urged armed revolt, and subsequently he was banished from each of those countries.

In 1899 he visited the United States, lecturing and editing an anarchist journal. After 1900 he lived more or less quietly in London for many years, taking time out to agitate for revolution in Italy in 1913–14. He returned permanently to Italy after an amnesty in 1919, engaging in political activity until the Fascists' rise to power in 1922.

Malatesta, Sigismondo Pandolfo (b. 1417—d. Oct. 9, 1468, Rimini [Italy]), feudal ruler and condottiere who is often regarded as the prototypical Italian Renaissance prince.

Sigismondo was one of three illegitimate sons of Pandolfo Malatesta, who had ruled over Brescia and Bergamo from *c.* 1404 to 1421. Sigismondo was legitimated by Pope Martin V, but he felt no loyalty toward the papacy, which deprived his family of many of their lands in 1430. From 1433 to 1463, Malatesta sold his military talents as a condottiere (mercenary captain) to all sides in the Italian wars of that period. As the feudal lord of Rimini, however, he was a generous and cultivated patron of writers and artists. He commissioned the architect Leon Battista Alberti to build the most famous monument in Rimini, the Church of San Francesco (also known as the Tempio Malatestiano).

Malatesta won popularity as a ruler and distinction as a mercenary captain, but he also gained a reputation for impiety, vice, and brutality. He owed part of this reputation to systematic defamation by his most powerful enemy, Pope Pius II. The most constant feature of Malatesta's character was impetuosity, which made him impatient of keeping faith with princes more powerful than himself. This was why, after years of feuds with his detested rival Federico di Montefeltro, Malatesta stood virtually alone when Pius II excommunicated him and sought his overthrow in 1461. By a peace agreement in 1463, Malatesta lost most of his dominions but was allowed to keep Rimini until his death.

Malathion, trade name for an organic phosphorus compound that is a general-purpose insecticide considerably less toxic to humans than parathion and is thus suited for the control of household and garden insects. It is important in the control of mosquitoes, flies, and lice. Malathion is a yellow-to-brown liquid with a characteristic unpleasant odour. It is generally prepared by combining *O,O′*-dimethyl phosphorodithioate with diethyl maleate. It is soluble in most organic solvents except paraffin hydrocarbons, and it is practically insoluble in water. Malathion is readily decomposed by alkalies.

Malatya, city, east-central Turkey. It lies in a fertile plain watered by the Tohma River (a tributary of the Euphrates) and is surrounded by high ranges of the eastern Taurus Mountains. The modern town was founded in 1838 near the sites of two earlier settlements: the ancient Hittite city of Milid, on the site of the present-day Arslantepe, 4 miles (6 km) north, and its successor, the Roman and medieval city of Melitene, now called Eski (Old) Malatya (6 miles [10 km] northeast).

An important garrison town and road junction of the eastern frontier of the Roman Empire, Melitene was granted city status by Emperor Trajan (reigned AD 98–117) and later served as the capital of Armenia Minor. It was occupied successively by the Persian Sāsānids, the Arabs, and the Armenians, and it came under the Seljuq Turks in the 12th century. The Seljuq Ulu Cami ("Great Mosque"), built on an earlier Arab foundation, and the *han* (caravansary) both date from the 13th century. In 1515 the city was incorporated into the Ottoman Empire under Sultan Selim I.

Now a busy industrial centre producing chiefly textiles, sugar, and cement, Malatya is also the regional market for agricultural goods including fruits, vegetables, cotton, tobacco, rice, and sugar beets. The locality also has deposits of chrome, lead, and copper. Malatya is a rail and road junction in which the line between Aleppo (in Syria) and Samsun (on the Black Sea) meets the line east to Elâzığ and Diyarbakır. İnönü University was founded at Malatya in 1975. Pop. (2000) 381,081.

Mālava (India): *see* Mālwa.

Malaŵi, officially REPUBLIC OF MALAŴI, formerly NYASALAND, landlocked country in southeastern Africa. Long and narrow in shape, Malaŵi stretches about 520 miles (837 km) from north to south and varies in width from 5 to 100 miles (8 to 160 km) from east to west. It is bordered by Tanzania to the north, Mozambique to the east and south, and Zambia to the west. The capital is Lilongwe. Area 45,747 square miles (118,484 square km). Pop. (2003 est.), 11,651,000.

A brief treatment of Malaŵi follows. For full treatment, *see* MACROPAEDIA: Southern Africa.

For current history and for statistics on society and economy, *see* BRITANNICA BOOK OF THE YEAR.

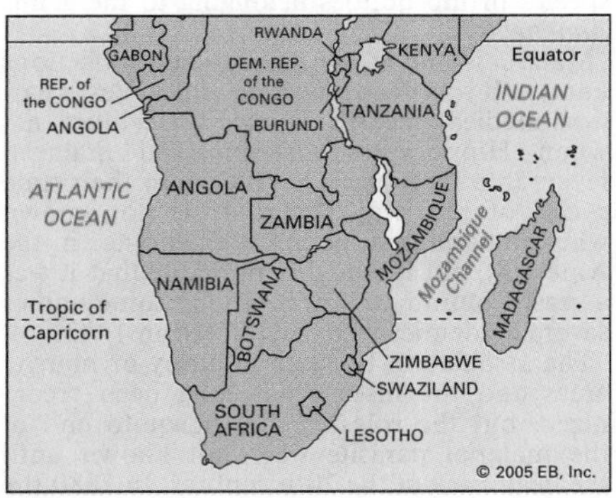

Malaŵi

The land. Malaŵi's terrain is characterized by dramatic highlands and extensive lakes. The country can be divided into four physiographic regions. The East African Rift Valley is Malaŵi's most prominent physical feature, running through the country from north to south and containing Lake Nyasa, known in Malaŵi as Lake Malaŵi (11,430 square miles [29,604 square km]), and the Shire River valley in the south. The broad plateaus of central Malaŵi have an elevation between 2,500 and 4,500 feet (760 and 1,370 m) and cover about three-fourths of the total land area. The highland areas consist chiefly of the Nyika and Viphya plateaus in the north, which rise to more than 8,000 feet (2,400 m), and the intensively cultivated Shire Highlands in the south. The fourth physiographic region consists of the isolated massifs of Zomba and Mulanje (9,849 feet [3,002 m] at Sapitwa peak, the country's highest point) in the south.

The Shire River, Lake Malaŵi's only outlet, is the country's principal river, flowing through adjacent Lake Malombe before joining the Zambezi River in Mozambique. Lake Malaŵi forms the border with Tanzania and Mozambique on the east. It is the third largest lake in Africa and is one of the largest and deepest lakes in the world; it also provides a rich harvest of fish, some of which is exported. The much smaller Lake Chilwa is in the southeast.

Malaŵi has an equatorial monsoonal climate with two main seasons: dry (May–October) and wet (November–April). The average temperature of October ranges from 69° F (21° C) in the highland region to 84° F (29° C) in the lowlands; the corresponding temperatures for July are 57° F (14° C) and 69° F (21° C). Annual precipitation ranges from 90 inches (2,300 mm) on the northern highlands to 50 inches (1,300 mm) on the plateaus and 30 inches (800 mm) in the lowlands.

Less than one-fourth of Malaŵi's total land area is cultivated. Tea plantations are found on the Shire Highlands, and tobacco is raised on the central plateau. Diverse forests and woodlands occupy about two-fifths of the total land area and range from savanna-type grasses and shrubs on the lowlands to grassland and evergreen forests on the highlands. The country's rich animal life includes game animals—antelope, buffalo, elephants, leopards, lions, rhinoceroses, and zebras—which are protected in several game reserves and national parks, of which Nyika and Kasungu national parks are the largest. Hippopotamuses live in Lake Malaŵi.

The people. Bantu-speakers constitute almost the entire population of Malaŵi, with Chewa and Maravi being the largest groups. There are also small minorities of Europeans and Asians. Chewa is spoken by more than half of the people. English is the language of state, and Chilomwe, Chiyao, and Chitumbuka are spoken as well. Religious practice is predominantly Christian, with about one-fifth of the population Protestant and somewhat fewer Roman Catholic. Another one-fifth are Muslim, and roughly one-tenth practice traditional systems.

Malaŵi's annual population growth rate is relatively high. Almost half of the population is under 15 years of age. The southern part of the country is the most densely populated. Only about one-tenth of the population lives in urban areas, although a rural-to-urban trend in internal migration continues.

The economy. Malaŵi has a developing mixed economy in which both the public and private sectors participate. The economy is based largely on agriculture, commercial and administrative services, and light industries. The gross national product (GNP) is growing slightly slower than the population, and GNP per capita is one of the lowest in the world.

Agriculture accounts for about one-third of the gross domestic product (GDP) but employs most of the workforce. Smallholders predominate and hold land under customary tenure. Corn (maize) is the chief staple and is typically grown with peanuts (groundnuts), beans, and peas. Tobacco, tea, sugarcane, and cotton are the principal cash crops.

Mineral industries are limited to the mining of coal and the quarrying of limestone. Sizable deposits of uranium are being exploited. Exploitation of the sizable bauxite reserve will require increased hydroelectric capacity. Manufacturing industries account for only about one-seventh of Malaŵi's GDP. Manufacturing industries have been a fast-growing sector of the economy, however, and centre on the production of sugar, beer, cigarettes, soap, chemicals, textiles, and blankets. All but a small fraction of Malaŵi's electricity is generated from hydroelectric power.

Malaŵi's external trade is dominated by exports of tobacco (as much as three-fourths of the total), tea, sugar, and cotton and by imports of transport equipment and petroleum products. Major trading partners include South Africa, the United Kingdom, and Germany.

Government and social conditions. Malaŵi has a multiparty system with free elections. The 1995 constitution places executive power in the hands of the president, who appoints the cabinet, and gives legislative power to the 193-member National Assembly. Both are elected by universal suffrage. A constitutional amendment to seat an upper house, the Senate, was put on hold in 2001. The judiciary comprises the Supreme Court of Appeal, the High Court, magistrates' courts, and traditional courts.

Malaŵi has a severe shortage of medical personnel that is most acute in rural areas. Public health facilities are generally inadequate. Malaria, gastrointestinal diseases, malnutrition, schistosomiasis, and trachoma are major health problems. By 2000 nearly one in seven adult residents was infected with HIV, which contributed to a drop in average life expectancy to 37 years for men and 38 years for women.

The educational system comprises eight-year primary schools, in which about half of the school-aged children are enrolled; four-year secondary schools; technical and teacher-training institutes; and the University of Malaŵi (founded in 1964). Malaŵi has an active and energetic print and broadcast media that is nonetheless subject to suppression and intimidation by the government and by special interests.

History. Prehistoric forebears of the early Twa and Fula inhabitants of Malaŵi date to the period between 8000 and 2000 BC. Bantu-speaking peoples entered the region between the 1st and 4th centuries AD. Early political states were established by Bantu speakers, and about 1480 the Maravi Confederacy was founded. The confederacy encompassed most of central and southern Malaŵi and influenced many adjacent peoples in the 17th century. In northern Malaŵi the Ngonde people founded a kingdom about 1600, and in the 18th century immigrants from the eastern shore of Lake Nyasa (or Lake Malaŵi) established the Chikulamayembe state.

The slave trade flourished in Malaŵi during the 18th and 19th centuries. Swahili-speaking peoples entered the region between 1830 and 1860 and, along with the Yao peoples, established spheres of influence. Both were involved in the slave trade. Islām spread into Malaŵi with the slave trade in the 1860s. Christianity was introduced about the same time by missionaries such as David Livingstone. In the 1880s and '90s missionaries from the Dutch Reformed Church of South Africa and the Roman Catholic church established missions in the region.

The British established colonial authority over the region in 1891, creating the Nyasaland Districts Protectorate. It became the British Central Africa Protectorate in 1893 and Nyasaland in 1907. The British colonial regime introduced the cultivation of cash crops by Europeans and constructed roads and railways. Little was done by the colonial administration to enhance the welfare of the people of Malaŵi. Indigenous African agriculture was not developed, and many persons left Malaŵi to seek employment in adjacent countries.

Between 1951 and 1953 the colonies of Northern and Southern Rhodesia and Nyasaland formed a federation. In 1963 the federation was dissolved, and the next year Malaŵi achieved independence as a member of the British Commonwealth; Hastings Kamuzu Banda of the Malaŵi Congress Party became prime minister. In 1966 Malaŵi became a republic, with Banda as president. In 1971 he was designated president for life, consolidating his almost complete political control. During the 1970s he adopted a foreign policy that was uncritical of South Africa but often critical of surrounding black African countries.

The economy prospered for much of the 1970s, owing in large part to foreign aid and capital investment in the country. In the early 1970s Malaŵi became a haven for antigovernment rebels from Mozambique. Malaŵi's first parliamentary elections since independence were held on June 29, 1978. In the early 1990s Malaŵi's close relationship with South Africa continued, with thousands of Malaŵian workers employed there, and Banda remained in power. His hold on the presidency was questioned, however, after a June 1993 referendum favouring creation of a multiparty state was approved by a wide margin. Banda's 30-year rule came to an end in May 1994, when he was defeated by Bakili Muluzi in multiparty presidential elections. Amid allegations of fraud, Malaŵi held its second free national elections in 1999.

Malaŵi, Lake (East Africa): *see* Nyasa, Lake.

Malay, Malay ORANG MELAYU ("Malay People"), any member of an ethnic group of the Malay Peninsula and portions of adjacent islands of Southeast Asia, including the east coast of Sumatra, the coast of Borneo, and smaller islands that lie between these areas. The Malay speak various dialects belonging to the Austronesian (Malayo-Polynesian) family of languages.

The Malay were once probably a people of coastal Borneo who expanded into Sumatra and the Malay Peninsula as a result of their trading and seafaring way of life. That this expansion occurred only in the last 1,500 years or so is indicated by the fact that the languages of the Malay group are all still very much alike, though very divergent from the languages of other peoples of Sumatra, Borneo, and other neighbouring lands. In the late 20th century the Malay constituted more than half of the population of Peninsular Malaysia (West Malaysia) and more than one-eighth of the population of East Malaysia (Sarawak and Sabah).

The Malay culture has been strongly influenced by that of other peoples, including the Siamese, Javanese, and Sumatran. The influence of Hindu India was historically great, and the Malay were largely Hinduized before they were converted to Islām in the 15th century. The population of the Malay Peninsula today includes large numbers of Indians and Chinese.

The Malay are mainly a rural people, living in villages rather than towns, where Chinese, Indians, and other groups predominate. Much of the Malay Peninsula is covered by jungle, and the villages, with populations from 50 to 1,000, are located along rivers and coasts or on roads. Houses are built on piling that raises them four to eight feet off the ground, with gabled roofs made of thatch; houses of the well-to-do have plank floors and tile roofs. The principal food crop is wet rice, and rubber is the main cash crop. The Malay Peninsula in the late 1970s produced more than two-fifths of the world's supply of natural rubber.

Traditionally the Malay had a somewhat feudal social organization with a sharp division between nobility and commoners. The head of a village was a commoner, but the chief of the district, to whom he reported, was a nobleman. The nobility has now been replaced by appointed and elected officials subject to a parliament and other elected bodies, but class distinctions are still marked.

Marriages have traditionally been arranged by the parents. The typical household consists of the husband and wife and their children. Marriage and inheritance are governed by Islāmic law.

The Malay religion is Islām of the school of Shāfiʿī. Muslim religious holidays are observed. Some Hindu ritual survives, as in the second part of the marriage ceremony and in various ceremonies of state. In rural areas the Malay have also preserved some of their old beliefs in spirits of the soil and jungle, which are partly Hindu in origin; they often have recourse to medicine men or shamans for the treatment of disease.

Malay Annals (15th or 16th century): *see* Sejarah Melayu.

Malay Archipelago, largest group of islands in the world, consisting of the more than 13,000 islands of Indonesia and the some 7,000 islands of the Philippines. The regional name "East Indies" is sometimes used as a synonym for the archipelago. New Guinea is usually arbitrarily included in the Malay Archipelago while the Andaman and Nicobar Islands in the northwest and the Bismarck Archipelago in the east are not. The principal islands and groups of the Republic of Indonesia include the Greater Sundas (Sumatra, Java, Borneo, and the Celebes), the Lesser Sundas, the Moluccas, and Irian Jaya (West New Guinea). The Philippines includes Luzon (north), Mindanao (south), and the Visayan Islands in between. Other political units in the archipelago are East Malaysia (Sabah and Sarawak), Brunei, and Papua New Guinea.

The archipelago extends along the Equator for more than 3,800 miles (6,100 km) and extends for 2,200 miles (3,500 km) in its greatest north-south dimension. Situated between the Pacific and Indian oceans, the islands of the archipelago enclose the Sulu, Celebes, Banda, Molucca, Sunda, Java, Flores, and Savu seas. They are separated from mainland Asia (west) by the Strait of Malacca and the South China Sea, from Taiwan (north) by the Bashi Channel, and from Australia (south) by the Torres Strait.

Structurally the archipelago divides into three parts: the Sunda Shelf, the Sahul Shelf (*qq.v.*), and the area of recent tectonic activity that lies between the two. The islands, with the exception of the northern Philippines, lie within 10 degrees of the Equator. Thus, they have high temperatures, averaging 80° F (21° C). The variable climatic element is rainfall, which ranges from more than 320 inches (8,100 mm) annually on slopes in Sumatra and Java to less than 20 inches (500 mm) in rain-shadow areas of western Celebes and the Lesser Sundas. Most of the archipelago averages more than 80 inches (2,000 mm), well distributed throughout the year, but the total decreases and the length of the dry season increases from central Java eastward through the Lesser Sundas and from Mindanao northward. Most of the islands receive rainfall from both the northeast (northern winter) and the southwest monsoons. Another climatic element is the typhoon, of which more than 20 arise each year in the southwestern Pacific (July to November) and then swing westward and northward, bringing violent winds and heavy rains to the Philippines. The flora and fauna of the archipelago are extremely rich and varied and reflect the character of the islands as a bridge between Asia and Australia.

Malayan peoples, who speak various languages belonging to the Austronesian, or Malayo-Polynesian, family of languages are the dominant population of the Malay Archipelago. Although two of the world's largest cities, Manila and Jakarta, are located there, the islands' economy is overwhelmingly rural and agricultural. The majority of the rural populace are sedentary cultivators, usually growing irrigated rice but sometimes corn (maize), yams, or cassava as their principal food crop. These sedentary smallholders grow many commercial crops, such as rubber and tobacco, as well as most of the region's sugar, copra, pepper, nutmeg, other spices, kapok, sago, and abaca fibre (Manila hemp). Plantations, introduced in the colonial period and located principally in Sumatra and Java, provide exports of rubber, palm oil, sisal, cinchona (quinine), and tea, as well as some coffee, tobacco, and copra. Nomadic hill cultivators still raise subsistence dry crops of rice and corn in more isolated localities.

Other important resources include the forests, which provide valuable timber, resins, rattans, and additional gathered products. Petroleum is the chief mineral resource, exploited in Sumatra, Indonesian Borneo, Brunei, and Irian Jaya. Tin mines on Singkep, Bangka, and Billiton islands, Indonesia, provide about 10 percent of the world's production. Deposits of bauxite are exploited in Borneo and the Riau Islands, and iron ore is mined in the central Philippines. Nickel is found in Celebes and gold, chrome, manganese, and copper in the Philippines. Although coal reserves are limited and of only fair quality, hydroelectric-power potential is great, but little developed.

Manufacturing is not greatly developed. Most important are handicraft industries and industries engaged in primary processing of agricultural and mineral products for export. Light manufacturing has expanded, with spinning mills, paper, glass, soap, and cigarette factories. There is some heavy industry.

Malay language, member of the Western, or Indonesian, branch of the Austronesian (Malayo-Polynesian) language family, spoken as a native language by more than 33,000,000 persons distributed over the Malay Peninsula, Sumatra, Borneo, and the numerous smaller islands of the area, and widely used in Malaysia and Indonesia as a second language. Malay shows the closest relationship to most of the other languages of Sumatra (Minangkabau, Kerintji, Rejang) and is clearly, but not so closely, related to the other Austronesian languages of Sumatra, Borneo, Java, and to the Cham languages of Vietnam.

Of the various dialects of Malay, the most important is that of the southern Malay Peninsula, the basis of standard Malay and of the official language of the Republic of Indonesia, Bahasa Indonesia, or Indonesian. A Malay pidgin called Bazaar Malay (*mĕlayu pasar,* "market Malay") was widely used as a lingua franca in the East Indian archipelago and was the basis of the colonial language used in Indonesia by the Dutch. The version of Bazaar Malay used in Chinese merchant communities in Malaysia is called Baba Malay. Languages or dialects closely related to Malay that are spoken on Borneo include Iban (Sea Dayak), Brunei Malay, Sambas Malay, Kutai Malay, and Banjarese.

Typical of Malay grammar is the use of affixes (particles attached to the beginning or end of a word or inserted within the word) and doubling, to mark changes in meaning or grammatical processes. Affixes are demonstrated in constructions such as *di-bĕli* "be bought" and *mĕm-bĕli* "buy" from the root form *beli* "buy!" and *kemauan* "desire" from *mau* "want." Doubling may be used to mark the plural—for example, *rumah* "house" and *rumah-rumah* "houses"—or to form derivative meanings, as in *kekuningkuningan* "tinted yellow" from *kuning* "yellow" and *bĕrlari-lari* "run around, keep running" from *bĕrlari* "run."

Modern Malay is written in two slightly differing forms of the Latin alphabet, one used in Indonesia and one in Malaysia, as well as in a form of the Arabic alphabet called Jawi, which is used in Malaya and in parts of Sumatra. The earliest written records in Malay are Sumatran inscriptions dating from the late 7th century and written in a Pallava (southern Indian) alphabet.

Malay literature effectively begins with the coming of Islām in the late 15th century; no literary works dating from the Hindu period (4th to late 15th centuries) have survived. Malay literature can be divided into that which was written in classical Malay, the written language of Malay-speaking Muslim communities scattered, from the 15th century, along all the coasts of Southeast Asia but based principally on the straits of Malacca; and modern Malaysian Malay, which, about 1920, began to replace classical Malay in Malaya.

Malay Peninsula, also called the KRA PENINSULA, in Southeast Asia, a long, narrow appendix of the mainland extending south for a distance of about 700 miles (1,127 km) through the Isthmus of Kra to Cape Balai, southernmost point of the Asian continent; its maximum width is 200 miles (322 km). It lies between the Andaman Sea of the Indian Ocean and the Strait of Malacca (west), the Singapore Strait (south), and the Gulf of Thailand and the South China Sea (east). Its central mountain range, rising to 7,175 feet (2,187 m) at Mount Tahan, divides the peninsula. The western coast is exposed to the southwest monsoons and the eastern coast to the northeast monsoons. Most of the western rivers have comparatively short courses, and navigation is limited by extensive silting near the sea. The eastern rivers are longer, with flatter gradients in their upper reaches. Politically the peninsula comprises the southwestern section of Thailand, Peninsular (or West) Malaysia, and Singapore. Known in ancient times as the Chersonesus Aurea ("Golden Chersonese," or "Golden Peninsula," from Greek *chersos,* "dry," and *nēsos,* "island"), it has formed a physical and cultural link between the mainland and the Malay Archipelago.

Malayalam language, also spelled MALAYĀLAM, language of the Dravidian family, spoken in southwestern India; it is the official language of the state of Kerala. Malayalam has three important regional dialects and a number of smaller ones. There is also some difference in dialect along caste lines and a distinction, called diglossia, between the formal, literary language and the colloquial tongue. Both the literary and colloquial languages use many words borrowed from Sanskrit. Closely related to Tamil, Malayalam differs from it in such aspects as the absence of personal endings on verbs. Like the Dravidian languages generally, Malayalam has a series of retroflex consonants (*e.g., ṭ, ḍ, ṇ;* sounds pronounced with the tongue tip curled back against the roof of the mouth), and it indicates such grammatical categories as tense, number, person, and case with suffixes.

Malayalam has a written tradition dating from the late 9th century, and the earliest literary work dates from the early 13th century. The language uses a script called Koleluttu (Rod script), which is derived from the Tamil writing system. The Tamil Grantha script also is used.

The history of Malayalam literature dates to the 13th century. Indigenous ballads and folk songs belong to the earliest times. Later literature was long influenced by Sanskrit, the language of scholarship, and by Tamil, the language of administration. All the branches of literature known in the West are cultivated today.

Malayan lar, species of gibbon (*q.v.*).

Malayan People's Anti-Japanese Army (MPAJA), guerrilla movement formed originally to oppose the Japanese occupation of Malaya during World War II. In December 1941 a rapid Japanese invasion commenced, and within 10 weeks it had conquered Malaya. British military forces had prepared for this possibility by training small Malayan guerrilla groups. Once war became a reality, the guerrillas organized the MPAJA. This army consisted primarily of Chinese Communists, with smaller numbers of Kuomintang (Nationalist) Chinese and some Malays. Because of the Chinese majority in the army, the Malayan Communist Party was able to infiltrate and indoctrinate the guerrillas and to stress that postwar Malaya would become Communist through their efforts.

Because the MPAJA was the only local resistance to the Japanese, Great Britain supplied it with officers and supplies. The army also received supplies and recruits from Chinese and Malays outside the jungle. The number of jungle fighters rose from about 3,000 in 1942 to 7,000 men and women in 1945. Upon British advice the MPAJA avoided large-scale action against the Japanese, but after the war its Communist-indoctrinated members emerged as heroes. This army attempted a brief, unsuccessful seizure of political power before the British military returned. The MPAJA officially disbanded when most of its members turned in their arms to the returning British forces. Its leadership, organization, and many of its arms remained underground, however, until the uprising of the Malayan Communist Party in 1948.

Malayan sun bear: *see* sun bear.

Malaysia, country of Southeast Asia, composed of two noncontiguous regions—Peninsular, or West, Malaysia and East Malaysia—separated by some 400 miles (650 km) of the South China Sea. Peninsular Malaysia (50,810 square miles [131,598 square km]) occupies the southern half of the Malay Peninsula; it is about 500 miles (800 km) long and 200 miles (325 km) wide and is bordered on the north by Thailand, on the south by Singapore, on the west by the Strait of Malacca, and on the east by the South China Sea. East Malaysia (76,510 square miles [198,160 square km]) occupies the northwestern part of the island of Borneo and is about 670 miles (1,075 km)

Malaysia

long and 240 miles (385 km) wide; it consists of the states of Sarawak and Sabah. It is bordered on the north and west by the South China Sea, on the east by the Sulu Sea and the Celebes Sea, and on the south by Kalimantan (Indonesian) Borneo; the small independent coastal sultanate of Brunei is surrounded on land by Sarawak. The capital of Malaysia is Kuala Lumpur. Area, including inland water, 127,584 square miles (330,442 square km). Pop. (2002 est.) 24,370,000.

A brief treatment of Malaysia follows. For full treatment, *see* MACROPAEDIA: Southeast Asia.

For current history and for statistics on society and economy, *see* BRITANNICA BOOK OF THE YEAR.

The land. Malaysia is unique in that it is the only country that has territory on both the mainland and insular regions of Southeast Asia. Peninsular Malaysia is largely mountainous (one-half of the total area is more than 500 feet [150 m] above sea level) and consists of several north–south-aligned mountain ranges dominated by the 300-mile- (500-kilometre-) long Main Range, with elevations rising to more than 7,000 feet (2,000 m). Bordering the mountainous core are coastal lowlands that are heavily populated on the west and are narrow, swampy, and densely forested on the east. In East Malaysia the coastal plains (10 to 20 miles [16 to 32 km] wide in the east and 20 to 40 miles [32 to 64 km] wide in the west) rise to a hill and valley region and then to a mountainous core that has elevations between 4,000 and 7,000 feet (1,200 and 2,000 m) and includes Mount Kinabalu (13,455 feet [4,101 m]) in the extreme northeast, the highest point in the country. The 270-mile- (435-kilometre-) long Pahang River is the principal river of Peninsular Malaysia, and in East Malaysia the Rajang and the Kinabatangan are the principal rivers of Sarawak and Sabah, respectively.

Malaysia's equatorial climate is strongly influenced by northeast (November or December to March) and southwest (June to September or early October) monsoons. Mean annual temperatures range between 77° and 86° F (25° and 30° C) in the lowlands and 72° and 83° F (22° and 28° C) on the interior mountains. The mean annual rainfall is very high and ranges from 100 inches (2,500 mm) in Peninsular Malaysia to 90 inches (2,300 mm) in Sarawak and to 130 inches (3,300 mm) in Sabah. Relative humidity is also high, averaging 80 to 85 percent.

The hot and humid climate favours dense tropical vegetation—up to three-fifths of the land is under forests, most of it evergreen rain forests, and vegetation includes bamboo, camphor, ebony, sandalwood, teak, palm, and mangrove forests. The country's varied animal life includes elephant, tiger, leopard, wild ox, sun (honey) bear, wild pig, orangutan, gibbon, and some rhinoceros. East Malaysia has one of the largest and most varied bird populations in the world, including hornbills, parrots, broadbills, swifts, pigeons, woodpeckers, and many other species. Tree crops, notably rubber and palm oil, are the country's most important cash crops.

Malaysia's tin reserves are the third largest in the world after those of Brazil and China. Its proven reserves of petroleum and natural gas are also important.

The people. Because it commands the Strait of Malacca, one of the major sea-lanes of the world, the Malay Peninsula has been the meeting place of peoples from other parts of Asia. This is reflected in the diversity of the country's population. Ethnic Malays constitute about two-thirds of Malaysia's inhabitants; they are usually Muslim and speak an Austronesian language called Malay (or Bahasa Malaysia), which is the country's official language. Chinese who migrated from southeastern China make up about three-tenths of the population, and Indians, Pakistanis, and Tamils (from Sri Lanka) account for most of the remainder. The Chinese are mostly Buddhists, Taoists, or Confucians, with some Christians. Most of the Indians and Sri Lankans are Hindus, and most of the Pakistanis are Muslim. Tamils speak either Dravidian or Indo-European languages. In Peninsular Malaysia the Orang Asli peoples, including the Jakun, Semang, and Senoi groups, practice traditional religions, and some are Muslims.

The population of East Malaysia is even more diverse than that of Peninsular Malaysia. The main groups are the Chinese (about one-third of the population) and some 25 ethnic groups, as well as smaller tribal subgroups that speak Austronesian languages. The Iban (Sea Dayak), who live in Sarawak, were formerly headhunters and continue to live in communal longhouses. The Bidayuh (Land Dayak) inhabit the hill country of western Sarawak. The Kadazan are the largest indigenous group in Sabah.

The annual rate of growth of Malaysia's population was once one of the highest in Asia but has decreased steadily since 1960. Peninsular Malaysia has about four-fifths of the country's population. Formerly high birth rates have dropped among the Chinese and Indian ethnic groups in particular. The population is young—about 37 percent are younger than 15 years of age. Health standards are good for a developing country, and the life expectancy is 69 years for men and 73 years for women. Approximately two-fifths of the population is urban, and the trend of migration is toward the cities.

The economy. Malaysia has a predominantly market economy that has been transformed from one heavily dependent on the production and export of raw materials to one that is much more diversified. The New Economic Policy and its successors, initiated after ethnic riots in 1970 against prosperous minority (usually Chinese or Indian merchant) communities, were designed to reduce poverty among Malays and other indigenous people. The gross national product (GNP) is growing more rapidly than the population; the GNP per capita is, after Singapore and Brunei, the third-highest in Southeast Asia.

Agriculture accounts for approximately one-fifth of the gross domestic product (GDP) and employs about one-fourth of the workforce. Land reform was initiated after 1955 but benefited relatively few peasants. Many Malays continue to depend on subsistence farming, and most smallholders live in poverty.

Malaysia's production of rice, the chief staple, meets nearly all of its domestic demand. Rubber, the main cash crop, is grown primarily on small farms and accounts for one-fourth of the world's production of this commodity. Private estates provide about one-half of palm-oil production and the Federal Land Development Authority, an organization of smallholders, accounts for one-third. Roundwood, exported to Japan, Taiwan, South Korea, and China, is a major source of foreign exchange. Extensive afforestation was initiated in 1981.

Malaysia's mineral industries are dominated by the production and export of petroleum, which the government controls, and tin, in whose exploitation it participates. Singapore, Japan, and South Korea are major markets for Malaysia's crude petroleum; its tin production is threatened by depletion of reserves and price fluctuations. Quantities of copper and bauxite are also mined and exported.

Manufacturing industries account for more than one-fourth of the GDP and employ about one-fifth of the workforce. The Chinese and other immigrants dominate most industries; foreign investment in domestic industries is encouraged. Rubber goods, cement, iron and steel products, and radio and television sets are important manufactures.

About two-thirds of Malaysia's roads are paved. Peninsular Malaysia has several highways, but Sabah and Sarawak have poor-quality roads. The rail network is well developed in Peninsular Malaysia, but Sarawak has no railway, and Sabah has only a short line for freight and passenger traffic. River transport continues to play a major role in East Malaysia. Kuala Lumpur is served by many international carriers, including Malaysia Airlines, a state-controlled line. There are five regional airports and numerous smaller airports located in Peninsular and East Malaysia.

The Malaysian Trade Union Congress, which was founded in 1949, encompasses most unions in the country.

Malaysia has enjoyed a positive balance of trade in recent years. Major trading partners are Japan, Singapore, the United States, the United Kingdom, and Germany.

Government and social conditions. Malaysia is a federation of states governed by a constitutional monarchy. The federal government is responsible for foreign affairs, defense, internal security, justice (except where Islāmic and native law prevail), federal citizenship, finance, commerce, industry, communications, and transportation. The state governments deal with immigration, civil service, and customs matters. Nine of the states are governed by hereditary rulers acting on the advice of State Executive Councils; the other four states are headed by appointed governors.

The nominal head of the federal government is the paramount ruler, who is elected to five-year terms by the Conference of Rulers, a body composed of the states' nine hereditary rulers. According to the country's constitution of 1957, however, real political power rests with the federal legislature, consisting of a Senate (Dewan Negara) and a House of Representatives (Dewan Rakyat). The Senate's 69 members include 43 appointed by the paramount ruler and 26 elected by legislative assemblies in the states. The powerful House of Representatives has 180 members elected to five-year terms by universal adult suffrage. The leader of the party with the most seats in the House of Representatives serves as prime minister and names a cabinet, whose members are appointed by the paramount ruler. The dominant political organization is the National Front, a coalition of parties representing the country's major ethnic groups.

Malaysia's social-welfare system provides employed persons with work injury, old age, and disability benefits. The general level of the country's health compares favourably with those of other developing nations. Malaysia is now free of many tropical diseases, but some diseases borne by animal vectors, such as malaria, are still a problem in rural areas. Health services are generally adequate in the towns and cities, and medical care is free for those who live near a government hospital or clinic, but there is a shortage of doctors and hospitals in the countryside.

Education is free, but non-compulsory for children between the ages of 6 and 15. It is estimated that almost 90 percent of all primary school age children attend the country's six-year primary schools. Graduates of this level may attend lower, and later upper, secondary school. Upper secondary graduates, upon certification, may enter one of the country's universities.

The nation's press is privately owned but restricted by laws that forbid the publishing of any matter considered harmful to the country's security, order, or morality. The broadcast media are government owned.

Cultural life. Malaysia, with its complex family of peoples and cultures, is a melting pot of traditions stemming from the Malay Archipelago as well as from China, India, and the West. Malay and Bornean cultures are indigenous to the area. The most important literary work in the Malay language is considered to be *Sejarah Melayu* ("Malay Annals") written about 1535. The work presents a detailed account of the medieval city-state of Malacca (modern Melaka city). The *pantunis* is a four-line verse spoken or sung at festivals and weddings. The nation's multifaceted culture is reflected in the National Museum in Kuala Lumpur, with traditional Chinese theatre scenes; the Malacca Museum features Chinese porcelain, furniture, and costumes; and the Sarawak Museum possesses a collection on Bornean ethnography.

History. Malaya has been inhabited for at least 6,000 to 8,000 years. Neolithic culture was well established by 2500–1500 BC. Small Malayan kingdoms existed in the 2nd or 3rd centuries AD, when adventurers from India arrived and initiated more than 1,000 years of Indian influence. Sumatran exiles founded Malacca (*c.* 1400) and secured Chinese protection for the city-state. Malacca entered a golden age as a commercial and Islāmic religious centre, but in 1511 it was captured by the Portuguese. When the Dutch captured Malacca in 1641, the port was no longer an important trading centre.

Minangkabau peoples from Sumatra migrated to Malaya during the late 17th century, bringing with them a matrilineal culture. In the 18th century the Buginese from the island of Celebes invaded Malaya and established the sultanates of Selangor and Johore.

The British founded a settlement on Singapore Island in 1819 and by 1867 had established the Straits Settlements—Malacca, Singapore, and Penang (now Pinang) Island. During the late 19th century Chinese began to migrate to Malaya. In 1896 the Malay states accepted British advisors, and Perak, Selangor, Negri Sembilan, and Pahang formed a federation.

From the 1890s the British invested heavily in Malaya, developing transportation and rubber plantations. In 1941 the Japanese invaded Malaya and captured Singapore in early 1942. After World War II the British tried unsuccessfully to organize Malaya into one state. This led to the birth of Malayan nationalism, which opposed a colonial status. In 1946 the United Malaya National Organization (UMNO) was established, and in 1948 the peninsula was federated with Penang Island. In the same year the Malayan Communist Party was formed. In 1955 the Malayan Chinese Association joined UMNO in an anticommunist, anticolonial coalition that won 51 of 52 parliamentary seats. The British relinquished their powers, and in 1957 Malayan independence was achieved.

In the 1960s membership in the federation shifted several times, finally settling into the present pattern in 1963, when Malaysia was established. Turbulence in the government went on into the early 1970s, when stability returned and the Malaysian economy began to prosper. Despite considerable regional and ethnic divisions, Malaysia has made significant gains in creating national unity.

Malbodius, Jan (Flemish painter): *see* Mabuse, Jan.

Malbone, Edward Greene (b. August 1777, Newport, R.I., U.S.—d. May 7, 1807, Savannah, Ga.), painter generally regarded as the greatest of American miniaturists.

Largely self-taught, Malbone began his professional career in Providence, R.I., at the age of 17 and quickly developed a remarkably fine technique. A man of agreeable manners, diligent, and blessed with what Washington Allston called "the happy talent . . . of elevating the character without impairing the likeness," Malbone was, during his short career, the most sought-after miniaturist of his day in Providence, Newport, Boston, New York City, Philadelphia, and Savannah. His career was cut short by tuberculosis. Many of his miniatures have survived and are highly prized for their delicacy of drawing, richness of colour, and convincing characterization. He had no formal pupils, but freely advised other artists, notably Charles Fraser, William Dunlap, and John Wesley Jarvis.

Malbork, German MARIENBURG, city, Elbląg *województwo* (province), northern Poland. It lies on the easternmost distributary of the Vistula River Delta known as the Nogat.

Malbork castle, Poland, dating from the 13th century
Elliott Erwitt—Magnum

The town was founded on the site of a medieval Prussian estate fortified by the Teutonic Knights in 1236 and once the residence of their grand master; the surrounding settlement received municipal rights in 1276. From the 13th to the 15th century the fortress was one of the most powerful in Europe. Incorporated into Poland in 1457, Malbork passed to the Prussians in 1772, and in 1920 Germany gained control of the town; it was returned to Poland after World War II.

Malbork is now a transportation centre located on major rail and highway routes. Local industry specializes in the processing of sugar and dairy products from the surrounding area. Pop. (1991 est.) 39,800.

Malchus (Neoplatonist philosopher): *see* Porphyry.

malcoha, also spelled MALKOHA, any of several species of cuckoos of southern Asia, especially members of the genus *Rhopodytes* (often placed in *Phaenicophaeus*). Malcohas

Red-faced malcoha (*Phaenicophaeus pyrrhocephalus*)
Painting by John P. O'Neill

are noted for having a long tail, a stout bill with bristly base, and bare skin around the eyes. They are forest birds that move in a squirrellike manner along branches in thick vegetation.

Malcolm, name of Scottish kings, grouped below chronologically and indicated by the symbol •.

• Malcolm I, also called MALCOLM MACDONALD (d. 954), king of the Picts and Scots (Alba).

Malcolm succeeded to the crown when his cousin Constantine II entered a monastery (943). He annexed Moray to the kingdom for the first time. After driving the Danes from York, the English king Edmund turned Cumbria over to Malcolm, apparently as a fief or seal of alliance. Later, when Norsemen again invaded the land, the Scots sent raids against the English, and in 954 the West Saxon king Eadred reunited the northern counties to his dominions. Malcolm was slain the same year.

• Malcolm II (b. *c.* 954—d. Nov. 25, 1034), king of Scotland from 1005 to 1034, the first to reign over an extent of land roughly corresponding to much of modern Scotland.

Malcolm succeeded to the throne after killing his predecessor, Kenneth III, and allegedly secured his territory by defeating a Northumbrian army at the battle of Carham (*c.* 1016); he not only confirmed the Scottish hold over the land between the rivers Forth and Tweed but also secured Strathclyde about the same time. Eager to secure the royal succession for his daughter's son Duncan, he tried to eliminate possible rival claimants; but Macbeth, with royal connections to both Kenneth II and Kenneth III, survived to challenge the succession.

• Malcolm III CANMORE (b. *c.* 1031—d. Nov. 13, 1093, near Alnwick, Northumberland, Eng.), king of Scotland from 1058 to 1093, founder of the dynasty that consolidated royal power in the Scottish kingdom.

The son of King Duncan I (reigned 1034–40), Malcolm lived in exile in England during part of the reign of his father's murderer, Macbeth (reigned 1040–57). Malcolm killed Macbeth in battle in 1057 and then ascended the throne. After the conquest of England by William the Conqueror, in 1066, Malcolm gave refuge to the Anglo-Saxon prince Edgar the Aetheling and his sisters, one of whom, Margaret (later St. Margaret), became his second wife.

Malcolm acknowledged the overlordship of William in 1072 but nevertheless soon violated his feudal obligations and made five raids into England. During the last of these invasions he was killed by the forces of King William II Rufus (reigned 1087–1100). Except for a brief interval after Malcolm's death, the Scottish throne remained in his family until the death of Queen Margaret, the Maid of Norway, in 1290. Of Malcolm's six sons by Margaret, three succeeded to the throne: Edgar (reigned 1097–1107), Alexander I (1107–24), and David I (1124–53).

• **Malcolm IV,** byname MALCOLM THE MAIDEN (b. 1141?—d. Dec. 9, 1165), king of Scotland (1153–65).

Malcolm ascended the throne at the age of 11. He was the eldest son of Henry, Earl of Huntingdon and of Northumberland (d. 1152), and succeeded his grandfather King David I. Under Malcolm's predecessors, the kingdom of Scotland had been extended to embrace the modern English counties of Northumberland and Cumbria. In 1157, by a treaty signed at Chester, England's King Henry II forced the boy king Malcolm to surrender these counties in return for confirming Malcolm's rights to the earldom of Huntingdon.

Malcolm died young, unmarried (thus his nickname, the Maiden) and without issue, and was succeeded by his brother, William I the Lion.

Malcolm X, original name MALCOLM LITTLE, Muslim name EL-HAJJ MALIK EL-SHABAZZ (b. May 19, 1925, Omaha, Neb., U.S.—d. Feb. 21, 1965, New York, N.Y.), black militant leader who articulated concepts of race pride and black nationalism in the early 1960s. After his assassination, the widespread distribution of his life story—*The Autobiography of Malcolm X* (1965)—made him an ideological hero, especially among black youth.

Growing up in Lansing, Mich., Malcolm saw his house burned down at the hands of the white supremacist Ku Klux Klan. Two years later his father was murdered, and Malcolm's mother was subsequently placed in a mental institution. Malcolm spent the following years in detention homes, and in his early teens he moved to Boston to live with his sister. In 1946, while in prison for burglary, he was converted to the Black Muslim faith (Nation of Islam); this sect professed the superiority of black people and the inherent evil of whites. Released from prison in 1952, Malcolm went to Nation of Islam headquarters in Chicago,

Malcolm X
AP/Wide World Photos

met the sect's leader, Elijah Muhammad, and embraced its rigorous asceticism. He changed his last name to "X," a custom among Nation of Islam followers who considered their family names to have originated with white slaveholders.

Malcolm X was sent on speaking tours around the country and soon became the most effective speaker and organizer for the Nation of Islam. He founded many new mosques and greatly increased the movement's membership. In 1961 he founded *Muhammad Speaks,* the official publication of the movement. He was eventually assigned to be minister of the important Mosque Number Seven in New York City's Harlem area.

Speaking with bitter eloquence against the white exploitation of black people, Malcolm developed a brilliant platform style, which soon won him a large and dedicated following. He derided the civil-rights movement and rejected both integration and racial equality, calling instead for black separatism, black pride, and black self-dependence. Because he advocated the use of violence (for self-protection) and appeared to many to be a fanatic, his leadership was rejected by most civil-rights leaders, who emphasized nonviolent resistance to racial injustice.

Malcolm X described the assassination of President John F. Kennedy (Nov. 22, 1963) as a "case of chickens coming home to roost"—an instance of the kind of violence that whites had long used against blacks. Malcolm's success had by this time aroused jealousy within the Black Muslim hierarchy, and, in response to his comments on the Kennedy assassination, Elijah Muhammad suspended Malcolm from the movement. In March 1964 Malcolm X left the Nation of Islam and announced the formation of his own religious organization. As a result of a pilgrimage he took to Mecca in April 1964, he modified his views of black separatism, declaring that he no longer believed whites to be innately evil and acknowledging his vision of the possibility of world brotherhood. In October 1964 he reaffirmed his conversion to orthodox Islām.

Growing hostility between Malcolm's followers and the rival Black Muslims manifested itself in violence and threats against his life. He was shot to death at a rally of his followers at a Harlem ballroom. Three Black Muslims were convicted of the murder.

The Autobiography of Malcolm X was written by Alex Haley after he had conducted numerous interviews with Malcolm X shortly before the latter's death. The book was immediately recognized as a classic of black American autobiography.

Articles are alphabetized word by word, not letter by letter

Malczewski, Antoni (b. June 3, 1793, Warsaw [Poland], or Knyaginino, near Dubna, Ukraine, Russian Empire—d. May 2, 1826, Warsaw), Polish Romantic poet.

A member of a wealthy military and landholding family, Malczewski was educated at the lycée of Krzemieniec in Volhynia and then served in the Napoleonic Polish army of the duchy of Warsaw. When in 1815 the major part of the duchy became the kingdom of Poland with the Russian tsar as its king, Malczewski was demobilized. He traveled in western Europe, returned, and eventually settled in 1821 in the Ukraine (formerly Volhynia), where he became entangled in an unhappy emotional affair with a beautiful woman from a neighbouring town who was suffering from a nervous illness. Compelled by social pressure Malczewski left, followed by her, and they settled in Warsaw, where in 1825 he published a long poem, *Maria,* which constitutes his only contribution to Polish poetry, but his rank is matched only by that of Adam Mickiewicz. In the poem, Wacław, a young husband, goes to fight the Tatars and, after routing the raiders, hurries home to his wife, Maria; but all he finds is a cold corpse. The poem makes use of diversified rhythms and carefully chosen rhymes; and its Byronic hero, as well as its picture of the Ukraine as a land of sombre charm, assured Malczewski both popularity and a high position in Polish literature.

Mālda, formerly OLD MĀLDA, also spelled MĀLDAH, town, north-central West Bengal state, northeastern India. It lies just east of the confluence of the Mahānanda and Kālindri rivers and is part of the English Bāzār urban agglomeration. The town rose to prominence as the river port of the Hindu capital of Pandua. During the 18th century it was the seat of prosperous cotton and silk industries. It remains an important distributing centre for rice, jute, and wheat. Historical monuments include the mosque Jāmi' Masjid (1566) and the landmark Nimasari tower across the river. Constituted a municipality in 1867, it has several colleges affiliated with the University of North Bengal. Rice, jute, legumes, and oilseeds are the chief crops in the surrounding area. Mulberry plantations and mango orchards occupy large areas; mango trade and silk manufacture are the main economic activities. Pop. (1981) town, 8,579.

Malden, city, Middlesex county, eastern Massachusetts, U.S. It lies along the Malden River, a branch of the Mystic River, just north of Boston. It is bounded by the towns of Melrose, Revere, Everett, and Medford and by Middlesex Fells Park (a state reservation). Settled in 1640, it became a part of Charlestown and was known as the Mystic Side. In 1649 it was incorporated as a town and named after Malden (now part of Kingston upon Thames), Eng. The city is now a residential, industrial, and shopping suburb of Boston. Its manufactures include rubber footwear, electronic parts, metal cans, paints, drugs, and clothing. The city's Bell Rock Memorial Park was named for the bell that in colonial times summoned the people to worship or sounded alarms in times of danger; there is a Civil War Soldiers and Sailors Monument atop the rock. Inc. city, 1881. Pop. (1990) 53,884.

Malden, Arthur Capel, Viscount: *see* Essex, Arthur Capel, 1st Earl of.

Malden Island, formerly INDEPENDENCE ISLAND, coral atoll in the Central and Southern Line Islands, part of Kiribati, southwestern Pacific Ocean. It is situated 1,700 miles (2,700 km) south of Honolulu. A level formation with a land area of 11 square miles (28 square km) and a large lagoon, it was first sighted in 1825 by a British naval officer, George Anson Byron. During the second half of the 19th century, when its guano deposits were being worked, the island was claimed by the United States under the Guano Act of 1856. Malden has remnants of an old Polynesian habitation. It was used (1956–64) as a viewing base by the British, who were testing nuclear weapons on nearby Kiritimati (Christmas) Atoll. The island became a part of the Gilbert and Ellice Islands Colony in 1972 and a part of independent Kiribati in 1979. It has no inhabitants.

Maldives, also called MALDIVE ISLANDS, formally REPUBLIC OF MALDIVES, Divehi DIVEHI JUMHURIYYA, independent island nation consisting of a chain of about 1,300 small coral islands and sandbanks (202 of which are inhabited), grouped in clusters, or atolls, in the Indian Ocean. The islands extend more than 510 miles (820 km) from north to south and 80 miles (130 km) from east to west. The northernmost atoll is about 370 miles (600 km) south-southwest of the Indian mainland, and the central area, including the capital island of Male, is about 400 miles (645 km) southwest of Sri Lanka. The population in 1991 was estimated at 220,700.

The land. The Maldive Islands, with a total land area of 115 square miles (298 square km), are built of coral on the crowns of an ancient, submerged volcanic mountain range. All of the islands are low-lying, none rising to more than 6 feet (1.8 m) above sea level. Barrier reefs protect the islands from the destructive effects of monsoons. The rainy season, from May to August, is brought by the southwest monsoon; from December to March, the northeast monsoon brings dry and mild winds. The average annual temperature varies from 86° to 76° F (30° to 24° C). Rainfall averages about 84 inches (2,130 mm) a year. The atolls have sandy beaches, lagoons, and a luxuriant growth of coconut palms, together with breadfruit trees and tropical bushes. Fish abound in the reefs, lagoons, and seas adjoining the islands; sea turtles are caught for food and for their oil, a traditional medicine.

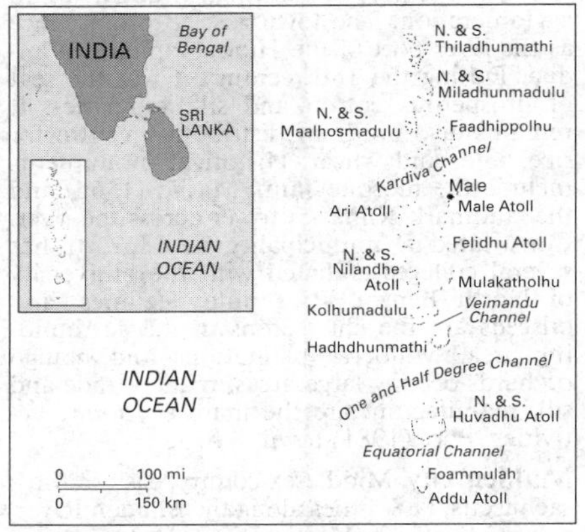

Maldives

The people. The Maldivians are a mixed people, speaking an Indo-European language called Divehi (the official language); Arabic, Hindi, and English are also spoken. Islām is the state religion. The first settlers, it is generally believed, were Dravidian and Sinhalese peoples from southern India and Sri Lanka. Traders from Arab countries, Malaya, Madagascar, Indonesia, and China visited the islands through the centuries. With the exception of those living in Male, the only relatively large settlement in the Maldives, the inhabitants of Maldives live in villages on small islands in scattered atolls. Only about 20 of the islands have more than 1,000 inhabitants, and the southern islands are more densely populated than are the northern ones. The birth rate is relatively high in Maldives, but the death rate is fairly low. More than two-fifths of the total population is under 15 years of age.

The economy. Maldives, one of the poorest countries in the world, has a developing economy based on fishing, tourism, boatbuilding, and boat repairing. The gross national product (GNP) per capita is among the lowest in the world. Most of the population subsist outside a money economy on fishing, coconut collecting, and the growing of vegetables and melons, roots and tubers (cassava, sweet potatoes, and yams), and tropical fruits. Cropland, scattered over many small islands, is minimal, and nearly all of the staple foods must be imported. Fishing, the traditional base of the economy, continues to be the most important sector, providing employment for approximately one-fourth of the labour force as well as accounting for a major portion of the export earnings. Tuna (tunny) is the predominant species caught, mostly by the pole-and-line method, although a good deal of the fishing fleet has been mechanized. Most of the fish catch is sold to foreign companies for processing and export.

The Maldives national shipping line forms the basis of one of the country's commercial industries. Tourism is a fast-growing sector of the economy. Resort islands and modern hotels in Male have attracted increasing numbers of tourists during the winter months. Industries are largely of the handicraft or cottage type, including the making of coir (coconut-husk fibre) and coir products, boatbuilding, and construction. Imports include consumer goods such as food (principally rice), textiles, medicines, and petroleum products. Fish, mostly dried, frozen, or canned skipjack tuna, account for the bulk of exports. The United States, Sri Lanka, the United Kingdom, and Japan are the main trading partners.

Boats provide the principal means of transport between the atolls, and scheduled shipping services link the country with Sri Lanka, Singapore, and India. There is a national airways, and the airport at Male island handles international traffic.

Government and social conditions. The head of state is the president, who, upon nomination by the Citizens' Council (*Majlis*), is elected by popular vote to a renewable five-year term. The unicameral Citizens' Council has 40 members elected to five-year terms—2 from Male island and 2 from each of the 19 atoll groups into which the country is divided for administrative purposes—and 8 who are appointed by the president. The president appoints all judges, who administer justice under the tenets of Islām.

Most Maldivians rely on traditional medical practices when ill; Male has a small hospital. Major illnesses include gastroenteritis, typhoid, cholera, and malaria. Life expectancy is about 65 years.

Three types of formal education are available in the Maldives, including traditional schools (*makthabs*) designed to teach the reading and reciting of the Qur'ān, Divehi-language schools, and English-language primary and secondary schools. The English-language schools are the only ones that teach a standard curriculum and offer secondary-level education. Students must go abroad for higher education. Only about two-thirds of the school-age population is enrolled in schools.

History. The archipelago was inhabited as early as the 5th century BC by Buddhist peoples who were probably from Sri Lanka and southern India. According to tradition, Islām was adopted in AD 1153. Ibn Baṭṭūṭah, a notable North African traveler, resided there during the mid-1340s and described conditions at that time, remarking disapprovingly on the freedom of the women—a feature that has been noticeable throughout Maldivian history. The Portuguese forcibly established themselves in Male from 1558 until their expulsion in 1573. In the 17th century the islands were a sultanate under the protection of the Dutch rulers of Ceylon, and, after the British took possession of Ceylon in 1796, they became a British protectorate, a status formalized in 1887. In 1932, before which time most of the administrative powers rested with sultans or sultanas, the first democratic constitution was proclaimed, the country remaining a sultanate. A republic was proclaimed in 1953, but later in that year the country reverted to a sultanate. In 1965 the Maldive Islands attained full political independence from the British, and in 1968 a new republic was inaugurated and the former sultanate was abolished. The last British troops left on March 29, 1976, the date thereafter celebrated in the Maldives as Independence Day. The Maldives became a member of the Commonwealth in 1982.

Maldon, town and district, county of Essex, England. The town site, on the south side of the Blackwater Estuary, was occupied in prehistoric times, and a burgh was established there by the Saxons. A battle, commemorated in an Old English poem, was fought between the English and the victorious Danes in the area in 991. Maldon remained a royal town, and Henry II granted its first charter in 1171. Several medieval buildings survive. The district surrounds the Blackwater Estuary and extends south to that of the River Crouch. Area 139 square miles (359 square km). Pop. (1991) town, 15,841; (2001) district, 59,433.

Maldonado, town, southeastern Uruguay. It lies near the Atlantic coast and is 67 miles (107 km) east of Montevideo. Founded in 1757, it was sacked by British forces in 1806, but many colonial buildings and ruins of Spanish fortifications remain. Especially noteworthy are the watchtower (El Vigía), fortifications on Gorriti Island (an island that shelters Maldonado's port), the parish church, and the Mazzoni Museum. Grains and wool are the principal trade commodities; the main industry is seal fishing at Lobos Island, a few miles south-southeast. Maldonado has a forestry school. Palm trees, maritime pines, and eucalyptus grow along Maldonado's shoreline. Tuna, black sea bass, mackerel, and anchovies are harvested from the Atlantic Ocean. Maldonado is linked by rail and highway to Montevideo, and it has an airfield. Pop. (1996) 48,936.

Male, island and atoll, capital of Maldives, Indian Ocean. It lies about 400 miles (645 km) southwest of Sri Lanka. As the seat of government for the Maldivians, it has central courts, a government hospital, public and private schools with instruction in English, and a vocational-training school focused on engineering. It is a trade and tourist centre and is connected with Sri Lanka and India by steamship lines. Male International Airport handles both domestic and international flights. Male's chief products are fish (bonito and tuna), coconuts, breadfruit, and woven palm mats. Pop. (2000) 74,069.

Malebo Pool, formerly STANLEY POOL, lakelike expansion of the lower Congo River above Livingstone Falls, between the Congo (west) and Zaire (east). It covers an area of 174 square miles (450 square km) and is divided into deep navigable channels by Bamu Island (70 square miles [181 square km]) in its centre. Its maximum depth is 52 feet (16 m). Brazzaville (Congo) and Kinshasa (Zaire) occupy its northwestern and southwestern shores, respectively.

Malebranche, Nicolas (b. Aug. 6, 1638, Paris, France—d. Oct. 13, 1715, Paris), French Roman Catholic priest, theologian, and major philosopher of Cartesianism, the school of philosophy arising from the work of René Descartes. His philosophy sought to synthesize Cartesianism with the thought of St. Augustine and with Neoplatonism.

Malebranche, engraving by de Rochefort, 1707
Archives Photographiques

Malebranche, the youngest child of the secretary to King Louis XIII, suffered all his life from malformation of the spine. After studying philosophy and theology at the Collège de la Marche and the Sorbonne, he joined the Congregation of the Oratory and in 1664 was ordained a priest. Chancing to read Descartes's

Traité de l'homme ("Treatise on Man"), he felt compelled to begin a systematic study of mathematics, physics, and the writings of Descartes.

Malebranche's principal work is *De la recherche de la vérité,* 3 vol. (1674–75; *Search After Truth*). Criticism of its theology by others led him to amplify his views in *Traité de la nature et de la grâce* (1680; *Treatise of Nature and Grace*). His *Entretiens sur la métaphysique et sur la religion* (1688; "Dialogues on Metaphysics and on Religion"), a series of 14 dialogues, has been called the best introduction to his system. His other writings include research into the nature of light and colour and studies in infinitesimal calculus and in the psychology of vision. His scientific works won him election to the Académie des Sciences in 1699. Also influential are his *Méditations chrétiennes* (1683; "Christian Meditations") and *Traité de morale* (1683; *A Treatise of Morality*).

Central to Malebranche's metaphysics is his doctrine that "we see all things in God." Human knowledge of both the internal and the external world is not possible except as the result of a relation between man and God. Changes, whether of the position of physical objects or of the thoughts of an individual, are directly caused not, as popularly supposed, by the objects or individuals themselves but by God. What are commonly called "causes" are merely "occasions" on which God acts to produce effects. This view, known as Occasionalism, hesitantly and inconsistently applied by Descartes, was more completely developed by Malebranche. Cartesian dualism between body and mind was also rendered compatible with orthodox Roman Catholicism by Malebranche. The inability of minds and bodies to interact is, according to Malebranche, simply a special case of the impossibility of interaction between created things in general.

With reference to sensation, Malebranche believed that sensory experiences have only a pragmatic value, appraising men of harm or benefit to their bodies. As aids in reaching knowledge, they are deceptive because they do not bear genuine witness to the actual nature of things perceived. Ideas alone are the objects of human thought processes. All such ideas are eternally contained in a single archetypal or model idea of the essence of matter called "intelligible extension." God's mind or reason contains ideas of all of the truths that men can discover. God's creation occurred after his contemplation of the same ideas, which are known only partially by men but are completely known to God. In contrast to Descartes's notion that men can directly perceive themselves, Malebranche declared that a person can know *that* he is but not *what* he is. He also reversed the Cartesian dictum that human existence can be known without demonstration, whereas God's requires demonstration; Malebranche held that man's own nature is completely unknowable, whereas God's is an immediate certainty needing no proof.

BIBLIOGRAPHY. Ralph W. Church, *A Study in the Philosophy of Malebranche* (1931, reprinted 1970); Beatrice K. Rome, *The Philosophy of Malebranche* (1963); Daisie Radner, *Malebranche: A Study of a Cartesian System* (1978).

Malecite, Algonkian-speaking Indians who occupied the Saint John Valley in what is now New Brunswick and also extended into the northeastern corner of Maine. Their language was closely related to that of the Passamaquoddy, and they were members of the Abnaki, a confederacy of Algonkian-speaking tribes organized for protection against the Iroquois League. The Malecite practiced corn (maize) cultivation, as well as hunting and fishing. Birch bark and wood were used for manufacture of utensils, tools, and weapons. A tribal council, consisting of the war chief, the civil chief, and representatives of each family decided most tribal questions; a general council of the entire tribe decided war matters.

Although the Malecite were probably encountered by English and French explorers as early as the middle of the 16th century, the first record of such contact dates from Samuel de Champlain's voyage of 1604. Fort La Tour, built on the Saint John River early in the 17th century, became a centre for the tribe, where they learned the use of firearms and other European implements. The few French settlers in this area intermarried with the Malecite, strengthening their alliance with the French and their hostility to the English. After the English gained control of the Malecite territory, there were disputes over land until 1776, after which certain lands were assigned to the Indians. By 1856 their territory was reduced to the Tobique River Valley and another small tract. The descendants of the Malecite live in New Brunswick, Quebec Province, and Maine.

Mālegaon, town, northwestern Mahārāshtra state, western India, on the Girna River, part of the Nāsik urban agglomeration, on the Bombay–Āgra highway. An important market for agricultural produce, it was an early centre of the handloom industry. It has rapidly industrialized and recorded remarkable growth since the 1940s. Cotton and silk goods are exported to Bombay, Pune (Poona), and Sātāra. The town has several colleges affiliated with the University of Poona. Pop. (1981) 245,883.

maleic acid, also called CIS-BUTENEDIOIC ACID ($HO_2CCH{=}CHCO_2H$), unsaturated organic dibasic acid, used in making polyesters for fibre-reinforced laminated moldings and paint vehicles, and in the manufacture of fumaric acid and many other chemical products. Maleic acid and its anhydride are prepared industrially by the catalytic oxidation of benzene.

Maleic acid shows reactions typical of both olefins and carboxylic acids. Commercially important reactions of the acid groups include esterification with glycols to polyesters and dehydration to the anhydride. The double bond is involved in conversions to fumaric acid, to sulfosuccinic acid (used in wetting agents), and to Malathion (an insecticide).

Maleic acid melts at 139–140° C (282–284° F); at higher temperatures it forms the anhydride, which, like the acid, is irritating to the skin and toxic.

Maleic anhydride is interchangeable with the acid in most applications.

Fumaric acid, or *trans*-butenedioic acid, the geometrical isomer of maleic acid, occurs in fumitory (*Fumaria officinalis*), in various fungi, and in Iceland moss. Like maleic acid, it is used in polyesters, and since it is nontoxic, unlike maleic acid, it is used as an acidulant in foods. It is produced by isomerization of maleic acid or by fermentation of molasses. Its reactions are generally similar to those of maleic acid, although it cannot form an intramolecular anhydride. It is very much less soluble in water and most other solvents than its isomer.

Malekula (Vanuatu): *see* Malakula.

Malenkov, Georgy Maksimilianovich (b. Jan. 13 [Jan. 8, Old Style], 1902, Orenburg, Russia—d. Jan. 14, 1988, near Moscow), prominent Soviet statesman and Communist Party official, a close collaborator of Joseph Stalin, and the prime minister (March 1953–February 1955) after Stalin's death.

Having entered the Red Army (1919) during the civil war that followed the 1917 October Revolution, Malenkov joined the Communist Party in 1920 and rose swiftly through the ranks. He became closely associated with Stalin and was deeply involved in the great party purge of the late 1930s. Named a candidate member of the Politburo in 1941, he served during World War II on the State Defense Committee, the small group that directed the Soviet war effort. After the war Malenkov won full membership on the Politburo (1946) and was appointed second secretary of the Central Committee and deputy prime minister.

In the postwar period he also became involved in a bitter rivalry with A.A. Zhdanov,

Malenkov, 1956
EB Inc.

as a result of whose charges Malenkov was relieved of one of his party posts (1946). But within two years he had regained his position as one of Stalin's chief lieutenants and, when Stalin died in March 1953, assumed the post of senior party secretary as well as chairman of the Council of Ministers (*i.e.,* prime minister). Although a few weeks later he was compelled to yield his top party post to Nikita S. Khrushchev, he worked for the next two years to reduce arms appropriations, increase the production of consumer goods at the expense of heavy industry, and provide more incentives for collective farm workers.

His programs were opposed by other party leaders, however, and in February 1955 he was forced to resign as prime minister. He retained his influential position on the party Presidium (formerly the Politburo) until 1957, when, after participating in the vain effort by the anti-party group to depose Khrushchev, he was expelled from the Presidium and Central Committee. In 1961 it was disclosed that he had also been expelled from the Communist Party. He was manager of a remote hydroelectric plant in Kazakh S.S.R. for some 30 years; he was never rehabilitated.

Maler Müller: *see* Müller, Friedrich.

Malesherbes, Chrétien Guillaume de Lamoignon de (b. Dec. 6, 1721, Paris—d. April 22, 1794, Paris), lawyer and royal administrator who attempted, with limited success, to introduce reforms into France's autocratic regime during the reigns of Kings Louis XV

Malesherbes, engraving by P.-M. Alix
By courtesy of the Bibliotheque Nationale, Paris

(ruled 1715–74) and Louis XVI (ruled 1774–92).

Malesherbes's father, Guillaume II de Lamoignon, was a prominent member of the *noblesse de robe* (judicial nobility). After completing his legal training Malesherbes was made a counsellor in the Parlement (high court of justice) of Paris in 1744. When his father became chancellor of France under Louis XV in 1750, Malesherbes was appointed president of the Cour des Aides in Paris and *directeur de la librairie* (director of the press), the chief censor of published material. The latter office, which he held until 1763, gave him the authority to allow the *philosophes* (writers of the Enlightenment) to publish many of their works. In particular, most of the volumes of Denis Diderot's *Encyclopédie*, which adopted a skeptical attitude toward Roman Catholic and feudal institutions, were published during this period.

Although Malesherbes recognized the need for reforms, his fear of royal absolutism caused him to side with the Parlements in their attempts to block the King's plans for financial reforms. Hence he opposed the suspension of several of the Parlements (1771) by the chancellor, René-Nicolas de Maupeou; as a consequence, Malesherbes was banished to his estates near Pithiviers.

When King Louis XVI ascended the throne in 1774, the Parlements were reinstated, and Malesherbes was again made president of the Cour des Aides. In July 1775 he became secretary of state for the royal household, thereby gaining control over the administration of a considerable part of the government of Paris and the provinces. He instituted prison reforms, put a stop to the misuse of *lettres de cachet* (royal orders for the arbitrary arrests of subjects), and supported the far-reaching economic reforms of the comptroller general, Anne-Robert-Jacques Turgot. Nevertheless, Malesherbes failed to win the King's support for his projects. He resigned in May 1776, a few days before Turgot was dismissed from office. During the next 13 years Malesherbes campaigned for civil rights for French Protestants.

The Revolution broke out in 1789, and in December 1792 Malesherbes emerged from retirement to help conduct the defense of Louis XVI, who was on trial for treason before the Convention (the revolutionary assembly). Arrested in December 1793 and condemned as a counterrevolutionary, Malesherbes was guillotined with his daughter and grandchildren.

BIBLIOGRAPHY. Henri Robert, *Malesherbes* (1927); John M.S. Allison, *Lamoignon de Malesherbes, Defender and Reformer of the French Monarchy* (1938).

Malet, Claude François de (b. June 28, 1754, Dole, Fr.—d. Oct. 29, 1812, Paris), French general who conspired against Napoleon and attempted an almost successful coup d'etat on Oct. 22–23, 1812.

Malet, detail from a lithograph by Gervais, *c.* 19th century

Giraudon—Art Resource/EB Inc.

The descendant of a noble family, Malet had his first military experience with the king's musketeers in 1771; when the Revolution broke out he enthusiastically supported it, though he was disinherited for his open apostasy. He joined the Revolutionary army in 1791 and was aide-de-camp to Gen. Charles de Hesse, serving on the Rhine. His military career for the next eight years was uneventful, but in August 1799 he was sent to defend the Little Saint Bernard Pass and was promoted to the rank of brigadier general for distinguished service.

An ardent republican, Malet accepted Napoleon's proclamation of the empire in May 1804 with great reluctance. After 1805 he served in Italy but was cashiered in May 1808 for dealing on the black market. The following year he was imprisoned in Paris on suspicion of belonging to the Société des Philadelphes, an anti-Bonapartist secret society. From July 1810 he was kept under house arrest in Paris but escaped on the night of Oct. 22–23, 1812. Assuming the identity of "Général Lamotte," he went to the barracks of the Second Paris Guard and proclaimed that Napoleon had died in Russia and that he had been named commandant of Paris by a "provisional government." The Guards believed him, and he was able to secure the release from prison of two pro-republican generals and to shoot the governor of Paris before being arrested.

A few days later Malet was court-martialled and shot. His conspiracy, which came very close to success, deeply disturbed Napoleon, who hastened his return from Russia. The events are treated in Guido Artom's *Napoleone è morto in Russia* (1968; "Napoleon Is Dead in Russia").

Malevich, Kazimir (Severinovich) (b. Feb 23 [Feb. 11, old style], 1878, near Kiev—d. May 15, 1935, Leningrad), Russian painter, who was the founder of the Suprematist school of abstract painting.

Malevich was trained at the Kiev School of Art and the Moscow Academy of Fine Arts. In his early work he followed Impressionism as well as Fauvism, and, after a trip to Paris in 1912, he was influenced by Picasso and Cubism. As a member of the Jack of Diamonds (*q.v.*) group, he led the Russian Cubist movement.

In 1913 Malevich created abstract geometrical patterns in a manner he called Suprematism (*q.v.*). From 1919 to 1921 he taught painting in Moscow and Leningrad, where he lived the rest of his life. On a 1926 visit to the Bauhaus in Weimar he met Wassily Kandinsky and published a book on his theory under the title *Die gegenstandslose Welt* ("The Nonobjective World"). Later, when Soviet politicians decided against modern art, Malevich and his art were doomed. He died in poverty and oblivion.

Malevich was the first to exhibit paintings composed of abstract geometrical elements. He constantly strove to produce pure, cerebral compositions, repudiating all sensuality and representation in art. His well-known "White on White" (1918; Museum of Modern Art, New York City) carries his Suprematist theories to their logical conclusion.

Malherbe, Daniel François (b. May 28, 1881, Paarl, Cape Colony, S.Af.—d. April 12, 1969, Bloemfontein, Orange Free State), South African novelist, poet, and dramatist whose work helped establish Afrikaans as the cultural language of South Africa. He published many volumes of poetry and drama but is known primarily as a novelist for such works as *Vergeet nil* (1913; "Don't Forget"), an extremely popular novel about the Boer War; *Die Meulenaar* (1936; "The Miller"); *Saul* (1933–37), a biblical trilogy; and *En die wawiele rol* (1945; "And the Wagon Wheels Roll On"), which describes the Great Trek. He served as professor of literature at the University of Bloemfontein (1922–42).

Malherbe, François de (b. 1555, in or near Caen, Fr.—d. Oct. 16, 1628, Paris), French poet who described himself as *un excellent arrangeur de syllabes* and theoretician whose insistence upon strict form, restraint, and purity of diction prepared the way for French Classicism.

François de Malherbe, engraving after an oil painting by Adrien Dumoutier

By courtesy of the trustees of the British Museum; photograph, J.R. Freeman & Co. Ltd.

Malherbe received a Protestant education at Caen and Paris and later at the universities of Basel (1571) and Heidelberg (1573) but was shortly converted to a lukewarm Catholicism.

In 1577 he went to Provence as secretary to the governor, Henri d'Angoulême. His first published poem was *Les Larmes de Saint Pierre* (1587; "The Tears of St. Peter"), a florid imitation of Luigi Tansillo's *Lagrime di San Pietro.* His friendship with two lawyers of Aix, the Stoic philosopher Guillaume du Vair and the extraordinarily learned Nicolas-Claude Fabri de Peiresc, developed his character and allowed his genius to mature. In 1600 an ode to the new queen, Marie de Médicis, made his name more widely known.

In 1605 Malherbe went to Paris, supported by his friends Peiresc and du Vair and by Cardinal Duperron. Henry IV was neither greatly interested in poetry nor notably generous, but Malherbe attained the position of court poet and a modest living from court patronage. He gathered a group of disciples, of whom Honorat de Bueil Racan and François Maynard are the best known, and much of his critical influence was exercised in the form of sharp verbal thrusts, some of them preserved in Racan's life of him and in the pages devoted to him in Gédéon Tallemant des Réaux's *Historiettes* (*c.* 1659; published 1834).

Malherbe's prose writings consist of translations of Livy and Seneca; about 200 letters to Peiresc, of interest for their picture of court life; and his commentary on the works of the poet Philippe Desportes. These notes are detailed and entirely negative, fastening critically on minute points of workmanship. Nevertheless, certain positive principles emerge by implication: verbal harmony, propriety, intelligibility, and, above all, the conception of the poet as craftsman rather than prophet.

Malherbe's own poetic work shows poverty of imagination; he wrote little and slowly, repeating his ideas, images, and rhymes. But there is a dignity and even grandeur in the harmony and strength of his best poems. In essentials, French verse retained the characteristics stamped on it by Malherbe up to the Romantic period and beyond.

Malheur River, river rising on the southern slopes of the Blue Mountains in the Malheur National Forest, Oregon, U.S., and flowing southeast, north, and northeast to join the Snake River at Ontario at the Idaho state line, after a course of 165 mi (266 km). Warm Springs Reservoir, formed by Warm Springs Dam (1919), is in the river's upper course, north of Riverside. The name is the French word for "misfortune," and the river is probably so called because a cache that the explorer Peter Skene Ogden had made near the stream (1826) was stolen.

Mali (people): *see* Mande.

Mali, trading empire that flourished in West Africa from the 13th to the 16th century. The Mali empire developed from the state of Kangaba, on the Upper Niger River east of the Fouta Djallon, and is said to have been founded before AD 1000. The Malinke inhabitants of Kangaba acted as middlemen in the gold trade during the later period of ancient Ghana. Their dislike of the Susu chief Sumanguru's harsh but ineffective rule provoked the Malinke to revolt, and in 1230 Sundiata, the brother of Kangaba's fugitive ruler, won a decisive victory against the Susu chief. (The name Mali absorbed the name Kangaba at about this time.)

In extending Mali's rule beyond Kangaba's narrow confines, Sundiata set a precedent for successive emperors. Imperial armies secured the gold-bearing lands of Bondu and Bambuk to the south, subdued the Diara in the northwest, and pushed along the Niger as far north as Lac Débo. Under Mansa Mūsā (1307–32?) Mali rose to the apogee of its power. He controlled the lands of the Middle Niger, absorbed into his empire the trading cities of Timbuktu and Gao, and imposed his rule on such south Saharan cities as Walata and on the Taghaza region of salt deposits to the north. He extended the eastern boundaries of his empire as far as the Hausa people, and to the west he invaded Takrur and the lands of the Fulani and Tukulor peoples. In Morocco, Egypt, and elsewhere he sent ambassadors and imperial agents and on his return from a pilgrimage to Mecca (1324) established Egyptian scholars in both Timbuktu and Gao.

By the 14th century the Dyula, or Wangara, as the Muslim traders of Mali came to be called, were active throughout West Africa. The tide that had carried Mali to success, however, impelled it ineluctably to decline. The empire outgrew its political and military strength: Gao rebelled (*c.* 1400); the Tuareg seized Walata and Timbuktu (1431); the peoples of Takrur and their neighbours (notably the Wolof) threw off their subjection; and the Mossi (in what is now Burkina Faso) began to harass their Mali overlord. By about 1550 Mali had ceased to be important as a political entity.

Mali, town, northern Guinea. Located on the Fouta Djallon plateau at an elevation of about 4,600 feet (1,400 m), it is the chief trading centre for the cattle, rice, millet, oranges, and peanuts (groundnuts) produced in the surrounding area. A hydroelectric plant (18 miles [29 km] south-southwest) on the Tantou River, a tributary of the Koumba, serves both the town and a cement factory at nearby Lébékéré. The surrounding region is mountainous and is mainly inhabited by the Muslim Fulani and Dialonke peoples. Pop. (1983 prelim.) 33,078.

Mali, officially REPUBLIC OF MALI, French RÉPUBLIQUE DU MALI, landlocked country in western Africa. Mali is bordered to the west by Senegal, to the northwest by Mauritania, to the northeast by Algeria, to the southeast by Niger and Burkina Faso, to the south by Côte d'Ivoire (Ivory Coast), and to the southwest by Guinea. The capital is Bamako. Area 482,077 square miles (1,248,574 square km). Pop. (1993 est.) 8,646,000.

A brief treatment of Mali follows. For full treatment, *see* MACROPAEDIA: Western Africa.

For current history and for statistics on society and economy, *see* BRITANNICA BOOK OF THE YEAR.

The land. Mali's terrain is largely flat and relatively monotonous, with plateaus and plains the only relief features. The plateaus

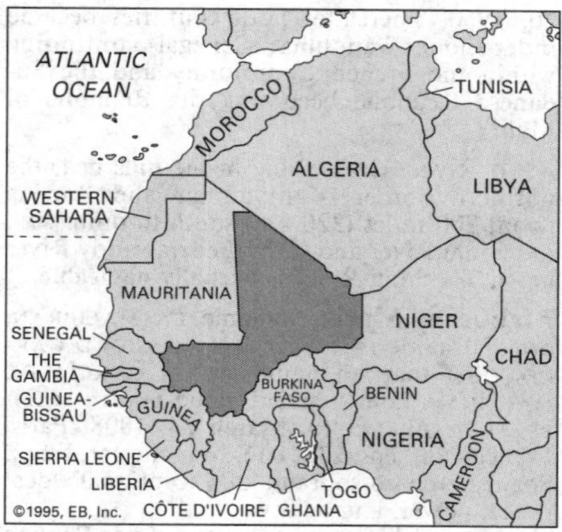

Mali

of the south and southwest rise to more than 2,100 feet (640 m) above sea level at Satadougou and are deeply notched by river valleys. The plateaus of the southeast and east are a series of small, broken hills lying at elevations between 1,000 and 2,000 feet (300 and 600 m). The vast plains of the Tanezrouft and Taoudenni in the northern part of the country lie within the Sahara (desert). Southwestern and south-central Mali are composed of the plains of the Upper Niger River basin, and nearly one-third of the total length of the Niger River flows through Mali, forming an interior delta. Periodic floods and the rich alluvial soils in the delta make the Niger valley an important agricultural region. The main headwaters of the Sénégal River rise in extreme western Mali.

Mali is situated within three climatic zones: the Sudanic, the Sahelian, and the Saharan. The Sudanic climate of southern Mali is characterized by an annual rainfall of between 20 and 55 inches (500 and 1,400 mm) and average temperatures of between 75° and 86° F (24° and 30° C). The Sahel, a semiarid area bordering the Sahara to the north, receives between 8 and 20 inches (200 and 500 mm) of rain a year and has average temperatures between 73° and 97° F (23° and 36° C). Northern Mali has a Saharan climate, which is marked by the virtual absence of rain and an extremely dry atmosphere. Temperatures exceed 117° F (47° C) during the day and reach 39° F (4° C) at night.

The Sudanic zone is dominated by herbaceous vegetation; its trees include bastard mahogany, kapok, and baobab. The incidence of the trees decreases to the north as the Sudanic zone merges into the Sahel. The latter is characterized by steppe vegetation; drought-resistant trees such as baobab, doum palm, and palmyra are found. Vegetation gradually disappears as one enters the Sahara region. Animal life in Mali includes lion, panther, hyena, gazelle and antelope, giraffe, elephant, crocodile, and a wide variety of monkeys, snakes, and birds.

About 2 percent of the country's total land area is considered arable, and about one-fourth of the total land area is available as pasture or rangeland. Mali's mineral reserves, which are largely unexploited, include iron ore, bauxite, petroleum, gold, nickel, copper, and manganese.

The people. Mali has so-called black and "white" populations. What is known as the white population includes nomadic groups of Berbers, such as the Tuareg, as well as the Arab-Berber group known as the Moors. These groups live mainly in the Sahelian zone of central Mali. The black population comprises various agricultural peoples, including the Bambara, the most numerous group, who constitute about one-third of the country's total population. The Fulani (Peul), the second largest group, are nomadic pastoralists of the Sahel and Macina. The agricultural Soninke (Sarakole) peoples are descended from the founders of the Ghana empire and live in the western Sahelian zone. The Malinke (Mandingo), bearers of the heritage of the Mali empire, live in the southwest, and the Songhai are settled in the Niger River valley from Djenné to Ansongo. The Dogon live in the plateau region around Bandiagara. Included in the Voltaic group are the Bwa (Bobo), the Senufo, and the Minianka, who occupy the east and the southeast.

French is the official language. There are several widely spoken indigenous languages and dialects, which correspond roughly to either ethnic groups or regions. The Moors speak Arabic. About 90 percent of the population are Muslims, some 9 percent are animists, and the rest are Christians.

Mali is sparsely populated: three-fourths of the population is rural, and about one-tenth of the population is nomadic. The relatively high birth and death rates are roughly equivalent to those of western Africa as a whole. Almost half of the population is less than 15 years of age.

The economy. Mali has a developing, mixed economy based largely on agriculture. Poor economic conditions were worsened during the 1970s and early '80s by drought, inflation, and rising oil prices. By the late 1980s the economy had recovered significantly. The gross national product (GNP) is increasing more rapidly than the population; the GNP per capita, however, is one of the lowest in the world.

Agriculture accounts for about half of the gross domestic product (GDP) and employs more than four-fifths of the workforce. Although production is largely subsistence farming and is subject to cyclical drought conditions, Mali is basically self-sufficient in foodstuffs. Staple crops include millet, sorghum, corn (maize), and rice. Cotton and peanuts (groundnuts) are the main cash crops. Livestock (including goats, sheep, and cattle) are numerous.

Fish are caught from rivers for both domestic consumption and export, and the government has established a fishery development program with foreign aid. Mining is limited to gold, marble, limestone, kaolin, and salt deposits.

Industry accounts for about 7 percent of the GDP and employs less than 2 percent of the workforce. Manufacturing is primarily small-scale and is dominated by food processing and the production of simple consumer goods. Most of Malian industry is state-owned. Foreign governments have contributed substantially to Mali's industrial development, and energy projects are almost entirely externally financed. Electricity is generated from both thermal and hydroelectric sources. Services, primarily in the public sector, account for one-third of the GDP and employ one-seventh of the workforce.

A primary obstacle to economic progress has been a chronic foreign-trade deficit. Mali is heavily dependent on foreign-aid funds as well as on remittances from emigrants working abroad. France, which supplies much of the foreign aid, is Mali's principal trading partner. Exports include raw cotton, cotton products, and live animals. Imports are mostly machinery, appliances, and transport equipment; food products; chemical products; petroleum products; and construction materials.

Government and social conditions. Following the overthrow of a military government in 1991, a new constitution was approved by referendum in 1992. It provides for a multiparty, democratic political system. Executive power is vested in the president, who is directly elected for no more than two five-year terms. The president appoints the prime minister. Legislative power is vested in the National Assembly, whose members are directly elected for terms of five years. The Supreme Court is the highest judicial authority; there is also a Constitutional Court.

Education is free and officially compulsory between the ages of 6 and 15 years. Less than one-fifth of the children of primary-school age actually attend school, however. Higher education is provided in state colleges; in addition, many students attend colleges and universities abroad, notably in France and Senegal. Despite its network of hospitals and medical centres, augmented by maternity clinics and various health centres, a shortage of personnel trained in Western medical techniques exists. Numerous traditional practitioners also provide health care for the country.

Cultural life. Situated between the Arab world to the north and the black African nations to the south, Mali has for centuries been one of the cultural crossroads of western Africa and has produced an original Sudanic culture. The music and dancing among the Malinke and Songhai peoples, wood carving among the Bambara and the Voltaic (Gur) groups, architecture in the Niger River valley, and jewelry of the Mandingo are especially noteworthy.

History. Evidence of prehistoric habitation of the Malian Sahara is provided by Paleolithic and Neolithic remains, including Asselar man, a human skeleton found north of Timbuktu in 1927 dating to around 5000 BC, and by rock paintings and carvings. Elsewhere in Mali numerous traces of late prehistoric civilizations have been found. Since approximately AD 300, caravan routes across the Sahara linked the bend of the Niger River to Morocco and southern Algeria and transported ivory, gum, ostrich feathers, gold, and slaves. At the origins of these routes were founded the Soninke empire of Ghana (4th to 11th century), between the Niger and Sénégal rivers, and the Malinke empire of Mali (12th to 16th century), from which the country derives its name, on the Upper and Middle Niger. In the 15th century the Songhai empire in the Timbuktu-Gao region spread its rule over much of Mali, extending eastward to the Hausa kingdoms. In 1591 the Moroccan army of Aḥmad al-Manṣūr, the 6th ruler of the Saʿdī dynasty, invaded the area, and Timbuktu remained under the Moors for two centuries. Thereafter, the Niger River valley was divided between the Tuareg in the region of Gao, the Fulani in Macina, and the Bambara in the kingdom of Ségou. In the middle of the 19th century the French conquered the area, and it became part of French West Africa. In 1946 the area, then called the French Sudan, became an overseas territory of the French Union.

In 1958 what is now Mali was proclaimed the Sudanese Republic, which a year later united with Senegal to form the Mali Federation. Owing to political differences, Senegal seceded, and on Sept. 22, 1960, the remnant of the federation was proclaimed the independent Republic of Mali. Modibo Keita became the first president. In 1968 a military junta overthrew Keita's government. Although a new constitution was adopted in 1974, the junta declared its intention to rule for five more years. Moussa Traoré, who had assumed power with the junta in 1968, reigned as a dictator until overthrown in a military coup in 1991. Civilian rule returned in 1992 and continued in the early 21st century.

Mali Federation, short-lived union between the autonomous territories of the Sudanese Republic and Senegal in West Africa. The federation took effect on April 4, 1959, achieved complete independence on June 20, 1960 (remaining within the French Community), and was dissolved by Senegal's secession on Aug. 20, 1960. Thereafter both countries became independent republics, Senegal continuing within the French Community and the Sudanese Republic becoming the Republic of Mali.

Mali River, river, rising in the hills near the northern border of Myanmar and flowing about 200 miles (320 km) south to unite with the Nmai River and form the Irrawaddy River (*q.v.*). The Mali River is partially navigable.

Malibran, Maria, byname LA MALIBRAN, original name MARÍA DE LA FELICIDAD GARCÍA, first married name MARÍA GARCÍA DE MALIBRAN, later married name MARIA MALIBRAN DE BÉRIOT (b. March 24, 1808, Paris, France—d. Sept. 23, 1836, Manchester, Eng.), Spanish mezzo-soprano of exceptional vocal range, power, and agility.

María and her mezzo-soprano sister Pauline Viardot were first instructed by their father, the tenor Manuel García, and at five years of age María sang a child's part in Ferdinando Paer's *Agnese* in Naples. She made her London debut at the King's Theatre in 1825 as Rosina in Gioacchino Rossini's *The Barber of Seville.* She performed with her father's company at the Park Theater in New York City for the next two years in operas by Rossini and W.A. Mozart and in two operas written for her by her father.

After a brief marriage to escape her father's control, Malibran made a sensational debut at the Théâtre-Italien, Paris, in Rossini's *Semiramide* in 1828. She then divided her time between Paris and London until she went to Italy in 1832 to sing in such operas as Vincenzo Bellini's *I Capuleti e i Montecchi* and *La sonnambula* and in the title role of *Maria Stuarda,* which she created for Gaetano Donizetti at La Scala in Milan. In 1836, a month after her marriage to the violinist Charles de Bériot and six months after her 28th birthday, she fell from a horse and soon died. Alfred de Musset wrote the poem *Stances* as a tribute to her, and in 1935 Robert Russell Bennett composed the opera *Maria Malibran* based on her life.

Malibú (people): *see* Mompox.

Malibu, city and beach community in Los Angeles county, southern California, U.S. It lies along the Pacific Coast Highway, just west-northwest of Santa Monica. Named by the Chumash Indians and located where the Santa Monica Mountains meet the ocean, it is well known as a beach colony of movie and television celebrities, whose homes line an unstable escarpment above a sandspit that extends into picturesque Santa Monica Bay. The Getty Villa (a reproduction of an ancient Roman villa), a branch of the J. Paul Getty Museum in Los Angeles, and the main campus of Pepperdine University are in Malibu, as is the Malibu Lagoon Museum, which preserves an early 20th-century mansion.

malignant pustule: *see* anthrax.

Malik, Adam (b. July 22, 1917, Pematangsiantar, North Sumatra, Dutch East Indies [now Indonesia]—d. Sept. 5, 1984, Jakarta, Indon.), Indonesian statesman and nationalist political leader.

Malik was jailed by the Dutch in the 1930s for being a member of the nationalist group that sought independence for the Dutch East Indies. In 1937 he founded the Indonesian news agency Antara, which originally served as an organ of the nationalist press. During World War II he was active in the Indonesian youth movement. In 1945 he was involved with the abduction of the Indonesian leaders Sukarno and Mohammad Hatta in order to "force" them to declare independence rather than receiving it as a gift from the Japanese, and in 1946 he was involved with the kidnapping of Sutan Sjahrir in order to protest a negotiated settlement with the Dutch.

After the Indonesian revolution ended in 1949, Malik served in various posts of the Sukarno government, including ambassador to the Soviet Union and to Poland. In 1962 he was the chief Indonesian delegate to the Washington, D.C., negotiations on the status of West Irian (Irian Jaya), which laid the groundwork for Indonesia's eventually securing this territory.

As foreign minister (1966–77) of the Suharto government, Malik was the architect of the new Indonesian foreign policy that restored relations with Malaysia, the Philippines, and China and regained the seat lost when Sukarno took Indonesia out of the UN in 1965. Malik also was able to obtain a 30-year extension on the $3 billion debt to creditor nations accumulated during the Sukarno years. As president of the United Nations 26th General Assembly (1971–72), Malik presided over the admission of the People's Republic of China to the UN. Later he served as vice president of Indonesia (1978–83).

Malik an-Nāṣir Ṣalāḥ ad-Dīn Yūsuf I, al- (Muslim sultan): *see* Saladin.

Malik aẓ-Ẓāhir Rukn ad-Dīn Baybars al-Bunduqdīrī, al-, also called AL-MALIK AẒ-ẒĀHIR RUKN AD-DĪN BAYBARS AṢ-ṢĀLIḤĪ: *see* Baybars I.

Mālik ibn Anas, in full ABŪ ʿABD ALLĀH MĀLIK IBN ANAS IBN AL-ḤĀRITH AL-AṢBAḤĪ (b. *c.* 715—d. 795, Medina, Arabia [now Saudi Arabia]), Muslim legist who played an important role in formulating early Islāmic legal doctrines.

Few details are known about Mālik ibn Anas' life, most of which was spent in the city of Medina. He became learned in Islāmic law and attracted a considerable number of students, his followers coming to be known as the Mālikī school of law. His prestige involved him in politics, and he was rash enough to declare during a rebellion that loyalty to the caliph was not a religious necessity, since homage to him had been given under compulsion. The caliph, however, was victorious, and Mālik received a flogging for his complicity. This only increased his prestige, and during later years he regained favour with the central government.

Mālik ibn Anas produced one major book—the *Muwaṭṭaʾ*. This is the oldest surviving compendium of Islāmic law.

Malik-Shāh (b. Aug. 6/16, 1055—d. November 1092, Baghdad [Iraq]), third and most famous of the Seljuq sultans.

Malik-Shāh succeeded his father, Alp-Arslan, in 1072 under the tutelage of the great vizier Niẓām al-Mulk, who was the real manager of the empire until his death. Malik-Shāh had first to overcome a revolt of his uncle Qāwurd (Kavurd) and an attack of the Qarakhanids of Bukhara on Khorāsān; thereafter he consolidated and extended his empire more through diplomacy and the quarrels of his enemies than by actual warfare. He suppressed the former vassal principalities of upper Mesopotamia and Azerbaijan, acquired Syria and Palestine, and established a strong protectorate over the Qarakhanids and a measure of control over Mecca and Medina, Yemen, and the Persian Gulf territories. His control of the Turkmen of Asia Minor was contested by a rival Seljuq dynasty.

Malik-Shāh displayed a great interest in literature, science, and art. His reign is memorable for the splendid mosques of his capital, Eṣfahān, for the poetry of Omar Khayyam, and for the reform of the calendar. His people enjoyed internal peace and religious tolerance.

However, there were shadows amidst this glory. His brother Takash, governor of Khorāsān, revolted and was imprisoned and blinded. Under the leadership of Ḥasan-e Ṣabbāḥ there arose the antiorthodox terrorist movement of the Assassins who murdered Niẓām al-Mulk in 1092. Before this he was partly estranged from his vizier who favoured the claims to succession of Malik-Shāh's eldest son by his first wife against those of a son by his second wife. Further, his relations deteriorated with the Caliph of Baghdad who had married Malik-Shāh's daughter and neglected her. He had ordered the Caliph to leave Baghdad when he himself died there suddenly, leaving his empire to disintegrate through internal quarrels.

Mālikīyah, also called MADHHAB MĀLIK, English MALIKITES, in Islām, one of the four Sunnī schools of law, formerly the ancient school of Medina. Founded in the 8th century and based on the teachings of the imam Mālik ibn Anas, the Mālikīyah stressed local Medinese community practice (*sunnah*), preferring traditional opinions (*ra'y*) and analogical reasoning (*qiyās*) to a strict reliance on Ḥadīth (traditions concerning the Prophet's life and utterances) as a basis for legal judgment. Ḥadīth, however, was always applied, though arbitrarily. The Mālikī school currently prevails throughout northern and western Africa, in The Sudan, and in some of the Persian Gulf states.

Malinche (Mexican princess): *see* Marina.

Malines (Belgium): *see* Mechelen.

Malinke, also called MANINKA, MANDINGO, or MANDING, a West African people occupying parts of Guinea, Ivory Coast, Mali, Senegal, The Gambia, and Guinea-Bissau. They speak a Mandekan language of the Mande branch of the Niger-Congo family.

The Malinke are divided into numerous independent groups dominated by a hereditary nobility, a feature that distinguishes them from most of their more egalitarian neighbours. One group, the Kangaba, has one of the world's most ancient dynasties; its rule has been virtually uninterrupted for 13 centuries. Beginning in the 7th century AD as the centre of a small state, Kangaba became the capital of the great Malinke empire known as Mali. (*See* Mali empire.) This was the most powerful and most renowned of all the empires of the western Sudan, now memorialized in the name of the Republic of Mali.

The contemporary Malinke are an agricultural people, cultivating such staples as millet and sorghum and tending small herds of cattle, kept primarily for trade, bride-price payments, and prestige. Houses are predominantly cylindrical, with thatched straw roofs, and are often grouped in substantial numbers and surrounded by a palisade. Descent, inheritance, and succession are patrilineal.

Malinovsky, Rodion Yakovlevich (b. Nov. 23 [Nov. 11, old style], 1898, Odessa, Ukraine, Russian Empire—d. March 31, 1967, Moscow), Soviet marshal prominent in World War II.

Malinovsky was drafted into the imperial army at the start of World War I and fought as a machine gunner throughout that conflict. Upon his return to Russia in 1919 he entered the Red Army, in which he fought against the White Guards and gradually advanced to battalion commander. He joined the Communist Party in 1926, graduated from the M.V. Frunze military academy in 1930, and was sent as an adviser to assist the Republican side during the Spanish Civil War (1936–39).

Commander of the 48th Rifle Corps at the start of the German invasion of the Soviet Union (1941), he was quickly put in charge of the Sixth Army and thereafter held various army and army-group commands on the southern front. As commander of the Second Guards Army, Malinovsky played an important role in the Battle of Stalingrad in December 1942. He commanded the Soviet drives into Romania in late 1944 and into Austria in the spring of 1945. From 1945 to 1955 he held important command positions in Soviet-held Manchuria and then in the Soviet Far East.

In 1956 Malinovsky advanced to first deputy minister of defense and commander in chief of ground forces; that same year he became a member of the Central Committee of the Communist Party. As minister of defense of the U.S.S.R. (1957–67), he oversaw the buildup of Soviet military power that began in the 1960s.

Malinowski, Bronisław (Kasper) (b. April 7, 1884, Kraków, Pol., Austria-Hungary—d. May 16, 1942, New Haven, Conn., U.S.), one of the most important anthropologists of the 20th century who is widely recognized as the founder of social anthropology and principally associated with field studies of the peoples of Oceania.

Malinowski
By courtesy of the Polish Library, London

Early life and studies. Malinowski was the son of Lucjan Malinowski, a professor of Slavic philology at the Jagiellonian University in Kraków and a linguist of some reputation who had studied Polish dialect and folklore in Silesia. Bronisław Malinowski's mother, Józefa, *née* Łącka, of a moderately wealthy land-owning family, was highly cultured and a good linguist. Early afflicted by the ill health that dogged him throughout life, Malinowski in his teens traveled extensively in the Mediterranean region with his mother, who was by then widowed. Although his early education was conducted largely at home, he subsequently attended the Jagiellonian University, completing his doctorate in 1908, with highest grade honours in philosophy, with physics and mathematics as subsidiaries. Happening upon Sir James Frazer's *Golden Bough,* an encyclopaedic treatment of religious and magical practices, Malinowski was enthralled and long afterward traced his enthusiasm for anthropology to it. After contact with the newer psychologies and economics in Leipzig, he came in 1910 to the London School of Economics and Political Science, where anthropology had been recently established as a discipline.

For the next quarter-century Malinowski's career was oriented toward London. A prolific writer, he soon published reinterpretations of Australian Aboriginal data from literature then very popular in anthropological circles. These gained him a reputation and promoted his plans for field research, and in 1914 he was able to go to New Guinea. Six months' work among the Mailu on the south coast produced a monograph that, while lacking theoretical development, was sufficient—along with his study of the Australian family—to earn him a doctor of science (D.Sc.) degree from the University of London in 1916. When he moved to the nearby Trobriand Islands, where he worked for two years in 1915–16 and 1917–18, Malinowski's talents flowered. Living in a tent among the people, speaking the vernacular fluently, recording "texts" freely on the scene of action as well as in set interviews, and observing reactions with an acute clinical eye, Malinowski was able to present a dynamic picture of social institutions that clearly separated ideal norms from actual behaviour. In later publications on ceremonial exchange; on agricultural economics; on sex, marriage, and family life; on primitive law and custom; and on magic and myth, he drew heavily on his Trobriand data in putting forward theoretical propositions of basic significance and stimulus in the development of social anthropology. Yet, while very rewarding, his field experience had its strains. Writing in Polish for his own private record, Malinowski kept field diaries in which he exposed very frankly his problems of isolation and of his relations with New Guinea people.

In 1919 Malinowski married Elsie Rosaline Masson, daughter of a professor of chemistry at the University of Melbourne; they had three daughters.

Mature career. After living in the Canary Islands and southern France, Malinowski returned in 1924 to the University of London as reader in anthropology; he became professor in 1927. As one of the most intellectually vigorous social scientists of his day, Malinowski had a stimulating and wide influence. His seminars were famous, and he attracted the attention of prominent scientists in other disciplines, such as linguistics and psychology, and collaborated or debated with them. Conversant with continental European social theory and especially acknowledging his debt to Émile Durkheim, Marcel Mauss, and others of the French sociological school, he rejected their abstract notions of society in favour of an approach that focused more on the individual—an approach that seemed to him more realistic. His functional theory, as he himself explained,

> insists . . . upon the principle that in every type of civilisation, every custom, material object, idea and belief fulfils some vital function, has some task to accomplish, represents an indispensable part within a working whole. ("Anthropology," in *Encyclopædia Britannica,* 13th ed., suppl., p. 133.)

Only by understanding such functions and interrelations, he held, can an anthropologist understand a culture. In keeping with his concept of culture as an expression of the totality of human achievement, he examined a wide range of cultural aspects and institutions, challenging existing propositions on kinship and marriage, exchange, and ritual.

Malinowski was active in sponsoring studies of social and cultural change and participated vigorously in educational programs for administrators, missionaries, and social workers. In the 1930s he became much interested in Africa; was closely associated with the International African Institute; visited students working among Bemba, Swazi, and other tribes in eastern and southern Africa; and wrote the introduction to Jomo Kenyatta's book *Facing Mount Kenya* (1938), prepared as a diploma thesis under his supervision. (Kenyatta became president of Kenya in 1964.)

In 1938 Malinowski went on sabbatical leave to the United States—which he had already visited in 1926 on a Laura Spelman Rockefeller Memorial Fellowship, in 1933 as a lecturer at Cornell University, and in 1936 as recipient of an honorary doctor of science degree at the Harvard University tercentenary celebrations. When World War II was declared, being by age and temperament unsuited for direct participation in the war effort, he became Bishop Museum Visiting Professor of Anthropology at Yale University, then accepted a tenured appointment there. His teaching career during those last years was less remarkable than before, but he was able to study peasant markets in Mexico in 1940 and 1941 and had plans for a study of social change in Mexican-Indian communities. A great believer in freedom, he had also been actively identified with the Polish partisan cause in the war. In 1940 Malinowski married again, to Anna Valetta Hayman-Joyce, an artist who painted under the name Valetta Swann and who assisted him in his Mexican studies and was primarily responsible for the publication of his *Scientific Theory of Culture* (1944) and other posthumous works. (R.W.Fi./Ed.)

MAJOR WORKS. *The Family Among the Australian Aborigines* (1913); *The Natives of Mailu* (1915); *Argonauts of the Western Pacific* (1922); *Myth in Primitive Psychology* (1926); *Crime and Custom in Savage Society* (1926); *The Father in Primitive Psychology* (1927); *Sex and Repression in Savage Society* (1927); *The Sexual Life of Savages in North-Western Melanesia* (1929); *Coral Gardens and Their Magic,* 2 vol. (1935); *The Foundations of Faith and Morals* (1936); posthumously published works include *A Scientific Theory of Culture* (1944); *Freedom and Civilization* (1944); *The Dynamics of Culture Change* (1945); *Magic, Science and Religion and Other Essays* (1948). *A Diary in the Strict Sense of the Term* (1967) is a translation of private field diaries kept in Polish during 1914–15 and 1917–18.

BIBLIOGRAPHY. Association of Polish University Professors and Lecturers in Great Britain, *Professor Bronislaw Malinowski: An Account of the Memorial Meeting Held at the Royal Institution in London on July 13th 1942* (1943); Raymond Firth (ed.), *Man and Culture: An Evaluation of the Work of Bronislaw Malinowski* (1957), analytical studies by former students and colleagues, with bibliography.

Malintzen (Mexican Indian princess): *see* Marina.

Malipiero, Gian Francesco (b. March 18, 1882, Venice—d. Aug. 1, 1973, Treviso, Italy), Italian composer whose music represented a fusion of modern techniques with the stylistic qualities of early Italian music.

Malipiero studied at the Vienna Conservatory and in Venice and Bologna, and subsequently he traveled to Paris, where he was influenced by contemporary French music. In 1921 he became professor of composition at the Parma Conservatory. Later he was director of the Istituto Musicale Pollini at Padua, and in 1939 he became director of the Liceo Benedetto Marcello in Venice.

Malipiero, with Alfredo Casella, played a leading part in Italian music in the 1920s. Rebelling against the realistic aesthetic of verismo that inspired Puccini, he rediscovered Italian pre-Romantic music. His work reflects the spirit of 17th- and 18th-century Venetian music, and his operas, that of Monteverdi. His music is characteristically contrapuntal, with some dissonance resulting from the counterpoint. Its tonality is based on free use of diatonic (as opposed to chromatic) material.

Malipiero's works include the operas *L'Orfeide* (1918–22; "The Orpheon") and *Venere prigioniera* (1957; "Captive Venus"); the cantata or "mystery" *San Francesco d'Assisi* (1922; "St. Francis of Assisi"); the oratorio *La Passione* (1935; "The Passion"); and several piano concerti. Among his orchestral works are *Pause del silenzio* (1917; "Pause of Silence"), which reflects the impact of World War I; *Impressioni dal vero* (three parts; 1910–22; "Impression of Truth"); *Fantasie di ogni giorni* (1954; "Fantasy of Every Day"); *Notturno di canti e balli* (1957; "Nocturne of Songs and Dances"); and nine symphonies. His chamber works include seven string quartets, of which the first, *Rispetti e strambotti* (1920; "Regards and Folderol") is particularly known; and works for various instruments.

Malipiero made important contributions to musical scholarship. He edited the complete works of Monteverdi, 16 vol. (1926–42), and collaborated in the collected edition of the works of Vivaldi. He also edited works of Corelli, Frescobaldi, and others and wrote numerous articles for scholarly journals.

malka (berry): *see* cloudberry.

Malkhed (India): *see* Mānyakheṭa.

malkoha (bird): *see* malcoha.

Mall, the, in Washington, D.C., broad promenade and greensward extending westward from the Capitol to the Potomac River beyond the Lincoln Memorial. The Mall is as wide (in the north–south dimension) as the grounds of the Capitol; it is bounded north by Constitution Ave. and south by Independence Ave., and it is crossed east–west by (from the north) Madison, Washington, Adams, and Jefferson drives. Set within the Mall or flanking it are numerous institutions: the National Gallery of Art, the National Museum of Natural History, the National Museum of American History, the Freer Gallery of Art, the Smithsonian Institution headquarters, the National Air and Space Museum, the Arts and Industries Building, and the Hirshhorn Museum and Sculpture Garden. West of 14th Street are the Washington Monument, the Sylvan Theater, a portion of the Tidal Basin, the Reflecting Pool, and the Lincoln Memorial.

mallard (*Anas platyrhyncos*), abundant "wild duck" of the Northern Hemisphere and ancestor of most domestic ducks. It belongs to the family Anatidae (order Anseriformes).

Of the several races, the common mallard (*A. p. platyrhynchos*) breeds throughout Europe, most of Asia, and northern North America; it winters as far south as North Africa, India, and southern Mexico. The drake has a metallic green head (purplish in some lights), reddish breast, and light-gray body; the hen is mottled yellowish brown. Both sexes have a yellow bill and a purplish-blue wing mark bordered front and rear with white.

Of the other races only one, the Greenland mallard (*A. p. conboschas*), shows the strong sexual difference in plumage. All others resemble, in both sexes, the hen of *A. p. platyrhynchos.* Two of these races are quite small and very rare: the Hawaiian duck (*A. p. wyvilliana*) and the Laysan teal (*A. p. laysanensis*); only a tiny population of the latter survives on Laysan Island, west of Hawaii. The remaining races are sometimes classified as races of the black duck (*A. rubripes*)—which may itself be merely another race of the mallard.

The mallard is a typical dabbling duck (*q.v.*) in its general habits and courtship display.

Mallarmé, François-René-Auguste (b. Feb. 25, 1755, Nancy, Fr.—d. July 25, 1835, Richemont), French revolutionist, briefly president of the Convention in 1793.

Mallarmé was brought up in his father's profession as a lawyer and, during the Revolution, was elected by the department of Meurthe as deputy to the Legislative Assembly and the Convention, where he joined the radical Montagnards and voted for the death of Louis XVI. He was made president of the Convention on May 30, 1793, and by his weakness contributed to the fall of the Girondins; he was forced to give up the post on June 2. In November he was sent to establish the revolutionary government in the departments of Meuse and Moselle. After Robespierre's fall he joined the Thermidorians (the anti-Jacobins) and was sent on a mission to the south of France, where he closed the Jacobin club at Toulouse but then set free a number of imprisoned "suspects." For this, on June 1, 1795, he was arrested, but soon set free. He held office both under the Directory and the Napoleonic Empire. Appointed subprefect of Avesnes during the Hundred Days, he was imprisoned by the Prussians in revenge for the sentence of death carried out by his orders on some young girls at Verdun who had offered flowers to the Prussians when they entered the town (1793). He lived in exile during the Restoration, returning to France after the Revolution of 1830.

Mallarmé, Stéphane (b. March 18, 1842, Paris—d. Sept. 9, 1898, Valvins, near Fontainebleau, Fr.), French poet, an originator (with Paul Verlaine) and a leader of the Symbolist movement in poetry.

Mallarmé enjoyed the sheltered security of family life for only five brief years, until the early death of his mother in August 1847. This traumatic experience was echoed 10 years later by the death of his younger sister Maria, in August 1857, and by that of his father in 1863. These tragic events would seem to explain much of the longing Mallarmé expressed, from the very beginning of his poetic career, to turn away from the harsh world of reality in search of another world; and the fact that this remained the enduring theme of his poetry may be explained by the comparative harshness with which adult life continued to treat him. After spending the latter part of 1862 and the early months of 1863 in London so as to acquire a knowledge of English, he began a lifelong career as a schoolteacher, first in provincial schools (Tournon, Besançon, and Avignon) and later in Paris. He was not naturally gifted in this profession, however, and found the work decidedly uncongenial. Furthermore, his financial situation was by no means comfortable, particularly after his marriage in 1863 and after the birth of his children, Geneviève (in 1864) and Anatole (in 1871). To try to improve matters he engaged in part-time activities, such as editing a magazine for a few months at the end of 1874, writing a school textbook in 1877, and translating another textbook in 1880. In October 1879, after a six-month illness, his son Anatole died.

Mallarmé, 1891
Archives Photographiques

Despite these trials and tribulations, Mallarmé made steady progress with his parallel career as a poet. His early poems, which he began contributing to magazines in 1862, were influenced by Charles Baudelaire, whose recently published collection *Les Fleurs du mal* ("The Flowers of Evil") was largely concerned with the theme of escape from reality, a theme by which Mallarmé was already becoming obsessed. But Baudelaire's escapism had been of an essentially emotional and sensual kind—a vague dream of tropical islands and peaceful landscapes where all would be "*luxe, calme et volupté*" ("luxury, calm, and voluptuousness"). Mallarmé was of a much more intellectual bent, and his determination to analyze the nature of the ideal world and its relationship with reality is reflected in the two dramatic poems he began to write in 1864 and 1865, respectively, *Hérodiade* ("Herodias") and *L'Après-midi d'un faune* ("The Afternoon of a Faun"), the latter being the work that inspired Claude Debussy to compose his celebrated *Prélude* a quarter of a century later.

By 1868 Mallarmé had come to the conclusion that, although nothing lies beyond reality, within this nothingness lie the essences of perfect forms. The poet's task is to perceive and crystallize these essences. In so doing, the poet becomes more than a mere descriptive versifier, transposing into poetic form an already existent reality; he becomes a veritable God, creating something from nothing, conjuring up for the reader, as Mallarmé himself put it, "*l'absente de tous bouquets*"—the ideal flower that is absent from all real bouquets. But to crystallize essences in this way, to create the notion of floweriness, rather than to describe an actual flower, demands an extremely subtle and complex use of all the resources of language, and Mallarmé devoted himself during the rest of his life to putting his theories into practice in what he called his *Grand Oeuvre* ("Great Work"), or *Le Livre* ("The Book"). He never came near to completing this work, however, and the few preparatory notes that have survived give little or no idea of what the end result might have been.

On the other hand, Mallarmé did complete a number of poems related to his projected *Grand Oeuvre,* both in their themes and in their extremely evocative use of language. Among these are several elegies—the principal ones being to Charles Baudelaire, Edgar Allan Poe, Richard Wagner, Théophile Gautier, and Paul Verlaine—that Mallarmé was commissioned to write at various times in his career. He no doubt agreed to do them because the traditional theme of the elegy—the man is dead but he lives on in his work—is clearly linked to the poet's own belief that, although beyond reality there is nothing, poetry has the power to transcend this annihilation. In a second group of poems, Mallarmé wrote about poetry itself, reflecting evocatively on his aims and achievements.

In addition to these two categories of poems, he also wrote some poems that run counter to his obsession with the ideal world, though they, too, display that magical use of language of which Mallarmé had made himself such a master. These are the dozen or so sonnets he addressed to his mistress, Méry Laurent, between 1884 and 1890, in which he expressed his supreme satisfaction with reality. At that time, life was becoming much happier for him, not only because his liaison was agreeable but also because a review of him in the series of articles entitled *Les Poètes maudits* ("The Accursed Poets") published by Verlaine in 1883 and the praise lavished on him by J.-K. Huysmans in his novel *À rebours* ("The Wrong Way") in 1884 led to his wide recognition as the most eminent French poet of the day. A series of celebrated Tuesday evening meetings at his tiny flat in Paris were attended by well-known writers, painters, and musicians of the time. All this perhaps decreased his need to seek refuge in an ideal world, and in *Un Coup de dés jamais n'abolira le hasard, poème* ("A Throw of Dice Will Never Abolish the Hazard, Poem"), the work that appeared in 1897, the year before his death, he found consolation in the thought that he had met with some measure of success in giving poetry a truly creative function. (C.Ch.)

MAJOR WORKS. *Poetry.* A number of poems contributed to two volumes (1866, 1869) of the anthology *Le Parnasse Contemporain* and to various magazines from 1862 onward; *Poésies* (1887), a collection of 35 poems selected by Mallarmé; *Album de vers et de prose* (1887), a selection of nine poems from *Poésies;* the book *Vers et prose* (1893), an expansion of the above to include 21 poems; and *Poésies,* 2nd enl. ed. (1899), to which Mallarmé had added about 12 poems—published six months after his death.

Prose poems. Various prose poems contained in the collections *Album de vers et de prose* (1887), *Pages* (1891), and *Vers et prose* (1893); *Un Coup de dés jamais n'abolira le hasard, poème,* published in the review *Cosmopolis* (1897).

Criticism. *Divagations* (1897), a collection of articles on such contemporaries as Verlaine, Villiers de l'Isle-Adam, and Wagner and a number of essays on literary matters.

Other works. *La Dernière Mode* (1874), eight issues of a fashion magazine; *Les Mots anglais* (1877), a study of English vocabulary; *Les Dieux antiques* (1880), a study of mythology.

BIBLIOGRAPHY. Mallarmé's writings are collected in *Oeuvres complètes,* ed. by Henri Mondor and G. Jean-Aubry (1945, reissued 1989). *Correspondance,* 11 vol. (1959–85), collects his letters; some of his letters have been translated in Rosemary Lloyd (ed. and trans.), *Correspondence* (1988). Biographies include Henri Mondor, *Vie de Mallarmé,* 2 vol. (1941–42), the standard biography of Mallarmé; and Gordan Millan, *A Throw of the Dice: The Life of Stéphane Mallarmé* (1994). Malcolm Bowie, *Mallarmé and the Art of Being Difficult* (1978), offers a unique analysis of form and content in Mallarmé's poetry. Austin Gill, *The Early Mallarmé,* 2 vol. (1979–86), is a commentary on the early poems. A.R. Chisholm, *Mallarmé's Grand Oeuvre* (1962), is a useful introduction to Mallarmé's work. Other critical studies are Charles Chadwick, *Mallarmé, sa pensée dans sa poésie* (1962); Pierre Olivier Walzer, *Essai sur Stéphane Mallarmé* (1963); Thomas A. Williams, *Mallarmé and the Language of Mysticism* (1970); Guy Michaud, *Mallarmé,* new ed. (1971); Leo Bersani, *The Death of Stéphane Mallarmé* (1982), a look at the contradictions in Mallarmé's thought; and F.C. St. Aubyn, *Stéphane Mallarmé* (1989).

Mallas, tribal people in the time of the Buddha (*c.* 6th–4th century BC), who settled in the northern parts of modern Bihār state, in India. Their two most important towns were at Kuśinagara (Kusinārā) and Pāvā (located east of modern Gorakhpur). The Mallas had a republican form of government, with an assembly. They lost their independence about the time of the Buddha and were annexed by the Magadha empire. A Malla dynasty ruled Nepal from the 10th century to 1769. The Mallas introduced the first legal and social code influenced by contemporary Hindu practices and were patrons of the arts and architecture.

Malle, Louis (b. Oct. 30, 1932, Thumeries, France—d. Nov. 23, 1995, Beverly Hills, Calif., U.S.), eclectic French motion-picture director whose films were noted for their emotional realism and stylistic simplicity.

Malle's wealthy family resisted his early interest in film but allowed him to enter the Institute of Advanced Cinematographic Studies in Paris in 1950. After studying at the institute, he worked as an assistant to filmmaker Robert Bresson and codirected the documentary *Le Monde du silence* (1956; *The Silent World*) with underwater explorer Jacques-Yves Cousteau.

Malle's first feature film, *Ascenseur pour l'échafaud* (1957; *Frantic*), was a psychological thriller. His second, *Les Amants* (1958; *The Lovers*), was a commercial success and established Malle and its star, Jeanne Moreau, in the film industry. The film's lyrical love scenes, tracked with exquisite timing, exhibit Malle's typically bold and uninhibited treatment of sensual themes. Social alienation and isolation was the subject of *Le Feu follet* (1963; *The Fire Within*), which was acclaimed by critics as Malle's most mature and sophisticated work. The sombre and keenly observed story of the last days of an alcoholic contemplating suicide demonstrated his versatility as a filmmaker. In Malle's next major film, *Le Voleur* (1967; *The Thief of Paris*), a gentleman is driven to become a thief out of hatred of himself and his bourgeois origins. Malle's other films of the 1960s include the zany comedy *Zazie dans le métro* (1960) and the musical satire *Viva Maria* (1965).

Malle's six-month-long stay in India resulted in a feature-length documentary, *Calcutta* (1969), and a seven-part television series, *L'Inde fantôme* (*Phantom India*), which was broadcast internationally to great acclaim. Two of his films of the early 1970s were notable for their moving simplicity: *Le Souffle au coeur* (1971; *Murmur of the Heart*), a tenderly treated comedy about an adolescent boy; and *Lacombe, Lucien* (1973), about a bored teenager who becomes an informer for the Gestapo during the German occupation of France.

Malle moved to the United States in 1975. In 1978 he directed *Pretty Baby,* the story of a 12-year-old resident of a brothel in New Orleans. His later films included the critically acclaimed *Atlantic City* (1980), a comedy-drama about the emotional renewal of a small-time criminal; *My Dinner with André* (1981), an unusual film consisting almost entirely of a dinner-table conversation between two characters; and *Au revoir les enfants* (1987; *Goodbye, Children*), an autobiographical reminiscence of life in a Roman Catholic boys' school in occupied France during World War II. Malle's last film was *Vanya on 42nd Street* (1994), in which a theatre ensemble gives a reading of Anton Chekhov's play *Uncle Vanya.*

Mallea, Eduardo (b. Aug. 14, 1903, Bahía Blanca, Arg.—d. Nov. 12, 1982, Buenos Aires), Argentine novelist, essayist, and short-story writer whose psychological novels won critical acclaim.

Mallea began as a short-story writer, first achieving recognition with *Cuentos para una inglesa desesperada* (1926; "Stories for a Desperate Englishwoman"). In 1931 he became editor of the weekly literary magazine of the Buenos Aires newspaper *La nación.* Soon, however, he found that the novel provided a suitable structure for his style of writing, enabling both psychological analysis of character and philosophical digression. Often set in Argentina, Mallea's novels were also concerned with national and regional problems, as in *La bahía de silencio* (1940; *The Bay of Silence*) and *Las águilas* (1943; "The Eagles"). In *Todo verdor perecerá* (1941; *All Green Shall Perish*), which many consider his greatest work, he explored—by the use of interior monologue and flashback techniques—the anguish of a woman living in the provinces.

Mallea also wrote several volumes of travel books and essays. His final works were published in the early 1970s.

Mallee, region of northwestern Victoria, Australia. It occupies about 16,000 square miles (41,000 square km) between the Wimmera and Murray rivers, and its climate is semiarid, with only 10–12 inches (250–300 mm) of rainfall annually. A narrow belt of irrigated land supports vineyards, citrus orchards, wheat fields, and dairy and sheep farming, but intensive irrigation has increased salinity and soil degradation. The name Mallee is said to be derived from an Aboriginal term denoting species of eucalyptus. The region's chief settlement is Mildura (*q.v.*).

mallee, also spelled MELLEE, a scrubland vegetation found in southern Australia. It is composed primarily of woody shrubs and trees of the genus *Eucalyptus.* These evergreen plants have leathery, thick leaves that prevent water loss during the hot dry season. Most scrubland growth occurs during the rainy season.

The extensive scrublands of southwestern Australia have a rich and varied vegetation, although only a few plant families are represented. Many of the approximately 1,000 species of shrubs found there have spiny branches or leaves, and most bear colourful flowers during the wet season.

Mallet-Joris, Françoise (b. July 6, 1930, Antwerp), Belgian author, one of the leading contemporary exponents of the traditional French novel of psychological love analysis. Her father was a statesman and her mother, Suzanne Lilar, an author and a critic.

At 19 Françoise won unanimous critical approval with her novel *Le Rempart des béguines* (1951; *The Illusionist,* 1952; *Into the Labyrinth,* 1953), the story of an affair between a girl and her father's mistress, described with clinical detachment in a sober, classical prose. After another novel, *La Chambre rouge* (1953; *The Red Room,* 1956), and a book of short stories in the same tone, *Cordélia* (1956; *Cordelia and Other Short Stories,* 1965), her style changed with *Les Mensonges* (Prix de la sélection des Libraires de France, 1956; *House of Lies,* 1957), which told of the struggle between a dying businessman and his illegitimate daughter, who remains true to her mother.

Françoise Mallet-Joris, *c.* 1969

Marc Garanger—J.P. Ziolo

In *L'Empire céleste* (1958; *Café Céleste,* 1959) and *Les Signes et les prodiges* (1966; *Signs and Wonders,* 1966), she pursued the search for a truth hidden beneath a proliferation of human activities. She turned to the historical novel with *Les Personnages* (1960; *The Favourite,* 1962), about the intrigues wrought by Cardinal de Richelieu around the love life of King Louis XIII, and with *Marie Mancini le premier amour de Louis XIV* (1964; *The Uncompromising Heart: A Life of Marie Mancini, Louis XIV's First Love* 1966). Bluntly candid about herself, Mallet-Joris has told of her personal life, her inner conflicts and her religious quests—she became a Roman Catholic convert—in her autobiographical writings, *Lettre à moi-même* (1963; *A Letter to Myself,* 1964) and *La Maison de papier* (1970) *The Paper House,* 1971). Among her later novels are *Le Jeu de souterrain* (1973; *The Underground Game,* 1974), *Allegra* (1976), and *Dickie-Roi* (1979) and *Un Chagrin d'amour et d'ailleurs* (1981; "A Sorrow of Love and More Besides"). She also wrote a biography of *Jeanne Guyon* (1978), the 17th-century French mystic. Her writings reveal an abundance of detail and colour that is reminiscent of Balzac.

Mallet-Stevens, Robert (b. March 24, 1886, Paris—d. Feb. 10, 1945, Paris), French architect known principally for his modernistic works in France during the 1920s and '30s.

Mallet-Stevens received his formal training at the École Speciale d'Architecture, Paris. He came to know the work of other young architects at the Salons d'Automnes of 1912–14, and after the war he emerged as a fashionable and even mildly avant-garde designer. His approach has been called "modernism à-la-mode."

One of his first commissions was for the villa of the Vicomte de Noailles at Hyères, Fr. The house was used by Man Ray as the set for his film *Les Mystères du Château du Dé.* The following year, Mallet-Stevens collaborated with the painter Fernand Léger and others on Marcel Lherbier's film *L'Inhumaine.* The house designed for the film and the villa de Noailles are representative of Mallet-Stevens' sophisticated synthesis of Cubist painting, Art Deco details, and other artistic modes of the time.

Typically, Mallet-Stevens drew artists, musicians, and others into his projects, as he did for the Tourism pavilion and so-called French embassy he designed at the Exposition des Arts Décoratifs et Industriels Modernes, Paris, 1925, the exposition that lent its name to the style termed "Art Deco." The musicians Francis Poulenc and Arthur Honegger and the painters Léger and Robert Delaunay worked on this project.

Mallet-Stevens was expert in the uses of metal framing and reinforced concrete; among the structures in which such techniques were applied is a block of apartments (1926–27) built on the rue Mallet-Stevens, Paris, so named in honour of the architect.

Malleus maleficarum, detailed legal and theological document (*c.* 1486) regarded as the standard handbook on witchcraft, including its detection and its extirpation, until well into the 18th century. Its appearance did much to spur on and sustain some two centuries of witch-hunting hysteria in Europe. The *Malleus* was the work of two Dominicans: Johann Sprenger, dean of the University of Cologne in Germany, and Heinrich (Institoris) Kraemer, professor of theology at the University of Salzburg, Austria, and inquisitor in the Tirol region of Austria. In 1484 Pope Innocent VIII issued the bull *Summis Desiderantes,* in which he deplored the spread of witchcraft in Germany and authorized Sprenger and Kraemer to extirpate it.

The *Malleus* codified the folklore and beliefs of the Alpine peasants and was dedicated to the implementation of Exodus 22:18: "You shall not permit a sorceress to live." The work is divided into three parts. In Part I the reality and the depravity of witches is emphasized, and any disbelief in demonology is condemned as heresy. Because of the nature of the enemy, any witness, no matter what his credentials, may testify against an accused. Part II is a compendium of fabulous stories about the activities of witches—*e.g.,* diabolic compacts, sexual relations with devils (incubi and succubi), transvection (night-riding), and metamorphosis. Part III is a discussion of the legal procedures to be followed in witch trials. Torture is sanctioned as a means of securing confessions. Lay and secular authorities are called upon to assist the inquisitors in the task of exterminating those whom Satan has enlisted in his cause.

The *Malleus* went through 28 editions between 1486 and 1600 and was accepted by Roman Catholics and Protestants alike as an authoritative source of information concerning satanism and as a guide to Christian defense.

Mallicolo (Vanuatu): *see* Malakula.

Mallorca (island, Spain): *see* Majorca.

Mallory, Molla, *née* BJURSTEDT (b. 1892, Oslo—d. Nov. 22, 1959, United States), Norwegian-born U.S. tennis player who was the only woman to win the U.S. singles championship eight times. She defeated Suzanne Lenglen of France for the U.S. title in 1921, the only loss in Lenglen's amateur career.

Mallory was known for her endurance and baseline game, relying on a strong forehand and defense designed to tire her opponents. She moved to New York City in 1914 and won her first national title in 1915, defeating three-time winner Hazel Hotchkiss Wightman. She repeated her victory each year through 1918. After marrying Franklin Mallory in 1919, she again won the championship from 1920 through 1922 and for the last time in 1926. During this period she played some of the greatest women stars of the game, including Helen Wills Moody. She was elected to the International Tennis Hall of Fame in 1958.

mallow, any of several flowering plants in the mallow family, Malvaceae, especially those of the genera *Hibiscus* and *Malva.* Hibiscus species include the desert rose mallow (*H. farragei*), from Australasia; the great rose mallow (*H. grandiflorus*), with large white to purplish flowers; the soldier rose mallow (*H. militaria*), a shrub that grows to a height of 2 metres (6 feet); and the common, or swamp, rose mallow (*H. moscheutos*).

Several *Malva* species are cultivated in gardens, especially the musk mallow (*M. moschata*), growing up to 1 m high, with rose-mauve or white flowers in early summer, and high mallow (*M. sylvestris*), the leaves and flowers of which have been used medicinally. Another musk mallow, the abelmosk (*Abelmoschus moschatus,* or *Hibiscus abelmoschus*), is widely cultivated in tropical Asia for its seeds.

The marsh mallow (*Althea officinalis*), a perennial plant native to eastern Europe and northern Africa, is naturalized in North America, especially in marshy areas near the sea; its root was formerly processed to make marshmallow confections.

Other mallows include the globe, or false, mallows (*Sphaeralcea*) such as the prairie, or red false, mallow (*S. coccinea*) and the trailing mallow (*S. philippiana*); Jew's mallow, or Tossa jute (*Corchorus olitorius*), from tropical Asia, a secondary source of jute; tree mallow (*Lavatera arborea*), up to 3 metres, from Europe but naturalized along coastal California; wax mallow (*Malvaviscus arboreus*), a reddish flowering ornamental shrub from South America; poppy mallow (*Callirhoe involucrata*), a hairy perennial, low-growing, with poppy-like reddish flowers; and Indian mallow, also called velvetleaf (*Abutilon theophrasti*), a weedy plant. Chaparral mallows (*Malacothamnus* species), a group of shrubs and small trees, are native to California and Baja California. The Carolina mallow (*Modiola caroliniana*) is a weedy, creeping wild flower of the southern U.S.

Mallowan, Sir Max (Edgar Lucien) (b. May 6, 1904, London—d. Aug. 19, 1978, Wallingford, Oxfordshire, Eng.), British archaeologist who made major contributions as an excavator and educator.

After receiving a degree in classics at New College, Oxford University, he began his long career as a field archaeologist. His excavations were carried out in the Near East, at first as assistant to Sir Leonard Woolley at Ur (1925–30) and to R. Campbell Thompson at Nineveh (1931–1932). He later directed excavations at Tall Arpachiyah, Iraq (1933); Chagar Bazar (1935–37), Tall Birāk (Tell Brak; 1937–38), and the Balīkh Valley (1938), Syria; and Nimrūd (1949–58).

At the British School of Archaeology, Baghdad, Mallowan was director (1947–61), chairman (1966–70), and president (1970–78). He was also professor (1947–62) and emeritus professor of western Asiatic archaeology at the University of London; fellow (1962–71) and emeritus fellow (1976) at All Souls College, Oxford; vice president (1961–62) of the British Academy; president (1961–78) of the British Institute of Persian Studies; and a trustee of the British Museum. He was knighted in 1968.

Mallowan married the novelist and playwright Agatha Christie (later Dame Agatha) in 1930. One year after her death in 1976, he married the archaeologist Barbara Parker. Mallowan's publications include *Early Mesopotamia and Iran* (1965), *Nimrud and Its Remains,* 3 vol. (1966), and *Elamite Problems* (1969). He also contributed (1967–68) to the *Cambridge Ancient History* and edited (1948–65) the Penguin series on the Near East and western Asia. His autobiography was published as *Mallowan's Memoirs* (1977).

Malmaison (France): *see* Rueil-Malmaison.

Malmédy, *commune,* Liège *province,* eastern Belgium. It is situated in the northern Ardennes, along the Warche River, southeast of Liège. Malmédy was established in the 7th century around a monastery founded by St. Remaclus, bishop of Maastricht. For more than 1,000 years thereafter, it (together with Stavelot) remained the seat of an ecclesiastical principality dependent on the Holy Roman Empire. It came under French rule from 1794 to 1814; and, together with the Eupen district, it was annexed to Prussia (1815) after the Congress of Vienna. Finally, it was awarded to Belgium (1920) after the Treaty of Versailles. Seized by Germany in World War II, it was heavily fought over during the Battle of the Bulge in December 1944. The town was the scene of the Malmédy Massacre (Dec. 17, 1944), in which advancing German SS troops murdered about 100 American soldiers who had surrendered to them.

Malmédy's economy depends on tourism and the manufacture of paper, beer, and tanning fluid. Pop. (2001 est.) 11,392.

Malmö, city and port, seat of Skåne *län* (county), southern Sweden. It is located across The Sound (Öresund) from Copenhagen, Den. The city was the capital of Malmöhus county until the county became part of Skåne county in 1997.

Malmö originally was known as Malmhaug ("Sandpile"). It was chartered in the late 13th century, and during the late Middle Ages its herring trade attracted German merchants from Lübeck, who settled there and named it Elbogen ("Elbow") for the curve of the coastline at that point. Following its union with Sweden in 1658, the city suffered an economic decline, owing in part to the loss of certain trading privileges that it had enjoyed under Danish rule, the many wars between Sweden and Denmark, and poor harbour facilities. By 1730 its population had dwindled to 282. With the building of the harbour in 1775, its fortunes revived somewhat, but it saw no large-scale economic development until the arrival of the railroad after 1800.

Since the mid-19th century, Malmö, now Sweden's third largest city, has been an industrial and transportation centre. Its diversified industries range from shipbuilding to food processing. Through its busy port pass a wide range of imports and exports. Factories and warehouses have been built on extensive landfill in The Sound. Malmö is connected by rail with Stockholm and Göteborg and via boat and train ferry with continental Europe; an international airport is located about 19 miles (31 km) east of the city, near Skurup. In 2000 the Öresund Link, a bridge and tunnel system connecting Malmö and Copenhagen, opened. Malmö's historic buildings include Malmöhus (a 16th-century castle and fortress that is now a museum) and the 14th-century St. Peter's Church (a fine example of early Baltic Gothic architecture). Pop. (2002) 265,481.

The town hall on the Stortorget park in Malmö, Swed., with the steeple of St. Peter's Church in the background

T. Lindebert—Ostman Agency

Malmöhus, former *län* (county) of extreme southern Sweden, bounded by the Baltic Sea, The Sound (Öresund), and the Kattegat (strait). Founded as a county in 1719, it was merged with the county of Kristianstad in 1997 to form Skåne county.

malnutrition, physical condition resulting either from a faulty or inadequate diet (*i.e.,* a diet that does not supply normal quantities of all nutrients) or from a physical inability to absorb or metabolize nutrients, owing to disease.

Malnutrition may be the result of several conditions. First, sufficient and proper food may not be available because of inadequate agricultural processes, imperfect distribution of food, or certain social problems, such as poverty or alcoholism. In these instances, the cause of malnutrition is most often found to be a diet quantitatively inadequate in calories or protein.

Malnutrition may also result when certain foods containing one or more of the essential vitamins or minerals are not included in the diet. This commonly leads to specific nutritional-deficiency diseases. Poor eating habits and food preferences may lead to malnutrition through the habitual consumption of certain foods to the exclusion of others or of large quantities of nonnutritious foods. In certain parts of Africa, for example, the practice of weaning breast-fed infants to a diet consisting chiefly of one kind of starchy food, such as cassava, may lead to protein deficiency. In parts of East Asia, a preference for white polished rice as a dietary staple has led to the prevalence of a deficiency of vitamin B_1 (thiamine), which is found mainly in grain husks. Multiple deficiencies are more likely to occur than single deficiencies, though the manifestations of one type usually predominate.

Malnutrition can also arise from acquired or inherited metabolic defects, notably those involving the digestive tract, liver, kidney, and red blood cells. These defects cause malnutrition by preventing the proper digestion, absorption, and metabolism of foodstuffs by organs and tissues. *See also* nutrition.

Malo, formerly ST. BARTHOLOMEW, island of Vanuatu, in the southwestern Pacific Ocean, 3 miles (5 km) south of Espiritu Santo. Volcanic in origin, it has a circumference of 34 miles (55 km) and occupies an area of about 70 square miles (180 square km). Its highest point is Malo Peak, 1,070 feet (326 m). Copra and cocoa are produced on Malo's plantations.

Malolos, town, south-central Luzon, Philippines. It lies at the head of the Pampanga River delta, near the northern shore of Manila Bay. During a revolt against U.S. administration, the insurgent congress met there in the Barasoain Church, where they framed the "Malolos Constitution" and proclaimed a republic on Jan. 23, 1899. The insurgent leader, Emilio Aguinaldo, established his headquarters in Malolos, which served as the revolutionary capital until it was captured by U.S. forces in March 1899.

The town is a trading centre for a rice- and vegetable-producing region, with major fishpond-culture areas to the south and west. It is situated on the main highway northward from Manila through the central plain and is bisected by the railway to the Lingayen Gulf (northwest). Bulacan College of Arts and Trades (1904) is located there. Pop. (2000) 175,291.

Malombe, Lake, lake fed and drained by the Shire River in southern Malaŵi. It lies in a broken depression running northwest from Lake Chilwa to Lake Nyasa, parallel to the Shire Rift Valley. The lake is fed by the Shire River 12 miles (19 km) below its efflux from Lake Nyasa and drains through that river's exit from Lake Malombe's southern shore. Malombe covers an area of 162 square miles (420 square km) and has a depth of 6–8 feet (2–2.5 m). Rice and corn (maize) are grown along the lake's marshy shores during the dry season, and commercial fishing is economically important.

Malone, Dumas (b. Jan. 10, 1892, Coldwater, Miss., U.S.—d. Dec. 27, 1986, Charlottesville, Va.), American historian, editor, and the author of an authoritative multivolume biography of Thomas Jefferson.

Malone was educated at Emory and Yale universities. He taught at Yale, Columbia, and the University of Virginia, where he was the Thomas Jefferson Foundation Professor of History. He edited the *Dictionary of American Biography* from 1929 to 1936 and the *Political Science Quarterly* from 1953 to 1958 and served as director of the Harvard University Press from 1936 to 1943. Malone's masterwork is *Jefferson and His Time,* a comprehensive, six-volume biography of Thomas Jefferson, consisting of: *Jefferson the Virginian* (1948); *Jefferson and the Rights of Man* (1951); *Jefferson and the Ordeal of Liberty* (1962); *Jefferson the President: First Term, 1801–1805* (1970); *Jefferson the President: Second Term, 1805–1809* (1974); and *The Sage of Monticello* (1981).

Malone's other writings include *The Public Life of Thomas Cooper* (1926); *Saints in Action* (1939); and *Empire for Liberty,* 2 vol. (1960, with Basil Rauch).

Malone, Edmund (b. Oct. 4, 1741, Dublin, Ire.—d. 1812, London, Eng.), Irish-born English scholar, editor, and pioneer in efforts to establish an authentic text and chronology of Shakespeare's works.

Edmund Malone, oil painting by Sir Joshua Reynolds, 1778; in the National Portrait Gallery, London

By courtesy of the National Portrait Gallery, London

After practicing in Ireland as a lawyer and journalist, Malone settled in London in 1777. There he numbered among his literary friends Samuel Johnson, Horace Walpole, and the ballad collector Bishop Percy. He also was an associate of the statesmen Edmund Burke and George Canning and of the dean of English painters, Sir Joshua Reynolds, who painted his portrait and whose literary works he collected and published (1797).

Malone's "An Attempt to Ascertain the Order in Which the Plays of Shakespeare Were Written" (1778) was the first such chronology. His three supplemental volumes (1780–83) to scholar George Steevens' edition of Johnson's Shakespeare—containing apocryphal plays, textual emendations, and the first critical edition of the sonnets—are landmarks in Shakespearean studies. Malone's *Historical Account of the Rise and Progress of the English Stage, and of the Economy and Usages of the Ancient Theatres in England* (1800) was the first treatise on English drama based on original sources. His own edition of Shakespeare in 11 volumes appeared in 1790. A new octavo edition, unfinished at his death, was completed by James Boswell, the son of Samuel Johnson's biographer, and published in 1821 in 21 volumes. This work, which included a memoir of Malone, was the standard edition of Shakespeare's writings for more than a century.

Malone also detected (1796) Shakespearean forgeries by William Henry Ireland, edited John Dryden's prose (1800), and helped Boswell revise his *Life of Samuel Johnson*.

Malone, Moses, in full MOSES EUGENE MALONE (b. March 23, 1955, Petersburg, Va., U.S.), American professional basketball player, a dominating centre who led the Philadelphia 76ers to a National Basketball Association (NBA) championship in 1983.

A formidable teenage athlete, Malone bypassed college to sign with the Utah Stars of the American Basketball Association (ABA) in 1974, becoming the first player to enter professional basketball directly from high school. When the ABA dissolved in 1976, he signed with the NBA Houston Rockets.

Noted for his all-around play, Malone was an outstanding offensive rebounder with a scoring touch. He was named the NBA's Most Valuable Player in 1979, 1982, and 1983, the latter with Philadelphia. He was a member of eight NBA teams during his 18 years in the league, setting records for most free throws made (8,531) and most offensive rebounds (6,731). He retired in 1994, having scored 27,409 points and collected 16,212 rebounds.

malonic acid, also called PROPANEDIOIC ACID ($HO_2CCH_2CO_2H$), a dibasic organic acid whose diethyl ester is used in syntheses of vitamins B_1 and B_6, barbiturates, and numerous other valuable compounds.

Malonic acid itself is rather unstable and has few applications. Its calcium salt occurs in beetroot, but the acid itself is usually prepared by hydrolyzing diethyl malonate. It undergoes the usual reactions of carboxylic acids as well as facile cleavage into acetic acid and carbon dioxide.

Diethyl malonate, $CH_2(CO_2C_2H_5)_2$, also called malonic ester, is prepared by the reaction of ethyl alcohol with cyanoacetic acid. Its utility in synthesis arises from the reactivity of its methylene (CH_2) group; a hydrogen atom is easily removed by sodium ethoxide or other strong base, and the resulting derivative reacts readily with an alkyl halide to form a diethyl alkylmalonate. A second alkyl group may be similarly introduced. The diethyl dialkylmalonates are converted by reaction with urea to barbiturates. Diethyl malonate is a colourless, fragrant liquid boiling at 181.4° C.

Małopolskie, *województwo* (province), southern Poland. It comprises the former provinces (1975–98) of Kraków, Tarnów, and Nowy Sącz, as well as portions of the former provinces of Bielsko-Biała, Katowice, Kielce, and Krosno. Dominated by the Tatra Mountains and other ranges, especially in the south, the province contains the highest peak in Poland. The main rivers are the Vistula (Wisła), Skawa, Raba, Prądnik, and Dunajec, which features the spectacular Dunajec River Gorge. Kraków, the provincial capital, is the hub of Polish culture, with more than 6,000 monuments of cultural and historical significance. Other large cities include Tarnów, Nowy Sącz, Olkusz, and Oświęcim, which in World War II was the site of the Auschwitz-Birkenau concentration camp, now a museum. The scenic beauty of the province draws tourists to its national parks, spa towns, and sporting centres. Two-thirds of the land is used for agriculture, but industry also is significant and quite diverse, including iron and steel production, zinc and lead metallurgy, chemicals, electronics, and petroleum refining. There is a port on the Vistula River at Kraków, as well as an international airport at Kraków-Balice. Area 5,847 square miles (15,144 square km). Pop. (2003 est.) 3,245,900.

Malory, Sir Thomas (fl. *c.* 1470), English writer whose identity remains uncertain but whose name is famous as that of the author of *Le Morte Darthur* (*q.v.*), the first prose account in English of the rise and fall of King Arthur and the fellowship of the Round Table.

Even in the 16th century Malory's identity was unknown, although there was a tradition that he was a Welshman. In the colophon to *Le Morte Darthur* the author, calling himself "Syr Thomas Maleore knyght," says that he finished the work in the ninth year of the reign of Edward IV (*i.e.,* March 4, 1469–March 3, 1470) and adds a prayer for "good delyueraunce" from prison. The only known knight at this time with a name like Maleore was Thomas Malory of Newbold Revell in the parish of Monks Kirby, Warwickshire. This Malory, like the author, was imprisoned, but it was on various occasions during the period from 1450 to 1460, rather than about 1470. A "Thomas Malorie (or Malarie), knight" was excluded from four general pardons granted by Edward IV to the Lancastrians in 1468 and 1470. This person is tentatively accepted as the author.

According to Sir William Dugdale's *Antiquities of Warwickshire* (1656), this Sir Thomas Malory served in the train of Richard Beauchamp, earl of Warwick, at the siege of Calais (presumably 1436, but possibly 1414); was knight of the shire in 1445; and died on March 14, 1471. He was buried in the Chapel of St. Francis at Grey Friars, near Newgate. (He had been imprisoned in Newgate in 1460.)

Maloti Mountains, Maloti also spelled MALUTI, mountain range, northern Lesotho. The term as generally used outside Lesotho refers to a particular range that trends off to the southwest from the Great Escarpment of the Drakensberg Range, which forms the northeastern arc of Lesotho's circumferential boundary with South Africa. Within Lesotho, *maloti* means merely "mountains," or "in the mountains," and as used in the country's western lowlands—all more than 3,300 feet (1,000 m) in elevation—it signifies the mountainous eastern two-thirds of Lesotho, containing the highest peaks in southern Africa.

The chain known outside Lesotho as the Maloti Mountains is properly the Front Range of the Maloti, sometimes called the Blue Mountains. It is a broad southwesterly spur from the Drakensberg Range near the northern tip of Lesotho and a few miles from its highest point, Mont aux-Sources. The Front Range is extended almost to Lesotho's southwestern border by another range, the Thaba Putsoa (Blue-Gray) Mountains; it is extended nearly to the southeastern border by the Central Range. All these mountains belong geologically to the Stormberg Series (Upper Triassic Period) of the Karoo System; they are composed of sandstone and shale overlain by basalt. Their rugged terrain causes visitors viewing them from the western plateaus to style Lesotho the Switzerland of Africa; the rough terrain has also prevented significant exploitation of the range's mineral resources. Winter (May–September) is usually dry, but winter precipitation in the *maloti* is virtually always snow; it snows in the mountains in every month of the year. This and the region's rivers make the place the source of much of southern Africa's water; the Front Range (Maloti Mountains) is the divide between the watersheds of the westward-draining Orange River and the eastward-draining Caledon River.

Malozi (people): *see* Lozi.

Malpeque Bay, arm of the Gulf of St. Lawrence, indenting the northwestern coast of Prince Edward Island, Canada. The inlet, 12 miles (19 km) long and up to 10 miles (16 km) wide, is protected from the ocean by Hog Island. Its shallow inshore waters form an ideal habitat for oysters. Several oyster farms operate in the bay from headquarters in Summerside, a town 4 miles (6 km) south, producing high-quality mollusks that bear the inlet's name, which is a French rendition of the Micmac Indian word *makpaak*, meaning "large bay."

Malpighi, Marcello (b. March 10, 1628, Crevalcore, near Bologna, Papal States [Italy]—d. Nov. 30, 1694, Rome), Italian physician and biologist who, in developing experimental methods to study living things, founded the science of microscopic anatomy. After Malpighi's researches, microscopic anatomy became a prerequisite for advances in the fields of physiology, embryology, and practical medicine.

Malpighi, detail of a painting attributed to the school of Bologna, 17th century; in the Putti Collection, Rizzoli Institute, Bologna, Italy
Fotofast

Life. Little is known of Malpighi's childhood and youth except that his father had him engage in "grammatical studies" at an early age and that he entered the University of Bologna in 1646. Both parents died when he was 21, but he was able, nevertheless, to continue his studies. Despite opposition from the university authorities because he was non-Bolognese by birth, in 1653 he was granted doctorates in both medicine and philosophy and appointed as a teacher, whereupon he immediately dedicated himself to further study in anatomy and medicine.

In 1656, Ferdinand II of Tuscany invited him to the professorship of theoretical medicine at the University of Pisa. There Malpighi began his lifelong friendship with Giovanni Borelli, mathematician and naturalist, who was a prominent supporter of the Accademia del Cimento, one of the first scientific societies. Malpighi questioned the prevailing medical teachings at Pisa, tried experiments on colour changes in blood, and attempted to recast anatomical, physiological, and medical problems of the day. Family responsibilities and poor health prompted Malpighi's return in 1659 to the University of Bologna, where he continued to teach and do research with his microscopes. In 1661 he identified and described the pulmonary and capillary network connecting small arteries with small veins, one of the major discoveries in the history of science. Malpighi's views evoked increasing controversy and dissent, mainly from envy, jealousy, and lack of understanding on the part of his colleagues.

Hindered by the hostile environment of Bologna, Malpighi accepted (November 1662) a professorship in medicine at the University of Messina in Sicily, on the recommendation there of Borelli, who was investigating the effects of physical forces on animal functions. Malpighi was also welcomed by Viscount Francavilla, a patron of science and a former student, whose hospitality encouraged him in furthering his career. Malpighi pursued his microscopic studies while teaching and practicing medicine. He identified the taste buds and regarded them as terminations of nerves, described the minute structure of the brain, optic nerve, and fat reservoirs, and in 1666 was the first to see the red blood cells and to attribute the colour of blood to them. Again, his research and teaching aroused envy and controversy among his colleagues.

After four years at Messina, Malpighi returned in January 1667 to Bologna, where, during his medical practice, he studied the microscopic subdivisions of specific living organs, such as the liver, brain, spleen, and kidneys, and of bone and the deeper layers of the skin that now bear his name. Impressed by the minute structures he observed under the microscope, he concluded that most living materials are glandular in organization, that even the largest organs are composed of minute glands, and that these glands exist solely for the separation or for the mixture of juices.

Malpighi's work at Messina attracted the attention of the Royal Society in London, whose secretary, Henry Oldenburg, extended him an invitation in 1668 to correspond with him. Malpighi's work was thereafter published periodically in the form of letters in the *Philosophical Transactions* of the Royal Society. In 1669 Malpighi was named an honorary member, the first such recognition given to an Italian. From then on, all his works were published in London.

At the peak of his fame, Malpighi could have left his tiring medical practice and research to accept one of the many highly remunerative positions offered to him. Instead, he chose to continue his general practice and professorship. These years at Bologna marked the climax of his career, when he marked out large areas of microscopy. Malpighi conducted many studies of insect larvae—establishing, in so doing, the basis for their future study—the most important of which was his investigation in 1669 of the structure and development of the silkworm. In his historic work in 1673 on the embryology of the chick, in which he discovered the aortic arches, neural folds, and somites, he generally followed William Harvey's views on development, though Malpighi probably concluded that the embryo is preformed in the egg after fertilization. He also made extensive comparative studies in 1675–79 of the microscopic anatomy of several different plants and saw an analogy between plant and animal organization.

During the last decade of his life Malpighi was beset by personal tragedy, declining health, and the climax of opposition to him. In 1684 his villa was burned, his apparatus and microscopes shattered, and his papers, books, and manuscripts destroyed. Most probably as a compensatory move when opposition mounted against his views, and in recognition of his stature, Pope Innocent XII invited him to Rome in 1691 as papal archiater, or personal physician, such a nomination constituting a great honour. In Rome he was further honoured by being named a count, he was elected to the College of Doctors of Medicine, his name was placed in the Roman Patriciate Roll, and he was given the title of honorary valet.

Assessment. Malpighi may be regarded as the first histologist. For almost 40 years he used the microscope to describe the major types of plant and animal structures and in so doing marked out for future generations of biologists major areas of research in botany, embryology, human anatomy, and pathology. Just as Galileo had applied the new technical achievement of the optical lens to vistas beyond the Earth, Malpighi extended its use to the intricate organization of living things, hitherto unimagined, below the level of unaided sight. Moreover, his lifework brought into question the prevailing concepts of body function. When, for example, he found that the blood passed through the capillaries, it meant that Harvey was right, that blood was not transformed into flesh in the periphery, as the ancients thought. He was vigorously denounced by his enemies, who failed to see how his many discoveries, such as the renal glomeruli, urinary tubules, dermal papillae, taste buds, and the glandular components of the liver, could possibly improve medical practice. The conflict between ancient ideas and modern discoveries continued throughout the 17th century. Although Malpighi could not say what new remedies might come from his discoveries, he was convinced that microscopic anatomy, by showing the minute construction of living things, called into question the value of old medicine. He provided the anatomical basis for the eventual understanding of human physiological exchanges.

(E.T./Al.R.)

BIBLIOGRAPHY. The definitive study of Malpighi is Howard Adelmann, *Marcello Malpighi and the Evolution of Embryology*, 5 vol. (1966). It contains a complete biography of Malpighi, translations from the Latin of Malpighi's chief works with Latin on facing pages, colour reproductions of Malpighi's illustrations, and detailed essays on structure based on embryologists of the 17th, 18th, and 19th centuries with extensive translations from French, German, and Latin. Ettore Toffoletto, *Discorso sul Malpighi* (1965), provides a critical analysis (in Italian) of Malpighi both as a man and as a scientist.

malpighian body (anatomy): *see* renal corpuscle.

malpighian tubule, in insects, any of the excretory organs that lie in the abdominal body cavity and empty into the junction between midgut and hindgut. In species having few malpighian tubules, they are long and coiled; in species with numerous (up to 150) tubules, they are short. The tubule cells actively transport initial urine constituents (potassium ions, water, urate ions, sugar, amino acids) into the tubule. In some species urine is acidified in the distal end of the tubule and an aqueous suspension of uric acid crystals is conducted into the rectum, where water and nutrients are reabsorbed. In other species the urine is acidified in the rectum. Certain tubule cells may have special functions, as in the secretion of the sticky substance that surrounds eggs of certain leaf beetles or in the secretion of silk by certain immature beetles.

Malplaquet, Battle of (Sept. 11, 1709), the duke of Marlborough's last great battle in the War of the Spanish Succession (1701–14). It was fought near the village of Malplaquet (now on the French side of the Franco-Belgian border), about 10 miles (16 km) south of Mons.

The battle was between an Anglo-Dutch-Austrian army of 100,000 men under the duke of Marlborough and Prince Eugene of Savoy, and a French army of 90,000 men under the marshal Claude-Louis-Hector, duc de Villars, and the marshal Louis-François, duc de Boufflers. The Allies began a siege of the fortress of Mons on September 4, and the French tried to break this siege by concentrating and entrenching nearby, at Malplaquet. The Allies were forced to attack to remove this threat to the siege operation. Marlborough and Eugene planned infantry attacks against the French flanks to force them to weaken their centre, which would then be charged and broken by the 30,000-man Allied cavalry. The plan was finally successful but only at the cost of very heavy losses. Desperate tree-to-tree infantry fighting, deadly French artillery fire, and repeated French cavalry counterattacks caused the Allies to suffer 22,000 killed and wounded to the 12,000 losses suffered by the French. The French withdrew in good order, and the Allies continued the siege of Mons, which they captured on October 26.

Malraux, André(-Georges) (b. Nov. 3, 1901, Paris—d. Nov. 23, 1976, Paris), French novelist, art historian, and statesman, who became an active supporter of General Charles de Gaulle and, after de Gaulle was elected president in 1958, served for 10 years as France's minister of cultural affairs. His major works include the novel *La Condition humaine* (1933; *Man's Fate*); *Les Voix du silence* (1951; *The Voices of Silence*), a history and philosophy of world art; and *Le Musée imaginaire de la sculpture mondiale* (1952–54; *Museum Without Walls*).

Malraux, 1967
Bruno Barbey—Magnum

Life. Malraux was born into a well-to-do family. The details of his early life and education are obscure, however. At the age of 21 he left France in search of a Khmer temple of whose discovery he had read in an archaeological bulletin. Plunging into the Cambodian forest, he reached the temple, which was not then being considered for restoration. He had some bas-reliefs removed from it and took them back to Phnom Penh, the capital of Cambodia. Arrested at once and sentenced to imprisonment, he appealed to Paris and was released. Malraux's mistreatment in jail by the French colonial authorities turned him into a fervent anticolonialist and an advocate of social change. While in Southeast Asia he organized the Young Annam League (the precursor of the Viet Minh, or Viet Nam League for Independence), became a leading writer and pamphleteer, and founded a newspaper, *L'Indochine Enchaînée* ("Indochina in Chains"). Crossing to China, he apparently participated in several Chinese revolutionary incidents and may possibly have met Mikhail Borodin, the Russian Communist adviser to Sun Yat-sen and then to Chiang Kai-shek.

Malraux was to return to the Far East several times. In 1929 he made important discoveries of Greco-Buddhist art in Afghanistan and Iran. In 1934 he flew over the Rubʿ al-Khali in Arabia and discovered what may have been the site of the Queen of Sheba's legendary city. After his second return from Indochina in 1926 he published his first novel, *La Tentation de l'Occident* (*The Temptation of the West*). His novels *Les Conquérants* (*The Conquerors*), published in 1928, *La Voie royale* (*The Royal Way*), published in 1930, and the masterpiece *La Condition humaine* in 1933 (awarded the Prix Goncourt) established his reputation as a leading French novelist and a charismatic, politically committed intellectual. Though he captivated Paris with his exceptional intelligence, lyrical prose, astonishing memory, and breadth of knowledge, it was not generally appreciated that his true life was elsewhere than in the literary salons or on the committee of *La Nouvelle Revue Française* or at literary congresses.

As fascism rose in the 1930s, Malraux recognized its threat and presided over committees pressing for the liberation of the international communists Ernst Thälmann and Georgi Dimitrov from their imprisonment under the Nazis. He simultaneously eschewed a rigid Marxism, participated in the National League Against Anti-Semitism, and in 1935—before the world in general had learned that concentration camps existed—published *Le Temps du mépris* (*Days of Wrath*), a short novel describing the brutal imprisonment of a communist by the Nazis. At the same time, he began to write his *Psychologie de l'art,* 3 vol. (1947–50; *The Psychology of Art*), an activity that bore a relationship to his other interests, for to Malraux aesthetic ideas, like the philosophy of action expressed in his own novels, would always be part of man's eternal questioning of destiny and his response to it.

Upon the outbreak of the Spanish Civil War in 1936, Malraux went to Spain, joined the Republican forces, and organized an international air squadron, becoming its colonel. After flying many missions, he visited the United States to collect money for medical assistance to Spain.

When World War II broke out, Malraux enlisted as a private in a French tank unit. He was captured but escaped to the free zone of France, where he joined the resistance. His life in that underground movement began in the Corrèze *département*. He was shot and captured (1944) by the Germans and made to undergo a mock execution. After his liberation by the French Forces of the Interior, he formed a Free French brigade that he commanded during the 1st French Army's campaign against Strasbourg in Alsace. At this time he abandoned his enthusiasm for revolutionary action and Marxism and rediscovered the sense of promise held out by Western culture.

On the Alsatian front he met General Charles de Gaulle, with whom his destiny was thenceforth to be linked. He was appointed temporary minister of information (November 1945–January 1946) in de Gaulle's first government and then followed de Gaulle into retirement, from which he emerged to deliver brilliant speeches as a national delegate to the Gaullist Rassemblement du Peuple Français, or RPF (French People's Rally). Withdrawing to his villa at Boulogne, he devoted himself to composing his monumental meditation on art, *Les Voix du silence* (1951).

When de Gaulle returned to power in France in 1958, he appointed Malraux minister of cultural affairs in the first cabinet of the Fifth Republic. For 10 years he was minister of cultural affairs and the intimate friend of de Gaulle. He proved an innovative and forceful cultural administrator.

Literary works. Between the acts of his dramatic and absorbing life, Malraux wrote several brilliant and powerful novels dealing with the tragic ambiguities of political idealism and revolutionary struggle. His first important novel, *Les Conquérants* (1928), is a tense and vivid description of a revolutionary strike in Canton. *La Voie royale* (1930) is a thriller set among the Khmer temples of Cambodia that Malraux himself explored. Malraux's masterpiece is *La Condition humaine* (1933), which made him known to readers all over the world. This novel is set in Shanghai during the crushing by Chiang Kai-shek and the Nationalists of their former Communist allies in 1927. Its main characters are several Chinese Communist conspirators and European adventurers who are betrayed both by the Nationalists and by emissaries of Soviet Russia. Each of these complex, introspective personalities is affected differently by the tragic fate awaiting him, but the brotherhood arising out of a common political activity seems to them the only antidote to the meaningless solitude that is the hallmark of the human condition. In the novel *Le Temps du mépris* (1935; *Days of Contempt,* or *Days of Wrath*), Malraux tells a story of the underground resistance to the Nazis within Hitler's Germany. Despite Malraux's evident Marxist sympathies and his bitter criticisms of fascism, this was the only one of his books that was allowed to be published inside the Soviet Union. His novel *L'Espoir* (1937; *Man's Hope*), based on his experiences in Spain, was his most pessimistic political novel. A motion-picture version of *L'Espoir* that Malraux produced and directed in Barcelona in 1938 was not shown in France until the end of World War II.

After 1945 Malraux virtually abandoned the writing of novels and turned instead to the history and criticism of art. *Les Voix du silence,* a revised version of his *Psychologie de l'art,* is a brilliant and well-documented synthesis of the history of art in all countries and through all ages. The work is also a philosophical meditation on art as a supreme expression of human creativity and as one that enables man to transcend the meaningless absurdity and insignificance of his own condition. Malraux continued to explore this approach in *La Métamorphose des Dieux,* 3 vol. (1957–76; *The Metamorphosis of the Gods*). He published his autobiography, *Antimémoires,* in 1967. After the death of his companion, the novelist Louise de Vilmorin, Malraux lived and worked in solitude at Verrières-le-Buisson, near Paris, where he was buried.

BIBLIOGRAPHY. Literary portraits include Jean Lacouture, *André Malraux* (1975); Violet M. Horvath, *André Malraux: The Human Adventure* (1969); Pierre Galante, *Malraux* (1971); Martine de Courcel (ed.), *Malraux: Life and Work* (1976), a collection of essays; James Robert Hewitt, *André Malraux* (1978); and Kenneth Murphy, *André Malraux: Man's Fate, Man's Hope* (1991). Critical studies in English of Malraux's works include R.W.B. Lewis (ed.), *Malraux* (1964), a collection of essays representing international contemporary critical opinion; W.M. Frohock, *André Malraux and the Tragic Imagination* (1952, reissued 1967), an important study of the writer by a leading American critic of modern French literature; Joseph Frank, *The Widening Gyre* (1963), a lucid exposition of Malraux's artistry and personal philosophy; Charles D. Blend, *André Malraux: Tragic Humanist* (1963), concentrating on the philosophy that underlies the novels; David O. Wilkinson, *Malraux: An Essay in Political Criticism* (1967); Denis Boak, *André Malraux* (1968), by a more severe critic who finds much pretentiousness in the writer's work; Cecil Jenkins, *André Malraux* (1972), an introductory work; T. Jefferson Kline, *André Malraux and the Metamorphosis of Death* (1973); James W. Greenlee, *Malraux's Heroes and History* (1975); and Jean-Francois Lyotard, *Soundproof Room: Malraux's Anti-Aesthetics,* trans. from the French by Robert Harvey (2001), in the series *Cultural Memory of the Present.* Herman Lebovics, *Mona Lisa's Escort: André Malraux and the Reinvention of French Culture* (1999), considers Malraux's efforts as the minister of cultural affairs.

malt, grain product that is used in beverages and foods as a basis for fermentation and to add flavour and nutrient value. Malt is prepared from cereal grain by allowing partial germination to modify the grains' natural food substances. Although any cereal grain may be converted to malt, barley is the chief grain used, with rye, wheat, rice, and corn used much less frequently.

The largest quantities of malt are used in the brewing of beer, and the flavour of beer is predominantly the result of the malt from which it was made. From 25 to 50 pounds (11 to 22 kg) of malt are used to make a barrel (31 U.S. gallons) of beer. The next most important use of malt is to make distilled alcohol for whiskey and other beverages. Malt extracts are also used for flavour, enzyme activity, and starch content in such food products as flour, malt vinegar, breakfast cereals, baby foods, confections, and baked goods.

The controlled germination of cereal grains that results in malt is initiated by adding moisture and is arrested by removing the moisture before the young plant grows out of its seed covering. The malting process itself consists of three stages: steeping, germination, and kilning.

In steeping, the grain is placed in a tank with water and absorbs moisture, awakening the embryo within the kernel. The dampened grain is then allowed to germinate, or sprout, and tiny rootlets grow out from the bottom of the kernel. During germination, enzymes are activated that the embryo plant uses to break down the starch in its kernel and build it into root and stem structures. These starch-splitting enzymes also permeate the seed's hard, brittle outer wall, converting it into a softer and more soluble form and giving it a characteristic malty flavour.

The germination process requires that cooled and moistened air move through the mass of sprouting grain, which must be gently moved to prevent matting of the rootlets. In modern malting procedures, germination usually takes place in revolving drums or in tanks equipped with agitators. This process has largely replaced floor malting, in which the moistened grain was spread on concrete floors and turned by shoveling.

When the desired biological modification in the grain has been attained, the germination process is stopped by kilning. In this stage, the germinated grain, called green malt, is dried by currents of heated air entering through perforations in the floor of a kiln. The timing and heat intensity applied in kilning affect the malt's flavour and colour development. The malt intended for Scotch whiskey is dried over a fire to which peat is added, whose smoke is absorbed by the malt.

The enzymes produced within the barleycorn during germination break down the starch stored in the seed kernel to simpler carbohydrates, chiefly malt sugar (maltose). Other enzymes are also produced in the grain that can break down proteins to simpler nitrogenous compounds. In brewing, malt is added to a cereal mash in order for the former's enzymes to convert the latter's starches into maltose. The maltose is subsequently fermented by yeast, resulting in the alcohol and carbon dioxide that give beer its distinctive qualities.

Consult
the
INDEX
first

Malta, small archipelago in the central Mediterranean Sea. Malta is an independent republic consisting of three inhabited islands, Malta, Gozo, and Comino, and two uninhabited islets, Comminotto and Filfla, lying nearly 60 miles (100 km) south of Sicily. This strategically important island group has played vital roles in the struggles of a succession of powers for domination of the Mediterranean. The capital is Valletta. Area 12 square miles (316 square km). Pop. (2003 est.) 399,000.

A brief treatment of Malta follows. For full treatment, *see* MACROPAEDIA: Malta.

For current history and for statistics on society and economy, *see* BRITANNICA BOOK OF THE YEAR.

The land. Malta island (comprising about 78 percent of the republic's land area) is essentially a 600-to-800-foot- (180-to-240-metre-) high coralline limestone upland in the west surrounded by clay slopes descending into 400-foot- (125-metre-) high areas of

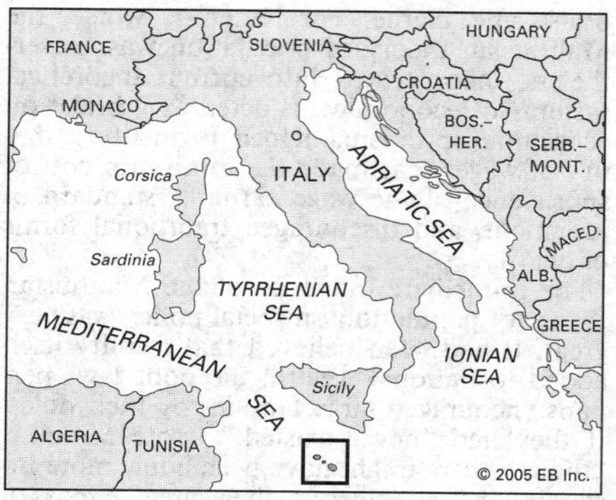

Malta

globigerina (marine protozoan) limestone in the south. These geologic formations have proved favourable for the percolation and underground storage of water. The coastline of Malta, and the other inhabited islands, is well-indented with harbours, bays, sandy beaches, and rocky coves. There are no permanent rivers or lakes on Malta island.

The islands' Mediterranean climate is characterized by hot, dry summers, cool, rainy winters, and the absence of any frost, snow, and fog. Rainfall averages about 20 inches (500 mm) per year. Because of high temperatures and the lack of regular drainage, soil formation has been slow and natural vegetation is sparse. Desalination plants have been built to alleviate a shortage of fresh water.

The people. Malta's ethnic composition is a mixture of Italian, Arab, British, and Phoenician heritages. Almost all of the population is native-born and Roman Catholic. The official languages are English and Maltese. The latter is a dialect of Arabic that is written in the Latin alphabet.

Malta's population has increased, although overall the natural growth rate is relatively low, being more typical of that of an industrial country. As is consistent with the low natural growth rate, Malta displays an older population profile. Improved health care has reduced the infant mortality rate to one that is typical of the more developed countries. A life expectancy of 78 years reflects this as well. Many emigrants from Malta chose to return there after 1975, thereby placing a burden on social and economic services. About nine-tenths of the population is urban.

The economy. Malta has a market economy that is largely based on tourism, light industry, shipping, and agriculture. The harbour at Marsaxlokk Bay has expanded the country's trade, particularly as a major Mediterranean transshipment centre. The gross national product (GNP) has grown rapidly, whereas the population has increased only slowly. The GNP per capita is among the highest of those of the world's developing countries.

About two-fifths of the total land area is arable, and most cultivation (including vegetables, cereals, potatoes, and citrus fruits) is conducted on small terraced strips of land. Agriculture accounts for only a tiny fraction of the gross domestic product (GDP), however, and Malta imports most of its food.

Mineral resources are poor, and the mining industry is limited to the production of building materials, principally of globigerina limestone. There are, however, proven offshore petroleum reserves.

Manufacturing accounts for about one-fourth of the GDP. Exports include textiles, garments, shoes, electrical equipment, and plastics. The government has promoted industrial development through the Malta Development Corporation.

Tourism is Malta's major industry and source of foreign exchange; most of the tourists come from the United Kingdom.

The country's infrastructure is highly developed, and virtually all roads are paved. Dry docks were nationalized in 1973, and the construction and repair of ships is an important industry. Malta's main harbour is at Valletta, and the international airport is at nearby Luqa.

The balance of payments was unfavourable from the 1970s into the '90s. Italy, Germany, the United Kingdom, and the United States are Malta's largest trading partners.

Government and social conditions. A 1974 revision of its 1964 constitution made Malta a republic within the Commonwealth. Legislative power is exercised by the unicameral Parliament. The president, the constitutional head of state, is elected by Parliament to a five-year term. The president appoints as prime minister the leader of the majority party. The principal political parties are the Malta Labour ("social-democratic") Party and the Nationalist ("Christian-democratic") Party. Maltese law, which was codified mainly between 1854 and 1873, is largely based on the Napoleonic Code.

The Maltese people enjoy a high standard of living. A series of social security acts ensures compensation for sickness and injury, unemployment, and invalidity; allowances for families and children; and pensions for old age and disability. Hospitalization and certain personal-health services are free in public institutions. The dimension of the housing shortage, which constituted a serious problem until the late 1970s, was considerably reduced by the transfer of residential and office quarters that had previously been used by the British military and their families.

Education is compulsory from age 6 to 16 and is free in public schools. The former Old and New universities were amalgamated in 1988 into the University of Malta.

For its small population, Malta has an extremely active press, publishing in both English and Maltese. Periodicals, many politically oriented, are especially numerous. Television is broadcast bilingually, and much of the programming is produced locally.

Cultural life. Folk traditions in Malta have evolved mainly around the *festa,* which is marked by processions and fireworks to celebrate the patron saint of a village. Apart from its unique Neolithic ruins, Malta contains important examples of its flourishing architectural school of the 17th and 18th centuries. The Italian artists Caravaggio and Mattia Preti spent several years in Malta, the latter's most important paintings embellishing many of the country's churches. Maltese literature has been enriched by the poetry of the national bard, Dun Karm.

History. The earliest archaeological remains on Malta date from about 3800 BC. At one time Malta's megalithic monuments were considered proof of Phoenician settlement, but modern archaeology has established that they were built by prehistoric humans and, indeed, are among the oldest human monuments in the Mediterranean basin. Evidence supports the landing of Carthaginians in the 8th or early 7th century BC; they apparently ruled harshly and levied high tribute upon the inhabitants. Malta was granted the privileges of a *municipium* after coming under Roman control in 218 BC.

In AD 60 the Apostle Paul was shipwrecked in the bay that bears his name; according to tradition, he converted the inhabitants to Christianity.

With the division of the Roman Empire in 395, Malta was assigned to the eastern portion dominated by Constantinople. Later, in 870, the Arabs made themselves Malta's masters. In 1091 the Norman noble Roger I, then master of Sicily, came to Malta with a small retinue and defeated the Arabs. The dominion of the Roman Catholic church was reestablished and bishops appointed. Gradually feudal customs asserted themselves, and Malta was ruled by a succession of feudal lords until the early 16th century.

In 1530 Malta was ceded to the religious military order known as the Hospitallers, or the Knights of Malta, as they subsequently became known. During the 16th to 18th centuries the Knights of Malta harassed Turkish commerce. Relations between these knights and the native Maltese were distant, as there was little social or economic contact between them. The rule of the Knights ended when, in June 1798, Napoleon took possession of the islands.

The 1802 Treaty of Amiens returned the islands to the Knights of Malta. The Maltese protested and acknowledged the king of Great Britain as the sovereign of Malta, stipulating that the Roman Catholic church be maintained and the Maltese Declaration of Rights be honoured. These conditions were accepted by the British and ratified in the 1814 Treaty of Paris.

Malta's political status under Britain underwent a series of vicissitudes in which constitutions were successively granted, suspended, and revoked. The Maltese economy became a function of British demands for Malta's military facilities, and the famous Dockyard developed into the economic mainstay of the islands.

During World War I the Maltese provided a local garrison and many naval seamen. Malta became self-governing in 1921, although Britain shared power and responsibility with Maltese ministers. In 1936 Malta reverted to a colonial regime.

After Italy entered World War II, Malta was subjected to severe aerial attacks from German and Italian bombers. On April 15, 1942, George VI awarded the George Cross, Britain's highest civilian decoration, to the islands, the first time that a medal was conferred upon any part of the Commonwealth.

On Sept. 21, 1964, Malta attained independence within the Commonwealth and later (in 1974) became a republic.

In 1979, when its alliance with Great Britain ended, Malta sought to guarantee its neutrality through other international agreements. In October 1981 the Soviet Union signed an agreement pledging to support the country's neutral status. In 2004, after lengthy debate, Malta joined the European Union.

Malta, Knights of: *see* Knights of Malta.

maltase, enzyme that catalyzes the hydrolysis of the disaccharide maltose to the simple sugar glucose. The enzyme is found in plants, bacteria, and yeast; in humans and other vertebrates it is thought to be synthesized by cells of the mucous membrane lining the intestinal wall. During digestion, starch is partially transformed into maltose by the pancreatic or salivary enzymes called amylases; maltase secreted by the intestine then converts maltose into glucose. The glucose so produced is either utilized by the body or stored in the liver as glycogen (animal starch).

Malte-Brun, Conrad, original name MALTE CONRAD BRUUN (b. Aug. 12, 1775, Thisted, Den.—d. Dec. 14, 1826, Paris, France), author and coauthor of several geographies and a founder of the first modern geographic society.

Exiled from Denmark in 1800 for his verses and pamphlets in support of the French Revolution, Malte-Brun established himself as a journalist and geographic writer in Paris. His works include the first six volumes of *Précis de la géographie universelle* (1810–29; "Précis of World Geography"). He was a founder and the first secretary of the Société de Géographie de Paris (1821). His son Victor Adolphe Malte-Brun, also a geographer, concerned himself with the course of African and Arctic exploration.

Maltese, breed of toy dog named for the island of Malta, where it may have originated about 2,800 years ago. Delicate in appearance but usually vigorous, healthy, affectionate, and lively, the Maltese was once the valued pet of the wealthy and aristocratic. It has a long, silky, pure-white coat, hanging ears, a compact body, and a plumed tail that curves over its back. It stands about 5 inches (13 centimetres) and weighs up to 7 pounds (3 kilograms).

Maltese lace, type of guipure lace (in which the design is held together by bars, or brides, rather than net) introduced into Malta in 1833 by Genoese laceworkers. It was similar to the early bobbin-made lace of Genoa and had geometric patterns in which Maltese crosses and small, pointed ears of wheat were incorporated. After 1851, when it was shown at the Great Exhibition, Maltese lace was widely copied at other lace centres, including Bedfordshire, Eng.

Maltese lace, early 19th century; in the Victoria and Albert Museum, London

By courtesy of the Victoria and Albert Museum, London

Maltese language, Maltese MALTI, Semitic language of the Southern Central group spoken on the island of Malta. Maltese developed from a dialect of Arabic and is closely related to the western Arabic dialects of Algeria and Tunisia. Strongly influenced by the Italian dialect spoken in Sicily, Maltese is the only form of Arabic to be written in the Latin alphabet.

Malthus, Thomas Robert (b. Feb. 14/17, 1766, Rookery, near Dorking, Surrey, Eng.—d. Dec. 23, 1834, St. Catherine, near Bath, Somerset), English economist and demographer, best known for his theory that population growth will always tend to outrun the food supply and that betterment of the lot of mankind is impossible without stern limits on reproduction.

Malthus was of a prosperous family. His father, a personal friend of the philosopher and skeptic David Hume, was an ardent disciple of Jean-Jacques Rousseau, whose book *Émile* may have been the source of the elder Malthus' liberal ideas about educating his son. The young Malthus was educated largely at home until his admission to Jesus College, Cambridge, in 1784. There he studied a wide range of subjects and took prizes in Latin and Greek, graduating in 1788. He took his master of arts degree in 1791, was elected a fellow of Jesus College in 1793, and took holy orders in 1797. He wrote a pamphlet in 1796 called "The Crisis" (not published), which, among other things, took a favourable view of newly proposed poor laws, which were to set up workhouses for the poor. This was a view that ran somewhat counter to his views on poverty and population published two years later.

Malthus, detail of an engraving after a portrait by J. Linnell, 1833

By courtesy of the trustees of the British Museum; photograph, J.R. Freeman & Company Ltd.

The opinions and teachings that Malthus developed reflect largely a reaction, amiably conducted, to his father's views and to the doctrines of the French Revolution and its supporters. The English radical philosopher William Godwin, for example, was being widely read for such works as *Political Justice* (1793), which took for granted the perfectibility of mankind and foresaw a millennium in which rational men would live prosperously and harmoniously without laws and institutions. Unlike Godwin (or, earlier, Rousseau), who viewed human affairs from a theoretical standpoint, Malthus was essentially an empiricist, and he began from the harsh realities of his time. His reaction developed in the tradition of British economics, which would today be called sociological.

In 1798 he published anonymously the first edition of *An Essay on the Principle of Population as it affects the Future Improvement of Society, with Remarks on the Speculations of Mr. Godwin, M. Condorcet, and other Writers.* The work received wide notice. Briefly, crudely, yet strikingly, Malthus argued that infinite human hopes for social happiness must be vain, for population will always tend to outrun the growth of production. The increase of population will take place, if unchecked, in a geometrical progression, while the means of subsistence will increase in only an arithmetical progression. Population will always expand to the limit of subsistence and will be held there by famine, war, and ill health. "Vice" (which included, for Malthus, contraception), "misery," and "self-restraint" alone could check this excessive growth.

Malthus was an economic pessimist, viewing poverty as man's inescapable lot. The argument in this first edition is essentially abstract and analytical. After further reading and travels in Europe, Malthus produced a subsequent edition (1803), expanding the long pamphlet of 1798 into a longer book, and adding much factual material and illustration to his thesis. At no point, even up to the final and massive sixth edition of 1826, did he ever adequately set out his premises or examine their logical status. Nor did he handle his factual and statistical materials with much critical or statistical rigour, even though during his lifetime the sophistication of statisticians was developing remarkably in both continental Europe and Great Britain. A remark by Kingsley Davis, a United States student of population, that Malthus' theories, apparently founded on so extensive an empirical base, are yet at their weakest with respect to empiricism and at their strongest as a tight and elegant theoretical formulation, has much truth in it as both praise and blame. For better or worse, the Malthusian theory of population was, nevertheless, incorporated into current theoretical systems of economics. It acted as a brake on economic optimism, helped to justify a theory of wages that made the minimum cost of subsistence of the wage earner a standard of judgment, and discouraged traditional forms of charity.

The immediate influence of the Malthusian theory of population on social policy was very great. It had been believed that fertility itself added to national wealth; the poor laws perhaps encouraged large families by their doles. If they had "never existed," wrote Malthus, "though there might have been a few more instances of severe distress, the aggregate mass of happiness among the common people would have been much greater than it is at present." These laws limited the mobility of labour, he said, and encouraged fecundity and should be abolished. For the most unfortunate it might be licit to establish workhouses, not "comfortable asylums," but they should be places in which "fare should be hard" and "severe distress . . . find some alleviation."

In 1804 Malthus married Harriet Eckersall and in 1805 became professor of history and political economy at the East India Company's college at Haileybury, Hertfordshire. It was the first time in Great Britain that the words political economy had been used to designate an academic office. He lived quietly at Haileybury for the remainder of his life, except for a visit to Ireland in 1817 and a trip to the Continent in 1825, for health reasons. In 1811 he met and became close friends with the economist David Ricardo.

Meanwhile, he continued publishing a variety of pamphlets and tracts on economics. In them he approached the problem of what determines price with a less rigorous analysis than Ricardo and in terms of an institutionally determined "effective demand," a phrase that he invented. In 1820 in his summary *Principles of Political Economy Considered with a View to Their Practical Application,* he went so far as to propose public works and private luxury investment, as palliatives for economic distress, that would increase effective demand and prosperity. He went further and criticized thrift as a virtue knowing no limit; to the contrary, he argued, "the principles of saving, pushed to excess, would destroy the motive to production." To maximize wealth, a nation had to balance "the power to produce and the will to consume." In fact, Malthus, as an economist concerned with what he called the problem of "gluts" or, as they would be called today, the problems of slump and depression, can be said to have anticipated the economic discoveries of John Maynard Keynes in the 1930s.

In 1819 Malthus was elected a fellow of the Royal Society; in 1821 he became a member of the Political Economy Club, the number of which included Ricardo and James Mill, and in 1824 he was elected one of the 10 royal associates of the Royal Society of Literature. Malthus was one of the cofounders, in 1834, of the Statistical Society of London. In 1833 he was elected to the French Académie des Sciences Morales et Politiques and to the Royal Academy of Berlin. During these later years, though he wrote various papers, he never added substantially to what he had gathered in *Essay on Population* and *Principles of Political Economy.* (D.G.MacR.)

BIBLIOGRAPHY. W. Otter, "Memoir," preface to the 2nd ed. of the *Principles of Political Economy* (1836), is still a basis for any biography. J. Ronar, *Malthus and His Work* (1885, reprinted and expanded 1924), is the major work of 19th-century scholarship, illuminated by very wide learning. John Maynard Keynes, "Robert Malthus: The First of the Cambridge Economists," in *Essays in Biography* (1933, new ed., 1957), is charming and of great importance in the rehabilitation of Malthus as a major economic theorist. D.V. Glass (ed.), *Introduction to Malthus* (1953), contains "A Summary View of the Principles of Population," an important letter on the Poor Laws by Malthus, a bibliography on the Malthusian question in the 19th century, and three useful essays. Also of interest are A. Flew, "The Structure of Malthus' Population Theory," *Australasian Journal of Philosophy,* 35:1–20 (1957), and the same author's edited version of Malthus' *An Essay on the Principle of Population* (1970); P.M. Hauser and O.D. Duncan (eds.), *The Study of Population: An Inventory and Appraisal* (1959), though partly out of date; K. Smith, *The Malthusian Controversy* (1951); and D.E.C. Eversley, *Social Theories of Fertility and the Malthusian Debate* (1959).

Malton, town, Ryedale district, administrative county of North Yorkshire, England. On the site of an early British settlement and later a Roman fort and town (Derventio) on the River Derwent, it was renamed Malton in Anglian times and was the site of a royal palace of the Kingdom of Derra. Its 11th-century castle was destroyed by Henry II (1135) but later rebuilt with a priory nearby. In Queen Anne's reign it became a busy river port; many elegant town houses and coaching inns of New Malton date from this period. It is no longer a port but retains a large livestock market and is an important service centre, with agricultural and other light industries. Well-known racing stables at the foot of the Wolds account for 20th-century development across the river at Norton. Pop. (1991) 4,294.

Maluku (Indonesian islands): *see* Moluccas.

Maluku, English MOLUCCAS, island group and *propinsi* (province) of eastern Indonesia. In 1999 the northern half of Maluku *propinsi* was made into a separate *propinsi* named North Maluku (Maluku Utara). The Moluccas group includes about 1,000 islands, among the largest of which are Halmahera, Morotai, Bacan, Obi, and the main islands of the Sula archipelago (all in North Maluku) and Ceram, Buru, Wetar, Babar, Ambon, and the main islands of the Aru, Tanimbar, Banda, Leti, and Kai archipelagos (in Maluku *propinsi*). North Maluku is bounded by the Pacific Ocean on the north, the Molucca Sea on the west, and Irian Jaya *propinsi* on the east. Maluku *propinsi,* which almost encircles the Banda Sea, is bounded on the east by the Ceram Sea and on the south by the Arafura Sea, East Timor territory, and the Timor Sea. The provincial capitals are Ambon (for Maluku) and Ternate (for North Maluku).

Commonly referred to as the Spice Islands by the early Indian, Chinese, and Arab traders, the Moluccas formed part of the Javanese Majapahit Empire and the Śrivijaya Empire (Sumatra) before Islām was introduced in the 15th century. The Portuguese entered the region in the early 16th century, and the Dutch, beginning in 1599, established settlements on some of the islands. The Dutch conquest was completed in 1667, when the sultan of Tidore Island recognized Dutch sovereignty. The islands were ruled by the British between 1796 and 1802 and again in 1810–17; they were occupied by the Japanese during World War II. The Moluccas formed part of the Dutch-inspired, temporary autonomous state of East Indonesia in 1945. The southern Moluccas, led by Christian Ambonese from Ambon, revolted against the Indonesian government in 1950 and formed the short-lived Republic of South Moluccas.

Surrounded by coral reefs and deep seas, the islands vary in size from tiny atolls to the large, mountainous islands of Halmahera and Ceram, each of which covers more than 6,600 square miles (17,100 square km). Ternate Island has an active volcano, which rises to 5,416 feet (1,651 m), and Mount Arpi on Banda emits fumes and smoke. Ambon Island has frequent earthquakes but no active volcanoes. The Aru Islands are low and swampy, and Babar and Wetar are hilly, with steep coasts. Many of the smaller islands are uninhabited. The slopes of the mountainous islands are covered with dense evergreen forests of pine, rhododendron, casuarina, and eucalyptus; mangrove and freshwater swamp forests line their coasts. The islands' lowlands are fertile because of the volcanic lava and ash that has been broken down and redistributed by small streams and wind action. Bird life includes honeyeaters; racket tailed kingfishers; giant redcrested Moluccan cockatoos; parakeets; black capped, purple, red, and green lories; and white fruit pigeons of Ceram. Opossums, civet-cats, wild pigs, and babirusas (wild East India swine) are also found.

Agriculture constitutes the mainstay of the economy of these sparsely populated islands. Rice, sago, coconut, spices (including cloves and nutmeg), tobacco, resin, ironwood, rattan, timber, coffee, and tortoiseshell are the chief products. Fish, ebony, rattan, copra, spices, and bird skins are exported. Crafts include wood carving, silver and gold filigree work, the making of bracelets and rings, and handloom weaving. Nickel is mined and oil is exploited on Ceram near Bula on the northeastern coast. Interisland traffic is mainly by steamer; inland transport on the larger islands is by roads that run parallel to the coasts. Halmahera has an airport at Jailolo. Ambon, Ternate, Namlea, Masohi, Tual, Soasiu, Morotai, and Labuha are important towns. The largest ethnic groups are Malay, who live mainly along the coasts, and Alfoer, who are concentrated inland. Less numerous groups include Tanimbarese on the southern islands; Ambonese on the central islands; and Ternatan, Tidorese, Makianese, Tobelorese, Batjan, and Sawai on the northern islands. Islām is the dominant religion, but a large number of Christians live in the central Moluccas. Area combined *propinsi,* 30,066 square miles (77,871 square km). Pop. (1995 est.) combined *propinsi,* 2,095,000.

Maluku, Laut (Pacific Ocean): *see* Molucca Sea.

Maʿlula, also spelled MAALULA, village in southern Syria about 30 miles (50 km) north of Damascus. The houses, which stand on the slopes of a huge cirque of rocks that encloses the village, are constructed of stones with flat beam roofs. Most of the houses have blue plaster on the outside, a Christian custom. The inhabitants are mainly Greek-Catholic and have preserved in their spoken language a dialect of Syriac. The Catholic monastery of Mar Sarkis (St. Sergius) has a Byzantine church and Byzantine-period tombs cut into the rock behind. There is also an Orthodox monastery, Mar Takla (St. Thecla).

Malus, Étienne-Louis (b. June 23, 1775, Paris—d. Feb. 23, 1812, Paris), French physicist who discovered that light, when reflected, becomes partially plane polarized; *i.e.,* its rays vibrate in the same plane. His observation led to a better understanding of the propagation of light.

Malus, engraving by A. Tardieu after a painting
By courtesy of the trustees of the British Museum; photograph, J.R. Freeman & Co. Ltd.

A member of the corps of engineers, Malus accompanied Napoleon's invasion of Egypt in 1798 and remained in the Near East until 1801. After he returned, he held official posts at Antwerp, Strasbourg, and Paris and did research in optics. He published a paper in 1809 on his discovery of the polarization of light by reflection and a memoir in 1810 on the theory of double refraction (bending) of light in crystals.

Maluti (Lesotho): *see* Maloti Mountains.

Malvaceae, the mallow family, a large group of flowering plants, in the order Malvales, containing about 95 genera of herbs, shrubs, and trees. Representatives occur in all except the coldest parts of the world but are most numerous in the tropics. Economically, the most important member of the family is cotton (*q.v.; Gossypium*). Several species of *Hibiscus* produce fibres that are of lesser importance. The green fruits of okra (*q.v.; H. esculentus*) are cooked and eaten, and the mucilage secreted in tissues of some species has been used in confections and for other purposes.

Rose mallow (*Hibiscus moscheutos*)
H. Oakman

Thirty genera supply many species valued as ornamentals, among which are hollyhock (*q.v.; Althaea*), rose mallow or rose of Sharon (*Hibiscus*), Indian mallow (*Sida*), checkerbloom (*Sidalcea*), poppy mallow (*Callirhoë*), flowering maple (*Abutilon*), false mallow (*Malvastrum*), tree mallow (*Lavatera*), wax mallow (*Malvaviscus*), and the genera *Kitaibelia* and *Malope*. Several species of the common mallow *Malva* are cultivated in gardens, including musk mallow (*M. moschata*) and curled mallow (*M. crispa*).

In the United States there are 27 genera; additional ones occur from Mexico into South America. Only three genera (*Malva, Althaea, Lavatera*) are native in Great Britain, but the family is well represented in the Mediterranean region, Africa, and Asia.

The family Malvaceae includes annual and perennial herbs, shrubs, and small trees. Their leaves, which alternate on the stem, are entire (smooth-margined), toothed, or palmately lobed or divided and mostly with deciduous stipules (small appendages at the base of the leafstalk). Stellate hairs, plant hairs with the upper ends branched into starlike patterns, commonly cover some or most vegetative parts and even occur in a few species on the parts of petals exposed in bud.

The flowers are regular, bisexual (sometimes

functionally either male or female), and often showy. Typically the flower has five sepals and five petals, with the petals tightly twisted in bud. The petals are fused to the staminal column (*i.e.,* the central columnar structure in the flower that bears the male structures, or stamens) at their bases and fall with the tube when the flower withers. A feature of the family is the central staminal column, surmounted by many kidney-shaped, one-celled anthers (pollen-producing structures) that open by terminal slits. The pollen grains are large, spherical, and ornamented with spines.

Pollination is by insects that seek the honey secreted in pits between the bases of the petals; self-pollination also occurs through the twisting of the stigmatic arms (female pollen-receptive structures) to touch the anthers. The carpels (*i.e.,* the ovule-bearing segments of the ovary) vary from two to many; when they number five the carpels are opposite the sepals (*Hibiscus*) or opposite the petals (*Abutilon*). In species having numerous carpels (*Malva, Lavatera, Sphaeralcea*), the carpels are arranged in a whorl around the top of the floral axis, with the stigmatic branches equaling or doubling the number of carpels and rising above the tip of the column. Each carpel produces from one ovule (*Malva, Malvastrum*) to several ovules (*Sphaeralcea, Wissadula, Gossypium, Hibiscus*).

The fruit is usually a one- to several-seeded schizocarp (fruit that breaks apart into one-seeded segments) but rarely, a berry in *Malvaviscus,* or a capsule in *Hibiscus* and *Gossypium.* Marginal hooks or elastic strands on the schizocarps, and mucilage or hairs on the seeds aid in dispersal.

The genera range in size from 10 or fewer species (*Anoda, Iliamna*) to more than 200 (*Sphaeralcea, Hibiscus*). Several genera are exclusively American (*Sidalcea, Callirhoë*); others are almost worldwide in distribution (*Abutilon, Hibiscus, Malva*). A few species are troublesome weeds, *Malva rotundifolia* (called cheeses for the shape of its fruit) being the most pernicious.

To make the best use of the Britannica, consult the INDEX *first*

Malvales, the mallow order of flowering plants, belonging to the class called dicotyledon (Magnoliopsida; characterized by two seed leaves). It includes five core families, together containing more than 250 genera and some 3,000 to 3,500 species. As many as five additional families are included in the order by some authorities. Representatives of this order grow in many different habitats in nearly all regions of the world. Many of its mostly woody, tropical members are commercially important.

A brief treatment of Malvales follows. For full treatment, *see* MACROPAEDIA: Angiosperms.

Members of the mallow family (Malvaceae) include several plants grown for their flowers, such as the hollyhock (*Alcea rosea,* or *Althaea rosea*) of temperate regions and the shrub Rose-of-China (*Hibiscus rosa-chinensis*), grown in most tropical regions. Economically important members include *Gossypium* (cotton, *q.v.*) and *Hibiscus esculentus* (okra).

The bombax, or kapok tree, family (Bombacaceae) includes several important tree genera. The baobab (*Adansonia digitata*) of tropical Africa is remarkable in that it becomes only moderately tall but increases its girth by a very active cambial layer of cells. Many specimens measure 9 m (30 feet) in circumference. Its young leaves are edible, the pulp of its fruit is made into a refreshing drink, and its bark yields fibre. Commercially important bombacaceous trees native to the Americas are planted in many tropical regions of the world. *Ochroma pyramidale* produces the lightest of all timbers, balsa wood. Kapok, or silk cotton, grows from the outer layers of seeds in the fruit of *Ceiba pentandra.*

Other important members of the Malvales include linden trees (*Tilia* in the Tiliaceae) and members of Sterculiaceae, whose seeds are the raw materials for beverages and confections important in world commerce. Fleshy fruits of *Theobroma cacao,* native from Brazil to Mexico, contain cacao nuts (seeds), which yield cocoa butter, cocoa, and chocolate. Kola "nuts" grow on *Cola nitida* and related species; their extracts are high in caffeine and the glucoside kolanin, which is used extensively in flavouring beverages.

Plants of the mallow order are perpetuated almost exclusively from seeds. In several families, flowers have the five-parted pattern with differing sepals and petals. Stamens are numerous. The pistil (female) component often conists of two or more carpels containing several ovules within the ovary.

Wind pollination occurs in some herbaceous representatives. The flowers of the sterculia family achieve pollination by attracting flies with their offensive odours. The flower of the wax mallow, a shrub of tropical America, is specialized for pollination by hummingbirds, and pollination by bats is the rule in the baobab and other members of the bombax family.

Typically, fruits ripen dry as capsules, but in the hollyhock 15 or more carpels develop as a ring in the centre of the flower. When ripe, the individual units separate into coin-shaped segments, each containing a seed. A few members of the mallow order produce fleshy fruits.

Malvana, Convention of (1597), agreement made between the Portuguese and the native chiefs of Ceylon (now Sri Lanka). The chiefs swore allegiance to the king of Portugal and, in return, were assured that their laws and customs would be left inviolate.

The convention also provided that the Ceylonese people should render all traditional services and taxes to their new sovereign. The purpose of the convention, summoned after the Portuguese had already assumed control of Ceylon, was to lend a guise of legality to the Portuguese seizure of Ceylon.

Malvern, locality, Malvern Hills district, county of Hereford and Worcester, England. The name Malvern is collectively applied to a number of former villages and hamlets on the eastern slopes of the Malvern Hills; Great Malvern is the main centre. Malvern Chase, a medieval administrative entity, was granted to the Earl of Gloucester by Edward I (reigned 1272–1307). Little Malvern, with the remains of a Benedictine priory (now the parish church), lies below Worcestershire Beacon, which is crowned by extensive and well-preserved Iron Age hill fortresses.

Malvern is now an educational and cultural centre, with Malvern College for boys (founded 1862), a further-education college, a school of art, a girls' college, and a theatre. Mineral springs and pleasant surroundings have also made it a popular resort. Pop. (1981 prelim.) 30,187.

Malvern (of Rhodesia and of Bexley), Godfrey (Martin) Huggins, 1st Viscount, also called (1941–55) SIR GODFREY HUGGINS (b. July 6, 1883, Bexley, Kent, Eng.—d. May 8, 1971, Salisbury, Rhodesia), prime minister of Southern Rhodesia (1933–53) and architect of the Federation of Rhodesia and Nyasaland, which he served as its first prime minister (1953–56).

After practicing medicine in London, Huggins migrated to Salisbury, Southern Rhodesia, in 1911 for reasons of health and soon established a reputation as a surgeon. When Southern Rhodesia became a self-governing colony in 1923, Huggins was elected to the Legislative Council. In 1933 his Reform Party won about half of the Assembly seats, and he became prime minister and also secretary of native affairs (until 1949). He was knighted in 1941.

His scheme to unite the two Rhodesias (Northern and Southern) and Nyasaland was finally realized in 1953, and a decisive victory at the polls by the Federal Party confirmed his premiership. He was created a viscount in 1955.

Malvern Hills, district, county of Hereford and Worcester, western England. The district was created in 1974 from parts of the former counties of Herefordshire and Worcestershire. Its dominant physical feature is the heath-covered Malvern Hills in the centre, trending north-south.

The name derives from *moel bryn* (Celtic: "bare hill"). The hills include a narrow ridge 9 miles (14 km) long that attains an elevation of 1,395 feet (425 m) and comprises granite and gneiss. The district is predominantly underlain by hard bands of Old Red Sandstone (a geologic formation of the Devonian Period), and to the west of the Malvern Hills the terrain is predominantly hills of red sandstone with occasional valleys. In the east a more fertile lowland is drained by the River Severn. Glaciers of the Pleistocene Epoch moving from the west deposited extensive amounts of unstratified drift (including sands, clays, and gravels) throughout the area. The district is noted for its orchards of apples (largely used for making cider) and pears. But the main agricultural activity is the breeding of cattle and sheep, and much of the county is permanent pasture. The two important communities of Malvern, the district seat, and Ledbury have industrial estates and are market centres. Ledbury, southwest of the Malvern Hills, has half-timbered houses from the 17th century and the mostly 14th-century Church of St. Michael. The poets Elizabeth Barrett Browning and John Masefield each lived as children near the town, as did the 14th-century author William Langland. The annual Malvern Festival (in Malvern) commemorates the composer Sir Edward Elgar and the playwright George Bernard Shaw. Area 347 square miles (900 square km). Pop. (1991 prelim.) 87,000.

Malvy, Louis-Jean (b. Dec. 1, 1875, Figeac, Fr.—d. June 9, 1949, Paris), French politician whose activities as minister of the interior led to his trial for treason during World War I.

Malvy entered the Chamber of Deputies in 1906 as a Radical; thereafter he served as under secretary under Ernest Monis (1911) and Joseph Caillaux (1911–12) and became minister of commerce under Gaston Doumergue (1913–14) and then minister of the interior under René Viviani. When World War I broke out, he remained minister under Aristide Briand and Alexandre Ribot (1915–17); but on July 22, 1917, Premier Georges Clemenceau charged Malvy with lax administration in dealing with defeatists and pacifists. Malvy resigned on August 31, and the Ribot cabinet fell. In October the royalist Léon

Malvy
By courtesy of the Bibliotheque Nationale, Paris

Daudet accused Malvy of high treason. At Malvy's request, he was tried on both charges by the Senate, sitting as a high court; on Aug. 6, 1918, he was acquitted of the charge of high treason but was found guilty of *forfaiture* (culpable negligence in the performance of his duties) and sentenced to banishment for five years. He spent his exile in Spain.

Pardoned and returned to the Chamber of Deputies in 1924, Malvy remained active in politics until his retirement in 1940.

Mālwa, Sanskrit MĀLAVA, historic province comprising a large portion of Madhya Pradesh state and parts of southeastern Rājasthān state, west-central India. Strictly, the name is confined to the hilly tableland bounded on the south by the Vindhya Range, but it has been extended to include the Narmada Valley. Traditionally a land of plenty, it is an area of fertile black soil drained by the Chambal, Siprā, Kāli Sindh, and Pārbati rivers. Cotton is a major crop.

As early as the 2nd century BC the area was known as Avanti; it was held by the Maurya and Gupta dynasties. The first recorded dynasty was the Paramāras, a Rājput (warrior caste) clan, who ruled (AD 800–1200) from their capital at Ujjain and, later, at Dhār. Invaded by the Muslims in 1235, the province became a strong independent state (1401–1531) with its capital at Māndu. Later annexed by the Mughals, it was one of the first provinces to be conquered by the Marāṭhās and was the headquarters of the Pindaris, or irregular plunderers. In 1817 the British restored order.

Mālwa Agency, a subdivision of the British Central India Agency, was created in 1895; it consisted of the princely states of Alīrājpur, Barwāni, Dhār, Jaora, Jhābua, Jobat, and Kathimau, and several petty states. Nimach was its headquarters.

Mālwa painting, 17th-century school of Rājasthānī miniature painting centred largely in Mālwa and Bundelkhand (in modern Madhya Pradesh state); it is sometimes referred to as Central Indian painting on the basis of its geographical distribution. The school was conservative, and little development is seen from the earliest examples, such as the *Rasikapriyā* (a poem analyzing the love sentiment) series dated 1636 and the *Amaru Śataka* (a Sanskrit poem of the late 17th century), now in the Prince of Wales Museum of Western India, Bombay. Little is known of the nature of the school in the 18th century.

Mālwa paintings show a fondness for rigorously flat compositions, black and chocolate-brown backgrounds, figures shown against a solid colour patch, and architecture painted in lively colour. The school's most appealing features are a primitive charm and a simple childlike vision.

An illustration from the *Rasarāja* series of the poet Puhakar, Mālwa school painting, 2nd half of the 17th century; in the National Museum of India, New Delhi
P. Chandra

Mālwa Plains, alluvial plains in central Punjab state, northern India, between the Ghaggar and Sutlej rivers south of the Bist Doab (plain). The Mālwa Plains are named for the Malloi peoples (Mālavas) who ruled the Punjab in the 4th century BC and offered stiff resistance to Alexander the Great. The Guptas supplanted the Mālavas in the 4th century AD. The region came under Muslim rule in the 10th century and, except for a short period of Rājput ascendancy *c.* 1030–1192, remained under Muslim rule until the decline of Mughal power.

The plains are bordered on the north by the Siwālik Hills. The terrain is slightly undulating, and there are occasional sand dunes and sand ridges in the southern part of the plains bordering the Great Indian (Thar) Desert. A few perennial rivers, including the Ghaggar, Patiāli, Dāngri, and Mārkanda, cross the plains, which are marked by former river channels. Scattered tropical dry deciduous forests, mostly of teak and dhak, are found. Agriculture dominates the economy of the plains; crops include cereals, pulse (legumes), cotton, sugarcane, and oilseeds. The region produces a surplus in food grains, particularly wheat. Small-scale industries produce machine tools, footwear, sewing machines and parts, plastic goods, and water pipes and fittings. Tractors, dry-cell batteries, polyester films, nylon, and automobile tires and tubes are manufactured on a large scale. The region has a network of roads and railways connecting the important towns.

Mālwa Plateau, plateau in north-central India, bounded by the Gujarāt Plains on the west, the Vindhya Range on the south, the Madhya Bhārat Plateau and Bundelkhand Upland on the north, and the Vindhya Range on the east. Of volcanic origin, the plateau comprises western Madhya Pradesh state and southeastern Rājasthān state. The name Mālwa is derived from the Sanskrit term Mālav and means "part of the abode of Lakṣmī (goddess of wealth)." The plateau was ruled successively by the Maurya, Gupta, and Paramāra dynasties; many Buddhist temples and monuments (*e.g.*, the Sānchi Stupas), noted for their architecture and sculpture, were built. The plateau was conquered by the Muslims in AD 1390 and became part of the Marāṭhā empire; then in 1817 it passed to the British.

The Mālwa Plateau has an elevation of 1,650 ft (500 m) to 2,000 ft; erosion has carved the lavas into isolated mesas found throughout the plateau, together with an occasional sandstone hill. The western part of the region is drained by the Māhi River, the middle section by the Chambal River, and the eastern part by the Betwa River and the headwaters of the Dhasān and Ken rivers. Other rivers include the Pārbati, Siprā, Chambal, Gambhīr, and Choti Kali Sindh, their valleys flanked by terraced slopes. Vegetation is of the savanna type with scattered teak and sal (*Shorea*) forests. The regional economy is mostly agricultural; cereals, pulse (legumes), oilseeds, and cotton are the main crops. Industries produce cotton textiles, ginned cotton, sugar, vegetable oil, lumber, and paper. The Chambal Valley Development Scheme provides water for irrigation and hydroelectric power. Ratlām has ceramic factories, Bhopāl and Ujjain have engineering industries, and Indore has a foundry.

Maly Kavkaz (mountains, Georgia): *see* Little Caucasus.

Mamaea, Julia: *see* Julia Mamaea.

Māmallapuram (India): *see* Mahābalipuram.

Mamaroneck, village, Westchester county, New York, U.S. It is located on Long Island Sound, just northeast of New Rochelle, astride the border separating the towns (townships) of Mamaroneck and Rye. Although considered part of the Dutch West India Company lands, the site was sold in 1661 by Wappinger Indians to an Englishman, John Richbell, who retained its Wappinger name meaning "where the fresh water meets the salt." Resold in 1698 to Caleb Heathcote, mayor of New York, it developed as a farming community. The writer James Fenimore Cooper married Susan De Lancey in 1811 at Heathcote Hill (De Lancey Manor House) in Mamaroneck and lived there until 1814.

The village was incorporated in 1895 through the consolidation of Mamaroneck Neck with Rye Neck. It is now a suburban enclave of New York City with some light manufacturing. Pleasure boating is popular in the area. Pop. (2002 est.) 18,833.

mamba (genus *Dendroaspis*), any of four species of large arboreal venomous snakes found in sub-Saharan Africa. Mambas are slender, agile, and quick and are active during the day. They have long front fangs and a powerful neurotoxic venom (*see* snakebite).

Green mamba (*Dendroaspis angusticeps*)
E.S. Ross

The "black," or black-mouthed, mamba (*Dendroaspis polylepis*) averages 2–2.5 m (6.6–8.2 feet) in length and ranges in colour from gray to dark brown but is never actually black. Its name derives from the inside of the mouth, which is black, in contrast to the white mouths of green mambas and other snakes. The black mamba is one of Africa's most dangerous snakes; most bites are fatal, but it is responsible for only a small number of deaths annually.

Mamberamo River, also called TARIKAIKEA, river in Indonesian Irian Jaya, northwestern New Guinea. Formed by the confluence of the Taritatu (Idenburg) and Tariku (Rouffaer) rivers, which converge in a large wild sago swamp, it flows generally northwest and empties into the Pacific Ocean near Tanjung (cape) D'Urville. After flowing placidly the first 20 mi (32 km), the river cuts through the Pegunungan (mountains) Van Rees in a series of rapids and gorges. Including its headstream, the Taritatu, the Mamberamo is about 500 mi long and forms the largest drainage system of Irian Jaya. It is navigable for 100 mi from its mouth, but the only settlements consist of small villages.

mambo, ballroom dance of Cuban origin, internationally popular in the late 1940s. It was performed as an offbeat rumba in which a step taken on the last beat of music in $\frac{4}{4}$ time was held through to the first beat of the following measure. Mambo foot patterns and breaks were essentially the same as in the rumba, the basic movement being step back, step front, close and hold (or front, back, close). In the mambo, couples more often abandoned the standard ballroom embrace position and danced holding one hand or without touching.

Mameli, Goffredo (b. Sept. 5, 1827, Genoa—d. July 6, 1849, Rome), Italian poet and patriot of the Risorgimento and author of the Italian anthem "Fratelli d'Italia" ("Brothers of Italy").

Giuseppe Mazzini, the republican leader, was a friend of his mother and inspired Mameli with his patriotic ideals. As a student Mameli began writing verses expressing patriotic sentiments. "Fratelli d'Italia," written in 1847 and set to music by Michele Novaro, overnight became the national hymn of revolution and independence. In 1848 Mameli volunteered for service in the war against the Austrians. In 1849 he was in Rome when the Roman Republic was proclaimed and sent Mazzini the famous summons: "Roma! Repubblica! Venite!" ("Rome! Republic! Come!"). Joining the patriot Giuseppe Garibaldi's force, he was wounded fatally while defending Rome against the French army sent by Louis-Napoléon Bonaparte.

mameluco (from *mamaruca,* Indian for "half-breed"), in colonial Brazil, especially in the São Paulo district, a person of mixed Indian and white ancestry. The reputation of *mamelucos* for cruelty toward Indians, supposedly reminiscent of the Mamlūks, a Muslim military caste of Southwest Asia and Egypt in medieval and early modern times, prompted the use of the term. *Mamelucos* usually worked on fazendas (plantations) or as artisans or traders and were comparable to the mestizos in Spanish America.

Mamet, David, in full DAVID ALAN MAMET (b. Nov. 30, 1947, Chicago, Ill., U.S.), American playwright, director, and screenwriter noted for his often desperate working-class characters and for his distinctive, colloquial, and frequently profane dialogue.

Mamet began writing plays while attending Goddard College in Plainfield, Vt. (B.A. 1969). Returning to Chicago, where most of his plays were first staged, he worked at various factory jobs, at a real-estate agency, and as a taxi driver; all these experiences would provide background for his plays. In 1973 he cofounded a theatre company in Chicago. He also taught drama at several colleges and universities.

Mamet's early plays include *Duck Variations* (produced 1972), in which two elderly Jewish men sit on a park bench and trade misinformation on various subjects. In *Sexual Perversity in Chicago* (produced 1974; filmed as *About Last Night . . .*, 1986), a couple's budding sexual and emotional relationship is destroyed by their friends' interference. *American Buffalo* (1976; filmed 1996) concerns dishonest business practices; *A Life in the Theatre* (1977) explores the teacher-student relationship; and *Speed-the-Plow* (1987) is a black comedy about avaricious Hollywood scriptwriters. *Glengarry Glen Ross* (1983; filmed 1992), a drama of desperate real-estate salesmen, won the 1984 Pulitzer Prize for drama. In all these works, Mamet used the rhythms and rhetoric of everyday speech to delineate character, describe intricate relationships, and drive dramatic development.

Mamet also wrote fiction, plays for children, and screenplays for a number of motion pictures, including *The Postman Always Rings Twice* (1981), *The Verdict* (1982), *Rising Sun* (1993), *Wag the Dog* (1997), and *Hannibal* (2001), all adaptations of novels. He both wrote and directed the motion pictures *House of Games* (1987), *Homicide* (1991), *Oleanna* (1994), *The Spanish Prisoner* (1998), and *State and Main* (2000).

Mamlūk, also spelled MAMELUKE, slave soldier, a member of one of the armies of slaves that won political control of several Muslim states during the Middle Ages. Under the Ayyūbid sulṭanate, Mamlūk generals used their power to establish a dynasty that ruled Egypt and Syria from 1250 to 1517. The name is derived from an Arabic word for slave.

The use of Mamlūks in Muslim armies became a distinct feature of Islāmic civilization as early as the 9th century AD. The practice was begun in Baghdad by the ʿAbbāsid caliph al-Muʿtaṣim (833–842), and it soon spread throughout the Muslim world. Moreover, the political result was almost invariably the same: the slaves exploited the military power vested in them to seize control over the legitimate political authorities, often only briefly but sometimes for astonishingly long periods of time. Thus, soon after al-Muʿtaṣim's reign the caliphate itself fell victim to the Turkish Mamlūk generals, who were able to depose or murder caliphs almost with impunity. Although the caliphate was maintained as a symbol of legitimate authority, the actual power was wielded by the Mamlūk generals; and by the 13th century, Mamlūks had succeeded in establishing dynasties of their own, both in Egypt and in India, in which the sultans were necessarily men of slave origin or the heirs of such men.

The Mamlūk dynasty. This process of usurping power was epitomized by and culminated in the establishment of the Mamlūk dynasty, which ruled Egypt and Syria from 1250 to 1517 and whose descendants survived in Egypt as an important political force during the Ottoman occupation (1517–1798). The Kurdish general Saladin, who gained control of Egypt in 1169, followed what by then constituted a tradition in Muslim military practice by including a slave corps in his army in addition to Kurdish, Arab, Turkmen, and other free elements. This practice was also followed by his successors. Al-Malik aṣ-Ṣāliḥ Ayyūb (1240–49) is reputed to have been the largest purchaser of slaves, chiefly Turkish, as a means of protecting his sultanate both from Ayyūbid rivals and from the crusaders. Upon his death in 1249 a struggle for his throne ensued, in the course of which the Mamlūk generals murdered his heir and eventually succeeded in establishing one of their own number as sultan. Thenceforth, for more than 250 years, Egypt and Syria were ruled by Mamlūks or sons of Mamlūks.

Historians have traditionally broken the era of Mamlūk rule into two periods—one covering 1250–1382, the other, 1382–1517. Western historians call the former the "Baḥrī" period and the latter the "Burjī," because of the political dominance of the regiments known by these names during the respective times. The contemporary Muslim historians referred to the same divisions as the "Turkish" and "Circassian" periods, in order to call attention to the change in ethnic origin of the majority of Mamlūks, which occurred and persisted after the accession of Barqūq in 1382, and to the effects that this change had on the fortunes of the state.

There is universal agreement among historians that the Mamlūk state reached its height under the Turkish sultans and then fell into a prolonged phase of decline under the Circassians. The principal achievements of the Turkish Mamlūks lay in their expulsion of the remaining crusaders from the Levant and their rout of the Mongols in Palestine and Syria; they thereby saved Arabic-Islāmic civilization from destruction. It is doubtful, however, that such a goal figured in their plans; rather, as rulers of Egypt they were seeking to reconstitute the Egyptian Empire. The Mamlūks also sought to extend their power into the Arabian Peninsula and into Anatolia and Little Armenia; to protect Egypt's rear, they strove to establish their presence in Nubia.

To consolidate their position in the Islāmic world, the Mamlūks revived the caliphate, which the Mongols had destroyed in 1258, and installed a caliph under their surveillance in Cairo. Their patronage of the rulers of the holy cities of Arabia, Mecca and Medina, served the same purpose. Spectacular success in war and diplomacy was underpinned economically by the Mamlūks' support of industries and crafts as well as by their restoration of Egypt as the principal trade and transit route between the Orient and the Mediterranean.

Among the most outstanding Mamlūk sultans were Baybars I (1260–77) and al-Malik an-Nāṣir (1293–1341). The Mamlūks' failure to find an able successor after the latter's death weakened the strength and stability of their realm. But the historians of the era date the beginning of the dynasty's decline from the accession of the first Circassian sultan (Barqūq) in 1382, claiming that thereafter, advancement in the state and the army was

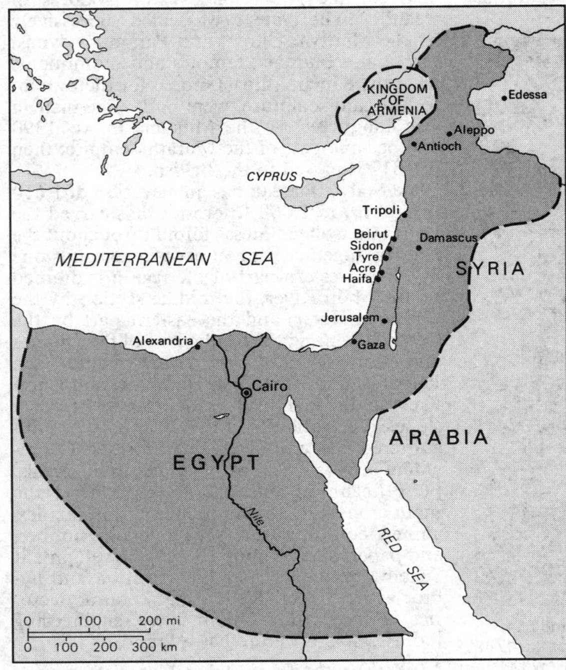

Mamlūk sultanate *c.* 1350

Adapted from Philip K. Hitti; *History of Syria,* Macmillan Company, New York, 1951

dependent on race (*i.e.*, Circassian descent) rather than on proved skill in the art of war, which had served as the chief criterion for promotion during the Turkish period. The increased importance assigned to ethnic affiliation was, however, only one cause of decline; equally or even more important were economic and other factors. Part of the explanation undoubtedly lies in the inability of the Mamlūks, split into hostile factions, to provide necessary safeguards against the Bedouins for the peaceful conduct of trade and agriculture. Furthermore, the demographic losses caused by plagues that raged in Egypt and elsewhere in the East contributed to economic decay. In such conditions the Mamlūks were unable to defend Syria against the Turkic conqueror Timur (Timur Lenk) in 1400. Under the rule of Sultan Barsbay (1422–38) internal stability was restored briefly and Mamlūk glory resuscitated by the conquest of Cyprus in 1426. Yet the increasingly higher taxes demanded to finance such ventures enlarged the Mamlūks' financial difficulties. The final economic blow fell with the Portuguese assault on trade in the Red Sea (*c.* 1500), which was accompanied by Ottoman expansion into Mamlūk territory in Syria. Having failed to adopt field artillery as a weapon in any but siege warfare, the Mamlūks were decisively defeated by the Ottomans both in Syria and in Egypt and from 1517 onward constituted only one of the several components that formed the political structure of Egypt.

Culturally, the Mamlūk period is known mainly for its achievements in historical writing and in architecture and for an abortive attempt at socio-religious reform. Mamlūk historians were prolific chroniclers, biographers, and encyclopaedists; they were not strikingly original, with the exception of Ibn Khaldūn, whose formative and creative years were spent outside Mamlūk territory in the Maghrib (North Africa). As builders of religious edifices—mosques, schools, monasteries and, above all, tombs—the Mamlūks endowed Cairo with some of its most impressive monuments, many of which are still standing; the Mamlūk tomb-mosques can be recognized by stone domes whose massiveness is offset by geometrical carvings. By far the most famous single religious figure of the period was Ibn Taymīyah, who was imprisoned by Mamlūk authorities because of his attempts to rid Mamlūk Islām of superstition and foreign accretions.

The Mamlūks under the Ottomans (1517–1798). With the Ottoman victories over the Mamlūks in 1516–17, Egypt and Syria reverted to the status of provinces within an empire. Although the Mamlūk sultanate was destroyed, the Mamlūks remained intact as a class in Egypt and continued to exercise considerable influence in the state. As had been the case during the Mamlūk dynasty, the Mamlūk elite continued to be replenished by purchases from slave markets. The slaves, after a period of apprenticeship, still formed the core of the army and were soon being appointed to offices in the Ottoman government. Thus, gradually the Mamlūks infiltrated the Ottoman ruling class and eventually were able to dominate it.

One major innovation changed the character of the Mamlūks. Earlier, during the era of the Mamlūk sultanate, the sons of Mamlūks had been excluded from serving in any but the nonslave regiments and from holding offices reserved for Mamlūks in the state. But under Ottoman rule the sons were no longer denied these privileges, so that the principles of Mamlūk loyalty and solidarity were undermined by ties of kinship. Consequently, rather than grouping themselves into military factions that lasted no longer than the lifetime of their individual members, the Ottoman Mamlūks formed "houses" that perpetuated themselves through their sons. The importance of these houses arose from the attempts of each house to dominate the others; thereby a new element of instability, perpetuated by heredity, was introduced into the Mamlūk institution.

To the degree that the Ottoman governors were able to exploit Mamlūk divisiveness, they were able to retain some degree of influence in the government of Egypt. But near the end of the 17th century, when Ottoman power was in decline throughout the empire, the Mamlūks once again held virtual control over the army, the revenues, and the government. Eventually, Istanbul was reduced to recognizing the autonomy of that faction of Mamlūks that would guarantee annual payment of certain sums to the Ottomans. And thus it was that when Napoleon invaded Egypt in 1798 he was confronted by Mamlūk armies and a Mamlūk state. Their power there was finally destroyed by Egypt's new ruler, Muḥammad 'Alī Pasha, in a massacre in 1811.

mammal, a member of the class Mammalia, a group of backboned animals in which the young are nourished with milk secreted by special glands (mammae) of the mother. Another unique mammalian feature is hair; all mammals possess hair at some point in life, though it is found only in the fetal stage of certain whales. Mammals are also warm-blooded and four-limbed (except in some aquatic varieties), but these features are not unique to the class. Mammals are an extremely diverse group, ranging in size from the largest animal that has ever lived, the 150-ton blue whale, to shrews that weigh only a few grams.

A brief treatment of mammals follows. For full treatment, *see* MACROPAEDIA: Mammals.

The primary developmental advance represented by mammals is the ability of their young to learn from the experience of their elders. The dependence of the young mammal on its mother for nourishment makes possible a period of training, and this in turn has brought about a degree of behavioral adaptability unknown in any other group of organisms.

Mammals first appeared in the Triassic Period (180,000,000 to 220,000,000 years ago). Their immediate ancestors were members of the reptilian order Therapsida. Therapsids were small, active carnivores equipped with several specialized types of teeth and with limbs that functioned close to the plane of the trunk (*i.e.*, the limbs were positioned more directly under the trunk as opposed to sprawling out to the sides). Both of these characteristics are prominent features of mammals.

For the past 70,000,000 years mammals have been the dominant animals in terrestrial ecosystems. Mammals have a decisive advantage over their reptilian ancestors because they are endotherms (warm-blooded), meaning that by physiological means they maintain a relatively constant body temperature independent of that of the environment. Endotherms are capable of longer terms of sustained activity than are cold-blooded organisms and can exploit environments that would be inhospitable to cold-blooded animals. Endothermy requires a high rate of metabolism, and many attributes of mammals are related to maintaining high metabolic levels. For example, the four-chambered heart and its resultant dual circulatory systems, red blood cells that lack nuclei, and the secondary palate (which permits breathing while chewing or sucking) are all features that assist in delivering large amounts of oxygen to the body tissues, where it is used to metabolize food. The mammalian hallmark of hair is also directly related to endothermy, as insulation is one of its chief functions. However, hair also serves for defense and in tactile sensation.

Today there are two surviving subclasses of mammals, the Prototheria (monotremes) and the Theria (marsupials and placentals). Another subclass, the Allotheria (multituberculates), is known only from the fossil record. Although primitive in some respects, the multituberculates early evolved into specialized herbivores with gnawing incisors and grinding cheek teeth. They were probably displaced from their ecological niche and driven to extinction by early forms of the rodent order.

The last surviving monotremes are the spiny anteaters (*Tachyglossus aculeatus* and *Zaglossus bruijni*) and the duckbilled platypus (*Ornithorhyncus anatinus*). Like the multituberculates, they are an ancient offshoot of the original mammal stock. Much about the monotremes seems out of character for mammals: they lay shelled eggs, which are incubated by the mother; they have no organized nipple (milk is secreted through ducts that open onto the fur covering the abdomen, where it is lapped up by the young); and they lack teeth altogether, substituting for them a horny beak. Their survival reflects the ancient geological isolation of Australia and New Guinea, which protected them from competition with later mammal forms.

The therians are the dominant mammalian group, and its members have invaded virtually every habitat on the planet, including the oceans, freshwater lakes and streams, the air, the trees, and even under the Earth. They are represented by approximately 4,000 species. Therians are classed according to their reproductive processes as either marsupials (literally meaning "pouched") or placentals.

Marsupials take their name from the teat-lined pouch in which their unweaned young are nurtured. Marsupial young are born in a near embryonic state; they must complete their development attached to the mother's teats. Marsupials were once a fairly widespread group, but they are now found only in the Americas and in Australia and nearby islands. It was in Australia that marsupials reached the apogee of their range, filling many of the ecological niches elsewhere occupied by such placental mammals as cats, wolves, moles, anteaters, and rats. The best known marsupials are kangaroos, koalas, wallabies, and opossums.

Reproductive patterns among placentals vary, but they all involve the preparation of the female's uterine wall by the hormone progesterone for the reception of a fertilized egg. The resulting complex of fetal and maternal tissues is a true placenta, and by means of it the young gestate within the mother's uterus for periods ranging from two weeks for the domestic hamster to 22 months for the African elephant. Among the 18 orders of placental mammals are the artiodactyls (pigs, cattle, giraffes, sheep, camels, hippopotamuses), carnivores (dogs, cats, foxes, bears, skunks, sea lions, seals), chiropterans (bats), edentates (armadillos, anteaters, sloths), insectivores (shrews, moles, hedgehogs), lagomorphs (rabbits, hares), perissodactyls (horses, zebras, rhinoceroses), primates (monkeys, apes, man), proboscids (elephants), rodents (mice, rats, squirrels, hamsters, beavers, porcupines), sirenians (sea cows), and cetaceans (whales).

Man has been dependent on other mammals for a large portion of his food and clothing throughout his cultural evolution. Domesticated mammals have provided transportation, heavy labour, and companionship as well. Many large mammals that competed directly with man for food or space have been rendered extinct or exist now only in captivity. Other types are now endangered by hunting or from the destruction of natural habitats.

mammalogy, scientific study of mammals. Human interest in nonhuman mammals dates far back in prehistory, and the modern science of mammalogy has its broad foundation in the knowledge of mammals possessed by all primitive peoples. The ancient Greeks were among the first to write systematically on mammalian natural history, and they knew many mammals not native to Greece; Aristotle recognized that although fishlike in form, whales and dolphins are mammals allied to terrestrial furbearers. Until the late 18th century much scientific work on mammals was devoted to taxonomy or to the practical matters of animal husbandry. The scientific explorations of the 19th century resulted in large collections of specimens from virtually all parts of the world. Most of the world's mammal species are believed to be known to science (with the possible exception of a good many bat species), but the biology of many species is totally unknown. Modern mammalogy is a multidisciplinary field, encompassing specialists in anatomy, paleontology, ecology, behaviour, and many other areas.

Mammalian taxonomy traditionally relied largely on museum collections of preserved skins (with their skulls), but by the second half of the 20th century additional information was being gained from other studies; *e.g.*, behaviour, cytogenetics, and biochemistry.

At mid-20th century a number of new techniques and instruments opened avenues of research to mammalogists that had previously been difficult or impossible. Telemetry, the use of minute radio transmitters to convey information to the researcher from a free-living animal, has been a particularly useful tool, allowing the tracking of the animal in its natural state and the monitoring of physiological information. The self-contained underwater breathing apparatus (SCUBA) has been important in many aspects of marine mammalogy.

mammary gland, milk-producing gland characteristic of all female mammals and present in a rudimentary and generally nonfunctional form in males. Mammary glands are regulated by the endocrine system and become functional in response to the hormonal changes associated with parturition.

In the primitive monotreme mammals (*e.g.*, platypus), milk is expressed directly from the ducts onto the fur, from which the young lap it up. Unique in monotremes, the mammae lack nipples and are functional in both sexes. In marsupial mammals (*e.g.*, kangaroo), the mammae are located on the ventral surface of the body and in some species are protected by a skin fold or by a pouchlike structure. The tiny newborn sucks the nipple, which then expands in its mouth and thus attaches the young to the female's body. It remains attached until it is fairly well developed, after which time it nurses at will, as do the more advanced mammals (*see* suckling). In cattle, horses, and whales, the mammary glands are located in the inguinal (groin) region; in primates, they are on the chest. Most small mammals have several pairs spread along the ventral surface.

Mammary glands are derived from a modification of sweat glands. They first appear in embryonic life as clumps of cells proliferating from a longitudinal ridge of ectoderm (the outermost of the three germ layers of the embryo) along the so-called milk line, from the buds, or beginnings, of the lower limbs to those of the upper limbs. The number of these clumps that ultimately become breasts, or mammae, varies with each mammalian species according to the size of its litter. In the human normally only one develops on each side of the chest. A lesser development of one or more breasts (polymastia) or nipples (polythelia) may, however, occur anywhere along the milk line.

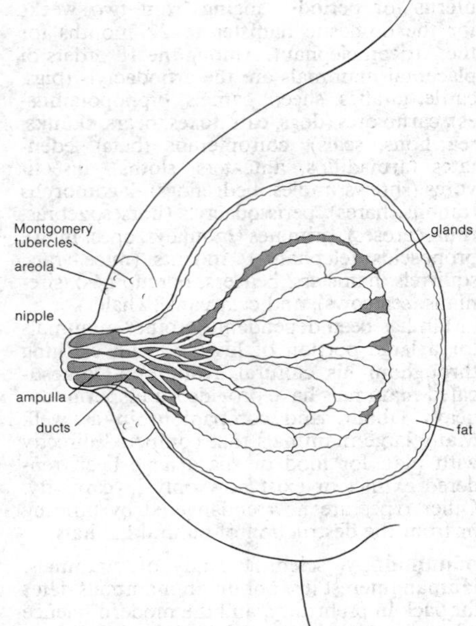

Lactating female breast

From C. Smout, F. Jacoby, and E. Little, *Gynecological and Obstetrical Anatomy;* H.K. Lewis and Co., Ltd., London

The human breast. The mammary gland of a woman who has not borne children consists of a conical disk of glandular tissue, which is encased in variable quantities of fat that give it its characteristic shape. The glandular tissue itself is made up of 15–20 lobes composed of solid cords of ductal cells; each lobe is subdivided into many smaller lobules, separated by broad fibrous suspensory bands (Cooper's ligaments), which connect the skin with the fascia, or sheet of connective tissue, that covers the pectoral muscles beneath the breast. Each lobe is drained by a separate excretory duct. These converge beneath the nipple, where they widen into milk reservoirs, before narrowing again to emerge as pinpoint openings at the summit of the nipple. Circular and radiating muscles in the areola, a circular disk of roughened pigmented skin surrounding the nipple, cause the nipple to become firm and erect upon tactile stimulation; this facilitates suckling. The areola also contains sebaceous glands to provide lubrication for the nipple during nursing.

Blood is supplied to the breast through the axillary, intercostal, and internal thoracic vessels. The nerve supply is from branches of the fourth, fifth, and sixth intercostal nerves.

For a depiction of the breast in human anatomy, shown in relation to other parts of the body, *see* the colour Trans-Vision in the PROPAEDIA: Part Four, Section 421.

Hormonal relationships. Under the primary influence of estrogens from the maturing ovary at puberty, the ductal cells proliferate and form branches. After ovulation, progesterone from the corpus luteum, an organ that develops in the ovary each time an ovum has been shed and has the function of preparing the uterus for receiving the developing embryo, causes the terminal ductal cells to differentiate into the milk-producing cells, which form acini. Interspersed with these cells are smooth muscle cells, which can contract and assist in the ejection of milk. The acini are collapsed or filled with desquamated epithelium (epithelium that has been shed), until the stimulus of pregnancy causes proliferation of all the epithelial cells. The breast becomes enlarged, tense, and sensitive, and the areola widened and more deeply pigmented. The actual secretion of milk is induced by hormones—prolactin from the pituitary and somatomammotropin from the placenta. At the end of lactation the mammary glands and areolae return almost but not completely to their state before pregnancy. After menopause the glands atrophy and are largely replaced by connective tissue and fat.

Diseases and abnormalities of the breast. The occurrence of supernumerary breasts and nipples has been mentioned. Absence of one or both breasts occurs, but rarely. Inequality in size is frequent, the left breast being larger more often than the right. Variations in size and shape are commonly of racial or genetic origin, but may be induced by a tight-fitting garment or by manipulation to cause elongation for the greater convenience of nursing an infant carried on the back.

Painful breasts may occur whenever estrogens are present in large amounts, as at puberty, during pregnancy, prior to menstruation, or after administration of the estrogens.

Fibrocystic disease, also called chronic cystic mastitis, may result in later reproductive life from the cumulative effect of the ebb and flow of endocrine stimulation with each menstrual cycle; this produces nodular fibrosis—or lumps of fibrous tissue—and cysts of various sizes. The condition can usually be distinguished from cancer because it is intermittently painful and tends to subside after menstrual periods. It may predispose to carcinoma, however. Early biopsy is indicated for any nodules that persist.

Endocrine disorders may cause precocious breast development or gynecomastia (enlargement of the breast in the male). Gynecomastia may also be an indication of a sex chromatin abnormality called Klinefelter's syndrome.

The only common infectious disease unique to the breast is acute mastitis, which occurs during lactation as the result of an invasion of pyogenic skin organisms through the nipple. The severe local inflammation, with high fever and prostration, responds promptly to antibiotics, usually without suppuration. Mastitis is ordinarily prevented by proper hygiene.

Benign tumours include fibroadenoma, more common in women under 30, and intraductal papilloma, which may cause bleeding from the nipple. These tumours should be removed. Malignant tumours may arise from any of the cell types contained in the breast, but sarcomas make up only 3 percent of all breast tumours.

Carcinoma of the female breast is the commonest form of malignant tumour in the Western world, afflicting about 4 percent of all adult women. Rare under the age of 25, it increases in incidence up to menopause and then levels off. Hereditary factors play a role, but their exact importance has not been clearly established. (The diagnosis and treatment of breast cancers is covered in the MACROPAEDIA: Cancer.)

mammee apple, also called MAMEY, or SAINT DOMINGO APRICOT, fruit of *Mammea americana,* a large, primarily West Indian tree of the garcinia family (Clusiaceae), with opposite, leathery, gland-dotted leaves; white, sweet-scented, short-stalked, solitary or clus-

Mammee apple (*Mammea americana*)

Walter Dawn

tered axillary flowers; and yellow or russet fruit, 7–15 cm (3–6 inches) in diameter. The bitter rind encloses a sweet, aromatic flesh, which is eaten raw and also used for preserves. Its one to four large, rough seeds are bitter and resinous and are used as an antiworming agent. An aromatic liqueur distilled from the flowers is called eau de Créole. The acrid, resinous gum has been used locally for destroying skin-infesting chigoe fleas.

Mammeri, Mouloud (b. Dec. 28, 1917, Taourirt-Mimoun, Alg.—d. Feb. 26, 1989, near Algiers), Kabyle novelist, playwright, and translator who depicted the changing realities of modern-day Algeria.

Mammeri was reared in the Kabylian mountains but was educated in Morocco, Paris, and Algiers, after which he was drafted into the French army to fight in World War II. He later became a professor at the University of Algiers.

In his first novel, *La Colline oubliée* (1952; "The Forgotten Hill"), Mammeri recorded the experiences of his Kabylian compatriots in a story of village youths who are stifled under the burden of traditional native customs. With *Le Sommeil du Juste* (1955; "The Sleep of the Just"), the scene shifts from Kabyle society to the larger world, where the protagonist is shocked at the confrontation of Berber and French culture, discovering hostility and indifference abroad and eventually suffering the trauma of World War II. In *L'Opium et le bâton* (1965; "Opium and the Stick"), Mammeri constructed a story of the Algerian war of independence, attempting to give the struggle meaning in terms of the essential problem of freedom. His later works included a play, *Le Banquet* (1973), which dealt with the destruction of the Aztecs, and *La Traversée* (1982; "The Crossing"), a novel that centred on an alienated journalist's attempt to return to his Berber roots.

mammillaria (genus *Mammillaria*), any member of a large genus (more than 200 species) of low-growing cacti, native to the Western Hemisphere but concentrated in Mexico. It includes pincushion, fishhook, snowball, bird's-nest, golden-star, thimble, old woman, coral, royal cross, feather, and lemon ball cacti, all of which are small plants suitable to pot culture in cold climates.

Mammillaria species bear tubercles arranged spirally on the cylindroid-to-globose stem; most species bear spines, either straight or hooked. Many small flowers, in a variety of colours, are borne in rings around the plant below the tip. Although some species may reach only 5 cm (2 inches) in height and only a few exceed 60 cm, most grow to less than 30 cm. A number of them, such as old woman cactus (*M. hahniana*) and feather cactus (*M. plumosa*), are woolly or hairy.

mammoth (genus *Mammuthus*), any member of an extinct class of elephants found as fossils in Pleistocene deposits over every continent except Australia and South America (the Pleistocene epoch began 1,600,000 years ago and ended 10,000 years ago). The woolly, Northern, or Siberian mammoth (*M. primigenius*) is by far the best-known of all mammoths. The relative abundance and, at times, excellent preservation of this species' carcasses found in the permanently frozen ground of Siberia has provided much information about mammoths' structure and habits. Fossil mammoth ivory was previously so abundant that it was exported from Siberia to China and Europe from medieval times.

Mammoths figured significantly in the art of primitive man; cave dwellers in Europe realistically depicted herds of these animals. Mammoths were sometimes trapped in ice crevasses and covered over; they were frozen, and their bodies were remarkably well preserved. In fact, cases have been reported in which sled dogs actually were fed the meat from frozen mammoth carcasses that had begun to thaw out of the ice that had held them for almost 30,000 years.

A variety of distinct species are included in the genus *Mammuthus*. Most mammoths were about as large as modern elephants. The North American imperial mammoth (*M. imperator*) attained a shoulder height of 4 m (14 feet). At the other extreme were certain dwarfed forms whose ancestors became isolated on various islands. Many mammoths had a woolly, yellowish brown undercoat about 2.5 cm (1 inch) thick beneath a coarser outer covering of dark brown hair up to 50 cm long. Under the extremely thick skin was a layer of insulating fat at times 8 cm thick. The skull in *Mammuthus* was high and domelike. The ears, small for an elephant, were probably adaptively advantageous for an animal living in a cold climate; the smaller amount of exposed surface area diminished heat losses. A mound of fat was present as a hump on the back. This structure is lacking in fossil remains, but evidence for its presence comes from cave paintings. The prominent tusks were directed downward and were very long; in older males they sometimes curved over each other. Remains of arctic plants have been found in the digestive tracts of frozen mammoth carcasses. It is clear that the mammoth was hunted by early North American hunters.

Mammoth (model)

By courtesy of the trustees of the British Museum (Natural History); photograph, Imitor

Mammoth Cave National Park, park containing an extensive system of limestone caverns, in west-central Kentucky, U.S. The park, authorized in 1926 but only fully established in 1941, occupies a surface area of 82 square miles (212 square km). In 1972 a passage was discovered linking the Mammoth Cave and the Flint Ridge Cave System; the explored underground passages of the multilevel system have a combined length of some 329 miles (530 km). The caves were formed by the dissolution of limestone by water, a continuing process, and their natural temperature is 54° F (12° C). They contain numerous unique geologic formations—to which descriptive names, such as Pillars of Hercules, have been given—and underground lakes and rivers. To the caves' natural entrance have been added three artificial ones, and five scenic routes through the caverns have been laid out for visitors.

Frozen Niagara, Mammoth Cave National Park, Kentucky

By courtesy of National Park Concessions, Inc.; photograph, W. Ray Scott

The caves are inhabited by various animals that have undergone evolutionary adaptation to the dark environment, including cave crickets, blindfish, and blind crayfish. Also found within the caves are fungi or related species; the park's aboveground area is mostly covered with hardwood forest.

Mummified Indian bodies, possibly of pre-Columbian origin, have been found in the caves.

mamo (species *Drepanis pacifica*), Hawaiian songbird of the family Drepanididae (order Passeriformes), which became extinct in about 1898. About 20 cm (8 inches) long, it was black with yellow touches and had a long, decurved bill for nectar-feeding. The native Hawaiian nobility killed mamos for their feathers, but the birds nevertheless remained fairly numerous until the Americans destroyed their mountain-forest habitat.

Mamo (*Drepanis pacifica*)

Painting by H. Jon Janosik

Mamoré River, Spanish RÍO MAMORÉ, river in north-central Bolivia. It is formed by headwaters, chiefly the Grande River, which arise in Andean cordilleras and drain the Moxos (Mojos) plain, an ancient lake bed. The Mamoré meanders generally northward to the Brazilian border, at which point it is joined by the Iténez River (Portuguese: Guaporé). It constitutes the Bolivia-Brazil frontier as far north as Villa Bella, where it joins the Beni River to form the Madeira. The Mamoré's importance as a transport route is diminished by the presence of rapids, but the river is navigable through the Moxos plain and tropical forest to Guajará-Mirim, Brazil, the southern terminus of the Madeira-Mamoré railway. Its total length is approximately 1,200 miles (1,900 km).

Mamou, town, west-central Guinea. Located on the Conakry-Kankan railway and at the intersection of roads from Kindia, Dalaba, Dabola, and Faranah, Mamou was founded in 1908 as a collecting point on the railroad from Conakry (125 miles [201 km] southwest). It is the chief trading centre for the rice, cattle, citrus fruits, bananas, tomatoes, and mangoes raised in the surrounding agricultural area. Mamou exports bananas, fruit juices, and orange essence; its industries include a food-processing plant and the nation's first sawmill. The town has several hospitals (general, psychiatric, leprosy), a secondary school, a meteorological station, a central mosque, and a Roman Catholic mission (1948).

The surrounding area, forming part of the Fouta Djallon plateau, is mostly savanna. It is inhabited by the Fulani (Peul), Dialonke (Djallonke), and Limba peoples. Timbo, the seat of the Fulani *almamys* (Muslim political, religious, and military leaders) of the 18th- and 19th-century state of Fouta Djallon, lies 26 miles (42 km) northeast of Mamou. Pop. (1983 prelim.) 35,748.

Mamoulian, Rouben (b. Oct. 8, 1897, Tiflis [now Tbilisi], Georgia, Russian Empire—d. Dec. 4, 1987, Los Angeles, Calif., U.S.), theatrical and motion-picture director noted for his contribution to the development of cinematic art at the beginning of the sound era. His achievements include the skillful blending of music and sound effects with an imaginative visual rhythm.

Born into an Armenian family, Mamoulian received a degree in law from the University of Moscow. While engaged in law studies, Mamoulian had become involved in acting, directing, and playwriting at the Moscow Art Theatre (now Moscow Academic Art Theatre). In 1918 he moved to London, where he directed grand opera, operettas, and musicals. Emigrating to the United States in 1923, he became the director of production for the Eastman Theatre, Rochester, N.Y.

Mamoulian
UPI

During the late 1920s he worked for the Theatre Guild and made a deep impression in American theatre with his production in 1927 of the American folk play *Porgy.* He directed a number of stage plays and one sound film, *Applause* (1929), before moving to Hollywood. For his work in *Applause,* he mounted wheels on the camera, which had had to be enclosed in a booth to block out noise for early sound films and had been thereby rendered stationary; this innovation brought him quick recognition. His noteworthy early films include *City Streets* (1931), a gangster picture; *Dr. Jekyll and Mr. Hyde* (1932); *The Song of Songs* (1933); *Queen Christina* (1933); *We Live Again* (1934); *Becky Sharp* (1935), the first picture in the new Technicolor process; *Golden Boy* (1939); *The Mark of Zorro* (1940); and *Blood and Sand* (1941).

Love Me Tonight (1932), an operetta that featured Maurice Chevalier and Jeanette MacDonald, was the first in a series of gay, imaginative musical comedies, including *The Gay Desperado* (1936), *High, Wide and Handsome* (1937), *Summer Holiday* (1948), and *Silk Stockings* (1957). Mamoulian's major stage works were colourful musicals, including *Porgy and Bess* (1935), *Oklahoma!* (New York, 1943; Europe, 1955), and *Carousel* (New York, 1945).

Mamprusi, also called MAMPRULI, a people who inhabit the area between the White Volta and Nasia rivers in northern Ghana. The Mamprusi speak different dialects of More-Gurma (Mõõre-Gurma) of the Gur (Voltaic) branch of the Niger-Congo language family. A few Mamprusi also live in northern Togo.

Mamprusi settlements usually consist of a grouping of circular compounds that are surrounded by farmland. The countryside of this area of northern Ghana is orchard bush (tropical uplands with open woodland). A dry season from about October to March is followed by a rainy season from April to October. Agriculture is central to the Mamprusi economy, and the Mamprusi are hoe cultivators. Principal crops include millet, corn (maize), yams, okra, hibiscus, rice, and tobacco. Men clear the land and plant yams, while women sow and harvest the grain and transport crops from the fields. Hunting and fishing are secondary activities.

The Mamprusi differ from some other peoples of northern Ghana in their traditional organization of a centralized state with four subdivisions and a king. They, like all the peoples of northern Ghana, believe in a supreme being. The earth is viewed in both its practical aspect and spiritually, and the "earth cult" maintains shrines at sacred places. The importance of ancestors for the Mamprusi is manifested in shrines and rituals devoted to them. Many Mamprusi have now adopted Islām, but traditional religious practices persist. In the late 20th century the Mamprusi numbered about 90,000.

Ma'mūn, al-, in full ABŪ AL-ʿABBĀS ʿABD ALLĀH AL-MAʾMŪN IBN AR-RASHĪD (b. 786, Baghdad—d. August 833, Tarsus, Cilicia), seventh ʿAbbāsid caliph (813–833), known for his attempts to end sectarian rivalry in Islām and to impose upon his subjects a rationalist Muslim creed.

Early years. The son of the celebrated caliph Hārūn ar-Rashīd and an Iranian concubine, al-Ma'mūn was born in 786, six months before his half-brother al-Amīn, the son of a legitimate wife of Arab blood. When it became necessary for ar-Rashīd to choose an heir, he is said to have hesitated before deciding finally in favour of al-Amīn. In 802, on the occasion of a pilgrimage to Mecca, the caliph formally announced the respective rights of the two brothers: al-Ma'mūn recognized al-Amīn as successor to the caliphate in Baghdad, but al-Amīn acknowledged his brother's almost absolute sovereignty over the eastern provinces of the empire, with his seat at Merv in Khorāsān (now in Turkmenistan).

Hārūn ar-Rashīd's death in March 809 nevertheless created discord that soon developed into armed conflict between the two brothers. Al-Ma'mūn, in effect stripped by al-Amīn of his rights to the succession, was supported by an Iranian, al-Faḍl ibn Sahl, whom he was to make his vizier, as well as by an Iranian general, Ṭāhir. Ṭāhir's victory over al-Amīn's army on the outskirts of the present Tehrān allowed al-Ma'mūn's troops to occupy western Iran. Al-Amīn appealed in vain to new troops recruited in part from among the Arabs of Syria. He was finally besieged in Baghdad in April 812. There was desperate resistance, and the city was taken only in September 813. Al-Amīn, who had in the meantime been declared deposed as caliph in Iraq and Arabia, wished to surrender but was killed, contrary, it seems, to al-Ma'mūn's orders. Thus ended one of the most merciless civil wars known to the Islāmic East.

The war had originated in Hārūn ar-Rashīd's ill-advised decision over the succession, but it also revealed internal divisions within the ʿAbbāsid empire. It was not merely a question of a personal rivalry between the two brothers—one of whom, al-Ma'mūn, was unquestionably of far-superior intelligence—it was also a question of a conflict between different politico-religious trends that had become apparent during the preceding reign; al-Amīn had emphasized traditionalism and Arab culture, while al-Ma'mūn, who was open to new movements of thought and outside influences, courted the support of Iranian figures and of the eastern provinces.

Caliphate. Al-Ma'mūn, having become caliph of the entire ʿAbbāsid empire, decided to continue to reside at Merv, assisted by his faithful Iranian vizier al-Faḍl. It was then that al-Ma'mūn, determined to put an end to the division of the Islāmic world between Sunnite and Shīʿite—between the adherents of the ʿAbbāsid caliphs, descendants of Muḥammad's uncle al-ʿAbbās, and the defenders of ʿAlī, the prophet's cousin and son-in-law, and his descendants—made a decision that was startling to his contemporaries and injurious to his own position. He designated as his heir not a member of his own family but instead ʿAlī ar-Riḍā, who was a descendant of ʿAlī. In an attempt visibly to reconcile the two rival families, al-Ma'mūn gave ʿAlī ar-Riḍā his own daughter as a wife. As a further symbol of reconciliation, he adopted the green flag in place of the traditional black flag of the ʿAbbāsid family.

But this spectacular measure did not achieve the anticipated result. It was not sufficient to pacify the Shīʿite extremists, while on the other hand it embittered the partisans of ʿAbbāsid legitimism and of Sunnism, particularly in Iraq. In Baghdad, declaring al-Ma'mūn deposed, they proclaimed as the new caliph the ʿAbbāsid prince Ibrāhīm, son of the third caliph, al-Mahdī. When news of this insurrection finally reached al-Ma'mūn, he abruptly decided to leave Merv for Baghdad. During the long journey, two dramatic events took place: the vizier al-Faḍl was assassinated in February 818, and ʿAlī ar-Riḍā died in August of the same year after a brief illness that chroniclers ascribed to poisoning. Thus, the man whose elevation to the position of heir presumptive had bedeviled the caliph's rule, as well as the vizier closely associated with that policy, were eliminated. Notwithstanding his denials, historians have generally attributed the deaths to al-Ma'mūn.

During the following 15 years, al-Ma'mūn showed himself to be a judicious sovereign. He closely controlled his ministers and did not again appoint an all-powerful vizier. He also tried to maintain strict control over the provincial governors but was forced to allow a relative degree of autonomy to his former general, Ṭāhir, who had been named governor of Khorāsān.

Support of Western philosophy and science. Although al-Ma'mūn, upon his arrival in Baghdad, abandoned his policy of reconciliation with the descendants of ʿAlī, which he symbolized by reinstating the traditional black ʿAbbāsid flag, he did not give up hope of attaining the same goal by means of a more circuitous path. He had already, at Merv, evidenced his sympathy for the representatives of the Muʿtazilī movement, those supporters of Islām who adopted rationalist methods and borrowed from the works of ancient Greek or Hellenistic philosophers the modes of reasoning that seemed to them best-suited for combating the influence of such doctrines as Manichaeism (a dualistic religion founded in Iran). Al-Ma'mūn encouraged the translation of Greek philosophical and scientific works and founded an academy called the House of Wisdom (Bayt al-Ḥikmah) to which the translators, most often Christians, were attached. He also imported manuscripts of particularly important works that did not exist in the Islāmic countries from Byzantium. Developing an interest in the sciences as well, al-Ma'mūn established observatories at which Muslim scholars could verify the astronomic knowledge handed down from antiquity.

Not content with extending his patronage to the translators and scientific research, al-Ma'mūn imposed on all his subjects the Muʿtazilī doctrine, characterized by a purified concept of divinity, belief in free will, and full human responsibility. One of the most innovative aspects of this theodicy was the affirmation of the created and not eternal character of the Qur'ān, the word of God. Such a doctrine was likely to diminish the influence of the learned doctors, the interpreters of the sacred text, who found themselves defending ʿAbbāsid legitimism; in addition, the doctrine demanded exceptional moral and religious qualities of the caliph, for it went so far as to authorize rebellion against a wicked sovereign. This tenet of the Muʿtazilī doctrine diverged from the traditional concept upon which the ʿAbbāsid caliphs had based their authority, and many adherents of the doctrine manifested an avowed sympathy for Shīʿah. Al-Maʾmūn, attracted by the intellectual rigour of Muʿtazilah, also saw in it the means of encouraging public opinion to accept a new, more flexible conception of the caliphate. In fact, when he announced his adherence to the thesis of the "created Qurʾān" in 827, al-Maʾmūn also asserted the superiority of ʿAlī over the other Companions of the Prophet. This position of al-Maʾmūn's manifested clear political implications.

Attempt to impose Muʿtazilī doctrine. At the beginning of 833 al-Maʾmūn decided to require adherence to Muʿtazilah from all his subjects. As the caliph was then on an expedition against the Byzantines in the region of Tarsus, he entrusted this task to his representative in Baghdad, the prefect of police Isḥāq ibn Ibrāhīm. The latter first called together the *qāḍīs* (judges) to urge them to recognize the Muʿtazilī doctrine; then it was the turn of the specialists in Ḥadīth Muslim tradition; but among this group protestations were raised that the caliph hoped to silence through the use of threats. Some resisted obstinately, refusing to pronounce the Qurʾān a "created" work. This was notably true of Aḥmad ibn Ḥanbal, the founder of the Ḥanbalī school of Islāmic law, who was to have been sent, under a heavy guard, before the caliph but was temporarily spared by the sudden death of al-Maʾmūn at Tarsus in 833. This episode, called the trial (*miḥnah*) by the traditionalists, showed that one portion of the public opinion resisted the beliefs that al-Maʾmūn had wished to impose. The strength of this opposition serves to explain why the caliphs, a few decades later, abandoning their attempt at reorienting religious beliefs, returned to traditional dogma.

Assessment. Possessed of a distinguished and sagacious mind, al-Maʾmūn set forth in the political domain very personal ideas that, in effect, ended in failure. He was never able to put an end to the divisions that were tearing the Muslim community apart; and the violence that he did not hesitate to employ at the end of his reign—to impose a doctrine he considered salutary for the Islāmic community—tarnished the image of an otherwise exceptionally open-minded ruler. (D.So.)

man, specifically, an adult human male and, generally, any extinct or living member, male or female, of the biological family Hominidae. *See* hominid; human being.

Consult the INDEX *first*

Man, town, western Côte d'Ivoire (Ivory Coast). The town is situated along the Ko River, in a mountainous area (Massif de Man) on the eastern edge of the Nimba Range. There are iron-ore reserves in the mountains east of Man. The chief trade centre (rice, cassava, livestock, and palm oil and kernels) for a forested region mainly inhabited by the Dan and the Ngere (or Guere) and Wobe peoples, it is also a major collecting point for coffee and timber, which are sent to the Atlantic coast for export. Man is the site of an agricultural research station and a government technical school. It is also a tourist centre. Local Dyula craftsmen have made the town a centre for ivory carvings. The Dan are noted for their wooden masks and for their dances. Pop. (1988) 88,294.

Man, Isle of, also spelled MANN, Manx-Gaelic ELLAN VANNIN, or MANNIN, Latin MONA, or MONAPIA, one of the British Isles, located in the Irish Sea off the northwest coast of England. The island lies roughly equidistant between England, Ireland, Scotland, and Wales. The Isle of Man is not part of the United Kingdom but rather is a crown possession (since 1828) that is self-governing in its internal affairs under the supervision of the British Home Office.

The Isle of Man is about 30 miles (48 km) long by 10 miles (16 km) wide, its main axis being southwest to northeast. It has an area of 221 square miles (572 square km). The island consists of a central mountain mass culminating in Snaefell (2,036 feet [621 m]) and extending north and south in low-lying agricultural land. Man's coastline is rocky and has fine cliff scenery. The grass-covered slate peaks of the central massif are smooth and rounded as a result of action during various glacial periods. The island's landscape is treeless except

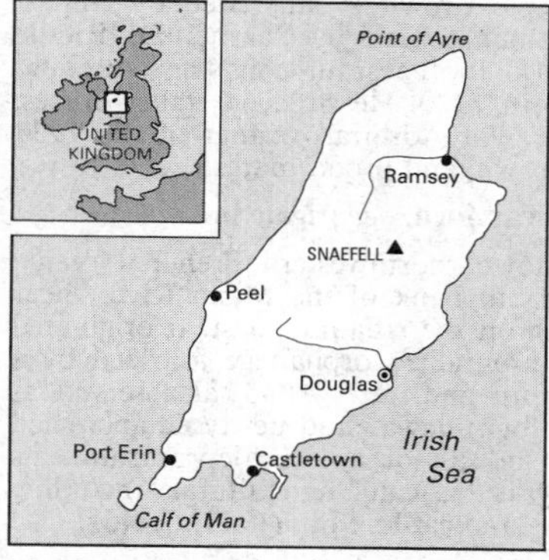

Isle of Man

in sheltered places. To the southwest lies an islet, the Calf of Man, with precipitous cliffs, which is administered by the Manx National Heritage as a bird sanctuary.

The climate is maritime temperate, with cool summers and mild winters. The average mean temperature in February is 41° F (4.9° C) and is 58° F (14.3° C) in August. The average annual rainfall is 45 inches (1,140 mm). The native flora and fauna are of little interest, but the domestic Manx cat, a distinctive tailless breed, is traditionally believed to have originated on the island.

The Isle of Man has been inhabited by humans since the Mesolithic Period. It became the home of many Irish missionaries in the centuries following the teaching of St. Patrick (5th century AD). Among its earliest inhabitants were Celts, and their language, Manx, which is closely related to Gaelic, remained the everyday speech of the people until the first half of the 19th century. The number of Manx speakers is now negligible, however. Norse (Viking) invasions began about AD 800, and the isle was a dependency of Norway until 1266. During this period Man came under a Scandinavian system of government that has remained practically unchanged ever since.

In 1266 the king of Norway sold his suzerainty over Man to Scotland, and the island came under the control of England in 1341. From this time on, the island's successive feudal lords, who styled themselves "kings of Mann," were all English. In 1406 the English crown granted the island to Sir John Stanley, and his family ruled it almost uninterruptedly until 1736. (The Stanleys refused to be called "kings" and instead adopted the title "lord of Mann," which still holds.) The lordship of Man passed to the dukes of Atholl in 1736, but in the decades that followed, the island became a major centre for the contraband trade, thus depriving the British government of valuable customs revenues. In response, the British Parliament purchased sovereignty over the island in 1765 and acquired the Atholl family's remaining prerogatives on the island in 1828.

The government consists of an elected president; a Legislative Council, or upper house; and a popularly elected House of Keys, or lower house. The two houses function as separate legislative bodies but come together to form what is known as the Tynwald Court to transact legislative business. The House of Keys constitutes one of the most ancient legislative assemblies in the world. The Isle of Man levies its own taxes.

Though fishing, agriculture, and smuggling were formerly important, offshore financial services, high-technology manufacturing, and tourism from Britain are now the mainstays of the island's economy. The island's annual Tourist Trophy motorcycle races (in June) attract many visitors. The island's farms produce oats, wheat, barley, turnips, and potatoes, and cattle and sheep graze on the pastures of the central massif. The principal towns are Douglas, the capital; Peel; Castletown (*qq.v.*); and Ramsey. There is an airport near Castletown, and packet boats connect Man with the British mainland. Pop. (1995 est.) 69,600.

Man-chou-li, Pinyin MANZHOULI, formerly (1910–49) LUPIN, city in the Inner Mongolian Autonomous Region, China. It is situated on the border opposite the Russian town of Zabaykalsk and lies 100 miles (160 km) west of Hailar and 20 miles (32 km) northwest of Lake Hu-lun. Man-chou-li was long a small Mongolian settlement in the Hu-lun-pei-erh League. It developed after 1900 when it became the western terminus of the Russian-built Chinese Eastern Railway and a junction with Russia's Siberian railway system. It rapidly grew as a customs station and as a market and communication centre.

After the fall of the Ch'ing (Manchu) dynasty in 1911, the city suffered from a Mongolian invasion. Chinese control was restored in 1914, but in 1920 the local Mongolians rebelled and attained some measure of local autonomy. In 1931, after coming under Japanese control, the city acquired some industry. There are coal (lignite) deposits in the vicinity. Pop. (1990 est.) 120,023.

man-eater, either of two dangerous sharks, the white shark (*q.v.*) of the family Isuridae or the Lake Nicaragua shark of the family Carcharhinidae. *See* carcharhinid.

man in the iron mask, the: *see* iron mask, the man in the.

man-made fibre, any raw, hairlike material that is used to produce yarns and fabrics and that includes fibres made by modifying natural materials (such as cellulose) and synthetic fibres made by chemical synthesis. Non-man-made fibres are called natural fibres.

A brief treatment of man-made fibres follows. For full treatment, *see* MACROPAEDIA: Industrial Polymers.

Cellulosic fibres are derived through chemical processing of short cotton fibres, or linters, and from wood pulp; they include rayon, acetate, and triacetate. Other materials modified to produce fibres include protein, glass, metals, and rubber. Synthetic fibres, produced from chemicals combined into large molecules called polymers, include such types as acrylic, modacrylic, nylon, polyester, and polyurethane. Individual manufacturers apply trademarked names to their own form of such fibres, such as Antron, Cumuloft, Qiana, Orlon, Dacron, and Lycra.

Man-made fibres are usually produced by converting the fibre-forming substance to a fluid state, either by melting or by employing a solvent, to form a spinning liquid. In the spinning, or extruding, operation, the liquid is fed through holes in a spinneret, a device performing much the same function as the spinneret of the silkworm. In the formation of man-made fibres, the term spinning applies to the process of forcing the liquid through the spinneret holes; the same word is applied to the production of yarn by twisting together either natural or man-made fibres or combinations of both.

The emerging liquid is hardened, forming a fibre having great length, called a filament, which is subjected to a stretching, or drawing, operation, increasing the alignment of its molecules. Variations and special properties can be introduced during the manufacturing process. Long filaments may be used to make yarn or may be cut into short, uniform lengths forming staple and then twisted together to form yarn.

As the variety of new man-made fibres increased, as various fibres were blended together, and as special finishes were applied, fabric care presented new problems to the consumer; a trend developed employing permanent labels specifying garment care. *Compare* natural fibre.

man-of-war fish (species *Nomeus gronovii*), small marine fish of the family Nomeidae (order Perciformes; sometimes placed in family Stromateidae), noted for living unharmed among the stinging tentacles of the Portuguese man-of-war jellyfish (*Physalia*). The man-of-war fish is usually found in the open sea, near its protector. It is striped or mottled, with large, black pelvic fins and is about 7.5 cm (3 inches) long.

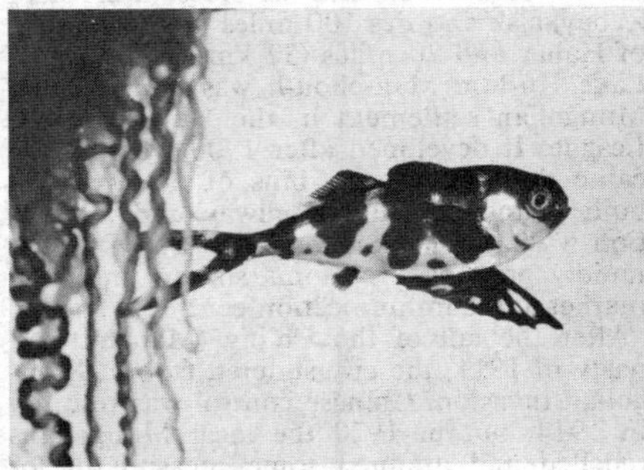

Man-of-war fish (*Nomeus gronovii*)
Des and Jan Bartlett—Bruce Coleman Inc./EB Inc.

man orchid (species *Aceras anthropophorum*), the only species in the genus *Aceras,* plant family Orchidaceae. It is native to grasslands of Great Britain, Eurasia, and northern Africa. The man orchid derives its name from the helmeted, humanlike shape of its flowers.

The flower spike, about 10 to 45 cm (4 to 18 inches) tall, may bear up to 90 greenish or yellowish flowers, which have an unpleasant odour. A man orchid has glossy leaves, short, thick roots, and two egg-shaped underground tubers.

Man orchid (*Aceras anthropophrum*)
G.E. Hyde—EB Inc.

Man o' War, byname BIG RED (foaled 1917), probably the most famous American racehorse (Thoroughbred), overwhelmingly voted, in an Associated Press poll taken in 1950, the greatest horse of the first half of the 20th century. In a brief career of only two seasons (1919–20), he won 20 of 21 races, finishing second to a horse named Upset on Aug. 13, 1919, at Saratoga, N.Y. He established five track records for speed over various distances and raced at odds as short as 1–100. In 1920 he won the Preakness Stakes and the Belmont Stakes, two of the U.S. Triple Crown races. (He did not run in the Kentucky Derby, the other Triple Crown event.) Bred by August Belmont but owned by Samuel D. Riddle from 1918, the chestnut colt was retired to stud late in 1920. He sired 64 stakes horses, including War Admiral, winner of the 1937 Triple Crown, and brood mares.

man-o'-war bird: *see* frigate bird.

Mana, town, northwestern French Guiana, on the south bank of the Mana River, near its mouth on the Atlantic coast. It originated in 1830 around an orphanage founded by a French nun and, after 1848, also served as a refuge for runaway and newly emancipated slaves. The site of a large leprosarium, its economy is basically agricultural, including sugarcane and cattle. Pop. (1999) 5,445.

Mana (ancient country): *see* Mannai.

mana, among Melanesian and Polynesian peoples, a supernatural force or power that may be ascribed to persons, spirits, or inanimate objects. Mana may be either good or evil, beneficial or dangerous. The term was first used in the 19th century in the West during debates concerning the origin of religion. It was first used to describe what apparently was interpreted to be an impersonal, amoral, supernatural power that manifested itself in extraordinary phenomena and abilities. Anything distinguished from the ordinary (*e.g.,* an uncommonly shaped stone) is so because of the mana it possesses.

Scholars in the 19th and early 20th centuries compared this portrait of mana to other religious phenomena they believed to be parallel, especially *wakan* and *orenda* among the Dakota (Sioux) and Iroquois Indians. From these anthropologists in the early part of the 20th century developed the theory that mana was a worldwide phenomenon that lay behind all religions but was later supplanted by personified forces and deities.

Subsequent scholarship has challenged both the original description of mana and the conclusions drawn from it. Mana is by no means universal; it is not even common to all of Melanesia; many of the parallels that have been adduced have been found to be specious. Mana is not impersonal. It is never spoken of by itself but always in connection with powerful beings or things. Thus, mana would seem to be descriptive of the possession of power and not itself the source of power. Rather than being an impersonal power, mana is inextricably related to belief in spirits.

Among contemporary scholars a functionalist and political interpretation has been offered. Mana is not found within relatively simple tribes but rather in the more highly organized Melanesian societies. It would seem to be a symbolic way of expressing the special qualities attributed to persons of status and authority in a society, of providing sanction for their actions, and of explaining their failures.

Manado, also spelled MENADO, *kotamadya* (municipality) and capital of Sulawesi Utara *provinsi* (province), Celebes island, Indonesia, located near the tip of the north-northeastern arm of Celebes island on an inlet of the Celebes Sea. Manado lies at the foot of Mount Klabat (6,634 feet [2,022 m]), about 600 miles (970 km) northeast of Ujung Padang. A trade centre for the surrounding agricultural and lumbering area, it exports coffee, sugarcane, nutmeg, and ebony and was a free port during the second half of the 19th century. Local handicrafts include bamboo and cane working, wood carving, and basketry. The city has a large Chinese population, and many of its residents are Christian. Manado has an airport and is linked by road with Amurang, Bolaang, Bitung, and Gorontalo. The remains of a fortress built by the Dutch in 1658 and the Sam Ratulangi University (founded 1961) are in the city. Pop. (1995 est.) 332,228.

managerial economics, application of economic principles to decision-making in business firms or of other management units. The basic concepts are derived mainly from microeconomic theory, which studies the behaviour of individual consumers, firms, and industries, but new tools of analysis have been added. Statistical methods, for example, are becoming increasingly important in estimating current and future demand for products. The methods of operations research and programming provide scientific criteria for maximizing profit, minimizing cost, and selecting the most profitable combination of products. Decision-making theory and game theory, which recognize the conditions of uncertainty and imperfect knowledge under which business managers operate, have contributed to systematic methods of assessing investment opportunities.

Where the same name may denote a person, place, or thing, the articles will be found in that order

---

Managua, city, capital of Nicaragua, lying amid small crater lakes on the southern shore of Lake Managua. One of Central America's warmest capitals, the city is only 163 feet (50 m) above sea level. Throughout the Spanish colonial period, Managua was recognized only as an Indian town, outranked by the relatively nearby Spanish cities of León and Granada. Its choice as a permanent capital in 1857 came after partisans of those two rival cities had exhausted themselves in internecine conflict. Much of Managua was rebuilt after 1931, when it was ravaged by earthquake and fire. After the disastrous earthquake of 1972, the business section was rebuilt 6 miles (10 km) away (to the south and west) from the former city centre. It was the scene in 1978–79 of general strikes against the Somoza government and of heavy fighting, particularly in the Sandinista-held slum areas. Notable landmarks include Darío Park, with its monument to Nicaragua's famed poet Rubén Darío; the National Palace; and the 20th-century cathedral. In 1952 the University of Managua became part of the National University of Nicaragua. Other universities are the Central American (1961) and the Polytechnic (1968; university status 1978).

Managua, the largest city in the country, is also its centre of commerce and culture. It produces a variety of small manufactures, including processed meat, furniture, metal, and textiles; it also has an oil refinery. Coffee and cotton are the principal crops grown in the agricultural hinterland. The city has railroad and highway connections with the Pacific port of Corinto and with the cities of León and Granada. The Pan-American Highway and an international airport tie it to other Central and North American cities.

The city is surrounded by rich agricultural lands devoted primarily to the cultivation of coffee, cotton, and corn (maize). The importance of sugarcane, rice, sorghum, cattle, and

Monument to the poet Rubén Darío in Managua, Nicaragua
Ewing Galloway

horses has been declining. Pop. (1995) city, 864,201.

Managua, Lake, Spanish LAGO DE MANAGUA, lake in western Nicaragua, in a rift valley at an elevation of 128 feet (39 m) above sea level. The lake, 65 feet (20 m) in depth, is 36 miles (58 km) from east to west and 16 miles (25 km) from north to south; its area is 400 square miles (1,035 square km). Also known by its Indian name, Xolotlán, the lake is fed by numerous streams rising in the central highlands and the Diriamba Highlands. It is drained by the Tipitapa River, which flows into Lake Nicaragua.

The lake is economically significant: its waters yield fish and alligators and are plied by shallow-draft vessels. Momotombo Volcano, reaching 4,199 feet (1,280 m) above sea level, is on the northwestern shore. Managua, the national capital, lies along the lake's southern shore.

Manahem (king of Israel): *see* Menahem.

Manakara, town, southeastern Madagascar. It is situated along the Indian Ocean and the Pangalanes Canal. An old fishing village, it became a thriving Indian Ocean port after a railway was constructed connecting it to Fianarantsoa (75 miles [120 km] northwest). Now it handles the coastal trade of coffee and cloves, and it has workshops serving the railway. Pop. (1998 est.) 24,970.

manakin, any of 59 species of small, stubby, short-billed birds of the American tropics (family Pipridae, order Passeriformes). Members range in size from 8.5 to 16 cm (3.5 to 6.5 inches) long. They are forest-dwelling and eat berries and insects. Males are mainly dark-

Golden-collared manakin (*Manacus vitellinus*)
John S. Dunning—Photo Researchers/EB Inc.

plumaged, with splashes of bright colour; females are greenish in hue. In many species the wing feathers are modified to produce rasping, snapping, or crackling sounds when vibrated.

Manakins are remarkable for their courtship displays. In *Manacus* species the males perform near one another, each in a cleared area of forest floor with one or two saplings that serve as perches for their acrobatics. Females may join the dance before mating. In *Pipra* species the males pose on low branches. Two or more males of the 9-centimetre (3.5-inch) blue-backed manakin (*Chiroxiphia pareola*) perform an intricate circular dance—momentarily afoot and in the air, like a rotating fireworks wheel. In the white-throated *Corapipo gutturalis,* the male bobs as he creeps toward the female. Males display throughout the breeding season; meanwhile, the female builds a cup nest on a forked twig near the ground and raises two young.

Manala, in Finnish mythology, the realm of the dead. The word is possibly derived from the compound *maan-ala,* "the space (or area) under the earth." It is also called Tuonela, the realm of Tuoni, and Pohjola, derived from the word *pohja,* meaning "bottom" and also "north."

The Finnish underworld and related concepts among other Finno-Ugric peoples, such as the Yabme-aimo of the Lapps, are the product of hundreds of years of various influences and, as a result, do not provide a consistent cosmology. Manala is often reached by crossing a fiery stream, the river of death, either over a narrow bridge or by a boat brought by a denizen of the otherworld. Manala itself is a dark, gloomy place but not a place of everlasting torment like the Christian hell. It is ruled by the goddess Louhi, who is a fierce haglike creature with several vaguely defined sons, daughters, and servants in her retinue. Pohjola is similarly found in various forms in the underworld, but it is also to the north and at the outer edges of the universe, outside the known world of man. In a more concrete sense the realm of the dead was where the dead were buried, and many of the descriptions of the underworld depict the coffins and funerary shelters erected at the burial sites.

Manama, Arabic AL-MANĀMAH, capital and largest city of the state and emirate of Bahrain.

Bahrain Monetary Agency, Manama, Bahrain
Aspect Picture Library/Peter Carmichael

It lies at the northeast tip of Bahrain island, in the Persian Gulf. About one-third of the emirate's population lives in the city. First mentioned in Islāmic chronicles about AD 1345, it was taken by the Portuguese (1521) and by the Persians (1602). It has been held, with brief interruptions, by the ruling Āl Khalīfah dynasty since 1783. Because Bahrain concluded a series of treaties (1861–1914) placing the country under increasing British protection, there was a British political agent stationed at Manama from 1900, subject to the political resident for the Persian Gulf, whose headquarters were long at Bushire, Iran. In 1946 the residency was moved to Manama, where it remained until the city became the capital of independent Bahrain in 1971.

Long an important commercial centre of the northern Persian Gulf, the traditional economy was based on pearling, fishing, boatbuilding, and import trade. Harbour facilities were poor; ocean vessels had to anchor in the open roadstead 2–4 miles (3–6 km) offshore. The discovery of petroleum on Bahrain (1932) revolutionized the city's economy and appearance, with the construction of many modern buildings. Manama developed as a trade, financial, and commercial centre; it is the seat of numerous banks. The headquarters of the Bahrain Petroleum Company (BAPCO), however, are at ʿAwālī, in the centre of Bahrain island. Manama was declared a free port in 1958, and the new deepwater port facilities of Mīnāʾ Salmān, in the protected bay of al-Qulayʿah Inlet, southeast of the built-up area of the city, were opened in 1962. With storage and refrigeration facilities, and equipment for docking and repair of large oceangoing vessels, it is now one of the most important ports of the Persian Gulf. The island and town of Al-Muḥarraq, Bahrain's second largest community, lies just northeast; the two cities are linked by a causeway 1.5 miles (2.5 km) long. Pop. (1999 est.) 162,000.

Mananjary, town, eastern Madagascar. It lies at the mouth of the Mananjary River. A port on the Indian Ocean and the Pangalanes Canal, it handles coastal shipments of coffee, vanilla, cacao, olives, and rice. It is at the end of a highway from Fianarantsoa (85 miles [137 km] northwest). Pop. (1998 est.) 19,474.

Manannán mac Lir (Celtic: "Manannán, Son of the Sea"), Irish sea god from whom the name of the Isle of Man allegedly derived. Manannán traditionally ruled an island paradise, protected sailors, and provided abundant crops. He gave immortality to the gods through his swine, which returned to life when killed; those who ate of the swine never died. He wore impenetrable armour and, carrying an invincible sword, rode over the waves in a splendid chariot. He and his Welsh equivalent, Manawydan, brother of the god Brân, apparently derived from an early Celtic deity.

Manapouri, Lake, lake, southwestern South Island, New Zealand, the deepest lake in the country. It is one of the Southern Lakes, found in the highland section of Fiordland National Park, which were formed by the glacial deepening of an existing stream valley accompanied by damming of the valley with a moraine (glacial debris). Manapouri derives its name from a Maori word meaning "lake of the sorrowing heart," with reference to a legend that its waters are the tears of dying sisters. It has a surface area of 55 square miles (142 square km) and a shoreline of 85 miles (137 km) extending into South, West, North, and Hope arms. From its surface, 608 feet (185 m) above sea level, the lake reaches to a depth of 1,455 feet (444 m). It drains a basin of 1,785 square miles (4,623 square km).

The lake empties into the Waiau River at

the town of Manapouri, a tourist centre and one of the few permanently inhabited places in the region. The Manapouri Lake Control Dam, which was completed in 1975, regulates the lake's water levels for hydroelectric power: a generating plant that was built on the shore, 700 feet (213 m) below ground, uses the lake's water discharged into the Tasman Sea via a tunnel.

Manās Wild Life Sanctuary, also called KĀMRŪP SANCTUARY, wildlife sanctuary in western Assam state, eastern India. It is situated at the foot of the Himalayas on the eastern bank of the Manās River, 92 miles (153 km) west of Gauhāti town. Established in 1928, it has an area of 151 square miles (391 square km) and lies in a dense, mixed semievergreen, evergreen, and wet deciduous forest region. The southern part of the preserve is grassland. Wildlife includes the great Indian rhinoceros, elephant, bison, deer, tiger, golden langur, black bear, and wild pig.

Manasā, folk goddess of snakes, worshiped mainly in Bengal and other parts of northeastern India, chiefly for the prevention and cure of snakebite and also for fertility and general prosperity. As the protector of children, she is often identified with the goddess Ṣaṣṭhī ("the Sixth," worshiped on the sixth day after birth). The antiquity of the goddess is a matter of conjecture. The written texts that contain her myth, the *Manasā-maṅgal*s, date from the 16th–17th century but are probably based on an earlier oral tradition. She is also celebrated in a variety of folk entertainment in the villages. Manasā is apparently a local goddess who was incorporated into the classical Hindu pantheon. She may be related to the *nāga*s, a legendary half-human, half-serpent race in India.

Mānasarowar (China): *see* Mapam Lake.

Manāslu I, also called KUTANG I, one of the world's highest mountains (26,781 feet [8,163 m]); it lies in the Himalayas of north Nepal, 38 miles (61 km) north of the town of Gurkha. The summit of this snow- and glacier-covered peak was first reached on May 9 and 11, 1956, by two separate Japanese parties.

Manassas, residential city, seat (1892) of Prince William county, northeastern Virginia,

Stonewall Jackson Monument, Manassas National Battlefield Park, Virginia
Milt and Joan Mann from CameraMann

U.S. It is situated near Bull Run, 30 miles (48 km) southwest of Washington, D.C. Originally known as Manassas Gap Junction and then Manassas Junction, the town was established in 1853, when the Manassas Gap and Orange and Alexandria railroads were joined, and was incorporated in 1873. During the American Civil War the junction afforded a direct connection between the Shenandoah Valley and the Washington-Richmond Railroad. In the Civil War, Confederate forces won the nearby battles of Bull Run, or First and Second Manassas (July 1861 and August 1862). The town was the trade centre for an agricultural area until after 1950, when transportation improvements resulted in an influx of residents commuting to Washington, D.C., as well as to the Quantico Marine Corps Reservation and other government installations. Inc. 1975. Pop. (1990) 27,957.

Manassas, battles of (American Civil War): *see* Bull Run, battles of.

Manasseh, one of the 12 tribes of Israel that in biblical times comprised the people of Israel. The tribe was named after a younger son of Joseph, himself a son of Jacob.

After the Exodus from Egypt and the death of Moses, the Israelites entered the Promised Land under the leadership of Joshua, who assigned a territory to each of the 12 tribes. The tribe of Manasseh settled in central Palestine—some to the east, some to the west of the Jordan River. When the independent kingdom of Israel, established by the 10 northern tribes after the death of King Solomon (10th century BC), was conquered by the Assyrians in the late 8th century BC, many Israelites were carried off into slavery. In time the tribe of Manasseh was assimilated by other peoples and thus became known in legend as one of the Ten Lost Tribes of Israel. Among the most illustrious members of the tribe of Manasseh was Gideon, a fearless warrior who served as judge for 40 years.

Manasseh, Prayer of, apocryphal work (noncanonical for Jews and Protestants), one of a collection of songs appended to the Old Testament book of Psalms in several manuscripts of the Septuagint (the Greek version of the Hebrew Bible). The Prayer of Manasseh, best known of the collection, is a penitential prayer written as an extension of 2 Chronicles 33:11–13, wherein Manasseh, successor to Hezekiah as king of Judah in the 7th century BC, repents his idolatrous worship of gods other than Yahweh.

Manasseh ben Israel, Manasseh also spelled MENASSEH, original name MANOEL DIAS SOEIRO (b. 1604, Lisbon? [Port.]—d. Nov. 20, 1657, Middelburg, Neth.), major Hebraic scholar of the Jewish community of Amsterdam and the founder of the modern Jewish community in England.

Manasseh was born into a family of Marranos (Jews of Spain and Portugal who publicly accepted Christianity but privately practiced Judaism). After his father appeared as a penitent in an auto da fé, the family escaped to Amsterdam, where Jewish settlement was officially authorized. Manasseh, a brilliant theological student, became the rabbi of a Portuguese Jewish congregation in Amsterdam in 1622. He founded that city's first Hebrew printing press in 1626, publishing his works in Hebrew, Latin, Spanish, and Portuguese.

Among his writings, *Conciliador,* 3 vol. (1632–51), was an attempt to reconcile discordant passages in the Bible; it established his reputation as a scholar in the Jewish and Christian communities. Manasseh maintained friendships with Hugo Grotius and Rembrandt, corresponded with Queen Christina of Sweden, and was an early teacher of Benedict de Spinoza.

Manasseh believed that the messiah would return to lead the Jews to the Holy Land only after their dispersal throughout the world was achieved. He considered immigrating to Brazil in 1640 and reported the alleged discovery in South America of the Ten Lost Tribes of Israel in *Esperança de Israel* ("Hope of Israel"). To support the settlement of Jews in Protestant England, where their presence had been officially banned since 1290, he dedicated the Latin edition of this work (1650) to the English Parliament.

Manasseh continued to plead for the formal recognition of Jewish settlement in England, and he appeared before Oliver Cromwell in London in 1655 to argue his cause. While in England he wrote *Vindiciae Judaeorum* (1656; "Vindication of the Jews") in answer to contemporary attacks on Jews, including William Prynne's *Short Demurrer*. He returned to Holland in 1657, believing his mission to have been unsuccessful. His efforts, however, initiated the unofficial English acceptance of Jewish settlement and led to the granting of an official charter of protection to the Jews of England in 1664, after Manasseh's death.

Manasses, Constantine (d. 1187), Byzantine chronicler, metropolitan of Naupactus, and the author of a verse chronicle (*Synopsis historike*) from the Creation to 1081. Written at the request of Emperor Manuel I's sister-in-law, Irene, the poem is in the so-called political (*i.e.,* 15-syllable) metre. His romance on Aristander and Calithea, also in "political" verse, survives in fragments only. He wrote a variety of other poems, as well as descriptive pieces in prose (some on works of art), and a number of orations, including an address to Manuel I and a funeral eulogy of Nicephorus Comnenus. Much of his work is unedited.

manatee (genus *Trichechus*), any of the three species of large aquatic mammals that constitute the family Trichechidae (order Sirenia). The manatee has a stout, tapered body ending

(Left) Juvenile and (right) adult female manatee (*Trichechus manatus*)
Jeff Foott

in a rounded flipper; the forelimbs are flippers close to the head; there are no hind limbs. The head is rather small, with a square, bristly snout. Adults range in length from 2.5 to 4.5 m (8 to 15 feet) and may reach nearly 700 kg (1,500 pounds) in weight.

Manatees are slow-moving creatures that feed on aquatic vegetation in shallow coastal waters, estuaries, and slow-flowing rivers. They live singly or in small family groups, sometimes forming herds of 15 to 20 individuals. Members of a group frequently communicate by muzzle-to-muzzle contact and, when alarmed, by chirplike squeaking. The sense of sight is very poorly developed.

All three species are declining in population. The Caribbean manatee (*T. manatus*) is found in Florida and sparsely along the Atlantic coast of the southeastern United States and the Gulf and Caribbean coasts to northern South America. The Amazonian manatee (*T. inunguis*), which inhabits rivers of the Amazon and Orinoco drainages, is listed in the *Red Data Book* as an endangered species. The West African manatee (*T. senegalensis*) is found in rivers in tropical West Africa.

Adult manatees have no natural enemies but in some areas are heavily hunted for meat, hides, and oil. Where boat traffic is heavy, manatees are often injured or killed by boat propellers. They are often protected by law because of their usefulness in keeping waterways clear of aquatic vegetation. The manatee or its relative, the dugong, may have given rise to the folklore of mermaids.

Manaus, city and river port, capital of Amazonas *estado* ("state"), northwestern Brazil. It lies along the north bank of the Negro River, 11 miles (18 km) above that river's influx into the Amazon River. Manaus is situated in the heart of the Amazon rainforest, 900 miles (1,450 km) inland from the Atlantic coast. The city, on a terrace overlooking the river, is traversed by several side channels called *igarapés* ("canoe paths") that are spanned by bridges and divide it into compartments.

The first European settlement on the site was a small fort (São José do Rio Negrinho) built in 1669 by Captain Francisco da Motta Falcão. The mission and village that later grew up were called Villa da Barra, or Barra do Rio Negro (*barra* referring to the sandbar at the mouth of the Negro). The town succeeded Barcelos in 1809 as capital of the Rio Negro captaincy general and in 1850 became the capital of Amazonas province (later state). Its name was then changed to Manáos (after an Indian river tribe); since 1939 it has been spelled Manaus. From 1890 to 1920 a regional economic boom based on the production of natural rubber from the tree *Hevea brasiliensis* brought prosperity to the city. Manaus' majestic buildings and homes, including the cathedral and ornate opera house (Teatro Amazonas, constructed in 1896 and renovated 1987–90), and the creation of port commerce date from that period. The city was made an episcopal see in 1892. In 1902 a British corporation began improvements to the port facilities, including a stone quay, storehouses, and floating wharves to allow for the annual rise and fall (up to 40 feet [12 m]) of the river.

Manaus is now a major inland port reached by oceangoing vessels from the Atlantic and is the chief collecting and distribution centre for the riverine areas of the entire upper Amazon basin. The port's principal exports include electrical equipment, petroleum, chemicals, rubber, Brazil nuts, and a host of minor forest products. In the late 1970s the Brazilian government and private companies began extensive deforestation to develop the mineral and agricultural wealth of the surrounding forested region. The government also installed a fishing terminal in Manaus. Manaus' industries include brewing, shipbuilding, soap manufacturing, the production of chemicals, the manufacture of electronics equipment, and petroleum refining. The scales of the piraracu (*Arapaima gigas*), a large South American fish, are exported for use as nail files. Tourism has become especially important since 1967, when the city was declared a duty-free zone.

Manaus has botanical and zoological gardens, and there is a natural jungle park on its outskirts. It is the seat of the National Research Institute for Amazonia (founded 1954), the University of the Amazon (1962), the Geographic and Historical Institute of the Amazon (1917), and a Salesian school for orphans. The city has an international airport. Pop. (1996) 1,150,193.

Teatro Amazonas, Manaus, Braz.
Art Resource

Manawatu River, river, in south-central North Island, New Zealand, rising on the east slopes of the Ruahine Range. The river, 113 miles (182 km) long, flows west and southwest for 30 miles (48 km) to Woodville and turns sharply northwest to pass between the Ruahine and Tararua ranges through the 4-mile- (6.4-kilometre-) long Manawatu Gorge. Emerging from the gorge at Ashhurst, the river runs southwest past Palmerston North, entering South Taranaki Bight of the Tasman Sea at Manawatu Heads, 60 miles (97 km) northeast of Wellington. The river's principal tributaries are the Mangatainoka, Tiraumea, Mangahao, Pohangina, and Oroua.

The Manawatu drains a basin 2,296 square miles (5,947 square km) in area. Periodic floods in its basin are contained by control works. In its lower reaches, the river crosses the wide Manawatu coastal plain, where it is deeply set between terraces. Four miles from the sea, the Manawatu becomes tidal.

Manawatu-Wanganui, local government region, southern North Island, New Zealand. It includes a major portion of one of the largest plains in the North Island and encompasses the Wanganui River valley. The region rises northward to the Kaimanawa Mountains and stretches along the Tasman Sea to include the Rangitikei River (noted for its steep-walled gorge) and the Manawatu River. The upper Wanganui River valley, which was an early centre of Maori settlement, is a national park noted for its scenic beauty. The region also extends the width of North Island to include the southern part of the inland Ruahine Range of mountains and a portion of the island's Pacific coast, south of Cape Turnagain.

Dairying is carried out on the western coastal plains, and the region's northeastern downlands are used for grazing sheep. Palmerston North, first settled in 1866, overlooks the Manawatu River. The port city of Wanganui lies northwest of Palmerston North. Pop. (1998) 231,700.

Mance, Sir Henry Christopher (b. 1840, London, Eng.—d. April 21, 1926, Oxford, Oxfordshire), British scientist and engineer who invented the heliograph, a signaling device that employs two mirrors to gather sunlight and send it to a prearranged spot as a coded series of short and long flashes.

Mance joined the Persian Gulf Telegraph Department of the government of India in 1863 and helped lay the first submarine telegraph cables in the Persian Gulf. He also invented the Mance method of detecting and localizing defects in submarine cables.

After his heliograph was successfully used in the second Anglo-Afghan War (1878–80), it was adopted by the British army in India and by the U.S. Army in campaigns against American Indians. Mance was knighted in 1885.

Manche, *département,* Basse-Normandie *région,* northwestern France, with a 200-mile (320-kilometre) coastline on the English Channel (French: La Manche) embracing the Cotentin peninsula. Its capital is Saint-Lô (*q.v.*).

The Manche area comprises several districts that were part of the historical province of Normandy (*q.v.*). Its west coast, facing the Channel Islands, stretches southward from the Cape of La Hague to the area near Avranches and Mont-Saint-Michel, where it turns westward. The 40-mile (64-kilometre) coast east from the Cape of La Hague to Point Barfleur contains the seaport and harbour of Cherbourg, the largest town in Manche. The east coast stretches down to Utah Beach, scene of one of the American landings in the Normandy Invasion during World War II, and to the tidal flat of Grand Veys Bay at the base of the peninsula.

The land is marshy and low-lying between the Cotentin peninsula and the rest of the *département,* which contains the hilly Bocage Normand farmland. Trees are ubiquitous in the bocage country, which consists of a patchwork of small fields bounded by hedges. The forested southeast around Mortain is especially picturesque. Some of the finest coastal scenery lies around the Cape of La Hague. Saint-Vaast-la-Hougue is noted for its oyster beds. Coutances, southwest of Saint-Lô, was seriously damaged in June 1944, but its fine Gothic cathedral was restored. Just inland from the coast north of Coutances stands the abbey church of Lessay, an outstanding example of Romanesque architecture, which was similarly damaged but was later restored. Mont-Saint-Michel is a picturesque Gothic abbey on a rocky islet attached to the shore by a long causeway. On the west coast, Granville, overlooked by its fortified old town on a rocky promontory, is a seaside resort. West of Cherbourg, at La Hague, was France's first uranium waste treatment plant.

The predominantly maritime climate is mild, damp, and regular, with 150 to 175 days of rain a year. The *département* is almost entirely devoted to agriculture, particularly cattle raising, dairy farming, and apple growing. Industry (metalworks, textile production, the reprocessing of nuclear waste, and the building of nuclear-powered submarines) is concentrated chiefly in the Cherbourg region. The *département* has four *arrondissements:* Avranches, Cherbourg, Coutances, and Saint-Lô. Area 2,293 square miles (5,938 square km). Pop. (1999) 481,471.

Manchester, city and metropolitan borough in the metropolitan county of Greater Manchester, northwestern England. Most of the city, including the historic core, is in the historic county of Lancashire, but it includes an area south of the River Mersey in the historic county of Cheshire. Manchester is the nucleus of the largest metropolitan area in the north of England, and it remains an important regional city, but it has lost the extraordinary vitality and unique influence that put it at the forefront of the Industrial Revolution.

A brief treatment of Manchester follows. For full treatment, *see* MACROPAEDIA: Manchester.

Manchester lies 180 miles (290 km) northwest of London and 35 miles (56 km) east of Liverpool. It stands at the junction of the Rivers Irwell, Irk, and Medlock and is separated from the adjacent city of Salford by the Irwell. The Manchester Ship Canal brings Mersey river traffic to the metropolitan area from the river's mouth to the west.

Manchester is the nucleus of Greater Manchester, comprising 10 metropolitan boroughs. Two large boroughs, Salford and Trafford, adjoin Manchester on the west and southwest; together the three form the chief concentration of commercial employment. The most important industrial zone bisects the metropolitan county from east to west.

There has long been a contrast between the economies of the core city and the textile towns that form the northern and eastern margins of the urban cluster. The core city has had a more diverse and stable economy, with more varied manufacturing (including printing and the production of engineering and electrical products, chemicals, and clothing), as well as a broad range of service activities. Manchester is a regional banking and financial centre housing the Northern Stock Exchange, the Cooperative Wholesale Society, and a branch of the Bank of England.

The University of Manchester (founded as

Owens College in 1851) has prospered and grown to become one of the more prominent institutions of higher education in Britain. The university's faculty of technology has become autonomous as the University of Manchester Institute of Science and Technology (1956). Manchester Metropolitan University (founded in 1970; university status in 1992) and the University of Salford (founded in 1896 as the Royal Technical Institute) also are important centres of higher learning. Manchester's Hallé Orchestra has an international reputation.

In 1996 the Irish Republican Army exploded a bomb in the city, devastating Manchester's city centre. By the beginning of the 21st century, the area was rebuilt.

Local transportation is provided by bus and commuter rail services. Railway lines radiate in all directions. Changing maritime trade and increases in the size of commercial ships have led to a decline in use of the Manchester Ship Canal. Manchester's international airport is located 10 miles (16 km) south at Ringway. Area city, 45 square miles (116 square km). Pop. (1999 est.) city, 404,861.

Manchester, urban town (township), Hartford county, central Connecticut, U.S. It lies east of Hartford on the Hockanum River. The area was settled in 1672, when it was purchased from the Mohegan Indians by the Puritan clergyman Thomas Hooker and his company. Originally a part of Hartford and called the Five-Mile Tract, it was organized as an ecclesiastical society called Orford Parish in 1772. In 1823 it was incorporated as a town and named for Manchester, Eng. It had sawmills and paper mills before the American Revolution. Subsequently, the Pitkin Glass Works, cotton mills, and especially silk mills (established in 1838) became important to the town's economy, along with the manufacture of grandfather clocks, soap, farm implements, and carriages. The town's modern industrial development is greatly diversified and includes aerospace and defense industries. Manchester Community-Technical College was opened in 1963. Pop. (2000) 54,740.

Manchester, city, Hillsborough county, southern New Hampshire, U.S. It lies along the Amoskeag Falls (named for the Amoskeag Indians) of the Merrimack River, the 55-foot (17-metre) drop of which provides hydroelectric power. Manchester is the state's largest city and the centre of a metropolitan area that includes Goffstown, Bedford, Londonderry, and Hooksett.

Settled in 1722–23, it was known for its fisheries. First called Old Harry's Town, it became Tyngstown after 1735, when it was granted to Captain William Tyng's men by the Massachusetts Bay colony. In 1751 it was incorporated as the town of Derryfield. It developed after one of America's first textile mills was built there in 1805 by Benjamin Prichard. The community was apparently renamed Manchester (1810) at the suggestion of Samuel Blodget, who had seen the barge canals at Manchester, Eng., and who constructed (1794–1807) the first canal around the falls. That canal, together with the Middlesex Canal in Massachusetts, opened navigation to Boston. Until the late 1930s the city's economy depended mainly on the Amoskeag Manufacturing Company's cotton-milling operations. The decline of the textile industry spurred planned industrial rehabilitation. Financial services are now the city's main economic activity, though manufacturing is important. The city's institutions include St. Anselm College (founded 1889), Notre Dame College (1950), New Hampshire College (1932), the University of New Hampshire at Manchester, the Manchester Institute of Arts and Sciences, and the Currier Gallery of Art (1929). Inc. city, 1846. Pop. (2000) city, 107,006; Manchester PMSA, 198,378.

Manchester, Edward Montagu, 2nd earl of, VISCOUNT MANDEVILLE, BARON KIMBOLTON OF KIMBOLTON (b. 1602—d. May 7, 1671, Whitehall, London, Eng.), Parliamentary general in the English Civil Wars.

Son of the 1st earl, Henry Montagu, he was educated at Sidney Sussex College, Cambridge. He sat in Parliament from 1624 to 1626 and in the latter year was raised to the peerage as Baron Kimbolton, but he was known generally by his courtesy title of Viscount Mandeville. At the beginning of the Long Parliament he was a leader of those opposed to King Charles I in the upper house, his name being joined with those of the five members of the House of Commons whom the king charged with treason in 1642.

At the outbreak of the Civil Wars, having succeeded his father in the earldom in November 1642, Manchester commanded a regiment in the army of the earl of Essex. In August 1643 he was appointed major general of the Parliamentary forces in the eastern counties, with Oliver Cromwell as his second in command. He became a member of the Committee of Both Kingdoms in 1644 and was in supreme command when the Royalist Army was defeated at Marston Moor (July 2, 1644); but later that year he disagreed with Cromwell and strongly expressed his disapproval of continuing the war. Cromwell brought his shortcomings before Parliament, and early in 1645 Manchester resigned his command.

He took a leading part in the frequent negotiations for an arrangement with Charles I and, with William Lenthall, was custodian of the great seal (1647–48). He opposed the trial and execution of the king and retired from public life during the Commonwealth; but after the Restoration, which he actively assisted, he was honoured by Charles II. In 1667 he was made a general.

Manchester, Greater (England): *see* Greater Manchester.

Manchester Ship Canal, waterway opened in 1894 linking Eastham, Merseyside, Eng., to the city of Manchester. The canal made Manchester accessible to large oceangoing vessels. It is 36 miles (58 km) long, 45–80 feet (14–24 m) wide, and varies in depth from 28 to 30 feet (about 9 m); it has five locks.

Manchester terrier, breed of dog developed in England from the whippet, a racing dog, and the black-and-tan terrier, a valued ratter, to combine the gaming talents of each. In 1860 the breed was named after the city of Manchester, but it was often called the black-and-tan terrier until the 1920s. A sleek, short-haired dog, the Manchester has a long, narrow head, small bright eyes, and a glossy black coat with tan on the head, chest, and legs. There are two varieties, the standard and the toy. The standard stands 35.5 to 40.5 cm (14 to 16 inches), weighs 5 to 10 kg (11 to 22 pounds), and has erect or folded (button) ears. The toy stands about 15 to 18 cm, weighs 5 kg or less, and has erect ears.

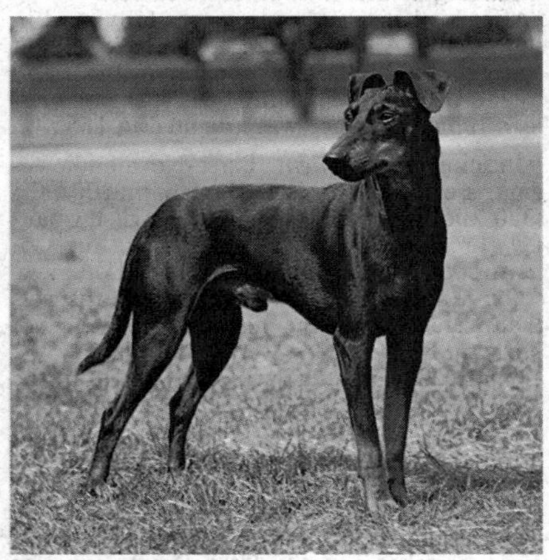

Manchester terrier
Sally Anne Thompson

manchineel, also called POISON GUAVA (*Hippomane mancinella*), tree of the genus *Hippomane,* of the spurge family (Euphorbiaceae), that is famous for its poisonous fruits. The manchineel is native mostly to sandy beaches of the Caribbean and Gulf of Mexico. Its attractive, single or paired yellow-to-reddish, sweet-scented, applelike fruits have poisoned Spanish conquistadores, shipwrecked sailors, and present-day tourists. The manchineel is a handsome, round-crowned tree that grows up to 12 m (40 feet) in height with a 60-centimetre- (2-foot-) thick trunk. It has long-stalked, lustrous, leathery, elliptic yellow-green leaves.

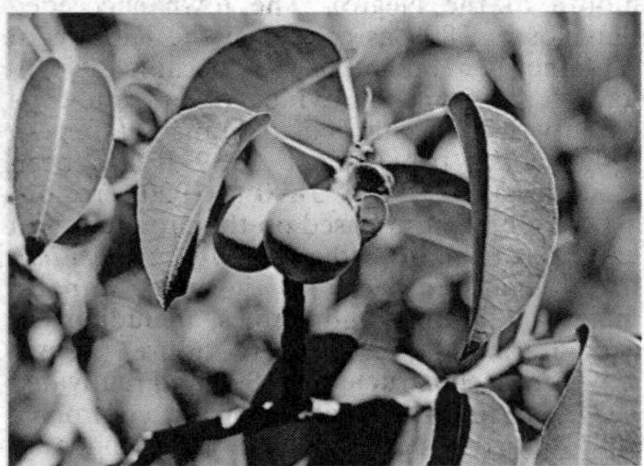

Manchineel (*Hippomane mancinella*)
W.H. Hodge

The manchineel is so poisonous that smoke from its burning wood irritates the eyes, and latex from its leaves and bark causes skin inflammation. Carib Indians used the sap to poison their arrows. The fruit contains a hard stone that encloses six to nine seeds. The tree's wood takes a good polish and is used for making furniture.

Manchu, also called MAN, people who lived for many centuries in Manchuria and adjacent areas and who in the 17th century conquered China and ruled that country for more than 250 years. The term Manchu dates from the 16th century, but it is certain that the Manchu are descended from a group of peoples collectively called the Tungus (the Even and Evenk are also descended from that group). The Manchu, under other names, had lived in northeastern Manchuria in prehistoric times. In early Chinese records they are known as the Tung-ihu, or "Eastern Barbarians"; in the 3rd century BC they were given the name of Su-shen, or I-lou; in the 10th century AD the Chinese historians speak of them as Nu-chi, or Ju-chi, an attempt to transliterate the native word *Juchen.* These Juchen established a kingdom of some extent and importance in Manchuria, and by AD 1115 their dynasty (called Chin in Chinese records) had secured control over northeastern China. The kingdom was annihilated by the Mongols in 1234, and the surviving Juchen were driven back into northeastern Manchuria. Three centuries later the descendants of these Juchen again came into prominence, but before long they dropped the name Juchen for Manchu. They regained control of Manchuria, moved south, and conquered Peking (1644); and by 1680 the Manchu had established complete control over all sections of China under the name of the Ch'ing dynasty (*q.v.*). The Manchu managed to maintain a brilliant and powerful government until about 1800, after which they rapidly lost energy and ability. It was not, however, until 1911/12 that the Ch'ing dynasty was overthrown.

Modern research shows that the Juchen-Manchu speak a language belonging to the sparse but geographically widespread Manchu-Tungus subfamily of the Altaic language family. At an early date, probably about the 1st century AD, various Manchu-Tungus-speaking tribes moved from their homeland in or near northeastern Manchuria to the north and west and eventually occupied most of Siberia between the Yenisey River and the Pacific Ocean. The Manchu became established in the south, while the Even, Evenk, and other peoples predominated in the north and west.

From the Chinese records it is evident that the I-lou, the Tungus ancestors of the Manchu, were essentially hunters, fishers, and food gatherers, though in later times they and their descendants, the Juchen and Manchu, developed a primitive form of agriculture and animal husbandry. The Juchen-Manchu were accustomed to braid their hair into a queue, or pigtail. When the Manchu conquered China they forced the Chinese to adopt this custom as a sign of loyalty to the new dynasty. Apart from this, the Manchu made no attempt to impose their manners and customs upon the Chinese. After the conquest of China, the greater part of the Manchu migrated there and kept their ancestral estates only as hunting lodges. Eventually these estates were broken up and sold to or occupied by Chinese (Han) immigrant farmers. By 1900 even in Manchuria the new Chinese settlers greatly outnumbered the Manchu.

The Manchu emperors—despite their splendid patronage of Chinese art, scholarship, and culture over the centuries—made strenuous efforts to prevent the Manchu from being absorbed by the Chinese. The Manchu were urged to retain their own language and to give their children a Manchu education. Attempts were made to prevent the intermarriage of Manchu and Chinese, so as to keep the Manchu strain ethnically "pure." Social intercourse between the two peoples was frowned upon. All these efforts proved fruitless. During the 19th century, as the dynasty decayed, efforts to preserve cultural and ethnic segregation gradually broke down. The Manchu began to adopt the Chinese customs and language and to intermarry with the Chinese. Few, if any, spoke the Manchu language by the end of the 20th century.

China's government, however, continues to identify the Manchu as a separate ethnic group (numbering about 10.5 million in the late 20th century), living in Liaoning, Kirin, Heilungkiang, and Hupeh provinces, in Peking, and in the Inner Mongolia Autonomous Region.

Manchu DYNASTY: *see* Ch'ing dynasty.

Manchu language, the most important of the Manchu-Tungus language group (a subfamily of the Altaic languages), formerly spoken by the Manchu people in Manchuria. Fewer than 100 Manchu are believed to still speak the Manchu language. However, there are several thousand speakers of Sibo (Pinyin: Xibe), a closely related language found in the I-li region of Sinkiang.

Vowel harmony, in which vowels are divided into two or three classes, with the restriction that suffixes added must use vowels of the same class, is generally typical of the Altaic languages but is not as strictly observed in Manchu as in, for example, Mongol. The Manchu verb, like that of Chinese, distinguishes neither person nor number. Manchu has no relative pronouns and expresses relative clauses by means of participles and gerunds. A peculiarity of Manchu is the indication of masculine and feminine, or strong and weak, in a certain group of words by the alternation of the vowels *a* and *e;* thus, *ama* 'father' becomes *eme* 'mother.' Manchu has been a written language since the 17th century, using a script borrowed from the Uighur alphabet.

Manchu-Tungus languages, also called TUNGUSIC LANGUAGES, the smallest of three subfamilies of the Altaic language family. The Manchu-Tungus languages are a group of 10 to 17 languages spoken by fewer than 70,000 people scattered across a vast region that stretches from northern China across Mongolia to the northern boundary of Russia. Apart from the moribund Manchu and the now-extinct Juchen (Jurchen) languages, these languages have not been written.

The best-known of the Manchu-Tungus languages is Manchu, which is now said to be spoken by fewer than 100 elderly individuals. Other languages include Sibo (Pinyin: Xibe) of China, Nanai (formerly called Gold and known in China as Ho-chen [Pinyin: Hezhe]), Oroch, Orok, Udihe, Evenk (Evenki), Even, Negidal, and Orochon (Pinyin: Oroqen).

Manchuria, also called NORTHEAST, Wade-Giles TUNG-PEI, Pinyin DONGBEI, historical region of northeastern China. Strictly speaking, it consists of the modern provinces (*sheng*) of Liaoning (south), Kirin (central), and Heilungkiang (north); often, however, the northeastern portion of the Inner Mongolia Autonomous Region also is included. Manchuria is bounded by Russia (northwest, north, and east), North Korea (south), and the province of Hopeh (southwest). The Chinese call Manchuria the Northeast, or the Northeast Provinces.

Manchuria to about 1900. Prior to the 17th century, the history of Manchuria was shaped by three converging ethnic groups: the Chinese, the people collectively known as the Tungus, and the Mongols and Proto-Mongols. The Tungus (from which several groups emerged) were forest and plain dwellers who had a mixed economy of primitive agriculture, fishing, hunting, and livestock breeding. Those in Manchuria were known in various historical periods by such names as Su-shen, I-lou, Fu-yu, Mo-ho, Juchen, and, finally, Manchu. The Mongols and Proto-Mongols were nomadic pastoralists who occupied the grasslands of the eastern rim of the Mongolian Plateau and the eastern slope of the Greater Khingan Range. They were known by such names as Hsien-pei, Wu-huan, Shih-wei, Khitan, and Mongol. The agricultural Chinese migrated from the north of China to cultivate the soil of the rich Liao Plain in south Manchuria. The successive hegemonies and kingdoms in Manchuria resulted from violent clashes among these ethnic groups.

Prehistoric Manchuria was the eastern terminus of a natural highway for nomadic peoples who moved across the great Eurasian plain from the Volga River to the Korean peninsula. As early as 1000 BC, certain Manchurian tribes are mentioned in Chinese sources. The earliest settlement of Chinese colonies in southern Manchuria began about the 3rd century BC. Chinese immigration into southern Manchuria accelerated during the following centuries: in the Han dynasty (206 BC–AD 220) some Manchurian lands were overrun by the Han, who organized these conquered territories into military commanderies. During the chaotic period following the collapse of the Han Empire, China was able to maintain only a loose hegemony over Manchuria.

Under the Sui (581–618) and T'ang (618–907) dynasties, China was able to reassert only a limited control over south Manchuria. In the late 7th century Manchuria's pastoral Tungus peoples asserted their independence, founding in 698 the Chen kingdom, which became the P'o-hai kingdom in 712. Centred in the modern province of Kirin, P'o-hai, at its height, covered nearly the whole of Manchuria and northern Korea. With the collapse of the T'ang dynasty in 907, the Mongol subgroup known as the Khitan gradually gained ascendancy in Manchuria and began expanding south against China and west against the Turkic nations. In 926 the Khitan forces overthrew P'o-hai. At the height of its power, the Khitan empire under its reigning Liao dynasty occupied practically the whole of Manchuria, part of northern Korea, part of North China, and the greater part of the Mongolian Plateau.

In the late 11th century there ensued a marked decline in the administrative efficiency and military prowess of the Khitan empire. The non-Khitan subjects staged frequent rebellions against their overlord. Of particular importance among these rebels were the Juchen tribes, a group of Tungus peoples who lived beyond the Liao frontier but were in a tributary relationship to the Liao court.

In 1115 A-ku-ta, the paramount chief of the Juchen, signalized the drastic decline of Khitan power by proclaiming the establishment of the Chin kingdom. An alliance between the Juchen Chin kingdom and the Chinese Sung dynasty succeeded in destroying the Liao empire in 1125. After the destruction of their common enemy, the Chin turned against the Sung. In 1127 the Juchen sacked the Sung capital, and the Sung court retreated to the south, where it existed as the Southern Sung dynasty. The Juchen decided to incorporate the occupied Sung territory into their own domain, and in 1214 their capital was moved from Manchuria to Yen-ching (modern Peking). By then, however, the formidable Chin military machine had become moribund and was an easy prey to the Mongols, who rose to power in the Mongolian Plateau in the 12th century.

In 1211 the Mongols invaded Chin under the leadership of the great Genghis Khan, and by 1234 Chin had succumbed to the combined pressure of the Mongols and the Sung Chinese. Occupying the whole of Manchuria, the Mongols made it one province, the Liaoyang. In 1280 the Mongols completed the conquest of China, having already established the Yüan dynasty. Eventually, however, the Mongols' harsh rule precipitated a series of rebellions among the Chinese, who overthrew the dynasty in 1368. The victorious Chinese established a native dynasty (the Ming), pursued the Mongols into the steppes, and reinstituted Chinese rule over Liaotung.

During the 15th and 16th centuries, the Mongols regained their strength and began pressing upon the Chinese frontier. As a result, the Ming position in Manchuria gradually deteriorated, and by the 17th century the Juchen were strong enough to challenge the Ming rule. It was the Chien-chou tribes, under the leadership of Nurhachi (1559–1626), who succeeded in forging a new and greater Juchen empire. Beginning in 1583, Nurhachi led a series of campaigns that ultimately brought all the Juchen tribes under his control. In 1616 he was proclaimed *han* ("emperor") by his subjects and allies. Nurhachi named his dynasty Chin in an attempt to rekindle the desire for imperial greatness among the Juchen people. After Nurhachi's death, his son and successor, Abahai, continued the task of territorial expansion. When Abahai died in 1643, Manchu arms had been carried east into Korea, north into the Amur and Ussuri river valleys, west to Inner Mongolia, and south to the Great Wall. Abahai adopted the name Manchu for his people and changed the dynastic designation from Chin to Ch'ing. In 1644 the Manchus, with the help of dissident Chinese, established themselves as the new rulers of China. Ch'ing dynastic rule of China lasted until 1911/12.

Although the Chinese had colonized the Liao Plain more than a thousand years before and had made it a centre of Chinese cultural influence, they had never been able to secure a foothold in central and north Manchuria, which remained predominantly a preserve of tribal groups. Paradoxically, it was during the period of Manchu ascendancy that the Chinese succeeded in penetrating the Sungari and Amur valleys. Until 1688 the Ch'ing government encouraged Chinese immigration to Liaotung in order to revive its economy. After 1688 Chinese immigration was restricted. But the Manchus soon had to modify their exclusion policy when they were forced to strengthen the thinly spread Manchu garrisons in the Amur Valley with Chinese recruits to counter the eastward march of Russian power in the area. Manchuria's natural resources attracted an unending stream of land-hungry peasants and other voluntary Chinese immigrants to Manchuria, despite the official ban. The flow of immigration became a flood tide in the 19th and 20th centuries as the Ch'ing government now actively sponsored planned colonization of virgin lands in Kirin and Heilungkiang. The growing Chinese presence helped the Manchurian economy develop from primitive self-sufficiency to an important centre of international trade. The great Manchuria frontier was thus inexorably Sinicized by Chinese colonists: the non-Manchu Tungus tribesmen of the Ussuri and Amur valleys declined in number year after year, and the Manchus soon merged imperceptibly into the Chinese population.

Manchuria since c. 1900. In the closing decades of the 19th century, foreign powers, particularly Russia and Japan, began to eye Manchuria as a fruitful field for imperialist expansion. The conflict between Russia and Japan for the control of Manchuria first raged over the possession of the Liaotung Peninsula. As the prize of its victory in the Sino-Japanese War of 1894–95, Japan demanded from China the cession of the Liaotung Peninsula. But Russia, backed by France and Germany, compelled Japan to abandon this claim. By means of intrigue and intimidation, Russia then (in 1898) acquired from China a 25-year lease of the Liaotung Peninsula and the right to build a connecting railway from the ports of Dairen and Port Arthur to the Chinese Eastern Railway. The clash of Russian and Japanese interests in Manchuria and Korea led to the outbreak of the Russo-Japanese War of 1904–05. After its defeat, Russia ceded to Japan all its interests in southern Manchuria.

After the Chinese Revolution of 1911, Manchuria came under the nominal control of the local warlord Chang Tso-lin, who was forced to grant the Japanese vast concessions in the region in return for their tacit military support. The notorious 21 Demands that Japan presented to China in 1915 compelled the Chinese to extend Japan's lease on the territory of Kwantung (at the tip of the Liaotung Peninsula) for 99 years and to grant Japanese far-reaching civil and commercial privileges in Manchuria. During the Chinese civil war Japan exercised a controlling influence in south Manchuria with the support of its Kwantung Army.

The overambitious Chang Tso-lin ran afoul of the Japanese and was assassinated in 1928. His more patriotic son and successor, Chang Hsüeh-liang, ignored Japanese warnings and decided to cast his lot with the Nationalist government in Nanking. On Sept. 18, 1931, Japanese military forces attacked the Chinese barracks in the city of Shenyang, and by the next day the Japanese had occupied the city. The Nanking government inexplicably directed the Manchurian leaders not to resist the Japanese, and this passive response enabled the Japanese to occupy all of Manchuria within five months.

On March 9, 1932, the Japanese created the puppet state of Manchukuo out of the three historic Manchurian provinces. The last Ch'ing (Manchu) emperor, P'u-i, was brought to Manchuria from his retirement in Tientsin and made "chief executive," and later emperor, of the new state. The Manchukuo government, though nominally in Chinese hands, was in fact rigidly controlled and supervised by the Japanese, who proceeded to transform Manchuria into an industrial and military base for Japan's expansion into Asia. The Japanese took over the direction, financing, and development of all the important Manchurian industries, with the fortunate result that by the end of World War II Manchuria was the most industrialized region in China. Manchuria was a land under Japanese colonial rule from 1932 to 1945. After the fall of Manchuria, many Manchurian soldiers, aided by armed civilians, cooperated with the Chinese Communist underground in organizing a vast anti-Japanese guerrilla movement.

At the Yalta Conference of February 1945, Soviet premier Joseph Stalin demanded the restoration of all former Russian rights and privileges in Manchuria as a price for Soviet entry into the Pacific war, an offer readily accepted by his fellow Allied heads of state. In May 1945, Soviet troops began to move from Europe to Asia. On August 8 the Soviet Union declared war on Japan and invaded Manchuria early on August 9. By August 15 the war was over, however. The next day, the Manchukuo emperor P'u-i was captured by the Russians. Having struck a good bargain for joining the war, the Soviets now plundered Manchuria as a conquered territory, systematically confiscating food, gold bullion, industrial machinery, and other stockpiles.

To the Nationalist (Kuomintang) government, the political damage of the Soviet occupation of Manchuria was even greater than the economic ravages. Under the protection of the Soviet Army, underground Chinese Communist guerrillas united with Communist troops from North China to form the United Democratic Army. Equipped with Japanese arms turned over to them by the Russians, the Communist force occupied much of Manchuria. Kuomintang progress in taking over the major Manchurian cities was exceedingly slow. It was June 1946 when the Kuomintang occupied Ch'ang-ch'un. By then the countryside was in the hands of the Communists. Nearly 500,000 of the elite Kuomintang troops found themselves surrounded by Communists in Ch'ang-ch'un, Shenyang, Chin-chou, and Ying-kou. By the end of 1948 the Kuomintang had suffered military defeat in Manchuria, an event that was the prelude to their loss of the entire Chinese mainland to the Communists in 1949.

The Communist rehabilitation of the Manchurian economy began with the land reform in 1946, and by the end of 1949 all the lands had been redistributed among the peasants. The power of the landlords was eliminated. Industrially, the initial task of the Communists was to reconstruct industrial plants so that Manchuria could serve as a major base for the further industrialization of China. During the First Five-Year Plan of 1953–57, Manchuria received the bulk of Chinese industrial investment. In August 1949 the Manchurian administration had been reorganized by the Communists as the Northeast People's Government. For the next several years it enjoyed considerable autonomy under its party head, the top-ranking Communist Kao Kang. Apparently conflicts developed between Kang and the central government, however, and in 1953 Peking abolished the Northeast People's Government, replacing it with a Manchuria formally divided into three provinces: Liaoning, Kirin, and Heilungkiang. Kao Kang was transferred to Peking and in 1955 was purged from the party. Since then Manchuria has been fully integrated into the political structure of China. Today it is still the industrial heartland of China.

Manchurian Incident (1931): *see* Mukden Incident.

Mancini, Pasquale Stanislao (b. March 17, 1817, Castel Baronia, Kingdom of the Two Sicilies—d. Dec. 26, 1888, Rome), leader of the Risorgimento in the Kingdom of the Two Sicilies, who played a prominent role in the government of united Italy.

Pasquale Stanislao Mancini
By courtesy of Camera dei Deputati, Rome

As a deputy in the Neapolitan parliament of 1848–49 and as a journalist and lawyer, Mancini fought for democracy and constitutionalism until forced into exile by the reactionary Bourbon government. Accepting a professorship at the University of Turin, he continued to be an active propagandist for national unity; after election to the parliament of Piedmont–Sardinia in 1860, he was sent (1861) to join the council presiding over the territory of his former homeland in the south, newly conquered by the Italian patriot Giuseppe Garibaldi. There he suppressed the religious orders, renounced the concordat with the papacy, and proclaimed the state's right to church property.

Returning to Turin, he sat with the centre in the first parliament of united Italy and served briefly in the cabinet. In 1865 he won a great personal triumph in convincing parliament to put substantial limitations on capital punishment. He served as minister of justice (1876–78) and as acting minister of public worship in 1878, when he gave the assurances necessary for a conclave of cardinals to elect a pope for the first time since Rome became a part of a united Italy (1871). He became minister of foreign affairs (1881) under Agostino Depretis. In an effort to gain support for Italian colonial expansion in Africa, he pursued a policy of rapprochement with Austria, leading to Italy's joining the Triple Alliance with Austria Hungary and Germany in 1882. Public discontent with the lack of immediate gains from his policy led to his resignation in June 1885.

Mandaeanism (from Mandaean *mandayya*, "having knowledge"), ancient Middle Eastern religion still surviving in Iraq and Khuzistan (southwest Iran). The religion is usually treated as a Gnostic sect; it resembles Manichaeism in some respects. Whereas most scholars date the beginnings of Mandaeanism somewhere in the first three centuries AD, the matter of its origin is highly conjectural. Some scholars, emphasizing the Babylonian elements in Mandaean magical texts, use of the Iranian calendar, and the incorporation of several Iranian words into the Mandaic language, argue that Mandaeanism originated in the area of southwestern Mesopotamia in early Christian or even pre-Christian times. Others argue for a Syro-Palestinian origin, basing their case on the quasi-historical Mandaean document, the *Haran Gawaita,* which narrates the exodus from Palestine to Mesopotamia in the 1st century AD of a group called Nasoreans (the Mandaean priestly caste as opposed to Mandaiia, the laity). They also call attention to certain Mandaean affinities to Judaism: familiarity with Old Testament writings; parallels to Jewish ethics, particularly the high value placed on marriage and procreation; concern for cultic purity; and the use of Hebrew angelology.

Like other dualistic systems, Mandaeanism stresses salvation of the soul through esoteric knowledge (gnosis) of its divine origin. In its cosmological superstructure, evil Archons (rulers) obstruct the ascent of the soul through the heavenly spheres to reunion with the supreme deity. Unlike many Gnostic systems, however, Mandaeanism strongly supports marriage and forbids sexual license.

The Mandaeans also developed an elaborate cultic ritual, particularly for baptism, which was not characteristic of any other known Gnostic sect. The Mandaeans viewed Jesus as a false messiah but revered John the Baptist, who performed miracles of healing through baptism, which the Mandaeans viewed as a magical process giving immortality, purification, and physical health.

Among the more important extant Mandaean writings are: the *Ginza* (*Book of Adam*), a cosmological treatise; the *Book of John*, describing the activities of John the Baptist; the *Book of the Zodiac*, a collection of magical and astrological texts; and the *Baptism of Hibil Ziwa*, describing the purification of the heavenly saviour of the Mandaeans.

mandala, Sanskrit MAṆḌALA ("circle"), in Hindu and Buddhist Tantrism, a symbolic diagram used in the performance of sacred rites and as an instrument of meditation. The mandala is basically a representation of the universe, a consecrated area that serves as a receptacle for the gods and as a collection point of universal forces. Man (the microcosm), by mentally "entering" the mandala and "proceeding" toward its centre, is by analogy guided through the cosmic processes of disintegration and reintegration.

Mandala of the Vairocana Buddha, Tibetan *thang-ka* painting, 17th century; in the Newark Museum, New Jersey

By courtesy of the Newark Museum, New Jersey

In China, Japan, and Tibet mandalas are basically of two types, representing different aspects of the universe: the *garbha-dhātu* (Sanskrit: "womb world"; Japanese: *taizō-kai*), in which the movement is from the one to the many; and the *vajra-dhātu* (Sanskrit: "diamond [or thunderbolt] world"; Japanese *kongō-kai*), from the many into one. Mandalas may be painted on paper or cloth, drawn on a carefully prepared ground with white and coloured threads or with rice powders (as for Buddhist Tantric ceremonies of initiation), fashioned in bronze, or built in stone, as at Borobuḍur, in central Java. There the circumambulation of the stupa (a commemorative monument) is tantamount to the ritual approach to the centre.

The mandala of a Tibetan tanka (cloth scroll painting) characteristically consists of an outer enclosure around one or more concentric circles, which in turn surround a square transversed by lines from the centre to the four corners. In the centre and the middle of each triangle are five circles containing symbols or images of divinities, most commonly the five "self-born" buddhas. Of the borders surrounding the mandala, the first is a ring of fire, which both bars entry to the uninitiated and symbolizes the burning of ignorance; next comes a girdle of diamonds, which stands for illumination; then a circle of eight graveyards, symbolizing the eight aspects of individuating cognition; next a girdle of lotus leaves, signifying spiritual rebirth; and, finally, at the centre, the mandala itself, where the images are set.

Similar ritual drawings have been found in cultures other than Hindu and Buddhist—for example, in the sand paintings of the North American Indians. The Swiss psychologist Carl Jung published studies of mandala-like drawings executed by his patients. In his view, the spontaneous production of a mandala is a step in the individuation process—a central concept in Jung's psychological theory—and represents an attempt by the conscious self to integrate hitherto unconscious material.

Mandalay, city, on the Irrawaddy River, central Myanmar (Burma). As the nation's second largest city (after Yangôn [Rangoon]), lying at the center of the country, it is the focus of interior communications and trade routes by rail, road, air, and river steamer.

Mandalay was built mainly in 1857–59 by King Mindon to replace Amarapura as his capital. It was the last capital of the Myanmar kingdom and fell to British troops in November 1885. During World War II, the city was occupied by the Japanese and was almost completely destroyed, sustaining the heaviest damage during a 12-day siege in March 1945, when it was retaken by the British 14th Army commanded by General Sir William Slim.

Buddhists are a majority in Mandalay, which is said to represent "the indestructible heart of Myanmar." As an important Buddhist religious centre, it is the home of large numbers of monks (*hpongyi*). The core of the city includes the moated citadel of Fort Dufferin, the ruins of the royal palace (Nandaw), numerous temples and monasteries, and the old British Government House. Mandalay Hill, northeast of the cantonment near the river, is the location of relatively recent monasteries, pagodas, and monuments. At its foot are the 730 pagodas, or Kuthodaw ("Works of Royal Merit"), Buddhist scriptures that are recorded on 729 white marble tablets and are regarded by Myanmar Buddhists as orthodox texts. Authorized by King Mindon as a result of the Fifth Buddhist Council, the tablets are set up in a square, each being protected by a small pagodalike structure. The 730th pagoda is a conventional temple occupying the centre of the square. The Mahamuni, or Arakan, pagoda, south of the city, is often considered Mandalay's most famous. Its brass Buddha (12 feet [3.7 m] high), believed to be of great antiquity, is one of numerous spoils of war brought from the Arakan Coast in 1784 by King Bodawpaya. The city proper, west of the palace, is laid out in a gridiron pattern. Its famous Zegyo bazaar is the largest of many markets that attract artisans and farmers from throughout the country. The Shwe Kyimyint pagoda, built by King Minshinsaw in 1167, is among the many fine pagodas in that part of the city.

Industries include tea packing, silk weaving, brewing and distilling, jade cutting, brass and copper casting, and gold-leaf work. Matches, wood carvings, and goldware and silverware are also produced. Mandalay is linked by train and air south to Yangôn and north to Myitkyinā and to Lashio, where the Burma Road begins. The nearby towns of Ava, Amarapura, and Sagaing are suburbs of Mandalay.

The Arts and Science University, formerly affiliated with Yangôn University, attained independent status in 1958. Other educational facilities include a teacher-training college, agricultural, medical, and technical institutes, a technical high school, and a school of fine arts, music, and drama. The city also has a museum and a modern hospital. The country's only daily newspapers outside Yangôn are published there.

The surrounding area is wooded (bamboo) and well watered by the Myitnge and Magyi (Madaya) rivers. The Saygin Hills near Madaya yield alabaster, which is carved into Buddha images in Mandalay. The plains area is part of Myanmar's Dry Zone. There is considerable irrigation; the Mandalay Canal irrigates 90,000 acres (36,400 hectares). Mingun, just north of Mandalay, has one of the world's largest ringing bells, weighing about 70 tons. Pop. (1983 prelim.) 532,895.

Mandalgovĭ, also spelled MANDAL GOBI, town, central Mongolian People's Republic. The town is located on the transition zone of scattered bunch grass of the great Gobi (desert) about 186 miles (300 km) south of Ulaanbaatar, the national capital. The area's economy is dominated by animal husbandry,

Mandalay Hill rising behind the Kuthodaw, Mandalay, Myanmar

© Van Bucher/Photo Researchers

as the terrain and climate are too harsh for agriculture. Sheep, cattle, and goats survive on the scanty vegetation. Light industry came to Mandalgovĭ in the 1960s with a program for building and improvement of the town's facilities. The town contains a palace of culture and an agricultural college. Pop. (latest census) 10,400.

mandamus, writ of, originally a formal order issued by the English crown commanding an official to perform a specific act within the duty of his office (Latin *mandamus,* "we command"). It later became a judicial writ issuing from the Court of King's (Queen's) Bench, in the name of the sovereign, at the request of individual suitors whose interests were alleged to be adversely affected by the failure of an official to act as his duty required. It is not awarded as a matter of right but rather at the discretion of the court and is thus largely controlled by equitable principles. The writ is not ordinarily granted when an alternative remedy is available, and it is never granted when the official to whom it would be directed has legal discretion either to perform the act demanded or to abstain from doing so. In Anglo-American legal systems, mandamus is used by courts of superior jurisdiction to compel the performance of a specific act refused by a lower court, such as the hearing of a case falling within the latter's authority.

Mandan, North American Plains Indian people of Siouan linguistic stock who lived along the Missouri River between the Heart and the Little Missouri rivers. They were linguistically related to the Winnebago, and a vague tradition suggested that they had once lived farther east. Mandan culture was one of the richest of the Plains.

In the 19th century the Mandan lived in dome-shaped, earth-covered lodges clustered in stockaded villages; they planted corn (maize), beans, pumpkins, and sunflowers, hunted buffalo seasonally, and made pottery and baskets. They had elaborate ceremonies, among them the sun dance and the Okipa, four-day festivals requiring long preparation. There were many other ceremonies that were performed by smaller groups; the bear ceremony was connected with healing and with war power.

Mandan villages consisted of from 12 to 100 lodges; they had three chiefs: one for war, one for peace, and one a village leader. Their social organization included age-graded warrior societies in which membership was obtained by purchase. There were also social, shamanistic, and women's societies. Mandan artists painted on buffalo robes, depicting heroic deeds of the tribe or of individuals.

In 1750 there were nine large Mandan villages, but recurrent epidemics of smallpox and cholera reduced them to two by 1800. In 1837 another smallpox epidemic left only 100–150 survivors. Some of them accompanied the Hidatsa to Fort Berthold in 1845; others following later. In the late 20th century the total Mandan population reported on the Fort Berthold Reservation in North Dakota was about 350.

"Bird's Eye View, Mandan Village," detail of painting by George Catlin, 1832; in the National Museum of American Art, Washington, D.C.

National Museum of American Art (formerly National Collection of Fine Arts), Smithsonian Institution, Washington, D.C., gift of Mrs. Sarah Harrison

Mandan, city, seat of Morton county, south-west-central North Dakota, U.S. It lies across the Missouri River from the state capital, Bismarck.

The settlement was established in 1873 with the survey for the Northern Pacific Railway and was named for the local Indian tribe. The community developed as a service centre for ranching, dry farming, and dairying. It is known for its livestock auctions. Industries include oil refineries, creameries, and the manufacture of building materials. The Northern Great Plains Research Center, one of the nation's largest agricultural research facilities, is just south of the city. There are lignite deposits in the area. Fort Lincoln State Park, 5 miles (8 km) to the south, includes reconstructed blockhouses of Fort Lincoln, which was commanded by Lieutenant Colonel George A. Custer before his "last stand" at the Battle of the Little Bighorn (1876). Inc. 1881. Pop. (1990) 15,177.

Mandara Mountains, French MONTS MANDARA, volcanic range extending about 120 miles (193 km) along the northern part of the Nigeria-Cameroon border from the Benue River (south) to Mora, Cameroon (north). The mountains rise to more than 3,500 feet (1,100 m) above sea level. During the colonial period they provided the border between the British and French Cameroons. The region is densely populated. People of the Chad language group predominate, living in dispersed homesteads or villages of small, circular huts. Sorghum is the principal crop. The major towns are Mokolo and Maroua in Cameroon and Mubi in Nigeria.

mandarin, Chinese (Wade-Giles) KUAN, or (Pinyin) GUAN, in imperial China, a public official of any of nine grades or classes that were filled by individuals from the ranks of lesser officeholders who passed examinations in Chinese literary classics. (The word comes through the Portuguese *mandarim* from Malay *mantri,* a counselor or minister of state; the ultimate origin of the word is the Sanskrit root *man-,* meaning to "think.") *See* Chinese civil service.

Consult the INDEX *first*

Mandarin language, also called NORTHERN CHINESE, Chinese (Wade-Giles) KUAN-HUA, or (Pinyin) GUANHUA ("Officials Language"), the most widely spoken form of Chinese. Mandarin Chinese is spoken in all of China north of the Yangtze River and in much of the rest of the country and is the native language of two-thirds of the population.

Mandarin Chinese is often divided into four subgroups: Northern Mandarin, centring on Peking and spoken in northern China and Manchuria (Northeast Provinces); Northwestern Mandarin, extending northward from the city of Pao-chi and through most of northwestern China; Southwestern Mandarin, centring in the area around Chungking and spoken in Szechwan and adjoining parts of southwestern China; and Southern, or Lower Yangtze, Mandarin, in an area with Nanking as its centre.

Mandarin Chinese in the form spoken in and around Peking forms the basis for Modern Standard Chinese—*Kuo-yü* (*Guoyu*), "national language," or *P'u-t'ung-hua* (*Putonghua*), "common language." Modern Standard Chinese is also spoken officially on Taiwan.

Mandarin uses four tones—level, rising, falling, and high-rising—to distinguish words or syllables that have the same series of consonants and vowels but different meanings; both Mandarin and the standard language have few words ending with a consonant. Mandarin, like all other varieties of Chinese, has mostly monosyllabic words and word elements, and, because there are neither markers for inflection nor markers to indicate parts of speech, it has a fixed word order.

Mandarin porcelain, ware produced in China for export in the late 18th century. It is called Mandarin because of the groups of figures in mandarin dress that appear in the decorative panels—painted mainly in gold, red, and rose pink and framed in underglaze blue—that characterize the ware. After 1800,

Village in the Mandara Mountains, Cameroon

Naud/Afrique—FPG/EB Inc.

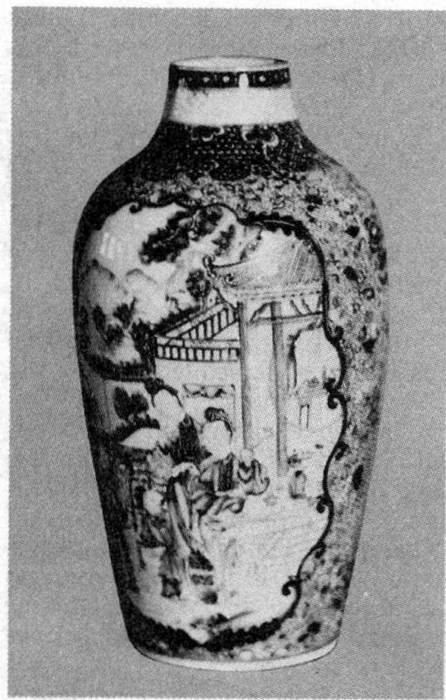

Mandarin porcelain vase, late 18th century, Ch'ing dynasty; in the Victoria and Albert Museum, London

By courtesy of the Victoria and Albert Museum, London

Mandarin porcelain was often copied by English potters.

mandate, an authorization granted by the League of Nations to a member nation to govern a former German or Turkish colony. The territory was called a mandated territory, or mandate.

Following the defeat of Germany and Ottoman Turkey in World War I, their Asian and African possessions, which were judged not yet ready to govern themselves, were distributed among the victorious Allied powers under the authority of Article 22 of the Covenant of the League of Nations (itself an Allied creation). The mandate system was a compromise between the Allies' wish to retain the former German and Turkish colonies and their pre-Armistice declaration (Nov. 5, 1918) that annexation of territory was not their aim in the war. The mandates were divided into three groups on the basis of their location and their level of political and economic development and were then assigned to individual Allied victors (mandatory powers, or mandatories).

Class A mandates consisted of the former Turkish provinces of Iraq, Syria, Lebanon, and Palestine. These territories were considered sufficiently advanced that their provisional independence was recognized, though they were still subject to Allied administrative control until they were fully able to stand alone. Iraq and Palestine (including modern Jordan and Israel) were assigned to Great Britain, while Turkish-ruled Syria and Lebanon went to France. All Class A mandates had reached full independence by 1949.

Class B mandates consisted of the former German-ruled African colonies of Tanganyika, parts of Togoland and the Cameroons, and Ruanda-Urundi. The Allied powers were directly responsible for the administration of these mandates but were subject to certain controls intended to protect the rights of the mandates' native peoples. Tanganyika (which is now part of Tanzania) was assigned to Britain, while most of the Cameroons and Togoland were assigned to France, and Ruanda-Urundi (now Rwanda and Burundi) went to Belgium.

Class C mandates consisted of various former German-held territories that mandatories subsequently administered as integral parts of their territory: South West Africa (now Namibia, assigned to South Africa), New Guinea (assigned to Australia), Western Samoa (New Zealand), the islands north of the Equator in the western Pacific (Japan), and Nauru (Australia, with Britain and New Zealand).

Theoretically, exercise of the mandates was supervised by the League's Permanent Mandates Commission, but the commission had no real way to enforce its will on any of the mandatory powers. The mandate system was replaced by the UN trusteeship system in 1946.

Mandaue, city, east-central Cebu island, Philippines. It lies along the coast of the Camotes Sea just northeast of the city of Cebu, which it serves as an industrial suburb. Mandaue guards the northern entrance to Cebu harbour opposite Mactan Island. It was founded by Jesuits in the 17th century. Mandaue has a brewery and a number of diversified manufacturing and processing industries in its industrial park, including sugar refining and food processing. Fishing is important to the economy, and there is a small boatbuilding industry as well. Inc. city, 1969. Pop. (1990) 180,000.

Mande, also called MALI, or MANDINGO, group of peoples of western Africa, whose various Mande languages form a branch of the Niger-Congo language family. The Mande are located primarily on the savanna plateau of the western Sudan, although small groups of Mande origin, whose members no longer exhibit Mande cultural traits, are found scattered elsewhere, as in the tropical rain forests of Sierra Leone, Liberia, and the Côte d'Ivoire. Some of the most typical Mande groups are the Bambara, Malinke, and Soninke (*qq.v.*).

The Mande peoples have been credited with the independent development of agriculture about 3000–4000 BC; and upon this agricultural base rested some of the earliest and most complex civilizations of western Africa, including the Soninke state of Ghana and the empire of Mali, which reached its height early in the 14th century.

Mande agriculture is based on shifting hoe cultivation. Staple crops are millet, sorghum, and rice; there are also a wide variety of other crops. Cattle are kept but are important mainly in terms of prestige and bride-price payments. Trade, both local and with distant Arab and other groups, has always been of great economic importance.

Descent, succession, and inheritance are patrilineal; marriage is polygynous, the incidence of polygyny varying considerably from group to group. The social structure, especially among Muslim groups, often exhibits a pronounced hierarchical ordering, from royalty and noble lineages to commoners, despised artisan castes, and, formerly, slaves.

Mande languages, group of Niger-Congo languages that are spoken in parts of Guinea, Mali, Sierra Leone, Liberia, Côte d'Ivoire, Burkina Faso, Ghana, and Nigeria. The most widely spoken of the Mande languages is Malinke (or Mandingo). Linguists often subdivide this language group into eastern and western subgroups; the important Mande languages (Malinke, Mende, Kpelle, and Vai) all belong to the western subgroup. The Mande languages are tonal languages (*i.e.*, they use pitch levels to differentiate words that are otherwise pronounced identically).

Mandeb, Strait of, Arabic BĀB EL-MANDEB, also spelled BĀB AL-MANDAB, strait between Arabia (northeast) and Africa (southwest) that connects the Red Sea (northwest) with the Gulf of Aden and the Indian Ocean (southeast). It is 20 miles (32 km) wide and is divided into two channels by Perim Island; the western channel is 16 miles (26 km) across, and the eastern is 2 miles (3 km) wide. With the building of the Suez Canal, the Strait of Mandeb assumed great strategic and economic importance, forming a portion of the link between the Mediterranean Sea and the Orient. The strait's Arabic name means "the gate of tears," so called from the dangers that formerly attended its navigation.

Mandel, Georges, original name LOUIS-GEORGES ROTHSCHILD (b. June 5, 1885, Chatou, France—d. July 7, 1944, Fontainebleau), French political leader noted for his hostility toward Nazi Germany.

Mandel, *c.* 1925

H. Roger-Viollet—Harlingue

A member of a prosperous Jewish family, though not related to the Rothschild banking dynasty, Mandel served on the personal staff of Premier Georges Clemenceau from 1906 to 1909 and again from 1917 to 1920. He also served as a deputy in the National Assembly from 1919 to 1924 and from 1928 to 1940. Mandel was a conservative and was strongly opposed to the policies of the left, but he was equally opposed to the pro-German policies of many conservatives between World Wars I and II. He served as minister of posts in four successive governments (1934–36) and as minister of colonies from April 1938 to May 1940, when Premier Paul Reynaud transferred him to the Ministry of the Interior. In May and June 1940 he supported Reynaud, who advocated continuing to fight the Germans from the French colonies in Africa.

Mandel was among the political leaders who vowed to refuse an armistice and, on June 21, 1940, sailed from Bordeaux to Africa aboard the *Massilia.* Arrested in Morocco, he was transported to France and imprisoned. Later he was delivered to the Germans in November 1942. After a stay at the concentration camps of Oranienburg and Buchenwald, he was sent back to Paris on July 4, 1944. Three days later he was shot on orders of Joseph Darnand, head of police of the French Vichy government.

Mandela, Nelson, in full NELSON ROLIHLAHLA MANDELA (b. July 18, 1918, Umtata, Cape of Good Hope, S.Af.), South African black nationalist and statesman whose long imprisonment (1962–90) and subsequent as-

Nelson Mandela, 1990

© Christopher Morris/Black Star

cension to the presidency (1994) symbolized the aspirations of South Africa's black majority. He led the country until 1999.

The son of Chief Henry Mandela of the Xhosa-speaking Tembu people, Nelson Mandela renounced his claim to the chieftainship to become a lawyer. He studied at the University College of Fort Hare and the University of Witwatersrand and in 1942 earned a law degree at the University of South Africa. Two years later he joined the African National Congress (ANC) (*q.v.*), a black-liberation group, and in 1949 became one of its leaders, helping to revitalize the organization and engaging in increasingly militant resistance against the government's apartheid (*q.v.*) policies. Mandela went on trial for treason in 1956-61 but was acquitted. During the extended court proceedings he divorced his first wife and married Nomzamo Winifred (Winnie Mandela); they divorced in 1996. After the massacre of unarmed Africans by police forces at Sharpeville in 1960 and the subsequent banning of the ANC, Mandela abandoned his nonviolent stance and began advocating acts of sabotage. In 1962 he was jailed and sentenced to five years in prison.

In 1963 the imprisoned Mandela and several other men were tried for sabotage, treason, and violent conspiracy in the celebrated Rivonia Trial, named after a fashionable suburb of Johannesburg where raiding police had discovered quantities of arms and equipment at the headquarters of the ANC's military wing, the underground Umkhonto We Sizwe ("Spear of the Nation"). Mandela had been a founder of the organization and admitted the truth of some of the charges that were made against him. On June 12, 1964, he was sentenced to life imprisonment.

From 1964 to 1982 Mandela was incarcerated at Robben Island Prison, off Cape Town. He was subsequently kept at the maximum-security Pollsmoor Prison until 1988, when he was hospitalized for tuberculosis. Mandela retained wide support among South Africa's black population, and his imprisonment became a cause célèbre among the regime's international opponents. The South African government under President F.W. de Klerk released Mandela from prison on Feb. 11, 1990. On March 2 Mandela was chosen deputy president of the ANC, and he became its president in July 1991. Mandela and de Klerk worked to end apartheid and bring about a peaceful transition to nonracial democracy in South Africa. In 1993 they were awarded the Nobel Prize for Peace for their efforts.

In April 1994 South Africa held its first all-race elections, which were won by Mandela and the ANC. As president, he established the Truth and Reconciliation Commission, which investigated human rights violations under apartheid, and introduced housing, education, and economic-development initiatives designed to improve the living standards of the country's black population. In 1996 he oversaw the enactment of a new democratic constitution. The following year Mandela resigned his post with the ANC and in 1999 did not seek a second term as South African president. After leaving office in June, he retired from active politics.

Mandela's writings and speeches were collected in *No Easy Walk to Freedom* (1965) and *I Am Prepared to Die,* 4th rev. ed. (1979). His autobiography, *Long Walk to Freedom,* was published in 1994.

BIBLIOGRAPHY. Mary Benson, *Nelson Mandela* (1986, reissued with additions, 1994); Fatima Meer, *Higher Than Hope* (1988, reprinted 1990).

Mandela, Winnie, original name NOMZAMO WINIFRED, original Xhosa name NKOSIKAZI NOBANDLE NOMZAMO MADIKIZELA (b. 1934/36?, Pondoland district, Transkei, S.Af.), South African social worker and black activist, the second wife of Nelson Mandela. The Mandelas separated in 1992 after her questionable behaviour and unrestrained militancy alienated fellow antiapartheid activists, including Nelson.

The daughter of a history teacher, Nomzamo Winifred attended high school and moved to Johannesburg in 1953 to study pediatric social work. She met Mandela in 1956, became his devoted coworker, and married him in 1958. After the start of her husband's long imprisonment (1962–90), Winnie Mandela was banned and for years underwent almost continual harassment by the South African government and its security forces; she spent 17 months in jail in 1969–70 and lived in internal exile from 1977 to 1985. During these years she did social and educational work and became a heroine of the antiapartheid movement. Her reputation was seriously marred in 1988–89, however, when she and her bodyguards were linked with the beating and kidnapping of four black youths, one of whom was murdered by her chief bodyguard.

After Nelson Mandela was released from prison in 1990, Winnie initially shared in his political activities and trips abroad. In May 1991 she was sentenced to six years in prison upon her conviction for the kidnapping, but the sentence was later reduced to a fine. She made a political comeback in 1993 with her election to the presidency of the African National Congress Women's League, and in 1994 she was appointed deputy minister of arts, culture, science and technology in South Africa's first multiracial government, which was headed by her husband. Winnie Mandela continued to provoke controversy by her attacks on the government and her strident appeals to radical young black followers, however, and in 1995 Nelson Mandela expelled her from his cabinet.

Mandelshtam, Osip Emilyevich, Mandelshtam also spelled MANDELSTAM (b. Jan. 3 [Jan. 15, New Style], 1891, Warsaw, Pol., Russian Empire [now in Poland]—d. Dec. 27, 1938?, Vtoraya Rechka, near Vladivostok, Russia, U.S.S.R. [now in Russia]), major Russian poet and literary critic. Most of his works went unpublished in the Soviet Union during the Stalin era (1929–53) and were almost unknown outside that country until the mid-1960s.

Mandelshtam grew up in St. Petersburg in a cultured Jewish household. After graduating from the elite Tenishev School in 1907, he studied at the University of St. Petersburg as well as in France at the Sorbonne and in Germany at the University of Heidelberg.

His first poems appeared in the avant-garde journal *Apollon* ("Apollo") in 1910. Together with Nikolay Gumilyov and Anna Akhmatova, Mandelshtam founded the Acmeist school of poetry, which rejected the mysticism and abstraction of Russian Symbolism and demanded clarity and compactness of form. Mandelshtam summed up his poetic credo in his manifesto *Utro Akmeizma* ("The Morning of Acmeism"). In 1913 his first slim volume of verse, *Kamen* ("Stone"), was published. During the Russian Civil War (1918–20), Mandelshtam spent time in the Crimea and Georgia. In 1922 he moved to Moscow, where his second volume of poetry, *Tristia,* appeared. He married Nadezhda Yakovlevna Khazina in 1922.

Mandelshtam's poetry, which was apolitical and intellectually demanding, distanced him from the official Soviet literary establishment. His poetry having been withdrawn from publication, he wrote children's tales and a collection of autobiographical stories, *Shum vremeni* (1925; "The Noise of Time"). A second edition of this work, augmented by the tale "Yegipetskaya marka" ("The Egyptian Stamp"), was published in 1928. That year, a volume of his collected poetry, *Stikhotvoreniya* ("Poems"), and a collection of literary criticism, *O poezii* ("On Poetry"), appeared. These were his last books published in the Soviet Union during his lifetime.

In May 1934 he was arrested for an epigram on Joseph Stalin he had written and read to a small circle of friends. In addition to describing Stalin's fingers as "worms" and his moustache as that of a cockroach, the draft that fell into the hands of the police called Stalin "the murderer and peasant slayer."

Shattered by a fierce interrogation, Mandelshtam was exiled with his wife to the provincial town of Cherdyn. After hospitalization and a suicide attempt, he won permission to move to Voronezh. Though suffering from periodic bouts of mental illness, he composed a long cycle of poems, the *Voronezhskiye tetradi* ("Voronezh Notebooks"), which contain some of his finest lyrics.

In May 1937, having served his sentence, Mandelshtam returned with his wife to Moscow. But the following year he was arrested during a stay at a rest home. In a letter to his wife that autumn, Mandelshtam reported that he was ill in a transit camp near Vladivostok. Nothing further was ever heard from him. Soviet authorities officially gave his death date as Dec. 27, 1938, although he was also reported by government sources to have died "at the beginning of 1939." It was primarily through the efforts of his widow, who died in 1980, that little of the poetry of Osip Mandelshtam was lost; she kept his works alive during the repression by memorizing them and by collecting copies. The two volumes of her memoirs, *Hope Against Hope* (1970) and *Hope Abandoned* (1974), were published in the West.

After Stalin's death the publication in Russian of Mandelshtam's works was resumed.

Mander, Carel van, Carel also spelled KAREL (b. May 1548, Meulebeke, Flanders, Spanish Netherlands [now in Belgium]—d. Sept. 2, 1606, Amsterdam [Neth.]), Dutch Mannerist painter, poet, and writer whose fame is principally based upon a biographical work on painters—*Het Schilder-boeck* (1604; "The Book of Painters")—that has become for the northern countries what Giorgio Vasari's *Lives of the Painters* became for Italy.

Mandeville, Bernard de (b. November 1670, Rotterdam, Neth.—d. Jan. 21, 1733, Hackney, London, Eng.), Dutch prose writer and philosopher who won European fame with *The Fable of the Bees.*

Mandeville graduated in medicine from the University of Leiden in March 1691 and started to practice but very soon went abroad. Arriving in England to learn the language, he "found the Country and the Manners of it agreeable" and settled in London. In 1699 he married an Englishwoman, with whom he had two children. His professional reputation in London was soon established, and he attracted the friendship and patronage of important persons.

Mandeville's first works in English were burlesque paraphrases from the 17th-century French poet Jean de La Fontaine and the 17th-century French writer Paul Scarron.

The 1714 edition of Mandeville's most important work, *The Fable of the Bees,* was subtitled *Private Vices, Publick Benefits* and consisted of a preface, the text of *The Grumbling Hive,* an "Enquiry into the Origin of Moral Virtue," and "Remarks" on the poem. The 1723 edition included an examination of "The Nature of Society" and provoked a long controversy. The 1729 edition remodeled the entire argument to suit Mandeville's philosophical commitment but nevertheless retained something of the original purpose of diverting readers.

Mandeville's argument in *The Fable,* a paradoxical defense of the usefulness of "vices," is based on his definition of all actions as equally vicious in that they are all motivated by self-interest. Yet while the motives must be vicious, the results of action are often socially beneficial, since they produce the wealth and comforts of civilization.

Mandeville, Edward Montagu, Viscount: *see* Manchester, Edward Montagu, 2nd Earl of.

Mandeville, Geoffrey de: *see* Essex, Geoffrey de Mandeville, 1st Earl of.

Mandeville, Sir John (fl. 14th century), purported author of a collection of travelers' tales from around the world, *The Voyage and Travels of Sir John Mandeville, Knight,* generally known as *The Travels of Sir John Mandeville*. The tales are selections from the narratives of genuine travelers, embellished with Mandeville's additions and described as his own adventures.

Sir John Mandeville, detail from a manuscript, early 15th century; in the British Library (MS. Add. 24,189)
Reproduced by permission of the British Library

The actual author of the tales remains as uncertain as the existence of the English knight Sir John Mandeville himself. The book originated in French about 1356–57 and was soon translated into many languages, an English version appearing about 1375. The narrator Mandeville identifies himself as a knight of St. Albans. Incapacitated by arthritic gout, he has undertaken to stave off boredom by writing of his travels, which began on Michaelmas Day (September 29) 1322, and from which he returned in 1356. The 14th-century chronicler Jean d'Outremeuse of Liège claimed that he knew the book's true author, a local physician named Jean de Bourgogne, and scholars afterward speculated that d'Outremeuse himself wrote the book. Modern historical research debunked the d'Outremeuse tradition but has yielded few more positive conclusions, and the actual author of the *Travels* remains unknown.

It is not certain whether the book's true author ever traveled at all, since he selected his materials almost entirely from the encyclopaedias and travel books available to him, including those by William of Boldensele and Friar Odoric of Pordenone. The author enriched these itineraries with accounts of the history, customs, religions, and legends of the regions visited, culled from his remarkably wide reading, transforming and enlivening the originals by his literary skill and genuine creative imagination. The lands that he describes include the realm of Prester John, the land of darkness, and the abode of the Ten Lost Tribes of Israel, all legendary. Although in his time "Mandeville" was famous as the greatest traveler of the Middle Ages, in the ensuing age of exploration he lost his reputation as a truthful narrator. His book, notwithstanding, has always been popular and remains extremely readable.

Mandhata (India): *see* Godarpura.

mandibulofacial dysostosis, also called TREACHER COLLINS SYNDROME, or FRANCHESCHETTI-KLEIN SYNDROME, a rare, genetic disorder, inherited as an autosomal-dominant trait and characterized by some or all of the following: underdevelopment of the cheek and jaw bones, widely separated eyes, malformation of the lower eyelid and lack of eyelashes, malformation of the ear auricle, lack of an external ear canal with resultant conductive deafness, and other, less common abnormalities. Respiratory problems may be present in the newborn. Intelligence is normal. Treatment includes correction of the deafness by use of a hearing aid or by surgical construction of an ear canal and, sometimes, plastic surgery to enlarge the jaw.

Mandingo (people): *see* Malinke; Mande.

Mandla, city, east-central Madhya Pradesh state, central India. It lies just north of the Narmada River. Formerly the capital of the Gaṛh-Mandla Goṇḍ kingdom, it was constituted a municipality in 1867. The city is a road junction and rail-spur terminus and is heavily engaged in agricultural trade. Sawmilling and the manufacture of hemp products and bell-metal vessels are also important. The city houses several colleges affiliated with the Dr. Harisingh Gour University in Saugar. Pop. (1991 prelim.) city, 38,390; metropolitan area, 47,601.

Mandogarh (India): *see* Māndu.

mandolin, also spelled MANDOLINE, small stringed musical instrument related to the lute. It evolved in the 18th century and was built in several varieties in different Italian towns, the Neapolitan mandolin becoming the representative type.

The instrument's form and proportions were strongly influenced by the maker Pasquale Vinaccia of Naples (1806–82). The mandolin has four pairs of steel strings tuned, by a machine head (as on a guitar), to violin pitch (g–d′–a′–e″). The pear-shaped body is deeply vaulted; the fingerboard, with 17 frets, is slightly raised. The strings are hitched to the instrument's end. At its widest part, where the bridge is set, the belly angles downward, increasing the pressure of the strings on the bridge to give a brilliant tone of great carrying power. Quick movement of the plectrum across each unison pair of strings produces a characteristic tremolo. A shell plate around the oval sound hole protects the belly from damage by the plectrum. In the 20th century the mandolin was built in a family of sizes from soprano to contrabass. Compositions for the mandolin include a concerto by Antonio Vivaldi and the serenade in W.A. Mozart's opera *Don Giovanni*.

The mandolin played in American bluegrass string bands is a shallow, flat-backed version of the instrument. The Milanese mandolin of the 18th century was a small, lutelike instrument with five or six courses of strings, a late variety of the medieval mandora.

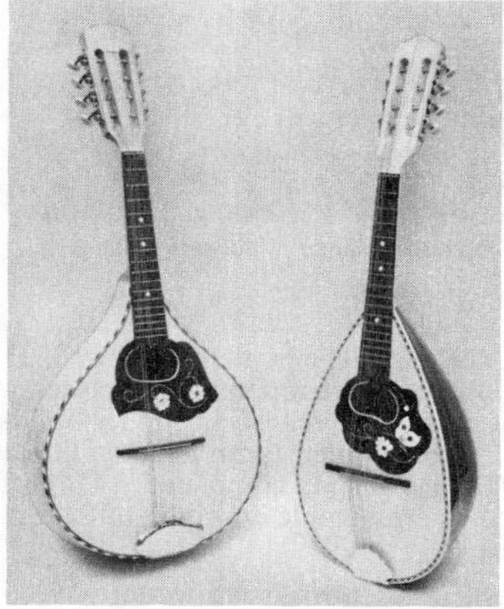

Neapolitan mandolins
By courtesy of Boosey & Hawkes Ltd.

mandora, also spelled MANDOLA, small, pear-shaped musical instrument of the lute family, played from about the 12th to the 18th century. Probably of Persian origin, it was known in the Middle Ages as the *guitarra morisca,* or *guitarra saracenica,* and shared with the guitarlike *guitarra latina* the name gittern.

Originally, the body and neck of the mandora were carved from a single piece of wood. It had a back-curving sickle-shaped pegbox with lateral tuning pegs. The four or five strings were hitched to the end of the instrument and were plucked with a plectrum. Tunings varied but frequently ran upward from middle C or the C below. The mandora was increasingly influenced by its larger cousin, the lute. By the 17th century it was finger-plucked and had acquired the frets, separate neck, and tension bridge (string holder placed on the belly) of the lute, although it retained its violin-like pegbox. A late variety was the 18th-century Milanese mandolin, which is distinct from the modern, or Neapolitan, mandolin. "Mandora" also denotes the tenor or alto Neapolitan mandolin.

mandorla (Italian: "almond"), in religious art, almond-shaped aureole of light surrounding the entire figure of a holy person; it was used in Christian art usually for the figure of Christ and is also found in the art of Buddhism. Its origins are uncertain. The Western mandorla first appears in 5th-century mosaics decorating the Church of Santa Maria Maggiore in Rome, where it surrounds certain Old Testament figures.

"Transfiguration," with a mandorla enclosing the figure of Christ; mosaic icon, early 13th century; in the Louvre, Paris
Giraudon—Art Resource

By the 6th century the mandorla had become a standard attribute of Christ in scenes of the Transfiguration (in which Christ shows himself to his Apostles transformed into his celestial appearance) and the Ascension (in which the resurrected Christ ascends to heaven) and, later, in other scenes involving the resurrected or celestial Christ, the death of the Virgin (in which, having descended from heaven, Christ stands by the deathbed of his mother), the descent into limbo, the Last Judgment, and the nonhistorical theme of Christ in majesty.

In the late Middle Ages the mandorla also occasionally enclosed the Virgin in scenes of the Last Judgment and of her Assumption into heaven, reflecting her increased popularity. In the 15th century, however, with the growth of naturalism in art, the mandorla became less popular, being incongruous in a naturalistic context, and it was abandoned by the painters of the Renaissance.

mandrake, any of six plant species belonging to the genus *Mandragora* (family Solanaceae) that are native to the Mediterranean region and the Himalayas. The best-known species, *M. officinarum,* has a short stem bearing a tuft of ovate flowers, with a thick, fleshy root that is often forked. The flowers are solitary, with a purple bell-shaped corolla, and the fruit is a fleshy orange-coloured berry.

The mandrake has long been known for its poisonous properties. In ancient times it was used as a narcotic and an aphrodisiac, and it was also believed to have certain magical powers. Its forked root, seemingly resembling the human form, was thought to be in the power of dark earth spirits. It was believed that the mandrake could be safely uprooted only in the moonlight, after appropriate prayer and ritual, by a black dog attached to the plant by a cord.

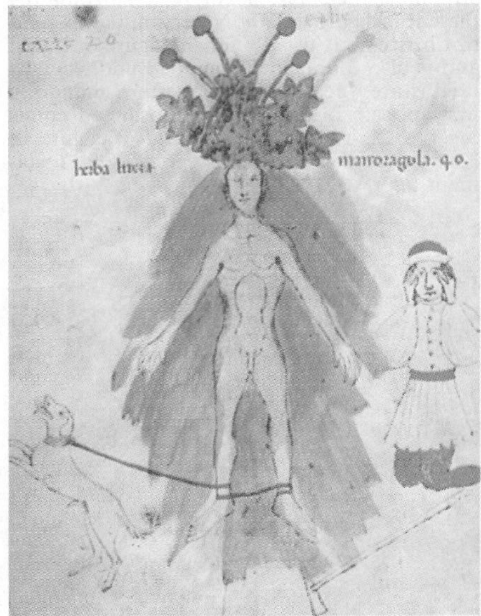

Mandrake root as conceived in a 15th-century manuscript illustration; in the University Library, Pavia, Italy (Aldini 211, fol. 20)

By courtesy of the Biblioteca Universitaria, Pavia, Italy

Human hands were not to come in contact with the plant. In medieval times it was thought that as the mandrake was pulled from the ground it uttered a shriek that killed or drove mad those who did not block their ears against it. After the plant had been freed from the earth, it could be used for beneficent purposes, such as healing, inducing love, facilitating pregnancy, and providing soothing sleep.

In North America, the name mandrake is often used for the mayapple (*q.v.*) of the order Ranunculales.

mandrill (*Mandrillus,* or *Papio, sphinx*), colourful Old World monkey, family Cercopithecidae, usually grouped with the related drill (*q.v.*) in the genus *Mandrillus* but sometimes placed with the baboons in the genus *Papio*. The mandrill is primarily terrestrial and inhabits the rain forests of equatorial Africa. It is stout-bodied and has a short tail, prominent brow ridges, and small, close-set, sunken eyes. The adult male has bare, coloured patches of skin on the face and buttocks: the cheeks are ribbed and bright blue to violet with scarlet on the bridge and end of the nose; and the buttock pads are pink to crimson, shading to bluish at the sides. The long body fur is olive to brown, and the small beard and the neck fur are yellow; the eyes are framed in black. The adult male is about 90 cm (3 feet) long including the tail stub and weighs about 19.5 kg (43 pounds). The female, also with bare face and buttocks, is duller in colour and considerably smaller.

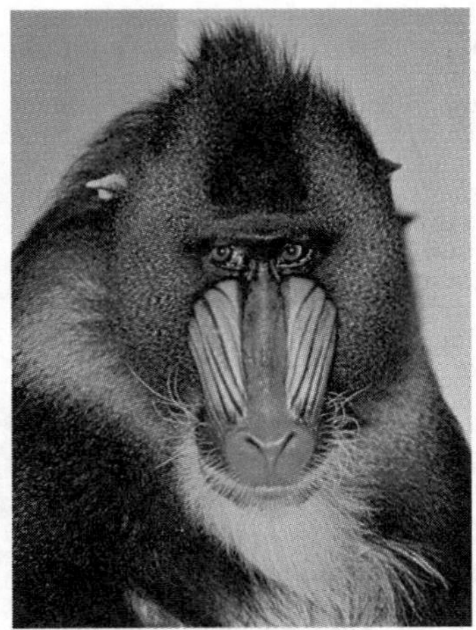

Mandrill (*Mandrillus sphinx*)

Russ Kinne—Photo Researchers

Mandrills feed on fruit, roots, insects, and small reptiles and amphibians. They are active on the ground during the day and retire to the trees at night. Mandrills live in troops headed by a dominant male and defend their territories from other troops. These primates are threatened by the deforestation of their habitat for agricultural and lumbering purposes.

Mandsaur (India): *see* Mandasor.

Māndu, also called MANDOGARH, ruined city, southwestern Madhya Pradesh state, central India. It lies 38 miles (60 km) southwest of the city of Indore. Said to have been founded in the 6th century AD, Māndu became famous as the 14th–15th-century capital of the Muslim Mālwa kingdom. The city reached its zenith under Hoshang Shāh (1405–34) and declined with the advent of the Mughals. Situated at an elevation of 2,079 feet (634 m), its ruins stretch for 8 miles (13 km) along the crest of the Vindhya Range. The battlemented wall, 23 miles (37 km) in circumference, encloses a number of palaces, mosques, and other buildings. The marble-domed tomb and the Great Mosque (Jāmiʿ Masjid; completed 1454) of Hoshang Shāh are notable examples of Pathān architecture.

The Great Mosque in Māndu, Madhya Pradesh, India

Art Resource

Mandurah, resort town, southwestern Western Australia. It lies at the entrance to Peel Inlet, 40 miles (65 km) south of Perth. Founded in 1895, it lies on the original land tract granted in 1829 to Thomas Peel, a cousin of the British prime minister Robert Peel, for a grandiose but unsuccessful colonization venture. The name Mandurah comes from the Aboriginal term *mandjar,* meaning "trading, watering, or meeting place." Serving a district of dairying, poultry farming, and fishing, Mandurah now functions mainly as a resort for the Perth metropolitan area, to which it is linked by road. Pop. (1991 prelim.) 26,841.

Manduria, town, Taranto *provincia,* Puglia (Apulia) *regione,* southeastern Italy. Of pre-Roman origin, it is the site of a well that was probably a pagan sanctuary and was named for Pliny the Elder, who mentioned it in his writings. The Imperiali and Giannuzzi palaces are notable monuments; the town's cathedral has a facade dating from 1532. Stockbreeding and farming are the economic mainstays. Pop. (1990 est.) mun., 32,737.

Mandya, city, southern Karnātaka (formerly Mysore) state, southwestern India. It lies about 26 miles (41 km) northeast of Mysore on the Chāmrājnagar-Bangalore Railway. The centre of a sugarcane region, its processing plants supply the sugar residues used in local paper manufacture and printing. Alcohol, tobacco, and vegetable-oil processing are other industries. Mandya has a government college and other colleges affiliated with the University of Mysore.

The surrounding area is part of the Deccan Plateau. The Cauvery River supplies the Visweswariah Canal, the main irrigation source; and millet, rice, tobacco, and cotton are grown. Silk is produced, and textile weaving is the main cottage industry. Pop. (1991 prelim.) 119,970.

mandyas, long, full, purple or blue cloak worn as a processional garment by bishops and some other dignitaries in the Eastern Orthodox churches. It is open down the front but fastened at the neck and at the hem. At the point where the neck and hem are fastened, the bishop's mandyas is decorated with *pōmata* (Greek: "beverages"), richly embroidered squares of material. Red and white stripes called *potamoi* (Greek: "rivers") flow out from the squares. The *pōmata* symbolize the New and Old Testaments, the sources of the doctrine that the bishop "pours out" on his congregation.

maned rat, also called CRESTED RAT (*Lophiomys imhausi*), large rodent of the family Cricetidae (order Rodentia), found in highland forests of eastern Africa. Long-haired and bushy-tailed, the maned rat is 25 to 35 cm (10 to 14 inches) long excluding its long tail. It has soft, thick fur, of an overall grayish colour, and has small ears and short legs. From head to tail, it has a mane of long hair that is erected when the animal is disturbed. The mane is set off from the rest of the animal's coat by a broad, white-bordered band of short hair covering a glandular area of skin. The maned rat is nocturnal and a good climber and lives

Maned rat (*Lophiomys imhausi*)

P.W. Hay from The National Audubon Society Collection/Photo Researchers among rocks or in a burrow under tree roots. It eats leaves and shoots, sitting up and manipulating its food with its forepaws.

maned wolf (species *Chrysocyon brachyurus*), rare, large-eared member of the dog family (Canidae) found in remote plains areas of central South America. The maned wolf has a foxlike head, long reddish brown fur, very long blackish legs, and an erectile mane. Its length ranges from 125 to 130 cm (50 to 52 inches), excluding the 30–40-centimetre tail. Its shoulder height is about 75 cm, and its weight is approximately 23 kg (50 pounds). A solitary

Maned wolf (*Chrysocyon brachyurus*)
Kenneth W. Fink—Root Resources

animal, the maned wolf is primarily nocturnal and feeds on small animals, insects, and plant material. It attacks sheep but generally avoids human contact.

Manes (Middle Eastern prophet): *see* Mani.

Manet, Édouard (b. Jan. 23, 1832, Paris, France—d. April 30, 1883, Paris), French painter who broke new ground by defying traditional techniques of representation and by choosing subjects from the events and circumstances of his own time. His "Déjeuner sur l'Herbe" ("Luncheon on the Grass"), exhibited in 1863 at the Salon des Refusés, aroused the hostility of critics and the enthusiasm of the young painters who later formed the nucleus of the Impressionist group. His other notable works include "Olympia" (1863) and "A Bar at the Folies-Bergère" (1882).

Early life and works. Édouard was the son of Auguste Manet, the chief of personnel at the Ministry of Justice, and Eugénie-Désirée Fournier. From 1839 he was a day pupil at Canon Poiloup's school in Vaugirard, where he studied French and the classics. From 1884 to 1848 he was a boarder at the Collège Rollin, then located near the Panthéon. A poor student, he was interested only in the special drawing course offered by the school.

Although his father wanted him to enroll in law school, Édouard could not be persuaded to do so. When his father refused to allow him to become a painter, he applied for the naval college but failed the entrance examination. He therefore embarked in December 1848 as an apprentice pilot on a transport vessel. Upon his return to France in June 1849, he failed the naval examination a second time, and his parents finally yielded to their son's stubborn determination to become a painter.

In 1850 Manet entered the studio of the classical painter Thomas Couture. Despite fundamental differences between teacher and student, Manet was to owe to Couture a good grasp of drawing and pictorial technique. In 1856, after six years with Couture, Manet set up a studio that he shared with Albert de Balleroy, a painter of military subjects. There he painted "The Boy with Cherries" (*c.* 1858) before moving to another studio, where he painted "The Absinthe Drinker" (1859). In 1856 he made short trips to The Netherlands, Germany, and Italy. Meanwhile, at the Louvre he copied paintings by Titian and Diego Velázquez and in 1857 made the acquaintance of the artist Henri Fantin-Latour, who was later to paint Manet's portrait.

During this period, Manet also met the poet Charles Baudelaire, at whose suggestion he painted "Concert in the Tuileries Gardens" (1862). The canvas, which was painted outdoors, seems to assemble the whole of Paris of the Second Empire—a smart, fashionable gathering composed chiefly of habitués of the Café Tortoni and of the Café Guerbois, which was the rendezvous of the Batignolles artists. As he created the work, passersby looked with curiosity at this elegantly dressed painter who set up his canvas and painted in the open air. At the Salon of 1861 Manet exhibited "Spanish Singer" (1860), dubbed "Guitarero" by the French man of letters Théophile Gautier, who praised it enthusiastically in the periodical *Le Moniteur universel.*

Mature life and works. From 1862 to 1865 Manet took part in exhibitions organized by the Martinet Gallery. In 1863 Manet married Suzanne Leenhoff, a Dutchwoman who had given him piano lessons and had given birth to his child before their marriage. That same year the jury of the Salon rejected his "Déjeuner sur l'Herbe," a work whose technique was entirely revolutionary, and so Manet instead exhibited it at the Salon des Refusés (established to exhibit the many works rejected by the official Salon). Although inspired by works of the Old Masters—Giorgione's "Pastoral Concert" (*c.* 1510) and Raphael's "Judgment of Paris" (*c.* 1517–20)—this large canvas aroused loud disapproval and began for Manet that "carnival notoriety" from which he would suffer for most of his career. His critics were offended by the presence of a naked woman in the company of two young men clothed in contemporary dress; rather than seeming a remote allegorical figure, the woman's modernity made her nudity seem vulgar and even threatening. Critics were also upset by how these figures were depicted in a harsh, impersonal light and placed in a woodland setting whose perspective is distinctly unrealistic.

At the Salon of 1865, his painting "Olympia," finished two years earlier, created a scandal. The painting's reclining female nude gazes brazenly at the viewer and is depicted in a harsh, brilliant light that obliterates interior modeling and turns her into an almost two-dimensional figure. This contemporary odalisque—which the French statesman Georges Clemenceau was to install in the Louvre in 1907—was called indecent by critics and the public. In his vexation, Manet left in August 1865 for Spain, but, disliking the food and frustrated by his total lack of knowledge of the language, he did not stay long. In Madrid he met Théodore Duret, who was later to be one of the first connoisseurs and champions of his work. The following year, "The Fifer" (1866), after having been rejected by the Salon jury under the pretext that its modeling was flat, was displayed along with others in Manet's studio in Paris.

When a large number of his works were rejected for the Universal Exposition of 1867, Manet, in imitation of Gustave Courbet, who had the same idea, had a stall erected at the corner of the Place de l'Alma and the Avenue Montaigne, where in May he exhibited a group of works, including his paintings of toreadors and bullfights. He showed about 50 paintings, but these were not received any more favourably than before. His work from this period was varied in character, but in general it seems to represent a greater concern with close relations of tone and complexities of illumination and atmosphere, sometimes exhibiting a freedom of handling comparable to that in "Concert in the Tuileries Gardens."

Much impressed by the naturalism of Manet's work, the young novelist Émile Zola undertook to praise it in a long and courageous article published in the *Revue du XIXe siècle* of Jan. 1, 1867. In the face of the hostility of the public, Zola saw Manet as representative of all artists of importance who begin by offending public opinion. Manet expressed his gratitude in his portrait of Zola shown at the Salon of 1868. Along with his portrait of Zola, Manet exhibited "The Balcony" (1869), in which there appeared for the first time—in the figure of the Spanish girl seated with her elbow on the railing—a portrait of the artist Berthe Morisot, whom he had met at the Louvre. From then on, Morisot, who was to become one of the leading female French Impressionists, was a frequent visitor to Manet's studio. He painted a series of portraits of her, until her marriage to his brother Eugène Manet.

After the positive reviews published by Zola, Duret, and the art critic Louis-Édmond Duranty, Manet at the Salon of 1870 received an homage in paint, Fantin-Latour's "The Studio in Batignolles," which served as a kind of manifesto on his behalf. This large canvas shows Manet painting, surrounded by those who were his defenders at the time: Zola, the

"A Bar at the Folies-Bergère," oil on canvas by Édouard Manet, 1882; in the Courtauld Institute Galleries, London
Courtauld Institute Galleries, London (Courtauld Collection)

painters Pierre-Auguste Renoir, Claude Monet, and Frédéric Bazille, and the sculptor Zacharie Astruc. The painting was caricatured in the *Journal amusant* under the title "Jesus Painting Among His Disciples."

During the Franco-German War (1870–71), Manet served as a staff lieutenant in the National Guard and witnessed the siege of Paris. In February 1871 he rejoined his family, returning to Paris shortly before the Commune. His studio there was half-destroyed, but he had taken care to store his canvases in a safe place, and he found them intact. The art dealer Paul Durand-Ruel bought almost everything that Manet's studio contained, paying 50,000 francs in the currency of the time. From about this time on, Manet and his friends met at the Café Nouvelle-Athènes, which had replaced the Guerbois. In 1872 he visited The Netherlands, where he was much influenced by the works of Frans Hals. As a result Manet painted "Le Bon Bock" (1873; "The Good Pint"), which achieved considerable success at the Salon exhibition of 1873.

Later life and works. The year 1874 was chiefly notable for the development of Manet's friendship with the young Impressionist painter Claude Monet, with whom he painted on the banks of the Seine (when they had first met in 1866, the relationship was rather cool). Manet painted his most luminous plein-air picture, "Boating" (1874), which was set in Le Petit Gennevilliers and depicted two figures seated in the sun in a boat. It was also at Argenteuil that Manet painted "Monet Working on His Boat in Argenteuil" (1874). Although he was friendly with Monet and the other Impressionists, Manet would not participate in their independent exhibitions and continued to submit his paintings to the official Salon. When "The Artist" and "The Laundress" were both rejected by the Salon in 1875, Manet exhibited them along with other paintings in his studio.

When painting "Nana" (1877), Manet was inspired by the character of a woman of the demimonde whom Zola first introduced in his novel *L'Assommoir* (1877; "The Drunkard"); in that same year he painted "The Plum," one of his major works, in which a solitary woman rests her elbow on the marble top of a café table. He followed these works with "The Blonde with Bare Breasts" (1878), in which the pearl-white flesh tones gleam with light, and "Chez le Père Lathuille" (1879), another of his major works, set in a restaurant near the Café Guerbois in Clichy. The latter depicts a coquette somewhat past her prime having lunch with her young lover in yet another of Manet's bold attempts to portray controversial subject matter in a decidedly modern manner. From then on, Manet did a large number of pastels. In broad, determined strokes he captured the features of George Moore (1879), an Irish would-be painter and later novelist who often joined Manet and Edgar Degas at the Café Nouvelle-Athènes.

In 1880 Manet had a one-man exhibition at the offices of the periodical *La Vie moderne* ("Modern Life"), but his legs were already affected by a malady that was to prove fatal. In 1881 he rented a villa at Versailles, and, by the following year, with his illness progressing at an alarming pace, he went to stay in a villa at Rueil. He took part in an important exhibition of French art that was held in London at Burlington House, and at the Salon he showed "A Bar at the Folies-Bergère" (1882), a daring composition that intensifies the exchange of glances between the image of the barmaid and the customer before her, allowing the viewer to stand in the customer's place. Radical in its obliteration of the boundary between the viewer and what is viewed, the "Bar" was Manet's last great contribution to the modern vision of painting. On April 6, 1883, after painting some roses and lilacs, Manet took to his bed. Gangrene developed in his left leg, which was subsequently amputated. He died not long after and was buried in the cemetery of Passy.

In January 1884 a posthumous exhibition of Manet's work was held in the Salle de Melpomène of the École des Beaux-Arts. True to his admiration for the artist, Zola wrote the preface to the catalog. It was after this memorial exhibition that Manet's paintings began to gain prominence.

Assessment. Manet's debut as a painter met with a critical resistance that did not abate until near the end of his career. Although the success of his memorial exhibition and the eventual critical acceptance of the Impressionists—with whom he was loosely affiliated—raised his profile by the end of the 19th century, it was not until the 20th century that his reputation was secured by art historians and critics. Manet's disregard for traditional modeling and perspective made a critical break with academic painting's historical emphasis on illusionism. This flaunting of tradition and the official art establishment paved the way for the revolutionary work of the Impressionists and Postimpressionists. Manet also influenced the path of much 19th- and 20th-century art through his choice of subject matter. His focus on modern, urban subjects—which he presented in a straightforward, almost detached manner—distinguished him still more from the standards of the Salon, which generally favoured narrative and avoided the gritty realities of everyday life. Manet's daring, unflinching approach to his painting and to the art world assured both him and his work a pivotal place in the history of modern art.

"Déjeuner sur l'Herbe" ("Luncheon on the Grass"), oil painting by Édouard Manet, *c.* 1863; in the Musée d'Orsay, Paris

BIBLIOGRAPHY. *Life and work.* The artist's life and work are treated in Françoise Cachin, Charles S. Moffett, and Juliet Wilson Bareau, *Manet, 1832–1883* (1983), a catalog published in conjunction with Manet's centenary exhibition. General biographies of the artist include Beth Archer Brombert, *Edouard Manet: Rebel in a Frock Coat* (1996); and Françoise Cachin, *Manet* (1991; originally published in French, 1990). Denis Rouart and Daniel Wildenstein, *Édouard Manet: catalogue raisonné*, 2 vol. (1975), provides a comprehensive survey of the artist's work. Manet's work in specific media is discussed in Sandra Orienti, *The Complete Paintings of Manet* (1967, reissued 1985), which also presents a concise biography and selections of contemporary criticism; Alain de Leiris, *The Drawings of Edouard Manet* (1969); and Jean C. Harris, *Édouard Manet, the Graphic Work: A Catalogue Raisonné*, rev. ed., edited by Joel M. Smith (1990). Essential among the early writings on Manet's career and contribution are Émile Zola, *My Hatreds* (1991; originally published in French, 1879); and Theodore Duret, *Manet,* trans. by J.E. Crawford Flitch (1937; originally published in French, 1902).

Themes and criticism. George Heard Hamilton, *Manet and His Critics* (1954, reprinted 1986), presents a wide survey of the contemporary reception of Manet's art. Many scholars have considered Manet's essential role in the emergence of modernism. A pioneering study is Anne Coffin Hanson, *Manet and the Modern Tradition* (1977, reprinted with corrections 1979). Also important are T.J. Clark, *The Painting of Modern Life: Paris in the Art of Manet and His Followers,* rev ed. (1999); Michael Fried, *Manet's Modernism: or, The Face of Painting in the 1860s* (1996); and Alan Krell, *Manet and the Painters of Contemporary Life* (1996). Studies of selected themes in Manet's art include Theodore Reff, *Manet: Olympia* (1976); Bradford R. Collins (ed.), *12 Views of Manet's Bar* (1996); Paul Hayes Tucker (ed.), *Manet's Le déjeuner sur l'herbe* (1998), a collection of essays by various authors; and Juliet Wilson-Bareau, *Manet, The Execution of Maximillian: Painting, Politics, and Censorship* (1992). (P.Co./Ed.)

Manetho, also spelled MANETHOS, or MANETHON (fl. *c.* 300 BC), Egyptian priest who wrote a history of Egypt in Greek, probably for Ptolemy I (305–282).

Manetho's history has not survived except for some fragments of narrative in Josephus' treatise "Against Apion" and tables of dynasties, kings, and lengths of reigns in the works of Julius Africanus, Eusebius, and George Syncellus. The fragments thus preserved showed that Manetho's work was based on good native sources. These fragments have been of much service to scholars in confirming the succession of kings where the archaeological evidence was inconclusive, and Manetho's division of the rulers of Egypt into 30 dynasties is still accepted.

Manfalūṭī, Muṣṭafā Luṭfī al- (b. Dec. 30, 1876, Manfalūṭ, Egypt—d. July 25, 1924, Cairo), essayist, short-story writer, and pioneer of modern Arabic prose.

Al-Manfalūṭī was born of a half-Turkish, half-Arab family claiming descent from Ḥusayn, grandson of the Prophet Muḥammad. He received the traditional Muslim theological education at al-Azhar University but was deeply influenced by pan-Islāmism, Egyptian nationalism, and the Syrian school of writers, who introduced him to Western, particularly French, learning.

It is uncertain whether he learned French, but his collected essays (*Nazarat,* 3 vol., 1902–10; *Mukhtarat,* 1912) and short stories (*ʿAbarat,* 1946) were adapted or translated from French and other European sources. His easy, flowing Arabic style, free from the then-fashionable ornamentation of rhymed prose (*sajʿ*), had a lustre not found in journalistic jargon; it formed the basis of the more accomplished modern Arabic narrative of succeeding generations of writers.

Manfred, Italian MANFREDI (b. *c.* 1232—d. Feb. 26, 1266, near Benevento, Kingdom of Naples), effective king of Sicily from 1258, during a period of civil wars and succession disputes between imperial claimants and the House of Anjou.

Manfred, detail of a manuscript illumination from the Manfred Bible, 13th century; in the Vatican Library (Ms. Vat. Lat. 36, fol. 522 v.)

By courtesy of the Biblioteca Apostolica Vaticana

The son of the Holy Roman emperor Frederick II, Manfred became vicar of Italy and Sicily for his half brother Conrad IV but soon began seeking the Sicilian crown for himself. On Conrad's death in 1254 a diet at San Germano ignored the imperial representative and elected Manfred. Pope Alexander IV, however, after having excommunicated Manfred twice, invested Edmund, son of Henry III of England, with the Sicilian kingdom in April 1255. A papal army entered the kingdom, but Manfred resisted successfully and was crowned king of Sicily at Palermo on Aug. 10, 1258.

As protector of the Italian Ghibellines, Manfred asserted himself also in Lombardy and Tuscany; and he further strengthened his position by the betrothal, in 1260, of his daughter Constance to the infante Peter of Aragon. Negotiations with the new pope, Urban IV, came to nothing; and Urban, considering Alexander IV's agreement with England void, offered the Sicilian crown to Charles of Anjou, who sailed for Rome in May 1265. Manfred, having failed to prevent Charles's army from joining him, was defeated near Benevento; he fell in battle.

Manfredonia, town and archiepiscopal see, Foggia province, Puglia (Apulia) region, east central Italy, on the southern slope of the Promontorio del Gargano at the head of the Golfo (gulf) di Manfredonia, northeast of Foggia. The Romanesque church of Sta. Maria di Siponto (1117), 2 mi (3 km) southwest, marks the site of the ancient Sipontum, conquered by the Romans in 217 BC and the see of a bishop from the 1st century AD. Abandoned in the 13th century because nearby stagnant lagoons had made the site unhealthy, Sipontum's inhabitants settled in Manfredonia, founded about 1260 by Manfred, king of Sicily. Although the town was destroyed by the Turks in 1620, the castle and the Romanesque church of S. Domenico remain. There is a museum housing many remains from Sipontum.

The chief occupations are agriculture, fishing, and commerce. Tourism is increasing, and a hydraulic works has been developed. Pop. (1999 est.) mun., 57,978.

mangabey (*Cercocebus*), any of several slender, rather long-limbed monkeys, belonging to the family Cercopithecidae, found in African rain forests. Mangabeys are fairly large, quadrupedal monkeys with large cheek pouches. They carry their long, tapering tails over their backs. Individual species range in head and body length from about 40 to almost 90 centimetres (15–35 inches) and weigh up to about 6 kilograms (13 pounds); their tails are about as long as the head and body. There are, depending on the authority, four or five species of mangabeys, most of which have vivid white on the eyelids or around the eyes. Features distinguishing the species from each other include contrasting caps, white markings, and tufts of hair or pointed crests on the head.

The white-collared (*C. torquatus*), sooty (*C. atys* or *C. torquatus atys*), and agile (*C. galeritus*) mangabeys are short-haired, primarily terrestrial animals with speckled, pale grayish-brown to dark-gray fur. The gray-cheeked (*C. albigena*) and black (*C. aterrimus*) mangabeys are more arboreal, long-haired monkeys whose fur is black and is not speckled. Little is known of the habits of wild mangabeys. They are social, reputedly quiet, and feed on seeds, fruit, and leaves. They are preyed on by leopards and crowned eagles (*Stephanoaetus coronatus*).

maṅgal-kāvya (Bengali: "auspicious poems"), a type of eulogistic verse in honour of a popular god or goddess in Bengal (India). The poems are sometimes associated with a Pan-Indian deity, such as Śiva, but more often with a local Bengali deity—*e.g.,* Manasā, the goddess of snakes, or Śītalā, the goddess of smallpox, or the folk god Dhama-Ṭhākur. These poems vary greatly in length, from 200 lines to several thousand, as in the case of the *Caṇḍī-maṅgal* of Mukundarāma Cakravartī, a masterpiece of 16th-century Bengali literature.

Maṅgal-kāvya are most often heard at the festivals of the deities they celebrate. There is some disagreement among scholars as to whether or not the poems actually constitute an essential part of the ritual, without which it would be incomplete and not efficacious. Some of them, however, such as the *Manasā-maṅgal,* have become so popular that village singers, or *gāyak*s, often sing them for the amusement and edification of a village audience.

Maṅgal poetry, unlike the texts of the Vedic tradition, is noncanonical literature and so has changed not only over the centuries but also from singer to singer, each performer being free to incorporate his own favourite legends and observations on the society around him. The texts are thus valuable not only as religious documents but also historically. The large number of variants, even among those texts that have been committed to writing, does, however, make dating extremely difficult.

*Maṅgal*s cannot be characterized by content, except by saying that they all tell the story of how a particular god or goddess succeeded in establishing his or her worship on Earth. The popular *Manasā-Maṅgal,* for example, tells how the Bengali snake goddess Manasā conquered the worshippers of other deities by releasing her powers of destruction in the form of snakes. The *Dharma-maṅgal,* which celebrates the merits of the folk god Dharma-Ṭhākur, also contains an account of the creation of the world.

*Maṅgal*s are similar in form despite the wide variance in length. They are written for the most part in the simple *payār* meter, a couplet form with rhyme scheme "aa bb," etc., an appropriate form for oral literature. Another characteristic of *maṅgal* poetry is its earthy imagery, drawn from village, field, and river, quite different from the elaborate and sophisticated imagery more typical of Sanskritic and court poetry. An exception is the 18th-century poem *Annadā-maṅgal* by Bhārat-candra, a court poet who used the *maṅgal* form not as an expression of faith but as a frame for a witty, elaborate, sophisticated tale of love.

Mangalore, town, administrative headquarters of Dakshin Kannaḍ district, southwestern Karnātaka (formerly Mysore) state, southern India, a port on the Arabian Sea. Lying on the backwaters formed by the Netrāvati and Gurpur rivers, it has long been a roadstead along the Malabar Coast. Engaged in Persian Gulf trade in the 14th century, Mangalore was occupied by the Portuguese in the mid-16th century. Under the Mysore sultans (1763) it became a strategic shipbuilding base, which was ceded to the British in 1799 after numerous sieges.

The town, heavily dotted with coconut plantations, has a deceptively rural appearance. It is a busy transshipment centre; ships must anchor 3 mi (5 km) offshore because of sandbars; a deepwater port, however, has been developed for the shipment of mineral ores. Cashew nuts, coffee, and sandalwood are brought from Mysore and Coorg districts; rice, areca nuts, coir yarn (coconut fibre), fish, and cardamom are local products. In the 19th century the German Basel Mission introduced cotton weaving and tile manufacture, and Mangalore remains an important producer of roofing tiles. Other industries include boatbuilding, coffee curing, pottery manufacture, and the making of brick kilns. The suburb of Ullal produces hosiery and coir yarn. Mangalore maintains a great bazaar near its coastal landing place.

The town is served by a diesel power station, an airport, and a national highway and is the terminus of the west-coast branch of the Southern Railway. Mangalore is the seat of a Roman Catholic bishopric and a Lutheran mission. It also is an educational centre, with government training and education colleges, an institute of social services, St. Aloysius College (founded by Jesuits in 1880), St. Agnes College, and St. Ann's College; all are affiliated with the University of Mangalore. The Koṅkaṇī language is associated with the town, and a large percentage of its inhabitants are Christian. Pop. (1991) town, 273,304; metropolitan area, 426,341.

Mangan (India): *see* Mangang.

Mangan, James Clarence (b. May 1, 1803, Dublin—d. June 20, 1849, Dublin), a prolific and uneven writer of almost every kind of verse whose best work, inspired by love of Ireland, ranks high in Irish poetry.

The son of an unsuccessful grocer, at the age of 15 Mangan became a copying clerk in a scrivener's office and remained one for 10 years. He then lived as best he could, contributing to the prestigious *Dublin University Magazine* and other literary periodicals,

Mangan, drawing by Sir Frederick William Burton, 1849; in the National Gallery of Ireland, Dublin

By courtesy of the National Gallery of Ireland, Dublin

though posts were found for him for brief periods in the library of Trinity College, Dublin, and the Ordnance Survey Office. His natural melancholy was aggravated by years of ill-paid drudgery and an acute disappointment in love. He became an opium addict and a chronic drunkard, and the last years of his life were spent in extreme neglect and wretchedness. When he died of cholera, only two persons attended his funeral.

Many of his poems are "translations" from the Irish, from German, and from various Eastern languages (which Mangan probably did not know), often so free that Mangan is in effect using the original as a vehicle for his own emotions. He often also described as translations poems that were, in fact, altogether his own. Much of his work has Irish history and legend for its theme, and his poems "The Nameless One" and "Dark Rosaleen," which achieve an extraordinary modern note of personal realism and a tragic sincerity of tone, are often anthologized.

manganese (Mn), chemical element, one of the silvery-white, hard, brittle metals of Group VIIb of the periodic table. It was recognized as an element (1774) by the Swedish chemist Carl Wilhelm Scheele while working with the mineral pyrolusite and was isolated the same year by his associate, Johan Gottlieb Gahn. Although it is rarely used in pure form, manganese is essential to steelmaking.

For detailed information on the extraction, refining, and applications of manganese, *see* MACROPAEDIA: Industries, Extraction and Processing.

Occurrence, uses, and properties. Manganese combined with other elements is widely distributed in the Earth's crust. The most important ores consist primarily of manganese dioxide (MnO_2) in the form of pyrolusite, psilomelane, and wad. Manganese is essential to plant growth and is involved in the reduction of nitrates in green plants and algae. It is an essential trace element in higher animals, in which it participates in the action of many enzymes. Lack of manganese causes testicular atrophy. An excess of this element in plants and animals is toxic.

More than 95 percent of the manganese produced is used in the form of ferromanganese and silicomanganese alloys for iron and steel manufacture. Manganese ores containing iron oxides are first reduced in blast furnaces or electric furnaces with carbon to yield ferromanganese, which in turn is used in steelmaking. Adding manganese, which has a greater affinity for sulfur than does iron, converts the low-melting iron sulfide in steel to high-melting manganese sulfide. Produced without manganese, steel breaks up when hot-rolled or forged. Steels generally contain less than 1 percent manganese. Manganese steel, also called Hadfield steel, is used for very rugged service; containing 12–14 percent manganese, it provides a hard, wear-resistant, and self-renewing surface over a tough unbreakable core. Pure manganese produced electrolytically is used mostly in the preparation of nonferrous alloys of copper, aluminum, magnesium, and nickel and in the production of high-purity chemicals. Practically all commercial alloys of aluminum and magnesium contain manganese to improve corrosion resistance and mechanical properties.

All natural manganese is stable isotope manganese-55. It exists in four allotropic modifications; the complex cubic structure of the so-called alpha phase is the form stable at ordinary temperatures. Manganese somewhat resembles iron in general chemical activity. The metal oxidizes superficially in air and rusts in moist air. It burns in air or oxygen at elevated temperatures, as does iron; decomposes water slowly when cold and rapidly on heating; and dissolves readily in dilute mineral acids with hydrogen evolution and the formation of the corresponding divalent salts.

Compounds. Of the wide variety of compounds formed by manganese, the most stable occur in oxidation states +2, +6, and +7. These are exemplified, respectively, by the manganese(II) (manganous) salts, the manganates, and the permanganates.

The principal industrial compounds of manganese include several oxides. Manganese(II) oxide, or manganese monoxide, MnO, is used as a starting material for the production of manganese(II) salts, as an additive in fertilizers, and as a reagent in textile printing. It occurs in nature as the green mineral manganosite. It also can be prepared commercially by heating manganese carbonate in the absence of air or by passing hydrogen or carbon monoxide over manganese dioxide.

The most important manganese compound is manganese(IV) oxide (manganese dioxide), and the black mineral pyrolusite is the chief source of manganese and all of its compounds. It is also widely used as a chemical oxidant in organic synthesis. Manganese dioxide is used as the cathode material in electric dry cells. It is produced directly from the ore, although substantial amounts are also prepared synthetically. The synthetic oxide is prepared by decomposition of manganese(II) nitrate; by reaction of manganese(II) sulfate, oxygen, and sodium hydroxide; or by electrolysis of an aqueous solution of manganese sulfate.

Various manganese salts also have commercial importance. Manganous sulfate ($MnSO_4$) is added to soils to promote plant growth, especially of citrus crops. In addition, it is a good reducing agent, particularly useful in the manufacture of paint and varnish driers. Manganous chloride ($MnCl_2$) is widely employed as a catalyst in the chlorination of organic compounds and as a feed additive. Potassium permanganate ($KMnO_4$) is used for disinfecting, deodorizing, and bleaching and as an analytical reagent.

atomic number	25
atomic weight	54.938
melting point	1,246° C (2,275° F)
boiling point	2,062° C (3,744° F)
density	7.21–7.44 (20° C)
valence	2, 3, 4, 6, or 7
electronic config.	2-8-13-2 or (Ar)$3d^5 4s^2$

manganese deficiency, condition in which an organism does not receive enough manganese, a trace metal found in body ash and thought to be an antisterility factor. Some evidence supports this claim in that infant mortality rates are lower when the manganese blood-chemistry level is maintained to a specific degree. Manganese is known to be a catalyst in the action of calcium and phosphorus in the system, and it is essential for normal bone structure. Principal food sources are legumes (peas), nuts, whole-grain cereal, tea, and green leafy vegetables.

Mangang, also spelled MANGEN, or MANGAN, village, Sikkim state, northeastern India, on the North Sikkim Highway. A trading centre,

A typical house in Mangang, Sikkim, India, with the family accommodation above that of the animals
Alice Kandell from Rapho/Photo Researchers

it lies on the east bank of the Tista River, south of where it joins the Talung. Mangang has a hospital, a rest house, and a small hydroelectric project. A monastery and higher secondary school are nearby. Pop. (1981) 780.

manganite, an ore mineral of manganese, basic manganese oxide [MnO(OH)] that forms dark gray to black crystal bundles or fibrous masses. Important deposits exist at Ilfeld, Ilmenau, Siegen, and Horhausen, Ger.; the Lauron and Aure valleys, in France; St. Just, Cornwall, Eng.; and Michigan and California, U.S. As a manganese ore it ranks after pyrolusite and psilomelane, to which it readily alters. For detailed physical properties, *see* oxide mineral (table).

Mangar (people): *see* Magar.

Mangareva Islands (French Polynesia): *see* Gambier Islands.

Mangas Coloradas (b. *c.* 1795 [probably in what is now southern New Mexico, U.S.]—d. January 1863, Fort McLane, N.M.), Mimbreño Apache chief noted for uniting the Apache nation.

Mangas Coloradas, an unusually tall and striking man, became chief of the Mimbreño in 1837, after his predecessor—together with a number of Mimbreño men, women, and children—had been betrayed and murdered by a group of trappers for the Mexican bounty on their scalps. Mangas Coloradas and his warriors avenged the treachery by slaughtering trapping parties, attacking supply trains to the region, and starving the citizens of Santa Rita, killing the remainder on their attempted escape. The area was for a time cleared of its white and Mexican inhabitants. When the Mexican-American War was declared, Mangas offered Apache aid to the American troops, but his offer was refused.

In 1848, when gold was discovered in California, the Apache were threatened by the incursions of heedless white fortune-seekers. In an incident at a mining camp, Mangas Coloradas was whipped, an act that resulted in his lasting enmity against white men. Though his son-in-law Cochise had long resisted fighting Americans, in 1861 he too was betrayed by white men and turned against them, and together Mangas Coloradas and Cochise depopulated southern New Mexico and Arizona. Wounded in battle in 1862, Mangas Coloradas eventually recovered. He was captured in January 1863 and killed allegedly while trying to escape.

Mangbetu, also spelled MONBUTTU, peoples of central Africa living to the south of the Azande in northeastern Zaire. They speak a Central Sudanic language of the Chari-Nile branch of the Nilo-Saharan family. They are a cluster of peoples who penetrated and now occupy the formerly Pygmy territory and who, in turn, subsequently absorbed waves of eastern Nigritic and Bantu peoples. They thus comprise a host of peoples of diverse cultural and linguistic strains.

The name Mangbetu refers strictly only to the aristocracy, which in the 19th century established a number of powerful kingdoms; in looser usage it denotes the whole amalgam of people whom they ruled. They subsist by hoe cultivation, with some fishing, hunting, and gathering. They also raise cattle; in contrast to other Sudanic peoples, among the Mangbetu only the men do the milking. Yams and plantains are the staple crops.

Bride-price includes a substantial gift of livestock. Polygynous marriage is everywhere accepted. Descent is patrilineal. Most settlements are composed of extended families that include several generations. Political organization today is simple, usually limited to local headmen and councils of elders.

The Mangbetu impressed early travelers with their political institutions and their arts, especially their remarkable skill as builders, potters, and sculptors. Contemporary Mangbetu continue to attract artistic interest with their exquisitely carved knives, wooden containers for honey, statues, musical instruments, and jars. They became renowned also for their cannibalism and for their practice of deforming the heads of babies by binding them tightly so that they retained through life a curiously elongated form.

mange, skin disease of animals caused by any of six varieties of mites, characterized by inflammation, itching, thickening of the skin, and hair loss. The most severe variety is caused by the mite *Sarcoptes scabiei,* which also causes human scabies. Some form of mange is known in all domestic animals, although most mange mites will infest only one species; they are transmitted between animals by direct contact and by objects that have been in contact with infested animals.

Manggarai, Indonesian people inhabiting western Flores, one of the Lesser Sunda Islands, in Indonesia. Numbering more than 400,000 in the mid-1980s, they are of Proto-Malay stock and speak a language in the Bima-Sumba subgroup of Indonesian languages. The Manggarai were historically ruled alternately by the Bimanese of Sumbawa and the Makassarese of Celebes. Their own political system is based on clans, led by the chief of the Todo clan. Manggarai descent is patrilineal, and the fundamental settlement pattern is the village, which is composed of at least two clans. Each clan traditionally existed in relationship with two others, one for wife-giving and one for wife-taking, but today marriage rules are quite flexible. The Manggarai practice swidden agriculture, growing rice and corn (maize); permanent rice terraces have become more common since 1960. They also grow coffee, onions, and mung beans for export and raise horses and water buffalo. As a result of the Dutch influx in the 20th century, most of the Manggarai are Roman Catholic.

Mangla Dam, embankment dam on the Jhelum River, Pakistan, completed in 1967. Mangla Dam is one of the two main structures in the Indus Basin project (the other is Tarbela Dam (*q.v.*). The Mangla Dam rises 453 feet (138 m) above ground level, is about 10,-300 feet (3,140 m) wide at its crest, and has a volume of 85,500,000 cubic yards (65,400,000 cubic m). Along with its three small subsidiary dams, it has an installed power capacity of at least 600 megawatts and impounds a reservoir with a gross capacity of 5,900,000 acre-feet (7,250,000,000 cubic m).

Mango, formerly SANSANNÉ-MANGO, town, northern Togo, western Africa, situated on the Oti River near the Kéran National Park. The town served as the principal locale of Savanes until the late 1970s, when Dapango (formerly Dapaong) assumed that position. Mango still functions as a centre for cattle and peanut (groundnut) trade within this sparsely populated area. The town lies on the country's main road going north to the country of Burkina Faso (formerly Upper Volta) and south to Lomé, the national capital. The Anoufo people inhabit Mango and the surrounding area. Pop. (1988) 17,000.

mango (species *Mangifera indica*), member of the cashew family (Anacardiaceae), one of the most important and widely cultivated fruits of the tropical world, considered indigenous to eastern Asia, Myanmar (Burma), and Assam state of India. The tree is evergreen, often reaching 15–18 m (50–60 feet) in height and attaining great age. Leaves are lanceolate, up to 30 cm (12 inches) long; the flowers, small, pinkish, and fragrant, are borne in large terminal panicles (loose clusters). They are polygamous; *i.e.,* some have both stamens and pistils, others stamens only.

The fruit varies greatly in size and character; the smallest mangoes are no larger than plums, while others may weigh 1.8 to 2.3 kg (4 to 5 pounds). Its form is oval, round, heart-shaped, kidney-shaped, or long and slender. Some varieties are vividly coloured with shades of red and yellow, while others are dull green. The single large seed is flattened,

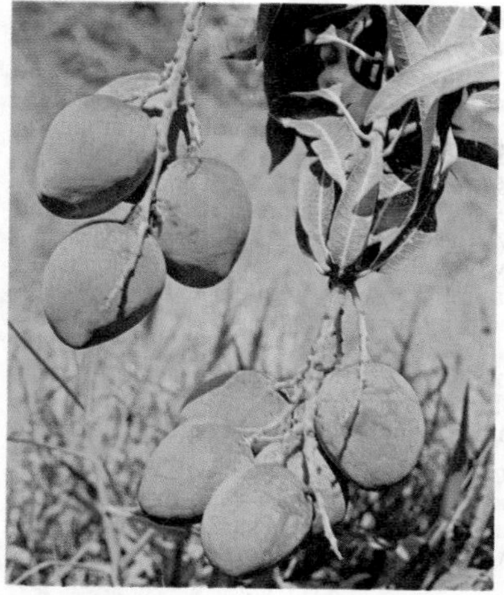

Mango (*Mangifera indica*)

Robert C. Hermes from The National Audubon Society Collection/Photo Researchers—EB Inc.

and the flesh that surrounds it is yellow to orange in colour, juicy, and of distinctive spicy flavour. Mangoes are a rich source of vitamins A, C, and D.

The mango is inextricably connected with the folklore and religious ceremonies of India. Buddha himself was presented with a mango grove that he might find repose in its grateful shade. The name mango, by which the fruit is known in English- and Spanish-speaking countries, is derived from the Tamil *man-kay* or *man-gay,* which the Portuguese adopted as *manga* when they settled in western India. Probably because of the difficulty in transporting seeds (they retain their viability a short time only), the tree was not introduced into the Western Hemisphere until about 1700, when it was planted in Brazil; it reached the West Indies about 1740.

The mango does not require any particular soil, but the finer varieties yield good crops only where there is a well-marked dry season to stimulate fruit production. In rainy areas a fungus disease known as anthracnose destroys flowers and young fruits and is difficult to control. Propagation is by grafting or budding. Inarching, or approach grafting (in which a scion and stock of independently rooted plants are grafted, and the scion later severed from its original stock), is widely practiced in tropical Asia but is tedious and relatively expensive. In Florida, more efficient methods—veneer grafting and chip budding—have been developed and are used commercially.

Mangoaela, Z(akea) D(olphin) (b. Feb. 1883, Hohobeng, Cape Colony [now Cape of Good Hope], S.Af.—d. Oct. 25, 1963), Southern Sotho writer and folklorist whose early work set the stage for much South African indigenous literature.

Mangoaela grew up in Basutoland (now Lesotho), where he received his primary education, later attending the Basutoland Training College, where he received a teaching certificate in 1902. As teacher and minister he worked at the Koeneng Mission School, meeting another early pioneer writer from Basutoland, E.L. Segoete, who was pastor there. From 1910 he taught and worked at Morija, a mission station, as a bookkeeper, translator, and later (1954–58) as editor of the journal *Leselinyana* ("The Little Light").

Quite early he had begun writing—first in a series of Sotho readers for schools, then at Morija a study of Lesotho under European rule, *Tsoe-lopele ea Lesotho* (1911; "The Progress of Lesotho"), and a collection of 54 hunting stories, *Har'a libatana le linyamat'sane* (1912; "Among Beasts and Animals"). He then contributed to a *Grammar of the Sesuto Language* (1917) and put together 82 praise songs under the title *Lithoko tsa marena a Basotho* (1921; "Praises of the Sotho Chiefs"), giving an early emphasis to an important genre in African oral literature.

Mangochi, formerly FORT JOHNSTON, town, south-central Malaŵi, on the Shire River below its efflux from Lake Nyasa (Malaŵi) and 5 miles (8 km) south of its entrance into Lake Malombe. The town began as a British colonial defense post founded by the colonial administrator Sir Harry Johnston in the 1890s on the littoral plain of the river's western shore. It developed as an agricultural centre and has marine-engineering shops. Local cash crops include tobacco, cotton, and peanuts (groundnuts). Rice and corn (maize) are intensively grown along the lakeshores, and commercial fishing is important. The surrounding region is mainly inhabited by the Yao people. Pop. (1998) township, 26,570.

mangosteen (species *Garcinia mangostana*), handsome tropical tree of the family Guttiferae, native to Southeast Asia, and its tart-sweet fruit. In Myanmar (Burma) it is called *men-gu.* Under favourable conditions, the slow-growing mangosteen tree can reach a height of 9.5 m (31 feet). Individual trees have been reported to yield more than 1,000 fruits in a season.

The tree has thick, dark green, glossy leaves, 15–25 cm (6–10 inches) long, and large, rose-pink flowers. The fruits are the size of a small orange, round or flattened on the ends. Mangosteens have a thick, hard, deep red rind surrounding snow-white flesh, in segments resembling those of a mandarin orange.

Highly valued for its juicy, delicate texture and slightly astringent flavour, the mango-

Mangosteen (*Garcinia mangostana*)

J.E. Cruise

steen has been cultivated in Java, Sumatra, Indochina, and the southern Philippines from antiquity. It is a common dooryard tree in Indonesia. The mangosteen was fruited in English greenhouses in 1855, and subsequently its culture was introduced into the Western Hemisphere, where it became established in several of the West Indian islands, notably Jamaica. It was later established on the mainland in Guatemala, Honduras, Panama, and Ecuador. The mangosteen generally does not prosper outside the tropics.

Because the fruit must ripen on the tree and keeps only a short time, it is found only in local markets. Seedlings take 8 to 15 years to bear fruit. Mangosteens usually produce good crops only in alternate years.

Mangrai, also spelled MENGRAI (b. Oct. 23, 1239, Chiang Saen [Thailand]—d. 1317, Chiang Mai), Thai founder of the city of Chiang Mai and the kingdom of Lan Na (reigned 1296–1317) in the north region of present Thailand, which remained an independent state until its capture by the Burmese in the 16th century.

Mangrai succeeded his father as ruler of the principality of Chiang Saen in 1259 and moved his state to Chiang Rai in 1262. He worked for more than a decade to prepare the conquest of the Chiang Mai region where Mon rulers had centred their kingdom of Haripunjaya since the 9th century. He captured Haripunjaya (now Lamphun) in 1281. In 1287 he made an alliance with Ramkhamhaeng of Sukhothai and the ruler of Phayao, hoping to take advantage of the Mongol capture of Pagan, the Burmese capital; and he may have assisted in the Shan conquest of Pagan in 1290. In 1296 he founded Chiang Mai, which became the capital of the kingdom of Lan Na (The Country of a Million Rice Fields), which remained a major power in the region until the 16th century.

mangrove, any of certain shrubs and trees, of the families Rhizophoraceae, Verbenaceae, Sonneratiaceae, and Arecaceae (Palmae), that grow in dense thickets or forests along tidal estuaries, in salt marshes, and on muddy coasts and characteristically have prop roots—*i.e.,* exposed, supporting roots. The term mangrove also applies to thickets and forests of such plants. Respiratory or knee roots (pneumatophores) are characteristic of many species; they project above the mud and have small openings (lenticels) through which air enters, passing through the soft, spongy tissue to the roots beneath the mud.

Mangrove flora along the Atlantic coast of tropical America and along the coast of the Gulf of Mexico to Florida consists chiefly of the common, or red, mangrove (*Rhizophora mangle*) of the family Rhizophoraceae and the black mangrove (*Avicennia nitida,* sometimes *A. marina*) of the family Verbenaceae. Mangrove formations in Southeast Asia include *Sonneratia* of the family Sonneratiaceae and the nipa palm (*Nypa fruticans*) of the family Arecaceae.

The trunks and branches of the common mangrove are typical of the growth habit of all mangroves. They constantly produce adventitious roots, which, descending in arched fashion, strike at some distance from the parent stem and send up new trunks. While the fruit is still attached to the parent branch, the long embryonic root emerges from the seed and grows rapidly downward. When the seed falls, the young root is in the correct position to be driven into the mud; the plant being thus rooted, the shoot makes its appearance. The young root may grow to such a length that it becomes fixed in the mud before the fruit separates from the parent tree.

The common mangrove grows to about 9 m (30 feet) tall. The leaves are 5 to 15 cm (2 to 6 inches) long, opposite, oval or elliptic, and smooth-edged; they are thick, have leathery surfaces, and are borne on short stems. The flowers are pale yellow.

Common mangrove (*Rhizophora mangle*)
Grant Heilman

The black mangrove, usually of moderate height, sometimes grows 18 to 21 m tall. The leaves are 5 to 7.5 cm long, opposite, oblong or spear-shaped; the upper surface is green and glossy, the lower surface whitish or grayish. The white flowers are small, inconspicuous, and fragrant and are frequented by honeybees for their abundant nectar.

The wood of some species is hard and durable. The astringent bark yields a water-soluble tanning substance. The fruit of the common mangrove is sweet and wholesome.

mangrove snake (genus *Boiga*), any of about 30 species (family Colubridae) of weakly venomous, rear-fanged snakes, ranging from tropical Africa to Australia and Polynesian islands. They are at home on the ground and in trees; many catch birds at night. Because they have elliptical pupils and may be green-eyed, they are sometimes referred to as cat, or cat-eyed, snakes. The head is short and broad, the body fairly stout.

Black-and-yellow mangrove snake (*Boiga dendrophila*)
Cy La Tour

The black-and-yellow mangrove snake (*B. dendrophila*) of the Malay Peninsula to the Philippines is black, with narrow yellow bars and yellow lips and throat. It may be 1.8 m (about 6 feet) long. The gamma (*B. trigonata*) of India and Central Asia is a 1.2-metre brown species that is chiefly arboreal. Like some others of the genus, the gamma defends itself by rearing into an S-curve, inflating the foreparts, and striking repeatedly. The brown tree snake (*B. irregularis*) is found in northern and eastern Australia; anchored to a bough, it can strike across a surprising distance.

Mangu (Mongol ruler): *see* Möngke.

Mangunkusumo, Tjipto (b. 1884—d. March 8, 1942, Djakarta, Java, Dutch East Indies [now Indonesia]), early 20th-century Indonesian nationalist leader whose resistance to Dutch colonial rule brought him exile and long imprisonment.

Tjipto Mangunkusumo was among the first Indonesian leaders to abandon the cultural approach of most early nationalist groups, which promoted distinctly Indonesian art, literature, and values. With E.F.E. Douwes Dekker and Suwardi Surjaningrat (later known as Ki Hadjar Dewantoro) he founded in 1911 the socialist Indies Party (Indische Partij), which was devoted to political action to attain independence. Two years later all three leaders were ordered out of the Dutch East Indies, although Tjipto Mangunkusumo was allowed to return in 1914. He resumed activity in Insulinde, the successor to the Indies Party, backing radical action such as the peasant resistance to taxes in the Solo princely lands. In 1918 he became a member of the Volksraad, a parliamentary body that included Indonesians but exercised very little power. In July 1927 he helped found the Indonesian Nationalist Party (Partai Nasional Indonesia), of which Sukarno was chairman. Shortly thereafter, however, Tjipto Mangunkusumo was sent into exile on a prison island for attempting to foment revolt among the Indonesians serving in the Dutch forces. He remained in exile for 11 years.

Mangyshlak, *oblast* (province), southwestern Kazakhstan, east of the Caspian sea. The *oblast* covers an area of 64,320 square miles (166,600 square km) and consists of vast flatlands, with some depressions (the Batyr Depression is 425 feet [130 m] below sea level). It is rich in petroleum and natural gas, especially in the Mangyshlak oil and gas region of the Mangyshlak Peninsula. The Mangyshlak Peninsula also contains deposits of phosphorites and coquina. The desert climate is continental and extremely dry, permitting virtually no crop farming and only limited raising of sheep, camels, and horses. The *oblast* is inhabited by Kazakhs, Russians, Ukrainians, Tatars, and other peoples. The only major city is the capital, Shevchenko, on the Caspian Sea, but for the various small communities there is a network of railroads, built since the 1960s. Pop. (1987 est.) 327,000.

Manhae (Buddhist leader): *see* Han Yongun.

Manhattan, city, Pottawatomie and Riley counties and seat of Riley county, northeastern Kansas, U.S., where the Big Blue and Kansas (Kaw) rivers meet, there dammed to form Tuttle Creek Lake, on the northern edge of the rolling Flint Hills. The village was founded in 1855 when the settlements of Poleska and Canton were consolidated as Boston, only to be renamed Manhattan the next year by mutual agreement between the Boston Association of Kansas and a party of colonists from Cincinnati, Ohio. The "Beecher Bible and Rifle" Church (1862) received its name from the proslavery and antislavery tumult, when rifles for the Abolitionist congregation arrived in crates marked "Bibles." Chiefly an educational centre, Manhattan is the home of Kansas State University (founded in 1858 as Bluemont College, one of the first land-grant colleges in the United States) and Manhattan Christian College (1927). It is a trading and processing centre for the surrounding agricultural area. Fort Riley (1852), headquarters of the 1st Infantry Division, is 8 miles (13 km) southwest. Inc. 1857. Pop. (1990) 37,712.

Manhattan, borough of New York City, coextensive with New York county, southeastern New York, U.S. The borough, mainly on Manhattan Island, spills over into the Marble Hill section on the mainland and includes a number of islets in the East River. It is bounded by the Hudson River (west), Harlem River and Spuyten Duyvil Creek (northeast), East River (east), and Upper New York Bay (south). Manhattan is often mistakenly deemed synonymous with New York City.

In 1626 Peter Minuit, the first director general of New Netherland province, is said to have purchased the island from the local Indians (the Manhattan, a tribe of the Wappinger Confederacy) with trinkets and cloth valued at 60 guilders, then worth about 1½ pounds (0.7 kg) of silver. The English took possession in 1664, the island having already been incorporated as the city of New Amsterdam in 1653. Renamed New York City when transferred to the British, it played a prominent role in the nation's early history, both militarily and politically. Congress met there (1785–90), and George Washington was inaugurated there in 1789 as the first U.S. president. In the 19th century, particularly following the opening of the Erie Canal in 1825, Manhattan developed as the heart of a prosperous and expanding metropolis. In 1898 Greater New York was formed when Manhattan was joined with the newly created boroughs of Brooklyn, Queens, Richmond, and the Bronx.

Manhattan is considered one of the world's foremost commercial, financial, and cultural centres. It is renowned for its many points of interest. Among these are Broadway (*q.v.*), one of the world's best-known streets; the financial district of Wall Street (*q.v.*); skyscrapers, such as the Empire State Building and the World Trade Center (*qq.v.*); Greenwich Village, Harlem, and Central Park (*qq.v.*); the United Nations headquarters; and various cultural and educational institutions, including the Metropolitan Museum of Art, the Metropolitan Opera House, the Museum of Modern Art, Columbia University, two branches of the City University of New York, and New York University. Pop. (2000) 1,537,195.

Manhattan Project, U.S. government research project (1942–45) that produced the first atomic bombs.

In 1939 American scientists, many of them refugees from Fascist regimes in Europe, took steps to organize a project to exploit the newly recognized fission process for military purposes. The first contact with the government was made by G.B. Pegram of Columbia University, who arranged a conference between Enrico Fermi and the Navy Department in March 1939. In the summer of 1939 Albert Einstein was persuaded by his fellow scientists to use his influence and present the military potential of an uncontrolled fission chain reaction to President Franklin D. Roosevelt. In February 1940, $6,000 was made available to start research under the supervision of a committee headed by L.J. Briggs, director of the National Bureau of Standards. On Dec. 6, 1941, the project was put under the direction of the Office of Scientific Research and Development, headed by Vannevar Bush. After the United States' entry into the war, the War Department was given joint responsibility for the project, since by mid-1942 it was obvious that a vast array of pilot plants, laboratories, and manufacturing facilities would have to be constructed by the U.S. Army Corps of Engineers so that the assembled scientists could carry out their mission. In June 1942 the Engineers' Manhattan District was initially assigned management of the construction work (because much of the early research had been performed at Columbia University, in Manhattan), and in September 1942 Brigadier General Leslie R. Groves was placed in charge of all Army activities (chiefly engineering activities) relating to the project. The "Manhattan Project" became the code name for research work that would extend across the country.

It was known in 1940 that German scientists were working on a similar project and that the British were also exploring the problem. In the fall of 1941 Harold C. Urey and Pegram visited England to attempt to set up a cooperative effort, and by 1943 a combined policy committee with Great Britain and Canada was established. In that year a number of scientists of those countries moved to the United States to join the project there.

If the project were to achieve success quickly, several lines of research and development had to be carried on simultaneously before it was certain whether any might succeed. The explosive materials then had to be produced and be made suitable for use in an actual weapon.

Uranium 235, the essential fissionable component of the postulated bomb, cannot be separated from its natural companion, the much more abundant uranium 238, by chemical means; the atoms of these respective isotopes must rather be separated from each other by physical means. Several physical methods to do this were intensively explored, and two were chosen—the electromagnetic process developed at the University of California at Berkeley under Ernest Orlando Lawrence and the diffusion process developed under Urey at Columbia University. Both of these processes, and particularly the diffusion method, required large, complex facilities and huge amounts of electric power to produce even small amounts of separated uranium 235. Philip Hauge Abelson developed a third method called thermal diffusion, which was also used for a time to effect a preliminary separation. These methods were put into production at a 70-square-mile tract near Knoxville, Tenn., originally known as the Clinton Engineer Works, later as Oak Ridge.

Only one method was available for the production of the fissionable material plutonium 239. It was developed at the metallurgical laboratory of the University of Chicago under the direction of Arthur Holly Compton and involved the transmutation in a reactor pile of uranium 238. In December 1942 Fermi finally succeeded in producing and controlling a fission chain reaction in this reactor pile at Chicago.

Quantity production of plutonium 239 required the construction of a reactor of great size and power that would release about 25,000 kilowatt-hours of heat for each gram of plutonium produced. It involved the development of chemical extraction procedures that would work under conditions never before encountered. An intermediate step in putting this method into production was taken with the construction of a medium-size reactor at Oak Ridge. The large-scale production reactors were built on an isolated 1,000-square-mile tract on the Columbia River north of Pasco, Wash.—the Hanford Engineer Works.

Before 1943 work on the design and functioning of the bomb itself was largely theoretical, based on fundamental experiments carried out at a number of different locations. In that year a laboratory directed by J. Robert Oppenheimer was created on an isolated mesa at Los Alamos, N.M., 34 miles (55 km) north of Santa Fe. This laboratory had to develop methods of reducing the fissionable products of the production plants to pure metal and fabricating the metal to required shapes. Methods of rapidly bringing together amounts of fissionable material to achieve a supercritical mass (and thus a nuclear explosion) had to be devised, along with the actual construction of a deliverable weapon that would be dropped from a plane and fused to detonate at the proper moment in the air above the target. Most of these problems had to be solved before any appreciable amount of fissionable material could be produced so that the first adequate amounts could be used at the fighting front with minimum delay.

By the summer of 1945, amounts of plutonium 239 sufficient to produce a nuclear explosion had become available from the Hanford Works, and weapon development and design were sufficiently far advanced so that an actual field test of a nuclear explosive could be scheduled. Such a test was no simple affair. Elaborate and complex equipment had to be assembled so that a complete diagnosis of success or failure could be had. By this time the original $6,000 authorized for the Manhattan Project had grown to $2,000,000,000.

The first atomic bomb was exploded at 5:30 AM on July 16, 1945, at a site on the Alamogordo air base 120 miles (193 km) south of Albuquerque, N.M. It was detonated on top of a steel tower surrounded by scientific equipment, with remote monitoring taking place in bunkers occupied by scientists and a few dignitaries 10,000 yards (9 km) away. The explosion came as an intense light flash, a sudden wave of heat, and later a tremendous roar as the shock wave passed and echoed in the valley. A ball of fire rose rapidly, followed by a mushroom cloud extending to 40,000 feet (12,200 m). The bomb generated an explosive power equivalent to 15,000 to 20,000 tons of TNT; the tower was completely vaporized and the surrounding desert surface fused to glass for a radius of 800 yards (730 m). The following month, two other atomic bombs produced by the project, the first using uranium 235 and the second using plutonium, were dropped on Hiroshima and Nagasaki.

Mani (Greece): *see* Maina.

Mani, also called MANES, or MANICHAEUS (b. April 14, 216, southern Babylonia—d. 274?, Gundeshapur), Iranian founder of the Manichaean religion, a church advocating a dualistic doctrine that viewed the world as a fusion of spirit and matter, the original contrary principles of good and evil, respectively.

Before Mani's birth, his father, Patek, a native of Hamadan, had joined a religious community practicing baptism and abstinence. Through his mother Mani was related to the Parthian royal family (overthrown in 224). Information about his life appears to derive from his own writings and the traditions of his church. He grew up at his birthplace, speaking a form of eastern Aramaic. Twice, as a boy and young man, he saw in vision an angel, the "Twin," who, the second time, called him to preach a new religion.

He traveled to India (probably Sind and Turan) and made converts. Favourably received on his return by the newly crowned Persian king, Shāpūr I, he was permitted to preach his religion in the Persian empire during that long reign. There is little information about Mani's life in those years. He probably traveled widely in the western parts of the empire, but later traditions that he visited the northeast seem unsound. Under the reign of the Persian king Bahrām I, however, he was attacked by Zoroastrian priests and was imprisoned by the king at Gundeshapur (Belapet), where he died after undergoing a trial that lasted 26 days.

mania, in psychiatric terminology, any abnormal or unusual state of excitement, as in the manic phase of a person with manic depression.

manic depression, also called BIPOLAR DISORDER, mental disorder characterized by severe and recurrent depression or mania with abrupt or gradual onsets and recoveries. The states of mania and depression may alternate cyclically, one mood state may predominate over the other, or they may be mixed or combined with each other.

A manic-depressive person in the depressive phase may be sad, despondent, listless, lacking in energy, unable to show interest in his surroundings or to enjoy himself, and may have a poor appetite and disturbed sleep. The depressive state can be either agitated—in which case sustained tension, overactivity, despair, and apprehensive delusions predominate—or retarded—in which case the patient's activity is slowed and reduced, he is sad and dejected, and he suffers from self-depreciatory and self-condemnatory tendencies. Mania is a mood disturbance that is characterized by abnormally intense excitement, elation, expansiveness, boisterousness, talkativeness, distractibility, and irritability. The manic person talks loudly, rapidly, and continuously and progresses rapidly from one topic to another; is extremely enthusiastic, optimistic, and confident; is highly sociable and gregarious; gesticulates and moves about almost continuously; is easily irritated and easily distracted; and is prone to grandiose notions and shows an inflated sense of self-esteem. The most extreme manifestations of these two mood disturbances are, in the manic phase, violence against others, and, in the depressive, suicide. As the name implies, a manic depression may also feature such psychotic symptoms as delusions and hallucinations. Depression is the more common symptom, and many patients never develop a genuine manic phase, although they may experience a brief period of overoptimism and mild euphoria while recovering from a depression.

Manic depression of varying severity affects about 1 percent of the general population and accounts for 10 to 15 percent of readmissions to mental institutions. Statistical studies have suggested a hereditary predisposition to the disorder, and this predisposition has now been linked to a defect on a dominant gene located on chromosome 11. In a physiological sense, it is believed that manic depression is caused by the faulty regulation of one or more naturally occurring amines at sites in the brain where the transmission of nerve impulses takes place; a deficiency of the amines results in depression, and an excess of them causes mania. The most likely candidates for the suspect amines are norepinephrine, dopamine, and 5-hydroxytryptamine. The ingestion of lithium carbonate on a long-term basis has been found effective in alleviating or even eliminating the symptoms of many persons with manic depression.

Manic depression was described in antiquity by the 2nd-century Greek physician Aretaeus of Cappadocia and definitively in modern times by the German psychiatrist Emil Kraepelin.

Manica (people): *see* Manyika.

Manichaeism, dualistic religious movement founded in Persia in the 3rd century AD by Mani (*q.v.*), who was known as the "Apostle of Light" and supreme "Illuminator." Although Manichaeism was long considered a Christian heresy, it was a religion in its own right that, because of the coherence of its doctrines and the rigidness of its structure and institutions, preserved throughout its history a unity and unique character.

Mani was born in southern Babylonia (now in Iraq). With his "annunciation" at the age of 24, he obeyed a heavenly order to manifest himself publicly and to proclaim his doctrines;

Fragment of wall painting presumably depicting (left) Mani, followed by members of the elect, from K'o-cha, China, 8th–9th century; in the Museum für Indische Kunst, Berlin

By courtesy of the Staatliche Museen Preussischer Kulturbesitz, Berlin

thus began the new religion. From that point on, Mani preached throughout the Persian Empire. At first unhindered, he later was opposed by the king, condemned, and imprisoned. After 26 days of trials, which his followers called the "Passion of the Illuminator" or Mani's "crucifixion," Mani delivered a final message to his disciples and died (sometime between 274 and 277).

Mani viewed himself as the final successor in a long line of prophets, beginning with Adam and including Buddha, Zoroaster, and Jesus. He viewed earlier revelations of the true religion as being limited in effectiveness because they were local, taught in one language to one people. Moreover, later adherents lost sight of the original truth. Mani regarded himself as the carrier of a universal message destined to replace all other religions. Hoping to avoid corruption and to ensure doctrinal unity, he recorded his teachings in writing and gave those writings canonical status during his lifetime.

The Manichaean Church from the beginning was dedicated to vigorous missionary activity in an attempt to convert the world. Mani encouraged the translation of his writings into other languages and organized an extensive mission program. Manichaeism rapidly spread west into the Roman Empire. From Egypt it moved across northern Africa (where the young Augustine temporarily became a convert) and reached Rome in the early 4th century. The 4th century marked the height of Manichaean expansion in the West, with churches established in southern Gaul and Spain. Vigorously attacked by both the Christian Church and the Roman state, it disappeared almost entirely from Western Europe by the end of the 5th century, and, during the course of the 6th century, from the eastern portion of the Empire.

During the lifetime of Mani, Manichaeism spread to the eastern provinces of the Persian Sāsānian Empire. Within Persia itself, the Manichaean community maintained itself in spite of severe persecutions, until Muslim ʿAbbāsid persecution in the 10th century forced the transfer of the seat of the Manichaean leader to Samarkand (now in Uzbekistan).

The religion's expansion to the East had already begun in the 7th century with the reopening of caravan routes there after China's conquest of East Turkistan. A Manichaean missionary reached the Chinese court in 694, and in 732 an edict gave the religion freedom of worship in China. When East Turkistan was conquered in the 8th century by the Uighur Turks, one of their leaders adopted Manichaeism and it remained the state religion of the Uighur kingdom until its overthrow in 840. Manichaeism itself probably survived in East Turkistan until the Mongol invasion in the 13th century. In China it was forbidden in 843, but, although persecuted, it continued there at least until the 14th century.

Teachings similar to Manichaeism resurfaced during the Middle Ages in Europe in the so-called neo-Manichaean sects. Groups such as the Paulicians (Armenia, 7th century), the Bogomilists (Bulgaria, 10th century), and the Cathari or Albigensians (southern France, 12th century) bore strong resemblances to Manichaeism and probably were influenced by it. However, their direct historical links to the religion of Mani are difficult to establish.

Mani sought to found a truly ecumenical and universal religion that would integrate into itself all the partial truths of previous revelations, especially those of Zoroaster, Buddha, and Jesus. However, beyond mere syncretism, it sought the proclamation of a truth that could be translated into diverse forms in accordance with the different cultures into which it spread. Thus, Manichaeism, depending on the context, resembles Iranian and Indian religions, Christianity, Buddhism, and Taoism.

At its core, Manichaeism was a type of Gnosticism—a dualistic religion that offered salvation through special knowledge (gnosis) of spiritual truth. Like all forms of Gnosticism, Manichaeism taught that life in this world is unbearably painful and radically evil. Inner illumination or gnosis reveals that the soul which shares in the nature of God has fallen into the evil world of matter and must be saved by means of the spirit or intelligence (nous). To know one's self is to recover one's true self, which was previously clouded by ignorance and lack of self-consciousness because of its mingling with the body and with matter. In Manichaeism, to know one's self is to see one's soul as sharing in the very nature of God and as coming from a transcendent world. Knowledge enables a person to realize that, despite his abject present condition in the material world, he does not cease to remain united to the transcendent world by eternal and immanent bonds with it. Thus, knowledge is the only way to salvation.

The saving knowledge of the true nature and destiny of humanity, God, and the universe is expressed in Manichaeism in a complex mythology. Whatever its details, the essential theme of this mythology remains constant: the soul is fallen, entangled with evil matter, and then liberated by the spirit or nous. The myth unfolds in three stages: a past period in which there was a separation of the two radically opposed substances—Spirit and Matter, Good and Evil, Light and Darkness; a middle period (corresponding to the present) during which the two substances are mixed; and a future period in which the original duality will be reestablished. At death the soul of the righteous person returns to Paradise. The soul of the person who persisted in things of the flesh—fornication, procreation, possessions, cultivation, harvesting, eating of meat, drinking of wine—is condemned to rebirth in a succession of bodies.

Only a portion of the faithful followed the strict ascetic life advocated in Manichaeism. The community was divided into the elect, who felt able to embrace a rigorous rule, and the hearers who supported the elect with works and alms.

The essentials of the Manichaean sacramental rites were prayers, almsgiving, and fasting. Confession and the singing of hymns were also important in their communal life. The Manichaean scriptural canon includes seven works attributed to Mani, written originally in Syriac. Lost after Manichaeism became extinct in the Middle Ages, portions of the Manichaean scriptures were rediscovered in the 20th century, mainly in Chinese Turkistan and Egypt.

manichord (musical instrument): *see* monochord.

Manicouagan River, also spelled MANIKUAGAN RIVER, French RIVIÈRE MANICOUAGAN, river in the Côte-Nord (North Shore) region, eastern Quebec province, Canada. Rising near the Labrador border, the river drains lakes Muskalagan and Manicouagan southward into the mouth of the St. Lawrence River near Baie-Comeau and Hauterive. It is more than 340 miles (550 km) long from the source of its longest headstream. The Manicouagan drains more than 16,000 square miles (41,000 square km) of the heavily forested region, hence its Indian name meaning "where there is bark." Long an important lumbering artery supporting the huge pulp and paper factories at Baie-Comeau, the river has become a major source of hydroelectric power; Hydro-Quebec has built several plants—including Daniel-Johnson Dam, one of the world's largest multiarch dams—which together have a generating capacity in the millions of kilowatts. A submarine cable, laid in 1954, carries electric power under the St. Lawrence to the copper-mining regions in the Gaspé Peninsula. Iron ore is mined in the upper Manicouagan Valley.

maniera (Italian: "manner," "style"), in art criticism, certain stylistic characteristics, primarily in Mannerist painting (*see* Mannerism). In the 14th and 15th centuries, *manière* in France and *maniera* in Italy designated refined, courtly manners and sophisticated bearing. The name was first applied to art—apparently to praise the grace of the art of the Italian court painter Pisanello—by a critic, either Agnolo Galli or Ottaviano Ubaldini, in

Urbino in 1442. Between about 1520 and 1550—first in Italy, then the French court (especially at Fontainebleau), and later in the Netherlands and other settings in the north of Europe—artists developed qualities of grace, novelty, and curiosity in their painting, at the same time adhering to older formal conventions and self-consciously displaying their abilities to resolve difficult artistic problems and to exercise license within rules derived from Classical art.

The Florentine painter and art historian Giorgio Vasari praised the productions of the Italians for exhibiting *bella maniera,* "beautiful style," in addition to satisfying more technical qualities. In the 17th century, critics condemned the same painters Vasari had praised because they had abandoned the study of nature and adulterated the arts with *maniera.*

Manifest Destiny, in U.S. history, the supposed inevitability of the continued territorial expansion of U.S. boundaries westward to the Pacific, and even beyond. The idea of "Manifest Destiny" was often used by American expansionists to justify U.S. annexation of Texas, Oregon, New Mexico, and California and later U.S. involvement in Alaska, Hawaii, and the Philippines.

John L. O'Sullivan coined the phrase in his *United States Magazine and Democratic Review* (July–August 1845) to prophesy "the fulfillment of our manifest destiny to overspread the continent allotted by Providence. . . ." Congressmen quickly adopted the term in their debates over the three territorial questions confronting the United States in 1845 and 1846—the annexation of Texas, the joint occupation of the Oregon Territory with England, and the prosecution of war with Mexico. Although chiefly a tenet of the Democrats, individual Whigs or Republicans also supported Manifest Destiny, which in the 1890s was revived as a Republican policy.

manifold, in mathematics, topological space equipped with a family of local coordinate systems that are related to each other by coordinate transformations belonging to a specified class. Manifolds occur in algebraic geometry, differential equations, and classical dynamics. They are studied for their global properties by the methods of analysis and algebraic topology, and they form natural domains for the global analysis of differential equations, particularly equations that arise in the calculus of variations.

Manikuagan River (Canada): *see* Manicouagan River.

Manila, capital and chief city of the Philippines. Located on Luzon island about 700 miles (1,100 km) southeast of Hong Kong, the city has for four centuries been the economic, political, social, and cultural centre of the Philippines. It is the focus of the country's industrial development, as well as the international port of entry. Area city, 15 square miles (38 square km); National Capital Region, 246 square miles (636 square km). Pop. (2000) city, 1,581,082; National Capital Region, 9,932,560.

The following article treats briefly the modern city of Manila. Fuller treatment is provided in the following MACROPAEDIA articles. For history and contemporary life, *see* Manila; for additional perspective on the city in its national context, *see* Philippines.

Manila and its contiguous cities and municipalities form a single unit known as Metropolitan Manila (National Capital Region). The city spreads along the eastern shore of Manila Bay, a large inlet with access to the sea to the southwest through a channel 12 miles (19 km) wide. It occupies the low, narrow deltaic plain of the Pasig River, which flows northwestward to Manila Bay out of a large lake, Laguna de Bay, southeast of the city. The city is an excellent port site because of its sheltered harbour, its access to inland agricultural areas by way of the river, and its relative proximity to the Asian mainland. Manila's tropical climate is characterized by a wet season (June to November), a dry season (December to May), and a year-round temperature of about 81° F (27° C).

Manila has experienced rapid economic development since its destruction in World War II and its subsequent rebuilding. Its diverse manufacturing activities include publishing and printing, food processing, and the production of textiles, paints, pharmaceuticals, aluminum articles, rope and cordage, shoes, tobacco goods, coconut oil, soap, and lumber. As the centre of trade and finance in the Philippines, Manila is the home of several major banks, government and private insurance companies, and the Manila Stock Exchange.

The heavily populated Tondo district on the northern shore of the Pasig River is the site of Manila North Harbor, the local port, while the international port, Manila South Harbor, is on the southern shore. The district of San Miguel is the site of Malacañang Palace, the presidential residence; Intramuros is renowned for its 16th-century San Agustin Church and other historical sites. Architectural styles reflect American, Spanish, Chinese, and Malay influences.

As the education centre of the country, Metropolitan Manila houses many of the major institutions of higher learning, including the University of the Philippines (with its main campus in Quezon City), the University of Manila, and the Polytechnic University of the Philippines. The heart of the country's performing arts activities is the Philippine Cultural Center. Other theatres include the Folk Arts, the historic Metropolitan, and an open-air theatre in Rizal Park. The many libraries and museums include the National Library, the National Museum, the National Institute of Science and Technology, the geological museum of the Bureau of Mines, and the archival Kamaynilaan (Manila City) Library and Museum.

Within Metropolitan Manila public transportation is provided by buses, jeepneys (small buses built on the chassis of jeeps), and taxis. Railways connect the city with northern and southeastern Luzon. Interisland and international transportation is provided by shipping and by air services. Manila Domestic Airport and Ninoy Aquino International Airport are both located about 6 miles (10 km) south of the city centre.

Manila Bay, bay of the South China Sea extending into southwestern Luzon Island, Philippines. Almost completely landlocked, it is considered one of the world's great harbours and has an area of 770 sq mi (2,000 sq km) with a 120-mi (190-km) circumference. Its widest diameter, from northwest to southeast, measures 36 mi. Corregidor Island, 30 mi west of Manila, divides the bay's 11-mi-wide entrance into two channels—the seldom used South Channel and the safer, 2-mi-wide North Channel between Bataan Peninsula and Corregidor.

The northern and northeastern shore of the bay adjoins Luzon's central plain. There the bay is shallow and lined by the mud flats and mangrove swamps of the delta of the Pampanga River, site of the most extensive commercial fishponds in the Philippines. Most of the bay is between 30 and 120 ft (10 and 40 m) deep; the tidal range is only moderate.

Tending fish traps, Manila Bay, Philippines

Ted Spiegel—Rapho/Photo Researchers

Manila Harbor, at the easternmost part of the bay, is divided into two sections: North Harbor for interisland ships and South Harbor for international shipping. Sangley Point is a U.S.–Filipino naval reservation near Cavite, on the southeastern shore, and Balanga, on the western shore, is the base of a small fishing fleet.

Manila Bay provides excellent protected anchorage, since it is sheltered by the mountains of Bataan Peninsula (west) and the Cordillera Central (east). Because of its location near the Southeast Asian mainland, it was already commercially important when, in 1571, Spanish colonizers began building fortifications at the site of present-day Manila. In 1574 the Chinese pirate Lim-ah-hong entered the bay with a force of nearly 3,000 but was repulsed by Spanish forces. Manila Bay was the western terminus of the Manila–Acapulco "galleon trade" between 1593 and 1815. The decisive naval battle of the Spanish–American War, the Battle of Manila Bay, took place there on May 1, 1898, when Commo. George Dewey's U.S. fleet destroyed the Spanish fleet off Cavite. During World War II many Philippine, American, and Japanese ships were sunk by aerial bombardment at Manila, Cavite, Corregidor, and other locations. In February–March 1945 Manila Bay was regained by U.S. forces.

Manila Bay, Battle of (May 1, 1898), defeat of the Spanish Pacific fleet by the U.S. Navy, resulting in the fall of the Philippines and contributing to the final U.S. victory in the Spanish–American War. After the United States had declared war (April 25), its Asiatic squadron was ordered from Hong Kong to "capture or destroy the Spanish fleet" then in Philippine waters. The U.S. Navy was well trained and well supplied, largely through the energetic efforts of the young assistant secretary of the Navy, Theodore Roosevelt, who had selected Commo. George Dewey for the command of the Asiatic squadron. In one morning's engagement (May 1), the guns of Dewey's squadron completely destroyed the Spanish ships anchored in Manila Bay. (Spanish casualties numbered 381; American, fewer than 10.) After token bombardment, Manila surrendered and was occupied by the U.S. Army on August 13. The Battle of Manila Bay made Commodore Dewey a national hero and helped establish the reputation of the United States as a major naval power.

Manila galleon, Spanish sailing vessel that made an annual round trip (one vessel per year) across the Pacific between Manila, in the Philippines, and Acapulco, in present Mexico, during the period 1565–1815. They were the sole means of communication between Spain and its Philippine colony and served as an economic lifeline for the Spaniards in Manila.

During the heyday of the galleon trade, Manila became one of the world's great ports, serving as a focus for trade between China and Europe. Though Chinese silk was by far the most important cargo, other exotic goods, such as perfumes, porcelain, cotton fabric (from India), and precious stones, were also transshipped via the galleon. After unloading at Acapulco, this cargo normally yielded a profit of 100–300 percent. On its return voyage, the vessel brought back huge quantities of Mexican silver and church personnel bearing communications from Spain.

The Spaniards in Manila came to depend on the annual vessel so much that when a ship went down at sea or was captured by English pirates, the colony was plunged into economic depression. The galleon trade had a negative effect on economic development in the Philippines, since virtually all Spanish capital was devoted to speculation in Chinese goods.

The importance of the trade declined in the late 18th century as other powers began to trade directly with China.

Manilius, Marcus (fl. early 1st century AD), last of the Roman didactic poets. Little of his life is known. He was the author of *Astronomica,* an unfinished poem on astronomy and astrology probably written between the years AD 14 and 27. Following the style and philosophy of Lucretius, Virgil, and Ovid, Manilius stresses the providential government of the world and the operation of divine reason. He exercises his amazing ability for versifying astronomical calculations to the extreme, often forcing unnecessarily complex constructions upon his lines. The poem's chief interest lies in the attractive prefaces to each book and in the mythological and moralizing digressions. The five extant books, consisting of 4,000 hexameters, are rarely read completely.

Manin, Daniele (b. May 13, 1804, Venice [Italy]—d. Sept. 22, 1857, Paris, Fr.), leader of the Risorgimento in Venice.

The son of a converted Jewish lawyer (who had taken his sponsors' historic name at baptism), Manin studied law at Padua, graduating at age 17. Early in his practice, he showed little interest in politics and disapproved of the conspiratorial activities of the Carbonari and other revolutionary groups. But in the late

Manin, detail of an oil painting by an unknown artist, 1848; in the Museum of the Risorgimento, Venice

By courtesy of the Civici Musei, Venice

1840s, Manin underwent a change and joined the patriot Niccolò Tommaseo in giving expression to the discontent of the Venetian people under Austrian rule.

When Manin presented a petition for home rule to the Congregation, the quasi-representative body of the Austrian province of Venetia, he was imprisoned along with Tommaseo (January 1848). After the rebellions of the following March, however, he was freed and made president of the Venetian republic, in which capacity he reluctantly accepted the project of union with the kingdom of Piedmont-Sardinia in the name of Italian unification. He led a heroic defense of Venice against an Austrian siege even after the defeat of the Piedmontese army at Novara; when cholera and bombardment finally forced surrender in August 1849, Manin was among those excepted from amnesty and was banished. For the remainder of his life he lived in Paris, where he strove to enlist French sympathy for the Italian cause. In 1868, 11 years after his death, his body was returned to liberated Venice for a state funeral.

Maning, Frederick, in full FREDERICK EDWARD MANING (b. July 5, 1811, Dublin, Ire.—d. July 25, 1883, London, Eng.), New Zealand author and judge, who was known for his histories of the British colony in New Zealand and for his service as a judge (1865–76) in land disputes, the key issue dividing settlers and the native Maoris.

The Maning family immigrated to Van Diemen's Land (now Tasmania) in 1824, and in 1833 Maning moved to Hokianga in the northern part of North Island, N.Z., where he worked as a trader in timber and flax. In 1837 he settled at Onoke, Hokianga, which became his home for the next 40 years, and married the sister of a Maori chief. Maning clashed with the colony's governor, William Hobson, and may have advised the Maoris against signing the Treaty of Waitangi (1840), which established British sovereignty. In an intertribal war (1845–46) involving the northern leader Hone Heke, Maning assisted Heke's victorious opponents. His account of the campaign, *The History of the War in the North Against the Chief Heke,* was published in 1862.

Maning's extensive knowledge of Maori culture led to his appointment in 1865 as judge in the native land court and also aided him in his decisions. For reasons not fully apparent, he developed an animosity for the Maori in later life. His account of his first years in the colony, *Old New Zealand* (1863), and his voluminous correspondence remain valuable chronicles of the colony's early history.

Manini: *see* Marín, Francisco de Paula.

Maninka (people): *see* Malinke.

manioc (plant): *see* cassava.

maniple, in early Christianity, narrow silk band worn over the left forearm, with ends hanging down on each side, and formerly used by clergy when celebrating or assisting at mass. It was about two to four inches wide and three to five feet long. Sometimes heavily embroidered, it was the same colour as the major vestments worn on the occasion. It was the symbol of work and service. The maniple was probably derived from a handkerchief or table napkin used by Romans, which evolved into a ceremonial napkin (*mappa*) worn by high Roman officials. In the church it was a functional napkin used during the liturgy until the 9th century, when it began changing gradually into a decorative band, which was universally accepted by the 12th century.

Manipur, constituent state of India located in the northeastern part of the country. It is bounded by the Indian states of Nāgāland to the north, Assam to the west, and Mizorām to the southwest and by Myanmar (Burma) to the south and east. The capital is Imphāl.

A brief treatment of Manipur follows. For full treatment, *see* MACROPAEDIA: India.

Little is known about Manipur's history prior to 1762, when a local raja (prince) requested British aid in repelling a Burmese invasion. The request was made again in 1824. Years of political turmoil followed, caused by disputed successions among local rulers. The British administered the area in the 1890s, abolishing slavery and forced labour and constructing roads. In 1907 a raja and durbar (council) took over, but a tribal uprising in 1917 led to a new system of government administered from Assam. In 1947 Manipur acceded to the Indian Union, and in 1949 its administration was taken over by the Indian government; the region was ruled as a union territory until it became a state in 1972.

The state's two main physical features are the Manipur River valley and a large surrounding tract of mountainous country. Running north and south, the valley covers about 695 square miles (1,800 square km). Its major feature is the reedy Logtāk Lake, which covers an area of about 40 square miles (100 square km) and is the source of the Manipur River, which flows southward through the valley into Myanmar. Mountain elevations range from 5,000 to 6,000 feet (1,500 to 1,800 m) above sea level. The highest peak, Tenipu, lies in the north at 9,826 feet (2,995 m). In the west the mountains are broken by the valley of the Surma River, known as the Barāk River in Manipur. The climate is temperate in the valley and cold in the hills. Rainfall is abundant, with about 100 inches (2,590 mm) of precipitation occurring annually in the Barāk River valley to about 40 inches (970 mm) annually in the central part of the state.

About one-half of Manipur's people are Meithei, mainly Hindus who occupy the Manipur River valley. The rest of the population is composed of indigenous hill tribes that are divided into numerous clans and sections—Nāgas in the north and Kukis in the south. Manipurī is the language of about two-thirds of the people and, together with English, is the state's official language. The hill people speak languages of the Tibeto-Burman family.

Agriculture and forestry are the main sources of income in Manipur. Rice is the major crop, and the rich soil also supports corn (maize), sugarcane, cotton, mustard, tobacco, tea, fruit orchards, and leguminous plants. Terracing is common in the hills, where farmers plow the ground with hand hoes. Among some of the hill people, domestic animals are kept only for meat and are not milked or used for hauling. Teak and bamboo are the major forest products; other trees include oak, pine, chestnut, magnolia, and chinquapin.

Manufacturing in Manipur is limited to several well-established cottage industries. The designed cloth produced on Manipurī handlooms is in demand throughout India. Other such industries include basket making, gold and silver jewelry, and wood carving. Manipur remains somewhat isolated from the rest of India and lacks a rail link with the rest of the country. There are air links from Imphāl to Silchar and Guwāhāti in Assam and to Calcutta in West Bengal. A highway connects Imphāl with Tamu in Myanmar.

Manipur has given birth to an indigenous form of classical dance known as *manipuri.* It is dissimilar to other Indian dance forms; hand movements are used decoratively rather than as pantomime, bells are not accentuated, and both men and women perform communally. More than two-fifths of the Manipur population is literate, and the state has a university at Imphāl and numerous colleges. Area 8,621 square miles (22,327 square km). Pop. (1991 prelim.) 1,826,714.

Manipuri (people): *see* Meithei.

manipuri, one of the six classical dance styles of India, the others being *bhārata-nāṭya, kathak, kathākali, kuchipudi,* and *oṛissī.* It is indigenous to Manipur and is characterized by a variety of forms that are linked to folk tradition and ritual. Themes are generally taken from episodes in the life of Krishna, the pastoral god. During the dance interpretations a narrator may chant dialogue and descriptive action, interspersed with choral singing. *Manipuri* is smooth and graceful and technically easier and more limited than the other classic styles. Although ankles are belled, the movement of the dance does not accentuate them, the steps being light and close to the floor. A flowing sway of the body and a liquid movement of the arms and hands characterize the women's style; stronger and more forceful movements are used by men. The *manipuri* was popularized throughout India when, in 1917, the poet Rabindranath Tagore saw demonstrations of the art and brought back dance teachers to serve in his Visva-Bharati University at Santiniketan.

Manisa, city, western Turkey. It lies in the valley of the Gediz River (ancient Hermus River), below Mount Sipylus (Manisa Dağı), 20 miles (32 km) northeast of İzmir. It was called Magnesia ad Sipylum (*q.v.*) in ancient times, and the Magnetes of Thessaly are thought to have been its first inhabitants in the 12th century BC. It was taken by Cyrus II the Great of Persia in the 6th century BC and in 190 BC it was the scene of a Roman victory over Seleucid Antiochus III the Great. Under the Attalids of Pergamum in the 1st century AD, it became a flourishing commercial centre, known first as Magnesiopolis and later as Magnesia. Emperor John III Ducas made it the seat of government in 1222. In 1313 Saruhan, a Turkmen tribal chief, captured Magnesia, renamed it Manisa, and made it the capital of his principality until the town was taken over by the Ottoman sultan Bayezid I in 1390. The principality was restored by the central Asian ruler Timur (Tamerlane) following his victory over the Ottomans (1402), but it again fell to the Ottomans about 1410. In the 18th century Manisa was ruled by the virtually independent Karaosmanoğlu governors until their power was broken in 1822.

Much favoured by the medieval Ottoman princes and sultans, Manisa has several buildings dating from that period. The mosque Muradiye Cami (built 1583–86), decorated with exquisitely worked marble, glazed tiles, and gilding, is particularly noteworthy. The *medrese* (religious school) attached to the mosque now houses a local archaeological museum. An important agricultural and commercial centre, Manisa is linked by rail with Afyon and İzmir.

The surrounding region includes the vast plain of Gediz (ancient Hyracanian Plain), north of Manisa, and is especially suited to vine growing. Other crops include olives, tobacco, sesame, and cotton. Some magnesite, zinc, and mercury are mined. Pop. (1985) 127,012.

Manises ware, in ceramics, a style that evolved at Manises, Spain, in the 14th and 15th centuries. It combined Arabic and Christian Gothic influences, the former evident in

Manises ware dish from Valencia painted in brownish lustre pigments, *c.* 1430; in the Victoria and Albert Museum, London

By courtesy of the Victoria and Albert Museum, London; photograph, Wilfrid Walter

rhythmic drawing, the latter in representing heraldic animals and foliage. The eagle of St. John and Spanish and Italian armorial emblems were favourite subjects.

Manistee, city, seat (1855) of Manistee county, northwestern Michigan, U.S., between Lake Michigan and Manistee Lake. The city is situated at the mouth of the Manistee River, 85 miles (137 km) north of Muskegon. Built on the river site that the Chippewa Indians called Manistee ("spirit of the woods"), it was one of the state's liveliest lumber camps in the mid-19th century but was largely destroyed by fire in 1871. When timber supplies were exhausted, Manistee developed as a health resort and as a leading producer of salt (based on local deposits). The surrounding area, which includes Manistee National Forest, is known for its fishing (salmon and trout) and deer hunting. Manufactures include clothing, chemicals, machinery, and wood and woodpulp products. The city is also an agricultural (fruit and potatoes) shipping point. Local landmarks are the Ramsdell Opera House, the Manistee County Historical Museum, and the Old Water Works Building. Orchard Beach State Park is nearby. Inc. city, 1869. Pop. (1990) 6,734.

Manitoba, most easterly of the three Prairie Provinces, central Canada. Manitoba was admitted to the Canadian Confederation in 1870 as the fifth province. It is bounded on the north by the territory of Nunavut, on the northeast by Hudson Bay, on the east by Ontario, on the west by Saskatchewan, and on the south by Minnesota and North Dakota in the United States. Area 250,947 square miles (649,950 square km). Pop. (1999 est.) 1,143,391.

A brief treatment of Manitoba follows. For full treatment, *see* MACROPAEDIA: Canada.

The province was first inhabited by Cree, Assiniboin, and Ojibwa Indians and along the Hudson Bay by Inuit (Eskimos). Europeans arrived in the 17th century, with Sir Thomas Button from England coming in 1612 and a Danish expedition in 1619. The Hudson's Bay Company, established in London in 1670, was responsible for the opening of Manitoba to European influence. The chief trading post of the company was the York Factory at the mouth of the Nelson, from which in 1691 Henry Kelsey explored southward to the region of The Pas and the prairies. In the 18th century there were clashes between British and French traders. From 1783, with Canada under the British flag, a fur trade war went on until 1821 between the Montreal-based North West Company and the Hudson's Bay Company, ending with the merger of the two companies. The first European settlement in 1812 was opposed on economic grounds by the Métis, a people derived from French-Indian intermarriage. The Métis resisted under the leadership of Louis Riel and refused to let government officials enter the territory until the officials made concessions in the Manitoba Act of 1870, which made Manitoba a province. In the mid- and late 19th century, steamboat and rail transportation opened the province to settlers from Europe and the United States. Provincial boundaries were extended westward in 1881, eastward in 1884, and northward in 1912 to give Manitoba its final dimensions. The westward expansion led to the Great Prairie grain fields, the northward expansion to the development of minerals and electric power.

Three-fifths of Manitoba's territory is covered by the ancient Canadian Shield, an area of rocks, forests, and rivers. It is drained by the Nelson and Churchill rivers into Hudson Bay. To the south of the area is the Manitoba Lowland, a former glacial basin and land of lakes. Extreme southern Manitoba is part of the fertile Saskatchewan plain. Manitoba's highest point is Baldy Mountain, at 2,730 feet (832 m). The climate is moderately dry with sharp seasonal temperature changes. Most of the precipitation occurs between May and September. About half of Manitoba's land area is heavily forested, and a seventh of its surface consists of rivers and lakes, including Lake Winnipeg, the 13th largest lake in the world. The province abounds in big game in the north and upland game birds and animals in the rest of the area. Government and private organizations cooperate in wildlife surveys and nature management programs.

Manitoba's ethnic composition is diverse, with large groups of Scotch-Irish, German, Scandinavian, Ukrainian, and Polish descent; the largest French-Canadian community in all of Canada outside of Quebec is in the town of St. Boniface. Members of various American Indian and Inuit groups are also present.

Manitoba's cultural life reflects the diversity of its people and their various traditional art forms. Its capital is the home of the renowned Royal Winnipeg Ballet, the Winnipeg Symphony Orchestra, and the Manitoba Theatre Centre. The city also boasts a downtown centennial building complex that includes concert and museum facilities.

Manitoba continues to draw most of its wealth from the exploitation and processing of the products of its primary industries—farming, lumbering, mining, and fishing—though Winnipeg is the focus of rapidly expanding manufacturing industries (foods and beverages, clothing, fabricated metal goods, chemicals, computers, and electrical equipment). The southern farmlands are a main resource. Wheat is the main crop, with barley, rapeseed (canola), flaxseed, rye, and vegetables also cultivated. The Canadian Shield area has about four-fifths of the mineral production in Manitoba. The major minerals are nickel, copper, gold, lead, silver, cadmium, and zinc. More than one-fourth of Manitoba's landmass supports valuable timber, although there has been some devastation from forest fires. The provincial government is moving into some areas of the private sector. In the early 1970s it implemented a compulsory government-operated automobile insurance program. The government's Manitoba Development Corporation acquired an interest in several businesses, including the forest complex in The Pas.

Manitoba derives its authority from two British statutes, the British North America Acts of 1867 and 1871, and one Canadian statute, the Manitoba Act of 1870. The provincial government consists of a unicameral legislative assembly, elected by universal adult suffrage to five-year terms; and an executive branch, consisting of the premier (who is the leader of the majority political party in the assembly and who chooses the executive council from the assembly) and the lieutenant governor, appointed by the Canadian governor-general to represent the British Crown. The judiciary is divided into two superior courts, the Court of Appeal and the Court of the Queen's Bench, and lower-level county, surrogate, provincial, small-debt, family, and juvenile courts. The province supervises medical and hospital insurance programs and provides all Manitobans with free medical insurance. The province also provides welfare, public health, care for the aged, and other services for the disadvantaged. Policing is done by the Royal Canadian Mounted Police together with municipal police forces.

Compulsory primary and secondary education to grade 12 as well as optional kindergarten are provided free. Private, mainly religious, schools have an insignificant portion of the primary enrollment and are government-subsidized. There has been considerable debate about the language of instruction. French-speaking Manitobans fought for their linguistic rights, and the availability of French as a language of instruction has been reinstated. The federal government provides schooling for the American Indian population. Vocational schools are based in Winnipeg, Brandon, and The Pas. The University of Manitoba (Winnipeg), the University of Winnipeg, and Brandon University provide higher and postgraduate education.

Manitoba, Lake, narrow, irregularly shaped lake in south-central Manitoba, Canada, 45 miles (72 km) northwest of Winnipeg. Fed by many small streams and by Crane Narrows (the outlet from Lake Winnipegosis [north]), it is drained northeastward into Lake Winnipeg via Lake St. Martin and the Dauphin River. Once part of the glacial Lake Agassiz, it was discovered in 1738 by the French voyageur La Vérendrye, who named it Lac des Prairies; the name Manitoba is believed to come from the Algonquian word *manito-bau* or *manito-wapau* ("the strait of the spirit"), applied to the lake's Narrows between Wapah (west) and Oakview (east). The lake has an area of 1,785 square miles (4,624 square km), is more than 125 miles (200 km) long, and is up to 28 miles (45 km) wide and 812 feet (248 m) deep. It is important for commercial fishing, though only fished in the winter.

Manitoulin Islands, archipelago in northern Lake Huron, straddling the U.S.-Canadian border and forming one of the prominent features of the Niagara Escarpment. The Ontario island of Manitoulin, the largest freshwater island in the world, has a length of 100 miles (160 km) and an area of 1,068 square miles (2,766 square km). Of the many other islands in the group, the Michigan island of Drummond and the Ontario islands of St. Joseph and Cockburn are the more important. The name Manitoulin is derived from an Algonquian Indian word for "spirit." The islands, first visited by Jesuit missionaries about 1650, are now noted for fishing, lumbering, dairying, and mixed farming; the region is popular with vacationists and sportsmen. A highway and a Canadian Pacific Railway line link the town of Little Current on Manitoulin Island, the chain's major centre, to the Ontario mainland. In 1990 Manitoulin Island was the site of a historic land-claim settlement brought against the provincial government by Indian groups in the region.

Manitowoc, city, seat (1851) of Manitowoc county, eastern Wisconsin, U.S., on the western shores of Lake Michigan at the mouth of the Manitowoc River. It adjoins the city of Two Rivers (northeast) and is located 77 miles (124 km) north of Milwaukee. In 1795 a trading post was established on the site by the North West Company. A permanent settlement was made in 1837, which developed as an industrial and shipping centre. The city is now a St. Lawrence Seaway port of entry with auto-ferry services across Lake Michigan to Ludington, Mich. Industries include shipbuilding and the manufacture of aluminumware. Vegetable canning and the processing of malt products are also important. A centre of the University of Wisconsin (1962) and Silver Lake College (Roman Catholic; 1869) are located there. The Rahr-West Museum focuses on Indian and pioneer history, and the Maritime Museum displays ship models and ship equipment. "Manitowoc" is from the Algonquian language and probably means "abode of the Great Spirit." Pop. (1990) 32,520.

Maniu, Iuliu (b. Jan. 8, 1873, Şimleu Silvaniei, Transylvania, Rom.—d. June 1953, Galaţi), statesman who served as prime minister of Romania (1928–30, 1930, 1932–33) and as head of the National Peasant Party. Maniu was one of the most important Romanian political leaders of the period.

Maniu, a native of Transylvania, was elected in 1906 to the Hungarian Parliament where he joined a small band of Romanian nationals urging equal rights for their minority. During World War I he served in the Austro-Hungarian army, but in May 1918 he organized a revolt of Romanian troops. In December 1918 he was elected president of the Transylvanian directing council (Consiliul Dirigent), which proclaimed union with Romania, a fait accompli later recognized by the Treaty of Trianon (June 1920).

From 1926 he headed the National Peasant Party, created in that year by the fusion of his Transylvanian Nationals with the Peasant Party of Ion Mihalache. Between November 1928 and October 1930 he served as prime minister of a National Peasant administration, which failed to fulfill its mandate for political and social reconstruction. He agreed to the return of the exiled king Carol II in June 1930 but resigned the following October, ostensibly over the king's continuing liaison with Magda Lupescu. From October 1932 to January 1933 he headed a second government and in 1937 formed an electoral alliance with the fascist Iron Guard in order to wrest political control from the king. During World War II he initially supported Romania's war effort against Russia. As the war progressed beyond the reclamation of national irredentas in Bessarabia and Bukovina, however, he became one of the principal resistance leaders and organizers of the coup of August 1944, which brought Romania into the war against Germany. After the installation of a communist regime in 1945, his position became increasingly precarious. He was imprisoned for espionage and treason in November 1947 and died in prison in 1953.

Manius (ancient Roman personal name, or praenomen): *see under* gens or family name or honorific (*e.g.,* under Dentatus for Manius Curius Dentatus).

Manizales, capital of Caldas *departamento,* central Colombia, situated on a commanding ridge of the Andean Cordillera (mountains) Central, 6,975 feet (2,126 m) above sea level. Its gray cathedral is visible for miles in all directions. Founded in 1848 by colonists from Antioquia *departamento,* it is the centre of Colombia's most important coffee-growing district. A cement plant is located in the city, as are factories producing agricultural machines, thread, textiles, refrigerators, dry batteries, furniture, and leather goods. The city is the site of the University of Caldas (1943). Manizales is the halfway point on the principal highway between Bogotá and Medellín and is also connected by highway and railroad with Quindío *departamento* and Cali. An aerial cableway across the crest of the Cordillera Central links Manizales with Mariquita and the Magdalena River. Pop. (1985) 275,067.

Manjhi (people): *see* Santāl.

Mañjuśrī, in Mahāyāna Buddhism, the bodhisattva ("Buddha-to-be") personifying supreme wisdom. His name in Sanskrit means "gentle, or sweet, glory"; he is also known as Mañjughoṣa ("Sweet Voice") and Vāgīśvara ("Lord of Speech"). In China he is called Wen-shu Shih-li, in Japan Monju, and in Tibet 'Jam-dpal.

Although sutras (Buddhist scriptures) were composed in his honour by at least AD 250, he does not seem to have been represented in Buddhist art before AD 400. He is most commonly shown wearing princely ornaments, his right hand holding aloft the sword of wisdom to cleave the clouds of ignorance and his left holding a palm-leaf manuscript of the *Prajñā-pāramitā*. He is sometimes depicted seated on a lion or on a blue lotus; and in paintings his skin is usually yellow in colour.

Mañjuśrī, basalt figure from Java, 1343; formerly in the Museum für Indische Kunst, Staatliche Museen, Berlin (missing from 1945)

By courtesy of the Museum fur Indische Kunst, Staatliche Museen, Berlin

His cult spread widely in China in the 8th century, and Mount Wu-t'ai in Shansi province, which is dedicated to him, is covered with his temples. Though he is usually considered a celestial bodhisattva, some traditions endow him with a human history. He is said to manifest himself in many ways—in dreams; as a pilgrim on his sacred mountain; as an incarnation of the monk Vairocana, who introduced Buddhism into Khotan; as the Tibetan reformer Atīśa; and as the emperor of China.

Mankato, city, seat of Blue Earth county, southern Minnesota, U.S., on the Minnesota River, opposite North Mankato, near the mouth of the Blue Earth River, in a mixed-farming and lake area, 80 miles (130 km) southwest of Minneapolis. Mankato was founded in 1852. Its name derives from a Sioux term for the blue clay along the riverbanks. The Sioux uprising of 1862 culminated in the mass hanging at Mankato of 38 Indians out of more than 400 who were tried for massacring white settlers at New Ulm. The execution spot is marked by a monument. Mankato State University (1867) and Bethany Lutheran College (1911) are in the city. The economy is centred on a prosperous hog market and many agricultural processing plants, and there are limestone quarries nearby. Inc. village, 1865; city, 1868. Pop. (1990) 31,477.

Mankiewicz, Herman (Jacob) (b. Nov. 7, 1897, New York, N.Y., U.S.—d. March 5, 1953, Los Angeles, Calif.), American screenwriter, journalist, playwright, and wit, notable as a member of the Algonquin Round Table and as the coauthor of the screenplay for *Citizen Kane* (1941).

Mankiewicz was the son of German immigrants. He grew up in Pennsylvania, where his father edited a German-language newspaper, and moved with his family to New York City in 1913. He graduated from Columbia University in 1917. Serving briefly in the Marine Corps, Mankiewicz held a variety of jobs, including work for the Red Cross press service in Paris. He returned for a short time to the United States, married, and then worked intermittently in Germany as a correspondent for a number of newspapers. He returned once again to New York City in 1922 and, among other activities, collaborated on two unsuccessful plays. He also became a member of the celebrated group of American critics, writers, and miscellaneous wits who met at the Algonquin Hotel and were known as the Algonquin Round Table. One of them, Alexander Woollcott, said that Mankiewicz was the funniest man in New York.

Mankiewicz worked at *The New Yorker* magazine until he was hired by Paramount Publix Studios in Hollywood, Calif. He began by writing titles for silent movies, and he was responsible for a distinct change in their tone. He is credited with the authorship or coauthorship of a number of sound motion pictures—including *The Royal Family of Broadway* (1931), *Dinner at Eight* (1933), *It's a Wonderful World* (1939, with Ben Hecht), *Pride of the Yankees* (1942), and *Citizen Kane* (1941, with Orson Welles). He took much of the story for *Citizen Kane* from his personal experience with William Randolph Hearst, whose guest he had been on many weekends during the 1930s. The screenplay won an Academy Award. Mankiewicz also produced, wrote, or doctored a number of scripts, some of them uncredited. He was involved, for example, in the Marx brothers' *Monkey Business* (1931) and *Horse Feathers* (1932). Plagued by alcoholism, he wrote his last film, *The Pride of St. Louis,* in 1952. His brother Joseph was also a screenwriter and director.

Manley, Mary de la Riviere (b. April 7, 1663, Jersey, Channel Islands—d. July 11, 1724, London), British writer who achieved notoriety through presenting political scandal in the form of romance. Her *Secret Memoirs . . . of Several Persons of Quality* (1709) was a chronicle seeking to expose the private vices of Whig ministers. After its publication she was arrested for libel but escaped punishment.

Her cousin John Manley married her bigamously in about 1688. In 1711 she succeeded Jonathan Swift as editor of *The Examiner* and in 1714 wrote her "fictitious autobiography," *The Adventures of Rivella. . . .*

Mann, Heinrich (b. March 27, 1871, Lübeck, Ger.—d. March 12, 1950, Santa Monica, Calif., U.S.), German novelist and essayist, a socially committed writer whose best known works are intemperate attacks on the authoritarian social structure of German society under William II.

Mann was the elder brother of Thomas Mann. He entered publishing, but, after the death (1891) of his father, a prosperous grain merchant, he became financially independent and lived in Berlin, spending long periods abroad, particularly in France. His early novels portray the decadence of high society (*Im Schlaraffenland* [1900; *In the Land of Cockaigne*]), and his later books deal with the greed

Heinrich Mann
Harlingue—H. Roger-Viollet

for wealth, position, and power in William's Germany. Mann's merciless portrait of a tyrannical provincial schoolmaster, *Professor Unrat* (1905; *Small Town Tyrant*), became widely known through its film version *Der blaue Engel* (1928; *The Blue Angel*). His *Kaiserreich* trilogy—consisting of *Die Armen* (1917; *The Poor*); *Der Untertan* (1918; *The Patrioteer*); and *Der Kopf* (1925; *The Chief*)—carries even further his indictment of the social types produced by the authoritarian state. These novels were accompanied by essays attacking the arrogance of authority and the subservience of the subjects. A lighter work of this period is *Die kleine Stadt* (1909; *The Little Town*).

After 1918 Mann became a prominent spokesman for radical democracy and published volumes of political essays, *Macht und Mensch* (1919; "Might and Man") and *Geist und Tat* (1931; "Spirit and Act"). He was forced into exile in 1933 when the Nazis came to power, and he spent the rest of his life in France and the United States. His novel *Henri Quatre* (two parts, 1935 and 1938) represents his ideal of the humane use of power.

Mann, Horace (b. May 4, 1796, Franklin, Mass., U.S.—d. Aug. 2, 1859, Yellow Springs, Ohio), U.S. educator, the first great American advocate of public education, who believed that, in a democratic society, education should be free and universal, nonsectarian, democratic in method, and reliant on well-trained, professional teachers.

Mann grew up in an environment ruled by poverty, hardship, and self-denial. He was taught briefly and erratically by comparatively poor teachers, but he managed to educate himself in the Franklin town library, and,

Horace Mann
By courtesy of Antioch College, Yellow Springs, Ohio

with the help of some tutoring by an itinerant schoolmaster, he gained admission at the age of 20 to the sophomore class at Brown University (Providence, R.I.). He did brilliant work at Brown, manifesting great interest in problems of politics, education, and social reform; his valedictory address, on the gradual advancement of the human race in dignity and happiness, was a model of humanitarian optimism, offering a way in which education, philanthropy, and republicanism could combine to allay the wants and shortcomings that beset mankind.

Upon graduation in 1819 Mann chose law as a career. He read law briefly with a Wrentham, Mass., lawyer, taught for a year at Brown, and then studied at Litchfield (Conn.) Law School, which led to his admission to the bar in 1823. He settled in Dedham, Mass., and there his legal acumen and oratorical skill soon won him a seat in the state House of Representatives, where he served from 1827 to 1833. There he led the movement that established a state hospital for the insane at Worcester, the first of its kind in the United States. In 1833 he moved to Boston, and from 1835 to 1837 he served in the Massachusetts Senate, in 1836 as president of it.

Of the many causes Mann espoused, none was dearer to him than popular education. Nineteenth-century Massachusetts could boast a public school system going back to 1647. Yet during Mann's own lifetime, the quality of education had deteriorated as school control had gradually slipped into the hands of economy-minded local districts. A vigorous reform movement arose, committed to halting this decline by reasserting the state's influence. The result was the establishment in 1837 of a state board of education, charged with collecting and publicizing school information throughout the state. Much against the advice of friends, who thought he was tossing aside a promising political career, Mann accepted the first secretaryship of this board.

Endowed with little direct power, the new office demanded moral leadership of the highest order and this Mann supplied for 11 years. He started a biweekly *Common School Journal* for teachers and lectured widely to interested groups of citizens. His annual reports to the board ranged far and wide through the field of pedagogy, stating the case for the public school and discussing its problems. Essentially his message centred on six fundamental propositions: (1) that a republic cannot long remain ignorant and free, hence the necessity of universal popular education; (2) that such education must be paid for, controlled, and sustained by an interested public; (3) that such education is best provided in schools embracing children of all religious, social, and ethnic backgrounds; (4) that such education, while profoundly moral in character, must be free of sectarian religious influence; (5) that such education must be permeated throughout by the spirit, methods, and discipline of a free society, which preclude harsh pedagogy in the classroom; and (6) that such education can be provided only by well-trained, professional teachers. Mann encountered strong resistance to these ideas—from clergymen who deplored nonsectarian schools, from educators who condemned his pedagogy as subversive of classroom authority, and from politicians who opposed the board as an improper infringement of local educational authority—but his views prevailed.

Mann resigned the secretaryship in 1848 to take the seat of former Pres. John Quincy Adams in the United States Congress. There he proved himself to be a fierce enemy of slavery. In 1853, having run unsuccessfully for the Massachusetts governorship a year before, he accepted the presidency of Antioch College in Yellow Springs, Ohio, a new institution committed to coeducation, nonsectarianism, and equal opportunity for Negroes. There, amidst the usual crises attendant upon an infant college, Mann finished out his years. Two months before he died, he had given his own valedictory to the graduating class: "I beseech you to treasure up in your hearts these my parting words: Be ashamed to die until you have won some victory for humanity."

(L.A.Cr.)

BIBLIOGRAPHY. The most comprehensive bibliography is Clyde S. King, *Horace Mann, 1796–1859: A Bibliography* (1966). The definitive biography is Jonathan Messerli, *Horace Mann* (1972). A recent popular biography is Louise Hall Tharp, *Until Victory: Horace Mann and Mary Peabody* (1953). Jonathan C. Messerli throws new light on Mann's early years in "Horace Mann at Brown," *Harvard Educational Review,* 33:285–311 (1963). Robert L. Straker deals authoritatively with the Antioch period in *The Unseen Harvest: Horace Mann and Antioch College* (1955). The standard work is Mary Tyler (Peabody) Mann (ed.), *Life and Works of Horace Mann,* rev. ed., 5 vol. (1891). Excerpts from the annual reports to the Massachusetts Board of Education are in L.A. Cremin (ed.), *Republic and the School: Horace Mann on the Education of Free Men* (1957).

Mann, Thomas (b. June 6, 1875, Lübeck, Ger.—d. Aug. 12, 1955, near Zürich), German novelist and essayist whose early novels—*Buddenbrooks* (1900), *Der Tod in Venedig* (1912;

Thomas Mann
Elliot Erwitt—Magnum

Death in Venice), and *Der Zauberberg* (1924; *The Magic Mountain*)—earned him the Nobel Prize for Literature in 1929.

Early literary endeavours. Mann's father died in 1891, and Mann moved to Munich, a centre of art and literature, where he lived until 1933. After perfunctory work in an insurance office and on the editorial staff of *Simplicissimus,* a satirical weekly, he devoted himself to writing, as his elder brother Heinrich had already done. His early tales, collected as *Der kleine Herr Friedemann* (1898), reflect the aestheticism of the 1890s but are given depth by the influence of the philosophers Schopenhauer and Nietzsche and the composer Wagner, to all of whom Mann was always to acknowledge a deep, if ambiguous, debt. Most of Mann's first stories centre in the problem of the creative artist, who in his devotion to form contests the meaninglessness of existence, an antithesis that Mann enlarged into that between spirit (*Geist*) and life (*Leben*). But while he showed sympathy for the artistic misfits he described, Mann was also aware that the world of imagination is a world of make-believe, and the closeness of the artist to the charlatan was already becoming a theme. At the same time, a certain nostalgia for ordinary, unproblematical life appeared in his work.

This ambivalence found full expression in his first novel, *Buddenbrooks,* which Mann had at first intended to be a novella in which the experience of the transcendental realities of Wagner's music would extinguish the will to live in the son of a bourgeois family. On this beginning, the novel builds the story of the family and its business house over three generations, showing how an artistic streak not only unfits the family's later members for the practicalities of business life but undermines their vitality as well. But, almost against his will, in *Buddenbrooks* Mann wrote a tender elegy for the old bourgeois virtues.

In 1905 Mann married Katja Pringsheim. There were six children of the marriage, which was a happy one. It was this happiness, perhaps, that led Mann, in *Royal Highness,* to provide a fairy-tale reconciliation of "form" and "life," of degenerate feudal authority and the vigour of modern American capitalism. In 1912, however, he returned to the tragic dilemma of the artist with *Death in Venice,* a sombre masterpiece. In this story, the main character, a distinguished writer whose nervous and "decadent" sensibility is controlled by the discipline of style and composition, seeks relaxation from overstrain in Venice, where, as disease creeps over the city, he succumbs to an infatuation and the wish for death. Symbols of eros and death weave a subtle pattern in the sensuous opulence of this tale, which closes an epoch in Mann's work.

World War I years. The outbreak of World War I evoked Mann's ardent patriotism and awoke, too, an awareness of the artist's social commitment. His brother Heinrich was one of the few German writers to question German war aims, and his criticism of German authoritarianism stung Thomas to a bitter attack on cosmopolitan litterateurs. In 1918 he published a large political treatise, *Reflections of an Unpolitical Man,* in which all his ingenuity of mind was summoned to justify the authoritarian state as against democracy, creative irrationalism as against "flat" rationalism, and inward culture as against moralistic civilization. This work belongs to the tradition of "revolutionary conservatism" that leads from the 19th-century German nationalistic and anti-democratic thinkers Paul Anton de Lagarde and H.S. Chamberlain, the apostle of the superiority of the "Germanic" race, toward National Socialism; and Mann later was to repudiate these ideas.

With the establishment of the German (Weimar) Republic in 1919, Mann slowly revised his outlook; the essays "Goethe und Tolstoi" and "Von deutscher Republik" ("The German Republic") show his somewhat hesitant espousal of democratic principles. His new position was clarified in the long novel *The Magic Mountain.* Its theme grows out of an earlier motif: a young engineer, Hans Castorp, visiting a cousin in a sanatorium in Davos, abandons practical life to submit to the rich seductions of disease, inwardness, and death. But the sanatorium comes to be the spiritual reflection of the possibilities and dangers of the actual world. In the end, somewhat skeptically but humanely, Castorp decides for life and service to his people: a decision Mann calls "a leave-taking from many a perilous sympathy, enchantment, and temptation, to which the European soul had been inclined." In this great work Mann formulates with remarkable insight the fateful choices facing Europe.

Political crisis and World War II. From this time onward Mann's imaginative effort was directed primarily to the novel, scarcely interrupted by the charming personal novella *Early Sorrow,* or by *Mario and the Magician,* a novella that, in the person of a seedy illusionist, symbolizes the character of Fascism. His literary and cultural essays began to play an ever-growing part in elucidating and communicating his awareness of the fragility of humaneness, tolerance, and reason in the face of political crisis. His essays on Freud (1929) and Wagner (1933) are concerned with this, as are those on Goethe (1932), who more and more became for Mann an exemplary figure in his wisdom and balance. The various essays on Nietzsche document with particular poignancy Mann's struggle against attitudes once dear to him. In 1930 he gave a courageous address in Berlin, "Ein Appell an die Vernunft" ("An Appeal to Reason"), appealing for the formation of a common front of the cultured bourgeoisie and the Socialist working class against the inhuman fanaticism of the National Socialists. In essays and on lecture tours in Germany, to Paris, Vienna, Warsaw, Amsterdam, and elsewhere during the 1930s, Mann, while steadfastly attacking Nazi policy, often expressed sympathy with Socialist and Communist principles in the very general sense that they were the guarantee of humanism and freedom.

When Hitler became chancellor early in 1933, Mann and his wife, on holiday in Switzerland, were warned by their son and daughter in Munich not to return. For some years his home was in Switzerland, near Zürich, but he travelled widely, visiting the United States on lecture tours and finally, in 1938, settling there, first at Princeton, and from 1941 to 1952 in southern California. In 1936 he was deprived of his German citizenship; in the same year the University of Bonn took away the honorary doctorate it had bestowed in 1919 (it was restored in 1949). In 1944 he became a U.S. citizen.

Mann visited both East Germany and West Germany several times after the war and received many public honours, but he refused to return to Germany to live. In 1952 he settled again near Zürich. His last major essays—on Goethe (1949), Chekhov (1954), and Schiller (1955)—are impressive evocations of the moral and social responsibilities of writers.

Later novels. The novels on which Mann was working throughout this period reflect variously the cultural crisis of his times. In 1933 he published *The Tales of Jacob* (U.S. title, *Joseph and His Brothers*), the first part of his four-part novel on the biblical Joseph, continued the following year in *The Young Joseph* and two years later with *Joseph in Egypt,* and completed with *Joseph the Provider* in 1943. In the complete work, published as *Joseph and His Brothers,* Mann reinterpreted the biblical story as the emergence of mobile, responsible individuality out of the tribal collective; of history out of myth; and of a human God out of the unknowable. In the first volume a timeless myth seems to be reenacted in the lives of the Hebrews. Joseph, however, though sustained by the belief that his life too is the reenactment of a myth, is thrown out of the "timeless collective" into Egypt, the world of change and history, and there learns the management of events, ideas, and himself. Though based on wide and scholarly study of history, the work is not a historical novel, and the "history" is full of irony and humour, of conscious modernization. Mann's concern is to provide a myth for his own times, capable of sustaining and directing his generation and of restoring a belief in the power of humane reason.

Mann took time off from this work to write, in the same spirit, his *Lotte in Weimar* (U.S. title, *The Beloved Returns*). Lotte Kestner, the heroine of Goethe's *The Sorrows of Young Werther,* his semi-autobiographical story of unrequited love and romantic despair, visits Weimar in old age to see once again her old lover, now famous, and win some acknowledgment from him. But Goethe remains distant and refuses to reenter the past; she learns from him that true reverence for man means also acceptance of and reverence for change, intelligent activity directed to the "demand of the day." In this, as in the Joseph novels, in settings so distant from his own time, Mann was seeking to define the essential principles of humane civilization; their spacious and often humorous serenity of tone implicitly challenges the inhuman irrationalism of the Nazis.

In *Doktor Faustus,* begun in 1943 at the darkest period of the war, Mann wrote the most directly political of his novels. It is the life story of a German composer, Adrian Leverkühn, born in 1885, who dies in 1940 after 10 years of mental alienation. A solitary, estranged figure, he "speaks" the experience of his times in his music, and the story of Leverkühn's compositions is that of German culture in the two decades before 1930—more specifically of the collapse of traditional humanism and the victory of the mixture of sophisticated nihilism and barbaric primitivism that undermine it. With imaginative insight Mann interpreted the new musical forms and themes of Leverkühn's compositions up to the final work, a setting of the lament of Doctor Faustus in the 16th-century version of the Faust legend, who once, in hope, had made a pact with the Devil, but in the end is reduced to hopelessness. The one gleam of hope in this sombre work, however, in which the personal tragedy of Leverkühn is subtly related to Germany's destruction in the war through the comments of the fictitious narrator, Zeitblom, lies in its very grief. No other literary work expresses the tragedy of Germany as this does.

The composition of the novel was fully documented by Mann in 1949 in *The Genesis of a Novel. Doktor Faustus* exhausted him as no other work of his had done, and *The Holy Sinner* and *The Black Swan,* published in 1951 and 1953, respectively, show a relaxation of intensity in spite of their accomplished, even virtuoso style. Mann rounded off his imaginative work in 1954 with *The Confessions of Felix Krull, Confidence Man,* the light, often uproariously funny story of a confidence man who wins the favour and love of others by enacting the roles they desire of him.

Mann's style is finely wrought and full of resources, enriched by humour, irony, and parody; his composition is subtle and many-layered, brilliantly realistic on one level and yet reaching to deeper levels of symbolism. His works lack simplicity, and his tendency to set his characters at a distance by his own ironical view of them has sometimes laid him open to the charge of lack of heart. He was, however, aware that simplicity and sentiment lend themselves to manipulation by ideological and political powers, and the sometimes elaborate sophistication of his works cannot hide from the discerning reader his underlying impassioned and tender solicitude for mankind.

Assessment. Mann was the greatest German novelist of the 20th century, and by the end of his life his works had acquired the status of classics both within and without Germany. His subtly structured novels and shorter stories constitute a persistent and imaginative enquiry into the nature of Western bourgeois culture, in which a haunting awareness of its precariousness and threatened disintegration is balanced by an appreciation of and tender concern for its spiritual achievements. Round this central theme cluster a group of related problems that recur in different forms—the relation of thought to reality and of the artist to society, the complexity of reality and of time, the seductions of spirituality, eros, and death. Mann's imaginative and practical involvement in the social and political catastrophes of his time provided him with fresh insights that make his work rich and varied. His finely wrought essays, notably those on Tolstoy, Goethe, Freud, and Nietzsche, record the intellectual struggles through which he reached the ethical commitment that shapes the major imaginative works. (Ro.Pa.)

BIBLIOGRAPHY. *Editions and correspondence.* The most complete edition is Mann's *Gesammelte Werke in zwölf Bänden,* ed. by Hans Buergin (1960); vol. 1–7 contain the novels, vol. 8 the *Novellen,* vol. 9–12 the essays, addresses, and speeches. There are several other collected editions and many editions of separate works. A full bibliography is included in Hans Buergin *et al., Das Werk Thomas Manns* (1959). There are many volumes of Mann's correspondence, the most complete being the three volumes selected and edited by his daughter Erika Mann, *Briefe: 1889–1936* (1961), *1937–1947* (1963), and *1948–1955* (1965). A good selection, translated, is given by Richard and Clara Winston, *Letters of Thomas Mann, 1889–1955,* 2 vol. (1970).

Biography and criticism. There is no definitive biography of Thomas Mann. Hans Buergin and Hans-Otto Mayer give a detailed chronicle of his life in *Thomas Mann: Eine Chronik seines Lebens* (1965; *Thomas Mann: A Chronicle of His Life*). The childhood home is described by his younger brother Viktor Mann in *Wir waren fünf* (1949). Richard Winston, *Thomas Mann* (1981), is an account of Mann's early years. *Thomas Mann: Autobiographisches,* ed. by Erika Mann (1968), contains Mann's autobiographical essays and his daughter's account (1956) of the last year of his life (trans. by Richard Graves as *The Last Year of Thomas Mann*); Nigel Hamilton, *The Brothers Mann* (1979), is particularly good on details of the lives of the brothers. Klaus W. Jonas gives a full account of critical studies on Mann in *Fifty Years of Thomas Mann Studies: A Bibliography of Criticism* (1955). Richard H. Thomas, *Thomas Mann: The Mediation of Art* (1956), is concerned with the relation of art and reality, the artist and the moralist in Mann. Erich Heller, *The Ironic German* (1958), finds the clue to the many ambiguities in Mann in his irony; while Kurt Sontheimer, *Thomas Mann und die Deutschen* (1961), is a more straightforward examination of the complex relationship of Mann to his fellow Germans. Jonas Lesser, *Thomas Mann in der Epoche seiner Vollendung* (1952), is a devoted study of the later Mann; while George Lukacs' Marxist essays *Thomas Mann* (1949; rev. ed., 1957; trans. by Stanley Mitchell as *Essays on Thomas Mann*), are shrewdly critical as well as admiring. Various essays in Charles Neider (ed.), *The Stature of Thomas Mann* (1947); and in Erich Kahler, *The Orbit of Thomas Mann* (1969), may be recommended; while his position in the history of the German novel is indicated in Roy Pascal, *The German Novel* (1956).

Mann, Tom, byname of THOMAS MANN (b. April 15, 1856, Foleshill, Warwickshire, Eng.—d. March 13, 1941, Grassington, Yorkshire), radical labour leader, founder and member of numerous British labour unions and organizations.

Mann joined the Amalgamated Society of Engineers in 1881 and in 1885 affiliated himself with the socialist movement. He first gained national prominence as coleader, with John Burns, of the great London dock strike in 1889. In the 1890s he served as secretary to James Keir Hardie's newly formed Independent Labour Party. During the first decade of the 20th century, Mann was active in Australia as a union organizer; after he returned to England, he helped the trade unionist Ben Tillett found the National Transport Workers' Federation in 1910. In the 1920s Mann was an important member of the British Communist Party.

manna, in biblical literature, one or more of the foods that sustained the Hebrews during the 40 years that intervened between their Exodus from Egypt and their arrival in the Promised Land. The word is perhaps derived from the question *man hu?* ("What is it?"), asked by the Hebrews when they first tasted the substances that they found growing or deposited by the wind on the arid land that they inhabited. The manna was gathered and was used in part to prepare bread, and it was therefore referred to as "bread from heaven."

In the interpretation of some Old Testament scholars, manna was miraculous in the sense that even in the desert food was available and that a double portion was available on Friday, freeing the Hebrews from the need to violate their Sabbath by gathering food. In the New Testament, Jesus spoke of himself as the "true bread from heaven" (John 6:32), and manna consequently is a Christian symbol for the Eucharist.

Consult the INDEX *first*

manna, in botany, any of a variety of plants and plant products. Manna is the common name for certain lichens of the genus *Lecanora* native to Turkey, especially *L. esculenta.* In the Middle East lichen bread and manna jelly are made from *Lecanora.* Manna also refers to resins produced by two plants called camel's thorns (*Alhagi maurorum* and *A. pseudalhagi*). Both are spiny-branched shrubs less than 1 m (about 3 feet) tall and are native to Turkey. An edible, white honeylike substance known as manna forms drops on the stem of a tamarisk tree, *Tamarix mannifera.* A scale insect either punctures the stem, triggering the exudation, or secretes the manna itself.

The flowering ash, or manna ash (*Fraxinus ornus*), is the source of a sugar-alcohol, mannitol, which has been used medicinally. The substance is obtained for commercial exploitation by slashing the branches of the tree and collecting the juice that extrudes and hardens. This sweetish material is sold in the form of flakes (flake manna), fragments (common manna), or thick droplets (fat manna).

Manna-heim (Norse mythology): *see* Midgard.

Mannai, also spelled MANNA, or MANA, ancient country in northwestern Iran, south of Lake Urmia. During the period of its existence in the early 1st millennium BC, Mannai was surrounded by three major powers: Assyria, Urartu, and Media. The Mannaeans are first recorded in the annals of the Assyrian king Shalmaneser III (reigned 858–824 BC) and are last mentioned in Urartu by Rusa II (reigned 685–645 BC) and in Assyria by Esarhaddon (reigned 680–669 BC). With the intrusion of the Scythians and the rise of the Medes in the 7th century, the Manneans lost their identity and were subsumed under the term Medes. Place-names and personal names in Mannai are thought to be in a dialect related to the Hurrian language of the Hittite empire.

Mannar, Gulf of, Mannar also spelled MANNĀR, inlet of the Indian Ocean, between southeastern India and western Sri Lanka. It is bounded on the northeast by Rāmeswaram (island), Adam's (Rama's) Bridge (a chain of shoals), and Mannar Island. The gulf is 80–170 miles (130–275 km) wide and 100 miles (160 km) long. It receives several rivers, including the Tāmbraparni (India) and the Aruvi (Sri Lanka). The port of Tuticorin is on the Indian coast. The gulf is noted for the pearl banks off Sri Lanka.

Mannar Island, dry, barren island that lies at the eastern end of Adam's Bridge, a chain of shoals off the northwestern coast of Sri Lanka. Mannar Island has an area of about 50 square miles (130 square km). Fishing is economically important. The small port of Mannar is on the southeastern shore. Pop. (1990 est.) 132,000.

Manner, Eeva Liisa (b. Dec. 5, 1921, Helsinki, Fin.—d. July 7, 1995, Tampere), lyrical poet and dramatist, a central figure in the Finnish modernist movement of the 1950s.

Manner's first publications as a lyrical poet appeared in the 1940s with *Mustaa ja punaista* (1944; "Black and Red") and *Kuin tuuli tai pilvi* (1949; "As Wind or Clouds"), but her breakthrough came in 1956 with *Tämä matka* ("This Journey"), perhaps the most influential collection of modernist poems of the 1950s in Finland. Her poems are technically advanced and have great richness of association and powerful images. They are also characterized by a rare musicality and harmony. Manner was deeply critical of the intellectuality of modern civilization and looked to primitive innocence as a source of renewal.

In a collection of essays, *Kävelymusiikkia pienille virahevoille* (1957; "Promenade Music for Small Hippopotamuses"), she pointed to Chinese Taoism as an example of balance between rigid organization and chaos. Oriental philosophy also plays a part in *Orfiset laulut* (1960; "Orphic Hymns"), which is otherwise characterized by a feeling of doom. In her next collection, *Niin vaihtuivat vuoden ajat* (1964; "Thus Changed the Seasons"), she moved away from the general theme of Western civilization and depicted with grace and simplicity the minute phenomena of nature as proof of an underlying cosmic harmony. A later book of poetry, *Kamala Kissa* (1976; "That Horrible Cat"), revealed her humorous side. She wrote an autobiography of her childhood entitled *Tyttö taivaan laiturilla* (1951; "The Girl on the Bridge to Heaven").

Manner was also known as a dramatist and wrote both verse dramas, such as *Eros ja Psykhe* (1959; "Eros and Psyche"), and traditional realistic plays, such as *Poltettu oranssi* (1968; "Burnt Orange").

Mannerheim, Carl Gustaf, in full CARL GUSTAF EMIL MANNERHEIM (b. June 4, 1867, Villnäs, Fin.—d. Jan. 27, 1951, Lausanne, Switz.), Finnish military leader and conservative statesman who successfully defended Finland against greatly superior Soviet forces during World War II and served as the country's president (1944–46).

Mannerheim
UPI

Mannerheim was of Swedish ancestry. He entered the Russian army in 1889 as a lieutenant in the cavalry. Finland was then a part of the Russian Empire, and Mannerheim distinguished himself during the Russo-Japanese War (1904–05) and World War I, rising to the rank of lieutenant general and corps commander in the Russian army. After the outbreak of the October (November) Russian Revolution in 1917 he returned to

Finland, which had declared its independence from Russia. A conservative aristocrat and monarchist, Mannerheim assumed command of the "White" (anti-Bolshevik) forces in January 1918 during the Finnish Civil War and, with German assistance, defeated the Finnish Bolsheviks and expelled Soviet forces in a bloody four-month campaign. He became regent of Finland in December 1918, holding this post for seven months until a republic was declared in 1919. From 1919 to 1931 he lived in semiretirement, concerning himself with volunteer health and social welfare causes in Finland.

Reentering public life in 1931, Mannerheim became chairman of the national defense council. During his eight-year tenure, Finland constructed the so-called Mannerheim Line of fortifications across the Karelian Isthmus facing Leningrad; this system of defenses was intended to block any potential aggressive moves by the Soviet Union. When Soviet forces attacked Finland in December 1939, he served as commander in chief, and his brilliant leadership won considerable successes against vast numerical superiority, but the end result was defeat, resulting in a relatively harsh peace settlement in 1940.

Hoping to win back some territory regarded by some as historically Finnish, Finland successfully joined Nazi Germany in its invasion of the Soviet Union in June 1941. Mannerheim was named the only marshal of Finland in June 1942. But as Russian strength grew and Germany weakened, Mannerheim's troops were forced to retreat. He was named president of the Finnish republic in August 1944 in the hope that he would be able to negotiate a separate peace with the Soviets, which he did, signing an armistice with them in September. The armistice ultimately led to a peace treaty by which Finland was forced to make concessions more extensive than those made after the winter war. Mannerheim remained president until ill health forced his retirement in 1946. He wrote *Erinnerungen* (1952; *Memoirs*).

Mannerism, Italian MANIERISMO (from *maniera,* "manner," or "style"), artistic style that predominated in Italy from the end of the High Renaissance in the 1520s to the beginnings of the Baroque style around 1590. The Mannerist style originated in Florence and Rome and spread to northern Italy and, ultimately, to much of central and northern Europe.

Mannerism originated as a reaction to the harmonious classicism and the idealized naturalism of High Renaissance art as practiced by Leonardo, Michelangelo, and Raphael in the first two decades of the 16th century. In the portrayal of the human nude, the standards of formal complexity had been set by Michelangelo, and the norm of idealized beauty by Raphael. But in the work of these artists' Mannerist successors, an obsession with style and technique in figural composition often outweighed the importance and innate meaning of the subject matter. The highest value was instead placed upon the apparently effortless solution of intricate artistic problems, such as the portrayal of the nude in complex and artificial poses.

Mannerist artists evolved a style that is characterized by artificiality and artiness, by a thoroughly self-conscious cultivation of elegance and technical facility, and by a sophisticated indulgence in the bizarre. The figures in Mannerist works frequently have graceful but queerly elongated limbs, small heads, and stylized facial features, while their poses seem difficult or contrived. The deep, linear perspectival space of High Renaissance painting is flattened and obscured so that the figures appear as a decorative arrangement of forms in front of a flat background of indeterminate dimensions. Mannerists sought a continuous refinement of form and concept, pushing exaggeration and contrast to great limits. The results included strange and constricting spatial relationships, jarring juxtapositions of intense and unnatural colours, an emphasis on abnormalities of scale, a sometimes totally irrational mix of classical motifs and other visual references to the antique, and inventive and grotesque pictorial fantasies.

Mannerist elements are already present in some of Raphael's later paintings done in Rome, notably the "Transfiguration" (1517–20; Vatican Museum). In the period from 1515 to 1524 the Florentine painters Rosso Fiorentino and Jacopo da Pontormo broke away from Renaissance classicism and evolved an expressive, emotionally agitated style in their religious compositions. Among the most notable of these early Mannerist works are Pontormo's Visdomini altarpiece (1518; Church of S. Michele Visdomini, Florence) and Rosso's "Deposition" (1521; Pinacoteca Comunale, Volterra). In the early 1520s Rosso journeyed to Rome, where he joined the artists Giulio Romano, Perino del Vaga, and Polidoro da Caravaggio, who had all been followers of Raphael in his work for the Vatican. The Mannerist style completely emerged in the paintings of these artists as well as in those of Parmigianino. The latter's "Madonna with the Long Neck" (1534; Uffizi, Florence), Rosso's "Dead Christ with Angels" (*c.* 1526; Museum of Fine Arts, Boston), and Pontormo's "Deposition" (1525–28; church of Sta. Felicità, Florence) are preeminent works of Mannerism's maturity. Michelangelo's huge fresco "The Last Judgment" (1533–41; Sistine Chapel, Vatican) shows strong Mannerist tendencies in its agitated composition, formless and indeterminate space, and in the tortured poses and exaggerated musculature of its bunches of nude figures.

The sophisticated Mannerism that developed in Rome before 1527 became the chief formative influence on the styles of a number of younger Italian painters who were active during the 1530s, '40s, and '50s. Among them were Giorgio Vasari, Daniele da Volterra, Francesco Salviati, Domenico Beccafumi, Federigo Zuccaro, Pellegrino Tibaldi, and most notably Il Bronzino, who was the pupil of Pontormo and who became the most important Mannerist painter in Florence at this time. Meanwhile, Mannerism had begun to spread outside Italy; Rosso took the style to France in 1530 and was followed there two years later by Francesco Il Primaticcio, who evolved an important French variant of Mannerism in his decorations done at the French royal court at Fontainebleau. Mannerism was transplanted and disseminated throughout central and northern Europe around mid-century through large numbers of engravings of Italian paintings and through the visits of northern artists to Rome to study. Bartholomaeus Spranger, Hendrik Goltzius, and Hans von Aachen became important Mannerist painters. Although the Dutch cities of Haarlem and Amsterdam became centres of the new style, the most ambitious patronage was practiced at Prague by the Emperor Rudolf II; Spranger and others who worked for Rudolf evolved a rather bizarre and exotic Mannerism that occasionally degenerated into the merely grotesque and inexplicable.

In sculpture, the serpentine complexity of Michelangelo's late sculptures, as epitomized in the sinuously spiraling form of his "Victory" (1532–34; Palazzo Vecchio, Florence), dominated Mannerist aspirations in this medium. The sculptors Bartolommeo Ammannati, Benvenuto Cellini, and, most importantly, Giambologna became the principal practitioners of Mannerism with their graceful and complexly posed statues.

Mannerism retained a high level of international popularity until the paintings of Annibale Carracci and of Caravaggio around 1600 brought the problematic style to an end and ushered in the long ascendancy of the Baroque. Mannerism was for long afterward looked down upon as a decadent and anarchic style that simply marked a degeneration of High Renaissance artistic production. But in the 20th century the style came to be appreciated anew for its technical bravura, elegance, and polish. Mannerism's spiritual intensity, its complex and intellectual aestheticism, its experimentation in form, and the persistent psychological anxiety manifested in it made the style attractive and interesting to the modern temperament, which saw affinities between it and modern expressionist tendencies in art.

manners, comedy of, witty, cerebral form of dramatic comedy that depicts and often satirizes the manners and affectations of a contemporary society. A comedy of manners is concerned with social usage and the question of whether or not characters meet certain social standards. Often the governing social standard is morally trivial but exacting. The plot of such a comedy, usually concerned with an illicit love affair or similarly scandalous matter, is subordinate to the play's brittle atmosphere, witty dialogue, and pungent commentary on human foibles.

The comedy of manners, which was usually written by sophisticated authors for members of their own coterie or social class, has historically thrived in periods and societies that combined material prosperity and moral latitude. Such was the case in ancient Greece when Menander (*c.* 342–*c.* 292 BC) inaugurated New Comedy, the forerunner of comedy of manners. Menander's smooth style, elaborate plots, and stock characters were imitated by the Roman poets Plautus (*c.* 254–184 BC) and Terence (186/185–159 BC), whose comedies were widely known and copied during the Renaissance.

One of the greatest exponents of the comedy of manners was Molière, who satirized the hypocrisy and pretension of 17th-century French society in such plays as *L'École des femmes* (1662; *The School for Wives*) and *Le Misanthrope* (1666; *The Misanthrope*).

In England the comedy of manners had its great day during the Restoration period. Although influenced by Ben Jonson's comedy of humours, the Restoration comedy of manners was lighter, defter, and more vivacious in tone. Playwrights declared themselves against affected wit and acquired follies and satirized these qualities in caricature characters with label-like names such as Sir Fopling Flutter (in Sir George Etherege's *Man of Mode,* 1676) and Tattle (in William Congreve's *The Old Batchelour,* 1693). The masterpieces of the genre were the witty, cynical, and epigrammatic plays of William Wycherley (*The Country-Wife,* 1675) and William Congreve (*The Way of the World,* 1700). In the late 18th century Oliver Goldsmith (*She Stoops to Conquer,* 1773) and Richard Brinsley Sheridan (*The Rivals,* 1775; *The School for Scandal,* 1777) revived the form.

The tradition of elaborate, artificial plotting and epigrammatic dialogue was carried on by the Anglo-Irish playwright Oscar Wilde in *Lady Windermere's Fan* (1892) and *The Importance of Being Earnest* (1895). In the 20th century the comedy of manners reappeared in the witty, sophisticated drawing-room plays of the British dramatists Noel Coward and Somerset Maugham and the Americans Philip Barry and S.N. Behrman.

Manners, John: *see* Granby, John Manners, 1st marquess of.

Manners, John James Robert: *see* Rutland, John James Robert Manners, 7th duke of.

manners, novel of, work of fiction that re-creates a social world, conveying with finely detailed observation the customs, values, and mores of a highly developed and complex society. The conventions of the society dominate the story, and characters are differentiated by the degree to which they measure up to the uniform standard, or ideal, of behaviour or fall below it. The range of a novel of manners may be limited, as in the works of Jane Austen, which deal with the domestic affairs of English country gentry families of the 19th century and ignore elemental human passions and larger social and political determinations. It may also be sweeping, as in the novels of Balzac, which mirror the 19th century in all its complexity in stories dealing with Parisian life, provincial life, private life, public life, and military life.

Notable writers of the novel of manners from the end of the 19th century into the 20th include Henry James, Evelyn Waugh, Edith Wharton, and John Marquand.

Mannes, Leopold (Damrosch) (b. Dec. 26, 1899, New York, N.Y., U.S.—d. Aug. 11, 1964, Vineyard Haven, Mass.), American musician and photographic technician known as a codeveloper of Kodachrome film (1935).

Mannes attended New York City's Riverdale School, where he met his future partner, Leopold Godowsky, Jr. They enjoyed a mutual interest in music and photography, and together they set up a small laboratory for experimentation with colour film. In 1917 Mannes went to Harvard University to study physics and musicology. After receiving his B.A. in music, he taught at the Mannes School of Music in New York City, an institution founded by his parents. Mannes continued his research in photography, however, and collaborated with Godowsky by mail.

In 1919 Mannes and Godowsky created a mediocre colour film, at which time they realized that the additive process they had been working with would not give them the true colours that they sought. It was at this point that Mannes and Godowsky switched to a multiple-layered subtractive-film approach that would eventually lead them to the development of Kodachrome. They opened their first real laboratory in New York City in 1922, and with the backing of Dr. C.E. Kenneth Mees of the Eastman Kodak Company in 1930, the duo moved to Rochester, N.Y., to work with assistants at the well-equipped Kodak Research Laboratories. On April 15, 1935, Kodachrome's development was announced as the earliest of the colour-subtractive films that proved a boon to colour photography. Though originally used for animated motion pictures, Kodachrome was later improved, and it remains a popular film today. Mannes returned to the Mannes School of Music, which he renamed the Mannes College of Music in 1953 after he became director, a position he held until his death.

Mannesmann AG, former German industrial corporation acquired by British telecommunications company Vodaphone Group PLC in April 2000.

Founded as Mannesmannroehren-Werke in 1890 by Reinhard Mannesmann (1856–1922), the company became a leading manufacturer of steel tubing. By the 1930s it had emerged as one of the six giant iron and steel works of the Ruhr. Although Mannesmann executives were not among the German industrialists to have promoted the rise of Adolf Hitler, the company did contribute significantly to the war effort and therefore was stripped of nearly all its directors under the terms of the war-crimes mandate. Following reorganization of Germany's basic industries, Mannesmann was split into three companies in 1952 but reintegrated by 1955.

During the 20th century, Mannesmann produced iron and steel, manufactured tubes and tube products, sold data processing equipment and precision instruments, and constructed industrial plants. It began acquiring telecommunications companies in 1995. A hostile bid by Vodaphone in 1999 led to Mannesmann's acquisition by that company in 2000.

Mannheim, city, Baden-Württemberg *Land* (state), southwestern Germany, on the right bank of the Rhine River opposite Ludwigshafen, at the mouth of the canalized Neckar River. Mannheim was mentioned as a village as early as 764. In 1606 it was laid out in a grid pattern of 136 rectangular blocks of houses and was fortified by Elector Frederick IV; it was chartered in 1607. The town was destroyed in the Thirty Years' War (1622) and again in 1689 in the succession struggle that led to the War of the Grand Alliance. It was rebuilt when the Palatine electors moved their residence there in 1720. The castle, the Jesuit church, the old town hall, the pilgrimage church, the warehouse, and the arsenal are among the noteworthy Baroque buildings of that period. The cylindrical water tower (*c.* 1888) is the emblem of the city of Mannheim. It is located in Friedrichsplatz, an art nouveau square constructed in 1907.

Water tower, Mannheim, Ger.
Klaus Hackenberg—ZEFA/EB Inc.

Mannheim became a cultural centre of high repute, with a school of conductors, violinists, and composers, an art gallery, and an academy of sciences. In 1778 the court moved to Munich. In the same year Germany's first National Theatre opened in Mannheim, and in 1782 it gave the first performance of Friedrich Schiller's play *Die Räuber* (*The Robbers*). Mannheim was destroyed again in 1795, and administrative control was transferred to the state of Baden in 1802. The city was rebuilt and became a centre of the revolutionary movement in 1848–49.

The construction of Mannheim's harbour on the Rhine in 1834 stimulated economic growth, and by 1900 it had become industrialized. Carl Benz produced his first two-stroke automotive engine (1879) in Mannheim. More than half of the city was destroyed in World War II, but most of the important buildings have been rebuilt. It is one of Europe's largest inland ports, and its trade in coal and iron is of particular economic importance. Manufactures include chemicals, textiles, fertilizer, and food products. Publishing and tourism are also important. Mannheim has remained a cultural centre with the National Theatre (rebuilt 1954–57) and schools of music and drama. The Reiss Museum and a city museum have collections of art. The University of Mannheim, founded in 1907 and reopened in 1946, regained university status in 1967. An annual folk festival is held in May. Pop. (1998 est.) 310,475.

Mannheim, Karl (b. March 27, 1893, Budapest [Hungary]—d. Jan. 9, 1947, London, Eng.), sociologist in Germany before the rise of Adolf Hitler and then in Great Britain, remembered for his "sociology of knowledge," for his study of science as a social organization having a sociological impact outside itself, and for his work on the problems of leadership and consensus.

After teaching at the universities of Heidelberg (1926–30) and Frankfurt am Main (1930–33), Mannheim lectured on sociology at the London School of Economics, University of London (1933–45), and was professor of the philosophy and sociology of education at that university's Institute of Education (1945–47).

In Mannheim's view, social conflict is caused by the diversity of individual ways of thought and personal criteria of truth. He believed these differences are more basic than economic disparity and class consciousness, which Marxist philosophers emphasize. He elaborated these ideas in *Ideologie und Utopie* (1929; 4th ed., 1965; *Ideology and Utopia: An Introduction to the Sociology of Knowledge*). He argued in favour of subjective beliefs (which to him were "knowledge") at the expense of verifiable facts. In the posthumously published *Freedom, Power, and Democratic Planning* (1950), Mannheim tried to reconcile his dislike of totalitarianism and his growing belief in the need for social planning.

Mannheim school, in music, a group of 18th-century composers who assembled themselves in the city of Mannheim, Ger., under the patronage of Duke Karl Theodor (reigned 1743–99), the elector palatine. They distinguished themselves particularly in their instrumental music, which proved to be of great significance in the development of the mature Classical style (as exemplified in the works of Joseph Haydn and W.A. Mozart). Many contemporary visitors to the Mannheim court, such as the famous 18th-century English music historian Charles Burney, wrote glowing accounts of the musical establishment there. Especially impressive to these travelers was the outstanding orchestra, which was famous throughout Europe for its highly disciplined virtuosity and its ability to produce certain novel and arousing effects. These effects, such as lengthy crescendos, abrupt dynamic changes, and swiftly ascending melodic figures (the famous "Mannheim rocket"), were particularly cultivated in the symphonic works of the Mannheim composers. More important historically than these compositional devices was the tendency of these composers (especially Johann Stamitz) to articulate the various components of the symphonic form to a greater degree than had previously been the case. Their role in the evolution of the Classical symphony is thus significant, although most scholars now agree that these changes occurred nearly simultaneously at various other centres, such as Berlin and Vienna.

The Mannheim school consists chiefly of two generations of composers. The first includes Johann Stamitz, who was the founder and inspired conductor of the orchestra; Ignaz Holzbauer; Franz Xaver Richter; and Carlo Giuseppe Toeschi. These men established the supremacy of the Mannheim school and, in their orchestral works, initiated many of the effects that were to popularize it. The composers of the second generation are Anton Filtz; Johann Christian Cannabich, who perfected the orchestra; Anton and Karl Stamitz; and Franz Beck.

mannikin, any of numerous birds of the tribe Amadini of the songbird family Estrildidae. This name is given particularly to certain species of the genus *Lonchura.* Mannikins are finchlike birds, mostly brownish and often with black throats and fine barring. Large flocks occur in open country from Africa to Australia. Many are popular cage birds. The 9-centimetre (3.5-inch) bronze mannikin (*L. cucullata*) has large communal roosts in Africa; it has been introduced into Puerto

Rico, where it is called hooded weaver. Abundant in southern Asia are the nutmeg mannikin (*L. punctulata*), also called spice finch or spotted munia, and the striated mannikin (*L. striata*), also called white-backed munia. The former is established in Hawaii, where it is called ricebird. A domestic strain of the latter is called Bengal finch.

For chestnut mannikin, *see* munia. For the South American manakins (family Pipridae), *see* manakin.

Manning, Henry Edward (b. July 15, 1808, Totteridge, Hertfordshire, Eng.—d. Jan. 14, 1892, London), member of the Oxford Movement, which sought a return of the Church of England to the High Church ideals of the 17th century, who converted to Roman Catholicism and became archbishop of Westminster.

Manning was the son of a banker and member of Parliament. He was associated with the Oxford Movement, was ordained priest in the Church of England (1833), and became archdeacon of Chichester (1840). Manning's attraction to Roman Catholicism was based on his opposition to government interference in ecclesiastical affairs. He was disturbed when the Privy Council overruled the refusal of a bishop to institute an Anglican divine, George C. Gorham, on grounds of unorthodoxy (1850). Manning was received into the Roman Catholic Church on April 6, 1851, and ordained priest (his wife had died in 1837) by Cardinal Nicholas Wiseman on June 15, 1851. He then studied theology at Rome. In 1857 he founded the Oblates of St. Charles. His rapid rise in the church culminated in his appointment as archbishop of Westminster (the Roman Catholic primatial see of England) in 1865 and his elevation to the rank of cardinal in 1875.

Cardinal Manning

By courtesy of the Gernsheim Collection, the University of Texas at Austin

As archbishop, Manning was a vigorous builder of Catholic schools and other institutions. An extreme Ultramontanist, he accused John Henry (later Cardinal) Newman of minimizing the authority of Rome, and in the debates on papal infallibility at the first Vatican Council advocated a less cautious definition than that eventually adopted. Manning won general public regard for his social concern and his successful intervention in the 1889 London dock strike. The *Life of Cardinal Manning, Archbishop of Westminster* by E.S. Purcell (1896) remains a primary source, citing documents nowhere else available. Other biographies are by V.A. McClelland, *Cardinal Manning, His Public Life and Influence* (1961), and E.E. Reynolds, *Three Cardinals* (1958).

Manning, James (b. Oct. 22, 1738, Piscataway, N.J.—d. July 29, 1791, Providence, R.I., U.S.), U.S. Baptist clergyman who founded Brown University, Providence, and served as its first president.

Manning, a graduate of Princeton in 1762, was ordained to the Baptist ministry the following year. Baptist authorities, intent on founding a college, put Manning, who had graduated second in his class, in charge of the project. A site was selected in Rhode Island, which was near the geographical centre of the colonies, and a charter was granted by the Rhode Island Assembly in March 1764. The next year the college opened in Warren, R.I., with Manning as its first president (1765–91). In 1770 it was moved to its present location in Providence, where Manning was also minister of the First Baptist Church. Although instruction was interrupted by the outbreak of the U.S. War of Independence, the college was firmly established by the end of Manning's administration. He also helped form the Warren Association, an organization of New England Baptists; represented Rhode Island in the Congress of the Confederation in 1786, which governed the U.S. until the Constitution went into effect; and drafted a report in 1791 urging the establishment of free public schools.

James Manning, detail from an oil painting by Cosmo Alexander, 1770; in University Hall, Brown University, Providence, R.I.

By courtesy of Brown University, Providence, R.I.

Manning, Olivia, married name MRS. R.D. SMITH (b. March 2, 1911, Portsmouth, Hampshire, Eng.—d. July 23, 1980, Ryde, Isle of Wight), British journalist and novelist, noted for her ambitious attempt to portray the panorama of modern history in a fictional framework.

Manning, the daughter of a naval officer, produced her first novel, *The Wind Changes,* in 1937. Two years later she married Reginald Donald Smith, drama writer and producer for the British Broadcasting Corporation. In 1951 she published *School for Love*, the story of a 16-year-old boy in war-ravaged Jerusalem, notable for its characterization of the central figure, the repellent Miss Bohun.

Manning's main body of work is the *Balkan Trilogy* (*The Great Fortune,* 1960; *The Spoilt City,* 1962; *Friends and Heroes,* 1965). These three books, set in Bucharest, trace the relationship between Guy Pringle, a British cultural representative, and his wife, Harriet, against a background of the shifting balance of power in Europe. A *Levant Trilogy* (*The Danger Tree*, 1978; *The Battle Lost and Won*, 1979; *The Sum of Things*, 1980) followed.

Mannix, Daniel (b. March 4, 1864, Charleville, County Cork, Ire.—d. Nov. 6, 1963, Melbourne), Roman Catholic prelate who became one of Australia's most controversial political figures during the first half of the 20th century.

Mannix studied at St. Patrick's College, Maynooth, County Kildare, where he was ordained priest in 1890 and where he taught philosophy (1891) and theology (1894); from 1903 to 1912 he served as president of the college. Consecrated titular archbishop of Pharsalus in 1912, he arrived in Melbourne in the following year as coadjutor archbishop, becoming archbishop of Melbourne in 1917.

Mannix's forthright demands for state aid for the education of Roman Catholics in return for their taxes and his opposition to drafting soldiers for World War I made him the subject of controversy. A zealous supporter of Irish independence, he made an official journey to Rome in 1920 via the United States, where his lengthy speechmaking attracted enthusiastic crowds. His campaign in behalf of the Irish, however, caused the British government to prevent him from landing in Ireland, which he finally visited in 1925.

After World War II Mannix sought to stop Communist infiltration of the Australian trade unions; he played a controversial part in the dissensions within the Australian Labor Party and backed the largely right-wing Catholic Democratic Labor Party, which broke away. A promoter of Catholic Action (*i.e.,* lay apostolic activity in the temporal society) and of the Catholic social movement, he is responsible for having established 181 schools, including Newman College and St. Mary's College at the University of Melbourne, and 108 parishes. F. Murphy's *Daniel Mannix, Archbishop of Melbourne* appeared in 1948.

Mannlicher, Ferdinand, Ritter von (knight of) (b. Jan. 30, 1848, Mainz, Rhenish Hesse—d. Jan. 20, 1904, Vienna), Austrian firearms designer who invented the cartridge clip, which allows loading a box magazine in one motion.

Mannlicher served as chief engineer of the Austrian Northern Railroad and then joined the Austrian Arms Company, Styr, in 1866. His first rifle design, a turning-bolt action, was not a notable success; but his subsequent designs incorporated many advanced innovations and came into wide use in Europe. His first straight-pull, bolt-action rifle (1884) led to the popular Model 1885 11-mm Austrian service rifle. In 1885 he developed the cartridge clip and used it in the Model 1885. Later, the clip was almost universally adopted for automatic-feeding pistols and rifles.

Mannlicher designed about 150 types of repeating guns, many of them automatic. Many of his designs were failures because they were more advanced than the ammunition and metals of their day.

Consult the INDEX *first*

Mannyng (of Brunne), Robert (fl. *c.* 1330), early English poet and author of *Handlyng Synne,* a poem of popular morality, and of the chronicle *Story of England.* The works are preserved independently in several manuscripts, none of certain provenance. The author is probably to be identified with a Sir Robert de Brunne, chaplain, named as executor in a Lincoln will of 1327; apart from this mention, his biography can only be reconstructed from his writings. He was at the University of Cambridge around 1300. For 15 years (*c.* 1302–*c.* 1317) Mannyng was a Gilbertine canon at Sempringham priory, Lincolnshire, where in 1303 he began *Handlyng Synne* and was still working at it after 1307. For many years he was engaged on the *Story of England,* which, he relates, was finished between 3 and 4 o'clock, on Friday, May 15, 1338.

Handlyng Synne is an adaptation in about 13,000 lines, in short couplets poorly versified, of the *Manuel des Péchés* ("Handbook of Sins"), which is usually ascribed to William of Waddington (or Widdington), an Englishman, probably a Yorkshireman, writing in Anglo-Norman between 1250 and 1270. Like Waddington, Mannyng aimed to provide a handbook that should serve to stimulate careful self-examination as preparation for confession.

Mannyng deals in turn with the Ten Commandments, the seven deadly sins and the sin of sacrilege, the seven sacraments, the 12 requisites of confession, and the 12 graces of confession. There is much direct instruction, exhortation, and didactic comment; each of the topics is illustrated by one or more tales. These exempla have sometimes been considered to provide the particular interest of the work. The whole work is designed for oral delivery. Mannyng's merit as a storyteller lies in his apt management of material and in his lucid, direct narration. Otherwise the literary merits of *Handlyng Synne* are negligible, although its documentary value for social history is great. It illustrates clearly the attitudes and values of the English minor clergy and peasantry in the early 14th century; throughout there is much comment on the social, domestic, parochial, and commercial scene.

Of similar literary quality is Mannyng's later work, the *Story of England*, but the basis of the *Story of England* is fiction. As history it is almost worthless. The work falls into two parts. The first tells the story from the biblical Noah to the death of the British king Caedwalla in 689. In the second part, he takes the story to the death of Edward I (1307).

Of particular interest is his incorporation of elements of popular romance, such as the story of Guy of Warwick's encounter with the giant Colbrand, which he inserts into his account of Athelstan. He works into his narrative several topical songs, mainly on the Scottish wars of Edward I's time.

Mano River, also called BEWA, or GBEYAR, river rising in the Guinea Highlands northeast of Voinjama, Liberia. With its tributary, the Morro, it forms more than 90 miles (145 km) of the Liberia–Sierra Leone border. The river and its affluents (including the Zeliba) drain a basin of 3,185 square miles (8,250 square km). It follows a 200-mile (320-kilometre) southwesterly course through the Gola National Forest in Liberia and empties into the Atlantic at Mano Salija, Sierra Leone. Intermittent rapids impede its navigability. The Mano River Bridge, completed in 1976, spans the river at Bo, Liberia, reducing the distance by road between the capitals of Liberia and Sierra Leone.

Manoello Giudeo: *see* Immanuel ben Solomon.

Manohar (fl. 1580–1620, India), a leading miniaturist of the Mughal school of painting in India, noted for his outstanding manuscript illustrations, portraits, and a few animal studies.

The son of the celebrated painter Basāvan, Manohar executed his work primarily between 1580 and 1620 and spanned the reigns of the emperors Akbar and Jahāngīr. He primarily depicts the richness of Mughal court life and etiquette. He was acquainted with Western painting and incorporated small sections in his earlier work. The splendid picture depicting Jahāngīr in the hall of private audience when encamped at the city of Ajmer is one of his great works (Victoria and Albert Museum, London). There is some speculation that he later entered the atelier of Prince Dārā Shikōh, the son of the emperor Shāh Jahān (reigned 1628–57/58).

Manolete, byname of MANUEL LAUREANO RODRÍGUEZ SÁNCHEZ (b. July 5, 1917, Córdoba, Spain—d. Aug. 29, 1947, Linares), bullfighter, generally considered the greatest Spanish successor to Joselito (José Gómez) and Juan Belmonte.

The son of a matador, Manolete became a professional at the age of 17. In the arena he was noted for his extreme economy of movement and his dispassionate demeanour. Although he was exceedingly popular with audiences in Spain and in Mexico, he frequently appeared arrogant to those who met him casually. After a career of 13 years he was gored to death in the ring.

Manolete

Barnaby Conrad

BIBLIOGRAPHY. Barnaby Conrad, *The Death of Manolete* (1958), was written by an American matador and aficionado.

Manolo (bullfighter): *see* Cordobés, El.

manor house, during the European Middle Ages, the dwelling of the lord of the manor or his residential bailiff and administrative centre of the feudal estate. The medieval manor was generally fortified in proportion to the degree of peaceful settlement of the country or region in which it was located. The manor house was the centre of secular village life, and its great hall was the scene of the manorial court and the place of assembly of the tenantry. The particular character of the manor

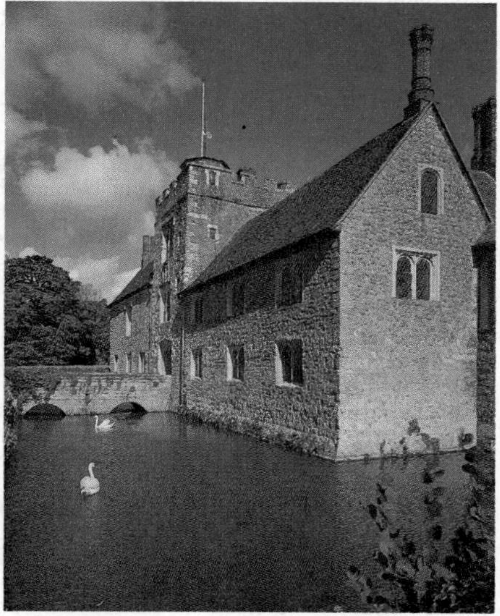

Gatehouse of the manor house at Ightham Mote, Kent, Eng.

A.F. Kersting

house is most clearly represented in England and France, but under different names similar dwellings of feudal overlords existed in all countries wherein the manorial system developed.

In England in the 11th century the manor house was an informal group of related timber or stone buildings consisting of the hall, chapel, kitchen, and farm buildings contained within a defensive wall and ditch. In the 12th century the hall, which throughout the medieval period was the major element of domestic architecture, was placed defensively at first-floor level and contained within a moated enclosure. Later it was planned at ground level, as in Oakham Castle, Rutland, within a more strongly defended enclosure. By the 14th century the manor-house plan was clearly defined, with private living apartments and service rooms at opposite ends of the great hall and with battlements, gatehouse, and moat—as at Ightham Mote, Kent. Ockwells Manor in Berkshire is a typical timber-framed manor house built in the 15th century without defensive elements.

In France, until the end of the Hundred Years' War in 1453, considerations of defense dominated manorial building. Such early manor houses as the 14th-century Camarsac Manor in Gironde consisted primarily of a rectangular fortified tower in a walled and moated enclosure. In Normandy the Ango Manor, near Dieppe, reveals some advance in domestic planning in the 15th century, the house standing at one end of a courtyard, flanked by farm buildings and defended by a gatehouse.

With increased prosperity and the desire for more commodious dwellings, the 16th-century manor house evolved into the Renaissance country house. In England more elaborate buildings were constructed, reflecting a new era of formality. The houses were frequently of regular quadrangular plan, with the hall diminished in size and importance. Later the hall was reduced to the status of an entrance, as at Ramsbury Manor, Wiltshire (*c.* 1680). The defended tower-house tradition persisted in France throughout the 16th century, generally retaining corner turrets and other defensive archaisms, as in the Tourelles Manor, near Troyes. In later years the title of manor house in England lost particular significance, having been adopted by large country mansions that had no manorial foundation.

manorial court, in feudal law, court through which a lord exercised jurisdiction over his tenants. The manorial court was presided over by the steward or seneschal, and it was there that various officials such as the reeve, who acted as general overseer, and the hayward, who watched over the crops and brought offenders to court, were appointed. The tenants were punished and often forced to pay fines for their offenses; the manorial court thus provided the lord with a convenient source of income. Through the court the tenants also registered land transactions between themselves when this was permitted, and through it they surrendered or took up holdings under the lord. *See also* court baron.

manorialism, also called MANORIAL SYSTEM, SEIGNORIALISM, or SEIGNORIAL SYSTEM, political, economic, and social system by which the peasants of medieval Europe were rendered dependent on their land and on their lord. Its basic unit was the manor, a self-sufficient landed estate, or fief, that was under the control of a lord who enjoyed a variety of rights over it and the peasants attached to it by means of serfdom (*q.v.*). The manorial system was the most convenient device for organizing the estates of the aristocracy and the clergy in the European Middle Ages, and it made feudalism (*q.v.*) possible. Under other names the manorial system was found not only in France, England, Germany, Italy, and Spain but also in varying degrees, in the Byzantine Empire, Russia, Japan, and elsewhere. The manorial system's importance as an institution varied in different parts of Europe at different times. In western Europe it was flourishing by the 8th century and had begun to decline by the 13th century, while in eastern Europe it achieved its greatest strength after the 15th century.

Manorialism had its origins in the late Roman Empire, when large landowners had to consolidate their hold over both their lands and the labourers who worked them. This was a necessity in the midst of the civil disorders, enfeebled governments, and barbarian invasions that wracked Europe in the 5th and 6th centuries AD. In such conditions, small farmers and landless labourers exchanged their land or their freedom and pledged their services in return for the protection of powerful landowners who had the military strength to defend them. In this way, the poor, defenseless, and landless were ensured permanent access to plots of land which they could work in return for the rendering of economic services to the lord who held that land. This arrangement developed into the manorial system, which in turn supported the feudal aristocracy of kings, lords, and vassals.

The typical western European manor in the 13th century consisted partly of the cottages, huts, and barns and gardens of its peasants, which were usually clustered together to form a small village. There might also be a church, a mill, and a wine or oil press in the village. Close by was the fortified dwelling, or manor house, of the lord, which might be inhabited by him or merely by his steward if the lord happened to hold more than one manor. The village was surrounded by arable land that was divided into three large fields that were farmed in rotation, with one allowed to lie fallow each year. There were also usually meadows for supplying hay, pastures for livestock, pools and streams for fishing, and forests and waste lands for wood gathering and foraging. Most of the latter and a portion of the cultivated land were held by the lord as his demesne, *i.e.,* that portion of a manor not granted to free tenants but either retained by the lord for his own use and occupation or occupied by his villeins (serfs) or leasehold tenants.

The lord would grant part of his land out to free tenants to hold at a rent or by military or other service. Below the lord and the free tenants came the villeins, serfs, or bondmen, each holding a hut or small dwelling, a fixed number of acre strips, and a share of the meadow and of the profits of the waste. Normally the peasant was unfree; he could not without leave quit the manor and could be reclaimed by process of law if he did. The strict contention of law deprived him of all right to hold property; and in many cases he was subject to certain degrading incidents, such as marchet (*merchetum*), a payment due to the lord upon the marriage of a daughter, which was regarded as a special mark of unfree condition. But there were certain limitations. First, all these incidents of tenure, even marchet, might not affect the personal status of the tenant; he might still be free, though held by an unfree tenure; second, even if unfree, he was not exposed to the arbitrary will of his lord but was protected by the custom of the manor as interpreted by the manor court. Moreover, he was not a slave, since he could not be bought and sold apart from his holding. The hardship of his condition lay in the services due from him. As a rule a villein paid for his holding in money, in labour, and in agrarian produce. In money he paid, first, a small fixed rent that was known as rent of assize and, second, dues under various names, partly in lieu of services commuted into money payments and partly for the privileges and profits enjoyed by him on the waste of the manor. In labour he paid more heavily. Week by week he was required to come with his own plow and oxen to plow the lord's demesne; when plowing was completed, he had to harrow, to reap the crops, to thresh and carry them, or to do whatever might be required of him, until his allotted number of days' labour in the year had been accomplished.

The most complicated structure in the system was the manor court, whose business was divided into criminal, manorial, and civil. Its powers under the first head depended on the franchises enjoyed by the lord in the particular manor; for the most part only petty offenses were triable, such as small thefts, breaches of the assize of bread and ale, assaults, and the like; except under special conditions, the justice of great offenses remained in the hands of the king or other territorial sovereign. But offenses against the custom of the manor, such as bad plowing, improper taking of wood from the lord's woods, and the like were of course the staple criminal business of the court. Under the head of manorial business, the court dealt with the choice of the manorial officers and had some power of making regulations for the management of the manor; but its most important function was the recording of the surrenders and admittances of the villein tenants. Finally, the court dealt with all suits as to land within the manor, questions of dower and inheritance, and those few civil suits not connected with land.

The revival of commerce that began in Europe in the 11th century signaled the decline of the manorial system, which could only survive in a decentralized and localized economy in which peasant subsistence farming was dominant. The reintroduction of a money economy into Europe and the growth of cities and towns in the 11th and 12th centuries created a market for the lords' agricultural produce and also provided luxuries for them to purchase. As a result, lords increasingly allowed their peasants to commute their (labour) services for money, and eventually to purchase their freedom with it as well. Agricultural surpluses could now be sold to the cities and towns, and it was found that free workers who paid rent or received wages farmed more efficiently (and produced more profits) than enserfed labourers. Owing to these and other economic reasons, the inefficient and coercive manorial system disintegrated in western Europe, gradually evolving into simpler and less onerous economic arrangements between landlords and rent-paying tenants.

Manorialism underwent a somewhat different evolution in central and eastern Europe. These areas had witnessed the decline of manorialism in the 12th and 13th centuries as vast areas of forest and wasteland were colonized by free German and Slavonic peasants. But the numerous wars fought between the Russians, Poles, Prussians, Lithuanians, and others in the 15th and 16th centuries reproduced the political instability and social insecurities that had led to peasant enserfment in western Europe centuries earlier. In addition, western Europe's growing demand for grain from the Baltic area gave nobles and other landlords there an additional incentive to enserf their peasants, since that was the best way to ensure labour services for grain-growing demesnes. So by the 16th century manorialism had been re-created on a large scale in eastern Europe, particularly in eastern Germany, Poland, and Russia. These reactionary manorial developments were not reversed in eastern Europe until the 19th century in most cases.

Manouel (Greek personal name): *see under* Manuel.

Manresa, town, Barcelona *provincia,* in the *comunidad autónoma* ("autonomous community") of Catalonia, northeastern Spain. It lies along the Cardoner River. The town—which probably originated as Minorisa, the Roman capital of Jacetani—was important during the European Middle Ages. Three bridges span the Cardoner, and on a rock above the oldest bridge stands the yellow Church of Santa María de la Seo (14th and 15th centuries). Below the 17th-century Church of San Ignacio is the cave where St. Ignatius of Loyola meditated. The municipal museum occupies the cloisters of San Ignacio. There is also a conservatory of music in Manresa. The town's industries include metallurgy and the making of textiles, tires, and glass. Pop. (1999 est.) mun., 63,688.

Manrique, Gómez (b. *c.* 1412, Amusco, Castile [now in Spain]—d. *c.* 1490, Toledo), soldier, politician, diplomat and poet, chiefly famous as one of the earliest Spanish dramatists whose name is known. He fought with the leagues of nobles against King Henry IV of Castile and in support of the claims to the crown of the king's half sister Isabella.

As a poet, Manrique is remembered for songs (some of which he wrote for Juana of Portugal, queen of Henry IV, before rising in opposition to the king), as well as elegies, satires such as the *Razonamiento de un rocín a un paje* ("Advice of a Horse to a Page"), and *Regimiento de príncipes* (1495; "Regiment of Princes") and other political poems. He is the only author of liturgical dramas in 15th-century Castile whose work survives. Among these is the *Representación del nacimiento de Nuestro Señor* ("Scenes of the Birth of Our Lord"), written at the request of his sister, an abbess, and consisting of a series of dramatic tableaux recounting the birth of Christ. A similar piece, entitled *Lamentaciones hechas para Semana Santa* ("Lamentations for Holy Week"), was a chronicle of the Crucifixion that achieved great popularity owing to its lyrical pathos.

Manrique, Jorge (b. 1440, probably at Paredes de Nava, Castile [now in Spain]—d. March 27, 1479, in front of Castle Garci-Muñoz, near Calatrava, Spain), Spanish soldier and writer, best known for his lyric poetry.

Manrique was born into an illustrious Castilian family that numbered among its members the statesman Pedro López de Ayala and the poets Gómez Manrique and the Marquess de Santillana. He entered the Castilian military service at an early age and by 1474 was made captain. He died in battle in the civil war, in which he supported the succession of Isabella of Castile as queen of a united Castile and Aragon.

Manrique's best-known literary work, *Coplas por la muerte de su padre* (1492; "Stanzas for the Death of His Father"), is a lyric poem in honour of his father, Rodrigo Manrique, Count de Paredes and grand master of the Military Order of Santiago. Written in *pie quebrado,* a 12-line stanza having 4 triplets of 8- , 8- , and 4-syllable lines and with a rhyme scheme of *abcabcdefdef,* the *Coplas* achieved a haunting, timeless quality. It was translated into English by Henry Wadsworth Longfellow as *Coplas de Don Jorge Manrique* (1833). Selections of Manrique's poetry appeared in Hernando de Castillo's anthology *Cancionero general* (1511).

Mans, Le (France): *see* Le Mans.

Mansa, formerly FORT ROSEBERY, town, northern Zambia. It is located between Lake Bangweulu to the east and the frontier with Zaire to the west. It lies in an agricultural and livestock-raising area, has a battery-manufacturing plant, and is the seat of a Roman Catholic bishopric. Pop. (1990) 37,900.

Mansa Mūsā (emperor of Mali): *see* Mūsā.

manṣabdār, member of the imperial bureaucracy of the Mughal Empire in India. The *manṣabdār*s governed the empire and commanded its armies in the emperor's name. Though they were usually aristocrats, they did not form a feudal aristocracy, for neither the offices nor the estates that supported them were hereditary. The system was organized by the emperor Akbar (reigned 1556–1605), who with its help turned a loose military confederation of Muslim nobles into a multiracial bureaucratic empire integrating Muslims and Hindus. The word is of Arabic origin, *dār* indicating the holder of an office or dignity and *manṣab* being a rank determined by the command of a specified number of men. There were 33 grades ranging from 10 to 5,000 (the highest for a subject) in a complicated system. For the maintenance of the men, the *manṣabdār*s received a salary, which Akbar paid in cash but which later emperors met by means of assignments on the revenues. The lands thus assigned were liable to transfer during a *manṣabdār*'s lifetime and were taken back at his death. To pay his way the *manṣabdār* was allowed advances from the treasury, which at death were recoverable in what amounted to a death duty of 100 percent.

*Manṣabdār*s held military commands and civil posts. The system provided an outlet for ambition and ability within the imperial service and formed the framework of the Mughal administration. The *manṣabdār*s were controlled by their dependence on salaries, by frequent transfer from one appointment to another, and by the diversion of revenue collection direct to the treasury. They had therefore little opportunity to build up either local connections or financial resources for raising private armies. For much of the Mughal period, the *manṣabdār*s were mostly of foreign origin or extraction, as were 70 percent of them toward the end of Akbar's reign. The remaining 30 percent were divided about equally between Muslims and Hindus, the latter mainly Rājputs.

Mansart, François, Mansart also spelled MANSARD (b. January 1598, Paris—d. September 1666), architect important for establishing classicism in Baroque architecture in mid-17th-century France. His buildings are notable for their subtlety, elegance, and harmony. His most complete surviving work is the château of Maisons.

Early years and works. Mansart was the grandson of a master mason and the son of a master carpenter. One of his uncles was a sculptor, another an architect. When his father died in 1610, Mansart's training was taken over by his brother-in-law, an architect and sculptor. Later, Mansart was apprenticed to and heavily influenced by Salomon de Brosse, a distinguished and successful architect during the reign of Henry IV and the regency of Marie de Médicis, mother of Louis XIII.

Château of Balleroy, near Bayeux, Fr., by François Mansart, *c.* 1626
Wayne Andrews

The 1600s, which saw the end of de Brosse's career and the beginning of Mansart's, could not have been more favourable for a young architect. Henry IV's entrance into Paris in 1594 as king of France signaled the beginning of a period of burgeoning political and social aspiration. Architecture reflected this aspiration, for the kings wanted their capital and their palaces to reflect the power of the crown; and the bourgeoisie commissioned châteaus (country houses) and hotels (town mansions) large enough for their coaches, stables of horses, and retinue of servants and splendid enough to receive the king and his entourage.

Most of Mansart's patrons were members of the middle class who had become rich in the service of the crown. They would have to have been very rich indeed to be Mansart's patrons. Not only did he draw up plans without regard to expense but he also refined and improved the plans—tearing down what had been built and rebuilding—as he went along. According to a contemporary, Mansart had cost one of his early patrons "more money than the Great Turk himself possesses."

Mansart's career can be traced from 1623, when he designed the facade of the chapel of the church of the Feuillants in the Rue Saint-Honoré in Paris (no longer standing). Of his early works, the only one that survives is the château of Balleroy (begun *c.* 1626), near Bayeux, in the *département* of Calvados. Built for Jean de Choisy, chancellor to Gaston, duc d'Orléans, the brother of Louis XIII, the château consists of three blocks—a massive, free-standing main building to which two small pavilions are subordinated. One of the facades of the main building overlooks a court, the other a garden. The materials and treatment of the walls are characteristic of much of the work built during the reign of Henry IV. The walls are mainly of rough, brownish yellow brick with little architectural ornament but emphasized by white stone quoins (corners) and white stone frames around the windows.

In 1635 Gaston commissioned Mansart to reconstruct his château at Blois, which had been built in the 15th and 16th centuries and used as a royal residence by three kings. Mansart proposed rebuilding it entirely, but only the north wing facing the gardens was reconstructed. The main building, flanked by pavilions, is subtly articulated by superimposed classical orders (Doric on the ground floor, Ionic on the first, and Corinthian on the second). The court entrance to the main building is approached on both sides by a curving colonnade. Mansart used the high-pitched, two-sloped roof that bears his name, mansard. (In fact, the roof had been used by earlier French architects.) The details are precise and restrained, the proportions of the masses harmonious.

In the same period, Phélypeaux de La Vrillière, an officer of the crown, commissioned Mansart to build a town house in Paris (rebuilt after Mansart's death). The building, known from engravings, was a fine example of Mansart's ability to arrive at subtle, ingenious, and dignified solutions to the problems of building on awkwardly shaped sites.

The château of Maisons. In 1642 René de Longeuil, an immensely wealthy financier and officer of the royal treasury, commissioned Mansart to build a château on his estate. The château of Maisons (now called Maisons-Laffitte, in the chief town of the *département* of Yvelines) is unique in that it is the only building by Mansart in which the interior decoration (graced particularly by a magnificent stairway) survives. The symmetrical design of the building (as well as the mansard roof) is similar to that of Mansart's earlier châteaus, but here there is a greater emphasis on relief. The central building is a free-standing block with a prominent rectangular frontispiece that projects from the main wall in a series of shallow steps. Two short wings, flanking the main building, stand out from it in clean, unbroken rectangular sections. Extending from each of the wings is a low, one-story block. The restrained play of subtly differentiated rectangular motifs lends grace and harmony.

Because it is now surrounded by roads and houses, one can only imagine how noble the château looked, in the setting of terraced gardens designed for it by Mansart, when it opened with a reception for Anne of Austria and her son, the boy-king Louis XIV. At times during the château's construction, de Longeuil must have been sorely tried by Mansart's stubborn, independent, generally difficult personality, but on this day he was surely pleased with the architect he had chosen.

Last years. Perhaps Mansart's personality was responsible for the setbacks he began to encounter, the first of which was a royal commission he received in 1645 and lost in 1646. Anne of Austria asked Mansart to draw up plans for the convent and church of the Val-de-Grâce in Paris, which the sovereign had vowed to build if she bore a son. When the costs of laying the foundation exceeded the funds provided, Mansart was replaced by Jacques Lemercier, who more or less followed the original plans.

Along with a large fortune, Mansart had accumulated many enemies who accused him of capriciousness in the building and rebuilding of his projects, of wild extravagance, and of dishonesty. In 1651 a pamphlet entitled "La Mansarade" (possibly written by political enemies of the prime minister, Cardinal Mazarin, for whom Mansart had worked) accused him of having made deals with contractors and charged him with profligacy. The attack did not prevent him from continuing to work for prominent people.

With the accession of Louis XIV to the throne in 1661, private patrons became fewer and fewer. Architects, painters, sculptors, and craftsmen were called upon to build, decorate, and furnish structures commissioned by the king. When, in 1664, Louis decided to complete the palace of the Louvre, his chief minister and *surintendant des bâtiments* (roughly, "superintendent of buildings"), Jean-Baptiste Colbert, asked Mansart to draw up plans for the east wing (the colonnaded wing). Possibly because he could not produce and keep to any final plan, Mansart lost the commission.

In 1665 Colbert again asked Mansart to produce designs—this time for a chapel for the tombs of the royal family of the Bourbons to be built at the end of the Saint-Denis basilica. Mansart planned his design (which was never executed) around a central, domed space, which later inspired his grandnephew Jules Hardouin-Mansart in his design for the dome of the church of Les Invalides.

When Mansart died the world was quite different from the one in which his career had begun. France had become the centre of Europe and Louis the centre of France—not only politically but also in matters of culture and taste. French architects, artists, and craftsmen were trained and employed by the crown for one end: the glorification of the state in the person of the king, who had declared himself to be the state. But the world was different, too, in that it had been enriched by the work of the independent and individualistic genius of François Mansart.

BIBLIOGRAPHY. Anthony Blunt, *Art and Architecture in France, 1500 to 1700,* 4th ed. (1981), contains an excellent discussion of Mansart. Allan Braham and Peter Smith, *François Mansart,* 2 vol. (1973), details his life and career.

Mansart, Jules Hardouin- (b. *c.* April 16, 1646 Paris, Fr.—d. May 11, 1708, Marly-le-Roi), French architect and city planner to King Louis XIV who completed the design of Versailles.

Mansart in 1668 adopted the surname of his granduncle by marriage, the distinguished architect François Mansart. By 1674, when he was commissioned to rebuild the château of Clagny for Louis XIV's mistress Madame de Montespan, he was already launched on a brilliant career. Among his earlier achievements were many private houses, including his own, the Hôtel de Lorges, later the Hôtel de Conti.

In 1675 Mansart became official architect to the king and from 1678 was occupied with redesigning and enlarging the palace of Versailles. He directed a legion of collaborators and protégés, many of whom became the leading architects of the following age. Starting from plans of architect Louis Le Vau, Mansart built the new Hall of Mirrors, the Orangerie, the Grand Trianon, and the north and south wings. At the time of his death he was working on the chapel. The vast complex, with an exquisite expanse of gardens designed by André Le Nôtre, was a harmonious expression of French Baroque classicism and a model that other courts of Europe sought to emulate.

Château de Dampierre, France, by Jules Hardouin-Mansart

Caisse Nationale des Monuments Historiques

Although occupied with this enormous project for much of his life, Mansart built many other public buildings, churches, and sumptuous houses. Thought to be most reflective of his individual ability to combine classical and Baroque architectural design is the chapel of Les Invalides, Paris. Admirable contributions to city planning include his Place de Vendôme and Place des Victoires, Paris.

Mansbridge, Albert (b. Jan. 10, 1876, Gloucester, Gloucestershire, Eng.—d. Aug. 22, 1952, Torquay, Devon), largely self-educated educator, the founder and chief organizer of the adult-education movement in Great Britain.

The son of a carpenter, Mansbridge had to leave school at the age of 14 owing to his family's limited financial resources. He became a clerical worker but simultaneously satisfied his acute desire for additional education by attending university extension classes at King's College in London. Eventually, he taught evening classes in industrial history, economics, and typing while supporting himself as a clerk during the day.

Albert Mansbridge, portrait by John Mansbridge (his son), 1947; National Portrait Gallery, London

By courtesy of the National Portrait Gallery, London

Mansbridge became distressed that the university extension system—created in 1873—appealed almost exclusively to the upper and middle classes. In 1903, therefore, he founded the Workers' Educational Association (WEA; originally called An Association to Promote the Higher Education of Working Men). The WEA was quickly recognized by most British universities, and in 1905 Mansbridge abandoned clerical work to become its full-time general secretary.

Under Mansbridge's administration, the WEA created a tutorial system and a scholarly library (National Central Library) for working people unaffiliated with an academic institution. He organized WEA branches in Australia, New Zealand, and Canada; and, after recovering from spinal meningitis, he established other adult-education groups: the World Association for Adult Education (1918), the Seafarers' Educational Service (1919), and the British Institute of Adult Education (1921). He delivered the Lowell Lectures in Boston in 1922 and the Earle Lectures for the Pacific School of Religion (in cooperation with the University of California) in 1926. His books include *An Adventure in Working-Class Education* (1920), *The Making of an Educationist* (1929), *Brick upon Brick* (1934), and his autobiography, *The Trodden Road* (1940). A selection of his essays and addresses appeared in 1944 as *The Kingdom of the Mind.*

Mānsehra, town, northeastern North-West Frontier Province, Pakistan. The town is situated at the southern end of the Pakhli Plain on the Bhut Stream, a tributary to the Siran River, at an elevation of 3,682 feet (1,122 m) above sea level. It is a market town surrounded by pine-covered hills and has a flour mill, a woolen-yarn mill, and an agricultural research centre. The nearby Aśokan rock edicts date to the 3rd century BC. The town is 12 miles (19 km) north of Ābbottābād city.

The surrounding region extends northwest from the Siran River valley to encompass the scenic Kāgān (Kāghān) Valley, formed by the Kunhār River. Kāgān Valley, a growing tourist area, is 96 miles (154 km) long by road, hemmed in by mountains with peaks rising to 17,000 feet (5,200 m), and is partly forested by *deodar* (East Indian cedar) and pine trees. Corn (maize), potatoes, *jowār* (sorghum), wheat, barley, rice, fruits, tobacco, and livestock are raised in the region. Jaba (Jabba), near Mānsehra, has a government sheep farm. Pop. (1981) town, 27,843.

Mansel, Henry Longueville (b. Oct. 6, 1820, Cosgrove, Northamptonshire, Eng.—d. July 30, 1871, Cosgrove), British philosopher and Anglican theologian and priest remembered for his exposition of the philosophy of the Scottish thinker Sir William Hamilton (1788–1856).

Educated at the University of Oxford, Mansel was elected Waynflete professor of moral and metaphysical philosophy there in 1859. In 1866 he was appointed regius professor of ecclesiastical history and canon of Christ Church. Two years later he became dean of St. Paul's.

Most of Mansel's philosophical works centre on the relation between human thought and human experience. For the eighth edition of the *Encyclopædia Britannica* (1857) he wrote an article on metaphysics in which he discussed this relationship and developed Hamilton's views. In his Bampton Lectures, *The Limits of Religious Thought* (1858), Mansel expounded Hamilton's doctrine that human knowledge is strictly limited to the finite and is "conditioned." In reply to attacks on this notion by John Stuart Mill and other critics, Mansel defended Hamilton's views in *The Philosophy of the Conditioned* (1866). His contention, however, that the human mind could not attain to any positive conception of the nature of God or his goodness provoked considerable controversy, and Mansel, who meant to attack deism, rather than theism, was accused of agnosticism. Concerned with problems of language and logic, Mansel discussed the verification of the meaning of different propositions and stressed the fundamental difficulty of arriving at particular truths. General knowledge, as his "Metaphysics" article indicated, is humanly possible, but specific truths are inscrutable. Consequently, faith is required in order to overcome the dilemma between the existence of evil and the goodness of God. Among Mansel's other writings are *Prolegomena logica: An Inquiry into the Psychological Character of Logical Processes* (1851) and *The Gnostic Heresies of the First and Second Centuries* (1875); with J. Veitch he edited Hamilton's *Lectures on Metaphysics and Logic,* 4 vol. (1859–60).

Mansfeld, (Peter) Ernst, Graf von (count of) (b. 1580, Luxembourg—d. Nov. 29, 1626, Rakovica, near Sarajevo, Bosnia), Roman Catholic mercenary who fought for the Protestant cause during the Thirty Years' War (1618–48); he was the Catholic League's most dangerous opponent until his death in 1626.

An illegitimate son of Peter Ernst, Fürst von Mansfeld, governor of the Spanish fortress in Luxembourg, Mansfeld entered the Habsburg army and fought in much of Europe. Although he was legitimized, the stigma of his birth adversely influenced his career, and during the first decade of the 17th century he gradually became an enemy of the house of Austria. At the outbreak of the Thirty Years' War (1618), Mansfeld was in the service of the

Protestant Union and, campaigning against the Habsburgs in Bohemia, captured Plzeň (Pilsen). He nevertheless failed to support the new Protestant Bohemian king, the elector Palatine Frederick V, who was subsequently defeated at the Battle of the White Mountain (November 1620). For the next two years, however, Mansfeld successfully defended the elector's Rhenish provinces against General Johann Tserclaes, Graf von Tilly, commanding the Catholic forces. By 1623, however, Frederick V's treasury was exhausted. After futile negotiations with Austria and the French Huguenots, Mansfeld and his ally, Christian of Brunswick, marched through Lorraine and Flanders to enter the service of the United Provinces of the Netherlands, conquering and holding East Frisia until 1624. Mansfeld then acquired English subsidies for the entry of Denmark into the war. While Christian IV of Denmark fought Tilly in Lower Saxony, Mansfeld opposed the imperial general Albrecht von Wallenstein at Dessau but was unable to dislodge him. Followed by Wallenstein, Mansfeld then marched to Hungary with a new army in French pay to join forces with Prince Gábor Bethlen of Transylvania, who was fighting the Austrians in the Balkans. Epidemics caused considerable loss to both sides, and, after Gábor Bethlen negotiated separately with Austria, Mansfeld decided to enter the Venetian service; he died on his way toward Venetian territory.

Mansfield, town and district, county of Nottinghamshire, England, on the River Maun. Mansfield was the chief town of Sherwood Forest (legendary base for the activities of Robin Hood, the medieval robber and popular hero), and the Forest court was held in the town's Moot Hall (built 1752). The population of Mansfield grew with the 19th-century expansion of coal mining and the hosiery industry, and both remain major local employers of labour. Hard red and white sandstone quarried near the town of Mansfield Woodhouse, 2 miles (3 km) north of Mansfield, was used to build the Houses of Parliament at Westminster. The district occupies 30 square miles (77 square km). Pop. (1981) town, 72,108; (1986 est.) district, 100,300.

Mansfield, town (township), Tolland county, eastern Connecticut, U.S. It lies along the Willimantic River, just north of Willimantic. It was originally a part of Windham and was known as Ponde Town. In 1702 it was incorporated as a separate town and was renamed for Major Moses Mansfield, an early settler. Once a busy manufacturing centre, Mansfield has become essentially a residential, agricultural, and educational community. It includes the villages of Gurleyville, Merrow, Eagleville, and Storrs (site of the University of Connecticut, founded 1881). Pop. (1990) 21,103.

Mansfield, city, seat (1808) of Richland county, north-central Ohio, U.S., on a fork of the Mohican River. Laid out in 1808, it was named for Jared Mansfield, U.S. surveyor general. The arrival of the Mansfield and Sandusky Railroad (1846; now Baltimore and Ohio), followed by the Pittsburg, Ft. Wayne, and Chicago Railway (1849; now Penn Central) and the Atlantic and Great Western Railway (1863; now Erie Lackawanna), stimulated Mansfield's economy. The city's diversified manufactures now include electric appliances, automotive parts, sheet steel, plumbing equipment, pumps, and thermostats. A branch of Ohio State University is in the city.

Notable features of Mansfield include Kingwood Center (the French Provincial mansion of industrialist Charles Kelly King) and Gardens; a log blockhouse from the War of 1812; a monument to John Chapman (Johnny Appleseed), who lived there for nearly 20 years; and the Richland County Museum. The nearby Malabar Farm (preserved within a state park) was created as an agricultural showcase by novelist Louis Bromfield (1896–1956), who was born in Mansfield. The city is a noted winter-sports centre and is the site of the annual Ohio Ski Carnival. The Mid-Ohio Sports Car Course is also nearby. Inc. town, 1828; city, 1857. Pop. (1990) city, 50,627; Mansfield MSA, 126,137.

Mansfield, Arabella, *née* BELLE AURELIA BABB (b. May 23, 1846, near Burlington, Iowa, U.S.—d. Aug. 2, 1911, Aurora, Ill.), educator who was the first woman admitted to the legal profession in the United States.

After graduating from Iowa Wesleyan University in 1866, Mansfield taught political science, English, and history at Simpson (Iowa) College, and at Iowa Wesleyan in Mount Pleasant. She subsequently studied law, along with her husband, John Melvin Mansfield, a professor of natural history, and applied for admission to the Iowa bar in 1869. The sympathetic examiners, saying that her examination gave "the very best rebuke possible to the imputation that ladies cannot qualify for the practice of law," certified Arabella Mansfield as the first female lawyer in the country. She never practiced law but continued to teach at Iowa Wesleyan, where she also earned an M.A. (1870) and an LL.B. (1872). In 1886 she began teaching at DePauw University in Greencastle, Ind., where she became dean of the schools of art and music by 1894.

Mansfield, Katherine, pseudonym of KATHLEEN MURRY, *née* KATHLEEN MANSFIELD BEAUCHAMP (b. Oct. 14, 1888, Wellington, N.Z.—d. Jan. 9, 1923, Gurdjieff Institute, near Fontainebleau, Fr.), New Zealand-born English master of the short story, who evolved a distinctive prose style with many overtones of poetry. Her delicate stories, focused upon psychological conflicts, have an obliqueness of narration and a subtlety of observation that reveal the influence of Anton Chekhov. She, in turn, had much influence on the development of the short story as a form of literature.

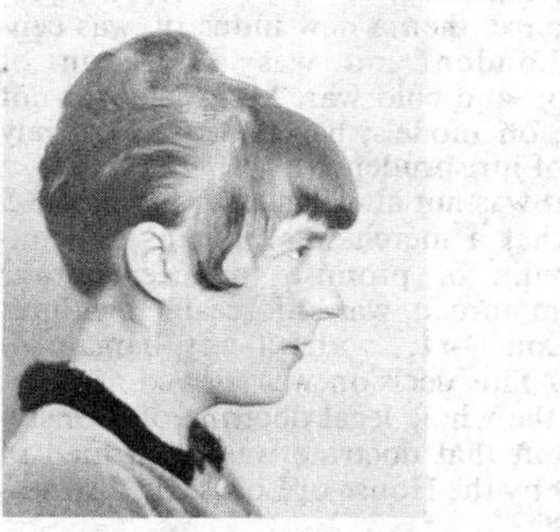

Katherine Mansfield
BBC Hulton Picture Library

After her education (in Wellington and London), Katherine Mansfield left New Zealand at the age of 19 to establish herself in England as a writer. Her initial disillusion appears in the ill-humoured stories collected in *In a German Pension* (1911). Until 1914 she published stories in *Rhythm* and *The Blue Review*, edited by the critic and essayist John Middleton Murry, whom she married in 1918 after her divorce from George Bowden. The death of her soldier brother in 1915 shocked her into a recognition that she owed what she termed a sacred debt to him and to the remembered places of her native country. *Prelude* (1918) was a series of short stories beautifully evocative of her family memories of New Zealand. These, with others, were collected in *Bliss* (1920), which secured her reputation and is typical of her art.

In the next two years Mansfield did her best work, achieving the height of her powers in *The Garden Party* (1922), which includes "At the Bay," "The Voyage," "The Stranger" (with New Zealand settings), and the classic "Daughters of the Late Colonel," a subtle account of genteel frustration. Her final work (apart from unfinished material) was published posthumously in *The Dove's Nest* (1923) and *Something Childish* (1924). From her papers, Murry edited the *Journal* (1927, rev. ed. 1954), and he also published with annotations her letters to him (1928, rev. ed. 1951). The last five years of her life were shadowed by tuberculosis.

Ian A. Gordon edited *Undiscovered Country: New Zealand Stories of Katherine Mansfield* (1974) and *The Urewara Notebook* (1979). A biography by Claire Tomalin, *Katherine Mansfield: A Secret Life,* appeared in 1988.

Mansfield, Michael J(oseph), byname MIKE MANSFIELD (b. March 16, 1903, New York City), Democratic Party majority leader in the U.S. Senate (1961–77) and U.S. ambassador to Japan from 1977 to 1988.

Reared by relatives in Montana, Mansfield dropped out of school before completing the eighth grade. He enlisted in the U.S. Navy at the age of 14 and served in military transport during World War I until his age was discovered and he was discharged. He then enlisted in the army and later the marine corps, serving in several remote outposts.

Mansfield spent most of the 1920s working in Montana copper mines, but his wife persuaded him to finish school, and in 1933 he earned both his high school and college diplomas (A.B., University of Montana, 1933). In 1934 he obtained his master's degree and joined the faculty of the University of Montana, eventually becoming a full professor of Far Eastern and Latin-American history.

In 1940 Mansfield made his first bid for elective office, running third in a three-candidate Democratic primary. But in 1942 he was elected to the House of Representatives and became an active member of the House Foreign Affairs Committee. He advised presidents Franklin D. Roosevelt and Harry S. Truman on U.S. foreign policy toward China and Japan and maintained a solidly liberal voting record on domestic issues.

In 1952 Mansfield won a seat in the Senate, despite the accusations of Senator Joseph R. McCarthy that he was soft on communism. A prominent member of the Senate Foreign Relations Committee, Mansfield in 1957 became majority whip. He succeeded Lyndon Johnson as Senate majority leader when Johnson became vice president in 1961.

Reelected to the Senate in 1958, 1964, and 1970, Mansfield refused Johnson's offer to run for vice president in 1964. Throughout the 1960s he became increasingly vocal in his criticism of U.S. involvement in the Vietnam War, and in 1971 he sponsored a bill calling for a ceasefire and the phased withdrawal of U.S. troops from Vietnam. In 1973 he backed the war powers bill, limiting presidential authority to engage the country in undeclared military conflicts abroad.

Mansfield became a persistent critic of President Richard Nixon, especially during the Watergate investigation. In 1976 he retired from the Senate, but he returned to government service early the next year as part of a commission seeking information about missing U.S. servicemen in Indochina. In 1977 President Jimmy Carter appointed Mansfield U.S. ambassador to Japan, and he kept the post during both terms of President Ronald Reagan, finally retiring in 1988.

Mansfield, Mount, highest point (4,393 feet [1,339 m]) in Vermont, U.S., standing 20 miles (30 km) northeast of Burlington in the Green Mountains, a segment of the Appalachians. The mountain is actually a series of summits that together resemble the profile of a face.

Individual peaks include the Adam's Apple, Forehead, Nose, Upper and Lower Lips, and Chin (highest point). On its western side, the

Mount Mansfield in the Green Mountains near Stowe, Vt.

Thomas B. Hollyman—Photo Researchers

mountain descends more than 4,000 feet (1,200 m) toward Lake Champlain. The mountain is the focus of a state forest and resort area noted for winter sports and was named for the town of Mansfield (annexed to Underhill and Stowe in 1839).

Mansfield, Sir Peter (b. Oct. 9, 1933, London, Eng.), English physicist who, with Paul Lauterbur, won the 2003 Nobel Prize for Physiology or Medicine for the development of magnetic resonance imaging (MRI), a computerized scanning technology that produces images of internal body structures.

Mansfield received a Ph.D. in physics from the University of London in 1962. Following two years as a research associate in the United States, he joined the faculty of the University of Nottingham, where he became professor in 1979. Mansfield was knighted in 1993.

Mansfield's prizewinning work expanded upon nuclear magnetic resonance (NMR), which is the selective absorption of very high-frequency radio waves by certain atomic nuclei subjected to a strong stationary magnetic field. A key tool in chemical analysis, NMR uses the absorption measurements to provide information about the molecular structure of various solids and liquids. In the early 1970s Lauterbur laid the foundations for MRI after realizing that if the magnetic field was made nonuniform, information contained in the signal distortions could be used to create two-dimensional images of a sample's internal structure. Mansfield turned Lauterbur's discoveries into a practical technology in medicine by developing a way to use the nonuniformities, or gradients, introduced in the magnetic field to identify differences in the resonance signals more precisely.

Mansfield, William Murray, 1st earl of, EARL OF MANSFIELD, BARON OF MANSFIELD, LORD MANSFIELD (b. March 2, 1705, Scone, Perthshire, Scot.—d. March 20, 1793, London, Eng.), chief justice of the King's Bench of Great Britain from 1756 to 1788, who made important contributions to commercial law.

Early life and career. William Murray, son of the 5th Viscount Stormont, was called to the bar at Lincoln's Inn in 1730. In Scotland he represented the city of Edinburgh when it was threatened with disfranchisement for the hanging of the English captain of the city guard by a mob. Yet his English practice remained scanty until 1737, when his eloquent speech to the House of Commons in support of a merchants' petition to stop Spanish assaults on their ships placed him in the front rank of his profession. In 1742 he was appointed solicitor general. In 1754 he became attorney general and acted as leader of the House of Commons under the duke of Newcastle. In 1756 he was appointed chief justice of the King's Bench and was made Baron Mansfield, becoming earl of Mansfield in 1776. Because of the limitations on the patent in 1776, he was granted a new patent in 1792, as the earl of Mansfield of Caen Wood.

Judicial decisions. Three cases reveal Mansfield's characteristic aloofness from personal or popular prejudices in rendering decisions. After the burning of his house and library in 1780 during anti-Catholic riots, Mansfield so fairly conducted the treason trial of the leader that an acquittal resulted. In another case involving the prosecution of the journalist John Wilkes, who had published works that were declared seditious libel by the House of Commons, Mansfield rose above both popular clamour and royal pressure through careful technical work on precedents. His investigations showed that the crown's case contained legal flaws, and he ultimately discharged Wilkes because due process so required. The legendary view that Mansfield abolished slavery in England with one judicial decision is unfounded. As a property-minded man of commerce, Mansfield sought to avoid any slavery issue. Even his judgment in the so-called Somersett case (1772), involving a slave who was bought in Virginia and attempted to flee after arriving in London, decided only that an escaping slave could not be forcibly removed from England for retributive punishment in a colony.

Mansfield's permanent stamp upon Anglo-American law lies in commercial law. When he mounted the bench, English law was land-centred and entrenched in professional tradition. Reform was imperative. Mansfield sought to make the international law of commerce not a separate branch but an integral part of the general law of England, both common law and equity. An important part of this brilliant venture succeeded.

In the area of bills of exchange (drafts), promissory notes, and the then still novel bank check, Mansfield, following standard international practice, shaped the law in sweeping judgments, each typically canvassing the whole relevant situation and its reasons. Marine insurance, then a new industry, was centred in London and was a weapon of competition and cold war. Mansfield did not build here on models; he created an entirely new area of jurisprudence.

Mansfield was not always successful. In 1765 he ruled that a merchant's or banker's confirmed credit, or promise to accept drafts drawn from abroad, was enforceable "without consideration"—*i.e.,* without any bargained-for return. This decision was viewed as a flat attack on the whole legal doctrine of "consideration," but that doctrine was reaffirmed in its entirety by the House of Lords. He also suffered a defeat in his effort to make documents transferring land interpretable by "plain intention," so that such intention could not be frustrated by technical rules giving unmeant effect to words. His decision in this area was reversed in 1772 (one of only six reversals during his 32 years of active service). But he triumphed in his expansion of the idea that a man should turn back or turn over any value received by mistake or wrongdoing or under other circumstances making it inequitable for him to retain it. The remedy he devised was a fictitious assumption of a "promise" to pay over (in modern times the fiction was discontinued and replaced by the term "restitution").

William Murray, 1st earl of Mansfield, detail of an oil painting by John Singleton Copley, 1783; in the National Portrait Gallery, London

By courtesy of the National Portrait Gallery, London

Three times during his career Mansfield held positions as a member of the cabinet. In 1783 he declined a cabinet office, preferring to serve as speaker of the House of Lords. He resigned as chief justice in 1788. (K.N.L./Ed.)

mansfieldite, arsenate mineral similar to scorodite (*q.v.*).

Manship, Paul (b. Dec. 25, 1885, St. Paul, Minn., U.S.—d. Jan. 31, 1966, New York, N.Y.), American sculptor, whose subjects and modern generalized style were largely inspired by antique classical sculpture. To a lesser degree he also was influenced by the East, especially India.

Paul Manship, 1933

Courtesy of Rockefeller Center, Inc.

Trained in the United States, Manship received a scholarship in 1909 to study at the American Academy in Rome. After three years abroad he settled in New York City and developed a style distinctive for its simplified modeling and rhythmical patterns.

Among his large decorative works—mostly in bronze—are "Dancer and Gazelles" (1916), of which there are versions in several museums, and the Prometheus Fountain (1934) in Rockefeller Center Plaza, New York City. He executed many portraits in marble; most striking are "Pauline Frances—Three Weeks Old" (1914) and "John D. Rockefeller" (1918). Manship's depictions of animals have charmed young and old; particularly famous is the Paul J. Rainey memorial gateway (1934) at the Bronx Zoo, New York City.

mansion, also called HOUSE, scenic device used in medieval theatrical staging. Individual mansions represented different locales in biblical stories and in scenes from the life of Christ as performed in churches. A mansion consisted of a small booth containing a stage with corner posts supporting a canopy and decorated curtains and often a chair and props to be used by the actors in that scene. Mansions were usually arranged elliptically in the nave of the church. Appropriate architectural features of the church were also used as mansions: the crypt served as the tomb of Christ or as hell and the choir loft was frequently used as heaven.

With the advent of outdoor staging, the booths were arranged in a row across the back of a raised stage. The mansions for heaven and hell occupied opposite ends, and those representing earthly locales were placed between them. In another arrangement, the mansions were placed around the periphery of a courtyard or city square, with heaven and hell on opposite sides. Mansion construction also grew more elaborate for outdoor performance, especially for those representing heaven and hell. The heaven mansion was often bi-level, with the Garden of Eden represented on the lower level. That representing hell was sometimes built to resemble a huge demonic head, the mouth of which served as an entrance, spewing smoke and fire during a performance.

manslaughter, in Anglo-American criminal law, a category of criminal homicide that generally carries a lesser penalty than the crime of murder. *See* homicide.

Manso River (Brazil): *see* Mortes River.

Manson, Charles (b. Nov. 12, 1934, Cincinnati, Ohio, U.S.), American criminal whose followers carried out several notorious murders in 1969.

Manson was born out of wedlock to a 16-year-old girl. After his mother was imprisoned for armed robbery, Manson lived with an aunt and uncle in West Virginia. Beginning at age 9 he spent much of his life in juvenile reformatories or in prison.

Following his release from prison in 1967, Manson moved to California, where his personal charisma brought him a devoted following. He became the leader of the "Family," a communal religious cult dedicated to studying and implementing his eccentric religious teachings, which were drawn from science fiction, the occult, and fringe psychology. He preached the imminent approach of a race war that would devastate the United States and leave the Family in a position of vast power.

Manson's hold over his followers was graphically illustrated in 1968–69, when the Family carried out several homicidal attacks on Manson's orders. The most famous victim was actress Sharon Tate, who was killed in her home along with three guests. The ensuing trials in 1970, which attracted national attention, were recounted in the best-selling book *Helter Skelter* (1974). In 1971 Manson was sentenced to death, but following the abolition of capital punishment in California by the state Supreme Court in 1972, his sentence was commuted to life in prison. (J.P.J./Ed.)

Manson, Sir Patrick (b. Oct. 3, 1844, Old Meldrum, Aberdeen, Scot.—d. April 9, 1922, London, Eng.), British parasitologist who founded the field of tropical medicine. He was the first to discover (1877–79) that an insect (mosquito) can be host to a developing parasite (the worm *Filaria bancrofti*) that is the cause of a human disease (filariasis, which occurs when the worms invade body tissues). His research, and Alphonse Laveran's discovery of the malarial parasite, facilitated Sir Ronald Ross's elucidation of the transmission of malaria by mosquitoes.

Sir Patrick Manson, detail of an oil painting by J. Young Hunter, 1912; in the Royal Society of Tropical Medicine and Hygiene, London

By courtesy of the Royal Society of Tropical Medicine and Hygiene, London

From 1866 to 1889 Manson practiced medicine in Hong Kong and other coastal Chinese cities, where he was one of the first to introduce vaccination. He instituted the Medical School of Hong Kong, which developed later (1911) into the University of Hong Kong. In 1890 he settled in London, where he organized the London School of Tropical Medicine (1899). He was knighted in 1903 and continued to practice medicine until his death. His textbook *Tropical Diseases* (1898) became a standard work.

Mansson, Olaf: *see* Magnus, Olaus.

Manstein, Erich von, original name ERICH VON LEWINSKI (b. Nov. 24, 1887, Berlin, Ger.—d. June 11, 1973, Irschenhausen, near Munich, W.Ger.), German field marshal who was perhaps the most talented German field commander in World War II.

The son of an artillery general, he was adopted by General Georg von Manstein after the untimely death of his parents. Manstein began his active career as an officer in 1906 and served in World War I on both the Western and Russian fronts. Rising through the ranks, he was promoted to major general in 1936 and to lieutenant general in 1938. At the start of World War II, he served as chief of staff to General Gerd von Rundstedt in the invasion of Poland (1939). Manstein had in the meantime devised a daring plan to invade France by means of a concentrated armoured thrust through the Ardennes Forest. Though this plan was rejected by the German High Command, Manstein managed to bring it to the personal attention of Adolf Hitler, who enthusiastically adopted it.

After leading an infantry corps in the assault on France in June 1940, Manstein was promoted to field marshal and general that month. He commanded the 56th Panzer Corps in the invasion of the Soviet Union (1941), and nearly captured Leningrad. Promoted to command of the 11th Army on the southern front (September 1941), Manstein managed to take 430,000 Soviet prisoners, after which he withstood the Soviet counteroffensive that winter and went on to capture Sevastopol in July 1942. He almost succeeded in relieving the beleaguered 6th Army in Stalingrad in December 1942–January 1943, and in February 1943 his forces succeeded in recapturing Kharkov, in the most successful German counteroffensive of the war. Thereafter he was driven into retreat, and in March 1944 he was dismissed by Hitler.

Manstein was captured by the British in 1945. He was tried for war crimes, and, though acquitted of the most serious charges, was imprisoned until his release in 1953 because of ill health. He subsequently advised the West German government on the organization of its army.

Manṣūr, also called USTĀD ("Master") MANṢŪR (fl. 17th century, India), a leading member of the 17th-century Jahāngīr studio of Mughal painters, famed for his animal and bird studies. The emperor Jahāngīr honoured him with the title Nādir-ul-ʿAsr ("Wonder of the Age"), and in his memoirs Jahāngīr praises Manṣūr as "unique in his generation" in the art of drawing. Manṣūr was primarily a natural history painter who avoided personal expression in his careful studies.

Manṣūr made many studies of natural life under the direct orders of his patron, who was passionately fond of recording the rare specimens that were brought before him. A turkey cock painted about 1612 (Victoria and Albert Museum, London) is attributed to Manṣūr and marks that bird's first appearance in India. Similarly, while on a trip to the Kashmir Valley, Jahāngīr ordered Manṣūr to paint as many varieties of local flowers as possible, stating in his memoirs that the number depicted exceeded 100.

Manṣūr, Abū ʿĀmir al-, in full MUḤAMMAD IBN ABŪ ʿĀMIR AL-MANṢŪR, Latin and Spanish ALMANZOR (b. *c.* 938—d. Aug. 10, 1002, Spain), the chief minister and virtual ruler of the Umayyad caliphate of Córdoba for 24 years (978–1002).

Manṣūr was descended from a member of the Arab army that conquered Spain. He began his career as a professional letter writer, becoming the protégé (and supposedly the lover) of the mother of the young caliph Hishām II (first reign 976–1009). In 978, with the aid of his father-in-law, General Ghālib, he overthrew and succeeded the vizier (chief minister). By giving African territories local independence under Umayyad suzerainty, Manṣūr reduced the drain on government resources. He replaced Slavs in the Cordoban army with Berber and Christian mercenaries and conducted a series of successful campaigns against the Christian states of northern Spain, including one against the great shrine of Santiago de Compostela in 997. In 981 he assumed the honorific title of al-Manṣūr bi-Allāh ("Made Victorious by God"), exercising supreme power in Córdoba, and in 994 he adopted the title of al-Malik al-Karīm ("Noble King"), while the caliph continued as nominal chief of state.

Manṣūr died on the way back from a campaign against Castile, the 50th of his expeditions, and was succeeded by his son; but his family, known as the ʿĀmirids, retained power for only a few more years.

Manṣūr, Abū Yūsuf Yaʿqūb al-, in full ABŪ YŪSUF YAʿQUB IBN ʿABD AL-MUʾMIN AL-MANṢŪR (b. *c.* 1160—d. Jan. 23, 1199, Marrakech, Mor.), third ruler of the Muʾminid dynasty of Spain and North Africa, who during his reign (1184–99) brought the power of his dynasty to its zenith.

When his father, Abū Yaʿqūb Yūsuf, died on July 29, 1184, Abū Yūsuf Yaʿqūb succeeded to the throne with minor difficulties. In November factious tribes in Algeria captured Algiers and other towns, but by 1188 he had pacified his African territories and returned to his Spanish possessions to check the encroachments of the Portuguese and Castilians. His efforts took seven years—until the Battle of Alarcos (July 18, 1195), when he decisively defeated the Castilian army of Alfonso VIII and took the title of al-Manṣūr ("the Victor"). The following year he advanced as far as Madrid but was unable to take it.

Having defeated all of his enemies, al-Manṣūr returned to Marrakech, where he went into partial retirement and appointed his son Muḥammad as his heir. Al-Manṣūr was a great builder of public works, many of which still stand.

Manṣūr, al-, in full ABŪ JAʿFAR ABD ALLĀH AL-MANṢŪR IBN MUḤAMMAD (b. 709–714, al-Ḥumaymah, Syria [Jordan]—d. Oct. 7, 775, near Mecca, Arabia [now in Saudi Arabia]), the second caliph of the ʿAbbāsid dynasty (754–775), generally regarded as the real founder of the ʿAbbāsid caliphate. He established the capital city at Baghdad (762–763).

Al-Manṣūr was born at al-Ḥumaymah, the home of the ʿAbbāsid family after their emigration from the Hejaz in 687–688. His father, Muḥammad, was a great-grandson of ʿAbbās; his mother was a Berber slave.

Shortly before the overthrow of the Umayyads, the first dynasty of caliphs, by an army of rebels from Khorāsān, many of whom were influenced by propaganda spread by the ʿAbbāsids, the last Umayyad caliph, Marwān II, arrested the head of the ʿAbbāsid family, al-Manṣūr's brother Ibrāhīm. Al-Manṣūr fled with the rest of the family to Kūfah in Iraq, where some of the leaders of the Khorāsānian rebels gave their allegiance to another brother of al-Manṣūr, Abū al-ʿAbbās as-Saffāḥ, Ibrāhīm having died in captivity. As-Saffāḥ was the first ʿAbbāsid caliph.

Because his brother died in 754, after only five years as caliph, it was upon al-Manṣūr that the main burden of establishing the ʿAbbāsid caliphate fell. Al-Manṣūr had played an important part in wiping out the last remnants of Umayyad resistance. During his brother's caliphate he led an army to Mesopotamia, where he received the submission of a governor after informing him of the death of the last Umayyad caliph. In Iraq itself, the last Umayyad governor had taken refuge with his army in a garrison town. Promised a safe-conduct by al-Manṣūr and the Caliph, he surrendered the town, only to be executed with a number of his followers.

A danger to al-Manṣūr's caliphate came from a number of revolts by ambitious army commanders. The most serious of these was the revolt in 754 of al-Manṣūr's uncle, ʿAbd Allāh, who thought he had better claims to the caliphate than his nephew. The danger was only averted with the help of Abū Muslim, one of the chief organizers of the revolt against the Umayyads.

Al-Manṣūr was largely responsible for cutting the ʿAbbāsids free from the movement that had brought them to power. While his brother was still caliph, al-Manṣūr was involved in the murder of several leading personalities in that movement. Upon becoming caliph himself, one of his first acts was to bring about the death of the man who had helped him become caliph, Abū Muslim. These acts served both to remove potential rivals and to dissociate the ʿAbbāsids from their "extremist" supporters.

Perhaps in reaction to this policy, a number of revolts broke out, in which some of the pre-Islāmic religions of Iran were involved. In 755 in Khorāsān, a certain Sunbadh, described as a magi (here probably meaning a follower of the Mazdakite heresy, not an orthodox Zoroastrian), revolted, demanding vengeance for the murdered Abū Muslim. Another group connected with the name of Abū Muslim, the Rāwandīyah, was charged with belief in the transmigration of souls and holding al-Manṣūr to be their god. Because of these excesses, al-Manṣūr had to suppress them, probably in 757–758. Finally, in 767 al-Manṣūr had to put down another revolt in Khorāsān, the leader of which was accused of claiming to be a prophet.

Probably the most frustrated of those who had worked against the Umayyads were those who had believed they were fighting for a leader from among the descendants of the Prophet Muḥammad's closest male relative, ʿAlī. When it became clear that the ʿAbbāsids had no intention of handing over power to an ʿAlid, these groups again moved into opposition. Al-Manṣūr's consequent harsh treatment of the ʿAlids led to a rebellion in 762–763, which was quickly put down.

Al-Manṣūr's achievement, however, was not based simply upon military power. His most lasting monument is the great city of Baghdad, upon which work began, at his command, in 762. The decision to build Baghdad was probably in part due to the restlessness of the chief towns in Iraq, Basra and, especially, Kūfah, but, in part, too, it was a statement by al-Manṣūr that the ʿAbbāsids had come to stay. It was significant that he considered taking some material for the construction of Baghdad from the ruins of Ctesiphon, the capital of the last native Iranian dynasty.

Another reason for the construction of the new capital was the need to house the rapidly growing bureaucracy, developed by al-Manṣūr under the influence of Iranian ideas in an attempt to provide a more stable basis for ʿAbbāsid rule.

By these political and military measures al-Manṣūr firmly established the ʿAbbāsid caliphate. Furthermore, he arranged the succession in favour of his son, al-Mahdī, and every future ʿAbbāsid caliph could trace his descent directly to al-Manṣūr.

Al-Manṣūr is described as a tall, lean man, with a brown complexion and a sparse beard. There are a number of anecdotes designed to illustrate the simplicity of his life, his tightfistedness, his love of poetry, and his objection to music. He died in 775 on his way to Mecca to perform the pilgrimage and was buried near the holy city. (G.R.H.)

BIBLIOGRAPHY. The only study of al-Manṣūr's caliphate as a whole is in Theodor Nöldeke, *Sketches from Eastern History* (1892, reprinted 1963). For a general survey of the ʿAbbāsid rise to power and the early years of their rule, see the article "ʿAbbāsids" by B. Lewis in the *Encyclopaedia of Islam*, new ed., vol. 1, pt. 1 (1960). The *Encyclopaedia of Islam* should also be consulted for more information on specific details of al-Manṣūr's life and caliphate (see especially the articles "Baghdād" and "al-Barāmika").

Manṣūrah, al-, also spelled EL-MANSURA, capital of ad-Daqahlīyah *muḥāfaẓah* (governorate) on the east bank of the Damietta Branch of the Nile Delta, Lower Egypt. It originated in AD 1219 as the camp of al-Malik al-Kāmil, nephew of the Saracen Ṣalāḥ ad-Dīn (Saladin). It was occupied briefly by crusaders, who in 1250 were decimated by the Muslim forces of Tūrān Shāh, who captured their leader, King Louis IX (later St. Louis) of France, and most of his knights and held them for ransom. The name al-Manṣūrah (Arabic: the Victory) apparently dates from this battle, which contributed significantly to the ultimate defeat of the Frankish expedition.

The modern city, on al-Baḥr aṣ-Ṣaghīr (canal linking the Damietta Branch with the lagoon of Buḥayrat al-Manzilah), is a market centre for the cotton, rice, and flax of the northeastern delta. Industrial activities include cotton ginning, cotton and rice processing, flour milling, and textile weaving. The al-Manṣūrah Polytechnical Institute was established in 1957, and al-Manṣūrah University in 1972; the Institute of al-Manṣūrah is a section of the al-Azhar University at Cairo. Historic structures include a fort named after Louis IX and the Sanga Mosque. Al-Manṣūrah is linked to Talkhā, on the west bank of the Damietta Branch, by a railway bridge. Pop. (1983 est.) 310,900.

Manta, port city, Manabí province, western Ecuador, on the Bahía (bay) de Manta. Originally known as Jocay (Golden Doors), it was inhabited in 3000 BC and was a Manta Indian capital by AD 1200. Under Spanish rule it was renamed Manta and was reorganized by the conquistador Francisco Pancheco in 1535. In 1565 families from Portoviejo were moved to the town, which was again renamed San Pablo de Manta (officially Manta in 1965). A commercial centre known primarily for the export of Panama hats, it also ships coffee, cacao, oilseeds, and tagua nuts (vegetable ivory). Processed food, lumber, leather, and cotton textiles are important. Deep-sea commercial fishing is based there, and Manta has a tuna cannery. Tourism has grown since seaside resort and fishing facilities were established. Pop. (1983 est.) 103,670.

manta ray: *see* devil ray.

Mantegna, Andrea (b. 1431?, near Vicenza, Republic of Venice—d. Sept. 13, 1506, Mantua, March of Mantua), painter and engraver, the first fully Renaissance artist of northern Italy. His best known surviving work is the Camera degli Sposi (Wedding Chamber; 1474), the painted room in the Palazzo Ducale, in

"St. James Led to Martyrdom," detail of fresco (destroyed in World War II), by Andrea Mantegna, 1453–55; formerly in the Eremitani Church, Padua, Italy

Anderson—Alinari from Art Resource/EB Inc.

which he developed a self-consistent illusion of a total environment. Mantegna's other principal works include the Ovetari Chapel frescoes (1448–55), Eremitani Church, Padua, and the "Triumph of Caesar" (begun *c.* 1486; Hampton Court Palace, England), the pinnacle of his late style.

Formative years in Padua. Mantegna's extraordinary native abilities were recognized early. He was the second son of a woodworker but was legally adopted by Francesco Squarcione by the time he was 10 years old and possibly even earlier. A teacher of painting and a collector of antiquities in Padua, Squarcione drew the cream of young local talent to his studio, which some of his protégés, such as Mantegna and the painter Marco Zoppo, later had cause to regret. In 1448, at the age of 17, Mantegna disassociated himself from Squarcione's guardianship to establish his own workshop in Padua, later claiming that Squarcione had profited considerably from his services without giving due recompense. The award to Mantegna of the important commission for an altarpiece for the church of Sta. Sofia (1448), now lost, demonstrates his precocity, since it was unusual for so young an artist to receive such a commission. Mantegna himself proudly called attention to his youthful ability in the painting's inscription: "Andrea Mantegna from Padua, aged 17, painted this with his own hand, 1448."

During the following year (1449), Mantegna worked on the fresco decoration of the Ovetari Chapel in the Eremitani Church in Padua. The figures of SS. Peter, Paul, and Christopher in the apse, his earliest frescoes in this chapel, show to what extent he had already absorbed the monumental figure style of Tuscany. In the "St. James Led to Martyrdom" in the lowest row on the left wall, painted sometime between 1453 and 1455, both Mantegna's mastery of *di sotto in su* (from below to above) perspective and his use of archaeologically correct details of Roman architecture are already apparent. The perspective scheme with a viewpoint below the lower frame of the composition exaggerates the apparent height of the scene with respect to the viewer and lends an aspect of grandiose monumentality to the triumphal arch.

In the two scenes from the life of St. Christopher united in a single perspective on the right-hand wall, Mantegna extended his experiments in illusionism to the framing element by painting a highly realistic column on the front plane. The meticulously detailed column divides the scene in two while appearing to exist in a realm totally apart from the pictorial space, a realm shared with the observer. This extension of illusionistic principles to the elements surrounding a picture anticipates Mantegna's S. Zeno altarpiece, where the carved half columns of the frame abut the painted piers (vertical members) on the front plane of the picture space, so that the frame architecture serves as the "exterior" of the temple-pavilion architecture depicted in the painting. In this way the sphere of intense ideality inhabited by the Virgin Mary is conjoined to the beholder's own space by a brilliant combination of physical and optical devices. Unfortunately, all Mantegna's frescoes in the Ovetari Chapel except "The Assumption" and "The Martyrdom of St. Christopher" episodes were destroyed by a bomb during World War II.

The environment of the city of Padua, where Mantegna lived during the major formative years of his life (from about age 10 to about age 30), exerted a strong influence on his interests, ideas, painting style, and concept of himself. Padua was the first centre of Humanism in northern Italy, the home of a great university (founded in 1222), and renowned as a centre for the study of medicine, philosophy, and mathematics. With the influx of scholars from all over Europe and Italy, an atmosphere of internationalism prevailed. From the time of the 14th-century poet Petrarch, Padua had experienced a rapidly growing revival of interest in antiquity, and many eminent Humanists and Latin scholars had resided there. Increasing interest in and imitation of the culture of ancient Rome produced a climate in which feverish collecting of antiquities and ancient inscriptions—even if only in fragmentary form—flourished. Mantegna's friendly relations with several Humanists, antiquarians, and university professors are a matter of record, and hence he may be seen as one of the earliest Renaissance artists to fraternize from a position of intellectual equality with such men. In this way Mantegna's life-style contributed to the early 16th-century ideal of the artist as a man so intimately familiar with antique history, mythology, and literature as to be able to draw easily from these highly respected sources.

The experience of the Paduan milieu was thus decisive for the formation of Mantegna's attitude toward the classical world, which may perhaps be characterized best as double faceted. On the one hand, Mantegna's search for accurate knowledge of Roman antiquity was reflected both in his depiction of specific monuments of Roman architecture and sculpture and in his creation of a vocabulary of antique forms that became the language of antique revival for more than a generation of northern Italian painters and sculptors after the mid-1450s. On the other hand, through a process of artistic synthesis, Mantegna sensed the forces and significances below the surfaces of Roman grandeur. The architectural backgrounds of pictures in the Ovetari Chapel such as the "St. James Before Herod" and the "St. James Led to Martyrdom," as well as of the two paintings of St. Sebastian in Vienna and Paris, were infused with a brooding harshness and severity against which the suffering of the Christian saints takes on the added tragic implication of an impending cultural clash that was to separate and alienate the Christian and pagan worlds. In Mantegna's century, overcoming the experience of alienation from antiquity through the study and revitalization of its architectural and sculptural vocabulary was an obsessive theme. That the Roman world still existed in Italy in ruins only served to increase the sudden sense of cultural loss that struck the 15th century. By his thoroughgoing description of antique forms coupled with an instinctive sense of the political realities that underlay their original creation, Mantegna lent great impetus to the antique revival movement at mid-century.

Mantegna's starting point had been a still earlier form of antique revival—the monumental Tuscan figure style brought to Venice by the Florentine painter Andrea del Castagno in 1442. Mantegna presumably saw Castagno's frescoes of evangelists and saints in the church of S. Zaccaria during a visit to Venice in 1447. His Venetian connections were strengthened by his marriage in 1453 to Nicolosia, daughter of Jacopo Bellini and sister of Giovanni and Gentile Bellini, who became the leading family of painters in Venice during the following decade. Jacopo Bellini's studies in perspective and drawings of fantastic architectural settings based on antique architecture would have interested his new son-in-law, who very likely had studied such drawings during his earlier visit to Venice.

Though Mantegna might have been expected to join the Bellini studio, he preferred to pursue his independent practice in Padua, where the overwhelming artistic influence on him for the preceding few years had come from the wealth of sculpture produced by the Florentine Donatello for the high altar of S. Antonio (finished by 1450). Giovanni Bellini's response to Mantegna's style has been termed a dialogue, but Mantegna's reaction to Donatello's works might more aptly be called a struggle or even a dialectic. The frame and painted architecture of Mantegna's S. Zeno altarpiece (1459) answered the challenge posed by Donatello's Padua altar, for example. Mantegna's art always retained echoes of Donatello's sculpture in its hard, even metallic, surfaces, revealing an essentially sculptural approach that was somewhat softened only in the 1490s.

Years as court painter in Mantua. Mantegna has been characterized as strongly jealous of his independence; yet by entering the service of the marquess of Mantua, Ludovico Gonzaga, in 1459, he was forced to submit to limitations on his freedom of travel and acceptance of commissions from other patrons. Despite such limitations, Mantegna journeyed to Florence and Pisa in 1466–67, where he renewed contact with works of art by Donatello, Fra Filippo Lippi, Paolo Uccello, and Andrea del Castagno. During this decade (1460–70) Mantegna produced his finest small-scale works, such as "The Circumcision" and the Venice "St. George."

The Gonzaga patronage provided Mantegna a fixed income (which did not always materialize) and the opportunity to create what became his best known surviving work, the so-called Camera degli Sposi (Wedding Chamber), or Camera Picta (Painted Room), in the Palazzo Ducale at Mantua.

Earlier practitioners of 15th-century perspective delimited a rectangular field as a transparent window onto the world and constructed an imaginary space behind its front plane. In the Camera degli Sposi, however, Mantegna constructed a system of homogeneous decoration on all four walls of the room, mainly by means of highly realistic painted architectural elements on walls and ceilings, which from ground level convincingly imitate three-dimensionally extended shapes. Though the ceiling is flat, it appears concave. Mantegna transformed the small interior room into an elegant open-air pavilion, to which the room's real and fictive occupants (actually one and the same, since the beholders must have been members of this very court) were transported from deep within an essentially medieval urban castle.

Directly above the centre of the room is a painted oculus, or circular opening to the sky, with putti (little angels) and ladies around a balustrade in dramatically foreshortened perspective. The strong vertical axis created by the oculus locates the spectator at a single point in the centre of the room, the point from which the observer's space blends with that of the frescoed figures that are thrust out toward him by the narrow shelf of space provided for them on the fireplace wall.

The realism of the perspective handling of the oculus made it the most influential illusionistic *di sotto in su* ceiling decoration of the early Renaissance. Its implications for the future of ceiling decoration were largely unrealized, however, until the time of Correggio, a major northern Italian painter of the early 16th century, who employed the same type of illusionism in a series of domes in Parma, Italy. Furthermore, the idea of total spatial illusion generated by Mantegna was not fully exploited until inventors of ingenious schemes of ceiling decoration in the Baroque era (the 17th century), such as Giovanni Lanfranco and Andrea Pozzo, utilized a basically identical concept of total illusion dependent upon the location of a hypothetical viewer standing at a single point in the room.

While at the Gonzaga court, Mantegna attained a position of great respect if not veneration. His close relations with his patron Ludovico were a unique phenomenon at such an early date. As one might expect, the signatures of Mantegna's paintings reveal intense pride in his accomplishments as a painter. Other than this there are only a few legal records of disputes with his neighbours (from which Ludovico had to rescue him) to provide tentative evidence for the painter's irascible and contentious personality during his later years. An empathetic viewer may draw many subjective conclusions as to Mantegna's thoughts and emotions by looking carefully at his paintings. But Ludovico died in 1478, followed soon after by Mantegna's son Bernardino, who had been expected to carry on his father's studio. Mantegna's financial situation was so bad that, in 1484, he was forced to ask for help from the powerful Florentine merchant prince Lorenzo de' Medici and even contemplated moving to Florence. Ludovico's son Federico outlived his father by only a few years, and, with the accession of young Francesco II in 1484, the financial conditions of patronage improved.

Though many of Mantegna's works for the Gonzaga family were subsequently lost, the remains of nine canvases depicting a Roman triumphal procession, the "Triumph of Caesar," begun around 1486 and worked on for several years, still exist. In these paintings, reflecting the classical tastes of his new patron, Francesco, Mantegna reached the peak of his late style. Perhaps it was this new imaginative synthesis of the colour, splendour, and ritualistic power of ancient Rome that brought about Pope Innocent VIII's commission to decorate his private chapel in the Belvedere Palace, Rome (destroyed 1780), which Mantegna carried out in 1488–90.

Notwithstanding ill health and advanced age, Mantegna worked intensively during the remaining years of his life. In 1495 Francesco ordered the "Madonna della Vittoria" to commemorate his supposed victory at the Battle of Fornovo. In the last years of his life, Mantegna painted the "Parnassus" (1497), a picture celebrating the marriage of Isabella d'Este to Francesco Gonzaga in 1490, and "Wisdom Overcoming the Vices" (1502), for Isabella's *studiolo* (a small room in the Gonzaga palace at Mantua embellished with fine paintings and carvings of mythological subjects intended to display the erudition and advanced taste of its patron). A third canvas intended for this program, with the legend of the god Comus (Louvre), was unfinished when Mantegna died and was completed by his successor at the Gonzaga court, Lorenzo Costa.

A funerary chapel in the church of S. Andrea at Mantua was dedicated to Mantegna's memory. Decorated with frescoes, including a dome painted (possibly by Correggio) with paradise symbols related to Mantegna's "Madonna della Vittoria," it was finished in 1516. No other 15th-century artist was dignified by having a funerary chapel dedicated to him in the major church of the city where he worked, which attests to the high stature Mantegna came to enjoy in his adopted city.

Assessment. Mantegna's art and his attitude toward classical antiquity provided a model for other artists, among them Giovanni Bellini in Venice and Albrecht Dürer in Germany. By placing the Virgin and saints of the S. Zeno altarpiece in a unified space continuous with its frame, Mantegna introduced new principles of illusionism into sacra conversazione paintings (*i.e.,* paintings of the Madonna and Child with saints).

Perhaps of even greater significance were his achievements in the field of fresco painting. Mantegna's invention of total spatial illusionism by the manipulation of perspective and foreshortening began a tradition of ceiling decoration that was followed for three centuries. Mantegna's portraits of the Gonzaga family in their palace at Mantua (1474) glorified living subjects by conferring upon them the over life-size stature, sculptural volume, and studied gravity of movement and gesture normally reserved for saints and heroes of myth and history. (W.S.Sh.)

MAJOR WORKS. *Paintings.* Ovetari Chapel frescoes (1448–55; Eremitani Church, Padua, Italy); "The Agony in the Garden" (*c.* 1450; National Gallery, London); "The Virgin with Sleeping Child" (*c.* 1450; Staatliche Museen Preussischer Kulturbesitz, Berlin); "The Man of Sorrows with the Virgin and Saints" ("The St. Luke Polyptych," 1454; Brera, Milan); "St. George" (*c.* 1455–60; Accademia, Venice); "Madonna Enthroned with Saints" (1456–59; S. Zeno Maggiore, Verona, Italy); "The Crucifixion" (1456–59; Louvre, Paris); "St. Sebastian" (*c.* 1459; Kunsthistorisches Museum, Vienna); "The Adoration of the Shepherds" (*c.* 1460; Metropolitan Museum of Art, New York City); "Portrait of Cardinal Lodovico Mezzarota" (*c.* 1460; Staatliche Museen Preussischer Kulturbesitz); "Portrait of a Man" (*c.* 1460; National Gallery of Art, Washington, D.C.); "Triptych with the Adoration of the Magi, the Circumcision, and the Ascension" (*c.* 1465; Uffizi, Florence); "The Death of the Virgin" (*c.* 1465; Prado, Madrid); "St. Sebastian" (*c.* 1465; Louvre); "The Dead Christ" (*c.* 1466; Jacob M. Heimann Gallery, New York); frescoes of the Camera degli Sposi (1473–74; Palazzo Ducale, Mantua, Italy); "The Mourning over the Dead Christ" (*c.* 1475?; Brera); "The Madonna of the Caves" (*c.* 1484?; Uffizi); "Triumph of Caesar" (begun *c.* 1486; Hampton Court Palace, England); "St. Sebastian" (*c.* 1490–1500; Ca d'Oro, Venice); "Madonna della Vittoria" (1495; Louvre); "Parnassus" (1497; Louvre); "Wisdom Overcoming the Vices" (1502; Louvre).

Engravings. "Battle of the Sea Gods" (*c.* 1490); "Bacchanal" (*c.* 1490); "Madonna and Child" (*c.* 1490); "The Entombment" (1490s); "The Risen Christ Between St. Andrew and Longinus" (1490s). Prints of all are in the British Museum.

BIBLIOGRAPHY. Paul Kristeller, *Andrea Mantegna* (1901), the first monograph on Mantegna in English, is a tremendous effort of scholarly achievement and synthesis. Many of Kristeller's conclusions remain unchallenged and all subsequent biographers have relied heavily on this book. Ilse Blum, *Andrea Mantegna und die Antike* (1936), is a thorough analysis of the appearance of antique motifs in Mantegna's work with identification of his sources. There is some subsequent work on this aspect in English but none supplanting this. Erica Tietze-Conrat, *Mantegna* (1955), is the best modern monograph in English, including a catalog of works, attributed works, drawings, and engravings (fully illustrated). Millard Meiss, *Andrea Mantegna As Illuminator: An Episode in Renaissance Art, Humanism and Diplomacy* (1957), an essential book for evaluating Mantegna's achievement in classical revival, explores hitherto uncharted areas such as the artist's activity in the field of miniature painting and his contributions to the revival of classical epigraphy. See also the same author's "Toward a More Comprehensive Renaissance Palaeography," *Art Bulletin,* 42:97–112 (1960), a continuation of his research in this area. Giovanni Paccagnini, *Mantegna: La Camera degli Sposi* (1957), is a monograph on Mantegna's best known work by the leading Italian authority, who also wrote *Andrea Mantegna* (1961), the catalog of the Mantegna show in the Palazzo Ducale, Mantua, 1961 (with a good bibliography through 1961). See also his article in the *Encyclopedia of World Art,* vol. 9, col. 486–498 (1964), an excellent summary of the artist's life and works including accounts of disagreement among scholars and a fair reflection of the latest consensus. Phyllis and Karl Lehmann, *Samothracian Reflections: Aspects of the Revival of the Antique* (1972), contains an essay on Mantegna's "Parnassus" that will most likely stand as the definitive analysis for many years to come.

mantel, also called MANTELPIECE, hood or other similar projection, usually ornamented, that surrounds the opening of a fireplace and directs smoke up to the chimney flue. *See* chimneypiece.

Mantell, Gideon Algernon (b. Feb. 3, 1790, Lewes, Sussex, Eng.—d. Nov. 10, 1852, London), British physician, geologist, and paleontologist, who discovered four of the five genera of dinosaurs known during his time. Mantell studied the paleontology of the Mesozoic Era (about 245,000,000 to 66,400,000 years ago), particularly in Sussex, a region he made famous in the history of geological discovery. He demonstrated the freshwater origin of the Wealden series of the Cretaceous Period (about 144,000,000 to 66,400,000 years ago), and from them he brought to light and described the remarkable dinosaurian reptiles known as *Iguanodon, Hylaeosaurus, Pelorosaurus,* and *Regnosaurus.* He also described the Triassic (about 245,000,000 to 208,000,000 years old) reptile *Telerpeton elginense.* Mantell's major works include *The Fossils of the South Downs, or Illustrations of the Geology of Sussex* (1822) and *Medals of Creation* (1844).

Mantell, detail of an engraving
The Mansell Collection

Manteuffel, Edwin (Hans Karl), Freiherr von (baron of) (b. Feb. 24, 1809, Dresden, Saxony [Germany]—d. June 17, 1885, Carlsbad, Bohemia, Austria-Hungary), Prussian field marshal, a victorious general and able diplomat of the Bismarck period.

A cavalryman from 1827, Manteuffel became aide-de-camp to Frederick William IV of Prussia during the revolution of 1848. In 1854, during the Crimean War, he went on two diplomatic missions to Vienna and one to St. Petersburg, where he persuaded Emperor Nicholas I to withdraw Russian troops from the Danubian principalities. He then returned to Vienna to dissuade Austria from joining the war against Russia. In 1857 he was appointed chief of the Prussian military Cabinet and in 1861 was promoted to the rank of lieutenant general.

Edwin, Freiherr von Manteuffel, *c.* 1855
By courtesy of the Staatsbibliothek Preussischer Kulturbesitz, Berlin

After service in the war against Denmark (1864), Manteuffel was made governor of Schleswig. During the Seven Weeks' War (1866) he occupied Holstein, led a division against the Hanoverians, and in July assumed command of the Army of the Main. Finally, he was delegated to explain Prussia's German policy to the Russians.

In the Franco-German War of 1870–71, Manteuffel led the I Corps and distinguished himself in the battles of Colombey-Neuilly and Noisseville. As commander of the 1st Army (from October 1870), he won the Battle of Amiens (November 27) and occupied Rouen (December 6). Commanding the newly formed Army of the South (January 1871), he quickly overcame resistance in the south of France. When this unit was disbanded, he became commander of the 2nd Army. From June 1871 to September 1873 Manteuffel commanded the Prussian occupation forces in France, exhibiting remarkable tact. He then was made a field marshal and military governor of Berlin.

After the Congress of Berlin in 1878 Manteuffel once more went on a diplomatic mission to Russia, and from 1879 he was German imperial governor of Alsace-Lorraine.

Manteuffel, Hasso, Freiherr von (baron of) (b. Jan. 14, 1897, Potsdam, Ger.—d. Sept. 24, 1978, Tyrol, Austria), German military strategist whose skillful deployment of tanks repeatedly thwarted Allied offensives in World War II.

Manteuffel was the descendant of a Prussian family noted in politics and military affairs; his granduncle was the Prussian field marshal Edwin, Freiherr von Manteuffel (1809–85).

A major at the outbreak of World War II, he earned rapid promotion and commanded a division at Tunis in North Africa, where his counterattack almost cut communications behind the Allies' front. In the Ukraine his 7th Panzer Division in November 1943 stemmed a victorious Soviet offensive, and in May 1944 his mobile defense checked Marshal I.S. Koniev's drive into Romania. He also commanded the 5th Panzer Army during the desperate and crucial Battle of the Bulge that took place in Belgium in December 1944. In that action Manteuffel almost succeeded in breaching the Allied front.

After the war, Manteuffel sat in the Bundestag (1953–57) as a Free Democrat, but in 1959 his military past was revived. A court sentenced him to 18 months in prison for ordering a 19-year-old shot for desertion in

1944. After serving four months, Manteuffel was released.

mantid, also called MANTIS, PRAYING MANTID, or PRAYING MANTIS, any large (about 5 centimetres [2 inches] long), slow-moving insect of the family Mantidae (order Mantodea). All of the approximately 2,000 species are characterized by an elongated prothorax (*i.e.*, first thoracic segment) and front legs modified so that the tibia of the lower leg fits into a spined groove in the femur of the upper leg. The mantid, which feeds exclusively on living insects, seizes its prey in a viselike grip. When alarmed the mantid assumes a "threatening" attitude: it raises and rustles its wings (if it is a winged species) and often displays bright warning coloration. Usually found among vegetation rather than on the ground, a mantid may be disguised to resemble green or brown foliage, a dried leaf, a slender twig, a lichen, a brightly coloured flower, or an ant. This camouflage hides it from predators and also makes it inconspicuous as it stalks or awaits victims. The female, who often eats the male after they mate, lays about 200 eggs in a large cocoon-like capsule (ootheca), which serves to protect the eggs during adverse weather conditions or from enemies. The nymph, which lacks wings but otherwise closely resembles the adult, emerges with other nymphs; often they eat each other.

Mantid (*Mantis religiosa*)
Lia E. Munson—Root Resources

The majority of the more than 1,500 mantid species are tropical or subtropical. Representative European genera are *Mantis* (*M. religiosa* is the most widespread), *Ameles, Iris*, and *Empusa*. North American genera include *Stagmomantis* (*S. carolina* is widely distributed), *Litaneutria* (*L. minor*, a small western species, is the sole mantid native to Canada), and *Thesprotia* and *Oligonicella* (both very slender forms). *M. religiosa, Iris oratoria, Tenodera angustipennis*, and *T. aridifolia sinensis* have been introduced into North America. The last species is the familiar Chinese mantid, which is native to many parts of eastern Asia and is the largest mantid in North America; it ranges from 7 to 10 cm in length.

The name mantis, which means "diviner," was given to this insect by the ancient Greeks because they believed that it had supernatural powers; its current name, mantid, or "soothsayer," also reflects this belief. Numerous myths and legends are associated with the mantid because it can remain motionless or sway gently back and forth, with head raised and front legs outstretched in an apparent attitude of supplication. According to superstition, the brown saliva of a mantid can cause blindness in a man, and a mantid, if eaten, can kill a horse or mule. The common name praying mantid and the scientific name *Mantis religiosa*—together with many other names such as *Gottesanbeterin* (German), *prie-Dieu* (French), *prega-Diou* (Provençal), and the West Indian "god-horse"—suggest piety. The names devil's horse and mule killer also are used. Since all mantids are ferocious carnivores, "preying" rather than "praying" may better describe them.

mantidfly (insect): *see* mantispid.

Mantineia, ancient Greek city of Arcadia, situated about eight miles north of modern Trípolis between Mt. Maínalon and Mt. Artemísion, mentioned as a source of soldiers in the catalog of ships in Book II of Homer's *Iliad*. It was the site of three ancient battles. Until the early 5th century BC, it had been a cluster of five villages, but, at the suggestion of Argos, the villages were merged into one city.

Mantineia generally sided with Sparta, especially during the revolt of the Messenian helots (464 BC). But in 420 it formed an alliance with Elis, Argos, and Athens against Sparta, only to be defeated at the first Battle of Mantineia in 418 by the Spartan forces of King Agis. In 362 the city was again prominent when the Theban army, cleverly outmanoeuvring the Spartan troops, won the battle and lost their commander, Epaminondas, in an encounter on the Mantineian Plain.

The last notable event at the site occurred in 207 BC, when Philopoemen, commanding the forces of the Achaean League, routed Machanidas, tyrant of Sparta, there. By the later Roman Empire, Mantineia had dwindled to a mere village, and from the 6th century AD until it disappeared under Ottoman rule it bore the Slavic name Goritza.

Mantiqueira Mountains, Portuguese SERRA DA MANTIQUEIRA, mountain range of eastern Brazil, rising abruptly from the northwestern bank of the Rio Paraíba do Sul and extending northeastward for approximately 200 mi (320 km), reaching a height of 9,255 ft (2,821 m) in the Pico (peak) das Agulhas Negras. The mountains, which eventually merge with the Serra do Espinhaço, were originally forest-covered except for the peaks that rise above the tree line. They provide charcoal and pasture for cattle; on the lower slopes there are several health resorts, including Campos do Jordão. The name Mantiqueira derives from an Indian word meaning "the place where the clouds lie."

To make the best use of the Britannica, consult the INDEX *first*

---

mantis (insect): *see* mantid.

mantis shrimp, any member of the marine crustacean order Stomatopoda, especially members of the genus *Squilla*. Mantis shrimps are so called because the second pair of limbs are greatly enlarged and shaped like the large grasping forelimbs of the praying mantid, or mantis, an insect.

Mantis shrimp (*Squilla*)
Jane Burton—Bruce Coleman Inc.

The mantis shrimp are a widely distributed group consisting of more than 250 species; they vary in size from 1 to 30 centimetres (0.4 to 12 inches). They occur in coastal waters but are sometimes found as deep as 1,300 metres (about 4,300 feet). Many species live in burrows. Both adults and larvae are excellent swimmers.

Squilla mantis, which grows to 20 centimetres (about 8 inches), is common in the Mediterranean Sea and in nearby regions of the Atlantic Ocean. It lives on muddy bottoms and among organic debris. *S. empusa,* which grows to 20 centimetres, is the commonest species on the Atlantic coast of North America. *Oratosquilla oratoria,* which also grows to 20 centimetres, is taken commercially in waters off the coast of Japan for human consumption.

mantispid, also called MANTISFLY, or MANTIDFLY, any insect of the neuropteran family Mantispidae, usually found in tropical and subtropical areas. The adult mantispid bears a superficial resemblance to the praying mantid (order Dictyoptera). The European mantispid (*Mantispa styriaca*) is 12 to 20 millimetres long and has a wingspread of about 25 millimetres.

The female fastens rose-coloured eggs to long, slender stalks. Two larval forms parasitize eggs and young of the spider genus *Lycosa*. One larval form is active and has well-developed legs and a squarish head; the second is a fat white grub with short legs. The fully grown larva (7 to 10 mm long) spins a silken cocoon before its first pupal stage; the second pupal stage, however, is active, and there is no cocoon. The larvae of the Brazilian mantispid (*Symphasis varia*) are parasitic on wasps and pupate in the wasp nest.

Mantispid
E.S. Ross

mantle, also called PALLIUM, plural PALLIA, or PALLIUMS, in biology, soft covering, formed from the body wall, of brachiopods and mollusks; also, the fleshy outer covering, sometimes strengthened by calcified plates, of barnacles, or the flexible body wall of tunicates.

The mantle of mollusks and brachiopods secretes the shell if one is present. It also forms a mantle cavity between itself and the body. The brachiopod mantle has a dorsal and a ventral lobe covered with small papillae (nipple-like projections) that penetrate into the shell. The molluscan mantle has a left and a right lobe and, as in bivalves, may be joined at the edge to form siphons for circulating water in the mantle cavity.

mantle, cloak fashioned from a rectangular piece of cloth, usually sleeveless, of varying width and length, wrapped loosely around the body. Usually worn as an outer garment in the ancient Mediterranean world, it developed in different styles, colours, and materials. The Greek chlamys (worn only by men) was a short mantle draped around the upper shoulders, pinned on the right shoulder with a brooch. It left the right arm free and was often used by travellers and military men. The Greek himation, draped in various ways, was a larger Greek mantle.

Some Christian religious vestments, such as

Aeschines wearing the Greek himation, late 4th century BC; in the National Museum, Naples
Alinari—Art Resource

the cope and the pallium, probably developed from the mantle.

mantle, that part of the Earth (*q.v.*) that lies beneath the crust and above the central core.

Mantle, Mickey, in full MICKEY CHARLES MANTLE (b. Oct. 20, 1931, Spavinaw, Okla., U.S.—d. Aug. 13, 1995, Dallas, Texas), professional American League baseball player for the New York Yankees (1951–68), who was a powerful switch-hitter (right- and left-handed) and who hit 536 home runs.

Mantle began playing baseball as a Little League shortstop and at Commerce (Okla.) High School. A football injury sustained in 1946 led to osteomyelitis, a bone-tissue infection, which required five operations before the disease was controlled.

Mantle played as an outfielder on Yankee farm clubs (1949–50) and joined the Yankees in 1951. He played with them mainly as an outfielder until he went to first base in 1967. He played much of his career heavily taped because of his earlier bone disease. He led the league in home runs for four seasons (1955–56, 1958, and 1960), and in 1961, when his teammate Roger Maris broke Babe Ruth's season home run record, Mantle hit a season high of 54. He led the league six times in runs scored (1954, 1956–58, 1960–61) and in runs batted in (RBI) in 1956, the year he won the league triple crown for home runs, RBI, and batting average (.353). In the 1980s his career 536 home runs placed him sixth among home-run hitters. He played in 12 World Series (1951–53, 1955–58, 1960–64), hitting a record 18 home runs in them. He was voted the American League's Most Valuable Player in 1956, 1957, and 1962.

After his retirement as a player Mantle coached for the Yankees and sold life insurance. In 1983 the baseball commissioner barred him from any connection with professional baseball because he had taken a public-relations position with an Atlantic City (N.J.) gambling casino. The ban was lifted in 1985. Mantle was elected to the Baseball Hall of Fame in 1974.

mantra, in Hinduism and Buddhism, a sacred utterance (syllable, word, or verse) that is considered to possess mystical or spiritual efficacy. Various mantras are either spoken aloud or merely sounded internally in one's thoughts, and they are either repeated continuously for some time or just sounded once. Most mantras are without any apparent verbal meaning, but they are thought to have a profound underlying significance and are in effect distillations of spiritual wisdom. Thus, repetition of or meditation on a particular mantra can induce a trancelike state in the participant and can lead him to a higher level of spiritual awareness. Besides bringing spiritual enlightenment, different kinds of mantras are used to work other psychic or spiritual purposes, such as protecting oneself from evil psychic powers. One of the most powerful and widely used mantras in Hinduism is the sacred syllable *om.* The principal mantra in Buddhism is *om maṇi padme hūṃ.*

Mantras continue to be an important feature of Hindu religious rites and domestic ceremonies. Initiation into many Hindu sects involves the whispering of a secret mantra into the ear of the initiate by the guru (spiritual teacher). Indeed, mantras are thought to be truly efficacious only when they are received verbally from one's guru or other spiritual preceptor.

Mantua, Italian MANTOVA, city, capital of Mantova *provincia,* Lombardia (Lombardy) *regione,* northern Italy. The city is surrounded on three sides by lakes formed by the Mincio River, southwest of Verona. It originated in settlements of the Etruscans and later of the Gallic Cenomani. Roman colonization began about 220 BC, and the great Latin poet Virgil was born at nearby Andes in 70 BC. In the 11th century, Mantua became a fief of Boniface of Canossa, marquis of Tuscany. After the death of Matilda of Tuscany in 1115, the city secured a communal government, and during that period (1167) Mantua joined the Lombard League (an alliance of northern Italian towns) against the policies of the Holy Roman emperor Frederick I Barbarossa. The Bonacolsi family gained control of Mantua in 1276. In 1328 the Bonacolsi were driven out by the Gonzagas, under whom the city enjoyed a long period of political prestige and cultural splendour that endured until the 17th century. The Gonzagas' rule of Mantua ended in 1707, when the city became a fief of the Austrian Habsburgs' empire and was heavily fortified as the southwest corner of the imperial "Quadrilateral." Napoleon took the city after a long siege in 1797, and Mantua was dominated by the French until it was returned to Austria in 1814. Mantua contributed to the cause of the Risorgimento (movement for national independence) and was joined to the Kingdom of Italy in 1866.

At the centre of the city stands its cathedral, which was rebuilt in the 16th century after designs by Giulio Romano. The vast ducal palace, also called the Reggia of the Gonzagas, stands opposite the cathedral. Its apartments contain many valuable works of art. The Church of San Andrea (begun 1472), which shares the privileges of the cathedral, was designed by Leon Battista Alberti. Other notable churches include the restored Rotonda of San Lorenzo (1082) and the churches of San Sebastiano (1460–70) by Alberti and of San Francesco (1304). Secular landmarks include the Castello di San Giorgio (1395–1406) by Bartolino da Novara with frescoes by Andrea Mantegna; the immense ducal palace (begun *c.* 1290); the famous Palazzo del Te (1525–35), designed by Romano; the 13th–15th-century Ragione Palace; and numerous other palaces and mansions. The city's cultural institutions include the Accademia Virgiliana, containing a Scientific Theatre designed by Antonio Bibiena (1769); the valuable library, founded in 1780 by the Austrian empress Maria Theresa; and the State Archives. The houses of the artists Andrea Mantegna and Giulio Romano have been preserved.

Mantua's economy is primarily concerned with the processing and shipping of agricultural products. The city is a centre of road, rail, and water transportation; its industrialization increased after World War II, and the population grew rapidly. Pop. (1993 est.) mun., 52,205.

Mantua, Siege of (June 4, 1796–Feb. 2, 1797), the crucial episode in Napoleon Bonaparte's first Italian campaign; his successful siege of Mantua excluded the Austrians from northern Italy. The city was easy to besiege: the only access to it was via five causeways over the Mincio River. The two Austrian commanders, Count Dagobert Siegmund Graf von Wurmser and Baron Josef Alvintzy, in four successive tries, repeated the same mistakes of giving priority to lifting the Siege of Mantua, rather than first trying to destroy Napoleon's 40,000-man Army of Italy, and of deploying their armies too far apart to coordinate their attacks effectively. Napoleon utilized his central position and greater mobility to "divide and conquer."

After a series of battles, Napoleon forced the surrender of Mantua on Feb. 2, 1797, and the French conquest of northern Italy was virtually completed.

Manu, in the mythology of India, the first man, and the legendary author of an important Sanskrit code of law, the *Manu-smṛti.* The name is cognate with the Indo-European "man" and also has an etymological connection with the Sanskrit verb *man-*, "to think." Manu appears in the Vedas as the performer of the first sacrifice. He is also known as the first king, and most rulers of medieval India traced their genealogy back to him, either through his son (the solar line) or his daughter (the lunar line).

In the story of the great flood, Manu combines the characteristics of Noah with those of Adam. The *Śatapatha Brāhmaṇa* recounts how he was warned by a fish, to whom he had done a kindness, that a flood would destroy the whole of humanity. He therefore built a boat, as the fish advised. When the flood came, he tied this boat to the fish's horn and was safely steered to a resting place on a mountaintop. When the flood receded, Manu, the sole human survivor, performed a sacrifice, pouring oblations of butter and sour milk into the waters. After a year there was born from the waters a woman who announced herself as "the daughter of Manu." These two then became the ancestors of a new human race to replenish the earth. In the *Mahābhārata* ("Great Epic of the Bharata Dynasty"), the fish is identified with the god Brahmā, while in the *Purāṇas* ("Ancient Lore") it is Matsya, the fish incarnation of the lord Vishnu.

In the cosmological speculations of later Hinduism, a day in the life of Brahmā is divided into 14 periods called *manvantara,* each of which lasts for 306,720,000 years. In every secondary cycle the world is recreated, and a new Manu appears to become the father of the next human race. The present age is considered the seventh Manu cycle.

Manu-smṛti (Sanskrit: "Tradition of Manu"), traditionally, the most authoritative of the books of the Hindu code (*Dharma-śāstra*) in India. *Manu-smṛti* is the popular name of the work, which is officially known as *Mānava-dharma-śāstra.* It is attributed to the legendary first man and lawgiver, Manu. In its present form, it dates from the 1st century BC.

The *Manu-smṛti* prescribes to the Hindu his dharma—*i.e.,* that set of obligations incumbent on him as a member of one of the four social classes (varnas) and engaged in one of the four stages of life (ashramas). It contains 12 chapters of stanzas, which total 2,694. It deals with cosmogony, the definition of the dharma, the sacraments (samskaras), initiation (*upanayana*) and study of the Veda, marriage, hospitality, obsequies, dietary restrictions, pollution and means of purification, the conduct of women and wives, and the law of kings. The last leads to a consideration of matters of juridical interest, divided under 18 headings, after which the text returns to religious topics, such as donations, rites of reparation, the doctrine of *karman,* the soul, and hell. The text makes no categorical distinction between religious law and practices and secular law in its treatment. Its influence has been monumental, and it has provided the caste Hindu with a system of practical morality.

Manua Islands, also spelled MANU'A, group of three islands (Tau, [Ta'u], Ofu, and Olosega), American Samoa, southwestern Pacific Ocean. Tau, the chief island, has an area of 15 sq mi (39 sq km). It is conical in shape, rising to Lata Mountain (3,179 ft [969 m]); the main village is Luma on the west coast. Ofu (3 sq mi) and Olosega (2 sq mi) are separated by a narrow channel, about eight miles northwest of Tau. Pop. (1990) 1,714.

Consult the INDEX *first*

Manual of Discipline, also called RULE OF THE COMMUNITY, one of the most important documents produced by the Essene community of Jews, who settled at Qumrān in the Judaean desert in the early 2nd century BC. They did so to remove themselves from what they considered a corrupt religion symbolized by the religiopolitical high priests of the Hasmonean dynasty centred in Jerusalem. The major portion of the scroll was discovered in Cave I at Qumrān in 1947, and fragments of 11 other versions of the *Manual* were found in Caves IV and V the same year. Modern scholars have suggested that, when the Qumrān sect was forced to abandon its community life because of the great Jewish revolt against Rome in AD 66–70, its members hid their library in nearby caves. The large number of preserved manuscripts indicate the importance of the *Manual* to the Essene community.

This scroll was probably intended for the Essene sect's leaders, including priests who supervised the sacrificial, liturgical, and possibly exegetical religious functions, and also guardians who controlled the admission and instruction of new members into the community. The document contains an explanation of the sect's religious and moral ideals, a description of its admission ceremony, a long catechetical discourse on its mystical doctrine of the primordial spirits of truth and perversity, organizational and disciplinary statutes, and a final hymn or psalm praising obedience and setting forth the sacred seasons. The first of two appendices, the *Rule of the Congregation,* or "Messianic Rule," contains additional statutes and instructions about a messianic feast. The second is a liturgical collection of benedictions: *Blessings.*

Although this work cannot be dated with precision, it was probably compiled after the community had settled in Qumrān. Some scholars have connected part of it to an enigmatic figure, the unknown Teacher of Righteousness, whose ministry within the community probably fell in the latter half of the 2nd century BC. *See also* Dead Sea Scrolls.

manucode, any of certain Australian bird-of-paradise species. *See* bird-of-paradise.

Manuel (personal name): *see under* Emmanuel, or Immanuel, except as below.

Manuel, Greek MANOUEL, name of rulers grouped below by country and indicated by the symbol •.

BYZANTINE EMPIRE

•Manuel I COMNENUS (b. *c.* 1122—d. Sept. 24, 1180), military leader, statesman, and Byzantine emperor (1143–80) whose policies failed to fulfill his dream of a restored Roman Empire, straining the resources of Byzantium at a time when the Seljuq Turks menaced the empire's survival.

The son of John II Comnenus (reigned 1118–43) and the Hungarian princess Irene, Manuel transformed the austere, conservative court of his father into a gay setting for tournaments and festivities imported from medieval western Europe.

Manuel devoted himself to affairs in the West at the beginning of his reign, practically ignoring the growing Turkish threat on the plains of Anatolia. He renewed his alliances in the West against his Norman rivals in both Sicily and Antioch. At the time of the Second Crusade he defended his Greek territory from Roger II of Sicily, whose fleet captured Corfu in 1147. With Venetian aid, the island was retaken two years later. In 1148 Manuel consolidated his alliance with Emperor Conrad III of Germany, whose sister-in-law he had earlier married. But Conrad died in 1152, and, despite repeated attempts, Manuel could not reach an agreement with his successor, Frederick I Barbarossa. When Roger II died in 1154, Manuel sent a fleet to attack Ancona (1155), capturing much of the region of Apulia. He was defeated in 1156 at Brindisi by a joint force of Germans, Venetians, and Normans, ending Byzantine influence in Italy.

Manuel next asserted his authority over the crusader states, established after the First Crusade. He campaigned in Cilicia (in modern Turkey) in 1158, regaining lost territory and forcing Renaud of Châtillon, prince of Antioch, and Baldwin III, king of Jerusalem, to recognize Byzantine suzerainty (1159).

Manuel I Comnenus, detail of a manuscript; in the Biblioteca Apostolica Vaticana (Cod. Vat. Gr. 1176)

By courtesy of the Biblioteca Apostolica Vaticana

Manuel was also successful in his dealings with the Serbs and Hungarians. In 1167 Dalmatia, Croatia, and Bosnia were incorporated into the empire. Interfering in Hungarian dynastic struggles, he was rewarded when his candidate, Bêla, was elected king in 1173. Elsewhere in the north his relations were not as successful. Relations between Venice and Constantinople were broken off for 10 years from 1171.

Manuel's activities elsewhere diverted his attention from the Turkish East. Although he had launched campaigns against the Sultan of Iconium in 1145, 1146, and 1160, there were no practical results. By the time he led a large-scale attack against the Turks in 1176, Manuel's dream of a restored Roman Empire had impaired his ability to measure the growth of Seljuq power. His defeat at Myriocephalon pointed toward the collapse of the Byzantine Empire.

•Manuel II PALAEOLOGUS (b. 1350—d. July 21, 1425), soldier, statesman, and Byzantine emperor (1391–1425) whose diplomacy enabled him to establish peaceful relations with the Ottoman Turks throughout his reign, delaying for some 50 years their ultimate conquest of the Byzantine Empire.

Manuel was a son of John V Palaeologus (reigned 1341–91 with interruptions) and was named his successor in 1373 after his older brother, Andronicus IV, led an unsuccessful revolt against their father. Manuel was crowned co-emperor in September 1373 and, in 1379, helped his father regain Constantinople and the throne, which Andronicus had seized in 1376. John V and Manuel had regained the throne with Turkish help and were forced to pay tribute to the Sultan and lend him military aid. In 1390 John VII, son of Andronicus IV, seized Constantinople and the throne, but the Turks again helped Manuel and John regain it. Manuel was forced to live at the court of Bayezid I as a submissive vassal, remaining there until he escaped to Constantinople after learning of his father's death in February 1391.

Manuel II Palaeologus, detail from a Greek manuscript, 15th century; in the Bibliothèque Nationale, Paris (MS. Suppl. Gr. 309)

By courtesy of the Bibliotheque Nationale, Paris

When the Turks overran Thessaly and the Peloponnese in 1396, Manuel made a journey to western Europe to appeal for help against them. He was graciously received in Rome, Milan, London, and Paris; he stayed in the French city for two years. His visit did much to promote cultural ties between Byzantium and the West, but military aid was not forthcoming.

Manuel arranged a peace treaty (1403) with Bayezid's successor, Mehmed I, recovering Thessalonica (modern Thessaloníki, Greece) and putting an end to tribute payments. Peaceful relations persisted until 1421, when Mehmed died, and Manuel withdrew from state affairs to pursue his religious and literary interests. His son and co-emperor, John VIII, ignored the tenuous bond that had been established and in 1421 supported a pretender, Mustafa, against the rightful heir to the Turkish throne, Murad II. Murad put down the revolt and in 1422 besieged Constantinople. The city survived, but the Turks overran the Peloponnese (1423). After being forced to sign a humiliating treaty, Manuel retired to a monastery.

PORTUGAL

•Manuel I, byname MANUEL THE FORTUNATE, Portuguese MANUEL O AFORTUNADO (b. May 31, 1469, Alcochete, Port.—d. December 1521, Lisbon), king of Portugal from 1495 to 1521, whose reign was characterized by religious troubles (all Moors and Jews refusing baptism were expelled), by a policy of clever neutrality in the face of quarrels between France and Spain, and by the continuation of overseas expansion, notably to India and Brazil.

Manuel was fortunate to have reigned at all; he was the ninth child of Dom Fernando, who was the younger brother of Afonso V. Manuel's father died a year after Manuel was born.

King Afonso had one of Manuel's sisters married to his heir, John II, and another to the powerful Duke of Bragança. On his accession John II had Bragança executed on a charge of treason and later murdered Manuel's only surviving brother on suspicion of conspiracy. But John extended his protection to the boy Manuel, making him Duke of Beja. On the death of his own legitimate son in 1491, John recognized Manuel as his heir. Although he later contemplated legitimizing his remaining son, Jorge, he finally left the crown to Manuel.

As king (from 1495), Manuel at once pardoned the banished Braganças and restored their confiscated estates. But the monarchy soon acquired vast new wealth as Vasco da Gama's voyage around Africa opened Portuguese trade with the East. In March 1500 Manuel sent Pedro Álvares Cabral with 13 ships to establish trade relations with the Indian princes. Cabral, sailing in the western Atlantic, sighted Brazil, sent back a ship to report the discovery, and continued around the Cape of Good Hope to India where he set up trading posts (*feitorias*) at Calicut, Cochin, and Cannanore, all on the Malabar coast of southwestern India. Although half his ships were lost, the venture was profitable. In 1502 da Gama took 20 ships and brought back gold as tribute from East Africa. Manuel was already wealthy by 1503. Meanwhile, João Fernandes Lavrador reached what was probably Labrador in 1499, and Gaspar Côrte-Real discovered Newfoundland in 1500. The Brazilian coast was explored, though trade was virtually confined to the dyewood (brazilwood [*Caesalpinia echinata*], called *pau-brasil* in Portuguese) after which Brazil is named.

Manuel's claims to these newly discovered lands were confirmed by the papacy and recognized by the Spanish, with whom Manuel maintained close relations. His three queens were Spanish. The first was Isabella, eldest daughter of cosovereigns Ferdinand and Isabella and widow of John II's heir. As a condition of the marriage, Manuel was to expel the Jews, many thousands of whom had been admitted by John II on their expulsion from Spain in 1492. Thus in December 1496 Manuel ordered Jews and free Muslims to quit Portugal within 10 months. On their assembly in Lisbon, every attempt was made to force their conversion. Some were allowed to leave, but the rest were "converted" under the promise that no inquiry should be made into their beliefs for 20 years.

Manuel and Isabella became heirs to the Spanish crowns on her brother's death. They visited Toledo and Saragossa to receive oaths of allegiance in 1498, but the possibility of the union of the crowns ended when Isabella died in the same year while giving birth to their son Miguel, who died in infancy. In October Manuel married Isabella's younger sister Maria, by whom he had nine children.

The consolidation of Portuguese influence in the East can be dated from the foundation of the fortress at Cochin in 1503 and its successful defense by Duarte Pacheco Pereira (1504). Manuel sent Dom Francisco de Almeida as the first viceroy of Portuguese India in 1505. Afonso de Albuquerque, who succeeded Almeida as governor, conquered Goa in 1510 and Malacca on the Malay Peninsula in 1511, bringing the distribution of oriental spices under Portuguese control. By 1513 the Portuguese had reached China.

The crusading aspect of the expansion reached its apogee with Albuquerque, who nourished grandiose schemes for blockading the Red Sea and capturing Mecca. Duarte Galvão's attempts to persuade other European courts to join a crusade met with little response. The arrival of an Abyssinian envoy at Manuel's court in 1514 suggested an alliance with the Christian negus (king) of that country, and Manuel appointed Galvão ambassador to Abyssinia. But the mission was delayed by Galvão's death, and the crusading vision faded with the death of Albuquerque off Goa (December 1515). Manuel was no warrior: it was the Duke of Bragança who conquered Azamor in Morocco (1513).

The Indian traffic added enormously to the size and splendour of Manuel's court. John II had cowed the ambitious nobles. Manuel converted them into a palace aristocracy, paying pensions to some 5,000 persons. Despite the brilliance of his age, Manuel appears in somewhat low relief. Most of the heroes of the day had made their mark under John II. Manuel was industrious, temperate, fond of music and display, and extravagant. He resided chiefly at Lisbon, where he built the waterside palace (near the present-day Terreiro do Paço), and at Sintra. The playwright-goldsmith Gil Vicente wrote for the court, which became a centre of minor poetry and painting. Manuel founded the palace-monastery of the Jerónimos at Belém and built the Tower of Belém; the architecture typical of the reign has been called "Manueline" only since the 19th century.

Under Manuel the public administration was increasingly centralized. A committee of royal officials revised town charters granted by previous rulers, standardized local privileges, and rationalized taxes. In 1515 Manuel ordered his council to revise the code of laws: his Ordenações Manuelinas were issued in 1512 and revised in 1521. The judiciary was enlarged, and royal *corregedores* were appointed to all districts. This carried forward the process of neo-Roman absolutism and assured the rise of the judicial class. Manuel also excepted the church and the military orders of knighthood from certain obligations. He severely punished those responsible for the massacre of Jews in 1506. Manuel married Eleanor of Austria, sister of the emperor Charles V, in 1518, and had one daughter by this marriage. He died at Lisbon in 1521 and was buried in the Jerónimos monastery. (H.V.L.)

BIBLIOGRAPHY. An outline of his reign can be found in Elaine Sanceau, *The Reign of the Fortunate King, 1495–1521* (1969).

Manuel II (b. Nov. 15, 1889, Lisbon, Port.—d. July 2, 1932, Twickenham, London, Eng.), king of Portugal from 1908 to 1910, when the republic was declared.

Manuel was the younger son of King Charles and Queen Maria Amalia. Charles supported the dictatorship of João Franco and was repudiated by most of the political leaders. On Feb. 1, 1908, Charles and his elder son, Luis Felipe, were assassinated by anarchists in the streets of Lisbon, and Manuel unexpectedly found himself king at the age of 18. Franco resigned, and Manuel asked Admiral Francisco Joaquim Ferreira do Amaral to head a government composed of equal numbers of the two main parties, the Regenerators and the Progressists, with one or two others. The admiral elected to play for calm, but the parties were deeply divided, neither of the party leaders appearing in the cabinet. Amaral proceeded with elections in Lisbon, which the republicans won. They intensified preparations for a revolution, while the monarchist parties formed ineffective coalitions, alternately advising the young king and blaming him for taking their advice. In the summer of 1910 Manuel went to Buçaco, but on his return the revolution, supported by the fleet on the Tagus River, broke out. His palace was shelled, and Manuel fled into exile.

The republic was proclaimed, and Manuel settled near London, at Richmond and later at Twickenham. On Sept. 4, 1913, he married Augusta Victoria, the daughter of Prince Wilhelm of Hohenzollern. He devoted himself to book collecting and published the indispensable *Early Portuguese Books, 1489–1600,* 3 vol. (1929–35). He left no issue.

Manuel, Niklaus, also (erroneously) called DEUTSCH (b. *c.* 1484, Bern [Switz.]—d. April 28, 1530, Bern), painter, soldier, writer, and statesman, notable Swiss representative of the

"The Judgment of Paris," tempera painting on canvas by Niklaus Manuel; in the Kunstmuseum, Basel, Switz.

Kunstmuseum Basel

ideas of the Italian and German Renaissance and the Reformation.

The art of Albrecht Dürer and Hans Baldung-Grien and of the painters of northern Italy prompted Manuel to eschew the prevailing late medieval style and to attempt new forms of expression in his drawings, portraits, and mythological and biblical paintings, most of which were done between 1515 and 1520. A self-assured, impulsive temperament permeates his vigorous, polemical anticlerical writings (mainly plays, written 1522–26). Later he spent his energies in political activities as a member of the Bern city councils. His paintings include the "Dance of Death" (1516–19, destroyed 1660), "Pyramus and Thisbe," and "The Beheading of John the Baptist." Among his literary works are *Der Ablasskrämer* (1526; "The Seller of Indulgences"), *Testament der Messe* (1528; "Testament of the Mass"), and *Fastnachtsspiele* (1540; "Carnival Play"). His *Sämtliche Dichtungen* ("Collected Works"), edited by J. Bächtold, appeared in 1878.

Manueline, Portuguese MANUELINO, particularly rich and lavish style of architectural ornamentation indigenous to Portugal in the early 16th century. Although the Manueline style actually continued for some time after the death of Manuel I (reigned 1495–1521), it is the prosperity of his reign that the style celebrates.

Portuguese wealth was dependent upon sea trade, and the vocabulary of Manueline decoration is decidedly nautical. When not made to resemble coral itself, moldings were encrusted with carved barnacles or covered with carved seaweed and algae. Stone ropes and cables form architectural string courses, and above the windows and doors heraldic shields, crosses, anchors, navigational instruments, and buoys are massed together in profusion. Contemporary ship accoutrements were turned into architectural motifs. Such vast building complexes as the church and convent of the Knights of Christ (original building, 12th century; rebuilt *c.* 1510–14) at Tomar or the Unfinished Chapels in the complex at Batalha are excellent examples of this unique style that existed for a few decades in the interval between the Gothic and the later High Renaissance and Mannerist domination of the arts in Portugal.

Window, ornamented in the Manueline style, from the exterior of the chapter house of the Convent of Christ Monastery, Tomar, Port., early 16th century
© Wayne Andrews/Esto

The profusion of dense ornament in Manueline architecture owes some debt to the contemporary Spanish, to the Flamboyant Gothic style of northern Europe, and to a revival of Moorish style.

Manuelito, original name BULLET (d. 1893, Navajo Reservation, New Mexico Territory, U.S.), Navajo Indian chief known for his strong opposition to the forced relocation of his people by the U.S. government.

Little is known of Manuelito's early life. He was already an established leader by 1864 when U.S. Army Colonel Kit Carson, after a war of attrition in which Navajo crops, homes, livestock, and equipment were destroyed, had

Manuelito; photograph, probably by C.M. Bell, 1874
Smithsonian Institution, National Anthropological Archives Photo No. 2390

8,000 Navajos confined to the Bosque Redondo, an arid, alkaline piece of land south of Santa Fe in New Mexico Territory. Manuelito and about 4,000 of his people would not surrender, however. Instead, they withdrew into the mountains and waged guerrilla warfare. Carson continued his policy of killing wild game and horses and destroying crops. By the autumn of 1866 Manuelito and his people were starving and so finally surrendered. They were taken to the Bosque Redondo. Conditions were so bad that by the spring of 1868 Manuelito and a few other leaders were permitted to go to Washington, D.C., to petition the government for a new reservation. He pleaded his cause successfully, and by that autumn the Navajos were allowed to move to a new reservation, located in the area that had been their traditional homeland.

manufacturer's liability, legal concept or doctrine that holds manufacturers or sellers responsible, or liable, for harm caused by defective products sold in the marketplace. Manufacturer's liability is usually determined on any of three bases: (1) negligence, which is the failure to exercise reasonable care to prevent product defects arising out of the manufacturing process, or which is the failure to give consumers appropriate warning of a danger attending the use of a manufactured product, (2) breach of warranty, which entails failure to fulfill the terms of a claim or promise concerning the quality or performance of a particular product, and (3) strict liability, in which a seller or manufacturer can be held liable for a defective product even if the conditions of negligence or breach of warranty do not apply. An active consumerism movement is credited with the courts' increasing acceptance of arguments based on manufacturer's liability.

manufacturing, any industry that makes products from raw materials by the use of manual labour or machinery and that is usually carried out systematically with a division of labour. (*See* industry.) In a more limited sense, manufacturing denotes the fabrication or assembly of components into finished products on a fairly large scale. Among the most important manufacturing industries are those that produce aircraft, automobiles, chemicals, clothing, computers, consumer electronics, electrical equipment, furniture, heavy machinery, refined petroleum products, ships, steel, and tools and dies.

Manufacturing is treated in a number of articles in the MACROPAEDIA. Some of the most important manufacturing industries are treated in Industries, Manufacturing. For treatments of other major manufacturing industries, *see* Beverage Production; Building Construction; Electronics; Energy Conversion; Food Processing; Industrial Ceramics; Industrial Glass; Industrial Polymers; Industries, Chemical Process; Industries, Extraction and Processing; Industries, Textile; Printing, Typography, and Photoengraving; Public Works. For treatment of manufacturing methods, processes, and organization, *see* Automation; Industrial Engineering and Production Management; Work and Employment. The utilization of energy in manufacturing is treated in Energy Conversion. For treatment of the tools and machines used in manufacturing, *see* Tools. For the application of measurement and control in industrial processes, *see* Analysis and Measurement, Physical and Chemical; Drafting. *See also* Engineering; Technology, History of.

For a description of the place of manufacturing in the circle of learning and for a list of both MACROPAEDIA and MICROPAEDIA articles on the subject, *see* PROPAEDIA: Part Seven.

For international statistical data on the manufacturing industry worldwide, *see* BRITANNICA BOOK OF THE YEAR.

Manukau, city, Auckland local government region, northern North Island, New Zealand. It is the third largest city in New Zealand with about one-third of its population made up of Maoris and other Pacific Islanders. Manukau lies 12 miles (19 km) southeast of Auckland city, on an isthmus separating Tamaki Strait (east) from Manukau Harbour (west). The latter is a shallow 150-square-mile (390-square-kilometre) inlet of the Tasman Sea.

In 1965 Manukau county and Manurewa borough were consolidated to form the city of Manukau. Some two-thirds of the area remains under active agricultural use, with the rest of the land devoted to industries and residences. Manukau produces such goods as transport equipment, electrical appliances, and machinery. The food and beverage, chemical, and paper and paper product industries are also important. The city is served by the North Island Main Trunk Railway and by Auckland International Airport at Mangere, built on land reclaimed from the bay. Pop. (1996) 254,577.

manul (mammal): *see* Pallas's cat.

manure, organic material that is used to fertilize land, usually consisting of the feces and urine of domestic livestock, with or without accompanying litter such as straw, hay, or bedding. Farm animals void most of the nitrogen, phosphorus, and potassium that is present in the food they eat, and this constitutes an enormous fertility resource. In some countries, human excrement is also used. Livestock manure is less rich in nitrogen, phosphorus, and potash than synthetic fertilizers and hence must be applied in much greater quantities than the latter. A ton of manure from cattle, hogs, or horses usually contains only 10 pounds of nitrogen, 5 pounds of phosphorus pentoxide, and 10 pounds of potash. But manure is rich in organic matter, or humus, and thus improves the soil's capacity to absorb and store water, thus preventing erosion. Much of the potassium and nitrogen in manure can be lost through leaching if the material is exposed to rainfall before being applied to the field. These nutrient losses may be prevented by such methods as stacking manure under cover or in pits to prevent leaching, spreading it on fields as soon as it is feasible, and spreading preservative materials in the stable. A green manure is a cover crop of some kind, such as rye, that is plowed under while still green to add fertility and conditioning to the soil.

The use of manure as fertilizer dates to the beginnings of agriculture. On modern farms manure is usually applied with a manure spreader, a four-wheeled self-propelled or two-wheeled tractor-drawn wagon. Home gardeners like to use well-rotted manure, since it is less odorous, more easily spread, and less likely to "burn" plants. *See also* fertilizer.

manus, in Roman law, autocratic power of the husband over the wife, corresponding to patria potestas of the father over his children. A daughter ceased to be under her father's potestas if she came under the manus of her husband. Marriage without manus, however, was by far the more common in all periods of Roman history except possibly the very earliest. By the time of the Twelve Tables (451–450 BC), it was possible to be married without manus, so that the wife remained under her father's potestas if he was still alive.

In marriage without manus, the property of the spouses remained distinct. Divorce, in marriage with manus, was always possible at the instance of the husband; in marriage without manus, either party was able to put an end to the relationship at will. *Compare* patria potestas.

Manus Island, also called GREAT ADMIRALTY ISLAND, largest of the Admiralty Islands, Papua New Guinea, 200 miles (320 km) north of the island of New Guinea in the southwestern Pacific Ocean. Measuring 50 by 20 miles (80 by 32 km) and having a total land area of 633 square miles (1,639 square km), the volcanic island is an extension of the Bismarck Archipelago. From a coast that alternates between mangrove-swamp-fringed bays and steep slopes, it rises to a well-dissected interior reaching 2,356 feet (718 m) at Mount Dremsel. Heavily forested and well watered, Manus is drained by numerous short, swift streams, whose valleys provide the only lowlands besides a narrow, densely populated east-coast plain.

Manus, perhaps visited by the Spaniard Álvaro Saavedra in 1528, was sighted by the Dutch navigator Willem Schouten in 1616. Navigational studies of the island were not made until 1875. The Germans established a post in 1912 at Lorengau, which came under Australian administration in 1914. Lorengau is the principal settlement. Manus was the site of a large U.S. naval base built in Seeadler Harbour in 1944.

Church near Lorengau, Manus Island, Papua New Guinea
Ira Spring

Exports, including copra, cocoa, and coffee, are sent from Seeadler Harbour, northeastern Manus. There is regular air service to Manus Island, but tourism is restricted to passengers aboard ships. Pop. (1989 est.) island (including adjoining islets), 29,700.

Manutius, Aldus, THE ELDER, Italian ALDO MANUZIO IL VECCHIO (b. 1449, Bassiano, Papal States [Italy]—d. Feb. 6, 1515, Venice), the leading figure of his time in printing, publishing, and typography, founder of a veritable dynasty of great printer-publishers, and organizer of the famous Aldine Press. Manutius produced the first printed editions of many of the Greek and Latin classics and is particularly associated with the production of small, excellently edited pocket-size books printed in inexpensive editions.

After studies in Rome and Ferrara, Manutius reached Venice in 1490 and gathered around him a group of Greek scholars and compositors. In March 1495 he issued his first dated book, the *Erotemata* of Constantine Lascaris. During 1495–98 he printed five volumes of Aristotle; in 1495, the *Idylls* of Theocritus and *De Aetna* of Pietro Bembo; in 1498, works by Aristophanes and Politian. Francesco Griffo, who was his type cutter, was responsible in 1500 for the first italic face, first regularly used in the Virgil of 1501. The *Hypnerotomachia Poliphili* (1499) of Francesco Colonna, with its outstanding woodcuts by an unknown artist, was Manutius' most famous book. In 1501 he printed Juvenal, Martial, and Petrarch's *Cose volgari;* in 1502, works by Catullus, Lucan, Thucydides, Sophocles, and Herodotus; in August 1502, *La divina commedia* of Dante, which first showed the famous colophon of the Aldine anchor and dolphin. In the Sophocles of 1502 occurred the first mention of the Aldine academy, an organization of scholars founded by Manutius to edit classical texts. Between 1503 and 1514 his production included works by Xenophon, Euripides, Homer, Aesop, Virgil, Erasmus, Horace, Pindar, and Plato.

Manutius married in 1505, and thereafter the name of his father-in-law, Andrea Torresani di Asola, appeared regularly with his in imprints. After Manutius' death, his brothers-in-law, the Asolani, carried on the Aldine Press until his third son, Paulus (*see* Manutius, Paulus), took over in 1533. Paulus went to Rome in 1561, leaving the Aldine Press to his son Aldus Manutius the Younger (*q.v.*). It is probable that the Aldine family printed 1,000 editions between 1495 and 1595.

Manutius, Aldus, THE YOUNGER, Italian ALDO MANUZIO IL GIOVANE (b. Feb. 13, 1547, Venice [Italy]—d. Oct. 28, 1597, Rome), last member of the Italian family of Manuzio to be active in the famous Aldine Press established by Aldus Manutius (1449–1515).

When only 14, Aldus the Younger wrote a work on Latin spelling, *Orthographiae ratio.* While in Venice superintending the Aldine Press after his father, Paulus (1512–74), had moved to Rome, he published his *Epitome orthographiae* (1575) and his commentary on Horace's *Ars poetica* (1576). At about the same time he was appointed professor of literature at the Cancelleria there. In 1585 Manutius moved to Bologna, where the next year he published his life of Cosimo de' Medici; in 1587 he went to Pisa, and in 1588 Sixtus V called him to Rome. Manutius married a daughter of the publisher Bernardo Giunta. Although he had children, none carried on the Aldine Press.

Manutius, Paulus, Italian PAOLO MANUZIO (b. June 12, 1512, Venice [Italy]—d. April 6, 1574, Rome), Renaissance printer, third son of Aldus Manutius, founder of the Aldine Press in Venice.

After the death of Aldus in 1515, his brothers-in-law, the Asolani, carried on the Aldine Press until 1533, when Paulus took it over. The Asolani attempted the duties of editing and dispensed with the services of competent collaborators. As a result, some of their editions, notably their Aeschylus of 1518, are very poor. Paulus, determined to remedy this situation, separated from his uncles in 1540. He was himself an excellent Latinist, especially dedicated to Cicero; he issued corrected editions of Cicero's letters and orations, his own Latin version of Demosthenes (1554), his epistles in a Ciceronian style (1560), and his four treatises on Roman antiquities. From 1558 he directed a press for the Accademia Veneta, but this had to close down for lack of funds in 1561, when Paulus was invited by Pius IV to Rome and was offered a yearly stipend of 500 ducats. In Rome Paulus printed about 50 books before 1571, dividing the profits with the Apostolic Camera.

Manuza (African emperor): *see* Mavura.

Manuzio FAMILY, Latin MANUTIUS, Venetian family of printers. *See* Manutius, Aldus, the Elder; Manutius, Aldus, the Younger; Manutius, Paulus.

Manx, breed of tailless domestic cat of unknown origin but presumed by tradition to have come from the Isle of Man. Noted for being affectionate, loyal, and courageous, the Manx is distinguished both by its taillessness

Red tabby Manx cat
John Gajda

and by its characteristic hopping gait. It is compactly built, with a rounded head; large, round eyes; and small, wide-set ears. The rump is also rounded and, because the hindlegs are considerably longer than the forelegs, is distinctly higher than the shoulders. The Manx may be born with a tail but ideally should be totally tailless with a hollow at the end of the backbone where the root of the tail should be. The double coat may be any solid, variegated, or tabby colour.

Manx language, a member of the Goidelic group of Celtic languages, formerly spoken on the Isle of Man but now extinct. Like Scottish Gaelic, Manx was an offshoot of Irish Gaelic, and it is closely related to the easternmost dialects of Irish and to Scottish. The earliest record of the Manx language is a version of the Anglican *Book of Common Prayer,* translated into Manx in 1610 by a Welsh bishop who used an orthography based on that of English. Manx was spoken by the majority of inhabitants of the Isle of Man until the 19th century, when it was displaced by English. There are no longer any native speakers of the Manx language.

Mānyakheṭa, modern MALKHAID, also spelled MALKHED, site of a former city in Karnātaka, India, about 85 miles (135 km) southwest of Hyderābād. The city was founded in the 9th century by the Rāṣṭrakūṭa ruler Amoghavarṣa I and became the capital of the dynasty.

In 972 it was sacked by the Paramāra ruler Sīyaka. After the downfall of the dynasty in the following year, it was taken by the Cālukyas (Chalukyas), who adopted it for some time as their capital. Thereafter it never regained its former glory and dwindled to the status of a village.

Manyara, Lake, lake in northern Tanzania, 60 miles (100 km) west-southwest of Arusha. It is 30 miles (50 km) long and 10 miles (16 km) wide and contains salt and rock phosphate deposits. Lake Manyara National Park, founded in 1960 and covering 124 square miles (320 square km), contains five distinct vegetation zones. Wildlife of the area includes buffalo, elephant, lion, leopard, rhinoceros, and many water birds, especially flamingos.

Manych Depression (Russia): *see* Kuma-Manych Depression.

Manyika, also spelled MANICA, also called WANYIKA, one of the cluster of Shona-speaking peoples inhabiting extreme eastern Zimbabwe and adjacent areas of interior Mozambique south of the Púnguè River. The Manyika have existed as an ethnic group discrete from other Shona groups only since the 1930s.

Historically, the Manyika recognized a hereditary headman who, assisted by family heads, arbitrated disputes and officiated at sacrifices to ancestral spirits. Although the earlier Manyika were divided into many small polities, Manyika-speaking peoples did make up the two kingdoms of Mutasa and Makoni, which are said to have existed from at least the early 17th century.

It was not until well into the colonial period that people of Mutasa and Makoni, in reaction to the activities of European missionaries and administrators, began to have the common feeling of being Manyika. Anglican, Methodist, and Roman Catholic missionaries established a written Manyika dialect with which they taught and evangelized. Educated, Christian Manyika were recognized as ardent workers and entrepreneurs and were given priority in hiring; being Manyika became profitable. Considerable rural-urban migration by Manyika has transformed social organization in rural areas. The Manyika were enthusiastic participants in the struggle for Zimbabwean independence. National leaders from their area include Herbert Chitepo and the Methodist bishop Abel Muzorewa.

Goldfields are found in Manicaland, Zimbabwe, and have been worked since the 17th century or earlier. Gold was an important trade item among peoples of the area and was taken eastward to coastal towns in Mozambique for trade with Indian, Arab, and Portuguese merchants there. Manyika work in the mines (gold, chromium, and tungsten) and local industries (lumber, distilleries, and food-preparation) of Zimbabwe and elsewhere in southern Africa. They are, however, largely an agricultural people who grow corn (maize) as a staple; raise cattle, goats, and chickens; and fish, hunt, and gather some wild foods. Rural Manyika reside in dispersed hamlets of family compounds, their round houses surrounding a communal cattle corral.

Man'yō-shū (Japanese: "Collection of Ten Thousand Leaves"), oldest (*c.* 759) and greatest of the imperial anthologies of Japanese poetry. Among the 4,500 poems are some from the 7th century and perhaps earlier. It was celebrated through the centuries for its "*man'yō*" spirit, a simple freshness and sincere emotive power not seen later in more polished and stylized Japanese verse. The poems, however, are far from naive; although the written language still contained certain technical crudities, and some Chinese stylistic influence may be seen, in the *Man'yō-shū* a sophisticated poetic tradition is already evident. The language of the *Man'yō-shū* has offered scholars technical difficulties almost from the time of its compilation; the unique *man'yō gana* writing system, a combination of Chinese characters used both phonetically and semantically, in both Japanese and Chinese syntax, posed many problems, some of which yet remain. Among the outstanding poets represented are Ōtomo Yakamochi, Kakinomoto Hitomaro, and Yamanoue Okura, all of whom flourished in the 8th century. The best English translation, by H.H. Fonda, was published in 1967.

Manzanar Relocation Center, an internment facility for Japanese-Americans during World War II. In March 1942 the U.S. War Relocation Authority was set up; it established 10 relocation centres for persons of Japanese ancestry, located in California, Arizona, Idaho, Utah, Wyoming, and Arkansas. The best known of these, and the first to be established, was the Manzanar Relocation Center near Lone Pine, Calif.; it operated from March 1942 to November 1945. During this time more than 11,000 persons were confined there.

Manzanillo, city, eastern Cuba. Founded in 1784, Manzanillo lies amid unhealthful swamplands at the head of the shallow Gulf of Guacanayabo. It is a commercial and manufacturing centre for the fertile agricultural district to the east and north, which produces sugarcane, fruit, rice, cattle, and a variety of other items. Manzanillo contains sugar refineries, sawmills, tanneries, canneries, and cigar factories. Zinc and copper deposits are located in the vicinity. The port handles mainly sugar products, tobacco, and hardwoods; fishing also contributes to the economy. Manzanillo is linked by railroad and highway to Santiago de Cuba and has an airfield. Pop. (1991) 109,471.

Manzanillo, city and port, western Colima *estado* ("state"), west-central Mexico. It lies on the Pacific Ocean between Manzanillo Bay and Cuyutlán Lagoon. In pre-Columbian times the site was occupied by the town of Tzalahua, and ships for Hernán Cortés' expedition (1533) to the Gulf of California were built there. The city's commercial and manufacturing activities are based on the products from the farmlands, forests, and waters of Colima and part of neighbouring Jalisco state, which are gathered into and shipped from Manzanillo. The chief exports include copra, corn (maize), bananas, lemons, fish, minerals, lumber, wine, and canned goods. Excellent beaches and deep-sea fishing make the city a popular resort. It is accessible by railroad and highway from Colima city, the state capital, to the northeast, and is served by domestic airlines. Pop. (2000 prelim.) 124,014.

manzanita, any of about 50 species of evergreen shrubs and trees of the genus *Arctostaphylos,* of the heath family (Ericaceae), native to western North America. The leaves are alternate and smooth-edged. The small, urn-shaped flowers are pink or white and are borne in terminal clusters. Except for one species, the bearberry (*A. uva-ursi*), which is found in Europe, Asia, and North America, species of

Manzanita (*Arctostaphylos manzanita*)
J.W. Wilburn

manzanita are native to western North America. Some species—*e.g., A. manzanita,* the common manzanita, and *A. stanfordiana,* the stanford manzanita—are cultivated for their showy, massive displays of flowers. The fruit of the manzanita is a smooth brown or red berry.

Manzhouli (China): *see* Man-chou-li.

Manzikert, Battle of (1071), battle in which the Byzantines under the emperor Romanus IV Diogenes were defeated by the Seljuq Turks led by the sultan Alp-Arslan. It was followed by Seljuq conquest of most of Anatolia.

Spurred by Seljuq raids and incursions into Byzantine-ruled Anatolia, Romanus assembled a large army to reestablish the security of the Byzantine Empire's eastern frontier there. In the spring of 1071 he led this army into parts of Turkish-held Armenia, entering Armenia along the southern branch of the Upper Euphrates River. Near the town of Manzikert (present Malazgirt, Tur.), he divided his army, which was composed of mercenaries that included a contingent of Turkmen, sending some ahead to secure the fortress of Akhlât on nearby Lake Van and taking others with him into Manzikert. Learning of the Byzantine foray into his territory, Alp-Arslan hastened to Manzikert, where he confronted the emperor's army.

Romanus abandoned Manzikert in an attempt to reunite his forces with the group besieging Akhlât. Trapped in a valley on the Akhlât road, he neglected to send out scouts to assess the enemy's position, and the Turks fell upon him. Romanus fought valiantly and might have won if his position had not been weakened by treachery within his ranks; his Turkmen troops went over to the enemy the night before the battle, and one of his generals, Andronicus Ducas, perceiving that the cause was lost, fled with his men. The Byzantine army was destroyed, and Romanus was taken prisoner.

Consult
the
INDEX
first

Manzil Bū Ruqaybah, also spelled MENZEL-BOURGUIBA, formerly FERRYVILLE, town, north-central Tunisia. It lies on the southwestern shore of Lake Banzart, 10 miles (16 km) southwest of Bizerte town and the Mediterranean Sea. Manzil Bū Ruqaybah, which is of modern origin, owes its development to the adjacent naval base and dockyard at Sīdī 'Abd Allāh (Sidi Abdallah) and was named after Tunisia's first president, Habib Bourguiba. Although its prosperity declined considerably following the French evacuation of naval installations in 1963, the town and its economy were greatly rejuvenated after the establishment of an iron and steel complex, an automobile assembly plant, and metallurgical and chemical industries. Roads and a railway link Manzil Bū Ruqaybah with Bizerte. Pop. (1989 est.) 47,340.

Manzini, formerly (until 1960) BREMERSDORP, town, central Swaziland. The Great Usutu River flows south of Manzini on its way east toward the Indian Ocean, and the Malkerns irrigation scheme is to the north. It was originally called Bremersdorp, for a trader who established a store there in 1887, but it was renamed in 1960. The first administrative centre of Swaziland from 1895 to 1899, it is now an important commercial, agricultural, and industrial centre. It lies in the heavily populated Middle Veld region, where the nucleus of the Swazi nation lives. They are agriculturists cultivating corn (maize), cotton, tobacco, and some fruit. Dairy and beef cattle are also raised, and Swaziland's main meat-processing plant, creamery, grain mill, cotton ginnery, and fruit-canning factory are located in and around Manzini. An international airport is 5 miles (8 km) away. Pop. (1986) 18,084.

Manzoni, Alessandro (b. March 7, 1785, Milan—d. May 22, 1873, Milan), Italian poet and novelist whose novel *I promessi sposi* (*The Betrothed,* 1952) had immense patriotic appeal for Italians of the nationalistic Risorgimento period and is generally ranked among the masterpieces of world literature.

After Manzoni's parents separated in 1792, he spent much of his childhood in religious schools. In 1805 he joined his mother and her lover in Paris, where he moved in radical circles and became a convert to Voltairian skepticism. His anticlerical poem "Il trionfo della libertà" demonstrates his independence of thought. When his mother's lover and his father died, the former left him a comfortable income, through his mother.

In 1808 he married Henriette Blondel, a Calvinist, who soon converted to Roman Catholicism, and two years later Manzoni himself returned to Catholicism. Retiring to a quiet life in Milan and at his villa in Brusiglio, he wrote (1812–15) a series of religious poems, *Inni sacri* (1815; *The Sacred Hymns*), on the church feasts of Christmas, Good Friday, and Easter, and a hymn to Mary. The last, and perhaps the finest, of the series, "La pentecoste," was published in 1822.

Manzoni, oil painting by Francesco Hayez; in the Brera Gallery, Milan
Alinari—Art Resource/EB Inc.

During these years, Manzoni also produced the treatise *Osservazioni sulla morale cattolica* (1819; "Observations on Catholic Ethics"); an ode on the Piedmontese revolution of 1821, "Marzo 1821"; and two historical tragedies influenced by Shakespeare: *Il conte di Carmagnola* (1820), a romantic work depicting a 15th-century conflict between Venice and Milan; and *Adelchi* (performed 1822), a richly poetic drama about Charlemagne's overthrow of the Lombard kingdom and conquest of Italy. Another ode, written on the death of Napoleon in 1821, "Il cinque maggio" (1822; "The Napoleonic Ode"), was considered by Goethe, one of the first to translate it into German, as the greatest of many written to commemorate the event.

Manzoni's masterpiece, *I promessi sposi,* 3 vol. (1825–27), is a novel set in early 17th-century Lombardy during the period of the Milanese insurrection, the Thirty Years' War, and the plague. It is a sympathetic portrayal of the struggle of two peasant lovers whose wish to marry is thwarted by a vicious local tyrant and the cowardice of their parish priest. A courageous friar takes up the lovers' cause and helps them through many adventures to safety and marriage. Manzoni's resigned tolerance of the evils of life and his concept of religion as the ultimate comfort and inspiration of humanity give the novel its moral dimension, while a pleasant vein of humour in the book contributes to the reader's enjoyment. The novel brought Manzoni immediate fame and praise from all quarters, in Italy and elsewhere.

Prompted by the patriotic urge to forge a language that would be accessible to a wide readership rather than a narrow elite, Manzoni decided to write his novel in an idiom as close as possible to contemporary educated Florentine speech. The final edition of *I promessi sposi* (1840–42), rendered in clear, expressive prose purged of all antiquated rhetorical forms, reached exactly the sort of broad audience he had aimed at, and its prose became the model for many subsequent Italian writers.

Manzoni's wife died in 1833; his second wife and most of his children also predeceased him. These calamities deepened rather than destroyed his faith. Revered by the men of his time, he was made a senator of Italy in 1860. A stroke followed the death of his oldest son in 1873, and he died that same year and was buried with a state funeral.

Manzù, Giacomo, original name GIACOMO MANZONI (b. Dec. 22, 1908, Bergamo, Italy—d. Jan. 17, 1991, Ardea), Italian sculptor who in the mid-20th century revived the ancient tradition of creating sculptural bronze doors for ecclesiastical buildings. His sober realism and extremely delicate modeling alternately achieved austere severity and sensuousness of form and surface, lending a new spirit of vitality to figurative bronze sculpture.

Manzù, who had to leave school at an early age to learn a trade, was apprenticed to local craftsmen who taught him to carve wood and to work in metal and stone. After service in the Italian army (1927–28), Manzù went to Paris to try his luck as a sculptor, but after three weeks he collapsed from hunger and was deported back to Italy. In those difficult years he began to concern himself with various themes, including diverse representations of Roman Catholic cardinals. Although Manzù generally made only one cast of each work, he executed numerous variants—often in vastly divergent sizes—of favourite themes. Ultimately, he produced more than 50 seated or standing cardinals. He also sculpted many tender figures of female nudes.

"Portrait of a Lady," bronze sculpture by Giacomo Manzù, 1946; in the Museum of Modern Art, New York City
By courtesy of the Museum of Modern Art, New York; A. Conger Goodyear Fund

In spite of the antifascist connotations of some of the works that he produced shortly before World War II, Manzù's reputation was sufficiently well established by 1940 for him to be appointed professor of sculpture at the Academy of Fine Arts in Milan, where he taught until 1954.

His most noteworthy work of the war years was "Francesca," a seated nude that won the Grand Prix of the Rome Quadriennale in 1942. In 1948 the artist was awarded the first prize for Italian sculpture at the Venice Biennale. Two years later he was commissioned to create a set of monumental bronze doors for St. Peter's in Rome; the portal was dedicated in 1964, after the death of Pope John XXIII, whose official portrait Manzù had executed. Among his other commissions were doors for Salzburg Cathedral (1958), the Church of Sankt-Laurents in Rotterdam (1969), and a relief of a "Mother and Child" (1965) for Rockefeller Center in New York City.

Mao, city, northwestern Dominican Republic. It lies near the Yaque del Norte River in the fertile Cibao Valley. The city was formerly called Valverde. Mao is principally a rice-growing and milling centre, although a variety of other crops are grown in the area. Lumbering and placer gold mining take place near the city. Mao can be reached by secondary highways linking Santo Domingo with Montecristi in the extreme northwest. Pop. (1981) 33,527.

Mao Ch'ang, Pinyin MAO CHANG (fl. 145 BC, Chao, China), Chinese scholar whose revision of and commentary on the great Confucian Classic the *Shih Ching* ("Classic of Poetry") became so famous that for the next 2,000 years this text was often referred to as the *Mao shih* ("Mao Poetry"). His work is still generally considered the authoritative version of that Classic.

During the interregnum when China came under the rule of the Ch'in dynasty (221–206 BC), a massive burning of books took place in which most copies of the Confucian Classics were destroyed. When the Han dynasty (206 BC–AD 220) followed the Ch'in, an intensive campaign was undertaken to replace the Classics; older scholars who had memorized these works entirely provided a chief source—and a reason—for the many conflicting versions of the different Classics available. In the midst of this confusion, Mao, who had supposedly received the *Shih Ching* from his father, prepared an edition of the work that was so well researched and documented that it is generally considered the version originally handed down by Confucius. Mao's explanation of the meaning of the text also had great influence, helping to define the Confucian beliefs that underlay most subsequent Chinese dynasties for the next 2,000 years.

Mao Dun, Wade-Giles romanization MAO TUN, pseudonym of SHEN YEN-PING, original name SHEN TE-HUNG (b. 1896, Ch'ing-chen, Chekiang province, China—d. March 27, 1981, Peking), editor and author, generally considered republican China's greatest realist novelist.

Forced to interrupt his schooling in 1916 because he ran out of money, Shen became a proofreader at the Commercial Press in Shanghai and was soon promoted to editor and translator. In 1920 he and several other young Chinese writers took over editorial control of the 11-year-old journal *Hsiao-shuo yüeh-pao* ("Short-Story Magazine"). The group revamped the magazine, began to promote new literature, and elected Shen as editor, a post he occupied until 1923.

In 1926 Shen joined the Northern Expedition as secretary to the propaganda department of the Kuomintang Central Executive Committee. When the Kuomintang broke with the Chinese Communist Party, Shen, pleading illness, fled the confusion to Kuling. In the next year he composed three novelettes, published as a trilogy under the title *Shih* (1930; "Eclipse"), using the pseudonym Mao Dun, the Chinese term for "contradiction." The work, dealing with a youth's involvement in the Northern Expedition, was an instant success and is considered by many Western critics to be Mao Dun's masterpiece because of its brilliant psychological realism. In China, however, *Shih* was attacked by Marxist critics, who berated it as "petty bourgeois." A later work, *Tzu-yeh* (1933; "Midnight"), was praised by Chinese Marxist critics for its social realism, while Western critics found it less vital than *Shih*.

In 1930 Mao Dun helped found the League of Left-Wing writers. During the Sino-Japanese War (1937–45), he continued his leftist literary activities, founding and editing two patriotic literary journals. After the establishment of the Communist government in 1949, Mao Dun was active on several literary and cultural committees, but he stopped writing works of fiction. He became minister of culture in 1949 but was dismissed in 1964. In the 1970s he became vice president of the Chinese Writers Association and edited a magazine of children's literature. In 1978 he was again publicly active in the Chinese Communist Party.

Mao-ming, Pinyin MAOMING, city in western Kwangtung *sheng* (province), China. Mao-ming is situated some 16 miles (25 km) inland, 50 miles (80 km) northeast of Chan-chiang city. Little more than a small market town and minor administrative centre until the 1950s, the whole area has undergone rapid growth since then; Mao-ming itself has been transformed into an industrial city on the basis of rich deposits of oil shale, the exploitation of which began in the late 1950s. Mao-ming was linked by rail with the line constructed from Chan-chiang to Kwangsi *sheng* in 1957. A refinery has been constructed to produce gasoline, diesel oil, and kerosene. In association with it, there are chemical plants recovering sulfur and producing large quantities of ammonium sulfate. Pop. (1988 est.) 149,700.

Mao Zedong, Wade-Giles romanization MAO TSE-TUNG (b. Dec. 26, 1893, Shao-shan, Hunan province, China—d. Sept. 9, 1976, Peking), principal Chinese Marxist theorist, soldier, and statesman who led his nation's communist revolution. Leader of the Chinese Communist Party from 1931, he was chairman (chief of state) of the People's Republic of China from 1949 to 1959 and chairman of the party until his death.

A brief treatment of Mao Zedong follows. For full treatment, *see* MACROPAEDIA: Mao Zedong.

Attracted to Chinese reformers and the nationalistic ideas of Sun Yat-sen, Mao enlisted in the revolutionary army in Hunan during the Chinese Revolution of 1911 that overthrew the Manchu dynasty. At Peking University (1919) he participated in the May Fourth Movement of students. Disillusioned with Western liberalism, he committed himself to Marxism and in 1921 helped to found the Chinese Communist Party. From 1927 to 1934 he organized Communist guerrilla units, composed mainly of peasants, to defend his bases in the countryside against the forces of General Chiang Kai-shek's Nationalist Party. Successful attacks by Chiang Kai-shek's armies prompted Mao in 1934–35 to lead the Red Army from its major base in southeastern China to northwestern China in a retreat known as the Long March. During the period 1936–40 he wrote his major theoretical and practical works on revolution and became the acknowledged leader of the Chinese Communists. His victory over the Nationalists at Nanking (April 1949) was decisive, and the Communist People's Republic of China was established. Mao became chairman of the Communist Party and of the republic. The failure of the Great Leap Forward (1958–60), his attempt to restructure the economy along communist lines, led to his retirement (1959) as chairman of the republic, but he remained chairman of the party. Mao reasserted his control in the upheaval known as the Cultural Revolution, which began in 1966 and did not officially end until 1976. Although the cult of Chairman Mao and his thought continued, Mao's final years were spent in declining health and virtual seclusion. His death in 1976 was followed by the abandonment of many of the radical socioeconomic policies he had promulgated.

Maoism, Chinese (Pinyin) MAO ZEDONG SIXIANG ("Mao Zedong Thought"), doctrine composed of the ideology and methodology for revolution developed by Mao Zedong and his associates in the Chinese Communist Party from the 1920s until Mao's death in 1976. Maoism has clearly represented a revolutionary method based on a distinct revolutionary outlook not necessarily dependent on a Chinese or Marxist-Leninist context.

The first political attitudes of Mao Zedong took shape against a background of profound crisis in China in the early 20th century. The nation was weak and divided, and the major national problems were the reunification of China and the expulsion of foreign occupiers. The young Mao was a nationalist, and his sentiments had been strongly anti-Western and anti-imperialist even before he became attracted to Marxism-Leninism about 1919–20. Mao's nationalism combined with a personal trait of combativeness to make him admire the martial spirit, which became a cornerstone of Maoism. Indeed, the army held an important position both in the process of creating the Chinese revolutionary state and in the process of nation building; Mao relied on army support in conflicts with his party in the 1950s and '60s.

Mao's political ideas crystallized slowly. He had a mentality that was opportunistic and wary of ideological niceties. The Marxist-Leninist tradition regarded peasants as incapable of revolutionary initiative and only marginally useful in backing urban proletarian efforts. Yet Mao gradually decided to base his revolution on the dormant power of China's hundreds of millions of peasants, for he saw potential energy in them by the very fact that they were "poor and blank"; strength and violence were, he thought, inherent in their condition. Proceeding from this, he proposed to instill in them a proletarian consciousness and make their force alone suffice for revolution. There was no significant Chinese proletariat, but by the 1940s Mao had revolutionized and "proletarianized" the peasantry.

For a time after the creation of the Chinese Communist state in 1949, Mao Zedong attempted to conform to the Stalinist model of "building Socialism." In the mid-1950s, however, he and his advisers reacted against the results of this policy, which included the growth of a rigid and bureaucratic Communist Party, and the emergence of managerial and technocratic elites—accepted in other countries, especially the Soviet Union, as concomitants of industrial growth. In 1955 the Maoists speeded up the process of agricultural collectivization. After this came the Great Leap Forward (*q.v.*), a refinement of the traditional five-year plans, and other efforts at mobilizing the masses into producing small-scale industries ("backyard steel furnaces") throughout China. The experiment faltered through waste, confusion, and inefficient management. In 1966 the party's leaders, at Mao's instigation, launched the Cultural Revolution (*q.v.*), designed again to quash emerging "bourgeois" elements—elites and bureaucrats—and to harness anti-intellectualism to galvanize popular will. The party leaders stressed egalitarianism and the value of the peasants' lack of sophistication; indeed, thousands of city workers were forced to receive "profound class education" through agricultural labour with the peasants.

Thus, Maoism's alternative to growth led by elites and bureaucracies was to be growth brought about by revolutionary enthusiasm and mass struggle. Maoism undertook to pit the collective will of human beings against the customary and rational dictates of economics and industrial management. The violent excesses of Maoism and its inability to achieve sustained economic growth led after the Chairman's death to a new emphasis on education and management professionalism, and by the 1980s Maoism appeared to be celebrated mainly as a relic of the late leader.

Maoke Mountains, Indonesian PEGUNUNGAN MAOKE, formerly SNOW MOUNTAINS, westernmost segment of the central highlands of New Guinea. It is located in the Indonesian part of New Guinea, known as Irian Jaya. The range extends for 430 miles (692 km), and much of it lies above 12,000 feet (3,660 m), with a number of peaks rising above the 14,500-foot (4,400-metre) snow line. It is composed of the Sudirman (west) and Jayawijaya (east) ranges, the former containing the island's highest point, 16,500-foot (5,000-metre) Puncak Jaya, formerly Puntjak Sukarno, and Mount Carstensz. These rugged mountains have their tree line at about 12,000 feet.

Maori, Polynesian people of New Zealand. Their traditional history describes their origins in terms of waves of migration beginning about AD 1150 and culminating in the arrival of a "great fleet" in the 14th century from Hawaiki, a mythical land usually identified as Tahiti. Although this tradition has largely been discounted by archaeological discoveries, which have dated habitations at least as early as AD 800 and possibly very much earlier, it still provided the basis for traditional Maori social organization. Members of each tribe (*iwi*) recognized a common ancestry (which might be traced through either or both parents) and common allegiance to a chief or chiefs (*ariki*). Traditionally, at the day-to-day level, the most important social groups were the *hapuu* (subtribe), the primary landholding group and the one within which marriage was preferred, and the extended family (*whaanau*).

This social order was in force when Abel Tasman, the first European contact, arrived off the coast of New Zealand in December 1642. He did battle with a group of Maori on the South Island and left the area largely unexplored. In 1769–70 Captain James Cook circumnavigated the two major islands and wrote about the intelligence of the Maori and the suitability of New Zealand for colonization. Whalers, sealers, and other Europeans seeking profit were initially welcomed by the Maori. With the introduction of muskets, disease, Western agricultural methods, and missionaries, Maori culture and social structure began to disintegrate. By the late 1830s New Zealand had been joined to Europe, and European settlers landed by the score.

After the British assumed formal control of New Zealand in 1840, European settlement and government began to alarm the Maori, especially in North Island. In 1845 some Maori chieftains began ravaging the Bay of Islands and other areas of the far north (in what has sometimes been called the First Maori War) and were not finally suppressed until 1847, by colonial forces under Governor Sir George Grey. His victories brought a peace that lasted from 1847 to 1860.

The so-called King Movement was a response to the increasing threat to the Maori land. In 1857 several tribes of the Waikato area of North Island elected as king Te Wherowhero, who reigned as Potatau I. In addition to electing a king, they established a council of state, a judicial system, and a police organization, all of which were intended to support Maori resolve to retain their land and to stop the intertribal warfare over the issue.

Not all Maori accepted the authority of the king, but the majority shared with the King Movement the resolve not to sell the land.

Until 1860 the Maori still owned most of the land of the North Island, but a large increase in the number of immigrants in the 1850s led to demands for greatly increased land purchase by the government. Many Maori were determined not to sell. In 1859 Te Teira, a Maori of the Taranaki area, sold his Waitara River land, without the consent of his tribe, to the colonial government, precipitating the First Taranaki War of 1860–61. Only the extremist wing of the King Movement joined in the First Taranaki War.

The war consisted essentially of a series of generally successful sieges of Maori *pa*s (fortified villages) by British troops and militia employing a sap trench procedure. The British were defeated during an attack (June 1860) on Puketakauere *pa* when the Maori executed a surprise counterattack; but the Maori were defeated at Orongomai in October and Mahoetahi in November. The war ended in a truce after the surrender of the Te Arei *pa* in late March 1861. The Maori remained in possession of the European-owned Tataraimaka block of land.

The fighting resumed in the Second Taranaki War in April 1863 after Governor Grey built an attack road into the Waikato area and drove the Taranaki Maori from the Tataraimaka block. While fighting raged in Taranaki once again, the Waikato War began in July 1863; and the Waikato River region, the centre of the King Movement tribes, became the main target of the Europeans. Once again the war was decided by sieges of Maori *pas*, but the Maori also began to employ guerrilla tactics. British troops were aided by gunboats and forest ranger units made up of colonial volunteers. The Europeans won notable victories at Meremere in October 1863 and at Rangiriri in November. The fall of the Orakau *pa* in early April 1864 essentially brought the Waikato War to an end.

The last of the wars, known to the Europeans as "the fire in the fern" and to the Maori as *te riri pakeha,* "the white man's anger," was fought from 1864 to 1872. Hostilities spread to virtually the whole of North Island. The main Maori combatants in the mid-60s were the Hauhau (*q.v.*) warriors. The British government wanted to conclude peace in 1864, but the colonial government, wishing to acquire more land, continued the war and assumed an increasing share of the fighting. In July 1865 Grey led the capture of Weroroa *pa* in southern Taranaki. European and supporting Maori forces (increasingly numerous after 1864) checked each new effort by the hostile tribes. From 1868 to 1872 the Hauhau were aided by a new warrior cult, Ringatu, founded and led by a guerrilla leader, Te Kooti.

All fighting ended in 1872. Great tracts of Maori land had been confiscated and Maori society permanently disrupted. The supporters of the King Movement retreated to King Country, in the west-central North Island. This area was closed to Europeans and remained under Maori control until 1881, when it was released to the government.

In the early part of the 21st century, about 14 percent of New Zealanders were classified as Maori, and more than four-fifths of these were urban dwellers. Urbanization has meant full exposure to an urban culture and increased contact with European New Zealanders. The rate of intermarriage between Maori and Europeans steadily increased, particularly in the younger age groups, between Maori men and European women. Economically, however, a disproportionate number remain in occupations of lower status and lower pay. This situation is largely the result of educational deficiencies, and in 1961 the Maori Education Foundation was set up with the aim of improving the standard of Maori education. Although this body has had some success, the educational achievement of most Maori children is still below that of other New Zealanders, with the result that few are able to enter occupations of higher status. There are, however, a sprinkling of Maori at all levels, and discrimination in jobs is minimal.

In other areas of social life, too, Maori are generally accepted by other New Zealanders, although some may have difficulty in finding housing in the cities and others may meet opposition if they wish to marry European New Zealanders. Prejudice is for the most part not deeply ingrained. Many Maori fear cultural domination more than discrimination and wish to maintain their identity as Maori. Nearly all have some European ancestry, and some who identify themselves as Maori actually have a predominance of European ancestry. Their identification is thus cultural rather than genetic.

To most Maori, being Maori means recognizing and venerating their Maori ancestors, having claims to family land, and having a right to be received as *taangata whenua* ("people of the land") in the village of their ancestors. It means the acceptance of group membership and the shared recognition, with members of the group, of distinctly Maori ways of thinking and behaving. There has been some revival of the teaching of the Maori language (*q.v.*), and in 1987 Maori was made an official language of New Zealand.

Many Maori cultural practices are kept alive in contemporary New Zealand. All formal Maori gatherings are accompanied by oratory in Maori; action songs; formal receptions of visitors, accompanied by the *hongi,* or pressing together of noses on greeting, and sometimes by ritual challenges; and cooking of food in earth ovens (*haangi*) on preheated stones. Carved houses, which serve as centres of meeting and ceremony in Maori villages, are still being erected.

For many Maori people the most significant issue in New Zealand remains that of the land. Acutely conscious of the injustices of European land dealings in the 19th century, they intensified efforts in the 1980s for the return of and compensation for lost natural resources, including land. Following the passage of the Treaty of Waitangi Act (1975), which established a tribunal to examine and make recommendations on Maori claims, the New Zealand government in 1993 began approving money and later land awards to the Maori. The government also apologized for the suffering and injustices inflicted on the Maori.

Maoris have played a role in the governing of New Zealand since the mid-19th century, when Maori members first entered Parliament. Seven seats are reserved for Maori in the New Zealand Parliament out of a total of 120. All voters who claim Maori ancestry may vote in a Maori electorate, but a Maori may register in either a Maori or non-Maori (general) electorate.

Maori language, Eastern Polynesian subgroup of the Eastern Austronesian (Oceanic) languages, spoken in the Cook Islands and New Zealand. Since the Maori Language Act of 1987, it has been one of the two official languages of New Zealand. Estimates of the number of Maori speakers range from 100,000 to 150,000.

As one of the marginal eastern Polynesian islands, New Zealand was one of the last of the Polynesian islands to be settled (about AD 800). Since that time the Maori language has developed independently of other Polynesian languages. European Christian missionaries developed Maori as a written language, and the first printed material in the Maori language was published in 1815.

The language contains 5 vowels (each of which can be either short or long) and 10 consonants (h, k, m, n, ng, p, r, t, w, and wh). Reduplication is frequently used, generally as a modification of intensity. Prefixes and suffixes are relatively rare, and the plurality of nouns and verb tenses is usually indicated by the syntax of a statement.

Maori Representation Act, original name NATIVE REPRESENTATION ACT (1867), legislation that created four Maori parliamentary seats in New Zealand, bringing the Maori nation into the political system of the self-governing colony. The Native Representation Act was originally intended to be temporary. When Maori landholdings were converted from tribal to individual ownership, the Maoris were to have joined the general electoral rolls. Because of the difficulty of dividing the Maori holdings, however, the act was made permanent in 1876. According to its terms, the Maoris received universal male suffrage 12 years before it was granted to the European colonists. The number of Maori parliamentary seats later increased, reaching seven in 2002.

map, graphic representation, drawn to scale and usually on a flat surface, of features—usually geographical, geological, or geopolitical—of an area of the Earth or of any other celestial body. Globes are maps represented on the surface of a sphere. Cartography is the art and science of making maps and charts.

A brief treatment of maps follows. For full treatment, *see* MACROPAEDIA: Mapping and Surveying.

Major types of maps include topographical maps, showing features of the Earth's land surface; nautical charts, representing coastal and marine areas; hydrographic charts, specifying ocean depths and the directions and intensities of oceanic currents; and aeronautical charts, detailing surface features and air routes.

History of cartography. The oldest known maps were drawn by Babylonians on clay tablets, dating to about 2300 BC. Nearly as old as these are certain Egyptian drawings and paintings discovered in early tombs. The Greek mathematician and astronomer Claudius Ptolemaeus (Ptolemy; AD 90–168) had a great influence on geography and cartography; his monumental eight-volume work, the *Guide to Geography* (*Geōgraphikē hyphēgēsis*), was an authoritative reference for almost 1,000 years.

Little progress was made in cartography until the age of exploration and commerce. Exploration encouraged the development of navigation, ship design and construction, instruments for astronomical and land observation, and general use of the compass—which in turn improved the accuracy of existing information for maps and encouraged further exploration and discovery.

The foremost cartographer of the age of discovery was Gerardus Mercator of Flanders, who developed a cylindrical projection, called the Mercator projection (*q.v.*), for representing the curved surface of the Earth on a flat map. In 1569 he published a map of the world based on this projection.

In the 18th and 19th centuries cartography was transformed by precision scientific instruments and more accurate detail. Principal among those instruments were the telescope, which helped raise the quality of astronomical observations, and the chronometer (an accurate timepiece), which made the computation of longitude much less laborious than before. Elaborate national surveys were begun in several countries, notably in France, Great Britain, and the United States. Even so, the rest of the world remained largely unmapped until the advent of aerial photography in World War II. The resulting World Aeronautical Charts provide generalized information for reconnaissance and other purposes.

Mapmaking design and technique. Designing maps is a twofold process. First, the requirements of the principal user must be determined, because they influence technical decisions as to map scale and content. Second, the content must be arranged to conform to standards of treatment, symbols, colours, style, and other factors.

Maps may be classified according to their scale, content, or derivation. Map scale refers to the size of the representation on the map as compared to the size of the object on the ground—and thus the level of detail shown. For maps it is usually convenient to express the scale by a representative fraction or ratio; for example, the ratio 1:63,360 means one inch on the map represents 63,360 inches (one mile) on the ground. In general, a large-scale map is one on which one inch represents a mile or less; on a small-scale map the ratio may be 1:1,000,000 (one inch to about 15 miles); and medium scale denotes the intermediate range.

A map's content is chosen to suit its primary purpose: thus the terms aeronautical chart, topographic map, road map, and weather map are self-descriptive. Maps may be derived or compiled from other maps, usually of larger scale; alternatively, they may be assembled from original surveys and photogrammetric compilations. Common road maps, for example, are compiled from road surveys, topographic maps, and aerial photographs.

Measurements for the map may be derived from a number of sources. Geodetic maps designed to depict large areas may rely in part on triangulation from satellites in orbit. Many mapping projects depend on numerous stereoscopic pairs of aerial photographs for accurate representation of the vertical relief of the terrain as well as much of the planimetric detail. Specialized detail maps may also rely on observations made by surveyors on the ground. Geological maps may incorporate information provided by infrared imagery or thematic mapping instruments aboard Earth-observation satellites.

Once the information is obtained, it must be accurately transferred to paper. For large-scale maps of small areas, that process is usually straightforward, but an accurate map of an area even a few tens of miles across must take into account the curvature of the Earth's surface. Several projections besides Mercator's have been developed for systematically depicting the curved meridians of longitude and parallels of latitude on a flat surface.

No matter what kind of projection is chosen, all maps are plotted with respect to the world standard geographic coordinate system; latitudes are measured north or south of the Equator and longitudes are measured east or west of the prime reference meridian of Greenwich, England. All geographical positions are stated in degrees, minutes, and seconds carried to the number of decimal places commensurate with the accuracy to which points have been located.

In many maps the symbols representing features are standardized by colour. Similarly, type style and size are also standardized, as are the specific symbols designating various features. The relative importance of the features is reflected in the sizes of lettering selected to label them.

map problem, four-colour: *see* four-colour map problem.

Mapa man, fossil fragments of an individual classified as *homo sapiens,* consisting of a frontal bone with parts of both eye sockets and part of the right half of the skull. The fragments were found in 1958 in a limestone cave at Ma-pa, Kwangtung Province, China. The skull is large, with rounded, capacious eye sockets and heavy browridges. The dating of the find is not conclusive, but it is believed the skull predates or is contemporaneous with Neanderthal man of Europe. It has been suggested this skull represents one member of an extinct population contemporaneous with, but distinct from, the Neanderthal peoples of Europe and western Asia.

Mapai, early and major labour party in Palestine–Israel that in 1930 became the central partner in the Israel Labour Party (*q.v.*).

Mapam, Hebrew abbreviation of MIFLEGET HA-POʿALIM HA-MEʾUḤEDET, English UNITED WORKERS' PARTY, left-wing labour party in Israel and in the World Zionist Organization, founded in 1948 by the ha-Shomer ha-Tzaʿir (Young Guard) and the Aḥdut ʿAvoda-Poʿale Tziyyon (Labour Unity-Workers of Zion), which were both Marxist Zionist movements. Mapam maintains a Marxist ideology and is influential in the left-wing section of the kibbutz (collective settlement) movement, from which it draws much of its strength. Differing from the more influential Israel Labour Party principally in matters of foreign policy, Mapam has historically been the most pro-Soviet of the Zionist parties, as well as the leader in the movement for Arab–Jewish rapprochement. In reaction to Soviet anti-Semitism and disagreement on policy toward the Arabs, a large number of Mapam dissidents left the party in 1954 to reform the Aḥdut ʿAvoda along pro-Western lines.

In 1969 Mapam formed an electoral alliance (ha-Maʿarakh) with the majority Israel Labour Party to contest the elections for the 6th Knesset (Parliament) and other national offices. The alliance continued to contest elections into the 1980s, although Mapam did not give up its autonomy or ideological program.

Mapam Lake, Wade–Giles romanization MA-FA-MU-TS'O, Pinyin MAFA MUCUO, conventional MĀNASAROWAR, lake, in western Tibet, to the south of the Kailas Range. Lying nearly 15,000 ft (4,570 m) above sea level, it is generally recognized as the highest body of fresh water in the world. The lake is prominent in Hindu mythology, and it has traditionally been one of the most important Hindu pilgrimage centres.

Mapimí Basin, Spanish BOLSÓN DE MAPIMÍ, enclosed depression in northern Mexico. Situated in the arid northern plateau region and averaging 3,000 ft (900 m) in elevation, it is structurally similar to the Basin and Range region of Arizona and New Mexico, in the United States. Although once considered unreclaimable desert, with irrigation it supports cotton, wheat, and alfalfa crops. The Laguna District lies in the southern portion of the basin. The chief cities, linked by railroad and highway, include Gómez Palacio, in Durango, and Torreón and San Pedro de las Colonias, in Coahuila.

maple (*Acer*), any of a large genus (about 200 species) of shrubs or trees in the family Aceraceae, widely distributed in the North Temperate Zone but concentrated in China. Maples constitute one of the most important groups of ornamentals for planting in lawns, along streets, and in parks. They offer a great variety of form, size, and foliage; many display striking autumn colour. Several yield maple syrup, and some provide valuable, dense hard

Silver maple (*Acer saccharinum*)
Walter Chandoha

wood for furniture and other uses. All maples bear pairs of winged seeds, called samaras or keys. The leaves are arranged oppositely on twigs. Many maples have lobed leaves, but a few have leaves separated into leaflets.

Among the popular smaller maples the hedge, or field, maple (*A. compestre*) and Amur, or ginnala, maple (*A. ginnala*) are useful in screens or hedges; both have spectacular foliage in fall, the former yellow and the latter pink to scarlet. The Japanese maple (*A. palmatum*), developed over centuries of breeding, provides numerous attractive cultivated varieties with varying leaf shapes and colours, many useful in small gardens. The vine maple (*A. circinatum*), of wide-spreading, shrubby habit, has purple and white spring flowers and brilliant fall foliage. The shrubby Siebold maple (*A. sieboldianum*) has seven- to nine-lobed leaves that turn red in fall.

Medium-sized maples, often more than 9 metres (30 feet) tall, include the big-toothed

Amur maple (*Acer ginnala*)
G.R. Roberts

maple (*A. grandidentatum*); some believe it to be a subspecies of sugar maple, a Rocky Mountain tree, often multistemmed, displaying pink to red fall foliage. Coliseum maple (*A. cappadocicum*) and Miyabe maple (*A. miyabei*) provide golden-yellow fall colour. The three-flowered maple (*A. triflorum*) and the paperbark maple (*A. griseum*) have tripartite leaves and attractive peeling bark, in the former tannish and in the latter copper brown.

The ash-leaved maple, or box elder (*q.v.*), is a fast-growing tree of limited landscape use. The Norway maple (*A. platanoides*), a handsome, dense, round-headed tree, has spectacular greenish-yellow flower clusters in early spring; many cultivated varieties are available with unusual leaf colour (red, maroon, bronze, or purple) and growth form (columnar, globular, or pyramidal).

Large maples, usually in excess of 30 metres high, that are much planted for shade include the sugar (*q.v.; A. saccharum*), silver (*A. saccharinum*), and red (*A. rubrum*) maples. The Oregon, or bigleaf, maple (*A. macrophyllum*) provides commercially valuable wood darker than that of other maples; it shows bright-orange fall foliage. The Sycamore maple (*A. pseudoplatanus*), an important shade and timber tree in Europe, has many ornamental varieties.

In one group of maples, the vertically striped silvery-white young bark provides an attractive winter landscaping feature. These trees are the striped maple (*A. pennsylvanicum*), the red snake-bark maple (*A. capillipes*), the Her's maple (*A. hersii*), and the David's maple (*A. davidii*). The chalk maple, with whitish bark, is sometimes classified as *A. leucoderme,* although some authorities consider it a subspecies of sugar maple.

The parlour maples, or flowering maples, are bedding and houseplants in the genus *Abutilon.*

Maple Creek, town, southwestern Saskatchewan, Canada, on Maple Creek, in the northern foothills of the Cypress Hills on the Trans-Canada Highway, near the Alberta border, 193 mi (311 km) west-southwest of Moose Jaw. Named for the maple trees that line the banks of the creek, the town originated after 1875, when a division of the North West Mounted Police established barracks (Fort Walsh, now restored within a national historic park) nearby. After the railroad arrived in 1882, Maple Creek grew as a ranching town and cattle-shipping station, and, in addition, it is now a grain and dairy centre. It has a historical museum and is a gateway to Cypress Hills Provincial Park, 18 miles (29 km) south. Inc. village, 1896; town, 1903. Pop. (1996) 2,307.

maple syrup, sweet-water sap of certain North American maple trees, chiefly the sugar maple, *Acer saccharum,* but also the black maple, *Acer nigrum.* It was utilized by the Indians of the Great Lakes and St. Lawrence River regions prior to the arrival of European settlers and is still produced solely in North America.

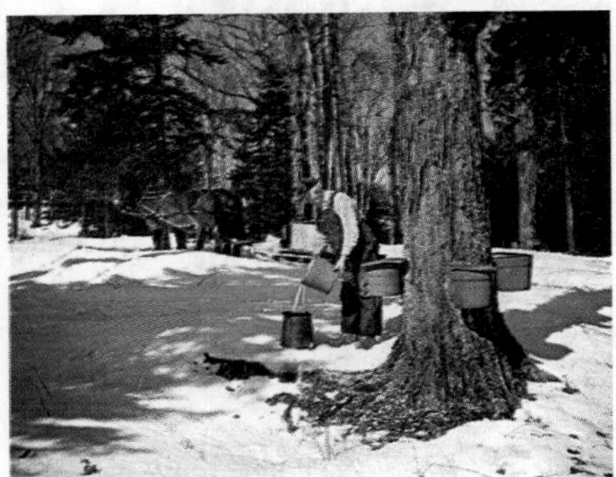

Tapping maple trees for syrup in Vermont
Bob Holland—Shostal

The sweet-water sap from which maple syrup is made is different from the circulatory sap of the growing tree. When the tree is dormant, the sap will flow from any wound in the sapwood, such as a taphole, each time a period of freezing is followed by a period of thawing. The sap contains 1½ to 3 percent solids, mostly sucrose, but does not contain the colour or flavour of maple syrup, which are imparted to the sap as it is concentrated by evaporation in open pans. About 30 to 50 gallons (115 to 190 litres) of sap yield one gallon of syrup.

Commercial quantities of maple syrup are produced, in order of amounts, in Quebec, Vermont, New York, Ontario, Wisconsin, Ohio, Michigan, New Hampshire, Pennsylvania, Massachusetts, and Maine. Maple products are similar in quality over the different areas. The major products are pure and blended brown table syrups, confections, toppings for ice cream, flavourings, and casing for tobacco. The best-known use of maple syrup is as a sweet topping for pancakes and waffles.

mapping, in mathematics, a function *f* between two topological spaces *A* and *B* that is continuous, meaning that the function sends points that were close together in *A* to points that are close together in *B. See* function.

Mapplethorpe, Robert (b. Nov. 4, 1946, New York, N.Y., U.S.—d. March 9, 1989, Boston, Mass.), American photographer who was noted for austere photographs of flowers, celebrities, and male nudes; among the latter were some that proved controversial because of their explicitly homoerotic and sadomasochistic themes.

Mapplethorpe attended the Pratt Institute in New York City (1963–70). By the mid-1970s he received critical attention for his elegant black-and-white photographs. During this period he pursued what were to remain his favourite subjects throughout his career: still lifes, flowers, portraits of friends and celebrities, such as poet and singer Patti Smith, and homoerotic depictions of the male body. His compositions were generally stark and his combination of cold studio light and precise focus created dramatic tonal contrasts. While these effects rendered still lifes with an almost Vermeer-like coolness, these same techniques rendered homosexual imagery in a manner that some found shocking. His muscular male models were generally framed against plain backdrops, sometimes engaged in sexual activity or posed with sadomasochistic props. His clear, unflinching style challenged viewers to confront this imagery. Moreover, the combination of his choice of subject matter with the photographs' formal beauty and grounding in artistic traditions created a tension for many between classifying the work as pornography or as art.

Mapplethorpe's reputation increased in the 1980s, and he began to focus more on flowers and celebrity portraits than on the overtly sexual subject matter of his earlier output. His work was exhibited internationally and featured in several major monographs. When he contracted the AIDS virus, Mapplethorpe chronicled his illness in a harrowing series of self-portraits.

A posthumous retrospective exhibition planned for the Corcoran Gallery in Washington, D.C., entitled "Robert Mapplethorpe: The Perfect Moment," stirred a political debate in 1990 that caused the museum to cancel the show. Because the exhibition was partly funded by a grant from the National Endowment for the Arts (NEA), the exhibit sparked a debate about government subsidies of "obscene" art and provoked Congress to enact restrictions on future NEA grants. Also in 1990, the director of the Contemporary Arts Center in Cincinnati, Ohio, was arrested but later acquitted of obscenity charges for displaying the same Mapplethorpe exhibition. Mapplethorpe's reptuation as one of his era's most talented—and most provocative—photographers continued into the turn of the 21st century.

mappō, in Japanese Buddhism, the age of the degeneration of the Buddha's law, which some believe to be the current age in human history. Ways of coping with the age of *mappō* were a particular concern of Japanese Buddhists during the Kamakura period (1192–1333) and were an important factor in the rise of new sects, such as Jōdo-shū and Nichiren and Zen Buddhism. These new sects taught a simpler, more immediate means of salvation than the more highly ritualistic, institutionalized forms of Buddhism that preceded them.

According to a view of cosmic history widely held in almost all Buddhist countries, the period following the death of the Buddha is divisible into three ages: the age of the "true law" (Sanskrit *saddharma,* Japanese *shōbō*); the age of the "copied law" (Sanskrit *pratirūpadharma,* Japanese *zōbō*); and the age of the "latter law," or the "degeneration of the law" (Sanskrit *paścimadharma,* Japanese *mappō*). A new period, in which the true faith will again flower, will be ushered in some time in the future by the bodhisattva (Buddha-to-be) Maitreya (Japanese Miroku).

The length of the three periods depends on the interpretation given various texts; according to some reckonings the first age lasted 1,000 years, the second age for another 1,000 years, and the third age will continue for 10,000 years. Assuming the date of the Buddha's death to be 949 BC, Japanese Buddhists calculated that the age of *mappō* began about AD 1052.

Mapu, Abraham (b. Jan. 10, 1808, near Kovno, Lithuania, Russian Empire—d. Oct. 9, 1867, Königsberg, East Prussia [now Kaliningrad, Russia]), author of the first Hebrew novel, *Ahavat Ziyyon* (1853; *Annou: Prince and Peasant*), an idyllic historical romance set in the days of the prophet Isaiah. Couched in florid biblical language, it artfully depicts pastoral life in ancient Israel; the book attained immediate popularity and was later translated into several languages.

A teacher of religion and German, Mapu was an influential advocate of the Haskalah, or Enlightenment, movement. Influenced stylistically by Victor Hugo and Eugène Sue, Mapu's novels romanticized a sovereign Israel and indirectly paved the way for the revival of Jewish nationalism and the Zionist movement. Other novels include *ʿAyiṭ tzavuaʿ* (1858–69; "The Hypocrite"), an attack on social and religious injustice in the ghetto; *Ashmat Shomron* (1865; "Guilt of Samaria"), a biblical epic about the hostility between Jerusalem and Samaria in the time of King Ahaz; and *Ḥoze ḥezyonot* (1869; "The Visionary"), an exposé of Ḥasidism, which was confiscated by religious authorities.

Mapuche, the most numerous group of Indians in South America. They numbered more than 1,400,000 at the turn of the 21st century. Most inhabit the Central Valley of Chile, south of the Bío-Bío River. A smaller group lives in Neuquén *provincia,* west-central Argentina. Historically known as Araucanians, the Mapuche were one of three groups—Picunche, Mapuche, Huilliche—identified by Spanish ethnographers. All Araucanians now identify themselves as Mapuche.

In the pre-Spanish period, the Mapuche lived in scattered farming villages throughout the Central Valley. Each settlement had a cacique, or chief, whose authority did not generally extend beyond his own village. They cultivated corn (maize), beans, squash, potatoes, chili peppers, and other vegetables and fished, hunted, and kept guinea pigs for meat. They kept llamas as pack animals and as a source of wool. A man's wealth was reckoned in terms of the size of his llama herd.

The Mapuche are famous for their 350-year struggle against Spanish and, later, Chilean domination. To resist the Spanish in the 16th, 17th, and 18th centuries, the Mapuche reorganized their traditional way of life. Widely separated villages formed military, political, and economic alliances; Mapuche warriors learned to use the horse against the Spanish; and Mapuche leaders such as Lautaro emerged as innovative and effective strategists.

In the 1800s, after Chile became independent of Spain, the Chilean government settled the Mapuche on reservations. For more than 100 years, the Mapuche held and farmed the reservation land collectively, and individual Mapuche could not lose their land to creditors. In the early 1980s, the Chilean government transferred ownership of reservation land to individual Mapuche, who now stand to lose their property and their means of livelihood if they are unable to repay debts. Since the Mapuche have never practiced a highly intensive or productive form of agriculture, they are often forced to go into debt for agricultural supplies and crop seeds.

Maputo, formerly (until 1976) LOURENÇO MARQUES, port city and capital of Mozambique. It lies along the north bank of Espírito Santo Estuary of Delagoa Bay, an inlet of the Indian Ocean. Maputo derived its former name from the Portuguese trader who first explored the region in 1544. The town developed around a Portuguese fortress completed in 1787. Created a city town in 1887, it superseded the town of Moçambique as the capital of Portuguese East Africa in 1907.

Maputo has a healthful climate, tempered by sea breezes. The city has a natural history museum and a university (1962). Its fine bathing beaches made it a popular resort for white South Africans and Rhodesians before Mozambique became independent in 1975; thereafter, revenues from tourism, once a major economic factor, virtually ended.

The port, one of the most important in East Africa, before independence handled transit trade from the mines and industries of South Africa, Swaziland, and Rhodesia, with which it has rail and road connections. After the frontier with Rhodesia was closed, and as Mozambique–South African relations became increasingly strained, the port suffered. Local industries include brewing, shipbuilding and repair, fish canning, iron working, and the manufacture of cement, textiles, and other goods. Pop. (2000 est.) 1,018,938.

Maputo River, Portuguese RIO MAPUTO, river formed by the confluence in southwestern Mozambique of the Great Usutu River (flowing from Swaziland) and the Pongola River (flowing from South Africa). From the confluence it flows about 50 miles (80 km) northeastward to enter Delagoa Bay, 14 miles (23 km) south-southeast of the city of Maputo. It is navigable along its entire course.

maqām (Arabic: "place of residence"), a spiritual stage that periodically marks the long path followed by Muslim mystics (Ṣūfīs) leading to the vision of and union with God. The Ṣūfī progresses by means of his own *mujāhadah* (work, or self-mortification) and through the help and guidance of the masters (sheikhs). In each *maqām* the Ṣūfī strives to purify himself from all worldly inclination and to prepare himself to attain an ever-higher spiritual level.

The order and number of the *māqams* are not uniform among all Ṣūfīs. The majority, however, agree on seven major *maqāms*: (1) the *maqām* of *tawbah* (repentance), which does not mean remembrance of sins and atonement for them but rather forgetting them along with everything that distracts from the love of God; (2) the *maqām* of *wara'* (fear of the Lord), which is not fear of hellfire but rather the dread of being veiled eternally from God; (3) the *maqām* of *zuhd* (renunciation, or detachment), which means that the person is devoid of possessions and his heart is without acquisitiveness; (4) the *maqām* of *faqr* (poverty), in which he asserts his independence of worldly possessions and his need of God alone; (5) the *maqām* of *ṣabr* (patience), the art of steadfastness; (6) the *maqām* of *tawakkul* (trust, or surrender), in which the Ṣūfī knows that he cannot be discouraged by hardships and pain, for he is in total submission to God's will and finds joy even in his sorrows; (7) the *maqām* of *riḍā* (satisfaction), a state of quiet contentment and joy that comes from the anticipation of the long-sought union.

maqām, plural MAQĀMĀT, in Islāmic music, a set of pitches and of characteristic melodic elements, or motives, and a traditional pattern of their use, forming a system for the melodic and tonal construction of performances. A *maqām* can be represented by a seven-tone scale. The number of *maqāmāt* in use has varied through history, with more than 100 described in the literature. The division of the octave into intervals has also varied historically.

A melodic motive is based within a unit, or span of four notes, and each *maqām* has a typical pattern of motion among the units. The tonal characteristics of the *maqām* serve as a guide for improvisation, which usually proceeds toward successively higher pitch levels.

The *maqām* is established during the solo prelude to an instrumental performance, before the accompanying instruments enter. Later in a piece, modulations to different *maqāmāt* are possible but with a final return to the original scale. In a suite, a common form in Arabic music, all sections are performed in the same *maqām*. By guiding the formation of melody, the *maqāmāt* set the moods of pieces and thus have traditionally been associated with the signs of the zodiac, the humours, and the elements. Present-day Arabic, Turkish, and Iranian music developed from the Islāmic tradition. *Compare dastgah.*

maqāmah (Arabic: "assembly"), Arabic literary genre in which entertaining anecdotes, often about rogues, mountebanks, and beggars, written in an elegant, rhymed prose (*saj'*), are presented in a dramatic or narrative context most suitable for the display of the author's eloquence, wit, and erudition.

The first collection of such writings, which make no pretense of being factual, was the *Maqāmāt* of al-Hamadhānī (d. 1008). It consists mainly of picaresque stories in alternating prose and verse woven round two imaginary characters. The genre was revived and finally established in the 11th century by al-Ḥarīrī of Basra (Iraq), whose *Maqāmāt,* closely imitating al-Hamadhānī's, is regarded as a masterpiece of literary style and learning.

Maqdisī, al-, in full MUḤAMMAD IBN AḤMAD AL-MAQDISĪ, also called AL-MUQADDASĪ (b. *c.* 946—d. *c.* 1000), Arab traveler, geographer, and author of a noted work based on personal observations of the populations, manners, and economic life of the various inhabitants of the lands of Islām, *Aḥson at-taqāsīm fi ma'rifat al-aqālīm* (985; "The Best of Classification for the Knowledge of Regions").

Maqtūl, al-: *see* Suhrawardī, as-.

maquiladora, any foreign-owned assembly plant in Mexico that imports and assembles duty-free components for export. The plant owner is thus able to take advantage of low-cost Mexican labour and to pay duty only on the "value added," that is, on the difference between the value of the finished product and the sum total value of the foreign-made components. The vast majority of *maquiladoras* are owned and operated by U.S. companies.

Maquiladoras originated in Mexico in the 1960s; by the late 20th century they employed hundreds of thousands of Mexican workers. Most of the plants are located in the border towns of northern Mexico. While they provided employment and significant foreign-exchange earnings for Mexico's troubled economy and helped U.S. manufacturers compete with the prices of goods produced by low-wage East Asian labour, they also created competition for a certain number of American workers. By the mid-1980s Japanese companies had begun to participate in the *maquiladora* system.

maquis, plural MAQUIS, Italian MACCHIA, plural MACCHIE, a scrubland vegetation of the Mediterranean region, composed primarily of leathery, broad-leaved evergreen shrubs or small trees. Garigue, or garrigue, a poorer version of this vegetation, is found in areas with a thin, rocky soil. Maquis occurs primarily on the lower slopes of mountains bordering the Mediterranean Sea. Many of the shrubs are aromatic, such as mints, laurels, and myrtles. Olives, figs, and other small trees are scattered throughout the area and often form open forests if undisturbed by humans.

Mar, EARLS OF, titled Scottish nobility, in the family Erskine, grouped below chronologically and indicated by the symbol •.

• Mar, John Erskine, 1st (and 18th) Earl of (d. Oct. 29, 1572, Stirling, Stirling, Scot.), Scottish lord who played a major role in deposing Mary Stuart, Queen of Scots (reigned 1542–67), and gaining the crown for her infant son James VI (later James I of England); Mar was regent for James in 1571–72.

Erskine's father, John, 5th Lord Erskine (d. 1555), was guardian for King James V (reigned 1513–42) during his minority and for Mary Stuart, the king's daughter and successor. A moderate Protestant, Erskine worked for a peaceful settlement during the armed struggle (1559–60) between Scotland's Protestant nobles and the regent, Mary of Lorraine, Mary Stuart's Roman Catholic mother (d. 1560). During the struggle he controlled the crucial Edinburgh Castle. Hence Mary Stuart appointed him to the Privy Council when she began her personal rule in Scotland in 1561.

In 1565 Erskine supported her ill-fated marriage to the treacherous Henry, Lord Darnley

1st Earl of Mar, portrait by an unknown artist; in the Scottish National Portrait Gallery, Edinburgh

By courtesy of the Scottish National Portrait Gallery, Edinburgh

(d. 1567). Mary granted him the earldom of Mar, thus substantiating the claims of his ancestors; and in 1566 she appointed him guardian of her newborn son, Prince James. Thereafter, he devoted himself to James's interests in the conflict between the supporters of James and Mary. Mar prevented James from falling into the hands of Mary's third husband, James Hepburn, 4th Earl of Bothwell, and he was a leader of the nobles who drove Bothwell from England (June 1567), deposed Mary (July 24), and made James king. Chosen regent of Scotland in 1571, he was succeeded upon his death by James Douglas, 4th Earl of Morton.

• Mar, John Erskine, 2nd (and 19th) Earl of (b. *c.* 1558—d. Dec. 14, 1634, Stirling, Stirling, Scot.), Scottish politician and friend of King James VI; he helped James govern Scotland both before and after James ascended the English throne (as James I) in 1603.

Erskine inherited the earldom of Mar in 1572 upon the death of his father, John, 1st (and 18th) Earl of Mar, who had become regent for the five-year-old James VI in 1571. Mar grew up with James at Stirling Castle, and in 1578 he made himself James's guardian. When his influence over the young king was challenged by Esmé Stewart, 1st Duke of Lennox, and James Stewart, Earl of Arran, Mar and several other lords seized James at Perth and took him to Ruthven Castle, Inverness. Ten months later, in June 1583, the king escaped. Arran then became ascendant; and in 1584 Mar, after a brief seizure of Stirling Castle in the

2nd Earl of Mar, portrait by an unknown artist, 1626; on loan to the Scottish National Portrait Gallery, Edinburgh

By courtesy of Rt. Hon. Lord Elibank

hope of prompting English intervention, was forced to flee to England, where he received the backing of Queen Elizabeth I. In November 1585 Mar returned to Scotland, banished Arran, and was reconciled with James, becoming one of the leading royal ministers. James made him guardian for his son, Prince Henry (1594–1612), in 1594.

After the death of Elizabeth and the accession of James to the English throne, Mar continued to exercise great influence in Scottish affairs. He served as treasurer of Scotland from 1616 to 1630.

• Mar, John Erskine, 6th earl of, LORD ERSKINE (b. February 1675, Alloa, Clackmannanshire, Scot.—d. May 1732, Aachen [Germany]), Scottish noble who led the Jacobite rebellion of 1715, an unsuccessful attempt to gain the British crown for James Edward, the Old Pretender, son of the deposed Stuart monarch James II. Because Mar shifted his political allegiances frequently, he earned the nickname "Bobbing John."

6th earl of Mar, detail of an india ink drawing by Sir Godfrey Kneller; in the Scottish National Portrait Gallery, Edinburgh

By courtesy of the Scottish National Portrait Gallery, Edinburgh

Mar inherited his father's earldom in 1689 and was secretary of state for Scotland and keeper of the signet under Queen Anne (reigned 1702–14). He turned to Jacobitism after he was dismissed from office on the accession of King George I in 1714. In August 1715 he traveled secretly to Scotland and organized an uprising in the Highlands. He proclaimed James king of Great Britain at Braemar on September 6 and promised that James would restore the traditional constitution of Scotland. Although some 10,000–12,000 men rallied to the pretender's cause, Mar, who had assumed the role of James's commander in chief, was defeated by a smaller army under John Campbell, 2nd duke of Argyll, at Sheriffmuir, in Perth county, on November 13. Although the pretender arrived in Scotland on December 22, the rebellion soon collapsed. In February 1716 Mar fled to France and then on to Rome with James Edward, who lavished him with titles, including that of duke of Mar (unrecognized in Britain). Despite these considerable attentions, Mar intrigued against James, and by 1725 he was no longer welcome at James's court in exile.

Mar, Serra do (Portuguese: "Mountain Range of the Sea"), great escarpment on the eastern margins of the Brazilian Highlands, which descend abruptly to the Atlantic coast. It extends for about 1,600 miles (2,600 km) from Rio Grande do Sul *estado* ("state") all the way northward to Bahia *estado* but is known as the Serra do Mar only in the southern section. The escarpment comprises such ranges as the Mantiqueira and Órgãos to the north of Rio de Janeiro, the Espinhaço and Aimorés mountains of Minas Gerais *estado,* and the Diamantina Upland of Bahia *estado.* Sections of these highlands also are known separately or collectively as the Geral Mountains. The range averages between 2,600 and 3,000 feet (800 and 900 m), but in Rio de Janeiro *estado* it is surmounted by the Órgãos Mountains (7,365 feet [2,245 m]), which overlook Guanabara Bay. Until the railroads passed over it in the 19th century, the Serra do Mar historically formed a major barrier to the development of Brazil's vast interior. The escarpment was originally covered by dense tropical and subtropical forests.

Sections of the railroad and highway that ascend the Serra do Mar between Santos and São Paulo, Braz.

Dilson Martins

Mar Chiquita, Lake, Spanish LAGUNA MAR CHIQUITA, saline lake at the southern edge of the Gran Chaco in northeastern Córdoba *provincia,* north-central Argentina. It is about 45 miles (70 km) long and 15 miles (24 km) wide with an area of almost 775 square miles (2,000 square km). Lake Mar Chiquita is fed by the rivers Primero and Segundo (from the southwest) and Dulce (from the north) during the flood season but has no outlet to the east. Several small islands, the largest of which is El Médano, lie in the lake. On the southern shore is the health resort of Miramar. To the north are vast expanses of saline marshes.

Mar del Plata, coastal city, southeastern Buenos Aires *provincia,* east-central Argentina. Juan de Garay, the second founder of Buenos Aires, first explored the coastal area of Mar del Plata in 1581. In 1746 Father Thomas Falkner and Father José Cardiel founded the Indian work mission Nuestra Señora del Pilar ("Our Lady of Pilar") at the site of the present-day city. Fear of attack by the Indian chief Cangapol caused the mission to be abandoned in 1751. The Portuguese explorer Jose Coelho Mierelles, granted land as *poblador* (settler) of Mar del Plata, colonized the region in 1856, establishing a fishing village, La Peregrina ("The Pilgrim"). Mierelles started the first meat-salting plant in the area in 1857. Meat salting remained important throughout the Buenos Aires region until the introduction of refrigeration in the late 19th century. Mar del Plata was founded in 1874, after Patriço Peralta Ramos acquired three landholdings from Mierelles in 1860 and promoted the sites as a seaside resort. In 1907 Mar del Plata was declared a city and has since that time developed as one of Argentina's foremost ocean-resort areas.

Beach and shoreline at Mar del Plata, Arg.

Ewing Krainin—Photo Researchers

Mar del Plata's primary commercial activities revolve around tourism. The city's 5 miles (8 km) of beaches attract huge crowds during the summer and a large number of people during the remainder of the year as well. The tourist season is from November to mid-April. Mar del Plata is famous for its luxurious casino, one of the largest in the world. After tourism, the chief economic activities are building construction, textiles, and commercial fishing and canning. The National University of Mar del Plata (1961) is located in the city. There are museums of art and natural science. The city is served well by highway, railway, and air transport to Buenos Aires and other major cities of Argentina. Pop. (1991) 519,707.

A list of the abbreviations used in the MICROPAEDIA *will be found at the end of this volume*

Mar-pa, also called MAR-PA OF LHOBRAG, or DVAGS-PO LHA-RJE ("Physician of Dvags-po") (b. 1012, Lhobrag, Tibet—d. 1096, Tibet), one of the foremost Tibetan translators of Indian Vajrayāna (or Tantric) Buddhist texts, a significant figure in the revival of Buddhism in Tibet.

The chief source of information on the life of Mar-pa is a 14th-century biography written by the "Mad Yogin of Tsang." According to it, Mar-pa was born of wealthy parents. He had a violent nature and was sent to a Tibetan monastery to study Buddhism. Eventually he went to India, where he studied for 10 years under the Indian yogi Nāropa. Mar-pa's return to Tibet was celebrated. He married, began to teach, and assumed the life of a wealthy farmer. He undertook another period of study with Nāropa in India, this time for six years. When he returned to Tibet, he gathered disciples, among them Mi-la ras-pa, who later founded the Bka'-brgyud-pa (Kagyupa; "Transmitted Command") sect. After a third stay in India, Mar-pa spent the remainder of his life in Tibet, integrating the management of his properties with the teaching of his disciples.

Among Mar-pa's notable translations are several works included in the *Bka'-'gyur* ("Translations of the Word of the Buddha") and the *Bstan-'gyur* ("Translations of Teachings"). He also introduced to Tibet the mystical songs (*dohās*) of the Indian Tantric tradition, later used with great skill by Mi-la ras-pa and his followers.

Mar Samuel (Jewish scholar): *see* Samuel of Nehardea.

Māra, the Buddhist "Lord of the Senses," who was the Buddha's temptor on several occasions. When the bodhisattva Gautama seated himself under the Bo tree to await Enlightenment, the evil Māra appeared first in the guise of a messenger bringing the news that a rival, Devadatta, had usurped the Śākya throne from Gautama's family. Next Māra sent forth a great storm of rain, rocks, ashes, and darkness, frightening away all the gods who had gathered to honour the future Buddha. He challenged Gautama's right to sit beneath the tree, provoking the future Buddha to call upon the earth to give witness to his previous charities (an act often represented in sculpture). Māra sent forth his three daughters, Tṛṣṇā, Rati, and Rāga (thirst, desire, and delight), to seduce Gautama, but to no avail. (Versions of the story differ in placing the temptation by the daughters before or after Buddha's Enlightenment.) After the Buddha had achieved supreme Enlightenment, he experienced doubt as to whether the truth could

Buddha assaulted by Māra and his demon horde, high-relief sculpture from Gandhara; in the Rijksmuseum voor Volkenkunde, Leiden, Neth.

By courtesy of Rijksmuseum voor Volkenkunde, Leiden, The Netherlands

be understood by men, and Māra pressed him to abandon any attempts to preach. But when the gods implored him to preach the law, the Buddha put aside his doubts.

mara, South American rodent, a species of cavy (*q.v.*).

Mara, Gertrud Elisabeth, *née* SCHMELING (b. Feb. 23, 1749, Kassel, Landgraviate Hesse-Kassel [Germany]—d. Jan. 20, 1833, Tallinn, Estonia, Russian Empire), German soprano of great technical ability, who was one of the few non-Italians of the time to gain a great international reputation.

A child prodigy, Schmeling gave violin recitals accompanied by her father, a violin maker, in Vienna and London, where at the age of 10 she played for the queen. At the advice of an attendant at court, she began to study voice under Pietro Paradisi in London. She sang in Johann Hiller's concerts in Leipzig in 1766, performed with the Dresden Opera, then moved to Berlin, where, overcoming Frederick II's dislike for German singers, she was engaged in 1771 by the court opera. In 1774 she married a cellist, Johann Baptist Mara, and the couple, seeking to escape the despotic prince's court, requested permission to leave the country. They escaped without retribution in 1779.

In 1780 Mara toured the continent, engaging in a fierce rivalry with Luiza Todi in Paris before moving to London in 1784. She was outstandingly successful there in 1787 as Cleopatra in George Frideric Handel's *Giulio Cesare*. She sang in Venice and Turin in 1788, then returned to London. She was praised for her performances in the oratorios of Handel and Joseph Haydn. In 1803 she moved to Moscow, where she acquired considerable property, only to lose it during the burning of the city in 1812. Her last years were spent in Tallinn, where she gave music lessons.

marabou, also called MARABOU STORK (*Leptoptilos crumeniferus*), large African bird of the stork family, Ciconiidae (order Ciconiiformes). The marabou is the largest stork, 150 cm (5 feet) tall with a wingspread of 2.6 m (8½ feet). Mainly gray and white, it has a naked pinkish head and neck, a pendant, reddish, inflatable throat pouch, and a straight,

Marabou stork (*Leptoptilos crumeniferus*)

M.P. Kahl

heavy bill. Marabous eat carrion, often feeding with vultures, which they dominate.

marabout, Arabic MURĀBIṬ ("one who is garrisoned"), originally, in North Africa, member of a Muslim religious community living in a *ribāṭ*, a fortified monastery, serving both religious and military functions. Men who possessed certain religious qualifications, such as the reciters of the Qur'ān (*qurrā'*), transmitters of Ḥadith (*muḥaddithūn*), jurists of Islāmic law (*fuqahā'*), and ascetics, lived in the *ribāṭ* and were held in honour by the common people. When Islām spread to western Africa in the 12th century, its propagators became known as al-Murābiṭūn (Almoravids), and every missionary who organized a group of disciples became known as a *murābiṭ*. In the 14th century, when Ṣūfism (mysticism) pervaded Muslim religious life, the *murābiṭ*, in the Maghrib, came to be the designation for any preacher calling for the formation of Ṣūfī fraternities according to the "order" (*ṭarīqah*) of Abū Madyan. Thus, the word lost all trace of its original literal meaning of military defense, and in Algeria *murābiṭ* came to be used for the tomb, usually domed, in which a pious man is buried.

Maracaibo, city, capital of Zulia *estado* ("state"), northwestern Venezuela, the country's second largest city and one of its largest seaports. On the western shore of the channel connecting Lake Maracaibo with the Gulf of Venezuela, it is in a basin surrounded by higher land that excludes the steady trade winds and suffers from high temperatures (average daily highs are in the 90s Fahrenheit [30s Celsius]) and high humidity. Founded in 1571 as Nueva Zamora, the city became a transshipment point for inland settlements after Gibraltar, at the head of the lake, was

Petroleum refinery in Maracaibo, Venezuela

Ray Halin—Photo Researchers/EB Inc.

destroyed by pirates in 1669. Although Maracaibo changed hands several times during Venezuela's struggle for independence from Spain, it was generally less involved in the wars than were eastern and central Venezuela.

Until petroleum was discovered in 1917, the city was a small coffee port. Within a decade it became the oil metropolis of Venezuela and South America. It has remained a city of contrasts—old Spanish culture and modern business, ancient Indian folklore and distinctive modern architecture. The dredging of the channel connecting the lake with the Caribbean in the late 1950s stimulated the economy of all of northwestern Venezuela and quickened the maritime life of the city. Important industries, other than the large and rapidly growing petrochemical industry, include construction, food, soaps, woven goods, beverages, and rope. The University of Zulia was established at Maracaibo in 1946. The city is linked by highway to each of the major urban centres of northern Venezuela; a bridge 5 miles (8 km) long spans the channel 3 miles (5 km) south of Maracaibo. Pop. (1987 est.) 1,124,432.

Maracaibo, Lake, Spanish LAGO DE MARACAIBO, large inlet of the Caribbean Sea, lying in the Maracaibo Basin of northwestern Venezuela. It covers an area of about 5,130 square miles (13,280 square km), extending southward for 130 miles (210 km) from the Gulf of Venezuela and reaching a width of 75 miles (121 km). Many rivers flow into the lake, the most important being the Catatumbo River, a transportation artery for products from the adjacent regions and from the Colombian-Venezuelan highlands. The lake water in the southern portion is fresh, but a stronger tidal influence makes the northern waters somewhat brackish. The lake is quite shallow, except toward the south, and it is surrounded by swampy lowlands. A bar at the mouth of the lake extending some 16 miles (26 km) for many years restricted navigation to vessels drawing less than 13 feet (4 m) of water. After constant dredging in the 1930s had increased the depth to 25 feet, a 2-mile-long stone breakwater and a 35-foot-deep channel were completed in 1957 to accommodate oceangoing ships and tankers.

Lake Maracaibo is one of the world's richest and most centrally located petroleum-producing regions. The first productive well was drilled in 1917, and the productive area has come to include a 65-mile strip along the eastern shore, extending 20 miles out into the lake. Thousands of derricks protrude from the water, and many more line the shore, while underwater pipelines transport the petroleum to storage tanks on the land. The lake's basin supplies about two-thirds of the total Venezuelan petroleum output. Most of the industry was developed by foreign (chiefly American, British, and Dutch) investment, with very few locally owned wells, but in 1975 the petroleum industry was nationalized. Natural gas is also obtained.

Maracay, city, capital of Aragua *estado* ("state"), northern Venezuela. In the central highlands at 1,500 feet (460 m) above sea level and 70 miles (110 km) southwest of Caracas, Maracay rose to fame when the dictator Juan Vicente Gómez determined to make the city the cultural and social centre of the nation. During his long reign (1908–35), Gómez initiated the construction of a number of projects, including a bullring (an exact replica of the Seville bullring), airports, and an opera house. In addition to being a commercial centre for the agricultural and pastoral hinterland, Maracay has become a major industrial centre and one of Venezuela's largest cities. Textiles, sugar, paper, rayon, rubber, foodstuffs, and cement are the principal manufactures. Maracay lies on the Pan-American Highway and has excellent transport facilities. Pop. (2001 prelim.) 394,000.

Maradi, town, south-central Niger, western Africa. The town is located on the banks of the Maradi, a seasonal stream, in a region consisting largely of a flat sandy plain (1,000 to 1,650 feet [300 to 500 m] in elevation) with isolated sandstone bluffs. Maradi was destroyed by floods in 1945 and subsequently was rebuilt on higher ground. It has peanut- (groundnut-) and cotton-processing industries. Leather tanning is also important—the Maradi School of Leather and Hides gives training in methods of skin dressing. The government-sponsored Maradi Training Centre supplies fertilizers and seed and imparts training in methods of agriculture. North of Maradi annual rainfall is generally less than 12 inches (300 mm), and thus the surrounding area marks the extreme northern limit of nonirrigated cultivation in Niger; peanuts, cassava, and cotton are grown in the relatively wet south, while less-important millet, sorghum, and sheep- and goat-raising are pursued in the drier north. The Maradi, Kaba, and Vallée de Tarka are the major seasonal streams (*goulbins*), flowing in a southwesterly direction, and aid cultivation in the area. The region is chiefly inhabited by the Hausa, sedentary farmers who are also skillful businessmen and traders. Maradi is a major junction on the all-weather trans-Niger (Niamey to Zinder) road opened in 1980. Pop. (2001 prelim.) 147,038.

Maradona, Diego Armando (b. Oct. 30, 1960, Lanus, Buenos Aires, Arg.), Argentine football (soccer) player, generally regarded as the top footballer of the 1980s and one of the greatest of all time. Renowned for his ability to control the ball and create scoring opportunities for himself and others, he led club teams to championships in Argentina, Italy, and Spain, and he starred on the Argentine national team that won the 1986 World Cup.

Maradona displayed football talent early, making his first division debut in 1976. The next year he debuted with the national team, becoming the youngest-ever Argentine international. However, he was excluded from the 1978 World Cup-winning squad because it was felt that he was still too young.

Maradona joined Boca Juniors in 1981 and immediately helped them gain the championship. He then moved to Europe, playing with Barcelona in 1982 (and winning the Spanish Cup in 1983), then Napoli (1984–91), where he enjoyed great success, raising the traditionally weak Naples side to the heights of Italian football. With Maradona the team won the league title and cup in 1987 and the league title again in 1990. Maradona's stint with Napoli came to an end when he was arrested in Argentina for cocaine possession and received a 15-month suspension from playing football. Next he played for Sevilla in Spain and Newell's Old Boys back in Argentina. In 1995 he returned to Boca Juniors and played his last match on Oct. 25, 1997.

Maradona's career with the Argentine national team included World Cup appearances in 1982, 1986, 1990, and 1994. He dominated the 1986 competition in Mexico. In a 2–1 quarterfinal victory over England, he scored two of the most memorable goals in World Cup history. The first was scored with his hand (the referee mistakenly thought the ball struck his head), a goal now remembered as the "Hand of God." The second saw Maradona dribble through a pack of English defenders and past the keeper before depositing the ball in the goal. He did not finish the 1994 World Cup because he tested positive for the drug ephedrine and was again suspended.

A tenacious midfielder, Maradona became a hero of the lower classes of Argentina (from which he hailed) and of southern Italy. An Internet poll conducted by the Fédération Internationale de Football Association named him the top player of the 20th century.

Marāgheh, also spelled MARĀGHAH, town in the Azerbaijan region of northwestern Iran. It lies in the shelter of Mount Sahand (12,100 feet [3,700 m]) in a well-watered valley. The town is the prosperous centre of a large fruit-growing area and exports dried fruits. Its modern development has been accelerated in recent decades. Once a Persian-speaking city, Marāgheh played a prominent role under several Turkish princes in the Middle Ages and also under the Mongol leader Hülegü (1256–65), whose capital it was. Five tomb towers dating from the 12th to the 14th century are the most notable monuments in the town; the earliest, the Sorkh Tomb (1147), is one of the finest examples of brickwork in Iran. West of the town are traces of an observatory (1259). The local building stone, known as Marāgheh marble, is of mainly yellow, pink, greenish, or milk-white colour, streaked with red and green veins; it is quarried mainly at Dehkhvāregān (Azar Shahr). Pop. (1996) 132,318.

Marais, Jean, in full JEAN-ALFRED VILLAIN-MARAIS (b. Dec. 11, 1913, Cherbourg, France—d. Nov. 8, 1998, Cannes), actor who was a protégé of French writer-director Jean Cocteau, and one of the most popular leading men in French films during the 1940s and '50s.

Marais was first attracted to the stage in high school but was turned down by the Paris Conservatory. After working as a photographer's apprentice, he began playing bit parts and walk-ons in film and on stage, making his motion-picture debut in 1933. Despite his handsome features, Marais had a thin voice and a limited acting ability that restricted the type and size of roles he played.

After meeting Jean Cocteau (1937), however, his career took an upward turn. Marais became Cocteau's male lead and made a notable appearance as an archetypal romantic hero, Tristan, in Cocteau's *L'Eternel retour* (1943; *The Eternal Return*).

Among the more than 70 films he appeared in are *La Belle et la bête* (1946; *Beauty and the Beast*), *Les Parents terribles* (1948; *The Storm Within*), *Orphée* (1950; *Orpheus*), and *Stealing Beauty* (1996), which was his last film.

Marais, Marin (b. March 31, 1656, Paris—d. Aug. 15, 1728, Paris), French composer who was also a virtuoso of the viola da gamba.

He studied viola da gamba and from 1685 played in the French royal orchestra. With Pascal Colasse he directed the orchestra of the Royal Academy of Music. He published several books of viol music, a genre in which he was the acknowledged master. He was also one of the first French composers to write trio sonatas. His instrumental music often bore descriptive titles like those used by François Couperin. His operas included *Ariane et Bacchus* (1696), *Alcyone* (1706), the most successful, and *Sémélé* (1709).

Marais's relationship with the composer Sainte-Colombe was fictionalized in the film *Tous les matins du monde* (1992).

Marais Theatre, French THÉÂTRE DU MARAIS, one of the major theatrical companies in 17th-century France. With the actor Montdory as its head, the company performed at various temporary theatres in Paris from 1629 before finding a permanent home in a converted tennis court in the Marais district in 1634. The Marais Theatre presented Pierre Corneille's early comedies and gave the first production of Corneille's *Le Cid* in 1637. It rapidly replaced the King's Players at the Hôtel de Bourgogne as the leading company of Paris. Bad health forced Montdory to leave the Marais Theatre in 1637, however, and under his successor, Floridor, the company turned increasingly to popular farces, usually featuring the comedian Jodelet.

The original Marais Theatre burned in 1644 and was rebuilt to accommodate the complex theatre machinery that had been growing increasingly popular in France. Floridor left the company in 1647 to join the Hôtel de Bourgogne troupe, and the actor Laroque assumed leadership. In an attempt to compete with the Bourgogne and Molière troupes, Laroque promoted spectacular productions, but little money was made, and in 1673 Louis XIV ordered the theatre closed. The Marais troupe was combined with the Molière troupe and moved to a theatre in the rue Guénégaud. In 1680 another royal order combined the Bourgogne troupe with that of the Guénégaud, creating the first modern national theatre—the Comédie-Française.

Marajó Island, Portuguese ILHA DE MARAJÓ, island, in the Amazon River delta, eastern Pará state, Brazil. It is the world's largest fluvial island (*i.e.,* one produced by sediments deposited by a stream or river). The island is 183 miles (295 km) long and 124 miles (200 km) wide, with an area of 15,500 square miles (40,100 square km). The main flow of the Amazon River passes to the north of Marajó, but numerous *furos,* or narrow channels, direct part of its water into the Pará River, an estuary that separates the island from the mainland to the south. Cattle and water buffalo graze in the savanna of eastern Marajó, which also contains a large number of archaeological mounds rich in pottery similar to that of pre-Columbian Andean cultures. Half of the island is flooded during the annual rainy season. Soure, a modern town and beach resort on the island's Atlantic coast, is linked to Belém, the state capital, by ferry.

Maramba (town, Zambia): *see* Livingstone.

Maran: *see* Karo, Joseph ben Ephraim.

Maranao, largest of the Muslim cultural-linguistic groups of the Philippines. Numbering almost 900,000 in the early 21st century, they live around Lake Lanao on the southern island of Mindanao. Rice farming is their main livelihood, along with metalworking and woodworking handicrafts.

Like the other Filipino Muslims, the Maranao differ markedly from the Christians, who make up the overwhelming majority of the country's population. Land is owned by the clan and controlled by local leaders known as *datus*. The customs of marriage and the family are Islāmic. The languages of all the Muslim groups are closely related to the languages of the central Philippines, which belong to the Austronesian (Malayo-Polynesian) family of languages.

Marandellas (town, Zimbabwe): *see* Marondera.

Maranhão, *estado* ("state") of northern Brazil, situated south of the equator and to the southeast of the Amazon River basin. About two-thirds of its area consists of a low, heavily wooded region, bordered by the Atlantic Ocean to the north. To the east and southeast lies Piauí state and to the west lie the states of Tocantins and Pará.

The higher plateaus in the southern section of the state are extensions of Brazil's northeastern massif (mountainous mass); the highest point, the Serra da Cinta, is 4,373 feet (1,333 m) in elevation. From these highlands a number of river systems run generally northeastward into the Atlantic. Several of them form a delta region around the capital city of São Luis, which stands on an island. The delta is bounded to the west by dense mangrove forests and to the east by areas of quicksand. The rivers in the state are navigable for much of their course, cutting through arable soils that support farming and cattle raising, the economic mainstays of Maranhão. The climate is hot and moist. There is a wet and a relatively dry season but never a rainless one.

Tupinambá Indians inhabited the Maranhão region when Europeans first explored the coasts in 1500 and when the region was included in land grants, known as captaincies, made by the Portuguese crown in 1534. In the decades that followed, rival European powers attempted to take possession of the territory. The first settlement was established by the French in 1594; later, in 1612, they also founded a colony on São Luis Island. The French were expelled by the Portuguese in 1615, but the Dutch succeeded in holding São Luis from 1641 to 1644.

In 1621 Maranhão and adjoining regions were united as the Estado do Maranhão, which remained independent of the southern captaincies and of Portuguese colonial administration until 1774, when the territory was formally made part of the Portuguese colony of Brazil. In 1823 Maranhão adhered to the newly independent empire of Brazil and, in 1889, to the newly proclaimed republic.

Maranhão was settled mainly by Jesuit missionaries, who introduced Roman Catholicism among the Tupinambás and introduced the pattern of agriculture and cattle raising that continues to characterize the local economy. The people of Maranhão represent a blend of Tupinambás, Europeans (mainly Portuguese), and the descendants of African slaves. There has been considerable racial intermarriage between these groups through the centuries, though in interior regions descendants of the original Indian population, known as caboclos, remain. Portuguese is the main written and spoken language, but it has been enriched by indigenous languages, just as Portuguese culture has been supplemented by local folklore. Most of the population is Roman Catholic.

Maranhão is an economically underdeveloped region, dependent largely on agriculture and cattle raising. The major industry is the extraction of oils and essences from plants. Palm oils from the babassu nut are a major export item, as is rice. Other important industries include food processing and steel manufacturing, centred in São Luis. There are bauxite deposits on Turiaçu Island, and petroleum discoveries have been made in the interior near the Tocantins border and in the northern part of the state. A hydroelectric facility was completed at Boa Esperança in 1970.

Itaqui Quay on São Luis Island is one of several modern shipping points on Maranhão's coasts, and the navigable river system permits extensive shipment from ports deep in the interior. A railway 250 miles (400 km) long links São Luis with Teresina, the capital of Piauí state. The road network is only partially paved. There are several commercial airports, of which the international airport at São Luis is by far the most important.

Medical facilities and health standards are relatively good. Occasional outbreaks of tropical disease rarely reach epidemic proportions. The state supports primary, secondary, and university education, in addition to which there are independent colleges, a number of technical institutes, and private educational institutions at lower levels.

Cultural institutions include the Historical and Artistic Museum of Maranhão and the Maranhão Historical and Geographical Institute. The best-known Maranhense writer was Antônio Gonçalves Dias (1823–64), a poet in the Romantic tradition versed in Maranhense lore, whose "Song of Exile" is renowned. Area 128,154 square miles (331,918 square km). Pop. (2003 est.) 5,873,655.

Marañón River, Spanish RÍO MARAÑÓN, headwater of the Amazon, rising in the snow-capped Andes above Lake Lauricocha in central Peru, about 100 miles (160 km) from the Pacific Ocean. It flows northwest across windswept plateaus 12,000 feet (3,650 m) high and carves a deep canyon between Andean ranges. As the Marañón passes through high jungle in its midcourse, it is marked by a series of unnavigable rapids and falls. Emerging from the most spectacular of these rapids, the Pongo de Manseriche, the river is only 575 feet (175 m) above sea level. For the rest of its 879-mile (1,415-km) course, it meanders eastward through hot, sparsely populated rain forest and receives the Huallaga River. It combines with the Ucayali River below Nauta to form the Amazon.

Marantaceae, the prayer plant family of the ginger order (Zingiberales), composed of about 31 genera and 550 species of rhizomatous perennial herbs that are native to moist or swampy tropical forests, particularly in the Americas. Members of the Marantaceae vary from plants with slender, reedlike stalks to leafy spreading herbs to dense bushes nearly 2 m (about 6.5 feet) high.

The smooth white rhizomes (underground stems) of some species, such as *Maranta arundinacea,* furnish the starch known as arrowroot. Other members of the family are popular ornamentals, such as the prayer plant (*M. leuconeura kerchoveana*), the water canna (*Thalia dealbata*), and species of the genus *Calathea. See also* prayer plant.

Maranville, Rabbit, byname of WALTER JAMES VINCENT MARANVILLE (b. Nov. 11, 1891, Springfield, Mass., U.S.—d. Jan. 5, 1954, Queens, New York, N.Y.), American professional National League baseball player (1912–35), who was rated as one of the finest shortstops of the game.

Maranville joined the Boston Braves in 1912, playing with them through the 1920 season. He batted and threw right-handed. The team in 1914 went from last place on the Fourth of July to win the pennant and the World Series. He played for the Pittsburgh Pirates (1921–24), the Chicago Cubs (1925), the Brooklyn Dodgers (1926), the St. Louis Cardinals (1927–28), and the Boston Braves (1929–35). He also managed parts of seasons for the Cubs (1925) and the Cardinals (1928) in the World Series. He was elected to the Baseball Hall of Fame in 1954.

Maranzano, Salvatore (b. 1868, Castellammare del Golfo, Sicily, Italy—d. Sept. 10, 1931, New York, N.Y., U.S.), American gangster of the Prohibition era, leader among the old-country-oriented Italians, known as "Moustache Petes," many of whom were former members of the Sicilian Mafia and Neapolitan Camorra.

Reared in Sicily, Maranzano immigrated to the United States after World War I and put together an organization of Sicilians with interests in bootlegging, gambling, and other rackets in New York City. In 1930–31 his gang and others headed by Castellammare-born mafiosi engaged in a bloody war—the Castellammare War—with New York's crime overlord, Joe (Giuseppe) Masseria. The internecine killings did not end until the execution of Masseria by his own men on April 15, 1931. Thereupon, Maranzano tried to establish himself as *capo di tutti capi* ("boss of all the bosses"). Each mob, or "family," already well-organized, would be reorganized with both a boss and an underboss and, under them, lieutenants and soldiers. Each family would respect the interests and territories of others, and disputes would be arbitrated. The system was adopted by the Five Families of New York City.

Maranzano himself survived only a few months. Killers hired by Lucky Luciano and Vito Genovese entered Maranzano's Park Avenue office and stabbed and shot him to death.

marasmus, a form of protein-calorie malnutrition, chiefly occurring among very young children. It is characterized by growth retardation (in weight more than in height) and progressive wasting of subcutaneous fat and muscle. Other symptoms include diarrhea; dehydration; behavioral changes; dry, loose skin; and dry, brittle hair. Marasmus can be treated with a high-calorie, protein-rich diet. Severe, prolonged marasmus may result in permanent mental retardation and impaired growth. *See also* kwashiorkor.

Marat, Jean-Paul (b. May 24, 1743, Boudry, near Neuchâtel, Switz.—d. July 13, 1793, Paris, France), French politician, physician, and journalist, a leader of the radical Montagnard faction during the French Revolution. He was assassinated in his bath by Charlotte Corday, a young Girondin conservative.

Marat, detail of a portrait by J. Boze, 1793; in the Museum of the History of Paris
Giraudon—Art Resource

Early scientific work. Marat, after obscure years in France and other European countries, became a well-known doctor in London in the 1770s and published a number of books on scientific and philosophical subjects. His *Essay on the Human Soul* (1771) had little success, but *A Philosophical Essay on Man* (1773) was translated into French and published in Amsterdam (1775–76). His early political works included *The Chains of Slavery* (1774), an attack on despotism addressed to British voters, in which (according to some) he first expounded the notion of an "aristocratic," or "court," plot; it would become the principal theme of a number of his great speeches and articles.

Returning to the Continent in 1777, Marat was appointed physician to the personal guards of the comte d'Artois (later Charles X), youngest brother of Louis XVI of France. At this time he seemed mainly interested in making a reputation for himself as a successful scientist. He wrote articles and experimented with fire, electricity, and light. His paper on electricity was honoured by the Royal Academy of Rouen in 1783. At the same time, he built up a practice among upper-middle-class and aristocratic patients. In 1783 he resigned from his medical post, probably intending to concentrate on his scientific career. In 1780 he published his *Plan de législation criminelle* ("Plan for Criminal Legislation"). Considered subversive, it was immediately suppressed by French authorities. It may be that this episode was the origin of his bitterness against the existing system, but he had already assimilated the ideas of such critics of the ancien régime as

Montesquieu and Jean-Jacques Rousseau and was corresponding with the American Revolutionary leader Benjamin Franklin. More serious, perhaps, was Marat's failure to be elected to the Académie des Sciences. Some historians, notably the American Louis Gottschalk, have concluded that he came to suffer from a "martyr complex," imagining himself persecuted by powerful enemies. Thinking that his work entitled him to a greater glory even than Sir Isaac Newton, he joined the opponents of the established social and scientific order. In the first weeks of 1789—the year that saw the beginning of the French Revolution—he published his pamphlet "Offrande à la Patrie" ("Offering to Our Country"), in which he indicated that he still believed that the monarchy was capable of solving France's problems. In a supplement published a few months later, though, he remarked that the king was chiefly concerned with his own financial problems and that he neglected the needs of the people; at the same time, Marat attacked those who proposed the British system of government as a model for France.

Attacks on the aristocracy. Beginning in September 1789, as editor of the newspaper *L'Ami du Peuple* ("The Friend of the People"), Marat became an influential voice in favour of the most radical and democratic measures, particularly in October, when the royal family was forcibly brought from Versailles to Paris by a mob. He particularly advocated preventive measures against aristocrats, whom he claimed were plotting to destroy the Revolution. Early in 1790 he was forced to flee to England after publishing attacks on Jacques Necker, the king's finance minister; three months later, he was back, his fame now being sufficient to give him some protection against reprisal. He did not relent but directed his criticism against such moderate revolutionary leaders as the marquis de Lafayette, the count de Mirabeau, and Jean-Sylvain Bailly, mayor of Paris (a member of the Academy of Sciences); he continued to warn against the émigrés, royalist exiles who were organizing counterrevolutionary activities and urging the other European monarchs to intervene in France and restore the full power of Louis XVI.

In July 1790 he declared to his readers:

> Five or six hundred heads cut off would have assured your repose, freedom, and happiness. A false humanity has held your arms and suspended your blows; because of this millions of your brothers will lose their lives.

The National Assembly sentenced him to a month in prison, but he went into hiding and continued his campaign. When bloody riots broke out at Nancy in eastern France, he saw them as the first sign of the counterrevolution.

Activities in the National Convention. In 1790 and 1791, Marat gradually came to the view that the monarchy should be abolished but did not say so publicly before the establishment of the Republic in September 1792. As a delegate to the National Convention (beginning also in September 1792), he advocated such reforms as a graduated income tax, state-sponsored vocational training for workers, and shorter terms of military service. Though he had often advocated the execution of counterrevolutionaries, Marat seems to have had no direct connection with the wholesale massacres of suspects that occurred in the same month. His articles in *L'Ami du Peuple* and his speeches before the Jacobin Revolutionary club encouraged a feeling of class consciousness among the ordinary people of Paris. He had opposed France's declaration of war against antirevolutionary Austria in April, but, once the war had begun and the country was in danger of invasion, he advocated a temporary dictatorship (probably under his fellow Parisian leader Georges Danton) to deal with the emergency.

Actively supported by the Parisian people both in the chamber and in street demonstrations, Marat quickly became one of the most influential members of the Convention. Attacks by the conservative Girondin faction early in 1793 made him a symbol of the Montagnards, or radical faction. In April the Girondins had him arraigned before a Revolutionary tribunal. His acquittal of the political charges brought against him (April 24) was the climax of his career and the beginning of the fall of the Girondins from power.

Assassination. On July 13, Charlotte Corday, a young Girondin supporter from Normandy, was admitted to Marat's room on the pretext that she wished to claim his protection and stabbed him to death in his bath (he took frequent medicinal baths to relieve a skin infection). Marat's dramatic murder at the very moment of the Montagnards' triumph over their opponents caused him to be considered a martyr to the people's cause. His name was given to 21 French towns and, later, as a gesture symbolizing the continuity between the French and Russian revolutions, to one of the first battleships in the Soviet Navy. (J.Vi.)

BIBLIOGRAPHY. Louis R. Gottschalk, *Jean Paul Marat: A Study in Radicalism* (1927, reissued 1967).

Marāṭhā, also spelled MAHRATTĀ, or MAHRATTĪ, a major people of India, famed in history as yeoman warriors and champions of Hinduism. Their homeland is the present state of Mahārāshtra, the Marāṭhī-speaking region that extends from Bombay to Goa along the west coast of India and inland about 100 miles (160 km) east of Nāgpur.

The term Marāṭhā is used in three overlapping senses: within the Marāṭhī-speaking region it refers to the single dominant Marāṭhā caste or to the group of Marāṭhā and Kunbī castes; outside Mahārāshtra, the term often loosely designates the entire regional population speaking the Marāṭhī language, numbering approximately 65,000,000; and, used historically, the term denotes the regional kingdom founded by the Marāṭhā leader Śivājī in the 17th century and expanded by his successors of many castes in the 18th century.

The Marāṭhā group of castes is a largely rural class of peasant cultivators, landowners, and soldiers. Some Marāṭhā and Kunbī have at times claimed Kshatriya (the warrior and ruling class) standing and supported their claims to this rank by reference to clan names and genealogies linking themselves with epic heroes, Rājput clans of the north, or historic dynasties. The Marāṭhā and Kunbī group of castes is divided into subregional groupings of coast, western hills, and Deccan Plains, among which there is little intermarriage. Within each subregion, clans of these castes are classed in social circles of decreasing rank. A maximal circle of 96 clans is said to include all true Marāṭhā, but the lists of these 96 clans are highly various and disputed.

Marāṭhā confederacy, alliance formed in the 18th century after Mughal pressure forced the collapse of Śivājī's kingdom of Mahārāshtra in western India. After the Mughal emperor Aurangzeb's death (1707), Marāṭhā power revived under Śivājī's grandson Shāhū. He confided power to the Brahman Bhat family, who became hereditary peshwas (chief ministers). He also decided to expand northward with armies under the peshwas' control. In Shāhū's later years the power of the peshwas increased. After his death (1749) they became the effective rulers. The leading Marāṭhā families—Sindhia, Holkar, Bhonsle, and Gaekwaḍ (Gaekwar)—extended their conquests in northern and central India and became more independent and difficult to control.

The effective control of the peshwas ended with the great defeat of Pānīpat (1761) at the hands of the Afghans and the death of the young peshwa Mādhav Rāo I in 1772. Thereafter the Marāṭhā state was a confederacy of five chiefs under the nominal leadership of the peshwa at Poona (Pune) in western India. Though they united on occasion, as against the British (1775–82), more often they quarreled. After he was defeated by the Holkar in 1802, the peshwa Bājī Rāo II sought protection from the British, whose intervention destroyed the confederacy by 1818. The confederacy expressed a general Marāṭhā nationalist sentiment but was divided bitterly by the jealousies of its chiefs.

Marāṭhā Wars (1775–82, 1803–05, 1817–18), three conflicts between the British and the Marāṭhā confederacy, resulting in the destruction of the confederacy.

The first war (1775–82) began with British support for Raghunath Rāo's bid for the office of peshwa (chief minister) of the confederacy. The British were defeated at Wadgaon (*see* Wadgaon, Convention of) in January 1779, but they continued to fight the Marāṭhā until conclusion of the Treaty of Salbai (May 1782); the sole British gain was the island of Salsette adjacent to Bombay.

The second war (1803–05) was caused by the peshwa Bājī Rāo II's defeat by the Holkars (one of the leading Marāṭhā clans) and his acceptance of British protection by the Treaty of Bassein in December 1802. The Sindhia and the Bhonsle families contested the agreement, but they were defeated, respectively, at Laswari and Delhi by Lord Lake and at Assaye and Argaon by Sir Arthur Wellesley (later the duke of Wellington). The Holkar clan then joined in, and the Marāṭhā were left with a free hand in central India and Rājasthān.

The third war (1817–18) was the result of an invasion of Marāṭhā territory in the course of operations against Pindari robber bands by the British governor-general, Lord Hastings. The peshwa's forces, followed by those of the Bhonsle and Holkar, rose against the British (November 1817), but the Sindhia remained neutral. Defeat was swift, followed by the pensioning of the peshwa and the annexation of his territories, thus completing the supremacy of the British in India.

Marāṭhī language, Indo-Aryan language of western and central India. Its range extends from north of Bombay down the western coast past Goa and eastward across the Deccan; in 1966 it became the official language of the state of Mahārāshtra. The standard form of speech is that of the city of Pune (Poona).

Descended from the Mahārāṣṭrī Prākrit, Marāṭhī has a significant literature. Books are printed in Devanāgarī script, which is also used for handwriting, for which there is also an alternate cursive form of Devanāgarī called Modi. Eastern Hindi is the Indo-Aryan language most closely related to Marāṭhī. Like Hindi, Marāṭhī has lost most of its inflectional system to indicate case, using instead postpositions (like prepositions, only following the word) with an oblique "case" to serve the function originally filled by inflection.

marathon, long-distance footrace first held at the revival of the Olympic Games in Athens in 1896. It commemorates the legendary Greek soldier who, in 490 BC, is supposed to have run from Marathon to Athens, a distance of about 40 km (25 miles), to bring news of the Athenian victory over the Persians; he then expired. Appropriately, in 1896 the first modern marathon winner was a Greek, Spyridon Louis.

In 1924 the Olympic marathon distance was standardized at 42,195 metres (26 miles 385 yards). This was based on a decision of the British Olympic Committee to start the 1908 Olympic race from Windsor Castle and finish it in front of the royal box in the stadium at

London. The marathon was added to the women's Olympic program in 1984.

One of the most coveted honours in marathon running is victory in the Boston Marathon, held annually since 1897. In 1972 it became the first major marathon to officially allow women to compete. Other premiere marathons are held in London, Chicago, Berlin, New York City, Tokyo, and Amsterdam. Marathons are not held on the track but on roads, and, despite the fact that courses are not of equal difficulty, the International Association of Athletics Federations (IAAF) does list world records for the marathon and also for the half-marathon. World-record times in the marathon steadily declined over the course of the 20th century from slightly under three hours to slightly more than two hours.

It was long considered necessary for a runner to prepare for a marathon by training over that distance. At the 1952 Olympic Games, however, Czech Emil Zátopek set an Olympic record even though he had never run the distance before. By the late 20th century, road racing, and marathon running in particular, had grown to become a recreational activity with broad appeal. Ultramarathons, which are neither Olympic nor IAAF events, are longer races based on a specific distance or an allotted time period for competition, such as a 12-hour race. For winners of the Boston Marathon and the New York Marathon, *see* Sporting Record: *Athletics.* For Olympic champions, *see* Olympic Games.

Marathon, Battle of (September 490 BC), in the Greco-Persian Wars, decisive battle fought on the Marathon plain of northeastern Attica in which the Athenians, in a single afternoon, repulsed the first Persian invasion of Greece. Command of the hastily assembled Athenian army was vested in 10 generals, each of whom was to hold operational command for one day. The generals were evenly divided on whether to await the Persians or to attack them, and the tie was broken by a civil official, Callimachus, who decided in favour of an attack. Four of the generals then ceded their commands to the Athenian general Miltiades, thus effectively making him commander in chief.

The Greeks could not hope to face the Persians' cavalry contingent on the open plain, but before dawn one day the Greeks learned that the cavalry were temporarily absent from the Persian camp, whereupon Miltiades ordered a general attack upon the Persian infantry. In the ensuing battle, Miltiades led his contingent of 10,000 Athenians and 1,000 Plataeans to victory over the Persian force of 15,000 by reinforcing his battle line's flanks and thus decoying the Persians' best troops into pushing back his centre, where they were surrounded by the inward-wheeling Greek wings. On being almost enveloped, the Persian troops broke into flight. By the time the routed Persians reached their ships, they had lost 6,400 men; the Greeks lost 192 men, including Callimachus. The battle proved the superiority of the Greek long spear, sword, and armour over the Persians' weapons.

According to legend, an Athenian messenger was sent from Marathon to Athens, a distance of about 25 miles (40 km), and there he announced the Persian defeat before dying of exhaustion. This tale became the basis for the modern marathon race. Herodotus, however, relates that a trained runner, Pheidippides (also spelled Phidippides, or Philippides), was sent from Athens to Sparta before the battle in order to request assistance from the Spartans; he is said to have covered about 150 miles (240 km) in about two days.

Marathon Oil Company, American petroleum company with a full range of operations from exploration and production to marketing and research; it became a subsidiary of the United States Steel Corp. (now USX Corp.) in 1981. Marathon Oil, founded in 1887 as the Ohio Oil Company, came under the control of the Standard Oil Trust in 1889. When the Standard Oil combine was broken up by the U.S. Supreme Court in 1911, the company again became independent, adopting the name of Marathon Oil Company in 1962. It operated mainly in North America, with additional production in Libya and Nigeria and additional refining and wholesaling in Europe. In 1976 its acquisition of Pan Ocean Oil Corporation brought mineral interests, chiefly in coal, fluorspar, and zinc.

Marathon orogeny, mountain-building event in the Marathon region of western Texas, U.S., during the Late Carboniferous Period (from 323 to 290 million years ago). Rocks of Early Permian age (from 290 to 256 million years old) that overlie the Pennsylvanian and older strata in this region exhibit great angular unconformities (*i.e.,* nonparallelism of strata) because the Marathon orogeny was an intense event, one associated with much thrust faulting and overriding of the geosynclinal deposits involved.

Maratta, Carlo, Maratta also spelled MARATTI (b. May 15, 1625, Camerino, Papal States [Italy]—d. Dec. 15, 1713, Rome), one of the leading painters of the Roman school in the later 17th century, and one of the last great masters of Baroque classicism, who (with Francesco Solimena) established the style known as the European Grand Manner.

Maratta went early to Rome, where he studied. His reputation was established with his first public work, the "Nativity" (1650; San Giuseppe dei Falegnami, Rome). A few years later he was noticed by Pope Alexander VII, and thereafter he secured an almost uninterrupted series of important commissions for altarpieces in Italian churches. Among these are "The Mystery of the Trinity Revealed to St. Augustine" (*c.* 1655; Santa Maria dei Sette Dolori, Rome), "The Appearance of the Virgin to St. Philip Neri" (*c.* 1675; Pitti Palace, Florence), and "The Virgin with SS. Charles and Ignatius" (*c.* 1685; Santa Maria in Vallicella, Rome). His many popular depictions of the Virgin earned him the nickname Carluccio delle Madonne ("Little Carlo of the Madonnas"). He also executed a number of decorative ceiling frescoes in Roman palaces and was one of the most distinguished portrait painters in Italy during this period.

"The Appearance of the Virgin to St. Philip Neri," painting by Carlo Maratta, *c.* 1675; in the Pitti Palace, Florence
SCALA—Art Resource

Maratta advocated classicism, at least in theory, in opposition to the Baroque painters Pietro da Cortona, Baciccia, and Padre Pozzo. But Maratta was only partly a classicist in practice. His work displays without restraint the Baroque quality of magnificence, and he was wholeheartedly engaged in the task of representing with the utmost splendour the dogmas of the Counter-Reformation.

Marattiaceae, the giant fern family, the only family of the fern order Marattiales, or, in some classification systems, one of four families in that order. The family contains as many as six genera and about 200 species of large tropical and subtropical ferns with stout, erect stems. The leaves (fronds) may be very large in some species, such as *Angiopteris evecta,* which may have a stem 60 to 180 cm (2 to 6 feet) in height and leaves 4.5 m (15 feet) or more in length.

Giant fern (*Marattia*)
G.R. Roberts

Genera are distinguished mainly by the disposition of the spore-producing structures (sporangia), which lie on the lower side of the leaves. *Angiopteris* and *Archangiopteris,* with 100 and 10 species, respectively, have separate sporangia. *Marattia* (60 species) has the sporangia united in clusters called synangia, which are paired along each side of certain leaf veins and open toward the leaflet axis in this genus. *Danaea* (30 species) has single synangia, sometimes extending from the midrib of the leaflet to the margin and open at the terminal end. The genus *Christensenia* (one species) is sometimes included in this group.

The genus of extinct ferns *Psaronius,* from Carboniferous and Permian times (354 to 248 million years ago), is to be either a member of the Marattiaceae or very closely related to it.

Maravi, cluster of nine Bantu-speaking peoples living in the tree-studded grasslands of Malaŵi and along the lower Zambezi River. The two largest groups are the Chewa (or Cewa) and the Nyanja. Their economy is based mainly on shifting agriculture, corn (maize) being the staple crop. Hunting, fishing, and trading are also important economically. The Maravi are thought to be of Congo origin, and, like other groups from that region, such as the Bemba, they are divided into matrilineal clans. Descent, succession, and inheritance are also matrilineal. Polygyny is practiced, the first wife enjoying special status; the typical family comprises a husband, his wives, and dependent children.

Maravi Confederacy, also called MARAVI EMPIRE, centralized system of government established in southern Africa about 1480. The members of the confederacy were related ethnolinguistic groups who had migrated from the north into what is now central and southern Malaŵi. The confederacy was ruled by a *karonga* (king), whose authority was passed down through the leaders of each clan.

The main body of the confederacy was settled in an area southwest of Lake Nyasa (Lake Malaŵi); two groups moved south into the Shire River valley during the 15th or 16th century, and other groups moved into territories now in Zambia and Mozambique. The confederacy reached its peak during the 17th century, administering a large area that stretched north of the Zambezi River to the Dwangwa River, west to the Luangwa River, and east to the Mozambique coast. Its decline began when clan leaders, who traded with the Portuguese and Arabs in ivory, slaves, and iron, became increasingly independent of the central authority of the *karonga.* By 1720 the confederacy had broken into several autonomous factions.

The Chewa and Nyanja peoples of modern Malaŵi are descendants of the original Maravi clans.

Marawi, formerly DANSALAN, chartered city, capital of Lanao del Sur province, north central Mindanao, Philippines. On the northern shore of Lake Lanao, 3,500 ft (1,100 m) above sea level, it is one of the largest cities in the Philippines inhabited by Muslims (Moros). An important trading centre specializing in Muslim handicrafts and bladed weapons, it is the seat of Mindanao State University (1961), Dansalan College, and Pangarungan Islam Colleges (1965). Camp Keithley, former U.S. military headquarters for Mindanao, is nearby. The 1972 Muslim rebellion began in Marawi. Inc. city, 1940. Pop. (2000) 131,090.

Marbeck, John, Marbeck also spelled MERBECKE (b. *c.* 1510—d. *c.* 1585), English composer, organist, and author, known for his setting of the Anglican liturgy.

Marbeck apparently spent most of his life at Windsor, where he was organist at St. George's Chapel. In 1544 he was sentenced to the stake for heresy but was pardoned through the intervention of Bishop Gardiner of Winchester. At that time Marbeck's "greate worke," his English *Concordance* to the Bible, was taken from him and destroyed. On his release he began it again, and in 1550, under Edward VI, it was published in abbreviated form. In 1550 he also published his setting of plainchant for the Anglican liturgy, *Booke of Common Praier Noted* (*i.e.*, set to musical notes). This setting was superseded in 1552, but interest in it revived during the Oxford Movement in the late 19th century, and it was printed in facsimile in 1939.

marble, granular limestone or dolomite (*i.e.*, rock composed of calcium-magnesium carbonate) that has been recrystallized under the influence of heat, pressure, and aqueous solutions. Commercially, it includes all decorative calcium-rich rocks that can be polished, as well as certain serpentines (verd antiques).

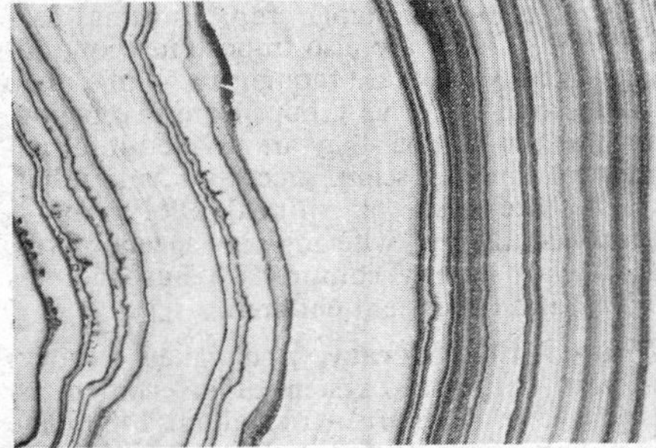

Concentric banding in onyx marble from Mexico
By courtesy of the Smithsonian Institution, Washington, D.C.

Petrographically marbles are massive rather than thin-layered and consist of a mosaic of calcite grains that rarely show any traces of crystalline form under the microscope. They are traversed by minute cracks that accord with the rhombohedral cleavage (planes of fracture that intersect to yield rhombic forms) of calcite. In the more severely deformed rocks, the grains show stripes and may be elongated in a particular direction or even crushed.

Marbles often occur interbedded with such metamorphic rocks as mica schists, phyllites, gneisses, and granulites and are most common in the older layers of the Earth's crust that have been deeply buried in regions of extreme folding and igneous intrusion. The change from limestones rich in fossils into true marbles in such metamorphic regions is a common phenomenon; occasionally, as at Carrara, Italy, and at Bergen, Nor., recrystallization of the rock has not completely obliterated the organic structures.

Most of the white and gray marbles of Alabama, Georgia, and western New England, and that from Yule, Colo., are recrystallized rocks, as are a number of Greek and Italian statuary marbles famous from antiquity, which are still quarried. These include the Parian marble, the Pentelic marble of Attica in which Phidias, Praxiteles, and other Greek sculptors executed their principal works, and the snow-white Carrara marble used by Michelangelo and Antonio Canova and favoured by modern sculptors. The exterior of the National Gallery of Art in Washington, D.C., is of Tennessee marble, and the Lincoln Memorial contains marbles from Yule, Colo., Alabama (roof transparencies), and Georgia (Lincoln statue).

Even the purest of the metamorphic marbles, such as that from Carrara, contain some accessory minerals, which, in many cases, form a considerable proportion of the mass. The commonest are quartz in small rounded grains, scales of colourless or pale-yellow mica (muscovite and phlogopite), dark shining flakes of graphite, iron oxides, and small crystals of pyrite.

Many marbles contain other minerals that are usually silicates of lime or magnesia. Diopside is very frequent and may be white or pale green; white bladed tremolite and pale-green actinolite also occur; the feldspar encountered may be a potassium variety but is more commonly a plagioclase (sodium-rich to calcium-rich) such as albite, labradorite, or anorthite. Scapolite, various kinds of garnet, vesuvianite, spinel, forsterite, periclase, brucite, talc, zoisite, wollastonite, chlorite, tourmaline, epidote, chondrodite, biotite, sphene, and apatite are all possible accessory minerals. Pyrrhotite, sphalerite, and chalcopyrite also may be present in small amounts.

These minerals represent impurities in the original limestone, which reacted during metamorphism to form new compounds. The alumina represents an admixture of clay; the silicates derive their silica from quartz and from clay; the iron came from limonite, hematite, or pyrite in the original sedimentary rock. In some cases the original bedding of the calcareous sediments can be detected by mineral banding in the marble. The silicate minerals, if present in any considerable amount, may colour the marble; *e.g.*, green in the case of green pyroxenes and amphiboles; brown in that of garnet and vesuvianite; and yellow in that of epidote, chondrodite, and sphene. Black and gray colours result from the presence of fine scales of graphite.

Bands of calc-silicate rock may alternate with bands of marble or form nodules and patches, sometimes producing interesting decorative effects, but these rocks are particularly difficult to finish because of the great difference in hardness between the silicates and carbonate minerals.

Later physical deformation and chemical decomposition of the metamorphic marbles often produces attractive coloured and variegated varieties. Decomposition yields hematite, brown limonite, pale-green talc, and, in particular, the green or yellow serpentine derived from forsterite and diopside, which is characteristic of the ophicalcites or verd antiques. Earth movements may shatter the rocks, producing fissures that are afterward filled with veins of calcite; in this way the beautiful brecciated, or veined, marbles are produced. Sometimes the broken fragments are rolled and rounded by the flow of marble under pressure.

The so-called onyx marbles consist of concentric zones of calcite or aragonite deposited from cold-water solutions in caves and crevices and around the exits of springs. They are, in the strict sense, neither marble nor onyx, for true onyx is a banded chalcedony composed largely of silicon dioxide. Onyx marble was the "alabaster" of the ancients, but alabaster is now defined as gypsum, a calcium sulfate rock. These marbles are usually brown or yellow because of the presence of iron oxide. Well-known examples include the *giallo antico* ("antique yellow marble") of the Italian antiquaries, the reddish-mottled Siena marble from Tuscany, the large Mexican deposits at Tecali near Mexico City and at El Marmol, Calif., and the Algerian onyx marble used in the buildings of Carthage and Rome and rediscovered near Oued-Abdallah in 1849.

Unmetamorphosed limestones showing interesting colour contrasts or fossil remains are used extensively for architectural purposes. The Paleozoic rocks (from 225,000,000 to 570,000,000 years in age) of Great Britian, for example, include "madrepore marbles" rich in fossil corals and "encrinital marble" containing crinoid stem and arm plates with characteristic circular cross sections. The shelly limestones of the Purbeck Beds, Eng., and the Sussex marble, both of Mesozoic Era (from 65,000,000 to 225,000,000 years ago), consist of masses of shells of freshwater snails embedded in blue, gray, or greenish limestone. They were a favourite material of medieval architects and may be seen in Westminster Abbey and a number of English cathedrals. Black limestones containing bituminous matter, which commonly emit a fetid odour when struck, are widely used; the well-known *petit granit* of Belgium is a black marble containing crinoid stem plates, derived from fossil echinoderms (invertebrate marine animals).

Uses. Marbles are used principally for buildings and monuments, interior decoration, statuary, table tops, and novelties. Colour and appearance are their most important qualities. Resistance to abrasion, which is a function of cohesion between grains as well as the hardness of the component minerals, is important for floor and stair treads. The ability to transmit light is important for statuary marble, which achieves its lustre from light penetrating from about 12.7 to 38 millimetres (0.5 to 1.5 inches) from where it is reflected at the surfaces of deeper lying crystals. Brecciated, coloured marbles, onyx marble, and verd antique are used principally for interior decoration and for novelties. Statuary marble, the most valuable variety, must be pure white and of uniform grain size. For endurance in exterior use, marble should be uniform and nonporous to prevent the entrance of water that might discolour the stone or cause disintegration by freezing. It also should be free from impurities such as pyrite that might lead to staining or weathering. Calcite marbles that are exposed to atmospheric moisture made acid by its contained carbon dioxide, sulfur dioxide, and other gases maintain a relatively smooth surface during weathering; but dolomite limestone may weather with an irregular, sandy surface from which the dolomite crystals stand out.

The principal mineral in marble is calcite, and the fact that this mineral varies in hardness, light transmission, and other properties in various directions has some practical consequences in the preparation of certain marbles. Calcite crystals are doubly refractive—they transmit light in two directions and more light in one direction; slabs prepared for uses in which translucency is significant are therefore cut parallel to that direction. Bending of marble slabs has been attributed to the directional thermal expansion of calcite crystals on heating.

Quarrying. The use of explosives in the quarrying of marble is limited because of the danger of shattering the rock. Instead, channeling machines that utilize chisel-edged steel bars make cuts about 5 cm (2 inches) wide and a few metres deep. Wherever possible, advantage is taken of natural joints already present in the rock, and cuts are made in the direction of easiest splitting, which is a consequence of the parallel elongation of platy or fibrous minerals. The marble blocks outlined by joints and cuts are separated by driving wedges into drill holes. Mill sawing into slabs is done with sets of parallel iron blades that move back and forth and are fed by sand and water. The marble may be machined with lathes and carborundum wheels and is then polished with increasingly finer grades of abrasive. Even with the most careful quarrying and manufacturing methods, at least half of the total output of marble is waste. Some of this material is made into chips for terrazzo flooring and stucco wall finish. In various localities it is put to most of the major uses for which high-calcium limestone is suitable.

marble, small, hard ball that is used in a variety of children's games and is named after the 18th-century practice of making the toy from marble chips. Marble games date from antiquity, and ancient games were played with sea-rounded pebbles, nuts, or fruit pits. The

A boy aiming his shooter at other marbles before him

Picture Partners/agefotostock

young Octavian (later the emperor Augustus), like other Roman children, played games with nut marbles, and engraved marbles have been dug up from the earthen mounds built by some early North American Indian tribes. Jewish children use filberts as marbles at Passover.

Marbles have been made out of a variety of materials, such as baked clay, steel, and agate, but by far the most common material is glass. Marbles vary in size from peewees at ⅛ inch (.31 cm) in diameter to the most common size used for play at ⅝ inch (1.58 cm) to the largest shooters at 1–3 inches (2.5–7.6 cm). Particular marbles may be named for their use (shooters may be called taws, a word of obscure origin), for their original material (alleys were once made of alabaster), or for their appearance (*e.g.,* "flints," "cat's eyes," "cloudies").

The object of marble games is to roll, throw, kick, drop, or knuckle marbles against an opponent's marbles, often to knock them out of a prescribed area. Further, the names and rules of marble games are as varied as the localities and countries where they are played, still, a few games may be mentioned. In taw, ringtaw, or ringer, players attempt to shoot marbles, sometimes arranged in a cross, out of a ring as much as 6 to 10 feet (about 2 to 3 m) in diameter. In hit and span, players try to shoot or roll marbles either against an opponent's marbles or a hand's span from them. In various pot games (a pot is a small hole in the ground), including moshie, the player tries to pitch his own marbles or knock his opponents' marbles into a hole. A Chinese marble game consists of kicking a marble against an opponent's to make the latter rebound in a specified direction. Local, regional, and national tournaments are held in a number of countries for various types of marble games. It must be noted that children do not play with marbles as commonly as they once did.

Marbles are small and often attractive objects and have always to some extent been collected. In many of the marble games, a player who won a marble by, for instance, shooting it out of the circle kept the marble won. Collections were built, and trades were effected among players. Collectors are now much more likely to be adults. The market for antique marbles is a thriving one, but there are also handmade "art" marbles made especially for the collector market. The Internet has facilitated this form of collecting.

Marble, Alice (b. Sept. 28, 1913, Plumes county, Calif., U.S.—d. Dec. 13, 1990, Palm Springs), American tennis player, known for her powerful serves and volleys, who dominated the women's game during the late 1930s.

The daughter of California ranchers, Marble attended school in San Francisco and began playing tennis at the age of 15. She won the California junior championship at 17 and the state's women's championship at 19. Illness from anemia and pleurisy limited her play in 1934–35, but thereafter she was almost invincible, winning four U.S. singles titles (1936, 1938–40) and one Wimbledon singles title (1939). During Wightman Cup play from 1936 to 1940, she lost only one match in singles and in doubles. Her record is extraordinary, as doctors had warned her not to play tennis again.

When World War II caused the temporary suspension of tournaments, Marble turned professional, touring with Don Budge and Bill Tilden. She was elected to the International Tennis Hall of Fame in 1964. Her autobiography, *The Road to Wimbledon,* appeared in 1946.

marble bone disease, also called OSTEOPETROSIS, or ALBERS-SCHÖNBERG DISEASE, rare congenital hereditary disorder in which the bones become extremely dense, hard, and brittle. The disease progresses as long as bone growth continues; the marrow cavities become filled with compact bone, and severe anemia results. In marble bone disease, bone-destroying cells called osteoclasts are reduced in number or are ineffective. Fractures are frequent; deafness and loss of vision may occur because cranial nerves become compressed by the narrowing of their passageways as bone is deposited in the skull. Severe cases may be fatal; individuals with mild cases of the disorder may have a normal life expectancy. Treatment may include gamma interferon, a protein that delays progression of the disease; bone marrow transplantation; or calcitriol, a vitamin D compound that stimulates osteoclasts to destroy bone.

marbled cat (species *Felis marmorata*), rare Southeast Asian cat, family Felidae, often referred to as a miniature version of the unrelated clouded leopard. The marbled cat is about the size of a domestic cat; it measures roughly 45–60 cm (18–24 inches) long, excluding a tail of approximately the same length. The coat is long, soft, and pale brown to brownish gray, with large, dark-edged blotches on the body and smaller dark spots on the legs and tail. The marbled cat is nocturnal and lives in jungles, and may feed on small animals and birds.

marbled pottery, a type of ware obtained by mixing clays of various colours to imitate natural marbles or agate. The working of marble pottery can be traced back at least as far as the 1st century AD in Rome, and samples of the ware were produced as far from Rome

Chinese marbled ware jar, T'ang dynasty (AD 618–907); in the Museum of Fine Arts, Boston

By courtesy of the Museum of Fine Arts, Boston, Hoyt Collection

as China. Techniques included the use of decorative bands of white-, brown-, and gray-marbled clay; tortoiseshell, obtained by mottling glazes with manganese brown; laying the slabs of variously coloured clay on each other and beating them out into a homogeneous mass (agate ware); and mingling coloured clay slips (liquid clay) on the surface of a clay form.

Marblehead, urban town ("township"), Essex county, northeastern Massachusetts, U.S. It lies on a rocky peninsula jutting into Massachusetts Bay, 18 miles (29 km) northeast of Boston. Its deep, narrow harbour is sheltered by Marblehead Neck, a promontory of marblelike rocks about 1.5 miles (2.5 km) long. Settled in 1629 by fishermen from the Channel Islands and Cornwall, Eng., it was set off from Salem and incorporated as a town in 1649. It developed as a fishing and shipbuilding centre and replaced Boston as the Massachusetts Colony port of entry after passage of the Boston Port Bill of 1774. It was home port for many privateering and colonial vessels. During the American Revolution the first American warship, *Hannah,* was commissioned there on Sept. 2, 1775, and the Marblehead schooner *Lee* captured the *Nancy,* a valuable British prize, in November 1775. General John Glover (1732–97) was a native of Marblehead, where he raised his famous amphibious regiment which ferried General George Washington and his soldiers across the Delaware River in 1776 to successfully attack British Hessian troops in Trenton.

Marblehead's port declined after the War of 1812 and the community turned to the manufacture of shoes, rope, glue, and paint. The town is now mainly residential with a few small manufacturing firms, commercial lobster fishing, and boatyard and yachting facilities.

Many colonial buildings survive, including the Jeremiah Lee Mansion (1768), St. Michael's Episcopal Church (1714), King Hooper Mansion (1628; with art exhibits), Old Town House (1727), and the Old Tavern (1680). Abbot Hall, the Victorian town hall, houses A.M. Willard's painting "The Spirit of '76." Ft. Sewall (1742) stands in a marine park overlooking the harbour, and the graves of hundreds of Revolutionary soldiers are on Old Burial Hill. Pop. (1990) 19,971.

Marbot, Jean-Baptiste-Antoine-Marcelin, baron de (b. Aug. 18, 1782, Altillac, Fr.—d. Nov. 16, 1854, Paris), general and author of memoirs of the Napoleonic period, whose book on war, *Remarques critiques,* prompted Napoleon to leave him a legacy.

Marbot, portrait by Dujardin, 1812
Giraudon—Art Resource

Entering the army at 17, Marbot was aide-de-camp successively to three of Napoleon's generals. Promoted to major and then to colonel of the Belgian light cavalry in 1812, he fought in the battles on the Dvina and Berezina rivers in Russia (1812) and on the Katzbach in Silesia (1813). After becoming colonel of hussars in 1815, he was promoted to general by Napoleon on the eve of the Battle of Waterloo. In exile after Waterloo, Marbot returned to France in 1819 and worked on his *Remarques critiques* (1820), a reply to Gen. Joseph Rogniat's treatise on war, in which Marbot effectively contrasted the human factor in war with Rogniat's pure theory. In 1826 he published a work on the new French Army. When Louis-Philippe became king in 1830, Marbot returned to service as aide-de-camp to Ferdinand, duc d'Orléans, with whom he saw action at the siege of Antwerp and in Algeria.

Marbot's *Mémoires* of the empire, written for his children, was not published until 1891 (Eng. trans., 1892). His memoirs revived interest in the incidents and personalities of the First Empire but are not always historically reliable.

Marburg, in full MARBURG AN DER LAHN, city, Hesse *Land* (state), central Germany, on the Lahn River. The name Marburg (meaning "frontier fortress"), was first used in 1130, when the site belonged to the landgraves of Thuringia. Chartered, according to tradition, in 1211, it became the seat of the first landgraves of Hesse in 1248. The city's early history is associated with St. Elizabeth of Hungary, who, arriving from the Wartburg in 1228, spent the remaining three years of her life there in charitable works. Until the Reformation her bones were preserved in the shrine in her honour, a masterpiece of the Rhenish goldsmiths' craft, in the church of St. Elizabeth (1235–83), which also contained the remains of Field Marshal Paul von Hindenburg during World War II. The city is dominated by the Gothic castle of the Hessian landgraves; its Rittersaal (Knights' Hall) and chapel were begun in 1277, and the building was completed in 1493. The Rittersaal was the scene of the Marburg disputations between Luther and Zwingli and other Protestant Reformers in 1529. The Philipps-Universität, founded (1527) in the city, was Europe's first Protestant university. In 1567 Marburg became the centre of independent Hesse-Marburg, which in 1604 was divided between Hesse-Darmstadt and Hesse-Kassel. German and other dramatic classics are produced annually at the Grauerholz Festival in the open-air theatre in the castle grounds.

Marburg's economy depends on tourist traffic and several industries in applied arts, particularly art potteries. Chemicals and precision instruments are manufactured, and the city is a popular conference and exhibition centre. Pop. (1989 est.) 70,905.

Marburg (Slovenia): *see* Maribor.

Marburg, Colloquy of, important debate on the Eucharist held in Marburg, Ger., on Oct. 1–4, 1529, between the Reformers of Germany and Switzerland. It was called because of a political situation. In response to a majority resolution against the Reformation by the second Diet of Speyer (April 1529), the landgrave Philip of Hesse wished to organize a federation of Protestants. Since the Lutherans insisted on a common confession as the basis of confederation, Philip called the colloquy to settle the controversy concerning the Eucharist, which had been dividing the Reformers since 1524.

The four participants, Martin Luther, Philipp Melanchthon, John Oecolampadius, and Huldrych Zwingli, held preliminary discussions and then held four sessions in the presence of the landgrave Philip, Duke Ulrich of Württemberg, delegates from participating territories, and up to 60 guests.

The point at issue in the debate concerned the question of Christ's Presence in the bread and wine of the Eucharist. Christ had said, "This is my body," when instituting the Eucharist, and Luther defended the literal understanding of the statement. Zwingli contended that the Eucharist was a symbolic memorial rite, but he was willing to accept the doctrine of the spiritual Presence of Christ in the sacrament. Luther and Zwingli believed that their differences could not be worked out, but Martin Bucer, a member of the delegation from Strassburg, who spoke at the end of the colloquy, believed that they could possibly be reconciled.

After discussions broke down on October 3, Luther, at the Landgrave's request, prepared the 15 Articles of Marburg, based on articles (later called the Articles of Schwabach) prepared at Wittenberg before Luther had departed for Marburg. The first 14 articles stated the usually accepted common doctrines of the German and Swiss Reformations, which had not been discussed at the colloquy. The 15th article stated that "at present we are not agreed as to whether the true body and blood [of Christ] are bodily present in the bread and wine." The articles were discussed, revised, and signed by the theologians and were accepted by the Landgrave as a statement of Protestant belief. Some material from these articles was later included in the Augsburg Confession of the Lutheran Church.

Marburg, Philipps University of, German PHILIPPS-UNIVERSITÄT MARBURG AN DER LAHN, coeducational institution of higher learning at Marburg, Ger. It was founded in 1527 by Philip the Generous of Hesse as a Protestant public institution. The university is financially supported by the state of Hesse. Departments include law, economics, social sciences, education, psychology, Protestant theology, history, classical studies, linguistics and philology, modern German literature and arts, modern languages and literature, non-European languages and literature, mathematics, physics, chemistry, pharmacy, biology, Earth sciences, geography, and medicine.

Marbury v. Madison (Feb. 24, 1803), landmark U.S. Supreme Court decision, the first instance in which the high court declared an act of Congress unconstitutional, thus establishing the doctrine of judicial review.

The Supreme Court's growing conflict with President Jefferson and the Republican Congress came to a head after Secretary of State Madison, on Jefferson's orders, withheld from William Marbury the commission of his appointment (March 2, 1801), by former President Adams, as justice of the peace in the District of Columbia. Marbury—one of the "midnight appointments" under the Judiciary Act of 1801—requested the Supreme Court to issue a writ of mandamus compelling Madison to deliver his commission. In denying his request, the Court held that it lacked jurisdiction because Section 13 of the Judiciary Act passed by Congress in 1789, which authorized the Court to issue such a writ, was unconstitutional and thus invalid. Chief Justice Marshall declared that in any such conflict between the Constitution and a law passed by Congress, the Constitution must always take precedence.

Marbut, Curtis Fletcher (b. July 19, 1863, Vernona, Mo., U.S.—d. Aug. 25, 1935, Harbin, China), U.S. geologist and authority on soils, who worked closely with experts from many countries to develop international classification systems for soil materials.

After earning a B.S. from the University of Missouri in 1889, Marbut worked for the Missouri Geological Survey before doing graduate work in geology and physiography at Harvard and in Europe. He returned to the University of Missouri, where he taught from 1895 to 1910, becoming increasingly interested in the composition of soils. In 1910 he was appointed chief of the Soil Survey of the U.S. Department of Agriculture, which mapped the soils of the country. He translated into English the German edition of a pioneering Russian work, *The Great Soil Groups of the World and Their Development* (1927), and wrote a basic text, *Soils of the U.S.* (1935). He was about to begin a preliminary study of the soils of China when he died of pneumonia.

Marc, Franz (b. Feb. 8, 1880, Munich—d. March 4, 1916, near Verdun, Fr.), German painter and printmaker, founding member of "The Blue Rider" group (*see* Blaue Reiter, Der), known for the intense nature mysticism of his paintings of animals.

"Blue Horses," oil painting by Franz Marc, 1911; in the Walker Art Center, Minneapolis, Minn.
By courtesy of the Walker Art Center, Minneapolis, Minn.

Marc's early works were done in a self-consciously academic style, but in 1903 his stolid naturalism was lightened by his exposure to French Impressionist painting and later to the sensuous, curvilinear art of Munich's Jugendstil movement.

In 1909 Marc joined a group of Expressionist artists known as the Neue Künstlervereinigung (New Artists' Association). There he met August Macke, whose idiosyncratic use of broad areas of rich colour led Marc to experiment with similar techniques.

In 1910 Marc met Wassily Kandinsky, with whom he edited *Der Blaue Reiter,* the journal that gave its name to the group of artists, led by Kandinsky, who split from the Neue Künstlervereinigung in the following year. Having long been interested in Eastern philosophies and religions, Marc responded enthusiastically to Kandinsky's almost mystical notion that art should lay bare the spiritual essence of natural forms instead of copying their objective appearance with exact verisimilitude. Under the influence of Kandinsky, Marc came to believe that spiritual essence is best revealed through abstraction. He believed that civilization destroys human awareness of the all-pervading spiritual force of nature. Consequently, he was passionately interested in the art of primitive peoples, children, and the mentally ill. But his own work consisted primarily of animal studies, since he considered nonhuman forms of life to be the most expressive manifestation of the vital natural force.

This philosophy is mirrored in Marc's "Blue Horses" (1911), in which the powerfully simplified and rounded outlines of the horses are echoed in the rhythms of the landscape background, uniting both animals and setting into a vigorous and harmonious organic whole. In this painting as in his other mature works, Marc used a well-defined symbology of colour.

In 1912 Marc's admiration for the works of Robert Delaunay and for the Italian Futurists made his art increasingly dynamic. He began to use the faceted space and forms of Delaunay's brightly coloured Cubistic compositions to express the brutal power and the timorous fragility of various forms of animal life.

Marc Anthony: *see* Antony, Mark.

Marca, also spelled MARKA, MERCA, or MERKA, port city, southern Somalia, on the Indian Ocean, about 45 miles (70 km) southwest of Mogadishu, the national capital and main port. The town, which was founded by Arab or Persian traders, was in existence by the 10th century. The first Somalis to settle near there arrived in the 13th century, and in the 17th century the town, its hinterland, and caravan routes from the interior were controlled by the Bimal, a subgroup of one of the four major Somali clans, who traded extensively in ivory, slaves, cattle, and hides. Offshore coral reefs make it necessary to carry goods by lighters between the port and ocean-going vessels, and they limit expansion of the port. The principal export is bananas. Pop. (latest est.) 62,000.

Marca-Relli, Conrad, original name CORRADO MARCARELLI (b. June 5, 1913, Boston, Mass., U.S.—d. Aug. 29, 2000, Parma, Italy), American artist associated with Abstract Expressionism. He was the first to raise the art of collage to a scale and complexity comparable to monumental painting, paving the way for the large "combine paintings" of the Neo-Dada artists of the 1960s.

The son of a news commentator and foreign correspondent, Marca-Relli grew up both in Boston and in Europe and took his first art lessons in Italy. In 1931, at age 18, he established his own studio in New York City. During the Great Depression, Marca-Relli worked for the WPA Federal Art Project (1935–38), creating paintings and murals, and he later taught at several universities, including Yale and the University of California at Berkeley. In the late 1990s Marca-Relli moved to Italy.

Marca-Relli was greatly influenced in his early career by the dreamlike imagery of the Surrealists. His experiments with collage began as a simple expedient one day in 1953 when he was out of paint. The technique provided the dense surface texture of impasto while maintaining the compositional clarity impasto often obscured. That same year he met Jackson Pollock and Willem de Kooning, leading painters of the Abstract Expressionist movement. Influenced by their method of intuitive painting, he began to work improvisationally, cutting and fixing the fragments of canvas spontaneously, scorching the canvas with a torch, and allowing the black fixative to ooze out between contiguous shapes.

Marca-Relli with one of his paintings
Hans Namuth

The early 1960s brought a new harmony and calm to his works, such as "The Blackboard" (1961), which is especially notable for its subdued but luminous colours. Seeking a more obdurate material than canvas to complement the new formal rigour of his compositions, he experimented with painted vinyl and cut aluminum. He then made the logical step to metal relief and finally to free-standing aluminum sculpture, but he returned in 1966 to painted canvas collages characterized by stark calligraphic designs.

Marcabru, also spelled MARCABRUN (b. Gascony [France]; fl. *c.* 1130–48), Gascon poet-musician and the earliest exponent of the *trobar clus,* an allusive and deliberately obscure poetic style in Provençal.

Unlike most successful troubadors, Marcabru was not of the aristocracy, and he served in several courts throughout southern France and Spain without finding a permanent patron. Marcabru's innovative technique and humour are evident in all his verse, and he was widely imitated and admired, despite his obscure imagery and difficult symbolism. More than 40 of his poems are extant, including Crusade songs, satires, romances, and a witty *pastourelle.* Marcabru's favourite subject, however, was the contrast of *fin' amors* (pure, perfect love) and *amars* (the sensual courtly love praised by his contemporaries). A vehement moralist, Marcabru criticized the nobility and other troubadours for distorting the true courtly virtues. Many of his finest poems are in direct response to works by other poets, including William IX, duke of Aquitaine, regarded as the first troubadour poet.

Marcantonio: *see* Raimondi, Marcantonio.

marcasite, an iron sulfide mineral that forms pale bronze-yellow orthorhombic crystals, usually twinned to characteristic cockscomb or sheaflike shapes; the names spear pyrites and cockscomb pyrites refer to the shape and colour of these crystals. Radially arranged fibres are also common.

Marcasite is found with lead and zinc minerals in metalliferous veins, as at Galena, Ill., U.S., and at Clausthal Zellerfeld and Linnich, Ger. Marcasite, which has the same chemical formula as pyrite (FeS_2) but crystallizes in the orthorhombic instead of the isometric system, alters upon weathering to ferrous sulfate and sulfuric acid. For detailed physical properties, *see* sulfide mineral (table).

Marceau(-Desgraviers), François-Séverin (b. March 1, 1769, Chartres, France—d. Sept. 21, 1796, Altenkirchen, Rhenish Palatinate [Germany]), French general, a notable young military hero of the early years of the French Revolutionary wars.

A lawyer's son, Marceau ran away to enlist in the infantry regiment of Savoy-Carignan in 1785 and took part in the attack on the Bastille in Paris in 1789. He joined the Chartres volunteers, who elected him lieutenant colonel, and they went to the Verdun garrison in the summer of 1792, but he left them in the disorder following capitulation to the Prussians on September 2. He obtained a cavalry captaincy when fighting the rebels of the Vendée in May 1793. A month later, in battle at Saumur, he again distinguished himself and was promoted. He was made a general at the Battle of Cholet on Oct. 16, 1793, and temporarily the commander in chief (November 27). Marceau's attractive heroism, guided by J.-B. Kléber's maturer talents, led to decisive victory over the Vendéan "grand army" in December.

Marceau was received with acclaim by the Convention in February 1794 and given a division in the Ardennes against the Austrians. His capture of Coblenz, the former capital of the émigrés, gave special pleasure in Paris (October 1794). In 1795 he was across the Rhine with Kléber; he then led a wing of 17,000 men west of the Rhine facing Mainz and held an exposed flank with prudence and skill. In 1796, when J.-B. Jourdan and the main army retreated, Marceau's corps was the all-important rear guard. In action at Altenkirchen on the Lahn River, Marceau was shot by a Tirolese sharpshooter.

Marceau, Marcel (b. March 22, 1923, Strasbourg, France), French mime of the 20th century whose silent portrayals are executed with eloquence, deceptive simplicity, and balletic grace. His most celebrated characterization is Bip, a character half-Pierrot, half-Charlie Chaplin's tramp, first presented in 1947.

Marcel Marceau, 1971
Horst Tappe—EB Inc.

Marceau served in the French army and in the Resistance during World War II, after which he studied at the School of Dramatic Art of the Sarah Bernhardt Theatre, Paris, and with pantomimist Étienne Decroux. After his first success, the role of Arlequin in *Baptiste*, a pantomime, he concentrated completely on pantomime and formed a mime troupe. Worldwide acclaim came in the 1950s with his production of a "mimodrama" of Gogol's *Overcoat* and with successful personal appearances. Thereafter he toured internationally.

Marcel, Étienne (b. *c.* 1316—d. July 31, 1358, Paris), bourgeois leader, a clothier and provost of the merchants of Paris, who played a major part in the Paris revolution of 1355–58 and was for a time able to coerce the government into considering reforms.

Marcel came of a family of cloth merchants, his grandfather having been the wealthy Pierre Marcel (d. 1305), whose commercial enterprises covered all Europe. After the death of his father, Simon (*c.* 1333), Marcel himself entered the family trade and, by 1350, had become provost of the Grande-Confrérie of Notre Dame and, by 1354, provost of all the Parisian merchants.

In November 1355, after King John II of France had called the Estates General to collect money for the continuing war against the English (the Hundred Years' War, 1337–1453), Marcel counteracted the King by proposing that the assembly administer the tax money. After John was captured at Poitiers (September 1356), Marcel in early 1357 led a hostile assembly that wanted to remove John's corrupt officials and that desired to have John's son, the Dauphin (later Charles V), placed under its tutelage. Later Charles was able to check some of the revolutionary furor, but he still needed money that the assembly controlled.

In November 1357, after helping Charles the Bad, king of Navarre, escape from imprisonment in the castle of Arleux, Marcel realized that with Charles the Bad's support he could force the Dauphin to submit. Marcel assassinated two of the Dauphin's marshals, frightening the Dauphin into believing that Marcel was the true head of government. After the Dauphin left Paris, Marcel began a defense of the city. In May 1358 he acted in concert with the Jacquerie (*q.v.*), who were revolting against the nobles; but when the revolt was put down in June, Marcel's popularity and power collapsed. In desperation he sought aid from the Flemish and even the English before he was assassinated that July.

His last objectives were far from the idealism of his early reforms: he desired to make himself king and to aid the interests of the King of Navarre. Marcel failed because he lacked a following outside Paris and could not make a moderate compromise that would have given him a wider base of support.

Marcel, Gabriel(-Honoré) (b. Dec. 7, 1889, Paris—d. Oct. 8, 1973, Paris), philosopher, dramatist, and critic, usually regarded as the first French Existential philosopher.

Early life and influences. Marcel was the only child of Henry Marcel, a government official, diplomat, and distinguished curator. Gabriel's mother died suddenly when he was four, leaving him with a sense of deep personal loss and yet of a continuing mysterious presence; the event made death and the irrevocable an early urgent concern for him. He was brought up by his maternal grandmother and his aunt—a devoted woman of stern upright character, who became his father's second wife and who had a major influence on his early development. He was, much to his distress, the centre of constant familial attention and care, and, despite his brilliant scholastic achievements, his family's incessant demands for ever better academic performance, together with the rigid, mechanical quality of his schooling, filled him with a lifelong aversion toward depersonalized, forced-fed modes of education. He found some consolation in travelling to foreign places on his vacations, and when his father became French minister to Sweden he accompanied him. These vacations were the beginning of his lifelong passion for travel and of the fulfillment of a deep inner urge to make himself at home in the new and to explore the unfamiliar. In later life he became versed in several foreign languages and literatures and played a significant role in making contemporary foreign writers known in France.

Gabriel Marcel, 1951

H. Roger-Viollet

Religion played no role in Marcel's upbringing. His father was a lapsed Catholic and cultured agnostic, who never bothered to have him baptized, and his aunt-stepmother, of nonreligious Jewish background, was converted to a liberal, humanist type of Protestantism. Reason, science, and the moral conscience were held to be sufficient guides, superseding traditional religion. Despite abundant parental love and solicitude, Marcel, in later life, looked back to this period as one of spiritual "servitude" and "captivity" that impelled him (without his knowing it) into a personal religious quest and to a philosophical inquiry into the conditions of religious faith.

Areas of his work. His search took three paths: music, drama, and philosophy. Hearing, playing, and composing music assumed an important role in the shaping of Marcel's mind from an early age, and composers such as J.S. Bach and Mozart played a more decisive role in his spiritual development than did great religious writers such as Augustine and Blaise Pascal. As a composer, his favourite mode was improvisation on the piano, for him a communion with a transcendent reality and not the mere expression of his private feelings and impressions. Only a small number of Marcel's improvisations have been transcribed or recorded; in 1945, however, he became a composer in the ordinary sense, devoting himself to the scored musical interpretation of poetry, ranging from that of Charles Baudelaire to that of Rainer Maria Rilke.

Playwriting provided another early and significant mode of expression. Henry Marcel frequently performed accomplished readings of dramatic works for his family. From an early age, Gabriel invented dialogues with imaginary brothers and sisters, and he wrote his first play at the age of eight. His own family situation had provided the living matrix for his later dramatic presentations of intertwined and irreconcilable aspirations, frustrations, and conflicts of definitely individual characters. The dramatic delineation of the chaotic and unpleasant aspects of human life complemented the expression of a transcendent harmony in his music, and both touched on key experiences and themes which were to be explored later in his philosophical meditations. They were unconsciously concrete illustrations of his philosphy before the fact, not deliberately contrived examples after the fact; they dealt with what were to be Marcel's main philosophical concerns as they emerged in the dramatic spiritual crises and relations of his full-dimensioned real-life characters, not with a disingenuous manipulation of animated concepts as in the conventional "play of ideas."

Marcel dealt with themes of spiritual authenticity and inauthenticity, fidelity and infidelity, and the consummation or frustration of personal relationships in his early plays, such as *La Grâce, Le Palais de sable, Le Coeur des autres,* and *L'Iconoclaste.* In *Le Quatuor en fa dièse* his musical, philosophical, and dramatic dispositions merge to render vividly the sense of the interpenetration of persons whose lives are bound up with one another. He appended one of his most significant philosophical essays ("On the Ontological Mystery") to the play *Le Monde cassé,* in which the "broken world" of the title is displayed in the empty life and relations of the charming, despairing, and yet still hoping woman who is its protagonist.

Philosophical development. Philosophy, an early passion with Marcel, was the only subject that aroused his whole-hearted participation during his preparatory education. At 18, he was at work on his thesis for a diploma in higher studies, "The Metaphysical Ideas of Coleridge in Their Relations with the Philosophy of Schelling," and he studied philosophy at the Sorbonne. Although he passed examinations to become a teacher of philosophy in secondary schools (1910), he never completed his doctoral dissertation—on the necessary conditions for the intelligibility of religious thought. He taught philosophy only intermittently, usually earning his living as a publisher's reader, editor, writer, and critic.

At first, philosophy for Marcel meant a highly abstract type of thought that sought to transcend the everyday empirical world. Gradually, over a long period of probing and searching, he came to shape a concrete philosophy that sought to deepen and restore the intimate human experience left behind by abstract thought. This philosophical "conversion" occurred when he was working for the French Red Cross, during World War I, trying to trace soldiers listed as missing. In place of the information on file cards he came to see real, though invisible, persons—presences—and to share in the agony of their grieving relatives. What Marcel called his "metapsychical" experiments—investigations of possible communications by means of telepathy, clairvoyance, prophecy, and spiritualism—also played a role in his philosophical conversion. For him these experiences convincingly challenged the conventional naturalistic and materialistic bent of contemporary philosophy, indicating a realm beyond that of ordinary sense-experience, and promising freedom from conformist biases and prohibitions in his philosophical quest.

Originally Marcel intended to express his philosophical reflections in the conventional treatise form, but as he came to see his philosophical vocation as essentially exploratory and the philosopher's situation to be always in search and en route (*homo viator*), he abandoned this format as too didactic. Instead he published his philosophical workbooks, his day-to-day journals of philosophical investigations (such as *Metaphysical Journal* and the later shorter philosophical diaries in *Being and Having* and *Presence and Immortality*). He also wrote essays on particular themes and occasions (as in *Homo Viator*); these were usually a more rounded development of themes explored initially in various journal entries, such as exile, captivity, separation, fidelity, and hope, which were also a response to the particular situation of the French people during the German occupation of 1940 to 1944.

The decisive event in Marcel's spiritual life

was his conversion to Roman Catholicism on March 23, 1929. The culmination of years of philosophical inquiry into the meanings and conditions of personal existence and faith, the action represented his realization that he had to choose a particular form of faith, that there is no faith in general. Despite his apparent affinity with Protestantism, which seemed more in keeping with his essentially nonconformist character and his need for intellectual freedom, he chose Catholicism, which he came to understand as a universal faith, not a special ecclesiastical institution or a partisan, exclusivist stance. After that decisive occasion he continued as an independent philosopher with a specific spiritual disposition, never as a theological apologist or spokesman for an official Catholic philosophy. And he continued in his plays, as well as in his philosophy, to explore and illuminate the dark and negative aspects of human existence.

Basic themes and method. Marcel's contribution to modern thought consisted of the exploration and illumination of whole ranges of human experience—trust, fidelity, promise, witness, hope, and despair—which have been dismissed by predominant schools of modern philosophy as not amenable to philosophical consideration. These explorations were buttressed by a remarkable reflective power and intellectual rigour, a metaphysical capacity par excellence.

His early central concept of "participation," the direct communion with reality, was gradually elaborated to elucidate everything from the elemental awareness of one's own body and sense-perception to the relation between human beings with ultimate being. The full, open relation between beings, thus conceived, is essentially "dialogical," the relation between an *I* and a *thou,* between the whole of a person and the fullness of what he confronts—another being, a "presence," and a "mystery," rather than an "object" of detached perception, thought, and expression. Such a relation requires an opening up to what is other than oneself, *disponibilité* (approximately "availability," "readiness," "permeability") and also an entering into, involvement, or *engagement*—dispositions demonstrable in everyday existence. The opposite is also ubiquitous—the refusal to open up and engage oneself, to give credit, to trust or hope, the disposition toward negation, despair, or even suicide. This possibility, for Marcel, is an essential characteristic of the human condition: man may deny as well as affirm his existence and either fulfill or frustrate his need to participate in being.

Marcel's method of thought and expression in dealing with these matters is an open, intuitive one. He probes the meaning of such terms as hope, fidelity, or witness and sketches the reality that they indicate through a sensitive description of the mind, action, and attitude of the hoper, faithful one, or witness. He makes use of concrete metaphors and real-life instances to evoke and embody the difficult-to-express experiences and realities he is exploring.

In his own unique way, Marcel was an outstanding example of one of the central emphases of mid-20th-century philosophy—Phenomenology. Marcel's use of this intuitive method was original and was developed independently of the work of the great German Phenomenologist Edmund Husserl and his followers, just as his notion of the *I–thou* relation was developed independently of Martin Buber and other dialogical thinkers, and just as his exploration of Existential themes occurred long before his reading of Kierkegaard and the bursting forth of Existential philosophy on the mid-20th-century European scene. Marcel may justly be called the first French Phenomenologist and the first French Existential philosopher (though he deprecated the term Existentialism).

Marcel was married in 1919 to Jacqueline Boegner (died 1947), whom he called "the absolute companion of my life." Their only child was an adopted son, Jean-Marie, the relation to whom may have inspired Marcel's later reflections on "creative paternity" and the spirit of adoption. (S.C./Ed.)

BIBLIOGRAPHY. *Biography.* Marie-Madeleine Davy, *Un Philosophe itinerant, Gabriel Marcel* (1959); Gabriel Marcel, "An Essay in Autobiography," in *The Philosophy of Existence* (1948).

Drama. Joseph Chenu, *Le Théâtre de Gabriel Marcel et sa signification métaphysique* (1948); Edgard Sottiaux, *Gabriel Marcel, philosophe et dramaturge* (1956).

Philosophy (in English). Seymour Cain, *Gabriel Marcel* (1963); Kenneth T. Gallagher, *The Philosophy of Gabriel Marcel* (1962); Sam Keen, *Gabriel Marcel* (1966); Vincent P. Miceli, *Ascent to Being: Gabriel Marcel's Philosophy of Communion* (1965); John B. O'Malley, *The Fellowship of Being: An Essay on the Concept of Person in the Philosophy of Gabriel Marcel* (1966). (in French): Michel Bernard, *La Philosophie Religieuse de Gabriel Marcel* (1952); Jean-Pierre Bagot, *Connaissance et amour* (1958); Etienne Gilson *et al., Existentialisme chrétien: Gabriel Marcel* (1947); Pietro Prini, *Gabriel Marcel et la méthodologie de l'invérifiable* (1953); Paul Ricoeur, *Gabriel Marcel et Karl Jaspers: Philosophie du mystère et philosophie du paradoxe* (1947); Roger Troisfontaines, *De l'Existence à l'Être,* 2 vol. (1953).

Bibliography. Troisfontaines' work (vol. 2, pp. 381–425), contains a complete list of Marcel's writings, published and unpublished, from 1897 to Jan. 1, 1953.

Marcellinus, SAINT (b. Rome?—d. October 304, Rome; feast day April 26), pope probably from 291/296 to 304, although the dates of his reign, as well as those of his predecessors Eutychianus and Gaius, are uncertain. His pontificate saw a long, tranquil period terminated by a renewed and bloody persecution of Christians, the last of its kind, by the Roman emperor Diocletian. It is believed that Marcellinus became an apostate during the persecution. St. Augustine of Hippo, however, discredits the charge. Marcellinus supposedly repented and was martyred, but his martyrdom is unproved.

A long period of crisis in the government of the church followed Marcellinus' death. Because of his alleged apostasy, peace was disturbed and was not restored until the election of Miltiades in July 311.

Marcello, Benedetto (b. July 24, 1686, Venice—d. July 24, 1739, Brescia, Rep. of Venice), Italian composer and writer, especially remembered for two works: the satirical pamphlet *Il teatro alla moda* (1720); and *Estro poeticoarmonico* (1724–26), a setting for voices and instruments of the first 50 psalms in an Italian paraphrase by G. Giustiniani. *Il teatro alla moda* is an amusing pamphlet in which Marcello vented his opinions on the state of musical drama at the time. The work was frequently reprinted and is an important document in the early history of opera.

Marcello was intended by his father for the law but turned to music instead. In 1711 he was a member of the Venetian Council of Forty and in 1730 went to Pola (Istria) as governor. After eight years he retired to Brescia as papal chamberlain. His compositions include operas, oratorios, cantatas, concerti, and sonatas. He was also a poet and translated John Dryden's *Timotheus* as a text for one of his own cantatas and wrote a libretto for G. Ruggeri's opera *Arato in Sparta* (1709).

The celebrated *Concerto in D Minor* for oboe and strings, long attributed to Benedetto, is now known to have been composed by his brother Alessandro (*c.* 1684–1750).

Marcellus I, SAINT (b. Rome—d. 309; feast day January 16), pope from May or June 308 to Jan. 16, 309. He succeeded St. Marcellinus after an interval of three or four years. The penances that he imposed on apostates resulting from the persecutions of Christians by the Roman emperor Diocletian led to rioting. In 309 he was banished from Rome by the Roman emperor Maxentius and died shortly afterward. His body was returned to Rome for burial.

Marcellus II, original name MARCELLO CERVINI (b. May 6, 1501, Montepulciano, Tuscany—d. May 1, 1555, Rome), pope from April 9/10 to May 1, 1555. He was made cardinal in December 1539 by Pope Paul III, for whom he served in numerous politico-ecclesiastical missions. With Cardinal Giovanni Maria Ciocchi del Monte (later Pope Julius III) and Cardinal Reginald Pole, he presided at the Council of Trent in 1545. A leader in church reform, he died less than a month after being elected pope.

Marcellus II, commemorative medallion by Giovanni Antonio de' Rossi

By courtesy of the National Gallery of Art, Washington, D.C., the Samuel H. Kress Collection

Marcellus, Marcus Claudius (b. *c.* 268 BC—d. 208, near Venusia, Apulia), Roman general who captured Syracuse during the Second Punic War (218–201). Although his successes have been exaggerated by the historian Livy, Marcellus deserved his sobriquet, "the sword of Rome."

In his first consulship (222) Marcellus fought the Insubres and won the *spolia opima* ("spoils of honour"; the arms taken by a general who killed an enemy chief in single combat) for the third and last time in Roman history. After the Roman defeat at Cannae (216), he commanded the remnant of the army at Canusium and saved Nola and southern Campania from Hannibal. From 214, when he was consul for the third time, to 211 he served in Sicily, where he stormed Leontini and, after a two-year siege, took Syracuse. His troops sacked the city and carried its art treasures to Rome. Marcellus was consul again in 210, and took Salapia in Apulia, which had revolted and joined forces with Hannibal. In 209 he fought Hannibal inconclusively near Venusia. In his fifth consulship (208) he was killed while reconnoitering enemy positions.

Marcellus, Marcus Claudius (d. May 45 BC), leading member of the Optimate (conservative senatorial aristocracy) and an uncompromising opponent of Julius Caesar. As consul in 51, Marcellus attempted to remove Caesar from his army command but was outmanoeuvred by the pro-Caesarian tribune Gaius Scribonius Curio. During the Civil War (Caesar against Pompey the Great and the Optimates, 49–45) Marcellus followed Pompey to Greece; after Pompey's death in 48 he retired to Mytilene, where he practiced rhetoric and studied philosophy. In 46 the Senate successfully appealed to Caesar to pardon Marcellus. It was on this occasion that Cicero delivered his speech *Pro Marcello.* Marcellus left for

Italy but was murdered in Piraeus, Achaea, by one of his own attendants.

Marcellus, Marcus Claudius (b. 42 BC—d. 23 BC, Baiae, Campania [Italy]), nephew of the emperor Augustus (reigned 27 BC–AD 14) and presumably chosen by him as heir, though Augustus himself denied it.

Marcellus was the son of Gaius Claudius Marcellus and Augustus' sister Octavia. In 25 he was married to the emperor's daughter Julia, an event that seemed to mark him as heir. His ambitions brought him into conflict with Agrippa. Marcellus served under Augustus in Spain in 25, but he died two years later, when he was a curule aedile. Great hopes had been built on him, and he was celebrated by many writers, especially by Virgil in a famous passage in the *Aeneid.* He was buried in the mausoleum of Augustus, and Augustus himself pronounced the funeral oration.

Marcellus, Theatre of, in Rome, building begun by Julius Caesar and completed by Augustus in 13 BC. It was dedicated in the name of Augustus' nephew, Marcus Claudius Marcellus (42–23 BC). According to Livy it was built on the site of an earlier theatre erected by Marcus Aemilius Lepidus—to the west of the Capitoline Hill. The theatre was restored by Vespasian. Complete foundations of the theatre's cunei (wedge-shaped sections of seats) exist under the Savelli Palace, and part of the external arcade, in Tuscan and Ionic orders, is well preserved. Estimates of the theatre's seating capacity range from 11,000 to 40,000.

March, third month of the Gregorian calendar. *See* month.

march, originally, musical form having an even metre with strongly accented first beats to facilitate military marching; many later examples, while retaining the military connotation, were not intended for actual marching. The march was a lasting bequest of the Turkish invasion of Europe, where it eventually consisted formally of an initial march alternating with one or more contrasting sections, or trios. One of the earliest examples, by Thoinot Arbeau, appeared in 1589. In 17th-century France, the military band of Louis XIV played marches, and France literally set the pace for march music all over Europe well into the 19th century. The French Revolutionary decade with its countless public rituals left a profound imprint on Ludwig van Beethoven's numerous marches, such as those in the *Piano Sonata in A Flat,* Opus 26, and the *Third Symphony* (*Eroica*). Similar events of the Napoleonic and post-Napoleonic eras are reflected in the pomp and circumstance of the march in Frédéric Chopin's *Piano Sonata in B Flat Minor* and the much-emulated "March to the Gallows" section of Hector Berlioz's *Symphonie fantastique.* In the 20th century, Sergey Prokofiev and Igor Stravinsky evoked the march for satirical purposes as well.

A relatively gentle tradition evolved in Austria from Wolfgang Amadeus Mozart and Franz Schubert to Gustav Mahler, whereas Britain excelled in marches that were theatrical rather than military in nature and as such were virtually unrivaled until the early 1900s when John Philip Sousa established America's preeminence in the field of band music.

March, EARLS OF, titled Scottish nobility of several creations, most notably in the family Dunbar, grouped below chronologically and indicated by the symbol •. The title derived from the Marches, or border regions, between Scotland and England.

•March, Patrick Dunbar, 2nd Earl of, 9TH EARL OF DUNBAR (b. 1285—d. 1369), Scottish noble prominent during the reigns of the Bruces Robert I and David II.

He gave refuge to Edward II of England after the Battle of Bannockburn and contrived his escape by sea to England. Later, he made peace with Robert de Bruce and by him was appointed governor of Berwick Castle, which he held against Edward III until the defeat of the Scots at Halidon Hill (July 19, 1333) made it no longer tenable. His countess, known in Scottish history and romance as "Black Agnes" (because of her swarthy complexion), daughter of Thomas Randolph, Earl of Moray, and grandniece of Robert de Bruce, is famous for her defense of Dunbar Castle against the English under the Earl of Salisbury in 1338, Salisbury being forced to abandon the attempt after a fierce siege lasting 19 weeks. The countess succeeded to the estates and titles of her brother, John Randolph, 3rd Earl of Moray. The earldom of Moray passed after her death to her second son, John Dunbar. The earldoms of March and Dunbar passed to a cousin of the 2nd earl, George Dunbar.

•March, Alexander Stewart, Earl of: *see* Albany, Alexander Stewart, Duke of.

March, EARLS OF, titled English nobility of several creations, most notably in the family Mortimer, grouped below chronologically and indicated by the symbol •. The title derived from the Marches, or border regions, between England and Wales.

•March, Roger Mortimer, 1st Earl of, 8TH BARON OF WIGMORE (b. 1287?—d. Nov. 29, 1330, Tyburn, near London, Eng.), lover of the English king Edward II's queen, Isabella of France, with whom he contrived Edward's deposition and murder (1327). For three years thereafter he was virtual king of England during the minority of Edward III.

The descendant of Norman knights who had accompanied William the Conqueror, he inherited wealthy family estates and fortunes, principally in Wales and Ireland, and in 1304 became 8th Baron of Wigmore on the death of his father, the 7th baron. He devoted the early years of his majority to obtaining effective control of his Irish lordships against his wife's kinsmen, the Lacys, who summoned to their aid Edward Bruce, brother of King Robert I of Scotland, when he was fighting to become king of Ireland. In 1316 Mortimer was defeated at Kells and withdrew to England, but afterward, as King Edward II's lieutenant in Ireland (November 1316), he was largely instrumental in overcoming Bruce and in driving the Lacys from Meath.

In 1317 he was associated with the Earl of Pembroke's "middle party" in English politics; but distrust of the Despensers (*see* Despenser, Hugh Le and Hugh Le) drove him, in common with other marcher lords, into opposition and violent conflict with the Despensers in South Wales in 1321. But, receiving no help from Edward II's other enemies, Roger and his uncle Roger Mortimer of Chirk made their submission in January 1322. Imprisoned in the Tower of London, Roger escaped in 1323 and fled to France, where in 1325 he was joined by Queen Isabella, who became his mistress. The exiles invaded England in September 1326; the fall of the Despensers was followed by the deposition of Edward II and his subsequent murder (1327), in which Mortimer was deeply implicated.

Thereafter, as the queen's paramour, Mortimer virtually ruled England. He used his position to further his own ends. Created Earl of March in October 1328, he secured for himself the lordships of Denbigh, Oswestry, and Clun, formerly belonging to the Earl of Arundel; the marcher lordships of the Mortimers of Chirk; and Montgomery, granted to him by the queen. His insatiable avarice, his arrogance, and his unpopular policy toward Scotland aroused against Mortimer a general revulsion among his fellow barons, and in October 1330 the young king Edward III, at the instigation of Henry of Lancaster, had him seized at Nottingham and conveyed to the Tower. Condemned for crimes declared to be notorious by his peers in Parliament, he was hanged at Tyburn as a traitor, and his estates were forfeited to the crown.

•March, Roger Mortimer, 2nd Earl of (b. Nov. 11, 1328, Ludlow, Shropshire, Eng.—d. Feb. 26, 1360, Rouvray, near Avallon, Burgundy [now in France]), a leading supporter of Edward III of England.

The eclipse of the Mortimer family's power following the death of the 1st Earl of March proved no more than temporary. Edward III's friendship with March's grandson Roger, 2nd Earl of March, enabled the latter in 1354 to recover his ancient patrimony. Royal support also lay behind a series of arbitrary decisions, thinly veiled as legal judgments, which restored to the young earl in addition many of the lands acquired by the 1st earl during his years of power, notably the lordship of Denbigh: the claims of the Earl of Salisbury were ignored, and the Earl of Arundel was pacified with the lordship of Chirk. By then, Roger had already served with the king at the Battle of Crécy (1346) and became one of the founder knights of the Garter. Later he accompanied Edward to Picardy in 1355 and, as constable, rode in the van of the great host that went to France in 1359.

•March, Edmund Mortimer, 5th Earl of, 3RD EARL OF ULSTER (b. Nov. 6, 1391, New Forest, Hampshire, Eng.—d. Jan. 19, 1425, Ulster, Ire.), friend of the Lancastrian king Henry V and an unwilling royal claimant advanced by rebel barons.

Son of Edmund (d. 1381), the 4th Earl of March, and Philippa, daughter and heiress of Edward III's second surviving son, Lionel of Clarence, he could be considered the heir presumptive of the childless Richard II. His position became dangerous after Henry IV's usurpation in 1399, for, by the ordinary rules of descent, he had a better title to the throne than the new king. Many people regarded him as the legitimate heir of Richard II, and it became the declared object of Owen Glendower and the English rebels to make him king of England. In February 1405 a bold attempt was made to abduct him and his brother, Roger, from Windsor, but they were soon recaptured. For this reason Edmund was kept under close supervision throughout Henry IV's reign, latterly by Henry, prince of Wales (the future Henry V). Edmund seems to have rewarded Henry V with persistent loyalty, and in August 1415 he revealed to the king a conspiracy formed by his own brother-in-law, Richard, Earl of Cambridge, and by Henry, Lord Scrope of Masham, to put him on the throne in Henry's place. He took part in the siege of Harfleur and thereafter served in all the French campaigns of Henry V's reign. Appointed lieutenant in Ireland in 1423, Edmund died of the plague there.

With the death of this childless earl, the male line of the Mortimers became extinct. His lands, his titles, and his potential claim to the throne passed to his nephew Richard (d. 1460), who became Duke of York in 1426 and who, in 1460, laid claim to the English throne in virtue of his descent through the Mortimers from Lionel of Clarence; his son Edward became king of England in 1461.

•March, Edward, Earl of: *see* Edward IV *under* Edward (England and Great Britain).

March, Ausias (b. 1397, Valencia, Spain—d. 1459, Valencia), first major poet to write in Catalan, whose verse greatly influenced other poets both of his own time and of the modern period.

As a young man March fought in Sicily, Sardinia, Corsica, and on Djorba under Alfonso V. March's verse describes the conflict between his sensuality and his passionate idealism, expressing an anguished contempt for the flesh and for his own weakness and that of his mistress, Teresa Bou, in yielding to it. Except for Petrarch, all the formative influences

Ausias March, detail of a lithograph
Archivo Mas, Barcelona

on March's poetry and on his attitude toward life—the Provençal troubadours, scholastic philosophy, and the Italian literary movement known as *dolce stil nuovo*—place him as a writer of the Middle Ages rather than of the Renaissance. March's poems, most fully published in 1543, are by convention divided into *Cants d'amor* and *Cants de mort* ("Songs of Love" and "Songs of Death," respectively before and after his mistress's death), *Cants morals* ("Moral Songs"), and the great *Cant espiritual* ("Spiritual Song"), in which he at last attains a measure of serenity in the face of death. An English translation by Arthur Terry was published in 1977.

March, Francis Andrew (b. Oct. 25, 1825, Millbury, Mass., U.S.—d. Sept. 9, 1911, Easton, Pa.), American language scholar and lexicographer who was a principal founder of modern comparative Anglo-Saxon (Old English) linguistics.

In 1857 March became professor of English language and comparative philology at Lafayette College, Easton, north of Philadelphia. He occupied this post, the first chair of its kind, until 1907.

March's monumental work was *A Comparative Grammar of the Anglo-Saxon Language* (1870; reprinted, 1977), based on 10 years of intensive research. He examined the relationship of Anglo-Saxon to Sanskrit, Greek, Latin, and five Germanic languages. It was immediately recognized in Europe and the United States as a front-ranking achievement, laying the cornerstone for subsequent historical studies of English. For a number of years he directed U.S. efforts contributing to the *New English Dictionary on Historical Principles* (*Oxford English Dictionary*). *The Spelling Reform* (1881) was his chief contribution to the reform of English orthography. With his son Francis Andrew March (1863–1928), he edited *A Thesaurus Dictionary of the English Language* (1903; 2nd ed., 1980).

March, Fredric, original name FREDERICK MCINTYRE BICKEL (b. Aug. 31, 1897, Racine, Wis., U.S.—d. April 14, 1975, Los Angeles, Calif.), versatile American stage and film actor, adept at both romantic leads and complex character roles.

March's early career, under his original name, included a part in the New York City production of *Deburau* (1920) and several performances in an Ohio stock company. His first professional engagement under the stage name Fredric March was in *The Melody Man* (1924). During the next four years March played various juvenile leads, married actress Florence Eldridge (1927), toured with her in a Theatre Guild series (1927–28), and eventually appeared in a West Coast production of *The Royal Family* (1928). The latter performance attracted the attention of Paramount Studios, which placed March under contract.

He made his film debut in *The Dummy* (1929). Several film roles followed before his appearance in the film version of *The Royal Family* (1930); as Anthony Cavandish, a character based on matinee idol and bon vivant John Barrymore, March created a nationwide following. He avoided Hollywood's penchant for typecasting, however; his reputation for versatility was firmly established two years later, when his portrayal of the starring role in *Dr. Jekyll and Mr. Hyde* won him his first Academy Award (1932). During his film career March appeared in more than 65 motion pictures; he won another Academy Award for *The Best Years of Our Lives* (1947) and was nominated for three more (*The Royal Family of Broadway,* 1931; *A Star Is Born,* 1937; and *Death of a Salesman,* 1951). His leading ladies included Greta Garbo (*Anna Karenina,* 1935) and Katharine Hepburn (*Mary of Scotland,* 1936) as well as his wife, with whom he appeared in many films, from *Studio Murder Mystery* (1929) to *Inherit the Wind* (1960).

After a hiatus of 10 years, March returned to the theatre to star with Eldridge in *Yr. Obedient Husband* (1938), and thereafter his activities were divided between stage and screen. Of his remaining stage roles, principal credits include Mr. Antrobus in *The Skin of Our Teeth* (1942), Major Joppolo in *A Bell for Adano* (1944), Nicholas in *The Autumn Garden* (1951), and his bravura performance as James Tyrone, to Eldridge's Mary Tyrone, in *Long Day's Journey into Night* (1956). For the latter roles, both he and Eldridge won the *Variety* New York Drama Critics Poll for best acting, and March received the Tony Award as best actor. His final performance was in the film version of *The Iceman Cometh* (1973).

March First Movement, also called SAMIL INDEPENDENCE MOVEMENT, series of demonstrations for Korean national independence from Japan that began on March 1, 1919, in the Korean capital city of Seoul and soon spread throughout the country. Before the Japanese finally suppressed the movement 12 months later, approximately 2,000,000 Koreans had participated in the more than 1,500 demonstrations. About 7,000 people were killed by the Japanese police and soldiers, and 16,000 were wounded; 715 private houses, 47 churches, and 2 school buildings were destroyed by fire. Approximately 46,000 people were arrested, of whom some 10,000 were tried and convicted.

The movement was begun by 33 Korean cultural and religious leaders who, after almost 10 years of Japanese rule, drew up a Korean "Proclamation of Independence" and then organized a mass demonstration in Seoul for March 1, 1919, their late emperor's commemoration day. On the appointed day, the 33 leaders, hoping to bring international pressure on Japan to end its colonial rule in Korea, signed and read their proclamation and had coconspirators read it in townships throughout the country. The suppressed anti-Japanese feelings of Koreans exploded, and mass demonstrations took place, forming the largest national protest rallies against foreign domination in Korean history.

Though the movement failed to bring about its paramount goal of national independence, it was significant in strengthening national unity, leading to the birth in Shanghai of the Korean Provisional Government (*q.v.*), and drawing worldwide attention. Finally, the failure of the March First Movement greatly enhanced the rise of the Korean communist party. Today, March 1 is a national holiday in both North and South Korea.

March fly, any stout, armoured insect of the family Bibionidae (order Diptera), with strong spurs on its legs. March flies are commonly seen around flowers during spring and early summer. The dark, short adults frequently have red and yellow markings. The larvae feed on the roots of plants and on decaying vegetation.

March Laws, also called APRIL LAWS, measures enacted by the Hungarian Diet at Pozsony (modern Bratislava) during the Revolution of 1848 that created a modern national Magyar state. After revolutions had broken out in Paris (Feb. 24, 1848) and in Vienna (March 13), liberal Hungarians, who dominated the lower house of the Diet, sought to avoid radical social revolution by emphasizing reform and national liberation.

On March 15 the liberals' leader Lajos Kossuth presented their program to the Diet; it was intended to preserve the gentry's power and to create an independent Magyar state united with the Austrian Empire only in the person of the emperor-king. This program, known subsequently as the March Laws, was adopted by both houses.

The Laws provided for a viceroy in Budapest to exercise the prerogatives of the emperor without answering to Vienna. They also stated that Hungary was to control its own national guard, budget, and foreign policy and that it was to have its own ministry responsible to the Hungarian parliament at Budapest; the parliament was to replace the feudal Diet at Pozsony, and suffrage was to be based on a property qualification. All the "lands of the crown of St. Stephen" were to be part of the Magyar state (including Transylvania and Croatia), but representatives to the parliament

Kossuth recruiting in Czegléd (Cegléd), September 1848
INTERFOTO MTI, Budapest

were required to speak the Hungarian language. The nobility's exemption from taxation was abolished, and feudalism was ended by abolishing the *robot* (the labour owed by the peasants to their landlords); the state was to compensate the landowners.

On April 11, 1848, the March Laws were constitutionally confirmed by Emperor Ferdinand I (reigned 1835–48), and the Hungarian Revolution was legalized. Although Austria denied the validity of the laws after the revolution was defeated (1849), Hungary continued to insist on their legality. Under the 1867 *Ausgleich* (Compromise), Hungary received full internal autonomy.

March on Rome (Mussolini coup): *see* Rome, March on.

Marchais, Georges (-René-Louis) (b. June 7, 1920, La Hoguette, France—d. Nov. 16, 1997, Paris), French politician, leader of the French Communist Party from 1972 to 1994.

As a young man Marchais worked as a mechanic and in 1946 became secretary of the union of metalworkers in Issy-les-Moulineaux. Marchais joined the Communist Party in 1947, and his rise through the hierarchy was rapid. In 1956 he became a member of the central committee, and in 1972 he became secretary general of the party. In 1972, with the Socialist leader François Mitterrand and the radical leader Robert Fabre, Marchais worked out a common political program between the leftist parties in France, to combine their electoral strength. Marchais was elected to the National Assembly in March 1973 and was continually reelected thereafter. He and his party supported Mitterrand as the unsuccessful candidate of the unified left in the presidential elections of 1974.

After the breakup of the Communist-Socialist alliance in 1977, Marchais abandoned his previous moderate Marxist stance and adopted a more pro-Soviet, hard-line policy. But his attempt to restore the Communists to their former dominance of the left by adopting an orthodox and dogmatic Communist stance alienated many sympathizers and drove them to the Socialist camp. In the first round of the presidential election in April 1981, Marchais ran against Mitterrand but dropped out after the first round, having polled only 15.3 percent of the vote, the worst showing for a Communist presidential candidate since 1935. In subsequent years support for the Communist Party declined further; in parliamentary elections held in 1986 and 1993 the party received less than 10 percent of the vote.

Throughout his career Marchais's wartime record was a subject of controversy. Opponents charged that during World War II he volunteered to work in an aircraft factory in Germany; Marchais claimed that he had been deported into forced labour.

Consult the INDEX *first*

Marchand, Jean-Baptiste (b. Nov. 22, 1863, Thoissey, France—d. Jan. 13, 1934, Paris), French soldier and explorer known for his occupation of Fashoda (now Kodok) in the Sudan in 1898.

After four years in the ranks, Marchand was sent to military school at St. Maxient and commissioned a sublieutenant in 1887. He saw active duty in West Africa in Senegal (1889), where he was wounded twice, and later at the capture of Diena, during which he was severely wounded. Subsequently, he was made a chevalier of the Legion of Honour. As early as 1890 he explored the sources of the Niger. Later he explored the western Sudan (1892) and the hinterland of the Ivory

Jean-Baptiste Marchand, detail from a portrait by Jacques-Fernand Humbert; in the National Museum of African and Oceanian Arts, Paris

Giraudon—Art Resource

Coast (1893–95). To prevent the British from linking the Sudan to Uganda, the French government in January 1897 sent Marchand on a march across Central Africa from Brazzaville, in the French Congo, to Fashoda on the White Nile, where he arrived with a small party in July 1898. His presence on the Nile provoked a crisis in Anglo-French relations. When his government withdrew its claims, Marchand returned to Paris and became the idol of the French nation. For his bravery in crossing Africa and confronting the British, he was promoted to commander of the Legion of Honour.

Marchand continued to serve with distinction during the Boxer Rebellion, the Chinese revolt (1900) against Western and Japanese expansion in China, in which he took part in the march on Peking. In World War I, he fought, as a general in command of the Colonial Division, in several major engagements on the Western Front. On retirement in 1919 he received the Grand Cross of the Legion of Honour.

Marchand, Marie-Françoise (French actress): *see* Dumesnil, Mademoiselle.

Marchantia, genus of liverworts (creeping ribbonlike plants) in the order Marchantiales, commonly found on moist clay or silty soils, especially on recently burned land throughout

Female *Marchantia polymorpha* bearing sexual reproductive structures (stalks with fingerlike projections)

By courtesy of the Field Museum of Natural History, Chicago

the Northern Hemisphere. *Marchantia polymorpha,* a well-known species, often is discussed as a representative liverwort in biology textbooks. Dark green *Marchantia* gametophytes (sexual plants) are branched and ribbonlike, about 1.3 cm (0.5 inch) wide and 5 to 13 cm long. The diamond-shaped markings on their upper surfaces, signs of interior air chambers, have a central pore through which air diffuses.

Male and female plants have umbrellalike, stalked reproductive structures. The male structures are disk-shaped with scalloped edges; the female structures have nine fingerlike projections. Sperm produced by male plants are splashed by raindrops onto female plants. Sporophytes (asexual plants) develop from fertilized eggs in the female structures. Vegetative reproduction occurs in both male and female plants by means of rounded, fringed gemmae (asexual buds) or by pieces of the plant body that may break off and grow.

Marche, French province before the Revolution of 1789 corresponding roughly to the modern *département* of Creuse, with a small fragment of Indre and much of northern Haute-Vienne.

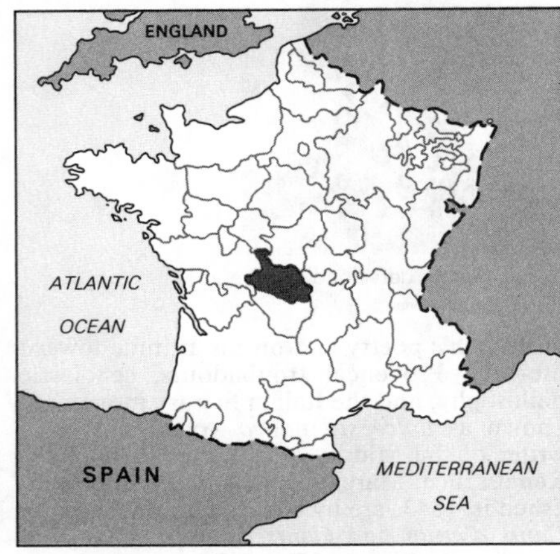

The *gouvernement* of Marche in 1789

In ancient times the country was part of Limousin, from which it was detached in the middle of the 10th century to form a separate frontier countship (march) to protect Poitou and the rest of the duchy of Aquitaine against invasion from the north. During the 12th and 13th centuries, a chain of fiefs depending directly on Poitiers, interspersed with ecclesiastical lordships, grew up to cut the countship practically into western and eastern halves, *basse* Marche and *haute* Marche. Held by a junior line of the Bourbons from 1342 to 1435 and by a junior line of the Armagnacs from 1435 to 1477, the countship later went to Pierre II, duc de Bourbon (sire de Beaujeu), and then to the constable Charles, duc de Bourbon. Confiscated by Francis I of France in 1527, it was granted successively to the widows of French kings from 1574 to 1643. From the late 17th century until the end of the ancien régime, the title was borne by the sons of the princes de Conti.

Administratively, *basse* Marche was from 1586 under the intendant of Limoges, and *haute* Marche was under the intendant of Moulins (Bourbonnais); judicially, the whole province depended on the Parlement of Paris.

Marche, English THE MARCHES, region in central Italy fronting on the Adriatic Sea and comprising the provinces of Ancona, Ascoli Piceno, Macerata, and Pesaro e Urbino; it has a total area of 3,742 square miles (9,692 square km). A region of mountains and hills, its only pieces of level land are scattered along river valleys and on the Adriatic shore northwest of Ancona. Its mountain backbone is the Umbrian-Marchigian section of the Apennines, rising to 8,130 feet (2,478 m) at Monte Vettore. The administrative boundary between Marche and neighbouring Umbria, on the west, is the watershed between the Tyrrhenian and Adriatic slopes.

Except for the northernmost part, the hills of Montefeltro, Marche is crossed by numerous rivers running from the Apennines east to the Adriatic; the most important are the Metauro, Foglia, Esino, Potenza, Chienti, and Tronto. In their upper sections these streams flow through narrow valleys and some deep gorges. In their lower sections they widen, and the valley floors are intensively cultivated, most of the lower slopes either in meadows or in well-tended fields.

The region, originally inhabited by the Gauls and the Picenes, was early incorporated into the domain of Rome and became a single administrative unit as early as AD 292. During the early Middle Ages the southern part was ruled by the Lombards; the northern section, the Maritime Pentapolis (Rimini, Pesaro, Fano, Senigallia, and Ancona) on the Adriatic coast, was controlled by the Byzantine exarchate of Ravenna. The modern name appeared during the 10th century when the region was divided into the imperial marches (border provinces) of Ancona, Camerino, and Fermo; shortly afterward numerous communes constituted themselves into independent units. With the emergence in the 12th and 13th centuries of such powerful feudal families as the Montefeltro of Urbino and the Malatesta of Pesaro (and Rimini), turbulent times set in—aggravated by the desire of the popes to reestablish their temporal authority, nominal in the area since the 8th century. This process, begun in the 14th century, was completed with the incorporation of the duchy of Urbino into the Papal States in 1631. Marche became part of the Kingdom of Italy in 1860.

The economy of Marche is primarily agricultural. Its principal products are wheat, corn (maize), fodder, olives, and wine. Livestock raising is extensive, and fishing is important in several of the Adriatic ports, particularly San Benedetto del Tronto and Ancona (*q.v.*), the capital and principal port. Industrial development is slight and includes shipbuilding at Ancona, paper at Fabriano, textiles at Iesi, musical instruments at Castelfidardo, and pottery at Pesaro and Recanati. The main artery of northwest–southeast traffic is the coastal railroad from Bologna to Foggia and Bari; also, a direct rail line runs from Ancona to Rome. Pop. (1983 est.) mun., 1,417,806.

Märchen, plural MÄRCHEN, folktale characterized by elements of magic or the supernatural, such as the endowment of a mortal character with magical powers or special knowledge; variations expose the hero to supernatural beings or objects. The German term *Märchen,* used universally by folklorists, also embraces tall tales and humorous anecdotes; although it is often translated as "fairy tale," the fairy is not a requisite motif.

Märchen usually begin with a formula such as "once upon a time," setting the story in an indefinite time and place. Their usual theme is the triumph over difficulty, with or without supernatural aid, of the one least likely to succeed. The characters are stylized—wicked stepmothers, stupid ogres, or handsome princes. The situations are familiar to the listeners; *i.e.,* European *Märchen* reflect the economic and domestic arrangements of peasants and simple workmen, such as millers, tailors, or smiths. Those of ancient origin may reflect archaic social conditions, such as matriarchy, primitive birth and marriage customs, or old forms of inheritance. The hero, however poor or friendless, has easy access to the king and may, through luck, cleverness, or magic information, win the king's daughter in marriage and automatically inherit the kingdom.

Versions of these stories, sometimes almost identical, have been found all over the world. Their origin is unknown. They have been subjected to literary reworking from very early times. Interest in the serious study of *Märchen* developed in the early 19th century. The first systematic attempt to transcribe and record them verbatim from oral tradition was the collection *Kinder-und Hausmärchen* (1812–15) of the Brothers Grimm, popularly known as *Grimm's Fairy Tales. See also* fairy tale.

Marchena Island, one of the smaller (area 45 sq mi [117 sq km]) of the Galápagos Islands, in the eastern Pacific Ocean, 600 mi (965 km) west of Ecuador. Called Bindloe in the 17th century by English pirates in honour of a member of the Jamaican council who condoned their activities, the island was renamed Torres in the late 18th century by the Spanish navigator Don Alonso de Torres, and finally by the Ecuadorian government as Marchena. The uninhabited island is dominated by a single volcanic crater.

Marchesi de Castrone, Mathilde, *née* MATHILDE GRAUMANN (b. March 24, 1821, Frankfurt am Main—d. Nov. 17, 1913, London), operatic soprano whose teaching transmitted the 18th-century bel canto style of singing to the 20th century.

She studied in Paris under Manuel García, the foremost teacher of singing of the 19th century, and made her debut as a singer in 1849. In 1854 she began teaching. She taught at the conservatories of Vienna and Cologne as well as in London and Paris. In 1852 she married the baritone Salvatore Marchesi (1822–1908), with whom she made concert tours.

Her teaching stressed the purity and precision and sound vocal technique taught by García, who was the central figure in the preservation of the bel canto style. Her own pupils included most of the leading female singers of the early 20th century, among them Nellie Melba, Emma Calvé, and Emma Eames. She published works on the technique of singing and, in 1897, reminiscences, *Marchesi and Music.* Her daughter, Blanche (1863–1940), was a Wagnerian singer and a teacher.

marchioness: *see* marquess.

Marchmont, Patrick Hume, 1st earl of: *see* Hume, Sir Patrick.

Marcian (b. 396, Thrace—d. early 457, Constantinople), Eastern Roman emperor from 450 to 457, the last ruler of the dynasty begun by the emperor Theodosius I (died 395). His relatively peaceful reign, which was later viewed as a golden age in the Eastern Roman Empire, provided a marked contrast to the violence that was destroying the Western Empire.

Beginning his career as a professional soldier, Marcian came to hold a high position in the service of Aspar, Theodosius II's powerful master of soldiers. After Theodosius' death in 450, Aspar and Theodosius' sister, Pulcheria, had Marcian appointed emperor (August 25). As part of this arrangement, Marcian was made the nominal husband of Pulcheria in order to formally perpetuate the Theodosian dynasty.

Marcian was an able administrator who left a well-filled treasury upon his death. He saved money by refusing to pay the annual tribute to the Huns and by carefully avoiding costly military ventures abroad. There were minor troubles with nomadic peoples in Syria and along the frontier of southern Egypt, but he refused to become entangled in war with the Vandals in Africa. The most notable event of his reign was the fourth ecumenical council assembled by Marcian at Chalcedon (modern Kadıköy, Tur.) in 451. This council upheld the orthodox Christian doctrine that Christ had two natures, divine and human, and rejected Monophysitism, which maintained that Christ had one divine nature. Marcian's daughter Euphemia was married to Anthemius, emperor of the West from 467 to 472. Leo I became emperor of the Eastern Empire upon Marcian's death.

Marciano, Rocky, byname of ROCCO FRANCIS MARCHEGIANO, also called THE BROCKTON BLOCKBUSTER (b. Sept. 1, 1923, Brockton, Mass., U.S.—d. Aug. 31, 1969, near Newton, Iowa), world heavyweight boxing champion from Sept. 23, 1952, when he knocked out champion Jersey Joe Walcott in 13 rounds in Philadelphia, to April 27, 1956, when he retired from the ring. Marciano was undefeated in 49 professional fights, scoring 43 knockouts. Among his victims were two former heavyweight champions other than Walcott: Joe Louis and Ezzard Charles.

First interested in a professional baseball career, Marciano began to box while in the U.S. Army during World War II. He had his first professional fight on March 17, 1947. Knockouts of Rex Layne, Louis, Lee Savold, and Harry (Kid) Matthews earned him a chance

Rocky Marciano (right) fighting Jersey Joe Walcott, 1952

UPI—EB Inc.

to win the championship. Marciano, knocked down by Walcott in the first round, was behind on points when, in the 13th round, he knocked the champion unconscious with a single punch.

Marciano, aged 32, retired after defending the championship six times. An unscientific but hard-punching and exceptionally durable fighter, he completely dominated the heavyweight division. He was killed in the crash of an airplane in which he was a passenger. Everett Skehan's biography was published in 1977.

Marcillac, François, prince de (writer): *see* La Rochefoucauld, François VI, duc de.

Marcionite, any member of a Gnostic sect that flourished in the 2nd century AD. The name derives from Marcion of Asia Minor who, sometime after his arrival in Rome, fell under the influence of Cerdo, a Gnostic Christian, whose stormy relations with the Church of Rome were the consequence of his belief that the God of the Old Testament could be distinguished from the God of the New Testament—the one embodying justice, the other goodness. For accepting, developing, and propagating such ideas, Marcion was expelled from the church in 144 as a heretic, but the movement he headed became both widespread and powerful.

The basis of Marcionite theology was that there were two cosmic gods. A vain and angry creator god who demanded and ruthlessly exacted justice had created the material world of which man, body and soul, was a part—a striking departure from the usual Gnostic thesis that only man's body is part of creation, that his soul is a spark from the true but unknown superior God, and that the world creator is a demonic power. The other god, according to Marcion, was completely ineffable and bore no intrinsic relation to the created universe at all. Out of sheer goodness, he had sent his son Jesus Christ to save man from the material world and bring him to a new home. One of Marcion's favourite texts with respect to Christ's mission was Letter of Paul to the Galatians 3:13: "Christ redeemed us." Christ's sacrifice was not in any sense a vicarious atonement for human sin but rather a legalistic act that cancelled the claim of the creator God upon men. In contrast to the typical Gnostic claim to a special revelatory gnosis, Marcion and his followers emphasized faith in the effect of Christ's act. They practiced stern asceticism to restrict contact with the creator's world while looking forward to eventual salvation in the realm of the extra-worldly God. They admitted women to the priesthood and bishopric. The Marcionites were considered the most dangerous of the Gnostics by the established church. When Polycarp met Marcion at Rome he is said to have identified Marcion as "the firstborn of Satan."

Marcion is perhaps best known for his treatment of Scripture. Though he rejected the Old Testament as the work of the creator God, he did not deny its efficacy for those who did not believe in Christ. He rejected attempts to harmonize Jewish biblical traditions with Christian ones as impossible. He accepted as authentic all of the Pauline Letters and the Gospel According to Luke (after he had expurgated them of Judaizing elements). His treatment of Christian literature was significant, for it forced the early church to fix an approved canon of theologically acceptable texts out of the mass of available but unorganized material.

Marcius, Ancus (Roman king): *see* Ancus Marcius.

Marco Polo Bridge Incident (July 7, 1937), conflict between Chinese and Japanese troops near the Marco Polo Bridge outside of Peiping (now Peking), which developed into the warfare between the two countries that was the prelude to the Pacific side of World War II.

In 1931 Japan occupied the former northeastern Chinese region of Manchuria (Northeast Provinces) and established the puppet state of Manchukuo, spending large sums to develop the region's industry. This violation of China's territorial integrity produced a growing anti-Japanese movement in China. By 1937 this movement had grown so strong that the Chinese Communists and Nationalists agreed to end their civil war and form a United Front against further Japanese aggression.

On the night of July 7, 1937, a small Japanese force on maneuvers near the Marco Polo Bridge demanded entry to the tiny walled town of Wan-p'ing in order to search for one of their soldiers. The Chinese garrison in the town refused the Japanese entry; a shot was heard; and the two sides began firing. The Chinese government, under strong anti-Japanese pressure, refused to make any concessions in the negotiation of the dispute. The Japanese, although not wanting to be involved in a land war in China that could leave them vulnerable to Soviet forces in the north, also maintained their position, fearing the new Chinese United Front and the growing anti-Japanese movement. As a result, the conflict, which no one seemed to desire, continued to grow.

As the fighting spread to central China, the Japanese scored successive victories. Under mounting public pressure not to retreat, the Japanese government decided to seek a quick victory in China, and the two sides plunged into what was to become World War II.

Marcomanni, also spelled MARCOMANI, a German tribe that settled in the Main River valley soon after 100 BC; they were members of the Suebi group (*see* Suebi). To escape Roman aggression in 9 BC they migrated east to Bohemia, where under their king Maroboduus they built a powerful confederation of tribes. The kingdom broke up after a war with the great German leader Arminius and in AD 19 Maroboduus became an exile in Roman territory. For many decades thereafter the Marcomanni and their neighbours the Quadi were clients of Rome, receiving frequent subsidies; and many Roman traders settled in their country. An attack by both tribes on the Romans in AD 88–89 was an isolated incident. But about 167 the Marcomanni with many allies invaded Roman territory and penetrated into Italy. The emperor Marcus Aurelius expelled them but was involved in war with them almost constantly until his death in 180, having apparently decided to annex their country. His plans were abandoned by his son Commodus. After that time surviving records do not mention the Marcomanni, but they probably formed part of the later Alemannic confederations.

Marconi, Guglielmo (b. April 25, 1874, Bologna, Italy—d. July 20, 1937, Rome), Italian physicist and inventor of a successful system of radio telegraphy (1896). In 1909 he received the Nobel Prize for Physics. He later worked on the development of shortwave wireless communication, which constitutes the basis of nearly all modern long-distance radio.

Education and early work. Marconi's father was Italian and his mother Irish. Educated first in Bologna and later in Florence, Marconi then went to the technical school in Leghorn, where, in studying physics, he had every opportunity for investigating electromagnetic wave technique, following the earlier mathematical work of James Clerk Maxwell and the experiments of Heinrich Hertz, who first produced and transmitted radio waves, and Sir Oliver Lodge, who conducted research on lightning and electricity.

In 1894 Marconi began experimenting at his father's estate near Bologna, using comparatively crude apparatus: an induction coil for increasing voltages, with a spark discharger controlled by a Morse key at the sending end and a simple coherer (a device designed to detect radio waves) at the receiver. After preliminary experiments over a short distance, he first improved the coherer; then, by systematic tests, he showed that the range of signaling was increased by using a vertical aerial with a metal plate or cylinder at the top of a pole connected to a similar plate on the ground. The range of signaling was thus increased to about 2.4 km (1.5 miles), enough to convince Marconi of the potentialities of this new system of communication. During this period, he also conducted simple experiments with reflectors around the aerial to concentrate the radiated electrical energy into a beam instead of spreading it in all directions.

Marconi, *c.* 1908
By courtesy of the Library of Congress, Washington, D.C.

Receiving little encouragement to continue his experiments in Italy, he went, in 1896, to London, where he was soon assisted by Sir William Preece, the chief engineer of the post office. Marconi filed his first patent in England in June 1896 and, during that and the following year, gave a series of successful demonstrations, in some of which he used balloons and kites to obtain greater height for his aerials. He was able to send signals over distances of up to 6.4 km on the Salisbury Plain and to nearly 14.5 km across the Bristol Channel. These tests, together with Preece's lectures on them, attracted considerable publicity both in England and abroad, and in June 1897 Marconi went to La Spezia, where a land station was erected and communication was established with Italian warships at distances of up to 19 km.

There remained much skepticism about the useful application of this means of communication and a lack of interest in its exploitation. But Marconi's cousin Jameson Davis, a practicing engineer, financed his patent and helped in the formation of the Wireless Telegraph and Signal Company, Ltd. (changed in 1900 to Marconi's Wireless Telegraph Company, Ltd.). During the first years, the company's efforts were devoted chiefly to showing the full possibilities of radiotelegraph. A further step was taken in 1899 when a wireless station was established at South Foreland, England, for communicating with Wimereux in France, a distance of 50 km; in the same year British battleships exchanged messages at 121 km.

In September 1899, Marconi equipped two U.S. ships to report to newspapers in New York City the progress of the yacht race for the America's Cup. The success of this demonstration aroused worldwide excitement and led to the formation of the American Marconi Company. The following year the Marconi International Marine Communication Company, Ltd., was established for the purpose of installing and operating services between ships and land stations. In 1900 also, Marconi filed his now-famous patent No. 7777 for Improvements in Apparatus for Wireless Telegraphy. The patent, based in part on earlier work in wireless telegraphy by Sir Oliver Lodge, enabled several stations to operate on different wavelengths without interference. (In 1943 the U.S. Supreme Court overturned patent No. 7777, indicating that Lodge, Nikola Tesla, and John Stone appeared to have priority in the development of radio-tuning apparatus.)

Major discoveries and innovations. Marconi's great triumph was, however, yet to come. In spite of the opinion expressed by some distinguished mathematicians that the curvature of the Earth would limit practical communication by means of electric waves to a distance of 161–322 km, Marconi succeeded in December 1901 in receiving at St. John's, Nfd., signals transmitted across the Atlantic Ocean from Poldhu in Cornwall, England. This achievement created an immense sensation in every part of the civilized world, and, though much remained to be learned about the laws of propagation of radio waves around the Earth and through the atmosphere, it was the starting point of the vast development of radio communications, broadcasting, and navigation services that took place in the next 50 years, in much of which Marconi himself continued to play an important part.

During a voyage on the U.S. liner *Philadelphia* in 1902, Marconi received messages from distances of 1,125 km (700 miles) by day and 3,200 km (2,000 miles) by night. He thus was the first to discover that, because some radio waves travel by reflection from the upper regions of the atmosphere, transmission conditions are sometimes more favourable at night than during the day. This circumstance is due to the fact that the upward travel of the waves is limited in the daytime by absorption in the lower atmosphere, which becomes ionized—and so electrically conducting—under the influence of sunlight. In 1902 also, Marconi patented the magnetic detector in which the magnetization in a moving band of iron wires is changed by the arrival of a signal causing a click in the telephone receiver connected to it. During the ensuing three years, he also developed and patented the horizontal directional aerial. Both of these devices improved the efficiency of the communication system. In 1910 he received messages at Buenos Aires from Clifden in Ireland over a distance of approximately 9,650 km (6,000 miles), using a wavelength of about 8,000 m (about 5 miles). Two years later, Marconi introduced further innovations that so improved transmission and reception that important long-distance stations could be established. This increased efficiency allowed Marconi to send the first radio message from England to Australia in September 1918.

In spite of the rapid and widespread developments then taking place in radio and its applications to maritime use, Marconi's intuition and urge to experiment were by no means exhausted. In 1916, during World War I, he saw the possible advantages of shorter wavelengths that would permit the use of reflectors around the aerial, thus minimizing the interception of transmitted signals by the enemy and also effecting an increase in signal strength. After tests in Italy (20 years after his original experiments with reflectors), Marconi continued the work in Great Britain and, on a wavelength of 15 m (49 feet), received signals over a range of 30–160 km (20–100 miles). In 1923 the experiments were continued on board his steam yacht *Elettra,* which had been specially equipped. From a transmitter of 1 kilowatt at Poldhu, Cornwall, signals were received at a distance of 2,250 km (1,400 miles). These signals were much louder than those from Caernarvon in Wales on a wavelength several hundred times as great and with 100 times the power at the transmitter. Thus began the development of shortwave wireless communication that, with the use of the beam aerial system for concentrating the energy in the desired direction, is the basis of most modern long-distance radio communication. In 1924 the Marconi company obtained a contract from the post office to establish shortwave communication between England and the countries of the British Commonwealth.

A few years later Marconi returned to the study of still shorter waves of about 0.5 m (1.6 feet). At these very short wavelengths a parabolic reflector of moderate size gives a considerable increase in power in the desired direction. Experiments conducted off the coast of Italy on the yacht *Elettra* soon showed that useful ranges of communication could be achieved with low-powered transmitters. In 1932, using very short wavelengths, Marconi installed a radiotelephone system between Vatican City and the pope's palace at Castel Gandolfo. In later work Marconi once more demonstrated that even radio waves as short as 55 cm (22 inches) are not limited in range to the horizon or to optical distance between transmitter and receiver.

Marconi received many honours and several honorary degrees. He was awarded the Nobel Prize for Physics (1909) for the development of wireless telegraphy; sent as plenipotentiary delegate to the peace conference in Paris (1919), in which capacity he signed the peace treaties with Austria and with Bulgaria; created marchese and nominated to the Italian senate (1929); and chosen president of the Royal Italian Academy (1930). (R.L.S.-R.)

BIBLIOGRAPHY. Degna Marconi, *My Father, Marconi* (1962); W.P. Jolly, *Marconi* (1972); W.J. Baker, *A History of the Marconi Company* (1970).

Marcos, Ferdinand E., in full FERDINAND EDRALIN MARCOS (b. Sept. 11, 1917, Sarrat, Phil.—d. Sept. 28, 1989, Honolulu, Hawaii, U.S.), Philippine lawyer and politician who, as head of state from 1966 to 1986, established an authoritarian regime in the Philippines that came under criticism for corruption and for its suppression of democratic processes.

Marcos attended school in Manila and studied law in the late 1930s at the University of the Philippines, near that city. Tried for the assassination in 1933 of a political opponent of his politician father, Marcos was found guilty in November 1939. But he argued his case on appeal to the Philippine Supreme Court and won acquittal a year later. He became a trial lawyer in Manila. During World War II he was an officer with the Philippine armed forces. Marcos' later claims of having been a leader in the Filipino guerrilla resistance movement were a central factor in his political success, but U.S. government archives revealed that he actually played little or no part in anti-Japanese activities during 1942–45.

From 1946 to 1947 Marcos was a technical assistant to Manuel Roxas, the first president of the independent Philippine republic. He was a member of the House of Representatives (1949–59) and of the Senate (1959–65), serving as Senate president (1963–65). In 1965 Marcos, who was a prominent member of the Liberal Party founded by Roxas, broke with it after failing to get his party's nomination for president. He then ran as the Nationalist Party candidate for president against the Liberal president, Diosdado Macapagal. The campaign was expensive and bitter. Marcos won and was inaugurated as president on Dec. 30, 1965. In 1969 he was reelected, the first Philippine president to serve a second term. During his first term he had made progress in agriculture, industry, and education. Yet his administration was troubled by increasing student demonstrations and violent urban-guerrilla activities.

On Sept. 21, 1972, Marcos imposed martial law. Holding that communist and subversive forces precipitated the crisis, he acted swiftly; opposition politicians were jailed, and the armed forces became an arm of the regime. Opposed by political leaders—notably Benigno Aquino, Jr., who was jailed and held in detention for almost eight years—Marcos was also criticized by church leaders and others. In the provinces Maoist communists (New People's Army) and Muslim separatists undertook guerrilla activities intended to bring down the central government. Under martial law the president assumed extraordinary powers, including the ability to suspend the writ of habeas corpus. Marcos announced the end of martial law in January 1981 but continued to rule in an authoritarian fashion under various constitutional formats. He won election to the newly created post of president against token opposition in June 1981.

Marcos' wife from 1954 was Imelda Romuáldez Marcos, a former beauty queen. Imelda became a powerful figure after the institution of martial law in 1972. She was often criticized for her appointments of relatives to lucrative governmental and industrial positions while she held the posts of governor of Metropolitan Manila (1975–86) and minister of human settlements and ecology (1979–86).

Marcos' later years in power were marred by rampant government corruption, economic stagnation, the steady widening of economic inequalities between the rich and the poor, and the steady growth of a communist guerrilla insurgency active in the rural areas of the Philippines' innumerable islands.

By 1983 Marcos' health was beginning to fail, and opposition to his rule was growing. Hoping to present an alternative to both Marcos and the increasingly powerful New People's Army, Benigno Aquino, Jr., returned to Manila on Aug. 21, 1983, only to be shot dead as he stepped off the plane. The assassination was seen as the work of the government and touched off massive antigovernment protests. An independent commission appointed by Marcos concluded in 1984 that high military officers were responsible for Aquino's assassination. To reassert his mandate, Marcos called for presidential elections to be held in 1986. But a formidable political opponent soon emerged in Aquino's widow, Corazon Aquino, who became the presidential candidate of the opposition. It was widely asserted that Marcos managed to defeat Aquino and retain the presidency in the election of Feb. 7, 1986, only through massive voting fraud on the part of his supporters. Deeply discredited at home and abroad by his dubious electoral victory, Marcos held fast to his presidency as the Philippine military split between supporters of his and of Aquino's legitimate right to the presidency. A tense standoff that ensued between the two sides ended only when Marcos fled the country on Feb. 25, 1986, at U.S. urging, and went into exile in Hawaii.

Evidence emerged that Marcos, his family, and his close associates had looted the Philippines' economy of billions of dollars through embezzlements and other corrupt practices. Marcos and his wife were subsequently indicted by the U.S. government on racketeering charges, but in 1990 (after Marcos' death) Imelda was acquitted of all charges by a federal court. She was allowed to return to the Philippines in 1991; in 1993 a Philippine court found her guilty of corruption.

Marcos DE NIZA: *see* Niza, Marcos de.

Marcus (ancient Roman personal name, or praenomen): *see under* gens or family name or honorific (*e.g.,* under Cicero for Marcus Tullius Cicero), except as below.

Marcus EREMITA: *see* Mark the Hermit.

Marcus, Rudolph A. (b. July 21, 1923, Montreal, Que., Can.), Canadian-born American chemist, winner of the 1992 Nobel Prize for Chemistry for his work on the theory of electron-transfer reactions in chemical systems. The Marcus theory shed light on diverse phenomena such as photosynthesis, cell metabolism, and simple corrosion.

Marcus received his doctorate from McGill University, Montreal, in 1946. From 1951 he worked at the Polytechnic Institute of Brooklyn. In 1964 he joined the faculty of the University of Illinois, leaving in 1978 for the California Institute of Technology.

Marcus began studying electron-transfer reactions in the 1950s. In a series of papers published between 1956 and 1965, he investigated the role of surrounding solvent molecules in determining the rate of redox reactions—oxidation and reduction reactions in which the reactants exchange electrons—in solution. Marcus determined that subtle changes occur in the molecular structure of the reactants and the solvent molecules around them; these changes influence the ability of electrons to move between the molecules. He further established that the relationship between the driving force of an electron-transfer reaction and the reaction's rate is described by a parabola. Thus, as more driving force is applied to a reaction, its rate at first increases but then begins to decrease. This insight aroused considerable skepticism until it was confirmed experimentally in the 1980s.

Marcus also did important work in areas such as transition-state theory, the theory of unimolecular reactions, and the theory of collisions and bound states.

Marcus, Siegfried (b. Sept. 18, 1831, Malchin, Mecklenburg [Germany]—d. June 30, 1898, Vienna, Austria), inventor who built four of the world's earliest gasoline-powered automobiles.

Marcus became an apprentice machinist at the age of 12, and five years later he joined an engineering company building telegraph lines. Within three years he invented a telegraphic relay system and moved to Vienna, where he was employed by several government and scientific organizations. In 1860 he established his own laboratory there. Marcus built his first automobile in 1864, a vehicle that was powered by a one-cylinder internal-combustion engine. Because the machine had no clutch, the rear wheels had to be lifted clear of the ground before the engine could be started. Dissatisfied with its performance after one test drive, he dismantled it.

Absorbed in other projects, Marcus did not return to his invention until 10 years later. His next vehicle, with a remarkably advanced electrical system, is preserved in the Technical Museum for Industry and Trade in

Vienna; it is probably the oldest gasoline-powered automobile extant. Because Marcus was a Jew, museum authorities had to hide the vehicle to prevent its destruction during the Nazi occupation. In 1949–50 it was overhauled and driven at about eight kilometres per hour (five miles per hour).

Marcus built two later autos, neither of which survives. He held about 76 patents (though none on his automobiles) in about a dozen countries. He also invented an electric lamp (1877), various other electrical devices, and a carburetor.

Marcus, (Harold) Stanley (b. April 20, 1905, Dallas, Texas, U.S.—d. Jan. 22, 2002, Dallas), American retail-store executive whose publicity campaigns gave the Neiman Marcus stores a reputation for luxury and fashion.

Stanley's father, Herbert Marcus, and his uncle, Al Neiman, opened the first Neiman Marcus store in Dallas in 1907. Their idea was to offer high-priced ready-to-wear clothing. At the time, women who could afford expensive clothes usually had them made by dressmakers. Neiman and Marcus hired a dressmaker to do alterations, and they did away with the fabric and piece-goods department. The founders and their sons waited on many of the customers themselves and had their sales clerks keep a "clientele book," recording information about customers' purchases and tastes.

Stanley Marcus earned a master's degree in business from Harvard in 1926 and began his career at the store as a floorman later that year. He set to work on building the store's image, insisting that no brand that they carried could be available in any other Dallas store. He made Neiman Marcus the first department store to hold fashion shows for its customers. By 1929 he was merchandising manager of all apparel divisions.

In 1934, at his suggestion, Neiman Marcus was the first specialty store to advertise in such national magazines as *Vogue* and *Harper's Bazaar.* Executive vice president from 1935 to 1950, Marcus introduced the Neiman Marcus Award, called the "Oscar of fashion," in 1938. He also selected a series of special displays of foreign merchandise and coordinated them with Dallas cultural events. Another of his attention-getting tactics was to offer outlandish products, such as windmills, camels, and airplanes. Such items helped make the store's catalogues, particularly the Christmas edition, internationally known.

Marcus served as cochairman for the Dallas Interracial Council for Business Opportunities and, in 1968, told suppliers that the store would favour affirmative-action employers. After the sale of Neiman Marcus to Broadway-Hale Stores, Inc. (from 1975, Carter Hawley Hale Stores, Inc.), in 1969, Marcus became a director of the corporation. He retired from the company in 1975, becoming chairman emeritus. In 1999 the Neiman Marcus Group, which included Neiman Marcus and the retailer Bergdorf Goodman, became a publicly held company. *Minding the Store* (1974) is Marcus' autobiography.

Marcus Aurelius, in full CAESAR MARCUS AURELIUS ANTONINUS AUGÚSTUS, original name (until AD 161) MARCUS ANNIUS VERUS (b. April 26, AD 121, Rome—d. March 17, 180, Vindobona [Vienna], or Sirmium, Pannonia), Roman emperor (AD 161–180), best known for his *Meditations* on Stoic philosophy. Marcus Aurelius has symbolized for many generations in the West the Golden Age of the Roman Empire.

Youth and apprenticeship. When he was born, his paternal grandfather was already consul for the second time and prefect of Rome, which was the crown of prestige in a senatorial career; his father's sister was married to the man who was destined to become the next emperor and whom he himself would in due time succeed; and his maternal grandmother was heiress to one of the most massive of Roman fortunes. Marcus thus was related to several of the most prominent families of the new Roman establishment, which had consolidated its social and political power under the Flavian emperors (69–96), and, indeed, the ethos of that establishment is relevant to his own actions and attitudes. The governing class of the first age of the Roman Empire, the Julio-Claudian, had been little different from that of the late Republic—it was urban Roman (despising outsiders), extravagant, cynical, and amoral; the new establishment, however, was largely of municipal and provincial origin—as were its emperors—cultivating sobriety and good works and turning more and more to piety and religiosity.

The child Marcus was, thus, clearly destined for social distinction. How he came to the throne, however, remains a mystery. In 136 the emperor Hadrian inexplicably announced as his eventual successor a certain Lucius Ceionius Commodus (henceforth L. Aelius Caesar), and in that same year young Marcus was engaged to Ceionia Fabia, the daughter of Commodus. Early in 138, however, Commodus died and later, after the death of Hadrian, the engagement was annulled. Hadrian then adopted Titus Aurelius Antoninus (the husband of Marcus' aunt) to succeed him as the emperor Antoninus Pius, arranging that Antoninus should adopt as his sons two young men, one the son of Commodus and the other Marcus, whose name was then changed to Marcus Aelius Aurelius Verus. Marcus thus was marked out as a future joint emperor at just under 17 years of age, though as it turned out he was not to succeed until his 40th year. It is sometimes assumed that in Hadrian's mind both Commodus and Antoninus Pius were merely to be "place warmers" for one or both of these youths.

The long years of Marcus' apprenticeship under Antoninus are illuminated by the correspondence between him and his teacher Fronto. Though the main society literary figure of the age, Fronto was a dreary pedant whose blood ran rhetoric, but he must have been less lifeless than he now appears, for there is genuine feeling and real communication in the letters between him and both of the young men. It was to the credit of Marcus, who was intelligent as well as hardworking and serious-minded, that he grew impatient with the unending regime of advanced exercises in Greek and Latin declamation and eagerly embraced the *Diatribai* ("Discourses") of a religious former slave, Epictetus, an important moral philosopher of the Stoic school. Henceforth, it was in philosophy that Marcus was to find his chief intellectual interest as well as his spiritual nourishment.

Marcus Aurelius, bas-relief depicting his triumphal entry into Rome in a *quadriga*; in the Palazzo dei Conservatori, Rome

Alinari—Art Resource/EB Inc.

There also was work to do at the side of the untiring Antoninus, with learning the business of government and assuming public roles. Marcus was consul in 140, 145, and 161. In 145 he married his cousin, the Emperor's daughter Annia Galeria Faustina, and in 147 the *imperium* and *tribunicia potestas,* the main formal powers of emperorship, were conferred upon him; henceforth, he was a kind of junior co-emperor, sharing the intimate counsels and crucial decisions of Antoninus. (His adoptive brother, nearly 10 years his junior, was brought into official prominence in due time.) On March 7, 161, at a time when the brothers were jointly consuls (for the third and the second time, respectively), their father died.

Roman emperor. The transition was smooth as far as Marcus was concerned; already possessing the essential constitutional powers, he stepped automatically into the role of full emperor (and his name henceforth was Imperator Caesar Marcus Aurelius Antoninus Augustus). At his own insistence, however, his adoptive brother was made co-emperor with him (and bore henceforth the name Imperator Caesar Lucius Aurelius Verus Augustus). There is no evidence that Lucius Verus had much of a following, so that a ruthless rival could have easily disposed of him, though to leave him in being as anything less than emperor might have created a focus for disaffection. It is most probable, however, that Marcus' conscience impelled him to carry out loyally what he believed to have been the plan by which alone he himself had eventually reached the purple. For the first time the Roman Empire had two joint emperors of formally equal constitutional status and powers, but, although the achievement of Lucius Verus has suffered by comparison with the paragon Marcus, it seems probable that the serious work of government was done by Marcus and was the more arduous in that it was done during most of his reign in the midst of fighting frontier wars and combatting the effects of plague and demoralization.

For constructive statesmanship or the initiation of original trends in civil policy, Marcus had little time or energy to spare. The field most congenial to him seems to have been the law. Numerous measures were promulgated and judicial decisions made, clearing away harshnesses and anomalies in the civil law, improving in detail the lot of the less-favoured—slaves, widows, minors—and giving recognition to claims of blood relationship in the field of succession. Marcus' personal contribution, however, must not be overstated. The pattern of ameliorating legislation was inherited rather than novel, and the measures were refinements rather than radical changes in the structure of law or society; Marcus was not a great legislator, but he was a devoted practitioner of the role of ombudsman. Moreover, there was nothing specifically Stoic about this legal activity, and in one respect the age of Antoninus Pius and Marcus signalizes a retrogression in the relationship of law to society, for under them there either began, or was made more explicit, a distinction of classes in the criminal law—*honestiores* and *humiliores,* with two separate scales of punishments for crime, harsher and more degrading for the *humiliores* at every point.

Marcus' claim to statesmanship has come under critical attack in numerous other ways; for example, in the matter of Christian persecution. Though Marcus disliked the Christians, there was no systematic persecution of them during his reign. Their legal status remained as it had been under Trajan and Hadrian: Christians were ipso facto punishable but not to be sought out. This incongruous position did little harm in times of general security and prosperity, but when either of these were threatened, the local population might denounce Christians, a governor might be forced to act, and the law, as the central authority saw it, must then run its course. The martyrdoms at Lyon in 177 were of this nature, and, though it appears that Christian blood flowed more profusely in the reign of Marcus the philosopher than it had before, he was not an initiator of persecution.

In 161 Syria was invaded by the Parthians, a major power to the East. The war that followed (162–166) was nominally under the command of Verus, though its successful conclusion, with the overrunning of Armenia and Mesopotamia, was the work of subordinate generals, notably Gaius Avidius Cassius. The returning armies brought back with them a plague, which raged throughout the empire for many years and—together with the German invasion—fostered a weakening of morale in minds accustomed to the stability and apparent immutability of Rome and its empire.

In 167 or 168 Marcus and Verus together set out on a punitive expedition across the Danube, and behind their backs a horde of German tribes invaded Italy in massive strength and besieged Aquileia, on the crossroads at the head of the Adriatic. The military precariousness of the empire and the inflexibility of its financial structure in the face of emergencies now stood revealed; desperate measures were adopted to fill the depleted legions, and imperial property was auctioned to provide funds. Marcus and Verus fought the Germans off with success, but in 169 Verus died suddenly, and doubtless naturally, of a stroke. Three years of fighting were still needed, with Marcus in the thick of it, to restore the Danubian frontier, and three more years of campaigning in Bohemia were enough to bring the tribes beyond the Danube to peace, at least for a time.

The Meditations. A more intimate contact with the thoughts pursued by Marcus during the troubling involvements of his reign, though not what would have been historically most valuable, his day-to-day political thoughts, can be acquired by reading the *Meditations.* To what extent he intended them for eyes other than his own is uncertain; they are fragmentary notes, discursive and epigrammatic by turn, of his reflections in the midst of campaigning and administration. In a way, it seems, he wrote them to nerve himself for his daunting responsibilities. Strikingly, though they comprise the innermost thoughts of a Roman, the *Meditations* were written in Greek—to such an extent had the union of cultures become a reality. In many ages these thoughts have been admired; the modern age, however, is more likely to be struck by the pathology of them, their mixture of priggishness and hysteria. Marcus was forever proposing to himself unattainable goals of conduct, forever contemplating the triviality, brutishness, and transience of the physical world and of man in general and himself in particular; otherworldly, yet believing in no other world, he was therefore tied to duty and service with no hope, even of everlasting fame, to sustain him. Sickly all through his life and probably plagued with a chronic ulcer, he took daily doses of a drug; the suggestion has been made that the apocalyptic imagery of passages in the *Meditations* betrays the addict. More certain and more important is the point that Marcus' anxieties reflect, in an exaggerated manner, the ethos of his age.

The *Meditations,* the thoughts of a philosopher-king, have been considered by many generations one of the great books of all times. Though they were Marcus' own thoughts, they were not original. They are basically the moral tenets of Stoicism, learned from Epictetus: the cosmos is a unity governed by an intelligence, and the human soul is a part of that divine intelligence and can therefore stand, if naked and alone, at least pure and undefiled, amidst chaos and futility. One or two of Marcus' ideas, perhaps more through lack of rigorous understanding than anything else, diverged from Stoic philosophy and approached that Platonism that was itself then turning into the Neoplatonism into which all pagan philosophies, except Epicureanism, were destined to merge. But he did not deviate so far as to accept the comfort of any kind of survival after death.

At the same time that Marcus was securing his trans-Danubian frontiers, Egypt, Spain, and Britain were troubled by rebellions or invasions. By 175, the general Avidius Cassius, who earlier had served under Verus, had virtually become a prefect of all of the eastern provinces, including control of the important province of Egypt. In that year, Avidius Cassius took the occasion of a rumour of Marcus' death to proclaim himself emperor. Marcus made peace in the north with those tribes not already subjugated and prepared to march against Avidius, but the rebel general was assassinated by his own soldiers. Marcus used the opportunity to make a tour of pacification and inspection in the East, visiting Antioch, Alexandria, and Athens—where, like Hadrian, he was initiated into the Eleusinian Mysteries (though that esoteric religious cult does not seem to have impinged at all upon his philosophical views). During the journey the empress Faustina, who had been with her husband in the Danubian wars as well, died. Great public honours were bestowed upon her in life and in death, and in his *Meditations* Marcus spoke of her with love and admiration. The ancient sources accuse her of infidelity and disloyalty (complicity, in fact, with Avidius Cassius), but the charges are implausible.

In 177 Marcus proclaimed his 16-year-old son, Commodus, joint emperor. Together they resumed the Danubian wars. Marcus was determined to pass from defense to offense and to an expansionist redrawing of Rome's northern boundaries. His determination seemed to be winning success when, in 180, he died at his military headquarters, having just had time to commend Commodus to the chief advisers of the regime.

Assessment. Marcus' choice of his only surviving son as his successor has always been viewed as a tragic paradox. Commodus turned out badly, though two things must be borne in mind: emperors are good and bad in the ancient sources according as they did or did not satisfy the senatorial governing class, and Commodus' rapid calling off of the northern campaigns may well have been wiser than his father's obsessive and costly expansionism. But those who criticize Marcus for ensuring the accession of Commodus are usually under the misapprehension that Marcus was reverting to crude dynasticism after a long and successful period of "philosophic" succession by the best available man. This is historically untenable. Marcus had no choice in the matter: if he had not made Commodus his successor, he would have had to order him to be put to death.

Marcus was a statesman, perhaps, but one of no great calibre; nor was he really a sage. In general, he is a historically overrated figure, presiding in a bewildered way over an empire beneath the gilt of which there already lay many a decaying patch. But his personal nobility and dedication survive the most remorseless scrutiny; he counted the cost obsessively, but he did not shrink from paying it. (J.A.Cr.)

BIBLIOGRAPHY. *Ancient sources.* Scriptores Historiae Augustae, *Vita M. Antonini philosophi,* the standard and reasonably reliable life from the set of late Latin biographies of emperors; Dio Cassius, book lxxi, which survives only in Byzantine excerpts; Fronto, *Epistulae,* which presents the correspondence (of which it is important to use the modern edition by M.P.J. Van den Hout, 1954); Eusebius, *Historia ecclesiastica,* v, 1—the account of the martyrs of Lyon; and A.S.L. Farquharson (ed.), *The Meditations of the Emperor Marcus Antoninus,* 2 vol. (1944), the full annotated edition.

Modern biographies. Farquharson's edition contains a brief biography (vol. 1, pp. 256–268); the fullest treatment (in German) is by P. von Rohden and H. von Arnim in *Pauly-Wissowa Real-Encyclopädie,* vol. 1, pp. 2279–2309 (1894), still fundamental in spite of its date. Anthony Birley, *Marcus Aurelius* (1966), is a more recent biography in English; A.S.L. Farquharson also produced a wider-ranging study: *Marcus Aurelius: His Life and His World,* ed. by D.A. Rees (1951). The general history of the principate by Albino Garzetti, *L'impero da Tiberio agli Antonini* (1960), places Marcus' reign in its historical setting and contains a useful bibliography. G.R. Stanton, "Marcus Aurelius, Emperor and Philosopher," *Historia,* 18:570–587 (1969), well represents a skeptical current in points of view about Marcus.

Chronological problems. For more detail on the controversial problems of the chronology of the reign, see the papers of C.H. Dodd in *Numismatic Chronicle,* 11:209–350 (1911), 13:162–199, 276–321 (1913), and 14:34–91 (1914); W. Zwikker, *Studien zur Markussäule* (1941); and J. Morris, "The Dating of the Column of Marcus Aurelius," in *Journal of the Warburg and Courtauld Institutes,* 15:33–47 (1952).

Consult the INDEX *first*

Marcus Island (Japan): *see* Minami-Tori-shima.

Marcus Julius Agrippa: *see* Herod Agrippa I.

Marcuse, Herbert (b. July 19, 1898, Berlin—d. July 29, 1979, Starnberg, W.Ger.), German-born U.S. political philosopher whose Marxist critical philosophy and Freudian psychological analyses of 20th-century Western society were popular among student leftist radicals, especially after the 1968 student rebellions in West Berlin, New York's Columbia University, and the Sorbonne in Paris.

Having become a member of the Social Democratic Party while a student at the University of Freiburg (Ph.D., 1922), Marcuse later conducted philosophical research there (1922–32) and was a co-founder of the Frankfurt Institut für Sozialforschung. He fled to Geneva in 1933 as Hitler rose to power, then went to the United States in 1934, where he taught at Columbia University and became a naturalized citizen in 1940. An intelligence analyst for the U.S. Army during World War II, he headed the Central European Section of the Office of Intelligence Research after the war. He returned to teaching in 1951 at Columbia and Harvard (to 1954), Brandeis University (1954–65), and the University of California at San Diego (1965–76), where after retirement he was honorary emeritus professor of philosophy until his death.

A Hegelian-Freudian-Marxist, Marcuse was wedded to the ideas of radicalization, vociferous dissent, and "resistance to the point of subversion." He believed that Western society was unfree and repressive, that its technology had bought the complacency of the masses with material goods, and that it had kept them intellectually and spiritually captive. However, although a frank exponent of resistance to the established order, Marcuse did not applaud the campus demonstrations. "I still consider the

American University an oasis of free speech and real critical thinking in the society," he said. "Any student movement should try to protect this citadel . . . [but] try to radicalize the departments inside the university."

Among his major writings are *Eros and Civilization* (1955), *One-Dimensional Man* (1964), *Counterrevolution and Revolt* (1972), and *Studies in Critical Philosophy* (1972).

Marcy, Mount, highest point (5,344 ft [1,629 m]) in New York, U.S., lying 12 mi (19 km) south-southeast of Lake Placid village in the Adirondack Mountains in the northeastern part of the state. The Hudson River's main headstream, the Opalescent River, originates on the mountain at Lake Tear of the Clouds. First ascended in 1837, the peak was named for William L. Marcy, then governor of New York who had instituted a geological survey of the Adirondack region.

Marcy, William L(earned) (b. Dec. 12, 1786, Southbridge, Mass., U.S.—d. July 4, 1857, Ballston Spa, N.Y.), U.S. politician, governor, and Cabinet member, remembered primarily for his remark: "To the victor belong the spoils of the enemy."

From 1823 to 1829 Marcy was comptroller of New York state and a leading member of the "Albany Regency," a group of powerful Democrats. After serving as an associate justice of the New York Supreme Court (1829–31), he entered the U.S. Senate, where, in a speech defending Secretary of State Martin Van Buren against an attack by Sen. Henry Clay, he made his remark and thereby became known as champion of the "spoils system." He resigned from the Senate (January 1833) to become governor of New York (1833–39). Marcy was secretary of war under Pres. James K. Polk (1845–49) and secretary of state under Pres. Franklin Pierce (1853–57).

Marcy
By courtesy of the Chicago Historical Society

In the latter office he secured approval of the Gadsden Treaty (1853), which settled the boundary dispute between Mexico and the United States; he also settled the Black Warrior case (1854), thus avoiding war with Spain.

Mardaïte, Arabic JURJUMĀNĪ, plural JARĀJIMA, member of a Christian people of northern Syria, employed as soldiers by Byzantine emperors. The Mardaïtes inhabited the Amanus (Gâvur) Mountains, in the modern Turkish province of Hatay, the 7th-century borderland between Byzantine and Muslim territory. In the period 660–680, allied with the Byzantine emperor Constantine IV, the Mardaïtes pushed southward into Arab-occupied Lebanon and northern Palestine. In the 690s Constantine's successor, Justinian II, by agreement with Caliph ʿAbd al-Malik of Damascus, resettled 12,000 Mardaïtes in various parts of Greece and Anatolia. Those remaining in Lebanon and Syria were subjected to Muslim rule and absorbed by other peoples.

Mardalsfossen, waterfall at the head of Eikesdalsvatnet (lake), east-southeast of Åndalsnes, Nor. It consists of two cataracts in Mardøla district of Møre og Romsdal *fylke* (county), western Norway. The falls rank among the highest in the world, with their total drop of 1,696 ft (517 m) and individual descents of 974 and 722 ft. During the period of maximum snow melting in the spring, the waterfalls, descending from a hanging (tributary) valley, appeared from the main valley below to be one long cataract. Hydroelectric development in recent years has dried out the waterfalls.

Mardān, town and district in Peshāwar division, North-West Frontier Province, Pakistan. The town, the district headquarters, lies just north of the Kalpāni River; it is connected by road and rail with Dargai (Malākand Pass), Nowshera, and Peshāwar, 30 mi (50 km) south-southwest. A growing industrial centre, it has textile and vegetable oil mills, a cigarette factory, and one of the largest sugar refineries in the Indian subcontinent. Mardān is the site of a government college. The Rock of Shāhbāzgarhi, 7 mi northeast of Mardān, bears one of the great inscriptions of Emperor Aśoka (3rd century BC).

Mardān district (area 1,211 sq mi [3,136 sq km]), until 1936 a part of Peshāwar district, extends north of the Kābul River, comprises the greater portion of the Yūsufzai plain, and has the largest concentration of irrigated land in Pakistan. The chief crops are wheat, corn (maize), sugarcane, tobacco, sugar beet, and fruit (peaches, plums, apples, apricots, and pears). Marble deposits are found in the hills. Pop. (1998 prelim.) town, 244,511; (1981 prelim.) district, 1,423,000.

Mardersteig, Giovanni, original name HANS MARDERSTEIG (b. Jan. 8, 1892, Weimar, Ger.—d. Dec. 27, 1977, Verona, Italy), printer and typographer who, as head of Officina Bodoni, created books exemplifying the highest standards in the art of printing.

He studied law at the universities of Bonn, Vienna, Kiel, and finally Jena, where he received his degree. After graduation he taught school for a time in the Swiss town of Zuoz. In 1917 he joined the publishing house of Kurt Wolff, in Leipzig, where he was in charge of the publication of a series of art books and edited the art journal *Genius*.

In 1922 Mardersteig moved to Montagnola, near Lugano, Italy, where he founded Officina Bodoni. His first book (1923) was an edition of Politian's *Favola d'Orfeo*; other early works included Shelley's *Epipsychidion*, Shakespeare's *Tempest*, and Dante's *Vita nuova*. These and other works were printed by Mardersteig alone, using his handpress, and they earned him an international reputation. Later, he acquired a few assistants. He received permission from the Italian government to cast type from Giambattista Bodoni's original matrices, and many of his editions used these Bodoni types.

As a result of winning a government competition in 1927, Mardersteig was assigned to print the Italian national edition of the works of Gabriele D'Annunzio. Mardersteig did the printing in Verona, near D'Annunzio's home, working on the 50-volume set for five years. He then spent a year in Scotland working for Collins Cleartype Press, where he designed a type that came to be known as Fontana.

Returning to Italy, Mardersteig again set up Officina Bodoni in Verona. The press specialized in small editions, printed with meticulous care on an old-fashioned handpress that occupied a room in his house. In addition to Fontana, he also designed the typefaces Dante, Griffo, and Zeno.

From 1947 Mardersteig also operated the Stamperia Valdonèga in Verona. This organization, continued after Mardersteig's death by his son Martino, became known for larger editions than those of the Officina Bodoni, but it, too, emphasized fine workmanship.

Mardi Gras (French: Fat Tuesday), festive day celebrated in France on the Tuesday (Shrove Tuesday; *q.v.*) before Ash Wednesday, which marks the close of the pre-Lenten season. In the United States the festival is most elaborately celebrated in New Orleans. *See* carnival.

Mardīkh, Tall (Syria): *see* Ebla.

Mardin, city, capital of Mardin *il* (province), southeastern Turkey. It lies on the southern slopes of a broad highland that rises to an altitude of 3,450 ft (1,052 m) and overlooks extensive limestone plateaus. The locality receives more rainfall than the lower plains and has hot summers and cold winters. A ruined Roman citadel, rebuilt in medieval times, crowns the summit of the highland as evidence of Mardin's earlier existence as the Marida (Marde, Maride, Merida) of antiquity. Marida was taken by the Seljuq Turks in the late 11th century and was incorporated into the Ottoman Empire by Sultan Selim I in 1516. The Ulu Cami (Great Mosque), dating from the Seljuq period, and the Sultan İsa Medresesi, a religious school built in the 14th century, are still standing.

Sultan İsa Medresesi, Mardin, Tur.
Josephine Powell, Rome

Mardin is an important regional trading centre on the east–west trade routes of southern Anatolia. It is connected by a branch line with the Istanbul–Baghdad railway and is linked by roads with Gaziantep (west), Aleppo (in Syria), Nusaybin (southeast), and Diyarbakır (northeast).

Mardin *il* (4,973 sq mi [12,879 sq km]), bordered on the south by Syria, is an agricultural area chiefly producing wheat, barley, and sesame. Angora goats are raised for mohair, and there is a small cotton- and woollen-weaving industry. In addition to the Turks, the *il* has a large population of Arabs and Kurds. Pop. (1997) city, 61,529; *il*, 646,826.

Mardonius (d. 479 BC, Plataea, Boeotia), Achaemenid general, a nephew of King Darius I and married to Darius' daughter Artazostra. In 492 BC he was sent to succeed the satrap (governor) Artaphernes in Ionia, with a special commission to attack Athens and Eretria. Contrary to the usual Achaemenid policy, he abolished the ruling "tyrants" and restored democracies in Ionia, thereby removing a major source of unrest. He then crossed the Hellespont and invaded Thrace and Macedonia. His fleet was wrecked off Mt. Athos with enormous loss, however, and because of this setback he was deprived of his command.

According to the Greek historian Herodotus, Mardonius was one of those who encouraged King Xerxes I, Darius' successor, to invade Greece. After the Achaemenid defeat at Salamis he persuaded Xerxes to return to

Asia and himself stayed behind with a large army. He unsuccessfully attempted to separate Athens from the other Greek allies, and, withdrawing from Attica, he finally was defeated and killed in battle at Plataea in September 479.

Marduk, in Mesopotamian religion, the chief god of the city of Babylon and the national god of Babylonia; as such he was eventually called simply Bel, or Lord. Originally he seems to have been a god of thunderstorms. A poem, known as *Enuma elish* and dating from the reign of Nebuchadrezzar I (1124–03 BC), relates Marduk's rise to such preeminence that he was the god of 50 names, each one that of a deity or of a divine attribute. After conquering the monster of primeval chaos, Tiamat, he became "lord of the gods of heaven and earth." All nature, including man, owed its existence to him; the destiny of kingdoms and subjects was in his hands.

Marduk's chief temples at Babylon were the Esagila and the Etemenanki, a ziggurat with a shrine of Marduk on the top. In Esagila the poem *Enuma elish* was recited every year at the New Year festival. The goddess named most often as the consort of Marduk was Zarpanit, or Zarbanit (She of the City Zarpan).

Marduk's star was Jupiter, and his sacred animals were horses, dogs, and especially the so-called dragon with forked tongue, representations of which adorn his city's walls. On the oldest monuments Marduk is represented holding a triangular spade or hoe, interpreted as an emblem of fertility and vegetation. He is also pictured walking, or in his war chariot. Typically, his tunic is adorned with stars; in his hand is a sceptre, and he carries a bow, spear, net, or thunderbolt. Kings of Assyria and Persia also honoured Marduk and Zarpanit on inscriptions and rebuilt many of their temples.

Marduk-apal-iddina II (king of Babylonia): *see* Merodach-Baladan II.

mare, plural MARIA, any flat, dark plain of lower elevation on the Moon. The term, which in Latin means "sea," was erroneously applied to such features by telescopic observers of the 17th century. In actuality, maria are huge basins containing lava flows marked by craters, ridges, faults, and straight and meandering valleys called rilles and are devoid of water. There are about 20 major areas of this type, most of them—and the largest ones—located on the side of the Moon that always faces Earth. Maria are the largest topographic features on the Moon and can be seen from Earth with the unaided eye. (Together with the bright lunar highlands, they form the face of the "man in the moon.")

Samples of lunar rock and soil brought back by Apollo astronauts proved that the maria are composed of basalt formed from surface lava flows that later congealed. The surface, down to approximately 5 metres (16 feet), shows effects of churning, fusing, and fragmenting as a result of several billion years of bombardment by small meteoroids. This debris layer, comprising rock fragments of all sizes down to fine dust, is called regolith. Before the first unmanned spacecraft landings on the Moon in the 1960s, some astronomers feared that the surface would be so pulverized that the machines might sink in. These missions—and the manned landings that followed—revealed that the regolith was only somewhat compressible and was firm enough to be supportive.

The maria basins were formed beginning about 3.9 billion years ago during a period of intense bombardment by asteroid-sized bodies. This was well after the lunar crust had cooled and solidified enough, following the Moon's formation, to retain large impact scars. Then, over a period lasting until perhaps three billion years ago, a long sequence of volcanic events flooded the giant basins and surrounding low-lying areas with magma originating hundreds of kilometres within the interior. Although the recognized giant impact basins are distributed similarly on the near and far sides of the Moon, most of the far-side basins were never flooded with lava to form maria. The reason remains to be clarified, but it may be related to an asymmetry of the Moon's crust, which appears to be about twice as thick on the far side as on the near side and thus less likely to have been completely ruptured by large impacts. Most maria are associated with mascons, regions of particularly dense lava that create anomalies in the Moon's gravitational field.

Maré, Île, formerly NENGONE ISLAND, southernmost of the Loyalty Islands, a raised coralline limestone and volcanic group in the southwestern Pacific Ocean that is part of the French overseas territory of New Caledonia. Rising to 300 ft (100 m), Maré is the highest in the group. It is 22 mi (35 km) long and 18 mi wide and has a total area of 248 sq mi (642 sq km). It was annexed by France in 1866 and was Christianized by indigenous teachers from Rarotonga and Samoa. Tadine (Tadinou), on the west coast, is the administrative centre and the site of an airfield. The islanders grow taro, yams, and bananas; copra and oranges are exported. Pop. (1996) 6,896.

Mare Orientale (Latin: "Eastern Sea"), circular, dark plain of basaltic material that fills the interior part of the multiringed Orientale Basin on the western limb of the Moon; it covers an area of about 50,000 square kilometres (19,300 square miles). The Orientale Basin is defined by a most conspicuous outer ring, the Montes Cordillera, 900 km (560 mi) in diameter. Other vast circular structures associated with the basin are the outer Montes Rook, 620 km (385 mi) in diameter; the inner Montes Rook, 480 km in diameter; and the inner ring that encloses Mare Orientale, 320 km in diameter. For years very little was known about Mare Orientale because it lies at the edge of the lunar surface that can be seen from Earth. Extensive explorations of the Moon by both manned and unmanned spacecraft during the 1960s and 1970s enabled scientists to make detailed observations of the feature and its surroundings.

Marechal, Leopoldo (b. June 11, 1900, Buenos Aires—d. September, 1970, Buenos Aires), Argentine writer and critic who was best known for his philosophical novels.

In the early 1920s, Marechal was part of the literary group responsible for *Martín Fierro* and *Proa,* Ultraista journals that revolutionized Argentine letters. His first book of poems, *Aguiluchos* (1922; "Eaglets"), employed Modernista techniques in the treatment of pastoral themes. In *Días como flechas* (1926; "Days Like Arrows") and *Odas para el hombre y la mujer* (1929; "Odes for Man and Woman"), his metaphors and images become more daring in expressing the Ultraista aesthetic. With *Cinco poemas australes* (1937; "Five Southern Poems"), *Sonetos a Sophia* (1940; "Sonnets to Sophia"), and *El centauro* (1940; "The Centaur"), his poetry was influenced by Neoplatonic philosophy and shows a search for balance and order in a chaotic world. This theme continued in the "Canciones Elbitences," love poems addressed to a quintessential woman, Elbiamor. These poems were included in *Antología poética* (1969).

Marechal's masterpiece is the novel *Adán Buenosayres* (1948), a work of technical complexity, stylistic innovations, and highly poetic language that was a precursor of the Latin American new novel. The mythical voyage of Adán, the hero, his descent into Hell, and his constant search for the ideal is at once autobiographical, a *roman à clef,* and a historicalization of Argentina from geologic times.

A socialist in his youth, Marechal became an ardent Peronist, and during the government of Juan Perón he occupied important government cultural posts. With Perón's fall he went into virtual seclusion but returned to public attention with the novels *El banquete de Severo Arcángelo* (1965; "The Banquet of Severo Arcángelo") and *Megafón o la guerra* (1970; "Megafón, or The War"). In these Marechal continued his explorations of mythology and idealism.

Maréchal, Pierre-Sylvain (b. Aug. 15, 1750, Paris—d. Jan. 18, 1803, Montrouge, Fr.), poet and publicist whose plan for a secular calendar, presented in his *Almanach des honnêtes gens* (1788; "Dictionary of Notables"), was subsequently the basis for the French Republican Calendar adopted in 1793.

By profession a lawyer and librarian, Maréchal was by philosophy a Materialist and an atheist. After writing some erotic poetry, he turned his talents to antireligious propaganda. He parodied the Bible in *Livre échappé au Déluge* (1784; "Book Salvaged from the Flood") and compiled his own *Dictionnaire des athées anciens et modernes* (1800; "Dictionary of Ancient and Modern Atheists"), in which he included Augustine, Pascal, and Bossuet. In the *Almanach* Maréchal substituted the names of famous people for those of saints. His proposed calendar divided the year into 36 decades; the French Republican Calendar divided the year into 12 months, each containing 3 decades of 10 days each, with the addition of 5 supplementary days in ordinary years and 6 in leap years.

Mareeba, town, northeastern Queensland, Australia, on the Barron River, 40 mi (65 km) west of the port of Cairns on the Coral Sea. It was the earliest European settlement on the Atherton Plateau; at its founding it was called Granite Creek and served as a stop for miners on their way to goldfields in the interior. Its present name is derived from an Aboriginal term meaning "meeting of the waters" or "place to meet." The town serves as the commercial centre of the Mareeba-Dimbulah Irrigation Area, the tobacco farms of which receive water from the Tinaroo Falls Reservoir. Other products shipped through Mareeba are bacon, beef (from the Gulf of Carpentaria region to the west), and timber. Pop. (2003 est.) 18,638.

Marées, Hans von (b. Dec. 24, 1837, Elberfeld, Prussia—d. June 5, 1887, Rome), painter of the so-called Idealist school in Germany.

In 1853 Marées went to Berlin, where he studied for two years. For the next eight years

"Self-portrait with Hildebrand and Grant," study for the Naples frescoes, oil on canvas by Hans von Marées, 1873; in the Von der Heydt-Museum, Wuppertal, Ger.

By courtesy of the Von der Heydt-Museum, Wuppertal, Ger.

he worked chiefly in Munich, coming under the influence of the historical school, and in 1864 he went to Italy, where he lived for about 20 years. In 1873 he received his most important commission, the painting of frescoes in the library of the zoological museum at Naples. Although ambitious, Marées lacked self-confidence and, in the latter part of his life, ceased to exhibit his work. He died a disappointed and practically unknown man. When his works were collected at the Munich exhibition in 1891, their value became apparent, as in "The Oarsmen," a subject he often painted.

Maremma, geographic region, largely within Tuscany (Toscana) *regione,* central Italy, extending along the Tyrrhenian coast from south of Livorno to Rome and inland to the Apennine foothills.

In Etruscan and Roman times the Maremma was well-settled and known for its farms, which were drained by subterranean canals. Among the Etruscan towns situated on hilltops, Populonia, Cosa, Tarquinii, and Caere were the largest; and several ports handled Etruria's foreign trade. During the later years of the Roman Empire, the region declined rapidly—drainage was neglected and malaria became endemic; the Maremma eventually was used only as a winter grazing ground for herds from the Apennines, in spite of reclamation efforts by the grand dukes of Tuscany in the 18th and early 19th centuries. Some reclamation and drainage of the swamps began in the 1930s, and beginning in 1951 the Maremma Land Reform Agency spent considerable sums on the region. New farms, roads, and rural service centres were built, changing the face of the Maremma beyond recognition. Much of that reclamation work was thwarted in 1966, however, when torrential rainstorms and the flooding of the Ombrone River inundated the land, with disastrous loss of livestock and equipment.

Marengo, Battle of (June 14, 1800), narrow victory for Napoleon Bonaparte in the War of the Second Coalition, fought on the Marengo Plain about 3 miles (5 km) southeast of Alessandria, in northern Italy, between Napoleon's approximately 28,000 troops and some 31,000 Austrian troops under General Michael Friedrich von Melas; it resulted in the French occupation of Lombardy up to the Mincio River and secured Napoleon's military and civilian authority in Paris.

Napoleon led his army across several Alpine passes in May and cut Melas off from communication with Austria. Melas concentrated his troops at Alessandria to meet the French. Napoleon mistakenly thought Melas was at Turin, more than 50 miles (80 km) to the west, and his troops were widely separated when Melas attacked. The initial French force of about 18,000 men was at first overpowered by the Austrians and was pushed back 4 miles (6.4 km) by 3 PM. Melas, believing victory was secured, gave the command to a subordinate and retired to Alessandria. The slow Austrian pursuit enabled Napoleon to hold his forces together until the arrival of some 10,000 reinforcements, mainly General Louis Desaix's corps. The furious French counterattack at 5 PM, in which Desaix was killed almost immediately, forced the Austrians into headlong retreat. Austrian losses included about 7,500 killed and wounded and some 4,000 captured, while French losses totaled about 6,000. The next day Melas signed an armistice.

marennes, popular edible variety of oyster (*q.v.*).

Marenzio, Luca (b. 1553, Coccaglio, near Brescia, Republic of Venice [now Italy]—d. Aug. 22, 1599, Rome), composer whose madrigals are considered to be among the finest examples of Italian madrigals of the late 16th century.

Marenzio published a large number of madrigals and villanelles and five books of motets. He developed an individual technique and was skilled in evoking moods and images suggested by the poetic texts of the madrigals. He exploited passages in a homophonic, or chordal, style in place of the polyphonic style characteristic of earlier madrigals. He was a daring harmonist: his chromaticism occasionally led to advanced enharmonic modulations, and he sometimes left dissonances unresolved for dramatic effect. He exerted a strong influence on Claudio Monteverdi, Don Carlo Gesualdo, and Hans Hassler and was much-admired in England, where his works were printed in N. Yonge's *Musica transalpina* (1588), a collection that stimulated the composition of English madrigals.

Marenzio was probably trained as a choirboy in Brescia, and he was in service with Cardinal Luigi d'Este in Rome from 1578 to 1586. In 1588 he went to Florence, where he worked with the circle of musicians and poets associated with Count Giovanni Bardi. Later he was in the service of Cardinal Cinzio Aldobrandini in Rome. In 1594 he visited Sigismund III of Poland, returned to Rome in 1595, and went again to Poland in 1596. In 1598 he was in Venice and later was appointed musician at the papal court.

mare's-tail, the aquatic plant *Hippuris vulgaris* or either of two other species of its genus, which constitute the water milfoil family (Hippuridaceae). Mare's-tail grows from submerged, stout rootstocks along the margins of lakes and ponds in temperate regions throughout the world. It resembles the unrelated horsetail (*Equisetum* species) in having whorls of small, linear leaves at intervals along the stem. The stems rise about 30 cm (12 inches) above the water to produce, in the upper angles between the stems and leaves, highly reduced, tiny, greenish, wind-pollinated bisexual flowers, each consisting of one male pollen-producing stamen and one female ovary with a single ovule. Mare's-tail plants are sometimes grown in bog or pond gardens.

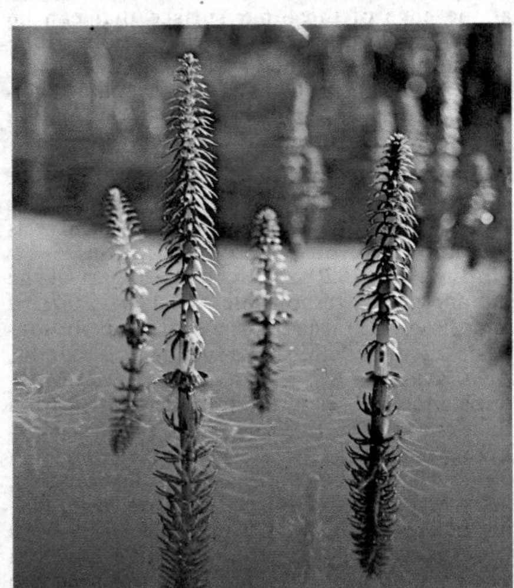

Mare's-tail (*Hippuris vulgaris*)
Ingmar Holmasen

Maret, Hugues-Bernard, DUC (duke) DE BASSANO (b. May 1, 1763, Dijon, Fr.—d. May 13, 1839, Paris), French diplomat and statesman of the Napoleonic period.

A journalist in the early stages of the French Revolution, Maret entered the diplomatic service in 1792. After the coup d'état of 18 Brumaire (Nov. 9, 1799), Napoleon appointed him secretary of state to the consuls. He grew in Napoleon's esteem and acted as his confidential adviser. From April 1811 to November 1813, Maret served as minister of foreign affairs; he concluded the treaties with Prussia (February 1812) and with Austria (March 1812) that preceded the French invasion of Russia. In 1815 he helped arrange Napoleon's return from Elba. Exiled during the second Bourbon Restoration, Maret returned to France in 1820 and was made a peer of France by Louis-Philippe. In November 1834 he was appointed prime minister but was unable to form a cabinet.

Maret, detail of a portrait by Robert Lefevre, 1807
H. Roger-Viollet

Marett, Robert R(anulph) (b. June 13, 1866, Jersey, Channel Islands—d. Feb. 18, 1943), English social anthropologist who, like Sir James George Frazer and Andrew Lang, came to anthropology with a strong background in classical literature and philosophy. Marett is best-known for his studies of the evolution of moral philosophy and religious beliefs and practices.

He studied at Victoria College in Jersey and Balliol College, Oxford, and, from 1891 until his death, held positions at Exeter College, Oxford, as a fellow, tutor of philosophy, examiner in *literae humaniores,* and rector. From 1910 to 1936 he was a reader in social anthropology.

Marett's views on primitive religion differed somewhat from those of Frazer and Sir Edward Burnett Tylor, generally acknowledged as the greatest anthropologists of his day; Marett opposed their rigid, rational categorizations and spoke of early man's "primitive logic of the heart." As opposed to Tylor's "animism," he postulated an impersonal religion, or "animatism," based on "awe," a feeling of "submissiveness tempered with admiration, hopefulness, and even love."

Marett's unusually broad intellectual accomplishments ranged from Plato's *Republic,* about which he gave a famous series of lectures, to prehistoric archaeology. He was gifted with a lucid writing style with which he was able to propagate the field of anthropology. In 1909 he helped found the Oxford University Anthropological Society. His major publications include: *The Threshold of Religion* (1900), *Anthropology* (1912), *Psychology and Folklore* (1920), *Faith, Hope and Charity in Primitive Religion* (1932), *Sacraments of Simple Folk* (1933), and *Head, Heart and Hands in Human Evolution* (1935).

Marey, Étienne-Jules (b. March 5, 1830, Beaune, Fr.—d. May 15, 1904, Paris), French physiologist who invented the sphygmograph, an instrument for recording graphically the features of the pulse and variations in blood pressure. His basic instrument, with modifications, is still used today.

Marey wrote extensively on the circulation of the blood, cholera, terrestrial and aerial locomotion, experimental physiology, and graphic methods in physiology. He also contributed to the development of the motion picture. To study the flight of birds, he invented a camera in 1882 with magazine plates that recorded a series of photographs; the pictures could be combined to represent movements. In 1894

Marey, photograph by Nadar (Gaspard-Félix Tournachon)

H. Roger-Viollet

he adapted the motion-picture camera to the microscope.

Marfan's syndrome, also called ARACHNODACTYLY, rare hereditary disorder of connective-tissue development in humans that affects several body systems, most notably the skeleton, heart, and eye. Affected individuals are tall, their limbs are long and thin, their fingers are long and may be described as spider-like, and there is a tendency to double-jointedness. The lens of the eye is dislocated (a diagnostic sign), and there is a high frequency of glaucoma or retinal detachment. The heart muscle has an abnormal composition, and a variety of malfunctions and malformations occur; rupture of the aorta is the commonest cause of death.

Depending on the degree of expression of the trait, affected individuals may die at an early age or may live essentially normal lives. Although the basic abnormality of connective tissue cannot be remedied, wound healing occurs normally and surgical correction of some of the defects is practicable.

mārga (Sanskrit: "path"), in Hinduism, the path, or way, of reaching salvation. In Hindu tradition three means are enumerated: *jñāna-mārga,* the way of knowledge, involving the study of philosophic texts and contemplation; *karma-mārga,* the way of action, the proper performance of one's religious and ethical duties; and *bhakti-mārga,* the way of devotion and self-surrender to God. (The three ways are also distinguished as the three yogas or "disciplines"; *i.e., jñāna-yoga, karma-yoga,* and *bhakti-yoga.*) In the *Bhagavadgītā* Lord Krishna (Kṛṣṇa) praised all three means, but he favoured *bhakti-mārga,* which was accessible to members of any social class or caste.

Margai, Sir Milton (Augustus Striery) (b. December 1895, Gbangbatok, Sierra Leone—d. April 28, 1964, Freetown), first prime minister of Sierra Leone, a conservative, pro-British politician who came to power with the backing of a coalition of traditional chiefs and elite modernists from the Protectorate—the part of Sierra Leone that became a British colony at the end of the 19th century.

The grandson of a paramount chief and the first physician from the Protectorate (1926), Margai worked in the government medical service until 1950, during which time he built up lasting contacts and loyalties. His active political career began after World War II, when he joined the Sierra Leone Organization Society, an antipopulist though moderately progressive party. In 1951 he founded the Sierra Leone People's Party, which gained the support of Protectorate chiefs, on whom he depended to assure the allegiance of the rural populations and whom he supported in turn against populist demands and pressures. As the majority leader in the Legislative Council he was appointed to the Executive Council and later, as minister of health, he became one of the first Africans to hold a ministerial post. In 1953–54 he was made chief minister (later premier) as well as minister of agriculture, health, and forests. Later in the 1950s he also held the posts of attorney general and minister for internal affairs.

Although he easily won the elections of 1957, Margai was challenged within the People's Party by his younger brother Albert, who accused him of being too moderate and cautious. In 1958 Albert left to form his own party, the People's National Party, which was defeated in district elections in 1959. That same year Margai formed a united front to hold talks in London for independence, which was granted in 1961. His coalition government, with many former opposition leaders in his Cabinet, lasted from 1959 until his death, after which he was succeeded by his brother Albert. Margai had been knighted in 1959.

Margam, locality, Afan district, West Glamorgan County, Wales. Situated inland of the sandy Margam Burrows at the base of Mynydd Margam and Moel Ton-mawr peaks, the community of Margam developed around a Cistercian abbey founded by Robert, Earl of Gloucester, in 1147. Margam Abbey dominated the area as the cultural and educational centre until its dissolution in 1537. During the region's industrial development in the 18th and 19th centuries, Margam grew into a modern industrial development closely associated with Port Talbot (named for a Margam Abbey family who pioneered the port's growth). In 1946 the Margam Abbey steelworks were established and quickly became the largest in Great Britain. The Margam Stones Museum, with early Christian memorial stones, is located on the old abbey site, and both the Afan-Argoed Country Park and the Margam Country Park are near the community of Margam. The M4 Motorway connects Margam with Cardiff to the east and with Swansea to the north, beyond Port Talbot.

Margão (India): *see* Madgaon.

Margaret, name of rulers grouped below by country and indicated by the symbol •.

Foreign-language equivalents:

Danish	Margrete, or Margrethe
Norwegian	Margrete, or Margrethe
Swedish	Margareta

DENMARK/NORWAY/SWEDEN

• Margaret I (b. 1353, Søborg, Den.—d. Oct. 28, 1412, Flensburg), regent of Denmark (from 1375), of Norway (from 1380), and of Sweden (from 1389), who, by diplomacy and war, pursued dynastic policies that led to the Kalmar Union (1397), which united Denmark, Norway, and Sweden until 1523 and Denmark and Norway until 1814.

Rise to power. The daughter of King Valdemar IV of Denmark, Margaret was only six years old when she was betrothed to Haakon, king of Norway and son of King Magnus Eriksson of Sweden and Norway. The betrothal, intended to counter the dynastic claims to the Scandinavian thrones by the dukes of Mecklenburg and the intrigues of certain aristocratic factions within the Scandinavian countries, was imperilled by the renewal in 1360 of the old struggle between Valdemar of Denmark and Magnus of Sweden. But military reverses and the opposition of his own nobility forced Magnus to suspend hostilities in 1363. The wedding of Margaret and Haakon took place in Copenhagen in the same year.

Haakon's aspirations to become king of Sweden were thwarted when he and his father were defeated soon afterward by Albert of Mecklenburg, who bore the Swedish crown from 1364 to 1389. Haakon, however, succeeded in keeping his Norwegian kingdom, and it was there that Margaret spent her youth, under the tutelage of Märta Ulfsdotter, a daughter of the Swedish saint, Bridget. Margaret early displayed her talent as a ruler: she soon overshadowed her husband and appears to have exercised the real power. The couple's only child, Olaf, was born in 1370.

Margaret I, detail of her tomb effigy (recumbent) in the cathedral of Roskilde, Den.

By courtesy of the Nationalmuseum Arkivet, Stockholm

After her father's death in 1375, Margaret—over the objections of the Mecklenburgian claimants—was successful in getting Olaf elected to the Danish throne. Following Haakon's death in 1380, Margaret also ruled Norway in her son's name. Thus began the Danish-Norwegian union that lasted until 1814. Margaret secured and extended her sovereignty: in 1385 she won back the economically important strongholds on the west coast of Scandia from the Hanseatic League, and for a time she was also able to safeguard Denmark's southern borders by agreement with the counts of Holstein.

Margaret and Olaf, who came of age in 1385, were on the point of making war on Albert to enforce their claims to the Swedish throne when Olaf died unexpectedly in 1387. Deploying all her diplomatic skill, Margaret consolidated her position, becoming regent of both Norway and Denmark and, in the absence of an heir, adopting her six-year-old nephew, Erik of Pomerania. She then joined forces with the Swedish nobles, who had risen against the unpopular king Albert in a dispute over the will disposing of the lands of Bo Jonsson Grip, the powerful chancellor. By the Treaty of Dalaborg of 1388, the nobles proclaimed Margaret Sweden's "sovereign lady and rightful ruler" and granted her the main portion of Bo Jonsson Grip's vast domains. Defeating Albert in 1389, Margaret took him captive and released him only after the conclusion of peace six years later. His supporters, who had allied themselves with pirate bands in the Baltic Sea, did not surrender Stockholm until 1398.

Congress of Kalmar. Margaret was now the undisputed ruler of the three Scandinavian states. Her heir, Erik of Pomerania, was proclaimed hereditary king of Norway in 1389 and was elected king of Denmark and Sweden (which also included Finland) in 1396. His coronation took place the following year in the southern Swedish town of Kalmar, in the presence of the leading figures of all the Scandinavian countries. At Kalmar the nobility manifested its opposition to Margaret's increasing exercise of absolute power. The two extant documents disclose traces of the struggle between two political principles: the principle of absolute hereditary monarchy, as expressed in the so-called coronation act, and the constitutional elective kingship preferred by some nobles, as expressed in the so-called union act. The Kalmar assembly was a victory for Margaret and absolutism; the union act—perhaps the medieval Scandinavian document most debated by historians—denoted a plan that failed.

Despite Erik's coronation, Margaret remained Scandinavia's actual ruler until her death. Her aim was to further develop a strong royal central power and to foster the growth of a united Scandinavian state with its centre of gravity located in Denmark, her old hereditary dominion. She succeeded in eliminating the opposition of the nobility, in curbing the powers of the council of state, and in consolidating the administration through a network of royal sheriffs. In order to secure her position economically, she levied heavy taxes and confiscated church estates and lands exempt from dues to the crown. That such a policy succeeded without fatal strife to the union testifies to her strong political position as well as to her diplomatic skills and her ruthlessness. By adroitly using her relations to the Holy See, she was able to strengthen her influence over the church and on the politically important episcopal elections.

Margaret's political acumen was also evident in foreign affairs. Her main goals were to put an end to German expansion to the north and to extend and secure Denmark's southern borders, goals she tried to achieve through diplomatic means. An armed conflict did, however, break out with Holstein, and during the war Margaret died unexpectedly in 1412.

Assessment. One of Scandinavia's most eminent monarchs, Margaret was able not only to establish peace in her realms but also to maintain her authority against the aspirations of German princes and against the superior economic power of the Hanseatic League. The united kingdom that she created and left as a legacy, whose cementing factor was a strong monarchy, remained in existence until 1523, albeit not without interruptions. (L.T.N.)

BIBLIOGRAPHY. The first study of Queen Margaret based on modern critical principles is Kristian Erslev, *Dronning Margrethe og Kalmarunionens Grundlaeggelse* (1882), still a work of great value. The most debated event during Margaret's reign was the foundation of the Kalmar Union in 1397. Among the contributions to this discussion the following titles are recommended: Lauritz Weibull, "Unionsmötet i Kalmar 1397," *Scandia,* pp. 185–222 (1930); Gottfrid Carlsson, "Kalmarunionen," *Svensk Historisk Tidskrift,* pp. 405–481 (1930); and *Sveriges historia till våra dagar,* vol. 3, pt. 1 (1941); Erik Lonnroth, *Sverige och Kalmarunionen 1397–1457* (1934); and Halvdan Koth, *Dronning Margareta og Kalmarunionen* (1950).

Margaret II: *see* Margrethe II.

SCOTLAND

Margaret, byname THE MAID OF NORWAY (b. 1282/83—d. September 1290, in the Orkney Islands), queen of Scotland from 1286 to 1290, the last of the line of Scottish rulers descended from King Malcolm III Canmore (ruled 1058–93).

Margaret's father was Eric II, king of Norway; her mother, Margaret, a daughter of King Alexander III of Scotland (ruled 1249–86), died in 1283. Because none of Alexander III's other children were alive at the time of his death (March 1286), the Scottish lords proclaimed the infant Margaret as their queen. In 1290 her great-uncle, King Edward I of England, arranged a marriage between Margaret and his son Edward, later King Edward II of England. On the voyage from Norway to England, however, Margaret fell ill and died. Although the marriage treaty had specified that Scotland was to maintain its independence of England, Edward now proclaimed himself overlord of Scotland; the Scots resisted, and for more than 20 years Scotland suffered foreign domination and civil war.

Margaret MAULTASCH, also called MARGARET OF TIROL, German MARGARETE MAULTASCH, or MARGARETE VON TIROL (b. 1318—d. Oct. 3, 1369, Vienna), countess of Tirol, whose efforts to keep Tirol in the possession of her family failed after two unsuccessful marriages, forcing her to cede her lands to the Austrian Habsburgs. (She was called

Margaret Maultasch, detail from an engraving

By courtesy of the Bild-Archiv, Osterreichische Nationalbibliothek, Vienna

Maultasch, "mouth pocket," because of her deformed jaw.)

The daughter of Henry, duke of Carinthia and count of Tirol, Margaret was married to the nine-year-old John Henry of Luxembourg in 1330. On her father's death (1335), she and her husband inherited Tirol but were forced to cede Carinthia to the House of Habsburg. The Tirolese, unhappy with the government of Charles (later the Holy Roman emperor Charles IV), brother of John Henry, allied themselves with Margaret, whose marriage was childless and unhappy, and in 1341 expelled John Henry. The emperor Louis IV the Bavarian annulled Margaret's first marriage in 1342 and gave her a new husband, his own son Louis, margrave of Brandenburg. These proceedings infuriated the papacy and aggrieved the House of Luxembourg as well as the Habsburgs (who still coveted Tirol). The Tirolese also rose against their rulers, but their rebellion was suppressed. After the deposition of Louis the Bavarian (1346), Charles IV was elected in his stead and acquiesced in the status quo in Tirol. Margaret's husband died in 1361 and her only son, Meinhard, in 1363. The Habsburg Rudolf IV thereupon induced Margaret to cede Tirol to his house. Retiring to Vienna, she died there six years later.

Margaret OF ANGOULÊME, also called MARGARET OF NAVARRE, French MARGUERITE D'ANGOULÊME, or DE NAVARRE, Spanish MARGARITA DE ANGULEMA, or DE NAVARRA (b. April 11, 1492, Angoulême, Fr.—d. Dec. 21, 1549, Odos-Bigorre), queen consort of Henry II of Navarre, who, as patron of Humanists and Reformers, and as an author in her own right, was one of the most outstanding figures of the French Renaissance.

Margaret of Angoulême, detail of a drawing by F. Clouet; in the Musée Condé, Chantilly, Fr.

By courtesy of the Musee Conde, Chantilly, Fr.; photograph, Giraudon—Art Resource/EB Inc.

Daughter of Charles de Valois-Orléans, comte d'Angoulême, and Louise of Savoy, she became the most influential woman in France, with the exception of her mother, when her brother acceded to the crown as Francis I in 1515.

After the death of her first husband, Charles, duc d'Alençon, in 1525, she married Henry II of Navarre (Henry d'Albret). Although she bore Henry a daughter, Jeanne d'Albret (mother of the future Henry IV of France), the couple was soon estranged. Margaret was, on the other hand, always devoted to her brother and is credited with saving his life when he became ill in prison at Madrid after his capture at Pavia during the disastrous French expedition into Italy in 1525.

Margaret extended her protection both to men of artistic and scholarly genius and to advocates of doctrinal and disciplinary reform within the church. François Rabelais, Clément Marot, Bonaventure Des Périers, and Étienne Dolet were all in her circle. Her personal religious inclinations tended toward a sort of mystical pietism, but she was also influenced by the Humanists Jacques Lefèvre d'Étaples and Guillaume Briçonnet, who saw St. Paul's Epistles as a primary source of Christian doctrine. Although Margaret espoused reform within the Catholic Church, she was not a Calvinist, and her relations with her daughter were therefore strained. She did, however, do her best to protect the Reformers and dissuaded Francis I from intolerant measures as long as she could. In the end, however, as persecution by the crown increased, she was unable to save Des Périers, Dolet, or Marot.

The most important of Margaret's own literary works is the *Heptaméron* (published posthumously, 1558–59). It is constructed on the lines of Boccaccio's *Decameron,* consisting of 72 tales (out of a planned 100) told by a group of travellers delayed by a flood on their return from a Pyrenean spa. The stories, illustrating the triumphs of virtue, honour, and quick-wittedness, and the frustration of vice and hypocrisy, contain a strong element of satire directed against licentious and grasping monks and clerics.

Although some of Margaret's poetry, including the *Miroir de l'âme pécheresse* (1531; trans. by the future Queen Elizabeth I of England as *A Godly Meditation of the Soul,* 1548), was published during her lifetime, her best verse, including *Le Navire,* was not compiled until 1896, under the title of *Les Dernières* Poésies ("Last Poems").

Margaret OF ANJOU (b. March 23, 1430, probably Pont-à-Mousson, Lorraine, Fr.—d. Aug. 25, 1482, near Saumur), queen consort of England's King Henry VI and a leader of the Lancastrians in the Wars of the Roses (1455–85) between the houses of York and Lancaster. Strong-willed and ambitious, she made a relentless, but ultimately unsuccessful, effort to obtain the crown for her son, Prince Edward (1453–71).

Margaret was the daughter of René I of Anjou, titular king of Naples. Her marriage to the ineffectual, mentally unbalanced Henry VI in April 1445 was arranged as part of a truce in the Hundred Years' War between France and England. Soon she became a key member of the King's party, which was bitterly opposed by the powerful Richard, duke of York. In May 1455 this factional dispute erupted into armed conflict with a Yorkist victory over the Lancastrians at St. Albans; Richard of York then controlled the government until the indomitable Margaret ousted him from power in 1456.

When hostilities again broke out in 1459, Margaret embittered the struggle by outlawing the Yorkist leaders. After the King was captured by the Yorkists at Northampton in July 1460, she upheld her son's claim to the royal succession and refused to accept the compromise by which York was declared Henry's heir. Her partisans killed York near Wakefield, Yorkshire, in December 1460 and freed the King from captivity at the second Battle of St. Albans in February 1461. But Edward of York, Richard's son, seized the throne as Edward IV on March 4 and crushed Margaret's army at the Battle of Towton, Yorkshire, on March 29. She fled to Scotland with her husband and son.

Margaret of Anjou, detail of a manuscript illumination, *c.* 1445; in the British Library (Royal MS. 15.E.VI)

In 1470 Margaret, then in France, became reconciled with her former Yorkist enemy, Richard Neville, earl of Warwick, who was plotting to overthrow Edward IV and restore Henry VI to the throne. Warwick successfully carried out his plan in October 1470, but Margaret did not return to England until April 14, 1471, the very day that Warwick was killed in battle against Edward IV. At Tewkesbury on May 4, 1471, Margaret was defeated by Edward IV, and her son was killed. Soon afterward her husband was murdered in the Tower of London. Margaret remained in custody in England until the French king Louis XI ransomed her in 1475. She returned to France, where she died in poverty. J.J. Bagley's biography, *Margaret of Anjou, Queen of England,* was published in 1948.

To make the best use of the Britannica, consult the INDEX *first*

Margaret OF ANTIOCH, SAINT, also called SAINT MARINA (fl. 3rd or 4th century, Antioch, Syria; Eastern feast day July 13; Western feast day July 20), virgin martyr and one of the 14 Holy Helpers (a group of saints jointly commemorated on August 8), who was one of the most venerated saints during the Middle Ages. Her story, generally regarded to be fictitious, is substantially that of the Eastern St. Marina of Antioch, whose feast day is July 17, and is related to that of St. Pelagia of Antioch, who is also known as Margaret or Marina.

During the reign (284–305) of the Roman emperor Diocletian, Margaret allegedly refused marriage with the prefect Olybrius at Antioch and was consequently beheaded after undergoing extravagant trials and tortures. Her designation as patron saint of expectant mothers (particularly in difficult labour) and her emblem, a dragon, are based on one of her trials: Satan, disguised as a dragon, swallowed Margaret; his stomach, however, soon rejecting her, opened, and let her out unharmed. In 1969 Margaret's feast day, formerly July 20, was eliminated in the revised calendar of the Roman Catholic Church because it is doubtful whether she ever existed. Nevertheless, during the medieval period she ranked among the most famous saints; her voice was among those attested to have been heard by St. Joan of Arc. A. Mabellini's *Leggenda di Santa Margherita* appeared in 1925.

Margaret OF AUSTRIA, Spanish MARGARITA DE AUSTRIA (b. Jan. 10, 1480, Brussels—d. Dec. 1, 1530, Mechelen, Spanish Netherlands), Habsburg ruler who, as regent of the Netherlands (1507–15, 1519–30) for her nephew Charles (later the Holy Roman emperor Charles V), helped consolidate Habsburg dominion there.

The daughter of the Habsburg archduke Maximilian (later the Holy Roman emperor Maximilian I) and his consort, Mary, duchess of Burgundy, Margaret was first betrothed in 1483 to the dauphin, later Charles VIII of France. After he repudiated her (1491), she married (April 1497) the infante John, heir to the Spanish kingdoms, who died only a few months later. Finally, in 1501, she married Philibert II, duke of Savoy, who died in 1504.

Margaret of Austria, detail of a painting attributed to Bernard van Orley, *c.* 1505; in Windsor Castle, Berkshire

In 1507 Maximilian appointed Margaret regent of the Netherlands for the infant Charles, the successor to her brother Philip I the Handsome, who had died in 1506. Her foreign policy was strongly pro-English, and she fought against France only when allied with Maximilian, England, and Spain. In both of her regencies, the Netherlands provinces were heavily taxed to support Habsburg military campaigns. In 1508 she represented Maximilian and her young nephew Ferdinand of Aragon (later Ferdinand I as Holy Roman emperor) at Cambrai, where disputes over French rights in the Burgundian Netherlands were resolved.

Although being declared of age to rule in 1515, Charles reappointed Margaret to govern in the Netherlands while he was securing the German Kingship and the imperial succession for himself. The last decade of her rule saw the extension of Habsburg dominion in the northeastern Netherlands, including the gradual subjection of Friesland (1515–24); the annexation of the bishop of Utrecht's lands (1528); and campaigns against Charles of Egmond, duke of Gelderland, who was allied with Charles V's archfoe, Francis I of France. As Charles's representative at Cambrai in 1529, she negotiated the "Ladies' Peace" with Louise of Savoy, who spoke for her son Francis I.

Margaret OF AUSTRIA, also called MARGARET OF PARMA, Spanish MARGARITA DE AUSTRIA, OR DE PARMA (b. 1522, Oudenaarde, Spanish Netherlands—d. Jan. 18, 1586, Ortona, Kingdom of Naples), duchess of Parma and Habsburg regent who, as governor general of the Netherlands (1559–67), attempted to appease the growing discontent with Spanish rule.

The illegitimate daughter of the Holy Roman emperor Charles V (Charles I of Spain) and Johanna van der Gheenst, Margaret was married in 1536 to Alessandro de' Medici, duke of Florence, who was murdered less than a year later. She then married (1538) Ottavio Farnese (duke of Parma after 1547) and was appointed governor of the Netherlands in 1559 by her half-brother, Philip II of Spain. Opposition to Spanish rule was already strong because of the presence of Spanish troops and especially because of the creation of new bishoprics in 1559 by a papal bull challenging local religious privileges.

Margaret's chief adviser, Antoine Perrenot de Granvelle, who benefitted from the church reorganization (archbishop of Mechelen in 1560 and cardinal in 1561), antagonized the higher nobles, led by William, prince of Orange (William I the Silent), and by Lamoraal, graaf van Egmond. As a result, she was forced to dismiss Granvelle in 1564. The initiative then passed to a faction of the lesser nobility, who called themselves Gueux (Beggars), and petitioned her, in 1566, for more moderate treatment of Protestants.

Margaret met some of the Gueux's requests, but she brought in a largely German mercenary army in early 1567 after Calvinist extremists had attacked Catholic churches in August 1566 ("breaking of the images"). Although peace was restored, Philip II then sent to the Netherlands the Duke of Alba, who assembled a Spanish army and enforced stern measures against dissident Protestants, precipitating an open revolt against Spanish rule. Alba's assumption of power led Margaret to resign in 1567. She returned to the Netherlands in 1580 to head the civil administration, while her son Alessandro Farnese served as commander in chief and then governor general. She retired to Italy in 1583.

Margaret OF FRANCE: *see* Margaret of Valois.

Margaret OF NAVARRE: *see* Margaret of Angoulême.

Margaret OF PROVENCE, French MARGUERITE DE PROVENCE (b. 1221—d. Dec. 21, 1295, Paris), eldest daughter of Raymond Berengar IV, count of Provence, whose marriage to King Louis IX of France on May 27, 1234, extended French authority beyond the Rhône.

Although Blanche of Castile, Louis IX's mother, had arranged the marriage, she was jealous of her daughter-in-law, whom she supervised strictly; Jean, Sire de Joinville, chronicler of Louis's reign, tells several stories of Blanche separating the royal couple, and Louis himself sometimes behaving brusquely toward Margaret.

Margaret accompanied Louis to Egypt on the crusade of 1248 and showed great courage at Damietta, reinspiring the crusaders after a defeat at al-Manṣūrah (February 1250), where Louis was captured by the Muslims. Blanche died in 1252; and Margaret, after returning to France, tried occasionally to meddle in politics. Though she was usually checked by the King's intransigence, she may have done something to improve relations between Louis and Henry III of England, who in 1236 had married her sister Eleanor. On the other hand, she resented the fact that her father (died 1245), by his will of 1238, left Provence to her youngest sister, Beatrice, who in 1246 was married to Charles of Anjou, a brother of Louis IX. After Louis IX's death (1270) Margaret did all she could to thwart Charles's ambitions.

Margaret OF SCOTLAND, SAINT (b. *c.* 1045, probably Hungary—d. Nov. 16, 1093, Edinburgh; canonized 1250; feast day June 10, Scottish feast day June 16), queen consort of Malcolm III Canmore and patroness of Scotland.

Margaret was brought up at the Hungarian court, where her father, Edward, was in exile. After the Battle of Hastings, Edward's widow and children fled for safety to Scotland. Her brother Edgar the Aetheling, defeated claimant to the English throne, joined her there. In spite of her leanings toward a religious life, Margaret married (*c.* 1070) Malcolm III Canmore, king of Scotland from 1057 or 1058 to 1093. Through her influence over her husband and his court, she promoted, in conformity with the Gregorian reform, the interests of the church and of the English population conquered by the Scots in the previous century. She died shortly after her husband was slain near Alnwick, Northumberland.

Margaret OF TIROL: *see* Margaret Maultasch.

Margaret OF VALOIS, also called MARGARET OF FRANCE, or QUEEN MARGOT, French MARGUERITE DE VALOIS, or DE FRANCE, or REINE MARGOT (b. May 14, 1553, Saint-Germain-en-Laye, Fr.—d. March 27, 1615, Paris), queen consort of Navarre known for her licentiousness and for her *Mémoires,* a vivid exposition of France during her lifetime.

The daughter of Henry II of France and Catherine de Médicis, she played a secondary part in the Wars of Religion (1562–98) from the moment she took her place at court in 1569. Her relations with her brothers Charles IX and the duc d'Anjou, the future Henry III, were often strained, and she had an early liaison with Henri, duc de Guise, the leader of the extremist Catholic party. On Aug. 18, 1572, she was married, at Paris, to the Protestant Henry de Bourbon, king of Navarre, the future Henry IV, in order to seal the peace between Catholics and Protestants. Five days later, however, the massacre of Protestants began on St. Bartholomew's Day.

Henry of Navarre had been able to escape death in the massacre by means of an expedient abjuration; despite her continued interest in other liaisons, Margaret refused to be parted from him. She used her influence to promote an understanding between him and her youngest brother, François, duc d'Alençon, a leader of the moderate Catholics. Her role in the ensuing conspiracies cost the life of her lover, the seigneur de La Môle (Joseph de Boniface), in 1574. Later Henry III banished her to the inaccessible castle of Usson in Auvergne (1586), but with Guise's help she was able to take control of the place.

Her husband's growing power and dynastic needs raised the possibility of an annulment of their childless marriage, but Margaret withheld her consent as long as Henry's mistress, Gabrielle d'Estrées, was alive. After the latter's death, she released Henry to marry Marie de Médicis (1600) but retained her royal title. Five years later she was allowed to return to Paris, where she lived in magnificent style, free to pursue her amours. In addition to her *Mémoires,* she wrote poems and letters.

Margaret TUDOR (b. Nov. 29, 1489, London—d. Oct. 18, 1541, Methven, Perth, Scot.), wife of King James IV of Scotland, mother of James V, and elder daughter of King Henry VII of England. During her son's minority, she played a key role in the conflict between the pro-French and pro-English factions in Scotland, constantly shifting her allegiances to suit her financial interests.

Margaret Tudor, detail of a miniature from the *Book of Hours* of James IV of Scotland; in the Österreichische Nationalbibliothek, Vienna

By courtesy of the Osterreichische Nationalbibliothek, Vienna

She married James IV in August 1503, but the scanty dowry provided by her father ruined any opportunity for improved relations between England and Scotland. James was killed fighting the English in 1513, and Margaret then ruled for her infant son, James V. Her marriage in 1514 to Archibald Douglas, earl of Angus, a partisan of England, gave the Scottish Parliament an excuse to replace her in the regency with John Stewart, duke of Albany, the leader of the pro-French party. For a time, Margaret was forced into exile in England, but she soon became estranged from Angus and actively sided with Albany against him. Shortly after obtaining an annulment in 1527, she married Henry Stewart, who was made Lord Methven when James assumed personal control of the government in 1528. For a time Margaret and Methven were James's most influential advisers. But in 1534 she fell out of royal favour after James discovered that she had betrayed state secrets to her brother, Henry VIII. Seven years later she died at Methven Castle. Margaret was the great-grandmother of King James VI of Scotland, who became James I of England in 1603.

Margareta (Swedish personal name): *see under* Margaret.

margarine, food product made principally from one or more vegetable or animal fats or oils in which is dispersed an aqueous portion containing milk products, either solid or fluid, salt, and such other ingredients as flavouring agents, yellow food pigments, emulsifiers, preservatives, vitamins A and D, and butter. It is used in cooking and as a spread. Nutritionally, margarine is primarily a source of calories.

The French chemist H. Mège-Mouriès developed margarine in the late 1860s and was given recognition in Europe and a patent in the United States in 1873. His manufacturing method was simplified in the United States into a process in which the melted fat blend was churned with milk and salt, chilled to solidify the mixture, kneaded to a plastic consistency, and packaged, all by means of the standard butter-working equipment of the time. The edible fats used have varied widely, the trend having been from the animal fats predominant in early use to the vegetable fats, principally cottonseed, soybean, coconut, peanut, and corn oils, and, more recently, palm oil. During the late 1950s an increased interest in the relation of polyunsaturated fats and oils to health hastened the shift to corn, safflower, and sunflower oils as the fat ingredients of margarine. Whale oil has been widely used in Europe but was never common in the United States.

Margarine was long subjected to severe restrictive legislation, particularly in the United States, because of the opposition of the dairy industry. But during the 1930s, margarine manufacturers learned to make margarine from domestic oils rather than the imported oils formerly used, thereby enlisting the support of U.S. cottonseed and soybean farmers. Repeal of federal and most state restrictions gradually followed, leading to the acceptance of margarine in the United States to an extent comparable with that in most European countries.

Margarita (Spanish personal name): *see under* Margaret.

Margarita Island, Spanish ISLA DE MARGARITA, island in the Caribbean Sea, 12 mi (19 km) north of the Península de Araya in northeastern Venezuela. Also known as the Isle of Pearls, Margarita is the largest of 70 islands comprising Nueva Esparta state. In reality two islands joined by a low, narrow isthmus, Margarita is about 40 mi (65 km) long, covers an area of 414 sq mi (1,072 sq km), and has a coastline of 198 mi, with many natural harbours. The island is generally low, but the highest elevation, in the Cerros (mountains) del Macanao, reaches 2,493 ft (760 m).

Harbour of Juangriego, Margarita Island, Venezuela

Robert Phillips

Isla de Margarita was discovered by Columbus in 1498 and quickly became known for its pearls. Through the centuries, settlements on the island were besieged by Indians (in reprisal for slave raids on the mainland) and by British pirates and Dutch forces. Its traders rendered invaluable assistance to the revolutionists in the struggle for independence from Spain. Simón Bolívar used the island as a base of operations in 1816, and the Spanish general Pablo Morillo was driven from its shores in 1817.

The population of Margarita is predominantly indigenous; the Spanish ancestry is traceable mainly to the Canary Islands. Since 1920 the island has attracted immigrants from abroad, but at the same time many islanders have migrated to the mainland in search of more favourable employment. Farming and grazing are carried on, but the island is a net importer of foodstuffs. The pearl industry is still important; fishing, the building of fishing boats, tourism (especially since World War II), and the manufacture of tile, ceramics, shoes, hats, and salt are additional sources of income. Although the capital is La Asunción (*q.v.*), the most important city is Porlamar, which is the centre of the pearl industry and has an airport; the largest port is at Pampatar. Pop. (latest est.) 117,700.

Margate, town, Thanet district, county of Kent, England. It lies east of the Thames River estuary. During the 18th century the town, which is endowed with sandy beaches, became a bathing resort. The large influx of summer visitors is presently Margate's mainstay. An industrial estate just to the south has attracted a considerable amount of light industry. Pop. (1991) 56,734.

margay, also called TIGER CAT, or TIGRILLO (*Felis wiedii*), species of small cat that ranges from South through Central America and, rarely, into the extreme southern United States. Like all cats, it is of the family Felidae. It lives in forests and presumably is nocturnal, feeding on small prey such as birds, frogs, and insects. It is largely arboreal and has specially adapted claws and feet that enable it to scamper up tree trunks and along branches

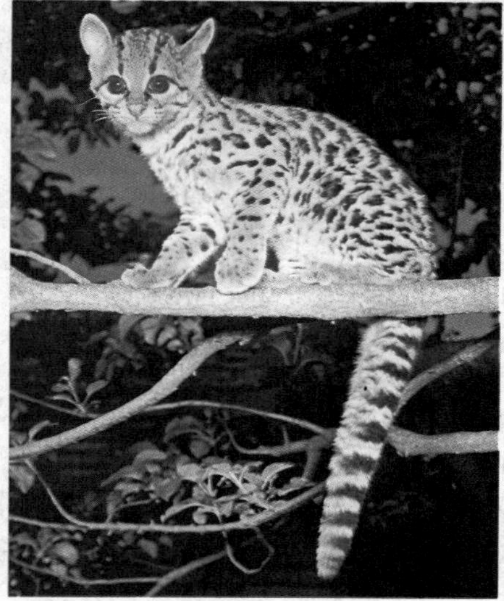

Margay (*Felis wiedii*)
John H. Gerard from the National Audubon Society Collection/Photo Researchers

with ease. The margay resembles the related ocelot but has a longer tail and fuller face, emphasized by large, dark eyes and rounded ears. The male attains a maximum length of about 1.1 m (3.5 feet), including a tail 46 cm (18 inches) long, and weighs up to about 16 kg (35 pounds). The female is generally smaller and has a relatively longer tail. Coloration varies from pale gray to deep brown with dark markings: spots, stripes, bands, and black-edged blotches. When hand reared as a kitten, the margay reportedly is easily tamed; as an adult, however, it may become unpredictable.

Marggraf, Andreas Sigismund (b. March 3, 1709, Berlin, Prussia [Germany]—d. Aug. 7, 1782, Berlin), German chemist whose discovery of beet sugar in 1747 led to the development of the modern sugar industry.

Marggraf served as assistant (1735–38) to his father, the court apothecary at Berlin, and as director of the chemical laboratory of the German Academy of Sciences of Berlin (1754–60). He distinguished between the oxides of aluminum (alumina) and calcium (lime) found in common clay, and he simplified the process for obtaining phosphorus from urine.

In 1747 Marggraf used alcohol to extract the juices from several plants, including one now known as the sugar beet (*Beta vulgaris*). He identified the sugar beet's dried, crystallized juice as identical with cane sugar by the use of a microscope, in what was perhaps the first such use of that instrument for chemical identification. His discovery of beet sugar was

Marggraf, engraving
Bavaria-Verlag

not acted on until 1786, four years after his death, and the first beet-sugar refinery began operations in 1802.

Margherita (Somalia): *see* Jamaame.

Margherita Peak, French PIC MARGUERITE, highest summit of the Ruwenzori Range in East Africa and the third highest in Africa (after Mounts Kilimanjaro and Kenya). Margherita Peak is the highest peak on Mount Stanley. It rises to 16,795 feet (5,119 m) between Lake Albert (Lake Mobutu Sese Seko) to the north and Lake Edward to the south on the Zaire-Uganda border. It was first climbed in 1906 by an expedition led by Luigi Amedeo Abruzzi and was named for Queen Margherita of Italy.

Marghiloman, Alexandru (b. July 4, 1854, Buzău, Rom.—d. May 10, 1925, Buzău), Romanian statesman and Conservative leader who greatly influenced Romania's role in World War I.

After studying law in Paris, Marghiloman was elected a deputy in Romania in 1884 and became a member of the government in 1888. As a member of the Young Conservative Junimist group, he favoured cooperation with Germany and Austria-Hungary but on the outbreak of war in 1914 advocated neutrality. In 1916, as leader of the Conservative Party, he refused a seat in Ion Brătianu's cabinet because he opposed Romania's entry into the war on the Allied side.

Marghiloman remained in Bucharest during the German occupation, acting as president of the Romanian Red Cross. He was a mediator between the occupying authorities and the population, rejecting German proposals that he should form a government in Bucharest in rivalry to King Ferdinand's government in Iaşi. After Romania's surrender in March 1918, he yielded to the king's request to become premier, signing a peace treaty with the Central Powers (May 7, 1918, never ratified). His cabinet fell on Nov. 8, 1918, with the defeat of the Central Powers.

Marghilon, formerly MARGILAN, city, eastern Uzbekistan. It lies 19 miles (30 km) north of Fergana. Originally known as Marginan, it probably dates back to the 2nd–1st century BC, when one branch of the great Silk Road to the Orient ran through the Fergana Valley. It was an important commercial town in the 10th–12th century AD, and one of the largest cities in the valley in the 16th century. It formed part of the khanate of Kokand in the 18th century, and in 1876 it was captured by the Russians. Marghilon has long been celebrated throughout Central Asia for its silks, and it is now the most important silk centre in Uzbekistan. Pop. (1993 est.) 129,000.

margin, in finance, the amount by which the value of collateral provided as security for a loan exceeds the amount of the loan. This excess represents the borrower's equity contribution in a transaction that is partly financed by borrowed funds; thus it provides a "margin" of safety to the lender over and above the collateral that is pledged. The size of the margin that is required varies with the type of collateral, the stability of its market price, expectations with regard to its future price, and the credit standing of the borrower.

The term margin is used especially in connection with transactions in securities and commodity futures. When securities are purchased "on margin," the buyer supplies only a percentage, or margin, of the purchase price and borrows the remainder from his broker, pledging the security as collateral for the loan. A fall in the price of the security subsequent to the purchase reduces the margin available to the lender, and the customer may be called upon to restore his margin to a prearranged level. This level is determined by the lending broker but may not be below minimum levels stipulated by the organized exchange in which the transaction takes place.

Minimum initial margin requirements on loans made for the purpose of purchasing securities are required in the United States by the Federal Reserve Board, under authority granted by the Securities Exchange Act of 1934. The purpose of the margin requirement is to prevent excessive use of credit for speculation in stocks. Dealings on margin are not allowed on British stock exchanges.

marginal-cost pricing, in economics, the practice of setting the price of a product to equal the extra cost of producing an extra unit of output. By this policy, a producer charges, for each product unit sold, only the addition to total cost resulting from materials and direct labour. The policy is used to maintain a low selling price or to keep a business operating during a period of poor sales. For example, a firm temporarily experiencing poor sales might want to keep its workers employed and ready for an expected upturn. Since fixed costs such as rent and building maintenance must be paid regardless of whether the workers are employed, the company can decide to remain in production and sell the product at marginal cost, thus losing no more money than it would if the workers were laid off and nothing was manufactured.

marginal efficiency of investment, in economics, expected rates of return on investment as additional units of investment are made under specified conditions and over a stated period of time. A comparison of these rates with the going rate of interest may be used to indicate the profitability of investment. The rate of return is computed as the rate at which the expected stream of future earnings from an investment project must be discounted to make their present value equal to the cost of the project.

As the quantity of investment increases, the rates of return from it may be expected to decrease because the most profitable projects are undertaken first. Additions to investment will consist of projects with progressively lower rates of return. Logically, investment would be undertaken as long as the marginal efficiency of each additional investment exceeded the interest rate. If the interest rate were higher, investment would be unprofitable because the cost of borrowing the necessary funds would exceed the returns on the investment. Even if it were unnecessary to borrow funds for the investment, more profit could be made by lending out the available funds at the going rate of interest.

The British economist J.M. Keynes used this concept, but a different term (the marginal efficiency of capital), in arguing the importance of profit expectations rather than interest rates as determinants of the level of investment. Statistical studies since the 1930s have tended to reinforce the idea that interest rates play a small role in investment decisions.

marginal productivity theory, in economics, a theory developed at the end of the 19th century by a number of writers, including John Bates Clark and Philip Henry Wicksteed, who argued that a business firm would be willing to pay a productive agent only what he adds to the firm's well-being or utility; that it is clearly unprofitable to buy, for example, a man-hour of labour if it adds less to its buyer's income than what it costs. This marginal yield of a productive input came to be called the value of its marginal product, and the resulting theory of distribution states that every type of input will be paid the value of its marginal product.

marginal utility, in economics, the additional satisfaction or benefit (utility) that a consumer derives from buying an additional unit of a commodity or service. The concept implies that the utility or benefit to a consumer of an additional unit of a product is inversely related to the number of units of that product he already owns.

Marginal utility can be illustrated by the following example. The marginal utility of one slice of bread offered to a family that has only seven slices will be great, since the family will be that much less hungry and the difference between seven and eight is proportionally significant. An extra slice of bread offered to a family that has 30 slices, however, will have less marginal utility, since the difference between 30 and 31 is proportionally smaller and the family's hunger has been allayed by what it had already. Thus, the marginal utility to a buyer of a product decreases as he purchases more and more of that product, until the point is reached at which he has no need at all of additional units. The marginal utility is then zero.

The concept of marginal utility grew out of attempts by 19th-century economists to analyze and explain the fundamental economic reality of price. These economists believed that price was partly determined by a commodity's utility—that is, the degree to which it satisfies a consumer's needs and desires. This definition of utility, however, led to a paradox when applied to prevailing price relations.

The economists observed that the value of diamonds was far greater than that of bread, even though bread, being essential to the continuation of life, had far greater utility than did diamonds, which were merely ornaments. This problem, known as the paradox of value, was solved by the application of the concept of marginal utility. Because diamonds are scarce and the demand for them was great, the possession of additional units was a high priority. This meant their marginal utility was high, and consumers were willing to pay a comparatively high price for them. Bread is much less valuable only because it is much less scarce, and the buyers of bread possess enough to satisfy their most pressing need for it. Additional purchases of bread beyond people's appetite for it will be of decreasing benefit or utility and will eventually lose all utility beyond the point at which hunger is completely satisfied.

The concept of marginal utility was augmented in the 20th century by the method of analysis known as indifference analysis (*see* indifference curve).

Margoliouth, David Samuel (b. Oct. 17, 1858, London, Eng.—d. March 22, 1940, London), English scholar whose pioneering efforts in Islāmic studies won him a near-legendary reputation among Islāmic peoples and Oriental scholars of Europe.

Margoliouth was professor of Arabic at the University of Oxford (1889–1937) and was briefly active as a minister of the Church of England. He spent considerable time traveling in the Middle East. At Baghdad and in the surrounding area, he came to be regarded as more knowledgeable on Islāmic matters than most Arab scholars.

His works on the history of Islām, which became the standard treatises in English for at least a generation, include *Mohammed and the Rise of Islam* (1905), *The Early Development of Mohammedanism* (1914), and *The Relations Between Arabs and Israelites Prior to the Rise of Islam* (1924). Particularly brilliant as an editor and translator of Arabic works, he made use of his remarkable talents in *The Letters of Abū'l-ʿAlā of Maʿarrat al-Nuʿmān* (1898), Yāqūt's *Dictionary of Learned Men,* 6 vol. (1907–27), and the chronicle of Miskawayh, prepared in collaboration with H.F. Amedroz under the title *The Eclipse of the ʿAbbasid Caliphate,* 7 vol. (1920–21).

Margot, QUEEN: *see* Margaret of Valois.

margrave, feminine MARGRAVINE: *see* marquess.

Margrete, also spelled MARGRETHE (Danish, Norwegian personal name): *see under* Margaret, except as below.

Margrethe II, in full MARGRETHE ALEXANDRINE THORHILDUR INGRID (b. April 16, 1940, Copenhagen, Den.), queen of Denmark since the death of her father, King Frederick IX, on Jan. 14, 1972.

Born a week after the Nazi invasion of Denmark, she spent the war years in Denmark and then attended school in Copenhagen. She continued her studies at the universities of Copenhagen, Århus in Jutland, Cambridge, the London School of Economics, and the Sorbonne. In 1953, following a change in the Danish constitution to permit female succession to the throne, Margrethe, the king's eldest daughter, assumed the title of "throne heiress" (*i.e.,* crown princess, although that title, in Denmark, had denoted the wife of a male heir to the throne). As such, from her 18th birthday she regularly took part in meetings of the Council of State in preparation for her future regal duties.

On June 10, 1967, she married Count Henri de Laborde de Monpezat, a French diplomat, who afterward took the title of Prince Henrik. Their first child, Crown Prince Frederik, was born on May 26, 1968, and a second son, Prince Joachim, on June 7, 1969.

Marguerite (French personal name): *see under* Margaret.

Marguerite, Pic (East Africa): *see* Margherita Peak.

Margunios, Maximus (b. Crete—d. 1602, Venice [Italy]), Greek Orthodox bishop and humanist exponent of Greek culture in Italy, whose attempt to reconcile the theologies of the Eastern and Western churches aroused in Byzantine churchmen suspicion of his orthodoxy.

After his education at the University of Padua, a centre for Greek scholars, Margunios became a monk in 1579, possibly at the monastery of St. Catherine, near Candia (Iráklion), Crete, where he first studied Greek literature. Later he was made bishop of Kíthira (Kythera), a Venetian-controlled island off western Greece. Prevented for many years by Venetian authorities from living in his diocese, he stayed chiefly with the Greek Orthodox community in Venice, where he became headmaster of the Greek College and assisted Greek scholars studying in Italian universities. He also was concerned with preserving the Eastern Orthodox religious tradition among his countrymen living in what he considered a materialistic milieu.

Margunios sought a theological compromise formula acceptable to both Latin and Greek churches for the disputed *Filioque* clause in the Latin version of the Nicene Creed. After his treatise on the subject, "On the Procession of the Holy Spirit," appeared in 1591, he was suspected of wavering on Eastern Orthodox doctrine and was obliged to send a statement to Constantinople assuring the Byzantine council on doctrine that he had not deviated from Orthodoxy.

A notable accomplishment in the advancement of learning was Margunios' collaboration with the Anglican classical scholar Sir Henry Savile in the 1613 standard edition of the complete works of St. John Chrysostom, the late 4th-century Greek church father. Savile publicly acknowledged that Margunios' cooperation was decisive in producing the critical Greek text, an edition that continues to be definitive.

Mari, Russian MARYTSY, formerly CHEREMIS, Russian CHEREMISY, European people, numbering about 670,000 in the late 20th century, who speak a language of the Finno-Ugric family and live mainly in Mari El, Russia, in the middle Volga River valley. There are also some Mari in adjacent regions and nearly 100,000 in Bashkortostan (Bashkiriya). Mari is their own name for themselves; Cheremis was the name applied to them by Westerners and pre-Soviet Russians.

The Mari and Chuvash have lived in a quasi-symbiotic relationship from about AD 700 to this day, though the period of most intense influence ended in 1236, when Tatar contacts became pressing. Tatar influences lasted until 1552, when the area came increasingly under the influence of Moscow. The process of Mari assimilation to Russian civilization accelerated during the 17th century, and the ever-mounting symptoms of social and economic change may be traced in many forms, including strong nativistic movements, among them Kuga Sorta (*q.v.*).

The principal source of subsistence among the Mari is agriculture (grain and flax) combined with dairy farming and stock raising. Yoshkar-Ola, the Mari El capital, boasts of training schools in subjects such as animal husbandry, forestry, optics, and papermaking. In handicrafts, the Mari are noted for their wood and stone carving and embroidery.

Mari, modern TALL AL-ḤARĪRĪ, ancient Mesopotamian city situated on the right bank of the Euphrates River in what is now Syria. Excavations, initially directed by André Parrot and begun in 1933, uncovered remains extending from about 3100 BC to the 7th century AD.

The most remarkable of the discoveries was the great palace of Zimrilim, a local king whose exceptionally prosperous rule of almost 30 years was ended when Hammurabi of Babylon captured and destroyed the city in the 18th century BC.

The palace contained nearly 300 rooms, within which were concentrated all of the most important administrative offices. Numerous wall murals and hundreds of small objects were uncovered; nothing, however, equaled the thousands of archives discovered in various scribal chambers. They consisted of diplomatic correspondence and reports sent in from all parts of the country as well as historical archives and letters exchanged between King Shamshi-Adad I of Assyria and his two sons shortly before 1800 BC. Economic and legal texts were also abundant. Altogether the texts have extended the knowledge of Assyrian geography and history and have given a graphic picture of life of the period.

Mari El, republic within Russia, in the basin of the middle Volga River.

Extending north from the left bank of the Volga and drained by its tributaries, the Vetluga, Bolshaya and Malaya Kokshaga, and Ilet, the republic consists of a level, often swampy, plain that rises gently toward the east, where it merges with the low Vyatka Hills. Winters are long and cold in the markedly continental climate, with an average January temperature of 9° F (−13° C), and incursions of Arctic air often result in temperature readings as low as −44° F (−42° C). Summers are mild, with a July average of 68° F (20° C). Precipitation is greatest in the summer and generally ranges from 18 to 20 inches (450 to 500 mm) annually. Forests, mostly spruce, birch, and pine, cover about one-half of the surface. Floodplain meadows line the Volga and other rivers, which are subject to annual flooding in the spring. Podzol-type soils prevail, except in the many peat bogs, marshes, and swampy forests that are scattered over the boulder clay (till) plain.

A Finno-Ugric people related to the Udmurt and Mordvin, the Mari were colonized by the Russians in the 16th century. Mari was first established as a Soviet autonomous oblast (province) in 1920 and became the Mari Autonomous Soviet Socialist Republic in 1936. After the dissolution of the Soviet Union in 1991 it became the republic of Mari El, part of the Russian Federation. The population, predominantly Russian and Mari with a scattering of other nationalities, is about two-thirds urban. Chief cities are Yoshkar-Ola (the capital), Volzhsk, and Kozmodemyansk.

The manufacture of electrical instruments and machinery, refrigeration equipment, machine tools, and other machinery is the principal economic activity, together with timber cutting and processing. Timber, floated down rivers to sawmills located along the railway to Yoshkar-Ola and to cities downstream on the Volga, is processed into prefabricated homes at Krasnogorsky, into furniture at Yoshkar-Ola, and into paper and pulp at Volzhsk. The wood-chemical industry produces turpentine and alcohol. Other industries are glassmaking and the manufacture of clothing, with food processing concentrated at Yoshkar-Ola.

Arable land constitutes about 30 percent of the total land area and is located mainly along the Volga and in the northeastern part of the Vyatka Hills. Most of this area is given over to grains (rye, oats, spring wheat, barley, buckwheat, and corn [maize] for silage). Other crops include flax, potatoes, and other vegetables. Cattle are raised for meat and milk, with sheep, goats, and pigs also kept. Roads connect Yoshkar-Ola with Orshanka and Yaransk in the Kirov oblast and with Sernur and Kozmodemyansk in the republic. The only railway is a branch line passing through Yoshkar-Ola. Area 9,000 square miles (23,200 square km). Pop. (1995 est.) 767,000.

Mari language, formerly CHEREMIS, member of the Finno-Ugric division of the Uralic language family, spoken primarily in the Mari El republic, Russia. The three major dialects of Mari are the Meadow dialect, spoken in Mari El and north of the Volga River; the Mountain (Hill) dialect, spoken mostly south of the Volga, between the Volga and Sura rivers (Chuvashiya republic); and the Eastern dialect, spoken around the Kama River. The Meadow and Mountain dialects are quite similar, but each has produced a distinct literary language. The linguistic and cultural history of Mari has been closely tied to that of its closest Uralic neighbours, Mordvin and the Permic languages—Udmurt, Komi, and Permyak. There were more than 500,000 Mari speakers in the late 20th century.

Maria (personal name): *see under* Mary, or Marie, except as below.

Maria I (b. Dec. 17, 1734, Lisbon, Port.—d. March 20, 1816, Rio de Janeiro, Brazil), the first queen regnant of Portugal (1777–1816).

Maria was the daughter of King Joseph. In 1760 she married her uncle who, as king consort after Maria's accession (February 1777), became Peter III. Maria attempted to correct the harshness of her father's minister, the marquês de Pombal, freeing his political prisoners and banishing him to Pombal; but an inquiry ended in his pardon. She abandoned some of his trading enterprises but developed small industries in Portugal and new crops in Brazil.

The deaths of Peter in 1786 and of Maria's elder son Joseph in 1788, combined with news of the excesses of the French Revolution, so affected Maria that she suffered a mental collapse in January 1792. She entrusted power to her second son, John (the future John VI), who assumed the title of prince regent in 1799, when her condition was deemed incurable. Maria proved incapable of resuming her duties, and when Napoleon's armies invaded Portugal in November 1807, she went with the rest of the royal family to Brazil, where she died.

Maria II, in full MARIA DA GLÓRIA (b. April 4, 1819, Rio de Janeiro, Brazil—d. Nov. 15, 1853, Lisbon, Port.), queen of Portugal (1834–53).

Maria was the daughter of Peter I of Brazil, IV of Portugal, who, on inheriting both countries from his father, entered a conditional abdication of Portugal in her favour (1826). His plan was that she should marry his younger brother Michael, who would accept and apply Peter's constitution, the Charter. But Michael seized power, declaring himself king; and only upon abdicating the Brazilian empire (1831) was Peter able to proceed to Europe, occupy the island of Terceira in the Azores, and launch an expedition to conquer the mainland in Maria's name. He seized Porto (Oporto) and took Lisbon in 1834, when Michael went into exile. Peter died (September 1834), and Maria was declared of age at 14. She was married and widowed almost at once; with her second husband, Ferdinand of Saxe-Coburg-Gotha, she had 11 children.

Maria regarded her father's Charter as the guarantee of her throne and depended on the Charter's champion, the duque de Saldanha. Her reign was marked by struggles between moderates and conservatives on the one hand, who supported the principle of constitutional monarchy established by the Charter, and democratic and radical elements on the other hand, who sought to reinstate an earlier, more democratic constitution. The conflict was not resolved until Saldanha, at the head of the reform movement known as the Regeneration, modified the Charter with the Additional Act (1852). This remained the Portuguese constitution until 1910.

Maria died in childbirth, leaving the throne to her eldest son, Peter V, to whose education she had devoted much care.

Maria DE JESÚS, SISTER (Spanish mystic): *see* Agreda, María de.

Maria Carolina (b. Aug. 13, 1752, Vienna [Austria]—d. Sept. 8, 1814, Vienna), queen of Naples and wife of King Ferdinand IV of Naples. She held the real power in Naples, and, under the influence of her favourite, Sir John Acton, 6th Baronet, who was reputed to be her lover, she adopted a pro-British, anti-French policy.

The daughter of the empress Maria Theresa of Austria, Maria Carolina married in 1768 Ferdinand IV, who allowed her to assume much of the power in the kingdom. By a clause in the marriage contract, she entered the council of state, the kingdom's ruling body, when she had given birth to a male heir (1777). She soon brought about the downfall of the liberal minister Bernardo Tanucci and changed the court's pro-Spanish policy to a pro-British one. Influenced mainly by Acton and possibly by the execution of her sister Marie Antoinette by the French, she took Naples into the first Austro-British coalition against the French Revolution and sent Neapolitan warships to join the British fleet near Toulon (1793).

Naples joined the second coalition against France, but Maria Carolina and Ferdinand had to flee before the French (December 1798), who seized Naples, making it the Parthenopean Republic. After the overthrow of the republic (June 1799), the king and queen returned to Naples, where a massacre of the republic's partisans, in violation of the peace agreement, took place, for which the royal couple must bear at least partial responsibility.

In 1805 Maria Carolina once more engaged Naples in a war with France, calling the British and Russian fleets to her aid, but the French again occupied the kingdom, forcing the royal family to flee to Sicily (January 1806). She is said to have encouraged plundering in Calabria by Cardinal Ruffo's army of brigands, whose former leader, Fra Diavolo, had received a pension and an estate from her. She finally quarreled with the British ambassador, Lord George Bentinck, who persuaded Ferdinand to exile her from the island (1811). She returned to Austria, where she died three years later.

María Cristina DE BORBÓN (b. April 27, 1806, Naples [Italy]—d. Aug. 23, 1878, Sainte-Adresse, France), queen consort of Ferdinand VII of Spain from 1829 to 1833 and queen regent from 1833 to 1840.

Maria was the daughter of Francis I, king of the Two Sicilies, and married Ferdinand in 1829. In 1830 Maria convinced her husband to change the law of succession to allow their daughter, Isabella, to become queen, an action that deprived the king's brother, Don Carlos (Carlos María Isidro; *q.v.*), of the Spanish throne and thus eventually precipitated the First Carlist War.

On the death of Ferdinand (Sept. 29, 1833), María Cristina became regent with absolute power, but within a few days the First Carlist War began. Maria's government proved unstable, since it did not entirely satisfy her liberal supporters and also failed to erase the suspicions of the absolutists. Moreover, Maria's secret morganatic marriage to Fernando Muñoz (1833) antagonized many of her supporters. On May 15, 1836, after a mutiny at La Granja, she was forced to accept the liberal constitution of 1812. The opposition of General Baldomero Espartero, whose victories over the Carlists had virtually ended the civil war, prompted María Cristina to resign the regency (1840). Her attempt to participate in the political life of the country during the reign of Isabella II failed, and María Cristina was compelled to go into exile in 1854.

María Cristina DE HABSBURGO-LORENA, in full MARÍA CRISTINA DESEADA ENRIQUETA FELICIDAD RANIERA (b. July 21, 1858, Gross Seelowitz, Austria—d. Feb. 6, 1929, Madrid, Spain), queen consort (1879–85) of Alfonso XII of Spain whose tact and wisdom as queen regent (1885–1902) for her son Alfonso XIII were instrumental in giving to Spain a degree of peace and political stability.

María Cristina began her rule by entrusting the government to the liberal leader Práxedes Mateo Sagasta and by granting freedom of the press and a generous amnesty to political prisoners. Under her regency the exercise of power was rotated between the conservative Antonio Cánovas del Castillo and the liberal Sagasta. She witnessed the end of the Spanish empire with the loss of Cuba, Puerto Rico, Guam, and the Philippines in the disastrous war with the United States (1898). On May 17, 1902, Alfonso XIII was declared of age, and María Cristina resigned the regency and devoted the rest of her life to social and charitable work.

Maria Island, island in the Tasman Sea, 4 mi ($6\frac{1}{2}$ km) off the east coast of Tasmania, Australia. Extending 12 mi north–south and up to 8 mi east–west, it comprises two sections, linked by a narrow sandy isthmus, and has an area of 23,906 ac (9,672 ha). It rises to 3,002 ft (915 m) near the rugged northeast

Maria Island in the distance as seen from Orford on the Tasmanian mainland

Frederick Ayer—Photo Researchers

coast. It was sighted in 1642 by Abel Tasman, the Dutch navigator, who named it after the wife of the governor general of the Dutch East Indies, Anthony van Diemen. A sealing and whaling centre early in the 19th century, the island was the site from 1825 to 1832 of the Darlington penal settlement. During the late 19th century wine and silk enterprises were established, and cement was manufactured in the 1920s from local limestone. In 1972 the island was made a national park.

Maria Legio, also called LEGIO MARIA, or LEGION OF MARY CHURCH, largest African, independent church with a Catholic background, which had a meteoric rise in the 1960s. The church should not be confused with a less successful predecessor in Kenya, the Dini ya Mariam (Religion of Mary) of the 1950s.

Maria Legio originated with two Catholics of the Luo group, Simeon Ondeto and Gaundencia Aoko, who claimed to have undergone prophetic experiences that directed them to reject traditional magic and divine healers and to form an all-African church to be named Maria Legio (after the Catholic Legion of Mary), which offered free healing by prayer and exorcism of evil spirits. The first year (1963) an estimated 90,000 fringe, or nominal, Catholics and non-Christians, mostly Luo, joined the church; by 1970 membership had dropped to about 50,000.

Catholic worship, symbols, and hierarchy have been imitated and pentecostal features added. The sect rejects Western and traditional medicines, alcohol, tobacco, and dancing but accepts polygamy and is strongly nationalistic. Internal tensions over the statues of the highly charismatic Gaundencia as Holy Mother and failure of the church to cooperate in Kenyan development plans have rendered the future of the church uncertain.

Maria Stella (b. April 16, 1773, Modigliana, Papal States—d. Dec. 28, 1843, Paris), Italian adventuress who contested the parentage of Louis Philippe, duc d'Orléans, upon his accession to the French throne in 1830.

Brought up as the daughter of Lorenzo Chiappini, constable of Modigliana, and his wife, Maria Stella was trained as a singer and dancer and appeared on the stage in Florence. When Lorenzo Chiappini died in 1821, he left a letter stating that Maria Stella's real father was not he but a nobleman who had exchanged her for Chiappini's son and had later died. Finding that in 1773 a couple travelling under the name of Comte and Comtesse de Joinville had been at Modigliana, Maria Stella built up the story that these two were the duc and duchesse de Chartres, Louis Philippe Joseph, later duc d'Orléans and named Louis Philippe Égalité, and his wife, Adélaïde de Bourbon-Penthièvre, and that the Duc had exchanged a daughter for Chiappini's son in order to keep the Penthièvre inheritance in his own house. The son whose parentage was thus contested was Louis Philippe, the duc d'Orléans and later king of the French. The ecclesiastical court of Faenza in 1824 accepted Chiappini's letter but rejected the identification of the nobleman with the Duc de Chartres.

The appearance of Maria Stella's apologia, *Maria Stella ou un`échange criminel d'une demoiselle du plus haut rang contre un garçon de la condition la plus vile* ("Maria Stella, or an Exchange of a Girl of Higher Rank for a Boy of Baser Station"), coincided with Louis-Philippe's accession. Its publication may have been arranged by partisans of the Duchesse de Berry as a counterblast to pamphlets (supposedly of Orleanist inspiration) casting doubt on the legitimacy of her son the Duc de Bordeaux, who was regarded by the Bourbon Legitimists as the rightful king Henry V.

María Teresa DE AUSTRIA: *see* Marie-Thérèse of Austria.

To make the best use of the Britannica, consult the INDEX *first*

Maria Theresa, German MARIA THERESIA (b. May 13, 1717, Vienna—d. Nov. 29, 1780, Vienna), archduchess of Austria and queen of Hungary and Bohemia (1740–80), wife and empress of the Holy Roman emperor Francis I (reigned 1745–65), and mother of the Holy Roman emperor Joseph II (reigned 1765–90). Upon her accession, the War of the Austrian Succession (1740–48) erupted, challenging her inheritance of the Habsburg lands. This contest with Prussia was followed by two more,

Maria Theresa, detail of an oil painting by Martin van Meytens; in Schönbrunn Palace, near Vienna

By courtesy of the Bild-Archiv, Osterreichische Nationalbibliothek, Vienna

the Seven Years' War (1756–63) and the War of the Bavarian Succession (1778–79), which further checked Austrian power.

Early life. Maria Theresa was the eldest daughter of the Holy Roman emperor Charles VI and Elizabeth of Brunswick-Wolfenbüttel. The death of an only son prompted Charles, the only living prince of his line, to promulgate the so-called Pragmatic Sanction, a royal act, eventually recognized by most powers, whereby female issue was entitled to succeed to the domains of the Habsburgs. (Since nearly every major European nation coveted some part of the Habsburg domains, their consent to the Pragmatic Sanction must be taken as nothing more than an act of convenience.) Maria Theresa thus became a pawn on Europe's political chessboard. In 1736 she married Francis Stephen of Lorraine. Because of French objections to the union of Lorraine with the Habsburg lands, Francis Stephen had to exchange his ancestral duchy for the right of succession to the Grand Duchy of Tuscany. The marriage was a love match, and 16 children were born to the couple, of whom 10 survived to adulthood.

War of the Austrian Succession. On Oct. 20, 1740, Charles VI died, and the war of succession he had striven so hard to forestall broke out before the end of the year. Charles left the Habsburg state at the lowest point of its prestige, its coffers empty, its capital beset by unrest. The naive courage with which Maria Theresa assumed her heritage (and made her husband co-regent) astounded Europe's chancelleries. Her refusal to negotiate with Frederick II (later the Great) of Prussia, who had invaded Silesia, her most prosperous province, appalled the senescent councillors of her late father. Her successful appearance before the refractory Hungarian Estates, ending with an appeal for a mass levy of troops, gave her a European reputation for diplomatic skill. When the elector Charles Albert of Bavaria—one of the princes who had joined Frederick in assaulting Habsburg territories—was elected emperor, Maria Theresa was mortified; that dignity, little more than titular by then, had in practice been hereditary in her family for 300 years. Upon the death of Charles Albert (1745), she secured for her husband, Francis, the imperial crown, which the law denied to women.

Domestic reforms. Realizing the need for a sizable standing army and in order to maintain one, Maria Theresa accepted the plans of Count Friedrich Wilhelm Haugwitz—the first in a succession of remarkable men of intellect she was to draw into her council. In the face of the opposition of many noblemen, she managed to reduce drastically (except in Hungary) the powers of the various dominions' estates, which had held the monarchy's purse strings since time immemorial. In the further process of abolishing tax exemptions held by the great landowners, who dominated those assemblies, she hit on the notion of a "God-pleasing equality." Yet she did not question the justice of the manorial lord's claim on the labour of his hereditary subjects. Only many years later did peasant riots in famine-stricken Bohemia, as well as the reported cruelty of Hungarian magnates, cause her to limit the use of forced labour. "The peasantry must be able to sustain itself as well as pay taxes . . . ," she wrote.

Practical, if not always fiscal, considerations, rather than doctrinaire humanitarianism, guided all of Maria Theresa's reforms. An enlarged central administration—from which the judiciary was separated in 1749—and a repeatedly reorganized treasury required knowledgeable civil servants and judges; and their training was, to her mind, the sole purpose of higher education. She approved drastic changes that her physician, the Dutchman Gerhard van Swieten, carried through at the universities (such as the introduction of textbooks, the linking of the medical school of the University of Vienna with the embryonic public health service, and the sovereign's right to veto the election of deans by the faculties) even as he took them out of the hands of the Jesuits, to whose Society she herself was devoted. (She was the last of the Catholic monarchs to close its establishments.) Deeply pious, strictly observant, and intolerant to the point of bigotry, she was moving, nonetheless, toward subordinating the church to the authority of the state.

Foreign relations. Neither the peace of 1745 (by which Austria ceded Silesia to Prussia) nor the peace of 1748 (which ended Maria

Theresa's war with the rest of her enemies) ended her efforts to modernize the army. The dazzling ideas of her new chancellor, Wenzel Anton von Kaunitz, fired her determination to recover Silesia, indeed, to destroy Prussia. In a famous "reversal of alliances" (1756) she threw over England, the old ally and "banker" of the Habsburgs, and allied herself with France, their ancient foe. Moreover, she had entered into a treaty with Russia, a newcomer to European rivalries. She paid but scant attention to the global ramifications of the ensuing Seven Years' War. When its end sealed the loss of Silesia and left the monarchy with a mountain of debts, she became a champion of peace. As late as 1779 she single-handedly frustrated another full-scale war with Prussia, risked by her self-opinionated firstborn, Joseph II, who on his father's demise had become co-regent in the Habsburg dominions (and been elected emperor).

Though Francis had not been a faithful husband, Maria Theresa never wavered in her love, and his sudden death in 1765 plunged her into prolonged grief. She emerged from it, her zeal for activity nowise impaired. A new public-debt policy, the settlement of the empty spaces of Hungary, the drafting of a penal code to supplant the tangle of local systems, and a kind of poor law—these were but some of the innovations in which she herself took a hand, with her common sense doing service for the book learning she lacked. In step with the enforced retreat of the church from secular affairs, she came to feel that it was incumbent on the state to control the intellectual life of its subjects. It was she who institutionalized government censorship; on the other hand, it was she, too, who launched plans for compulsory primary education.

Late years. Although Maria Theresa pedantically supervised her children's upbringing and education, she was to experience many disappointments in connection with them. Of her sons, only Leopold of Tuscany (later Emperor Leopold II), though difficult as a child, lived up to her hopes. Her special affection belonged to Maria Christina, who was allowed to marry for love and on whom Maria Theresa showered vast gifts of money. Three of her daughters, married off to unprepossessing Bourbons—in Parma, Naples, and France—again and again irritated their mother with their strong will or their follies; to her dying day she bombarded one of these, Queen Marie-Antoinette of France, with practical advice, moral exhortations, and dire warnings of the future.

But it was the running conflict with her son Joseph that clouded the years of her widowhood most. His flirting with the "new philosophy" of the Enlightenment frightened her, his admiration of Frederick the Great offended her, and his foreign enterprises filled her with trepidation. There were threats of abdication on both his part and hers. When Joseph, supported by Kaunitz, pressured her into agreeing to share in the (first) partition of Poland in 1772, she loudly bewailed the immorality of the action. And while she had shrugged off ridicule on such occasions as her setting up a public morals squad (the "chastity commission" of popular parlance) or, prude though she was, her enlisting the help of Louis XV's mistress, Mme de Pompadour, in order to obtain the French alliance, the accusation of "lachrymose hypocrisy" raised in foreign courts during the Polish affair distressed her. Grown enormously stout and in poor health, she spent more and more of her time in suburban Schönbrunn, whose palace owed its reconstruction to her initiative. She was still trying to hold off the appproach of the new age. Ironically, her own pragmatic reforms had smoothed the road to the enlightened despotism that was to mark the reign of her son and successor, Joseph II. She died in November 1780.

Assessment. Maria Theresa was a key figure in the power politics of 18th-century Europe. To the Habsburg monarchy, a dynastic agglomeration of disparate lands, she gave a measure of unity. A princess of engaging naturalness, she was one of the most capable rulers of her house and, according to one historian, "the most human of the Habsburgs."

(R.Pi.)

BIBLIOGRAPHY. A. von Arneth, *Geschichte Maria Theresias,* 10 vol. (1863–79), is a basic chronicle. *Empress Maria Theresa,* by Robert Pick (1966), covers her life up to 1757 and contains a valuable bibliography. Sentimental biographies abound; the most informative is Eugen Guglia, *Maria Theresia: Ihr Leben und ihre Regierung,* 2 vol. (1917). J.F. Bright's primarily diplomatic study, *Maria Theresa* (1897), is useful. By far the most judicial appraisal of Maria Theresa's domestic policies is to be found on pp. 1–118 of C.A. Macartney, *The Habsburg Empire 1790–1918* (1968). Prince J.J. Khevenhuller's diaries, 1748–73, published as *Aus der Zeit Maria Theresias,* 7 vol., ed. by Khevenhuller and Schlitter (1907–25), are indispensable. So are two memoirs of Maria Theresa reissued as *Maria Theresias politisches Testament* (1952). The various collections of Maria Theresa's surviving letters to her children, her friends, and some of her servants—notably *Marie Antoinette: Correspondance secrète entre Marie-Thérèse et le Cte. de Mercy-Argenteau, avec les lettres de Marie-Thérèse et de Marie-Antoinette,* ed. by Arneth and Geoffroy, 3 vol. (1874–75)—offer splendid views of her behaviour and her thinking.

María Trinidad Sánchez, coastal province, northern Dominican Republic, facing the Atlantic Ocean (northeast) and rising to a rugged, though not mountainous, interior (maximum elevation 3,091 ft [942 m]). The province, 505 sq mi (1,310 sq km) in area, is little developed except along the coastal plains, especially southeast of Nagua, the provincial capital. The province is one of the wettest in the republic, rainfall exceeding 85 in. (2,160 mm) annually, for the most part drained seaward by short torrential streams, of which the Río Nagua is the most significant. Mixed agriculture and livestock raising predominate, the chief crops being peanuts (groundnuts), cacao, bananas, and tobacco. These are processed in the coastal towns, such as Cabrera and Río San Juan in the north and Nagua in the southeast, all of which are connected via a coastal road. There are port facilities and an airport at Cabrera. Pop. (1993) 124,957.

mariachi, Mexican string orchestra composed of violins, guitars (large and small), harps, mandolins, and double basses; brass wind instruments are sometimes included. The size of the orchestra varies from 3 to 12 players, and the instrumentation changes from performance to performance. The *mariachi* accompanies folk music in the city streets and plays both traditional and recently composed popular music. The ensemble's early use at weddings explains the derivation of its name, which is perhaps a Mexican-Spanish variation from French *mariage,* "marriage." The word *mariachi* also refers to an individual folk singer.

Mariamne (*c.* 57–29 BC), Jewish princess, a popular heroine in both Jewish and Christian traditions, whose marriage (37 BC) to the Judean king Herod the Great united his family with the deposed Hasmonean royal family (Maccabees) and helped legitimize his position. At the instigation of his sister Salome and Mariamne's mother, Alexandra, however, Herod had her put to death for adultery. Later, he also executed her two sons, Alexander and Aristobulus.

Mariana, city, east central Minas Gerais state, Brazil, on the Rio do Carmo in the Rio Doce Basin, at 2,287 ft (697 m) above sea level. Formerly known as Vila de Albuquerque and Vila de Carmo, the settlement was made a seat of a municipality in 1711 and attained city status in 1745. The state's oldest city, Mariana was once renowned as a mining centre and since 1905 has been the seat of a bishopric. The old prison (*gadeia*), the Carmo and São Francisco de Assis churches, the Palace of Governors, and other colonial buildings remain. Agriculture and livestock raising are now the principal economic activities, yielding beef, milk, poultry, coffee, rice, corn (maize), *feijão* (beans), sugarcane, garlic, and sorghum. The nearby Minas da Passagem, one of the largest gold mines in Minas Gerais, is still economically significant. Mariana is accessible by railroad and highway from Rio de Janeiro and from Belo Horizonte, the state capital (50 mi [80 km] northwest). Pop. (2000 prelim.) 46,565.

Mariana, Juan de (b. 1536, Talavera de la Reina, Spain—d. Feb. 16, 1624, Toledo), historian, author of *Historiae de rebus Hispaniae* (1592), a history of Spain from its earliest times.

After studying in Alcalá, Mariana entered the Jesuit order and was ordained in 1561. For the next 14 years he taught theology in Rome, Sicily, and Paris, where his expositions of the writings of Thomas Aquinas attracted large audiences. Returning to Spain in 1574,

Mariana, detail of an engraving
Archivo Mas, Barcelona

he spent the rest of his life in Toledo, studying and writing.

A man of liberal mind, Mariana disturbed his superiors with his defense of the heretic Arioso Montano and with his *De rege et regis institutione* (1598; *The King and the Education of the King,* 1948), a treatise on government that argued that the overthrow of a tyrant was justifiable under certain conditions. When his *Tractus VII* (1607), a series of seven treatises on political and moral subjects, was published, it was banned by the Inquisition, and Mariana was imprisoned for a year and forced to do penance. Although he remained a Jesuit throughout his life, his criticism of the order, *Discurso de los grandes defectos que hay en la forma del Govierno de lo Jesuitas* (1626), severely censured the Jesuits for many injustices and inequities.

The first edition of *Historiae de rebus Hispaniae* was published in 1592; Mariana appended several supplements during his lifetime and recast the work into Spanish, the first Spanish edition (*Historia general de España*) appearing in 1601. Further editions, updated by various authors, were published as late as 1841; one of these was translated into English as *The General History of Spain* (1699). It is less a great history than a work of art, combining history, anecdote, and legend in a fluid and readable prose that makes it a work of sustained interest.

Mariana Islands, series of volcanic and uplifted coral formations in the western Pacific Ocean, 1,500 mi (2,400 km) east of the Philippines. They are divided politically into Guam (an organized unincorporated territory of the

United States) and an island chain, the Northern Marianas, which comprises a U.S. commonwealth. (It was part of the U.S.-administered United Nations Trust Territory of the Pacific Islands from 1947 to 1986.) The Northern Marianas extend 450 miles (725 km) north of Guam and have a total area of about 184 square miles (477 square km). The more important islands are Saipan, Tinian, Agrihan, and Rota (*qq.v.*). Pagan, Asuncion, and Farallon de Pajaros are active volcanoes. Guam occupies 209 square miles (541 square km). The climate is tropical.

After their European discovery by Ferdinand Magellan (1521), the Portuguese navigator sailing for Spain, the Marianas were visited frequently but were not colonized until 1668, when their name was changed by Jesuit missionaries from Ladrones Islands (Thieves Islands) to honour Mariana of Austria, then regent of Spain. The Jesuits then began to forcibly convert the native Chamorro to Catholicism. Guam was ceded to the United States following the Spanish-American War (1898), and the Northern Marianas were sold to Germany in 1899. Occupied by Japan in 1914, the Northern Marianas became a Japanese mandate from the League of Nations after 1919. Seized by the United States in World War II, they were prepared as forward bases for the invasion of Japan but were never used as such. The islands were part of a trusteeship granted to the United States by the United Nations in 1947; in 1978 they chose to become a self-governing commonwealth and achieved this formal status upon the dissolution of the trust territory in 1986.

The economy of the Marianas is largely based on subsistence agriculture, with some income from copra and services to U.S. military installations; cattle are also raised. The population is descended from the pre-Spanish Chamorro with considerable intermingling of Spanish, Mexican, Philippine, German, and Japanese blood. Spanish cultural traditions are strong. *See also* Guam. Pop. (1992 est.) Northern Marianas, 44,800; Guam, 139,000.

Mariana Trench, submarine trench in the floor of the western North Pacific Ocean, situated east of the Mariana Islands. It is the deepest such trench known. An arcing depression, the trench stretches for more than 1,580 miles (2,550 km) with a mean width of 43 miles (69 km). There is a smaller steep-walled valley on the floor of the main trench. In 1899 Nero Deep (31,693 feet [9,660 m]) was discovered southeast of Guam. This sounding was not exceeded until a 32,197-foot (9,813-metre) hole was found in the vicinity 30 years later. In 1957, during the International Geophysical Year, the Soviet research ship *Vityaz* sounded a new world record depth of 36,056 feet (10,990 m). This was later increased to 36,201 feet (11,034 m). On Jan. 23, 1960, the French-built U.S. Navy-operated bathyscaphe *Trieste,* with the inventor's son, Jacques Piccard, aboard, made a record dive to 35,800 feet (10,911 m) in the trench.

Marianao, city, Ciudad de la Habana *provincia,* west-central Cuba. Situated in a slightly hilly area along the northern coast, Marianao was founded in 1726. Since 1900, with the growth of Havana (10 miles [16 km] to the northeast by highway and railroad), Marianao has become the capital's principal residential suburb. Exclusive residential sections have developed near La Playa beach and in the country club area. Additional entertainment facilities include a casino, yacht club, and racetrack. The city also contains numerous and varied industries, notably beer, pharmaceuticals, cloth, and tobacco. Cuba's chief military encampment, Camp Columbia, is in Marianao. Pop. (1989 est.) 133,016.

Marianist, member of SOCIETY OF MARY (S.M.), a religious congregation of the Roman Catholic church founded by William Joseph Chaminade at Bordeaux, Fr., in 1817. The Marianists, including the Brothers of Mary, developed from the sodality (a devotional association of the laity) of the Blessed Mother organized in 1800 by Chaminade. The Institute of the Daughters of Mary, or Marianist Sisters, was also a product of this sodality. The male congregation, which is spread throughout western Europe, the Americas, Asia, Africa, and Australia, is engaged primarily in Christian education. To the usual religious vows of poverty, chastity, and obedience, the Marianists add a fourth vow of stability, faithfulness to the congregation, and special consecration to Mary. As an outward sign of this fourth vow, they wear a gold ring on their right hand.

Mariánské Lázně, German MARIENBAD, spa and town, Západočeský *kraj* (region), western Czech Republic. It is situated on the edge of the wooded hills southwest of Karlovy Vary.

Spa colonnade in Mariánské Lázně, Czech Republic

K. Krahulec—Bruce Coleman Inc.

Its more than 40 mineral springs were long the property of the Premonstratensian Abbey (12th century) at Teplá, a few miles east of the town. When Josef Nehr, the abbey's doctor, demonstrated the therapeutic properties (efficacious for rheumatism and digestive disorders) of the peat and springs in the early 19th century, the monks subsidized the spa, which adopted its German name (Marienbad) in 1808. It received its town charter in 1868.

Situated in a forested and enclosed basin at an elevation of 2,000 feet (600 m), Mariánské Lázně is one of Europe's most scenic spas. Well-known patrons have included the English king Edward VII, the composers Frédéric Chopin and Richard Wagner, and the writers Johann Wolfgang von Goethe, Franz Kafka, and Henrik Ibsen. During the period of communist rule in Czechoslovakia (1948–89), many of the town's once-luxurious hotels and cure houses became dilapidated. Pop. (1991 prelim.) 15,378.

Marianus Scotus, original name MOELBRIGTE (Gaelic: "Servant of Bridget") (b. 1028, Ireland—d. Dec. 22, 1082 or 1083, Mainz, Franconia [now in Germany]), chronicler who wrote a universal history of the world from creation to 1082 that disputed the chronology of the Pascal calendar formulated by Dionysus Exiguus, a 6th-century theologian. His *Chronicon,* written in Germany, maintains that the Pascal calendar incorrectly dated Christ's birth 22 years too early. Marianus' chronological system never replaced the Pascal calendar, however.

Becoming a Benedictine monk (1052) in northern Ireland, he assumed the name Marianus Scotus. He was banished from Ireland (1056) for an infringement of monastic rules and then journeyed to Cologne, where he entered an Irish monastery. Ordained priest in 1059 at Würzburg, he spent the rest of his life as an incluse at Fulda and then at Mainz.

The *Chronicon* is valuable not only as a world chronicle but also as a history of the Irish monastic movement in 10th- and 11th-century Germany. It was popular with other medieval chroniclers because it was based on many ancient and early medieval scholarly works. The chronicler should not be confused with another Irish monk, Marianus Scotus, abbot of St. Peter's, Regensburg (d. 1088).

Marías Islands, archipelago in the Pacific Ocean, off the coast of west-central Mexico. Lying approximately 100 miles (160 km) northwest of Cape Corrientes and about 230 miles (370 km) southeast of the tip of Baja California, the islands are administered by the state of Nayarit, Mexico. They consist of several rocky, rugged islands. Largest of the Marías is northernmost María Madre, 44 square miles (114 square km) in area and rising to an elevation of 2,011 feet (613 m). Nearby María Magdalena is second in area (32 square miles [83 square km]); María Cleofas, approximately 10 miles (16 km) to the southeast, totals only 9 square miles (23 square km). A fourth island, tiny San Juanito, is also included in the group. Lacking water, the islands are uninhabited except for a government penal colony and lighthouse on María Madre. The Marías are of some economic value for their guano and salt deposits, maguey (source of pulque), and lumber.

Marias River, river, formed by the confluence of Cut Bank Creek and Two Medicine River, in Glacier county, northwestern Montana, U.S. It flows generally southeast and is joined by several creeks. The river is impounded by the Tiber Dam to form Lake Elwell, an irrigation and recreation reservoir. Beyond the dam it flows for 50 miles (80 km) to enter the Missouri River at Loma. The Marias, used by pioneer and trading expeditions, was named in 1804 by the explorer Meriwether Lewis for his cousin Maria Wood. In 1806 Lewis proceeded up the river to a point near the site of Cut Bank, where Fort Piegan, an American Fur Company trading post, was later established (1831). The Marias receives its principal tributary, the Teton River, near its junction with the Missouri.

Mariátegui, José Carlos (b. June 14, 1895, Lima, Peru—d. April 16, 1930, Lima), political leader and essayist who was the first Peruvian intellectual to apply the Marxist model of historical materialism to Peruvian problems.

The Leguía dictatorship in Peru (1919–30) sought to rid itself of one of its most ardent critics by sending the hitherto self-educated Mariátegui to study in Italy in 1919. While there, he established strong ideological ties with some of the leading Socialist thinkers of the time, among them Henri Barbusse, Antonio Gramsci, and Maxim Gorky. He returned to Lima in 1923 and became a strong supporter of Víctor Raúl Haya de la Torres' Alianza Popular Revolucionaria Americana (APRA). After a dispute with Luis Alberto Sánchez, a leading Aprista, he left the Alliance to establish the Peruvian Communist Party (in 1928). Though paralyzed and confined to a wheelchair, Mariátegui also founded *Amauta* (1926–30), a Marxist cultural and literary journal that published avant-garde writing. In essays in *La escena contemporánea* (1925; "The Contemporary Scene"), Mariátegui attacked Fascism and defined the responsibilities of the intellectual in countries where social oppression reigns. César Vallejo, Peru's greatest poet, was deeply influenced by him.

Mariátegui's masterpiece is the collection of essays *Siete ensayos de interpretación de la realidad peruana* (1928; *Seven Interpretive Essays on Peruvian Reality*). While emphasizing the economic aspects of Marxism, Mariátegui nonetheless does not repudiate the value of religion and myth in his treatment of the Indians. His views on literature, signaling the importance of indigenous themes and language while adhering to avant-garde artistic tendencies, provided the means to reevaluate Peruvian culture. His *Obras completas* ("Complete Works") were published in 1959.

Mariazell, town, Steiermark *Bundesland* (federal state), east-central Austria, in the Salza River valley amid the north Styrian Alps north of Kapfenberg. Founded in 1157 by the monks of St. Lambrecht's Abbey, it is the most famous pilgrimage place in Austria. In the Gnaden Church (rebuilt 1644–83) is a 12th-century limewood statue of the Virgin Mary (24 inches [61 cm] high), regarded as miraculous by many thousands of pilgrims who visit the shrine annually. Mariazell is also a summer resort and winter-sports centre. Pop. (1981) 1,927.

Ma'rib, town and historic site, north-central Yemen. It is famous as the location of the ancient fortified city of Ma'rib and its associated dam, principal centre of the pre-Islāmic state of Saba' (950–115 BC). Sabaean civilization reached its peak with the transfer of power from the *mukarrib*s (priest-kings) to autocratic monarchs (7th century BC). The ancient city, in a fertile oasis irrigated by the impounded waters of the Ma'rib Dam, has been called "the Paris of the ancient world." It was on one of the principal caravan routes that linked the Mediterranean world and the Arabian Peninsula, and it prospered especially because of its trading monopoly of frankincense and myrrh from Yemen and the southern coastal region of Hadhramaut.

Ma'rib Dam (Arabic: Sadd Ma'rib) was built to regulate the waters of the Wadi (watercourse) Sadd, called Wadi Saba' in antiquity. The ancient dam, about 1,800 feet (550 m) long and pyramidal in cross section, was of fine stone-and-masonry construction, with sluice gates to control the flow of water. It irrigated more than 4,000 acres (1,600 hectares) and supported a densely settled agricultural region, dependent on careful water conservation. Successive generations of Sabaean and Ḥimyarite rulers improved the works, though there were breaks in it in the 5th and 6th centuries AD. Its final destruction, perhaps by earthquake or volcanic eruption, took place possibly in the 7th century. As the "flood of Arim" (Arabic *sayl al-ʿarim*), it is mentioned in the Qur'ān (Koran); sometimes translated "the flood of the dike" or the "bursting of the dike," it is a favourite topic in Islāmic myth and legend.

The contemporary small town of Ma'rib, principally constructed of stones from the ancient Sabaean ruins and standing upon a *tall* (a stratified archaeological mound), is a centre for Bedouin tribesmen, who pasture flocks of camels, sheep, and goats. Some of the country's finest horses are raised in the district. The town's citadel, which stored many inscriptions and statues of the pre-Islāmic Sabaean period, and the finely built ancient temple of the moon god were severely damaged in the Yemeni civil war of 1962–70.

The surrounding region borders the southern Arabian desert known as Rubʿ al-Khali ("Empty Quarter"), mostly in Saudi Arabia. Although there are several wadis such as Ḥarīb and al-Jawf, the region has the poorest agricultural productivity in the country. The land slopes eastward from 6,000 to 3,000 feet (2,000 to 1,000 m) where it merges with the Rubʿ al-Khali. Sheep, goats, cattle, and donkeys are raised; and dates are cultivated. Pop. (1986) town, 1,457.

Maribo, city, Storstrøms *amtskommune* (county commune), central Lolland Island, Denmark, on Maribo Lake. The city (chartered 1416) grew up around an early 15th-century Bridgettine convent, the chapel of which survives as the cathedral of the Lolland-Falster diocese. The Diocesan Museum displays prehistoric and medieval artifacts and a collection of Danish paintings. The region is famous for its cheese and has old-established sugar refineries. Pop. (1986 est.) city, 5,510; (1988 est.) metropolitan area, 11,527.

Maribor, German MARBURG, industrial town and the political and economic centre of northern Slovenia, on the Drava River near the Austrian border. A popular resort and winter-sports centre, it lies between the Pohorje and Slovenske mountains. Though it is the centre of a fertile region specializing in apple and grape growing, it is one of the largest industrial cities in Slovenia. Heavy industry is dominant: chemicals, engineering, electrical and aluminum industries, truck and bus manufacture.

A settlement existed in Roman times, but the present town grew from the 12th century, being first documented in 1147. From 1209 it developed as a Habsburg trade centre, and it has a long history as a focal point of German culture and as a Christian bastion against the Turks. With the building of the Vienna-Trieste railway in the 1840s, Maribor was revitalized. During World War II the town was subjected to an intense program of Germanization until its liberation in 1945 by Yugoslav Partisans.

Historic structures include a 12th-century cathedral with many later additions, a 15th-century fortress famous for its sculptures and frescoes, the St. Madeleine Church (1288; rebuilt 1788), and a monument recalling the great plague of 1680. A new university was opened in Maribor in 1975. Pop. (1981) 106,113.

Marica (Europe): *see* Maritsa River.

Marīcī, Japanese MARISHI-TEN, Tibetan 'OD-ZER-CAN-MA, in Mahāyāna Buddhist mythology, the goddess of the dawn. Marīcī (Sanskrit: "Ray of Light") is usually shown riding on seven pigs and with three heads, one of which is that of a sow. In Tibet she is invoked at sunrise and, though not as popular a goddess as Tārā, has many shrines dedicated to her. Each of the abbesses of the convent of Samding (Bsam-l ding) on Lake Yamdok are said to be successive incarnations of Marīcī. She is also known in Tibet in several terrifying and hideous forms, with three or six heads and wearing ornaments of skulls.

Marie (personal name): *see under* Mary, or Maria, except as below.

Marie I (adventurer): *see* David de Mayrena, Marie-Charles.

Marie DE FRANCE (fl. late 12th century), earliest known French woman poet, creator of verse narratives on romantic and magical themes that perhaps inspired the musical lais of the later trouvères, and author of Aesopic and other fables, called *Ysopets*. Her works, of considerable charm and talent, were probably written in England. What little is known about her is taken or inferred from her writings and from a possible allusion or two in contemporary authors.

From a line in the epilogue to her fables, Claude Fauchet (1581) drew the name by which she has since been known. The same epilogue states that her fables were translated from, or based on, an English source for a Count William, usually identified as William Longsword, Earl of Salisbury, or sometimes as William Marshal, Earl of Pembroke. Her lais were dedicated to a "noble" king, presumably Henry II of England, though it is sometimes thought that this was Henry's son, the Young King. Her version of *L'Espurgatoire Seint Patriz* ("St. Patrick's Purgatory") was based on the Latin text (*c.* 1185) of Henry of Saltrey. Every conjecture about her has been hotly debated.

Her lais varied in length from the 118 lines of *Chevrefoil* ("The Honeysuckle"), an episode in the Tristan story, to the 1,184 lines of *Eliduc,* a story of the devotion of a first wife whose husband brings a second wife from overseas.

Marie DE MÉDICIS, Italian MARIA DE' MEDICI (b. April 26, 1573, Florence [Italy]—d. July 3, 1642, Cologne [Germany]), queen consort of King Henry IV of France (reigned 1589–1610) and, from 1610 to 1614, regent for her son, King Louis XIII (reigned 1610–43).

Marie was the daughter of Francesco de' Medici, grand duke of Tuscany, and Joanna

Marie de Médicis, detail of a portrait by Peter Paul Rubens; in the Prado, Madrid

H. Roger-Viollet

of Austria. Shortly after Henry IV divorced his wife, Margaret, he married Marie (October 1600) in order to obtain a large dowry that would help him pay his debts. In 1601 Marie gave birth to the dauphin Louis (the future Louis XIII), and during the following eight years she bore the king five more children. Nevertheless, their relationship was strained. Marie resented Henry's endless infidelities, and the king despised her unscrupulous Florentine favourites, Concino Concini and his wife Leonora. Upon the assassination of Henry IV (May 14, 1610) the Parlement of Paris proclaimed Marie regent for young King Louis XIII.

Guided by Concino (now the Marquis d'Ancre), Marie reversed Henry's anti-Spanish policy. She squandered the state's revenues and made humiliating concessions to the rebellious nobles. Although Louis XIII came of age to rule in September 1614, Marie and Ancre ignored him and continued to govern in his name. On April 24, 1617, Louis's favourite, Charles d'Albert de Luynes, had Ancre assassinated. Marie was then exiled to Blois, but in February 1619 she escaped and raised a revolt. Her principal adviser, the future Cardinal de Richelieu, negotiated the peace by which she was allowed to set up her court at Angers. Richelieu again won favourable terms for her after the defeat of her second rebellion (August 1620). Readmitted to the king's council in 1622, Marie obtained a cardinal's hat for Richelieu, and in August 1624 she persuaded Louis to make him chief minister. Richelieu, however, did not intend to be dominated by Marie. He enraged her by rejecting the Franco-Spanish alliance and allying France with Protestant powers. By 1628 Marie was the cardinal's worst enemy. In the crisis known as the Day of the Dupes (Nov. 10, 1630), she demanded that Louis dismiss the minister. Louis stood by Richelieu and in February 1631 banished Marie to Compiègne. She fled to Brussels in the Spanish Netherlands in July 1631 and never returned to France. Eleven years later she died destitute.

Marie de Médicis built the Luxembourg Palace in Paris, and in 1622–24 the Flemish artist Peter Paul Rubens decorated its galleries with 21 paintings, portraying the events of her life, that rank among his finest work.

Marie (-Catherine) LESZCZYŃSKA, Polish MARIA KAROLINA LESZCZYŃSKA (b. June 23,

1703, Breslau, Silesia—d. June 24, 1768, Versailles, Fr.), queen consort of King Louis XV of France (ruled 1715–74). Although she had

Marie Leszczyńska, detail from a pastel by Jean de la Tour; in the Louvre, Paris
Giraudon—Art Resource/EB Inc.

no direct influence on French politics, her Polish dynastic connections involved France in a European conflict that resulted in the eventual annexation of Lorraine by France.

Marie's father, Stanisław Leszczyński, was elected King Stanisław I of Poland in 1704. After he was deposed in 1709, he settled with Marie at Wissembourg. In the hope of quickly obtaining an heir to the French throne, Louis XV's chief minister, the Duc de Bourbon, betrothed the 15-year-old king to Marie in 1725. The marriage took place at Fontainebleau on September 5. Marie bore Louis 10 children between 1727 and 1737, but only one of her two sons—the dauphin Louis—survived infancy. In 1733 France entered the War of the Polish Succession against Austria in support of Stanisław's claims to the Polish throne; Stanisław was made duke of Lorraine by the treaty that ended the conflict (1738). Meanwhile, Louis XV, having lost interest in his queen, was lavishing his attentions on a succession of mistresses. Marie's marital unhappiness was intensified by the death of the Dauphin in 1765. In accordance with the treaty of 1738, Lorraine became a part of France when her father died in the following year. A biography, A. Leroy's *Marie Leczinska*, appeared in 1940.

Consult the INDEX *first*

Marie, Pierre (b. Sept. 9, 1853, Paris—d. April 13, 1940, Paris), French neurologist whose discovery that growth disorders are caused by pituitary disease contributed to the modern science of endocrinology.

A student of the neurologist Jean Charcot at the Salpêtrière Hospital, Paris (1885), Marie published the first description of acromegaly (1886), a condition characterized by overgrowth of bone tissue such as that of the nose, jaws, fingers, and toes, and traced the disease to a tumour of the pituitary gland, at the base of the brain.

He first described pulmonary osteoarthropathy (1890; inflammation of the bones and joints of the four limbs, often secondary to chronic conditions of the lungs and heart); hereditary cerebellar ataxia, also known as Marie's ataxia (1893; a disease in young adults characterized by a failure of muscular coordination caused by an atrophy of the cerebellum); and (with Charcot) a type of progressive muscular atrophy known as the "Charcot–Marie type." He served as professor of neurology at the University of Paris from 1907 to 1925.

Marie-Antoinette, in full MARIE-ANTOINETTE-JOSÈPHE-JEANNE D'AUTRICHE-LORRAINE (Austria-Lorraine), original German MARIA ANTONIA JOSEPHA JOANNA VON ÖSTERREICH-LOTHRINGEN (b. Nov. 2, 1755, Vienna—d. Oct. 16, 1793, Paris), queen consort of King Louis XVI of France (1774–93). Frivolous, imprudent, and prodigal and an enemy of reform, she contributed to the popular unrest that led to the Revolution and to the overthrow of the monarchy in August 1792.

The 11th daughter of the Holy Roman emperor Francis I and Maria Theresa, Marie-Antoinette was married in 1770 to the dauphin Louis, grandson of France's King Louis XV. The timid, uninspiring Louis proved to be an inattentive husband; and by the time he ascended the throne in 1774, Marie-Antoinette had withdrawn into the companionship of a small circle of frivolous court favourites.

Her extravagant court expenditures contributed—though to a minor degree—to the huge debt incurred by the French state in the 1770s and 1780s, and her close associations with the more dissipated members of the court aristocracy prompted her enemies to circulate

Marie-Antoinette, detail of a portrait by Élisabeth Vigée-Lebrun; in the Château de Versailles
Cliche Musees Nationaux

slanderous reports of her alleged extramarital affairs. These vilifications culminated in the Affair of the Diamond Necklace (1785–86), in which the Queen was unjustly accused of having formed an immoral relationship with a cardinal. The scandal discredited the monarchy and encouraged the nobles to oppose vigorously (1787–88) all the financial reforms advocated by the King's ministers.

During these crises, as in those to come, Marie-Antoinette proved to be stronger and more decisive than her husband. After a crowd stormed the Bastille on July 14, 1789, the Queen failed to convince Louis to take refuge with his army at Metz. In August–September, however, she successfully prodded him to resist the attempts of the revolutionary National Assembly to abolish feudalism and restrict the royal prerogative. As a result, she became the main target of the popular agitators, who attributed to her the celebrated and callous remark on being told that the people had no bread: "Let them eat cake!" ("Qu'ils mangent de la brioche!"). In October 1789 popular pressure compelled the royal family to return from Versailles to Paris, where they became hostages of the Revolutionary movement. Six months later Marie-Antoinette opened secret communications with the Comte de Mirabeau, a prominent member of the National Assembly who hoped to restore the authority of the crown. Nevertheless, her mistrust of Mirabeau prevented the King from following his advice. After Mirabeau died in April 1791, she turned for assistance to a group of émigrés. They arranged for the King and Queen to escape from Paris on the night of June 20, but Revolutionary forces apprehended the royal couple at Varennes (June 25) and escorted them back to Paris.

Marie-Antoinette then attempted to shore up the rapidly deteriorating position of the crown by opening secret negotiations with Antoine Barnave, leader of the constitutional monarchist faction in the Assembly. Barnave persuaded the King to publicly accept the new constitution (September 1791); but the Queen undermined Barnave's position by privately urging her brother, the Holy Roman emperor Leopold II, to conduct a counterrevolutionary crusade against France. Leopold avoided acceding to her demands. After France declared war on Austria in April 1792, Marie-Antoinette's continuing intrigues with the Austrians further enraged the French. Popular hatred of the Queen provided impetus to the insurrection that overthrew the monarchy on Aug. 10, 1792.

Marie-Antoinette spent the remainder of her life in Parisian prisons. Louis XVI was executed on orders from the National Convention in January 1793, and in August the Queen was put in solitary confinement in the Conciergerie. She was brought before the Revolutionary tribunal on Oct. 14, 1793, and guillotined two days later.

BIBLIOGRAPHY. Charles Kunstler, *La Vie privée de Marie-Antoinette* (1938; *The Personal Life of Marie-Antoinette*, 1940); André Castelot, *Marie-Antoinette* (1957).

Marie Byrd Land, unclaimed region of Antarctica, bordering on the South Pacific Ocean and extending from the Ross Sea and Ice Shelf (west) to Ellsworth Land (east). The barren, ice-capped region averages 2,600–6,500 ft (800–2,000 m) above sea level in altitude, except along its mountainous coast, where in the Flood and Executive Committee ranges there are several peaks more than 11,000 ft. Discovered in 1929 by the U.S. naval commander and explorer Richard E. Byrd and named by him in honour of his wife, it was first mapped and surveyed by a co-worker, Paul A. Siple, in 1935. The U.S. research base, Byrd Station, was opened in 1959 and has from 20 to 30 people working there in the warmer months.

Marie-Galante, island in the middle of the windward group of the Lesser Antilles in the Caribbean Sea and a dependency of Guadeloupe, an overseas *département* of France. It lies 16 mi (30 km) southeast of the island of Guadeloupe. Marie-Galante is of coral and limestone structure and is round in shape, measuring some 10 mi across; it has an area of about 61 sq mi (158 sq km). The chief town is Grand-Bourg. Marie-Galante suffers occasional droughts. The island was discovered in 1493 by Christopher Columbus, who named it after his ship "Maria Galanda." It was first settled by the French and, after frequent changes of ownership between them and the British, remained French from 1816. Sugarcane is the main crop. Pop. (1982) 3,983.

Marie-Louise, in full MARIE-LOUISE-LÉOPOLDINE-FRANÇOISE-THÉRÈSE-JOSÉPHINE-LUCIE, German MARIA-LUISE-LEOPOLDINA-FRANZISKA-THERESIA-JOSEPHA-LUZIA VON HABSBURG-LOTHRINGEN, also called (1817–47) MARIA LUIGIA D'ASBURGO-LORENA, DUCHESSA DI PARMA, PIACENZA, E GUASTALLA (b. Dec. 12, 1791, Vienna—d. Dec. 17, 1847, Parma, Italy), Austrian archduchess who became empress of the French (*impératrice des Français*), as the second wife of the emperor Napoleon I; she was later duchess of Parma, Piacenza, and Guastalla.

Marie-Louise, a member of the House of Habsburg, was the eldest daughter of the Holy

Marie-Louise, detail of a portrait by Joseph Franque; in the Château de Versailles

Alinari—Art Resource

Roman emperor Francis II (Francis I of Austria) and Maria Theresa of Naples-Sicily and niece of Marie-Antoinette, queen of France. Klemens von Metternich, the Austrian statesman, seems to have suggested her to Napoleon, who was looking for a wife with royal blood and had already decided to dissolve his childless marriage with the empress Joséphine. The match was arranged in February 1810. Marie-Louise was married to Napoleon at Paris on April 1–2. On March 20, 1811, she bore him the long-desired heir, the king of Rome and the future Duke von Reichstadt (*see* Reichstadt, Napoléon-François-Charles-Joseph Bonaparte, Herzog von).

While Napoleon was campaigning in Russia, Marie-Louise served as regent for him in Paris. After his first abdication (signed at Fontainebleau, April 11, 1814), however, she returned to Vienna with her son. The Treaty of Fontainebleau awarded her the duchies of Parma, Piacenza, and Guastalla with full sovereignty. She ignored Napoleon's entreaties to join him in his exile in Elba and became completely estranged from him when he threatened to abduct her forcibly. During the Hundred Days (1815) she remained in Austria, showing no interest in the success of Napoleon in France. The Congress of Vienna ratified her accession to Parma, Piacenza, and Guastalla, despite Bourbon opposition; but her son's right of succession was overruled (1817), the duchies being secured to her for her lifetime only.

In September 1821, following Napoleon's death that May, Marie-Louise married Adam Adalbert, Count von Neipperg, having already borne him two children. Together they governed the duchies more liberally than did most other princes in Italy, though some authorities suggest that this resulted more from weakness of character than from policy. Josef von Werklein, however, who became secretary of state in Parma after Neipperg's death (1829), pursued a more reactionary policy, and in 1831 a rebellion in Parma forced the duchess to take refuge with the Austrian garrison in Piacenza. Restored to power by the Austrians, she ruled thenceforward in accordance with their prescriptions.

In 1832 Marie-Louise visited the dying Duke von Reichstadt in Vienna. In February 1834 she contracted a second morganatic marriage, with Charles René, Count de Bombelles (1784–1856). She died in Parma and was buried in the Capuchin church in Vienna.

Marie-Thérèse OF AUSTRIA, French MARIE-THÉRÈSE D'AUTRICHE, Spanish MARÍA TERESA DE AUSTRIA (b. Sept. 10, 1638, El Escorial, Spain—d. July 30, 1683, Versailles, Fr.), queen consort of King Louis XIV of France (reigned 1643–1715).

As the daughter of King Philip IV of Spain and Elizabeth of France, Marie-Thérèse was betrothed to Louis by the Peace of the Pyrenees (1659), which ended a 24-year war between France and Spain. Under the terms of the pact, she agreed to renounce her claim to succession to the Spanish throne in return for a large dowry. The couple was married in June 1660. On the death of Philip IV and the accession of young Charles II to the Spanish throne in 1665, Louis XIV claimed that since Marie-Thérèse's dowry had never been paid, her renunciation was void. Accordingly, he conquered part of the Spanish Netherlands in his wife's name (War of Devolution, 1667–68). Meanwhile, Marie-Thérèse had proved unable to hold Louis's affection. A year after their marriage he took the first of a succession of royal mistresses. The queen suffered his infidelities in silence, and on her death Louis is reported to have said, "This is the only trouble she has ever caused me." Of Marie-Thérèse's five children, only one, the dauphin Louis (d. 1711), lived to maturity.

Marieberg pottery, Swedish pottery produced at the factory of Marieberg on the island of Kungsholmen, not far from Stockholm, from about 1759 until 1788. When the Marieberg factory, founded by Johann Eberhard Ludwig Ehrenreich, encountered finan-

Rococo "terrace vase" of Marieberg faience, Henrik Sten period (1769–88); in a private collection

Christie's, London; photograph, A.C. Cooper

cial difficulties in 1766, Ehrenreich was succeeded by the Frenchman Pierre Berthevin. In 1769 Berthevin left and Henrik Sten became director. In 1782 Marieberg was sold to its rival Rörstrand, and in 1788 it closed.

The Marieberg factory was famous particularly for its faience (tin-glazed earthenware) and porcelain. Unlike Rörstrand, Marieberg faience from the very beginning used brilliant overglaze colours. One of its specialties was a marbled glaze in unusual colours such as black, blue, violet, red, yellow, and brown. Transfer printing, which was introduced by Anders Stenman, who had come from Rörstrand, was mainly in evidence during the period when Sten was manager. The factory produced tureens with applied fruit and flowers. Its most original faience production, almost verging on the eccentric, is the Rococo "terrace vase," which is supposed to have been the creation of Ehrenreich himself; it is a vase decorated with applied flowers, standing on a base consisting of a flight of steps set on rocks, at the foot of which an animal (commonly a rabbit) was sometimes lying. Marieberg produced a cream-coloured earthenware, or creamware, called *Flintporslin,* which closely resembled that of Wedgwood.

Porcelain was made at Marieberg for only about 20 years, from the time Pierre Berthevin became manager in 1766 until 1788. It is even more reminiscent of French porcelain than the faience produced by Marieberg during the same period, because Berthevin had come from the Mennecy factory, near Paris, which made a soft-paste porcelain of a particularly light and transparent quality, almost like *milchglas.* Soft-paste porcelain was made by Marieberg until 1777, when, with the help of Jacob Dortu, a hard-paste porcelain was produced.

Mariehamn, Finnish MAARIANHAMINA, port city and capital of Ahvenanmaan autonomous *lääni* (province), southwestern Finland. It is situated on the island of Åland in the Baltic Sea, west of Helsinki. Founded in 1861, it is the chief port and the only city of the province. Its Swedish-speaking inhabitants depend on fishing and shipping for their livelihood. A renowned local fleet, once numbering 30 ships involved mainly in the grain trade with Australia, greatly diminished after World War II. The two bays—Svibyviken and Slemmern—have remained active ports, serving steamers to Turku (Swedish Åbo) and Stockholm. The city has become a resort area that abounds with gardens, parks, and beaches. Pop. (1992 est.) mun., 10,278.

Marienbad (Czech Republic): *see* Mariánské Lázně.

Marienburg (Poland): *see* Malbork.

Mariental, town, south-central Namibia. It lies at an elevation of 3,576 feet (1,090 m) and is situated 145 miles (232 km) north of Keetmanshoop and 170 miles (274 km) southeast of Windhoek, the national capital. The town and the surrounding area are in a hot, arid region. The eastern sections of the region overlap the western limits of the Kalahari sandveld, where groundwater is difficult to obtain. Near Mariental the sandveld merges with the hardveld (rocky plain) of the Central Highland, an area commonly grazed by Karakul sheep. Named by local Rhenish (German Lutheran) missionaries, Mariental was founded in 1912 as a railway stop between Windhoek and Keetmanshoop. It was proclaimed a town in 1920 and a municipality in 1946. An important economic function of the town is the processing and transport of Karakul skins. The Hardap Dam on the Fish River, 14 miles (22 km) northwest of Mariental, is Namibia's first large earth-fill dam and supplies electricity and water to the area. Vegetables and citrus fruits are grown in the floodplain below the dam, and its reservoir has been developed as a recreational area for campers, water-skiers, and anglers. Pop. (1988 est.) 6,500.

Marietta, city, seat (1834) of Cobb county, north-central Georgia, U.S., 20 miles (32 km) northwest of Atlanta, in the Blue Ridge foothills. It was probably named for Judge Thomas W. Cobb's wife. Its growth was stimulated in the 1840s by the arrival of the Western and Atlantic Railroad. The Kennesaw Mountain National Battlefield Park marks the

The Kolb House on Kolb Farm, Kennesaw Mountain National Battlefield Park, near Marietta, Ga.

Milt and Joan Mann from CameraMann

site of a major American Civil War battle (June–July, 1864), and thousands of soldiers are buried in the Marietta National and Confederate cemeteries. The city's industrial development was boosted in 1942 with the opening of a B-29 bomber plant (reactivated in 1951 by Lockheed Aircraft Corporation for jet aircraft production). The city is the seat of Kennesaw College (1966) and Southern Technical Institute (1948), an affiliate of the Georgia Institute of Technology. Dobbins Air Force Base is adjacent to the Lockheed plant. Inc. 1852. Pop. (1990) 44,129.

Marietta, city, seat (1788) of Washington county, southeastern Ohio, U.S. It lies at the confluence of the Ohio and Muskingum rivers, opposite Williamstown, W.Va. Shortly after the construction (1785) there of Fort Harmar, the American Revolutionary war general Rufus Putnam and his pioneer group, the Ohio Company of Associates, made the first permanent white settlement in Ohio (April 7, 1788); it was named to honour Queen Marie Antoinette of France. On July 15, 1788, General Arthur St. Clair was installed there as the first governor of the Northwest Territory, of which Marietta became the first capital.

The city is now an important agricultural centre with some diversified industrial development; manufactures include chemicals (especially plastics), metal alloys, grindstones, safes, concrete, and office equipment. Marietta College was established in 1835, and Washington Technical College in 1971. The Campus Martius State Memorial Museum includes the restored home of Putnam, the Ohio Company Land Office (1788), and the Ohio River Museum. Inc. 1800. Pop. (1990) city, 15,026; Parkersburg-Marietta MSA, 149,169.

Mariette, Auguste (-Ferdinand-François) (b. Feb. 11, 1821, Boulogne, Fr.—d. Jan. 19, 1881, Cairo), French archaeologist who conducted major excavations throughout Egypt, revealing much about the earlier periods of Egyptian history.

Mariette
H. Roger-Viollet

Mariette joined the Egyptian department of the Louvre in 1849 and in the following year traveled to Egypt to obtain ancient manuscripts. Instead, he began excavating at Ṣaqqārah, an area that included part of the burial grounds of ancient Memphis. There he unearthed the Avenue of the Sphinxes and the Sarapeum, a temple containing the tombs of sacred bulls, making Ṣaqqārah a focus for archaeological study. He remained in Egypt four years, continuing excavations and dispatching most of what he found to the Louvre, where he became curator upon his return to France.

Accepting the position of conservator of monuments from the Egyptian government, Mariette in 1858 settled in Egypt, where he remained for the rest of his life. He eliminated unauthorized excavation, thereby securing a virtual monopoly on archaeological investigation, and he restricted the sale and export of antiquities in order to preserve new discoveries for the Egyptian nation. In 1859 Mariette succeeded in persuading the Ottoman viceroy of Egypt to establish a museum at Būlāq, near Cairo, to house what became the world's foremost repository of Egyptian antiquities, the Egyptian Museum.

Among his discoveries was one of the finest examples of Egyptian temple architecture, the temple of Seti I. He also studied the pyramid fields of Ṣaqqārah and the burial grounds of Maydūm, Abydos, and Thebes. He unearthed the great temples of Dandarah and Edfu and carried out excavations at Karnak, Dayr al-Baḥrī, Tanis, and, in the Sudan, Jabal Barkal. Under his direction the great Sphinx was bared to the rock level; the wall paintings found in a tomb at Ṣaqqārah provided a detailed panorama of life in the Old Kingdom (*c.* 2575–*c.* 2130 BC).

His published works include *Abydos* (1869), *Aperçu de l'histoire d'Égypte* (1874; "Survey of the History of Egypt"), and *Les Mastabas de l'Ancien Empire* (1889, ed. by Gaston Maspero; "The Mastabas of the Old Kingdom"). Mariette also suggested the plot for Giuseppe Verdi's opera *Aida.*

Marignac, Jean-Charles-Galinard de (b. April 24, 1817, Geneva—d. April 15, 1894, Geneva), Swiss chemist whose work with atomic weights suggested the possibility of isotopes and the packing fraction of nuclei and whose study of the rare-earth elements led to his discovery of ytterbium in 1878 and codiscovery of gadolinium in 1880.

After studying at the Paris Polytechnic School and School of Mines, he worked for a year with Justus von Liebig at Giessen, in Germany. He became professor of chemistry (1841) and of mineralogy (1845) at Geneva, posts he held until his retirement (1878) from the university. In establishing the formula of silica as SiO_2, he made a substantial contribution to mineralogy. His preparation of silicotungstic acid was one of the first examples of a complex inorganic acid.

Marignano, Battle of (Sept. 13–14, 1515), Franco-Venetian victory over Swiss mercenaries in the first Italian campaign of Francis I of France. Fought near the village of Marignano (modern Melegnano), 10 miles (16 km) southeast of Milan, the battle resulted in the French recovery of Milan and in the conclusion of the peace treaty of Geneva (Nov. 7, 1515) between France and the Swiss Confederation.

Determined to conquer the duchy of Milan, Francis I allied himself with Venice and crossed the Alps via the previously unexploited route Col de l'Argentière (Col de Larche; Maddalena). The French forces seized Novara and proceeded toward Milan, which was defended by its Swiss allies. On September 13 the Swiss advanced against the French position near Marignano and attacked across the marshy ground separating the armies but withdrew somewhat by midnight. The next day, after eight hours of inconclusive fighting, the French were reinforced by Venetian cavalry and forced the Swiss to retreat.

Marignolli, Giovanni dei (b. before 1290, Florence, fl. 1338–57), Franciscan friar and one of four legates sent to the court of the Mongol emperor of China, Togon-Temür, at Khanbaliq (Peking). Marignolli's notes on the journey, though fragmentary, contain vivid descriptions that established him among the notable travelers to the Far East in the 14th century.

The mission left the papal city of Avignon in December 1338 and spent the winter of 1339–40 at the court of Muḥammed Uzbek, khan of the Golden Horde (the autonomous western region of the Mongol empire). From the khan's capital at Sarai on the Volga, near modern Volgograd, Russia, the legates crossed the steppes to Almarikh (now Kuldja, Sinkiang Uighur Autonomous Region, China), where they built a church, and reached Khanbaliq in May or June 1342. There Marignolli remained for three or four years, after which he traveled through eastern China until his departure in December 1347. He reached Coilum (modern Quilon, now in Kerala, India) during Easter Week, 1348, and founded a Roman Catholic church there. He visited the shrine of St. Thomas, near Madras, as well as the kingdom of Saba', which he identified with the biblical Sheba but which seems to have been Java. Detained in Ceylon, he was stripped of the gifts and Eastern rarities that he was carrying home but nevertheless was able to gather information on the country and its inhabitants. He returned to Avignon (1353) by way of the Persian Gulf city of Hormuz, now in Iran, also visiting Mesopotamia, Syria, and Jerusalem. In 1354–55, while serving as chaplain to the emperor Charles IV, he was engaged in revising the Annals of Bohemia, interpolating them with recollections of his Asian travel. An English translation of his recollections appears in Sir Henry Yule, *Cathay and the Way Thither* (1866).

Marigny, Enguerrand de (b. 1260, Lyons-la-Forêt, in Normandy, Fr.—d. April 11/30, 1315, Paris), powerful chamberlain to the French king Philip IV the Fair, who depended heavily on Marigny's advice on foreign policy and on relations between king and church. Marigny was described as the man who knew all the king's secrets and who encouraged Philip to make drastic departures from his father's foreign policy.

At first a courtier, Marigny rose rapidly after 1302. Knighted, and later created Count de Longueville, he became grand chamberlain to the king, was sent to preside over the Norman exchequer in 1306, and subsequently became superintendent of finances and buildings and captain of the Louvre. His power peaked in the years 1313–14, when he was in charge of the royal treasury and of the newer auditing department, the *chambre des comptes,* imposing on them a unified rule.

Marigny was generally unpopular, both with the nobility and with the bourgeoisie, and he was associated with the policy of heavy taxation and debasement of the coinage. He also incurred the special enmity of the king's brother, Charles of Valois. Charged toward the end of Philip's reign with corruption in his financial administration, Marigny was first cleared and then imprisoned. The new king, Louis X, was inclined merely to banish Marigny; but Charles of Valois then accused the minister of sorcery, and immediate execution was ordered.

marigold, any plant of the genus *Tagetes* of the family Asteraceae, consisting of about 30

French marigold (*Tagetes patula*)
Robert Bornemann—Photo Researchers

species of annual herbs native to southwestern North America, tropical America, and South America. The name marigold also refers to the pot marigold (genus *Calendula*) and unrelated plants of several families.

African marigold (*T. erecta*), French marigold (*T. patula*), and several other species are grown as garden ornamentals, although most species have strong-scented leaves. Members of the genus *Tagetes* have attractive yellow, orange, or dark red flowers that are solitary or clustered; leaves opposite each other on the stem that usually are finely cut; and bracts (leaflike structures) that form a cup-shaped base below each flower head.

Mariinsky Ballet, also spelled MARYINSKY, Russian MARIINSKY BALET, formerly (1935–91) KIROV BALLET, prominent Russian ballet company, part of the Mariinsky Theatre of Opera and Ballet in St. Petersburg. Its traditions, deriving from its predecessor, the Imperial Russian Ballet, are based on the work of such leading 19th-century choreographers as Jules Perrot, Arthur Saint-Léon, and Marius Petipa and such dancers as Marie Taglioni, Olga Preobrajenska, Mathilde Kschessinskaya, Anna Pavlova, Vaslav Nijinsky, Tamara Karsavina, Michel Fokine, George Balanchine, and Maria Danilova.

Marijampolė, formerly (1955–90) KAPSUKAS, administrative centre of a *rayon* (sector), Lithuania. Marijampolė lies along both banks of the Šešupė River. The settlement developed as a monastic centre in the 18th century, when it was known as Starapolė, and achieved urban status in 1758. After World War II it developed as an industrial city, specializing in equipment for the food industry, automotive parts, furniture, building materials, textiles, and foodstuffs. There is a teacher-training school, a museum, and a theatre. Pop. (1999 est.) 52,020.

marijuana, also spelled MARIHUANA, the Indian hemp plant, *Cannabis sativa* (cannabis), or the crude drug composed of its leaves and flowers. It is usually dried and crushed and put into pipes or formed into cigarettes (joints) for smoking. The drug—known by a variety of other names, including pot, tea, grass, and weed—can also be added to foods and beverages. The active ingredient, tetrahydrocannabinol (THC), is present in all parts of both the male and female plants but is most concentrated in the resin (cannabin) in the flowering tops of the female. Hashish, a more powerful form of the drug, is made by collecting and drying this resin and is about eight times as strong as the marijuana typically smoked in the United States.

Mentioned in a Chinese herbal dating from 2700 BC, marijuana long has been considered valuable as an analgesic, an anesthetic, an antidepressant, an antibiotic, and a sedative. Although it was usually used externally (*e.g.*, as a balm or smoked), in the 19th century its tips were sometimes administered internally to treat gonorrhea and angina pectoris. Marijuana's effects vary, depending upon the strength and amount consumed, the setting in which it is taken, and the experience of the user. Psychological effects tend to predominate, with the user commonly experiencing a mild euphoria. Alterations in vision and judgment result in distortions of time and space. Acute intoxication may occasionally induce visual hallucinations, anxiety, depression, extreme variability of mood, paranoid reactions, and psychoses lasting from four to six hours. Marijuana's physical effects include reddening of the eyes, dryness of the mouth and throat, moderate increase in the rapidity of the heartbeat, tightness of the chest (if the drug is smoked), drowsiness, unsteadiness, and muscular incoordination. Chronic use does not establish physical dependence, nor does the regular user suffer extreme physical discomfort after withdrawal. However, the use of marijuana may be psychologically habituating.

The worldwide use of marijuana and hashish (*q.v.*) as intoxicants has raised various medical and social questions, especially since the mid-1960s, when THC was first isolated and produced synthetically. Research was directed toward identifying the short- and long-term physical effects of marijuana. In the late 20th century, medical research revealed various therapeutic effects of marijuana and THC. They were found to be useful in lowering internal eye pressure in persons suffering from glaucoma and in alleviating nausea and vomiting caused by chemotherapeutic drugs used to treat cancer patients and those with AIDS. Marijuana also reduces the muscle pain associated with multiple sclerosis and prevents epileptic seizures in some patients. In the late 1980s researchers discovered a receptor for THC and THC-related chemicals in the brains of certain mammals, including humans. This finding indicated that the brain naturally produces a THC-like substance that may perform some of the same functions that THC does. Such a substance subsequently was found and named anandamide, from the Sanskrit *anada* ("bliss").

International trade in marijuana and hashish was first placed under controls during the International Opium Convention of 1925. By the late 1960s most countries had enforced restrictions on trafficking and using marijuana and had imposed generally severe penalties for its illegal possession, sale, or supply. Beginning in the 1970s, some countries and jurisdictions reduced the penalty for the possession of small quantities. The Netherlands has long tolerated the sale of small amounts of marijuana, and in 1999 its legislature debated the decriminalization of the drug. In 1998 Swiss voters overwhelmingly rejected a broad referendum that would have decriminalized many illegal drugs, including marijuana, heroin, and cocaine, but the government took steps to legalize marijuana two years later.

In the United States, several states passed legislation in the late 1970s and early '80s to fund research on or to legalize the medicinal use of marijuana, though some of these statutes were later repealed or lapsed. Renewed decriminalization efforts in the 1990s led to the legalization of medicinal marijuana in seven states. In 2001, however, the U.S. Supreme Court ruled against the use of marijuana for medicinal purposes. Canada passed legislation in 2001 easing restrictions on medicinal marijuana and licensing growers to produce the drug.

Marília, city, west-central São Paulo *estado* ("state"), Brazil, lying between the Aguapeí and Peixe rivers in the highlands at 2,139 feet (652 m) above sea level. Founded in 1611, it was made the seat of a municipality and given city status in 1928. Agriculture (rice, coffee, cotton), livestock raising, and lumbering are regional activities. Marília's industries include the extraction of nonferrous minerals, the processing of foodstuffs, and the production of liquor, chemicals, and pharmaceuticals. These goods are shipped to São Paulo, the state capital, about 320 miles (515 km) southeast, and to other cities in the state, by rail, road, and air. Pop. (2000 prelim.) 189,533.

Marillac, Saint Louise de (b. Aug. 12, 1591, Paris/Ferrières, France—d. March 15, 1660, Paris; canonized March 11, 1934; feast day March 15), cofounder with St. Vincent de Paul of the Daughters of Charity of St. Vincent de Paul, a congregation of laywomen dedicated to teaching and hospital work.

Louise was a member of the powerful de Marillac family and was well educated. Poor health prevented her from joining the strict order of Poor Clares, and in 1613 she married Antoine Le Gras (secretary to Queen Marie de Médicis of France), by whom she had a son, Michel. Widowed in 1625, she had already chosen Vincent de Paul as her spiritual guide, and he encouraged her to undertake charitable works. She trained girls in the spiritual life and taught them to assist in visiting, feeding, and nursing the needy.

In 1633 Vincent de Paul founded the Daughters of Charity with Louise as their superior. Because they were neither enclosed nor called nuns, their concept pioneered in bringing women into religious service outside the cloister. By the late 20th century the Daughters of Charity became the Roman Catholic church's largest congregation of women.

marimba, any of several varieties of xylophone. Marimba is one of many African names for the xylophone, and, because

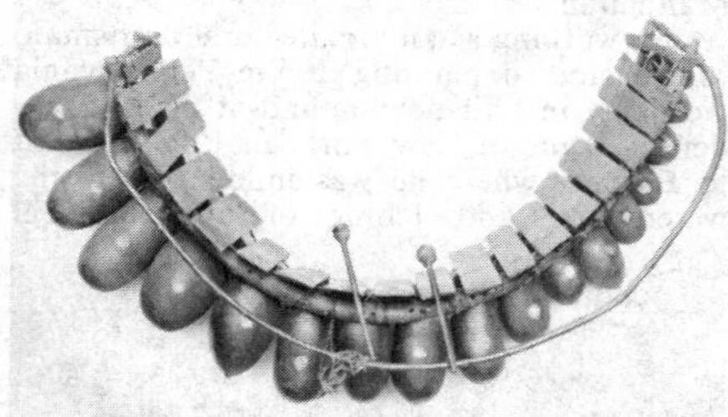

African marimba with gourd resonators, made by the Chokwe people, Angola; collected in 1931
By courtesy of The Field Museum, Chicago (Neg. A90911)

African instruments bearing this name frequently have a tuned calabash resonator for each wooden bar, some ethnomusicologists use the name marimba to distinguish gourd-resonated from other xylophones.

The xylophone was taken to Latin America by African slaves (or possibly originated through pre-Hispanic contact), became known there as "marimba," and has remained a popular folk instrument in Central America. The wooden bars are affixed to a frame supported by legs or hung at the player's waist. Large, deep-toned instruments up to 6½ octaves in range are sometimes played by four musicians. Marimba keys have tubular or gourd resonators, and, as in Africa, a buzzing membrane is frequently set in the resonator wall, adding a sharp edge to the instrument's sound.

The orchestral marimba is a tube-resonated instrument pitched an octave below the orchestral xylophone; its range varies, but 3½ octaves upward from the C below middle C is common. Extremely large marimbas are known as xylorimbas. Compositions for marimba include a concertino by the American composer Paul Creston (1940) and a concerto by the French composer Darius Milhaud (1947).

Marín, Francisco de Paula, byname MANINI (b. 1774, Jerez, Spain—d. Oct. 30, 1837, Honolulu, Hawaiian Islands [U.S.]), horticultural experimenter who introduced numerous plant species to the Hawaiian Islands.

Marín acquired his horticultural knowledge as a youth working in the Andalusian vineyards of Spain. He was taken to California and then to the Hawaiian Islands, then known as the Sandwich Islands, sometime between 1791 and 1794, after having been shanghaied, according to his own account, from the port of San Francisco.

The Spaniard was befriended by King Kamehameha I, who gave Marín land for his agricultural experiments. Marín also served as Kamehameha's interpreter, and, as the king aged, the Spaniard assumed many government duties. He began to experiment with island herbs and developed a wealth of pharmacological lore. From Spanish colonies all over the world, Marín requested and received foreign seeds and plants and devised the best means, time, and soil type in which to plant them. Peaches, oranges, olives, and others arrived; in exchange, Marín sent coconuts. Much of the diversity of Hawaii's island flora today is due to Marín's careful studies. He became known for his flourishing gardens and vineyards and also for his reluctance to bestow his bountiful crops on friends and acquaintances. The Hawaiian corruption of his name, "Manini," has become a slang word in the modern island vocabulary, meaning miserly.

Marin, John (b. Dec. 23, 1870, Rutherford, N.J., U.S.—d. Oct. 1, 1953, Cape Split, Maine), American painter and printmaker, especially known for his expressionistic watercolour seascapes of Maine and his views of Manhattan.

After working as an architectural draftsman, Marin studied painting at the Pennsylvania Academy in Philadelphia and at the Art Students League of New York. In 1905 he went to Europe, where he was influenced by the watercolours and etchings of James McNeill

"Maine Islands," watercolour by John Marin, 1922; in the Phillips Collection, Washington, D.C.
By courtesy of the Phillips Collection, Washington, D.C.

Whistler. But he remained unaware of the new movements of European art until 1910, when he returned to New York. There, at Alfred Stieglitz' "291" Gallery and at the Armory Show in 1913, he became familiar with Cubism and the various schools of German Expressionism. Influenced by those movements, his own style matured into a very personal form of expressionism, exemplified by such works as "The Singer Building" (1921), "Lower Manhattan" (1920), and "Maine Islands" (1922).

Watercolour is usually employed to produce only delicate, transparent effects, but Marin's brilliant command of the medium enabled him to render the monumental power of the city and the relentless surge of the sea on the Maine coast. Although semiabstract, his works were always based on objective reality. His concern with force and motion, however, led him to produce such works as "Lower Manhattan" (1922; Museum of Modern Art, New York City) and "Off York Island, Maine" (1922; Philadelphia Museum of Art), in which objective reality is hardly recognizable.

Marin's oil paintings, such as "Tunk Mountains, Maine" (1945; Phillips Collection), often employ the watercolour technique of dragging a nearly dry brush across the canvas to achieve an effect of lightness and transparency.

Marín, Luis Muñoz (Puerto Rican statesman): *see* Muñoz Marín, Luis.

Marina, original name MALINTZIN, also called MALINCHE or DOÑA MARINA (b. *c.* 1501, Painalla, Mex.—d. 1550, Spain), Mexican Indian princess, one of a group of female slaves given as a peace offering to the Spanish conquistadors by the Tabascan Indians (1519); she became mistress, guide, and interpreter to Hernán Cortés during his conquest of Mexico. The success of his ventures was often directly attributable to her services.

Renouncing her Indian name, Malintzin, on her conversion to Christianity, Doña Marina served her adopted countrymen with dedication. Her intelligence and tact and her knowledge of the Maya language of the coast and the Nahuatl language of the interior extricated the Spaniards from many perilous situations. She bore Cortés a son, Martín, and later married one of his soldiers, Juan de Jaramillo.

Marina (island, Vanuatu): *see* Espiritu Santo.

Marina, SAINT: *see* Margaret of Antioch, Saint.

Marinatos, Spyridon, in full SPYRIDON NIKOLAOU MARINATOS (b. Nov. 4, 1901, Lixoúrion, Greece—d. Oct. 1, 1974, Thera), Greek archaeologist whose most notable discovery was the site of an ancient port city on the island of Thera, in the southern Aegean Sea. The city, the name of which was not discovered, apparently had about 20,000 inhabitants when it was destroyed by the great volcanic eruption of 1500 BC. Among the finds made at the site were the finest frescoes discovered in the Mediterranean region to that time, surpassing even those found at Knossos in Crete.

Marinatos, educated at the universities of Athens, Berlin, and Halle, became professor at the University of Athens and inspector general of the archaeological services of Greece. He was the discoverer of the site of the Battle of Thermopylae (480 BC) and the burial ground associated with the Battle of Marathon (490 BC). He wrote *Crete and Mycenae* (1959) and, beginning in 1968, a series of annual reports on the excavations at Thera.

Marinduque, island, Philippines, in the Sibuyan Sea, south of Luzon and east of Mindoro. A substantial part of the hilly, oval-shaped island is devoted to agriculture (coconuts, rice). There are also cattle ranches and rich fishing grounds, and iron ore and copper mining are important. Boac, the provincial capital, is on the northwestern coast of the island. Other coastal settlements include Santa Cruz, Buenavista, Gasan, and Torrijos. The inhabitants are mostly Tagalogs. The annual Moriones Festival features street pageants performed through the Holy Week of Easter. Pop. (2000) 217,392.

Marinduque Island, Philippines
John Lewis Stage—Photo Researchers

marine, member of a military force especially recruited, trained, and organized for service at sea and in land operations incident to naval campaigns. The use of marines goes far back in history. The 5th-century-BC Greek historians Herodotus and Thucydides referred to *epibatai,* or heavy-armed sea soldiers in the Greek fleets, while Polybius, in the 3rd–2nd century BC, described *milites classiarii* ("soldiers of the fleet"), a category of Roman soldier organized and specially armed for duty aboard warships. During the Middle Ages, ordinary soldiers in Europe were frequently embarked aboard ship to provide a fighting backbone, but not until the naval wars of the 17th century was the distinct and organized role of marines almost simultaneously rediscovered by the British and Dutch, who raised the first two modern corps of marines—the Royal Marine (1664) and the Koninklijke Nederlandse Corps Mariniers (1665), respectively. The United States Marine Corps (*q.v.*), organized in 1775, has become the most famous organization of the kind, but other countries also maintain marine corps.

marine (musical instrument): *see* trumpet marine.

Marine Biological Laboratory, an independent research and educational organization founded at Woods Hole, Mass., U.S., in 1888. It was established by the Women's Educational Association of Boston, the Boston Society of Natural History, and other organizations and was modeled after the Naples Zoological Station (1872) in Italy. The laboratory's summer research program played a vital role in furthering American research and teaching in the biological sciences in the early 20th century. The laboratory is still a leading centre for research in marine biology and supports both visiting scientists and a permanent staff. The Woods Hole Oceanographic Institution, an offshoot of the laboratory, was established in 1930.

marine biology, the science that deals with animals and plants that live in the sea. It also deals with air-borne and terrestrial organisms that depend directly upon bodies of salt water for food and other necessities of life. In the broadest sense it attempts to describe all vital phenomena pertaining to the myriads of living things that dwell in the vast oceans of the world. Some of its specialized branches concern natural history, taxonomy, embryology, morphology, physiology, ecology, and geographical distribution. Marine biology is closely related to the science of oceanography because of the relationship of the physical features of the oceans to the living organisms that dwell in them. It aids in the understanding of marine geology through the study of those organisms that contribute their skeletal remains to the floors of the oceans or that elaborate the vast coral reefs of the tropic seas.

A principal aim of marine biology is to discover how ocean phenomena control the distribution of organisms. Marine biologists study the way in which particular organisms are adapted to the various chemical and physical properties of the seawater, to the movements and currents of the ocean, to the availability of light at various depths, and to the solid surfaces that make up the seafloor. Special attention is given to determining the dynamics of marine ecosystems, particularly to the understanding of food chains and predator-prey relationships. Marine biological information on the distribution of fish and crustacean populations is of great importance to fisheries. Marine biology is also concerned with the effects of certain forms of pollution on the fish and plant life of the oceans, particularly the effects of pesticide and fertilizer runoff from land sources, accidental spills from oil tankers, and silting from coastline construction activities.

During the second half of the 19th century, when the emphasis was on the collection, description, and cataloging of marine organisms, methods evolved for the capture and preservation of specimens for study. Marine biologists adapted traditional dredges and trawls to collect specimens from the ocean floor; and hoop nets were used to secure free-swimming animals. New instruments for collecting water samples and obtaining temperature information at any desired depth were developed.

Late in the 19th century, the focus began to shift from collecting and cataloging to the systematic analysis of marine ecosystems and the ecological roles and behaviour of marine life. By the early 20th century, oceanographers had begun to intensively study fishing grounds and other localities of economic importance. This research combined studies of marine flora and fauna, ocean currents, water temperature, salinity, and oxygen levels, and other factors in an effort to understand the relationship between marine animals and their environment.

Since World War II, direct observation of marine organisms in their natural habitats has been made possible by underwater cameras, television, improved diving equipment, and submersible craft, or submarines, that can descend to great depths. Underwater television provides the observer with a continuous picture of events that occur within the field of the submerged camera. The development of self-contained diving equipment made it possible for the investigator to inspect marine organisms in their natural habitat.

Morphological and taxonomic studies of marine organisms are generally performed on preserved materials in connection with the work in museums and universities. Physiological and embryological investigations requiring the use of living material are generally pursued at biological stations. These are situated on the seacoast, thus facilitating the rapid transfer of specimens to the laboratory where they may be maintained in seawater provided by special circulating systems.

marine cable: *see* undersea cable.

Marine Corps, United States: *see* United States Marine Corps, The.

marine geology, also called GEOLOGIC OCEANOGRAPHY, scientific discipline that is concerned with all geological aspects of the continental shelves and slopes and the ocean basins. In practice, the principal focus of marine geology has been on marine sedimentation and on the interpretation of the many bottom samples that have been obtained through the years. The advent of the concept of seafloor spreading in the 1960s, however, broadened the scope of marine geology considerably. Many investigations of midoceanic ridges, remanent magnetism of rocks on the seafloor, geochemical analyses of deep brine pools, and of seafloor spreading and continental drift may be considered within the general realm of marine geology.

marine geophysics, scientific discipline that is concerned with the application of geophysical methods to problems of marine geology. Each of the principal branches of geophysical knowledge is involved: heat-flow data are obtained from ocean floors and from the midoceanic ridges; seismic reflection and refraction techniques are used to determine sediment thickness and the thickness of the oceanic crust; geomagnetics has been applied to samples of the oceanic crustal rocks in paleomagnetic investigations; and gravity measurements are made over the oceans (as on land) to complete knowledge of the global gravity distribution. Marine geophysics is intimately associated with the concepts and problems of seafloor spreading, continental drift, and plate tectonics.

Marine Highway (Pacific Ocean): *see* Inside Passage.

marine insurance, contract whereby, for a consideration stipulated to be paid by one interested in a ship or cargo that is subject to the risks of marine navigation, another undertakes to indemnify him against some or all of those risks during a certain period or voyage.

Marine insurance is the oldest form of insurance known. Indeed, the institution of general average (*q.v.*), under which the participants in a maritime venture contribute to losses incurred by some for the benefit of all, may itself be looked on as a primitive form of self-insurance. Marine insurance in a discernibly modern form made its appearance in the Middle Ages in Europe; many of the medieval sea codes contained regulatory provisions.

Until the 20th century it was a characteristic of marine insurance that a substantial number of risks could not be covered, and this remains to some degree true in cargo policies customarily written to exclude losses under stated percentages. The theoretical basis for exclusion of certain risks is often said to be the furnishing of an inducement to the owner of property to look after it himself, as in the case of the deductible feature in the familiar automobile collision-insurance policy. Pressures from shipowners for comprehensive coverage have, however, gradually led to the inclusion of almost all risks: "collision and running down" clauses, war-risk riders, and "P. and I." (protection and indemnity) insurance.

An appreciation of the part played by marine insurance is essential to an understanding of the shipping industry. With certain exceptions, such as claims for death and personal injury and claims of seamen for wages, the great majority of claimants have insured themselves. The shipowner carries hull insurance on his own ship and protects himself against claims by third parties under a variety of arrangements. Any case of property damage to a ship or its cargo or to ships in collision resolves itself into a settlement between insurance carriers.

marine phosphorescence, heatless light generated chemically by marine plants and animals. Bioluminescence is exhibited by a wide variety of oceanic organisms, from bacteria to large squids and fish. The light is emitted when a flavin pigment, luciferin, is oxidized in the presence of luciferase, an enzyme also produced by the organism (the chemical system is like that of fireflies). The light produced is usually blue-green, near the point in the spectrum of maximum transmission for seawater and most visible for many deep-sea organisms. Most of the homogeneous phosphorescence of the sea, the glowing wakes, is caused by the presence of blooming phytoplankton, notably the microscopic dinoflagellate *Noctiluca miliaris,* as well as some jellyfish. Many small crustaceans, such as the *Cypridina hilgendorfii,* which is 3 to 4 mm (about 1/6 inch) long, also emit phosphorescence when disturbed. Many squids emit luminous clouds when threatened. Some species of fish emit light in distinctive patterns or at regular intervals, permitting individuals to form or maintain schools. Some deep-sea fish, notably the angler fish, possess lights in or near the mouth with which to attract and illuminate prey.

marine sediment, any deposit of insoluble material, primarily rock and soil particles, transported from land areas to the ocean by wind, ice, and rivers, as well as the remains of marine organisms, products of submarine volcanism, chemical precipitates from seawater, and materials from outer space (*e.g.,* meteorites) that accumulate on the seafloor.

A brief treatment of marine sediments follows. For full treatment, *see* MACROPAEDIA: Oceans.

Although systematic study of deep-ocean sediments began with the HMS *Challenger* expeditions between 1872 and 1876, intensive research was not undertaken until nearly 100 years later. Since 1968 American scientists, in collaboration with those from the United Kingdom, the Soviet Union, and various other countries, have recovered numerous sedimentary core samples from the Atlantic and Pacific oceans through the use of a specially instrumented deep-sea drilling vessel called the *Glomar Challenger.*

Marine sediments deposited near continents cover approximately 25 percent of the seafloor, but they probably account for roughly 90 percent by volume of all sediment deposits. Submarine canyons constitute the main route for sediment movement from continental shelves and slopes onto the deep seafloor. In most cases, an earthquake triggers a massive slumping and stirring of sedimentary material at the canyon head. Mixed with seawater, a dense liquid mass forms, giving rise to a density current that flows down the canyon at speeds of several tens of kilometres per hour. After reaching the base of the continental slope, the sediment-laden mass moves out onto the continental rise at the base of the slope. Deposits from turbidity currents (*i.e.,* short-lived density currents caused by suspended sediment concentrations) can build outward for hundreds and sometimes thousands of kilometres across the ocean bottom. Large sediment-built plains commonly occur in the Atlantic Ocean, where turbidity currents flow from the base of a continent to the Mid-Atlantic Ridge.

Deposits produced by turbidity currents are called turbidites. Most of them consist of sands and silts, but a few are composed of gravels. Turbidites tend to have distinct boundaries between adjacent units. Each of these units is formed by a separate flow and often exhibits a systematic change in grain size from coarsest at the bottom to finest at the top. Turbidites characteristically contain the remains of shallow-water organisms mixed with deep-water varieties. The shallow-water organisms came from areas where the density current originated, whereas the deep-water forms existed in the area traversed by the current or where it finally deposited its load.

The sediments deposited on continental shelves and rises, frequently referred to as hemipelagic sediments, ordinarily accumulate too rapidly to react chemically with seawater. In most cases, individual grains thus retain characteristics imparted to them in the area where they formed. As a rule, sediments deposited near coral reefs in shallow tropical waters contain abundant carbonate material. Calcareous, reef-derived muds, for example, occur around atolls at the northwestern end of the Hawaiian Island chain. Near volcanoes, sediments contain ash—*e.g.,* silicate glass and fine volcanic-rock fragments.

Roughly 75 percent of the deep seafloor is covered by slowly accumulating deposits known as pelagic sediments. Because of its great distance from the continents, the abyssal plain does not receive turbidity currents and their associated coarse-grained sediments. Moreover, since relatively little land-derived sediment consisting of silicate mineral and rock fragments reach the ocean bottom, deposits there show a predominance of biogenic constituents (*i.e.,* the skeletal remains of marine organisms). In areas where surface waters are fertile, opal from diatoms (algae) and radiolarians (protozoans) and calcium carbonate from such organisms as foraminiferans, coccolithophorids, and pteropods are supplied to the sediment. If the biological constituents exceed 30 percent by volume, then the deep-ocean sediments are usually classified on the basis of their biogenic components. For example, a mud containing 30 percent by volume of foraminiferal tests (external hard parts) is called a foraminiferal mud or ooze. When one genus dominates, it is frequently referred to by the generic name, such as *Globigerina* ooze. Diatomaceous and radiolarian muds are named on the same basis. Where biogenic constituents compose less than 30 percent of the total, the deposit is called a deep-sea clay, brown mud, or red clay.

The deep-ocean bottom is continually renewed through seafloor spreading (*see* seafloor spreading hypothesis). Oceanic crust is created at the mid-oceanic ridges as a consequence of extrusive igneous activity and moves away, carrying along overlying sediments. Over time, the crust and the associated sedimentary material are destroyed at the oceanic trenches. The sedimentary core samples recovered by the "Glomar Challenger" strongly support the seafloor-spreading hypothesis. No deep-sea sediments older than 150,000,000 years were discovered, indicating that the seafloor is relatively young. Furthermore, the sediments become progressively older and thicker with increasing distance from the ridge crests.

Sources of marine sediments

source of particulate matter	production	
	grams/yr	metric tons*/yr
lithogenous		
river transported	2×10^{16}	20,000,000,000
biogenic sediments		
calcareous†	1.2×10^{14}	120,000,000
siliceous†	0.4×10^{14}	40,000,000
cosmogenic		
meteorites (primarily chondrite)	7×10^{8}	700
cosmic dust	2.5×10^{12}	2,500,000

*Metric ton = 2,204.6 pounds. †Assuming that all the silicon and calcium brought to the ocean each year are removed by organisms.

marine style, an innovation in the embellishment of Cretan pottery, developed around 1500 BC and characterized by the depiction of octopuses and other sea creatures. Possibly originating at Knossos, marine style pottery began to rival older plant and flower designs and was exported from Crete all over the Cyclades and the Greek mainland, where its freshness eventually gave place to a somewhat debased formalism.

Cretan marine style painted terra-cotta vase, Late Minoan, *c.* 1500 BC; in the Archaeological Museum, Iráklion, Crete

By courtesy of the Iraklion Museum, Crete

marine terrace, a rock terrace formed where a sea cliff, with a wave-cut platform (*q.v.*) before it, is raised above sea level. Such terraces are found in California, Oregon, Chile, and Gibraltar and in New Zealand and other islands of the Pacific.

marine worm, any of the segmented worms constituting the class Polychaeta. *See* polychaete.

Marineland, world's first large oceanarium, located near St. Augustine, Fla., U.S. This privately owned, commercial facility was opened to the public in 1938. Its major attractions are display tanks containing marine mammals, where porpoises perform acrobatic feats. These mammals are also used in basic research on animal learning processes and have been the source of many of the major scientific discoveries about learning behaviour in such marine creatures. Marineland is best noted for its mammal exhibits, but it also has a large saltwater fish collection consisting of about 2,500 specimens of 125 species. Most of the fishes, together with marine invertebrates, are displayed in wall aquarium units. A big rectangular tank contains larger species such as tarpons, sharks, stingrays, moray eels, and sea turtles. Visitors are able to observe these specimens through a series of glass windows situated at different levels of the tank.

Marineland of the Pacific, also called HANNA-BARBERA MARINELAND, former large, commercially operated oceanarium at Rancho Palos Verdes near Los Angeles. It was opened in 1954 following the overwhelming success of Marineland in Florida. The aquarium had the world's largest holding tank, with a circumference of 76 metres (250 feet) and a capacity of close to 3,800,000 litres (1,000,000 gallons). This and other tanks housed an impressive array of fishes (4,000 specimens of 250 species) and marine mammals (more than 110 specimens of 11 species). These marine mammals, which included Pacific pilot whales, were featured in numerous acrobatic shows and were also used in behavioral research on the learning capabilities of such animals. Marineland of the Pacific closed in 1987.

Mariner, any of a series of unmanned U.S. space probes sent to the vicinities of Venus, Mars, and Mercury. Mariners 2 (1962) and 5 (1967) passed Venus within 22,000 miles and 2,500 miles (13,700 and 1,500 kilometres), respectively, and made measurements of temperature and atmospheric density. Mariners 4 (1965), 6 and 7 (1969), and 9 (1971–72) obtained striking photographs of the Martian surface and made significant analyses of the atmosphere of that planet. Mariner 10 (1973–75), which flew by Mercury three times, passed within 200 miles of the planet on its third pass and radioed back to Earth the first close-up pictures of the surface, as well as analyses of the atmosphere and magnetic field.

marinera (Peruvian folk dance): *see* cueca.

Mariners Museum, museum in Newport News, Va., founded in 1930 by the author Archer M. Huntington and devoted to the "culture of the sea." Its notable collections include hundreds of ship models and ornaments and examples of sailors' crafts.

The museum has a graphic arts collection of more than 13,000 pieces and a library containing 60,000 volumes, 6,000 maps, and 160,000 photographs. It also contains native boats and canoes, relics of sunken warships, and marine coins, medals, and postage stamps.

Marines, François de Créquy, marquis de: *see* Créquy, François, chevalier de.

Marinette, city, seat (1879) of Marinette county, northeastern Wisconsin, U.S., port of entry at the mouth of the Menominee River, opposite Menominee, Mich., on Green Bay of Lake Michigan. A trading post established in 1795 by Stanislaus Chappu, an American Fur Company agent, formed the nucleus of the original settlement, which was named for Marinette Chevalier, the daughter of a Menominee Indian chief, who married William Farnsworth, a noted fur trader of the 1820s. Logging was the main occupation, but after about 1900 it gave way to diversified manufacturing. Principal products include chemicals and wood, paper, and auto parts. A Great Lakes port, the city is in the "Near North" resort area and is known for its smelt fishing. A centre of the University of Wisconsin is located there. Inc. 1887. Pop. (2000) 11,749.

Marinetti, Filippo Tommaso (Emilio) (b. Dec. 22, 1876, Alexandria—d. Dec. 2, 1944, Bellagio, Italy), Italian-French prose writer, novelist, poet, and dramatist, the ideological founder of Futurism (*q.v.*), an early 20th-century literary, artistic, and political movement.

Marinetti was educated in Egypt, France, Italy, and Switzerland and began his literary career working for an Italian-French magazine in Milan. During most of his life his base was in France, though he made frequent trips to Italy and wrote in the languages of both countries. Such early poetry as the French *Destruction* (1904) showed the vigour and anarchic experimentation with form characteristic of his later work. Futurism had its official beginning with the publication of his "Manifeste de Futurisme" in the Paris newspaper *Le Figaro* (Feb. 20, 1909). His ideas were quickly adopted in Italy, where the writers Aldo Palazzeschi, Corrado Govoni, and Ardengo Soffici were among his most important disciples.

Marinetti's manifesto was also endorsed by Futurist painters, who published a manifesto of their own in 1910. Such painters and sculptors as Umberto Boccioni, Giacomo Balla, and Gino Severini carried out Marinetti's ideas.

Marinetti's later works reiterated the themes introduced in his 1909 manifesto. In 1910 he published a chaotic novel (entitled *Mafarka le Futuriste* in France and *Mafarka il futurista* in Italy), which illustrated and elaborated on his theory. He also applied Futurism to drama in such plays as the French *Le Roi bombance* (performed 1909; "The Feasting King") and the Italian *Anti-neutràlità* (1912; "Anti-Neutrality") and summed up his dramatic theory in a prose work, *Teatro sintetico futurista* (1916; "Synthetic Futurist Theatre").

In a volume of poems, *Guerra sola igiene del mundo* (1915; "War the Only Hygiene of the World"), Marinetti exulted over the outbreak of World War I and urged that Italy be involved. He became an active Fascist, an enthusiastic backer of Mussolini, and argued in *Futurismo e Fascismo* (1924), that Fascism was the natural extension of Futurism. Although his views helped temporarily to ignite Italian patriotism, Marinetti lost most of his following by the second decade of the 20th century.

Maringá, city, northwestern Paraná state, southern Brazil, on the Paraná Plateau, at 169 ft (52 m) above sea level. Maringá grew rapidly after its founding in 1947. Many of its residents are Japanese. Much of the local economic activity is based on coffee growing. Other important crops include corn (maize), *feijão* (beans), rice, wheat, and sugarcane. The Universidade Estadual de Maringá is located there. The city is accessible by air, road, and rail from Curitiba, the state capital, to the southeast, and from São Paulo. Pop. (2000 prelim.) 288,465.

Marini, Marino (b. Feb. 27, 1901, Pistoia, Italy—d. Aug. 6, 1980, Viareggio), Italian artist who was instrumental in the revival of the art of portrait sculpture in Italy during the first half of the 20th century.

At the Accademia di Belle Arti in Florence, Marini immersed himself in the study of ancient Italian sculpture, and his sensitivity to form and surface owes much to Etruscan and Roman works. The inner tension of his bold, straining figures, however, reflects the influence of German Gothic sculpture. Fate and the human capacity for self-destruction are his pervasive themes; most of his works are in bronze.

Marini consistently refined and penetrated two major images—the earthbound woman and the horse and rider—and in each case the differences between individual pieces can be extremely subtle. The "Dancer" series of the 1940s and '50s is especially notable for the enrichment of the surface with chisel work and corrosive dyes.

Marini

Through the surfaces of his elementary forms, Marini sought to reveal the spiritual substratum of his subjects; the portrait of Igor Stravinsky (1950) is a striking example. His later work is characterized by a heightened, almost architectural sense of scale and an increased sensitivity to planes at the expense of volume.

Marini was professor of sculpture at the Accademia Brera in Milan from 1940 until his retirement in 1970. He was also known for his graphic works.

Marīnid DYNASTY, also called BANŪ MARĪN, Berber dynasty that replaced Almohad rule in Morocco and temporarily in other parts of northern Africa during the 13th–15th centuries.

The Marīnids were a tribe of the Zanātah group—traditional allies of the Umayyad caliphs of Córdoba. The Marīnids had been established in eastern Morocco for more than a century when, in 1248, their ruler, Abū Yaḥyā, captured Fez (Fès) and made it the Marīnid capital. With the defeat of the last of the Almohads and the capture of Marrakech in 1269, the Marīnids, under Abū Yūsuf Yaʿqūb, became masters of Morocco. In order to fulfill the duties of Muslim sovereignty and to acquire religious prestige, they conducted a *jihād* (holy war) in Spain until the mid-14th century. Although the war helped the Muslim Naṣrid dynasty of Granada to consolidate its position and the fighting slowed down the Christian advance toward the Strait of Gibraltar, no territory was recaptured from the Christians, nor were any permanent conquests made in Africa, where the Marīnids tried to reestablish the Almohad empire. The greatest of the Marīnid sultans, Abū al-Ḥasan, captured the ʿAbd al-Wādid capital of Tilimsān (Tlemcen) in 1337, but neither he nor his successor, Abū ʿInān, were able to shake Ḥafṣid rule in Tunisia. The campaigns, however, depleted the resources of the dynasty, and, by the 15th century the Marīnid realm was in a state of anarchy. A collateral branch of the Marīnids, the Waṭṭāsids (Banū Waṭṭās), assumed rule over Morocco in 1465, but it collapsed when the Saʿdī *sharīf*s, descendants of Muḥammad, took Fez in 1548.

Marinism, also called SECENTISMO (Italian: "17th century"), style of the 17th-century poet Giambattista Marino (*q.v.*) as it first appeared in part three of *La lira* (1614; "The Lyre"). Marinism, a reaction against classicism, was marked by extravagant metaphors, hyperbole, fantastic word play, and original myths, all written with great sonority and sensuality, and with the aim to startle. The style appeared in sonnets, madrigals, and narrative poems. Marino's imitators carried his stylistic conceits to excess, and the term came ultimately to be pejorative by the end of the 17th century when it died out along with the Baroque period of which it was a part. Other European movements like it were Gongorism in Spain, *préciosité* in France, and metaphysical poetry in England, notably in the work of George Herbert, Richard Crashaw, and Andrew Marvell. A revival of interest in the Baroque generally after World War II led to both a resurgence in interest and a reassessment of Marino and Marinism.

Marinković, Vojislav (b. May 13 [May 1, old style], 1876, Belgrade—d. Sept. 18, 1935, Belgrade), influential statesman and eloquent spokesman for Serbia and later Yugoslavia in the early 20th century.

Marinković entered the Serbian Parliament as a Progressist (1906), represented Serbia at the Paris Conference (1913) for the financial settlement of the Balkan Wars, and became minister of national economy (1914–17). As the leader of the Progressists from 1915, he took part in the drafting of the Corfu Declaration calling for a South Slav state in 1917. In 1919, when Yugoslavia attained nationhood, he became its first minister of trade and merged the Progressists with the second most powerful political party in the new state, the Democratic Party. As minister of the interior (1921–22), Marinković organized the electoral law. He later served twice as minister of foreign affairs (1924, 1927–32) and as prime minister from April 4 to July 29, 1932.

Marinković

As foreign minister Marinković signed a treaty of friendship with France (1927), ratified the Nettuno Conventions concluded in 1925 to improve economic and cultural relations with Italy (1928), represented Yugoslavia at the assemblies of the League of Nations, and was a member of the League Council (1929–32) and its president (1930). At the League of Nations in Geneva in 1931, he so energetically opposed the formation of an Austro-German customs union that the Austrians had to disavow their signature to the agreement. Marinković also took part in the negotiations for establishing the Balkan Entente and for the new statute of the Little Entente; but both were signed (1934 and 1933, respectively) after his resignation.

Marino, town, Roma province, Lazio (Latium) region, central Italy, in the Colli Albani (Alban Hills) near Lago (lake) Albano, southeast of Rome. Near the site of the ancient Castrimoenium, the town became a possession of the Orsini family in 1370 and passed to the Colonna in the early 15th century. Notable monuments include the Fontana dei Quattro Mori (Fountain of the Four Moors), commemorating the Battle of Lepanto (1571), at which allied Christian forces defeated the Turks and in which many of the town's inhabitants took part; a Turkish shield captured in the battle is kept in the 17th-century church of S. Barnaba. The 16th-century Palazzo Colonna was heavily damaged in World War II. Marino is a vacation resort noted for its wine. Pop. (1981 prelim.) mun., 30,024.

Marino, Giambattista, Marino also spelled MARINI (b. Oct. 18, 1569, Naples—d. March 25, 1625, Naples), Italian poet, founder of the school of Marinism (later Secentismo), which dominated 17th-century Italian poetry. Marino's own work, praised throughout Europe, far surpassed that of his imitators, who carried his complicated word play and elaborate conceits and metaphors to such extremes that Marinism became a pejorative term. His work was translated all over Europe.

Marino trained for the law because of parental pressure but refused to practice his profession. His life after 1590 consisted of wild living, wandering between Italian and French courts, frequent money problems, brushes with the law, and immense success with the poetry that he managed to get published despite censorship. Much of his early work was circulated, with great acclaim, in manuscript and published later in his life. In 1596 he wrote *La sampogna* ("The Syrinx"), a series of sensual idylls using mythological and pastoral subjects, but he was unable to publish it until 1620.

After serving for a while as secretary to a Neapolitan prince, Marino was arrested in 1598 and 1600 for immorality, each time obtaining release through powerful admirers. He went to Rome and attached himself to Cardinal Pietro Aldobrandini, a nephew of the Pope. Together they visited several Italian cities. Marino tried to publish some of his voluptuous poems in Parma but was halted by the Inquisition. Finally he was able to publish his early poetry as *Le rime* (1602; "The Rhymes") and under the title *La lira,* 2 vol. (1608 and 1614; "The Lyre").

At Torino (Turin) from 1608 to 1615 he enjoyed the patronage of the duke of Savoy but was resented for his satirical poems against a rival poet, Gaspare Murtola (*La Murtoleide,* 1619; "The Murtoliad"). Murtola had him imprisoned for this offense and others; and, though his friends secured his release, Marino left Torino for Paris in 1615, where he stayed until 1623 under the patronage of Marie de Médicis and Louis XIII.

Before leaving Paris Marino published his most important work, a labour of 20 years, *Adone* (1623; definitive ed. by R. Balsamo-Crivelli, 1922; *Adonis* [selections]). *Adone,* an enormous poem (45,000 lines), relates, with many digressions, the love story of Venus and Adonis and shows the best and worst of Marino's style. The best is found in brilliant passages, written in a masterly style; the worst, in excessive conceits and metaphors, word play, and hyperbole. On returning to Italy in 1623, Marino encountered new difficulties with censorship, but he stayed in Naples until his death.

Other works for which Marino is remembered are *La galeria* (1620; "The Gallery"), an attempt to recreate works of art poetically, and *La strage degli innocenti* (1632; *The Slaughter of the Innocents*). His correspondence was published as *Lettere* ("Letters") in 1627.

Marinot, Maurice (b. 1882, Troyes, Fr.—d. 1960, Troyes), French painter and glassmaker who was one of the first 20th-century glassworkers to exploit the aesthetic qualities of weight and mass and one of the first to incorporate bubbles and other natural flaws as elements of design.

Marinot went to Paris in 1901 to study painting at the École des Beaux-Arts. There he became acquainted with the Fauves and exhibited his works with theirs at the annual Salons des Indépendants. In 1911, while in Troyes, Marinot began to learn the art of glassmaking and became immediately fascinated with the new medium. He abandoned painting (although he returned to it after 1937) and devoted himself to mastering the techniques of glassblowing, molding, and cold carving, experimenting with the decorative uses of enamels and etching. With simple tools he bent and manipulated the glass but, to a certain extent, allowed the nature of the material to determine its own form. This spontaneity represented a dramatic departure from the technical precision of earlier glassmakers, just as his massive, chunklike works departed from the traditional values of delicacy, fragility, and perfection.

As Marinot's technical facility grew, his works became increasingly abstract and innovative. Although they shocked the refined tastes of glass connoisseurs, his rough-hewn pieces, with their random globules and irregular shapes, contributed significantly to the development of glass as a medium for modern art.

Marinus, name of two Roman Catholic popes, grouped below chronologically and indicated by the symbol •. They were sometimes erroneously called Martin; *see* Martin (II) *under* Martin (Papacy).

• **Marinus I** (b. Tuscany—d. May 15, 884, Rome), pope from 882 to 884. He was a deacon when, in 869, Pope Adrian II sent him as emissary to the fourth Council of Constantinople, which condemned Patriarch St. Photius of Constantinople for defending Eastern traditions against the Roman Church. Marinus was made bishop of Caere, now Cerveteri, Italy, by Pope John VIII, who appointed him ambassador to Constantinople to negotiate the schism following Photius' condemnation. Upon John's assassination, Marinus was elected pope in December 882. He continued discussing the issue of Photius, and he absolved and restored Cardinal Bishop Formosus (later pope) of Porto, Italy, whom John had deposed.

• **Marinus II** (b. Rome—d. April/May 946, Rome), pope from 942 to 946. He was a priest when nominated by the senator Alberic II, marquess of Spoleto. Marinus' pontificate was subsequently dictated by Alberic. He managed, however, to work for church reform, contributing mainly to discipline and monasticism.

Marinus, Rabbi (Hebrew grammarian): *see* Ibn Janāḥ.

Mario, Giovanni Matteo, original name MARIO CAVALIERE DI CANDIA (b. Oct. 17, 1810, Cagliari, Sardinia—d. Dec. 11, 1883, Rome), Italian romantic tenor, known for his striking good looks, grace, and charm as well as for the beauty and range of his voice.

He was of a noble family and was trained as an officer in the Piedmontese Guard, where his father was a general. At the age of 26 he left the army for political reasons, travelled to Paris, and began to study voice with Giovanni Marco Bordogni at the Paris Conservatory. Before his debut in 1838 at the Paris Opéra in the title role of Giacomo Meyerbeer's *Robert le diable,* he was instructed by the composer. He was immediately successful, signed his contract simply "Mario," and was popularly known thereafter by that name alone.

In 1839 Mario made a triumphant debut in London as Gennaro in Gaetano Donizetti's *Lucrezia Borgia* opposite Giulia Grisi, a famous Italian soprano who later became his wife, and in Paris as Nemorino in Donizetti's *L'elisir d'amore.* For the next 25 years he was a principal singer of romantic parts in Paris and London, also appearing at St. Petersburg (Russia), New York City, and Madrid. His most admired early roles were Nemorino, Ernesto, and Gennaro. Later he was acclaimed for his Almaviva, which he sang more than 100 times in London, the Duke of Mantua, Raoul, and Faust. In 1871 he gave his farewell performance as Fernand in Donizetti's *La favorita* at Covent Garden in London, and after a concert tour of the United States he retired to Rome where his fortunes so declined that friends arranged a benefit recital for him in 1880.

Mariology, in Christian, especially Roman Catholic, theology, the study of doctrines concerning Mary, the mother of Jesus; the term also refers to the content of these doctrines.

The primary methodological problem of Mariology lies in the very limited mention of Mary made in the New Testament and in the relative, although not complete, silence about Mary in the early church. Although Mary is mentioned in some early apocryphal (noncanonical) writings and baptismal creeds, theological disputes were the most significant factor in bringing Mary to theological prominence. At various times, it was denied both that Jesus was authentically human and that he was fully divine. To the first charge, the assertion that he had a human mother was considered a convincing refutation; with regard to the second, the affirmation by the Council of Ephesus (431) that Mary was Theotokos (*q.v.*; Greek: God-bearer) became the principle upon which devotion to Mary in the East has primarily rested. In both Eastern and Western liturgical traditions, various feast days in her honour were established.

Suppliants in front of the cave of St. Bernadette at Lourdes, Fr.

Paul Popper Ltd., London

The tradition that she remained a virgin though she gave birth to Jesus was generally accepted in the early church. A further appreciation of her holiness led to the doctrine that she was so favoured by God's grace that she could not have sinned and, in the view of some theologians, that she was even free from the effect of the disobedience of Adam. The latter doctrine, known as the Immaculate Conception, was formally proclaimed a matter of Roman Catholic belief by Pope Pius IX in 1854. The association of Mary in the work of Jesus developed into the view of Mary as everyone's spiritual mother and as co-redemptrix—*i.e.,* the partner with Jesus in the redemption of human beings. Her role in redemption was extended to her intercession in heaven and to the application of Christ's merits to individual persons. The doctrine that after death Mary's body was assumed into heaven was proclaimed by Pope Pius XII in 1950.

Post-Reformation Roman Catholic Mariology has generally been characterized by a sensitivity to Protestant criticisms. Popular piety was reflected in the establishment of lay groups and communities of priests or nuns devoted to Mary and the building of shrines at places (such as Lourdes in France and Fátima in Portugal) where Mary was said to have appeared. In the 20th century the teachings of several successive popes encouraged numerous pilgrimages in her honour and congresses devoted to her.

Marion, city, seat of Perry county, west central Alabama, U.S., near the Cahaba River. Settled in 1817, it was known as Muckle Ridge until renamed to honour Francis Marion, a soldier in the Revolutionary War who was known as the Swamp Fox. A resolution adopted by the Baptist State Convention meeting in Marion in 1845 separated the Baptists into Northern and Southern factions. Light industry is the economic mainstay. Judson College was founded in 1838, and Marion Military Institute was established in 1842. Nearby are the Talladega National Forest (Oakmulgee Division) and a U.S. fish hatchery. Pop. (1990) 4,211.

Marion, city, seat (1831) of Grant county, north central Indiana, U.S., on the Mississinewa River, 66 mi (97 km) northeast of Indianapolis. Settled in 1826, it was named for Gen. Francis Marion of the Revolutionary War. It developed as an agricultural town, but local oil and gas booms at the turn of the century attracted industry which continued after the wells ran out. Manufactures now include auto, radio, and television parts, and plastics, wire, glass, and foundry products. U.S. troops fought Miami Indians nearby at the Battle of Mississinewa in 1812. Salamonie and Mississinewa recreation areas are north of the city. Marion Collge was founded in 1920. Inc. 1889. Pop. (1990) 32,618.

Marion, city, seat (1824) of Marion county, north central Ohio, U.S., 45 mi (72 km) north of Columbus. Laid out *c.* 1820, it was first called Jacob's Well (for Jacob Foos, who dug for water there). Renamed in 1822 for Gen. Francis Marion of Revolutionary War fame, it was incorporated as a village in 1830. Industrial development began in 1865 when Edward Huber, a German mechanic, founded a farm equipment factory there. The community soon became preeminent in the manufacture of excavating machinery (now the leading industry). The steam shovel was introduced in 1874 and earned Marion the title "Shovel City." Varied manufactures now include road construction, conveying and handling equipment, signposts, air-conditioning units, household appliances, and processed foods. Surrounding farms specialize in popcorn growing, and limestone quarries are nearby. Marion Technical College opened in 1970, and a campus of Ohio State University is also in the city.

Warren G. Harding (1865–1923) was born on a farm in nearby Blooming Grove (then Corsica) and became the owner and publisher of the *Marion Star* in 1884 before entering state politics and later being elected as U.S. president. His home on Mt. Vernon Avenue is preserved as a museum, and the Harding Memorial contains the President's tomb and that of his wife, Florence. Inc. city, 1890. Pop. (1990) 34,075.

Marion, Francis, byname THE SWAMP FOX (b. *c.* 1732, Winyah, S.C.—d. Feb. 26, 1795, Berkeley County, S.C., U.S.), colonial American soldier in the U.S. War of Independence (1775–83), nicknamed by the British for his elusive tactics.

Marion gained his first military experience fighting against the Cherokee Indians in 1759. Then, serving as a member of the South Carolina Provincial Congress (1775), he was commissioned a captain. It was after the surrender of Gen. Benjamin Lincoln to the British at Charleston, S.C. (1780), that he slipped away to the swamps, gathered together his band of guerrillas, and then began leading his bold raids. Marion and his irregulars often defeated larger bodies of British troops by the surprise and rapidity of their movement over swampy terrain. For a daring rescue of Americans surrounded by the British at Parkers Ferry, S.C. (August 1781), Marion received the thanks of Congress. He was then appointed a brigadier general, and after the war he served in the senate of South Carolina (1782–90).

Marion Island, one of the two Prince Edward Islands in the southern Indian Ocean, about 1,190 miles (1,920 km) southeast of Cape Town. In 1947 South Africa proclaimed sovereignty of the islands and established a meteorological station on Marion Island in 1948. The islands are otherwise uninhabited. A sub-Antarctic island of volcanic origin, Marion is 115 square miles (298 square km) in area and has a low, domelike shape rising to President Swart Peak (3,890 feet [1,186 m]). The coastline, exposed and rugged, has steep cliffs rising 500 feet (150 m) high. The climate is cool (mean annual temperature, 40° F [4.4° C]) and stormy, with prevailing westerly winds that bring heavy rain (100 inches [2,500 mm] annually) and snow; cloudless days are rather exceptional. Plants include the Kerguelen cabbage, mosses, and ferns. Birdlife is extensive. Prince Edward Island lies 12 miles (19 km) to the northeast.

marionette, also called STRING PUPPET, any of several types of puppet figures manipulated from above by strings or threads attached to a control. In a simple marionette, the strings are attached in nine places: to each leg, hand, shoulder, and ear and at the base of the spine. By adding strings, more sensitive control of movement is achieved. Among European puppets, marionettes are considered the most delicate and difficult to master; some are capable of imitating almost every human and animal action.

Scheherezade, snake charmer, and snake, marionettes by Bil Baird

By courtesy of the Bil Baird Collection; photograph, Zbigniew Gajda

Although this type of puppet was not fully developed until the mid-19th century, examples of marionettes controlled by an iron rod instead of strings still survive in Sicily and elsewhere. In the 18th century marionette operas, acting out the works of well-known composers, were extremely popular.

Mariotte, Edme (b. *c.* 1620, Dijon, Fr.—d. May 12, 1684, Paris), French physicist and plant physiologist who, independent of Robert Boyle, discovered the law that states that the volume of a gas varies inversely with its pressure. Although widely known as Boyle's law, this basic tenet of physics and chemistry is called Mariotte's law in France.

Mariotte, a Roman Catholic priest and prior of Saint-Martin-sous-Beaune, was in 1666 one of the founding members of the Academy of Sciences, in Paris. In his *Discours de la nature de l'air* (1676; "Discourse on the Nature of Air"), in which he coined the word barometer, Mariotte stated Boyle's law and went further by noting that the law holds only if there is no change in temperature.

From his studies of plants, he concluded that they synthesize materials by chemical processes that vary from plant to plant—a theory verified long after his time. He also observed the pressure of sap in plants and compared it to blood pressure in animals. The first volume of the *Histoire et mémoires de l'Académie* (1733; "History and Memoirs of the Academy") contains many papers by him on such subjects as the motion of fluids, the nature of colour, and the notes of the trumpet.

Mariotte's law (physics): *see* Boyle's law.

mariposa lily (genus *Calochortus*), tuliplike perennial plants of the lily family (Liliaceae), consisting of about 40 species native to western North America. They have simple or somewhat branched stems, 15 to 130 cm (0.5 foot to 4 feet) tall, rising from corms (bases of modified underground stems) and bearing a few narrow leaves and showy white, yellow, lilac, or bluish flowers, often spotted or marked in the centre. The three large broad petals, 2.5 to 5 cm long, usually bear a conspicuous basal gland.

Mariposa lily (*Calochortus*)

John Kohout from Root Resources

Several species are in cultivation, among them the sego lily (*Calochortus nuttallii*), native to dry soil from South Dakota to Washington and south to Oregon and California. Its white flowers are variously marked with yellow, purple, and lilac. The edible roots of the sego lily were used for food by the early Mormon settlers in the Salt Lake Valley.

Mariposan (California Indians): *see* Yokuts.

Maris, Jacob, in full JACOBUS HENDRICUS MARIS (b. Aug. 25, 1837, The Hague, Neth.—d. Aug. 7, 1899, Karlsbad, Bohemia, Austria-Hungary [now Karlovy Vary, Czech Republic]), Dutch landscape painter who, with his brothers Matthijs and Willem, formed what has come to be known as the Hague school of painters, influenced by both the 17th-century Dutch masters and the Barbizon school.

Maris was the son of an etcher and lithographer. He first studied at the Antwerp Academy and then in Paris (1865–71). His early work contained figures (children, young women), but he is best known for the landscapes he began painting about 1872. These include scenes from the Dutch countryside of bridges and windmills, old quays, massive towers, and level banks, against misty skies or chasing clouds. In all his paintings, whether in watercolour or oil, and in his etchings, the subject is subordinate to the atmospheric effect, as in the "Grey Tower, Old Amsterdam" and "Landscape near Dordrecht." He was a notable influence on his contemporaries.

Maris, Matthijs, Matthijs originally MATTHIAS, also called THIJS (b. Aug. 17, 1839, The Hague, Neth.—d. Aug. 22, 1917, London, Eng.), Dutch painter, brother of Jacob and Willem Maris, noted for his movement away from the realism of the Hague school toward a more symbolic expression. He was without doubt the most gifted of the brothers.

Maris received a royal subsidy and for some time (1861–68) lived and worked with his elder brother Jacob, on whom his more spiritual and mystical nature had a refining influence. Matthijs himself gradually began to soften the realistic style of his paintings; the contours of objects became more vague, his colours dominated by gray, and his subjects nearer to dream-visions than to actual scenes from life. From 1869 to 1875 he worked in Paris, and from 1877 he lived in London, where he remained for the rest of his life. He was influenced by the Pre-Raphaelites. In addition to painting, Maris made etchings in limited editions and lithographs.

Maris, Roger, original name ROGER EUGENE MARIS (b. Sept. 10, 1934, Hibbing, Minn., U.S.—d. Dec. 14, 1985, Houston, Texas), American professional baseball player whose one-season total of 61 home runs (1961) was the highest ever recorded in the major leagues. As this feat was accomplished in a 162-game schedule, the commissioner of baseball Ford C. Frick ruled that Maris had not broken Babe Ruth's record of 60 home runs, set during a 154-game schedule in 1927; not until 1991 was Maris recognized without dispute as the official record-holder.

Maris entered the major leagues with the Cleveland Indians in 1957. From 1960 through 1966 he played for the New York Yankees, Ruth's former team; like Ruth, Maris was an exceptional defensive outfielder as well as a powerful hitter. Maris won the Most Valuable Player Award for the American League in 1960 and 1961. He retired with a career total of 275 home runs after playing for the St. Louis Cardinals in 1967 and 1968.

Mariscal Estigarribia, town, northern Paraguay. It lies in the sparsely settled Chaco Boreal region, on the bank of Mosquitos Creek, which drains into the Paraguay River. Until 1945 it was a military outpost known as López de Filippis; it was renamed to honour the general whose strategy in the Chaco War (1932–35) established Paraguayan control over the area. The town is now a commercial centre for the surrounding region, the main product of which is quebracho, yielding hardwood and tannin. Pop. (1985 est.) 6,525.

Marishi-ten (Buddhist mythology): *see* Marīcī.

Marisol, in full ESCOBAR MARISOL (b. May 22, 1930, Paris, Fr.), American sculptor of boxlike figurative works combining wood and other materials and often grouped as tableaux.

Marisol was born in Paris of Venezuelan parents and spent her youth in Los Angeles and Paris. In 1950 she moved to New York City, where she studied at the Art Students League and the Hans Hofmann School. From her earliest, roughly carved figures, she worked mainly in wood. She gained wide recognition in the 1960s for her mixed-media figure groups; the juxtaposition of blockish, inert forms and their painted, cast-plaster, or found-object features and accoutrements lend the works a deadpan irony. Her portrait groups of public figures are particularly satirical.

Marist Brother, member of LITTLE BROTHERS OF MARY (F.M.S.), a Roman Catholic congregation of teaching brothers founded near Lyon, Fr., on Jan. 2, 1817, by Marcellin Champagnat for the Christian education of French youth. In 1836 several brothers accompanied the first Marist Fathers to the mission field of the South Pacific islands. Since then, more than 100 schools have been opened in 23 mission territories.

The congregation staffs schools in countries around the world, providing education at the elementary, secondary, college, and university levels. They maintain academic, agricultural, technical, and vocational schools.

Marist Father, member of SOCIETY OF MARY (S.M.), a Roman Catholic religious congregation founded in 1816 in the diocese of Belley, Fr., by Jean-Claude Courveille and Jean-Claude-Marie Colin to undertake all ministerial works—parishes, schools, hospital chaplaincies, and the foreign missions—while stressing the virtues of the Virgin Mary. Its foreign missions, the acceptance of which was the chief reason for its approval by Rome in 1836, embrace the islands of the South Pacific (the congregation's original mission field), Japan, Algeria, Peru, and Venezuela. Stemming from the Marist Fathers are the Marist Brothers, the Marist Sisters, the Missionary Sisters of the Society of Mary, and the Marist Third Order.

Maritain, Jacques (b. Nov. 18, 1882, Paris—d. April 28, 1973, Toulouse, Fr.), Roman Catholic philosopher, respected both for his interpretation of the thought of St. Thomas Aquinas and for his own Thomist philosophy.

Reared a Protestant, Maritain attended the Sorbonne in Paris, where he was attracted by

Maritain
John Howard Griffin

teachers who claimed that the natural sciences alone could resolve human questions about life and death. There, however, he also met Raissa Oumansoff, a Russian-Jewish student, who began to share his quest for truth. Both became disillusioned with the Sorbonne's scientism and began to attend lectures by the intuitionist philosopher Henri Bergson. From him, they came to realize their need for "the Absolute," and in 1906, two years after their marriage, they converted to Catholicism.

After studying biology at Heidelberg (1906–08) Maritain studied Thomism at Paris and in 1913 began teaching at the Institut Catholique, serving as professor of modern philosophy (1914–39). From 1932 he also taught annually at the Pontifical Institute of Mediaeval Studies in Toronto and was a visiting professor at Princeton (1941–42) and Columbia (1941–44). He returned as professor of philosophy at Princeton (1948–60) after serving as French ambassador to the Vatican (1945–48). In 1958, at the University of Notre Dame, Ind., the Jacques Maritain Center was established to further studies along the lines of his philosophy.

Maritain's thought, which is based on Aristotelianism and Thomism, incorporates features from other classical and modern philosophers and draws upon anthropology, sociology, and psychology. The dominant themes in his more than 50 books include the contentions that (1) science, philosophy, poetry, and mysticism are among many legitimate ways of knowing reality; (2) the individual person transcends the political community; (3) natural law expresses not only what is natural in the world but also what is known naturally by human beings; (4) moral philosophy must take into account other branches of human knowledge; and (5) people holding different beliefs must cooperate in the formation and maintenance of salutary political institutions.

Referring to Thomism as Existentialist Intellectualism, Maritain believed that to exist is to act. His philosophy contained elements of humanism; he emphasized the importance of the individual as well as the Christian community.

Some critics have regarded Maritain as the most important modern interpreter of St. Thomas. A man of acute sensibility and known as a friend of numerous painters, poets, and other artists, Maritain devoted much attention to developing a philosophy of the arts. Among his major works are *Art et scolastique* (1920; 4th ed., 1965; *Art and Scholasticism,* 1930); *Distinguer pour unir, ou les degrés du savoir* (1932; *The Degrees of Knowledge,* 1937); *Frontières de la poésie et autres essais* (1935; *Art and Poetry,* 1943); *Man and the State* (1951); and *La Philosophie morale . . .* (1960; *Moral Philosophy,* 1964).

BIBLIOGRAPHY. G. Phelan, *Jacques Maritain* (1937); H. Bars, *Maritain et notre temps* (1959); J. Evans (ed.), *Jacques Maritain: The Man and His Achievement* (1965).

marital exchange, system of mate recruitment in which specific families, groups of families, tribes, or segments of a tribe are designated as those groups from which one must choose a spouse. *See* exchange marriage; cross-cousin.

Maritime, economic *région,* southern Togo, West Africa, bordering the Plateaux *région* on the north, Benin on the east, the Gulf of Guinea on the south, and Ghana on the west. The *région*'s relief consists of coastal sandbars with inland lagoons backed by low-lying plains. Maritime's area of 2,470 sq mi (6,395 sq km) encompasses the *préfectures* of Golfe, Lacs, Yoto, Vo, and Zio. The *région* has a warm climate, with two rainy seasons annually. A fertile area near the coast supports the growth of oil palms, sugarcane, and rice; cassava and corn (maize) are grown throughout. Maritime's industry is the most fully developed among the country's five *régions*; important manufactures include palm oil, beer, processed meat and sugar, and steel. The administrative centre is Lomé, Togo's capital and largest city. Railways and the major north–south road from Lomé link Maritime with the country's central and northern *régions.* The Ewe, Ouatchi, and Ane (Mina) peoples compose Maritime's population, which is the largest among Togo's *régions.* Pop. (1981 est.) 1,300,000.

maritime air mass, vast body of air of oceanic origin; also, an air mass (*q.v.*) that has had a long trajectory over water and has been so modified that it has the characteristics of an air mass of oceanic origin.

Maritime Alps, Italian ALPI MARITTIME, French ALPES MARITIMES, segment of the Western Alps extending in an arc along the French–Italian border for 120 mi (190 km) between two passes, the Colle di Cadibona (east) and Colle della Maddalena (west). Punta Argentera (10,817 ft [3,297 m]) is the highest point. The mountains are bounded east by the Appenino Ligure (Ligurian Appennines) and north by the Cottian Alps (*q.v.*), and they include the Alpi Liguri (Ligurian Alps, between Colle di Cadibona and Colle di Tenda) and the Provence Alps (*q.v.*; lower western spurs spreading toward the Rhône River Valley).

Maritime Atlas (North Africa): *see* Tell Atlas.

maritime law, also called ADMIRALTY LAW, or ADMIRALTY, the body of legal rules that governs ships and shipping.

A brief treatment of maritime law follows. For full treatment, *see* MACROPAEDIA: Transportation Law.

The transportation of goods and passengers by water is one of the earliest forms of commercial activity on record, and scattered references in ancient documents to maritime regulations are known. The 6th-century Byzantine compilation known as the Digest of Justinian includes references to such regulations, several of which indicate that the island of Rhodes had anciently had an important and influential maritime code. Rome appears to have borrowed heavily from the Rhodian maritime laws, and from Rome's contributions there gradually evolved a uniform body of maritime law for the Mediterranean region. Eventually, certain Italian cities formulated their own maritime codes, which interrupted for a time the uniformity of the laws of the area. The next major body of maritime laws was compiled at Barcelona in the 13th century, called the Consolat de Mar ("Consulate of the Sea"). This extensive maritime code was soon adopted throughout other places in the Mediterranean, restoring a measure of uniformity.

Owing in part to the rise of nationalism and to greater expansion of shipping, maritime law began to become more diverse in the late Renaissance. Separate maritime codes were enacted in Sweden (1667), France (1681), and Denmark (1683). In England an admiralty court was established around 1360. Modern British Admiralty courts, operating without a jury, still try cases involving marine collisions and salvage; however, other types of cases involving marine actions are usually tried in the Commercial Court. The United States has no equivalent type of court; maritime cases fall within the jurisdiction of the federal district courts. A claimant is also free to sue in a state court, provided that the defendant is a citizen of the same state.

Several features are characteristic of maritime law. One is the lien, or claim on the vessel and cargo as security. Most types of maritime claims, whether arising from breach of contract, injury or damage, or salvage service, give rise to such liens. Maritime claim pleadings, called libels in maritime terminology, are of two types: *in personam,* or *in rem.* Libels brought *in personam* are directly enforceable against an individual, usually the shipowner. More distinctive of maritime law, however, are libels brought *in rem,* enforceable against the ship or cargo. Maritime liens arise in all cases in which a ship is involved whether stemming from negligent navigation, from the negligence of ship personnel, or from the unseaworthiness of the ship.

Another characteristic feature of maritime law is that a shipowner is permitted to limit his liability in most cases to the value of the ship. The idea of liability limitation is an ancient one and appeared long before the advent of any form of insurance. It is probably a recognition of the extreme risks involved in shipping, designed to protect the shipowner from the often prohibitive burden of liability that he would otherwise be forced to bear. The effect was that a shipowner could satisfy his liability by turning over the ship and cargo to the claimants. If the ship was a total loss, the claimants therefore received nothing. This limitation of liability has been modified somewhat in modern maritime codes.

Collision is another matter addressed by maritime law. A colliding vessel is responsible for damage to another ship or structure only if the collision is caused by negligence, intent, or fault of the vessel. In certain circumstances there is a presumption of fault, as when a moving vessel collides with a stationary object or vessel. Regulations differ on how compensation is determined when the colliding vessels share blame.

Salvage is another subject of maritime law. When a maritime property is saved from loss or damage from the sea, the salvager is entitled to a reward, the amount depending upon a number of factors. A related idea is that of "general average," referred to in the Digest of Justinian; if part of a cargo must be jettisoned to save the remainder, the loss is "averaged" or shared by the owners of the property that was saved.

Marine insurance—the oldest-known form of insurance—plays a critical role in the shipping industry and comprises an extremely complex branch of maritime law. Shipowners carry hull insurance to cover damage to their ships. To protect themselves against claims by third parties, they carry "protection and indemnity" insurance.

Maritime law has a distinctive status with respect to other types of law. In some ways it is a species of international law, for uncertain courts of one nation often look to the practice of other nations for guidance. It is also based heavily on long-established traditions, in the process preserving some practices whose rationale is not entirely clear. Although nations can and do adopt their own laws (and many have codified their own maritime laws in the 20th century), there is an increasing tendency to make maritime laws uniform. Many international conferences have been convened on specific parts of maritime law. The chief organization overseeing maritime law is the International Maritime Committee (or Comité Maritime International), composed of the maritime law associations of several nations.

maritime log (measurement): *see* log.

Maritime Provinces, the Canadian Atlantic Coast–Gulf of St. Lawrence provinces of New Brunswick, Nova Scotia, and Prince Edward Island. With Newfoundland they form the Atlantic Provinces. During the French period much of the region was known as Acadia, which was ceded to the British by the Treaty of Utrecht (1713).

Maritsa River, also called MARICA, Greek ÉVROS, Turkish MERIÇ, river in Bulgaria, rising in the Rila Mountains southeast of Sofia on the north face of Musala Peak. It flows east and southeast across Bulgaria for 170 miles (275 km), forms the Bulgaria–Greece frontier for a distance of 10 miles (16 km), and then becomes the Greece–Turkey frontier for another 115 miles (185 km). At Edirne it changes direction, flowing south and then southwest to enter the Aegean Sea. Major tributaries are the Arda, Stryama, Topolnitsa, and Tundzha. The area of its drainage basin is 20,000 square miles (53,000 square km).

The Maritsa River valley forms part of the route for the Sofia–Istanbul railway. The fertile valley soils support extensive fruit and vegetable growing, especially for export. Several large hydroelectric and irrigation schemes have been developed on tributaries of the Maritsa.

Maritsa River, Battle of the (Sept. 26, 1371), Ottoman Turk victory over Serbian forces that allowed the Turks to extend their control over southern Serbia and Macedonia. After the Ottoman sultan Murad I (reigned 1360–89) advanced into Thrace, conquered Adrianople, and thereby gained control of the Maritsa River valley, which led into the central Balkans, the Christian states of the Balkans formed an alliance to drive him back. Their early efforts ended in defeat, and the Bulgarians were compelled to become vassals of the sultan (1366). Another campaign to resist Turkish expansion was organized in 1371 by Vukašin, the king of the southern Serbian lands, who gathered an army of 70,000 men and marched into the Maritsa valley. While halting at Chernomen (Chirmen; located between Philippopolis and Adrianople), however, his forces were surprised by a much smaller Turkish army, which slaughtered large numbers of Serbs, including Vukašin, and drove many of the survivors into the river to be drowned.

The battle involved such carnage that the field was later referred to as "the Serbs' destruction." It confirmed Bulgaria's status as a vassal-state to the Turks and destroyed the independent South Serbian kingdom, whose new ruler, Marko Kraljević, became a vassal of the sultan. Macedonia and ultimately the remainder of the Balkan Peninsula were exposed to Turkish conquest.

Maritz, Salomon Gerhardus, also called GERRIT MARITZ (b. 1876, Kimberley, Griqualand West [now in South Africa]—d. Dec. 19, 1940, Pretoria, S.Af.), general and rebel who was an ardent believer in the Boer nationalist cause in South Africa. He fought against the British in the South African War (Boer War; 1899–1902) and led a rebellion against British rule during World War I.

During the Boer War, Maritz carried out a daring raid on the British Cape Colony, shortly before the Boer surrender in 1902. In 1914 he was commander of South African troops on the border of German South West Africa. When World War I began Maritz defected to the German side with his troops and precipitated a general rebellion of Boer troops throughout South Africa. When the rebellion was put down in 1915, he fled to Europe but returned to South Africa in 1923. In the 1930s he established an anti-Semitic, pro-fascist movement in South Africa.

Mariupol, formerly (1948–89) ZHDANOV, city, Donetsk *oblast* (province), Ukraine. It lies along the estuary of the Kalmius and Kalchik rivers, 6 miles (10 km) from the Sea of Azov. The original 18th-century settlement of Pavlovsk was renamed Mariupol by Greek settlers in 1779. In 1882 it was connected by rail to the Donets Coal Basin and developed as a major port for the basin, a role it maintains. The town was renamed Zhdanov in 1948 for Andrey Zhdanov, a native who died that year, though the city's earlier name was restored in 1989. Modern Mariupol exports coal, steel, machinery, and grain. It is the base of a fishing fleet, and a dredged channel leads to the open sea. Mariupol also has large and important iron and steel works and associated coke-chemical and machine-building works; other industries include ship repairing, fish canning, and flour milling. The city also has a metallurgical institute. Pop. (1991 est.) 521,800.

Marius, Gaius (b. *c.* 157 BC, Cereatae, near Arpinum [Arpino], Latium [now in Italy]—d. Jan. 13, 86 BC, Rome), Roman general and politician, consul seven times (107, 104–100, 86 BC), who was the first Roman to illustrate the political support that a successful general could derive from the votes of his old army veterans.

Early career. Gaius Marius was a strong and brave soldier and a skillful general, popular with his troops, but he showed little flair for politics and was not a good public speaker. As an equestrian, he lacked the education in Greek normal to the upper classes. He was superstitious and overwhelmingly ambitious, and, because he failed to force the aristocracy to accept him, despite his great military success, he suffered from an inferiority complex that may help explain his jealousy and vindictive cruelty. As a young officer-cadet, along with Jugurtha (later king of Numidia), on Scipio Aemilianus' staff in the Numantine War in Spain (134 BC), he, like Jugurtha, made an excellent impression on his commanding officer. Marius' family enjoyed the patronage of more than one noble family, in particular the distinguished and inordinately conceited Caecilii Metelli, then at the height of their political power. They backed his candidacy for tribune (defender) of the plebs (common people) in 119. As tribune, Marius proposed a bill affecting procedure in elections and legislative assemblies by narrowing the bridges—the gangway across which each voter passed to fill in and deposit his ballot tablet—as a result of which there was no longer room on the gangway for observers, normally aristocrats, who abused their position to influence an individual's vote. When the two consuls tried to persuade the Senate to block the bill, Marius threatened them with imprisonment, and the bill was carried.

Marius showed himself no unprincipled candidate for popular favour, for he vetoed a popular grain bill, and the following years offered him little promise of a conspicuous career. He failed to secure the aedileship (control of markets and police) and was only just elected praetor (judicial magistrate) for the year 115 after bribing heavily, for which he was lucky to escape condemnation in court. The next year he governed Further Spain, campaigned successfully against bandits, and laid a foundation for great personal wealth through mining investments. After that, he made a good marriage into a patrician family that, after long obscurity, was on the point of strong political revival. His wife was Julia, the aunt of Julius Caesar.

Election to the consulship. The command in the war against Jugurtha (who was now Numidian king) was given to Quintus Metellus, and Marius was invited to join Metellus' staff. After defeating Jugurtha in pitched battle, Metellus was less successful in later guerrilla warfare, and this failure was exaggerated by Marius in his public statements when at the end of 108 he returned to Rome to seek the consulship (chief magistracy). Marius was elected on the equestrian and popular vote and, to Metellus' bitter chagrin, appointed by a popular bill to succeed Metellus at once in the African command.

In recruiting fresh troops, Marius broke with custom, because of a manpower shortage, by enrolling volunteers from outside the propertied classes, which alone had previously been liable for service. In Africa he kept Jugurtha on the run, and in 105 Jugurtha was captured, betrayed by his ally, King Bocchus of Mauretania—not to Marius himself but to Sulla, considered a rather disreputable young aristocrat, who had joined Marius' staff as quaestor in 107. Sulla had the incident engraved on his seal, provoking Marius' jealousy.

The victory, however, was Marius', and he was elected consul again for 104—at the start of which year he celebrated a triumph and Jugurtha was executed—in order to take command against an alarming invasion of the Cimbri and Teutones, who had defeated a succession of Roman armies in the north, the last in disgraceful circumstances in 105. For this war, Marius used fresh troops raised by Rutilius Rufus, consul in 105, and excellently trained in commando tactics by gladiatorial instructors. With them, Marius defeated the Teutones at Aquae Sextiae (modern Aix-en-Provence, Fr.) in 102 and in 101 came to the support of the consul of 102, Quintus Lutatius Catulus, who had suffered a serious setback; together they defeated the Cimbri at the Vercellae, near modern Rovigo in the Po River valley, and the danger was over. This was the apex of Marius' success. He had been consul every year since 104, and he was elected again the year 100. With Catulus he celebrated a joint triumph, but already there was bad feeling between them. Marius claimed the whole credit for the victory; Catulus and Sulla gave very different accounts of the event in their memoirs.

Marius had always had equestrian support, not only because his origins lay in that class but also because wars were bad for trade, and Marius had brought serious wars to an end. The Roman populace liked him because he was not an aristocrat. He had the further support of his veterans, for it was in their interest to stick closely to their general. Marius perhaps did not realize the potency of their force, one that Sulla, Caesar, and Octavian employed with overpowering effect later.

Fall from power. The year 100 saw Marius fail disastrously as a politician. Saturninus was tribune for the second time, and Glaucia was praetor; given the poverty of surviving sources, it is extremely difficult to understand either their political aims or Marius' relationship to them. The three shared a common hatred of Metellus, who, as censor in 102, had tried to remove Saturninus and Glaucia from the Senate, and in 103 Saturninus had carried a bill, evidently in Marius' interest, for the settlement of veterans in Africa. Now, with the inevitability of civil disorder—for the Roman populace opposed his measures—Saturninus introduced bills for land distribution of Cimbric territory in the north to Romans living in the country, and probably to Italians, and for the settlement of veterans, evidently including allied troops, in colonies overseas. This bill may have included a powerful command for Marius to supervise the resettlement of the veterans—empowering him to give Roman citizenship to a certain number of the new settlers in each colony.

Marius had already violated the law by granting citizenship on the battlefield to two cohorts of Italians (Camertes) who fought under him against the Cimbri in 101, and conceivably Saturninus and Marius were agreeable to a program of extensive enfranchisement of Italians by means of the new colonial settlements. A breach between them occurred, possibly because Marius, in his jealous way, thought that Saturninus was stealing some of his own thunder or possibly because Saturninus' lawlessness had reached a pitch that no self-respecting consul could tolerate.

First the land and colonial bill was passed, but with blatant illegality; it required senators to take an oath within five days to observe it. After misleading statements about his own intention, Marius took the oath. Metellus refused, however, presumably because of the way in which the bill had been carried, and, forestalling condemnation in the treason court, he retired to Greece; later he was officially exiled. At the tribunician elections for 99, Saturninus was reelected together with a pretender who, already heavily discredited, claimed to be the son of Tiberius Gracchus. At the consular elections, with Glaucia as a candidate, Marcus Antonius, the orator, was elected, and Gaius Memmius, a man with an excellent popular record, was murdered. In the ensuing pandemonium the Senate passed the "last decree," calling on the consuls to save the state. Through Marius' action Saturninus and Glaucia were captured on the Capitol and imprisoned in the Senate house; then a mob stripped off the roof and stoned them to death. Although this was no responsibility of Marius, he was smeared as a man who betrayed not only his enemies but also his friends.

Later years. Rather than attend the inevitable recall of Metellus from exile, Marius went to the east in 99 and there met Mithradates VI of Pontus. He was elected to a priesthood (the augurship) but wisely withdrew his candidature for the censorship of 97. He acted as a background figure in the not fully unraveled politics of the 90s and successfully opposed an attempt in 95 to disenfranchise men to whom he had given citizenship under the terms of Saturninus' colonial bill, though the law itself had been shelved. In 92 he supported the scandalous prosecution and condemnation of his old associate Rutilius Rufus (in fact a model administrator) for alleged misgovernment of Asia.

Marius was now beginning to show his age. In an Italian rebellion (the Social War) of 90–88, he campaigned under the consul Rutilius Lupus, a soldier far his inferior. In 88, when the tribune Sulpicius Rufus proposed the transfer of the Asian command from the consul Sulla to Marius, presumably on the ground that Marius alone was sufficiently experienced to conduct such a critical war, there was violent public opposition to Sulla in Rome. Sulla went to his army in Campania and marched with it on Rome. Sulpicius' measures were rescinded, and Marius was exiled.

After a series of near catastrophes, all much embroidered in the telling, Marius escaped safely to Africa. In 87, when Sulla was fighting in Greece, disorder in Rome led to the consul Cinna being dismissed. Marius landed in Etruria, raised an army, sacked Ostia, and, by joining forces with Cinna, captured Rome; both Marius and Cinna were elected consuls for 86, Marius for the seventh time. Hideous massacre followed as Marius ordered the deaths of Marcus Antonius, Lutatius Catulus, Publicus Licinius Crassus, and other distinguished men whom he considered to have behaved with treacherous ingratitude toward him. By this time he was hardly sane, and his death, in 86, was a godsend for enemies and friends alike. If the outcome of his proscriptions was considered to be less disastrous than that of the later proscriptions of Sulla, it was only because they lasted for a shorter time.

Marius' only son died as consul fighting against Sulla in 82. His widow survived until 69 and received the unusual honour, for a woman, of a public funeral oration by her nephew Julius Caesar, who later won great popularity by restoring to the Capitol Marius' trophies, which Sulla had removed.

Marius was commemorated by the name Mariana given to Uchi Majus and Thibaris (two African settlements) and to a colony in Corsica, and by the Fossa Mariana, a canal dug by his soldiers at the mouth of the Rhône River. (J.P.V.D.B.)

BIBLIOGRAPHY. E. Badian, *Foreign Clientelae* (1958, reissued 1984), gives a general account of the period. Thomas Francis Carney, *A Biography of C. Marius* (1961), is a brief work, strongly biased in Marius' favour. Ronald Syme, *Sallust* (1964), discusses Sallust's account of the war against Jugurtha.

Marius, Simon (Latin), German SIMON MAYR, MAIR, or MAYER (b. Jan. 10, 1573, Gunzenhausen, Bavaria [Germany]—d. Dec. 26, 1624, Anspach), German astronomer who named the four largest moons of Jupiter: Io, Europa, Ganymede, and Callisto. He and Galileo both claimed to have discovered them, about 1610, and it is likely both did so independently. A dispute over priority resulted in unwarranted obloquy for Marius.

Marius studied briefly with Tycho Brahe and later became one of the first astronomers to use a telescope. He was the first to publish, in 1611, the telescopic observation of the great spiral nebula in Andromeda, describing the sight as "like a candle seen at night through a horn" (referring to horn lanterns, then common). He was also among the first to observe sunspots.

Marius Servius Honoratus (Latin grammarian): *see* Servius.

Marivaux, Pierre (Carlet de Chamblain de) (b. Feb. 4, 1688, Paris, Fr.—d. Feb. 12, 1763, Paris), French dramatist, novelist, and journalist whose comedies are, after those of Molière, the most frequently performed in today's French theatre.

His wealthy, aristocratic family moved to Limoges, where his father practiced law, the same profession for which the young Marivaux trained. Most interested in the drama of the courts, at 20 he wrote his first play, *Le Père prudent et équitable, ou Crispin l'heureux fourbe* ("The Prudent and Equitable Father"). Such early writings showed promise, and by

Marivaux, detail of an oil painting by L.M. Van Loo, 1753; in the Comédie-Française, Paris
Cliche Musees Nationaux

1710 he had joined Parisian salon society, whose atmosphere and conversational manners he absorbed for his occasional journalistic writings. He contributed *Réflexions . . .* on the various social classes to the *Nouveau Mercure* (1717–19) and modeled his own periodical, *Le Spectateur Français* (1720–24), after Joseph Addison's *The Spectator.*

The loss of his fortune in 1720, followed a few years later by the death of his young wife, caused Marivaux to take his literary career more seriously. He was drawn into several fashionable artistic salons and received a pension from Mme de Pompadour. He became a close associate of the *philosophes* Bernard de Fontenelle and Montesquieu and of the critic and playwright La Motte.

Marivaux's first plays were written for the Comédie-Française, among them the five-act verse tragedy *Annibal* (1727). But the Italian Theatre of Lelio, sponsored in Paris by the regent Philippe d'Orleans, attracted him far more. The major players Thomassin and Silvia of this commedia dell'arte troupe became Marivaux's stock lovers: Harlequin, or the valet, and the ingenue. *Arlequin poli par l'amour* (1723; "Harlequin Brightened by Love") and *Le Jeu de l'amour et du hasard* (1730; *The Game of Love and Chance*) display typical characteristics of his love comedies: romantic settings, an acute sense of nuance and the finer shades of feeling, and deft and witty wordplay. This verbal preciousness is still known as *marivaudage* and reflects the sensitivity and sophistication of the era. Marivaux also made notable advances in realism; his servants are given real feelings, and the social milieu is depicted precisely. Among his 30-odd plays are the satires *L'Île des esclaves* (1725; "Isle of Slaves") and *L'Île de la raison* (1727; "Isle of Reason"), which mock European society after the manner of *Gulliver's Travels*. *La Nouvelle colonie* (1729; "The New Colony") treats equality between the sexes, while *L'École des mères* (1724; "School for Mothers") studies mother-daughter rapport.

Marivaux's human psychology is best revealed in his romance novels, both unfinished. *La Vie de Marianne* (1731–41), which preceded Samuel Richardson's *Pamela* (1740), anticipates the novel of sensibility in its glorification of a woman's feelings and intuition. *Le Paysan parvenu* (1734–35; "The Fortunate Peasant") is the story of a handsome, opportunistic young peasant who uses his attractiveness to older women to advance in the world. Both works concern struggles to arrive in society and reflect the author's rejection of authority and religious orthodoxy in favour of simple morality and naturalness. His attitude won him the whole-hearted admiration of Jean-Jacques Rousseau. Though Marivaux was elected to the French Academy in 1743 and became its director in 1759, he was not fully appreciated during his lifetime. He died quite impoverished and remained without real fame until his work was reappraised by the critic Charles-Augustin Sainte-Beuve in the 19th century. Marivaux has since been regarded as an important link between the Age of Reason and the Age of Romanticism.

Marj, Al- (Arabic: "The Meadows"), formerly BARCE, or BARCA, town, northeastern Libya, on Al-Marj plain at the western edge of the Akhḍar Mountains, near the Mediterranean coast. Site of the 6th-century-BC Greek colony of Barce, it was taken by the Arabs in about AD 642. The present town grew around a Turkish fort built in 1842 and now restored. The Italians developed the town (1913–41) as an administrative and market centre and hill resort; it was the site of a Bedouin concentration camp (1930). Destroyed by earthquake in 1963, it was rebuilt on firm ground 3 miles (5 km) distant. The new town is divided into districts, each with housing, shops, a dispensary, a cinema, and public gardens. There are also a large general hospital and a maternity and child health centre. Al-Marj is the commerical centre for the surrounding plain, which has 16 inches (400 mm) of rain per year and produces cereals (barley and wheat), fruits, and vegetables. It is connected by a road with Banghāzī, Tūkrah, and Zāwiyat al-Bayḍā'. The Marzotti Livestock Centre promotes the improvement of local herds. Pop. (latest est.) 15,063.

Marj ʿUyūn, also spelled MARJAYOUN, MERDJAYOUNE, MERJAYUN, or MERJ ʿUYŪN, town, southern Lebanon, lying on a fertile plain east of Al-Līṭānī River, at an elevation of 2,500 feet (760 m) above sea level. Marj ʿUyūn is an agricultural market centre serving a tobacco-, cereal-, grape-, and orange-growing region. The nearby town of Ḥāṣbayyā contains the principal sanctuary of the Druze, who practice a form of Islām. Pop. (1998 est.) 14,900.

marjoram, also called SWEET MARJORAM (species *Majorana hortensis*), perennial herb of the mint family (Lamiaceae, or Labiatae) or its fresh or dried leaves and flowering tops, used to flavour many foods. Its taste is warm, aromatic, slightly sharp, and bitterish. A herb of many culinary uses, marjoram is particularly appreciated for the taste it lends to sausages, meats, poultry, stuffings, fish, stews, eggs, vegetables, and salads. Native to the Mediterranean region and western Asia, marjoram is also cultivated as an annual in northerly climates where winter temperatures kill the plant. Marjoram contains about 2 percent essential oil, the principal components of which are terpinene and terpineol.

Various other aromatic herbs or undershrubs of the genera *Origanum* and *Majorana* of the Lamiaceae family are called marjoram. Pot marjoram, *Majorana onites,* is also cultivated for its aromatic leaves and is used to flavour food. Wild marjoram, *Origanum vulgare,* is a perennial herb native to Europe and Asia that is commonly found in England and has been naturalized in the United States.

mark, former German monetary unit. In the 19th century the mark was a common small coin in the German states, but its value varied between states. In 1873, soon after the creation of the German Empire, the gold mark, equal to 100 pfennigs, was adopted as the standard of value and the money of account for the empire. In 1948 the deutsche mark (DM; "German mark") was introduced in West Germany, and in 1990 it became the currency of reunified Germany. In 2002, however, the DM ceased to be legal currency after the euro, the monetary unit of the European Union, became the country's sole currency.

The early history of the term can be traced back at least to the 11th century, when the mark was mentioned in Germany as a unit of weight (approximately eight ounces) most commonly used for gold and silver. As a unit of account, it was employed during the Middle Ages for payment of large sums; the small silver coins of varying size and quality were melted and cast into lumps on which were stamped the weight and purity of the silver. The latter were called Usualmark.

Mark (THE EVANGELIST), SAINT (fl. 1st century AD; b. Jerusalem?—d. traditionally Alexandria, Egypt; Western feast day April 25, Eastern feast day September 23), traditional author of the second Synoptic Gospel. Data on his life found in the New Testament are fragmentary, and most of their historicity has been questioned by critical investigation. The only unquestionably reliable information is in Philemon 24, where a certain Mark is mentioned as one of St. Paul's fellow workers who sends greetings from Rome to the Christians of Colossae (near modern Denizli, Tur.), but the identity of this person is not indicated. That Mark was St. Barnabas' cousin in Colossians 4:10 may also be authentic.

"St. Mark," fresco by the School of Ghirlandajo, late 15th century; in Santa Maria Novella, Florence
Alinari—Art Resource/EB Inc.

Except for being referred to as John in Acts 12:25, 13:5; 13, and 15:37, elsewhere in the New Testament he is consistently called by his Latin surname Mark. According to Acts, his mother's house in Jerusalem was a centre of Christian life (12:12), and he accompanied Barnabas and Paul to Antioch (12:25), now Antakya, Tur., where he became their assistant on a mission journey (13:5). When they arrived at Perga (near modern İhsaniye, Tur.), Mark left them and returned to Jerusalem (13:13). Mark's leaving caused Barnabas and Paul to separate, for Paul declined Barnabas' insistence on giving Mark another chance (15:37–39). Subsequently, Mark sailed to Cyprus with Barnabas, never to be mentioned again in Acts. The dependability of the Acts account is questionable, for its author is particularly interested in explaining the breach between Paul and Barnabas, probably introducing Mark for this reason. In this, he contradicts Paul's account of their breach in Galatians 2:11–14.

In 2 Timothy 4:11, Paul requests St. Timothy to bring Mark, "for he is very useful in serving me," but this is believed to be falsely deduced from Acts and Colossians. A close relationship between Mark and St. Peter is suggested by the greetings from "my son Mark" in 1 Peter 5:13; furthermore, the Apostolic Father Papias of Hierapolis says that Mark's treatise (presumably the Gospel) was based on Peter's teaching about Jesus. Later tradition assumes that Mark was one of the 72 disciples appointed by Jesus (Luke 10:1) and identifies him with the young man fleeing naked at Jesus' arrest (Mark 14:51–52). The Egyptian church claims Mark as its founder, and, from the 4th century AD, the see of Alexandria has been called *cathedra Marci* ("the chair of Mark"). Other places attributing their origin to Mark are the Italian cities of Aquileia and Venice, of which he is the patron saint. His symbol is the lion.

Mark, SAINT, Latin MARCUS (b. Rome [Italy]—d. Oct. 7, 336, Rome; feast day October 7), pope from Jan. 18 (?) to Oct. 7, 336. He is credited with having given the bishops of Ostia the right to consecrate new popes. He may have been the founder of the present Church of San Marco, Rome, and also of another that is situated over the catacomb of Balbina on the Via Ardeatina.

Mark THE HERMIT, Latin MARCUS EREMITA (d. after 430), theological polemicist and author of works on Christian asceticism notable for their psychological insight and for their influence on later monastic history and literature. To some scholars, elements of his doctrine suggest aspects of 16th-century Reformation theology.

Probably an abbot of a monastery in Ancyra (modern Ankara, Tur.), Mark later undertook the solitary life in the Syrian and Palestinian wilderness. Except for references to his scholarly and spiritual acumen by theological writers of the 7th and 8th centuries, nothing else is known of his life. With the publication in 1891 of a Jerusalem manuscript of his theological polemic *Contra Nestorianos* ("Against the Nestorians"), written about 430, Mark's importance in 5th-century doctrinal controversies and his specific authorship of other writings were finally recognized. Resembling the Christological doctrine of St. Cyril of Alexandria, spokesman for 5th-century orthodoxy, *Contra Nestorianos* refutes the heretical Nestorian doctrine holding that Jesus was human and the Christ divine but denying that both natures were united in the one Person of Jesus Christ. Arguing principally from the Scriptures and from the primitive Christian baptismal creed, Mark declares that only if Christ's humanity were indivisibly united, although not combined, with the divine Logos (Greek: "Word") could the salvation of humanity have been effected, because the atoning deeds of a mere mortal could not have achieved this end.

The richest source for Mark's ascetical and doctrinal theology consists of his treatise *De Baptismo* ("On Baptism"). Rejecting other traditional explanations for personal sin, Mark asserts that following baptism every sin is the result of human choice. Christ's atonement, by virtue of its reconciliation of alienated man to God, restores perfect freedom of the will to the baptized. Good works, however, are attributable to God's grace and not to human effort. Moreover, human mortality, Mark observes, derives from Adam's sin and consequent condemnation to death. The Christian has to die, however, in order to be fulfilled, because a mortal nature is not capable of achieving unchanging perfection.

In several tracts, including *De Baptismo,* Mark disputes against the Messalians, an unorthodox mystical sect advocating ceaseless prayer to expel the demon present in all. He repudiates their equation of ascetic contemplation with salvation, arguing that one cannot be the author of his own redemption. The treatise *De lege spirituali* ("On the Spiritual Law"), delineating a monastic program, describes Christian perfection as knowledge of the Divine Presence and Providence, which begins with man knowing his limited self. Asceticism, the purpose of which is simply to dispose one to this state of awareness, negates itself if egocentrism persists. The essence of sin is to forget God.

Mark's general theological position is consonant with the doctrine of St. John Chrysostom, the 4th-century Byzantine patriarch and bulwark of orthodoxy. More oriented toward the practical rather than the speculative, Mark felt it was more important to keep the commandments of Christ than to intellectualize the mysteries of God. Mark's works are contained in *Patrologia Graeca,* ed. J.-P. Migne (1857–66).

Mark, The Gospel According to, also called THE HOLY GOSPEL OF JESUS CHRIST ACCORDING TO ST. MARK, second of the four New Testament Gospels (narratives recounting the life and death of Jesus Christ), and, with Matthew and Luke, one of the three Synoptic Gospels (*i.e.,* those presenting a common view). It is attributed to John Mark (Acts 12:12; 15:37), an associate of Paul and a disciple of Peter, whose teachings the Gospel may reflect. It is the shortest and the earliest of the four Gospels, presumably written during the decade preceding the destruction of Jerusalem in AD 70. Most scholars agree that it was used by Matthew and Luke in composing their accounts; more than 90 percent of the content of Mark's Gospel appears in Matthew's, and more than 50 percent in the Gospel of Luke. Although the text lacks literary polish, it is simple and direct; and, as the earliest Gospel, it is the primary source of information about the ministry of Jesus.

Mark's explanations of Jewish customs and his translations of Aramaic expressions suggest that he was writing for Gentile converts, probably especially for those converts living in Rome. After an introduction (1:1–13), the Gospel describes Jesus' ministry in and around Galilee (1:14–8:26); his journey to Jerusalem (11–13); the Passion (14–15); and the Resurrection (16). The final passage in Mark (16:9–20) is omitted in some manuscripts, including the two oldest, and a shorter passage is substituted in others. Many scholars believe that these last verses were not written by Mark, at least not at the same time as the balance of the Gospel, but were added later to account for the Resurrection. Mark's Gospel stresses the deeds, strength, and determination of Jesus in overcoming evil forces and defying the power of imperial Rome. Mark also emphasizes the Passion, predicting it as early as chapter 8 and devoting the final third of his Gospel (11–16) to the last week of Jesus' life.

One of the most striking elements in the Gospel is Mark's characterization of Jesus as reluctant to reveal himself as the Messiah. Jesus refers to himself only as the Son of Man, and while tacitly acknowledging Peter's declaration that Jesus is the Christ, he nevertheless cautions his followers not to tell anyone about him.

Consult
the
INDEX
first

mark system, penal method developed about 1840 by Alexander Maconochie at the English penal colony of Norfolk Island (located east of Australia). Instead of serving fixed sentences, prisoners there were held until they had earned a number of marks, or credits, fixed in proportion to the seriousness of their offenses. A prisoner became eligible for release when he had obtained the required number of credits, which were accumulated for good conduct, hard work, and study and could be denied or subtracted for indolence or misbehaviour. The mark system symbolized the decline of the "let the punishment fit the crime" theory of correction and presaged the use of indeterminate sentences, individualized treatment, and parole. Above all, it emphasized training and performance as the chief mechanisms of reformation.

Markelius, Sven (Gottfrid) (b. Oct. 25, 1889, Stockholm, Swed.—d. Feb. 27, 1972), eminent Swedish architect who introduced the International Style into Sweden in the 1920s.

Markelius studied at the Institute of Technology and the Academy of Fine Arts in Stockholm and opened his own architectural office in Stockholm in 1915. From the early years of his practice, Markelius won numerous important design competitions throughout Sweden. His prize-winning design for a

Markelius, 1965

concert-hall complex at Hälsingborg (1925) is perhaps his major work; its spare, rectilinear forms, with their white walls and broad glazing, reflect the bold anonymity that was coming to characterize academic European design. Among his more experimental works is the so-called Collective House (1925) in Stockholm, which provided communal kitchens, restaurants, nurseries, and other domestic facilities to accommodate families in which both parents worked outside the home.

Markelius achieved international recognition with his design for the Swedish Pavilion at the New York World's Fair in 1939. His own home in Kevinge, a low-roofed, sprawling villa among rocks and trees, became a prototype for informal, "site-conscious" houses throughout the world. As director of planning for the city of Stockholm (1938–54) he supervised the design of Vallingby, a satellite community established in 1953.

Marken, island and *gemeente* (commune), Noordholland *provincie,* west-central Netherlands, within the IJsselmeer. Lying some 11 miles (17 km) northeast of Amsterdam, Marken was separated from the mainland in the 13th century during the formation of the Zuiderzee. The 2-mile- (3-kilometre-) long island has an area of 1 square mile (2.5 square km) and lies about 1.5 miles (2.5 km) offshore. Since 1957 it has been connected to the mainland by a causeway. Before the Zuiderzee was made into the IJsselmeer by the 19-mile (30-kilometre) Afsluitdijk, the inhabitants of Marken and its neighbouring island of Volendam made their living from eel fishing. Their houses were grouped on small mounds and built on piles to protect against high tides. The island has retained much of the atmosphere of past days. During tourist season the residents enhance this effect by dressing in traditional regional costumes. Tourism is now an important economic factor. Pop. (1989 est.) 2,055.

marker bed, also called KEY BED, a bed of rock strata that are readily distinguishable by reason of physical characteristics and are traceable over large horizontal distances. Stratigraphic examples include coal beds and beds of volcanic ash. The term marker bed is also applied to sedimentary strata that provide distinctive seismic reflections.

market, a means by which the exchange of goods and services takes place as a result of buyers and sellers being in contact with each other, either directly or through mediating agents or institutions. The term originally denoted and still sometimes denotes a particular place where products are bought and sold, as in an open-air market. In a wider sense a market can be any arena, however abstracted from physical actuality, in which buyers and sellers can deal with each other; transactions may take place on a global scale. The commodities markets in London or in the United States, for example, are international markets in which dealers from all over the world buy and sell through telephone and telex links as well as by direct contact. One may also talk about financial markets because shares, securities, government bonds, and currencies change hands through organized stock markets or foreign exchange markets.

A brief treatment of markets follows. For full treatment, *see* MACROPAEDIA: Markets.

In free markets, prices are determined by the interaction of demand and supply. Classical economists, relying on the virtues of laissez-faire, developed the theory of perfect competition. The market environment is assumed to be one in which the commodity traded is homogeneous, there is a large number of buyers and sellers, buyers and sellers are in touch with each other, and the commodity is easily transferable. Under these conditions each producer accounts for a tiny proportion of the total output of the product or commodity. Consequently, on his own he is unable to influence the price by expanding or contracting output. Similarly, each buyer accounts for only a small part of the total exchange in the market and thus cannot influence price by buying more or less. The price, therefore, is given, and the supplier can sell as much as he can produce—his increase in production does not lead to a reduction in price since his total output is a small portion of the total. Although no real markets match the exact conditions of this model, a number approximate it closely. The markets for agricultural commodities are the classic example. These goods are produced under competitive conditions by a large number of widely distributed small producers, who generally have to sell their entire offering regardless of the price level. By and large the total output of such goods does not vary in the short term with changes in price (demand). Supply, on the other hand, is subject to the vagaries of the weather, and greater fluctuations in price occur in response to changes in supply.

Since the 1930s, increased attention has been given to imperfect competition, a model that more nearly matches the actual, world markets for manufactured goods. In imperfect competition the number of sellers, buyers, or both may be limited, rival products are typically differentiated (by design, quality, brand names, etc.), and entry into the market by new producers is limited by various factors. In this type of market, supply is usually very responsive to demand in the short term; prices, on the other hand, tend to respond slowly and may not come down in response to a decline in demand, while they may rise more freely if demand permits. Many markets have become more imperfectly competitive in recent decades owing to the increasingly active role of government in influencing markets through fiscal and monetary policies such as tax incentives to encourage new investment in preferred industries or in preferred locations.

Market Harborough, market and manufacturing town, Harborough district, county of Leicestershire, Eng., on the River Welland. General and cattle markets for a wide agricultural area have been held there since 1203. Several timbered buildings survive, notably Robert Smythe's grammar school (1614) raised on wooden pillars above street level. Industries include rubber, textiles, and light engineering. The town is a noted fox-hunting centre. Pop. (1981) 15,966.

market research, study of the requirements of various markets, the acceptability of products, and methods of developing or exploiting new markets. A variety of techniques is employed, depending on the purpose of the research: salesmen's expectations may be used as a guide to future demand for a product; past sales may be projected forward; surveys may be made of consumer attitudes and product preferences, either generally or in particular regions; and new or altered products may be introduced experimentally into designated test-market areas.

Formal market research dates back to the 1920s in Germany and the 1930s in Sweden and France. After World War II, American firms probably led in the use and refinement of market-research techniques, which spread throughout much of western Europe and Japan. Whereas the information obtained through market research in industrialized economies is fairly specific, relating to particular products or individual firms, in less-developed countries more general information is sought.

By the 1980s market research was being used in Communist countries in planning the production of consumer goods, particularly as the variety of these goods increased. The Soviet Union had established a Market Research Institute in 1965 to study long-term trends in consumer interests and expenditures.

market socialism, also called LIBERAL SOCIALISM, economic system representing a compromise between socialist planning and free enterprise, in which enterprises are publicly owned but production and consumption are guided by market forces rather than by government planning. A form of market socialism was adopted in Yugoslavia in the 1960s in distinction to the centrally planned socialism of the Soviet Union. A similar development occurred in Hungary during the late 1960s and early 1970s.

Consult the INDEX *first*

marketing, the sum of activities involved in directing the flow of goods and services from producers to consumers.

A brief treatment of marketing follows. For full treatment, *see* MACROPAEDIA: Marketing and Merchandising.

In advanced industrial economies, marketing considerations play a major role in establishing corporate policies. Where once corporate marketing departments were primarily concerned with increasing sales through advertising and other promotional techniques, they now typically concern themselves with credit policies, product development, customer support, personal sales, distribution, and corporate communications.

Consumer goods, those whose final sale is to individual users, are sold through a variety of channels. Retail stores, which may be chain stores (with many branches under a single owner or franchiser), offer great economies of scale that can translate into lower prices and a wider variety of products offered. Direct marketing; which is a form of retailing, operates through catalogs and broadcast advertisements. Wholesalers sell merchandise in large quantities to retail stores or other users at prices below the final selling price. Manufacturers may wholesale their own goods, or they may rely on agents, brokers, or regional distributors.

Goods sold for the purpose of manufacturing other goods or providing services are known as industrial products. They include raw materials such as ores and crude oil, partly processed goods such as textiles, and capital equipment such as computers and machinery. Such sales are frequently consummated at high levels of corporate management.

Marketers may make psychological and demographic studies of a potential market for goods, may experiment with various marketing approaches, and may conduct informal interviews with target audiences. Marketing may be used to increase sales of an existing product (by suggesting new uses for it or redefining its image). New products may be marketed in many ways—*e.g.*, to appeal to a user's status or vanity or to be seen as a solid bargain. Products may be aimed at audiences of a particular age or income level. Credit arrangements and guarantees are frequently an important part of marketing.

marketing board, organization set up by a government to regulate the buying and selling of a certain commodity within a specified area. An example is the former Cocoa Marketing Board of Nigeria (which, after 1977, functioned as the Nigerian Cocoa Board and controlled marketing of tea and coffee, as well). The powers of marketing boards range from advisory and promotional services to full control over output and sales.

The simplest type of board is one established to carry out market research, promote sales, and furnish information; it is usually financed by a fee levied on all sales of the products concerned. Examples of this type include the Tea Propaganda Board of Sri Lanka and the Tobacco Export Promotion Council of Zimbabwe. Other boards are empowered to regulate terms and conditions of sale, usually by establishing packing standards and quality analysis.

The prime motive in the establishment of most marketing boards is to stabilize producer prices, particularly in the case of products designed primarily for those export markets in which price fluctuations are most violent. Marketing boards are also used for domestically consumed products whose perishability requires that outlets be set up in advance.

The boards may stabilize and raise average prices through the manipulation of commodity flows, with the objective of maintaining reasonably high levels of demand in all markets at all times. This approach is characteristic of marketing programs for fruits, vegetables, and nuts in California.

In economies in which this approach is administratively difficult, other means of stabilization have been tried. In the Middle East and Latin America, for example, marketing boards and branches of public banks or development institutes have been furnished with capital in order to purchase basic grains, to maintain buffer stocks, and to sell on open markets alongside other traders. The objective, in these cases, has been to increase incentives to producers by buying to maintain a minimum price level and to protect low-income consumers by selling from accumulated stocks when prices are rising.

Where products are produced primarily for export, the boards may seek protection from fluctuating world prices. In one approach, practiced widely in West Africa, a reserve fund is accumulated when export prices are high and is drawn upon to maintain prices to farmers when they are low. In countries in which this type of marketing board operates, the board is granted a monopoly of all export sales, and domestic purchases are made through licensed agents and the board's own buying stations. *Compare* cartel.

Markham, Beryl, *née* CLUTTERBUCK (b. Oct. 26, 1902, Leicester, Leicestershire, Eng.—d. Aug. 3, 1986, Nairobi, Kenya), professional pilot, horse trainer and breeder, writer, and adventurer, best-known for her memoir *West with the Night* (1942; reissued 1983).

At age four Markham went with her father to British East Africa, where she received a spotty education while hunting with African tribesmen and learning to speak Swahili and several African dialects. She remained in Kenya alone when her father's fortune was lost and he left for Peru. At age 18 she became the first woman in Africa to receive a race-horse-trainer's license. While in her late 20s, Markham learned to fly and became a commercial pilot, doing free-lance transporting of goods, people, and mail. She made a historic solo flight (1936) across the North Atlantic from England to Cape Breton Island, Canada.

Beryl Markham, 1937
UPI/Bettmann Newsphotos

In 1942 she wrote *West with the Night* (possibly with the help of others), and, her reputation having preceded her, she was invited to Hollywood. In addition to occasionally writing short stories, Markham trained six Kenya Derby winners. Though *West with the Night* had not been a great success when it was published, popular interest in colonial Africa and the complex relationships among the white settlers there—including Isak Dinesen, Bror Blixen, and Denys Finch Hatton—rekindled interest in the period during the late 20th century.

Markham, Edwin, original name CHARLES EDWARD ANSON MARKHAM (b. April 23, 1852, Oregon City, Ore., U.S.—d. March 7, 1940, New York City), American poet and lecturer, best-known for his poem of social protest, "The Man with the Hoe."

The youngest son of pioneer parents, Markham grew up on an isolated valley ranch in the Suisun hills in central California. After graduation from college, he became first a teacher and then a school administrator. In 1899 he gained national fame with the publication in the *San Francisco Examiner* of "The Man with the Hoe." Inspired by Jean-François Millet's painting, Markham made the French peasant the symbol of the exploited classes throughout the world. Its success enabled Markham to devote himself to writing and lecturing—in which he concerned himself with social and industrial, as well as poetic, problems.

Edwin Markham, 1907
By courtesy of the Library of Congress, Washington, D.C.

His first book of verse, *The Man with the Hoe and Other Poems* (1899), was followed in 1901 by *Lincoln and Other Poems*, the dignified title piece of which found almost as much favour as "The Man with the Hoe." Succeeding volumes—*Shoes of Happiness* (1915),

Gates of Paradise (1920), *New Poems: Eighty Songs at Eighty* (1932), and *The Star of Araby* (1937)—have the commanding rhetoric but lack the passion of the early works.

Markham River, river in eastern Papua New Guinea. The swift but shallow and unnavigable stream rises on the Finisterre Range and receives the Erap River, coursing south from the Saruwaged Range, and the Watut River, flowing north from the Bulolo Valley. Flowing southeast through the great Central Depression, the Markham traces a 110-mile (180-kilometre) course to the Huon Gulf, Solomon Sea, 3 miles (5 km) south of Lae. Its wide, sparsely populated valley holds a considerable amount of level agricultural land in the lower reaches. Once an area of cocoa plantations, it has been developed for peanut (groundnut) cultivation and cattle farming. Two roads ascend the valley; one leads to the Bulolo Valley, the other to the central highlands.

markhor (*Capra falconeri*), large wild goat, family Bovidae (order Artiodactyla), formerly found throughout the mountains from Kashmir and Turkestan to Afghanistan but now greatly reduced in population and range. Several subspecies are considered endangered. The markhor stands about 102 cm (40 inches) at the shoulder and has long, corkscrew-shaped horns. Its coat is reddish brown in summer and long, gray, and silky in winter. The male has a long, heavy fringe on its throat and chest.

Markhor (*Capra falconeri*)
Emil Muench—Ostman Agency

Marko KRALJEVIĆ (b. *c.* 1335—d. May 17, 1395, Rovine, Serbia), king of Serbia from 1371 to 1395 and a hero in the literature and traditions of the South Slavic peoples.

Marko Kraljević ("Mark, the King's Son") was a member of the powerful Macedonian family allied to that of Balšić, which ruled in northern Albania and along the Adriatic. When his father, King Vukašin, was slain in battle with the Turks in 1371, Marko succeeded him as a vassal to the sultan. He is known to have completed a monastery at Sušica, near Skopje, and to have died fighting at the Battle of Rovine (1395) during a war between the Turks and the Walachian prince Mircea the Old, but otherwise his life is sparsely documented. More colourful details have been preserved in Romanian, Bulgarian, and Albanian folk songs as well as in Serbian ballads and epic poetry. Joyous, just, strong, incredibly brave, and chivalrous to a fault, Marko is portrayed as an implacable foe of the Turks and a prodigious drinker of wine.

Markov, Andrey Andreyevich (b. June 14, 1856, Ryazan, Russia—d. July 20, 1922, Petrograd [now St. Petersburg]), Russian mathematician who helped to develop the theory of stochastic processes, especially those called Markov chains. Based on the study of the probability of mutually dependent events, his work has been developed and widely applied to the biological and social sciences.

Markov taught at St. Petersburg University from 1886 and became a member of the Russian Academy of Sciences in 1896. His early work was devoted to number theory and analysis, mainly concerning continued fractions, the limits of integrals, the approximation theory, and the convergence of series. After 1900 he was chiefly occupied with probability theory. Under fairly general assumptions, he proved the central limit theorem, which states that the sum of a large number of independent random variables approximates the asymptotically normal, or Gaussian, distribution. He then turned to the study of mutually dependent variables, introducing the important notion of chained events. Markov extended several classical results concerning independent events to certain types of chains.

Markov process, sequence of possibly dependent random variables ($x_1, x_2, x_3, \ldots$)—identified by increasing values of a parameter, commonly time—with the property that any prediction of the value of x_n, knowing $x_1, x_2, \ldots, x_{n-1}$, may be based on x_{n-1} alone. That is, the future value of the variable depends only upon the present value and not on the sequence of past values.

These sequences are named for A.A. Markov, who was the first to study them systematically. Sometimes the term Markov process is restricted to sequences in which the random variables can assume continuous values, and analogous sequences of discrete-valued variables are called Markov chains. *See also* stochastic process.

Markova, Dame Alicia, original name LILIAN ALICIA MARKS (b. Dec. 1, 1910, London), English ballerina noted for the ethereal lightness and poetic delicacy of her dancing.

Markova studied with Serafima Astafieva and Enrico Cecchetti and, after her debut at 14 with the Diaghilev Ballet, was soon dancing leading roles. In 1931 she joined the Vic-Wells Ballet and was both its first prima ballerina (1933–35) and the first English dancer to dance the lead in *Giselle* and the full-length *Swan Lake.* Markova appeared as a ballerina of Ballet Rambert, Ballet Russe de Monte-Carlo, and Ballet Theatre and as guest artist with the Metropolitan Opera. With Anton Dolin she headed the Markova-Dolin Ballet (1935–38) and London's Festival Ballet (1949–52). In addition to *Giselle,* her favourite role, and *Swan Lake,* she excelled in *Les Sylphides,* as Taglioni (with whom she has been compared) in the Dolin *Pas de quatre,* and as the Sugar Plum Fairy in *The Nutcracker.* A versatile artist, she excelled not only in the classics but also in early jazz ballets, in Massine's symphonic *Rouge et Noir* (1939), as a Gypsy in *Aleko* (1942), as Juliet in Antony Tudor's *Romeo and Juliet* (1943), and in Ruth Page's *Vilea* (1953). In 1963 she retired from the stage, was appointed director of the Metropolitan Ballet in New York City (a post she held until 1969), and was created Dame of the British Empire. Dame Alicia, in retirement as a dancer, taught, coached, lectured, and occasionally staged traditional ballets for various companies.

Alicia Markova as Juliet with Hugh Laing as Romeo in *Romeo and Juliet*, Ballet Theatre, 1944
Fred Fehl

Marković, Svetozar (b. Sept. 21 [Sept. 9, Old Style], 1846, Jagodina, Serbia, Ottoman Empire [now in Yugoslavia]—d. March 10, 1875, Trieste, Austro-Hungarian Empire [now in Italy]), political writer who was largely responsible for introducing socialism into Serbia. He was a skilled popularizer of political ideas, a courageous fighter, and a strong influence on the realist trend in Serbian literature.

Marković studied in Belgrade, in St. Petersburg, and in Zürich, where he first was influenced by Marxism. A member of the Socialist International, he edited the first Serbian socialist newspaper, *Radnik* ("The Worker"; founded 1871), which was more concerned with economics than with politics. When the Serbian government took repressive measures, Marković went into exile briefly. He returned to edit the newspaper *Javnost* ("Public Opinion"; 1873), which placed greater emphasis on politics than on economics, and then *Glas Javnosti* ("The Voice of Public Opinion"; 1874). After a nine-month term of imprisonment for his writings, he edited the newspaper *Oslobodjenje* ("Liberation") until poor health forced his retirement.

Marković had a marked influence on the literary and political development of Serbia. His realistic writings (eight volumes) were published between 1891 and 1912 and were reissued by the Tito government of Yugoslavia.

Markovnikov, Vladimir Vasilyevich (b. Dec. 22, 1838, Nizhny Novgorod, Russia—d. February 1904, Moscow), Russian organic chemist who contributed to structural theory and to the understanding of the ionic addition (Markovnikov addition) of hydrogen halides to the carbon-carbon double bond of alkenes.

After studying at the universities of Kazan and St. Petersburg, Markovnikov taught at the universities of Kazan, Odessa, and Moscow (1873–98). Through his experiments he showed that butyric and isobutyric acids have the same chemical formula but different structures; *i.e.,* they are isomers. In 1869, while developing his theory of the mutual influence of atoms in chemical compounds, he noted that when hydrogen halides are added to an alkene, the hydrogen attaches to the carbon with more hydrogens already attached, whereas the halogen attaches to the carbon with fewer hydrogens attached. Why hydrogen bromide exhibited both Markovnikov as well as reversed-order, or anti-Markovnikov, addition, however, was not understood until Morris Selig Kharasch offered an explanation in 1933.

Markovnikov rule, in organic chemistry, a generalization, formulated by Vladimir Vasilyevich Markovnikov in 1869, stating that in addition reactions to unsymmetrical alkenes, the electron-rich component of the reagent adds to the carbon atom with fewer hydrogen atoms bonded to it, while the electron-deficient component adds to the carbon atom with more hydrogen atoms bonded to it. Thus, hydrogen chloride (HCl) adds to propylene ($CH_3CH=CH_2$) to produce 2-chloropropane ($CH_3CHClCH_3$) rather than the isomeric 1-chloropropane ($CH_3CH_2CH_2Cl$). The rule is useful in predicting the molecular structures of products of addition reactions.

Markowitz, Harry M. (b. Aug. 24, 1927, Chicago, Ill., U.S.), American finance and economics educator, cowinner (with Merton H. Miller and William F. Sharpe) of the 1990 Nobel Memorial Prize in Economic Science for theories on evaluating stock-market risk and reward and on valuing corporate stocks and bonds.

Markowitz studied at the University of

Chicago (Bachelor of Philosophy, 1947; M.A., 1950, Ph.D., 1954) and then was on the research staff of Rand Corporation, Santa Monica, Calif. (1952–60, 1961–63), where he met Sharpe. He then held various positions with Consolidated Analysis Centers, Inc., Santa Monica (1963–68), the University of California at Los Angeles (1968–69), Arbitrage Management Company, New York City (1969–72), and IBM's T.J. Watson Research Center, Yorktown Hills, N.Y. (1974–83) before becoming a professor of finance at Baruch College of the City University of New York (from 1982).

The research that earned Markowitz the Nobel Prize involved his "portfolio theory," which sought to prove that a diversified, or "optimal," portfolio—that is, one that mixes assets so as to maximize return and minimize risk—could be practical. His techniques for measuring risk associated with various assets and his techniques for mixing assets became routine investment methods. He also developed a computer language called Simscript, used to write economic-analysis programs.

Marks and Spencer Group PLC, nickname MARKS AND SPARKS, major British purveyor of food and clothing. It is headquartered in London.

Marks & Spencer started in 1884 as a stall in an open market in Leeds, Yorkshire. Then known as Marks' Penny Bazaar, it was the household goods, haberdashery, toy, and sheet-music business of Michael Marks, a Jewish refugee from Poland. His sign read, "Don't ask the price—it's a penny." In 1894 he took Thomas Spencer as a business partner. Marks' son Simon transformed the business from a number of outdoor stalls in various markets in northern England to a number of indoor shops. It purchased Brooks Brothers, the oldest U.S. clothing retailer, in 1988 but sold that division in 2001. By this time the company operated more than 300 retail outlets in the United Kingdom, with an additional 150 stores in 27 other countries.

Marl, city, North Rhine–Westphalia *Land* (state), western Germany, situated in the Ruhr industrial district, just northwest of Recklinghausen. First mentioned about 800 as a relatively large settlement, the Marl district was sold to the archbishops of Cologne about 1000 and thereafter was part of the "Vest Recklinghausen" of the prince-electors. After 1802 it passed to the dukes of Arenberg, who held it as a fief of Prussia from 1815. It grew with the development of coal and iron-ore mining in the late 19th century, and the town was chartered in 1936. Chemical factories supplement its mining economy. Pop. (1998 est.) 93,642.

marl, earthy mixture of fine-grained minerals. The term is applied to a great variety of sediments and rocks with a considerable range of composition. Calcareous marls grade into clays, by diminution in the amount of lime, and into clayey limestones. Greensand marls contain the green, potash-rich mica mineral glauconite; widely distributed along the Atlantic coast in the United States and Europe, they are used as water softeners.

Both marine and freshwater marls most commonly are of a white, gray, or brownish colour; red and black marls also occur. In calcareous marine marls, some lime is present in the form of shells, whereas in others it is a fine impalpable powder mixed with clay and siliceous silt. Freshwater marl may be similar in composition to marine marl. Much of the calcium carbonate in lake deposits is precipitated by algae, but some lake marls contain numerous shell fragments from freshwater snails and bivalves. Large deposits of freshwater marl that contain from 80 to 90 percent calcium carbonate and less than 3 percent magnesium carbonate have been used in the manufacture of insulating material and portland cement. Marl also is used as a liming material and in making bricks.

Marlborough, town ("parish"), Kennet district, administrative and historic county of Wiltshire, Eng. It lies on the River Kennet in a valley of the Marlborough Downs (hills).

Traces of Neolithic and Roman occupation have been found in the vicinity of the Castle Mound, former site of an 11th-century royal castle. John, later king, was married at the castle chapel in 1189. He granted the town its first charter in 1204; the present charter dates from 1575. During the English Civil Wars the town, which supported Parliament, was besieged and captured. In 1653 a great fire destroyed much of Marlborough, and other fires occurred in 1679 and 1690, but the present broad High Street is still flanked with houses dating from the 16th century. The town's trade is largely based on its role as a rural service centre for the surrounding farming area. Pop. (1991) 6,429.

Marlborough, also spelled MARLBORO, city, Middlesex county, east-central Massachusetts, U.S., in an area of ponds and reservoirs, 27 miles (43 km) west of Boston. Originally part of Sudbury, it was set off as Whipsuferadge Plantation in 1656 and was incorporated as a town in 1660 and named for Marlborough, Eng. The adjoining Indian plantation of Okammakamefit was annexed in 1718. Shoe manufacturing was begun in 1812. Other products include paper boxes, sporting goods, chemicals, computers, electronic equipment, and metal stampings. Inc. city, 1890. Pop. (2000) 36,255.

Marlborough, unitary authority, northeastern South Island, New Zealand. It is bounded by Cook Straight (north), the South Pacific Ocean (east), Christchurch local government region (southeast and south), and Tasman and the city of Nelson unitary authorities (west). The Wairau River rises in western Marlborough in the Spenser Mountains, the source of headwaters of many smaller rivers as well. The Wairau flows northeast, south of the Richmond Range, into Cloudy Bay. Other important rivers are the Awatere and Flaxbourne.

The first whaling stations were established in the 1830s along Port Underwood (a bay) and Queen Charlotte Sound. The New Zealand Company's efforts to acquire the Wairau Plains in 1843 led to the Wairau Affray, a battle between them and local Maori chiefs.

There is mixed arable farming around Blenheim and Seddon, and sheep and dairy farming in the Rai River valley. Industries include food processing, clothing and textiles, metals and engineering, nearly all of it in the vicinity of Blenheim. There are road and rail ferries between the town of Picton and Wellington (on North Island), and air freight is handled through Woodbourne, near Blenheim, and Rongotai in Wellington. Pop. (2001) 39,555.

Marlborough, John Churchill, 1st Duke of, MARQUESS OF BLANDFORD, EARL OF MARLBOROUGH, BARON CHURCHILL OF SANDRIDGE, LORD CHURCHILL OF EYEMOUTH, REICHSFÜRST (Imperial Prince) (b. May 26, 1650, Ashe, Devon, Eng.—d. June 16, 1722, Windsor, near London), one of England's greatest generals, who led British and allied armies to important victories over Louis XIV of France, notably at Blenheim (1704), Ramillies (1706), and Oudenaarde (1708).

Military career. John Churchill was the son of Sir Winston Churchill, member of Parliament, who possessed only a moderate property but was sufficiently influential at the court of Charles II to be able to provide for his sons there and in the armed forces. John, the eldest, advanced rapidly both at court and in the army but, marrying for love, remained throughout his life dependent upon his career in the public service for financial support.

Churchill received a commission in the foot guards in 1667 and served at Tangier from about 1668 to 1670. In the third Dutch War (1672–74), he served with the allied fleet that was defeated at Solebay on May 28, 1672, and

John Churchill, 1st Duke of Marlborough, painting attributed to J. Closterman; in the National Portrait Gallery, London

By courtesy of the National Portrait Gallery, London

was promoted captain. He went with the English troops sent in December 1672 to assist Louis XIV against the Dutch and distinguished himself at Maastricht with the Duke of Monmouth. He was appointed colonel of the English regiment by Louis XIV in 1674 and served with distinction at Enzheim.

After his marriage to Sarah Jennings, an attendant upon Princess (later Queen) Anne, Churchill rose rapidly. On the accession of James II in 1685, he was made a lieutenant general and effective commander in chief, in addition to a peer of the realm. He demonstrated his political acumen by surviving the expulsion of the Roman Catholic James II in 1688, transferring his allegiance to the Dutch prince of Orange (who was to become William III, three weeks after his landing in England), having already given William assurances that he would in all circumstances stand by the Protestant religion. He was rewarded by William with the earldom of Marlborough, membership of the Privy Council, confirmation of his military rank, and a succession of commands in Flanders and in Ireland between 1689 and 1691, in which he was uniformly successful.

Marlborough seemed on the threshold of great achievements when, suddenly, at the end of 1691, he was removed from all his appointments. The next May he was imprisoned on suspicion of being implicated in the intrigues to restore James II, with the support of a French invasion to be launched from Cherbourg in the summer of that year. He was released soon afterward but remained wholly out of favour at court for three years and out of employment for the remainder of the war. Responsible contemporaries, however, never suspected him of treason. Although Marlborough certainly acted like all leading politicians of his age by making comforting assurances to the contender for the throne, as an insurance lest the regime be overthrown again, as it had been twice already in Marlborough's lifetime, his quarrel with William did not originate in any suspicion of treason. He was dismissed, rather, because he led a substantial English faction opposed to the favours William bestowed on his Dutch associates.

In 1701 Louis XIV made it clear that he was again intent on advancing, through war, his claims upon the now-vacant throne of

Spain and the Spanish empire. William III, now a sick man and in what turned out to be the last year of his life, appointed Marlborough to be, in effect, his successor in the struggle against the ambitions of Louis XIV, to which, in England as in Holland, William had devoted his life. On her accession, Queen Anne confirmed the appointment, and Marlborough crossed to the European continent to undertake the first of 10 successive campaigns in command of the English and Dutch forces and their auxiliaries. In this first campaign he captured Kaiserswerth in 1702 and cleared the territory between the Rhine and Meuse rivers. For these services a grateful sovereign created him duke of Marlborough.

Bavaria had entered the war and joined the French in the attack on the heart of the Holy Roman Empire while the Austrian armies were engaged on the Rhine and in Italy. Without assistance to Austria the war would be lost, but Marlborough knew that the Dutch would oppose a distant campaign; therefore he attacked on the Moselle River, deceiving both friend and foe, and he deceived them again by a feint against Alsace. After a fierce struggle he took the Schellenberg fortress and opened the crossing of the Danube River at Donauwörth. On Aug. 13, 1704, he engaged the main enemy force at Blenheim; a quarter (about 12,000) of his troops were killed or wounded, but the enemy casualties exceeded three times that number. On his return to the Netherlands, Marlborough took Trier and Trarbach. These victories altered the whole balance of power in Europe and put France firmly on the defensive.

In 1705 Marlborough was confident that the French could be beaten in any but the strongest of positions. The Dutch and Austrians, however, were less keen to cooperate after a year's success, and by their lack of support they prevented Marlborough from exploiting his successes. Louis XIV had concluded that peace was necessary and that he could only get satisfactory terms by an assault on all fronts. Consequently, when Marlborough threatened to move between Namur and the French army, he was challenged near Ramillies. Feinting an attack upon the right, Marlborough concentrated his main attack upon the left, to the south of the village of Ramillies. The result was a crushing victory in which the French losses may have been five or six times those of the allies. With this and his later victory at Oudenaarde, he secured a reputation unrivaled until Napoleon's rise.

Political rise and fall. At home Marlborough was an important political figure whose support was indispensable to any ministry. The key to this influence lay with his wife, who had been Anne's firm companion and guide through all the political upheavals of the past two decades. Anne, though a woman with decided views and prejudices of her own, was, for the time being, content to leave her affairs in the hands of Sarah's husband and his friend and political ally Sidney, Earl of Godolphin, whom Anne made lord treasurer and, in effect, prime minister.

Both Marlborough and Godolphin were Tories of a traditional kind and so were staunch supporters of the crown and the court as well as of the church. They allied themselves at first with Robert Harley, later the 1st Earl of Oxford, leader of a new breed of Tory hostile to the financial interests nurtured by the war. This alliance provided backing for the war against Louis XIV that produced the great victories of Blenheim and Ramillies, but increasingly, as the old Tories left the government one by one, Marlborough and Godolphin could find effective and consistent support for the war only from the Whigs. Sarah strongly advocated a Whig alliance, with the result that her influence over Anne, among whose prejudices was a strong dislike of the Whig leaders, rapidly declined. A political crisis in January 1708 resulted in Harley's dismissal, and Marlborough and Godolphin were now entirely dependent upon the Whigs. Although Marlborough continued to win his battles, the Whigs proved unable to secure peace, and, by now weary of war, the people endorsed Anne's dismissal of Godolphin and his Whig colleagues in the general election of 1710. Marlborough, who had already found himself increasingly isolated and without influence during the Whig predominance, was left in command of the army for another year, but when he endeavoured to take a political stand over the terms of peace being negotiated by the new government, he was dismissed in December 1711 from all his appointments after charges of misuse of public money had been made in the House of Commons. He took no further part in public life under Anne, retiring abroad when condemned by the Commons for misappropriation of public money. Although restored to favour under George I, Marlborough was already a sick man and lived in retirement up to his death. (I.F.B./Ed.)

Marlborough, Sarah Jennings, Duchess of, also called (1689–1702) COUNTESS OF MARLBOROUGH (b. May 29, 1660, Sandridge, Hertfordshire, Eng.—d. Oct. 18, 1744, London), wife of the renowned general John Churchill, 1st Duke of Marlborough; her close friendship with Queen Anne bolstered her husband's career and served to aid the Whig cause.

Duchess of Marlborough, oil painting by Bernard Lens, 1720; in the Victoria and Albert Museum, London

By courtesy of the Victoria and Albert Museum, London

As a child, Sarah Jennings formed a friendship with the Princess Anne (the future queen of Great Britain) and entered the household of Anne's father, the Duke of York (the future James II) in 1673. Her romance with John Churchill, who was also at court, began late in 1675. Churchill's parents opposed an unremunerative match, but with the assistance of the Duchess of York the couple were married secretly during the winter of 1677–78. Sarah was devoted to the Princess Anne, who came to depend upon her; they addressed each other as Mrs. Morley and Mrs. Freeman; and, upon Anne's marriage in 1683, Sarah became one of the ladies of the bedchamber. Sarah escorted Anne to meet the Prince of Orange in 1688 and persuaded her to accept the statutory settlement of the succession. Upon Marlborough's disgrace in 1692, Queen Mary compelled Anne to dismiss Sarah from her offices and excluded her from court; but after Mary's death in 1694, Anne and William III were reconciled and the Marlboroughs returned to favour.

After Anne's accession, the Marlboroughs enjoyed great favour. But Sarah's favour was in the balance: for the queen had High Church sympathies, while Sarah was a strong Whig. This difference came to a head after 1705; the high Tories had fallen from office but the queen, supported by Robert Harley (later Earl of Oxford), stoutly resisted taking in the Whigs. Sarah persistently urged her to bring the Earl of Sunderland into office in 1706, and mutual irritation showed that the friendship of Anne and Sarah was cooling. Harley was clearly using Mrs. (later Lady) Abigail Masham to supplant Sarah in Anne's affections by 1707. When Anne's husband, the Prince of Denmark, died in 1708, relations between Anne and Sarah temporarily improved, but Mrs. Masham's power grew.

The Whigs and Sarah thoroughly lost influence in 1710. Anne dismissed her, and they never met again.

Marley, Bob, in full ROBERT NESTA MARLEY (b. Feb. 6, 1945, Nine Miles, St. Ann, Jamaica—d. May 11, 1981, Miami, Fla., U.S.), Jamaican singer-songwriter who attained international fame with music influenced by reggae, rock, and ska forms.

Marley grew up amidst poverty—his poetic worldview was shaped by the countryside, his music by the tough West Kingston ghetto streets. As a youngster, he was exposed to ska and American pop music; his first records, including "Judge Not" (1961) and "One Cup of Coffee" (1963), reflected his diverse influences. About the same time, Marley formed his band, the Wailers, and recorded the song "Simmer Down," a raw, urgent anthem from the shantytown precincts of Kingston. The record was an enormous hit and helped engender pride within Jamaica's urban poor. The Wailers had continued success throughout the 1960s, with much of their music reflecting their Rastafarian faith.

Marley attained international stardom with the release of the album *Catch a Fire* (1972); his fame spread further when Eric Clapton released his version of the Wailers' "I Shot the Sheriff" in 1974. Throughout the 1970s, Marley's music transcended all stylistic roots on such notable recordings as "No Woman No Cry," "Exodus," "Could You Be Loved," "Jamming," and "Redemption Song," and on such landmark albums as *Natty Dread* (1974), *Live!* (1975), *Rastaman Vibration* (1976), *Exodus* (1977), and *Uprising* (1980).

Marley died of cancer in May 1981, a month after the Jamaican government awarded him the Order of Merit. His death increased his popularity, evidenced by the release of *Legend* (1984), a retrospective of his work that became the best-selling reggae album of all time.

marlin, any of several species of large, long-nosed marine fishes of the family Istiophoridae (order Perciformes) characterized by an elongated body, a long dorsal fin, and a rounded spear extending from the snout. They are wanderers, found worldwide near the surface of the sea, and are carnivorous, feeding largely on other fishes. They are consumed as food and are highly prized by sport fishermen.

A number of species of marlins have been named; four are generally accepted as valid: the blue, black, striped, and white marlins.

Black marlin (*Makaira indica*)

Painted especially for *Encyclopaedia Britannica* by Tom Dolan, under the supervision of Loren P. Woods, Chicago Natural History Museum

The blue marlin (species *Makaira nigricans*), found worldwide, is a very large fish, sometimes attaining a weight of 450 kg (1,000 pounds) or more. It is deep blue with a silvery belly and is often barred with lighter vertical stripes. The black marlin (*M. indica,* or *Istiompax indicus*) grows as large or larger than the blue. It is known to reach a weight of more than 700 kg (1,500 pounds). An Indo-Pacific species, it is blue or blue gray above and lighter below; its distinctive, stiff pectoral fins are set at an angle and cannot be flattened against the body without force. The striped marlin (*M.*, or *Tetrapterus, audax*), another Indo-Pacific fish, is bluish above and white below, with pale vertical bars; it normally does not exceed 125 kg (275 pounds). The white marlin (*M. albida*, or *T. albidus*) is limited to the Atlantic and is blue green with a paler belly and with pale vertical bars on its sides. Its maximum weight is about 45 kg (100 pounds).

Marlow, parish (town), Wycombe district, county of Buckinghamshire, England, on the River Thames. The parish Church of All Saints was built in 1835 on the site of a church that dated from the 12th century. The Sir William Borlase Boys School was founded at Marlow in 1624. Marlow Place (1720) was built for George II (reigned 1727–60) when he was Prince of Wales. Marlow is a residential town, but in summer its boating facilities and regatta attract visitors. Medmenham Abbey, about 3 miles (5 km) southwest, is built on the site of a Cistercian monastery, founded *c.* 1200. Pop. (1991) 17,771.

Marlowe, Christopher (baptized Feb. 26, 1564, Canterbury, Kent, Eng.—d. May 30, 1593, Deptford, near London), Elizabethan poet and Shakespeare's most important predecessor in English drama, noted especially for his establishment of dramatic blank verse.

Detail of a portrait thought to be of Christopher Marlowe, dated 1585, artist unknown; in the collection of Corpus Christi College, Cambridge

By courtesy of The Master, Fellow and Scholars of Corpus Christi College, Cambridge; photograph, Edward Leigh

Early years. Marlowe was the second child and eldest son of John Marlowe, a Canterbury shoemaker. Nothing is known of his first schooling, but on Jan. 14, 1579, he entered the King's School, Canterbury, as a scholar. A year later he went to Corpus Christi College, Cambridge. Obtaining his bachelor of arts degree in 1584, he continued in residence at Cambridge—which may imply that he was intending to take Anglican orders. In 1587, however, the university hesitated about granting him the master's degree; its doubts (arising from his frequent absences from the university) were apparently set at rest when the Privy Council sent a letter declaring that he had been employed "on matters touching the benefit of his country"—apparently in Elizabeth I's secret service.

Last years and literary career. After 1587 Marlowe was in London, writing for the theatres, occasionally getting into trouble with the authorities because of his violent and disreputable behaviour, and probably also engaging himself from time to time in government service. Marlowe won a dangerous reputation for "atheism," but this could, in Elizabeth I's time, indicate merely unorthodox religious opinions. In Robert Greene's deathbed tract, *Greenes Groatsworth of Wit . . .*, Marlowe is referred to as a "famous gracer of Tragedians" and is reproved for having said, like Greene himself, "There is no god" and for having studied "pestilent Machiuilian pollicie." There is further evidence of his unorthodoxy, notably in the denunciation of him written by the spy Richard Baines and in the letter of Thomas Kyd to the lord keeper in 1593 after Marlowe's death. Kyd alleged that certain papers "denying the deity of Jesus Christ" that were found in his room belonged to Marlowe, who had shared the room two years before. Both Baines and Kyd suggested on Marlowe's part atheism in the stricter sense and a persistent delight in blasphemy. Whatever the case may be, on May 18, 1593, the Privy Council issued an order for Marlowe's arrest; two days later the poet was ordered to give daily attendance on their lordships "until he shall be licensed to the contrary." On May 30, however, Marlowe was killed by Ingram Friser, in the dubious company of Nicholas Skeres and Robert Poley, at a tavern in Deptford, where they had spent most of the day and where, it was alleged, a fight broke out between them over the tavern bill.

In a playwriting career that spanned little more than six years, Marlowe's achievements were diverse and splendid. Perhaps before leaving Cambridge he had already written *Tamburlaine the Great* (in two parts, both performed by the end of 1587). Almost certainly during his later Cambridge years, Marlowe had translated Ovid's *Elegies* and the first book of Lucan's *Pharsalia* from the Latin. About this time he also wrote the play *Dido, Queen of Carthage* (published in 1594 as the joint work of Marlowe and Thomas Nashe). With the production of *Tamburlaine* he received recognition and acclaim, and playwriting became his major concern in the few years that lay ahead. Both parts of *Tamburlaine* were published anonymously in 1590, and the publisher omitted certain passages that he found incongruous with the play's serious concern with history; even so, the extant *Tamburlaine* text can be regarded as substantially Marlowe's. No other of his plays or poems or translations was published during his life. His unfinished but splendid poem *Hero and Leander*—which is almost certainly the finest nondramatic Elizabethan poem apart from those produced by Edmund Spenser—appeared in 1598.

There is argument among scholars concerning the order in which the plays subsequent to *Tamburlaine* were written. It is not uncommonly held that *Faustus* quickly followed *Tamburlaine* and that then Marlowe turned to a more neutral, more "social" kind of writing in *Edward II* and *The Massacre at Paris.* His last play may have been *The Jew of Malta,* in which he signally broke new ground. It is known that *Tamburlaine, Faustus,* and *The Jew of Malta* were performed by the Lord Admiral's Men, a company whose outstanding actor was Edward Alleyn, who most certainly played Tamburlaine, Faustus, and Barabas, the Jew.

Works. In the earliest of Marlowe's plays, the two-part *Tamburlaine the Great* (*c.* 1587; published 1590), Marlowe's characteristic "mighty line" (as Ben Jonson called it) established blank verse as the staple medium for later Elizabethan and Jacobean dramatic writing. It appears that originally Marlowe intended to write only the first part, concluding with Tamburlaine's marriage to Zenocrate." But the popularity of the first part encouraged Marlowe to continue the story to Tamburlaine's death. This gave him some difficulty, as he had almost exhausted his historical sources in part I; consequently the sequel has, at first glance, an appearance of padding. Yet the effort demanded in writing the continuation made the young playwright look more coldly and searchingly at the hero he had chosen, and thus part II makes explicit certain notions that were below the surface and insufficiently recognized by the dramatist in part I.

The play is based on the life and achievements of Timur (Timurlenk), the bloody 14th-century conqueror of Central Asia and India. Tamburlaine is a man avid for power and luxury and the possession of beauty: at the beginning of part I he is only an obscure Scythian shepherd, but he wins the crown of Persia by eloquence and bravery and a readiness to discard loyalty. He then conquers Bajazeth, emperor of Turkey, he puts the town of Damascus to the sword, and he conquers the sultan of Egypt; but, at the pleas of the sultan's daughter Zenocrate, the captive whom he loves, he spares him and makes truce. In part II Tamburlaine's conquests are further extended; whenever he fights a battle, he must win, even when his last illness is upon him. But Zenocrate dies, and their three sons provide a manifestly imperfect means for ensuring the preservation of his wide dominions; he kills Calyphas, one of these sons, when he refuses to follow his father into battle. Always, too, there are more battles to fight: when for a moment he has no immediate opponent on earth, he dreams of leading his army against the powers of heaven, though at other times he glories in seeing himself as "the scourge of God." Certainly Marlowe feels sympathy with his hero, giving him magnificent verse to speak, delighting in his dreams of power and of the possession of beauty, as seen in the following of Tamburlaine's lines:

> Nature, that fram'd us of four elements
> Warring within our breasts for regiment,
> Doth teach us all to have aspiring minds:
> Our souls, whose faculties can comprehend
> The wondrous architecture of the world,
> And measure every wandering planet's course,
> Still climbing after knowledge infinite,
> And always moving as the restless spheres,
> Wills us to wear ourselves and never rest,
> Until we reach the ripest fruit of all,
> That perfect bliss and sole felicity,
> The sweet fruition of an earthly crown.

But, especially in part II, there are other strains: the hero can be absurd in his continual striving for more demonstrations of his power; his cruelty, which is extreme, becomes sickening; his human weakness is increasingly underlined, most notably in the onset of his fatal illness immediately after his arrogant burning of the Qur'ān. In this early play Marlowe already shows the ability to view a tragic hero from more than one angle, achieving a simultaneous vision of grandeur and impotence.

Marlowe's most famous play is *The Tragicall History of Dr. Faustus;* but it has survived only in a corrupt form, and its date of composition has been much-disputed. It was first published in 1604, and another version appeared in 1616. *Faustus* takes over the dramatic framework of the morality plays in its presentation of a story of temptation, fall, and damnation and its free use of morality figures such as the good angel and the bad angel and the seven deadly sins, along with the devils Lucifer and Mephistopheles. In *Faustus* Marlowe tells the story of the doctor-turned-necromancer Faustus, who sells his soul to the devil in exchange for knowledge and power. The devil's intermediary in the play, Mephistopheles, achieves tragic grandeur in his own right as a fallen angel torn between satanic pride and dark despair. The play gives eloquent expression to this idea of damnation in the lament of Mephistopheles for a lost heaven and in Faustus' final despairing entreaties to be saved by Christ before his soul is claimed by the devil:

The stars move still, time runs, the clock
 will strike,
The devil will come, and Faustus must
 be damn'd.
O, I'll leap up to my God!—Who pulls
 me down?—
See, see, where Christ's blood streams in
 the firmament!
One drop would save my soul, half a drop:
 ah, my Christ!—
Ah, rend not my heart for naming of my Christ!
Yet will I call on him: O, spare me, Lucifer!—
Where is it now? 'tis gone: and see, where God
Stretcheth out his arm, and bends his
 ireful brows!
Mountains and hills, come, come, and fall
 on me,
And hide me from the heavy wrath of God!

Just as in *Tamburlaine* Marlowe had seen the cruelty and absurdity of his hero as well as his magnificence, so here he can enter into Faustus' grandiose intellectual ambition, simultaneously viewing those ambitions as futile, self-destructive, and absurd. The text is problematic in the low comic scenes spuriously introduced by later hack writers, but its more sober and consistent moments are certainly the uncorrupted work of Marlowe.

In *The Famous Tragedy of the Rich Jew of Malta,* Marlowe portrays another power-hungry figure in the Jew Barabas, who in the villainous society of Christian Malta shows no scruple in self-advancement. But this figure is more closely incorporated within his society than either Tamburlaine, the supreme conqueror, or Faustus, the lonely adventurer against God. In the end Barabas is overcome, not by a divine stroke but by the concerted action of his human enemies. There is a difficulty in deciding how fully the extant text of *The Jew of Malta* represents Marlowe's original play, for it was not published until 1633. But *The Jew* can be closely associated with *The Massacre at Paris* (1593), a dramatic presentation of incidents from contemporary French history, including the Massacre of St. Bartholomew's Day, and with *The Troublesome Raigne and Lamentable Death of Edward the Second* (published 1594), Marlowe's great contribution to the Elizabethan plays on historical themes.

As *The Massacre* introduces in the duke of Guise a figure unscrupulously avid for power, so in the younger Mortimer of *Edward II* Marlowe shows a man developing an appetite for power and increasingly corrupted as power comes to him. In each instance the dramatist shares in the excitement of the pursuit of glory, but all three plays present such figures within a social framework: the notion of social responsibility, the notion of corruption through power, and the notion of the suffering that the exercise of power entails are all prominently the dramatist's concern. Apart from *Tamburlaine* and the minor work *The Tragedie of Dido Queene of Carthage* (of uncertain date, published 1594 and written in collaboration with Thomas Nashe), *Edward II* is the only one of Marlowe's plays whose extant text can be relied on as adequately representing the author's manuscript. And certainly *Edward II* is a major work, not merely one of the first Elizabethan plays on an English historical theme. The relationships linking the king, his neglected queen, the king's favourite, Gaveston, and the ambitious Mortimer are studied with detached sympathy and remarkable understanding: no character here is lightly disposed of, and the abdication and the brutal murder of Edward show the same dark and violent imagination as appeared in Marlowe's presentation of Faustus' last hour. Though this play, along with *The Jew* and *The Massacre,* shows Marlowe's fascinated response to the distorted Elizabethan idea of Machiavelli, it more importantly shows Marlowe's deeply suggestive awareness of the nature of disaster, the power of society, and the dark extent of an individual's suffering.

In addition to translations (Ovid's *Amores* and the first book of Lucan's *Pharsalia*), Marlowe's nondramatic work includes the poem *Hero and Leander.* This work was incomplete at his death and was extended by George Chapman: the joint work of the two poets was published in 1598.

An authoritative edition of Marlowe's works was edited by Fredson Bowers, *The Complete Works of Christopher Marlowe,* 2nd ed., 2 vol. (1981). (Cl.L./Ed.)

BIBLIOGRAPHY. Biographies include Frederick S. Boas, *Christopher Marlowe: A Biographical and Critical Study* (1940, reprinted 1966); J. Leslie Hotson, *The Death of Christopher Marlowe* (1925, reprinted 1967); Philip Henderson, *Christopher Marlowe,* 2nd ed. (1974); and Gerald Pinciss, *Christopher Marlowe* (1975, reissued 1984). Works of criticism include Paul H. Kocher, *Christopher Marlowe: A Study of His Thought, Learning, and Character* (1946, reissued 1974); Harry Levin, *The Overreacher: A Study of Christopher Marlowe* (1952, reissued 1974); F.P. Wilson, *Marlowe and the Early Shakespeare* (1953, reissued 1973); J.B. Steane, *Marlowe: A Critical Study* (1964, reprinted 1974); Clifford Leech, *Christopher Marlowe: Poet for the Stage* (1986); and Roger Sales, *Christopher Marlowe* (1991). Anthologies of critical essays include Clifford Leech (ed.), *Marlowe: A Collection of Critical Essays* (1964); Judith O'Neill (comp.), *Critics on Marlowe* (1969); and Kenneth Friedenreich, Roma Gill, and Constance B. Kuriyama (eds.), *"A Poet and a Filthy Play-Maker"* (1987).

Marlowe, Julia, original name SARAH FRANCES FROST (b. Aug. 17, 1866, near Keswick, Cumberland, Eng.—d. Nov. 12, 1950, New York, N.Y., U.S.), English-born American actress, one of the great romantic actresses of her day, known especially for her interpretations of William Shakespeare.

Julia Marlowe as Viola in William Shakespeare's *Twelfth Night*
Culver Pictures

Her family moved to the United States in 1870, and at the age of 11 she toured the Midwest in a juvenile *H.M.S. Pinafore.* Her New York debut was in 1887. Her first financially successful role was that of the sister of Henry VIII in *When Knighthood Was in Flower,* a play she also directed. She dominated this immensely popular 1900 production, adapted especially for her by Paul Kister from Charles Major's novel; it ran for two seasons. In 1904 she teamed with Edward Hugh Sothern (whom she married in 1911), and together they became the leading couple of Shakespearean actors of their day. Among Marlowe's greatest roles were Viola in Shakespeare's *Twelfth Night* and Julia in James Sheridan Knowles's play *The Hunchback.* She retired because of poor health in 1916 but appeared sporadically until 1924.

Marma, also called MAGH, or MOGH, Mongoloid people of the Chittagong Hills region of Bangladesh. The Marma numbered approximately 210,000 in the late 20th century. One group, the Jhumia Marma, have long settled in this southeastern region of Bengal; the other group, the Rakhaing Marma, are recent immigrants, having come from Arakan toward the end of the 18th century, when their kingdom was conquered by the Burmese.

Most of them came under Bengali influence, but in the south of the Chittagong Hills region, where their culture remains comparatively pure, the script and dress are Burmese and the language an Arakanese dialect. Elsewhere the Bengali dress and language prevail. The religion of the Arakanese-speaking Marma is animistic Buddhism. The people are divided into endogamous clans, and in modern times there were still strong traces of a political organization under clan chiefs. In the hills, shifting cultivation was still preferred to plow agriculture in modern times, but the villages, containing from 10 to 50 houses, were invariably built on the banks of streams. The houses were flimsy structures on bamboo piles, and a relic of the communal house for men was sometimes found in the form of a roofed platform built at the end of the village street.

marmalade tree: *see* sapote.

Marmara, Sea of, Turkish MARMARA DENİZİ, historically PROPONTIS, inland sea partly separating the Asiatic and European parts of Turkey. It is connected through the Bosporus on the northeast with the Black Sea and through the Dardanelles on the southwest with the Aegean Sea. It is 175 miles (280 km) long from northeast to southwest and nearly 50 miles (80 km) wide at its greatest width. Despite its small area, 4,382 square miles (11,350 square km), its average depth is about 1,620 feet (494 m), reaching a maximum of 4,446 feet (1,355 m) in the centre. It has no strong currents. Salinity, which averages 22 parts per thousand, is greatest at the end nearest the Dardanelles. The sea was formed as a result of crustal movements that occurred approximately 2,500,000 years ago, in the Late Pliocene Epoch. It is an area of frequent earthquakes.

The sea has two distinct island groups. The first is the Kızıl Islands in the northeast near Istanbul; these islands are primarily resort areas. The second group consists of the Marmara islands proper in the southwest, off Kapıdagı Peninsula; these have granite, slate, and marble that have been quarried since antiquity—hence the sea's name (Greek *marmaros,* "marble").

Mármol, José (Pedro Crisólogo) (b. Dec. 2, 1817, Buenos Aires, Arg.—d. Aug. 9, 1871, Buenos Aires), Argentine poet and novelist whose outspoken denunciation in verse and prose of the Argentine dictator Juan Manuel de Rosas earned him the title of "*verdugo poético de Rosas*" ("poetic hangman of Rosas"), and whose best-known work, *Amalia*

(1851–55; *Amalia: A Romance of the Argentine,* 1919), is considered by many critics to be the first Argentine novel. He was highly influential on the development of the realistic novel in Latin America.

Mármol, outspoken from his youth in his opposition to Rosas and to tyranny in any form, was imprisoned in 1839 for his political views and eventually was forced to flee the country. He wrote most of his works during his years of exile in Montevideo and in Rio de Janeiro. *Amalia* dramatically depicts the horrors of the Rosas regime with a highly romantic plot of love set against a background of contemporary events. In poetry such as *Rosas: El 25 de mayo de 1850* (1850) Mármol also spoke out against the dictator with a forcefulness that made him the hero of liberals throughout Latin America.

In 1852, after the overthrow of Rosas, Mármol returned home to Argentina as a national hero. An important public figure, he served as a senator and as director of the National Library, a post he held from 1858 until his death.

Marmont, Auguste-Frédéric-Louis Viesse de, DUC (duke) DE RAGUSE (b. July 20, 1774, Châtillon-sur-Seine, Fr.—d. March 2, 1852, Venice), marshal of France whose distinguished military career ended when, as Napoleon's chief lieutenant in a battle under the walls of the city, he surrendered Paris (March 30, 1814) and a few days later took his troops into the Allied lines.

Marmont, detail from a portrait by Paulin Guérin; in the Musée de Versailles

Giraudon—Art Resource/EB Inc.

Marmont entered the artillery in 1792. At the Siege of Toulon (1793) he was noticed by Bonaparte and soon became his aide-de-camp. Marmont was so prominent in the Italian campaign (1796) that he was made a colonel at the age of 22. Two years later Bonaparte made him a general on the voyage to Egypt, and on July 7, 1806, he appointed him governor of Dalmatia. There Marmont forced the Russians to lift the siege of Ragusa in September and secured control of the Adriatic coast. As governor, he built roads and introduced a modern administration. He was made duc de Raguse in 1808 but lamented the "cruel obscurity" of a provincial command.

In the war of 1809 against Austria, Marmont again saw action, and, after the Battle of Wagram (July 5–6), he was made a marshal. With Austria's defeat he was appointed governor general of the Illyrian Provinces, a state newly created by Napoleon that included Dalmatia and other conquered territory. Marmont was called to command the French army in Portugal in May 1811 but had little success against the British; he was severely wounded in the Battle of Salamanca (July 22, 1812). The following year he commanded a corps in Germany, where his successes led to his becoming Napoleon's chief lieutenant.

At the restoration of Louis XVIII, Marmont was rewarded for his desertion of Napoleon and was made a peer of France. During the revolution of July 1830, when his troops failed to hold Paris for Charles X, he was accused of treachery. His name was stricken from the list of marshals, and he went into exile. His *Mémoires* appeared in nine volumes in 1856–57.

Marmontel, Jean-François (b. July 11, 1723, Bort-les-Orgues, Fr.—d. Dec. 31, 1799, Normandy), French poet, dramatist, novelist, and critic who is remembered for his autobiographical work, *Mémoires d'un père* (1804, "Memoirs of a Father").

In 1745, encouraged by Voltaire, Marmontel settled in Paris, where good management made his career more brilliant than his talent warranted. He was a mediocre dramatist, composing short-lived tragedies in the manner of Voltaire, and libretti of operas for composers Jean-Philippe Rameau, André-Ernest-Modeste Grétry, Niccolò Piccinni, and Luigi Cherubini. His *Contes moraux* (1761; "Moral Stories") are more original. He first published them separately in the *Mercure de France,* which he edited between 1758 and 1760. Sentimental and edifying, insipidly elegant in content and style, these tales were widely appreciated and imitated. The publication of two philosophical romances, *Bélisaire* (1767) and *Les Incas* (1777), considerably enhanced his reputation. The first was condemned by the Sorbonne because of its plea for religious toleration; the second denounced the evils of fanaticism.

Marmontel, detail of an engraving by Augustin de Saint-Aubin, 1765, after a portrait by C.N. Cochin

H. Roger-Viollet

Marmontel derived from Voltaire the brand of liberal Classicism he expounded in his *Éléments de littérature* (1787; "Elements of Literature") and in articles for the *Encyclopédie.* He was elected to the Académie Française in 1763 and became its permanent secretary in 1783. He was appointed royal historiographer in 1771. During the Revolution he retired to the country, where he wrote his only really lasting work, *Mémoires d'un père.*

Marmor Parium (ancient Greek document): *see* Parian Chronicle.

marmoset, any of the small, long-tailed, South American monkeys constituting the family Callitrichidae. Marmosets are squirrel-like tree dwellers and move in a quick, jerky manner. They are active during the day; live in small groups; and, as an aid to scampering along branches, have claws on all digits except the big toe. Unlike other American primates, they lack the last (third) molar teeth in both jaws. Marmosets have been kept as pets since the early 17th century, but they require some care to remain healthy. They are primarily insect eaters but take fruit as well as other small animals. The gestation period is about 145 days, and the females generally bear twins.

Marmosets fall into two groups: those with short lower canines (short-tusked) are commonly called marmosets, and those with relatively long lower canines (long-tusked) are known as tamarins. Pygmy marmosets (*Cebuella pygmaea*) are the smallest members of the family. Their head and body are about 14 centimetres (6 inches) long, the tail somewhat longer. Adults weigh only about 90 grams (3 ounces), whereas other members of the family attain weights of up to 1 kilogram (2.2 pounds). Marmosets of the genus *Callithrix* are more common. These animals are about 15–25 cm long, excluding their 25–40-cm tails. Their fur is dense and silky and generally forms tufts on the ears. Colour varies among the eight species from white to reddish or blackish, and it may be grizzled or otherwise marked, as with rings on the tail.

About 25 species of tamarins are placed

Comparative taxonomy of the marmosets and tamarins

	Simpson 1945	Hershkovitz 1949a	Cabrera 1957	Hill 1957	Hill 1960	Hershkovitz 1966a and b
marmosets: (short-tusked; *i.e.,* with elongated lower incisors and incisiform lower canines)						
typical marmosets	*Callithrix*		*Callithrix*	*Hapale*	*Hapale*	*Callithrix*
bare-eared marmosets	*Callithrix*		*Callithrix*	*Mico*	*Mico*	*Callithrix*
pygmy marmosets	*Callithrix*		*Cebuella*	*Cebuella*	*Cebuella*	
tamarins: (long-tusked; *i.e.,* with normal lower canine-incisor relationship)						
black-faced hairy-faced tamarins	*Leontocebus*	*Marikina (Tamarin)*	*Leontocebus (Tamarin)*	*Tamarin*	*Tamarin*	*Saguinus*
white-moustached hairy-faced tamarins	*Leontocebus*	*Marikina (Tamarin)*	*Leontocebus (Tamarin)*	*Tamarinus*	*Leontocebus*	*Saguinus*
bare-faced tamarins	*Leontocebus*	*Marikina (Marikina)*	*Leontocebus (Marikina)*	*Marikina*	*Marikina*	*Saguinus*
crested bare-faced tamarins or pinches	*Leontocebus*	*Marikina (Oedipomidas)*	*Leontocebus (Oedipomidas)*	*Oedipomidas*	*Oedipomidas*	*Saguinus*
golden lion tamarins	*Leontocebus*	*Leontocebus*	*Leontideus*	*Leontocebus*	*Leontideus*	

Source: J.R. Napier and P.H. Napier, *A Handbook of Living Primates.*

in the genera *Leontopithecus* (*Leontideus* of some authorities) and *Saguinus*. Tamarins are about 20–35 cm long, excluding the 30–40-cm tail. One of the most striking forms is the golden lion tamarin or marmoset (*L. rosalia*),

Common marmoset (*Callithrix jacchus*)
Art Wolfe/Tony Stone Images

which has a thick, lionlike mane; black face; and long, silky, golden fur. Another species, the emperor tamarin (*S. imperator*), has long, grizzled, gray fur; a reddish tail; and long white moustaches. The three species of *Leontopithecus* are all listed as critically endangered in the *Red Data Book*. Goeldie's marmoset (*Callimico goeldii*) is a small, rare, black monkey of the upper Amazon. It is generally placed with the Callitrichidae (sometimes as the subfamily Callimiconinae), but certain of its features are like those of the other New World monkeys (family Cebidae).

Depending on the authority, tamarins and marmosets may be placed in various different genera. (*See* Table.)

marmot, any of about 14 species of heavy-set, ground-dwelling rodents constituting the genus *Marmota,* and belonging to the squirrel family, Sciuridae. Marmots are coarse-furred

Olympic marmot (*Marmota olympus*)
E.R. Degginger

and have small ears, short tails, and strong feet and claws adapted for digging. They are 30 to 60 cm (12 to 24 inches) long without the 10- to 25-centimetre tail and weigh from 3 to 7.5 kg (about 6.5 to 16.5 pounds). The coat may be yellowish brown, brown, reddish brown, or a hoary mixture of white and black.

Marmots are found in North America and from the European Alps through Asia, north of the Himalayas. They inhabit open country, in the mountains or plains, and live in burrows or among boulders on talus slopes. They frequently sit upright, keeping watch, and when alarmed they emit a sharp, whistling call. Some, such as the Alpine marmot (*M. marmota*) of Eurasia, are gregarious and live in colonies. Others, such as the woodchuck (*q.v.; M. monax*) of North America, are essentially solitary. Marmots are diurnal and feed almost entirely on green plants, sometimes causing considerable crop damage. They hibernate in winter, living on fat reserves accumulated during the summer. The hoary marmot (*M. caligata*) of the North American northwest and Siberia may hibernate for as long as nine months. Marmots mate soon after they emerge from hibernation. The young (generally four or five) are born in a nest in the burrow; gestation is about a month.

The yellow-bellied marmot (*M. flaviventris*) is an inhabitant of rocky hills and mountains in the western United States and British Columbia. It is yellowish brown with a yellowish belly and white markings between its eyes. An agricultural pest in some areas, it may also carry the ticks that transmit Rocky Mountain spotted fever.

The hoary marmot lives high in the mountains of Siberia and northwestern North America. Also known as the whistler because of its piercing alarm call, it is distinguished by the mixed black and white of its head and shoulders and by its black "boots." The hoary marmot is eaten locally and is hunted for its hide (for shoelaces) and its fur.

Marne, *département*, Champagne-Ardenne *région,* northeastern France, established from part of the historical province of Champagne (*q.v.*). It is bisected from southeast to west by the Marne River, which makes a sweeping arc of 105 miles (170 km) and passes through Châlons-sur-Marne (*q.v.*), its capital. In the east, the Perthois region, where the Marne enters the *département,* is wooded and hilly. The Aisne, which flows northwest, has its source in the heights of the Argonne forest, which extends into neighbouring Meuse *département*. In central and southwestern Marne is the slightly undulating Champagne Pouilleuse, a barren, chalky plain with an average altitude of 300 feet (90 m) that occupies about half the *département.* The countryside is thinly populated except in the Marne and other valleys. Pine forests have been planted in the poor soil, which in some areas has been enriched with humus for farming. A military camp and artillery range is above Châlons. In the western sector, in the area of Épernay, the Marne enters high country covered with forests and the vineyards from which champagne is produced. The cathedral city of Reims, the largest town, is watered by the Vesle River, a tributary of the Aisne, and is linked with Châlons by canal.

The climate is fairly temperate, and there is abundant rainfall in areas of higher elevation. The champagne industry is of great importance around Épernay and Reims, but at Reims itself engineering, food-processing, glass, textile, and electronic industries have been developed. The statesman Jean-Baptiste Colbert (1619–83) was born in Reims, and Dom Pierre Pérignon (1638–1715), who discovered how to make champagne sparkle, was born in Sainte-Menehould. Several of the towns were severely damaged in the two world wars. The *département* has five *arrondissements*—Châlons-sur-Marne, Reims, Épernay, Menehould, and Vitry-le-François. It is in the educational division of Reims. Area 3,151 square miles (8,162 square km). Pop. (1999) 565,229.

Marne, First Battle of the (September 6–12, 1914), an offensive during World War I by the French army and the British Expeditionary Force (BEF) against the advancing Germans who had invaded Belgium and northeastern France and were within 30 miles (48 km) of Paris.

By early September, one month after the outbreak of war, the German army had advanced deep into northeastern France, Paris was preparing for a siege, and the French troops were exhausted from their 10–12 day retreat to the south of the Marne River. The French commander in chief, General Joseph Joffre, decided to risk a counterattack. The French 6th Army under General Michel-Joseph Maunoury attacked the flank of the German general Alexander von Kluck's 1st Army on the morning of September 6. When Kluck turned to oppose them, a 30-mile-wide gap was opened between his troops and the German 2nd Army. The Allies immediately exploited this gap by sending in the French 5th Army and troops of the British Expeditionary Force. On September 7 and 8, Maunoury's forces were reinforced by 6,000 infantrymen who were transported to the battle from Paris by 600 taxis, the first automotive transport of troops in the history of war. On September 8 General Franchet d'Espery's 5th Army made a surprise night attack on the German 2nd Army and widened the gap. On the 10th the Germans began a general retreat that ended north of the Aisne River, where they dug in, and the trench warfare that was to typify the Western Front for the next three years began. In the Battle of the Marne the French threw back the massive German advance that had threatened to overrun their country and thwarted German plans for a quick and total victory on the Western Front.

Marne, Prieur de la: *see* Prieur, Pierre-Louis.

Marne, Second Battle of the (July 15–18, 1918), last large German offensive of World War I.

Following the success of his four major offensives in France from March to June 1918, the chief of the German supreme command, General Erich Ludendorff, conceived another offensive as a diversion to draw French troops away from the Flanders front, against which he planned to direct his final decisive offensive. In the diversionary attack, he intended to capture Reims and split the French armies. But the French general Ferdinand Foch had foreseen the coming offensive, and the Germans consequently met unexpected French resistance and counterattacks. German troops did cross the Marne River at several points but were able to advance only a few miles. British, American, and Italian units assisted the French in their defense. In the southwest the Germans advanced only 6 miles (10 km) under heavy fire before realizing that they were trapped. On July 18 the German offensive was called off just as a great Allied counteroffensive began that same day. Allied troops attacked the Germans' large Marne salient (*i.e.,* a bulge protruding into the Allied lines), taking the Germans by surprise. Three days later the Allies crossed the Marne, and the Germans withdrew from the Marne salient and retreated to their former Aisne-Vesle lines.

Marne-la-Vallée, new town (French *ville nouvelle*), occupying parts of the *départements* of Seine-et-Marne, Seine-Saint-Denis, and Val-de-Marne and located approximately 6 miles (10 km) east of Paris in north-central France. Marne-la-Vallée is one of several new towns developed outside Paris since 1965 and is intended as an urban centre to collect the population in the immediate area. Pop. (latest est.) 26,867.

Marne River, river, northern France, 326 miles (525 km) long, rising 4.5 miles (7.2 km) south of Langres on the Langres Plateau. Flowing north-northwest in a wide valley past Chaumont and Saint-Dizier, it then turns west before veering northwest to skirt Vitry-le-François and Châlons-sur-Marne; it then flows west to Épernay, where it crosses undulating wine-growing country. After flowing through Château-Thierry, it meanders through grain-growing lands and passes La Ferté-sous-

Jouarre and Meaux before making a wide loop southeast of Paris and entering the Seine River at Charenton, an eastern suburb of Paris. Its drainage basin covers some 5,000 square miles (13,000 square km) in all. Important canalization works, entailing the submerging of three villages in the Saint-Dizier area, have been undertaken to regulate the flow of the Marne as well as that of the Seine. The Marne is accompanied by a canal from its source to a lock northwest of Épernay, where its own channel is canalized. At Vitry-le-François two canals separate, one leading toward the Saône River, the other toward the Rhône River; both are ancient and in disrepair. The Marne River valley saw heavy fighting in World War I.

Marnia (Algeria): *see* Maghnia.

Marnix, Philips van, HEER (lord) VAN SINT ALDEGONDE (b. 1540, Brussels [now in Belgium]—d. Dec. 15, 1598, Leiden, Neth.), Dutch theologian and poet whose translation of the Psalms is considered the high point of religious literature in 16th-century Holland. In exile (1568–72) and a prisoner of the Roman Catholics (1573–74), Marnix was in the thick of the political and religious struggles of the time.

His first main work was *Den byencorf der H. Roomsche Kercke* (1569; "The Beehive of the Roman Catholic Church"), a polemical tract in prose in which the author, affecting to defend Roman Catholicism, in fact ridicules it.

Marnix's Psalm translations were first published in 1580, but he spent many years improving them. His constant fidelity to the original Hebrew did not inhibit his poetic nature—the language of his version is often moving and powerful. His identification with the Israelites through his own persecution and exile is strongly evident.

Maro, Publius Vergilius (Roman poet): *see* Virgil.

Maroboduus (d. AD 37, Ravenna [Italy]), king of the Marcomanni who organized the first confederation of German tribes.

A Marcomannian noble, Maroboduus spent his youth in Italy and received a Roman education. On his return to Germany, he emerged as leader of the Marcomanni. About 9 BC, to escape the threat of Roman domination, he and his people migrated from the Main River valley in west-central Germany to Bohemia, now part of the Czech Republic, where he founded a kingdom and formed a powerful confederacy with neighbouring German tribes in what is now Silesia and Saxony. After a period of hostility, the Romans recognized his kingdom in AD 6. In AD 9, Maroboduus refused to support the Cherusci leader Arminius in his war against Rome. Defeated by Arminius in 17, he was deposed in 19 and spent the rest of his life as an exile in Italy.

Marondera, formerly MARANDELLAS, town, northeastern Zimbabwe. It originated in 1890 as a rest house on the road from Harare (formerly Salisbury) to Mutare (formerly Umtali) and was named for Marondera, chief of the ruling Barozwi people. Destroyed in the Shona resistance of 1896, the town was moved 4 miles (6 km) north to the Harare-Beira railway line. During the Boer War it was used by the British as a staging point for military operations into the Transvaal, and in World War II it was a refuge for displaced Poles. Marondera services a large forestry and farming district and markets timber, tobacco, corn (maize), beef, and dairy products. It is an educational centre and the site of the Grasslands Research Station. Constituted a village in 1913, it became a town in 1943. Pop. (1982) 19,971.

Maroni River, Dutch MAROWIJNE RIVIER, river forming the boundary between French Guiana and Suriname (formerly Dutch Guiana), in South America. It rises on the northern slopes of the Tumuc-Humac Mountains, near the Brazilian border, and descends generally northward through dense tropical rain forests, to enter the Atlantic Ocean at Point Galibi, Suriname, about 19 miles (30 km) below the river ports of Saint-Laurent-du-Maroni, French Guiana, and Albina, Suriname. For much of its 450-mile (725-kilometre) length the river divides French

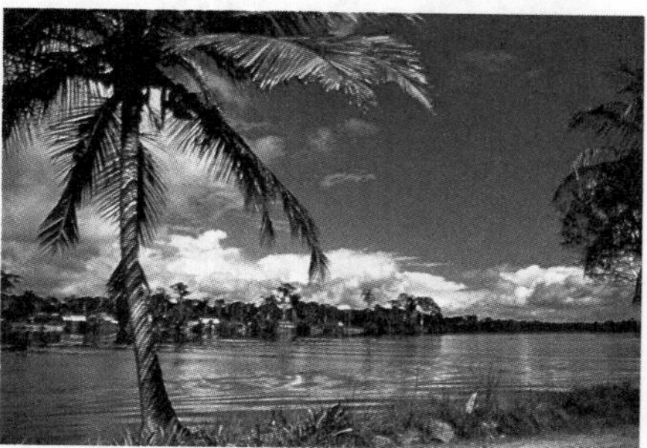

Maroni River near the village of Cottica, Suriname
Carl Frank

Guiana on the east from Suriname on the west. Its upper course is known as the Litani in Suriname, or Itany in French Guiana; its middle course, along which there is placer gold mining, is called the Lawa, or Aoua. Shallow-draft vessels can penetrate 60 miles (100 km) upstream from the river's mouth; beyond that point there are many waterfalls and rapids. The river's chief tributary is the Tapanahoni, in Suriname, from the southwest.

Maronite Church, one of the largest Eastern-rite communities of the Roman Catholic church, prominent especially in modern Lebanon; it is the only Eastern-rite church that has no non-Catholic or Orthodox counterpart. The Maronites trace their origins to St. Maron, or Maro (Arabic Mārūn), a Syrian hermit of the late 4th and early 5th centuries, and St. John Maron, or Joannes Maro (Arabic, Yūḥanna Mārūn), patriarch of Antioch in 685–707, under whose leadership the invading Byzantine armies of Justinian II were routed in 684, making the Maronites a fully independent people.

Though their traditions assert that the Maronites were always orthodox Christians in union with the Roman see, there is evidence that for centuries they were Monothelites, followers of the heretical doctrine of Sergius, patriarch of Constantinople, who affirmed that there was a divine but no human will in Christ. According to the medieval bishop William of Tyre, the Maronite patriarch sought union with the Latin patriarch of Antioch in 1182. A definitive consolidation of the union, however, did not come until the 16th century, brought about largely through the work of the Jesuit John Eliano. In 1584 Pope Gregory XIII founded the Maronite College in Rome, which flourished under Jesuit administration into the 20th century and became a training centre for scholars and leaders.

Hardy, martial mountaineers, the Maronites valiantly preserved their liberty and folkways. The Muslim caliphate (632–1258) could not absorb them, and two caliphs of the Umayyad dynasty (661–750) paid them tribute. Under the rule of the Ottoman Turks, the Maronites maintained their religion and customs under the protection of France, largely because of their geographic isolation. In the 19th century, however, the Ottoman government incited a neighbouring mountain people of Lebanon, the Druzes, against the Maronites, a policy that culminated in the great Maronite massacre of 1860. As a result of this incident, the Maronites achieved formal autonomy within the Ottoman Empire under a nonnative Christian ruler. In 1920, following the dissolution of the Ottoman Empire, the Maronites of Lebanon became self-ruling under French protection. Since the establishment of a fully independent Lebanon in 1943, they have constituted one of the two major religious groups in the country. The government is run by a coalition of Christian, Muslim, and Druze parties, but the president is always Maronite.

The immediate spiritual head of the Maronite church after the pope is the "patriarch of Antioch and all the East," residing in Bkirkī, near Beirut. The church retains the ancient West Syrian liturgy, even though the vernacular tongue of the Maronites is Arabic. Contact with Rome has been close and cordial, but it was not until after the second Vatican Council that the Maronites were freed of papal efforts to Latinize their rite. French Jesuits conduct the University of St. Joseph, at Beirut.

Maronites are also found in southern Europe and North and South America, having emigrated in the 19th century under the pressure of persecutions. The émigrés keep their own liturgy and have their own clergy, some of whom are married, but are subject to the local Latin-rite bishops.

Maroochydore, resort town, southeastern Queensland, Australia. It lies at the mouth of the Maroochy River and at the foot of Buderim Mountain; the southern part of Maroochydore merges with the township of Mooloolaba. The Maroochy River was sighted by Andrew Petrie in 1862, and Petrie took the name for the river and the district from an Aboriginal word meaning "water where the black swan lives." The town of Maroochydore, founded in 1900 as a port serving inland districts and for timber exports from the nearby Blackall Ranges, took its name from the district. It is now mainly a holiday resort, offering surfing, swimming, boating, and fishing to visitors from the state capital, Brisbane, 75 miles (120 km) to the south. Some sugarcane is grown in the area. Nearby Mooloolah National Park is a major lowland coastal reserve. Pop. (1986) including Mooloolaba, 20,635.

Maros River (Romania): *see* Mureș River.

Marosvásárhely (Romania): *see* Tîrgu Mureș.

Marot, Clément (b. 1496?, Cahors, Fr.—d. September 1544, Turin, Savoy [now in Italy]), one of the greatest poets of the French Renaissance, whose use of the forms and imagery of Latin poetry had marked influence on the style of his successors. His father, Jean, was a poet and held a post at the court of Anne de Bretagne and later served Francis I.

In 1514 Marot became page to Nicolas de Neufville, seigneur de Villeroi, secretary to the king. Wishing to follow in his father's footsteps by obtaining a place as court poet, he entered the service of Margaret of Angoulême, sister of Francis I and later queen of Navarre. On his father's death, he became valet de chambre to Francis I, a post he held, except for his years of exile (1534–36), until 1542.

Marot was arrested in 1526 for defying Lenten abstinence regulations, behaviour that put him under suspicion of being a Lutheran. A short imprisonment inspired some of his best-known works, especially "L'Enfer" ("The Inferno"), an allegorical satire on justice, and an epistle to his friend Lyon Jamet (1526). In 1527 he was again imprisoned, this time for attacking a prison guard and freeing a prisoner; an epistle, addressed to the king and begging for his deliverance, won his release. In 1531 Marot was again arrested for eating meat during Lent, but this time he avoided imprisonment. By 1530, in any event, his fame had become firmly established, and his many poems seem to have enjoyed a wide circulation.

After the Affaire des Placards, when placards attacking the Mass were posted in the major cities and on the door of the king's bedchamber (1534), Marot fled to Navarre, where he was protected by Margaret. When persecution of the Protestants increased, he again fled, this time to the court of Renée de France in Ferrara, Italy. Marot subsequently returned to Paris in 1537 after Francis I had stopped the persecutions.

When he was not engaged in writing the official poems that his duties at the French court compelled him to write, Marot spent most of his time translating the Psalms; a first edition of some of these appeared in 1539, the *Trente Pseaulmes de David* in 1542. These translations were notable for their sober and solemn musicality. Their condemnation by the Sorbonne caused Marot to go into exile again. But they were greatly admired by John Calvin, who gave Marot sanctuary in Geneva. Marot's behaviour became unacceptable in that strict and sober city, however, and he was forced to return to Italy.

Clément Marot, oil painting by an unknown artist; in the Bibliothèque Protestante, Paris

E. Bulloz

Although Marot's early poems were composed entirely in the style of the late medieval poets known as *rhétoriqueurs,* he soon abandoned the established genres of that school as well as its conceits, its didactic use of allegory, and its complicated versification. Instead, his knowledge of the Latin classics and his contacts with Italian literary forms enabled him to learn to imitate the styles and themes of antiquity. He introduced the elegy, the eclogue, the epigram, the epithalamium (nuptial poem), and the one-stanza Italian satiric *strambotto* (French *estrabot*) into French poetry, and he was one of the first French poets to attempt the Petrarchan sonnet form. His epigrams and epistolary poems (*épîtres*), in particular, display those qualities of wit, intellectual refinement, and sincerity and naturalness that were to characterize the French use of these genres for the next two centuries. He was also a master of the chant royal and infused some Horatian wit into the old forms of the ballade and the rondeau.

Marot attempted to create new or to improve existing lyrical forms, composing chansons and *cantiques* and originating the *blason* (1536), a satiric verse describing, as a rule, some aspect of the female body in minute detail. The *blason* found immediate popularity and was so widely imitated that it was possible to publish an anthology in 1555. Marot translated Catullus, Virgil, and Ovid and edited the works of François Villon and the *Roman de la rose.* He added grace, elegance, and personal warmth to French light verse. Much of his achievement was temporarily eclipsed by La Pléiade, a group of poets who dominated the literary scene for a period shortly after his death. But the influence of Marot was evident in England among the Elizabethans, notably Edmund Spenser, and was revived in France in the 17th century.

Marot, Daniel (b. 1661, Paris—d. June 4, 1752, The Hague), French-born Dutch architect, decorative designer, and engraver whose opulent and elaborate designs contributed to

Etching of a design for a table by Daniel Marot, *c.* 1700

By courtesy of the Victoria and Albert Museum, London

European styles of decoration in the late 17th and early 18th centuries. His many engravings provide an excellent record of the fashions of the times, including the beginnings of European interest in Oriental motifs.

Trained by his father, Jean Marot, an architect and engraver, Daniel was influenced by the French designers Jean Lepautre and Jean Berain. A Protestant, he left France in 1685, the year in which the Edict of Nantes was revoked, thus depriving French Protestants of the religious and civil rights formerly granted to them. Emigrating to Holland, he entered the service of the Prince of Orange and also worked for private clients. In 1694 he followed the prince, by that time William III of England, to London, returning about 1698 to Holland, where he continued to work for both the princely family and private patrons until his death.

In the Netherlands Marot's designs for William III included the chamber later known as the Armistice, or Truce, Hall at The Hague (*c.* 1697) and apartments and gardens at Het Loo, a palace built as a hunting lodge in the province of Gelderland (*c.* 1692). At Hampton Court, the palace occupied by William in England, Marot was involved in the design and layout of the gardens. He was also probably consulted in the decoration and furnishing of the palace interiors and designed such delftware as tulip vases and tiles. After his return to Holland, his work there included designs for the houses of various private patrons, the Portuguese synagogue, and the present royal library.

Marot, Jean (b. *c.* 1619—d. Dec. 15, 1679, Paris), French architect and engraver who was one of a large family of Parisian craftsmen and artists.

Although he was a Protestant, Marot was named architect of the king. He was also the architect of various private houses, including the Hôtel de Pussort, Hôtel de Mortemart, and Hôtel de Monceau, but he is chiefly renowned for his two great series of architectural engravings known as "Le Petit Marot" and "Le Grand Marot," which are essential for the study of French 17th-century architecture. In addition he engraved a large number of ornamental designs for chimneys, ceilings, etc., a practice in which he was followed by his son Daniel Marot, who became a celebrated decorative designer.

Maroteaux-Lamy syndrome, also called MUCOPOLYSACCHARIDOSIS VI, uncommon hereditary metabolic disease characterized by dwarfism, hearing loss, and progressive skeletal deformity. Onset of the disease is usually in early childhood, with some coarsening of facial features evident by the first birthday. Eye changes, consisting of corneal opacification and hypertelorism, or unusual widening of the space between the eyes, and enlargement of the liver and spleen are also features of the disease. Intelligence is normal, but the lifespan is greatly shortened; affected persons seldom survive beyond age 20. Like other mucopolysaccharidoses, Maroteaux-Lamy syndrome is caused by a defect in one of the enzymes that govern mucopolysaccharide metabolism, which is important in the development of connective tissue. The disorder is inherited as a recessive trait.

Maroua, also spelled MARUA, town, northern Cameroon, west-central Africa. It is situated in the foothills of the Mandara Mountains, along the Mayo ("river") Kaliao. An important marketing centre, it lies at the intersection of roads from Mokolo (northwest), Bogo (northeast), and Garoua (southwest). The town's agricultural exports are shipped by road to Garoua and then by boat on the Benue (Bénoué) River to Nigeria. A textile research institute,

Market in Maroua, Cameroon

Salmer/Plessner—Keystone

a cotton factory to the south, and an agricultural school reinforce Maroua's position as a major trade centre. The town is a handicraft centre (embroidery, leatherwork and metalwork, jewelry, pottery) and also contains an ethnographic museum. It has a hospital, a customs station, a veterinary station, a Protestant church, and several mosques. Waza National Park is nearby to the north. Pop. (1985 est.) 100,176.

Consult the INDEX *first*

Marowijne River (South America): *see* Maroni River.

Marprelate Controversy, brief but well-known pamphlet war (1588–89) carried on by English Puritans using secret presses; they attacked the episcopacy as "profane, proud, paltry, popish, pestilent, pernicious, presumptious prelates." The tracts, of which seven survive, never had the support of Puritan leaders and ceased when the presses were discovered by government agents. The identity of the author, who signed himself "Martin Marprelate gentleman" and "Martin junior," is still a mystery; perhaps more than one individual was involved. Anonymous replies appeared in 1589, and in February of that year Richard Bancroft delivered a sermon against the tracts at Paul's Cross, London, which is considered the first statement of the "divine right" of episcopacy in Anglican apologetics.

Marpurg, Friedrich Wilhelm (b. Nov. 21, 1718, Marpurgsdorf, near Seehausen, Brandenburg—d. May 22, 1795, Berlin), German composer and writer remembered for his theoretical and critical writings on music.

Nothing is known of his musical education. In 1746 he was secretary to a Prussian general in Paris, where he met Voltaire and the composer Jean Rameau. He later lived in Berlin and Hamburg and from 1763 to 1795 directed the Prussian state lottery. Particularly important among his works are the *Historisch-kritische Beyträge* (1754–58) and his introductions to different branches of music, notably the fugue in *Abhandlung von der Fuge* (1753–54). These works are valuable to students of 18th-century music history, theory, and practice. His compositions include *6 Sonaten für das Cembalo* (1756) and *Fughe e caprice* (1777).

Marquand, J(ohn) P(hillips) (b. Nov. 10, 1893, Wilmington, Del., U.S.—d. July 16, 1960, Newburyport, Mass.), U.S. novelist who recorded the shifting patterns of middle and upper class U.S. society in the mid-20th century.

Marquand grew up in New York City and suburban Rye in comfortable circumstances until his father's business failure, when he was sent to live with relatives in Newburyport. This experience of reduced status and security—sharpened by attending Harvard on a scholarship obtained by agreeing to study a subject he despised (chemistry)—made him acutely conscious of social gradations and their psychological corollaries.

After about 15 years devoted to writing popular fiction, including the widely read adventures of the Japanese intelligence agent Mr. Moto, Marquand wrote his three most characteristic novels, satirical but sympathetic studies of a crumbling New England gentility: *The Late George Apley* (1937), *Wickford Point* (1939), and *H.M. Pulham, Esquire* (1941), in which a conforming Bostonian renounces romantic love for duty. He wrote three novels dealing with the dislocations of wartime America—*So Little Time* (1943), *Repent in Haste* (1945), and *B.F.'s Daughter* (1946)—but in these his social perceptions were somewhat less keen. He came back to his most able level of writing in his next novel, *Point of No Return* (1949), a painstakingly accurate social study of a New England town much like Newburyport. Two social types particularly important in the 1950s were depicted in *Melville Goodwin, U.S.A.* (1951), about a professional soldier, and *Sincerely, Willis Wayde* (1955), a sharply satiric portrait of a big business promoter. His last important novel, *Women and Thomas Harrow* (1958), is about a successful playwright and is partly autobiographical.

Marqués, René (b. Oct. 4, 1919, Arecibo, Puerto Rico—d. March 22, 1979, San Juan), playwright, short-story writer, critic and Puerto Rican nationalist whose work shows deep social and artistic commitment.

Marqués was graduated in 1942 from the College of Agricultural Arts of Mayaguez. He studied at the University of Madrid in 1946 and later studied writing at Columbia University in New York City.

His best known play, *La Carreta* (1956; "The Wagon"; Eng. trans. *The Oxcart*, 1966), concerns a rural Puerto Rican family who emigrate to New York City in search of their fortune but fail and subsequently return to Puerto Rico, where they find it hard to adapt. In 1959 he published three plays together in the collection *Teatro* ("Theatre"). These were *La muerte no entrará en palacio* ("Death Will Not Enter the Palace"), a political allegorical play in which a governor betrays his youthful ideals by succumbing to foreign imperialism, *Un niño azul para esa sombra* ("A Blue Child for That Shadow"), and *Los soles truncos* ("Maimed Suns"). In *Los soles truncos*, one of his most successful plays, Marqués re-creates the closed environment and lives of three patrician sisters unable to cope with the onslaught of modernization. In most of his plays, Marqués calls for developing a sense of national identity; an acceptance of foreign values leads only to alienation.

This theme is expressed in the short-story collections *Otro día nuestro* (1955; "Another of Our Days"), *En una ciudad llamada San Juan* (1960; "In a City Called San Juan"), and *Inmersos en el silencio* (1976; "Immersed in Silence"), as well as in the novels *La víspera del hombre* (1959; "The Eve of Man") and *La mirada* (1975; "The Glance").

A collection of his essays, *Ensayos* (1966; some included in *El puertorriqueño dócil,* (1967; *The Docile Puerto Rican,* 1976), is also concerned with the problem of national identity in relation to the language, literature, and prevailing social conditions of Puerto Rico.

Marquesas Islands, French ÎLES MARQUISES, pair of volcanic clusters in French Polynesia in the central South Pacific, 740 mi (1,200 km) northeast of Tahiti. The southeastern group includes Hiva Oa (*q.v.*), largest and most populated and the burial place of the French artist Paul Gauguin; Fatu Hiva and Tahuata, each about 23 sq mi (60 sq km) and both rising to about 3,300 ft (1,005 m); and the uninhabited

Governor's residence on Nuku Hiva, one of the Marquesas Islands, French Polynesia
John Yates—Photographic Library of Australia

Motane and Fatu Huku. The northwestern group comprises the picturesque Nuku Hiva (*q.v.*), Ua Pu, Ua Huka, Eiao, and Hatutu.

The southeastern islands were sighted in 1595 by the Spanish explorer Álvaro de Mendaña de Neira, who named them for the Marquesa de Mendoza. Capt. James Cook visited Fatu Huku in 1774. In 1791 the American sea captain Joseph Ingraham sighted the northwestern group and named them Washington Islands. The whole group, annexed by the French in 1842, now forms a *circonscription* (administrative division) of French Polynesia, with headquarters at Hakapehi (Tai-o-hae) on Nuku Hiva. Because the islands lack coastal plains and coral reefs, habitation is largely restricted to the narrow valleys where streams run down from the mountains. Chief products are copra, taros, breadfruit, coffee, and vanilla. Most of the residents are Roman Catholic. Pop. (1981 est.) 6,100.

marquess, also spelled MARQUIS, feminine MARCHIONESS, also called (in Germany) MARGRAVE, feminine MARGRAVINE, a European title of nobility, ranking in modern times immediately below a duke and above a count, or earl. Etymologically the word marquess or margrave denoted a count or earl holding a march, or mark, that is, a frontier district; but this original significance has long been lost.

In western Europe the Carolingian *marchiones* or margraves had been royal officials whose duty of defending a frontier might justify an exception being made to the normal rule that no count should hold more than one countship or county. Their authority was thus not much less than that of a duke; indeed the term *Markherzog* ("mark duke") is occasionally found instead of *Markgraf* ("mark count"). But as conditions on the frontiers or the frontiers themselves were changed, the special importance of the old marches diminished.

France. As the great French feudatories' power grew at the expense of the king's, the old *marquisats* were practically lost in the great duchies or countships. Then, with the multiplication of little fiefs, minor counts holding several such lordships took to assuming the style of marquis to distinguish themselves. The rank of a marquis, always inferior to that of a duke, was thus in a controversial relation to that of a count. Sometimes a count's nobility was better established and his fief greater than that of any marquis; sometimes a marquis with a royal patent should obviously have precedence. These ambiguities served to bring the title into disrepute in the 17th and 18th centuries, as being too often self-made or pretentious; and after the Revolution had abolished it Napoleon did not see fit to revive it. Louis XVIII, reviving it after the Restoration, gave its holders definitive precedence between dukes and counts.

Germany. At the end of the Carolingian era, the German kings of the Saxon dynasty, Otto I, Otto II, and Otto III, created a new system of marks in the 10th century, giving particular attention to their eastern frontier. A margrave was expected not only to secure the frontier but also to push it forward into Slav or pagan territory, as did Gero, the Billungs, the margraves of Meissen, and Albert I the Bear. Some of the margraviates grew into hereditary principalities; thus, the Bavarian Ostmark became the duchy of Austria, the Steiermark became the duchy of Styria, and the Saxon Nordmark became the electorate of Brandenburg. Later, however, the margraves of Baden were so styled simply because their ancestor had held the mark of Verona in 11th-century Italy; the Hohenzollern margraves of Ansbach and of Bayreuth likewise echoed their ancestor's title to Brandenburg.

Italy. The frontier mark in Italy long survived as a major territorial unit, though the original Carolingian demarcations were considerably altered. By the 14th century, however, barons and *signori* had begun to erect their fiefs into *marchesati,* after which the title grew to have much the same fate as the French *marquisat.*

Spain. The remnant of the original Carolingian Marca Hispanica was merged in the countship of Barcelona. The first Castilian *marquesado* was that of Villena (on the Valencian frontier), created for Don Alonso of Aragon in 1376; the Pacheco family, who acquired it from the crown in 1445, subsequently became dukes of Escalona. The next senior *marquesado* was that of Santillana (1445).

The British Isles. In England the Late Latin term *marchiones* was early applied to the lords of the Welsh marches, but it was there used in a sense descriptive only of their lordships' location near the frontier without implying that they were superior to other earls. In 1385, however, Robert de Vere, 9th earl of Oxford, was created marquess of Dublin with precedence between dukes and earls; the other earls resented this creation, and the patent of the marquessate was revoked in 1386, after its holder had been created duke of Ireland. John Beaufort, earl of Somerset, was created marquess of Dorset and of Somerset in 1397, but he was degraded to his former earldom in 1399. When the commons petitioned for his restoration as marquess of Dorset in 1402, he objected because of the strangeness of the term in England. In 1443, however, his son Edmund Beaufort was raised to be marquess of Dorset, after which the title retained its place in the peerage. As earlier creations became extinct or were raised to dukedoms, the premier marquessate of England in the 20th century was that of Winchester, created in 1551.

Marquess, marchioness
foreign-language equivalents

	masculine	feminine
Czech	markrabě	markraběnka
French	marquis	marquise
German	Markgraf	Markgräfin
Hungarian	örgróf	örgrófnö
Italian	marchese	marchesa
Japanese	kōshaku	kōshaku-fujin
Portuguese	marquês	marquesa
Spanish	marqués	marquesa

Marquess of Queensberry rules, code of rules that most directly influenced modern boxing. Written by John Graham Chambers, a member of the British Amateur Athletic Club, the rules were first published in 1867 under the sponsorship of John Sholto Douglas, ninth marquess of Queensberry, from whom they take their name. The rules are as follows:

Rule 1—To be a fair stand-up boxing match in a 24-foot ring, or as near that size as practicable.

Rule 2—No wrestling or hugging allowed.

Rule 3—The rounds to be of three minutes' duration, and one minute's time between rounds.

Rule 4—If either man falls through weakness or otherwise, he must get up unassisted, 10 seconds to be allowed him to do so, the other man meanwhile to return to his corner, and when the fallen man is on his legs the round is to be resumed and continued until the three minutes have expired. If one man fails to come to the scratch in the 10 seconds allowed, it shall be in the power of the referee to give his award in favour of the other man.

Rule 5—A man hanging on the ropes in a helpless state, with his toes off the ground, shall be considered down.

Rule 6—No seconds or any other person to be allowed in the ring during the rounds.

Rule 7—Should the contest be stopped by any unavoidable interference, the referee to name the time and place as soon as possible for finishing the contest; so that the match must be won and lost, unless the backers of both men agree to draw the stakes.

Rule 8—The gloves to be fair-sized boxing gloves of the best quality and new.

Rule 9—Should a glove burst, or come off, it must be replaced to the referee's satisfaction.

Rule 10—A man on one knee is considered down and if struck is entitled to the stakes.

Rule 11—No shoes or boots with springs allowed.

Rule 12—The contest in all other respects to be governed by revised rules of the London Prize Ring. *See* London Prize Ring rules.

To make the best use of the Britannica, consult the INDEX *first*

marquetry, thin sheets of wood, metal, or organic material, such as shell or mother-of-pearl, cut into intricate patterns according to a preconceived design and affixed to the flat surfaces of furniture. The process became popular in France in the late 16th century and received an enormous stimulus in the two following centuries as the European economy started to expand and created a demand for luxurious domestic furniture. The work of André-Charles Boulle, in the late 17th and early 18th centuries, achieved such beauty that furniture adorned with marquetry patterns is sometimes known as boulle work.

To produce the desired effect, the *ébéniste,* or specialist in marquetry, either drew the pattern directly on the base wood or affixed a paper pattern onto the wood. The thin sheets were then cut out with a burin or, later, sometimes with a saw, the pattern assembled and glued onto the carcass. Boulle initiated an ingenious method for use with contrasting materials, such as ebony and ivory. Two sheets of identical thickness were glued together and the pattern cut out. When the sheets were taken apart, it was then possible to decorate two panels of the same size with identical patterns in contrasting materials. As marquetry-work tends to splinter, vulnerable places such as the outer edges of the design and keyholes were often protected with mounts of bronze or other metals, often of an intricate shape, which add to the decorative richness of the piece of furniture. Marquetry patterns became more and more complex and, though often floral, they could also include narrative subjects and the like. The range of materials used also became more varied, including not only rare tropical woods and metals such as silver, bronze, and brass but also a wide range of other materials of a semiprecious nature.

Marquette, city, seat (1851) of Marquette county, Upper Peninsula of Michigan, U.S., on Lake Superior, overlooked by Sugar Loaf Mountain (north), 66 mi (106 km) north-northwest of Escanaba. Founded in 1849 as Worcester and renamed for Jacques Marquette, it became an important iron ore and lumber port. Manufactures include foundry and wood products and mining machinery. Other economic factors are the tourist trade and Northern Michigan University (1899). Marquette is a Roman Catholic diocesan seat (St. Peter's Cathedral, 1933). The city's Presque Isle Park is on a small wooded peninsula extending into the lake. Inc. village, 1859; city, 1871. Pop. (1990) 21,977.

Marquette, Jacques, byname PÈRE (Father) MARQUETTE (b. June 1, 1637, Laon, Fr.—d. May 18, 1675, Ludington, Mich.), French Jesuit missionary explorer who, with Louis Jolliet, travelled down the Mississippi River and reported the first accurate data on its course.

Marquette arrived in Quebec in 1666. After a study of Indian languages, he assisted in founding a mission at Sault Ste. Marie (now in Michigan) in 1668, and another at St. Ignace (now in Michigan) in 1671. In mid-May 1673 he left St. Ignace with Jolliet, who had been commissioned by Louis, comte de Frontenac, governor of New France, to find the direction and the mouth of the Mississippi. They travelled westward to Green Bay (now in Wisconsin), ascended the Fox River to a portage that crossed to the Wisconsin River, and entered the Mississippi near Prairie du Chien on June 17. Following it to the mouth of the Arkansas River, they learned that the Mississippi flowed through hostile Spanish domains, and in mid-July they turned homeward by way of the Illinois River. Marquette was exhausted when he reached Green Bay, and he remained there while Jolliet continued on to Canada.

In 1674 Marquette set out to found a mission among the Illinois Indians, but, caught by the winter, he and two companions camped near the site of the city of Chicago, and thus became the first Europeans to live there. Marquette reached the Indians (near what is now Utica, Ill.) in the spring, but illness forced his return. While en route to St. Ignace he died at the mouth of a river now known as Père Marquette.

Márquez, Gabriel García: *see* García Márquez, Gabriel.

marquis (title): *see* marquess.

Marquis, Don, byname of DONALD ROBERT PERRY MARQUIS (b. July 29, 1878, Walnut, Ill., U.S.—d. Dec. 29, 1937, New York City), U.S. newspaperman, poet, and playwright, creator of the literary characters Archy, the cockroach, and Mehitabel, the cat, wry, down-and-out philosophers of the 1920s.

Educated at Knox College, Galesburg, Ill., Marquis worked as a reporter on *The Atlanta Journal.* When in 1907 Joel Chandler Harris established the *Uncle Remus's Magazine,* Marquis became his associate editor. Harris gave him his own department with a by-line.

In 1912 Marquis left Atlanta for New York City, where he became one of the best known of literary journalists. He wrote his columns "The Sun Dial" for *The Sun* and "The Lantern" for the *Tribune.* Archy and Mehitabel first appeared in "The Sun Dial." Archy's poetic reflections on the world and the racy misadventures of Mehitabel were related in first person and lowercase by Archy, who supposedly could not press down the typewriter's shift key.

Among Marquis' published collections of humorous poetry, satirical prose, and plays are *Danny's Own Story* (1912), *Dreams and Dust* (1915), *Hermione* (1916), *The Old Soak* (1916; made into a play, 1926), *Sonnets to a Red Haired Lady* (1922), *The Dark Hours* (1924), and *Out of the Sea* (1927). After Marquis' death *archy and mehitabel* (1927) was combined with several sequels into an omnibus, *the lives and times of archy and mehitabel* (1940), illustrated by George Herriman. In 1957 some of the Archy and Mehitabel stories were made into a musical by George Kleinsinger and Joe Darion. *The Best of Don Marquis* (1946) has an introduction by Marquis' friend Christopher Morley; Edward Anthony's *O Rare Don Marquis* (1962) is a biography.

Marquises, Îles (French Polynesia): *see* Marquesas Islands.

Marr, Nikolay Yakovlevich (b. Jan. 6, 1865 [Dec. 25, 1864, old style], Kutaisi, Georgia, Russian Empire—d. Dec. 20, 1934, Leningrad [St. Petersburg]), Russian linguist, archaeologist, and ethnographer specializing in the languages of the Caucasus.

A professor at St. Petersburg University from 1900, Marr published numerous collections of old Georgian and Armenian literature and attempted to prove a relationship between the Caucasian and Semitic-Hamitic and Basque languages. Marr took his ideas further in 1924, proposing a monogenetic theory of language: all languages evolved from one original made up of four basic elements (*sal, ber, yon, rosh*). Each language of the world had attained its own stage of evolution. Languages themselves were the products of the underlying socio-economic structure and were therefore class-related and not national phenomena. Marr's ideas lent themselves to Marxist theory; and became the "official" linguistic approach until 1950, when Stalin denounced it. After his death in 1934, Marr's ideas were adopted and expanded by the Institute of Language and Thought.

Marr's discredited theory has obscured his legitimate accomplishment: exciting interest in the many non-Indo-European languages within republics of the former Soviet Union.

Marrah, Jabal, English MARRA MOUNTAINS, mountain range, a rugged volcanic chain extending for 100 mi (160 km) west-southwest of al-Fāshir, in west-central Sudan. The highest point of the Nile-Lake Chad watershed, the mountains reach heights of more than 10,000 ft (3,000 m). Some intermittent tributaries of the Baḥr al-ʿArab rise on the southern flanks.

Marrakech, also spelled MARRAKESH, chief city of southern Morocco. One of Morocco's four imperial cities, it lies in the centre

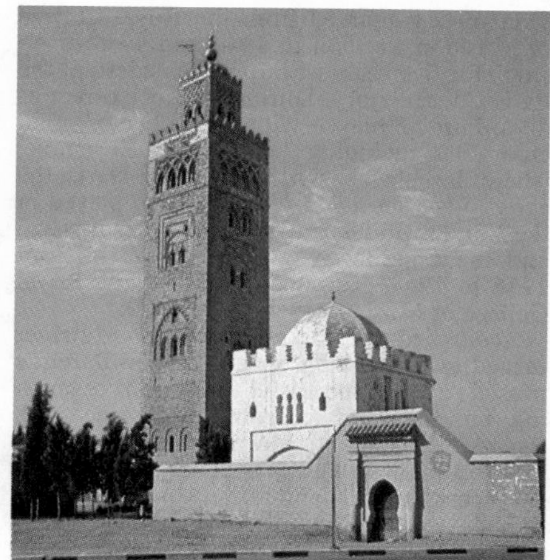

Koutoubia Mosque, Marrakech, Mor.
Jean Bottin

of the fertile, irrigated Haouz plain, south of the Wadi Tensift.

Marrakech, misnamed Morocco by Europeans, gave its name to the kingdom of which it was for long the capital. It was founded in 1062 by Yusuf ibn Tāshufīn of the dynasty of the Almoravids and served as the Almoravid capital until it fell to the Almohads in 1147. In 1269 Marrakech passed to the control of the Marinids, whose preferred capital was Fès. Although Marrakech served as the capital under the Saʿadians in the 16th century, the succeeding ʿAlawīd rulers resided more often at Fès or Meknès. In 1912 Marrakech was captured by the Saharan insurgent al-Hiba, who was defeated and driven out by French forces commanded by Colonel C.M.E. Mangin. Under the French protectorate (1912–56) Marrakech was for many years administered by the Glaoua family, the last of whom, Haj Thami al-Glaoui, was the chief instigator of the deposition of Sultan Muḥammad ben Yusuf (Muḥammad V) in 1953.

Surrounded by a vast palm grove, the medina (or ancient Moorish town) in Marrakech is called the "red city" because of its buildings and ramparts of beaten clay; its heart is the Place Jema al-Fna, a colourful marketplace. Just east is the 12th-century Koutoubia Mosque with its 220-foot (67-metre) minaret, built by Spanish captives. The 16th-century Saʿdī Mausoleum, the 18th-century Dar el-Beïda Palace (now a hospital), and the 19th-century Bahia royal residence reflect the city's historical growth. The modern quarter, called Gueliz, to the west of the medina, developed under the French Protectorate. Marrakech is famous for its parks, especially the Menara olive grove and the walled, 1,000-acre (405-hectare) Agdal gardens. Popular for tourism and winter sports, the city is a commercial centre for the Haut (High) Atlas and Saharan trade and has an international airport. It is connected by railway and road to Safi and Casablanca. Pop. (2000 est.) 822,000.

Marrano, in Spanish history, a Jew who converted to the Christian faith to escape persecution but who continued to practice Judaism secretly. It was a term of abuse and also applies to any descendants of Marranos. The origin of the word *marrano* is uncertain.

In the late 14th century, Spanish Jewry was threatened with extinction by mobs of fanatical Christians. Thousands of Jews accepted death, but tens of thousands found safety by converting to Christianity. The number of converts is estimated at more than 100,000. By the mid-15th century the persons who had been baptized but continued to practice Judaism in secret—Marranos—formed a compact society. The Marranos began to grow rich and to rise to high positions in the state, the royal court, and the church hierarchy. They intermarried with the noblest families. The hatred directed against them, ostensibly because they were suspected of being untrue to their converted faith, was in fact directed indiscriminately against all conversos, or Jewish converts.

In March 1473, riots against Marranos broke out in Córdoba, with pillage and carnage lasting for three days. The massacres spread from city to city, carried out by fanatical mobs. In 1480 the Inquisition was introduced to provide institutional control over the persecution of the Marranos. In the Inquisition's first year, more than 300 Marranos were burned, their estates reverting to the crown. The number of victims grew into tens of thousands.

To the Jews, the Marranos were pitiful martyrs. The Jews maintained religious bonds with the Marranos and kept strong their faith in the God of Israel. The Inquisition finally became convinced, however, that only the total expulsion of the Jews from Spain could end Jewish influence in the national life. Purity of faith became the national policy of the Catholic sovereigns, and thus came about the final tragedy, the edict of expulsion of all the Jews from Spain on March 31, 1492. Portugal promulgated an edict of expulsion in 1497 and Navarre in 1498.

A considerable minority of Jews saved themselves from expulsion by baptism, thus adding strength and numbers to the Marranos, but the mass of Spanish Jews refused conversion and went into exile. The physical separation of the Marranos from their spiritual sympathizers, however, did not make them more amenable to inquisitorial discipline. The Jewish religion remained deeply rooted in their hearts, and they continued to transmit their beliefs to the succeeding generations. Many Marranos did eventually choose emigration, however, principally to North Africa and to other western European countries. Marranism had disappeared in Spain by the 18th century owing to this emigration and to gradual assimilation within Spain. *See also* converso.

marriage: *see under* descriptive word (*e.g.,* exchange marriage; group marriage), except as below.

marriage, a legally and socially sanctioned union, usually between a man and a woman, that is regulated by laws, rules, customs, beliefs, and attitudes that prescribe the rights and duties of the partners and accords status to their offspring (if any). The universality of marriage within different societies and cultures is attributed to the many basic social and personal functions for which it provides structure, such as sexual gratification and regulation, division of labour between the sexes, economic production and consumption, and satisfaction of needs for affection, status, and companionship. Perhaps the most important function concerns procreation and child rearing and the regulation of lines of descent.

In 2000 The Netherlands became the first country to legalize same-sex marriages. Belgium passed a similar law in 2003, except that it limited marriageable partners to those whose national laws allowed such marriages. Court decisions made same-sex marriages legal in the U.S. state of Massachusetts (2004) and in some Canadian provinces (2002–04). Some Scandinavian countries extended benefits and obligations to same-sex couples by means of a registered domestic partnership or civil union, both of which terms meant different things in different contexts. This type of union was also recognized by some U.S. states.

In the biological evolutionary scale, the more complex the species, the longer the offspring is dependent on its mother for survival from the time of birth to maturity. Human beings, at the top of the evolutionary scale, require the most time of all species to reach maturity. This imposes increased duties on human parents for the care of their children, and marriage traditionally has been seen as the institution best suited to fulfill these parental duties and responsibilities.

Marital customs and laws. Some form of marriage has been found to exist in all human societies, past and present. Its importance can be seen in the elaborate and complex laws and rituals surrounding it. Although these laws and rituals are as varied and numerous as human social and cultural organizations, some universals do apply.

The main legal function of marriage is to ensure the rights of the partners with respect to each other and to ensure the rights and define the relationships of children within a community. Marriage has historically conferred a legitimate status on the offspring, which entitled him or her to the various privileges set down by the traditions of that community, including the right of inheritance. In most societies marriage also established the permissible social relations allowed to the offspring, including the acceptable selection of future spouses.

Until the late 20th century, marriage was rarely a matter of free choice. In Western societies love between spouses came to be associated with marriage, but even in Western cultures romantic love was not the primary motive for matrimony in most eras, and one's marriage partner was carefully chosen.

Endogamy, the practice of marrying someone from within one's own tribe or group, is the oldest social regulation of marriage. When the forms of communication with outside groups are limited, endogamous marriage is a natural consequence. Cultural pressures to marry within one's social, economic, and ethnic group are still very strongly enforced in some societies.

Exogamy, the practice of marrying outside the group, is found in societies in which kinship relations are the most complex, thus barring from marriage large groups who may trace their lineage to a common ancestor.

In societies in which the large, or extended, family remains the basic unit, marriages are usually arranged by the family. The assumption is that love between the partners comes after marriage, and much thought is given to the socioeconomic advantages accruing to the larger family from the match. By contrast, in societies in which the small, or nuclear, family predominates, young adults usually choose their own mates. It is assumed that love precedes (and determines) marriage, and less thought is normally given to the socioeconomic aspects of the match.

In societies with arranged marriages, the almost universal custom is that someone acts as an intermediary, or matchmaker. This person's chief responsibility is to arrange a marriage that will be satisfactory to the two families represented. Some form of dowry or bridewealth is almost always exchanged in societies that favour arranged marriages.

In societies in which individuals choose their own mates, dating is the most typical way for people to meet and become acquainted with prospective partners. Successful dating may result in courtship, which then usually leads to marriage.

Marriage rituals. The rituals and ceremonies surrounding marriage in most cultures are associated primarily with fecundity and validate the importance of marriage for the continuation of a clan, people, or society. They also assert a familial or communal sanction of the mutual choice and an understanding of the difficulties and sacrifices involved in making what is considered, in most cases, to be a lifelong commitment to and responsibility for the welfare of spouse and children.

Marriage ceremonies include symbolic rites, often sanctified by a religious order, which are thought to confer good fortune on the couple. Because economic considerations play an essential role in the success of child rearing, the offering of gifts, both real and symbolic, to the married couple are a significant part of the marriage ritual. Where the exchange of goods is extensive, either from the bride's family to the bridegroom's or vice versa, this usually indicates that the freedom to choose one's marital partner has been limited and determined by the families of the betrothed.

Fertility rites intended to ensure a fruitful marriage exist in some form in all ceremonies. Some of the oldest rituals still to be found in contemporary ceremonies include the prominent display of fruits or of cereal grains that may be sprinkled over the couple or on their nuptial bed, the accompaniment of a small child with the bride, and the breaking of an object or food to ensure a successful consummation of the marriage and an easy childbirth.

The most universal ritual is one that symbolizes a sacred union. This may be expressed by the joining of hands, an exchange of rings or chains, or the tying of garments. However, elements in marriage rituals vary greatly among different societies, and components such as time, place, and the social importance of the event are often fixed by tradition and habit.

marriage and wardship: *see* wardship and marriage.

marriage law, the body of legal specifications and requirements and other laws that regulate the initiation, continuation, and validity of marriages. Marriage is a legally sanctioned union usually between one man and one woman. At the beginning of the 21st century, marriage between people of the same sex was legally recognized in two countries—The Netherlands (2000) and Belgium (2003)—in the U.S. state of Massachusetts (2004), and in some Canadian provinces (2002–04). Civil unions or domestic partnerships between persons of the same sex, which entailed many of the rights and obligations assumed by married couples, were recognized in numerous other jurisdictions, including several European countries and some U.S. states. Other U.S. jurisdictions, while not recognizing civil unions or domestic partnerships, granted a range of legal rights to same-sex couples.

Because marriage is viewed as a contractual agreement subject to legal processes, a newly married couple assumes certain legal rights and obligations to each other. In many societies, these obligations include living together in the same or nearby dwellings, the provision of domestic services such as child rearing, cooking, and housekeeping, and the provision of food, shelter, clothing, and other means of support. The rights of marriage include the shared ownership and inheritance of each other's property to varying degrees and, in monogamous marriages, the exclusive right to sexual intercourse with each other.

These generalizations notwithstanding, every past or present society has had its own concept of marriage. Ancient Roman law recognized three forms of marriage: *confarreatio,* usually reserved for patrician families, was marked by a highly solemnized ceremony involving numerous witnesses and animal sacrifice; *coemptio,* used by many plebeians, was effectively marriage by purchase; and *usus,* the most informal variety, was marriage simply by mutual consent and evidence of extended cohabitation. Roman law generally placed the woman under the control of her husband and on the same footing as children.

The canon law of the Roman Catholic church was the only law governing matrimonial relations between Christians in western Europe until the Reformation. The church historically regarded marriage as a lifelong and sacred union that could be dissolved only by the death of one of the spouses. This exalted view of marriage envisaged the husband and wife as made of "one flesh" by the act of God. In canon law the free and mutual consent of the parties was essential to marriage. Marriage was regarded as completed between baptized persons by consent and then consummation. Canon law held a marriage to be null and void in cases in which the parties were within prohibited degrees of close blood relationship (consanguinity and affinity).

Marriage law as it developed in England specified the requisites of marriage as follows: each party shall have attained a certain age; each shall be sexually competent and mentally capable; each shall be free to marry; each shall give his or her consent to marry; the parties shall be outside the prohibited degrees of blood relationship to each other; and the marriage ceremony shall conform with the statutory formalities.

The marriage law of most western European nations and that of the United States (which is itself based on English marriage law) is the product of canon law that has been greatly modified by the changed cultural and social conditions of modern life. Modern marriage law regards marriage as a civil transaction and allows only monogamous unions. In general, the legal capacity of a person to marry is the same in most of the Western world and is subject to constraints only regarding consanguinity and affinity, age, and mental capacity. In the United States the federal Defense of Marriage Act (1996) defines marriage as a legal union between one man and one woman only and allows states to refuse to recognize same-sex marriages performed in other states. Many states have passed laws similar to the Defense of Marriage Act or have amended their constitutions to the same effect.

Divorce is almost universally allowed. Restrictions in Roman Catholic countries have gradually been relaxed. In Russia only registered civil marriage is recognized. Monogamy is strictly enforced there, and marriage must be completely voluntary between the parties, who must be over 18 years of age. Caste and social standing continue to influence the incidence of divorce in areas of South Asia.

In Muslim countries, the prevailing Islāmic law regards marriage as a contract between the two spouses for the "legalization of intercourse and the procreation of children," though it is also regarded as a gift from God or a kind of service to God. The terms of the marriage depend on the will of the consenting parties, and it may be constituted without any ceremonial. The essential requirement of marriage is offer and acceptance, expressed at one meeting. Islāmic law has historically permitted the practice of polygamy, but its incidence was always limited and was waning in virtually all Muslim countries by the late 20th century.

Polygamous marriages are still permitted in many African nations, but there is a growing tendency toward monogamy. Many developing nations in Africa and elsewhere are markedly different from Western nations in that there is no uniform marriage law; the regulation of marital relations is based either on religion or on the customary laws of the territory. This leads to a diversity of laws within one territorial unit and often gives rise to complex problems in the case of tribal, ethnic, or religious intermarriage.

In Japan polygamous marriage is prohibited, and age limits of 18 years for men and 16 years for women are specified before marriage can take place. Consanguinity to a close degree is prohibited, and all marriages must be registered in accordance with law. Polygamy is also forbidden in China. Formality in the marriage celebration has been abandoned, but the civil marriage must be duly registered.

Marriner, Sir Neville (b. April 15, 1924, Lincoln, Lincolnshire, Eng.), British violinist, teacher, and conductor who in 1959 organized the Academy of St. Martin-in-the-Fields, a London chamber ensemble that won popular and critical acclaim.

Marriner graduated from the Royal College of Music in London in 1944 and went on to study for five years with René Benedetti at the Paris Conservatory. During his early career as a violinist he played with a number of small ensembles, including the Jacobean Ensemble, where he played with Thurston Dart, the early-music specialist. Marriner also played in the London Philharmonia from 1952 to 1956 and the London Symphony Orchestra from 1956 to 1968. He taught violin at the Royal College of Music from 1949 to 1959.

Encouraged by Pierre Monteux, Marriner turned to conducting, specializing in Baroque music. After 10 successful years spent organizing, building, and recording extensively with the Academy of St. Martin-in-the-Fields, he went on to direct and conduct major symphony orchestras throughout the world, including the Los Angeles Chamber Orchestra (1969–77; founded by Marriner), the Minnesota Symphony (1979–86), and the Stuttgart Radio Symphony Orchestra, Germany (1983–89). He also served as guest conductor for a number of ensembles. Marriner was knighted in 1985.

Marriott, J(ohn) Willard (b. Sept. 17, 1900, Marriott, Utah, U.S.—d. Aug. 13, 1985, Wolfeboro, N.H.), American businessman who founded one of the largest hotel and restaurant organizations in the United States.

The son of a Mormon rancher, Marriott worked his way through Wheeler State College and the University of Utah at Ogden, graduating in 1926. He opened a small root beer and barbecue stand in Washington, D.C., in 1927 and by 1932 had expanded his Hot Shoppe chain of inexpensive family restaurants to seven in the area. By the end of World War II his restaurant chain had spread over the entire East Coast, and Marriott had started an airline catering service as well. In 1957 Marriott opened his company's first motel, and during the 1950s and '60s Marriott-Hot Shoppes, Inc., as the company was then called, became known as the fastest growing and most profitable organization in the American food and lodging business.

Marriott's son J. Willard Marriott, Jr., succeeded his father as president of the renamed Marriott Corporation in 1964 and became the corporation's chief executive officer in 1972; his father remained chairman of the board until his death. By the time of the elder Marriott's death in 1985, the Marriott Corporation had 140,000 employees in 26 countries, operated 1,400 restaurants and 143 hotels and resorts in 95 cities, and had total annual sales of $3,500,000,000. Although the company's stock was offered to the public in 1952, the Marriott family retained a controlling share of it.

Marriott, Sr., was an active supporter of Republican Party presidential candidates. He was awarded (posthumously) the Presidential Medal of Freedom in 1988.

marrow, bone: *see* bone marrow.

Marrucini, ancient tribe that occupied a small area around Teate (modern Chieti) on the east coast of Italy. The Marrucini, though Samnite kinsmen, were probably not members of the Samnite league; they did, however, come into conflict with the Romans during the Second Samnite War, at the end of which they entered the Roman alliance (304 BC). They revolted in 91 BC and were thereafter enrolled in the Roman tribe Arnensis. Their language is known from an inscription, the "Bronze of Rapino" (*c.* 250 BC). It is written in the Latin alphabet but in a dialect of the Northern Oscan group, which included the Paeligni and Vestini.

Marryat, Frederick (b. July 10, 1792, London—d. Aug. 9, 1848, Langham, Norfolk, Eng.), naval officer and the first important English novelist after Tobias Smollett to make full and amusing use of his varied experience at sea.

Marryat entered the Royal Navy at the age

Marryat, detail of an oil painting by J. Simpson, *c.* 1835; in the National Portrait Gallery, London
By courtesy of the National Portrait Gallery, London

of 14 and served with distinction in many parts of the world before retiring in 1830 with a captain's rank. He then began a series of adventure novels marked by a lucid, direct narrative style and an unfailing fund of incident and humour. These included *The King's Own* (1830), *Peter Simple* (1834), *Mr. Midshipman Easy* (1836), and *Poor Jack* (1840). He also wrote a number of children's books, among which *The Children of the New Forest* (1847), a story of the English Civil Wars, is a classic of children's literature. A *Life and Letters* was prepared by his daughter Florence (1872).

BIBLIOGRAPHY. Oliver Warner, *Captain Marryat: A Rediscovery* (1953, reprinted 1979).

Mars, ancient Roman deity, in importance second only to Jupiter. Little is known of his original character, and that character (chiefly from the cult at Rome) is variously interpreted. It is clear that by historical times he had developed into a god of war; in Roman literature he was protector of Rome, a nation proud in war.

Mars's festivals at Rome occurred in the spring and the fall—the beginning and the end of both the agricultural and the military seasons. The month of March was especially

Mars, bronze statuette, Etruscan; in the Museo Archeologico, Florence
Alinari—Art Resource

filled with festivals wholly or partially in his honour; the members of the ancient priesthood of the Salii, who were particularly associated with Jupiter, Mars, and Quirinus, came out several times during the month to dance their ceremonial war dance in old-fashioned armour and chant a hymn to the gods. October was also an important month for Mars. At the festival of the October Horse on October 15, a two-horse chariot race was held in the Campus Martius, and on October 19 the Armilustrium marked the purification of the arms of war and their storage for the winter. The god was invoked in the ancient hymn of the Arval Brothers, whose religious duties had as their object to keep off enemies of all kinds from crops and herds.

Until the time of Augustus, Mars had only two temples at Rome: one was in the Campus Martius, the exercising ground of the army; the other was outside the Porta Capena. Within the city there was a *sacrarium* ("shrine," or "sanctuary") of Mars in the *regia,* originally the king's house, in which the sacred spears of Mars were kept; upon the outbreak of war the consul had to shake the spears saying, "*Mars vigila*" ("Mars, wake up!").

Under Augustus the worship of Mars at Rome gained a new impetus; not only was he traditional guardian of the military affairs of the Roman state but, as Mars Ultor ("Mars the Avenger"), he became the personal guardian of the emperor in his role as avenger of Caesar. His worship at times rivaled that of Capitoline Jupiter, and about AD 250 Mars became the most prominent of the *di militares* ("military gods") worshiped by the Roman legions. In literature and art he is hardly distinguished from the Greek Ares.

Mars, in astronomy, fourth major planet from the Sun, named after the Roman god of war because of its reddish colour.

A brief treatment of Mars follows. For full treatment, *see* MACROPAEDIA: Solar System.

Mars's mean distance from the Sun is 228 million km, about half as far again as is Earth. Owing to its relatively elongated orbit, its solar distance varies considerably. A Martian day, or sol, is 24.6 Earth hours, and a Martian year is approximately 687 Earth days. The planet has two small moons, Phobos and Deimos (*qq.v.*).

Like Earth, Mars has seasons because of an oblique axis of rotation and the presence of an atmosphere. It is, however, much colder: the mean surface atmospheric temperature is only −63° C (−82° F). Mars is a small planet, having a mean diameter of 6,779 km, about half that of Earth. Also, its density, 3.94 grams per cubic centimetre, is lower than that of Earth; this suggests that its iron core is fairly small or mixed with a less dense substance like sulfur. No magnetic field has been detected on Mars. Mars's thin atmosphere is 95 percent carbon dioxide; nitrogen, argon, and traces of water vapour are also present. The planet's polar caps, which consist of frozen carbon dioxide, grow and shrink with the seasons. The northern cap disappears each summer, exposing a residual water-ice cap.

Telescopic observations from Earth established the existence but not the nature of Mars's atmosphere, polar caps, light and dark markings, and moons. The first spacecraft images of the planet were obtained during flybys of the planetary probes Mariner 4 (1965) and 6 and 7 (1969); they showed a cratered surface, similar to that of the Moon, in the southern hemisphere. The first Mars-orbiting spacecraft was Mariner 9 (1971–72), which photographed much of the Martian surface. These images revealed a stark difference between the southern and northern hemispheres. The southern hemisphere is old and cratered, whereas most of the older terrain in the north has been buried by younger materials, probably of volcanic and wind-blown origin.

During the late 1970s two Viking spacecraft photographed the Martian surface from orbit in greater detail. Their companion landing craft performed various experiments on the surface, including tests designed to detect the presence of life forms such as microbes, but these yielded no positive results. More than two decades later Mars was visited successively by a lander and two orbiters. Mars Pathfinder, which set down in 1997, deployed a robotic, wheeled rover on the surface. Starting in 1999, Mars Global Surveyor systematically mapped the topography and other properties of the entire planet from orbit for several years. In 2001 Mars Odyssey entered orbit and began making complementary maps of such properties such as the surface chemical composition and the distribution of near-surface ice.

Among surface features first revealed by the Mariner and Viking probes were volcanoes, craters, extensive lava plains, and various types of channels and canyons. Many of these are large by terrestrial standards. Olympus Mons, for example, is the largest known volcano in the solar system, having a diameter of 540 km and a height of roughly 21 km. Other large volcanoes occur nearby on the Tharsis rise, an extensive volcanic province bulging as much as 12 km higher than the surrounding northern plains. Valles Marineris is a gigantic equatorial system of interconnected canyons more than 4,000 km long.

Some of the impact craters on Mars resemble those found on Mercury and the Moon, but other types may be unique to Mars. Among the latter are rampart craters, so called because the ejecta blanket (*i.e.,* the material thrown out from the crater and extending around it) is bordered by a low ridge. This suggests that the ejecta had a mudlike consistency, possibly as a result of the mixing of impact-created debris with water present under the surface.

Wind is an important element on Mars. Wind-formed deposits such as dunes and crater streaks are common, and global dust storms occasionally obscure almost all of the surface. The largest known dune field forms a ring around the north polar cap. Dust devils have been seen from Mars orbit and at the landing site of Mars Pathfinder.

One kind of major channel system on Mars consists of networks of small valleys that resemble drainage systems on Earth cut by flowing water. Scientists speculate that they were created by runoff of rainfall on the surface or erosion from seeping groundwater. Also prominent are large flood channels, termed outflow channels, incised into the surface in several areas. Generally tens of kilometres across and hundreds of kilometres long, they emerge from rubble-filled depressions and continue downslope into basins and plains. They appear to have once carried enormous water flows. The presence of such channels and much other evidence indicate that ancient Mars had a denser, warmer atmosphere and much more water than at present. Images from Mars Global Surveyor showing small, fresh-appearing gullies on steep slopes suggest that some liquid water may have flowed near the surface even in relatively recent times, although this interpretation is disputed.

Spacecraft images show Mars's moons, Phobos and Deimos, to be irregular, cratered lumps of rock. They may be residue from Mars's formation or asteroids that were captured by the planet early in its history.

Mars, canals of, apparent systems of rectilinear markings on the surface of Mars that are now known to be illusions caused by the chance alignment of large craters and other features of the Martian surface. They were the subject of much controversy in the late 19th and early 20th centuries. The Italian astronomer and statesman Giovanni Virginio Schiaparelli observed about 100 of them, from 1877, and described them as *canali* (Italian: "channels"). Others had earlier noted similar markings, but Schiaparelli's writings first drew wide attention to the subject. The U.S. astronomer Percival Lowell became the leader of those who believed the markings to be bands of vegetation, kilometres wide, bordering irrigation ditches dug by intelligent beings to carry water from the polar caps. Lowell and others described canal networks, studded with dark intersections called oases and covering much of the surface of the planet. Occasionally the lines were perceived as doubled; *i.e.*, two parallel lines became visible where only a single canal had been seen before. Most astronomers could see no canals, and many doubted their reality. The controversy was finally resolved only when pictures were made from several hundred kilometres above the surface of Mars by the Mariner 6 and 7 spacecraft in 1969. These showed many craters and other features but nothing resembling a network of channels.

Mars, Field of: *see* Campus Martius.

Mars-la-Tour and Gravelotte, Battles of (Aug. 16–18, 1870), two major engagements of the Franco-German War in which the 130,000-man French Army of the Rhine, under Marshal Achille-François Bazaine, failed to break through the two German armies under General Helmuth von Moltke and were bottled up in the fortress of Metz. It was followed by the Count de Mac-Mahon's abortive attempt to rescue Bazaine, which ended in Mac-Mahon's crushing defeat at Sedan.

The French Army had been in retreat and its command in shock since German victories in the first week of August. Bazaine was given command of the Army of the Rhine on August 12, as it was falling back from Metz toward Verdun. He was intercepted on August 16 by the German general Constantine von Alvensleben's III Corps of 30,000 men near Vionville, east of Mars-la-Tour. Alvensleben, with one-quarter the troops of Bazaine, captured and secured Vionville, thus blocking the French escape route toward the west. The resulting Battle of Mars-la-Tour included the last major cavalry engagement in western Europe. Each side suffered about 16,000 casualties.

Bazaine withdrew his army on the 17th to a line of hills running north–south, between the walled village Saint-Privat-la-Montagne and Gravelotte, a few miles west of Metz. The French were now facing west, toward their intended line of retreat. The Germans were not aware, early on the 18th, that the French lay on their right flank as they deployed parallel to the road from Mars-la-Tour to Metz, facing north. When the French dispositions were discovered, several German units turned 90° to the east to face the French lines. Moltke was forced to send his troops directly against the excellent French position, and only the conservatism of Bazaine permitted Moltke to turn what initially seemed a draw into a victory.

The northern sector of the French line, around Saint-Privat, inflicted heavy losses on the Germans in house-to-house fighting before being forced to retire toward Metz at nightfall. The southern sector of the French line, situated behind a deep ravine and prepared trenches, virtually pulverized the German assaults directed against it. Moltke was therefore astonished when, instead of counterattacking in order to reopen the road to Verdun, Bazaine used the night to pull back to Metz.

The German loss of more than 20,000 men at Gravelotte outnumbered the French loss of 13,000, but the Germans had accomplished their purpose of trapping the French Army. Moltke then used part of his forces to confine Bazaine's troops in Metz and was able to use the remainder to overwhelm Mac-Mahon at Sedan on September 1.

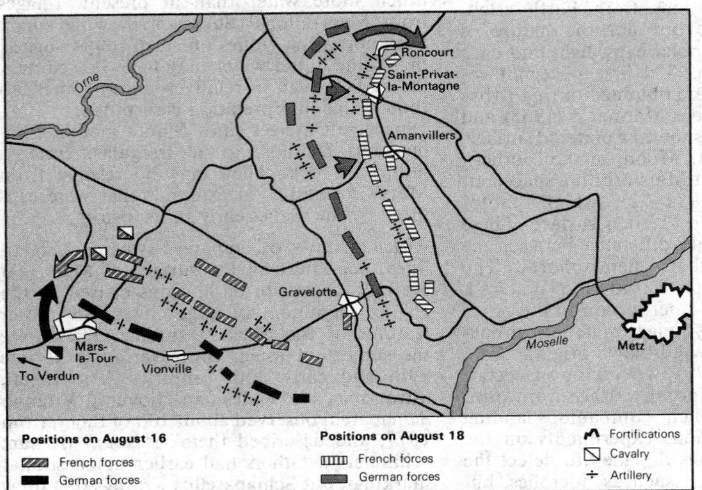

The Battles of Mars-la-Tour and Gravelotte

From David Chandler (ed.), *A Guide to the Battlefields of Europe*, vol. 1, copyright 1965 by Hugh Evelyn, Ltd.; published by Dimension Books, Denville, New Jersey

Marsā al-Burayqah, also spelled MARSA EL-BREGA, Mediterranean port on the Gulf of Sidra, northeastern Libya. The site, which was located by a small fishing village destroyed during World War II, contained nothing but land mines when it was chosen as the terminal for Libya's first oil pipeline, running from Zalṭan, 105 miles (169 km) south. After 1960 a new port and town were built from prefabricated materials, including breakwaters and a wharf for supply ships, undersea pipes and floating berths for oil tankers, a power plant, housing, paved streets, and trees to hold back the sand. The first oil flowed there for shipment in 1961, and a refinery and a natural-gas liquefaction plant were subsequently opened. The coastal highway connecting Tripoli with Banghāzī and Cairo passes through the town. Pop. (1990 est.) 8,000.

Marsā Maṭrūḥ, town and capital of Maṭrūḥ *muḥāfaẓah* (governorate), on the Mediterranean coast, Western Desert, in northwestern Egypt. The town serves as a market and distribution centre for the surrounding agricultural region. Olives, barley, and fruits are grown, and there are vineyards as well. Sheep and goats are raised. Winter rains (5–8 inches [125–200 mm]) provide most of the water needed in the coastal zone, which is 12–20 miles (19–32 km) wide. Wells provide additional supplies.

Maṭrūḥ's climate and fine beaches have made it a vacation and resort centre. The town has port facilities and has become a transshipment centre with the growth of mineral exploration in various parts of the *muḥāfaẓah.* A railway and highway link the town to Alexandria 168 miles (270 km) east and the Libyan border to the west. There is also a road to Siwa Oasis. Pop. (1996) 52,247.

Marsala, Latin LILYBAEUM, town, Trapani province, western Sicily, Italy. It is situated on the Boeo Cape, also called Lilibeo, south of Trapani. It originated as Lilybaeum, which was founded by the Carthaginians in 397–396 BC after the destruction of the offshore island of Motya (modern San Pantaleo) by Dionysius the Elder, tyrant of Syracuse. Serving as the Carthaginians' principal stronghold in Sicily, it successfully resisted sieges by Pyrrhus, king of Epirus, and by the Romans but surrendered to the latter in 241 BC at the end of the First Punic War. Its present name dates from its occupation by the Saracens, who regarded the town's harbour so highly that they called it Marsa ʿAlī ("Harbour of ʿAlī"), or Mars el-Allah ("Harbour of Allah"). The town declined in the 16th century after Emperor Charles V destroyed its old harbour to prevent its occupation by pirates. On May 11, 1860, the town was the site of the landing of Giuseppe Garibaldi and 1,000 of his "Redshirts" in their campaign to conquer the Kingdom of the Two Sicilies. Roman baths in the vicinity have been excavated. The town's Baroque cathedral, dedicated to St. Thomas à Becket, contains fine Flemish tapestries.

The town is surrounded by vineyards, and its chief industry is that of Marsala wine, a blended wine of high alcoholic content that was first produced in the area in 1773. Pop. (1999 est.) 80,798.

Marsalis, Wynton (b. Oct. 18, 1961, New Orleans, La., U.S.), trumpet virtuoso known primarily as the leading figure in American jazz from the 1980s; he also garnered acclaim for his work in classical music.

Marsalis was born into one of New Orleans's most illustrious musical families. He began playing trumpet at age six and was a member of the New Orleans Civic Orchestra while in his teens. He attended the Juilliard School of Music at age 17 and made his first recordings in 1980 as a member of Art Blakey's Jazz Messengers. By age 19, Marsalis was hailed as the "saviour" of jazz and was the music's most prominent spokesman. He also made his first classical recordings in the early 1980s and was praised as one of the finest classical trumpeters of all time, although Marsalis always maintained that he was primarily a jazz musician who dabbled in classical. In 1983 he became the first artist in history to win Grammy awards in both the jazz and classical categories, a feat he repeated the following year.

Among the noted recordings of Marsalis's early career were *Hot House Flowers* (1984), *Black Codes from the Underground* (1985), and *J Mood* (1985). Also notable were the series of *Standard Time* albums on which Marsalis interpreted well-known numbers from the American popular songbook. In the 1990s, he evolved as a composer and featured his extended, Duke Ellington-influenced compositions on such albums as *Blue Interlude* (1992) and *Citi Movement* (1992).

Marsalis was a highly active and articulate spokesman for jazz; as such, he generated great controversy for his dismissal of such contemporary music as jazz fusion, avant-garde jazz, and rap. Yet, even his harshest critics who disagreed with his traditionalist opinions acknowledged his virtuosic abilities as a musician.

Marsalis was the leader of Lincoln Center's prestigious jazz orchestra, which he cofounded in 1987. He was the first jazz musician to be awarded the Pulitzer Prize for music, which he received for his epic oratorio on slavery, *Blood on the Fields* (1997).

Marschner, Heinrich August (b. Aug. 16, 1795, Zittau, Saxony—d. Dec. 14, 1861, Hannover, Hanover), composer who helped establish the style of German Romantic opera.

Marschner studied law at Leipzig, but, encouraged by Ludwig van Beethoven, whom he met in Vienna in 1817, and others, he turned to composing. In 1820 his close friend Carl Maria von Weber produced Marschner's opera *Heinrich IV und d'Aubigné* at Dresden. Marschner was later appointed director of the Dresden opera. In 1827 he became Kapellmeister of the Leipzig City Theatre, where he produced his operas *Der Vampyr* (1828) and *Templer und Jüdin* (1829; libretto after Sir Walter Scott's *Ivanhoe*). In 1831 he became court Kapellmeister at Hannover. His most successful opera, *Hans Heiling*, was produced in Berlin in 1833; it remains in the operatic repertory in Germany. He produced five further operas, but none of them achieved the success of his earlier works. Stylistically, Marschner exhibits both the musical flavour and the interest in the supernatural of Weber and the early Romantics and the expanded 19th-century orchestration with its wider emotional range that was to characterize the works of Richard Wagner.

Marsden, William (b. Nov. 16, 1754, Verval, Wicklow, Ire.—d. Oct. 6, 1836, Aldenham, Herefordshire, Eng.), British historian, linguist, and numismatist, pioneer of the scientific study of Indonesia.

Marsden was preparing to enter Trinity College, Dublin, when in 1770 he was persuaded to follow his brother John into the service of the East India Company in western Sumatra. Arriving there at the age of 16, he was appointed a writer on the Fort Marlborough Establishment but rapidly gained more senior posts, becoming secretary before finally leaving for England in 1779. Throughout his nearly 10 years in Bencoolen (Bangkahulu) in Sumatra, he engaged in intensive study of the languages and peoples there.

When Marsden returned to England, he was encouraged by Sir Joseph Banks and others of the Royal Society to prepare his material for publication. The *History of Sumatra* that resulted (London, 1783) was the first detailed account of Sumatra to appear in any language. It contained copious material on flora and fauna, economic products, social organization, religion, language, and much else, all arranged on the current scientific principles. Marsden was elected a fellow of the Royal Society in 1783. At intervals he operated an East Asian agency house, and from 1795 to 1807 he served as second and then first secretary of the Admiralty, meanwhile continuing to produce scholarly materials on Southeast Asia. His *Dictionary* and *Grammar of the Malayan Language*, begun in 1786, were published in 1812 and form the basis of all subsequent Sumatran linguistics. Marsden's scholarly work earned him many honours and distinctions.

Marseillaise, La, French national anthem, composed in one night during the French Revolution (April 24, 1792) by Claude-Joseph Rouget de Lisle, a captain of the engineers and amateur musician.

After France declared war on Austria on April 20, 1792, P.F. Dietrich, the mayor of Strasbourg (where Rouget de Lisle was then quartered), expressed the need for a marching song for the French troops. "La Marseillaise" was Rouget de Lisle's response to this call. Originally entitled "Chant de guerre de l'armée du Rhin" ("War Song of the Army of the Rhine"), the anthem came to be called "La Marseillaise" because of its popularity with volunteer army units from Marseille. The spirited and majestic song made an intense impression whenever it was sung at Revolutionary public occasions. The Convention accepted it as the French national anthem in a decree passed on July 14, 1795. "La Marseillaise" was banned by Napoleon during the empire and by Louis XVIII on the Second Restoration (1815) because of its Revolutionary associations. Authorized after the July Revolution of 1830, it was again banned by Napoleon III and not reinstated until 1879.

The original text of "La Marseillaise" had six verses, and a seventh and last verse (not written by Rouget de Lisle) was later added. Only the first and sixth verses of the anthem are customarily used at public occasions. The text of these two verses follows, along with an English translation:

Allons, enfants de la patrie,
Le jour de gloire est arrivé.
Contre nous, de la tyrannie,
L'étendard sanglant est levé; l'étendard
  sanglant est levé.
Entendez-vous, dans les campagnes
Mugir ces féroces soldats?
Ils viennent jusque dans nos bras
Égorger nos fils, nos compagnes.
  Aux armes, citoyens!
  Formez vos bataillons,
  Marchons, marchons!
  Qu'un sang impur
  Abreuve nos sillons.
Amour sacré de la Patrie,
Conduis, soutiens nos bras vengeurs.
Liberté, liberté chérie,
Combats avec tes défenseurs; combats
  avec tes défenseurs.
Sous nos drapeaux, que la victoire
Accoure à tes mâles accents;
Que tes ennemis expirants
Voient ton triomphe et notre gloire!
  Aux armes, citoyens! *etc.*

(Let us go, children of the fatherland,
Our day of glory has arrived.
Against us the bloody flag of tyranny
is raised; the bloody
  flag is raised.
Do you hear in the countryside
The roar of those savage soldiers?
They come right into our arms
To cut the throats of our sons, our comrades.
  To arms, citizens!
  Form your battalions,
  Let us march, let us march!
  That their impure blood
  Should water our fields.
Sacred love of the fatherland,
Guide and support our vengeful arms.
Liberty, beloved liberty,
Fight with your defenders; fight
  with your defenders.
Under our flags, so that victory
Will rush to your manly strains;
That your dying enemies
Should see your triumph and glory!
  To arms, citizens! *etc.*)

Marseille, also spelled MARSEILLES, ancient MASSILIA, or MASSALIA, city, capital of Bouches-du-Rhône *département* and of Provence-Alpes-Côtes d'Azur *région*. Marseille is the second largest city in France and is one of the Mediterranean's major seaports. Area city, 93 square miles (240 square km); metropolitan area, 362 square miles (946 square km). Pop. (1999) city, 807,071; metropolitan area, 1,349,772.

A brief treatment of Marseille follows. For full treatment, *see* MACROPAEDIA: Marseille.

Settled by Greeks from Asia Minor during the 7th century BC, Marseille is the oldest of France's major cities. It was annexed by the Romans, who called it Massilia, in the 1st century BC; after the decline of the Roman Empire, it deteriorated almost to extinction but was revived as an important commercial port of departure during the Crusades (11th through 14th century AD).

Situated along the northern shoreline of the Mediterranean Sea, Marseille has mean monthly temperatures averaging about 72° F (22° C) during the warm summer period and 45° F (7° C) during the winter. Its climate is somewhat uncharacteristic of the region, with most of the annual rainfall of 22 inches (560 mm) coming in the spring and autumn rather than in the winter.

Marseille's Old Port (Vieux-Port) is a natural harbour and one of the most westerly of the inlets along the northeastern Mediterranean. Great impetus was lent to Mediterranean shipping through Marseille by the French conquest of Algeria (1830), which eliminated the Barbary pirates, and by the completion of the Suez Canal (1869); thereafter Marseille's development as an important port city was rapid. Although the port facilities were largely destroyed by German mines during World War II, they were rebuilt and expanded afterward. In 1968 the huge port-industrial complex of Fos-sur-Mer opened some 23 miles to the northwest. The combined port facilities of Marseille, Fos, and other industrial suburbs such as Lavéra have made the area the centre of the large Provence-Alpes-Côtes d'Azur *région*. Regional planning has replaced programs on the municipal level, and construction projects such as the Sud-European oil pipeline (linking the industrial zone to Germany and Switzerland), steelworks, and chemical plants have brought a major shift of heavy industry to Marseille's periphery.

Despite the city's rapid growth following the war and the loss of much of its quaintness, the Old Port is still reminiscent of the colourful past. Fishermen hawk their daily catch (including such local delicacies as squid and eel), and the port entrance is guarded by the 18th-century command post Fort-Saint-Jean. On a hill overlooking the port is the Basilica of Notre-Dame-de-la-Garde (dating from the 8th century and rebuilt in 1853). Other historic buildings dotting the Old Port are the Cathédrale de la Major, dating primarily from the 12th century, and the Hospice de la Vieille Charité, a hospital built between 1660 and 1750.

During the century preceding 1953, no important thoroughfare was constructed in Marseille (the width of older streets averages 19½ feet [6 m]). Since then, widened thoroughfares, elevated highways, a subway system, and road tunnels (including one under the Old Port) have been built. The Marseille-Provence Airport is France's third-ranking airport for passenger traffic.

Marseille faience, tin-glazed earthenware made in Marseille in the 18th century. The Joseph Clérissy factory, active in 1677–1733, produced wares usually in blue with purple outlines. The Fauchier factory excelled in trompe l'oeil work and landscapes. The factory of the Veuve Perrin was famous for its enameled "bouillabaisse" decor that included

Marseille faience tureen, probably from the Robert factory, *c.* 1760; in the Victoria and Albert Museum, London

By courtesy of the Victoria and Albert Museum, London

all the ingredients of that famous local fish soup, rendered realistically. The factory of Joseph-Gaspard Robert was known for its faience and, from 1777, for porcelain with elaborate floral decoration. The greatest technical feat was a decoration entirely in gold, which is unique in French pottery.

marsh, type of wetland ecosystem characterized by poorly drained mineral soils and by plant life dominated by grasses. The latter characteristic distinguishes a marsh from a swamp (*q.v.*), whose plant life is dominated by trees.

Marshes are common at the mouths of rivers, especially where extensive deltas have been built. The river brings a steady supply of water. The gradient of the river approaches zero at the sea, where flow is sluggish. Because the delta is deposited by sediment settling from the river water, the land that is built will be poorly drained at its driest and will often be underwater. Sediment supplied by the river has often been eroded from the surface soils of the drainage basin and is thus very rich. The combination of water supplied steadily at a low rate over a waterlogged but rich soil creates a perfect environment for marsh grasses.

Fibrous-rooted grasses bind the muds together and further hinder water flow, thus encouraging the spread of both the delta and the marsh. Marshes occur in the deltas of most of the world's great rivers. In Europe well-known river-mouth marshes include those of the Camargue in the Rhône Delta, the Guadalquivir in Spain, and the Danube in Romania, all of which are famous as bird sanctuaries. In the Middle East, both the Nile Delta and the delta of the Tigris–Euphrates have extensive marshes of historical importance. The marsh dwellers of the Iranian marshes have developed a unique culture adapted to life in the wetlands. Marshes occur in the deltas of the Mekong in Vietnam and the Amazon in Brazil. In the United States, the most extensive delta marshes are those of the Mississippi River.

Some low-lying areas with poor drainage at the heads of more extensive drainage patterns contain wetlands. A well-known example is the Pripet Marshes and fens that historically have served as the natural boundary between Poland and Russia. In some places basin-like depressions in the Earth's surface trap waters and make wetlands. Most such areas are drained someplace along their rim by a river that is impeded at that point sufficiently to dam water at times of high flow and create marshes and swamps. The world's two largest rivers, the Amazon and the Congo, fall into this category. Both of the great basins named after these rivers have extensive wetlands. The papyrus marshes of the upper Nile in southern Sudan lie above dams of resistant rocks of the cataracts.

The Okavango Marshes east of the Kalahari desert in Botswana are perhaps the best example of marshes formed in an interior, closed basin that has no drainage. Other basins without outlets like that of the Great Salt Lake in Utah have accumulated too much salt for marsh growth.

The Florida Everglades constitutes a unique marsh–swamp combination growing on a limestone base. Because the region is near sea level the water from the abundant rains does not drain but remains on the surface. The Everglades is similar to a huge, shallow, slowly flowing river. The area is an ideal marsh habitat but the Everglades is different from usual marshes. The soils are alkaline because of the limy base, and the water is clear.

Some areas, such as the northern Great Plains of the United States, have so many small marshes that they are a characteristic of the landscape. These small marshes formed because the landscape left by the retreat of glacial ice was so irregular and so poorly drained that countless little depressions were filled with water each spring. As snow melted, the depressions supported the growth of temporary marshes, which then dried up during the summer. Larger depressions were occupied by ponds. These gradually became marshy as they filled in with sediment.

The number of plant species in marshes is few compared to the numbers that grow on well-watered but not waterlogged land. Grasses, grasslike sedges, and reeds or rushes are of major importance. Wild rice is of some commercial importance, but true rice is undoubtedly by far the most important marsh plant and supplies a major portion of the world's grain.

Salt marshes, which are extensive along the east coast of the United States and are also common in the Arctic, northern Europe, Australia, and New Zealand, are formed by seawater flooding and draining, which exposes flat areas of intertidal land. Salt-marsh grasses will not grow on permanently flooded flats; growth is also prevented where the flooded land is subject to strong currents and is therefore unstable.

Animals have adapted to the limited supplies of oxygen in salt-marsh water in various ways. Rat-tailed maggots (*Tubifera*), for example, survive in shallow marshes by means of a telescoping, tail-breathing tube that they extend to the water surface for air. Some larvae of shore flies (Ephydridae) and some nematodes take advantage of the air spaces in plants and obtain oxygen from that source. Many small marsh animals have great resistance to lack of oxygen; for example, many nematodes can live indefinitely in the complete absence of oxygen. This ability is essential for such minute animals that would otherwise be limited in distribution to a thin layer a fraction of an inch deep at the mud surface.

Salt-marsh animals living at or in the ground are largely derived from marine ancestors and have a problem in resisting fresh water from rains rather than salt. Some, such as worms, merely hide in the mud until the freshwater has run off the marsh surface. Others, such as fiddler crabs, have developed the ability to control their osmotic concentration in freshwater for periods of up to several days. Insects are the principal land animals found on marshes. Although they can withstand short periods of saltwater immersion, they often avoid saltwater by moving up the plants or flying away.

Salt marshes are among the most productive natural systems. Productivities of more than 3,000 grams per square metre per year have been reported for the most productive parts of salt marshes, the tall *Spartina alterniflora* stands growing along tidal creeks. These values correspond to nearly 30 tons per acre per year and are equal to the highest values that have been achieved in agriculture.

Marsh, Sir Edward Howard (b. Nov. 18, 1872, London—d. Jan. 13, 1953, London), man of letters and art collector who influenced the development of contemporary British art by patronizing artists who were not yet established. He was also an editor, translator, and biographer well known in British literary circles of the early 20th century.

Marsh entered the civil service in 1896; beginning in 1905 he served for more than 20 years as private secretary to Winston Churchill. By 1904 an important private collector of English old masters, he later turned to contemporary artists, helping popularize such painters as Duncan Grant, Stanley Spencer, and R.O. Dunlop; his London flat was famous as a miniature gallery. He was knighted on his retirement in 1937.

Marsh edited the five volumes of *Georgian Poetry* (1912–22). Other literary works include translations of La Fontaine's *Fables* (1931) and of *The Odes of Horace* (1941); *The Collected Poems of Rupert Brooke* (1918), a memoir; and a series of reminiscences entitled *A Number of People* (1939).

Marsh, George Perkins (b. March 15, 1801, Woodstock, Vt., U.S.—d. July 23, 1882, Vallombrosa, Italy), U.S. diplomat, scholar, and conservationist whose greatest work, *Man and Nature* (1864), was one of the most significant advances in geography, ecology, and resource management of the 19th century.

Educated at Dartmouth College, Hanover, N.H., Marsh developed a successful law practice, but his wide-ranging mind led him into the study of classical literature, languages (he was fluent in 20 by the age of 30), and the applied sciences of silviculture and soil conservation. In 1842 he was elected to Congress, where he was greatly influenced by former president John Quincy Adams, a fellow congressman whose foresight and ideas of government's role in natural resource preservation and management anticipated those of Theodore Roosevelt. After serving a second term in Congress, Marsh was appointed minister to Turkey by Pres. Zachary Taylor, during which assignment he studied Middle Eastern and Mediterranean geography and agricultural practices. He sent many specimens to the Smithsonian Institution in Washington, D.C., before his recall in 1852. Marsh was a lecturer in English philology and etymology at Columbia University and the Lowell (Mass.) Institute. He became a member of the Republican Party in 1856. In 1861 Pres. Abraham Lincoln made him the first minister to Italy, a position he held until his death. During that period he summarized his accumulated knowledge and experience in *Man and Nature, or Physical Geography as Modified by Human Action* (1864).

Marsh, Ngaio, in full DAME EDITH NGAIO MARSH (b. April 23, 1899, Christchurch, N.Z.—d. Feb, 18, 1982, Christchurch), one of New Zealand's most popular 20th-century authors, known especially for her many mystery stories featuring Inspector Roderick Alleyn of Scotland Yard.

Originally an artist and then an actress in a touring Shakespearean company in Australia and New Zealand, she went to England in 1928 and wrote her first novel, *A Man Lay Dead* (1934). She returned to New Zealand, where she produced plays (Shakespearean repertory theatre) from 1938 to 1964. She wrote about New Zealand and about the theatre in addition to writing such famed detective novels as *Overture to Death* (1939), *Death of a Fool* (1956), and *Dead Water* (1963). Her autobiography, *Black Beech and Honeydew,* was published in 1966. In 1948 she was made Dame of the Order of the British Empire.

Marsh, Othniel Charles (b. Oct. 29, 1831, Lockport, N.Y., U.S.—d. March 18, 1899, New Haven, Conn.), U.S. paleontologist who made extensive scientific explorations of the western U.S. and contributed greatly to knowledge of extinct North American vertebrates.

Marsh spent his entire career at Yale University (1866–99) as the first professor of vertebrate paleontology in the U.S. In 1870 he organized the first Yale Scientific Expedition, which explored the Pliocene (from 2,500,000 to 7,000,000 years ago) deposits of Nebraska and the Miocene (from 7,000,000 to 26,000,000 years ago) deposits of northern Colorado. Marsh continued to sponsor similar parties nearly every year thereafter until his death. In 1871 his party discovered the first pterodactyl (a flying reptile) found in the U.S. In 1882 he was placed in charge of the U.S. Geological Survey's work in vertebrate paleontology, aggravating a fierce rivalry that existed between him and the U.S. paleontologist Edward Cope. Credited with the discovery of more than a thousand fossil vertebrates and the description of at least 500 more, Marsh published major works on toothed birds, gigantic horned mammals, and North American dinosaurs. He also wrote *Fossil Horses in America* (1874) and *Introduction and Succession of Vertebrate Life in America* (1877).

Marsh, Reginald (b. March 14, 1898, Paris—d. July 3, 1954, Bennington, Vt., U.S.), U.S.

painter and printmaker who was noted for his satirical and realistic depiction of New York City life.

After graduation from Yale University (1920) Marsh worked as a freelance artist in New York City and from 1922 to 1925 was on the staff of the New York *Daily News,* where he produced a daily column of drawings of the vaudeville acts in music halls and nightclubs.

Marsh was an original member of the staff of *The New Yorker* magazine (founded in 1925), for which he drew humorous illustrations and

"Tattoo and Haircut," egg tempera painting by Reginald Marsh, 1932; in the Art Institute of Chicago
By courtesy of the Art Institute of Chicago

metropolitan scenes. After 1931 he was an occasional contributor to the magazine and to *Vanity Fair* and *Harper's Bazaar.* In 1925–26 and again in 1928, Marsh studied in Europe. Back in the United States again, in 1929, he began to paint the life around him in New York City. He walked the streets of the city, sketching the neighbourhoods, crowds, girls, subways, elevated trains, and movie and burlesque houses. In particular he was attracted to Coney Island Beach, with its tangled masses of humanity. Another favourite subject was the derelicts of the Bowery. These paintings suggest not so much social protest as a love of life. Among his more important paintings are "Why Not Use the 'L'?" (1930; Whitney Museum of American Art, New York City), "Tattoo and Haircut" (1932; Art Institute of Chicago), and "Twenty-Cent Movie" (1936; Whitney Museum of American Art).

Marsh taught at the Art Students League of New York from 1934 until his death and also at the Moore Institute of Art, Science and Industry, in Philadelphia, from 1949.

marsh cress, also called YELLOW CRESS, any of the 70 plant species of the genus *Rorippa* of the mustard family (Brassicaceae). Most members of the genus are found in the Northern Hemisphere. The genus has at times been included with the genera *Nasturtium* and *Radicula.* Iceland watercress, or marsh yellow cress (*R. islandica,* sometimes *Nasturtium palustre*), grows, like others of the genus, in marshy ground. It bears small, four-petaled, yellow flowers in clusters at the top of the flowering spikes. Iceland watercress is annual, but greater yellow cress (*R. amphibia*) is perennial. The latter is often used in aquariums. Creeping yellow cress, or water rocket (*R. sylvestris*), is a perennial that grows from a rootstock.

marsh frog (*Rana ridibunda*), large aquatic frog (family Ranidae), similar in appearance and habits to the closely related pool frog (*R. lessonae*) and the edible frog (*R. esculenta*). In Europe they are all called green frogs. The marsh frog inhabits marshes, river banks, and lake edges in Europe and western Asia. About 9 to 13 cm (3.5 to 5 inches) long, it is brown or green, with or without irregular black spots

Marsh frog (*Rana ridibunda*)
Eric Hosking

on the back. During the day the marsh frog often basks in the sun. It emerges onto land but seldom strays far from water.

marsh grass: *see* cordgrass.

marsh hawk, common name for the best-known harrier species. *See* harrier.

marsh mallow (*Althaea officinalis*), perennial herbaceous plant of the mallow family (Malvaceae), native to eastern Europe and northern Africa. It has also become established in North America. The plant is usually found

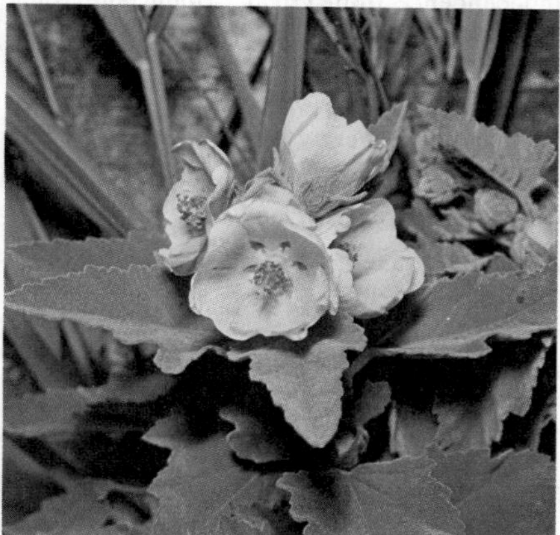

Marsh mallow (*Althaea officinalis*)
G.E. Hyde

in marshy areas, chiefly near the sea. It has strongly veined heart-shaped or oval leaves. The pinkish flowers, borne on stalks about 1.8 m (6 feet) tall, are about 5 cm (2 inches) in diameter. The root was formerly used to make marshmallows, a confection.

marsh marigold, also called COWSLIP (*Caltha palustris*), perennial herbaceous plant of the

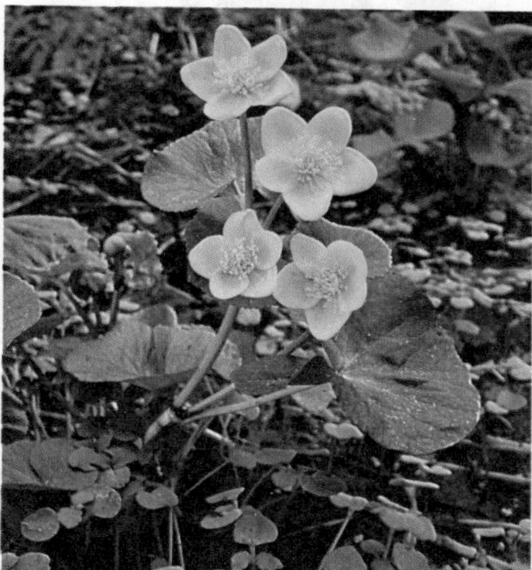

Marsh marigold (*Caltha palustris*)
G.J. Chafaris

buttercup family (Ranunculaceae) native to wetlands in Europe and North America. It is grown in boggy wild gardens.

The stem of a marsh marigold is hollow, and the leaves are kidney-shaped, heart-shaped, or round. The glossy flowers are 2.5 to 5 cm (1 to 2 inches) across and have pink, white, or yellow sepals. Petals are absent. The stems, leaves, and roots are sometimes cooked and eaten as a vegetable, although the fresh plant is poisonous. The cooked and pickled flower buds are a substitute for capers.

marsh treader, also called WATER MEASURER, any insect of the family Hydrometridae (order Heteroptera), so named because of its slow, deliberate manner of moving as it walks along the surface of a pond or crawls among shore vegetation. Marsh treaders, worldwide in distribution, are usually found among the cattails in marshy ponds containing algae. More than 100 species of the insect have been described.

Marsh treader (*Hydrometra stagnorum*)
M. Tweedie—Bruce Coleman Inc.

The marsh treader, about 8 mm (0.3 inch) long, is recognized by its sticklike body and long, thin, threadlike legs. Its slender head is almost as long as the thorax, and the antennae, extending in front of the head, resemble another pair of legs. The body is covered with fine, velvety hairs. Marsh treaders feed on small crustaceans and insect larvae, especially mosquito larvae.

The female lays beautifully sculptured eggs and glues each one to a plant just above the water line. Each egg is about one fourth the length of the female.

marshal, also called FIELD MARSHAL, in some past and present armies, including those of Britain, France, Germany, Russia or the Soviet Union, and China, the highest ranking officer. The rank evolved from the title of *marescalci* (masters of the horse) of the early Frankish kings. The importance of cavalry in medieval warfare led to the marshalship being associated with a command position; this rank came to include the duties of keeping order at court and in camp and of deciding questions of chivalry. As a military leader the marshal was originally subordinate to the constable in the various states of western Europe. By the 13th century, however, the marshal was rapidly coming to prominence as a commander of the royal forces and a great officer of state.

The office of marshal of France (*marescallus Franciae*) was instituted under King Philip II (d. 1223), and the marshal became one of the great officers of the crown. The number of French marshals gradually increased, from two (13th century) to four (16th century) until there were as many as 20 (18th century). The office was abolished in 1793, during the French Revolution, but in 1804 Napoleon created 18 marshals of the empire, among them Michel Ney, Nicolas Soult, Jean Bernadotte, and Joachim Murat. Napoleon's successors converted the title to *maréchal de France* ("marshal of France") and reduced the number of officers who held it. Later the title lapsed and was revived as a rare honour normally conferred only in time of war.

The office of marshal was already well established in England by the 12th century, but the modern military title of field marshal was introduced into the British army in 1736 by King George II, who imported it from Germany. In Britain the rank came to be bestowed only upon a few senior army officers, notably the chief of Britain's Imperial General Staff. In the army of the former Soviet Union the rank was generally held by officers commanding army groups or higher commands.

The title of marshal also has various applications in the British and American judicial systems. In the United States, marshals are the executive officers of the federal courts, with one marshal serving each court district. The marshal's duties are to open and close the sessions of the district and circuit courts, serve warrants, and generally execute the orders of the court.

Marshal, William: *see* Pembroke, William Marshal, 1st Earl of.

Marshall, city, seat (1842) of Harrison county, northeastern Texas, U.S. The city lies 34 miles (55 km) west of Shreveport, La. Founded in 1841 by Isaac Van Zandt, it was named for Chief Justice John Marshall. It served as the temporary Confederate capital of Missouri during the Civil War when Governor C.F. Jackson, unable to induce Missouri to secede from the Union, moved the official seal and state records to Marshall.

Situated on the Texas and Pacific Railway, the city has repair shops and serves as the centre of a farming area with considerable oil production. Its manufactures include petrochemicals, plastics, and carbon. Marshall is the seat of East Texas Baptist University (1912) and Wiley College (1873). Caddo Lake State Park is a nearby refuge for water-sport and fishing enthusiasts. Inc. town, 1843; city, 1848. Pop. (1994 est.) city, 23,324; Longview-Marshall MSA, 201,336.

Marshall, Alfred (b. July 26, 1842, London, Eng.—d. July 13, 1924, Cambridge, Cambridgeshire), one of the chief founders of the school of English neoclassical economists and first principal of University College, Bristol (1877–81).

Educated at Merchant Taylors' School and at St. John's College, Cambridge, Marshall was a fellow and lecturer in political economy at Balliol College, Oxford, from 1883 to 1885 and professor of political economy at the University of Cambridge from 1885 to 1908. He thereafter devoted himself to his writings. From 1891 to 1894 he was a member of the Royal Commission on Labour.

Marshall's magnum opus, *Principles of Economics* (1890), was his most important contribution to economic literature. It was distinguished by the introduction of a number of new concepts, such as elasticity of demand, consumer's surplus, quasi-rent, and the representative firm, all of which played a major role in the subsequent development of economics. His *Industry and Trade* (1919) was a study of industrial organization; *Money, Credit and Commerce* was published in 1923. Writing at a time when the economic world was deeply divided on the theory of value, Marshall succeeded, largely by introducing the element of time as a factor in analysis, in reconciling the classical cost-of-production principle with the marginal-utility principle formulated by William Jevons and the Austrian school. Marshall is often considered to have been in the line of descent of the great English economists—Adam Smith, David Ricardo, and J.S. Mill.

Consult the INDEX *first*

Marshall, David Saul (b. March 12, 1908, Singapore—d. Dec. 12, 1995, Singapore), politician, lawyer, and diplomat who was the chief minister (1955–56) of Singapore's first elected government.

Marshall was the son of Baghdadi Jewish immigrants who moved to the polyglot and multiracial city-state of Singapore. He enjoyed a highly successful career at the bar as a criminal lawyer before entering Singapore politics in the early 1950s, during the struggle for independence from Great Britain. He organized the socialist Labour Front party and was elected to the Legislative Assembly in April 1955 under Singapore's new constitution. He formed a centre-left coalition government composed of the Labour Front and several other parties and thus became the state's first elected chief minister.

Marshall led an unsuccessful mission to London late in 1955 for talks on obtaining full independence from Great Britain, and when a second mission in 1956 also failed, he resigned as chief minister. In 1962 he founded and became president of the Workers' Party, which, however, was unsuccessful at the polls. Though subsequently much less involved in political life, he remained a major public figure and served as Singapore's ambassador to France from 1978 to 1993.

Marshall, George C., in full GEORGE CATLETT MARSHALL (b. Dec. 31, 1880, Uniontown, Pa., U.S.—d. Oct. 16, 1959, Washington, D.C.), general of the army and U.S. Army chief of staff during World War II (1939–45) and later U.S. secretary of state (1947–49) and of defense (1950–51). The European Recovery Program he proposed in 1947 became known as the Marshall Plan. He received the Nobel Prize for Peace in 1953.

George C. Marshall
EB Inc.

Marshall was descended on both sides of his family from settlers who had been in Virginia since the 17th century. His father, a prosperous coke and coal merchant during his younger son's boyhood, was in financial difficulties when George entered the Virginia Military Institute, Lexington, in 1897.

After a poor beginning at the institute, Marshall's record steadily improved, and he soon showed proficiency in military subjects. Once he had decided on a military career, he concentrated on leadership, ending his last year at the institute as first captain of the corps of cadets.

Marshall finished college in 1901. Immediately after receiving his commission as second lieutenant of infantry in February 1902, he married Elizabeth Carter Coles of Lexington and embarked for 18 months' service in the Philippines. Marshall early developed the rigid self-discipline, the habits of study, and the attributes of command that eventually brought him to the top of his profession. Men who served under him spoke of his quiet self-confidence, his lack of flamboyance, his talent for presenting his case to both soldiers and civilians, and his ability to make his subordinates want to do their best.

After his first service in the Philippines (1902–03), he advanced steadily through the ranks, ultimately becoming general of the army in December 1944. In World War I he served as chief of operations of the 1st Division, first to go to France in 1917, and then as the chief of operations of the 1st Army during the Meuse-Argonne offensive in 1918. After the war he served for five years as aide to General John J. Pershing (1919–24) and for five years as assistant commandant in charge of instruction at the infantry school, Fort Benning, Georgia (1927–33), where he strongly influenced army doctrine as well as many officers who were to become outstanding commanders in World War II.

He was sworn in as chief of staff of the U.S. Army on Sept. 1, 1939, the day World War II began with Germany's invasion of Poland. For the next six years, Marshall directed the raising of new divisions, the training of troops, the development of new weapons and equipment, and the selection of top commanders. When he entered office, the United States forces consisted of fewer than 200,000 officers and men. Under his direction it expanded in less than four years to a well-trained and well-equipped force of 8,300,000. Marshall raised and equipped the largest ground and air force in the history of the United States, a feat that earned him the appellation of "the organizer of victory" from the wartime British prime minister, Winston Churchill. As the chief representative of the U.S. chiefs of staff at the international conferences at Casablanca, Washington, Quebec, Cairo, and Tehrān, Marshall led the fight for an Allied drive on German forces across the English Channel, in opposition to the so-called Mediterranean strategy of the British.

A few days after Marshall resigned as chief of staff on Nov. 21, 1945, President Harry Truman persuaded him to attempt, as his special representative, to mediate the Chinese Civil War. Though his efforts were unsuccessful, in January 1947 he was appointed secretary of state. In June of that year he proposed a European Recovery Program, which, known as the Marshall Plan, played a decisive role in the reconstruction of war-torn Europe. Also significant during his secretaryship were the provision of aid to Greece and Turkey, the recognition of Israel, and the initial discussions that led to the establishment of the North Atlantic Treaty Organization (NATO). Marshall left his position because of ill health in 1949. Then, in 1950, when he was nearly 70, President Truman called him to the post of secretary of defense, in which he helped prepare the armed forces for the Korean War by increasing troop strength and matériel production and by raising morale.

After 1951 General Marshall remained on the active-duty list as the highest ranking general of the army, available for consultation by the government. In 1953 he was awarded the Nobel Prize for Peace in recognition of his contributions to the economic rehabilitation of Europe after World War II and his efforts to promote world peace and understanding. He died at Walter Reed General Hospital, Washington, D.C., in 1959. (F.C.P.)

BIBLIOGRAPHY. The authorized biography of General Marshall is a projected four- or five-volume work by Forrest C. Pogue of which three volumes, *Education of a General, 1880–1939* (1963), *Ordeal and Hope, 1939–42* (1966), and *Organizer of Victory, 1943–45* (1973), have appeared. Robert H. Ferrell, *George C. Marshall* (1966), a volume in the "American Secretaries of State Series," written without access to unpublished State Department files, is a valuable summary of the period. John Robinson Beal, *Marshall in China* (1970), contains excerpts of the diary of an American news adviser to Chiang Kai-shek during the Marshall mission. H.L. Stimson and McGeorge Bundy, *On Active Service in Peace and War* (1947), draws heavily on Stimson's manuscript diary for the period 1941–45 in relation to Marshall. His papers are held in the George C. Marshall Library, Lexington, Va.

Marshall, John (b. Sept. 24, 1755, near Germantown, Va.—d. July 6, 1835, Philadelphia), fourth chief justice of the United States and principal founder of the U.S. system of constitutional law, including the doctrine of judicial review. The first of Marshall's great cases in more than 30 years of service was *Marbury* v. *Madison* (1803), which established the Supreme Court's right to state and expound constitutional law. His most important decision in exercising this authority was in *McCulloch* v. *Maryland* (1819), which upheld the authority of Congress to create the Bank of the United States. During his tenure Marshall participated in more than 1,000 decisions, writing 519 of them himself.

John Marshall, crayon portrait by Févret de Saint-Mémin; in the Duke University Law School, Durham, N.C.

By courtesy of Duke University, Durham, N.C.

Youth. John Marshall was the eldest of 15 children of Thomas Marshall and Mary Keith Marshall. His childhood and youth were spent in the near-frontier region that in 1759 became Fauquier County, Va., and he later lived in the more extensive properties his father acquired in the Blue Ridge mountain area. His education appears to have been largely the product of his parents' efforts, supplemented only by the instruction afforded by a visiting clergyman who lived with the family for about a year and by a few months of slightly more formal training at an academy in Westmoreland County.

Early career. When political debate with England was followed by armed clashes in 1775, John Marshall, as lieutenant, joined his father in a Virginia regiment of minutemen and participated in the first fighting in that colony. Joining the Continental Army in 1776, he served under Washington for three years in New Jersey, New York, and Pennsylvania, including in this service the harsh winter of 1777–78 at Valley Forge. When the term of service of his Virginia troops expired in 1779, Marshall returned to Virginia and thereafter saw little active service prior to his discharge in 1781.

Marshall's career in law dates from 1780. His only formal training was a brief course of lectures given by George Wythe that he attended at William and Mary College early in that year. Licensed to practice in August 1780, he returned to Fauquier County and was elected to the Virginia House of Delegates in 1782 and 1784. Attending the sessions of the legislature in the capitol at Richmond, he established there both a law practice and a home, after marriage to Mary Ambler in January 1783.

For the next 15 years Marshall's career was marked by increasing stature at the brilliant bar of Virginia. He had not, in 1787, achieved a public position that would have sent him as a delegate to the Constitutional Convention in Philadelphia, but he was an active, if junior, proponent of the Constitution in the closely contested fight for ratification. Marshall was elected to the legislature that took the first step toward ratification by issuing a call for a convention to consider ratifying; he was also elected a delegate to the convention. His principal effort on the floor of the convention was, perhaps prophetically, a defense of the judiciary article. He then used his acknowledged popularity to gain or hold the narrow margin by which Virginia's ratification of the Constitution was won.

With the new government under the Constitution installed, Pres. George Washington offered Marshall appointment as United States attorney for Virginia. Marshall declined. In 1789, however, he sought and obtained a further term in Virginia's House of Delegates as a supporter of the national government. As party lines emerged and became defined in the 1790s, Marshall became recognized as one of the leaders of the Federalist Party in Virginia. In 1795 Washington tendered him an appointment as attorney general. This, too, was declined, but Marshall returned to the state legislature as a Federalist leader.

His first federal service came when Pres. John Adams appointed him member of a commission, with Elbridge Gerry and Charles C. Pinckney, to seek improved relations with the government of the French Republic. The mission was unsuccessful. But reports then were published disclosing that certain intermediaries, some shadowy figures known as X, Y, and Z, had approached the commissioners and informed them that they would not be received by the French government unless they first paid large bribes; the reports further revealed that these advances had been rebuffed in a memorial prepared by Marshall. Marshall thereupon became a popular figure, and the conduct of his mission was applauded by one of the earliest American patriotic slogans, "Millions for defense, but not one cent for tribute."

Returned from France, Marshall declined appointment to the Supreme Court to succeed Justice James Wilson but was persuaded by Washington to run for Congress. He was elected in 1799 as a Federalist from the Richmond district, though his service in the House of Representatives was brief. His chief accomplishment there appears to have been the effective defense of the President against a Republican attack for having honoured a British request under the extradition treaty for the surrender of a seaman charged with murder on a British warship on the high seas. In May 1800 President Adams requested the resignation of his secretary of war and offered the post to Marshall. Marshall declined. The President next dismissed his secretary of state and tendered the vacant place in his Cabinet to Marshall.

In an administration harassed by dissension and with uncertain prospects in the forthcoming election, the appeal of the invitation must have been addressed principally to Marshall's loyalty. After some hesitation he accepted and almost immediately became the effective head of government when the President retired to his home in Massachusetts for a stay of a few months. In the autumn of 1800, Chief Justice Oliver Ellsworth resigned because of ill health. Adams, defeated in the election of November, tendered reappointment to John Jay, the first chief justice. Jay declined. The President then turned to his secretary of state and in January 1801 sent to the Senate the nomination of John Marshall to be chief justice. The last Federalist Senate confirmed the nomination on Jan. 27, 1801. On February 4, Marshall accepted the appointment but, at the President's request, continued to act as secretary of state for the last month of the Adams administration.

Chief justice of the United States. It fell to Marshall, and to the Supreme Court under and beginning with Marshall, to set forth the main structural lines of the government. Whether the Constitution had created a federation or a nation was not a matter on which agreement could have been won at the beginning of the 19th century. Though judicial decisions could not alone dispel differences of opinion, they could create a body of coherent, authoritative, and disinterested doctrine around which opinion could mass and become effective. To the task of creating such a core of agreement Marshall brought qualities that were admirably adapted for its accomplishment. His own mind had apparently a clear and well-organized concept of the effective government that he believed was needed and was provided by the Constitution. He wrote with a lucidity, a persuasiveness, and a vigour that gave to his judicial opinions a quality of reasoned inevitability that more than offset an occasional lack in precision of analysis. The 35 years of his magistracy gave opportunity for the development of a unified body of constitutional doctrine. It was the first aspect of Marshall's accomplishment that he and the court he headed did not permit this opportunity to pass unrecognized.

Prior to Marshall's appointment, it had been the custom of the Supreme Court, as it was in England, for each justice to deliver an opinion in each significant case. This method may be effective where a court is dealing with an organized and existing body of law, but with a new court and a largely unexplored body of law, it created an impression of tentativeness, if not of contradiction, which lent authority neither to the court nor to the law it expounded. With Marshall's appointment, and presumably at Marshall's instance, this practice changed. Thereafter, for some years, it became the general rule that there was only a single opinion from the Supreme Court. This change of practice alone would have contributed to making the court a more effective institution. And when the opinions were cast in the mold of Marshall's clear and compelling statement, the growth of the court's authority was assured.

Marbury v. *Madison* (1803) was the first of Marshall's great cases and the case that established for the court its power to state and expound constitutional law in disregard of federal statutes that it found in conflict with the Constitution. President Adams had appointed a number of justices of the peace for the District of Columbia shortly before his term expired. Their commissions had been signed and the seal of the United States affixed in the office of the secretary of state, but some of them, including that of William Marbury, remained undelivered. Pres. Thomas Jefferson is believed to have ordered that some of them not be delivered.

After unsuccessful application at the Department of State, Marbury instituted suit in the Supreme Court against James Madison, the new secretary. Though the matter was not beyond question, the Court found that Congress had by statute authorized that such suits be started in the Supreme Court rather than in a lower court. But the Supreme Court, speaking through Marshall, held that Article III of the Constitution did not permit this and that the court could not follow a statute that was in conflict with the Constitution. It thereby confirmed for itself its most controversial power, the function of judicial review, of finding and expounding the law of the Constitution.

Once the power of judicial review had been established, Marshall and the court followed with decisions that assured that it would be exercised, and the whole body of federal law determined, in a unified judicial system with the Supreme Court at its head. *Martin* v. *Hunter's Lessee* (1816) and *Cohens* v. *Virginia* (1821) affirmed the Supreme Court's right to review and overrule a state court on a federal question. *McCulloch* v. *Maryland* (1819) asserted the doctrine of "implied powers" granted Congress by the Constitution (in this instance, that Congress could create a bank of the United States, even though such a power was not expressly given by the Constitution).

McCulloch v. *Maryland* well illustrated that judicial review could have an affirmative aspect as well as a negative; it may accord an authoritative legitimacy to contested government action no less significant than its restraint of prohibited or unauthorized action. *Fletcher* v. *Peck* (1810) and *Dartmouth College* v. *Woodward* (1819) established the inviolability of a state's contracts. *Gibbons* v. *Ogden* (1824) established the federal government's right to regulate interstate commerce and to override state law in doing so. It must be clearly noted, however, that many of Marshall's decisions dealing with specific restraints upon government have turned out to be his less-enduring ones, particularly in later eras of increasing governmental activity and control. It is in this area, indeed, that judicial review has evoked its most vigorous critics.

There was only one term of the Supreme Court each year, generally lasting about seven or eight weeks (a little longer after 1827). Each justice, however, also conducted a circuit court—Marshall in Richmond, Va., and Raleigh, N.C. It was in Richmond in 1807 that he presided at the treason trial of former Vice President Aaron Burr, during which he successfully frustrated President Jefferson's efforts toward a runaway conviction; Burr was freed. With hardly more than three months annually engaged in judicial duties, Marshall had much time to devote to private life. He early completed a five-volume *Life of George Washington* (1804–07). He cared for an invalid wife, who bore him 10 children, 4 of whom died in early life. He enjoyed companionship, drinking, and debating with fellow lights in Richmond. In general, for the first 30 years of his service as chief justice, his life was largely one of contentment.

In the autumn of 1831, at the age of 76, he underwent the rigours of surgery for the removal of kidney stones and appeared to make a rapid and complete recovery. But the death of his wife on Christmas of that year was a blow from which his spirits did not so readily recover. In 1835 his health declined rapidly, and on July 6 he died in Philadelphia. He was buried in Richmond.

BIBLIOGRAPHY. Albert J. Beveridge, *The Life of John Marshall,* 4 vol. (1916–19), is the standard biography of Marshall and the most detailed and comprehensive account of his life and career; it is, however, pervasively laudatory and almost completely uncritical. James Bradley Thayer, *John Marshall* (1901, reprinted 1967), is a biographical essay, keenly perceptive in its appraisal of Marshall's career and work as chief justice. Charles Warren, *The Supreme Court in United States History,* rev. ed., 2 vol. (1937), which is a study of the Supreme Court as an institution of government, appropriately gives great emphasis to the court and the chief justiceship of John Marshall.

Marshall, Sir John Hubert (b. March 19, 1876, Chester, Cheshire, Eng.—d. Aug. 17, 1958, Guildford, Surrey), English director general of the Indian Archaeological Survey (1902–31) who in the 1920s was responsible for the large-scale excavations that revealed Harappā and Mohenjo-daro, the two largest cities of the previously unknown Indus Valley Civilization.

Marshall was educated at Dulwich College and at King's College, Cambridge. He took part in excavations on Crete under the auspices of the British School at Athens, where he studied from 1898 to 1901. Despite his youth, he was appointed director general of archaeology in India in 1902. Marshall reorganized the Indian Archaeological Survey and greatly expanded its scope of activity. Initially, his chief task was to save and conserve the standing Indian temples, sculptures, paintings, and other ancient remains, many of which had been long neglected and were in a sad state of decay. His energetic efforts resulted in the preservation of ancient buildings all over British India.

In addition to monument conservation, Marshall presided over an ambitious program of excavation. He devoted much attention to the ancient region of Gandhāra, in modern Pakistan, and particularly to the excavation of one of its principal cities, Taxila. Here were found vast quantities of jewelry and domestic artifacts that helped make possible a vivid reconstruction of ancient everyday life. *Taxila* (1951) is one of Marshall's most valuable works. The sites of Sānchi and Sārnāth, important for their connection with the history of Buddhism, were also excavated and restored, and Marshall published *The Monuments of Sanchi,* 3 vol. (1939).

Until the final 10 years of his directorship, virtually no attempt was made to examine Indo-Pakistani prehistoric remains. Then came the dramatic finds at Harappā (1921) and Mohenjo-daro (1922), in present-day Pakistan. The Indian Archaeological Survey's excavations of these and other sites revealed an ancient civilization that flourished from about 2500 to 1750 BC over an area covering much of Pakistan and corners of India and Afghanistan. Eight years after his retirement, Marshall completed editing *Mohenjo-Daro and the Indus Civilization,* 3 vol. (1931). He was knighted in 1914.

Marshall, Sir John Ross (b. March 5, 1912, Wellington, N.Z.—d. Aug. 30, 1988, England), lawyer, politician, and statesman who was prime minister of New Zealand (1972) and a leading figure in the economic planning of the Commonwealth for more than two decades.

A member of Parliament (1946–75), he also held several Cabinet posts, including minister of health (1951–54), minister of justice (1954–57), and minister of commerce and industry (1960–69), and in 1972 he was prime minister. Marshall was also a representative to the United Nations (1970), chairman of the National Development Council (1969–72), and a director of several companies. He was knighted in 1974.

Marshall, Louis (b. Dec. 14, 1856, Syracuse, N.Y., U.S.—d. Sept. 11, 1929, Zürich, Switz.), lawyer and leader of the American Jewish community who worked to secure religious, political, and cultural freedom for all minority groups.

Marshall attended Columbia Law School (1876–77) and was admitted to the New York bar (1878). Marshall successfully argued cases in which the U.S. Supreme Court declared unconstitutional state statutes forbidding private and parochial elementary and secondary schools (*Pierce* v. *Society of Sisters of the Holy Name,* 1925) and excluding black voters from primary elections (*Nixon* v. *Herndon,* 1927). At the Paris Peace Conference after World War I (1919), Marshall advocated treaty provisions that were intended to protect minority rights and were accepted by Romania, Poland, and other eastern European nations. His opposition hastened the discontinuance of Henry Ford's anti-Semitic newspaper, the *Dearborn* (Michigan) *Independent.*

Marshall, Stephen (b. *c.* 1594, Godmanchester, Huntingdonshire, Eng.—d. Nov. 19, 1655, London), Presbyterian minister and popular Puritan leader. He was an influential preacher to the English Parliament and a participant in the formulation of his church's creed.

By 1629 Marshall had become a vicar at Finchingfield, Essex, a position he held until 1651, when personal dissatisfaction caused him to move to Ipswich as town preacher. From 1640 he was also lecturer at St. Margaret's, Westminster. The following year he joined in an attack, published under the name Smectymnuus (*q.v.*), on the policies of church government and liturgy.

In 1643 Marshall became a member of the Westminster Assembly, a body of clerics and laymen convened by Parliament to determine the nature and doctrine of the English church. When in 1646 Parliament ordered that Presbyterianism be established in England, he was nominated to serve as an elder in his local classis, or district ruling body.

Marshall was influential primarily through his sermons. Though he never held an official position in London, his ability as a spokesman enabled him to win support in the House of Commons for liturgical and episcopal reforms. He was also active in the preparation of the Shorter Westminster Catechism (1647), still a major statement of Presbyterian belief.

Marshall, Thomas R(iley) (b. March 14, 1854, North Manchester, Ind., U.S.—d. June 1, 1925, Washington, D.C.), 28th vice president of the United States (1913–21), who served in the Democratic administration of President Woodrow Wilson. He was the first vice president in almost a century to serve two terms in office. A popular public official, he was heard to make the oft-quoted remark during a tedious debate: "What this country needs is a really good five-cent cigar."

Marshall was admitted to the Indiana bar in 1875 and practiced law for almost 35 years in Columbia City (1875–1909). A forceful and entertaining speaker, he was elected governor of Indiana in 1908 and during the next four years sponsored an extensive program of social legislation. Largely because of his record in office, his name was presented as a favourite-son candidate for president at the Democratic National Convention of 1912. When Wilson won, Marshall received the vice-presidential nomination.

Marshall's personal influence on legislation was a powerful aid to the Wilson administration. He advocated strict neutrality prior to World War I (a stand he later regretted), supported the League of Nations, and opposed woman suffrage. His homespun philosophy and humour are recorded in *Recollections*

Thomas Marshall
Culver Pictures

of Thomas R. Marshall, Vice-President and Hoosier Philosopher: A Hoosier Salad (1925).

Marshall, Thurgood (b. July 2, 1908, Baltimore, Md., U.S.—d. Jan. 24, 1993, Bethesda, Md.), first black member of the U.S. Supreme Court. As an attorney he successfully argued before the U.S. Supreme Court the case of *Brown* v. *Board of Education of Topeka* (1954), in which racial segregation in American public schools was declared unconstitutional.

Thurgood Marshall
Harris and Ewing

Marshall graduated from Lincoln University, Pennsylvania (1930), and Howard University Law School, Washington, D.C. (1933, ranking first in his class). From 1936 he worked for the National Association for the Advancement of Colored People (NAACP), and in 1940 he became chief of its legal staff. He won 29 of the 32 cases that he argued before the Supreme Court. Among them, in addition to *Brown,* were cases in which the court declared unconstitutional a Southern state's exclusion of black voters from primary elections (*Smith* v. *Allwright,* 1944), state judicial enforcement of racial "restrictive covenants" in housing (*Shelley* v. *Kraemer,* 1948), and "separate but equal" facilities for black professionals and graduate students in state universities (*Sweatt* v. *Painter* and *McLaurin* v. *Oklahoma State Regents,* both 1950).

In September 1961, Marshall was nominated to the U.S. Court of Appeals for the Second Circuit by President John F. Kennedy, but opposition from Southern senators delayed his confirmation for several months. President Lyndon B. Johnson named Marshall U.S. solicitor general in July 1965 and nominated him to the Supreme Court in June 1967. Marshall was a steadfast liberal during his tenure on the court, and he maintained his previous views concerning the need for equitable and just treatment of the nation's minorities by the state and federal governments. By the time he retired in 1991, he was one of the last remaining liberal members of a Supreme Court dominated by a conservative majority.

Marshall Field & Co., a department store on State Street in Chicago that was for a time the largest in the world. In its 73 acres of floor space the store had larger book, china, shoe, and toy departments than any other department store.

The store was founded by Marshall Field (1834–1906) and Levi Zeigler Leiter (1834–1904) in 1865. After buying out his partner (1881), Field introduced many merchandising concepts that were revolutionary at the time. Placing strong emphasis on total customer service, Field made his store a complete shopping world, providing virtually every product and service routinely needed, and many not so routine. This was the first store to have a restaurant for shoppers.

Marshall Field department stores are located in many American cities, as well as in other shopping centres in the Chicago area. In 1982 Marshall Field & Co. was acquired by BATUS Inc., an American subsidiary of London-based B.A.T Industries PLC. The Dayton Hudson Corporation purchased Marshall Field & Co. from BATUS in 1990.

Marshall Islands, officially REPUBLIC OF THE MARSHALL ISLANDS, Marshallese MAJŌL, independent republic of the central Pacific Ocean. It is composed of two parallel chains of coral atolls, the Ratak, or Sunrise, to the east and the Ralik, or Sunset, to the west. The chains lie about 125 miles (200 km) apart and extend some 800 miles (1,290 km) northwest to southeast. The islands and islets number more than 1,200. The capital is Majuro. Area 70 square miles (181 square km). Pop. (1992 est.) 50,000.

A brief treatment of the Marshall Islands follows. For information about regional aspects of the Marshall Islands, *see* MACROPAEDIA: Pacific Islands.

For current history and for statistics on society and economy, *see* BRITANNICA BOOK OF THE YEAR.

None of the 29 low-lying coral atolls and the 5 coral islands in the Marshall group rises to more than 20 feet (6 m) above high tide. The islands are coral caps set on dome volcanoes rising from the ocean floor. The island units of the Marshalls are scattered over about 770,000 square miles (2,000,000 square km) of the Pacific. The largest atoll is Kwajalein, consisting of about 90 islets (with a total land area of 6 square miles [16 square km]); the islets surround a 665-square-mile (1,722-square-kilometre) lagoon. Bikini and Enewetak atolls served as testing grounds for U.S. nuclear weapons (1946–58), and much of Kwajalein atoll today is used as a missile-testing range by the U.S. military.

The climate is tropical with little seasonal variation in daily temperatures, which generally peak at about 89° F (32° C) in the mid-afternoon and fall to about 75° F (24° C) at night. Relative humidity is always high, averaging about 85 percent. Annual rainfall varies from 20 to 30 inches (500 to 800 mm) in the north to 160 inches (4,100 mm) in the southern atolls. The typical Marshallese atoll is about 50 miles (80 km) in circumference and consists of an irregular, oval-shaped coral reef surrounding a lagoon; the islets lie along the coral reef. Soils are generally sandy and low in fertility.

The indigenous people are Micronesians. The most populous atolls are Majuro and Kwajalein, together having about two-thirds of the country's total population. The people live mostly in traditional villages and are predominantly Christian. Marshallese and English are spoken. Subsistence farming, fishing, and the raising of pigs and poultry are the principal economic activities. Coconuts, pandanus, breadfruit, taro, and arrowroot are major foods. The production of copra cake and coconut oil for export and the leasing of land for the U.S. missile range on Kwajalein are the major sources of revenue. Majuro has a commercial dock complex, and many of the atolls have good anchorage within their lagoons. Majuro and Kwajalein have international airports.

The government consists of a president elected by a 33-member parliament known as the Nitijela. The 12-member Council of Iroji ("Chiefs") has mainly a consultative function, concerned with traditional laws and customs.

Sighted in 1529 by the Spanish navigator Álvaro Saavedra, the Marshalls lacked the wealth to encourage exploitation. In 1885 Germany declared the islands a protectorate. Japan seized them in 1914 and later (after 1919) administered them as a League of Nations mandate. Occupied by the United States in World War II, after heavy fighting at Kwajalein and Enewetak, the Marshall Islands were made part of the United Nations Trust Territory of the Pacific Islands under U.S. jurisdiction in 1947. Nuclear testing ceased in 1958, and clean-up efforts were completed; but Bikini and Enewetak remained too badly contaminated for the return of their populations.

A constitution was approved by the Marshallese people, and the country became an internally self-governing republic in 1979. The Marshall Islands, in 1982, signed a Compact of Free Association with the United States, which was endorsed by referendum in 1983. The document required that the United States be responsible for external security and defense and provide financial assistance to the republic. The compact came into effect in 1986, terminating the islands' Trust Territory status, and the Republic of the Marshall Islands became fully self-governing in free association with the United States. In 1991 the country was admitted to the United Nations.

Marshall Plan, formally EUROPEAN RECOVERY PROGRAM (April 1948–December 1951), U.S.-sponsored program designed to rehabilitate the economies of 17 western and southern European nations in order to create stable conditions in which democratic institutions could survive. The United States feared that the poverty, unemployment, and dislocation of the postwar period were reinforcing the appeal of communist parties to voters in western Europe. On June 5, 1947, in an address at Harvard University, Secretary of State George C. Marshall advanced the idea of a European self-help program, to be financed by the United States. On the basis of a unified plan for western European economic reconstruction presented by a committee representing 16 countries, the U.S. Congress authorized the establishment of the European Recovery Program. Aid was originally offered to almost all the European countries, including those under military occupation by the U.S.S.R. The U.S.S.R. early on withdrew from participation in the plan, however, and was soon followed by the other eastern European nations under its influence. This left the following countries to participate in the plan: Austria, Belgium, Denmark, France, Greece, Iceland, Ireland, Italy, Luxembourg, The Netherlands, Norway, Portugal, Sweden, Switzerland, Turkey, the United Kingdom, and western Germany.

Under Paul G. Hoffman the Economic Cooperation Administration (ECA), a specially created bureau, distributed over the next four years some $13 billion worth of economic aid, helping to restore industrial and agricultural production, establish financial stability, and expand trade. Direct grants accounted for the vast majority of the aid, with the remainder in the form of loans. To coordinate the European participation, 16 countries, led by the United Kingdom and France, established the Committee of European Economic Cooperation, to suggest a four-year recovery program. This organization was later replaced by the permanent Organisation for European Economic Cooperation (OEEC), to which West Germany was ultimately admitted.

The Marshall Plan was very successful; the several western European countries experienced a rise in their gross national products of 15 to 25 percent during this period. The plan contributed greatly to the rapid renewal of the western European chemical, engineering, and steel industries. The Marshall Plan concept of economic aid was so successful that President Harry S. Truman extended it to less developed countries throughout the world under the Point Four Program, initiated in 1949.

marshmallow, aerated candy that originated as a versatile medicinal syrup and ointment; it was made from root sap of the marsh mallow (*Althaea officinalis*), sugar, and egg white.

The modern marshmallow candy is made

from corn syrup, dextrose, gelatine, and egg albumen. A mixture of these ingredients is heated to around 240° F (115° C), whipped to twice or three times its original volume, and flavoured.

Finished marshmallow ranges in consistency from chewy to semi-liquid. The firmer candy is shaped into the traditional bite-sized "pillows" dusted with rice flour or powdered sugar before packaging; these are sometimes used as a garnish in cooking and are popularly toasted on sticks over open fires. More elastic marshmallow is often coated with chocolate. The softest marshmallow is used as a base for icings, fudges, and puddings, and as a topping for ice cream.

To make the best use of the Britannica, consult the INDEX *first*

Marsi, ancient people of Italy, located on the eastern shore of Lake Fucinus (now drained) in the modern province of L'Aquila. They are principally known for their prominent part in the Social War against Rome. In 304 BC the Marsi and their allies, the Vestini, Paeligni, and Marrucini (*qq.v.*), made an alliance with Rome that lasted until the Social War (91 BC onward). This war ended when the allies were finally given Roman citizenship.

The earliest pure Latin inscriptions of the Marsi are dated to about 150 BC, whereas the earliest inscriptions in the local dialect date from about 300 to 150 BC. The Marsi were among those who worshipped Angitia, a goddess of healing, and because they practiced primitive medicine, their country was held by the Romans to be the home of witchcraft. The name of the tribe is derived from the god Mars.

Marsi was also the name of an ancient Germanic tribe located between the Ruhr and Lippe rivers. Defeated during the Roman campaigns in AD 14–16, they then disappeared from history.

Marsileaceae, only family of the fern order Marsileales. The three genera and about 70 species of small aquatic ferns root in mud or grow in shallow water. The family is typified by spore-bearing structures (sporangia) in hard cases (sporocarps) produced at or beneath ground level at the bases of the leaves. The genera are widely distributed. *Marsilea* (water clover; *q.v.*), with 60 species, has clover-like leaves with four leaflets. *Pilularia* (pillwort), with six species, has threadlike (filiform) leaves without leaflets. *Regnellidium,* with one species, has leaves with two leaflets.

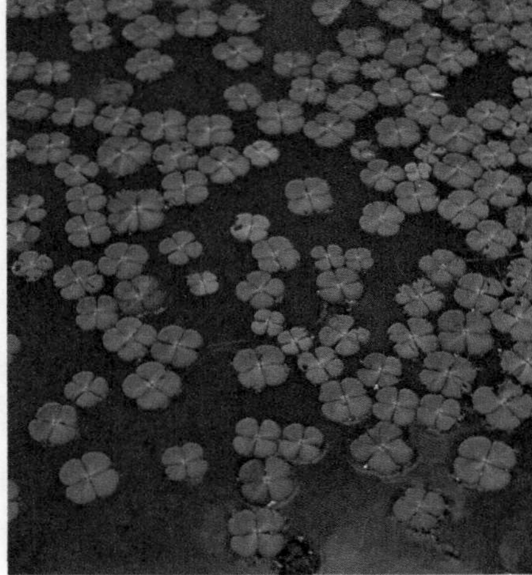

Water clover (*Marsilea quadrifolia*)
W.H. Hodge

Marsilius OF PADUA, Italian MARSILIO DA PADOVA (b. *c.* 1280, Padua, Kingdom of Italy—d. *c.* 1343, Munich), Italian political philosopher whose work *Defensor pacis* ("Defender of the Peace"), one of the most original treatises on political theory produced during the Middle Ages, significantly influenced the modern idea of the state. He has been variously considered a forerunner of the Protestant Reformation and an architect both of the Machiavellian state and of modern democracy.

After a brief period as professor and rector at the University of Paris (*c.* 1312–14), Marsilius served in Italy as political consultant to the Ghibellines (the pro-Imperial, anti-papal party). He wrote *Defensor pacis* in Paris between 1320 and 1324. When his authorship of the work, which was severely critical of papal politics, became known (1326), he fled to the Nürnberg court of King Louis IV of Bavaria and later was condemned as a heretic in Italy (1327). While accompanying Louis on his Italian expedition (1327–28), he joined in declaring Pope John XXII a heretic, installing Nicholas V as anti-pope, and crowning Louis emperor (Rome, 1328), with the authority to dissolve marriages. He remained at Louis's court in Munich for the rest of his life.

In *Defensor pacis,* a political polemic, as well as a tract on political theory, Marsilius, applying principles of Aristotle, evolved a secular concept of the state. The unity of the state must be preserved, he holds, by limiting the power of the church hierarchy. The state's principal responsibility is the maintenance of law, order, and tranquillity. The source of all political power and law is the people, among whose rights is the right to choose their ruler. The church's supreme authority in morals and doctrine, he concluded, should be vested in a general council representative of all believers—people and clergy.

Marsman, Hendrik (b. Sept. 30, 1899, Zeist, near Utrecht, Neth.—d. June 21, 1940, at sea in the English Channel), one of the outstanding Dutch poets and critics active between World War I and World War II.

Marsman studied law and practiced in Utrecht, but after 1933 he travelled in Europe and devoted himself to literature. Under the influence of the German Expressionists, Marsman made his literary debut about 1920 with rhythmic free verse, which attracted notice for its aggressive independence. The collection *Verzen* (1923; "Verses") expresses an antihumanist, anti-intellectual rebelliousness, which the poet called "vitalism." As editor of the periodical *De Vrije bladen* ("The Free Press"), he became in 1925 the foremost critic of the younger generation. His next collection of verse appeared in 1927 with the English title *Paradise Regained* and was greeted as a major artistic achievement. Another cycle, *Porta Nigra,* dominated by the idea of death, appeared in 1934. His last book of verse, *Tempel en kruis* (1940; "Temple and Cross"), an autobiographical account of the poet's development, reaffirms humanistic ideals. Marsman was drowned during World War II when his ship was torpedoed in the English Channel.

Marston, John (baptized Oct. 7, 1576, Oxfordshire, Eng.—d. June 25, 1634, London), English dramatist, one of the most vigorous satirists of the Shakespearean era, whose best known work is *The Malcontent* (1604), in which he rails at the iniquities of a lascivious court. He wrote it, as well as other major works, for the companies of boy actors popular at the time.

Marston began his literary career in 1598 with *The Metamorphosis of Pigmalions Image and Certaine Satyres,* a callow, erotic poem that was severely criticized. In the same year, the roughhewn, obscure verses of *The Scourge of Villainie,* in which Marston referred to himself as a "barking satirist," was widely acclaimed.

In 1599 Marston turned to writing for the theatre, producing *Histriomastix* (published in 1610), based on an anonymous earlier work. In his character Chrisoganus, a "Master Pedant" and "translating scholler," the audience was able to recognize the learned Ben Jonson. A brief, bitter literary feud developed between Marston and Jonson—part of "the war of the theatres." Jonson paid him back in *The Poetaster* (1601) by depicting Marston as Crispinus, a character with red hair and small legs who was given a pill that forced him to disgorge a pretentious vocabulary.

For the Children of Paul's, a theatre company, Marston wrote *The History of Antonio and Mellida* (1602), its sequel, *Antonios Revenge* (*c.* 1602), and *What You Will* (1607). The most memorable is *Antonios Revenge,* a savage melodrama of a political power struggle. Although *What You Will* satirized Jonson, that same year Marston and Jonson collaborated on *Love's Martyr.*

In 1604 Marston became a shareholder in the Children of the Chapel, another theatre company, for whom he wrote his remaining plays. *The Dutch Courtezan* (1603–04) as well as *The Malcontent* (1604) earned him his place as a dramatist. The former, with its coarse, farcical counterplot, was considered one of the cleverest comedies of its time. In *The Malcontent,* although he uses all the apparatus of contemporary revenge tragedy, Marston does not allow his wronged hero to kill any of his tormentors.

In 1605 Marston again collaborated with Jonson and with George Chapman on *Eastward Hoe,* a comedy of the contrasts within the life of the city. But the play's satiric references to opportunistic Scottish countrymen of the newly crowned James I gave offense, and all three authors were imprisoned.

After another imprisonment in 1608, Marston left unfinished *The Insatiate Countesse,* his most erotic play, and entered the Church of England. He took orders in 1609, married the daughter of James I's chaplain, and in 1616 accepted an ecclesiastical post in Christchurch, Hampshire. In 1633 he apparently insisted upon the removal of his name from the collected edition of six of his plays, *The Works of John Marston,* which was reissued anonymously the same year as *Tragedies and Comedies.*

Marston Moor, Battle of (July 2, 1644), the first major Royalist defeat in the English Civil War. In June 1644, King Charles I ordered a force under Prince Rupert of the Palatinate to relieve the Royalist garrison at York, then under siege by the Parliamentarians. Rupert outmanoeuvred the besiegers, relieved York, and pursued the Parliamentary forces seven miles west to Long Marston. There the parliamentary armies under Sir Thomas Fairfax (later 3rd Baron Fairfax of Cameron), and a Scottish Army under Alexander Leslie, the 1st earl of Leven, surprised Rupert with an early-evening attack. The left wing of the Parliamentary forces under Oliver Cromwell scattered Rupert's cavalry, then reformed and went to Fairfax's aid on the right, enveloping the Royalist centre. The Royalists suffered heavy losses—3,000 to 4,000 killed, many prisoners taken, and most of their cannon captured. With the fall of York, the King lost control of the north, and Oliver Cromwell emerged as the leading Parliamentary general.

marsupial, a member of the mammalian superorder (or order—authorities differ) Marsupialia, which includes a diversity of primitive mammals that undergo premature birth and complete their development outside the mother's body while attached to her nipples. Most are also characterized by a pouch, or marsupium, a flap of skin that lies over the nipples, but this is not always present; in some species there is merely a fold of skin encircling the nipples and in others there may be no such feature at all.

A brief treatment of marsupials follows. For full treatment, *see* MACROPAEDIA: Mammals.

Living marsupials are limited in distribution to the Australasian region, where about 175 species are found primarily in Australia, New Guinea, Timor, and Celebes; and to the New World, where more than 70 species inhabit South and Central America, although a few range into southern North America and one, the common opossum (*Didelphis marsupialis*), extends into southern Canada. They range in size from the great gray kangaroo (*Macropus giganteus*), 3 m (9 feet) long and 2 m (6 feet) tall, down to the planigale (*Planigale ingrami*), a 12-centimetre (5-inch) marsupial mouse.

The earliest-known marsupials are from the Cretaceous Period some 100 million years ago. Many of these early forms were members of the still extant family Didelphidae (the opossums). Marsupials originated in the New World and are presumed to have crossed to Australia by an early land bridge at some time preceding the rise of the placental mammals. No fossil marsupials have been found in Africa or Asia. By the beginning of the Tertiary Period (about 66.4 million years ago) Australia had become isolated from the other continents, and its marsupial fauna was able to diversify widely, free from competition from other mammals. Various members of this superorder developed forms or habits similar to those of many of the orders of placental mammals (a phenomenon known as convergent evolution). Thus the grazing kangaroos (Macropodidae) occupy the ecological niche filled on other continents by various hoofed mammals, the predatory dasyures (Dasyuridae) are equivalent to small cats, and the marsupial mole (*Notoryctes*) has converged remarkably in both form and habit on the true moles. Other Australian marsupials resemble, in form or habit, bears, squirrels, wolves, and mice. In the New World only two families of marsupials survive, the Didelphidae and the Caenolestidae (rat opossums). These animals are for the most part generalized omnivores, which has aided their survival in competition with placental mammals. More specialized groups, such as the large predatory Borhyaenidae, were unable to compete with the influx of placental competitors. One fact which undoubtedly contributed to the demise of many marsupials is that their brains are relatively much smaller than those of similar-sized placentals.

In many marsupials the hind legs are noticeably larger than the forelegs, a feature most apparent in kangaroos but appearing throughout the Marsupialia. Unique to this superorder are the epipubic, or marsupial, bones associated with the pelvic girdle, which were once thought to help support the pouch. Where a pouch occurs, it tends to open anteriorly in upright and climbing forms and posteriorly in quadrupedal, ground-dwelling species. The dentition of marsupials also differs from that of other mammals. The number of teeth ranges from 22 in the honey possum (*Tarsipes spenserae*) to 52 in the numbat (*Myrmecobius fasciatus*). Typically there are three premolars and four molars in each jaw, contrasting with the placental four premolars and three molars.

As marsupials evolved into diverse forms, they came to occupy various habitats. Several forms are highly arboreal, including the koala (*Phascolarctos cinereus*) and the tree kangaroos (*Dendrolagus*). The greater glider (*Schoinobates volans*) has membranes that stretch between the fore and hind limbs and enable it to glide from tree to tree in the manner of the flying squirrels. Only one marsupial has taken to an aquatic life-style; this is the New World water opossum (*Chironectes minimus*).

Many marsupials are herbivorous. The kangaroos are mainly grazers, the wombats (Vombatidae) live on roots, fungi, and grass, and the honey possum feeds on nectar. The most highly specialized is the koala, which can survive only on the leaves of certain species of eucalyptus trees. The numbat lives on ants and termites, which it ingests with its long tongue. The possums and bandicoots are generally omnivorous, living on a variety of plant matter and invertebrates. Many of the marsupial mice and the smaller native cats (Dasyuridae) live on insects and various small vertebrates such as lizards and mice. Larger carnivores such as the Tasmanian devil (*Sarcophilus harrisii*) prey on birds and other mammals.

The most remarkable characteristic of marsupials is their mode of reproduction. Gestation is relatively short, ranging from 8 to 40 days, and the young are born blind and in a very embryonic condition. In spite of this they must travel unassisted over the mother's body from the birth canal to the pouch or teat. The young are equipped for this purpose with relatively large forelimbs, with which they grasp the mother's fur as they squirm and wriggle their way to the pouch. Once inside the pouch each young clamps onto a nipple, which becomes engorged within its mouth. The young marsupial remains in the pouch and continues to develop for weeks to months. After several weeks, the growing young are able to leave the pouch for short intervals, but they will remain with the mother for some time thereafter, often clinging to her fur.

Marsupials are typically solitary animals, exhibiting minimal sociability outside of breeding season, although kangaroos often travel and graze in groups known as mobs; these lack, however, the leadership and cohesion found in herds of placental mammals. Marsupials seldom vocalize, a trait that, like their unsocial nature, may derive from their relatively low intelligence.

marsupial mole, either of the two species of small marsupial mammals of the genus *Notoryctes,* comprising the family Notoryctidae. Found in hot sandy wastes of south-central and northwestern Australia, the 18-centimetre (7-inch) *N. typhlops* and the 10-centimetre (4-inch) *N. caurinus* (by some not separated from *N. typhlops*) are remarkably like true moles. The forefeet bear triangular claws used in digging, and the skin of the blunt snout and stubby tail is leathery. The eyes are poorly developed and virtually hidden in the long silky fur, which is silvery to yellowish red or pinkish, with an iridescent sheen—much like that of the golden moles of Africa. These creatures are intensely active one moment, then suddenly fall asleep. They burrow just beneath the soil surface, hunting for grubs and earthworms. Unlike true moles, they do not leave tunnels behind them when feeding; they therefore often come up for air.

Marsupial mole (*Notoryctes typhlops*)
Painting by H. Douglas Pratt

marsupial mouse, any of many small rat- or mouselike animals, belonging to the family Dasyuridae (order Marsupialia), found in Australia and New Guinea. The species vary in body length from 5 to 22 cm (2 to 9 inches), and all have tails, often brushlike, that are about as long as their bodies. Their coat is generally solid gray, buff, or brown; a few species are speckled. All marsupial mice are predatory, most are nocturnal, and they are really more like shrews than mice.

They subsist on insects and small vertebrates, although the broad-footed marsupial mice (*Antechinus* species) are also known to eat nectar. The fat-tailed dunnart (*Sminthopsis crassicaudata*) stores excess fat in its tail. Members of all genera except *Antechinus* will go into torpor when food is scarce. The crest-tailed marsupial mouse, or mulgara (*Dasycercus cristicauda*), an arid-land species valued for killing house mice, gets all of its water from the bodies of its prey.

Reminiscent of jerboas—long-tailed and big-eared with stiltlike hind legs—are the two species of *Antechinomys,* also of the Australian outback. The two species of brush-tailed marsupial mice, or tuans (*Phascogale*), are grayish above and whitish below in colour; the distal half of the long tail is thickly furred and resembles a bottle brush when the hairs are erected. Tuans are arboreal but may raid poultry yards. In both appearance and behaviour the flat-skulled marsupial mice, or planigales (*Planigale*), are similar to the true shrews (*Sorex*). The Red Data Book lists the eastern jerboa marsupial, or kultarr (*Antechinomys laniger*), of Australia as endangered; several other marsupial mice are considered rare.

Marsyas, legendary Greek figure of Anatolian origin. According to the usual Greek version, Marsyas found the oboe that the goddess Athena had invented and, after becoming skilled in playing it, challenged Apollo to a contest with his lyre. When King Midas of Phrygia, who had been appointed judge, declared in favour of Marsyas, Apollo punished Midas by changing his ears into ass's ears. In another version the Muses were the judges, and they awarded the victory to Apollo, who tied Marsyas to a tree and flayed him. In Rome a statue of Marsyas, a favourite art subject, stood in the Forum; this was imitated by Roman colonies and came to be considered a symbol of autonomy.

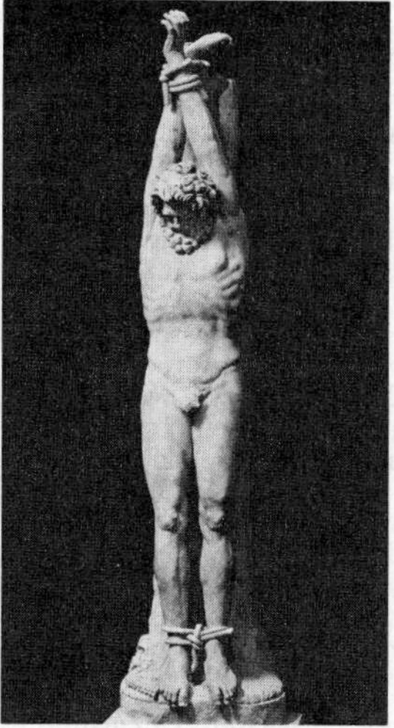

Marsyas about to be flayed, antique sculpture; in the Museo Nuovo, Rome
Alinari—Art Resource/EB Inc.

Marsyas Painter (fl. *c.* 350–325 BC), Greek painter of the late Classical period, known for a pelike (wine container), now in the British Museum, of "Peleus Taming Thetis," and for a "Nuptial Lebes" (the bringing of gifts to the newly wed bride), now in the Hermitage at St. Petersburg. Both vases date from 340–330 BC, and both are in the so-called Kerch style, of which the Marsyas Painter is a key representative. (Kerch refers to the area north of the Black Sea where many of the vessels were excavated.) The Kerch style is recognized by slender, mannered forms; elaborate

"Peleus Taming Thetis," pelike by the Marsyas Painter, *c.* 340–330 BC; in the British Museum
By courtesy of the trustees of the British Museum

decoration; and polychrome effects, achieved through the heavy use of white paint and sometimes gilding. It is thought to be the last major style of Attic red-figure painting.

Martel, Charles: *see* Charles Martel.

Martel, Édouard-Alfred (b. 1859, Pontoise, Fr.—d. 1938, Montbrison), French geographer and speleologist, known for his pioneer work in 1894 on the physiography and accessibility of caves.

As founder of speleology, or the scientific exploration of caverns, he explored the limestone caves of Cévennes and, with others, made descents into previously unknown caves of France, Ireland, Austria, Majorca, and Greece. In 1895 he founded the Society of Speleology in France. Martel was the tribunal of commerce in Paris from 1886 until 1899, when he became a professor of subterranean geography at the Sorbonne; he was appointed a member of the staff of the Department of Geological Maps of France in 1901.

marten, any of several weasel-like carnivores of the genus *Martes* (family Mustelidae), found in Canada and parts of the United States and in the Old World from Europe to the Malay region. Differing in size and coloration according to species, they have lithe, slender bodies, short legs, rounded ears, bushy tails, and soft, thick coats that are valuable in the fur trade. Martens are forest dwelling and usually solitary; they climb easily and feed rapaciously on animals, fruit, and carrion. A litter contains one to five young; the gestation period, especially in northern areas, may last 290 days or more because of a delay before implantation of the fertilized egg in the wall of the uterus.

Stone marten (*Martes foina*)
Reinhard/Reiser—Bavaria-Verlag

Animals commonly called "marten" but better known by other names include the Pennant's, big, or fisher marten (*see* fisher) and the foul marten (*see* polecat).

The best known species of *Martes* are the following:

The American marten (*M. americana*) is a North American species of northern wooded regions. It is also called pine marten; its fur is sometimes sold as American, or Hudson Bay, sable. Its adult length is 35–43 centimetres (14–17 inches), exclusive of the 18–23-cm tail. It weighs 1–2 kilograms (2–4 pounds) and has a yellowish-brown coat deepening to dark brown on tail and legs, with a pale whitish or yellowish throat patch.

The pine marten (*M. martes*) of European and Central Asian forests is also called baum marten and sweet marten. It has a dark brown coat with an undivided yellowish throat patch. Its head and body length is 42–52 cm, with a 22–27-cm long tail. Its shoulder height is 15 cm, its weight, 1–2 kg.

The stone marten, or beech marten (*M. foina*), inhabits wooded country in Eurasia. It has grayish-brown fur with a divided, white throat bib. It weighs 1–2.5 kg, is 42–48 cm long, and is 12 cm high at the shoulder.

The yellow-throated marten (*M. flavigula*), of the subgenus *Charronia*, is also called honey dog for its fondness for sweet food. It is found in southern Asia. Its head and body length is 56–61 cm, and its tail is 38–43 cm long. It has a brown coat that darkens toward and on the tail, and its throat and chin are orange.

Marten, Henry, also called HARRY MARTEN (b. 1602, Oxford—d. Sept. 9, 1680, Chepstow Castle, Monmouth, Eng.), a leading Parliamentary judge in the trial of King Charles I of England and the signer of his death warrant.

Educated at University College, Oxford, Marten first became prominent in 1639 when he refused to contribute to the general loan for the Scottish war, and in April and again in November 1640 he was returned to Parliament as a member for Berkshire. There he spoke in favour of the proposed bill of attainder against the Earl of Strafford and used such frank language about the King that Charles demanded his trial for high treason. When rebellion broke out, Marten did not take the field, although he was appointed governor of Reading, but in Parliament he was very active. In 1643, on account of some remark about extirpating the royal family, he was expelled from Parliament, but in the following year was made governor of Aylesbury. Allowed to return to Parliament in 1646, Marten again spoke against the King, attacked the Presbyterians, and supported the army against the Parliament. He was one of the most prominent of the King's judges and signed the death warrant. In 1649 he was chosen a member of the Council of State, but he took no part in public life during the Protectorate. He resumed his seat in the Long Parliament in 1659 and surrendered himself as a regicide in June 1660. He was imprisoned and died at Chepstow Castle.

Marten published several pamphlets and in 1662 *Henry Marten's Familiar Letters to His Lady of Delight,* containing letters to his mistress, Mary Ward.

martenot (musical instrument): *see* ondes martenot.

Martens, Fyodor Fyodorovich, French FRÉDÉRIC DE MARTENS, German FRIEDRICH VON MARTENS (b. Aug. 27 [Aug. 15, old style], 1845, Parnu, Livonia—d. June 20 [June 7, O.S.], 1909, St. Petersburg, Russia), Russian jurist and diplomat, international arbitrator, and historian of European colonial ventures in Asia and Africa.

After serving four years in the Russian foreign ministry, Martens taught public law in St. Petersburg from 1872 to 1905. He helped to

Fyodor Fyodorovich Martens
H. Roger-Viollet

settle the controversy between Great Britain and France over Newfoundland (1891) and a Mexican–U.S. dispute that was the first case determined by the Permanent Court of Arbitration, The Hague (1902). During the Russo-Japanese War (1904–05), he took part in the negotiations that led to the peace treaty of Portsmouth, N.H. (Sept. 5, 1905). Representing Russia at the second international conference at The Hague (1907), he served as president of the maritime law committee.

Martens wrote books on the right of private property in war (1869); the expansion of Russia and Great Britain in Central Asia (1879); international law (1882); and the Berlin conference of 1884–85, concerning European spheres of influence in Africa, the Middle East, China, and the Pacific (1887). His most ambitious work of editing, *Recueil des traités et conventions conclus par la Russie* . . . (15 vol., 1874–1909), contains not only the texts of treaties between Russia and other countries but also histories (based on unpublished Russian documents) of the diplomatic conditions necessitating the treaties. It was printed in Russian and French in parallel columns.

To make the best use of the Britannica, consult the INDEX *first*

Martens, Georg Friedrich von (b. Feb. 22, 1756, Hamburg—d. Feb. 21, 1821, Frankfurt am Main), Hanoverian diplomat, professor of jurisprudence at the University of Göttingen from 1783, the original editor of what remains the largest collection of treaties in the world. He singlehandedly edited *Recueil des traités,* covering treaties from 1761, through the first seven volumes (1791–1801) and collaborated with his nephew Karl von Martens in editing four additional volumes (1802–08). The Martenses and numerous later scholars prepared *Nouveau recueil général des traités,* dealing with treaties from 1808 (112 vol., 1817–1944).

Martha's Vineyard, island off the southeastern coast of Massachusetts, U.S., 4 mi (6 km) across Vineyard Sound from the mainland (Cape Cod). Of glacial origin, it is nearly 20 mi long, 2 to 10 mi wide, and 308 ft (94 m) above sea level at its highest point. Its coastline is characterized by numerous inlets and ponds sealed by sand spits from the sea. It was probably sighted by many early navigators but was first recorded in 1602 by Bartholomew Gosnold and named by his

Menemsha Harbor, in Chilmark, Martha's Vineyard, Massachusetts
Arthur Griffin

coexplorer Gabriel Archer for its many vines (the source of the "Martha" appellation is unknown). Purchased by Thomas Mayhew in 1641 and settled the following year, it was considered part of New York but was ceded in 1692 to Massachusetts and incorporated into Dukes county (along with the Elizabeth Islands, Chappaquiddick, and No Man's Land). Early attempts at farming, brickmaking, and fish smoking gave way in the 18th and 19th centuries to the development of whaling and fishing enterprises based at Edgartown (inc. 1671), the county seat, which once boasted the world's largest sperm-oil candle factory. The summer yachting and tourist trade is now the economic mainstay. Chief resorts are Vineyard Haven (the port for island steamers and ferries), Tisbury, Oak Bluffs, Edgartown, West Tisbury, Chilmark, and Gay Head (named for the multicoloured cliffs found there). Much of the island makes up Martha's Vineyard State Forest. Pop. (1992 est.), Dukes county, 11,869.

Martí, José Julián, in full JOSÉ JULIÁN MARTÍ Y PÉREZ (b. Jan. 28, 1853, Havana, Cuba—d. May 19, 1895, Dos Ríos), poet and essayist, patriot and martyr, who became the symbol of Cuba's struggle for independence from Spain. His dedication to the goal of Cuban freedom made his name a synonym for liberty throughout Latin America. As a patriot, Martí organized and unified the movement for Cuban independence and died on the battlefield fighting for it. As a writer, he was distinguished for his personal prose and deceptively simple, sincere verse on themes of a free and united America.

Martí
By courtesy of the Organization of American States

Educated first in Havana, Martí had published several poems by the age of 15, and at age 16 he founded a newspaper, *La patria libre* ("The Free Fatherland"). During a revolutionary uprising that broke out in Cuba in 1868, he sympathized with the patriots, for which he was sentenced to six months of hard labour and, in 1871, deported to Spain. There he continued his education and his writing, receiving both an M.A. and a degree in law from the University of Zaragoza in 1874 and publishing political essays. He spent the next few years in France, in Mexico, and in Guatemala, writing and teaching, and returned to Cuba in 1878.

Because of his continued political activities, however, Martí was again exiled from Cuba to Spain in 1879. From there he went to France, to New York City, and, in 1881, to Venezuela, where he founded the *Revista Venezolana* ("Venezuelan Review"). The politics of his journal, however, provoked Venezuela's dictator, Antonio Guzmán Blanco, and Martí returned that year to New York City, where he remained, except for occasional travels, until the year of his death.

Martí continued to write and publish newspaper articles, poetry, and essays. His regular column in *La nación* of Buenos Aires made him famous throughout Latin America. His poetry, such as the collection *Versos libres* (1913; "Free Verses"), written between 1878 and 1882 on the theme of freedom, reveals a deep sensitivity and an original poetic vision. Martí's essays, which are considered by most critics his greatest contribution to Spanish-American letters, helped to bring about innovations in Spanish prose and to promote better understanding among the American nations. In essays such as *Emerson* (1882), *Whitman* (1887), *Nuestra América* (1881; "Our America"), and *Bolívar* (1893), Martí expressed his original thoughts about Latin America and the United States in an intensely personal style that is still considered a model of Spanish prose. His writings reflect his exemplary life, his kindness, his love of liberty and justice, and his deep understanding of human nature. Collections of English translations of Martí's writings are *Inside the Monster: Writings on the United States and American Imperialism* (1975); *Our America: Writings on Latin America and the Cuban Struggle for Independence* (1978); and *On Education* (1979)—all edited by Philip Foner.

In 1892 Martí was elected *delegado* ("delegate"; he refused to be called president) of the Partido Revolucionario Cubano ("Cuban Revolutionary Party") that he had helped to form. Making New York City the centre of operations, he began to draw up plans for an invasion of Cuba. He left New York for Santo Domingo on Jan. 31, 1895, accompanied by the Cuban revolutionary leader Máximo Gómez and other compatriots. They arrived in Cuba to begin the invasion on April 11. Martí's death a month later in battle on the plains of Dos Ríos, Oriente province, came only seven years before his lifelong goal of Cuban independence was achieved.

Martial, Latin in full MARCUS VALERIUS MARTIALIS (b. March 1, AD 38–41, Bilbilis, Hispania [Spain]—d. *c.* 103), Roman poet who brought the Latin epigram to perfection and provided in it a picture of Roman society during the early empire that is remarkable both for its completeness and for its accurate portrayal of human foibles.

Life and career. Martial was born in a Roman colony in Spain along the Salo River. Proudly claiming descent from Celts and Iberians, he was, nevertheless, a freeborn Roman citizen, the son of parents who, though not wealthy, possessed sufficient means to ensure that he received the traditional literary education from a grammarian and rhetorician. In his early 20s, possibly not before AD 64, since he makes no reference to the burning of Rome that occurred in that year, Martial made his way to the capital of the empire and attached himself as client (a traditional relationship between powerful patron and humbler man with his way to make) to the powerful and talented family of the Senecas, who were Spaniards like himself. To their circle belonged Lucan, the epic poet, and Calpurnius Piso, chief conspirator in the unsuccessful plot against the emperor Nero in AD 65. After the latter incident and its consequences, Martial had to look around for other patrons. Presumably the Senecas had introduced him to other influential families, whose patronage would enable him to make a living as a poet. Yet precisely how Martial lived between AD 65 and 80, the year in which he published *Liber Spectaculorum* (*On the Spectacles*), a small volume of poems to celebrate the consecration of the Colosseum, is not known. It is possible that he turned his hand to law, although it is unlikely that he practiced in the courts either successfully or for long.

When he first came to Rome, Martial lived in rather humble circumstances in a garret on the Quirinal Hill (one of the seven hills on which Rome stands). He gradually earned recognition, however, and was able to acquire, in addition to a town house on the Quirinal, a small country estate near Nomentum (about 12 miles [19 km] northeast of Rome), which may have been given to him by Polla, the widow of Lucan. In time Martial gained the notice of the court and received from emperors Titus and Domitian the *ius trium liberorum,* which entailed certain privileges and was customarily granted to fathers of three children in Rome. These privileges included exemption from various charges, such as that of guardianship, and a prior claim to magistracies. They were therefore financially profitable and accelerated a political career. Martial was almost certainly unmarried, yet he received this marital distinction. Moreover, as an additional mark of imperial favour, he was awarded a military tribuneship, which he was permitted to resign after six months' service but which entitled him to the privileges of an *eques* (knight) throughout his life, even though he lacked the required property qualification of an *eques*.

From each of the patrons whom Martial, as client, attended at the morning levee (a reception held when arising from bed), he would regularly receive the "dole" of "100 wretched farthings." Wealthy Romans, who either hoped to gain favourable mention or feared to receive unfavourable, albeit oblique, mention in his epigrams, would supplement the minimum dole by dinner invitations or by gifts. The poverty so often pleaded by the poet is undoubtedly exaggerated; apparently his genius for spending kept pace with his capacity for earning.

Martial's first book, *On the Spectacles* (AD 80), contained 33 undistinguished epigrams celebrating the shows held in the Colosseum, an amphitheatre in the city begun by Vespasian and completed by Titus in 79; these poems are scarcely improved by their gross adulation of the latter emperor. In the year 84 or 85 appeared two undistinguished books (confusingly numbered XIII and XIV in the collection) with Greek titles *Xenia* and *Apophoreta;* these consist almost entirely of couplets describing presents given to guests at the December festival of the Saturnalia. In the next 15 or 16 years, however, appeared the 12 books of epigrams on which his renown deservedly rests. In AD 86 Books I and II of the *Epigrams* were published, and between 86 and 98, when Martial returned to Spain, new books of the *Epigrams* were issued at more or less yearly intervals. After 34 years in Rome, Martial returned to Spain, where his last book (numbered XII) was published, probably in AD 102. He died not much over a year later in his early 60s.

The chief friends Martial made in Rome—Seneca, Piso, and Lucan—have already been mentioned. As his fame grew, he became acquainted with the literary circles of his day and met such figures as the literary critic Quintilian, the letter writer Pliny the Younger, the satirist Juvenal, and the epic poet Silius Italicus. Whether he knew the historian Tacitus and the poet Valerius Flaccus is not certain.

Poetry. Martial is virtually the creator of the modern epigram, and his myriad admirers throughout the centuries, including many of the world's great poets, have paid him the homage of quotation, translation, and imitation. He wrote 1,561 epigrams in all. Of these, 1,235 are in elegiac couplets, each of which consists of a six-foot line followed by a five-foot line. The remainder are in hendecasyllables (consisting of lines 11 syllables long) and other metres. Though some of the epigrams are devoted to scenic descriptions, most are about people—emperors, public officials, writers, philosophers, lawyers, teachers, doctors, fops, gladiators, slaves, undertakers, gourmets, spongers, senile lovers, and revolting debauchees. Martial made frequent use of the mordant epigram bearing a "sting" in its tail—*i.e.,* a single unexpected word at the poem's end that completes a pun, antithesis, or an ingenious ambiguity. Poems of this sort would later greatly influence the use of the epigram in the literature of England, France, Spain, and Italy. Martial's handling of this type of epigram is illustrated by I:28, where the apparent contradiction of an insult masks an insult far more subtle: "If you think Acerra reeks of yesterday's wine, you are mistaken. He invariably drinks till morning." Puns, parodies, Greek quotations, and clever ambiguities often enliven Martial's epigrams.

Martial has been charged with two gross faults: adulation and obscenity. He certainly indulged in a great deal of nauseating flattery of the emperor Domitian, involving, besides farfetched conceits dragging his epigrams well below their usual level, use of the official title "my Lord and my God." Furthermore, Martial cringed before men of wealth and influence, unashamedly whining for gifts and favours. Yet, however much one despises servility, it is hard to see how a man of letters could have survived long in Rome without considerable compromise. As for the charge of obscenity, Martial introduced few themes not touched on by Catullus and Horace (two poets of the last century BC) before him. Those epigrams that are indescribably obscene constitute perhaps one-tenth of Martial's total output. His references to homosexuality, "oral stimulation," and masturbation are couched, at least, in a rich setting of wit, charm, linguistic subtlety, superb literary craftsmanship, evocative description, and deep human sympathy. Martial's poetry is generally redeemed by his affection toward his friends and his freedom from both envy of others and hypocrisy over his own morals. In his emphasis on the simple joys of life—eating, drinking, and conversing with friends—and in his famous recipes for contentment and the happy life, one is reminded continually of the dominant themes of Horace's *Satires, Epistles,* and *Second Epode.*

The most convenient complete translation of Martial with the Latin on the facing page is in the "Loeb Classical Library," *Martial,* by W.C.A. Ker, 2 vol. (1919–20). A good selection may be found in *Martial's Epigrams: Translations and Imitations,* by A.L. Francis and H.F. Tatum (1924); and *Epigrams, with an English Translation,* by W.C.A. Ker, 2 vol. (1961). (H.H.Hu.)

BIBLIOGRAPHY. Studies and commentaries include Paul Nixon, *Martial and the Modern Epigram* (1927, reissued 1963), which discusses Martial's literary influence; A.G. Carrington, *Aspects of Martial's Epigrams* (1960), a useful general work; Peter Howell, *A Commentary on Book One of the Epigrams of Martial* (1980), which includes a short introduction on Martial and his work; N.M. Kay, *Martial, Book XI: A Commentary* (1984); and J.P. Sullivan, *Martial, the Unexpected Classic: A Literary and Historical Study* (1991), with a lengthy bibliography.

martial art, any of various fighting sports or skills, mainly of East Asian origin, such as kung fu, judo, karate, and kendō.

Martial arts can be divided into the armed and unarmed arts. The former include archery, spearmanship, and swordsmanship; the latter, which originated in China, emphasize striking with the feet and hands or grappling. In Japan, traditionally a warrior's training emphasized archery, swordsmanship, unarmed combat, and swimming in armour. Members of other classes interested in combat concentrated on arts using the staff, everyday work implements (such as thrashing flails, sickles, and knives), and unarmed combat. Perhaps the most versatile practice was *ninjutsu,* which was developed for military spies in feudal Japan and also included training in disguise, escape, concealment, geography, meteorology, medicine, and explosives. In modern times, derivatives of some of the armed martial arts, such as kendō (fencing) and kyūdō (archery), are practiced as sports. Derivatives of the unarmed forms of combat, such as judo, sumo, karate, and tae kwon do, are practiced, as are self-defense forms, such as aikido, hapkido, and kung fu. Simplified forms of T'ai Chi ch'uan, a Chinese form of unarmed combat, are popular as healthful exercise, quite divorced from martial origins. Derivatives of many of the armed and unarmed forms are practiced as a means of spiritual development.

The primary unifying aspect of the East Asian martial arts, which sets them apart from other martial arts, is the influence of Taoism and Zen Buddhism. This influence has resulted in a strong emphasis on the mental and spiritual state of the practitioner, a state in which the rationalizing and calculating functions of the mind are suspended so that the mind and body can react immediately as a unit, reflecting the changing situation around the combatant. When this state is perfected, the everyday experience of the dualism of subject and object vanishes. Since this mental and physical state is also central to Taoism and Zen, and must be experienced to be grasped, many of their adherents practice the martial arts as a part of their philosophical and spiritual training. Conversely, numerous practitioners of the martial arts take up the practice of these philosophies.

martial law, temporary rule by military authorities of a designated area in time of emergency when the civil authorities are deemed unable to function. The legal effects of a declaration of martial law differ in various jurisdictions, but they generally involve a suspension of normal civil rights and the extension to the civilian population of summary military justice or of military law. Although temporary in theory, a state of martial law may in fact continue indefinitely.

In the English legal system, the term is of dubious significance; in the words of the English jurist Sir Frederick Pollock, "so-called 'martial law,' as distinct from military law, is an unlucky name for the justification by the common law of acts done by necessity for the defence of the Commonwealth when there is war within the realm."

Such "acts done by necessity" are limited only by international law and the conventions of civilized warfare. Further, the regular civil courts do not review the decisions of tribunals set up by the military authorities, and very little authority exists on the question of remedies against abuse of powers by the military. In Great Britain and many other jurisdictions, such questions are of little significance in view of the modern practice of taking emergency or special powers by statute.

Martignac, Jean-Baptiste-Sylvère Gay, Viscount (Vicomte) **de** (b. June 20, 1778, Bordeaux, France—d. April 3, 1832, Paris), French politician, magistrate, and historian who, as leader of the government in 1828–29, alienated King Charles X with his moderate policy.

In 1798 Martignac was secretary to the abbé Sieyès, a publicist and Revolutionary leader. After service in the army, Martignac wrote several light plays. During the reign of Napoleon I (1804–14), he was a successful advocate in Bordeaux, where he belonged to a secret society of ultraroyalists, the Chevaliers de la Foi ("Knights of the Faith"). In 1818 he was appointed advocate general of the *cour royale* ("royal court"), and in 1819 he became *procureur général* ("attorney general") at Limoges. In 1821 he was elected to the Chamber of Deputies, where he supported the conservative politician the Count de Villèle.

In 1822–24 Martignac received important appointments and was made a viscount. His contact with practical politics and the currents of the time modified his views in the direction of the centre. When the Villèle administration fell (1827), Charles X chose Martignac to carry out a compromise policy. On Jan. 4, 1828, Martignac was appointed minister of the interior and became virtual head of the cabinet. He succeeded in abolishing Villèle's laws censoring the press and in gaining for the state some control over religious houses of education. In 1829 a coalition of the extreme right and the extreme left defeated him in the Chamber. Martignac's willingness to make even small concessions to the left had consistently galled the king, who replaced him with the Prince de Polignac, an ultraroyalist. Martignac's last public appearance was to defend Polignac in the Chamber of Peers in December 1830.

Martigues, town, Bouches-du-Rhône *département,* Provence-Alpes-Côte-d'Azur *région,* southeastern France, northwest of Marseille. The town is at the eastern end of the Canal de Caronte, which connects the Étang de Berre, a salt lagoon, to the Mediterranean Sea. Probably the site of the Roman camp Maritima Avaticorum, it was founded (1232) by Ramon Berenguer IV, count of Provence. It has three museums and several old churches, including Saint-Louis (14th century), Saint-Genès (17th century), and the Annunciade

Martigues, Fr., on the Mediterranean coast
Club Iris

Chapel. A fishing port and summer resort frequented by artists, Martigues also has oil refineries and fish-processing plants. Charles Maurras (1868–1952), leader of the extreme right-wing Action Française, was born there. Pop. (1990) 42,922.

Martin, name of rulers grouped below by country or papacy and indicated by the symbol •.

Foreign-language equivalents:

Italian	Martino
Latin	Martinus
Spanish	Martín

PAPACY

• **Martin I,** SAINT (b. Todi, Tuscany [Italy]—d. Sept. 16, 655, Cherson, Crimea [now Kherson, Ukraine]; feast day April 13), pope from 649 to 655.

Martin succeeded Theodore I in July 649. Martin's pontificate occurred during an extensive controversy that had strained relations between the Eastern and Western churches—namely monothelitism, a heresy maintaining that Christ had only one will. To bring an end to the controversy, Martin convoked and presided over the Lateran Council of 649 that condemned monothelitism and the Typos, an order by the Byzantine emperor Constans II Pogonatus that forbade discussion on Christ's wills. Constans, who had not approved Martin's election, ordered the pope's arrest. Martin was taken to Constantinople (Sept. 17, 654), publicly humiliated, and banished to the Crimea in May 655. He was honoured as a martyr.

A list of the abbreviations used in the MICROPAEDIA *will be found at the end of this volume*

• **Martin (II),** nonexistent pope. In the 13th century the papal chancery misread the names of the two popes Marinus as Martin, and as a result of this error Simon de Brie in 1281 assumed the name of Pope Martin IV instead of Martin II. The enumeration has not been corrected, and thus there exist no Martin II and Martin III.

• **Martin (III):** *see* Martin (II) (Papacy).

• **Martin IV,** original name SIMON DE BRION, or BRIE (b. *c.* 1210–20, Brie?, France—d. March 28, 1285, Perugia, Papal States [Italy]), pope from 1281 to 1285.

Of noble birth, Martin was a member of the council of King Louis IX of France and, in 1260, chancellor and keeper of the great seal. Pope Urban IV created him cardinal about 1261. He was elected pope on Feb. 22, 1281, assuming the name of Martin IV instead of Martin II because of a 13th-century error that misread the names of the two popes Marinus as Martin II and III.

Soon after his coronation at Orvieto, on March 23, Martin began to reverse the policy of his predecessor, Pope Nicholas III, by restoring Charles of Anjou, king of Naples and Sicily, as Roman senator and by favouring his interests in every possible way, even at the expense of union with the Greeks. (Charles apparently had convinced Martin that the only guarantee of a permanent union between East and West was the conquest of the Byzantine Empire.) Martin excommunicated the Byzantine emperor Michael VIII Palaeologus for lack of sincerity in the union's cause shortly before Michael's death (1282). This led to a new break (1283) between the churches of Constantinople and Rome under the Byzantine emperor Andronicus II.

After the War of the Sicilian Vespers (a massacre of the French in Sicily with which the Sicilians began their revolt in 1282 against Charles) had deprived Charles of possession of Sicily, and the Sicilians had chosen King Peter III the Great of Aragon as ruler, Martin spent the remainder of his pontificate in vain attempts to dislodge him and reinstate Charles. He excommunicated Peter and declared that he had forfeited the kingdom of Aragon, which had been a papal fief since the 11th century. Martin invited Charles's nephew, King Philip III the Bold of France, to take control of Aragon.

Martin's political enterprises, however, were destined for disaster. A Roman uprising against Charles cost him his senatorship, and a great sea battle between the Aragonese and Angevin fleets resulted in Charles's defeat and in the capture of his son, the future king Charles II of Naples. Philip's campaign in Aragon likewise ended calamitously, followed by Martin's death.

• **Martin V,** original name ODDO, or ODDONE, COLONNA (b. 1368, Genazzano, Papal States [Italy]—d. Feb. 20, 1431, Rome), pope from 1417 to 1431.

A cardinal subdeacon who had helped organize the Council of Pisa in 1409, he was unanimously elected pope on Nov. 11, 1417, in a conclave held during the Council of Constance (1414–18), which had been called to end the Great Schism (1378–1417), a split in the Western church caused by multiple claimants to the papacy.

As pope, Martin faced enormous difficulties, for he had to restore the Western church, the papacy, and the Papal States. The Council of Constance accepted his proposal (January 1418) that ecclesiastics rule lands and cities belonging to the church, but he found it necessary to establish himself in these places diplomatically rather than forcibly. Immediately after the Council of Constance, he condemned the widely held "conciliar theory" which would make the pope subject to a council, and he forbade any appeal from papal judgment on matters of faith. After the council adopted seven church reform decrees, leaving their execution to Martin, he concluded concordats on other points with the principal countries involved, chiefly methods of taxation and some modifications in favour of national demands for the reform of abuses in the papacy's central bureaucracy.

Although the French offered him Avignon for the papal residence, where it had been situated from 1309 to 1377, Martin chose Rome. He remained a year in Florence, however, for Rome—which he finally entered in 1420—was in ruins. Martin restored some of its churches and fortifications and tried to recover control of the Papal States. His chief difficulty was with the ambitious Italian soldier Braccio da Montone, whom in 1420 he had made vicar of the papal territories of Perugia and Umbria. Not content, Braccio sought further dominion in southern Italy but was defeated in the Battle of Aquila (June 2, 1424). Thereafter, Martin was able to make headway in Italy. By obtaining the grant of fiefs for his influential family in southern Italy, he increased the Colonnas' power and enriched them with vast estates in papal territory.

In non-Italian affairs he advanced papal interests and aimed to retrieve the authority of the Curia in the church as a whole. He worked to mediate the Hundred Years' War between France and England and to organize crusades against the Hussites, followers of the Bohemian religious reformer Jan Hus. Against the English government he fully asserted his determination to obliterate the Statute of Provisors of 1390, which had outlawed the papacy's conferring of an office or benefice. In the Spanish kingdoms he similarly emphasized the rights of the church against the crown.

Martin V, detail from a bronze monument by Simone di Giovanni Ghini; in the Basilica of St. John Lateran, Rome

Alinari—Anderson from Art Resource

Although he dreaded councils for fear that they would revive the conciliar theory, Martin called the Council of Pavia in 1423. Yet he soon strove to abort the council, which, because of a plague, moved to Siena. He refused to attend in person and in 1424 manipulated its dissolution. In short, he asserted papal supremacy in all matters ecclesiastical.

Martin neglected the opportunity offered by councils for church reform, toward which his own efforts were halfhearted and ineffective. He died shortly after calling the Council of Basel in 1431.

BIBLIOGRAPHY. Peter Partner, *The Papal State Under Martin V* (1958).

SICILY

• **Martin I,** byname MARTIN THE YOUNGER, Italian MARTINO IL GIOVANE (b. 1374—d. July 25, 1409, Cagliari, Sardinia [Italy]), prince of Aragon, king of Sicily (1392–1409), and skilled soldier, who had to subdue a popular revolt to maintain his reign on the island.

The son of Martin the Humanist of Aragon, Martin married Queen Mary of Sicily in November 1391. He was crowned at Palermo in May 1392, without having requested investiture by the pope. Baronial opposition to the Aragonese mounted, and when Martin condemned and executed as a traitor a nobleman who had been accused by an ambitious Aragonese rival, a rebellion broke out all over the island, later spreading to Messina and Catania. Martin proved himself to be a skilled and courageous soldier in quelling the rebels, who were supported by the pope.

Having restored order, Martin called a general parliament at Syracuse in 1398, which reformed the administration of the kingdom. Having lost his wife and son in 1402, he married Blanche of Navarre the following year. He then set out to bring Sardinia under his father's rule. When he died there, leaving no heir, he was succeeded by his father.

• **Martin II:** *see* Martin (Spain: Aragon).

SPAIN: ARAGON

• **Martin,** also called (until 1395) MARTÍN, DUKE (duque) DE MONTBLANCH (b. 1356, Gerona, Catalonia [Spain]—d. May 31, 1410, Barcelona), king of Aragon from 1396 and of Sicily (as Martin II). He was the son of Peter IV and brother of John I of Aragon.

Martin's life was marked chiefly by the continued Aragonese intervention in Sicily. When Frederick III of Sicily died in 1377, leaving a daughter, Mary, as his heiress, there ensued a long period of disorder. Peter IV of Aragon, on the grounds that females were excluded from succession to the Sicilian crown, claimed it for himself as the nearest male heir; and Mary underwent a series of abductions. Peter, however, in the face of objections from the papacy and the Angevins, in 1380 ceded his pretensions to his son, Martin, whose own son Martin was to marry Mary. Peter IV died in 1387, leaving Aragon to his elder son John I; the queen of Sicily was brought to Spain in 1388, and her marriage to the younger Martin took place in 1390. In 1392 the couple landed in Sicily with Martin of Montblanch and began to reign as queen and king-consort, despite strong local opposition. Mary died in 1401, leaving her widower to reign alone as Martin I of Sicily; but meanwhile Martin de Montblanch had become king of Aragon as Martin I in 1395 through the death of John I. When Martin I of Sicily died without legitimate issue in 1409, he left his kingdom, with his second wife, Blanche of Navarre, as regent, to his father, who thus became Martin II.

Martin, who had no surviving children of his own, intended that Sicily at least, if not Aragon too, should go to his grandson

Fadrique (Frederick) de Luna, a bastard of Martin I of Sicily. On Martin's death, however, in 1410, this succession was contested; and Ferdinand of Antequera, son of Peter IV's daughter Leonor, having been chosen king of Aragon as Ferdinand I in 1412, defeated Fadrique's partisans and reestablished Blanche's authority as his regent in Sicily. Thenceforward the Aragonese (later the Spanish) and the Sicilian crowns were to remain united for nearly 300 years (until the War of the Spanish Succession).

martin, any of several swallows belonging to the family Hirundinidae (order Passeriformes). In America the name refers to the purple martin (*Progne subis*) and its four tropical relatives—at 20 cm (8 inches) long, the largest American swallows. The sand martin,

House martin (*Delichon urbica*)
Bruce Coleman Ltd.

or bank swallow (*Riparia riparia*), a 12-cm (5-inch) brown and white bird, breeds throughout the Northern Hemisphere; it makes nest burrows in sandbanks. The house martin (*Delichon urbica*), blue-black above and white-rumped, is common in Europe. The African river martin (*Pseudochelidon eurystomina*) of the Congo River is black, with red eyes and bill; it is sometimes placed in a separate family, Pseudochelidonidae. The bee-martin, or bee bird, is not a martin but a kingbird (*q.v.*).

Martin FAMILY, French lacquerware artists of the period of Louis XV. The four brothers—Guillaume (d. 1749), Julien (d. 1752), Robert (b. 1706—d. 1765), and Étienne-Simon (d. 1770)—are remembered for perfecting the composition and application of vernis Martin, a lacquer substitute named after them, patented by Guillaume and Robert in 1730. In 1748 their factory became part of the Royal Factory of Furnishings to the Crown. Among their commissions were coaches and rooms at Versailles. Their name is also associated with vernis Martin fans, although it is not known if they actually made these fans. Robert's son Jean-Alexandre (b. 1738) worked for Prussia's Frederick II the Great at Potsdam.

Martin OF TOURS, SAINT (b. *c.* AD 316, Sabaria, Pannoni [now Szombathely, Hung.]—d. Nov. 8, 397, Candes, Gaul [France]; Western feast day, November 11; Eastern feast day November 12), patron saint of France, father of monasticism in Gaul, and the first great leader of Western monasticism.

Of pagan parentage, Martin chose Christianity at age 10. As a youth he was forced into the Roman army, but later—according to his disciple and biographer Sulpicius Severus—he petitioned the Roman emperor Julian the Apostate to be released because "I am Christ's soldier: I am not allowed to fight." When charged with cowardice, he is said to have offered to stand in front of the battle line armed only with the sign of the cross. He was imprisoned but was soon discharged.

On leaving the Roman army, Martin settled at Poitiers, under the guidance of Bishop Hilary. He became a missionary in the provinces of Pannonia and Illyricum (now in the Balkan Peninsula), where he opposed Arianism, a heresy that denied the divinity of Christ. Forced out of Illyricum by the Arians, Martin went to Italy, first to Milan and then to the island of Gallinaria, off Albenga. In 360 he rejoined Hilary at Poitiers. Martin then founded a community of hermits at Ligugé, the first monastery in Gaul. In 371 he was made bishop of Tours, and outside that city he founded another monastery, Marmoutier.

As bishop, Martin made Marmoutier a great monastic complex to which European ascetics were attracted and from which apostles spread Christianity throughout Gaul. He himself was an active missionary in Touraine and in the country districts where Christianity was as yet barely known. In 384/385 he took part in a conflict at the imperial court in Trier, France, to which the Roman emperor Magnus Maximus had summoned Bishop Priscillian of Ávila, Spain, and his followers. Although Martin opposed Priscillianism, a heretical doctrine renouncing all pleasures, he protested to Maximus against the killing of heretics and against civil interference in ecclesiastical matters. Priscillian was nevertheless executed, and Martin's continued involvement with the case caused him to fall into disfavour with the Spanish bishops. During his lifetime, Martin acquired a reputation as a miracle worker, and he was one of the first nonmartyrs to be publicly venerated as a saint.

Martin, A(rcher) J(ohn) P(orter) (b. March 1, 1910, London, Eng.—d. July 28, 2002, Llangarron, Herefordshire), British biochemist who was awarded (with R.L.M. Synge) the Nobel Prize for Chemistry in 1952 for development of partition chromatography, a quick and economical analytical technique permitting extensive advances in chemical, medical, and biological research.

Martin obtained a Ph.D. from the University of Cambridge in 1936 and worked as a research chemist for the Wool Industries Research Association in Leeds from 1938 to 1946. He then became head of biochemical research at the Boots Pure Drug Company, Nottingham, and held the post until 1948, when he was appointed to the staff of the British Medical Research Council. From 1959 to 1970 he was director of Abbotsbury Laboratories, Ltd.

Martin and Synge invented paper partition chromatography in 1944. Partition chromatography depends on the partition, or distribution, of each component of a mixture between two immiscible liquids. One of the liquids is held stationary by strong adsorption on the surface of a finely divided solid while the other flows through the interstices of the solid particles. Any substance that preferentially dissolves in the mobile liquid is more rapidly transported in the direction of flow than is a substance that has greater affinity for the stationary liquid. In 1953 Martin and A.T. James helped perfect gas chromatography, the separation of chemical vapours by differential absorption on a porous solid.

Martin, Billy, byname of ALFRED MANUEL MARTIN (b. May 16, 1928, Berkeley, Calif., U.S.—d. Dec. 25, 1989, near Fenton, N.Y.), American professional baseball player and manager whose leadership transformed teams on the field, but whose outspokenness and pugnacity made him the centre of controversy.

At age 18 Martin began playing baseball in the minor leagues. He batted and threw right-handed and in 1950 joined the American League New York Yankees, where he played mainly at second base. Not an outstanding player, he was, however, aggressive and a great player in crucial games, such as the 1952–53 World Series won by the Yankees. After being traded to the Kansas City Athletics (later the Oakland Athletics) in 1957, he played with five different clubs up to 1961.

From 1962 to 1964 Martin was a scout for the American League Minnesota Twins, the last team he played for, and a coach (1965–67). He then managed the Twins to first place in their division (1969) but was fired by the owner for insubordination. Martin then managed the American League Detroit Tigers to second, first, and third place in their division (1971–73) but again was fired for differences with management. Managing the American League Texas Rangers (1973–75), Martin brought the team from last place in 1973 to second place in 1974 but was again fired in mid-season 1975 in a dispute with management over trading policy. He managed the New York Yankees in five separate periods over a number of years, winning the World Series in 1977. Martin's volatility and frequent contretemps with principal Yankee owner George Steinbrenner resulted in his five firings (the last in 1988). From 1980 to 1982 Martin managed the Oakland Athletics, bringing the team from last place in 1979 to second place in 1980 and to first and second place in 1981 (the season was split because of a players' strike).

Martin, Frank (b. Sept. 15, 1890, Geneva, Switz.—d. Nov. 21, 1974, Naarden, Neth.), one of the foremost Swiss composers of the 20th century.

In the middle and late 1920s Martin was associated with Émile Jaques-Dalcroze. Martin was president of the Swiss Musicians' Union from 1943 to 1946, and in the latter year he settled in The Netherlands. Active as a teacher and lecturer, he was also a pianist and harpsichordist and toured widely, performing his own music. Martin evolved a strong personal style that incorporated elements of German music, particularly J.S. Bach, and of French Impressionism. In the 1930s he employed the 12-tone method in several works, such as the oratorio *Le Vin Herbé* (1938–41). Other major works include the opera *Der Sturm* (1952–55), the oratorio *Golgotha* (1945–48), and the *Requiem* (1971–72). He also produced a large quantity of instrumental music, including orchestral works and chamber music. Perhaps his best-known work is *Petite symphonie concertante* (1945).

Martin, Glenn L(uther) (b. Jan. 17, 1886, Macksburg, Iowa, U.S.—d. Dec. 4, 1955, Baltimore, Md.), American airplane inventor whose bombers and flying boats played important roles in World War II.

In Santa Ana, Calif., before World War I, Martin designed his first powered airplane and leased an abandoned church as his first factory. He became one of the outstanding barnstorming flyers (from about 1910 to 1914) and used his experience to develop several successful types of military aircraft. The first Martin bomber, designated the MB, appeared

Glenn L. Martin
By courtesy of the National Air and Space Museum, Smithsonian Institution, Washington, D.C.

in 1918–19, too late for active use in World War I, but its success in the hands of Colonel "Billy" Mitchell established Martin as one of the leading military airplane manufacturers of the United States. He built a factory in Cleveland and in 1929 moved his manufacturing facilities to Middle River, Md., near Baltimore. Toward the end of his life Martin took great interest in civic affairs, education (he gave large sums to the engineering school of the University of Maryland), and wildlife conservation.

Martin, Gregory (b. *c.* 1540, Maxfield, Sussex, Eng.—d. Oct. 28, 1582, Reims, Fr.), Roman Catholic biblical scholar, principal translator of the Latin Vulgate into English (Douai-Reims Bible). His version, in Bishop Richard Challoner's third revised edition (1752), was the standard Bible for English Roman Catholics until the 20th century, and his phraseology influenced the Anglican translators of the Authorized, or King James, Version (1611).

One of the earliest students at St. John's College, Oxford, Martin became proficient in Greek and Hebrew and befriended Edmund Campion, who was converted to Roman Catholicism partly because of Martin's influence. Martin was tutor (1569–70) to the 4th Duke of Norfolk's sons, studied theology at William (afterward Cardinal) Allen's English Roman Catholic college at Douai, Fr., and was ordained priest in 1573. He taught intermittently at that college until 1582 and aided Allen in founding the English College in Rome (1576–78). Though he worked under Allen's direction and was assisted by other Oxford-educated scholars, Martin prepared most of the Douai-Reims translation himself. He died of tuberculosis as his New Testament was being printed in 1582; his translation of the Old Testament was not published until 1609–10.

Martin, (Bon-Louis-)Henri (b. Feb. 20, 1810, Saint-Quentin, Fr.—d. Dec. 14, 1883, Paris), author of a famous history of France that included excerpts from the chief chroniclers and historians, with original expository passages filling the gaps.

The *Histoire de France,* 15 vol. (1833–36), rewritten and further elaborated (fourth ed., 16 vol. and index, 1861–65), won Martin the first prize of the Académie Française in 1856, and in 1869 the grand biennial prize of 20,000 francs. A popular abridgment in seven volumes was published in 1867. This work, together with the continuation, *Histoire de France depuis 1789 jusqu'à nos jours,* 6 vol. (1878–83; "History of France from 1789 to Our Time"), gives a complete history of France and superseded earlier such works. Martin was a staunch republican and sat in the National Assembly as deputy for Aisne in 1871, but he left no mark as a politician.

Martin, Homer Dodge (b. Oct. 28, 1836, Albany, N.Y., U.S.—d. Feb. 12, 1897, St. Paul, Minn.), landscape painter who was one of the first to introduce Impressionism into American painting.

Martin studied briefly with James Hart, and his early work is akin to that of the Hudson River school. In 1862 he moved to New York City, where he was able to study the landscapes of John Frederick Kensett. His early works show an interest in carefully observed detail, as well as the larger forms of landscape such as the shape of land masses and trees silhouetted against the sky.

Martin made two trips to Europe. The first, in 1876, was inspired by the works of Camille Corot and the Barbizon school, which were just beginning to appear in the United States. On the second, in 1882, he lived primarily in Normandy and Brittany, saw the work of the Impressionists, but did practically no painting himself. His best work, such as "The Harp of the Winds" (1895; Metropolitan Museum of Art, New York City), in which he borrowed the broken colour of the Impressionists but not their high-keyed palette, was done after his return to the United States. Martin's painting is generally characterized by its spacious design, brilliant colour, and an underlying gravity or gentle melancholy. He became a member of the National Academy of Design in 1874 and in 1877 was one of the founders of the Society of American Artists.

"The Harp of the Winds," oil painting by Homer Dodge Martin, 1895; in the Metropolitan Museum of Art, New York City

By courtesy of the Metropolitan Museum of Art, New York City, gift of several gentlemen, 1897

Martin, Joseph William, Jr. (b. Nov. 3, 1884, North Attleboro, Mass., U.S.—d. March 6, 1968, Fort Lauderdale, Fla.), U.S. Republican congressional leader and speaker of the House of Representatives (1947–49; 1953–55).

A newspaper reporter, Martin became the owner and publisher of the North Attleboro *Evening Chronicle*, a position he held until his death. In 1911 Martin won a seat in the Massachusetts House of Representatives; three years later he was elected to the state Senate. He first won election to the U.S. House of Representatives in 1924. During the 1930s, Martin emerged as a leader of forces opposed to President Franklin D. Roosevelt's New Deal programs, which Martin likened to both fascism and socialism. For two decades from 1939 he led the Republicans in the House, urging his colleagues to adhere to traditional conservative principles. From 1947 to 1949 and again from 1953 to 1955, Martin was speaker of the House. In 1959 he was deposed as House Republican leader. Martin's power waned steadily, and in 1966 he lost a primary election for his congressional seat.

Martin, Luther (b. Feb. 9, 1744/48, New Brunswick, N.J. [U.S.]—d. July 10, 1826, New York, N.Y.), American lawyer best known for defending Supreme Court Justice Samuel Chase at his impeachment trial and Aaron Burr at his treason trial and for arguing the losing side in *McCulloch* v. *Maryland*.

Martin graduated with honours in 1766 from the College of New Jersey (now Princeton University). He taught in Maryland before moving to Virginia in 1770 to become superintendent of a grammar school. He studied law and in 1771 was accepted into the Virginia bar. He moved back to Maryland, where he enjoyed a lucrative practice there.

A patriot in the years preceding the American Revolution, Martin became attorney general of Maryland in 1778 and vigorously prosecuted loyalists. He was a member of Congress in 1785 and was a delegate to the Constitutional Convention in 1787. An anti-Federalist, he opposed the plan for a strong central government and walked out of the Convention without signing the Constitution. He fought vainly to prevent Maryland from ratifying.

Martin defended Associate Justice Chase in 1804, saving the Federalist judge from conviction on impeachment charges. In 1807 Martin defended Burr, the former vice president, against treason charges following his mysterious adventure on the Mississippi River. Having resigned as Maryland attorney general in 1805, Martin took up that position once again in 1818 after having been a judge from 1813 to 1816. As the state attorney general, he argued Maryland's right to tax the Bank of the United States in *McCulloch* v. *Maryland* (1819). He lost the case, a landmark decision in the contest between federal authority and states' rights. In 1822, two years after suffering a stroke, Martin resigned his office.

Martin, Mary (Virginia) (b. Dec. 1, 1913, Weatherford, Texas, U.S.—d. Nov. 3, 1990, Rancho Mirage, Calif.), American singer and actress.

Martin began her professional career as co-owner of a dancing school in Weatherford, Texas, in the 1930s. Late in the decade she ventured to Hollywood, where her initial attempts as a singer and actress were unsuccessful. In 1938, however, in New York City, she obtained a small part in the musical *Leave It to Me,* in which her rendition of the song "My Heart Belongs to Daddy" won wide acclaim. After appearing in several motion-picture musicals in Hollywood, she returned to Broadway and played her first starring role in *One Touch of Venus* (1943). In 1948 Martin created the role of Nellie Forbush in the Broadway musical *South Pacific,* which firmly established her career. In the 1950s she starred in the title role of *Peter Pan,* playing it both on the stage and on television. In 1959 she created the lead role in another hit stage musical, *The Sound of Music.* For her performances she won numerous awards. Her son, Larry Hagman, became a successful television actor.

Martin, Paul, in full PAUL JOSEPH MARTIN, JR. (b. Aug. 28, 1938, Windsor, Ont., Can.), Canadian politician who became prime minister of Canada in 2003.

His father, Paul Joseph Martin, served as a minister in four Liberal governments and was a leading architect of Canada's post-World War II social policy. The younger Martin attended the University of Toronto, graduating from its law school in 1964. He soon joined Canada Steamship Lines, a Montreal firm, and built it into a strong multinational company. In 1981 he purchased the firm.

In 1988 Martin won election to the House of Commons. Two years later he made a bold bid for leadership of the Liberal Party but lost to Jean Chrétien. When the Liberals won the 1993 election, Chrétien appointed Martin minister of finance. Martin eliminated a large budget deficit, achieved five consecutive budget surpluses, and secured the largest tax cut in Canadian history.

Martin was dropped from Chrétien's cabinet in 2002 after refusing to abandon his ambition for leadership. In 2003, however, when Chrétien announced his impending retirement, Martin was chosen to succeed him. Martin called early federal elections for June 2004 in an effort to win a public mandate. Although the Liberals lost one-quarter of their seats and their majority in the House of Commons, Martin continued as prime minister in a minority administration. He sought to foster economic growth and introduced progressive social policies.

Martin, Pierre-Émile (b. Aug. 18, 1824, Bourges, Fr.—d. May 23, 1915, Fourchambault), French engineer who invented the Siemens–Martin (open-hearth) process, which produced most of the world's steel until the development of the basic oxygen process.

While the chemistry of steelmaking was already familiar in 1856, the only practical method, the Bessemer process, had many serious drawbacks. In that year the English engineer Sir William Siemens invented the open-hearth furnace, which could produce and sustain much higher temperatures than any other furnace. Martin obtained a license to build such furnaces and developed a method of producing steel by using scrap steel and pig iron. His steel products were awarded a Gold Medal at the Paris Exhibition of 1867.

Pierre-Émile Martin

H. Roger-Viollet

Although Siemens developed his own method of steel production with his open-hearth furnace, the Siemens-Martin process eventually became the most widespread.

Martin's patents on his process were challenged, and the ensuing litigation reduced him to virtual poverty. Others were making large profits using his process, however, and finally, when Martin was 83 years old, the Comité des Forges de France ("Ironworkers Guild of France") instituted a fund for him that was supported by all of the principal steelmaking countries. Barely one week before Martin's death, the Iron and Steel Institute, London, honoured him with its Bessemer Gold Medal.

Martin du Gard, Roger (b. March 23, 1881, Neuilly-sur-Seine, France—d. Aug. 22, 1958, Bellême), French author and winner of the 1937 Nobel Prize for Literature. Trained as a paleographer and archivist, Martin du Gard brought to his works a spirit of objectivity and a scrupulous regard for details. For his concern with documentation and with the relationship of social reality to individual development, he has been linked with the realist and naturalist traditions of the 19th century.

Martin du Gard first attracted attention with *Jean Barois* (1913), which traced the development of an intellectual torn between the Roman Catholic faith of his childhood and the scientific materialism of his maturity; it also described the full impact of the Dreyfus affair on French minds. He is best known for the eight-part novel cycle *Les Thibault* (1922–40; parts 1–6 as *The Thibaults;* parts 7–8 as *Summer 1914*). This record of a family's development chronicles the social and moral issues confronting the French bourgeoisie from the turn of the 19th century to World War I. Reacting against a bourgeois patriarch, the younger son, Jacques, renounces his Roman Catholic past to embrace revolutionary socialism, and the elder son, Antoine, accepts his middle-class heritage but loses faith in its religious foundation. Both sons eventually die in World War I. The outstanding features of *Les Thibaults* are the wide range of human relationships patiently explored, the graphic realism of the sickbed and death scenes, and, in the seventh volume, *L'Été 1914* ("Summer 1914"), the dramatic description of Europe's nations being swept into war.

Martin du Gard

© Harlingue-Viollet/Roger-Viollet

Other works by Martin du Gard include *Vielle France* (1933; *The Postman*), biting sketches of French country life, and *Notes sur André Gide* (1951; *Recollections of André Gide*), a candid study of the author, who was his friend. Martin du Gard also wrote a somber drama about repressed homosexuality, *Un Taciturne* (1931; "A Silent Man"), and two farces of French peasant life, *Le Testament du père Leleu* (1914; "Old Leleu's Will") and *La Gonfle* (1928; "The Swelling"). In 1941 he began work on *Le Journal du colonel de Maumort*, a vast novel that he hoped would prove to be his masterpiece, but it was still unfinished at his death.

Martín García Island, Spanish ISLA MARTÍN GARCÍA, island, historically a strategic control point in the estuary of Río de la Plata, near the mouth of the Uruguay and Paraná rivers, between Argentina and Uruguay. The island (0.7 square mile [2 square km]) is a part of Buenos Aires province, Argentina. In March 1814 it was taken from the Spaniards by the forces of the Argentine admiral Guillermo Brown. Prisoners from the Indian Wars of 1879 were interned on the rocky island, which was also a place of exile for various presidents of Argentina, including Hipólito Irigoyen (1930), Juan Perón (1945), and Arturo Frondizi (1962). An agreement reached by Argentina and Uruguay in 1973 reaffirmed Argentine jurisdiction over Martín García (which is actually on the Uruguayan side of the boundary), ending a century-old dispute between the two countries over the island. According to the terms of the agreement, Martín García was to be devoted exclusively to a natural preserve.

Martin-Harvey, Sir John: *see* Harvey, Sir John Martin.

Martin Marietta Corporation, diversified American corporation (incorporated 1961) that was primarily involved in the production of aerospace equipment and defense systems for the U.S. government. In 1995 it merged with another major aerospace firm, the Lockheed Corporation, to form the Lockheed Martin Corporation (*q.v.*).

Martín-Santos, Luis (b. Nov. 11, 1924, Larache, Morocco—d. Jan. 21, 1964, San Sebastian, Spain), Spanish psychiatrist and novelist.

Martín-Santos received a medical degree from the University of Salamanca and, in 1947, a doctorate in psychiatry from the University of Madrid. From 1951 until his death, he was director of the Psychiatric Sanitorium in San Sebastián. He tried to develop a psychology of the whole person, and he published his ideas in *Dilthey, Jaspers y la comprensión del enfermo mental* (1955; "Dilthey, Jaspers, and the Understanding of Mental Illness"). In 1962 he published his novel *Tiempo de silencio* ("Time of Silence"), the first of a projected trilogy. The novel is about a medical student, Pedro, thrust among inhabitants of the Madrid slums and confronted with their often violent adaptation to severe conditions. Events force him to confess to a crime of which he is innocent and to face in silence the consequences—even after his innocence has been proved. The novel has been compared in structure and style to James Joyce's *Ulysses.* The sequel, *Tiempo de destrucción* (1975; "Time of Destruction"), was unfinished when Martín-Santos was killed in an automobile accident in 1964.

Martina Franca, town, Taranto *provincia,* Puglia (Apulia) *regione,* southeastern Italy. It has numerous Baroque buildings, such as the Church of San Martino, the Corte palace, and particularly the civic centre, a former ducal palace (1669). In 1529, during the war against the Holy Roman emperor Charles V, the town repelled the besieging French troops of Francis I. An agricultural centre, it is also noted for hosiery manufacture. Pop. (1993 est.) mun., 45,713.

Martineau, Harriet (b. June 12, 1802, Norwich, Norfolk, Eng.—d. June 27, 1876, near Ambleside, Westmorland), essayist, novelist, and economic and historical writer who, despite deafness, heart disease, and other disabilities, was prominent among English intellectuals of her time. Perhaps her most scholarly work is *The Positive Philosophy of Auguste Comte, Freely Translated and Condensed,* 2 vol. (1853), her version of Comte's *Cours de philosophie positive,* 6 vol. (1830–42).

Harriet Martineau, detail of an engraving

BBC Hulton Picture Library

Martineau first gained a large reading public with an extensive series of anecdotes and dialogues popularizing classical economics, especially the ideas of Thomas Robert Malthus and David Ricardo: *Illustrations of Political Economy,* 25 vol. (1832–34), *Poor Laws and Paupers Illustrated,* 10 vol. (1833–34), and *Illustrations of Taxation,* 5 vol. (1834). After a visit to the United States (1834–36), concerning which she wrote *Society in America* (1837) and *Retrospect of Western Travel* (1838), she espoused the then unpopular Abolition Movement and repudiated laissez-faire economics in favour of a more utopian system. Her best-known novels, including *Deerbrook* (1939) and *The Hour and the Man* (1841), were also written during this period.

A trip to the Middle East (1846) led her to study the evolution of religions and to become increasingly skeptical of religious beliefs, including her own liberal Unitarianism. Her chief historical work, *The History of the Thirty Years' Peace, A.D. 1816–1846* (1849), was a widely read popular treatment. She also contributed to several periodicals, and her *Biographical Sketches* (1869, enlarged 1877) was a collection of articles written for the *Daily News* on various well-known contemporaries, including Charlotte Brontë. Her candid *Autobiography,* edited by Maria Weston Chapman, was published posthumously (3 vol., 1877).

BIBLIOGRAPHY. Valerie Kossew Pichanick, *Harriet Martineau* (1980); Gillian Thomas, *Harriet Martineau* (1985); Susan Hoecker-Drysdale, *Harriet Martineau, First Woman Sociologist* (1992).

Martineau, James (b. April 21, 1805, Norwich, Norfolk, Eng.—d. Jan. 11, 1900, London), English Unitarian theologian and philosopher whose writings emphasized the individual human conscience as the primary guide for determining correct behaviour. He was a brother of Harriet Martineau.

From 1828 to 1832 Martineau served as junior minister at Eustace Street (Unitarian) Church, Dublin, leaving on the death of his senior for a position in Liverpool. There he began to question the traditionally authoritative role of Scripture, and in his *Rationale of Religious Inquiry* (1836) he declared that "the last appeal in all researches into religious truth must be to the judgment of the human mind." Appointed professor of mental and moral philosophy at Manchester New College in 1840, Martineau taught there (and from 1869 served as principal) until 1885, searching for an alternative to biblical authority, especially in such later works as *Types of Ethical Theory* (1885), *A Study of Religion* (1888), and *The Seat of Authority in Religion* (1890).

Martinez, city, seat (1850) of Contra Costa county, western California, U.S., on the south shore of Carquinez Strait (between Suisun and San Francisco bays) near Oakland. It was named for Ignacio Martínez, commandant of the San Francisco presidio and grantee (1829) of the Rancho El Pinole, which was part of the original townsite (laid out in 1849 by Col. William E. Smith). The completion of the Contra Costa Canal (1947) to its Martinez Reservoir terminus and the opening of the Benicia–Martinez Bridge (1962) across the strait boosted the city's port and industrial development (petroleum, chemicals, steel, and copper). The home of John Muir, the naturalist, is preserved as a national historic site. Inc. 1864. Pop. (1990) 31,808.

Martínez, Rafael Arévalo: *see* Arévalo Martínez, Rafael.

Martínez Campos, Arsenio (b. Dec. 14, 1831, Segovia, Spain—d. Sept. 23, 1900, Zarauz), general and politician whose *pronunciamiento* on Dec. 29, 1874, restored Spain's Bourbon dynasty. He was a competent soldier and negotiator.

Martínez Campos was given a military education and after 1852 served on Spain's general staff. He took part in the international expedition of Gen. Juan Prim to Mexico (1861) and fought Cuban rebels (until 1872). On his return to Spain, he briefly taught military science and then was sent to put down rebellions in Valencia (1872), Alicante, and Cartagena.

After Alfonso XII, the son of the deposed Isabella II, had declared for a constitutional monarchy (Nov. 24, 1874), and other generals disillusioned with the republic had rallied to him, Alfonso took the throne following Martínez Campos' *pronunciamiento.* Martínez Campos then took command of Alfonso's forces against the Carlists, made the fighting less brutal by signing agreements protecting the lives of the wounded and prisoners, and brought about the end of the civil war (February 1876). His humane policy, which he then applied in Cuba, ended the 10-year rebellion there on Feb. 10, 1878, with the Peace of El Zanjón.

On his return from Cuba, Martínez Campos served briefly as prime minister in 1879 and two years later as minister of war. After war broke out in Morocco (September 1893), he was put in command and succeeded in negotiating the Treaty of Marrakech (Jan. 29, 1894). The following year he was sent to Cuba again but failed to win over the rebels. He resigned and returned to Spain (1896).

Martínez de la Rosa (Berdejo Gómez y Arroyo), Francisco de Paula (b. March 10, 1787, Granada, Spain—d. Feb. 7, 1862, Madrid), Spanish dramatist, poet, and conservative statesman.

He became a professor of philosophy at the University of Granada in 1705. His play *La conjuración de Venecia* ("The Conspiracy of Venice"), written during his political exile in France (1823–31) and staged in Madrid shortly after he became prime minister of the new government (1834), was the first success of the Romantic theatre in Spain. His importance is purely historical. He later served as ambassador to Paris (1844) and Rome (1848).

Martínez Estrada, Ezequiel (b. Sept. 14, 1895, San José de la Esquina, Arg.—d. Nov. 4, 1964, Bahía Blanca), leading Argentine writer of the Post-modernist generation who influenced many younger writers.

He worked for 30 years (1916–46) at the Buenos Aires post office while also teaching initially in a preparatory school and later at the university there. He began his literary career with essays in the journal *Nosotros* (1917). His first book of poems, *Oro y piedra* (1918; "Gold and Stone"), was followed by *Nefelibal* (1922), *Motivos del cielo* (1924; "Heaven's Reasons"), *Argentina* (1927), and *Humoresca* (1929). These displayed very complex techniques. Language and imagery are often tinted with humour, conveying a satirical view reminiscent of Quevedo, the master satirist of Spain's Golden Age.

His view of the political and economic crises of the early 1930s and of what he saw as factors contributing to moral and social decay in Argentina led him to write *Radiografía de la pampa* (1933; *X-Ray of the Pampa*, 1971), a comprehensive psychological study of the Argentine character laden with fatalistic overtones. *La cabeza de Goliat: microscopia de Buenos Aires* (1940; "The Head of Goliath: A Microscopic Study of Buenos Aires") treats the people of Buenos Aires and continues the themes of *Radiografía.*

His many studies of literary figures and texts made him a respected critic. His analyses include those of the 19th-century Argentine narrative poem by José Hernández, *Martín Fierro, Muerte y transfiguración del Martín Fierro,* 2 vol. (1948; "The Death and Transfiguration of Martin Fierro"), *El mundo maravilloso de Guillermo Enrique Hudson* (1951; "The Wonderful World of Guillermo Enrique Hudson"), and *El hermano Quiroga* (1957; "Brother Quiroga"). From 1960 to 1962, he worked with the Cuban government publishing house Casa de las Américas. Two studies of Martínez Estrada are P.G. Earle, *Prophet in the Wilderness* (1971), and A. Marsala, *Martínez Estrada* (1973).

Martínez Montañés, Juan (de): *see* Montañés, Juan (de) Martínez.

Martínez Ruiz, José: *see* Azorín.

Martínez Sierra, Gregorio (b. May 6, 1881, Madrid—d. Oct. 1, 1947, Madrid), poet and playwright whose dramatic works contributed significantly to the revival of the Spanish theatre.

Martínez Sierra's first volume of poetry, *El poema del trabajo* (1898; "The Poem of Work"), appeared when he was 17. Short stories reflecting the Modernist concern with individuality and subjectivity and freedom from archaic forms followed. He turned to drama in 1905 with his *Teatro de ensueño* ("Theatre of Dreams"). His masterpiece, *Canción de cuna* (1911; "Song of the Cradle"), was popular in both Spain and Spanish America. The most marked feature of his drama, his insight into his female characters, has been attributed to his wife, María de la O Lejárraga, who collaborated with him and wrote a book on their collaboration, *Gregorio y yo* (1953; "Gregory and I").

A man of enormous energy, Martínez Sierra also edited several important Modernist periodicals in Madrid and operated Renacimiento, a publishing house that introduced a host of foreign playwrights into Spain, including George Bernard Shaw, James Barrie, and Luigi Pirandello. Martínez Sierra himself translated the works of Shakespeare and the Belgian playwright Maurice Maeterlinck. His most important contribution to the Spanish theatre was his introduction of the art theatre while he was director of the Eslava Theatre in Madrid (1917–28). His work there is described in his book *Un teatro de arte en España* (1926; "An Art Theatre in Spain"). His popularity waned after his death.

Martini, Arturo (b. Aug. 11, 1889, Treviso, Italy—d. March 22, 1947, Milan), leading Italian sculptor of the period between the World Wars, whose figurative works encompass a wide variety of styles and materials.

Martini was trained in goldsmithing and in ceramics and worked for a time as a potter. In 1905 he began sculpting and studied the nude at classes in Treviso, Venice, and Munich. He first exhibited his works in Paris in 1912. During World War I he served in the Italian Army. In 1931 he won the grand prize for sculpture at the first Quadriennale in Rome.

Martini's works range from delicate terra-cottas (*e.g.,* "Moonlight," 1932) to dramatic figures in stone ("Thirst," 1934). He was particularly adept at conveying the tension and movement of physical activity (*e.g.,* "Girl Swimming Under Water," 1941). His high relief of "Corporate Justice" (1937) is perhaps the pinnacle of his achievement. *La scultura, lingua morta* (1945; "Sculpture: A Dead Language") provides an autobiographical account of his career.

Martini, Francesco Maurizio di Giorgio: *see* Francesco di Giorgio.

Martini, Giovanni Battista, byname PADRE MARTINI (b. April 24, 1706, Bologna, Papal States—d. Oct. 4, 1784, Bologna), Italian composer and music theorist who was internationally renowned as a teacher.

Martini was educated by his father, a violinist; by Luc'Antonio Predieri (harpsichord, singing, organ); and by Antonio Riccieri (counterpoint). He was ordained in 1722 and became chapelmaster of San Francesco in Bologna in 1725. He opened a school of music, and his fame as a teacher made Bologna a place of pilgrimage. Among his pupils were Sarti, J.C. Bach, Mozart, Gluck, Jommelli, and Grétry.

Giovanni Martini, engraving by Carlo Faucci, 1776
J.P. Ziolo

Martini was a zealous collector of musical literature; his library, estimated at 17,000 volumes by the 18th-century music historian Charles Burney, passed at his death to the Imperial Library at Vienna and to the city of Bologna. He was a prolific composer of sacred and secular music. His works include the *Litaniae* (1734), 12 *Sonate d'intavolatura* (1742), 6 *Sonate d'intavolatura per l'organo ed il cembalo* (1747), *Duetti da camera* (1763), and masses and oratorios. His most important literary works are the *Storia della musica* (1757–81; incomplete) and the *Saggio di contrappunto* (1774–75).

Martini, Simone (b. *c.* 1284, Siena, Republic of Siena—d. 1344, Avignon, Provence), important exponent of Gothic painting who did more than any other artist to spread the influence of Sienese painting.

Martini was very possibly a pupil of Duccio di Buoninsegna, from whom he probably inherited his love of harmonious, pure colours

"St. Martin Abandoning His Arms," detail from fresco series by Simone Martini, *c.* 1325–26; in the lower Church of San Francesco, Assisi, Italy
SCALA—Art Resource

and most of his early figure types. To these he added a gracefulness of line and delicacy of interpretation that were inspired by French Gothic works that the young artist studied in Italy. He carried to perfection the decorative line of the Gothic style and subordinated volume to the rhythm of this line.

Simone's earliest documented painting is the large fresco of the "Maestà" in the Sala del Mappamondo of the Palazzo Pubblico, Siena. The fresco depicts the enthroned Madonna and Child with angels and saints. This painting, which is signed and dated 1315 but was retouched by Simone himself in 1321, is a free version of Duccio's "Maestà" of 1308–11. But the hierarchic structure of Duccio's work has been replaced by a growing interest in illusionary perspective, and the abstract character and lack of setting of the earlier work has given way to concrete concepts: Simone's Virgin, crowned and splendidly attired, is a Gothic queen who holds court beneath a Gothic canopy.

About 1317 the artist painted, in Naples, the highly spiritual altarpiece "St. Louis of Toulouse Crowning His Brother, King Robert of Anjou." Two years later he composed for the Church of Santa Caterina, Pisa, a colouristically magnificent Madonna polyptych. Perhaps in the middle of the 1320s he began the 10 scenes, full of chivalrous ideals, from the life of St. Martin of Tours in this saint's chapel in the lower Church of San Francesco, Assisi. His equestrian portrait (1328) representing Guidoriccio da Fogliano, general of the Sienese republic, was perhaps the first Sienese work of art that did not serve a religious purpose. It was also an important precedent for the numerous equestrian portraits of the Renaissance. On the other hand, the "Annunciation" triptych, painted for the Siena Cathedral, but now in the Uffizi, Florence, is deliberately unreal. Simone signed this work in 1333 with his brother-in-law, the Sienese painter Lippo Memmi, an associate for many years. The exquisite rhythm of the lines and dematerialized forms of Gabriel and Mary in the central portion of the "Annunciation" led a number of artists to imitation, but none of them achieved such vibrant contours and such spirited forms as did Simone in this great masterpiece.

In 1340 the painter settled at the papal court in Avignon, where he made the acquaintance of Petrarch. He executed for the poet a portrait (now lost) of his beloved Laura, a fact known from two of Petrarch's sonnets in which Simone is eulogized.

Simone was the most important Sienese painter after Duccio. His influence in Siena was great in the 14th century and considerable in the 15th. His art was imitated by local painters in Naples, Pisa, Orvieto, Assisi, and Avignon.

Martinique, officially DEPARTMENT OF MARTINIQUE, French DÉPARTEMENT DE LA MARTINIQUE, island in the Lesser Antilles chain and the smallest of all the French overseas *départements,* situated about 4,400 miles (7,100 km) from France in the eastern Caribbean Sea. The island is some 50 miles (80 km) long from north to south and at its widest extends about 22 miles (35 km) from east to west. The capital is Fort-de-France. Area 436 square miles (1,128 square km). Pop. (1992 est.) 369,000.

For information about regional aspects of Martinique, *see* MACROPAEDIA: West Indies.

For current history and for statistics on society and economy, *see* BRITANNICA BOOK OF THE YEAR.

The land. The island is largely mountainous and is composed of volcanic rocks. Its average elevation is more than 3,000 feet (900 m) above sea level. The highest point, Mount Pelée (4,583 feet [1,397 m]), in the north, is an active volcano. Its catastrophic eruption in 1902 destroyed the town of Saint-Pierre, killing an estimated 30,000 people. The Lamentin Plain (the Lézarde River basin) in the central southwest is the only flat land on the island except for the narrow coastal plains. Rivers are numerous but small, and few are navigable. The coastline is so indented that no part of the island is more than 7 miles (11 km) from the sea.

Martinique's climate is tropical, with an annual average temperature of 79° F (26° C). Rainfall is abundant and ranges from 160 to 200 inches (4,000 to 5,000 mm) in the mountainous northern region to less than 40

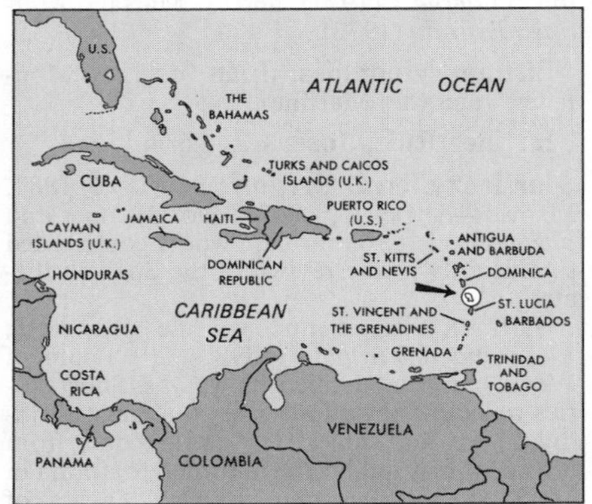

Martinique

inches (1,000 mm) in the south. The fertile volcanic soils and abundant rainfall produce luxuriant vegetation ranging from mangrove swamps on the southern coast to tropical rain forests (palm, rosewood, logwood, breadfruit, mahogany, oleander, ferns, and orchids) on the mountain slopes. Wildlife is limited and includes mongoose (introduced), rabbit, turtledove, and pigeon. Some carbonate of lime is quarried for local use in cement making.

The people. The racial composition of Martinique is extremely mixed, although the mulatto element predominates. French is the official language, though a local creole is widely spoken, and Roman Catholicism is the religion with the most adherents. Since the early 1980s the average annual growth rate of Martinique's population has been the lowest in the Caribbean, primarily because of the extensive emigration of young people and the resultant low birth rate. Most emigration is to France or to other Caribbean islands. More than one-fifth of the population is younger than 15 years of age, and almost one-third of the islanders live in Fort-de-France.

Economy. Martinique has a developing market economy that is based largely on agriculture and tourism. Despite substantial economic growth, the economy remains heavily dependent on France. The standard of living is one of the highest in the Caribbean. The gross national product (GNP) is growing more rapidly than the population; the GNP per capita is about average for a Caribbean country.

Agriculture accounts for approximately one-twelfth of the gross domestic product (GDP) and employs a comparable fraction of the work force. Bananas and other tropical fruits are the main agricultural exports, while yams and cassava are the chief food crops. Sugarcane, the major agricultural crop, is utilized largely for the manufacture of rum, another export. Banana production declined drastically after the destruction of most of the island's banana plantations by a hurricane in 1980, but by the mid-1980s production had returned to normal.

Forests, which include both European and tropical species, cover more than one-third of the island's area and provide some potential for exploitation. Fish and freshwater prawns are caught for domestic consumption.

Industry is relatively undeveloped in Martinique, with most activity concentrated in construction and public works, which are largely funded by France. Manufacturing is dominated by food processing, rum distilling, and the production of consumer goods for the domestic market. France also maintains a petroleum refinery on the island for processing crude oil, primarily from Venezuela and Trinidad and Tobago, into petroleum products for use by the French Caribbean possessions. Five industrial zones have been established, and a number of tax incentives are in operation to encourage industrial and commercial development. Electricity is generated thermally from imported fuels.

The service sector accounts for approximately three-fourths of the GDP and employs more than half of the work force. The growing tourist industry is extremely important to the island's economy. As one of the most popular tourist areas in the Caribbean, Martinique has a flourishing cruise-ship business that brings in large numbers of tourists, mainly from France, the United States, and Canada.

The French government spends more money on Martinique than it raises in local taxes in pursuing its goals of bringing overseas territories up to the economic level of metropolitan France. The minimum wage has been raised to match that of metropolitan France, but unemployment remains high, and many islanders emigrate to France and other Caribbean islands each year. The island's total imports vastly exceed the value of exports. Trade with France accounts for about two-thirds of the total.

Government and social conditions. Martinique is an overseas *département,* or administrative district, of France. A prefect functions as the executive authority on the island. A measure of legislative authority rests with the 45-member General Council and the 41-member Regional Council. The councils' representatives are elected for terms of up to six years. Martinique sends four deputies to the French National Assembly and two senators to the French Senate. The Court of Appeal is the highest court; lower courts serve both Martinique and French Guiana.

Martinique has general and maternity hospitals. There is an excellent system of primary and secondary schools, and attendance is almost 100 percent. There are several newspapers, including a daily, and the press is free. The French government operates the broadcast media. The annual carnival of Fort-de-France is a major island event.

History. Martinique was inhabited by the Carib Indians in 1502 when Christopher Columbus visited the island during his fourth voyage to the New World. The Carib had migrated to the island from South America, driving out the earlier Arawak inhabitants. The island remained unoccupied by Europeans until 1635, when a Frenchman, Pierre Bélain d'Esnambuc, established a colony there. In 1674 it became a domain of the French crown. In 1762 the island was captured and held for a year by the British, and it was in British hands twice again during the Napoleonic Wars (1794–1802 and 1809–14). Slavery was abolished on Martinique in 1848, and some 74,000 slaves were freed.

After World War II, Martinique was made a *département* of France. From the 1950s through the 1980s, Martinique was plagued by high unemployment, underdevelopment, and overpopulation. In order to ease the social suffering that was brought on by these problems, the French government encouraged island residents to migrate to France. Local leftists and communists in Martinique began to advocate self-determination and independence, causing numerous strikes and demonstrations in the 1970s. France proved unwilling to consider independence for the island, however.

Martino (Italian personal name): *see under* Martin.

Martins, Peter (b. Oct. 27, 1946, Copenhagen, Den.), Danish dancer and choreographer, known principally for his work with the New York City Ballet.

Martins began his dance training at the Royal Danish Ballet School in 1953, became a corps de ballet member in 1965, and was made a soloist two years later. George Balanchine, artistic director of the New York City Ballet (NYCB), arranged several guest appearances for him with the NYCB, and in 1969 Martins left Denmark to become a principal dancer in Balanchine's company.

Martins had several roles in dances created for him, among which are Jerome Robbins' *Goldberg Variations* (1971) and *In G Major* (1975) and Balanchine's *Violin Concerto* (1972) and *Duo Concertante* (1972). In 1977 Martins made his debut as a choreographer, creating *Calcium Light Night* for the NYCB. He subsequently created several other works, including *L'Histoire du soldat* (1981). In 1982 his autobiography, *Far from Denmark,* was published. In 1983, shortly before the death of Balanchine, Martins was named director of daily operations and, with Jerome Robbins, ballet master in chief of the NYCB. In January 1990, upon Robbins' resignation, Martins became sole director of the New York City Ballet.

Martins Ferry, city, Belmont county, eastern Ohio, U.S. It lies along the Ohio River (there bridged to Wheeling, W.Va.). Squatters in the 1770s and '80s formed settlements (Hoglin's, or Mercer's, Town and Norristown) on the site. In 1795 Absalom Martin of New Jersey laid out a town called Jefferson, which was later abandoned; his son Ebenezer replanned the site as Martinsville in 1835, but it was later renamed for his father's ferry. It developed as a farming community and prior to the American Civil War was a station on the Underground Railroad for escaping slaves. The arrival of the Cleveland and Pittsburgh (later called Penn Central) Railroad in 1852 and the discovery of coal in the locality gave impetus to the town's industrial growth. Its manufactures include fabricated metals, castings, ferroalloys, and pipe couplings. A port authority was established in 1966. The novelist William Dean Howells (1837–1920) was born at Martins Ferry, where the Western writer Zane Grey set some of his early works. Inc. village, 1865; city, 1885. Pop. (1990) 7,990.

Martinsburg, city, seat (1772) of Berkeley county, eastern panhandle of West Virginia, U.S. It lies 16 miles (26 km) southwest of Hagerstown, Md. Settled in 1732, it was laid out by Adam Stephen, later a Revolutionary War general, and was named for Colonel Thomas B. Martin. The town developed after 1837 with the arrival of the Baltimore and Ohio Railroad. During the American Civil War it was in turn occupied by both sides, and, after a Confederate raid (1861) destroyed the railroad, engines were hauled by horses over muddy roads from Martinsburg to Winchester, Va. (18 miles [29 km] southwest). In 1877 federal troops were used in the city for the first time in the nation's history to put down a strike and riot threat by railroad firemen.

Martinsburg is located in a rich fruit-growing region (apples, peaches) and has diversified manufacturing (glassware, hosiery, auto parts, and paper products). It was the early home of Confederate spy Belle Boyd, who was once jailed at the old courthouse. Colonial relics include the Tuscarora Presbyterian Church (organized 1740–45) and nearby Bunker Hill village, one of the oldest recorded (*c.* 1729) European settlements in West Virginia. Sleepy Creek Public Hunting Area is a few miles west. Inc. town, 1778; city, 1868. Pop. (1991 est.) 14,131.

Martinson, Harry (Edmund) (b. May 6, 1904, Jämshög, Swed.—d. Feb. 11, 1978, Stockholm), Swedish novelist and poet who was the first self-taught, working-class writer to be elected to the Swedish Academy (1949). With Eyvind Johnson he was awarded the Nobel Prize for Literature in 1974.

Martinson spent his childhood in a series of foster homes and his youth and early adulthood as a merchant seaman, labourer, and vagrant. His first book of poetry, *Spökskepp* ("Ghost Ship"), much influenced by Rudyard Kipling's *Seven Seas,* appeared in 1929. His early experiences are described in two autobiographical novels, *Nässlorna blomma* (1935; *Flowering Nettle*) and *Vägen ut* (1936; "The Way Out"), and in original and sensitive travel sketches, *Resor utan mål* (1932; "Aimless Journeys") and *Kap Farväl* (1933; *Cape Farewell*). Among his best-known works are *Passad* (1945; "Trade Wind"), a collection of poetry; *Vägen till Klockrike* (1948; *The Road*), a novel that sympathetically examines the lives of tramps and other social outcasts; and *Aniara* (1956; *Aniara, A Review of Man in Time and Space*), an epic poem about space travel that was turned into a successful opera in 1959 by Karl Birger Blomdahl. Martinson's language is lyrical, unconstrained, innovative, and sometimes obscure; his imagery, sensuous; his style, often starkly realistic or expressionistic; and his philosophy, primitivistic. He was married to another noted Swedish writer, Moa Martinson, from 1929 to 1940.

Martinson, Moa, original name HELGA SWARTZ (b. Nov. 2, 1890, Vardnass, Swed.—d. Aug. 5, 1964, Södertälje), Swedish novelist who was among the first to write about the agricultural labourer, the landless worker of the Swedish countryside known as *statare.* The first half of her life was filled with poverty and misery, yet she retained an ability to write about the life of the workers with warmth and humour.

The mother of five children, she was widowed at 25 and struggled to support her family. After her second marriage, to the proletarian writer Harry Martinson (divorced 1940), she began a literary career and took the name Moa Martinson. Her most successful work is the autobiographical trilogy *Mor gifter sig* (1936; "Mother Gets Married"), *Kyrkbröllop* (1938; "Church Wedding"), and *Kungens rosor* (1939; "The King's Roses"). Her later novels were about proletarian characters of the 18th and 19th centuries.

Martinů, Bohuslav (b. Dec. 8, 1890, Polička, Bohemia, Austria-Hungary [now in Czech Republic]—d. Aug. 28, 1959, Liestal, Switz.), modern Czech composer whose works exhibit a distinctive blend of French and Czech influences.

Martinů studied violin from age six, attended and was expelled from the Prague Conservatory, and in 1913 joined the Prague Philharmonic Orchestra. After the success of his ballet *Istar* and symphonic poem *Mizející půlnoc* (*Vanishing Midnight*), both in 1922, he studied under Josef Suk, a leader of the movement toward nationalism in Czech music. In 1923 he went to Paris to study under the French composer Albert Roussel. In 1940 Martinů fled the German invasion of France and settled in the United States, where he taught at Princeton University and at the Berkshire Music Center at Tanglewood, Mass. He returned to Prague in 1946 and taught at the conservatory there. In 1957 he was in Rome as composer in residence at the American Academy.

His orchestral works *Polička* (*Half-Time,* 1925) and *La Bagarre* (1928) were inspired by contemporary events, respectively a Czech-French football (soccer) game and the crowds that met Charles Lindbergh's plane as it ended its transatlantic flight. Of his later works, the *Concerto grosso* for chamber orchestra (1941) uses the alternation between soloists and full orchestra found in the Baroque concerto grosso and shows Martinů's skill in polyphonic writing. The *Double Concerto* for two string orchestras (1940) is a powerful work expressing Czech suffering after the partition of Czechoslovakia (1938). His *Memorial to Lidice* (1943) is a short symphonic poem commemorating Czechs killed by the Nazis during their destruction of the village of Lidice in 1942. Martinů's other works include six symphonies; violin, piano, cello, and flute concerti; six string quartets; and compositions for piano, for harpsichord, for voice, and for unaccompanied cello and violin.

Martinů was a prolific composer whose works varied greatly in quality; at its best his music shows vitality, charm, and originality. He assimilated the rhythmic and melodic traits of Czech folk music into a modern, Neoclassical idiom that shows a clarity and precision characteristic of French music.

Martinus (Latin personal name): *see under* Martin.

Martinus GOSIA (b. *c.* 1100, Bologna [Italy]—d. *c.* 1166), jurist, one of the "four doctors" of the Bologna Law School, and an important successor of Irnerius, although probably not his pupil.

Martinus, who advocated a more liberal interpretation of the law than did his Bolognese contemporary Bulgarus, gave considerable weight to equity; critics called his approach the equity of the purse (*aequitas bursalis*). Like Bulgarus, he was an adherent of the Holy Roman emperor Frederick I Barbarossa and supported imperial claims at the Diet of Roncaglia (1158). Martinus, whose opinions were quoted in imperial and papal documents of his time, wrote a commentary on the Corpus Juris Civilis, or Code of Justinian.

Martinuzzi, György, original name JURAJ UTJE-ŠENOVIĆ, byname BROTHER, or FRIAR, GEORGE, Latin-Hungarian FRATER GYÖRGY, Latin FRATER GEORGIUS (b. 1482, Kamicic, Croatia—d. Dec. 17, 1551, Alvinc, Transylvania, Hung.), Hungarian statesman and later cardinal who worked to restore and maintain the national unity of Hungary.

Martinuzzi, detail of a painting by an unknown artist; in the Historical Gallery of the Hungarian National Museum, Budapest

By courtesy of the Magyar Nemzeti Muzeum, Budapest

Born of a Croatian father and a mother of the patrician Venetian family of Martinuzzi, György became a Paulist friar at the age of 28 after a brief military career. A skilled diplomat, he later became the close adviser to King John of Hungary in his struggle against the rival claims of Ferdinand of Austria to the Hungarian throne.

Martinuzzi was in 1534 consecrated bishop of Nagyvárad in Transylvania. In 1538 he concluded with Ferdinand the Treaty of Nagyvárad, which left John with the royal title and most of Hungary and Ferdinand as successor to the Hungarian crown.

On his deathbed, however, John repudiated the treaty. The Turks recognized John Sigismund, the infant son of John, as king, but occupied Buda, the capital of Hungary; Martinuzzi, as guardian and regent, managed to retain Transylvania as an independent principality under Turkish suzerainty. Fighting off the intrigues of Isabella, the mother of John Sigismund, Martinuzzi returned to the original plan of unification of Hungary under the Austrian Habsburg dynasty in order to resist Turkish expansion. He finally concluded the agreement with Ferdinand in 1551, by which he continued to be governor of Transylvania and was rewarded with the archbishopric of Esztergom (Gran) and a cardinal's hat. To forestall attack by the Turks, Martinuzzi resumed payment of tribute to the Porte in December 1551. Ferdinand, however, suspected the cardinal's loyalty and had him killed.

Martius, Karl Friedrich Philipp von (April 17, 1794, Erlangen, Bavaria—d. Dec. 13, 1868, Munich), German botanist best known for his work on Brazilian flora.

Martius studied medicine at Erlangen University and was an *élève* of the Royal Bavarian Academy (1814–17). On April 2, 1817, Martius left from Trieste with an Austrian expedition to Brazil. In December 1820 he presented the Munich herbarium with 6,500 plant species, enriching the botanical garden with Brazilian plants and seeds. Appointed a member of the academy, he became the conservator of its botanical gardens (1832) and a professor in Munich (1826). Among his prominent students were the plant physiologist Hugo von Mohl and the botanists Alexander Braun and Karl Schimper.

In his *Historia naturalis palmarum*, 3 vol. (1823–50; with others), Martius observed that leaves on a plant stem appear to form distinct arrangements, or phyllotaxis, and seem to be arranged in a spiral pattern which follows fixed geometric rules. Martius published numerous other studies, most notably *Flora Brasiliensis*, 15 vol. (1840–1906), and *Die Kartoffel-epidemie* (1842). He became the secretary of the academy's physico-mathematical section in 1840.

Martos, city, Jaén province, in the autonomous community (region) of Andalusia, southern Spain, southwest of Jaén city, on a western peak of the Sierra Jabalcuz. Identified with the Roman Colonia Augusta Gemella, Martos was taken from the Moors by Ferdinand III in 1225 and given to the Order of the Knights of Calatrava. The Peñon de los Carvajales, a height above the city, is traditionally known as the place from which the Carvajal brothers—commanders of the order who were falsely accused of murder—were hurled to their deaths, under a decree of Ferdinand IV of Castile (1312). The largest olive-growing centre in Spain, Martos produces olive oil, flour, and pottery. In the area are sulfurous springs with bathing establishments. Pop. (1981) 21,672.

Martov, L., pseudonym of YULY OSIPOVICH TSEDERBAUM (b. Nov. 24, 1873, Constantinople—d. April 4, 1923, Berlin), leader of the Mensheviks, the non-Leninist wing of the Russian Social Democratic Workers' Party.

Martov served his revolutionary apprenticeship in Vilna as a member of the Bund, a Jewish Socialist group. In 1895 he and Vladimir Ilich Lenin formed the St. Petersburg Union of Struggle for the Liberation of the Working Class. Martov was arrested in 1896 and spent three years in Siberia. On his return he left Russia for Switzerland, where he joined Lenin as an editor of *Iskra*, the voice of Russian social democracy.

At the second Congress of the Russian Social Democratic Party in Brussels (1903), Martov spoke for those who were subsequently known as Mensheviks. They opposed Lenin's attempt to limit party membership to "professional revolutionaries" and favoured the establishment of a mass party on the west European model. Martov later became the leader of the Menshevik faction (1905–07), frequently clashing with other Menshevik leaders as well as with Lenin; during World War I he called for a peace without victory, while Lenin hoped for the transformation of the "imperialist" war into a revolutionary war.

After the Bolshevik Revolution in Russia (October 1917, old style), Martov opposed many of the new regime's dictatorial measures, but he supported the government in its battle against White Russian forces. In 1920 Martov left Soviet Russia and edited the *Socialist Courier* in Berlin until his death.

Martyn, Edward (b. Jan. 30, 1859, Tulira, County Galway, Ire.—d. Dec. 5, 1923, Tulira), Irish dramatist who with William Butler Yeats and Lady Gregory formed the Irish Literary Theatre (1899), which was part of the nationalist revival of interest in Ireland's Gaelic literary history.

Martyn's admiration of the craftsmanship and intellectualism of Ibsen caused him to emulate continental drama and to advocate its production.

During its three-year existence, the Irish Literary Theatre presented plays by Yeats, George Moore, and Martyn (*The Heather Field* and *Maeve;* both 1899), among others, in order to develop a Celtic and Irish school of dramatic literature. After the theatre closed, Martyn broke with the mainstream of Irish Revivalism, which led to the Abbey Theatre, because of personal conflicts and his dislike of "peasant plays" and "Celtic twilight romanticism." In 1914 Martyn helped found the Irish Theatre in Dublin to produce "non-peasant" plays, Irish-language plays, and great continental dramas. The aims of both theatres were successfully realized in the Gate Theatre (established 1928).

In addition to his dramatic writing and related activities, Martyn was an ardent Catholic and nationalist. He established the Palestrina Choir in Dublin, was president of Sinn Fein from 1904 to 1908, and promoted various educational movements.

martyr, one who voluntarily suffers death rather than deny his religion by words or deeds; such action is afforded special, institutionalized recognition in most major religions of the world. The term may also refer to anyone who sacrifices his life or something of great value for the sake of principle.

Judaism. The universality of persecution throughout its history has engendered in Judaism an explicit ideal of martyrdom. It begins with Abraham, who according to legend was cast into a lime kiln and saved from the fire by divine grace. The tradition was continued by Isaac, who consented to be sacrificed by his father, and by Daniel, whose example compelled the popular imagination. Readiness for martyrdom became a collective Jewish ideal during the Antiochene persecution and the Maccabean rebellion of the 2nd century BC. The best known episode was that of the mother and her seven sons (II Maccabees 7). Martyrdom was preferred to the desecration of the Sabbath by the early *Ḥasidim.* In Hadrian's time, pious Jews risked death to circumcise their children, and Rabbi Akiba embraced martyrdom to assert the right to teach the Law publicly. The Talmud cites the majority opinion that one should prefer martyrdom to three transgressions—idolatry, sexual immorality, and murder.

The Midrash on Lamentations 2:2 contains what is probably the oldest Jewish martyrology, the list of the Ten Martyrs. It was repeated in later *midrashim* and formed the theme of several liturgical elegies, including the *Eleh Ezkerah,* found in the Yom Kippur service. During the European persecutions of the later Middle Ages, chronological registers of martyrs were drawn up for use in synagogue commemorative services. In 1296 Isaac ben Samuel of Meiningen began to collect these in the *Memorbuch* published in 1898, covering the years 1096–1349.

In a sense, Jewish life was a nearly continuous training in martyrdom. Martyrs are honoured as *kedoshim* ("the holy ones"). Rabbi Shneur Zalman of Lyady, founder of Ḥabad Ḥasidism, considered the spirit of martyrdom (*mesirut nefesh*) to be the distinguishing quality of the Jewish people.

The deliberate execution of 6,000,000 Jews by the Nazis during World War II dwarfed all previous ordeals of martyrdom. In current Jewish literature, the Six Million are regarded as martyrs since they died for the sole reason of being Jews. In contrast to previous occasions, they were not given the alternative of saving their lives by abjuring their faith. In Israel the library of Yad Veshem contains most of the extant records of the holocaust (*q.v.*).

Christianity. The original meaning of the Greek word *martys* was "witness"; in this sense it is often used in the New Testament. Since the most striking witness that Christians could bear to their faith was to die rather than deny it, the word soon began to be used in reference to one who was not only a witness but specifically a witness unto death. This usage is present, at least implicitly, in Acts 22:20 and Revelation 2:13.

The first Christian martyrs were St. Stephen and St. James. Of the apostles the most important martyrs were SS. Peter and Paul, both put to death at Rome. Clement of Rome describes them as God's athletes, contending for the heavenly prize, and mentions a "great multitude" executed at the same time. Early in the 2nd century, Ignatius of Antioch described his own prospective martyrdom as a way of "attaining to God" and urged the Roman Christians not to make any effort to have him spared. In the sporadic persecutions of the first two centuries, martyrdoms were not especially frequent, but the martyrs were highly regarded by Christians. The Roman emperor Marcus Aurelius, by contrast, viewed their constancy as theatrical. The government's position was not entirely clear. Were Christians to be condemned as Christians because of specific criminal charges or because of crimes inherent in the profession of Christianity? In any event, they were ordered to prove their abandonment of Christianity by offering sacrifices to the Roman gods; when they refused to do so, they were executed.

With the passage of time and with a fresh emphasis on martyrdom (often regarded as a substitute for baptism) in the persecutions under Decius (AD 250) and Diocletian (AD 303–311), the authentic acts of the early martyrs were often replaced by legendary accounts (for instance, none of the versions of the death of Ignatius is genuine). The earliest surviving Christian martyrologies are the Syrian *Breviarium Syriacum* (AD 411) and the Hieronymian (mid-5th century), which purports to be by St. Jerome, a claim rejected by critics.

Islām. The Islāmic designation *shahīd* (Arabic: "witness") is equivalent to and in a sense derivative of the Judaeo-Christian concept of martyr. The full sense of "witness unto death" does not appear in the Qur'ān but receives explicit treatment in the subsequent Ḥadīth literature, in which it is stated that martyrs, among the host of heaven, stand nearest the throne of God.

While details of the status accorded by martyrdom (*e.g.,* whether or not a martyr is exempt from certain rituals of burial) have been debated among dogmatists, it is generally agreed that the rank of *shahīd* comprises two groups of the faithful: those killed in jihad, or holy war, and those killed unjustly. The term is used informally to venerate anyone who dies in a pitiable manner (*e.g.,* in childbirth; in a strange land). Among the Shīʿite branch, the martyr par excellence is Ḥusayn ibn ʿAlī (*c.* 629–680), whose death at the hands of the rival Sunnite faction under Yazīd is commemorated every year during the first 10 days of the month of Muḥarram.

Buddhism. While distinctly lacking a history of persecution or of violent conflict with other faiths, Buddhism does recognize among its adherents a venerable class of martyrs. The Jātaka *(q.v.)* commentary on the former lives of the Buddha is in a sense a martyrology of the bodhisattva ("buddha-to-be") and his disciples, recounting their continual self-sacrifice and repeated deaths. In Mahāyāna (Greater Vehicle) Buddhism, the decision by one destined to become a buddha in this or another life to postpone his own enlightenment to alleviate the suffering of others is regarded as martyrdom (*see* bodhisattva).

Martyrdom of Polycarp, letter that describes the death by burning of Polycarp, bishop of Smyrna in Asia Minor. It was sent to the Christian church in Philomelium, Asia Minor, from the church in Smyrna (modern İzmir, Tur.) and is the oldest authentic account of an early Christian martyr's death. Establishing the exact date of the death of Polycarp is difficult and has been the subject of much debate among scholars. The date suggested by the letter itself is 155; but the date given by Eusebius, bishop of Caesarea (d. *c.* 340), in his *Ecclesiastical History* is 167–168.

The account of the martyrdom was quoted extensively in the *Ecclesiastical History.* Unfortunately, the letter as presented in extant Greek manuscripts, the oldest of which dates from the 10th century, is somewhat different from the account given by Eusebius, so that probably the work has undergone interpolation. The later manuscripts include an elaborate comparison of the death of Polycarp with that of Christ.

Marua (Cameroon): *see* Maroua.

Marugame, city, Kagawa *ken* (prefecture), Shikoku, Japan, on the coast of the Inland Sea. Founded as a castle town in 1597, Marugame flourished from the Tokugawa period (1603–1867) to the early Meiji period (1868–1912) as a sea terminal for pilgrims coming from the Kyōto and Ōsaka areas to worship at the Kompira Shrine in Kotohira, located about 10 miles (16 km) south of Marugame. The port's importance declined with the opening of the railway between Matsuyama and Takamatsu (stopping at Kotohira) in 1889 and the more recent development of bus and air service linking Kotohira with major cities. Marugame occupies the centre of an alluvial plain that produces rice and barley under a well-organized irrigation system. The city's industries produce chemicals, textiles, fans, and salt. Large coastal salt fields were reclaimed from the sea to stimulate further industrialization in the early 1980s. Pop. (1990) 75,607.

Marulić, Marko (b. Aug. 18, 1450, Split, Dalmatia [now in Croatia]—d. Jan. 6, 1524, Split), Croatian moral philosopher and poet whose vernacular verse marked the beginnings of Croatian literature.

The scion of a noble family, Marulić studied classical languages and literature and philosophy at Padua before returning to his native Split and a life of scholarship. At the age of 60 he withdrew to a Franciscan monastery on the island of Šolta but returned to Split, disillusioned by the experience, two years later.

Marulić's didactic moral works were written in Latin and translated into many European languages. They stressed practical Christianity and reflected an appreciation of Stoic thought. His most important vernacular poem was *Istorija svete udovice Judit u versih hrvacki složena* (1521; "The History of the Holy Widow Judith"). The first printed Croatian literary work, *Judit* is an epic in six cantos in which Marulić sought by the example of an Old Testament heroine to strengthen his people in their struggles against the Turks.

Marusthali, sand-dune-covered eastern portion of the Great Indian (Thar) Desert in western Rājasthān state, northwestern India, extending over about 24,000 square miles (62,000 square km), north of the Lūni River. Marusthali (Sanskrit: "Land of the Dead") was populated as early as the 5th century AD and became part of the Mauryan empire and later of the Gurjara-Pratihāra dynasty. It passed next to the Mughals and then later to the Marāṭhā kingdom. The Arāvalli Range, the area's most striking feature, defines the Marusthali's eastern limits. The sand dunes in the region's northern half are ridges of densely packed, coarse sand. Short, discontinuous sand levees strike northeast-southwest on a plateau, enclosing small playas between them. The southern half of the Marusthali forms a vast bowl, rimmed by flat-topped hills of sand, rocks, and limestone. Scattered shrubs of spurge and acacia survive in the region. The Lūni River, its channels often obliterated by windblown sand, is the major river and forms the southern boundary of the Marusthali. The soils are mostly loamy sands.

Livestock raising and dry-desert and irrigated farming are the principal occupations of the Marusthali's inhabitants. Cereals, gram (chickpea), cotton, sugarcane, peanuts (groundnuts), and oilseeds are grown, though the local agriculture is hampered by frequent locust invasions. Small-scale industries process local raw materials, and lignite and gypsum are mined. Bīkaner, Jaisalmer, and Barmer are the important communities; road and railway transport is hampered by shifting sand, and parts of the region remain virtually inaccessible.

Mārūt (Islāmic myth): *see* Hārūt and Mārūt.

Marut, Ret (American author): *see* Traven, B.

Maruyama school (Japanese art): *see* Shijō school.

marvel-of-Peru (plant): *see* four-o'clock.

Marvell, Andrew (b. March 31, 1621, Winestead, Yorkshire, Eng.—d. Aug. 18, 1678, London), English poet whose political reputation overshadowed that of his poetry until the 20th century. He is considered to be one of the best secular Metaphysical poets.

Marvell was educated at Hull grammar school and the University of Cambridge, taking his B.A. in 1639. His father's death in 1641 may have ended Marvell's promising academic career. He was abroad for at least five years (1642–46), presumably as a tutor. In 1651–52 he was tutor to Mary, daughter of Lord Fairfax, the Parliamentary general, at Nun Appleton, Yorkshire, during which time he wrote his notable poems "Upon Appleton House" and "The Garden."

Although earlier opposed to Oliver Cromwell's Commonwealth government, he wrote "An Horatian Ode upon Cromwell's Return from Ireland" (1650), and from 1653 to 1657 he was a tutor to Cromwell's ward William Dutton. In 1657 he became assistant to John Milton as Latin secretary in the foreign office. "The First Anniversary" (1655) and "On the Death of O.C." (1659) showed his continued and growing admiration for Cromwell. In 1659 he was elected member of Parliament for Hull, an office he held until his death, serving skillfully and effectively.

After the restoration of Charles II in 1660, Marvell turned to political verse satires—the most notable was *Last Instructions to a Painter,* against Lord Clarendon, Charles's lord chancellor—and prose political satire, notably *The Rehearsal Transpos'd* (1672–73).

At Marvell's death, his housekeeper-servant Mary Palmer claimed to be his widow, although this was undoubtedly a legal fiction. The first publication of his poems in 1681 resulted from a manuscript volume she found among his effects.

While Marvell's political reputation has faded and his reputation as a satirist is on a par with others of his time, his small body of lyric poems, first recommended in the 19th century by Charles Lamb, has since appealed to many readers, and in the 20th century he came to be considered one of the most notable poets of his century. Marvell was eclectic: his "To His Coy Mistress" is a classic of Metaphysical poetry; the Cromwell odes are the work of a classicist; his attitudes are sometimes those of the elegant Cavalier poets; and his nature poems resemble those of the Puritan Platonists. In "To His Coy Mistress," which is one of the most famous poems in the English language, the impatient poet urges his mistress to abandon her false modesty and submit to his embraces before time and death rob them of the opportunity to love:

Had we but world enough, and time,
This coyness, lady, were no crime....
But at my back I always hear
Time's wingèd chariot hurrying near;
And yonder all before us lie
Deserts of vast eternity...
The grave's a fine and private place,
But none, I think, do there embrace....

BIBLIOGRAPHY. The standard text is H.M. Margoliouth (ed.), *The Poems and Letters of Andrew Marvell,* 3rd rev. ed., 2 vol. (1971). Studies of his life and works include Pierre Legouis, *Andrew Marvell: Poet, Puritan, Patriot,* 2nd ed. (1968); John Dixon Hunt, *Andrew Marvell* (1978); and Annabel M. Patterson, *Marvell and the Civic Crown* (1978).

Marwān I ibn al-Hakam (b. 623—d. 685), first of the Marwānid caliphs of the Umayyad dynasty (reigned 684–685).

A governor of Medina and the Hejaz under the caliph Muʿāwiya I, where he showed unusual vigour, Marwān I was an old man in poor health when he ascended the throne himself in 684. He died of illness less than a year later. His short reign was a period of continuous battle between various factions for the caliphate. Marwān I was able to arrange the succession of his son ʿAbd al-Malik by eliminating all other contenders for the caliphate. He strengthened the foundations of the Umayyad house and concentrated more power in the hands of the caliph.

Marwān II (b. *c.* 684—d. 750, Egypt), last of the Umayyad caliphs (reigned 744–750). He was killed while fleeing the forces of Abū al-ʿAbbās as-Saffāḥ, the first caliph of the ʿAbbāsid dynasty.

The grandson of Marwān I, Marwān II was governor of Armenia and other territories for 12 years, gaining military experience which later led him to reorganize the Islāmic army. In place of a clumsy system of divisions based on tribal loyalties, Marwān II created smaller, more mobile divisions of paid troops under professional commanders. Ascending to the throne in 744, he completed the reconquest of Syria by 746. However, the ʿAbbāsid rebellion broke out in 747, and a combined force of ʿAbbāsids, Persians, Iraqis, and Shīʿites decisively defeated the Umayyad army at the Battle of the Great Zab River in 750. The subsequent death of Marwān II marked the end of the Umayyad dynasty.

Marwell Zoological Park, zoo in Winchester, Hampshire, Eng., that is known for its large breeding groups of hoofed stock and carnivores. It was opened in 1972 and occupies 99 acres (40 hectares) of attractive parkland. Its animal collection, comprising more than 960 specimens of some 145 species, is arranged zoogeographically. Most of the animals are exhibited in large enclosures, ungulates being kept in mixed species groups wherever possible. The zoo maintains large breeding herds of most members of the horse family, including the goatlike goral, all three zebra species, and the impala and other varieties of antelope.

marwysgafn (Welsh: "deathbed song"), religious ode in which the poet, sensing the approach of death, confesses his sins and prays for forgiveness. The *marwysgafn* was popular during the period of the Welsh court poets, called *gogynfeirdd* in the 12th–14th centuries.

Marx, Karl, in full KARL HEINRICH MARX (b. May 5, 1818, Trier, Rhine Province, Prussia [Germany]—d. March 14, 1883, London, Eng.), political theorist, sociologist, and economist, from whom the movement known as Marxism derives its name and many of its ideas. He published (with Friedrich Engels) *The Communist Manifesto* (1848) and wrote the classic *Das Kapital* (1867, 1885, 1894).

A brief treatment of Karl Marx follows. For full treatment, *see* MACROPAEDIA: Marxism, Marx and.

During his student days at the universities of Bonn and Berlin, Marx studied history and philosophy and was strongly influenced by the works of G.W.F. Hegel. In 1841 he received a doctor's degree from the University of Jena. His liberal political views led him to consider journalism as a career and in 1842 he became an editor of the *Rheinische Zeitung* in Cologne. The *Economic and Philosophical Manuscripts,* which Marx wrote in 1844, show an aversion to everything that impairs man's liberty, a tendency that did not survive with the same strength in his later writings.

In 1843 Marx married Jenny von Westphalen, a close friend of his boyhood and the daughter of a high government official. This marriage survived the vicissitudes of all the subsequent years. Shortly after his marriage, Marx's newspaper was suppressed and he emigrated to Paris with his wife. There he became acquainted with French socialist writers and established his lifelong friendship with Engels.

In 1847, at a new place of exile in Brussels, Marx wrote *Misère de la philosophie* (1847; *The Poverty of Philosophy*), in which he developed the fundamental propositions of his economic interpretation of history. Against the utopian socialists' quest for the most morally desirable social order he put his own search for a system that would inevitably and by necessity result from the operation of historical forces. Another even more important document originated from Marx's (and Engels') pen during the stay in Brussels—*Manifest der Kommunistischen Partei* (1848), commonly known as *The Communist Manifesto,* which contains a summary of his whole social philosophy. It was written to serve as the platform of the Communist League. *The Communist Manifesto* appeared at a moment most favourable to its effectiveness: on the eve of the February (1848) revolution in France during which socialism showed its power.

The revolutionary atmosphere in Germany in 1848 enabled Marx to return to Cologne and revive his newspaper, now under the title of *Neue Rheinische Zeitung,* but in 1849 he was expelled. He then settled in London, where he spent most of the remainder of his life, studying in the British Museum. His most important theoretical work was *Das Kapital* (1867), an analysis of the economics of capitalism. He also became the leading spirit of the International Working Men's Association, subsequently known as the First International. Most of Marx's life was spent in poverty that was only partially alleviated by the benefactions of friends and relatives. After his death his unpublished writings were edited by Engels. His works were the intellectual basis of much of late 19th-century European socialism and 20th-century communism.

Marx, Roberto Burle: *see* Burle Marx, Roberto.

Marx, Wilhelm (b. Jan. 15, 1863, Cologne, Prussia [Germany]—d. Aug. 5, 1946, Bonn, Ger.), German statesman, leader of the Roman Catholic Centre Party, and twice chancellor during the Weimar Republic.

Marx studied law and rose from a judgeship to the presidency of the senate of the Court of Appeal at Berlin (1922). He founded and was first president of the Catholic Schools Organization (Düsseldorf, 1911) and he became president of the People's Union for Catholic Germany after World War I.

After joining the Centre Party, Marx served as a deputy in the Prussian Landtag (1899–1918) and the Reichstag (1910–32). From 1921 to 1928, he was the party's chairman and its leader in the Reichstag. He first served as chancellor from November 1923 until December 1924, during which time his government secured the acceptance of the Dawes Plan for war reparations payments. After a period as prime minister of Prussia (February–April 1925), Marx lost his bid for the presidency of Germany to Paul von Hindenburg. In May 1926, he returned as chancellor but resigned in 1928 after the successes of the Social Democrats. In December 1928 Marx resigned from the chairmanship of the Centre Party and withdrew from politics.

Marx BROTHERS, American comedy team that was popular on stage, screen, and radio for 30 years. They were celebrated for their inventive attacks on the socially respectable and upon ordered society in general. Five Marx brothers became entertainers: Chico (Leonard; b. March 1887, New York, N.Y., U.S.—d. Oct. 11, 1961, Hollywood, Calif.), Harpo (Adolph Arthur; b. Nov. 23, 1888, New York City—d. Sept. 28, 1964, Hollywood), Groucho (Julius Henry; b. Oct. 2, 1890, New York City—d. Aug. 19, 1977, Los Angeles, Calif.), Gummo (Milton; b. Oct. 23, 1892, New York City—d. April 21, 1977, Palm Springs, Calif.), and Zeppo (Herbert; b. Feb. 25, 1901, New York City—d. Nov. 29, 1979, Palm Springs). Encouraged by their mother, Minnie, the brothers formed vaudeville acts such as "The Four Nightingales" (1908–10), "The Six Musical Mascots," and later "The Four Marx Brothers." They adopted their distinctive nicknames in 1914, the same year they began their successful comedy show *Home Again.* Zeppo replaced Gummo in the act in 1918. Their first play on Broadway, *I'll Say She Is* (1924), was a huge success and was followed by *The Cocoanuts* (1925) and *Animal Crackers* (1928).

Groucho, Harpo, and Chico Marx
The Bettmann Archive

The brothers initiated a series of screen comedies in the late 1920s. These, at first film versions of their stage successes, soon developed into a skillful cinematic blend of visual and verbal humour. Among their best-known pictures were *The Cocoanuts* (1929), *Animal Crackers* (1930), *Monkey Business* (1931), *Duck Soup* (1933), *A Night at the Opera* (1935), *A Day at the Races* (1937), and *Room Service* (1938). These films were characterized by perfect comic interplay between the brothers, with Groucho supplying a running commentary of pungent asides to the audience as counterpoint to the frantic activities of the silent Harpo and the Italian-accented Chico. Groucho, a master of the wisecrack and the non sequitur delivered in an anarchic, unpredictable style, customarily walked with bent knees, gliding across the floor with a furtive air and casting predatory looks at women. The actress Margaret Dumont, who was most often the recipient of these looks, played a statuesque lady whose aplomb was seldom ruffled by the amorous attacks of her admirer or by the chaos that the brothers created. Harpo played the harp (with great skill) and Chico the piano, on at least one occasion demolishing it as he played.

In the late 1930s Zeppo became a theatrical agent, and Chico was a band leader during World War II. In 1947 Groucho began the radio show "You Bet Your Life." After the brothers' last film together, *Love Happy* (1950), Groucho appeared independently in several motion pictures, wrote his memoirs, and achieved success as the quiz master on a long-lived television version of "You Bet Your Life."

Marxism, a body of doctrine developed by Karl Marx and, to a lesser extent, by Friedrich Engels in the middle of the 19th century and consisting originally of three interrelated ideas: a philosophical view of man, a theory of history, and an economic and political program. During his lifetime Marx strove to keep these various aspects consistent and coherent; in later years—and especially after his death—various interpretations imposed on his doctrines, as well as political pressures generated by the adoption of Marxism as the official creed of the Soviet Union from 1917 to 1990/91, led to many compromises and adjustments. Today the term can refer either to the doctrine of the former Soviet government (often called Marxism-Leninism) or of Communist or Socialist parties in other nations on the one hand, or on the other hand to a number of loosely related perspectives on philosophical or social problems as developed by certain Western thinkers inspired by Marx.

A brief treatment of Marxism follows. For full treatment, *see* MACROPAEDIA: Marxism, Marx and.

The philosophical view of Marxism is that creativity, that is, the ability to exert labour on objects of nature in order to satisfy one's needs, is the defining characteristic of humanity. Further, one labours not merely for the individual but for the species. All human works, from food to art, houses to governments, form the human world, which consists of the various forms of the objectification of humanity's productive powers as a species. Man is a species being, and the species as a whole should enjoy the objectifications of its labour.

Owing to various historical events not entirely within the control of mankind, however, this ideal situation is not achieved. Under capitalism, one class of individuals (the proletariat) invests its creative energies, or labour, while another class (the bourgeoisie) appropriates the products of this energy in exchange for wages. This means that the human world created by the proletariat does not belong to them, but is instead owned by a class of non-labouring owners. To describe this situation—the ownership by one class of the objectified labour of another—Marx used the word "alienation." When and if the workers could repossess the fruits of their labour, then this alienation would be overcome and all class divisions would cease.

The ideas of both class struggle and classless community were already familiar in Marx's time. The notion that economic interests in society necessarily are in conflict has been traced as far back as Thucydides, while the first decades of the 19th century were rife with sundry socialist critiques of the existing economic order and attempts to found utopian, classless communities. Marx coupled these two ideas in a novel way. The problem of every utopian writer is not to describe what his utopia looks like but to suggest how one achieves it. In his theory of history, Marx adopted the idea of the class struggle as the driving mechanism in the sequence of events that would culminate in the classless society.

The form in which this theory of history was most influential was expressed in the *Communist Manifesto,* published by Marx and Engels in 1848. "The history of all hitherto existing society is the history of class struggles" is its famous first sentence. All history is a protracted struggle between an exploiting class and an exploited class. While previous historians had considered the essential stuff of history to consist of battles, discoveries, inventions, treaties, intrigues, and the like—or so Marx claimed—these were only surface phenomena. The real motor of history was the developing means of production, the methods by which individuals in a society provide themselves with food, shelter, and other commodities.

This is the core of Marx's historical materialism. Human existence requires—is—a material life. To preserve this material life, man must interact with nature through a set of relations called the means of production. These relations are chosen for humanity at each historical stage—there are no capitalists in the 14th century, nor barons in the 20th. Historical stages themselves evolve in a dialectical manner, each stage being succeeded by a contrasting one with which it interacts, creating a synthesis of the two that constitutes a next stage, and so on. In any stage the prevailing means of production stipulate at once a set of relationships between man and nature and between man and man. In certain of these sets of relationships, human beings are deprived of their humanity.

The most recent historical stage is that of capitalism. Capitalism's success is based on its ability to increase productive capacity in a worldwide system that generates enormous quantities of surplus value, which are then appropriated by capitalists. But capitalism is beset by numerous internal contradictions and cannot survive. Most importantly, capitalism turns an entire class of human beings into commodities, dehumanizing them. In so doing, it prepares the way for its own destruction. Capitalism brings the class struggle to its critical point, where the proletariat are so thoroughly deprived of their humanity by such manifest exploitation that they are at last able to unite behind a common goal. The victory of the proletariat is therefore imminent, and the classless society is about to be realized. The interests of the proletariat are therefore the interests of humanity as a whole, and its victory will heal the division within humanity that has plagued it since the introduction of the division of labour.

The failure of the 1848 revolutions, and, much later, the awareness that an increasingly complex social structure was no longer described by Marx's analysis, led to refinements and elaborations of this basic doctrine. These revisions grew more extensive following Marx's death. Engels, followed by Karl Kautsky and others of the so-called orthodox school, transformed Marx's doctrine from a revolutionary program tied to the uniqueness of a particular historical moment to a more peaceful anticipation of eventual evolutionary triumph. In the hands of Vladimir Lenin, Marxism underwent a further transformation. The working class is not able to bring about the revolution by itself, according to Lenin, and must be guided by a professional class of revolutionaries. Lenin also altered Marx's historical analysis to allow for the possibility of revolution occurring in nonindustrialized nations. This fusion of traditional Marxism with an efficient party organization became known as Marxism-Leninism. An Austrian school led by Otto Bauer, called Austro-Marxism, attempted a return to the ethical basis of socialism, against the amorality of those who wished to push the class struggle to its extreme. Marxism as practiced by communist states frequently departed from orthodox Marxism, not only in the Soviet Union but also in states such as China and Cuba. Contemporary intellectuals have often appropriated Marxism as an instrument with which to criticize technological society; a notable example is Jean-Paul Sartre, who fused Marxism with existentialism in the *Critique of Dialectical Reason.*

The transformation of the U.S.S.R. into a body of loosely knit republics, the independence of the Baltic states, the dissolution of the Warsaw Pact, and other related events that characterized the last decades of the 20th century made the future of Marxism as a government dynamic uncertain.

Mary (personal name): *see under* Maria, or Marie, except as below.

Mary, also called SAINT MARY, or VIRGIN MARY (fl. beginning of the Christian Era), the mother of Jesus, an object of veneration in the Christian church since the apostolic age, and a favourite subject in Western art, music, and literature. Mary is known from biblical references, which are, however, too sparse to construct a coherent biography. The development of the doctrine of Mary can be traced through titles that have been ascribed to her in the history of the Christian communions—guarantee of the incarnation, virgin mother, second Eve, mother of God, ever virgin, immaculate, and assumed into heaven.

Her humility and obedience to the message of God have made her an exemplar for all ages of Christians. Out of the details supplied in the New Testament by the Gospels about the maid of Galilee, Christian piety and theology have constructed a picture of Mary that fulfills the prediction ascribed to her in the Magnificat (Luke 1:48): "Henceforth all generations will call me blessed."

Biblical references. The first mention of Mary is the story of the Annunciation, which reports that she was living in Nazareth and was betrothed to Joseph (Luke 1:26 ff.); the last mention of her (Acts 1:14) includes her in the company of those who devoted themselves to prayer after the ascension of Jesus into heaven. She appears in the following incidents in the Gospels: the Annunciation; the visit with Elizabeth, her kinswoman and the mother of John the Baptist, the precursor of Jesus (Luke 1:39 ff.); the birth of Jesus and the presentation of him in the Temple (Luke 2:1 ff.); the coming of the Magi and the flight to Egypt (Matthew 2:1 ff.); the Passover visit to Jerusalem when Jesus was 12 years old (Luke 2:41 ff.); the marriage at Cana in Galilee, although her name is not used (John 2:1 ff.); the attempt to see Jesus while he was teaching (Mark 3:31 ff.); and the station at the cross, where, apparently widowed, she was entrusted to the disciple John (John 19:26 ff.). Even if one takes these scenes as literal historical accounts, they do not add up to an integrated portrait of Mary. Only in the narratives of the Nativity and the Passion of Christ is her place a significant one: her acceptance of the privilege conferred on her in the Annunciation is the solemn prologue to the Christmas story; not only does she stand at the foot of the Cross, but in the Easter story "the other Mary" who came to the tomb of Jesus (Matthew 28:1) is not she—according to traditional interpretations, because, having kept in her heart what he was to be, she knew that the body of Jesus would not be there. On the other hand, the three incidents that belong to the life of Jesus contain elements of a pronouncedly human character, perhaps even the suggestion that she did not fully understand Jesus' true mission.

Since the early days of Christianity, however, the themes that these scenes symbolize have been the basis for thought and contemplation about Mary. Christian communions and theologians differ from one another in their interpretations of Mary principally on the basis of where they set the terminal point for such development and expansion—that is, where they maintain that the legitimate development of doctrine may be said to have ended. To a considerable degree, therefore, a historical survey of that development is also an introduction to the state of contemporary Christian thought about Mary.

Dogmatic titles. Probably the earliest allusion to Mary in Christian literature is the phrase "born of woman" in Galatians 4:4, which was written before any of the Gospels. As parallels such as Job 14:1 and Matthew 11:11 suggest, the phrase is a Hebraic way of speaking about the essential humanity of a person. When applied to Jesus, therefore, "born of woman" was intended to assert that he was a real man, in opposition to the attempt—later seen in various systems of Gnosticism, a 2nd-century dualistic religion—to deny that he had had a completely human life; he was said by some Gnostics to have passed through the body of Mary as light passes through a window. It seems unwarranted to read anything further into the phrase, as though "born of woman" necessarily implied "but not of a man and a woman." Thus, the phrase made Mary the sign or the guarantee that the Son of God had truly been born as a man. For the ancient world, one human parent was necessary to assure that a person was genuinely human, and from the beginning the human mother of Jesus Christ, the Son of God, has been the one to provide this assurance. Some scholars have even maintained that the primary connotation of the phrase "born of the Virgin Mary" in the Apostles' Creed was this same insistence by the church upon the authentic manhood of Jesus. That insistence has been the irreducible minimum in all the theories about Mary that have appeared in Christian history. Her role as mother takes precedence over any of the other roles assigned to her in devotion and in dogma. Those who deny the virgin birth usually claim to do so in the interest of true humanity, seeing a contradiction between the idea of Jesus as the human son of a human mother and the idea that he did not have a human father. Those who defend the virgin birth usually maintain that the true humanity was made possible when the Virgin accepted her commission as the guarantee of the Incarnation (Luke 1:38): "Let it be to me according to your word." This is the original source of the title Coredemptrix—indicating some participation with Christ in the redemption of mankind—assigned to Mary in Roman Catholic theology, though the term has come to connote a more active role by her; the precise nature of this participation is still a matter of controversy among Catholic theologians.

By far the most voluminous narratives about Mary in the New Testament are the infancy stories in the Gospels of Matthew and Luke. In their present form, both accounts make a point of asserting that Jesus was conceived in the womb of Mary without any human agency (Matt. 1:18 ff.; Luke 1:34 ff.); yet the many textual variants in Matt. 1:16, some of them with the words "Joseph begat Jesus," have caused some scholars to question whether such an assertion was part of Matthew's original account. The passages in Matthew and in Luke seem to be the only references to the matter in the New Testament. The Apostle Paul nowhere mentions it; the Gospel According to Mark begins with Jesus as an adult; and the Gospel According to John, which begins with his prehistorical existence, does not allude to the virgin birth, unless a variant of John 1:13, which reads ". . . who was born" rather than ". . . who were born," is followed. Matthew does not attach any theological significance to the miracle, but it is possible that the words of the angel in Luke 1:35 are intended to connect the holiness of the child with the virginity of the mother. In postbiblical Christian literature the most voluminous discussions of Mary have been those dealing with her virginity. On the basis of the New Testament, it was the unanimous teaching of all the orthodox Fathers of the Church that Mary conceived Jesus with her virginity unimpaired, a teaching enshrined in the early Christian Creeds and concurred in by the 16th-century Reformers as well as by most Protestant churches and believers since the Reformation.

One of the interpretations of the person and work of Jesus Christ in the New Testament is the formulation of parallels between him and Adam: "As in Adam all die, so also in Christ shall all be made alive" (First Letter of Paul to the Corinthians 15:22). Decisive in the parallel is the contrast between the disobedience of Adam, by which sin came into the world, and the obedience of Christ, by which salvation from sin was accomplished (Letter of Paul to the Romans 5:12–19). Whether or not the story of the Annunciation in the first chapter of the Gospel According to Luke is intended to suggest a similar parallel between Eve and Mary, this did soon become a theme of Christian reflection. Writing at about the end of the 2nd century, the Church Father Irenaeus elaborated the parallel between Eve, who, as a virgin, had disobeyed the word of God, and Mary, who, also as a virgin, had obeyed it;

> for Adam had necessarily to be restored in Christ, that mortality be absorbed in immortality, and Eve in Mary, that a virgin, become the advocate of a virgin, should undo and destroy virginal disobedience by virginal obedience.

Irenaeus did not argue the point; he seems rather to have taken the parallel for granted, and this may indicate that it was not his own invention but belonged to tradition, for which he had a high respect. In any case, the parallel did ascribe to Mary and to her obedience an active share in the redemption of the human race: all men had died in Adam, but Eve had participated in the sin that brought this on; all men were saved in Christ, but Mary had participated in the life that made this possible.

The first widespread theological controversy over Mary had to do with the propriety of applying to her the title of Theotokos, meaning "God-bearer" or "mother of God." The title seems to have arisen in devotional usage, probably in Alexandria, sometime in the 3rd or 4th century; it was a logical deduction from the doctrine of the full deity of Christ, which was established as a dogma during the 4th century, and those who defended that dogma were also the ones who drew the inference. Perhaps, as the 19th-century English theologian Cardinal John Henry Newman supposed, the determination of the Council of Nicaea in 325 that Christ was not merely the highest of creatures but belonged on the divine side of the line between Creator and creature was even responsible for the rapid growth of devotion and speculation attached to Mary as the highest of creatures. By the end of the 4th century, the Theotokos had successfully established itself in various sections of the church. Because it seemed to him that the supporters of the title were blurring the distinction between the divine and the human in Christ, Nestorius, the patriarch of Constantinople, objected to its use, preferring the less explicit title Christotokos, meaning "Christ-bearer" or "mother of Christ." Along with other aspects of his teaching, Nestorius' objections were condemned at the Council of Ephesus in 431.

Various corollaries could be deduced from the New Testament's assertion of Mary's virginity in the conception of Jesus, including the doctrine that she had remained a virgin in the course of his birth (the *virginitas in partu*) and the doctrine that she had remained a virgin after his birth and until the end of her life (the *virginitas post partum*). The Apostles' Creed appears to teach at least the *virginitas in partu* when it says "born of the Virgin Mary." Although this teaching about how Mary gave birth to Jesus occurs for the first time in the 2nd-century apocryphal, or noncanonical, *Protevangelium of James,* its origins and evolution are not easy to trace, and Roman Catholic and Protestant historians have come to contradictory conclusions. The growth of the ascetic ideal in the church helped to give support to this view of Mary as the model of the ever virgin. The doctrine is neither asserted nor denied but is simply ignored in the New Testament, and Old Testament passages adduced in support of it by Church Fathers (such as Ezekiel 44:2 and Song of Solomon 4:12) were probably convincing only to those who already accepted the doctrine.

As the doctrine of the perpetual virginity of Mary implied an integral purity of body and soul, so, in the opinion of many theologians, she was also free of other sins. Attempting to prove the universality of sin against Pelagius (whose teaching was condemned as heretical by the Christian Church but who did maintain the sinlessness of Mary), Augustine, the great theologian and bishop from northern Africa, spoke for the Western Church when he wrote:

> We must except the holy Virgin Mary. Out of respect for the Lord, I do not intend to raise a single question on the subject of sin. After all, how do we know what abundance of grace was granted to her who had the merit to conceive and bring forth him who was unquestionably without sin?

It was, however, the distinction between original sin (*i.e.,* the sin that all men are born with) and actual sin (*i.e.,* the sins that men commit during their life), firmly established in Western theology by the same Augustine, that eventually compelled a further clarification of what the sinlessness of Mary meant. Certain Eastern theologians in the 4th and 5th centuries were willing to attribute actual sins to her, but most theologians in both East and West came to accept the view that she never did anything sinful, a view that found expression even among the 16th-century Reformers. But was she free from original sin as well? And if so, how? Thomas Aquinas, the most important medieval theologian in the West, took a representative position when he taught that her conception was tarnished, as was that of all men, but that God suppressed and ultimately extinguished original sin in her, apparently before she was born. This position, however, was opposed by the doctrine of the Immaculate Conception, systematized by Duns Scotus, a 13th-century British Scholastic theologian, and finally defined as Roman Catholic dogma by Pope Pius IX in 1854. According to this dogma, Mary was not only pure in her life and in her birth, but

> at the first instant of her conception was preserved immaculate from all stain of original sin, by the singular grace and privilege granted her by Almighty God, through the merits of Christ Jesus, Saviour of mankind.

When the Immaculate Conception was promulgated, petitions began coming to the Vatican for a definition regarding the Assumption of the Virgin into heaven, as this was believed by Roman Catholics and celebrated in the Feast of the Assumption. During the century that followed, more than 8,000,000 persons signed such petitions; yet Rome hesitated, because the doctrine was difficult to define on the basis of Scripture and early witnesses to the Christian tradition. No account of the place and circumstances of Mary's death was universally accepted in the church (although paintings depicting her "dormition," or "falling asleep," in the ancient Ionian city of Ephesus were quite common); no burial place was acknowledged (although there was a grave in Jerusalem that was said to be hers); and no miracles were credited to relics of her body (although the physical remains of far lesser saints had performed many). Such arguments from silence, however, did not suffice to establish a dogma, and on the positive side even the earliest doctrinal and liturgical testimony in support of the idea has appeared relatively late in history. Finally, in 1950 Pope Pius XII made the dogma official, declaring that "the Immaculate Mother of God, the ever Virgin Mary, when the course of her earthly life was run, was assumed in body and soul to heavenly glory."

Cultural importance. In addition to these official prerogatives and titles given to her by Catholic Christianity, the Virgin Mary has achieved great cultural importance. Popular devotion to Mary—in such forms as feasts, devotional services, and the rosary—has played a tremendously important role in the lives of Roman Catholics and the Orthodox; at times, this devotion has pushed other doctrines into the background. Modern Roman Catholicism has emphasized that the doctrine of Mary is not an isolated belief but must be seen in the context of two other Christian doctrines: the doctrine of Christ and the doctrine of the church. What is said of Mary is derived from what is said of Jesus: this was the basic meaning of Theotokos. She has also been known as "the first believer" and as the one in whom the humanity of the church was representatively embodied.

Mary's cultural importance, however, far transcends any dogmatic or institutional boundaries. In ways that she could never have anticipated, all generations have indeed called her blessed. (J.J.Pe./Ed.)

BIBLIOGRAPHY. Hilda Graef, *Mary: A History of Doctrine and Devotion,* 2 vol. (1963–65), is especially instructive about the early development of the doctrine. Juniper Carol (ed.), *Mariology,* 3 vol. (1955–61), deals successively with the sources of Marian doctrine, theology, and devotions. Raymond E. Brown *et al.* (eds.), *Mary in the New Testament: A Collaborative Assessment by Protestant and Roman Catholic Scholars* (1978), reports many matters on which agreement was reached. Modern theological treatments by Roman Catholics include René Laurentin, *La Question mariale* (1963; *The Question of Mary,* 1965); and E. Schillebeeckx, *Maria, moeder van de verlossing,* 3rd rev. ed. (1957; *Mary Mother of the Redemption,* 1964). Critical but sympathetic treatments by Protestants are Giovanni Miegge, *La Vergine Maria* (1950; *The Virgin Mary,* 1955); and Max Thurian, *Marie, Mère du Seigneur, figure de l'Eglise* (1962; *Mary, Mother of All Christians,* 1964).

Mary, name of rulers grouped below by country and indicated by the symbol •.

Foreign-language equivalents:

French .... Marie
Portuguese .... Maria

BURGUNDY

• Mary, also called MARY OF BURGUNDY, French MARIE DE BOURGOGNE (b. Feb. 13, 1457, Brussels—d. March 27, 1482, Brugge [Bruges], Flanders), duchess of Burgundy (1477–82), daughter and heiress of Charles the Bold, duke of Burgundy; her crucial marriage to the archduke Maximilian (later Maximilian I), son of the Habsburg emperor Ferdinand III, resulted in Habsburg control of the Netherlands.

Betrothed to Maximilian in 1476, Mary found herself faced with French invasion when she became duchess of Burgundy on her father's death at Nancy early in 1477. She resisted French pressure to marry the future Charles VIII and became Maximilian's wife on August 18, 1477. Through her own marriage and the subsequent match that was made between her son, Philip the Handsome, and Joanna the Mad of Spain, daughter of Ferdinand of Aragon and Isabella of Castile, the Netherlands came to be joined with Spain and with the Habsburg's own Austrian possessions in the hands of her famous grandson, the emperor Charles V.

ENGLAND/GREAT BRITAIN

• Mary I, also called MARY TUDOR, byname BLOODY MARY (b. Feb. 18, 1516, Greenwich, near London—d. Nov. 17, 1558, London), the first queen to rule England (1553–58) in her own right. She was known as Bloody Mary for her persecution of Protestants in a vain attempt to restore Roman Catholicism in England.

Early life. The daughter of King Henry VIII and the Spanish princess Catherine of Aragon, Mary as a child was a pawn in England's bitter rivalry with more powerful nations, being fruitlessly proposed in marriage to this or that potentate desired as an ally. A studious and bright girl, she was educated by her mother and a governess of ducal rank.

Betrothed at last to the Holy Roman emperor, her cousin Charles V (Charles I of Spain), she was commanded by him to come to Spain with a huge cash dowry. This demand ignored, he presently jilted her and concluded a more advantageous match. Made princess of Wales in 1525, she held court at Ludlow Castle while new betrothal plans were made. Mary's life was radically disrupted, however, by her father's new marriage to Anne Boleyn.

Mary I, detail of a painting on wood by Sir Anthony More, 1553; in the Prado, Madrid

By courtesy of the Museo del Prado, Madrid

As early as the 1520s Henry had planned to divorce Catherine in order to marry Anne Boleyn, claiming that, since Catherine had been his deceased brother's wife, her union with Henry was incestuous. The Pope, however, refused to recognize Henry's right to divorce Catherine, even after the divorce was legalized in England. In 1534 Henry broke with Rome and established the Church of England. The allegation of incest, in effect, made Mary a bastard. Anne Boleyn, the new queen, bore the King a daughter, Elizabeth (the future queen), forbade Mary access to her parents, stripped her of her title of princess, and forced her to act as lady-in-waiting to the infant Elizabeth. Mary never saw her mother again, though, despite great danger, they corresponded secretly.

Anne's hatred pursued Mary so relentlessly that she feared execution, but, having her mother's courage and all her father's stubbornness, she would not admit to the illegitimacy of her birth. Nor would she enter a convent when ordered to do so.

After Anne fell under Henry's displeasure, he offered to pardon Mary if she would acknowledge him as head of the Church of England and admit the "incestuous illegality" of his marriage to her mother. She refused to do so until her cousin, the emperor Charles, persuaded her to give in, an action she was to regret deeply.

Henry was now reconciled to her and gave her a household befitting her position and again made plans for her betrothal. She became godmother to Prince Edward, his son by Jane Seymour, the third queen.

She was now the most important European princess. Although plain, she was a popular figure, with a fine contralto singing voice and great linguistic ability. She was, however, not able to free herself of the epithet of bastard, and her movements were severely restricted. Husband after husband proposed for her failed to reach the altar. When Henry married Catherine Howard, however, Mary was granted permission to return to court, and in 1544, although still considered illegitimate, she was granted succession to the throne after Edward and any other legitimate children who might be born to Henry.

Edward VI succeeded his father in 1547 and, swayed by religious fervour and overzealous advisers, made English rather than Latin compulsory for church services. Mary, however, continued to celebrate mass in the old form in her private chapel and was once again in danger of losing her head.

Mary as queen. Upon the death of Edward in 1553, she fled to Norfolk, as Lady Jane Grey had seized the throne and was recognized as queen for a few days. The country, however, considered Mary the rightful ruler, and within some days she made a triumphal entry into London. A woman of 37 now, she was forceful, sincere, bluff, and hearty like her father but, in contrast to him, disliked cruel punishments and the signing of death warrants.

Insensible to the need of caution for a newly crowned queen, unable to adapt herself to novel circumstances, and lacking self-interest, she longed to bring her people back to the church of Rome. To achieve this end, she was determined to marry Philip II of Spain, the son of the emperor Charles V and 11 years her junior, though most of her advisers advocated her cousin Courtenay, earl of Devon, a man of royal blood.

Those English noblemen who had acquired wealth and lands when Henry VIII confiscated the Catholic monasteries had a vested interest in retaining them, and Mary's desire to restore Roman Catholicism as the state religion made them her enemies. Parliament, also at odds with her, was offended by her discourtesy to their delegates pleading against the Spanish marriage: "My marriage is my own affair," she retorted.

When in 1554 it became clear that she would marry Philip, a Protestant insurrection broke out under the leadership of Sir Thomas Wyat. Alarmed by Wyat's rapid advance toward London, Mary made a magnificent speech rousing citizens by the thousands to fight for her. Wyat was defeated and executed, and Mary married Philip, restored the Catholic creed, and revived the laws against heresy. For three years rebel bodies dangled from gibbets, and heretics were relentlessly executed, some 300 being burned at the stake. Thenceforward the Queen, now known as Bloody Mary, was hated, her Spanish husband distrusted and slandered, and she herself blamed for the vicious slaughter. An unpopular, unsuccessful war with France, in which Spain was England's ally, lost Calais, England's last toehold in Europe. Still childless, sick, and grief stricken, she was further depressed by a series of false pregnancies. She died on Nov. 17, 1558, in London, and with her died all that she did. (E.N.S.)

BIBLIOGRAPHY. H.F.M. Prescott, *Mary Tudor* (1940, reprinted 1970), considered the best biography; Frederic Madden (ed.), *Privy Purse Expenses of the Princess Mary* (1831); John E. Paul, *Catherine of Aragon and Her Friends* (1966); Eric N. Simons, *The Queen and the Rebel* (1964), a detailed account of the Wyat rebellion; J.M. Stone, *The History of Mary I, Queen of England* (1901), good but dated; Godfrey Turton, *The Dragon's Breed: The Story of the Tudors* (1970), contains a short account of Mary I; R.B. Wernham, *Before the Armada* (1966); B.M.I. White, *Mary Tudor* (1935), considered the next best life to Prescott's; Carolly Erikson, *Bloody Mary* (1978), a readable biography concentrating on Mary's personal life; a scholarly and detailed account of her monarchy is D.M. Loades, *The Reign of Mary Tudor: Politics, Government, and Religions in England 1553–38* (1979).

• Mary II (b. April 30, 1662, London—d. Dec. 28, 1694, London), queen of England (1689–94) and wife of King William III. As the daughter of King James II, she made it possible for her Dutch husband to become co-ruler of England after he had overthrown James's government.

Although her father and mother were converts to Roman Catholicism, Mary was brought up a Protestant. In November 1677 she was married to her cousin William of Orange, stadholder of Holland and champion of Protestantism in Europe. She then settled in Holland. Her inability to bear children and

Mary II, detail of an oil painting after Willem Wissing; in the National Portrait Gallery, London
By courtesy of the National Portrait Gallery, London

William's infidelity made the early years of her marriage unhappy, but eventually they became a devoted couple.

During the quarrel (1687–88) between James II and William over James's pro-Catholic policies, Mary felt it her religious duty to side with her husband. Hence, she agreed to support William's invasion of England in November 1688. James fled the country in December, and two months later Mary arrived in London. At once Mary rejected proposals, advanced particularly by the Earl of Danby, that she become sole ruler to the exclusion of her husband, and on April 11, 1689, she and William were crowned joint sovereigns of England. While her husband was directing military campaigns in Ireland and on the Continent, Mary administered the government in her own name, but she relied entirely on his advice. In the periods when William was in England she willingly retired from politics. She was, however, actively concerned with ecclesiastical appointments.

Mary enjoyed great popularity, and her Dutch tastes had a marked influence on English pottery, landscape gardening, and interior decoration. She never settled down happily to life in England, however, and continued to be deeply troubled by her estrangement from her deposed father. Mary died of smallpox at the age of 32. Modern biographies of Mary include H.W. Chapman, *Mary II, Queen of England* (1953) and H. and B. van der Zee, *William and Mary* (1973).

PORTUGAL

• **Mary I–II:** *see* Maria I–II.

SCOTLAND

• **Mary,** byname MARY QUEEN OF SCOTS, original name MARY STUART, or STEWART (b. Dec. 8, 1542, Linlithgow Palace, Lothian, Scot.—d. Feb. 8, 1587, Fotheringhay Castle, Northamptonshire, Eng.), queen of Scotland (1542–67) and queen consort of France (1559–60). Her unwise marital and political actions provoked rebellion among the Scottish nobles, forcing her to flee to England, where she was eventually beheaded as a Roman Catholic threat to the English throne.

Early life. Mary Stuart was the only child of King James V of Scotland and his French wife, Mary of Guise. The death of her father six days after her birth left Mary as queen of Scotland in her own right. Although Mary's great-uncle King Henry VIII of England made an unsuccessful effort to secure control of her (Mary inherited Tudor blood through her grandmother, a sister of Henry VIII of England), the regency of the kingdom was settled in favour of her mother.

Her mother saw to it that Mary was sent to France at the age of five. There she was brought up at the court of King Henry II and his queen Catherine de Médicis with their own large family, assisted by relations on her mother's side, the powerful Guises. Despite a charmed childhood of much luxury, including frequent hunting and dancing (at both of which she excelled), Mary's education was not neglected, and she was taught Latin, Italian, Spanish, and some Greek. French now became her first language, and indeed in every other way Mary grew into a Frenchwoman rather than a Scot.

By her remarkable beauty, with her tall, slender figure (she was about 5 feet 11 inches), her red-gold hair and amber-coloured eyes, and her taste for music and poetry, Mary summed up the contemporary ideal of the Renaissance princess at the time of her marriage to Francis, eldest son of Henry and Catherine, in April 1558. Although it was a political match aimed at the union of France and Scotland, Mary was sincerely fond of her boy husband, though the marriage was probably never consummated.

The accession of Elizabeth Tudor to the throne of England in November 1558 meant that Mary was, by virtue of her Tudor blood, next in line to the English throne. Those Catholics who considered Elizabeth illegitimate because they regarded Henry VIII's divorce from Catherine of Aragon and his marriage to Anne Boleyn invalid even looked upon Mary as the lawful queen. Mary's father-in-law, Henry II of France, thus claimed the English throne on her behalf. The death of Henry in 1559 brought Francis to the French throne and made Mary a glittering queen consort of France, until Francis' premature death in December 1560 made her a widow at the age of 18.

Queen of Scotland. Returning to Scotland in August 1561, Mary discovered that her sheltered French upbringing had made her ill-equipped to cope with the series of problems now facing her. Mary's former pretensions to the English throne had incurred Elizabeth's hostility. She refused to acknowledge Mary as her heiress, however much Mary, nothing if not royal by temperament, prized her English rights. While Mary herself was a Roman Catholic, the official religion of Scotland had been reformed to Protestantism in her absence, and she thus represented to many, including the leading Calvinist preacher John Knox, a foreign queen of an alien religion.

Mary Queen of Scots, detail of a drawing by François Clouet, 1559; in the Bibliothèque Nationale, Paris
Giraudon—Art Resource/EB Inc.

Most difficult of all were the Scottish nobles; factious and turbulent after a series of royal minorities, they cared more for private feuds and self-aggrandizement than support of the crown. Nevertheless, for the first years of her rule, Mary managed well, with the aid of her bastard half-brother James, earl of Moray, and helped in particular by her policy of religious tolerance. Nor were all the Scots averse to the spectacle of a pretty young queen creating a graceful court life and enjoying her progresses round the country.

It was Mary's second marriage in July 1565 to her cousin Henry Stewart (Stuart), earl of Darnley, son of Matthew Stewart, 4th earl of Lennox, that started the fatal train of events culminating in her destruction. Mary married the handsome Darnley recklessly for love. It was a disastrous choice because by her marriage she antagonized all the elements interested in the power structure of Scotland, including Elizabeth, who disapproved of Mary marrying another Tudor descendant, and her halfbrother James, who, jealous of the Lennox family's rise to power, promptly rebelled. Nor did Darnley's character measure up to the promise of his appearance—he was weak, vicious, and yet ambitious. The callous butchery of her secretary and confidant, David Riccio (Rizzio), in front of her own eyes, in March 1566, by Darnley and a group of nobles, convinced Mary that her husband had aimed at her own life. The birth of their son James in June did nothing to reconcile the couple, and Mary, armed now with the heir she had craved, looked for some means to relieve an intolerable situation.

The next eight months constitute the most tangled and controversial period of Mary's career. According to Mary's detractors, it was during this period that she developed an adulterous liaison with James Hepburn, 4th earl of Bothwell, and planned with him the death of Darnley and their own following marriage. There is, however, no contemporary evidence of this love affair, before Darnley's death, except the highly dubious so-called Casket Letters, poems and letters supposedly written by Mary to Bothwell but now generally considered to be inadmissible evidence by historians. But Mary did undoubtedly consider the question of a divorce from Darnley, after a serious illness in October 1566, which left her health wrecked and her spirits low. On the night of Feb. 9, 1567, the house at Kirk o' Field on the outskirts of Edinburgh where Darnley lay recovering from illness was blown up, and Darnley himself was strangled while trying to escape. Many theories have been put forward to explain conflicting accounts of the crime, including the possibility that Darnley, plotting to blow up Mary, was caught in his own trap. Nevertheless, the most obvious explanation—that those responsible were the nobles who hated Darnley—is the most likely one.

Whatever Mary's foreknowledge of the crime, her conduct thereafter was fatally unwise and showed how much she lacked wise counsellors in Scotland. After three months, she allowed herself to be married off to Bothwell, the chief suspect, after he abducted and ravished her. If passion is rejected as the motive, Mary's behaviour can be ascribed to her increasing despair, exacerbated by ill health, at her inability to manage the affairs of tempestuous Scotland without a strong arm to support her. But in fact Bothwell as a consort proved no more acceptable to the jealous Scottish nobility than Darnley had been. Mary and Bothwell were parted forever at Carberry Hill on June 15, 1567, Bothwell to exile and imprisonment where he died in 1578, and Mary to incarceration on the tiny island of Loch Leven, where she was formally deposed in favour of her one-year-old son James. After a brief fling of liberty the following year, defeat of her supporters at a battle at Langside put her once more to flight. Impulsively, Mary sought refuge in England with her cousin Elizabeth. But Elizabeth, with all the political cunning Mary lacked, employed a series of excuses connected with the murder of Darnley to hold Mary in English captivity in a series of prisons for the next 18 years of her life. In the meantime, Mary's brother Moray flourished as regent of Scotland.

Captivity in England. Mary's captivity was long and wearisome, only partly allayed by the consolations of religion and, on a more mundane level, her skill at embroidery and her love of such little pets as lap dogs and singing birds. Her health suffered from the lack of physical exercise, her figure thickened, and her beauty diminished, as can be seen in the best known pictures of her in black velvet and white veil, dating from 1578. Naturally, she concentrated her energies on procuring release from an imprisonment she considered unjustified, at first by pleas, and later by conspiracy. Unfortunately for her survival, Mary as a Catholic was the natural focus for the hopes of those English Catholics who wished to replace the Protestant queen Elizabeth on the throne. It was the discovery in 1586 of a plot to assassinate Elizabeth and bring about a Roman Catholic uprising that convinced Queen Elizabeth that, while she lived, Mary would always constitute too dangerous a threat to her own position.

Despite the fact that she was the sovereign queen of another country, Mary was tried by an English court and condemned; her son, James, who had not seen his mother since infancy and now had his sights fixed on succeeding to the English throne, raised no objections. Mary was executed in 1587 in the great hall at Fotheringhay Castle, near Peterborough; she was 44 years old. It was a chilling scene, redeemed by the great personal dignity with which Mary met her fate. Her body ultimately came to rest in Westminster Abbey in a magnificent monument James I raised to his mother, after he finally ascended the throne of England.

A romantic and tragic figure to her supporters, a scheming adulteress if not murderess to her political enemies, Mary aroused furious controversy in her own lifetime, during which her cousin Queen Elizabeth aptly termed her "the daughter of debate." Her dramatic story has continued to provoke argument among historians ever since, while the public interest in this 16th-century femme fatale remains unabated. (A.Fr.)

BIBLIOGRAPHY. Antonia Fraser, *Mary Queen of Scots* (1969), comprehensive biography taking into account modern research, replaces T.F. Henderson, *Mary Queen of Scots,* 2 vol. (1905); Prince Labanoff (ed.), *Lettres et mémoires de Marie, Reine d'Ecosse,* 7 vol. (1844), collected edition of the letters, also a useful reference book; P. Stewart Mackenzie, *Queen Mary's Book* (1905), text and translation of all Mary's writings; Claude Nau, *Memorials of Mary Stewart,* ed. by J. Stevenson (1883), Mary's own story dictated to her secretary while in captivity; D. Hay Fleming, *Mary Queen of Scots from Her Birth till Her Flight into England* (1898), a well-documented account, extremely hostile; S. and M. Tannenbaum, *Marie Stuart: Bibliography,* 3 vol. (1944), in which references to more specialized studies may be found.

Mary, *oblast* (province), southeastern Turkmenistan, having an area of 33,500 square miles (86,800 square km). It includes the basin of the Murgab River, which diminishes in the Kara-Kum Desert in the north. In the south, on the Afghanistan frontier, are spurs of the Selseleh-ye Safīd Kūh (Paropamisus Mountains). The climate is continental and dry. The economy is based on irrigated agriculture, particularly cotton cultivation, in the Murgab oasis and along the Kara-Kum Canal; the breeding of Karakul sheep in the desert; and the large Mayskoye and Shatlyk natural-gas deposits, the latter being one of the largest in Central Asia and the entire continent. The cities are Mary, the *oblast* centre, Bayram-Ali, Iolotan, and Kyshka. In 1979 the population was one-third urban. Pop. (1991 est.) 859,500.

Mary, city and administrative centre of Mary *oblast* (province), Turkmenistan, on the Murgab River, at the intersection of the Kara-Kum Canal and the Balkhan–Tashkent railway. It was founded in 1884 on the site of a former Turkmen fort, 19 miles (30 km) west of the ruined city of Merv, and was known by that name until 1937. It is now a centre for the huge Shatlyk gas field and a transport junction. It also has a large gas-fired power station, a plastic works, and various food-processing and light industries. Pop. (1991 est.) 94,900.

Mary Magdalene, Saint, also called MARY OF MAGDALA (fl. 1st century AD, Palestine; feast day July 22), one of Jesus' most celebrated disciples, famous, according to Mark 16:9–10 and John 20:14–17, for being the first person to see the resurrected Christ.

The unchallenged facts about her life establish that Jesus cleansed her of seven demons (Luke 8:2 and Mark 16:9), probably implying that he cured her of a physical disorder rather than the popular notion that he freed her of sins. She was one of the women who accompanied and aided Jesus in Galilee (Luke 8:1–2), and all four canonical Gospels attest that she witnessed Jesus' crucifixion and burial; John 19:25–26 further notes that she stood by the cross, near the Virgin Mary and the unidentified Apostle whom Jesus loved. Having seen where Jesus was buried (Mark 15:47), she went with two other women on Easter morning to the tomb to anoint the corpse. Finding the tomb empty, Mary ran to the disciples. She returned with St. Peter, who, astonished, left her. Christ then appeared to Mary and, according to John 20:17, instructed her to tell the Apostles that he was ascending to God.

The Gospels reveal her to be of practical character. Origen and other early textual interpreters usually viewed her as distinct from the mystical Mary of Bethany, who anointed Jesus' feet and wiped them with her hair (John 12:3–7), and from the penitent woman whose sins Jesus pardoned for anointing him in a like fashion (Luke 7:37–48). The Eastern Church also distinguishes between the three, but after they were identified as one and the same by Pope St. Gregory I the Great, Mary Magdalene's cult flourished in the West. This identification has since been challenged, and modern scholars feel that the three women are distinct.

Gnostics, pre-Christians and early Christians who believed that matter is evil and redemption is attained by an enlightened elite through faith alone, regarded her as a medium of secret revelation, so described in their *Gospel of Mary, Gospel of Philip,* and *Pistis Sophia.* According to Eastern tradition, she accompanied St. John the Evangelist to Ephesus (near modern Selçuk, Tur.), where she died and was buried. French tradition spuriously claims that she evangelized Provence (now southeastern France) and spent her last 30 years in an Alpine cavern. Medieval legend relates that she was John's wife. H.C. Koehler's English translation of Peter Ketter's *Magdalene Question* appeared in 1935, followed by H. Hansel's *Maria-Magdalena-Legende* (1937; "The Mary Magdalene Legend").

Mary of Burgundy: *see* Mary *under* Mary (Burgundy).

Mary of Guise: *see* Mary of Lorraine.

Mary of Lorraine, also called MARY OF GUISE, French MARIE DE LORRAINE, or DE GUISE (b. Nov. 22, 1515, Bar-le-Duc, Lorraine, Fr.—d. June 11, 1560, Edinburgh), regent of Scotland for her daughter, Mary Stuart, during the early years of the Scottish Reformation. A Roman Catholic, she pursued pro-French policies that involved her in civil war with Scotland's Protestant nobles.

Mary of Lorraine, detail of an oil painting by an unknown artist; in Hardwick Hall, Derbyshire

By courtesy of the National Trust, Hardwick Hall; photograph, R. Wilsher

Mary was the eldest child of Claude de Lorraine, 1er duc de Guise of Lorraine. By her first marriage, to Louis d'Orléans, 2e duc de Longueville, on Aug. 4, 1534, she had one son, François, 3e duc de Longueville. Widowed in 1537, she married King James V of Scotland in 1538, frustrating the hopes of England's King Henry VIII for her hand. But James died on Dec. 14, 1542, a few days after the birth of their daughter, Mary Stuart.

In April 1554, James, 2nd earl of Arran, resigned, and Mary of Lorraine replaced him as regent for her 12-year-old daughter. At first she reconciled the religious factions under her rule, arranging, with Protestant support, her daughter's marriage in 1558 to the Dauphin (later King Francis II) of France. Apparently, however, pressure from France caused her to abandon her policy of religious toleration and to attempt the suppression of Protestantism in Scotland. By initiating legal proceedings against a number of reformist preachers in 1559, she sparked an uprising at Perth. The Protestant lords then drove Mary from Edinburgh and on Oct. 21, 1559, proclaimed that she was deposed. With French assistance she recaptured Edinburgh, but an English army helped the Protestants by besieging Leith in April 1560. The ailing regent took refuge in Edinburgh Castle and on her deathbed urged the nobles of both parties to dismiss the armies of France and England and pledge to support her daughter. Her wishes were fulfilled soon after her death, but ultimately Mary Stuart proved unable to rule Scotland.

Mary of Modena, original name MARIE BEATRICE D'ESTE (b. Oct. 5, 1658, Modena,

Mary of Modena, detail of an oil painting by Willem Wissing, *c.* 1685; in the National Portrait Gallery, London

By courtesy of the National Portrait Gallery, London

Modena—d. May 7, 1718, Saint-Germain-en-Laye, Fr.), second wife of King James II of England; it was presumably on her inducement that James fled from England during the Revolution of 1688.

The daughter of Alfonso IV, duke of Modena, she grew up a devout Roman Catholic. The match with James was arranged through French diplomatic channels; they were married by proxy in September 1673, and she arrived in England in November. Although the English public regarded her as an agent of French and papal interests, her influence on her Roman Catholic husband's political thinking appears to have been negligible.

Between 1675 and 1682 she gave birth to five children, none of whom survived—with the blame popularly assigned to James's affliction with venereal disease in the 1660s. When her second son, James Francis Edward, was born on June 10, 1688, a month earlier than anticipated, it was widely, and falsely, rumoured that the child was not really hers but had been imposed upon the nation to ensure a Catholic succession to the throne. This suspicion gave the Protestant ruler William of Orange, stadholder of Holland, a pretext to invade England in November 1688. Mary escaped to France with her son on December 11, and James followed shortly afterward. Carola Oman's *Mary of Modena* was published in 1963.

Mary OF ORANGE, byname of MARY HENRIETTA STUART, Dutch MARIA VAN ORANJE, or MARIA HENRIETTE STUART (b. Nov. 4, 1631—d. Dec. 24, 1660 [Jan. 3, 1661, new style], London), eldest daughter of the English king Charles I and wife of the Dutch stadholder William II of Orange. The marriage to Prince William took place in London on May 2, 1641, and in 1642 she crossed over to Holland.

In 1647 her husband succeeded his father as stadholder, but three years later, just after his attempt to capture Amsterdam, he died; a son, afterward the English king William III was born a few days later (Nov. 14, 1650). Mary was unpopular with the Dutch owing to her sympathies with her kinsfolk, the Stuarts; and at length, public opinion having been further angered by the hospitality that she showed to her brothers, the future Charles II and James II, she was forbidden to receive her relatives. From 1654 to 1657 the Princess passed most of her time away from Holland. In 1657 she was appointed regent on behalf of her son for the principality of Orange, but the difficulties of her position led her to implore the assistance of Louis XIV, and the French king answered by seizing Orange himself. The position of both Mary and her son in Holland was greatly bettered through the restoration of Charles II in Great Britain. In September 1660 Mary journeyed to England. She was taken ill of smallpox and died in London.

Mary OF TECK, in full VICTORIA MARY AUGUSTA LOUISE OLGA PAULINE CLAUDINE AGNES (b. May 26, 1867, Kensington Palace, London—d. March 24, 1953, London), queen consort of King George V of Great Britain and the mother of kings Edward VIII (afterward duke of Windsor) and George VI.

Mary was the only daughter of Prinz (Prince; or, after 1871, Herzog [Duke]) von Teck, who was a member of the royal house of Württemberg. She was also a great-granddaughter of George III of Great Britain.

In 1891 Mary became engaged to Albert Victor, duke of Clarence (elder son of the Prince of Wales, afterward King Edward VII), but he died a few weeks before the marriage was to have taken place. Later, she was engaged to and, on July 6, 1893, married the Duke's younger brother, George, duke of York, prince of Wales from 1901 and king from 1910.

Her intellect, good sense, and artistic taste fitted her to be the wife of a sovereign, and her concern with the welfare of servicemen in World Wars I and II helped to make her popular with all classes of the British people.

Mary OF THE INCARNATION, original name BARBE-JEANNE AVRILLOT, MME ACARIE (b. Feb. 26, 1566, Paris—d. April 18, 1618, Pontoise, Fr.), mystic whose activity and influence in religious affairs inspired most of the leading French ecclesiastics of her time.

Although Mary wished to be a nun, her parents insisted that she marry (1582) Pierre Acarie, vicomte de Villemore. With the aid of King Henry IV of France and his wife, Marie de Médicis, she brought the Carmelite nuns to Paris, leading to the introduction into France in 1604 of the Discalced Carmelites, an order of meditative, cloistered nuns. She helped to reform the French Benedictine convents and worked for the expansion of the Ursulines, the first order of nuns dedicated to the education of girls. She encouraged her cousin Cardinal Pierre de Bérulle to found (1611) the Oratory, a congregation of priests that played an important part in the religious development of France in the 17th century.

After Pierre's death (1613), she entered the Carmelite convent at Amiens, Fr., where she made her vows in 1615, taking the name of Mary of the Incarnation. She was beatified in 1791 by Pope Pius VI, and her traditional feast day is April 18.

Mary QUEEN OF SCOTS: *see* Mary *under* Mary (Scotland).

Mary TUDOR (b. March 1495/96—d. June 24, 1533, Westhorpe, Suffolk, Eng.), English princess, the third wife of King Louis XII of France; she was the sister of England's King Henry VIII (ruled 1509–47) and the grandmother of Lady Jane Grey, who was titular queen of England for nine days in 1553.

Mary's father, King Henry VII (ruled 1485–1509) betrothed her to Archduke Charles (later the Holy Roman emperor Charles V) in 1507. In 1514, however, political considerations caused King Henry VIII to renounce this engagement and arrange a match between his beautiful, charming sister, Mary, and Louis XII, a broken man of 52. Since Mary was already in love with Charles Brandon, 1st duke of Suffolk, she made Henry promise that after Louis died she would be allowed to wed the man of her choice.

The marriage with Louis took place on Oct. 9, 1514, and Mary treated her husband with affection until he died on January 1 of the following year. Before Henry or Louis's successor, King Francis I, could involve her in another political marriage, Mary secretly wed Suffolk in Paris, probably in late February. Henry was infuriated at the news, but Suffolk regained the King's favour by paying him a large sum of money and perhaps by the intercession of Cardinal Wolsey. One of Mary's daughters by Suffolk became the mother of Lady Jane Grey. Walter C. Richardson's biography, *Mary Tudor* was published in 1970.

Mary, Society of: *see* Marianist; Marist Father.

Mary Gregory glass, variety of glass produced in the United States toward the end of the 19th century in imitation of the then popular English cameo glass. It was named for Mary Gregory, an employee in the decorating department of the Boston and Sandwich Glass Company in Sandwich, Mass. Both transparent and coloured, the glass was decorated with white enamel designs that were painted on the surface instead of being carved, as the genuine cameo glass was. Such cheap copying of the real cameo glass eventually ruined the market for both the genuine and the copies alike, since the greatest part of the English genuine cameo glass produced in the 1880s was exported to the United States.

Mary Gregory glass pitcher, the Boston and Sandwich Glass Company, Sandwich, Mass., *c.* 1880; in the Sandwich Glass Museum, Massachusetts

By courtesy of the Sandwich Glass Museum

Mary Immaculate, Oblates of (O.M.I.), one of the largest missionary congregations of the Roman Catholic Church, inaugurated at Aix-en-Provence, Fr., on Jan. 25, 1816, as the Missionary Society of Provence by Charles-Joseph-Eugène de Mazenod. By preaching to the poor, especially in rural areas, Mazenod hoped to renew the life of the church after the French Revolution. On Feb. 17, 1826, Pope Leo XII gave approval to the congregation, henceforth known as the Oblates of Mary Immaculate. In 1831 a general chapter (legislative meeting) voted to begin work in the foreign missions. The first mission foundations were made in Canada in 1841 and a year later in the United States.

In addition to the three vows of poverty, chastity, and obedience, the Oblates take a vow of perseverance by which they promise to remain in the congregation until death. A superior general in Rome directs the activities of the members, who are located on every continent; their principal apostolate (religious activity) is still to the poor. Where the church has been long established, the task of the congregation is to strengthen the faith, especially by preaching parish missions and retreats, teaching, and directing shrines dedicated to Mary. In Africa, South America, the Orient, and the Arctic it is engaged in pioneering missionary efforts.

Mary Kathleen, district and former mining settlement, northwestern Queensland, Australia, in the Selwyn Range. In 1954 a major deposit of uranium ore was discovered there near the Corella River. The town, named for the wife of Norman McConachy, who, with Clem Walton, discovered the ores, was built to house workers and their families; a processing plant was completed, and production begun in 1958. The closest railhead is Cloncurry (38 mi [61 km] east). When the original U.K. Atomic Energy Commission's contract was terminated in 1962, only a token maintenance force remained in residence. Mining was resumed in the 1970s but ceased in 1982. The following year, the contents of the town, including the buildings, were sold by public auction. Pop. (1981) 830.

Maryborough, city, southeastern Queensland, Australia, 20 mi (32 km) above the mouth of Mary River. Founded in 1843 and named after the river, which was named after Mary, the wife of Gov. Sir Charles Fitz Roy, it was proclaimed a town in 1861, when it was primarily a wool-shipping point; it became a city in 1905. Maryborough later developed as a marketing centre for a mixed farming region. Manufactures include boats, heavy machinery, locomotives, and furniture. It is linked by rail to Urangan, its nearest deepwater port, and there are seaside resorts at nearby Wide Bays and Hervey. Pop. (2001 prelim.) 25,145.

Maryborough, city, central Victoria, Australia. It lies along the Pyrenees Highway and is connected by rail to Melbourne (southeast). Located on the northern slopes of the Eastern Highlands and originating (1839) as a sheep run known as Simson's or Charlotte Plains, the town was founded in 1854 during a gold rush. It was renamed after the Irish birthplace of the local police commissioner and was proclaimed a municipality in 1857. Maryborough is the market for a district of grain farming and livestock raising and is also a lumbering and manufacturing centre. It was declared a city in 1961. Pop. (2001 prelim.) 7,163.

Maryborough (Ireland): *see* Portlaoihise.

Maryland, constituent state of the United States of America lying in the south Atlantic region of the country.

A brief treatment of Maryland follows. For full treatment, *see* MACROPAEDIA: United States of America: *Maryland.*

Maryland lies astride the northern reaches of Chesapeake Bay, which is an arm of the Atlantic Ocean. On its eastern shore Maryland shares the Delmarva Peninsula with Delaware and Virginia. On its western shore, the Potomac River forms the state's southern boundary with Virginia and West Virginia. The Mason and Dixon Line forms the state's northern border with Pennsylvania. The District of Columbia occupies a small enclave along the left (north) bank of the Potomac River. The state capital is Annapolis.

The earliest inhabitants of Maryland were late Ice Age hunters who roved the area about 10,000 BC. At the time of initial European contact, the main Indian groups were the Nanticoke and Piscataway tribes of the Algonkian family. The warlike Susquehanna tribe of the Iroquois family exerted heavy pressure from the north on the colonists until peace was negotiated in 1652.

Captain John Smith from Virginia charted the Chesapeake Bay region in 1608. Maryland was included in a charter given by the British king Charles I to Cecil Calvert, the second Lord Baltimore. Leonard Calvert, his younger brother, founded the first settlement in 1634 at St. Marys City, the first capital. The Roman Catholic Calvert family stipulated a strict policy of religious freedom for their colony, though only within the bounds of trinitarian Christianity. The colony became a haven for persecuted English Catholics and dissidents from sectarian rigidity in other colonies. The primary economic interest of the early settlers was cultivating tobacco, which was accomplished by the labours of indentured servants and African slaves. As more farms were cleared, the population centre shifted rapidly to the north and west. The capital of the colony was moved to Annapolis in 1694, and the city of Baltimore was founded in 1729.

The Treaty of Paris (1783) ending the American Revolution and acknowledging the independence of the colonies was ratified by the Continental Congress sitting at Annapolis. In 1788 Maryland became the seventh state to ratify the U.S. Constitution. The state ceded the District of Columbia as the site for a new federal capital in 1791. In 1814 the British, who had burned the government buildings at Washington, D.C., were repulsed by the guns of Fort McHenry in their attempt to inflict similar punishment on Baltimore.

With the reestablishment of peace, Maryland turned toward development and built the National Pike across the Appalachians, the Chesapeake & Ohio and Chesapeake & Delaware canals, and the first intercity telegraph line, from Baltimore to Washington, D.C. The U.S. Naval Academy was founded at Annapolis in 1845. During the American Civil War, Maryland remained loyal to the Union, but strong Southern sentiments resulted in the imposition of martial law throughout. Maryland was the site of several major Civil War military campaigns and battles.

Physiographically Maryland can be divided into three main regions: (1) the Atlantic Coastal Plain, which is penetrated by the long, broad Chesapeake estuaries; (2) the Piedmont Plateau, which has excellent farming soils; and (3) the Appalachians, which largely consist of forested ridges and valleys. The boundary between the Coastal Plain and the Piedmont is the Fall Line, or limit of navigation, of the rivers. Settlements often developed at that site on each river. Most of Maryland drains toward Chesapeake Bay, but in the extreme west the Youghiogheny River flows northward into the Ohio system, and in the extreme east a narrow portion of the Delmarva Peninsula drains directly into the Atlantic.

The climate of eastern Maryland is humid and subtropical. Summer temperatures are as high as 107° F (42° C), and relative humidity approaches 100 percent for extended periods. Winters are generally ice- and snow-free. In the far west, the climate is continental, with warm summers and cold winters. Rainfall averages more than 40 inches (1,000 mm), with the greatest concentration falling in the summer. Forests cover some two-fifths of the land.

The early settlement of Maryland was primarily by British farmers and tradesmen. African slaves were brought to work in Maryland under the first Calverts. Baltimore, the largest city in the state, was a major immigration centre for Europeans in the 19th century. Most of Maryland lies within the great population complex of the Eastern Seaboard, and four-fifths of its inhabitants live in areas classified as urban. The Baltimore and Washington, D.C., metropolitan areas contain more than four-fifths of the state's population.

The economy of Maryland is based primarily on government service and manufacturing. Department of Defense installations and several large federal agencies, such as the Bureau of the Census and the Food and Drug Administration, are among the largest employers in the state. In addition, thousands of Maryland suburbanites commute daily to government jobs in Washington, D.C. The city of Baltimore has about one-third of the state's manufacturing establishments. The largest manufacturing payrolls are in the primary metals, electronic and electrical equipment, food products, and transportation equipment industries.

The main agricultural products are chickens, corn (maize), soybeans, and tobacco. The fishing industry's most important catch is crab; other Maryland seafood products include other types of shellfish and perch and other finfish. The major mineral resources are bituminous coal, stone, and sand and gravel.

Multiple routes of the interstate highway system radiate from Baltimore and Washington, D.C., both of which have circular beltways to divert through-traffic from their central-city areas. Amtrak provides passenger rail service to Baltimore, and Montgomery and Prince George's counties are served by Washington D.C.'s Metro subway. The Port of Baltimore is one of the nation's largest in volume of foreign traffic handled. Baltimore–Washington International Airport is located midway between the two cities.

Virtually all towns, cities, and rural areas of Maryland are marked by relics of the past—landmarks, monuments, museums, festivals—or by products of Chesapeake Bay or sporting or artistic events. Antietam Battlefield, Assateague Island, the Chesapeake and Ohio Canal, and Fort McHenry are among the areas administered by the National Park Service. The state presents annual subsidies to Baltimore's symphony orchestra, art museum, public library, and resident theatre. The University of Maryland is the largest university; other institutions of note include Johns Hopkins University, St. John's College, and Goucher College. Area 10,460 square miles (27,092 square km). Pop. (2000) 5,296,486.

Marylebone Cricket Club (MCC), former governing body of cricket, founded in London in 1787. Marylebone soon became the leading cricket club in England and, eventually, the world authority on laws. The MCC headquarters are at Lord's Cricket Ground in London. The Cricket Council is now the final arbiter in England, as are boards of control in other countries, with the International Cricket Conference exercising advisory jurisdiction over world cricket affairs.

Marysville, city, seat (1850) of Yuba county, north-central California, U.S. It is situated in the Central Valley, at the junction of the Feather and Yuba rivers, 50 miles (80 km) north of Sacramento. It was established as a trading post in 1842 by Theodore Cordua on land leased from Captain John Sutter. The site was purchased by Charles Covillaud and Company, and the town was laid out (1849–50) by Auguste Le Plongeon and named for Covillaud's wife.

Stimulated by the gold rush and connected to Sacramento by river steamer, Marysville grew as a miners' supply depot and collection point. After a controversy over hydraulic mining, dikes were built (after 1875) to protect the city from flooding. It became a trade centre for a mixed-farming (especially peach-orchard) region. There was some industrial development after World War II. Yuba (junior) College was founded in 1927. The Chinese Bok Kai Temple dates from the mining era. Beale Air Force Base (1942) is 15 miles (24 km) east. Inc. 1851. Pop. (2000) 12,268.

Maryūṭ (Egypt): *see* ʿĀmirīyah, Al-.

Maryville, city, seat (1845) of Nodaway county, northwestern Missouri, U.S. It lies north of St. Joseph. Founded in 1845, it was named after Mary Graham, the first girl born there. The community's agricultural-based economy depends on corn (maize), wheat, and livestock raised in the surrounding area. Maryville is the seat of Northwest Missouri State University (established 1905). The first incorporation (1856) of Maryville was annulled, and the city was reincorporated in 1869. Pop. (2000) 10,581.

Maryville, city, seat (1795) of Blount county, eastern Tennessee, U.S., 16 miles (26 km) south of Knoxville, and a gateway to Great Smoky Mountains National Park. The settlement was founded in 1790 around Fort Craig (built in 1785). It was named for the wife of William Blount, governor of the Territory South of the River Ohio. A few miles northeast of the city is a restored log cabin (1794) where Sam Houston, who later became president of the Republic of Texas, taught school in 1812. Maryville College was founded in 1819. In

Sam Houston Schoolhouse, near Maryville, Tenn.
Dean Stone

1910 the first of a series of power dams was begun on the nearby Little Tennessee River and its tributaries. The purchase of these dams by the Aluminum Company of America (Alcoa) led to the procurement of land north of Maryville for a plant site. This area was incorporated as Alcoa in 1919. The city's economy now depends mainly on the aluminum industry. Other activities include the manufacture of building materials and textiles. Maryville College was founded in 1819. Pop. (2000) 23,120.

marzipan, a malleable confection of crushed almonds or almond paste, sugar, and whites of eggs. Soft marzipan is used as a filling in a variety of pastries and candies; that of firmer consistency is traditionally modeled into fanciful shapes, such as miniature fruits, vegetables, and sea creatures, and coloured realistically.

Marzūq, also spelled MURZUK, oasis, southwestern Libya. It lies on the northern edge of the Ṣaḥrā' Marzūq ("Sea of Sand"). An ancient assembly place for caravans to Lake Chad and the Niger River, it was the traditional capital of the Fezzan province (16th–19th century) and a centre of the Arab slave and arms trade. Once called the "Paris of the Desert," it was a base for Saharan explorers, including Frederick Hornemann in 1798 and Gustav Nachtigal in 1870–71. After the caravan tracks closed and motor and air travel began, Marzūq declined. Extensive ruins remain, including the old Turkish fort. The Italian fort now serves as a police station. The town is linked to Sabhā, 85 miles (137 km) northeast, by sand track and remains a local trade centre. Pop. (1990 est.) 40,500.

Masaccio, byname of TOMMASO DI GIOVANNI DI SIMONE GUIDI (b. Dec. 21, 1401, Castel San Giovanni [now San Giovanni Valdarno, Italy]—d. autumn 1428, Rome, Papal States), important Florentine painter of the early Renaissance whose frescoes in the Brancacci Chapel of the Church of Santa Maria del Carmine in Florence (*c.* 1427) remained influential throughout the Renaissance. In the span of only six years, Masaccio radically transformed Florentine painting. His art eventually helped create many of the major conceptual and stylistic foundations of Western painting. Seldom has such a brief life been so important to the history of art.

Early life and works. Tommaso di Giovanni di Simone Guidi was born in what is now the town of San Giovanni Valdarno, in the Tuscan province of Arezzo, some 40 miles (65 km) southeast of Florence. His father was Ser Giovanni di Mone Cassai, a notary, while his mother, Monna Iacopa, was the daughter of an innkeeper. Masaccio's brother Giovanni was also an artist; called lo Scheggia ("the Splinter"), he is known only for several inept paintings. According to the biographer Giorgio Vasari (who is not always reliable), Tommaso himself received the nickname Masaccio (loosely translated as "Big Tom," or "Clumsy Tom") because of his absentmindedness about worldly affairs, carelessness about his personal appearance, and other heedless—but good-natured—behaviour.

In the Renaissance, art was often a family enterprise passed down from father to son. It is curious, therefore, that Masaccio and his brother became painters even though none of their immediate forebears were artists. Masaccio's paternal grandfather was a maker of chests (*cassoni*) which were often painted. It was perhaps through his grandfather's connection with artists that he became one.

One of the most tantalizing questions about Masaccio revolves around his artistic apprenticeship. Young boys, sometimes not yet in their teens, would be apprenticed to a master. They would spend several years in his workshop learning all the necessary skills involved in making many types of art. Certainly Masaccio underwent such training, but there remains no trace of where, when, or with whom he studied. Knowing who taught Masaccio would reveal much about his artistic formation and his earliest work.

From his birthdate in 1401 until Jan. 7, 1422, absolutely nothing is known about Masaccio. On the latter date he entered the Florentine Arte dei Medici e Speziali, the guild to which painters belonged. It is safe to assume that by his matriculation, he was already a full-fledged painter ready to supervise his own workshop. Where he had been between his birth and his 21st year remains, like so much about him, a tantalizing mystery.

Masaccio's earliest extant work is a small triptych dated April 23, 1422, or about three months after he matriculated in the Florentine guild. This triptych, consisting of the Madonna enthroned, two adoring angels, and saints, was painted for the Church of San Giovenale near San Giovanni Valdarno and is now in the Uffizi Gallery in Florence. It displays an acute knowledge of Florentine painting, but its eclectic style, strongly influenced by Giotto and Andrea Orcagna, does not allow us to discern whether Masaccio trained in San Giovanni Valdarno or Florence before 1422. The triptych, nonetheless, is a powerfully impressive demonstration of the skill of the young, but already highly accomplished, artist. Compared to the lyrical, elegant art of Lorenzo Monaco and Gentile da Fabriano, the leading painters of the International Gothic style, Masaccio's forms are startlingly direct and massive. The triptych's tight, spare composition and the unidealized and vigorous portrayal of the plain Madonna and Child at its centre does not in the least resemble contemporary Florentine painting. The figures do, however, reveal a complete understanding of the revolutionary art of Donatello, the founder of the Florentine Renaissance sculptural style, whose early works Masaccio studied with care. Donatello's realistic sculptures taught Masaccio how to render and articulate the human body and provide it with gestural and emotional expression.

After the Giovenale Triptych, Masaccio's next important work was a sizable, multipaneled altarpiece for the Church of Santa Maria del Carmine at Pisa in 1426. This important commission demonstrates his growing reputation outside Florence. Unfortunately, the Pisa altarpiece was dismantled in the 18th century and many of its parts lost, but 13 sections of it have been rediscovered and identified in museums and private collections. The altarpiece's images, which include the "Madonna and Child" (National Gallery, London) originally at its centre, amplify the direct, realistic character of the 1422 triptych. Ensconced in a massive throne inspired by classical architecture, the Madonna is viewed from below and seems to tower over the spectator. The contrast between the bright lighting on her right side and the deep shadow on her left impart an unprecedented sense of volume and depth to the figure.

Originally placed beneath the Madonna, the rectangular panel depicting the "Adoration of the Magi" (Staatliche Museums, Berlin) is notable for its realistic figures, which include portraits, most likely those of the donor and his family. Like the "Madonna and Child," the palette of the "Adoration of the Magi" is notable for its deep, vibrant hues so different from the prevailing pastels and other light colours found in contemporary Florentine painting. Unlike his fellow artists, Masaccio used colour not as pleasing decorative pattern but to help impart the illusion of solidity to the painted figure.

The Brancacci Chapel. Shortly after completing the Pisa Altarpiece, Masaccio began working on what was to be his masterpiece—the frescoes of the Brancacci Chapel (*c.* 1427) in the Florentine Church of Santa Maria del Carmine. He was commissioned to finish painting the chapel's scenes of the stories of St. Peter after Masolino (1383–1447) had abandoned the job, leaving only the vaults and several frescoes in the upper registers finished. Previously, Masaccio and Masolino were engaged in some sort of loose working relationship. They had already collaborated on a "Madonna and Child with St. Anne" (Uffizi Gallery, Florence) in which the style of Masaccio, who was the younger of the two, had a profound influence on that of Masolino. It has been suggested, but never proven, that both artists were jointly commissioned to paint the Brancacci Chapel. The question of which painter executed which frescoes in the chapel posed one of the most discussed artistic problems of the 19th and 20th centuries.

Detail from "Expulsion of Adam and Eve," fresco by Masaccio, *c.* 1427; in the Brancacci Chapel, Santa Maria del Carmine, Florence, Italy

Scala/Art Resource, New York City

It is now generally thought that Masaccio was responsible for the following sections: the "Expulsion of Adam and Eve" (or "Expulsion from Paradise"), "Baptism of the Neophytes," "The Tribute Money," "St. Peter Enthroned," "St. Peter Healing the Sick with His Shadow," "St. Peter Distributing Alms," and part of the "Resurrection of the Son of Theophilus." (A cleaning and restoration of the Brancacci Chapel frescoes in 1985–89 removed centuries of accumulated grime and revealed the frescoes' vivid original colours.)

The radical differences between the two painters are seen clearly in the pendant frescoes of the "Temptation of Adam and Eve" by Masolino and Masaccio's "Expulsion of Adam and Eve," which preface the St. Peter stories. Masolino's figures are dainty, wiry, and elegant, while Masaccio's are highly dramatic, volumetric, and expansive. The shapes of Masaccio's Adam and Eve are constructed not with line but with strongly differentiated areas of light and dark that give them a pronounced three-dimensional sense of relief. Masolino's figures appear fantastic, while Masaccio's seem to exist within the world of the spectator illuminated by natural light. The expressive movements and gestures that

Masaccio gives to Adam and Eve powerfully convey their anguish at being expelled from the Garden of Eden and add a psychological dimension to the impressive physical realism of these figures.

The boldness of conception and execution—the paint is applied in sweeping, form-creating bold slashes—of the "Expulsion of Adam and Eve" marks all of Masaccio's frescoes in the Brancacci Chapel. The most famous of these is "The Tribute Money," which rivals Michelangelo's "David" as an icon of Renaissance art. "The Tribute Money," which depicts the debate between Christ and his followers about the rightness of paying tribute to earthly authorities, is populated by figures remarkable for their weight and gravity. Recalling both Donatello's sculptures and antique Roman reliefs that Masaccio saw in Florence, the figures of Christ and his apostles attain a monumentality and seriousness hitherto unknown. Massive and solemn, they are the very embodiments of human dignity and virtue so valued by Renaissance philosophers and humanists.

The figures of "The Tribute Money" and the other frescoes in the Brancacci Chapel are placed in settings of remarkable realism. For the first time in Florentine painting, religious drama unfolds not in some imaginary place in the past but in the countryside of Tuscany or the city streets of Florence, with St. Peter and his followers treading the palace-lined streets of an early 15th-century city. By setting his figures in scenes of such specificity, Masaccio sanctified and elevated the observer's world. His depiction of the heroic individual in a fixed and certain place in time and space perfectly reflects humanistic thought in contemporary Florence.

The scene depicted in "The Tribute Money" is consistently lit from the upper right and thus harmonizes with the actual lighting of the chapel, which comes from a window on the wall to the right of the fresco. The mountain background of the fresco is convincingly rendered using aerial perspective; an illusion of depth is created by successively lightening the tones of the more distant mountains, thereby simulating the changes effected by the atmosphere on the colours of distant objects. In "The Tribute Money," with its solid, anatomically convincing figures set in a clear, controlled space lit by a consistent fall of light, Masaccio decisively broke with the medieval conception of a picture as a world governed by different and arbitrary physical laws. Instead, he embraced the concept of a painting as a window behind which a continuation of the real world is to be found, with the same laws of space, light, form, and perspective that obtain in reality. This concept was to remain the basic idiom of Western painting for the next 450 years.

The Trinity. "The Trinity," a fresco in the Church of Santa Maria Novella, also embodies important contemporary influences. Painted about 1427, it was probably Masaccio's last work in Florence. It represents the Trinity (Father, Son, and Holy Spirit) set in a barrel-vaulted hall before which kneel two donors. The deep coffered vault is depicted using a nearly perfect one-point system of linear perspective, in which all the orthogonals recede to a central vanishing point. This way of depicting space may have been invented in Florence about 1410 by the architect Filippo Brunelleschi. Masaccio's "Trinity" is the first extant example of the systematic use of one-point perspective in a painting. One-point perspective fixes the spectator's viewpoint and determines his relation with the painted space. The architectural setting of "The Trinity" is derived from contemporary buildings by Brunelleschi which, in turn, were much influenced by classical Roman structures. Masaccio and Brunelleschi shared a common artistic vision that was rational, human-scaled and human-centred, and inspired by the ancient world.

Influence. Documentation suggests that Masaccio left Florence for Rome, where he died about 1428. His career was lamentably short, lasting only about six years. He left neither a workshop nor any pupils to carry on his style, but his paintings, though few in number and done for patrons and locations of only middling rank, made an immediate impact on Florence, influencing an entire generation of important artists. Masaccio's weighty, dignified treatment of the human figure and his clear and orderly depiction of space, atmosphere, and light renewed the idiom of the early 14th-century Florentine painter Giotto, whose monumental art had been weakened by the succeeding generations of painters. Masaccio carried Giotto's more realistic style to its logical conclusion by utilizing contemporary advances in anatomy, chiaroscuro, and perspective. The major Florentine painters of the mid-15th century—Filippo Lippi, Fra Angelico, Andrea del Castagno, and Piero della Francesca—were all inspired by the rationality, realism, and humanity of Masaccio's art. But his greatest impact came only 75 years after his death, when his monumental figures and sculptural use of light were newly and more fully appreciated by Leonardo da Vinci, Michelangelo, and Raphael, the chief painters of the High Renaissance. Some of Michelangelo's earliest drawings, for example, are studies of figures in "The Tribute Money," and through his works and those of other painters, Masaccio's art influenced the entire subsequent course of Western painting.

(B.C.)

BIBLIOGRAPHY. Giorgio Vasari, *The Lives of the Artists*, trans. by Julia Conaway Bondanella and Peter Bondanella (1991; originally published in Italian, 1550), provides an early biography; a modern work is John T. Spike, *Masaccio* (1995). The artist's work is examined in Bruce Cole, *Masaccio and the Art of Early Renaissance Florence* (1980); and Andrew Ladis, *The Brancacci Chapel, Florence* (1993). Paul Joannides, *Masaccio and Masolino: A Complete Catalogue* (1993), includes over 450 plates and a bibliography of studies on the works of both artists. Bernard Berenson, *The Italian Painters of the Renaissance* (1952, reissued 1980); and Bruce Cole, *Italian Art, 1250–1550: The Relation of Renaissance Art to Life and Society* (1987), place Masaccio's work in historical context.

Masada, Hebrew ḤORVOT MEẒADA ("Ruins of Masada"), ancient mountaintop fortress in southeastern Israel, site of the Jews' last stand against the Romans after the fall of Jerusalem in AD 70.

Masada occupies the entire top of an isolated mesa near the southwest coast of the Dead Sea. The rhomboid-shaped mountain towers 1,424 feet (434 m) above the level of the Dead Sea. It has a summit area of about 18 acres (7 hectares). Some authorities hold that the site was settled at the time of the First Temple (*c.* 900 BC), but Masada is renowned for the palaces and fortifications of Herod the Great (reigned 37–4 BC), king of Judaea under the Romans, and for its resistance to the Roman siege in AD 72–73.

The site was first fortified either by Jonathan Maccabeus (d. 143/142 BC) or by Alexander Jannaeus (reigned 103–76 BC), both of the Hasmonean dynasty. Masada was chiefly developed by Herod, who made it a royal citadel. His constructions included two ornate palaces (one of them on three levels), heavy walls, defensive towers, and aqueducts that brought water to cisterns holding nearly 200,000 gallons (750,000 l). After Herod's death (4 BC), Masada was captured by the Romans, but the Zealots, a Jewish sect that staunchly opposed domination by Rome, took it by surprise in AD 66. The steep slopes of the mountain made Masada a virtually unassailable fortress.

Following the fall of Jerusalem and the destruction of the Second Temple (AD 70), the Masada garrison—the last remnant of Jewish rule in Palestine—refused to surrender and was besieged by the Roman legion X Fretensis under Flavius Silva. Masada's unequaled defensive site baffled even the Romans' highly developed siegecraft for a time. It took the Roman army of almost 15,000, fighting a defending force of less than 1,000, including women

Aerial view of the ruins at Masada, Israel

and children, almost two years to subdue the fortress. The besiegers built a sloping ramp of earth and stones to bring their soldiers within reach of the stronghold, which fell only after the Romans created a breach in the defenders' walls. The Zealots, however, preferred death to enslavement, and the conquerors found that the defenders, led by Eleazar ben Jair, had taken their own lives (April 15, AD 73). Only two women and five children—who had hidden in a water conduit—survived to tell the tale. Masada was briefly reoccupied by the Jews in the 2nd century AD and was the site of a Byzantine church in the 5th–6th century. Thereafter, it was abandoned until the 20th century.

A general survey of the ruins was made by Israeli archaeologists in 1955–56, and the entire mountaintop was excavated by Yigael Yadin in 1963–65, assisted by thousands of volunteers from around the world. Descriptions by the Jewish historian Josephus, until then the only detailed source of Masada's history, were found to be highly accurate; the palaces, storehouses, defense works, and Roman camps and siege works were all revealed and cleared, as was the winding trail (the "Snake Path") on the mesa's northeastern face. A synagogue and ritual bath discovered on Masada are the earliest yet found in Palestine. Among the most interesting discoveries is a group of potsherds inscribed with Hebrew personal names. These may be lots cast by the last defenders to determine who should die first.

In the 20th century Masada became a symbol of Jewish national heroism, and it is now one of Israel's most popular tourist attractions. The difficult ascent of its footpaths is regularly performed by Israeli youth groups, while a cablecar provides tourists with a less rigorous access route.

Masaddiq, Mohammad (Iranian political leader): *see* Mosaddeq, Mohammad.

Masai, also spelled MAASAI, nomadic pastoralists of East Africa. Masai is essentially a linguistic term, referring to speakers of this Eastern Sudanic language (sometimes called Maa) of the Chari-Nile branch of the Nilo-Saharan family. These include the pastoral Masai who range along the Great Rift Valley of Kenya and Tanzania, the Samburu of Kenya, and the semipastoral Arusha and Baraguyu (or Kwafi) of Tanzania.

Masai warrior in the Great Rift Valley, Kenya
J.B. Davidson, Survival Anglia

The pastoral Masai are fully nomadic, wandering in bands throughout the year and subsisting almost entirely on the meat, blood, and milk of their herds. Their kraal, consisting of a large circular thornbush fence around a ring of mud-dung houses, holds four to eight families and their herds. Polygyny is common among older men; wife-lending occurs between men of the same age-set. Marriage involves a substantial bride-price in livestock.

The Masai have a number of patrilineal clans grouped into two classes, or moieties. The basic institution of social integration, however, is the system of age-sets. Under this system, groups of the same age are initiated (circumcised) into adult life during the same open-initiation period; the age-class thus formed is a permanent grouping, lasting the life of its members. They move up through a hierarchy of grades, each lasting approximately 15 years, including those of junior warriors, senior warriors, and junior elders, until they become senior elders authorized to make decisions for the tribe. Masai society is remarkably egalitarian; slaves have never been kept.

Between the ages of about 14 and 30, young men are traditionally known as morans. During this life stage they live in isolation in the bush, learning tribal customs and developing strength, courage, and endurance—traits for which Masai warriors are noted throughout the world.

Ceremonial events are directed by a ritual expert (*oloiboni*) who, although he has no political power, is religious head of his people.

The Kenyan and Tanzanian governments are encouraging the Masai to make permanent agricultural settlements and to give up moranism as a way of life, in favour of formal education and greater assimilation.

Masai Amboseli Game Reserve (Kenya): *see* Amboseli National Park.

Masaka, town, southern Uganda, situated about 80 miles (130 km) southwest of Kampala (the national capital), at an elevation of 4,300 feet (1,310 m). Roads connect it with Mbirizi, Lyantonde, and Mbarara. It is a market town and important commercial centre for the surrounding rich coffee-growing area. Its industries produce processed meat and fish, beverages, footwear, furniture, bakery products, glass, clay products, and milled grain. The town is the site of historic Fort Mosaka. About 24 miles (39 km) to the east is the small Lake Victoria port of Bukakata. Pop. (1991 prelim.) 49,070.

Masamune Hakuchō, pseudonym of MASAMUNE TADAO (b. March 3, 1879, Bizen, Okayama prefecture, Japan—d. Oct. 28, 1962, Tokyo), writer and critic who was one of the great masters of Japanese naturalist literature. Unlike others of that school, he seems to have had a basically unsentimental and skeptical view of human society that gave a notably disinterested tone to his writing.

Early influenced by Christianity, Masamune went to Tokyo in 1896 to enter Tokyo Senmon Gakkō (later Waseda University); he was baptized the following year. In 1903 he began writing literary, art, and cultural criticism for the newspaper *Yomiuri*. The novels *Doko-e* (1908; "Whither?") and *Doro ningyō* (1911; *The Mud Doll*) brought him attention as a writer of fiction, although he was already known for his distinctive criticism. These are stories of people living in a gray world devoid of all ambition and hope; *Ushibeya no nioi* (1916; "The Stench of the Stable") and *Shisha seisha* (1916; "The Dead and the Living") are similar works. Masamune also devoted some time to writing plays, the best known of which is perhaps *Jinsei no kōfuku* (1924; "The Happiness of Human Life").

It is in criticism that Masamune is often considered to have done his best work. In 1932 he published the influential *Bundan jimbutsu hyōron* ("Critical Essays on Literary Figures"). Other outstanding critical works are *Shisō mushisō* (1938; "Thought and Non-Thought") and *Bundanteki jijoden* (1938; "A Literary Autobiography").

Masan, city, Kyŏngsang-nam *do* (province), southeastern South Korea. It is located on Masan Bay, across from Chinhae Bay, 22 miles (35 km) west of Pusan, with which it is connected by rail and road. After 1899 Masan developed as an open port, but it was closed in 1908 because it lay in a fortified naval zone. Masan's port was opened again in 1967. The city is the market centre for agricultural products from the Kimhae plain and the Nam-ch'ŏn River valley and for marine products. Masan is also a service centre for the surrounding area. The main industries were formerly the manufacturing of marine products and the brewing of liquor; further industrial development has occurred with the construction of a thermoelectric plant and of machine, chemical, and textile factories. Masan has become one of the largest commercial and industrial cities in the province. The port has a free export zone. Pop. (1990 prelim.) 496,639.

Masaniello, byname of TOMMASO ANIELLO (b. June 1620, Naples [Italy]—d. July 16, 1647, Naples), leader of a popular insurrection in Naples against Spanish rule and oppression by the nobles.

Masaniello, oil painting attributed to D. Gargiulio; in the National Museum and Gallery of Capodimonte, Naples
Alinari—Art Resource

Masaniello was a young fisherman in 1647 when he was chosen to lead a protest against a new tax on fruit, levied by the nobility to raise money to pay the tribute demanded by Spain. The insurrection against the nobles was successful, but Masaniello became intoxicated and urged the people to slaughter the nobles. Shortly thereafter, he was murdered by assassins hired by the nobles. His brief, sensational career was the subject of an opera, *La Muette de Portici* (1828; also called *Masaniello*), by D.-F.-E. Auber and Eugène Scribe.

Masaoka Shiki, pseudonym of MASAOKA TSUNENORI (b. Oct. 14, 1867, Matsuyama, Japan—d. Sept. 19, 1902, Tokyo), poet, essayist, and critic who revived the haiku and tanka, traditional Japanese poetic forms.

Masaoka was born into a samurai (warrior) family. He went to Tokyo to study in 1883 and began to write poetry in 1885. After studying at Tokyo Imperial University from 1890 to 1892, he joined a publishing firm. During his brief service with the Japanese army as a correspondent during the Sino-Japanese War, the tuberculosis he had first contracted in 1889 became worse, and from that time on he was almost constantly an invalid. Nevertheless, he maintained a prominent position in the literary world, and his views on poetry and aesthetics, as well as his own poems, appeared regularly.

As early as 1892 Masaoka began to feel that a new literary spirit was needed to free poetry from centuries-old rules prescribing topics and vocabulary. In an essay entitled "Jojibun" ("Narration"), which appeared in the newspaper *Nihon* in 1900, Masaoka introduced the word *shasei* ("delineation from nature") to describe his theory. He believed that a poet should present things as they really are and should write in the language of contemporary speech. Through his articles Masaoka also stimulated renewed interest in the 8th-century poetry anthology *Man'yō-shū* ("Collection of Ten Thousand Leaves") and in the haiku poet Buson. Masaoka frequently wrote of his illness, both in his poems and in such essays as "Byōshō rokushaku" (1902; "The Six-foot Sickbed"), but his work is remarkably detached and almost entirely lacking in self-pity.

Consult the INDEX *first*

Masaryk, Jan (Garrigue) (b. Sept. 14, 1886, Prague, Bohemia, Austria-Hungary [now in Czech Republic]—d. March 10, 1948, Prague), statesman and diplomat who served as foreign minister in both the Czechoslovak émigré government in London during World War II and the postwar coalition government of Czechoslovakia.

The son of the statesman Tomáš Masaryk, Jan served in a Hungarian regiment during World War I, entered the foreign office of the newly independent Czechoslovakia in 1919, and served in Washington, D.C., and London before becoming secretary to the foreign minister Edvard Beneš in 1921. From 1925 to 1938 Masaryk was ambassador to Great Britain. During World War II he was foreign minister of the Czechoslovak émigré regime in London. A leading spokesman for that government, Masaryk made wartime broadcasts to occupied Czechoslovakia, published in English in 1944 under the title *Speaking to My Country,* and became a popular figure at home. Retaining the portfolio of foreign minister after his government's return to Prague in 1945, he accompanied Beneš to Moscow and also participated in the inauguration of the United Nations in San Francisco. He was convinced that Czechoslovakia must remain friendly to the Soviet Union, and he was greatly disappointed by the Soviet veto of Czechoslovak acceptance of postwar U.S. reconstruction aid under the Marshall Plan.

At the request of President Beneš, Masaryk remained at his post after the Communist takeover of Feb. 25, 1948, but a few weeks later he either committed suicide by throwing himself out of a window at the foreign office or was murdered by being thrown out.

Masaryk, Tomáš (Garrigue) (b. March 7, 1850, near Göding, Moravia, Austrian Empire [now Hodonín, Czech Republic]—d. Sept. 14, 1937, Lány, Czech.), chief founder and first president (1918–35) of Czechoslovakia.

Tomáš Masaryk, painting by Vojtěch Hynais, 1919; in the Národní Galerie, Prague
From the collections of the National Gallery in Prague

Early life. Masaryk's father was a Slovak coachman; his mother, a maid, came from a Germanized Moravian family. Though he was trained to be a teacher, he briefly became a locksmith's apprentice but then entered the German Hochschule in Brno in 1865. Continuing his studies at the University of Vienna, he obtained his doctorate in 1876. He studied for a year in Leipzig, where he met an American student of music, Charlotte Garrigue, whom he married in 1878. He was appointed lecturer in philosophy in Vienna in 1879, and he became professor of philosophy in the Czech university of Prague in 1882.

Masaryk was a Neo-Kantian, but he was also strongly influenced by the English puritan ethics and the austere teaching of the Hussites. At the same time, he showed a critical interest in the self-contradictions of capitalism—*e.g.,* in his first major work, a study of suicide as a mass phenomenon of modern civilization.

Masaryk's early works on the Czech Reformation and the Czech revival of the early 19th century were intended to remind the Czechs of the "religious meaning" of their heritage. His treatise on the work of the Czech historian František Palacký, who favoured equal rights for Slavs within the Austrian state, was a profound analysis of Austrian-Czech tensions. Masaryk founded two periodicals, in one of which he proved after a bitter debate that two ostensibly early medieval Czech poems, regarded as Slavic counterparts of the German *Nibelungenlied,* were in fact patriotic forgeries by an early 19th-century Czech poet.

In 1889 Masaryk entered upon his political career after transforming a journal into a political review. In the early 1890s he began to turn his attention to the Slovaks in northern Hungary. By criticizing both the feudal nature of Hungarian sovereignty and the antiquated Pan-Slav tendencies of the Slovak politicians, he became the idol of the young Slovak progressives who played a decisive role in the Czech-Slovak union in 1918–19. After unmasking the forged medieval Czech poems, he demonstrated his willingness to risk unpopularity in pursuit of moral righteousness once again when he succeeded in 1899 in proving the innocence of Jews accused in a ritual-murder case. Although deeply involved in political controversies, Masaryk published two monumental works before 1914. In his work on Marxism (1898), he discussed the immanent contradictions of both capitalism and socialism. In *Russia and Europe* (1913) he provided a critical survey of the Russian religious, intellectual, and social crises—the contradictions and confusions of the "Byzantine" retardation of Russian society by the Orthodox church and reactionary ideas.

As a politician Masaryk was at first an adherent of the federative Austro-Slavism envisioned in 1848. But as a democrat he gradually became estranged from the loyal, conservative, and Roman Catholic concept of the Old Czech Party and accepted the invitation of the liberal, bourgeois Young Czech Party. In 1891 he was elected to the Austrian Reichsrat, but, after disagreeing with the Young Czechs' emotional nationalism, he resigned his seat in 1893. In March 1900 he founded his own Realist Party, and, after his reelection in a more democratic Reichsrat, he became an outstanding figure of the left Slav opposition there. In both the Reichsrat and the standing committee of the Austrian and Hungarian parliaments, he attacked Austria-Hungary's alliance with Germany and its imperialistic politics in the Balkans. He defended the rights of the Serbs and Croats—especially at the time of the annexation of Bosnia and Hercegovina by Austria.

Fight for Czech and Slovak independence. In early 1915, after the outbreak of World War I, Masaryk made his way to western Europe, where he was recognized as the representative of the underground Czech liberation movement and conducted a vigorous campaign against Austria-Hungary and Germany. His British and French friends helped him to establish contact with the Allied leaders, to whom he delineated the Czech aims: restitution of Bohemia's independence on a democratic basis; establishment of Czech-Slovak unity; dismemberment of Austria-Hungary according to ethnic principles; and establishment of new states between Germany and Russia as a *cordon sanitaire* ("sanitary line," or line drawn around an infected spot) against German imperialism.

After the overthrow of the autocratic tsarist regime in 1917, Masaryk transferred his activities to Russia in order to organize the Czechoslovak Legion, formed by Czechoslovak war prisoners, and to develop contacts with the new government. After the Bolshevik Revolution, he set out for the United States, where he was welcomed by Czech and Slovak groups and where he negotiated the terms of Czechoslovak independence with President Woodrow Wilson and Secretary of State Robert Lansing. The Lansing Declaration of May 1918 expressed the sympathy of the U.S. government with the Czechoslovak freedom movement, and Czechoslovakia's liberation became one of Wilson's Fourteen Points for the post-World War I peace settlement. Masaryk also concluded the so-called Pittsburgh Convention with the Slovak associations in the United States, which promised the Slovaks a large measure of home rule; the interpretation of this declaration led to controversies between the Slovak opposition and the Czechoslovak government during the life of the first Czech republic.

On June 3, 1918, Czechoslovakia was recognized as an Allied power, and its frontiers were demarcated according to Masaryk's outline. As Masaryk had promised, the new multinational state respected the minority rights of its large German and Hungarian ethnic groups. On Nov. 14, 1918, he was elected president of Czechoslovakia, and he was reelected in 1920, 1927, and 1934. As a true "liberator" and "father of his country," he was constantly occupied in settling the crises resulting from the conflicts between the Czech and the Slovak parties, as well as from Slovakia's minority status. A philosopher and democrat, Masaryk was among the first to voice his anxiety over central Europe's fate after the Nazis came to power in Germany in 1933. He resigned his post in December 1935 and died nearly two years later. (L.v.G.)

BIBLIOGRAPHY. Studies of Masaryk's life and politics include Zbyněk Zeman, *The Masaryks: The Making of Czechoslovakia* (1976, reissued 1990); Roman Szporluk, *The Political Thought of Thomas G. Masaryk* (1981); and *T.G. Masaryk (1850–1937),* 3 vol. (1989–90), ed. by Stanley B. Winters, Robert B. Pynsent, and Harry Hanak, respectively.

Masaya, city, southwestern Nicaragua, at the eastern foot of Masaya Volcano, just east of the small Lake Masaya in the rift valley between Lakes Nicaragua and Managua. Masaya serves as a commercial and manufacturing centre for the rich agricultural hinterland. The large Indian population is known for its handicraft industries and festivals; other manufactures include rope, hammocks, palm hats, jams, and cassava starch. Masaya is accessible by highway and railroad from Managua, the national capital, and Granada city. It was a scene of heavy fighting between the Sandinista guerrillas and government troops in 1978–79, leaving much of the centre of the city in ruins. Pop. (1985 est.) 74,946.

Masbate, island and town, central Philippines, part of the Visayas group, bordered by the Sibuyan (west), Visayan (south), and Samar (east) seas. The island, 30 miles (48 km) southwest of the southern tip of Luzon, is V-shaped, with the open end of the V forming the Asid Gulf on the south; it has an area of 1,262 square miles (3,269 square km). The discontinuous highlands that stretch along both arms of the V represent the major structural arcs of the Philippine archipelago. Masbate's interior consists of rolling hills; grasslands cover two-thirds of the island. Agriculture (corn [maize], rice, and root crops) is the dominant economic activity. The island has several livestock ranches and a government cattle-breeding station. Commercial fishing is concentrated in the southwest near Balud. Gold was mined for centuries near Aroroy in the north; operations declined in the 1960s, but substantial reserves remain. Copper is found in the southeast.

Masbate town, located on the northeastern coast of the island, is the commercial centre, with trade in copra, corn, fish, and cattle; the town has an airport. Cataingan, Placer, Milagros, and Dimasalang are other important towns. Pop. (1980) island, 435,269; (1990) mun., 58,714.

Mascagni, Pietro (b. Dec. 7, 1863, Livorno, Kingdom of Italy—d. Aug. 2, 1945, Rome, Italy), Italian operatic composer, one of the principal exponents of *verismo,* a style of opera writing marked by melodramatic, often violent plots with characters drawn from everyday life.

Mascagni studied at the conservatory at Milan, but, unable to submit to the discipline of his master, Amilcare Ponchielli, he left to join a traveling opera company. In 1889 he won the first prize in a competition with his one-act opera *Cavalleria rusticana,* based on a Sicilian melodrama by Giovanni Verga. Produced at the Teatro Costanzi, Rome, on May 17, 1890, it was an instant success and subsequently maintained its popularity, usually being given with Ruggero Leoncavallo's one-act *Pagliacci*. *Le maschere* (1901), reviving the commedia dell'arte, is musically superior, though it had little success. He succeeded Arturo Toscanini as musical director of La Scala, Milan, in 1929. Among Mascagni's other operas are *L'amico Fritz* (1891), *Iris* (1898), and *Nerone* (1935), the last glorifying Benito Mussolini.

Mascara, also called (after 1981) MOUASKAR, town, northwestern Algeria, situated about 40 miles (60 km) south of the Mediterranean coast. Spread across two hills separated by the Wadi Toudman, it lies on the southern slope of the Beni Chougran Range of the Atlas Mountains. Mascara (meaning "mother of soldiers") was founded as a Turkish military garrison in 1701. In about 1790 the town was abandoned by the Spanish Muslims who had settled there and was returned to the Turks, who settled a Jewish community there. In 1832 Abdelkader, an Algerian patriot who was born in the vicinity, chose Mascara as his headquarters. The town was laid in ruins by the French in 1835, but total control was contested until 1841. Now an administrative, commercial, and market centre, Mascara has expanded beyond the ruins of its ancient ramparts. The main French-built town is to the northeast, and the Muslim town is to the northwest, overlooking the well-cultivated Ghriss Plain. There is much trade in leather goods, grains, and olive oil, but the region's main industry is the production of wine of high repute. Pop. (1998 prelim.) 80,797.

Mascarene Islands, French ÎLES MASCAREIGNES, collectively, the islands of Réunion, Mauritius, and Rodrigues, which are situated in a line along a submarine ridge, the Seychelles–Mauritius Plateau, 400 to 500 miles (640 to 800 km) northeast from southern Madagascar in the western Indian Ocean. All are volcanic in origin. The name Mascarene is taken from the 16th-century Portuguese explorer Pedro de Mascarenhas. The islands now form the two separate Indian Ocean states of Réunion and Mauritius (Rodrigues Island is a dependency of Mauritius), and all face problems of extreme population pressure. Pop. (1998 est.) 1,851,700.

Mascarene Plateau (Indian Ocean): *see* Seychelles–Mauritius Plateau.

Masdevallia, genus of about 300 species of tropical American orchids, family Orchidaceae, that have brightly coloured flowers with unusual shapes. Most species grow on other plants.

They have short stems and erect or slightly spreading leaves. The sepals are united at their bases and have one or more long taillike extensions.

Masdevallia
Walter Dawn

Masefield, John (b. June 1, 1878, Ledbury, Herefordshire, Eng.—d. May 12, 1967, near Abingdon, Berkshire), poet, best known for his poems of the sea, *Salt-Water Ballads* (1902, including "Sea Fever" and "Cargoes"), and for his long narrative poems, such as *The Everlasting Mercy* (1911), which shocked literary orthodoxy with its phrases of a colloquial coarseness hitherto unknown in 20th-century English verse.

Educated at King's School, Warwick, Masefield was apprenticed aboard a windjammer that sailed around Cape Horn. He left the sea after that voyage and spent several years living precariously in the United States. His work there in a carpet factory is described in his autobiography, *In the Mill* (1941). He returned to England, worked for a time as a journalist for the *Manchester Guardian,* and settled in London. After he succeeded Robert Bridges as poet laureate in 1930, his poetry became more austere.

Other of Masefield's long narrative poems are *Dauber* (1913), which concerns the eternal struggle of the visionary against ignorance and materialism, and *Reynard the Fox* (1919), which deals with many aspects of rural life in England. He also wrote novels of adventure—*Sard Harker* (1924), *Odtaa* (1926), and *Basilissa* (1940)—sketches, and works for children. His other works include the poetic

Masefield, 1961
Camera Press

dramas *The Tragedy of Nan* (1909) and *The Tragedy of Pompey the Great* (1910) and a further autobiographical volume, *So Long to Learn* (1952). Masefield was awarded the Order of Merit in 1935.

Constance Babington Smith's biography of Masefield was published in 1978.

maser, device that produces and amplifies electromagnetic radiation mainly in the microwave region of the spectrum. The maser operates according to the same basic principle as the laser (the name of which is formed from the acronym for "light amplification by stimulated emission of radiation") and shares many of its characteristics. The first maser was built by the American physicist Charles H. Townes and his colleagues in 1953. The name is an acronym derived from "microwave (or molecular) amplification by stimulated emission of radiation."

A maser oscillator requires a source of excited atoms or molecules and a resonator to store their radiation. The excitation must force more atoms or molecules into the upper energy level than in the lower, in order for amplification by stimulated emission to predominate over absorption. For wavelengths of a few millimetres or longer, the resonator can be a metal box whose dimensions are chosen so that only one of its modes of oscillation coincides with the frequency emitted by the atoms; that is, the box is resonant at the particular frequency, much as a kettle drum is resonant at some particular audio frequency. The losses of such a resonator can be made quite small, so that radiation can be stored long enough to stimulate emission from successive atoms as they are excited. Thus, all the atoms are forced to emit in such a way as to augment this stored wave. Output is obtained by allowing some radiation to escape through a small hole in the resonator.

The first maser used a beam of ammonia molecules that passed along the axis of a cylindrical cage of metal rods, with alternate rods having positive and negative electric charge. The nonuniform electric field from the rods sorted out the excited from the unexcited molecules, focusing the excited molecules through a small hole into the resonator. The output was less than one microwatt (10^{-6} watt) of power, but the wavelength, being determined primarily by the ammonia molecules, was so constant and reproducible that it could be used to control a clock that would gain or lose no more than a second in several hundred years. This maser can also be used as a microwave amplifier. Maser amplifiers have the advantage that they are much quieter than those that use vacuum tubes or transistors; that is, they add very little noise to the signal being amplified. Very weak signals can thus be utilized. The ammonia maser amplifies only a very narrow band of frequencies and is not tunable, however, so that it has largely been superseded by other kinds, such as solid-state ruby masers.

Solid-state and traveling-wave masers. Amplification of radio waves over a wide band of frequencies can be obtained in several kinds of solid-state masers, most commonly crystals such as ruby at low temperatures. Suitable materials contain ions (atoms with an electrical charge) whose energy levels can be shifted by a magnetic field so as to tune the substance to amplify the desired frequency. If the ions have three or more energy levels suitably spaced, they can be raised to one of the higher levels by absorbing radio waves of the proper frequency.

The amplifying crystal may be operated in a resonator that, as in the ammonia maser, stores the wave and so gives it more time to interact with the amplifying medium. A large amplifying bandwidth and easier tunability are obtained with traveling-wave masers. In these, a rod of a suitable crystal, such as ruby, is positioned inside a wave-guide structure that is designed to cause the wave to travel relatively slowly through the crystal.

Solid masers have been used to amplify the faint signals returned from such distant targets as satellites in radar and communications. Their sensitivity is especially important for such applications because signals coming from space are usually very weak. Moreover, there is little interfering background noise when a directional antenna is pointed at the sky, and the highest sensitivity can be used. In radio astronomy, masers made possible the measurement of the faint radio waves emitted by the planet Venus, giving the first indication of its temperature.

Gas masers. Generation of radio waves by stimulated emission of radiation has been achieved in several gases in addition to ammonia. Hydrogen cyanide molecules have been used to produce a wavelength of 3.34 mm. Like the ammonia maser, this maser uses electric fields to select the excited molecules.

One of the best fundamental standards of frequency or time is the atomic hydrogen maser introduced by American scientists N.F. Ramsey, H.M. Goldenberg, and D. Kleppner in 1960. Its output is a radio wave whose frequency of 1,420,405,751.786 hertz (cycles per second) is reproducible with an accuracy of one part in 30×10^{12}. A clock controlled by such a maser would not get out of step more than one second in 100,000 years.

In the hydrogen maser, hydrogen atoms are produced in a discharge and, like the molecules of the ammonia maser, are formed into a beam from which those in excited states are selected and admitted to a resonator. To improve the accuracy, the resonance of each atom is examined over a relatively long time. This is done by using a very large resonator containing a storage bulb. The walls of the bulb are coated so that the atoms can bounce repeatedly against the walls with little disturbance of their frequency.

Another maser standard of frequency or time uses vapour of the element rubidium at a low pressure, contained in a transparent cell. When the rubidium is illuminated by suitably filtered light from a rubidium lamp, the atoms are excited to emit a frequency of 6.835 gigahertz (6.835×10^9 hertz). As the cell is enclosed in a cavity resonator with openings for the pumping light, emission of radio waves from these excited atoms is stimulated.

(Ar.L.S./Ed.)

Maseru, capital and only urban centre of Lesotho. It is on the left bank of the Caledon River near the border with Free State, Republic of South Africa. In 1869 the chief of the Basotho (Sotho) nation, Mshweshwe I, founded the town near his mountain stronghold of Thaba Bosiu; few of the 19th-century buildings remain. Lesotho is linked with the South African railway system by a short line from Maseru to Marseilles on the Bloemfontein-Natal main line, thus providing an outlet for farm produce, trade, and the transport of labourers. Maseru, in turn, is linked by road and airstrips to other areas of mountainous Lesotho and by scheduled air service to Johannesburg.

The National Assembly chamber buildings and the High Court buildings of Lesotho are there, as are Radio Lesotho, an African high school, a technical school, and the Lesotho Agricultural College, founded in 1955. The town of Roma, 15 miles (24 km) southeast of Maseru, is the site of the National University of Lesotho (established 1975). Pop. (1996 est.) city, 160,100; (1999 est.) Maseru-Roma-Morija metropolitan area, 373,000.

A handicraft centre, Maseru, Lesotho
Authenticated News International

Consult the INDEX *first*

Masham, Abigail, BARONESS MASHAM OF OTES, *née* HILL (d. Dec. 6, 1734), favourite of Queen Anne of England. That she turned against both her patrons—Sarah Jennings, Duchess of Marlborough, and Robert Harley, Earl of Oxford—has led historians to speak harshly of her, but Jonathan Swift, who knew her intimately, spoke highly of her character and abilities.

She was the daughter of Francis Hill, a Levant merchant, who was ruined by speculation; he left four children, for whom their cousin Lady Churchill (the future Duchess of Marlborough) sought to provide. Through her influence Abigail Hill entered the household of Queen Anne and began, by compliant temper and Tory views, to supplant the Duchess of Marlborough in the queen's affection. In June 1707 the Duke of Marlborough suspected her of using her influence with the queen in order to further the political ends of her cousin Robert Harley. Already Abigail Hill had been married secretly in the queen's presence to Samuel Masham (1679?–1758), a groom of the bedchamber to Anne's consort, Prince George of Denmark. Gradually an irreparable breach developed between the duchess and Mrs. Masham. After Harley fell from office (February 1708), he contrived to negotiate with the queen through Mrs. Masham, and in 1710 he arranged through her for the queen to dismiss her ministers. Mrs. Masham succeeded to the charge of the privy purse; her brother Jack became colonel, and her husband was among the 12 Tory peers created in 1712 to secure approval of the Treaty of Utrecht. (Her husband's title was Baron Masham of Otes.)

Lake Kariba (right), on the Zambezi River at Kariba, Mashonaland, Zimbabwe
E. Streichan—Shostal Associates

Soon, however, Lady Masham quarreled with Oxford and set herself to foster by all the means in her power the queen's growing personal distaste for her minister. Oxford's vacillation between the Jacobites and the adherents of the Hanoverian succession to the crown probably strengthened the opposition of Lady Masham, who now warmly favoured the Jacobite party led by Viscount Bolingbroke and Francis Atterbury. Altercations took place in the queen's presence between Lady Masham and the minister; and finally, on July 27, 1714, Anne dismissed Oxford from his office of lord high treasurer and, three days later, gave the post to the Duke of Shrewsbury. Anne died on August 1, and Lady Masham then retired to private life.

Masham (of Swinton), Samuel Cunliffe Lister, 1st Baron (b. Jan. 1, 1815, Calverley Hall, near Bradford, Yorkshire, Eng.—d. Feb. 2, 1906, Swinton Park, Yorkshire), English inventor whose contributions included a wool-combing machine that helped to lower the price of clothing and a silk-combing machine that utilized silk waste.

In 1838 Samuel and his brother John opened a worsted mill in Manningham. He had worked on a machine to comb wool so that the long hairs would be separated from the short, thus allowing their use for different kinds of textiles, and eventually he evolved a successful machine from an earlier, inefficient device built by another inventor. Its success contributed greatly to the development of Australian sheep farming. In time he had nine combing mills operating at once—five in England, one in Germany, and three in France. In 1855 he began to direct his efforts toward the utilization of waste silk. After 10 years and great expense, he developed a machine for making silk waste into goods that could compete with those manufactured from the perfect cocoon; moreover, the products could be sold at many times the cost of production. His velvet loom for making piled fabrics was another important textile machine.

He was created Baron Masham in 1891.

Mashhad (Iran): *see* Meshed.

Mashonaland, traditional region in northeastern Zimbabwe, bordering Zambia to the north and Mozambique to the northeast and east. It is the traditional homeland of the Shona (*q.v.*), a Bantu-speaking people who are subsistence farmers, live in villages, and raise some cattle.

Mashonaland consists largely of the northeastern part of Zimbabwe's Middle Veld, a wide plateau lying at an elevation of between 3,000 and 4,000 feet (900 and 1,200 m) that slopes down northward to the Zambezi River valley. The region is drained by tributaries of the Zambezi River. The northern part of man-made Lake Kariba, on the Zambezi, is located in western Mashonaland. The region is predominantly savanna (tropical grassland) country with some savanna woodland.

Mashonaland was given its name by Europeans in the mid-19th century. In 1890 the British South Africa Company, a mercantile company based in London, established a fort at the spot where the Company's Pioneer Column halted its march northward into Mashonaland. The fort (later to become the city of Salisbury [now Harare]) was named for Lord Salisbury, then British prime minister, and used as a foothold for further British occupation of the territory. Later in the 1890s, what is now Zimbabwe was divided by the British South Africa Company into two provinces, Mashonaland in the east and Matabeleland (the lands inhabited by the Ndebele people) in the west. Mashonaland, part of self-governing Southern Rhodesia after 1923, became part of independent Zimbabwe in 1980.

Mashrafah, Al- (Syria): *see* Katna.

Mashriq, geographic region extending from the western border of Egypt to the western border of Iran. It includes the modern states of Egypt, The Sudan, Saudi Arabia, Yemen, Oman, Kuwait, United Arab Emirates, Israel, Jordan, Lebanon, Syria, and Iraq and covers an area of approximately 2,700,000 square miles (7,000,000 square km).

The Mashriq comprises two major physical regions. One consists of barren desert areas that are dominated by the great plateau of the Arabian Peninsula and that support the nomadic Bedouin people. Average summer temperatures in this region exceed 120° F (48.9° C). The other region consists of the rich and fertile territory that is generally defined by the Fertile Crescent. Long considered to have been the "cradle of civilization," the Fertile Crescent extends in an arc from the Nile River valley through Israel, Lebanon, Jordan, and Syria and into Iraq. At either tip of the crescent is a river valley—that of the Tigris and Euphrates in the east and that of the Nile in the west—that is annually flooded and replenished with alluvium.

mashriq al-adhkār (Arabic: "place where the uttering of the name of God arises at dawn"), temple or house of worship in the Bahā'ī faith. The *mashriq* is characterized by a nine-sided construction, in keeping with the Bahā'ī belief in the mystical properties of the number

The Bahā'ī house of worship, Wilmette, Ill.
By courtesy of the National Baha'i Public Information Office

nine. Free of ritual and clergy, the *mashriq* is open to adherents of all religions and offers a simple service consisting of readings from the sacred Bahā'ī writings and the holy books of other faiths. The Bahā'ī faithful envision a *mashriq* in every sizeable community, serving as the focal point of a social centre that would include a hospital, orphanage, dispensary, and school.

The first *mashriq* was completed in 1907 in 'Ishqābād, modern Turkmenistan. In 1928, however, it was appropriated by the Soviet government and leased to the temple organization. Ten years later it was seized and converted into an art gallery. In 1963, having suffered severe damage in a 1948 earthquake, the structure was demolished. By the 1970s, however, several other temples had been built, including those in Wilmette, Ill., U.S.; Frankfurt am Main; Sydney; Kampala, Uganda; and Panama City, Panama.

Mashtots (monk): *see* Mesrob, Saint.

Masina (Africa): *see* Macina.

Masinissa, also spelled MASSINISSA (b. *c.* 240 BC—d. 148), ruler of the North African kingdom of Numidia, and an ally of Rome in the last years of the Second Punic War (218–201). His influence was lasting because the economic and political development that took place in Numidia under his rule provided the base for later development of the region by the Romans.

Masinissa was the son of the chieftain of a Numidian tribal group, the Massyli. Brought up in Carthage, of which his father was an ally, he fought for Carthage against the Romans in Spain from 212 to 206. When the Carthaginians were driven from Spain in 206, Masinissa switched sides and assisted Rome in the invasion of Carthaginian territory in Africa. Meanwhile, his father had died; the Romans thereafter supported his claim to the Numidian throne against Syphax, pro-Carthaginian ruler of the Massaesyli tribe.

After the defeat of Syphax and the Carthaginians, Masinissa became king of both the Massyli and the Massaesyli. He showed unconditional loyalty to Rome, and his position in Africa was strengthened by a clause in the peace treaty of 201 between Rome and Carthage prohibiting the latter from going to war even in self-defense without Roman permission. This enabled Masinissa to encroach on the remaining Carthaginian territory as long as he judged that Rome wished to see Carthage weakened.

Masinissa's chief aim was to build a strong and unified state from the semi-nomadic Numidian tribes. To this end he introduced Carthaginian agricultural techniques and forced many Numidians to settle as peasant farmers. Any hopes he may have had of extending his rule across North Africa were dashed when a Roman commission headed by the elderly Marcus Porcius Cato came to Africa about 155 to decide a territorial dispute between Masinissa and Carthage. Animated probably by an irrational fear of a Carthaginian revival, but possibly by suspicion of Masinissa's ambitions, Cato thenceforward advocated, finally with success, the destruction of Carthage. Masinissa showed his displeasure when the Roman army arrived in Africa in 149, but he died early in 148 without a breach in the alliance.

Maṣīrah, also spelled MASIRA, island of Oman, in the Arabian Sea, off the country's southeastern coast. The island is separated from the mainland by the narrow Tur'at (channel) Maṣīrah. There is an airfield, occupied by the British until the late 1970s, at the northern tip. The Gulf of Masira lies between the island (north) and the Ra's (cape) al-Madrakah (south). Maṣīrah is the habitat of large colonies of turtles. There are several very small towns on the island's coast.

Masjed Soleymān, also spelled MASJID-I SULAIMAN, town, southwestern Iran. Oil was discovered at Masjed Soleymān in 1908, and the town early became one of Iran's leading

Oil tank and pipelines at Masjed Soleymān, Iran
Fred J. Maroon—Photo Researchers

oil centres. Pipelines, built in 1909–10, link the town with Abadan, 125 miles (200 km) southwest. Pop. (1986) 104,787.

masjid: *see* mosque.

Masjid-i-Jami: *see* Eṣfahan, Great Mosque of.

mask, type of disguise, commonly an object worn over or in front of the face to hide the identity of the wearer. The features of the mask not only conceal those of the wearer but also project the image of another personality or being. This dual function is a basic characteristic of masks.

A brief account of masks follows. For full treatment, *see* MACROPAEDIA: Masks.

Men have made and used masks imbued with symbolism and ascribed spiritual power since the Stone Age. The greatest range of mask forms and functions occurs in Africa and in Oceania. It is only since the end of the 19th century, however, that masks began to be exhibited and collected as art objects in their own right or as cultural artifacts.

Masks vary widely in materials, construction techniques, appearance, colour, and sophistication. They can be made of wood, stone, leather, paper, ivory, cloth, or even silver or gold and are often adorned with paint, mosaic, shells, or carving. Frequently, they are part of an entire costume that covers the body of the wearer. Masks may derive their features from human or animal forms. In most cases, as for example among various African cultures, the form of the mask is dictated by tradition, and many restrictions and taboos limit the mask designer. The spirit represented by the mask is usually thought to exist in its image, and for this reason the mask maker is obliged to adhere to conventional and symbolic forms and imagery. The completed mask is thought to have supernatural or spirit power quite separate from the maker or the wearer. Within the traditional imagery and convention, the mask maker can exercise his skill as an artist and craftsman to give his own creative interpretation to the standardized forms. The mask wearer is like an actor who loses his own identity when he dons the mask. For cultures without written histories, the mask often gives a sense of continuity with the past, as its imagery and symbolism refer back to earlier times. The mask forms part of a traditional ritual that associates the spectators psychologically with the past. The spirits represented by masks may be respected and powerful or evil and harmful. They may provoke emotions ranging from pleasure to terror. The ritual meaning of a mask can be appreciated only with a knowledge of its particular cultural context, though the aesthetic qualities may be enjoyed without any understanding of the mask's social and cultural function.

In primitive societies, masks are frequently associated with the ritual of secret societies or with the high priest or medicine man. The practice of totemism, whereby a natural object such as an animal or bird is adopted as the emblem of a family line, has led to the evolution of totem masks. These have been used by the Indians of the northwestern coast of the United States and also by some African cultures.

Funerary masks and death masks were used in ancient Egypt and were associated with the return of the spirit to the body. Such masks were generalized portraits and, in the case of nobility, were made of precious metals. Gold death masks also occur in Asia and in the Inca civilization. From Roman times onward, death masks were sometimes made and kept as portraits of the dead person.

Some masks have been primarily designed to provide physical protection. Mask helmets with frightening expressions were worn by Japanese samurai (warriors). Fencers and other sportsmen may wear masks to protect their faces.

Masks are also worn on festive occasions, such as Halloween and Mardi Gras. Festival masks commonly have comic or satiric features and are conducive to good-natured license and ribaldry.

Masks as theatrical devices, to represent characters, evolved from religious traditions of ancient Greek civilization. In medieval mystery plays, papier-mâché masks portrayed evil and grotesque spirits such as sin and the devil. In the Italian Renaissance, the mask became an important feature of the commedia dell'arte, in which the actors were masked to hide their identities. The small black mask worn over the eyes, often called the masquerade mask, originates from this tradition. Wooden masks coated with plaster and painted white, red, or black (the different colours symbolizing such concepts as corruption, righteousness, and villainy) are still important aspects of the Nō drama of Japan. Nō masks are rigidly conventional and stylized. In China and in the Kabuki theatre of Japan, the actual face of the actor is painted to resemble a mask—as is that of the circus clown in the West.

mask (theatre): *see* masque.

Maskelyne, John Nevil (b. Dec. 22, 1839, Cheltenham, Gloucestershire, Eng.—d. May 18, 1917, London), British magician whose inventions and patronage of new performers greatly influenced the development of the art of producing illusions by sleight of hand.

Trained as a watchmaker, Maskelyne became famous in 1865 when he exposed the Davenport Brothers as fraudulent spiritualists. For eight years he and George A. Cooke toured with a show featuring Maskelyne's box trick, juggling, and automata. After Cooke died in 1904, Maskelyne took as a partner David Devant, the most famous magician in England. He and Devant collaborated on *Our Magic* (1911), an important source book on the theory of magic.

A list of the abbreviations used in the MICROPAEDIA *will be found at the end of this volume*

Maskelyne, Nevil (b. Oct. 6, 1732, London—d. Feb. 9, 1811, Greenwich, London), British astronomer noted for his contribution to the science of navigation.

Maskelyne was ordained a minister in 1755, but his interest in astronomy had been aroused by the eclipse of July 25, 1748. In 1758 he was admitted to the Royal Society of London, which in 1761 sent him to the island of St. Helena to observe a transit of Venus.

Maskelyne, detail from an engraving by E. Scriven after a portrait by Vanderburgh

By courtesy of the trustees of the British Museum; photograph, J.R. Freeman & Co. Ltd.

During the voyage he experimented with the determination of longitude by observations of the Moon's position and introduced this method into navigation by publishing *The British Mariner's Guide* (1763). Succeeding Nathaniel Bliss as astronomer royal in 1765, he published the first volume of the *Nautical Almanac* in 1766 and continued the supervision of the almanac until his death.

Maskelyne suggested to the Royal Society an experiment for determining the Earth's density with the use of a plumb line. He carried out the experiment two years later in Scotland on Schiehallion Mountain, North Perthshire. From his observations, it was found that the Earth's density is approximately 4.5 times that of water. He was also the first to make time measurements that were accurate to the nearest tenth of a second.

Maskhūṭah, Tall al- (ancient Egyptian city): *see* Pithom.

Maslow, Abraham H(arold) (b. April 1, 1908, New York City—d. June 8, 1970, Menlo Park, Calif., U.S.), U.S. psychologist and philosopher best known for his self-actualization theory of psychology, which argued that the primary goal of psychotherapy should be the integration of the self.

Maslow studied psychology at the University of Wisconsin and Gestalt psychology at the New School for Social Research in New York City before joining the faculty of Brooklyn College in 1937. In 1951 he became head of the psychology department at Brandeis University (Waltham, Mass.), where he remained until 1969.

In his major works, *Motivation and Personality* (1954) and *Toward a Psychology of Being* (1962), Maslow argued that each person has a hierarchy of needs that must be satisfied, ranging from basic physiological requirements to love, esteem, and, finally, self-actualization. As each need is satisfied, the next higher level in the emotional hierarchy dominates conscious functioning; thus, people who lack food or shelter or who cannot feel themselves to be in a safe environment are unable to express higher needs. Maslow believed that truly healthy people satisfied even the highest psychological needs and were self-actualizers, fully integrating the components of their personality, or self. His papers, published posthumously, were issued in 1971 as *The Farther Reaches of Human Nature.*

Maso DI BANCO (fl. *c.* 1325–53), Florentine painter who was the most talented of Giotto's pupils. Maso's work displays a style that effectively and intelligently incorporated the teachings of the master. It was the work of Maso that Ghiberti singled out in the 15th century for praise. Maso is mentioned in connection with the Bardi family in a document of 1341. It was a member of this family that provided for the foundation of a chapel bearing the family name. The Bardi di Vernio chapel in Sta. Croce was largely decorated by Maso di Banco. The frescoes representing five scenes from the legend of St. Sylvester possess clarity of design and harmony of colour. The architectural settings and figures in the "St. Sylvester Resurrecting the Ox" and "St. Sylvester Resurrecting the Two Magi Killed by a Dragon" anticipate the monumental style of Masaccio and Piero della Francesca.

Maso's elegance, the suaveness of his contours, and his use of colour display elements of Sienese and Florentine influence, yet his style always remained severe and monumental like that of Giotto. He became a distinguished master in Florence, though he had few followers.

masochism, psychosexual disorder in which erotic release is achieved through having pain inflicted on oneself. The term derives from the name of Chevalier Leopold von Sacher-Masoch, an Austrian who wrote extensively about the satisfaction he gained by being beaten and subjugated. The amount of pain involved can vary from ritual humiliation with little violence to severe whipping or beating; generally the masochist retains some control over the situation and will end the abusive behaviour before becoming seriously injured. While pain may cause a certain amount of sexual excitement in many persons, for the masochist it becomes the chief end of sexual activity. The term is frequently used in a looser social context in which masochism is defined as the behaviour of one who seeks out and enjoys situations of humiliation or abuse.

Masochism as an isolated trait is fairly rare. More commonly, the association of pain with sexual pleasure takes the form of both masochism and sadism (*q.v.*), the obtaining of sexual pleasure through inflicting pain on others. Often, an individual will alternate roles, becoming aroused through the experience of pain in one instance and through the infliction of pain in another.

Masolino, original name TOMMASO DI CRISTOFORO FINI (b. 1383, Panicale, near Perugia, Romagna—d. probably 1440–47, Florence), painter who achieved a compromise between the International Gothic manner and the advanced early Renaissance style of his own day and who owes his prominence in the history of Florentine art not to his innovations but to his lyrical style and his unfailing artistry.

Masolino came from the same district of Tuscany as his younger contemporary Masaccio (*q.v.*), with whom his career was closely linked. Trained in a Florentine studio, possibly that of Gherardo Starnina, he appears before 1407 to have been a member of the workshop of Lorenzo Ghiberti. His earliest works include the "Madonna of Humility" (Alte Pinakothek, Munich), probably painted *c.* 1424, and a "Virgin and Child" (Kunsthalle, Bremen), dated 1423. In 1424 he received payment for frescoes in S. Stefano at Empoli (in large part destroyed).

The first known work to display the fundamental antithesis between the decorative late Gothic style of Masolino and the more progressive early Renaissance style of Masaccio is a "Virgin and Child with St. Anne" (*c.* 1420; Uffizi, Florence). It is thought that this work may be the result of a collaboration of the two artists.

The influence on Masolino of the stronger and more decisive personality of Masaccio reached its climax in the frescoes of scenes from the life of St. Peter in the Brancacci Chapel in the Church of the Carmine in Florence. There have been many opinions about the respective shares of the two artists in this important cycle. It is likely that the frescoes were commissioned from Masolino about

"Baptism of Christ," fresco by Masolino, completed 1435; in the Baptistery, Castiglione Olona, Italy

SCALA—Art Resource/EB Inc.

1425 and that at this time he painted some lost scenes in the upper register of the chapel walls. Thereafter he worked in Hungary, from which he returned in 1427 to undertake, jointly with Masaccio, the remaining frescoes in the chapel. By this time the balance of emphasis within the studio had shifted toward Masaccio, and Masolino was responsible for only one fresco, that of "St. Peter Preaching," on the altar wall, and three scenes on the right wall, the "Fall of Adam and Eve," the "Healing of the Lame Man," and the "Raising of Tabitha," where the perspective scheme seems to have been worked out and in part realized by Masaccio.

Work on the Brancacci frescoes was abandoned in 1428, and probably at this time Masolino received the commission for a fresco cycle in the Chapel of St. Catherine in S. Clemente in Rome and possibly executed his double-sided triptych for Sta. Maria Maggiore in Rome. The two central panels of this altarpiece, representing the foundation of Sta. Maria Maggiore and the Assumption of the Virgin (Museo e Gallerie Nazionali di Capodimonte, Naples), are among Masolino's most distinguished panel paintings. The death of Masaccio in Rome in the autumn of 1428 marks a turning point in Masolino's career, and the story of his later development is that of a progressive return to the International Gothic idiom of his youth. This is evident initially in the S. Clemente frescoes (where the space construction is once more decorative and systematized) and subsequently in a frescoed "Virgin and Child" in S. Fortunato at Todi (1432) and in fresco cycles in the Baptistery (completed 1435) and Collegiata at Castiglione Olona. The extensive panoramas in the backgrounds of the "Crucifixion" on the altar wall in S. Clemente and the "Baptism of Christ" at Castiglione Olona are milestones in the history of landscape painting. With their light tonality and elegant, rhythmical figures, the scenes by Masolino in the Baptistery and Collegiata form two of the most fascinating fresco cycles of the 15th century.

Mason, an adherent of Freemasonry (*q.v.*).

Mason, Daniel Gregory (b. Nov. 20, 1873, Brookline, Mass., U.S.—d. Dec. 4, 1953, Greenwich, Conn.), composer in the German-influenced Boston group of U.S. composers.

Mason was the grandson of the music publisher and educator Lowell Mason and the son of Henry Mason, a founder of the Mason

Daniel Mason, 1938

By courtesy of the Library of Congress, Washington, D.C.

& Hamlin Co. piano firm. He studied with John K. Paine at Harvard and with Vincent d'Indy in Paris. From 1910 to 1942 he taught at Columbia University. His music was conservative in form and shows strong influence of the German Romantic composers. He also employed some devices of French Impressionism and Russian Modernism. His works include three symphonies, chamber works, and the overture *Chanticleer*, for which he is best remembered. He published several books of essays and teaching guides.

Mason, George (b. 1725, Fairfax County, Va.—d. Oct. 7, 1792, Fairfax County, Va., U.S.), American patriot and statesman who insisted on the protection of individual liberties in the composition of both the Virginia and U.S. Constitutions (1776, 1787); he was

George Mason, detail of an oil painting by L. Guillaume after a portrait by J. Hesselius; in the collection of the Virginia Historical Society

By courtesy of the Virginia Historical Society

ahead of his time in opposing slavery and in rejecting the constitutional compromise that perpetuated it.

As a landowner and near neighbour of George Washington, Mason took a leading part in local affairs. He also became deeply interested in Western expansion and was active in the Ohio Company, organized in 1749 to develop trade and sell land on the upper Ohio River. At about the same time, Mason helped to found the town of Alexandria, Va. Because of ill health and family problems, he generally eschewed public office, though he accepted election to the House of Burgesses in 1759. Except for his membership in the Constitutional Convention at Philadelphia, this was the highest office he ever held—yet few men did more to shape U.S. political institutions.

A leader of the Virginia patriots on the eve of the American Revolution (1775–83), Mason served on the Committee of Safety and in 1776 drafted the state constitution, his declaration of rights being the first authoritative formulation of the doctrine of inalienable rights. Mason's work was known to Thomas Jefferson and influenced his drafting of the Declaration of Independence. The model was soon followed by most of the states and was also incorporated in diluted form in the federal Constitution. He served as a member of the Virginia House of Delegates from 1776 to 1788.

As a member of the Constitutional Convention, Mason strenuously opposed the compromise permitting the continuation of the slave trade until 1808. Although he was a Southerner, Mason castigated the trade as "disgraceful to mankind"; he favoured manumission and education for bondsmen and supported a system of free labour. Because he also objected to the large and indefinite powers vested in the new government, he joined several other Virginians in opposing adoption of the new document. A Jeffersonian Republican, he believed that local government should be kept strong and central government weak. His criticism helped bring about the adoption of the Bill of Rights to the Constitution.

Soon after the Convention, Mason retired to his home, Gunston Hall.

Mason, James (b. May 15, 1909, Huddersfield, Yorkshire, Eng.—d. July 27, 1984, Lausanne, Switz.), British stage and motion-picture actor best known for his urbane characterizations. During his 50-year acting career he played in 106 films.

Mason studied architecture before trying for a theatrical career. Following four years as a stage actor, his first film was *Late Extra* (1935). From then on he became one of the busiest of motion-picture actors. He proved to have great depth as an actor, as shown in *The Seventh Veil* (1945) and *Odd Man Out* (1947).

Having expressed dissatisfaction with the British film industry, he began to make motion pictures in the United States, where he again often found himself at odds with the industry establishment. His memorable voice and good looks aided in his development as an actor adept in portraying flawed individuals. He is well remembered for his performances in *Madame Bovary* (1949), *The Desert Fox* (1951), *Five Fingers* (1952), *Julius Caesar* (1953), *A Star Is Born* (1954), *North by Northwest* (1959), *Lolita* (1962), *Georgy Girl* (1966), *The Boys from Brazil* (1978), and *The Verdict* (1982).

Mason, James Murray (b. Nov. 3, 1798, Fairfax County, Va., U.S.—d. April 28, 1871, Alexandria, Va.), antebellum U.S. senator from Virginia and, later, Confederate diplomat taken prisoner in the Trent Affair.

Although raised a Tidewater aristocrat, Mason graduated from the University of Pennsylvania and, after studying law at the College of William and Mary, set up his practice in the Virginia back country. He served in the state legislature from 1826 to 1832 (except for 1827) and one term in the U.S. House of Representatives (1837–39) before being appointed in 1847 to fill an unexpired Senate term.

Reelected for terms beginning in 1849 and 1855, Mason allied himself closely with other states'-rights Southern Democrats in the Senate. With Abraham Lincoln's election in 1860, Mason advocated Southern secession and resigned his Senate seat to join the Confederacy. He accepted appointment by Pres. Jefferson Davis to serve as Confederate commissioner to England. Accompanied by John Slidell, he sailed for England aboard the British ship "Trent." The "Trent" was captured at sea by a U.S. naval vessel, and the two Confederate diplomats were imprisoned for two months in Boston.

The Trent Affair nearly caused a severance of diplomatic relations between the U.S. and Great Britain. But on Jan. 1, 1862, Pres. Lincoln ordered the release of Mason and Slidell, and the two emissaries made their way to Europe. In England, however, Mason was able to make little progress in winning official support for the Confederate cause.

Mason did not return to North America until 1866, and he stayed in Canada—afraid of being arrested as an important official of the defeated Confederacy—until 1868. Following Pres. Andrew Johnson's second proclamation of amnesty in 1868, however, Mason returned to Virginia, where he lived his final years.

Mason, John Mitchell (b. March 19, 1770, New York City—d. Dec. 26, 1829, New York City), U.S. minister and educator, who is best known for his work in raising standards of Protestant theological education in the U.S. He also was noted for his prowess as an orator.

Mason developed a plan for theological education and in 1804 founded a seminary of the Associate Reformed Presbyterian Church in New York City. He believed that the entire student—body, mind, and spirit—should be strengthened, that Scriptures should be studied in their original languages, that a teacher should aid the student in making up his own mind, and that intellectual creativity was more important than the absorption of inflexible dogma. His collected writings were published in four volumes (1832; enlarged 1849).

Mason became president of Dickinson College, Carlisle, Pa. (1821–24); he was also a trustee (1795–1811, 1812–24) and provost (teacher and administrator) of Columbia College (1811–16). In addition, he served as pastor of two churches in New York City.

Mason, Lowell (b. Jan. 8, 1792, Medfield, Mass., U.S.—d. Aug. 11, 1872, Orange, N.J.), hymn composer, music publisher, and one of the founders of public-school music-education in the United States.

Mason went to Savannah, Ga., as a bank clerk and became choirmaster at the Independent Presbyterian Church in that city. In 1822 he returned to Boston and published his famous and profitable *The Handel and Haydn Society's Collection of Church Music*. Between 1829 and 1869 he published about 20 similar collections of hymns. These collections favoured adaptations of tunes by prominent European composers rather than the traditional rural hymn tunes.

In 1832 he founded the Boston Academy of Music, and in 1838 he established in Boston the first public-school music program in the United States. He was also influential in the training of music teachers. His compositions include the hymn tunes for "From Greenland's Icy Mountains," "Nearer, My God, to Thee," and "My Faith Looks Up to Thee."

Mason, Max (b. Oct. 26, 1877, Madison, Wis., U.S.—d. March 23, 1961, Claremont, Calif.), American mathematical physicist, educator, and science administrator.

Mason completed his undergraduate work at the University of Wisconsin (1898) and received his Ph.D. degree from the University of Göttingen in 1903. His first position, as an instructor in mathematics at the Massachusetts Institute of Technology, Cambridge (1903–04), ended with an appointment as an assistant professor of mathematics at the Sheffield Scientific School at Yale (1904–08). Mason then returned to his alma mater as professor of mathematical physics (1908–25). During World War I he invented several devices for submarine detection. He served as president of the University of Chicago (1925–28), then as director of natural sciences of the Rockefeller Foundation (1928–29), and as president of the foundation (1929–36). Mason's last major appointment was as a member of the executive council of the California Institute of Technology and chairman of its council to direct construction of the Palomar Observatory (completed in 1948).

Mason's special interest and contributions lay in mathematics (differential equations, calculus of variations), physics (electromagnetic theory), invention (acoustical compensators, submarine-detection devices), and the administration of universities and foundations. He was the author of *The New Haven Mathematical Colloquium* (1910) and contributed numerous papers on mathematical research and electromagnetic field theory to scientific journals.

Max Mason
The University of Chicago Archives

Mason and Dixon Line, originally the boundary in the United States between Maryland and Pennsylvania. In the pre-Civil War period it was regarded, together with the Ohio River, as the dividing line between slave states south of it and free-soil states north of it. Between 1765 and 1768 the 233-mile (375-kilometre) line was surveyed along the parallel 39°43′ by two Englishmen, Charles Mason and Jeremiah Dixon, to define the long-disputed boundaries of the overlapping land grants of the Penns, proprietors of Pennsylvania, and the Baltimores, proprietors of Maryland. The term "Mason and Dixon Line" was first used in congressional debates leading to the Missouri Compromise (1820). Today the Mason and Dixon Line still serves figuratively as the political and social dividing line between the North and the South.

Mason City, city, seat (1855) of Cerro Gordo county, north-central Iowa, U.S. It lies along the Winnebago River, 119 miles (192 km) north of Des Moines. Settled by Freemasons in 1853, its earlier names were Shibboleth and Masonic Grove. The city is underlain by deposits of clay and limestone and also has deposits of sand and gravel available, hence it supports a substantial cement industry. It also has one of the largest brick and drain-tile plants west of the Mississippi. Other industries in the city are farm-based. Mason City was the hometown of the composer Meredith Willson and was the "River City" of his highly successful Broadway musical *The Music Man* (1957). The city is the home of the North Iowa Area Community College (founded 1918). The resort area of Clear Lake is 10 miles (16 km) west. Inc. town, 1870; city, 1881. Pop. (1990) 29,040.

Mason ware, a sturdy English pottery known as Mason's Patent Ironstone China. It was first produced by C.J. Mason & Company in 1813 to provide a cheap substitute for Chinese porcelain, especially the larger vases. The decoration was a kind of chinoiserie, or hybrid Oriental. Mason specialties were vases, some more than 3 feet (1 m) high, with flowers in high relief and handles and knobs shaped like dragons; exceptionally large dinner services; and a typical hexagonal jug with snake handle made in various sizes. Mason also made chimneypieces.

masonry, the art and craft of building and fabricating in stone, clay, brick, or concrete block. Construction of poured concrete, reinforced or unreinforced, is often also considered masonry.

The art of masonry originated when early man sought to supplement his valuable but rare natural caves with artificial caves made from piles of stone. Circular stone huts, partially dug into the ground, dating from prehistoric times have been found in the Aran Islands, Ireland. By the 4th millennium BC, Egypt had developed an elaborate stonemasonry technique, culminating in the most extravagant of all ancient structures, the pyramids.

The choice of masonry materials has always been influenced by the prevailing geological formations and conditions in a given area. Egyptian temples, for example, were constructed of limestone, sandstone, alabaster, granite, basalt, and porphyry quarried from the hills along the Nile River. Another ancient centre of civilization, the area of western Asia between the Tigris and Euphrates, lacked stone outcroppings but was rich in clay deposits. As a result, the masonry structures of the Assyrian and Persian empires were constructed of sun-dried bricks faced with kiln-burned, sometimes glazed, units.

Stone and clay continued to be the primary masonry materials through the Middle Ages and later. A significant development in masonry construction in ancient times was the invention of concrete by the Romans. Although well-cut blocks of stone masonry could be erected without benefit of mortar, the Romans recognized the value of cement, which they made from pozzolanic tuff, a volcanic ash. Mixed with water, lime, and stone fragments, the cement was expanded into concrete. Walls of this concrete, faced with various stone or fired-clay materials, were more economical and faster to erect than walls made of stone blocks.

Because it provided more freedom in shaping structures, concrete helped the Romans develop the arch into one of the great basic construction forms. Prior to the arch, all builders in stone had been handicapped by the stone's fundamental lack of tensile strength—that is, its tendency to break under its own weight when supported on widely separated piers or walls. The Egyptians had roofed temples with stone slabs but had been forced to place the supporting columns close together. The Greeks had used wooden roof beams covered with thin stone; such beams were subject to weather and fire. The Roman arch avoided tension entirely, keeping all the masonry in compression, from the keystone to the piers. Stone in compression has great strength, and the Romans built huge arched bridges and aqueducts in large numbers. Extending their arch into a tunnel, they invented the barrel vault, with which they successfully roofed such buildings as the Temple of Venus in Rome. Several arches intersecting at a common keystone could be used to form a dome, such as that of the Pantheon in Rome. Two intersecting barrel vaults gave rise to the groin vault, which was used in some of the great Roman public baths.

The Roman arch underwent a significant modification in the Middle Ages in the evolution of the pointed arch, which provided a strong skeleton resting on well-spaced piers. The massive, rigid masonry structures of the Romans gave way to soaring vaults supported by external flying buttresses (external bracing). The use of smaller-sized stones and thick mortar joints created an elastic, slender structure that stressed the masonry to its fullest. The bearing of unit upon unit required the use of mortar to distribute the contact stresses.

With the advent of Gothic forms, masonry construction in a historic sense had solved the problem of spanning space entirely by material in compression, the only design formula suitable to stone. With the advent of the truss in the 16th century, the rise of scientific structural analysis in the 17th century, and the development of high-tensile resistant materials (steel and reinforced concrete) in the 19th century, the importance of masonry as a practical material for spanning space declined. It owes its revival largely to the invention of portland cement, the principal ingredient of concrete, which in the 20th century returned unit masonry to its essentially pre-Roman role of forming vertical wall enclosures, partitions, and facings.

Masonry construction begins with extractive materials, such as clay, sand, gravel, and stone, usually mined from surface pits or quarries. The most widely used rocks are granite (igneous), limestone and sandstone (sedimentary), and marble (metamorphic). In addition to rocks, clays of varying types are manufactured into bricks and tiles. Concrete blocks are fabricated from cement, sand, aggregate, and water.

For the shaping and dressing of stone a great variety of tools can be used. These range from such hand-held tools as hammers, mallets, chisels, and gouges to machines including frame and circular saws, molding and surfacing machines, and lathes. There are also various appliances for handling stone at the building site, ranging from different forms of light hand tackle to machine-driven cranes.

Many architects value masonry for its colour, scale, texture, pattern, and look of permanence. In addition to its aesthetic appeal, masonry has a number of other desirable properties, such as its value in controlling sound, resisting fire, and insulating against daily fluctuations in temperature.

In 20th-century housing, masonry is frequently used over wood-stud construction. Cavity walls, highly resistant to moisture, are often built of two vertical layers of masonry separated by a layer of insulating material. Foundations may be built of concrete blocks, and many building codes require the use of masonry in fire walls.

Masoretic text (from Hebrew *masoreth,* "tradition"), traditional Hebrew text of the Jewish Bible, meticulously assembled and codified, and supplied with diacritical marks to enable correct pronunciation. This monumental work was begun around the 6th century AD and completed in the 10th by scholars at Talmudic academies in Babylonia and Palestine, in an effort to reproduce, as far as possible, the original text of the Hebrew Old Testament. Their intention was not to interpret the meaning of the Scriptures but to transmit to future generations the authentic Word of God. To this end they gathered manuscripts and whatever oral traditions were available to them.

The Masoretic text that resulted from their work shows that every word and every letter was checked with care. In Hebrew or Aramaic, they called attention to strange spellings and unusual grammar and noted discrepancies in various texts. Since texts traditionally omitted vowels in writing, the Masoretes introduced vowel signs to guarantee correct pronunciation. Among the various systems of vocalization that were invented, the one fashioned in the city of Tiberias, Galilee, eventually gained ascendancy. In addition, signs for stress and pause were added to the text to facilitate public reading of the Scriptures in the synagogue.

When the final codification of each section was complete, the Masoretes not only counted and noted down the total number of verses, words, and letters in the text but further indicated which verse, which word, and which letter marked the centre of the text. In this way any future emendation could be detected. The rigorous care given the Masoretic text in its preparation is credited for the remarkable consistency found in Old Testament Hebrew texts since that time. The Masoretic work enjoyed an absolute monopoly for 600 years, and experts have been astonished at the fidelity of the earliest printed version (late 15th century) to the earliest surviving codices (late 9th century). The Masoretic text is universally accepted as the authentic Hebrew Bible.

Masovia (Poland): *see* Mazovia.

Maspero, Gaston(-Camille-Charles) (b. June 23, 1846, Paris—d. June 30, 1916, Paris), French Egyptologist and director general of excavations and antiquities for the Egyptian government, who was responsible for locating a collective royal tomb of prime historic importance.

Maspero taught Egyptian language at Paris, from 1869 until his appointment as professor at the Collège de France in 1874. In November 1880 he went to Egypt as head of an archaeological mission that grew into the French Institute of Oriental Archaeology.

Succeeding Auguste Mariette as director general of excavations and antiquities (1881–86) for the Egyptian government, he recorded scenes and inscriptions from important tombs and continued Mariette's museum work and excavation of the pyramids at Ṣaqqārah. In 1881 his suspicion that a royal tomb had been discovered by grave robbers led to the apprehension of a thief who revealed a tomb secreted in a cliff near Dayr al-Baḥrī. It contained 40 mummies, including those of the pharaohs Seti I, Amenhotep I, Thutmose III, and Ramses II, in inscribed sarcophagi, as well as a profusion of decorative and funerary artifacts. Maspero's intensive study of these findings was published in *Les Momies royales de Deir-el-Bahari* (1889; "The Royal Mummies of Dayr al-Baḥrī").

After a period in Paris (1886–89), he returned to Egypt and began arranging and cataloging the now-vast collection of antiquities that he and his predecessor Mariette had amassed at a museum in the Būlāq district of Cairo. This collection became the nucleus of the Egyptian Museum, which Maspero helped found in 1902. During his second, long tenure as director general (1899–1914), Maspero regulated excavations, tried to prevent illicit trade in antiquities, sought to preserve and strengthen monuments, and directed the archaeological survey of Nubia. His writings include *Histoire ancienne des peuples de l'Orient classique,* 3 vol. (1895–97; "Ancient History of the Peoples of the Classic Orient"), *L'Archéologie égyptienne* (1887; "Egyptian Archaeology"), *Les Contes populaires de l'Égypte ancienne* (4th ed. 1914; "Popular Tales of Ancient Egypt"), and *Causeries d'Égypte* (1907; *New Light on Ancient Egypt*).

Maspero
H. Roger-Viollet

masque, also spelled MASK, festival or entertainment in which disguised participants offer gifts to their host and then join together for a ceremonial dance. A typical masque consisted of a band of costumed and masked persons of the same sex who, accompanied by torchbearers, arrived at a social gathering to dance and converse with the guests. The masque could be simply a procession of such persons introduced by a presenter, or it could be an elaborately staged show in which a brief lyrical drama heralded the appearance of masquers, who, having descended from their pageant to perform figured dances, reveled with the guests until summoned back into their pageant by farewell speeches and song. The theme of the drama presented during a masque was usually mythological, allegorical, or symbolic and was designed to be complimentary to the noble or royal host of the social gathering.

Most likely originating in primitive religious rites and folk ceremonies known as disguising, or mummery, masques evolved into elaborate court spectacles that, under various names, entertained royalty throughout Europe. In Renaissance Italy, under the patronage of Lorenzo de Medici, the *intermezzo* became known for its emphasis on song, dance, scenery, and stage machinery. No matter how literary, the *intermezzi* invariably included a dance or masked ball where the guests mingled with the actors. A nondramatic form, the *trionfe,* or triumph, evolved from these Italian court masques and, arriving in France, gave rise to the *ballet de cour* and the more spectacular masquerade.

During the 16th century the European continental masque traveled to Tudor England, where it became a court entertainment played before the king. Gorgeous costumes, spectacular scenery with elaborate machinery to move it on- and offstage, and rich allegorical verse marked the English masque. During the reign of Elizabeth I the masque provided a vehicle for compliments paid to the queen at her palace and during her summer tours through England. Under the Stuarts the masque reached its zenith when Ben Jonson became court poet. He endowed the form with great literary as well as social force. In 1605 Jonson and the scene designer Inigo Jones produced the first of many excellent masques, which they continued to collaborate on until 1634. Jonson invented the antimasque—also known as the antemasque, the false masque, and the antic masque—and produced the first in 1609. It took place before the main masque and concentrated on grotesque elements, in direct contrast to the elegance of the masque that followed. In later years the masque developed into opera, and the antimasque became primarily a farce or pantomime. After Jonson's retirement, masques lost their literary value and became mainly vehicles for spectacle. Masque entertainments in England ceased with the beginning of the Civil War, and later revivals never equaled their precursors. Although not treated as part of the history of drama itself, the masque's influence on ballet, opera, and pantomime make it important to theatre history.

Detail of a design by Inigo Jones for a procession in *The Mask of Augures* by Ben Jonson, 1622; in the Devonshire Collections, Chatsworth House, Derbyshire
Reproduced by permission of the Trustees of the Chatsworth Settlement

mass, the celebration of the Eucharist (*q.v.*) in the Roman Catholic church. The term mass is derived from the rite's Latin formula of dismissal, *Ite, missa est* ("Go, it is ended"). According to Roman Catholic teaching, the mass is a memorial in which the death and Resurrection of Jesus Christ are sacramentally reenacted; it is a true sacrifice in which the body and blood of Jesus, under the appearances of bread and wine, are offered to God; and it is a sacred meal in which the community symbolically expresses its unity and its dependence upon God and seeks nourishment in its attempt to bring the gospel message to all men. The mass consists of two parts: the liturgy of the Word, which includes readings from Scripture and the homily (sermon), and the liturgy of the Eucharist, which includes the offertory, the eucharistic prayer (canon), and the communion. The rite was changed greatly after the second Vatican Council (1962–65), most conspicuously in the use of vernacular languages in place of the traditional Latin.

mass, in music, the setting, either polyphonic or in plainchant, of the liturgy of the Eucharist. The term most commonly refers to the mass of the Roman Catholic church, whose Western traditions used texts in Latin from about the 4th century to 1966, when the use of the vernacular was mandated. The Anglican mass, commonly called communion service, contains the same elements but has usually been sung in the English translation from the Book of Common Prayer. The Lutheran mass consists of the first two elements of the Roman mass, the Kyrie and the Gloria. In modern times other Protestant churches have borrowed freely from musical masses for their own liturgical uses and for special music. (For the Eastern traditions *see* Byzantine chant; Armenian chant; Ethiopian chant; Coptic chant; Syrian chant.)

The Ordinary. The Ordinary of the mass employs texts that remain the same for every mass. Those sung by the choir are, in the Latin mass, the Kyrie, Gloria, Credo, Sanctus (sometimes divided into Sanctus and Benedictus), and Agnus Dei, although the intonations of Gloria and Credo are sung by the celebrant.

The earliest musical settings of the mass were plainchant (one voice part, in free rhythm) melodies. From the 9th to the 16th centuries some plainchants were expanded by means of tropes; *i.e.,* the grafting of new music and new texts onto the original chants.

Organum, the simultaneous combination of more than one melody, was developed in about the 9th century. The *Winchester Troper,* a manuscript from about the 11th century, contains 12 Kyries and 8 Glorias in two-part organum; the notation, however, cannot be deciphered. In the 12th and 13th centuries further developments of organum took place in the *Magnum Liber Organi.*

In about 1300, polyphonic cycles of the Ordinary (having two or more sections musically related to one another) appeared. The French composer Guillaume de Machaut (d. 1377) wrote the first complete Ordinary cycle, the *Messe de Notre Dame.*

The secular music style of the 14th century manifested itself in Ordinary settings, which at that time were rarely based on plainsong melodies. The music is basically in descant or treble-dominated style: a melodically and rhythmically elaborated upper part over two slower moving parts, usually for instruments.

In the 15th and 16th centuries numerous composers chose the Ordinary as a chief means of musical expression. Masters of the 15th century were the Englishman John Dunstable and the Burgundian Guillaume Dufay. Both applied the treble-dominated style of plainsong. Dufay brought to completion the developments of cantus firmus mass, in which each section of the Ordinary is based on a precomposed melody, or cantus firmus (*q.v.*), usually either a plainchant melody or a secular song. The celebrated Flemish composer Josquin des Prez (d. 1521), among his several other innovations, perfected the parody mass: the borrowing and free elaboration of two or more parts of another sacred or secular composition within a new setting of the Ordinary texts. He also standardized the use of melodic imitation by having each voice begin in turn with the same motif.

The works of the Italian composer Giovanni da Palestrina (d. 1594) summarize the techniques of his era. His style was later termed the *stile antico,* the ancient polyphonic style, in contrast to the *stile moderno,* the 17th-century modern solo style. In the 17th century these two styles are found, sometimes even juxtaposed, in the Ordinary of the mass settings, along with the use of the concertato principle: one or more solo voices or instruments, in running scale passages, that contrast with the whole choral and instrumental ensemble. In such settings the text is separated into smaller units to permit varied settings and instrumental interludes.

In the 18th century, the Neapolitan Alessandro Scarlatti continued the operatic approach, as did Haydn and Mozart. Beethoven's *Missa Solemnis* (completed 1823) flows from the contemplation of the liturgy, as does J.S. Bach's *Mass in B Minor* (1724–46), but neither was meant to accompany it.

Near the beginning of the 19th century in Germany there arose a renewed interest in plainchant and 16th-century polyphony, ideals that in 1868 initiated the Cecilian movement for reform in Roman Catholic liturgical music. But composers still wrote settings for orchestra, chorus, and soloists, notable examples being Franz Liszt, Charles-François Gounod, and Anton Bruckner.

In 20th-century style are the Ordinary settings of Igor Stravinsky, the Hungarian Zoltán Kodály, the French composer Francis Poulenc, and the British composers Ralph Vaughan Williams, Benjamin Britten, and William Walton. A kind of troped Ordinary is the American Leonard Bernstein's *Mass.*

The Proper. The Proper of the mass includes the scriptural texts that change daily with the liturgical calendar. The Proper texts sung by the choir, with the participation of soloists, are the Introit, Gradual, Alleluia or Tract, Sequence, Offertory, and Communion.

As with the Ordinary, the earliest settings are in plainchant, and troping also existed in the Propers. The *Winchester Troper* includes 3 Introits, 53 Alleluias, 19 Tracts, and 7 Sequences in undecipherable note-against-note organum. Around 1200, two of the composers of Notre-Dame Cathedral, Paris, Léonin and Pérotin, wrote the *Magnus Liber Organi,* a compilation including settings of 59 Graduals and Alleluias in two to four voices. Some pieces have an unmeasured melismatic (many notes per syllable) upper voice over prolonged notes of the chant; others have measured, regular, recurring rhythmic patterns in all of the voices.

Around 1430 Dufay reawakened interest in settings of the Proper. Much later, collections of polyphonic Proper settings for the liturgical year are found in the German Heinrich Isaac's *Choralis Constantinus* (begun 1550, completed 1555 by Ludwig Senfl) and in the German Georg Rhau's publications for the Lutheran Church in 1539 and 1545.

Within the Roman Catholic Church, the liturgical reforms of the Council of Trent (1545–63) gave new impetus to Proper settings. Starting with Giovanni Contino in 1560, numerous Italian composers wrote settings of the Proper. In 1605 and 1607 appeared the two books of the English composer William Byrd's *Gradualia,* a collection of polyphonic Propers for major feasts.

Systematic development of the Propers in music was rare from the Baroque era on.

mass, in physics, quantitative measure of inertia, a fundamental property of all matter. It is, in effect, the resistance that a body of matter offers to a change in its speed or position upon the application of a force. The greater the mass of a body, the smaller the change produced by an applied force. Although mass is defined in terms of inertia, it is conventionally expressed as weight. By international agreement the standard unit of mass, with which the masses of all other objects are compared, is a platinum-iridium cylinder of one kilogram. This unit is commonly called the International Prototype kilogram. In countries that continue to favour the English system of measurement over the International System of Units (SI), the current version of the metric system, the avoirdupois pound is used instead. Another unit of mass, one that is widely employed by engineers, is the slug, which equals 32.17 pounds.

Weight, though related to mass, nonetheless differs from the latter. Weight essentially constitutes the force exerted on matter by the gravitational attraction of the Earth, and so it varies from place to place. In contrast, mass remains constant regardless of its location under ordinary circumstances. A satellite launched into space, for example, weighs increasingly less the further it travels away from the Earth. Its mass, however, stays the same.

For years it was assumed that the mass of a body always remained invariable. This notion, expressed as the theory of conservation of mass, held that the mass of an object or collection of objects never changes, no matter how the constituent parts rearrange themselves. If a body split into pieces, it was thought that the mass divided with the pieces, so that the sum of the masses of the individual pieces would be equal to the original mass. Or, if particles were joined together, it was thought that the mass of the composite would be equal to the sum of the masses of the constituent particles. But this is not true.

With the advent of the special theory of relativity by Einstein in 1905, the notion of mass underwent a radical revision. Mass lost its absoluteness. The mass of an object was seen to be equivalent to energy, to be interconvertible with energy, and to increase significantly at exceedingly high speeds near that of light (3×10^8 metres per second, or 186,000 miles per second). The total energy of an object was understood to comprise its rest mass as well as its increase of mass caused by high speed. The mass of an atomic nucleus was discovered to be measurably smaller than the sum of the masses of its constituent neutrons and protons. Mass was no longer considered constant, or unchangeable. In both chemical and nuclear reactions, some conversion between mass and energy occurs, so that the products generally have smaller or greater mass than the reactants. The difference in mass, in fact, is so slight for ordinary chemical reactions that mass conservation may be invoked as a practical principle for predicting the mass of products. Mass conservation is simply invalid, however, for the behaviour of masses actively involved in nuclear reactors, in particle accelerators, and in the thermonuclear reactions in the Sun and stars. The new conservation principle is the conservation of mass-energy. *See also* energy, conservation of.

mass action, law of, fundamental law of chemical kinetics, formulated in the years 1864 to 1879 by the Norwegian scientists Cato M. Guldberg and Peter Waage. The law states that the rate, or velocity, of any simple chemical reaction is proportional to the product of the masses of the reacting substances, each raised to a certain power. The magnitude of the exponent of each mass is equal to the corresponding number of molecules taking part in the reaction. Thus, the reaction for the reacting compounds X, Y, and Z, which form the product compound P, in which α, β, and γ represent the numbers of reacting molecules, is represented by the balanced chemical equation $\alpha X + \beta Y + \gamma Z \rightarrow P$; the reaction rate ($r$) is given by $r = k(C_X)^\alpha (C_Y)^\beta (C_Z)^\gamma$. In the equation, k represents a proportionality constant called the specific reaction rate or the velocity constant, and the C's represent concentrations—*e.g.,* moles per litre—of X, Y, and Z, respectively. All quantitative expressions of the rates of chemical reactions are based on the law of mass action.

mass-energy equation: *see* Einstein's mass-energy theory.

mass flow, also called PRESSURE FLOW, in botany, the most widely accepted explanation for the movement of sugars and other nutrient solutes through the phloem. The mass-flow hypothesis explains how foods move from source areas, where they are manufactured (mainly in the leaves) or stored (such as in the storage tissues of stems and roots), to sink areas, where they are metabolized or stored. (Storage tissues, it should be noted, can serve as either a source or sink, depending on the direction of the nutrient flow.)

According to the mass-flow hypothesis, dissolved nutrients (primarily sugars) move from a source into the sieve tubes of the phloem via active transport—that is, by a process that involves the expenditure of energy. This inflow of solutes causes the contents of the sieve elements (sieve-tube cells) in the region of the source to become hypertonic, and water flows into these cells by osmosis. This influx of water raises the osmotic pressure in the sieve elements; eventually, the increased pressure causes the fluid contents of the cells to flow into adjacent sieve elements. This mass flow carries the nutrient solutes with it, and, thus, the receiving sieve elements now become hypertonic and the process repeats itself. The mass flow proceeds along the length of the sieve tube until the sink is reached; at this point, nutrient molecules are removed from the sieve tube by active transport. Their removal makes the sink tissue hypertonic, and water osmotically flows out of the phloem into the sink. The mechanism of food translocation as envisioned in the mass-flow hypothesis thus involves active transport at each end of the sieve tube, with the passive movement of foods through the tube by means of osmotic pressure build-up and resultant bulk flow.

The mass-flow hypothesis does not satisfy objections that much higher turgor pressures (internal pressure in plant cells caused by osmosis) should exist within the sieve tubes than has been shown; that pressure gradients from sources to sinks should be more clear-cut; that the observed rates of transport are higher than mass flow can explain; that transport is often simultaneously bidirectional; and that low temperature and lack of oxygen depress transport. These observations suggest that the movement of substances in sieve elements is under more control by the living cytoplasm of the cell than the mass-flow hypothesis allows for. Despite these objections, mass flow remains the best explanation for nutrient movement in plants.

mass movement, also called MASS WASTING, bulk movements of soil and rock debris down slopes in response to the pull of gravity, or the rapid or gradual sinking of the Earth's ground surface in a predominantly vertical direction. Formerly, the term mass wasting referred to a variety of processes by which large masses of earthen material are moved by gravity from one place to another. More recently, the term mass movement has been substituted to include mass wasting processes and the sinking of confined areas of the Earth's ground surface. Mass movements on slopes and sinking mass movements are often aided by water and the significance of both types is the part each plays in the alteration of landforms.

A brief treatment of mass movement follows. For full treatment, *see* MACROPAEDIA: Geomorphic Processes.

The variety of downslope mass movements reflects the diversity of factors that are responsible for their origin. Such factors include: weathering or erosional debris cover on slopes, which is usually liable to mass movement; the character and structure of rocks, such as resistant permeable beds prone to sliding because of underlying impermeable rocks; the removal of the vegetation cover, which increases the slope's susceptibility to mass movement by reducing its stability; artificial or natural increases in the slope's steepness, which will usually induce mass movement; earthquake tremors, which affect the slope equilibrium and increase the likelihood of mass movement; and flowing ground water, which exerts pressure on soil particles and impairs slope stability. These factors affecting slope conditions will often combine with climatic factors such as precipitation and frost activity to produce downslope mass movement.

The types of mass movements caused by the above factors include: the abrupt movement and freefall of loosened blocks of solid rock, known as rockfalls; several types of almost imperceptible downslope movement of surficial soil particles and rock debris, collectively called creep; the subsurface creep of rock material, known as bulging: the multiplicity of downslope movements of bedrock and other debris caused by the separation of a slope section along a plane of least resistance or slip surface, collectively called landslides; the separation of a mass along a concave head scarp, moving down a curved slip surface and accumulating at the slope's foot, known as a slump; the saturation of debris and weathered material by rainfall in the upper section of a slope or valley, increasing the weight of the debris and causing a slow downslope movement, called an earthflow; a rapidly moving earthflow possessing a higher water content, known as a mudflow; a fast-moving earthflow in a mountainous region, called a debris flow or avalanche; and the downslope movement of moisture-saturated surficial material, known as solifluction, over frozen substratum material, occurring in sub-Arctic regions during seasonal periods of surface thaw.

Sinking mass movements occur in relatively rapid fashion, known as subsidence, and in a gradual manner, called settlement. Subsidence involves a roof collapse or breakdown of a subsurface cavity such as a cave. Extensive subsidence is evident in areas where coal, salt, and metalliferous ores are mined. Marine erosion sometimes causes the roof collapse of sea caves. Regions of karst topography will exhibit widespread subsidence in the form of sinkholes caused by underground drainage. Other types of subsidence caused by underground solutions have been found in chalk, gypsum, anhydrite, and halite (salt) terrains. The melting of ground ice also contributes to subsidence such as the formation of glacial kettles and depressions following the seasonal surface thaw of perennially frozen land. The chemical decomposition of subsurface rocks and ores is also a cause of subsidence. Another form of subsidence is the steep-walled depression, known as a volcanic sink, formed following the withdrawal of magma from below the ground surface.

The gradual settlement of confined areas of earth material occurs through consolidation of soil and rock by the squeezing or removal of fluids from the pore spaces, and by the collapse of the grain structure. The most widespread cause of consolidation is by surface loading such as the continued deposition of sediments in sea and lake beds or by loads imposed on land by glacial ice sheets or outwash deposits. Human-made structures also cause surface loading, consolidation, and settlement. Consolidation is also caused by the lowering of the ground water table. The extraction of pressurized water or oil from deep beneath the surface will cause a collapse of the pore spaces and consolidation of rock material. Grain structure collapse usually occurs from the wetting of rock materials such as clays and sands, which causes the structure of the grains to shift and settle in a more compact and dense configuration.

mass number, in nuclear physics, the sum of the numbers of protons and neutrons present in the nucleus of an atom. The mass number is commonly cited in distinguishing among the isotopes of an element, all of which have the same atomic number (number of protons) and are represented by the same literal symbol; for example, the two best known isotopes of uranium (those with mass numbers 235 and 238) are designated uranium-235 (symbolized ^{235}U) and uranium-238 (^{238}U).

mass production, the application of the principles of specialization, division of labour, and standardization of parts to the manufacture of goods. The use of modern methods of mass production has brought such improvements in the cost, quality, quantity, and variety of goods available that the largest global population in history is now sustained at the highest general standard of living.

A brief treatment of mass production follows. For full treatment, *see* MACROPAEDIA: Industrial Engineering and Production.

A moving conveyor belt installed in a Dearborn, Mich., automobile plant in 1913 cut the time required to produce flywheel magnetos from 18 minutes to 5 and was the first instance of the use of modern integrated mass production techniques. In designing their manufacturing operation, Henry Ford and his colleagues drew on a history of ideas and examples of the benefits obtainable by dividing a manufacturing process into a sequence of tasks, each of which is performed by a worker specially trained for it. Eli Whitney, inventor of the cotton gin, demonstrated the usefulness of specially designed and standardized tools in eliminating the need for highly trained artisans when, in 1798, he produced 10,000 flintlock guns using a work force of relatively unskilled boys. The great precision of the Ford conveyor belt operation was made possible by time and motion studies pioneered by F.W. Taylor and Frank and Lillian B. Gilbreth in the late 19th and early 20th centuries.

The requirements for mass production of a particular commodity include the existence of a market for quantities of the commodity sufficient to justify a large investment; a product design amenable to the use of standardized parts and processes; a physical plan that minimizes material handling; division of labour into simple, short, repetitive steps; continuous flow of work; and tools designed specifically for the tasks to be performed.

Each worker in a modern mass production operation performs one or a small number of tasks over and over, many times per shift. The placement and action of the tools used, the height of the conveyor belt or work table, and all other details of the workplace are designed to allow the worker to accomplish the task by a series of movements that time and motion studies have demonstrated to be natural (and therefore easily learned) and to involve a minimum of waste motion or need for mental or physical readjustment. From this calculated economy of labour derives much of the savings in manufacturing costs in mass production. Carefully designed workplaces make possible the close estimates of worker productivity necessary for the coordination of a multistage, high-volume production operation.

In order for each worker to be able to perform a task the same way each time, the machines used in mass production are precisely tailored to the task, and parts are interchangeable among final products. In industries such as automobile manufacture, where various models are offered for sale, the use of interchangeable components in as many models as possible allows production to respond flexibly to market demand for each model. Standardization of parts is also economical in that it makes possible production (or purchase) of the parts in large quantities.

Design of a production line begins with consideration of the most economical division of work functions between workers and machines. Then special tools and workplaces are designed, workers are trained, and arrangements are made for the delivery and handling of raw materials. A pilot line may be set up to study the actual performance of the line, and based on its results adjustments may be made. There is an optimum rate of production for any given manufacturing process or set of facilities; producing at lower than the ideal rate wastes trained labour and machinery, while producing at a higher rate causes fatigue of workers and machine breakdowns. Adjustments may be required to avoid bottlenecks that prevent the optimum rate from being achieved. Finished items may come off a production line either in batches (as in the chemical industry) or one after another in a continuous line. In many operations, some components are produced in batches and then delivered to an appropriate stage for integration into a continuous production main line. To cite just one of thousands of examples, with such integrated production techniques a factory employing 8,000 workers can produce 8,000,000 telephone sets annually, in 1,000 varieties and colour combinations, using materials from more than 3,000 different suppliers.

To the savings in the utilization of labour already mentioned should be added other "economies of scale." These include large-lot purchasing of raw materials and supplies, the benefits of long production runs over short ones in which much time is lost to setup and other nonproductive steps, and the observed fact that, with increased experience of both workers and production engineers, production becomes progressively more efficient and unit costs decline.

The rise of mass production has had implications for both the nature of work and the nature of ownership. The repetitive nature of the work produces boredom and fatigue, which may lead to inefficiency, error, or injury. It has been found that often positive measures must be taken to encourage workers to identify with a finished product to which they may have contributed only a tiny and invisible part. The great amounts of capital necessary for creating mass production operations can seldom be supplied by individuals; as a result, in modern large manufacturing firms, ownership has passed from the hands of individuals to a corporate body.

mass spectrometry, also called MASS SPECTROSCOPY, analytic technique by which chemical substances are identified by the sorting of gaseous ions in electric and magnetic fields. A device that performs this operation and uses electrical means to detect the sorted ions is called a mass spectrometer; one that uses photographic or other nonelectrical means is called a mass spectrograph; either may be called a mass spectroscope.

A brief treatment of mass spectrometry follows. For full treatment, *see* MACROPAEDIA: Analysis and Measurement, Physical and Chemical.

Using mass spectrometry with a suitable choice of experimental conditions, it is possible to measure precisely the mass of ions, to show the presence of different isotopes, and to measure the relative abundance of ions in a mixture. Organic chemicals can be made to produce a spectrum of ions from the fragmenting of the parent molecule; by identifying the fragments according to their masses and relative abundances, the structure of the original molecule can be established.

Mass spectrometry developed from experiments conducted by J.J. Thomson and others on the behaviour of charged particles in electrical and magnetic fields. Thomson built a form of mass spectrometer known as a parabola spectrograph in 1913. With such a device F.W. Aston demonstrated in 1919 the existence of isotopes by showing that ions of mass 22 found in samples of air were in fact a heavy form of neon (thitherto thought of as mass 20).

Mass spectrometers, which operate under high vacuum, consist of four basic parts: a handling system to introduce the unknown sample into the equipment; an ion source, in which a beam of particles characteristic of the sample is produced; an analyzer, in which the particles in the beam are separated according to mass; and a detector, in which the separated ion components are collected and characterized. The most widely used ionization method is electron bombardment, in which electrons striking the sample molecules supply the energy needed to convert them to ions. Separation of the ions is accomplished by mass analyzers, including the magnetic, time-of-flight, and quadrupole analyzers. In magnetic analysis, the ions are accelerated by an electric field and passed into a magnetic field. A charged particle traveling at high speed in a magnetic field follows a curved path, the radius of which depends on the speed of the particle and on its mass-to-charge ratio (m/z). By changing the accelerating voltage (hence the speed of the particle) or the magnetic field strength, ions of different m/z can be collected and measured, yielding a plot of numbers of ions at various masses, or a mass spectrum. A powerful method for the analysis of mixtures containing unknown constituents is the use of mass spectrometry to analyze products of a separation accomplished by liquid or gas chromatography (*q.v.*).

Mass spectrometry is widely used to measure the masses and relative abundances of different isotopes and to determine their relative abundances in various natural or enriched samples. Many compounds are available in which the molecules have an enhanced proportion of a particular isotope, notably the heavy isotopes ^{2}H, ^{13}C, ^{15}N, ^{17}O, and ^{18}O. These are used to label substances involved in biological processes, making possible precise chemical studies of such complex reactions as metabolism, photosynthesis, plant respiration, enzymatic reactions, phosphate-transfer reactions, and the direct application of oxygen in physiological oxidation. The products of such processes are analyzed by mass spectrometry, and the details of the metabolic pathways involved can be worked out from the distribution of heavy isotopes in the resulting molecular fragments.

Mass spectroscopy is also used in gas analysis. In particular, the method is widely used for hydrocarbon gases; with the addition of automatic recording, continuous gas analysis is possible for process control in chemical plants. Mass spectrometry can be used as a sensitive method for testing vacuum tightness in high-vacuum equipment. Apparatus under test is connected to a mass spectrometer tuned to detect a particular tracer gas, and this gas (usually helium) is then applied to the apparatus; the spectrometer reading shows where leakages occur. Another mass spectroscopic technique can be used to measure the geologic age of minerals. Since radioactive disintegration of uranium and thorium results in the formation of different lead isotopes, analysis of the proportions of the latter makes possible accurate estimates of the age of the minerals in which they occur.

In accelerator mass spectrometry, high-energy particle accelerators are coupled with electrostatic and magnetic mass analyzers to measure rare, low-abundance isotopes. This method has greatly improved the range of radiocarbon dating, enabling the use of much smaller sample sizes.

mass transit, also called MASS TRANSPORTATION, or PUBLIC TRANSPORTATION, transportation system, usually publicly but sometimes privately owned and operated, designed to move large numbers of people in various types of vehicles, along fixed and nonfixed routes in cities, suburbs, and larger metropolitan areas. Modern mass transit is an outgrowth of industrialization and urbanization and is an important feature of the separation of industrial from residential areas. Peak periods of mass transit use are the morning and evening rush hours when commuters journey to and from workplaces. The frequency of mass transit service declines and in some cases ends completely following peak periods of use.

While historically many systems were privately owned and operated, increasing complexity and expense of operation have resulted in government takeover of services in many cases. Fixed-route mass transit is usually associated with rail and trolley travel of some type and can be divided into below-surface (subway), surface, or above-surface (elevated) modes. Nonfixed-route mass transit refers to passenger travel along streets and highways. Air travel may be included when it comprises frequently scheduled helicopter or plane service within a metropolitan area. Boat, hydroplane, or hovercraft commuting exists where waterways, suitable climate, and commuter traffic exist, as for instance in Venice, English Channel ports, Hong Kong, and New York City's Staten Island. Nonfixed-route travel is generally the most common mode of mass transit in the United States, and buses are the most widespread type of vehicle used.

Buses drawn by horses traversed the cobblestone streets of New York City in the 1830s but were soon replaced by fixed-rail horse-drawn trolleys. Motorized buses appeared in Europe and North America in the late 19th century, but the modern bus, mounted on a specially designed chassis, did not appear until the 1920s. Since the '20s bus technology has continually undergone change as manufacturers have sought a smoother-riding bus and have increased carrying capacity by introducing articulated buses. Even though buses provide greater scheduling and routing flexibility, their tendency to be slower than fixed-rail mass transit—because of frequent stopping and congested traffic—offsets that flexibility by time costs. The institution in the 1970s of express buses and highway and street lanes reserved for bus traffic were addressed to this deficiency.

The use of minibuses and vans in dial-a-ride systems, which are not tied to designated street routes, offers more flexibility than does ordinary bus service and is especially suited for serving the disabled and elderly, who telephone the dispatcher for service. Taxis are a component of mass transit systems for many cities but generally serve only passengers who can afford the higher rates. In cities where the automobile is the primary mode of passenger travel (and mass transit is limited), share-a-ride systems (car pooling) have been advocated whereby personal automobiles or other vehicles are used by several persons with destinations in close proximity. Fares in both dial-a-ride and share-a-ride systems are usually lower than for individual-passenger private taxis because the expense of the ride is shared by the users, the service is not operating continuously, and government subsidies or reduced road, bridge, and tunnel tolls lower the operating costs. These for-hire, low-capacity services are known as paratransit, a mode of transit that provides greater scheduling and routing flexibility than do bus or rail systems. Paratransit generates higher labour costs than a comparable multitrip bus system because it requires more vehicle operators.

The 19th century saw a fairly rapid transition in surface, medium-capacity systems—from horsecars to steam-powered cable during the 1880s and by the end of the century to the widespread use of electric traction. Electric power for the streetcar (or tram) was gathered by a small carriage, or troller (hence the term *trolley car*), running along electrical wire overhead. Many street rail systems in the United States and Great Britain were dismantled as the use of the automobile increased and trolley tracks were found to impede automobile traffic; but some cities replaced them with trolleybuses, themselves in turn replaced by motor buses in many cases. Although tramway systems remained popular in many cities throughout the world, by the mid-1980s many cities in North America were turning to light rail transit. Light rail vehicles (LRVs), the technological descendants of streetcars, are more segregated from street traffic than are tramways but may be interrupted by vehicle or pedestrian crossings.

Heavy local rail service, also called rapid transit, is another fixed-route form of mass transit and includes subways, surface lines or elevated trains, and commuter railways. Early elevated steam-powered lines were erected in New York City in Manhattan (1867) and expanded subsequently to Brooklyn, the Bronx, and Queens. In 1895 the electric-powered Chicago West Side Elevated Railway was opened, and in 1897 the city's South Side Elevated converted to electricity, as did Brooklyn's elevated in 1898. The first subway was constructed in London (1863), followed by subways in Glasgow (1886), and by 1900 Budapest, Boston, and Paris had followed suit. In 1904 the first section of the New York City subway opened, and it was progressively expanded into the 1940s as subways replaced elevated lines in Manhattan. Underground mass transit spread during the first half of the 20th century to Tokyo (1927), Buenos Aires (1928), and Moscow (1935). The largest existing rapid-transit systems are in New York City (263 miles [423 km]), London (260 miles [418 km]), Paris (157 miles [253 km]), Tokyo (122 miles [196 km]), and Moscow (102 miles [164 km]). The most used rapid-transit system is Moscow's, followed by those of Tokyo, Paris, New York City, and London. Five of the most recently constructed subway systems in the United States and Canada are found in San Francisco, Atlanta, Washington, D.C., Montreal, and Toronto, and others were being built in the 1980s, for instance, in Cairo and Calcutta. Many cities combine elevated trains with subways (Chicago, Boston, New York City, and London), but Chicago retains the largest elevated system.

Commuter railroads are another type of heavy-rail service, developed mainly along existing railroad lines to serve growing suburban communities. Major cities such as New York, Chicago, Philadelphia, Paris, London, Cairo, and Tokyo possess commuter railroads linked with their other forms of mass transit.

Long-distance (250 miles [400 km] or more) corridor rail service is a type of commuter railroad found since the 1970s in regions of the world with closely spaced metropolitan areas. This type of rail service started with the development of trains attaining speeds of 100–200 miles per hour (160–320 km/h), the speeds necessary to permit convenient daily commuting over such distances. The famous "Bullet Train" (Shinkansen) of Japan travels the Tokaido line between Tokyo and Ōsaka at 130 mile/h (210 km/h) and, in the early 1980s, linked Hokkaido and Kyushu islands as well. France's Train à Grande Vitesse (TGV) reaches a speed of about 168 mile/h (270 km/h) between Paris and Lyon. The only rail corridor in the United States generally capable of providing this service is the Boston–Washington route, but in the early 1980s another privately sponsored system between Los Angeles and San Diego was being developed with Japanese expertise.

A more recent form of fixed-route mass transit is the people mover, which consists of unmanned automated vehicles moving along fixed guideways and rights-of-way. During the early 1980s monorails in Germany, having automated cars varying in size, provided a good example of a people mover. People movers also exist in the United States but are found mainly in airports, zoos, and amusement parks and comprise moving walkways, rubber belts on rollers, as well as monorails.

The effect of the automobile on mass transit has been more severe in the United States than elsewhere. Following World War II, mass-transit ridership declined steadily as private automobile ownership rose, and public-transit systems had to raise fares owing to escalating operations and equipment costs; the 1970 total ridership fell to less than that of 1910. In the 1970s, U.S. ridership began to increase as gasoline prices sharply rose, but increasing transit fares tended to counter this trend. Many pre-World War II commuter lines and rapid-transit systems are in need of rehabilitation, requiring large capital outlays. Many rapid-transit systems have been coordinated into regional authorities, linking rapid transit, light-rail transit, and bus lines and making the systems eligible for state, provincial, or regional aid. In many nations the public-transport systems are government-subsidized, keeping fares low, whereas in the United States the involvement of state legislatures in the funding process has often led to rural–urban political conflict over the level of support to be extended, causing fluctuations in fare structure and declining public confidence in the systems. The need for mass transit in developing countries could increase if population growth, industrialization, and urbanization continue. *See also* streetcar; subway.

mass wasting: *see* mass movement.

Massa, city, capital of Massa-Carrara *provincia,* Toscana (Tuscany) *regione,* north-central Italy. Massa lies in the Frigido Valley at the foot of the Apuan Alps near the Ligurian coast, just southeast of Carrara and La Spezia. Mentioned in the 9th century, it was a possession of the bishops of Luni and passed through numerous hands before falling to the Malaspina family in 1421. It became the seat of the principate (duchy from 1633) of Massa-Carrara in 1568. Notable landmarks in the city include the 15th- to 16th-century fortress, the 17th-century ducal palace, and the 15th-century cathedral. With Carrara, the city specializes in the processing and export of marble, and it also manufactures office furniture. Pop. (2001 est.) 68,141.

Massachuset, an Algonquian-speaking Indian tribe that in the early 17th century may have numbered 3,000 living in more than 20 villages distributed along what is now the Massachusetts coast. The cultivation of corn (maize) and other vegetables, hunting, and fishing were the basis of their subsistence. They moved seasonally between fixed sites to exploit their food resources. The tribe was divided into bands, each ruled by a subchief, or sachem. Before colonial settlement began, they were greatly reduced in number by warfare with their northeastern neighbours and by a pestilence in 1617, followed in 1633 by smallpox that wiped out most remaining members of the tribe, including the chief. Christian missionaries, notably John Eliot, gathered the Massachuset and converts from other tribes into separate villages, in which they lost their tribal identity. The state of Massachusetts is named after the Indian tribe.

Massachusetts, officially THE COMMONWEALTH OF MASSACHUSETTS, constituent state of the United States of America, located in New England, in the northeastern U.S. Massachusetts is bounded on the north by Vermont and New Hampshire; on the east by the Atlantic Ocean; on the south by the Atlantic Ocean, Rhode Island, and Connecticut; and on the west by New York. The state capital is Boston.

A brief treatment of Massachusetts follows. For full treatment, *see* MACROPAEDIA: United States of America: *Massachusetts.*

The original Indian inhabitants of Massachusetts coexisted with the first permanent European settlement from 1620, when the *Mayflower* left its intrepid band of Pilgrims at Plymouth. Ten years later, the first wave of English Puritans arrived at the newly founded town of Boston. Their establishment of a Puritan commonwealth had far-reaching effects on the development of American religious, political, and social institutions. Massachusetts was a hotbed of revolutionary activity in the years preceding the American Revolution, and the Revolution's first skirmish was fought on the green at Lexington (1775). Massachusetts led the struggle for the abolition of slavery in the 19th century and in the second half of the 19th century became the first truly industrialized state in the Union.

The indented coasts of Massachusetts were formed by great glaciers that disappeared some 11,000 years ago. Hard, flat land stretches out behind the coasts, becoming stony upland pasture near the central part of the state and bulging into gently hilly country in the west. Cape Cod, in the southeast, juts 65 miles (105 km) into the ocean. Central Massachusetts comprises rolling plains fed by many streams. Beyond the plains lie the fertile Connecticut Valley, the Berkshire Hills, and the Taconic and Hoosac ranges. There are 19 main river systems and more than 1,100 ponds or lakes. The climate is basically temperate but is colder and drier in the west. July is the hottest month, averaging about 71° F (22° C), in contrast to the 26° F (−3° C) average for January.

During its first two centuries of European settlement, Massachusetts was solidly English and Protestant (the Congregational Church was not disestablished there until 1833); but in the 19th century, immigration and industrialization greatly altered the ethnic composition. Today the state's population is largely Roman Catholic, a legacy of the great numbers of Irish and Italian immigrants who came there throughout the 19th century. In 1980 the state was no more than 4 percent black, but Boston's population was more than one-fifth black. Boston, like most large northern cities, continued to lose population to its suburbs in the early 1980s. The state population as a whole has one of the lowest growth rates of all the 50 states.

Agriculture has never been central to the economy of Massachusetts. The generally rocky soils support only truck gardening, although southeastern Massachusetts is one of the world's major producers of cranberries. Greenhouse and nursery products, followed by dairy products, are the main source of agricultural income. Fishing in the surrounding Atlantic waters has always been a primary component of the economy, but the once-prosperous whaling industry died out at the beginning of the 20th century.

Massachusetts has long been an industrial state. The first saltworks and ironworks date from the 1640s. Though the once-flourishing textile industry is no more, Massachusetts is still known for its watches, cutlery, guns, and leather goods. The presence of such major educational institutions as Harvard University, the Massachusetts Institute of Technology, and Boston University stimulated the growth of electronics, communications, and other high-technology facilities in Massachusetts in the 1980s, thus revitalizing the state's declining industrial base. Tourism also features prominently in the state's economy.

Massachusetts was responsible for the famous clipper ships of the 1850s and also had the nation's first railroad. Brockton had the first electric street railway and Boston the first passenger subway. Today the state is served by a network of major highways and railroads. Boston is a major sea and air port.

Boston has long been a cultural centre, not only of Massachusetts but of the nation. Both Boston and Massachusetts have nourished a lively literary tradition, from Jonathan Edwards to Ralph Waldo Emerson, Henry David Thoreau, Nathaniel Hawthorne, Henry W. Longfellow, and Emily Dickinson. From the founding of Harvard in 1636, Massachusetts has led the nation in education, both public and private. Area 8,284 square miles (21,456 square km). Pop. (2000) 6,349,097.

Massachusetts Bay, inlet of the North Atlantic Ocean, extending southward for 65 miles (105 km) from Cape Ann to Cape Cod, Massachusetts, U.S. It includes Boston, Plymouth, and Cape Cod bays and Gloucester and Salem harbours. The Atlantic Intracoastal Waterway enters the bay through the Cape Cod Canal and reaches its northernmost point at Boston. Late in 1620, the Pilgrims explored Cape Cod Bay and at Plymouth founded a colony that remained distinct from the Puritan group around Boston (the Massachusetts Bay Colony) until 1691. Coastal activities include industry, shipping, fishing, and tourism.

Massachusetts Bay Colony, one of the original English settlements in present Massachusetts, settled in 1630 by a group of about 1,000 Puritan refugees from England under Governor John Winthrop. In 1629 the Massachusetts Bay Company had obtained from Charles a charter empowering the company to trade and colonize in New England between the Charles and Merrimack rivers. Omitted from the charter was the usual clause requiring the company to hold its business meetings in England, a circumstance that the Puritan stockholders used to transfer control of the colony to America. The Puritans established a theocratic government with the franchise limited to church members. Growing estrangement between the colony and England resulted in the annulment of the company's charter in 1684 and the substitution of royal government under a new charter granted in 1691. The charter of 1691 merged the Plymouth colony and Maine into the Massachusetts Bay Colony. *See also* Plymouth.

Massachusetts Institute of Technology (MIT), privately controlled coeducational institution of higher learning famous for its scientific and technological training and research. It was chartered by the state of Massachusetts in 1861 and became a land-grant college in 1863. William Barton Rogers, MIT's founder and first president, had worked for years to organize an institution of higher learning devoted entirely to scientific and technical training, but the outbreak of the American Civil War delayed the opening of the school until 1865, when 15 students enrolled for the first classes, held in Boston. MIT moved to Cambridge, Mass., in 1916; its 146-acre (59-hectare) campus is located along the Charles River.

MIT offers both graduate and undergraduate education. There are five academic schools—the School of Architecture and Planning, the School of Engineering, the School of Humanities and Social Sciences, the Sloan School of Management, and the School of Science—and the Whitaker College of Health Sciences and Technology. While MIT is perhaps best known for its programs in engineering and the physical sciences, other areas—notably economics, political science, urban studies, linguistics, and philosophy—are also strong. Admission is extremely competitive, and students are often able to pursue their own original research.

MIT has numerous research centres and laboratories. Among its facilities are a nuclear reactor, a computation centre, geophysical and astrophysical observatories, a linear accelerator, a space research centre, supersonic wind tunnels, an artificial intelligence laboratory, a centre for cognitive science, and an international studies centre. MIT's library system is extensive and includes a number of specialized libraries; there are also several museums.

massage, in medicine, systematic and scientific manipulation of body tissues, performed with the hands for therapeutic effect on the nervous and muscular systems and on systemic circulation. It was used more than 3,000 years ago by the Chinese. Later, the Greek physician Hippocrates used friction in the treatment of sprains and dislocations and kneading to treat constipation. Early in the 19th century, Per Henrik Ling, a doctor in Stockholm, devised a system of massage to treat ailments involving joints and muscles. Others later extended the treatment to relieve deformities of arthritis and re-educate muscles following paralysis.

Massage is used to relieve pain and reduce swelling, to relax muscles, and to speed the healing process following strain and sprain injuries. Massage, however, cannot prevent loss of muscle strength nor reduce fat deposits.

There are three forms of hand manipulation employed in therapeutic massage. They are: light or hard stroking (effleurage), which relaxes muscles and improves circulation to the small surface blood vessels and is thought to increase the flow of blood toward the heart; compression (petrissage), which includes kneading, squeezing, and friction and is useful in stretching scar tissue, muscles, and tendons so that movement is easier; and percussion (tapotement), in which the sides of the hands are used to strike the surface of the skin in rapid succession to improve circulation. *See also* physical medicine and rehabilitation.

Massalia (France): *see* Marseille.

massasauga (*Sistrurus catenatus*), small North American rattlesnake of the family Viperidae, found in prairies, swamps, and woodlands from the Great Lakes to Arizona. It is about 45 to 75 cm (18 to 30 inches) long.

The massasauga may be totally black but is more commonly gray or tan with rows of black or brown spots on its back and sides. It is a venomous snake, usually secretive and unaggressive, that can deliver a painful but rarely fatal bite.

Massasauga (*Sistrurus catenatus*)
William B. Allen, Jr., from The National Audubon Society Collection/Photo Researchers

Massasoit (b. *c.* 1590, near present Bristol, R.I., U.S.—d. 1661, near Bristol), Wampanoag Indian chief who throughout his life maintained peaceful relations with English settlers in the area of the Plymouth Colony, Mass.

Massasoit was the grand sachem (intertribal chief) of all the Wampanoag Indians, who inhabited parts of present Massachusetts and Rhode Island, particularly the coastal regions. In March 1621—several months after the landing of the *Mayflower* at Plymouth—Massasoit journeyed to the colony with his colleague Samoset, who had already made friendly overtures to the Pilgrims there. Convinced of the value of a thriving trade with the newcomers, Massasoit set out to ensure peaceful accord between the races—a peace that lasted as long as he lived. In addition, he and his fellow Indians shared techniques of planting, fishing, and cooking that were essential to the settlers' survival in the wilderness. When Massasoit became dangerously ill in the winter of 1623, he was nursed back to health by the grateful Pilgrims. The colonial leader, Governor Edward Winslow, was said to have traveled several miles through the snow to deliver nourishing broth to the chief.

Massasoit was able to keep the peace for many decades, but new waves of land-hungry Europeans created tension as the Indians' native land was steadily taken over by the whites. When he died, goodwill gradually dissolved, culminating in the bloody King Philip's War (1675), led by Massasoit's second son.

Massawa, also spelled MITSIWA, port city, Eritrea, in the Bay of Massawa on the Red Sea. It is connected to Asmera, the national capital, on the hinterland plateau (40 miles [64 km] west-southwest) by road, railroad, air, and aerial tramway. The town rests on the islands of Tawlad (Taulud) and Massawa (the site of the modern harbour) and on the Gerar and Abdel Kader peninsulas, which are linked to each other by causeways. Massawa is one of the world's hottest places, with an annual average temperature of 86° F (30° C). It was an Ethiopian port in the 16th century and came under Ottoman control in 1557. It changed hands intermittently for the next 300 years and became an Italian possession in 1885, functioning as the capital of Eritrea colony until 1900. Conquered by British forces in 1941, Massawa remained under British administration until the federation of Eritrea with Ethiopia in 1952. The city was badly damaged in 1990, during the war for Eritrean independence.

The port exports agricultural products (chiefly oilseeds, nuts, hides, and coffee), salt, fish, and pearls and imports industrial goods. Local industries include a saltworks, fish- and meat-processing enterprises, a cement plant, and an ice factory. Massawa is a significant tourist centre whose architecture shows both Italian and Arab influence. Most of the inhabitants are Muslim. Pop. (1989 est.) 19,404.

Massena, village and town (township), St. Lawrence county, northern New York, U.S., 68 miles (109 km) southwest of Montreal; it is the location of the St. Lawrence Seaway Development Corporation Headquarters and the focal point of Seaway power projects. The village (area 3.7 square miles [9.6 square km]) is surrounded by the town (area 52 square miles [135 square km]) with a small section overlapping into Louisville township.

The first European settler, Amable Faucher (1792), named the site after André Massena, one of Napoleon's marshals. The village, a health spa in the 19th century, was incorporated in 1886. It grew after 1900 when a power canal linking the St. Lawrence and Grass rivers was dug and attracted industry, notably the Aluminum Company of America. Main Seaway structures (completed by the early 1960s) are the Moses-Saunders Power Dam (owned jointly by Ontario and New York, with the U.S.-Canadian boundary running through its centre), Long Sault Spillway Dam, Iroquois Dam, Massena Intake, Eisenhower and Snell locks, and the Seaway International Bridge (across the Seaway Channel to Cornwall Island, Ontario).

Massena remains a major centre for aluminum production. Engine blocks and auto components are also made. St. Lawrence State Park on Barnhart Island overlooks the power-navigation complex. Pop. (1992 est.) 11,801.

Masséna, André, DUKE (DUC) DE RIVOLI, PRINCE D'ESSLING (b. May 6, 1758, Nice, France—d. April 4, 1817, Paris), leading French general of the Revolutionary and Napoleonic wars.

Masséna enlisted in the Royal Italian regiment in the French service in 1775. At the outbreak of the French Revolution in 1789, he was a sergeant at Antibes. He soon became a captain in the Revolutionary government's army of Italy at Nice, and in December 1793 he was made general of a division.

During the next two years in campaigns against the Austrians in Italy, Masséna displayed a genius for maneuvering his forces over difficult terrain. Becoming Napoleon's most trusted lieutenant during the Italian campaign of 1796–97, he won the Battle of Rivoli (Jan. 14, 1797), a key victory in the successful drive against Mantua. After Rome fell to the French in February 1798, Masséna was sent as an assistant to the French commander there; a week after his arrival, his troops

Masséna, lithograph by F.-S. Delpech, 19th century, after portrait by Maurin
By courtesy of the Bibliotheque Nationale, Paris

mutinied and forced his recall. Nevertheless, in March 1799 he was made commander of the French army in Switzerland. He defeated a large Russian army in the Second Battle of Zürich on September 25 and then prevented another Russian army from advancing into Italy. These victories saved France from the immediate threat of invasion.

Shortly after Napoleon came to power, Masséna was sent to command the badly demoralized army of Italy. He restored his troops' fighting spirit, and, by holding out against Austrian besiegers at Genoa from April 21 to June 4, he enabled Napoleon to maneuver into position behind the enemy and win the Battle of Marengo (June 14), forcing the Austrians to evacuate most of northern Italy.

Although he was made a marshal in 1804, Masséna had little respect for Napoleon's imperial regime. He reconquered Calabria from the British in 1806 and in 1808 was made duc de Rivoli. In 1809 he displayed stunning heroism in two important battles against the Austrians—at Aspern-Essling (near Vienna) on May 21–22 and at Wagram on July 5–6. Napoleon rewarded him with the title prince d'Essling in January 1810. Three months later Masséna, in poor health, was given command of the French forces that were fighting the British in Portugal. The British commander, Arthur Wellesley, duke of Wellington, defeated him at Buçaco, Port., on Sept. 27, 1810, and at Fuentes de Oñoro, Spain, on May 5, 1811. Masséna was then relieved of his command. He was in Paris in 1815 but took no part in the Hundred Days of Napoleon; instead he supported the restoration of King Louis XVIII to the French throne.

Massenet, Jules (-Émile-Frédéric) (b. May 12, 1842, Montaud, near Saint-Étienne, France—d. Aug. 13, 1912, Paris), leading French opera composer of his generation, whose music is admired for its lyricism, sensuality, occasional sentimentality, and theatrical aptness.

Massenet entered the Paris Conservatory at the age of 11, subsequently studying composition under the noted opera composer Ambroise Thomas. In 1863 he won the Prix de Rome with his cantata *David Rizzio.* With the

Massenet, photograph by Nadar (Gaspard-Felix Tournachon)
J.P. Ziolo

production in 1867 of his opera *La Grand' Tante* (*The Great Aunt*), he embarked on a career as a composer of operas and incidental music. His 24 operas are characterized by a graceful, thoroughly French, melodic style. *Manon* (1884; after Antoine François Prévost) is considered by many his masterpiece. The opera, marked by sensuous melody and skilled personification, uses leading themes and motifs to identify and characterize the protagonists and their emotions. In the recitatives (dialogue) it employs the unusual device of spoken words over a light orchestral accompaniment. Also among his finest and most successful operas are *Le Jongleur de Notre-Dame* (1902), *Werther* (1892; after J.W. von Goethe), and *Thaïs* (1894). The famous "Méditation" for violin and orchestra from *Thaïs* remains part of the standard violin repertory.

Several of Massenet's operas reflect the succession of contemporary operatic fashions. Thus, *Le Cid* (1885) has the characteristics of French grand opera; *Le Roi de Lahore* (1877; *The King of Lahore*) reflects the taste for Oriental exoticism; *Esclarmonde* (1889) shows the influence of Wagner; and *La Navarraise* (1894; *The Woman of Navarre*) is influenced by the end-of-the-century style of *verismo,* or realism. Also prominent among Massenet's operas are *Hérodiade* (1881) and *Don Quichotte* (1910).

Of Massenet's incidental music, particularly notable is that for Leconte de Lisle's play *Les Érinnyes* (1873; *The Furies*), which contains the widely performed song "Élégie." In 1873 he also produced his oratorio, *Marie-Magdeleine,* later performed as an opera. This work exemplifies the mingling of religious feeling and eroticism often found in Massenet's music. Massenet also composed more than 200 songs, a piano concerto, and several orchestral suites.

As a teacher of composition at the Paris Conservatory from 1878, Massenet was highly influential. His autobiography was entitled *Mes Souvenirs* (1912; *My Recollections*).

Masses, The, American monthly journal of arts and politics, socialist in its outlook. It was known for its innovative treatment of illustration and for its news articles and social criticism.

The Masses was founded in 1911 in New York City by the Dutch immigrant Piet Vlag, but he and the magazine's first editor quit within 18 months. From 1912 Max Eastman was editor; during his tenure the magazine followed a more radical socialist policy. It published poems, stories, and political commentary by writers such as Sherwood Anderson, Carl Sandburg, and Louis Untermeyer; the radical journalists John Reed and Floyd Dell were staff members and regular contributors. The artists John Sloan and Art Young were also staff members; under their leadership *The Masses* published some of the best illustrations of the period, including, in addition to drawings by Sloan and Young, works by George Bellows, Stuart Davis, and Boardman Robinson.

During World War I *The Masses* took an antiwar stand, and in July 1917 the U.S. postmaster general declared the August 1917 issue "unmailable" under the Espionage Act of 1917; the magazine's second-class mailing permit was later revoked, and it ceased publication at the end of 1917. In 1918 Eastman and several other editors twice stood trial under the Espionage Act; both trials produced hung juries.

masseter (from Greek *masasthai,* "to chew"), prominent muscle of the jaw. It arises from the zygomatic bone (cheekbone) and is inserted at the rear of the mandible (jawbone). Its contraction raises the mandible, and it is particularly used in chewing food. The masseter can be easily felt at the side of the jaw when the teeth are clenched.

Massey, Vincent, in full CHARLES VINCENT MASSEY (b. Feb. 20, 1887, Toronto, Ont., Can.—d. Dec. 30, 1967, London, Eng.), statesman who was the first Canadian to serve as governor-general of Canada (1952–59).

Massey lectured in modern history at the University of Toronto from 1913 to 1915 until he was appointed associate secretary of the cabinet war committee during World War I (1914–18). After the war he operated a farm-equipment business until 1925, when he became minister without portfolio in W.L. Mackenzie King's Liberal cabinet. In 1926 he was appointed Canada's first minister to the United States, where he stayed until 1930.

From 1932 to 1935 Massey served as president of the National Liberal Federation before being appointed high commissioner for Canada in the United Kingdom, at which post he served until 1946. The following year he became chancellor of the University of Toronto. In 1949, as chairman of the Royal Commission on National Development in Arts, Letters, and Sciences, Massey spoke of Canada's need to break away culturally from the United States. He was named Canadian governor-general in 1952. His younger brother, Raymond, achieved prominence as an actor on the stage and in films.

Massey, William Ferguson (b. March 26, 1856, Limavady, County Londonderry, Ire.—d. May 10, 1925, Wellington, N.Z.), New Zealand statesman, prime minister (1912–25), lifelong spokesman for agrarian interests, and opponent of left-wing movements.

William Massey, detail from an oil painting by W. Orpen, 1919; in the National Portrait Gallery, London
By courtesy of the National Portrait Gallery, London

After immigrating to New Zealand in 1870, Massey farmed near Auckland and assumed leadership in farmers' organizations. He entered Parliament in 1894 as a conservative and from 1894 to 1912 was a leader of the conservative opposition to the Liberal ministries. He became prime minister in 1912 and promptly signed legislation enabling freeholders to buy their land at its original value. The first years of his ministry saw labour strikes by miners in Waihi in 1912 and wharf workers in Wellington in 1913; his harsh repression of them gave impetus to the formation of the Labour Party in 1916. He also improved federal administration by putting civil service positions under a nonpolitical commission.

A coalition with the Liberal Party led by Sir Joseph Ward enabled Massey to continue his ministry in 1915. He participated in the Imperial War Cabinet (1917–18) and signed the Treaty of Versailles at the Paris Peace Conference of 1919, making New Zealand a founding member of the League of Nations. He opposed separate sovereign status for dominions within the British Commonwealth.

Following the war, farmers were troubled by depressed prices resulting from the sharply reduced British demand for their products, and they also faced inflation in land prices, aggravated by increased demand for land by returned servicemen. Massey responded to these problems by establishing the Meat Control Board (1922) and the Dairy Export Control Board (1923), but rural and urban unrest resulting from rising prices continued to mount in the final years of his ministry.

massicot, one of the two forms of lead oxide (PbO) that occurs as a mineral (the other form is litharge). Massicot forms by the oxidation of galena and other lead minerals as soft, yellow, earthy or scaly masses that are very dense. It has been found in significant quantities at Badenweiler, Ger.; La Croix-aux-Mines, Fr.; the Transvaal, S.Af.; Perote, Mex.; and Leadville, Colo., U.S. For detailed physical properties, *see* oxide mineral (table).

Massif Central, upland area in south-central France. Bordered by the lowlands of Aquitaine and the Loire Basin on the west and northwest, by the Rhône–Saône Valley on the east, and by the Mediterranean coastlands of Languedoc on the south, it is conventionally demarcated by the 1,000 feet- (305 m-) above-sea-level contour. Occupying about one-sixth of France (35,006 square miles [90,665 square km]), the massif, for the most part, consists of plateaus lying between 2,000 and 3,000 feet (610 and 910 m). The highest peaks are the Puy de Sancy (6,184 feet [1,885 m]) and the Plomb de Cantal (6,096 feet [1,858 m]).

About three-quarters of the region is underlain by crystalline rocks, mainly granite, gneiss, and schist, produced by the Hercynian earth movements of the Carboniferous and Permian periods. Sedimentary deposits of a later age have been denuded in most areas but are evident in the Jurassic limestones of the Causses and the Tertiary sands and clays of the upper Loire and Allier river valleys. Uplifting and tilting during the Mid-Tertiary Period, together with intense volcanic activity beginning in the Pliocene Epoch, produced the area's volcanic cones and the extensive plateaus now deeply dissected by gorgelike valleys formed by glacial waters. These Tertiary uplifts also determined the two great trenches of the Loire and the Limagne, and they caused the tilting of the massif, which inclines gently to the west and north, then rises abruptly from the valley of the Rhône and from the sill of Naurouze, especially in the Cévennes.

Physiographically, seven areas can be distinguished: the Morvan on the northeast; the eastern margins, extending the length of the Rhône–Saône Valley and including Cévennes; the central uplands, characterized by volcanic cones and plateaus (notably, the Chaîne des Puys and Dore Mountains); the Grands-Causses, a permeable limestone region trenched by imposing gorges of the Tarn and Lot rivers; the southwestern uplands of the Ségalas, Lacaune, and Noires Mountains; Limousin, comprising the plateaus of La Montagne and a series of lower plateaus; and the northern basins of the Loire and Allier rivers.

Land use reflects the diverse topography and the differences that exist between the massif's interior and its periphery. Cattle are raised on the interior upland meadows; sheep occupy the more barren areas of the periphery. In the central uplands of Auvergne, distinctive cheeses, such as Cantal and Bleu Saint-Nectaire, are produced; in the Grands-Causses, Roquefort cheese is made from ewes' milk. On the favoured slopes a variety of fruits and wine grapes are produced; on arable lands, grains, potatoes, sugar beets, and fodder crops are grown, with market gardening important near the larger towns.

The mining of coal at Saint-Étienne, Alès, and Blanzy has furthered the development of steelworks and metallurgical industry in the Saint-Étienne region, at Le Creusot, and Montluçon. The Michelin Tire Company produces rubber at Clermont-Ferrand; Limoges has long been famous for its fine porcelain; and various textile plants are widespread. Other industries, often using local raw materials, manufacture bricks, tiles, furniture, paper, leather goods, and lace. A nuclear power plant at the confluence of the Loire and Vienne rivers and hydroelectric stations on the Dordogne, Cère, Truyère, Lot, and Tarn rivers generate a significant portion of the nation's electric power.

Population is unevenly distributed over the massif. The largest conurbations centre around Saint-Étienne, Clermont-Ferrand, and Limoges. In contrast there are some plateau areas more than 3,000 feet (9,800 m) above sea level and parts of the Causses that are virtually uninhabited. A number of market towns are dispersed through the more agriculturally productive areas. Tourist centres include Vichy, Le Puy in the upper Loire Valley, and Millau in the Grands-Causses.

Massiliensis, Johannes: *see* Cassian, Saint John.

Massillon, city, Stark county, northeastern Ohio, U.S., just west of Canton, on the Tuscarawas River. Settled (1811) by New Englanders, it developed from two villages named Kendal and Brookfield and was named (1826), after its founding by James Duncan, for Bishop Jean-Baptiste Massillon, preacher and writer at the French court of Louis XIV. The Ohio and Erie Canal (completed 1832) led to the community's early development as the wheat-shipping capital of the state. Although now industrialized, it remains a shipping centre for a wide agricultural region. Manufactures include surgical equipment, wire products, housewares, steel castings and roller bearings, cans, and meat products. The Massillon Museum, connected with the public library, is housed in Duncan's home (1830). Inc. town, 1853; city, 1868. Pop. (1990) 31,007.

Massim style, type of stylized, curvilinear carving found in the Massim region, one of the major stylistic areas of Papua New Guinea. The Massim region, located in the southeast, includes the Trobriand, D'Entrecasteaux, and Woodlark islands; the Louisiade Archipelago; and the easternmost tip of the mainland.

Shallow-relief wood carving is the most widespread medium for this style, which combines human and animal forms with abstract motifs such as scrolls, chevrons (V-shaped patterns), circles, and meanders. Some motifs are purely decorative; others represent everyday objects and natural phenomena. Some motifs represent matters important in Massim belief systems, but this symbolism is poorly understood outside Massim culture. Among the most commonly decorated objects are canoe prows and splashboards, fishnet floats, clubs, war shields, drums, dance paddles, ceremonial staffs, ax handles, bowls, lime spatulas, and betel mortars. In the Trobriands, the houses and yam stores of chiefs carry decorated gable boards. Independent figure sculpture is comparatively rare. Particularly significant are canoe prows and splashboards with rich surface decorations including representations of cultural heroes, human figures, animals, canoes, and stars. The surface carving on canoe prows, gable boards, and dance paddles is enhanced with red, white, and black paint. Most numerous in Massim art are the lime spatulas used in betel chewing to lift powdered lime from a gourd to the mouth. Most spatulas are carved in ebony, some in bone or turtle shell. The decorative incisions on the wooden spatulas are filled in with powdered lime, creating an attractive black-and-white contrast. Some spatula handles carry abstract designs, but most represent human figures, animals, plants, and artifacts, thus showing much that is important in Massim culture.

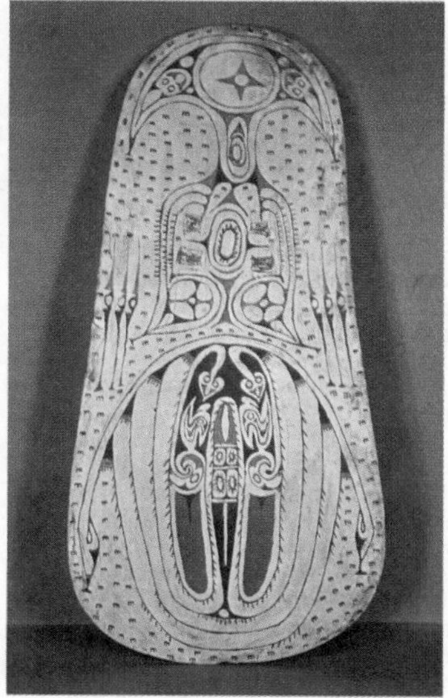

Wooden war shield from the Trobriand Islands, painted with serpents, birds, and stars in typical Massim style; in the British Museum

Holle Bildarchiv, Baden-Baden, Ger.

Massine, Léonide, original name LEONID FYODOROVICH MIASSIN (b. Aug. 9 [July 28, Old Style], 1896, Moscow—d. March 15, 1979, Cologne, W.Ger.), dancer and innovative choreographer of more than 50 ballets, one of the most important figures in 20th-century dance.

He studied acting and dancing at the Imperial School in Moscow and had almost decided to become an actor when Sergey Diaghilev, seeking a replacement for Vaslav Nijinsky, invited Massine to join his company. After a few months of study under Italian dancer and teacher Enrico Cecchetti, Massine made his Paris debut in *La Légende de Joseph* in 1914 and received favourable comment on his dramatic dance ability and commanding stage personality. Diaghilev supervised his artistic education, taking him to museums and con-

Massine as the Peruvian in *Gaîté Parisienne*, with members of the Ballet Russe de Monte Carlo, 1942

Fred Fehl

certs and introducing him to such people as the Russian painter Mikhail Larionov, the conductor Ernest Ansermet, and the composer Igor Stravinsky, all of whom influenced Massine's approach to dance. Diaghilev also encouraged his choreographic talent. Massine's first work as a choreographer, *Le Soleil de nuit,* was produced in 1915 and was eventually followed by such masterpieces as *La Boutique fantasque* (1919), *Le Tricorne* (1919; *The Three-Cornered Hat*), *Le Beau Danube* (1924), and *Gaîté Parisienne* (1938). Massine extended Michel Fokine's choreographic reforms by enriching and clarifying narration and characterizations. His ballets incorporated both folk dance and the demi-caractère dance, a style that uses classical technique to perform character dance. He added variety and complexity by including synchronized yet individual or small-group dance patterns within the corps de ballet.

From 1932 until 1938 Massine was principal dancer and choreographer of Colonel de Basil's Ballet Russe de Monte Carlo. In 1933 he created his first symphonic ballet, *Les Présages,* using Peter Ilich Tchaikovsky's *Fifth Symphony.* Although dancers such as Isadora Duncan had previously used symphonic music, Massine's choreography more completely paralleled the structure of the music. The symbolic characterizations of *Les Présages* were innovative because they relied on dance itself rather than costuming or props to convey their identity. *Choreartium,* first performed in London (1933) and danced to Johannes Brahms's *Fourth Symphony,* created even greater controversy; its second movement was close to modern dance in movement style. Critics declared it was both blasphemous and redundant to add dance to these musical masterpieces. With their eventual acceptance, Massine's symphonic ballets effected a choreographic revolution and in turn led to reforms in costuming and sets. *Rouge et Noir* (1939), set to Dmitry Shostakovich's First Symphony, had scenery and costumes by Henri Matisse. *Nobilissima Visione, St. Francis* (1938) had libretto and music by Paul Hindemith and decor by Pavel Tchelichew. Surrealist painter Salvador Dalí designed three major experimental ballets. Because of disagreements with de Basil, Massine resigned and formed his new Ballet Russe de Monte Carlo, which he headed until 1942. Later he appeared with the Ballet Theatre and the Royal Ballet. In 1966 he joined the newly formed Ballet de Monte Carlo as choreographer and artistic director. He also choreographed and danced in such films as *The Red Shoes* (1948) and *Tales of Hoffmann* (1951). Massine's publications include *My Life in Ballet* (1968) and *Massine on Choreography* (1976).

Consult the INDEX *first*

Massinger, Philip (b. 1583, near Salisbury, Wiltshire, Eng.—d. March 1639/40, London), English Jacobean and Caroline playwright noted for his gifts of comedy, plot construction, social realism, and satirical power.

Baptized at St. Thomas' Church, Salisbury, on Nov. 24, 1583, Massinger attended St. Alban Hall, Oxford, in 1602, but nothing certain is known about his life from then until 1613, though he may have been an actor. After an indefinite period of apprenticeship—during which he wrote for the theatrical manager Philip Henslowe and collaborated, from about 1613, with fellow playwrights, including John Fletcher—Massinger began about 1620 to work as an independent author. In 1625 he succeeded Fletcher, some of whose plays he revised, as the chief playwright of the King's Men, a well-known theatrical company. Though apparently not as successful as Fletcher, he remained with the King's Men until his death.

Massinger, engraved frontispiece to "Three New Playes," 1655

By courtesy of the trustees of the British Museum; photograph, J.R. Freeman & Co. Ltd.

Among the plays Massinger collaborated on with Fletcher is *The False One* (*c.* 1620), a treatment of the story of Caesar and Cleopatra. Two other important plays written in collaboration are *The Fatal Dowry* (1616–19, with Nathaniel Field), a domestic tragedy in a French setting, and *The Virgin Martyr* (1620?, with Thomas Dekker), a historical play about the persecution of Christians under the Roman emperor Diocletian. Fifteen plays written solely by Massinger have survived, but many of their dates can only be conjectured. The four tragedies are *The Duke of Milan* (1621–22) and *The Unnatural Combat* (1624?)—both skillfully told mystery stories of a melodramatic type—and *The Roman Actor* (1626) and *Believe As You List* (1631)—each a historical tragedy in a classical setting. *The Roman Actor* is considered his best serious play. *The Bondman* (1623), about a slave revolt in the Greek city of Syracuse, is one of Massinger's seven tragicomedies and shows his concern for state affairs. *The Renegado* (1624), a tragicomedy with a heroic Jesuit character, gave rise to the unaccepted theory that he became a Roman Catholic. Another tragicomedy, *The Maid of Honour* (1621?), combines political realism with the courtly refinement of later Caroline drama. The tendency of his serious plays to conform to Caroline fashion, however, is contradicted by the mordant realism and satirical force of his two great comedies—*A New Way to Pay Old Debts,* his most popular and influential play, in which he expresses genuine indignation at economic oppression and social disorder, and *The City Madam* (1632?), dealing with similar evils but within a more starkly contrived plot that curiously combines naturalistic and symbolic modes. A standard edition in five volumes, *Plays and Poems,* by Philip Edwards and Colin Gibson, was published in 1976.

Massinissa (Numidian ruler): *see* Masinissa.

Masson, André, in full ANDRÉ-AIMÉ-RENÉ MASSON (b. Jan. 4, 1896, Balagny, Oise, Fr.—d. Oct. 28, 1987, Paris), noted French Surrealist painter and graphic artist.

Masson studied painting in Brussels and then in Paris. He fought in World War I and was severely wounded. He joined the emergent Surrealist group in the mid-1920s after one of his paintings had attracted the attention of the movement's leader, André Breton. Masson soon became the foremost practitioner of automatic writing, which, when applied to drawing, was a form of spontaneous composition intended to express impulses and images arising directly from the unconscious. Masson's paintings and drawings from the late 1920s and the '30s are turbulent, suggestive renderings of scenes of violence, eroticism, and physical metamorphosis. A natural draftsman, he used sinuous, expressive lines to delineate biomorphic forms that border on the totally abstract. Masson lived in Spain from 1934 to 1936 and in the United States during World War II. His work was the subject of major retrospective exhibitions in Basel, Switz. (1950) and New York City (1976).

Masson, Frédéric (b. March 8, 1847, Paris, Fr.—d. Feb. 19, 1923, Paris), French historian and academician best known for his books on Napoleon I.

In *Napoléon inconnu* (1895; "The Unknown Napoleon"), Masson, with Guido Biagi, brought out the unpublished writings (1786–93) of Napoleon before he became emperor: notes; extracts from historical, philosophical, and literary books; and personal reflections. His other works include several books on Josephine; *Napoléon et sa famille,* 13 vol. (1897–1919; "Napoleon and His Family"); *Napoléon et son fils* (1904; "Napoleon and His Son"); and *Napoleon à Sainte-Hélène, 1815–1821* (1912).

Masson, Robert Le: *see* Le Maçon, Robert.

Massys, Quentin, Massys also spelled MATSYS, METSYS, or MESSYS (b. *c.* 1465/66, Louvain, Brabant [now in Belgium]—d. 1530, Antwerp), Flemish artist, the first important painter of the Antwerp school.

Trained as a blacksmith in his native Louvain, Massys is said to have studied painting after falling in love with an artist's daughter. In 1491 he went to Antwerp and was admitted into the painters' guild.

"The Money Changer and His Wife," painting by Quentin Massys, 1514; in the Louvre, Paris

Lauros—Giraudon/Art Resource, New York City

Among Massys' early works are two pictures of the Virgin and Child. His most celebrated paintings are two large triptych altarpieces, "The Holy Kinship," or "St. Anne Altarpiece," ordered for the Church of Saint-Pieter in Louvain (1507–09), and "The Entombment of the Lord" (*c.* 1508–11), both of which exhibit strong religious feeling and precision of detail. His tendency to accentuate individual expression is demonstrated in such pictures as "The Old Man and the Courtesan" and "The Money Changer and His Wife." "Christus Salvator Mundi" and "The Virgin in Prayer" display serene dignity. Pictures with figures on a smaller scale are a polyptych, the scattered parts of which have been reassembled, and a later "Virgin and Child." His landscape backgrounds are in the style of one of his contemporaries, the Flemish artist Joachim Patinir; the landscape depicted in Massys' "The Crucifixion" is believed to be the work of Patinir. Massys painted many notable portraits, including one of his friend Erasmus.

Although his portraiture is more subjective and personal than that of Albrecht Dürer or Hans Holbein, Massys' painting may have been influenced by both German masters. Massys' lost "St. Jerome in His Study," of which a copy survives in Vienna, is indebted to Dürer's "St. Jerome," now in Lisbon. Some Italian influence may also be detected, as in "Virgin and Child" (Nationalmuseum, Poznań, Pol.), in which the figures are obviously copied from Leonardo da Vinci's "Virgin of the Rocks" (Louvre).

Massys' two sons were artists. Jan (1509–75), who became a master in the guild of Antwerp in 1531, was banished in 1543 for his heretical opinions, spent 15 years in Italy or France, and returned to Antwerp in 1558. His early pictures were imitations of his father's work, but a half-length "Judith with the Head of Holofernes" of a later date, now in the Museum of Fine Arts, Boston, shows Italian or French influence, as does "Lot and His Daughters" (1563; Kunsthistorisches Museum, Vienna). Cornelis Massys (1513–79), Quentin's second son, became a master painter in 1531, painting landscapes in his father's style and also executing engravings.

mast, in botany, nuts or fruits of trees and shrubs, such as beechnuts, acorns, and berries, that accumulate on the forest floor, providing forage for game animals and swine. Mast has also been used as human food and to fatten poultry. The phrase "a good mast year" refers to a period in which there is a heavy crop of wild nuts.

mast cell, type of cell of the immune system of vertebrate animals. Mast cells mediate inflammatory responses such as hypersensitivity and allergic reactions. They are scattered throughout the connective tissues of the body, especially beneath the surface of the skin, near blood vessels and lymphatic vessels, within nerves, throughout the respiratory system, and in the digestive and urinary tracts. Mast cells store a number of different chemical mediators—including histamine, interleukins (IL-4 and IL-5), proteoglycans (*e.g.,* heparin), and various enzymes—in coarse granules found throughout the cytoplasm of the cell. Upon stimulation by an allergen, the mast cells release the contents of their granules (called degranulation) into the surrounding tissues. The chemical mediators produce local responses characteristic of an allergic reaction, such as increased permeability of blood vessels (*i.e.,* inflammation and swelling), contraction of smooth muscles (*e.g.,* bronchial muscles), and increased mucus production.

mastectomy, surgical removal of a breast, usually to remove a malignancy but also performed in the treatment of other conditions (*e.g.,* cystic breast disease) and for other medical reasons. Mastectomy is most effective when the cancerous tumour is discovered at an early stage and the malignant cells are localized. In order to best ensure the removal of all cancerous tissue, however, a margin of tissue surrounding a tumour and, sometimes, other nearby structures are also removed. Thus, there are several types of mastectomy, the selection of procedure depending on the location and extent of the disease (determined by X ray, thermography, and other diagnostic techniques) and the nature of the cancerous cells (determined by biopsy).

The procedure known as the standard radical mastectomy consists of the removal of the entire breast, the supporting pectoral muscles, and the axillary lymph nodes. A supraradical mastectomy is a standard radical mastectomy plus the removal of the internal mammary and supraclavicular nodes. An extended radical mastectomy is the standard radical mastectomy plus the removal of the internal mammary nodes. In the modified radical mastectomy, the procedure involves removal of the breast but preservation of the pectoralis major muscle. The extent of preservation of the pectoralis minor and axillary nodes varies.

In the 1970s and '80s there was increasing clinical evidence that the standard radical mastectomy differed little from the modified radical mastectomy in terms of morbidity, mortality, and survival rates. For this reason, the modified procedure came to be preferred in many cases. It also offered cosmetic and functional advantages.

Other mastectomy methods include simple mastectomy, or the removal of only the breast; simple mastectomy with axillary lymph node dissection; and local incision, sometimes called "lumpectomy," in which only the tumour is removed.

Master E.S. (fl. 1440–1468, Germany), unidentified late Gothic German goldsmith and engraver who signed many of his engravings with the monogram E.S. and who was one of the outstanding early printmakers of Europe.

His line engravings are especially known for their use of crosshatching and their subtlety of tonal effect. He produced over 300 prints of religious, profane, and fantastic subjects. It is believed that he came from the same Upper Rhineland region as the Master of the Playing Cards, whose influence is evident in his work. His own output also includes playing cards, but his best engravings were of religious subjects and his most popular work was "The Man of Sorrows with Four Angels."

Master of Moulins: *see* Moulins, Master of.

Masters, Edgar Lee (b. Aug. 23, 1869, Garnett, Kan., U.S.—d. March 5, 1950, Philadelphia, Pa.), American poet and novelist, best known as the author of *Spoon River Anthology* (1915).

Masters grew up on his grandfather's farm near New Salem, Ill., studied in his father's law office, and attended Knox College, Galesburg, Ill., for one year. He was admitted to the bar in 1891 and developed a successful law practice in Chicago.

Edgar Lee Masters

By courtesy of the Library of Congress, Washington, D.C.; photograph, Arnold Genthe

A volume of his verses appeared in 1898, followed by *Maximilian,* a drama in blank verse (1902), *The New Star Chamber and Other Essays* (1904), *Blood of the Prophets* (1905), and a series of plays issued between 1907 (*Althea*) and 1911 (*The Bread of Idleness*).

If Masters had continued to write along these lines, he would not be remembered, but in 1909 he was introduced to *Epigrams from the Greek Anthology*. Masters was seized by the idea of composing a similar series of free-verse epitaphs in the form of monologues. The result was *Spoon River Anthology,* in which the former inhabitants of Spoon River speak from the grave of their bitter, unfulfilled lives in the dreary confines of a small town. The community of Spoon River was fictitious; it was compounded of Petersburg and Lewistown, Ill., which Masters had known as a boy. In 1963 a staging of *Spoon River Anthology* was presented on Broadway.

Though Masters continued to publish volumes of verse almost yearly, the quality of his work never again rose to the level of the *Spoon River Anthology*.

Among his novels are *Mitch Miller* (1920) and *The Nuptial Flight* (1923). Masters wrote biographies of Abraham Lincoln (*Lincoln the Man,* 1931, in which Masters' attacks on Lincoln were poorly received by critics and historians), Walt Whitman (1937), and Mark Twain (1938). His best effort in this form is *Vachel Lindsay: A Poet in America* (1935), a study of his friend and fellow poet. Also notable are his autobiography, *Across Spoon River* (1936), and *The Sangamon* (1942), a volume in the "Rivers of America" series.

Masters, William H(owell); and Johnson, Virginia E(shelman), Johnson *née* ESHELMAN (respectively b. Dec. 27, 1915, Cleveland, Ohio, U.S.—d. Feb. 16, 2001, Tucson, Ariz.; b. Feb. 11, 1925, Springfield, Mo.), American research team, and, respectively, physician and psychologist, noted for their studies of human sexuality.

Masters was educated at Hamilton College, Clinton, N.Y. (B.S.), and the School of Medicine and Dentistry of the University of Rochester (M.D., 1943) and in 1947 joined the faculty of the School of Medicine of Washington University in St. Louis. Johnson, who had studied at Drury College (Springfield, Mo.), the University of Missouri, Columbia, and the Kansas City Conservatory of Music but had never earned a degree (she later received two honorary D.Sc. degrees), began work with Masters as a research associate in 1957, assisting him in the sex research that he had begun in 1954. In 1964 they established the Reproductive Biology Research Foundation in St. Louis, Mo. In 1973 they became codirectors of the Masters & Johnson Institute, also in St. Louis. They were married in 1971 and continued to collaborate after their divorce in 1993.

Their book *Human Sexual Response* (1966) was considered by many to be the first comprehensive study of the physiology and anatomy of human sexual activity under laboratory conditions—much of it the result of actual research observation. Biochemical equipment, such as electrocardiographs and electroencephalographs, was used in recording sexual stimulations and reactions. The two also conducted much clinical marriage counseling, dealing with problems of sexual performance. A second important study, *Human Sexual Inadequacy,* appeared in 1970. *Homosexuality in Perspective,* a report on the clinical treatment of the sexual problems of homosexuals, was published in 1979. Other works, cowritten with Robert C. Kolodny, include *Human Sexuality* (1982) and *Heterosexuality* (1994).

master's degree, a type of academic degree. *See* degree.

Masters Tournament, invitational golf competition held annually since 1934 at the Augusta National Golf Club, Augusta, Ga., on a course designed by the former U.S. amateur champion Bobby Jones and the Scottish golf-course architect Alister MacKenzie. It is 72 holes of stroke play (the player with the lowest score wins). The Masters is one of the world's most prestigious golf contests, and golfers are invited to compete on the basis of their past achievements. Most of the entrants are professionals, although some amateurs are also invited. *See* Sporting Record: *Golf.*

Masterson, Bat, byname of BARTHOLOMEW MASTERSON, pseudonym WILLIAM BARCLAY MASTERSON (b. Nov. 27, 1853, Henryville,

Canada East [Quebec]—d. October 25, 1921, New York, N.Y., U.S.), gambler, saloon-keeper, lawman, and newspaperman who made a reputation in the old American West.

Born in Canada, Masterson grew up on successive family farms in New York, Illinois, and Kansas. Leaving home at 19, he eventually became a buffalo hunter and Indian scout, working out of Dodge City, Kan. (1873–75). In January 1876 in Sweetwater, Texas, he killed a man and a dance-hall girl in a quarrel and fled back to Dodge City. There, except for brief intervals, he spent the next decade, becoming sometime Ford county sheriff (1877–79) and deputy U.S. marshal (1879) identified with the local town bosses known as "the Gang," but working mostly as saloonkeeper and gambler. He made occasional visits to other western towns, including Tombstone, Ariz., where he briefly worked with Wyatt Earp at the Oriental Saloon. He ended his Western days in plush Denver gambling houses (1887–1902), until reform-minded citizens asked him to leave.

Masterson's final years were spent in New York City, where he was successively deputy U.S. marshal for the southern district of New York (appointed by President Theodore Roosevelt), feature writer for *Human Life Magazine,* and a prominent sports editor for the *New York Morning Telegraph.* In 1921 he died at his desk of a heart attack.

Masterton, town ("district"), Wellington local government region, southern North Island, New Zealand, on the Ruamahanga River (a tributary of the Wairarapa), 55 miles (89 km) northeast of Wellington. The town was established in 1854 and named after Joseph Masters, founder of the Wairarapa Small Farms Association.

Masterton lies on the rail line that passes through the Rimutaka Range tunnel to Wellington and serves an area of sheep, dairy, fruit, and cereal farms. The town has dairy, lime, and meat-freezing works; woolen mills and sawmills; and furniture, clothing, home appliance, agricultural implements, and plastic and concrete products factories. Pop. (1991 prelim.) 22,927.

mastic, also spelled MASTICH, aromatic resin, obtained as a soft exudation from incisions in mastic trees. It is used chiefly to make pale varnishes for protecting metals and paintings. When dispersed in bodied (thickened by heating) linseed oil, mastic is known as megilp and is used as a colour vehicle. Mastic is also used as an adhesive in dental work.

The mastic, or lentisc, tree, *Pistacia lentiscus,* an evergreen shrub of the sumac family (Anacardiaceae), is indigenous to the Mediterranean coast region from Syria to Spain, and particularly the Greek archipelago, but grows also in Portugal, Morocco, and the Canary Islands. Since about AD 50, production of the resin has been confined almost exclusively to the Greek island of Khíos in the Aegean Sea.

The resin is contained in the bark and not in the wood, and in order to collect it numerous vertical incisions are made, during June, July, and August, in the stem and chief branches. The resin speedily exudes and hardens into oval tears, which are collected every 15 days. The collection is repeated several times between June and September. Mastic is usually marketed in the form of roundish tears about the size of peas. These are transparent, with a glassy fracture, of a pale yellow or faint greenish tinge, which darkens slowly.

Other trees yield resins that are referred to as mastic. In Algeria, *Pistacia atlantica* yields a solid resin. Cape mastic is the produce of *Euryops multifidus,* the resin bush, or *harpuis bosch* of the Boers—a plant of the family Compositae. Dammar resin is sometimes sold under the name of mastic. The West Indian mastic tree is *Bursera gummifera,* and the Peruvian mastic, or California pepper tree, is *Schinus molle.* The name mastic tree is also applied to a timber tree, *Sideroxylon mastichodendron,* family Sapotaceae, which grows in the West Indies and on the coast of Florida.

The term mastic is also used for various pasty materials used as protective coatings (for example, in thermal insulation and in waterproofing) and as cements (for example, in setting tile or wall panels).

mastication (biology): *see* chewing.

mastiff, breed of large working dog used as a guard and fighting dog in England for more than 2,000 years. Dogs of this type are found in European and Asian records dating back to 3000 BC. The Roman invaders of England sent the mastiff to compete in the arenas of ancient Rome, where the dog was pitted against bears, lions, tigers, bulls, other dogs, and human gladiators. The breed also fought in the later bullbaiting and bearbaiting rings of England.

(Top) Mastiff; (bottom) bull mastiff
Sally Anne Thompson

A powerful but characteristically gentle dog, the mastiff has a broad head, drooping ears, a broad, short muzzle, and a short, coarse coat. Colour, as specified by the breed standard, is apricot, silver fawn, or brindled fawn and black. Ears and muzzle are dark. The mastiff stands 70 to 76 cm (28 to 30 inches) and weighs 75 to 84 kg (165 to 185 pounds).

The bull mastiff, a cross between the mastiff and the bulldog, was developed in 19th-century England; it was used chiefly to discourage poaching on estates and game preserves and was known as the "gamekeeper's night-dog." The bull mastiff is a tan, reddish brown, or brindled dog, with black on the face and ears. It stands 61 to 69 cm and weighs 50 to 54 kg. It is frequently used as a police and guard dog.

mastiff bat, any of several bat species otherwise known as the bulldog bat and the free-tailed bat (*q.v.*).

Mastigophora, protozoan superclass whose members are characterized, at some time in the life cycle, by the possession of hairlike structures called flagella. *See* flagellate.

mastitis, inflammation of the breast in women or of the udder in sheep, swine, and cattle. Acute mastitis in women is a sudden infectious inflammation caused usually by the bacterium *Staphylococcus aureus,* or sometimes by streptococcus organisms. It begins almost exclusively during the first three weeks of nursing and is limited to the period of lactation (milk production). The bacterial organisms invade the breast through cracks in the nipples, the exposed lymphatic ducts, or the milk ducts. Irregular nursing, which leads to overfilling of the breasts, increases the effects of infections. The breasts become swollen, painful, reddened, hardened, and tender. The infection may be in one or both breasts; it can be localized or spread over an area. Purulent discharges may occur; frequently the discharge indicates abscess formation. Abscesses may remain internal or they may involve the skin. The lymphatic system's nodes and vessels are commonly enlarged and tender also. Acute mastitis accompanied by abscesses is often mistaken for acute inflammatory carcinoma (cancer) of the breasts. In a female child, after birth and during puberty, there may be brief episodes of breast inflammation; these are usually hormone induced and are not caused by bacterial infection.

Chronic mastitis is usually a secondary effect of systemic diseases such as tuberculosis, fungal infections, yeast infections, or syphilis. A relatively uncommon type of mastitis, called plasma cell mastitis, occurs most frequently in older women who have had a number of children and have a history of difficulty in nursing. It is sometimes difficult to distinguish from cancer of the breast. In this disease lymphatic fluids stagnate in the breast, and the stagnated fluids are treated by the body as foreign objects. Plasma cells, white blood cells, and fatty acid crystals accumulate, and fatty tissue suffers degeneration. A hard lump forms under part of the nipple; there may be distortion of the nipple because of the lesion. The nipple area is painful, tender, and inflamed and may exude a cloudy discharge. The milk ducts and lymph nodes are commonly thickened and enlarged. As the condition progresses, small areas of the breast become hardened as the original tissue is destroyed and replaced by fibrous or granular tissue.

Injury to the breast tissue is sometimes followed by inflammation and necrosis (death) of the fatty tissue resulting in a hard fixed lump with no skin discoloration. The symptoms of mastitis may be present for many years or may arise after a disease of the breast that involves purulent discharges and abscesses.

Economically, bacterial mastitis is a serious disease of dairy cattle. It is spread by milking machines, by the hands of milkers, and by flies. An afflicted animal may develop gangrene, characterized by discoloration of the teats or udder.

mastodon, any of several extinct elephantine mammals (family Mastodontidae, genus *Mastodon* [also called *Mammut*] that first appeared in the early Miocene and continued in

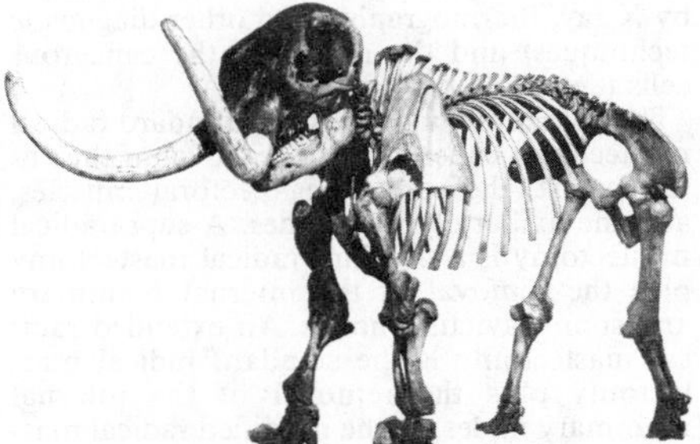

Mastodon skeleton, of Pleistocene age, found in Licking county, Ohio
By courtesy of the Cleveland Museum of Natural History

various forms through the Pleistocene Epoch (from 2,500,000 to 10,000 years ago). In North America, mastodons probably persisted into post-Pleistocene time and were thus contemporaneous with historic North American Indian groups. Mastodons had a worldwide distribution; their remains are quite common and are often very well preserved.

A characteristic feature of the mastodons, which appear to have fed upon leaves, is the distinctive nature of the grinding teeth, which in many respects are relatively primitive. They are low-crowned, large, and strongly rooted, with as many as four prominent ridges separated by deep troughs; the teeth are much smaller and less complex, however, than those in the true elephants. The prominent upper tusks were long and grew parallel to each other with an upward curvature. Short lower tusks were present in males but absent in females.

Mastodons were shorter than modern elephants but were heavily built. Although the skull was lower and flatter and of generally simpler construction than that of the modern elephants, it was similar in appearance. The ears were smaller and not as prominent as those of elephants. The body was relatively long, and the legs were short, massive, and pillarlike. Mastodons were covered with long, reddish brown hair. The reasons for their extinction are not certain, but, in North America at least, human hunting may have played a role.

mastoid process, the smooth pyramidal or cone-shaped bone projection at the base of the skull on each side of the head just below and behind the ear in humans. The mastoid process is important to students of fossil humans because it occurs regularly and in the specific form described only in hominids (*i.e.,* members of the genera *Homo* and *Australopithecus*). The development of the mastoid process is apparently related to the upright posture of hominids and the consequent evolutionary realignment of the head in relation to the neck.

mastoiditis, inflammation of the mastoid process, which is a projection of the temporal bone just behind the ear. Mastoiditis is almost invariably secondary to acute or chronic otitis media (inflammation of the middle ear). In some instances the inflammation may spread into the mastoid antrum and cells, small cavities within the process, but when the infection is very severe, the whole middle ear cleft, which includes the mastoid region, is infected simultaneously.

The narrow drainage channels from the antrum and cells are obstructed readily, and the degree to which the products of inflammation are penned within the mastoid antrum and cells determines the severity of the mastoid symptoms. The chief symptom is pain behind the ear and over the side of the head, and there may be a rise of temperature and pulse rate. Tenderness over the mastoid bone may be marked, and, as the condition develops, there is increased swelling of the tissues overlying the mastoid bone. The swelling may continue until a fluctuant abscess develops; this indicates that the infection has eroded the bone and destroyed its cortex (outer layer).

In some circumstances the mastoiditis, instead of coming to the surface, may involve structures within the cranium and so give rise to complications. The most important of these are abscess without or within the dura mater covering the brain; infection and thrombosis (blood clot formation) of the lateral sinus (the large blood channel emptying into the internal jugular vein); and infection of the labyrinth (the inner ear) containing the balance and hearing apparatus. In addition, meningitis is a serious danger.

Mastoiditis is treated by the early administration of antibiotics. At one time a frequent and dangerous disease, it is now rare because modern drugs can effectively arrest the preceding otitis media. In the few cases that do not respond to these remedies, surgical drainage with wide removal of diseased bone is necessary.

Chronic mastoiditis results from unresolved attacks of acute mastoiditis and may produce any of the symptoms and signs already described. It can be treated during surgery for the cure of chronic otitis media.

Mastroianni, Marcello (b. Sept. 28, 1924, Fontana Liri, Italy—d. Dec. 19, 1996, Paris, France), actor who became the preeminent leading man in Italian cinema during the 1960s. An attractive man whose acting style projected a mood of casual affability, he achieved international fame as the screen symbol of the modern European.

Mastroianni enrolled at the University of Rome after World War II. He began an acting career in amateur theatricals sponsored by the university, and in 1948 he joined Italy's leading theatrical troupe. Having made his film debut in 1947, Mastroianni had become a well-known actor in Italy by the mid-1950s. As the star of *Le notti bianche* (1957; *White Nights*), he was noticed by the Italian director Federico Fellini who cast him in the leading role of the world-weary journalist in *La dolce vita* (1960; "The Sweet Life"), the award-winning film that established Mastroianni's international reputation. It was followed by other outstanding pictures—*e.g., La notte* (1960; *The Night*), in which Mastroianni portrays a novelist who experiences emotional aridity in his marriage; *Divorzio all'italiana* (1961; *Divorce—Italian Style*), a satiric farce about a debonair baron's attempts to free himself from an unwanted wife; and *Otto e mezzo* (1963; *8½*), an Academy Award-winning film also directed by Fellini, with Mastroianni as a creative film director.

The comedies *Ieri, oggi, domani* (1964; *Yesterday, Today, and Tomorrow*) and *Matrimonio all'italiana* (1964; *Marriage—Italian Style*) were two of the many films in which he costarred with the Italian actress Sophia Loren. He also appeared with Loren in *I girasoli* (1969; *Sunflower*), *La moglie del prete* (1970; *The Priest's Wife*), and *Una giornata speciale* (1977; *A Special Day*). Mastroianni continued to act until his death and held starring roles in about 120 films over the course of his long career.

masturbation, manipulation of the genital organs for pleasure, usually to orgasm. The term masturbation generally connotes self-manipulation, but it can also be used to describe manipulation of or by a sexual partner, exclusive of sexual intercourse. Once the object of extravagant superstitions and severe taboos, masturbation by adults was frowned upon in the majority of premodern societies. Christian moral teaching condemned it as the sin of Onan, who in the Old Testament was censured for spilling his seed; and the Roman Catholic church still officially condemns masturbation as a mortal sin.

The American researcher Alfred Kinsey and others estimated that at mid-20th century at least 92 percent of all American males and 70–80 percent of all females have indulged in masturbation, and European studies show comparable figures.

The stigma against masturbation is decreasing, and many students of sexual behaviour extoll its virtues as being healthy, pleasurable, sedative, and a release of tension. Masturbation is a widely used element in sex therapy.

Masuda, city, Shimane *ken* (prefecture), western Honshu, Japan. It lies in the basin of the Takatsu River, near the Sea of Japan. The commercial hub of the surrounding agricultural region, Masuda has a few rural industries such as tatami mat production, silk manufacture and spinning, and lumbering. It is also a small trade centre for charcoal and lumber. The San-in Line (railway) between Kyōto and Shimonoseki runs through the city. Pop. (1990) 52,408.

Masʿūdī, al-, in full ABŪ AL-ḤUSAYN ʿALĪ IBN AL-ḤUSAYN AL-MASʿŪDĪ (b. 9th century, Baghdad, Iraq—d. 957, al-Fusṭāṭ, Egypt), historian and traveler, known as the "Herodotus of the Arabs." He was the first Arab to combine history and scientific geography in a large-scale work, *Murūj adh-dhahab wa maʿādin al-jawāhir* ("The Meadows of Gold and Mines of Gems"), a world history.

As a child, al-Masʿūdī showed an extraordinary love of learning, an excellent memory, a capacity to write quickly, and a boundless curiosity that led him to study a wide variety of subjects, ranging from history and geography—his main interests—to comparative religion and science. He was not content to learn merely from books and teachers but traveled widely to gain firsthand knowledge of the countries about which he wrote. His travels extended to Syria, Iran, Armenia, the shores of the Caspian Sea, the Indus Valley, Ceylon (now Sri Lanka), Oman in Arabia, and the east coast of Africa as far south as Zanzibar, at least, and, possibly, Madagascar.

The titles of more than 20 books attributed to him are known, including several about Islāmic beliefs and sects and even one about poisons, but most of his writings have been lost. His major work was *Akhbār az-zamān* ("The History of Time") in 30 volumes. This seems to have been an encyclopaedic world history, taking in not only political history but also many facets of human knowledge and activity. A manuscript of one volume of this work is said to be preserved in Vienna; if this manuscript is genuine, it is all that has remained of the work. Al-Masʿūdī followed it with *Kitāb al-awsaṭ* ("Book of the Middle"), variously described as a supplement to or an abridgment of the *Akhbār az-zamān.* The *Kitāb* is undoubtedly a chronological history. A manuscript in the Bodleian Library, Oxford, may possibly be one volume of it.

Neither of these works had much effect on scholars—in the case of *Akhbār az-zamān,* possibly because of its daunting length. So al-Masʿūdī rewrote the two combined works in less detail in a single book, to which he gave the fanciful title of *Murūj adh-dhahab wa maʿādin al-jawāhir* ("The Meadows of Gold and the Mines of Gems"). This book quickly became famous and established the author's reputation as a leading historian. Ibn Khaldūn, the great 14th-century Arab philosopher of history, describes al-Masʿūdī as an imam ("leader," or "example") for historians. Though an abridgment, *Murūj adh-dhahab* is still a substantial work. In his introduction, al-Masʿūdī lists more than 80 historical works known to him, but he also stresses the importance of his travels to "learn the peculiarities of various nations and parts of the world." He claims that, in the book, he has dealt with every subject that may be useful or interesting.

The work is in 132 chapters. The second half is a straightforward history of Islām, beginning with the Prophet Muḥammad, then dealing with the caliphs down to al-Masʿūdī's own time, one by one. While it often makes interesting reading because of its vivid description and entertaining anecdotes, this part of the book is superficial. It is seldom read now, as much better accounts can be found elsewhere, particularly in the writings of aṭ-Ṭabarī.

The first half, in contrast, is of great value, though somewhat sprawling and confused in its design. It starts with the creation of the world and Jewish history. Then it intersperses chapters describing the history, geography, social life, and religious customs of non-Islāmic lands, such as India, Greece, and Rome, with accounts of the oceans, the calendars of various nations, climate, the solar system, and great temples. Among particularly interesting sections are those on pearl diving in the Persian Gulf, amber found in East Africa, Hindu burial customs, the land route to China, and navigation, with its various hazards, such as storms and waterspouts. The relative positions and characteristics of the seas are also explained.

Al-Masʿūdī's approach to his task was original: he gave as much weight to social, economic, religious, and cultural matters as to politics. Moreover, he utilized information obtained from sources not previously regarded as reliable. He retailed what he learned from merchants, local writers (including non-Muslims), and others he met on his travels. He displayed interest in all religions, including Hinduism and Zoroastrianism, as well as Judaism and Christianity. But he tended to reproduce uncritically what he heard; thus, his explanations of natural phenomena are often incorrect. Yet he was no worse, in this respect, than medieval European travelers such as Marco Polo and Sir John Mandeville.

Al-Masʿūdī had no settled abode for most of his adult life. In 945 he settled in Damascus. Two years later, he left there for al-Fusṭāṭ (old Cairo), where he remained until his death in 957. It was there, in the last year of his life, that he wrote *Kitāb at-tanbīh wa al-ishrāf* ("The Book of Notification and Verification"), in which he summarized, corrected, and brought up-to-date the contents of his former writings, especially the three historical works.

(J.A.H.)

Masukagami, historical epic about the Kamakura period (1192–1333) and one of the four best-known *kagami* (records) of Japanese history. The document, which is attributed to Nijō Yoshimoto, was written sometime between 1333 and 1376 and narrates the historical events occurring from the birth of the emperor Go-Toba (1180) to the return of the emperor Go-Daigo from exile on the Oki Islands (1334). It includes descriptions of the Mongol invasions of Japan (1274, 1281). Quoting numerous court records and diaries of noblemen, and writing in an elegant, classical style, the author narrates with pathos the declining power of the court nobility and the rising status of the warrior class, all seen from the perspective of a court nobleman.

Masulipatam, formerly MASULIPATNAM, also called MACHILĪPATNAM, or BANDAR, city, eastern Andhra Pradesh state, southern India. Masulipatam was the first British trading settlement (1611) on the Bay of Bengal. From 1686 to 1759 the city was held by the French and Dutch, until it was finally ceded to the British, who captured the city and fort from the French in 1759. The ruined fort is still a point of interest. The city received its present name in 1949.

Masulipatam is a railroad terminus and a seaport; it is connected to Vijayawāda, to the northwest, by the Bandar Canal. The city's main industries include carpet weaving, rice and oilseed milling, and the manufacture of scientific instruments. The headquarters of the All-India Spinners' Association, several colleges affiliated with Andhra University, and an engineering institute are located there. Pop. (1991 prelim.) 159,007.

Masulipatam, Treaty of (Feb. 23, 1768), agreement by which the state of Hyderābād, India, submitted to British control. The First Mysore War began in 1767 and concerned the East India Company's attempts to check the expansionary policies of the ruler of Mysore, Hyder Ali. Although originally allied to the British, the nizam of Hyderābād soon deserted his British allies and then finally made peace with them at Masulipatam when the British recognized the nizam as ruler of Balaghat. At the conclusion of the war in 1769, however, the British recognized the sovereignty of Mysore over Hyderābād. The double cross eventually prompted the nizam to join in a confederacy with Hyder Ali against the British in 1779, but the subsequent war ended in the solidification of British control over both Mysore and Hyderābād.

Masur, Kurt (b. July 18, 1927, Brieg, Ger. [now Brzeg, Pol.]), German conductor who rose to prominence in East Germany in the 1970s.

Masur studied piano and cello at the National Music School in Breslau, Ger. (now Wrocław, Pol.), from 1942 to 1944. He then studied conducting, piano, and composition at the Leipzig Conservatory in 1946–48. He spent the next seven years conducting in regional East German opera houses before becoming conductor of the Dresden Philharmonic in 1955. He was subsequently music director of the Mecklenburg State Theatre (1958–60), music director of the Comic Opera in Berlin (1960–64), and conductor at Dresden again from 1967 to 1972. During his long tenure as conductor of the Leipzig Gewandhaus Orchestra (from 1970), Masur became internationally known and toured widely throughout the world. He was noted for his comprehensive repertoire, which spanned German Romanticism from the works of Ludwig van Beethoven to those of Gustav Mahler.

A prestigious cultural figure in East Germany, Masur participated in the popular agitation that led to the fall of the communist government in late 1989. He became music director of the New York Philharmonic in 1991.

Masurian Lakeland, Polish POJEZIERZE MAZURSKIE, lake district, northeastern Poland. It is a 20,000-square-mile (52,000-square-kilometre) area immediately to the south of the Baltic coastal plains and extends 180 miles (290 km) eastward from the lower Vistula River to the Poland-Belarus border. It includes the *województwa* (provinces) of Elbląg, Olsztyn, Suwałki, Toruń, Ostrołęka, and Łomża. There are more than 2,000 lakes, originally formed by meltwaters from the Vistula ice sheet, in the district. Shallow proglacial stream valleys in the region contain marshes and sand dunes. The morainal Dylewska Hills, which rise to about 1,000 feet (300 m), are southwest of the city of Olsztyn.

Fertile black and brown soils are found in the western part of the district and produce wheat and sugar beets; sandy soils in the eastern part of the district produce potatoes and rye. The principal urban centres are Elbląg, Olsztyn, and Ełk.

Masvingo, formerly FORT VICTORIA, town, south-central Zimbabwe. It was founded in 1890 near the Macheke and Mshangashe rivers and became a municipality in 1953. A fort was built there and named for Queen Victoria. Located on the road between Harare (formerly Salisbury) and Pretoria and the terminus of a railway spur from Bulawayo, the town is a commercial centre for cattle ranching and agriculture (grain, cotton, tobacco, fruit, and sugar). There is gold and asbestos mining in the vicinity. Masvingo is a tourist base for the Kyle National Park, the Mushandike National Park, and the Zimbabwe (Bantu: "Stone Dwelling"), or Great Zimbabwe, ruins. These ruins, the oldest of which date from the 8th century, are a significant archaeological site. Long considered by Western archaeologists to be the handiwork of King Solomon, the Phoenicians, or the Arabs, the ruins at last have been recognized as the remains of the great inland empire of the Karanga people. Pop. (1982) 30,523.

Mata Hari, byname of MARGARETHA GEERTRUIDA MACLEOD, *née* ZELLE (b. Aug. 7, 1876, Leeuwarden, Neth.—d. Oct. 15, 1917, Vincennes, near Paris, Fr.), dancer and courtesan whose name has become a synonym for the seductive female spy. She was shot by the French on charges of spying for Germany during World War I, although the nature and extent of her espionage activities remain uncertain.

The daughter of a prosperous hatter, she attended a teachers' college in Leiden. In 1895 she married an officer of Scottish origin, Captain Campbell MacLeod, in the Dutch colonial army, and from 1897 to 1902 they lived in Java and Sumatra. The couple returned to Europe but later separated, and she began to dance professionally in Paris in 1905 under the name of Lady MacLeod. She soon called herself Mata Hari, said to be a Malay expression for the sun (literally, "eye of the day"). Tall, extremely attractive, superficially acquainted with East Indian dances, and willing to appear virtually nude in public, she was an instant success in Paris and other large cities. Throughout her life she had numerous lovers, many of them military officers.

Mata Hari
H. Roger-Viollet—Harlingue

The facts regarding her espionage activities remain obscure. According to one account, in the spring of 1916, while she was living in The Hague, a German consul is said to have offered to pay her for whatever information she could obtain on her next trip to France. After her arrest by the French, she acknowledged only that she had given some outdated information to a German intelligence officer.

According to Mata Hari's story, she had agreed to act as a French spy in German-occupied Belgium. She did not bother to tell French intelligence of her prior arrangement with the Germans. She later said that she had intended to secure for the Allies the assistance of Ernest Augustus, Duke of Brunswick-Lüneburg in Germany and heir to the dukedom of Cumberland in the British peerage.

Apparently, British sources informed French intelligence of Mata Hari's negotiations with the German official in The Hague. French suspicion of her duplicity increased, and on Feb. 13, 1917, she was arrested in Paris. She was imprisoned, tried by a military court on July 24–25, 1917, sentenced to death, and shot by a firing squad.

Matabele (people): *see* Ndebele.

Matabeleland, traditional region in southwestern Zimbabwe, inhabited mainly by the Bantu-speaking Ndebele people. It includes the southwestern portion of Zimbabwe's High and Middle velds, plateau country that ranges in elevation from 3,000 to 5,000 feet (900 to 1,500 m). The region slopes downward to the north and south; it is drained by tributaries of the Zambezi River to the north and by affluents of the Limpopo River to the south. Matabeleland consists mostly of savanna (tropical grassland) with wooded savanna to the northwest of the city of Bulawayo.

The Ndebele were originally an offshoot of the Nguni people of Natal (now part of the Republic of South Africa) who migrated northward in 1823 after their leader, Mzilikazi, an Nguni military commander under the orders of Shaka, king of the Zulu, fell foul of his master. The Matabele (as they were then known) settled in about 1840 in what is now southwestern Zimbabwe, a region that was given the name of Matabeleland by Europeans in the mid-19th century. The British South Africa Company, a mercantile company based in London, established itself in the region in 1890. The Matabele were defeated by the British in a war in 1893; later in the 1890s what is now Zimbabwe was divided by the British South Africa Company into two provinces, Matabeleland in the west and Mashonaland (the traditional homeland of the Shona people) in the east. Matabeleland, part of self-governing South Rhodesia after 1923, became part of independent Zimbabwe in 1980.

The contemporary Ndebele live in hamlets primarily around the city of Bulawayo, Zimbabwe's industrial centre. They raise corn (maize), peanuts (groundnuts), and cattle. Gold, coal, and tin are mined in the region.

Mataco, self-designation WICHI, South American Indians of the Gran Chaco, who speak an independent language and live mostly between the Bermejo and Pilcomayo rivers in northeastern Argentina. The Mataco are the largest and most important group of the Chaco Indians. They combine limited agriculture with fishing, hunting, and gathering of wild foods.

The Mataco were discovered by Europeans in 1628. They were originally peaceful but resisted European attempts at Christianization and colonization. Many were massacred, placed on reservations, or incorporated into government colonies. Today, the Mataco are being assimilated into the mestizo (mixed-blood) population of the Chaco. Many work as lumberjacks or migrate annually to employment on the sugar plantations of Jujuy and Salta—which indicates that they no longer sustain their traditional social organization and that their culture is disappearing.

Matadi, port city, extreme western Congo (Kinshasa). It lies along the Congo River opposite the town of Vivi. Matadi is situated 93 miles (150 km) upstream from the Atlantic port of Banana and is the farthest point up the river reached by oceangoing ships; cataracts prevent navigation farther upstream. It is the nation's principal port, with one of the largest harbours in central Africa and a mile-long waterfront that is cut in granite. Located at the base of the Cristal Mountains, the city takes its name from the Kikongo word for stone. In 1879 the British-American explorer Sir Henry Morton Stanley opened a trading station there. Between 1890 and 1908 the first Congo railroad was built from Matadi past the cataract region to Léopoldville (now Kinshasa), the national capital (210 miles [338 km] northeast). The Inga Falls, 25 miles (40 km) upstream, have been developed for hydroelectric power. Pop. (1994 est.) 172,730.

Port of Matadi on the Congo River, Congo (Kinshasa)
Tomas D.W. Friedmann—Photo Researchers/EB Inc.

matador, in bullfighting, the principal performer, who works the capes and attempts to dispatch the bull with a sword thrust between the shoulder blades.

The techniques used by modern matadors date from about 1914, when Juan Belmonte revolutionized the ancient spectacle. Formerly, the main object of the fight had been only to prepare the bull for the sword thrust. But Belmonte, a small, frail Andalusian, emphasized the danger to the man by close and graceful capework, and the kill became secondary. He worked closer to the bull's horns than had ever been believed possible and became an overnight sensation.

The possibility of death and the matador's disdain and skillful avoidance of injury thrills a crowd. The audience judges the matador according to his skill, grace, and daring. Therefore, a bullfight, or corrida, is viewed by many people as not so much a struggle between a man and a bull but rather a contest between a man and himself: how close will he dare to let the horns come, how far will he go to please the crowd.

Matador performing a close pass
By courtesy of Barnaby Conrad from Rodriguez/Boetticher Collection; photograph, Michael Christmas

Joselito (José Gómez), Belmonte's great friend and rival, considered one of the greatest bullfighters of all time, was killed in the ring in 1920. Almost every matador is gored at least once a season in varying degrees of severity. Belmonte was gored more than 50 times. Of the major matadors (since 1700), more than 40 have been killed in the ring; this does not include the beginning matadors or the *banderilleros* or picadors who have been killed.

The greatest matadors of the 20th century were the Mexicans Rodolfo Gaona, Armillita (Fermín Espinosa), and Carlos Arruza and the Spaniards Belmonte, Joselito, Domingo Ortega, Manolete (Manuel Rodríguez), and El Cordobés (Manuel Benítez). Cristina Sánchez of Spain became a matador in 1996, but she retired after three successful seasons, citing crowd hostility and harassment by male matadors.

Matagalpa, city, west-central Nicaragua, situated in a highland valley 2,237 feet (682 m) above sea level. One of the older and more picturesque cities of the nation, it contains a colonial church. It is the leading commercial and manufacturing centre of the region.

Except for the valleys of the Río Grande de Matagalpa and its tributaries, most of the region around Matagalpa is mountainous. The surrounding region produces a substantial portion of the country's coffee, as well as corn (maize), beans, rice, other vegetables, tobacco, and fruits. Gold and silver are mined in the region, and cattle and pigs are raised. In addition, processed foodstuffs, furniture, leather goods, and clay products are manufactured in the city. Matagalpa is accessible from Sébaco, via the Pan-American Highway; secondary roads lead to the smaller towns in the region. Pop. (1995) 59,397.

Matale, town, central Sri Lanka (Ceylon), 14 miles (23 km) north of Kandy. A Buddhist monastery and rock temple (Aluvihara) are near the town. Matale's intermediate elevation and moderate rainfall abet the cultivation of spices. It is a cattle centre, and there are extensive tea, rubber, and cacao plantations in the vicinity. Pop. (1994 est.) 43,000.

Matamba, historic African kingdom of the Mbundu people, situated on the west bank of the Kwango River northeast of Luanda, Angola. In the early 16th century it was a well-established state, independent but paying occasional tribute to the Kongo kingdom to the north. The dominant feature of Matamba's history from the 16th to the 19th century was conflict with the Portuguese colonists of Angola. In the 1590s Matamba joined with Ndongo, Kongo, and the Jaga to battle against the Portuguese, successfully blocking their advance inland but failing to capture the Portuguese forts at Luanda and Massangano. In about 1630 Matamba was conquered by Nzinga (also called Ana de Sousa), *ngola* (ruler) of Ndongo, who had been expelled from her homeland after attempting to halt the European advance there. Nzinga built Matamba into a strong power base for her continuing struggle against Portuguese Angola.

Angola's eastward expansion was stopped in the 1670s at the borders of Matamba and Kasanje (southeast of Matamba). A treaty of 1684 between Matamba and the Portuguese remained in effect, despite continual skirmishes, for 60 years. In 1744 the murder of a white trader in Matamba served as the excuse for a Portuguese invasion that won for Angola a bit of Matamba's territory. Further territorial losses followed in the 1830s, supplying land for Angolan coffee plantations. The remainder of Matamba, assigned to Angola by European treaties of 1870–1900, remained in fact a self-governing kingdom until Portuguese troops finally occupied it in the early 20th century.

Matamoros, in full IZÚCAR DE MATAMOROS, city, southwestern Puebla state, south-central Mexico. Formerly known as Matamoros de Izúcar, the city is situated at 4,350 feet (1,326 m) above sea level on the Nexapa River, which descends through the Sierra Nevada. Livestock raising and crop growing (mainly sugarcane, rice, corn [maize], beans, and fruits) are found in the hinterland. Sugar, cheese, butter, and canned goods are the city's principal products. Beekeeping is also practiced in the area. The main highway linking Oaxaca with Mexico City passes through Matamoros, as does the narrow-gauge Mexico City–Río Balsas railroad. Pop. (2000 prelim.) 70,532.

Matamoros, in full HEROICA MATAMOROS, city, northern Tamaulipas state, Mexico, on the southern bank of the Rio Grande (Río Bravo del Norte), 28 miles (45 km) from the Gulf of Mexico and across from Brownsville, Texas. Matamoros, founded in 1824, was the scene of bitter fighting in the Mexican War and was occupied by U.S. troops in 1846. It is now one of Mexico's chief ports of entry for tourists and for the import and export of goods. The manufacturing and commercial centre of an extensive cotton- and sugarcane-growing area, it has tanneries, cotton mills, and distilleries. Air, rail, and highway connections link Matamoros to Monterrey and Mexico City. Pop. (2000 prelim.) 416,428.

Matane, city, Bas-Saint-Laurent region, eastern Quebec province, Canada. It lies on the south bank of the St. Lawrence River, at the mouth of the Matane River.

A transportation, commercial, and industrial centre, Matane is a pulp-shipping port and eastern terminus of the Canada and Gulf Terminal Railway. Lumbering, woodworking, furniture making, flour milling, and tanning are its main industries, while dairying, market gardening, ranching, and shrimp and salmon fishing are important in the surrounding rural area. Matane is 32 miles (51 km) from Métis Gardens (Jardins de Métis), a former private estate with formal gardens that include 4,000 plant species from varied climates. Pop. (1996) 12,364.

Matanzas, *provincia,* west-central Cuba, bounded on the north by the Straits of Florida, on the northeast by Villa Clara province, on the southeast by Cienfuegos province, on the southwest by the Caribbean Sea, and on the west by La Habana province. It was established in 1879. Much of northern Matanzas is covered by fertile plains, but much of the south is covered by mangrove swamps and marshy lowlands, especially the Zapata Peninsula in the southwest. Both coasts are dotted with offshore islands and indented with bays.

Vineyards in northern Matanzas province, Cuba
Atlas Photo

The province produces sugarcane, citrus fruits, rice, and livestock. Sugar, rum, fertilizer, and paper are manufactured. Matanzas city and Cárdenas, the main population centres and sugar ports, lie in the north. Matanzas city is also the provincial capital and a major centre of tourism. Major highways and railroads link Matanzas city and Colón with Havana. Area 4,625 square miles (11,978 square km). Pop. (1998 est.) 654,516.

Matanzas, city, capital of Matanzas *provincia,* west-central Cuba. Founded in 1693 on an excellent bay (on the Straits of Florida) known to the Spanish since 1508 and used by pirates, it was by 1860 the second city of Cuba, but its growth was slowed as the sugarcane industry expanded into the eastern part of the island.

Matanzas has been called the Athens of Cuba because of its active cultural institutions and because of the many scholars and artists who have worked there. It has scenic drives, plazas, and monuments; historic buildings include the Castillo (castle) de San Severino (17th century) and the San Carlos cathedral (1730). It is one of Cuba's chief ports, handling mainly sugar and henequen fibre, and it is an industrial centre, manufacturing rayon, rope, shoes, fertilizers, and matches. A thermal-power plant is located nearby. The city is linked to Havana by two railroads and by the central highway. Pop. (1994 est.) 123,843.

Matanzas National Monument, Fort (Florida, U.S.): *see* Fort Matanzas National Monument.

Matapa, a southern African empire ruled by a line of kings known as the Mwene Matapa (*q.v.*).

Matapédia Valley, most important valley in the Gaspé Peninsula, lying in Bas-Saint-Laurent region, eastern Quebec province, Canada. Extending in a northwest-southeast direction for some 60 miles (100 km), it forms a direct lowland route through the Notre Dame Mountains from the St. Lawrence River to Chaleur Bay on the Atlantic. The valley is drained by the Matapédia River, which flows 50 miles (80 km) from Lake Matapédia (14 miles [23 km] long by 2 miles [3 km] wide) to the Restigouche River (Matapédia is Indian for "joining of two rivers"); both the river and the lake are noted for their salmon fishing and scenic beauty. Part of the valley's interior lies within Gaspesian Provincial Park.

The valley floor is a fertile dairying and mixed-farming area, the centres of which are the agricultural market towns of Sayabec, Amqui, and Causapscal. In addition to its attraction for farmers, tourists, and sportsmen, the valley serves as an important transportation route between the Maritime Provinces and the Canadian mainland; through it passes the Canadian National Railway and a main provincial highway. New settlements in the interior include Saint-Thomas de Cherbourg and Saint-Jean de Cherbourg.

Matara, town, southern Sri Lanka (Ceylon). It lies at the mouth of the Nilwala River on the island's southern coast. Its name, meaning Great Ford, arose from its location at a river crossing. The Portuguese held the town in the 17th century, and the Dutch in the 18th. Under both countries it was an important commercial centre, and Dutch fortifications can still be seen. Matara is now the trade centre of a productive agricultural region. It is linked by rail with Colombo and is a road junction. Pop. (1994 est.) 48,000.

Mataram, large kingdom in Java that lasted from the late 16th century to the 18th century, when the Dutch came to power in Indonesia. Mataram was originally a vassal of Pajang, but it became powerful under Senapati (later known as Adiwijoyo), who defeated Pajang and became the first king of Mataram. Senapati attempted to unite eastern and central Java without much success.

Under Sultan Agung, who came to power in 1613, as the Dutch entered the region, Mataram was able to expand its territory to include most of Java. After capturing several port cities of northern Java, especially Surabaya and Madura, he attempted to seize Batavia from the Dutch East India Company. He launched two unsuccessful attacks, one in 1628 and the other in 1629. The sultan also launched a "holy war" against Bali and against Balambangan in extreme eastern Java. He then concentrated on the internal development of Mataram. He moved the inhabitants of central Java to the less populated Krawang (in western Java) and encouraged interisland trade. He also adapted Islām to the Hindu-Javanese tradition and introduced a new calendar in 1633 based on Islāmic and Javanese practice. The arts during Sultan Agung's reign were a mixture of Islāmic and Hindu-Javanese elements.

Mataram began to decline after the death of Sultan Agung (1645) and, in the mid-18th century, lost both power and territory to the Dutch East India Company. It had become a vassal state of the company by 1749. Wars of succession took place in Mataram, resulting in the division of the eastern and western regions in 1755 (*see* Gianti Agreement); two years later Mataram was divided into three regions.

Mataram, city, capital of Nusa Tenggara Barat *provinsi* ("province"), Lombok island, Indonesia. It is located on the western coast, east of Bali. Until the end of the 18th century, it was the chief city of the Muslim kingdom of Mataram on Lombok. Brought under Balinese rule by Agung Dahuran in the early 19th century, the city subsequently became the capital of the Balinese sultans. Mataram was occupied by the Dutch in 1894 and by the Japanese during World War II. Its population is mostly Sassaks, who are Muslims of Malayan stock.

Mataram is a trade centre for agricultural goods via the nearby port of Ampenan. Small-scale industry consists of food processing, boatbuilding, and rice milling. The city is linked by road to Tanjung in the north and to Praya and Selong in the east; it also has an airport. Mataram University (founded 1962) is located at Ampenan. A number of palaces built by the Balinese sultan are in the vicinity. Pop. (1990) 275,089.

Mataró, port town, Barcelona *provincia,* in the *comunidad autónoma* ("autonomous community") of Catalonia, northeastern Spain, on the Mediterranean coast. The town originated as the Roman Iluro and is divided into an older, Moorish sector on a rise surrounded by walls and a modern sector. The first railway in Spain was built (1848) between Mataró and Barcelona city, 18 miles (29 km) southwest. Its church of Santa María has a Baroque altar and fine paintings by Antonio Viladomat and Pedro Montana. Wine, carnations, and potatoes are produced and exported; hosiery and underwear, knitting machinery, soap, paper, chemicals, and bus and truck bodies are manufactured. Nearby is the carbonated mineral spring of Argentona. Pop. (1999 est.) 104,095.

Mataura River, river, South Island, New Zealand. It rises in the Eyre Mountains south of Wakatipu Lake and flows south past Gore and Mataura to enter the Pacific Ocean at Foveaux Strait, 20 miles (32 km) east of Bluff, after a course of 149 mi (240 km). Together with the Oreti and Aparima rivers, the Mataura has created the Murihiku (Southland) Plain and drains an area of 281 square miles (728 square km). The river derives its name from a Maori term meaning "reddish, glowing face," referring to the red glow of the river surface when swamp water, coloured red by iron oxide, drains into it.

match, splinter of wood, strip of cardboard, or other suitable flammable material tipped with a substance ignitable by friction.

A match consists of three basic parts: a head, which initiates combustion; a tinder substance to pick up and transmit the flame; and a handle. There are two main types of modern friction matches: (1) strike-anywhere matches and (2) safety matches. The head of the strike-anywhere match contains all the chemicals necessary to obtain ignition from frictional heat, while the safety match has a head that ignites at a much higher temperature and must be struck on a specially prepared surface containing ingredients that pass ignition across to the head. The substance commonly used for obtaining combustion at the temperature of frictional heat is a compound of phosphorus. This substance is found in the head of strike-anywhere matches and in the striking surface of safety matches.

In addition to the phosphoric igniting agent, three other main groups of chemicals are found in the match: (1) oxidizing agents, such as potassium chlorate, which supply oxygen to the igniting agent and the other combustible materials; (2) binders, such as animal glue, starches and gums, and synthetics, which bind the ingredients and are oxidized during combustion; post-combustion binders, such as ground glass, which fuse and hold the ash together, must also be used; and (3) inert materials, such as diatomaceous earth, which provide bulk and regulate the speed of reaction.

Before the invention of matches, it was common to use specially made splinters tipped with some combustible substance, such as sulfur, to transfer a flame from one combustible source to another. An increased interest in chemistry led to experiments to produce fire by direct means on this splinter. Jean Chancel discovered in Paris in 1805 that splints tipped with potassium chlorate, sugar, and gum could be ignited by dipping them into sulfuric acid. Later workers refined this method, which culminated in the "promethean match" patented in 1828 by Samuel Jones of London. This consisted of a glass bead containing acid, the outside of which was coated with igniting composition. When the glass was broken by means of a small pair of pliers, or even with the user's teeth, the paper in which it was wrapped was set on fire. Other early matches, which could be both inconvenient and unsafe, involved bottles containing phosphorus and other substances. An example was François Derosne's *briquet phosphorique* (1816), which used a sulfur-tipped match to scrape inside a tube coated internally with phosphorus.

These first matches were extremely difficult to ignite, and they frequently erupted in a shower of sparks. In addition, the smell was particularly offensive, and the warning printed on Jones's box ("Persons whose lungs are delicate should by no means use the Lucifers") seems well founded.

Economic conditions between 1825 and 1835 seem to have favoured the manufacture of matches as an industrial proposition, although the first suppliers fell back on nonphosphoric formulas—*i.e.,* those based mostly on potassium-chlorate mixtures. The first friction matches were invented by John Walker, an English chemist and apothecary, whose ledger of April 7, 1827, records the first sale of such matches. Walker's "Friction Lights" had tips coated with a potassium chloride–antimony sulfide paste, which ignited when scraped between a fold of sandpaper. He never patented them. Nonphosphoric friction matches were being made by G.-E. Merkel of Paris and J. Siegal of Austria, among others, by 1832, by which time the manufacture of friction matches was well established in Europe.

In 1831 Charles Sauria of France incorporated white, or yellow, phosphorus in his formula, an innovation quickly and widely copied. In 1835 Jànos Irinyi of Hungary replaced potassium chlorate with lead oxide and obtained matches that ignited quietly and smoothly.

The discovery by the Austrian chemist Anton von Schrötter in 1845 of red phosphorus, which is nontoxic and is not subject to spontaneous combustion, led to the safety match, with its separation of the combustion ingredients between the match head and the special striking surface. J.E. Lundström of Sweden patented this method in 1855.

Although safety matches became widely accepted, white phosphorus matches continued to be popular because of their keeping qualities and resistance to climatic conditions. However, at the end of the 19th century serious toxic effects of white phosphorus ("phossy jaw") were discovered in the factory workers who made such matches. Phosphorus sesquisulfide, much less toxic, was first prepared by the French chemist Georges Lemoine in 1864 but was not used in matches until E.-D. Cahen and H. Sevène of the French government match monopoly filed a patent in 1898; within a few years white phosphorus was outlawed nearly everywhere.

Modern safety matches usually have antimony sulfide, oxidizing agents such as potassium chlorate, and sulfur or charcoal in the heads, and red phosphorus in the striking surface. Nonsafety matches usually have phosphorus sesquisulfide in the heads.

matchlock, in firearms, a device for igniting gunpowder developed in the 15th century, a major advance in the manufacture of small arms. The matchlock was the first mechanical firing device. It consisted of an S-shaped arm, called a serpentine, that held a match, and a trigger device that lowered the serpentine so that the lighted match would fire the priming powder in the pan attached to the side of the barrel. The flash in the pan penetrated a small port in the breech of the gun and ignited the main charge.

In the matchlock all the working elements were protected inside the lock. The device also freed the hand of the user or his aide. Early matchlock guns had a number of names including harquebus, hacquebut, hagbutt, hachbuss, caliver, and musket. Slow and somewhat clumsy, the matchlock was difficult to use in wind or rain, and its glow presented a hazard at night or in ambush. Matchlock guns, however, remained primary military firearms in Europe even after other ignition systems were invented.

maté, also called YERBA MATÉ, PARAGUAY TEA, or BRAZILIAN TEA, tealike beverage, popular in many South American countries, brewed from the dried leaves of an evergreen shrub or tree (*Ilex paraguariensis*) related to holly. It is a stimulating drink, greenish in colour, containing caffeine and tannin, and is less astringent than tea.

Silver vessel for the preparation and serving of maté; in a private collection
Librairie Larousse

Although maté is an ancient Indian beverage, the plant, growing wild in Paraguay and southern Brazil, was first cultivated by Jesuit missionaries. In the wild state the plant becomes a round-headed tree; under cultivation, which improves the quality of the brew, it remains a small, multi-stemmed shrub, requiring a minimum of two years between harvests for regrowth.

Drying methods vary. In Brazil the leafy branches are placed on a six-foot square of beaten earth, called a *tatacua,* and a fire is kindled around the area, providing preliminary roasting; the branches are next heated on an arch of poles over a fire; and the dried leaves, placed in pits in the earth, are ground into coarse powder, producing a maté called *caa gazu,* or *yerva do polos.* In Paraguay and parts of Argentina the leaves, with midribs removed before roasting, are made into a maté called *caa-míri. Caa-cuys,* a Paraguayan maté of superior quality, is made from leaf buds. In a newer method, similar to the Chinese procedure for drying tea leaves, the leaves are heated in large cast-iron pans.

In brewing maté, the dried leaves (*yerba*), placed in dried hollow gourds, are covered with boiling water and steeped. The gourds, called matés or *culhas,* are decorated, sometimes silver mounted; the vessel may even be made entirely of silver. The tea is sucked from the gourd with a *bombilla,* a tube about 6 inches (15 cm) long, often made of silver, with a strainer at one end to keep leaf particles from the mouth. Maté, usually served plain, is sometimes flavoured with milk, sugar, or lemon juice. When tightly covered, it retains flavour during storage.

Matehuala, city, northern San Luis Potosí *estado* ("state"), northeastern Mexico. It is situated on the interior plateau, 5,955 feet (1,815 m) above sea level, in the Salado Valley, east of the Sierra del Catorce. Some corn (maize) is cultivated in the area, but it is primarily a mining (gold, silver, lead, and copper) and industrial (large copper smelters) centre. In addition, there are tanneries, and liquor and fibres are extracted from maguey (American aloe). The city is linked by highway with San Luis Potosí, the state capital, to the south-southwest, and with Saltillo, the capital of Coahuila state, to the north-northwest. Matehuala also has an airfield. Pop. (1990 prelim.) mun., 70,283.

Matera, city, capital of Matera *provincia,* Basilicata *regione,* southern Italy. It lies above a deep ravine, northwest of Taranto. Of obscure origin, the town formed part of the duchy of Benevento and of the principality of Salerno and was occupied successively by the Normans, the Aragonese, and the Orsini. In the old part of the city on the slope of the ravine, people inhabit cavelike houses cut into the rock with only an opening for the door, a system dating from prehistoric times. The modern part of the city consists of more ordinary dwellings. Matera is an archiepiscopal see, and important monuments are the Apulian-Romanesque cathedral (1268–70) and the churches of San Francesco (rebuilt 1670), San Giovanni Battista (13th century), and San Pietro Caveoso, carved out of rock. There is a museum with a collection of local artifacts.

The population is engaged in agriculture, tufa quarrying, and the manufacture of terracotta and artistic ceramics. Pop. (1991 prelim.) mun., 53,775.

materialism, in philosophy, the view that all facts (including facts about the human mind and will and the course of human history) are causally dependent upon physical processes, or even reducible to them.

A brief treatment of materialism follows. For full treatment, *see* MACROPAEDIA: Philosophical Schools and Doctrines, Western.

The many materialistic philosophies that have arisen from time to time may be said to maintain one or more of the following theses: (1) that what are called mental events are really certain complicated physical events, (2) that mental processes are entirely determined by physical processes (*e.g.,* that "making up one's mind," while it is a real process that can be introspected, is caused by bodily processes, its apparent consequences following from the bodily causes), (3) that mental and physical processes are two aspects of what goes on in a substance at once mental and bodily (this thesis, whether called "materialistic" or not, is commonly opposed by those who oppose materialism), and (4) that thoughts and wishes influence an individual's life, but that the course of history is determined by the interaction of masses of people and masses of material things, in such a way as to be predictable without reference to the "higher" processes of thought and will.

Materialism is thus opposed to philosophical dualism or idealism and, in general, to belief in God, in disembodied spirits, in free will, or in certain kinds of introspective psychology. Materialistic views insist upon settling questions by reference to public observation and not to private intuitions. Since this is a maxim which scientists must profess within the limits of their special inquiries, it is natural that philosophies which attach the highest importance to science should lean toward materialism. But none of the great empiricists have been satisfied (at least for long) with systematic materialism.

The Greek atomists of the 5th century BC (Leucippus and Democritus) offered simple mechanical explanations of perception and thought—a view that was condemned by Socrates in the *Phaedo*. In the 17th century Thomas Hobbes and Pierre Gassendi, inspired by the Greek atomists, used materialistic arguments in defense of science against Aristotle and against the orthodox tradition, and in the next century the materialists of the Enlightenment (Julien de Lamettrie, Paul d'Holbach, and others) attempted to provide a detailed account of psychology.

During the modern period, the question of materialism came to be applied on the one hand to problems of method and interpretation in science (Henri Bergson, Samuel Alexander, A.N. Whitehead) and on the other hand to the interpretation of human history (G.W.F. Hegel, Auguste Comte, Karl Marx). Marx offered a new kind of materialism, dialectic and not mechanistic, and embracing all sciences (*see* dialectical materialism).

In the 20th century materialistic thought faced novel developments in the sciences and in philosophy. In physics, relativity and quantum theory modified, though they did not abandon, the notions of cause and of universal determinism. In psychology, J.B. Watson's behaviourism, an extreme form of materialism, did not find general acceptance; and researches both in psychology and in psychoanalysis made it impossible to hold any simple direct view of the mind's dependence on the processes and mechanisms of the nervous system. In philosophy, further reflection suggested to many that it is futile to try to erect a system of belief, whether materialistic or otherwise, on the basis of the concepts of science and of common sense (especially those of cause and of explanation).

materials handling, the movement of raw goods from their native site to the point of use in manufacturing, their subsequent manipulation in production processes, and the transfer of finished products from factories and their distribution to users or sales outlets.

In early systems of handling materials, goods were handled as single units in a discontinuous manner. These early methods treated the three basic stages of handling—materials collection, manufacturing, and product distribution—as discrete steps, and materials were moved in individual rather than bulk units.

Modern materials-handling systems, by contrast, emphasize the integrated flow of goods from the source of raw materials to final user. This can be achieved by transporting goods in large quantities and in standardized units; by handling procedures using cranes, conveyor belts, and other machines; and by the careful coordination of the movement of goods with production, processing, and distribution schedules. Recent developments in bulk transport have been directed toward keeping materials in units as long as possible, minimizing unit costs, and reducing the amount of handling necessary at all stages.

Materials that are capable of being moved in liquid or gaseous form in large quantities, such as petroleum and natural gas, are most often moved through pipelines from mining sites to storage tanks and refineries, and in turn to distribution facilities. Piping networks are also used to transport slurries, which are solids (such as coal) suspended in water. The compression of natural gas and the use of large-capacity tankers have also facilitated the transportation of these materials over long distances and through major waterways. Materials handled in bulk that cannot flow through pipelines are restricted to shipping, trucking, and rail transport. Such commodities include unprocessed minerals and building materials. A third type of material consists of machine parts and other manufactured goods that can be transported in bulk to assembly lines or distributors.

Materials handling equipment ranges from the simplest carts and wheelbarrows to a specialized variety of highly sophisticated cranes. Power trucks and forklifts are used for lifting bulky or heavy loads, often in connection with trailers that transport the materials along a particular route for distribution. Conveyors and monorails, powered artificially or by gravity, are also widely used in the short-distance transfer of materials within a plant and for sorting and assembly line production. Containers that range from boxes and bins to truck-size proportions help to reduce the amount of handling needed for materials and parts and to maximize efficiency through transportation in large units. Frames are also used, with or without pallets, as a way of optimizing the use of vertical storage space.

Generally, optimal efficiency of handling involves a balance between the desired speed of an individual shipment and its size, weight, and composition. Innovations in trucking have produced specialized equipment for transporting refrigerated goods, bulk liquids, and gases and have developed loading methods that use pallets and wide platforms to minimize handling labour. The rail industry has produced rail cars that can be loaded from the side, flatcars, trilevel cars for shipping automobiles, and unit trains consisting of a chain of cars that carry a single bulk commodity. These trains can be loaded efficiently by cranes, hoppers, and conveyors and are capable of transporting large quantities of goods over long distances at lowered costs. Efficient transoceanic conveyance of bulk materials is typically accomplished by large cargo freighters and conference carriers. Supertankers are capable of carrying larger loads, but they also involve an increased risk of severe economic loss in case of accidents or, in transporting petroleum, of potentially destructive environmental hazards. General-cargo vessels are used for moving packaged goods along well-traveled water routes. Of all methods of transport, air travel offers the greatest advantage in speed of delivery, but it is also the highest in cost and the least capable of handling bulky or heavy shipments. Nevertheless, equipment has been developed to reduce loading time, and special containers help to maximize the efficient use of air cargo space.

materials processing, the series of operations that transforms industrial materials from a raw-material state into finished parts or products. Industrial materials are defined as those used in the manufacture of "hard" goods, such as more or less durable machines and equipment produced for industry and consumers, as contrasted with disposable "soft" goods, such as chemicals, foodstuffs, pharmaceuticals, and apparel.

Materials processing by hand is as old as civilization; mechanization began with the Industrial Revolution of the 18th century, and in the early 19th century the basic machines for forming, shaping, and cutting were developed, principally in England. Since then, materials-processing methods, techniques, and machinery have grown in variety and number.

The cycle of manufacturing processes that converts materials into parts and products starts immediately after the raw materials are either extracted from minerals or produced from basic chemicals or natural substances. The processes used to convert raw materials into finished products perform one or both of two major functions: first, they form the material into the desired shape; second, they alter or improve the properties of the material.

Forming and shaping processes may be classified into two broad types—those performed on the material in a liquid state and those performed on the material in a solid or plastic condition. The processing of materials in liquid form is commonly known as casting when it involves metals, glass, and ceramics; it is called molding when applied to plastics and some other nonmetallic materials. Most casting and molding processes involve four major steps: (1) making an accurate pattern of the part, (2) making a mold from the pattern, (3) introducing the liquid into the mold, and (4) removing the hardened part from the mold. A finishing operation is sometimes needed.

Materials in their solid state are formed into desired shapes by the application of a force or pressure. The material to be processed can be in a relatively hard and stable condition and in such forms as bar, sheet, pellet, or powder, or it can be in a soft, plastic, or puttylike form. Solid materials can be shaped either hot or cold. Processing of metals in the solid state can be divided into two major stages: first, the raw material in the form of large ingots or billets is hot-worked, usually by rolling, forging, or extrusion, into smaller shapes and sizes; second, these shapes are processed into final parts and products by one or more smaller scale hot or cold forming processes.

After the material is formed, it is usually further altered. In materials processing, a "removal" process is one that eliminates portions of a piece or body of material to achieve a desired shape. Although removal processes are applied to most types of materials, they are most widely used on metallic materials. Material can be removed from a workpiece by either mechanical or nonmechanical means.

There are a number of metal-cutting processes. In almost all of them, machining involves the forcing of a cutting tool against the material to be shaped. The tool, which is harder than the material to be cut, removes the unwanted material in the form of chips. Thus, the elements of machining are a cutting device, a means for holding and positioning the workpiece, and usually a lubricant (or cutting oil). There are four basic noncutting removal processes: (1) in chemical milling the metal is removed by the etching reaction of chemical solutions on the metal; although usually applied to metals, it can also be used on plastics and glass, (2) electrochemical machining uses the principle of metal plating in reverse, as the workpiece, instead of being built up by the plating process, is eaten away in a controlled manner by the action of the electrical current, (3) electrodischarge machining and grinding erodes or cuts the metal by high-energy sparks or electrical discharges, (4) laser machining cuts metallic or refractory materials with an intense beam of light from a laser.

Another further alteration may be "joining," the process of permanently, sometimes only temporarily, bonding or attaching materials to each other. The term as used here includes welding, brazing, soldering, and adhesive and chemical bonding. In most joining processes, a bond between two pieces of material is produced by application of one or a combination of three kinds of energy: thermal, chemical, or mechanical. A bonding or filler material, the same as or different from the materials being joined, may or may not be used.

The properties of materials can be further altered by hot or cold treatments, by mechanical operations, and by exposure to some forms of radiation. The property modification is usually brought about by a change in the microscopic structure of the material. Both heat-treating, involving temperatures above room temperature, and cold-treating, involving temperatures below room temperature, are included in this category. Thermal treatment is a process in which the temperature of the material is raised or lowered to alter the properties of the original material. Most thermal-treating processes are based on time-temperature cycles that include three steps: heating, holding at temperature, and cooling. Although some thermal treatments are applicable to most families of materials, they are most widely used on metals.

Finally, "finishing" processes may be employed to modify the surfaces of materials in order to protect the material against deterioration by corrosion, oxidation, mechanical wear, or deformation; to provide special surface characteristics such as reflectivity, electrical conductivity or insulation, or bearing properties; or to give the material special decorative effects. There are two broad groups of finishing processes, those in which a coating, usually of a different material, is applied to the surface and those in which the surface of the material is changed by chemical action, heat, or mechanical force. The first group includes metallic coating, such as electroplating; organic finishing, such as painting; and porcelain enameling.

materials salvage, also called RECYCLING, recovery and reuse of materials from spent products. The principal motives for recycling have been the increasing scarcity and cost of natural resources, such as oil, gas, coal, mineral ores, and trees, and the pollution of air, water, and land by waste materials.

Historically, the earliest salvage was probably military in nature. After a battle, the victors claimed the weapons of the vanquished. Almost equally ancient is the recovery of ships and their cargoes. Ships sunk in shallow harbours or broken up on the rocks of a coast often contained easily salvageable objects and materials. Later, the development of suitable equipment made deep marine-cargo salvage possible, so that such operations now can be carried out at depths of several hundred feet.

There are two types of materials-salvage operations: internal and external. Internal salvage or recycling is the reuse in a manufacturing process of materials that are a waste product of that process. Internal recycling is common in the metals industry. The manufacture of copper tubing results in a certain amount of waste in the form of tube ends and trimmings; this material is remelted and recast. External salvage or recycling is the reclaiming of materials from a product that has been worn out or rendered obsolete. An example of external recycling is the collection of old newspapers and magazines for the manufacture of newsprint or other paper products.

Whether the recycling or salvage operation is internal or external is of little technological significance but of considerable economic importance. The cost of reprocessing waste or recycled material must be less than the cost of processing new raw material.

Ferrous metals. Ferrous products can be salvaged by both internal and external methods. Internally, metal cuttings or imperfect products are recycled by remelting, recasting, and redrawing entirely within the steel mill. Most iron and steel manufacturers produce their own coke. By-products from the coke oven include many organic compounds, hydrogen sulfide, and ammonia. The organic compounds are purified and sold. The ammonia is sold as an aqueous solution or combined with sulfuric acid to form ammonium sulfate, which is subsequently dried and sold as fertilizer.

During its manufacture, steel is pickled (treated with sulfuric or hydrochloric acid) to remove scale formed in the high-temperature drawing and rolling operations. The acid slowly attacks the scale and removes it, forming iron compounds in solution. These solutions can be transformed into iron oxide and reprocessed to make more steel. Unconsumed acid can also be reclaimed for future pickling operations. Blast furnace slag and, to some extent, steel slag are used by the construction industry as all-purpose aggregates for road building and in various types of concrete products. Refuse from preparation of taconite ore has been converted into a foamed building material; similar potential exists for refuse from copper, lead, and zinc mining.

In the ferrous-metals industry there are also many applications of external salvage or recycling. Scrap steel makes up a significant percentage of the feed to the open-hearth furnace, the Bessemer converter, or the basic oxygen furnace. The scrap comes from a variety of manufacturing operations that use steel as a basic material and from discarded or obsolete goods made from iron and steel.

The average junked automobile contains about 62 percent iron and steel, 28 percent nonferrous metals, and 10 percent rubber, plastics, and textiles. Salvage operations on automobiles actually begin before they reach the reprocessor; parts such as carburetors and electrical components can be removed, rebuilt, and resold. In a process developed in Belgium, liquid nitrogen (at a temperature of −320° F [−196° C]) is sprayed on the auto body before shredding. At such temperatures, steel becomes brittle; nonferrous metals such as copper and aluminum do not. The steel parts of a superchilled auto body break in the shredder much as a glass bottle breaks if thrown on a concrete floor. The nonferrous metals tend to agglomerate and are therefore much more easily removed from the ferrous metals after shredding. The same basic procedures apply to washing machines, refrigerators, or other large, bulky steel or iron items.

Nonferrous metals. At present, manual sorting seems to be the only practical method of separating pieces of nonferrous scrap materials, the most important of which are aluminum, copper, lead, and silver.

Secondary aluminum reprocessing is a large industry, involving salvage of machine turnings, rejected castings, siding, and even aluminum covered with decorative plastic. They are thrown into a reverberatory furnace (in which heat is radiated from the roof into the material treated) and melted while the impurities are burned off. The resulting material is cast into ingots and resold for drawing or forming operations.

The primary source of used lead is discarded electric storage batteries. Battery plates may be smelted to produce antimonial lead (a lead-antimony alloy) for manufacture of new batteries, or pure lead and antimony as separate products.

Photographic paper and X-ray film contain small but valuable quantities of silver, and recycling methods utilizing incineration have been developed. Most of the silver salts used in photographic papers are volatile, and the vent gas from their incineration can be cooled by water sprays and then passed into an electrostatic precipitator where the silver salts are almost completely recovered. The silver may then be recycled and used for coating more photographic paper.

Rubber. Though much used rubber was formerly burned, in most countries burning has been greatly curtailed to prevent air pollution. Internal recycling is common in most rubber plants; the reprocessed product can be used wherever premium-grade rubber is not needed. External salvage has proved a problem over the years; the cost of recycling old or worn-out tires has far exceeded the value of the reclaimed material. Destructive distillation of scrap rubber products may, however, allow reclamation of valuable chemicals, including a liquid oil that can be used in manufacturing other chemicals, a combustible gas valuable as a fuel, and a carbonaceous residue useful as a filter char or binder in concrete or asphalt roadways.

Chemicals. The chemical industry produces hundreds of waste products, many of which cannot be recovered economically. To prevent air and water pollution, however, recovery has become necessary.

Many plastics-manufacturing processes liberate solvent vapours, such as methyl ethyl ketone and toluene or plasticizers such as dioctyl phthalate. These materials can be salvaged by passing the air-solvent mixture through a granular bed of activated carbon or charcoal. The bed removes between 95 and 99 percent of the solvent from the airstream. Once saturated, the bed is treated with steam, which flushes out almost all the solvent from the activated carbon. Condensation forms a mixture of solvent and water that can be separated by distillation or decantation.

Manufacture of many insecticides, herbicides, and plastics results in residues that contain toxic compounds of chlorine. Since most of these wastes are combustible, they are often burned; hydrogen chloride is one of the products of combustion. Hydrogen chloride is extremely toxic, but it is soluble in water: it can be separated out by water scrubbing, a process that then presents the problem of disposing of dilute hydrochloric acid. Several processes have been developed that involve reclamation of the hydrochloric acid either as commercial-grade muriatic acid or as anhydrous hydrogen chloride gas. Both of these products can profitably be recycled.

Domestic refuse. Once glass, plastics, and metals have been removed from domestic refuse, what remains is essentially organic waste that lends itself to one of several salvage operations. Upon burial or composting, the biological action of the earth degrades the residue and returns its elements to the soil. Pyrolysis (incineration with a deficiency of air) permits recovery of certain fuel gases and chemicals. Incineration appears especially promising in the light of two environmental dilemmas: a worldwide demand for more electric energy—which can be produced from the liberated heat—and the need to dispose of growing mountains of organic wastes and garbage.

Paper and other cellulose products. Trees, vines, grasses, and straws are about one-third cellulose by weight; thus vast quantities accumulate as waste products from food processing, lumbering, papermaking, and grain harvesting. Municipal and industrial wastepaper, rags, boxes, wood, grass, and leaves also contribute to the enormous volume of cellulose waste products. Wallboard, door cores, and mulch have been made from cereal grain straws and bagasse (a waste product of sugarcane). Chemical-grade cellulose has been made from cotton linters, wood, and similar fibres. Animal feed has been made from pea vines and other fibrous vegetable materials. Animal bedding has been made from oat, rice, and wheat straw. Chemicals have been produced from bagasse and corncobs.

Newsprint, bond, coated stock, and other paper products constitute a significant portion of municipal solid waste; these papers must be sorted by the user before recycling. Most recycled paper is used to make new paper and paperboard, though small amounts are made into cellulose insulation and other building products. Paper intended for printing-grade products must be de-inked (often using caustic soda) after pulping; for some uses the stock is bleached before pressing into sheets.

Bark, wood chips, and lignin from sawmills, pulp mills, and paper mills are returned to the soil as fertilizers and soil conditioners. The kraft process of papermaking produces a variety of liquid wastes that are sources of such valuable chemicals as turpentine, methyl alcohol, dimethyl sulfide, ethyl alcohol, and acetone. Sludges from pulp and paper manufacture and phosphate slime from fertilizer manufacture can be made into gypsum wallboard.

Glass. Though enormous numbers of glass containers are used throughout the world, most are not recycled. Even those that are returned by consumers in their original form sooner or later become damaged or broken. The chief problems in recycling glass are separating it from other refuse and sorting it by colour. About 15 percent cullet (broken or refuse glass) is used in new glass production, but because the raw materials are so inexpensive there has been scant economic motive to see how much glass could be recycled.

By running molten waste glass into cold water, frit, or finely divided, glass can be formed. Frit is used as landfill or a soil conditioner, or it can be mixed with asphalt for the surfacing of roads; it may be substituted in a number of building materials that have been based on sand.

Plastics. Plastic containers and other household products are increasingly recycled, and, like paper, these must be sorted at the source before processing. Thermoplastics (such as polyethylene and polypropylene) may be remelted and reformed into new products. Thermosetting plastics (such as polyurethane and epoxy resins) cannot be remelted; these are usually ground or shredded for use as fillers or insulating materials. So-called biodegradable plastics include starches that degrade upon exposure to sunlight (photodegradation), but a fine plastic residue remains and the degradable additives preclude recycling of these products.

Water. Domestic waste water goes to a sewage treatment plant, where it is purified and recycled to the household; much industrial waste water, however, is funneled into a river, stream, or ocean for subsequent recycling by nature. Though nature can handle small quantities of certain wastes, temporary or permanent damage has resulted from widespread disposal of this type. In some cases, legislation has prohibited the disposal of harmful wastes, while in others, pretreatment has been required.

materials science, study of the properties of solid materials and how these properties arise from a material's structure. The study encompasses the entire range of properties, including mechanical, thermal, chemical, electric, magnetic, and optical behaviour. The optimal use of materials in applications such as packaging, construction, magnets, batteries, engines, automobile bodies, insulation, catalytic cracking, electronics, and computers depends on the intelligent exploitation of these properties.

A brief treatment of materials science follows. For full treatment, *see* MACROPAEDIA: Materials Science.

The properties of materials are determined by their internal structure—that is, the way in which the fundamental parts of the materials are put together. Thus, the atomic structure is the arrangement of the atoms in space, the electron structure is the distribution of the electrons in space and in energy, the defect structure is the distribution of crystal flaws (such as impurities, vacant atomic sites, and dislocations), and the microscopic structure is the size and arrangement of microscopic grains and precipitates. These structures, and their interactions, are responsible for the behaviour of materials. For example, the combination of atomic and electronic structures controls the ease with which electrons can move in or through a solid and therefore determines whether it will be an insulator, a conductor, or a semiconductor; the atomic and defect structures control the ease with which a mechanical disturbance can move through a solid and therefore determine its degree of ductility or brittleness; and the distribution of spinning electrons gives rise to magnetic properties.

After World War II economic progress and national defense needs required the development of sophisticated materials, and it was soon apparent that an integration of the knowledge and methods of metallurgy, chemistry, and physics was essential for their development. The field of semiconductor electronics was a prime example of this. The basic work was originally done by physicists, who were oriented toward the analysis of electronic properties of pure, simple solids. But the successful production of good semiconductor devices required a knowledge of defect structure, traditionally the province of the metallurgist, and the importance of impurity control was in many respects a problem of chemistry.

By 1960 the integration of the three fields into a new activity was well under way. In the late 1950s the Advanced Research Projects Agency of the U.S. Department of Defense, in cooperation with research universities, sponsored an open competition to establish government-supported research laboratories at a limited number of universities to pursue the integrated study of materials and to educate graduate students in the new field. A dozen such facilities were set up in the United States.

The methods of materials science have been extended to the study of polymers, glasses, ceramics, amorphous metals, and even biological materials such as bone. The simple concept of relating properties to structure has resulted in an astonishing variety of advanced materials of great utility. (L.A.G.)

maternal school, French ÉCOLE MATERNELLE, a French school for children between two and six years old. Private schools for young children were founded in France around 1779, under the influence of Jean-Jacques Rousseau's *Émile*. The central government took over most of them in 1833 and named them maternal schools, hoping that the care would be like that of a mother. Pauline Kergomard, general inspector of schools from 1879 to 1917, abolished fees in 1881. In 1886 she issued guidelines advocating that children should be offered challenging toys and games and allowed to move about. By 1911 every French child had access to either a specially housed maternal school or to an infants school in a primary-school building, and about 60 percent attended such a school or a similar private school.

Maternal schools are voluntary and are open six days a week for many hours each day. Most private maternal schools charge no fees and adhere closely to government guidelines in return for generous subsidies. Children are supervised in games, exercises, and other recreational activities and are given rudimentary instruction in speaking, singing, drawing, general knowledge, and basic ethics. Efforts are made to improve perception and language skills, to broaden experience, and to instill moral sensitivity. Researchers have found that maternal schools help poor children greatly with exercise and nutrition but are hampered in raising intellectual skills, because of a high pupil-teacher ratio.

Mateus da Graça, José Vieira: *see* Vieira, Luandino.

mathematical model, either of two decidedly different kinds of mathematical representation. Physical mathematical models include reproductions of plane and solid geometric figures made of cardboard, wood, plastic, or other substances; models of conic sections, curves in space, or three-dimensional surfaces of various kinds made of wire, plaster, or thread strung from frames; and models of surfaces of higher order that make it possible to visualize abstract mathematical concepts.

The usage of the term in the theoretical or analytical sense denotes, perhaps, the more important kind of model. Essentially, any real situation in the physical and biological world, whether natural or involving technology and human intervention, is subject to analysis by modeling if it can be described in terms of mathematical equations. Thus, optimization and control theory may be used to model industrial processes, traffic patterns, sediment transport in streams, and other situations; information and communication theory may be used to model message transmission, linguistic characteristics, and the like; and dimensional analysis and computer simulation may be used to model atmospheric circulation patterns, stress distribution in engineering structures, the growth and development of landforms, and a host of other processes in science and engineering.

mathematical programming, theoretical tool of management science and economics in which management operations are described by mathematical equations that can be manipulated for a variety of purposes. It is used on problems for which calculus is unsuitable. If the basic descriptions involved take the form of linear algebraic equations, the technique is described as linear programming. If more complex forms are required, the term nonlinear programming is applied. Mathematical programming is used in planning production schedules, in transportation, in military logistics, and in calculating economic growth, by inserting assumed values for the variables in the equations and solving for the unknowns. Computers are widely used in arriving at solutions.

mathematicism, the effort to employ the formal structure and rigorous method of mathematics as a model for the conduct of philosophy. Mathematicism is manifested in Western philosophy in at least three ways: (1) General mathematical methods of investigation can be used to establish consistency of meaning and completeness of analysis. This is the revolutionary approach introduced in the first half of the 17th century by René Descartes. The perfection of this approach led to the Age of Analysis in the first half of the 20th century. (2) Descartes also pioneered the subjection of metaphysical systems, expressing the nature of ultimate reality, to axiomatization—*i.e.,* to a procedure that deduces tenets from a set of basic axioms, on the model of Euclid's axiomatization of geometry. The method was elaborately used later in the 17th century by Benedict de Spinoza. (3) Calculi, or syntactic systems, on the model of mathematical logic, have been developed by several 20th-century analytic philosophers, among them Bertrand Russell, Ludwig Wittgenstein, and Rudolf Carnap, to represent and to explicate philosophical systems, as well as to solve and to dissolve metaphysical problems.

Descartes gave four rules of method in philosophy based on mathematical procedure: (1) accept as true only indubitable (self-evident) propositions, (2) divide problems into parts, (3) work in order from simple to complex, and (4) make enumerations and reviews complete and general. When a philosopher approaches metaphysical problems in this way, it may appear to be natural or useful for him to organize his philosophical knowledge in the form of definitions, axioms, rules, and deduced theorems. In this way he can assure consistency of meaning, correctness of inference, and a systematic way to discover and to exhibit relationships.

mathematics, the science of structure, order, and relation that has evolved from elemental practices of counting, measuring, and describing the shapes of objects. It deals with logical reasoning and quantitative calculation, and its development has involved an increasing degree of idealization and abstraction of its subject matter. Since the 17th century, mathematics has been an indispensable adjunct to the physical sciences and technology, and in more recent times it has assumed a similar role in the quantitative aspects of the life sciences.

In many cultures—under the stimulus of the needs of practical pursuits, such as commerce and agriculture—mathematics has developed far beyond basic counting. This growth has been greatest in societies complex enough to sustain these activities and to provide leisure for contemplation and the opportunity to build on the achievements of earlier mathematicians. For full treatment of this aspect of mathematics, *see* MACROPAEDIA: Mathematics, The History of.

All mathematical systems (for example, Euclidean geometry) are combinations of sets of axioms and theorems that can be logically deduced from the axioms. Inquiries into the logical and philosophical basis of mathematics reduce to questions of whether the axioms of a given system ensure its completeness and its consistency. For full treatment of this aspect, *see* MACROPAEDIA: Mathematics, The Foundations of.

The substantive branches of mathematics are treated in several articles in the MACROPAEDIA. *See* Algebra; Analysis (in Mathematics); Arithmetic; Combinatorics and Combinatorial Geometry; Game Theory; Geometry; Number Theory; Numerical Analysis; Optimization, The Mathematical Theory of; Probability Theory; Set Theory; Statistics; Trigonometry.

For a description of the place of mathematics in the circle of learning and a list of MACROPAEDIA and MICROPAEDIA articles on the subject, *see* PROPAEDIA: Part Ten, Division II.

Mather, Cotton (b. Feb. 12, 1663, Boston, Massachusetts Bay Colony [U.S.]—d. Feb. 13, 1728, Boston), American Congregational minister and author, supporter of the old order of the ruling clergy, who became the most celebrated of all New England Puritans. He combined a mystical strain (he believed in the existence of witchcraft) with a modern scientific interest (he supported smallpox inoculation).

The son of Increase Mather and the grandson of John Cotton and Richard Mather, Cotton Mather lived all his life in Boston. He entered Harvard at the age of 12, easily passing entrance requirements to read and write Latin and to "decline the Greek nouns and verbs." He devoted himself unremittingly to study and prayer. At 18 he received his M.A. degree from the hands of his father, who was president of the college.

Cotton Mather, portrait by Peter Pelham; in the collection of the American Antiquarian Society, Worcester, Mass.

By courtesy of the American Antiquarian Society, Worcester, Mass.

Mather once noted that his life was "a continual conversation with heaven," but he spent agonizing hours convinced that he was damned and equal time in ecstasies that he was not. For a while, he feared he could not enter the ministry because of a speech impediment, and he considered becoming a physician; the subject of medicine was of lifelong interest to him. After a friend persuaded him "to oblige himself to a dilated Deliberation in speaking," he conquered his weakness and returned to religious studies. He preached his first sermon in his father's church in August 1680 and in October another from his grandfather John Cotton's pulpit. He was formally ordained in 1685 and became his father's colleague.

He devoted his life to praying, preaching, writing, and publishing and still followed his main purpose in life of doing good. His book, *Bonifacius, or Essays to Do Good* (1710), instructs others in humanitarian acts, some ideas being far ahead of his time: the schoolmaster to reward instead of punish his students, the physician to study the state of mind of his patient as a probable cause of illness. He established societies for community projects.

He joined his father in cautioning judges against the use of "spectre evidence" (testimony of a victim of witchcraft that he had been attacked by a spectre bearing the appearance of someone he knew) in the witchcraft trials and in working for the ouster of Sir Edmund Andros as governor of Massachusetts. He was also a leader in the fight for inoculation against smallpox, incurring popular disapproval. When Cotton inoculated his own son, who almost died from it, the whole community was wrathful, and a bomb was thrown through his chamber window. Satan seemed on the side of his enemies; various members of his family became ill, and some died. Worst of all, his son Increase was arrested for rioting.

Mather's interest in science and particularly in various American phenomena—published in his *Curiosa Americana* (1712–24)—won him membership in the Royal Society of London. His account of the inoculation episode was published in the society's transactions. He corresponded extensively with notable scientists, such as Robert Boyle. His *Christian Philosopher* (1721) recognizes God in the wonders of the earth and the universe beyond; it is both philosophical and scientific and, ironically, anticipates 18th-century Deism, despite his clinging to the old order.

Cotton Mather wrote and published more than 400 works. His magnum opus was *Magnalia Christi Americana* (1702), an ecclesiastical history of America from the founding of New England to his own time. His *Manuductio ad Ministerium* (1726) was a handbook of advice for young graduates to the ministry: on doing good, on college love affairs, on poetry and music, and on style. His ambitious 20-year work on biblical learning was interrupted by his death.

He died only five years after his father, whose colleague he had been for 40 years. Of 15 children by his three wives—Abigail Phillips, Elizabeth (*née* Clark) Hubbard, and Lydia (*née* Lee) George—only two survived him.

Cotton Mather's heritage from his two grandfathers, Richard Mather and John Cotton, was both fortunate and unfortunate. Like them, he had an active mind and the will to use it. He lived in the shadow of their greatness and expected to carry on the tradition and to assume their role in the Puritan community. Unfortunately, he could not see that the old order was passing. As colonial communities became more secure from earlier hardships of settlements, they also became more complacent and less in need of a confining spiritual leadership. Cotton fought for the continuance of the old order of the ruling clergy, sometimes with frustration, sometimes in anger. His *Diary* was edited by W.C. Ford (1911–12).

BIBLIOGRAPHY. Barrett Wendell, *Cotton Mather* (1891, reprinted 1980); David Levin, *Cotton Mather: The Young Life of the Lord's Remembrancer, 1663–1703* (1978); Kenneth Silverman, *The Life and Times of Cotton Mather* (1984).

Mather, Increase (b. June 21, 1639, Dorchester, Massachusetts Bay Colony [U.S.]—d. Aug. 23, 1723, Boston), Boston Congregational minister, author and educator, who was a determining influence in the councils of New England during the crucial period when leadership passed into the hands of the first native-born generation. He was the son of Richard Mather, son-in-law of John Cotton, and father of Cotton Mather.

Increase Mather, portrait by Jan van der Spriet, 1688; in the collection of the Massachusetts Historical Society, Boston

By courtesy of the Massachusetts Historical Society, Boston

He entered Harvard at the age of 12 and received his bachelor's degree at 17. At graduation, his attack on Aristotelian logic, basic to the Harvard curriculum, shocked the faculty and nearly resulted in his dismissal. On his 18th birthday he preached his first sermon in a village near his home and his second in his father's church in Dorchester. Soon he left for Dublin, where he entered Trinity College and received a master's degree the following June. At his commencement, he refused to wear a cap and gown, but the assembled scholars were so impressed with him that they hummed their approval of him. Chosen a fellow at Trinity, he refused the post. He preached at various posts in England and was at Guernsey when the Puritan Commonwealth ended and Charles II was proclaimed king (May 8, 1660). He refused to drink the king's health or sign papers expressing rejoicing. On the appointment of a new governor for Guernsey, unsympathetic to Nonconformists, Increase left a comfortable living and in a few months sailed for New England, where he became minister of North Church, Boston, in 1661, and married his stepsister, Maria Cotton, in 1662. Maria died in 1714, and in 1715 he married Ann Cotton, widow of his nephew John.

In 1683 Charles delivered an ultimatum to the Massachusetts colonists: to retain their charter with absolute obedience to the king or to have it revoked. Before an assembly of freemen, Mather proclaimed that an affirmative vote would be a sin against God, for only to him should one give absolute obedience. The colonists refused submission, and the charter was subsequently revoked in 1686.

While James II was king, in 1688, Mather was sent as the representative of the colonists to thank him for his declaration of liberty to all faiths. He remained in England for several years, and, on the accession of William and Mary in 1689, he obtained from them the removal of the hated governor of Massachusetts, Sir Edmund Andros, and his replacement by Sir William Phipps. Increase's petition for the restoration of the old charter proved unsuccessful, but he was able to get a new charter in 1691. Both the new governor and the new charter, however, turned out to be unpopular. In 1685 Increase had been made president of Harvard but resigned in 1701, in part because of opposition to the new colonial charter. He received the honorary degree of doctor of divinity in the same year.

Among his books is *An Essay for the Recording of Illustrious Providences* (1684), a compilation of stories showing the hand of divine providence in rescuing people from natural and supernatural disasters. Some historians suggest that this book conditioned the minds of the populace for the witchcraft hysteria of Salem in 1692. Despite the fact that Increase and Cotton Mather believed in witches—as did most of the world at the time—and that the guilty should be punished, they suspected that evidence could be faulty and justice might miscarry. Witches, like other criminals, were tried and sentenced to jail or the gallows by civil magistrates. The case against a suspect rested on "spectre evidence" (testimony of a victim of witchcraft that he had been attacked by a spectre bearing the appearance of someone he knew), which the Mathers distrusted because a witch could assume the form of an innocent person. When this type of evidence was finally thrown out of court at the insistence of the Mathers and other ministers, the whole affair came to an end.

Increase's *Case of Conscience Concerning Evil Spirits Personating Men* (1693) is a clear vindication of the Mathers' part in the witchcraft trials. Yet their enemies, such as William Douglass and Robert Calef, spread denigrating rumours about them. This enmity, together with the Mathers' part in a campaign for inoculation against smallpox and the failure of their protégé Phipps to measure up to expectations, contributed to the decline of the Mathers' influence in the last decade of the century. Changing times, more than anything else, had their impact; for people like the Mathers were losing touch with the younger generation.

BIBLIOGRAPHY. Kenneth B. Murdock, *Increase Mather, the Foremost American Puritan* (1925, reissued 1966); Michael G. Hall, *The Last American Puritan: The Life of Increase Mather, 1639–1723* (1988).

Mather, Richard (b. 1596, Lowton, Lancashire, Eng.—d. April 22, 1669, Dorchester, Massachusetts Bay Colony [U.S.]), English-born American Congregational minister, father of Increase Mather and three other Puritan ministers. After joining the Great Migration of Puritans from England to New England (1635), he was elected "teacher" minister at Dorchester, Mass., and became locally celebrated as a preacher and formulator of Congregational creed and policy.

At age 15 he decided to enter the ministry and entered Brasenose College, Oxford, where he greatly enjoyed the pursuit of learning. In 1618, at the request of the people of Toxteth, he left the university to become their minister

Richard Mather, mid-19th-century painting after a contemporary portrait, *c.* 1660–69; in the collection of the American Antiquarian Society, Worcester, Mass.

By courtesy of the American Antiquarian Society, Worcester, Mass.

and, bowing to their wishes, was ordained by the Bishop of Chester.

As a thorough Puritan, Richard Mather had rejected all pomp and ceremony retained by the Church of England from its Catholic origins, and he preached at Toxteth without a surplice for 15 years before authorities discovered it. Suspended, and then reinstated, he returned to his dissenting practices and was tried before a court, before which he admitted without apology the matter of the surplice.

Permanently "silenced from Publick Preaching the Word," he retired to private life and resolved to leave for America, where he would be free to preach and do good according to his own convictions. He and his wife (Katherine Holt, whom he had married in 1624) and their four sons sailed for America in June 1635 and arrived at Boston in August. His journal of the voyage is one of his best written works. His reputation had preceded him to New England, where several towns asked for his services. He chose Dorchester, Mass., a post he held until his death. Two more sons, Eleazar and Increase, were born there.

Of Richard Mather's six sons, four became ministers. Samuel and Nathaniel, after being educated at Harvard College, returned to the British Isles in 1650, where Samuel received a degree, became a fellow at Trinity College, Dublin, and later became minister in Dublin, a post he held until his death. Nathaniel preached at Barnstaple and later succeeded Samuel in Dublin. Eleazar became minister of Northampton. Richard's first wife, Katherine, died in 1655; a year later he married Sarah Cotton, the widow of John Cotton, an eminent Puritan minister.

Richard's most respected work is his summation of principles as adopted at the Cambridge Synod of 1648 and considered to be the clearest statement of Puritan Congregationalism.

He is remembered for his part, with other ministers, in the literal translation of the Psalms for the *Bay Psalm Book* (1640), which were set to already accepted tunes; in his preface to that work, Richard excused the terrible results by explaining that the editors would not take "poeticall licence to depart from the true and proper sence of David's words."

On his deathbed, Richard Mather was troubled about two things: he was not back in his study, and he had not convinced his son Increase of the rightness of the so-called Half-Way Covenant, a plan that provided modified church membership for those who were unable to meet the rigorous tests for full membership.

Mathesius, Vilém (b. Aug. 3, 1882, Pardubice, Bohemia, Austria-Hungary [now in Czech Republic]—d. April 12, 1945, Prague, Czech.), Czech linguist and scholar of English language and literature. He was president of the Prague Linguistic Circle, famous for its influence on structural linguistics and for its phonological studies. Mathesius taught at Charles University in Prague, beginning in 1909 after he had received his degree in Germanic and Romance studies. He became its first professor of Anglistics in 1912.

Three periods of intellectual activity mark Mathesius' life. Highlighting the first period is his 1911 lecture, "O potenciálnosti jevů jazykových" ("On the Potentiality of Language Phenomenon"), anticipating the Saussurean distinction between "langue" and "parole" and emphasizing the importance of synchronic (nonhistorical) language study. He also published a two-volume history of English literature (*Dějiny anglické literatury;* 1910–15) and several Shakespearean studies. From 1926 to 1936 Mathesius' interest turned to syntax and semantics. In phonology he did research on the load and combining capability of phonemes. From 1936 on, his interest was in functional syntax and the sentence.

Mathew, Theobald (b. Oct. 10, 1790, Thomastown, County Tipperary, Ire.—d. Dec. 8, 1856, Cobh, County Cork), Irish priest and orator known as the "Apostle of Temperance."

Ordained in 1814, Mathew entered the Capuchin order, of which he was made provincial in 1822. Concurrently, the earliest European temperance organizations were forming in Ireland; Mathew joined the movement at Cork. Between 1838 and 1842 he traveled throughout Ireland. People flocked to hear him, and whole crowds took the temperance pledge. The number of abstainers in Ireland alone in 1841 was estimated to be 4,647,000, and in three years the consumption of spirits dropped approximately 50 percent—much of this decrease attributable to Mathew's efforts. He went to England in 1843 and to the United States in 1849, where, despite failing health, he preached in 25 states. Incapacitated by illness, he returned to Ireland two years later, where he remained relatively inactive for the remainder of his life.

Mathews, Charles (b. June 28, 1776, London, Eng.—d. June 28, 1835, Plymouth, Devon), prominent English stage personality and theatre manager who, renowned for his genius at mimicry and for his wit, was among the leading comedians of his day.

Charles Mathews, detail from a mezzotint by C. Turner, 1825, after an oil painting by James Lonsdale

By courtesy of the Victoria and Albert Museum, London

The son of a bookseller, Mathews was educated at Merchant Taylors School, Crosby, Lancashire. After acting in the provinces, primarily at York, he first appeared on the stage in Dublin in 1794 and made his London debut in 1803 in the role of Lingo in *The Agreeable Surprize,* by the English dramatist Samuel Foote. From that time, Mathews' career was an uninterrupted triumph. He is credited with having created some 400 new parts, appearing at London's finest theatres. Among his most notable roles was Sir Fretful Plagiary in Richard Brinsley Sheridan's *Critic.* His first wife, Eliza Kirkham Strong, died in 1802, and he married the actress Anne Jackson, who later wrote the popular and diverting *Memoirs of Charles Mathews* (4 vol., 1838–39).

In 1808 Mathews conceived a personal form of entertainment known as "At Homes," involving one-man shows with comic songs and impersonations of eccentric characters. It was in such performances that he revealed his great art of mimicry. In 1817 the English dramatist George Colman (the Younger) wrote *The Actor of All Work* for Mathews, enabling him to play a fantastically varied group of characters. Among the sketches he devised for himself are "Mr. Mathews and His Youthful Days" and "The Trip to America." He toured the United States in 1822 and 1834. Already in poor health, he died shortly after his return to England. From 1827 he had co-managed the Adelphi Theatre, London, with a fellow actor, Frederick Henry Yates.

Mathews, Charles James (b. Dec. 26, 1803, Liverpool—d. June 24, 1878, Manchester), writer of comic sketches and one of the best high comedians ever to appear on the English stage.

Mathews was the son of the celebrated entertainer Charles Mathews and his wife, the actress Anne Jackson. Although he possessed much of his parents' theatrical talents and enjoyed dabbling in amateur productions, Mathews evidently had no early desire for a stage career. He studied architecture under Augustus Pugin, travelled in France and Italy, and worked as an architect for a Welsh coal company before entering the London office of architect John Nash.

His theatrical career did not begin in earnest until 1835, when, upon the death of his father, he took over the elder Mathews' part in the management of the Adelphi Theatre. Later that year he made his debut in his own play, *The Humpbacked Lover,* followed by *The Old and Young Stager.* In 1838 he married the actress-dancer-singer known as Madame Vestris (Elizabeth Lucia Mathews). The newly married couple made an unsuccessful appearance in the United States. Upon their return to London they assumed the management of Covent Garden Theatre, where they produced many entertainments, including a highly popular but financially disastrous production of *London Assurance* with Mathews playing one of his best roles, Dazzle. They moved to the Lyceum, producing light comedies that eventually cost them bankruptcy. Two years after retiring in 1854, Elizabeth died.

Mathews continued acting and made a second and more successful tour of the United States. He married the actress Lizzie Davenport (1858), and they lived a productive and financially stable life together. In 1870 he began an extensive tour, which included appearances in Australia and India, returning once more to New York City (1871) in a remarkably popular six-week run at Daly's Theatre. His most memorable roles included Mr. Affable Hawk in *The Game of Speculation* (an adaptation of Balzac's *Mercadet*) and Plumper in *Cool as a Cucumber.* He and his wife also performed in an entertainment reminiscent of his father's work entitled *Mr. & Mrs. Mathews at Home.*

A biography of Mathews, with a selection of his correspondence, edited by Charles Dickens, was published in 1879.

Mathews, Shailer (b. May 26, 1863, Portland, Maine, U.S.—d. Oct. 23, 1941, Chicago), leader of the Social Gospel movement of the late 19th and early 20th centuries in the United States, which interpreted the Kingdom of God as requiring social as well as individual salvation.

Educated at Colby College, Waterville, Maine; Newton Theological Institution, Newton, Mass.; and the University of Berlin, Mathews taught at Colby from 1887 to 1894. Thereafter he taught in the divinity school of the University of Chicago, of which he was dean from 1908 until his retirement in 1933.

Mathews published more than a score of books and hundreds of articles, among them *The Messianic Hope in the New Testament* (1905), *The Spiritual Interpretation of History* (1916), *The Faith of Modernism* (1924), and *Creative Christianity* (1935). His autobiography, *New Faith for Old* (1936), is a significant document for the history of the Social Gospel movement in the United States.

Mathewson, Christy, byname of CHRISTOPHER MATHEWSON (b. Aug. 12, 1880, Factoryville, Pa., U.S.—d. Oct. 7, 1925, Saranac Lake, N.Y.), U.S. professional baseball pitcher, one of the first five players chosen for the Baseball Hall of Fame at Cooperstown, N.Y. (1936).

Mathewson, 1909
Culver Pictures

Also known as "Matty" and "Big Six," he pitched in the National League for the New York Giants from 1900 to 1916 and for the Cincinnati Reds in 1916; he also managed Cincinnati from 1916 to 1918. From 1923 until his death he was president of the Boston Braves in the National League.

Mathewson was one of the first college men to enter the major leagues, having been a football and baseball player at Bucknell University, Lewisburg, Pa. For the Giants he won more than 20 games in each of 13 seasons (12 consecutive, 1903–14) and 30 or more on 3 or 4 occasions (29 or 30 in 1903; many old baseball records are in dispute). In 1908 he scored 35 or 37 victories, 11 or 12 of them shutouts. He won 367, 372, or 373 regular-season games in his career while losing only 186 or 188. In four World Series he won five games, pitching three shutouts against the Philadelphia Athletics in the 1905 Series and another shutout against the Athletics in 1913.

A right-handed thrower and batter, Mathewson was a master of the fadeaway pitch, later called the screwball. Testifying to the pitcher's exceptional control, a Giants' catcher said he could "catch Matty in a rocking chair." Mathewson was an intelligent, proud, reticent man with great powers of concentration.

Mathiassen, Therkel (b. Sept. 5, 1892, Favrbo, Den.—d. 1967), Danish archaeologist and ethnographer whose excavations during 1921–23 to the west and north of Hudson Bay revealed the existence of the Thule prehistoric Eskimo culture.

His doctoral dissertation for the University of Copenhagen, *Archaeology of the Central Eskimos* (1927), laid the groundwork for further study of Eskimo archaeology. Between 1929 and 1955 he conducted six expeditions to Greenland, where he continued his work with Eskimo remains. Mathiassen served as curator (1941–46) and as chief curator (1946–62) of the prehistoric department of the Danish National Museum, Copenhagen.

Mathieu, Claude-Louis (b. Nov. 25, 1783, Macon, Fr.—d. March 5, 1875, Paris), French astronomer and mathematician who worked particularly on the determination of the distances of the stars.

After a brief period as an engineer, Mathieu became an astronomer at the Observatoire de Paris and at the Bureau des Longitudes in 1817. He later served as professor of astronomy at the Collège de France, Paris, and from 1829 was professor of analysis at the École Polytechnique, Paris. He represented Macon in the Chamber of Deputies (1834–48). For many years he edited the work on population statistics, *L'Annuaire du Bureau des Longitudes,* and published *L'Histoire de l'astronomie au XVIIIe siècle* (1827; "The History of Astronomy of the 18th Century").

Mathif al-Baladīyah al-Iskandarī (Alexandria, Egypt): *see* Alexandria Municipal Museum.

Mathif al-Miṣrī, al- (Cairo): *see* Egyptian Museum.

Mathura, formerly MUTTRA, town, administrative headquarters of Mathura district, Uttar Pradesh state, northern India, on the Yamuna River, northwest of Āgra. The site of Mathura was inhabited before the 1st century AD. In the 2nd century the town was a stronghold of Buddhists and Jainas. In 1017–18, Maḥmūd of Ghazna pillaged Mathura, and between 1500 and 1757 it was sacked four times. The town fell under British rule in 1804.

Situated at a major junction of roads and rail lines, it is an agricultural trade centre with some industry. Two colleges, a state veterinary college, and the Curzon Museum of Archaeology are located in the town. Mathura is the traditional birthplace of the god Krishna and has long been a centre of Hindu worship. There are a number of temples and *ghāṭs,* or bathing stairs, along the river.

Mathura district, 1,466 sq mi (3,797 sq km)

Bathing *ghāṭ* on the Yamuna River, at Mathura, Uttar Pradesh, India
Globe

in area, straddles the Yamuna River and is irrigated by the Āgra and Ganges canals. Crops include grains, sugarcane, and cotton. Pop. (1981) town, 147,493; metropolitan area, 159,498; district, 1,560,447.

Mathurā art, style of Buddhist visual art that flourished in the trading and pilgrimage centre of Mathura, Uttar Pradesh, India, from the 2nd century BC to the 12th century AD; its most distinctive contributions were made during the Kushān and Gupta periods (1st–6th century AD). Images in the mottled red sandstone from the nearby Sīkri quarries are found widely distributed over north central India, attesting to Mathurā's importance as an exporter of sculpture.

A *yakṣī* (female nature spirit) holding tray and pitcher, red sandstone relief from Mathura, Uttar Pradesh, India, 2nd century AD; in the Archaeological Museum, Mathura
P. Chandra

The Mathurā school was contemporaneous with a second important school of Kushān art, that of Gandhāra in the northwest, which shows strong Greco-Roman influence. About the 1st century AD each area appears to have evolved separately its own representations of the Buddha. The Mathurā images are related to the earlier *yakṣa* (male nature deity) figures, a resemblance particularly evident in the colossal standing Buddha images of the early Kushān period. In these, and in the more representative seated Buddhas, the overall effect is one of enormous energy. The shoulders are broad, the chest swells, and the legs are firmly planted with feet spaced apart. Other characteristics are the shaven head; the *uṣṇīṣa* (protuberance on the top of the head) indicated by a tiered spiral; a round smiling face; the right arm raised in *abhaya-mudrā* (gesture of reassurance); the left arm akimbo or resting on the thigh; the drapery closely molding the body and arranged in folds over the left arm, leaving the right shoulder bare; and the presence of the lion throne rather than the lotus throne. Later, the hair began to be treated as a series of short flat spirals lying close to the head, the type that came to be the standard representation throughout the Buddhist world.

Jaina and Hindu images of the period are carved in the same style, and the images of the Jaina Tīrthaṅkaras, or saints, are difficult to distinguish from contemporary images of the Buddha, except by reference to iconography. The dynastic portraits produced by the Mathurā workshops are of special interest. These rigidly frontal figures of Kushān kings are dressed in Central Asian fashion, with belted tunic, high boots, and conical cap, a style of dress also used for representations of the Hindu sun god, Sūrya.

The female figures at Mathura, carved in high relief on the pillars and gateways of both Buddhist and Jaina monuments, are frankly sensuous in their appeal. These delightful nude or seminude figures are shown in a variety of toilet scenes or in association with trees, indicating their continuance of the *yakṣī* (female nature deity) tradition seen also at other Buddhist sites, such as Bhārhut and Sānchi. As auspicious emblems of fertility and abundance they commanded a popular appeal that persisted with the rise of Buddhism.

Matías de Gálvez (Guatemala): *see* Santo Tomás de Castilla.

Matilda, also called MAUD, German MATHILDE (b. 1102, London—d. Sept. 10, 1167, near Rouen, Fr.), consort of the Holy Roman emperor Henry V and afterward claimant to the English throne in the reign of King Stephen.

She was the only daughter of Henry I of England by Queen Matilda and was sister of William the Aetheling, heir to the English and Norman thrones. Both her marriages were in furtherance of Henry I's policy of strengthening Normandy against France. In 1114 she was married to Henry V; he died in 1125, leaving her childless, and three years later she was married to Geoffrey Plantagenet, effectively count of Anjou.

Her brother's death in 1120 made her Henry I's sole legitimate heir, and in 1127 he compelled the baronage to accept her as his successor, though a woman ruler was equally unprecedented for the kingdom of England and the duchy of Normandy. The Angevin marriage was unpopular and flouted the baron's stipulation that she should not be married out of England without their consent. The birth of her eldest son, Henry, in 1133 gave hope of silencing this opposition, but he was only two when Henry I died (1135), and a rapid coup brought to the English throne Stephen of Blois, son of William I the Conqueror's daughter Adela. Though the church and the majority of the baronage supported Stephen, Matilda's claims were powerfully upheld in England by her half brother Robert of Gloucester and her uncle King David I of Scotland. Matilda and Robert landed at Arundel in September 1139, and she was for a short while besieged in the castle. But Stephen soon allowed her to join her brother, who had gone to the west country, where she had much support; after a stay at Bristol, she settled at Gloucester.

Matilda, detail of a miniature from *Vita Mathildis* by Donizo of Canossa, 12th century; in the Vatican Library (Vat. Lat. 4922)
By courtesy of the Biblioteca Apostolica Vaticana

She came nearest to success in the summer of 1141, after Stephen had been captured at Lincoln in February. Elected "lady of the English" by a clerical council at Winchester in April, she entered London in June; but her arrogance and tactless demands for money provoked the citizens to chase her away to Oxford before she could be crowned queen. Her forces were routed at Winchester in September 1141, and thereafter she maintained a steadily weakening resistance in the west country. Her well-known escape from Oxford Castle over the frozen River Thames took place in December 1142.

Normandy had been in her husband's possession since 1144, and she retired there in 1148, remaining near Rouen to watch over the interests to her eldest son, who became duke of Normandy in 1150 and King Henry II of England in 1154. She spent the remainder of her life in Normandy exercising a steadying influence over Henry II's continental dominions.

Matilda OF CANOSSA, byname MATILDA THE GREAT COUNTESS, Italian MATILDE DI CANOSSA, or MATILDE LA GRAN CONTESSA (b. 1046, Lucca, Tuscany—d. July 24, 1115, Bondeno, Romagna), countess of Tuscany remembered for her role in the conflict between the papacy and the Holy Roman emperor. The climax of this struggle, the confrontation of the emperor Henry IV and Pope Gregory VII, took place at Matilda's castle of Canossa.

The assassination in 1052 of her father, Boniface of Canossa, and the deaths of her older brother and sister left her the sole surviving heir to the extensive holdings of the House of Attoni, founded by her grandfather Atto Adalbert. Two years later Matilda's mother, Beatrice, married Godfrey, duke of Upper Lorraine, an enemy of the emperor Henry III. Henry seized Beatrice and Matilda as hostages in 1055 and took them to Germany, but the following year he became reconciled with Godfrey and released them a few months before his own death.

When Godfrey died in 1069, Matilda married his son Godfrey the Hunchback, with whom she resided in Lorraine. After the death of their child in infancy, she returned to Italy, reigning with her mother until Beatrice's death in 1076. Matilda's father, for many years a supporter of the German emperors, had moved toward the papal (Guelf) side in the factional struggle dividing Italy, and Matilda remained loyal to the popes. She became a close friend of Pope Gregory VII, lending him important support in his struggle against the emperor Henry IV, and it was at her castle at Canossa that in January 1077 Gregory received the barefoot penance of the Emperor that marked an apogee of papal prestige. After Henry's excommunication in 1080, Matilda was intermittently at war with him until his death (1106), sometimes donning armour to lead her troops in person. In 1082 she sent part of the famous treasure of Canossa to Rome to finance the Pope's military operations.

In 1089, at the age of 43, Matilda married the 17-year-old Welf V, duke of Bavaria and Carinthia, a member of the Este family. They separated six years later, Henry IV taking the Este side in the resulting quarrel. Matilda encouraged Henry's son Conrad to rebel against his father in 1093 and seize the crown of Italy. She finally made peace with Henry IV's son and successor, Henry V, in 1110, willing her nonfeudal possessions to him, although she had already donated them to the papacy, an act that later provoked controversy between papacy and empire.

Buried near Mantua, she was held in such high regard by succeeding popes that her remains were removed to Rome in 1634 by Pope Urban VIII and reinterred in St. Peter's.

Matilda OF FLANDERS, French MATHILDE, or MAHAULT, DE FLANDRE (d. 1083), queen consort of William I the Conqueror, whom she married *c.* 1053. During William's absences in England, the duchy of Normandy was under her regency, with the aid of their son, Robert Curthose (*q.v.*), except when he was in rebellion against his father. The embroidery of the Bayeux tapestry was once wrongly attributed to her.

Matisse, Henri(-Émile-Benoît) (b. Dec. 31, 1869, Le Cateau, Picardy, Fr.—d. Nov. 3, 1954, Nice), artist often regarded as the most important French painter of the 20th century. The leader of the Fauvist movement around 1900, Matisse pursued the expressiveness of colour throughout his career. His subjects were largely domestic or figurative, and

"Decorative Figure on an Ornamental Background," oil painting by Henri Matisse, 1925–26; in the Musée National d'Art Moderne, Paris

a distinct Mediterranean verve presides in the treatment.

Formative years. Matisse, whose parents were in the grain business, displayed little interest in art until he was 20 years old. From 1882 to 1887 he attended the secondary school in Saint-Quentin; after a year of legal studies in Paris, he returned to Saint-Quentin and became a clerk in a law office. He began to sit in on an early-morning drawing class at the local École Quentin-Latour, and, in 1890, while recovering from a severe attack of appendicitis, he began to paint, at first copying the coloured reproductions in a box of oils his mother had given him. Soon he was decorating the home of his grandparents at Le Cateau. In 1891 he abandoned the law and returned to Paris to become a professional artist.

Although at this period he had, in his own words, "hair like Absalom's," he was far from being a typical Left Bank bohemian art student. "I plunged head down into work," he said later, "on the principle I had heard, all my young life, expressed by the words 'Hurry up!' Like my parents, I hurried up in my work, pushed by I don't know what, by a force which today I perceive as being foreign to my life as a normal man." This 19th-century gospel of work, derived from a middle class, northern French upbringing, was to mark his entire career, and soon it was accompanied by a thoroughly bourgeois appearance—gold-rimmed spectacles; short, carefully trimmed beard; plump, feline body; conservative clothes—which was odd for a leading member of the Parisian avant-garde.

Matisse did not, however, become a member of the avant-garde right away. In 1891, in order to prepare himself for the entrance examination at the official École des Beaux-Arts, he enrolled in the privately run Académie Julian, where the master was the strictly academic Adolphe-William Bouguereau, then at the peak of a since-departed fame as a painter of bevies of naked, mildly provocative nymphs. That Matisse should have begun his studies in such a school may seem surprising, and he once explained the fact by saying that he was acting on the recommendation of a Saint-Quentin painter of hens and poultry yards. But it must be remembered that he himself was for the moment a provincial with tastes that were old-fashioned in a Paris already familiar with the Postimpressionism of Paul Cézanne, Paul Gauguin, and Vincent van Gogh. His earliest canvases are in the 17th-century Dutch manner favoured by the French Realists of the 1850s.

In 1892 he left the Académie Julian for evening classes at the École des Arts Décoratifs and for the atelier of the Symbolist painter Gustave Moreau at the École des Beaux-Arts, without being required to take the entrance examination. Moreau, a tolerant teacher, did not try to impose his own style on his pupils but encouraged them rather to develop their personalities and to learn from the treasures in the Louvre. Matisse continued, with some long interruptions, to study in the atelier until 1899, when he was forced to leave by Fernand Cormon, an intolerant painter who had become the professor after Moreau's death. After that, although he was nearing 30, he frequented for a time a private academy where intermittent instruction was given by the portraitist Eugène Carrière.

In 1896 Matisse exhibited four paintings at the backward-looking Salon de la Société Nationale des Beaux-Arts and scored a triumph; he was elected an associate member of the Salon society, and his "Woman Reading" (1894) was purchased by the government. From this point onward he became increasingly confident and venturesome, both as an artist and as a man. During the next two years he undertook expeditions to Brittany, met the veteran Impressionist Camille Pissarro, and discovered the series of Impressionist masterpieces in the Gustave Caillebotte Collection, which had just been donated—amid protests from conservatives—to the French nation. His colours became, for a while, lighter in hue and at the same time more intense. In 1897 he took his first major step toward stylistic liberation and created a minor scandal at the Salon with "The Dinner Table" ("La Desserte"), in which he combined a Renoir kind of luminosity with a firmly classical composition in deep red and green.

In 1898 he married a young woman from Toulouse, Amélie Parayre, and left Paris for a year, visiting London, where he studied the paintings of J.M.W. Turner, and working in Corsica, where he received a lasting impression of Mediterranean sunlight and colour.

Revolutionary years. During 1898, Paul Signac, the theoretician and actively proselyting leader (after the death of Georges Seurat) of the Neo-Impressionists, or Pointillists, published in the literary review *La Revue Blanche* his principal manifesto, "D'Eugène Delacroix au Néo-Impressionnisme." Matisse, back in Paris in 1899, read the articles and, without turning into an immediate convert, became interested in the Pointillist idea of obtaining additive mixtures of colour on the retina by means of juxtaposed dots (*points* in French) on the canvas. He furthered his research into new techniques by buying, from the well-known modernist dealer Ambroise Vollard, a painting by Paul Cézanne, "The Three Bathers"; one by Paul Gauguin, "Boy's Head"; and a drawing by Vincent van Gogh. Often accompanied by his close friend Albert Marquet, who was also interested in the problem of pure colour, he began to paint outdoor scenes in the Luxembourg Gardens in Paris, in suburban Arcueil, and from the open window of his apartment overlooking the Seine.

He also purchased from Vollard the plaster model of the bust of Henri Rochefort by Auguste Rodin, and during 1899 he began to attend an evening class in sculpture. His early work in three dimensions, the first of some 60 pieces he executed during his lifetime, reveals the influence not only of Rodin but also of Antoine-Louis Barye, generally considered the greatest French sculptor of animals.

After 1899 he ceased to exhibit at the Salon and gradually became a familiar figure in the Parisian circles where modern art was being produced and ardently discussed. In 1901 he showed for the first time in the juryless, eclectic Salon des Indépendants, which had been founded in 1884 as a refuge for painters unacceptable to the official exhibition juries. In 1902 he was in a group show at the small gallery of Berthe Weill, and the next year he and a number of his old classmates from Moreau's atelier and the Académie Carrière were the progressive contingent in the liberal, newly created Salon d'Automne. But in spite of such recognition, he was often on the brink of financial disaster. In 1900 he was obliged to accept work on the decoration of the Grand Palais, which was being erected to house part of the new Exposition Universelle in the Champs-Élysées quarter. His wife opened a dress shop in the hope of helping to make ends meet. In 1901 an attack of bronchitis forced him to take a long rest. During part of 1902 he had to return to Bohain with his three children—Marguerite, Jean, and Pierre—and Mme Matisse. He was past 34 when, in June 1904, at Vollard's gallery, he had his first one-man show, and it was a failure.

He spent the summer of 1905 with André Derain at Collioure, a small French fishing port on the Mediterranean, near the Spanish border. In the dazzling sunshine he rapidly freed himself from what he called "the tyranny" of Pointillism. The carefully placed little dabs required by the additive-mixture approach turned into swirls and slabs of spontaneous brushwork, and the theoretically realistic colours exploded into an emotional display of complementaries: red against green, orange against blue, and yellow against violet. Representative of this new freedom were "Open Window," which was finished at Collioure, and "Woman with the Hat," a portrait of his wife painted back in Paris in September. That fall, the two pictures were exhibited at the Salon d'Automne alongside works by a number of artists who also had been experimenting with violent colour. The Paris critic Louis Vauxcelles called the group *les fauves* ("the wild beasts"), and thus Fauvism, the first of the important "isms" in 20th-century painting, was born. Almost immediately Matisse became its acknowledged leader.

Almost immediately, too, his financial situation altered for the better. The Stein family in Paris—Gertrude, her brothers Leo and Michael, and the latter's wife, Sarah—became Matisse collectors. In 1906 the artist had a show at the Galerie Druet in Paris in addition to exhibiting again at the Salons des Indépendants and d'Automne. In 1907 a group of admirers, who included Sarah Stein and Hans Purrmann, organized for him a Left Bank art school, in which he taught off and on until 1911. In 1908 he exhibited in New York City, Moscow, and Berlin.

Fauvism was too undisciplined to last long, and soon its adherents were moving, according to their temperaments, toward Expressionism, Cubism, or some kind of neo-traditionalism. Matisse had no liking for these directions, and if "Fauve" is taken to mean simply a painter with a passion for pure colour, he can be said to have remained one all his life. He had, however, too much rationalism in his outlook not to wish for some order in a stylistic situation that threatened to become chaotic, and his search for chromatic equilibrium and linear economy can be followed in a series of major works produced between the revelation of Fauvism in 1905 and the end of World War I. In 1906 he painted "Joy of Life"; in 1908, "The Dessert, a Harmony in Red"; in 1911, "The Red Studio"; in 1915, "Goldfish"; in 1916, "Piano Lesson"; and in 1918, "Montalban, Large Landscape."

In such works, the list of which should be much longer, the main characteristics of Matisse's mature painting style recur constantly. The forms tend to be outlined in flowing, heavy contours and to have few interior details; the colour is laid on in large, thin, luminous, carefully calculated patches; shadows are practically eliminated; and the depicted space is either extremely shallow or warped into a flatness that parallels the plane of the canvas and defies academic rules for perspective and foreshortening. The total effect, although too intense and freehand to be merely decorative, may recall the patterns of the rugs, textiles, and ceramics of the Islāmic world. The choice and treatment of subject matter imply optimism, hedonism, intelligence, a fastidious sensuality, and, in spite of the many studies of both clothed and unclothed women, scarcely a trace of conventional sentiment.

Riviera years. In 1912 Matisse's sculpture was on view in New York City and his painting in both Cologne and London. In 1913 he was represented by 13 pictures in the much-discussed, much-lambasted New York Armory Show, and when the exhibition arrived in Chicago he was given some useful publicity by the burning, happily merely in effigy, of his "Blue Nude." But middle age, growing affluence, an established international reputation, the disruptions of World War I, and a distaste for public commotion gradually combined to isolate him from the centres of avant-gardism. He began to winter on the French Riviera, and by the early 1920s he was mostly a resident of Nice or its environs. His pictures became less daring in conception and less economical in means. Like many of the painters and composers during these years (notably Pablo Picasso and Igor Stravinsky), Matisse relaxed into a rather modernized sort of classicism and into a rather evident attempt to please an art public that was a bit tired of attempts to shock it. Such typically Nice-period works as the "Odalisque with Magnolias" and "Decorative Figure on an Ornamental Background," however, are masterpieces that deserve their popularity.

Prosperity did not make him less industrious. In 1920 he did the sets and costumes for Sergey Diaghilev's production of *Le Chant du Rossignol.* He returned to sculpture, which he had neglected for several years, and by 1930 he had completed his fourth and most nearly abstract version of "The Back," a monumental female nude in relief, on which he had been working at intervals since 1909. He relaxed, as he had always done, by traveling: to Étretat, on the coast of Normandy, in 1921; to Italy in 1925, and to Tahiti, by way of New York City and San Francisco, in 1930. During 1933 he visited Venice and Padua (Italy), and in Merion, Pa., completed and installed the final version of his large mural, "The Dance II" (Barnes Foundation).

Matisse had been interested in etching, drypoint, lithography, and allied printmaking techniques since his first years in Paris and had produced a number of occasional prints. In 1932 he had published, as illustrations for an edition of Stéphane Mallarmé's *Poésies,* 29 etchings, in which his talent for supple contours and linear economy was subtly attuned to the "purity of means" evident in the poems. After the outbreak of World War II, he became increasingly active as a graphic artist, notably with his illustrations for Henry de Montherlant's *Pasiphaé* (published in 1944), Pierre Reverdy's *Visages* (1946), the *Lettres portugaises* (1946), Charles Baudelaire's *Fleurs du mal* (1947), Pierre de Ronsard's *Florilège des Amours* (1948), and Charles d'Orléans' *Poèmes* (1950). Along with these books in mostly black and white techniques, he published *Jazz* (1947), a book consisting of his own reflections on art and life, with brilliantly coloured illustrations made by a technique he called "drawing with scissors": the motifs were pasted together after being cut out of sheets of coloured paper (hand-painted with gouache in order to get the desired hue).

During the last years of his life, he was a rather solitary man who was separated from his wife and whose grownup children were scattered. After 1941, when he underwent an operation for an intestinal disorder, he was bedridden much of the time; after 1950 he suffered from asthma and heart trouble. Cared for by a faithful Russian woman who had been one of his models in the early 1930s, he lived in a large studio in the Old Hôtel Regina at Cimiez, overlooking Nice. Often he was obliged to work on his mural-sized projects from a studio bed with the aid of a crayon attached to a long pole. But there are no signs of flagging creative energy or of sadness in his final achievements; on the contrary, these works are among the most daring, most accomplished, and most serenely optimistic of his entire career.

At Vence, a Riviera hill town where Matisse had a villa from 1943 to 1948, he completed in 1951, after three years of planning and execution, his Chapelle du Rosaire for the local Dominican nuns, one of whom had nursed him during his nearly fatal illness in 1941. He had begun by agreeing to design some stained-glass windows, had gone on to do murals, and had wound up by designing nearly everything inside and outside, including vestments and liturgical objects. Before the chapel was finished, he was at work on the huge coloured-paper cutouts—amplifications of what he had done in the illustrations for *Jazz*—that made him in many respects the "youngest" and most revolutionary artist of the early 1950s. He died in 1954. (R.McMu./Ed.)

MAJOR WORKS. *Paintings.* "The Dinner Table" ("La Desserte"; 1897; Stavros S. Niarchos Collection, London); "Compote and Glass Pitcher" (1899; Baltimore Museum of Art); "La Coiffure" (1901; Philadelphia Museum of Art); "Carmelina" (1903; Museum of Fine Arts, Boston); "Luxe, calme, et volupté" (1904–05; private collection, Paris); "Joy of Life" (1905–06; Barnes Foundation, Merion, Pa.); "Open Window" (1905; John Hay Whitney Collection, New York City); "Woman with the Hat" (1905; Walter A. Haas Collection, San Francisco); "The Blue Nude" (1907; Baltimore Museum of Art); "Le Luxe" (1907; Musée National d'Art Moderne, Paris); "The Dessert, a Harmony in Red" (1908; Hermitage, St. Petersburg); "Red Madras Headdress" (1908; Barnes Foundation); "Dance" (1909; Museum of Modern Art, New York City); "The Red Studio" (1911; Museum of Modern Art); "Goldfish and Sculpture" (1911; Museum of Modern Art); "The Blue Window" (1911; Museum of Modern Art); "Goldfish" (1912; Barnes Foundation); "Goldfish" (1915; Samuel A. Marx Collection, Chicago); "Piano Lesson" (1916; Museum of Modern Art); "Interior with a Violin Case" (1917–18; Museum of Modern Art); "Montalban, Large Landscape" (1918; private collection); "Odalisque with Magnolias" (1924; private collection); "Decorative Figure on an Ornamental Background" (1927; Musée National d'Art Moderne); "The Dance I" (1931–32; Musée d'Art Moderne de la Ville de Paris); "The Dance II" (1932–33; Barnes Foundation); "The Pink Nude" (1935; Baltimore Museum of Art); "Lady in Blue" (1937; Mrs. John Wintersteen Collection, Philadelphia); "La Musique" (1939; Albright–Knox Art Gallery, Buffalo); "Dancer and Armchair, Black Background" (1942; private collection); "Large Interior in Red" (1948; Musée National d'Art Moderne); Chapelle du Rosaire (1951; Vence, Fr.; entire decoration designed by Matisse); "Sorrows of the King" (1952; Musée National d'Art Moderne); "Souvenir of Oceania" (1953; Museum of Modern Art).

Sculpture (all bronze, several examples of each). "Jaguar Devouring a Hare" (1899; private collection); "The Slave" (1900–03; Baltimore Museum of Art, and elsewhere); "Madeleine I" (1901; Baltimore Museum of Art and elsewhere); "Small Head" (1906–07); "Two Negresses" (1908); "The Back I–IV" (1909–30); "Jeanette I–V" (1910); "Seated Nude" (1925).

BIBLIOGRAPHY. Lawrence Gowing, *Matisse* (1979), a general introduction to his art; Alfred H. Barr, Jr., *Matisse: His Art and His Public* (1951, reprinted 1974), an excellent critical analysis; John Russell *et al., The World of Matisse, 1869–1954* (1969), a general work; Pierre Schneider (ed.), *Exposition Henri Matisse* (1970), the catalog of the Paris retrospective show of 1970; Louis Aragon, *Henri Matisse, roman,* 2 vol. (1971), a poetic evocation by a perceptive French contemporary of the painter; Jack D. Flam (ed.), *Matisse on Art* (1973), a collection and analysis of many statements by Matisse on art.

Matlock, locality, Derbyshire Dales district, county of Derbyshire, England. It consists of a group of settlements extending along the River Derwent. The locality is noted for its beautiful valleys and rugged hills. Between Cromford (site of Sir Richard Arkwright's first water-powered mill, 1771) and Matlock Bridge (16th century), the River Derwent runs through a narrow gorge. Matlock was once famous for its hydropathic treatment, but the largest establishment (1852) in the locality now houses the county offices. Pop. (1981) 13,867.

Mato Grosso, inland *estado* ("state") of Brazil, situated in the Grande Região Centro-Oeste (Grand Central-West Region). It is bounded on the northwest by the states of Rondônia and Amazonas, on the northeast by Pará, on the east by Tocantins and Goiás, on the south by Mato Grosso do Sul, and on the southwest and west by Bolivia. Mato Grosso, whose name means "great woods," is one of the remaining great frontier regions of the world. It has an area of 340,156 square miles (881,001 square km). The state capital is Cuiabá.

Mato Grosso was settled first by pioneering gold seekers from São Paulo after they had been forced to retreat by the *emboabas* (Portuguese colonists) of Minas Gerais in the so-called war of the *emboabas* in 1708, over mining rights in gold fields. With the founding in 1719 of Cuiabá, where rich placer mines had been found, Mato Grosso became a district of the captaincy of São Paulo, and in 1748 it became an independent captaincy. In 1761 the capital was transferred to Vila Bela, on the Guaporé River, but in 1820 it was returned to Cuiabá. During the colonial period and until deposits were largely exhausted, the region's placer mines supplied substantial quantities of gold and some diamonds. After the decline of mining, cattle ranching emerged as the principal activity. Mato Grosso became a province of the empire in 1822 and a state of the federal union in 1889.

The entire area's overall growth and development was long retarded by its isolation and lack of access to the sea. Until the railroad was built across southern Mato Grosso in 1914, the only means of communication except by overland trails was by way of the Paraguay and Paraná rivers, 2,000 miles (3,000 km) eastward to the Atlantic Ocean. Only in the second half of the 20th century have highways and airplanes begun to offer more widespread communications. The expedition of the Brazilian explorer Marshal Cândido Mariano da Silva Rondon in the early part of the 20th century furnished the first complete, accurate data about Mato Grosso; some sections of the state, however, remained virtually uninvestigated in the late 20th century.

Most of Mato Grosso lies on the western extension of the Brazilian Plateau, across which runs the watershed that separates the Amazon River basin to the north from the basin of the Río de la Plata system to the south. This elevated region is known as the Mato Grosso Plateau, and its elevation is about 3,000 feet (900 m). Its northern slope, drained by the Xingu, Tapajós, and Madeira rivers, descends to the valley of the Amazon. The valley of the Araguaia River, an affluent of the Tocantins River, marks the eastern border of the state. The southern portion of the state drains southward through a multitude of streams flowing into the Paraguay River to the southwest. The northern region of Mato Grosso is drained by a dendritic system of streams that flows north into tributaries of the Amazon River. The western part of the state, chiefly a floodplain, is among Brazil's best grazing lands, and it ranks as one of the great tropical grazing lands of the world.

The state's lowlands are hot and humid, and its highlands are hot and dry. The average temperature is 79° F (26° C). Average annual rainfall is 50 to 60 inches (1,300 to 1,500 mm). There is a distinct dry season from May to September.

Natural vegetation includes expanses of grassland, densely wooded areas, and, in the highlands, extensive plains, or *campos,* with scrub growth and light forest.

Mato Grosso had a high rate of population growth in the 20th century. Despite this, the state as a whole has one of the lowest population densities of any Brazilian state. Ethnically, the state includes a relatively high proportion of mestizos (persons of mixed European and Indian ancestry), as do other areas of the interior.

The population is chiefly rural, and there are few cities, the principal ones being Cáceres, Rondonópolis, and the state capital, Cuiabá. The influx of new settlers has been distributed about equally between rural and urban areas, expanding both segments of the population.

Social conditions are those of an expanding frontier. Public health and welfare services are limited in the growing cities and developing rural areas of the south and even more limited in the sparsely settled expanses in the north. Elementary education is free and compulsory, by law, but there are insufficient numbers of schools and teachers to supply it. The Federal University of Mato Grosso (founded 1970) is located in Cuiabá.

Livestock raising and agriculture are the principal economic activities of Mato Grosso. The state supports several million head of cattle, the principal market being São Paulo. Mato Grosso has important deposits of iron ore, manganese, tin, and limestone. Rice, sugarcane, corn (maize), oranges, and *feijão* (beans), the main commercial crops, are produced in that order.

The state's traditions have been those of the cattle ranch and the farm, being transformed in the second half of the 20th century by the infusion of immigrants, many from similar parts of Brazil. Pop. (1988 est.) 1,660,000.

Mato Grosso do Sul, inland *estado* ("state") of Brazil, situated in the Grande Região Centro-Oeste (Grand Central-West Region). It is bounded on the north by the state of Mato Grosso, on the northeast by the state of Goiás, on the east by Minas Gerais and São Paulo, on the southeast by Paraná, and on the west and south by Bolivia and Paraguay. Mato Grosso do Sul has an area of 135,347 square miles (350,548 square km). The state capital is Campo Grande.

The area now known as Mato Grosso do Sul was scarcely settled before the mid-1900s. Initial settlement was mainly by pioneering gold seekers who migrated west from São Paulo in the early 18th century. Mato Grosso, the mother state, became a district of the captaincy of São Paulo in 1719 and a state of the federal union in 1889. Mato Grosso do Sul was created in 1979 from the southern portion of Mato Grosso state.

After the exploitation of the region's gold- and diamond-rich placer mines declined, cattle ranching became prominent, but nonetheless the area's growth and development was long impeded by its isolation and insufficient means of communication. A railroad across southern Mato Grosso (now Mato Grosso do Sul) opened in 1914 and was a significant advancement, but only in the latter part of the 20th century has wider settlement been permitted by highway and air transport. Such expansion was facilitated by the development-minded move of the national capital from Rio de Janeiro to inland Brasília in the 1960s. The population density of Mato Grosso do Sul remains, however, one of the lowest in Brazil.

About half of the state lies on a southwestern extension of the Brazilian Plateau. The rest of the state lies in relative lowland. Its eastern boundary is formed by the Paraná River; the Paraguay River valley defines part of its western boundary, and the Taquari and Mirando tributaries cut across its western part. The Paraguay drainage area is essentially a floodplain that ranks as one of the world's best tropical grazing lands.

The average annual temperature of the state is 79° F (26° C). The highlands are much drier than the lowlands, with the average overall rainfall being 50 to 60 inches (1,300 to 1,500 mm). The period from May to September constitutes the dry season.

The population of Mato Grosso do Sul is largely urban, with the principal cities being the capital of Campo Grande, Dourados, Corumbá, Três Lagoas, Pontao Porã, and Coxim. Mestizos (persons of mixed European and Indian ancestry) compose a large percentage of the state's population.

Social conditions have continued to improve with increasing development. Public health and welfare services are limited in the growing cities and rural settlements, however. Though elementary education is free and compulsory, its quality is hampered by a lack of schools and teachers.

Despite continuing political and financial difficulties, Mato Grosso do Sul has been, since its formation, one of the most solid areas of socioeconomic development in Brazil. Its vast mineral deposits of iron ore and manganese form the foundation of an active mining industry. Livestock raising and agriculture are also important, the chief crops being cotton, peanuts (groundnuts), rice, beans, corn (maize), and soybeans. Pop. (1988 est.) 1,729,000.

Consult the INDEX *first*

Mato Grosso Plateau, Portuguese PLANALTO DE MATTO GROSSO, part of the Brazilian Highlands of inland Brazil. It is an ancient erosional plateau that occupies much of central Mato Grosso state and extends from the border of Goiás state westward to the Serra dos Parecis, which lies near the Bolivian border. In the south it gives way to floodplains called the Pantanal; this arca consists of often-inundated but rich grazing lands that make up a basin of the upper Paraguay and Cuiabá rivers. The Mato Grosso Plateau, with an average elevation of approximately 2,000 feet (600 m) above sea level, forms the divide between the Amazon River basin to the north and the Paraguay River basin to the south. The plateau is covered with a mixture of savanna grasslands and woodland. The area was explored and partially settled by 17th-century miners, who combed the region in search of gold, diamonds, and other minerals. Although mining is still important in portions of the Mato Grosso Plateau, the primary economic activity is cattle raising. The transportation network is poorly developed, although there are a few highways. Cuiabá, the state capital of Mato Grosso, is the principal urban centre.

Matoaka (Powhatan Indian princess): *see* Pocahontas.

Matoniaceae, family of ferns dating from the Mesozoic era (245 million to 66.4 million years ago) and distinguished by an umbrella-shaped membranous covering over clusters (sori) or spore-bearing structures (sporangia). The leaves are fan-shaped and lobed in narrow segments or have long midribs that aid the plant in a climbing habit. The family now includes only two genera (*Matonia,* 2 species; and *Phanerosorus,* 2 species). Although once widespread in the tropics, the family's members now occur only in the Malayan regions, mainly on open ridgetops at higher elevations, on mountain summits, and on limestone.

Matopo Hills, Matopo also spelled MATOPOS, mass of granite hills, southeast of Bulawayo, Zimbabwe, formed by river erosion and weathered into fantastic shapes and deep valleys. The hills are associated with folklore and tradition, some being venerated as dwelling places of the spirits of departed Ndebele chiefs. The hills contain gigantic caves (notably Bambata, Nswatugi, and Silozwane) with Khoisan paintings, and there are Stone and Iron Age archaeological sites. The name may have originated from *matombe* or *madombe,* meaning "the rocks," or from *matobo,* "bald heads."

Matopo Hills, Zimbabwe
Art Resource—EB Inc.

The hills, with average heights of 5,000 feet (1,500 m), cover an area of about 1,200 square miles (3,100 square km) and extend (east to west) for 50 miles (80 km). They are well watered by the Limpopo River's tributaries, which are dammed for irrigation, recreation, and water supply. Vegetation ranges from the lichens of the desertlike hilltops to the luxuriant growth of valley swamps. Animal life includes a wide variety of insects and birds, lizards, monkeys and baboons, antelopes, and leopards.

The Rhodes Matopos National Park was founded in 1902 as an estate with pastoral and arable land leased to private farmers or the government, an extensive experimental farm, and a game park. Accessible by road from Bulawayo, 5½ mi north, the national park, 106,750 acres (43,200 hectares), includes the scenic View of the World Hill, or Malindidzimu (4,700 feet [1,400 m]), where Cecil Rhodes (and others) are buried.

Matos, Luis Palés: *see* Palés Matos, Luis.

Matos Guerra, Gregório de, also called GREGÓRIO DE MATTOS E GUERRA (b. 1636? Salvador, Brazil—d. Oct. 19, 1696, Recife), poet who was the most colourful figure in early Brazilian literature. He was called the Brazilian Villon.

Born into the slave-owning gentry, Matos studied law at Coimbra, Port., and advanced to a high position in Lisbon until he fell into disfavour for using his caustic wit at the expense of court society. Returning to Bahia while in his 40s, he practiced law after his own fashion, sometimes defending the poor without charge. His sarcastic epigrams (directed chiefly against the ruling classes, though he did not spare the blacks, mulattoes, or Indians) became increasingly bitter. His satirical verses, recited to guitar accompaniment and circulated in manuscript, earned him the additional nickname *bôca do inferno* ("devil's mouthpiece"). Though he married, his private life was a scandal, and he was soon at odds with the clergy, government, and respectable society.

Exiled to the African colony of Angola, Matos composed a farewell to his native land in which he compared Brazilians to beasts of burden toiling to support Portuguese rascals. He was later permitted to return to Pernambuco on condition that he refrain from making verses and from associating with musicians, idlers, and low company, which conditions he ignored.

Matos' poetical works were not printed until 1882. Though he produced no single great work, his was the first native Brazilian poetic voice. He mixed the religious and the sensual in Baroque fashion. Matos was the first to write in a bold, informal style using national slang and idioms. His rebellious spirit has made him one of the cultural heroes of Brazil.

Matosinhos, also spelled MATOZINHOS, town and *concelho* (township), Porto *distrito* ("district"), northwestern Portugal. The town, a northwestern suburb of Porto city, lies at the mouth of the Leça River along the Atlantic Ocean.

Originally known as Matusiny (1258), it received its charter from King Manuel I in 1514 and, by decree of Queen Maria II, became a town in 1853. In the Church of Bom Jesus de Bouças is a crucifix reputedly carved by the Nicodemus who, according to the Bible, helped to bury Jesus; it inspires annual pilgrimages. The town's artificial harbour, the Porto de Leixoes, serves as the principal (wine export) port of Porto and northern Portugal. Situated in a beach resort area, Matosinhos is also an important fishing harbour for large local canneries. Pop. (1981) town, 26,426; (1987 est.) *concelho,* 144,800.

Mátra Mountains, the highest range in northern Hungary, and part of the region's central highland belt. The range's maximum elevation is reached at Mount Kékes (3,327 feet [1,014 m]). The Mátra is a sharply defined volcanic mass consisting in large part of lava and measuring approximately 25 miles (40 km) east-west between the Tarna and Zagyva rivers and 9 miles (14 km) north-south across the range's spine. The north slopes shelve sharply into the Nógrád basin; to the south are the Mátra foothills, a series of fingerlike projections onto the Great Alföld. The fingerlike pattern of the foothills was created by the erosive action of the several tributaries of the Tarna River system, flowing south.

The Mátras have a rich and varied vegetation, beech and oak predominating. The climate is mild, especially on the south-facing slopes, and on the high points long hours of summer sunshine have favoured popular resorts and sanatoriums, such as those at Kékestető, Galyatető, Ágasvár, and Parádfürdő.

The industrial basin in the Mátra foothills (centred on the Gyöngyös River) developed rapidly in the 1970s. The Kisterenye-Nagybátony coalfield is important, and there are small deposits of nonferrous metals around the range's volcanic core.

Maṭraḥ, also spelled MUTRAH, OR MUTTRAH, town in Oman, on the Gulf of Oman coast, just west of Muscat. Maṭraḥ has traditionally been the country's chief commercial centre and port. Port Qābūs, the town's new port facilities, were completed during the 1970s. Port al-Faḥl, 3 miles (5 km) to the west, is Oman's oil terminal and is connected by pipelines to the oil fields in the south. Maṭraḥ has a large fish market, selling fresh fish for domestic use and processing frozen fish for export. The town is a departure point for caravans traveling inland with fruit, fish, pearls, and other commodities. Shipbuilding and ship repair are also economically important. Pop. (early 1970s est.) 15,000.

matriarchy, hypothetical social system in which familial and political authority is wielded by women. Under the influence of Charles Darwin's theories of evolution and, more particularly, the work of the Swiss anthropologist J.J. Bachofen, some 19th-century historians and anthropologists believed that matriarchy followed a stage of general promiscuity and preceded male ascendancy in human society's evolutionary sequence. Like other elements of the so-called evolutionist view of human culture, the view of matriarchy as constituting a stage of cultural development is now generally discredited. Furthermore, the consensus among modern anthropologists and sociologists is that a strictly matriarchal society never existed.

matrix, a set of numbers arranged in rows and columns so as to form a rectangular array. The numbers are called the elements, or entries, of the matrix. Matrices have wide applications in engineering, physics, economics, and statistics as well as in various branches of mathematics. Historically, it was not the matrix but a certain number associated with a square array of numbers called the determinant that was first recognized. Only gradually did the idea of the matrix as an algebraic entity emerge. The term matrix was introduced by the 19th-century English mathematician Arthur Cayley, who developed the algebraic aspect of matrices.

If there are m rows and n columns, the matrix is said to be an "m by n" matrix, written "$m \times n$." For example,

$$\begin{bmatrix} 1 & 3 & 8 \\ 2 & -4 & 5 \end{bmatrix}$$

is a 2×3 matrix. A matrix with n rows and n columns is called a square matrix of order n. An ordinary number can be regarded as a 1×1 matrix; thus, 3 can be thought of as the matrix [3].

In a common notation, a capital letter denotes matrix and the corresponding small letter with a double subscript describes an element of the matrix. Thus, a_{ij} is the element in the ith row and jth column of the matrix A. If A is the 2×3 matrix shown above, then $a_{11} = 1$, $a_{12} = 3$, $a_{13} = 8$, $a_{21} = 2$, $a_{22} = -4$, and $a_{23} = 5$. Under certain conditions, matrices can be added and multiplied as individual entities, giving rise to important mathematical systems known as matrix algebras.

Matrices occur naturally in systems of simultaneous equations. In the following system for the unknowns x and y,

$$2x + 3y = 7$$
$$3x + 4y = 10,$$

the array of numbers

$$\begin{bmatrix} 2 & 3 \\ 3 & 4 \end{bmatrix}$$

is a matrix whose elements are the coefficients of the unknowns. The solution of the equations depends entirely on these numbers and on their particular arrangement. If 7 and 10 were interchanged, the solution would not be the same.

Two matrices A and B are equal to one another if they possess the same number of rows and the same number of columns and if $a_{ij} = b_{ij}$ for each i and each j. If A and B are two $m \times n$ matrices, their sum $S = A + B$ is the $m \times n$ matrix whose elements $s_{ij} = a_{ij} + b_{ij}$. That is, each element of S is equal to the sum of the elements in the corresponding positions of A and B.

A matrix A can be multiplied by an ordinary number c, which is called a scalar. The product is denoted by cA or Ac and is the matrix whose elements are ca_{ij}.

The multiplication of a matrix A by a matrix B to yield a matrix C is defined only when the number of columns of the first matrix A equals the number of rows of the second matrix B. To determine the element c_{ij}, which is in the ith row and jth column of the product, the first element in the ith row of A is multiplied by the first element in the jth column of B, the second element in the row by the second element in the column, and so on until the last element in the row is multiplied by the last element of the column; the sum of all these products gives the element c_{ij}. In symbols, for the case where A has m columns and B has m rows,

$$c_{ij} = a_{i1}b_{1j} + a_{i2}b_{2j} + \ldots + a_{im}b_{mj}.$$

The matrix C has as many rows as A and as many columns as B.

Unlike the multiplication of ordinary numbers a and b, in which ab always equals ba, the multiplication of matrices A and B is not commutative. It is, however, associative and distributive over addition. That is, when the operations are possible, the following equations always hold true: $A(BC) = (AB)C$, $A(B + C) = AB + AC$, and $(B + C)A = BA + CA$.

A matrix O with all its elements 0 is called a zero matrix. A square matrix A with ones on the main diagonal (upper left to lower right) and zeros everywhere else is called a unit matrix. It is denoted by I, or I_n to show that its order is n. If B is any square matrix and I and O are the unit and zero matrices of the same order, it is always true that $B + O = O + B = B$ and $BI = IB = B$. Hence O and I behave like the 0 and 1 of ordinary arithmetic. In fact, ordinary arithmetic is the special case of matrix arithmetic in which all matrices are 1×1.

Associated with each square matrix A is a number that is known as the determinant of A, denoted det A. For example, for the 2×2 matrix

$$A = \begin{bmatrix} a & b \\ c & d \end{bmatrix},$$

det $A = ad - bc$. A square matrix B is called nonsingular if det $B \neq 0$. If B is nonsingular, there is a matrix called the inverse of B, denoted B^{-1}, such that $BB^{-1} = B^{-1}B = I$. The equation $AX = B$, in which A and B are known matrices and X is an unknown matrix, can be solved uniquely if A is a nonsingular matrix, for then A^{-1} exists and both sides of the equation can be multiplied on the left by it: $A^{-1}(AX) = A^{-1}B$. Now $A^{-1}(AX) = (A^{-1}A)X = IX = X$; hence the solution is $X = A^{-1}B$. A system of m linear equations in n unknowns can always be expressed as a matrix equation $AX = B$ in which A is the $m \times n$ matrix of the coefficients of the unknowns, X is the $n \times 1$ matrix of the unknowns, and B is the $n \times 1$ matrix containing the numbers on the right-hand side of the equation.

A problem of great significance in many branches of science is the following: given a square matrix A of order n, find the $n \times 1$ matrix X, called an n-dimensional vector, such that $AX = cX$. Here c is a number called an eigenvalue, and X is called an eigenvector.

matrix, in geology, the material in which something is embedded, either the natural rock that holds crystals, fossils, pebbles, mineral veins, and the like, or the fine-grained materials that surround larger grains in a rock—*e.g.,* silt and clay particles in a sandstone or tiny crystals in a crystalline rock, sometimes called groundmass.

Matronalia, also called MATRONALES FERIAE, in Roman religion, ancient festival of Juno, the birth goddess, celebrated annually by Roman matrons on March 1, the day on which a temple was dedicated to Juno. According to tradition, the cult was established by Titus Tatius, king of the Sabines. The Matronalia symbolized not only the sacredness of marriage but also the peace that followed the first marriages between Romans and Sabine women. The festival consisted of a procession of married women to the temple, where they made offerings to Juno. At home, offerings were supplemented by prayers for marital felicity. Wives received gifts from their husbands and gave a feast for their female slaves.

Maṭrūḥ, desert *muḥāfaẓah* (governorate) of Egypt that includes all of Egypt west of al-Jīzah governorate and north of latitude 26°20′ N. Only one percent of its area is inhabited. It is mostly a plateau area of sedimentary rock such as limestone, averaging 700–800 feet (215–245 m) in elevation and nowhere surpassing 1,500 feet (460 m). Surface dissection results from wind erosion on the stone-covered wastes and sandy plains. Longitudinal belts of parallel sand dunes occur, rising to 200 feet (60 m) in the Great Sand Sea extending south from the Siwa Oasis. Light rain falls only along the coastal plain, but underground aquifers provide water for Siwa Oasis. The Qattara Depression reaches 435 feet (133 m) below sea level and occupies 7,000 square miles (18,000 square km), extending southward 35 miles (56 km) from the coast at al-ʿAlamayn.

The governorate's natural resources include petroleum, with fields at al-ʿAlamayn, Abū al-Gharādiq, and in the Qattara Depression, and natural gas at Abū al-Gharādiq. The population is concentrated along the small coastal strip, where Roman ruins are located, and in Siwa Oasis. A railway connects the small ports of Marsā Maṭrūḥ (*q.v.*), the capital of the governorate, and as-Sallūm to Alexandria. Area 81,897 square miles (212,112 square km). Pop. (2004 est.) 262,200.

Matshangana-Tsonga (South Africa): *see* Gazankulu.

Matshikiza, Todd (b. 1920/21, Queenstown, S.Af.—d. March 4, 1968, Lusaka, Zambia), journalist, writer, and musician noted for his score for the musical play *King Kong* (1960) and for his short stories.

Matshikiza divided his career from the start between musical and literary activities. Trained as a teacher at Lovedale, near the University College of Fort Hare, he wrote a monthly column for *Drum* magazine and also worked as a jazz critic. His choral music was widely performed by South African choirs and won him a commission for the Johannesburg Festival in 1956. When he and his family accompanied the *King Kong* cast to London in 1961, he decided to stay; there he collaborated with the white South African writer Alan Paton on the musical *Mkumbane,* presented radio programs for the British Broadcasting Corporation, and wrote autobiographical short stories of his life in London and South Africa.

Matson, Randy, byname of JAMES RANDEL MATSON (b. March 5, 1945, Kilgore, Texas, U.S.), American shot-putter who, in 1965, was the first man to put the shot more than 21 m, with a distance of 21.52 m (70 feet 7.25 inches).

Matson's weight-throwing ability was recognized when he was in the eighth grade, and he set state high school records in both the shot put and discus. After his freshman year at Texas A & M University (College Station), he won the silver medal in the shot put at the 1964 Summer Olympic Games. He bettered his 1965 record in 1967 with a put of 21.78 m (71 feet 5.5 inches) and won the James E. Sullivan Award that year as the country's outstanding amateur athlete. At the 1968 Summer Olympics he won the gold medal with a put of 20.54 m. He also won United States Track and Field Association shot-put titles (1969–71). Matson retired from competition in 1972 after failing to make the U.S. Olympic team. He later was an executive of alumni relations for Texas A & M University.

Matsu Island, Chinese (Wade-Giles) MA-TSU TAO, or (Pinyin) MAZU DAO, also called NANKAN, small island under the jurisdiction of Taiwan in the East China Sea, lying off the Min River estuary of mainland China and about 130 miles (210 km) northwest of Chi-lung (Keelung), Taiwan. Matsu is the main island of a group of 19, the Matsu Islands, which constitute Lien-kiang (Lienchiang) *hsien* (county). The island has a hilly terrain of igneous rock and a monsoonal subtropical climate. Fishing is the main economic activity. The islanders also raise vegetables, grain, hogs, and chickens, aided by an extensive system of reservoirs and wells.

Once part of the mainland's Fukien province, Matsu and the other islands were occupied by the Nationalist Chinese when they were driven from the mainland to Taiwan in 1949. Thereafter, Matsu and Quemoy Island to the south were central to the ongoing tension between Taiwan and the mainland, and both subsequently came under periodic artillery bombardment by communist forces on the mainland. One such incident, in 1958, provoked an international diplomatic crisis when the communists combined a heavy bombardment with the demand that the Nationalists surrender. The standoff was diffused only after the United States had interposed the 7th Fleet between the mainland and Taiwan. The island group remained under military rule until 1992. Area Matsu Island, 4 square miles (10 square km). Pop. (2003 est.) county, 8,732.

Matsudaira Sadanobu (b. Jan. 25, 1759, Edo [now Tokyo], Japan—d. June 14, 1829, Edo), Japanese minister who instituted the Kansei reforms (*q.v.*), a series of conservative fiscal and social measures intended to reinvigorate Japan by recovering the greatness that had marked the Tokugawa shogunate from its inception in 1603. Although traditional historians have paid tribute to them, Matsudaira's reforms are now generally considered to have been a vain resuscitation of an outdated system and to have hindered any adjustment to changes already taking place in society.

Matsudaira was a member of the reigning Tokugawa family and had early been considered for adoption as heir to the shogun, or hereditary military dictator of Japan. Instead he was made the daimyo, or lord, of an important fief not under the shogun's direct rule. There his vigorous measures reordered finances and administration.

When the shogun Tokugawa Ieharu died in 1786, Matsudaira's influence secured the nomination of Tokugawa Ienari (reigned 1787–1837) as successor. Under the new administration, Matsudaira, a firm believer in the anti-commerce, ruler-oriented philosophy of the 12th-century Chinese thinker Chu Hsi, accomplished the dismissal of the chief minister, Tanuma Okitsugu, who had headed a notoriously corrupt administration but had encouraged the development of trade and industry.

Having then succeeded Tanuma as chief minister, Matsudaira tried to proscribe unorthodox thought. He dismissed numerous corrupt officials and instituted qualifying examinations for new appointees. He sought to foster the traditional agricultural economy by curtailing foreign trade and severely restricting the growth of the merchant class, while limiting fiscal expenditure through a vigorous program of economy. His policies gave some aid to the government in its financial difficulties, and his measures to alleviate famine temporarily averted serious peasant unrest, but such solutions proved to be only temporary.

After a minor policy dispute with the shogun had caused his retirement in 1793, Matsudaira devoted himself to Confucian studies and writing. He was considered—and styled himself—a model Confucian ruler.

Matsudaira Tsuneo (b. April 17, 1877, Tokyo, Japan—d. Nov. 11, 1949, Tokyo), Japanese diplomat and statesman who helped secure an increase in the naval strength allotted to Japan at the 1930 London Naval Conference. The increase, however, was not large enough to satisfy the Japanese Navy. From 1936 to June 1945, as imperial household minister, Matsudaira was an adviser to the emperor. As such he initially tried unsuccessfully to influence Japanese policy, which seemed headed for a collision with the United States, in a moderate direction. After World War II he became first chairman of the Diet (parliament) under the new constitution (1947).

Matsudaira Yoshinaga, also called MATSUDAIRA KEIEI (b. Oct. 10, 1828, Edo [now Tokyo], Japan—d. June 2, 1890, Tokyo), one of the primary Japanese political figures in the events preceding the Meiji Restoration—*i.e.,* the 1868 overthrow of the feudal Tokugawa shogunate and the establishment of a centralized regime under the Japanese emperor.

Matsudaira was born into a collateral branch of the Tokugawa clan, the family that controlled the office of shogun, or hereditary military dictator of Japan. In 1838 he succeeded his father as daimyo (feudal lord) of the Fukui fief in central Japan, where he established a Western-style arms factory, encouraged education, and developed medical facilities.

As one of the more important daimyos of the country, he was called upon by the shogun to act as an advisor when the government was confronted with the crisis resulting from U.S. Commodore Matthew C. Perry's demand (1853) that Japan open its doors to trade and intercourse with the outside world. Matsudaira at first took a firm stand for continued seclusion, but by the time of the Harris Treaty in 1858 he had reversed his position.

In 1858 Matsudaira was placed under house arrest by the powerful state councillor Ii Naosuke because of Matsudaira's and others' attempts to determine the succession of the shogunate. After Ii was assassinated in 1860, Matsudaira was pardoned and released, and in 1862 he became an important shogunal adviser under a new administrative structure. Influenced by his famous adviser Yokoi Shōnan, Matsudaira attempted to appease the other daimyos, abolishing the *sankin kōtai,* or alternate attendance system, by which the Tokugawa house had controlled Japan's most powerful lords. Under that costly system, the daimyos were required to live in the capital city in alternate years, leaving their wives and children as hostages while they returned to their fiefs.

A strong believer in national solidarity, Matsudaira also attempted to give the emperor more power in the government. In 1864 he even joined a council of great lords appointed to advise the court and thus bring the Imperial house and the shogunate together. But when this group broke up, Matsudaira went back to serving the Tokugawa family, waiting for the inevitable conflict between the two factions. Since Matsudaira was known to be an Imperial supporter, he later served for a while in high positions in the Meiji government.

Matsudo, city, Chiba Prefecture (*ken*), Honshu, Japan, on the Jōban Line (railway), east of the centre of Tokyo. During the Tokugawa era (1603–1867), Matsudo was a post town on the Mito-kaidō (Mito Highway) and a port on the Tone-gawa (Tone River) and the Edo-gawa. After World War II it became a residential and industrial suburb of the Tokyo–Yokohama Metropolitan Area, its factories including ironworks and engineering works. Pop. (1983 est.) 418,490.

Cycling stadium in Matsudo, Japan
Design-Uni—FPG/EB Inc.

Matsue, capital, Shimane Prefecture (*ken*), southwestern Honshu, Japan, on Shinji-ko (Lake Shinji) and the Tenjin-gawa (Tenjin River), near the Sea of Japan. Known as the "city built on water," Matsue retained its feudal character into the 1970s. Many of the buildings were designed by the feudal lord Fumai, who promoted the lacquer ware and pottery industries and the daily practice of the tea ceremony. During the 1970s Matsue was designated a "New Industrial City" by the Japanese government in a program designed to utilize underdeveloped areas and to relieve the congestion in larger industrial areas. The city is a meeting point for land and sea communications and has an important commercial centre south of the river. The 17th-century Matsue Castle contains a giant rope made of rice straw to honour the Shintō harvest god. Matsue also has the residence of the 19th-century Irish-American writer and educator Lafcadio Hearn, who lived and wrote there and became a naturalized Japanese subject. Pop. (1983 est.) 138,199.

The residence of Lafcadio Hearn in Matsue, Japan
Kenji Narumiya—Bon

Matsukata Masayoshi, KOSHAKU (Duke, or Prince) (b. April 3, 1834, Kagoshima, Japan—d. July 2, 1924, Tokyo), statesman whose financial reforms stabilized and restored Japanese government finances in the 1880s, giving Japan the capital with which to modernize.

In the new Imperial government that followed the overthrow (1868) of the Tokugawa family, which had ruled Japan for 264 years, and restored power to the emperor, Matsukata held various important positions. By 1881 he was named minister of finance. As such, he became the major advocate and executor of financial reform.

The government had met the severe financial strain of modernization by printing paper money. In the 1880s currency was badly depreciated, specie was being hoarded, and revenues, because of the fixed tax on land, were declining in value. Under Matsukata's regime government expenses were cut; newly built factories were sold to private buyers, paper money was redeemed, and the Bank of Japan was founded with the right to issue convertible notes. In a period of three years the currency was stabilized and government finances restored to health.

In 1891, and again in 1896, Matsukata was named prime minister, but each time he retired shortly after his appointment because of widespread opposition brought on by his harsh dealings with the Diet (parliament). He was minister of finance again in 1897, when Japan adopted the gold standard. After 1902 he was one of the elder statesmen (genro) whose advice the government relied upon in formulating policy.

Matsumoto, city, Nagano Prefecture (*ken*), central Honshu, Japan, in a mountain basin on the Narai-gawa (Narai River). It is noted for its silk industry, which dates from feudal times. Mulberry and fruit trees are grown on terraces encircling the floor of the basin. The city is a tourist centre with hot springs and skiing resorts in the surrounding mountains. Near Matsumoto are two castles where governors of the historic province lived before the Tokugawa era (1603–1867), when the castles were passed to various daimyo families. Pop. (1983 est.) 193,829.

Castle at Matsumoto, Japan
W.H. Hodge

Matsunaga Teitoku, original name MATSUNAGA KATSUGUMA, also called SHŌYUKEN, or CHOZUMARU (b. 1571, Kyoto—d. Jan. 3, 1654, Kyoto), renowned Japanese scholar and haikai poet of the early Tokugawa period (1603–1867) who founded the Teitoku (or Teimon) school of haikai poetry. Teitoku raised haikai—comic *renga* (linked verses) from which the more serious 17-syllable haiku of Bashō were derived—to an acceptable literary standard and made them into a popular poetic style.

Teitoku was the son of a professional *renga* poet, and he received an excellent education from some of the best poets of the day. After making the acquaintance of the Neo-Confucian scholar Hayashi Razan, Teitoku began giving public lectures on Japanese classics. In about 1620 he opened the Teitoku school in his home; at first he concentrated on educating children, but gradually he became more interested in tutoring aspiring poets.

Throughout this time he had been composing poems, primarily serious *waka* and *renga* but also lighter haikai. Although reluctant at first, he allowed one of his students to publish a number of his haikai in the anthology *Enoko-shū* (1633; "Puppy Collection"). This volume established him as the leading poet of the early to mid-17th century, and numerous poets were inspired to compose haikai. Several other collections of his poems were published, including *Taka tsukuba* (1638) and *Shinzo inu tsukuba-shu* (1643). Teitoku also set down the rules he had formulated for writing haikai in *Gosan* (1651).

Matsuo Bashō, pseudonym of MATSUO MUNEFUSA (Japanese poet) *see* Bashō.

matsuri (Japanese: "festival"), in general, any of a wide variety of civil and religious ceremonies in Japan; more particularly, the shrine festivals of the Shintō religion. *Matsuri* vary according to the shrine, the *kami* (god or sacred power) worshipped, and the purpose and occasion of the ceremony and often are performed in accordance with traditions of great antiquity. The term *matsuri-goto,* which literally means "affairs of religious festivals," in common usage also means "government." This is in accordance with the tradition that the ceremonies of Shintō were the proper business of the state, and that all important aspects of public just as of private life were the occasions for prayers and reports to the *kami.* The *matsuri* ceremonies generally fall into two parts: the solemn ritual of worship, followed by a joyous celebration.

The participants first purify themselves (*see* harai) by periods of abstinence, which may vary from a number of hours to days, and by bathing (*misogi*), preferably in salt water. The *kami* is then requested to descend into its symbol or object of residence (*shintai*) in an invocatory rite that consists of opening the inner doors of the shrine, beating a drum or ringing bells, and calling the *kami* to descend. Next the food offerings (*shinsen*) are presented and on occasion other offerings, *heihaku* (literally, cloth, but in modern usage including also paper, jewels, weapons, money, and utensils). Prayers (*norito*) are recited by the priests. Individual worshippers present offerings of branches of a sacred tree (*tamagushi*), and ceremonial music and dancing (*gagaku*) are performed. The offerings are then withdrawn and the *kami* respectfully requested to retire.

The celebrations usually include a feast (*naorai*) in which the consecrated offerings of food and drink are consumed by priests and laymen, dancing, theatrical performances, divination, and athletic contests, such as sumo wrestling, archery, either on foot or on horseback, and boat races. The *kami* is frequently taken out in a procession in a portable shrine (*mi-koshi*); thus its presence blesses the locations along its route. Accompanying it in the procession, which may commemorate some local historical event, are priests of the temple in full ceremonial dress; delegations of parishioners, musicians, and dancers dressed in ancient costumes; and floats (*dashi*). The floats are beautifully decorated cars shaped like mountains, shrines, or perhaps boats, either drawn by men or oxen or carried on men's shoulders.

Matsushita Electric Industrial Company, Ltd., Japanese MATSUSHITA DENKI SANGYŌ KK, major Japanese manufacturer of electric appliances and consumer electronics products. Headquarters are in Kadoma, near Ōsaka.

The company was founded in 1918 by Matsushita Konosuke to manufacture and market the electric lamp sockets and plugs he designed. It was incorporated in 1935, when it took its present name, and began expanding rapidly into a number of varied electrical product lines. During the 1930s it added such electrical devices as irons, radios, phonographs, and light bulbs. In the 1950s it began producing transistor radios, television sets, tape recorders, stereo equipment, and large household appliances. During the next decade it added microwave ovens, air conditioners, and videotape recorders. Most of its products are marketed under the brand names Panasonic, Quasar, National, Technics, Victor, and JVC.

Nonconsumer products include minicomputers, telephone equipment, electric motors, chemical and solar batteries, and cathode-ray tubes. The company also has developed and marketed electronic measuring and timing instruments, copy machines, automatic traffic control devices, office automation equipment, and products in the communications, broadcasting, and solar energy fields. The company is noted for its heavy investment in research and development; in addition to its main research laboratories, each Matsushita manufacturing division is backed by its own research team.

The bulk of the company's sales comes from foreign markets in Europe and North America, among other regions. It has manufacturing and sales subsidiaries in a number of overseas markets, and handles exports and imports through the Matsushita Electric Trading Company, Ltd.

Matsushita Konosuke (b. Nov. 27, 1894, Wakayama prefecture, Japan—d. April 27, 1989, Ōsaka), Japanese industrialist who founded the Matsushita Electric Industrial Co., Ltd., the largest manufacturer of consumer electric appliances in the world.

His parents having died, Matsushita began work at age 9 as an errand boy. At age 16 he began working for the Ōsaka Electric Light Company, and he quit his job as an inspector there at age 23 to start a company that would sell electric plug attachments of his own design. His inventive marketing strategies helped the Matsushita Electric grow, and in 1935 he reorganized the company under the name it still holds. Matsushita managed to prevent his company from being broken up by the U.S. occupation authorities after World War II, and by the 1950s the Matsushita Electric Industrial Co. was the chief manufacturer of washing machines, refrigerators, and television sets for Japanese homes. In the decades that followed, the company became internationally famous for such products as electrical equipment, computer chips, and videocassette recorders under such brand names as Panasonic, Quasar, and National.

Matsushita was president of the company until 1961, at which time he became chairman of the board of directors. His influential business philosophy, which called for the production of essential consumer goods in abundance at the lowest possible prices, was widely adopted in the egalitarian, consumer-oriented society that emerged in Japan in the second half of the 20th century.

Matsuwaka-Maru: *see* Shinran.

Matsuyama, capital, Ehime *ken* (prefecture), northwestern Shikoku, Japan. It is a seaport that faces the Inland Sea and lies on the fertile Dōgo Plain. Matsuyama is the largest city on Shikoku, covering an area of 80 square miles (207 square km). Its industries produce textiles, petrochemicals, paper, and machinery. The city is also a trade centre for local handicrafts (pottery, handweaving, and dolls) and the cultivation of mandarin oranges. Katsu Hill, rising in the city centre, is crowned by a 17th-century castle that now contains a military museum. Matsuyama was the headquarters of an important warrior clan during Japan's feudal era (1185–1867). Many haiku poetry masters came from the area. To the northeast, Dōgo Spa is one of the oldest and largest hot-spring resorts established in Japan, housing public baths in a three-story facility. Pop. (1989 est.) 441,464.

Castle at Matsuyama, Japan
Orion Press, Tokyo

Matsuzaka, city, Mie *ken* (prefecture), Honshu, Japan, facing Ise Bay. It was a castle town and commercial centre during the Tokugawa era (1603–1867), when cotton spinning was introduced there. Agricultural products of the surrounding Ise-wan plain include rice, wheat, sweet potatoes, and tea. The city's modern industries produce glass, electrical machinery, ships, and yarn. Matsuzaka is well known in Japan for its production of beef cattle, and mulberries are grown for sericulture (silkworm raising). Points of historic interest include the 17th-century castle and the home of the eminent scholar and poet Motoori Norinaga (1730–1801). Pop. (1989 est.) 118,466.

Matsya (Sanskrit: "Fish"), first of the 10 avatars (incarnations) of the Hindu god Vishnu. In this appearance Vishnu saved the world from a great flood. Manu, the first man, caught a little fish that grew to giant size and revealed himself as the god. When the flood approached, Manu saved himself by tying his boat to the horn on the fish's head. Some early accounts refer to the fish-saviour as Prajāpati (whose identity is later merged with that of Brahmā), an illustration of how the legends of the avatars incorporate existing myths.

Matsya, Rajasthani painting, late 17th century; in a private collection
Pramod Chandra

Matsya may be depicted either in animal form or in a combined human-animal form. In the latter case the man is shown as the upper half, and the fish as the lower half. Matsya is generally represented with four hands, one holding the conch shell, one the discus (chakra), one in the pose of conferring a boon (*varada-mudrā*), and one in the protection-affording pose (*abhaya-mudrā*). According to the canons of sculpture, the man-half should be shown as wearing all the ornaments usually associated with Vishnu.

Matsyendranātha, also called MĪNANĀTHA (fl. 10th century?, India), first human guru, or spiritual teacher, of the Nātha cult, a popular Indian religious movement combining elements of Hinduism, Buddhism, and Haṭha Yoga, a form of yoga that stresses breath control and physical postures.

Matsyendranātha's name appears on both the lists of the 9 *nātha*s ("masters") and the 84 *mahāsiddha*s ("great accomplished ones") common to Hinduism and Buddhism. He was given semidivine status by his followers and identified with Avalokiteśvara-Padmapāni (a bodhisattva, or buddha-to-be) by his Buddhist followers in Nepal and with the god Śiva by his Hindu devotees. In Tibet he was known as Lui-pa. The name Mīna-nātha ("Fish-Lord") refers, according to one legend, to his receipt of spiritual instruction from Śiva while in the form of a fish and in another legend to his rescue of a sacred text from the belly of a fish.

The historical details of Matsyendranātha's life are lost in the legends that have grown up around him. Though an ascetic he succumbed, according to one legend, to enchantments of two queens of Ceylon and had two sons, Pārosenāth and Nīmnāth, who were leaders of the Jaina religious sect. His leading disciple, Gorakhnāth, is commonly regarded as the founder of the Kānphaṭa Yogis, an order of religious ascetics who stress the practice of Haṭha Yoga.

Consult the INDEX *first*

Matsys, Quentin (Flemish artist): *see* Massys, Quentin.

Matta, Joaquim Dias Cordeiro da (Angolan writer): *see* Cordeiro da Matta, Joaquim Dias.

Mattāncheri, former township in Kerala state, southwestern India. It lies adjacent to the city of Cochin on the Arabian Sea coast. In 1970 Mattāncheri township was incorporated with the Cochin urban agglomeration. The township is notable chiefly for the impressive Pardesī synagogue of the Jewish community as well as for the palace of the rajas of Cochin.

The synagogue was built in 1568 and was restored after partial destruction by the Portuguese in 1664. It includes a Dutch-style clock tower built in 1761, Torah scrolls decorated in silver and gold, and many valuable ritual objects. Among the latter are ancient inscribed copper plates that were presented to the Jews by King Bhāskara Ravi Varma in the 4th century and are regarded by them as the charter of their community. Mattāncheri's Jewish community has dwindled considerably in the second half of the 20th century because of emigration to the state of Israel.

The palace, dating from 1555, was the residence of the rajas of Cochin. It houses exquisite mural paintings that depict the entire story of the *Rāmāyaṇa,* the shorter of the two great epic poems of India.

Mattathias (d. *c.* 166 BC), Jewish priest and landowner of Modein, near Jerusalem, who in 167 defied the decree of Antiochus IV Epiphanes of Syria to Hellenize the Jews; he fled to the Judaean hills with his five sons and waged a guerrilla war against the Syrians, being succeeded by his son Judas Maccabeus. Because, according to Josephus, Mattathias' great-great-grandfather was called Hasmoneus, the family is often designated Hasmonean rather than Maccabee.

matte, crude mixture of molten sulfides formed as an intermediate product of the smelting of sulfide ores of metals, especially copper, nickel, and lead. Instead of being smelted directly to metal, copper ores are usually smelted to matte, preferably containing 40–45 percent copper along with iron and sulfur, which is then treated by converting in a Bessemer-type converter. Air is blown into the molten matte, oxidizing the sulfur to sulfur dioxide and the iron to oxide that combines with a silica flux to form slag, leaving the copper in the metallic state. Smelting of nickel sulfide ores yields a matte in which nickel and copper make up about 15 percent, iron about 50 percent, and sulfur the rest; the iron is removed in a converting furnace, and the sulfides of copper and nickel are separated before being reduced to the metals. Smelting of lead sulfide ores produces a liquid layer of copper sulfide matte that can be decanted, along with slag and speiss, from the lead bullion.

Matteo (SERAFINI) DA BASCIO, also called MATTEO DI BASSI (b. *c.* 1495, Bascio, Papal States [Italy]—d. Aug. 6, 1552, Venice), founder of the Order of Friars Minor Capuchin, commonly called Capuchins, the chief order of friars among the permanent offshoots of the Franciscans.

After entering the Observant Franciscans about 1511 at Montefalcone, Matteo was ordained priest about 1520. Eager to return to his order's primitive simplicity of poverty as founded by St. Francis of Assisi, Matteo secretly left for Rome, where Pope Clement VII informally granted him permission to do so.

Convinced that the habit worn by the Franciscans was not the kind Francis had worn, he accordingly made himself a pointed, or pyramidal, hood; in addition, he grew a beard and traveled barefoot. Others followed his example, resulting in a recognized order (*c.* 1525). Their life approached Francis' ideal as nearly as was practicable. On July 3, 1528, Clement, in his bull *Religionis Zelus,* gave the order canonical approbation. Matteo was elected first vicar general of the Capuchins in 1529 but soon resigned to continue his apostolic missionary work. He achieved the reputation of a great preacher, contributing especially to the Italian Catholic reformation.

In 1546 Pope Paul III dispatched Matteo to Germany to accompany the papal troops that assisted the Holy Roman emperor Charles V in his campaign against the Schmalkaldic League, a defensive organization of imperial Protestant estates in Germany. Charles declared war on John Frederick I, elector of Saxony. At the Battle of Mühlberg on April 24, 1547, Matteo reportedly spurred the Catholic soldiers to victory, and John Frederick was taken prisoner. Matteo returned to Venice, where he continued his preaching.

BIBLIOGRAPHY. An account of his life is found in Father Cuthbert, *The Capuchins,* 2 vol. (1928, reprinted 1971).

Matteo DI PASTI (b. 1420, Verona, Republic of Venice [Italy]—d. 1467/68, Rimini, Papal States), artist who was one of the most accomplished medalists in Italy during the 15th century, also a prestigious sculptor and architect.

At the beginning of his career Matteo worked as an illuminator, illustrating Petrarch's *Trionfi* (1441) and other works. The medals he executed for Sigismondo Malatesta and Isotta degli Atti (the first ones dating from 1446) are especially important for their refinement. Matteo moved from Verona to Rimini about 1449. Between the years 1460 and 1464 he apparently visited Constantinople (now Istanbul) at the request of Mahomet II.

As an architect, Matteo was given the responsibility by Malatesta for reconstructing the interior spaces of the Tempio Malatestiano in Rimini, and it is assumed that he executed many of its exquisite and sensitive reliefs. Other reliefs known to have been produced by Matteo in the Tempio were at the Chapel of the Planets and at the Arca degli Antenati.

Matteotti, Giacomo (b. May 22, 1885, Fratta Polesine, Italy—d. June 10, 1924, Rome), Italian Socialist leader whose assassination by Fascists shocked world opinion and shook Benito Mussolini's regime. The Matteotti Crisis, as the event came to be known, initially threatened to bring about the downfall of the Fascists but instead ended with Mussolini as the absolute dictator of Italy.

After graduating from the University of Bologna law school, Matteotti entered law practice and joined the Italian Socialist Party. He was elected to the Chamber of Deputies in 1919 and reelected in 1921 and 1924, by which time he had become secretary general of his party. In the meantime, Mussolini, who had succeeded in gaining power, was conducting terroristic attacks on leftists. On May 30, 1924, Matteotti addressed a ringing denunciation of the Fascist Party to the Chamber. Less than two weeks later (June 10) six Fascist *squadristi* kidnapped Matteotti in Rome, murdered him, and hastily buried his body outside the city near Riano Flaminio.

Matteotti's disappearance created a sensation, as did the discovery of his body a few weeks later. The Italian public had no doubt that Fascists were implicated in the crime and reacted against Fascist rule. Fascist party badges disappeared overnight; the antechamber of Mussolini's office, usually full, stood empty.

The opposition deputies withdrew from the Chamber, in an action known as the Aventine secession, to protest the murder and to work for the overthrow of Mussolini. But the parliamentary forces, powerless before in the events leading to Mussolini's seizure of power in 1922, proved ineffective in keeping public opinion aroused and failed to take decisive action against Mussolini. Despite a prolonged judicial inquiry, the six suspects arrested for the murder were allowed to go free.

Mussolini, at first taken aback by his loss of public favour, decided to take the offensive. On Jan. 3, 1925, in a speech to the Chamber, he took full responsibility for the murder as head of the Fascist party (although whether he gave a direct order for the murder remains uncertain) and dared his critics to prosecute him for the crime, a challenge that never was made since they were too weak to take it up.

The Matteotti Crisis marked a turning point in the history of Italian Fascism. Mussolini abandoned any plan of working with Parliament and took steps to create a totalitarian state, including suppression of the opposition press, exclusion of non-Fascist ministers, and formation of a secret police.

After World War II the democratic regime instituted a new inquiry, and the surviving three assassins were sentenced to 30 years in prison.

matter, material substance that constitutes the observable universe and, together with energy, forms the basis of all objective phenomena.

A brief treatment of matter follows. Articles providing fuller treatment appear in the MACROPAEDIA. For the properties, states, varieties, and behaviour of matter, *see* Matter; for its basic constituents and structure, *see* Atoms; for the relationship between matter and energy, *see* Physical Sciences, Principles of.

The basic building blocks of matter are atoms. All matter shares certain fundamental properties. Every physical entity has gravitation, the property by which it attracts every other entity. Another inherent and permanent property of matter is inertia, which causes a body to resist any change in its condition of rest or its motion. The mass of a body is a measure of its inertia, though it is commonly taken as a measure of the amount of material contained in the body.

Matter in bulk may have several states, the most familiar of which are the gaseous, liquid, and solid states. Less clearly definable but also referred to as states of matter are plasma, clusters, and amorphous conditions such as the glassy state. Each such state exhibits properties that distinguish it from the others. Moreover, these general states can be subdivided into groups according to particular types of properties. Solids, for example, may be divided into metallic, ionic, covalent, or molecular based on the kinds of bonds that hold together the constituent atoms.

According to Albert Einstein's special theory of relativity, matter (as mass) and energy are equivalent. Accordingly, matter can be converted into energy and energy into matter. The transformation of matter into energy, for instance, results during nuclear fission, which involves the splitting of a nucleus of uranium or another heavy element into two fragments of almost equal mass.

Matter, Herbert (b. April 25, 1907, Engelberg, Switz.—d. May 8, 1984, Southampton, N.Y., U.S.), Swiss-born American advertising designer and photographer known for his pioneering use of photomontage in commercial art.

Matter studied under the painters Fernand Léger and Amédée Ozenfant in Paris, where he later assisted the graphic artist Adolphe Mouron Cassandre and the architect Le Corbusier. His own international reputation was firmly established from 1932 to 1936, when he made travel posters for the Swiss National

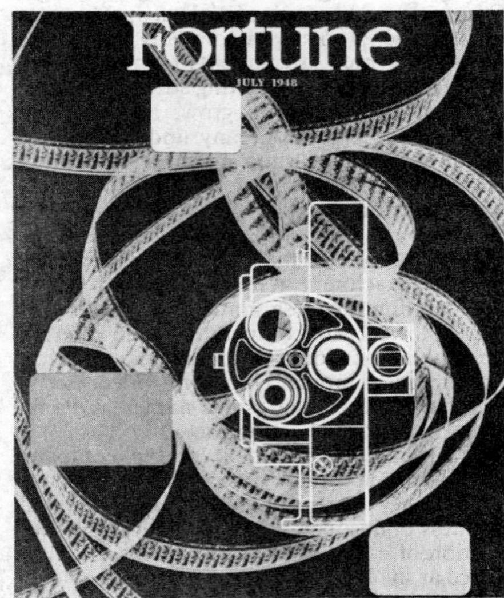

Cover of *Fortune* magazine designed by Herbert Matter, July, 1948; in the Museum of Modern Art, New York City

By courtesy of the Museum of Modern Art, New York, Study Collection, and Fortune Magazine, © 1948 Time Inc.; photograph, Sandak, Inc.

Tourist Office in Zürich. These posters were among the earliest effective uses of photomontage, the technique of constructing a picture from parts of more than one photograph.

In 1936 Matter moved to New York City to work as a photographer for such fashion magazines as *Harper's Bazaar* and *Vogue,* a pursuit he continued until 1957. He also collaborated on the design work of the Swiss and Corning Glass pavilions of the New York World's Fair of 1939 and was closely associated with the Solomon R. Guggenheim Museum in New York City and the Museum of Fine Arts in Houston, Texas, from 1958 to 1968. He also made a film on the work of the sculptor Alexander Calder (1949) for the Museum of Modern Art in New York City. He was a professor of graphic arts and photography at Yale University from 1952 to 1976.

matter and form (philosophy): *see* hylomorphism.

matter wave (physics): *see* de Broglie wave.

Matterhorn, French MONT CERVIN, Italian MONTE CERVINO, one of the best-known mountains (14,692 feet [4,478 m]) in the Alps, straddling the frontier between Switzerland and Italy, 6 miles (10 km) southwest of the village of Zermatt, Switz. Though from the Swiss side it appears to be an isolated horn-shaped peak, it is actually the butt end of a ridge; and the Swiss slope is not nearly so steep or difficult to climb as the grand terraced walls of the Italian slope.

The Matterhorn reflected in one of the Riffel lakes, Switzerland
Ewing Galloway

After a number of attempts, chiefly on the Italian side, the Matterhorn was first conquered from the Swiss *arête* (ridge) on July 14, 1865, by the British explorer Edward Whymper (*q.v.*); but four of his party fell to their deaths on the descent. Three days later it was scaled from the Italian side by a party of men from the village of Valtournanche, Italy, led by the Italian guide Giovanni Antonio Carrel. It is frequently ascended in summer, especially from Zermatt (*q.v.*), the town after which the peak was named.

Matteucci, Pellegrino (b. Oct. 13, 1850, Ravenna [Italy]—d. Aug. 8, 1881, London, Eng.), Italian explorer who was the first European to traverse the whole of the African continent north of the equator from Egypt to the Gulf of Guinea. The journey took him through many parts of Africa that had been only marginally explored by Europeans. While his crossing is well remembered as an exploit, Matteucci failed to compile any significant geographical observations.

A doctor who was struck with a passion for exploring, Matteucci made his first expedition to Africa in 1877, traveling up the Blue Nile until he was turned back by hostile tribesmen in southern Sudan. Two years later he led an expedition to Ethiopia to investigate its commercial possibilities. His journey across the continent, which began in February 1880, took him from Egypt through the Sudan and the Wadai (or Ouadai) district of Chad, into northeastern Nigeria and down the Niger River to the west coast of Africa, where he arrived in July 1881. He died of a fever contracted during his travels.

Matthay, Tobias (b. Feb. 19, 1858, London, Eng.—d. Dec. 15, 1945, High Marley, Surrey), English pianist, teacher, and composer noted for his detailed examination of the problems of piano technique, the interpretation of music, and the psychology of teaching.

Matthay studied at the Royal Academy of Music and then taught there from 1876 to 1925, when he left to devote his full attention to the piano school that he had founded in 1900. His teaching method stressed development of proper piano touch and was based on a detailed analysis of arm movements. His books include *The Act of Touch* (1903), *The First Principles of Pianoforte Playing* (1905), *Relaxation Studies* (1908), *Musical Interpretation* (1913), and *On Method in Teaching* (1921). Together with his own teaching, his books brought him international fame and many pupils of distinction, including Myra Hess.

Matthes, François-Emile (b. March 16, 1874, Amsterdam, Neth.—d. June 21, 1948, Berkeley, Calif., U.S.), Dutch-born American geologist and topographer whose mapping of some of the most rugged and scenic features of the western United States was instrumental in the establishment of several notable national parks.

His education, begun in The Netherlands, Switzerland, and Germany, was continued at Massachusetts Institute of Technology and Harvard University. He became a U.S. citizen in 1896; and as topographer with the U.S. Geological Survey (1896–1913) mapped the Bighorn Mountains and Glacier National Park in Wyoming and Montana, the Grand Canyon in Arizona, Yosemite Valley in California, Mount Rainier in Washington, and other western areas. His beautiful sketching of these maps probably never has been equaled. Following the 1906 California earthquake, he was assigned by the investigatory commission to map the San Andreas fault.

Matthes later concentrated on geologic problems and attained distinction as a geomorphologist and glacialist. His investigations in the Sierra Nevadas, California, culminated in his classic *Geologic History of the Yosemite Valley* (1930). He organized the program of systematic glacier observations in North America, part of a worldwide study of climatic fluctuations as indicated by changes in existing glaciers. Highly artistic, he was also a writer of rare excellence.

Mattheson, Johann (b. Sept. 28, 1681, Hamburg [Germany]—d. April 17, 1764, Hamburg), composer and scholar whose writings are an important source of information about 18th-century German music.

Mattheson studied under Michael Praetorius and befriended George Frideric Handel while serving as a singer and conductor at the Hamburg Opera. In 1706 he became secretary to the English ambassador, and he later served as ambassador *ad interim.* He was cantor and organist at Hamburg cathedral from 1715 to 1728, when his deafness forced him to resign.

Mattheson, detail of an engraving by J.J. Haid after a painting by J.S. Wahl
The Andre Meyer Collection—J.P. Ziolo

Mattheson's compositions include oratorios, operas, and instrumental works, but his influence lies mainly in his scholarly writings. Most notable is a biographical dictionary, *Grundlage einer Ehrenpforte* (1740; "Foundation of a Triumphal Arch"), with lives of 148 composers. Also among his writings are two works on the thorough bass and *Der vollkommene Kapellmeister* (1739; "The Complete Chapel-Master"), an encyclopaedia of his musical ideas. He advocated the merging of the separate Italian, French, and German styles into an integrated musical style and felt that sacred music could be revitalized by the inclusion of secular elements (*e.g.,* operatic elements in church cantatas). His translations from English to German include John Mainwaring's biography of Handel and Daniel Defoe's *Moll Flanders.*

Matthew (THE EVANGELIST), SAINT, also called LEVI (fl. 1st century AD, Palestine; Western feast day September 21, Eastern feast day November 16), one of the Twelve Apostles, traditional author of the first Synoptic Gospel.

According to Matthew 9:9 and Mark 2:14, Matthew was sitting by the customs house in Capernaum (near modern Almagor, Israel, on the Sea of Galilee) when Jesus called him into his company. Assuming that the identification of Matthew with Levi is correct, Matthew (probably meaning "Yahweh's Gift") would appear to be the Christian name of Levi (called by Mark "Levi the son of Alphaeus"), who had been employed as a tax collector in the service of Herod Antipas, tetrarch of Galilee. Because Levi's occupation was one that earned distrust and contempt everywhere, the scribes of the Pharisees criticized Jesus on seeing him eat with tax collectors and sinners; whereupon Jesus answered, "I came not to call the righteous, but sinners" (Mark 2:15–17). According to Luke 5:29, the aforementioned dinner was given by Levi in his house after his call.

Other than naming Matthew in the list of Apostles, usually pairing him with St. Thomas, the New Testament offers scanty and uncertain information about him. Outside the New Testament, a statement of importance about him is the passage from the Apostolic Father Papias of Hierapolis preserved by Bishop Eusebius of Caesarea: "So then Matthew composed the Oracles in the Hebrew language, and each one interpreted them as he could." The Gospel According to Matthew was certainly written for a Jewish-Christian church in a strongly Jewish environment, but that this Matthew is definitely the synoptic author is seriously doubted. Tradition notes his ministry in Judaea, after which he supposedly missioned to the East, suggesting Ethiopia and Persia. Legend differs as to the scene of his missions and as to whether he died a natural or a martyr's death. Matthew's relics were reputedly discovered in Salerno (Italy) in 1080. His symbol is an angel.

Matthew BASARAB, Romanian MATEI BASARAB (d. April 1654), enlightened prince of Walachia (in present Romania) whose reign (1632–54) was marked by cultural development and advances in government.

A last scion of the ancient Basarab dynasty, Matthew spent much of his reign combating the designs of the rival prince of Moldavia, Basil the Wolf, on the Walachian throne. He successfully repulsed invasions by Basil in 1637 and 1639, and in 1653 decisively defeated his rival. He was, however, unable to reassert Walachian independence against the Turks and remained throughout his reign a vassal of the Ottoman Empire. Concerned with the welfare of his subjects, he accomplished economic, cultural, and legislative reforms and improvements, including the introduction of the printing press (1634), the first codification of Walachian law (1652), and the liberal endowment of art and religion.

Matthew, Gospel According to, first of the four New Testament Gospels (narratives recounting the life and death of Jesus Christ), and, with Mark and Luke, one of the three so-called Synoptic Gospels (*i.e.*, those presenting a common view). It has traditionally been attributed to Matthew, one of the 12 Apostles, described in the text as a tax collector (10:3). The Gospel was composed in Greek, probably sometime after AD 70, with evident dependence on the earlier Gospel According to Mark. There has, however, been extended discussion about the possibility of an earlier version in Aramaic. Numerous textual indications point to an author who was a Jewish Christian writing for Christians of similar background. The Gospel consequently emphasizes Christ's fulfillment of Old Testament prophecies (5:17) and his role as a new lawgiver whose divine mission was confirmed by repeated miracles.

After tracing the genealogy of Jesus back to Abraham, the evangelist mentions certain details related to the infancy of Christ that are not elsewhere recorded; *e.g.*, Joseph's perplexity on learning that Mary is pregnant, the homage of the Wise Men, the flight into Egypt to escape Herod's soldiers, the massacre of the innocents, and the return of the holy family from Egypt. Matthew then describes the preaching of John the Baptist, the call of the Apostles, and major events in the public ministry of Jesus. The final section describes the betrayal, Crucifixion, burial, and Resurrection of Christ.

Exegetes view the main body of the Gospel as five extended sermons, one of which includes the memorable Sermon on the Mount (chapters 5–7). Numerous parables are recorded, some very well known but not set down by the other evangelists. One passage, "And I tell you, you are Peter, and on this rock I will build my church" (16:18), has become the basis of Roman Catholic belief in the divine institution of the papacy. Matthew's version of the Lord's Prayer (6:9–15) is used in the liturgies of the Christian churches.

Matthew, William Diller (b. Feb. 19, 1871, Saint John, N.B., Can.—d. Sept. 24, 1930, San Francisco), Canadian-American paleontologist who was an important contributor to modern knowledge of mammalian evolution.

From 1895 to 1927 Matthew worked in the department of vertebrate paleontology at the American Museum of Natural History, New

William Diller Matthew

By courtesy of the American Museum of Natural History, New York

York City. He became curator of the department in 1911 and divisional curator in chief in 1922. During this period he made an exhaustive study of the fossil collections of pioneer paleontologist Edward Cope and published 240 papers. Most important among them was "Climate and Evolution" (*Annals of the New York Academy of Sciences,* vol. 24, 1915). In this work, Matthew argued for a relative permanency of the great ocean basins and continental masses and against the existence of former land bridges across what are now abyssal depths. He proposed a theory of transport by natural rafts to explain the existence of closely related species on landmasses separated by such depths. His principal contention was that most mammalian orders and families originated in the Northern Hemisphere, subsequently spreading southward. Isolation of species in more remote southern areas, such as Australia, accounted for the extraordinary primitive faunas there.

Matthew Island, active volcano in the southwestern Pacific Ocean, within the French overseas territory of New Caledonia but disputed by Vanuatu. It was sighted in 1788 by the English mariner Thomas Gilbert and was named for one of his close associates. Because of the volcano's continuing eruption and the opposing forces of erosion, the island varies in size and height.

Matthews, (James) Brander (b. Feb. 21, 1852, New Orleans—d. March 31, 1929, New York City), essayist, drama critic, novelist, and first U.S. professor of dramatic literature.

Educated at Columbia University, Matthews was admitted to the bar but never practiced, turning instead to writing and the study of literature. He was professor of literature at Columbia, 1892–1900, and of dramatic literature, 1900–24. A prominent figure in New York literary groups, he was the founder of both the Authors' and Players' clubs. Matthews was the author of many short stories and critical essays, was a regular critic for *The New York Times* for a long period, and was the author or editor of more than 40 books. *A Confident Tomorrow* (1899) is considered his best novel. His sound scholarship was revealed in such works as *Molière: His Life and His Works* (1910); *Shakspere as a Playwright* (1913), a work notable for its consideration of Shakespeare as a theatrical rather than a literary figure; and *French Dramatists of the 19th Century* (1881). His collections and mementoes are the foundation of the Brander Matthews Dramatic Museum at Columbia University, New York City.

Matthews, Stanley (b. July 21, 1824, Cincinnati, Ohio, U.S.—d. March 22, 1889, Washington, D.C.), associate justice of the United States Supreme Court (1881–89).

After studying law in Cincinnati, Matthews was admitted to the bar in 1842 and began to practice law in Columbia, Tennessee, while also editing a weekly paper (*Tennessee Democrat*) in the interests of James K. Polk, the future president. After his return to Cincinnati in 1844 he continued to divide his time between journalism (as editor of the antislavery *Cincinnati Morning Herald*) and the law and was soon appointed assistant prosecuting attorney. He served briefly as clerk of the Ohio House of Representatives and then as a judge of common pleas but returned to private practice until 1858, when he was appointed U.S. attorney for Ohio's southern district. In this capacity he was obliged to prosecute a reporter, W.B. Connelly, under the Fugitive Slave Law, generating an ironic notoriety that dogged his professional career.

He joined the Union Army, but during the Civil War he was elected to the Cincinnati Superior Court and resigned his commission to serve. He returned to private practice after the war but again gained national notice in 1877 as counsel before the electoral commission that decided the Hayes–Tilden presidential contest. That same year he was elected to the U.S. Senate, in which he introduced the "Matthews Resolution" making silver legal tender.

In 1881 Pres. Rutherford B. Hayes nominated Matthews to the U.S. Supreme Court. The Senate refused to confirm him, citing his past support of Hayes, his prosecution of Connelly, and the fact that he had served as attorney for powerful railroad and corporation interests. The opposition to Matthews continued into the James A. Garfield administration, when his name was again submitted to fill the still vacant seat and he was approved by only a one-vote majority.

Matthews joined with the bloc of justices that were bringing about an extension of federal powers by liberal interpretation of the Constitution, particularly in the areas of commerce and federal borrowing. He gave the court's opinion in the Virginia Coupon Cases, which struck down prohibitions against the use of state bond coupons in payment of taxes. In *Bowman* v. *Chicago and North Western Railway Company* he declared that a state prohibition of common carriers transporting liquor into the state was unconstitutional because it constituted state regulation of interstate commerce. His most important opinion, given for the court in *Yick Wo* v. *Hopkins* (1866), held that even a law fair and impartial on its face was unconstitutional if its operations denied 14th Amendment guarantees of equal protection to citizens.

Matthews, Sir Stanley (b. Feb. 1, 1915, Hanley, Stoke-on-Trent, Eng.—d. Feb. 23, 2000, Newcastle-under-Lyme, Staffordshire), association football (soccer) player, an outside right considered by many the greatest dribbler in the history of the sport, and the first British footballer to be knighted (1965).

Matthews began his professional career in 1931 and played at various times for the Stoke City and Blackpool teams. By 1938 he was representing England in international matches, and, when he retired in 1965, he had played in 54 full international contests. In 1953 he led Blackpool to the Football Association Cup championship. An autobiography, *The Stanley Matthews Story,* appeared in 1960.

Matthias, name of rulers grouped below by country and indicated by the symbol •.

Foreign-language equivalents:
German . . . . Matthias
Hungarian . . . . Mátyás

AUSTRIA

•**Matthias:** *see* Matthias (Germany/Holy Roman Empire).

GERMANY/HOLY ROMAN EMPIRE

•**Matthias** (b. Feb. 24, 1557, Vienna—d. March 20, 1619, Vienna), Holy Roman emperor from 1612, who, in a reversal of the policy of his father, Maximilian II, sponsored a Catholic revival in the Habsburg domains that, despite his moderating influence, eventually led to the outbreak of the Thirty Years' War.

The third son of the archduke Maximilian of Austria (later emperor), Matthias received no territories on his father's death. This incapable and unreliable Habsburg ruler was

Matthias, detail from an engraving by Egidius Sadeler, 1616

By courtesy of the Bild-Archiv, Osterreichische Nationalbibliothek, Vienna invited by the Catholic nobility of the Spanish Netherlands to replace Don Juan of Austria as governor general (1577). Unable to arrange a compromise peace between Spain and the Protestant faction headed by William of Orange, he returned to Germany in 1581. Appointed governor of Austria in 1593 by his oldest brother, the emperor Rudolf II, Matthias continued the Emperor's policy of backing the Counter-Reformation, suppressing several peasant rebellions (1595–97) caused by the government's attempts to suppress Protestantism, though not without being forced to grant concessions. In about 1598 he met Melchior Klesl, a cleric who became his principal adviser and was to play an important role in imperial affairs.

When, by the turn of the century, Rudolf became increasingly unbalanced and unable to conduct the affairs of state, the archdukes of the House of Habsburg pressed for a succession settlement. In 1606 they recognized Matthias, whose elder brother Ernest had died in 1595, as head of the family and as heir to the throne. He now began a struggle against Rudolf that lasted until the Emperor's death in 1612.

Matthias had been imperial commander in chief against the Turks in 1594–95 and 1598–1601. In 1606 he was able to sign an armistice, reaffirmed in 1615, that brought peace to the Turkish frontier for a half century. He also ended a Hungarian rebellion by negotiating a peace in 1606 that granted the estates religious freedom and some measure of political autonomy. When, in 1608, the estates of Hungary, Austria, and Moravia allied themselves with Matthias against the Emperor, Rudolf suffered a major blow. Matthias gained the Hungarian crown (as Matthias II), to which he added that of Bohemia in 1611, but was in both cases compelled to grant further concessions to the Protestants.

After his succession to the imperial throne on Rudolf's death in 1612, Matthias increasingly withdrew from public life, leaving Klesl in charge of most affairs of state. The imperial Diet had been paralyzed since 1608 over disputes between Protestant and Catholic princes, but Matthias and Klesl failed in their attempts to reconcile both parties, while the younger Habsburg archdukes encouraged Germany's Catholic princes to further intransigence. The archdukes decided that the archduke Ferdinand of Styria (the future emperor Ferdinand II) should succeed Matthias, who was old, ill, and childless, as emperor. Ferdinand was accepted as king of Bohemia in 1617 and crowned king of Hungary in 1618 but met with Protestant resistance in Bohemia. Matthias and Klesl advised concessions to the Protestants, but Ferdinand refused compromise. The resulting Bohemian Revolt of 1618 became the first hostile act of the Thirty Years' War. Matthias died the following year.

Hungary

• **Matthias I,** byname MATTHIAS CORVINUS, Hungarian MÁTYÁS CORVIN, original name MÁTYÁS HUNYADI (b. Feb. 24, 1443, Kolozsvár, Transylvania—d. April 6, 1490, Vienna), king of Hungary (1458–90), who attempted to reconstruct the Hungarian state after decades of feudal anarchy, chiefly by means of financial, military, judiciary, and administrative reforms. His nickname, Corvinus, derived from the raven (Latin *corvus*) on his escutcheon.

Election as king. Matthias was the second son of a military leader, János Hunyadi (*q.v.*). After the death of his father and elder brother, Matthias became heir to a vast landed propriety and to a great name glorified by the chroniclers of the war against Turkish conquerors. After the death of King Ladislas Posthumus of Austria (Habsburg), and despite dynastic claims of his uncle, the Holy Roman emperor Frederick III, and other pretenders to the

Matthias I, detail from the gate tower of Ortenburg Castle, Bautzen (now in Germany), 1486

By courtesy of the Magyar Nemzeti Muzeum, Budapest

throne, a general Diet held in Buda and Pest in January 1458 elected Matthias king. This was the first time in the medieval Hungarian kingdom that a member of the nobility, without dynastic ancestry and relationship, mounted the royal throne, although it happened contemporaneously in the neighbouring Bohemian kingdom. Such elections upset the usual course of dynastic succession. Crossing the plans of the Habsburg dynasty (and partly those of the Jagiełłos of Poland), they caused a long series of controversies in that part of Europe. In the Czech and Hungarian states they heralded a new era, characterized by the supremacy of the "estates and orders," a dietal system, and a tendency to centralization.

After struggles to stabilize his reign against repeated attacks, mostly from baronial opposition and the foreign dynastic pretenders, Matthias held back Turkish invaders, who had annexed the Serbian and Bosnian territories on his southern frontiers. He reorganized a defensive system against the Turks, taking his lack of forces into consideration.

He did everything he could to increase state incomes and to improve the modern elements of his army and his warfare. One of his first steps was a reform of finances and taxes (1467), ending special exemptions to large proprietors. A few years later the treasury was developed into a well-organized office, collecting regularly the "extraordinary" taxes (originally intended in case of urgent necessity, mostly under the pressure of the Turkish peril). As a result the state income reached a considerable sum. The high taxation burdened mostly the peasants.

The financial reforms were not easily accepted. Revolts endangered the government, occasionally even the reign of Matthias. The opposition, stimulated by foreign forces, won over some old counsellors of the King. But Matthias always succeeded, by force and diplomacy, in calming the opposition and in reestablishing, even reinforcing, the political and social conditions of his sovereignty. Some historians have characterized him as an early representative of modern absolutism, but this was far beyond his possibilities. He increased the influence of the lower nobility against the barons; he tried to repress or at least to moderate feudal anarchy; he protected merchants and small proprietors and even peasants, not against their own lords but against other troubles; and he tried to improve the system of central government (without disturbing local autonomies), mainly by increasing the governmental role of the chancellors, the royal secretaries, and other offices. His jurists began a great work of codification; a royal decree of 1486 was intended to summarize the main principles of law "for all times." This meant, together with the further development of the standing army, a certain degree of centralization, within the limits of an essentially feudal state.

Foreign successes. Successes in foreign politics, diplomacy, and warfare contributed to the stabilization of his own authority and his country's position. His diplomacy grew more active during the second and third decades of his reign. He maintained constant diplomatic relations with the papacy, with Venice, Naples, and other Italian states and repeatedly exchanged ambassadors with France, Burgundy, Switzerland, and many German territories; later he tried to establish regular contacts with Russia and, occasionally, with Persia and Egypt. His main purpose may have been the creation of a system of alliances against actual or possible rivals and enemies. His diplomatic activity varied with the varying aims of his foreign policy. After gaining suzerainty over Bosnia (1463), Matthias tried to occupy the Bohemian kingdom. This was a grave error; the Jagiełło dynasty intervened, and a 10-year struggle was followed by a peace that left the Bohemian crown to Vladislav II, while Matthias retained the Moravian and Silesian territories with the royal title.

An almost continuous rivalry with the emperor Frederick III ran through Matthias' reign. He tried repeatedly, but without success, to induce (or coerce) the Emperor to renounce his claims to the Hungarian throne. Following the Polish-Bohemian war, Matthias tried to annihilate the main base of Frederick's dynastic power. After a long series of military successes, aided by the Emperor's German and Austrian adversaries, he occupied Vienna and a considerable part of the Habsburg family possessions. But he could not diminish the Habsburg influence in the German Empire or in central and western Europe. Indeed, Habsburg power began to increase as a result of events in Burgundy. Until his death (1490) Matthias remained in possession of his conquests; thereafter, all of them were lost.

Assessment. Matthias' political relations with the papacy and the Italian states were connected with the interests in Turkish wars. But they were connected also with the special rights of Hungarian kings concerning the distribution of ecclesiastical dignities in their country. This complicated the relations between church and kingdom. After the second marriage of Matthias (1476), to Beatrice of Aragon, princess of Naples, the King's diplomacy became a factor in Italian state affairs. His connections with Florence, Milan, and other Italian states and cultural centres reflected his interest in Italian art and humanistic culture.

Matthias deserved his reputation, mentioned by contemporaries, for being "a friend of the Muses." The knowledge of many languages, classic latinity, modern humanistic ideas, and ancient books and the support of new art and science were all familiar to him since childhood. His education took place partly on battlefields, partly under the control of prominent humanists. He never ceased to read and to learn. Supporting all kinds of art, he founded a considerable library—the famous Corvina. He trusted, like the majority of his contemporaries, in astrology and other semi-scientific beliefs of his age, but he supported many real scientists and participated eagerly in the discussions of philosophers invited to his court.

Matthias possessed high personal qualities, as reported by friends and enemies alike. He tried to strengthen his state, not without success. His name became later—during centuries of Turkish occupation and Habsburg oppression—a symbol of strength and independence. His memory was glorified by statesmen and military leaders as well as by students of cultural progress. And, despite the heavy taxes, it was also glorified by the people, who were reported, a few years after the King's death, as being willing to pay still more, "if only he could rise again." This could be explained by the general decline of the country after Matthias' death but also by a popular saying: "Matthias is dead—justice is lost."

(L.El.)

BIBLIOGRAPHY. There is no modern English-language biography of Matthias I. Imre Lukinich (ed.), *Mátyás Király Emlékkönyv*, 2 vol. (1940), contains articles analyzing his family relations, personality, and political, military, and cultural activities. Vilmos Fraknoi, *Hunyadi Mátyás király, 1440–1490* (1890); and Elemer Malyusz, "Matthias Corvinus," in *Menschen die Geschichte machten*, vol. 2, pp. 187–191 (1931), are two classic biographies; Lajos Elekes, *Mátyás és kora* (1956), is an essay on the social and political background of the King's activities.

• **Matthias II:** *see* Matthias (Germany/Holy Roman Empire).

Articles are alphabetized word by word, not letter by letter

Matthias, SAINT (fl. 1st century AD, Judaea; d. traditionally Colchis, Armenia; Western feast day February 24, Eastern feast day August 9), the disciple who, according to the biblical Acts of the Apostles 1:21–26, was chosen to replace Judas Iscariot after Judas betrayed Jesus.

Jesus' choice of 12 Apostles points to a consciousness of a symbolic mission—originally there were 12 tribes of Israel—that the community maintained after the Crucifixion. Acts reveals that Matthias accompanied Jesus and the Apostles from the time of the Lord's Baptism to his Ascension and that, when it became time to replace Judas, the Apostles cast lots between Matthias and another candidate, St. Joseph Barsabbas. St. Jerome and the early Christian writers Clement of Alexandria and Eusebius of Caesarea attest that Matthias was among the 72 disciples paired off and dispatched by Jesus. Soon after his election, Matthias received the Holy Spirit with the other Apostles (Acts 2:1–4). He is not mentioned again in the New Testament.

It is generally believed that Matthias ministered in Judaea and then carried out missions to foreign places. Greek tradition states that he Christianized Cappadocia, a mountainous district now in central Turkey, later journeying to the region about the Caspian Sea, where he was martyred by crucifixion and, according to other legends, chopped apart. His symbol, related to his alleged martyrdom, is either a cross or a halberd. St. Helena, mother of the Roman emperor Constantine the Great, reputedly transported Matthias' relics from Jerusalem to Rome.

Matthías Jochumsson (Icelandic writer): *see* Jochumsson, Matthías.

Matthisson, Friedrich von (b. Jan. 23, 1761, Hohendodeleben, near Magdeburg, Saxony—d. March 12, 1831, Wörlitz, Anhalt-Dessau), German poet whose verses were praised for their melancholy sweetness and pastoral descriptive passages.

After studying philology at the University of Halle, Matthisson was appointed (1781) master at the once-famous Philanthropin, a seminary in Dessau, and then accepted a travelling tutorship (1784). Appointed reader and travelling companion to Princess Louisa of Anhalt-Dessau, he entered the service of the king of Württemberg (1812), who made him counsellor of legation and intendant of the court theatre and, later, a member of the nobility (1818) and knight of the crown of Württemberg.

Matthisson's poems, which brought him great popularity in his time, were published as *Gedichte* in 1787; their melodious verse exhibits a vigour and warmth combined with delicacy and style. His poem "Adelaide" was set to music as a song by Beethoven. A complete, eight-volume edition of his works, *Schriften*, was published in 1825–29.

Mattioli, Pietro Andrea Gregorio (b. March 23, 1500, Siena, Italy—d. January/February 1577, Trento), Italian physician and botanist whose *Di Pedacio Dioscoride Anazarbeo libri cinque* (1544) is an Italian translation, with critical commentary, of Dioscorides' classical 1st-century Greek herbal. It served as one of the bases for the development of modern botany.

Mattioli received a medical degree from the University of Padua in 1523. His first work, *De morbi gallici curandi ratione, dialogus* (1530), was a traditional examination of the origins and treatment of syphilis. He served as physician and adviser to Bernardo Cardinal Clesio, bishop of Trento; in 1554 he became physician to Holy Roman Emperor Ferdinand I, and later to Maximilian II.

Di Pedacio Dioscoride provided physicians, apothecaries, and herbalists with a practical scientific treatise in Italian; its commentary allowed them to identify and use medicinal plants. Mattioli's Latin version of the text, published in 1554, made Dioscorides accessible to many European scholars. It included extensive annotations and commentary based on Mattioli's own observations and those of others, carefully detailed illustrations, and plant-name synonyms in several languages.

Matto Grosso, Planalto de (Brazil): *see* Mato Grosso, Plateau.

mattock, digging implement, one of the oldest tools of agriculture. *See* hoe.

Mattoon, city, Coles county, east central Illinois, U.S., on the Lincoln National Memorial Highway, near the Little Wabash River (impounded to form Lake Mattoon). It was founded in 1854 at the junction of the Illinois Central and New York Central railroads and named for William B. Mattoon, a railroad official. A bronze tablet near the Illinois Central rail depot commemorates the mustering into service of Mattoon's unruly 21st Illinois Infantry (June 1861) by Ulysses S. Grant, then in the military service of the state. The city developed as a rail and agricultural centre. Oil, discovered locally in 1940, and manufacturing, notably photo lamps, have boosted its economic growth. Lake Land (junior) College was established in 1966 in Mattoon. Shiloh Cemetery, where Abraham Lincoln's father and stepmother are buried, and the Lincoln Log Cabin State Park are a few miles southeast. Inc. village, 1857; city, 1861. Pop. (1990) 18,441.

Matura diamond, colourless variety of the gemstone zircon (*q.v.*).

Māturīdī, Abū Manṣūr Muḥammad al-, in full ABŪ MANṢŪR MUḤAMMAD IBN MAḤMŪD AL-ḤANAFĪ AL-MUTAKALLIM AL-MĀTURĪDĪ AS-SAMARQANDĪ (d. 944, Samarkand, titular head of the Māturīdīyah school of theology, which came to be one of the most important foundations of Islāmic doctrine.

Except for the place and time of Māturīdī's death, almost nothing is known about the details of Māturīdī's life. He lived during a time when the Muʿtazilites, a Muslim sect, were using the techniques of Greek logical argument to attack what had come to be accepted as orthodox Muslim theology. Māturīdī seized the offensive by using these same arguments as a means of defending orthodox theology. In fact, such use of logic was widespread, and it is not clear why Māturīdī came to be accepted as a protagonist of such thought or why reference to him came to supersede reference to Abū Ḥanīfah (d. 767), the Muslim theologian who seems to have been the first to adopt the methods of the Muʿtazilites. Māturīdī is also noted for his emphasis on the morality of human responsibility, which contributed to the "humanization" of orthodoxy that occurred in the following centuries.

Māturīdīyah, a Muslim orthodox school of theology named after its founder Abū Manṣūr Muḥammad al-Māturīdī (d. 944). The Māturīdīyah is similar in basic outlook to another orthodox school, that of al-Ashʿarī (d. 935), the Ashʿarīyah, that has received more attention and praise as the champion of the true faith. The Māturīdīyah claims more popularity in the area known historically as Transoxania, where it was founded.

The Māturīdī school is characterized by its reliance on the Qurʾān (Islāmic scripture) without reasoning or free interpretation. Its members argued that since Muḥammad himself had not used reason in this respect, it is an innovation (*bidʿah*) to do so, and every innovation is a heresy according to a well-known prophetic saying. The later Māturīdīyah, however, acknowledged the possibility of fresh problems for which there was no precedent in either the Qurʾān or Ḥadīth (accounts of sayings of the Prophet Muḥammad), and modified this rigid rule, allowing for rational inferences when necessary.

The Māturīdīyah entered the discussion of "compulsion" and "free will," which was at its peak in theological circles at the time of its founding. They followed a doctrine similar to that of the Ashʿarīyah, emphasizing the absolute omnipotence of God and at the same time allowing man a minimum of freedom to act so that he may be justly punished or rewarded. In the later stages of its development, however, the Māturīdīyah took an independent course and stated unequivocally that man has the utmost freedom to act, a point of view derived directly from many verses in the Qurʾān and the Ḥadīth.

The Māturīdīyah differed also from the Ashʿarīyah on the question of the "assurance of salvation." They held that a Muslim who sincerely performed his religious duties as prescribed by God in the Qurʾān, and as explained and taught by his prophet, is assured of a place in heaven. The Ashʿarīyah maintained that one is not saved unless God wills him to be saved, and that no one knows whether he is a believer or not, for only God can make such a decision.

Maturín, city, capital of Monagas state, northeastern Venezuela, on the Río Guarapiche, between the easternmost outliers of the Andean highlands and the Orinoco Delta. Founded in 1710 by Capuchin missionaries, the city is a commercial and manufacturing centre for an agricultural and pastoral region that produces cattle, cacao, cotton, and cereals. Oil from nearby fields to the north and west is piped through the city, which is accessible by highway from Carúpano, in Sucre state, and from the Barcelona–Puerto La Cruz area in northeastern Anzoátegui state. A road leads south from Maturín to Barrancas, on the Orinoco River. The city also has an international airport. Pop. (1981 est.) 181,000.

Maturin, Charles Robert (b. 1782, Dublin—d. Oct. 30, 1824, Dublin), Irish Roman Catholic clergyman, dramatist, and author of Gothic romances. He has been called "the last of the Goths," as his best known work, *Melmoth the Wanderer* (1820), is considered the last of the classic English Gothic romances.

Educated at Trinity College, Maturin became curate of St. Peter's in Dublin in 1804. His first popular success was the verse tragedy *Bertram* (1816), produced at Drury Lane with Edmund Kean in the title role, but he soon exhausted his gains from this and his next two plays were failures. He returned to novels, producing his masterpiece, *Melmoth*, the adventures of an Irish Faust. The author's ingenuous delight in the novel's bizarre improbabilities contributes to its freshness and force. The book captured the fancy of many British writers and was especially admired in France. Honoré de Balzac wrote an ironic sequel to it. Oscar Wilde, in exile, chose the name "Sebastian Melmoth" for a pseudonym.

Matveyev, Artamon Sergeyevich, Matveyev also spelled MATVEEV (b. 1625—d. May 15 [May 25, New Style], 1682, Moscow, Russia), Russian diplomat and statesman who was a friend and influential adviser of Tsar Alexis of Russia (ruled 1645–76) and did much to introduce western European culture into Russia.

Son of an obscure government clerk, Matveyev rose through the ranks to become chief of the Moscow *streltsy* (household troops) in 1654. In that year he also was entrusted with the negotiations with the Poles that resulted in their surrender of Smolensk to Russia. In 1669 Matveyev became head of the department for Ukrainian affairs, and in 1671 he was appointed head of the foreign department.

In addition to his activities as a statesman, Matveyev was intensely concerned with western European cultural affairs. He imitated Western custom by holding social gatherings at which his wife participated in the discussions; he also taught his son Latin and Greek. As a well-educated man with broad intellectual interests, he enjoyed the confidence of Tsar Alexis, and in 1671 he gave his ward Natalya Kirillovna Naryshkina in marriage to the tsar. Subsequently, he arranged the first theatrical performance to be presented at the Russian court (1672). Despite Matveyev's low birth, Alexis honoured him by raising him to the rank of boyar.

When Alexis died in 1676, Matveyev advocated the succession of Natalya's son Peter. But Fyodor III, Alexis' eldest son by his first wife, ascended the throne, and Matveyev as a consequence of his indiscretion was accused of black magic and fraud. As head of the government department on pharmacy, he had been preparing a book on drugs and medicines, the text of which was found when his house was searched for incriminating evidence. Matveyev was deprived of his rank and possessions and exiled to the far northeastern section of Russia, where he lived until 1682, when he was pardoned and allowed to live at Lukh. After Peter I the Great succeeded Fyodor (April 1682), Matveyev was recalled to Moscow. Four days after his return, however, he was killed by rebellious *streltsy,* who were intervening in the contest between Peter and his half brother Ivan for possession of the throne.

Mátyás (Hungarian personal name): *see under* Matthias.

Matzeliger, Jan Ernst (b. Sept. 15, 1852, Paramaribo, Dutch Guiana [now Suriname]—d. Aug. 24, 1889, Lynn, Mass., U.S.), inventor best known for his shoe-lasting machine that mechanically shaped the upper portions of shoes.

Son of a Dutch father and a black Surinamese mother, Matzeliger began work as a sailor on a merchant ship at the age of 19 and after about six years settled in Lynn, where he found employment in a shoe factory and became interested in the possibilities of lasting shoes by machine. Working alone and at night for six months, he produced a model in wood and on March 20, 1883, received a patent. His invention won swift acceptance and within two years had largely supplanted hand methods in Lynn. Matzeliger received several other patents for shoe-manufacturing machinery, including an improved model of his first lasting machine.

matzeva, also spelled MAẒẒEVAH (Hebrew: "tombstone," "monument"), plural MATZEVOT, or MAẒẒEVOTH, a stone pillar erected on elevated ground beside a sacrificial altar. It was considered sacred to the god it symbolized and had a wooden pole (*ashera*) nearby to signify a goddess. After conquering the Canaanites, early Israelites used these symbols as their own until their use was outlawed as idolatrous (*e.g.,* Deuteronomy 16:21).

In the Old Testament (Genesis 28:18–22; 2 Samuel 18:18; Joshua 4:20–23) *matzeva* is used to designate a stone memorial, or monument, or, more specifically, as in the case of Rachel, a tombstone resting upright on a grave (Genesis 35:20). This latter meaning is retained in modern Hebrew.

matzo, also spelled MATZOH, MATZA, or MATZAH, plural MATZOS, MATZOT, MATZOTH, MATZAS, or MATZAHS, unleavened bread eaten by Jews during the holiday of Passover (Pesaḥ) in commemoration of their Exodus from Egypt. The rapid departure from Egypt did not allow for the fermentation of dough, and thus the use of leavening of any kind is proscribed throughout the week-long holiday.

The Passover ritual requires that Jews eat matzos at least on the first night of the celebration. Among observant Jews it is customary, however, to eat matzos throughout Passover.

Mau Escarpment, steep natural rampart along the western rim of the Great Rift Valley in western Kenya, west and south of the town of Nakuru; it rises to more than 10,000 feet (3,000 m) on the Equator. Its crest is covered with a vast forest. To the south the woods are more open, and the plateau falls to an open country drained toward the Dogilani plains.

Mau Mau, militant African nationalist movement that originated in the 1950s among the Kikuyu people of Kenya. The Mau Mau (origin of the name is uncertain) advocated violent resistance to British domination in Kenya; the movement was especially associated with the ritual oaths employed by leaders of the Kikuyu Central Association to promote unity in the independence movement.

In October 1952, after a campaign of sabotage and assassination attributed to Mau Mau terrorists, the British Kenya government declared a state of emergency and began four years of military operations against Kikuyu rebels. By the end of 1956, more than 11,000 rebels had been killed in the fighting, along with about 100 Europeans and 2,000 African loyalists. More than 20,000 other Kikuyu were put into detention camps, where intensive efforts were made to convert them to the political views of the government, *i.e.,* to abandon their nationalist aspirations. Despite these government actions, Kikuyu resistance spearheaded the Kenya independence movement, and Jomo Kenyatta, who had been jailed as a Mau Mau leader in 1953, became prime minister of an independent Kenya 10 years later.

Maubeuge, town, Nord *département,* Nord-Pas-de-Calais *région,* northern France, on the Sambre River, near the Belgian frontier, south of Mons. Maubeuge (Latin: Malbodium, signifying "bad place or dwelling") grew up around the monastery of Sainte-Aldegonde (7th century). Part of the medieval county of Hainaut, and later of the Spanish Netherlands, the town was ceded to France by the Peace of Nijmegen (1678). It has 17th-century fortifications and a monument commemorating the Battle of Wattignies (1793), fought nearby. Blast furnaces, breweries, and chemical and glass works support the town's economy.

The Flemish painter Jan Gossaert (*c.* 1478–*c.* 1532) was a native of Maubeuge, from which he derived the name by which he is best known—Jan Mabuse. There is a zoological garden; and the Porte de Mons still stands, a vestige of 17th-century fortifications built by Sébastien Le Prestre de Vauban. Pop. (1990) 35,225.

Mauch, Karl, in full KARL GOTTLIEB MAUCH (b. May 7, 1837, Stetten, Württemberg [Germany]—d. April 4, 1875, Stuttgart, Ger.), explorer who made geologic and archaeological discoveries in southern Africa, notably goldfields in Hartley Hills (1867) and the ruins of the ancient city of Zimbabwe.

After an unsatisfying few years as a private tutor, Mauch gave up teaching and hired on with a shipping company. He arrived in South Africa in 1865, found a Swedish patron, and began the first of a long series of journeys into the uncharted interior in May 1866. Though not formally trained in geology, Mauch was a keen observer, noting in his journals geologic and botanical data (including the distribution of the tsetse fly and the elevations of mountains) that have contributed to the paleontology of southern Africa. His charts of the area were the first maps of southeast Africa in the more than 200 years since the Portuguese had undertaken the mapping of Mozambique.

Mauch began the search for the Zimbabwe ruins (which he wrongly believed were those of the ancient biblical city of Ophir, the capital of the Queen of Sheba) and finally sighted and mapped the city in 1871 after a long and trouble-plagued journey.

Mauch Chunk, borough of Pennsylvania that was merged with a neighbouring borough to create the town of Jim Thorpe (*q.v.*).

maucherite, a nickel arsenide mineral with chemical composition approximating Ni_3As_2 or $Ni_{11}As_8$, assigned to the group of sulfide minerals. It often occurs with niccolite (to which it alters), as at Mansfeld, Ger.; Los Jarales, Málaga, Spain; and Ontario, Can. Its crystals belong to the tetragonal system. It is identical to the furnace product placodine. For chemical formula and detailed physical properties, *see* sulfide mineral (table).

Mauchline, village closely associated with the Scottish national poet Robert Burns, situated near the River Ayr in the Strathclyde region of Scotland. Mauchline is the site of the Burns National Memorial and has many links with the poet, who lived (1784–88) with his brother Gilbert at nearby Mossgiel. In Castle Street stands a house, now a museum, in which Burns and his mistress Jean Armour once stayed. Mauchline churchyard was the scene of "The Holy Fair"; the Jolly Beggars met at Poosie Nansie's, still a popular inn.

Modern industries include coal mining and agricultural engineering. Pop. (1981) 3,663.

Mauchly, John W., in full JOHN WILLIAM MAUCHLY (b. Aug. 30, 1907, Cincinnati, Ohio, U.S.—d. Jan. 8, 1980, Ambler, Pa.), American physicist and engineer, coinventor in 1946, with John P. Eckert, of the Electronic Numerical Integrator and Calculator (ENIAC), the first general-purpose electronic computer.

After completing his education, Mauchly entered the teaching profession, eventually becoming an associate professor of electrical engineering at the University of Pennsylvania, Philadelphia. During World War II Mauchly and Eckert, a graduate engineer, were asked to devise ways to accelerate the recomputation of artillery firing tables for the U.S. Army. They accordingly proposed the construction of a general-purpose digital computer that would handle data in coded form; by 1946 they completed the ENIAC, a huge machine (containing more than 18,000 vacuum tubes) that incorporated features developed by J.V. Atanasoff. The ENIAC was first used by the U.S. Army at its Aberdeen Proving Ground in Maryland in 1947 for ballistics tests.

The following year Mauchly and Eckert formed a computer-manufacturing firm, and in 1949 they announced the Binary Automatic Computer (BINAC), which used magnetic tape instead of punched cards. In 1950 the Eckert–Mauchly Computer Corporation was acquired by Remington Rand, Inc. (later Sperry Rand Corporation), Mauchly becoming director of special projects. The third computer after BINAC was UNIVAC I, specially designed to handle business data. Mauchly continued his work in the computer field, winning many honours. He served as president (1959–65) and chairman of the board (1965–69) of Mauchly Associates, Inc., and as president of Dynatrend Inc. (1968–80) and of Marketrend Inc. (1970–80).

Maud (Holy Roman empress): *see* Matilda.

Maudslay, Henry (b. Aug. 22, 1771, Woolwich, Kent, Eng.—d. Feb. 14, 1831, London), British engineer and inventor of the metal lathe and other devices.

The son of a workman at the Woolwich Arsenal, Maudslay was apprenticed to Joseph Bramah, who manufactured locks. Maudslay soon became Bramah's foreman, but, when refused an increase in pay, he left to go into business for himself. His first job was construction of machinery for the ship block (pulley) factory of Sir Marc Isambard Brunel. Over the next 30 years he invented machines of fundamental importance to the Industrial Revolution; of these the metal lathe is perhaps the most outstanding. He also invented methods for printing calico cloth and for desalting seawater for ships' boilers, and he perfected a measuring machine that was accurate to 0.0001 inch. He was the first to realize the critical importance in a machine shop of accurate plane surfaces for guiding the tools; he produced for his workmen standard planes so smooth that they adhered when placed atop each other and could be separated only by sliding. He also designed and built a great number of stationary and marine engines.

Several of the outstanding British engineers of the Victorian period, notably James Nasmyth and Sir Joseph Whitworth, learned their profession in Maudslay's shop.

Mauer, Pleistocene locality on the Neckar River of Germany and the name of a Pleistocene deposit, the Mauer Sands (the Pleistocene epoch began about 1,600,000 years ago and ended about 10,000 years ago). The Mauer Sands are about 64 feet (20 m) thick and contained the fossil remains of the sabre-toothed cat, bear, horse, hippopotamus, and extinct elephant; Germany's oldest human fragment, the Heidelberg, or Mauer, jaw was discovered there in 1907. The faunal evidence supports the view that the Mauer Sands were deposited during a relatively moderate climatic phase of the Pleistocene, probably the Günz-Mindel Interglacial Stage.

Mauer jaw: *see* Heidelberg jaw.

Maugham, Robin, byname of ROBERT CECIL ROMER MAUGHAM, 2ND VISCOUNT MAUGHAM OF HARTFIELD (b. May 17, 1916, London, Eng.—d. March 13, 1981, Brighton), English novelist, playwright, and travel writer, who achieved some fame and no little notoriety with his first novel, *The Servant* (1948).

The only son of the 1st Viscount, Lord Chancellor Herbert Romer Maugham (whom he succeeded in 1939), Robin Maugham was educated at Eton and Trinity College, Cambridge. He served as an intelligence officer in World War II but was severely wounded in 1944 and retired from active service. Two nonfiction books based on his war experiences are *Come to Dust* (1945) and *Nomad* (1947).

The Servant, though denounced as obscene by Maugham's father, who demanded that publication be halted, convinced Robin's uncle, W. Somerset Maugham, of his nephew's literary ability. The novel became very popular, and it was filmed in 1965. Much of Maugham's work is about homosexuals: a play, *Enemy* (1970), which brings a British and a German soldier into confrontation alone in the desert, charts their doomed friendship; and *The Last Encounter* (1972), which portrays Charles George ("Chinese") Gordon of Khartoum as a man as unsure of his destiny as of his sexual orientation.

Maugham wrote several memoirs, including *Somerset and All the Maughams* (1966) and *Conversations with Willie: Recollections of W. Somerset Maugham* (1978). His autobiographies include *Escape from the Shadows* (1972) and *Search for Nirvana* (1975).

Maugham, W. Somerset, in full WILLIAM SOMERSET MAUGHAM (b. Jan. 25, 1874, Paris, France—d. Dec. 16, 1965, Nice), English novelist, playwright, and short-story writer whose work is characterized by a clear unadorned style, cosmopolitan settings, and a shrewd understanding of human nature.

W. Somerset Maugham
Michael Ochs Archives/Venice, Calif.

Maugham was orphaned at the age of 10; he was brought up by an uncle and educated at King's School, Canterbury. After a year at Heidelberg, he entered St. Thomas' medical school, London, and qualified as a doctor in 1897. He drew upon his experiences as an obstetrician in his first novel, *Liza of Lambeth* (1897), and its success, though small, encouraged him to abandon medicine. He traveled in Spain and Italy and in 1908 achieved a theatrical triumph—four plays running in London at once—that brought him financial security. During World War I he worked as a secret agent. After the war he resumed his interrupted travels and, in 1928, bought a villa on Cape Ferrat in the south of France, which became his permanent home.

His reputation as a novelist rests primarily on four books: *Of Human Bondage* (1915), a semi-autobiographical account of a young medical student's painful progress toward maturity; *The Moon and Sixpence* (1919), an account of an unconventional artist, suggested by the life of Paul Gauguin; *Cakes and Ale* (1930), the story of a famous novelist, which is thought to contain caricatures of Thomas Hardy and Hugh Walpole; and *The Razor's Edge* (1944), the story of a young American war veteran's quest for a satisfying way of life. Maugham's plays, mainly Edwardian social comedies, soon became dated, but his short stories have increased in popularity. Many portray the conflict of Europeans in alien surroundings that provoke strong emotions, and Maugham's skill in handling plot, in the manner of Guy de Maupassant, is distinguished by economy and suspense. In *The Summing Up* (1938) and *A Writer's Notebook* (1949) Maugham explains his philosophy of life as a resigned atheism and a certain skepticism about the extent of man's innate goodness and intelligence; it is this that gives his work its astringent cynicism.

Mauguin, Charles, in full CHARLES-VICTOR MAUGUIN (b. Sept. 19, 1878, Provins, France—d. April 25, 1958, Villejuif), French mineralogist and crystallographer who first studied the structure of the mica group of minerals by X-ray-diffraction analysis. His work was one of the earliest contributions to the systematic study of the silicate minerals.

Mauguin was educated at the École Normale Supérieure in Paris, and in 1919 he joined the Faculty of Sciences of the University of Paris, where he served (1933–48) as professor of mineralogy. His study of the micas enabled him to explain their characteristic tendency to split into thin sheets on the basis of their internal atomic structure. His modification of an earlier system of symbols for designating the symmetry properties of crystals was adopted (1935) as the international standard.

Maui, volcanic island, Maui county, Hawaii, U.S., separated from Molokai (northwest) and Hawaii (southeast) islands by the Pailolo and Alenuihaha channels. With an area of 728 square miles (1,886 square km), the island is the second largest of the Hawaiian chain (after Hawaii Island). It takes its name from a Polynesian demigod and was created by two volcanoes, Puu Kukui and Haleakala, which constitute east and west peninsulas connected by a valleylike isthmus 7 miles (11 km) wide. This isthmus has earned Maui the nickname of the "valley isle." The port of Lahaina on the west coast was an early whaling centre. Other important towns are Wailuku (the county seat), Kahului, and Hana. The county consists of Maui, Kahoolawe, Lanai, and Molokai islands. Ranching and sugar and pineapple cultivation are major economic activities. Area county, 1,160 square miles (3,004 square km). Pop. (2003 est.) county, 135,605.

Mauldin, Bill, byname of WILLIAM HENRY MAULDIN (b. Oct. 29, 1921, Mountain Park, N.M., U.S.—d. Jan. 22, 2003, Newport Beach, Calif.), American cartoonist who gained initial fame for his sardonic drawings of the life of the World War II combat soldier and who later became well known for editorial cartoons dealing with a wide range of political and social issues.

After studying cartooning at the Chicago Academy of Fine Arts, Mauldin returned to the Southwest, where he worked as a cartoonist before enlisting in the U.S. Army (September 1940). He was sent to Fort Sill, Okla., for infantry training. In 1943 he shipped with his division to Sicily, where he joined the Mediterranean edition of the U.S. Army newspaper *Stars and Stripes.* He covered the fighting in Sicily, at Salerno (where he was wounded), and at other locations in Italy, France, and Germany. His cartoons of that period have appeared in several collections, the best known being *Up Front* (1945), which also contained a prose description of his experiences. He received a Pulitzer Prize in 1945 for a cartoon showing battle-weary troops quite the opposite of the description given in the caption: "Fresh American troops flushed with victory . . . ." Many of his cartoons featured Willie and Joe, a pair of disheveled enlisted men who managed to retain their humanity though caught between the horrors of war and an unrealistic and often fatuous army hierarchy.

After his discharge in June 1945, Mauldin drew cartoons expressing the soldier's difficult transition back to civilian life. A new phase of his career began in 1958, when he joined the *St. Louis Post-Dispatch* as an editorial cartoonist. In 1959 he won a second Pulitzer Prize for his cartoon dealing with the suppression of civil liberties in the Soviet Union. In 1962 Mauldin joined the *Chicago Sun-Times,* where his cartoons dealt with national and international issues and were widely syndicated. His illustrations also appeared in magazines such as *Life* and *Sports Illustrated.*

Maule, *región,* central Chile. It faces the Pacific Ocean on the west and borders Argentina on the east. Created in 1974, it comprises Curicó, Talca, and Linares *provincias.* Its area spans coastal mountains, the Central Valley, and the Andean cordillera. The region is drained in the north by the Mataquito River, the tributaries of which (the Teno and Lontué rivers) rise in the Andes, and by the Maule River in the central part, which is said to have been the southern limit of the Inca empire. Most of the inhabitants live in rural areas, particularly in the river valleys, and practice agriculture. Wheat, wine grapes, rice, barley, potatoes, vegetables, and forage crops are grown, and Talca leads all Chilean *provincias* in wine making. Pine trees are grown on plantations, and cattle, sheep, horses, and pigs are also important to the economy. The Pan-American Highway and the main north-south railroad run through the Central Valley, in which are situated Talca (*q.v.*), the regional capital, Curicó, and Linares, all market centres. Area 11,700 square miles (30,302 square km). Pop. (1992 prelim.) 834,053.

Maumee River, river formed near Fort Wayne, Ind., U.S., by the confluence of the St. Joseph and St. Marys rivers. It flows northeast into Ohio, past Defiance and on to Toledo, where it enters Lake Erie through Maumee Bay. About 130 miles (210 km) long, the Maumee is navigable for about 12 miles (19 km) from its mouth and serves as the harbour of Toledo. It receives the Auglaize River, its chief tributary, at Defiance. The name Maumee is a derivative of Miami, in reference to the Indian tribe.

Maun, village, northwestern Botswana. It lies at the southern edge of the Okavango Swamp, northeast of Lake Ngami. The traditional capital of the Tswana people, Maun is the centre of the safari and game industry for the Okavango River delta and the Moremi Game Reserve. Pop. (1991) 26,768.

Mauna Kea, dormant volcano in north-central Hawaii Island, Hawaii, U.S., and the focus of a state park (500 acres [202 hectares]). It is the highest point in the state (13,796 feet [4,205 m] above sea level), and its name means "white mountain," so-called because it is often snowcapped. The dome is 30 miles (48 km) across, with numerous cinder cones, and is the site of a major astronomical observatory. Lava flows from Mauna Kea have buried the southern slopes of the Kohala Mountains (to the northwest), whereas its own western and southern slopes are covered with lava from Mauna Loa, its still-active neighbour. During the Ice Age a glacier about 250 feet (75 m) thick covered the peak and formed Lake Waiau at 13,020 feet (3,970 m). High on the slopes (12,400 feet [3,780 m]) several caves have been discovered where ancient Hawaiians quarried the basalt for adzes and other cutting tools. Pohakuloa (8,000 feet [2,440 m]) is a base camp for skiers and hunters.

Mauna Kea Observatory, astronomical observatory in Hawaii, U.S., that has become one of the most important in the world owing to its outstanding observational conditions. The Mauna Kea Observatory is operated by the University of Hawaii and lies at an elevation of 4,205 m (13,796 feet) atop the peak of Mauna Kea, a dormant volcano on north-central Hawaii Island.

The observatory was founded in 1964 at the urging of the influential American astronomer Gerard Kuiper, and a 2.2-metre (88-inch) reflector used for planetary studies went into service there in 1970. Mauna Kea subsequently became the site of the world's most important collection of telescopes designed for observations in the infrared range. Three large reflectors, the 3.8-metre (150-inch) United Kingdom Infrared Telescope, the 3.6-metre (142-inch) Canada-France-Hawaii Telescope, and the 3-metre (118-inch) NASA Infrared Telescope Facility, went into service there in 1979. In addition, a 15-metre British-Dutch submillimetre- and millimetre-wavelength telescope was completed in the late 1980s, and a similar 10.4-metre millimetre wave telescope owned by the California Institute of Technology (Caltech) was completed early in the '90s. The Keck telescope, a 10-metre multimirror telescope operated jointly by Caltech and the University of California, was completed at Mauna Kea in 1992; it is the largest reflector in the world and is used for both optical and infrared observations. Another Keck telescope was planned to go into operation on Mauna Kea in 1996.

Mauna Kea is the site of many major telescopes because its viewing conditions are the finest of any Earth-based observatory. The site lies at an elevation almost twice that of any other major observatory and above 40 percent of the Earth's atmosphere; there is thus less intervening atmosphere to obscure the light from distant stellar objects. A high proportion of nights at Mauna Kea are clear, calm, and cloudless owing to local weather peculiarities and the fact that the mountaintop lies above cloud cover most of the time. The high elevation and extremely dry, clear air make the site ideal for observing astronomical objects that emit radiation at far-infrared wavelengths, which are easily blocked by atmospheric water vapour.

Mauna Loa, volcano, south-central Hawaii Island, Hawaii, U.S., and a part of Hawaii Volcanoes National Park (established as Hawaii National Park in 1916). One of the largest single mountain masses in the world, Mauna Loa (meaning "long mountain") rises to 13,678 feet (4,169 m) above sea level. Its dome is 75 miles (120 km) long and 64 miles (103 km) wide, and its lava flows occupy more than 2,000 square miles (5,120 square km) of the island. Mokuaweoweo, its pit crater, has an area of nearly 4 square miles (10 square km) and a depth of 500–600 feet (150–180 m). Frequently snowcapped in winter, Mauna Loa has averaged one eruption every 3½ years since 1832. Many of its eruptions are confined within Mokuaweoweo Crater; others are lower flank eruptions along northeast or southwest fissure zones. In the eruption of 1935, U.S. Army planes dropped bombs in the path of a lava flow that threatened Hilo. In June 1950 a 23-day flow from a 13-mile (21-kilometre) fissure in the southwest rift destroyed a small village. Substantial eruptions at the summit occurred in 1975 and 1984.

Maundy Thursday, also called HOLY THURSDAY, the Thursday before Easter, observed in commemoration of Jesus Christ's institution of the Eucharist. The name is taken from an anthem sung in Roman Catholic churches on that day: "Mandatum novum do vobis" ("a new commandment I give to you"; John 13:34). In the early Christian church the day was celebrated with a general communion of clergy and people. At a special mass the bishop consecrated the holy oils in preparation for the anointing of the neophytes at the Baptism on Easter night. Since 1956 Maundy Thursday has been celebrated in Roman Catholic churches with a morning liturgy for the consecration of the holy oils for the coming year and an evening liturgy in commemoration of the institution of the Eucharist, with a general communion. During the evening liturgy the hosts are consecrated for the communion on Good Friday (when there is no liturgy), and the ceremony of the washing of feet is performed by the celebrant, who ceremonially washes the feet of 12 men in memory of Christ's washing the feet of his disciples. Eastern Orthodox churches also have a ceremony of foot washing and blessing of oil on this day.

In England, alms are distributed to the poor by the British sovereign in a ceremony held at a different church each year. This developed from a former practice in which the sovereign washed the feet of the poor on this day. In most European countries Maundy Thursday is known as Holy Thursday; other names are Green Thursday (Gründonnerstag; common in Germany), from the early practice of giving penitents a green branch as a token for completing their Lenten penance, and Sheer Thursday (clean Thursday), which refers to the ceremonial washing of altars on this day.

Maunick, Édouard J., in full ÉDOUARD JOSEPH MARC MAUNICK (b. Sept. 23, 1931, Mauritius), African poet, critic, and translator.

Maunick grew up on Mauritius Island, where, as a métis (mulatto), he experienced social discrimination from both blacks and whites. After working briefly as a librarian in Port-Louis, he settled in Paris in 1960, writing, lecturing, and directing for Coopération Radiophonique. He published frequently in *Présence Africaine* and other European journals.

In his first poetry collection, *Les Oiseaux du sang* (1954; "The Birds of Blood"), Maunick introduced a perspective that became characteristic of his later work; he rejected the sentimental search for roots to establish his individual identity. In *Les Manèges de la mer* (1964; "Taming the Sea"), he lamented his lonely exile and the persecution of his people. *Mascaret ou le livre de la mer et de la mort* (1966; "Mascaret or The Book of the Sea and of Death") reiterated his sense of isolation. Outraged by blacks killing blacks in Nigeria, Maunick published *Fusillez-moi* (1970; "Shoot Me"), a cry of anguish at the martyrdom of the Biafran Igbos.

Maunick's later collections include *Africaines du temps jadis* (1976; "African Women of Times Gone By") and *En mémoire du mémorable suivi de Jusqu'en terre Yoruba* (1979; "A Memory of the Memorable, Followed by As Far as the Land of the Yoruba").

Maupassant, Guy de, in full HENRY-RENÉ-ALBERT-GUY DE MAUPASSANT (b. Aug. 5, 1850, Château de Miromesnil?, near Dieppe, France—d. July 6, 1893, Paris), French naturalist writer of short stories and novels who is by general agreement the greatest French short-story writer.

Early life. Maupassant was the elder of the two children of Gustave and Laure de Maupassant. His mother's claim that he was born at the Château de Miromesnil has been disputed. The couple's second son, Hervé, was born in 1856.

Both parents came of Norman families, the father's of the minor aristocracy, but the marriage was a failure, and the couple separated permanently when Guy was 11 years old. Al-

Maupassant, photograph by Nadar (Gaspard-Félix Tournachon), *c.* 1885
Archives Photographiques

though the Maupassants were a free-thinking family, Guy received his first education from the church and at age 13 was sent to a small seminary at Yvetot that took both lay and clerical pupils. He felt a decided antipathy for this form of life and deliberately engineered his own expulsion for some trivial offense in 1868. He moved to the lycée at Le Havre and passed his baccalaureate the following year. In the autumn of 1869 he began law studies in Paris, which were interrupted by the outbreak of the Franco-German War. Maupassant volunteered, served first as a private in the field, and was later transferred through his father's intervention to the quartermaster corps. His firsthand experience of war was to provide him with the material for some of his finest stories.

He was demobilized in July 1871 and resumed his law studies in Paris. His father came to his assistance again and obtained a post for him in the Ministry of Marine, which was intended to support him until he qualified as a lawyer. He did not care for the bureaucracy but was not unsuccessful and was several times promoted. His father managed to have him transferred, at his own wish, to the Ministry of Public Instruction in 1879.

Apprenticeship with Flaubert. Maupassant's mother, Laure, was the sister of Alfred Le Poittevin, who had been a close friend of Gustave Flaubert, and she herself remained on affectionate terms with the novelist for the rest of his life. Laure de Maupassant sent her son to make Flaubert's acquaintance at Croisset in 1867, and when he returned to Paris after the war, she asked Flaubert to keep an eye on him. This was the beginning of the apprenticeship that was the making of Maupassant the writer. Whenever Flaubert was staying in Paris, he used to invite Maupassant to lunch on Sundays, lecture him on prose style, and correct his youthful literary exercises. He also introduced him to some of the leading writers of the time, such as Émile Zola, Ivan Turgenev, Édmond de Goncourt, and Henry James. "He's my disciple and I love him like a son," Flaubert said of Maupassant. It was a concise description of a twofold relationship: if Flaubert was the inspiration for Maupassant the writer, he also provided the child of a broken marriage with a foster father. Flaubert's sudden and unexpected death in 1880 was a grievous blow to Maupassant.

Zola described the young Maupassant as a "terrific oarsman able to row fifty miles on the Seine in a single day for pleasure." Maupassant was a passionate lover of the sea and of rivers, which accounts for the setting of much of his fiction and the prevalence in it of nautical imagery. In spite of his lack of enthusiasm for the bureaucracy, his years as a civil servant were the happiest of his life. He devoted much of his spare time to swimming and to boating expeditions on the Seine. One can see from a story like "Mouche" (1890; "Fly") that the latter were more than merely boating expeditions and that the girls who accompanied Maupassant and his friends were usually prostitutes or prospective prostitutes. Indeed, there can be little doubt that the early years in Paris were the start of his phenomenal promiscuity.

When Maupassant was in his early 20s, he discovered that he was suffering from syphilis, one of the most frightening and widespread maladies of the age. The fact that his brother died at an early age of the same disease suggests that it might have been congenital. Maupassant was adamant in refusing to undergo treatment, with the result that the disease was to cast a deepening shadow over his mature years and was accentuated by neurasthenia, which had also afflicted his brother.

During his apprenticeship with Flaubert, Maupassant published one or two stories under a pseudonym in obscure provincial magazines. The turning point came in April 1880, the month before Flaubert's death. Maupassant was one of six writers, led by Zola, who each contributed a short story on the Franco-German War to a volume called *Les Soirées de Médan.* Maupassant's story, "Boule de suif" ("Ball of Fat"), was not only by far the best of the six; it is probably the finest story he ever wrote. In it, a prostitute traveling by coach is companionably treated by her fellow French passengers, who are anxious to share her provisions of food, but then a German officer stops the coach and refuses to let it proceed until he has possessed her; the other passengers induce her to satisfy him, and then ostracize her for the rest of the journey. "Boule de suif" epitomizes Maupassant's style in its economy and balance.

Mature life and works. As soon as "Boule de suif" was published, Maupassant found himself in demand by newspapers. He left the ministry and spent the next two years writing articles for *Le Gaulois* and the *Gil Blas.* Many of his stories made their first appearance in the latter newspaper. The 10 years from 1880 to 1890 were remarkable for their productivity; he published some 300 short stories, six novels, three travel books, and his only volume of verse.

La Maison Tellier (1881; "The Tellier House"), a book of short stories on various subjects, is typical of Maupassant's achievement as a whole, both in his choice of themes and in his determination to present men and women objectively in the manifold aspects of life. His concern was with *l'humble vérité*—words which he chose as the subtitle to his novel *Une Vie* (1883; *A Woman's Life*). This book, which sympathetically treats its heroine's journey from innocent girlhood through the disillusionment of an unfortunate marriage and ends with her subsequent widowhood, records what Maupassant had observed as a child, the little dramas and daily preoccupations of ordinary people. He presents his characters dispassionately, foregoing any personal moral judgment on them but always noting the word, the gesture, or even the reticence that betrays each one's essential personality, all the while enhancing the effect by describing the physical and social background against which his characters move. Concision, vigour, and the most rigorous economy are the characteristics of his art.

Collections of short stories and novels followed one another in quick succession until illness struck Maupassant down. Two years saw six new books of short stories: *Mademoiselle Fifi* (1883), *Contes de la bécasse* (1883; "Tales of the Goose"), *Clair de lune, Les Soeurs Rondoli* ("The Rondoli Sisters"), *Yvette,* and *Miss Harriet* (all 1884). The stories can be divided into groups: those dealing with the Franco-German War, the Norman peasantry, the bureaucracy, life on the banks of the Seine River, the emotional problems of the different social classes, and—somewhat ominously in a late story such as "Le Horla" (1887)—hallucination. Together, the stories present a comprehensive picture of French life from 1870 to 1890.

Maupassant's most important full-length novels are *Une Vie, Bel-Ami* (1885; "Good Friend"), and *Pierre et Jean* (1888). *Bel-Ami* is drawn from the author's observation of the world of sharp businessmen and cynical journalists in Paris, and it is a scathing satire on a society whose members let nothing stand in the way of their ambition to get rich quick. Bel-Ami, the amiable but amoral hero of the novel, has become a standard literary personification of an ambitious opportunist. *Pierre et Jean* is the tale of a man's tragic jealousy of his half-brother, who is the child of their mother's adultery.

Maupassant prospered from his best-sellers and maintained an apartment in Paris with an annex for clandestine meetings with women, a house at Étretat, a couple of residences on the Riviera, and several yachts. He began to travel in 1881, visiting French Africa and Italy, and in 1889 he paid his only visit to England. While lunching in a restaurant there as James's guest, he shocked James profoundly by pointing to a woman at a neighbouring table and asking James to "get" her for him.

The French critic Paul Léautaud called Maupassant a "complete erotomaniac." His extraordinary fascination with brothels and prostitution is reflected not only in "Boule de suif" but also in stories such as "La Maison Tellier." It is significant, however, that as the successful writer became more closely acquainted with women of the nobility there was a change of angle in his fiction: a move from the peasantry to the upper classes, from the brothel to the boudoir. Maupassant's later books of short stories include *Toine* (1886), *Le Horla* (1887), *Le Rosier de Madame Husson* (1888; "The Rose-Bush of Madame Husson"), and *L'Inutile Beauté* (1890; "The Useless Beauty"). Four more novels also appeared: *Mont-Oriol* (1887), on the financing of a fashionable watering place; *Pierre et Jean; Fort comme la mort* (1889; "As Strong as Death"); and *Notre coeur* (1890; "Our Heart").

Although Maupassant appeared outwardly a sturdy, healthy, athletic man, his letters are full of lamentations about his health, particularly eye trouble and migraine headaches. With the passing of the years he had become more and more sombre. He had begun to travel for pleasure, but what had once been carefree and enjoyable holidays gradually changed, as a result of his mental state, into compulsive, symptomatic wanderings until he felt a constant need to be on the move.

A major family crisis occurred in 1888. Maupassant's brother was a man of minimal intelligence—today one would call it arrested development—and could work at nothing more demanding than nursery gardening. In 1888 he suddenly became violently psychotic, and he died in an asylum in 1889. Maupassant was reduced to despair by his brother's death; but though his grief was genuine, it cannot have been unconnected with his own advanced case of syphilis. On Jan. 2, 1892, when he was staying near his mother, he tried to commit suicide by cutting his throat. Doctors were summoned, and his mother agreed reluctantly to his commitment. Two days later he was removed, according to some accounts in a straitjacket, to Dr. Blanche's nursing home in Paris, where he died one month before his 43rd birthday.

Maupassant's work is thoroughly realistic. His characters inhabit a world of material desires and sensual appetites in which lust, greed, and ambition are the driving forces, and any higher feelings are either absent or doomed to cruel disappointment. The tragic power of many of the stories derives from the fact that Maupassant presents his characters, poor people or rich bourgeois, as the victims of ironic necessity, crushed by a fate that they have dared to defy yet still struggling against it hopelessly.

Because so many of his later stories deal with madness, it has been suggested that Maupassant himself was already mentally disturbed when he wrote them. Yet these stories are perfectly well balanced and are characterized by a clarity of style that betrays no sign of mental disorder. The lucid purity of Maupassant's French and the precision of his imagery are in fact the two features of his work that most account for its success.

By the second half of the 20th century, it was generally recognized that Maupassant's popularity as a short-story writer had declined and that he was more widely read in the English-speaking countries than in France. This does not detract from his genuine achievement—

the invention of a new, high-quality, commercial short story, which has something to offer to all classes of readers. (M.Tu./R.Dum.)

BIBLIOGRAPHY. Biographies include Francis Steegmuller, *Maupassant: A Lion in the Path* (1949), the most satisfactory biography in English; and Michael Lerner, *Maupassant* (1975), a later biographical study. Criticism includes Artine Artinian, *Maupassant Criticism in France, 1880–1940* (1941), a bibliography; E.D. Sullivan, *Maupassant the Novelist* (1954), and *Maupassant: The Short Stories* (1962), useful studies; and Martin Turnell, *The Art of French Fiction* (1959, reprinted 1970).

Maupeou, René-Nicolas-Charles-Augustin de (b. Feb. 25, 1714, Paris, France—d. July 29, 1792, Thuit), chancellor of France who succeeded in temporarily (1771–74) depriving the Parlements (high courts of justice) of the political powers that had enabled them to block the reforms proposed by the ministers of King Louis XV. By rescinding Maupeou's measures, King Louis XVI (reigned 1774–92) lost his opportunity to institute fundamental reforms that might have prevented the outbreak of the French Revolution.

Maupeou was born into a prominent family of the *noblesse de robe* (judicial nobility). Trained in law, he became president of the Parlement of Paris in 1763, when his father, René-Charles de Maupeou, was made keeper of the seals. The elder Maupeou resigned within 24 hours after assuming the chancellorship on Sept. 15, 1768, and René-Nicolas was then appointed chancellor in his place.

In the following year Maupeou brought the abbé Joseph-Marie Terray into the ministry as controller general of finances. Terray's plans to stabilize royal finances by levying taxes on the privileged classes were certain to meet with vigorous opposition from the Parlements. Hence Maupeou took the offensive by provoking the judges of the Parlement of Paris into calling a judicial strike. On the night of Jan. 19–20, 1771, he ordered the magistrates of the Parlement to resume their duties. When nearly all the judges refused to comply, Maupeou exiled 130 of them to remote provinces and deprived them of their offices. The following month he established six regional courts that were to handle judicial matters in most of the vast area over which the Parlement of Paris had exercised jurisdiction. In April he set up a smaller version of the Parlement of Paris, but limited its activities to trying crown cases and registering royal edicts. Louis XV allowed Maupeou to suppress only two of the seven provincial Parlements.

Nevertheless, Maupeou's decrees amounted to a coup d'état against the hereditary *noblesse de robe,* which he began to replace with appointed, salaried judges. Most important, he had denied the Parlement of Paris the right to veto royal edicts. As a result, Terray was able to proceed with his plans for tax reform.

Maupeou, detail of an engraving by G.E. Petit, 1753, after a painting by J. Chevallier, 1745

By courtesy of the Bibliotheque Nationale, Paris

Since Maupeou hoped to establish an enlightened royal despotism, his measures aroused the fury of the nobles and wealthy bourgeoisie whose interests had been protected by the Parlements and who, however desirous of reform, were by 1771 unwilling to accept it from the hands of the king and his ministers. Nevertheless, by the end of Louis XV's reign, the chancellor's new judicial system was operating successfully. After the accession of King Louis XVI in May 1774, however, Maupeou's enemies gained the upper hand. Louis XVI restored the Parlements to their former powers and privileges in August, and Maupeou was forced into retirement. The failure of Maupeou prefigured the failure of Anne-Robert-Jacques Turgot and, with it, the fall of the monarchy itself in the Revolution.

Maupertuis, Pierre-Louis Moreau de (b. Sept. 28, 1698, Saint-Malo, France—d. July 27, 1759, Basel, Switz.), French mathematician, biologist, and astronomer who helped popularize Newtonian mechanics.

Maupertuis, detail of an engraving

By courtesy of the trustees of the British Museum; photograph, J.R. Freeman & Co. Ltd.

Maupertuis became a member of the Academy of Sciences in Paris in 1731 and soon became the foremost French proponent of the Newtonian theory of gravitation. In 1736 he led an expedition to Lapland to measure the length of a degree along the meridian. His measurement verified the Newtonian view that the Earth is an oblate spheroid (a sphere flattened at the poles). The success of his expedition gained him favour with Frederick the Great, who called him to Berlin. He became a member of the Berlin Academy of Sciences in 1741 and served as its president from 1745 to 1753.

In 1744 Maupertuis enunciated the principle of least action, later published in his *Essai de cosmologie* (1750; "Essay on Cosmology"). It states simply that "in all the changes that take place in the universe, the sum of the products of each body multiplied by the distance it moves and by the speed with which it moves is the least [that is] possible." The German mathematician Samuel Koenig accused Maupertuis of having plagiarized Gottfried Wilhelm Leibniz's work in this principle. In the ensuing controversy, Leonhard Euler came to the support of Maupertuis, but Voltaire, once his proselyte, satirized the "earth flattener" so mercilessly that Maupertuis left Berlin in 1753.

Maupertuis' *Système de la nature* (1751) contained theoretical speculations on the nature of biparental heredity based on his careful study of the occurrences of polydactyly, or extra fingers, in several generations of a Berlin family. He demonstrated that polydactyly could be transmitted by either the male or female parent, and he presciently explained the trait as the result of a mutation in the "hereditary particles" possessed by them. He also calculated the mathematical probability of the trait's future occurrence in new members of the family. In this research Maupertuis produced the first scientifically accurate record of the transmission of a dominant hereditary trait in humans.

Maura, Antonio, in full ANTONIO MAURA Y MONTANER (b. May 2, 1853, Palma, Majorca, Spain—d. Dec. 13, 1925, Torrelodones), statesman and five times prime minister of Spain whose vision led him to undertake a series of democratic reforms to prevent revolution and foster a constitutional monarchy. His tolerance and lack of knowledge of human nature, however, tended to obscure his otherwise brilliant political career.

Maura was elected to the Cortes (Spanish parliament) of 1881 and in 1890 became minister for the colonies in the Liberal cabinet of Práxedes Mateo Sagasta. He resigned when his reforms that would have granted autonomy to Cuba failed to pass (1894). Later, as minister of the interior (1902), he conducted elections notable for their honesty.

Maura first became premier in December 1903 but resigned a year later in protest against what he thought was an attempt to seize personal power by King Alfonso XIII. During his second tenure (1907–09) as premier, Maura was able to pass some of his projects, such as reforming local governments and making education compulsory. His attempt to promote Spanish political influence and commercial interests in Morocco, however, provoked the Rif War, which set off a general strike (July 1909) and anticlerical violence in Barcelona. After the execution of the propagandist Francisco Ferrer, Maura reestablished the constitutional guarantees in Barcelona and Gerona. He was forced to resign, however, in October.

In December 1912 Maura resigned his seat in the Cortes as well as his post of Conservative Party leader. He headed three more short-lived governments in periods of crisis: March–November 1913, April–July 1919, and August 1921–March 1922.

Maurel, Victor (b. June 17, 1848, Marseille, France—d. Oct. 22, 1923, New York, N.Y., U.S.), French operatic baritone and outstanding singing actor, admired for his breath control and dramatic artistry.

Maurel studied voice at the School of Music in Marseille then continued at the Paris Conservatoire, where in 1867 he won first prize. In the following year he made his debut at the Paris Opéra as the Count de Nevers in Giacomo Meyerbeer's *Les Huguenots,* and thereafter he appeared at La Scala, Milan, in the premiere of Antonio Carlos Gomes' *Il Guarany* and at Covent Garden, London, in English premieres of Richard Wagner's *Lohengrin, Tannhäuser,* and *The Flying Dutchman.*

In 1873 Maurel made his U.S. debut in the American premiere of Giuseppe Verdi's *Aida* in New York City. He then withdrew from the stage before rejoining the Paris Opéra in 1879, where he remained one of its reigning baritones for 15 years. Maurel's most memorable achievements were as Iago and Falstaff in the respective world premieres of Verdi's *Otello* (1887) and *Falstaff* (1893). He sang at the Metropolitan Opera in 1894 and again in 1899. After an attempt at legitimate acting he returned to the operatic stage in 1904, but five years later retired to New York City to become a singing teacher.

Maurel was the author of several books on singing and staging operas as well as an autobiography, *Dix Ans de carrière* (1897).

Maurepas, Jean-Frédéric Phélypeaux, Count (comte) **de** (b. July 9, 1701, Versailles, France—d. Sept. 21, 1781, Versailles), secretary of state under King Louis XV and chief royal adviser during the first seven years of the reign of King Louis XVI. By dissuading

Louis XVI from instituting economic and administrative reforms, Maurepas was partially responsible for the governmental crises that eventually led to the outbreak of the French Revolution.

Maurepas, engraving by Dupin de Franlieu, 18th century
Giraudon—Art Resource

Maurepas's father was a secretary of state under King Louis XIV. In 1718 Maurepas was made secretary of state for the king's household, thereby gaining authority over ecclesiastical affairs and the administration of Paris. Appointed to the additional office of secretary for the marine in 1723, he undertook the immense task of reorganizing the severely demoralized French navy.

Maurepas remained in office until 1749, when, as a result of a personal quarrel with Louis XV's mistress, Madame de Pompadour, he was disgraced and banished to his estates. In 1774 he was recalled from exile and made chief adviser to the newly crowned young monarch, Louis XVI. Maurepas proved unwilling to continue the reforming trend that had begun with the abolition of the political powers of the Parlements (high courts of justice) in 1771, and he persuaded Louis to restore the full authority of the Parlements (1774), which sought to protect the interests of the nobles and the wealthy bourgeoisie. Although Maurepas secured the appointment of Anne-Robert Turgot as controller general of the finances, he refused to support Turgot's efforts to shift the burden of taxation to the privileged orders. In 1776 he persuaded Louis to dismiss Turgot. Maurepas then had Jacques Necker put in charge of government finances, but he became jealous of Necker's popularity and forced him to resign in 1781.

Mauretania, region of ancient North Africa corresponding to present northern Morocco and western and central Algeria north of the Atlas Mountains.

Its native inhabitants, seminomadic pastoralists of Berber stock, were known to the Romans as the Mauri (*i.e.,* Moors) and the Massaesyli. From the 6th century BC the Phoenicians and Carthaginians also settled at points along the coast. Beginning in the late 2nd century BC, the kings of Mauretania became Roman vassals. About 42 AD the area was annexed to Rome and divided into two provinces: Mauretania Tingitana, with its capital at Tingis (modern Tangier); and Mauretania Caesariensis, with its capital at Caesarea (modern Cherchell, Alg.). Roman influence was mostly confined to the coast, and Rome ruled much of the province's vast interior through local chieftains. Mauretanians made effective light cavalrymen in the Roman legions, however.

In the late 3rd century another province, Sitifensis, was formed out of the eastern part of Caesariensis. When the Vandals arrived in Africa in 429, much of Mauretania became virtually independent. Christianity had spread rapidly there in the 4th and 5th centuries but was extinguished when the Arabs conquered the region in the 7th century.

Mauretania, transatlantic passenger liner of the Cunard Line, called the "Grand Old Lady of the Atlantic." It was launched in 1906 and made its maiden voyage in 1907; thereafter, it held the Atlantic Blue Riband for speed until 1929, challenged only by its sister ship, the *Lusitania* (sunk by a German submarine on May 7, 1915). During World War I the *Mauretania* worked as a transport and hospital ship. During its long career the ship made 269 double crossings of the Atlantic, exclusive of war work. Its last crossing was made in 1934, and it was broken up in 1935.

Mauriac, Claude (b. April 25, 1914, Paris, France—d. March 22, 1996, Paris), French novelist, journalist, and critic, a practitioner of the avant-garde school of *nouveau roman* ("new novel") writers, who, in the 1950s and '60s, spurned the traditional novel.

A son of the novelist François Mauriac, he was able to make the acquaintance of many notable French writers at his father's house and later during his career as a journalist. He worked as Charles de Gaulle's private secretary from 1944 to 1949 and was a columnist and film critic for the newspapers *Le Figaro* and *Le Figaro Littéraire* from 1946 to 1977.

Claude Mauriac, 1972
Jimmy Fox © 1972

Mauriac established his own reputation as a novelist with four works published under the general title *Le Dialogue intérieur*: *Toutes les femmes sont fatales* (1957; *All Women Are Fatal*), *Le Dîner en ville* (1959, Prix Médicis; *The Dinner Party*), *La Marquise sortit à cinq heures* (1961; *The Marquise Went Out at Five*), and *L'Agrandissement* (1963; "The Enlargement"). These books deal with the adventures of Bertrand Carnéjoux, the hero and narrator, who is both an irresistible womanizer and a cold-hearted egoist. These highly experimental novels focus on characters' states of mind and their varying experiences of time within a general atmosphere of sexual intrigue.

Mauriac's best-known work, the 10-volume *Le Temps immobile* (1974–88; "Time Immobilized"), consists of excerpts from letters, documents, and parts of other writers' works interspersed with entries from his own diaries. These books paint a rich picture of 50 years of French intellectual life, with separate volumes devoted to his father, de Gaulle, and Marcel Proust. Mauriac is also known for *L'Alittérature contemporaine* (1958; *The New Literature*), a collection of essays on 20th-century writers.

Mauriac, François (b. Oct. 11, 1885, Bordeaux, France—d. Sept. 1, 1970, Paris), novelist, essayist, poet, playwright, journalist, and winner in 1952 of the Nobel Prize for Literature. He belonged to the lineage of French Catholic writers who examined the ugly realities of modern life in the light of eternity. His major novels are sombre, austere psychological dramas set in an atmosphere of unrelieved tension. At the heart of every work Mauriac placed a religious soul grappling with the problems of sin, grace, and salvation.

François Mauriac
EB Inc.

Mauriac came from a pious and strict upper-middle-class family. He studied at the University of Bordeaux and entered the École Nationale des Chartes at Paris in 1906, soon deserting it to write. His first published work was a volume of delicately fervent poems, *Les Mains jointes* (1909; "Joined Hands"). Mauriac's vocation, however, lay with the novel. *L'Enfant chargé de chaînes* (1913; *Young Man in Chains*) and *La Robe prétexte* (1914; *The Stuff of Youth*), his first works of fiction, showed a still uncertain technique but, nevertheless, set the pattern for his recurring themes. His native city of Bordeaux and the drab and suffocating strictures of bourgeois life provide the framework for his explorations of the relations of characters deprived of love. *Le Baiser au lépreux* (1922; *The Kiss to the Leper*) established Mauriac as a major novelist. Mauriac showed increasing mastery in *Le Désert de l'amour* (1925; *The Desert of Love*) and in *Thérèse Desqueyroux* (1927; *Thérèse*), whose heroine is driven to attempt the murder of her husband to escape her suffocating life. *Le Noeud de vipères* (1932; *Vipers' Tangle*) is often considered Mauriac's masterpiece. It is a marital drama, depicting an old lawyer's rancour toward his family, his passion for money, and his final conversion. In this, as in other Mauriac novels, the love that his characters seek vainly in human contacts is fulfilled only in love of God.

In 1933 Mauriac was elected to the French Academy. His later novels include the partly autobiographical *Le Mystère Frontenac* (1933; *The Frontenac Mystery*), *Les Chemins de la mer* (1939; *The Unknown Sea*), and *La Pharisienne* (1941; *A Woman of the Pharisees*), an analysis of religious hypocrisy and the desire for domination. In 1938 Mauriac turned to writing plays, beginning auspiciously with *Asmodée* (performed 1937), in which the hero is a heinous, domineering character who controls weaker souls. Such is also the theme of the less successful *Les Mal Aimés* (1945; "The Poorly Loved").

A highly sensitive man, Mauriac felt compelled to justify himself before his critics. *Le Romancier et ses personnages* (1933; "The Novelist and His Characters") and the four volumes of his *Journal* (1934–51), followed by three volumes of *Mémoires* (1959–67), tell much of his intentions, his methods, and his reactions to contemporary moral values. Mauriac tackled the difficult dilemma of the Christian writer—how to portray evil in human nature without placing temptation before his readers—in *Dieu et Mammon* (1929; *God and Mammon,* 1936).

Mauriac was also a prominent polemical writer. He intervened vigorously in the 1930s, condemning totalitarianism in all its forms and denouncing Fascism in Italy and Spain. In World War II he worked with the writers of the Resistance. After the war he increasingly engaged in political discussion. He wrote *De Gaulle* (1964; Eng. trans., 1966), having officially supported him from 1962. Though Mauriac's fame outside France spread slowly, he was regarded by many as the greatest French novelist after Marcel Proust.

Maurice, name of rulers grouped below by country and indicated by the symbol •.

Foreign-language equivalents:

Dutch	Maurits
German	Moritz
Greek	Mauricios, or Maurikios
Latin	Mauricius

BYZANTINE EMPIRE

• Maurice, Latin in full MAURICIUS FLAVIUS TIBERIUS (b. *c.* 539, Cappadocia—d. 602, Constantinople), outstanding general and emperor (582–602) who helped transform the shattered late Roman Empire into a new and well-organized medieval Byzantine Empire.

Maurice first entered the government as a notary but in 578 was made commander of the imperial forces in the East. Distinguished by his successes against the Persians, he was selected by the emperor Tiberius II as his successor. On Aug. 5, 582, he was made emperor and betrothed to Tiberius' daughter Constantina. He was crowned on August 13, the day preceding Tiberius' death.

In the East, Maurice led his armies against Persia, reaching a satisfactory peace settlement after helping Khosrow II gain the Persian throne. With peace restored, Maurice could turn to the North, where nomadic Slavs and Avars were establishing permanent settlements in the empire. His campaign had some success, for in 602 the Avars went over to the imperial side. In the West, Maurice is credited with establishing a new kind of civil administration in war-torn Italy. He appointed military governors for Rome and Ravenna—the exarchate of Ravenna—when he realized that the civil authorities were unable to protect remaining Byzantine territory from the advancing Lombards. He later created an exarchate at Carthage, in North Africa, designed to withstand the attacks of Berber tribesmen. The two exarchates were provinces whose civil administration was placed in the hands of military officials. They are believed to have been the basis for the system of provincial rule (themes) used in the later Byzantine Empire.

Maurice's campaigns against Persians, Slavs, Avars, and Lombards drained the imperial treasury and necessitated the collection of high taxes. Dissatisfaction grew within the army, and, when he ordered some troops to set up winter quarters on the far side of the Danube River, a revolt broke out. The mutinous soldiers rallied behind Phocas, one of their junior officers, and marched on Constantinople. The citizens revolted, Maurice was overthrown, and Phocas was crowned emperor.

NETHERLANDS

• Maurice, in full MAURICE, PRINCE OF ORANGE, COUNT OF NASSAU, Dutch MAURITS, PRINS VAN ORANJE, GRAAF VAN NASSAU (b. Nov. 13, 1567, Dillenburg, Nassau—d. April 23, 1625, The Hague), hereditary stadholder (1585–1625) of the United Provinces of the Netherlands, or Dutch Republic, successor to his father, William I the Silent. His development of military strategy, tactics, and engineering made the Dutch army the most modern in the Europe of his time.

Youth and rise to power. Maurice was the second son of William the Silent. Although known as the prince of Orange, he did not actually inherit that principality until 1618, on the death of his elder half brother. A child of William's disastrous marriage to the schizophrenic Anna of Saxony and delicate as a youth, Maurice was shuffled from place to place during the years of his father's struggle against Spanish tyranny. His boyhood was further overshadowed by the desertion and betrayal of his father by former allies and finally by William's assassination in 1584. It was hardly surprising that these experiences deepened his natural reserve, leaving him suspicious of friends as well as of enemies.

At the time of his father's death, Maurice was still a student at the newly founded University of Leiden, but the States of Holland swiftly invested him as stadholder (chief executive). He later also became stadholder of Zeeland, Utrecht, Overijssel, and Gelderland. The years 1584–86 were critical. English help for the Netherlands revolt had finally materialized in the person of the Earl of Leicester, who headed an English expeditionary force, temporarily strengthening the provinces' defenses but imperilling the cause of the rebels by political blunders. Fortunately for Maurice, he had the assistance of the master politician Johan van Oldenbarnevelt, *landsadvocaat* (pensionary) of Holland. With Maurice's cousin and loyal supporter, William Louis, stadholder of Friesland, Oldenbarnevelt and Maurice formed a powerful triumvirate. Under the three, the northern provinces steadily consolidated their position against Spain, grew progressively richer by trade and shipping, and prepared themselves for independence.

Military career. Oldenbarnevelt took control of domestic and foreign affairs; Maurice, as federal commander in chief, attended to military matters with the aid of William Louis. Mathematics, ballistics, and military engineering had fascinated Maurice since childhood; now he was in a position to put his theories to the test. His first task was to reduce the army's size and improve its organization. He did his best to remove the perpetual curse of all contemporary armies—mutiny—by ensuring that his soldiers were properly and promptly paid, equipped with better arms, given improved and more regular training, and instructed in the science of fortification and siege warfare. The secret of Maurice's military planning was to bring to the art of siege warfare—the dominant type of warfare of his century—those habits of steady, close observation and attention to detail so characteristic of the Dutch in all the arts and sciences of the time. He was also greatly helped by the advice of Simon Stevin—the great mathematician and philosopher of Bruges, then living in Holland—whose lectures attracted his attention.

Maurice, detail of a painting by Michiel Janszoon van Mierrelt; in the Rijksmuseum, Amsterdam

By courtesy of the Rijksmuseum, Amsterdam

The fruits of his efforts were harvested in the 1590s. Beginning with Breda (the Nassau family seat), Maurice captured one enemy stronghold after another. In a series of actions, remarkable less for their audacity than for cool and systematic planning, the Spanish front lines were pushed back to the north, east, and south until the republic's territory began to assume something very much like its modern shape. Joyfully the Holland towns paid homage to their saviour; Maurice was hailed (literally) as the engineer of victory.

He had less success in the south. With great reluctance, Maurice was persuaded by the impatient Oldenbarnevelt to try to reunite the northern and southern Netherlands, divided by Spanish conquests. His attempt to invade Flanders and rouse it to repel its Spanish conquerors failed completely. After an initial victory at Nieuwpoort in 1601, Maurice was compelled to withdraw. Later, Oostende had to be surrendered. Oldenbarnevelt's optimism had proved totally misplaced. The southerners were apathetic, even hostile, to the appeals of the Hollanders. Even Maurice, with his doubts about the wisdom of undertaking such a campaign, was taken by surprise by its outcome. The defeat revealed that there was one department of military reform he had overlooked—intelligence. Unwillingly, and with bitterness, Maurice had to bow to facts. He agreed first to an armistice (1607) and then a 12-year truce with Spain (1609). The division of the Netherlands was to continue.

Rivalry with Oldenbarnevelt. The problems of war had brought out the strength of Maurice's character. An English visitor noted that he was "of great forwardness, good presence and courage, flaxen haired, endued with a singular wit." With growing confidence, he stood up for his own interests as well as those of his people against the English queen, Elizabeth I, and her emissaries as well as those of France. As Maurice's stature grew to match his responsibilities, he increasingly resented the continual interference by Oldenbarnevelt in military matters. The unsuccessful foray into Flanders was a special cause of friction, and the long siege of Oostende put a heavy strain on their relations. Estrangement was made worse by the negotiations for the truce; Maurice suspected Oldenbarnevelt of sacrificing Dutch independence in his anxiety for a peace with Spain, while Oldenbarnevelt suspected Maurice of attempting to acquire sovereign power.

During the decade after the truce, the partnership turned into a war, as yet private and undeclared, for supremacy. Maurice's mastery of strategy again stood him in good stead. While Oldenbarnevelt was more deeply drawn into the bitter theological politics of the times, Maurice patiently waited for his moment, quietly consolidating his support in Zeeland and Amsterdam. Oldenbarnevelt, confident of his power in the Holland states, emerged as the champion of Erastianism (which advocated dominance of the state over the church) and of those moderate Protestants who wanted religious toleration, in opposition to the intolerance of the orthodox Dutch Calvinists.

It was 1617 before Maurice came out publicly as protector of the Calvinists (the so-called Counter-Remonstrants). When Oldenbarnevelt obtained authority for his supporters in the towns to raise levies of professional soldiers (*waardgelders*), Maurice acted swiftly. Marching to the Brill (in South Holland) on September 28–29, he disbanded the levies. Next, he took advantage of his legal right to approve appointments in the local governments in order to purge each *vroedschap* (council) of his opponents. By the summer of 1618 he had forcibly dismissed all the *waardgelders.* It then only remained to remove Oldenbarnevelt. On Aug. 29, 1618, the old statesman was arrested, and on May 13, 1619, he was executed. The long political trial was marked by persistent bias, petty spite, and inexcusable cruelty and injustice. Maurice did not himself dictate the sentence, but he ostentatiously refrained from exercising his prerogative of pardon, and he personally endorsed the demand for the probably illegal forfeiture of Oldenbarnevelt's property. The trial and execution of his old ally remain a blot upon his character and career.

After this victory, Maurice wielded unprecedented power. In all but name the Stadholder was king. Yet, having forged his alliance with orthodox Calvinism, created an Orangist Party, and packed local, provincial, and federal offices with his supporters, Maurice pressed his "revolution" no further. In 1621 he ended with a flourish the truce with the Spanish that he had detested for 12 long years. Ironically, the Calvinist hero was quickly faced by a Habsburg threat so dangerous that he was compelled to conclude an alliance with Roman Catholic France. Just before he died (of a liver complaint) in 1625, Breda, the scene of his first spectacular victory against the Spanish, was again lost to the enemy.

Assessment. The last 10 years of his life added nothing to Maurice's reputation. He was a great soldier but not a great statesman. In peace he had few of the sympathetic qualities that had drawn men to his father to settle issues by advice and discussion. His greatest claim to fame was his repulsion of the Spanish from 1590 to 1609 and the extension and securing of the frontiers of the Dutch Republic. Yet his achievement fell short of reunifying the whole of the Netherlands, and his vindictive pursuit of Oldenbarnevelt helped to divide the republic permanently into Orangists and anti-Orangists. For the latter, Oldenbarnevelt's martyrdom provided a focus and a rallying cry down to the French Revolution.

Maurice's was an involuted and contradictory character. The circumstances of his childhood left him vulnerable to fears, suspicions, and resentments; yet he was also a man of great courage, capable of magnanimity on the battlefield. His natural caution did not inhibit his capacity for swift and decisive action. Coldly logical, he enjoyed a joke, albeit a sarcastic one. His lack of passion may have prevented him from marrying but did not prevent him from fathering a brood of illegitimate children. (C.H.Wi.)

BIBLIOGRAPHY. G. Groen van Prinsterer, *Maurice et Barnevelt* (1875), remains the classic Dutch biography. The outstanding recent work that assesses Maurice's contribution to history is Jan den Tex, *Oldenbarnevelt,* 3 vol. (1960; Eng. trans., 2 vol., 1972). A shrewd appreciation of Maurice appears in *The Dutch Nation* by G.J. Renier (1944). J.L. Motley, *The Life and Death of John of Barneveld,* 2 vol. (1874), and his *History of the United Netherlands,* 4 vol. (1861–68), contain much valuable information.

Saxony

• **Maurice** (b. March 21, 1521, Freiberg, Saxony—d. July 9, 1553, Sievershausen, Saxony), duke (1541–53) and later elector (1547–53) of Saxony, whose clever manipulation of alliances and disputes gained the Albertine branch of the Wettin dynasty extensive lands and the electoral dignity.

Maurice succeeded his father, Duke Henry of Saxony, in 1541. Although a Protestant, he aided the Roman Catholic emperor Charles V against the Turks (1542), Cleve (1543), and France (1544). In 1545, he was dissuaded from supporting the Lutheran Schmalkaldic League by an imperial promise of the Saxon electorship, held by John Frederick the Magnanimous of the rival Ernestine branch of the Wettin dynasty; Maurice returned to Charles's camp and conquered electoral Saxony. Ousted in 1547, he returned after John Frederick's defeat in the Battle of Mühlberg (April 24, 1547) and received the electoral dignity and sizable lands.

Maurice, portrait by Lucas Cranach the Younger; in the Gemäldegalerie, Dresden, Ger.

By courtesy of the Staatliche Kunstsammlungen, Dresden, Ger.; photograph, Deutsche Fotothek Dresden

Soon, however, Maurice began to resent Charles's plans to reintroduce Catholicism in Germany's Protestant territories and the continued imprisonment of his father-in-law, Philip the Magnanimous, landgrave of Hesse, whose freedom Charles had guaranteed. Commissioned to capture the rebellious Lutheran city of Magdeburg (1550), Maurice seized the occasion to raise an army and signed anti-Habsburg compacts with France and Germany's Protestant princes. In March 1552 the rebels overran southern Germany and parts of Austria, forcing the Emperor to flee and release Philip. In August 1552 the Lutheran position was provisionally guaranteed by the Treaty of Passau. Again returning to the Emperor's camp, Maurice campaigned against the Turks in Hungary. Finally, in northwestern Germany, he confronted his former ally Albert II Alcibiades of Brandenburg, who had rejected the Passau armistice. He defeated Albert at Sievershausen but was himself killed in the battle.

Maurice, SAINT (d. *c.* 286, Agaunum, near Geneva; feast day September 22), Christian soldier whose alleged martyrdom, with his comrades, inspired a cult still practiced today. Among those martyred with him were SS. Vitalis, Candidus, and Exuperius.

Their story was recorded in the *Passio martyrum Acaunensium* ("The Passion of the Martyrs of Agaunum"), by the 5th-century French bishop St. Eucherius, who believed that the Theban Legion was a group of Egyptian Christians serving in the Roman army under the command of Maurice (Latin Mauritius). Ironically, they were sent by Maximian (later Roman emperor) to help quash a revolt of Christian peasants in Gaul. The legion met Maximian at Octodurum (now Martigny, Switz.), but they refused to fight against their brethren and withdrew in protest to Agaunum. There Maximian twice had one man in 10 executed, and finally the entire group was put to death.

Study of the legend was stimulated by excavations (1944–49) at Saint-Maurice-en-Valais. In 1956 an analysis of the *Passio* by D. van Berchem, a specialist in the history of the Roman army, appeared, claiming that the prime source for the author of the *Passio* was an oral account given by a 4th-century Oriental bishop, Theodore of Octodurum, who brought from the East the legend of one St. Maurice who suffered martyrdom with 70 soldiers under his command. Van Berchem claimed that the soldiers were neither Thebans nor an entire legion.

The cult of St. Maurice and the Theban Legion is found in Switzerland, along the Rhine, and in northern Italy. Around Theodore's basilica, supposedly built by Theodore of Octodurum, was founded the Abbey of St. Maurice, presumably by *c.* 524. Prince St. Sigismund of Burgundy ordered that the *laus perennis*, or unbroken chant, be practiced there. In devotion to Maurice the *laus perennis* has become a tradition at the present-day abbey. Maurice's relics are preserved at the Abbey of St. Maurice at Brzeg, Pol., and at Turin, Italy.

Maurice OF NASSAU: *see* Maurice *under* Maurice (Netherlands).

Maurice, (John) Frederick Denison (b. Aug. 29, 1805, Normanston, Suffolk, Eng.—d. April 1, 1872, London), major English theologian of 19th-century Anglicanism and prolific author, remembered chiefly as a founder of Christian Socialism.

Prevented from graduation in law at Cambridge by his refusal to subscribe to the Thirty-nine Articles, the Anglican confession of faith, Maurice reversed his position by 1830 and attended Oxford. In the interim he had worked for several years in London as a writer and an editor for literary journals and in 1834 published his only novel, *Eustace Conway.* That same year he was ordained and soon afterward became chaplain at Guy's Hospital in London. Elected professor of English literature and modern history at King's College, Cambridge, in 1840, he became professor of divinity and accepted the chaplaincy at Lincoln's Inn, the London academy of law, six years later. His reputation as a theologian was enhanced with the publication of his book *The Kingdom of Christ* (1838), in which he held the church to be a united body that transcended the diversity and partiality of individual men, factions, and sects. That view—subsequently regarded as presaging the 20th-century ecumenical movement—aroused the suspicions of orthodox Anglicans. Their misgivings were intensified in 1848, when he joined the moderate Anglicans Charles Kingsley, John Malcolm Ludlow, and others to found the Christian Socialist movement.

Frederick Denison Maurice, detail from a portrait by Samuel Laurence, 1871; in the National Portrait Gallery, London

By courtesy of the National Portrait Gallery, London

Opposition to Maurice progressed after his *Theological Essays* of 1853 revealed his disbelief in the eternity of hell, and that year he was dismissed from his King's College post. Combining his skill as an educator with his interest in improving the status of workers, Maurice planned and became the first principal of the Working Men's College (1854). He also organized cooperative associations among workers.

In 1860 Maurice left the chaplaincy at Lincoln's Inn to serve St. Peter's Church, where admirers of his preaching called him "the Prophet." Elected to the Knightsbridge professorship of moral philosophy at Cambridge in 1866, he lectured on ethical subjects and wrote his celebrated *Social Morality* (1869). To this position, which he held until his death, he added the chaplaincy of St. Edward's Church at Cambridge in 1870.

After World War II, considerable interest in his work revived, and, though some critics have viewed his teachings as dated and obscure, he remains a versatile and creative source for students of Christian Socialism. Noteworthy among his numerous works are *Moral and Metaphysical Philosophy* (1850–62), *What Is Revelation?* (1859), and *The Claims of the Bible and of Science* (1863).

BIBLIOGRAPHY. Studies of Maurice's life and thought include Michael Ramsey, *F.D. Maurice and the Conflicts of Modern Theology* (1951); Alexander R. Vidler, *F.D. Maurice and Company* (1966); Olive J. Brose, *Frederick Denison Maurice, Rebellious Conformist* (1972); Frank M. McClain, *Maurice: Man and Moralist* (1972); and Torben Christensen, *The Divine Order: A Study in F.D. Maurice's Theology* (1973).

Maurice, Furnley, pseudonym of FRANK LESLIE THOMPSON WILMOT (b. April 6, 1881, Collingwood, Vic., Australia—d. Feb. 22, 1942, Melbourne), Australian poet, best known for his book *To God: From the Warring Nations* (1917), a powerful indictment of the waste, cruelty, and stupidity of war. He was also the author of lyrics, satirical verses, and essays.

At age 14 Wilmot worked in a Melbourne bookshop, rising to the position of manager. When the business was dissolved in 1929, he operated as an independent bookseller for three years but, finding this unprofitable, became manager of the Melbourne University Press, a post he held until his death.

He began to write poetry before he was 20, contributing his earliest work to the *Tocsin,* a Melbourne labour paper. His first book, *Some Verses,* was published in 1903 under his real name, and a year later *More Verses* appeared but was withdrawn shortly after publication. Neither of these books attracted much attention, and so their embarrassed author took the pen name Furnley Maurice. *Unconditioned Songs* (1913) caused a small stir, but it was not until *To God: From the Warring Nations* appeared in 1917 that critics began to take an interest in Wilmot's work. In the same year, he brought out *The Bay and Padie Book: Kiddie Songs,* highly successful children's verse that went through three editions in the next nine years. *Eyes of Vigilance* (1920) contained what is considered some of his best poetry. Of his later volumes, *Melbourne Odes* (1934) contains the ode that won him the Melbourne centenary prize in 1934.

Maurienne, high Alpine valley, about 80 miles (130 km) long, in southeastern France. Drained by the Arc River, a tributary of the Isère, it consists of a succession of large basins and narrow, wild gorges that are cut through outcrops of heavily folded and overthrust rocks. Twenty-four hydroelectric stations in the valley generate power for electrochemical plants, aluminum refining, and electric, steel, and alloy production. In the Haute-Maurienne, spruce is logged for fuel and timber. Stock breeding, dairying, and cheese production are the main agricultural activities. The northerly trans-Alpine railway follows the Maurienne to Modane, Fr., whence the line runs southwest to Turin, Italy, through the Mont Cenis Tunnel. A road system, stretching southward from Lake Geneva to Nice crosses the Maurienne to give motor access to the outside world. Modane (the centre of tourism), Saint-Jean (the site of a major aluminum plant), and Saint-Michel are the chief towns in the Maurienne valley.

Maurier, Sir Gerald Hubert Edward Busson du: *see* Du Maurier, Sir Gerald (Hubert Edward Busson).

Maurist, member of a congregation of French Benedictine monks founded in 1618 and devoted to strict observance of the Benedictine Rule and especially to historical and ecclesiastical scholarship. Dom Gregory Tarrisse (1575–1648), the first president, desired to make scholarship the congregation's distinguishing feature; he organized schools of training and set up their headquarters at Saint-Germain-des-Prés in Paris, which soon became a rendezvous for many scholars. Each Maurist monk made his religious profession not for his own monastery but for the congregation, so that promising students could be selected and work at studies apportioned by the superiors. Tarrisse found in Jean-Luc d'Achéry an excellent organizer of his designs. The golden age of the Maurists lay between the arrival of Jean Mabillon in 1664 and the death of Bernard de Montfaucon in 1741. The Maurists excelled both as editors and as historians, and many of their texts remain the best available; they were pioneers in critical medieval history, and their work has attached the adjective "learned" to the Benedictines. The congregation numbered 180 monasteries in 1700 but was suppressed during the French Revolution in 1789. It formally ceased to exist in 1817.

Consult
the
INDEX
first

Mauritania, officially ISLĀMIC REPUBLIC OF MAURITANIA, Arabic MŪRĪTĀNIYĀ, or AL-JUMHŪRĪYAH AL-ISLĀMĪYAH AL-MŪRĪTĀNĪYAH, French MAURITANIE, or RÉPUBLIQUE ISLAMIQUE DE MAURITANIE, country of northwestern Africa, covering an area of 398,000 square miles (1,030,700 square km). The capital is Nouakchott. Mauritania is bordered to the west by the Atlantic Ocean, to the northwest and north by Western Sahara, to the northeast by Algeria, to the east and southeast by Mali, and to the southwest by Senegal. The population in 2002 was estimated to be 2,656,000.

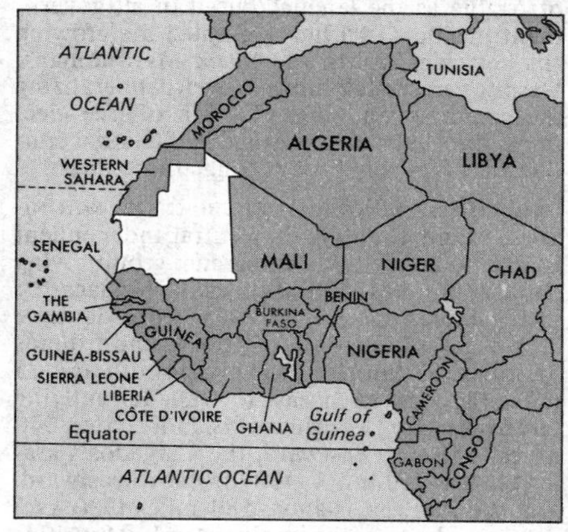

Mauritania

A brief treatment of Mauritania follows. For full treatment, *see* MACROPAEDIA: Western Africa.

For current history and for statistics on society and economy, *see* BRITANNICA BOOK OF THE YEAR.

The land. Most of Mauritania is made up of low-lying desert that forms the westernmost part of the Sahara. The coastal plains are less than 150 feet (45 m) above sea level, and the higher plains of the interior range from 600 to 750 feet (180 to 230 m). The flat interior plains are diversified by escarpments that sometimes reach 900 feet (270 m) or by numerous inselbergs (isolated peaks), of which the highest is Kediet Ijill (3,002 feet [915 m]). Sand dunes cover about 50 percent of the country. Drainage in Mauritania is mostly inland, except where the Sénégal River and its tributaries flow southward and westward. The dry inland plateaus are cut by a number of wadis that are subject to occasional flash flooding.

The climate throughout Mauritania is hot and, except for certain sections in the south, dry. Southern Mauritania has a Sahelian climate; there is one rainy season from July to October, but it delivers only about 25 inches (635 mm) of precipitation a year. Afternoon temperatures in the summer months exceed 100° F (38° C) at most stations, and daily highs of 115° F (46° C) are not uncommon in the interior. Temperatures drop considerably at night, however, especially inland. Nighttime lows in the winter range from 45° to 55° F (7° to 13° C), while daytime highs range from 86° to 102° F (30° to 36° C).

The frequency of vegetation increases from north to south. The Sudanic savanna, located in the country's extreme south, is studded with baobab trees and palmyra (rônier) palm trees. The savanna gradually gives way in the south-central region to a discontinuous belt of Sahelian vegetation that includes an occasional acacia tree. The rest of the country northward to the borders with Western Sahara and Algeria is arid desert. Antelope, lion, and elephant are found in the southern savanna. The Sahelian steppes in the south-central region are frequented by gazelle, ostrich, warthog, panther, hyena, and lynx; crocodile are found in the permanent streams.

Although only a tiny fraction of Mauritania is considered arable, it is cultivated exhaustively. It supplies only about half of Mauritania's needs, however. Almost 40 percent of the land is rangeland or pasture, and the nomadic herding of goats, sheep, and camels still occupies a large portion of the population. Mauritania has substantial reserves of iron ore, copper, and gypsum. Titanium and phosphate reserves have also been identified.

The people. The Moors (of mixed Arab-Berber and Sudanic black descent, all speaking Ḥassānīyah, an Arabic-based dialect) constitute the overwhelming majority of the population. The remainder is almost entirely black and consists of the Tukulor people, who live in the Sénégal River valley; the Fulani, who are dispersed throughout the south; and the Wolof, who live in the vicinity of Rosso in coastal southwestern Mauritania. The Tukulor and the Fulani speak Fulfulde, and the other groups have retained their respective traditional languages. Virtually all Mauritanians are Muslims. The population density of Mauritania is extremely low.

The economy. Mauritania has a developing mixed economy based largely on agriculture and mineral exports. The gross national product (GNP) is not growing as rapidly as the population, and the GNP per capita is relatively low.

Agriculture accounts for approximately one-third of the gross domestic product (GDP) and employs two-thirds of the work force, largely in subsistence-level farming. Millet, sorghum, rice, and other cereals are grown along the Sénégal River, and dates are grown in the oases. The production of livestock is the country's most important agricultural activity. Cyclical drought conditions can drastically lower output, and the construction of the Gorgol irrigation project on the Sénégal River was designed to improve this situation.

Fish are caught in the Atlantic; they are sold domestically and are also Mauritania's main export. The government allows foreign vessels to fish Mauritanian waters, provided they land and process their catches in Mauritania, thus boosting exports.

Mauritania's other principal source of wealth is derived from iron-ore production, which accounts for about one-eighth of the GDP but employs less than 5 percent of the work force. Development is under the Complexe Minier du Nord, or Cominor, which was formed from the nationalized holdings of a European company in 1974. A petroleum refinery was completed in 1978, and a company has been formed to reopen the copper mine at Akjoujt. Prospecting for petroleum, tungsten, iron, phosphates, and uranium is carried out by the state-owned Société Nationale Industrielle et Minière–Société d'Economie Mixte, which was opened to private participation in 1978. There is almost no significant industrial development outside the mining sector.

Services account for about one-fifth of the GDP and employ about one-fourth of the work force. The transportation system, outside the mineral shipment network, is generally poor, but the situation was improved in 1985 with the completion of the Trans-Mauritania highway linking Nouakchott with the more populous southeastern regions of the country.

Mauritania operated under a chronic budget deficit, and spending was boosted in the late 1970s by military involvement in Western Sahara, from which Mauritania withdrew in 1978 and relinquished its territorial claims in 1979. A trade deficit appeared as world demand for iron ore slackened in the early 1980s. The rapid growth of the fishing sector in the mid-1980s resulted in a trade surplus during the rest of the decade, though this also led to overharvesting by the late 1990s. Principal trading partners include France, Japan, Spain, Algeria, and Italy.

Government and social conditions. Mauritania has been a one-party military regime since a coup d'état in 1978. The 1960 constitution was suspended and replaced by a provisional constitution promulgated in 1980 by the Military Committee for National Salvation; this constitution was abandoned in 1981. In February 1980 Islāmic principles were adopted as the basis for the legal system. Despite the official abolition of slavery in July 1980, it was reported by the London-based Anti-Slavery Society that at least 100,000 people still lived in slavery. Slavery remained a volatile topic at the beginning of the 21st century, and human rights activists were occasionally harassed and imprisoned in Mauritania.

Even though Mauritania is a poor country, its social-welfare system provides old-age and maternity benefits; but benefits for unemployment and illness are inadequate or nonexistent. Infant mortality is high (about 80 per 1,000 births) and life expectancy low (about 50 years), though both rates are gradually improving. Even though the numbers and proportions of eligible students enrolled in primary and secondary schools have been increasing, illiteracy remains high, at more than 60 percent of the adult population. The University of Nouakchott was founded in 1981.

The food supply is considered adequate during normal years, but periodic droughts create pockets of malnutrition, promoting the spread of such life-threatening diseases as malaria, tuberculosis, measles, and influenza. The only major hospital is located in Nouakchott; most of the country's doctors also practice there.

Mauritania's news media, owned and operated by the government, are dominated by the national radio network (there is also a fledgling television station). Its single daily newspaper has a circulation of only 1,000, and there are fewer than 15,000 telephones.

The National Library at Nouakchott (founded in 1965 and the country's largest) has more than 10,000 volumes and a large collection of early manuscripts. The Arab and Muslim heritage of Mauritania's Moorish society is reflected in its arts. Its architecture is influenced by that of the Maghrib (region of North Africa bordering the Mediterranean Sea). Goldsmithing is among the country's fine-art traditions.

History. Mauritania's earliest inhabitants were blacks and Sanhadja Berbers. In the 11th and 12th centuries it was the cradle of the Berber Almoravid movement, which imposed Islām upon many of the neighbouring peoples of northwestern Africa. A caravan route that linked Morocco with Mauritania became an immigration route for Arab tribes moving southward in the 15th century; they eventually submerged the Berbers' power. The nomadic Arab tribes formed several powerful confederations: Trarza and Brakna, which dominated the Sénégal River region; Kunta in the east; and Rigaibāt (Regeibat) in the north. In the 15th century the Portuguese visited Mauritania and founded the fort of Arguin. The coastal territory was disputed among traders of different European nations and ultimately recognized as a French sphere of influence in the Senegal treaty of 1817. In 1903 a formal protectorate was extended over the territory, and in 1904 it was added to French West Africa; it was made a colony in 1920. In 1960 Mauritania achieved independence and left the French Community. A year later Mauritania was admitted to the United Nations. The country's first president, Moktar Ould Daddah, was ousted in a coup in 1978, and a military government was established. In 1979 Mauritania signed a peace accord with the Polisario Front in Algiers, which was seeking independence for Western Sahara, and the following year renounced its sovereignty over the Tiris el Gharbia region, which Morocco subsequently annexed. In 1980 slavery of blacks, practiced by northern nomads, was officially abolished, but an increasing policy of government Arabization—reflected in the adoption of Arabic as the language used in all government business in 1990—revealed the growing rift between Moors and black Mauritanians. Despite successful moves toward liberalizing the economy and the adoption of free elections, the 1990s were marked by factional conflict that typically broke along ethnic lines.

Mauritius, officially REPUBLIC OF MAURITIUS, island country, the central independent island state of the Mascarene group, lying about 500 miles (800 km) east of Madagascar in the Indian Ocean. It is situated at latitude 20°18′ S and longitude 57°36′ E and extends 35 miles (55 km) from north to south and 25 miles (40 km) from east to west. Its outlying territories are Rodriques Island, lying 340 miles (550 km) eastward, the Cargados Carajos Shoals, 250 miles (400 km) northeastward, and the Agalega Islands, 580 miles (930 km) northward from the main island. Mauritius also claims sovereignty over Diego Garcia in the Chagos Archipelago, some 1,200 miles (1,930 km) to the northeast, although this claim is disputed by Britain. The capital is Port Louis. Area 788 square miles (2,040 square km). Pop. (2000 est.) 1,184,000.

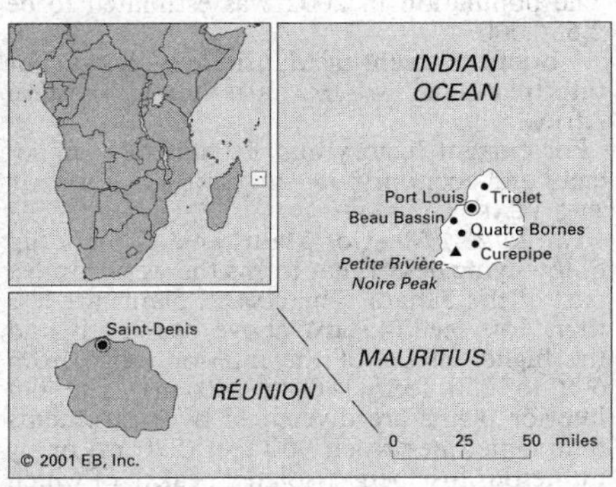

Mauritius

For current history and for statistics on society and economy, *see* BRITANNICA BOOK OF THE YEAR.

The land. Mauritius is volcanic in origin and almost surrounded by coral reefs. The northern part is a plain and rises to a central plateau, varying in elevation from about 900 to 2,400 feet (270 to 730 m) above sea level. The plateau is bordered by small mountains that may have formed the rim of an ancient volcano; the highest point (2,711 feet [826 m]) is the Petite Rivière–Noire Peak in the southwest. The two major rivers, the Grand River South East (about 25 miles [40 km] long) and Black River are also the major sources of hydroelectric power. Lake Vacoas, one of the major reservoirs, is the chief source of water.

The climate is maritime subtropical with fairly uniform temperature throughout the year. Mean temperatures vary from 74° F (23° C) at sea level to 67° F (19° C) on the high plateau. Two seasons are recognized: hot (December to April) and cool (June to September). Annual rainfall varies from 35 inches (900 mm) on the west coast to 60 inches (1,525 mm) on the southeast coast and about 200 inches (5,080 mm) on the central plateau. The vegetation includes 600 indigenous species, even though little original forest is now left. The fauna comprises samber (a long-tailed, dark brown deer), tenrec (a spiny insectivore), and mongoose, as well as a variety of birds and insects.

More than half of the country's area is arable. Sugarcane is the major crop.

The people. Approximately two-thirds of the population is of Indo-Pakistani origin, about one-fourth is Creole (of mixed French and African descent), and there are small numbers of Chinese and Franco-Mauritian descent. Half of the population is Hindu, about one-third Christian, and the rest are Muslims. The number of languages in use among the various ethnic groups is large, but English is the official language, and Creole has become the lingua franca of the country.

The population density is one of the highest in the world. Overpopulation became a serious problem after eradication of malaria in the 1960s. Driven by government policy, the rate of natural increase dropped rapidly in the last decades of the 20th century. Emigration, primarily to Britain and France, also helped slow the annual growth rate.

Economy. Mauritius has a mixed developing economy based on manufactured exports, agriculture, and tourism. Government efforts to diversify have been successful, and thus the island is no longer solely dependent on sugar production. The gross national product (GNP) grew much more rapidly than the population in the 1990s.

The agricultural sector accounts for only a small fraction of the gross domestic product (GDP) and employs roughly one-tenth of the work force. Sugar production, generating one-fifth of export earnings, occupies about nine-tenths of the total arable land, and the country depends heavily on food imports, mainly rice. Tea production has expanded; other important crops include potatoes, tomatoes, coconuts, and bananas. Technical assistance from Japan and Australia is regenerating the fishing industry.

The industrial sector accounts for approximately one-fourth of the GDP but employs two-fifths of the work force. There has been a steady increase in manufacturing. The Mauritius Export Processing Zone, which concentrates on labour-intensive processing of imported raw materials or semifinished goods for the export market, has successfully attracted foreign investment. Economically important manufactures include textiles, electronics, plastic and leather goods, and synthetic gemstones. Electricity is largely generated from imported petroleum.

Services account for about one-eighth of the GDP and employ one-third of the population.

Significant growth in the tourism industry from the 1970s made tourism a major earner of foreign exchange. An offshore banking facility began operations in 1989.

Imports, largely of manufactured goods, machinery, and foodstuffs, outweigh exports of clothing and textiles, sugar, processed diamonds and synthetic stores, and fish. Leading trading partners are the countries of the European Union and the United States.

Government and social conditions. Under the constitution adopted in 1968, Mauritius was a constitutional monarchy with the British monarch as head of state. In 1991 a constitutional amendment was passed, providing for a republican form of government, with a president as head of state. The amendment went into effect in 1992. Legislative power is vested in a Legislative Assembly elected every five years and consisting of 62 elected and 4 appointed members. The president and vice president are elected by the Legislative Assembly for terms of five years. Executive power is exercised by a Council of Ministers headed by the prime minister. The Supreme Court is the highest judicial authority.

The social welfare system comprises a network of hospitals and dispensaries, and community centres have been set up in areas not served by social welfare centres. Old age pensions, family allowances, and other measures for social protection are also provided. Overcrowding is prevalent in urban areas, and government provides loans to local authorities for urban housing schemes.

Virtually all children of primary-school age receive primary education. The standard of secondary education is very high, and the University of Mauritius (founded in 1965) has faculties of agriculture, technology, education, and administration.

The Mauritius Broadcasting Corporation transmits foreign radio and television broadcasts and also locally produced radio and television programs. School broadcasting constitutes an important part of the service. There are numerous daily newspapers and weekly publications published in English, French, Chinese, and other languages.

Cultural life. Interest in arts and letters and the sciences is promoted by voluntary associations. The island has produced talented poets and novelists. Representational and abstract painting flourishes. The national cultural institutions are the Mauritius Institute and the Mauritius Archives. The theatre is popular, and performances of comparatively high quality are given by local amateur groups. There are both public and institutional libraries.

History. Mauritius was probably known to Arab seafarers from the 10th century, or earlier. It was visited by the Portuguese in the early 16th century, but they did not settle the island. The Dutch took possession from 1598 to 1710, called it Mauritius for the *stadhouder* (governor) Maurice of Nassau, and attempted to settle the island in 1638–58 and again in 1664–1710; abandoning their attempts, they left it to pirates. In 1721 the French East India Company occupied Mauritius, which was renamed Île de France. Settlement proceeded slowly over the next 40 years. Until 1767, when the French Ministry of marine took over the administration, it was governed by the French East India Company. The French authorities brought African slaves to the island, sugar planting was the main industry, and the colony prospered. At the beginning of the 19th century, when England and France were at war, privateers based on Île de France were a continual threat to British and Indian merchant vessels. In 1810 the British captured the island, and, upon the restoration of peace in 1814, it was confirmed to the British by the Treaty of Paris. The customs, laws, and language remained French, but the name Mauritius was reinstated. Slavery was abolished in 1835, and the slaves were replaced by Indian indentured labourers. Mauritius prospered in the 1850s, but competition from beet sugar caused a decline. The malaria epidemic of 1866–68 drove shipping away from Port Louis, which further declined after the opening of the Suez Canal in 1869. During World War I, when sugar prices rose, the economy prospered, but the depression of the 1930s changed the situation drastically, culminating in labour unrest in 1937. World War II did not improve the economic situation, and after 1945 economic reforms were introduced. Political and administrative reforms were also initiated, which led to the 1968 independence of Mauritius within the Commonwealth. The effects of a devastating cyclone in late 1979 and of falling world sugar prices in the early 1980s led the government to initiate a vigorous program of agricultural diversification and to develop the processing of imported goods for the export market. Mauritius emerged as a political success story after independence with an open multiparty system, free elections, and a competitive political process. This political stability and a balmy climate allowed the country to grow into a major tourist destination by the end of the 20th century, although the general prosperity this generated did not penetrate to all levels of society.

Mauritius hemp (species *Furcraea gigantea*), Portuguese PITEIRA, French ALOE, plant of the family agave (Agavaceae), and its fibre, belonging to the leaf fibre (*q.v.*) group. Despite its name, it is not a true hemp.

Although the plant is native to Brazil, commercial production of the fibre did not begin there until about 1875. The plant was introduced to Mauritius in the late 18th century. Fibre from the highland is referred to as "aloe malgache," and from the lower areas as "aloe creole." Cultivation was established in East Africa, Ceylon (now Sri Lanka), and St. Helena late in the 19th century.

The plant has lance-shaped leaves growing directly from the short plant stalk to form a dense rosette. The gray-green leaves are 4 to 7 feet (1.2 to 2.1 m) long and about 8 inches (20 cm) across the widest portion. In some varieties they are edged with thorns. The flower stalk, which appears near the end of the plant's life span, some 8 to 10 years after planting, grows up to 40 feet (12.2 m) and bears white flowers about 1.5 inches (3.8 cm) long.

Mauritius hemp, which is cultivated mainly on large plantations, produces leaves suitable for harvest within 3 to 4 years after planting and each 18 to 36 months thereafter, yielding about 25–30 leaves at each harvest. Fibre is usually obtained by machine decortication, a scraping process that is sometimes preceded by several days of retting. Processing is completed by washing and drying, and the fibre is sometimes brushed, which adds softness and lustre.

Careful processing of the fibre strands, about 4 to 7 feet long, yields creamy-white fibre with fair lustre. Mauritius hemp is not as strong as the leaf fibres sisal and henequen but is softer and finer. It has an affinity for dyestuffs and is fairly resistant to deterioration in fresh water but is subject to damage in salt water. The fibre is made into bagging and other coarse fabrics and is sometimes mixed with other fibres to improve colour in rope.

Mauritshuis, in full KONINKLIJK KABINET VAN SCHILDERIJEN (MAURITSHUIS) (Dutch: Royal Gallery of Paintings [Mauritshuis]), picture gallery in The Hague housed in a palace (1633–44) designed by Jacob van Campen and built by Pieter Post for Prince John Maurice of Nassau. The collection, opened to the public in 1820, is especially noted for its Flemish and Dutch paintings from the 15th to the 17th century.

Maurois, André, pseudonym of ÉMILE HERZOG (b. July 26, 1885, Elbeuf, France—d. Oct. 9, 1967, Paris), biographer, novelist, essayist, and prominent personality in French letters for 50 years.

Born into a prosperous family of textile manufacturers, Maurois came under the influence of the French philosopher and teacher Alain (Émile-Auguste Chartier). He was a liaison officer in the British army during World War I, and his first literary success was a humorous commentary on warfare and the British character in *Les Silences du Colonel Bramble* (1918; *The Silence of Colonel Bramble*). His novels, including *Bernard Quesnay* (1926) and *Climats* (1928; *Whatever Gods May Be*), focus on middle-class provincial life. As a historian he demonstrated a broad culture in his popular histories: *Histoire de l'Angleterre* (1937; "History of England"), and *Histoire des États-Unis* (1943; "History of the United States"). Maurois is best known, in both France and the English-speaking world, for biographies that maintain the narrative interest of novels. *À la Recherche de Marcel Proust* (1949; *The Quest for Proust*) is considered his finest biography.

Maurois
Harlingue—H. Roger-Viollet

Mauropous, John (b. *c.* 1000, Paphlagonia, Byzantine Empire [now in Turkey]—d. after *c.* 1075–81, Constantinople), Byzantine scholar and ecclesiastic, author of sermons, poems and epigrams, letters, a saint's life, and a large collection of canons, or church hymns (many unpublished).

The chronology of Mauropous' life is uncertain. He was a private tutor in Constantinople in the first quarter of the 11th century and was at court in Constantine IX's reign (1042–55) at the instigation of his friend and pupil Michael Psellus. About 1050 he became metropolitan of Euchaita in Asia Minor; later he became a monk.

Maurras, Charles (-Marie-Photius) (b. April 20, 1868, Martigues, France—d. Nov. 16, 1952, Tours), French writer and political theorist, a major intellectual influence in early 20th-century Europe whose "integral nationalism" anticipated some of the ideas of fascism.

Maurras was born of a Royalist and Roman Catholic family. In 1880, while he was engaged in studies in the Collège de Sacré-Coeur at Aix-en-Provence, he contracted an illness that left him permanently deaf, and he took refuge in books. Having lost the religious faith of his parents, he built his own conception of the world, aided by the great poets from Homer to Frédéric Mistral, as well as the Greek and Roman philosophers.

In 1891, soon after his arrival in Paris, Maurras founded, with Jean Moréas, a group of young poets opposed to the Symbolists and later known as the *école romane.* The group favoured classical restraint and clarity over what they considered to be the vague, emotional character of Symbolist work. After the "Dreyfus affair," which polarized French opinion of the right and left, Maurras became an ardent monarchist. In June 1899 he was one of the founders of *L'Action française,* a review devoted to integral nationalism, which emphasized the supremacy of the state, and advocated the primacy of the interests of France in its relations with other nations. In 1908, with the help of Léon Daudet, the review became a daily newspaper, the organ of the Royalist Party. Over a period of 40 years, its causes were often reinforced by public demonstrations and riots, spectacular lawsuits and trials.

Maurras also acquired a reputation as the author of *Le Chemin de paradis* (1895), philosophical short stories; *Anthinea* (1900), travel essays chiefly on Greece; and *Les Amants de Venise* (1900), dealing with the love affair of George Sand and Alfred de Musset. *Enquête sur la monarchie* (1900; "Enquiry Concerning Monarchy") and *L'Avenir de l'intelligence* (1905; "The Future of Intelligence") give a comprehensive view of his political ideas. After World War I, he was still admired in literary quarters as the poet of *La Musique intérieure* (1925), the critic of *Barbarie et poésie* (1925), and the memorialist of *Au signe de Flore* (1931). But he lost some of his political influence when on Dec. 29, 1926, the Roman Catholic church placed some of his books and *L'Action française* on the Index, thus depriving him of many sympathizers among the French clergy. The reason given for the ban was the movement's subordination of religion to politics.

Maurras was received into the Académie Française in 1938. During the German occupation in World War II, he became a strong supporter of the Pétain government. He was arrested in September 1944 and the following January was sentenced to life imprisonment and excluded from the Académie. In 1952 he was released on grounds of health from the prison at Clairvaux and entered the St. Symphorien clinic in Tours. Reconciled with the Roman Catholic church, he produced the poems of *La Balance intérieure* (1952) and a book on Pope Pius X, *Le Bienheureux Pie X, sauveur de la France* (1953).

Maurus Servius Honoratus: *see* Servius.

Maury, Matthew Fontaine (b. Jan. 14, 1806, Spotsylvania county, Va., U.S.—d. Feb. 1, 1873, Lexington, Va.), U.S. naval officer, pioneer hydrographer, and one of the founders of oceanography.

Maury entered the navy in 1825 as a midshipman, circumnavigated the globe (1826–30), and in 1836 was promoted to the rank of lieutenant. In 1839 he was lamed in a stagecoach accident, which made him unfit for active service. In 1842 he was placed in charge of the Depot of Charts and Instruments, out of which grew the U.S. Naval Observatory and Hydrographic Office. To gather information on maritime winds and currents, Maury distributed to captains specially prepared logbooks from which he compiled pilot charts, enabling ships to shorten the time of sea voyages. In 1848 he published maps of the main wind fields of the Earth. Maury's work inspired the first international marine conference, held in Brussels in 1853. He was U.S. representative at the meeting that led to the establishment of the International Hydrographic Bureau. Provided with worldwide information, Maury was able to produce charts of the Atlantic, Pacific, and Indian oceans. He also prepared a profile of the Atlantic seabed, which proved the feasibility of laying a transatlantic telegraph cable. In 1855 he published the first modern oceanographic text, *The Physical Geography of the Sea.* In that year his *Sailing Directions* included a section recommending that eastbound and westbound steamers travel in separate lanes in the North Atlantic to prevent collisions.

On the outbreak (1861) of the American Civil War, Maury returned to Virginia to become head of coast, harbour, and river defenses for the Confederate Navy, for which he attempted to develop an electric torpedo. In 1862 he went to England as a special agent of the Confederacy, and at the war's end (1865) he went to Mexico, where the emperor Maximilian made him imperial commissioner of immigration so that Maury could establish a Confederate colony there. In 1866, when the emperor abandoned this scheme, Maury went back to England. He returned to the United States in 1868 and accepted the professorship of meteorology at Virginia Military Institute, a post he held until his death. Maury Hall at Annapolis, Md., is named in his honour, and his birthday is a school holiday in Virginia.

BIBLIOGRAPHY. Charles Lee Lewis, *Matthew Fontaine Maury: The Pathfinder of the Seas* (1927, reprinted 1980); Francis Leigh Williams, *Matthew Fontaine Maury: Scientist of the Sea* (1963).

Mauryan empire (*c.* 321–185 BC), in ancient India, a state centred at Pāṭaliputra (later Patna) near the junction of the Son and Ganges rivers. In the wake of Alexander the Great's death, Candra Gupta, its dynastic founder, carved out the majority of an empire that encompassed most of the subcontinent except for the Tamil south. The Mauryan empire was an efficient and highly organized autocracy with a standing army and civil service. This bureaucracy and its operation was the model for the *Artha-śāstra* ("Treatise on the Aims of Life"), a work of political economy similar in tone and scope to Machiavelli's *The Prince.*

Much is known of the reign of the Buddhist Mauryan emperor Aśoka (reigned *c.* 265–238 BC, or *c.* 273–232 BC) from the exquisitely executed stone edicts that he had erected throughout his realm. These comprise some of the oldest deciphered original texts of India. Aśoka campaigned little to expand the realm; rather, his conquest consisted of sending many Buddhist emissaries throughout Asia and commissioning some of the finest works of ancient Indian art.

After Aśoka's death the empire shrank because of invasions, defections by southern princes, and quarrels over ascension. The last ruler, Bṛhadratha, was killed in 185 BC by his Brahman commander in chief, Puṣyamitra, who then founded the Śuṅga dynasty, which ruled in central India for about a century.

Mauser rifle, any of a family of bolt-action rifles designed by Peter Paul Mauser (1838–1914), a German who had worked in an arms plant before entering the German army in 1859. Mauser's first successful design was a single-shot, 11-millimetre, bolt-action rifle that became the forerunner of many important designs. In 1880 Mauser applied a tubular magazine to his rifle, and the result was selected (1884) by the Prussian government as a basic infantry weapon.

The tubular magazine, which held eight rounds, proved not entirely successful, and Mauser adjusted the design until he devised a five-round box-style magazine located within the forearm. This became the basic infantry weapon of the German army in 1898, and its bolt action was widely—virtually universally—copied around the world. It has been chambered in a wide variety of calibres, but original German Mausers were all made in 7.92 mm.

mausoleum, large and impressive sepulchral monument. The word is derived from Mausolus, ruler of Caria, in whose memory his widow Artemisia raised a splendid tomb at Halicarnassus *c.* 353–*c.* 350 BC. Some remains of this monument are now in the British Museum. Probably the most ambitious mausoleum is the famous white marble Tāj Mahal at Āgra, in India, built by the Mughal emperor Shāh Jahān for his favourite wife, who died in 1631. He originally intended to build another in black marble, opposite the Tāj Mahal, but died before work could begin. Other notable examples include the mausoleum called Hadrian's Tomb, now the Castel Sant'Angelo, Rome; that of Frederick William III and Queen Louisa of Mecklenburg-Strelitz at Charlottenburg, near Berlin; of Napoleon III at Farnborough, Hampshire, Eng.; and of Vladimir Lenin at Moscow.

Mausolus (d. 353/352 BC), Persian satrap (governor), though virtually an independent ruler, of Caria, in southwestern Anatolia, from 377/376 to 353. He is best known from the name of his monumental tomb, the so-called Mausoleum—considered one of the Seven Wonders of the Ancient World—a word now used to designate any large and imposing burial structure.

By moving his capital from Mylasa in the interior to Halicarnassus on the coast, Mausolus indicated that he would attempt to make Caria an expansionist power. In 362 he joined the revolt of the satraps of Anatolia against the Persian king Artaxerxes II (reigned 404–359/358) but abandoned the struggle just in time to keep from going down in defeat with his allies. Thereafter Mausolus was a nearly autonomous ruler who absorbed part of Lycia, immediately to the southeast, and several Ionian Greek cities northwest of Caria. He backed the islands of Rhodes, Cos, and Chios (all off the west coast of Anatolia) and their allies in their war against Athens (the Social War of 357–355), and the victory of this coalition brought Rhodes and Cos into his sphere of influence.

The planning of his great tomb was begun by Mausolus; after his death, Artemisia, who was both his sister and his widow, directed the construction. Although now a ruin, the tomb was an enormous structure containing colossal figures of the Carian king and his queen. It was designed by the famous Greek architect Pythius and decorated with works by the Greek sculptors Scopas, Bryaxis, Timotheus, and Leochares.

Mauss, Marcel (b. May 10, 1872, Épinal, Fr.—d. Feb. 10, 1950, Paris), French sociologist and anthropologist whose contributions include a highly original comparative study of the relation between forms of exchange and social structure. His views on the theory and method of ethnology are thought to have influenced many eminent social scientists, including Claude Lévi-Strauss, A.R. Radcliffe-Brown, E.E. Evans-Pritchard, and Melville J. Herskovits.

Mauss was the nephew of sociologist Émile Durkheim, who contributed much to his intellectual formation and whom he assisted in the preparation of a number of works, notably *Le Suicide.* Mauss also assisted, and eventually succeeded, Durkheim as editor of the journal *L'Année Sociologique* ("The Sociological Year"). In 1902 he began his career as professor of primitive religion at the École Pratique des Hautes Études ("Practical School of Higher Studies"), Paris. He was a founder of the Ethnology Institute of the University of Paris (1925) and also taught at the Collège de France (1931–39). He possessed an encyclopaedic mind familiar with an exceptional breadth of ethnographic and linguistic knowledge. His lectures were described as abounding in new and productive ideas that inspired books and theses. A political activist for many years, he supported Alfred Dreyfus in his famed court battle, aligned himself with the socialist leader Jean Jaurès, and assisted in founding the socialist daily *L'Humanité* (1904).

Although he never did fieldwork, Mauss turned the attention of French sociologists, philosophers, and psychologists toward ethnology. He took pains to distinguish points of view in nonliterate societies, thus preserving their freshness and specificity and, at the same time, strengthening the link between psychology and anthropology. Among his earliest works is "Essai sur la nature et la fonction du sacrifice" (1899; *Sacrifice: Its Nature and Function*). His most influential work is thought to be *Essai sur le don* (1925; *The Gift*); concentrating on the forms of exchange and contract in Melanesia, Polynesia, and northwestern North America, the work explores the religious, legal, economic, mythological, and other aspects of giving, receiving, and repaying. This study provides an excellent example of Mauss's approach to method in its concern with a limited segment of social phenomena viewed in its systematic entirety. Mauss also wrote on magic, the concept of self, mourning rites, and other topics. *Sociologie et anthropologie* (1950) is a collection of essays he published between 1904 and 1938.

Mauthausen, one of the most notorious of Nazi concentration camps, located near the village of Mauthausen, on the Danube, 12 miles (20 km) east of Linz, Austria. It was established in April 1938, shortly after Austria was annexed to Nazi Germany. Starting as a satellite of Dachau, it became an independent camp in the spring of 1939, acquiring satellites of its own throughout Austria, all collectively called Mauthausen. The camps became the main centre for the imprisonment of anti-Nazis drawn from all over Europe, including 10,000 Spanish Republicans; in November 1941 Soviet prisoners of war began arriving. All categories were officially designated *Rückkehr unerwünscht* ("return not desired"), and the prisoners were thus subjected to the most grueling work, especially in the local quarries, and starved and beaten. Unruly prisoners or captured escapees of other camps were delivered to Mauthausen for punishment by beating, hard labour, shooting, or gassing. The main camp was liberated by U.S. troops in May 1945. Of the estimated 335,000 prisoners who passed through Mauthausen and its satellites, more than 122,000 died there by execution or privation.

Mauthner, Fritz (b. Nov. 22, 1849, Hořice, Bohemia—d. June 29, 1923, Meersburg, Ger.), German author, theatre critic, and exponent of philosophical Skepticism derived from a critique of human knowledge.

Though his novels and popular parodies of German classical poems brought him moderate literary fame, he spent most of the time between 1876 and 1905 as a theatre critic for *Berliner Tageblatt*. As a philosopher he was preoccupied with the implications of language. He had read Friedrich Nietzsche and Otto Ludwig's *Shakespeare-Studien,* and he admired Bismarck for combining a life of action with a contempt for words and ideologies. Mauthner believed that words have pragmatic social value, but, because they are applied subjectively and are ever changing, they represent sense experience only (and that imperfectly). Further, words cannot adequately express concepts, and they necessarily misrepresent reality.

Such considerations led Mauthner to philosophical Skepticism and the postulation of a criterion of truth based on personal experiences shaped by cultural influences. Mauthner applied linguistic analysis in both his major works: *Wörterbuch der Philosophie,* 2 vol. (1910; "Dictionary of Philosophy"), and *Der Atheismus und seine Geschichte im Abendlande,* 4 vol. (1921–23; "Atheism and Its History in the West"). His Skepticism was not new, but his approach to epistemology through language was unique.

Mauve, Anton (b. Sept. 18, 1838, Zaandam, Neth.—d. Feb. 5, 1888, Arnhem), Dutch Romantic painter who, like his friends Jozef Israëls and the three Maris brothers, was profoundly influenced by the French landscape painter Camille Corot and the Barbizon school. Mauve's work consists largely of landscapes and scenes of rural life in The Netherlands.

Mauve settled at The Hague around 1870, painting in the neighbouring fishing village of Scheveningen. In 1885 he went to live in the country at Laren, near Hilversum, where he brought together a group of landscape painters who came to be known as the "Dutch Barbizon." Mauve's pictures are subdued in colour and close to Corot in their harmonies of grays and blues. Major pictures include "Cows in Meadow" and "Dune Landscape." He was an accomplished watercolourist. His wife was a cousin of Vincent van Gogh, to whom Mauve gave advice about oil painting in 1881 and 1882.

Mavrokordátos, Aléxandros (b. Feb. 11, 1791, Constantinople [now Istanbul, Tur.]—d. Aug. 18, 1865, Aegina, Greece), statesman, one of the founders and first political leaders of independent Greece.

The scion of a Greek Phanariot house (living in the Greek quarter of Constantinople) long distinguished in the Turkish imperial service, Mavrokordátos was secretary (1812–17) to Ioannis Karadja, hospodar (prince) of Walachia (now in Romania), and later went into exile with his master. In 1821, however, Mavrokordátos joined the revolutionaries in Greece who had just rebelled against the Turks; despite their suspicions of his Phanariot origins, he soon established himself as head of a regional government at Missolonghi, in western Greece. During December 1821–January 1822 he presided over the first National Assembly, at Epidaurus, and led in the drafting of a constitution.

Mavrokordátos was elected first president of the Hellenic republic, but the new government exercised little actual power, and he soon returned to Missolonghi, where he conducted a successful defense against the Turks (November 1822–January 1823). He represented the national government as governor-general (1823–25) at Missolonghi, receiving there Lord Byron, the famous English poet-partisan of the Greek cause. He later became the principal leader of the pro-English party, though he did not approve of the Greek demand for British protection (June–July 1825).

Mavrokordátos, painting by an unknown artist; in the Ethnological Museum, Athens
Dimitri Papadimos

Ignored during the presidency of the Russophile Count Ioánnis Kapodístrias (1827–31), Mavrokordátos was appointed minister of finance (1832) and then prime minister (1833) under Greece's first king, Otto. He later served as Greek envoy in Munich, Berlin, London, and finally Constantinople. Recalled from London by the king in February 1841 to head the foreign ministry, Mavrokordátos was soon charged with the formation of a government with himself as minister of the interior (July 1841); but his reformist administration soon foundered in the face of royal absolutism, and on Aug. 20, 1841, he was forced to resign. After the revolution of 1843 he was again prime minister (1844, 1854–55).

Mavura, also called MANUZA (fl. mid-17th century), African emperor who was installed as the ruler of the great Mwene Matapa empire by the Portuguese. His conversion to Christianity enabled the Portuguese to extend their commercial influence into the African interior from their trading base in Mozambique on the East African coast.

Mavura enlisted Portuguese aid in deposing his uncle Kapranzine as emperor in 1629. Converting to Christianity, he took the name Filipe and swore vassalage to the king of Portugal. In 1631, again with Portuguese assistance, he decisively defeated his uncle and ruled with complete authority as long as he lived. During his reign Portugal established missionary and trading stations in central Africa for the first time.

Consult the INDEX *first*

Māwardī, al- (d. 1058, Baghdad), Muslim jurist who played an important role in formulating orthodox political theory as to the nature of the authority of the caliph.

As a young man al-Māwardī entered the service of the caliph and soon came to be entrusted with the conduct of important negotiations with neighbouring princes. When the Būyid emirs, who since 946 had subjected the caliphs of Baghdad to their temporal authority, were weakened by internal dissensions and military revolts, the moment seemed ripe for an attempt to reassert caliphal authority, and al-Māwardī was commissioned to write an exposition of the prerogatives of the caliph sanctioned by religious law. His *Ordinances of Government* became an influential statement of Muslim political theory. Although it is essentially theoretical (as a design for the restoration of the Sunnite caliphate), the work was not, as some scholars have suggested, an abstract description of caliphal authority; it did, however, adjust the orthodox ideal of caliphal power to the realities of the time, treating such subjects as the rights, duties, and preferred characteristics of the caliph.

mawlā, also spelled MAWLĀY (Muslim title): *see* mullah.

Mawlānā (Persian poet): *see* Jalāl ad-Dīn ar-Rūmī.

Mawlawīyah, Turkish MEVLEVIYAH, fraternity of Ṣūfīs (Muslim mystics) founded in Konya (Qonya), Anatolia, by the Persian Ṣūfī poet Jalāl ad-Dīn ar-Rūmī (d. 1273), whose popular title *mawlānā* (Arabic: "our master") gave the order its name. The order, propagated throughout Anatolia, controlled Konya and environs by the 15th century and in the 17th century appeared in Constantinople (Istanbul). European travelers identified the Mawlawīyah as dancing (or whirling) dervishes, based on their observations of the order's ritual prayer (dhikr), performed spinning on the right foot to the accompaniment of musical instruments.

After the dissolution of all Ṣūfī brotherhoods in Turkey by a decree of September 1925, the Mawlawīyah survived in a few monasteries in Aleppo, Syria, and a scattering of small towns in the Middle East. Special permission granted by the Turkish government in 1954 allowed the Mawlawī dervishes of Konya to perform their ritual dances for tourists during two weeks of every year. Despite government opposition the order continued to exist in Turkey as a religious body into the late 20th century. The tomb of ar-Rūmī at Konya, although officially a museum, attracted a steady stream of devotees.

mawlid, also spelled MAWLŪD, or MĪLĀD, in Islām, the birthday of a holy figure, especially the birthday of the Prophet Muḥammad (Mawlid an-Nabī).

Muḥammad's birthday, arbitrarily fixed by tradition as the 12th day of the month of Rabīʿ I, *i.e.,* the day of Muḥammad's death, was not celebrated by the masses of Muslim faithful until about the 13th century. At the end of the 11th century in Egypt, the ruling Shīʿite Fāṭimids (descendants of ʿAlī, the fourth caliph, through his wife Fāṭimah, Muḥammad's daughter) observed four *mawlid*s, those of Muḥammad, ʿAlī, Fāṭimah, and the ruling caliph. The festivals, however, were simple processions of court officials, held in daylight hours, that culminated in the recitation of three sermons (khutbahs) in the presence of the caliph.

Sunnites, who constitute the major branch of Islām, regard a *mawlid* celebration held in 1207 as the first *mawlid* festival. That occasion was organized by Muẓaffar ad-Dīn Gökburi, brother-in-law of the Egyptian sultan Saladin, at Irbīl, near Mosul (Iraq). It closely parallels the modern *mawlid* in form. The actual day of Muḥammad's birth was preceded by an entire month of merrymaking. Musicians, jugglers, and assorted entertainers attracted people from as far away as Baghdad and Niṣībīn (modern Nusaybin, Turkey); and Muslim scholars, jurists, mystics, and poets began arriving as much as two months in advance. Two days before the formal *mawlid* a large number of camels, sheep, and oxen were sacrificed, and on the eve of *mawlid* a torchlight procession passed through the town. On the morning of the *mawlid,* the faithful and the soldiery assembled in front of a specially erected pulpit to hear the sermon. The religious dignitaries were then honoured with special robes, and all those attending were invited to feast at the prince's expense.

The *mawlid* festival quickly spread throughout the Muslim world, partly because of a contemporary corresponding enthusiasm for Ṣūfism (Islāmic mysticism), which allowed Islām to become a personal experience. Even in Arabia, where the Prophet's birthplace and tomb had been simply the sites of pious but not required pilgrimage, the *mawlid* celebrations took hold. Many Muslim theologians could not accept the new festivities, branding them *bidʿah*s, innovations possibly leading into sin. The *mawlid,* indeed, betrayed a Christian influence; Christians in Muslim lands observed Christmas in similar ways, and Muslims often participated in the celebration. Modern fundamentalist Muslims such as the Wahhābīyah still view the *mawlid* festivities as idolatrous.

*Mawlid*s, however, continue to be celebrated and have been extended to popular saints and the founders of Ṣūfi brotherhoods. The *mawlid* poems, which relate Muḥammad's life and virtues, are also widely popular outside the times of regular feasts. *Mawlid*s are also recited in commemoration of deceased relatives.

Mawson, Sir Douglas (b. May 5, 1882, Shipley, Yorkshire, Eng.—d. Oct. 14, 1958, Adelaide, S. Aus., Australia), Australian geologist and explorer whose travels in the Antarctic earned him worldwide acclaim.

Mawson received a bachelor's degree in mining engineering from Sydney University in 1902, and his field investigations in the Broken Hill mining area of west-central New South Wales earned him a doctorate in science from the university in 1909. A member of the scientific staff of Sir Ernest Henry Shackleton's Antarctic Expedition (1907), Mawson, together with T.W.E. David, reached the south magnetic pole on the high ice plateau of Victoria Land on Jan. 16, 1909. The two men made this landmark journey by sledge. From 1911 to 1914 Mawson led the Australasian Antarctic Expedition and from 1929 to 1931 directed the combined British, Australian, and New Zealand Antarctic Expedition. His explorations enabled Australia to claim some 2,500,000 square miles (6,475,000 square km) of the Antarctic continent. For his achievements as an explorer and scientist, he was knighted in 1914. In addition to his other activities, Mawson edited and contributed to the 22-volume *Reports of Australasian Antarctic Expeditions.* Another of his most notable works was the book *The Home of the Blizzard* (1915).

Max, Adolphe (b. Dec. 30, 1869, Brussels, Belg.—d. Nov. 6, 1939, Brussels), Belgian Liberal statesman who as burgomaster of Brussels at the beginning of World War I gained national fame for his resistance to the German occupation.

Max
© A.C.L., Brussels

Max studied at the Free University of Brussels and obtained a law degree in 1889. He held office in the governments of Brabant and Brussels from 1896 and between 1903 and 1909 worked as a journalist. He was elected burgomaster of Brussels in 1909, and in August 1914, when the German troops entered Brussels, he refused to perform his duties under the authority of the German-appointed governor and demanded complete freedom of action. He worked to reduce the taxes and requisitions that were imposed by the Germans on Brussels, and he formed a national committee to provide supplies to the Belgian population.

Max was arrested by the Germans in September 1914 and was imprisoned in the fortress of Namur before being sent to Germany for the duration of the war. Shortly after his celebrated return to Brussels in November 1918, he was appointed minister of state and was elected to the chamber of representatives the following year. He remained as burgomaster of Brussels until his death in 1939.

Max Planck Society for the Advancement of Science, German MAX-PLANCK-GESELLSCHAFT ZUR FÖRDERUNG DER WISSENSCHAFTEN, official scientific research organization of Germany. It is headquartered in Munich. It was founded in 1911 as the Kaiser Wilhelm Society (Kaiser-Wilhelm Gesellschaft), but its name was changed in 1948 to honour the great German physicist Max Planck (1858–1947), the originator of the quantum theory. The society is funded by the government and does research in areas of particular scientific importance and in highly specialized or interdisciplinary fields. Studies in such fields often require specialized facilities as well as funds and staff that cannot be supplied by the universities alone, and so the society brings together the necessary ingredients for productive, long-term research. The society supports more than 35 research institutes throughout Germany, each of which is devoted to a separate field or group of fields covering the medical and biological sciences, chemistry, physics, and technology. There are Max Planck institutes devoted to such disciplines as molecular genetics, biochemistry, plasma physics, and radio astronomy.

Maxakali, South American Indians speaking related languages of the Maxakali branch of the Macro-Ge language family. The tribes—Maxakali, Macuní, Kumanaxo, Kapoxo, Pañame, and Monoxo—live in the mountains near the border between the Brazilian *estados* ("states") of Minas Gerais and Bahia, near the headwaters of the Itanhêm River. Over the past century the Maxakali have moved progressively eastward from their original home along the upper Mucuri River. The Maxakali numbered about 400 in the late 20th century.

At the time of the first contact between the Maxakali and the Portuguese, the Maxakali were established agriculturists. They raised corn (maize), sweet potatoes, and beans; some of the groups raised cassava and cotton, which they harvested with simple weighted digging sticks. The Maxakali supplemented their agricultural produce by hunting a variety of forest animals and birds and by gathering fruits, nuts, seeds, and the like.

Traditionally, the Maxakali lived in dome-shaped single-family houses made of palm fronds matted over a framework of branches anchored in the ground. They made fibre from the inner bark of the embauba tree and used it to make nets, baskets, bags, hammocks, and cord. They made and used bows and arrows, as well as an assortment of other weapons. They were familiar with and used a wide variety of pharmacologically active substances, including fish poisons and hallucinogens.

Maxamed Cabdulle Xasan, SAYYID, also spelled MOHAMMED ABDULLAH HASSAN (b. April 7, 1864, Dulbahante area, British Somaliland [now Doli Bahanta, Somalia]—d. Dec. 21, 1920, Imi, Eth.), Somali religious and nationalist leader (called the "Mad Mullah" by the British) who for 20 years led armed resistance to the British, Italian, and Ethiopian colonial forces in Somaliland. Because of his active resistance to the British and his vision of a Somalia united in a Muslim brotherhood transcending clan divisions, Sayyid Maxamed is seen as a forerunner of modern Somali nationalism.

Maxamed's father belonged to a clan from the Ogaden region of Ethiopia, but he was raised among his mother's Dulbahante clan. At a young age he showed great learning in the Qur'ān, and, during a pilgrimage to Mecca in 1894, he joined the Ṣaliḥīyah, a militant, reformist, and puritanical Ṣūfī order. Soon after his return to Somaliland, he began urging the expulsion of the English "infidels" and their missionaries and a strict observance by all Somalis of the Islāmic faith. Through his stirring oratory and didactic verse (some of his poems are considered classics in Somalia), Maxamed attracted a fanatical group of followers who became known as dervishes. In 1899 he declared a holy war (jihad) on the colonial powers and their Somali collaborators. Between 1900 and 1904, four major British, Ethiopian, and Italian expeditions were made against Maxamed. By 1905 he was forced to conclude a truce, under which he and his followers constructed a small theocratic state in the Italian protectorate. In 1908 he began his holy war again, winning a major victory at Dulmadobe in 1913. Early in 1920, however, the dervish stronghold at Taalex (Taleh) was bombed, and Maxamed escaped to the Ogaden, where he died of influenza. With his death the dervish rebellion ceased.

Maxentius, Basilica of, also called BASILICA OF CONSTANTINE, large, roofed hall in Rome, begun by the emperor Maxentius and finished by Constantine about AD 313. This huge building, the greatest of the Roman basilicas, covered about 7,000 square yards (5,600 square m) and included a central nave that was 265 feet (80 m) long and 83 feet (25 m) wide.

The basilica followed in construction and plan the great hall of the Roman baths. The vaults over the bays on the north side are still to be seen overhanging without support, a striking testimony to the marvelous cohesion and enduring strength of Roman concrete construction.

Maxentius, Marcus Aurelius Valerius (d. 312), Roman emperor from 306 to 312. His father, the emperor Maximian, abdicated with Diocletian in 305. In the new tetrarchy (two augusti with a caesar under each) that was set up after these abdications, Maxentius was passed over in favour of Flavius Valerius Severus, who was made a caesar, and then, in 306, an augustus. But discontent with the policies of Severus at Rome caused Maxentius to be proclaimed augustus there on Oct. 28, 306.

Maximian, recalled to the throne to support Maxentius, defeated and killed Severus in 307. Shortly thereafter, however, father and son quarreled, and Maximian sought refuge with Constantine, who had been designated an augustus by Maximian. Maxentius at first controlled Italy, Spain, and Africa, but in 308 the vicar of Africa, Lucius Domitius Alexander, revolted and proclaimed himself augustus. Two years later Constantine annexed Spain. Africa was recovered by Maxentius in 311, but he was killed by Constantine at the Battle of the Milvian Bridge in 312.

Because the sources from this period reflect the propaganda of Constantine, they represent Maxentius as a brutal tyrant, although in actuality he stopped the persecution of the Christians. He built a huge basilica, which Constantine renamed after himself, and a temple to his son Romulus in the Roman Forum.

Maxia school (Chinese painters): *see* Mahsia school.

Maxillaria, genus of more than 300 species of tropical American orchids, family Orchidaceae, that grow on other plants or on soil at high altitudes. Some species are less than 5 cm (2 inches) tall, but others may grow to nearly a metre (about 3 feet).

Maxillaria curtipes
Walter Chandoha

Pseudobulbs (bulblike stems) vary in position, shape, and size, depending on the species, but usually are flattened and spaced along a creeping underground stem. The leaves are thick and leathery. Most species bear a single flower or a cluster of several flowers.

Maxim, Hiram Percy (b. Sept. 2, 1869, Brooklyn, N.Y., U.S.—d. Feb. 17, 1936, La Junta, Colo.), American inventor and manufacturer known especially for the "Maxim silencer" gun attachment.

Son and nephew of famous inventors, Maxim graduated from Massachusetts Institute of Technology, then in Boston, at age 16 and by 1890 was superintendent of the American Projectile Company plant at Lynn, Mass. While bicycling from Salem to Lynn, he conceived the idea for a gasoline-powered tricycle, which he built by 1895, leading to his employment by the Pope Manufacturing Company of Hartford, Conn. There he supervised production of the vehicle and also designed an electric automobile, the Columbia, which the company manufactured for several years.

His efforts to improve the gasoline-powered automobile led to research on the exhaust muffler, which in turn brought the discovery of the principle that made possible the famous "silencer." This invention brought him fame, and even notoriety, as editors, writers, and the general public mistakenly assumed that the device could be attached to the pistols of criminals; in actuality, it was usable only on a sealed-breech rifle and never found wide demand. The ensuing furor led to its prohibition in many states in the United States and in several other countries and caused Maxim to stop its manufacture in 1930. He adapted the principle to mufflers, safety valves, air compressors and blowers, and other devices.

In his later years Maxim became a champion of the rights of amateur radio operators and was instrumental in opening shortwave and ultra-shortwave radio to them.

Maxim, Sir Hiram (Stevens) (b. Feb. 5, 1840, Sangerville, Maine, U.S.—d. Nov. 24, 1916, London, Eng.), prolific inventor best known for the Maxim machine gun.

The eldest son of a farmer who was a locally notable mechanic, Maxim was apprenticed at 14 to a carriage maker. Exhibiting an early genius for invention, he obtained his first patent in 1866, for a hair-curling iron. His iron was followed by a device for generating illuminating gas and a locomotive headlight; in 1878 he was hired as chief engineer of the United States Electric Lighting Company, the first such company in the United States. In that post he produced a basic invention, a method of manufacturing carbon filaments. In 1881 he exhibited an electric pressure regulator at the Paris Exposition.

His interest in the problem of automatic weapons led him to settle in London, where in 1884 he produced the first satisfactory fully automatic machine gun, employing the recoil of the barrel for ejecting the spent cartridges and reloading the chamber. To improve its efficiency, he developed his own smokeless powder, cordite. Within a few years every army was equipped with Maxim guns or adaptations.

In the 1890s Maxim experimented with airplanes, producing one powered by a light steam engine that successfully rose from the ground; he recognized that the real solution to flight was the internal-combustion engine but did not attempt to develop it. His hundreds of patents in the United States and Great Britain included a mousetrap, an automatic sprinkling system, an automatic steam-powered water pump, vacuum pumps, engine governors, and gas motors.

His Maxim Gun Company, founded in 1884, was later absorbed into Vickers, Ltd., of which he became a director. In 1900 he became a naturalized British subject, and in 1901 he was knighted by Queen Victoria.

Maxim, Hudson (b. Feb. 3, 1853, Orneville, Maine, U.S.—d. May 6, 1927, Landing Post Office, N.J.), American inventor of explosives extensively used in World War I.

Maxim's study of chemistry at Wesleyan Seminary in Kent's Hill, Maine, led to a hypothesis concerning the compound nature of atoms not unlike the atomic theory later accepted. In 1888, as a member of the gun and ammunition company founded by his brother, Hiram Maxim, he experimented with explosives and in 1890 built a dynamite and powder factory at Maxim, N.J. There, with R.C. Schupphaus, he developed the Maxim-Schupphaus smokeless powder, the first in the United States and the first adopted by the U.S. government. He next invented a smokeless cannon powder, with cylindrical grains so perforated that it burned more rapidly, which was widely used during World War I. In 1897 he sold his factory and patents to E.I. du Pont de Nemours & Company but remained with them as consulting engineer until his death.

Maxim invented maximite, a high explosive bursting powder 50 percent more powerful than dynamite, which, when placed in torpedoes, resisted the shock of firing and the still greater shock of piercing armour plate without bursting. This powder was then set off by a delayed-action detonating fuse, also Maxim's invention. Later, he perfected a new smokeless powder, called stabillite because of its high stability, and motorite, a self-combustive substance to propel torpedoes.

During World War I Maxim served as chairman of the committee on ordnance and explosives of the naval consulting board and donated several inventions to the government.

Maxim machine gun, first fully automatic machine gun (*q.v.*), developed by engineer and inventor Hiram Maxim in about 1884, while he was residing in England. It was manufactured by Vickers and was sometimes known as the Vickers-Maxim and sometimes just Vickers. These guns were used by every major power. The Maxim gun was recoil-operated and was cooled by a water jacket surrounding the barrel. The Maxim was in large part responsible for the epithet "the machine gun war" for World War I.

A list of the abbreviations used in the MICROPAEDIA *will be found at the end of this volume*

Maximian, Latin in full MARCUS AURELIUS VALERIUS MAXIMIANUS (b. Sirmium, Pannonia Inferior—d. 310), Roman emperor with Diocletian from AD 286 to 305.

Born of humble parents, Maximian rose in the army, on the basis of his military skill, to become a trusted officer and friend of the emperor Diocletian, who made him caesar in 285 and augustus the following year. Maximian thus became in theory the colleague of Diocletian, but his role was always subordinate. Assigned the government of the West, Maximian failed to suppress revolts in Gaul and Britain; Constantius Chlorus, appointed caesar under Maximian in 293, took charge of these areas while Maximian continued to govern Italy, Spain, and Africa. Although long viewed by Christians as a persecutor of their religion, Maximian seems to have done no more than obediently execute in his part of the empire the first edict of Diocletian, which ordered the burning of the Scriptures and the closing of the churches. On May 1, 305, the same day that Diocletian abdicated at Nicomedia, Maximian abdicated, evidently reluctantly, at Mediolanum. As the new tetrarchy (two augusti with a caesar under each) that succeeded them began to break down, Maximian reclaimed the throne to support his son Maxentius' claim to be caesar. Persuaded to abdicate once more by Diocletian in 308, he lived at the court of Constantine, who had recently married his daughter Fausta. Maximian died, either by murder or by suicide, shortly after the suppression of a revolt raised by him against Constantine.

Maximianus, Gaius Galerius Valerius: *see* Galerius.

Maximilian, name of rulers grouped below by country and indicated by the symbol •.

Foreign-language equivalents:

German . . . . Maximilian
Hungarian . . . . Miksa
Spanish . . . . Maximiliano

AUSTRIA

• Maximilian I–II: *see* Maximilian I–II (Germany/Holy Roman Empire).

BAVARIA

• Maximilian I (b. April 17, 1573, Munich—d. Sept. 27, 1651, Ingolstadt, Bavaria), duke of Bavaria from 1597 and elector from 1623, an effective champion of the Roman Catholic side during the Thirty Years' War (1618–48).

After a strict Jesuit education, Maximilian succeeded to the ducal throne on his father's abdication in 1597. Bavaria, debt-ridden and ill-administered, was soon restored to solvency and sound government by the energetic young duke. He revised the law code, built an effective army, and tightened control over his lands and the church. To counteract the newly created Protestant Union, Maximilian formed the defensive Catholic League in February 1610. His Catholic faith did not prevent him from being a rival of the Habsburgs; yet after

Maximilian I, detail from a portrait by Nikolaus Prugger; in the Bayerisches Nationalmuseum, Munich

By courtesy of the Bayerisches Nationalmuseum, Munich

reorganizing the league to curb that dynasty's power, he came to the aid of Austria in 1619, defeating the Bohemians and their Protestant king Frederick (the Palatine elector Frederick V) in 1620. Austria had promised Maximilian the Palatine electorship and territories, and from 1622–23 the duke's general, Johann von Tilly, conquered both the Upper and Rhenish Palatinates and the electorship for Maximilian, whose army then drove the Danes from northern Germany (1626). Maximilian's position as leader of the Catholic coalition became threatened, however, by the creation of an independent imperial army under Albrecht von Wallenstein. The elector forced the general's dismissal (1630) and the disbanding of his army; but with Sweden's entry into the conflict, Wallenstein was reinstated. Maximilian then engineered Wallenstein's downfall in 1634. Bavaria fell to the Swedes (1632) but was liberated again after the Battle of Nördlingen (1634); and Maximilian, now reasonably secure, was content to defend his realm. Defeated by France and Sweden, he concluded a separate armistice (1647). By the Peace of Westphalia (1648) kept the electorship and the Upper Palatinate, restoring only the Rhenish lands to Frederick V's heir.

• Maximilian II Emanuel (b. July 11, 1662, Munich—d. Feb. 26, 1726, Munich), elector of Bavaria from 1679 and an able soldier whose quest for dynastic aggrandizement led him into a series of wars, first as an ally of the House of Habsburg, later against it, an enmity that nearly cost him his holdings.

Maximilian Emanuel, the son of the elector Ferdinand Maria, came of age in 1680 and

Maximilian II Emanuel, engraving by Karl Gustav Amling, 1682

By courtesy of the Staatliche Graphische Sammlung, Munich

three years later joined Austria in its war against the Turks. The capture of Belgrade (1688) made his reputation. During the War of the Grand Alliance (1689–97), a coalition of most European powers against Louis XIV of France, he once again ranged himself on the Habsburgs' side, and was appointed governor of the Spanish Netherlands (1692). Through his marriage to Maria Antonia (died 1692), a daughter of the emperor Leopold I, Maximilian Emanuel exercised some claim to the Habsburg succession; and his son, Joseph Ferdinand, was expected to inherit most of the Spanish possessions. After Joseph Ferdinand's death in 1699 destroyed such hopes, Maximilian Emanuel for a number of years still hoped to retain the Spanish Netherlands, but his efforts were to remain futile. Although his marriage to Teresa Kunigunda Sobieska (1694) opened the possibility of the Polish succession after the death of John III (Jan Sobieski) in 1696, Maximilian Emanuel decided to remain in western Europe.

The War of the Spanish Succession (1701–13) found the elector on the French side in the hope that his dynasty, the Wittelsbachs, could supplant the Habsburgs on the imperial throne. After defeat of the French and Bavarians at Blenheim (1704), Maximilian Emanuel was driven from his country, and, after the Battle of Ramillies (1706), he also lost the Netherlands and became a refugee at the French court. Restored to Bavaria after the Treaty of Utrecht (1713), he returned to Munich in 1715. In 1724 he organized the Wittelsbach House Union to coordinate actions in German affairs. His eldest son, Charles Albert, finally realized Maximilian Emanuel's dreams and became emperor in 1742.

• Maximilian I, also called (as elector of Bavaria) MAXIMILIAN IV JOSEPH (b. May 27, 1756, Mannheim, Palatinate—d. Oct. 13, 1825, Munich), first Wittelsbach elector of Bavaria (1799–1806) and first king of Bavaria (1806–25), whose alliance with Napoleon gained him a monarch's crown and enabled him to turn the scattered, poorly administered Bavarian holdings into a consolidated, modern state.

Maximilian Joseph, the second son of Prince Frederick Michael of Palatinate-Zweibrücken, served in the French regiment of Alsace from 1777 to the outbreak of the French Revolution, developing the affinity for France that he was to retain for the rest of his life. In 1795, when he succeeded his older brother as duke of Zweibrücken, France was already in possession of the duchy; but on the death of the elector Charles Theodore of Bavaria and the Palatinate in 1799, he inherited all of the Wittelsbach territories as Maximilian IV Joseph. Widely scattered and ill-administered, most of them were occupied by Austria. With his able minister Maximilian, Graf von Montgelas, the new elector was to make Bavaria into an efficient, liberal state.

Forced by Austrian pressure to enter the war against France (1799), Maximilian IV Joseph signed a separate peace in 1801, which, though formalizing the loss of his lands west of the Rhine, guaranteed compensation elsewhere. Distrustful of Austria, which tried repeatedly to annex Bavarian territories, the elector remained faithful to his French alliance for more than a decade. In 1803 he received Würzburg, Bamberg, Freising, Augsburg, and other lands. In 1805 Ansbach was added, and on Jan. 1, 1806, the elector crowned himself king of Bavaria as Maximilian I. Bavaria's membership in the Confederation of the Rhine—the league of German princes sponsored by Napoleon—and contributions to the French war effort against Austria (1805), Prussia and Russia (1806–07), and, again, Austria (1809), led to the acquisition of most of Western Austria. Thirty thousand men of the Bavarian contingent fought with Napoleon in Russia, but after the French defeat there Maximilian entered into an alliance with Austria in return for a guarantee of the integrity of his kingdom. After returning sections of Western Austria in 1814 and 1816, Bavaria received sizable territories on the west bank of the Rhine.

With the restoration of peace (1815), Maximilian reorganized his administration. He dismissed Montgelas (1817) largely on the insistence of his son, the future Louis I; and the kingdom, which already had received a liberal constitution in 1808, was granted a new charter in 1818, providing for a bicameral parlia-

Maximilian I, miniature by an unknown artist; in the Gemäldegalerie, Dresden, Ger.

By courtesy of the Staatliche Kunstsammlungen, Dresden, Ger.; photograph, Deutsche Fotothek Dresden

ment. These measures made Bavaria one of Germany's most liberal states during the last years of Maximilian's reign.

• Maximilian II (b. Nov. 28, 1811, Munich—d. March 10, 1864, Munich), king of Bavaria from 1848 to 1864, whose attempt to create a "third force" in German affairs by an alliance of smaller states led by Bavaria, foundered on the opposition of the two dom-

Maximilian II, detail from an engraving, 1859

By courtesy of the trustees of the British Museum; photograph, J.R. Freeman & Co. Ltd.

inant states, Prussia and Austria, and of the German parliament.

Maximilian, the eldest son of King Louis I and Therese of Saxe-Hildburghausen, received a thorough education at Göttingen and Berlin. He inclined to intellectual pursuits for the rest of his life, surrounding himself with scholars and artists, most notable among them the historian Leopold von Ranke.

With the abdication of his father (March 1848), Maximilian succeeded to the throne at a time of revolutionary fervour throughout Germany. His proposal of a triad, a league of smaller territories as a counterweight to the two large conservative German states, was opposed not only by Austria and Prussia, but by the Frankfurt National Assembly, whose efforts were directed toward a single, unified German state. Although Prussia aided Bavaria in the suppression of a revolt in the Palatinate (1849), Maximilian refused an alliance with the northern power. In fact, with the elevation of Ludwig von der Pfordten to the post of chief minister (1849), Bavaria assumed a pro-Austrian stance.

On his accession, the King liberalized Bavarian life through the introduction of freedom of the press and ministerial responsibility, although he preferred to leave politics in the hands of his ministers. He made Munich a centre of Germany's intellectual and artistic life, calling many notable scholars to the Bavarian capital. Departments of the sciences, technology, and history were established at the Bavarian Academy of Sciences and research projects initiated. The King kept in close personal touch with his intellectual acquaintances, the latter even occasionally serving as advisers on policy matters.

Maximilian firmly backed the hereditary prince Frederick of Augustenburg in the long dispute over the duchies of Schleswig and Holstein, which again erupted in the early 1860s between Denmark and Prussia. His aggressive stand was not supported by the other European powers. He died before the German states were able to settle the issue by force.

• **Maximilian III Joseph** (b. March 28, 1727, Munich—d. Dec. 30, 1777, Munich), elector of Bavaria (1745–77), son of the Holy Roman emperor Charles VII. By the Peace of Füssen signed on April 22, 1745, he obtained restitution of his dominions lost by his father—on condition, however, that he formally acknowledge the Pragmatic Sanction and not seek the imperial title. He was a man of the Enlightenment, did much to encourage agriculture, industries, and the exploitation of minerals, founded the Academy of Sciences at Munich, and abolished the Jesuit censorship of the press. At his death, without issue, the Bavarian line of the Wittelsbachs became extinct, and the succession passed to Charles Theodore, the elector Palatine.

GERMANY/HOLY ROMAN EMPIRE

• **Maximilian I** (b. March 22, 1459, Wiener Neustadt, Austria—d. Jan. 12, 1519, Wels), archduke of Austria, German king, and Holy Roman emperor (1493–1519), who made his family, the Habsburgs, dominant in 16th-century Europe. He added vast lands to the traditional Austrian holdings, securing the Netherlands by his own marriage, Hungary and Bohemia by treaty and military pressure, and Spain and the Spanish empire by the marriage of his son Philip. He also fought a series of wars against the French, mostly in Italy. His grandson succeeded to the vast Habsburg realm and the imperial crown as Charles V.

Territorial expansion. Maximilian was the eldest son of the emperor Frederick III and Eleanor of Portugal. By his marriage in 1477 to Mary, daughter of Charles the Bold, duke of Burgundy, Maximilian acquired the vast Burgundian possessions in the Netherlands and along the eastern frontier of France. He

Maximilian I, charcoal drawing by Albrecht Dürer, 1518; in the Albertina, Vienna

By courtesy of the Albertina, Vienna

successfully defended his new domains against the attacks of Louis XI of France, defeating the French at the Battle of Guinegate in 1479. After Mary's death (1482) Maximilian was forced to allow the States General (representative assembly) of the Netherlands to act as regent for his infant son Philip (later Philip I the Handsome, of Castile); but, having defeated the States in war, he reacquired control of the regency in 1485. Meanwhile, by the Treaty of Arras (1482), Maximilian was also forced to consent to the betrothal of his daughter Margaret of Austria to Charles VIII of France.

In 1486 he was elected king of the Romans (heir to his father, the emperor) and crowned at Aachen on April 9. With the military help of Spain, England, and Brittany, he continued his war against France and the rebellious Netherlands. In order to surround France, Maximilian in 1490 married Duchess Anne of Brittany by proxy but could not forestall an invasion of Brittany by the French. A dramatic setback occurred when Charles VIII sent his fiancée Margaret back to her father and required Anne to sever her marriage with Maximilian and to become the queen of France.

Through the archduke Sigismund, his cousin, Maximilian obtained the Tirol. Because of its favourable situation politically as well as its silver mines, its chief city, Innsbruck, became his favorite centre of operations.

By 1490 he regained control of most of his family's traditional territories in Austria, which had been seized by Hungary. He then became a candidate for the vacant Hungarian throne. When Vladislav (Ulászló) II of Bohemia was elected instead, he waged a successful campaign against Vladislav. By the Treaty of Pressburg in 1491 he arranged that the succession to Bohemia and Hungary would pass to the Habsburgs if Vladislav left no male heir.

The Treaty of Senlis (1493) ended the conflict against the Netherlands and France and left the Duchy of Burgundy and the Low Countries secure in the possession of the House of Habsburg.

Consolidation of power. On the death of Frederick III in 1493, Maximilian had become sole ruler over the German kingdom and head of the House of Habsburg; he then drove the Turks from his southeast borders, married Bianca Maria Sforza of Milan (1494), and handed over the Low Countries to his son Philip (1494), reserving, however, the right of joint rule. The flourishing culture of the Low Countries influenced literature, art, government, politics, and military methods in all the other Habsburg possessions.

Charles VIII's invasion of Italy (1494) upset the European balance of power. Maximilian allied himself with the pope, Spain, Venice, and Milan in the so-called Holy League (1495) to drive out the French, who were conquering Naples. He campaigned in Italy in 1496, but, although the French were expelled, he achieved little benefit. More important were the marriages of his son Philip to the Spanish infanta Joan (the Mad), in the same year, and of his daughter Margaret to the Spanish crown prince, in 1497. These marriages assured him of the succession in Spain and the control of the Spanish colonies.

At a meeting of the Reichstag (Imperial Diet) at Worms in 1495 Maximilian sought to strengthen the empire. Laws were projected to reform the Reichskammergericht (Imperial Chamber) and taxation and to give permanency to the public peace; however, no solution was forthcoming for many military and administrative problems. The princes would permit no strengthening of the central authority, and this limitation of power neutralized imperial policies. To thwart the opposition, which was led primarily by the lord chancellor Berthold, archbishop of Mainz, Maximilian set up his own extra-constitutional judicial and financial commissions.

In 1499 Maximilian fought an unsuccessful war against the Swiss Confederation and was forced to recognize its virtual independence by the Peace of Basel (September 22). At the same time, the French moved back into Italy, in cooperation with Spain, and occupied the imperial fief of Milan.

In 1500 the imperial princes at the Reichstag in Augsburg withdrew considerable power from Maximilian and invested it in the Reichsregiment, a supreme council of 21 electors, princes, and others. They even considered deposing him, but the plan miscarried because of their own apathy and Maximilian's effective countermeasures. He strengthened his European position by an agreement with France, and he regained prestige within the empire by victories in a dynastic war between Bavaria and the Rhenish Palatinate (1504). At the same time, the death of Berthold of Mainz rid him of one of his main opponents. Credit arrangements with south German business firms, such as the Fuggers, assured Maximilian of funds for foreign and domestic needs; and a campaign against Hungary in 1506 strengthened the Habsburg claim to the Hungarian throne. Though he was German king, he had not been crowned as emperor by the pope, as was customary. Excluded from Italy by the hostile Venetians, he was unable to go to Rome for his coronation and had to content himself with the title of Roman emperor elect that was bestowed on him with the consent of Pope Julius II on Feb. 4, 1508.

To oppose Venice, Maximilian entered into the League of Cambrai with France, Spain, and the pope in 1508. Their aim was to partition the Republic of Venice. In the war that followed, Maximilian was labelled an unreliable partner because of his lack of funds and troops. Pope Julius' severe illness prompted Maximilian to consider accepting the office of pope, which the schismatic Council of Pisa offered him. At times pious, at other times antipapal, he thought he might win financial help from the German Church if he were a rival pope; but in the end he let himself be dissuaded from this by Ferdinand II the Catholic, of Aragon. Turning away from his French alliance, he entered into a new Holy League (1511) with the pope, Spain, England, and their allies; with the help of England he scored a victory against the French in the Battle of the Spurs (1513), while his allies concentrated on regaining Milan and Lombardy. The French were victorious in Italy at the Battle of Marignano in 1515, and Maximilian's efforts to re-win Milan failed miserably. The Treaty of Brussels granted Milan to the French and

Verona to the Venetians, leaving Maximilian with only the territorial boundaries of Tirol.

In the east, by making overtures to Russia, he was able to put pressure on Poland, Bohemia, and Hungary to acquiesce in his expansionist plans. In 1515 advantageous marriages were arranged between members of the Habsburg family and the Hungarian royal house, thus strengthening the Habsburg position in Hungary and also in Bohemia, which was under the same dynasty. His intricate system of alliances, embracing both central Europe and the Iberian Peninsula, made Maximilian a potent force in European affairs.

On Jan. 12, 1519, having spent the previous year trying to have his grandson Charles elected emperor and to raise a European coalition against the Turks, he died at Wels in Upper Austria. He was buried in Georgskirche at Wiener Neustadt. (His magnificent tomb at the Hofkirche in Innsbruck was completed later.) His plans did come to fruition when his grandson, already king of Spain, became emperor as Charles V later the same year.

Assessment. Great as Maximilian's achievements were, they did not match his ambitions; for he had hoped to unite all of western Europe by reviving the empire of Charlemagne. Adhering more often to medieval patterns of thought, he was nevertheless open to new ideas, enthusiastic about promoting science as well as the arts. He not only planned a Latin autobiography but wrote two poetical allegories, *Weisskunig* ("White King") and *Teuerdank* (both largely autobiographical), and the *Geheimes Jagdbuch,* a treatise on hunting, and kept a bevy of poets and artists busy with projects that glorified his reign. His military talents were considerable and led him to use war to attain his ends. He carried out meaningful military and administrative reforms, but he was ignorant of economics and was financially unreliable. (H.Wi.)

BIBLIOGRAPHY. R.W. Seton-Watson, *Maximilian I, Holy Roman Emperor* (1902); and Christopher Hare (pseud. of Marian Andrews), *Maximilian the Dreamer: Holy Roman Emperor, 1459–1519* (1913), are the most important of the older presentations in English. Glenn Elwood Waas, *The Legendary Character of Kaiser Maximilian* (1941, reissued 1966), is primarily concerned with his character and personality and offers an imposing bibliography. Gerhard Benecke, *Maximilian I (1459–1519)* (1982), describes the ruler's career and character and presents the social history of the land he governed.

•**Maximilian II** (b. July 31, 1527, Vienna, Austria—d. Oct. 12, 1576, Regensburg [Germany]), Holy Roman emperor from 1564, whose liberal religious policies permitted an interval of peace between Roman Catholics and Protestants in Germany after the first struggles of the Reformation. A humanist and patron of the arts, he largely failed to achieve his political goals, both at home and abroad.

Maximilian, the eldest son of the future emperor Ferdinand I and the nephew of the emperor Charles V, received his education in Spain. In a dispute over the Habsburg succession order, he was at first placed behind Charles V's son Philip (the future Philip II of Spain), but, by a 1553 agreement, he displaced Philip as heir to the empire and remained hostile to the Spanish branch of the Habsburgs.

Maximilian's sympathies for Lutheranism, formed in his youth, eventually caused sufficient scandal in Habsburg circles for his father to threaten him with exclusion from the succession in 1559. Henceforth, although he paid lip service to Roman Catholicism, he remained basically a humanist Christian who favoured compromise between the rival confessions.

Already Bohemian king (from September 1562) and king of the Romans, or successor-

Maximilian II, detail from an engraving, *c.* 1575

By courtesy of Bild-Archiv, Osterreichische Nationalbibliothek, Vienna

designate to the empire (from November 1562), Maximilian became Hungarian king in 1563 and succeeded to the imperial throne in 1564. His refusal to invest Protestant administrators of bishoprics with their imperial fiefs disappointed the hopes of Germany's Protestant princes. Yet he proved his personal liberalism by granting freedom of worship to the Protestant nobility of Austria (1568), promising to respect religious liberty in Bohemia (1575), and working for the reform of the Roman Catholic church. His efforts to gain the right of marriage for priests failed, largely because of the opposition of Spain.

In the Netherlands, Maximilian advised compromise between Catholics and Protestants but was again frustrated by Spanish intransigence. After fighting an unsuccessful campaign against the Turks, who remained a threat to the empire, he was compelled by a peace concluded in 1568 to continue to pay tribute to the sultan. His proposed army reform of 1570, by which the emperor would have controlled the army and would have had to grant his consent before foreign powers could recruit on German soil, was defeated by Germany's Protestant princes, who suspected an attempt to prevent them from assisting coreligionists abroad and were less willing to grant greater powers to the emperor.

Maximilian's religious neutrality was largely a policy of political expediency in maintaining peace in the empire. Yet, although he preserved the right of his subjects to worship according to their beliefs, he succeeded in few of his political aims.

Hungary

•**Maximilian:** *see* Maximilian II (Germany/Holy Roman Empire).

Mexico

•**Maximilian,** in full FERDINAND MAXIMILIAN JOSEPH (b. July 6, 1832, Vienna, Austria—d. June 19, 1867, near Querétaro, Mex.), archduke of Austria and the emperor of Mexico, a man whose naive liberalism proved unequal to the international intrigues that had put him on the throne and to the brutal struggles within Mexico that led to his execution.

The younger brother of Emperor Francis Joseph I, he served as a rear admiral in the Austrian navy and as governor-general of the Lombardo-Venetian kingdom. In 1863 he accepted the offer of the Mexican throne, falsely believing that the Mexican people had voted him their king; in fact, the offer was the result of a scheme between conservative Mexicans, who wished to overturn the liberal government of President Benito Juárez, and the French emperor Napoleon III, who wanted to collect a debt from Mexico and further his imperialistic ambitions there. Backed by a pledge of support from the French army, Maximilian sailed for Mexico with his wife Carlota, daughter of Leopold I, king of the Belgians.

Crowned emperor on June 10, 1864, Maximilian intended to rule with paternal benevolence, viewing himself as the protector of the Indian peasants. He upheld Juárez' sweeping reforms (to the indignation of the landed proprietors) and was determined to abolish peonage, and he antagonized the Roman Catholic hierarchy by refusing to restore vast church holdings confiscated by Juárez. The treasury was so bare, however, that he had to use his own inherited income for daily expenses.

Maximilian

By courtesy of the Library of Congress, Washington, D.C.

By April 1865 the French army had successfully supported Maximilian by driving Juárez northward almost into Texas. But that month the American Civil War ended, and the United States demanded the withdrawal of French troops from Mexico on the grounds that their presence was a violation of the Monroe Doctrine. Carlota rushed to Europe to seek aid for her husband from Napoleon III and Pope Pius IX, only to suffer a profound emotional collapse when her efforts failed. The French forces withdrew in March 1867, and Juárez and his army moved back into Mexico City. Refusing to abdicate, feeling that he could not honorably desert "his people," Maximilian was made supreme commander of the imperial army by his conservative Mexican backers. At Querétaro, Maximilian's small force was surrounded, starved, and finally betrayed into capitulation (May 15, 1867). Even though Victor Hugo, Giuseppe Garibaldi, and many of the crowned heads of Europe petitioned Juárez to save Maximilian's life, he was executed on a hill outside Querétaro the following month.

Consult the INDEX *first*

Maximilian, PRINCE OF BADEN, byname MAX, German MAXIMILIAN, PRINZ VON BADEN (b. July 10, 1867, Baden-Baden, Baden [Germany]—d. Nov. 6, 1929, Schloss Salem, Baden, Ger.), chancellor of Germany, appointed on Oct. 3, 1918, because his humanitarian reputation made the emperor William II think him capable of bringing World War I expeditiously to an end.

Maximilian, prince of Baden, *c.* 1900

By courtesy of the Bildarchiv Preussischer Kulturbesitz BPK, West Berlin

The son of the grand duke Frederick I's brother Prince William of Baden, Maximilian in 1907 became heir presumptive to the grand duchy because his cousin the grand duke Frederick II (d. 1928) had no children. In the first years of World War I he devoted himself to the Red Cross and to work for the welfare of prisoners of war (on both sides). On Oct. 3, 1918, when Germany was on the verge of collapse, he was appointed chancellor of the empire and prime minister of Prussia in succession to Georg Hertling. He hastily superintended the constitutional changes whereby a genuine parliamentary system was at last brought into being in Germany, began negotiations for an armistice, and secured the dismissal of Army Chief of Staff Erich Ludendorff—but too late to save the monarchy. When the emperor William II would give no definite answer to Max's demands that he should abdicate in the face of the danger of Communist revolution, Max finally himself announced the abdication of the Emperor on Nov. 9, 1918. He then resigned the chancellery to the leader of the Majority Social Democratic Party, Friedrich Ebert.

Max published *Völkerbund und Rechtsfriede* (1919), *Die moralische Offensive* (1921), and *Erinnerungen und Dokumente* (1927; *Memoirs*, 1928).

Maximinus, original name GAIUS JULIUS VERUS MAXIMINUS, also called MAXIMIN (d. 238), first soldier who had started from the ranks to become Roman emperor (235–238). His reign marked the beginning of a half century of civil war in the empire. Originally from Thrace, he is said to have been a shepherd before enlisting in the army. There his

Maximinus, plaster bust; in the Capitoline Museum, Rome
BBC Hulton Picture Library

immense strength attracted the attention of Septimius Severus (emperor 193–211).

Under Severus Alexander (emperor 222–235), Maximinus held high command in the Army of the Rhine, and, when Severus was murdered, he was proclaimed emperor by the Rhine army. Maximinus spent most of his reign fighting invading tribes along the Danube and the Rhine. The numerous milestones displaying his name attest to his energetic reconstructions of the roads in these regions.

When in 238 a group of landowners in Africa, discontented with imperial taxation, rebelled, killed their tax collectors, and proclaimed the aged Gordian emperor, Maximinus quickly suppressed the revolt; but he himself was soon deposed by the Senate at Rome. Maximinus and the army crossed the Alps and besieged Aquileia, in northeast Italy. The city resisted, and after several months of stalemate Maximinus was killed by his own soldiers. Gordian's grandson, Gordian III, emerged as Maximinus' successor.

Maximinus, Galerius Valerius, original name DAIA (d. 313, Tarsus, Cilicia), Roman emperor from 310 to 313 and a persistent persecutor of the Christians. He was a nephew of Galerius, one of the two men named au-

Galerius Valerius Maximinus, marble bust; in the Egyptian Museum, Cairo
Alinari—Art Resource/EB Inc.

gustus after the abdication of Diocletian and Maximian.

Originally a shepherd, Maximinus joined the army and advanced rapidly through the ranks. On May 1, 305, the date of the abdications, he was proclaimed caesar to Galerius and assigned to rule Syria and Egypt. After Galerius elevated Licinius to the rank of augustus in 308, Maximinus also claimed and obtained the same title.

In 306 and again in 308 Maximinus ordered a general sacrifice to the pagan gods; Christian recusants were mutilated and sent to the mines and quarries. In 311 he grudgingly accepted Galerius' edict of toleration for Christians but still endeavoured to organize and revitalize paganism. Cities and provinces were encouraged to petition for expulsion of Christians from their territories, and the *Acts of Pilate*, an anti-Christian forgery, was taught in the schools. In the autumn of 312 Maximinus relaxed his persecutions somewhat, and shortly before his death in 313 he granted full toleration and the restoration of the confiscated church property.

On Galerius' death in 311, Maximinus occupied Asia Minor. In 313 he invaded Licinius' dominions in Thrace but, defeated at Tzurulum, was forced to retreat into Asia Minor, where he died of disease.

Maximus OF EPHESUS (d. 370), Neoplatonist philosopher and theurgic magician whose most spectacular achievement was the animation of a statue of Hecate. Through his magic he gained a powerful influence over the mind of the future Roman emperor Julian, and Maximus was invited to join the court in Constantinople when Julian succeeded to the throne in 361. He was imprisoned by the emperor Valens after Julian's death, was released, and was finally executed for complicity in an assassination plot against Valens.

Maximus THE CONFESSOR, SAINT (b. *c.* 580, Constantinople—d. Aug. 13, 662, Lazica), the most important Byzantine theologian of the 7th century, whose commentaries on the early 6th-century Christian Neoplatonist Pseudo-Dionysius the Areopagite and on the Greek Church Fathers considerably influenced the theology and mysticism of the Middle Ages.

A court secretary of the Eastern Roman emperor Heraclius I, Maximus became a monk *c.* 613 at a monastery near Chrysopolis in Bithynia. Fleeing to North Africa because of the Persian invasion of 626, he took part at Carthage (near modern Tunis) in the Monothelite controversy over the doctrine that Christ, while having two distinct natures, divine and human, in his one Person (a doctrine firmly established) nonetheless had only one will and one operation. Arguing for a dual-will faculty in Christ, Maximus was called to Rome, where he supported the condemnation of Monothelitism by a regional church council under Pope Martin I in 649. Maximus and Martin were arrested by the emperor Constans II in an intricate theological–political tactic, and, after imprisonment from 653 to 655, Maximus was later tortured and exiled; he died in the wilderness near the Black Sea.

Throughout his approximately 90 major works Maximus developed a Christocentric theology and mysticism. His *Opuscula theologica et polemica* ("Short Theological and Polemical Treatises"), *Ambigua* ("Ambiguities" in the works of Gregory of Nazianzus), and *Scholia* (on Pseudo-Dionysius the Areopagite), mostly authentic, express Maximus' teaching on the transcendental, nonpredicable nature of the divinity, his intrinsic Trinitarian existence, and his definitive communication in Christ. In his *400 Capita de caritate* ("Four Hundred Chapters on Charity"), Maximus counselled a Christian humanism, integrating asceticism with ordinary life and active charity.

Maximus' attempt to achieve balance in spiritual theory and practice was not always furthered by later theologians; he thus remains an independent and original thinker in the history of Christian speculation.

Maximus THE GREEK, also called MAXIMUS THE HAGIORITE (b. 1480, Árta, Greece—d. 1556, near Moscow), Greek Orthodox monk, Humanist scholar, and linguist, whose principal role in the translation of the Scriptures and philosophical–theological literature into the Russian language made possible the dissemination of Byzantine culture throughout Russia.

Maximus was educated in Paris, Venice, and Florence. A friend of prominent Humanist scholars and editors in Italy, he was later influenced by the ascetical reformer Girolamo Savonarola of the Dominican Order in Florence. So great was his reputation as a scholar that when the Russian Church requested from the patriarchate of Constantinople an expert to correct church texts that were used in Russia, Maximus was chosen for the mission. In Moscow, with the assistance of Russian secretaries, he translated original Greek canonical, liturgical, and theological texts into the Russian language. The great literary output inspired a Slavic cultural movement and laid the groundwork for later Russian theology.

While in Moscow Maximus became involved in the factional controversy that disturbed the Russian Church throughout most of the 16th century. This was between the Nonpossessors (or Transvolgans), who believed that monasteries should not own property and who had liberal political views, and the Possessors (or Josephites), who held opposite opinions on monastic property and strongly supported the monarchy, including its autocratic aspects. The Nonpossessors came to be led by Maximus and Nil Sorsky, the Possessors by Joseph of Volokolamsk. Among his many activities, Maximus took part in the preparation of a corrected and critical edition of the *Kormchaya kniga,* a Slavic version of the Byzantine ecclesiastical laws collected as the *Nomocanon.* In this work, he supported the ideas of the Nonpossessors, holding that the Church should practice poverty and desist from feudal exploitation of the peasantry. In 1525 Maximus was arrested on the charge of heresy by Daniel, metropolitan of Moscow and a Possessor. After a series of trials, he was condemned in 1531 and imprisoned for 20 years in the monastery of Volokolamsk, near Moscow, of which Joseph was abbot. While in detention, Maximus continued to produce theological works. When he emerged in 1551, his personal prestige was immense. Tsar Ivan IV the Terrible paid him public honour, but his political views were suppressed. The last five years of his life, he retired to the Troitse-Sergiyeva Monastery, where he was buried and was subsequently venerated as a saint.

Among the written works credited to him are commentaries on the Psalms and on the Acts of the Apostles and an anti-Latin church treatise entitled "Eulogy for the Holy Apostles Peter and Paul." The "Eulogy" includes a criticism of Western Christianity for fostering the doctrine of the existence of purgatory, a belief in a requisite period of spiritual cleansing after death to enable union with God.

Maximus, Magnus (d. Aug. 28, 388), usurping Roman emperor who ruled Britain, Gaul, and Spain from AD 383 to 388.

A Spaniard of humble origin, Maximus commanded the Roman troops in Britain against the Picts and Scots. In the spring of 383, Maximus' British troops proclaimed him emperor, and he at once crossed to the European continent to confront his rival, the Western emperor Gratian. Maximus won over Gratian's advancing troops; Gratian fled but was overtaken and killed (Aug. 25, 383).

Maximus took up residence at Trier (in present-day Germany) and entered into negotiations with the Eastern emperor, Theodosius I, who decided to recognize Maximus rather than fight a war in the West. Maximus elevated his son Flavius Victor to be coruler with him.

In the summer of 387 Maximus invaded Italy, forcing Valentinian to flee to Thessalonica. War broke out in 388 between Maximus and Theodosius, whose position had been strengthened by a treaty with the Persians. When his troops were defeated near Siscia and at Petovio, in Illyricum (in the Balkans), Maximus was captured and executed.

Maximus, Petronius (b. 396—d. May 31, 455, Rome [Italy]), Western Roman emperor from March 17 to May 31, 455. He was not recognized as emperor by the Eastern empire.

Maximus was prefect of Rome in 420 and twice served as consul. In 454 he and the eunuch Heraclius engineered the assassination of the powerful patrician Aetius. Proclaimed emperor the day after the emperor Valentinian III was murdered, Maximus immediately forced Valentinian's widow, Eudoxia, to marry him. At the same time, a Vandal fleet, perhaps invited by Eudoxia, was approaching Rome; Maximus tried to escape but was caught by the enraged Roman populace and torn limb from limb.

maxixe, ballroom dance that evolved in Brazil about 1870 and became an international craze in the years before World War I. A fusion of elements from the habanera, the polka, and rural Afro-Brazilian dance, it was related to the tango and was the precursor of the ballroom version of the samba.

Maxwell, Gavin (b. July 15, 1914, Elrig, near Mochrum, Wigtown, Scot.—d. Sept. 6, 1969, Inverness, Inverness), Scottish author and naturalist.

Maxwell was educated at Stowe School and the University of Oxford, then became a freelance journalist, though ornithology remained his special interest. He served with the Scots Guard in World War II. In 1945 he bought the island of Soay and described in *Harpoon at a Venture* (1952; also published as *Harpoon Venture*) his attempt to establish a shark fishery there. The best-selling *Ring of Bright Water* (1960) describes his life with two pet otters in his seaboard cottage in the west Highlands of Scotland; *The Rocks Remain* (1963) is a sequel. Maxwell's prolonged stay in Sicily resulted in two fine books, *God Protect Me from My Friends* (1956; also published as *Bandit*), about the bandit Salvatore Giuliano, and *The Pains of Death* (1959), on the poverty-stricken lives of the islanders. *A Reed Shaken by the Wind* (1957; also published as *People of the Reeds*) is an account of his travels among the marsh dwellers of southern Iraq.

Consult the INDEX *first*

Maxwell, James Clerk (b. June 13, 1831, Edinburgh, Scot.—d. Nov. 5, 1879, Cambridge, Cambridgeshire, Eng.), Scottish physicist best known for his formulation of electromagnetic theory. He is often ranked with Sir Isaac Newton for the fundamental nature of his contributions to science.

A brief treatment of James Clerk Maxwell follows. For full treatment, *see* MACROPAEDIA: Maxwell.

Maxwell's first scientific paper, *On the Description of Oval Curves,* was published when he was but 14 years of age. He attended the University of Edinburgh for three years but obtained a mathematics degree from Trinity College, Cambridge, in 1854. He became professor of natural philosophy at Marischal College, Aberdeen, Scot., in 1856 and in 1860 was appointed to King's College, London. During the next five years he published his two classic papers on the electromagnetic field. He retired in 1865. In 1871 he became the first Cavendish Professor of Physics at Cambridge.

Maxwell's interests ranged from colour vision (he produced one of the first colour photographs) and the nature of Saturn's rings to mechanics and the kinetic theory of gases. His publications include *Theory of Heat* (1870) and *Treatise on Electricity and Magnetism* (1873). The electromagnetic unit of magnetic flux in the centimetre-gram-second system of units was named maxwell in his honour.

Maxixe
Brown Brothers

Maxwell, William, original name WILLIAM MAXWELL KEEPERS, JR. (b. Aug. 16, 1908, Lincoln, Ill., U.S.—d. July 31, 2000, New York, N.Y.), American editor and author of spare, evocative short stories and novels, many of which are about small-town life in the American Midwest in the early 20th century.

Educated at the University of Illinois (B.A., 1930) and Harvard University (M.A., 1931), Maxwell taught English at the University of Illinois before joining the staff of *The New Yorker* magazine, where he worked from 1936 to 1976, mainly as a fiction editor. Among the writers he edited were John Cheever, J.D. Salinger, Eudora Welty, and Mavis Gallant. Maxwell's first novel, *Bright Center of Heaven,* was published in 1934. *They Came Like Swallows* (1937) tells how an epidemic of influenza affects a close family. *The Folded Leaf* (1945), perhaps Maxwell's best-known work, describes the friendship of two small-town boys. In *Time Will Darken It* (1948) a long visit from relatives disrupts a family; in *The Château* (1961) American travelers encounter postwar French culture.

Maxwell also published several collections of short stories, including *Over by the River, and Other Stories* (1977) and *All the Days and Nights* (1995). His 1980 novel, *So Long, See You Tomorrow,* returns to the subject of a friendship between two boys. Involving murder and suicide, it is darker than most of Maxwell's work but eschews sensationalism, as do all his books.

Maxwell-Boltzmann distribution law, a description of the statistical distribution of the energies of the molecules of a classical gas. This distribution was first set forth by the Scottish physicist James Clerk Maxwell in 1859, on the basis of probabilistic arguments, and gave the distribution of velocities among the molecules of a gas. Maxwell's finding was generalized (1871) by a German physicist, Ludwig Boltzmann, to express the distribution of energies among the molecules. The law can be derived in several ways, none of which is absolutely rigorous. All systems observed to date appear to obey Maxwell-Boltzann statistics provided that quantum-mechanical effects are not important.

Maxwell Davies, Peter: *see* Davies, Peter Maxwell.

Maxwell (of Terregles), Sir John: *see* Herries, John Maxwell, 4th Baron.

Maxwell's demon, hypothetical intelligent being (or a functionally equivalent device) capable of detecting and reacting to the motions of individual molecules. It was imagined by James Clerk Maxwell in 1871, to illustrate the possibility of violating the second law of thermodynamics. Essentially, this law states that heat does not naturally flow from a cool body to a warmer; work must be expended to make it do so. Maxwell envisioned two vessels containing gas at equal temperatures and joined by a small hole. The hole could be opened or closed at will by "a being" to allow individual molecules of gas to pass through. By passing only fast-moving molecules from vessel A to vessel B and only slow-moving ones from B to A, the demon would bring about an effective flow from A to B of molecular kinetic energy. This excess energy in B would be usable to perform work (*e.g.,* by generating steam), and the system could be a working perpetual motion machine. By allowing all molecules to pass only from A to B, an even more readily useful difference in pressure would be created between the two vessels. About 1950 the French physicist Léon Brillouin exorcised the demon by demonstrating that the decrease in entropy resulting from the demon's actions would be exceeded by the increase in entropy in choosing between the fast and slow molecules.

Maxwell's equations, four equations that, together, form a complete description of the production and interrelation of electric and magnetic fields. The physicist James Clerk Maxwell in the 19th century based his description of electromagnetic fields on these four equations, which express experimental laws.

The statements of these four equations are, respectively: (1) electric field diverges from electric charge, an expression of the Coulomb force, (2) there are no isolated magnetic poles, but the Coulomb force acts between the poles of a magnet, (3) electric fields are produced by changing magnetic fields, an expression of Faraday's law of induction, and (4) circulating magnetic fields are produced by changing electric fields and by electric currents, Maxwell's extension of Ampère's law (*q.v.*) to include the interaction of changing fields. The most compact way of writing these equations in the metre-kilogram-second (mks) system is in terms of the vector operators div (divergence) and curl. In these expressions the Greek letter rho, ρ, is charge density, $\boldsymbol{J}$ is current density, $\boldsymbol{E}$ is the electric field, and $\boldsymbol{B}$ is the magnetic field; here, $\boldsymbol{D}$ and $\boldsymbol{H}$ are field quantities that are proportional to $\boldsymbol{E}$ and $\boldsymbol{B}$, respectively. The four Maxwell equations, corresponding to the four statements above, are: (1) div $\boldsymbol{D} = \rho$, (2) div $\boldsymbol{B} = 0$, (3) curl $\boldsymbol{E} = -d\boldsymbol{B}/dt$, and (4) curl $\boldsymbol{H} = d\boldsymbol{D}/dt + \boldsymbol{J}$.

May, fifth month of the Gregorian calendar. *See* month.

May, Karl (Friedrich) (b. Feb. 25, 1842, Hohenstein-Ernstthal, Saxony [Germany]—d. March 30, 1912, Radebeul, Ger.), German author of travel and adventure stories for young people, dealing with desert Arabs or with American Indians in the wild West, remarkable for the realistic detail that the author was able to achieve.

May was a weaver's son. He was an elementary school teacher until arrested for petty theft. He later was twice arrested for fraud and spent several years in prison, where he is said to have read voraciously. After his release in 1874 May wrote short stories that were serialized in various periodicals. His popularity soared upon the appearance of his short-story collections and novels in the early 1890s.

Some of the best known of his more than 60 works are *Der Schatz im Silbersee* (1894; "The Treasure in the Silver Lake"), *Durch die Wüste* (1892; *In the Desert*), *Winnetou*, 3 vol. (1893; Eng. trans., 1977); *Ardistan und Dschinnistan* (1909; *Ardistan and Djinnistan*), and the autobiography *Mein Leben und Streben* (1910; "My Life and Struggle"). In his memory there have been established a publishing house, the Karl May Verlag in Bamberg, Ger. (originally in Radebeul); the

Karl May, 1910
Historia-photo

Karl May Museum in Bamberg, containing North American Indian collections; and the Karl May Freilichtspiele, open-air theatres in Bad Segeberg and Elspe. Though virtually unknown in the United States, he is widely read in Europe and is one of the world's all-time fiction best-sellers.

May, Phil, byname of PHILIP WILLIAM MAY (b. April 22, 1864, Wortley, near Leeds, Yorkshire, Eng.—d. Aug. 5, 1903, London), British social and political caricaturist whose most popular works deal with lower- and middle-class London life in the late Victorian period.

His father, an engineer, died when May was nine years old. Three years later he began to earn his living; he worked as a timekeeper in a foundry, as a jockey, and then on the stage. When he was 16 he went to London, finally obtaining work as a designer with a theatrical costumer. He also drew posters and cartoons and for about two years worked for *St. Stephen's Review.* After a period in Australia, where he worked for the *Sydney Bulletin,* he returned to London in 1892 and resumed his work for *St. Stephen's Review.* May's studies of the London "guttersnipe" and the coster girl rapidly made him famous. His overflowing sense of fun, his sympathy with his subjects, and his kindly wit were on a par with his artistic ability. The economy of line characteristic of his drawings was the result of a laborious process in which he made numerous

"Self-portrait," pen and ink drawing by Phil May; in the National Portrait Gallery, London
By courtesy of the National Portrait Gallery, London

preliminary sketches. His later work included some excellent political portraits. He became a member of the staff of *Punch* in 1896, and from then on his services were retained entirely for that magazine and for the *Graphic.*

May, Thomas (b. 1595—d. Nov. 13, 1650, London), English man of letters known for his historical defense of the English Parliament in its struggle against King Charles I.

After graduating from Cambridge, May began the study of law at Gray's Inn (1615). He later abandoned law for literature. *The Heir* (1620), a comedy and his first dramatic work, was followed by another comedy and three tragedies and by translations of Virgil and Martial and (in 1627) of Lucan's historical poem *Pharsalia.* This last impressed Charles I, who requested May to compose verse histories of the reigns of Henry II and Edward III. Disappointment at the rewards from Charles may have contributed to May's sympathy with the Parliamentarians. As joint secretary "for the Parliaments" from 1646, he was in effect their propagandist. His *History of the Parliament of England, Which Began Nov. the Third, 1640* (1647) and his *Breviary of the History of the Parliament of England* (1650), although impartial in tone, were, in fact, skillful defenses of the Parliamentarian position.

May beetle: *see* June beetle.

May Day, in medieval and modern Europe, day (May 1) for traditional springtime celebrations, probably originating in pre-Christian agricultural rituals. Though local usage varied widely, these celebrations commonly included the carrying in procession of trees, green branches, or garlands; the appointment of a May king and May queen; and the setting up of a May tree or Maypole. Originally such rites were intended to ensure fertility to the crops, and by extension to cattle and human beings, but in most cases this significance was gradually lost, and the practices survived merely as popular festivities. A widespread superstition held that washing the face in the May Day morning dew would beautify the skin.

May Day was designated as an international labour day by the International Socialist congress of 1889. It was a major holiday in the Soviet Union and other Communist countries, and elsewhere it was the occasion for important political demonstrations.

May Fourth Movement, intellectual revolution and sociopolitical reform movement that occurred in China in 1917–21. The movement was directed toward national independence, emancipation of the individual, and rebuilding society and culture.

In 1915, in the face of Japanese encroachment on China, young intellectuals, inspired by "New Youth" (*Hsin Ch'ing-nien*), a monthly magazine edited by the iconoclastic intellectual revolutionary Ch'en Tu-hsiu, began agitating for the reform and strengthening of Chinese society. As part of this New Culture Movement, they attacked traditional Confucian ideas and exalted Western ideas, particularly science and democracy. Their inquiry into liberalism, pragmatism, nationalism, anarchism, and Socialism provided a basis from which to criticize traditional Chinese ethics, philosophy, religion, and social and political institutions. Moreover, led by Ch'en and the American-educated scholar Hu Shih, they proposed a new naturalistic vernacular writing style (*pai-hua*), replacing the difficult 2,000-year-old classical style (*wen-yen*).

These patriotic feelings and the zeal for reform culminated in an incident on May 4, 1919, from which the movement took its name. On that day, more than 3,000 students from 13 colleges in Peking held a mass demonstration against the decision of the Versailles Peace Conference, which drew up the treaty officially ending World War I, to transfer the former German concessions in northeastern Shantung Province to Japan. The Chinese government's acquiescence to the decision so enraged the students that they burned the house of the minister of communications and assaulted China's minister to Japan, both pro-Japanese officials. Over the following weeks, demonstrations occurred throughout the country; several students died in these incidents, and more than 1,000 were arrested. In the big cities, strikes and boycotts against Japanese goods were begun by the students and lasted more than two months. For one week, beginning June 5, merchants and workers in Shanghai and other cities went on strike in support of the students. Faced with this growing tide of unfavourable public opinion, the government acquiesced; three pro-Japanese officials were dismissed, the Cabinet resigned, and China refused to sign the peace treaty with Germany.

As a part of this movement, a campaign had been undertaken to reach the common people; mass meetings were held throughout the country, and more than 400 new publications were begun to spread the new thought. As a result, the decline of traditional ethics and the family system was accelerated, the emancipation of women gathered momentum, a vernacular literature emerged, and the modernized intelligentsia became a major factor in China's subsequent political developments. The movement also spurred the successful reorganization of the Kuomintang, the Nationalist Party later ruled by Chiang Kai-shek, and stimulated the birth of the Chinese Communist Party as well.

May Thirtieth Incident (1925), in China, a nationwide series of strikes and demonstrations precipitated by the killing of 13 labour demonstrators by British police in Shanghai. This was the largest anti-foreign demonstration China had yet experienced, and it encompassed people of all classes from all parts of the country. The Chinese Communist Party greatly benefitted by the anti-imperialist sentiment prevalent in the movement, and party membership swelled from a few hundred to more than 20,000.

The incident began early in 1925 when the terms of agreement decided upon between members of a mediation board and striking workers at a Japanese cotton mill in Shanghai were rejected by the company. On May

15 the workers sent eight representatives to negotiate with the management, but a melee resulted in which one worker was killed and the other seven wounded. The foreign-controlled Shanghai Municipal Council not only did not prosecute the Japanese who had opened fire but arrested several of the workers for disturbing the police. This led to a series of worker-student demonstrations, culminating in a mass demonstration on May 30 in which the British municipal police opened fire and killed 13 demonstrators and wounded many more. Following the incident a rash of nationalistic demonstrations erupted in all parts of the country. Chinese of all classes were outraged, and boycotts and strikes against British and Japanese goods and factories were organized by merchants and workers throughout the country. The unrest lasted almost seven months, until the British fired the police officials in charge and paid an indemnity to the families of the dead and wounded.

Consult the INDEX *first*

Maya, also called MAYAN, Meso-American Indians occupying a nearly continuous territory in southern Mexico, Guatemala, and northern Belize. Before the Spanish conquest of Mexico and Central America, the Maya possessed one of the greatest civilizations of the Western Hemisphere. They practiced agriculture, built great stone buildings and pyramid temples, worked gold and copper, and made use of a form of hieroglyphic writing that has now largely been deciphered.

A brief treatment of Mayan history and culture follows. For full treatment, *see* MACROPAEDIA: Pre-Columbian Civilizations.

As early as 1500 BC the Maya had settled in villages and had developed an agriculture based on the cultivation of corn (maize), beans, and squash. They began to build ceremonial centres, and by AD 200 these had developed into cities containing temples, pyramids, palaces, courts for playing ball, and plazas. They also developed a system of hieroglyphic writing and highly sophisticated calendrical and astronomical systems. The ancient Maya quarried immense quantities of building stone, which they cut using harder stones such as volcanic glass. They practiced mainly slash-and-burn agriculture, but they also used advanced techniques of irrigation and terracing. The Maya made paper from the inner bark of wild fig trees and wrote their hieroglyphs on books made from this paper; surviving books are called codices. They also developed an elaborate and beautiful tradition of sculpture and relief carving. Architectural works and stone inscriptions and reliefs are the chief sources of knowledge about the Maya. Early Mayan culture showed the influence of the earlier Olmec civilization.

The rise of the Maya began about AD 250, and what is known to archaeologists as the Classic period of Mayan culture lasted until about AD 900. At its height Mayan civilization consisted of more than 40 cities, each with a population of from 5,000 to 50,000. Among the principal cities were Tikal, Uaxactún, Copán, Bonampak, Palenque, and Río Bec. The peak Mayan population may have reached 2,000,000 people, most of whom were settled in the lowlands of what is now Guatemala. After AD 900, however, the classical Mayan civilization declined precipitously, leaving the great cities and ceremonial centres vacant and overgrown with jungle vegetation. The causes of this decline are uncertain; some scholars have suggested that armed conflicts and the exhaustion of agricultural land were responsible. During the Post-Classic period (900–1519), cities such as Chichén Itzá, Uxmal, and Mayapán in the highlands of the Yucatán Peninsula continued to flourish for several centuries after the great lowland cities had become depopulated. By the time the Spaniards conquered the area in the early 16th century, most of the Maya were mere village-dwelling agriculturists who practiced the religious rites of their forebears.

The major extant Mayan cities and ceremonial centres feature a variety of pyramidal temples or palaces overlaid with limestone blocks and richly ornamented with narrative, ceremonial, and astronomical reliefs and inscriptions that have ensured the stature of Mayan art as premier among Indian cultures. But the true nature of Mayan society, the meaning of its hieroglyphics, and the chronicle of its history remained unknown to scholars for centuries after the Spaniards discovered the ancient Mayan building sites.

Systematic explorations of the Mayan sites were first undertaken in the 1830s, and a small portion of the writing system was deciphered in the early and mid-20th century. These discoveries shed some light on Mayan religion, which was based on a pantheon of nature gods, including those of the sun, the moon, rain, and corn. A priestly class was responsible for an elaborate cycle of rituals and ceremonies. Closely related to Mayan religion, indeed inextricable from it, was the impressive development of mathematics and astronomy. In mathematics, positional notation and the use of the zero represented a pinnacle of intellectual achievement. Mayan astronomy underlay a complex calendrical system involving an accurately determined solar year (18 months of 20 days, plus an unlucky 5-day period), a sacred year of 260 days (13 cycles of 20 named days), and a variety of longer cycles culminating in the Long Count, based on a zero date in 3114 BC. Mayan astronomers compiled precise tables of positions for the Moon and Venus and were able to predict solar eclipses.

Based on these discoveries, scholars in the mid-20th century mistakenly thought that Mayan society was composed of a priestly class of peaceful stargazers and calendar keepers supported by a devout peasantry. The Maya were thought to be utterly absorbed in their religious and cultural pursuits, in favourable contrast to the more warlike and sanguinary Indian empires of central Mexico. But the progressive decipherment of nearly all of the Mayan hieroglyphic writing has provided a truer if less elevating picture of Mayan society and culture. Many of the hieroglyphs depict the histories of the Mayan dynastic rulers, who waged war on rival Mayan cities and took their aristocrats captive. These captives were then tortured, mutilated, and sacrificed to the Mayan gods. Indeed, torture and human sacrifice were fundamental religious rituals of Mayan society; they were thought to guarantee fertility, demonstrate piety, and propitiate the gods, and if such practices were neglected, cosmic disorder and chaos were thought to result. The drawing of human blood was thought to nourish the gods and was thus necessary to achieve contact with them; hence the Mayan rulers, as the intermediaries between the Mayan people and the gods, had to undergo ritual bloodletting and self-torture.

The present-day Mayan peoples can be divided on linguistic and geographic grounds into the following groups: the Yucatec Maya, inhabiting the Mexican Yucatán Peninsula and extending into northern Belize and northeastern Guatemala; the Lacandones, very few in number, occupying a territory in southern Mexico between the Usumacinta River and the Guatemalan border, with small numbers in Guatemala and Belize; the Quichéan peoples of the eastern and central highlands of Guatemala (Kekchí, Picomohi, Pocomam, Uspantec, Quiché, Cakchiquel, Tzutujil, Sacapultec, and Sipacapa); the Mamean peoples of the western Guatemalan highlands (Mam, Teco, Aguacatec, and Ixil); the Kanjobalan peoples of Huehuetenango in the same region and adjacent parts of Mexico (Motozintlec, Tuzantec, Jacaltec, Acatec, Tojolabal, and Chuj); the Tzotzil and Tzeltal peoples of Chiapas in southern Mexico; the Cholan peoples, including the Chontal and Chol speakers in northern Chiapas and Tabasco and the linguistically related Chortí of the extreme eastern part of Guatemala; and the Huastec of northern Veracruz and adjoining San Luís Potosí in eastern-central Mexico. The chief division in Mayan cultural type is between highland and lowland cultures. Yucatec, Lacandón, and Chontal-Chol are lowland groups. The Huastec are a linguistically and geographically isolated group who never were Mayan culturally, and the other Mayan peoples live in highlands across Guatemala.

The modern Maya are basically agricultural, raising crops of corn, beans, and squash. They live in communities organized around central villages, which may be permanently occupied but more commonly are community centres with public buildings and houses that generally stand vacant; the people of the community live on farm homesteads except during fiestas and markets. Cultivation is with the hoe and, where the soil is tough, the digging stick. The Yucatec usually keep pigs and chickens and, rarely, oxen that are used for farming. Industries are few, and crafts are oriented toward domestic needs. Usually some cash crop or item of local manufacture is produced for sale outside the region in order to provide cash for items not otherwise obtainable.

Dress is largely traditional, particularly for women; men are more likely to wear modern ready-made clothing. Domestic spinning and weaving, once common, is becoming rare, and most clothing is made of factory-woven cloth.

Almost all Maya are nominal Roman Catholics, but their Christianity is generally overlaid upon the native pagan religion. Its cosmology is typically Mayan, and Christian figures are commonly identified with Mayan deities. Public religion is basically Christian, with masses and saint's-day celebrations; but the native pre-Columbian religion is observed in domestic rites.

Māyā (mother of the Buddha): *see* Mahā Māyā.

maya (Sanskrit: "wizardry," or "illusion"), a fundamental concept in Hindu philosophy, notably, in the Advaita (Nondualist) school of the orthodox system of Vedānta. Maya originally denoted the power of wizardry with which a god can make human beings believe in what turns out to be an illusion; by extension it later came to mean the powerful force that creates the cosmic illusion that the phenomenal world is real. For the Nondualists, maya is thus that cosmic force that presents the infinite Brahman (the supreme being) as the finite phenomenal world. Maya is reflected on the individual level by human ignorance (*ajñāna*) of the real nature of the self, which man has mistaken for the empirical ego but which is in reality identical with Brahman.

Maya languages, also called MAYAN, family of Meso-American Indian languages spoken in southern Mexico, Guatemala, and Belize; Maya languages were also formerly spoken in western Honduras and western El Salvador. The family may be subdivided into the Huastec, Yucatec, Western Maya, and Eastern Maya groups. The most important Eastern Maya languages are Quiché and Cakchiquel; but there are also Mam, Teco, Aguacatec, Ixil, Uspantec, Sacapultec, Sipacapa, Pocomam, Pocomchí, and Kekchí. The largest Western Maya language is Tzeltal, spoken in Chiapas, Mex., but other Western Maya languages include Chontal, Chol, Chortí, Tzotzil, Tojolabal, Chuj, Kanjobal, Acatec, Jacaltec, and Motozintlec. The Yucatec languages, including Yucatec, Lacandón, Itzá, and Mopán, are sometimes also classed as Western Maya languages; Yucatec, the most important, is spoken in Yucatán, northern Guatemala, and Belize. The Huastec group is composed of the Huastec and Chicomuceltec languages. *See also* Yucatec language; Quiché language.

For a detailed treatment of Maya languages, *see* MACROPAEDIA: Languages of the World; *Meso-American Indian Languages.*

Maya Mountains, Spanish MONTAÑAS MAYAS, range of hills mostly in southern Belize, extending about 70 miles (115 km) northeastward from across the Guatemalan border into central Belize. The range falls abruptly to the coastal plain to the east and north but more gradually to the west, becoming the Vaca Plateau, which extends into eastern Guatemala. Both the range and the plateau are extensively dissected and of uniform elevation throughout, the highest point being reached at Victoria Peak (3,680 feet [1,122 m]) in the transverse Cockscomb Range, which extends seaward perpendicularly from the main divide. The mountains take their name from the Maya people, who retreated into the mountains before the Spaniards, leaving great centres, such as Lubaantun on the mountains' southeastern periphery, deserted behind them.

Mayagüez, city and municipality, western Puerto Rico. Created in 1760 as Nuestra Señora de la Candelaria de Mayagüez, it was elevated to the royal status of *villa* in 1836 and to a city in 1877. In 1918 the city and port were ravaged by an earthquake and tidal wave, but they were quickly rebuilt. Mayagüez has been one of the most progressive cities of Puerto Rico and, since the late 19th century, has been a centre of political activity.

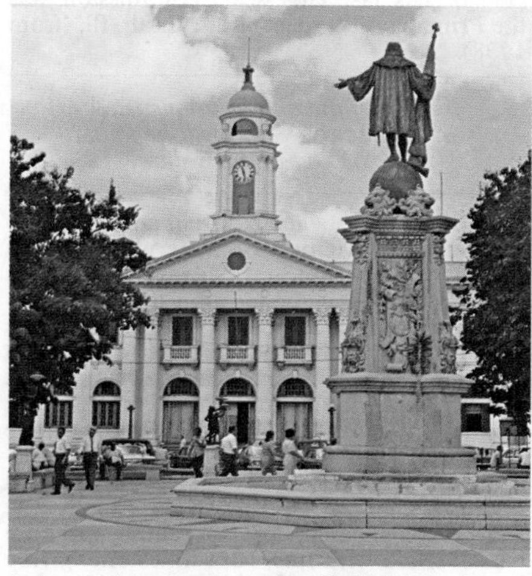

Statue of Columbus facing the City Hall in the Plaza Mayagüez, Mayagüez, Puerto Rico
Peter Arnold

With its excellent deepwater harbour, Mayagüez has long been the chief shipping port of western Puerto Rico and the centre of the island's needlework industry. The establishment of the Mayagüez Foreign Trade Zone, with heavy rent and tax subsidies, has fostered assembly and electronics industries, creating products for reexport. Other products include foods, beer, liquor, furniture, clothing, tiles, soap, cigars, and agricultural tools. The city is linked by rail and by commercial flights to San Juan. The U.S. Department of Agriculture's experimental station at Mayagüez is said to have the largest collection of tropical plants in the Western Hemisphere.

Among the city's educational institutions is the Mayagüez Campus of the University of Puerto Rico. There are some nuclear research facilities associated with the campus.

Mayagüez municipality, with an area of 77 square miles (200 square km), contains 5 urban or partly urban and 13 rural barrios (wards), including offshore Mona Island in the centre of the Mona Passage between Puerto Rico and the Dominican Republic. Agricultural products of the district include sugarcane, tobacco, coffee, and fruits and vegetables. Minerals include the Las Mesas limonite (iron-ore) deposits. Pop. (2000) city, 78,647; (1999 est.) mun., 100,463.

Mayakovsky, Vladimir Vladimirovich (b. July 19 [July 7, Old Style], 1893, Bagdadi, Georgia, Russian Empire—d. April 14, 1930, Moscow), the leading poet of the Russian Revolution and of the early Soviet period.

At the age of 15 Mayakovsky joined the Russian Social-Democratic Workers' Party and was repeatedly jailed for subversive activity. He started to write poetry during solitary confinement in 1909. On his release he attended the Moscow Art School and joined, with David Burlyuk and a few others, the Russian Futurist group and soon became its leading spokesman. In 1912 the group published a manifesto, *Poshchochina obshchestvennomuvkusu* ("A Slap in the Face of Public Taste"), and Mayakovsky's poetry became conspicuously self-assertive and defiant in form and content. His poetic monodrama *Vladimir Mayakovsky* was performed in St. Petersburg in 1913.

Between 1914 and 1916 Mayakovsky completed two major poems, "Oblako v shtanakh" (1915; "A Cloud in Trousers") and "Fleytapozvonochnik" (written 1915, published 1916; "The Backbone Flute"). Both record a tragedy of unrequited love and express the author's discontent with the world in which he lived. Mayakovsky sought to "depoetize" poetry, adopting the crude language of the man in the street and using the most daring technical innovations. Above all, his poetry is declamatory, for mass audiences.

When the Russian Revolution broke out, Mayakovsky was wholeheartedly for the Bolsheviks. Such poems as "Oda revolutsi" (1918; "Ode to Revolution") and "Levy marsh" (1919; "Left March") became very popular. So too did his *Misteriya-buff* (first performed 1921; "Mystery-Bouffe"), a drama representing a universal flood and the subsequent joyful triumph of the "Unclean" (the proletarians) over the "Clean" (the bourgeoisie).

As a vigorous spokesman for the Communist Party, Mayakovsky expressed himself in many ways. From 1919 to 1921 he worked in the Russian Telegraph Agency as a painter of posters and cartoons, which he provided with apt rhymes and slogans. He poured out topical poems of propaganda and wrote didactic booklets for children, while lecturing and reciting all over Russia. In 1924 he composed a 3,000-line elegy on the death of Lenin. After 1925 he traveled in Europe, the United States, Mexico, and Cuba, recording his impressions in poems and in a booklet of caustic sketches,

Mayakovsky
Novosti Press Agency

Moye otkrytiye Ameriki (1926; "My Discovery of America"). He also found time to write scripts for motion pictures, in some of which he acted. In his last three years he completed two satirical plays: *Klop* (performed 1929; *The Bedbug*), lampooning the kind of philistine that emerged with the New Economic Policy in the Soviet Union, and *Banya* (performed in Leningrad on Jan. 30, 1930; "The Bathhouse"), a persiflage of bureaucratic stupidity and opportunism under Stalin.

Mayakovsky's poetry was saturated with social meaning, but no amount of social propaganda could stifle his personal need for love, which burst out again and again because of repeated romantic frustrations. After his early lyrics this need came out particularly strongly in two poems, "Lyublyu" (1922; "I Love") and "Pro eto" (1923; "About This"). To make things worse, during a stay in Paris in 1928, he fell in love with a refugee, Tatyana Yakovleva, whom he wanted to marry but who refused him. At the same time, he had misunderstandings with the dogmatic Russian Association of Proletarian Writers and with Soviet authorities. Nor was the production of his *Banya* a success. Disappointed in love, increasingly alienated from Soviet reality, and denied a visa to travel abroad, he committed suicide in Moscow.

Mayakovsky was, in his lifetime, the most dynamic figure of the Soviet literary scene, but much of his utilitarian and topical poetry is now out of date. His predominantly lyrical poems and his technical innovations, however, influenced a number of Soviet poets, and outside Russia his impress has been strong, especially in the 1930s, after Stalin declared him the "best and most talented poet of our Soviet epoch."

Mayan calendar, dating system of the ancient Mayan civilization of Meso-America. The calendar was based on a ritual cycle (tzolkin) of 260 named and numbered days running concurrently with a 365-day civil year (haab). The Maya divided the tzolkin into 13 periods of 20 days each and the haab into 18 months (uinals) of 20 days plus one month of 5 "nameless" days. The nameless days were considered extremely unlucky, causing the Maya to observe them with fasting and sacrifices to deities.

Each ordinary day had a fourfold designation—day name and day number in the 260-day cycle and month name and month number within the month. Every 52 years the interlocked 260-day and 365-day cycles returned to the same positions relative to each other. Modern scholars call this period of more than half a century the Calendar Round. Every one of the 18,980 days in the Calendar Round had a different combination of day number, day name, month number, and month name (*e.g.,* 12 Caban 15 Ceh).

The Maya erected stelae—*i.e.,* stone slabs or pillars—on which they carved representative figures and important dates and events in their rulers' lives. To describe accurately a given date, the Maya instituted the "Long Count," a continuous marking of time from a base date. The base date, 4 Ahau 8 Cumku (3113 BC), was considered by them to be the beginning of the Mayan era.

Mayan hieroglyphic writing, system of writing used by the people of the Mayan Indian civilization of Meso-America from about the 3rd century AD until about the end of the 17th century, 200 years after the Spanish conquest of Mexico. It was the only true writing system developed in the pre-Columbian Americas. Mayan inscriptions are found on stelae (standing stone slabs), stone lintels, sculpture, and pottery, as well as on the few surviving Mayan books, or codices.

The Mayan system of writing contains more than 800 characters, many of which are hieroglyphic; *i.e.,* they are recognizable pictures of real objects. The signs are pictorial, representing animals, people, and objects of daily life. Until the mid-20th century, very little Mayan writing could be deciphered except for the symbols representing numbers, dates, and rulers' names and denoting such events as birth, death, and capture. In the 1960s, however, the first groups of glyphs describing the life histories of Mayan dynastic rulers were translated by Tatiana Proskouriakoff of the Carnegie Institution. It was increasingly recognized that the writing system used both logograms and phonetic symbols. More and more logograms and phonetic symbols were subsequently deciphered, until by the early 1990s readings had been established for a substantial proportion of the glyphs. Scholars were able to read many inscriptions, and these have provided new information about ancient Mayan culture and society.

Books in Mayan hieroglyphs, called codices, existed before the Spanish conquest of Yucatán about 1540, but most works written in the script were destroyed as pagan by Spanish priests. Only four Mayan codices are known to survive: the Dresden Codex, or Codex Dresdensis, probably dating from the 11th or 12th century, a copy of earlier texts of the 5th to 9th century AD; the Madrid Codex, or Codex Tro-Cortesianus, dating from the 15th century; the Paris Codex, or Codex Peresianus, probably slightly older than the Madrid Codex; and the

Mayan hieroglyphic inscriptions on stone tablet, 6th century, from Yaxchilan, Chiapas, Mexico
By courtesy of the Museo Nacional de Antropologia, Mexico City

Grolier Codex, discovered in 1971 and dated to the 13th century AD. The codices were made of fig-bark paper folded like an accordion; their covers were of jaguar skin.

Mayan languages: *see* Maya languages.

Mayapán, ruined ancient Mayan city, located about 35 miles (55 km) southeast of modern Mérida, Yucatán state, Mex. It became one of the most important cities of that region in the early Postclassic period (*c.* AD 900–1519). The art and architecture of the city were imitative of, but inferior to, that of Chichén Itzá, especially in the use of colonnades. The city was walled and built around a large well (cenote). About 3,600 buildings have been uncovered, most of them dwellings. There is a large pyramid, the Castillo, on the great plaza; to the south of it is a circular temple and to the east a temple with a serpent column. The two main groups of buildings each are arranged around a quadrangular court and were connected by a causeway, parts of which remain. Mayapán belonged to a league with the cities of Uxmal and Chichén Itzá; after the latter's decline, Mayapán became the dominant political power and religious centre of Yucatán from about 1200 to 1450. The despotic Cocom rulers of Mayapán were finally overthrown about 1450, when the city was abandoned.

mayapple, also called MAYFLOWER, or MANDRAKE (*Podophyllum peltatum*), perennial herbaceous plant of the family Podophyllaceae (order Ranunculales) native to eastern North America, most commonly in shady areas on moist, rich soil.

Its plant is 30 to 45 cm (12 to 18 inches) tall. Its dark green, umbrella-like leaves, nearly 30 cm across, have five to seven lobes. The cup-shaped flower, with six to nine white petals, is 2.5 to 5 cm (1 to 2 inches) across and appears from April to June. The fruit is an edible

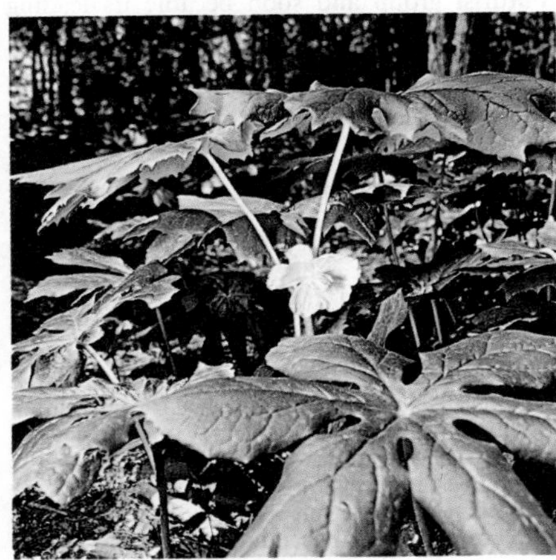

Mayapple (*Podophyllum peltatum*)
Grant Heilman

yellow berry that is sometimes used in jams or beverages. The dried rhizomes (fleshy underground stems) are sometimes used medicinally as a purgative. The plant is a coarse but attractive specimen for the shady wild garden.

Maybach, Wilhelm (b. Feb. 9, 1846, Heilbronn, Württemberg [Germany]—d. Dec. 29, 1929, Stuttgart, Ger.), German engineer and industrialist who was the chief designer of the first Mercedes automobiles (1900–01).

From 1883 Maybach was associated with Gottlieb Daimler in developing efficient internal-combustion engines; their first important product, a relatively light four-stroke engine, was patented in 1885. In 1890 Daimler and Maybach formed the Daimler-Motoren-Gesellschaft, in Cannstatt, to manufacture automobiles; from 1895 Maybach was the firm's technical director. His design for a carburetor was widely used from 1893 and was the subject of litigation (successful in England) over infringement of his patents. In 1909 Maybach and his son Carl organized a company at Friedrichshafen to build aircraft engines, including the power plants for airships constructed by the Zeppelin organization, to which the Maybachs' firm was subsidiary. Automobiles bearing the Maybach marque were produced from 1922 to 1939.

For the earliest Mercedes cars Maybach greatly improved an existing design for a 24-horsepower engine, providing mechanical inlet valves that could be throttled by the driver. He was at least in part responsible for the development of a light pressed-steel chassis with a honeycomb radiator; the initial conception perhaps should be credited to Paul Daimler, Gottlieb's son.

Maybeck, Bernard (Ralph) (b. Feb. 7, 1862, New York City—d. Oct. 3, 1957, Berkeley, Calif., U.S.), American architect whose work in California (from 1889) exhibits the versatility attainable within the formal styles of early 20th-century architecture.

First Church of Christ, Scientist, Berkeley, Calif., by Bernard Maybeck, begun 1910
Sandak, Inc.

Educated at the École des Beaux-Arts, Paris (1880–86), Maybeck worked briefly in New York City and Kansas City, Mo., before going to San Francisco. He joined the faculty of the University of California, Berkeley, as a drawing instructor (1894) and served as the university's first professor of architecture (1898–1903). For the university he designed Hearst Hall (1899; destroyed by fire, 1922), using for the first time the laminated-wood arch; the Town and Gown Club (1899), a brick building with a wood "outrigger" cornice; and the Men's Faculty Club (1900), a free treatment of the Spanish mission style. Among his other public buildings are the free-Gothic First Church of Christ, Scientist, Berkeley (1910), and the Neoclassical Palace of Fine Arts for the Panama-Pacific Exposition, San Francisco (1915). His last large-scale commission was the Principia College campus, Elsah, Ill. (from 1938).

A list of the abbreviations used in the MICROPAEDIA *will be found at the end of this volume*

Maydūm, also spelled MEDUM, ancient Egyptian site near Memphis on the west bank of the Nile River in Banī Suwayf *muḥāfaẓah* (governorate). It is the location of the earliest-known pyramid complex with all the parts of a normal Old Kingdom (*c.* 2575–*c.* 2130 BC) funerary monument. These parts included the pyramid itself, a mortuary temple, and a sloping causeway leading to a valley temple built near the Nile River. The Maydūm pyramid was originally a seven-stepped pyramid to which another step was added. Finally, the steps were filled in, and the entire structure was overlaid with fine Tura limestone, giving it the appearance of a true pyramid. Most scholars agree that the pyramid was probably begun by Huni, the last king of the 3rd dynasty (*c.* 2650–*c.* 2575), but was apparently completed by his successor, Snefru, the first king of the 4th dynasty (*c.* 2575–*c.* 2465). Late in its reconstruction under Snefru, the outer casing and fill of the pyramid began to collapse. The work was abandoned, and the

The Maydūm pyramid
H. Roger-Viollet

mortuary chapel remained uninscribed. The collapse produced the present appearance of the pyramid.

Mayekawa Kunio (Japanese architect): *see* Maekawa Kunio.

Mayence (Germany): *see* Mainz.

Mayenne, *département,* Pays de la Loire region, northwestern France, south of Normandie and east of Bretagne (Brittany). Its area of 1,997 sq mi (5,171 sq km) comprises the western part of the historic province of Maine (*q.v.*) and a strip of northwestern Anjou. The *département* is watered by the Mayenne River, which flows into the Loire via the Maine. The Mayenne, bisecting the *département* north–south and navigable for 55 mi, passes through Mayenne, an ancient town; Laval (*q.v.*), the capital; and Château-Gontier, a picturesque town founded in the 9th century. The *département* was ravaged by insurrections after the French Revolution, and the town of Mayenne was captured in 1793.

Mayenne is predominantly wooded and hilly, its climate chiefly oceanic. The Haut-Maine range, which reaches 1,368 ft (417 m) in the extreme northeast at Mont des Avaloirs, slopes southwestward. The hills in the south are little more than 300 ft high. During the 19th and 20th centuries, many wooded areas were cleared for agriculture, predominantly for grazing and apple growing. The cattle market at Château-Gontier is one of the most important in France, but the once thriving linen industry practically disappeared in the mid-19th century. Some cotton looms and a few foundries remain, as well as printing works and food-processing plants. Picturesque sites include the fortified town of Sainte-Suzanne on a rocky promontory dominating the Erve River in the southeast. The *département* has three *arrondissements*—Laval, Château-Gontier, and Mayenne. It is in the educational division of Rennes. Pop. (1999) 285,377.

Mayenne, Charles de Lorraine, duc de (duke of) (b. March 26, 1554, Alençon, Fr.—d. Oct. 13, 1611, Soissons), leader (1589–95) of the Holy League in France and opponent of Henry of Navarre's claims to the French throne.

During the first religious wars in France, Mayenne participated in several military actions against the Huguenots. After the assassinations (1588) of his brothers, Henri, duc de Guise, and Louis, cardinal de Lorraine, Mayenne emerged as the leader of the Catholic party. In 1589 he assumed the presidency of the general council of the Holy League, and, after the assassination of Henry III, Mayenne supported the old Cardinal de Bourbon as "Charles X" in his bid for the crown in opposition to the Huguenot claimant, Henry of Navarre (King Henry IV, 1589–1610). Although he wanted a Catholic ruler for France, Mayenne curbed the extremists who sought to put the Spanish infanta Isabella on the French throne; in 1593 he summoned a meeting of the States General in Paris, which upheld the principles of the Salic law of succession against Isabella's claim. In September 1595 Mayenne finally submitted to Henry IV; by the Articles of Folembray (January 1596) Mayenne retained Chalon, Seurre, and Soissons for six years, his followers kept the honours and offices he had granted them, his own debts were settled up to 35,000 crowns, and his son was made governor of Île-de-France. Thereafter he remained on excellent terms with Henry IV.

Mayenne, engraving 16th century
By courtesy of the Bibliotheque Nationale, Paris

Mayenne River, river in northwestern France; its headwaters are west-northwest of Alençon in Forêt de Multonne, Orne *département*. It flows southward for 121 miles (195 km) to its confluence with the Sarthe above Angers. The combined rivers, called the Maine River (*q.v.*), flow through Angers into the Loire. The Mayenne is canalized for 73 mi, having 45 dams and locks.

Mayer, Johann Tobias (b. Feb. 17, 1723, Marbach, Württemberg—d. Feb. 20, 1762, Göttingen), German astronomer who developed lunar tables that greatly assisted navigators in determining longitude at sea. Mayer also discovered the libration (or apparent wobbling) of the Moon.

A self-taught mathematician, Mayer had already published two original geometrical works when, in 1746, he entered the employ of a cartographic establishment in Nürnberg. Mayer published his calculations of the Moon's libration and equatorial inclination in the transactions of the Nürnberg Cosmographic Society, thereby gaining a scientific reputation that led to his appointment to the chair of economy and mathematics at the University of Göttingen in 1751. He became superintendent of the university observatory in 1754.

Mayer began calculating lunar and solar tables in 1753. Two years later he submitted to the British government an amended body of tables, which were found to be sufficiently accurate to determine longitude at sea within about half a degree. A London edition of the tables (1770) also contained Mayer's method of determining longitude by lunar distances (the angular separation between the Moon and another celestial object), as well as a formula for correcting errors in longitude caused by atmospheric refraction.

Mayer, Louis B(urt), original name ELIEZER, or LAZAR, MAYER (b. July 4, 1885, Minsk, Russian Empire—d. Oct. 29, 1957, Los Angeles), most powerful motion-picture executive in Hollywood for 30 years. As the head of Metro-Goldwyn-Mayer, the largest and most prestigious film studio, he created the star system during the 1920s and '30s and had under contract the outstanding screen personalities of the day.

The son of immigrant parents, Mayer worked in his father's ship-salvaging and scrap-iron business from the age of 14. In 1907 he opened his first small nickelodeon in Haverhill, Mass., and by 1918 owned the largest chain of motion-picture theatres in New England. To increase the supply of pictures for his theatres, he opened in Hollywood Louis B. Mayer Pictures and the Metro Pictures Corporation. Six years later MGM was formed by a merger with Goldwyn Pictures Corporation, with Mayer as the controlling head of the new company.

Under Mayer's influence, MGM productions seldom dealt with controversial subject matter. They were characterized, rather, by elaborate sets, gorgeous costuming, and pretty girls. The emphasis was on the glamorous stars, many of whom, such as Greta Garbo, Joan Crawford, Rudolph Valentino, and Clark Gable, were Mayer discoveries. Such pictures as *Ben Hur* (1926), *Grand Hotel* (1932), *Dinner at Eight* (1933), and *The Good Earth* (1937) gained MGM the reputation for entertaining films of consistently high quality. Mayer relinquished control of the studio in 1948 and retired completely three years later.

Mayer, Maria Goeppert (b. June 28, 1906, Kattowitz, Ger.—d. Feb. 20, 1972, San Diego, Calif., U.S.), German physicist, joint winner, with J. Hans Daniel Jensen of West Germany and Eugene P. Wigner of the U.S., of the Nobel Prize for Physics in 1963 for their explanation of the detailed properties of atomic nuclei in terms of a structure of shells occupied by the protons and neutrons.

In 1930 Goeppert received her Ph.D. from the University of Göttingen and married U.S. chemical physicist Joseph E. Mayer and went with him to Johns Hopkins University, Baltimore. In 1939 she went to Columbia University, where she worked on the separation of uranium isotopes for the atomic bomb project, and in 1945 to the Institute for Nuclear Studies at the University of Chicago. The great stability and abundance of nuclei that have a particular number of neutrons (such as 50, 82, or 126) and the same special number of protons was explained by Mayer in 1949 in terms of the nuclear shell theory. She and Jensen jointly wrote *Elementary Theory of Nuclear Shell Structure* (1955).

Mayer, Simon: *see* Marius, Simon.

Mayer, Werner (composer): *see* Egk, Werner.

Mayerling, village on the Schwechat River in eastern Lower Austria (Niederösterreich), 24 kilometres (15 miles) southwest of Vienna. It is the site of a hunting lodge (now a Carmelite convent) where the Habsburg crown prince, Archduke Rudolf, and his paramour Mary Vetsera committed suicide under mysterious circumstances in January 1889. *See* Rudolf, Archduke and Crown Prince of Austria.

Mayet (Egyptian goddess): *see* Maʿat.

Mayfield, city, seat of Graves county, southwestern Kentucky, U.S., 25 mi (40 km) west of Kentucky Lake. It was settled about 1820 and named for a local creek into which according to legend a George Mayfield fell, mortally wounded by robbers. The New Orleans and Ohio Railroad arrived in 1854 and boosted its development as a market centre for dark-leaf tobacco, livestock, and grain. Light industry and extensive local deposits of ball clay (used for ceramics and china) have broadened its economic base. A monument marks the site of Camp Beauregard (1861), a Confederate Civil War base captured (1862) along with the city by Federal forces. Inc. 1823. Pop. (2000) 10,349.

mayflower, either of two spring-blooming wild flowers native to eastern North America. *Podophyllum peltatum* is more often called mayapple (*q.v.*) and *Epigaea repens* is the trailing arbutus (*q.v.*).

To make the best use of the Britannica, consult the INDEX *first*

Mayflower, in American colonial history, the ship that carried the Pilgrims from England to Plymouth, Mass., where they established the first permanent New England colony in 1620. Although no detailed description of the original vessel exists, marine archaeologists estimate that the square-rigged sailing ship weighed about 180 tons and measured 90 feet (27 m) long. Some of the Pilgrims were brought from Holland on the *Speedwell,* a smaller vessel that accompanied the *Mayflower* on its initial departure from Southampton, Eng., on August 15. When the *Speedwell* proved unseaworthy and was twice forced to return to port, the *Mayflower* finally set out alone from Plymouth, Eng., a month later, after taking on some of the smaller ship's passengers and supplies. Among the *Mayflower's* most distinguished voyagers were William Bradford and Captain Myles Standish.

Chartered by English merchants called the London Adventurers, the *Mayflower* was prevented by rough seas and storms from reaching the territory that had been granted in Virginia. Instead, after a 66-day voyage, it first landed November 21 on Cape Cod at what is now Provincetown, Mass., and the day after Christmas deposited its 102 settlers nearby at the site of Plymouth. The ship remained in port until the following April, when it left for England. In 1957 the historic voyage of the *Mayflower* was commemorated when a replica of the original ship was built in England and sailed to Massachusetts in 53 days.

Mayflower Compact (Nov. 21 [Nov. 11, Old Style], 1620), document signed by 41 of the male passengers on the *Mayflower* prior to their landing at Plymouth, Mass. The compact resulted from the fear that some members of the company might leave the group and settle on their own. The Mayflower Compact bound the signers into a body politic for the purpose of forming a government and pledged them to abide by any laws and regulations that would later be established. The document was not a constitution but rather an adaptation of the usual church covenant to a civil situation. It became the foundation of Plymouth's government.

mayfly, any slender, small to medium-size (up to 4 cm [1.6 inches]) insect of the order Ephemeroptera usually found around streams and ponds. The approximately 2,000 species are characterized by triangular membranous fore wings, smaller round hind wings, and two or three long, threadlike tails. The mayfly is

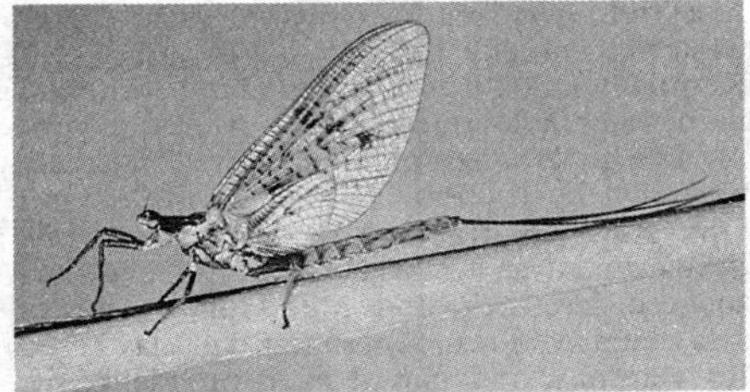

Female mayfly (*Ephemera danica*)
G.E. Hyde

the only insect to molt after its wings become functional. Wings are held vertically when at rest rather than in the rooflike position typical of most other insects. Chewing mouthparts in the aquatic larvae are vestigial in the adult, which lives just long enough to mate and reproduce. Males "dance" in large swarms to attract the females. The frantic activity of the adult mayfly has long been of interest to both the poet and the angler: the poet uses it as a symbol of life's ephemeral nature; and the angler, using lures that resemble mayflies, tries to mimic it.

mayhem, in Anglo-American law, offense against the person in which the offender violently deprives his victim of a member of his body, thus making him less able to defend himself. The disabling of an arm, hand, finger, leg, foot, or eye are examples of mayhem. In a number of jurisdictions, mere disfigurement or maiming is considered mayhem. To be guilty of the criminal offense, one must intend to dismember the victim or must assault him so recklessly as to create the danger of dismemberment even though not intending to cripple.

Some jurisdictions do not distinguish between mayhem and other types of battery. Japan treats all batteries similarly. Most criminal systems, however, divide batteries into two classes, reserving the more severe penalties for "aggravated" batteries including mayhem. The terminology varies from country to country. Thus, Indian law divides bodily harms into "hurts" and "grievous hurts." *See also* assault and battery.

Mayhew, Henry (b. 1812, London, Eng.—d. July 25, 1887, London), English journalist and sociologist, a founder of the magazine *Punch* (1841), who was a vivid and voluminous writer best known for *London Labour and the London Poor,* 4 vol. (1851–62). His evocation of the sights and sounds of London in this work influenced Charles Dickens and other writers.

Henry Mayhew, engraving after a photograph
BBC Hulton Picture Library

The son of a solicitor, Mayhew ran away to sea and made a voyage to India. Upon his return he studied law with his father but soon turned to journalism. He helped to found the periodicals *Figaro in London* (1831) and *The Thief* (1832) before organizing the highly successful *Punch,* of which he was coeditor (with Mark Lemon) for two years. He also wrote plays, farces, fairy tales, and novels, some in collaboration with his brother Augustus Septimus Mayhew (1826–75). Short of money in his later years, he produced much hackwork and died in obscurity.

Mayhew had a genius for lively and sensitive reportage of people, including social outcasts and nomads, and of contrasting ways of life; and he was able to combine his observation with penetrating economic and social analysis, some of it with a Marxist flavour. *London Labour and the London Poor* was based on letters he wrote to the *London Morning Chronicle* in 1849–50, at the end of a stormy decade in British social history. Responding to the newspaper's desire for "trustworthy information" on the great social problems of the day, Mayhew prepared three volumes that were published in 1851; the fourth volume, *The Criminal Prisons of London,* was written in collaboration with John Binny and did not appear until 1862. A revised complete edition was published in 1864.

Mayhew, Jonathan (b. Oct. 8, 1720, Martha's Vineyard, Mass. [U.S.]—d. July 9, 1766, Boston), vigorous Boston preacher whose outspoken political and religious liberalism made him one of the most controversial men in colonial New England.

The Mayhew family had arrived in the American colonies in 1631. After a boyhood on Martha's Vineyard, young Mayhew attended Harvard College (1740–44). In 1747 he was ordained pastor of Boston's West Church, where he remained—outspoken, controversial, and at odds with most of the local clergy—until his death. His sermons were printed in New England and in London. He carried on a lively correspondence with several British clergymen and became, to the English, one of the best-known Americans.

In theology Mayhew was an Arminian—he saw divine will in terms of the power of love rather than of unmitigated force. Rejecting both Calvinistic dogmatism and Anglican authoritarianism, he preached a "true primitive religion" of strong belief in individual responsibility and private judgment. He believed that resistance to tyranny was a Christian duty, and he was an outspoken defender of civil liberties. When the British imposed the Stamp Act on the colonists early in 1765, he opposed it so zealously that he was accused of inciting the Stamp Act riots of that August, but he denied the charges and continued his vigorous opposition to the act.

Maykop, also spelled MAIKOP, city and capital of the republic of Adygeya, Krasnodar *kray* (region), Russia, on the right bank of the Belaya River. Maykop (from the Adygey *myequape* meaning "valley of apple trees") was founded in 1857 as a Russian fortress. Food processing is the city's leading industry; metalworking, machine building, timber working, and tannin extracting are also important. The Maykop oil fields lie southwest of the city. In 1950 a hydroelectric plant was completed on the Belaya. The many mineral springs in the neighbourhood have given Maykop some importance as a spa. The city has a teacher-training institute and an institute of the Adygey language, history, and literature. Pop. (1991 est.) 170,400.

Maymūn ibn Qays al-Aʿshā: *see* Aʿshā, al-.

Maymyo, town, central Myanmar (Burma). It lies at the head of a shallow valley, at an elevation of about 3,450 feet (1,050 m). The town, named for Colonel (later Major General) James May of the 5th Bengal Infantry stationed there in 1886, served as the summer capital during the British administration. Although the Myanmar government does not leave Yangôn (Rangoon), the national capital, the head of state maintains a summer residence in Maymyo, which is also a training centre for army officers. The town is spaciously laid out in broad roads lined with eucalyptus, silver oak, and pine. The flowers, fruits, and vegetables produced in its many large gardens are widely distributed. Maymyo is reached by road from Mandalay and rail and air from Yangôn. It has notable botanical gardens, and there is a hunting reserve nearby. The town has a technical high school. Pop. (latest est.) 31,479.

Maynard, François, Maynard also spelled MAINARD (b. 1582/83, Toulouse, Fr.—d. Dec. 28, 1646), French poet, leading disciple of François de Malherbe and, like him, concerned with the clarification of the French language. He is commonly confused with François Ménard (1589–1631) of Nîmes, also a poet.

Maynard obtained a post with Marguerite de Valois in 1605 and began writing pastoral poetry. *Philandre* belongs to this period, although it was not printed until 1619. He attached himself to Malherbe and helped to spread the latter's ideas on the necessity of a standard grammar, the elimination of personal sentiments in writing, and an objective treatment of the subject matter.

Maynard held office in the presidial court of Aurillac from 1611 to 1628. He failed to win the esteem of Cardinal de Richelieu, however, and spent many years in the country in retirement. He was made a member of the French Academy in 1634. Returning to Paris after Richelieu's death, he found that literary fashion had changed; he retired to the country again.

As a poet, Maynard is inferior to Honorat de Racan, another Malherbian disciple. Yet he is noted for carrying on the tradition of clarity, power, and perfection of form.

Mayne, Cuthbert (b. 1544, Youlston, Devon, Eng.—d. Nov. 30, 1577, Launceston, Cornwall), Roman Catholic martyr executed during the persecution of Roman Catholics under the English queen Elizabeth I.

Mayne was raised and ordained (1561) in the Church of England. While at the University of Oxford he was befriended by Edmund Campion (who was to become perhaps the most famous of the English Catholic martyrs) and Gregory Martin (later the principal translator of the Douai-Reims Bible). Under their influence, Mayne also converted to Roman Catholicism. He fled to the European continent; was ordained a Roman Catholic priest at the English College at Douai, Fr.; and returned in 1576 as a missionary to Cornwall. He disguised himself as the steward of a local landowner but was discovered and put to death at Launceston on Nov. 30, 1577, on charges of denying the queen's spiritual supremacy, saying Mass, and possessing an Agnus Dei (a type of Roman Catholic devotional medallion). Mayne was the first of the Douai-trained priests to be martyred and, with 39 other British martyrs (the Forty Martyrs of England and Wales), was canonized by Pope Paul VI in 1970, on October 25, the day designated as their feast day.

Maynooth, village, County Kildare, Ireland, 15 miles (24 km) west of Dublin. Historic remains in the locality include those of a castle built by Gerald FitzMaurice (d. 1203) and an early manorial church that has been incorporated into the Church of Ireland. St. Patrick's College at Maynooth is the largest Roman Catholic seminary in the British Isles; it was established in 1795 on the site of a college founded by the Earl of Kildare in the 16th century and is now a college of the National University of Ireland. At the east end of the town is the scenic Carton estate, the former residence of the dukes of Leinster. Carton House, designed in classic style, was built about 1740. Pop. (1986) 4,768.

Mayo, Indian people centred in southern Sonora and northern Sinaloa states on the west coast of Mexico. They speak a dialect of the Cahita language, which belongs to the Uto-Aztecan language family.

The history of the Mayo people prior to the Spanish conquest of Mexico is obscure. In the early 17th century they readily allied themselves with the Spaniards against their northern neighbours, the Yaqui. But gradual Spanish encroachment on their land drove the Mayo to revolt in 1740 and subsequently before they were permanently pacified in the 1880s by Mexico's central government.

The Mayo are concentrated in the fertile irrigated valleys of the Mayo and Fuerte rivers, which are set in the midst of semidesert terrain that supports thorny scrubland and cactus. The Mayo are settled agriculturalists whose traditional crops of corn (maize), beans, and squash have given way in part to such crops as cotton, wheat, and safflower (for oil). The Mayo combine Roman Catholicism with aboriginal religious practices. They numbered about 80,000 in the late 20th century.

Mayo, Irish MAIGH EO ("Plain of the Yew Trees"), county in the province of Connaught, western Ireland. With an area of 2,084 square miles (5,398 square km), it is bounded by the Atlantic Ocean (north and west) and by Counties Sligo (northeast), Roscommon (east), and Galway (southeast and south). Mayo's extensive coastline is wild and broken, with many inlets from Killala Bay in the north to Killary Harbour in the southwest. Westport and Ballina are port towns, and there are numerous islands and inland lakes. Stretching east and north from Lough (lake) Carrowmore is the largest expanse of bog in Ireland, 200 square miles (520 square km) in area. The principal rivers in Mayo are the Moy and the Errif. The low peaks of Nephin (2,646 feet [807 m]) and Croagh Patrick (2,510 feet [765 m]) dominate the landscape; and Mweelrea (2,688 feet [819 m]), to the north of Killary Harbour, is the highest mountain in Connaught.

At the close of the 12th century the territory that now constitutes County Mayo was granted by King John of England to the Norman William de Burgh, but Mayo remained loosely subject to the Gaelic overlordship of O'Donnell, chief of Tyrconnell. In the 14th century the land passed to a branch of the de Burgh family known as MacWilliam Iochtair. In 1603 Theobald Burke, of the MacWilliam Iochtair, surrendered his lands and received them back to hold with the title of Viscount Mayo.

The county is rich in Neolithic remains and has strong associations with the early Irish ministry of St. Patrick. There are round towers at Killala and Turlough. Ballintober Abbey, founded in 1216, is still in use as a church. Monastic ruins are widespread.

Castlebar is the county town (seat) and an urban district, as are Ballina and Westport. Ballina is the seat of the Roman Catholic bishop of Killala.

In the rugged mountains of the north and west, the farms are small, and most of the population supplements its earnings by migration to Great Britain. Cattle for the British market and sheep and pigs are raised extensively. Tourism is developing, and the area is particularly attractive to fishermen and bird hunters. The county's industries include those in Ballina (flour milling), Westport (clothing), Foxford (woolens), Castlebar (bacon), and Belmullet (toys). Pop. (1986) 115,184.

Mayo FAMILY, the most famous group of physicians in the United States. Three generations of the Mayo family, pioneers in the practice of group medicine, established the world-renowned Mayo Clinic and the Mayo Foundation for Medical Education and Research at Rochester, Minn.

William Worrall Mayo
By courtesy of the Mayo Clinic, Rochester, Minn.

William Worrall Mayo (b. May 31, 1819, near Manchester, Eng.—d. March 6, 1911, Rochester, Minn., U.S.) was the father of the doctors Mayo who developed a large-scale, world-renowned practice of medicine.

Mayo attended Owens College in Manchester, majoring in chemistry, and, after immigrating to the United States in 1845, studied medicine with a private physician in Lafayette, Ind., subsequently receiving degrees from Indiana Medical College, La Porte, and the University of Missouri, Columbia. In 1863 he moved to Rochester, where he soon had an extensive surgical practice. After taking care of the casualties of a disastrous tornado in Rochester, with the assistance of the Sisters of St. Francis, Mayo, his two sons, and the sisters planned to erect a new hospital. St. Mary's Hospital was opened on Oct. 1, 1889, and Mayo and his two sons became responsible for care of the patients. After the father retired, the work at the hospital was continued by his sons.

William James Mayo (b. June 29, 1861, Le Sueur, Minn.—d. July 28, 1939, Rochester) was the eldest son of William Worrall Mayo. He received his M.D. degree in 1883 from the University of Michigan, Ann Arbor, and then

William James Mayo
By courtesy of the Mayo Clinic, Rochester, Minn.

engaged at Rochester in the private practice of medicine and surgery with his father and later with his younger brother Charles Horace Mayo. Though William J. Mayo became the administrator in the practice, no important decisions were made without the full agreement of both brothers. He and his brother performed all the surgery at St. Mary's Hospital until about 1905. From this surgical partnership of the two brothers evolved the cooperative group clinic, later known as the Mayo Clinic. William James Mayo, who became a specialist in surgery of the abdomen, pelvis, and kidney, remained active in surgery at the clinic until 1928 and in administration until 1933.

Charles Horace Mayo (b. July 19, 1865, Rochester—d. May 26, 1939, Chicago, Ill.) was the younger son of William Worrall Mayo and was characterized as a "surgical wonder." He received an M.D. degree from the Chicago Medical College (later part of Northwestern University Medical School) in 1888 and in the same year began private practice of surgery with his father and brother.

Charles Mayo had the ability to work in all surgical fields; he originated modern proce-

Charles Horace Mayo
By courtesy of the Mayo Clinic, Rochester, Minn.

dures in goitre surgery and in neurosurgery; he performed highly successful operations for cataract of the eye and originated procedures for several orthopedic operations. In 1930 he retired from surgery at the clinic and three years later from administration. He was professor of surgery at the University of Minnesota Medical School from 1919 to 1936 and at the University of Minnesota Graduate School from 1915 to 1936. William J. Mayo said about his brother, "Charlie has . . . an intuitive mind, from his knowledge of physiology and anatomy and his understanding of the personality of the patient." At one time he was a member of the advisory board of *Encyclopædia Britannica.* With his brother, he alternated as chief consultant for all surgical services in the U.S. Army during World War I, serving with the rank of colonel. After the war, each brother was commissioned a brigadier general in the medical-corps reserve.

Charles William Mayo (b. July 28, 1898, Rochester—d. July 28, 1968, Rochester) was the son of Charles Horace. He was a skilled surgeon and member of the board of governors of the Mayo Clinic, chairman of the Mayo Association, and a member (chairman 1961–67) of the board of regents of the University of Minnesota. He is noted for a speech he gave in 1953 as a member of the United States delegation at the United Nations.

The clinic began to grow in size in the early 1900s, when many young physicians began to apply for positions as interns and assistants. At the same time, outstanding scientists in basic medical subjects were added to the clinic's training and research programs. In 1919 the Mayo brothers transferred property and capital to the Mayo Properties Association, later called the Mayo Foundation, a charitable and educational corporation having a perpetual charter. About 1900 the Mayo Clinic was changed from a partnership to a voluntary association of physicians and specialists in allied fields. In the late 20th century the clinic's staff included about 500 physicians, treating more than 200,000 patients annually.

In 1915 the Mayo brothers gave $1,500,000 to the University of Minnesota to establish the Mayo Foundation for Medical Education and Research at Rochester in connection with the clinic. The foundation, which is part of the University of Minnesota Graduate School, offers graduate training in medicine and related subjects.

In 1986 the Mayo Clinic merged with the nearby St. Mary's Hospital and Rochester Methodist Hospital. The Mayo Foundation also began a national expansion program that year, opening the Mayo Clinic Jacksonville in Florida; the Mayo Clinic Scottsdale in Arizona opened in 1987. (T.E.K./Ed.)

BIBLIOGRAPHY. Studies of their lives and work include Helen B. Clapesattle, *The Doctors Mayo,* 3rd ed. (1989), an authoritative work based on printed sources and interviews; Lucy Wilder, *The Mayo Clinic,* 2nd ed. (1955), by the wife of a prominent Mayo physician; Gunther W. Nagel, *The Mayo Legacy* (1966), written by a doctor trained in surgery at the Mayo Clinic; and William F. Braasch, *Early Days in the Mayo Clinic* (1969), by the pioneer urologist of the Mayo Clinic.

Mayo, Elton, in full GEORGE ELTON MAYO (b. Dec. 26, 1880, Adelaide, Australia—d. Sept. 7, 1949, Polesden Lacey, Surrey, Eng.), Australian-born psychologist who became an early leader in the field of industrial sociology in the United States, emphasizing the dependence of productivity on small-group unity. He extended this work to link the factory system to the larger society.

After teaching at the universities of Queensland in Brisbane (1919–23) and Pennsylvania in Philadelphia (1923–26), Mayo served as professor of industrial research at the Harvard Graduate School of Business Administration (1926–47). *The Human Problems of an Industrial Civilization* (1933) is probably his most important book.

In 1927 Mayo initiated a pioneering industrial research project at the Western Electric Company's Hawthorne Works, Chicago; his associates F.J. Roethlisberger and William J. Dickson summarized the results in *Management and the Worker* (1939). Parts of this study—those concerning the collection of data, labour-management relations, and informal interaction among factory employees—continued to be influential. Mayo also advocated a personnel-counseling program that would address the particular needs of industrial workers unable to derive satisfaction from employment in large organizations.

Mayo, Richard Southwell Bourke, 6th Earl of, VISCOUNT MAYO OF MONYCROWER, BARON NAAS OF NAAS, also called (1849–67) LORD NAAS (b. Feb. 21, 1822, Dublin, Ire.—d. Feb. 8, 1872, Port Blair, Andaman Islands), Irish politician and civil servant best known for his service as viceroy of India, where he improved relations with Afghanistan, conducted the first census, turned a deficit budget into a surplus, and created a department for agriculture and commerce.

The eldest son of the 5th earl, Richard Bourke spent 1838–39 traveling in Europe with his parents before graduating from Trinity College, Dublin. In 1845 he traveled in Russia and published a two-volume account of his journey, *St. Petersburg and Moscow,* in 1846. As a member of Parliament in 1847–67, he successively represented Kildare, Coleraine, and Cockermouth and was chief secretary for Ireland in three administrations, from 1852, 1858, and 1866.

Mayo became viceroy of India in January 1869 and in March received Shīr ʿAlī Khān, emir of Afghanistan, at Ambāla to negotiate a closer alliance that would decrease Russian influence. Generally maintaining domestic peace, he sanctioned an expedition against the raiding Lushai tribes of the northeastern border in 1871–72. He initiated the policy of decentralization of finances and promoted the development of public works, railways, forests, irrigation schemes, and port defenses. The European-oriented Mayo College at Ajmer was founded for the education of young native chiefs, with £70,000 being subscribed by the chiefs themselves. In 1869–70 he hosted the Duke of Edinburgh (Queen Victoria's second son). On an inspection tour of the convict settlement in the Andaman Islands, he was stabbed to death by an Afghan prisoner, who was hanged five weeks later for the crime.

Mayon Volcano, active volcano, southeastern Luzon, Philippines, dominating the city of Legaspi. Called the world's most perfect cone, it has a base 80 miles (130 km) in circumference and rises to 7,943 feet (2,421 m) from the shores of Albay Gulf. Popular with climbers and campers, it is the centre of Mayon Volcano National Park (21 square miles [55 square km]). There are large abaca plantations on its lower slopes. There have been more than 30 eruptions recorded since 1616; an eruption in 1993 caused 75 deaths. Its most destructive eruption was in 1814, when the town of Cagsawa was buried.

Mayon Volcano, Luzon, Philippines
Ted Spiegel—Rapho/Photo Researchers

mayonnaise, cold sauce originating in French cuisine, an emulsion of raw egg yolks and vegetable oil. As the yolks are continuously beaten, oil is added little by little until a thick cream results. Plain mayonnaise is flavoured with lemon juice, mustard, or vinegar.

This rich, somewhat bland sauce serves as the base of dozens of variations such as *mayonnaise verte* (with puréed green herbs), *sauce rémoulade* (with anchovies, pickles, and capers), *sauce aïoli* (a Provençal mayonnaise flavoured with a great deal of garlic), and salad dressings such as Thousand Island and Russian dressings.

The term mayonnaise is also used to denote cold dishes and salads that are dressed with this sauce, as egg mayonnaise or lobster mayonnaise.

The etymology of the word *mayonnaise* is uncertain. It may be a corruption of *moyeunaise, moyeu* being an old French word denoting the yolk of an egg. The French chef Antonin Carême thought that it derived from the verb *manier,* meaning "to stir." Another possibility is that it was named after the victory of the Duke de Richielieu at Mahon in Minorca in 1757.

mayor, in modern usage, the head of a municipal government. As such, the mayor is almost invariably the chairman of the municipal council and of the council executive committee. In addition he may fulfill the roles of chief executive officer, ceremonial figurehead, and local agent of the central government. In another, more recent, system of municipal management—the council-manager system—the mayor's role is much reduced; he serves essentially only as head of the council. Whatever the form of local government, the mayor's role may be said to rest largely on his relationship to the council and to the central government.

Mayors are either appointed or elected. In Europe, until about the middle of the 19th century, most mayors were appointed by the central government. With the rise of representative government, more and more countries adopted the practice of electing the mayor. This practice takes a variety of forms. In most European countries the mayor is elected by the local council from among its members; usually he is the leader of the majority party or of one of the largest parties. In Switzerland, Canada, New Zealand, the Philippines, and Japan, most mayors are popularly elected.

In countries where the mayor is an agent of the central government, as in France, the mayor is usually the actual as well as the nominal head of the local government. In other words, his position is generally determined by the central government, and he has much greater executive powers than the council. As an agent of the central government, the mayor is the mainspring of the municipal administration and the focal point of policy.

With the development of popularly elected municipal councils, most mayors have taken on a dual role, serving not only as chief executive officer of the municipal administration but also as agents of the central government charged with such functions as maintaining public order, security, and health.

In the United States the central government never did control the cities directly and mayors were either elected by the populace at large or chosen by a city council whose members were also so elected. Among the reform measures of the early 20th century was the so-called council-manager system, in which the mayor, whether chosen by the council or by the electorate at large, merely presided over the council while most executive powers were exercised by a city manager (*q.v.*) hired by the council.

mayor and council system, municipal government in which a locally elected council is headed by a mayor, either popularly elected or elected by the council from among its members. In strict usage, the term is applied only to two types of local governmental structure in the United States. In the weak-mayor and council form, the mayor is merely council chairman and has largely only ceremonial and parliamentary functions. In the strong-mayor and council form, the mayor acts as real chief executive of the city or town, with the prerogative to veto actions of the council.

mayor of the palace, official of the western European kingdoms of the 6th–8th century, whose status developed under the Merovingian Franks from that of an officer of the household to that of regent or viceroy. The Merovingian kings adopted the system by which great landowners of the Roman Empire had employed a *major domus* (mayor, or supervisor, of the household) to superintend the administration of numerous, often scattered, estates. The Merovingians appointed a *major palatii* (mayor of the palace) to perform a similar function. The mayor gradually acquired further duties and powers: he obtained authority over court personnel, advised the king on the appointment of counts and dukes, protected the *commendati* (persons commended to the king) and the king's wards, and eventually even came to command the royal army.

It was probably a long series of Merovingian child kings from the late 6th century onward that enabled the mayors of the palace, as tutors of the young rulers, to gain control of the government. Eventually, they maintained it even when the kings had come of age. At first liberal to, and thus supported by, the landowning aristocracy, some mayors later became strong enough to act severely toward them.

From the second quarter of the 7th century, members of the Carolingian family usually held the mayoral power in the Frankish kingdom of Austrasia. After Pepin II (Pepin of Herstal) had defeated the Neustrians at Tertry in 687, the three Frankish kingdoms of Austrasia, Neustria, and Burgundy were united under his de facto rule as mayor of the palace. His grandson Pepin III the Short set aside the Merovingian king Childeric III in 751 and had himself elected king, becoming the first of the Carolingian dynasty.

Consult the INDEX *first*

Mayor Pablo Lagerenza, formerly INGAVI, or FORTÍN INGAVI, town, in extreme northwestern Paraguay. The town, located on the Timane River, was the site of the last major battle in 1935 of the Chaco War, fought with Bolivia. Mayor Pablo Lagerenza is a market town of a region that is largely scrub desert populated by Guaraní Indians engaged in subsistence agriculture and cattle raising. Pop. (1982 prelim.) 286.

Mayotte, in full TERRITORIAL COLLECTIVITY OF MAYOTTE, French COLLECTIVITÉ TERRITORIALE DE MAYOTTE, also called MAHORÉ, southeasternmost island of the Comoros archipelago and a French dependency, situated in the Mozambique Channel of the Indian Ocean, about 193 miles (310 km) northwest of Madagascar. Pamandzi, an islet lying about 1.5 miles (2.5 km) east of Mayotte, is connected by a 1.2-mile causeway to the rocky outcrop known as Dzaoudzi, site of the capital city and port. Area 144 square miles (373 square km). Pop. (1991 est.) 85,800.

For current history and for statistics on society and economy, *see* BRITANNICA BOOK OF THE YEAR.

A volcanic mountain range forms a north-south chain on Mayotte island, with summits of from 1,600 to 2,000 feet (500 to 600 m) in elevation. Protected waters for shipping and fishing are created by surrounding coral reefs some distance from the shore. The climate is warm, humid, and maritime, and average monthly temperatures range from 75° F (24° C) in August to 81° F (27° C) in December. The island's average annual rainfall is 200 inches (5,000 mm). The vegetation comprises lush green tropical forest.

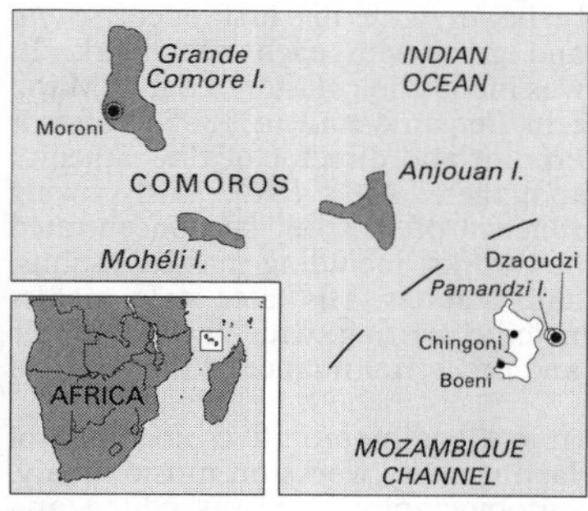

Mayotte

The people. Most of the people are Moharais of Malagasy origin and are Muslim, strongly influenced by French culture; there is a substantial Roman Catholic minority. French is the official language, but most of the people speak Comorian (closely allied to Swahili); there are some villages along the Mayotte coast in which a Malagasy dialect is the main language. Births greatly exceed deaths and the population is growing rapidly. Moreover, about 50 percent of the population is less than 15 years of age, portending high rates of natural increase well into the 21st century. The principal towns are Dzaoudzi and Mamoudzou, the largest town and capital designate.

The economy. Agriculture is the principal occupation on Mayotte and is confined to central and northeastern plains; cash crops include vanilla, ylang-ylang, coconuts, and coffee. Cassava, bananas, corn (maize), and rice are grown for subsistence. The island's main exports are ylang-ylang extract, vanilla, coffee, and copra. Rice, sugar, flour, clothing, building materials, hardware, cement, and transport equipment are imported. Mayotte's major trading partner is France, and the territory's economy is in large part dependent on French aid. A road system links the principal towns on Mayotte island, and an interisland airport is located on the islet of Pamandzi, southwest of Dzaoudzi.

Government and social conditions. Mayotte has had a special status with France since 1976 as a *collectivité territoriale* (territorial collectivity), conceived as being midway between an overseas territory and an overseas *département.* It is represented in the French National Assembly by a deputy and in the French Senate by a senator. The territory is administered by a commissioner and an elected 17-member General Council. The judiciary is modeled on the French system.

Mayotte has several small hospitals and some dispensaries. Major illnesses include malaria, parasitic diseases, and tuberculosis. The educational system includes both traditional Islāmic schools, in which the Qur'ān is studied, and primary and secondary schools established by the French.

History. In the 15th century, Arabs invaded the island and converted its inhabitants, who were probably descendants of earlier Bantu and Malayo-Indonesian peoples, to Islām; in the 16th century, the Portuguese and French visited Mayotte. At the end of the 18th century, the Sakalava, a Malagasy tribe from Madagascar, invaded and populated the island, bringing a Malagasy dialect. The French gained colonial control over Mayotte in 1843, and, together with the other islands of the Comoros archipelago and Madagascar, Mayotte became part of a single French overseas territory in the early 20th century.

The French have administered Mayotte separately from the remainder of the Comoros since 1975, when the three northernmost and predominantly Muslim islands of the Comoros unilaterally declared independence, and the Muslim and Christian inhabitants of Mayotte chose to remain with France. In 1976 the French government introduced a special status of *collectivité territoriale* for the island. The population of Mayotte demanded the status of a *département* for the island, but this was rejected by the French government. In December 1979 the French National Assembly voted to prolong the island's special status for five years, after which time the population's wishes would again be consulted. In the same year, the United Nations passed a resolution affirming the sovereignty of the Comoros over Mayotte.

Mayow, John (b. May 24, 1640, London, Eng.—d. October 1679, London), English chemist and physiologist who, about a hundred years before Joseph Priestley and Antoine-Laurent Lavoisier, identified *spiritus nitroaereus* (oxygen) as a distinct atmospheric entity.

Mayow, detail of an engraving
BBC Hulton Picture Library

Though a doctor of law from the University of Oxford (1670), Mayow made medicine his profession. His writings include a remarkably correct anatomical description of respiration and a recognition of the role of oxygen in the combustion of metals.

maypole dance, ceremonial folk dance performed around a tall pole garlanded with greenery or flowers and often hung with ribbons that are woven into complex patterns by the dancers. Such dances are survivals of ancient dances around a living tree as part of spring rites to ensure fertility. Typically performed on May 1, they also occur at midsummer in Scandinavia and at other festivals elsewhere. They are widely distributed through Europe—*e.g.,* "Sellenger's Round" in England, the *baile del cordón* of Spain—and also are found in India. Similar ribbon dances were performed in pre-Columbian Latin America and were later integrated into ritual dances of Hispanic origin. Maypoles may also appear in

Mayday, with peasants dancing around a maypole, detail of an English embroidery, first quarter of the 18th century, anonymous; in the Irwin Untermeyer Collection

By courtesy of Irwin Untermeyer; photograph, Helga Abramczyk

other ritual dances, as in the Basque *ezpata dantza,* or sword dance.

Mayr, Ernst (b. July 5, 1904, Kempten, Ger.), German-born American biologist known for his work in avian taxonomy, population genetics, and evolution.

Two years after receiving the Ph.D. degree from the University of Berlin (1926), Mayr, then a member of the university staff, led the first of three expeditions to New Guinea and the Solomon Islands, where he was profoundly impressed with the effects of geographic distribution among various animal species. His early studies of the ability of one species to separate or subdivide into daughter species (speciation) and of those populations that were established by a small number of founders (founder populations) made him one of the leaders in the development of the modern synthetic theory of evolution. This theory encompasses the biological processes of gene mutation and recombination, changes in the structure and function of chromosomes, reproductive isolation, and natural selection.

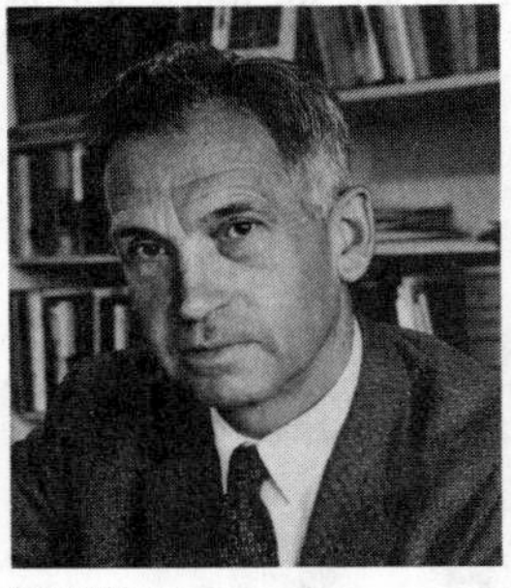

Ernst Mayr

By courtesy of the Department of Library Services, The American Museum of Natural History, New York City, neg. no. 334102

Mayr continued his studies as the curator of birds at the American Museum of Natural History in New York (1932–53), where he wrote more than 100 papers on avian taxonomy, including *Birds of the Southwest Pacific* (1945). He proposed in 1940 a definition of species that won wide acceptance in scientific circles and led to the discovery of a number of previously unknown species. In 1953 he became Alexander Agassiz professor of zoology at Harvard University and in 1961 became director of the Museum of Comparative Zoology, retiring in 1970. His works include *Methods and Principles of Systemic Zoology* (with E.G. Linsley and R.L. Usinger; 1953), *Animal Species and Evolution* (1963), and *The Growth of Biological Thought* (1982).

Mayr, (Johannes) Simon, also spelled GIOVANNI SIMONE MAYR (b. June 14, 1763, Mendorf, Bavaria [Germany]—d. Dec. 2, 1845, Bergamo, Lombardy, Austrian Empire [now in Italy]), Italian operatic and liturgical composer of German origin who was one of the first composers to use the orchestral crescendo technique made famous by Gioacchino Rossini.

As a youth Mayr entered the University of Ingolstadt to study theology, but while there he learned to play several instruments. He later studied music in Bergamo and in Venice, where he had several oratorios produced. His popularity began with his first opera, *Saffo* (1794), and grew with each new work. In 1802 he was made choirmaster of Santa Maria Maggiore in Bergamo and in 1805 professor of counterpoint and director of the cathedral choir school there. After 1815, partly owing to the influence of Rossini, he concentrated on religious works, including masses, psalms, motets, and cantatas. His later style merges Italian melodic writing with the harmonic richness and orchestral nuance of the German tradition.

Mayr wrote a commemorative biography of Joseph Haydn, many works on music theory, and an autobiography that was edited and published posthumously, and he founded two institutions for poor and elderly musicians. Of his more than 60 operas, the best-remembered include *La Lodoiska* (1796), *Ginevra di Scozia* (1801), *Medea in Corinto* (1813), and *La rosa bianca e la rosa rossa* (1813; "The White Rose and the Red Rose").

Mayrena, Marie-Charles David de: *see* David de Mayrena, Marie-Charles.

Mays, Willie (Howard) (b. May 6, 1931, Westfield, Ala., U.S.), American professional National League baseball player who was notable for his batting and fielding.

Both Mays's father and grandfather had been baseball players. Willie, who batted and fielded right-handed, played semiprofessional baseball when he was 16 years old and joined the Birmingham Black Barons of the Negro National League in 1948, playing only on Sunday during the school year. The National League New York Giants paid the Barons for his contract when he graduated from Fairfield Industrial High School in 1950. After two seasons in the minor leagues, Mays went to the Giants in 1951. He became known first for his spectacular leaping and diving catches before he established himself as a hitter. He served in the army (1952–54), and in the 1954 season, when the Giants won the National League pennant and the World Series, Mays led the league in hitting (.345) and had 41 home runs. In 1966 his two-year contract with the Giants (moved to San Francisco in 1958) gave him the highest salary of any baseball player of that time. He was traded to the New York Mets midseason in 1972 and retired after the 1973 season. Late in his career he played in the infield, mainly at first base. His career home run total was 660 and his batting average .302. He led the league in home runs in 1955, 1962, and 1964–65.

Mays

UPI

After retiring as a player, Mays was a part-time coach and did public relations work for the Mets. In 1979 Mays took a public relations job with a company that was involved in gambling concerns, with the result that he was banned from baseball-related activities just three months after he was elected into the Baseball Hall of Fame. In 1985 the ban was lifted, and in 1986 Mays became a full-time special assistant to the Giants.

Maysville, city, seat (1848) of Mason county, northeastern Kentucky, U.S., on the Ohio River, bridged (1931) to Aberdeen, Ohio. The town was established as Limestone in 1787 at the site of a tavern operated (1786–89) by Daniel Boone and his wife, Rebecca. It was laid out by Simon Kenton and John May (for whom it was later renamed). By 1792 it had become a landing point for pioneers. General Ulysses S. Grant attended school there, and the birthplace of Confederate General Albert Sydney Johnston is preserved as a historic shrine at nearby Old Washington. Maysville is a river port with a balanced farm–industrial economy and is an important burley tobacco marketing centre. Maysville Community College opened in 1967. Blue Licks Battlefield State Park is 25 miles (40 km) southwest. Inc. city, 1833. Pop. (1990) 7,169.

Maysvillian stage, time division of the Ordovician period in North America (the Ordovician period began about 505,000,000 years ago and lasted about 67,000,000 years); the Maysvillian stage follows the Edenian stage and precedes the Richmondian stage. In eastern North America, Maysvillian rocks consist largely of shales and sandstones; a portion of the Martinsburg Shale and the Pulaski Sandstone are notable examples. These sediments reflect deposition during the progressive uplift of the Appalachian highlands in Ordovician time.

Mayumba, town and Atlantic seaport of southwestern Gabon, central Africa, at the tip of a spit of land sheltering the long, narrow Mbanio Lagoon. The port handles lumber exports from the region's equatorial forest. Offshore oil has been exploited between Mayumba and Port-Gentil, 230 miles (370 km) to the northwest, since the 1960s. Net fishing is a significant industry in the Mbanio Lagoon, where abundant fish include tarpon weighing 150 pounds (70 kg) or more.

Expansive white sand beaches stretch between the ocean and the forest, which shelters elephants, buffalo, gorillas, sitatungas (antelope), crocodiles, and multicoloured birds. Rare butterflies (Anthinacus and Xalmoxys) swarm in the trees. Tourism (by bathers, fishermen, and hunters) is increasing as Mayumba becomes more accessible to other parts of Gabon. A highway connects it with Libreville, the national capital, and there is an airport. Pop. (1985 est.) 17,700.

Maywood, Augusta, original name AUGUSTA WILLIAMS (b. 1825, New York City—d. Nov. 3, 1876, Lwów, Pol., Austrian Empire [now Lviv, Ukraine]), first American ballerina to achieve international renown.

Maywood acquired the name of her stepfather, the theatrical manager Robert Campbell Maywood, when she was three. She studied with the French-Belgian Paul Hazard and made her debut in Philadelphia at 12 in *The Maid of Cashmere,* an English version of Auber's opera-ballet *Le Dieu et la Bayadère*.

Study in Paris led to her debut at the Paris Opéra in *Le Diable Boiteux* in 1839. She was acclaimed by French critics including Théophile Gautier, but after only a year at the Opéra she left Paris with the dancer Charles Mabille, whom she later married. In Lisbon and Vienna she starred in several ballets, including *Giselle* and *La Sylphide.* At the age of 23 she became prima ballerina at La Scala in Milan, where she remained until her retirement in 1862.

Mazama Ash, volcanic ash deposit widely distributed in the northwestern United States and southwestern Canada. The ash was released by the eruption of Mount Mazama, the event that produced Crater Lake in Oregon.

The eruption was a cataclysmic event dated at about 6,600 years ago. Great thicknesses of pumice were deposited on the flanks of Mount Mazama, while finer material was blown over great distances by the winds.

The widespread distribution of the Mazama Ash has made it useful in archaeological studies as a horizon, or time, marker. Studies of sediments formed in relation to the ash deposits suggest that the ash formed at a time when generally drier climates prevailed in the regions in which the ash occurs. The mineralogical composition of the ash is distinctive and allows it to be distinguished from other volcanic ash deposits.

Māzandarān, also spelled MAZANDERAN, historic region of northern Iran, bordering the Caspian Sea on the north.

A stream running through a section of the Elburz Mountains in Māzandarān *ostan,* Iran
Robert Harding Picture Library

An early Iranian civilization flourished at the beginning of the 1st millennium BC in Tabarestan (Māzandarān). It was overrun about AD 720 by the Arab general Yazīd ibn al-Muhallab and was the last part of Iran to be converted to Islām. Its insecure eastern and southeastern borders were crossed by Mongol invaders in the 13th and 14th centuries. Cossacks attacked the region in 1668 but were repulsed. It was ceded to the Russian Empire by a treaty in 1723, but the Russians were never secure in their occupation. The area was restored to Iran under the Qājār dynasty.

The northern section of the region consists of a lowland along the Caspian and an upland along the north slopes of the Elburz Mountains. Marshlands dominate the coastal plain, and extensive gravel fans fringe the mountains. The climate is subtropical and humid, with hot summers. The highland slopes rise abruptly in the west and more gently in the east. Forests have been largely destroyed; the higher parts are cultivated summer pasture studded with villages partly deserted in winter. Wild boar, deer, and birds are numerous; the tiger, formerly found in the lowland, has disappeared. There are many rivers, including the Chālūs, Heris, Talar, Tajan, and Nekā, which are well stocked with trout and salmon.

The population is Iranian with a large admixture of Turkic tribes (especially Turkmen), Armenians, and Russian immigrants. The smaller Indo-Iranian-speaking ethnic minorities include the Qadikolahi and the Palavi. The Qājārs, from whom came the royal family that Reza Shah dethroned in 1925, form an enclave among the Māzandarāni. Some are settled farmers; others retain their original nomadic way of life.

Agriculture dominates the economy. Crops include rice, wheat, barley, tobacco, cotton, oilseeds, jute, tea, fruits, and vegetables. The buffalo is widely used as a draft animal. Māzandarān is still famous for its Arab or Turkmen horses. Agribusinesses, established under the agricultural reforms of the mid-1970s, undertook large-scale and mechanized farming. More than 247,000 acres (100,000 hectares) of land were developed for the production of rice. Major dams constructed were the Taleqan, Tangue Soleiman, and Voshmguir. The oil boom of the 1970s encouraged industrial investment and the development of major industries, including cement, textiles and cotton ginning, fisheries, food processing (including rice and flour mills), and wood processing. Coal is mined and stone is quarried.

The coastal plains and Gorgān are prosperous, being connected with the interior by the Trans-Iranian Railway and three roads; but the coast lacks good natural harbours. The artificially created port of Now Shahr, north of Tehrān, cannot compare with Bandar-e Anzalī (formerly Bandar-e Pahlavī) farther west, and silting and a falling water level have rendered other ports useless.

Mazār-e Sharīf, town, northern Afghanistan, 35 miles (56 km) south of the border with Uzbekistan, at an elevation of 1,250 feet (380 m). The town derives its name (meaning "Tomb of the Saint") from the reputed discovery there of the tomb of the caliph ʿAlī, son-in-law of the Prophet Muḥammad, in the 15th or (according to Afghan legend) 12th century. A blue-tiled mosque and a shrine mark the location of the tomb, which is venerated by all Muslims, especially Shīʿites. Mazār-e Sharīf's growth and the corresponding decline of the much older town of Balkh, a few miles to the west, date from this discovery. Mazār-e Sharīf came under Afghan rule in 1852 and became the political hub of Afghan Turkistan in 1869. After their military intervention in 1979, Soviet forces established a military command in the town. It was later the site of brutal fighting and atrocities between competing Afghan factions and changed hands several times. The city was controlled by the Taliban (*q.v.*) from 1998 to late 2001, when it was taken with little violence by a coalition of Afghan, U.S., and allied forces; a subsequent uprising at a prison there holding Taliban troops and their allies, however, left hundreds dead.

The Blue Mosque at Mazār-e Sharīf, Afg.
Christa Armstrong from Rapho/Photo Researchers

Mazār-e Sharīf is located in one of Afghanistan's most fertile regions, extensively irrigated by the Balkh River and producing cotton, grain, and fruit. The town's industries include flour milling and the manufacturing of silk and cotton textiles. It is connected by road and air with Kabul, 200 miles (320 km) southeast, and other Afghan cities and is the nation's chief transit point for Soviet trade. A well-known Islāmic theology school is located there. The inhabitants of Mazār-e Sharīf are mainly Uzbek, Tajik, and Turkmen. Pop. (latest est.) 127,800.

Mazara del Vallo, Mazara also spelled MAZZARA, Latin MAZARA, town and episcopal see, Trapani *provincia,* western Sicily, Italy, at the mouth of the Mazaro River south of Trapani city. Of Phoenician origin, the town was later colonized by Greeks from nearby Selinus (modern Selinunte). It fell to the Carthaginians in 409 BC and subsequently to the Romans, Saracens, and Normans. The first Norman parliament in Sicily met there in 1097. Notable buildings are the cathedral (1075; rebuilt 1694), the Norman church of San Nicolò, and the palace of the Knights of Malta, housing a civic museum of art and archaeology.

One of the most important fishing (tunny, coral) ports in Italy, it also has a busy export trade in Marsala wine and local agricultural produce. Pop. (2001 prelim.) 48,156.

Mazarin, Jules, Cardinal, original Italian in full GIULIO RAIMONDO MAZZARINO, or MAZARINI (b. July 14, 1602, Pescina, Abruzzi, Kingdom of Naples [now in Italy]—d. March 9, 1661, Vincennes, Fr.), first minister of France after Cardinal de Richelieu's death in 1642. During the early years of King Louis XIV, he completed Richelieu's work of establishing France's supremacy among the European powers and crippling the opposition to the power of the monarchy at home.

Mazarin, detail of a portrait by Philippe de Champaigne; in the Musée Condé, Chantilly, Fr.
By courtesy of the Musee Conde, Chantilly, Fr.; photograph, Giraudon—Art Resource

Service as papal diplomat. Born a papal subject at Pescina, in the Abruzzi, near Rome, Giulio Mazzarino spent his childhood in a region whose temperament, ways of thought, and Roman Catholic outlook were to permeate his whole existence. His father, Pietro, was a Romanized Sicilian in the household of the constable Filippo I Colonna; his mother, Ortensia Bufalini, of a noble Tuscan family, was related to the Colonna house by marriage. From the beginning Mazzarino recognized the benefits of having powerful patrons and learned to exploit them to his advantage. Thus, in spite of financial difficulties and the expenses of a large family (another son, who became a monk, and four daughters), the Mazzarinos were able to send Giulio to the Jesuit school in Rome, where he was an excellent student.

Accompanying a young member of the Colonna family to Spain, he completed his education at the university at Alcalá de Henares (now the University of Madrid), where he studied law and then returned to Rome eager to learn more about aristocratic ways of life and secular affairs. From the Colonna he obtained a captaincy in the papal army in 1624, and, while serving in Loreto, on Christmas night 1625 he underwent an unusual mystical religious experience, or "tranquility of soul," which was to exert a certain influence on his life. He entered the diplomatic service of the Holy See and in 1628 was appointed secretary to the papal legate of Milan, G.F. Sacchetti; in this post he had his first opportunity to play an active political role.

In January 1630, during the war between Spain and France over the succession to the crown of Mantua, Sachetti's successor, Antonio Cardinal Barberini, sent Mazarin to France to negotiate with the great cardinal de Richelieu. The young man was fascinated by the powerful minister: "I resolved," he wrote, "to devote myself to him entirely." Soon afterward the young secretary acquired an international reputation when he dramatically galloped between the two opposing armies about to do battle at Casale in Monferrato on Oct. 26, 1630, shouting "Peace, peace!" as if peace had been concluded. For the rest of his life he would be remembered as the intrepid knight who risked his life between two armies in order to stop the fighting. Though the Spaniards raised their siege at Casale, much remained to be done in order to bring about a general settlement. By the Treaty of Cherasco (June 19, 1631), negotiated by Mazarin, the French candidate was installed in Mantua, but the agreement settled only the differences between France and Savoy.

Mazarin's resolution to devote himself to Richelieu did not prevent him from also obtaining the patronage of Cardinal Barberini, the youngest nephew of Pope Urban VIII. After Mazarin's return to Rome in 1632, Barberini included him in a circle of artists, painters, and musicians, before obtaining for him a mission as extraordinary nuncio (ambassador) to the French court in 1634. There, at Richelieu's side, Mazarin acquired the favour of those in power and became devoted to the French nation, whose "openness of heart and of mind" impressed him. He did not forget his mission, however, which was to negotiate the peace between Spain and France sought by Urban VIII; hence it was with despair that he watched Richelieu bring France openly into the Thirty Years' War in May 1635.

Recalled to Avignon in his capacity as legate, then to Rome (December 1636), he continued to exert an influence on French politics through his correspondence with Richelieu and his adviser, Father Joseph. With his friends cardinals Barberini, Nicholas Bagni, and Alessandro Bichi, Mazarin directed the French faction within the papal court. Louis XIII of France rewarded his efforts by recommending him as the royal candidate for a cardinalate in 1638, gave him ecclesiastical pensions and benefices (in order to be eligible for them Mazarin was granted French naturalization papers in 1639), and finally invited him to return to Paris, where he arrived on Jan. 5, 1640. Disappointed because his ambitions in Rome had been frustrated by the Spanish faction, Mazarin left the papal service to enter the service of France. It was to France and, in particular, to Richelieu that he owed the cardinal's hat bestowed upon him by the Pope on Dec. 16, 1641, though Urban VIII had himself been favourably impressed by the efforts his former subject was making in favour of the general peace.

Career as first minister of France. Mazarin's ambition was to put an end to the rivalry between the Catholic powers of Europe. On Richelieu's death, however (Dec. 4, 1642), and especially after that of Louis XIII (May 14, 1643), he became first minister of France, an office that the regent, Anne of Austria, entrusted to his experience and his ability in the name of the child Louis XIV. Mazarin used this new power to promote the peace negotiations that opened at Münster, in Westphalia, on April 10, 1644, although he now had to subordinate his ideal of peace to French foreign policies and ambitions. He was aided by a good diplomatic team, over which he exercised firm control, and by extremely competent generals, Louis II de Bourbon, prince de Condé, and Henri de Turenne. Their brilliant victories over the Spanish and imperial troops helped bring about the Peace of Westphalia (October 1648), a general European settlement that established peace in Germany.

As the war between France and Spain still continued and as grave issues were developing in the north and east, Germany could easily have been involved again in a general war. No one believed in the power of the Emperor to safeguard the empire from this danger. Mazarin took advantage of the weakened imperial power of the Habsburgs to organize a defensive alliance between France and the German states closest to the French frontier (the League of the Rhine, August 1658). Spain, however, encouraged by the defection of the United Provinces of the Netherlands, who had signed a separate peace in January 1648, refused to agree to the peace. In order to force Spain to make a settlement, Mazarin continued the war and formed an alliance with England (March 23, 1657), surrendering to the English the fort of Dunkirk, which had been captured from the Spaniards after the Battle of the Dunes (June 14, 1658).

Peace with Spain was finally negotiated in a general treaty signed on Nov. 7, 1659, at the Pyrenees frontier. Mazarin completed this settlement by arbitrating the "northern peace" (the treaties of Oliva and of Copenhagen on May 3 and June 6, 1660) and by returning Lorraine to its duke (Treaty of Paris, Feb. 28, 1661). Thus, at his death, the former diplomat of the Holy See could rejoice at having "returned peace to Christendom." He would have liked to have seen Europe take advantage of this peace by uniting in a crusade against the Turks and, above all, to have "let these peoples enjoy the fruits of the tranquility" they had regained now that fighting had ended in their home territory.

France, indeed, needed a rest. Mazarin therefore had to limit his activities within the realm to thwarting intrigues at court and multiplying financial expedients to meet war expenditures. The new taxes imposed upon leading Parisians contributed to the discontent that precipitated the revolts known as the Fronde. These rebellions, which lasted more than five years, originated in the judicial oligarchy of the Parlement of Paris; they spread to the upper nobility and soon found popular support even in the provinces largely because of "Mazarinades," inflammatory pamphlets written against the Cardinal. Mazarin was obliged to leave the court twice and was only able to maintain his post because he was in favour with Anne of Austria and the boy king Louis XIV, whose education he had carefully directed.

The Fronde was finally suppressed in 1653, and Louis XIV was crowned the following year. Mazarin increasingly involved the young sovereign in affairs of government, encouraging him to stand firm against the Parlement and helping him train a staff of great administrators for his reign: Jean-Baptiste Colbert, Nicholas Fouquet, Hughes de Lionne, and Michel Le Tellier. He reestablished the role of the intendants or commissaries of the king, who administered the provinces; they gradually assumed the power of the provincial governors who had shown themselves to be unreliable during the rebellions. He thus succeeded in sustaining order through a policy of moderation, which he applied even to popular revolts such as the peasant uprising of Sologne in 1658.

Reputation and character. Mazarin's enemies reproached him for his greed. He had accumulated offices and benefices and had sometimes confused royal income with his own. Yet, on several occasions, when the state faced desperate financial situations, he put his own fortune at its disposal. A lover of the arts, he acquired fine collections, decorated his Parisian mansion (today the home of the Bibliothèque Nationale) with works by Italian artists, and brought the Roman opera into favour in France. His library remains in the palace (now called the Institut de France) that he ordered built to house the College of the Four Nations, intended for the education of young men from the four provinces that had been acquired by France during his ministry: Alsace, Roussillon, Flanders-Artois, and the region of Pinerolo. He founded the Royal Academy of Painting and Sculpture (1648) and gave pensions to several men of letters.

According to the Roman tradition of nepotism, Mazarin offered rich dowries and arranged noble marriages for his nephews and especially for his Mancini and Martinozzi nieces. Yet he did not allow his affection as an uncle to win out over political considerations; thus, he thwarted the desire of Louis XIV, who by treaty was bound to marry the Spanish infanta, to marry Marie Mancini. Anne of Austria felt a strong attraction for him: he was a handsome man, eloquent and charming; devoid of political experience herself, she accepted his advice unquestioningly. The "Mazarinades" accused them of having an illicit relationship, but the evidence is conflicting. The hypothesis of a secret marriage between the Regent and her minister is also unlikely, for the cardinalate, even that of a layman, implied the obligation of celibacy. Mazarin was not an ordained priest (in 1632 he had received only minor orders), though he thought of entering the priesthood on several occasions, especially in 1651 and even in 1660 shortly before his death. Faithful to the Catholicism as he had practiced it in his youth, he had defended Roman orthodoxy against the heterodox Jansenist movement, yet without advocating persecution of the Jansenists. (G.Det.)

BIBLIOGRAPHY. Mazarin's correspondence while minister was published by Adolphe Chéruel, *Lettres du Cardinal Mazarin pendant son ministère,* 9 vol. (1872–1906); this monumental edition is supplemented by fragmentary publications, the most important of which are those of M. Ravenel, *Lettres du Cardinal Mazarin à la Reine . . . en 1651 et 1652* (1836), and the letters of the young Mazarin, translated from the Italian, as an appendix to Georges Dethan, *Mazarin et ses amis* (1968; *The Young Mazarin,* 1977). The *Carnets,* or notebooks, in which Mazarin wrote brief reflections and guides for his conduct at court and his relations with the Queen, have only been published in incomplete form by Victor Cousin in *Journal des Savants* (1854–56).

Standard works on Mazarin include: Victor Cousin, *La Jeunesse de Mazarin* (1865); and especially Adolphe Chéruel, *Histoire de France pendant la minorité de Louis XIV,*4 vol. (1879–80), a monumental work; *Histoire de France sous le ministère de Mazarin (1651–1661),* 3 vol. (1882). Recent works of synthesis include: *Mazarin* (1959), a collective work with articles by Georges Mongrédien, Pierre du Colombier, Maurice Schumann, and Georges Dethan; *Mazarin* (1961), the catalog of the *Exposition Mazarin* of the Bibliothèque Nationale; and Georges Dethan (*op. cit.*). The chief works in English are Arthur Hassall, *Mazarin* (1903); and James B. Perkins, *France Under Mazarin,* 2 vol. (1886).

Mazaruni River, river in north central Guyana. Its headstreams arise in the Pakaraima Mountains of western Guyana and flow generally northward. Descending from the Guiana Highlands, the river turns southeastward as far as Issano and then curves northeastward to Bartica, where it is joined by the Cuyuni River, just upstream from its confluence with the Essequibo. Although the Mazaruni is approximately 350 miles (560 km) long, only short stretches are navigable, the rest being marked by intermittent rapids. It flows through sparsely inhabited, dense tropical rain forests. It is economically significant, however, because it is Guyana's main source of alluvial diamonds.

Mazatec, Middle American Indians of northern Oaxaca in southern Mexico. The region is mostly mountainous, with small valleys, and its flora and fauna are diverse. The Mazatec language is most closely related to those of the Chocho, Ixcatec, and Popoloca. The people are agricultural, depending primarily on corn (maize), beans, squash, and chilies. Meat and eggs are considered luxuries. Cultivation is done mainly with digging stick and hoe. Houses are rectangular, with thatched roofs; they are congregated in towns and villages. Crafts such as weaving and pottery are dying out, their products replaced by commercial goods. Women still wear the huipil (a long, loose cotton tunic) and ankle-length underskirt; men wear white cotton pants and shirts. Cloth is industrially woven.

The Mazatec elect their own municipal authorities at two-year intervals; candidates must have the approval of the council of elders. Townspeople are also eligible for compulsory communal labour. The Mazatec are Roman Catholic with syncretistic elements. A mayordomo is elected or appointed in each town to take care of the patron saint and to organize and partially to finance the saint's annual fiesta. Spirits of caves, hills, and springs are also reverenced, however, and witchcraft is widely believed in.

Mazatenango, town, southwestern Guatemala. It lies along the southward-flowing Sis River, on the southern piedmont of the central highlands, at an elevation of 1,217 feet (371 m) above sea level. Mazatenango is an important commercial and manufacturing centre for the Pacific coastal lowlands it overlooks. Cotton, coffee, sugarcane, cacao, tropical fruits, and rubber are the principal crops. Cotton and its seed are processed for textiles and oil. Mazatenango lies about 120 miles (190 km) from Guatemala City, with which it is connected by road and rail, and is a transportation centre for traffic from the Pacific ports. Pop. (1994 prelim.) 30,350.

Mazatlán, Pacific port and resort, southwestern Sinaloa state, western north-central Mexico. It occupies a peninsula overlooking Olas Altas Bay, on the Gulf of California. It is Mexico's largest Pacific Ocean port, and its island-studded harbour is known for its fine sandy beaches. Lying diagonally across the gulf from the tip of Baja California, it provides a chief communications link between the peninsula and the mainland. It is also accessible by railroad, highway, and air. Mazatlán, called Pearl of the Pacific, is a fishing and hunting centre and a popular tourist resort. Pop. (2000 prelim.) 380,265.

Beach at Mazatlán on Olas Altás Bay, Mexico
Shostal

Mazdā (Zoroastrian god): *see* Ahura Mazdā.

Mazda Motor Corporation, formerly (1927–84) TŌYŌ KŌGYŌ COMPANY, Japanese automotive manufacturer, maker of Mazda passenger cars, trucks, and buses. The company is affiliated with the Sumitomo group. It is headquartered at Hiroshima.

Founded in 1920 as a cork plant, the company acquired its Tōyō Kōgyō name in 1927. In 1931 it began manufacturing its first vehicles, a line of three-wheel trucks, producing some 200,000 in the next 25 years. During World War II, it provided the Japanese armed forces with these trucks as well as with rifles. The company's factory survived the atomic bombing of Hiroshima because it lay shielded behind a hill.

The company entered the passenger-car market in 1960 with the production of a coupe model; two years later, sedans and station wagons came on line, and in 1964 it introduced a line of cars that were marketed in the United States. In 1967 the company committed itself to producing automobiles with the rotary-piston Wankel engine. By the early 1970s, more than half of all Mazdas were equipped with the new engine. The major drawback of the Wankel engine, however, was its relatively poor fuel efficiency. With the rise in the price of gasoline in the 1970s, sales of Mazdas dropped sharply.

Since then the company gradually has regained its fortunes. By reducing its work force through attrition, greatly improving productivity, and turning to conventional, more fuel-efficient engines for its cars, the company has become one of the largest automobile manufacturers in Japan. In 1981 it brought out a more fuel-efficient Wankel engine for some of its models. Also important to its recovery has been its relationship with the Ford Motor Company. Mazda supplies axles for Ford and ships a ready-to-assemble car that Ford markets. The company also manufactures rock drills, machine tools, and gauge blocks. The company changed its name from Tōyō Kōgyō Company to Mazda Motor Corporation in 1984.

Mazdakism, dualistic religion that rose to prominence in the late 5th century in Iran from obscure origins. According to some scholars, Mazdakism was a reform movement seeking an optimistic interpretation of the Manichaean dualism. Its founder appears to have been one Zaradust-e Khuragan; a connection has been sought between him and a Persian, Bundos, who preached a divergent Manichaeism in Rome under Diocletian at the end of the 3rd century. Other scholars see it as an internal development within Iranian religion. After the 5th century the religion came generally to be called after Mazdak (fl. late 5th century AD, Persia), its major Persian proponent. No Mazdakite books survive. Knowledge of the movement comes from brief mentions in Syrian, Persian, Arabic, and Greek sources.

According to Mazdakism, there exist two original principles, Good (or Light) and Evil (or Darkness). Light acts by free will and design; Darkness, blindly and by chance. By accident the two became mixed, producing the world. There are three Light elements: water, fire, and earth. The god of Light, who is to be worshiped, is enthroned in paradise, having before him four powers—perception, intelligence, memory, and joy. These rule over 7 "viziers" and 12 "spiritual beings"—identical with the 7 planets of antiquity and the 12 signs of the zodiac. The 4 powers are united in man; the 7 and 12 control the world.

By his actions man should seek to release the Light in the world; this is accomplished through moral conduct and ascetic life. He may not kill or eat flesh. He is to be gentle, kind, hospitable, and clement to foes. To encourage brotherly helpfulness and reduce causes of greed and strife, Mazdak sought to make property and women common. He converted to his faith the Sāsānid king Kavadh I (488–496 and 499–531), who introduced social reforms inspired by its tenets. These appear to have involved some liberalizing of marriage laws and of measures concerning property. These actions aroused the hostility of the nobles and the orthodox Zoroastrian clergy and led to the eventual suppression of Mazdakism. Nevertheless, the religion survived in secret into Islāmic times (the 8th century).

maze: *see* labyrinth.

Mazeikiai, town and centre of a *rayon* (district), northwestern Lithuania. It lies along the Virvyčia River. The first oil refinery in the Baltic states began operation in 1980 about 12 miles (20 km) northwest of the town, processing crude oil brought by a pipeline completed in 1977. The refinery was designed to supply fuel for a thermal power station at Elektrenai (1972). Mazeikiai, a small town of about 13,500 people in 1970 just before refinery construction began, nearly doubled in size during the construction period. The town is a road and rail junction with diversified manufacturing, including food-processing and electronics industries. It has a theatre and a museum. Pop. (1999 est.) 45,875.

Mazepa, Ivan Stepanovich (b. *c.* 1644, Mazepintsy, near Bila Tserkva, Pol. [now Belaya Tserkov, Ukraine]—d. Sept. 8 [Aug. 28, Old Style], 1709, Bendery, Moldavia [now Moldova]), hetman (leader) of the Cossacks in the Russian Ukraine who turned against the Russians and joined the Swedes during the Great Northern War (1700–21).

Having served as a page at the court of the Polish king John Casimir, Mazepa was educated in western Europe but returned to his native land and in 1663 entered the service of Pyotr Doroshenko, the Cossack hetman of Ukraine west of the Dnieper River.

During the 1660s and 1670s Mazepa's transfer of loyalty between rival hetmans contributed to the complex and prolonged warfare (that continued into the 1680s) among the Turks, Russians, Poles, and various Cossack factions for control of the Ukraine.

Mazepa subsequently succeeded the established hetman of the Ukraine (1687) and fought against the Crimean Tatars (1689). When Peter I the Great took power, Mazepa managed to win Peter's favour and retain his position in the Ukraine.

Peter, however, alienated Mazepa and the Cossacks, ordering them to perform uncustomary duties and allowing the Russian army to mistreat the Ukraine's civilian population.

Mazepa, detail from a lithograph by D. Kitchenko
Novosti Press Agency

Consequently, when the Great Northern War began (1700), Mazepa entered into secret negotiations with Charles XII of Sweden. When Charles led his forces into the Ukraine seeking supplies and reinforcements, Mazepa and 5,000 of his Cossacks joined the Swedes instead of going to the aid of the Russians (October 1708). Mazepa, however, was able neither to inspire the Ukrainian population to revolt against the Russians nor to supply the Swedes with enough Cossacks to prevent the Russians from inflicting a major defeat upon them at Poltava (June 1709). After that battle, Mazepa escaped with Charles into Turkish-controlled Moldavia, where he died.

mazer, medieval drinking bowl of turned (shaped on a lathe) wood, usually spotted maple. The oldest extant examples, dating from the early 14th century, are mounted with silver or silver-gilt bands around the lip and foot and have an engraved or enameled embossed medallion, called a print or boss, in the centre of the inside of the bowl. During the

Mazer bowls, maplewood mounted with silver gilt; (left) 1510, (right) *c.* 1460
By courtesy of the Worshipful Company of Goldsmiths

15th century the bowls became shallower, and their mounts, which became wider, displayed inscriptions of a religious or secular character; more elaborate versions of the simple prototype were also made, including the double-mazer, which has a small bowl inverted on a larger one, and the standing mazer, which has an unusually high silver foot. Mazers are extremely rare after the 16th century.

Mazia, Daniel (b. Dec. 18, 1912, Scranton, Pa., U.S.—d. June 9, 1996, Monterey, Calif.), American cell biologist who was notable for his work in nuclear and cellular physiology, especially the mechanisms involved in mitosis (the process by which the chromosomes within the nucleus of a cell double and divide prior to cell division).

Mazia was educated at the University of Pennsylvania (Ph.D., 1937) and taught at the University of Missouri (1938–50) and the University of California at Berkeley (1951–79).

Throughout his career Mazia's research focused on various aspects of cell reproduction, including division and regulation. He is best known for isolating the mitotic apparatus, the structure responsible for cell division, research that he carried out with the Japanese biologist Katsuma Dan in 1951.

Mazovia, also spelled MASOVIA, Polish MAZOWSZE, lowland territory in east-central Poland, located west of Podlasia in the basin of the middle Vistula and lower Bug rivers. Mazovia includes the Płock-Ciechanów region (to which the name Mazovia originally referred) as well as the regions of Sochaczew, Grójec (formerly Grodziec), and Czersk. It was incorporated into the Polish state in the first half of the 10th century. After 1138, when Bolesław III the Wry-Mouthed (ruled Poland 1102–38) divided his realm among his sons, it became one of the major principalities within the disintegrating Polish kingdom and developed a distinctive social structure charac-

Mazovia, *c.* 1320

terized by a large, if not wealthy, gentry class (which constituted 25 percent of the population in the 16th century). During the 13th and 14th centuries, however, Mazovia was subdivided; the region did not become completely reincorporated into the reunified Polish state until after all its princely houses (which were descended from Ziemowit I, a great-grandson of Bolesław III and the ruler of Mazovia from 1248 to 1262) became extinct in 1526.

When Poland was partitioned late in the 18th century, Mazovia became part of Prussia; but it was transferred to the Duchy of Warsaw (1807), created during the Napoleonic Wars, and then incorporated into Russian Poland (1815). It rejoined Poland in 1918.

Mazovian Lowland, Polish NIZINA MAZOWIECKA, valley district, east-central Poland. Located in the eastern part of the central lowlands, it is directly south of the Masurian Lakeland and west of the Podlasian Lowland along the border with Belarus. The distinctive feature of this sinuous valley is its marshy floodplain, which is bordered by dry fertile river terraces. The valley widens in places, especially in the ancient lake basin of Warsaw, where water was once dammed up in front of a glacial ice sheet. The Vistula River follows a serpentine course through the broad valley. Elsewhere in the lowland, sand deposits have piled up and ruined the soil for cultivation.

Mazowiecki, Tadeusz (b. April 18, 1927, Płock, Pol.), Polish journalist, Solidarity official, and premier (1989–91), the first noncommunist premier of an eastern European country since the late 1940s.

After graduating in law from the University of Warsaw, Mazowiecki entered journalism and became prominent among Poland's liberal young Roman Catholic intellectuals in the mid-1950s. In 1958 Mazowiecki cofounded the independent Catholic monthly journal *Wieź* ("Link"), which he edited until 1981. In the 1970s he forged links with the Workers' Defense Committee, which protected anticommunist labour activists in Poland from government persecution.

When strikes in the Lenin Shipyard in Gdańsk sparked the birth of the Solidarity labour movement there in August 1980, Mazowiecki became one of the principal advisers to the strikers and helped mobilize Polish intellectuals in support of them. In 1981 Solidarity's leader, Lech Wałęsa, appointed Mazowiecki the first editor of *Tygodnik Solidarność* ("Solidarity Weekly"), the new Solidarity newspaper. His ties to Wałęsa only deepened during the government's suppression of the Solidarity movement from 1981 to 1988.

In early 1989 Mazowiecki served as the mediator in talks between the government and Solidarity that resulted in Solidarity's legalization and the holding of the freest national elections in Poland since 1947. Solidarity's stunning victory in those elections in June prompted Poland's communist president, General Wojciech Jaruzelski, to appoint Mazowiecki as prime minister of a coalition government in August on the advice of Wałęsa.

As prime minister, Mazowiecki undertook free-market economic reforms. His government greatly reduced price controls, subsidies, and centralized planning while simultaneously privatizing businesses, creating a stable convertible currency, and restraining wage increases in order to reduce inflation. Through these means Mazowiecki was successful at stabilizing Poland's finances, but only at the cost of sharply rising unemployment and a fall in real wages. Popular discontent with these negative effects led to the election of Wałęsa as president in December 1990; Mazowiecki finished third.

Mazowieckie, *województwo* (province), east-central Poland. It is made up of the former provinces (1975–98) of Warsaw, Ostrołęka, Radom, Płock, Ciechanów, and Siedlce, as well as portions of Skierniewice, Łomża, and Biała Podlaska. A low-lying region, it is crossed by the Vistula (Wisła), Bug, and Narew rivers. The economy is dominated by Warsaw, the provincial and national capital. Other large cities are Radom, Płock, Siedlce, and Ostrołęka. In addition to government services and state-owned businesses, leading enterprises are automobile manufacturing, steel production, food processing, and financial services. Despite being highly industrialized, Mazowieckie is a leading producer of potatoes, and rye, sugar beets, fruits, and vegetables are also grown. Tourists visit the many cultural institutions of Warsaw, as well as outlying Kampinos National Park, one of the country's largest. Transportation is well-developed, and Okęcie international airport in Warsaw is Poland's busiest. Situated on the middle course of the Vistula, the region has long been a major component of the Polish state. Though sections of historic Warsaw remain intact, the city was largely rebuilt after being destroyed during the German occupation of World War II. Area 13,745 square miles (35,598 square km). Pop. (2003 est.) 5,128,400.

Mazu Island: *see* Matsu Island.

mazurka, Polish MAZUREK, Polish improvisatory folk dance for a circle of couples, characterized by stamping feet and clicking heels and traditionally danced to the music of bagpipes. The music is in $\frac{3}{4}$ time with a forceful accent on the second beat. The dance has no set figures, and more than 50 different steps exist.

The mazurka originated in the 16th century among the Mazurs of east-central Poland and was quickly adopted at the Polish court, yet it remained a peasant dance. It eventually spread to Russian and German ballrooms and by the 1830s had reached England and France. As a ballroom dance intended for four or eight couples or for single couples, the mazurka retains room for improvisation. The volume of mazurkas for piano composed by Frédéric Chopin (1810–49) reflects the dance's popularity in his day. The varsoviana is a 19th-century couple dance that evolved from a simple mazurka step. The smooth kujawiak and the energetic oberek are Polish dances that are closely related to the mazurka.

Mazurka
Press-Photo Agency CAF

Mazyadid DYNASTY, Muslim Arab dynasty that ruled central Iraq from its capital at al-Ḥillah in the period from about 961 to 1150. The Mazyad family, which belonged to the Bedouin tribe of Asad, had settled along the Euphrates River, between Hīt and Kūfah, in the middle of the 10th century; soon afterward the Būyid Sulṭān ad-Dawlah in Baghdad recognized ʿAlī I ibn Mazyad as emir of the area. ʿAlī died in 1018, leaving behind three sons, each of whom was eager to assume power, although Dubays I (reigned 1018–81) officially succeeded his father. Dubays' brother al-Muqallad soon attempted to oust him but, failing, turned to the ʿUqaylid capital of Mosul for help. In 1030, supported by ʿUqaylid and Būyid forces, al-Muqallad routed Dubays. Dubays, however, was allowed to return to his capital, provided that he pay a sizable tribute to the Būyid Jalāl ad-Dawlah. Meanwhile, the third brother, Thābit, enlisted the aid of Arslān al-Basāsīrī of Baghdad in his bid for power and defeated Dubays twice in about 1033, forcing him to relinquish parts of the province to him. About 1057 Dubays himself allied with al-Basāsīrī against an invasion by the Seljuqs under Toghril Beg.

The brief rule of Manṣūr (1081–86) was followed by a period of heightened Mazyadid activity. Having allied himself first with the Seljuq ruler Berk-yaruq, then from about 1101 with Berk-yaruq's brother Muḥammad, the Mazyadid ruler Ṣadaqah I (reigned 1086–1108) gradually assumed control of most of Iraq, seizing Hīt, Wāsiṭ, Basra, and Takrīt. In 1102 he expanded and fortified his capital city of al-Jāmiʿān and renamed it al-Ḥillah. Ṣadaqah, however, proved to be too threatening to Muḥammad, and the Mazyadid ruler was killed in a battle with Seljuq armies sent out against him early in 1108.

Dubays II (reigned 1108–35) succeeded to the throne on his father's death and distinguished himself as a great warrior against the crusaders and as a generous patron of Arabic poetry. After Dubays' death, Mazyadid strength was reduced by his three brothers' efforts to displace one another from power. The dynasty finally submitted to the Seljuq sultan Masʿūd in 1150, and al-Ḥillah was given to one of the sultan's generals.

Mazzei, Philip (b. Dec. 25, 1730, Poggio a Caiano, Tuscany [Italy]—d. March 19, 1816, Pisa, Italy), Italian physician, merchant, and author, ardent supporter of the U.S. War of Independence, and correspondent of Thomas Jefferson.

Mazzei studied medicine in Florence and practiced in Turkey before moving in 1755 to London, where he became a wine merchant. In 1773 Mazzei set sail for the American colonies, intending to launch the development of olive and grape growing in Virginia. He established an experimental farm next to Jefferson's Monticello. Mazzei soon became enveloped in the independence movement, and he strongly favoured Virginia's strides toward religious and political freedom. In 1779 he accepted a commission from Patrick Henry, the Virginia governor, to seek a loan from the Grand Duke of Tuscany. After being captured by the British and imprisoned for three months, Mazzei arrived in Europe—only to find his every effort blocked by Benjamin Franklin, who believed that the national government alone could contract foreign debts.

Mazzei remained in Europe until late 1783, collecting political and military information for Jefferson. He returned to the United States briefly in quest of a foreign service post, but when that effort failed he went back to Europe. In 1788 his four volumes on America, *Recherches historiques et politiques sur les États-Unis de l'Amérique septentrionale* ("Historical and Political Studies of the United States of America"), were published in Paris.

In 1789 Mazzei became an adviser to Stanisław II, last king of an independent Poland, and in 1802 he began to receive a pension from Russia. He continued for many years to correspond with Jefferson and other Virginians. One of Jefferson's letters to him—criticizing the Federalists and, by implication, George Washington—created a controversy when American newspapers reprinted it.

Three years before his death, Mazzei completed an account in Italian of his remarkable life and travels; it was published in two volumes in 1845–46.

maẓẓevah (Judaism): *see* matzeva.

Mazzini, Giuseppe (b. June 22, 1805, Genoa [Italy]—d. March 10, 1872, Pisa, Italy), Genoese propagandist and revolutionary, founder of the secret revolutionary society Young Italy (1832), and a champion of the movement for Italian unity known as the Risorgimento. An uncompromising republican, he refused to participate in the parliamentary government that was established under the monarchy of the House of Savoy when Italy became unified and independent (1861).

Education and exile. Giuseppe Mazzini was a doctor's son; his birthplace, formerly a republic, was annexed to the Kingdom of Piedmont in 1814. As a child, he gave promise of high intellectual ability, fully confirmed when he entered the University of Genoa at 14. Two years later, strongly influenced by seeing a patriot fleeing from Italy after an unsuccessful insurrection, he began to think "that we Italians *could* and therefore *ought* to struggle for the liberty of our country."

On graduating in law in 1827, he practiced as a "poor man's lawyer," wrote articles for progressive reviews, and hoped to become a dramatist or historical novelist. But his life was already shaping itself differently. His love of freedom led him to join the Carbonari, a secret society pledged to overthrow absolute rule in Italy. In 1830 he was betrayed to the police, arrested, and interned at Savona, where for three months he reviewed his political beliefs and conceived the outlines of a new patriotic movement to replace the decaying Carbonari.

When released early in 1831, he was ordered either to leave Piedmont or to live in some small town. He chose exile and went to Marseille, where his slight figure, handsome olive features, black hair and beard, and black velvet suit were soon familiar to the other Italian exiles, who accepted him as their leader. His first public gesture was an "open letter" to Charles Albert, the king of Piedmont, urging him to give Piedmont constitutional government, to lead a national movement, and to expel the Austrians from Lombardy-Venetia and their other Italian strongholds. The letter was circulated in Italy, but Charles Albert's only reaction was to threaten Mazzini with arrest if he returned to Piedmont. As a lifelong republican, Mazzini was afterward censured for this friendly approach to an autocratic sovereign; he explained that he had meant to expose Charles Albert as one who would never fight for Italian freedom.

Foundation of Young Italy. At Marseille Mazzini spent two of his most rewarding years. He founded his patriotic movement for young men and called it Giovine Italia (Young Italy). It was designed as a national association for liberating the separate Italian states from foreign rule and fusing them into a free and independent unitary republic. Its methods were education and insurrection, and it had a moral basis derived from Mazzini's own belief in God (though he was not a Christian) and in permanent laws of progress, duty, and sacrifice. It was the first Italian democratic movement embracing all classes, for Mazzini believed that only a popular initiative could free Italy. "Neither pope nor king," he declared. "Only God and the people will open the way of the future to us."

Mazzini, detail of an oil painting by Luigi Zuccoli, 1865; in the Museo del Risorgimento, Milan
By courtesy of the Museo del Risorgimento, Milan

The new movement captured the imagination of Italian youth. Branches were secretly formed in Genoa and other cities; by 1833 there were 60,000 members. Mazzini edited the propagandist journal *Giovine Italia,* which was smuggled into Italy with other revolutionary pamphlets. He also became the lover of a fellow exile, the beautiful Modenese widow Giuditta Sidoli.

Young Italy's attempted insurrections were failures. A projected rising in Piedmont in 1833 was discovered before it had begun; 12 conspirators were executed, one committed suicide, and Mazzini was tried in absence and condemned to death. He said prophetically, "Ideas ripen quickly when nourished by the blood of martyrs." A few months later, when he had moved to Switzerland to escape from the French police, he tried to rally 1,000 volunteers to invade Savoy (then part of the kingdom of Piedmont). Only 200 could be mustered, and the force was disbanded.

These failures destroyed Young Italy as an organization, though its spirit lived on. Mazzini turned to wider revolutionary plans, based on his faith in the brotherhood of man and his hopes for a world republican federation. He founded Young Europe and helped to establish Young Germany, Young Switzerland, and Young Poland, but his three years in Switzerland were unhappy and frustrated. Giuditta Sidoli had gone back to Italy to rejoin her children; he suffered an emotional crisis through doubts and disillusionment. In 1837 he went with a few Italian friends to live in London.

Stay in England. England was now his real home. He lived in modest London lodgings, surrounded by books, papers, and the tame birds in which he delighted; he studied at the British Museum and wrote for English periodicals. Though he had little money, he started a school for Italian boys in London and a newspaper, *Apostolato popolare* ("Apostleship of the People"), in which he published part of his essay "On the Duties of Man." In 1840, with the help of Giuseppe Lamberti in Paris, he revived Young Italy, primarily as a means of building up a national consciousness among Italians everywhere. He wrote innumerable letters to his new agents in Europe and North and South America; he also became acquainted with Thomas and Jane Welsh Carlyle and other notable people.

In 1844 he was in touch with the Bandiera brothers, who made an ill-fated attempt to start a revolt in Calabria. After their execution, he told two friends who were members of Parliament of his fears that the British government was opening his letters and had passed on information about the Bandieras' plans to the Neapolitan authorities. The matter was raised in Parliament, and the government was compelled to admit that it opened private letters. There was much public indignation and widespread sympathy with Mazzini. The affair made him better known in England and brought him into contact with a notable liberal family, the Ashursts. Many English liberals supported him when he founded the People's International League in 1847.

In that year he wrote an "open letter" to the new pope, Pius IX, who had introduced liberal reforms in the Papal States. He urged the pope to unify Italy, but Pius made no comment. Mazzini returned to Italy for the first time in the revolutionary year of 1848, when the Milanese drove out their Austrian masters and Piedmont began a war to expel the Austrians from Italy. Milan welcomed him, but he was soon unpopular because he wanted Lombardy to become a republic and he thought that union with the kingdom of Piedmont, as proposed by the Milanese provisional government, was the wrong kind of pattern for the future Italy. When the Piedmontese armies withdrew and the Austrians reentered Milan, he served briefly with an irregular force under Giuseppe Garibaldi before returning to England.

Triumvir of republican Rome. Mazzini was again in Italy in 1849, first in Tuscany and then in Rome, where a revolution had driven out the pope and a republic had been proclaimed. He had long believed that the imperial and papal Romes would be followed by a third Rome—a Rome of the people; now his dream had come true. He was acclaimed as a great patriot, was elected a triumvir of the republic, and became the effective head of the government, showing great administrative talent in ecclesiastical and social reforms. His rule was short-lived. The pope appealed to Catholic countries for help, and a French army landed in Italy; after heroic resistance, the republic was crushed, and Mazzini left Rome.

Back in London, he founded another society—the Friends of Italy—in 1851 and was soon involved in new revolutionary activities. In 1853 he backed the Milanese workers in their unsuccessful rising against the Austrians. In 1853–54 he sent Felice Orsini on two unproductive missions to raise a revolt in Carrara. In 1856 he went secretly to Genoa to plan a number of simultaneous insurrections. The only one that was seriously attempted was Carlo Pisacane's disastrous landing in Calabria in 1857. Even the apparently futile conspiracies of this period had the useful effect, however, of keeping Italian problems before the governments of Europe. For these plots Mazzini was reviled in Piedmont, where the new moderate party was working for orderly progress without revolution. Count Cavour, the prime minister, called him "chief of the assassins," but this charge was unfair; Mazzini's plots were for insurrection, not assassination, and he expressly disclaimed the "theory of the dagger."

In 1858 Mazzini founded another journal in London: this was *Pensiero ed azione* ("Thought and Action"), a title reflecting his view that thought is only of value when it results in action. He did not participate in the Franco-Piedmontese war against Austria in 1859, by which Cavour with the help of Napoleon III vainly sought to free Italy from the Alps to the Adriatic; nor did he belong to the "party of action," which sponsored Giuseppe Garibaldi's expedition to Sicily in 1860. Yet this expedition has been called "Mazzini's gift to the 'party of action,' " for it followed plans devised by him in earlier years. Mazzini went to Naples during Garibaldi's brief dictatorship of southern Italy but was back in London when the new united Kingdom of Italy (excluding Venice and Rome) was proclaimed in 1861.

Impractical schemes for seizing Venice and Rome occupied Mazzini's mind in the 1860s. This was the decade of the Socialist First International; he had early contact with its members but soon withdrew, since the moral and religious basis of his own political thought prevented him from accepting either Karl Marx's communism or Mikhail Bakunin's anarchism. Messina repeatedly elected him as its parliamentary deputy, but the elections were quashed by the Italian government. In 1870 he misguidedly agreed to lead a republican rising in Sicily. He was arrested on his way there and interned at Gaeta but was released and pardoned after the occupation of Rome by Italian troops.

Accomplishments and reputation. Mazzini's life was ending in disappointment, even though both Venice (acquired in 1866) and Rome were now part of the new kingdom. Italy had been united by fusion, as he had always advocated against strong opposition, rather than by federation, but it was a monarchy and not the republic he had wanted. "I thought I was awakening the soul of Italy, and I see only the corpse before me," he said.

In his last years he founded another paper, *Roma del popolo* ("Rome of the People"), which he edited from Lugano, and made plans for an Italian workingmen's congress. He died from pleurisy at Pisa in 1872. He had never married.

Mazzini's reputation has fluctuated greatly. In his earlier years, he was an almost legendary hero in his own country, but he was later denounced by many of his compatriots as an enemy of the state. For two generations after his death, most historians considered that his useful work ended in 1849 and that he should then have withdrawn from conspiracy.

A different view, however, prevails among modern historians. Many believe that all his plots were valuable, since they held out a permanent threat of violent revolution if Italy were not freed and united. By spurring on the Piedmontese government, and later the Italian government, to work for the national cause, he is now considered to have played an indispensable part in the making of modern Italy. (E.C.H.)

BIBLIOGRAPHY. Bolton King, *Mazzini* (1902, reissued with title *The Life of Mazzini,* 1938); and Gwilym O. Griffith, *Mazzini: Prophet of Modern Europe* (1932, reprinted 1970), are the best general biographies. E.E.Y. Hales, *Mazzini and the Secret Societies* (1956), is an excellent detailed study of the earlier years.

To make the best use of the Britannica, consult the INDEX *first*

M'ba, Léon, M'ba also spelled MBA (b. February 1902, Libreville, French Congo [now in Gabon]—d. Nov. 28, 1967, Paris, Fr.), first president of independent Gabon, whose regime, after an abortive 1964 coup, came to depend on French government and business support.

Considered a troublemaker by the French colonial administration before World War II and even exiled by it from 1933 to 1946, M'ba entered politics shortly after his return to Gabon. In 1952 he was elected to the Territorial Assembly, and in 1956 he became mayor of the Gabon capital, Libreville. After the victory of his party, the Gabon Democratic Bloc, in the important 1957 elections, M'ba was made vice president of the Gabon Executive Council (the highest post then held by an African). He soon afterward became council president and prime minister of the Republic of Gabon, which had opted to remain within the French community in the referendum of September 1958.

By the time Gabon gained independence two years later, M'ba was already coming under attack from members of his own party as being too conservative and pro-French, and he imprisoned several of them. He was elected president in 1961 and became increasingly paternalistic and authoritarian, stressing both the need for unity and Gabon's dependence on France. In early 1964, just before an election, he unilaterally decided to establish a one-party regime; in the resulting military uprising he was momentarily captured by the Gabonese army. French troops, however, restored him to power. With more tacit French backing, he remained president until his death in 1967.

Mbabane, capital and largest town of Swaziland. Located in the Highveld of western Swaziland, Mbabane developed near the cattle kraal of the Swazi king Mbandzeni in the late 19th century. The actual town traces its foundation to 1902, when the British assumed control of Swaziland and established an administrative headquarters there. A Mozambican railway link near Mbabane was established in 1964, primarily to export iron ore extracted from the Ngwenya iron-ore mine in the Highveld region. Production of this ore had virtually ceased by the late 1970s. Pop. (1998 est.) 60,000.

Mbale, town, southeastern Uganda. It lies at the western foot of the volcano Mount Elgon, 75 miles (120 km) northeast of Jinja. Located in a fertile coffee-growing region, Mbale is an agricultural (cotton, bananas, vegetables, grain) trade centre and the site of one of Uganda's principal dairies. The town is the terminus for an improved road offering a scenic route around the north of Mount Elgon to Kitale, Kenya. Pop. (1991) 53,600.

Mbalmayo, town, south-central Cameroon. It lies along the Nyong River south of Yaoundé. Located within the forest zone, it has a major plywood factory, powered by electricity from the hydroelectric complex at Edéa. It is also a commercial centre because of its position at the junction of three transportation routes: it lies on the main road south from Yaoundé, is the southeastern terminus of the railway from Douala, and serves as a river port on the Nyong River, which is seasonally navigable for 155 miles (250 km) from Mbalmayo east to Abong Mbang. Pop. (1992 est.) 43,858.

Mbandaka, formerly (until 1966) COQUILHATVILLE, city, northwestern Congo (Kinshasa). It lies on the equator about 435 miles (700 km) northeast of Kinshasa. It was a colonial administrative centre from 1886. It is now a busy river port situated at the junction of the Congo (Zaïre) and Ruki rivers midway on the Kinshasa-Kisangani shipping route. In addition to shipping, Mbandaka's economic activities centre on agriculture and forestry (rubber, coffee, rice, lumber). The city also is the site of a national museum, a teacher-training college, and a botanical garden. It has an airport. Pop. (1994 est.) 169,841.

Mbangala (African people): *see* Imbangala.

M'banza Congo, also spelled MBANZA KONGO, formerly SÃO SALVADOR DO CONGO, town, northwestern Angola. It is situated on a low plateau about 100 miles (160 km) southeast of Nóqui, which is the nearest point on the Congo River. It was the capital of the Kongo kingdom from the 16th to the 18th century and was known as M'banza or Bonza Congo until renamed São Salvador by the Portuguese after a cathedral was built there in 1534. The idea of a Kongo kingship with a throne at São Salvador survived in the minds of African leaders in Angola and Zaire, even after the destruction of the Kongo domain by Europeans in the 19th century, and it influences modern central African politics. The intermittent rebellion of the area's Kongo peoples because of forced labour and land eviction led to Portuguese reprisals and mass migration of the Kongo from 1961 to 1974 to neighbouring Zaire. The town's original name was restored after Angola attained its independence from Portugal in 1975. Pop. (latest est.) 4,000.

Mbari Mbayo Club, club established for African writers, artists, and musicians at Ibadan and Oshogbo in Nigeria. The first Mbari Club was founded in Ibadan in 1961 by a group of young writers with the help of Ulli Beier, a teacher at the University of Ibadan. *Mbari,* an Igbo word for "creation," refers to the traditional painted mud houses of the area, which must be renewed periodically. The Ibadan club operated an art gallery and theatre and published works by Nigerian artists and *Black Orpheus,* a journal of African and African American literature.

Duro Ladipo, a Yoruba playwright, was inspired to start a similar club in Oshogbo, then a city of 250,000 people, about 50 miles (80 km) northeast of Ibadan. With the help of Beier, he converted his father's house into an art gallery and a theatre, where he produced his plays. The Oshogbo club became more than a meeting place for intellectuals. Because it was on the main road, the club attracted women on the way to the market, hunters, chiefs, kings, schoolchildren, farmers, politicians, and the unemployed, and it became a vital part of Oshogbo life. The name of the club was inadvertently altered when the Igbo word *mbari* was mistaken for the Yoruba phrase *mbari mbayo,* meaning "when we see it we shall be happy." To reach the local, mostly Yoruba audience, Ladipo drew upon Yoruba mythology, drumming, dance, and poetry and soon developed a kind of Yoruba opera.

Beier organized art workshops in Ibadan in 1961 and 1962 and at Oshogbo in 1962 to attract unemployed primary-school dropouts. The school was run to give the artists a committed, critical audience on the theory that their art would degenerate if subjected only to undiscerning tourists. The young artists drew on their traditions and their contemporary environment and rapidly created a fresh, sophisticated art. The problem of how to protect these artists from the easy tourist market was solved by social acceptance of the Mbari Mbayo Club, which provided a lively, local, outspoken audience; soon local groups commissioned palace murals, stage sets, church doors, and an Esso gasoline station. With this firm local support, the artists were able to sell to European collectors and send exhibits abroad without compromising their art.

A number of well-known artists emerged from the Mbari Mbayo Club in Oshogbo, among them Twins Seven Seven (dancer, drummer, and graphic artist), Jimoh Buraimoh (mosaicist), Samuel Ojo (appliqué artist), Ashiru Olatunde (whose aluminum panels are found on Nigerian banks, churches, and bars as well as in private collections in Europe and America), Yemi Bisiri (lost-wax brass figures for the Ogboni cult), Jinadu Oladepo (brass figures, bracelets, and pendants), and Senabu Oloyede and Kikelomo Oladepo (cloth dyeing, an art traditionally reserved for women).

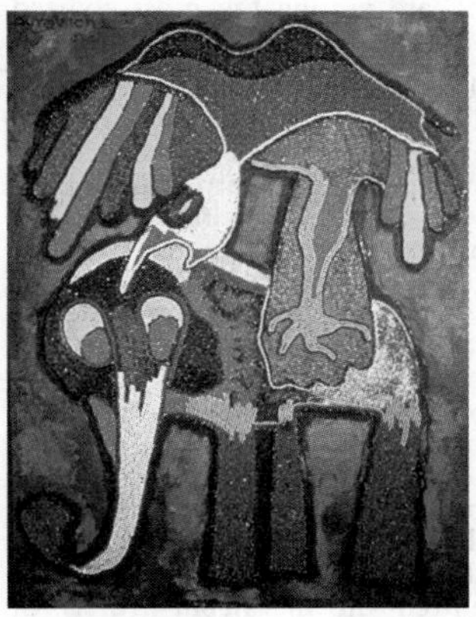

"Bird and Elephant," bead mosaic by Jimoh Buraimoh; in the David Welch Collection
Maude Wahlman

The success of the Mbari Mbayo Club lies as much in the artists it has produced as in its social impact on Oshogbo, for the club helped reaffirm the traditional interdependence between African art and African society.

Mbayá, also called CADUVEO, or GUAYCURÚ, South American Indians of the Argentine, Paraguayan, and Brazilian Chaco, speakers of a Guaycuruan language. At their peak of expansion, they lived throughout the area between the Bermejo and Pilcomayo rivers in the eastern Chaco. At one time nomadic hunters and gatherers, the Mbayá became feared warlike horsemen shortly after they encountered the Spanish and their horses.

The pre-Spanish, pre-horse Mbayá had already given up their primary dependence on hunting, gathering, and horticulture and relied on tribute extracted from the Guaná, groups of settled agriculturalists whom the Mbayá had conquered. The Guaná, successful farmers, weavers, and potters, provided the Mbayá with labour, agricultural produce, and manufactured goods; the Mbayá, in turn, protected the Guaná from other predatory Chaco tribes.

The Mbayá first became familiar with horses during the late 16th and early 17th centuries, when the Spanish were expanding from their coastal strongholds into the interior reaches of the Gran Chaco. By the mid-17th century, less than 100 years after the arrival of the Spanish, the Mbayá had become skilled horsemen, and their culture was undergoing drastic changes. The range and intensity of their raids on Spanish and Indian villages alike increased, Mbayá horsemen expanded the variety and quantity of game animals that they hunted, and they were able to raid herds of Spanish cattle and horses more effectively. Mbayá society became more stratified than it had been in the pre-horse days.

The 21st-century Mbayá are sedentary farmers, noted for their elaborately decorated pottery and textiles.

M.B.E., member of the British Empire, member of a British order of knighthood, though this rank does not confer knighthood. *See* British Empire, The Most Excellent Order of the.

Mbeki, Thabo (b. June 18, 1942, Idutywa, Transkei [now S.Af.]), politician who became the president of South Africa in 1999.

Mbeki's father, a leader in the Eastern Cape African National Congress (ANC), was imprisoned (1964–87) with fellow ANC member Nelson Mandela. In 1956 the younger Mbeki joined the ANC Youth League, and three years later he led a student strike that resulted in his expulsion from school. He continued his studies at home and remained active in the ANC after it was banned in South Africa in 1960. In 1962 he left South Africa illegally and attended the University of Sussex in England, graduating with an M.A. in economics in 1966.

Moving rapidly up the ANC hierarchy while working abroad, Mbeki became in 1975 the youngest member of the organization's national executive, and three years later he was named political secretary to ANC Pres. Oliver Tambo (1978). Mbeki played a key role in the discussions that led to negotiations between the ANC and South African Pres. F.W. de Klerk. The negotiations, in which Mbeki was also involved, led to the adoption of a new interim constitution that marked the end of apartheid. In 1994 Mbeki was appointed South Africa's deputy president by President Mandela. Following the ANC's electoral victory in 1999, Mbeki became president of South Africa. His administration faced challenges in continuing the transition from apartheid, halting the dramatic increase in crime, and combating the spread of AIDS. In 2004 the ANC won nearly 70 percent of the vote, and Mbeki was elected to a second term.

Mbembe, group of peoples living along the middle Cross River in Nigeria. Numbering about 100,000 in the late 20th century, they speak a language of the Benue-Congo branch of the Niger-Congo family.

The Mbembe cultivate yams, rice, cocoyams (taro), and cassava. In modern times wage labourers generally clear the fields and cultivate the yams. The land is either fallowed after one year or planted with cassava by women, who receive the profits from its sale. Compact settlements of wattle-and-daub houses with mat or thatched roofs range in size from 100 to 3,000 inhabitants.

The Mbembe trace descent through both matrilineal and patrilineal lines. Movable property (such as yams, money, and clothing) is inherited matrilineally. The matrilineage is collectively responsible for its members in jural matters. Rights to land and houses are inherited patrilineally, and lineage members usually live together. Age sets cutting across kinship ties are formed in each village. Of village associations that function as agents of social control, the *okwa,* the most powerful, has certain authority over women and authority to issue orders in such matters as public works. Members of the *okwa* also select the village chief.

Mbembe religion includes belief in a creator god and spirits who serve as intermediaries between the living and the dead. Many Mbembe are Christians.

Mbomou River (Africa): *see* Bomu River.

Mboya, Tom, in full THOMAS JOSEPH MBOYA (b. Aug. 15, 1930, Kilima Mbogo, near

Nairobi, Kenya—d. July 5, 1969, Nairobi), major political leader in Kenya until his assassination six years after his country had achieved independence.

A member of the Luo people and a graduate of mission schools, Mboya first worked as a sanitary inspector in Nairobi and almost immediately became involved in the nascent Kenyan trade-union movement. He was a key nationalist figure in the days of the Mau Mau rebellion by the Kikuyu tribe against European ownership of land. From 1953 to 1963 he was general secretary of the Kenya Federation of Labour (KFL), an especially important post since no strictly political African national organizations were allowed in Kenya until 1960.

Although the KFL was not able to participate overtly in politics, Mboya won the 1957 legislative council elections as a workers' candidate, becoming one of only eight elected African members on the council. Unlike most of his colleagues, he opposed the policy of multiracial political representation put forward by the British colonial government in the late 1950s. He helped form the Kenya independence movement in the council and the People's Convention Party in Nairobi. In the critical preindependence decade he also spent a year at the University of Oxford and twice visited the United States. In 1959 he helped found the African-American Students Foundation to raise money to send East African (originally only Kenyan) university students to the United States on charter flights, thus making it possible for many more students to study abroad.

Mboya was a founder-member of the Kenya African National Union (KANU) in 1960 and was minister of labour in the coalition government before independence. Although his importance declined after the release from prison (1961) of nationalist leader Jomo Kenyatta, he participated in Kenyatta's government as minister of justice and constitutional affairs in 1963 and minister for economic planning and development in 1964–69. His assassination in 1969 shocked the nation and exacerbated tensions between the dominant Kikuyu and other ethnic groups, especially Mboya's own Luo.

Mbuji-Mayi, formerly (until 1966) BAKWANGA, city, south-central Zaire. It is situated on the Mbuji-Mayi River. It was developed by Europeans as a mining town after diamonds were found in the area in 1909. The region in which Mbuji-Mayi is situated annually produces one-tenth in weight of the world's industrial diamonds, with mining managed by the Société Minière de Bakwanga. The city had only 30,000 inhabitants in 1960, but during the next 15 years massive immigration from neighbouring areas increased the city's population nearly ninefold. There is a teacher-training college in the city, which is accessible from Kananga (100 miles [160 km] west-northwest) by road and from Kinshasa, Lubumbashi, and Kananga by air. Pop. (1991 est.) 613,027.

mbulu-ngulu, tomb figure of carved wood covered with a sheet of copper or brass, created by the Kota tribe of Gabon, Africa, to protect the dead. Its traditional function, as a guardian figure standing against a wall, had a direct influence upon its form.

Carved in a highly stylized fashion, the figures consist of an abstracted fan-shaped head bisected vertically and horizontally by metal bands placed on top of a pounded metal sheet covering the head. The head is placed on a copper-covered, cylindrical neck, resting on schematically represented bent arms supported by a short base. The *mbulu-ngulu* figures, which exhibit a serene, curious sense

Kota *mbulu-ngulu,* engraved and embossed copper and metal sheet on a wooden base, Gabon; in the Ethnographical Collection, Zürich
Holle Bildarchiv, Baden-Baden, Ger.

of detachment, are among the most stylized of all African figures.

Mbundu, also called KIMBUNDU, second largest ethnolinguistic group of Angola, comprising a diversity of peoples who speak Kimbundu, a Bantu language. Numbering about 2,420,000 in the late 20th century, they occupy much of north-central Angola and live in the area from the coastal national capital of Luanda eastward, between the Dande (north) and Kwanza (Cuanza; south) rivers. They are distinct from the more populous Ovimbundu, their neighbours who occupy the Benguela Highlands to the south.

In the 16th century the Mbundu were organized into tribal groups that had loose political connections. In response to pressure from the Kongo Kingdom to the north, the Mbundu leadership centred on the *ngola* (ruler) of the Ndongo tribe. This centralization was destroyed by the Portuguese, who from the late 16th to the late 17th century provoked warfare and slaving among the peoples of the region.

The small amount of ethnological study of the Mbundu shows them to be related linguistically to the Ovimbundu and culturally to the Kongo, their neighbours to the north. Their cultural diversity has been reinforced by a traditional restraint on intertribal marriage and by long contact with the Portuguese and other Europeans. The Mbundu include many acculturated persons in the Luanda area as well as the staunchly conservative Dembo (Ndembo) of the interior. Major tribes of the Mbundu are the Mbaka, Ndongo, and Mbondo. In the 1970s the Mbundu peoples provided the main ethnic support for the Marxist-oriented Popular Movement for the Liberation of Angola, which assumed power in 1976 after the end of Portuguese colonial rule in 1975.

Mbuti, also called BAMBUTI, a group of Pygmies of the Ituri Forest of Zaire. They are the shortest group of Pygmies in Africa, averaging under 4 feet 6 inches (137 cm) in height, and are perhaps the most famous. Much lighter in colour than their Bantu and Sudanic neighbours, they also differ in blood type and other physical characteristics and are probably the earliest inhabitants of the area.

The Mbuti are nomadic hunters and gatherers living in small bands that vary in composition and size throughout the year but are generally formed into patrilineal groups of from 10 to 25 individual families. The tropical rain forest provides all their basic needs—food, fresh water from innumerable streams and springs, firewood, and clothing. They make huts simply by forming a beehive-shaped frame of sticks covered with phrynium leaves. A group lives in a camp for about a month and then abandons it.

Their technology is limited to the necessities of a hunting-and-gathering economy. One eastern group, the Efe, hunt with bow and arrow; elsewhere nets and spears are used to capture and kill game.

The Mbuti have no chiefs or any formal councils of elders; they settle their problems and disputes by general discussion. They believe in a benevolent forest deity, and important occasions, including the maturity of boys and girls, marriage, and death, are marked by special songs designed "to rejoice the forest." The Mbuti's music is complex in rhythm and harmony, but visual art is virtually nonexistent among them. Music, dance, and mime provide a means of reinforcing accepted values and form the basis of religious expression.

Marriage among the Mbuti is by sister exchange. Few Pygmies are polygynous, and family bonds are strong and lasting. The Mbuti show little concern with afterlife; the dead are buried in or near their hut, and the camp is then abandoned.

The Mbuti have a loose exchange relationship with neighbouring Bantu tribes and have apparently adopted some of their customs. Such acculturation is superficial, however, in spite of the use of a common language.

Archaeological evidence is lacking, but early Egyptian records show that the Mbuti were living in the same area 4,500 years ago.

Mdina, also called NOTABILE, or CITTÀ VECCHIA, town, west-central Malta, adjoining Rabat, west of Valletta. Possibly Bronze Age in origin, it has Punic, Greek, and Roman ruins. The name derives from the Arabic word *madīnah* ("town," or "city"). It was also named Notabile in the 15th century, possibly by the Castilian rulers who made it the Maltese capital until the mid-16th century, when Valletta was nearly completed; it was then referred to as Città Vecchia ("Old City"). Mdina retains intact its remarkable fortifications with a complete wall and contains many 15th-, 16th-, and 17th-century Maltese palaces. Its chief building is St. Paul's, the cathedral church of Malta (restored after an earthquake in 1693), said to occupy the site of the house of the Roman governor Publius, whose father was cured by the Apostle Paul. Beneath both Mdina and Rabat are catacombs, partly pre-Christian, showing early Christian burials. Some damage occurred during World War II, but the town retains its Renaissance atmosphere. Pop. (1992 est.) 418.

Mdo-stod (Tibet): *see* Khams.

Me 109, abbreviation of MESSERSCHMITT 109, also called BF 109, fighter aircraft of Nazi Germany, used to great effect in World War II. Originally designated the Bf 109 for Bayerische Flugzeugwerke (BFW; Bavarian Airplane Company) when it was first designed in 1934, it received its better-known designation after BFW foundered and its designer, Willy Messerschmitt, founded a firm to take over production. After the Me 109 was put into action in the Spanish Civil War, various modifications continued to be made. The Me 109E is probably the best-known model because of its wide use in the Battle of Britain. Powered by a fuel-injected Daimler-Benz engine of 1,150 horsepower, this single-seat, single-engine low-wing monoplane had a top speed of 350 miles (570 km) per hour and a ceiling of 36,000 feet (11,000 m). It was armed with two 20-millimetre cannons and two machine guns.

As many as 35,000 Me 109s were built. It was Germany's premier fighter, faster in a dive or at climbing than the British Spitfire and Hurricane but less maneuverable. Also, its range was severely limited by a small fuel capacity. By 1944, improved Allied fighters outstripped it.

Me-baragesi (Mesopotamian ruler): *see* Enmebaragesi.

mead, also called METHEGLIN, alcoholic beverage fermented from honey and water; sometimes yeast is added to accelerate the fermentation. Strictly speaking, the term metheglin (from the Welsh *meddyglyn,* "physician," for the drink's reputed medicinal powers) refers only to spiced mead made with the addition of such spices and herbs as cloves, ginger, rosemary, hyssop, and thyme; often, however, the terms are interchanged. Mead can be light or rich, sweet or dry, or even sparkling; in the Middle Ages it was usually similar to sparkling table wine.

Alcoholic drinks made from honey were common among the ancients of Scandinavia, Gaul, Teutonic Europe, and Greece and in the European Middle Ages, particularly in northern countries where grapevines do not flourish; the hydromel of the Greeks and Romans was probably like the mead drunk by the Celts and Anglo-Saxons, although the Roman *mulsum,* or mulse, was not mead but wine sweetened with honey. In Celtic and Anglo-Saxon literature, such as the writings of Taliesin and in the *Mabinogion* and *Beowulf,* mead is the drink of kings and thanes. Chaucer's miller drank mead, but by the 14th century, spiced ale and pyment (a sweetened wine similar to *mulsum*) were superseding it in popularity. The rules that King Howel the Great laid down for making mead in the 10th century are proof that the Welsh took great interest in mead. They preferred spiced mead, and it was from the early 16th century (when the Tudors brought elements of Welsh culture into England) that the word metheglin was often used for plain and spiced mead alike. Nonetheless, mead, once the most common alcoholic drink of England, had lost ground to ales and beers (since the earliest days of improved medieval agriculture) and also to wines (imported from Gascony for the wealthy, from the 12th century onward). Finally, when West Indian sugar began to be imported in quantity (from the 17th century), there was less incentive to keep bees, and the essential honey became scarcer.

Mead is made in modern times as a sweet or dry wine of low alcoholic strength, such as the homemade mead of the Pennsylvania Dutch region in Pennsylvania, or in Finland, where it is known as *sima.*

Mead, George Herbert (b. Feb. 27, 1863, South Hadley, Mass., U.S.—d. April 26, 1931, Chicago), American philosopher prominent in both social psychology and the development of Pragmatism.

Mead studied at Oberlin College and Harvard University. During 1891–94 he was instructor in philosophy and psychology at the University of Michigan. In 1894 he went to the University of Chicago, where he remained until his death.

To social psychology, Mead's main contribution was his attempt to show how the human self arises in the process of social interaction. He thought that spoken language played a central role in this development. Through language the child can take the role of other persons and guide his behaviour in terms of the effect his contemplated behaviour will have upon others. Thus Mead's psychological approach was behaviouristic.

In philosophy, Mead was one of the major thinkers among the American Pragmatists. In common with a number of his contemporaries, he was much-influenced by the theory of relativity and the doctrine of emergence. His philosophy might be called objective Relativism. Just as some objects are edible, but only in relation to a digestive system, so Mead thought of experience, life, consciousness, personality, and value as objective properties of nature which emerge only under (and hence are relative to) specific sets of conditions. John Dewey acknowledged his own great indebtedness to Mead's philosophy.

Mead never published his work. After his death his students edited four volumes from stenographic recordings and notes on his lectures and from unpublished papers: *The Philosophy of the Present* (1932); *Mind, Self, and Society* (1934); *Movements of Thought in the Nineteenth Century* (1936); and *The Philosophy of the Act* (1938).

Mead, Lake, reservoir of Hoover Dam, one of the largest man-made lakes in the world, on the Arizona–Nevada border, 25 miles (40 km) east of Las Vegas, Nev., U.S. Formed by the damming of the Colorado River, Lake Mead extends 115 miles (185 km) upstream, is from 1 to 10 miles (1.6 to 16 km) wide, and has a capacity of 31,047,000 acre feet (38,296,-200,000 cubic m) with 550 miles (885 km) of shoreline and a surface area of 229 square miles (593 square km). It was named after Elwood Mead, commissioner of reclamation (1924–36).

Lake Mead National Recreation Area, established in 1936, has an area of 2,338 square miles (6,055 square km) and extends 240 miles (386 km) along the Colorado River, from the western end of Grand Canyon National Monument to below Davis Dam (1950). It includes Lake Mohave and part of the Hualpai Indian Reservation.

Mead, Margaret (b. Dec. 16, 1901, Philadelphia—d. Nov. 15, 1978, New York City), American anthropologist whose great fame owed as much to the force of her personality and her outspokenness as it did to the quality of her scientific work. As an anthropologist, she was best-known for her studies of the nonliterate peoples of Oceania, especially with regard to various aspects of psychology and culture, the cultural conditioning of sexual behaviour, natural character, and culture change. As a celebrity, she was most notable for her forays into such far-ranging topics as women's rights, childrearing, sexual morality, nuclear proliferation, race relations, drug abuse, population control, environmental pollution, and world hunger.

In 1923 Mead entered the graduate school of Columbia University, where she studied with and was greatly influenced by anthropologists Franz Boas and Ruth Benedict (a lifelong friend). Mead obtained a Ph.D. in 1929. During a 1925 field trip in Samoa she gathered material for the first of her 23 books, *Coming of Age in Samoa* (1928; new ed., 1968), a perennial bestseller and a characteristic example of her reliance on observation rather than statistics for data. This book clearly indicated her belief in cultural determinism, a position that caused some later 20th-century anthropologists to question both the accuracy of her observations and the soundness of her conclusions.

Margaret Mead
Cornell Capa—Magnum

Other works include *Growing Up in New Guinea* (1930; new ed., 1975), *Sex and Temperament in Three Primitive Societies* (1935; reprinted, 1968), *Balinese Character: A Photographic Analysis* (1942, with her then husband Gregory Bateson), *Continuities in Cultural Evolution* (1964), and *A Rap on Race* (1971, with James Baldwin).

During her many years with the American Museum of Natural History in New York City, she successively served as assistant curator (1926–42), associate curator (1942–64), curator of ethnology (1964–69), and curator emeritus (1969–78). Her contributions to science received special recognition when, at the age of 72, she was elected to the presidency of the American Association for the Advancement of Science. In 1979 Margaret Mead was posthumously awarded the Presidential Medal of Freedom, the United States' highest civilian honour.

Some of her other works are *Male and Female* (1949; new ed., 1975), *Anthropology: A Human Science* (1964), *Culture and Commitment* (1970), a biography of Ruth Benedict, and an autobiography of her early years, *Blackberry Winter* (1972). *Letters from the Field* (1977) is a selection of Mead's correspondence written during the Samoa expedition.

Mead, Richard (b. Aug. 11, 1673, London—d. Feb. 16, 1754, London), leading 18th-century British physician who contributed to the study of preventive medicine.

A graduate of the University of Padua (M.D., 1695) and of Oxford (M.D., 1707) and a staff member of St. Thomas' Hospital and Medical School, London (1703–15), Mead attended some of the foremost personalities of the day, including King George I, Queen Anne, King George II, the British prime minister Sir Robert Walpole, Sir Isaac Newton, and the poet Alexander Pope.

He wrote on the prevention and treatment of plague, smallpox, measles, and scurvy; his *Mechanical Account of Poisons* (1702) includes original observations on the action of snake venom. Mead was also known as a prodigious collector and scholar; his library—one of the best in England at the time—numbered nearly 10,000 volumes.

Richard Mead, detail of a 19th-century engraving by H. Cook after a portrait by Allan Ramsay, 18th century
BBC Hulton Picture Library

Meade, George G(ordon) (b. Dec. 31, 1815, Cádiz, Spain—d. Nov. 6, 1872, Philadelphia), American army officer who played a critical role in the American Civil War by defeating the Confederate Army at Gettysburg, Pa. (July 1863). As commander of the 3rd Military District in the south, Meade was noted for his firm justice, which helped to make the Reconstruction period following the war less painful.

The son of a U.S. naval agent in Spain, Meade graduated from the U.S. Military Academy at West Point, N.Y., in 1835. He was commissioned in the artillery but resigned after a

Meade
By courtesy of the Library of Congress, Washington, D.C.

year's service to work for a time as a surveyor. He reentered the army in 1842 and in August 1861 was commissioned brigadier general of volunteers in command of the 2nd Brigade of the Pennsylvania Reserves. After the disastrous Union defeat at Fredericksburg, Va., he was assigned the V Corps, which participated in the Chancellorsville, Va., campaign (April–May 1863).

On June 28, 1863, President Lincoln appointed Meade to replace General Joseph Hooker in command of the Army of the Potomac. Meade repulsed General Robert E. Lee at Gettysburg (July 1–3) with great tactical skill; however, he has been criticized by some for allowing Lee's army to escape after this decisive victory. Although Meade retained command of the Army of the Potomac until the end of the war, his independence of action was sharply curtailed after March 1864, when General Ulysses S. Grant was placed in command of all Union forces. Meade was respected by his associates though he engaged in frequent quarrels. He was promoted to major general in the regular army (August 1864), and after the war he commanded several military departments.

Meade, James Edward (b. June 23, 1907, Swanage, Dorset, Eng.—d. Dec. 22, 1995, Cambridge, Cambridgeshire), British economist whose work on international economic policy procured him (with Bertil Ohlin) the Nobel Prize for Economics in 1977.

Meade was educated at Malvern College and at Oriel College, Oxford, where he earned first-class honours in 1928. In 1930–31 he spent a postgraduate year at Trinity College, Cambridge, where he became involved in discussions of John Maynard Keynes's *Treatise on Money* that led to the development of Keynes's *General Theory of Employment, Interest, and Money* (1936). It was perhaps this period that gave Meade's policy work its distinctly Cambridge and somewhat leftist flavour. He served as a war economist during World War II and was the leading economist in the Labour government (1946–47). He held chairs at the London School of Economics (1947–57) and at Cambridge (1957–68).

Meade's early important work resulted in *The Theory of International Economic Policy,* which was published in two volumes—*The Balance of Payments* (1951) and *Trade and Welfare* (1955). In the first of these books he sought to synthesize Keynesian and neoclassical elements in a model designed to show the effects of various monetary and fiscal policies on the balance of payments. In the second volume Meade explored the effects on economic welfare of various kinds of trade policy, providing a detailed analysis of the welfare effects of regulation of trade. Meade's work also led to later work on trade discrimination and effective protection.

meadow grasshopper, any member of the long-horned grasshopper subfamily Conocephalinae (family Tettigoniidae). The slender, small to medium-sized grasshoppers are found in grassy meadows near lakes and ponds. When disturbed, they enter the water, cling to underwater plants, and can remain submerged for several minutes.

Orchelimum, one of the most abundant and widespread types of meadow grasshoppers, has large orange eyes; the top of the insect is brown, the bottom green. *Conocephalus* (sometimes called *Xiphidium*) is smaller and has a weak song. The meadow grasshopper

Meadow grasshopper (*Orchelimum*)
William E. Ferguson

produces a song, consisting of clicks and buzzes, during the day or at night.

meadow mouse, any of the numerous species of voles in the genus *Microtus. See* vole.

meadow rue, any of approximately 100 species of perennial herbaceous plants constituting the genus *Thalictrum* of the buttercup family (Ranunculaceae). They occur in the North Temperate Zone and in South America and Africa, in wooded as well as in sunny, open areas.

The plants' compound leaves consist of three stalked leaflets. The small fuzzy flowers, which grow in clusters, are often greenish, yellow, or purple, with four or five sepals; petals are absent.

Early meadow rue (*Thalictrum dioicum*)
Kitty Kohout from Root Resources

The native American species, such as *T. dioicum,* also called quicksilver weed, and *T. polygomum,* also called muskrat weed, are grown as ornamentals in the wild garden. Some of the Eurasian species, however, are more showy, notably *T. aquilegiofolium* and *T. delavayi*.

meadowlark, any member of the genus *Sturnella,* belonging to the family Icteridae (order Passeriformes). Meadowlarks are sharp-billed plump birds, 20 to 28 cm (8 to 11 inches) long. The two species in North America look alike: streaked brown above, with

Western meadowlark (*Sturnella neglecta*)
Allan D. Cruickshank—The National Audubon Society Collection/Photo Researchers

yellow breast crossed by a black V and a short tail with distinctive white outer feathers. The eastern, or common, meadowlark (*S. magna*) ranges from eastern Canada to Brazil, the western meadowlark (*S. neglecta*) from western Canada to Mexico (introduced to Hawaii). The former has a simple four-note whistle and the latter an intricate fluting. Meadowlarks consume insects in summer and weed seeds in fall and winter. The nest is a grass dome hidden in a field.

The red-breasted meadowlark (*Pezites militaris*), which occurs from Ecuador southward, and a subtropical relative (*P. defilippi*) are sometimes grouped with red-breasted blackbirds.

Meadows, Earle (b. June 29, 1913, Corinth, Miss., U.S.), American pole-vaulter who, tied with Bill Sefton, set the world record in 1937 of 4.54 m (14 feet 11 inches). Meadows and Sefton were nicknamed "the Heavenly Twins."

Both vaulters competed for the University of Southern California (Los Angeles). They tied for the event in the 1935 Amateur Athletic Union (AAU) meet with vaults of 4.23 m and at the National Collegiate Athletic Association (NCAA) meet the same year with vaults of only a 1/4-inch difference. In the 1936 Olympic Games at Berlin, Meadows won the gold medal with a vault of 4.35 m (14 feet 3 1/4 inches). In the 1937 AAU meet, Sefton won and Meadows came in third. Later in the same year, Meadows tied with Sefton again, as did George Varoff and Cornelius Warmerdam, the vaults being 4.45 m (14 feet 7 5/8 inches). Still later, Meadows and Sefton tied for the world record. Meadows won the AAU pole vault in 1940 and 1941, and at the age of 35 he could still clear 4.27 m.

Meads, Colin Earl, byname PINE TREE (b. June 3, 1936, Cambridge, N.Z.), New Zealander rugby player and former team captain (1971) whose outstanding performance as a lock forward made him a national figure. Meads was a farmer before becoming an athlete, and he played for King County from 1955 until his retirement in 1972. His appearance in 55 Test (international) matches is a record for the New Zealand All Blacks club.

Meadville, city, seat of Crawford county, Pennsylvania, U.S., on the French Creek, 87 miles (140 km) north of Pittsburgh. The oldest settlement in the northwestern part of the state, it was founded by David Mead and other settlers from New England in 1788. Meadville developed as the commercial centre of a fertile dairy region; oil and natural-gas deposits are nearby. Since 1923 the manufacture of slide fasteners (zippers) has been a major industry. The city is the seat of Allegheny College (1815). Conneaut Lake, the state's largest natural lake, is 10 miles (16 km) west, and the Erie National Wildlife Refuge is 10 miles east. Inc. borough, 1823; city, 1866. Pop. (1992 est.) 14,212.

Consult the INDEX *first*

Meagher, Thomas Francis (b. Aug. 23, 1823, Waterford, County Waterford, Ire.—d. July 1, 1867, near Fort Benton, Mont., U.S.), Irish revolutionary leader and orator who served as a Union officer during the American Civil War (1861–65).

Meagher became a member of the Young Ireland Party in 1845 and in 1847 was one of the founders of the Irish Confederation, dedicated to Irish independence. In 1848 he was involved, with William Smith O'Brien, in an abortive attempt to mount an insurrection against English rule. Arrested for high treason, he was condemned to death, but his sentence was commuted to life imprisonment in Van Diemen's Land (now Tasmania).

He escaped in 1852 and made his way to the United States. After a speaking tour of U.S. cities, he settled in New York City, studied law, and was admitted to the bar in 1855. He soon became a leader of the Irish in New York and, from 1856, edited the *Irish News*.

At the outbreak of the Civil War, Meagher became a captain of New York volunteers and fought at the First Battle of Bull Run (July 1861). He then organized the Irish Brigade, and in February 1862 was elevated to the rank of brigadier general. After his brigade was decimated at the Battle of Chancellorsville (May 1863), Meagher resigned his commission, but in December he returned to command the military district of Etowah, with headquarters at Chattanooga, Tenn.

At the close of the war, he was appointed secretary of Montana Territory, where in the absence of a territorial governor he served as acting governor until his accidental death by drowning in the Missouri River.

mealybug, any small sap-sucking insect of the family Pseudococcidae (order Homoptera). They are worldwide in distribution and attack citrus trees and potted plants. Observed most frequently is the ovoid, sluggish mature female, about 1 cm (0.4 inch) long.

The name mealybug is descriptive of the insect's body, which is covered by a white sticky powder resembling cornmeal. The females and "crawlers" (the active young) cluster along the veins and on the undersides of leaves; the males are active two-winged fliers. Common members of the Pseudococcidae family are the citrus mealybug (*Pseudococcus citri*) and the citrophilus mealybug (*P. gahani*). Biological control and organic insecticides have been effective against these pests.

mean, in mathematics, quantity that has a value intermediate between those of the extreme members of some set. Several kinds of mean exist, and the method of calculating a mean depends upon the relationship known or assumed to govern the other members. The arithmetic mean, denoted $\bar{x}$, of a set of n numbers $x_1, x_2, \ldots, x_n$ is defined as the sum of the numbers divided by n:

$$\bar{x} = \frac{x_1 + x_2 + \cdots + x_n}{n}.$$

The arithmetic mean represents a point about which the numbers balance. For example, if unit masses are placed on a line at points with coordinates $x_1, x_2, \ldots, x_n$, then the arithmetic mean is the coordinate of the centre of gravity of the system. In statistics, the arithmetic mean is commonly used as the single value typical of a set of data. For a system of particles having unequal masses, the centre of gravity is determined by a more general average, the weighted arithmetic mean. If each number x_i is assigned a positive weight w_i, the weighted arithmetic mean is defined as the sum of the products $w_i x_i$ divided by the sum of the weights. In this case,

$$\bar{x} = \frac{w_1x_1 + w_2x_2 + \cdots + w_nx_n}{w_1 + w_2 + \cdots + w_n}.$$

The weighted arithmetic mean also is used in statistical analysis of grouped data; each number x_i is the midpoint of an interval; and each corresponding value of w_i is the number of data points within that interval.

For a given set of data, many possible means can be defined, depending on which features of the data are of interest. For example, suppose five squares are given, with sides 1, 1, 2, 5, and 7 inches. Their average area is $(1^2 + 1^2 + 2^2 + 5^2 + 7^2)/5$, or 16 square inches, the area of a square of side 4 inches. The number 4 is the quadratic mean (or root mean square) of the numbers 1, 1, 2, 5, 7 and differs from their arithmetic mean, which is $3\frac{1}{5}$. In general, the quadratic mean of n numbers $x_1, x_2, \ldots, x_n$ is the square root of the arithmetic mean of their squares,

$$\sqrt{(x_1^2 + x_2^2 + \cdots + x_n^2)/n}.$$

The arithmetic mean gives no indication of how widely the data are spread or dispersed about the mean. Measures of the dispersion are provided by the arithmetic and quadratic means of the n differences $x_1 - \bar{x}, x_2 - \bar{x}, \ldots, x_n - \bar{x}$. These are called the variance and the standard deviation of $x_1, x_2, \ldots, x_n$.

The arithmetic and quadratic means are the special cases $p = 1$ and $p = 2$ of the pth-power mean, M_p, defined by the formula

$$M_p = \left(\frac{x_1^p + x_2^p + \cdots + x_n^p}{n}\right)^{1/p}$$

where p may be any real number except zero. The case $p = -1$ is also called the harmonic mean. Weighted pth-power means are defined by

$$M_p = \left(\frac{w_1x_1^p + w_2x_2^p + \cdots + w_nx_n^p}{w_1 + w_2 + \cdots + w_n}\right)^{1/p}.$$

If $\bar{x}$ is the arithmetic mean of x_1 and x_2, the three numbers $x_1, \bar{x}, x_2$ are in arithmetic progression. If h is the harmonic mean of x_1 and x_2, the numbers x_1, h, x_2 are in harmonic progression. A number g such that x_1, g, x_2 are in geometric progression is defined by the condition that $x_1/g = g/x_2$, or $g^2 = x_1x_2$; hence $g = \sqrt{x_1x_2}$. This g is called the geometric mean of x_1 and x_2. The geometric mean of n numbers $x_1, x_2, \ldots, x_n$ is defined to be the nth root of their product; $g = \sqrt[n]{x_1x_2 \ldots x_n}$.

All the means discussed are special cases of a more general mean. If f is a function having an inverse f^{-1}, the number

$$f^{-1}\left(\frac{f(x_1) + f(x_2) + \cdots + f(x_n)}{n}\right)$$

is called the mean value of $x_1, x_2, \ldots, x_n$ associated with f. When $f(x) = x^p$ the inverse is $f^{-1}(x) = x^{1/p}$ and the mean value is the pth-power mean, M_p. When $f(x) = \log_e x$, the inverse is $f^{-1}(x) = e^x$ and the mean value is the geometric mean.

mean free path, average distance an object will move between collisions. The actual distance a particle, such as a molecule in a gas, will move before a collision, called free path, cannot generally be given because its calculation would require knowledge of the path of every particle in the region. The probability (dP) that a molecule will move a distance between two points (x and $x + dx$) without collision is proportional to an exponential factor; that is, $dP = e^{-x/\mu}dx$, in which e is the base of natural logarithms. The constant μ is the mean free path and is the average (mean) distance traveled by a molecule between collisions. The mean free path of an oxygen gas molecule under a pressure of 1 atmosphere at 0° C is about 6×10^{-6} cm (2×10^{-6} inch).

mean life, in radioactivity, average lifetime of all the nuclei of a particular unstable atomic species. This time interval may be thought of as the sum of the lifetimes of all the individual unstable nuclei in a sample, divided by the total number of unstable nuclei present. The mean life of a particular species of unstable nucleus is always 1.443 times longer than its half-life (time interval required for half the unstable nuclei to decay). Lead-209, for example, decays to bismuth-209 with a mean life of 4.69 hours and a half-life of 3.25 hours.

mean-value theorem, theorem in mathematical analysis dealing with a type of average useful for approximations and for establishing other theorems, such as the fundamental theorem of calculus.

The theorem states that the slope of a line connecting any two points on a smooth curve is the same as the slope of some line tangent to the curve between the two points. In symbols, if $g(x)$ represents the function, x_0 and x_1 the two given points, and c_1 the point between, then $[g(x_1) - g(x_0)]/(x_1 - x_0) = g'(c_1)$, in which $g'(c_1)$ represents the slope of the tangent line at c_1, as given by the derivative. Although the mean-value theorem seems obviously geometrically, proving the result without reference to diagrams involves deep properties of real numbers and continuous functions. Other mean-value theorems can be obtained from this basic one by letting $g(x)$ be some special function.

meander, extreme U-bend in a stream, usually occurring in a series. Meanders are most often formed in alluvial materials (stream-deposited sediments) and thus freely adjust their

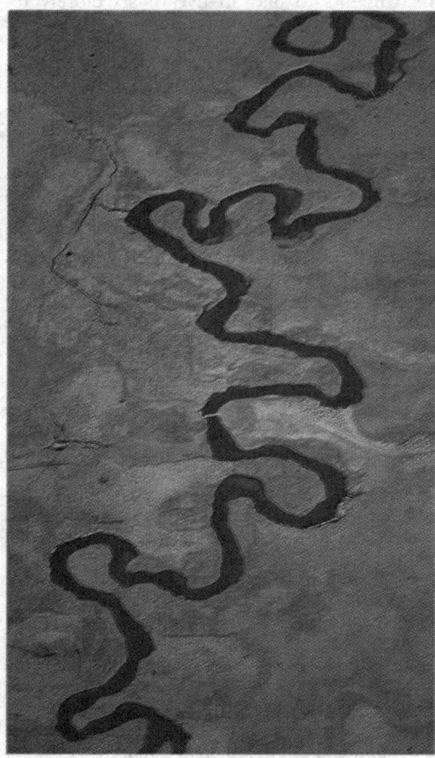

Meanders, Owens River, near Mammoth Lakes, Calif.

shapes and shift downstream according to the slope of the alluvial valley. A meandering channel commonly is about one and one-half times as long as the valley, and it exhibits pools in the meander bends and riffles in the reaches between the meanders. The length of a meander generally ranges from seven to ten times the channel width.

The uneven resistance to erosion of nonhomogenous material causes irregularities in a meandering stream, such as the stacking of meanders upstream of an obstruction. This commonly causes a meander to constrict and form a gooseneck, an extremely bowed meander. A cutoff may form through the gooseneck and allow the former meander bend to be sealed off as an oxbow lake. Silt deposits will eventually fill the lake to form a marsh or meander scar.

Subjected to rapid uplift, a meandering stream may cut into bedrock surfaces to produce entrenched or incised meanders. The rock walls thus formed are commonly quite steep and sometimes are symmetrical on both sides of the meander beds.

Many explanations have been proposed for meanders, including changes in river stages, local obstructions, rotation of the Earth, and enlargement of previous bends in the channel. Although they are not completely understood as yet, meanders are considered a form of wave phenomenon. They represent the most probable channel shape because they minimize such variables as the angle of deflection of the current, the water-surface slope, and the total work of turning done by the river. The latter is the crucial point because natural systems always tend to do least work; water flows downhill rather than uphill and follows a meandering path even on ice, glass (automobile windshields), and within water bodies, such as the Gulf Stream in the Atlantic Ocean.

meantone temperament, system of tuning keyboard instruments, prevalent from *c.* 1500 through the 18th century. It enabled keyboard instruments to play in five or six closely related keys, rather than in only one key. The system supposedly used in medieval monophonic (melody-only) music, just intonation, derived the proper tuning of all the intervals in the scale by various additions and subtractions of perfect natural fifths and thirds (in tune with the fifths and thirds found in the natural harmonic series, perceivable as faint overtones above a fundamental note). This process resulted in whole tones of two sizes. When an instrument tuned, say, in C was played in G, the large and small whole tones were in the wrong order, and the instrument sounded sourly out of tune. Meantone tuning substituted a single, mean whole tone, hence its name.

Meantone tuning accomplished this by making the fifth slightly smaller than a natural fifth (by 16 cents; 1 cent = 1/1200 octave). When a series of four meantone fifths was tuned (C–G; G–d; d–a; a–e′) and the excess octaves (here, between C and e′) were removed, the result was a pure, or natural, major third (c–e′). Various combinations of meantone fifths were used to determine the correct tuning of each of the keyboard's 12 notes per octave. The result was a notably pleasing sonority for triads (the predominant chord type, consisting of a root, a third, and a fifth, as c–e–g).

In the tuning of the black keys, however, notes such as F♯ and G♭, which share the same key, did not have the same pitch. A given black key could thus serve only for one of its two possible notes, the usual choices being C♯, E♭, F♯, G♯, and B♭. If an instrument was played in a key requiring an alternative note, say A♭ instead of G♯, a strong dissonance, known as the "wolf," resulted. This disadvantage led, in the 18th century, to the replacement of meantone tuning by equal temperament (*q.v.*); it persisted in England, however, into the mid-19th century, and it has been revived in the 20th for specialized use.

Meany, George (b. Aug. 16, 1894, New York City—d. Jan. 10, 1980, Washington, D.C.), U.S. labour leader, president of the American Federation of Labor-Congress of Industrial Organizations (AFL-CIO) from the time of merger of the two unions in 1955 until 1979, when he retired.

A plumber's son and a plumber himself by trade, Meany joined the United Association of Plumbers and Steam Fitters of the United States and Canada in 1915 and was elected business agent of a New York local in 1922. In 1932 he was elected a vice president of the New York State Federation of Labor and served as its president, 1934–39. In 1939 he was elected secretary-treasurer of the American Federation of Labor, and, upon the death of William Green in 1952, he became the AFL's president. One of Meany's greatest accomplishments was the merger of two competitive and dissimilar labour organizations (the AFL organized by crafts, the CIO by industries).

Meany's long tenure as president of the combined AFL-CIO established him as the leading spokesman for U.S. labour, and he used his power vigorously. Overall he transformed U.S. labour from a basically radical movement to a conservative one.

In 1957 he expelled the Teamsters Union, led by Jimmy Hoffa, from the AFL-CIO and, after disputes with its president Walter Reuther, lost the United Auto Workers in 1967. Though considered tardy in supporting equal job opportunities, the program that Meany eventually approved became the cornerstone of the Civil Rights Act of 1964.

Feisty and often dictatorial, Meany exerted considerable influence in the Democratic Party. In 1972, however, he opposed the presidential candidacy of George S. McGovern; he returned to the Democratic fold in 1976, during the campaign of Jimmy Carter.

A fervent opponent of Communism, Meany helped to lead the United States out of the International Labor Organization in 1977 when it refused to criticize repressive Communist policies.

Mearns, The (Scotland): *see* Kincardine.

measles, also called RUBEOLA, contagious disease caused by a virus, with community outbreaks taking place about every two to four years. Measles is commonest in children but may appear in older persons who have escaped it earlier in life. Infants are immune up to four or five months of age if the mother has had the disease. Immunity to measles following an attack is usually lifelong.

Measles is so highly communicable that the slightest contact with an active case may infect a susceptible person. Infectivity is greatest just before the eruption appears and subsides as the rash fades. Uncomplicated measles is seldom fatal; deaths attributed to measles usually result from secondary bronchopneumonia caused by bacterial organisms entering the inflamed bronchial tree.

After an incubation period of about 10 days, the patient develops fever, redness and watering of the eyes, profuse nasal discharge, and congestion of the mucous membranes of the nose and throat—symptoms often mistaken for those of a severe cold. This period of invasion lasts for 48 to 96 hours. The fever increases with appearance of a blotchy rash, and the temperature may rise as high as 104° to 106° F (about 40° C) when the rash reaches its maximum. Twenty-four to 36 hours before the rash develops, there appear in the mucous membranes of the mouth typical maculae, called Koplik spots—bluish-white specks surrounded by bright red areas about 1/32 inch (0.75 millimetre) in diameter. After a day or two the rash becomes a deeper red and gradually fades, the temperature drops rapidly, and the catarrhal symptoms disappear.

Measles must be differentiated from other disorders accompanied by an eruption. In roseola infantum, a disease seen in babies, a measles-like rash appears after the child has had a high temperature for two or three days, but there is no fever at the time of the rash. German measles (rubella) can be superficially differentiated from measles by the shorter course of the disease and mildness of the symptoms. Sometimes the rashes of scarlet fever, serum reactions, and other conditions may, on certain parts of the body, look like measles. Drugs that may produce rashes similar to measles are phenobarbital, diphenylhydantoin, the sulfonamides, phenolphthalein, and penicillin.

Mortality caused by measles declined steadily in the 20th century as the health of children and infants improved and effective treatment of complications became possible through the use of sulfonamide and antibiotic drugs. No drug is effective against measles; the only treatment required is rest in bed, protection of the eyes, care of the bowels, and sometimes steam inhalations to relieve irritation of the bronchial tree.

The widespread use of measles vaccine, beginning in the late 1960s, raised hopes for the eventual eradication of the disease; but, contrary to expectations, the incidence of measles continued to rise worldwide. One of the great problems with the measles vaccine is that it is a live vaccine that rapidly becomes inert if exposed to warm temperatures; 10 minutes in sunlight is sufficient to kill it. This sensitivity is a great hindrance to its use in tropical areas. Research is currently directed toward development of a more stable vaccine.

Me'assef (Hebrew: Collector), first Hebrew publication of the Haskala cultural movement within central and eastern European Jewry in the late 18th and 19th centuries. Founded in Königsberg, Prussia, by pupils of Moses Mendelssohn, it appeared as a quarterly from 1784 to the end of the century. Devoted to increased use of the Hebrew language and the preparation of Jews for emancipation from ghetto life, *Me'assef* became the prototype for later organs of the Haskala.

measure, in mathematics, generalization of the concepts of length and area to arbitrary sets of points not composed of intervals or rectangles. Abstractly, a measure is any rule for associating with a set a number having the properties of being non-negative and additive; *i.e.,* the measure of the union of two non-overlapping sets is equal to the sum of their individual measures. The measure of an elementary set composed of a finite number of rectangles can be defined simply as the sum of their areas found in the usual manner.

For other sets, such as curved regions or vaporous regions with missing points, the concepts of outer and inner measure must first be defined. The outer measure of a set is the number that is the lower bound of the area of all elementary rectangular sets containing the given set, while the inner measure of a set is the upper bound of the areas of all such sets contained in the region. If the inner and outer measures of a set are equal, this number is called its measure, and the set is said to be measurable.

The measure of a set of points on a line is defined similarly using intervals in place of rectangles. For example, the set of rational numbers from 0 to 1 is not composed of a finite number of intervals, and so no length is defined for it. It has a measure, however, that can be found in the following way: The rational numbers are countable, and each successive number can be covered by intervals of length $1/8$, $1/16$, $1/32$, . . . etc., the total sum of which is $1/4$, calculated as the sum of the infinite geometric series. The rational numbers could also be covered by intervals of lengths $1/16$, $1/32$, $1/64$, . . . etc., the total sum of which is $1/8$. By starting with smaller and smaller intervals, the total length of intervals covering the rationals can be reduced to smaller and smaller values approaching the lower bound of zero, and so the outer measure is zero. The inner measure is always less than or equal to the outer measure, so it must also be zero. Therefore, the rationals are measurable with measure zero.

Where the same name may denote a person, place, or thing, the articles will be found in that order

---

measurement, the process of associating numbers with physical quantities and phenomena. Measurement is fundamental to the sciences; to engineering, building, and other technical matters; and to much everyday activity. For that reason the elements, conditions, limitations, and theoretical foundations of measurement have been much studied.

A brief treatment of measurement follows. For full treatment, *see* MACROPAEDIA: Analysis and Measurement, Physical and Chemical; Measurement Systems.

Measurements may be made by unaided human senses—in which case they are often called estimates—or, more usually, by the use of instruments, which may range in complexity from simple rules for measuring lengths to highly sophisticated systems designed to detect and measure quantities entirely beyond the capabilities of the senses, such as radio waves from a distant star or the magnetic moment of a subatomic particle. (*See* instrumentation.)

Measurement begins with a definition of the measurand, the quantity that is to be measured, and it always involves a comparison of the measurand with some known quantity of the same kind. If the measurand is not accessible for direct comparison, it is converted or "transduced" into an analogous measurement signal. Since measurement always involves some interaction between the measurand and the observer or observing instrument, there is always an exchange of energy, which, although in everyday applications is negligible, can become considerable in some types of measurement and thereby limit accuracy.

In general, measuring systems comprise a number of functional elements. One element is required to discriminate the measurand and sense its dimensions or frequency. This information is then transmitted throughout the system by physical signals. If the measurand is itself active, such as water flow, it may power the signal; if passive, it must trigger the signal by interaction either with an energetic probe, such as a light source or X-ray tube, or with a carrier signal. Eventually the physical signal is compared with a reference signal of known quantity that has been subdivided or multiplied to suit the range of measurement required. The reference signal is derived from measurands of known quantity by a process called calibration. The comparison may be an analogue process in which signals in a continuous dimension are brought to equality. An alternative comparison process is quantization by counting, *i.e.,* dividing the signal into parts of equal and known size and adding up the number of parts.

Other functions of measurement systems facilitate the basic process described above. Amplification ensures that the physical signal is strong enough to complete the measurement. In order to reduce degradation of the measurement as it progresses through the system, the signal may be converted to coded or digital form. Magnification, enlarging the measurement signal without increasing its power, is often necessary to match the output of one element of the system with the input of another, such as matching the size of the readout meter with the discerning power of the eye.

One important type of measurement is the analysis of resonance, or the frequency of variation within a physical system. This is determined by harmonic analysis, commonly exhibited in the sorting of signals by a radio receiver. Computation is another important measurement process, in which measurement signals are manipulated mathematically, typically by some form of analogue or digital computer. Computers may also provide a control function in monitoring system performance.

Measuring systems may also include devices for transmitting signals over great distances (*see* telemetry). All measuring systems, even highly automated ones, include some method of displaying the signal to an observer. Visual display systems may comprise a calibrated chart and a pointer, an integrated display on a cathode-ray tube, or a digital readout. Measurement systems often include elements for recording. A common type utilizes a writing stylus that records measurements on a moving chart. Electrical recorders may include feedback reading devices for greater accuracy.

The actual performance of measuring instruments is affected by numerous external and internal factors. Among external factors are noise and interference, both of which tend to mask or distort the measurement signal. Internal factors include linearity, resolution, precision, and accuracy, all of which are characteristic of a given instrument or system, and dynamic response, drift, and hysteresis, which are effects produced in the process of measurement itself. The general question of error in measurement raises the topic of measurement theory.

Theory of measurement. Measurement theory is the study of how numbers are assigned to objects and phenomena, and its concerns include the kinds of things that can be measured, how different measures relate to each other, and the problem of error in the measurement process. Any general theory of measurement must come to grips with three basic problems: error; representation, which is the justification of number assignment; and uniqueness, which is the degree to which the kind of representation chosen approaches being the only one possible for the object or phenomenon in question.

Various systems of axioms, or basic rules and assumptions, have been formulated as a basis for measurement theory. Some of the most important types of axioms include axioms of order, axioms of extension, axioms of difference, axioms of conjointness, and axioms of geometry. Axioms of order ensure that the order imposed on objects by the assignment of numbers is the same order attained in actual observation or measurement. Axioms of extension deal with the representation of such attributes as time duration, length, and mass, which can be combined, or concatenated, for multiple objects exhibiting the attribute in question. Axioms of difference govern the measuring of intervals. Axioms of conjointness postulate that attributes that cannot be measured empirically (for example, loudness, or intelligence, or hunger) can be measured by observing the way their component dimensions change in relation to each other. Axioms of geometry govern the representation of dimensionally complex attributes by pairs of numbers, triples of numbers, or even n-tuples of numbers.

The problem of error is one of the central concerns of measurement theory. At one time it was believed that errors of measurement could eventually be eliminated through the refinement of scientific principles and equipment. This belief is no longer held by most scientists, and almost all physical measurements reported today are accompanied by some indication of the limitation of accuracy or the probable degree of error. Among the various types of error that must be taken into account are errors of observation (which include instrumental errors, personal errors, systematic errors, and random errors), errors of sampling, and direct and indirect errors (in which one erroneous measurement is used in computing other measurements).

Measurement theory dates back to the 4th century BC, when a theory of magnitudes developed by the Greek mathematicians Eudoxus of Cnidus and Thaeatetus was included in Euclid's *Elements.* The first systematic work on observational error was produced by the English mathematician Thomas Simpson in 1757, but the fundamental work on error theory was done by two 18th-century French astronomers, Joseph-Louis, Count de Lagrange, and Pierre-Simon, Marquess de Laplace. The first attempt to incorporate measurement theory into the social sciences also occurred in the 18th century, when Jeremy Bentham, a British utilitarian moralist, attempted to create a theory for the measurement of value. Modern axiomatic theories of measurement derive from the work of two German scientists, H.L.F. von Helmholtz and L.O. Hölder, and contemporary work on the application of measurement theory to psychology and economics derives in large part from the work of Oskar Morgenstern and John von Neumann.

Since most social theories are speculative in nature, attempts to establish standard measuring sequences or techniques for them have met with limited success. Some of the problems involved in social measurement include the lack of universally accepted theoretical frameworks and thus of quantifiable measurands, sampling errors, problems associated with the intrusion of the measurer on the object being measured, and the subjective nature of the information received from human subjects. Economics is probably the social science that has had the most success in adopting measurement theories, primarily because many economic variables (like price and quantity) can be measured easily and objectively. Demography has successfully employed measurement techniques as well, particularly in the area of mortality tables.

Weights and measures. Measurement is accomplished through the comparison of a measurand with some known quantity of the same kind. The term weights and measures signifies those standard quantities by which such comparisons are achieved. Standard quantities may be established arbitrarily or by reference to some universal constant. Standards for different kinds of quantities may develop separately or may be integrated into logical systems of units. Originally standard measures were four in number: those for mass (weight), volume (liquid or dry measure), length, and area. To these have been added standard measurements of temperature, luminosity, pressure, electric current, and others.

The earliest standard measurements appeared in the ancient Mediterranean cultures and were based on parts of the body, or on calculations of what man or beast could haul, or on the volume of containers or the area of fields in common use. The Egyptian cubit is generally recognized to have been the most widespread unit of linear measurement in the ancient world. It came into use around 3000 BC and was based on the length of the arm from the elbow to the extended finger tips. It was standardized by a royal master cubit of black granite, against which all cubit sticks in Egypt were regularly checked. One of the earliest known weight measures was the Babylonian mina. Two surviving examples vary widely—one weighs 640 g (about 1.4 pounds), the other 978 g (about 2.15 pounds).

The terms ounce, inch, pound, and mile come from the Roman adoption of earlier Greek measuring units. The Roman system of measurement persisted into the Middle Ages in Europe, but there was great diversity of standards. Thereafter various national governments made efforts to standardize their systems, producing a welter of often confusing units and standards. The British Imperial and U.S. Customary are two of the most elaborate such systems.

The first proposal for what would later become the metric system was made by a French clergyman, Gabriel Mouton, around 1670. He suggested a standard linear measurement based on the length of the arc of one minute of longitude on the Earth's surface and divided decimally. Mouton's proposal was much discussed and refined, but it was not until 1795 that France officially adopted the metric system. Its spread throughout the rest of Europe was accelerated by the military successes of the French Revolution and Napoleon, but in many places it took a long time to overcome the nonrational customary systems of weights and measures that had been used for centuries.

Now the standard system in most nations, the metric system has been modernized to take into account 20th-century technological advances. In Paris in 1960 an international convention agreed on a new metric-based system of units. This was the Système Internationale (SI). Six base units were adopted: the metre (length), the kilogram (mass), the second (time), the ampere (electric current), the degree Kelvin (temperature), and the candela (luminosity). Each was keyed to a standard value. The kilogram was represented by a cylinder of platinum-iridium alloy kept at the International Bureau of Weights and Measures in Sèvres, France, with a duplicate at the U.S. National Bureau of Standards. The kilogram is the only one of the six units represented by a physical object as a standard. In contrast, the metre was set to be 1,650,763.73 wavelengths in vacuum of the orange-red line of the spectrum of krypton-86, and the other units were related to similarly derived natural standards.

Other units derived from basic SI units include the coulomb (charge), joule (energy), newton (force), hertz (frequency), watt (power), ohm (resistance), and cubic metre (volume).

Conversion factors

Instructions:
To convert U.S. Customary units (a) into SI (metric) units (c), multiply by factor (b).
To convert SI units (c) into U.S. Customary units (e), multiply by factor (d).

U.S. Customary (a)	(b)	metric (c)	(d)	U.S. Customary (e)
length				
inch	25.4000	mm	0.0394	inch
inch	2.5400	cm	0.3937	inch
foot	0.3048	m	3.2808	foot
yard	0.9144	m	1.0936	yard
rod	5.0292	m	0.1988	rod
statute mile	1.6093	km	0.6214	statute mile
nautical mile	1.8520	km	0.5400	nautical mile
area				
square inch	6.4516	square cm	0.1550	square inch
square foot	0.0929	square m	10.7639	square foot
square yard	0.8361	square m	1.1960	square yard
acre	0.0040	square km	247.1054	acre
acre	40.4686	are (square dekametre)	0.0247	acre
acre	0.4047	hectare (square hectometre)	2.4711	acre
square mile	2.5900	square km	0.3861	square mile
square mile	258.9988	hectare	0.0039	square mile
volume				
cubic inch	16.3871	cubic cm	0.0610	cubic inch
cubic foot	0.0283	cubic m	35.3147	cubic foot
cubic yard	0.7646	cubic m	1.3080	cubic yard
acre-foot	1,233.4818	cubic m	0.0008	acre-foot
board foot	2,359.7372	cubic cm	0.0004	board foot
board foot	0.0024	cubic m	423.7760	board foot
capacity				
liquid measure				
barrel*				
gallon (U.S.)	3.7854	litre	0.2642	gallon (U.S.)
gallon (British)	4.5460	litre	0.2200	gallon (British)
quart (U.S.)	0.9463	litre	1.0567	quart (U.S.)
quart (British)	1.1365	litre	0.8799	quart (British)
pint (U.S.)	0.4732	litre	2.1134	pint (U.S.)
pint (British)	0.5682	litre	1.7598	pint (British)
fluid ounce (U.S.)	0.0296	litre	33.8150	fluid ounce (U.S.)
fluid ounce (British)	0.0284	litre	35.1961	fluid ounce (British)
cubic inch	0.0164	litre	61.0255	cubic inch
cubic foot	28.3161	litre	0.0353	cubic foot
dry measure				
barrel*				
bushel (U.S.)	35.2381	litre	0.0284	bushel (U.S.)
bushel (U.S.)	0.0353	cubic m	28.3776	bushel (U.S.)
bushel (British)	36.3677	litre	0.0275	bushel (British)
bushel (British)	0.0369	cubic m	27.4962	bushel (British)
peck (U.S.)	8.8095	litre	0.1135	peck (U.S.)
peck (British)	9.0919	litre	0.1100	peck (British)
quart (U.S.)	1.1012	litre	0.9081	quart (U.S.)
quart (U.S.)	1,101.2209	cubic cm	0.0009	quart (U.S.)
pint (U.S.)	0.5506	litre	1.8162	pint (U.S.)
pint (U.S.)	550.6105	cubic cm	0.0018	pint (U.S.)
weight				
short ton (2,000 pounds)	0.9072	metric ton	1.1023	short ton
short ton	907.1847	kg	0.0011	short ton
long ton (2,240 pounds)	1.0160	metric ton	0.9842	long ton
long ton	1,016.0469	kg	0.0010	long ton
short hundredweight (cental; 100 pounds U.S.)	45.3592	kg	0.0220	short hundredweight
short hundredweight	0.0454	metric ton	22.0462	short hundredweight
long hundredweight (112 pounds British)	50.8023	kg	0.0197	long hundredweight
pound	453.5924	g	0.0022	pound
pound	0.4536	kg	2.2046	pound
pound	0.0005	metric ton	2,204.6226	pound
ounce avoirdupois	28.3495	g	0.0353	ounce avoirdupois
ounce troy	31.1035	g	0.0322	ounce troy

*Measures given in barrels vary with the commodity, and, in the case of liquids, with the specific gravity.

measuring worm, also called LOOPER, CANKERWORM, or INCHWORM (family Geometridae), larva of any member of a large, cosmopolitan class of moths (order Lepidoptera). Because it lacks the middle pair of legs, it moves in a characteristic "inching," or "looping," gait by extending the front part of the body and bringing the rear up to meet it. The larvae resemble twigs or leaf stems, feed on foliage, and often seriously damage or destroy trees. The spring cankerworm (species *Paleacrita vernata*) and the fall cankerworm (*Alsophila pometaria*) attack fruit and shade trees, skeletonizing the leaves and spinning threads between the branches. Pupation usually occurs in the soil without a cocoon. Because of their distinctive larvae, the name measuring worm moth is sometimes applied to certain members of the Geometridae (*see* geometrid moth).

Omnivorous looper (*Sabulodes caberata*) larva
William E. Ferguson

meat, the flesh or other edible parts of animals (usually domesticated cattle, swine, and sheep) used for food, including not only the muscles and fat but also the tendons and ligaments.

A brief treatment of meat and meat processing follows. For full treatment, *see* MACROPAEDIA: Food Processing.

Meat is valued as a complete protein food containing all the amino acids necessary for the human body. The fat of meat, which varies widely with the species, quality, and cut, is a valuable source of energy and also influences the flavour, juiciness, and tenderness of the lean. Parts such as livers, kidneys, hearts, and other portions are excellent sources of vitamins and of essential minerals, easily assimilated by the human system.

Meat digests somewhat slowly, but 95 percent of meat protein and 96 percent of the fat are digested. Fats tend to retard the digestion of other foods; thus, meat with a reasonable proportion of fat remains longer in the stomach, delaying hunger and giving "staying power." Extractives in meat cause a flow of saliva and gastric juices, creating the desire to eat and ensuring ease of digestion.

The most widely consumed meat is beef, the flesh of mature cattle that normally weigh from 450 to 540 kg (1,000 to 1,200 pounds) and yield between 55 and 60 percent of their weight in meat. Veal, the flesh of calves of cattle, is much less fatty than beef.

The pig is the world's second largest provider of meat. When taken to slaughter, pigs generally weigh between 90 and 135 kg (200 and 300 pounds) and provide about 70 to 74 percent of that weight in meat.

Meat from lambs and sheep is produced on a much smaller scale than either beef or pork (less than one-tenth of that provided by cattle, for example). They ordinarily weigh between 45 and 70 kg (100 and 150 pounds), although the most select lambs may weigh no more than 14 to 18 kg (30 to 40 pounds) and yield about 48 to 50 percent of their weight in meat.

The meat-products industry, though called meat packing, includes the slaughtering of animals. The steps in this process generally include stunning, bleeding, eviscerating, and skinning. Carcasses are then inspected and graded according to government-set standards of quality.

The usual methods of preserving meat from bacteria and decay are refrigerating, freezing, curing, freeze-drying, and canning.

Meats are marketed as fresh or processed goods or become ingredients of various meat products, including many types of sausages and luncheon meats. They also yield a number of important by-products.

Meath, Irish AN MHÍ, originally MIDE, county in the province of Leinster, Ireland. It is bounded by Counties Monaghan (north), Louth (northeast), Dublin (southeast), Kildare (south), Offaly (southwest), Westmeath (west), and Cavan (northwest); the Irish Sea lies on the east coast. Navan is the county town (seat).

Crops and pasture cover virtually the entire county, and there are a few patches of woodland, some peat bogs in the southwest, and small areas of hill pasture around Slieve na Calliagh in the northwest. The landscape of the county consists almost entirely of glacial drift. The rivers include the Blackwater and the Boyne. Many eskers, or long glacial gravel ridges, and deep deposits of rich glacial loam extend over a great part of Meath and north Kildare, giving the area rich agricultural and grazing lands.

This deep, workable soil favoured prehistoric settlement. At Newgrange is a vast Neolithic burial place in the shape of a mound over a circular chamber that is entered by a passage walled with blocks of stone. Nearby are the two big tumuli, or grave mounds, of Dowth and Knowth. At Ceanannus Mór (formerly, Kells), the Book of Kells (*c.* 800) may have been inscribed and illuminated. There are round towers at Ceanannus Mór and Donaghmore. The hill of Tara is the traditional seat of the high kings of Ireland (*árd rí Éireann*).

Meath, "the middle kingdom," originally consisted of the present Meath and Westmeath, with parts of Cavan and Longford. The present county came into existence in the 13th century and was defined in the 16th century. In 1172 Henry II of England bestowed Meath as an earldom to Hugh de Lacy, who built strong castles at Trim, Ceanannus Mór, and elsewhere and enfeoffed 18 baronies, creating an English territorial nobility that lasted into the 17th century. As the English hold in Ireland deteriorated in the 13th and 14th centuries, only part of Meath remained inside the English Pale (territory) and under direct rule from Dublin. Meath's northern boundary, west of Drogheda, was the scene of the Battle of the Boyne (1690), in which William III defeated James II and asserted English Protestant rule over Ireland.

Navan, Ceanannus Mór, and Trim are urban districts. Meath is administered by a county council and a county manager. Most towns are small market centres and together have less than one-fourth of the county's population, but Drogheda in County Louth serves a large area of Meath. Navan has clothing, farm-tool, carpet, and furniture factories; important lead and zinc deposits, discovered in 1970, are exploited nearby. Ceanannus Mór has a boot-making factory, and Trim has a factory making office supplies.

Meath is well-favoured agriculturally; it specializes in fattening cattle (mostly bought from areas west of the River Shannon) or keeping them for export. The farms are highly productive, and three-fourths of the farmed area is in permanent pasture. One-sixth is under crops: wheat and oats, barley, potatoes, and some sugar-beet and other root and green crops. There are a number of demesnes (tenant farms) in Meath, some of which belong to Irish-speaking people of the poor west country. Area 902 square miles (2,336 square km). Pop. (1996) 109,732.

Meath, Hugh de Lacy, 1st Lord of (d. July 25, 1186, Durrow, Leinster, Ire.), one of the Anglo-Norman justiciars of Ireland who went to Ireland with England's King Henry II in 1171.

Hugh de Lacy was granted (*c.* March 1172) the lordship of Meath for the service of 50 knights and was left as constable of Dublin and justiciar when Henry returned to England in April 1172. Hugh de Lacy returned to England later in the same year; in 1173 he fought for Henry in Normandy, defending Verneuil. He was appointed to succeed William Fitz Audlin as procurator-general of Ireland in 1177 but was removed from office in May 1181, perhaps because he had married a daughter of Roderic, king of Connaught, without seeking Henry's permission. Apparently restored during the winter of 1181–82, he was finally suspended from office in 1184. Henry's son John, who had been created lord of Ireland in 1177, visited Ireland in 1185 and subsequently complained that Hugh de Lacy had intrigued against him.

According to Giraldus Cambrensis, Hugh de Lacy was an able and resolute governor but physically unprepossessing, swarthy, short, and ill-proportioned. He built many castles in his territory; the construction of one, at Durrow, had involved the demolition of an ancient and venerated monastery. While inspecting the building on July 25, 1186, Hugh de Lacy was decapitated by an assassin. His son Walter de Lacy (d. 1241) became 2nd Lord of Meath; a younger son, Hugh de Lacy (d. *c.* 1242), became 1st Earl of Ulster (1205).

Meaux, town, Seine-et-Marne *département,* Île-de-France *région,* northern France, east-northeast of Paris. Situated in a loop of the Marne River in an intensively cultivated region, it has been an agricultural market centre since medieval times. The most outstanding building, Saint-Étienne Cathedral (12th to 16th century), has a Flamboyant Gothic facade, which has suffered from crumbling. The cathedral contains the tomb and two statues of Jacques-Bénigne Bossuet, a 17th-century French writer and religious orator. The former episcopal palace (12th to 17th century) houses a Bossuet museum.

First called Latinum by the Romans, later Meldi, the name of a Gaulish tribe, Meaux became an episcopal see in the 4th century. From 923 to 1361 it belonged to the counts of Champagne. Meaux was the first diocese in France to shelter Protestant Reformers during the Wars of Religion in the late 16th century and was much fought over. It was the scene of some of the massacres of Huguenots (French Protestants) on St. Bartholomew's Day in 1572. Industries include metallurgy, chemical manufacturing, food processing, and electrical-machinery manufacturing. Pop. (1999) city, 49,421; agglomeration, 67,956.

Mecca, Arabic MAKKAH, ancient BAKKAH, or MACORABA, city, western Saudi Arabia. Mecca is the most holy city of Islām; it was the birthplace of the Prophet Muḥammad, to whom the religion of Islām was revealed, and is a religious centre to which Muslims attempt a pilgrimage, or hajj, during their lifetime. Area city, 10 square miles (26 square km). Pop. (1991 est.) 630,000.

A brief treatment of Mecca follows. For full treatment, *see* MACROPAEDIA: Mecca and Medina.

Mecca is located in the Ṣirāt Mountains, 45 miles (70 km) inland from the Red Sea port of Jiddah. The city is situated in the dry beds of the Wādī Ibrāhīm and several of its short tributaries. Temperatures are high and precipitation low, but, because of Mecca's relatively low-lying position, it is threatened by seasonal flash floods.

Mecca has developed supplementary industries to diversify its economy, once largely based on income from pilgrimages. The city's growing industrial base includes the manufacture of textiles, furniture, and utensils; pottery making is also important. The overall economy, however, is commercial. Transportation and facilities related to pilgrimages are the main service industries. Because arable land and water are scarce, Mecca must import most of its food.

Mecca centres upon the Al-Ḥaram Mosque. In the mosque's central courtyard is the Kaʿbah, the holiest shrine of Islām. The Kaʿbah, according to tradition, was built by Abraham and his son Ishmael as a replica of God's house in heaven. The Ḥaram has been renovated extensively over the centuries; the most recent refurbishment during the 1980s and '90s made the enclosure a modern, up-to-date complex.

The compact built-up area around the mosque constitutes the old city, which stretches to the north and southwest but is limited on the east and west by the nearby mountains. Since World War II, Mecca has expanded along the roads through the mountain gaps. Areas in the old city have been renovated, and Mecca has been transformed into a modern city.

During the month of pilgrimage (the Islāmic month of Dhū al-Ḥijjah), Mecca's population swells with the addition of about two million pilgrims. Only Muslims are permitted to enter the city at that time. Mecca has two university-level colleges (for the study of jurisprudence and for teacher training) and a number of cultural clubs and public libraries.

Mecca has no airport and no rail services. It is well served, however, by Jiddah's seaport and international airport, which was built in the early 1980s, as well as by truck, bus, and taxi services. A well-developed transport network carries pilgrims to religious destinations. Paved roads link Mecca with Medina and other Saudi Arabian cities and with neighbouring countries.

Mechain, Pierre (-François-André) (b. Aug. 16, 1744, Laon, Fr.—d. Sept. 20, 1804, Castellón de la Plana, Spain), French astronomer and hydrographer who, with Jean Delambre, measured the meridian arc from Dunkirk, Fr., to Barcelona. The measurement was made between 1792 and 1798 to establish a basis for the unit of length in the metric system called for by the French national legislature. Mechain also discovered 11 comets and calculated the orbits of these and other known comets.

Born the son of a master ceiling plasterer,

Mechain early in life showed mathematical prowess and worked as a hydrographer for the Naval Map Archives at Versailles during the 1770s. He turned to astronomy, and in 1782 his work with comets won him admission to the Académie Royale des Sciences. In addition, Mechain discovered numerous nebulae that were later incorporated by Charles Messier into his famous catalog of clusters and nebulae.

mechanical advantage, force-amplifying effectiveness of a simple machine, such as a lever, an inclined plane, a wedge, a wheel and axle, a pulley system, or a jackscrew. The theoretical mechanical advantage of a system is the ratio of the force that performs the useful work to the force applied, assuming there is no friction in the system. In practice, the actual mechanical advantage will be less than the theoretical value by an amount determined by the amount of friction.

mechanical efficiency, measure of the effectiveness with which a mechanical system performs. It is usually the ratio of the power delivered by a mechanical system to the power supplied to it, and, because of friction, this efficiency is always less than one. For simple machines, such as the lever and the jackscrew, the efficiency is the actual load lifted divided by the theoretical force delivered.

mechanical energy, sum of the kinetic energy, or energy of motion, and the potential energy, or energy stored in a system by reason of the position of its parts. Mechanical energy is constant in a system that has only gravitational forces or in an otherwise idealized system—that is, one lacking dissipative forces, such as friction and air resistance, or one in which such forces can be reasonably neglected. Thus, a swinging pendulum has its greatest kinetic energy and least potential energy in the vertical position, in which its speed is greatest and its height above the Earth least; it has its least kinetic energy and greatest potential energy at the extremities of its swing, in which its speed is zero and its height is greatest. As the pendulum moves, energy is continuously passing back and forth between the two forms. Neglecting friction at the pivot and air resistance, the sum of the kinetic and potential energies of the pendulum, or its mechanical energy, is constant. Actually the mechanical energy of the system is diminished at the end of each swing by the tiny amount of energy transferred out of the system by the work done by the pendulum in opposition to the forces of friction and air resistance. The mechanical energy of the Earth-Moon system is nearly constant as it is rhythmically interchanged between its kinetic and potential forms. When the Moon is farthest from the Earth in its nearly elliptical orbit, its speed is least. Its kinetic energy has become least, and its potential energy is greatest. When the Moon is closest to the Earth, it travels fastest; some potential energy has been converted to kinetic energy.

mechanical engineering, the branch of engineering concerned with the design, manufacture, installation, and operation of engines, machines, and manufacturing processes.

A brief treatment of mechanical engineering follows. For full treatment, *see* MACROPAEDIA: Energy Conversion; Engineering; Technology, History of.

Mechanical engineering involves the application of the principles of dynamics, control, thermodynamics and heat transfer, fluid mechanics, strength of materials, material science, tribology, mathematics, and computation. Increasingly a knowledge of electronics and, in particular, of microprocessors is required.

Originally engineering meant military engineering, and it was not until the end of the 18th century that nonmilitary engineering, or what became known as civil engineering, was recognized. The Institution of Civil Engineers, the first professional engineering society, was founded in 1818 in Great Britain with Thomas Telford as its first president. In 1847 a group of railway engineers, who felt that the Institution of Civil Engineers was uninterested in the new breed of engineers resulting from the development of railways, formed the Institution of Mechanical Engineers, again in Great Britain, with George Stephenson as its first president.

If the Industrial Revolution could be said to have started at any particular date, a logical year to pick would be 1712, when Thomas Newcomen produced the first practical steam engine for pumping water out of mines. James Watt was responsible for developing the double-acting steam engine and introducing the separate condenser that greatly improved the engine's thermodynamic efficiency; he also produced the first rotative engines. Richard Trevithick's development of the high-pressure steam engine in 1802 opened the way for his construction of the first locomotive in 1803. The locomotive was further developed by other engineers, including George and Robert Stephenson. Steam locomotives have been largely replaced in the second half of the 20th century by diesel- and electric-powered locomotives.

Steam engines were developed for powering pumping stations, factories, ships, traction vehicles, and the first electric generators. Late in the 19th century Sir Charles Parsons invented the steam turbine, which largely replaced the reciprocating steam engine in most applications. Coal was used to fire the boilers for raising steam, although from the mid-19th century it was increasingly replaced by oil. With increasing scarcity of oil, nuclear power for electrical-power generation partially replaced other sources of thermal energy. The first nuclear-power station to produce power commercially went into operation in Great Britain in 1957.

Steam was used for the steam-traction engines and some early automobiles, but it was replaced by the more convenient and compact internal-combustion engine pioneered by Siegfried Marcus, Gottlieb Daimler, and Carl Benz that remains the main power plant for automobiles. The internal-combustion engine was also extensively developed for aircraft propulsion, but for large aircraft it has been replaced by the gas-turbine jet engine, which resulted from the pioneering efforts of Sir Frank Whittle. Gas turbines are also used for standby power generation, pumps and compressors on oil and gas lines, and the propulsion of warships. Yet another form of internal-combustion engine, the diesel engine, is used extensively for bus and truck engines, ship propulsion, standby power generation, and increasingly for automobile engines because of its high thermal efficiency.

Mechanical engineering is concerned with textile machinery, packaging machines, printing machinery, metalworking machines, machine tools, welding, air conditioning, refrigerators, agricultural machinery, and a multitude of other machines and processes that are essential to an industrial economy. There has been a great increase in the understanding and application of new materials such as high-strength steels, aluminum alloys, titanium, plastics, and composite materials such as glass fibre and carbon-reinforced resins.

The computer, particularly the microprocessor, is increasingly used by mechanical engineers to speed and control design and manufacturing. Computer-aided design and drafting enables the designer to express ideas on a video screen and carry out the necessary analyses for stresses, fluid flow, heat transfer, etc., and then to produce a final dimensional drawing. Computer-aided manufacture allows the transfer of final design of components directly from the computer to the workshop, where the components are manufactured on computer-controlled machines. Machine tools, transfer devices, and robots are increasingly being controlled directly from a central computer that can, for instance, decide on the allocation of work to particular machines and the particular tools to be used and can keep an inventory of stocks of material and tooling. This is known as a flexible manufacturing system.

Articles are alphabetized word by word, not letter by letter

mechanics: *see under* descriptive word (*e.g.,* fluid mechanics, statistical mechanics), except as below.

mechanics, the science of the action of forces upon material bodies. It forms a central part of all physical science and engineering; indeed, the enunciation of the laws of mechanics by Isaac Newton in the 17th century initiated the development of modern science. Newton's theory does not correctly describe the behaviour of particles at the atomic scale or of systems that move at speeds close to that of light or in intense gravitational fields. In these cases the more modern theories of quantum mechanics and relativity are needed.

A brief treatment of mechanics follows. For full treatment, *see* MACROPAEDIA: Mechanics.

Classical mechanics. Newton's theory of mechanics is today referred to as classical mechanics because it accurately represented the effects of forces under all conditions known in his time, even though it has been superseded by quantum mechanics and the relativistic mechanics of Albert Einstein. Nevertheless, the Newtonian theory remains unchallenged for almost all practical applications to large-scale (*i.e.,* not atomic) systems.

Classical mechanics may be divided into statics and dynamics. In statics, interest centres on the topic of equilibrium, in which any number of forces balance each other and thereby cancel. A rigid framework, such as a bridge, a vehicle chassis, or the timber frame of a house or roof, will experience various stresses according to the loading characteristics. The study of statics is important for determining the loading limits of such structures.

If the forces acting on a system do not cancel, motion will result; the analysis of this situation falls within the province of dynamics. Before the work of Galileo and Newton, ideas about the motion of material bodies were vague and inaccurate. There was a common belief that, in the absence of forces, all bodies eventually achieve a state of rest. Forces were thus required to act continuously to produce any sort of motion. This led to difficulties in explaining how, for example, an arrow can continue to fly through the air when the only evident source of propulsion is the bow. Problems also arose in accounting for the Earth's continuing motion around the Sun.

Newton produced the first systematic set of mathematical laws to describe the motion of bodies. Newton maintained that mere motion does not require force: only accelerated motion needs a mechanism. Uniform motion in a straight line is "natural" and will continue indefinitely unless some agency interferes. This is the essential content of Newton's first law of motion. Thus, a vehicle slows to rest only because frictional forces sap its energy. In space, there is no friction to restrain the Earth's motion within the solar system.

Newton's second law relates the acceleration of a body to the forces acting on it. Specifically, the acceleration is proportional to the force, the constant of proportionality being the body's mass, which is a measure of its inertia. Newton's third law, expressing the equality of action and reaction, frames a principle that is exploited in the case of the rocket, in which the backward expulsion of gases causes a reactive force that drives the payload forward. These laws of classical mechanics embody the laws of conservation of energy, momentum, and angular momentum, which play a central part in understanding all isolated mechanical systems.

Applications of Newton's mechanics include the study of continuous media, such as fluids and elastic solids; discrete particles, as in the case of projectiles and planetary bodies; and chains of coupled particles, such as crystal lattices.

In the 19th century, classical mechanics was reformulated within a very general mathematical framework by Joseph-Louis Lagrange and Sir William Rowan Hamilton. Their equations form the starting point of most modern applications of the subject.

Celestial mechanics. Newton verified his new laws of mechanics by showing that they correctly explained the motion of the planets in the solar system. Although no mechanism is required to explain the Earth's motion as such, the curvature of its orbit constitutes an acceleration in the direction of the Sun, and Newton attributed this to the force of the Sun's gravity. His laws actually underlie those advanced earlier by Johannes Kepler to explain the sizes and shapes of the planetary orbits.

Subsequently, the study of the solar system was greatly refined to include the tiny perturbations of planetary orbits produced by the gravitational fields of the other planets, investigations of the stability of the entire system, and speculations about its origin. Important work by Lagrange, Pierre-Simon Laplace, and Friedrich Wilhelm Bessel in the 19th century maintained the tradition of celestial mechanics as the great proving ground of physical theory, but the subject declined in importance in the 20th century as classical mechanics was superseded by quantum mechanics and relativistic mechanics at the forefront of physical theory.

Quantum mechanics. Classical mechanics fails on the scale of atoms and molecules. The realization that Newton's laws could explain neither the structure and behaviour of atoms nor the emission and absorption of light led to one of the 20th century's major scientific revolutions—quantum mechanics.

The quantum theory, which was developed mainly by Niels Bohr, Erwin Schrödinger, Werner Heisenberg, and Max Born, not only replaces classical mechanics with an entirely new set of laws but also requires a completely different conceptual framework, which is abstract and can be properly described only mathematically. Central to quantum mechanics are the notions of uncertainty and unpredictability, which imply, for example, that there is a definite limitation upon the precision with which qualities (such as location and momentum) of an atom or subatomic particle can be specified. The theory is formulated entirely in terms of probabilities.

These strange properties are embodied in the concept of wave-particle duality, which holds that a particle such as an electron moves according to the principles that apply to wave propagation and therefore can display phenomena such as diffraction and interference. According to this picture, the observed discrete energy levels in atoms can be envisaged as standing waves of different wavelengths.

Quantum mechanics led to a drastic reappraisal of the concept of objective reality. It is also, however, an intensely practical subject. At a stroke, it explained the structure of atoms, atomic nuclei, and molecules; the behaviour of subatomic particles; the nature of chemical bonds; the properties of crystalline solids; nuclear energy; and the forces stabilizing collapsed stars. It led directly to the development of the laser, the electron microscope, the transistor, and the superconductor, and it remains the framework for much of 20th-century physical science, from the study of elementary particles to the investigation of the early evolution of the universe.

mechanics' institute, a voluntary organization common in Britain and the United States between 1820 and 1860 for educating manual workers. Ideally such an institute was to have a library, a museum, a laboratory, public lectures about applied science, and courses in various skills, but few had all of these. Mechanics of different trades were to learn from each other—a denial of guild exclusiveness—and to add to human knowledge.

A forerunner of such institutes was the Birmingham Brotherly Society founded in England in 1796. In Glasgow, George Birkbeck collected information about different trades and offered lectures at the Andersonian University (also called Anderson's University) from 1800 to 1804. He then moved to London, where in 1809 he helped to found the London Institute for the Diffusion of Science, Medicine, and the Arts, while Andrew Ure continued his work in Glasgow. Timothy Claxton founded the Mechanical Institution in London in 1817; it offered lecture-discussions for three years, until Claxton left London in 1820. The New York Mechanic and Scientific Institution, founded in 1822, was the first of many short-lived efforts in New York.

The Glasgow Mechanics' Institute—considered a model because of its library, museum, and lecture program—was founded in 1823. The same year, Birkbeck helped organize the London Mechanics' Institute. The Franklin Institute of the State of Pennsylvania for the Promotion of the Mechanic Arts was founded in Philadelphia in 1824, and the Maryland Institute for the Promotion of the Mechanic Arts in Baltimore in 1825. Timothy Claxton, who had moved to Boston, founded the Boston Mechanics' Institute in 1826, but its reliance on lectures doomed it. Claxton tried again, founding the Boston Mechanics' Lyceum in 1831. In Cincinnati the Ohio Mechanics' Institute opened in 1829. In France, Baron Charles Dupin founded several institutes before 1826, beginning at La Rochelle and Nevers.

From 1830 to 1860 hundreds of institutes were founded in the United States and Britain. Britain's Society for the Diffusion of Useful Knowledge (founded 1825) provided a central organization unknown in the United States. But many institutes were short-lived, and some of the more successful were taken over by non-mechanics with money, leisure, and the desire to hear lectures. Rules requiring mechanic majorities on governing boards were disregarded. The Franklin Institute early became a centre for advanced research in applied science, publishing reports which few mechanics could understand. The Ohio Mechanics' Institute became a school, offering courses and certificates in skills. The Maryland Institute fell dormant after its building burned in 1835 but was revived in 1847. Some institutes became lyceums; others, public libraries; others, exhibiting agencies.

After 1860 mechanics' institutes largely disappeared. But the Franklin Institute has remained an important research centre; the Ohio Mechanics' Institute was an independent school until 1969, when it became part of the University of Cincinnati (O.M.I. College of Applied Science); and the Manchester Mechanics' Institute offered courses until it became a municipal trade school in 1892. The Maryland Institute opened a School of Design in 1850; that school gradually became the focus of the Institute, which became the Maryland Institute, College of Art.

mechanism, in mechanical construction, the means employed to transmit and modify motion in a machine or any assemblage of mechanical parts. The chief characteristic of the mechanism of a machine is that all members have constrained motion; *i.e.,* the parts can move only in a determinate manner relative to one another. The nature of these relative motions is determined largely by the number of parts and the way in which they are connected.

Regardless of its complexity, the mechanism of a machine can always be analyzed as an assemblage of simple basic mechanisms, each of which contains members or links that transmit motion from one moving link to another with or without modification in degree or kind. In general, there are three ways in which this can be done: by a wrapping connector such as a chain (*q.v.*) or belt (*see* belt drive); by direct contact as in a cam or gear (*qq.v.*); or by a pin-connected link (*see* linkage).

mechanism, in philosophy, the predominant form of Materialism, which holds that natural phenomena can and should be explained by reference to matter and motion and their laws. Upholders of this philosophy were mainly concerned with the elimination from science of such unobservables as substantial form and occult qualities that could not be related to the mathematical method. It rejected the notion of organisms by reducing biological functions to physical and chemical processes, thus putting an end to spirit–body dualism. The 17th-century chemist Robert Boyle raised the question whether mechanism could be combined with the assumption that nature has "designs."

mechanoreception, the ability of an animal to detect and respond to certain kinds of stimuli—notably touch, sound, and changes in pressure or posture—in its environment.

A brief treatment of mechanoreception follows. For full treatment, *see* MACROPAEDIA: Sensory Reception.

Mechanoreception depends upon a slight deformation of a mechanoreceptive nerve cell, which causes an electrical charge at the outer surface of the cell, thus activating the nerve fibre to an appropriate response.

The mechanoreceptors in humans are located in "pain spots," or pressure points, in the skin, which are probably clusters of free nerve endings. The receptors in these pain spots respond to a wide range of stimuli, sometimes with reflexive speed, *e.g.,* a pricked finger may be withdrawn before the brain has even registered the pain. Depending on location, the pain spots may have a greater or lesser ability to distinguish among stimuli. For example, the separate stimuli of a two-pronged prick on a fingertip can be distinguished if the two prongs are only two millimetres apart. On the back of the hand the same stimuli would be felt as a single prong. At the tip of the tongue, where there are about 200 pressure points per square centimetre, the double prong can be detected as such if the two are only 1 mm apart.

The lateral-line organs of many fishes are an example of highly specialized mechanoreceptors. From head to tail along part of the spine and in certain areas of the face, fish have visible mechanoreceptor organs along a lateral line. These organs can detect very slight, local displacements of the water such as are produced by movements of other animals. The receptors, therefore, can anticipate touch at a distance. Each of these receptor organs, called neuromasts or sense-hillocks, is made up of a cluster of sensory cells surrounded by long, slender, supporting cells, topped with hairs that project into a jellylike substance called the cupula which bends in response to currents in the water. The cupula projects into the water and is replaced continuously from below to compensate for the wearing away of its outer surface by water; thus it maintains its high degree of sensitivity.

Frogs and other amphibians have a lateral-line system in the embryonic and tadpole stage; as they metamorphose into adult, largely terrestrial animals, the lateral-line system disappears. In most fishes the lateral-line system begins a series of grooves, forming a canal filled with a watery fluid. Disturbances in the outside water are transmitted into the canal system through pores. The neuromasts react, registering the disturbances and passing on the information via electrical nerve impulses.

There are other types of mechanoreceptors. Some animals living on or near the water's surface use ripples to locate prey nearby; still others use bottom currents or even air currents to orient themselves or to detect the movement of other animals. The structures in the body that respond to vibrations in the surrounding air—sound—are mechanoreceptors. Other structures, often associated with sound receptors, allow the organism to sense its orientation with respect to gravity. Still others inform the brain of the extension and translation of limbs or the state of various muscles.

Mechelen (Flemish), French MALINES, municipality, Antwerp *province,* north-central Belgium. It lies along the Dijle River, a few miles north-northeast of Brussels. St. Rumoldus (Rombold) was said to have come there in 756. In the Middle Ages it was called Machlina (Mechlinia) and belonged to the prince-bishops of Liège (915–1333) and the counts of Flanders (1333–69). It passed to the Burgundians (1369), and Charles the Bold made it the seat of the Grand Council (1473), the supreme court of the Low Countries. Mechelen reached its zenith as capital of the Netherlands and as a centre of culture under the regency of Margaret of Austria, who held a brilliant court there from 1507 to 1530. Since 1559 Mechelen has been the see of Belgium's only archbishopric. Mechelen suffered greatly in the wars of the 16th, 17th, and 18th centuries and was captured several times by the Spanish, English, and French. It was heavily damaged in World Wars I and II.

Long renowned for lace making, Mechelen is also one of western Europe's principal vegetable markets and has railway repair shops. Its industries include brewing, the manufacture of furniture and textiles, and various handicrafts, in particular tapestry making.

Medieval churches include the Cathedral of St. Rumoldus (13th–15th century), containing a 49-bell carillon and Anthony Van Dyck's "Crucifixion"; St. John's, with Peter Paul Rubens' "Adoration of the Magi"; and Notre Dame (Onze Lieve Vrouw), (with Rubens' "Miraculous Draught of Fishes." Notable civic landmarks include the Renaissance palace of Margaret of Austria (law courts since 1796), the 14th-century Cloth Hall, and the town hall, which is composed of three distinct structures: the Palace of the Grand Council (1526), the cadre of halls (1311–26), and a Renaissance building (17th century). Of four museums in Mechelen, the most notable are the Stadsmuseum (art and antiquities) and the diocesan museum. Pop. (1991) mun., 75,313.

Mechitarist, also spelled MEKHITARIST, member of CONGREGATION OF BENEDICTINE ARMENIAN ANTONINE MONKS, a congregation of Roman Catholic Armenian monks, widely recognized for their contribution to the renaissance of Armenian philology, literature, and culture early in the 19th century and particularly for the publication of old Armenian-Christian manuscripts.

The congregation, whose constitution is based on the Rule of St. Benedict, was founded in Constantinople (now Istanbul) in 1701 by the Armenian priest Mekhitar Petrosian of Sivas. Driven from Constantinople in 1703, the Mechitarists moved to Modon in Morea (1703–15) and finally settled in 1717 on the island of San Lazzaro, Venice, which was given to them by the Venetian state. This community, known as the Ordo Mechitaristarum Venetiarum, argued over a revised constitution set up by Abbot Stephen Melkonen, and in 1772 a group of dissidents left Venice for Trieste, establishing a separate branch (Ordo Mechitaristarum Vindobonensis) in Vienna (*c.* 1810).

The Armenian Academy at San Lazzaro, which was set up in Rome by the Venetian Mechitarists in the early 19th century, quickly became a centre of Armenian learning. The academy introduced the scientific and literary journal *Pazmaveb* in 1843, pioneered a dictionary of the Armenian language (1836), and continues to publish many classics and original works of scholarship in Armenian. The Venetian branch of the congregation maintains five religious houses, two colleges, and four schools, as well as the publishing house.

The Viennese Mechitarists are active missionaries. They worked among the Armenians under the Austro-Hungarian Empire and established parishes in Budapest, Cambridge (Mass.), and Los Angeles. Their motherhouse in Vienna incorporates a school, library, museum of ancient Armenian art, and a publishing house that issues *Handés Amsorya* (1887), a journal of Armenian philology. They also run colleges in Istanbul and Beirut.

Mechnikov, Ilya Ilich: *see* Metchnikoff, Élie.

Meckel, Johann Friedrich (b. Oct. 17, 1781, Halle, Prussia [Germany]—d. Oct. 31, 1833, Halle), German anatomist who first described the embryonic cartilage (now called Meckel's cartilage) that ossifies to form part of the lower jaw in fishes, amphibians, and birds. He also described a pouch (Meckel's diverticulum) of the small intestine.

Meckel, also known as Meckel the Younger, came from a family of physicians. He studied medicine at the universities of Halle and Göttingen, graduating in 1802 after writing a doctoral dissertation on congenital abnormalities of the heart. He was the author of numerous papers and several multivolume treatises, including one on pathological anatomy, and an atlas depicting human abnormalities.

Mecklenburg, historic region of northeastern Germany, located along the Baltic Sea coastal plain, from the Bight of Lübeck about 100 miles (160 km) eastward. It is now included in the German *Land* (state) of Mecklenburg–West Pomerania (*q.v.*).

By the 7th century AD the Slavic Obodrites and the Lutycy (Lyutichi) in the west and east, respectively, had replaced the area's earlier Germanic inhabitants. In 1160, under Henry the Lion, duke of Saxony, Christianity and German domination were introduced. Przybysław (Přibislav), son of the vanquished Obodrite ruler Niklot, became Henry's vassal and founded the Mecklenburg dynasty. In a series of partitions, four separate lines were established by Przybysław's great-grandsons in the 13th century: Mecklenburg (named from the family castle, Mikilinborg, south of Wismar), Rostock, Güstrow (or Werle), and Parchim. In 1436 the Mecklenburg line reabsorbed the whole inheritance. Meanwhile, it had acquired the lordship of Stargard in 1292 and the countship of Schwerin in 1358. The German king Charles IV in 1348 made the Mecklenburgs dukes and princes of the empire.

Mecklenburg became Lutheran during the Protestant Reformation, and in the 16th and early 17th centuries the region was recurrently divided into two duchies, Mecklenburg-Schwerin (the west) and Mecklenburg-Güstrow (the east). During the Thirty Years' War, Albrecht von Wallenstein in 1627–31 ousted the dukes who had sided with Christian IV of Denmark, but the dukes were restored by the Swedes. By the Peace of Westphalia (1648) Sweden acquired Wismar and its environs, which it held until 1803.

With the extinction of the Güstrow line in 1695, Mecklenburg was again reunited but then was permanently divided by the Treaty of Hamburg (1701). Most of the territory went to Mecklenburg-Schwerin, while Mecklenburg-Strelitz comprised the principality of Ratzeburg in the northwest and the lordship of Stargard in the southeast. In 1808 both duchies joined the Confederation of the Rhine set up by Napoleon I; the Congress of Vienna in 1814–15 recognized them as grand duchies and members of the German Confederation. They sided with Prussia in the Seven Weeks' War (1866) and joined the North German Confederation in 1867 and the German *Reich* in 1871. After World War I, under the Weimar Constitution, the grand ducal regimes were abolished in favour of elected governments. The Nazi government in 1934 merged the two states into one *Land* (state) of Mecklenburg, which, after World War II, with some territorial adjustments, was briefly (1949–52) a *Land* of the German Democratic Republic (East Germany) before it was dissolved into the *Bezirke* (districts) of Rostock, Schwerin, and Neubrandenburg. Before the unification of East and West Germany in 1990, the former *Land* was reconstituted from these districts as Mecklenburg–West Pomerania.

Mecklenburg–West Pomerania, German MECKLENBURG-VORPOMMERN, *Land* (state), northeastern Germany. It extends about 100 miles (160 km) along the Baltic Sea coastal plain, from the Bight of Lübeck on the west to the Darss Peninsula on the east, with a hinterland that stretches southward to the lower Elbe River in the west and beyond the sources of the Havel River in the east. Mecklenburg–West Pomerania *Land* is coterminous with the historic region of Mecklenburg (*q.v.*). The *Land* was re-created just before the unification of East and West Germany in 1990 from the East German *Bezirke* (districts) of Rostock and most of Schwerin and Neubrandenburg. It covers the northernmost one-fifth of what was formerly East Germany. The capital is Schwerin.

Most of Mecklenburg–West Pomerania drains into the Baltic. The central part of the *Land* is traversed from west to east by a plateau of hilly country covered by fertile soil and beech forests and having more than 600 lakes, the largest being Lake Müritz in the south. The southwest, between the plateau and the Elbe, has poor sandy soils, pine forests, and marshy valleys. In the north the plateau has good clay soils. Along the coast, steep cliffs alternate with beaches and dunes. The *Land* lies wholly within the North European Plain.

Agriculture is the most important economic activity in Mecklenburg–West Pomerania. The chief crops are rye, wheat, sugar beets, potatoes, and hay. Smaller areas are devoted to corn (maize), peas, rape, hemp, and flax. The region's pastures support herds of sheep, cattle, and horses, and fishing is carried on in the inland lakes. Mecklenburg is relatively sparsely populated, and its only significant urban centres are Rostock, Schwerin, and Neubrandenburg. Area 9,202 square miles (23,835 square km). Pop. (1991 est.) 1,924,000.

Meconopsis, genus of about 45 species of herbaceous plants of the poppy family (Papaveraceae) native to Eurasia, several of which are grown for their poppylike flowers. The only European representative is the Welsh poppy (*M. cambrica*), a 38-centimetre- (15-inch-) tall, somewhat hairy, yellow-flowering perennial; it has orange-flowered and double-flowered varieties. The blue poppy (*M. betonicifolia*), with blue-violet flowers, and the satin poppy (*M.

Welsh poppy (*Meconopsis cambrica*)

G.E. Hyde—EB Inc.

napaulensis), with nodding pale blue to purple flowers, are often cultivated.

medal, piece of metal struck with a design to commemorate a person, place, or event. Medals can be of various sizes and shapes ranging from large medallions to small plaques, or plaquettes. Most medals are made of gold, silver, bronze, or lead, the precious metals being used for the finer productions. Medals are produced by a variety of techniques: they

Henry IV and Marie de Medicis portrayed on the obverse side of a bronze-gilt medal by Guillaume Dupré, 1603; in the National Gallery of Art, Washington, D.C.

By courtesy of the National Gallery of Art, Washington, D.C., Samuel H. Kress Collection

are cast from a model of wax, wood, or sometimes stone; they are struck from a die engraved in intaglio, the design impressed on the medal by pressure; or they can be produced by the repoussé process, in which two separately worked, interlocking molds containing the blank are brought together under pressure. A positive punch, or hub, can be cut in hard metal and the design stamped into a softer metal, which is then hardened to form a die (thus many dies can be made from one hub). Machine cutters, introduced in the 19th century, copied mechanically an enlarged electrotype of the original design; but this technique, by eliminating hand cutting, took away much of the medalist's art.

Although some Roman medallions of bronze and other metals are known, it is generally accepted that the art of the medalist began in 1438 with a bronze medal of the Byzantine emperor John VIII Paleologus—the first of a series of fine portrait medals. Italian medalists were responsible for a number of innovations, including the development by the Renaissance architect Donato Bramante of a press for leaden seals, which eliminated the damaging hammer blows otherwise needed to force the impression onto the medal. Some of the most beautiful 16th-century medals were made by Benvenuto Cellini. German medalists gained a justified reputation in the first half of the 16th century with the work of Peter Flötner and other artists of the Nürnberg school. In the 17th century, French medalists such as Guillaume Dupré, the Warin brothers, and François Briot, with his fine medal of King Louis XIII struck in 1610, brought the French school to prominence. In England during the 17th century, Thomas Rawlins and the brothers Simon produced medals of considerable quality; a fine example is a gold medal depicting General George Monck made in 1660 by Thomas Simon.

Important medalists of the 18th and early 19th centuries include the Englishman John Croker and the Italian Benedetto Pistrucci. In general, however, this was a period of sterility in the medalist's art. In spite of the development of mechanical techniques, the 19th century saw a revival of the art with the work of Hubert Ponscarme and Jules-Clément Chaplain in France and the Wyon family in England. Medalists of the 20th century often returned to the older techniques of hand cutting and casting.

Medal of ——: *see under* substantive word (*e.g.,* Honor, Medal of).

medallion carpet, any floor covering on which the decoration is dominated by a single geometric centrepiece, such as a star-shaped, circular, quatrefoiled, or octagonal figure. The name, however, is sometimes also given to a carpet on which the decoration consists of several forms of this kind or even of rows of medallion figures.

Among Persian carpets, particularly those of the classic period, the medallion may represent an open lotus blossom with 16 petals as seen from above, a complex star form, or a quatrefoil with pointed lobes. Toward each end of the carpet there may be added to this centrepiece a cartouche form (an oval or oblong ornate frame), placed transversely, and

Northwest Persian medallion carpet, 17th century; in the Metropolitan Museum of Art, New York City

By courtesy of the Metropolitan Museum of Art, New York City, gift of J.F. Ballard; photograph, Otto E. Nelson—EB Inc.

a finial or pendant that sometimes is very large. In each corner of the field there may appear a quarter-medallion, which may or may not have the same contour and the same appendages as the central medallion. Such combinations are still used in the decoration of modern Persian carpets.

Among the 15th- and 16th-century Mamlūk carpets of Egypt, star, octagonal, and octofoiled centrepieces were preferred, without the other elements mentioned. In Ottoman Turkish and Egyptian classic carpets, the lobed circle was the most common medallion form, as in more recent Chinese carpets. Ottoman weavers used the quarter-medallion cornerpiece, but the Chinese preferred to balance against the central figure complete smaller roundels near the corners.

European carpet designers of the 18th and 19th centuries invented fanciful new medallion contours, often including architectural elements and other Renaissance details. Their products have found imitators in commercial carpets from several Persian centres and from India and Japan.

Medan, *kotamadya* (municipality) and capital, Sumatera Utara *provinsi* ("province"), Indonesia. It lies along the Deli River in northeastern Sumatra. Medan's harbour is Belawan, 12 miles (19 km) north on the Strait of Malacca. The chief historical building is the sultan of Deli's palace, built for him by

The Post Office in Medan, Sumatra, Indon.

Don North—Nancy Palmer Agency

the Dutch in the 19th century. There is also a large mosque and a tobacco-research facility. The University of North Sumatra (1952) and the Islāmic University of North Sumatra are in Medan. A railway carries agricultural products to Medan from the interior, and there is an international airport. The city's light industry produces bricks, tile, and machinery.

Once the occasional home of the sultan of Deli, Medan became, after the introduction of tobacco plantations to the area in 1873, the centre of a vast region of export-crop agriculture (tobacco, tea, palm products, rubber). The population comprises descendants of Chinese traders, Malay plantation workers (the indigenous population), Javanese contract workers, and Bataks, who have immigrated in large numbers since independence ended the power of the old Malay nobility.

Contemporary Medan supplies the oil and gas fields of northern Sumatra and continues the traditional export of plantation crops. Pronounced a city by the Dutch in 1886, it became a municipality in 1909 and was briefly the capital of East Sumatra after the Japanese occupation during World War II. Pop. (1987 est.) 1,715,670.

Medawar, Sir Peter B(rian) (b. Feb. 28, 1915, Rio de Janeiro—d. Oct. 2, 1987, London), British zoologist who received (with Sir Macfarlane Burnet) the Nobel Prize for Physiology or Medicine in 1960 for the discovery of acquired immunological tolerance when he found (1953) that adult animals injected with foreign cells early in life accept skin grafts from the original cell donor.

Medawar was born in Brazil, to which his parents had been transferred on business. He attended Magdalen College, Oxford, from which he received a degree in zoology. His involvement with transplant research began in earnest in 1949, when Burnet advanced the hypothesis that during embryonic life and immediately after birth, cells gradually acquire the ability to distinguish between their own tissue substances and unwanted cells and foreign material. Medawar lent support to this theory when he found that fraternal cattle twins accept skin grafts from each other, indicating that certain substances known as antigens "leak" from the yolk sac of each embryo twin into the sac of the other. In a series of experiments on mice, he produced evidence indicating that each animal cell contains certain genetically determined antigens important to the immunity process, because the recipient injected as an embryo with the donor's cells will accept tissue from all parts of the donor's body and from the donor's twin.

Medawar, 1960
Keystone

Medawar was professor of zoology at the universities of Birmingham (1947–51) and London (1951–62), director of the National Institute for Medical Research, London (1962–71), professor of experimental medicine at the Royal Institution (1977–83), and president of the Royal Postgraduate Medical School (1981–87). He was knighted in 1965 and awarded the Order of Merit in 1981. Medawar's work resulted in a shift of emphasis in the science of immunology from one that attempts to deal with the fully developed immunity mechanism to one that attempts to alter the immunity mechanism itself, as in the attempt to suppress the body's rejection of organ transplants.

Medawar's works include *The Uniqueness of the Individual* (1957), *The Future of Man* (1960), *The Art of the Soluble* (1967), *The Hope of Progress* (1972), *Life Science* (1977), *Pluto's Republic* (1982), and his autobiography, *Memoir of a Thinking Radish* (1986).

Medb, also spelled MEDHBH (Celtic: "Drunken Woman"), legendary queen of Connaught (Connacht) in Ireland. In the Irish epic tale *Táin Bó Cuailnge,* she led her forces against those of Ulster and fought in the battle herself with weapons, unlike the other war goddesses, who influenced its outcome by means of their magical powers. Medb was not a historical queen but a fierce goddess with an insatiable sexual appetite. The list of her mates is impressive; at the time of the battle against Ulster, the king Ailill was her mate, but she also had an affair with the mighty hero Fergus, distinguished for his prodigious virility. Medb had a sacred tree, *bile Medb,* and was often represented with a squirrel and a bird sitting on her shoulders.

Mede, one of an Indo-European people, related to the Persians, who entered northeastern Iran probably as early as the 17th century BC and settled in the plateau land that came to be known as Media (*q.v.*).

Medea, in Greek mythology, an enchantress who helped Jason, leader of the Argonauts, to obtain the Golden Fleece from her father, King Aeetes of Colchis. She was perhaps a goddess and had the gift of prophecy. She married Jason and used her magic powers and advice to help him.

The *Medea* of Euripides takes up the story at a later stage, after Jason and Medea had fled Colchis with the fleece and had been driven out of Iolcos because of the vengeance taken by Medea on King Pelias of Iolcos (who had sent Jason to fetch the fleece). The play is set during the time that the pair lived in Corinth, when Jason deserted Medea for the daughter of King Creon of Corinth; in revenge, Medea murdered Creon, his daughter, and her own two sons by Jason and took refuge with King Aegeus of Athens.

Ovid in his *Metamorphoses* carried the story further. After fleeing Corinth, Medea became the wife of Aegeus, who later drove her away after her unsuccessful attempt to poison his son Theseus. The Greek historian Herodotus related that from Athens Medea went to the region of Asia subsequently called Media, whose inhabitants thereupon changed their name to Medes.

Medea also is the heroine of Seneca's *Medea,* a tragedy based on Euripides' drama, and a number of contemporary settings including plays by Franz Grillparzer and Jean Anouilh and an opera by Luigi Cherubini.

Médéa, also called LEMDIYYA, town, north-central Algeria. It is situated 56 miles (90 km) south of Algiers, on a plateau separating the Tell Atlas and the Kabylie. Shadowed by Mount Nador (3,693 feet [1,126 m]) to the northwest, the town is surrounded by fertile, well-watered soil that forms the watershed for the Wadis Chelif, Chiffa, and Isser. Located on the site of Lambdia, a Roman military post, Médéa was founded in the 10th century by Yūsuf Buluggin I ibn Zīrī and became capital of the Turkish beylik of Titteri in the 14th. It was occupied by Abdelkader, the Algerian national leader, in 1835 and taken by the French in 1840. Médéa was the birthplace of the French poet and playwright Jean Richepin (1849–1926).

The town is French in character, with a rectangular city plan, public gardens, and red-tile-roofed buildings. The neighbouring hills are covered with vineyards and orchards, and the surrounding plains yield high-grade cereals. Médéa's chief products include pumps and irrigation equipment, wines, and varied handicrafts. Pop. (1987 prelim.) mun., 84,062.

Medeba (Jordan): *see* Ma'dabā.

Medellín, city, capital of Antioquia *departamento,* northwestern Colombia. It lies along the Porce River (a tributary of the Cauca) at an elevation of 5,000 feet (1,500 m) above sea level, in the steep, temperate Aburrá Valley of the Cordillera Central. It is one of the nation's largest cities and is heavily industrialized, particularly in the steel industry. Medellín was founded in 1675 as a mining town, but few colonial buildings survive. It is a well-ordered city, laid out on modern planning lines. Medellín has developed a wide industrial base that includes food processing, woodworking, metallurgy, automobiles, chemicals, and rubber products; it is known as "Colombia's Manchester," because of its textile mills and clothing factories.

After 1914, the completion of the Panama

Cathedral of Villanueva on Parque Bolívar, Medellín, Colom.
Ralph Mandol—DPI

Canal and the arrival of the railroad from Cali led to the rapid growth of Medellín, which became an important transportation crossroads. The city is connected by road to the Caribbean littoral and has an international airport. Medellín has long been one of Colombia's largest commercial centres of the coffee industry. A new international airport at nearby Rionegro was completed in the mid-1980s. Medellín became a centre for the illegal international distribution of Colombian-grown cocaine in the late 20th century. Pop. (1985) 1,418,554.

Medelpad, *landskap* (province) in the administrative *län* (county) of Västernorrland, northeastern Sweden. Its land area of 2,725 square miles (7,058 square km) is bounded on the south by the *landskap* of Hälsingland, on the west by that of Härjedalen, on the north by those of Jämtland and Ångermanland, and on the east by the Gulf of Bothnia. Fertile cultivated fields are found along the two principal rivers, Ljungan and Indalsälven, former logging routes that are now sources of hydroelectric power. The area between the two river valleys abounds in forests, mountains, and lakes. Artifacts from the Stone and Bronze ages indicate that Medelpad was one of the earliest-inhabited parts of the region of Norrland. Finds of Arabic, Anglo-Saxon, and German coins from Viking times attest to its early importance as a commercial and trading area, where the Ljungan and Indalsälven served as lines of communication between the east and west coasts of the Scandinavian Peninsula. Agriculture is practiced along the deeply indented coast, as well as in the river valleys. Leading industries are sawmilling and wood processing. The major town is the port of Sundsvall. Pop. (1988 est.) 123,855.

Médenine (Tunisia): *see* Madanīyīn.

Medford, city, Middlesex county, northeastern Massachusetts, U.S. It lies along the Mystic River, just north of Boston. It was founded in 1630, when Mathew Cradock, first governor of Massachusetts, settled a plantation there; its English place-name is descriptive of a "middle ford." Farming and fishing were early enterprises. Shipbuilding in Medford began in 1631 with *Blessing of the Bay,* one of the first oceangoing ships to be built in America. Later, the city's merchants were active in the "Triangular Trade" by which rum made from West Indian sugar was traded for African slaves, who in turn were sold to the West Indies. Medford is now primarily residential with some light manufacturing. It is the site of Tufts University, founded in 1852. Several colonial buildings are preserved, including Royall House, furnished with period pieces. Inc. town, 1684; city, 1892. Pop. (1990) 57,407.

Medford, city, seat (1926) of Jackson county, southwestern Oregon, U.S., in the Rogue River valley, on Bear Creek. Founded in 1883 as a depot on the Oregon and California (now Southern Pacific) Railroad, it was named for

Medford, Mass., and grew as a shipping point for pears and lumber. The heart of a resort region that includes Crater Lake National Park and Oregon Caves National Monument, it is headquarters for the Rogue River National Forest and a trading centre for fruit, dairy, and truck-farm produce. Timber, pears, and tourism are its economic mainstays. Jacksonville (*q.v.*), Oregon's most picturesque historical settlement, is 5 miles (8 km) west. Inc. 1885. Pop. (1994 est.) city, 52,611; (1995 est.) Medford-Ashland MSA, 166,060.

Media, ancient country of northwestern Iran, generally corresponding to the modern regions of Azerbaijan, Kurdistan, and parts of Kermanshah. Media first appears in the texts of the Assyrian king Shalmaneser III (858–824 BC), in which peoples of the land of "Mada" are recorded. The inhabitants came to be known as Medes.

Although Herodotus credits "Deioces son of Phraortes" (probably *c.* 715) with the creation of the Median kingdom and the founding of its capital city at Ecbatana (modern Hamadan), it was probably not before 625 BC that Cyaxares, grandson of Deioces, succeeded in uniting into a kingdom the many Iranian-speaking Median tribes. In 614 he captured Ashur, and in 612, in alliance with Nabopolassar of Babylon, his forces stormed Nineveh, putting an end to the Assyrian empire. The victors divided the Assyrian provinces among themselves, with the Median king taking over a large part of Iran, northern Assyria, and parts of Armenia.

In many respects the internal organization of the Median empire probably resembled that of Assyria, but little is actually known. Few identifiable "Median" objects have been found, but the Medes apparently favoured rich ornamentation and also received a strong artistic influence from Assyria. Since no Median written documents of any kind have ever been uncovered, their spiritual and economic life is also a matter of conjecture.

By the victory in 550 of the Persian chief Cyrus II the Great over his suzerain, Astyages of Media, the Medes were made subject to the Persians. In the new Achaemenian Empire they retained a prominent position; in honour and war they stood next to the Persians, and their court ceremonial was adopted by the new sovereigns, who in the summer months resided in Ecbatana.

Alexander the Great occupied Media in 330, and in the partition of his empire, southern Media was given to the Macedonian commander Peithon and eventually passed to the Seleucids, but the north was left to Atropates, a former general of Darius III, who succeeded in founding an independent kingdom, named Atropatene, with its capital at Gazaca. In later times Atropatene came under the control of Parthia, Armenia, and Rome.

Southern Media remained a province of the Seleucid empire for a century and a half, and Hellenism was introduced everywhere. About 152 BC, however, Media was taken by the Parthian king Mithradates I, and it remained subject to the Arsacids until about AD 226, when it passed, together with Atropatene, to the Sāsānians. By that time the Medes had lost their distinctive character and had been amalgamated into the one nation of the Iranians.

Mediaş, city, Sibiu *judeţ* (county), central Romania, on the Tîrnava Mare River. It was founded by German colonists in the 13th century on the site of a Roman camp called Media. Formerly a part of Austria-Hungary, Mediaş was united with Romania in 1919. The city centre is a large, tree-filled square, surrounded by old houses with tiled roofs. There is still a tower with an entrance gate and remnants from the walls of the 14th-century fortress. The Church of St. Margaret dates from the 17th century.

Church of St. Margaret, Mediaş, Romania
By courtesy of Editura Enciclopedica Romana

Mediaş has become an important industrial centre, utilizing nearby natural gas deposits. Its chief products are enameled kitchen utensils, glassware and window panes, textiles, and footwear. The city is surrounded by famous local vineyards. Pop. (1992 prelim.) 64,488.

mediastinitis, inflammation of the tissue around the heart, aortic artery, and entrance (hilum) to the lungs, located in the middle chest cavity. The mediastinum is essentially the space between the left and right lung; it contains all the organs and major structures of the chest except the lungs themselves. Inflammation of the mediastinum can be caused by physical injuries, infections, or tumour growths.

Most cases of acute mediastinal infection arise as complications of perforation of the esophagus. The wall of the esophagus can be penetrated by tumour growths or foreign objects, such as chicken or fish bones, glass, pins, or small toys swallowed by children. While attempts are being made to remove lodged objects, the wall can be injured by surgical instruments.

Most persons with cases of mediastinitis show symptoms of severe pain under the breastbone, or sternum. The pain can radiate toward the neck or mid-back. Chills, high fever, and laboured breathing are common. Treatment of infections is with antibiotics. Cysts, abscesses, and tumours require either surgical drainage or removal.

mediastinum, the anatomic region located between the lungs that contains all the principal tissues and organs of the chest except the lungs. It extends from the sternum, or breastbone, back to the vertebral column and is bounded laterally by the pericardium, the membrane enclosing the heart, and the mediastinal pleurae, membranes that are continuous with those lining the thoracic cage. The mediastinum is a division of the thoracic cavity; it contains the heart, thymus gland, portions of the esophagus and trachea, and other structures. For clinical purposes it is traditionally divided into the anterior, middle, posterior, and superior regions.

mediation, a practice under which, in a conflict, the services of a third party are utilized to reduce the differences or to seek a solution. Mediation differs from "good offices" in that the mediator usually takes more initiative in proposing terms of settlement. It differs from arbitration in that the opposing parties are not bound by prior agreement to accept the suggestions made.

In many countries there are standard procedures for mediating industrial disputes. In labour disputes, if the conflict does not fall within a labour-management agreement, or if it exceeds the capacity of such machinery to settle, the government usually provides a mediator. The U.S. federal government (as well as many U.S. state and local governments) and the majority of the governments of western Europe maintain labour mediation or conciliation services. In the great majority of situations in which labour mediation agencies have been created by a governmental unit, these agencies have the power to intervene in a dispute when in their judgment the public interest is threatened.

Mediation procedures are less fully developed in international conflicts, though there are several examples of successful mediation from as early as the 19th century: for example, of Great Britain in 1825 between Portugal and Brazil; of the great powers in 1868–69 between Greece and Turkey when relations were strained over Crete; and of Pope Leo XIII in 1885 between Germany and Spain in the matter of the Caroline Islands. Further important moves toward creating mediation machinery were made in the Hague conventions of 1899 and 1907 and in the League of Nations Covenant. Under the Charter of the United Nations, especially, members assumed a much larger obligation than heretofore to settle their disputes in a peaceful manner. Article 2, paragraph 3, states inter alia that all members "shall settle their international disputes by peaceful means." Under Article 33 the parties to any dispute likely to endanger the maintenance of international peace and security are enjoined first to "seek a solution by negotiation, inquiry, mediation, conciliation, arbitration, judicial settlement, resort to regional agencies or arrangements or other peaceful means of their own choice." Should they fail to settle it by these means, they are called upon under Article 37 to refer it to the Security Council. The Council, or the General Assembly if the dispute is referred to it, then undertakes the form of settlement that it believes suited to the particular case.

Following discussion in the Council or in the Assembly, the dispute may be submitted to mediation. In May 1948, for instance, the General Assembly appointed a mediator in Palestine. In the winter and spring of 1949 a later appointee was able to conclude armistice agreements between Israel and the four neighbouring Arab states. Several commissions appointed by the Security Council and by the General Assembly have had mediatory functions: for example, the commission on Indonesia, the India-Pakistan commission, the Palestine conciliation commission, and the commission on Korea. The secretaries-general, especially Dag Hammarskjöld, have exercised a great deal of personal diplomacy that can be characterized as mediatory.

medical association, professional organization or learned society developed to promote high standards in medical education and practice, science, and ethics. The medical association also works to promote and protect the interests of its physician members. The largest such organization is the World Medical Association, which has more than 60 member associations. It was founded in 1947.

A prime example of a medical association is the influential American Medical Association (*q.v.;* AMA), founded in 1847. Its major publication is the *Journal of the American Medical*

Association. With the rise of speciality boards and associations, however, the AMA lost its place as the exclusive forum for American medicine, and other highly respected publications—such as *The New England Journal of Medicine*—gained prominence. Other examples include the three major medical associations in Great Britain: the Royal College of Physicians of London, the Royal College of Surgeons of England, and the British Medical Association (BMA). The latter association, formed in 1832, initially represented rural physicians and specifically excluded London doctors or those associated with the Royal Societies. Now it chiefly represents general practitioners and has had great influence in shaping the provisions of the National Health Service.

medical imaging: *see* diagnostic imaging.

medical jurisprudence, also called LEGAL MEDICINE, science that deals with the relation and application of medical facts to legal problems. Medical persons giving legal evidence may appear before courts of law, administrative tribunals, inquests, licensing agencies, boards of inquiry or certification, or other investigative bodies.

Doctors in most countries are legally obligated to certify persons for workers' compensation or other national insurance plans, to certify the occurrence of a birth or the cause of a death, to notify the authorities of any cases of specified infectious diseases, and to determine when mentally disturbed persons need to be detained to protect themselves or others. These routine acts constitute the most frequent tasks of medical jurisprudence.

Less frequent but perhaps more significant are the uses of the doctor as a witness. When doctors appear in court merely to relate facts that they have observed, they are governed by the rules applicable to an ordinary witness. If they have to interpret those facts with their medical knowledge, they are known as "expert" witnesses and are expected to present their opinions fairly and without bias toward the litigant by whom they have been called. Despite this expectation, conflicts of medical opinion in court are common, perhaps because the human body and its ailments are less controlled by rule than is the law.

Medicine and the law do not always work in harmony. The most common source of conflict is medical confidentiality. Some doctors claim that any information received from a patient during a medical consultation is subject ethically to absolute confidentiality and can in no circumstances be revealed without the patient's permission. Without such a rule, they believe, patients sometimes would not give doctors all the information needed to treat them. Other doctors (a majority in most countries) believe that occasionally, though very rarely, their obligations to society override their obligations to their patients. Many, but not all, would report to the police a patient with severe epilepsy who, despite a warning from them, persisted in driving a car. This conflict with the law arises because, in most countries, courts, while recognizing legal privilege (the confidentiality of exchanges between lawyers and their clients), do not extend the same recognition to medical consultants.

Law and medicine come together more harmoniously in forensic medicine, a medical specialty that assists in the detection of crime. Specialists in forensic medicine also assist courts—including the coroner's court in Anglo-Saxon law—to determine the cause of sudden and unexpected deaths. In these cases the main investigation that a forensic specialist employs is a postmortem examination of the body, involving a careful examination of every organ and its contents, with sections of some organs being studied microscopically and subjected to chemical and DNA tests. Forensic medicine commonly involves estimating the time of a person's death or measuring alcohol level in the blood of a motorist and thus establishing the degree of impaired judgment.

Medicare and Medicaid, two U.S. government programs that guarantee health insurance for the elderly and the poor, respectively. They were formally enacted in 1965 as amendments (Titles XVIII and XIX, respectively) to the Social Security Act (1935) and went into effect in 1966.

The Medicare program covers most persons aged 65 or older and consists of two related health insurance plans: a hospital insurance plan (called Part A) and a supplementary medical insurance plan (Part B). The hospital plan, which is financed through Social Security payroll taxes, helps pay the cost of inpatient hospital care, skilled nursing home care, and certain home health services. The plan meets most of the cost of hospital bills for up to 90 days for each episode of illness. (An episode of illness is termed a "benefit period" and lasts from a patient's admittance to a hospital or nursing facility until he has been out of such facilities for 60 consecutive days.) The patient must pay a one-time fee called a deductible for hospital care for the first 60 days in a benefit period, and an additional, daily fee called a co-payment for hospital care for the following 30 days; Medicare covers the rest of the expenses.

The hospital plan also pays for skilled care in a nursing care facility for 100 days if such care follows a period of hospitalization within 30 days. This nursing care is free for the first 20 days after hospitalization, with the patient required to make a co-payment for any of the next 80 days. A person is thus eligible for 90 days of hospitalization and 100 days of nursing care in any benefit period. In addition, home health visits by nurses or medical technicians are covered by Medicare, as is hospice care for the terminally ill.

A patient becomes eligible for Medicare benefits again anytime he has gone for 60 consecutive days without receiving skilled care in a hospital or nursing facility; his reentry into such a facility marks the start of a new benefit period. In addition, each person has a "lifetime reserve" of 60 more hospital days that can be used at any time (including times when the 90 days covered in a benefit period have been exhausted), though a sizable co-payment is required.

Medicare's supplementary medical insurance plan supplements the benefits provided by the hospital plan and is available to most persons 65 years or older. Persons who enroll in the plan pay a small deductible for any medical costs incurred above that amount and then pay a regular monthly premium. If these requirements are met, Medicare pays 80 percent of any bills incurred for physicians' and surgeons' services, diagnostic and laboratory tests, and other services. Almost all people entitled to the hospital plan also enroll in the supplementary medical plan. The latter is financed by general tax revenues and members' payments.

The legislation enacting Medicare was passed in 1965 under the administration of President Lyndon B. Johnson and represented the culmination of a 20-year legislative debate over a program originally sponsored by President Harry S. Truman. Amendments to the program passed in 1972 extended coverage to long-term disabled persons and those suffering from chronic kidney disease. The program's rapid and unanticipated growth spurred the federal government to legislate various cost-containment measures beginning in the 1970s, notably one in 1983 that set standard payments for the care of patients with a particular diagnosis.

Medicaid is a health insurance program established for low-income persons under age 65 and persons over that age who have exhausted their Medicare benefits. The program is jointly funded by the federal government and the states. To participate in the plan, states are required to offer Medicaid to all persons on public assistance. Aside from this, and within broad federal guidelines, the individual states determine the eligibility guidelines for enrollment in their own programs, with Medicaid generally offered to persons whose incomes and assets fall below a certain level. The federal government pays the states from 50 to about 80 percent of their Medicaid costs. Hospital care, physicians' services, skilled nursing facility care, home health services, family planning, and diagnostic screening are covered by the plan.

Like Medicare, Medicaid quickly grew larger than originally expected, and in 1972 the federal government instituted the first of several sets of cost-containment measures in an effort to reduce the program's expenditures. From the early 1980s, increasing numbers of physicians refused to treat Medicaid patients because of the low reimbursement levels involved.

Medicean-Laurentian Library, Italian BIBLIOTECA MEDICEO-LAURENZIANA, collection of books and manuscripts gathered during the 15th century in Florence by Cosimo the Elder and Lorenzo the Magnificent, both members of the Medici family. Part of the collection was open to the public before 1494, but in that year the Medici were overthrown and their palace was sacked. What remained of the library was taken to Rome, where it was kept by Lorenzo's son Giovanni, who was elected pope (Leo X) in 1513. When Lorenzo's nephew Giulio was elected pope (Clement VII) in 1523, he returned the library to Florence and commissioned Michelangelo to construct a suitable building. The first drawings for the building were made in 1523. Michelangelo's designs for the staircase of the library were finished by Bartolomeo Ammanati and Giorgio Vasari in 1559.

Though it was unfinished, the library was opened in 1571. Its principal importance lies in its 10,500 manuscripts, more than 700 of which date from before the 11th century. Some are among the most valuable codices in the world—a famous Virgil of the 4th or 5th century, the Justinian Pandects of the 6th, a Horace of the 10th, many other very early classical and biblical texts, approximately 100 codices of Dante, a *Decameron* copied by a contemporary from Giovanni Boccaccio's own manuscript, and Benvenuto Cellini's manuscript of his autobiography.

Medici FAMILY, French MÉDICIS, Italian bourgeois family that ruled Florence and, later, Tuscany, during most of the period from 1434 to 1737, except for two brief intervals (from 1494 to 1512 and from 1527 to 1530). It provided the church with four popes (Leo X, Clement VII, Pius IV, and Leon XI) and married into the royal families of Europe (most notably in France, in the persons of queens Catherine de Médicis and Marie de Médicis).

Three lines of Medici successively approached or acquired positions of power (see the Table). The line of Chiarissimo II failed to gain power in Florence in the 14th century. In the 15th century the line of Cosimo the Elder set up a hereditary principate in Florence but without legal right or title, hence subject to sudden overthrow; crowns burgeoned, however, on the last branches of their genealogical tree, for two of them were dukes outside Florence, their last heir in a direct line became queen of France (Catherine de Médicis), and their final offspring, Alessandro, a bastard, was duke of Florence. In the 16th century a third line renounced republican notions and imposed its tyranny, and its members made themselves a dynasty of grand dukes of Tuscany.

The differences between these three collateral lines are due essentially to circumstances, for there was, in all the Medici, an extraordinary persistence of hereditary traits. In the first place, not being soldiers, they were constantly confronting their adversaries with bribes of gold rather than with battalions of armed men. In addition, the early Medici resolutely courted favour with the middle and poorer classes in the city, and this determination to be *popolani* ("plebeian") endured a long time after them. Finally, all were consumed by a passion for arts and letters and for building. They were more than beneficent and ostentatious patrons of the arts; they were also enlightened and were probably the most magnificent such patrons that the West has ever seen.

Line of Chiarissimo II. The Medici were originally of Tuscan peasant origin, from the village of Cafaggiolo in the Mugello, the valley of the Sieve, north of Florence. Some of these villagers, in the 12th century perhaps, became aware of the new opportunities afforded by commerce and emigrated to Florence. There, by the following century, the Medici were counted among the wealthy notables, although in the second rank, after leading families of the city. After 1340 an economic depression throughout Europe forced these more powerful houses into bankruptcy. The Medici, however, were able to escape this fate and even took advantage of it to establish themselves among the city's elite. But their policy of consolidating their position by controlling the government—the work of the descendants of Chiarissimo II (himself the grandson of the first known Medici)—resulted in 50 years of serious misfortunes for the family (1343–93).

His grandson Salvestro took up his policy of alliance with the *popolo minuto* ("common people") and was elected gonfalonier, head of the *signoria,* the council of government, in 1378. Salvestro more or less willingly stirred up an insurrection of the *ciompi,* the artisans of the lowest class, and, after their victory,

The Three Branches of the Medici Family

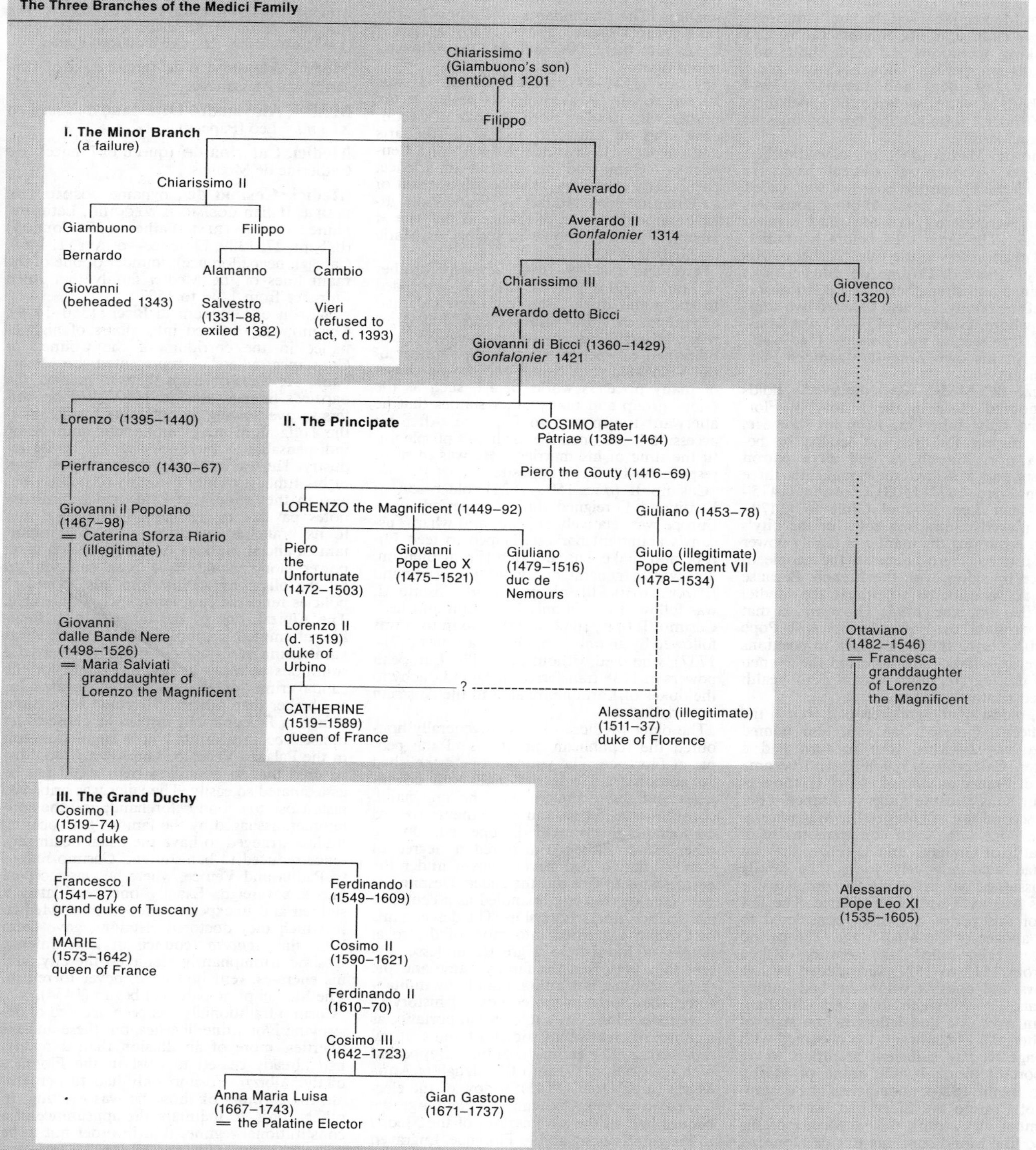

was not above reaping substantial monetary and titular advantages. But in 1381, when the popular government fell, he had to go into exile. His memory, however, was still alive in 1393, when the *popolo magro* ("lean people") once more thought it possible to take over the *signoria.* The mob hastened to seek out his first cousin, Vieri, who was, however, able to fade away without losing face. With Vieri this branch of the Medici was to disappear definitively from history.

Line of Cosimo the Elder. A distant cousin of Salvestro was Averardo de' Medici (or Bicci), whose progeny became the famous Medici of history. His son Giovanni di Bicci de' Medici (1360–1429), considered the first of the great Medici, inherited the family business based on cloth and silk manufacturing and on banking operations and made the family powerfully prosperous. Giovanni's two sons, Cosimo (1389–1464) and Lorenzo (1394–1440), both of whom acquired the appellation of "the Elder," founded the famous lines of the Medici family.

Cosimo de' Medici (*q.v.*), the older brother, established the family's political base. He served on the Florentine board of war, called the Dieci (The Ten), and held other posts. His two sons were Piero (1416–69) and Giovanni (1424–63). The latter died before his father, who in death received the title "Father of His Country." Piero di Cosimo de' Medici (*q.v.*) maintained and strengthened the political fortunes of the family. He also fathered two sons, one of whom, Giuliano (1453–78) was assassinated. The second son, Lorenzo (1449–92), became in his own time Il Magnifico (The Magnificent).

Lorenzo de' Medici (*q.v.*) deservedly holds an honoured place in the history of Florence and Italy. Inheriting from his forebears a deep respect for arts and letters, he became a poet himself as well as a patron of artists and a skilled statesman. His three children, Piero (1472–1503), Giovanni (1475–1521)—later Leo X—and Giuliano (1479–1516), played contrasting roles in the city's history. Assuming the mantle of family power from Lorenzo, Piero alienated the people of Florence by siding with the French. Because of this act, considered a betrayal, the Medici had to flee Florence (1494). Giovanni, at that time a cardinal, used his influence with Pope Julius II to bring the family back to positions of power. Giuliano, who received the French title of duc de Nemours, was in poor health and died relatively young.

Piero, oldest of the children of Lorenzo the Magnificent, fathered one son, also named Lorenzo (1492–1519), who in turn had a daughter, Catherine (1519–89), who became queen of France as wife of Henry II; three of her four sons became kings of France. Giovanni, second son of Lorenzo the Magnificent, became Pope Leo X. In commemoration of the deaths of Giuliano and Lorenzo, the two who had died relatively young, the family commissioned Michelangelo to complete the famous Medici Tombs in Florence. The few years of this period are often considered to be the apogee of the Medici age. The period has even been called "the century of Leo X." From 1513 to 1521, surrounded by five nephews and cousins whom he had named cardinals, Leo X reigned less over Christianity than over arts and letters in the style of his father, the Magnificent, too occupied with patronage to pay sufficient attention to an unimportant monk by the name of Martin Luther. By the 1520s, nonetheless, the descendants of Cosimo the Elder had become few in number. To ensure that a Medici of the Cosimo line would continue to rule Florence, Pope Clement VII, nephew of Lorenzo the Magnificent, installed Alessandro (1511–37), reputedly his own illegitimate son, as hereditary duke of Florence. In the same year, 1532, Clement VII abolished the city's old constitution.

Alessandro (*q.v.*) proved to be cruel and brutally authoritarian. He ruled for five years. In 1537 he was assassinated by a companion who was also a relative.

The grand dukes of Tuscany. Alessandro's death did not terminate the Medici family's power in Florence. A younger branch of the family, descendants of the Lorenzo who had been the brother of Cosimo the Elder, now came forward. Cosimo de' Medici (1519–74), great-great-grandson of Lorenzo, became duke of Florence, then grand duke of Tuscany (1569), and reigned as Cosimo I (*q.v.*). He established a new dynasty that perpetuated the family's traditional regard for the arts and sciences. The descendants of Cosimo I, who ruled over Florence and Tuscany as grand dukes into the 1700s, included the following major figures.

Francis (1541–87), son of Cosimo I, was known equally as a suspicious despot, a tax master who nearly ruined the nation's economy, and an estimable patron of the arts and sciences. He favoured the goldsmith Benvenuto Cellini; and his interest in science, particularly chemistry, led to establishment of a Florentine porcelain factory. Francis' daughter became the queen of France as the wife of Henry IV and is known in history as Marie de Médicis (*q.v.*).

Ferdinand I (1549–1609), younger brother of Francis and a cardinal when he succeeded to the grand duchy, showed more tact and experience in administration and, during his reign, brought Tuscany to new heights of stability and prosperity. He was the founder of the Villa Medici at Rome and the purchaser of many priceless works of art, such as the Niobe group and many other statues that he afterward transported to Florence. After his accession he retained the cardinal's purple until the time of his marriage. He was in most respects his brother's opposite.

Cosimo II (*q.v.*; 1590–1621), older son of Ferdinand I, reigned during a period when Europe was relatively at peace and when Tuscany's abundant harvests helped to feed Europe and make Tuscany rich. From then on, however, a general decay set in. Ferdinand II (*q.v.*; 1610–70), oldest son of Cosimo II, was followed by his only living son and heir, Cosimo III (*q.v.*; 1642–1723), who in turn was followed by an only son, Gian Gastone (1671–1737), who died without issue. The European powers in 1738 transferred the grand duchy to the dukes of Lorraine, related to the Austrian imperial house.

The older Medicean line had generally honoured the republican ambitions of the people of Florence. The younger line established an authoritarian rule that had both advantages and disadvantages. On the one hand, constitutional forms and movements toward democratic government disappeared. On the other hand, Florence acquired a degree of stability that it had never known under the descendants of Cosimo the Elder. Despite the new stability, the city dwindled as a centre of art, science, and scholarship. The descendants of Cosimo I married into most of the royal houses of Europe; to a greater or lesser extent they preserved the family name and the family fortune; but, ruling mainly by military force, they seem in the context of history to have reduced the city's role and importance as a centre of creative artistic effort and cultural renaissance. The grand ducal line disappeared with the death of Cosimo III's daughter Anna Maria Luisa (1667–1743), widow of the elector palatine John William of Neuburg; she bequeathed all the art treasures of the Medici to the grand duchy and to Florence. Engraved on her tomb in the Cappella dei Principi (Chapel of the Princes) are the words *Ultima della stirpe reale dei Medici* ("Last of the royal Medici line").

BIBLIOGRAPHY. Among many historians and memorialists contemporary with the Medici, Niccolò Machiavelli, Francesco Guicciardini, and, to a lesser degree, Scipione Ammirato cannot be dispensed with. Modern works, for a general view, include G.F. Young, *The Medici,* 2 vol. (1909, reprinted 1933; Italian trans. 1935; French trans. 1969), dated but still useful; Albert Jourcin, *Les Médicis* (1968; German trans. 1969); Gaetano Pieraccini, *La stirpe de' Medici di Cafaggiolo,* 2nd ed., 3 vol. (1947), extensive researches on the hereditary features and diseases that run in the Medici family; and Marcel Brion, *Le Siècle des Médicis* (1969; *The Medici: A Great Florentine Family,* 1969). On institutions and banking, Nicolai Rubinstein, *The Government of Florence Under the Medici, 1434 to 1494* (1966), based on a masterly examination of the Florentine archives, is fundamental; while Raymond de Roover, *The Rise and Decline of the Medici Bank, 1397–1494* (1963), excellently clears up a difficult matter.

Medici, Alessandro de' (grand duke of Tuscany): *see* Alessandro.

Medici, Alessandro Ottaviano de': *see* Leo XI *under* Leo (Papacy).

Medici, Caterina de' (queen of France): *see* Catherine de Médicis.

Medici, Cosimo de', byname COSIMO THE ELDER, Italian COSIMO IL VECCHIO, Latin byname PATER PATRIAE (Father of His Country) (b. Sept. 27, 1389, Florence—d. Aug. 1, 1464, Careggi, near Florence), founder of one of the main lines of the Medici family that ruled Florence from 1434 to 1537.

The son of Giovanni di Bicci (1360–1429), Cosimo was initiated into affairs of high finance in the corridors of the Council of Constance, where he represented the Medici bank. He went on from there to manage the papacy's finances and in 1462 filled his coffers to overflowing by obtaining from Pius II the Tolfa alum mines monopoly, alum being indispensable to Florence's famed textile industry. He was certainly the wealthiest man of his time, not only in terms of bullion but also in the amount of bank and promissory notes payable to his bank in Florence and to its branches operating in all the important financial markets of Europe. Such great power alone would have been sufficient to set the oligarchy against him; his "popular" policies rendered him completely intolerable. The Albizzi, one of the other leading families, attempted a coup. In 1431 Cosimo was vacationing in Cafaggiolo when he received a summons to reply to his indictment for the capital crime "of having sought to elevate himself higher than others." He could have taken refuge in Bologna, but instead he chose to let himself be incarcerated in a small dungeon in the Palazzo Vecchio. The Albizzi soon discovered that so wealthy a man could not be assassinated so easily. The jailer was bribed to taste Cosimo's food beforehand, and the gonfalonier, assuaged by the famous gold-bearing mules, arranged to have the usual death sentence reduced to banishment. Cosimo retired to Padua and Venice, where he was received like a sovereign. Exactly one year later, a sudden and unexpected move by the Medici, in which they doctored elections, gave them back the *signoria* (council of government). Cosimo triumphantly reentered the city; and his enemies went into exile, never to return. The Medici principate had begun (1434).

Cosimo traditionally has been accused of destroying Florentine liberties; but these ancient liberties, more of an illusion than a reality, had already ceased to exist in the Florence of the Albizzi. Cosimo only had to perpetuate the formula of those he was evicting, in other words, to maintain the appearance of a constitutional regime. But, in order not to be taken by surprise like the Albizzi, he perfected the system. He made no changes in the law's actual administration, but in the spirit of the law he changed everything. Previously, it was the rule to fill high official positions by drawing lots. The process was now manipulated so that only the names of men who could be depended upon were drawn. The independent mood of the two municipal assemblies was neutralized by making an exceptional procedure the rule: dictatorial powers were now granted for a fixed term that was always renewed. He also made an alliance with the Sforzas of Milan, who, for gold, provided him with troops. This alliance permitted Cosimo to crush the rising opposition by a coup d'état in August 1458 and to create a Senate composed of 100 loyal supporters (the Cento, or Hundred); thus he was able to live out the last six years of his life in security.

Cosimo required undivided power in order to carry out his plans as well as to satisfy his passions, above all his passion for building. Brunelleschi completed the "marble hat" of his famous cupola at the time of Cosimo's return in 1434; in addition, he almost completed the work on S. Lorenzo and on the Sagresta Vecchia and began work on the strange rotunda of Sta. Maria degli Angeli. He drew up plans for a princely palace for Cosimo; but the latter preferred the less lofty plans of Michelozzo, although Michelozzo's Medici Palace (the modern Palazzo Medici-Riccardi) was only slightly less grandiose and provided the first break with the family's traditional stance of humility. Under the patronage of Cosimo, Michelozzo also built the convent of S. Marco, the Medici Chapel at Sta. Croce, and a chapel at S. Miniato. In addition to architects, Cosimo gathered around him all the masters of an age abounding in geniuses: the sculptors Lorenzo Ghiberti and Donatello and the painters Andrea del Castagno, Fra Angelico, and Benozzo Gozzoli. He not only assured these artists of commissions but also treated them as friends at a time when people still looked upon them as manual workers.

Cosimo also organized a methodical search for ancient manuscripts, both within Christendom and even, with Sultan Mehmed II's permission, in the East. The manuscripts picked up by his agents form the core of the incomparable library that is rather unjustly called the Laurentian (Laurenziana), after his grandson. He opened it to the public and employed copyists in order to disseminate scholarly editions compiled by, among others, the Humanists Poggio and Marsilio Ficino.

In short, he was well prepared for the singular opportunity that came his way in 1439, when he succeeded in enticing the ecumenical council from Ferrara to Florence. The Council of Florence, Cosimo's most important success in foreign relations, deluded itself into believing it had finally ended the schism with the Eastern Church. As for Cosimo, he assiduously attended the lectures delivered by the Greek scholars, and at the age of 50 he became an ardent admirer of Plato. He then re-created Plato's ancient academy in his villa of Careggi, where Marsilio Ficino became the Platonic cult's high priest. At the same time the University of Florence, with conspicuous success, resumed the teaching of Greek, which had been unknown in the West for 700 years. Thus Cosimo was one of the mainsprings of Humanism.

In 1440 Cosimo prematurely lost his brother, who had been his staunchest supporter. In 1463 he had to face the loss of his most gifted son, Giovanni, thus leaving the succession to Piero, born in 1416, who was sickly and almost constantly bedridden. The future seemed dark to the old man as he roamed through his palace, sighing, "Too big a house for such a small family." He died in Careggi in 1464, and a huge crowd accompanied his body to the tomb in S. Lorenzo. The following year, the *signoria* conferred upon him the deserved title of Pater Patriae (Father of His Country).

Medici, Cosimo de' (grand duke of Tuscany): *see* Cosimo I; Cosimo II; Cosimo III.

Medici, Ferdinando de' (grand duke of Tuscany): *see* Ferdinand I; Ferdinand II *under* Ferdinand (Tuscany).

Medici, Francesco de' (grand duke of Tuscany): *see* Francis (I) *under* Francis (Tuscany).

Medici, Gian Gastone de' (grand duke of Tuscany): *see* Gian Gastone.

Medici, Giovanni Angelo de' (pope): *see* Pius IV.

Medici, Giovanni de': *see* Leo X *under* Leo (Papacy).

Medici, Giovanni de', original name LODOVICO, byname GIOVANNI DALLE BANDE NERE (Italian: Giovanni of the Black Bands) (b. April 6, 1498, Forlì, Papal States—d. Nov. 30, 1526, Mantua, Marquisate of Mantua), the most noted soldier of all the Medici.

Giovanni belonged to the younger, or cadet, branch of the Medici, descended from Lorenzo, brother to Cosimo the Elder. Always in obscurity and, until the 16th century, held in check by the elder line, this branch first entered the arena of history when the other was on the point of extinction. Its first major figure, in fact, was this valiant captain of the papal forces, Giovanni de' Medici. His father was Giovanni, son of Pierfrancesco, who was the son of Lorenzo. Though christened Lodovico, the child took his father's name of Giovanni, his father having died soon after his birth. Trained to arms from his earliest years, this youth inherited all the energy of his mother, Caterina, whose Sforza blood seemed to infuse new life into the younger branch of the Medici. Having first fought for Pope Leo X against Francesco Maria della Rovere (1516–17) and against the French (1521), he took service with the French in 1522, went over to the Emperor's side in 1523, but returned to the French service in 1525 (before the Battle of Pavia). In 1526 he entered the army of the League of Cognac against the Emperor but was mortally wounded in battle near Mantua on November 25 and died five days later. His *bande nere* or "black bands" were named from the black banners that they began to carry in mourning for Leo X.

Giovanni was married to Maria Salviati, by whom he had one son, Cosimo (1519–74), who became the first grand duke of Tuscany (as Cosimo I) and indeed the founder of the grand duchy and the new Medicean dynasty.

Medici, Giuliano de', DUC (duke) DE NEMOURS (b. 1479—d. March 17, 1516, Florence), ruler of Florence from 1512 to 1513, after the Medici were restored to power.

The republicans of Florence, with the aid of the French, had driven out Giuliano's brother Piero di Lorenzo de' Medici in 1494. The republicans, however, fought among themselves; and the French alliance, to which the republic remained faithful, led to the political isolation of Florence when Pope Julius II organized his Holy League against France's king Louis XII. In 1512 the Pope demanded that Florence enter the league, dismiss its current leaders, and allow the exiled Medici to return. Florence was forced to submit by a Spanish army, which sacked Prato. Giuliano, who returned with his Medici kin in September 1512, used harsh measures to suppress a conspiracy but generally showed moderation during his short reign. In 1513, however, his older brother Cardinal Giovanni became pope as Leo X; and Giuliano, himself a cardinal and appointed gonfalonier of the Holy Roman Church, went to join him in Rome. In 1515 he received the French title of duc de Nemours.

Medici, Giulio de' (pope): *see* Clement VII.

Medici, Ippolito de' (b. 1509, Urbino, Duchy of Urbino—d. Aug. 10, 1535, Itri, Papal States), one of the pawns in the civil strife of Florence in the 1520s and 1530s.

Only seven years of age on the death of his natural father, Giuliano de' Medici, duc de Nemours, Ippolito was cared for by his uncle Pope Leo X, who, however, died just five years later. In 1524 Pope Clement VII sent him to Florence to be installed as a member of the government and destined, when of age, to rule Florence as his father had—meanwhile, living under the regency of Silvio, Cardinal Passerini. In 1527 a republican uprising drove out Passerini and the Medici; and Clement VII and the Holy Roman emperor Charles V, heretofore at odds, had to come to terms to restore order on the Italian peninsula.

By the end of 1529, Clement VII was scheming to supplant Ippolito with the more ruthless Alessandro de' Medici as ruler of Florence and, to this effect, entered into a secret treaty with Charles V at Bologna (December 1529). Charles had already sent an army against Florence, which capitulated after a seige of 11 months (August 1530), and Alessandro was installed as head of state for Florence in October 1530 (becoming duke of Florence in May 1532). Ippolito, meanwhile, had been compelled to become a cardinal and was kept out of the way on missions to Hungary and elsewhere.

Alessandro's tyrannical rule proved so unpopular that a group of Florentine exiles selected Ippolito as their ambassador to petition Charles V for Alessandro's removal. While waiting at Itri for a boat to Tunis, where Charles was on an expedition, Ippolito was poisoned, presumably at the instigation of Alessandro. His assassin, Giovanni Andrea, escaped to Florence and the protection of Alessandro's palace but later, on a visit to his hometown of Borgo San Sepolcro, was seized by the populace and stoned to death.

Medici, Lodovico de': *see* Medici, Giovanni de'.

Medici, Lorenzino de', Lorenzino also spelled LORENZACCIO (b. March 23, 1514, Florence—d. Feb. 26, 1548, Venice), assassin of Alessandro, grand duke of Tuscany. He was one of the more noted writers of the Medici family.

He was the son of one Pierfrancesco of a younger, cadet branch of the Medici family. He was a writer of considerable elegance, the author of several plays, one of which, the *Aridosio,* was held to be among the best of his age, and he was a worshipper of Greco-Roman antiquity. Notwithstanding these tastes, when in Rome he knocked off the heads of some of the finest statues of the age of Adrian, an act by which Pope Clement VII was so incensed that he threatened to have him hanged. Thereupon Lorenzino fled to Florence, where he became the friend of Alessandro and his partner in the most licentious excesses. They went together to brothels and violated private dwellings and convents. They often showed themselves in public mounted on the same horse.

On the evening of Jan. 5, 1537, Lorenzino led the Duke to his own lodging and left him there, promising shortly to return with the wife of Leonardo Ginori. Alessandro, worn out by the exertions of the day, fell asleep on the couch while awaiting Lorenzino's return. Before long the latter came, accompanied by one Scoronconcolo, who aided him in falling on the sleeper. Roused by their first thrusts, the Duke fought for his life and was only killed after a violent struggle. Disappointed at the Florentines' failure to rise against tyrannical government, Lorenzino fled first to Bologna, to await the result of the exiles' attack on Florence. When this was defeated, he went to Turkey, to France, and finally to Venice, where he was murdered in 1548.

Lorenzino wrote an *Apologia*, in which he defended himself with great skill and eloquence, saying that he had been urged to the deed solely by love of liberty. For this reason alone he had followed the example of Brutus and played the part of friend and courtier. The tone of this *Apologia* is straightforward, sometimes even eloquent and lofty, but his subsequent career completely gave the lie to his vaunted nobility of purpose. By Alessandro's death the elder branch of the Medici became extinct, and thus the appearance of the younger line, which would provide the grand dukes of Tuscany, was heralded by a bloody crime.

Medici, Lorenzo de', byname LORENZO THE MAGNIFICENT, Italian LORENZO IL MAGNIFICO (b. Jan 1, 1449, Florence—d. April 9, 1492, Careggi, near Florence), Florentine statesman,

Lorenzo de' Medici, terra-cotta bust by Andrea del Verrocchio, *c.* 1485; in the National Gallery of Art, Washington, D.C.

By courtesy of the National Gallery of Art, Washington, D.C., Samuel H. Kress Collection, 1943

ruler, and patron of arts and letters, the most brilliant of the Medici. He ruled Florence with his younger brother, Giuliano (1453–78), from 1469 to 1478 and, after the latter's assassination, was sole ruler from 1478 to 1492.

Upon the death of his father, Piero de' Medici, and his own accession to power Lorenzo immediately let it be known that he intended to follow his father's and grandfather's example and "use constitutional methods as much as possible." In saying this, he was, however, keeping up appearances. In 1471 the popular assemblies lost their financial powers. According to the historian Francesco Guicciardini's apt definition, Lorenzo's regime was "that of a benevolent tyrant in a constitutional republic." It was, moreover, a tyranny tempered by the festivals that Florentines always loved passionately: carnivals, balls, tournaments, weddings, and princely receptions.

The Pazzi Conspiracy in 1478 thus came as a rude shock to a carefree city. The Pazzi bank, in the course of a treacherous war in which the adversaries did not scruple to use the most devious methods, had taken the business affairs of the papacy away from the Medici. Sixtus IV, his nephew Riario, and Francesco Salviati, the archbishop of Pisa, supported the Pazzi and in the end formed a conspiracy with them. They decided to assassinate Lorenzo and Giuliano in the cathedral during Easter mass on April 26, while the Archbishop was to take over the *signoria* (the council of government). Giuliano was indeed killed in front of the altar, but Lorenzo succeeded in taking refuge in a sacristy. The Archbishop clumsily accosted the Medici gonfalonier, a harsh and suspicious man who immediately had him hanged from a window of the Palazzo Vecchio wearing his episcopal robes. The crowd stood by the Medici, seized the conspirators, and tore them limb from limb. Sixtus IV, forgetting the murder in the cathedral—in which two priests had taken part—refused to consider anything else than the hanging of a prelate and threatened Florence with interdiction unless it handed over Lorenzo to him. The city and its clergy rejected the proposal. The situation was all the more critical because Ferdinand I, king of Naples, was supporting the papacy. Florence's ruler could count on nothing more than very limited aid from Milan and the encouragement of the King of France. Lorenzo thereupon went, alone, to Naples. In his situation it required unusual audacity to present himself before one of the cruelest rulers of the century. But Lorenzo's boldness was crowned with success. Ferdinand, disconcerted, perhaps intimidated, yielded and concluded a peace; and Sixtus IV, now isolated, could only comply with it.

Lorenzo emerged from the conflict with greatly increased prestige. From then on he was considered the Wise, "the needle on the Italian scales." He did not take advantage of his position by imitating the Sforza and making himself a duke. He contented himself with creating a Council of Seventy that he hoped would be even more manageable than the old Cento (Hundred). This amazed Europe, for he had all the attributes of a true sovereign. His new villa, at Poggio a Caiano, had all the majesty of a royal residence.

Thus, step by step, the Medici were approaching the status that they continued to refuse. Lorenzo married an Orsini, of the high Roman nobility. His daughter Maddalena was married to a son of Pope Innocent VIII (born before his father's entry into religious orders), and his eldest son, Piero, married another Orsini. When his son Giovanni was 13, Lorenzo obtained a cardinal's hat for him from Innocent VIII. To be sure, Lorenzo remained a simple citizen, and yet he was called "the Magnificent." In Italy during this period, this was a title of commonplace obsequiousness used in addressing the great; but it was Lorenzo who raised it to its current high stature.

There was, however, one difference between Lorenzo and titled kings, who are able to live in pomp and ceremony even when their treasury is empty. Lorenzo could not do so, and the stream of florins that fed his munificence was becoming less abundant. This was partially his own fault for, with the Medici, the aptitude for business diminished as the thirst for power increased. In addition, economic conditions were deteriorating. New competitors were appearing in Europe, and the branches in London, Bruges, and Lyon became insolvent. But the recurrent accusation that the Medici bank was kept solvent at the expense of the public treasury is not borne out by the facts. The movement of funds between the Medici bank and the treasury of the *signoria* was the equivalent of that occurring between private and public banks in modern states. The family's patronage of artists, architects, and writers also imposed a considerable burden upon its resources. He himself contributed more than anyone to the flowering of Florentine genius during the second half of the 15th century. He continued collecting ancient texts, and in his villas in Careggi, Fiesole, and Poggio a Caiano he assembled what is called the Platonic Academy but was more like a circle of good friends: his teacher Marsilio Ficino, the Humanist Pico della Mirandola, and the man who was always closest to his heart, Politian (Angelo Poliziano), the poet, who had saved his life on the day of the Pazzi Conspiracy.

Lorenzo's reputation did not rest on lavish hospitality alone. He was also respected as a poet of great talent. His preference for the Tuscan dialect over Latin was remarkable for this time. Equally rare was his custom of treating artists with "the affectionate and warm-hearted familiarity that allows a protégé to stand erect at the side of his protector, as man to man." The artists under his protection included Giuliano da Sangallo, Botticelli, Verrocchio, and Verrocchio's pupil Leonardo da Vinci. Toward the end of his life, Lorenzo opened a school of sculpture in his garden of San Marco. There a 15-year-old pupil attracted his attention and was brought up in the palace like a son of the family; it was Michelangelo.

On the recommendation of Pico della Mirandola, Lorenzo permitted the Dominican monk Girolama Savonarola to preach at San Marco in 1490. He mounted the pulpit on August 1 and launched an unceasing deluge of denunciations of the Medici, the papacy, and the whole of Christianity. The Florentines, who had grown weary of festivities, listened to his appeals for asceticism and to his terrifying prophecies, among which was the imminent death of the "tyrant." But it was easy for him to be thus prophetic, for Lorenzo's health had been declining for three years, and the secret had not been well kept. From his deathbed he sent for Savonarola, who, according to a doubtful tradition, called upon him to "give Florence back her freedom" and, in the face of the dying man's silence, refused to grant him absolution. Lorenzo's obsequies were simple, as he had requested; but the presence of the entire population of Florence, sincerely moved by his premature death—he was 43—took on the character of a plebiscite. He was buried in S. Lorenzo, where the grandiose tomb that his son Giovanni, who later became Pope Leo X, had planned was never executed. His tombstone passes almost unnoticed at the side of the monuments erected by Michelangelo to Giuliano, one of his sons, and to his grandson Lorenzo, both very insignificant persons.

Lorenzo the Magnificent died at the very moment when a new historical era was beginning. Six months later Christopher Columbus was to reach the new world. And two years later the foolish Italian expedition of the French king Charles VIII was to plunge the peninsula into a half century of suffering.

To make the best use of the Britannica, consult the INDEX *first*

Medici, Lorenzo di Piero de', DUCA (duke) DI URBINO (b. Sept. 12, 1492, Florence—d. May 4, 1519, Florence), ruler of Florence from 1513 to 1519, to whom Niccolò Machiavelli addressed his treatise *The Prince,* counselling him to accomplish the unity of Italy by arming the whole nation and expelling its foreign invaders.

Lorenzo's father, Piero, son of Lorenzo the Magnificent, was driven out of Florence by the republicans, who were aided by the French, when Lorenzo was but two years of age. The papal-led Holy League, aided by the Spanish, however, finally defeated the rebels in 1512, and the Medici and Lorenzo the Magnificent's constitution were restored to Florence.

Lorenzo's uncle Cardinal Giuliano ruled in Florence for one year but then, in August 1513, turned the lordship over to Lorenzo. Lorenzo, being of more ambitious temper, was by no means content to remain at the head of the Florence government hampered by many restrictions imposed by republican institutions and subject to the incessant control of the pope. In his eagerness to aggrandize his kinsmen, the Pope nevertheless decided to give Lorenzo the Duchy of Urbino and formally invested him in its rights, after expelling on false pretenses its legitimate lord, Francesco Maria della Rovere. Francesco Maria, however, soon returned to Urbino, where he was welcomed by his subjects, and Lorenzo regained possession only by a protracted war, in which he was wounded. In 1519 he died, worn out by disease and excess. By his marriage with Madeleine de la Tour d'Auvergne, he had one daughter, Caterina de' Medici (known in France as Catherine de Médicis), who was married in 1533 to Henry, duke d'Orléans, afterward king of France, as Henry II.

Medici, Maria de' (queen of France): *see* Marie de Médicis.

Medici, Piero di Cosimo de', byname PIERO THE GOUTY, Italian PIERO IL GOTTOSO (b. 1416—d. Dec. 2, 1469), ruler of Florence for five years (1464–69), whose successes in war helped preserve the enormous prestige bequeathed by his father, Cosimo the Elder.

Afflicted by gout (a hereditary ailment of the Medici), Piero was so badly crippled that he was often able to use only his tongue. In 1466 he detected a plot to overthrow his rule, and, showing more courage than he was supposed to possess, he had himself borne on a litter to Florence, where he defeated his enemies. On Venice's launching a new war against Florence, he made an alliance with Milan and Naples, defeated the condottiere Bartolomeo Colleoni at Imola, and, under the peace of 1468, acquired Sarzana and Sarzanello.

Piero's wife, Lucrezia Tornabuoni, was highly intelligent; and his sons, Lorenzo (the Magnificent) and Giuliano (1453–78), received an exceptional literary and artistic education. Piero himself acted as patron of the Platonic Academy and provided work for such great artists as Donatello, Andrea del Verrocchio, and Sandro Botticelli.

Medici, Piero di Lorenzo de', byname PIERO THE UNFORTUNATE, or THE FATUOUS, Italian PIERO IL SFORTUNATO, or IL FATUO (b. 1472—d. Dec. 28, 1503, Garigliano River, Italy), son of Lorenzo the Magnificent who ruled in Florence for only two years (1492–94) before being expelled.

Upon the death of his father, Piero came to power at age 21 without difficulty. He was endowed with beautiful features and proved to be a good soldier, but he was painfully lacking in political sense, and he owes his surname of "the Unfortunate" mainly to his own errors of judgment. Threatened domestically by the reformer Girolamo Savonarola's denunciations and by the intrigues of the younger branch of the Medici family and threatened abroad by the imminence of a French invasion of Italy, he made the foolish and dangerous decision to abandon the old French alliance in favour of one with Naples. Suddenly realizing the danger when the "barbarians" from beyond the Alps poured into Tuscany under Charles VIII, Piero thought he could save the day by imitating his father and hastened to meet the invader. The disastrous agreement—the only one possible under the circumstances—that he obtained from Charles aroused a wave of indignation in Florence. A revolt broke out, and Piero was forced to flee the city while the populace sacked the Medici Palace.

Piero henceforth led the restless life of an exile. He never again saw Florence. His various plots (in 1496, 1497, and 1498) to reinstate himself in Florence were all unsuccessful. At last he went to the south of Italy with the French forces of Louis XII, was drowned at the passage of the Garigliano River in 1503, and was buried in the cloister of Monte Cassino.

Medici, Villa (1574–80), important example of Mannerist architecture designed by Annibale Lippi and built in Rome for Cardinal Ricci di Montepulciano. It was later purchased by Cardinal A. de Medici. In 1801 Napoleon bought the building, and in 1803 the Villa Medici became the headquarters of the French Academy in Rome. It also houses the recipients of the Prix de Rome.

Medici Chapel, Italian CAPPELLA MEDICEA, chapel housing monuments to members of the Medici family, in the New Sacristy of the Church of San Lorenzo in Florence. The funereal monuments were commissioned in 1520 by Pope Clement VII (formerly Cardinal Giulio de' Medici), executed largely by Michelangelo from 1520 to 1534, and completed by Michelangelo's pupils after his departure.

The two monumental groups (for the tombs of Lorenzo, duke di Urbino, and Giuliano, duke de Nemours) are each composed of a seated armed figure in a niche, with an allegorical figure reclining on either side of the sarcophagus below. The seated figures, representing the two dukes, are not treated as portraits but as types. Lorenzo, whose face is shaded by a helmet, personifies the reflective man; Giuliano, who is holding the baton of an army commander, portrays the active man. At his feet recline the figures of "Night" and "Day." "Night," a giantess, is twisting in uneasy slumber; "Day," a herculean figure, looks wrathfully over his shoulder. Just as imposing, but far less violent, are the two companion figures reclining between sleep and waking on the sarcophagus of Lorenzo. The male figure is known as "Dusk," the female figure as "Dawn."

Lorenzo the Magnificent and his brother Giuliano the Elder were buried at the entrance wall, and over them was set up a marble group consisting of a "Madonna and Child" and the Medici patron saints Cosmas and Damian. The "Madonna" is a work of imposing majesty, completely by Michelangelo's own hand; the saints are the work of pupils after models by the master.

Medici porcelain, first European soft-paste porcelain, made in Florence between about 1575 and 1587 in workshops under the patronage of Francis I (Francesco de' Medici). It is thought that the body of Medici porcelain

Medici soft-paste porcelain bottle, Florence, *c.* 1580; in the Victoria and Albert Museum, London

By courtesy of the Victoria and Albert Museum, London

consists of glass, powdered rock crystal, and sand, as well as clay from Vicenza and white earth from Faenza. The ware, heavily potted, was covered with a rather cloudy, bubble-pitted glaze. Production was probably limited; most of the wares were made as gifts for European princes. The rare surviving examples (about 60) include utilitarian objects such as flasks, jugs, bowls, and plates, in addition to purely decorative ones such as plaques. Medici porcelain reflects the influence of Persian pottery, Chinese porcelain, and indigenous maiolica. The decoration is generally blue and white, but occasionally manganese is added. The mark of Medici porcelain, which is blue, represents the dome of the cathedral of Florence, with the letter *F* below.

medicinal leech, any of certain leech species, particularly *Hirudo medicinalis,* once used in the treatment of human diseases. *See* leech.

medicinal poisoning, also called DRUG POISONING, harmful effects on health of certain therapeutic drugs, resulting either from overdose or from the sensitivity of specific body tissues to regular doses (side effects).

Until about the 1920s, there were few effective medications at the disposal of the physician. By mid-century, however, a vast array of synthetic chemical agents had come into use as medicines, and many of these were undeniably potent, therapeutically beneficial, and, in many cases, unquestionably dangerous.

Commonly, the margin between dose and overdose is fairly narrow; what was intended as a curative dose may in fact prove toxic in certain people or over time.

In the United States and some other countries, a series of safeguards have been adopted to avoid medicinal poisoning. First, a new drug is subjected to pharmacological and toxicity testing in large numbers of animals, and its actions and limitations are provisionally assessed. Next, it is given in successive doses to volunteers, whose responses are carefully checked. Then it undergoes clinical trials in patients. Only after this stage is it released for general clinical use. Monitoring for further reactions continues, and from these data a drug's uses, contraindications, and limitations can be outlined. All of this work devolves primarily upon the pharmaceutical companies responsible for producing new drugs. Their efforts, nonetheless, are supervised and checked by official bodies, such as the Food and Drug Administration in the United States.

The sale and supply of drugs unsafe for self-medication are limited to a doctor's order or prescription. Each country has its own laws regulating this arrangement. In addition, educational campaigns are promoted by pharmaceutical companies, professional associations, and medical journals in order to induce doctors to prescribe judiciously and discriminatingly and, further, to convince the public that the misuse of medicines can have tragic consequences. Despite all of this activity, however, probably more poisoning is due to medicines than to any other cause.

medicine: *see under* descriptive word (*e.g.,* preventive medicine), except as below.

medicine, the science concerned with the maintenance of health and the prevention, alleviation, or cure of disease.

The subject of medicine is treated in a number of articles in the MACROPAEDIA, the principal of which is Medicine. For a treatment of general considerations and current techniques in the diagnosis and treatment of disease, *see* Diagnosis and Therapeutics. For fields of medicine linked to environmental and occupational conditions, *see* Occupational Diseases and Disorders; Radiation. For articles dealing with the major systems of the human body, as well as the broad fields of pathology associated with them, *see* Blood; Circulation and Circulatory Systems; Digestion and Digestive Systems; Endocrine Systems; Excretion and Excretory Systems; Integumentary Systems; Metabolism; Muscles and Muscle Systems; Nerves and Nervous Systems; Reproduction and Reproductive Systems; Respiration and Respiratory Systems; Sensory Reception; Supportive and Connective Tissues.

Specific ailments are dealt with in such articles as Cancer; Childhood Diseases and Disorders; Infectious Diseases; Poisons and Poisoning. For the use of drugs in the treatment of disease and the general principles of their medicinal properties, as well as a description of various groups of drugs, *see* Drugs and Drug Action. For articles dealing in whole or in part with microorganisms that cause disease, *see* Bacteria and Other Monerans; Viruses. For a treatment of the role of diet and health, *see* Nutrition. For medical aspects related specifically to women and childbirth, *see* Reproduction and Reproductive Systems. For a summation of the principles used in the identification of disease and major factors influencing it, *see* Disease.

For articles on the maintenance of health, *see* Exercise and Physical Conditioning; Immunity. For articles on the interconnection of physiological and psychological factors, *see* Behaviour, Development of Human; Learning and Cognition, Human; Perception, Human; Sex and Sexuality; Sleep and Dreams. For articles discussing the maladjustment of these two sets of factors, *see* Alcohol and Drug Consumption; Mental Disorders and Their Treatment. For problems of aging and development, *see* Growth and Development, Biological.

For articles dealing with fundamental aspects of living organisms, *see* Life; Death; Biochemical Components of Organisms. For some of the underlying principles of medicine, *see* Cells: Their Structures and Functions; Genetics and Heredity, Principles of. Much of the science of medicine is inseparable from related fields such as microbiology, biochemistry, and biophysics. For a discussion of related fields, *see* Biological Sciences; Science, History of.

For a description of the place of medicine in the circle of learning and for a list of both MACROPAEDIA and MICROPAEDIA articles on the subject, *see* PROPAEDIA: Part Four, Division II.

For international statistical data on health, *see* BRITANNICA BOOK OF THE YEAR.

Medicine Bow Mountains, northwestern section of the Front Range, in the central Rocky Mountains, U.S. Comprising a generally dissected upland with an average height of 10,000 feet (3,050 m), the mountains run southeastward for about 100 miles (160 km) from Medicine Bow, Wyo., to near Cameron Pass (10,285 feet [3,135 m]), Colorado, just northwest of Rocky Mountain National Park. The highest summit, Medicine Bow Peak (12,014 feet [3,662 m]), is on a 5-mile-long, 12,000-foot-high quartzite ridge (known locally as the Snowy Range) west of Centennial, Wyo. Medicine Bow and Roosevelt national forests embrace parts of the mountain region, which was the setting for Owen Wister's popular novel, *The Virginian.* The name is thought to be derived from the gathering of Indians in the area for the purpose of collecting wood for bows and holding ceremonial, or "medicine," dances.

Medicine Hat, city, southeastern Alberta, Canada. It lies at the foot of the Cypress Hills, along the South Saskatchewan River, 164 miles (264 km) southeast of Calgary. It originated as a settlement around a North West Mounted Police post (1882) and a railroad construction camp (1883). The site, according to one legend, marks the spot in the river where a cowardly Cree medicine man lost his hat (*saamis*) after deserting his tribe and fleeing from Blackfoot warriors. The community's economic growth can be attributed mainly to its location in the centre of one of the world's largest natural-gas fields. This and the city's position on the Trans-Canada Highway and the Canadian Pacific Railway have attracted diversified industries, including glassblowing and pottery manufactures; the local economy, however, still remains heavily dependent upon agriculture, particularly ranching and vegetable growing. Medicine Hat has a notable historical museum, holds an annual (July) stampede and exhibition, and is the gateway to Cypress Hills Provincial Park. Medicine Hat College (1965) is affiliated with the University of Calgary. Inc. town, 1898; city, 1906. Pop. (1991) 43,625.

Medicine Lodge, city, seat of Barber county, southern Kansas, U.S. It lies 70 miles (113 km) west-southwest of Wichita, along the Medicine Lodge River. The site was regarded as sacred by the Plains Indians, who peacefully shared a "lodge" on the banks of the river, which they believed had curative powers. There in 1867 the Five Tribes met with U.S. commissioners to negotiate a treaty that opened the area to white settlement and railroads and fixed the southern boundary of Kansas. The town was laid out in 1873 and was incorporated as a city in 1879. Carry Nation (1846–1911), the hatchet-wielding temperance crusader, lived in Medicine Lodge, where she attacked her first saloon with an umbrella; her home is preserved as a shrine and museum. The city is now a shipping point for wheat and cattle and is the site of a large gypsum plant based on the nearby Gypsum Hills, a scenic area of canyons, towering mesas, and buttes. A pageant reenacting the peace treaty is held every three years. Pop. (1990) 2,453.

medicine man, member of a nonliterate society who is knowledgeable about the magic potencies of various substances (medicines) and skilled in the rituals in which they are administered, particularly for healing. The term has been used most widely in the context of indigenous American cultures.

Some medicine men (women may perform this function in some societies) undergo rigorous initiation to gain supernormal powers, while others are essentially learned experts. The medicine man commonly carries a kit of objects—such as feathers of valued birds, suggestively shaped or marked stones, or hallucinogenic plants—that have magical associations; in some cases, the stones are considered to have been embedded in the body of the medicine man at his initiation. Correspondingly, the work of healing often involves the extraction, by sucking, pulling, or other means, of offending substances from the patient's body.

Because nonliterate societies often attribute illness and other distressing situations to the activities of witches or sorcerers, the term witch doctor, denoting a person who diagnoses and treats such conditions, was coined by 18th-century Western observers; in the late 20th century the term was generally considered pejorative. *See also* shaman.

medicine society, in popular literature, any of various complex healing societies and rituals of many American Indian tribes. More correctly, the term is used as an alternative name for the Grand Medicine Society, or Midewiwin, of the Ojibwa Indians of North America.

According to the origin myth, the rituals were first performed by various gods to comfort Minabozho, a culture hero and intercessor between the Great Spirit and man, on the death of his brother. Minabozho, having pity on the suffering of man, transmitted the ritual to the otter and, through him, to man.

The Grand Medicine Society was an esoteric group consisting at times of more than 1,000 members, including the tribal shamans, prophets, and seers, as well as anyone else who could afford the initiation fee. The Society was thus both a centre of spiritual knowledge and a source of social prestige.

Possessing a complex series of four degrees of initiation held within an especially constructed medicine lodge, the Society's central act of initiation was the ritual death and rebirth of the initiate. The powers of an initiate include not only those of healing and causing death but also those of obtaining food for the tribe and victory in battle.

Médicis FAMILY: *see* Medici family.

Médicis, Catherine de (queen of France): *see* Catherine de Médicis.

Médicis, Marie de (queen of France): *see* Marie de Médicis.

Medill, Joseph (b. April 6, 1823, near Saint John, N.B., Can.—d. March 16, 1899, San Antonio, Texas, U.S.), Canadian-born American editor and publisher who from 1855 built the *Chicago Tribune* into a powerful newspaper. He was the grandfather of three newspaper publishers: Robert R. McCormick of the *Chicago Tribune,* Joseph M. Patterson of the *New York Daily News,* and Eleanor M. Patterson of the *Washington* (D.C.) *Times-Herald.*

After publishing newspapers in Ohio (Coshocton, 1849–51, and Cleveland, 1851–55), Medill joined a partnership that acquired the *Chicago Tribune* (founded 1847), and from the first he largely determined the paper's editorial policy. He wrote antislavery editorials and worked for Abraham Lincoln's nomination by the Republican Party (which Medill had helped to found in 1854 and may have named) and for his election as president in 1860. He supported Lincoln's administration throughout the American Civil War (1861–65) and favoured the Radical Republicans' program for reconstruction of the defeated South.

Medill, detail of a lithograph by J.O. Ottomann Company, 1893

By courtesy of the Library of Congress, Washington, D.C.

In November 1871, a month after the great Chicago fire, Medill was elected mayor of the city. Taking emergency powers, he reorganized the municipal government, especially its finances. He also was instrumental in establishing the Chicago Public Library (1872–74). In 1874, after resigning as mayor, he purchased a controlling interest in the *Chicago Tribune* and became editor in chief, advocating a free hand for business and fighting liberal reformers and labour unions. Strongly nationalistic in foreign policy, the *Chicago Tribune* was in the forefront of interventionist newspapers during the Cuban crisis preceding the Spanish-American War of 1898. Medill helped to obtain for Chicago the World's Columbian Exposition of 1893. His family endowed the Medill School of Journalism at Northwestern University, Evanston, Ill.

Medina, district (borough), county of Isle of Wight, England, with an area of 45 square miles (117 square km). It comprises the northeastern portion of the island and includes the towns of Newport, Cowes, and Ryde. Newport is the administrative centre for the island and is important for its manufacturing and service industries. Cowes has long been associated with shipbuilding and is famous for its yachting competitions. Ryde is the island's principal tourist town. With less than one-third of the area of the island county, Medina includes more than half of its total population. The rest of the island constitutes the South Wight district.

Medina, Arabic AL-MADĪNAH, formally AL-MADĪNAH AL-MUNAWWARAH ("The Luminous City"), or MADĪNAT RASŪL ALLĀH ("City of the Messenger of God [*i.e.,* Muḥammad]"), ancient YATHRIB, one of the two most sacred cities of Islām, situated in the Hejaz region of western Saudi Arabia about 100 miles (160 km) inland from the Red Sea and some 280 miles (450 km) from Mecca by road. Pop. (1991 est.) 400,000.

A brief treatment of Medina follows. For full treatment, *see* MACROPAEDIA: Mecca and Medina.

The city developed from an oasis, probably settled by Jews about AD 135. In 622 the Prophet Muḥammad arrived at Medina from Mecca. This flight, known as the Hegira, marks the beginning of the Muslim calendar. Soon afterward Muḥammad drove out the Jews who had controlled the oasis. Thereafter known as Medina, the city prospered as the administrative capital of the steadily expanding Islāmic state, a position it maintained until 661, when it was superseded in that role by Damascus. After the sack of the city in 683 by the caliphs for its fractiousness, the native emirs enjoyed a fluctuating measure of independence, interrupted by the aggressions of the sharifs of Mecca or by periods under the intermittent Egyptian protectorate.

The Ottomans, following their conquest of Egypt, held Medina after 1517 with a firmer hand, but their rule weakened and was almost nominal long before the Wahhābīs, an Islāmic revivalist sect, first took the city in 1804. An Ottoman-Egyptian force retook it in 1812, and the Ottomans remained in effective control until the revival of the Wahhābī movement

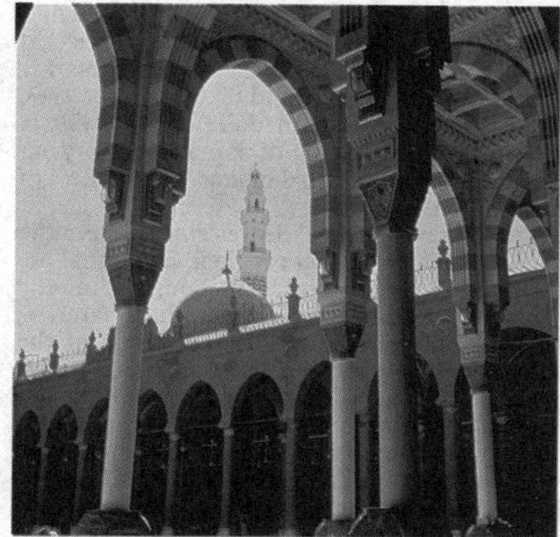
Dome and interior courtyard of the Prophet's Mosque in Medina, Saudi Arabia
By courtesy of Middle East Airlines

under Ibn Saʿūd after 1912. Between 1904 and 1908 the Ottomans built the Hejaz railroad to Medina from Damascus in an attempt to strengthen the empire and ensure Ottoman control over the hajj, the obligatory Muslim pilgrimage to the nearby holy city of Mecca. Ottoman rule ceased during World War I, when the sharif Ḥusayn ibn ʿAlī, ruler of Mecca, revolted and, with the assistance of the British officer T.E. Lawrence (Lawrence of Arabia), put the railroad out of commission. Ḥusayn later came into conflict with Ibn Saʿūd, and in 1925 Medina fell to the Saʿūdī dynasty.

Medina is second only to Mecca as the holiest place of Muslim pilgrimage; the tomb of Muḥammad in the Prophet's Mosque is among the most sacred shrines in the Islāmic world. The first two orthodox caliphs, Abū Bakr and ʿUmar, are also believed to be buried there. The mosque has been renovated extensively over the centuries, most recently in the 1980s and '90s. Other religious features of the oasis include the mosque of Qubāʾ, the first in Islāmic history, from which the Prophet was vouchsafed a view of Mecca; the Mosque of the Two Qiblahs at ar-Rimāḥ, commemorating the change of the prayer direction from Jerusalem to Mecca; the tomb of Ḥamzah, uncle of the Prophet, and of his companions who fell in the Battle of Uḥud (625), in which the Prophet was wounded; and the cave in the flank of Uḥud, in which the Prophet took refuge on that occasion. Other mosques commemorate where he donned his armour for that battle; where he rested on the way thither; where he unfurled his standard for the Battle of the Ditch; and the ditch itself, dug around Medina by Muḥammad. In addition, the city is also the site of the Islāmic University, established in 1961.

To supplement the income derived from accommodating pilgrims, Medina has an economy based on the cultivation of fruits, vegetables, and cereals and on pottery making. The city is famous for its date palms, the fruits of which are processed and packaged for export at a plant built in 1953. Roads link Medina with Jiddah, Mecca, and Yanbuʿ al-Baḥr (Medina's port on the Red Sea); another road extends north through the Hejaz and connects Medina to Jordan. Al-Jiladain airport nearby provides transportation to Saudi Arabian centres and has links to Jordan, Lebanon, and Syria.

Medina, Bartolomé de (b. 1528, Medina de Ríoseco, Spain—d. 1580, Salamanca), Spanish Dominican theologian who developed the patio process for extracting silver from ore.

Medina developed the patio process, an intricate amalgamation process utilizing mercury, while mining in Pachuca, Mex., in 1557. The process proved especially useful in America, where fuel and waterpower were scarce. It was introduced into Hungary in 1786 and thence to other parts of Europe. The patio process was effective even with low-grade ores and was used widely up to the 20th century.

From 1576 to 1580 Medina taught theology at the University of Salamanca, where he was a zealous exponent of Thomism and where he formulated the casuistical theory of probabilism, a means of settling moral questions.

Medina, Constitution of, document based upon two agreements concluded between the clans of Medina and the Prophet Muḥammad soon after the Hegira, or emigration to Medina in AD 622. The agreements established the muhajirun, *i.e.,* the early Muslims who followed Muḥammad, on a par with the eight clans of Medina (called the ansar, or "helpers"); collectively, the nine tribes formed the first Muslim community (*ummah*). The agreements also regulated the relations of the Muslims with the Jews of Medina.

Medina, River, river, Isle of Wight, England. The Medina drains much of the island, rising on the high sandstone ground near the south coast and flowing 12 miles (19 km) north through a gap in the chalk ridge that forms the backbone of the island. Past Newport at the head of its estuary it flows into The Solent on the English Channel. There Cowes and East Cowes lie on either side of its mouth.

Medina del Campo, Treaty of (1489), treaty between Spain and England, which, although never fully accepted by either side, established the dominating themes in Anglo-Spanish relations in the late 15th and early 16th centuries. It was signed at Medina del Campo, in northern Spain, on March 27 and ratified by Ferdinand of Aragon and Isabella of Castile the following day. It settled the details of a proposed marriage between the infanta Catherine, the youngest daughter of Ferdinand and Isabella, and Arthur (d. 1502), the eldest son of the English king Henry VII. It also effected a mutual reduction of tariffs between the two countries and attempted to arrive at a common policy in opposition to France. The terms of the anti-French alliance were unacceptable to Henry VII, who ratified it (Sept. 23, 1490) with amendments that were in turn rejected by Spain. The marriage was renegotiated in 1496 on terms similar to those proposed in 1489.

Medina-Sidonia, Alonso Pérez de Guzmán, duke (duque) **de** (b. Sept. 10, 1550—d. 1619, Sanlúcar, Spain), commander in chief of the Spanish Armada of 1588.

A member of the noble and illustrious house of Guzmán, Medina-Sidonia became the seventh bearer of the ducal title in 1555 on the death of his father; he became master of one of the greatest fortunes in Europe on the death of his grandfather, Juan Alonso de Guzmán, in 1559. Philip II of Spain regarded him with confidence and appointed him captain general of the coast of Andalusia in January 1588.

In February 1588 the Marquess de Santa Cruz (Alvaro de Bazán) died; and Medina-Sidonia was nominated in his place to command the Armada against England. He protested forcefully but in vain at being chosen for this post; and, in the event, his inexperience and lack of seamanship were among the causes of the failure of the enterprise. Even so, royal favour was not withdrawn from him: he was appointed captain general of the Ocean sea in 1595 and remained in practical control of the Spanish navy under Philip III, notwithstanding further disasters (the sacking of Cádiz by the English in 1596 and the destruction of a squadron by the Dutch off Gibraltar in 1606).

Medina worm: *see* guinea worm.

Medinipur (India): *see* Midnapore.

meditation, private devotion or mental exercise consisting in any of innumerable techniques of concentration, contemplation, and abstraction, regarded as conducive to heightened spiritual awareness or somatic calm.

The practice of meditation has occurred worldwide since ancient times in a variety of contexts. It may serve purely quietistic aims, as in the case of certain reclusive mystics; it may be viewed as spiritually or physically restorative and enriching to daily life, as in the case of numerous religious orders and the majority of secular practitioners; or it may serve as special, potent preparation for a particular, usually physically or otherwise strenuous activity, as in the case of the warrior before battle or the musician before performance. In recent medical and psychological studies, meditational techniques have proved effective in skilled practitioners in controlling pulse and respiratory rates and effective to varying degrees in the symptomatic control of migraine headache, hypertension, and hemophilia, among other conditions.

Meditation in some form has been systematized in most great religions of the world. The Hindu philosophical school of Yoga prescribes a highly elaborated process for the purification of body, mind, and soul. One aspect of Yoga practice, dhyana (Sanskrit: "concentrated meditation"), became the focus of a school of its own among the Buddhists, in China as Ch'an and, subsequently, in Japan as Zen. In numerous religions, spiritual purification may be sought through the verbal or mental repetition of a prescribed efficacious syllable, word, or text (*e.g.,* the Hindu and Buddhist mantra; Islāmic dhikr; Christian Jesus prayer). The focusing of attention upon a visual image (*e.g.,* a flower, a distant mountain) is a common technique in informal contemplative practice and has been formalized in several traditions. Tantric Buddhists of Tibet, for example, regard the mandala (Sanskrit: "circle") diagram as a collection point of universal forces, accessible to man by meditation. Tactile and mechanical devices, such as the rosary and the prayer wheel, and music play a highly ritualized role in many contemplative traditions.

In the West in the 20th century, disenchantment with materialistic values led to an awakening of interest in Eastern philosophies and practices, which were seen as holistic and humane. The teaching and practice of numerous techniques of meditation, most based on esoteric Eastern tradition, became a widespread phenomenon. *See also* prayer.

Mediterranean anemia: *see* thalassemia.

Mediterranean fever: *see* brucellosis.

Mediterranean flour moth: *see* flour moth.

Mediterranean fruit fly, also called MED FLY, particularly destructive and costly insect pest, a species of fruit fly (*q.v.*).

Mediterranean Sea, an intercontinental sea situated between Europe to the north, Africa to the south, and Asia to the east. It covers an area, including the Sea of Marmara but excluding the Black Sea, of about 970,000 square miles (2,512,000 square km).

A brief treatment of the Mediterranean Sea follows. For full treatment, *see* MACROPAEDIA: Atlantic Ocean.

To the west the Mediterranean Sea is connected to the Atlantic Ocean by the Strait of Gibraltar, which at its narrowest point is only 8 miles (13 km) wide and has a relatively shallow channel. To the northeast the Dardanelles, the Sea of Marmara, and the strait of the Bosporus link the Mediterranean Sea to the Black Sea. The Suez Canal connects it with the Red Sea to the southeast. The Mediterranean's greatest recorded depth is in the Ionian Basin south of Greece at 16,800 feet (5,121 m) below sea level.

A submarine ridge between the island of Sicily and the African coast divides the Mediterranean Sea into eastern and western parts. The western Mediterranean has three submarine basins separated from each other by submerged ridges, including from west to east, the Alborán, the Algerian, and the Tyrrhenian basins. The Ionian Basin (northwest of which is the Adriatic Sea) and the Levantine Basin (northwest of which is the Aegean Sea) compose the eastern part of the Mediterranean Sea. Majorca, Corsica, Sardinia, Sicily, Crete, Cyprus, and Rhodes are the largest islands in the Mediterranean.

The Mediterranean once was thought to be a remnant of the Tethys Sea, which formerly girdled the Eastern Hemisphere; it is now known to be a structurally younger basin. The sea's continental shelves are relatively narrow. The widest shelf, off the Gulf of Gabes (Qābis) on the eastern coast of Tunisia, extends 170 miles (275 km); the bed of the Adriatic Sea is also mostly continental shelf. The floor of the Mediterranean consists of sediments made up of lime, clay, and sand, under which is blue mud. The sea's coasts are generally steep, rocky, and deeply indented. The Rhône, Po, and Nile rivers have formed the only large deltas in the Mediterranean Sea. The continuous inflow of surface water from the Atlantic Ocean is the sea's major source of replenishment. The most constant component of circulation in the Mediterranean Sea is the current formed by this inflow from the Strait of Gibraltar along the north coast of Africa. The whole Mediterranean basin is tectonically active, and earthquakes are common.

The climate is characterized by mild, wet winters and hot, dry summers. The air flow into the Mediterranean is through gaps in the mountain ranges, except over its southern shores east of Tunisia. Much of North Africa rarely receives more than 10 inches (250 mm) of rainfall annually, whereas on the rugged Dalmatian coast of Croatia, some areas receive 100 inches (2,500 mm).

The low concentration of phosphates and nitrates, necessary for marine pastures, limits the quantity of marine life in the Mediterranean. Small-scale fishing operations predominate, with the most important species including hake, flounder, sole, turbot, sardine, anchovy, bluefin tuna, bonito, and mackerel; shellfish, corals, sponges, and seaweed are also harvested. Overexploitation of the sea's marine resources remains a serious problem.

Petroleum deposits have been found off Spain, Sicily, Libya, and Tunisia, and natural gas has been discovered in the Adriatic Sea. Specialty crops of the region include olives, citrus fruits, grapes, and cork. Tourism is a major source of income for many of the countries bordering the Mediterranean.

Mediterranean vegetation, any scrubby, dense vegetation composed of broad-leaved evergreen shrubs, bushes, and small trees usually less than 2.5 m (about 8 feet) tall and growing in regions lying between 30° and 40° north and south latitudes. These regions have a climate similar to that of the Mediterranean area, which is characterized by hot, dry summers and mild, wet winters. Around the Mediterranean Sea this vegetation is called macchie, maquis, or garigue; it is known as chaparral in southwestern North America, as Cape flora in southern Africa, and as mallee in southwestern Australia. *See also* chaparral; maquis; mallee.

medium, in occultism, a person reputedly able to make contact with the world of spirits, especially while in a state of trance. A spiritualist medium is the central figure during a séance (*q.v.*) and sometimes requires the assistance of an invisible go-between, or control. During a séance, disembodied voices are said to speak, either directly or through the medium. Materialization of a disembodied spirit or of a specific part of a human body can allegedly take shape from a mysterious, viscous substance called ectoplasm that exudes from the medium's body and subsequently disappears by returning to its original source. At times the medium, or a material object, appears to float in the air (levitation).

Medjerda, Oued (river, Tunisia): *see* Majardah, Wadi.

medlar (species *Mespilus germanica*), tree of the rose family (Rosaceae), closely allied to the genus *Pyrus,* in which it is sometimes included. A native of Europe from The Netherlands southward and of western Asia, it occurs in middle and southern England as a small, much-branched, deciduous, spinous tree. The flowers are white or pink-tinged, with five petals. The fruit is globular but depressed above, with leafy, persistent sepals, and contains stones of a hemispheric shape. It is not fit to eat until it begins to decay; then it takes on an agreeable acid and somewhat astringent flavour. Several varieties are cultivated.

Médoc, wine-producing district, southwestern France, on the left bank of the Gironde River estuary, northwest of Bordeaux. An undulating plain extending for about 50 miles (80 km) to Grave Point, the Médoc is renowned for its *crus* (vineyards). The grapes are grown especially along a strip of gravelly soil between the estuary and Landes Forest, which separates the estuary from the Bay of Biscay.

The land of the Médoc was early used for rye production, and, on land surrounding priories and feudal seigniories, for growing grapes. Dutch engineers drained the northern marshy lowlands in the early part of the 17th century to make the land more suitable for agriculture. In the second half of that century, the seigniories became the great estates of the gentry. As the practice of viticulture developed, the connection between the region's gravelly soil and the wine it produced became clear. The Médoc was perfectly suited to wine production, and virtually all the vineyards of Médoc were planted by 1760.

Most of these were wiped out a century later by grape phylloxera (a small greenish-yellow insect), mildew, and fungus. Though vintners struggled to recover, restructuring their vineyards and importing American graft-stocks, the region only regained and surpassed its former reputation in the mid-20th century.

The Médoc produces many of the best-known Bordeaux red wines, notably Cabernet Sauvignon and Cabernet Franc. Some Merlot and Petit Verdot grapes are also grown.

medulla oblongata, also called MEDULLA, the lowest part of the brain and the lowest portion of the brain stem. The medulla oblongata is connected by the pons to the midbrain and is continuous posteriorly with the spinal cord, with which it merges at the opening (foramen magnum) at the base of the skull.

For a depiction of the medulla oblongata in human anatomy, shown in relation to the other parts of the body, *see* the colour Trans-Vision in the PROPAEDIA: Part Four, Section 421.

Like the cerebrum and cerebellum, the medulla oblongata consists of both myelinated (white matter) and unmyelinated (gray matter) nerve fibres. In the medulla, however, the normal anatomic relationship of the two is reversed, with the white matter on the outside and the gray matter lying on the inside, around the fourth ventricle (a fluid-filled cavity formed by the expansion of the central canal of the spinal cord upon entering the brain).

A complex network of medullary nerve cells and processes from elsewhere in the central nervous system enables the medulla to carry on complex integrative functions. The medulla also contains several functional centres that control autonomic nervous activity, regulating respiration, heart rate, and digestive processes. Other activities of the medulla include control of movement, relaying of somatic sensory information from internal organs, and control of arousal and sleep.

The last seven cranial nerves emerge from the medulla, which influences their functional activities. Injuries or disease affecting the middle portion of the medulla may produce paralysis of the opposite side of the body, loss of the senses of touch and position, or partial paralysis of the tongue. Injuries or disease of the lateral medulla may cause loss of pain and temperature sensations, loss of the gag reflex, difficulty in swallowing, vertigo, vomiting, or loss of coordination.

Medusa, in Greek mythology, the most famous of the monster figures known as Gorgons. She was usually represented as a winged female creature having a head of hair consisting of snakes. Unlike the other Gorgons, she was sometimes represented as very beautiful. Medusa was the only Gorgon who was mortal; hence her slayer, Perseus, was able to kill her by cutting off her head. From the blood that spurted from her neck sprang Chrysaor and Pegasus, her two sons by Poseidon. The severed head, which had the power of turning into stone all who looked upon it, was given to Athena, who placed it in her shield; according to another account, Perseus buried it in the marketplace of Argos.

Heracles (Hercules) is said to have obtained a lock of Medusa's hair (which possessed the same powers as the head) from Athena and given it to Sterope, the daughter of Cepheus, as a protection for the town of Tegea against attack; when exposed to view, the lock was supposed to bring on a storm, which put the enemy to flight. *See also* Gorgon; Perseus.

medusa, in zoology, one of two principal body types occurring in members of the invertebrate animal phylum Cnidaria. It is the typical form of the jellyfish. The medusoid body is bell- or umbrella-shaped. Hanging downward from the centre is a stalklike structure, the manubrium, bearing the mouth at its tip. The mouth opens into the main body cavity, or enteron, which connects with radial canals extending to the outer rim of the bell. The medusa is a free-swimming form; it moves by rhythmic muscular contractions of the bell, providing a slow propulsive action against the water. The other principal body type of the adult cnidarian is the polyp, a stalked, sessile (attached) form. *Compare* polyp.

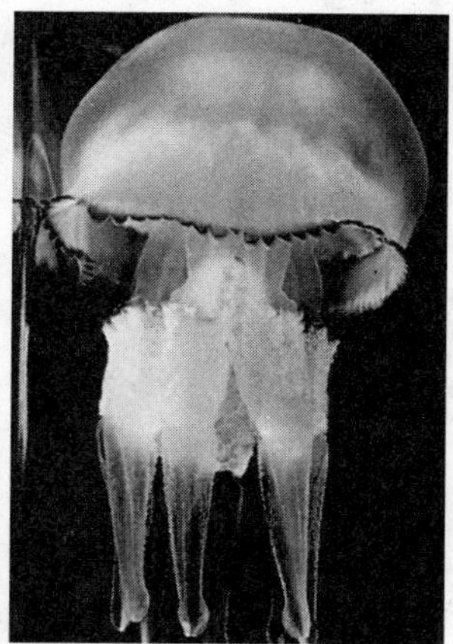

Medusa stage of a jellyfish
Tom McHugh—Photo Researchers

Medvedev, Roy Aleksandrovich (b. Nov. 14, 1925, Tbilisi, Georgia, U.S.S.R. [now in Georgia]), Soviet historian and dissident who was one of his country's foremost historiographers in the later 20th century.

Roy was the identical twin brother of the biologist Zhores Medvedev. Their father was arrested in 1938 during one of Joseph Stalin's purges, and he died in a labour camp in 1941. This tragedy sparked Roy Medvedev's lifelong interest in the Soviet political system and its history. He graduated from Leningrad State University in 1951 and earned the equivalent of a Ph.D. degree from the Academy of Pedagogical Sciences in Moscow in 1958. Medvedev then worked as a history teacher, a secondary-school administrator, and an editor before serving as a senior researcher at the Academy of Pedagogical Sciences in the 1960s. He was a member of the Communist Party from 1956 until his expulsion from the party in 1969. From 1971 he worked as a freelance writer based in Moscow and had his works published abroad. Roy was less severely harassed by the Soviet authorities than was his brother Zhores.

As a historian, Medvedev examined Soviet politics and its leading personalities from the period of the Russian Revolution to the 1960s. Perhaps his most important book, *Let History Judge* (1971), is a comprehensive historical study of Stalinism, with particular attention paid to that movement's origins and consequences. His books *Khrushchev: The Years in Power* (1976; coauthored with Zhores), *Khrushchev* (1983), and *Khrushchev: A Political Biography* (1986) are landmark biographies of that Soviet leader, while *All Stalin's Men* (1984) presents biographies of six of Stalin's lieutenants. In *On Socialist Democracy* (1975), Medvedev presented his own political views, calling for democratic reforms within the Soviet system of state socialism.

With the easing of censorship under the reforms of Mikhail Gorbachev in the late 1980s, Medvedev's books were published in his own country for the first time.

Medvedev, Zhores Aleksandrovich (b. Nov. 14, 1925, Tbilisi, Georgia, U.S.S.R. [now in Georgia]), Soviet biologist who became an important dissident historian in the second half of the 20th century.

Zhores was the identical twin brother of the Soviet historian Roy Medvedev. He graduated from the Timiriazev Academy of Agricultural Sciences in Moscow in 1950 and received his master's degree in biology that same year from the Moscow Institute of Plant Physiology. He conducted research at the Timiriazev Academy from 1951 to 1962, becoming a senior scientist there and winning an international reputation for his work on protein biosynthesis and the physiology of aging.

In the 1960s Medvedev wrote a history of Soviet science with the aim of discrediting the doctrines of T.D. Lysenko, the charlatan who dominated Soviet biology during the reign of Joseph Stalin (1929–53) and whose assaults on classical genetics crippled Soviet biology for decades. The Soviet authorities refused to publish Medvedev's book, which was circulated in *samizdat* (the Soviet literary underground) until its publication in the West under the title *The Rise and Fall of T.D. Lysenko* in 1969. The Soviet government denied Medvedev opportunities to attend scientific conferences abroad despite his growing reputation as a scientist, and he underwent constant harassment from the KGB from the mid-1960s on. He detailed his travails, which included a brief forced stay in a mental hospital, in the books *The Medvedev Papers* (1970) and *A Question of Madness* (1971), the latter coauthored with his brother Roy.

While in London in 1973, Medvedev was stripped of his Soviet citizenship. He settled in England and continued to document the underside of Soviet science in such works as *Soviet Science* (1978), *Soviet Agriculture* (1987), and *The Legacy of Chernobyl* (1990). His book *The Nuclear Disaster in the Urals* (1979) provided the West with the first details of a major nuclear disaster that had occurred in the Soviet Union in 1957. His Soviet citizenship was restored in 1990, and his books began to be published in the Soviet Union. Medvedev also produced more than 200 papers and articles on gerontology, genetics, biochemistry, and other topics.

Medwall, Henry (fl. 1490), author remembered for his *Fulgens and Lucrece,* the first known secular play in English.

Medwall was chaplain to Cardinal John Morton, archbishop of Canterbury, and was the rector of Balynghem in the English marches of Calais, in France. The first note of him is in Morton's register at Lambeth, London, in 1490; in 1501 he seems to have been granted letters of protection allowing him to go abroad; a few months later he resigned, and no later reference to him is known.

Medwall's dramatic works were written for the entertainment of the cardinal and his guests. A morality play, *Nature,* a good example of the allegorical type of early drama, displays Medwall's talent for realistic dialogue and his skill as a versifier.

Medway, unitary authority, geographic and historic county of Kent, southeastern England. The unitary authority is named for, and lies around the mouth of, the River Medway where it flows into the estuary of the Thames. It comprises the ports of Chatham and Gillingham and the town of Rainham south of the Medway and the historic cathedral city of Rochester north of the Medway. The areas along the Medway are largely industrialized. From the 15th century until 1984 Chatham had one of Britain's major naval dockyards. Besides the oil refinery at Grain, there are numerous engineering plants lining the river frontage of the Medway. Area 79 square miles (205 square km). Pop. (1998 est.) 242,600.

Meegeren, Han van, byname of HENRICUS ANTONIUS VAN MEEGEREN (b. Oct. 10, 1889, Deventer, Neth.—d. Dec. 30, 1947, Amsterdam), Dutch painter, best known for his successful and complex scheme of forging and selling paintings attributed to Dutch masters.

Van Meegeren's activities as a forger first came to light after World War II, when an Allied art commission was established to identify and restore to their owners the works of art that had been collected by Nazi leaders. Puzzled at the discovery of a painting called "Christ and the Woman Taken in Adultery" by Jan Vermeer among the collection amassed by Hermann Göring, the commission traced the sale of the painting to van Meegeren, an eccentric and wealthy Amsterdam painter. Arrested in 1945 and faced with charges of collaboration, van Meegeren confessed to having forged the reputed Vermeer and other paintings, stating that his original intention had been to reveal his authorship of them after the paintings had been acclaimed by critics. Of van Meegeren's 14 known forgeries of works by Vermeer and Pieter de Hooch, 9 had been sold before the war at enormous profit, including the painting entitled "Christ and the Disciples at Emmaus," which had been proclaimed by scholars as a masterpiece by Vermeer.

Meekatharra, town, west-central Western Australia. Founded in the 1890s, it became the centre of the Murchison goldfield, but with the exhaustion of gold it became the focal point of a large pastoral region. Once the terminus of the Canning Stock Route and Madman's (cattle) Track, Meekatharra now receives livestock trucked south down the Great Northern Highway from as far away as Broome. Meekatharra is the site of a Royal Flying Doctor Service and the first regular School of the Air (public education by radio for outback children). The town is also a base for mining in the region. The name Meekatharra is said to derive from an Aboriginal term for "bad watering place." Pop. (1991) 1,414.

Meer, Simon van der (b. Nov. 24, 1925, The Hague, Neth.), Dutch physical engineer who in 1984, with Carlo Rubbia, received the Nobel Prize for Physics for his contribution to the discovery of the massive, short-lived subatomic particles designated *W* and *Z* that were crucial to the unified electroweak theory posited in the 1970s by Steven Weinberg, Abdus Salam, and Sheldon Glashow.

After receiving a degree in physical engineering from the Higher Technical School in Delft, Neth., in 1952, van der Meer worked for the Philips Company. In 1956 he joined the staff of CERN (the European Organization for Nuclear Research), near Geneva, where he remained until his retirement in 1990.

The electroweak theory provided the first reliable estimates of the masses of the *W* and *Z* particles—nearly 100 times the mass of the proton. The most promising means of bringing about a physical interaction that would release enough energy to form the particles was to cause a beam of highly accelerated protons, moving through an evacuated tube, to collide with an oppositely directed beam of antiprotons. CERN's circular particle accelerator, four miles in circumference, was the first to be converted into a colliding-beam apparatus in which the desired experiments could be performed. Manipulation of the beams required a highly effective method for keeping the particles from scattering out of the proper path and hitting the walls of the tube. Van der Meer, in response to this problem, devised a mechanism that would monitor the particle scattering at a particular point on the ring and would trigger a device on the opposite side of the ring to modify the electric fields in such a way as to keep the particles on course.

meerkat, also spelled MIERKAT, certain carnivores of the civet family (Viverridae), specifically the suricate (*q.v.*) and various mongoose (*q.v.*) species.

Meersch, Jean-André van der (b. Feb. 10, 1734, Menen, Austrian Netherlands [now in Belgium]—d. Sept. 14, 1792, Dadizeele), military leader of the Belgian revolt against Austrian rule in 1789.

Meersch joined the French army in 1757 during the Seven Years' War and rose to lieutenant colonel in 1761. He later served in the Austrian army and retired in 1779.

In the 1789 revolt, which was precipitated by Austrian attempts to replace traditional Belgian autonomy with centralized authority, Meersch accepted (August 1789) the leadership of the forces of the Belgian rebel Jean-François Vonck. He defeated an Austrian detachment at Turnhout on October 24, won further successes, and concluded an armistice with the Austrian general Richard d'Alton in December. The hostility of Vonck's rival Henri van der Noot resulted in Meersch's arrest in April 1790. On the restoration of Austrian authority in Belgium in December 1790, Meersch fled to France, but, later amnestied, he returned to Brussels and then retired to Dadizeele.

meerschaum: *see* sepiolite.

Meerut, town, northwestern Uttar Pradesh state, northern India. It lies northeast of Delhi, at the junction of several roads and rail lines. Meerut is a trade centre for agricultural products and has a considerable amount of industry, including manufacturing, smelting, handicrafts, and the milling of sugar, cotton, flour, and oilseeds. Meerut University (1965) is located in the town; Meerut College (1892) and several other colleges are affiliated with the university. The town also has a 12th-century mausoleum and old temples and mosques. Meerut is an important army headquarters. The initial uprising of the 1857 Indian Mutiny occurred there. Pop. (2001 prelim.) city, 1,074,229; metropolitan area, 1,167,399.

Megabyzus (fl. early 5th century BC), one of the greatest generals of the ancient Achaemenid Empire of Persia.

He was the son of Zopyrus and the brother-in-law of King Xerxes I. Sent to quell an uprising in Babylon (482), Megabyzus quickly seized and devastated the city, carrying off the huge gold statue of Bel-Marduk. By melting down the statue, he thus prevented any future Babylonian ruler from legitimizing his position, which was done by grasping the hands of the god's image at the Babylonian Akitu (New Year) festival. Megabyzus accompanied Xerxes on his invasion of Greece, but he later became one of the co-conspirators in the assassination of Xerxes (465).

Under the new king, Artaxerxes I, Megabyzus was appointed satrap (governor) of Syria and was sent with a large army to restore Achaemenid rule in Egypt. Successful, he promised safety to Inaros, the leader of the Egyptian revolt, who thus surrendered. But after his pledge to Inaros was broken through the intrigues of the Achaemenid queen mother, Amestris, Megabyzus returned to Syria and rebelled. Although he and Artaxerxes became reconciled, he later offended the king on a hunting trip and was exiled to Cyrtae on the Persian Gulf. After five years he feigned leprosy and was allowed to return; through the intercession of the royal court, he and Artaxerxes became friends once more.

Megacles (fl. mid-6th century BC), the leader of one of the parties that struggled for control of Athens during the period between the archonship of Solon and the establishment of Peisistratus' tyranny.

Megacles was grandson to that Megacles who directed the slaughter of Cylon and his supporters on the Acropolis (612 BC). That bloody act resulted in the banishment of his family. The elder Megacles' son Alcmaeon may have taken refuge at this time in Sicyon under Cleisthenes' protection. That tyrant's daughter Agariste was married to Alcmaeon's son Megacles, who thus won out over other suitors from all parts of Greece. Though the Alcmaeonids were subsequently allowed to return to Athens, the family was still considered stained by blood-guilt.

Among the Athenian political parties, Megacles' faction was known as the party of the Coast. The party of the Plain was led by Lycurgus. The unsettled political conditions that resulted from these parties' factional struggles tempted Peisistratus to seize power in 560/559 BC, but the two parties promptly combined to expel him.

Within five years Peisistratus had achieved a reconciliation with Megacles, who not only helped to restore his power in Athens but gave to Peisistratus his daughter Coesyra. The tyrant mistreated his wife, however, and the Alcmaeonids and Lycurgus once more threw him out. This time Peisistratus assembled an army and invaded Attica. Megacles and his clan were once more banished; and, though he and, after him, his son Cleisthenes continued to plot against Peisistratus, they did not succeed during the tyrant's lifetime.

megacolon, massive enlargement and dilation of the large intestine (colon). The two main types of the syndrome are congenital megacolon, or Hirschsprung's disease, and acquired megacolon. In congenital megacolon, the lowermost portion of the large intestine is congenitally lacking in normal nerve fibres; thus, peristalsis, or involuntary contractions, of the muscles of this part of the intestine cannot occur, and the bowel's contents are not pushed onward. The area of normal intestine above the abnormal part works harder to push on the fecal contents, with the result that the muscular walls of that part of the intestine become enlarged and thickened. The entire colon eventually becomes thick and distended. Congenital megacolon's symptoms are a distended abdomen and severe constipation in infants born with the disorder. Various surgical procedures are used to correct the condition.

Acquired megacolon in children characteristically results from a combination of faulty toilet training and emotional disturbances. Mentally retarded or psychotic children are also vulnerable to the syndrome, which results from a child's refusal to try to defecate. The administration of increasingly larger doses of laxatives fails to permanently solve the problem, and over time the child's rectum becomes filled with impacted feces and the colon becomes progressively enlarged. Once the distended bowel has been emptied, the treatment for this disorder is primarily psychiatric and involves persuading the child to accept bowel training.

megalith, huge, often undressed stone used in various types of Neolithic and Early Bronze Age monuments.

Although some aspects of the spread and development of megalithic monuments are still under debate, in Spain, Portugal, and the Mediterranean coast the most ancient of the cyclopean stone tombs was probably the dolmen. The dolmen consisted of several upright supports and a flat roofing slab, all covered by a protective mound of earth that in most cases has weathered away. In northern and western Europe, two principal plans developed

Megalith at Avebury stone circle, Wiltshire

J. Allan Cash

from the dolmen: one, the passage grave, was formed by the addition of a long stone-roofed entrance passage to the dolmen itself; and the other, the long, coffinlike cist or covered gallery grave, consisted of a long, rectangular burial chamber with no distinct passageway. Hybrid versions have also been discovered, for example, in the Hebrides. Many round and long barrows also were found to contain megalithic burial chambers.

Another form of the megalithic monument was the menhir (from Breton *men,* "stone," and *hir,* "long"), which may or may not occur in connection with a megalithic grave. Menhirs were simple upright stones, sometimes of great size, and were erected most frequently in western Europe, especially Brittany. Often menhirs were placed together, forming circles, semicircles, or vast ellipses. Many were built in England, the best-known sites being Stonehenge and Avebury in Wiltshire. Megalithic menhirs were also placed in several parallel rows, called alignments. The most famous of these are the Carnac, Fr., alignments, which include 2,935 menhirs. The alignments were probably used for ritual processions, and often a circle or semicircle of megaliths stood at one end.

The conception underlying the building of megalithic monuments is still unknown, but all of the monuments share certain architectural and technical features, demonstrating that the disseminators of the megalith idea came to dominate the local populations of many areas. The similarity of magical symbols carved on many of the monuments also shows an underlying unity of beliefs.

In most areas the megalith builders were superseded by the Beaker folk at the beginning of the Early Bronze Age. The newcomers, however, carried on the megalithic tradition by building round barrows for single burials, in contrast to the collective tombs of the Neolithic builders.

Megalopolis, Modern Greek MEGALÓPOLIS, ancient and modern settlement, *nomós* (department) of Arkadhía, of the Peloponnese, Greece, just northwest of which lay an ancient city of the same name at 1,400 feet (427 m) above sea level on the Akhíllion plain. Spreading extensively on both banks of the Helisson (Elísson) River just above its junction with the Alpheus (Alfiós), the ancient community (the name means "large city," or "great city") was founded on a grandiose scale (371–368 BC) by Epaminondas of Thebes as the seat of the Arcadian League and as a bastion for the southern Arcadians' containment of Sparta. Megalopolis on the Helisson was populated by the wholesale transfer of inhabitants from 40 local villages and by contingents from Tegéa, Mantineia, and other locations. Encompassed by strong walls, the city reached about 5.5 miles (9 km) in circumference; its territory, extending 24 miles (39 km) northward, was the greatest of any city-state in Arcadia. Spartan attempts to take the city, which had been weakened by the failure of the Arcadian League, were foiled in 353 and 331—as well as after 234, when Megalopolis joined the Achaean League. In 223, however, Cleomenes III of Sparta plundered it, and with the coming of Rome in 146, the city declined rapidly; in the 2nd century AD the Greek traveler Pausanias noted that it was a heap of ruins. The only great historical figures it produced were the Achaean soldier-statesman Philopoemen (*c.* 252–182 BC) and the historian Polybius (*c.* 200–after 118 BC).

Excavation by the British School at Athens in 1890–93 revealed municipal buildings north of the river that were grouped around a square agora; buildings to the south of the river included the main federal buildings, a theatre that was the largest in ancient Greece, and an adjoining Thersilion, or assembly hall.

Megalopolis is at the centre of a rich lignite-bearing region that has been exploited since the early 1970s to fuel several thermal-power stations. Pop. (1981) 4,875.

megalosaur (genus *Megalosaurus*), carnivorous dinosaur (suborder Theropoda) found in fossils of the Early to Late Jurassic Period (208 to 144 million years ago) in Europe and North Africa. One of the first dinosaur finds of the early 19th century (by William Buckland), the megalosaur was orginally described on the basis of a lower jaw fragment with some daggerlike teeth. It was later determined to be a middle- to large-sized obligatory biped and predator with short arms and clawed grasping hands. The jaws carried long serrated blade-like teeth, much like those in the allosaur (*Allosaurus*) and other large theropods, to which it must have been closely related.

megapode, also called MOUND BUILDER, or INCUBATOR BIRD (family Megapodiidae), any of 12 species of Australasian chickenlike birds (order Galliformes) that bury their eggs to hatch them. Most species rely on fermenting plant matter to produce heat for incubation, but some use solar heat and others the heat produced by volcanic action.

Megapodes are of three kinds: scrub fowl; brush turkeys (not true turkeys); and mallee fowl, or lowan (*Leipoa ocellata*), which frequent the mallee, or scrub, vegetation of southern interior Australia. The mallee fowl, the best known of the group, is 65 cm (25.5 inches) long and has white-spotted, light brown plumage. The male builds a mound of decaying vegetation, which may require 11 months to construct. The result is a low mound, about 1 m (3 feet) in the ground and up to 4.5 m across, consisting of leaves and twigs soaked with rain and covered with 0.5 m of sandy soil. When the heat of fermentation inside the mound reaches 33° C (91° F), the female lays the first of about 35 eggs in a central chamber. The male maintains a mound temperature astonishingly close to 33° C even in the face of daily and seasonal weather variation. The eggs hatch in seven weeks, and the hatchlings dig upward through the mound and run off on their own. They can fly one or two days after hatching.

Mallee fowl (*Leipoa ocellata*)
Painting by Murrell Butler

Megara, Modern Greek MÉGARA, ancient and modern settlement on the Saronic Gulf within Attica *nomós* (department) of Greece. Modern Megara sits on the southern slopes of two hills that served as the acropolises (citadels) of the ancient town.

The early inhabitants were annihilated during the Dorian invasion (*c.* 1100–*c.* 1000 BC). In the 8th century BC, Megarian commercial colonies were established on Sicily. Megara also colonized northward and eastward on the Bosporus River and Sea of Marmara at Chalcedon (676) and Byzantium (660), the latter being the most significant in later history. The chief colonies, however, were Astacus and Heraclea in Bithynia in northwestern Asia Minor and a second Heraclea in the Crimea.

The history of Megara after 630 BC is largely that of its losing conflict with its powerful neighbour, Athens, to which it lost the island of Salamís about 570. Forced to accept Athenian defensive assistance after 461, it revolted in 446 and in 432 suffered an Athenian trade embargo throughout its empire. Though its surrounding territory was subjugated by Athens during the Peloponnesian War (431–404 BC), the citadel of Megara itself did not fall. In the 4th century BC Megara recovered some of its prosperity but remained politically insignificant. The city survived the Roman period, but in the 2nd century AD the Greek traveler Pausanias noted that Megarians were the only people whom the emperor Hadrian (117–138) could not make thrive. Although Megara continued as a prominent place for several more centuries, in 1500 it was depopulated by the Venetians. Megara was the birthplace of the Sophist philosopher Eucleides (*c.* 450–*c.* 380 BC), who founded the Megarian school of philosophy, which influenced Stoic thought. Modern Megara is a major centre for farming and poultry-raising and has benefited from the rapid industrialization of the coastal areas from Piraeus to Corinth. Pop. (1991 prelim.) 26,562.

Megarian school, school of philosophy founded in Greece at the beginning of the 4th century BC by Eucleides of Megara. It is noted more for its criticism of Aristotle and its influence upon Stoic logic than for any positive assertions. Although Eucleides was a pupil of Socrates and the author of Socratic dialogues, only imperfect glimpses of his thought survive. He is said to have held that "the good is one, though it is called by many names, sometimes wisdom, sometimes God, and sometimes reason" and that "the contrary to the good has no reality."

The Megarians, at least under Eucleides, had an ethical and educational purpose, and it was in this spirit that they defended the unity of goodness. They were, nevertheless, men of theory, as compared with other self-styled followers of Socrates, such as the Cyrenaics and Cynics. The Megarians consciously cultivated dialectical skills, and it was the Socratic method of questions and answers, rather than any positive doctrine, that linked them together. After Eucleides' death (*c.* 380 BC), practical and dialectical interests diminished; one wing of the school propounded and studied paradoxes in the manner of Zeno and otherwise approached an independent treatment of logic.

Among Eucleides' successors was Eubulides of Miletus, who took the lead in Megarian criticism of Aristotle's doctrine of categories, his definition of (and belief in) movement, and his concept of potentiality. (For Megarians, only what is now actual is possible.) Some passages in Aristotle's writings are probably retorts to Megarian criticism. Whereas Aristotelian logic was applicable to predicates (noun expressions) or classes, the Megarians specialized in a logic of whole propositions.

Other Megarians were Diodorus Cronus and Stilpon, a representative of the older tradition inasmuch as he subordinated dialectic to a moral purpose. He taught the Stoic Zeno of Citium, and Menedemus, leader of the Eretrian school. The Megarian school died out at the beginning of the 3rd century BC.

megaron, in ancient Greece and the Middle East, architectural form consisting of an open porch, a vestibule, and a large hall with a central hearth and a throne. The megaron was found in all Mycenaean palaces and was also built as part of houses. It seemingly originated in the Middle East, attaining a peculiarly Aegean aspect because of its open porch, which was usually supported by columns. Early Greek architecture used the megaron, and it also became an important element in the Classical temple. A typical megaron plan is that of the palace of Nestor at Pylos, where the large main unit apparently served as royal living quarters. It faced onto the usual courtyard, which was entered through a decorative gateway with fluted columns on either side.

megass (natural fibre): *see* bagasse.

Megasthenes (b. *c.* 350 BC—d. *c.* 290), ancient Greek historian and diplomat, author of an account of India, the *Indica,* in four books. An Ionian, he was sent by the Hellenistic king Seleucus I on embassies to the Maurya emperor Candra Gupta. Though credulous and inaccurate, he gave the most complete account of India then known to the Greek world.

Megatherium, largest of the ground sloths, an extinct group of mammals that underwent a highly successful evolutionary radiation in South America in the Cenozoic Era (beginning 66.4 million years ago). The size of these animals approximated that of a modern elephant, and they were equipped with large claws and teeth; the latter were confined to the sides of the jaw, because the animal fed largely on the leaves of trees and bushes. Ground sloths appeared briefly in North America during the Pleistocene Epoch (1,600,000 to 10,000 years ago), when a land connection was established between the American continents.

Meghālaya, constituent state of India, lying in the northeast corner of the country. Occupying a mountainous plateau of great scenic beauty, it is bounded on the south and west by Bangladesh and on the north and east by the Indian state of Assam. The capital is Shillong.

A brief treatment of Meghālaya follows. For full treatment, *see* MACROPAEDIA: India.

The tribal hill people of Meghālaya trace their origins to pre-Aryan times in India. Over the centuries—despite being driven from the plains by Aryan invaders—they have managed to maintain their identity largely intact and in seclusion. They accepted nominal British rule in the 19th century, but the British never really conquered them and left the tribes alone. Included in the state of Assam (along with other tribal areas), the area received special protection under the Indian constitution. With the introduction of Assamese as the official language in 1960, agitation for autonomy began, and the area was made a state in 1972.

From west to east in Meghālaya, the Gāro Hills rise abruptly from the Brahmaputra River valley to about 1,000 feet (300 m), merging with the Khāsi Hills and Jaintia Hills. Eastward-trending ridges reach heights of 4,000 to 6,000 feet (1,220 to 1,830 m). A central plateau is a watershed for the many rivers and streams traversing the state. The most important of these rivers is Umiam-Barapani. The state's climate is generally mild.

Most of the inhabitants of Meghālaya are of Tibeto-Burman (Gāros) or Mon-Khmer (Khāsis) origin. The predominately rural population is mostly Hindu and Christian, with some Muslims and a few Sikhs and Buddhists.

Farming is the primary economic activity. Crops include rice, millet, corn (maize), pepper, potatoes, chilies, cotton, ginger, jute, betel nuts, oranges, mangoes, bananas, pineapples, and numerous varieties of vegetables. Traditional farming practices—*jhum* cultivation (burning trees and planting the cleared areas in rotation)—have eroded the soil.

The state's abundant mineral resources are mostly untapped. It has coal, limestone, kaolin, feldspar, quartz, mica, gypsum, and bauxite. Almost 100 percent of India's sillimanite (a source of high-grade ceramic clay) is produced in Meghālaya. Despite these resources, Meghālaya has few industries, and—except for Shillong, Jowai, Nongthymmai, and Tura—few urban centres. Light manufacturing encompasses construction materials, electronics, and beverages. There is little communication between the hill districts of Meghālaya, and even within the districts the valleys remain isolated. The state has no railways and a few thousand miles of roads, divided among surfaced, graveled, and earth.

Though literacy is low, Meghālaya has several local newspapers. The North-Eastern Hill University is at Shillong. Area 8,660 square miles (22,429 square km). Pop. (2001 prelim.) 2,306,069.

Meghna River, major watercourse of the Ganges-Brahmaputra delta, in Bangladesh. The name is properly applied to a channel of the Old Brahmaputra downstream from Bhairab Bāzār, after it has received the Surma (Barāk) River. Flowing almost due south, the Meghna receives the combined waters of the Padma (Ganges) and Jamuna (Brahmaputra) rivers near Chāndpur. After a course of about 164 miles (264 km) it enters the Bay of Bengal by four principal mouths—the Tetulia, Shāhbāzpur, Hātia, and Bāmni. Major tributaries are the Dhaleswari, Gumti, and Fenny. A river of great depth and velocity, the Meghna is sometimes split up into several channels. It is navigable, but dangerous, all year. At spring tide the sea rushes upriver in a single 20-foot (6-metre) wave.

Megiddo, modern TEL MEGIDDO, important town of ancient Palestine, overlooking the Plain of Esdraelon (Valley of Jezreel). It lies about 18 miles (29 km) southeast of Haifa in northern Israel. Megiddo's strategic location at the crossing of two military and trade routes gave the city an importance far beyond its size. It controlled a commonly used pass on the trading route between Egypt and Mesopotamia, and it also stood along the northwest-southeast route that connected the Phoenician cities with Jerusalem and the Jordan River valley. It is thought that the word *Armageddon* is derived from Megiddo, since the prefix *har* means "hill" in Hebrew; hence, *Armageddon* means "Hill of Megiddo."

Excavations of the site were conducted by archaeologists of the Deutsche Orientgesellschaft (1903–05) and of the Oriental Institute of the University of Chicago (1925–39). The excavations have shown that the first town there was built in the early 4th millennium BC. Megiddo was captured by the Egyptian king Thutmose III about 1468 BC. The Israelites eventually took Megiddo, along with other cities of the area, and King Solomon rebuilt the city as a military centre; a number of the stables that have been excavated at Megiddo probably date to this time. A mutilated inscribed stele records the occupation of Megiddo by Sheshonk I, who became king of Egypt about 935 BC. King Ahaziah of Judah died at Megiddo about 842 BC, and King Josiah of Judah also died there (609 BC) while opposing the advance of the Egyptian king Necho II toward Assyria. The last traceable remains at Megiddo are from about 450 BC. Nearly 400 Phoenician ivories have been found at the site, showing influences from various culture areas of the Middle East.

Remains of the stables at Megiddo
By courtesy of the Oriental Institute, University of Chicago

In modern times Megiddo gave its name to an important battle won by the British general Edmund Allenby, who commanded the British forces in Palestine during the latter part of World War I. In September 1918, at a number of points near Megiddo, Allenby's cavalry cut off the northward retreat of the Turkish 7th and 8th armies after his infantry had defeated them in the coastal plain. His well-conceived operations led to the final defeat of the Turks in the Middle East.

Megillah, also spelled MEGILLA, Hebrew MEGILLAH ("Scroll"), plural MEGILLOT, or MEGUILLOTH, in the Hebrew Bible, any of the five sacred books of the Ketuvim (the third division of the Old Testament), in scroll form, that are read in the synagogue in the course of certain festivals. The Song of Solomon (Song of Songs) is read on the Sabbath of Passover week, the Book of Ruth on Shabuoth, Lamentations of Jeremiah on Tisha be-Av, Ecclesiastes on the Sabbath of the week of Sukkoth, and the Book of Esther on Purim. The reading of Esther on Purim is prescribed in the Mishna; other readings were introduced in post-Talmudic days. The parchment scrolls, especially that of Esther, are handwritten by scribes and often richly illuminated.

Scroll of Esther in a silver case embossed with vignettes showing scenes from the story of Esther, German, 17th century; in the Jewish Museum, London
By courtesy of the Jewish Museum, London; photograph, A.C. Cooper

Megiste (Greece): *see* Kastellórizon.

Megrelian language: *see* Mingrelian language.

Mehābād (Iran): *see* Mahābād.

Mehedinți, *județ* (county), southwestern Romania. It is bounded to the west and south by Serbia and Montenegro and by Bulgaria. The mountain ranges of Cernei and Almăj, part of the Transylvanian Alps (Southern Carpathians), and the sub-Carpathians rise above settlement areas in the valleys. The Danube River, flowing southeastward, marks the county's southern border, and the Motru and Cerna rivers and several tributaries drain the area southward. Drobeta-Turnu Severin, a centre for machinery and timber production, serves as the county seat. Textiles and foodstuffs are produced in several towns within the county. Stone quarries have been worked near Gura Vaii since Roman times. The county's agricultural activities consist of livestock raising and cereal growing.

Electricity for the county is supplied by the Iron Gate I hydroelectric project, which was built between 1964 and 1971 on the Danube. Construction of the Iron Gate II project began during the late 1970s and was completed in 1984. The island of Ada Kaleh, long a fortified port of the Ottoman Empire, was submerged when the Iron Gate I hydroelectric project was built. By legend, the island was the place from which the Argonauts brought the olive that they introduced to Greece. Historic remnants in Mehedinți county include a Roman castrum found at the port of Orșova and a Roman sundial discovered near Ogradina. Built in 1429, the castle of Trikule is situated near Svinița, a small coal-mining town. A nature reserve at Mount Babele contains rare species of irises, dianthus, and fig trees. Highway and railway connections in the county extend through Drobeta-Turnu Severin, Vînju Mare, and Strehaia. Area 1,905 square miles (4,933 square km). Pop. (2002) 306,118.

Mehemet (Arabic or Turkish personal name): *see under* Mahmud, Mehmed, Muḥammad, or Mohammed.

Meher Baba, also called THE AWAKENER, original name MERWAN SHERIAR IRANI (b. Feb. 25, 1894, Poona, India—d. Jan. 31, 1969, Ahmednagar), spiritual master in western India with a sizable following both in that country and abroad. Beginning on July 10, 1925, he observed silence for the last 44 years of his life, communicating with his disciples at first through an alphabet board but increasingly with gestures. He observed that he had come "not to teach but to awaken," adding that "things that are real are given and received in silence."

He was born into a Zoroastrian family of Persian descent. He was educated in Poona and attended Deccan College there, where at the age of 19 he met an aged Muslim woman, Hazrat Babajan, the first of five "perfect masters" (spiritually enlightened, or "God-realized," persons) who over the next seven years helped him find his own spiritual identity. That identity, Meher Baba said, was as the avatar of this age, interpreting that Vedantic term to mean the periodic incarnation of God in human form. He placed himself among such universal religious figures as Zoroaster, Rama, Krishna, Gautama Buddha, Jesus, and Muḥammad. "I am the same Ancient One come again into your midst," he told his disciples, declaring that all major religions are revelations of "the One Reality which is God."

Meher Baba's cosmology may be summarized as follows: the goal of all life is to realize the absolute oneness of God, from whom the universe emanated as a result of the whim of unconscious divinity to know itself as conscious divinity. In pursuit of consciousness, evolution of forms occurs in seven stages: stone or metal, vegetable, worm, fish, bird, animal, and human. Every individualized soul must experience all of these forms in order to gain full consciousness. Once consciousness is attained, the burden of impressions accumulated in these forms prevents the soul from realizing its identity with God. To gain this realization the individual must traverse an inward spiritual path, eliminating all false impressions of individuality and eventuating in the knowledge of the "real self" as God.

Meher Baba saw his work as awakening the world through love to a new consciousness of the oneness of all life. To that end he lived a life of love and service which included extensive work with the poor, the physically and mentally ill, and many others, including such tasks as feeding the poor, cleaning the latrines of untouchables, and bathing lepers. He saw a responsibility to give spiritual help to "advanced souls," and travelled throughout the Indian subcontinent to find such persons.

These outward activities Meher Baba saw as indications of the inner transformation of consciousness that he came to give the world. He established and later dismantled many institutions of service, which he compared to scaffolding temporarily erected to construct a building that really was within the human heart. He said that a "new humanity" would emerge from his life's work, and that he would bring about an unprecedented release of divine love in the world.

Between 1931 and 1958 he made many visits to the United States and Europe, on one such trip in 1952 establishing the Meher Spiritual Center in Myrtle Beach, S.C. A similar centre, Avatar's Abode, was created at Woomby, Queensland, Australia in 1958.

From the mid-1960s Meher Baba was in seclusion, and during that period several U.S. drug experimenters were drawn to him in a quest for spiritual truth. Through them his admonitions against the non-medical use of psychedelic and other drugs came to the attention of the news media in the U.S. and the West. He warned young people explicitly that "drugs are harmful mentally, physically, and spiritually," trying to draw them away from drugs and toward a spiritual life.

Meher Baba never sought to form a sect or proclaim a dogma; he attracted and welcomed followers of many faiths and every social class with a message emphasizing love and compassion, the elimination of the selfish ego, and the potential of realizing God within themselves. Although his equation of the several manifestations of God was syncretic, he won many followers from sects and denominations that repudiated syncretism, and encourged those followers to be strong in their original faiths. After his death his followers heeded his wish that they not form an organization, but continued to gather informally and often to discuss and read his works and express through music, poetry, dance, or drama their reflections on his life. His tomb at Meherabad, near Ahmednagar, has become a place of pilgrimage for his followers throughout the world. His books include *Discourses* (5 vol., 1938–43; the earliest dictated on an alphabet board, the others by gesture), *God Speaks: The Theme of Creation and Its Purposes* (1955), and *The Everything and the Nothing* (1963).

Where the same name may denote a person, place, or thing, the articles will be found in that order

Mehmed (Arabic or Turkish personal name): *see under* Muḥammad, Mohammed, or Mahmud, except as below.

Mehmed, also spelled MOHAMMED, or MUḤAMMAD, name of Ottoman sultans grouped below chronologically and indicated by the symbol •.

•Mehmed I, also called ÇELEBI SULTAN MEHMED (d. May 26, 1421, Edirne, Ottoman Empire), Ottoman sultan who reunified the

Mehmed I, miniature from a 16th-century manuscript illustrating the dynasty; in the Istanbul University Library (Ms. Yildiz 2653/261)

By courtesy of Istanbul University Library

dismembered Ottoman territories following the defeat of Ankara (1402). He ruled in Anatolia and, after 1413, in the Balkans as well.

Timur (Tamerlane), victorious over the Ottoman sultan Bayezid I at Ankara, restored to the Turkmen their principalities that had been annexed by the Ottomans and divided the remaining Ottoman territory among three of Bayezid's sons. Thus Mehmed ruled in Amasya, İsa in Bursa, and Süleyman in Rumelia (Balkan lands under Ottoman control). Mehmed defeated İsa and seized Bursa (1404–05), then sent another brother, Mûsa, against Süleyman. Mûsa was victorious over Süleyman (1410) but then declared himself sultan in Edirne and undertook the reconquest of the Ottoman territories in Rumelia. Mehmed, assisted by the Byzantine emperor Manuel II Palaeologus, defeated Mûsa in 1413 at Camurlu (in Serbia) and declared himself sultan in both Anatolia and Rumelia, with his capital at Edirne.

During his reign Mehmed pursued a policy of relative restraint in the Balkans, although he reduced Walachia to vassal status (1416), made territorial gains in Albania (1417), and conducted raids into Hungary. In Anatolia he reestablished Ottoman control over much of the western provinces and reduced the Karaman principality (in Konya) to submission. He was successful in crushing a socio-religious revolt (1416) inspired by Bedreddin, who had been chief judge under Mûsa. Mehmed also overcame a threat from a pretender, who claimed to be his brother, Mustafa.

•Mehmed II, byname MEHMED FATIH (Turkish: Mehmed the Conqueror) (b. March 30, 1432, Adrianople, Thrace, Ottoman Empire—d. May 3, 1481, Hunkârçayırı, near Maltepe, near Constantinople), Ottoman sultan from 1444 to 1446 and from 1451 to 1481. A great military leader, he captured Constantinople and conquered the territories in Anatolia and the Balkans that comprised the Ottoman Empire's heartland for the next four centuries.

Early years and first reign. Mehmed was the fourth son of Murad II by a slave girl; at the age of 12 he was sent, as tradition required, to Manisa (Magnesia) with his two tutors. The same year, his father set him on the throne at Edirne and abdicated. During his first reign (August 1444–May 1446), Mehmed had to face grave external and internal crises. The King of Hungary, the Pope, the Byzantine Empire, and Venice—all eager to take advantage of the accession of a child to the Ottoman throne—succeeded in organizing a crusade. Edirne was the scene of violent rivalry between the powerful grand vizier Çandarlı Halil, on the one hand, and the viziers Zaganos and Şihâbeddin, on the other, who claimed that they were protecting the rights of the child sultan. In September 1444 the army of the crusaders crossed the Danube. In Edirne this news triggered a massacre of the Christian-influenced Hurūfī sect and conjured up an atmosphere of panic and arson. When the crusaders laid siege to Varna, the reigning sultan's father was urged to come back from retirement in Bursa and lead the army. The Ottoman victory at Varna under Murad II (Nov. 10, 1444) put an end to the crises. Mehmed II, who had stayed in Edirne, maintained the throne, and after the battle his father retired to Manisa. Zaganos and Şihâbeddin then began to incite the child sultan to undertake the capture of Constantinople, but Çandarlı engineered a revolt of the Janissaries and called Murad II back to Edirne to resume the throne (May 1446). Mehmed was sent once more to Manisa with Zaganos and Şihâbeddin, newly appointed as his tutors. There Mehmed continued to consider himself the legal sultan.

Second accession in 1451. On his father's death, Mehmed ascended the throne for the second time in Edirne (Feb. 18, 1451). His mind was filled with the idea of the capture of Constantinople. Europe and Byzantium, remembering his former reign, were then not concerned much about his plans. Neither was his authority firmly established within the empire. But he was not long in showing his

Mehmed II, miniature by Sinan Bey, late 15th century; in the Topkapı Sarayı Museum, Istanbul

By courtesy of the Topkapi Sarayi Museum, Istanbul

stature by severely punishing the Janissaries who had dared to threaten him over the delay of the customary gift of accession. Yet he reinforced this military organization, which was destined to be the instrument of his future conquests. He devoted the utmost care to all the necessary diplomatic and military preparations for the capture of Constantinople. To keep Venice and Hungary neutral, he signed peace treaties favourable to them. He spent the year 1452 mainly in building the fortress of Boğazkesen (later Rumeli Hisarı) for the control of the Bosporus, in building a fleet of 31 galleys, and in casting new cannon of large calibre. He made the Hungarian master gunsmith, Urban, cast guns of a size unknown as yet even in Europe. Meanwhile, the grand vizier Çandarlı argued against the enterprise and during the siege of Constantinople (April 6–May 29, 1453), the opposing views were voiced in two war councils convened at critical moments. Zaganos vehemently rejected the proposal to raise the siege. He was given the task of preparing the last great assault. The commander in chief, Mehmed II himself, on the day of the attack personally directed the operations against the breach opened in the city wall by his cannon. The day after the capture of the city, Çandarlı was arrested and soon afterwards was executed in Edirne. He was replaced by Zaganos, who had become Mehmed's father-in-law. Mehmed had had to consent to a three-day sack of the city, but, before the evening of the first day after its capture, he countermanded his order. Entering the city at the head of a procession, he went straight to Hagia Sophia and converted it into a mosque. Afterward he established charitable foundations and provided 14,000 gold ducats per annum for the upkeep and service of the mosque.

One of the tasks on which Mehmed II set his heart was the restoration of the city, now popularly called Istanbul, as a worthy capital of a worldwide empire. To encourage the return of the Greeks and the Genoese of Galata (the trading quarter of the city), who had fled, he returned their houses and provided them with guarantees of safety. In order to repopulate the city, he deported Muslim and Christian groups in Anatolia and the Balkans and forced them to settle in Constantinople. He restored the Greek Orthodox Patriarchate (Jan. 6, 1454) and established a Jewish grand rabbi and an Armenian patriarch in the city. In addition, he founded, and encouraged his viziers to found, a number of Muslim institutions and commercial installations in the main districts of Constantinople. From these nuclei, the metropolis developed rapidly. According to a survey carried out in 1478, there were then in Constantinople and neighbouring Galata 16,324 households and 3,927 shops. Fifty years later, Constantinople had become the largest city in Europe.

Mehmed's empire. The capture of Constantinople bestowed on Mehmed incomparable glory and prestige and immense authority in his own country, so that he began to look upon himself as the heir of the Roman Caesars and the champion of Islām in holy war. It is not true that he had preconceived plans for his conquests, but it is certain that he was intent upon resurrecting the Eastern Roman Empire and upon extending it to its widest historic limits. His victory over the Turkmen leader Uzun Ḥasan at the Battle of Bashkent in Erzincan (Aug. 11, 1473) marked in Mehmed's life a turning point as important as the capture of Constantinople, and it sealed his domination over Anatolia and the Balkans.

Mehmed had assumed the title of Kayser-i Rum (Roman Caesar) and, at the same time, described himself as "the lord of the two lands and the two seas" (*i.e.,* Anatolia and the Balkans, the Aegean and the Black seas), a designation that reflected his idea of the empire. During the quarter-century after the fall of Constantinople, he undertook a series of campaigns or expeditions in the Balkans, Hungary, Walachia, Moldavia, Anatolia, the island of Rhodes, and even as far as the Crimea and Otranto in southern Italy. This last enterprise (1480) indicated that he intended to invade Italy in a new attempt at founding a world empire. The following spring, having just begun a new campaign in Anatolia, he died 15½ miles (25 kilometres) from Constantinople. Gout, from which he had suffered for some time, in his last days had tortured him grievously, but, there are indications that he was poisoned.

During the autocrat's last years, his relations with his eldest son Bayezid became very strained, as Bayezid did not always obey his orders. Mehmed's financial measures resulted, toward the end of his reign, in widespread discontent throughout the country, especially when he distributed as military fiefs about 20,000 villages and farms that had previously belonged to pious foundations or the landed gentry. Thus, at his death, the malcontents placed Bayezid on the throne, discarding the Sultan's favourite son, Cem (Jem), and initiated a reaction against Mehmed's policies.

Achievements. The conqueror reorganized the Ottoman government and, for the first time, codified the criminal law and the laws relating to his subjects in one code, whereas the constitution was elaborated in another, the two codes forming the nucleus of all subsequent legislation. In the utterly autocratic personality of the conqueror, the classical image of an Ottoman padishah (emperor) was born. He punished with the utmost severity those who resisted his decrees and laws, and even his Ottoman contemporaries considered him excessively hard.

Nevertheless, Mehmed may be considered the most broadminded and freethinking of the Ottoman sultans. After the fall of Constantinople, he gathered Italian Humanists and Greek scholars at his court; he caused the patriarch Gennadius II Scholarios to write a credo of the Christian faith and had it translated into Turkish; he collected in his palace a library of works in Greek and Latin. He called Gentile Bellini from Venice to decorate the walls of his palace with frescoes as well as to paint his portrait (now in the National Gallery, London). Around the grand mosque that he constructed, he erected eight colleges, which, for nearly a century, kept their rank as the highest teaching institutions of the Islāmic sciences in the empire. At times, he assembled the *'ulamā',* or learned Muslim teachers, and caused them to discuss theological problems in his presence. In his reign, mathematics, astronomy, and Muslim theology reached their highest level among the Ottomans. And Mehmed himself left a divan (a collection of poems in the traditional style of classical Ottoman literature). (H.I.)

BIBLIOGRAPHY. Franz Babinger, *Mehmed der Eroberer und seine Zeit* (1953), is the most detailed account of the subject by an authority, reviewed by Halil Inalcik, "Mehmed the Conqueror (1432–1481) and His Time," in *Speculum,* 35:408–427 (1960). See also *Cambridge History of Islam,* pp. 295–308 (1970); and Steven Runciman, *The Fall of Constantinople, 1453* (1965). The main sources on the subject are given in H. Inalcik, "Mehmed II," in *Islam Ansiklopedisi,* 7:506–535 (in Turkish).

•Mehmed III (b. 1566, Manisa, Ottoman Empire—d. Dec. 22, 1603, Constantinople), Ottoman sultan (1595–1603) whose reign saw a long and arduous conflict with Austria and serious revolts in Anatolia.

At the outset of Mehmed's reign, the war against Austria, already in progress for two years, was accelerated by an alliance between Austria and the Danubian principalities of Moldavia, Transylvania, and Walachia. Following the Ottoman loss of Gran (Esztergom, Hung.) in 1595 to the Christian allies, Mehmed himself participated in the campaign of 1596, which saw the Ottoman conquest of Erlau (Eger) and victory at Hachova (Mező-Kersztes). In 1601, following a continuous war of sieges, the Ottomans took the fortress of Kanizsa.

Meanwhile, in Anatolia, the decline of Ottoman institutions, particularly the land-tenure system, resulted in extensive revolts by the *sipahiyan* (cavalry based on quasi-feudal land units) and by the peasants, who were oppressed by taxes. While the Ottoman government struggled to suppress these revolts, war with Iran broke out in 1603.

•Mehmed IV Avcı (Hunter) (b. Jan. 2, 1642, Constantinople—d. Jan. 6, 1693, Edirne, Ottoman Empire), Ottoman sultan whose reign (1648–87) was marked first by administrative and financial decay and later by a period of revival under the able Köprülü viziers. Mehmed IV, however, devoted himself to hunting rather than to affairs of state.

Mehmed succeeded his mentally ill father, İbrahim, at the age of six. Power was exercised by factions led by his grandmother and mother while the chiefs of the Janissary corps dominated the state administration. During this period revolts broke out in Constantinople and Anatolia, and a series of grand viziers sought in vain to solve the empire's financial crisis. The emergence of the Köprülüs as grand viziers offered temporary domestic relief and ushered in a period of victories against Venice in the Mediterranean and against Austria and Poland in the Balkans.

Mehmed IV participated in the military campaigns against Austria (1663) and Poland (1672); his primary interest, however, remained the pursuit of new hunting grounds. He opposed his grand vizier Merzifonlu Kara Mustafa Paşa's grandiose scheme to conquer Vienna but was unable to prevent him from entering into a disastrous war with Austria. The subsequent Ottoman defeats led to Mehmed's deposition (Nov. 7, 1687). He spent the last three years of his life in retirement in Edirne.

•Mehmed V, original name MEHMED REŞAD (b. Nov. 2, 1844, Constantinople—d. July 3, 1918, Constantinople), Ottoman sultan from 1909 to 1918, whose reign was marked by the absolute rule of the Committee of Union and Progress and by Turkey's defeat in World War I.

Mehmed V
EB Inc.

Having lived in seclusion most of his life, Mehmed Reşad became sultan after his brother Abdülhamid II was forced to abdicate. A kind and gentle man, educated in traditional Islāmic subjects and Persian literature, he showed a keen interest in Ottoman and Islāmic history; nevertheless, he lacked the ability to govern. Attempting to rule as a constitutional monarch, he surrendered all authority to the Committee of Union and Progress, the liberal–nationalist organization of the Young Turk movement.

On the advice of the committee, the Sultan went on a goodwill tour of Thrace and Albania (1911). In the two Balkan Wars during 1912–13, however, the Ottomans lost almost all their European possessions, and, in the war with Italy (1911–12), Tripoli was lost. Although Mehmed was opposed, the Ottoman Empire entered World War I on the side of Germany and Austria-Hungary, and, as caliph, he declared holy war and invited all Muslims, especially those under the rule of the Allies, to rally to the support of Ottomans. By the time of Mehmed's death, most of the empire had fallen to the Allies, and six months later Constantinople was under military occupation.

• **Mehmed VI,** original name MEHMED VAHIDEDDIN (b. Jan. 14, 1861—d. May 16, 1926, San Remo, Italy), the last sultan of the Ottoman Empire, whose forced abdication

Mehmed VI, portrait by an unknown artist
By courtesy of the Topkapi Saray Muzesi Mudurlugu, Istanbul

and exile in 1922 prepared the way for the emergence of the Turkish Republic under the leadership of Mustafa Kemal Atatürk within a year.

Clever and perceptive, Mehmed VI became sultan July 4, 1918, and attempted to follow the example of his elder brother Abdülhamid II (reigned 1876–1909) by assuming personal control of the government. After the Armistice of Mudros (Oct. 30, 1918) and the establishment of the Allied military administration in Istanbul on Dec. 8, 1918, the nationalist–liberal Committee of Union and Progress had collapsed, and its leaders had fled abroad. The Sultan, opposed to all nationalist ideologies and anxious to perpetuate the Ottoman dynasty, acceded to the demands of the Allies. On December 21 he dissolved Parliament and undertook to crush the nationalists.

The nationalists, however, who were organizing in Anatolia under the leadership of Mustafa Kemal, sought the Sultan's support in their struggle for territorial integrity and national independence. After negotiations, the Sultan agreed to elections, which were held late in 1919, and the nationalists won a majority in the new parliament. The Allies, alarmed at the prospect of Turkish unity, extended the occupied area in Constantinople and arrested and exiled the nationalists.

The Sultan dissolved the Parliament (April 11, 1920), and the nationalists set up a provisional government in Ankara. Mehmed's signing of the Treaty of Sèvres (Aug. 10, 1920), however, reduced the empire to little but Turkey itself and served to strengthen the nationalist cause. After their defeat of the Greeks, the nationalists were in solid control of Turkey. The Grand National Assembly on Nov. 1, 1922, abolished the sultanate. Sixteen days later Mehmed VI boarded a British warship and fled to Malta. His later attempts to install himself as caliph in the Hejaz failed.

Mehmed Ağa, Ağa also spelled ĀGHĀ (fl. late 16th century and early 17th century, Turkey), an architect whose masterpiece is the Sultan Ahmed Cami (Blue Mosque) in Istanbul.

Sultan Ahmed Cami (Blue Mosque), Istanbul, by Mehmed Ağa, 1609–16
Shostal—EB Inc.

Mehmed went to Constantinople (Istanbul) in 1567 and began the study of music but later switched to architecture. He became a pupil of Sinan, Turkey's most celebrated architect. In 1606 Mehmed Ağa was named royal architect to the Ottoman court.

From 1609 until 1616 he worked on the Sultan Ahmed Cami, called the Blue Mosque because of the colour of its tile work. The design of the mosque was based on the Hagia Sophia (Church of Holy Wisdom), the masterpiece of Byzantine architecture built in the 6th century, and on the work of his master, Sinan. The design of the mosque is perfectly symmetrical, with a great centre dome buttressed by four semidomes and surrounded by a number of smaller domes.

Mehmed had a book on architecture theory written for him by Cafer Efendi. In it he explained the methods of work and the architectural training of the period.

Mehmed Es'ad: *see* Gâlib Dede.

Mehmed Fuat Köprülü, also known as KÖPRÜLÜZADE (b. Dec. 5, 1890, Constantinople—d. June 28, 1966, Istanbul), scholar, historian, and statesman who made important contributions to the history of Turkey and its literature.

A descendant of the famous 17th-century Ottoman prime ministers (grand viziers), Köprülü began teaching at the famous Galatasaray Lycée (secondary school) in Constantinople and in 1913 occupied the chair of Turkish literature at Istanbul University. Later he became dean of the Faculty of Letters there and founder and first director of the *Tükiyat Enstitüsü* (Institute of Turkology).

Turning to politics in 1936, he became a member of Parliament and finally foreign minister (1950–54). A brilliant and prolific scholar, he exerted influence in Turkish intellectual circles even after his death. He wrote many books on Turkish literature and history, among them *Türk edebiyatında ilk mutasavvıflar* (1919; "The First Mystics in Turkish Literature"), a penetrating analysis of the confluence of Central Asian and Islāmic streams of mysticism and its subsequent effect on Turkish literature; and a masterly revision of earlier American and European historians' theories of the rise of the Ottoman Empire, *Les Origines de l'empire Ottoman* (1935; "The Origins of the Ottoman Empire").

Mehmed Siyah-Kalem (fl. 15th century, Turkestan or Iran), artist known solely by the attribution of his name to a remarkable series of paintings preserved in the Imperial Ottoman Palace Library (Topkapı Saray).

Nothing is known of his life, but his work indicates that he was of Central Asian (presumably Turkish) origin, and thoroughly familiar with camp and military life. The paintings appear in the "Conqueror's Albums," so named because two portraits of Sultan Mehmed II the Conqueror are present in one of them. The albums are made up of miniatures taken from manuscripts of the 14th, 15th, and early 16th centuries, and one series of paintings is inscribed "work of Master Muḥammad Siyah Kalem." Something of the style and techniques of Chinese paintings is apparent in these, and an acquaintance with Buddhist art, particularly in the depictions of grotesque demonic figures. There also is evident a mordant humour and a personal vision of men or animals as little better than devils, and this may be the origin of the painter's name Siyah-Kalem (Black Pen). These paintings show a pessimistic forcefulness and realism wholly lacking in Persian art of the 15th century, and it is possible that they provided a major influence on Turkish painting, which departed from the idyllic, languid, and romantic path taken by Persian art.

Mehmed Talât Paşa: *see* Talât Paşa.

Mehmet (Arabic or Turkish personal name): *see under* Mahmud, Mehmed, Muḥammad, or Mohammed.

Mehring, Franz (b. Feb. 27, 1846, Schlawe, Pomerania—d. Jan. 28, 1919, Berlin), radical journalist, historian of the German Social Democratic Party, and biographer of Karl Marx.

Originally a middle-class democrat, he moved gradually leftward, for a time with the General German Workers' Union of Ferdinand Lassalle, then (1883–88) at the head of the left-liberal newspaper *Berliner Volkszeitung,* and finally to his affiliation with the Social Democrats in 1890. Thereafter, he edited the Socialist *Leipziger Volkszeitung* and served on the staff of the party's official *Neue Zeit* ("New Age"). In 1914 he joined with his radical left colleagues, Rosa Luxemburg and Karl Liebknecht, in opposing Germany's participation in World War I and in 1916 sided with the revolutionary-pacifist Spartacists. His contributions to the historical literature of German Socialism include *Geschichte der deutschen Sozialdemocratie*, 4 vol. (1897–98; "History of German Social Democracy") and *Karl Marx: Geschichte seines Lebens* (1918; "Karl Marx: A Biography").

Mehsāna, town, administrative headquarters of Mehsāna district, Gujarāt state, west central

Surya (Sun god) temple in Modhera, Mehsāna district, Gujarāt, India
Baldev—Shostal Assoc./EB Inc.

India, in the lowlands between the Arāvalli Range and the Little Rann of Kutch. Founded in the 12th to the 14th century by the Chāvada Rājputs, the old town is believed to have had four gates, of which only one remains. Rājmahal, built by the Marāṭhā ruler of Baroda (now Vadodara), Sayaji Rao III, is an imposing structure. The town is a centre of marketing and manufacturing. It is a major junction of the Western Railway and several highways. Pop. (1981) 72,872.

Mehta, Sir Pherozeshah (b. Aug. 4, 1845, Bombay, India—d. Nov. 5, 1915, Bombay), Indian political leader, planner of Bombay's municipal charter and founder of the English-language newspaper *Bombay Chronicle* (1913).

The son of a middle-class Parsi foreign trader, Mehta studied law in England for four years, was called to the bar in 1868, and then returned home. During a legal defense of a Bombay commissioner, Arthur Crawford, he noted the need for municipal government reforms and later drew up the Municipal Act of 1872, for which he was called the "father of municipal government in Bombay." He became a commissioner himself in 1873 and served as chairman in 1884–85 and in 1905. A member of the Bombay Legislative Council from 1886, he was elected to the governor-general's Supreme Legislative Council in 1893. He presided over the sixth session of the Indian National Congress in 1890. He was knighted in 1904. After a trip to England in 1910, Mehta was appointed a vice chancellor of the University of Bombay. In 1911 he helped found the Central Bank of India, financed and controlled by Indian interests.

Mehta, Zubin (b. April 29, 1936, Bombay, India), orchestral conductor, musical director of the Los Angeles Philharmonic Orchestra (1962–78), the New York Philharmonic Orchestra (1978–91), and the Israel Philharmonic (from 1968).

Mehta's father, Mehli Mehta, a violinist, helped found the Bombay String Quartet and the Bombay Symphony Orchestra, and Zubin was surrounded by Western music as a child. He studied at the Vienna Academy of Music. In 1958 he won first prize in the Liverpool International Conductor's Competition and became assistant conductor of the Royal Liverpool Philharmonic for a year. His reputation grew swiftly. He made guest appearances all over the world, and he was musical director of the Montreal Symphony from 1961 to 1967. He served in the same position for the Los Angeles Philharmonic from 1962, making him the first conductor to direct two major North American orchestras simultaneously. In 1965 he made his debut at the Metropolitan Opera in New York City with a performance of *Aida;* his London opera debut occurred in 1977 (*Otello*). In 1968 he became chief music adviser to the Israel Philharmonic Orchestra.

Zubin Mehta, 1986
Bachrach

In 1978 Mehta replaced Pierre Boulez as musical director of the New York Philharmonic Orchestra. He expressed special interest in the late Romantic and early modern composers. Mehta was a flamboyant conductor whose gestures provided musical cues for the audience.

Méhul, Étienne-Nicolas (b. June 22, 1763, Givet, Ardennes, Fr.—d. Oct. 18, 1817, Paris), composer who influenced the development of French opera and who was one of the principal composers in the late 18th- and early 19th-century style.

Méhul, lithograph by A. Maurin
J.P. Ziolo

In 1782 Méhul produced a cantata at the Concert Spirituel on a text by Jean-Jacques Rousseau. Influenced by Christoph Gluck and Luigi Cherubini, he turned to dramatic music and between 1787 and 1822 composed more than 40 operas, produced mainly at the Opéra-Comique. His first performed opera was *Euphrosine et Coradin, ou le tyran corrigé* (1790; *Euphrosine and Coradin, or the Tyrant Corrected*). His most successful works were *Le Jeune Henri* (1797), *Les Deux Aveugles de Tolède* (1806; *The Two Blind Men of Toledo*), *Uthal* (1806), and *Joseph* (1807). He also wrote patriotic works, demanding great choral and orchestral resources, to mark festive occasions of the French Revolution, such as the *Hymne à la raison* (1793).

Méhul had a bold sense of harmony and original gifts as a dramatist and orchestrator, although he was poorly served by his librettists. His operas emphasized the orchestra's role in opera; frequently he chose a theme that was developed symphonically as the dramatic action progressed. Besides writing operas he wrote piano sonatas, chamber works, and symphonic works. His influence on younger composers was considerable.

Mei-chou, Pinyin MEIZHOU, formerly MEI-HSIEN, Pinyin MEIXIAN, city in northeastern Kwangtung *sheng* (province), China. It is situated on the north bank of the Mei River, a tributary of the Han River, which discharges into the sea at Swatow. A county was established there in the late 5th century. It became the seat of a prefecture (*chou*) in the early 10th century and received the name Mei in 971; the prefecture was abolished in 1368. The Ch'ing dynasty (1644–1911), however, established a superior prefecture (*fu*) there under the name Chia-ying. In 1912 it reverted to county status and took the name Mei-hsien. It received its new name, Mei-chou, in 1991. Mei-chou is the chief collecting centre for the produce of the Mei River basin, which lies behind the coastal ranges of Kwangtung; this produce is exported to Swatow. The city lies in an area mostly inhabited by the Hakka. Pop. (1989 est.) 125,300.

Mei Lanfang, Wade-Giles romanization MEI LAN-FANG (b. 1894, T'ai-chou, Kiangsu province, China—d. August 1961, Peking), Chinese theatrical performer, one of the greatest singer-actor-dancers in Chinese history.

The son and grandson of noted opera singers, Mei began studying at the Peking Opera at the age of 8 and made his debut onstage at 12, playing a weaving girl. Thereafter he played mostly female roles, becoming especially known for his portrayal of the "Flower-shattering Diva"; his style of dance won such acclaim over the years that it came to be known as the "Mei Lanfang school." At age 14 he had joined the Hsi-lien-ch'eng Theatrical Company and, through performances in Shanghai and elsewhere, acquired a national reputation. He toured Japan in 1919 and 1924, the United States in 1930, and the Soviet Union in 1932 and 1935.

After the outbreak of the Sino-Japanese War he settled in Hong Kong (1937) but returned to Shanghai following the Japanese seizure of the territory and withdrew from the theatre for five years, resuming his career only in 1946. Thereafter he did both stage and film work and served as director or member of several cultural organizations. He was also active in the Chinese Communist Party.

mei p'ing, Pinyin MEI PING, English PRUNUS VASE, type of Chinese pottery vase popular especially during the Sung (960–1279) and Ming (1368–1644) periods, the shape inspired by the youthful female breast. Often a tall celadon vase with a short, narrow neck, it was meant to hold a single branch of plum tree blossoms. Most Ming examples are white porcelain painted in underglaze blue.

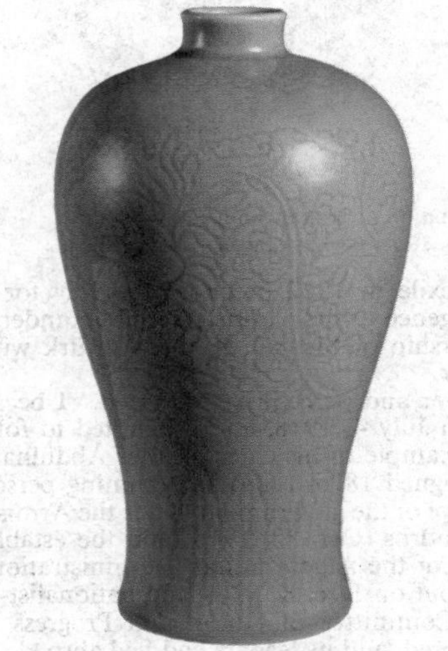
Mei p'ing porcelain vase with a celadon glaze decorated with incised floral motifs, Ch'ing dynasty, reign of Yung-cheng (1722–35); in the Victoria and Albert Museum, London
By courtesy of the Victoria and Albert Museum, London

Mei Yao-ch'en, Pinyin MEI YAOCHEN, courtesy name (*tzu*) SHENG-YÜ (b. 1002, Hsüan-ch'eng, China—d. 1060, Kaifeng), a leading Chinese poet of the Northern Sung dynasty whose verses helped to launch a new poetic style linked with the *ku-wen,* or "ancient literature," revival.

Although Mei entered government service through the examination system like other statesmen-poets of the Sung, his political career was undistinguished. While in office, however, he met and became friends with Ou-yang Hsiu (1007–1072), then a minor official and leading advocate of the *ku-wen* movement. Deeply influenced by Neo-Confucian ideals, proponents of this movement felt that literature should mirror and comment on contemporary life. Mei thus made social and political issues the focus of his poetry and sought subjects in commonplace events and people. Rejecting the then-fashionable *tz'u* poetry, which derived from romantic ballads and employed elaborate conceits and hyperbole, Mei returned to the old *lü-shih,* or "regulated poetry," perfecting a plainer, more prosaic style to gain what he called an "easygoing" voice better suited to his themes and subjects.

Meidias Painter (fl. late 5th and early 4th centuries BC), Greek vase painter known for his theatrical "florid" style and for his "flying drapery." A large hydria (water vessel), dating from *c.* 410 BC, now in the British Museum,

"Phaon in a Bower with Demonassa," hydria by the Meidias Painter, *c.* 410 BC; in the Museo Archeologico, Florence
SCALA—Art Resource/EB Inc.

is representative of his work. Painted on it are scenes from the stories of the "Rape of the Daughters of Leucippus" and "Heracles in the Garden of the Hesperides." Also attributed to him are a hydria with "Adonis Seated on the Lap of Aphrodite" (now in Florence), and a toilet box cover with "Women and Cupids" (now in the Ashmolean Museum at Oxford).

Meier, Richard, in full RICHARD ALAN MEIER (b. Oct. 12, 1934, Newark, N.J., U.S.), American architect noted for his refinements of and variations on classic Modernist principles.

Meier graduated from Cornell University in Ithaca, N.Y.; his early experience included work with the firm of Skidmore, Owings and Merrill in New York City and with Marcel Breuer, a noted exponent of the International Style of architecture. In 1963 Meier formed his own firm. Early on he received critical acclaim for the Smith House (1965–67) in Darien, Conn., the first of his so-called white buildings, which clearly built upon the pristine Modernism of Le Corbusier's work in the 1920s and '30s. During this period he formed a loose association with a group of young architects, known as the "New York Five," who advocated a return to Modernist, rational architecture. He received more attention for his Douglas House (1971–73), an archetypal example of his work located in Harbor Springs, Mich. Like much of his work, it features intersecting planes and, in its crisp geometric whiteness, it provides a sharp contrast to the natural setting that surrounds it.

Building upon the success of his series of spectacular private residences, starting in the mid-1970s Meier began to receive large public commissions, including the Athenaeum (1975–79) in New Harmony, Ind.; the Museum of Decorative Arts (1979–85) in Frankfurt am Main, Ger.; the High Museum of Art (1980–83) in Atlanta, Ga.; and the Museum of Contemporary Art (1987–95) in Barcelona, Spain. These structures are characterized by geometric clarity and order, which is often punctuated by curving ramps and railings, and by a contrast between the light-filled transparent surfaces of public spaces and the solid white surfaces of interior, private spaces. While some critics have found these structures too austere and reminiscent of past architectural achievement, others have applauded their formal beauty and welcomed their purity in the midst of the often jumbled forms of Postmodernist architecture.

From 1985 to 1997, Meier focused much of his attention on the Getty Center in Los Angeles. Comprising six principal buildings that house the Getty collection and educational facilities, the centre reflects Meier's lifelong explorations with pure form and light.

Meier received numerous awards from the American Institute of Architects (AIA) and other architectural associations. In 1984 he won the prestigious Pritzker Prize.

Meighen, Arthur (b. June 16, 1874, near Anderson, Ont., Can.—d. Aug. 5, 1960, Toronto), Conservative Party leader and the youngest prime minister of Canada (1920–21; 1926).

Elected to Parliament in 1908 from Portage la Prairie, Man., where he practiced law, in 1913 Meighen became solicitor general and subsequently held Cabinet posts in Robert (later Sir Robert) Borden's government. When the Conservatives and some Liberals formed a Union Government in 1917, Meighen became minister of the interior. Meighen worked effectively to implement the controversial policies of the Borden government, which enlarged Canada's role in world affairs. During his first term as prime minister, he waged a successful campaign in 1921 against renewal of the Anglo-Japanese alliance. Convinced that the chief threat to Canada's national existence came from the economic power of the U.S., he advocated a protective tariff system. Meighen's second term was cut short by his party's defeat in the House of Commons and the subsequent general election. When the Liberal Party was in power, Meighen served intermittently as leader of the opposition.

Meigs, Montgomery C(unningham) (b. May 3, 1816, Augusta, Ga., U.S.—d. Jan. 2, 1892, Washington, D.C.), U.S. engineer and architect, who, as quartermaster general of the Union Army during the American Civil War, was responsible for the purchase and distribution of vital supplies to Union troops. As U.S. quartermaster general in the years before and after the war, he supervised the construction of numerous buildings and public works projects in the Washington, D.C., area.

After graduation from the University of Pennsylvania (1831) and the U.S. military academy (1836), Meigs was assigned to the Army corps of engineers. In this capacity he supervised several important government projects, including the construction of the wings and dome of the Capitol and the expansion of the Post Office. His most substantial contribution, however, was the Washington Aqueduct, which extended 12 miles (19 kilometres) from the Great Falls on the Potomac to a distribution reservoir west of Georgetown. The Cabin John Bridge (1852–60), designed to carry Washington's main water supply and vehicular traffic, is an engineering masterpiece. Until the 20th century it was, at 220 feet, the longest single masonry arch in the world. The other major bridge forming part of the aqueduct system was Meigs's cast-iron Pennsylvania Avenue Bridge (replaced by the present Rock Creek Bridge in 1916).

Meigs's best known architectural work in Washington, D.C.—undertaken after his official retirement—is the Old Pension Building (1883) in Judiciary Square, originally intended as a pension distribution centre for veterans of the Union Army. Modelled after the Farnese Palace in Rome, the structure is essentially a huge brick shell, covering a rectangular interior space of about 30,000 square feet. The exterior is decorated with a terra-cotta frieze in low relief depicting Union forces in battle. The building was used for the inaugural festivities of presidents Cleveland, Harrison, McKinley, Roosevelt, and Taft.

It was Meigs who suggested to Abraham Lincoln that Arlington would be an appropriate site for a national cemetery. Meigs himself is buried there.

Meiji, in full MEIJI TENNŌ, personal name MUTSUHITO (b. Nov. 3, 1852, Kyōto—d. July 30, 1912, Tokyo), emperor of Japan from 1867 to 1912, during whose reign Japan was dramatically transformed from a feudal country into one of the great powers of the modern world.

The second son of the emperor Kōmei, Mutsuhito was declared crown prince in 1860; following the death of his father in 1866 he was raised to the throne (1867). In 1868 his coronation ceremony was carried out, and he took the name Meiji, by which the era of his reign is also known. Meiji's accession to the throne coincided with the end of the Tokugawa Shogunate and the restoration to the emperor of supreme executive authority in the country. Unlike Kōmei, he supported the growing popular consensus on the need for modernization of Japan along Western lines that had developed as a result of the country's resumption of contact with other nations after a 250-year period of cultural and economic isolation. In 1868 Meiji took the "Charter Oath of Five Principles," which launched Japan on the course of Westernization. As emperor he ordered, though he did not initiate, the abolition of the feudal land system (1871), the creation of a new school system (1872), adoption of the cabinet system of government (1885), promulgation of the Meiji Constitution (1889), and

Meiji Tennō, portrait by G. Molinari, 1897
By courtesy of the Consulate General of Japan, New York

opening of the Diet (1890). He played active roles in the prosecution of the Sino-Japanese War (1894–95) and the Russo-Japanese War (1904–05). In 1910 he issued an edict proclaiming the annexation of Korea to Japan.

Meiji himself epitomized the superimposition of Western ideas and innovations onto a base of Japanese culture; he wore Western clothes and ate Western-style food but also managed to compose 100,000 poems in the traditional Japanese style during his lifetime.

Meiji Restoration, in Japanese history, the political revolution that brought about the fall of the Tokugawa Shogunate and returned control of the country to direct Imperial rule under the emperor Meiji, beginning an era of major political, economic, and social change known as the Meiji period (1868–1912). This revolution brought about the modernization and Westernization of Japan.

The leaders of the restoration, mostly young samurai from feudal domains historically hostile to Tokugawa authority, were motivated by growing domestic problems and the threat of foreign encroachment. Adopting the slogan "wealthy country and strong arms" (*fukoku-kyōhei*), they sought to create a nation-state capable of standing equal among Western powers. As expressed in the Charter Oath of 1868, the first goal of the new government, relocated to Tokyo (formerly Edo), was the dismantling of the old feudal regime. This was largely accomplished by 1871, when the domains were officially abolished and replaced by a prefecture system. All feudal class privileges were also abolished. In the same year, a national army was formed, which was further strengthened in 1873 by a universal conscription law. The new government also carried out policies to unify the monetary and tax systems, with the agricultural tax reform of 1873 providing its primary source of income.

The revolutionary changes carried out by restoration leaders acting in the name of the emperor faced increasing opposition in the mid-1870s. Disgruntled samurai participated in several rebellions against the government, the most famous being led by the former restoration hero Saigō Takamori. These uprisings were repressed only with great difficulty by the newly formed army. Peasants, distrustful of the new regime and dissatisfied by its agrarian policies, also took part in revolts that reached their peak in the 1880s. At the same time, a growing popular rights movement, encouraged by the introduction of liberal Western ideas, called for the creation of a constitutional government and wider participation through deliberative assemblies. Responding to these pressures, the government issued a statement in 1881 promising a constitution by 1890. In 1885 a Cabinet system was formed, and in 1886 work on the constitution began. Finally in 1889 the constitution, presented as a gift from the emperor to the people, was officially promulgated. It established a bicameral parliament, called the Diet (*gikai*), to be elected through a limited voting franchise. The first Diet was convened the following year, 1890.

Economic and social changes paralleled the political transformation of the Meiji period. Although the economy remained dependent on agriculture, industrialization was the primary goal of the government, which directed the development of strategic industries, transportation, and communications. The first railroad was built in 1872, and by 1890 there were more than 1,400 miles (2,250 km) of rail. The telegraph linked all major cities by 1880. Private firms were also encouraged by government financial support and aided by the institution of a European-style banking system in 1882. These efforts at modernization required Western science and technology, and under the banner of "Civilization and Enlightenment" (*bunmei kaika*) Western culture, from current intellectual trends to clothing and architecture, was widely promoted. Wholesale Westernization was somewhat checked in the 1880s, however, when a renewed appreciation of traditional Japanese values emerged. Such was the case in the development of a modern educational system which, though influenced by Western theory and practice, stressed the traditional values of samurai loyalty and social harmony. The same tendency prevailed in art and literature, where Western styles were first imitated, and then a more selective blending of Western and Japanese tastes was achieved.

By the early 20th century, the goals of the Meiji Restoration had been largely accomplished. Japan was well on its way to becoming a modern industrial nation. The unequal treaties that had granted foreign powers judicial and economic privileges through extraterritoriality were revised in 1894; and with the Anglo-Japanese Alliance of 1902 and its victory in two wars (over China in 1895 and Russia in 1905), Japan gained respect in the eyes of the Western world, appearing for the first time on the international scene as a major world power. The death of the emperor Meiji in 1912 marked the end of the period.

Consult the INDEX *first*

Meikle, Andrew (b. 1719, Scotland—d. Nov. 27, 1811, Houston Mill, near Dunbar, East Lothian), Scottish millwright and inventor of the threshing machine for removing the husks from grain.

During most of his life Meikle was a millwright at Houston Mill. In 1778 he constructed his first threshing machine, probably basing its design on a device patented in 1734 by Michael Menzies. The machine was a failure, as was a second, developed from a Northumberland model. Meikle analyzed these threshers and constructed a strong drum with fixed beaters that beat rather than rubbed the grain. The drum that made Meikle's machine a success may have been copied from the flax-scutching machine used to beat the fibres from flax plants. He took out a patent in 1788 and probably began manufacture a year later; he does not seem to have realized a fortune from his invention, inasmuch as a subscription for his relief was started in 1809. Meikle also devised a method for rapidly furling the sails of windmills to prevent damage from storms.

Meillet, Antoine (b. Nov. 11, 1866, Moulins, Fr.—d. Sept. 21, 1936, Châteaumeillant), one of the most influential linguists of his time. Using a comparative method of utmost precision, he clearly explained the early Indo-European linguistic system and traced its history. He steadily emphasized that any attempt to account for linguistic change must recognize that language is a social phenomenon. He also explored the psychological factors in sound changes.

In 1891 Meillet became director of comparative Indo-European studies at the School of Advanced Studies in Paris and taught Armenian from 1902 until 1906, when he was appointed a professor at the Collège de France. In 1903 he published what is generally considered his most important work, *Introduction à l'étude comparative des langues indo-européennes* ("Introduction to the Comparative Study of the Indo-European Languages"), which explained the relationships of the languages to one another and to the parent Indo-European tongue. Advancing a theory of linguistic differentiation, he suggested that languages that developed farther away from a centre of common origin are less disturbed by changes initiated at the point of origin and may retain archaic characteristics in common. Around the early 1900s he produced his authoritative *Esquisse de la grammaire comparée de l'arménien classique* (1902; "Outline of a Comparative Grammar of Classical Armenian") and also made the first of his notable contributions to Slavic studies. Part of his prodigious effort went into studies of the Germanic, Baltic, and Celtic languages; he made fundamental contributions to Old Iranian, notably with a grammar (1915), and produced two outstanding works (1913 and 1928) on the historical contexts and significance of Greek and Latin. In a number of articles he related sociological factors to changes in word meanings and other linguistic phenomena.

Mein Kampf (German: "My Struggle"), political manifesto written by Adolf Hitler. It was his only complete book and became the bible of National Socialism (Nazism) in Germany's Third Reich. It was published in two volumes in 1925 and 1927, and an abridged edition appeared in 1930. By 1939 it had sold 5.2 million copies and had been translated into 11 languages.

The first volume, entitled *Die Abrechnung* ("The Settlement [of Accounts]," or "Revenge"), was written in 1924 in the Bavarian fortress of Landsberg am Lech, where Hitler was imprisoned after the abortive Beer Hall Putsch of 1923. It treats the world of Hitler's youth, the First World War, and the "betrayal" of Germany's collapse in 1918; it also expresses Hitler's racist ideology, identifying the Aryan as the "genius" race and the Jew as the "parasite," and declares the need for Germans to seek living space (*Lebensraum*) in the East at the expense of the Slavs and the hated Marxists of Russia. It also calls for revenge against France.

According to Hitler, it was "the sacred mission of the German people . . . to assemble and preserve the most valuable racial elements . . . and raise them to the dominant position." "All who are not of a good race are chaff," wrote Hitler. It was necessary for Germans to "occupy themselves not merely with the breeding of dogs, horses, and cats but also with care for the purity of their own blood." Hitler ascribed international significance to the elimination of Jews, which "must necessarily be a bloody process," he wrote.

The second volume, entitled *Die Nationalsozialistische Bewegung* ("The National Socialist Movement"), written after Hitler's release from prison in December 1924, outlines the political program, including the terrorist methods, that National Socialism had to pursue both in gaining power and in exercising it thereafter in the new Germany.

In style, *Mein Kampf* has been appropriately deemed turgid, repetitious, wandering, illogical, and, in the first edition at least, filled with grammatical errors—all reflecting a half-educated man. It was skillfully demagogic, however, appealing to many dissatisfied elements in Germany—the ultranationalistic, the anti-Semitic, the antidemocratic, the anti-Marxist, and the military.

Postwar German law banned the sale and public display of books espousing Nazi philosophy. Even at the end of the 20th century, the foreign publication of *Mein Kampf* brought condemnation both in Germany and in the countries where the book was published, not least because of its popularity with neo-Nazi groups, especially those that arose in Germany in the 1990s. There also was great concern in some circles over the availability of this book from Internet-based booksellers.

Meinecke, Friedrich (b. Oct. 30, 1862, Salzwedel, Prussia—d. Feb. 6, 1954, Berlin), the leading German historian of the first half

Meinecke, 1942

Archiv fur Kunst und Geschichte, Berlin

of the 20th century and, together with his teacher Wilhelm Dilthey, a founding father of modern intellectual historiography.

Meinecke was a professor at Strassburg (1901), Freiburg im Breisgau (1906), and Berlin (1914–28) and was editor of the *Historische Zeitschrift,* Germany's most important historical journal, from 1896 until he was dismissed during the Nazi regime in 1935.

Meinecke's development from an admirer of Bismarck and the power state to a moderate liberal who emphasized Humanist values in the German past is reflected in his works. In *Weltbürgertum und Nationalstaat* (1908; *Cosmopolitanism and the National State*), he optimistically traced Germany's emergence from the cosmopolitanism of the 18th century to the nationalism of the 19th. His *Idee der Staatsräson in der neueren Geschichte* (1924; *Machiavellism; the Doctrine of Raison d'État and Its Place in Modern History*) has been read as both a handbook and a condemnation of power politics. In it he questioned the validity of the notion that the sovereign state is the embodiment of the highest ethical values and that political necessity justifies the breaking of moral laws. The book reflects the contradiction between power and morality in which Meinecke found himself involved as a result of World War I. He saw that war as a demonstration of the bankruptcy of the German ruling class and, acknowledging the necessity of a thorough change, became an unenthusiastic but loyal defender of the Weimar Republic.

Die Entstehung des Historismus (1936; *Historism*) traces the rise of historicism from Giambattista Vico to Leopold von Ranke. Meinecke's emphasis on the importance of the private concerns of individuals implied a clear opposition to the Nazis, who valued a person only as an instrument of the state's aims. In a smaller work, *Die deutsche Katastrophe* (1946; *The German Catastrophe*), Meinecke criticized forces and entities such as the Prussian state for preparing the groundwork for Hitler and the Nazis. After World War II he became the first president of the Free University of Berlin. In his later years he wrote a number of essays on the problems of historical theory, disclaiming any notion, however, of attempting to formulate a system of historical philosophy.

Meinesz, Felix Andries Vening (Dutch geodesist): *see* Vening Meinesz, Felix Andries.

Meinhof, Carl (b. July 23, 1857, Barzwitz, near Schlawe, Pomerania, Prussia [now in Pol.]—d. Feb. 10, 1944, Greifswald, Ger.), German scholar of African languages and one of the first to give them scientific treatment. He studied primarily the Bantu languages but also Hottentot, Bushman, and Hamitic. Alice Werner published a popularization of his ideas in *The Language-Families of Africa* (1915).

Meinhof was first a secondary school teacher, then for 17 years a pastor at Zizow, when his meetings with African natives on missions sparked his interest in African languages. When a Duala man came to him for tutoring in German, he was convinced instead to teach the Duala language to Meinhof. In 1899 Meinhof published *Grundriss einer Lautlehre der Bantusprachen* ("Outline of the Phonetics of the Bantu Languages"), detailing the sound-shifting laws of six modern Bantu languages and postulating a Proto-Bantu that was their predecessor. In 1902 Meinhof went to Zanzibar on a government stipend, and from 1903 to 1909 he taught at the Seminar für Orientalische Sprachen in Berlin. His second principal publication appeared in 1906, *Grundzüge einer vergleichenden Grammatik der Bantusprachen* ("Principles of the Comparative Grammar of the Bantu Languages"), a study of the morphology of the Bantu languages. From 1909 until his death Meinhof was on the staff of the Kolonial-institut in Hamburg.

Meiningen, city, Thuringia *Land* (state), Germany. It lies along the Werra River, between the Thüringer Wald (forest) and the Rhön. First mentioned in 982 and chartered in 1344, it belonged to the bishops of Würzburg (after 1008) and the counts of Henneberg (after 1542) before it passed in 1583 to Saxony. It was the capital of the Duchy of Saxe-Meiningen from 1680 to 1919. A major fire in 1874 spared the ducal castle (1509–11), containing art, coin, and historical collections. In the late 19th century the town was noted for its dramatic academy and stock-company theatre and for its orchestra, conducted (1880–85) by Hans von Bülow and (1911–14) by Max Reger. The town has railway repair shops and some metal, paper, and textile production. Pop. (1990 est.) 25,474.

Meiningen Company, German MEININGER HOFTHEATERTRUPPE ("Meiningen Court Theatre Troop"), experimental acting group begun in 1866 and directed by George II, duke of Saxe-Meiningen, and his morganatic wife, the actress Ellen Franz. It was one of the first companies in which the importance of the director was stressed.

Inspired by the English theatre, particularly by the work of actor Charles Kean, the "Theatre Duke" sought to create a production style that unified the conception, interpretation, and execution of dramatic works. Assisted by the actor Ludwig Chronegk, who conducted it on tour, the duke instituted many reforms, among which were an emphasis upon historical accuracy and authenticity in costumes and sets; the use of steps and platforms to keep the action moving fluidly on many different levels; the division of groups in crowd scenes into organic yet distinct vocal entities; the introduction of long, carefully planned rehearsals (anticipating Konstantin Stanislavsky's method); and the displacement of stage scenery (paintings) by settings in which the actor became a natural part of his environment.

The company's first public performance was in 1874 at Berlin. In 1881 the Meiningen Company went to London, where it presented three plays by Shakespeare and a number of German and non-German classics. Thereafter, the ensemble performed in more than 35 European cities, including Moscow and Brussels. In 1890, feeling the work of the company had been done, the duke closed it.

Its realistic productions profoundly affected the thinking of the Russian director Stanislavsky and the French director André Antoine, the two major proponents of stage realism, and provided the impetus for the further exploration and development of naturalistic theatre, which found its greatest expression and perfection in the work of the Moscow Art Theatre.

Meinong, Alexius (b. July 17, 1853, Lemberg, Galicia, Austrian Empire [now Lviv, Ukraine]—d. Nov. 27, 1920, Graz, Austria), Austrian philosopher and psychologist remembered for his contributions to axiology, or theory of values, and for his *Gegenstandstheorie,* or theory of objects.

Meinong

By courtesy of the Department of Philosophy, Karl-Franzens-Universitat Graz, Austria

After studying under the philosophical psychologist Franz Brentano from 1875 to 1878 in Vienna, he joined the faculty of philosophy at the University of Graz, where he remained as a professor from 1889 until his death. With Brentano he helped promote the Austrian school of values but eventually dissented from Brentano's views on epistemology.

In his major work, *Über Annahmen* (1902; "On Assumptions"), Meinong discussed the assumptions men make in believing they know or do not know a particular truth. Like Brentano, Meinong considered intentionality, or the direction of attention to objects, to be the basic feature of mental states. Yet he drew his own distinction between two elements in every experience of the objective world: "content," which differentiates one object from another, and "act," by which the experience approaches its object.

Anticipating the work of the Phenomenologists, Meinong maintained that objects remain objects and have a definite character and definite properties (*Sosein*) even if they have no being (*Sein*). Thus, "golden mountain" is an object existing as a concept, even though no golden mountains exist in the world of sense experience. Bertrand Russell was among those influenced by this aspect of Meinong's thought. Like every other type of object knowable by different mental states, values could also be classified as objects existing independently of the experience of values and of the world of sense experience. Two examples of value feeling are *Seinsfreude,* the experience of joy in the existence of a particular object, and *Seinsleid,* the experience of sadness at the object's existence.

Meinong's *Gegenstandstheorie* is discussed in his *Gesammelte Abhandlungen,* 2 vol. (1913–14; "Collected Treatises"), and in John N. Findlay, *Meinong's Theory of Objects* (1933). His other important writings include *Über Möglichkeit und Wahrscheinlichkeit* (1915; "On Possibility and Probability") and *Über emotionale Präsentation* (1917).

meiofauna (zoology): *see* mesofauna.

meiosis, also called REDUCTION DIVISION, division of a germ cell involving two fissions of the nucleus and giving rise to four gametes, or sex cells, each possessing half the number of chromosomes of the original cell.

A brief treatment of meiosis follows. For a full treatment, *see* MACROPAEDIA: Cells: Their Structures and Functions.

The process of meiosis is characteristic of organisms that reproduce sexually. Such species have in the nucleus of each cell a diploid (double) set of chromosomes, consisting of two haploid sets (one inherited from each parent). These haploid sets are homologous—*i.e.,* they contain the same kinds of genes, but not necessarily in the same form. In humans, for example, each set of homologous chromosomes contains a gene for blood type, but one set may have the gene for blood type A and the other set the gene for blood type B.

Prior to meiosis, each of the chromosomes in the diploid germ cell has replicated and thus consists of a joined pair of duplicate chromatids. Meiosis begins with the contraction of the chromosomes in the nucleus of the diploid cell. Homologous paternal and maternal chromosomes pair up along the midline of the cell. Each pair of chromosomes—called a tetrad, or a bivalent—consists of four chromatids. At this point, the homologous chromosomes exchange genetic material by the process of crossing over (*see* linkage group). The homologous pairs then separate, each pair being pulled to opposite ends of the cell, which then pinches in half to form two daughter cells. Each daughter cell of this first meiotic division contains a haploid set of chromosomes.

The chromosomes at this point still consist of duplicate chromatids.

In the second meiotic division, each haploid daughter cell divides. There is no further reduction in chromosome number during this division, as it involves the separation of each chromatid pair into two chromosomes, which are pulled to the opposite ends of the daughter cells. Each daughter cell then divides in half, thereby producing a total of four different haploid gametes. When two gametes unite during fertilization, each contributes its haploid set of chromosomes to the new individual, restoring the diploid number. *See also* mitosis.

Meïr (Hebrew: "the Enlightener") (fl. 2nd century AD), rabbi who was among the greatest of the tannaim, the group of some 225 masters of the Jewish Oral Law that flourished in Palestine for roughly the first 200 years AD. He continued the work of his teacher, Rabbi Akiba, in compiling by subject the Halakhot (laws) that came to be incorporated into the Mishna made by Rabbi Judah ha-Nasi, who took Meïr as his master.

Meïr was born in Asia Minor, and his real name may have been Nehorai or Mesha. When Rabbi Akiba was killed by the Romans during the persecutions that followed the Bar Kokhba revolt (AD 132–135), Meïr fled Palestine but later returned to the city of Usha. There he helped reestablish the Jewish high court known as the Sanhedrin. He also established Jewish academies in other cities. When Simeon, the patriarch of the Sanhedrin, threatened him with excommunication over a question of protocol, Meïr openly defied his authority and then left Palestine to return to Asia Minor.

He was known for his great dialectical skill in analyzing the pros and cons of a Halakha; the Talmud states that he could give 150 reasons to prove a thing clean and 150 to prove it unclean. He is cited by name in the Mishna more than 300 times. He was also renowned as a fabulist, holding his audiences spellbound with his learned lectures enlivened by anecdotes. His wife, Beruriah, is often cited in the Talmud as a model of generosity and faith. During the Middle Ages, legends of Meïr's thaumaturgic powers sprang up, so that he is sometimes known as Ba'al ha-Nes, or Miracle Worker. A tomb marks his reputed burial place in Tiberias (Ṭeverya, Israel).

Meir OF ROTHENBURG, original name MEIR BEN BARUCH (b. *c.* 1215, Worms, Franconia [Germany]—d. May 2, 1293, Ensisheim Fortress, Alsace), great rabbinical authority of 13th-century German Jewry and one of the last great tosaphists (writers of notes and commentary) of Rashi's authoritative commentary on the Talmud.

Meir studied in Germany and later in France, where he witnessed, in 1242 or 1244, the public burning of 24 cartloads of Talmudic manuscripts, a disaster that inspired him to write a moving poem. On returning to Germany, he was rabbi in many communities but probably spent the longest time in Rothenburg, where he opened a Talmudic school. He became famous as an authority on rabbinic law and for nearly half a century acted as the supreme court of appeals for Jews of Germany and surrounding countries. In practice he was a strict Talmudist.

In 1286, in addition to the other persecutions German Jews endured, Emperor Rudolph I attempted to abrogate their political freedom by making them *servi camerae* ("serfs of the treasury"). Many Jews tried to escape from Germany, including Rabbi Meir. While leading his family and a group of followers through Lombardy, he was apprehended and imprisoned for the rest of his life in an Alsatian fortress. Although the Jews raised a large ransom, it is generally believed that Meir refused it for fear of encouraging the government to imprison more rabbis for ransom. Fourteen years after his death, upon payment of a large ransom, his body was finally delivered for burial.

Although Meir wrote no single major work, his 1,500 or so extant responsa (authoritative answers to questions regarding Jewish law and ritual) are rich with information about the community organization and social customs of medieval German Jewry. He also wrote many erudite Talmudic tosaphoth (notes). His main teachings, however, were included in numerous literary compositions by his disciples, such as the famous codifier Asher ben Jehiel. These compositions became classical textbooks of law and ritual for Ashkenazic Jews (those of German–Polish descent) of all subsequent generations.

Meir, Golda, original name GOLDIE MABOVITCH, later GOLDIE MYERSON (b. May 3, 1898, Kiev—d. Dec. 8, 1978, Jerusalem), a founder and fourth prime minister (1969–74) of the State of Israel.

In 1906 Goldie Mabovitch's family emigrated to Milwaukee, Wis., where she attended the Teachers' Seminary and later became a leader in the Milwaukee Labor Zionist Party. In 1921 she and her husband, Morris Myerson, emigrated to Palestine and joined the Merḥavya kibbutz. She became the kibbutz's representative to the Histadrut (General Federation of Labour), the secretary of that organization's Women's Labour Council (1928–32), and a member of its executive committee (1934 until World War II). During the war, she emerged as a forceful spokesman for the Zionist cause in negotiating with the British mandatory authorities. In 1946, when the British arrested and detained many Jewish activists, including Moshe Sharett, head of the Political Department of the Jewish Agency, Goldie Myerson provisionally replaced him and worked for the release of her comrades and the many Jewish war refugees who had violated British immigration regulations by settling in Palestine. Upon his release, Sharett took up diplomatic duties, and she officially took over his former position. She personally attempted to dissuade King Abdullah of Jordan from joining the invasion of Israel decided on by other Arab states.

Golda Meir
Dennis Brack—Black Star/EB Inc.

On May 14, 1948, Goldie Myerson was a signatory of Israel's independence declaration and that year was appointed minister to Moscow. She was elected to the Knesset (Israeli parliament) in 1949 and served in that body until 1974. As minister of labour (1949–56), she carried out major programs of housing and road construction and vigorously supported the policy of unrestricted Jewish immigration to Israel. Appointed foreign minister in 1956, she Hebraized her name to Golda Meir. She promoted the Israeli policy of assistance to the new African states aimed at enhancing diplomatic support among uncommitted nations. Shortly after retiring from the Foreign Ministry in January 1966, she became secretary general of the Mapai Party and supported Prime Minister Levi Eshkol in intraparty conflicts. After Israel's victory in the Six-Day War (June 1967) against Egypt, Jordan, and Syria, she helped merge Mapai with two dissident parties into the Israel Labour Party.

Upon Eshkol's death on Feb. 26, 1969, Meir, the compromise candidate, became prime minister. She maintained the coalition government that had emerged in June 1967. Meir pressed for a peace settlement in the Middle East by diplomatic means. She traveled widely, her meetings including those with Nicolae Ceaușescu in Romania (1972) and Pope Paul VI at the Vatican (1973). Also in 1973, Meir's government was host to Willy Brandt, chancellor of West Germany.

Her efforts at forging a peace with the Arab states were halted by the outbreak in October 1973 of the fourth Arab–Israeli war, called the Yom Kippur War. Israel's lack of readiness for the war stunned the nation, and Meir formed a new coalition government only with great difficulty in March 1974 and resigned her post as prime minister on April 10. She remained in power as head of a caretaker government until a new one was formed in June. Although in retirement thereafter, she remained an important political figure. Upon her death it was revealed that she had had leukemia for 12 years. Her autobiography, *My Life,* was published in 1975.

Meireles, Cecília (b. Nov. 7, 1901, Rio de Janeiro—d. Nov. 9, 1964, Rio de Janeiro), poet, teacher, and journalist, whose lyrical and highly personal poetry, often simple in form yet containing complex symbolism and imagery, earned her an important position in 20th-century Brazilian literature.

Orphaned at an early age and brought up by her grandmother, Meireles began to write poetry at the age of nine. She became a public school teacher at 16 and two years later established her literary reputation with the publication of *Espectros* (1919; "Visions"), a collection of sonnets in the Symbolist tradition.

The 1920s were a time of revolution in Brazilian literature, but Meireles' work of the period showed little affinity with the prevailing nationalistic tendencies or the radical technical innovations in free verse and colloquial language. Her poetry is considered by most critics to have found its best expression in such traditional forms as the sonnet.

Between 1925 and 1939 Meireles concentrated on her career as a teacher, writing several books for children and in 1934 founding the Biblioteca Infantil in Rio de Janeiro, the first children's library in Brazil. That year she lectured on Brazilian literature in Portugal at the universities of Lisbon and Coimbra; in 1936 she was appointed lecturer at the new Federal University in Rio de Janeiro.

Meireles reestablished her reputation as a poet after 14 years of silence with *Viagem* (1939; "Journey"), considered by many critics to mark her attainment of poetic maturity and individuality. From that time she devoted herself to her literary career, continuing to publish collections of poetry regularly until her death. Much of her work is collected in *Obra Poética* (1958; "Poetic Work"), and several of her poems have been translated into English for anthologies.

Meirionnydd, English MERIONETH, historic region and former county in Wales, on Cardigan Bay north of the Dovey Estuary, and since 1974 a district of Gwynedd county. Meirionnydd is one of the oldest regional names in Wales. It represents the territory of Meirion, grandson of Cunedda, who conquered northern and western Wales in the 5th century AD. In the post-Roman centuries, shut off by hills on all sides, Meirionnydd experienced little Saxon, Scandinavian, or early Norman influence. In pre-Norman times the county was largely under the princes of Gwynedd. A Norman attempt to enter the county was repulsed in 1096. During the next 300 years there were many battles in the neighbourhood of Corwen, which commanded the entrance to the county at the Bala cleft. The seclusion of the region made it a gathering ground of Welsh resistance to the English, and there are traditions that Owen Glendower's parliaments sat at Dolgellau.

Meirionnydd was traditionally a sheep-rearing county, with important flannel and woollen industries. In the 18th century, Dolgellau was famous for its production of a Welsh tweed cloth, and at Bala stockings and woollen caps were made. The slate industry had its origins in the 16th century and came into prominence in the 18th; by the 19th century there were quarries at Ffestiniog, Corris, Aberllefenni, Pennal, Abergynolwyn, and Arthog. There are records of gold mines in the Mawddach Valley from early times, and copper and lead have been mined in the Ardudwy and Dyfi valleys respectively.

Meirionnydd district, covering 586 sq mi (1,517 sq km) of mountainous terrain and coastline, lies almost entirely within Snowdonia National Park. It is bordered by the districts of Dwyfor, Aberconwy, and Colwyn to the north, Glyndŵr and Montgomery to the east, and Ceredigion to the south. The town of Dolgellau serves as the administrative seat. Pop. (1981) 32,027.

Meiron (Israel): *see* Meron.

Meissen, city, Saxony *Land* (state), southeastern Germany, on the Elbe River, just northwest of Dresden. It grew out of the early

The cathedral and (left) the Albrechtsburg Castle overlooking Meissen, Ger.

©Caio Garrubba—Madeline Grimoldi

Slav settlement of Misni and was founded as a German town by King Henry I in 929. In 968 it became the seat of the margraviate of Meissen, which passed in 1089 to the House of Wettin, electors of Saxony after 1423. The bishopric of Meissen, established in 968 and suppressed in 1581 after the diocese accepted the Reformation (1559), was re-created in 1921 with its seat at Bautzen. Meissen was chartered in 1205, when it was a bastion of the German colonization of the East. The city is dominated by the group of 13th- and 14th-century Gothic cathedral buildings and by the Albrechtsburg Castle (1471–85).

Meissen is famous for the manufacture of porcelain, based on extensive local deposits of china clay and potter's earth. Ceramics, metalware, and leather are also manufactured, and wine is produced. Pop. (1989 est.) 36,767.

Meissen, Heinrich von: *see* Frauenlob.

Meissen porcelain, also called DRESDEN PORCELAIN in England and PORCELAINE DE SAXE in France, German hard-paste, or true, porcelain produced at the Meissen factory, near Dresden in Saxony (now Germany), from 1710 until the present day. It was the first successfully produced true porcelain in Europe and dominated the style of European

Meissen hard-paste porcelain bird, *c.* 1750; in the Victoria and Albert Museum, London

By courtesy of the Victoria and Albert Museum, London; photograph, EB Inc.

porcelain manufactured until about 1756, after which the leadership ultimately passed to French Sèvres porcelain. The secret of true porcelain, similar to that produced in China, was discovered in about 1707 by Johann Friedrich Böttger, an alchemist, and Ehrenfried Walter von Tschirnhaus, a physicist, whose research into porcelain had earlier produced a stoneware that is the hardest known substance of its kind. The earliest porcelain was smoky in tone and not highly translucent, but improvements to it were subsequently made.

The high point of the Meissen factory was reached after 1731 in the modelling of the sculptor Johann Joachim Kändler. An underglaze blue decoration called *Zwiebelmuster,* or onion pattern, was introduced in about 1739 and was widely copied. Meissen porcelain is marked with crossed blue swords.

Meissner, Alexander (b. Sept. 14, 1883, Vienna—d. Jan. 3, 1958, Berlin), Austrian engineer whose work in antenna design, amplification, and detection advanced the development of radio telegraphy.

Meissner studied at the Vienna College of Engineering, earning the doctor of technical science degree in 1902. In 1907 he joined the Telefunken Company of Berlin, where he conducted research on radio problems. He improved the design of antennas for transmitting at long wavelengths, devised new vacuum-tube circuits and amplification systems, and developed the heterodyne principle for radio reception. In 1911 Meissner designed the first rotary radio beacon to aid in the navigation of the Zeppelin airships. In 1913 he was the first to amplify high-frequency radio signals by using feedback in a vacuum triode; this principle made it possible to build radio receivers more sensitive than any earlier type. After 1928 Meissner served as a professor at the Technical University of Berlin.

Meissner corpuscle, also called TACTILE CORPUSCLE, oval, encapsulated sensory nerve ending, believed to be a touch receptor. Meissner corpuscles are found in hairless skin, as in the palms. They were named for the 19th–20th-century German physiologist Georg Meissner, who first described them. *See also* pacinian corpuscle; Ruffini ending.

Meissner effect, the expulsion of a magnetic field from the interior of a material that is in the process of becoming a superconductor, that is, losing its resistance to the flow of electrical currents when cooled below a certain temperature, called the transition temperature, usually close to absolute zero. The Meissner effect, a property of all superconductors, was discovered by the German physicists W. Meissner and R. Ochsenfeld in 1933.

As a superconductor in a magnetic field is cooled to the temperature at which it abruptly loses electrical resistance, all or part of the magnetic field within the material is expelled. Relatively weak magnetic fields are entirely repulsed from the interior of all superconductors. The term interior includes all the material within the superconductor except a surface layer about one-millionth of an inch thick. The external magnetic field may be made so strong, however, that it prevents a transition to the superconducting state, and the Meissner effect does not occur.

Generally, ranges of intermediate magnetic-field strengths, which are present during cooling, produce a partial Meissner effect as the original field is reduced within the material but not wholly expelled. Some superconductors, called type I (tin and mercury, for example), can be made to exhibit a complete Meissner effect by eliminating various chemical impurities and physical imperfections and by choosing proper geometrical shape and size. Other superconductors, called type II (vanadium and niobium, for example), exhibit only a partial Meissner effect at intermediate magnetic-field strengths no matter what their geometrical shape or size. Type II superconductors show incomplete expulsion of the external magnetic field except in relatively weak magnetic fields and gradually less expulsion of the magnetic field as its strength increases until they abruptly cease being superconductors in relatively strong magnetic fields.

Meissonier, (Jean-Louis-)Ernest (b. Feb. 21, 1815, Lyon—d. Jan. 31, 1891, Paris), French painter and illustrator of military and

"1814," oil on canvas by Jean-Louis-Ernest Meissonier, 1864; in the Louvre, Paris

By courtesy of the Musee du Louvre, Paris; photograph, Marc Garanger

historical subjects, especially of Napoleonic battles.

Meissonier studied first under Jules Potier, then in the studio of Léon Cogniet. In his early years Meissonier spent much time making illustrations for the publishers Curmer and Hetzel, but beginning in 1834 he exhibited regularly at the French Salon and received the highest official honours from the middle of the 1840s onward.

The greater part of Meissonier's painting is on a small scale and is concerned with military subjects or with genre in a historical setting. Meissonier's minute and scrupulous technique was largely derived from the study of Dutch painters of the 17th century, but the documentary approach of his preparatory study of costume and armour and of his detailed observation of nature (such as his systematic analysis of the movements of horses) links him with the 19th century. Among his major works are "Napoleon III at Solferino" (1863; Louvre) and "1814" (1864; Louvre).

Meissonier, Juste-Aurèle (b. 1693/95, Turin, Savoy—d. July 31, 1750, Paris), French goldsmith, interior decorator, and architect, often considered the leading originator of the influential, though short-lived, Rococo style in the decorative arts.

Early in his career Meissonier migrated to Paris, receiving his warrant as master goldsmith from King Louis XV in 1724 and his appointment as designer for the King's bedchamber and cabinet in 1726. He had a powerful and fertile imagination; his fantastic grottoes and swirling, animated, asymmetrical metalwork designs combined contrasting and original motifs. As a goldsmith, he was remarkable for the boldness of his conceptions for such objects as snuffboxes, watch cases, sword hilts, and tureens. He prepared three fine sets of sketches for interior decoration, furniture, and goldsmith designs. He also developed a plan for the facade of the church of Saint-Sulpice, Paris, in 1726, but few of his architectural ideas were realized.

Consult the INDEX *first*

meistersinger, any of certain German musicians and poets, chiefly of the artisan and trading classes, in the 14th to the 16th century. They claimed to be heirs of 12 old masters, accomplished poets skilled in the medieval *artes* and in musical theory; the minnesinger Heinrich von Meissen, called Frauenlob, was said to be their founder. In a sense, then, they represent the bourgeois inheritance of the courtly minnesinger. Their true predecessors, however, likely were fraternities of laymen, trained to sing in church and elsewhere. Later, when music and poetry became "crafts" to be taught, these fraternities became *Singschulen* ("song schools"), organized like craft guilds. Their main activity became the holding—still in church—of singing competitions. Composition was restricted to fitting new words to tunes ascribed to the old masters; subject matter, metre, language, and performance were governed by an increasingly strict code of rules (*Tablatur*). These deadening restrictions led Hans Folz, a barber-surgeon from Worms (d. *c.* 1515), to persuade the Nürnberg Singschule to permit a wider range of subjects and the composition of new tunes. These reforms, adopted elsewhere, restored some life to the *Singschulen;* henceforth, a member, having passed through the grades of *Schüler, Schulfreund, Singer,* and *Dichter,* became a "master" by having a tune of his own approved by the *Merkern,* or adjudicators. In this freer atmosphere, Hans Sachs flourished—though some regard the 16th century as a period of decline rather than of florescence.

Nevertheless, music, form, and subject matter remained remarkably constant through the centuries. The music, derived from Gregorian chant, folksong, and other sources, determined the metre (*Ton* meant both metre and melody). Each stanza, or *Gesätz,* consisted of two musically identical *Stollen* (together forming an *Aufgesang*) and an *Abgesang,* with its separate metrical scheme—a form derived from the *Minnesang* and sometimes termed *Bar* form (*q.v.*). Verses were based on syllable counting regardless of stress or quantity; rhyme schemes were often elaborate. Three stanzas or a multiple of three constituted a song, or *Bar* (the musical *Bar* form provided music for one stanza). For large subjects, several *Töne* were used. Songs were unaccompanied solos. For the *Singschulen* in church, a wide range of religious subjects was versified; after the Reformation the text of Luther's Bible was rigidly adhered to. From the 15th century, secular subjects also were used. At the *Zechsingen,* held afterward at a tavern (perhaps not an official part of the *Singschule*), subjects were humorous, sometimes obscene.

From the earliest centres, Mainz, Worms, and Strassburg, the movement spread all over southern Germany and to Silesia and Bohemia; northern Germany had individual meistersingers but no *Singschulen.* The best documented centre is Nürnberg. The meistersingers were not popular figures, as Richard Wagner's opera *Die Meistersinger* (1868) suggests; they were largely ignored by professional men, humanists, and the general populace, and their songs were not published. They produced few outstanding songs or artists. Their importance lies rather in their devotion to their art in a troubled age and in their constant efforts to inculcate religious and moral principles. After the year 1600, attempts—mostly unsuccessful—at modernization were made; but the *Singschulen* slowly declined and disappeared, although the last one, at Memmingen, was not disbanded until 1875.

Meit, Conrat (b. *c.* 1475, Worms, Bishopric of Worms—d. 1550/51, Antwerp), Flemish sculptor and medalist known for the realistic portraits that he produced during the Northern Renaissance. Meit was a central figure in the art of his period, and his sculptures made from bronze, wood, and other materials demonstrate a fusion of Italian idealism with solid German realism.

Educated under Hans Seyfer, Meit knew Albrecht Dürer, who apparently respected his work. He served Frederick the Wise before 1511 and was court sculptor to Margaret of Austria, who gave him most of her commissions. He lived in Antwerp after 1534.

Meit's small, realistic figures and portraits are especially natural for their time. "Adam and Eve" (first half of the 16th century) reveals the decline in popularity of the historical concept of the Fall; Meit's subjects, such as "Judith" (1520), are markedly human and contemporary. Meit is perhaps best known for the tombs of the family of Margaret of Austria (1526–31) in Brou, in which he blends Gothic structure with Italianate detail.

Meithei, also called MANIPURI, dominant population of Manipur in northeastern India. The area was once inhabited entirely by peoples resembling such hill tribes as the Nāga and the Mīzo. Intermarriage and the political dominance of the strongest tribes led to a gradual merging of ethnic groups and the formation finally of the Meithei, numbering about 780,000. They are divided into clans, the members of which do not intermarry.

Although they are genetically Mongol and speak a Tibeto-Burman language, they differ culturally from the surrounding hill tribes by following Hindu customs. Before their conversion to Hinduism they ate meat, sacrificed cattle, and practiced headhunting, but now they abstain from meat (though they eat fish), do not drink alcohol, observe rigid rules against ritual pollution, and revere the cow. They claim high-caste status. The worship of Hindu gods, with especial devotion to Krishna, has not precluded the cult's worship of many pre-Hindu indigenous deities and spirits.

Meithei warriors, Manipur, India
The Times, London—Pictorial Parade/EB Inc.

Rice cultivation on irrigated fields is the basis of their economy. They are keen horse breeders, and polo is a national game. Hockey, boat races, theatrical performances, and dancing (well known throughout India as the Manipuri style) are other pastimes.

Meitner, Lise (b. Nov. 7, 1878, Vienna—d. Oct. 27, 1968, Cambridge, Cambridgeshire, Eng.), German physicist who shared the Enrico Fermi Award (1966) with the chemists Otto Hahn and Fritz Strassmann for their joint research that led to the discovery of uranium fission.

After receiving her doctorate at the University of Vienna (1906), Meitner attended Max Planck's lectures at Berlin in 1907 and joined Hahn in research on radioactivity. During three decades of association, she and Hahn were among the first to isolate the isotope protactinium-231 (which they called protactinium), studied nuclear isomerism and beta decay, and in the 1930s (along with Strassmann) investigated the products of neutron bombardment of uranium. Because she was Jewish, she left Nazi Germany in the summer of 1938 to settle in Sweden. After Hahn and Strassmann had demonstrated that barium appears in neutron-bombarded uranium, Meitner, with her

Lise Meitner
EB Inc.

nephew Otto Frisch, elucidated the physical characteristics of this division and in January 1939 proposed the term fission for the process. She retired to England in 1960.

Meixian (China): *see* Mei-hsien.

Mékambo, town, northeastern Gabon. It lies along the south bank of the Djadié River (a tributary of the Ogooué). Mékambo is the trading centre for a substantial mining district. The hills along the plateau, extending for about 100 miles (160 km) from Mékambo to Makokou, contain some of the world's richest iron-ore deposits; notable reserves are located at Belinga, 60 miles (97 km) west-northwest of Mékambo, and at Bokaboka, 30 miles (48 km) southwest.

There is also farming in the vicinity. Coffee and cocoa from the hinterland are shipped by road, river, and rail to either Pointe-Noire, Congo, or Owendo, Gabon, for export. Mékambo also has a Roman Catholic church, a government medical centre, a rubber market, and a school for carpentry and ironsmithing. Pop. (1993) 2,800.

Mekele, also spelled MAKALLE, town, northern Ethiopia. Situated 6,778 feet (2,066 m) above sea level overlooking the salt mines of the Danakil Plain, Mekele is the principal centre of Ethiopia's inland salt trade. Newer industries include the production of incense and resin. An airport serves the town. Nearby are the ruins of prehistoric settlements. Pop. (1994) 96,938.

Mekhitarist (monks): *see* Mechitarist.

Meknès, city, north-central Morocco. It lies about 70 miles (110 km) from the Atlantic Ocean and 36 miles (58 km) southwest of Fès. One of Morocco's four imperial cities, it was founded in the 10th century by the Zanātah tribe of the Meknassa Berbers as Meknassa ez-Zeitoun ("Meknès of the Olives"), a group of villages among olive groves; it grew around Takarart, an 11th-century Almoravid citadel. Meknès became the Moroccan capital in 1673 under Maulāy Ismā'īl, who built palaces and mosques that earned for Meknès the name "Versailles of Morocco." His city wall, fortified by four-cornered towers and pierced by nine ornamented gates, still stands. After his death the city declined. In 1911 it was occupied by the French, who built a new quarter, separated from the old by the Bou Fekrane River. Meknès has massive buildings of a heavy splendour, the Roua (stables said to have housed 12,000 horses), and celebrated gardens irrigated by water from a 10-acre (4-hectare) artificial lake.

Towered gate in the city wall, Meknès, Mor.
Richard Abeles

Meknès is a commercial centre for the surrounding fertile agricultural plateau region and is also a market for fine embroidery and carpets, woven chiefly by Berber women of the Moyen Atlas mountains. The city is linked by road to Rabat and by rail with Fès, Tangier (Tanger), and Casablanca. The ruins of the Roman Volubilis and the holy city of Idrīs, who founded the Idrīsid dynasty, are nearby.

Grapes, cereals (primarily wheat), citrus fruits, olives, sheep, goats, and cattle are raised in the surrounding region. Fluorite is also mined near Meknès. Pop. (1994) 459,958.

Mekong River, Cambodian MÉKÔNGK, Wade-Giles romanization LAN-TS'ANG CHIANG, Pinyin LANCANG JIANG, Laotian MÈNAM KHONG, Thai MAE NAM KHONG, Vietnamese SÔNG TIÊN GIANG, longest river in Southeast Asia, having a length of approximately 2,700 miles (4,350 km).

A brief treatment of the Mekong River follows. For full treatment, *see* MACROPAEDIA: Asia.

The Mekong River drains more than 313,000 square miles (810,600 square km) of land. The headwaters, known as the Ang-ch'ü and the Cha-ch'ü, rise at elevations of more than 16,000 feet (4,900 m) in the T'ang-ku-la Mountains on the southern border of Tsinghai province in China. The upper Mekong, comprising roughly one-fourth of the total length, descends in a southerly direction across the highlands of Yunnan province in a long, narrow, deeply cut valley. It then forms part of the international border between Myanmar (Burma) and Laos, as well as between Laos and Thailand, and flows successively through Laos, Cambodia, and Vietnam before entering the South China Sea in a wide delta south of Ho Chi Minh City (formerly Saigon) in Vietnam.

South of the Myanmar-Laos border, the lower Mekong basin receives the drainage of the Khorat Plateau of Thailand, from most of Cambodia, and from the western slopes of the Annamese Cordillera (Chaîne Annamitique) in Laos and Vietnam, before the river divides into two streams—the Mekong and the Bassac—in its delta section. South of Yunnan, most of these drainage areas have similar landforms, soils, and tropical broadleaf vegetation. Vientiane, the capital of Laos, and Phnom Penh, the capital of Cambodia, stand on the banks of the Mekong.

The mean annual discharge of the river at Krâchéh in central Cambodia is about 500,000 cubic feet (14,000 cubic m) per second. Flow comes chiefly from rainfall in the lower basin and reflects the variation in seasonal rainfall caused by monsoon winds. When the wet southwesterly monsoon winds blow from July to October, the highest water levels are reached, coming as early as August or September in the upper reaches of the Mekong and as late as October in the southern reaches. The lowest levels occur during the dry weather caused by the northeasterly monsoon winds from November to May.

The lower Mekong River basin is home to about one-third of the combined population of Cambodia, Laos, Thailand, and Vietnam. About nine-tenths of these people are engaged in agriculture and produce rice, the chief crop of the basin. Rice cultivation, however, is impossible during the long dry period without irrigation. In 1957 the Mekong River Development Project was initiated by the United Nations. The project called for cooperation between Laos, Thailand, Cambodia, and South Vietnam in building facilities for the generation of hydroelectric power and for improvements in irrigation, flood control, drainage, and navigation.

Mekran (coastal area, Pakistan and Iran): *see* Makran.

Mekri carpet, floor covering handwoven in the Turkish town of Mekri (modern Fethiye), noted for its unusual prayer rugs. They are sometimes called Rhodes carpets, even though there is no evidence that carpets were ever made on that island. Mekri carpets are mainly small prayer rugs that have two central fields and two mihrabs (arched designs characteristic of prayer rugs). They are called "brothers' rugs," presumably because two people may use each carpet for prayer simultaneously. The two central fields of brothers' rugs usually have contrasting colours and decorative motifs of stylized flowers. Most Mekri carpets dating from the 18th and 19th centuries are made entirely of coarse wool.

Mela, Pomponius (b. Tingentera, Baetica [Roman Spain]; fl. AD 43), author of the only ancient treatise on geography in classical Latin, *De situ orbis* ("A Description of the World"), also known as *De chorographia* ("Concerning Chorography"). Written about AD 43 or 44, it remained influential until the beginning of the age of exploration, 13 centuries later. Though probably intended for the general reader, Mela's geography was cited by Pliny the Elder in his encyclopaedia of natural science as an important authority.

Though the work was largely a borrowing from Greek sources and contained information that was frequently obsolete, it was unique among the ancient geographies in that it divided the Earth, which Mela placed at the centre of the universe, into five zones: a northern frigid zone, a northern temperate zone, a torrid zone, a southern temperate zone, and a southern frigid zone. The two temperate zones were habitable, but only one, the northern, was known. The southern was unattainable by people of the north because of the necessity of passing through the unbearable heat of the intervening torrid zone in order to reach it. According to Mela, the ocean surrounding the Earth cut into it in four seas, the most important being the Mediterranean. He avoided technical details, such as distances, but usually included short phrases describing the places mentioned. Less was said of familiar regions than of distant countries, where even fabulous material was included.

melaconite, noncrystalline variety of the mineral tenorite (*q.v.*).

Melaka, formerly MALACCA, town and port, West Malaysia (Malaya), on the Strait of Malacca, at the mouth of the sluggish Melaka River. The city was founded about 1400, when Paramesvara, the ruler of Tumasik (now Singapore), fled from the forces of the Javanese kingdom of Majapahit and found refuge at the site, then a small fishing village. There he founded a Malay kingdom the kings of which, aided by the Chinese, extended their power

Christ Church in Melaka city, Malaysia
Jan Moline—Photo Researchers/EB Inc.

over the peninsula. The port became a major stopping place for traders to replenish their food supplies and obtain fresh water from the hill springs. Malay rule ended in 1511, when Alfonso d'Albuquerque, viceroy of the Portuguese Indies, conquered Malacca. During the 16th century Malacca developed into the most important trading port in Southeast Asia. Indian, Arab, and European merchants regularly visited there, and the Portuguese realized enormous profits from the especially lucrative spice trade that passed through the port.

A period of Dutch rule, which began in 1641, was interrupted by the British in 1795. The rivalry was settled in favour of the British by the Anglo-Dutch Treaty of London (1824), and Malacca became one of the original Straits Settlements (with Penang and Singapore) in 1826.

Heavy silting of the Malacca estuary, combined with the rise of Singapore, led to Malacca's decline. Modern harbour facilities are limited to offshore anchorage. The river's mouth is protected against silting by two groynes (low walls) projecting outward for ½ mile (0.8 km). Melaka remains significant, however, as an exporter of rubber from its hinterland and as an importer of general cargo (sugar and rice).

The surrounding region has a number of fruit and coconut small holdings, but rubber is its primary export. Rubber has come under highly commercialized production because of Malacca's early overseas-trading economy. Malaccan Chinese were the first to venture into commercial rubber production (1898), and there are now large Chinese estates and smallholdings in the region.

The town of Melaka presents a sleepy, unhurried atmosphere; its single-storied houses include many dating from the Dutch and Portuguese colonial periods. Its residents are mostly Chinese, many of whom have, through intermarriage, adopted the dress and speech of the Malays. This mixed strain, known as Baba Chinese, together with Malay-Portuguese-Dutch admixtures, is unique in Malaysian ethnography.

A low hill on the river's southern bank is occupied by the ruins of the Old Fort, designed by Albuquerque. The Portuguese also built St. Paul's Church (1521), now a ruin, which held the body of St. Francis Xavier until its removal in 1553 to Goa, India. The Stadthuys (Town Hall) is an example of mid-17th century Dutch architecture. Christ Church, St. John's Fort, a cultural museum, Cheng Hoon Teng Temple, and a Chinese cemetery with graves dating from the Ming dynasty are also there. The town has an airport and road links to Kuala Lumpur and Singapore. Pop. (1991) 74,962.

melamine, also called CYANURAMIDE, or TRIAMINOTRIAZINE, a colourless, crystalline substance belonging to the family of heterocyclic organic compounds, which are used principally as a starting material for the manufacture of synthetic resins.

Melamine is manufactured by heating dicyandiamide under pressure. Its most important reaction is that with formaldehyde, forming resinous compounds of high molecular weight. These resins form under the influence of heat but, once formed, are insoluble and infusible. Usually formulated with fillers and pigments, they are molded into dishes, containers, utensils, handles, and the like or used as laminating agents or coating materials for wood, paper, and textiles. Formica and Melmac are well-known trade names for products based on melamine resins.

Butylated melamine resins, made by incorporating butyl alcohol into the melamine-formaldehyde reaction mixture, are fluids used as ingredients of paints and varnishes.

Melampus, in Greek mythology, a seer who as a child received the understanding of the language of birds after two young snakes, whose lives he had saved, licked his ears when he was asleep. He later helped his brother Bias to marry Pero, daughter of King Neleus of Pylos. According to another legend, Melampus cured the insanity of the daughters of Proitus, prince of Tiryns; he and Bias then married two of the daughters. According to Pausanias (2nd century AD), there was a shrine to Melampus at Aegosthena (Megarid) and an annual festival.

melancholia, a mental condition characterized by extreme depression (*q.v.*) and feelings of hopelessness and worthlessness. It is especially a part of manic-depressive psychosis (*q.v.*).

Melanchthon, Philipp, original name PHILIPP SCHWARTZERD (German: "Black Earth"; in Greek, Melanchthon) (b. Feb. 15, 1497, Bretten, Palatinate [Germany]—d. April 19, 1560, probably Wittenberg, Saxony [Germany]), German author of the Confession of Augsburg of the Lutheran Church (1530), humanist, Reformer, theologian, and educator. He was a friend of Martin Luther and defended his views. In 1521 Melanchthon published the *Loci communes,* the first systematic treatment of evangelical doctrine. Because of his academic expertise he was asked to help in founding schools, and he virtually reorganized the whole educational system of Germany, founding and reforming several of its universities.

Melanchthon, engraving by Albrecht Dürer, 1526

By courtesy of the Staatliche Museen Kuperstichkabinett, Berlin

Early life and education. Melanchthon inherited from his parents, Barbara Reuter and Georg Schwartzerd, a deep sense of piety that never left him. From his Bretten surroundings (where five citizens were burned as witches in 1504) he absorbed a sense of the occult that combined later with biblical references to stars, dreams, and devils to make him a firm believer in astrology and demonology. In 1508, within a period of 11 days, both his grandfather Reuter and his father died, his father after four years of invalidism.

Humanism predominated in Melanchthon's education, his studies having been directed by a great-uncle, Johannes Reuchlin, who was a famed Hebraist and humanist. Philipp's first tutor instilled in him a lifelong love of Latin and classical literature, and, at the Pforzheim Latin school, he received further humanistic training and had his name changed from Schwartzerd to its Greek equivalent, Melanchthon.

While at the universities of Heidelberg (1509–11, B.A.) and Tübingen (1512–14, M.A.), Melanchthon explored Scholastic thought in depth, steeped himself in the rhetoric of the Dutch humanist Rudolf Agricola and the Nominalism of the English philosopher William of Ockham and the ecclesiastical reformer John of Wesel, studied Scripture, and read classical works with a fellow student. On receiving the M.A. degree, he lectured, with conspicuous success, on the classics and soon had six books to his credit, including "Rudiments of the Greek Language" (1518), a grammar that was to go through many editions. He was praised by the great Dutch humanist Erasmus, and his name became known in England. In the best tradition of the time, Melanchthon was a humanist.

In 1518 Melanchthon accepted an invitation, relayed through Reuchlin, to become the University of Wittenberg's first professor of Greek. Only four days after his arrival, he addressed the university on "The Improvement of Studies," boldly setting forth a humanistic program and calling for a return to classical and Christian sources in order to regenerate theology and rejuvenate society.

Luther and the Reformation. Luther, the founder of the Protestant Reformation, and Melanchthon responded to each other enthusiastically, and their deep friendship developed. Melanchthon committed himself wholeheartedly to the new evangelical cause, initiated the previous year when Luther nailed his Ninety-five Theses to the door of the castle church in Wittenberg. By the end of 1519 he had already defended scriptural authority against Luther's opponent Johann Eck, rejected (before Luther did) transubstantiation—the doctrine that the substance of the bread and wine in the Lord's Supper is changed into the body and blood of Christ—made justification by faith the keystone of his theology, and openly broken with Reuchlin.

During this time he had also published seven more small books and had earned the Bachelor of Theology degree at Wittenberg. His energy was phenomenal. He began his day at 2:00 AM, with lectures, often to as many as 600 students, at 6:00. In addition, he found time to court Katherine Krapp, whom he married in 1520 and who bore him four children—Anna, Philipp, Georg, Magdalen.

At Luther's urging, Melanchthon lectured on Paul's Letter to the Romans and in 1521 published the *Loci communes,* the first systematic treatment of evangelical doctrine. Sin, law, and grace were the principal topics, with free will, vows, hope, confession, and other doctrines subsumed. Drawing on Scripture, Melanchthon argued that sin is more than an external act; it reaches beyond reason into man's will and emotions so that man cannot simply resolve to do good works and earn merit before God. Original sin is a native propensity, an inordinate self-concern tainting all man's actions. But God's grace consoles man with forgiveness, and man's works, though imperfect, are a response in joy and gratitude for divine benevolence. Three editions of the *Loci* appeared before the end of the year and 18 editions by 1525, in addition to printings of a German translation. The last edition in 1558 was much enlarged and changed. Luther declared that the *Loci* deserved a place in the canon of Scriptures; the University of Cambridge in England later made it required reading, and Queen Elizabeth I (1533–1603) virtually memorized it so she could converse about theology.

Despite an imperial decree of death to those who supported Luther, in 1521 Melanchthon sharply answered the Sorbonne's condemnation of 104 statements of Luther with "Against the Furious Decree of the Parisian Theologasters." His "Passion of Christ and Antichrist," in the same year, utilized woodcuts by Lucas Cranach (1472–1553) in a scathing criticism of the pope's life-style as diametrically opposed to Christ's. When Melanchthon hesitated to publish his lectures on Corinthians, Luther stole a copy and published them in 1521 with a preface saying, "It is I who publish these annotations of yours, and send you to yourself." In 1523 Luther did the same with Melanchthon's notes on John.

In 1521, during Luther's confinement in the Wartburg, Melanchthon was the leader of the Reformation cause at Wittenberg. After the First Diet of Speyer (1526), where a precarious peace was patched up for the Reformed faith, Melanchthon was deputed as one of the 28 commissioners to visit the Reformed imperial states and regulate the constitution of the churches. In 1528 this resulted in the publication of *Unterricht der Visitatoren* ("Instructions for Visitors"), a set of instructions for the commissioners. In addition to a statement of evangelical doctrine, it contained an outline of education for the elementary grades, which was enacted into law in Saxony to establish the first real Protestant public-school system. Melanchthon's educational plan was widely copied throughout Germany, and at least 56 cities asked his advice in founding schools. Through him, his textbooks, and the teachers he trained, virtually the whole educational system in Germany was reorganized. He helped found the universities of Königsberg, Jena, and Marburg and reformed those of Greifswald, Wittenberg, Cologne, Tübingen, Leipzig, Heidelberg, Rostock, and Frankfurt an der Oder. His efforts earned him the title "Preceptor of Germany."

The Augsburg Confession. Melanchthon was present when the protest, from which the term *Protestant* originated, was lodged in the name of freedom of conscience against the Roman Catholic majority at the Second Diet of Speyer (1529). At the Diet of Augsburg (1530) Melanchthon was the leading representative of the Reformation, and it was he who prepared the Augsburg Confession, which influenced every subsequent major credal statement in Protestantism. In the Confession he sought to be as inoffensive to the Catholics as possible but forcefully stated the evangelical stance. In the ensuing negotiations over adoption of the confessional statement, he seemed to compromise, but the vigour of his Apology of the Confession of Augsburg (1531) belied any change. The Apology and Confession quickly became official Lutheran symbols (authoritative statements of faith), as did one other Melanchthon treatise, his "Appendix on the Papacy," which was an addition to the Schmalkald Articles of 1536–37, another Lutheran confessional statement. In the "Appendix," Melanchthon refuted historically and theologically any papal primacy by divine right but accepted papal jurisdiction as a human right for the sake of peace, if the Gospel were permitted. After the Diet of Augsburg further attempts were made to settle the Reformation controversies by compromise, and Melanchthon, from his conciliatory spirit and facility of access, appeared to the defenders of Roman Catholicism as the fittest of the Reformers with whom to deal. Despite frequent charges of collaboration with Roman Catholicism, Melanchthon staunchly upheld the evangelical doctrines of justification by faith and scriptural authority.

Later years. The year after Luther's death, when the Battle of Mühlberg (1547) had given a seemingly crushing blow to the Protestant cause, an attempt was made to unite the evangelicals and Roman Catholics in the provisional agreements of the Augsburg Interim. Melanchthon refused to accept the Interim until justification by faith was ensured as a fundamental doctrine. Then, for the sake of order and peace, he declared that those principles which did not violate justification by faith might be observed as adiaphora, or nonessentials. He allowed the necessity of good works to salvation, but not in the old sense of meriting righteousness; and he accepted the seven sacraments, but only as rites that had no inherent efficacy to salvation. Melanchthon was bitterly criticized by fellow Protestants for his conciliatory stand on the Interim. His later years were occupied with controversies within the evangelical church and fruitless conferences with his Roman Catholic adversaries. He died in 1560 and was buried in Wittenberg beside Luther.

Doctrinal thought. Melanchthon's literary facility, clear thought, and elegant style of expression made him the scribe of the Reformation and the representative of the evangelicals at numerous colloquies. He never attained entire independence of Luther, though he gradually modified some of his positions. These modifications centred on the Eucharist, man's part in conversion, and the place of good works.

As late as 1530 Melanchthon agreed with Luther on the Lord's Supper, but by 1529 his own views had begun to shift from Luther's, and the changes that Melanchthon introduced in 1540 in the 10th article of the Augsburg Confession indicated that his view on the Eucharist paralleled Calvin's.

Melanchthon also came to believe that man has a part in conversion. At first, following Luther's cardinal doctrine of grace, Melanchthon seemed to reject free will, and he pushed the Augustinian doctrine of irresistible grace close to fatalism. However, his *Commentary on Colossians* (1527) implied a rejection of predestination, and by 1532 in the *Commentary on Romans* he spoke of man's struggle to accept or reject the love of God. In the 1535 edition of *Loci* he pointed out that man must at least accept the gift of God's salvation and that man is therefore responsible for his destiny. This view is clearly expressed in *De Anima* (1540). "God draws, but he draws him who is willing."

Because of his interest in ethics, Melanchthon increasingly emphasized good works as the inevitable fruits of faith. Luther was disposed to make faith itself the principle of sanctification, but Melanchthon laid more stress on law. In his "Instructions for Visitors" articles of 1528 he urged pastors to instruct people in the necessity of repentance and to bring the threat of the law to bear upon men in order to instill faith. This brought upon him the opposition of the antinomian Johann Agricola. In the *Loci* of 1535 Melanchthon sought to put the fact of the coexistence of justification and good works in the believer on a secure basis by declaring the latter "necessary" to eternal life. For the sake of public order Melanchthon was led to lay more and more stress upon the law and moral ideas, but his evangelical position was that man is saved by faith and that good works are the "necessary" expression of faith, for good works flow from faith.

(C.L.Ma.)

BIBLIOGRAPHY. C.L. Manschreck, *Melanchthon: The Quiet Reformer* (1958), is the most complete biography; see also R. Stupperich, *Der unbekannte Melanchthon* (1961; Eng. trans. by R.H. Fischer, *Melanchthon,* 1965). M. Rogness, *Philip Melanchthon: Reformer Without Honor* (1969), contains aspects of Melanchthon's thought. His basic works and letters may be found in K.G. Bretschneider and E. Bindseil (eds.), *Corpus Reformatorum,* 28 vol. (1834–60); W. Pauck (ed.), *Melanchthon and Bucer* (1969), contains the 1521 *Loci;* and C.L. Manschreck (ed.), *Melanchthon on Christian Doctrine* (1965), the 1555 *Loci.* For information on Lutheran symbols, see T.G. Tappert (ed.), *The Book of Concord* (1959); for educational endeavours, C. Hartfelder, *Philipp Melanchthon als Praeceptor Germania* (1889), with bibliography. W. Hammer, *Die Melanchthonforschung im Wandel der Jahrhunderte,* 2 vol. (1967–68), has a good bibliography to 1965; for a discussion of Melanchthon's relation to patristics, see P. Fraenkel, *Testimonia Patrum* (1961).

Melanesia, one of the traditional ethnogeographic groupings of the Pacific Islands, including (generally from west to east) the island of New Guinea, the Admiralty Islands, and the Bismarck and Louisiade archipelagoes; the Solomon Islands and the Santa Cruz Islands; New Caledonia and the Loyalty Islands; Vanuatu (formerly New Hebrides); Fiji; Norfolk Island; and numerous smaller islands. The island group is separated from Polynesia in the east by the Andesite Line of extreme volcanic and earthquake activity and from Micronesia in the north (along the equator); it is bounded by the Tropic of Capricorn and Australia in the south. Melanesia's name was derived from the Greek *melas,* "black," and *nēsoi,* "islands."

A brief treatment of Melanesia follows. For full treatment, *see* MACROPAEDIA: Pacific Islands.

The third voyage of Jules-Sébastien-César Dumont d'Urville resulted in an extensive revision of the charts of the South Sea Islands that first designated the division of island groups into the traditional regions of Melanesia, Polynesia, and Micronesia. Since his early 19th-century explorations, however, both linguistic and archaeological evidence have rendered the designation "Melanesian" at least imprecise, if not obsolete, for two distinct populations and cultures can be readily distinguished.

Papuans, the earliest people in the region, occupied the Sahul continent (which later partially submerged to become the island of New Guinea) at least 40,000 years ago. By 30,000 years ago, the Bismarck Archipelago east of New Guinea had been occupied by speakers of Papuan languages. Perhaps partly through indirect contact with developments in Southeast Asia, Papuan peoples developed one of the earliest agricultural complexes—based on root crops and sugarcane cultivation—as much as 9,000 years ago. Modern descendents of these early populations speak languages categorized as Papuan.

Not until about 4,000 years ago did another culture appear. About that time seafaring peoples with a Southeast Asian cultural tradition began to move into areas north of New Guinea; archaeological evidence—particularly the appearance of the distinctive pottery and associated tools and shell ornaments of the Lapita culture—points to their settlement and occupation of the islands of the Bismarck

Coconut palms growing along the lagoon at Savusavu, Vanua Levu Island, Fiji, Melanesia

Archipelago by about 3,500 years ago. Their language was apparently of the Austronesian family, related to languages of the Philippines and the Indonesian archipelago, and their culture was based on root- and tree-crop cultivation and maritime technology.

The speakers of Austronesian languages established coastal communities and associated trade systems in the southeastern Solomons, Vanuatu, New Caledonia, and Fiji. That these widely spread communities were politically associated is suggested by the wide distribution of trade goods, such as Lapita obsidian and shell ornaments. It is believed that Fiji was initially colonized by Lapita-making peoples and later was settled by dark-skinned, culturally Melanesian peoples after Fiji had been a springboard to the settlement of western Polynesia. Linguistically, the Austronesian peoples were clearly dominant; virtually all of the languages spoken by dark-skinned peoples in the Pacific east of the Bismarcks are classified as Oceanic Austronesian.

The societies of precolonial New Guinea and island Melanesia (the zone east of New Guinea) were characteristically organized in kinship- and descent-based local groups, who were linked together by intermarriage. Such local groups, usually including from 20 to 100 members, were relatively autonomous political units. They characteristically held corporate title to lands (although domestic groups or individuals held rights over gardens and cultivated trees). Chains of descent determined land rights. Patrilineal descent systems prevail in most of lowland New Guinea, northern Vanuatu, and New Caledonia; matrilineal descent systems prevail in much of the Massim—what is now Milne Bay province in Papua New Guinea (taking in the D'Entrecasteaux Islands, the Louisiades, and nearby islands)—and the Bismarck Archipelago and in much of the Solomons and the Banks Islands.

In many areas, local groups were dispersed through territories in scattered homesteads and hamlets. Often occupation of these settlements was of short duration, the period determined by cultivation cycles. Communities clustered more closely when there was danger of surprise attack; in interior areas they were usually established on ridges and peaks for defensive purposes.

Settlement patterns varied widely. In parts of the Sepik plains of New Guinea, descent-based local groups gathered in huge villages (some with populations of more than 1,000 people). In the agricultural heartland of northern Kiriwina, in the Trobriands (Massim), villages of up to 200 people were centred on a central dance ground; villages at least that size inhabited small coral platforms in the lagoons of northern Malaita (Solomons). Generally speaking, larger villages settled over several generations were characteristic of coastal-strand environments, and smaller, shifting settlements were characteristic of interior areas.

The polarization of the sexes was remarkable, and residental separation of the sexes was common. Men's houses or clubhouses, a focus of ritual or military solidarity or both, were common in many areas of New Guinea and island Melanesia, especially in the Sepik River basin of New Guinea and on the southern Papuan coast. Women and children occupied domestic dwellings.

Leadership of local groups, both in Papuan-speaking New Guinea and Austronesian-speaking island Melanesia, often has been referred to as that of the "Big Man," because it is based largely on status achieved through entrepreneurial success and the influence and obligations attendant to it. In the early stage of European penetration of island Melanesia, many societies were led by hereditary chiefs. This form of government was also characteristic of parts of Austronesian-speaking coastal New Guinea (*e.g.,* Mekeo, Motu), parts of the Solomons (*e.g.,* Rugara, Buka, Shortlands, Small Malaita), parts of Vanuatu (Aneityum), and most of New Caledonia. In some other areas, leadership was based on rank but also involved a complex interplay of hereditary right and demonstrated ability.

Swidden horticulture (a practice of shifting cultivation whereby rain-forest gardens are cleared, planted, harvested, and then left fallow for periods of up to a generation) forms the basis of the ancient root-crop cultivation systems of Papuan and Austronesian cultural traditions. Forests were cleared with ground stone tools (and, in some coral-island areas, shell tools) and sometimes by means of fire. Using digging sticks for cultivation, the islanders planted primarily taro and yams (*Dioscorea*), with supplementary crops of plantains, sago, pandanus, leafy greens such as *Hibiscus manihot,* and sugarcane.

In addition to the cultivation of roots and trees, the islanders raised domestic pigs, fished, and hunted marsupials and birds. Sometimes they also gathered insects and grubs. Gathering of wild-vegetable foods, including tubers, greens, nuts (notably the canarium almond), and fruits augmented diets or provided emergency rations.

Both Papuan-speaking and Austronesian-speaking zones of Melanesia developed notable exchange systems; these were typified by prestige feasts in which surpluses of pigs and root crops were used and ceremonial valuables (such as objects made of shell, dolphin teeth, dog teeth, and other material objects) were exchanged. In some areas at least, competitive exchanges replaced warfare (and in some instances they seem to have grown out of homicide compensations).

Another notable feature of the islands around the eastern end of New Guinea is the elaborate regional trading system. In the Massim, the trade of pottery from the Amphletts, canoe timber and greenstone blades from Murua (Woodlark), carved platters and canoe prow boards, and other specialized products was complemented by yams and pigs from resource-rich areas to smaller, ecologically less favoured, islands.

Religions of Papuan-speaking New Guinea are diverse. Among such montane peoples as the Telefol, Bimin Kuskusmin, and Baktamin, highly complex male initiatory cults progressively reveal cosmic secrets to initiates. In New Guinea as in island Melanesia, fear of sorcery is widespread; and, among such peoples as the Fore of the highlands, accusations of sorcery are a major cause of hostility between groups and of blood feuding.

In Austronesian-speaking Melanesia ancestral ghosts and other spirit beings are participants in daily social life. These invisible beings provide sure support for mere human effort in the uncertain projects of war, gardening, and the pursuit of prestige. The presence and effects of invisible ghosts and spirits were manifested in dreams, revealed in divination, and inferred from human success or failure, prosperity or disaster, health or death. Island Melanesian societies had no full-time religious intermediaries. Some forms of everyday magic—for gardening, fishing, attracting valuables or lovers—were widely known; other forms, for powers of fighting or theft, were closely guarded.

Christianity has gradually replaced the forms of religion that were prevalent in precolonial Melanesia. One fascinating phenomenon of the early colonial period was the emergence of cargo cults (*q.v.*) in coastal New Guinea and island Melanesia. These movements, which in some respects resemble Christian millennial movements, promoted belief in a new age to be precipitated by the arrival of "cargo" (meaning European material goods) sent by supernatural sources.

Like religion, the art of Melanesia is highly varied. The body itself is the focus for much of the art of highland New Guinea, with face and body painting, wigs and headdresses, and elaborate costumes. In lowland New Guinea, ebullient art traditions like those of the Sepik region and those of the Massim are world-renowned. The Christianization of much of Melanesia led to the early abandonment of many forms of music and dance, and much of its variety and significance is a matter of conjecture. Music ranges from dirges at wakes and love songs to highly complex forms such as the polyphonic panpipe music, with as many as eight contrapuntal voices, played by orchestras on Malaita in the Solomons. Storytelling in the form of epic narrative, myth, folktales, and oratory, redolent with metaphor and allusion, is also characteristic of the region.

Most of the indigenous peoples of the Melanesian region are now subjected to pressures of Christianization and westernization. In some areas such forces have been at work for more than a century. In some interior areas, however, particularly in the rugged and virtually impenetrable mountains of New Guinea, contact with Western culture was not made until the 1930s or even later. Today even the most remote regions of Melanesia have become accessible, and they have been transformed. One significant change is the transformation of Melanesia's once classless societies into class-stratified groups.

The countries of modern Melanesia show increasing polarization between metropolitan centres and village hinterlands. The rapid growth of squatter settlements around urban centres and increasing movement into towns have begun to link village and urban life. The more remote villages are poor and have little access to the educational, medical, and economic services of the state. As might be expected, it is in the areas of least contact with the Western world that traditional culture tends to be the most resilient.

Capitalist enterprise, such as cash cropping of coffee and other high-value crops, is evident even in the hinterlands. Roads and airfields now connect once-isolated areas to regional networks.

Melanesian languages, languages belonging to the Eastern, or Oceanic, branch of the Austronesian (Malayo-Polynesian) language family and spoken in the islands of Melanesia. The Melanesian languages, of which there are about 400, are most closely related to the languages of Micronesia and Polynesia; most have a few hundred or a few thousand speakers, and the total number of speakers of Melanesian tongues is fewer than 1,000,000. With few exceptions, these languages are only slightly documented.

The most important Melanesian language is Fijian, spoken by about 334,000 persons and widely used in Fiji in newspapers, in broadcasting, and in government publications. Other Melanesian languages of note are Motu, in the form of Police Motu (a pidgin), used widely as a lingua franca in Papua New Guinea; Roviana, the language of the Methodist Mission in the Solomon Islands; Bambatana, a literary language used by the Methodists on Choiseul Island; Bugotu, a lingua franca on Santa Isabel (Ysabel Island); Tolai, a widely used missionary language in New Britain and New Ireland; Yabêm and Graged, lingua francas of the Lutheran Mission in the Madang region of Papua New Guinea; and Mota, a widely used lingua franca and literary language of the Melanesian Mission in northern Melanesia in the 19th century.

Melanesian Pidgin, also called MELANESIAN PIDGIN ENGLISH, NEO-MELANESIAN, BEACH-LA-MAR, or SANDALWOOD ENGLISH, an English-based pidgin that is used widely in Melanesia as a trade and mission language; in some areas it has become established as a creole (*i.e.,* it has become the native language of some communities). Melanesian Pidgin has also become the lingua franca of Papua New Guinea, where several hundred native languages are spoken, most of them being mutually incomprehensible.

The vocabulary of Melanesian Pidgin is originally derived primarily from English; about 1,500 English words make up approximately 90 percent of the language's small basic vocabulary, although words have in many cases widened or shifted their meanings, and compound words and other new constructions further enlarge the vocabulary. Grammar and syntax are also based on English patterns, although they have been much simplified and then somewhat modified through usage and through the influence of native Melanesian languages. Pronunciation and stress have clearly been affected by contact with non-English languages. Stress has been shifted to the first syllable of the word in all cases, resulting in forms such as *bíkos* "because," and *másin* "machine"; and the sound system has altered in that the sounds *f* and *p,* and *s, sh,* and *ch* are not distinguished (resulting in *dispela* "this fellow," *pinis* "finish," *sap* "sharp," and *sok* "chalk"). *Th* is not pronounced as in English (it becomes *t* or *d* or occasionally *r: dispela* "this fellow," *tri* "three," *arapela* "other fellow"). Also, between two vowels, *b* and *d* often become *mb* and *nd,* respectively: *tambak* for *tabak* "tobacco" and *sindaun* for *sidaun* "sit, sit down, set."

melanin, a dark biological pigment (biochrome) found in skin, hair, feathers, scales, eyes, and some internal membranes; it is also found in the peritoneum of many animals (*e.g.,* frogs), but its role there is not understood. Formed as an end product during metabolism of the amino acid tyrosine, melanins are conspicuous in dark skin moles of humans; in the black dermal melanocytes (pigment cells) of most dark-skinned peoples; and as brown, diffuse spots in the epidermis.

Melanism refers to the deposition of melanin in the tissues of living animals. The chemistry of the process depends on the metabolism of the amino acid tyrosine, the absence of which results in albinism, or lack of pigmentation. Melanism can also occur pathologically, as in a malignant melanoma, a cancerous tumour composed of melanin-pigmented cells.

Melanic pigmentation is advantageous in many ways: (1) It is a barrier against the effects of the ultraviolet rays of sunlight. On exposure to sunlight, for example, the human epidermis undergoes gradual tanning as a result of an increase in melanin pigment. (2) It is a mechanism for the absorption of heat from sunlight, a function that is especially important for cold-blooded animals. (3) It affords concealment to certain animals that become active in twilight. (4) It limits the incidence of beams of light entering the eye and absorbs scattered light within the eyeball, allowing greater visual acuity. (5) It provides resistance to abrasion because of the molecular structure of the pigment. Many desert-dwelling birds, for example, have black plumage as an adaptation to their abrasive habitat.

"Industrial" melanism has occurred in certain moth populations, in which the predominant coloration has changed pale gray to dark-coloured individuals. This is a striking example of rapid evolutionary change; it has taken place in less than 100 years. It occurs in moth species that depend for their survival by day on blending into specialized backgrounds, such as lichened tree trunks and boughs. Industrial pollution, in the form of soot, kills lichens and blackens the trees and ground, thus destroying the protective backgrounds of light-coloured moths, which are rapidly picked off and eaten by birds. Melanic moths, by their camouflage, then become selectively favoured. "Industrial" melanic moths have arisen from recurrent mutations and have spread via natural selection. *See* coloration; integument.

melanoma, a spreading and frequently recurring malignant cancer of specialized skin cells (melanocytes) that produce the protective skin-darkening pigment melanin. In the United States melanoma represents less than 5 percent of all cases of skin cancer, yet it is responsible for nearly three-quarters of all skin cancer deaths and is increasing in frequency.

Like all cancers, melanoma is caused by changes in a cell's DNA that alter the cell's ability to control its growth. The most common cause of DNA damage is ultraviolet radiation from sunlight. People who have fair skin, freckle easily, or have a large number of moles or several very large moles are at increased risk of developing this cancer. A family history of melanoma also increases the risk. Risk is greatly reduced by avoiding exposure to ultraviolet light. Exposure can be reduced by staying out of direct sunlight during periods of peak intensity, protecting the skin with clothing, or using a strong sunscreen. Children should be particularly careful to avoid sunburns, as an increased risk of developing melanoma has been linked to severe sunburns during childhood.

Moles that are asymmetrical, have irregular edges or colour, or are greater than 5–6 mm (about ¼ inch) in diameter are suspect. Any mole that changes in size, shape, or colour should be examined by a physician immediately. A sample of the skin is examined under a microscope for signs of cancer growth and for measurement of the thickness of the growth. Several treatment options are available, depending on the stage of the disease. Stage 0 through stage II melanomas are confined to the skin, and most can be cured by excision of the tumour, especially if caught early. Stage III melanoma has spread to nearby lymph nodes, and surgical removal of the cancerous nodes is required. Stage IV melanoma has spread beyond the regional lymph nodes to other tissues in the body and is extremely serious. Disease progression may be delayed by surgery or chemotherapy, but the survival rate for persons with stage IV melanoma is extremely low.

Melas carpet, floor covering handwoven in the neighbourhood of Milâs (Melas) on the Aegean coast of southwestern Turkey. Normally of small size and 19th century in date, Melas carpets have unusually wide borders in relation to their narrow fields. In the prayer rugs the arch (which indicates the direction of Mecca, the Holy City) is straight-sided, with a triangular indentation below it on each side, the local reminiscence of a lobed-arch form used in the Ottoman court prayer rugs of the 16th and 17th centuries.

Melas prayer rug from Western Anatolia, 19th century; in the Philadelphia Museum of Art

By courtesy of the Philadelphia Museum of Art, The Samuel S. White, III, and Vera White Collection; photograph, Otto E. Nelson—EB Inc.

Their colour scheme is unique: the field is usually a strong red, and yellow and violet are used often, together with a light blue that is quite variable owing to uneven dyeing. Examples that predate the use of chemical dyes are considered to be among the most attractive Turkish carpets.

Consult the INDEX *first*

melatonin, the only hormone secreted by the pineal gland. (The pineal gland is a tiny endocrine gland situated at the centre of the brain.) Melatonin was discovered in 1958 by Aaron B. Lerner and other researchers working at Yale University. Melatonin, a derivative of the amino acid tryptophan, is produced in humans, other mammals, birds, reptiles, and amphibians. It is present in very small amounts in the human body.

Melatonin was previously known to cause the skins of amphibians to blanch, but its functions in mammals remained uncertain until research discoveries in the 1970s and '80s suggested that it regulates sleeping cycles. Secretion of melatonin is increased whenever the sympathetic nervous system is stimulated. The pineal gland's production of melatonin varies both with the time of day and with age; production of melatonin is dramatically increased during the nighttime hours and falls off during the day, and nighttime melatonin levels are much higher in children under age seven than in adolescents and are lower still in adults. Melatonin also seems to play an important role in regulating sleeping cycles; test subjects injected with the hormone become sleepy, suggesting that the increased production of melatonin coincident with nightfall acts as a fundamental mechanism for making people sleepy. With dawn the pineal gland stops producing melatonin, and wakefulness and alertness ensue. The high level of melatonin production in young children may explain their tendency to sleep longer than adults.

In mammals other than humans melatonin possibly acts as a breeding and mating cue, since it is produced in greater amounts in response to the longer nights of winter and less so during summer. Animals who time their mating or breeding to coincide with favourable seasons (such as spring) may depend on melatonin production as a kind of biological clock that regulates their reproductive cycles on the basis of the length of the solar day.

Melba, Dame Nellie, original name HELEN ARMSTRONG, *née* MITCHELL (b. May 19, 1861, Richmond, near Melbourne, Australia—d. Feb. 23, 1931, Sydney), coloratura soprano, a singer of great popularity.

She sang at Richmond (Australia) Public Hall at the age of six and was a skilled pianist and organist, but she did not study singing until after her marriage to Charles Nesbitt Armstrong in 1882. She appeared in Sydney in 1885 and in London in 1886 and then studied in Paris. She made her operatic debut as Gilda in Verdi's *Rigoletto* in 1887 at Brussels under the name Melba, derived from that of the city of Melbourne. Until 1926 she sang in the principal opera houses of Europe and the United States, particularly Covent Garden and the Metropolitan Opera, excelling in Delibes' *Lakmé,* as Marguerite in Gounod's *Faust,* and as Violetta in Verdi's *La traviata.* Her marriage was dissolved in 1900. She was created a Dame of the British Empire in 1918.

Nellie Melba, engraving, 1894

By courtesy of the trustees of the British Museum; photograph, J.R. Freeman & Co. Ltd.

In 1925 she published *Melodies and Memories.* She returned in 1926 to Australia, where she became president of the Melbourne Conservatorium. Melba toast and peach Melba were named for her.

Melbourne, city, capital of the state of Victoria, Commonwealth of Australia. Situated on the southeastern coast of Australia at the head of Port Phillip Bay, Melbourne is the world's southernmost urban area of more than 1,000,000 people. Formerly (1901–27) the capital of Australia, Melbourne is rivaled in size and importance only by the city of Sydney. Area Inner Melbourne, 33.2 square miles (85.9 square km); statistical division, 2,970 square miles (7,695 square km). Pop. (1999 est.) Inner Melbourne, 241,623; statistical division, 3,413,894.

A brief treatment of Melbourne follows. For full treatment, *see* MACROPAEDIA: Melbourne.

For census and planning purposes, the sprawling city of Melbourne has two boundaries. The outer boundary, defining the Melbourne Statistical Division, includes all areas in close economic and social contact with the central city; the division contains nearly three-fourths of Victoria's population. The inner boundary encloses the Melbourne metropolitan area, which occupies a flat site at the northern end of the bay and is drained by the Yarra River and its main tributaries. The city's climate is temperate; average daily maximum temperatures vary from 55° F (13° C) in July to 79° F (26° C) in January, and the average annual rainfall is 26 inches (657 mm).

Melbourne dominates the economic life of Victoria and is the centre of major financial institutions. The city's most important industries include metal processing, engineering, textile and clothing manufacture, food processing, papermaking and printing, and the manufacture of chemicals and building materials. The inner city has been declining in industrial importance as newer activities—production of automobiles, rubber goods, chemicals, and refined oils—have become established in the outer suburbs. Large regional shopping centres have been constructed in the rapidly growing eastern and southern suburbs. The main imports passing into Melbourne's fine sheltered harbour include newsprint and paper, iron and steel, chemicals, motor vehicles, and textiles; chief exports include wool, petroleum products, and food products.

The heart of Melbourne is on the northern bank of the Yarra, 3 miles (5 km) from the bay. It is dissected into square blocks by long main streets. Commercial areas include Swanston, Bourke (both now closed to automobiles), Elizabeth, Collins, and Queen streets. The city is circled by parks, notably the Royal Botanic Gardens, and by sports fields. A concentrated program of revitalizing and repurposing older buildings has brought new life to the city centre and helped preserve Melbourne's architectural heritage. The Docklands development, begun in the 1990s, has been transforming a 500-acre (200-hectare) industrial site into a business, entertainment, and residential enclave.

The University of Melbourne (1853), La Trobe University, the Royal Melbourne Institute of Technology, Deakin University, and Monash University are the main centres of higher education. The public library has a collection of rare books of the earliest European printers. A major cultural facility is the Victorian Arts Centre (1968), which houses art galleries, theatres, auditoriums, studios, and study areas; the performing arts are well-represented in the city.

Melbourne's public transport is provided by electric trains, buses, and old-fashioned but efficient tramcars. An underground loop extending the service of the suburban electric railways was opened in 1981. Traffic congestion has risen with the increasing popularity of automobile travel, necessitating a major overhaul of the road network. Melbourne's port serves overseas passengers in addition to a high tonnage of freight. An international airport is located to the northwest near suburban Tullamarine.

Melbourne, city, Brevard county, east-central Florida, U.S. It lies on the Intracoastal Waterway along the Indian River (a lagoon) about 60 miles (95 km) southeast of Orlando. The site, originally known as Crane Creek, was settled in 1878, and the community was soon renamed for Melbourne, Australia. Tourism (yachting and sport fishing), truck farming, citrus growing, and cattle raising provided the town's early economic base.

Since 1950 Melbourne's growth has been influenced by the space complex at Cape Canaveral to the north and a subsequent influx of aerospace industries. The economy is based on tourism, high-technology industries, the military, and services (especially health care). The city is the site of the Florida Institute of Technology (1958). In 1969 Melbourne consolidated with Eau Gallie, just to the north. Patrick Air Force Base is nearby. Melbourne is home to the Brevard Museum of Art and Science and the Brevard Zoo. The John F. Kennedy Space Center, at Cape Canaveral, has a visitor complex with exhibits on space exploration. The Melbourne bone beds, a series of deposits along the east coast, contain important fossil remains of extinct animals. Inc. town, 1888; city, 1913. Pop. (2000) city, 71,382; Melbourne–Titusville–Palm Bay MSA, 476,230.

Melbourne, University of, coeducational institution of higher learning in Melbourne, financed by both the Commonwealth of Australia and Victoria governments. One of the oldest universities in Australia, it was founded by the Victoria legislature in 1853 and at first offered a liberal arts course. A law school was added in 1857, engineering instruction in 1860, and a medical school in 1862; a music conservatory, now the faculty of music, was opened in 1895. Between 1904 and 1924, schools of dentistry, agriculture, veterinary science, education, architecture, and commerce were established. Its faculties also include arts and business, and a school of graduate studies was established in 1994. Women were admitted to the arts and sciences courses in 1881 and to the medical school in 1887.

The university underwent rapid expansion after World War II. There are four campuses and six regional campuses of the Institute of Land and Food Resources.

Melbourne (of Kilmore), William Lamb, 2nd Viscount, LORD MELBOURNE, BARON OF KILMORE, BARON MELBOURNE OF MELBOURNE (b. March 15, 1779, London—d. Nov. 24, 1848, Brocket, near Hatfield, Hertfordshire, Eng.), British prime minister from July 16 to Nov. 14, 1834, and from April 18, 1835, to Aug. 30, 1841. He was also Queen Victoria's close friend and chief political adviser during the early years of her reign. Although a Whig and an advocate of political rights for Roman Catholics, he was essentially conservative. Not believing that the world could be bettered through politics, he was always more interested in literature and theology.

Lamb's mother, Elizabeth (*née* Milbanke), was a confidante of the poet Lord Byron and an aunt of Byron's future wife Anne Isabella Milbanke. It was widely believed that the 1st Viscount Melbourne was not Lamb's real father. In June 1805 Lamb married Lady Caroline Ponsonby, the eccentric daughter of Frederic Ponsonby, 3rd earl of Bessborough. The marriage had failed even before Lady Caroline's affair with Byron in 1812–13, and, after several estrangements and reconciliations, it ended in separation in 1825. Subsequently, Lamb was named as corespondent in two unsuccessful divorce suits, the second, in 1836, involving the poet Caroline Norton.

Melbourne, detail of an oil painting by J. Partridge, 1844; in the National Portrait Gallery, London

By courtesy of the National Portrait Gallery, London

Called to the bar in 1804, Lamb entered the House of Commons in 1806. From 1822 he was an avowed supporter of the conservatism of George Canning. From April 1827 to May 1828, in the governments of Canning and Arthur Wellesley, 1st duke of Wellington, he served as chief secretary for Ireland. In 1829 he succeeded to the viscountcy. As home secretary in the 2nd Earl Grey's ministry (Nov. 16, 1830–July 8, 1834), he reluctantly supported the parliamentary Reform Act of 1832 but forcibly repressed agrarian and industrial radicals, notably the Tolpuddle Martyrs in 1834, and he opposed, while prime minister, the reduction of duties on imported grain.

Melbourne's first administration ended with his dismissal by William IV, who was offended by Whig plans for church reform. But Sir Robert Peel's Conservatives failed to win a parliamentary majority, and Melbourne took office as prime minister once more. After Victoria's accession he also became her private secretary. Their mutual affection led to Victoria's Whig partisanship. On May 7, 1839, during the "bedchamber question" crisis (the Queen insisted her attendants be Whig ladies), Melbourne resigned but soon resumed office when Peel could not form a government.

By early 1840, Great Britain was divided over industrial depression and Chartism (a working-class radical movement) and was fighting wars in China and Afghanistan. Later that year the firm stand of Melbourne and his foreign secretary, Lord Palmerston, averted war with France over Syria. As his parliamentary support dwindled, Melbourne tried to prepare the Queen for dealing with a Conservative government unwelcome to her and wisely insisted that she permit her husband, Prince Albert, to assume state responsibilities. He left office after the Conservatives had won the general election of 1841 and was permanently weakened by a stroke on Oct. 23, 1842. He died without children, and the viscountcy went to his brother Frederick James Lamb.

Biographies include Bertram Newman's *Lord Melbourne* (1930) and Lord David Cecil's studies, *The Young Melbourne* (1939; 2nd ed., 1948) and *Lord M* (1954).

Melchiades, SAINT (pope): *see* Miltiades, Saint.

Melchior, Johann Peter (b. Oct. 12, 1742, Lindorf, near Düsseldorf, Berg—d. June 13, 1825, Nymphenburg, Bavaria), modeller in porcelain, best known of the artists associated with the great German porcelain factory at Höchst. As a child he showed an interest in drawing, painting, and sculpture, and a relative apprenticed him to a sculptor in Düsseldorf. He became sufficiently well known to be named *Modellmeister* at the Höchst factory, a position he held from 1767 to 1779.

Melchior's best work is considered to be transitional between the Rococo and Neoclassical styles. His graceful and often sentimental works include religious groups, pastoral scenes, and characters from mythology, but he is particularly noted for his warmly animated figures of children. He later worked at the porcelain factories at Frankenthal (1779–93) and Nymphenburg (1797–1822), where his style became increasingly Neoclassical and less sentimental; his chief interest was portrait reliefs, which he executed in biscuit (marble-like, unglazed) porcelain.

Melchite, also spelled MELKITE, any of the Christians of Syria and Egypt who accepted the ruling of the Council of Chalcedon (451) affirming the two natures—divine and human—of Christ. Because they shared the theological position of the Byzantine emperor, they were derisively termed Melchites—that is, Royalists or Emperor's Men (from Syriac *malkā:* "king")—by those who rejected the Chalcedonian definition and believed in only one nature in Christ (the Monophysite heresy). While the term originally referred only to Egyptian Christians, it came to be used for all Chalcedonians in the Middle East and finally, losing its pejorative tone, came to designate the faithful of the patriarchates of Alexandria, Jerusalem, and especially Antioch.

The Melchite community generally consisted of Greek colonists and the Arabicized populations of Egypt and Syria. They adopted the Byzantine rite and thus followed Michael Cerularius, patriarch of Constantinople, into schism with Rome in 1054. For several centuries afterward, the patriarch of Antioch attempted reunification with Rome, and a small number of Melchite Catholics emerged. Final union came in 1724, when Cyril VI, a Catholic, was elected patriarch of Antioch; he was followed by several bishops and a third of the faithful. The Orthodox who opposed union elected their own patriarch, Silvester, and obtained the legal recognition from the Ottoman government that assured them autonomy. About 100 years later, after much persecution and religious difficulties with Jesuits and Lebanese Maronites, the Catholics also received autonomous status from the Ottoman Turks, which allowed for normal activity and growth.

While there had been some few conversions to Catholicism in the patriarchates of Alexandria and Jerusalem, there is only one Catholic Melchite "patriarch of Antioch, Alexandria, Jerusalem and all the East." In each patriarchate he has his own diocese (Damascus, Jerusalem, Alexandria) and is helped by a patriarchal vicar. There are seven archdioceses—Aleppo, Homs, and Latakia (all in Syria), Beirut and Tyre (both in Lebanon), Basra (in Iraq), and Petra-Philadelphia (Jordan). There are six dioceses, in Acre (Israel) and Baalbek, Baniyas, Saïda, Tripolis, and Zahleh-Furzol (all in Lebanon). The number of Catholic Melchites, who observe the Byzantine liturgy in their vernacular Arabic, totals about 250,000 with an additional 150,000 abroad, mainly in Brazil, Argentina, the United States, and Canada.

Melchizedek, also spelled MELCHISEDECH, in the Old Testament, a figure of importance in biblical tradition because he was both king and priest, was connected with Jerusalem, and was revered by Abraham, who paid a tithe to him. He appears as a person only in an interpolated vignette (Gen. 14:18–20) of the story of Abraham rescuing his kidnapped nephew, Lot, by defeating a coalition of Mesopotamian kings under Chedorlaomer.

In the episode, Melchizedek meets Abraham on his return from battle, gives him bread and wine (which has been interpreted by some Christian scholars as a precursor of the Eucharist, so that Melchizedek's name entered the canon of the Roman mass), and blesses Abraham in the name of "God Most High" (in Hebrew El ʿElyon). In return, Abraham gives him a tithe of the booty.

Melchizedek is an old Canaanite name meaning "My King Is [the god] Sedek" or "My King Is Righteousness" (the meaning of the similar Hebrew cognate). Salem, of which he is said to be king, is very probably Jerusalem. Psalm 76:2 refers to Salem in a way that implies that it is synonymous with Jerusalem, and the reference in Gen. 14:17 to "the King's Valley" further confirms this identification. The god whom Melchizedek serves as priest is "El ʿElyon," again a name of Canaanite origin, probably designating the high god of their pantheon. (Later, the Hebrews adapted another Canaanite name as an appellation for God.)

For Abraham to recognize the authority and authenticity of a Canaanite priest-king is startling and has no parallel in biblical literature. This story may have reached its final formulation in the days of King David, serving as an apologia for David's making Jerusalem his headquarters and setting up the priesthood there. Abraham's paying tribute to a Jerusalem priest-king then would anticipate the time when Abraham's descendants would bring tithes to the priests of Jerusalem ministering in the sanctuary at the Davidic capital. The story may also relate to the conflict between the Levite priests descended from Abraham and the Zadokite priests of Jerusalem, who later changed their allegiance to Yahweh, the Hebrew god. The Zadokites monopolized the Jerusalem priesthood until forcibly taken away to Babylon, at which time Levite priests asserted their own hegemony; the Melchizedek episode could reveal the reascendancy of Zadokite power.

The biblical account also poses textual problems. Abraham paying a tithe to Melchizedek is an interpretation, though a likely one, of the original biblical text, in which the matter is ambiguous; it seems incongruous that Abraham gives a tenth of the booty to Melchizedek and then refuses to take any of it for himself (verses 22–23). Again, some scholars have asserted that it would be unusual for an author of Davidic times to construct a narrative with a Canaanite protagonist.

Psalm 110, in referring to a future messiah of the Davidic line, alludes to the priest-king Melchizedek as a prototype of this messiah. This allusion led the author of the Letter to the Hebrews in the New Testament to translate the name Melchizedek as "king of righteousness" and Salem as "peace," so that Melchizedek is made to foreshadow Christ, stated to be the true king of righteousness and peace (Heb. 7:2). According to the analogy, just as Abraham, the ancestor of the Levites, paid tithes to Melchizedek and was therefore his inferior, so the Melchizedek-like priesthood of Christ is superior to that of the Levites. Furthermore, just as the Old Testament assigns no birth or death date to Melchizedek, so is the priesthood of Christ eternal.

Melchizedek priesthood, in the Mormon church (Church of Jesus Christ of Latter-day Saints), the higher of the two priesthoods, concerned with spiritual rather than secular matters. *See* Mormon.

Melcombe, George Bubb Dodington, 1st Baron: *see* Bubb Dodington, George.

Meleager, in Greek mythology, the leader of the Calydonian boar hunt. The *Iliad* relates how Meleager's father, King Oeneus (*q.v.*) of Calydon, had omitted to sacrifice to Artemis, who sent a wild boar to ravage the country. Meleager collected a band of heroes to drive it away and eventually killed it himself. The Calydonians and the Curetes (neighbouring

Meleager, bronze and gold statue by Antico; in the Victoria and Albert Museum, London

By courtesy of the Victoria and Albert Museum, London

warriors who aided in the hunt) then quarrelled over the spoils, and war broke out between them. At one point the Curetes besieged Calydon and were ready to take it when Meleager finally repulsed them. The *Iliad* does not describe Meleager's death, though it mentions that it occurred before the Trojan War. A variant tradition relates that Meleager's mother, Althea, caused his death by burning the log whose span of existence was coterminous with his.

Meleager forms the subject of the *Meleager* of Euripides, of which only fragments survive.

Meleager (fl. 1st century BC), Greek poet from Gadara in Syria, who compiled the first large anthology of epigrams. This was the first of the collections that made up what is known as the Greek Anthology (*q.v.*). Meleager's collection contained poems by 50 writers and many by himself; an introductory poem compared each writer to a flower, and the whole was entitled *Stephanos* ("Garland"). Meleager's own poems do not rank particularly high, though they are held to be neatly constructed, and they treat erotic themes with cleverness. He lived in Tyre and, in old age, on the Aegean island of Cos.

mêlée, also spelled MELLAY, ancient and medieval game, a predecessor of modern football, in which a round or oval object, usually the inflated bladder of an animal, was kicked, punched, carried, or driven toward a goal. Its origins are not known, but, according to one British tradition, the first ball used was the head of an enemy Dane. The games were played by large numbers of people with few rules and often became violent. By the 11th century in Britain, Shrove Tuesday, a day of festival before Lent, had become the day on which most of the *mêlées* took place; among the more notable were those at Chester, Derby, Corfe Castle, Alnwick, Bromford, Cross of Scone, and Midlothian. The term *mêlée* is also used as part of the chivalric tournament (*q.v.*).

melegueta pepper (*Aframomum melegueta*): *see* grains of paradise.

Melekess (Russia): *see* Dimitrovgrad.

Meléndez Valdés, Juan (b. March 11, 1754, Ribera de Fresno, Spain—d. May 24, 1817, Montpellier, France), poet and politician. The representative poet of the Spanish Neoclassic period, he is considered by many critics to be the only genuinely readable poet of that period.

After studying law and classics at Salamanca, Meléndez Valdés was appointed a professor at the university in 1778 through the auspices of a statesman and author, Gaspar Melchor de Jovellanos. In Salamanca, Meléndez Valdés belonged to a circle of literati who formed what came to be described as the second Salmantine school of literature. He entered the judiciary, again with the aid of Jovellanos. When France invaded Spain in 1808, he barely escaped execution as a traitor by the Spanish forces but survived to become director of public instruction in the Napoleonic government. Forced to flee Spain when the French withdrew, he died in poverty in France.

Meléndez Valdés wrote very eclectic poetry, much influenced by French, Italian, and classical models. He had a genuine feeling for nature and, at his best, displayed a considerable gift.

A list of the abbreviations used in the MICROPAEDIA *will be found at the end of this volume*

Meletios Pegas, Meletios also spelled MELETIUS (b. 1549, Candia [Iráklion], Crete—d. Sept. 14, 1601, Alexandria), Greek Orthodox patriarch of Alexandria who strove by theological arguments and ecclesiastical diplomacy to maintain the position and prestige of Greek Orthodoxy in the Middle East and Eastern Europe.

A monastic superior at Candia, Meletios studied at Padua and Venice, from which he was sent into exile. Soon after 1575 he entered the service of the patriarchal courts at Alexandria and Constantinople and in 1590 was consecrated patriarch of Alexandria. In the exercise of this office he participated in various Eastern Orthodox councils, notably at Constantinople in 1593 and 1597, dealing with the patriarchate of Moscow that had been established in 1589, to which Meletios gave reluctant support in 1592.

He was vigorously opposed to the negotiations between Ukrainian and Belorussian Orthodox, living in Polish Lithuania, and the Roman Catholic church, and to the Union of Brest-Litovsk (1596), by which they submitted to Rome. His writings include his correspondence with King Sigismund III of Poland, denying claims of papal supremacy and condemning the union; miscellaneous writings delineating his theology of the church; a polemic (1596) against the Latin church's formulation of the Trinitarian relations between Father, Son, and Spirit; and an apology of the Christian religion, addressed to the Jews (1593).

Meletius OF ANTIOCH, SAINT (d. 381, Constantinople [now Istanbul, Turkey]; feast day February 12), bishop of Antioch whose name is attached to the Meletian schism that split the church of Antioch in the 4th century.

Meletius, who was by origin Armenian, became bishop of Sebaste in 358. He was elected bishop of Antioch in late 360 or 361 when that church, tired of ecclesiastical strife over Arianism, was eager to choose a moderate person, not deeply involved in either camp. His views, however, soon incurred the displeasure of the Arian emperor Constantius II, who exiled him to Armenia. His departure from Antioch had a double effect: an Arian bishop was appointed, and an orthodox party supporting Meletius was formed. This confused situation continued until an attempt was made (362) to secure peace during the reign of the emperor Julian the Apostate. But Paulinus, a famous ascetic, was consecrated as bishop, and, Meletius' followers refusing to accept any other bishop, the schism continued. The death of Julian and the accession of the emperor Jovian (363) brought Meletius back from exile. He refused all compromise with Paulinus, however, and Paulinus was recognized as bishop and the Meletian party remained. Jovian was succeeded (364) in the East by the Arian Valens, and the anti-Arians were again exiled. In 378 the orthodox Gratian became sole emperor and in 379 appointed Theodosius, also orthodox, emperor in the East. Again the exiled anti-Arian bishops, among them Meletius, returned to their sees. It was proposed at first that Paulinus and Meletius rule together, but when Paulinus refused to agree, Meletius was declared bishop. He presided at the Council of Constantinople (381), which accepted the Nicene Creed and ended Arianism in the empire and during which Meletius died. The schism persisted at Antioch for another 20 years.

Meletius OF LYCOPOLIS (fl. early 4th century), bishop of Lycopolis, in Upper Egypt, near Thebes, who formed an ascetic, schismatic Christian church holding a rigorous attitude in readmitting apostates who had compromised their faith during pagan persecutions, particularly the violent repression decreed by the Eastern Roman emperor Diocletian (AD 284–305).

For presuming to ordain clergy and bishops for Christian communities deprived of their pastors by the general persecution, Meletius was deposed about 306 by Peter, bishop of Alexandria, who formerly had fled arrest and whom Meletius charged with abandoning the community of the faithful. Meletius, however, was accused of fomenting discord by his criticism of the light penances imposed by Peter on "lapsed" Christians. When the persecution was resumed in 308 by the Eastern Roman emperors Galerius and Maximinus, Meletius was condemned to the mines in Palestine, and on his return, in 311, with his prestige enhanced by the title of "confessor" for having endured punishing exile, he was excommunicated by Peter after refusing to abdicate his jurisdiction and ministerial authority. Several of Peter's own clergy sided with Meletius, considering the penalty outrageous. The Council of Nicaea in 325 ruled on the schism and restricted Meletius' jurisdiction.

On Athanasius' accession as bishop of Alexandria in 328, Meletius, accompanied by Arians and a community of Coptic (Egyptian Christian) followers terming themselves the "church of the martyrs," went into permanent schism. After his death his followers pursued an ascetic, monastic regimen that endured probably to the 8th century.

Melfi, town and episcopal see, Potenza *provincia,* Basilicata *regione,* southern Italy, at the foot of the volcanic mass of Monte Vulture, at an elevation of 1,742 feet (531 m), north of Potenza. Of Roman origin, the town was taken from the Byzantines by the Normans, who, for a period, made it their capital. It was a favourite residence of the Holy Roman emperor Frederick II, who there assembled the Parliament that passed the Constitutions of Melfi. The town later declined, passing successively to the Caracciolo, Philip of Orange, the Doria, and the Kingdom of the Two Sicilies, before becoming part of the Kingdom of Italy in 1861. Although it suffered from several earthquakes and was rebuilt after that of 1851, some important monuments remain. These include the Romanesque cathedral with its campanile (1153; rebuilt 1281) and the 13th-century Norman castle.

Melfi is an important agriculture, forestry, and tourist centre, producing cereals, olive oil, wine, and fruit, especially apples. Pop. (1991 prelim.) mun., 15,751.

Meliaceae, the mahogany family of flowering plants, of the order Sapindales, comprising 51 genera and about 575 species of trees and (rarely) shrubs, native to tropical and subtropical regions. Most members of the family have large compound leaves, with the leaflets arranged in the form of a feather, and branched flower clusters. The fruit is fleshy and coloured or a leathery capsule. The China tree (*Melia azedarach*), also called chinaberry, bead tree, and Persian lilac, is an ornamental Asian tree with round yellow fruits, often cultivated in many tropical and warm temperate areas. Trees of the genus *Swietenia* and *Entando phragma,* commonly called mahogany, and of the genus *Cedrela* (especially the cigar-box cedar, *C. odorata*) are economically important timber trees. The neem, or nim, tree, also called the margosa tree (genus *Azadirachta*), grown throughout the Old World tropics, notably in India and Southeast Asia, is a source of timber and medicinal oils and resins.

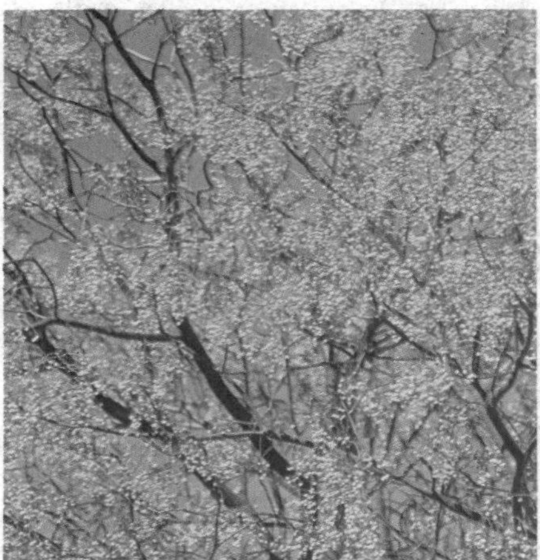

China tree (*Melia azedarach*)
H. Oakman

Méliès, Georges (b. Dec. 8, 1861, Paris, France—d. Jan. 21, 1938, Paris), early French experimenter with motion pictures, the first to film fictional narratives.

When the first genuine movies, made by the Lumière brothers, were shown in Paris in 1895, Méliès, a professional magician and manager-director of the Théâtre Robert-Houdin, was among the spectators. The films were scenes from real life having the novelty of motion, but Méliès saw at once their further possibilities. He acquired a camera, built a glass-enclosed studio near Paris, wrote scripts, designed ingenious sets, and used actors to film stories. With a magician's intuition he discovered and exploited the basic camera tricks: stop motion, slow motion, dissolve, fade-out, superimposition, and double exposure.

Méliès
Rene Dazy—J.P. Ziolo

From 1899 to 1912 Méliès made more than 400 films, the best of which combine illusion, comic burlesque, and pantomime to treat themes of fantasy in a playful and absurd fashion. He specialized in depicting extreme physical transformations of the human body (such as the dismemberment of heads and limbs) for comic effect. His films included pictures as diverse as *Cléopâtre* (1899; "Cleopatra"), *Le Christ marchant sur les eaux* (1899; "Christ Walking on the Waters"), *Le Voyage dans la lune* (1902; "A Trip to the Moon"), *Le Voyage à travers l'impossible* (1904; "The Voyage Across the Impossible"); and *Hamlet* (1908). He also filmed studio reconstructions of news events as an early kind of newsreel. It never occurred to him to move the camera for close-ups or long shots. The commercial growth of the industry forced him out of business in 1913, and he died in poverty.

melilite, any member of a series of silicate minerals that consist of calcium silicates of aluminum and magnesium; gehlenite is the aluminous end-member and åkermanite the magnesian end-member. These minerals crystallize from calcium-rich, alkaline magmas and from many artificial melts and blast-furnace slags. They occur in thermally metamorphosed limestones at contact zones and in impure carbonate rocks altered to feldspathoidal rocks by basic magmas. For chemical formulas and detailed physical properties, *see* silicate mineral (table).

Melilla, chief town of a Spanish *plaza* (enclave) on the northern coast of Morocco. The town is located on the eastern side of the Cap des Trois Fourches, a rocky peninsula that extends approximately 25 miles (40 km) into the Mediterranean Sea. Though physically contiguous with Morocco, Melilla is administered by Spain.

Colonized by the ancient Phoenicians (later Carthaginians) and Romans under the name of Rusaddir, it fell as a Berber town to Spain in 1497 and remained Spanish thereafter despite a long history of attack and siege. After acquiring the adjacent area in about 1909, Spain modernized Melilla's port and made the town into a garrison post for Spanish Morocco. In 1921 during the Rif War, Moroccan tribes under the leadership of Abd el-Krim almost captured the town. Melilla was the first Spanish town to rise against the Popular Front government in July 1936, thus helping precipitate the Spanish Civil War. Melilla was retained by Spain as an enclave when Morocco attained independence in 1956. In 1995 the Spanish government approved statutes of autonomy for Melilla, replacing the city council with an assembly similar to those of Spain's other autonomous communities.

The port exports iron ore that is transported by rail from mines in the Rif of the adjacent (Moroccan) hinterland. Melilla is also the site of an important Spanish military base. Two-thirds of the enclave's population is Roman Catholic, while the remainder is mostly Muslim. Area 5 square miles (12 square km). Pop. (1991 prelim.) 56,497.

Melilla, War of (1919–1926): *see* Rif War.

Méline, Félix-Jules (b. May 20, 1838, Remiremont, France—d. Dec. 20, 1925, Paris), French politician and premier (1896–98).

In 1872 Méline was elected to the National Assembly and was reelected in 1876, when he served as undersecretary for justice. He became minister of agriculture (1883–85) and later president of the Chamber of Deputies (1888–89). He was a fierce opponent of the nationalistic adventurer General Georges Boulanger. He demanded protection for French industries and played a major role in drafting the protectionist legislation of the years 1890–1902 (the "Méline tariffs").

Méline, *c.* 1920
Harlingue—H. Roger-Viollet

As premier and minister of agriculture from April 29, 1896, to June 14, 1898, Méline refused to allow a rehearing of the controversial Dreyfus case (1897). He worked to form a coalition of moderate republicans and conservatives against the leftist parties in the Chamber. Méline was elected to the Senate in 1903 and was again minister of agriculture in 1915–16.

melioidosis, a bacterial infection in humans and animals caused by *Pseudomonas pseudomallei*. Transmission to humans occurs through contact of a skin abrasion with contaminated water or soil rather than through direct contact with a contaminated animal. Inhalation of the pathogen also is suspected as a route of infection. The term *melioidosis,* from the Greek, means "a similarity to distemper of asses." Mostly observed in humans in Southeast Asia, the disease may be acute or chronic. Acute melioidosis, which can be fatal, is characterized by fever, chills, cough, bloody and purulent sputum, diarrhea, and abdominal pain. Physical examination may reveal signs of lung inflammation and pus formation, jaundice, and enlargement of the liver and spleen. Chronic melioidosis may follow the acute phase of the disease or may sometimes develop without it. It is associated with inflammation of the bones and lymph nodes and with the formation of abscesses beneath the skin and inside the lungs and abdominal organs. The diagnosis of melioidosis is established by the isolation of *Pseudomonas pseudomallei* in the sputum, blood, urine, or pus. Long-term treatment with sulfonamides or antibiotics is usually successful, along with surgical drainage of abscesses.

Melissus OF SAMOS (fl. 5th century BC), Greek philosopher who was the last significant member of the Eleatic school of philosophy, which adhered to Parmenides' doctrine of reality as a single, unchanging whole. Although Melissus defended Parmenides, he differed from him in that he held reality to be boundless and of infinite duration (having a past and a present). He is also known as the commander of the Samian fleet, which was victorious over the Athenians in 441/440 BC.

Melito OF SARDIS (fl. 2nd century), Greek bishop of Sardis in Lydia (now in Turkey), whose rediscovered theological treatise on Easter, "The Lord's Passion," verifies his reputation as a notable early Christian spokesman.

The 4th-century chronicles of Eusebius of Caesarea identify Melito as a bishop who addressed a discourse to the Roman emperor Marcus Aurelius, arguing that Christianity should be made the state religion of the Roman Empire. Eusebius gives the titles of 20 of Melito's books, which were in Greek. Only fragments of these books survive, except for the almost complete text of his homily on the Passion of Christ. This work was first published in 1940 after a papyrus discovery and was fully published in 1960. In it, eternity and time, Christ's divine and human nature, and the Jews and the Christian church are contrasted in highly rhetorical antitheses.

Melitopol, also spelled MELITOPOL', city, Zaporozhye *oblast* (province), Ukraine, on the Molochnaya River. The settlement of Novo-Aleksandrovka grew up in the late 18th century, and in 1841 it became the city of Melitopol. The centre of a fruit-growing area, modern Melitopol has engineering plants and light industries. Pop. (1993 est.) 178,000.

Melk, town, *Bundesland* ("federal state") Niederösterreich, northeastern Austria. It lies at the confluence of the Danube and Melk rivers, west of Sankt Pölten. The town was the site of a Roman garrison and was the castle-residence of the Babenberg rulers of Austria from 976 to 1101. The castle and surrounding lands were given in 1111 to the huge Benedictine abbey of Melk (founded in 1089), which dominates the city. The abbey was enlarged and fortified in the 14th century, but most of its palatial buildings date from its Baroque reconstruction (1702–36). Melk also has some notable Renaissance houses, notably Schallaburg castle. The locality is well known for its wines. Pop. (1991) 5,139.

The Benedictine abbey in Melk, Austria
Michel Serraillier from Rapho/Photo Researchers

Melkart (god): *see* Melqart.

Melkite (Christianity): *see* Melchite.

mellay (game): *see* mêlée.

mellee (Australian scrubland vegetation): *see* mallee.

Mellitus OF CANTERBURY, SAINT (d. April 24, 624, Canterbury, Kent [England]; feast day April 24), first bishop of London and the third archbishop of Canterbury (619–624), known for his missionary work and his diplomatic efforts between the Roman church and the churches of Britain.

Mellitus, a Roman and the son of a noble family, may have been the abbot of St. Andrew's monastery in Rome before he was summoned to the missionary field by Pope

St. Gregory I the Great. In 601 he was sent to England by Gregory to assist Augustine, the archbishop of Canterbury and the head of Gregory's first mission to the Saxons. The pope also sent a letter instructing Mellitus to tell Augustine and his fellow missionaries to destroy the Saxons' idols but to convert their pagan places of worship into churches (rather than destroy them) and to preserve local pagan festivals by turning them into Christian observances. These measures helped to make Christianity more acceptable and, consequently, greatly furthered the cause of the church in England.

Consecrated as a bishop (*c.* 604), Mellitus was directed to preach in the kingdom of the East Saxons. He baptized their king, Saberht, but failed to convert Saberht's sons. After Saberht's death, Mellitus was eventually banished by his sons, supposedly when he refused to give them the bread of Communion because they were unbelievers. After a brief exile in Gaul, he was recalled by Laurentius (Lawrence), archbishop of Canterbury, whom he succeeded in that office in 619. According to legend, Mellitus saved Canterbury from destruction by fire, the strength of his prayers summoning a great wind that drove the flames away from the city.

mellohorn: *see* mellophone.

Mellon, Andrew W., in full ANDREW WILLIAM MELLON (b. March 24, 1855, Pittsburgh, Pa., U.S.—d. Aug. 26, 1937, Southampton, N.Y.), American financier, philanthropist, and secretary of the Treasury (1921–32) who reformed the tax structure of the U.S. government in the 1920s. His benefactions made possible the building of the National Gallery of Art in Washington, D.C.

After completing his studies at Western University (now the University of Pittsburgh), Mellon entered his father's banking house in 1874 and proved so capable that in 1882 his father transferred the bank's ownership to him. In the next three decades Mellon built up a financial-industrial empire by supplying capital for Pittsburgh-based corporations to expand in such fields as aluminum, steel, oil, coal, coke, and synthetic abrasives. Mellon's keen judgment of new technologies and potentially successful firms and entrepreneurs enabled him to help found the Aluminum Company of America (Alcoa) and the Gulf Oil Company. In alliance with Henry Clay Frick, he helped found the Union Steel Company, which later merged with United States Steel Corporation. He and Frick were also the principal organizers (in 1889) of the Union Trust Company, which became Mellon's principal financial instrument and acquired his family's bank. By the early 1920s Mellon had become one of the richest men in the United States.

Mellon
EB Inc.

Mellon was appointed to head the U.S. Treasury by President Warren G. Harding in 1921. In discussions concerning reduction of the national debt, which totaled $24,000,000,000 in 1920 as a result of World War I expenditures, Mellon held that continuance of the high wartime tax rates would discourage business expansion and hence reduce revenue. He also advocated reduction of the surtax rates on incomes. Largely through his efforts Congress repealed the excess-profits tax and gradually lowered the income tax rate until in 1926 the maximum surtax was reduced from 50 to 20 percent. Further reductions in tax rates were later made; by June 30, 1928, the national debt had fallen to $17,604,000,000. As chairman ex officio of the World War I foreign debt commission, Mellon also played a prominent part in formulating U.S. policy concerning the funding of war debts owed to the United States by foreign governments. Mellon's policies helped stimulate the American economic boom of the 1920s, and he continued to head the Treasury under presidents Calvin Coolidge and Herbert Hoover. His popularity declined after the Great Depression began in 1929, however, and in 1932 he resigned to serve as U.S. ambassador to England for a year.

One of the nation's foremost art collectors, Mellon gave a collection valued at $25,000,000 to the U.S. government in 1937. It included Raphael's "Alba Madonna," 23 Rembrandts, and 6 Vermeers. Mellon donated $15,000,000 to build the National Gallery of Art, opened in 1941, to house the collection. The Andrew W. Mellon Foundation supports higher education, the arts, and cultural affairs.

Mellon Financial Corporation, American banking and financial services corporation and a longtime leader in individual asset management. Its headquarters are in Pittsburgh, Pa.

The original bank, T. Mellon and Sons Bank, was founded in 1869 by Thomas Mellon (1813–1908), a native of Ireland. One of his four sons, Andrew W. Mellon (1855–1937), joined the business in 1874 and proved so capable that the elder Mellon transferred the bank's ownership to him in 1882. With the bank as the cornerstone of his financial empire, Andrew Mellon (later treasury secretary in the Warren G. Harding, Calvin Coolidge, and Herbert Hoover administrations) helped establish Pittsburgh's leading industrial companies, including the Aluminum Company of America (Alcoa) and Gulf Oil Company. In 1902 the bank was reorganized as Mellon National Bank and became a subsidiary of Andrew Mellon's Union Trust Company. The two companies merged completely in 1946 to become Mellon National Bank and Trust Company. Andrew's younger brother Richard B. Mellon and the latter's son Richard K. Mellon successively headed the bank until 1967.

The bank's holding company, formed in 1972, was renamed Mellon Bank Corporation in 1984. In the 1960s it led in the application of data-processing technology to banking transactions. Mellon diversified into financial services in the 1980s, purchasing the Girard Company in 1982 and merging with Commonwealth National Financial Corporation in 1985. Some of its key acquisitions in the 1990s included the Boston Company, Inc., in 1993 and the Dreyfus Corporation in 1994.

Mellon continued to build its investment management business and in 1999 changed its name to Mellon Financial Corporation. Such acquisitions as Buck Consultants, Inc., in 1997 and the consulting division of Unifi Network in 2002 made Mellon a leading provider of human resources consulting.

mellophone, also called BALLAD HORN, CONCERT HORN, MELLOHORN, or TENOR COR, a brass musical instrument, an alto horn built in coiled form, often used in marching bands as a substitute for the French horn. It is pitched in E♭ or F, with a compass from the second A or B below middle C to the second E♭ or F above, derived from the orchestral horn.

The mellophone, a circular tenor horn (althorn), is usually built right handed and looks like a French horn. It bears no relationship to the mélophone, a free-reed instrument.

Melo, city, northeastern Uruguay. It lies along the Arroyo (stream) de los Conventos, an affluent of the Tacuarí River, near the Brazilian border. It was founded in 1795 by Captain Agustín de la Rosa as a Spanish military post and was named for Pedro de Melo, then viceroy of the Río de la Plata territory. Melo serves as a distribution centre for wool, hides, textiles, meats, liquor, and dairy goods. One of the city's colonial-era buildings houses a museum dedicated to the gaucho. Pop. (1996) 46,883.

Melo, Francisco Manuel de (b. Nov. 23, 1608, Lisbon, Port.—d. Oct. 13, 1666, Alcântara, near Lisbon), Portuguese soldier, diplomat, and courtier who won fame as a poet, moralist, historian, and literary critic in both the Spanish and Portuguese languages.

Born of aristocratic parents, he studied classics and mathematics at the Jesuit College of Santa Antão and chose a military career. Since Portugal was then under Spanish rule, he spent some time at the brilliant court of Madrid, where he formed a friendship with the satirist Quevedo y Villegas, the foremost Hispanic literary figure of the day. At the outbreak of the Catalan rebellion he was chief of staff to the commander of the royal forces, out of which experience came his classic history of the origin and first year of the war, *Historia de la Guerra de Cataluña* (1645; "History of the Catalan War"). When Portugal declared its independence from Spain, Melo offered his services to the new Portuguese monarch, John IV, and traveled to Holland to equip a fleet for Portugal, which he brought safely to Lisbon in October 1641. For reasons still obscure he was arrested on Nov. 19, 1644, and was in prison or under police supervision for 11 years. In 1655 his sentence was commuted to exile in Brazil, where he remained for three years, writing and restoring his fortunes by participation in the sugar trade.

During his imprisonment, he wrote constantly; he finished his history of the Catalan war and published some verse in 1649 and a popular, much-reprinted discourse on marriage, *Carta de Guia de Casados* (1650; *The Government of a Wife*). He himself never married. He edited 500 letters, most of which are a record of his experiences and thoughts in prison. They were published as *Cartas Familiares* (1664; "Personal Letters"). Many are addressed to Quevedo. In 1665 he published his *Obras Métricas* ("Poetic Works"), which includes Spanish verse betraying the Baroque conceits and Latinisms conventional in the period, and Portuguese sonnets and verse epistles that are notable for their power, sincerity, and perfection of form.

melodeon, also spelled MELODIUM, also called REED ORGAN, or AMERICAN ORGAN, keyboard instrument sounded by the vibration of free reeds by wind. It is an American development of the harmonium, from which it differs in two principal respects. Its foot-operated bellows draw the air in past the reeds by suction, rather than forcing it out by pressure; and the characteristic size and form of the reeds and resonators result in a more even dynamic level throughout the compass. It was slower to respond than the harmonium but sounded more organlike and had a softer tone.

mélodie (French: "melody"), the accompanied French art song of the 19th and 20th centuries. Following the model of the German *Lied,* the 19th-century *mélodie* was usually a setting of a serious lyric poem for solo voice and piano that recognizably combined and unified the poetic and musical forms. The earliest use of the word *mélodie* for this type of song was in the 1820s, when it was applied to the popular French translations and adaptations of Schubert's *lieder*. Berlioz was the first major composer to write in this style, which freed itself of the rigid strophic form and predominantly lighter mood of the earlier French *romance.* Other first-rank composers, recognizing the versatility and musical quality of French poetry—and inspired by the poetry of Verlaine and Baudelaire—molded the *mélodie* into a typically French tradition of song. Meyerbeer, Liszt, Gounod, Bizet, Massenet, Saint-Saëns, Lalo, and Franck all contributed to the development of the *mélodie,* although in Franck's case, his importance in this field is more noteworthy as teacher. One of Franck's pupils was Henri Duparc, whose 16 songs (composed between 1868 and 1877) became the cornerstone for one of the most important and cherished genres of French music. At about the same time, Fauré began to write songs, many forming song cycles (*La Bonne Chanson, La Chanson d'Eve, Le Jardin clos, L' Horizon chimérique,* and others) and all possessing the essence of the ideals inherent in French art and culture. Fauré's influence on the younger generation, including Ravel, was considerable and signalled the decisive turning away from the path set by the *Lied* and anticipating the French Impressionist style, exemplified by Debussy's startling and exciting *Chansons de Bilitis* (1897). The songs of Ravel and of Albert Roussel generally follow this trend, but later 20th-century vocal compositions reflect the reaction of contemporary artists and writers against various forms of Romanticism and Impressionism. Neoclassicism, jazz, and music-hall (and other pseudo-popular) styles were often employed, although the apparent gaiety was just as often only superficial, a mask for deeper and more sombre feelings. Francis Poulenc and Darius Milhaud, two members of Les Six (the Parisian group of composers that came into existence after World War I), both made important contributions to the *mélodie.* More recently, the character of French art songs has become more eclectic, and 12-note techniques have extended to athematic serialism.

melodrama, in Western theatre, sentimental drama with an improbable plot that concerns the vicissitudes suffered by the virtuous at the hands of the villainous but ends happily with virtue triumphant. Featuring stock characters such as the noble hero, the long-suffering heroine, and the cold-blooded villain, the melodrama focusses not on character development but on sensational incidents and spectacular staging. In music, melodrama signifies lines spoken to a musical accompaniment.

Stock poster for *Under the Gaslight,* a popular 19th-century melodrama

By courtesy of the Mander and Mitchenson Theatre Collection, London

The melodramatic stage play is generally regarded as having developed in France as a result of the impact of Jean-Jacques Rousseau's *Pygmalion* (1762; first performed 1770) on a society torn by violent political and social upheaval and exposed to the influences of the English Gothic novel and of Sturm und Drang (Storm and Stress) and Romanticism from Germany. The pioneer and prime exponent of the 18th-century French melodrama with its music, singing, and spectacular effects was Guilbert de Pixérécourt. His *Coelina, ou l'enfant de mystère* (1800) was translated as *A Tale of Mystery* (1802) by Thomas Holcroft and established the new genre in England. It was not utterly new to England, however; the restrictions of the Licensing Act of 1737 had been habitually evaded by combining drama with music, singing, and dancing.

Another prominent dramatist whose melodrama influenced other countries was the German August von Kotzebue. His *Menschenhass und Reue* (1789) became tremendously popular in England as *The Stranger* (1798); he also provided the original of Richard Brinsley Sheridan's *Pizarro* (1799). In the early 19th century, melodrama spread throughout the European theatre; in Russia the authorities welcomed it as diverting attention from more serious issues.

During the 19th century, music and singing were gradually eliminated. As technical developments in the theatre made greater realism possible, more emphasis was given to the spectacular—*e.g.,* snowstorms, shipwrecks, battles, train wrecks, conflagrations, earthquakes, and horse races. Among the best known and most representative of the melodramas popular in England and the United States are *The Octoroon* (1859) and *The Colleen Bawn* (1860), both by Dion Boucicault. More sensational were *The Poor of New York* (1857), *London by Night* (1844), and *Under the Gaslight* (1867). The realistic staging and the social evils touched upon, however perfunctorily and sentimentally, anticipated the later theatre of the Naturalists.

With the growing sophistication of the theatre in the early 20th century, the theatrical melodrama declined in popularity. It was a vigorous form, though, in motion picture adventure serials until the advent of sound. The exaggerated gestures, dramatic chases, emotional scenes, simple flat characters, and impossible situations were later revived and parodied. Melodrama makes up a good part of contemporary television drama.

melody, in music, the aesthetic product of a given succession of pitches in musical time, implying rhythmically ordered movement from pitch to pitch. Melody in Western music by the late 19th century was considered to be the surface of a group of harmonies. The top tone of a chord became a melody tone; chords were chosen for their colour and sense of direction relative to each other and were spaced so that a desired succession of tones lay on top. Any melody, then, had underlying chords that could be deduced. Thus, a good guitarist, analyzing mentally, can apply chords to a melody.

But melody is far older than harmony. The single line of melody was highly developed—*e.g.,* in medieval European and Byzantine plainchant, in the melodies of the trouvères and troubadours, and in the ragas and *maqāmāt* (melody types) of Indian and Arab music. Combining several lines of melody at once is polyphony; varying a melody in different ways in simultaneous performance is heterophony; combining melody and chords is homophony.

A melodic line has several characteristics that, taken together, describe it:

1. It has contour, an overall line that rises, falls, arches, undulates, or moves in any other characteristic way. For example, the first line of "My Bonnie Lies Over the Ocean" rises with a leap, then descends more or less stepwise. Melodic motion may be disjunct, using leaps, or conjunct, moving by steps; motion helps form the melody's contour.

2. Melody also has range: it occupies a certain space within the spectrum of pitches the human ear can perceive. Some primitive melodies have a range of two notes; the soprano solo in the "Kyrie Eleison" of Mozart's *Mass in C Minor* (K. 427) has a range of two octaves.

3. It has a scale. In musically sophisticated cultures, scales are formally recognized as systems of tones from which melody can be built. Melody, however, antedates the concept of scale. Scales may be abstracted from their melodies by listing the tones used in order of pitch. The intervals of a melody's scale contribute to its overall character. When children sing the ditty found throughout Europe, "It's raining, it's pouring" (g–g–e–a–g–e), they sing a melody that uses a scale of three tones; two intervals are used, a wide one (minor third) and a narrow one (major second). The harmonic minor scale of western Europe contains an interval not found in the major scale—an augmented second, as A♭–B—which contributes to the distinctive quality of many minor melodies. African and European melodies sometimes consist of chains of intervals, *e.g.,* of thirds or fourths.

Composers and improvisers draw from a number of melodic resources:

1. A theme is a melody that is not necessarily complete in itself except when designed for a set of variations but is recognizable as a pregnant phrase or clause. A fugue subject is a theme; the expositions and episodes of a sonata are groups of themes.

2. Figures or motives, small fragments of a theme, are grouped into new melodies in the "development" of a sonata. In a fugue, they carry on the music when the subject and countersubject are silent.

3. In a sequence, a figure or group of chords is repeated at different levels of pitch.

4. Ornaments, or graces (small melodic devices such as grace notes, appoggiaturas, trills, slides, tremolo, and slight deviations from standard pitch), may be used to embellish a melody. Melodic ornamentation is present in most European music and is essential to Indian, Arabic, Japanese, and much other non-Western music.

Some musical systems have complex formulaic structures called modes or melody types with which melodies are built.

melon, any of the varieties of *Cucumis melo,* a trailing vine grown for its edible, often musky-scented fruit. Melons are members of the horticulturally diverse gourd family (Cucurbitaceae). They are frost-tender annuals, native to central Asia, and widely grown in many cultivated varieties in warm regions around the world. The species has soft, hairy trailing stems, large round to lobed leaves, and yellow flowers about 2.5 centimetres (1 inch) across. The fruits of the numerous cultivated varieties differ greatly in size, shape, surface texture, and flesh colour and flavour: they weigh from 1 to 4 kilograms (2 to 9 pounds).

Seven groups of melons are cultivated:

Reticulatis group, the netted, or nutmeg, melons, including the small muskmelons and Persian melons, with net-ribbed rind and sweet orange flesh;

Cantalupensis group, the cantaloupes (named for Cantalupo, near Rome, where these melons were early grown from southwestern Asian stock), characterized by rough warty rind and sweet orange flesh;

Inodorus group, the winter melons, including the large, smooth-skinned, mildly flavoured, and light green- to white-fleshed honeydew and casaba melons;

Flexuosus group, the snake or serpent melons, up to 7 cm in diameter and about 1 metre (3 feet) long, with slightly acid cucumber-like flesh;

Conomon group, the Oriental pickling melons, with greenish flesh, neither musky nor sweet;

Chito group, the mango melons, with fruit usually the size and shape of a lemon or orange, and flesh whitish and cucumber-like;

Dudaim group, sometimes called the stinking melons, characterized by orange-sized, highly fragrant and ornamental fruit.

Cantaloupes are commonly grown commercially in Europe; the melons sold as "cantaloupes" in the U.S. are a variety of melons, especially the netted types. The familiar dessert melons in North America are the netted and winter melons. Chito, Conomon, and Flexuosus melons, grown for making preserves and pickles, and Dudaim melons, grown for their ornamental and perfumed fruits, are of commercial importance only locally.

Cantaloupes and netted melons are ripe when they give off a sweet fruity odour, at which time they "slip" or break readily at the union of fruit and stalk. Honeydews and casabas are ripe when they turn yellow, at which time they are cut from the vine; they are called the winter melons because they ripen late and mature slowly in storage for many weeks, becoming softer but not noticeably sweeter.

Plants resembling true melons include the watermelon (*q.v.*); the Chinese watermelon (*see* wax gourd); the melon tree (*see* papaya); and the melon shrub, or pear melon (*Solanum muricatum*), with purple fruit and yellow aromatic flesh, native to the Andes.

melon cactus, the genus *Melocactus,* containing about 36 species, in the family Cactaceae, native to the West Indies, Central America, and tropical South America, and distinguished by a cephalium—*i.e.,* a woolly and bristly mass topping the plant. The cephalium forms when the plant reaches a certain age, varying with the species. The common names Turk's head or Turk's cap refer to them. *Melocactus* species are also called melon-cacti or melones for their size and shape. Carmine to pink flowers, which push up through the cephalium, only the tips being visible, are followed by fruits, usually pink. Jamaican species *M. communis* is up to 100 centimetres (about 3 feet) tall and 30 cm wide.

Melon cactus (*Melocactus*)
Buzz Atkins—Photo Researchers

melorheostosis, a rare disorder of bone in which cortical bone overgrowth occurs along the main axis of a bone in such a way as to resemble candle drippings; pain is the major symptom, and stiffness and deformity may ensue. Usually only one limb and the nearest hip or shoulder are affected. The disease progresses in childhood but ceases with maturity; adults have no symptoms beyond residual disability caused by crippling.

Meloria, rocky islet in the Ligurian Sea, off the coast of Tuscany, north central Italy, opposite Livorno. Meloria is known as the site of two 13th-century naval battles, both features of the long-standing rivalry between Pisa and Genoa. In the first battle (1241) the fleets of the Holy Roman emperor Frederick II and of Pisa attacked a Genoese squadron and captured the English, French, and Spanish prelates on their way to the Lateran Council summoned by Pope Gregory IX. In the second battle in August 1284 two Genoese squadrons, commanded by Oberto Doria and Benedetto Zaccaria, crushingly defeated a numerically superior Pisan fleet under Albertino Morosini, Ugolino della Gherardesca, and Andreotto Saraceno. After this Pisa never recovered its naval power.

Melos, Modern Greek MÍLOS, island, most southwesterly of the major islands of the Greek Cyclades in the Aegean Sea. The greater portion of the 58.1-sq-mi (150.6-sq-km) island, of geologically recent volcanic origin, is rugged, culminating in the west in Mt. Profítis Ilías (2,464 ft [751 m]).

Its obsidian exports to Phoenicia helped to make it an important centre of early Aegean civilization. The bay, 165–330 ft deep, is a submerged crater created out of a violent volcanic eruption that left an isthmus approximately 1.5 mi (2.4 km) wide on the south. Mílos, the capital and chief town, lies just north of the chief port, Adhámas. Southwest of the town are catacombs in which early Christians from the Greek mainland sought refuge. On the ancient acropolis of Adamanda the famous Venus (Aphrodite) of Milo was found in 1820.

The British School at Athens excavated (1896–99) the ancient acropolis of Klima (1000–800 BC) above Mílos, uncovering a palace and a gymnasium and a Roman theatre of later date. The most significant civilization uncovered on Melos by the British School, however, was that of Phylakopi, a site near Apollonia, the second port of Melos, on the promontory of Pláka. Phylakopi was a flourishing settlement at the time of the late Bronze Age eruption of neighbouring Thera. Evidence discovered at Phylakopi in 1974 tended to reverse earlier assumptions that the eruption had destroyed the island: no break in continuity was established. The oldest city dates from between 2300 and 2000 BC. On the same site a second city rose (from 2000 to 1550 BC). The third city (1550–1100), dating largely from the Mycenaean Age, represents the fullest flowering of Melos' Cycladic civilization. Phylakopi was destroyed about 1100 by Dorian settlers.

The Athenian outrage of slaying the entire male population (416) in reprisal for the islanders' neutrality during the Peloponnesian War inspired the playwright Euripides to write and stage before his fellow Athenians his work *Trojan Women,* an anti-war play that continues as part of modern dramatic repertories. The historian Thucydides, in his "Melian Dialogue," preserved the speeches made in negotiations between the Athenians and Melians which preceded the military action. The Spartan soldier-statesman Lysander (died 395 BC) restored the island to its Dorian possessors, but it never recovered its prosperity. Under Frankish rule the island formed part of the duchy of Naxos.

In classical times Melos' sulfur, alum, and obsidian mines gave it wide commercial prominence; the Melian earth was used as a pigment by painters. Bentonite, perlite, kaolin, barium, gypsum, millstones, and salt are exported, and oranges, olives, grapes, cotton, and barley are cultivated. The island is no longer famous for the ornamental vases and the goldsmiths' art produced in the 7th century BC. Pop. (1981) town, 735; island, 4,554.

Melozzo DA FORLÌ (b. 1438, Forlì, near Ravenna—d. Nov. 8, 1494, Forlì), early Italian Renaissance painter of the Umbrian school who was one of the great fresco artists of the 15th century. He is mentioned in Forlì in 1460 and 1464 and between 1465 and 1475 probably was active at Urbino, where he came into contact with Piero della Francesca, the main source of his pictorial style; the architect Bramante; and the Flemish and Spanish painters employed by Federico da Montefeltro. Melozzo may have worked with Justus of Ghent and Pedro Berruguete on the decorations of the *studiolo* of the ducal palace at Urbino. About 1475 Melozzo moved from Urbino to Rome, where he may also have worked temporarily somewhat earlier. His first major work in Rome (completed 1477) was a fresco showing the investiture of Platina as librarian to the Pope, painted in the library of Sixtus IV in the Vatican. Records of payments of 1480 and 1481 relate to subsidiary frescoes and decorative paintings in the library. In 1478 Melozzo became a member of the Guild of St. Luke and about 1480 completed one of his most important works, a fresco of "The Ascension" in the SS. Apostoli. The athletic figures in this work amply account for the reputation Melozzo enjoyed among Giovanni Santi and other contemporary writers as an exponent of perspective and foreshortening. Melozzo seems to have left Rome in 1484, on the death of Pope Sixtus IV, after completing the decoration of a chapel (destroyed) in Sta. Maria in Trastevere, and returned there in 1489. Probably during this second Roman period he prepared cartoons for mosaics in Sta. Croce in Gerusalemme. In 1493 he was painting in the Palazzo Comunale at Ancona and later in the year returned to Forlì. Little of his work has been preserved, and none of his great decorative schemes survives intact.

"Sixtus IV Investing Platina as a Prefect of the Vatican Library," fresco (transferred to canvas) by Melozzo da Forlì, *c.* 1475–77; in the Vatican Museum
SCALA—Art Resource/EB Inc.

Melpomene, in Greek religion, one of the nine Muses, patron of tragedy and lyre play-

Melpomene, terra-cotta figurine found at Tanagra, Greece, *c.* 300 BC; in the Staatliche Museen zu Berlin, Ger.
By courtesy of the Staatliche Museen zu Berlin, Ger.

ing. In Greek art her attributes were the tragic mask and the club of Heracles. According to some traditions, the half-bird, half-woman Sirens were born from the union of Melpomene with the river god Achelous.

Melqart, also spelled MELKART, or MELKARTH, Phoenician god, chief deity of Tyre and of two of its colonies, Carthage and Gadir (Cádiz, Spain). He was also called the Tyrian Baal. Under the name Malku he was equated with the Babylonian Nergal, god of the underworld and death, and thus may have been related to the god Mot of Ras Shamra (ancient Ugarit). Melqart was usually depicted as a bearded figure, wearing a high, rounded hat and a kilt and holding an Egyptian ankh, symbol of life, and, as a symbol of death, a fenestrated ax. His sanctuary in Tyre, described by the Greek historian Herodotus (who called the temple that of Heracles), was the scene of annual winter and spring festivals and is believed to have been the model for Solomon's temple in Jerusalem.

Melqart was probably equated with the sun, and Baal Hammon (Baal Amon), "Lord of the Incense Altar," was perhaps his title in that capacity. Baal Hammon was also the name of the chief god of Carthage, consort of the goddess Tanit.

Consult the INDEX *first*

Melrhir, Chott, lake in northeastern Algeria. Lying almost entirely below sea level, the Chott Melrhir is a marshy, saline lake that fluctuates in area with the seasons; usually, it is more than 80 miles (130 km) wide east–west. The Melrhir occupies the westernmost of a series of depressions extending into the Sahara from the Gulf of Gabès, Tunisia. The lowest point in Algeria, 131 feet (40 m) below sea level, is near the lake's centre.

Melrose, small burgh, Ettrick and Lauderdale district, Borders region, Scotland, on the right bank of the River Tweed. It lies 33 miles (53 km) southeast of Edinburgh. The original Columban monastery was founded nearby in the 7th century at Old Melrose. It was burned in 839 during the wars between the Scots and Angles, and, although it was rebuilt, it was deserted in the mid-11th century. In 1136 an abbey was founded a little higher up the Tweed. The abbey was frequently attacked and was destroyed in 1322 and again in 1385 and was finally reduced to ruin by the English in 1545. In 1822 the ruins were repaired under the supervision of the Scottish novelist Sir Walter Scott, whose country home was located at nearby Abbotsford. The work was carried out for the owner, the Duke of Buccleuch, who subsequently presented the restored ruins to the nation. The southern front of the abbey is still impressive, but the western front and much of the nave have disappeared. The heart of Robert I the Bruce, the Scottish national leader who won the throne in 1306, was buried at the high altar.

Melrose Abbey, Scotland
Kenneth Scowen

The town of Melrose grew and prospered under the auspices of the abbey. Since the death of Sir Walter Scott (1832), Melrose, with its literary and historical associations, has attracted many tourists. Near Newstead, an eastern suburb, was the Roman fort of Trimontium. Melrose is now an agricultural market town. Pop. (1981) 2,345.

melting: *see* thermal fusion.

melting point, temperature at which the solid and liquid forms of a pure substance can exist in equilibrium. As heat is applied to a solid, its temperature will increase until the melting point is reached. More heat then will convert the solid into a liquid with no temperature change. When all the solid has melted, additional heat will raise the temperature of the liquid. The melting temperature of crystalline solids is a characteristic figure and is used to identify pure compounds and elements. Most mixtures and amorphous solids melt over a range of temperatures.

The melting temperature of a solid is generally considered to be the same as the freezing point (*q.v.*) of the corresponding liquid; because a liquid may freeze in different crystal systems and because impurities lower the freezing point, however, the actual freezing point may not be the same as the melting point. Thus, for characterizing a substance, the melting point is preferred. *See also* thermal fusion.

Melton, district (borough), county of Leicestershire, south-central England, occupying an area of 186 square miles (482 square km) in the northeastern part of the county. Melton district is a slightly elevated (about 400 feet [120 m]), partly wooded, rolling countryside dotted with stone-built villages. The only parish (town) of consequence, Melton Mowbray, has an important cattle market and is the administrative seat in the district's centre. The rich pastureland is grazed by New Leicester sheep (first bred locally), cattle (both beef and dairy), and pigs. During World War II a considerable amount of the district's land was plowed for the first time in centuries, but since then much of it has reverted to pasture. Pies made of pork and Stilton cheese have long been associated with Melton Mowbray.

Industries in the parish produce hosiery, knitwear, and processed pet foods. Horses and dogs are trained in the vicinity for use by the military, and ironstone is extracted at Holwell and Asfordby, north of Melton Mowbray. Extensive coal deposits were discovered in 1976 under the Vale of Belvoir in the northeast, but their exploitation was delayed by its potentially unfavourable environmental impact and labour–management disagreements. Melton Mowbray has the cruciform Church of St. Mary (built 1280–1330) that contains rare double-aisled transepts. Fox hunting is a popular local sport in Melton; sites such as Belvoir in the district and its vicinity have particular hunts named after them. Pop. (1986 est.) 42,900.

Melun, town, capital of Seine-et-Marne *département,* Île-de-France *région,* northern France. It lies 28 miles (45 km) south-southeast of Paris. Like Paris, it is situated on both banks of the Seine, and its ancient church of Notre-Dame stands on an island between two branches of the river. Built in the 11th century, the church underwent several alterations before being completely restored in the 19th century. The fine 17th-century château of Vaux-le-Vicomte stands 4 miles (6 km) northeast of the town. Melun, which was called Melodunum by the Romans, became the favourite residence of the kings of France in medieval times. It was seriously damaged by bombing in World War II.

Located on the northern edge of the Fontainebleau Forest, the town is a commercial centre for the agricultural district of southern Brie. It holds an annual fair in May. Industries include mechanical, aeronautical, and food-processing plants. The future growth of the city is assured by the construction of a new town, Melun-Senart, just to the north. Pop. (1982) 34,379.

Melun-Sénart, new town (French *ville nouvelle*), located immediately north of Melun in the *départements* of Seine-et-Marne and Essonne, north-central France. Melun-Sénart, which is southeast of Paris, is one of several new towns developed outside the capital since 1965. The agglomeration of Melun-Sénart includes Melun and the communes of Boissettes, Dammarie-Les-Lyes, Livry-sur-Seine, Le Mée-sur Seine, La Rochette, Rubelles, and Vaux-le-Pénil. The new town of Évry is nearby. Pop. (1982) agglomeration, 81,732.

Melville, Andrew (b. Aug. 1, 1545, Baldovie, Angus, Scot.—d. 1622, Sedan, Fr.), scholar and Reformer who succeeded John Knox as a leader of the Scottish Reformed Church, giving that church its Presbyterian character by replacing bishops with local presbyteries, and gaining international respect for Scottish universities.

Andrew Melville, engraving
By kind permission of the Church of Scotland; photograph, Scottish National Portrait Gallery, Edinburgh

After attending Scottish universities and the University of Paris, Melville left for Geneva in 1569, where he studied under the Protestant Reformer Theodore Beza. Returning to Scotland in 1574, Melville set out to reform its schools. As principal of the University of Glasgow (1574–80), as visitor to Aberdeen (1575), and as principal of St. Mary's College at St. Andrews in Edinburgh (1580–1606), he introduced educational methods he had learned from European scholars. Under his influence, new students came from at home and abroad, and many foreign students trained in Scotland returned to teach in Reformed institutions overseas. In Scotland a vacuum had been left in Reformed Church governance after the death in 1572 of its principal leader, John Knox, and Melville in 1574 began to act in his stead, his major concern being the preservation of the independence of the church from state control. The *Second Book of Discipline* (1578), largely his work, was incorporated in the act of religious settlement of 1592, but only after he had suffered virtual banishment for it in 1584–85.

In 1597, when King James VI of Scotland began to undermine the charter he had earlier granted, Melville led the resistance against royal attacks upon the newly legitimated liberties. Despite royal prohibition, a general assembly met at Aberdeen in 1605, but then respected a royal order of dismissal by simply fixing the date of the next meeting and conducting no other business. That act brought imprisonment or banishment to 14 ministers, and in 1606 Melville was summoned to London with seven other ministers by James, then James I of England, to help resolve the crisis. Melville's group spoke in behalf of a new assembly, but his satiric Latin poem composed to combat constant Anglican pressures on him turned his own career in another direction. Imprisoned in the Tower of London for four years for his intransigence, Melville was released only to accept a chair in France, that of biblical theology at the University of Sedan, where he remained until his death.

Melville, George Wallace (b. July 31, 1841, New York City—d. March 17, 1912, Philadelphia), U.S. explorer and naval engineer who led the sole surviving party from George Washington De Long's tragic North Polar expedition.

Melville entered the U.S. Navy in 1861 and in 1879 joined De Long's crew on the "Jeanette." When the vessel became lodged in the ice off northeastern Siberia, Melville's engineering skill helped keep it afloat for almost two years until it was finally crushed. After a long, arduous journey by boat and sledge, Melville and a group of men reached the Siberian shore and obtained help at the mouth of the Lena River. He then led an expedition that found the remains of De Long and his party the following spring. The incredible hardships the searchers endured on their 500-mile (800-kilometre) trek are modestly told in Melville's *In the Lena Delta* (1884). He was again chief engineer aboard the "Thetis" on a mission that in June 1884 rescued the survivors from Adolphus Washington Greely's Arctic expedition.

George Melville

By courtesy of the Library of Congress, Washington, D.C.

In 1887 Melville became engineer in chief of the U.S. Navy. During a period when a modern navy was being built, he designed machinery for 120 ships of more than 700,000 horsepower. For a decade, two of them were the fastest warships afloat. He introduced various engineering improvements, including the triple screw (a propellor system) and the vertical boiler. Before his retirement as rear admiral in 1903, he brought about a general reform of the naval engineering department.

Melville (of Melville), Henry Dundas, 1st Viscount, Baron Dunira (b. April 28, 1742, Arniston, Midlothian, Scot.—d. May 28, 1811, Edinburgh), British careerist politician who held various ministerial offices under William Pitt the Younger and whose adroit control of Scottish politics earned him the nickname "King Harry the Ninth." Educated at the University of Edinburgh, he became a member of the faculty of advocates in 1763 and soon acquired a leading position at the bar; but after his appointment as lord advocate in 1775, he gradually relinquished his legal practice to devote his attention more exclusively to public business. In 1774 he was returned to Parliament for Midlothian and joined the party of Lord North; and, notwithstanding his provincial dialect and ungraceful manner, he soon distinguished himself by his clear and argumentative speeches.

After holding subordinate offices under the Marquess of Lansdowne and Pitt, he entered the Cabinet in 1791 as home secretary. From 1794 to 1801 he was secretary at war under Pitt, who conceived for him a special friendship. In 1802 he was elevated to the peerage as Viscount Melville and Baron Dunira. Under Pitt in 1804 he again entered office as first lord of the Admiralty, when he introduced numerous improvements in the details of the department. Suspicion had arisen, however, as to the financial management of the Admiralty, of which Dundas had been treasurer between 1782 and 1800; in 1802 a commission of inquiry was appointed, which reported in 1805. The result was the impeachment of Lord Melville in 1806 for the misappropriation of public money; and though it ended in an acquittal, and nothing more than formal negligence lay against him, he never again held office. An earldom was offered in 1809 but declined.

Melville, Herman (b. Aug. 1, 1819, New York City—d. Sept. 28, 1891, New York City), American novelist, short-story writer, and poet, best known for his novels of the sea, including his masterpiece, *Moby Dick* (1851).

Heritage and youth. Melville's heritage and youthful experiences were perhaps crucial in forming the conflicts underlying his artistic vision. He was the third child of Allan and Maria Gansevoort Melvill, in a family that was to grow to four boys and four girls. His forebears had been among the Scottish and Dutch settlers of New York and had taken leading roles in the American Revolution and in the fiercely competitive commercial and political life of the new country. One grandfather, Maj. Thomas Melvill, was a member of the Boston Tea Party in 1773 and was subsequently a New York importer. The other, Gen. Peter Gansevoort, was a friend of James Fenimore Cooper and famous for leading the defense of Ft. Stanwix, in upstate New York, against the British.

Herman Melville, detail of an oil painting by Joseph Oriel Eaton; in the Houghton Library, Harvard University

By courtesy of the Harvard College Library

In 1826 Allan Melvill wrote of his son as being "backward in speech and somewhat slow in comprehension . . . of a docile and amiable disposition." In that same year, scarlet fever left the boy with permanently weakened eyesight, but he attended Male High School. When the family import business collapsed in 1830, the family returned to Albany, where Herman enrolled briefly in Albany Academy. Allan Melvill died in 1832, leaving his family in desperate straits. The eldest son, Gansevoort, assumed responsibility for the family and took over his father's felt and fur business. Herman joined him after two years as a bank clerk and some months working on the farm of his uncle, Thomas Melvill, in Pittsfield, Mass. About this time, Herman's branch of the family altered the spelling of its name. Though finances were precarious, Herman attended Albany Classical School in 1835 and became an active member of a local debating society. A teaching job in Pittsfield made him unhappy, however, and after three months he returned to Albany.

Wanderings and voyages. Young Melville had already begun writing, but the remainder of his youth became a quest for security. A comparable pursuit in the spiritual realm was to characterize much of his writing. The crisis that started Herman on his wanderings came in 1837, when Gansevoort went bankrupt and the family moved to nearby Lansingburgh (later Troy). In what was to be a final attempt at orthodox employment, Herman studied surveying at Lansingburgh Academy to equip himself for a post with the Erie Canal project. When the job did not materialize, Gansevoort arranged for Herman to ship out as cabin boy on the "St. Lawrence," a merchant ship sailing in June 1839 from New York City for Liverpool. The summer voyage did not dedicate Melville to the sea, and on his return his family was dependent still on the charity of relatives. After a grinding search for work, he taught briefly in a school that closed without paying him. His uncle Thomas, who had left Pittsfield for Illinois, apparently had no help to offer when the young man followed him west. In January 1841 Melville sailed on the whaler "Acushnet," from New Bedford, Mass., on a voyage to the South Seas.

In June 1842 the "Acushnet" anchored in the Marquesas Islands in present-day French Polynesia. Melville's adventures here, somewhat romanticized, became the subject of his first novel, *Typee* (1846). In July Melville and a companion jumped ship and, according to *Typee,* spent about four months as guest-captives of the reputedly cannibalistic Typee people. Actually, in August he was registered in the crew of the Australian whaler "Lucy Ann." Whatever its precise correspondence with fact, however, *Typee* was faithful to the imaginative impact of the experience on Melville. Despite intimations of danger, Melville represented the exotic valley of the Typees as an idyllic sanctuary from a hustling, aggressive civilization.

Although Melville was down for a 120th share of the whaler's proceeds, the voyage had been unproductive. He joined a mutiny that landed the mutineers in a Tahitian jail, from which he escaped without difficulty. On these events and their sequel, Melville based his second book, *Omoo* (1847). Lighthearted in tone, with the mutiny shown as something of a farce, it describes Melville's travels through the islands, accompanied by Long Ghost, formerly the ship's doctor, now turned drifter. The carefree roving confirmed Melville's bitterness against colonial and, especially, missionary debasement of the native Tahitian peoples.

These travels, in fact, occupied less than a month. In November he signed as a harpooner on his last whaler, the "Charles & Henry," out of Nantucket, Mass. Six months later he disembarked at Lahaina, in the Hawaiian Islands. Somehow he supported himself for more than three months; then in August 1843 he signed as an ordinary seaman on the frigate "United States," which in October 1844 discharged him in Boston.

The years of acclaim. Melville rejoined a family whose prospects had much improved. Gansevoort, who after James K. Polk's victory in the 1844 presidential elections had been appointed secretary to the U.S. legation in London, was gaining political renown. Encouraged by his family's enthusiastic reception of his tales of the South Seas, Melville wrote them down. The years of acclaim were about to begin for Melville.

Typee provoked immediate enthusiasm and outrage, and then a year later *Omoo* had an identical response. Gansevoort, dead of a brain disease, never saw his brother's career consolidated, but the bereavement left Melville head of the family and the more committed to writing to support it. Another responsibility came with his marriage in August 1847 to Elizabeth Shaw, daughter of the chief justice of Massachusetts. He tried unsuccessfully for a job in the U.S. Treasury Department, the first of many abortive efforts to secure a government post.

In 1847 Melville began a third book, *Mardi* (1849), and became a regular contributor of reviews and other pieces to a literary journal. To his new literary acquaintances in New York City he appeared the character of his own books—extrovert, vigorous, "with his cigar and his Spanish eyes," as one writer described him. Melville resented this somewhat patronizing stereotype, and in her reminiscences his wife recalled him in a different aspect, writing in a bitterly cold, fireless room in winter. He enjoined his publisher not to call him "the author of *Typee* and *Omoo*," for his third book was to be different. When it appeared, public and critics alike found its wild, allegorical fantasy and medley of styles incomprehensible. It began as another Polynesian adventure but quickly set its hero in pursuit of the mysterious Yillah, "all beauty and innocence," a symbolic quest that ends in anguish and disaster. Concealing his disappointment at the book's reception, Melville quickly wrote *Redburn* (1849) and *White-Jacket* (1850) in the manner expected of him. In October 1849 Melville sailed to England to resolve his London publisher's doubts about *White-Jacket.* He also visited the Continent, kept a journal, and arrived back in America in February 1850. The critics acclaimed *White-Jacket,* and its powerful criticism of abuses in the U.S. Navy won it strong political support. But both novels, however much they seemed to revive the Melville of *Typee,* had passages of profoundly questioning melancholy. It was not the same Melville who wrote them. He had been reading Shakespeare with "eyes which are as tender as young sparrows," particularly noting sombre passages in *Measure for Measure* and *King Lear.* This reading struck deeply sympathetic responses in Melville, counterbalancing the Transcendental doctrines of Ralph Waldo Emerson, whose general optimism about human goodness he had heard in lectures. A fresh imaginative influence was supplied by Nathaniel Hawthorne's *Scarlet Letter,* a novel deeply exploring good and evil in the human being, which Melville read in the spring of 1850. That summer, Melville bought a farm, which he christened "Arrowhead," near Hawthorne's home at Pittsfield, and the two men became neighbours physically as well as in sympathies.

Melville had promised his publishers for the autumn of 1850 the novel first entitled *The Whale,* finally *Moby Dick.* His delay in submitting it was caused less by his early-morning chores as a farmer than by his explorations into the unsuspected vistas opened for him by Hawthorne. Their relationship reanimated Melville's creative energies. On his side, it was dependent, almost mystically intense—"an infinite fraternity of feeling," he called it. To the cooler, withdrawn Hawthorne, such depth of feeling so persistently and openly declared was uncongenial. The two men gradually drew apart. They met for the last time, almost as strangers, in 1856, when Melville visited Liverpool, where Hawthorne was American consul.

Moby Dick was published in London in October 1851 and a month later in America. It brought its author neither acclaim nor reward. Basically its story is simple. Captain Ahab pursues the white whale, Moby Dick, which finally kills him. At that level, it is an intense, superbly authentic narrative of whaling. In the perverted grandeur of Captain Ahab and in the beauties and terrors of the voyage of the "Pequod," however, Melville dramatized his deeper concerns: the equivocal defeats and triumphs of the human spirit and its fusion of creative and murderous urges. In his private afflictions, Melville had found universal metaphors.

Increasingly a recluse to the point that some friends feared for his sanity, Melville embarked almost at once on *Pierre* (1852). It was an intensely personal work, revealing the sombre mythology of his private life framed in terms of a story of an artist alienated from his society. In it can be found the humiliated responses to poverty that his youth supplied him plentifully and the hypocrisy he found beneath his father's claims to purity and faithfulness. His mother he had idolized; yet he found the spirituality of her love betrayed by sexual love. The novel, a slightly veiled allegory of Melville's own dark imaginings, was rooted in these relations. When published, it was another critical and financial disaster. Only 33 years old, Melville saw his career in ruins. Near breakdown, and having to face in 1853 the disaster of a fire at his New York publishers that destroyed most of his books, Melville persevered with writing.

Israel Potter, plotted before his introduction to Hawthorne and his work, was published in 1855, but its modest success, clarity of style, and apparent simplicity of subject did not indicate a decision by Melville to write down to public taste. His contributions to *Putnam's Monthly Magazine*—"Bartleby the Scrivener" (1853), "The Encantadas" (1854), and "Benito Cereno" (1855)—reflected the despair and the contempt for human hypocrisy and materialism that possessed him increasingly.

In 1856 Melville set out on a tour of Europe and the Levant to renew his spirits. The most powerful passages of the journal he kept are in harmony with *The Confidence-Man* (1857), a despairing satire on an America corrupted by the shabby dreams of commerce. This was the last of his novels to be published in his lifetime. Three American lecture tours were followed by his final sea journey, in 1860, when he joined his brother Thomas, captain of the clipper "Meteor," for a voyage around Cape Horn. He abandoned the trip in San Francisco.

The years of withdrawal. Melville abandoned the novel for poetry, but the prospects for publication were not favourable. With two sons and daughters to support, Melville sought government patronage. A consular post he sought in 1861 went elsewhere. On the outbreak of the Civil War, he volunteered for the Navy, but was again rejected. He had apparently returned full cycle to the insecurity of his youth, but an inheritance from his father-in-law brought some relief and "Arrowhead," increasingly a burden, was sold. By the end of 1863, the family was living in New York City. The war was much on his mind and furnished the subject of his first volume of verse, *Battle-Pieces and Aspects of the War* (1866), published privately. Four months after it appeared, an appointment as a customs inspector on the New York docks finally brought him a secure income.

Despite poor health, Melville began a pattern of writing evenings, weekends, and on vacations. In 1867 his son Malcolm shot himself, accidentally the jury decided, though it appeared that he had quarrelled with his father the night before his death. His second son, Stanwix, who had gone to sea in 1869, died in a San Francisco hospital in 1886 after a long illness. Throughout these griefs, and for the whole of his 19 years in the customs house, Melville's creative pace was understandably slowed.

His second collection of verse, *John Marr, and Other Sailors; With Some Sea-Pieces,* appeared in 1888, again privately published. By then he had been in retirement for three years, assisted by legacies from friends and relatives. His new leisure he devoted, he wrote in 1889, to "certain matters as yet incomplete." Among them was *Timoleon* (1891), a final verse collection. More significant was the return to prose that culminated in his last work, the novel *Billy Budd,* which remained unpublished until 1924. Provoked by a false charge, the sailor Billy Budd accidentally kills the satanic master-at-arms. In a time of threatened mutiny he is hanged, going willingly to his fate. Evil has not wholly triumphed, and Billy's memory lives on as an emblem of good. Here there is, if not a statement of being reconciled fully to life, at least the peace of resignation. The manuscript ends with the date April 19, 1891. Five months later Melville died. His life was neither happy nor, by material standards, successful. By the end of the 1840s he was among the most celebrated of American writers, yet his death evoked but a single obituary notice.

In the internal tensions that put him in conflict with his age lay a strangely 20th-century awareness of the deceptiveness of realities and of the instability of personal identity. Yet his writings never lost sight of reality. His symbols grew from such visible facts, made intensely present, as the dying whales, the mess of blubber, and the wood of the ship, in *Moby Dick.* For Melville, as for Shakespeare, man was ape and essence, inextricably compounded; and the world, like the "Pequod," was subject to "two antagonistic influences . . . one to mount direct to heaven, the other to drive yawingly to some horizontal goal." It was Melville's triumph that he endured, recording his vision to the end. After the years of neglect, modern criticism has secured his reputation with that of the great American writers.

(D.E.S.M./Ed.)

MAJOR WORKS. *Novels. Typee: A Peep at Polynesian Life* (1846); *Omoo: A Narrative of Adventures in the South Seas* (1847); *Mardi and a Voyage Thither* (1849), a political and philosophical allegory; *Redburn, His First Voyage* (1849); *White-Jacket; or, The World in a Man-of-War* (1850); *Moby Dick; or, The Whale* (1851, as *Moby Dick; or, The White Whale* in some later 19th-century editions); *Pierre; or The Ambiguities* (1852); *Israel Potter: His Fifty Years of Exile,* (1855), a historical novel of the American Revolution; *The Confidence-Man: His Masquerade* (1857), a satirical allegory; *Billy Budd, Foretopman,* a short novel written 1888–91 and found after Melville's death; first published in *Billy Budd, and Other Prose Pieces* (1924).

Other stories, sketches, and journals. The Piazza Tales (1856), includes "The Piazza," "Bartleby the Scrivener," "Benito Cereno," "The Encantadas, or, Enchanted Isles," and "The Lightning-Rod Man"; *The Apple-Tree Table and Other Sketches* (1922), contains 10 sketches first published in periodicals, 1850–56; *Journal up the Straits, October 1, 1856–May 5, 1857* (1935); *Journal of Melville's Voyage in the Clipper Ship, "Meteor"* (1929).

Verse. Battle-Pieces and Aspects of the War (1866); *Clarel: A Poem and Pilgrimage in the Holy Land* (1876); *John Marr, and Other Sailors; With Some Sea-Pieces* (1888); *Timoleon* (1891), a collection. Poems unpublished during Melville's lifetime are included in later collections and selections.

BIBLIOGRAPHY. Studies of the author's life and work include Edward H. Rosenberry, *Melville* (1979), an introductory survey; Edwin H. Miller, *Melville* (1975), a psychobiography; Raymond M. Weaver, *Herman Melville, Mariner and Mystic* (1921, reissued 1968), interesting as the first biography; Lewis Mumford, *Herman Melville,* rev. ed. (1963), a little outmoded, but a sensitive appreciation of the man; Newton Arvin, *Herman Melville* (1950, reprinted 1976), a judicious critical biography; Leon Howard, *Herman Melville: A Biography* (1951, reissued 1967), a complete factual account of Melville's life, perceptively analytic; Jay Leyda, *The Melville Log: A Documentary Life of Herman Melville, 1819–1891,* 2 vol. (1951, reissued 1969), a fascinating collection of documents, photographs, and letters; William H. Gilman, *Melville's Early Life and Redburn* (1951, reissued 1972), a thorough record of Melville's youth and the relationships between fact and fiction in *Redburn;* and Tyrus Hillway, *Herman Melville,* rev. ed. (1979), a concise analytical biography. For literary criticism, see William E. Sedgwick, *Herman Melville: The Tragedy of Mind* (1944, reissued 1972), one of the best studies of Melville's ideas as they appear in his novels; A.R. Humphreys, *Melville* (1962), an excellent introductory study; and Kerry McSweeney, *Moby-Dick: Ishmael's Mighty Book* (1986), a compact but insightful and readable analysis of key points of the work and of its place among Melville's other works.

Melville, James (b. July 26, 1556, near Montrose, Angus, Scot.—d. Jan. 13, 1614, Berwick-upon-Tweed, Northumberland, Eng.), Scottish Presbyterian reformer and educator.

Melville studied at the University of St. Andrews, where he heard John Knox preach, in 1571–72. He taught at the University of Glasgow (1575–80) and at St. Andrews (1581–84), helping his uncle Andrew Melville, who had succeeded John Knox as leader of the Scottish Reformed Church, in his efforts to preserve the church from state control. As moderator of the Church of Scotland's general assembly (1589), he opposed any effort to establish conformity with the church government in England. In May 1606 he and his uncle and other ministers were called to London to confer with King James I on church affairs in Scotland. After his uncle was imprisoned in the Tower of London, James Melville was detained in England at Newcastle-on-Tyne until 1613 for his continued refusal to accept the king's policy.

Melville, Jean-Pierre, pseudonym of JEAN-PIERRE GRUMBACH (b. Oct. 20, 1917, Paris—d. Aug. 2, 1973, Paris), French motion-picture director whose early films strongly influenced the directors of the New Wave, the innovative French film movement of the late 1950s.

Grumbach's enthusiasm for American culture prompted him to change his name to that of his favourite writer, Herman Melville. He served in the Free French forces during World War II, founded his own film production company in 1946, and built his own studio in 1949. Melville's early films, such as *Le Silence de la mer* (1947; "The Silence of the Sea"), were made on small budgets and used character actors instead of established stars. His other early films were *Les Enfants terribles* (1948; "The Little Terrors"), a brilliant screen adaptation of the novel by Jean Cocteau; *Bob le flambeur* (1955), his first gangster film; and *Deux hommes à Manhattan* (1958; "Two Men in Manhattan"). Melville's use of location shooting, natural lighting, and improvisational acting in these films strongly influenced such later directors as Claude Chabrol, François Truffaut, and Jean-Luc Godard.

The stylized decor of Melville's later, more commercial works is strongly reminiscent of the Hollywood products of the 1930s. *Léon Morin, prêtre* (1961; "Leon Morin, Priest") was his first major commercial production. It was followed by a series of highly stylized, Hollywood-inspired gangster films: *Le Doulos* (1962; *Doulos—The Finger Man*), *Le Deuxième Souffle* (1966; "Second Wind"), and *Le Samourai* (1967; "The Samurai").

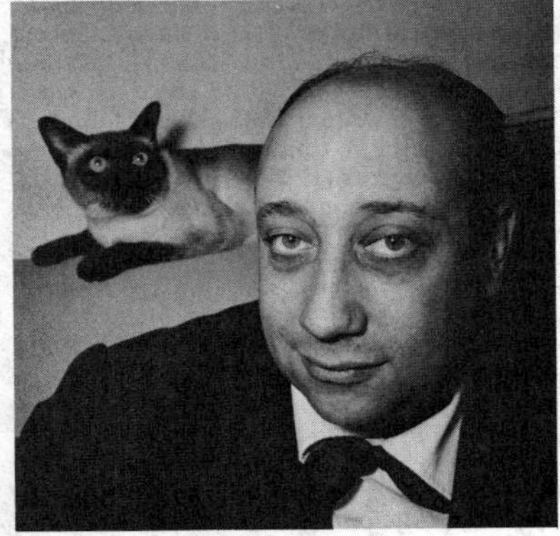

Jean-Pierre Melville
H. Roger-Viollet

Melville Island, island in the Timor Sea, 16 miles (26 km) off the coast of Arnhem Land, Northern Territory, Australia. It is separated from the Australian mainland by Clarence Strait. Measuring about 80 by 55 miles (130 by 88 km), it has an area of 2,240 square miles (5,800 square km) and rises from sandy beaches and shoreline mangrove swamps to low wooded hills. It is divided from Bathurst Island (west) by the narrow Apsley Strait and from Coburg Peninsula (east) by the Dundas Strait. The island, sighted in 1644 by the Dutch navigator Abel Tasman, was named in 1818 by Captain Phillip Parker King in honour of Robert Saunders Dundas, 2nd Viscount Melville, first lord of the Admiralty. The island was the site (1824–29) of Fort Dundas, the first British attempt to settle Australia's north coast. Populated chiefly by Aborigines, with a government settlement and Catholic missions, the island produces some pearls, trepang (sea cucumbers), and timber. Large herds of wild buffalo, descended from introduced Asian stock that infested the island, have recently been exterminated. Melville Island, known to Aborigines as Yermalner, is one of the few areas in Australia still occupied by its original Aboriginal peoples, the Tiwi, and in 1978 ownership of the island passed from the Australian government to the Tiwi Land Council. Pop. (1981) 554.

Melville Island, one of the largest of the Parry Islands, in the Arctic Ocean, Baffin region, Northwest Territories, Canada. Separated from Victoria Island (south) by Viscount Melville Sound and from Banks Island (southwest) by McClure Strait, Melville Island is about 200 miles (320 km) long and 30–130 miles (50–210 km) wide with an area of 16,274 square miles (42,149 square km). Deeply indented by Hecla Eldridge and Griper bays on the north coast and by Liddon Gulf on the southwest, the island rises in the northwest to 3,500 feet (1,067 m). It has no human habitation but supports musk-oxen and has natural-gas deposits. Discovered (1819) by Sir William Parry, it was named after Robert Saunders Dundas, 2nd Viscount Melville, then first lord of the Admiralty.

Melville Sound (Arctic Ocean): *see* Viscount Melville Sound.

membrane, in biology, the thin layer that forms the outer boundary of a living cell or of an internal cell compartment. The outer boundary is the plasma membrane, and the compartments enclosed by internal membranes are called organelles. Biological membranes have a dual function: (1) they separate vital but incompatible metabolic processes conducted in the organelles and keep toxic substances out of the cell; and (2) they allow specific nutrients, wastes, and metabolic products to pass between organelles and between the cell and the outside environment.

A brief treatment of biological membranes follows. For full treatment, *see* MACROPAEDIA: Cells: Their Structures and Functions.

Membranes consist largely of a lipid bilayer, which is a double wall of phospholipid, cholesterol, and glycolipid molecules containing chains of fatty acids. Lipids give cell membranes a fluid character, with a consistency approaching that of a light oil. The fatty-acid chains allow many small, fat-soluble molecules, such as oxygen, to permeate the membrane, but they repel large, water-soluble molecules, such as sugar, and electrically charged ions, such as calcium.

Embedded in the lipid bilayer are large proteins, many of which transport ions and water-soluble molecules across the membrane. Some proteins in the plasma membrane form open pores, called membrane channels, which allow the free diffusion of ions into and out of the cell. Others bind to specific molecules on one side of a membrane and, in a process that is not clearly understood, transport the molecules to the other side. Sometimes one protein simultaneously transports two types of molecules in opposite directions. Most plasma membranes are about 50 percent protein by weight, while the membranes of some metabolically active organelles are 75 percent.

Attached to proteins on the outside of the plasma membrane are long carbohydrate molecules. Although their exact functions are unknown, they are believed to act in the recognition of substances from the extracellular environment and from other cells.

Many cellular functions, including the uptake and conversion of nutrients, synthesis of new molecules, production of energy, and regulation of metabolic sequences, take place in the organelles. The nucleus, containing the genetic material of the cell, is surrounded by a double membrane with large pores that permit the exchange of materials from within and outside the cell. The nuclear membrane is an extension of the membrane of the endoplasmic reticulum, which synthesizes the lipids for all cell membranes. Proteins are synthesized by ribosomes that are either attached to the endoplasmic reticulum or suspended freely in the cell contents. The mitochondria, the oxidizing and energy-storing units of the cell, have an outer membrane readily permeable to many substances, and a less-permeable inner membrane studded with transport proteins and energy-producing enzymes.

membranophone, any of a class of musical instruments in which a stretched membrane vibrates to produce sound. Besides drums, the basic types include the mirliton, or kazoo, and the friction drum (sounded by friction produced by drawing a stick back and forth through a hole in the membrane).

According to shape, drums are classified as barrel, conical, cylindrical, footed, frame, goblet, long, vessel, and waisted. The names membranophone and idiophone (instruments whose solid, resonant body vibrates to produce sound) replace the looser term percussion instruments when an acoustically based classification is required. *Compare* aerophone; chordophone; electrophone; idiophone.

Memel (Lithuania): *see* Klaipėda.

Memel dispute, Memel also called KLAIPĖDA, post-World War I dispute regarding sovereignty over the former German Prussian territory of Memelland. Its seizure by Lithuania was eventually approved by the great powers.

Before World War I, Memelland, an area on the Baltic Sea located to the north of the Neman (Memel) River, belonged to Prussia.

Memelland

From A. Senn, *The Emergence of Modern Lithuania*

A large portion of its population, particularly outside the port city of Memel, however, was Lithuanian; and after the war the newly formed state of Lithuania requested that the Allied Powers at the Paris Peace Conference grant it possession of the Memel territory (March 24, 1919). The Allied Powers did detach Memelland from Germany (Versailles Treaty; Article 99); but rather than annex the region to Lithuania, whose political situation was then unstable, they assumed direct control over the area, appointed a French administration to rule it, and only in the fall of 1922 created a special commission to review the status of Memelland. When that commission displayed sympathy for a plan, supported by German and Polish interest groups, to transform Memelland into a free state, Lithuanian inhabitants of the region formed a Committee for the Salvation of Lithuania Minor, gained the support of numerous volunteers from Lithuania proper, and on Jan. 9, 1923, announced at Šilutė (Heydekrug) that they were taking over the government of Memelland in order to unite the region, as an autonomous unit, with Lithuania. By January 15 the Lithuanian forces had gained control over the entire district, including the city of Memel. The Allied Powers sent formal notes to Lithuania protesting against this action, but their Ambassadors' Conference decided on February 16 to place Memelland under Lithuanian control. The subsequent negotiations concerning the nature of the union and control of the port continued inconclusively until December; and only after the matter was referred to the League of Nations did Lithuania reach an accord with Great Britain, France, Italy, and Japan (the member states of the Ambassadors' Conference) and sign the Memel Statute, which officially made Memelland an autonomous region within Lithuania, outlined the governmental structure of the territory, and also established an administrative body for the port of Memel, renamed Klaipėda.

The Memel Statute remained in effect until March 23, 1939, when Lithuania was forced to accept a German ultimatum demanding the return of Memelland. At the close of World War II, it was returned to Lithuania, which by then had become part of the U.S.S.R.

Memling, Hans, Memling also spelled MEMLINC (b. *c.* 1430/35, Seligenstadt, near Frankfurt am Main—d. Aug. 11, 1494, Bruges), leading Flemish painter of the Bruges school during the period of the city's political and commercial decline. The number of his imitators and followers testified to his popularity throughout Flanders. His last commission, which has been widely copied, is a Crucifixion panel from the "Passion Triptych" (1491).

Memling, born in the region of the Middle Rhine, was apparently first schooled in the art of Cologne and then travelled to the Netherlands (*c.* 1455–60), where he probably trained in the workshop of the painter Rogier van der Weyden. He settled in Bruges (Brugge) in 1465; there he established a large shop and executed numerous altarpieces and portraits. Indeed, he was very successful in Bruges: it is known that he owned a large stone house and by 1480 was listed among the wealthiest citizens on the city tax accounts. Sometime between 1470 and 1480 Memling married Anna de Valkenaere (died 1487), who bore him three children.

A number of Memling's works are signed and dated, and still others allow art historians to place them easily into a chronology on the basis of the patron depicted in them. Otherwise it is very difficult to discern an early, middle, and late style for the artist. His compositions and types, once established, were repeated again and again with few indications of any formal development. His Madonnas gradually become slenderer and more ethereal and self-conscious, and a greater use of Italian motifs such as putti, garlands, and sculptural detail for the settings marks the later works. His portraits, too, appear to develop from a type with a simple neutral background to those enhanced with a loggia or window view of a landscape, but these, too, may have been less a stylistic development than an adaptation of his compositions to suit the tastes of his patrons.

A good example of the difficulties of dating encountered by scholars is the triptych of "The Virgin and Child with Saints and Donors" that Memling executed for Sir John Donne (National Gallery, London), which until recently had been dated very early—around 1468—because it was believed that the patron commissioned the work while visiting Bruges for the wedding of Charles the Bold (duke of Burgundy) to Margaret of York and that he died the following year (1469) in the Battle of Edgecote. It is now known that Sir John lived until 1503 and that it is probably his daughter Anne (born 1470 or later) who is portrayed as the young girl kneeling with her parents in the central panel, thus indicating that the painting was commissioned about 1475.

"Diptych with Madonna and Martin van Nieuwenhove" (left wing), oil on panel by Hans Memling, 1487; in the Memling-Museum, Brugge, Bel.

By courtesy of the Memling-Museum, Brugge, Bel., photograph, © A.C.L., Brussels

Memling's art clearly reveals the influence of contemporary Flemish painters. He borrowed, for example, from the compositions of Jan van Eyck, the famed founder of the Bruges school. The influence of Dirck Bouts and Hugo van der Goes can also be discerned in his works—for example, in a number of eye-catching details such as glistening mirrors, tile floors, canopied beds, exotic hangings, and brocaded robes. Above all, Memling's art reveals a thorough knowledge of, and dependence on, compositions and figure types created by Rogier van der Weyden. In Memling's large triptych (a painting in three panels, generally hinged together) of the "Adoration of the Magi" (Prado, Madrid), one of his earliest works, and in the altarpiece of 1479 for Jan Floreins (Memling-Museum, Brugge), the influence of Rogier's last masterpiece, the "Columba Altarpiece" (1460–64; Alte Pinakothek, Munich), is especially noticeable. Some scholars believe that Memling himself may have had a hand in the production of this late work while still in Rogier's studio. He also imitated Rogier's compositions in numerous representations of the half-length Madonna with the Child, often including a pendant with the donor's portrait (the "Madonna and Martin van Nieuwenhove"; Memling-Museum, Brugge). Many devotional diptychs (two-panel paintings) such as this were painted in 15th-century Flanders. They consist of a portrait of the "donor"—or patron—in one panel, reverently gazing at the Madonna and Child in the other. Such paintings were for the donor's personal use in his home or travels.

Most of Memling's patrons were those associated with religious houses, such as the Hospital of St. John in Bruges, and wealthy businessmen, including burghers of Bruges and foreign representatives of the Florentine Medicis and the Hanseatic League (an association of German merchants dealing abroad). For Tommaso Portinari, a Medici agent, and his wife, Memling painted portraits (Metropolitan Museum of Art, New York City) and an unusual altarpiece that depicts more than 22 scenes from the Passion of Christ scattered in miniature in a panoramic landscape encompassing a view of Jerusalem (Galleria Sabauda, Turin). Such an altarpiece, perhaps created for new devotional practices, became very popular at the end of the 15th century. His best known work with extensive narration is the sumptuous Shrine of St. Ursula in the Hospital of St. John. It was commissioned by two nuns, Jacosa van Dudzeele and Anna van den Moortele, who are portrayed at one end of the composition kneeling before Mary. This reliquary, completed in 1489, is in the form of a diminutive chapel with six painted panels filling the areas along the sides where stained glass would ordinarily be placed. The narrative, which is the story of Ursula and her 11,000 virgins and their trip from Cologne to Rome and back, unfolds with charm and colourful detail but with little drama or emotion. Other patrons of the same hospital commissioned Memling to paint a large altarpiece of St. John with the mystical marriage of St. Catherine to Christ as the central theme (Memling-Museum, Brugge). Elaborate narratives appear behind the patron saints John the Baptist and John the Evangelist painted on the side panels, while the central piece is an impressive elaboration of the enthroned Madonna between angels and saints (including Catherine) that one finds in innumerable other devotional pieces attributed to Memling.

Because Memling's work was so strongly influenced by that of other painters, it often has been harshly dealt with by 20th-century critics. Yet in his own lifetime he was acclaimed. Recording his death, the notary of Bruges described him as "the most skillful painter in the whole of Christendom." (J.E.Sn.)

MAJOR WORKS. "The Martyrdom of St. Sebastian" (*c.* 1470; Musées Royaux des Beaux-Arts, Brussels); "Portinari Triptych" (*c.* 1470; Metropolitan Museum of Art, New York City); "Portrait of Gilles Joye" (1472; Sterling and Francine Clark Art Institute, Williamstown, Mass.); "The Last Judgment" (*c.* 1473; Marienkirche, Gdańsk, Pol.); "Triptych: The Virgin and Child with Saints and Donors" (*c.* 1475; National Gallery, London); "The Deposition" (*c.* 1475; Museo de la Capilla Real, Granada, Spain); "The Virgin and Child" (*c.* 1475; Museo de la Capilla Real); "The Mystic Marriage of St. Catherine of Alexandria" (*c.* 1475; Louvre, Paris); "Christ Surrounded by Angel Musicians" (*c.* 1475; Musée Royal des Beaux-Arts, Antwerp); "Mystic Marriage of St. Catherine of Alexandria" (1479; Memling-Museum, Brugge); "Adoration of the Magi" (1479; Memling-Museum); "The Descent from the Cross" (1480; Memling-Museum); "Scenes from the Life of Christ and the Virgin" (*c.* 1480; Alte Pinakothek, Munich); "Madonna and Child with Angels" (*c.* 1480–85; National Gallery of Art, Washington, D.C.); "Moreel Triptych" (1484; Groeninge Museum, Brugge); "Bathsheba" (*c.* 1485; Staatsgalerie, Stuttgart, Ger.); "Diptych with Madonna and Martin van Nieuwenhove" (1487; Memling-Museum); "St. Benedict" (1487; Uffizi, Florence); "Portrait of Benedetto Portinari" (1487; Uffizi); "The Virgin and Child" (1487; Staatsliche Museen Preussischer Kulturbesitz, Berlin); St. Ursula Shrine (1489; Memling-Museum); "Resurrection" (*c.* 1490; Louvre); "Passion Triptych" (Crucifixion Panel, 1491; St.-Annen-Museum, Lübeck, Ger.).

BIBLIOGRAPHY. Lengthy bibliographies on the artist appear in A. Wurzbach, *Niederländisches Künstler-Lexikon,* vol. 2 (1909); and V. Denis, *Encyclopedia of World Art,* vol. 9, col. 729–735 (1964). Among the earlier studies of Memling, see especially J.A. Crowe and G.B. Cavalcaselle, *The Early Flemish Painters* (1857); L.J. Krämmerer, *Memling* (1899); F. Bock, *Memling Studien* (1900); W.H.J. Weale, *Hans Memling* (1901); and K. Voli, *Memling* (1909). For the relationships with Rogier van der Weyden, see especially G. Hulin de Loo "Hans Memling in Rogier van der Weyden's Studio," *Burlington Magazine,* 52:160–177 (1928); and M.J. Friedländer, "Noch etwas über das Verhältnis Roger van der Weydens zu Memling," *Oud-Holland,* 61:11–19 (1946). The standard references are L. von Baldass, *Hans Memling* (1942); M.J. Friedländer, *Memling* (1950) and his *Die altniederländisch Malerei,* vol. 6 (1928; *Early Netherlandish Painting,* vol. 6, 1971); and Georges Henri Dumont, *Hans Memling* (1966; Eng. trans. 1967); also see the discussions of Memling's works that have appeared in the series *Les Primitifs flamands,* especially vol. 9, J. Bialostocki, *Les Musées de Pologne* (1966); and vol. 11, M. Davies, *The National Gallery-London-III* (1970).

Memmi, Albert (b. 1920, Tunis), French-language Tunisian novelist and author of numerous sociological studies treating the subject of human oppression.

Memmi was the product of a poor Jewish section of the capital city of Tunisia, but he studied at an exclusive French secondary school there. He thus found himself, early in his life, in the anomalous position of a Jew among Muslims, an Arab among Europeans, a ghetto dweller among the bourgeoisie, and an *évolué* (one "evolved" in French culture) among tradition-bound family and friends. It was this tension of living in several worlds at once that became the subject of Memmi's autobiographical first novel, *La Statue de sel* (1953; "The Pillar of Salt"), a work for which he received the Prix de Carthage and the Prix Fénéon. Subsequent novels included *Agar* (1955), which deals with the problem of mixed marriage; *Le Scorpion* (1969), an intricately structured tale of psychological introspection; and *Le Désert* (1977), in which violence and injustice are seen as age-old responses to the pain and uncertainty of the human condition.

Memmi's most influential sociological work was *Portrait du colonisé* (1957; "Portrait of the Colonized"), an analysis of the situations of both the colonizer and the colonized, who contribute to their own entrapment in their respective roles. Among Memmi's other studies of human oppression are his two-part *Portrait d'un Juif* (1962 and 1966; "Portrait of a Jew") and *L'Homme dominé* (1968; "Dominated Man"), a collection of essays examining the situations of women, blacks, and other traditionally dominated groups. Memmi contributed to North African literature as a critic as well as an author, in part through his establishment and direction of a research group on North African literature at the École Pratique des Hautes Études in Paris, where he also taught sociology at the Université de Paris.

Memmingen, city, Bavaria *Land* (state), southern Germany, on the Ach River (a small tributary of the Iller), south of Ulm. First mentioned in 1128, it was founded as a town by Duke Welf VI in 1160; it later belonged to the Hohenstaufens. It was a free imperial city from 1286 until it was absorbed by Bavaria in 1803. Historic landmarks include remains of the fortifications, the Protestant pilgrimage church of St. Martin with finely carved Gothic choir stalls, and the Church of Our Lady with notable late-Gothic wall paintings. The Renaissance town hall dates from 1568–89 and there are old patrician, guild, and burghers' houses. The Baroque Hermannsbau (1766) incorporates the municipal museum. Ottobeuren, just southeast, has an enormous Benedictine abbey, first founded in 764, with 250 rooms, 20 halls, and six courts. A rail junction, Memmingen's industries include brewing and the manufacture of textiles, chemicals, electrical machinery, and metal products. Pop. (1989 est.) 37,942.

Memminger, Christopher G(ustavus) (b. Jan. 9, 1803, Nayhingen, Württemberg—d. March 7, 1888, Charleston, S.C., U.S.), Confederate secretary of the treasury, generally held responsible for the collapse of his government's credit during the American Civil War.

Soon after his father's death while a soldier in Germany, Memminger immigrated to the United States and settled with his mother in Charleston, S.C. In 1819 Memminger was graduated from South Carolina College, began to study law, and subsequently went on to become a successful attorney. By 1830 he was emerging as a prominent public figure, notable for his opposition to the nullification movement in South Carolina. Elected to the state legislature in 1836, he served as chairman of the finance committee and actively sought to force banks to maintain specie payments. During his legislative career, Memminger gained a reputation as a sound financier.

Although dissatisfied with the Compromise of 1850, Memminger opposed unilateral opposition by South Carolina. He sided with the conservatives in his state, but, following the John Brown raid in January 1860, he counselled joint defensive measures in the South against Northern antislavery agitation. After Abraham Lincoln's election, he wholeheartedly backed secession and served in South Carolina's secession convention.

Memminger helped draft the provisional constitution of the Confederate states and then accepted appointment by Pres. Jefferson Davis to become secretary of the treasury for the new Confederate government. He initially planned sparing use of treasury notes, but the financial obligations of the Confederacy dictated their massive issuance. By 1863 the currency had depreciated greatly, and, as the notes fell in value, more were printed to cover governmental expenditures. Military defeats and the effective Union blockade of Southern ports made the financial plight of the South desperate by early 1864. On June 15, 1864—following the collapse of Confederate credit—Memminger resigned.

He retired to Flat Rock, N.C., and lived there until after the Civil War was over. Then he returned to Charleston and, granted a presidential pardon, began to practice law once again. During the final two decades of his life, he was involved in chemical manufacturing and in assisting the public school system in Charleston.

Memnon, in Greek mythology, son of Tithonus (son of Laomedon, legendary king of Troy) and Eos (Dawn) and king of the Ethiopians. He was a post-Homeric hero, who, after the death of the Trojan warrior Hector, went to assist his uncle Priam, the last king of Troy, against the Greeks. He performed prodigies of valour but was slain by the Greek hero Achilles. According to tradition, Zeus, the king of the gods, was moved by the tears of Eos and bestowed immortality upon Memnon. His companions were changed into birds, called Memnonides, that came every year to fight and lament over his grave. The combat between Achilles and Memnon was often represented by Greek artists, and the story of Memnon was the subject of the lost *Aethiopis* of Arctinus of Miletus (fl. *c.* 650 BC).

In Egypt the name of Memnon was connected with the colossal (70-foot [21-metre]) stone statues of Amenhotep III near Thebes, two of which still remain. The more northerly of these was partly destroyed by an earthquake in 27 BC, resulting in a curious phenomenon. Every morning, when the rays of the rising sun touched the statue, it gave forth musical sounds like the twang of a harp string. This was supposed to be the voice of Memnon responding to the greeting of his mother, Eos. After the restoration of the statue by the Roman emperor Septimius Severus (AD 170) the sounds ceased; they were attributed to the passage of air through the pores of the stone, caused chiefly by the change of temperature at sunrise.

memoir, history or record composed from personal observation and experience. Closely related to, and often confused with, autobiography, a memoir usually differs chiefly in the degree of emphasis placed on external events; whereas writers of autobiography are concerned primarily with themselves as subject matter, writers of memoir are usually persons who have played roles in, or have been close observers of, historical events and whose main purpose is to describe or interpret the events. The English Civil Wars of the 17th century, for example, produced many such reminiscences, most notable of which are the *Memoirs* of Edmund Ludlow and Sir John Reresby. The French have particularly excelled at this genre; one of the greatest memoirists of his time was the Duc de Saint-Simon, whose *Mémoires* (covering the early 1690s through 1723), famous for their penetrating character sketches, provide an invaluable source of information about the court of Louis XIV. Another of the great French memoirists was François-René, vicomte de Chateaubriand, who devoted the last years of his life to his *Mémoires d'outre-tombe* (1849–50; "Memoirs from Beyond the Tomb"). In the 20th century, many distinguished statesmen and military men have described their experiences in memoirs. Notable reminiscences of World War II are the memoirs of England's Viscount Montgomery (1958) and Charles De Gaulle's *Mémoires de guerre* (1954–59; *War Memoirs,* 1955–60).

memoria technica: *see* mnemonic.

Memorial Day, also called DECORATION DAY, public legal holiday in the United States and its territories and among its armed forces, honouring U.S. citizens who have died in war. Originally commemorating soldiers killed in the American Civil War, the observance was later extended to all U.S. war dead. Most states conform to the federal practice of observing the holiday on the last Monday in May, which began in 1971, but a few retain the long-established day of celebration, May 30. National observance is marked officially by the placing of a wreath on the Tomb of the Unknown Soldier in Arlington National Cemetery in Virginia.

The custom itself of honouring the graves of the war dead began before the close of the Civil War. In the South, the town of Columbus, Miss., claims origination of a formal observance for both the Union and the Confederate dead in 1866. Waterloo, N.Y., is cited as the birthplace of the observance in the North in the same year. There was no fixed day of national celebration, however, until 1868, when Commander in Chief John A. Logan of the Grand Army of the Republic issued a general order designating May 30, 1868, "for the purpose of strewing with flowers or otherwise decorating the graves of comrades who died in defense of their country during the late rebellion."

In addition to the national holiday, Confederate memorial days continue to be celebrated in some Southern states. Similar commemorations are observed in numerous other countries.

memory, the retention and retrieval in the human mind of past experiences.

A brief treatment of memory follows. For full treatment, *see* MACROPAEDIA: Memory.

The function of remembering and its converse, forgetting, are normally adaptive. Learning, thought, and reasoning could not occur without remembering. On the other hand, forgetting has many functions, including time orientation by virtue of the tendency of memories to fade over time; adaptation to new learning by the loss or suppression of old patterns; and relief from the anxiety of painful experiences.

Some theorists believe memory is best described as a single storage and retrieval system. Others conceptualize a short-term memory where a limited amount of information (about five–nine items) can be held for a few seconds, after which it is either coded into a separate long-term system or lost. Organic evidence is adduced in favour of the two-system theory: persons who have suffered damage to an area of the brain called the hippocampus can retain short-term memory functions but are apparently unable to store any new long-term memory.

Measuring retention. The ability to recall information and the ability to recognize something previously encountered are two measurable indications of retention. In a simple memory test, a subject is given a list to study and is later asked to recall as many items from the list as possible, either in sequence or in random order. In recognition tests the subject is asked to pick out from a new list those items which were also on the studied list. Once the subject is able to recall or recognize a certain quota (predetermined by the test designer) of items from a list, he is considered to have learned it. Then, the difference between this basic rate of retention and the amount of information still retained at a later quiz determines the rate of forgetting over the interval between the two quizzes. A third indication of retention is the ability to do something more quickly when one has already done it once, and some tests (called "relearning tests") measure retention as a function of subjects' increased efficiency in accomplishing some task previously learned. Rates of retention vary according to whether subjects are asked to recall, recognize, or relearn. For instance, after six months a subject may be able to recall nothing but may perform a task significantly faster.

Encoding. Research into the physiological and behavioral bases for memory has attempted to describe mechanisms for encoding information (transforming it into a storable state), as well as decoding and retrieving it. One avenue of study has sought to identify a neurochemical code which may be responsible for creating a memory trace (engram) in the nervous system.

A research method commonly employed in the investigation of encoding mechanisms has been the manipulation of characteristics of words. Words related by some feature (*e.g.*, functional or structural similarity, same part of speech, acoustic similarity, etc.) are presented together in successive lists. Theoretically, if the related feature (*e.g.*, furniture pieces) is of importance to the encoding process, a decrease in recall performance will be seen until a new feature (*e.g.*, mammals) is added. If performance does not improve with the presentation of the new feature, it is assumed that the initial manipulated characteristic was not important to the process of encoding.

All memory traces are thought to consist of clusters of attributes—*e.g.*, "cat," "Siamese," "blue eyes," etc.—any of which may serve as clues in decoding and retrieving. The more closely the circumstances in which something was learned are duplicated, the more likely it is to be recalled. Any attribute or association may be used to encode information, though some are more likely to be used than others: animal, vegetable, or mineral, for instance, are more likely to be used than grammatical class. Errors made in recognition tests frequently suggest ways the subjects may have encoded the information given them; for instance, if a subject shown the word "sea" later mistakenly claims to recognize the word "see," it may be supposed that he encoded phonetically.

Forgetting. It has been theorized that as time passes, the physiological bases of memory tend to change; specifically, the neural engram is thought to decay or lose its clarity. A preeminent theory of forgetting at the behavioral level is anchored in the phenomenon of interference, or inhibition, in the encoding and decoding processes of memory. In proactive inhibition, old memories interfere with the retention of new ones; and in retroactive inhibition, learning interferes with retention of the old. These phenomena suggest the hypothesis that a balance is maintained between memory input (learning) and output (forgetting). Memory research indicates that rates of forgetting are uniform with respect to degree of learning for all normal individuals. That is, one person's memory is as good as another's, provided they have both learned as well.

The interference theory of forgetting, which is currently prevalent and supported by behavioral evidence, is compatible with the single-system model of memory.

Abnormalities of memory. The concepts and techniques used in the investigation of memory disorders date from the expansion of medical knowledge that took place in the late 19th century. Three pioneers in the study of these disorders illustrate the cross-disciplinary nature of the phenomena: Théodule Armand Ribot, a French psychologist; Sergey Sergeyevich Korsakov (Korsakoff), a Russian psychiatrist; and Pierre Janet, a French neurologist.

The collective contributions of these men can be summarized thus: that memory loss, though related to brain functioning, may be present without organic damage (*e.g.*, in hysterics) and need not involve a dementia (loss of the ability to reason). Memory loss may, in fact, be due to emotional anxiety, as Sigmund Freud was to demonstrate.

Memory defects are among the most frequently observed symptoms of impaired brain function and may be transitory (as after an epileptic seizure) or enduring (as after severe head injury). When a person has impaired ability to store new memories, he or she is suffering from anterograde amnesia; an exaggerated loss of old memories is termed retrograde amnesia. The two may, but do not necessarily, appear together. Even in the most severe amnesias, immediate (short-term) memory is intact, leading scientists to speculate that new experiences are initially registered and comprehended long enough to allow a response. Many psychologists who distinguish short-term from long-term storage systems therefore locate memory problems in the transfer of information from one system to the other.

This suggestion requires a few qualifications. Some patients with Korsakoff's syndrome (anterograde amnesia without loss of reason or judgment) learn new manual skills even when new verbal information is poorly remembered. Also, as Korsakoff noted, some new learning may be implicit, as when a patient cannot name the hospital where he lives but, when asked to guess, can select it from a list of names. Evidently the problem in this case lies in a selective inability to call forth what was originally registered; it should be noted that a recognition task may succeed where voluntary recall fails. Finally, most memory, normal and abnormal, is strongly affected by the current concerns and goals which motivate a person so that when these are affected by injury or illness, a consequent memory loss should be no surprise.

Diseases and disorders. Korsakoff's syndrome, which is now known to be caused by many physical problems in addition to alcoholism, can produce a retrograde amnesia for periods prior to the disorder; however, its central, identifying psychological feature is the anterograde loss of the ability to assimilate new phenomena. This loss can be so severe, and consciousness so restricted, that some patients report no connection between one moment and the next. Patients sometimes confabulate, unconsciously reconstructing false pictures of the past by drawing from fantasy rather than from fact, and sometimes deny that they have a memory problem. Certain forms of encephalitis produce a similar disorder which, however, does not typically include confabulation or denial.

A physical trauma resulting in loss of consciousness can leave the awakened victim disoriented for days. When recovered, he is often unable to recall anything from this period and may also show a retrograde amnesia for earlier events. Similarly, psychiatric patients treated by electroshock therapy, the application of electrical currents which often bring on convulsions, are sometimes left in a confused state which they later find difficult to recall. A series of such treatments can cause complaints of a diminished ability to remember daily events. Once treatment is over, the difficulties clear up within weeks in most cases. Surgical removal of a portion of the temporal lobes of the brain, undertaken to control epilepsy, can also produce memory problems. When only the dominant lobe is involved, the patient can have a problem learning new verbal material for up to three years after surgery. In the rare cases when both lobes are involved, a severe memory impairment (similar to a post-encephalic amnesia) results.

Brief irregularities in blood flow to specific brain regions can produce transient global, or total, amnesia. During the attack, no new memories are formed. There is also a retrograde amnesia which then diminishes during recovery, leaving only an empty period surrounding the attack. Memory defects may also be an early sign of cerebral arteriosclerosis or senility.

Psychological oddities of memory. Accounts of hypnosis indicate that the trance state is imperfectly remembered and that a suggestion from the hypnotist can effectively block memory more completely, only to restore it by a later suggestion if he wishes. Some types of hysterical amnesia may also be relieved by a suggestion made under hypnosis. Hysterical memory losses, unlike organically based amnesias, seem to target specific, emotionally important groups of memories and can be effectively interpreted in terms of the patient's motives. Fugue states, periods during which a person temporarily forgets his identity and wanders away from home, have been explained by both psychogenic and organic models. Although many accounts of remarkable superior memory capacity (hypermnesia) exist, very little is known about the processes which underlie this skill. Paramnesia, the falsification of memory, includes (in addition to confabulation, which occurs unconsciously) retrospective falsification, a purposeful embellishment of memory; déjà vu, a mysterious feeling of having experienced something before; and jamais vu, a false unfamiliarity with a certain experience.

memory, computer: *see* computer memory.

Memphis, city and capital of ancient Egypt during the Old Kingdom (*c.* 2575–*c.* 2130 BC), located south of the Nile delta, on the west bank of the river. It lies about 15 miles (25 km) south of Cairo. Closely associated with the ancient city's site are the cemeteries, or necropolises, of Memphis, where the famous pyramids of Egypt and the Great Sphinx are located. From north to south, the main pyramid fields are: Abū Ruwaysh, Giza, Zawayet el-Aryan, Abū Ṣīr, Ṣaqqārah, and Dahshūr.

Foundation and Early Dynastic Period. According to a commonly accepted tradition, Memphis was founded about 2925 BC by Menes, who supposedly united the two prehistoric kingdoms of Upper and Lower Egypt. The precise historical identity of this king is still in question, but there is little doubt as to his connection with Memphis or of the importance of the city from the earliest period. The site had obvious political advantages, being located at the junction of the boundaries of the two formerly separate kingdoms. The local god of Memphis was Ptah, patron of craftsmen and artisans and, in some contexts, a creator god as well. The Great Temple of Ptah was one of the city's most prominent structures. According to an Egyptian document known as the Memphite Theology, Ptah created mankind through the power of his heart and speech; the concept, having been shaped in the heart of the creator, was brought into existence through the divine utterance itself. In its freedom from the conventional physical analogies of the creative act and in its degree of abstraction, this text is virtually unique in Egypt, and it testifies to the philosophic sophistication of the priests of Memphis.

The original name of the city was the White Wall, and the term may have referred originally to the king's palace, whose walls would have been built of whitewashed brick. The colour also had significance politically; white was the colour of the Lower Egyptian crown.

No remains of the period of Menes have come to light in the city site itself, but the evidence of the Memphite necropolises confirms the traditional age of the city. The large, elaborately niched tombs of the 1st and 2nd dynasties (*c.* 2925–*c.* 2650 BC) found at Ṣaqqārah have been claimed as royal tombs, but some scholars doubt that Memphis was the sole, or even the primary, capital of Egypt under those dynasties. According to the 3rd-century-BC historian Manetho, the 1st and 2nd dynasties originated at Tjene, or Thinis, in Upper Egypt. Thinis is near Abydos, and excavations at Abydos uncovered rectangular cut-stone tombs (mastabas) of this period that were long believed to be the royal burials of the first dynasties. To complicate the matter still further, there are equally important tombs of the period at other sites, such as Tarkhan and Abū Ruwaysh. Scholars disagree as to which of these are actually royal tombs, which are simply memorials, and which are tombs of important courtiers.

The Old Kingdom. By the 3rd dynasty the preeminence of Memphis is unquestioned. Manetho calls the 3rd and 4th dynasties (*c.* 2650–2465) Memphite, and the huge royal pyramid tombs of this period, in the necropolises of Memphis, confirm this. Djoser, the second king of the 3rd dynasty, was the builder of the Step Pyramid of Ṣaqqārah, the first large monument to be constructed entirely of stone. Imhotep, the king's architect and adviser, is credited with this architectural feat; his reputation as a wise man and physician led, in later times, to his deification and his identification with the Greek god Asclepius.

The remains of several unfinished or badly ruined pyramids near Memphis have been attributed to other 3rd-dynasty kings. The first king of the 4th dynasty, Snefru, built two pyramid tombs at Dahshūr. The three great pyramids of Giza belong to Khufu, Khafre, and Menkaure, later 4th-dynasty monarchs. The Great Sphinx at Giza dates from the time of Khafre. The last legitimate king of this dynasty, Shepseskaf, built his tomb at South Ṣaqqārah. It was not a pyramid but a distinctive oblong structure with sloping sides, now called the Maṣṭabat Firʿawn.

The royal pyramids are surrounded by large cemeteries where the courtiers and officials who had served the king during his lifetime were buried. The beautiful reliefs in certain of these tombs include scenes of daily life and thus give some idea of the crafts, costumes, and occupations of the royal court of Memphis. Since little has survived of domestic architecture and household furnishings, these reliefs are a valuable source of information on such subjects. A notable exception to the general rule of loss and destruction is the hidden tomb of Queen Hetepheres, the mother of Khufu, which was discovered near the Great Pyramid of Giza. Though the queen's body was unaccountably missing from her sarcophagus, her funerary equipment and furniture survived. The exquisite taste and craftsmanship of these objects testify, as do the splendid low reliefs of the tombs, to the high development of the arts and crafts of the period. Indeed, it is believed by some scholars that the Old Kingdom, influenced by the craftsmen of the Memphite court and the philosopher-theologians of Ptah, reached a peak of "classic" culture that was never surpassed in Egypt.

The kings of the 5th dynasty (*c.* 2465–*c.* 2325) moved south of Giza to build their funerary monuments; their pyramids, at Abū Ṣīr, are much smaller than those of the 4th dynasty, but the pyramid temples and causeways were decorated with fine reliefs. This dynasty was probably marked by a decline of Memphite influence paralleling the rise of a sun cult centred at Heliopolis. The major monuments of the period are not the pyramids but the sun temples, which were, however, also part of the so-called Memphite pyramid area, not far from Abū Ṣīr.

During the 6th dynasty (*c.* 2325–*c.* 2150), which Manetho also designates as Memphite, the funerary monuments in the pyramid field of Ṣaqqārah continue to decline in size and workmanship; a curious fact is that the modern name of Memphis is ultimately derived from Men-nefer, the name of the pyramid city of the 6th-dynasty king Pepi I. This relatively small and obscure pyramid thus gave its name to the entire region. At this time the influence of the centralized government at Memphis began to wane, as is indicated by the increased prominence of provincial cities and the number of fine tombs located away from the Memphis area. This process of decentralization ended in the First Intermediate Period, a time of internal breakdown. Manetho's 7th and 8th dynasties are both called Memphite, but it is believed that both dynasties together comprised a very short period and that the old Memphite house lost its control over the provincial princes soon after the end of the 6th dynasty.

Later history. Memphite influence continued during the Middle Kingdom (1938–*c.* 1600?), when Egypt was once more reunited, but the official residence of the 12th dynasty (1938–1756) was at Lisht, near the entrance to al-Fayyum. Several 12th-dynasty monarchs erected pyramids at Dahshūr, the southernmost of the Memphite pyramid fields, but the majority of Middle Kingdom monuments were located nearer to Lisht. Yet the predominant artistic and administrative influences during this period seem to be Memphite, and virtually every 12th-dynasty ruler added to the Great Temple of Ptah.

Another period of political and social chaos followed the 12th dynasty. This Second Intermediate Period (*c.* 1630–1540) is characterized by the presence in Egypt of the Asian Hyksos peoples. According to the 1st-century-AD historian Josephus, the Hyksos king, whom he calls Salitis, made his capital at Memphis and from there ruled both Upper and Lower Egypt. Inscriptional and archaeological evidence, though it is scanty, tends to confirm the assumption that the invaders controlled northern Egypt, but their capital is generally supposed to have been located at Avaris, near Tanis, in the Nile delta. Records left by Kamose, the 17th-dynasty king who initiated the reconquest of Egypt from the Hyksos, describe his holdings as extending from Elephantine to Hermopolis Magna but note that he "could not pass by (the invader) as far as Memphis."

With the final expulsion of the Hyksos and the restoration of a united kingdom under the 18th dynasty, based at Thebes in Upper Egypt, Memphis entered on a new period of prosperity. Some scholars claim that Memphis never lost its political preeminence and that during the New Kingdom, as in earlier times, the city was the actual political capital of Egypt, with Thebes merely the religious centre. Such a hypothesis is impossible to prove, and it may well be that such distinctions, with their rigidity and exclusiveness, are meaningless in terms of Egyptian culture.

The importance of Memphis was based to a considerable extent upon its venerable religious role. Certain of the coronation ceremonies were traditionally enacted in Memphis, as was the Sed festival, a reenactment of the coronation that restored and restated the supernatural powers of the kingship.

During the New Kingdom (1539–1075), Memphis probably functioned as the second, or northern, capital of Egypt. At one time it seems to have been the principal residence of the crown prince. Several 18th-dynasty (1539–1292) inscriptions mention royal hunting parties in the desert near the Sphinx. Amenhotep II (reigned ?1426–1400) was born at Memphis and held the office of high priest there. Both he and his son, Thutmose IV (reigned 1400–1390), left inscriptions at Giza.

Despite the rise of the god Amon of Thebes, Ptah remained one of the principal gods of the pantheon. The Great Temple was added to or rebuilt by virtually every king of the 18th dynasty. Chapels were constructed by Thutmose I and Thutmose IV and by Amenhotep III. Amenhotep III's son, the religious reformer Akhenaton, built a temple to his god, Aton, in Memphis. A number of handsome private tombs dating from this period in the Memphite necropolis testify to the existence of a sizable court.

During the New Kingdom the city shared the increasingly cosmopolitan character of the nation, as trade, foreign conquest, and travel developed. Though Memphis was not on the Nile, it was connected with it by a canal, and it was probably important as a commercial centre. Specific quarters of the city were named after the foreign colonies—slaves, prisoners of war, or merchants—who resided there. A section called the "Field of the Hittites" is known, as are, in later periods, sections inhabited by Carians and Phoenicians.

Under the 19th dynasty (1292–1190) a new royal residence was built farther north at Per-Ramessu in the Delta, but Memphis continued to be important. The Great Temple was rebuilt. The kings of that period pillaged the monuments of their predecessors for building materials, and some of the reused blocks come not only from structures in the city but also from temples and pyramid complexes in the Memphite necropolises. Ramses II (reigned 1279–13) erected several colossuses in the temple. The Sarapeum, dedicated to the cult of Apis, the bull-god, and built in the form of a labyrinth, was begun under the son of Ramses II, Khaemwese, high priest of Ptah.

By the end of the 20th dynasty the united kingdom had begun to break down once again. The official capitals were Tanis and Thebes, but the royal palace at Memphis continues to be mentioned. The growing popularity of the Apis cult led to further enlargement of the Sarapeum. In the 8th century BC, the Nubian king Piankhi conquered Egypt and restored its unity. Nubia (or Kush), to the south of Egypt, had been under Egyptian political and cultural influence for centuries. An inscription describing Piankhi's campaign has survived, and it mentions a siege of Memphis. The city had fortified walls and was surrounded by water, presumably from its encircling canals. Piankhi took the city, but it was left to his brother and successor, Shabaka, to claim the royal title. There are some indications that this king made Memphis his capital. But the Kushite dynasty was overthrown shortly thereafter, when the Assyrians invaded Egypt. Records left by the Assyrian king Esarhaddon (680–669 BC) refer to the siege and destruction of Memphis, the royal residence of one Tarku, king of Egypt, who is probably to be identified with Taharqa, who became pharaoh in 690 BC. After the death of Esarhaddon, Taharqa regained Memphis, but he was driven out of the city again by Ashurbanipal of Assyria, in 667 BC.

The collapse of Assyria (612 BC) led to brief Egyptian independence under the 26th dynasty, but it was not long before new invaders appeared. The Persian Cambyses took Memphis by siege in 525 BC. After years of Persian rule Egypt was ready to welcome Alexander the Great in 332 BC. The conqueror used Memphis as his headquarters while making plans for his new city of Alexandria. After his death at Babylon, his body was brought to Egypt and was laid to rest temporarily in Memphis before being buried at Alexandria.

Under the Hellenistic Ptolemaic dynasty (304–30 BC), Memphis retained its cosmopolitan character and had a sizable Greek population. Some of the diversified racial types to be found in the city during Greco-Roman times are depicted in a series of striking terracotta heads dating from this period.

At the beginning of the Roman period (1st century BC), Memphis was still considered an important provincial capital. The serious decay of the ancient city began after the rise of Christianity, when zealots of that faith defaced and destroyed the remaining pagan temples. In the 5th century AD the Christian monastery of Apa Jeremias rose among the venerable tombs of Ṣaqqārah. The capital continued to deteriorate, receiving its death blow during the Muslim conquest of Egypt in AD 640. A garrison and fort called Babylon occupied the eastern end of the bridge that crossed the Nile from Memphis, and after a long siege the fortress was taken by the Arab general ʿAmr ibn al-ʿĀṣ. Memphis was abandoned, and later the few remaining structures were dismantled so that the stone might be reused in the neighbouring villages and in Cairo, after that city's foundation in the 10th century.

Archaeology. The ancient city of Memphis lies near the modern village of Mīt Ruhaynah. At the beginning of the 20th century some ruined walls were still to be seen, but these have now disappeared, and the only monument above ground is a colossal statue of Ramses II, which once adorned the Great Temple of Ptah. Few city sites in Egypt have been excavated; and, like so many other ancient Egyptian sites, Memphis is known primarily from the exploration of its necropolises, which tend to yield more dramatic finds than the city itself.

The first archaeologist to work at the city site for any prolonged period was Flinders Petrie, who excavated between 1908 and 1913, uncovering sections of the Great Temple of Ptah. These remains, left exposed, soon disappeared under the depredations of the nearby villagers. A University of Pennsylvania expedition worked at the site in 1917, finding foundations of a palace of Merneptah (1213–04 BC) east of the temple of that king. The university sponsored further digging in 1955 and 1956, excavating parts of the Great Temple and a small temple of Ramses II.

For the past century there has hardly been a season when archaeological activity was not proceeding at one or another of the pyramid sites. Almost all of the pyramids, and a majority of the large private tombs, were entered by treasure hunters before the beginning of scholarly excavation. One of the earliest scholars to work in the Memphite area was Auguste Mariette, who discovered the Sarapeum in 1851. Among the most important of Mariette's successors were G.A. Reisner and Hermann Junker, who excavated at Giza; Ludwig Borchardt, who excavated the sun temples and the 5th-dynasty pyramids at Abū Ṣīr; Ahmad Fakhry, who worked in the pyramids of Snefru at Dahshūr; and Zakaria Goneim, who discovered a previously unknown pyramid, probably of the 3rd dynasty, to the southwest of the Step Pyramid at Ṣaqqārah. Also noteworthy are the excavations of J.P. Lauer in the Step Pyramid complex. In the 1930s, W.B. Emery began the excavations that uncovered the great 1st-dynasty tombs. His work in the archaic cemetery disclosed another huge labyrinth resembling that of the Sarapeum, the precise function of which is as yet undetermined. (B.G.M.)

BIBLIOGRAPHY. Dorothy J. Crawford, Jan Quaegebeur, and Willy Clarysse, *Studies on Ptolemaic Memphis* (1980), describes the interaction between rulers and priests in Memphis in cultural and political terms. Dorothy J. Thompson, *Memphis Under the Ptolemies* (1988), studies all aspects of the city during the Hellenistic period.

Memphis, city, seat (1819) of Shelby county, extreme southwestern Tennessee, U.S., the state's largest city. It lies on the Chickasaw bluffs above the Mississippi River where the borders of Arkansas, Mississippi, and Tennessee meet. Aside from West Memphis, Ark., Memphis's main suburbs in Tennessee include Bartlett, Lakeland, Collierville, Arlington, Millington, and Germantown.

Spanish explorer Hernando de Soto visited the area in 1541. French (1739) and Spanish (1795) forts briefly existed on the site; in 1797 the U.S. built Fort Adams there. Memphis was founded in 1819 on land previously inhabited by Chickasaw Indians and was named for the ancient Egyptian city (meaning "Place of Good Abode"). Andrew Jackson, later U.S. president, was one of its founders.

Memphis grew rapidly with the expansion of cotton growing in the South and because of its transportation facilities by railroad and river. It was incorporated in 1826. A Confederate military centre early in the American Civil War, it was captured by a Union gunboat force on June 6, 1862, and remained occupied until the end of the war. One of the country's worst race riots took place there in May 1866.

Memphis subsequently became a centre of trade for the South's cotton. In the 1870s yellow fever devastated the city, killing more than 5,000 residents. The city became bankrupt; its population declined, and in 1879 it surrendered its charter. Drastic sanitary reforms, continued cotton trading, and the growth of a market in hardwood contributed to its economic recovery, and a new city charter was granted in 1893. Economic development was accelerated after World War II. During the 1960s the civil rights movement greatly affected the city. On April 4, 1968, civil rights leader Martin Luther King, Jr., visiting the city in support of a sanitation workers' strike, was killed on the balcony of the Lorraine Motel by a sniper's bullet. James Earl Ray was convicted of the murder. The motel became the National Civil Rights Museum in 1991; exhibits trace the history of the civil rights struggle, and King's room is preserved.

Memphis's central location has helped make it one of the largest distribution centres in the United States. Its international airport is the world's busiest cargo airport, and the city is among the nation's largest inland river ports. Extensive rail and highway facilities and the headquarters of major freight corporations contribute to the importance of the industry. Memphis is a major world cotton market and a world leader in hardwood trading and processing and soybean processing. The city serves an agricultural area noted for livestock, cotton, soybeans, corn (maize), feed grains, and forest products and has agricultural research and food processing industries. It is an important wholesale centre. Manufactures include electronics, medical products and equipment, and paper products. Services (including health care, banking and finance, government, and education), tourism and convention business, and high-technology industries also contribute to the economy. Educational institutions in Memphis include Rhodes College (1848; Presbyterian), LeMoyne-Owen College (1871), Christian Brothers University (1871; Roman Catholic), University of Memphis (1912), Southwest Tennessee Community College (established in 2000 by the merger of the State Technical Institute at Memphis and Shelby State Community College), Memphis College of Art (1936), and the health science centre of the University of Tennessee.

Memphis is one of the birthplaces of blues music and is associated particularly with composer W.C. Handy, who immortalized the city's Beale Street in one of his songs. Handy's home is preserved as a museum, and modern Beale Street is a popular entertainment district with nightclubs, restaurants, shops, live music, and other attractions. A blues festival is held annually in August, and other events throughout the year celebrate the city's musical heritage. Memphis is also known as the birthplace of rock and roll; Elvis Presley was one of many musicians who launched careers from Memphis's Sun Studio. After Presley's death in 1977 Graceland, his city mansion and burial site, became a shrine (opened to the public for tours in 1982). Memphis has a symphony orchestra, ballet troupe, and opera company, as well as several theatre organizations. The Memphis Brooks Museum of Art (1916) is the state's oldest; the Memphis Pink Palace Museum includes a planetarium and cultural and historical exhibits. Historic sites include the Hunt-Phelan Home (1828) and the Burkle Estate/Slavehaven (1849), an Underground Railroad station. The Center for Southern Folklore is devoted to the people and culture of the South. A park on Mud Island, in the Mississippi, includes a five-block-long scale model of the river. The Pyramid is a 32-story stainless-steel arena that hosts sports events, concerts, and shows. The Memphis in May International Festival is an annual month-long event devoted to a different country each year; Africa in April is an annual festival celebrating African American culture.

A U.S. Navy facility is at Millington to the north. Chucalissa, a prehistoric Native American village and archaeological museum, is in T.O. Fuller State Park, and Meeman-Shelby Forest State Park is north of the city. Pop. (2000) city, 650,100; Memphis MSA, 1,135,614.

Memphis Race Riot (May 1866), in the U.S. post-Civil War period, attack by members of the white majority on black residents of Memphis, Tenn., illustrating Southern intransigence in the face of defeat and indicating unwillingness to share civil or social rights with the newly freed blacks. In the attack, which occurred a little more than a year after the Confederate surrender, 46 blacks (most of them Union veterans) were murdered, more than 70 wounded, 5 black women raped, and 12 churches and 4 schools burned. Such unprovoked violence aroused sympathy in the U.S. Congress for the freedmen, drawing attention to the need for legal safeguards in their behalf and thus helping to win passage (June 13, 1866) of the Fourteenth Amendment to the U.S. Constitution.

Memphite DYNASTY, either of the first two dynasties of Egypt (*c.* 2925–*c.* 2650 BC), the first founded by Menes (*q.v.*), who initially unified Egypt and built his capital at Ṣaqqārah, later called Memphis.

Memphremagog, Lake, elongated finger lake that crosses the United States–Canadian border 5 miles (8 km) north of Newport, Vt., U.S. Extending about 27 miles (43 km) from Newport to Magog, Que., the lake forms a small part of the northern boundary of Vermont. It is only 1–2 miles (1.5–3 km) wide for most of its length but has several large embayments; these include Fitch Bay on the eastern shore and Sargents Bay on the west. Depths average 50–75 feet (15–23 m) with shallows at the southern end. A small-scale hydroelectric development has been established at the northern end of the lake where it drains by way of the Magog and St.-François rivers into the St. Lawrence. The lake is surrounded by hills and mountains, the loftiest being Owl's Head (3,360 feet [1,024 m]), on the western shore. The name Memphremagog comes from the Algonquian, meaning "where there is a big expanse of water."

Men, moon god worshiped widely in Asia Minor during Roman times and also in Attica from the 3rd century BC. Little is known of his origin, but he may have been connected with the Persian moon god Mao. His name was usually written together with a cult title, often an adjective denoting a locality, and his most frequent attributes were the pine cone, bucranium (ox skull), and chicken. He was represented as a male figure with a crescent moon behind his shoulders. A temple of Men has been excavated at Antioch in Pisidia (modern Yalvaç, Tur.).

Men of God (Islām): *see* Ahl-e Ḥaqq.

Men Shen, in Chinese mythology, the two door gods whose separate martial images are

Men Shen, Chinese painting on paper; in the Musée Guimet, Paris

Giraudon—Art Resource/EB Inc.

posted on the two halves of the double front door of private homes to guarantee protection from evil spirits. One tradition reports that two T'ang-dynasty generals stood guard at the imperial gates during a serious illness of T'ai Tsung (reigned AD 626–649), who was grievously troubled by evil spirits. Their presence was so effective that the emperor ordered their pictures to be posted permanently on the gates—with salutary effects. At a later date another Men Shen was added and given custody of the rear door. The custom of having Men Shen standing guard at one's door quickly spread throughout China. During the New Year celebration, the images are refurbished in brilliant colours.

Mena, Juan de (b. 1411, Córdoba—d. 1456, Torrelaguna, Castile), poet who was a forerunner of the Renaissance in Spain.

Mena belonged to the literary court of King John II of Castile, where he was renowned for the Latin erudition he had acquired at the University of Salamanca and in Italy. He is best known for his poem *El laberinto de Fortuna* (1444; "The Labyrinth of Fortune"), also called *Las trescientas* ("The Three Hundreds") for its length; it is a complex work that owes much to Lucan, Virgil, and Dante. Writing in *arte mayor,* lines of 12 syllables that lend themselves to stately recitation, Mena sought to make the Spanish language a literary vehicle adequate to his epic vision of Spain and her mission. His themes are medieval, but his use of Latinisms and rhetorical devices and his references to classical personages suggest an affinity to the new manner of expression that came to be associated with the Renaissance.

Mena (y Medrano), Pedro de (b. August 1628, Granada, Spain—d. Oct. 13, 1688, Málaga), Spanish sculptor who created many statues and busts of polychromed wood for churches in Spain and Latin America and whose work typifies the late Baroque.

Beginning as a student of his father, the sculptor Alonso de Mena, Pedro worked in the studio of Alonso Cano from 1652 to 1657. After Cano departed for Madrid, Pedro went in 1658 to Málaga to begin work on 40 choir stalls for the cathedral there, a project that took four years to complete. Establishing a studio in Málaga, he remained there the rest of his life, except for a visit to Madrid and Toledo in 1663, when he was named sculptor of the Toledo cathedral. His studio produced innumerable works for local churches and for churches in Madrid, Granada, and Córdoba.

Mena's style is heavily indebted to Cano but is more theatrical and realistic. Unfortunately, many of his sculptures at Málaga were destroyed in the riots of 1931. Among these was his masterful "Virgin of Bethlehem" in the Church of Santo Domingo, which combined dignity and playfulness, seriousness and extroverted grace, typical of Andalusia. Works that

"St. Francis," polychrome wood sculpture by Pedro de Mena, 1663–64; in the treasury of the cathedral, Toledo, Spain

Joseph Martin—SCALA, from Art Resource/EB Inc.

have survived include the simple but very moving statue of "St. Francis of Assisi in His Tomb" in the Toledo cathedral, and a "Dolorosa" at Cuenca cathedral and another "Dolorosa" (1673, Madrid, Descalzas Reales), both expressing their motif with remarkable poignancy.

Menabé, historic kingdom of the Sakalava people in southwestern Madagascar, situated roughly between the Mangoky and Manambalo rivers. It was founded in the 17th century by King Andriandahifotsy (d. 1685), who led a great Sakalava migration into the area from the southern tip of Madagascar. Under his son Andramananety, the kingdom became known as Menabé, to distinguish it from a second Sakalava kingdom—Boina—founded by Adramananety's brother farther north.

At the height of their power, in the 18th century, Menabé and Boina together controlled nearly all of western Madagascar and were recognized as overlords by other kingdoms on the island, including Merina, their principal rival. Menabé's eminence was short-lived, however. By the mid-19th century, it had been absorbed into the expanding Merina empire.

Menado (Indonesia): *see* Manado.

Menadra (Indo-Greek king): *see* Menander.

List of Abbreviations

A.B.	Bachelor of Arts (Latin *Artium Baccalaureus*); Army Base
Ac	actinium
AC	alternating current
A.C.T.	Australian Capital Territory
AD	in the year of the Lord (Latin *anno Domini*)
A.F.B.	Air Force Base
Afg.	Afghanistan
A.F.S.	Air Force Station
Ag	silver (Latin *argentum*)
AG	Limited-liability Company (German *Aktiengesellschaft*)
AH	in the year of the Hegira, or Muslim era (Latin *anno Hegirae*)
Al	aluminum, aluminium
Ala.	Alabama
Alb.	Albania
Alg.	Algeria
Alta.	Alberta
Am	Americium
AM	before noon (Latin *ante meridiem*)
AM	amplitude modulation
A.M.	Master of Arts (Latin *Artium Magister*)
Amer.	American
Ant.B.	Antigua and Barbuda
Ar	argon
Arg.	Argentina
Ariz.	Arizona
Ark.	Arkansas
Arm.	Armenia
Arpt.	Airport
As	arsenic
A.S.	Air Station
A.S.S.R.	Autonomous Soviet Socialist Republic
At	astatine
Au	gold (Latin *aurum*)
Aug.	August
Austl.	Australia
Av.	Avenida (Spanish: "Avenue")
Ave.	Avenue
Azer.	Azerbaijan
b.	born
B	boron
Ba	barium
B.A.	Bachelor of Arts
Bah.	The Bahamas
Bangl.	Bangladesh
Barb.	Barbados
BC	before Christ
B.C.	British Columbia
BCE	before the Common Era, or Christian era
Be	beryllium
B.Ed.	Bachelor of Education
Bela.	Belarus
Belg.	Belgium
Bfld.	Battlefield
Bge.	Bridge
Bi	bismuth
Bk	berkelium
Bldg.	Building
Bldgs.	Buildings
Blvd.	Boulevard
Bol.	Bolivia
Bos.-Her.	Bosnia and Hercegovina
Bots.	Botswana
BP	before the present
Br	bromine
Braz.	Brazil
Brit.	British
B.S.	Bachelor of Science
B.Sc.	Bachelor of Science
Bulg.	Bulgaria
Burk.	Burkina Faso
c.	about, approximately (Latin *circa*)
C	carbon; Celsius
C.	Cape
Ca	calcium
C.A.R.	Central African Republic
Calif.	California
Camb.	Cambodia
Camer.	Cameroon
Can.	Canada
Cay.Is.	Cayman Islands
Cb	columbium
Cd	cadmium
C.d'I.	Côte d'Ivoire
Ce	cerium
CE	Common era, Christian era
cf.	compare (Latin *confer*)
Cf	californium
cg	centigram(s)
Cia.	Company (Italian *Compagnia;* Portuguese *Companhia;* Spanish *Compañia*)
Cie.	Company (French *Compagnie*)
Cl	chlorine
cm	centimetre(s)
Cm	curium
CMSA	consolidated metropolitan statistical area
Co	cobalt
Co.	Company; County
Colo.	Colorado
Colom.	Colombia
Conn.	Connecticut
Cord.	Cordillera
Corp.	Corporation
cos	cosine
cot	cotangent
Cr	chromium
C.Rica	Costa Rica
Cro.	Croatia
Cs	cesium
csc	cosecant
Cu	copper (Latin *cuprum*)
Czech.	Czechoslovakia
Cz.Rep.	Czech Republic
d.	died
DC	direct current
D.C.	District of Columbia
Dec.	December
Del.	Delaware
Den.	Denmark
Dept.	Department
D.F.	Federal District (Spanish *Distrito Federal*)
Djib.	Djibouti
D.Litt.	Doctor of Letters (Latin *Doctor Litterarum*)
Dom.Rep.	Dominican Republic
Dr.	Doctor; Drive
Dy	dysprosium
E	east
Ecua.	Ecuador
ed.	edited; edition; editor
Ed.	*Britannica* editor, or editors
eds.	editors
e.g.	for example (Latin *exempli gratia*)
E.Ger.	East Germany
El Salv.	El Salvador
Eng.	England; English
Eq.Guin.	Equatorial Guinea
Er	erbium
Es	einsteinium
est.	estimate; estimated
Est.	Estonia
et al.	and others (Latin *et alli,* or *aliae*)
et seq.	and following page(s) (Latin *et sequens, sequentese,* or *sequentia*)
etc.	and so forth (Latin *et cetera*)
Eth.	Ethiopia
Eu	europium
Expwy.	Expressway
F	Fahrenheit; fluorine
Fe	iron (Latin *ferrum*)
Feb.	February
ff.	and following pages
Fig.	Figure
Fin.	Finland
fl.	flourished (Latin *floruit*)
Fm	fermium
Fla.	Florida
FM	frequency modulation
Fr	francium
Fr.	France
Fr.Guia.	French Guiana
Fr.Poly.	French Polynesia
Ft.	Fort
g	gram(s)
Ga	gallium
Ga.	Georgia (U.S.)
Gd	gadolinium
Ge	germanium
Geo.	Georgia (country)
Ger.	Germany
Gib.	Gibraltar
GmbH	Company with Limited Liability (German *Gesellschaft mit beschränkter Haftung*)
Green.	Greenland
Gren.	Grenada
Guad.	Guadeloupe
Guat.	Guatemala
Guin.Bis.	Guinea-Bissau
h	hour(s)
H	hydrogen
Ha	hahnium
Hbr.	Harbour
He	helium
Hf	hafnium
Hg	mercury (Latin *hydrargyrum*)
H.K.	Hong Kong
HMS	His, or Her, Majesty's Ship, or Service
Ho	holmium
Hond.	Honduras
Hosp.	Hospital
Hung.	Hungary
Hwy.	Highway
I	iodine
I.	Island
ibid.	in the same place (Latin *ibidem*)
Ice.	Iceland
i.e.	that is (Latin *id est*)
Ill.	Illinois
In	indium
Inc.	Incorporated
Ind.	Indiana
Ind. Res.	Indian Reservation
Indon.	Indonesia
Inst.	Institute
Intl.	International
Ir	iridium
Ire.	Ireland
Is.	Islands
Jam.	Jamaica
Jan.	January
Jr.	Junior
K	potassium (Latin *kalium*); Kelvin; Köchel catalog number
Kazakh.	Kazakhstan
Kan.	Kansas
kg	kilogram
KG	Limited Partnership (German *Kommandit Gesellschaft*)
Kiri.	Kiribati
Kitts/N.	Saint Kitts and Nevis
KK	Limited-liability Company (Japanese *Kabushiki Kaisha*)
km	kilometre(s)
Kr	krypton
Ky.	Kentucky
Kyrgyz.	Kyrgyzstan
L.	Lake
La	lanthanum
La.	Louisiana
Leb.	Lebanon
Leso.	Lesotho
Liech.	Liechtenstein
Lith.	Lithuania
LL.B.	Bachelor of Laws (Latin *Legum Baccalaureus*)
LL.D.	Doctor of Laws (Latin *Legum Doctor*)
log	logarithm
Lr	lawrencium
Ltd.	Limited
Lu	lutetium
Lucia	Saint Lucia
Lux.	Luxembourg
m	metre(s)
MA	metropolitan area
M.A.	Master of Arts
Maced.	Macedonia
Madag.	Madagascar
Malay.	Malaysia
Mald.	Maldives
Man.	Manitoba
Marsh.Is.	Marshall Islands
Mart.	Martinique
Mass.	Massachusetts
Maurits.	Mauritius
mbH	Limited; with Limited Liability (German *mit beschränkter Haftung*)
Md.	Maryland
M.D.	Doctor of Medicine (Latin *Medicinae Doctor*)
Mem.	Memorial
Mex.	Mexico
mg	milligram(s)
Mg	magnesium
Mich.	Michigan
Micron.	Micronesia
Mil.	Military
min	minute(s)
Minn.	Minnesota
Miss.	Mississippi
Mlle	Mademoiselle
mm	millimetre(s)
Mme	Madame
Mn	manganese
Mo	molybdenum
Mo.	Missouri
Moldv.	Moldova
Mon.	Monument
Mong.	Mongolia
Mont.	Montana
Monts.	Montserrat
Mor.	Morocco
Mozam.	Mozambique
MP	member of Parliament
Mr.	Mister
Mrs.	"Missus"
M.S.	Master of Science
MSA	metropolitan statistical area
M.Sc.	Master of Science
Mt.	Mount
Mtania.	Mauritania
Mtn.	Mountain
Mts.	Mountains
mun.	municipality
Mus.	Museum
MV	Motor Vessel
Myan.	Myanmar
N	nitrogen; north
Na	sodium (Latin *natrium*)
NA	National Association
Namib.	Namibia
Natl.	National
Natl. Pk.	National Park
Nat. Res.	Nature Reserve
Nb	niobium
N.B.	New Brunswick; Naval Base
N.C.	North Carolina
Nd	neodymium
N.D.	North Dakota
Ne	neon
NE	northeast

Neb.	Nebraska
NECMA	New England county metropolitan area
Neth.	The Netherlands
Neth.Ant.	Netherlands Antilles
Nev.	Nevada
New Cal.	New Caledonia
Nfd.	Newfoundland
N.H.	New Hampshire
Ni	nickel
Nic.	Nicaragua
N.Ire.	Northern Ireland
N.J.	New Jersey
N.Kor.	North Korea
N.M.	New Mexico
no.	number
No	nobelium
Nor.	Norway
Nov.	November
Np	neptunium
NS	Nuclear Ship
N.S.	New Style (calendar)
N.S.W.	New South Wales
N.Terr.	Northern Territory
NV	Limited-liability Company (Dutch *Naamloze Vennootschap*)
NW	northwest
N.W.Terrs.	Northwest Territories
N.Y.	New York
N.Y.C.	New York City
N.Z.	New Zealand
O	oxygen
Oct.	October
Okla.	Oklahoma
Ont.	Ontario
op.	opus
Ore.	Oregon
Os	osmium
O.S.	Old Style (calendar)
p.	page
P	phosphorus
pA	Limited (Italian *per Azioni*)
Pa	protactinium
Pa.	Pennsylvania
Pak.	Pakistan
Pal.	Palace
Pan.	Panama
Para.	Paraguay
Pb	lead (Latin *plumbum*)
Pd	palladium
P.E.I.	Prince Edward Island
Pen.	Peninsula
perf.	performed; performance
pH	potential of hydrogen (acidity-alkalinity factor)
Ph.D.	Doctor of Philosophy (Latin *Philosophiae Doctor*)
Phil.	Philippines
Pk.	Park; Peak
Pkwy.	Parkway
Pl.	Place
Plat.	Plateau
PLC	Public Limited Company
Pm	promethium
PM	afternoon (Latin *post meridiem*)
PMSA	primary metropolitan statistical area
P.N.G.	Papua New Guinea
Po	polonium
Pol.	Poland
pop.	population
Port.	Portugal
pp.	pages
Pr	praseodymium
P.R.	Puerto Rico
prelim.	preliminary (census)
Prov.	Province
Prov. Pk.	Provincial Park
Pt	platinum
Pt.	Point
Pu	plutonium
qq.v.	which see (plural; Latin *quae vide*)
Que.	Quebec
Queen.	Queensland
q.v.	which see (singular; Latin *quod vide*)
R	Rankine
R.	River
Ra	radium
Rb	rubidium
Rd.	Road
Re	rhenium
Res.	Reservoir; Reservation
rev.	revised; revision
Rf	rutherfordium
Rh	rhodium
R.I.	Rhode Island
Rn	radon
Rom.	Romania
Ru	ruthenium
s	second(s)
S	South; sulfur
SA	Limited-liability Company (French *Société Anonyme;* Italian *Società Anònima;* Portuguese *Sociedade Anónima;* Spanish *Sociedad Anónima*)
S.Af.	South Africa
Sask.	Saskatchewan
Saud.Ar.	Saudi Arabia
S.Aus.	South Australia
Sb	antimony (Latin *stibium*)
Sc	scandium
S.C.	South Carolina
Scot.	Scotland
SCSA	standard consolidated statistical area
S.D.	South Dakota
Se	selenium
SE	southeast
sec	secant; second(s)
Seneg.	Senegal
Sept.	September
Seych.	Seychelles
S.F.S.R.	Soviet Federated Socialist Republic
Si	silicon
sin	sine
Sing.	Singapore
S.Kor.	South Korea
Slvk.	Slovakia
Slvn.	Slovenia
Sm	samarium
Sn	tin (Latin *stannum*)
Solo.Is.	Solomon Islands
Som.	Somalia
SpA	Limited-liability Company (Italian *Società per Azioni*)
Spr.	Spring
Sprs.	Springs
Sq.	Square
Sr	strontium
Sr.	Senior
Sri L.	Sri Lanka
SS	Steamship
SS.	Saints
S.S.R.	Soviet Socialist Republic
St.	Saint; State; Street
St. Pk.	State Park
Ste.	Saint (French *Sainte*)
S.Tomé/P.	São Tomé and Príncipe
Str.	Strait
Strs.	Straits
Suri.	Suriname
SW	southwest
Swaz.	Swaziland
Swed.	Sweden
Switz.	Switzerland
Ta	tantalum
Tajik.	Tajikistan
tan	tangent
Tanz.	Tanzania
Tas.	Tasmania
Tb	terbium
Tc	technetium
Te	tellurium
Tenn.	Tennessee
Terr.	Territory; Terrace
Terrs.	Territories
Th	thorium
Thai.	Thailand
Ti	titanium
Tl	thallium
Tm	thulium
Tpk.	Turnpike
trans.	translated; translation; translator(s)
Trin.	Trinidad
Trin./Tob.	Trinidad and Tobago
Tun.	Tunisia
Tur.	Turkey
Turkm.	Turkmenistan
U	uranium
U.A.E.	United Arab Emirates
Ugan.	Uganda
U.K.	United Kingdom
Ukr.	Ukraine
UN	United Nations
Univ.	University
Uru.	Uruguay
U.S.	United States
USGPO	United States Government Printing Office
USS	United States Ship
U.S.S.R.	Union of Soviet Socialist Republics
Uzbek.	Uzbekistan
v.	versus
V	vanadium
Va.	Virginia
var.	variant
Venez.	Venezuela
Vic.	Victoria
Viet.	Vietnam
Vinc./G.	Saint Vincent and the Grenadines
Vir.Is.	Virgin Islands
vol.	volume(s)
Vol.	Volcano
Vt.	Vermont
W	west; tungsten (wolfram)
Wash.	Washington
W.Aus.	Western Australia
W.Ger.	West Germany
Wis.	Wisconsin
W.Samoa	Western Samoa
W.Va.	West Virginia
Wyo.	Wyoming
Xe	xenon
Y	yttrium
Yb	ytterbium
Yugos.	Yugoslavia
Zamb.	Zambia
Zimb.	Zimbabwe
Zn	zinc
Zr	zirconium

Table of Measurement Conversions

To convert	Into	Multiply by
acres	hectares	0.40468564
Celsius (centigrade)	Fahrenheit	(C° × 9/5) + 32
centimetres	inches	0.3937008
cubic feet	cubic metres	0.028316847
cubic metres	cubic feet	35.31467
Fahrenheit	Celsius (centigrade)	5/9(F° − 32)
feet	metres	0.3048
gallons (U.S. liquid)	litres	3.785412
grams	ounces (troy)	0.032150747
hectares	acres	2.471054
inches	centimetres	2.54
inches	millimetres	25.4
kilograms	pounds	2.2046226
kilometres	miles (nautical)	0.5399568
kilometres	miles (statute)	0.6213712
litres	gallons (U.S. liquid)	0.26417205
metres	feet	3.2808399
metres	yards	1.093613298
miles (nautical)	kilometres	1.852
miles (statute)	kilometres	1.609344
millilitres	ounces (U.S. fluid)	0.03381402
millimetres	inches	0.03937008
newtons	pounds (of force)	0.224809
ounces (troy)	grams	31.1034768
ounces (U.S. fluid)	millilitres	29.57353
pounds	kilograms	0.45359237
pounds (of force)	newtons	4.44822
square kilometres	square miles	0.38610216
square miles	square kilometres	2.58998811
yards	metres	0.9144